# The INTERNATIONAL STANDARD BIBLE ENCYCLOPEDIA

# The INTERNATIONAL STANDARD BIBLE ENCYCLOPEDIA

VOLUME THREE • K-P

GENERAL EDITOR

**GEOFFREY W. BROMILEY**
*Church History and Doctrine*

ASSOCIATE EDITORS

**EVERETT F. HARRISON**
*New Testament*

**ROLAND K. HARRISON**
*Old Testament*

**WILLIAM SANFORD LASOR**
*Biblical Geography and Archeology*

CONSULTING EDITOR

**LAWRENCE T. GERATY**
*Archeology*

PROJECT EDITOR

**EDGAR W. SMITH, JR.**

FULLY REVISED • ILLUSTRATED • IN FOUR VOLUMES

WILLIAM B. EERDMANS PUBLISHING COMPANY
GRAND RAPIDS, MICHIGAN

255 Jefferson Ave. S.E., Grand Rapids, MI 49503


Printed in the United States of America

*Publication History:*

First published 1915; copyright 1915 by the Howard-Severance Company, Chicago. New and revised edition, edited by Melvin Grove Kyle, copyright 1929 by the Howard-Severance Company. Copyright renewed, 1956, by William B. Eerdmans Publishing Company. Completely revised and reset.
Volume III: first printing, 1986

**Library of Congress Cataloging in Publication Data**

Main entry under title:

International standard Bible encyclopedia.

1. Bible—Dictionaries. I. Bromiley, Geoffrey William
BS440.16 1979 220.3 79-12280
ISBN 0-8028-8163-7
ISBN 0-8028-8160-2 (set)



Printed and Bound at Eerdmans Printing Company, Grand Rapids.

# CONTRIBUTORS †

ADAMS, KIMBERLY VAN ESVELD
B.A., M.A., Former Editorial Assistant, *ISBE* Revision Project.

ALDEN, ROBERT L.
B.A., M.Div., Ph.D., Professor of Old Testament, Denver Conservative Baptist Seminary, Denver, Colorado.

ALLEN, GEORGE H.*
Ph.D., Editor of *Forum Conche*, or *Fuero De Cuenca*, the Medieval Charter and Bylaws of the city of Cuenca, Spain.

ALLEN, RONALD B.
B.A., Th.M., Th.D., Professor of Hebrew Scripture and Chairman of the Department of Old Testament, Western Conservative Baptist Seminary, Portland, Oregon.

ANGUS, S.*
M.A., Ph.D., Professor of New Testament and Historical Theology, St. Andrew's College, University of Sydney, Australia

ARMERDING, CARL EDWIN
A.B., B.D., M.A., Ph.D., Principal and Professor of Old Testament, Regent College, Vancouver, British Columbia, Canada.

AUNE, DAVID E.
B.A., M.A., M.A., Ph.D., Professor of Religion, Saint Xavier College, Chicago, Illinois.

BALCHIN, JOHN A.
M.A., B.D., Pastor, First Presbyterian Church, Papakura, New Zealand.

BALL, EDWARD
M.A., Lecturer in Old Testament, St. John's College, Nottingham, England.

BANDSTRA, ANDREW J.
A.B., B.D., Th.D., Professor of New Testament, Calvin Theological Seminary, Grand Rapids, Michigan.

BANDSTRA, BARRY L.
B.A., B.D., M.A., Ph.D., Assistant Professor of Religion, Hope College, Holland, Michigan.

BARKER, GLENN W.
A.B., A.M., Ph.D., Late Provost and Professor Christian Origins, Fuller Theological Seminary, Pasadena, California.

BAUR, WILLIAM*
D.D., Professor of Church History, Eden Seminary, St. Louis, Missouri.

BEECHER, WILLIS JUDSON*
M.A., D.D., Professor of Hebrew Language and Literature, Auburn Theological Seminary, Auburn, New York.

BIRCH, BRUCE C.
B.A., B.D., M.A., M.Phil., Ph.D., Professor of Old Testament, Wesley Theological Seminary, Washington, D.C.

BLOCK, DANIEL I.
B.Ed., B.A., M.A., Ph.D., Associate Professor of Old Testament, Bethel Theological Seminary, St. Paul, Minnesota.

BLOMBERG, CRAIG L.
B.A., M.A., Ph.D., Assistant Professor of Religion, Palm Beach Atlantic College, West Palm Beach, Florida.

BORCHERT, GERALD L.
B.A., LL.B., M.Div., Th.M., Ph.D., Professor of New Testament Interpretation, Southern Baptist Theological Seminary, Louisville, Kentucky.

BOWER, ROBERT K.
B.S., M.A., B.D., Ph.D., Late Professor of Practical Theology and Pastoral Counseling, Fuller Theological Seminary, Pasadena, California.

BOYD, JAMES O.*
Ph.D., Assistant Professor of Oriental and Old Testament Literature, Princeton Theological Seminary, Princeton, New Jersey.

BREMER, PAUL L.
A.B., B.D., Ph.D., Professor of Bible and Greek Language, Reformed Bible College, Grand Rapids, Michigan.

BRISCO, THOMAS V.
B.A., Ph.D., Assistant Professor of Biblical Backgrounds and Archaeology, Southwestern Baptist Theological Seminary, Fort Worth, Texas.

BROMILEY, GEOFFREY W.
M.A., Ph.D., Emeritus Professor of Church History and Historical Theology, Fuller Theological Seminary, Pasadena, California.

†An asterisk (*) indicates a contributor to the 1915/1929 *ISBE* whose work has been retained with editorial changes.

CONTRIBUTORS

BROWN, COLIN
B.A., B.D., M.A., Ph.D., Professor of Systematic Theology, Fuller Theological Seminary, Pasadena, California.

BROWNLEE, WILLIAM H.
Th.M., Ph.D., Late Professor of Religion, Claremont Graduate School, Claremont, California.

BRUCE, FREDERICK FYVIE
M.A., D.D., F.B.A., Emeritus Professor of Biblical Criticism and Exegesis, University of Manchester, England.

BUEHLER, WILLIAM W.
B.S., B.D., D.Th., Professor of Biblical and Theological Studies, Gordon College, Wenham, Massachusetts.

BULLARD, REUBEN
B.A., Th.B., M.A., M.S., Ph.D., Professor of History and Science, Cincinnati Bible Seminary, Cincinnati, Ohio.

BURDICK, DONALD W.
A.B., B.D., Th.M., Th.D., Professor of New Testament, Denver Conservative Baptist Seminary, Denver, Colorado.

BURKE, DAVID G.
A.B., B.D., Th.M., Ph.D., Director, Office on Studies, Lutheran World Ministries, New York, New York.

BUSH, FREDERIC W.
B.A., M.Div., Th.M., M.A., Ph.D., Associate Professor of Old Testament, Fuller Theological Seminary, Pasadena, California.

CALDECOTT, W. SHAW*
M.R.A.S., Minister of the Wesleyan Conferences of Great Britain and South Africa.

CARMIGNAC, JEAN
D.Th., Editor, *Revue de Qumrân,* Paris, France.

CARPENTER, EUGENE E.
A.B., M.Div., Ph.D., Professor of Old Testament Literature and Languages, Asbury Theological Seminary, Wilmore, Kentucky.

CARR, G. LLOYD
B.Th., B.A., M.Div., Th.M., Ph.D., Professor of Biblical and Theological Studies and Chairman of the Division of Humanities, Gordon College, Wenham, Massachusetts.

COOK, EDWARD M.
B.A., M.Div., M.A., Adjunct Faculty, Fuller Theological Seminary, Pasadena, California.

COUGHENOUR, ROBERT A.
B.S., M.Div., M.A., Ph.D., Professor of Old Testament, Western Theological Seminary, Holland, Michigan.

CRAIGIE, PETER C.
M.A., Dip.Th., M.Th., Ph.D., Late Professor of Religious Studies and Vice President (Academic), University of Calgary, Calgary, Alberta, Canada.

DAANE, JAMES
A.B., Th.B., Th.D., Late Professor of Theology and Ministry, Fuller Theological Seminary, Pasadena, California.

DANKER, FREDERICK W.
B.D., M.Div., Ph.D., Christ Seminary–Seminex Professor of New Testament, Lutheran School of Theology, Chicago, Illinois.

DEHOOG, JOHN W.
A.B., Former Project Editor, *ISBE* Revision.

DEVRIES, CARL E.
B.S., M.A., B.D., Ph.D., Former Research Associate (Associate Professor), Oriental Institute of the University of Chicago, Chicago, Illinois.

DONALDSON, TERENCE L.
B.Sc., M.Rel., Th.M., Th.D., Professor of New Testament Language and Literature, College of Emmanuel and Saint Chad, Saskatoon, Saskatchewan, Canada.

DUGAN, ROBERT P., JR.
B.A., M.Div., Director, Office of Public Affairs of the National Association of Evangelicals, Washington, D.C.

EARLE, RALPH
A.B., B.D., M.A., Th.D., Emeritus Professor of New Testament, Nazarene Theological Seminary, Kansas City, Missouri.

EASTON, BURTON SCOTT*
D.D., Ph.D., Professor of the Interpretation and Literature of the New Testament, General Theological Seminary, New York, New York.

ELLENS, J. HAROLD
A.B., B.D., Th.M., Ph.D., Executive Director, Christian Association for Psychological Studies, International; Editor-in-Chief, *Journal of Psychology and Christianity,* Farmington Hills, Michigan.

ELLIS, E. EARLE
Ph.D., Visiting Professor of Theology, Southwestern Baptist Theological Seminary, Fort Worth, Texas.

ENGELHARD, DAVID H.
A.B., B.D., M.A., Ph.D., Professor of Old Testament, Calvin Theological Seminary, Grand Rapids, Michigan.

EVANS, MORRIS O.*
D.D., Ph.D., Lecturer on English Bible and Literature, Congregational College, Bangor, North Wales.

EWING, WILLIAM*
M.C., M.A., D.D., Minister, Grange United Free Church, Edinburgh, Scotland.

FAGAL, HAROLD E.
Th.B., M.A., M.Div., M.Th., Ph.D., Professor of New Testament and Associate Dean of the College of Arts and Sciences, Loma Linda University, Riverside, California.

FENSHAM, F. CHARLES
B.A., B.D., M.A., D.D., Ph.D., Professor of Semitic Languages and Head of the Department, University of Stellenbosch, Republic of South Africa.

FOXVOG, DANIEL A.
B.A., M.A., Ph.D., Lecturer in Assyriology and Ancient Near Eastern History and Literature, University of California, Berkeley, California.

FREND, W. H. C.
T.D., D.D., F.S.A., Professor of Ecclesiastical History, The University, Glasgow, Scotland.

FRITSCH, CHARLES T.
A.B., Th.B., Ph.D., Emeritus Professor of Old Testament Literature, Princeton Theological Seminary, Princeton, New Jersey.

CONTRIBUTORS

FULTON, A. S.*
M.A., M.R.A.S., Assistant Keeper, Department of Oriental Books and Manuscripts, British Museum, London, England.

GAEBELEIN, PAUL W., JR.
B.A., Ph.D., Ph.D., Adjunct Professor of Semitic Languages, Fuller Theological Seminary, Pasadena, California.

GARBER, PAUL LESLIE
Th.M., Ph.D., Professor Emeritus of Bible and Religion, Agnes Scott College, Decatur, Georgia.

GARLAND, DAVID E.
B.A., M.Div., Ph.D., Associate Professor of New Testament, Southern Baptist Theological Seminary, Louisville, Kentucky.

GASQUE, W. WARD
B.A., B.D., M.Th., Ph.D., Vice Principal and Professor of New Testament, Regent College, Vancouver, British Columbia, Canada.

GERATY, LAWRENCE T.
B.A., M.A., M.Div., Ph.D., President and Professor of Archaeology and History of Antiquity, Atlantic Union College, South Lancaster, Massachusetts.

GERSTNER, JOHN H.
B.A., M.Div., M.Th., Ph.D., Professor-at-Large, Ligonier Ministries, Orlando, Florida.

GHIRSHMAN, ROMAN
Late Member of the Académie des Inscriptiones et Belles-Lettres, Paris, France.

GIBBS, JOHN G.
A.B., M.Div., Th.M., Ph.D., Acquisitions Editor, John Knox Press, Atlanta, Georgia.

GLASSER, ARTHUR
C.E., B.D., S.T.M., Dean Emeritus and Senior Professor of Theology, School of World Missions, Fuller Theological Seminary, Pasadena, California.

GOLD, VICTOR ROLAND
B.A., B.D., Ph.D., Professor of Old Testament, Pacific Lutheran Theological Seminary, Berkeley, California.

GOODSPEED, EDGAR J.*
Ph.D., Professor of Biblical and Patristic Greek, Chairman of the New Testament Department, University of Chicago, Chicago, Illinois.

GORDON, VICTOR R.
A.B., M.Div., Ph.D., Chaplain and Assistant Professor of Biblical Studies, Wheaton College, Wheaton, Illinois.

GRAYBILL, JOHN B.
B.A., B.D., Ph.D., Emeritus Professor, Department of Bible and Theology, Barrington College, Barrington, Rhode Island.

GREEN, NORMAN
B.A., L.Th., Former Assistant Director, McLaughlin Planetarium, Toronto, Ontario, Canada.

GRIDER, J. KENNETH
A.B., B.D., Th.B., M.A., M.Div., Ph.D., Professor of Theology, Nazarene Theological Seminary, Kansas City, Missouri.

GUINAN, MICHAEL D.
B.A., S.T.B., S.T.L., M.A., Ph.D., Professor of Old Testament and Semitic Languages, Franciscan School of Theology, Berkeley, California.

GUTHRIE, DONALD
B.D., M.Th., Ph.D., Senior Lecturer in New Testament, London Bible College, London, England.

GWINN, RALPH A.
B.A., B.D., Ph.D., Former Professor of Religion and Philosophy, Tarkio College, Tarkio, Missouri.

HAGNER, DONALD A.
B.A., B.D., Th.M., Ph.D., Professor of New Testament, Fuller Theological Seminary, Pasadena, California

HAMMOND, PHILIP C.
B.A., B.D., M.A., Ph.D., Professor of Anthropology, University of Utah, Salt Lake City, Utah.

HARRIS, BRUCE F.
M.A., B.A., B.D., Ph.D., Associate Professor of History, Macquarie University, North Ryde, New South Wales, Australia.

HARRIS, MURRAY J.
M.A., Dip.Ed., B.D., Ph.D., Warden, Tyndale House, Cambridge, England.

HARRIS, WILLIAM R.
B.A., M.Div., Freelance Writer and Editor in Biblical Studies, Grand Rapids, Michigan.

HARRISON, EVERETT F.
B.A., Th.B., M.A., Ph.D., Th.D., Professor Emeritus of New Testament, Fuller Theological Seminary, Pasadena, California.

HARRISON, ROBERT T.
B.A., M.Div., M.A., Assistant Professor of History, Biola University, La Mirada, California.

HARRISON, ROLAND K.
B.D., M.Th., Ph.D., D.D., Bishops Frederick and Heber Wilkinson Professor of Old Testament, Wycliffe College, Toronto, Ontario, Canada.

HARTLEY, JOHN E.
B.A., B.D., M.A., Ph.D., Chair of Department of Biblical Studies and Professor of Old Testament, Graduate School of Theology, Azusa Pacific University, Azusa, California.

HARVEY, DOROTHEA WARD
B.A., B.D., Ph.D., Professor of Religion, Urbana University, Urbana, Ohio.

HASEL, GERHARD F.
M.A., B.D., Ph.D., Professor of Biblical Theology and Dean, Andrews University Theological Seminary, Berrien Springs, Michigan.

HAWTHORNE, GERALD F.
B.A., M.A., Ph.D., Professor of Greek, Wheaton College, Wheaton, Illinois.

HAYDEN, ROY E.
B.A., B.D., Th.M., M.A., Ph.D., Professor of Biblical Literature and Chairman, Department of Theology, Oral Roberts University, Tulsa, Oklahoma.

HEIDEL, WILLIAM ARTHUR*
M.A., Ph.D., Research Professor of Greek Language and Literature, Wesleyan University, Middletown, Connecticut.

HELMBOLD, ANDREW K.
B.A., B.D., Ph.D., Former Professor of Humanities, Tidewater Community College, Portsmouth, Virginia.

HEMER, COLIN J.
M.A., Ph.D., Research Fellow in New Testament History, Tyndale House, Cambridge, England.

HENRY, CARL F. H.
A.B., M.A., Th.D., Ph.D., Lecturer-at-Large, World Vision International.

HERION, GARY
B.A., M.A., Ph.D., Lecturer in Biblical Studies, University of North Carolina, Chapel Hill, North Carolina.

HERR, LARRY G.
B.A., Ph.D., Associate Professor of Religion, Canadian Union College, College Heights, Alberta, Canada.

HIGUCHI, SHINPEI
M.Div., President and Professor of Old Testament, Tokyo Christian College, Tokyo, Japan.

HILL, ANDREW E.
B.A., M.A., M.Div., Ph.D., Assistant Professor of Old Testament Studies, Wheaton College, Wheaton, Illinois.

HIRSCH, FRANK E.*
M.A., President, Charles City College, Charles City, Iowa.

HOCH, CARL B., JR.
B.S., Th.M., Th.D., Professor of New Testament, Grand Rapids Baptist Seminary, Grand Rapids, Michigan.

HOEHNER, HAROLD W.
B.A., Th.M., Th.D., Ph.D., Chairman and Professor of New Testament Literature and Exegesis, Dallas Theological Seminary, Dallas, Texas.

HOFFINE, JAMES E.
B.A., M.A.B.S., M.A., Former Editorial Associate, *ISBE* Revision Project.

HOFFMEIER, JAMES K.
A.A., B.A., M.A., Ph.D., Assistant Professor of Archaeology and Old Testament Studies, Wheaton College, Wheaton, Illinois.

HOLWERDA, DAVID E.
A.B., B.D., D.Th., Professor of New Testament, Calvin Theological Seminary, Grand Rapids, Michigan.

HORSNELL, MALCOLM J. J.
B.A., B.D., Th.M., Ph.D., Associate Professor of Old Testament Interpretation, McMaster Divinity College, Hamilton, Ontario, Canada.

HOVEY, BARRY
B.A., B.D., Th.M., Software Support Representative, Sperry Univac, Blue Bell, Pennsylvania.

HOWARD, DAVID M., JR.
B.S., M.A., A.M., Instructor of Old Testament, Bethel Theological Seminary, St. Paul, Minnesota.

HUBBARD, DAVID A.
B.A., B.D., Th.M., Ph.D., President and Professor of Old Testament, Fuller Theological Seminary, Pasadena, California.

HUGENBERGER, GORDON P.
B.A., M.Div., Adjunct Professor of Old Testament, Gordon-Conwell Theological Seminary, South Hamilton, Massachusetts; Pastor, Lanesville Congregational Church, Gloucester, Massachusetts.



HUGHES, JOHN J.
B.A., M.Div., Freelance Editor and Author in Biblical Studies, Whitefish, Montana.

HUGHES, ROBERT J., III
D.V.M., M.Div., Th.M., Professor of Science and Chairman of the Division of General Studies, Fort Wayne Bible College, Fort Wayne, Indiana.

HUNT, LESLIE
B.A., B.D., M.Th., D.D., Principal Emeritus and Professor of New Testament, Wycliffe College, Toronto, Ontario, Canada.

HURTADO, LARRY W.
B.A., M.A., Ph.D., Associate Professor of Religion, University of Manitoba, Winnipeg, Manitoba, Canada.

HUTCHISON, JOHN*
M.A., Rector of the High School, Glasgow, Scotland.

IRVIN, DOROTHY
B.A., M.A., D.Theol., Consultant and Lecturer in Scripture and Women's Studies, Durham, North Carolina.

JEWETT, PAUL K.
B.A., Th.B., Th.M., Ph.D., Professor of Systematic Theology, Fuller Theological Seminary, Pasadena, California.

JOHNSTON, ROBERT H.
B.S., M.A., Ph.D., Dean and Professor, College of Fine and Applied Arts, Rochester Institute of Technology, Rochester, New York.

JUDGE, EDWIN A.
M.A., M.A., Professor of History, Macquarie University, North Ryde, New South Wales, Australia.

JUNG, KURT GERHARD
Th.D., U.S. Army Chaplain, Berlin, Germany.

KAUTZ, JAMES R., III
B.A., B.D., Ph.D., Planning Analyst, Division of Policy, Planning and Evaluation, Department of Health and Human Resources, Baton Rouge, Louisiana.

KELLY, DAVID J.
B.A., M.Div., Th.M., Ph.D., Minister, Aldersgate and Lefler United Methodist Churches, South Omaha Parish, Omaha, Nebraska.

KEOWN, GERALD L.
B.S., M.Div., Ph.D., Assistant Professor of Old Testament Interpretation, Southern Baptist Theological Seminary, Louisville, Kentucky.

KILMER, ANNE D.
B.A., Ph.D., Professor of Assyriology and Ancient Near Eastern History and Literature, University of California, Berkeley, California.

KITCHEN, KENNETH A.
B.A., Ph.D., Reader in Egyptian and Coptic, School of Archaeology and Oriental Studies, University of Liverpool, England.

KLOOSTER, FRED H.
A.B., B.D., Th.M., Th.D., Professor of Systematic Theology, Calvin Theological Seminary, Grand Rapids, Michigan.

KNAPP, GARY L.
B.A., M.Div., Th.M., Editorial Associate, *ISBE* Revision Project.

KNUTSON, F. BRENT
B.S., M.A., Ph.D., Associate Professor of Philosophy and Religion, University of Arkansas, Little Rock, Arkansas.

KROEGER, CATHERINE CLARK
A.B., M.A., Co-Director, North Central Center for Christian Studies, St. Paul, Minnesota.

KROEGER, RICHARD CLARK
B.A., M.Div., S.T.M., Co-Director, North Central Center for Christian Studies, St. Paul, Minnesota.

KROEZE, GEORGE
B.A., B.D., Ph.D., Professor of Biblical Studies, Reformed Bible College, Grand Rapids, Michigan.

LAARMAN, EDWARD
B.A., B.D., Ph.D., Minister of Education and Witnessing, Calvin Christian Reformed Church, Grand Rapids, Michigan.

LADD, GEORGE ELDON
Th.B., B.D., Ph.D., Late Professor of New Testament Exegesis and Theology, Fuller Theological Seminary, Pasadena, California.

LASOR, WILLIAM SANFORD
A.B., A.M., Th.B., Th.M., Ph.D., Th.D., Emeritus Professor of Old Testament, Fuller Theological Seminary, Pasadena, California.

LEE, GARY A.
B.A., M.T.S., Editor, Reference Books, William B. Eerdmans Publishing Company.

LEES, JOHN A.*
Pastor, St. James' Congregational Church, Hamilton, Scotland.

LEWIS, ARTHUR H.
B.A., M.A., B.D., Ph.D., Professor of Old Testament, Bethel College, St. Paul, Minnesota.

LIEFELD, WALTER L.
Th.B., M.A., Ph.D., Professor of New Testament, Trinity Evangelical Divinity School, Deerfield, Illinois.

LINTON, CALVIN D.
A.B., M.A., Ph.D., Professor Emeritus of English and Dean Emeritus, Columbian College of Arts and Sciences, The George Washington University, Washington, D.C.

LIVERANI, MARIO
Professor of Ancient Oriental History, University of Rome, Italy.

LONGENECKER, RICHARD N.
B.A., M.A., Ph.D., Ramsay Armitage Professor of New Testament, Wycliffe College, University of Toronto, Toronto, Ontario, Canada.

LUERING, HEINRICH LUDWIG EMIL*
Ph.D., Professor of Dogmatic Theology and New Testament Greek, Martin Theological Seminary of the Methodist Episcopal Church, Frankfurt-am-Main, Germany.

MAAHS, KENNETH H.
B.A., M.Div., Th.M., Ph.D., Professor of Religion, Eastern College, Saint Davids, Pennsylvania.

MACK, EDWARD*
Ph.D., McCormick Professor of Old Testament Interpretation, Union Theological Seminary, Richmond, Virginia.

MACLEOD, MURDO A.
M.A., Director and General Secretary, Christian Witness to Israel, Kent, England.

MADVIG, DONALD H.
A.B., B.D., Th.M., M.A., Ph.D., Senior Pastor, Ravenswood Evangelical Covenant Church, Chicago, Illinois.

MALONY, H. NEWTON
A.B., M.Div., M.A., Ph.D., Professor of Psychology, Fuller Theological Seminary, Pasadena, California.

MARTIN, BRICE L.
B.A., M.Div., Th.M., Ph.D., Pastor, Bedford Park Chapel, Toronto, Ontario, Canada.

MARTIN, RALPH P.
B.A., M.A., Ph.D., Professor of New Testament and Director of the Graduate Studies Program, Fuller Theological Seminary, Pasadena, California.

MASTERMAN, ERNEST W. G.*
M.D., F.R.C.S., F.R.G.S., Honorary Secretary of the Palestine Exploration Fund, London, England.

MCCOMISKEY, THOMAS EDWARD
B.A., M.Div., Th.M., M.A., Ph.D., Professor of Old Testament and Semitic Languages, Trinity Evangelical Divinity School, Deerfield, Illinois.

MCCREADY, WAYNE O.
B.A., M.Rel., M.A., Ph.D., Associate Professor of Religious Studies, University of Calgary, Calgary, Alberta, Canada.

MCKENNA, JOHN
A.B., M.Div., Teaching Fellow in Hebrew, Adjunct Faculty, Fuller Theological Seminary, Pasadena, California.

MCKIM, DONALD K.
B.A., M.Div., Ph.D., Associate Professor of Theology, University of Dubuque Theological Seminary, Dubuque, Iowa.

MEYE, ROBERT P.
B.A., B.D., Th.M., D.Th., Dean and Professor of New Testament Interpretation, Fuller Theological Seminary, Pasadena, California.

MEYER, MARVIN W.
A.B., M.Div., Ph.D., Assistant Professor of Religion, Chapman College, Orange, California.

MICHAELS, J. RAMSEY
B.A., B.D., Th.M., Th.D., Professor of Religious Studies, Southwest Missouri State University, Springfield, Missouri.

MILLARD, ALAN RALPH
M.A., M.Phil., Reader in Hebrew and Ancient Semitic Languages, University of Liverpool, England.

MILLER, PATRICK D., JR.
A.B., B.D., Ph.D., Professor of Old Testament Theology, Princeton Theological Seminary, Princeton, New Jersey.

MONTGOMERY, JOHN WARWICK
B.A., B.D., B.L.S., LL.B., M.A., Th.M., M.Phil., Ph.D., D.Théol., Barrister at Law, Dean and Professor of Jurisprudence, The Simon Greenleaf School of Law, Anaheim, California and Strasbourg, France.

MORRIS, LEON
B.Sc., M.Sc., M.Th., Ph.D., Former Principal, Ridley College, Melbourne, Australia.

MOULDER, WILLIAM J.
B.A., M.Div., Ph.D., Associate Professor of Bible, Trinity College, Deerfield, Illinois.

MOUNCE, ROBERT H.
B.A., B.D., Th.M., Ph.D., President, Whitworth College, Spokane, Washington.

MOUNCE, WILLIAM D.
B.A., M.A., Ph.D., Associate Professor of New Testament, Azusa Pacific University, Azusa, California.

MOYER, JAMES C.
A.B., M.Div., M.A., Ph.D., Professor and Head of the Department of Religious Studies, Southwest Missouri State University, Springfield, Missouri.

NORTH, ROBERT
B.A., M.A., S.S.D., Editor, *Elenchus Bibliographicus Biblicus;* Professor of Archeology, Pontificio Istituto Biblico, Rome, Italy.

OMANSON, ROGER L.
B.A., M.Div., Ph.D., Assistant Professor of New Testament Interpretation, Southern Baptist Theological Seminary, Louisville, Kentucky.

OPPERWALL, NOLA J.
A.B., M.Div., Editorial Associate, *ISBE* Revision Project.

ORR, JAMES*
M.A., D.D., Professor of Apologetics and Theology, Theological College of United Free Church, Glasgow, Scotland.

PACKER, JAMES I.
M.A., D.Phil., Professor of Historical and Systematic Theology, Regent College, Vancouver, British Columbia, Canada.

PALMER, EDWIN H.
B.A., Th.B., Th.D., Late Executive Secreatry, NIV Committee on Bible Translation; General Editor, NIV Study Bible.

PATCH, JAMES A.*
B.S., Professor of Chemistry, American University of Beirut.

PATTEN, B. REBECCA
B.S., B.A., M.A., Ph.D., Professor of New Testament and Academic Dean, Patten College, Oakland, California.

PATTEN, PRISCILLA CARLA
B.S., B.A., M.A., Ph.D., President and Professor of New Testament, Patten College, Oakland, California.

PAYNE, DAVID F.
B.A., M.A., Academic Registrar, London Bible College, Northwood, Middlesex, England.

PECOTA, DANIEL B.
B.A., M.Div., Th.M., D.Min., Professor of Greek and Theology, Northwest College, Kirkland, Washington.

PERKIN, HAZEL W.
B.A., M.A., Principal, St. Clement's School, Toronto, Ontario, Canada.

PICCIRILLO, MICHELE
S.Th.L., S.S.L., Dottore in Lettere e Filosophia, Professor of Biblical Geography and History, Director of the Archaeological Museum, Franciscan Biblical Institute, Jerusalem, Israel.

CONTRIBUTORS

PINCHES, CHARLES
B.A., Ph.D., Assistant Professor of Philosophy, University of Central Arkansas, Conway, Arkansas.

PIPER, OTTO A.
Ph.D., Late Professor of New Testament, Princeton Theological Seminary, Princeton, New Jersey.

POLLARD, EDWARD BAGBY*
M.A., D.D., Ph.D., Professor of Homiletics, Crozer Theological Seminary, Chester, Pennsylvania.

PRATICO, GARY
B.A., M.Div., Th.D., Assistant Professor of Old Testament, Gordon-Conwell Theological Seminary, South Hamilton, Massachusetts; Assistant Curator of the Semitic Museum of Harvard University, Cambridge, Massachusetts.

PRICE, JAMES R.
A.B., M.Div., A.M., Late Pastor, Faith United Methodist Church, Joliet, Illinois.

RAINEY, ANSON F.
B.A., M.A., B.D., M.Th., Ph.D., Professor of Ancient Near Eastern Cultures and Semitic Languages, Tel Aviv University, Tel Aviv, Israel.

RASMUSSEN, CARL
B.A., B.D., Th.M., Th.D., Associate Professor of Old Testament, Bethel College, St. Paul, Minnesota.

REICKE, BO
D.Th., Professor Emeritus of New Testament, University of Basel, Switzerland.

REID, W. STANFORD
B.A., M.A., Th.B., Th.M., Th.D., Emeritus Professor of History, University of Guelph, Guelph, Ontario, Canada.

RENWICK, A. M.
M.A., B.D., D.L.H., D.D., Late Professor of Church History, Free Church of Scotland College, Edinburgh, Scotland.

RIDDERBOS, NICHOLAS H.
D.D., Late Professor of Old Testament, The Free University, Amsterdam, Netherlands.

SAARISALO, AAPELI A.
Th.D., Emeritus Professor of Oriental Literature, Helsinki University, Helsinki, Finland.

SALLER, SYLVESTER
Sacrae Theologiae Lector, Late Professor of Archaeology, Franciscan Biblical Institute, Jerusalem, Israel.

SANDERSON, JUDITH E.
B.A., Zertifikat und Diplom, M.Div., M.A., M.A., Ph.D., Assistant Professor of Old Testament, Princeton Theological Seminary, Princeton, New Jersey.

SAYCE, ARCHIBALD HENRY*
D.D., Litt.D., LL.D., Professor of Assyriology, Oxford University, England.

SCHOVILLE, KEITH N.
B.A., M.A., Ph.D., Professor of Hebrew and Semitic Studies, University of Wisconsin, Madison, Wisconsin.

SCHREINER, THOMAS
B.S., M.Div., Th.M., Ph.D., Assistant Professor of New Testament, Azusa Pacific University, Azusa, California.

SCHULTZ, SAMUEL J.
A.B., B.D., S.T.M., Th.D., Emeritus Professor of Biblical Studies and Theology, Wheaton College and Graduate School, Wheaton, Illinois.

SCOTT, JULIUS J., JR.
A.B., B.D., Ph.D., Professor of Biblical and Historical Studies, Wheaton College Graduate School, Wheaton, Illinois.

SEALE, MORRIS S.
B.A., Ph.D., Former Professor, Near East School of Theology, Beirut, Lebanon.

SHEA, WILLIAM H.
B.A., Ph.D., Professor and Chairman, Department of Old Testament, Andrews University Theological Seminary, Berrien Springs, Michigan.

SHERIFFS, ROBERT J. A.
B.A., B.D., Ph.D., Former Lecturer in Old Testament, Rhodes University, Grahamstown, Cape Province, South Africa.

SHERWIN-WHITE, A. N.
M.A., Reader in Ancient History (Retired), Oxford University; Fellow and Tutor in Ancient History, St. John's College, Oxford, England.

SMICK, ELMER
B.A., Th.B., S.T.M., Ph.D., Professor of Old Testament, Gordon-Conwell Theological Seminary, South Hamilton, Massachusetts.

SMITH, EDGAR W., JR.
B.A., B.D., Ph.D., Project Editor, *ISBE* Revision.

SMITH, GARY V.
B.A., M.A., Ph.D., Associate Professor of Old Testament, Bethel Theological Seminary, St. Paul, Minnesota.

SMITH, ROBERT HOUSTON
B.A., B.D., Ph.D., Fox Professor of Religion and Chairman, Department of Religious Studies, The College of Wooster, Wooster, Ohio.

SODERLUND, SVEN K.
B.A., M.A., M.C.S., Ph.D., Assistant Professor of Biblical Studies, Regent College, Vancouver, British Columbia, Canada.

SPARKS, IRVING ALAN
A.B., B.D., S.T.M., Ph.D., Professor and Chairperson, Department of Religious Studies, San Diego State University, San Diego, California.

STEIN, ROBERT H.
B.A., B.D., S.T.M., Ph.D., Professor of New Testament, Bethel Theological Seminary, St. Paul, Minnesota.

STEWART, ROY A.
M.A., B.D., M.Litt., Retired Church of Scotland Minister and Biblical Scholar, Edinburgh, Scotland.

STRANGE, JAMES F.
B.A., M.Div., Ph.D., Professor of Religious Studies and Dean of the College of Arts and Letters, University of South Florida, Tampa, Florida.

STRATTON-PORTER, GENE*
Author and Illustrator; Special Writer on Birds and Nature.

STUART, DOUGLAS
B.A., Ph.D., Professor of Old Testament, Gordon-Conwell Theological Seminary, South Hamilton, Massachusetts.

STUART, STREETER S., JR.
B.S., M.Div., M.A., S.T.M., M.A., Ph.D., Professor of Biblical Studies, United Wesleyan College, Allentown, Pennsylvania.

SUNDSMO, ALLEN
B.A., M.A., Bookstore Manager, William B. Eerdmans Publishing Company, Grand Rapids, Michigan.

THOMPSON, JOHN ALEXANDER
A.B., M.Div., Th.M., Ph.D., Research Consultant, Translations Department, American Bible Society.

THOMPSON, JOHN ARTHUR
B.A., B.Ed., M.Sc., M.A., Ph.D., B.D., Former Reader, Department of Middle Eastern Studies, University of Melbourne, Australia.

THOMSON, J. E. H.*
M.A., D.D., Missionary to the Jews in Palestine.

TIPPETT, ALAN R.
L.Th., M.A., Ph.D., Research Fellow, St. Mark's Library, Canberra, Australia.

TREVER, JOHN C.
B.D., Ph.D., Director, Dead Sea Scrolls Project, School of Theology at Claremont, Claremont, California.

TURNER, GEORGE A.
A.B., B.D., S.T.B., S.T.M., Ph.D., Professor Emeritus of Biblical Literature, Asbury Theological Seminary, Wilmore, Kentucky.

VAN BROEKHOVEN, HAROLD, JR.
B.A., M.A., M.Div., Th.M., Pastor, Tabernacle Baptist Church, Hope, Rhode Island; Faculty, Biblical Studies, Barrington College, Barrington, Rhode Island.

VANELDEREN, BASTIAAN
A.B., B.D., M.A., Th.D., Professor of New Testament, The Free University, Amsterdam, Netherlands.

VAN SELMS, ADRIANUS
D.Th., Emeritus Professor of Semitic Languages, University of Pretoria, South Africa.

VERHEY, ALLEN D.
B.A., B.D., Ph.D., Associate Professor of Religion, Hope College, Holland, Michigan.

VOS, CLARENCE J.
A.B., Th.B., Th.M., Th.D., Professor of Religion and Theology, Calvin College, Grand Rapids, Michigan.

VOS, GEERHARDUS*
D.D., Ph.D., Professor of Biblical Theology, Princeton Theological Seminary, Princeton, New Jersey.

VOS, HOWARD F.
B.A., Th.M., Th.D., M.A., Ph.D., Professor of History and Archaeology, The King's College, Briarcliff Manor, New York.

VRIEND, JOHN
B.Th., M.A., Freelance Religious Writer and Translator, Grand Rapids, Michigan.

WALHOUT, EDWIN
Th.B., Th.M., D.Min., Minister, Christian Reformed Church; Freelance Writer, Grand Rapids, Michigan.

WALLACE, DAVID H.
B.A., B.D., Th.M., Ph.D., Retired Professor of Biblical Theology, Newport Beach, California.

WALLACE, RONALD STEWART
B.S., M.A., Ph.D., Professor Emeritus of Biblical Theology, Columbia Theological Seminary, Decatur, Georgia.

WARING, DAWN E.
B.S., M.A., Ph.D., Adjunct Faculty and Interim Director for Women's Concerns, Fuller Theological Seminary, Pasadena, California.

WATTS, JOHN D. W.
B.A., Th.M., Ph.D., Professor of Old Testament Interpretation, Southern Baptist Theological Seminary, Louisville, Kentucky.

WEAD, DAVID W.
A.B., B.Th., B.D., Th.D., Minister, First Christian Church, Nashville, Tennessee.

WEBB, ROBERT ALEXANDER*
B.A., D.D., LL.D., Professor of Apologetics and Systematic Theology, Louisville Presbyterian Theological Seminary, Louisville, Kentucky.

WEBSTER, JOHN HUNTER*
M.A., D.D., Professor of Greek Exegesis and New Testament Literature, Xenia Theological Seminary, St. Louis, Missouri.

WEDDLE, FOREST
A.B., M.S., Ph.D., Late Professor of Biblical Archaeology and History, Fort Wayne Bible College, Fort Wayne, Indiana.

WELCH, E. DOUGLAS
B.S., M.Div., M.A., Ph.D., Scholar in Biblical and Ancient Near Eastern Studies.

WENHAM, GORDON J.
M.A., Ph.D., Senior Lecturer in Religious Studies, The College of Saint Paul and Saint Mary, Cheltenham, Gloucester, England.

WESTERHOLM, STEPHEN
M.A., D.Th., Assistant Professor of Religious Studies, McMaster University, Hamilton, Ontario, Canada.

WIEAND, DAVID JOHN
B.A., M.A., B.D., Ph.D., Emeritus Professor of Biblical Literature, Bethany Theological Seminary, Oak Brook, Illinois.

WILSON, GERALD H.
B.A., M.A., M.Div., M.A., Ph.D., Assistant Professor of Religion, University of Georgia, Athens, Georgia.

WILSON, MARVIN R.
B.A., M.Div., M.A., Ph.D., Ockenga Professor of Biblical Studies, Gordon College, Wenham, Massachusetts.

WILSON, R. MCL.
M.A., B.D., Ph.D., D.D., F.B.A., Emeritus Professor of Biblical Criticism, St. Mary's College, University of St. Andrews, Scotland.

WISEMAN, DONALD J.
M.A., D.Lit., F.B.A., Emeritus Professor of Assyriology, University of London, England; Chairman and Former Director, British School of Archaeology in Iraq.

WOLF, HERBERT M.
B.A., Th.M., Ph.D., Associate Professor of Old Testament, Wheaton Graduate School, Wheaton, Illinois.

WOOD, ARTHUR SKEVINGTON
B.A., Ph.D., Principal Emeritus, Cliff College, Derbyshire, England.

WYATT, ROBERT J.
B.A., M.A., Ph.D., Former Editorial Associate, *ISBE* Revision Project; Instructor in Biblical Studies, Bethel College, St. Paul, Minnesota.

WYPER, GLENN
B.A., B.D., Th.M., Registrar and Chairman of the Department of Biblical Studies, Ontario Bible College, Willowdale, Ontario, Canada.

YAMAUCHI, EDWIN M.
B.A., M.A., Ph.D., Professor of History, Miami University, Oxford, Ohio.

YOUNG, FREDERICK E.
A.B., B.D., Ph.D., Dean and Professor of Old Testament, Central Baptist Theological Seminary, Kansas City, Kansas.

YOUNGBLOOD, RONALD F.
B.A., B.D., Ph.D., Professor of Old Testament and Hebrew, Bethel Theological Seminary, West Campus, San Diego, California.

# PUBLISHERS' NOTES TO VOLUME THREE

Like Volume II, Volume III includes the Abbreviations (with a few more additions), the Transliteration Scheme, and the Pronunciation Key, as well as its own list of Contributors.

The publishers' staff has seen further changes. While the work of some of those mentioned in Volumes I and II — Smith, Lee, Prus, Beversluis, and Bauer — has continued, Nola J. Opperwall and Gary L. Knapp have replaced Robert J. Wyatt and James E. Hoffine as Editorial Associates; Catherine Rollins-Page has done the work with photographs and the proofreading formerly done by Kimberly Adams; and Genevieve Barney has done much of the typesetting of the latter stages of the volume.

THE PUBLISHERS

# Abbreviations

## GENERAL

| | |
|---|---|
| A | Codex Alexandrinus (*See* Text and MSS of the NT I.B) |
| abbr. | abbreviated, abbreviation |
| act. | active |
| Akk. | Akkadian |
| Amer. Tr. | J. M. P. Smith and E. J. Goodspeed, *The Complete Bible: An American Translation* |
| Am.Tab. | el-Amarna Letters (*See* Amarna Tablets) |
| Apoc. | Apocrypha |
| Apost. Const. | Apostolic Constitutions |
| Aq. | Aquila's Greek version of the OT (*See* Septuagint) |
| Arab. | Arabic |
| Aram. | Aramaic |
| art. | article |
| Assyr. | Assyrian |
| ASV | American Standard Version |
| AT | Altes (or Ancien) Testament |
| AV | Authorized (King James) Version |
| b. | born |
| B | Codex Vaticanus (*See* Text and MSS of the NT I.B) |
| Bab. | Babylonian |
| bk. | book |
| Boh. | Bohairic (dialect of Coptic) |
| *ca.* | *circa,* about |
| Can. | Canaanite |
| cent., cents. | century, centuries |
| CG | Coptic Gnostic (*See* Nag Hammadi Literature) |
| ch., chs. | chapter(s) |
| Chald. | Chaldean, Chaldaic |
| col., cols. | column(s) |
| comm., comms. | commentary, commentaries |
| Copt. | Coptic |
| d. | died |
| D | Deuteronomist (*See* Criticism II.D.4); also Codex Bezae (*See* Text and MSS of the NT I.B) |
| diss. | dissertation |
| DSS | Dead Sea Scrolls |
| E | Elohist (*See* Criticism II.D.4); east |
| E.B. | Early Bronze (Age) |
| ed., eds. | editor, edition, edited (by), editors, editions |
| Egyp. | Egyptian |
| E.I. | Early Iron (Age) |
| *Einl.* | *Einleitung* (Introduction) |
| Eng. tr. | English translation |
| ERV | English Revised Version (1881-1885) |
| esp. | especially |
| *et al.* | and others |
| Eth. | Ethiopic, Ethiopian |
| f., ff. | following |
| fem. | feminine |
| fig. | figuratively |
| ft. | foot, feet |
| gal., gals. | gallon(s) |
| gen. | genitive |
| Ger. | German |
| Gk. | Greek |
| gm. | gram(s) |
| H | Law of Holiness (Lev. 17–26; *See* Criticism II.D.5) |
| ha. | hectare(s) |
| Heb. | Hebrew |
| Hist. | History |
| Hitt. | Hittite |
| Hom. | Homily |
| impf. | imperfect (tense) |
| in. | inch(es) |
| *in loc.* | at/on this passage |
| inscr. | inscription |
| intrans. | intransitive |
| intro., intros. | introduction(s) |
| J | Yahwist (*See* Criticism II.D.4) |
| JB | Jerusalem Bible |
| *K* | *kethibh* (*See* Text and MSS of the OT) |
| km. | kilometer(s) |
| l. | liter(s) |
| L | Lukan source (*See* Gospels, Synoptic V) |
| Lat. | Latin |
| L.B. | Late Bronze (Age) |
| lit. | literally |
| *loc. cit.* | in the place cited |
| LXX | Septuagint |
| m. | meter(s) |
| M | Matthaean source (*See* Gospels, Synoptic V) |
| masc. | masculine |
| M.B. | Middle Bronze (Age) |
| mg. | margin |
| mi. | mile(s) |
| mid. | middle voice |

| | |
|---|---|
| Midr. | Midrash |
| Mish. | Mishnah (*See* TALMUD I) |
| Moff. | J. Moffatt, *A New Translation of the Bible* (1926) |
| MS, MSS | manuscript(s) |
| MT | Mas(s)oretic Text (*See* TEXT AND MSS OF THE OT) |
| N | north |
| n., nn. | note(s) |
| NAB | New American Bible |
| NASB | New American Standard Bible |
| n.d. | no date |
| NEB | New English Bible |
| neut. | neuter |
| N.F. | *Neue Folge* (New Series) |
| NIV | New International Version |
| NJV | New Jewish Version |
| no., nos. | number(s) |
| N.S. | New Series |
| NT | New (Neues, Nouveau) Testament |
| Onk. | Onkelos (Targum) |
| *op. cit.* | in the work quoted |
| OT | Old Testament |
| Oxy. P. | Oxyrhynchus papyrus |
| *p* | papyrus (used only with superscript number of the papyrus) |
| P | Priestly Code (*See* CRITICISM II.D.5) |
| par. | (and) parallel passage(s) |
| para. | paragraph |
| part. | participle |
| pass. | passive |
| Pent. | Pentateuch |
| Pers. | Persian |
| Pesh. | Peshito, Peshitta (*See* VERSIONS) |
| pf. | perfect (tense) |
| Phoen. | Phoenician |
| pl. | plural |
| prob. | probably |
| pt., pts. | part(s) |
| Q | *Quelle* (*See* GOSPELS, SYNOPTIC V) |
| *Q* | *qere* (*See* TEXT AND MSS OF THE OT) |
| repr. | reprinted |
| rev. | revised (by) |
| RSV | Revised Standard Version |
| RV | Revised Version (ERV or ASV) |
| S | south |
| Sah. | Sahidic (dialect of Coptic) |
| Sam. | Samaritan |
| Sem. | Semitic |
| sing. | singular |
| sq. | square |
| subst. | substantive |
| Sum. | Sumerian |
| supp. | supplement(ary) |
| *s.v.* | *sub voce* (*vocibus*), under the word(s) |
| Symm. | Symmachus' Greek version of the OT (*See* SEPTUAGINT) |
| Syr. | Syriac |
| Talm. | Talmud |
| T.B. | Babylonian Talmud |
| Tg., Tgs. | Targum(s) |
| Th. | Theodotion's revision of the LXX (*See* SEPTUAGINT) |
| T.P. | Palestinian (Jerusalem) Talmud |
| TR | Textus Receptus (*See* TEXT AND MSS OF THE NT IV) |
| tr. | translation, translated (by) |
| trans. | transitive |
| Ugar. | Ugaritic |
| v., vv. | verse(s) |
| *v.* | *versus* |
| var. | variant |
| vb., vbs. | verb(s) |
| viz. | namely |
| vol., vols. | volume(s) |
| Vulg. | Vulgate (*See* VERSIONS) |
| W | west |
| yd., yds. | yard(s) |

## SYMBOLS

| | |
|---|---|
| ℵ | Codex Sinaiticus (*See* TEXT AND MSS OF THE NT I.B) |
| < | derived from (etymological) |
| = | is equivalent to |
| * | theoretical or unidentified form |
| § | section |

## PUBLICATIONS

| | |
|---|---|
| *AASOR* | *Annual of the American Schools of Oriental Research* |
| *AB* | *Anchor Bible* |
| *ADAJ* | *Annual of the Department of Antiquities of Jordan* |
| *AfO* | *Archiv für Orientforschung* |
| *AJSL* | *American Journal of Semitic Languages and Literatures* |
| Alf. | Henry Alford, *Greek Testament* (4 vols., 1857-1861) |
| *ANEP* | J. B. Pritchard, ed., *The Ancient Near East in Pictures* (1954; 2nd ed. 1969) |
| *ANET* | J. B. Pritchard, ed., *Ancient Near Eastern Texts Relating to the Old Testament* (1950; 3rd ed. 1969) |
| *ANT* | M. R. James, *The Apocryphal New Testament* (1924; repr. 1953) |
| *AOTS* | D. W. Thomas, ed., *Archaeology and Old Testament Study* (1967) |
| *AP* | W. F. Albright, *The Archaeology of Palestine* (1949; rev. 1960) |
| *APC* | L. Morris, *Apostolic Preaching of the Cross* (3rd ed. 1965) |
| *APOT* | R. H. Charles, ed., *The Apocrypha and Pseudepigrapha of the Old Testament* (2 vols., 1913; repr. 1963) |
| *ARAB* | D. D. Luckenbill, ed., *Ancient Records of Assyria and Babylonia* (2 vols., 1926-1927) |
| *ARI* | W. F. Albright, *Archaeology and the Religion of Israel* (4th ed. 1956) |
| *ARM* | *Archives Royales de Mari* (1941–) |
| *ATD* | *Das Alte Testament Deutsch* |
| *ATR* | *Anglican Theological Review* |
| *BA* | *The Biblical Archaeologist* |
| *BANE* | G. E. Wright, ed., *The Bible and the Ancient Near East: Essays in Honor of William Foxwell Albright* (1961; repr. 1965, 1979) |
| *BASOR* | *Bulletin of the American Schools of Oriental Research* |
| Bauer | W. Bauer, *A Greek-English Lexicon of the New Testament,* tr. W. F. Arndt and F. W. Gingrich (1957; rev. ed. |

[tr. F. W. Gingrich and F. W. Danker from 5th Ger. ed.] 1979)

*BC* — F. J. Foakes Jackson and K. Lake, eds., *The Beginnings of Christianity* (5 vols., 1920-1933)

BDB — F. Brown, S. R. Driver, and C. A. Briggs, *Hebrew and English Lexicon of the Old Testament* (1907)

BDF — F. Blass and A. Debrunner, *A Greek Grammar of the New Testament*, tr. and rev. R. W. Funk (1961)

*BDTh* — *Baker's Dictionary of Theology* (1960)

*BH* — R. Kittel, ed., *Biblia Hebraica* (3rd ed. 1937)

*BHS* — K. Elliger and W. Rudolph, eds., *Biblia Hebraica Stuttgartensia* (1967-1977)

*BhHW* — *Biblisch-historisches Handwörterbuch* (1962–)

*BHI* — J. Bright, *A History of Israel* (1959; 2nd ed. 1972; 3rd ed. 1981)

*Bibl.* — *Biblica*

*BJRL* — *Bulletin of the John Rylands Library*

*BKAT* — *Biblischer Kommentar, Altes Testament*

Bousset-Gressmann — W. Bousset, *Die Religion des Judentums im späthellenistischen Zeitalter*, rev. H. Gressmann (*HNT*, 21, 1926)

*BZ* — *Biblische Zeitschrift*

*BZAW* — *Beihefte zur Zeitschrift für die alttestamentliche Wissenschaft*

*BZNW* — *Beihefte zur Zeitschrift für die neutestamentliche Wissenschaft*

*CAD* — I. J. Gelb, *et al.*, eds., *Assyrian Dictionary of the Oriental Institute of the University of Chicago* (1956–)

*CAH* — *Cambridge Ancient History* (12 vols., rev. ed. 1962; 1970)

*CBC* — *Cambridge Bible Commentary on the New English Bible*

*CBP* — W. M. Ramsay, *Cities and Bishoprics of Phrygia* (1895-1897)

*CBQ* — *Catholic Biblical Quarterly*

*CBSC* — *Cambridge Bible for Schools and Colleges*

*CCK* — D. J. Wiseman, *Chronicles of Chaldaean Kings* (1956)

*CD* — K. Barth, *Church Dogmatics* (Eng. tr., 4 vols., 1936-1962)

CD — See Biblical and Extrabiblical Literature: Dead Sea Scrolls

*CERP* — A. H. M. Jones, *Cities of the Eastern Roman Provinces* (1937)

*CG* — P. Kahle, *The Cairo Geniza* (2nd ed. 1959)

*CGT* — *Cambridge Greek Testament* (20 vols., 1881-1933)

*CHAL* — W. L. Holladay, *A Concise Hebrew and Aramaic Lexicon of the Old Testament* (1971)

*CIG* — *Corpus Inscriptionum Graecarum* (1825-1859; index 1877)

*CIL* — *Corpus Inscriptionum Latinarum* (1862–)

*ConNT* — *Coniectanea Neotestamentica*

*CRE* — W. M. Ramsay, *The Church in the Roman Empire Before A.D. 170* (1903)

*DBSup.* — L. Pirot, *et al.*, eds., *Dictionnaire de la Bible: Supplement* (1928–)

*DCG* — J. Hastings, *Dictionary of Christ and the Gospels* (2 vols., 1906, 1908)

Deiss.*LAE* — G. A. Deissmann, *Light from the Ancient East* (Eng. tr., 2nd ed. 1927 [from German 4th ed.]; repr. 1978)

Dessau — H. Dessau, ed., *Inscriptiones Latinae Selectae* (3 vols., 2nd ed. 1954-1955)

*DJD* — *Discoveries in the Judean Desert*

*DNTT* — C. Brown, ed., *Dictionary of New Testament Theology* (3 vols., Eng. tr. 1975-1978)

*DOTT* — D. W. Thomas, ed., *Documents from Old Testament Times* (1958)

*DTC* — *Dictionnaire de Théologie Catholique* (15 vols., 1903-1950)

*EAEHL* — M. Avi-Yonah and E. Stern, eds., *Encyclopedia of Archaeological Excavations in the Holy Land* (4 vols., Eng. tr. 1975-1978)

*EB* — T. K. Cheyne and J. S. Black, eds., *Encyclopaedia Biblica* (4 vols., 1899)

*Enc.Brit.* — *Encyclopaedia Britannica*

*EQ* — *Evangelical Quarterly*

*ERE* — J. Hastings, *Encyclopaedia of Religion and Ethics* (12 vols., 1908-1926)

*EtB* — *Études Bibliques*

*EvTh* — *Evangelische Theologie*

*Expos.* — *The Expositor*

*Expos.B.* — *The Expositor's Bible* (3rd ed. 1903; rev. 1956)

*Expos.G.T.* — *The Expositor's Greek Testament*

*Expos.T.* — *Expository Times*

*FRLANT* — *Forschungen zur Religion und Literatur des Alten und Neuen Testaments*

*FSAC* — W. F. Albright, *From the Stone Age to Christianity* (2nd ed. 1957)

*GAB* — L. H. Grollenberg, *Atlas of the Bible* (1956)

*GB* — D. Baly, *Geography of the Bible* (1957; 2nd ed. 1974)

*GJV* — E. Schürer, *Geschichte des jüdischen Volkes im Zeitalter Jesu Christi* (3 vols., 4th ed. 1901-1909) (Converted to *HJP* when possible; but Eng. tr. not complete)

GKC — W. Gesenius, E. Kautzsch, and A. E. Cowley, *Gesenius' Hebrew Grammar* (2nd ed. 1910)

*GP* — F.-M. Abel, *Géographie de la Palestine* (2 vols., 2nd ed. 1933-1938)

*GTTOT* — J. Simons, *Geographical and Topographical Texts of the Old Testament* (1959)

*HAT* — *Handbuch zum Alten Testament*

*HBD* — M. S. Miller and J. L. Miller, eds., *Harper's Bible Dictionary* (1952; 2nd ed. 1961; 8th ed. [rev.] 1973)

*HDB* — J. Hastings, ed., *Dictionary of the Bible* (4 vols., 1898-1902, extra vol., 1904; rev. one-vol. ed. 1963)

*HGHL* — G. A. Smith, *Historical Geography of the Holy Land* (rev. ed. 1932)

*HibJ* — *The Hibbert Journal*

*HJP* — E. Schürer, *A History of the Jewish People in the Time of Jesus Christ* (Eng. tr. [of Ger. *3rd* ed.] 1892-1901)

*HJP*² — E. Schürer, *The History of the Jewish People in the Age of Jesus Christ*, ed. G. Vermes and F. Millar (Eng. tr. and rev. 1973–)

*HNT* — *Handbuch zum Neuen Testament*

*HNTC* — *Harper's New Testament Commentaries = Black's New Testament Commentaries*

ABBREVIATIONS

*HNTT* R. H. Pfeiffer, *A History of New Testament Times with an Introduction to the Apocrypha* (1949)
HR E. Hatch and H. A. Redpath, *Concordance to the Septuagint* (1897)
H-S E. Hennecke and W. Schneemelcher, eds., *New Testament Apocrypha* (2 vols., Eng. tr. 1963, 1965)
*HST* R. Bultmann, *History of the Synoptic Tradition* (Eng. tr., 2nd ed. 1968)
*HTK* *Herders Theologischer Kommentar zum Neuen Testament*
*HTR* *Harvard Theological Review*
*HUCA* *Hebrew Union College Annual*
*IB* *Interpreter's Bible* (12 vols., 1952-1957)
*ICC* *International Critical Commentary*
*IDB* *Interpreter's Dictionary of the Bible* (4 vols., 1962; Supplementary Volume, 1976)
*IEJ* *Israel Exploration Journal*
*ILC* J. Pedersen, *Israel: Its Life and Culture* (vols. I-II, Eng. tr. 1926; III-IV, Eng. tr. 1940)
*Interp.* *Interpretation: A Journal of Bible and Theology*
*IOTG* H. B. Swete, *Introduction to the Old Testament in Greek* (1902)
*IP* M. Noth, *Die israelitischen Personennamen in Rahmen der gemeinsemitischen Namengebung* (1928)
*ISBE* J. Orr, *et al.*, eds., *International Standard Bible Encyclopedia* (2nd ed. 1929)
*JAOS* *Journal of the American Oriental Society*
Jastrow M. Jastrow, *Dictionary of the Targumim, the Talmud Babli, and the Midrashic Literature* (2 vols., 1950)
*JBL* *Journal of Biblical Literature*
*JBR* *Journal of Bible and Religion*
*JCS* *Journal of Cuneiform Studies*
*JEA* *Journal of Egyptian Archaeology*
*JETS* *Journal of the Evangelical Theological Society*
*Jew.Enc.* *Jewish Encyclopedia* (12 vols., 1901-1906)
*JJS* *Journal of Jewish Studies*
*JNES* *Journal of Near Eastern Studies*
*JPOS* *Journal of the Palestinian Oriental Society*
*JQR* *Jewish Quarterly Review*
*JR* *Journal of Religion*
*JSOT* *Journal for the Study of the Old Testament*
*JSS* *Journal of Semitic Studies*
*JTS* *Journal of Theological Studies*
*KAI* H. Donner and W. Röllig, *Kanaanäische und Aramäische Inschriften* (3 vols., 2nd ed. 1966-1968)
*KAT* E. Schrader, ed., *Die Keilinschriften und das Alte Testament* (3rd ed. 1903)
KD K. F. Keil and F. Delitzsch, *Commentary on the Old Testament* (Eng. tr. 1864-1901; repr. 1973)
*KEK* *Kritisch-exegetischer Kommentar über das Neue Testament*
KoB L. Koehler and W. Baumgartner, *Lexicon in Veteris Testamenti Libros* (1953)
*KS* A. Alt, *Kleine Schriften zur Geschichte des Volkes Israel* (3 vols., 1953-1959)
*KZAT* *Kommentar zum Alten Testament*
*KZNT* *Kommentar zum Neuen Testament*
Lange Lange Commentaries
*LAP* J. Finegan, *Light from the Ancient Past* (1946; rev. 1959)
*LBHG* Y. Aharoni, *Land of the Bible: A Historical Geography* (Eng. tr. 1967)
*LCC* *Library of Christian Classics*
*LCL* *Loeb Classical Library*
*LSC* W. M. Ramsay, *Letters to the Seven Churches of Asia* (1905)
LSJ H. G. Liddell, R. Scott, H. S. Jones, *Greek-English Lexicon* (9th ed. 1940)
*LTJM* A. Edersheim, *Life and Times of Jesus the Messiah* (8th ed., rev., 1904; repr. 1977)
*LTK* Herder, *Lexicon für Theologie und Kirche* (2nd ed. 1957–)
MM J. M. Moulton and G. Milligan, *The Vocabulary of the Greek New Testament* (1930)
*MNHK* E. R. Thiele, *The Mysterious Numbers of the Hebrew Kings* (1965 ed.)
*MNTC* *Moffatt New Testament Commentary*
*MPB* H. N. and A. L. Moldenke, *Plants of the Bible* (1952)
MSt J. McClintock and J. Strong, *Cyclopaedia of Biblical, Theological and Ecclesiastical Literature* (1891)
*NBC* F. Davidson, ed., *New Bible Commentary* (1953; 2nd ed. 1954; 3rd ed. [ed. D. Guthrie, *et al.*] 1970
*NBD* J. D. Douglas, ed., *New Bible Dictionary* (1962)
*NCBC* *New Century Bible Commentary*
*NHI* M. Noth, *History of Israel* (Eng. tr. 1958; 2nd ed. 1960)
*NICNT* *New International Commentary on the New Testament*
*NICOT* *New International Commentary on the Old Testament*
*NIGTC* *New International Greek Testament Commentary*
*Nov.Test.* *Novum Testamentum: An International Quarterly*
*NTD* *Das Neue Testament Deutsch*
*NTS* *New Testament Studies*
*ODCC* *Oxford Dictionary of the Christian Church* (1957; 2nd ed. 1974)
*ORHI* W. O. E. Oesterley and T. H. Robinson, *History of Israel* (2 vols., 1932)
*OTG* H. B. Swete, *The Old Testament in Greek According to the Septuagint* (4th ed. 1912)
*OTL* *Old Testament Library*
*OTMS* H. H. Rowley, ed., *The Old Testament and Modern Study* (1951)
Pauly-Wissowa A. Pauly and G. Wissowa, eds., *Real-Encyclopädie der classischen Altertumswissenschaft*
*PEF* *Palestine Exploration Fund Memoirs*
*PEQ* *Palestine Exploration Quarterly*
*PG* J. P. Migne, ed., *Patrologia Graeca* (162 vols., 1857-1866)
*PIOT* R. H. Pfeiffer, *Introduction to the Old Testament* (1952 [1957] ed.)
*PJ* *Palästinajahrbuch*
*PL* J. P. Migne, ed., *Patrologia Latina* (221 vols., 1844-1864)

| | |
|---|---|
| *PSBA* | *Proceedings of the Society of Biblical Archaeology* |
| *QHJ* | A. Schweitzer, *The Quest of the Historical Jesus* (1906; Eng. tr., 2nd ed. 1936) |
| *RAC* | *Reallexikon für Antike und Christentum* |
| *RB* | *Revue Biblique* |
| *RGG* | *Religion in Geschichte und Gegenwart* (5 vols., 3rd ed. 1957-1965) |
| *RGJ* | K. L. Schmidt, *Der Rahmen der Geschichte Jesu* (1919) |
| *RHR* | *Revue de l'histoire des religions* |
| *RQ* | *Revue de Qumran* |
| *RRAM* | D. Magie, *Roman Rule in Asia Minor* (2 vols., 1950) |
| *RTWB* | A. Richardson, ed., *A Theological Word Book of the Bible* (1950) |
| SB | H. L. Strack and P. Billerbeck, *Kommentar zum Neuen Testament aus Talmud und Midrasch* (5 vols., 1922-1961) |
| *SBT* | *Studies in Biblical Theology* |
| Sch.-Herz. | *The New Schaff-Herzog Encyclopedia of Religious Knowledge* (2nd ed. 1949-1952) |
| *SE* | *Studia Evangelica* |
| *SJT* | *Scottish Journal of Theology* |
| *SPT* | W. Ramsay, *St. Paul the Traveller and Roman Citizen* (1920) |
| *SQE* | K. Aland, ed., *Synopsis Quattor Evangeliorum* (2nd ed. 1964) |
| *SSW* | G. Dalman, *Sacred Sites and Ways* (Eng. tr. 1935) |
| *ST* | *Studia Theologica* |
| *SVT* | *Supplements to Vetus Testamentum* |
| *SWP* | C. R. Conder, *et al.*, eds., *Survey of Western Palestine* (9 vols., 1881-1888) |
| *TDNT* | G. Kittel and G. Friedrich, eds., *Theological Dictionary of the New Testament* (10 vols., Eng. tr. 1964-1976) |
| *TDOT* | G. J. Botterweck and H. Ringgren, eds., *Theological Dictionary of the Old Testament* (1974–) |
| *THAT* | E. Jenni and C. Westermann, eds., *Theologisches Handwörterbuch zum Alten Testament* (2 vols., 1971-1976) |
| Thayer | Thayer's *Greek-English Lexicon of the New Testament* |
| *ThHK* | *Theologischer Handkommentar zum Neuen Testament mit Text und Paraphrase* (7 vols., 1928-1939; rev. 1957–) |
| *TLZ* | *Theologische Literaturzeitung* |
| *Torch* | *Torch Bible Commentaries* |
| *TR* | *Theologische Rundschau* |
| *TU* | *Texte und Untersuchungen zur Geschichte der altchristlichen Literatur* |
| *TWOT* | R. L. Harris, *et al.*, eds., *Theological Wordbook of the Old Testament* (2 vols., 1980) |
| *UT* | C. Gordon, *Ugaritic Textbook* (*Analecta Orientalia*, 38, 1965) |
| *VC* | *Vigiliae Christianae* |
| *VE* | *Vox Evangelica* |
| *VT* | *Vetus Testamentum* |
| *WA* | Luther's *Werke*, Weimar Ausgabe (1883–) |
| Wace | H. Wace, ed., *Apocrypha* (*Speaker's Commentary*, 1888) |
| *WBA* | G. E. Wright, *Biblical Archaeology* (rev. ed. 1962) |
| *WC* | *Westminster Commentaries* |
| *WHAB* | G. E. Wright and F. V. Filson, eds., *Westminster Historical Atlas to the Bible* (1956) |
| *WMANT* | *Wissenschaftliche Monographien zum Alten und Neuen Testament* |
| *WTJ* | *Westminster Theological Journal* |
| *ZAW* | *Zeitschrift für die alttestamentliche Wissenschaft* |
| *ZDPV* | *Zeitschrift des deutschen Palästina-Vereins* |
| *ZNW* | *Zeitschrift für die neutestamentliche Wissenschaft* |
| *ZTK* | *Zeitschrift für Theologie und Kirche* |

## ANCIENT AUTHORS AND DOCUMENTS

| | |
|---|---|
| Appian *Syr.* | *Syrian Wars* |
| Aquinas *Summa Theol.* | *Summa Theologica* |
| Aristotle *De an.* | *De anima* (*On the Soul*) |
| *Eth. Nic.* | *Nicomachaean Ethics* |
| *Eth. Eud.* | *Eudemaean Ethics* |
| *Meta.* | *Metaphysics* |
| *Phys.* | *Physics* |
| *Pol.* | *Politics* |
| *Anal. post.* | *Posterior Analytics* |
| *Anal. pr.* | *Prior Analytics* |
| *Rhet.* | *Rhetoric* |
| *Poet.* | *Poetics* |
| Augustine *Civ. Dei* | *De civitate Dei* (*The City of God*) |
| *Conf.* | *Confessiones* |
| *De trin.* | *De trinitate* |
| *Ench.* | *Enchiridion* |
| *Ep.* | *Epistulae* |
| *Retr.* | *Retractiones* |
| Calvin *Inst.* | *Institutes of the Christian Religion* |
| Chrysostom | |
| *Hom. in Gen.* | Homily on Genesis |
| *Hom. in Heb.* | Homily on Hebrews |
| *Hom. in Jn.* | Homily on John |
| *Hom. in Mt.* | Homily on Matthew |
| Clement of Alexandria | |
| *Misc.* | *Miscellanies* (*Stromateis*) |
| *Paed.* | *Paedagogus* |
| Curtius Rufus | Quintus Curtius Rufus |
| *Digest* | *See* ROMAN LAW II.G |
| Dio Cassius *Hist.* | *Roman History* |
| *Hist. Epit.* | Epitome of the *History* |
| Diodorus | Diodorus Siculus, *Library of History* |
| Diogenes | Diogenes Laertius, *Vitae philosophorum* |
| Epiphanius *Haer.* | *Adversus lxxx haereses* (*Panarion*) |
| Eusebius *HE* | *Historia ecclesiastica* |
| *Onom.* | *Onomasticon* |
| *Praep. ev.* | *Praeparatio evangelica* |
| *HE* | *Historia ecclesiastica* (*Church History*) |
| Herodotus | Herodotus *History* |

ABBREVIATIONS

| | |
|---|---|
| Hippolytus *Ref.* | *Refutatio omnium haeresium (Philosophoumena)* |
| Homer *Il.* | *Iliad* |
| *Od.* | *Odyssey* |
| Irenaeus *Adv. haer.* | *Adversus omnes haereses* |
| Jerome *Ep.* | *Epistula(e)* |
| *De vir. ill.* | *De viris illustribus* |
| *Adv. Pelag.* | *Dialogi adversus Pelagianos* |
| Josephus *Ant.* | *Antiquities of the Jews* |
| *BJ* | *Bellum Judaicum (The Jewish War)* |
| *CAp* | *Contra Apionem* |
| *Vita* | *Life* |
| Justin Martyr *Apol.* | *Apologia* |
| *Dial.* | *Dialogus contra Tryphonem* |
| Livy *Epit.* | Epitomes of *Annals of the Roman People* |
| Origen *De prin.* | *De principiis* |
| Orosius | Orosius *Historiae* |
| Pliny (the Elder) *Nat. hist.* | *Naturalis historia* |
| Pliny (the Younger) *Ep.* | *Epistulae* |
| Ptolemy *Geog.* | *Geography* |
| Sallust | *Bellum Catilinae* |
| Strabo *Geog.* | *Geography* |
| Sulpicius Severus *Chronicorum* | *Historia sacra* |
| Tacitus *Ann.* | *Annals (Annales ab excessu divi Augusti)* |
| *Hist.* | *Histories* |
| Tertullian *Adv. Judaeos* | *Adversus Judaeos* |
| *Adv. Marc.* | *Adversus Marcionem* |
| *Adv. Prax.* | *Adversus Praxeam* |
| *Apol.* | *Apologeticum* |
| *De orat.* | *De oratione* |
| *De praescr. haer.* | *De praescriptione haereticorum* |
| *De res.* | *De resurrectione carnis* |
| Vergil *Aen.* | *Aeneid* |

## BIBLICAL AND EXTRABIBLICAL LITERATURE

### OLD TESTAMENT

| | |
|---|---|
| Gen. | Genesis |
| Ex. | Exodus |
| Lev. | Leviticus |
| Nu. | Numbers |
| Dt. | Deuteronomy |
| Josh. | Joshua |
| Jgs. | Judges |
| | Ruth |
| 1, 2 S. | 1, 2 Samuel |
| 1, 2 K. | 1, 2 Kings |
| 1, 2 Ch. | 1, 2 Chronicles |
| Ezr. | Ezra |
| Neh. | Nehemiah |
| Est. | Esther |
| Job | Job |
| Ps. | Psalm(s) |
| Prov. | Proverbs |
| Eccl. | Ecclesiastes |
| Cant. | Canticles (Song of Songs) |
| Isa. | Isaiah |
| Jer. | Jeremiah |
| Lam. | Lamentations |
| Ezk. | Ezekiel |
| Dnl. | Daniel |
| Hos. | Hosea |
| | Joel |
| Am. | Amos |
| Ob. | Obadiah |
| | Jonah |
| Mic. | Micah |
| Nah. | Nahum |
| Hab. | Habakkuk |
| Zeph. | Zephaniah |
| Hag. | Haggai |
| Zec. | Zechariah |
| Mal. | Malachi |

### NEW TESTAMENT

| | |
|---|---|
| Mt. | Matthew |
| Mk. | Mark |
| Lk. | Luke |
| Jn. | John |
| | Acts |
| Rom. | Romans |
| 1, 2 Cor. | 1, 2 Corinthians |
| Gal. | Galatians |
| Eph. | Ephesians |
| Phil. | Philippians |
| Col. | Colossians |
| 1, 2 Thess. | 1, 2 Thessalonians |
| 1, 2 Tim. | 1, 2 Timothy |
| Tit. | Titus |
| Philem. | Philemon |
| He. | Hebrews |
| Jas. | James |
| 1, 2 Pet. | 1, 2 Peter |
| 1, 2, 3 Jn. | 1, 2, 3 John |
| | Jude |
| Rev. | Revelation |

### APOCRYPHA

| | |
|---|---|
| 1, 2 Esd. | 1, 2 Esdras |
| Tob. | Tobit |
| Jth. | Judith |
| Ad. Est. | Additions to Esther |
| Wisd. | Wisdom of Solomon |
| Sir. | Sirach (Ecclesiasticus) |
| Bar. | Baruch |
| Ep. Jer. | Epistle (Letter) of Jeremiah |
| Song Three | Song of the Three Young Men |
| Sus. | Susanna |
| Bel | Bel and the Dragon |
| Pr. Man. | Prayer of Manasseh |
| 1, 2 Macc. | 1, 2 Maccabees |

## PSEUDEPIGRAPHA

| | |
|---|---|
| Asc. Isa. | Ascension of Isaiah |
| Asm. M. | Assumption of Moses |
| 2 Bar. | 2 (Syriac Apocalypse of) Baruch |
| 3 Bar. | 3 (Greek Apocalypse of) Baruch |
| 1, 2 En. | 1, 2 Enoch |
| Jub. | Jubilees |
| Ps. Sol. | Psalms of Solomon |
| Sib. Or. | Sibylline Oracles |
| XII P. | Testaments of the Twelve Patriarchs |
| T. Reub. | Testament of Reuben |
| T. Sim. | Testament of Simeon |
| T. Levi | Testament of Levi |
| T. Jud. | Testament of Judah |
| T. Iss. | Testament of Issachar |
| T. Zeb. | Testament of Zebulun |
| T. Dan | Testament of Dan |
| T. Naph. | Testament of Naphtali |
| T. Gad | Testament of Gad |
| T. Ash. | Testament of Asher |
| T. Jos. | Testament of Joseph |
| T. Benj. | Testament of Benjamin |

## APOSTOLIC FATHERS

| | |
|---|---|
| Barn. | Epistle of Barnabas |
| 1 Clem. | 1 Clement |
| 2 Clem. | 2 Clement |
| Did. | Didache |
| Ign. | Ignatius of Antioch |
| Eph. | Epistle to the Ephesians |
| Magn. | Epistle to the Magnesians |
| Trall. | Epistle to the Trallians |
| Rom. | Epistle to the Romans |
| Philad. | Epistle to the Philadelphians |
| Smyrn. | Epistle to the Smyrnaeans |
| Polyc. | Epistle to Polycarp |
| Polyc. Phil. | Polycarp of Smyrna, Epistle to the Philippians |



| | |
|---|---|
| M. Polyc. | Martyrdom of Polycarp |
| Shep. Herm. | Shepherd of Hermas |
| Vis. | Visions |
| Mand. | Mandates |
| Sim. | Similitudes |
| Diogn. | Epistle to Diognetus |

## DEAD SEA SCROLLS

Initial arabic numeral indicates cave number; Q = Qumrân; p = pesher (commentary).

| | |
|---|---|
| CD | Damascus Document (Zadokite Fragment) |
| 1QapGen | Genesis Apocryphon |
| 1QH | Thanksgiving Hymns |
| 1QIsa[a] | First copy of Isaiah from Qumrân Cave 1 |
| 1QIsa[b] | Second copy of Isaiah |
| 1QM | War Scroll |
| 1QpHab | Pesher (Commentary) on Habakkuk |
| 1QpMic | Pesher on Micah |
| 1QpPs | Pesher on Psalms |
| 1QS | Manual of Discipline |
| 1Q*34*[bis] | Prayer for the Feast of Weeks (Fragment of Liturgical Prayer Scroll = 1Q Prayers) |
| 1QDM (or 1Q*22*) | Sayings of Moses |
| 3QInv (or 3Q*15*) | Copper (Treasure) Scroll |
| 4QFlor | Florilegium (eschatological midrashim) from Cave 4 |
| 4QPBless | Patriarchal Blessings |
| 4QpIsa[a, b, c, d] | Copies of Isaiah pesher from Cave 4 |
| 4QpNah | Pesher on Nahum |
| 4QpPs37 | Pesher on Ps. 37 |
| 4QSam[a, b, c] | Copies of Samuel |
| 4QTestim | Testimonia text from Cave 4 |
| 6QD (or 6Q*15*) | Fragments of the Damascus Document |

**KAB** kab [Heb. *qaḇ*–'something hollowed out'] (2 K. 6:25); AV CAB. A Hebrew dry and liquid measure equal to about one quart. *See* WEIGHTS AND MEASURES.

**KABZEEL** kab'zə-el [Heb. *qaḇṣᵉʾēl*–'may 'El gather']. A city in the Negeb, described as being "in the extreme South" (Josh. 15:21). Benaiah the son of Jehoiada, one of David's mighty men, came from Kabzeel (2 S. 23:20; 1 Ch. 11:22). In Neh. 11:25 Jekabzeel is located in the same general area and is doubtless the same place.

Aharoni originally suggested that Kabzeel be identified with Khirbet Gharrah, "a large town surrounded by a casemate wall . . . mid-way between Beersheba and Arad" (*LBHG*, p. 295), but apparently withdrew this suggestion in the revised edition (1975), which identifies Hormah with Khirbet Gharrah (p. 216). Abel suggested identification with Khirbet Ḥōra, which he did not further describe (*GP*, II, 89). W. S. L. S.

**KADES** (Jth. 1:9, AV). *See* KADESH **1.**

**KADESH** kā'dəsh [Heb. *qāḏēš*; Gk. *Kadēs*].

**1.** Also **KADESH-BARNEA** bär-nē'ə [Heb. *qāḏēš barnē(a)ʿ*; Gk. *Kadēs barnē*]; **KEDESH** ke'dəsh [Heb. *qeḏeš*] (Josh. 15:23); **ENMISHPAT** en-mish'pat [Heb. *ʿên mišpāṭ*–'fountain of judgment'] (Gen. 14:7); AV also CADES-BARNE (Jth. 5:14); NEB also CADESH-BARNEA (Jth. 5:14); AV also KADES (Jth. 1:9); NEB also CADESH (Jth. 1:9). An oasis in northeast Sinai on the southern border of the Wilderness of Zin.

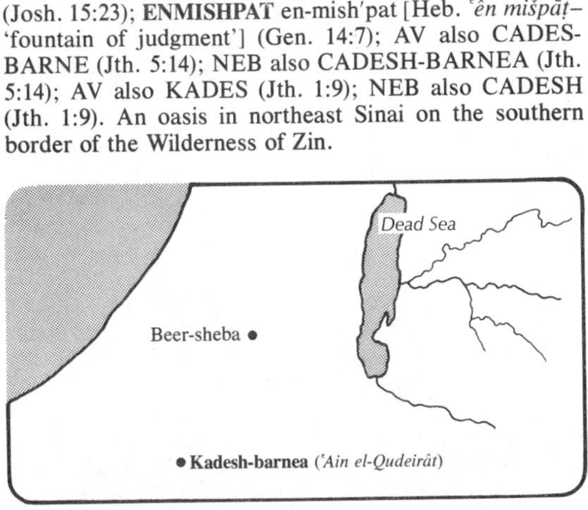


When Chedorlaomer's forces marched through Transjordan they penetrated Edomite territory as far as El-paran, turned back to the northwest, and came to Kadesh, called by its alternative name Enmishpat (Gen. 14:7). There they subdued the Amalekites before returning northeast to defeat the kings of the cities of the plain. In the narrative concerning Hagar, the well Beer-lahai-roi was located "between Kadesh and Bered" (16:14) on the way to the wilderness region of Shur in the northwest Sinai isthmus, E of the present Suez canal and W of the Wâdī el-ʿArîsh.

The Israelites visited Kadesh-barnea more than once in their wanderings (Nu. 13:26; 20:1), and the site seems to have been their headquarters for thirty-eight years (Dt. 2:14). It was an eleven-day journey from Horeb or Sinai to Kadesh via Mt. Seir (1:2). Moses sent spies into Canaan from Kadesh (Nu. 13:17), and there Israel was condemned to wander in the wilderness for a generation because they had doubted God's ability to give them the Promised Land (14:26-35). At Kadesh-barnea Miriam died and was buried (20:1), and from there messengers were sent in vain to the Edomite king (v. 14). When the oases dried up, Moses was provoked into offending God, and the occasion was commemorated in the name of Meribath-kadesh (Heb. *mᵉrîḇaṯ qāḏēš*), "contention of Kadesh" (27:14).

Kadesh-barnea was to be the southern corner of the southwest boundary of Judah (Nu. 34:4); Ezekiel included it as part of the southern border of his ideal land (Ezk. 47:19; 48:28). The meaning of the word "Barnea," appended to Kadesh to distinguish it from other places with similar names, is unknown. It may be a personal name like Bera and Birsha (Gen. 14:2).

Kadesh-barnea has often been identified with ʿAin Qedeis, one of several springs in a locality 78 km. (49 mi.) SW of Beer-sheba. The water supply there, however, is too limited to have met the needs of the wandering Israelites, and in addition there is doubt concerning the connection of the name Qedeis with Kadesh. The neighboring ʿAin Qeṣeimeh also has an inadequate water supply. A more suitable location for Kadesh-barnea is at ʿAin el-Qudeirât, a spring 8 km. (5 mi.) NW of ʿAin Qedeis. Although these three springs are close to one another, and the wandering Israelites probably used each on occasion, the vegetation near ʿAin el-Qudeirât and its ample supply of water suit very well the topographical requirements of the wilderness narratives.

See *EAEHL*, III, *s.v.* "Kadesh-Barnea" (M. Dothan).

R. K. H.

**2.** Same as KEDESH **3.**

**3.** Kadesh on the Orontes, mentioned only in 2 S. 24:6 [Heb. *taḥtîm ḥoḏšî*; corrected by the LXX (Lucian) to Gk. *eis tēn gēn Chetieim Kadēs*–'to the land of the Hittites, toward Kadesh' (cf. RSV, NEB)]; AV TAHTIM-HODSHI. An important Hittite stronghold on the Upper Orontes, just S of Lake Homs, the ancient Lake Kadesh. It was strategically located at the gateway to the plains of Syria.

In the 15th cent. the king of Kadesh, leading a coalition of Canaanite monarchs against the Egyptians at Megiddo, was defeated by Thutmose III, who later captured the city of Kadesh itself. Two hundred years later Ramses II fought against the Hittites at Kadesh and claimed a glorious victory, even though he failed to occupy the city. The Battle of Kadesh is graphically and extensively portrayed on the monuments of Ramses II.

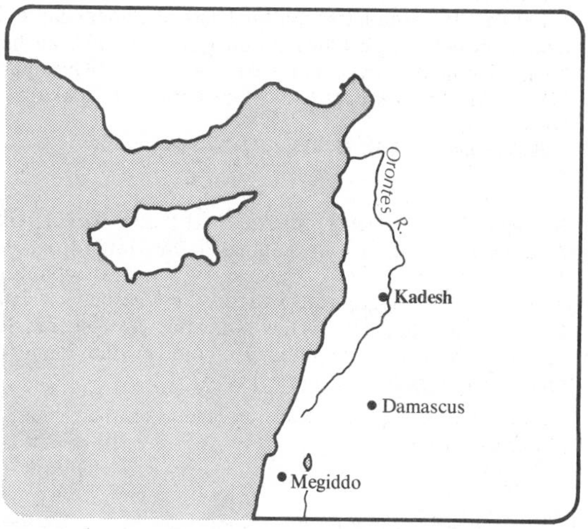


J. Simons (*GTTOT*, §§ 111f., pp. 41-43) contended that the context of 2 S. 24:6 requires a Kadesh near Dan; Kadesh on the Orontes is too far north to be included in the census of David. His conjecture, following Ewald, would restore the text to read Heb. *taḥaṯ ḥermôn,* "at the foot of Hermon" (cf. Josh. 11:3; 13:5; Jgs. 3:3).

A third suggestion, proposed by Guthe and Klostermann, emends the evidently corrupted MT of 2 S. 24:6 to refer to Kadesh of Naphtali, a solution that does not account at all for Heb. *taḥtîm.*

The inclusion of Hittite Kadesh on the Orontes in David's census is unlikely but not historically impossible. The Davidic conquests made tributaries of Damascus and other regions near Kadesh bordering on the state of Hamath (2 S. 8:6-8). A. H. LEWIS

**KADMIEL** kad'mē-əl [Heb. *qaḏmî'ēl*–'El is ancient'?; AV CADMIEL; NEB CADMIELUS, CADOEL in parallel lists in 1 Esd. 5:26, 58; omitted in LXX B; A reads Gk. *kaí Kadmiēlon*]. A Levite (Ezr. 2:40; Neh. 7:43), founder of a family whose descendants returned from captivity with Zerubbabel (Ezr. 2:1; Neh. 7:43; 12:1, 8). He is named among those who praise God for the return (Neh. 9:4f.; 12:24) and those who "took the oversight of" restoring the Lord's house (Ezr. 3:9; 1 Esd. 5:26, 58). He is again mentioned with those who "seal" the new covenant (Neh. 10:28-39 [MT 29-40]) after the reestablishment of worship (vv. 1, 9 [MT 2, 10]).

**KADMONITE** kad'mən-īt [Heb. *qaḏmōnî*–'easterners'; Gk. *Kedmonaioi*]. The Kadmonites are mentioned in Gen. 15:19 along with the Kenites and Kenizzites of Edom and are doubtless the same as "the people of the east," whose wisdom was celebrated (1 K. 4:30 [MT 5:10]). Kedemah (Heb. *qēḏᵉmâ,* "the East") was a son of Ishmael (Gen. 25:15; cf. v. 6). In an Egyptian story, a political refugee who fled from Egypt in the time of the 12th Dynasty found a refuge in Canaan in the land of Kaduma or Kedem, apparently an area of the Syrian desert E of Byblos.

A. H. SAYCE

**KAIN** kān [Heb. *qayin*] (Nu. 24:22); AV THE KENITE; NEB CAIN. The singular form of the clan name KENITES.

**KAIN** kān [Heb. *haqqayin*–'the Kenite, smith'(?)]. A city in the southern hill country of Judah, in a grouping of "ten cities and their villages" that were part of the tribal allotment of Judah (Josh. 15:57). Included in the group are a number of places that can be located SE of Hebron (*see* JUDAH, TERRITORY OF). Kain has therefore been tentatively identified with Khirbet Yaqîn, 3 km. (2 mi.) NE of Ziph. The LXX (15:56) combines two names into one, reading *Zakanaïm* (B) or *Zanōakim* (A; this is more clearly from *Zanoah* + *Kain*), and emends "ten" to "nine." If this reading is accepted, the place should be called "Zanoah of the Kenites." Simons's argument that the figure "ten" opposes this reading (*GTTOT,* § 319, p. 150) is not convincing. A stronger argument may be found in Jgs. 4:11, translating "and Heber the Kenite [*haqqênî*] separated himself from Kain [*miqqayin*]," but it is not established that Heber came from Kain since this word is also a proper or a clan name. W. S. L. S.

**KAIWAN** kā'wän, kī'wän [Heb. *kîyûn*]; AV Chiun (following MT vocalization); NEB "pedestals" (relating *kîyûn* to *kûn*–'be firm, establish'). The name of a god in Am. 5:26. The vocalization by the Masoretes is probably meant to draw the reader's attention to the word *siqqûṣ,* "detested thing," or *gillûl,* "idol" (cf. the similar phenomenon with the god-name Molech [2 K. 23:10; Jer. 32:35], a deliberate misvocalization of the consonants *mlk* with the vowels of the word "shame" [*bōšeṯ*]). Kîyûn is apparently the same as Bab. *kayawânu,* the god-name given to the planet Saturn (cf. Pesh. *ke'wān*). The RSV rearranges the MT and translates "Kaiwan your star-god," which removes a grammatical difficulty (see comms.) and accords well with the identification with the Babylonian god. The first part of the verse mentions SAKKUTH, another name for the Assyrian god Ninurta (= Saturn); this lends credence to the identification of this form (i.e., *kywn*) with the Babylonian god. The LXX translation of the word is *Raiphan,* which many authorities regard as an inner Greek corruption of an original *Kaiphan.* The quotation of Am. 5:26 in Acts 7:43, apparently in dependence on the LXX, has *Raiphan* (or a similar term). The apparent meaning of the verse is that the Israelites will carry the images of their gods into exile beyond Damascus; the images of Saturn are mentioned as representatives. (For alternate views and discussion of the many problems in this verse, see comms.) H. F. VOS

**KALCOL** kal'kol (1 K. 4:31, NEB). *See* CALCOL.

**KALLAI** kal'ī [Heb. *qallay* < *qal*–'swift']. A priest among those who returned with Zerubbabel (Neh. 12:1). He represented the family of Sallai (v. 20).

**KAMON** kā'mən [Heb. *qāmôn*]; AV CAMON. The city, possibly in Gilead (Josephus *Ant.* v.7.6 [254]), where Jair was buried (Jgs. 10:3-5). It may be the Gk. *Kamous* of Polybius (v.70) and has been identified with Qamm, 4 km. (2½ mi.) N of eṭ-Ṭaiyibeh in ʿAjlûn. See Abel, *GP,* II, 412.

W. S. L. S.

**KANAH** kā'nə [Heb. *qānâ*–'reed'].

**1.** The name of a brook (wadi, NEB "gorge") forming part of the boundary between Ephraim and Manasseh (Josh. 16:8; 17:9). The border of Ephraim extended west from Tappuah to the brook Kanah, ending at the sea; the border of Manasseh from Tappuah "went down to the brook Kanah, south of the brook." There seems to be no good reason to doubt the identification of "the brook Kanah" with the modern Wâdī Qânah. The stream reaches the sea about 6 km. (4 mi.) N of Jaffa.

**2.** A town in the Lebanon foothills, on the northern border of Asher (Josh. 19:28), probably identical with modern Qânah about 11 km. (7 mi.) SE of Tyre (not to be confused with NT Cana).

See E. Danelius, *PEQ*, 1958, pp. 32-43.

R. P. DUGAN

**KAPH** käf [כ]. The eleventh letter of the Hebrew alphabet (sometimes rendered caph or kaf), transliterated as *k* when with daghesh and as *ḵ* when without. It also came to be used for the number twenty. For name, etc., *see* WRITING.

**KAREAH** kə-rē'ə [Heb. *qārē(a)ḥ*–'bald head']; AV also CAREAH (2 K. 25:23). The father of the Johanan and Jonathan who after the fall of Jerusalem joined Gedaliah at Mizpah (2 K. 25:23; Jer. 40:8, 13-16; 41:11-16; 42:1, 8; 43:2-5).

**KARKA** kär'kə [Heb. *haqqarqaʿ*–'the floor, ground']. A location on the southern border of Judah, mentioned between Hazar-addar and Azmon, on the way to Wâdī el-ʿArîsh (Josh. 15:3). Hazar-addar has been identified with ʿAin Qudeirât, hence the suggestion that Karka was located at the confluence of Wâdī el-ʿAin and Umm Hašîm, where a well-built pool has been discovered (*GP*, II, 47). The AV form "Karkaa" was based on a misreading of the locative ending as part of the place name.

W. S. L. S.

**KARKOR** kär'kôr [Heb. *qarqōr*]. An unidentified place where Gideon surprised and overwhelmed the remnants of the army of Zeba and Zalmunnah (Jgs. 8:10f.). According to v. 11 the place was on or near a well-known desert highway running N-S, which may have followed roughly the same line as the present pilgrims' highway from Damascus to Mecca and therefore have passed "east of . . . Jogbehah." Thus Qarqar, some 400 km. (250 mi.) from Jogbehah, can hardly be considered a probable location.

B. HOVEY

**KARNAIM** kär-nā'əm [Heb. *qarnāyim*] (Am. 6:13); AV HORNS; NEB POWER; cf. NEB mg. A city in north Gilead; modern Sheikh Saʿd, Syria, perhaps identical with Ashteroth-karnaim of Gen. 14:5 and Carnaim of 1 Macc. 5:26, 43f.; 2 Macc. 12:21, 26. The NEB rendering underlines the play on the meanings of Karnaim, "horns" (symbolizing power; cf. Dt. 33:17), and Lo-debar, "a nothing."

G. WYPER

**KARTAH** kär'tə [Heb. *qartâ*] (Josh. 21:34). One of the four Levitical cities from the tribal allotment of Zebulun, the others being Jokneam, Dimnah, and Nahalal, each "with its pasture lands." Ramses II mentioned a *qrt*, and the Pilgrim of Bordeaux referred to *mutatio Certha*, leading to the identification of Kartah with Athlit. If this identification is correct, it indicates a westward expansion of Zebulun to the sea at a much earlier period than is generally accepted. The territory of Zebulun is generally thought to have lain N of the Kishon, on the basis of Josh. 19:10-16.

***Bibliography.***–*GP*, II, 22, 63, 414; *GTTOT*, § 337, no. 38.

W. S. L. S.

**KARTAN** kär'tən, kär'tan [Heb. *qartān*]. A city in Naphtali given to the Levites (Josh. 21:32). In the parallel passage (1 Ch. 6:76 [MT 61]) Kartan is not mentioned, but Kiriathaim seems to replace it; hence the two are usually identified. Neither name occurs in Josh. 19:32, 38, which instead have Chinnereth. Some scholars have taken this as the original name and suggested that Kartan and Kiriathaim are textual corruptions. Both names, however, begin with *qôp*, a distinctly different sound from the *kap* in Chinnereth. Moreover, *qiryāṯayim* and *qartān* have the same meaning, "double city" (the latter, on the basis of Phoenician evidence, possesses an alternate dual ending). Kartan has been identified provisionally with Khirbet el-Qureiyeh, NE of ʿAin Ibl in Upper Galilee, possibly the Rakkath of Josh. 19:35.

***Bibliography.***–*GP*, II, 49, 415; *GTTOT*, § 337, no. 36.

W. S. L. S.

**KASSITES** kas'īts [Akk. *kaššu*, Nuzi dialect *kuššu*; Gk. *Kossaioi*]. A people who dominated Babylonia from the 16th to 12th cents. B.C. Like so many other mountain peoples who invaded Mesopotamia, the Kassites left little trace of their presence. They were the most successful invaders, however, maintaining a hold on Babylonia for almost half a millennium (*ca.* 1595-1157 B.C.).

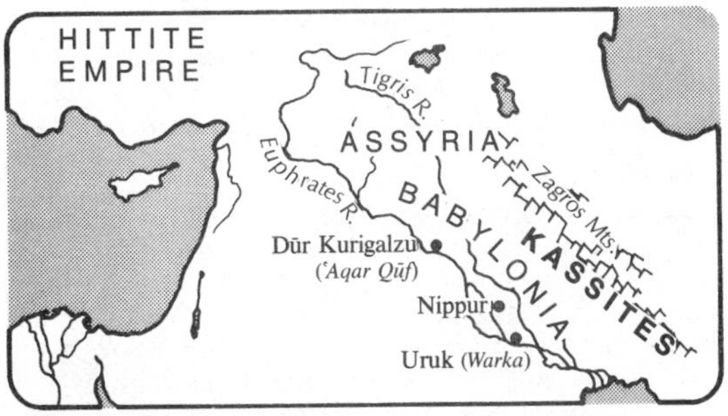


The Kassites' opportunity to seize the throne of Babylon came when a sudden raid by the Hittites toppled the Hammurabi dynasty *ca.* 1595 B.C. Since the Hittites could not hold so distant a realm, the Kassites took the kingdom. In fact, the Kassites may have played some part in the raid as allies of the Hittites, for there is evidence of Kassite rule over the state of Khana on the mid-Euphrates a little before Babylon fell, and the conquerors apparently removed the statue of Marduk, patron deity of Babylon, to this district. There had been Kassite settlers, migrants from their Zagros homeland, in Babylonia for decades, and Hammurabi's son had repelled Kassite bands from his territory. Now larger contingents arrived, driven, perhaps, by pressure from the first Indo-European movements into western Iran.

A dark age covered Babylonia for two centuries; later scribes seem to have known very little about the period, and few inscriptions are extant. This lack of documentation prevents the compilation of a precise chronology for the reigns of the first twenty-one of the thirty-six Kassite kings named in the Babylonian King List. Some of the earliest rulers probably overlapped the last years of the Hammurabi dynasty. That the early Kassites were not uncouth barbarians is shown by two dedicatory texts, preserved in later copies. One (a problematic document for the historian) is for the restoration of a shrine in Babylon by Gandash, the first Kassite king, the other for the return of Marduk's statue from Khana by Agum-kakrime, a later king, who claimed to rule most of Babylonia (*ca.* 1550 B.C.).

A separate kingdom had emerged in the 17th cent. B.C.

in the Sea-Land, the marshes of southern Iraq. The Kassites extinguished it soon after 1500 B.C. Their state grew to a position of respectability during the two dark centuries and shortly after 1400 B.C. it had a fraternal relation with Egypt. The Amarna Letters record the marriage of a Babylonian princess to the pharaoh and an exchange of gifts. Kassite kings sent horses, having introduced them in Babylonia for general use, and lapis lazuli, demanding gold in return, a current mode of state trading. One letter, in which Burnaburiaš II complains that Akhenaten of Egypt had slighted him by according recognition to Assyria, Babylon's supposed vassal, marks a turning point in Babylonian history. Burnaburiaš or his son did, in fact, marry a daughter of the Assyrian king Aššur-uballiṭ I (*ca.* 1365-1330 B.C.), an action possibly signifying the inferiority of the girl's father. When the son of this union was murdered for being too pro-Assyrian, Aššur-uballiṭ, whose power had been increasing, invaded Babylonia and installed as king his great-grandson Kurigalzu II (*ca.* 1345-1324 B.C.). The remainder of the Kassite era saw continual warfare between the two states; the Kassites normally held their ground but seldom achieved even fleeting victory over the Assyrians. Tukulti-Ninurta I of Assyria (*ca.* 1244-1208 B.C.) ruled Babylon for seven years (*ca.* 1234-1228 B.C.), and ten years later an Elamite king ruled there briefly. Finally, *ca.* 1160 B.C., a raid by the Elamite Šuttruk-Naḫḫunte gave the death blow to the tottering Kassite rule.

The earliest group of texts from the Kassite period dates from *ca.* 1370 B.C., the majority stemming from Nippur in the south, another collection coming from Dūr Kurigalzu, now ʿAqar Qūf, near Baghdad. These texts are in the Babylonian language and are dated by the year of the king's reign, an innovation. They display occasional Kassite words, notably in texts concerning horses. Personal and divine names and an ancient, fragmentary Kassite-Babylonian "dictionary" are the only other sources for knowledge of the Kassite tongue. The later rulers of the dynasty bore Babylonian names. Parts of an inscribed statue of Kurigalzu I (*ca.* 1400 B.C.) indicate reverence for the local deities and continuing use of the Sumerian tongue for religious texts.

Amarna Letter (*ca.* 1350 B.C.) in which Burnaburiaš II complains that Akhenaten slighted him by recognizing Assyria (Trustees of the British Museum)

There is evidence that Babylonian scribes copied the "classical" works of the previous age, revising and systematizing them. Several later scribes trace their ancestry to the Kassite period. The famous "Babylonian Job" poem, *I Will Praise the Lord of Wisdom* (W. G. Lambert, *Babylonian Wisdom Literature* [1960], pp. 21-62), and a few other pieces were composed at this time. Some changes are apparent in architecture, although it is hard to attribute any of them to Kassite influence. The remarkable facade of molded and glazed brick figures from Warka (Uruk) is now seen to have Babylonian antecedents (H. Frankfort, *Art and Architecture of the Ancient Orient* [1958], plate 70A). Glass and glazed earthenware were inventions that spread throughout the Fertile Crescent *ca.* 1500 B.C. (although findings at Metsamor suggest an earlier origin). Engraved on the cylinder seals called Kassite are a number of lengthy prayers for the owners — a symptom, perhaps, of an insecure society.

The country was divided into regions; some were large towns, some were tribal territories, and each was administered by an army of officials under a governor responsible to the king. Grants of tax-free land to loyal subjects and the harsh financial and physical penalties for infringement were recorded on boundary stones. Symbols of the gods were carved on the stones to give extra protection. These land donations, coupled with the regional system, aided the breakup of the state at the end of the Kassite dynasty and the settlement of Aramean and Chaldean tribes in the heart of Babylonia.

The Kassites are not mentioned in the Bible, unless "the land of Cush" of Gen. 2:13 is Kassite territory (see E. A. Speiser, *Oriental and Biblical Studies* [1967], pp. 25-28).

***Bibliography.***–K. Balkan, *Kassitenstudien* (1954); *CAH* (3rd ed.), II/1 (1973), chs. 18, 25, 31; J. A. Brinkman, *Materials and Studies for Kassite History* (1976); "Kassiten" (in English), in *Reallexicon der Assyriologie,* V (1980), 464-473.

A. R. MILLARD

**KASTELLION.** *See* MIRD.

**KATTATH** kat'əth, kat'äth [Heb. *qaṭṭāṯ*; Gk. *Katanath,* A *Kattath,* Lucian *Kottath*]. One of twelve cities of Zebulun, mentioned in Josh. 19:15. The name is believed, on the basis of the Gk. *Katanath,* to have developed from **qaṭnaṯ*. Since it is named next to Nahalal in Joshua, and Kitron is named next to Nahalol in Jgs. 1:30, Kattath is commonly identified with KITRON. In T.P. *Megillah* i.1, Kattath is identified with Qeṭonith, which was still standing in the time of Rabbi Yosi ben Ḥaninah. On this basis, the site of Kattath/Kitron is located at Khirbet Qoṭeina, 8 km. (5 mi.) SW of Jokneam. According to Simons (*GTTOT,* § 329, p. 182), this location argues against the identification. Abel (*GP,* II, 423) suggested a location at Tell Fâr, on the eastern edge of the plain of Zebulun, about 4 km. (2½ mi.) NE of Kefr Ḥasidim. No scholar has given a certain identification of the site.

W. S. L. S.

**KEBAR** (Ezk. 1:1, NEB). *See* CHEBAR.

**KEDAR** kē'där [Heb. *qēḏār*–'black, swarthy'; Gk. *Kēdar*]. The second son of Ishmael (Gen. 25:13; 1 Ch. 1:29) and, eponymously, a people and a country in the East.

*I. Location*.–The descendants of Ishmael "dwelt from Havilah to Shur" (Gen. 25:18), i.e., in the northern Arabian peninsula and into the Sinai. Isa. 21:13-17, an oracle concerning Arabia, mentions Teman (a brother of Kedar; cf. Gen. 25:15) and the "archers" of Kedar. In a prophecy against Israel Jer. 2:10 uses Kittim (RSV "Cyprus") and Kedar to represent "west" and "east," respectively, and in 49:28 "Kedar" and "the people of the east" occur in parallel strophes. Nebuchadrezzar's attack on "Kedar and the kingdoms of Hazor" (49:28) is probably to be identified with that king's plundering of the "Arabs" in his sixth year (BM 21946 rev. 9f.; Wiseman, *CCK*, pp. 70f.). Ezk. 27:21 associates "Arabia and all the princes of Kedar."

Ashurbanipal referred to Ammuladi and Iauta' son of Hazael as kings of Kedar (*qi-id-ri*), who marched against the kings of the Amurru and whom Ashurbanipal defeated. Iauta' was an Assyrian vassal who "roused the people of Arabia to revolt with him"; he was captured and taken to Nineveh, where, Ashurbanipal recorded, "I put a dog chain upon him and made him guard a kennel" (*ARAB*, II, §§ 820, 869). A comparison of statements in Esarhaddon's and Ashurbanipal's annals seems to indicate that "Kedar" was almost synonymous with "Arabia" (cf. *ANET*, pp. 291f., 298-300). Old South Arabic inscriptions mention *qdrn* (Qadirân or Qadrân), either as a person or as a people (*Corpus Inscriptionum Himyariticarum* [ = *CIS*, IV], 493.2; cf. K. Conti Rossini, *Chrestomathia arabica meridionalis ephigraphica* [1931], p. 229). According to an Aramaic inscription from Tell el-Maskhuta in Egypt, Geshem the Arabian (cf. Neh. 2:19; 6:1f., 6) was King of Kedar, and Kedarites lived on the eastern border of Egypt in the 5th cent. B.C. (cf. I. Rabinowitz, *JNES*, 15 [1956], 1-9). A conclusion that Kedar was a prominent Arabian tribe living SE of Damascus and E of Transjordan is thus reasonable.

*II. Description*.–The Kedarites were possibly of two general types: nomads (Arab. *wabarîya*), who lived in tents (Jer. 49:29), and sedentary people (Arab. *ḥaḍarîya*), who lived in villages (*ḥᵃṣērîm*, Isa. 42:11; cf. BDB, p. 347). In the references to the "tents of Kedar" in Ps. 120:5 and Cant. 1:5 Heb. *qēḏār* could also be translated "black," with no specific reference to Kedar (although the Arabs often made tents of black sheep's wool). The people of Kedar are described as "a nation at ease, that dwells securely" (Jer. 49:31). Isa. 21:16f. refers to their pomp and their warrior activities, particularly their skill with the bow, which are confirmed by the Assyrian records of their raids against the Amurru (the "Westerners"). Their flocks, including lambs, rams, goats, and camels, are mentioned in Isa. 60:7, Jer. 49:29, and Ezk. 27:21. That these items were part of an extensive commerce is indicated in Ezekiel's lament over Tyre (27:21). Since Kedar was closely related to other tribes in the Arabian peninsula (according to both Gen. 25:13-18 and linguistic studies), and since the prophets, particularly Ezekiel, include other tribes in parallel with it, possibly Kedar also traded in "all kinds of spices, and all precious stones, and gold" (Ezek. 27:22). Note Ashurbanipal's references to booty from Arabia and Kedar, which consisted of "cattle, sheep, asses, camels, slaves" in "countless numbers," and his record of yearly tribute of gold and precious stones (*ARAB*, II, §§ 869f.).

A. S. FULTON W. S. L. S.

**KEDEMAH** ked'ə-mä, kə-dē'mə [Heb. *qēḏᵉmâ*–'eastward']. Son of Ishmael (Gen. 25:15), head of a clan (1 Ch. 1:31). *See* KADMONITE.

**KEDEMOTH** kĕd'ə-mōth [Heb. *qᵉḏēmôṯ*]. A priestly city in the territory of Reuben (Josh. 13:18; 21:37), probably on the Arnon. From the wilderness of Kedemoth Moses sent messengers to Sihon king of Heshbon asking for permission to pass peaceably through his land (Dt. 2:26-29). The city was allotted to Reuben (Josh. 13:18) and then assigned to the Merarites (21:37; 1 Ch. 6:79 [MT 64]).

F. P. W. Buhl identified it with Umm er-Reṣāṣ (*Geographie des alten Palästina* [1896], 268), but more recently it has been identified either with Khirbet er-Remeil (*GP*, II, 415), 4 km. (2½ mi.) WSW of el-Medeiyineh (*GP*, II, 217 n. 2), or with Qaṣr ez-Za'ferân (N. Glueck, *BASOR*, 65 [Feb. 1937], 27), 4 km. (2½ mi.) NW of el-Medeiyineh. Cf. *WHAB*, plate IX.

W. S. L. S.

**KEDESH** kē'desh [Heb. *qeḏeš*–'sacred place, sanctuary'; Gk. *Kadēs*].

**1.** A town in Judah, described in Josh. 15:23 as "toward the border of Edom in the south" and probably to be identified with Kadesh-barnea (*see* KADESH **1**).

**2.** A town located in the territory of Issachar and given to the Gershonite Levites (1 Ch. 6:72 [MT 57]). In Josh. 21:28 it is called Kishion (AV, NEB, Kishon); the AV rendering may be more correct since the town was spelled *qsn* in the list of conquered cities compiled under Thutmose III. The entry in the list in 1 Ch. 6:72, "Kedesh with her suburbs," may have arisen through misreading Kishon for Kedesh. The town has been tentatively identified with the modern Tell Abû Qedeis, nearly 5 km. (3 mi.) SE of Megiddo, although the tribal claims of Issachar perhaps did not extend so far south.

**3.** Also **KEDESH (IN) NAPHTALI** [Heb. *qeḏeš naptālî*; Gk. *Kedes Naphtali*] (Jgs. 4:6; Tob. 1:2); **KEDESH IN GALILEE** [Heb. *qeḏeš baggālîl*] (Josh. 20:7; 21:32; 1 Ch. 6:76); **KADESH IN GALILEE** (1 Macc. 11:63); AV CADES; NEB KADESH-IN-GALILEE. A famous refuge city in the east Galilee uplands assigned to the Gershonite Levites (1 Ch. 6:76).

From its name ("holy") it is thought to have been a pre-Israelite pagan sanctuary, and prior to the Conquest period it was a Canaanite royal city (Josh. 12:22). It recovered some of its ancient character when it was designated as a city of refuge (20:7). It was the home of Barak and the place where he and Deborah assembled their followers for the battle against Sisera (Jgs. 4:1-10).

Tiglath-pileser III captured Kedesh in the time of Pekah of Israel and deported its inhabitants (2 K. 15:29). The great battle between Jonathan Maccabeus and Demetrius was fought near Kedesh (1 Macc. 11:63ff.); in the days of Josephus it belonged to the Phoenicians (*Ant*. xiii.5.6 [154]; *BJ* ii.18.1 [459]; iv.2.3 [105]; etc.). It is the modern Tell Qades, NW of Lake Huleh, and dates from the Early Bronze Age.

R. K. H.

**KEDORLAOMER** ked-ər-lā'ō-mər (Gen. 14:1, 4f., etc., NEB). *See* CHEDORLAOMER.

**KEDRON** ked'rən, kē'drən [Gk. *Kedrōn*]; AV CEDRON. A place fortified by Cendebeus in obedience to Antiochus Sidetes (1 Macc. 15:39-41). Later, when Cendebeus was defeated, he fled there, hotly pursued by John and Judas (sons of Simon the Maccabee), who burned the city (16:4-10). The context locates Kedron near Jamnia (15:40) and Modein (16:4). The site has been located tentatively at Qaṭrā, a village about 40 km. (25 mi.) W of Jerusalem, near the modern towns of Gaderah (cf. Josh. 15:36) and Qidron. Simons believed that the name Qaṭrā is derived from Qiṭrôn, the Hebrew name behind the Kedron of 1 Macc. 15:39–16:10 (*GTTOT,* § 318, p. 147).

For Jn. 18:1, NEB, *see* KIDRON. W. S. L. S.

**KEEPER** [Heb. *'îš*] (Gen. 46:32, 34); [*nāṭar*] (Cant. 1:6; 8:11f.); NEB GUARDIANS; [*nāṣar*] (Isa. 27:3); [*rā'â*] (Gen. 4:2); NEB SHEPHERD; [*śar*] (Gen. 39:21-23); NEB GOVERNOR; [*šāmar*] (Gen. 4:9; 1 S. 17:20, 22; 2 K. 22:4, 14; 1 Ch. 9:19; Neh. 2:8; Ps. 121:5; Eccl. 12:3; etc.); NEB also GUARD, "picket," QUARTERMASTER, "those on duty," etc.; [*šā'ar*] (2 Ch. 31:14); AV PORTER; [Gk. *neōkóros*] (Acts 19:35); AV "worshipper"; NEB WARDEN.

In the OT keepers were custodians or guardians of a variety of things. Some served as herders of cattle (Gen. 46:32, 34) or sheep (4:2; 1 S. 17:20). Some tended vineyards (Cant. 1:6; 8:11f.); Yahweh is depicted as tending His vineyard Israel (Isa. 27:3). Besiegers of Jerusalem are described as men who watch over a field (Jer. 4:17). Other keepers were guardians of a house (Eccl. 12:3), guards (2 Ch. 21:14; Neh. 3:29), or temple officials responsible for the threshold (2 K. 22:4; 23:4; 25:18; 1 Ch. 9:19; 2 Ch. 34:9; Jer. 35:4; 52:24), entrance (1 Ch. 9:19), and wardrobe (2 K. 22:14; 2 Ch. 34:22). Some were prison wardens (Gen. 39:21-23) or forest rangers (Neh. 2:8). When David visited his brothers on the battlefield, he left the things he brought with him in the care of the custodian of the baggage (1 S. 17:22). Cain asked if he were responsible for Abel's whereabouts (Gen. 4:9). The psalmist confessed that Yahweh is mankind's protector (Ps. 121:5).

In Acts 19:35 the town clerk stated that Ephesus was the custodian of the temple of Artemis. J. R. PRICE

**KEHELATHAH** kē-hə-lā'thə, kə-hel'ə-thə [Heb. *qᵉhēlāṯâ*–'gathering, assembly']. An Israelite camp during the wilderness wanderings, between Rissah and Mt. Shepher (Nu. 33:22f.). The location is unknown.

**KEILAH** kə-ī'lə [Heb. *qᵉ'îlâ*]. The Garmite, grandson of Hodiah (1 Ch. 4:19).

**KEILAH** kə-ī'lə [Heb. *qᵉ'îlâ*]. A fortified city of Judah in the Shephelah, about 13.5 km. (8.5 mi.) NW of Hebron, named with Nezib, Achzib, and Mareshah in Josh. 15:43f. It was very high for a city in the Shephelah, being over 450 m. (1500 ft.) above the Mediterranean Sea. The city had gates and bars (1 S. 23:7).

During the Amarna period, Šuwardata prince of Hebron and Abdu-Ḫeba prince of Jerusalem sent numerous letters to Akhenaten pharaoh of Egypt (*ca.* 1369-1353) complaining of his unlawful occupation of Keilah. Apparently Keilah was a boundary city between the two ruling princes in Canaan. The reputed strength of the city in the Amarna area is seen in its repeated listing in the Amarna Tablets with such formidable cities as Rabbah, Gezer, and Gath.

During the monarchy David delivered Keilah from the roving bands of Philistines who had come to rob its threshing floors. He made it his military headquarters for a short time. When informed by the oracle of Abiathar the priest that the treacherous citizens of Keilah planned to hand him over to Saul (1 S. 23:7-13), he and his men quickly left the city and hid in the Wilderness of Ziph.

Exiles returning from Babylon resettled Keilah in the 5th cent. B.C., and some helped to rebuild the wall of Jerusalem under the supervision of Nehemiah. "Next to him Hashabiah, ruler of half the district of Keilah, repaired for his district. After him their brethren repaired: Bavvai the son of Henadad, ruler of half the district of Keilah" (Neh. 3:17f.).

According to an early Christian tradition, the sixth-century-B.C. prophet Habakkuk was buried in Keilah (Eusebius *Onom.*).

Today the site is called Khirbet Qîlā. The hill is covered with ruins, but the terraced slopes surrounding it are covered with grainfields. F. E. YOUNG

**KEILAN** (1 Esd. 5:15, NEB). *See* KILAN.

**KELAIAH** kə-lā'yə, kə-lī'ə [Heb. *qēlāyâ*; Gk. *Kōlios*; LXX B *Kōnos*]; AV, NEB Apoc., Colius, Calitas. One of the priests who had a foreign wife (Ezr. 10:23; also KELITA; cf. 1 Esd. 9:23). He was present when Ezra promulgated the law (Neh. 8:7; 1 Esd. 9:48), and was one of those who signed the covenant (Neh. 10:10 [MT 11]). Kelaiah gave up his foreign wife at the behest of Ezra (Ezr. 10:23).

**KELITA** kel'i-tə, kə-lī'tə [Heb. *qᵉlîṭā'*–'dwarf']; AV, NEB Apoc., Calitas. This is apparently an allusion to the crippled physical condition of KELAIAH and was his nickname.

**KEMOSH.** *See* CHEMOSH.

**KEMUEL** kem'u-el, kə-mū'el [Heb. *qᵉmû'ēl*–'God's mound'(?)].

**1.** Nephew of Abraham (Gen. 22:21), father of Aram, whom H. G. A. Ewald identified with Ram of Job 32:2. But cf. Gen. 10:21f., where Aram is described as one of the children of Shem. They may not have been the same person.

**2.** A chieftain of Ephraim, one of the land commissioners who divided Canaan (Nu. 34:24).

**3.** A Levite, father of Hashabiah, one of the tribal princes of David's time, a ruler among the Levites (1 Ch. 27:17).

**KENAN** kē'nən [Heb. *qēnan*; Gk. *Kainan*]. A son of Enosh the son of Seth (Gen. 5:9f., 12-14 [AV Cainan]; 1 Ch. 1:2).

**KENATH** ke'nəth [Heb. *qᵉnāṯ*]. A city in northern Transjordan taken from the Amorites by Nobah, who gave it his own name (Nu. 32:42). It was recaptured by Geshur and Aram (1 Ch. 2:23) and apparently regained its original name.

Abel (*GP,* II, 417) identified it with Kerak-Kanata 20 km. (12½ mi.) W of Suweida in the fertile plain of the Nuqra (see map IX in *GP*), on the basis of an inscription recording the adduction of waters *eis Kanata,* "to Kanata." Other scholars have identified Kenath with modern Qanawât in the Hauran, 26 km. (16 mi.) NE of Bozrah. Kenath (*qanū,* Am.Tab. 197:14) is mentioned as a city-state in the Amarna Letters. See *WHAB,* plates IV, VIII; Y. Aharoni and M. Avi-Yonah, *Macmillan Bible Atlas* (1968), maps 34, 38, 249, 250.

W. S. L. S.

**KENAZ** kē'naz, kə-naz' [Heb. *qᵉnaz*–'hunting'].

**1.** A "chief" of Edom, grandson of Esau (Gen. 36:11, 15, 42; 1 Ch. 1:36, 53). He was the eponymous ancestor of the KENIZZITE clan.

**2.** Father of Othniel (Josh. 15:17; Jgs. 1:13; 3:9, 11; 1 Ch. 4:13).

**3.** Grandson of Caleb through Elah (1 Ch. 4:15), though the text is obscure here. Elsewhere Caleb's Kenizzite connections are traced through Jephunneh (Nu. 32:12; Josh. 14:6, 14). *See* UKNAZ.

**KENEZITE.** *See* KENIZZITE.

**KENITES** ken'īts [Heb. *haqqênî,* also *qayin* (Nu. 24:22; Jgs. 1:16; 4:11); Gk. *Kenaioi, Kinaioi*]; NEB CAIN (Nu. 24:22). A tribe of nomads, named in association with various other peoples. They are first mentioned, along with Kadmonites and Kenizzites, among the peoples whose land was promised to Abram (Gen. 15:19). Balaam, in the days of the Exodus, punned upon their name *qayin* as he observed them from the heights of Moab. *Qayin* resembles *qēn,* the word for "nest," and Balaam prophesied the Kenites' destruction even though their nest was "set in a rock" (a reference to their mountain home, possibly the city Sela). The name *qayin,* however, means "smith" or "metalworker." Evidence of such artisans is a tomb painting at Beni-hasan, Egypt, of Semites (*see* picture in BELLOWS). They are shown with donkeys and other animals, a lyre, and weapons and possibly a metalworking implement, thus combining all the arts of Lamech's three sons (Gen. 4:19-22): herding (Jabal), playing of musical instruments (Jubal), and metalworking (Tubal-cain, or Tubal, a smith).

Hebrew *qayin* is related to Arab. *qayn,* "worker in iron," and to Aram. *qênāʾâ,* "metalworker." These similarities provide further linguistic evidence that the Kenites were smiths of some kind. That is not unlikely, since there were deposits of copper ore in what apparently was the Kenites' area — the mountains S of the Dead Sea and in the Sinai Peninsula. It has been conjectured that Moses learned the art of metalworking from the Kenites. But they were evidently not workers in iron, for the Philistines had a monopoly on this trade (1 S. 13:19f.).

Moses' father-in-law, known by three names — Jethro, Reuel, and Hobab (one of these may have been a tribal name) — is called a priest of Midian in Ex. 2:16-21; 3:1; 18:1 and a Midianite in Nu. 10:29 but a Kenite in Jgs. 1:16; 4:11. These passages suggest that the Kenites and Midianites had a close relationship.

The descendants of Jethro the Kenite went up with the people of Judah into the wilderness of Judah in the Negeb near Arad (Jgl:16). The MT, which reads "they settled with the people [*hāʿām*]," has an alternative reading in some of the versions, "they settled with the Amalekites [*hāʿamālēqî*]." The LXX may have been influenced by 1 S. 15:6, where Saul, before attacking the city of Amalek, warns the Kenites to leave the city lest they be destroyed; there is apparently a tradition that some Kenites lived among the Amalekites at that time. One of the Kenite families, that of Heber, migrated north to the Galilee region, indicating that the Kenites were a nomadic group (Jgs. 4:11). The Canaanite general Sisera sheltered in Heber's tent because Heber was at peace with Sisera's king (v. 17), but Heber's wife Jael slew the general (5:24-26). Kenites were not only living again among the Israelites but even killing Israel's enemies.

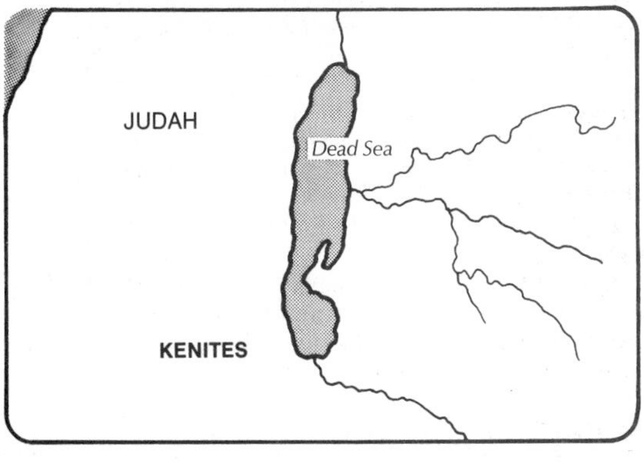


In general, the Kenites were to be found in the southern Judean territories. They were living there when Saul attacked the Amalekites (1 S. 15:6). A little later, when David was a vassal of the Philistines, he attacked Judah's enemies in these southern areas, although he told the Philistines that he was attacking Judahites, Jerahmeelites, and Kenites (27:10). David later sent Judah and its friends part of the booty of his raids (30:29). Some commentators have suggested that two of David's wives, Abigail of Carmel and Ahinoam of Jezreel (25:42f.), were Kenites because the two villages of Jezreel and Carmel are listed in the same group as Kain (Heb. *qayin*) in Josh. 15:55-57. The claim is tenuous, however; geographical proximity does not presuppose familial identity. Another proposal to link David with the Kenites comes from David's being a musician, like the Kenites, but this proposal is also tenuous, since all kinds of people can produce music.

The Kenites seem to have been a recognizable element in the population in postexilic times, for in 1 Ch. 2:55 Kenite descendants of Hammath, father of the Rechabites, lived near Jabez. By then the Kenites had given up their nomadic ways and their metalworking and become scribes. The Rechabites, who were originally of Kenite stock, were also active in postexilic times. The Rechabite Malchijah, ruler of the district of Beth-haccherem, repaired the Dung Gate of Jerusalem in Nehemiah's day (Neh. 3:14).

According to the so-called Kenite hypothesis Moses learned the name Yahweh from the Kenite-Midianite priest Jethro (Ex. 2:16; 3:1-6; 18:1), who worshiped Yahweh. Support for the theory is found in the unusual zeal for Yahweh displayed by the Rechabites, descended from the Kenites. Further, Jethro's sacrifices to God (18:12) are said to have taught Moses how to worship Yahweh. But it is clear from vv. 10-12 that Jethro was learning of God from Moses. The Kenite hypothesis is not now generally accepted, since the arguments supporting it are of very doubtful validity.

Josephus referred to the Kenites as *Kenetides,* but in his retelling of 1 S. 15 (*Ant.* vi.7.3 [140]) the Kenites appear as "the race of the Sikimites [Shechemites]."

*See also* KAIN.

***Bibliography.***–S. Abramsky, *Eretz Israel,* 3 (1954), 116-124; W. F. Albright, *CBQ,* 25 (1963), 3-9; *Yahweh and the Gods of Canaan* (1968), pp. 33-37; Y. Kaufmann, *Religion of Israel* (Eng. tr. 1961), pp. 242-44; *LBHG,* pp. 185, 198, 259, 298; B. Mazar, *JNES,* 24 (1965), 297-303; T. J. Meek, *Hebrew Origins* (1936), pp. 93ff.; H. H. Rowley, *From Moses to Qumran* (1963), pp. 48ff.; *From Joseph to Joshua* (1950), pp. 149ff.; H. Schmökel, *JBL,* 52 (1933), 219-229; R. de Vaux, *Eretz Israel,* 9 (1969), 28ff.

JOHN ARTHUR THOMPSON

**KENIZZITE** ken'ə-zīt [Heb. $q^{e}$*nizzi*; Gk. *Kenezaios*]; AV also KENEZITE (Nu. 32:12; Josh. 14:6, 14). A prominent Edomite clan that claimed Eliphaz, eldest son of Esau (Gen. 36:11, 15, 42; 1 Ch. 1:36, 53), as ancestor. The name is a gentilic adjective derived from the clan's eponymous ancestor, KENAZ, Eliphaz's youngest son. The territory where they lived, along with the holdings of nine other nations, had been promised by God to Abraham (Gen. 15:19). Jephunneh the father of Caleb was a Kennizite (Nu. 32:12; Josh. 14:6, 14). The tribe apparently migrated to the Negeb area in the Late Bronze Age, but to what extent they were in contact with the Kenites at this period is unknown. During the Settlement period they began to be absorbed into the tribe of Judah. R. K. H.

**KENOSIS** ken-ō'sis [Gk. *kenṓsis* < *kenóō*–'empty']. An early Christian theological term relating to the Incarnation of Christ. Few Christian doctrines have been more discussed and less understood. The main cause of this difficulty lies in the mystery of the incarnation and death of the Son of God, who became a man without ceasing to be God. Great theological interest therefore has centered on Paul's declaration that the divine Christ "emptied himself," made Himself "nothing" or "no account," when He assumed the "form of a servant" and thus existed in the form of a man. Although the Gk. *kenóō* is used in this sense only in Phil. 2:7, the idea appears in 2 Cor. 8:9 in Paul's assertion, "Though he was rich, yet for your sake he became poor, so that by his poverty you might become rich." It may also be reflected in Jesus' description of His death upon the cross as His being "treated with contempt" (Mk. 9:12).

Although Scripture teaches and the Christian faith confesses that a divine person became a man and then actually died, both ideas elude the profoundest probings of theological reflection. Moreover, both the manner in which and the purpose for which Paul presents his assertion about the self-emptying of Christ in Phil. 2:5-11 suggest that he himself did not regard his assertion as a special illumination that would throw a brighter light on the general biblical teaching about the incarnation and death of the Son of God, or as a passage of special theological interest.

Appeals to the kenosis have varied with the particular interests of a dogmatic period. In the 19th cent., especially among Lutherans and particularly within the context of the problems raised by their *communicatio idiomatum,* i.e., the transference of the divine attributes to the human nature of Christ, the idea of kenosis was employed to support varying explanations of the human quality of Christ's life on earth. Thomasius held that the Christ retained His divine moral attributes but divested Himself of such attributes as omnipotence, omniscience, and omnipresence and resumed them at the Resurrection. Martensen suggested that during His earthly life Christ lived out of two noncommunicating centers, first as the Son of God within the trinity and then out of a human center where He possessed only ordinary human powers. Earlier Lutherans had suggested that the earthly Christ possessed the divine attributes but used them only on occasion, or concealed them and used them only secretly. None of these views, however, appears to do justice to the self-emptying of Christ.

Modern kenosis theology is far more drastic. Christ is reduced to being no more than the "man for others." In its crudest form the divine self-emptying means that God was in Christ but died when Christ died. Altizer averred that the death of God is a historical event in that through the Incarnation God lost His transcendence (T. J. J. Altizer and W. Hamilton, *Radical Theology and the Death of God* [1966]). Such notions as these, however, do not relate to traditional kenotic theologies.

Theologians in an age of epistemological concern appealed to the kenosis to account for the limitation of Christ's knowledge clearly implied in statements that He "advanced" in wisdom (Lk. 2:52), "learned" obedience (He. 5:8), and was ignorant of the exact time of the Parousia (Mt. 24:36). Yet essentially the same problem of limitation emerges in every aspect of Jesus' human life. That the Christ as incarnate deity possesses limited knowledge is no greater mystery than that He was a helpless baby needing care, food, and clothing to avoid death or that He required rest and sleep throughout His life. These, too, are expressions of the kenosis.

Is the subject of Gk. *ekénōsen* the divine Christ, so that the idea of diminution refers to deity, or is the subject the incarnate Christ, so that the diminution refers to Christ's humanity? The language of Phil. 2 makes it plain that the immediate reference is to the preexistent divine Christ, to Him who existed in "the form of God" (v. 6) but did not regard "equality with God" something to be tenaciously grasped.

Nevertheless, the force and idea of *ekénōsen* also appears in that "being born in the likeness of men" (Phil. 2:7) He as the incarnate man "humbled himself" by becoming "obedient unto death, even death on a cross" (v. 8). This giving over of Himself to death was no less an act of humiliation than that act by which He who existed in the form of God gave Himself over to the existence of a human servant. In each instance, what was more became less, what was rich became poor, and what was something was "set at nought" (Mk. 9:12, AV, ASV); each instance was one of self-emptying. Thus the self-emptying moves from existence as God to the loss of existence in death. From the reality of Christ, Paul's kenotic perspective moves backward to Christ's taking on His servant-human form and to His dying.

This clearly indicates that what Paul declared in the kenosis is not that Christ emptied Himself of His deity in becoming a man. Phil. 2 does not clarify the theological problem of kenosis. This is further substantiated by recognition of Paul's ethical and pastoral purpose in the passage. He is urging the Philippians all to have the "same love" and to be of "one mind" — which they can do only if they act not through "selfishness or conceit" but through a humble estimate of themselves, each counting the others as better than himself. Paul thus exhorts the Philippians, "Have this mind among yourselves, which you have in Christ Jesus" (v. 5) and then describes this mind in the statement that Christ "emptied himself" in becoming man and dying for mankind on the cross as a servant.

Here one approaches the mystery of Christ and of the divine love and grace for sinners without which none can see the kingdom of God. By every rational, commonsense standard of human values, the kenosis of Christ on its levels of both deity and humanity was an unwarranted expenditure that can be justified only in the name of Christian love. Certainly, some Christians are better than others; Paul himself suggests this when he claims he is the chief of sinners. Is Paul the worst sinner that ever lived? Is every Christian at Philippi, is every Christian throughout the world, in objective fact a lesser Christian than all others, and must therefore so regard himself? In terms of objective reality and worth, as well as in terms of logic, obviously not. Yet the Christian must, says Paul, so regard himself and, acting upon this self-estimation, "not look only to his own interests, but also [as Christ did] to the interests of others" (Phil. 2:4). Thus the Christian will have that self-humbling mind of Christ which empties itself for the sake of others. For, says Paul to the Philippians, "it has been granted to you that for the sake of Christ you should not only believe in him, but also suffer for his sake" (1:29), a suffering that is "a clear omen . . . of your salvation" (v. 28) and an inducement to "work out your own salvation with fear and trembling" (2:12).

From the preceding discussion it is clear that the mind of Christ expressed in the kenosis has no special reference to Christ's emptying Himself of His deity. Rather, it exemplifies with that self-emptying of Christ's humanity in death for sinners, the mind of Christ that must characterize all Christians and will unite them all together in one mind and one love, even as it united the divine Christ with mankind both in His humanity and in mankind's sin and death. If the self-emptying of Christ refers only to His action by which He as divine became man, it and the mind of Christ could not be held up as a requirement of the Philippian Christian. J. DAANE

**KEPHAR-AMMONI** (Josh. 18:24, NEB). *See* CHEPHAR-AMMONI.

**KEPHIRAH.** *See* CHEPHIRAH.

**KERAS** (1 Esd. 5:29, NEB). *See* KEROS.

**KERCHIEF** (Ezk. 13:18, 21, AV). *See* VEIL.

**KEREN-HAPPUCH** ker-ən-hap'ək [Heb. *qeren happûḵ*–'horn of antimony,' i.e., a cosmetics case; LXX Gk. *Amaltheias kéras*]. Job's third daughter born after his restoration from affliction (Job 42:14). Antimony, producing a brilliant black, was used in the ancient Near East for coloring the edges of the eyelids, making the eyes large and lustrous. Thus this name suggests a little horn or receptacle for the eye paint.

**KERETHITES** (1 S. 30:14; 2 S. 15:18; etc., NEB). *See* CHERETHITES.

**KERIOTH** ker'ē-oth [Heb. *$q^{e}$rîyôṯ*–'cities'] (Jer. 48:24, 41; Am. 2:2); AV also KIRIOTH (Am. 2:2). A region in the Mishor (tableland) of Moab (Jer. 48; cf. Eusebius *Onom.* 120, *en chṓra Mōab*). The use of the definite article in two of the word's three occurrences (Jer. 48:41; Am. 2:2) seems to support the translation "the cities" (cf. Am. 2:2, LXX: *tṓn póleōn autḗs,* "of its cities"). The word is translated as the proper noun *Kariōth,* however, in the LXX renderings of the Jeremiah passages (LXX 31:24, 41 [*Akkarioth* in MS A, v. 41]). Moreover, the boast of the king of Moab (Mesha Inscription line 13), that he dragged the altar hearth of Ataroth before Chemosh in Kerioth (*lpny kmš bqryt*), suggests that Kerioth was the site of a sanctuary to the Moabite deity.

Attempts to locate the site differ considerably. Aharoni (*LBHG,* pp. 307f.) placed it at el-Qereiyat, S of Ataroth (Khirbet ʿAṭṭārûs). Simons (*GTTOT,* § 1382, p. 450) tentatively proposed Sâliyeh, SE of Beth-gamul. E. D. Grohman (*IDB,* III, 8) suggested AR, particularly in light of Am. 2:2. BDB (p. 901) records Buhl's identification of Kerioth with Rabbah (Rabbath Moab), 17½ km. (11 mi.) S of the Arnon. Abel (*GP,* II, 422) made the likely proposal that, besides the city of this name, the term with the article refers to the region between the Arnon and the Waleh, where numerous important ruins have been found, most notably at Sâliyeh.

W. S. L. S.

**KERIOTH-HEZRON** ker'ē-əth hez'rən [Heb. *$q^{e}$rîyôṯ ḥeṣrôn*]. A place in southern Judah, further identified by the phrase "which is Hazor" (Josh. 15:25). The AV takes the Hebrew as indicating two places, Kerioth and Hezron. The verse presents several problems. Kerioth is plural in form and appears to mean "cities." The Hebrew text reads, "And Ḥaṣor-ḥadatta and [(or) even] Qeriot [(or) the cities of] Ḥeṣron, which is Ḥaṣor" (literal translation). The word *$ḥ^{a}$dattâ* has been taken by some scholars as the Aramaic form of the adjective "new," so that it and the preceding word yield "New Hazor." No explanation is given for why an Aramaic word would occur in a name either in this location or in this text. The LXX reads *kaí hai póleis Aserōn (haútē Asōr),* "and the cities of Aseron (which is Asor [= Hazor])." (Codex Alexandrinus reads *pólis,* "city.") The opening words of the Hebrew verse are not found in the Greek, and Kerioth is taken as a common noun, whether singular or plural. Attempts to identify the site at Khirbet el-Qaryatein, 7 km. (4.4 mi.) S of Maʿîn (Maon) or 8 km. (5 mi.) N of Arad (*GTTOT,* § 317, p. 143), or at Hazar-addar (*GP,* II, 345) are not convincing in view of the problems of the text.

W. S. L. S.

**KERNEL** [Gk. *kókkos*] (1 Cor. 15:37); AV, NEB, GRAIN. The term occurs only here in the RSV, other uses of Gk. *kókkos* being translated "seed." For the whole concept, and for Nu. 6:4, AV, *see* SEED.

**KEROS** kē'ros [Heb. *qērōs*–'fortress'] (Ezr. 2:44; Neh. 7:47); [Gk. *Kēras*] (1 Esd. 5:29); AV also CERAS; NEB also KERAS. One of the NETHINIM, an order appointed to the liturgical offices of the temple.

**KERUB** (Ezr. 2:59; Neh. 6:1, NEB). *See* CHERUB.

**KERYGMA** kə-rig'mə, ke'rig-mə [Gk. *kḗrygma*]. A systematic statement of the theology of the primitive Church as revealed in its preaching. The kerygma was the "proclamation of the death, resurrection, and exaltation of Jesus that led to evaluation of His person as both Lord and Christ, confronted man with the necessity of repentance and promised the forgiveness of sins" (Mounce, p. 84).

The noun *kḗrygma* occurs eight times in the NT. Its basic meaning is "that which is prewched, the message." In some verses, however, it seems to indicate the activity of preaching: e.g., in Tit. 1:3 Paul speaks of God bringing His word to light through "the preaching [*en kērýgmati*]" entrusted to him. Normally the act of preaching would be *kḗryxis* (not found in the NT). *Kḗrygma* belongs to the word group including *kḗryx,* "herald," and *kerýssō,* "to announce, proclaim." In the classical period the *kḗryx* held an important place in the royal court. It was his responsibility to call out in a clear and loud voice whatever needed to be made known publicly. He was often a confidant and attendant to the prince. In later periods he served the state rather than the king. It is significant that while the *kḗryx* was everywhere to be found in Hellenistic literature, the designation occurs only four times in the LXX and three times in the NT. At the same time the verb *kērýssō* is found 29 times in the LXX and 61 times in the NT. L. Coenen reasons that this shift makes it clear that the NT witnesses "avoided identifying themselves or the messengers of Jesus with the Gk. institution of the *kḗryx,* open as it was to such a wide variety of interpretation. . . . it is not the institution or the person to which importance is attached, but only the effective act of proclamation" (*DNTT,* III, 52).

*Kērýssō* does not mean to deliver an edifying discourse but to declare an event. It is through the proclamation itself that divine intervention takes place. Friedrich notes that "the preaching of the apostles is part of God's saving plan for men, like the death and resurrection of Christ" (*TDNT,* III, 709). At the heart of the *kḗrygma* is God's saving action in and through Jesus Christ. John the Baptist proclaimed the imminence of God's rule (Mt. 3:1). The Synoptists summarize the ministry of Jesus as "teaching . . . and preaching [*kērýssō*] . . . and healing" (Mt. 4:23; Mk. 1:39; Lk. 4:44; cf. Mt. 9:35; 11:1; Lk. 8:1). Like his forerunner, Jesus calls for repentance and declares that the kingdom of heaven is at hand (Mt. 4:17; Mk. 1:15). When we move into the preaching of the primitive Church we find the message no longer to be the kingdom but the king. What is preached is Christ — crucified (1 Cor. 1:23), raised (1 Cor. 15:12), Lord (2 Cor. 4:5). The shift from kingdom to Christ is accounted for by the simple yet central fact that Christ *is* the kingdom. He is the power of God let loose redemptively in time and space. The apostolic heralds could now focus the overarching concept of God's sovereign control onto the One through whom He established forever His reign over humanity.

Any survey of the kerygma in modern thought must acknowledge the major contribution of C. H. Dodd, specifically his work in *Apostolic Preaching and Its Developments.* By examining the fragments of primitive Christian tradition embedded in the Pauline epistles and comparing these with the early speeches in Acts, Dodd arrived at a resultant kerygma as "a proclamation of the death and resurrection of Jesus Christ, in an eschatological setting from which those facts derive their saving significance" (p. 24). Dodd's approach met with opposition from redaction critics. Nineham, for instance, held that the Gospel account (Mark) is made up of such disconnected units that no basis for a chronology can be derived ("The Order of Events in St. Mark's Gospel — an Examination of Dr. Dodd's Hypothesis," in D. E. Nineham, ed., *Studies in the Gospels* [R. H. Lightfoot, Festschrift, 1955] pp. 223-241). Wilckens demonstrated to the satisfaction of many that the early speeches in Acts do not reveal any pattern of Jewish-Christian missionary preaching (*Die Missionsreden der Apostelgeschichte* [1961]). Others questioned the items included by Dodd in the kerygma (T. F. Glasson, *HibJ*, 51 [1952/53] 129-132) or objected to defining it in terms of content rather than form (W. Baird, *JBL*, 76 [1957], 181-191). Critical methodologies tend to wax and wane. The lasting significance of Dodd's crucial insights will be determined by the validity of his critical methodology.

*See also* GOSPEL; PREACH.

***Bibliography.***–*DNTT*, III (1978), 44-68; C. H. Dodd, *Expos.T.*, 43 (1931/32), 396-400; *Apostolic Preaching and Its Developments* (1936); C. F. Evans, *JTS*, N.S. 7 (1956), 25-41; A. M. Hunter, *Paul and His Predecessors* (1940); R. H. Mounce, *Essential Nature of NT Preaching* (1960); B. Reicke, "A Synopsis of Early Christian Preaching" in A. Fridrichsen, *et al.*, *Root of the Vine* (1953), pp. 128-160; J. M. P. Sweet, *Expos.T.*, 76 (1964/65), 143-47; *TDNT*, III, *s.v.* κῆρυξ κτλ. (Friedrich).

R. H. MOUNCE

**KESALON** (Josh. 15:10, NEB). *See* CHESALON.

**KESIL** (Josh. 15:30, NEB). *See* CHESIL.

**KESULLOTH** (Josh. 19:18, NEB). *See* CHESULLOTH.

**KETAB** kē'tab [Gk. *Kētab*] (1 Esd. 5:30); AV CETAB. An ancestor of a family of NETHINIM, not found in the parallel lists in Ezr. 2:46; Neh. 7:48.

**KETTLE.** In the RSV this term occurs only in 1 S. 2:14 for Heb. *dûḏ*, a vessel in which meat from the sacrificial animal could be stewed, and Mic. 3:3 for Heb. *sîr*, a cooking pot (cf. AV, NEB).

**KETURAH** kə-too͞'rə [Heb. *qᵉṭûrâ*; Gk. *Chettoura*–'incense']. The second wife of Abraham (Gen. 25:1). In 1 Ch. 1:32f. she is called his concubine. According to the biblical tradition, he contracted this second marriage after the death of Sarah (cf. Gen. 23) and very likely after the marriage of Isaac (cf. Gen. 24). Possibly, as some writers have suggested, Abraham remarried to overcome the loneliness caused by Isaac's marriage.

In 1 Ch. 1:32 (and also Gen. 25:6) Keturah is not accorded the same dignity as Sarah who, indeed, was the mother of the son of promise. For obvious reasons the sons of Abraham's concubines were separated from Isaac. She was the mother of six sons representing Arab tribes S and E of Palestine (Gen. 25:1-6), so that through the offspring of Keturah Abraham became "the father of many nations."

W. BAUR

**KEY** [Heb. *maptē(a)ḥ*; Gk. *kleís*]. In Mt. 16:19 the expression "keys of the kingdom" is employed to denote the authority committed by Jesus Christ to His disciples (cf. Mt. 18:18; Jn. 20:22f.). In the book of Revelation He is depicted as holding "the key of David" and "the keys of hell and of death" (Rev. 1:18; 3:7; cf. 9:1; 20:1). The rabbis spoke of four keys in the hand of God alone, including that of death. In Isa. 22:22 Eliakim prefigures Christ as being entrusted with "the key of the house of David." It is laid upon his shoulder, where the long and heavy keys of the past were carried (cf. P. Haupt, ed., *Sacred Books of the OT* [1893], pt. 10, p. 160 for an illustration of a Cairene merchant in more recent times).

What Isaiah had in mind no doubt is the grand vizier or majordomo, into whose hands is committed "unlimited authority over the royal household, carrying with it a similar influence in all affairs of state" (J. Skinner, *Isaiah* [1915], I, 170). Jewish commentaries usually interpreted the Eliakim passage as referring to the Messiah. It speaks of Him as "the Heir and Lord of the abiding theocracy" and is clearly related to Rev. 3:7; the reference in each to opening and shutting makes the identification complete. 3:7 and the other verses in Revelation that mention the keys imply that the supreme power and the one true key belong to Christ alone. Only He possesses the key by right. He may, however, bestow it on others for use (Rev. 9:1; 20:1).

That the keys have a connection with doctrine as well as with the destiny of souls is evident from Lk. 11:52. There Jesus castigates the lawyers because they have "taken away the key of knowledge" — that is, of the Scriptures, which are able to make men wise to salvation (2 Tim. 3:15). The function of the scribes was to unlock the Word, so that others might be brought to a knowledge of the truth. Instead, by their concentration on the secondary and the peripheral, they locked the book and threw away the key (G. B. Caird, *Luke* [1964], p. 159). The delivery of a key was part of the scribe's ordination.

The authenticity of Mt. 16:18f. was first questioned by H. J. Holtzmann. By the end of the 19th cent. it was widely rejected by radical scholars, many of whom approached the text with the presupposition that Jesus did not intend to found a Church. Harnack denied only the sentence referring to the Church, but his attempt to prove that it is an interpolation made in Rome about the time of Hadrian (A.D. 117-138) is groundless. No Greek MS or ancient version omits it (K. L. Schmidt, "Die Kirche im NT," in *Festgabe für Adolf Deissmann* [1927], p. 283). In recent years there has been a considerable revision of opinion in favor of its genuineness, although some, like Stauffer, Cullmann, and Weiss, would assign it to a different context. Most conservative scholarship maintains the integrity of the saying in its Matthaean setting.

The recipient of the keys is undoubtedly Peter. The crucial question concerns the capacity in which Peter received the keys and whether his was an exclusive monopoly or a shared trusteeship. Mt. 18:18 and Jn. 20:22f. indicate that what is committed to Peter is also delegated to the rest of the disciples. There is no hint of any restriction of this prerogative to Peter alone. Nor can Mt. 18:18 necessarily be confined to the Twelve; indeed, the implication, reinforced by the verses immediately preceding and following, is that every disciple of Christ is similarly invested. R. Glover rightly concluded in his comment on Mt. 16:18: "The words are misunderstood when applied to men of a particular office rather than to men of a particular spirit" (*Teacher's Comm. on the Gospel of Matthew* [1889], p. 187).

The time factor is not to be overlooked. "I will give" in Mt. 16:19 is parallel with "I will build" in v. 18. Neither had started yet, as v. 20 confirms. As soon as Christ began to build His Church, Peter and the rest would exercise the power of the keys. And throughout the period in which Christ goes on building His Church (i.e., until His return) Christians, of whom Peter was the first representative, will go on exercising the power of the keys. It should be noted that v. 19 concerns the kingdom and v. 18 the Church. The precise relationship between the two is not easy to define, but the NT cannot be interpreted as postponing the kingdom to the end of the age. Whatever its weaknesses, the "realized-eschatology" school has established that the kingdom was inaugurated with the first advent of Christ and will continue to grow throughout the age of grace. That it is to be consummated at the end should not overshadow its present reality. Scholars have tended to speak rather of an eschatology that is being realized; even C. H. Dodd accepted this interpretation which confirms the use of the keys before the end has come.

What, then, do the keys entrusted to Peter, and to all believers since him, signify? As Flew brought out, there are two possible interpretations that may be justified by the biblical use of the metaphor. The key of the grand vizier in Isa. 22:22 is undoubtedly the authority given to Christ Himself. But Flew argued that the whole history of the Church denies that this authority was transferred to Peter. Peter's leadership was shared with others and even questioned by Paul in one matter (Gal. 2:11; Acts 11:3). There is no trace of any authoritarian attitude on his part.

Flew preferred to interpret the power of the keys as knowledge, based upon Mt. 23:13 and Lk. 11:52. In Scripture *gnōsis* is not merely an intellectual awareness, but "a spiritual possession resting on revelation" (*TDNT,* I, *s.v.* γινώσκω [Bultmann]). In Lk. 1:77 it is linked with salvation and the remission of sins. "The key is the spiritual insight which will enable Peter to lead others in through the door of revelation through which he has passed himself. . . . And this key is not the exclusive possession of Peter, though on the day of Pentecost by common consent he was the first to use it. It belongs to every confessor of the Son of God" (R. N. Flew, *Jesus and His Church* [1956], pp. 132f.).

The allusion to binding and loosing in the remainder of Mt. 16:19 cannot be detached from the promise concerning the keys, although, if the interpretation favored above is correct, the two concepts are not identical. If the power of the keys is exercised primarily through preaching the gospel, then it has a vital connection with the remission of sins, and Jn. 20:22f. may be used to throw light on Mt. 16:19. But there are significant differences; A. Plummer warned not to read the full meaning of the Johannine saying into this (comm. on Matthew [2nd ed. 1910], p. 231). In the passage in Matthew it is "whatsoever"; in John it is "whosesoever." In Matthew it is binding and loosing; in John it is remitting and retaining.

*See also* KEYS, POWER OF THE; LOCKS AND KEYS.

A. S. WOOD

## KEYS, POWER OF THE.

*I. Problem.*–The reference in Mt. 16:19 to the giving of the keys of the kingdom of heaven to Peter has given rise to considerable debate about what the power of the keys is. On the one side Roman Catholicism insists, on the strength of this saying, that the Roman communion to which Peter came as the first bishop has inherited his prerogative; it is the church in which forgiveness is validly proclaimed, entrance to the kingdom insured, and binding ecclesiastical rules established. On the other side, the churces of the Reformation contend that Peter represents the apostles and that the keys refer to the total apostolic mission, being used to convey the message of remission of believers' sins and to order rightly the Church's life and ministry.

*II. Statements.*–In Mt. 16:19 Jesus makes two clear statements: first, that He will give the keys to Peter, and second, that whatever Peter binds or looses on earth will be bound or loosed in heaven. The second statement finds a direct parallel in Mt. 18:18, where all the disciples are told that whatever they bind or loose on earth is bound or loosed in heaven. A further parallel has been seen in Jn. 20:22f., where the Lord breathes the Spirit on the disciples and connects with this the pronouncement that if they forgive the sins of any these sins are forgiven, and if they retain the sins of any these sins are retained. To be compared with the first statement are the other sayings about keys in the NT, especially in the book of Revelation. The key of death and Hades is in the hands of the First and the Last (1:1). The key of David is held by the True and Holy One who irresistibly opens and shuts (3:7). The key of the bottomless pit is given to angels (20:1). In Lk. 11:52 the lawyers are condemned because they have taken away the key of knowledge, neither entering the kingdom themselves nor letting others do so.

*III. Interpretation of the Statements.*–All authorities agree, of course, that the statements in Mt. 16:19 are metaphorical. The image of the delivery of a key is sometimes connected with the giving of the "key of knowledge" to a scribe at ordination (cf. Lk. 11:52; *HDB, s.v.* "Binding and Loosing"). In Isa. 22:22, Eliakim, at his appointment as steward, has the key of the house of David placed on his shoulder, and it is stated that no one will be able to shut what he opens or opens what he shuts. A relation of the thoughts of scribe and steward with Mt. 16:19 may be that the scribe exercises good stewardship when he imparts knowledge of God's word and work and thereby opens the door of heaven to those he instructs. Binding and loosing may well represent releasing and nonreleasing from offenses, although some scholars prefer to see here again an agreement with rabbinic usage and thus to equate binding and loosing with ecclesiastical rulings on what is right or wrong according to the law of God.

*IV. Relation of the Statements.*–The relation of the two statements in Mt. 16:19 to each other and to v. 18 has also been debated. There can be no doubt that v. 19 is part of a series of sayings to Peter arising out of his confession in v. 16. Whether building the church on this rock parallels giving the keys of the kingdom to Peter may, however, be debated. The first and second clauses in v. 19 seem to be integrally related. Some scholars have argued that the keys denote a special authority that might also embrace civil matters and that is conferred on Peter alone and (at least by implication) the bishops of Rome as his successors. In contrast, binding and loosing is more general, being elsewhere conferred on all the apostles and finding its counterpart in the common or individual absolving that is the function of every priest. Over against this view one should note that here the two statements are both addressed to Peter and that in the light of the key metaphor they obviously have an inner relation; if in other passages the binding and loosing are related to all the apostles, the same may be said of the keys of the kingdom, too.

*V. Role of Peter.*–Whether the power of the keys was vested in Peter alone depends in part on the nature of his confession in Mt. 16:16. Since Jesus asked all the disciples who they said He is, Peter most likely made his famous confession not only for himself but for the others, too. Thus one might infer that the reply of Jesus applied to Peter representatively rather than individually. Even if it applied individually, the question arises whether it applied to him as a private person or as a member of the community. Also, if it was spoken exclusively to Peter, the further question arises whether it extended beyond him to those who would succeed him in a specific office (and, if so, what that specific office is). The thesis that the bishops of Rome succeeded to this office, and are thus vested with the keys as Peter was, depends on particular answers that lack convincing support.

*VI. Question of Power.*–Whether the keys have the primary signification of power may also be debated. Jesus' role as the holder of the key of death and Hades suggests that just as Peter and the apostles can be the Church's foundation only because Jesus Himself is the one foundation, so they have the authority of the keys only as His authorized stewards. Stewardship, however, implies responsibility or obligation as well as power. The papacy itself implicitly recognizes this when it claims to be Christ's vicar on earth, for the stress in vicariate lies more on accountability than on privilege.

*VII. NT Examples.*–The NT gives no direct examples of the use of the keys or the exercise of binding and loosing. Nevertheless the opening of doors in Acts seems to correspond to the use of the keys, for with the preaching of the gospel and its offer of forgiveness the door is opened to the kingdom. Peter initiated the apostolic mission in Jerusalem by proclaiming in the name of Jesus the remission of sins (Acts 2). Philip took the message to Samaria (ch. 8), men of Cyprus and Cyrene to Antioch (ch. 11), Paul and Barnabas to Asia Minor (ch. 13), and Paul and Silas to Europe (ch. 16). In this connection one reads not only of the opening of doors to locations but also of the opening of a door of faith to the Gentiles (14:27).

Examples of binding and loosing might also be cited. Peter condemned Ananias and Sapphira in Acts 5 and Simon Magus in ch. 8 and decided to baptize Cornelius and his household in Caesarea (ch. 10). Paul in the Spirit passed judgment on Elymas in ch. 13, ruled in the case of the twelve at Ephesus in ch. 19, ordered the Corinthians to turn over the incestuous person to Satan in 1 Cor. 5:5 (cf. 1 Tim. 1:20), and later urged the restoration of this (or another) person to fellowship on the basis of the divine remission (2 Cor. 2:5-11). An instance of binding and loosing in the sense of giving a ruling might be seen in 1 Cor. 7, where Paul accepts the binding nature of marriage but declares release when a believer is deserted by an unbelieving spouse (vv. 10-15).

***VIII. Nature, Agent, and Scope of the Power.***–From the NT data one may conclude that the power of the keys is not a special privilege or extraordinary authority reserved for one person or group of people. It has no magical, mystical, or arbitrary features, nor is it ecclesiastical or official in a purely institutional sense. The keys undoubtedly relate to the ministry, but only insofar as it is understood as the proclamation of Jesus Christ and the forgiveness that is mediated through Him, which open to believers the door to the kingdom. The gospel, however, is not a message that Christians devise. It has been divinely given and has received a normative form in the apostolic writings of the NT. It is not something that Christian ministers may arbitrarily choose either to pass on or to withhold. They have a sacred responsibility and even a duty to transmit it to others and may pronounce the door closed only to those who will not repent and turn to Christ for salvation.

Peter did receive the keys, but as a representative of the apostles and indeed of all who join in his confession of Christ as the Son of the living God. All confessing believers may thus exercise the "power" of the keys as they offer forgiveness to others through faith in the crucified and risen Jesus. They do this in concert with others, participating in the ministry of the whole Church, which is more specifically committed to those who are called and set apart for the purpose. The declaration of forgiveness may be continually made to Christians themselves as they acknowledge their ongoing sinfulness, but in terms of entry into the kingdom it has first an evangelistic and missionary function. On the basis of Christ's saving work and the divine commission, ministers of God's Word can boldly state that those who respond in faith to the gospel will have forgiveness, whereas those who do not will still be under the divine judgment unless and until they convert and believe.

Since the use of the keys relates to evangelical ministry, it obviously has nothing to do with political authority. Not before Christ's second coming will the kingdoms of this world be His kingdom. The keys bear no relation to hierarchical structure in the church; although church government involves an external gradation of functions, no greater "power" of the keys lies with those higher in the structure. The evangelical pronouncement has unique boldness and validity because the authority behind it is God's, not man's. Thus it is removed from the sphere of human valuation. Divine authority prevents the manipulation of the keys for the attainment of influence or prestige and allows impregnable ground for confidence in what might otherwise seem to be an arbitrary human evaluation.

Binding and loosing primarily refer to the remitting and nonremitting of sins according to the acceptance or rejection of the gospel by those who hear it. Yet the gospel includes instruction in a new life of discipleship as well as an initial act of faith. Certain things are enjoined and others forbidden, not by arbitrary ecclesiastical judgments, but according to the Scriptures. Hence binding and loosing might involve a broader reference to the rulings (or canons) by which Christians may do some things and not do others. These rulings were first made by Jesus and the apostles and have been embodied in Holy Scripture. Neither the whole Church nor individual Christians can claim the right to change dominical and apostolic rulings or to give the same ongoing validity to new ones in new situations. Church canons, or ecclesiastical rulings in indifferent matters, will always be relative and reformable in distinction from the absolute and irreformable binding and loosing of Jesus and the apostles.

*See* ABSOLUTION; KEY; PETER I.C; ROCK.

***Bibliography***–Comms.; J. A. Burgess, *History of the Interpretation of Matt. 16:17-19 from 1781 to 1965* (1976); H. J. Cadbury, *JBL*, 58 (1939), 251-54; J. Calvin, comms.; *Inst.* iv.2; H. von Campenhausen, *EvTh*, 4 (1937), 143-169; *ERE*, *s.v.* "Discipline"; R. N. Flew, *Jesus and His Church* (1938); *TDNT*, III, *s.v.* κλείς, esp. pp. 749-753 (J. Jeremias).

G. W. BROMILEY

**KEZIAH** kə-zī'ə [Heb. *qᵉṣîʿâ*–'cassia'; Gk. *Kasia*]; AV KEZIA. The second daughter born to Job after his restoration from affliction (Job 42:14). The word cassia became a feminine noun from the fragrance of the flower.

**KEZIZ.** *See* EMEK-KEZIZ.

**KHIRBET** kēr'bət [Arab. *ḫirba*, construct *ḫirbat*]. A lowlying ruin. The term often is part of a place name for an ancient site (e.g., Khirbet Qumrân, "ruins of Qumrân"). It is sometimes abbreviated *Kh*. The Hebrew equivalent is *ḥorbâ*.

**KIBROTH-HATTAAVAH** kib'rəth-ha-tā'-ə-və [Heb. *qiḇrôṯ hatta'ᵃwâ*–'the graves of greed'; LXX *Mnḗmata tḗs epithymías*–'graves of desire' (Nu. 11:34)]. The first stopping-place of the Israelites after leaving Sinai (Nu. 33:16). Here they craved meat, and the Lord sent a strong wind that brought a great quantity of quails, which they ate greedily. Then the Lord smote them "with a very great plague," and many were buried at the place, hence the name (Nu. 11:31-34; cf. Dt. 9:22). Since the next stopping-place was Hazeroth (ʿAin Khaḍrā?), the location of Kibroth-hattaavah must be about halfway between Mt. Sinai (generally identified with Jebel Mûsā) and Hazeroth. A reasonable suggestion is Rueis el-Ebeirig, about ten hours' march from Sinai (*GP*, II, 214; *GTTOT*, § 1632, p. 255). W. S. L. S.

**KIBZAIM** kib-zā'əm. *See* JOKMEAM.

**KICK** [Heb. *bāʿaṭ*; LXX *apolaktízō*–'kick off (or) away'; Syr. *bᵉʿat*–'kick'] (Dt. 32:15); NEB GROW . . . UNRULY; [Gk. *laktízō*] (Acts 26:14).

Hebrew *bāʿaṭ,* which occurs only once else in the OT (1 S. 2:29, if the MT is correct; but see P. K. McCarter, *1 Samuel* [*AB,* 1980], p. 87), is of uncertain meaning in Dt. 32:15. Late Hebrew has two homonyms with this spelling, one meaning "kick" and the other "swell, bulge" (M. Jastrow, *Dictionary* [2nd ed. 1926], p. 180). Either meaning would fit the context. If "kick" is the correct rendering, the imagery of the first line of this verse is that of a domestic animal, probably an ox, that becomes too heavy to work and thus rebels when its master attempts to drive it with a GOAD. If "swell" (which would fit the context very well) is correct, then the imagery could again be that of an overweight animal; alternatively, becoming fat could simply be a metaphor for spiritual indifference. Another possible meaning for *bāʿaṭ* here is "despise," suggested by C. Rabin on the basis of an Arabic cognate (*SVT,* 16 [1967], 228-230). If this is correct, the implied object would be God.

"Kick" appears only once in the NT (Acts 26:14), in a proverb addressed to Paul by Christ. This proverb, which has close parallels in Greek literature (e.g., Euripides *Bacchae* 794f.; cf. also Ps. Sol. 16:4; Philo *Decalogue* 87), refers to the pain experienced by an animal when it kicks against the goad. In this context it thus probably means, "It is futile for you to resist your destiny (of becoming My apostle)" (I. H. Marshall, *Acts of the Apostles* [*Tyndale,* 1980], p. 395). Some scholars (e.g., F. F. Bruce, *Acts of the Apostles* [1951], p. 444) have interpreted the goads to be Paul's conscience, which would have been bothering him since he had begun persecuting the Christians.

J. E. H.

**KID.** The English versions differ very little in their translations of the terms for "kid" (Heb. *gᵉḏî,* "kid"; *gᵉḏî ʿizzîm, bᵉnê ʿizzîm,* "kid(s) from the flock"; Gk. *ériphos,* "kid"). The meat of a kid was very desirable and was frequently prepared for small feasts (Gen. 27:9; Jgs. 6:29), although the fatted calf was even more desirable and more expensive (Lk. 15:23, 27-29). The kid was used in sacrifices (*ʿēz,* Nu. 15:11; *bᵉnê ʿizzîm,* 2 Ch. 35:7). The one figurative use of "kid" is Isa. 11:6, which tells that the leopard will lie down with the kid and the wolf with the lamb, an indication of a future hope of peace.

The prohibition against boiling a kid in its mother's milk (Ex. 23:19; 34:26; Dt. 14:21) led to the Jewish dietary laws, practiced today, of not eating meat with milk. The biblical prohibition has been explained as an attempt in Israel to prevent the unorthodox fertility festivals of its neighbors. This interpretation may be correct, but caution must be exercised, for Craigie showed several problems with the Ugaritic text (*UT* 52:14) that is translated "Cook a kid in milk." This rendering rests on a tenuous reconstruction (*ṭb[ḫ g]d*), and refers only to milk, not mother's milk; moreover, "cook" (Ugar. *ṭbḫ,* "slaughter"; cf. Heb. *ṭbḥ*) is a questionable translation (cf. J. C. L. Gibson, *Canaanite Myths and Legends* [rev. ed. 1978], p. 123). Therefore this text is not a real contrast to the biblical prohibition, although it has often been so cited, and the reason for the prohibition remains unknown.

A very difficult passage is Isa. 5:17. Both the RSV and NEB translations are based on an emendation that follows the LXX, making "kids" parallel "lambs." But the MT *gārîm,* "aliens," does not have to be emended if it is connected to Akk. *gūrū,* "ewe," which also preserves the parallelism with "lambs" (*TDOT,* II, 386).

*See also* GOAT.

*Bibliography.*–P. C. Craigie, *Tyndale Bulletin,* 28 (1977), 155-169; *TDOT,* II, *s.v.* "gᵉdhî" (Botterweck).

J. C. MOYER

**KIDNAPERS** [Gk. *andrapodistḗs*]; AV MENSTEALERS. The term occurs only in 1 Tim. 1:10, in a catalog of vices that (beginning with the fourth term) corresponds to the Decalogue (Ex. 20:1-17; Dt. 5:6-21). In this passage kidnaping corresponds with the eighth commandment, "You shall not steal" (Ex. 20:15; Dt. 5:19). This should not appear odd when one considers that rabbinic exegesis included under this commandment kidnaping for the purpose of selling a person as a slave (SB, I, 210ff.; cf. Ex. 21:17; Dt. 24:7). In the OT, kidnaping for sale carried the death penalty (Ex. 21:17; Dt. 24:7; cf. Gen. 37:28; 40:15; cf. also Code of Hammurabi, § 14).

**KIDNEYS** kid'nēz [always in the pl.; Heb. *kᵉlāyôṯ*; Gk. *nephroí*; Lat. *renes,* whence the English "reins"]. "Reins" and "kidneys" are synonyms, but the AV undertook a distinction by using the former word in the figurative and the latter in the literal passages. In figurative uses the RSV generally translates "heart," "inward parts," "mind," or "soul." The ancient Hebrews assigned specific emotional functions to the major organs of the body, regarding the kidneys as the seat of passion and anger; they apparently did not understand the organs' physiological action.

The kidneys were important in the sacrificial rituals because of the adipose tissue surrounding them. This fat was remarkably pure and in literary use became synonymous with excellence, prosperity, and the like (cf. Job 15:27; Isa. 25:6; Ezk. 34:3; etc.). Being readily combustible, the abdominal fat served sacrificial purposes well and so was credited with a particular sanctity (Lev. 7:22-33; 1 S. 2:16). The kidneys and their accompanying fat were burned in every sacrifice in which the entire animal was not consumed, whether in peace (Lev. 3:4ff.; 9:19), sin (Ex. 29:13; Lev. 4:9; 8:16; 9:10), or guilt (Lev. 7:4) offerings. In Isa. 34:6 the fat of rams' kidneys was equated in importance with the blood of lambs and goats in the sacrificial system. Being rather inaccessible, the kidneys represented dramatically the more remote parts of a person (Ps. 139:13; RSV "inward parts"). Thus to have the kidneys slashed open was tantamount to complete destruction of the individual (cf. Job 16:13).

In a psychosomatic sense, the kidneys were credited with an ability to instruct the mind (Ps. 16:7; RSV "heart") or to challenge motivation (73:21; RSV "heart"). Similarly, God was held to withdraw from those who were governed by the emotions associated with the kidneys (Jer. 12:2; RSV "heart"). Proper control of the passions could bring rejoicing (Prov. 23:16; RSV "soul"); venting them would result in distress (2 Esd. 5:34) or anger (1 Macc. 2:24). God's sovereignty over mankind enables Him to "try the minds and hearts" (Ps. 7:9 [MT 10]; 26:2; Jer. 11:20; 17:10; 20:12; Wisd. 1:6; Rev. 2:23) to determine motivations.

*See also* FAT; SACRIFICES AND OFFERINGS IN THE OT.

R. K. H.

**KIDON** (1 Ch. 13:9, NEB). *See* CHIDON.

**KIDRON, BROOK; KIDRON VALLEY** kid'ron, kid'rən [Heb. *naḥal qiḏrôn*; Gk. *ho cheimárrous toú Kedrōn* (Jn. 18:1)]; AV also CEDRON; NEB also KEDRON. A valley E of Jerusalem, separating it from the Mt. of Olives. The valley results from the confluence of several valleys NE of Jerusalem, probably the most important of which is

Village of Silwan in the Kidron Valley (W. S. LaSor)

Wâdī ej-Jôz, with which it is sometimes identified. It ends, strictly speaking, where it joins the Hinnom Valley to form the Wâdī en-Nâr, with which it is alternatively identified. Locally the Kidron is known successively, from north to south, as Wâdī Sittī Maryam ("the valley of our Lady Mary"), Wâdī Ṭanṭur Farʿûn ("the valley of the tomb of Pharaoh['s Daughter]"), and Wâdī Silwân ("the valley of Siloam"). The Kidron is a seasonal watercourse, i.e., it only carries water in the rainy season; hence it is called a *wâdī* in Arabic, a *nahal* in Hebrew (the only valley in the Jerusalem area so called in the OT), and a *cheimárrous* ("winter-flowing") in the LXX and the Gospel of John. In fact, because of the great quantities of debris, the Kidron seems to have no water at all, even in the rainy season. Its present bed, SE of Jerusalem, is about 12 m. (39 ft.) higher and 27 m. (89 ft.) farther east than the original location.

Near the confluence of the Kidron and the Hinnom is a region of luxuriant growth, suggesting that the "king's garden" (Neh. 3:15) was in this location. There are also references to a watering system in or along the Kidron. The water for such projects came from Spring Gihon, not from the Kidron (*see* JERUSALEM III.C.2.g; D.5.t).

The Kidron Valley is mentioned in the OT only in the period of the kings, and then in only two kinds of references. First, it was the eastern boundary of Jerusalem and, apparently, of the king's direct authority. Thus when David fled from Jerusalem at the time of Absalom's conspiracy, he "crossed the brook Kidron" (2 S. 15:23) and was beyond the reach of the plotters. Again, when Shimei was under "house arrest" in Jerusalem, he was warned by Solomon, "on the day you go forth, and cross the brook Kidron, know for certain that you shall die" (1 K. 2:37). "Crossing the brook Kidron" may have been an idiom for attempting to leave the city by any route, as is perhaps indicated by the sequel to the account in v. 42. The principal gates to the city at that time were on the Kidron side.

Second, the Kidron is the place where images and altars to other deities were destroyed. There Asa burned the idol of his mother Maacah (1 K. 15:13). There Hezekiah destroyed the "uncleanness" that was found in the house of the Lord (2 Ch. 29:16) and the altars for burning incense that were found in Jerusalem (30:14). There Josiah had Hilkiah the high priest burn the Asherah from the house of the Lord (2 K. 23:6) and the altars that the kings of Judah had erected on the roof of the upper chamber of Ahaz and that Manasseh had made in the two courts of the house of the Lord (23:12). Hilkiah also burned in "the fields of the Kidron" the vessels made for Baal, for Asherah, and for all the host of heaven. The word for "fields" is *šᵉḏēmâ,* used only in the plural. In other passages it appears to mean "cultivated fields" (BDB, p. 995). However, it may have a different meaning in 2 K. 23:4 and Jer. 31:40, in light of the ancient versions. The LXX translates — rather, transliterates — the words in 2 K. 23:4, *en sadēmōth Kedrōn,* but Lucian translates the words *en tǭ empyrismǭ,* "in the burning-place." In the Jeremiah passage, *K* reads *šᵉrēmôṯ,* emended in *Q* to *šᵉḏēmôṯ,* and the LXX (38:40) follows *K,* reading *Asarēmōth.* The Vulg. translates the phrase *regionem mortis,* "region of the dead," suggesting that it read the Hebrew as *śᵉḏê māweṯ,* dividing the consonants into two words and vocalizing them accordingly. These facts indicate that an area along the Kidron may have been set apart for such acts of iconoclasm, much as took place in the Hinnom Valley.

In the NT, the word Kidron occurs only in Jn. 18:1. Even there, textual variants suggest that the name was not familiar, and manuscripts have *tou Kedrou, tōn Kedrōn,* and *tṓn dendrṓn,* whereas only Codex Alexandrinus (supported by a few later MSS, the Vulg., and the Syr.) has the correct reading *tou Kedrōn.*

In modern books on eschatology, the Kidron has been given a disproportionately large place. According to Ezk. 47:1-12 a stream of water shall issue from the temple, flow toward the east, and ultimately reach the (Dead) Sea. It shall turn the waters of the sea sweet, so that they become abundant in fish, and the banks of the river shall be lined with trees whose fruit shall be for food and whose leaves for healing. Modern interpreters of this passage often associate the new river with the Kidron Valley and the Wâdī en-Nâr. Likewise, in Joel 3:18 (MT 4:18) a fountain flows from the house of the Lord and waters the valley of Shittim, which is taken to mean the Kidron (more specifically, Wâdī en-Nâr). In Zec. 14:4, 8, however, the living waters flow eastward from Jerusalem through a new opening made in the Mt. of Olives. The spiritual intent of these promises of living water has often been overlooked by such interpreters.

Because of such prophecies and such interpretations, a somewhat fantastic set of identities has developed around the Kidron Valley, beginning about the 4th cent. A.D. It has become the Valley of Jehoshaphat of Joel 3:2 (MT 4:2), the scene of the last judgment. As a result, Jewish, Christian, and Moslem belief in this interpretation has led to a very great number of graves on the slopes of the Kidron, particularly that portion E of the temple mount. The Valley of Hinnom of Jer. 7:31-33 has sometimes been located in the same area, and the distinction between the Hinnom and the Kidron has thus been lost. Even the valley of Baca ("weeping") of Ps. 84:6 (MT 7), because of the promise to make it a "place of springs," has been identified with the Kidron. Doubtless because of such manipulative exegesis, even the name "torrent of Kidron" has come into the vocabulary (cf. *GP,* I, 401 n. 3).

***Bibliography.***–*GP,* I, 83f., 400f.; *GTTOT,* § 139; *Jerusalem in the OT* (1952), pp. 9f.; G. A. Smith, *Jerusalem* (1907), I, 39-41.

W. S. LASOR

**KILAN** kī'lən [Gk. *Kilan*]; AV CEILAN; NEB KEILAN. Head of a family whose sons returned with Zerubbabel after the Exile (1 Esd. 5:15). The sons' names do not appear in the lists of Ezra and Nehemiah.

**KILL** [Heb. *hārag* (e.g., Gen. 4:8), hiphil of *mûṯ* (e.g., Ex. 1:16), hiphil of *nāḵâ* (e.g., Gen. 4:15), *šāḥaṭ* (e.g., Ex. 12:6), *rāṣaḥ* (e.g., Ex. 20:13; Dt. 5:17), *zāḇaḥ, ṭāḇaḥ, ḥālal, qāṭal*]; AV also SLAY, SMITE, PUT TO DEATH; NEB also MURDER, SLAUGHTER, LET DIE, etc.; [Gk. *apokteínō* (e.g., Mt. 10:28); *phoneúō* (e.g., Mt. 5:21), *anairéō* (e.g., Acts 5:33), *thýō* (e.g., Lk. 15:23), *diacheirízō* (Acts 5:30; 26:21), *thanatóō* (Rom. 9:36; 2 Cor. 6:9), *apothnḗskō* (He. 11:37), *phthóra* (noun, 2 Pet. 2:12)]; AV also DO MURDER, PUT TO DEATH, SLAY, etc.; NEB also (COMMIT) MURDER, PUT TO DEATH, MASSACRE, etc.

I. In the OT
  A. Hebrew Terms
  B. Sixth Commandment
II. In the NT

***I. In the OT.–A. Hebrew Terms.*** Although each of the three major Hebrew verbs for killing has its distinctive meaning — *hārag,* "take (someone's) life, kill"; *mûṯ* (hiphil), "put to death"; *nāḵâ* (hiphil), "smite, strike (a mortal blow)" — they are sometimes used as synonyms in the Hebrew Bible. 2 S. 14:7 is especially instructive in that it combines all three: "Give up the man who struck [hiphil of *nāḵâ*] his brother, that we may kill [hiphil of *mûṯ*] him for the life of his brother whom he slew [*hārag*]." Various passages use *hārag* and *mûṯ* (hiphil) interchangeably. In 1 K. 18:12-14 *hārag* represents the penalty for Obadiah's subversive action against Queen Jezebel, yet in v. 9 this same penalty is *mûṯ* (hiphil). Cf. also Gen. 37:18, 20; 2 K. 17:25f.

Hebrew *hārag,* "take life, kill," has Old South Arabic and Moabite cognates, both of which by their usage suggest that the term originated from the vocabulary of holy war — the killing of enemies according to sworn oath. *Hārag* occurs 165 times in the Hebrew Bible, spanning the literature from the earliest texts (e.g., Gen. 49:6; RSV "slay") to the latest (e.g., the Chronicler's history). *Hārag* appears most often in narrative texts and least often in legal texts (see *TDOT,* III, 449f.). Usually the subjects and objects of *hārag* are persons, whether individuals (e.g., Cain in Gen. 4:8; an Egyptian taskmaster in Ex. 2:14), groups (e.g., Simeon and Levi in Gen. 34:25; heirs of Ahab in 2 Ch. 22:8), or nations (e.g., Israel against Midian in Nu. 31:17; Israel in Ex. 5:21). In some instances God Himself is the subject of *hārag* (e.g., Ex. 4:23 [RSV "slay"]; Nu. 11:15). In a few exceptional cases the subject is nonhuman — e.g., lions in 2 K. 17:25 and the viper's tongue in Job 20:16. Of the fifty-five times that the RSV translates *hārag* as "kill," only twice is the object nonhuman: Lev. 20:15f., an animal used in bestiality; Nu. 22:29, Balaam's ass (cf. also Isa. 22:13, oxen [RSV "slaying"]). The killing of animals is elsewhere consistently expressed through the terminology of sacrifice or of meat preparation (esp. *šāḥaṭ, zāḇaḥ,* and *ṭāḇaḥ*; see below). The LXX normally uses *apokteínō,* "kill (someone)," to translate *hārag* (e.g., Neh. 4:11 [MT 5]).

The earliest meaning of *hārag* appears to be "kill enemies in battle or in exercising the ban [Heb. *ḥērem*]." In Nu. 31:17, e.g., *hārag* functions as the equivalent of the hiphil of Heb. *ḥāram,* "put to the ban," in the narration of the ritual destruction of Midian under the rubrics for the conduct of holy war. See also Gen. 34:25; "slay," in 49:6; "slaughtering" in Josh. 8:24-26.

A later usage of *hārag* is for the killing of political opponents (esp. in throne successions, coups, revolutions, etc. [2 Ch. 22:8]), who were often also religious opponents (1 S. 22:21 [cf. the hiphil of *mûṯ* in v. 18]; 1 K. 18:13; Neh. 4:11; 6:10; "slay" in Est. 3:13; 8:11; 9:6, 15f.). *Hārag* designates the penalty for (assumed) treason in 1 S. 16:2; 1 K. 18:12-14, for apostasy in Dt. 13:9, and for regicide in 2 S. 4:12 (David's order of execution for the assassins of Saul's legitimate heir; cf. "slew," v. 10).

*Hārag* also denotes the killing of (nonpolitical) rivals or opponents. Thus it expresses the violent intent of Esau toward Jacob (Gen. 27:41f.) and of the brothers toward Joseph (37:20), and the violent result of the sibling rivalry between Cain and Abel (the notorious first murder, Gen. 4:8; cf. "have slain," v. 23). See also *TDOT,* III, 453f. Occasionally *hārag* refers in legal texts to a crime. Ex.

21:12-14 distinguishes homicide (understood neutrally, v. 13) from murder (v. 14, *lᵉhorgô ḇᵉʿormâ,* "to kill him treacherously"). *Hārag* in this usage remains neutral; the qualifier *bᵉʿormâ* makes it wilful murder that disqualifies the killer from refuge. Cf. Ps. 94:6, where the wicked "slay [*hārag*] the widow and the sojourner, and murder [*rāṣaḥ*] the fatherless."

*Hārag* appears in Ex. 22:24 as a mode of divine retribution (by the sword). In Job 5:2 the simple person "slays" himself through an outburst of anger (par. the hiphil of *mûṯ*). The RSV translates *hārag* "slay" or "slaughter" in numerous other passages.

Hebrew *mûṯ* in the causative stem properly means "put to death" (cf. Lev. 20:4; 2 S. 21:4), but in sixty occurrences the RSV translates "kill." It is used to designate homicidal intent (Gen. 37:18; 1 S. 19:1f.; 1 K. 11:40) as well as homicidal action (Ex. 1:16; 1 S. 17:50f.; 2 S. 3:30). The RSV also renders the hiphil of *mûṯ* as "kill" in contexts of regicide and political assassination (1 K. 15:28; 16:10; 2 K. 21:23; 25:25 par.).

In its primary sense of "cause to die," the hiphil of *mûṯ* appears in the complaint of the people in the wilderness, in combination with *rāʿaḇ* in Ex. 16:3 (NEB "starve to death"), and with *ṣāmāʾ* in Ex. 17:3 (NEB "die of thirst"). In Nu. 14:15f. Moses strives to convince God that it is in His own best interest not to "kill" (*mûṯ* [hiphil]; NEB "put to death") all His timorous people because the other nations would infer that He lacked power to fulfil His divine promises and could thus only slay (*šāḥaṭ*, "slaughter, sacrifice") them in the wilderness. The hiphil of *mûṯ* is also used in Moses' encounter at Midian with the Lord, who sought to "kill" him even though He had only recently called Moses to leadership of His people (Ex. 4:24). This enigmatic story at least underscores the vital significance of the rite of circumcision and thus the seriousness of Moses' oversight (see further Childs, pp. 95ff.). In a similar vein, the faith affirmation that it is the Lord who kills and who makes alive appears in the songs of Moses (Dt. 32:39) and Hannah (1 S. 2:6) as well as on the lips of the king of Israel in the Naaman story (2 K. 5:7); in each instance the verb for "kill" is the hiphil of *mûṯ*. See also the reference in 1 Clem. 59:3 to God as *ho apokteínōn kaí zḗn poiṓn,* "the one who kills and makes alive." The hiphil of *mûṯ* also denotes the ox's fatal goring of a person (Ex. 21:29). The hophal of *mûṯ* is used in the conclusion of the same verse to represent the penalty for the negligent owner (RSV "be put to death"). In the sardonic view of the sage, the hiphil of *mûṯ* is used for the death that the sluggard brings upon himself when his desire finally stirs him to unaccustomed action (Prov. 21:25).

Hebrew *nāḵâ* (hiphil) is the major term for "smite, strike down, attack" in the Hebrew Bible (occurring 480 times in the hiphil stem; usually translated by *patássō,* "strike," in the LXX; translated "kill" thirty-six times in the RSV). The hiphil of *nāḵâ* very often refers to the striking of a mortal blow (Ex. 2:12; 1 S. 21:9; 2 S. 21:12; 1 K. 15:27, 29). Since very few cases of smiting and striking down are not fatal (a rare example appears in 2 K. 8:28; RSV "wounded"), the hiphil of *nāḵâ* is easily translated "kill." It may, for example, refer to homicide (Nu. 35:11, 15, 30; Lev. 24:17, 21), violent assault (1 K. 20:36), or defeat in battle (Josh. 7:15; 9:18; Jgs. 3:29; 14:29; 1 S. 17:9). The hiphil of *nāḵâ* is also used in Gen. 4:15 to indicate the mortal attacks that the outlaw fratricide Cain expected to receive from all sides.

The hiphil of *nāḵâ* is frequently combined with the hiphil of *mûṯ* for the more descriptive "struck down and killed" (1 K. 16:10; 2 K. 15:10) or "attacked and killed" (2 K. 25:25 par. Jer. 41:2). In Ex. 22:2 (MT 1) the same combination is translated "struck so that he dies" (cf. NEB "fatally injured"). *Nāḵâ* (hiphil) in the RSV is most frequently translated "smite." *See also* SMITE, STRIKE.

Hebrew *šāḥaṭ* properly means "slaughter (animals as sacrifice)," "kill (so as to drain the blood)" and has clear Akkadian and Arabic cognates with a similar meaning (cf. Ex. 29:16; Ezk. 16:21; 23:39). Although clearly a cultic term, *šāḥaṭ* is simply translated "kill" fifty-three times by the RSV. In most of these occurrences *šāḥaṭ* refers to the slaughter of animals for sacrifice and food (e.g., Ex. 29:11, 20; Lev. 1:5; cf. for Passover Ex. 12:6, 21; 2 Ch. 30:17; 35:6; Ezr. 6:20). It occurs as a sacrificial term in Leviticus altogether thirty-six times. The sole RSV exception, in which a human is the object, is Elijah's killing of the Baal prophets on Mt. Carmel (1 K. 18:40). See the use of *šāḥaṭ* for child sacrifice in Ezk. 16:21; 23:39 (RSV, NEB, "slaughtered") and for Jehu's massacre of the heirs of Ahab in 2 K. 10:7, 14 (RSV "slew"). In Isaiah's indictment of Jerusalem's wrongheaded response to the siege of Sennacherib — celebrating with merriment and sacrifice the completion of its vaunted antisiege defense system instead of issuing a call to repentance — *šāḥaṭ* is paired synonymously with *hārag* (Isa. 22:13, "slaying oxen and killing sheep").

Although Heb. *rāṣaḥ* and its participial forms usually appear as "murder," "manslayer" in the RSV, it is also translated simply as "kill" in five instances. Two of these represent the eventually definitive appearance of the term in the commandment against killing (Ex. 20:13; Dt. 5:17), and one occurrence is in Hosea's charge against Samaria (Hos. 4:2), which strongly echoes the Mosaic commandment. It is particularly enlightening that *rāṣaḥ* is the verb used for Ahab's heinous crime against the life of Naboth (1 K. 21:19; RSV "killed"), for it connotes more strongly than other synonyms the intentional malicious violence of the act (see also I.B below on the sixth commandment as prohibiting murder). The RSV also has "kills" for *rāṣaḥ* in Dt. 4:42 in connection with the provision for refuge for the accidental murderer. *See also* MURDER; MANSLAYER.

The familiar Hebrew paradigm verb, *qāṭal,* "kill," is actually translated "kill" only once by the RSV, in reference to the murderer (*rôṣē(a)ḥ,* from *rāṣaḥ*) who rises early to "kill" the poor and needy (Job 24:14).

Hebrew *ḥālal,* "pierce, wound," is twice translated "kill" in the RSV. (Otherwise [Job 13:15; Ps. 139:19] God is the subject of this verb, and the RSV translates "slay.") Since in military terminology *ḥālal* is a technical term for the "wounded" in battle (e.g., 1 K. 11:15; RSV "slain"), in Jgs. 20:31, 39 *ḥᵃlālîm* possibly refers to wounded soldiers (cf. LXX *traumatías*), so that the Benjaminites were beginning their sortie by "smiting" and "killing" those few wounded, the survivors of earlier battles, who were still lying in the open field or along the roads. *See also* WOUND.

Hebrew *zāḇaḥ,* "slaughter, sacrifice," although occurring 113 times in the Hebrew Bible, is translated "kill" only three times in the RSV, always to indicate the sacrificial slaughter of food animals. *Zāḇaḥ* may refer both to the routine work of the butcher in preparing cuts of meat and to the whole ritual procedure of preparing and offering an animal in sacrifice. In contrast with the regulations of the Holiness Code (Lev. 17:3-9), Dt. 12:21 allows those who live far from the temple to slaughter animals at home rather than at the sanctuary. In 1 S. 28:24f. the medium of Endor, after stupefying Saul with her feat of necromancy, "killed" a fatted calf and prepared a meal for Saul before his departure. In his lavish attempt to induce Jehoshaphat to join him against Ramoth-gilead, Ahab "killed" an abundance of sheep and oxen (2 Ch. 18:2). In each of these three instances the LXX has Gk. *thýō,* "sacrifice, immolate," for Heb. *zāḇaḥ,* underscoring the ritual character of this preparation of food animals. Indeed, the act of slaughtering became sacrifice in that, while much of each animal was consumed as food, the blood, fat, and certain other parts were set aside for God. The RSV also translates *zābaḥ* "sacrifice" (e.g., in 1 S. 6:15; Hos. 6:6; cf. LXX *thýō* in both).

The verb *ṭābaḥ* occurs only eleven tims in the Hebrew Bible, always applied to food animals in the sense of "slaughter, butcher" (cf. the similar meaning of the cognate *ṭbḥ* in both Akkadian and Ugaritic). *Ṭābaḥ* is twice translated "kill" in the RSV. It has its usual noncultic sense of preparing meat for cooking and eating in 1 S. 25:11 (LXX *thýō*) and in Ex. 22:1 (MT 21:37), the regulation covering one who "kills" (LXX *sphágō*, "slaughter") a stolen food animal, obviously to eat it. *Ṭābaḥ* occurs in poetic parallelism with *zābaḥ* in Isa. 34:6. See further *TDOT,* V, *s.v.* "tabhach" (Hamp).

*B. Sixth Commandment.* Underlying the prohibition against killing is the deeply ingrained Hebrew conviction of the utter sanctity of human life. The precise nature and scope of "killing" that are signified by the Hebrew verb *rāṣaḥ,* however, have been intensely debated. *Rāṣaḥ* is not as common as *hārag* or the hiphil of *mûṯ* (46 occurrences, compared with 165 and 201, respectively). This relatively sparse use alone has suggested that *rāṣaḥ* has a special meaning, understood by numerous commentators as "murder." Some modern translations have thus understood the prohibition as forbidding the committing of murder and have so translated the term (e.g., NEB "commit murder," NIV, NASB, "murder," Ex. 20:13). The great advantage of this rendering is the elimination of the tension between what appears to be an all-inclusive prohibition against killing in any form and a number of OT passages that sanction the taking of human life either in battle or as punishment for crime (e.g., Ex. 21:12-17; Dt. 20:10-18).

B. Childs, following Stamm and Reventlow, has contended that *rāṣaḥ* was originally part of the vocabulary of blood vengeance and has its earliest definition in such passages as Nu. 35:16-21, where the formula *rōṣē(a)ḥ hûʾ* (RSV "he is a murderer") delineates these actions that constitute *rāṣaḥ.* Originally the term functioned objectively to define the acts against persons that could not in fairness be allowed to go unrequited by the vengeance of the *gôʾēl,* the kinsman of blood. For cases of unintentional homicide the system of refuge cities was devised to provide sanctuary for the innocent (vv. 6, 22-28). At some later point (before the 8th cent.) *rāṣaḥ* came less and less to be a neutral term for homicide and began more specifically to denote the malicious killing of a person (cf. v. 20). Thus as it now stands the sixth commandment prohibits such acts of intentional and malicious violence against another person (see Childs, pp. 419ff.).

***II. In the NT.***–Greek *apokteínō,* "kill (someone), put to death," has seventy-four occurences in the NT, and the RSV translates sixty-three of them "kill" (e.g., Mt. 10:28, "those who kill the body but cannot kill the soul"; 21:38 par.; 26:4 par. [NEB "put to death"]; Jn. 5:18; Rom. 11:3). *Apokteínō* occurs and is translated "kill" most often in the Gospels and in Revelation (fifty-three times). Its objects most often are those who represent or speak for God (e.g., Mt. 23:27). In Jn. 16:2 the unfortunate, yet ever recurring, notion that killing an'unbeliever" may constitute a service to God is expressed with *apokteínō.* It may also have the sense "condemn to death" (thus NEB in 2 Cor. 3:6). In the sole NT example of the figurative use of *apokteínō* (Eph. 2:16) the RSV translates "bringing . . . to an end."

In the active voice Gk. *anairéō* means "do away with, destroy (someone)," usually by violent means (combat, assassination, murder, or the like). It is translated "kill" in sixteen instances by the RSV, fifteen of which are in Acts (cf. Acts 9:24; 16:27; 23:15 [NEB "do away with"]). The RSV also translates *anairéō* as "put to death" (e.g., Paul in Acts 26:10; Jesus in Lk. 22:2).

Greek *phoneúō,* "murder," is translated "kill" by the RSV in ten of its eleven NT occurrences. This is the verb that appears whenever Jesus cites the commandment against killing (Mt. 5:21 par. 19:18) and, similarly, in Paul's summary of the law (Rom. 13:9) and in James's interpretation of the commandments (Jas. 2:11).

Greek *thýō,* "sacrifice, immolate," is translated "kill" by the RSV seven times. The specialized ritual character of this verb (preparation of animals for sacrifice and food) may be seen in the circumstances of its use: the "killing" of the fatted calf (Lk. 15:23, 27, 30), of oxen and fat calves for the marriage feast (Mt. 22:4), of the flock by the thief (Jn. 10:10), and of a variety of animals in Peter's Caesarea vision (Acts 10:13; 11:7). Cf. also Tob. 7:8; Ex. 12:21 (of the Passover lamb). The RSV also translates *thýō* "sacrifice" (the Passover, Lk. 22:7; Christ as the paschal lamb, 1 Cor. 5:7). Paul's discussions in 1 Cor. 8:4-13; 10:25-30 are instructive on the close relation between sacrifice and the slaughtering of food animals in the ancient Mediterranean world.

Greek *diacheirízomai,* "handle violently," easily possessses the extended sense "kill" and is so translated by the RSV in both its NT occurrences. This is the verb that characterizes the "killing" of Jesus on the cross in the preaching of Peter and John (Acts 5:30; NEB "had done to death") as well as the intentions of the opposition, to which Paul referred in his defense speech before Herod Agrippa (Acts 26:21; NEB "do away with"); see also Josephus *Ant.* xv.6.1 (173).

Greek *thanatóō,* "deliver up unto death, kill," familiar in the LXX as the equivalent of the Hebrew verbs *hārag* and *mûṯ* (hiphil), appears twice as "kill" in the RSV NT. Paul discovered that it is characteristic of the paradoxical servant life that "we are treated . . . as dying, and behold we live; as punished, and yet not killed" (2 Cor. 6:9; NEB "not done to death"). Rom. 8:36 quotes Ps. 43:22 (= LXX Ps. 44:22 [MT 23]), "For thy sake we are being killed all the day long" (Heb. *hārag*), a clear use of hyperbole for constantly being in danger of death. The RSV more commonly translates *thanatóō* as "put to death" (e.g., in Mt. 27:1; Mk. 13:12; 14:55; 1 Pet. 3:18; cf. also 1 Clem. 12:2).

Greek *apothnḗskō,* "die (of natural causes)," in one instance is translated "killed" by the RSV: the fearful catalog of sufferings borne by faithful martyrs in Heb. 11:37 includes "[being] killed with the sword" (NEB "put to the sword").

2 Peter 2:12 warns against the false teachers who are like "irrational animals . . . born to be caught and killed." Here Gk. *phthóra,* translated "killed," is actually a noun meaning "ruin, dissolution," often having the moral connotation of depravity or corruption (cf. Mic. 2:10, LXX, where *phthóra* represents Heb. *ṭomʾâ,* "impurity, uncleanness"; 2 Pet. 1:4; 2:19, RSV "corruption").

*See also* DEATH I.A; SLAUGHTER, SLAY.

***Bibliography.***–B. S. Childs, *Book of Exodus* (*OTL,* 1974); H. G. Reventlow, *Gebot und Predikt im Dekalog* (1962); J. J. Stamm and M. E. Andrew, *Ten Commandments in Recent Research* (*SBT,* 2/2, 1967), pp. 98f.; *TDOT,* III, *s.v.* "haragh" (Fuhs); IV, *s.v.* "chalal II" (Dommershausen); "zabhach" (Bergman, Ringgren, Lang); V, *s.v.* "ṭabhach" (Hamp); R. de Vaux, *Ancient Israel,* I (Eng. tr. 1961), 158-163.

D. G. BURKE

**KILN.** *See* FURNACE; POTTER.

**KIN; KINS(WO)MAN; KINSFOLK** [Heb. *ʾāḥ*–'brother,' *qārôḇ*–'near' (Job 19:14; Ps. 38:11 [MT 12]), *gôʾēl*–'redeemer' (Nu. 5:8; 1 K. 16:11), *môḏaʿ* (*Q*; *K m$^{e}$yuddāʿ*) and *môḏaʿaṯ* (Ruth 2:1; 3:2), *ʿam*– 'people' (Jgs. 5:14), *ḥay*– 'life' (1 S. 18:18), *š$^{e}$ʾēr*–'flesh' (Jer. 51:35), *dôḏ*–'uncle' (Am. 5:10); Gk. *syngenḗs, syngenís* (Lk. 1:36)]; AV also BROTHER (e.g., Gen. 14:14), LIFE (1 S. 18:18), UNCLE (Am. 6:10), COUSIN (Lk. 1:36), etc.; NEB also BROTHER (e.g., Jgs. 9:18), UNCLE (Am. 6:10), etc.; **KINDRED** [Heb. *môleḏeṯ*–'descendants,' *mišpāḥâ*–'clan, family' (Gen. 24:38, 40f.; Josh. 6:23), *ʿam* (Gen. 25:17); Gk. *syngéneia*]; AV also PEOPLE (Gen. 25:17); NEB also FAMILY (e.g., Gen. 24:38); **NEAR (OF) KIN, NEXT OF KIN, NEAR KINSMAN, etc.** [Heb. *š$^{e}$ʾēr, š$^{e}$ʾēr bāśār*–'flesh of flesh' (Lev. 18:6; 25:49), *š$^{e}$ʾēr haqqārôḇ* (21:2), *gōʾēl haqqārôḇ*– 'the nearest (kinsman-)redeemer' (25:25), *gōʾēl*–'one who redeems=next of kin' (Ruth 2:20; 3:9, 12; 4:1, 3, 6, 8, 14), *gāʾal*–'redeem=do the part of next of kin' (3:13), *qārôḇ* (2 S. 19:42 [MT 43])].

*I. OT Terms.*–The Hebrew terms discussed below indicate various degrees of kinship, from close blood relationship to intertribal relationships according to the tradition that the twelve tribes of Israel were the descendants of Jacob's twelve sons. (For evaluations of this tradition cf. Gottwald; R. de Vaux, *Early History of Israel* [Eng. tr. 1978], pp. 717-749; G. Mendenhall, *Tenth Generation* [1973], pp. 174-197; *see also* PATRIARCHS; TRIBE.) On Albright's theory that *paḥaḏ yiṣḥāq* should be translated "kinsman of Israel," *see* FEAR II.C.

*A. Kin, Kinsfolk, Kinsman.* These terms most frequently translate Heb. *ʾāḥ*. Although *ʾāḥ* is usually rendered "brother," it can also denote a nephew (Gen. 13:8; 14:14, 16; 29:12, 15), a more distant relative (Ruth 3:2; 4:3), any relative at all (Gen. 16:12; 1 Ch. 9:6, 9, 13), or one descended, according to tradition, from a common ancestor (1 K. 12:24; 1 Ch. 7:5; 2 Ch. 28:8; Jer. 7:15; 29:16). Cf. *TDOT,* I, 190-92.

Other general terms for kin are:

(1) *Gōʾēl,* twice used of distant relatives (Nu. 5:8; 1 K. 16:11; see further below).

(2) *Qārôḇ* (<*qāraḇ*, "draw near, approach"), used in a wordplay ("near"–"far") in Ps. 38:11.

(3) *Môḏaʿ* (the *kethibh* may be preferable; cf. E. Campbell, *Ruth* [*AB,* 1975], pp. 88-90; J. Sasson, *Ruth* [1979], p. 39) and *môḏaʿaṯ* — both from *yāḏaʿ*, "know." These terms are used of Boaz in the book of Ruth, apparently designating a general relative; only when Boaz assumes the kinsman-redeemer role is he called a *gōʾēl* (see below).

(4) *Š$^{e}$ʾēr,* also used generally in Jer. 51:35, although textual uncertainty allows a more literal interpretation (see J. A. Thompson, *Jeremiah* [*NICOT,* 1980], p. 761 n. 4; see further below).

(5) *Dôḏ* iam. 6:10, probably referring to a close relative, although the text is problematic (see the comms.).

(6) *ʿAm,* which, according to J. Gray (*Joshua, Judges and Ruth* [*NCBC,* 1977], p. 222), "denotes a tribal ancestor or senior relative," but the context makes R. Boling's translation, "troops," more likely (*Judges* [*AB,* 1975], p. 102; cf. also *ILC,* I-II, 55f.).

(7) *Ḥay,* which usually means "life, living" but one time (1 S. 18:18) denotes some kind of relative, apparently a member of David's immediate family. *Ḥay* is usually explained on the basis of Arab. *ḥayy,* "tribe" (see W. R. Smith, *Kinship and Marriage in Ancient Arabia* [2nd ed. 1903], pp. 41-46; S. R. Driver, *Notes on the Hebrew Text and Topography of the Books of Samuel* [2nd ed. 1913], p. 153). But Gottwald (pp. 260f.) noted that the feminine form, *ḥayyâ* (2 S. 25:13), refers to a Philistine fighting unit, and thus he suggested that *ḥay* means a specific social unit, probably a military organization, not just "kinsmen."

*B. Kindred.* This is another vague term for relatives. In Gen. 12:1 the progression from country to kindred (Heb. *môleḏeṯ* <*yālaḏ,* "bear [children]") to father's house sets the limits of the term. Thus *môleḏeṯ* does not mean the immediate family (father's house) or just a countryman, but, as G. Wenham (*Leviticus* [*NICOT,* 1979], p. 257) suggested"patrilineage" or "extended family" (cf. also *môleḏeṯ* in Gen. 24:4 and *ʾāḥ* in v. 27).

Gottwald has provided a thorough treatment of *mišpāḥâ,* which he said was composed of "'kinsmen' (not implying common descent as such but basically a community of shared interests) . . . [who] lived together in the same village or neighborhood" (p. 257). Thus he suggested the translation "protective association of extended families" (p. 258; cf. further pp. 301-315; *ILC,* I-II, 46-60). In Gen. 24:38, 40f.; Josh. 6:23, however, *mišpāḥâ* appears to refer to the immediate family (cf. Gottwald, p. 258).

In Gen. 25:17 the RSV arbitrarily translates Heb. *ʿam* "kindred"; *ʿam* in every other occurrence of this expression is rendered "people" (cf. esp. v. 8; *see* GATHER).

*C. Near (of) Kin, Next of Kin, Near Kinsman, etc.* Except for 2 S. 19:24 these terms appear exclusively in Leviticus and Ruth as the translation of various combinations of *š$^{e}$ʾēr, bāśār, qārôḇ,* and *gōʾēl*. According to *CHAL,* p. 357, and *TDOT,* II, 318, *š$^{e}$ʾēr* is a synonym of *bāśār,* "flesh." Ugaritic evidence suggests that there are two distinct roots, *ṯʾr,* "kinsman," and *šʾr,* "flesh" (see *UT,* pp. 487, 500), but scholars have disagreed about the meaning of *ṯʾr* (see A. Caquot, M. Sznycer, and A. Herdner, *Textes Ougaritiques,* I [1974], 123f.; M. Dietrich and O. Loretz, "Das Porträt einer Königin in KTU 1.14 I 12-15," *Ugarit-Forschungen,* 12 [1980], 199-204, esp. p. 202). If Ugar. *ṯʾr* does mean "kinsman," then Heb. *šʾr,* "flesh," *šʾr,* "kinsman," and *šʾr,* "remain," are all from distinct roots, and some of the texts discussed below must be interpreted differently. In several texts, however, *bāśār,* which usually means "flesh," does mean "relative" (see BDB, p. 142; *TDOT,* II, 319); thus the one root *šʾr* may also mean both "flesh" and "relative."

The RSV translation of *š$^{e}$ʾēr,* "near kin(sman/woman)," reflects a close family relationship in Lev. 18:12f.; 20:19 (aunts); and 18:17 (stepdaughter and stepgranddaughter); cf. Eng. "flesh and blood" as an expression of biological relationship. In 18:6; 25:49 the unusual expression *š$^{e}$ʾēr bāśār* (lit. "flesh of flesh"), recalling Gen. 2:23 (*bāśār mibb$^{e}$śārî*; cf. *TDOT,* II, 319, 327f.), seems to mean a close relative (so G. Wenham, *Leviticus* [*NICOT,* 1979], p. 253). Wolff, however (p. 29), interpreted 18:6 in a way that distinguishes *š$^{e}$ʾēr* from *bāśār* ("Here *š$^{e}$ʾēr,* as the physiological term for flesh . . . is clearly thrown into relief against [*bāśār*] as the legal term for a member of the family"; cf. W. Eichrodt, *Theology of the OT,* II [Eng. tr., *OTL,* 1967], 146f.). But Wolff's distinction is made questionable by 25:49, where the same expression *š$^{e}$ʾēr bāśār* clearly means a close relative, one in the same *mišpāḥâ* ("family"), who, after brother (v. 48), uncle, and cousin, is next in line to act as redeemer (*gōʾēl*) for a family member who has sold himself into slavery (see also Gottwald, p. 264).

*Š$^{e}$ʾēr* is also used with *qārôḇ* in referring to the immediate family: mother, father, son, daughter, brother, (unmarried) sister (Lev. 21:2f.). Scholars have disagreed about the interpretation of *š$^{e}$ʾērô haqqārōḇ ʾēlāyw mimmišpaḥtô* (lit. "his flesh, the one near to him from his family") in Nu. 27:11. According to Gottwald (p. 265) this expression means "the nearest relative of his *mišpāḥāh*" and refers to "all further degrees of kinship," which have been merged "into one indistinguishable mass"; this interpretation is reflected in most translations (e.g., AV, RSV, NIV). But the NEB's "nearest survivor in his family" reflects the derivation of *š$^{e}$ʾēr* from another Hebrew root *š'r*, "remain" (cognate to Arab. *ṯ'r*; the first-mentioned Hebrew root *š'r* is cognate to Arab. *s'r*). Although either reading is possible in this context, the NEB's is less likely because of the use of *šᵉ'ēr* and *qārôḇ* mentioned above.

In 2 S. 19:42 *qārôḇ* occurs by itself and means "near (of kin)," referring perhaps to David as a member of the tribe of Judah.

As noted above, the book of Ruth, which is very important for any study of relationships in ancient Hebrew society, has several different terms for relatives. Especially significant are derivatives of the root *g'l*. The part. *gō'ēl*, which eight times in Ruth is used for "next of kin," indicates a relative whose responsibility is to "redeem" his kin, i.e., protect and defend them (cf. *TDOT*, II, 351f.; de Vaux, I, 21f.; on the problem of Ruth see H. H. Rowley, "Marriage of Ruth," in *Servant of the Lord and Other Essays on the OT* [1952], pp. 161-186; Gottwald, pp. 261-64; and esp. the comms. by J. Sasson [1979] and E. F. Campbell [*AB*, 1975]). As the widow of a Hebrew, Ruth had the right to receive full support from her nearest kinsman (cf. Sasson, pp. 90-92, who saw Naomi as the one who would benefit from the kinsman-redeemer's action). In 3:12f. Boaz explains to Ruth that there is a kinsman (*gō'ēl*) nearer to her than he, but that if the other kinsman "will not do the part of the next of kin [*gā'al*]" then Boaz himself will (cf. Lev. 25:25, which tells of the responsibility of the *gō'ēl haqqārôḇ*, "next of kin").

*II. NT Terms*.–The three NT Greek words denoting kinship are all based on *syn*, "with," + *génos*, "race, stock." Gk. *syngenḗs* in Mk. 6:4 seems to designate distant relatives (note the progression country–kin–house). It may have the same meaning in Luke, especially in 21:16, where the progression is parents–brothers–kinsmen–friends (note also the links with "neighbor" in 1:58, "acquaintances" in 24:4, and "friends, brothers, and neighbors" in 14:12; cf. Acts 10:24). In Lk. 1:36 Gabriel calls Elizabeth Mary's kinswoman (*syngenís*), but the women's exact relationship cannot be deduced from this imprecise Greek term.

In Rom. 9:3 Paul calls the Israelites "my brethren, my kinsmen by race [*katá sárka*, "according to the flesh"]," reflecting the Hebrew notion that all Israelites are relatives. But in 16:7 Paul calls Andronicus and Junias simply "kinsmen," no doubt meaning fellow Jews (cf. vv. 11, 21; E. Käsemann, *Comm. on Romans* [Eng. tr. 1980], p. 414, translating "fellow-countrymen"). Cf. *TDNT*, VII, 740-42.

*See also* RELATIONSHIPS, FAMILY.

***Bibliography***.–N. Gottwald, *Tribes of Yahweh* (1979); R. de Vaux, *Ancient Israel* (2 vols., Eng. tr. 1961); H. Wolff, *Anthropology of the OT* (Eng. tr. 1974).

G. A. LEE

**KINAH** kī'nə, kē-nä' [Heb. *qînâ*]. A city allotted to the tribe of Judah during the Conquest (Josh. 15:22). It probably received its name from the KENITES, who established settlements in southern Judah (cf. 1 S. 27:10). The city list in Josh. 15 locates it "in the extreme South, toward the boundary of Edom," and some modern authorities have identified it with Khirbet Ṭaiyib, about 5½ km. (3½ mi.) NNE of biblical Arad (modern Tell ʿArâd; cf. *LBHG*, p. 406). This identification has some plausibility because a nearby wadi is named el-Qeini and Kinah is mentioned with ARAD in the Arad ostraca (Y. Aharoni, *Arad Inscriptions* [1975], pp. 48-51; *BASOR*, 197 [Feb. 1970], 16-28; cf. *GP*, I, 273; II, 88, 149; *GTTOT*, §§ 76, 143). J. E. H.

**KIND** [Heb. *mîn*] (Gen. 1:11f., 21, 25; 6:20; 7:14; Lev. 11:14ff.; Dt. 14:14); [*kil'ayîm*–'two kinds'] (Lev. 19:19); [Gk. *génos*] (Mt. 13:47). In these passages "kind" represents a general classification differentiating animal from animal and plant from plant, and not the precise designation of modern biological species or varieties. Cf. SORT in Gen. 6:19; etc.

**KINDNESS** [Heb. *ḥeseḏ*] (Gen. 19:19; 20:13; 40:14; Jgs. 8:35; Ruth 2:20; 3:10; 1 S. 15:6; Job 6:14; Hos. 4:1; etc.); AV also MERCY, LOVINGKINDNESS; NEB also LOYALTY, DEVOTION, "keep faith"; [Gk. *epieíkeia*] (Acts 24:4); AV CLEMENCY; NEB INDULGENCE; [*philanthrōpía*] (Acts 28:2); [*chrēstótēs*] (Rom. 2:4; 11:22; 2 Cor. 6:6; Gal. 5:22; Eph. 2:7; Col. 3:12; Tit. 3:4); AV also GOODNESS, GENTLENESS; NEB also KINDLINESS; [*chrēstós*–'kind'] (1 Pet. 2:3); AV GRACIOUS; NEB GOOD; **KIND** [Heb. *ḥāsîḏ*] (Ps. 145:17); AV "holy"; NEB "unchanging"; [*ḥāsed* (pausal)] (Prov. 11:17); AV MERCIFUL; NEB LOYAL(TY); [polel of *ḥānan*–'take pity on'] (Prov. 14:21, 31; 19:17; 28:8); AV HAVE MERCY ON, PITY; NEB BE GENEROUS TO; [*lᵉṭôḇ*–'for good'] (2 Ch. 10:7); NEB "well-disposed"; [Gk. *chrēstós*] (Lk. 6:35; Eph. 4:32); NEB also GENEROUS; [*chrēsteúomai*] (1 Cor. 13:4); [*poiéō kalṓs*–'do well'] (Acts 10:33; Phil. 4:14); AV "well done"; [*agathós*–'good'] (Tit. 2:5; 1 Pet. 2:18); AV "good"; **KINDLY** [Heb. *ḥeseḏ*] (Josh. 2:12, 14; Jgs. 1:24; Ruth 1:8; 1 S. 20:8); AV also MERCY; NEB "(keep) faith," "honestly," "(see that you come to) no harm" (Jgs. 1:24); [*ʿal lēḇ*–'to the heart'] (Jgs. 19:3; Ruth 2:13; 2 S. 19:7 [MT 8]); AV FRIENDLY, "comfortably"; NEB also "(appeal) to her" (Jgs. 19:3), "(give) . . . encouragement" (2 S. 19:7 [MT 8]); [*ṭôḇôṯ*–'good things'] (2 K. 25:28; Jer. 52:32); [*agathós*] (1 Thess. 3:6); AV GOOD; [*ḗpion*–'gentle'] (2 Tim. 2:24); AV GENTLE.

"Kindness" in the RSV of the OT is always a translation of Heb. *ḥeseḏ*; this term is also once rendered "kind" and five times "kindly." *Ḥeseḏ* is a rich word that has no satisfactory English equivalent. Its etymological origins are not certain. In the OT it basically denotes an attitude and a behavior that display faithfulness to an obligation to a relative, friend, host, guest, master, subject, etc. (*TDNT*, II, 479). This concept became prominent in the history of Israel particularly in relation to the covenant (see Snaith, p. 98).

Ancient Israel shared with Arabia a tradition in which family and tribal bonds had primary importance. The term *ḥeseḏ* was used to designate behavior that fulfilled obligations to those in the family or tribal relationship. Scripture contains numerous examples of these kinds of relationships.

A basic relationship was marriage. Abraham, traveling in Egypt and afraid for his life because of his beautiful wife, reminded Sarah of her duties to him, saying, "This is the kindness you must do me: at every place to which we come, say of me, 'He is my brother'" (Gen. 20:13). Though she risked the danger of being taken by the Egyptians, she was obligated to show the loyalty and duty that the marriage relationship required. Naomi said that Boaz by letting Ruth glean in his fields showed *ḥeseḏ*, an awareness of his familial obligations as one of the nearest kin of their deceased husbands (Ruth 2:20). Ruth showed *ḥeseḏ* by turning to Boaz to fulfil the next-of-kin's obligation to marry a deceased brother's wife (the levirate law of Dt. 25:5-10). He blessed her for having "made this last kindness greater than the first, in that you have not gone after young men, whether poor or rich" (Ruth 3:10), meaning that the *ḥeseḏ* she showed to her deceased husband by leaving her home and following Naomi to her husband's homeland was even surpassed by the loyalty she showed him in marrying his near kinsman (see Glueck, p. 40).

Obligation between related tribes is seen in Israel's treatment of its neighbors and "relatives" (by Moses' marriage), the Kenites (Jgs. 1:16; 4:11). This tribe had shown *ḥeseḏ* to the Israelites in their exodus from Egypt and were shown *ḥeseḏ* in return when Saul spared them while fighting the Amalekites who lived around them (1 S. 15:6).

The rights and duties between host and guest, who became "brothers" with reciprocal responsibilities for protection, are illustrated by Lot's offer of his virgin daughters to the men of Sodom who wanted the strangers (angels) visiting him. Because the host's duty to his guests was so sacred that he had to risk his life for their safety if necessary, Lot protected them in his house (Gen. 19). The strangers in turn showed *ḥeseḏ* to Lot by protecting him from the men and foretelling the city's destruction so that he and his family might flee to safety in the mountains (see Glueck, p. 44).

In ancient Israel the relationship of allies was of the greatest importance, and *ḥeseḏ* was the only possible mode of conduct within it. In 2 S. 9:1, 3, 7 David wished to show *ḥeseḏ* to Saul's house for the sake of his friendship with Saul's son Jonathan. This loyal love had the quality of brotherliness but was based on the mutual responsibilities of friendship.

Rulers and subjects also had mutual rights and obligations. As 2 Ch. 24:22 shows, *ḥeseḏ* was sometimes violated. Joash the king did not remember "the kindness [*ḥeseḏ*] which Jehoiada, Zechariah's father, had shown him," and so he had Zechariah killed.

*Ḥeseḏ* sometimes took the form of "mutual aid," as in Gen. 40:14, where the imprisoned Joseph asked the chief butler to return his *ḥeseḏ* by asking Pharaoh to release him. This request was based on the service that Joseph had rendered in interpreting the butler's dream favorably. Jgs. 8:35 is an example of this relationship broken — the people of Israel did not show to the house of Gideon the *ḥeseḏ* they owed "in return for all the good he had done to Israel."

The meaning of *ḥeseḏ* is greatly expanded in the prophetic literature, where it comes to represent the kind of loving conduct toward all people that pleases God and demonstrates faithfulness to Him (see Glueck, p. 56). In Hosea it "does not reside in the punctilious offering of sacrifices . . . but in ethical and religious behavior and the devoted fulfillment of the divinely ordained ethical commandments" (Glueck, p. 57). Thus there is a reciprocal relationship between God and Israel. "God provides for his people [Hos. 2:10f.], grants peace and rest [2:20], stands by to help [12:10], and is full of benevolence [11:3f.; 3:1]. The people, on the other hand, must obey the divine commandments, heed his demands, and remain faithful in thought and deed" (Glueck, pp. 56f.). In Hos. 4:1 and Mic. 6:1 God has a "controversy" (*rîḇ*) with the people because they have not fulfilled their side of the covenant relationship. In Mic. 6:8 the moral responsibilities for the human side of this relationship are pointed out, the use of *ḥeseḏ* showing that "every man becomes every other man's brother" (Glueck, p. 61). Job 6:14 uses *ḥeseḏ* in the same sense, saying that "he who withholds kindness from a friend forsakes the fear of the Almighty." The obligation appears again in Zec. 7:9: "Thus says the Lord of hosts, Render true judgments, show kindness and mercy each to his brother." The pious man in Ps. 109:12, 16 asks the Lord not to show *ḥeseḏ* to the wicked, for they have not fulfilled their obligations but oppressed the poor and needy.

A praiseworthy woman speaks according to *ḥeseḏ* (Prov. 31:26), and a good man's kind rebuke is not resented (Ps. 141:5). But perhaps the greatest consequence of showing *ḥeseḏ* is found in Prov. 21:21, "He who pursues righteousness and kindness will find life and honor."

In the NT the main word translated by "kindness" is Gk. *chrēstótēs*. It describes human goodness and generosity in 2 Cor. 6:6; Gal. 5:22; Col. 3:12 and conveys the thought of knowing another's need and helping to fulfil it. When used of God in Rom. 2:4 it is linked with both *anochḗ* ("forbearance") and *makrothymía* ("patience"); in 11:22 it appears with its opposite *apotomía* ("severity") as Paul urged the Roman Christians to persevere in showing "kindness" so that God's "kindness" might be shown to them (cf. Eph. 2:7). In Tit. 3:4 *chrēstótēs* describes God and is linked with *philanthrōpía*, which itself is translated "kindness" in Acts 28:2. When used of God the latter term refers to His "love to mankind at large" but usually denotes "love toward individuals in distress" (Guthrie, p. 204). In Acts 28:2 it describes the special hospitality of the natives of Malta toward Paul when he was shipwrecked there. The term *epieíkeia*, which Paul used in addressing Felix, is only a "polite phrase" (Haenchen, p. 653) and occurs in the papyri in the same sense of complimentary address to officials (MM, p. 238). *Chrēstós* is used in Jer. 24:2-5 (LXX) of "good" figs and in Lk. 5:39 of "good" wine, thus meaning "delicious to the taste" (Kelly, p. 86). This same "deliciousness" means "loving" and "benevolent" when applied to God, as His people have "tasted the kindness of the Lord" (1 Pet. 2:3).

*See also* Steadfast Love.

***Bibliography.***–E. D. Burton, *Galatians* (*ICC*, 1921), pp. 315f.; C. H. Dodd, *The Bible and the Greeks* (1935), pp. 59ff.; N. Glueck, *"Ḥesed" in the Bible* (Eng. tr. 1967); D. Guthrie, *Pastoral Epistles* (*Tyndale*, 1957); E. Haenchen, *Acts of the Apostles* (Eng. tr. 1971); J. N. D. Kelly, *First Peter* (HNTC, 1969); *RTWB, s.v.* "Lovingkindness" (Snaith); K. D. Sakenfeld, *Meaning of "Ḥesed" in the Hebrew Bible: A New Inquiry* (1978); N. H. Snaith, *Distinctive Ideas of the OT* (1964); *TDNT*, II, *s.v.* ἔλεος (Bultmann).

D. K. McKim

**KINE** (Gen. 41:2f.; 1 S. 6:7, 10, 12; etc., AV). An archaic plural of "cow" used in the AV. *See* Cattle; Cow.

**KING; KINGDOM.**

I. Introduction
 A. Biblical Terms
 B. Application of "King"
 C. Application of "Kingdom"
II. Historical Survey
 A. Hebrew Kings
 B. Hasmoneans
 C. Herod and His Family
III. Nature of Kingship
 A. General Conception
 B. The Israelite King
 C. Saul and David
 D. Messianic Hope
 E. Character of the Kings
 F. Marks of Royalty
 G. Throne Names
 H. Functions and Officers
 I. Succession
IV. Divine Kingship
 A. General Conception
 B. Israel's Theocracy
 C. Enthronement Ceremony

***I. Introduction.***–*A. Biblical Terms.* The biblical words for "king" are Heb. and Aram. *meleḵ*; Gk. *basileús*. The root sense of the Hebrew word was probably "counselor," since the cognate Aramaic verb *meḻaḵ* means "advise, counsel." But if this is the derivation, little sign of it remains in biblical usage. An alternative original sense is "possessor"; cf. Arab. *malaka*, "possess."

Hebrew has three words for "kingdom," all derived from *meleḵ*. They are *mamlāḵâ*, *malᵉḵûṯ*, and *mamlāḵûṯ*. The other words are Aram. *malᵉḵû* and Gk. *basileía*.

*B. Application of "King."* The title "king" is freely

given in the Bible to a considerable variety of rulers. Princes of small city-states are thus designated (e.g., Achish of Gath, 1 S. 27:2), and so are emperors of vast realms such as Cyrus (Ezr. 1:1). In NT times the Roman emperor is given the same title (Acts 17:7; 1 Pet. 2:17). The rulers of many small states, whether independent or tributary, are called kings; this category includes the Hebrew kings, and in NT times Herod the Great and several of his family.

It is also a divine title, applied frequently to God and to Christ, who are viewed as reigning over the kings of the earth (Rev. 1:5). Pagan deities were also sometimes styled kings by their worshipers (cf. Am. 5:26, RSV, NEB). Names of gods such as Milcom, Molech, and Melkart reveal the same Semitic root, and make it clear that those who revered them viewed them in the same light.

*C. Application of "Kingdom."* The word "kingdom" usually means the territory ruled by a king, or else more specifically his subjects. In NT times the application of the term to the vast Roman empire gave the word almost a cosmic connotation; it implied the political allegiance of a wide diversity of nations and faiths to the one ruling power, vested in one man. Such an understanding of the word "kingdom" may well underlie the NT conception of the kingdom of God (or "of heaven"), which is viewed as having no territorial limits, in a sense embracing diverse elements. Jesus Himself, however, stressed the spiritual as opposed to the political nature of this kingdom. There are strong eschatological elements in the NT portrait of the kingdom of God, and it is not easily decided to what extent Jesus inaugurated the kingdom and to what extent it still awaits its future consummation. *See* ESCHATOLOGY; CHRIST, OFFICES OF IV; KINGDOM OF GOD.

***II. Historical Survey.**–A. Hebrew Kings.* The first Hebrew king was Saul, who took the throne under circumstances of Philistine aggression *ca.* 1020 B.C. David was his successor, and Solomon, David's son, was the third king. During the latter two reigns the kingdom reached its greatest power and extent. After the death of Solomon, however, the northern ten tribes broke away, refusing to give allegiance to the dynasty of David, and thereafter had their own kings, Jeroboam being the first. No one dynasty long held the throne in the northern kingdom (Israel). The last king was Hoshea; in 722 B.C. his kingdom fell to the Assyrians under Sargon II. Meanwhile Judah and Benjamin maintained their own kingdom (Judah), under the Davidic dynasty. The last Davidic king was Zedekiah, deposed and deported to Babylon by Nebuchadrezzar in 587 B.C. Thus ended the kingdom of Judah.

*B. Hasmoneans.* For some centuries the Jews had no independence and no kings of their own. But the revolt against the Seleucid king Antiochus Epiphanes in 166 B.C., headed by Judas Maccabeus, saw the rise of a militant Jewish nationalism. The family of Judas, correctly called Hasmoneans, gradually won independence for Judea; they were undoubtedly the leaders in this struggle, and eventually they claimed royal title. The first to do so seems to have been Aristobulus I (104-103 B.C.). In 63 B.C. the Romans divested the Hasmoneans of their royal position, but the family remained influential.

*C. Herod and His Family.* An important Idumean who married into the Hasmonean family, Herod (the Great), was in 37 B.C. given by Rome the position of king of Judea (with Samaria, Galilee, and some territory in Transjordan), with a large measure of independence. After his death in 4 B.C., none of his sons or descendants seemed to display the same abilities, and though several were given tetrarchies, none was given the title of king and set over Judea except Herod Agrippa I (A.D. 41-44), whose realm was as extensive as that of his grandfather Herod the Great. Lesser members of the family such as Herod Antipas are called kings in the NT, though technically their rank was not that high (e.g., Mk. 6:14).

***III. Nature of Kingship.**–A. General Conception.* A great deal of research into the nature of kingship has been carried out in recent years. It is now recognized that in the ancient world generally, kingship was sacral — a sacred, cultic office as well as a political position. The king was, in fact, universally acknowledged as a mediator between god(s) and people. This inevitably led to his being considered at least a semidivine person. In Egypt, indeed, the king was accorded full divine honors; he was a god in human form. In Babylonia, on the other hand, the king was recognized as a human being, elevated to near-divine status. In Egypt the king was a god incarnate; in Babylon he was a mere man whose office conferred deity upon him. Despite the differences, in both areas the king was pivotal in the cultic beliefs and practices. No doubt the Canaanites followed a similar pattern; in the Râs Shamrah tablets the Canaanite king Keret (Kirta, Kirtu) is styled both the "servant of [the deity] El" and the "son of El." Before the Israelites ever entered Canaan, the enigmatic figure of Melchizedek was acting both as king and as priest of 'El 'Elyon, God Most High (Gen. 14:18-24).

*B. The Israelite King.* It is specifically stated in 1 S. 8:5 that when the Israelites felt they should have a king, they were influenced by the practices of neighboring peoples. It is no surprise, therefore, that the nature of the Israelite kingship was again sacral. Each king was anointed — a sacred ceremony indicating that he had been chosen by Yahweh. As Yahweh's anointed, his person was sacrosanct (cf. 1 S. 26:9). The so-called royal Psalms speak of the throne as "divine" (Ps. 45:6 RSV) and view the king as Yahweh's son (Ps. 2:7). Some of the kings played a part in the cultic ritual (cf. 2 S. 6:17-20; 8:18); David so embedded the kingship in the cultus that his descendants were assured of the throne (of Judah, at least) as a divine right for four centuries. This "Davidic covenant" (cf. Ps. 89:3f. [MT 4f.]) can have had no counterpart in the northern kingdom.

On the other hand, it must be observed that the Israelite king was subject to a measure of control, in matters both moral and cultic. The prophets were prepared to guide the king and moreover to comment on his actions as they felt necessary; thus Nathan fearlessly rebuked David for committing adultery and murder (2 S. 12:1-15), and Elijah denounced Ahab for condoning idolatry and murder (1 K. 21:17-22). For presumptuous actions in cultic affairs Saul was sternly rebuked by Samuel (1 S. 13:8-14), while Uzziah was challenged by the priesthood, and his leprosy was understood to be a punishment for his presumption (2 Ch. 26:16-21). It is quite possible that the priestly functions exercised by David and his immediate successors were related to their position as king in Jerusalem rather than as king of Israel; that would explain the importance attached to Melchizedek — Ps. 110:4 shows that the king's priestly functions were considered to be "after the order of Melchizedek." Possibly the Aaronic priesthood resented the king's assumption of their prerogatives and gradually deprived the ruler of them, the dispute with Uzziah marking the culmination of their efforts.

*C. Saul and David.* Sacral elements in the Israelite kingship can be granted, then. But it is not clear that such elements were very strong in the case of Saul, the first king. The reasons for his promotion to royal office were purely political: the Philistine menace and Israel's desperate need of strong military leadership. Samuel, as Yahweh's representative, anointed Saul, to be sure; but the narrative indicates that there was also a considerable measure of religious misgiving and opposition (1 S. 8:6ff.). Saul's person was considered sacrosanct by David (1 S. 26:9-11), but David's men evidently did not share their leader's views (v. 8). It is conceivable that the nature of the kingship was sacral not so much because Israel followed the pattern of neighboring states, but because David deliberately fostered this conception of kingship, both before and during his reign. Even so, the pattern he chose to follow was probably based on earlier practice, the practice of Jerusalem in particular, as has been indicated (see III.B above).

*D. Messianic Hope.* David's reign was afterward remembered as a golden age. When, later on, kings of Judah proved weak or wicked, the longing arose for another David. This hope received fresh impetus after the Exile when there were kings no longer, and when the state had lost its independence. The expected king was called simply "the anointed" (Heb. *māšî[a]ḥ*), a frequent title for the Israelite king in the Psalter (e.g., Ps. 2:2). The Aramaic word for this was *mᵉšîḥā'*, which was transliterated in Greek as *Messias* or was translated as *Christos*. Jesus claimed to be the Davidic Messiah but stressed that His kingdom was not political, and He interpreted His messianic office in terms of the "Suffering Servant" of Isa. 53. (*See* MESSIAH.) The book of Hebrews emphasizes the priestly character of Christ's kingship; Melchizedek again figures as the prototype (He. 5; 6:20–7:28).

*E. Character of the Kings.* The OT consistently portrays the Persian rulers as thoroughly autocratic, and no doubt the kings of Assyria and Babylon were scarcely less so. But it is clear that the Israelite kings were unable to act in too autocratic and tyrannous a fashion. This is patent in the story of Naboth's vineyard (1 K. 21); King Ahab's wishes were defied by an obstinate landowner, but the king had no intention of taking action to secure what he wanted. His acceptance of the situation elicited from his queen Jezebel the significant remark, "Do you now govern Israel?" (v. 7). Evidently the Phoenician kings of whom Jezebel was the daughter would not have brooked opposition from such a minor individual as Naboth.

The prophets were those chiefly responsible for keeping the king's actions in check. Even so, the Israelite monarchs were guilty of a variety of faults (cf. Dt. 17:16-20; 1 S. 8:11-18); tyrannical behavior and oriental luxury are deprecated. Solomon, in particular, was guilty of the latter, having a huge harem and a most ornate palace and court. The books of Samuel and Kings, however, pronounce judgment on the various kings on the basis of their fidelity to Yahweh; so Solomon is condemned not so much for the size of his harem as for the idolatrous practices he tolerated in order to please his wives (1 K. 11:1ff.).

The character of the ideal king is described in Ps. 101. Dt. 17:14-17 indicates some of the vices of royalty.

*F. Marks of Royalty.* The Israelite kings were always anointed. Two of them at least, Saul and David, were privately anointed first (by the prophet Samuel) and were later anointed a second time at a public ceremony. The fullest description of such a ceremony is given in 2 K. 11:9-12 (2 Ch. 23:9-11). The usual mode of address to royalty was "Long live the king!" (*yᵉḥî hammelek̠*).

The royal insignia were the crown or diadem, the scepter, and the throne. Saul held a spear (1 S. 18:10) and wore an armlet (2 S. 1:10). From the reign of David onward, the Israelite kings had palaces and personal troops. Most of the kings of Judah were buried at Jerusalem in the royal tombs.

*G. Throne Names.* A feature of the Hebrew royalty was the use of regnal names, by which most of the kings are regularly known. Here and there the personal name is mentioned; the most explicit instance is Zedekiah, whose personal name was Mattaniah (2 K. 24:17). David's personal name may have been Elhanan (cf. 2 S. 21:19), Solomon's Jedidiah (cf. 2 S. 12:24f.), Uzziah's Azariah (cf. 2 K. 15:1-7 with 2 Ch. 26). The practice was by no means confined to Israel and Judah; the Assyrian king Tiglath-pileser III held the throne of Babylon under the name Pul (or *Pulu*) and appears with both names in 1 Ch. 5:26.

Detail of a monument in the palace courtyard at Nimrûd (Calah). In the text (*ANET*, pp. 558-560) Ashurnasirpal II (883-859 B.C.; here surrounded by astral symbols of Assyrian gods) describes how he built the city and the (impossibly) large banquet he held upon its completion (Consulate General, Republic of Iraq)

*H. Functions and Officers.* It was the duty of the king to promote the well-being of his subjects in all respects (indeed, the welfare of the nation was generally thought of as integrally connected with the well-being of the monarch). He was therefore responsible for military, fiscal, and legal administration. Apart from sacral functions, it devolved upon him to promote the worship of Yahweh and to put down idolatrous cults, necromancy, and the like. Of course, the king could and did delegate authority, and several lists of royal officers are given in the OT (2 S. 8:15-18; 20:23-26; 1 K. 4:1-19). David seems to have followed an Egyptian pattern in his appointing of officers.

*I. Succession.* In the case of Saul and David, who both came to the throne in a way unprecedented in Israel, selection for royal office was due to the "charismatic" qualities they exhibited; both were possessed at times by the "Spirit of Yahweh" (1 S. 11:6; 16:13), which enabled them to be effective leaders in battle. Both were capable of ecstatic actions (1 S. 10:9-13; 2 S. 6:14). In these respects Saul and David resembled their predecessors the "judges." After David, however, the succession was hereditary. Usually the eldest son succeeded to the throne, but not always. David chose Solomon as successor, even though Solomon had an elder brother living, Adonijah (who indeed made every effort to become king). The last king of Judah, Zedekiah, was the uncle of his predecessor Jehoiachin. In the northern kingdom there were frequent usurpations, and only two dynasties outlasted the second generation. The only usurpation in Judah was that of the queen mother Athaliah, and it was only temporary; a counterrevolution placed a Davidic king on the throne once again.

***IV. Divine Kingship.****–A. General Conception.* It was a commonplace in the ancient world that gods were understood as ruling like kings over their territories (see I.B above). The human rulers were usually closely associated with them. In Babylon there was an annual ceremony (at the new year) at which the king ritually handed back his royal position to the god Marduk and was then redesignated king by the god for the following year. This was called the Akitu ceremony. There were similar new year rituals elsewhere, and the regular feature was that a god, frequently represented by a human ruler, ritually died and rose again (symbolizing the "death" of vegetation in autumn and its rebirth in spring); a sacred marriage ensued, and the god was reenthroned.

*B. Israel's Theocracy.* As has been shown, Israel to some extent followed the pattern of its neighbors. Certainly one of its oldest and most basic concepts was that Yahweh was its King. The very early poem in Ex. 15:1-18 concludes with the words "Yahweh will reign for ever and ever." The ark of the covenant, which undoubtedly antedated the conquest of Canaan, was viewed as the throne of Yahweh (cf. 1 S. 4:4; Ps. 99:1). Numerous Psalms speak of the kingship of Yahweh (e.g., Ps. 5:2 [MT 3]). But whereas other peoples had human kings as mediators between them and the god(s), the Israelites were convinced that to appoint a human monarch would be tantamount to rejecting Yahweh's rule over them. This was the attitude throughout the period of the judges (cf. Jgs. 8:22f.; 1 S. 8:7). It was only urgent political necessity that brought Israel a monarchy. After the era of the kings had ended, the theocratic concept again came to the fore, especially in Isa. 40–55 (e.g., 41:21). When the Hasmonean rulers took upon themselves the title of king at the end of the 2nd cent. B.C., the fact was resented by the more devout Jews; but this was probably not so much because of the theocratic concept as because the kingship was thought to belong solely to the house of Judah and the lineage of David.

*C. Enthronement Ceremony.* In view of the autumnal New Year ceremonies in Babylon and elsewhere, it is fair to ask whether such a ritual ever took place among the Israelites, a ritual including the ceremonial reenthronement of Yahweh (perhaps represented by the king). Yahweh is frequently portrayed as the husband of Israel (cf. Hos. 3:16ff.), which may be an allusion to a ritual marriage annually celebrated between Yahweh and His people. But as noted above, Israel's theocratic concept differed somewhat from that of other nations, and it cannot be taken for granted that such a ceremony was adopted by the Israelites. Certainly there is little hint in the OT that Yahweh was understood to die and revive in the manner of pagan fertility gods.

A number of scholars (particularly the so-called Myth and Ritual School, headed by S. H. Hooke) have contended that such a ritual did take place in Israel; their chief evidence is Zec. 14:16-19, which links references to the Feast of Tabernacles (the New Year Festival) with the thought of the kingship of Yahweh. Also adduced are the Psalms that depict Yahweh as king (e.g., Ps. 93). A recurring phrase in these so-called kingship Psalms is *YHWH mālaḵ*, which is perhaps to be translated "Yahweh has become king" rather than "Yahweh reigns." These Psalms may have been liturgical poems used at such an enthronement ceremony. The phrase, however, may not have this connotation at all; J. Bright suggested the translation "It is Yahweh who reigns." Certainly there is no direct evidence that the Feast of Tabernacles included any such ritual. The hypothesis merits attention, but it is far from proven.

***Bibliography***–A. Bentzen, *King and Messiah* (Eng. tr. 1955); *BHI; DNTT;* J. H. Eaton, *Kingship and the Psalms* (*SBT,* 2/32, 1976); I. Engnell, *Studies in Divine Kingship in the Ancient Near East* (1943, repr. 1967); H. Frankfort, *Kingship and the Gods* (repr. 1978); J. H. Hayes and J. M. Miller, eds., *Israelite and Judaean History* (*OTL,* 1977); S. H. Hooke, ed., *Myth, Ritual and Kingship* (1958); A. R. Johnson, *Sacral Kingship in Ancient Israel* (rev. ed. 1967); S. Mowinckel, *He That Cometh* (Eng. tr. 1956); *NHI;* M. Noth, *Laws in the Pentateuch and Other Studies* (Eng. tr. 1966); *ORHI; La regalità sacra/The Sacral Kingship* (*Studies in the History of Religions,* 4, 1959); J. A. Soggin, *Das Königtum in Israel* (1967); *TDNT,* I, *s.v.* βασιλεύς κτλ. (Kleinknecht, von Rad, Kuhn, K. L. Schmidt); R. de Vaux, *Ancient Israel* (Eng. tr. 1961); G. Widengren, *Sakrales Königtum im AT und im Judentum* (1955).

D. F. PAYNE

**KING, CHRIST AS.** *See* **CHRIST, OFFICES OF** IV.

**KING JAMES VERSION.** *See* ENGLISH VERSIONS V.

**KING OF THE JEWS** [Gk. *ho basileús tṓn Ioudaíōn*]. A title used of Jesus in the Passion narratives both as an insult (Mk. 15:18, etc.) and as an official notice (Gk. *aitía,* Mk. 15:26 par. Mt. 27:37; *titlós,* Jn. 19:19) giving the reason for his execution (cf. Bauer, rev., pp. 26, 180; MM, pp. 15, 637). According to Jn. 19:20, the notice was written in Aramaic, Greek, and Latin (cf. R. Brown, *Gospel According to John,* II [*AB,* 1970], 900-902; J. Blinzler, *Der Prozess Jesu* [3rd ed. 1960], pp. 270f.). *See also* JESUS CHRIST, ARREST AND TRIAL OF V.

The title is used of Jesus more positively in Mt. 2:2, where it not only gives the reasons for Herod's suspicion and violence but also expresses Matthew's emphasis on the Davidic descent of Jesus.

**KINGDOM OF GOD** [Gk. *hē basileía toú theoú*].

I. Terminology
II. Eschatology and History
III. Prophetic Hope
IV. Messiah, Son of Man, Suffering Servant

- V. The NT Fulfillment
  - A. Gospels
  - B. Acts
  - C. Pauline Epistles
  - D. Revelation

*I. Terminology.*–According to all three Synoptics, the kingdom of God was the central theme of the preaching and teaching of Jesus. The phrase occurs fourteen times in Mark, thirty-two times in Luke, but only four times in Matthew (12:28; 19:24; 21:31, 43). In its place, Matthew substitutes "the kingdom of heaven" (lit. "the kingdom of the heavens," Gk. *hē basileía tōn ouranōn*). Although dispensational theology has customarily made a theological distinction between these two terms, the simple fact is that they are quite interchangeable (cf. Mt. 19:23 with v. 24; Mk. 10:23). In Jewish rabbinic literature, the common phrase is "the kingdom of the heavens" (Dalman, pp. 91ff.). In Jewish idiom, "heaven" or some similar term was often used in place of the holy name (see Lk. 15:18; Mk. 14:61).

"The kingdom of God" is a rare expression in literature antedating our Gospels. It does not occur in the OT, although the idea is found throughout the Prophets, and it appears only a few times in intertestamental literature (references in Ladd, *Presence of the Future,* pp. 46, 130f.).

Scholars have differed about the basic meaning of the term, whether it conveys an "abstract" idea of God's rule or reign, or a "concrete" idea of the realm over which He will reign — in this case, the age to come. It is established, however, that the meaning of the Heb. *malkûṯ,* which provides the historical background for Jesus' teaching, was the abstract idea of reign, rule. "They shall speak of the glory of thy kingdom and tell of thy power. . . . Thy kingdom is an everlasting kingdom, and thy dominion endures throughout all generations" (Ps. 145:11, 13). "The Lord has established his throne in the heavens, and his kingdom rules over all" (103:19).

The abstract idea appears in the NT and seems to be the root meaning of the Gk. *basileía* (*TDNT,* I, *s.v.* [Schmidt]). The secondary sense is that of the realm over which a king rules.

Both uses appear in the NT. The RSV renders *basileía* in Jn. 18:36 by "kingship." God's kingdom is His rule, by which He overcomes His enemies and brings to His people the benefits of His reign. In the Lord's Prayer, the petition "thy kingdom come" (Mt. 6:10) is similar to the Jewish prayer "And may He set up His sovereignty in your lifetime, and in your days, and in the lifetime of the whole house of Israel, (yea) speedily, and in a time that is near" (Dalman, p. 99). The coming of God's kingdom is an eschatological event when the kingly reign of God, which is His *de jure,* will be manifested on earth *de facto,* so that His will is done on earth as it is in heaven. This means two things: negatively, the judgment of the wicked and the subjugation of every hostile power; positively, the salvation of the righteous and the redemption of a fallen creation from the burden of evil.

This abstract use of *basileía* is found not only as something eschatological but also as something present (Lk. 17:21). It is the rule of God, which people must receive as little children here and now (Mk. 10:15). It is something that people must seek not only in the future but in their present existence (Mt. 6:33 par. Lk. 12:31), for it has actually come among them in the person and works of Jesus (Mt. 12:28).

Other sayings refer to the kingdom as the eschatological order to be established when God manifests His kingly rule. In such sayings, the kingdom is interchangeable with the age to come (Mk. 9:47; 10:23-25; 14:25; Mt. 8:1[illegible] par. Lk. 13:28). A further group of sayings refers to the kingdom as a present realm of blessings that is here among people because of the mission of Jesus. Mt. 11:11 contrasts the old order of the prophets that ended with John the Baptist with a new order inaugurated by Jesus, called the "kingdom of heaven." The least in this new order is greater than John, even though John was the greatest of the prophets, because he is the recipient of blessings mediated through the ministry of Jesus that John had not experienced. Jesus said to the priests and elders who rejected His message of the kingdom, "The tax collectors and the harlots go into the kingdom of God before you" (Mt. 21:31). To the Pharisees, who also opposed Him, He said, "You shut the kingdom of heaven against men; for you neither enter yourselves, nor allow those who would enter to go in" (23:13).

*II. Eschatology and History.*–A future rule, a present rule; a future realm, a present realm; eschatology and history: this is the rather confusing picture presented in the Gospels. Many scholars have insisted that these two kinds of sayings are mutually exclusive and that the critical scholar must accept one and explain away the other. Liberalism rejected the eschatological sayings as the time-conditioned husk that encased the real kernel of Jesus' religious-ethical teaching (A. Harnack). Scholars who represent a fundamentally liberal viewpoint eliminated eschatology in one way or another and interpreted Jesus' message primarily in religious or ethical terms (see C. J. Cadoux, F. C. Grant, H. B. Sharman, W. Manson, possibly J. W. Bowman). Other scholars have insisted that the essence of Jesus' teaching was eschatology. He was a Jewish apocalyptic prophet who (mistakenly) proclaimed the imminent end of the world and the inauguration of the age to come (A. Schweitzer, E. F. Scott, M. S. Enslin, R. H. Fuller, R. Hiers). This consistent eschatology was accepted by R. Bultmann as the correct description of Jesus' message. Instead of merely setting aside this eschatological message as the "husk," however, Bultmann thought of it as a mythological way of describing an important existential truth: the nearness of God. Therefore he "demythologized" the eschatological message and argued that it *means* that God is near, that God is confronting people with the challenge to decision. The overwhelming sense of the nearness of God caused history to seem to fall away and be at an end.

C. H. Dodd made a new kind of interpretation with his "realized eschatology." He accepted the sayings of the present as the most meaningful and interpreted eschatological language as symbolizing the inbreaking of the eternal into the temporal, the wholly other into the historical. He claimed that in the person of Jesus all that the prophets had hoped for and predicted has been realized. In this interpretation "eschatology" assumes new meanings. Traditionally it designates the things that will happen at the end of the world in the consummation of history. For Dodd, the event that belongs at the end of history has happened in the midst of history. Therefore the person and mission of Jesus are both historical and eschatological — historical outwardly, but eschatological in their inner meaning.

Many scholars have accepted both the present and future sayings as authentic and have combined them in one way or another. They have recognized positive elements in each of the schools of thought described above. Jesus' teaching is spiritual and ethical, but it includes an eschatological consummation. The mission of Jesus is a fulfillment of the OT hope (Dodd). The kingdom is both present and future (see Jeremias, Kümmel, Wilder, Hunter, Schnackenburg, Ridderbos, Ladd). For the history of interpretation, see Lundström and Perrin.

*III. Prophetic Hope.*–While the prophets did not talk about the kingdom of God, its reality was constantly in their prophesying. In the OT the kingdom of God is largely a matter of hope (Bright). The heart of the OT faith is the revelatory and redeeming acts of God in history (G. E. Wright, *God Who Acts* [*SBT,* 1/8, 1952]). Because God has revealed Himself in history, He has shown Himself to be the Lord of history. History is the scene of the divine activity. History, therefore, has a direction and a goal — the kingdom of God. The certainty of the future kingdom springs from faith in God's work of salvation in the history of Israel. This is the source of Israel's eschatology. The Israelite view of history and eschatology is unique (T. C. Vriezen, *Outline of OT Theology* [1958], p. 229).

The prophetic hope of the kingdom of God is expressed in different forms, but there are several constants. God's rule will be established only as a result of a divine visitation. The God revealed in the OT is "the God who comes." Some scholars have found two different eschatologies in Hebrew-Jewish thought: a truly Hebraic concept of an earthly kingdom that arises out of history, and an apocalyptic concept that despairs of history and sees the kingdom as a completely new and different order (S. Mowinckel, *He That Cometh* [Eng. tr. 1956]). This critical reconstruction cannot be sustained from the biblical texts. The earliest prophetic hope looked for a divine visitation when the whole physical order would be shaken in a cosmic catastrophe (Am. 8:7-9; 9:5f.). This is even more vividly expressed in the prophecy of Zephaniah. The prophetic expectation cannot be described as "historical" or "this-worldly" in the sense that it looks for the kingdom of God to be the product of historical forces. The source of God's kingdom is suprahistorical; God Himself must visit His people. "There is no eschatology without rupture" (E. Jacob, *Theology of the OT* [Eng. tr. 1958], p. 318).

Though the kingdom comes from outside of history — from God — it is always an earthly kingdom. The degree of continuity and discontinuity between the present order and the new eschatological order is differently expressed, but both elements are always present. Sometimes the new order of God's kingdom is pictured as the perfecting of the present earthly order (Am. 9:13-15); sometimes the transformation is more radically pictured, involving a complete disruption of the present order (Isa. 51:6; 34:4) so that a new order may be established (65:17). But the new order is always an earthly one. Behind this is the theology of man as creature who stands in solidarity with the world. Not only man but the whole creation stands in need of the redemption that will be realized in the Day of the Lord. Salvation does not mean deliverance from creaturehood, but the perfecting of the entire creation.

An outstanding characteristic of the prophetic hope is the tension between the acts of God in history and the final act of God to establish His kingdom — between history and eschatology. The prophets were scarcely interested in the chronology of the future; they were interested in God and His acting both in history and at the end of history. The Day of the Lord in Amos is *both* the historical judgment when Israel will be taken into judgment beyond Damascus (5:18-26) and a day of eschatological judgment (7:4; 8:8f.; 9:5). Zephaniah describes the Day of the Lord (1:7, 14) as a historical disaster at the hands of some unnamed foe (1:10-12, 16f.; 2:5-15) but also in terms of a worldwide catastrophe in which all creatures are swept off the face of the earth (1:2f.) and nothing remains (1:18). Yet out of universal conflagration emerges a redeemed remnant (2:3, 7, 9), and beyond judgment is salvation both for Israel (3:11-20) and for the Gentiles (3:9f.). Joel prophesies the visitation of the Day of the Lord as a fearful plague of locusts and drought (1:4-12) and also as a universal eschatological judgment (2:10f.; 3:11-15).

In such prophecies, history and eschatology are so blended as to be inseparable and practically indistinguishable. Behind this blending stands a profound theology. The purpose of prophecy is not to give a scheme of future events but to confront Israel with God — with the God of both judgment and salvation. The God who acts in history both to save and judge His people will also act at the end of history in final judgment and salvation. Both the present and the future will witness the redemptive acts of the same God. The prophetic picture of the future often has height and breadth but not depth. The present and the future are blended together because God will act redemptively both in the immediate and in the more remote future. The purpose of prophecy is not to give a chronological scheme of future events; it is to let the light of God's future shine in the present (2 Pet. 1:19).

The OT hope is always expressed in terms of Israel's future. Israel has been called to be God's people; God acts in history both to judge and bless His people; and God will finally bring His people into the salvation of His kingdom. This salvation is formulated in theocratic terms, with the nation Israel restored to the land. It is never the nation as a whole, however, but a faithful redeemed remnant that is the true people of God (Am. 9:8; Isa. 4:2-4; 10:20-22; 37:20-32; Mic. 2:12; 5:7). The Gentiles participate in this salvation, sometimes by way of subjugation to converted Israel (Am. 9:12; Mic. 5:9; 7:16; Isa. 45:14-16; 49:23; 60:12, 14), sometimes by way of conversion (Zeph. 3:9, 20; Isa. 2:2-4; 42:6f.; 60:1-14; Zec. 8:20-23; 14:16-19). The prophets do not envision what may be called a universalistic kingdom; Israel in the form of a purified, converted remnant is the center of the prophetic hope.

*IV. Messiah, Son of Man, Suffering Servant.*–The administration of the kingdom is pictured in very diverse terms that are not synthesized in the OT. Sometimes there is no messianic figure (Amos, Habakkuk, Zephaniah). In other prophecies, it is God alone who reigns over His people (Isa. 2). The most prevalent concept is that of a Davidic king who will be endued with divine power and authority to punish the wicked and bless the righteous (Isa. 9:6f.; 11:1-5; Jer. 33:14-26; Mic. 5:2f.). Although this Davidic king is not called "Messiah" in the OT, he came to be known as such in Jewish thought (Ps. Sol. 17) and in rabbinic literature (J. Klausner, *Messianic Idea in Israel* [Eng. tr. 1955], pp. 458ff.).

A very different figure appears in Dnl. 7, where one like a son of man comes with the clouds of heaven to the throne of God to receive an everlasting kingdom (7:13f.). If in Daniel this is a symbolic figure representing the saints of God, as many critics have thought, in Jewish thought the Son of man becomes a preexistent, supernatural heavenly figure who comes from heaven to earth to set up a throne of glory, judge the wicked, and gather the righteous under his rule in the kingdom of God (1 En. 37–71). This kingdom is described as a radically new order, a transformed heaven and earth (45:4), which are the "world to come" (71:15), in contrast to this world of unrighteousness (48:7). While this Son of man is called "Messiah" in two places (48:10; 52:4), the Son of man and the Messiah are two distinct concepts that are only later conflated (2 Esd. 12:32; 13:3, 26, 37f.). The Messiah is an earthly, human Davidic king who arises from among men to establish the kingdom; the

Son of man is a preexistent, heavenly, supernatural being who comes from heaven to establish the kingdom.

A third figure appears in the OT — that of a humble servant who redeems his people by his own sufferings (Isa. 53). He is not identified; he is a solitary figure, neither messianic king nor heavenly Son of man, who suffers for his people to make them righteous. The OT does not conflate these three figures, and later Judaism seldom understood the suffering servant in messianic terms.

*V. The NT Fulfillment.-A. Gospels.* John the Baptist appeared as a prophet among his people with the proclamation, "The kingdom of heaven is at hand" (Mt. 3:2). It is clear from John's own words that he understood this to be an apocalyptic event. God was about to send a person — designated neither as Messiah nor as Son of man — who would be the agent of the eschatological judgment. He would gather the wheat into the barn and burn the chaff with unquenchable fire (3:12). When "the deeds of the Christ" did not turn out as John had announced, he was perplexed and sent emissaries to Jesus to ask if He really was the one that John had predicted (11:2f.).

Jesus' message is summarized by the same words: "Repent, for the kingdom of heaven is at hand" (Mt. 4:17). He went through all Galilee preaching "the gospel of the kingdom" (4:23). What He meant by this announcement must be decided from His total message. It is a complex idea that involves both fulfillment and radical reinterpretation of the OT hope.

By the kingdom of God, Jesus meant the new eschatological order to be established by a divine visitation. A new terminology emerges in the Gospels that became common in Jewish and rabbinic literature — that of the two ages: this age and the age to come (Ladd, *Jesus and the Kingdom,* pp. 86ff.). Although this terminology is not found in the OT, it is an easy development of the prophetic theology of the kingdom of God. This age is the time of sinfulness, evil, and rebellion against God; the age to come will see the perfect establishment of God's rule in the world and the purging of all sin, evil, and rebellion. The NT interprets the evil of this age in terms of satanic and demonic power. Satan is the "god of this age" (2 Cor. 4:4) who has been allowed in the sovereign wisdom of God to exercise great power in human affairs (Mt. 4:9). Satan is a spirit hostile to God who does all he can to frustrate the will of God. Allied with him are evil spirits — demons — who are capable of taking possession of the human personality. From one point of view, the theology of the entire NT can be understood in terms of a titanic conflict between God and Satan, between the powers of light and the hosts of darkness. The ultimate enemies of God are not sinful people or pagan nations but evil spiritual powers. Since this conflict involves the destiny of individuals and of human history as a whole, however, the conflict is waged on the scene of human history. This is one of the fundamental presuppositions of the Bible — that there is a real invisible spiritual world of both good and evil that impinges upon and determines human existence and destiny. The theology of Satan and demons affirms their existence: evil is not merely human ignorance, failure, or error; nor is it blind fate or irrational chance. Evil has its roots in personality, and it is greater than man and stronger than man. It is God's purpose finally to subdue and destroy these evil powers and deliver people from their enslavement.

This divine victory will be achieved only in the age to come, which will witness the kingdom of God. In fact, it is the coming of His kingdom that will inaugurate the age to come. The term "kingdom of God" is used of the divine visitation (Mt. 6:10; see Rev. 12:10); but in the Gospels it is used more often of the new era to be inaugurated by the coming of God's reign. In this sense, the kingdom of God and the age to come are interchangeable terms.

This is proven by the incident of the rich young ruler. When he asked Jesus how he might inherit eternal life, he was asking about life in the age to come — the life of the resurrection (Dnl. 12:2). In His reply, Jesus spoke about entering the kingdom of God (Mk. 10:23ff.), about being saved (v. 26), and also about receiving eternal life in the age to come (v. 30). Thus Mk. 9:47 tells of entering the kingdom of God, while Mt. 18:9 tells of entering life. Usually this future age is spoken of simply as the kingdom of God into which the righteous will enter and from which the unrighteous will be excluded (Mt. 5:20; 7:21; Mk. 9:47).

This age will end and the new age of God's kingdom will be inaugurated by the coming of the heavenly Son of man. The early Church certainly believed that Jesus taught that He was Himself destined to be the heavenly Son of man who would inaugurate the kingdom of God. Mt. 24:3 reports that the disciples asked what would be the sign of His parousia and the consummation of the age. The discourse that follows speaks at length of the coming of the heavenly Son of man with power and great glory to gather the elect into the kingdom of God (vv. 30f.). The Son of man will come in His glory to sit upon the throne of judgment to decide the destiny of everyone. The righteous will inherit the kingdom of God (25:34), which again means to enter into eternal life (v. 46), while the wicked will suffer the judgment of eternal punishment. The parable of the weeds and wheat teaches that the Son of man will send His angels to gather all causes of sin and all evildoers out of His kingdom; then the righteous will shine like the sun in the kingdom of God (13:41f.). The future destiny of individuals will be decided by the Son of man on the basis of the relationship of individuals to Jesus (Lk. 12:8; the parallel in Mt. 10:32 does not refer to the Son of man but only to Jesus in both His historical and eschatological mission).

The parable of the judgment of the nations implies that it will be the eschatological mission of the Son of man to win the final victory over the demonic powers of evil, for the place of condemnation is called the eternal fire prepared for the devil and his angels (Mt. 25:41). The coming of the kingdom of God will witness the complete expurgation of evil from God's creation.

Life in the eschatological kingdom of God — life in the age to come — will be resurrection life. Although the Gospels say little about resurrection, Luke reports a saying that equates attaining to the age to come with the resurrection (Lk. 20:34f.). Resurrection life will mean a transformed existence very different from the life of this age. There will be no more death; therefore the need for procreation will no longer exist.

The Gospels say very little about the conditions in the kingdom of God. That it will involve a transformation of the whole created order is reflected in Mt. 19:28. The "new world" (RSV) is literally the "regeneration" of the world. Although the word belongs to the world of Hellenistic Judaism and not to Aramaic idiom, it expresses the theology of resurrection and world renewal (*TDNT,* I, 688).

In their treatment of the age to come, the Gospels' primary interest is its soteriological dimension — the restoration of fellowship with God. The pure in heart will see God (Mt. 5:8) and enter into the joy of their Lord (25:21, 23). The harvest will take place and the grain will be gathered into the barn (13:30, 39; Mk. 4:29; cf. Mt. 3:12; Rev. 14:15). The sheep will be separated from the goats and brought safely into the fold (Mt. 25:32). The most common picture is that of a feast or table fellowship.

perhaps near the "king's wine presses" (Zec. 14:10). Josephus located it near En-rogel (*Ant.* ix.10.4 [225]). The garden was in the Kidron Valley, probably on a lower slope of the City of David, where it could have been watered by the overflow from the pool of Siloam (cf. Neh. 3:15), and so flourish all year round. *See also* JERUSALEM III.D.5.t; F.2.f; JERUSALEM maps in I. 1011, 1020.

See J. H. Negenman, *New Atlas of the Bible* (Eng. tr. 1969), pp. 66, 109. P. L. GARBER R. K. H.

**KING'S HIGHWAY** [Heb. *derek̠ hammelek̠*]. A road or routes in Edom and northern Moab, mentioned in Nu. 20:17; 21:22 (cf. Dt. 2:27).

Since the publication of N. Glueck's exploration of the Transjordan (*Other Side of the Jordan* [1940]), *derek̠ hammelek̠* has been considered a reference to an ancient way roughly identical with the Roman *Via Nova* and the Turkish "Sultan's Highway." The route of this road follows the narrow strip of highland between the rocky, arid desert and the scarp of the Jordan Rift Valley and connects such prominent sites as Damascus, Gerasa, Rabbath-ammon, Heshbon, Dibon, Kir-hareseth, Bosra, and Petra.

Presumably it connected south Arabia and Elath with Damascus and Mesopotamia. Fortresses along this route from as early as E.B. IV-M.B. I and Iron I seem to confirm its identification with the King's Highway. The description in Gen. 14 of Chedorlaomer's foray seems to assume such a route.

*Derek̠ hammelek̠* may not signify a single, named route, however. First, the term may be an appellative (e.g., "the royal road," or any road that the king designated), as early commentators assumed. Second, since Nu. 20:17 describes Moses asking permission to pass through Edomite territory from Kadesh-barnea, and 21:22 shows a quest for passage N of the Arnon, different routes may be indicated. Third, no pattern of Iron Age sites that conforms to the modern or Roman road has been discovered in recent surveys.

North-south routes through Transjordan are likely, however, especially when political stability permitted interregional trade. Control of such trade probably motivated many of the wars and alliances that involved the peoples of Transjordan, such as the Davidic campaigns and the wars of the Omrides (*see* MOAB).

*Bibliography.–GB* (2nd ed. 1974), p. 97; *LBHG* (rev. ed. 1979), pp. 54-57; J. M. Miller, *Perspectives in Religious Studies* 8 (1981), pp. 219-229. J. R. KAUTZ, III

**KING'S MOTHER.** The queen mother had a very important position at the courts of the kings of Israel. Her authority may have reflected the influence of the ancient Egyptian matriarchate. Examples are: Bathsheba (1 K. 2:19); Maacah (15:13); Athaliah (2 Ch. 22:2); and Nehushta (2 K. 24:8; Jer. 13:18). *See* QUEEN; QUEEN MOTHER.

**KING'S POOL** [Heb. *b^erēk̠aṯ hammelek̠*] A name occurring only in Neh. 2:14. It is apparently another name for the Pool of Shelah (*see* SILOAM) of 3:15 and the "pool that was made" (AV) or "artificial pool" (RSV, NEB) of 3:16.

Ruins of a Roman military camp on a possible route of the King's Highway along the Arnon in northern Moab (A. D. Baly)

**KING'S VALLEY** [Heb. *ʿēmeq hammeleḵ*] (Gen. 14:17; 2 S. 18:18); AV KING'S DALE; NEB also KING'S VALE (2 S. 18:18); **VALLEY OF SHAVEH** shä'və [Heb. *ʿēmeq šāwēh*–'valley of a plain'(?)] (Gen. 14:17). The place where Abraham, after defeating the coalition of kings, met the king of Sodom (Gen. 14:17); later Absalom built a monument there (2 S. 18:18). Although Gen. 14:17 identifies the King's Valley with the Valley of Shaveh, many scholars have rejected that identification (see below). Geographical and exegetical problems leave the location in doubt.

The geographical problem is that no exact location is given for this valley, although sources and traditions point to possibilities N, E, and SE of Jerusalem. Gen. 14:17f. suggests a locale near Jerusalem (if Salem = Jerusalem, which is doubtful; *see* JERUSALEM I.B), and Josephus (*Ant.* vii.10.3 [243]) stated that it was two stades from Jerusalem. J. Mauchline (*1 and 2 Samuel* [*NCBC*, 1971], p. 287) noted that a "Valley of the Kings" is located about 1 km. (½ mi.) N of the Damascus Gate, but this is a post-Christian name given to the site of the tombs of the first-century Queen Helena (of Adiabene) and her sons. Similarly, in the Kidron Valley just below Gethsemane is the "tomb of Absalom," which a late tradition identifies with Absalom's monument (2 S. 18:18). It was built in late Hellenistic times (probably in the 1st cent. A.D.), however, and according to A. Dillmann (comm. on Genesis [Eng. tr. 1897], II, 48) and J. Simons (*GTTOT*, § 364) a locale in the Kidron Valley is ruled out because the Kidron is always called a *naḥal* ("brook, wadi"), not an *ʿēmeq*. The supposition that the KING'S GARDEN, which is thought to have been near the southeast corner of Jerusalem, was in the vicinity of the King's Valley has little to commend it (*contra* G. A. Barrois, *IDB*, IV, *s.v.* "Shaveh, Valley of"; cf. B. Mazar, *Mountain of the Lord* [Eng. tr. 1975], p. 156, who located the King's Valley near En-rogel, apparently also on the supposition that the King's Valley and the king's garden were near one another). The gloss in 1QapGen 22:13 identifies the Valley of Shaveh as the Valley of Beth-haccerem (Ramat Raḥel, about 3 km. [2 mi.] S of Jerusalem), but no other evidence supports this identification.

The exegetical problem concerns the phrase *ʿēmeq šāwēh*, which makes little literal sense. Since no place called Shaveh was known in Israel (the Shawe mentioned in Papyrus Anastasi I [cf. *ANET*, p. 477] was just N of Byblos), various reconstructions have been proposed. Simons (*GTTOT*, § 364) thought that the text originally read *šāwēh hammeleḵ*, "plain of the king," but that reading hardly helps to locate the place. B. Vawter (*On Genesis* [1977], pp. 196f.) connected the Valley of Shaveh with SHAVEH-KIRIATHAIM (cf. v. 5), where the battle was fought in Transjordan; this is a more likely locale. The phrase "that is, the King's Valley" is generally recognized as a gloss (note the RSV's use of parentheses).

A. Wieder's attempt (*JBL*, 74 [1965], 160-62), followed by C. Gordon (*UT*, p. 501), to relate Heb. *šāwēh* to Ugar. *ṯwy* has three problems. Wieder assumed that the gloss in Gen. 14:17 ("that is, the King's Valley") reflects the meaning of *ʿēmeq šāwēh* and that therefore the root *šwh* must approximate the meaning of *mlk*, "rule, be king." Unfortunately, no evidence supports this assumption. Second, Ugar. *ṯwy* occurs in only three contexts and thus is difficult to define; most scholars have translated it "live, abide." Third, Arab. *ṯwy*, "live," seems to be the cognate of Ugar. *ṯwy*, and Arab. *swy*, "even, level," the cognate of Heb. *šwh*.

For a well-documented summary of this problem, see W. Schatz, *Genesis 14: Eine Untersuchung* (1972), pp. 186f.

G. A. LEE

**KINNERETH** (Nu. 34:11; Dt. 3:17; etc., NEB). *See* CHINNERETH; GALILEE, SEA OF.

**KINSFOLK; KINSMAN; KINSWOMAN.** *See* KIN.

**KIR** kir, kēr [Heb. *qîr*–'wall'; cf. Moabite *qr*–'city' (Moabite Stone, lines 11f., 24)]. A place to which Tiglath-pileser, the Assyrian king, deported the Arameans of Damascus (2 K. 16:9f.); it is traditionally considered to have been in Mesopotamia. Am. 1:5 ("and the people of Syria shall go into exile to Kir") is taken to refer to the same or a similar event. (Some scholars have considered this stich to be an editorial gloss [cf. M. C. Astour, *IDB Supp.*, p. 524], but this cannot be supported by the structure of 1:5, which when compared with v. 8 shows that a fourth stich is required to complete the poetic arrangement.) The Kir mentioned in Isa. 22:6 may be identical with the two mentioned above. According to Am. 9:7, the Arameans ("Syrians") originated in Kir. Tiglath-pileser III recorded ". . . 5,400 captives of the city of Dîr I settled in . . . the land of Unki" (*ARAB*, I, § 772). Unki is to be identified with ʿAmuk, where the KaraSu and Orontes rivers form a broad plain. Since no "Kir" is known in Mesopotamia, some have suggested that Heb. *qîr*, "wall," is to be equated with Assyr. *dêr*, "wall," a variant form of the more common *dûru* (cf. *CAD*, III, 197), used as a place name in *di-i-ri i-li*, "wall of god." This suggestion is ingenious, but if the Dîr of Tiglath-pileser's account was located in the ʿAmuk plain, it cannot be equated with Dêr(ili), for that was in Gutium, on the road from Babylon to Elam.

The early versions give no help, for in the pertinent texts the LXX has various readings, none of them place names, and the Vulg. follows Symm. and translates Kir as "Crete." The identification of the place must therefore await further evidence.

W. S. LASOR

**KIR** kir, kēr **OF MOAB** [Heb. *qîr môʾāḇ*]. A city of Moab, apparently the capital, mentioned in an Isaianic oracle (15:1). In parallel stichs Isaiah, repeating the same words, uses the names Ar and Kir, possibly suggesting that these are identical. The LXX has Gk. *tó teíchos*, "the wall, fortress," for the latter, instead of treating the word as a proper noun. In Moabite, *qr* (pl. *qrn*) means "city" (Moabite Stone 11f., 24, 29). In Hebrew, except in this passage, *qîr* means "wall," the customary word for city being Heb. *ʿîr* (pl. *ʿārîm*). In Nu. 21:28 *ʿār môʾāḇ*, "Ar of Moab," is mentioned, and in passages pertaining to the Israelite journey through Moab (Nu. 21:15; Dt. 2:9, 18, 29), Heb. *ʿār*, "city," occurs.

These facts raise the question whether *ʿr* and *qr* may have been dialectal variants in Moabite, just as *ʾrʿ* and *ʾrq*, "land," were in Aramaic (cf. Jer. 10:11; Moabite exhibits other similarities to Aramaic, as would be expected since the Moabites lived near the Arameans). If so, then Ar of Moab and Kir of Moab would be identical terms, "the city of Moab," meaning the capital city. AR OF MOAB, however, is generally identified with Rabba (Rabbath Moab), about 12 km. (7.5 mi.) further north. Kir of Moab, if the capital city, is probably to be identified with Kir-hareseth (modern el-Kerak).

W. S. L. S.

**KIRAMA** ki-rā'mə (1 Esd. 5:20, NEB). *See* RAMAH **1**.

**KIR-HARESETH** kir-här'ə-seth, kir-hä-rē'seth [Heb. *qîr ḥ^areśeṯ*]; AV also KIR-HARASETH (pausal form in MT, 2 K. 3:25); **KIR-HERES** kir-he'rəs [*qîr ḥereś*]; AV also KIR-HARESH (pausal form incorrectly pointed as in MT, Isa. 16:11). A Moabite city, probably the capital.

The LXX reads *toís katoikoúsin Deseth,* "to the inhabitants of Deseth," in Isa. 16:7; *hōseí teíchos hó enekaínisas,* "as a wall that you have renewed," in 16:11; and *Kiradas* (= Heb. *qîr ḥādāš,* "new city"?) in Jer. 48:31, 36 (LXX 31:31, 36). The problem of identifying various cities of Moab is difficult, as the LXX readings suggest. *See* AR; CITY OF MOAB; KIR OF MOAB.

When the kings of Israel, Judah, and Edom went to war against Moab in the days of Elisha, the Israelites slaughtered the Moabites, overthrew the cities, and devastated the land "till only its stones were left in Kir-hareseth" (2 K. 3:25). In an oracle against Moab, Isaiah once put "Moab" and "Kir-hareseth" in parallel stichs (Isa. 16:7) and another time used the word "Kir-heres" in a similar parallel (v. 11). Jeremiah, in a judgment oracle against Moab, put "Moab" and "men of Kir-heres" in parallel stichs (Jer. 48:31, 36). In all these prophecies it seems that Kir-hareseth (or Kir-heres) is synonymous with Moab and therefore probably its chief city or capital. The biblical contexts do not add geographical details but only suggest that the city was inland from where the Israelite forces first engaged the Moabites (2 K. 3:25).

The LXX translations suggest that some Hebrew MSS may have had a *d* instead of an *r* in the second element of the name. (Both in the old Phoenician characters and in later Aramaic square letters the *daleth* and the *resh* were remarkably similar and sometimes confused.) For example, Gk. *Deseth* in Isa. 16:7, the words "as a wall that you have renewed" (= Heb. *ḥaddaštâ*) in v. 11, and Gk. *Kiradas* in Jer. 48:31, 36 all suggest a form with a *d.* The remaining occurrence of Kir-hareseth (2 K. 3:25) is translated by the LXX *héōs toú katalipeín toús líthous toíchou kathērēménous,* "until the torn-down stones of the wall remained," which neither supports nor disproves an *r* in the Hebrew text.

If the suggestion of an original Heb. *qîr ḥādāš* (which requires reading *š* for *ś,* as well as *d* for *r*) is accepted, then the name of the Moabite city was "New Town" or "Newburg" — a common enough name for cities. ("Carthage" is almost certainly Phoen. *qart ḥadašt,* "new city.") The presence of a "New Town" suggests the previous existence of an old town, which in turn may suggest how to identify the various cities of Moab whose names all can be translated "city of Moab."

At the time the tribes passed through Moab on the way to the Promised Land, the "city" of Moab seems to have been Ar. The term "Ar" was synonymous with "Moab" (Dt. 2:9; cf. vv. 8, 29); the Moabites dwelt in Ar (v. 29). The "seat of Ar" is in parallel with "the border of Moab" (Nu. 21:14f.). It seems virtually certain that the chief city of Moab at that time was Ar, even though it lay on the northern boundary. The Israelites were told when they were about to enter the land of the Ammonites N of Moab, "This day you are to pass over the boundary of Moab (at) Ar" (Dt. 2:18). Ar is described as "in the valley," perhaps meaning on the very edge of the Arnon gorge (v. 36). "Ar of Moab" is described as "the lords of the heights of the Arnon" (Nu. 21:28). "The city of Moab" (*ʿîr môʾāḇ*) also is described as "on the boundary formed by the Arnon, at the extremity of the border" (22:36). There seems to be no compelling reason to distinguish between this city and Ar.

The identification of Ar with Rabbath Moab (modern Khirbet er-Rabbah), 21.7 km. (13.5 mi.) S of the Arnon, was made at the beginning of the 4th cent. A.D. (The name Rabbath Moab is not biblical.) Rabbath Moab was also known as Areopolis, and Jerome (comm. on Isaiah, 15:1) suggested that this name preserved the biblical name Ar. It is clear, however, both from the image of Mars (= Ares) on coins and from Eusebius *Onom.* 36.26 that the name Areopolis came from the worship of Ares. A little over 3 km. (2 mi.) NW of Rabbath Moab is the site el-Miṣnaʿ, occupied from 2200 to 1800 B.C., which is sometimes, but unconvincingly in light of the previous facts, identified as the location of Ar.

During the Israelite monarchial period, however, the principal city of Moab was Kir-hareseth. Ar is mentioned only once, in a poetic prophecy by Isaiah (Isa. 15:1) where it is paralleled with Kir of Moab. It is perhaps better to regard Ar as the name of the earlier capital transferred to the new capital, "New Town" or Kir-hareseth, than to identify it with Rabbath Moab. (But *see* KIR OF MOAB.)

Kir-hareseth is generally identified with the modern city of Kerak, located 27 km. (17 mi.) S of the Arnon gorge. The Targum renders *Qîr* by *Karak* and *Qîr-Môab* by *Keraka de-Moab.* In the Byzantine era, Gk. *Charachmōba,* "Characmoba" (i.e., Kerak [of] Moab) appears as the name of the episcopal see. When the Moabite territory extended northward to the Jabbok, Ar on the Arnon was not an objectionable site for the principal city. But when the Amorites pushed the Moabite boundary southward to

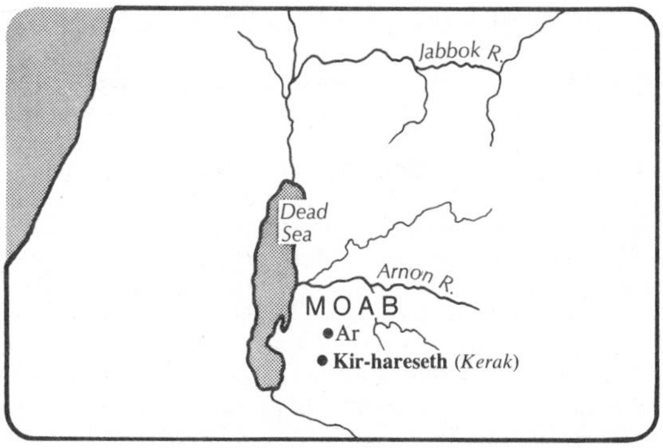


Crusader fortress on a rocky plateau overlooking the valley at Kir-hareseth (Kerak) (A. D. Baly)

the Arnon, it became necessary to relocate the capital farther inland away from the border. Kerak, standing on a rocky plateau protected on all sides by valleys, was a splendid choice. The Crusaders, who always recognized a strategic location, built a fortress at Kerak, which, though today in ruins, is still magnificent.

*Bibliography.*–*AASOR*, 14 (1934), 14, 62, 65; 15 (1935), 5; *GP*, II, 69, 248, 418f.; *HGHL*, pp. 379ff. W. S. L. S.

**KIR-HERES.** *See* KIR-HARESETH.

**KIRIATHAIM** kir-i-ə-thā'əm [Heb. *qiryāṯayim*–'two cities']; AV also KIRJATHAIM.

**1.** A city in the uplands of Moab that was assigned to the tribe of Reuben (Nu. 32:37; Josh. 13:19) and appears in the prophecies against Moab (Jer. 48:1, 23; Ezk. 25:9). The city is often identified with modern el-Qereiyât, 8 km. (5 mi.) NW of Dibon.

**2.** A city in the territory of Naphtali assigned to the Gershonites (1 Ch. 6:76), probably corresponding to Kartan in Josh. 21:32.

**KIRIATH-ARBA** kir-i-ath-är'bə. *See* HEBRON.

**KIRIATHARIM** kir-i-ath-är'əm (Ezr. 2:25; 1 Esd. 5:19). *See* KIRIATH-JEARIM.

**KIRIATH-BAAL** kir-i-ath-bā'əl. *See* KIRIATH-JEARIM.

**KIRIATH-HUZOTH** kir-i-ath-ho͞o'zoth [Heb. *qîryaṯ ḥuṣôṯ*–'city of streets'; Gk. *póleis epaúleōn*–'city of residences,' suggesting an original Heb. *qîryaṯ ḥᵃṣērôṯ*–'city of courts']; AV KIRJATH-HUZOTH. The place to which Balak and Balaam went after their meeting (Nu. 22:39). The "city of Moab" (v. 36) was probably KIR OF MOAB; hence Kiriath-huzoth was not far from Kir in Moab. Tg. Jonathan identifies it with *Bîrôšâ*, possibly el-Barrishî near Rabbah, but the location does not seem to fit the description in Numbers. Abel (*GP*, II, 421) suggested el-Qeryeh, 12 km. (7.5 mi.) NE of Dibon. W. S. L. S.

**KIRIATHIARIUS** kir-i-ath-ē-âr'ē-əs (1 Esd. 5:19, AV). *See* KIRIATH-JEARIM.

**KIRIATH-JEARIM** kir-i-ath-je-är'əm [Heb. *qiryaṯ-yeʿārîm, -hayyeʿārîm*–'city of (the) forests']; AV KIRJATH (Josh. 18:28), KIRJATH-JEARIM; also **KIRIATHARIM** kir-i-əth-är'əm [Heb. *qiryaṯ ʿārîm*] (Ezr. 2:25); AV KIRJATH-ARIM; **BAALAH** bā'ə-lə [Heb. *baʿᵃlâ*] (Josh. 15:9; 1 Ch. 13:6); **BAALE-JUDAH** bā'ə-lə jo͞o'də [Heb. *baʿᵃlê yehûḏâ*] (2 S. 6:2); AV BAALE OF JUDAH; NEB BAALATH-JUDAH; **KIRIATH-BAAL** kir-i-ath-bā'əl [Heb. *qiryaṯ-baʿal*] (Josh. 15:60; 18:14); AV KIRJATH-BAAL; **JAAR** [Heb. *yaʿar*] (Ps. 132:6); AV "the wood" (cf. *GTTOT*, §§ 666-68, 1708); Apoc. **KIRIATHARIM** [Gk. *Kariathiarios*] (1 Esd. 5:19); AV KIRIATHIARIUS; NEB CARIATH-IARIUS. A town on the boundary between Judah and Benjamin.

The site of the ancient town is now identified as Tell el-Azhar, 14 km. (9 mi.) W of Jerusalem along the road to Jaffa. It is just NW of Abū Ghôsh. The biblical indications appear to place Kiriath-jearim E of Beth-shemesh (Tell er-Rumeileh; cf. 1 S. 6–7) and on higher terrain ("up," 6:21; 7:1). The house of Abinadab, where the ark was kept in Kiriath-jearim, was "on the hill" (7:1).

Kiriath-jearim was the southernmost of the Hivite league of four cities (with Gibeon, Chephirah, and Beeroth [Josh. 9:17]), whose representatives from Gibeon successfully deceived Joshua into making a covenant with them. After

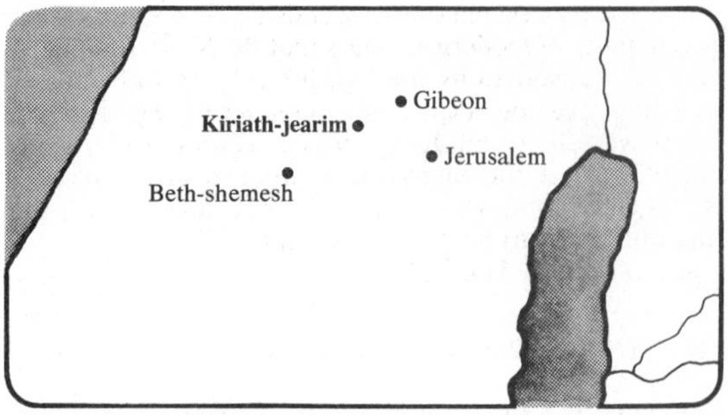


discovering the deception, Joshua made the inhabitants of these cities servants of Israel (vv. 16-27). When a confederation of five kings attacked the Hivite league, the league appealed to the Israelites, who honored their alliance and with divine aid defeated the attackers (ch. 10). In migrating to its later northern location the tribe of Dan camped "at Kiriath-jearim in Judah" (Jgs. 18:12; the site was called MAHANEH-DAN, "the camp of Dan," described as *ʾaḥᵃrê* ["behind," AV; "west of," RSV, NEB] Kiriath-jearim; cf. 13:25, which places it "between Zorah and Eshtaol"). After the Philistines returned the ark of the covenant to Israel, the people of Beth-shemesh passed it on to Kiriath-jearim, where it remained "some twenty years" (1 S. 6:21–7:2). David's first attempt to transfer the ark from Kiriath-jearim to Jerusalem ended in the death of Uzzah and the housing of the ark in the home of Obed-edom (1 Ch. 13:5-14), but later David brought the ark to Jerusalem and placed it in a tent he had prepared for it (2 S. 6:12-17; 1 Ch. 15).

In the last days of the Judean kingdom, the prophet Uriah, "the son of Shemaiah of Kiriath-jearim" (Jer. 26:20), prophesied against Jerusalem and Judah with a message similar to Jeremiah's. When Uriah fled to Egypt to escape the wrath of King Jehoiakim, the king sent men to Egypt to bring him back and the prophet was put to death (vv. 20-23). The exiles who returned from Babylon included men of Kiriath-jearim, Chephirah, and Beeroth (Neh. 7:29; Ezr. 2:25; 1 Esd. 5:19). In the genealogy of Judah, Kiriath-jearim also appears as a descendant of Caleb and Ephrathah (1 Ch. 2:50, 53; cf. Ps. 132:6).

*Bibliography.*–F. D. Cooke, *AASOR*, 5 (1923/24), 105-120; *LBHG*, pp. 224-27, 287, 301. C. E. DEVRIES

**KIRIATH-SANNAH** kir-i-ath-san'ə [Heb. *qiryaṯ sannâ*]. A city in southern Judah, probably to be identified with KIRIATH-SEPHER, since (1) it is identified as Debir (Josh. 15:49), and (2) the LXX translates Kiriath-sannah, just as it does Kiriath-sepher, as *pólis grammátōn*. *See* DEBIR **1.** W. S. L. S.

**KIRIATH-SEPHER** kir-i-ath-sē'fər [Heb. *qiryaṯ sēp̱er*–'city of book(s)'; cf. LXX *pólis grammátōn*, but more reasonably "city of the scribe(s)"]. A city in southern Judah (Josh. 15:15f.; Jgs. 1:11f.). Caleb occupied the city by the agency of Othniel (Josh. 15:17), and since Caleb's daughter (who had been given to Othniel as a reward for his valor) referred to the place as "in the Negeb" (v. 19), it is perhaps to be identified with "the Negeb of Caleb" (1 S. 30:14). Kiriath-sepher, however, was not in the Negeb proper, but rather was a "Negeb" (i.e., a comparatively dry location) in the hill country SW of Hebron (Josh. 15:49, emending Kiriath-sannah to Kiriath-sepher, since it is called Debir). For the location of Kiriath-sepher, *see* DEBIR **1.** Caleb was a Kenizzite (Nu. 32:12; Josh. 14:6), a member of a subtribe of the Edomites who occupied the area that later became southern Judah. It is therefore held by a number of modern scholars that the Kenizzites, who were later absorbed by the Israelite tribe of Judah, were an earlier invasion stage of the "conquest." The story of Caleb, who along with Joshua was one of the twelve spies (Josh. 14:7), is too thoroughly ingrained in the biblical account of the movement toward, and invasion of, the land of Canaan to be dismissed lightly.

See *GTTOT,* § 514. W. S. L. S.

**KIRIOTH** (Am. 2:2, AV). *See* KERIOTH.

**KIRJATH, KIRJATH-.** AV form for Kiriath-.

**KISAEUS** (Ad. Est. 11:2, NEB). *See* KISH **5**.

**KISH** kish [Heb. *qîš*; Gk. *Kis* (Acts 13:21), *Kisaios* (Ad. Est. 11:2)].

**1.** The son of Abiel and the father of Saul the first king of Israel. He was of the tribe of Benjamin, of the family of the Matrites (1 S. 9:1; 14:51; 1 S. 10:21; cf. Acts 13:21, AV CIS). 1 Ch. 8:33; 9:39 suggest that Abiel was actually his grandfather and Ner his father, since the term "son" is the equivalent of "descendant" and does not necessarily imply the next generation. Ner had another son named Abner (1 S. 14:51; 1 Ch. 26:28), so Kish would have been Abner's brother. 1 Ch. 12:1 also mentions Kish as the father of Saul. The sepulchre of Kish was located in Zela in the country of Benjamin (2 S. 21:14). He seems to have resided at Gibeah.

**2.** The son of Jeiel and his wife Maacah (1 Ch. 8:30, 33; 9:36, 39). His relationship to Saul's father has not yet been determined.

**3.** A Levite, the son of Mahli the Merarite (1 Ch. 23:21f.; cf. 24:29).

**4.** Another Merarite Levite in the time of Hezekiah (2 Ch. 29:12).

**5.** The great-grandfather of Mordecai, of the tribe of Benjamin (Est. 2:5; Ad. Est. 11:2, AV CISAI, NEB KISAEUS).

**KISHI** kish'ī, kē'shē [Heb. *qîšî*–'trapper'(?), 'gift'(?)]. Father of Ethan, one of the singers that David "put in charge of the service of song" in the house of the Lord (1 Ch. 6:31); the Kushaiah of 1 Ch. 15:17.

**KISHION** kish'i-on, kish'yən [Heb. *qišyôn*]; AV, NEB, also KISHON (Josh. 21:28). A town in the territory of Issachar (Josh. 19:20) given to the Gershonites (21:28) and undoubtedly identical with KEDESH **2**. The site is unknown but has been often identified with Tell el-Muqarqash (Albright) or with Tell el-ʿAjjûl (Simons) in the vicinity of Endor.

*Bibliography.*–W. F. Albright, *ZAW,* 3 (1926), 231; *GP,* II, 422f.; *LBHG,* pp. 160, 280 n. 111, 303, 438; J. Simons, *GTTOT,* § 330.

W. W. BUEHLER

**KISHON** kī'shon, kish'on [Heb. *qîšōn*–possibly 'bending' or 'winding']; AV also KISON (Ps. 83:9 [MT 10]). The river along whose banks Israel, led by Deborah and Barak, fought the army of Sisera (Jgs. 4:7, 13; 5:21). In the AV it is also called a "brook" (1 K. 18:40; Ps. 83:9); the RSV calls it a "torrent" in Jgs. 5:21, a "brook" in 1 Kings; except in Josh. 19:11 ("gorge") the NEB always refers to it as a "torrent." The Song of Deborah calls the Kishon "the waters of Megiddo" (Jgs. 5:19). Later the river appears as the scene of Elijah's slaughter of the prophets of Baal (1 K. 18:40). It is first mentioned in connection with the boundary of Zebulun, as "the brook which is east of Jokneam" (Josh. 19:11).

The river, modern Nahr el-Muqaṭṭaʿ, rises in the hills of northern Samaria near Megiddo, drains all of the plain of Esdraelon, and then flows NW to the Mediterranean Sea through the plain of Acre, emptying at the foot of Mt. Carmel. In the summer the water from the springs is largely used in irrigation, and the upper portion of the river, which is in the plain, becomes dry. The bed runs along the bottom of a trench 6 m. (20 ft.) deep, which quickly fills in times of heavy rain, making the soft soil of the plain on either side marshy and miry. Apparently mire caused by a heavy storm hampered the movement of Sisera's cavalry and chariots and led to his downfall (Jgs. 5:20f.).

*Bibliography.*–*GB*; *GP,* I, 158f.; *LBHG.*

W. W. BUEHLER

**KISLEV** (Neh. 1:1; Zec. 7:1, NEB). *See* CHISLEV.

**KISLON** (Nu. 34:21, NEB). *See* CHISLON.

**KISLOTH-TABOR** (Josh. 19:12, NEB). *See* CHESULLOTH.

**KISS** [*nāšaq*] (Gen. 27:26f.; 29:11, 13; 31:28; etc.); NEB also "join hands," SMOTHER, etc.; [*n^ešîqâ*] (Prov. 27:6; Cant. 1:2); [*ḥēḵ*–'palate'] (Cant. 7:9); AV "roof of . . . mouth"; NEB WHISPERS; [Gk. *philéō*] (Mt. 26:48; Mk. 14:44); [*phílēma*] (Lk. 7:45; Rom. 16:16; 1 Cor. 16:20; 2 Cor. 13:12; 1 Thess. 5:26; 1 Pet. 5:14); [*kataphiléō*] (Mt. 26:49; Mk. 14:45; Lk. 7:38, 45; 15:20; 22:47f.; Acts 20:37). To touch with the lips, a gesture of affection or homage usually devoid of erotic content in the Bible.

The OT mentions the kiss most often in the context of the family. The son kissed his father in the story of Jacob's deceiving Isaac to obtain his blessing (Gen. 27:26f.; cf. 50:1). In this instance it may be that "Isaac's desire to kiss concealed the secret intention to smell in order to be quite sure [that his uncertainty was unfounded]" (G. von Rad, *Genesis* [Eng. tr., *OTL,* 1961], p. 272). A man (Jacob) kissed his cousin (Rachel) and his uncle (Laban) in 29:11, 13. An older man kissed his children and grandchildren in 31:28, 55 [MT 32:1]; 48:10. At the dramatic reconciliation of Jacob and Esau (33:4) the two brothers wept and embraced, with Esau kissing Jacob as a sign of forgiveness, a point missed by a late Jewish midrash that replaced the words "he kissed him" with "he bit him" (von Rad, p. 322). Other examples of brothers kissing each other occur when Joseph made himself known to his brothers in Egypt (Gen. 45:15) and when Moses and Aaron met in the wilderness (Ex. 4:27). In Ex. 18:7 a man kissed his father-in-law. Naomi kisses her daughters-in-law Ruth and Orpah in Ruth 1:9 (cf. v. 14; these are the only biblical examples of women kissing each other). David kissed his son Absalom as a token of full reconciliation after Absalom's murder of his brother Amnon (2 S. 14:33). Elisha's kissing of his parents was essential to a proper leave-taking (1 K. 19:20).

Examples of kisses exchanged by nonrelations include those exchanged by the weeping David and Jonathan when Jonathan told David to leave his hiding place and flee from Saul (1 S. 20:41). David kissed King Barzillai when the latter returned to Gilead (2 S. 19:39 [MT 40]). The crafty politician Absalom kissed those who "came near to do obeisance to him" and thus "stole the hearts of the men of Israel" (15:5f.). Kissing to feign affection is most vividly seen when, during Sheba's rebellion, Joab seized Amasa's beard in his right hand as if to kiss him but used the opportunity for murder by striking him with the sword drawn by his left hand (20:9f.). Joab's stratagem has been called the "Old Testament kiss of Judas" (H. W. Hertzberg, *Samuel* [Eng. tr., *OTL,* 1965], p. 372; cf. Prov. 27:6).

Limestone relief of Nefertiti and Akhenaten, who is kissing one of their daughters (Tell el-Amarna; 14th cent. B.C.) (Ägyptisches Museen, Staatliche Museen zu Berlin, DDR)

The kiss was used ceremonially in pagan worship, as when worshipers kissed the idol of their affections (Hos. 13:2), e.g., Baal (1 K. 19:18). The reference in Job 31:27 is to throwing kisses to the moon, a practice mentioned only here in the OT but known from other sources. When Samuel ceremonially anointed Saul (1 S. 10:1) he kissed the new king, probably as a sign of his personal affection rather than of loyalty. It is possible, however, that this was related to the act of kissing the feet of a king, signifying self-humiliation and homage, well known from Babylonian and Egyptian documents (A. Weiser, *The Psalms* [Eng. tr., *OTL*, 1962], p. 115; A. A. Anderson, *Psalms (1-72)* [*NCBC*, 1972], pp. 69f.; cf. Isa. 49:23; Mic. 7:17 [lit. "lick the dust"]; esp. Ps. 2:12). In Ps. 85:10 [MT 11] the phrase "righteousness and peace will kiss each other" personifies these spiritual powers in a profound vision of God bowing down from heaven to meet earth and earth reaching up to Him, foretelling the glory of salvation for the people.

The ceremonial or conventional nature of the kiss is further seen in its associations with a greeting, particularly after a long absence (e.g., Gen. 33:4; 45:15; Ex. 4:27), when departure is near (e.g., Gen. 31:28, 55 [MT 32:1]; Ruth 1:9, 14), or when death is at hand (e.g., Gen. 27:26f.; 2 S. 19:39). Yet the kisses were more than conventional; they were enacted with great emotion, as is seen by the frequent accompaniment of embracing, bowing, and weeping. The expressly erotic aspects of the kiss are mentioned in the OT only in the seductive kiss of the immoral woman in Prov. 7:13 and in the romantic kisses of the lovers in Cant. 1:2; 7:9; 8:1. Prov. 24:26 says, "He who gives a right answer kisses the lips," meaning "a straightforward answer is as good as a kiss of friendship" (NEB).

The kiss in the NT is very similar to that in the OT. The father in the parable of the Prodigal Son embraced his son and kissed him when he returned home (Lk. 15:20). The sinful woman wept and kissed Christ's feet out of reverence and gratitude (7:38). In Jewish practice a host was required to place his hand on any guest's shoulder and give him the kiss of peace, a gesture neglected when Jesus dined with Simon the Pharisee (7:45; Daniel-Rops, p. 303). In bidding Paul farewell, the Ephesian elders, out of sorrow and affection, wept while embracing and kissing him (Acts 20:37). The most terrible example of the "kisses of an enemy" (Prov. 27:6) is the "kiss of Judas" (Mt. 26:48f. par. Mk. 14:44f.; Lk. 22:47f.), the customary salutatory kiss of a rabbi by his pupil (SB, I, 996), which became the sign enabling the Roman soldiers to recognize and seize Jesus.

The remaining NT references are in the closing Pauline injunctions to "greet one another with a holy kiss" (*phílēma hágion*; Rom. 16:16; 1 Cor. 16:20; 2 Cor. 13:12; 1 Thess. 5:26) and in the "kiss of love" (*phílēma agápēs*, 1 Pet. 5:14). By this kiss the early Christians expressed the intimate fellowship of the reconciled community (Bauer, rev., p. 859). It developed as a liturgical form in the Church and as the "kiss of peace" is maintained in the liturgy of the Eastern Church. The church order known as the *Testimony of the Lord* calls it "The Peace" (i.23, 30; ii.4, 9). The earliest reference to the kiss as a regular feature of Christian worship is in Justin's *Apol.* i.65, where he reported that in eucharistic worship, "when we have ceased from our prayers, we greet one another with a kiss." Tertullian (*De orat.* 14) spoke of the "holy kiss which is a sign of speech" and asked whether any prayer could be complete "separate from the holy kisses." According to E. G. Selwyn, "by the middle of the second century it was in regular use in the liturgy at the conclusion of the prayers and immediately before the offertory" (*First Epistle of Peter* [1946], p. 244). The "holy kiss" seems also to have been used at baptisms, ordinations of bishops, and marriages (J. B. Lightfoot, *Notes on the Epistles of St. Paul* [1895], p. 91). It became abused, however, and Clement of Alexandria wrote, "Love is judged not in a kiss but in good will. Some do nothing but fill the Churches with noise of kissing" (*Paed.* iii.11). Thus the practice was regulated (*Apost. Const.* ii.57.12) and gradually died out in the West after the 13th century.

***Bibliography.***–H. Daniel-Rops, *Daily Life in the Times of Jesus* (1964); L. Friedlander, *Roman Life and Manners* (Eng. tr., 7th ed. 1965), IV, 58ff.; *TDNT*, IX, 118-127, 138-146 (G. Stählin).

D. K. MCKIM

**KITCHENS** [Heb. *bêṯ ham$^e$ḇašš$^e$lîm*] (Ezk. 46:24); AV "places of them that boil." Ezekiel's vision of the temple included four small courts at the corners of the larger courtyard. Here sacrifices that the common people were permitted to eat were boiled on the hearths. The Bible does not mention separate rooms in private houses for preparing food, which, in any case, would have been found only in the houses of the rich. G. WYPER

**KITE** [Heb. *ʾayyâ*; Gk. *iktínos*; Lat. *Milvus ictinus* or *regalis*] (Lev. 11:4; Dt. 14:13). A medium-sized member of the hawk family. This bird is 69 cm. (27 in.) long, is bright reddish-brown, and has sharply pointed wings and a deeply forked tail. It is supposed to have exceptionally piercing eyes. It eats moles, mice, young game birds, snakes, and frogs as well as carrion. Its head and facial expression are unusually like the eagle. It was common in Palestine in winter but less visible in summer, since it bred in the hills of Galilee and rough mountainous places. It is listed among the birds of abominations. The Palestinian kites included members of the genera *Milvus* and *Elanus*.

G. STRATTON-PORTER

**KITHLISH** (Josh. 15:40, AV, NEB). *See* CHITLISH.

**KITRON** kit'rən, kit'ron [Heb. *qiṭrôn*–'enclosed'(?); Gk. *Kedrōn*, A *Chebrōn*]. A Canaanite enclave in Zebulun named in Jgs. 1:30. Josh. 19:15, an apparently parallel passage, gives the name Kattath, thus suggesting that these are identical locations. Abel (*GP,* II, 423), following Alt, identified it with Tell el-Fâr on the eastern edge of the plain of Zebulun, about 4 km. (2½ mi.) NE of Kefr Ḥasidim. Another suggested location is Khirbet Qṭeina, 8 km. (5 mi.) SW of Jokneam (*GP,* II, 63). Simons (*GTTOT,* § 329, p. 182) thought that this location argues against the identification. If the identification of Kitron with Kattath is accepted, it may be significant that Rabbi Yosi ben Ḥaninah equated Kitron with Qeṭonith (T.P. *Megillah* I.1), still standing in his day but now unknown. W. S. L. S.

**KITTIM** kit'əm, ki-tēm' [Heb. *kittîm, kittîyîm* (Gen. 10:4; Nu. 24:24; 1 Ch. 1:7; Isa. 23:12; Jer. 2:10; Ezk. 27:6; Dnl. 11:30), DSS *kittî'îm*–probably refers to nationals (Kittites or Kittians) of a place Kit or Kitti]; RSV also CYPRUS (Isa. 23:1, 12; Jer. 2:10; Ezk. 27:6); AV also CHITTIM; NEB also "the west" (Dnl. 11:30). A city on Cyprus, called by the Phoenicians KTY (= *Kitti*). Its Greek name was *Kition,* the name by which the Hebrews designated the island as a whole and then the Mediterranean peoples generally or even certain nations specifically, such as Macedonia and Rome. According to Josephus (*Ant.* i.6.1 [128]), "the name Chethim [was] given by the Hebrews to all islands and to most maritime countries" (cf. "the isles of Kittim" [Jer. 2:10]).

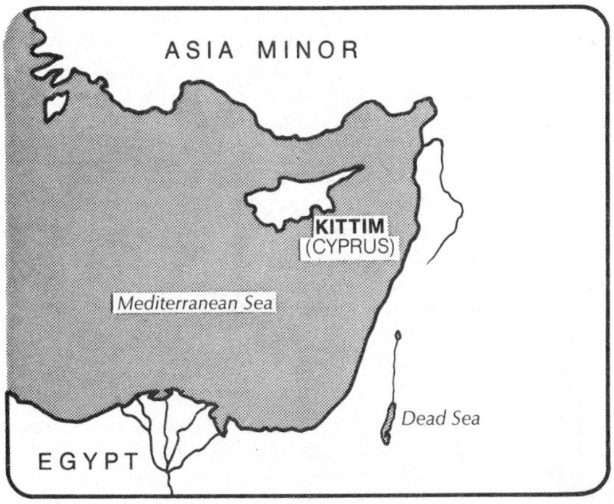


In Gen. 10:4 Kittim is one of the four sons of Javan (= Ionia, or Greece), the others being Elishah, Tarshish, and Rodanim (cf. 1 Ch. 1:7); Elishah may be another city-state of Cyprus. Ezk. 27:6f. also differentiates Kittim from Elishah. Josephus seems to be wrong in identifying Elishah with the Aeolians and Kittim with the whole of Cyprus. The biblical derivation of these islands from Javan is historically correct, as shown by the vast migrations from the north in the second half of the 2nd millennium B.C. In these the aborigines of Greece and Ionia were displaced southward into the islands of the Mediterranean, where they in turn both displaced and mingled with the natives. See *ANET,* pp. 262f.

The oracles of Balaam conclude with the prophecy (Nu. 24:23f.):

"Sea-peoples shall gather from the north;
and ships, from the district of Kittim.
I look, and they afflict Eber;
but they too shall perish forever!"

(This reading follows [in part] W. F. Albright, who has shown that a more exact form of the original text can be obtained through a knowledge of ancient orthography; cf. JB). The final phase of the migrations of sea-peoples mentioned in v. 23 was the coming of the Philistines to Palestine in the 12th cent. B.C. The eponym Eber is here employed as a poetic term for the Hebrews (so the versions) in their homeland. Dramatically, Balaam did at last please Balak by predicting Philistine oppression of the Hebrews, but his last statement gives them their freedom again through the destruction of the Philistines.

Later misreading of v. 24b produced the traditional text:

And they shall afflict Asshur
and they shall afflict Eber;
but they too shall come to destruction.

Cyprus never did subdue Asshur (= Assyria); instead, the Assyrian king Sargon II placed his stele at Kition in 712 B.C. His successors Sennacherib and Esarhaddon strengthened Assyrian rule there, the latter claiming tribute from all the isles from Cyprus to Tarshish (*ANET,* p. 290). References to Kittim in Isa. 23:1, 12 (RSV Cyprus) probably relate to the Assyrian period (despite v. 13). Verse 12 refers to Luli king of Sidon, who sought refuge in Cyprus from Sennacherib but there met his doom (*ANET,* p. 288). Kittim as mercenary soldiers of Judah appear on the ostraca of Arad (*see* Arad III).

Lacking any literal fulfillment, the Kittian oppression of Assyria and Eber became a mysterious prophecy of the future. Some Jews may have seen in the conquest by

Hebrew ostracon from Arad (*ca.* 600 B.C.) in which Eliashib is ordered to give wine and flour to the Kittim, who were apparently mercenaries in the Judean army (Israel Museum, Jerusalem)

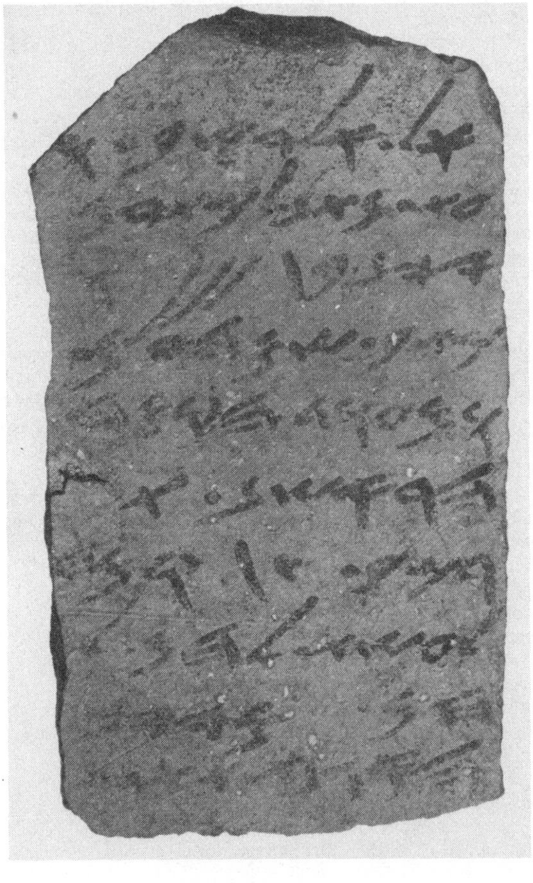

Alexander the Great a fulfillment of this prophecy, with Kittim denoting Macedonia (as in 1 Macc. 1:8; 8:5) and Asshur denoting the Persian empire. An even more intricate interpretation is implied by Dnl. 11:30: "For ships of Kittim shall come against him, and he shall be afraid and withdraw, and be enraged and take action against the holy covenant." The setting of this verse is Antiochus Epiphanes' invasion of Egypt in 168 B.C. Rome intervened by sending its commissioner Gaius Popilius Laenas, who (backed by the Roman navy) successfully demanded the withdrawal of the Syrians.

Cowed but resentful, Antiochus vented his rage on the Jews in a fearsome persecution. According to H. L. Ginsberg (*Studies in Daniel* [1948], p. 72), Daniel interpreted Nu. 24:24b to mean: "The Kittim (= Romans) shall afflict Asshur (= Syria); and they (the Syrians) shall afflict Eber (= Hebrews)."

In the Qumrân Scrolls, the Kittim are the great eschatological foe, the last great earthly empire to precede the messianic kingdom. Since these people have already arrived on the scene of history, the messianic age is not far off. Some scholars have identified these Kittim with Seleucid Syria. This identification fits well the book of Jubilees, a work found among the Qumrân fragments but probably of pre-Qumrânian composition. Jub. 24:28f. predicts punishment of the Philistines by both Kittim and Jews, with probable allusion to ravages of the Palestinian coastal towns by both Seleucids and Maccabees. The mention of Kittim in 37:10 may allude to Seleucid oppression of the Jews. Though some students of the DSS have seen allusions to the Seleucids and Ptolemies in the phrases "Kittim of Assyria" and "Kittim in Egypt" in the War Scroll (1 QM 1:2, 4), these are probably only geographic, not national, distinctions.

The Kittim are generally portrayed as world conquerors and oppressors but not specifically as persecutors of the sect of the Scrolls. According to 1QpHab 9:5ff. the wealth of the "last priests of Jerusalem" (the persecutors of the sect) will in the last days be given up to the army of the Kittim. 4QpIsa[a] 3:7f., however, explains Isa. 10:34 to mean: "They are the Kittim wh[o] will f[all] by the hand of Israel, when the oppressed of [Judah subdue] all the nations." Probably this refers to the expected eschatological war, in which the Sons of Light will defeat the Kittim and all other nations. This "war of the Kittim" (3:11) is elaborately described in 1QM (the War Scroll).

Most descriptions of the Kittim in 1QpHab are general, applying equally well to the Seleucids and the Romans, although giving the impression of a world empire like Rome. Other depictions are clearly more apt for the Romans. "From afar they will fly as an eagle" (Hab. 1:8) is amplified: "From afar they will come, from remote shores of the sea, to devour all the peoples as an eagle" (1QpHab 13:10f.). The Hebrew lacks a word for "remote," but the idea is implicit in the appositional relationship. The reference to the eagle may allude to the worship of military standards and insignia (including the eagle emblem) mentioned in 6:4f. and well attested for the Roman legions but not for the Seleucids. Paleographic study places this MS more than a century earlier than the incident mentioned by Josephus (*BJ* vi.6.1 [316]). The Kittim have *môšᵉlîm* (rulers, governors, and commanders), but not *mᵉlāḵîm* (kings); but see below. The annual succession of provincial governors, appointed by the Roman senate ("their house of guilt"), is probably referred to in 4:10-13.

The most conclusive proof for the Roman identification is 4QpNah, which after noting the failure of "[Deme]trius, king of Greece . . . to enter Jerusalem" states that God had never given the city "into the power of the kings of Greece from the time of Antiochus until the rulers of the Kittim arose." The clear chronological distinction placing the rise of the "rulers of the Kittim" after the time of the "kings of Greece" (Syria) points conclusively to the Romans as the Kittim. Yet after 44 B.C., when Caesar became a virtual king, one could speak of "the king of the Kittim" (1QM 15:2).

The identification of the Kittim with the Romans in late Jewish thought is well supported by the versions: Nu. 24:24 (Onk., Vulg.); Ezk. 27:6 (Tg. Jonathan, Vulg.); Dnl. 11:30 (LXX, Tg. Jonathan, Vulg.).

***Bibliography.***–Y. Aharoni, *IEJ*, 16 (1966), 1-7; W. F. Albright, *JBL*, 63 (1944), 207-233; G. R. Driver, *The Judaean Scrolls* (1965) (Zealot hypothesis, Kittim = Romans); A. Dupont-Sommer, *The Jewish Sect of Qumran and the Essenes* (1954), pp. 14-37 (Kittim = Romans); R. Goossens, *Nouvelle Clio*, 4 (1952), 137-170 (Kittim = Romans); M. P. Horgan, *Pesharim: Qumran Interpretations of Biblical Books* (1979); H. H. Rowley, *PEQ*, 88 (1956), 92-109 (Kittim = Seleucids); E. Stauffer, *TLZ*, 76 (1951), 667-674 (Kittim = Seleucids); G. Vermes, *Discovery in the Judean Desert* (1956), pp. 81-85 (Kittim = Romans); Y. Yadin, *Scroll of the War of the Sons of Light Against the Sons of Darkness* (1962) (Kittim = Romans).

W. H. BROWNLEE

**KNEADING.** *See* BREAD IV.

**KNEE** [Heb. *bereḵ*; Aram. *'arḵubbâ*; Gk. *góny*]; **KNEEL** [Heb. *bāraḵ*; Aram. *bᵉraḵ*; Gk. *gonypetéō*]. The knee is the most complex joint of the human body, and in the ancient world it was considered the place of affection and devotion (Jgs. 16:19; cf. 2 K. 4:20; Isa. 66:12). Egyptian sculptures commonly represent this idea by showing the king as an infant seated on the knees of a goddess (*see* picture in NURSE). In Job 3:12 the knees symbolize the place where the newborn infant receives its first care. In another figurative use common in Mesopotamia of the Middle Bronze Age, the knees were a symbol of adoption. When a concubine gave birth to a child, it was delivered "on the knees" of the legal wife so that it was in effect recognized as her own adopted child and therefore as a legitimate member of the family. Rachel became the "mother" of Bilhah's children in this manner (Gen. 30:3), and in an analogous fashion Jacob adopted Ephraim and Manasseh so that they became two separate eponymous ancestors of Israelite tribes. A form of paternal adoption is described in Gen. 50:23, where Joseph received Machir's children in the traditional manner as they were born.

Weakness of the knees resulted from fear (cf. Job 4:4; Isa. 35:3f.; Ezk. 7:17f.; Nah. 2:10; etc.) but also from fasting (Ps. 109:24) or physical disease (Dt. 28:35; *see* BOIL; DISEASE III.I).

The close relationship between the word for "knee" and that for "bless," "praise" (Heb. *bāraḵ*) suggests kneeling as the original posture for these functions. People presenting petitions frequently knelt (cf. Dnl. 6:10 [MT 11]; Acts 9:40; etc.) to acknowledge the superior status of the one being petitioned (cf. 2 K. 1:13; Mt. 17:14; Mk. 1:40; etc.). The Hebrews more often prayed standing than kneeling, a posture in which the individual is most defenseless, but kneeling was nevertheless a recognized part of worship, whether of true (cf. 1 K. 8:54; 2 Ch. 6:13; Ps. 95:6; Isa. 45:23) or false (1 K. 19:18) gods. In the NT kneeling was more commonly associated with prayer (Lk. 5:8; Rom. 11:4; 14:11; Eph. 3:14; Phil. 2:10), though again was not the normative procedure. (In Acts 7:60 Stephen is dying as he kneels and prays.) *See* PRAYER; pictures in GESTURE; JEHU.

R. K. HARRISON

**KNIFE** [Heb. *ma'ᵃḵeleṯ*–lit. an instrument for eating, but the term is used of large knives for slaying animals, cutting

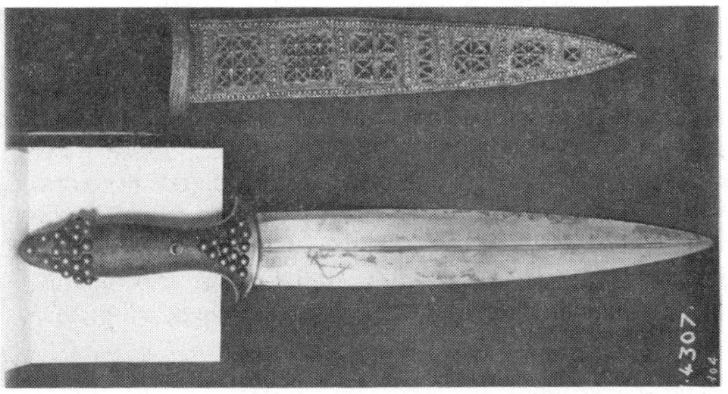

Gold dagger and sheath from a grave at Ur (25th cent. B.C.) (The State Antiquities Organization, Republic of Iraq)

Detail of an alabaster relief from the palace of Ashurnasirpal II (883-859 B.C.) at Nimrûd showing hilts of two daggers over an ornamental border of the king's garment (Staatliche Museen zu Berlin, DDR)

up a carcass or a sacrificial victim (Gen. 22:6, 10; Jgs. 19:29; Prov. 30:14); *ḥereḇ*–'sword,' but in Josh. 5:2f. it is used of stone knives for circumcision (cf. Ex. 4:25) and of probably similar knives in 1 K. 18:28 that were used by Baal prophets to gash themselves; *taʿar*–'razor,' in combination with *hassōp̄ēr*–'knife of the writer' or 'penknife' (Jer. 36:23; *see* PEN); *śakkîn* (Prov. 23:2), cf. Aram. *sakkînāʾ*–'knife']. The earliest knives were made of flint, and such artifacts have been recovered in quantity from Near Eastern sites. Flint was superior to metal, which could not maintain a sharp cutting edge; as a result flint knives continued to be used alongside bronze and iron knives for many centuries, for both religious and secular purposes (*see* picture in FLINT). The most common length for knives was 15 to 25 cm. (6 to 10 in.), and the blade was generally straight with a central ridge. A limestone mold found at Tell Beit Mirsim was designed for an iron knife 40 cm. (16 in.) long. Small knives were worked or cast in one piece, but larger ones, especially those of copper, bronze, or iron, had wooden handles attached, sometimes not very securely. Knives were not generally used at meals; meats were cut into bits before being served and bread was broken into fragments. Herod attempted suicide with a knife that he was using for paring apples (Josephus *Ant.* xvii.7.1 [183]; *BJ* i.33.7 [662]).

E. B. POLLARD

**KNIT** [Heb. niphal of *qāšar*–'bind' (1 S. 18:1), *(lēḇāḇ) leyaḥaḏ*–'(a heart) for union' (1 Ch. 12:17 [MT 18]), *sāḵaḵ*–'interweave' (Job 10:11 [polel]; Ps. 139:13), pual of *śārag*–'intertwine' (Job 40:17); Gk. *symbibázō*–'bring together' (Eph. 4:16; Col. 2:2, 19)]; AV also "fenced," "covered," "wrapped," "compacted"; NEB also "give," "join," "unity."

The Heb. *qāšar* is used figuratively of the soul. Also figurative is the RSV's paraphrase of the Hebrew in 1 Ch. 12:17 (lit. "I have toward you a heart for union"). Both *sāḵaḵ* and *śārag* are Hebrew terms for the close connections of parts of the body, the former being used only for prenatal development. The Gk. *symbibázō* is used in both literal (Eph. 4:16; Col. 2:19) and figurative (Col. 2:2) senses. See also *TDNT*, VII, *s.v.* συμβιβάζω (Delling).

G. A. L.

**KNOCK** [Heb. hiphil of *nāp̄al*] (Ex. 21:27); [*dāp̄aq*] (Cant. 5:2); [Aram. *neqaš*] (Dnl. 5:6); AV also SMITE; [Gk. *kroúō*] (Mt. 7:7f.; Lk. 11:9f.; 12:36; 13:25; Acts 12:13, 16; Rev. 3:20).

In Ex. 21:27 the hiphil of *nāp̄al* means "cause [a tooth] to fall," i.e., "knock [it] out." The essential meaning of *dāp̄aq* in the OT is "beat vigorously" (cf. Gen. 33:13 [of driving cattle]; Jgs. 19:22 [of men beating themselves against a door]), but in Cant. 5:2 it simply means "knock [on the door]." The basic meaning of Gk. *kroúō* is "strike"; in the NT it always refers to knocking on a door. "Knock" in Lk. 11:9f. occurs in an instruction about prayer and clearly means "be persistent in prayer" (cf. the similar phraseology in T.B. *Megillah* 12b: "Mordecai knocked at the doors of mercy, and they were opened to him"; also *Pesikta* 176a: "If a man knocks, it will be opened to him" [concerning study of the Mishnah]). The same verb occurs in the parallel Mt. 7:7f., but there the context is different and it is hard to find any connection between vv. 7-11 and what precedes or follows. It seems clear, however, that the meaning is again "be persistent in prayer" (cf. v. 11), and D. Hill is probably correct in supposing that the situation presupposed is that described in Lk. 11:5-8 (*Gospel of Matthew* [*NCBC*, 1972], p. 148). It is possible that the divergent placement of these sayings by Matthew and Luke is a result of their having different recensions of Q material before them (I. H. Marshall, *Comm. on Luke* [*New International Greek Testament Comm* , 1978], p. 463). In Lk. 12:36; 13:25 the metaphor is merely a detail of the parables and does not correspond to any specific theological meaning. In Rev. 3:20 Christ's knocking connotes His desire for a closer fellowship with the Laodicean church, based on their repentance (v. 19).

(Some commentators interpret Cant. 5:2 with reference to this verse.)

*Bibliography.*–*DNTT,* II, pp. 881f.; S. Safrai, "Home and Family," in S. Safrai and M. Stern, eds., *Jewish People in the First Century,* II (1976), 734; *TDNT,* III, *s.v.* κρούω (Bertram).

A. L. SUNDSMO

**KNOP.**

**1.** AV translation of Heb. *kaptôr* in Ex. 25:31, 33-36; 37:17, 19-22. *See* CAPITAL.

**2.** AV translation of Heb. *p<sup>e</sup>qāʿîm* in 1 K. 6:18; 7:24. *See* GOURD **2.**

**KNOW, KNOWLEDGE.**

I. Terminology
II. OT
III. NT
IV. Revelation and Truth

*I. Terminology.*–The Hebrew terms for "know" are mainly *yāḏaʿ* and *nāḵar,* though the latter often has the force of "recognize" (Ruth 3:14). "Knowledge" in the OT is usually expressed by several cognate forms of the verb *yāḏaʿ*. Such terms as *daʿaṯ* can allude to general knowledge (Prov. 24:4), to particular knowledge about an event or a characteristic (Job 10:7), in a negative sense to describe an accidental, nonpurposive activity such as involuntary manslaughter (Dt. 4:42; 19:4; Josh. 20:3, 5) or technical ability (Ex. 31:3; 35:31; 1 K. 7:14, where in each case the technical expertise was linked with wisdom [Heb. *ḥoḵmâ*], one early sense of which was "ability to perform skilled tasks").

In the sense of cognition *daʿaṯ* was applied in Balaam's fourth oracle to knowing God (Nu. 24:16), and in the Garden of Eden narrative to the knowledge of the entire range of morality (Gen. 2:17; *see also* TREE OF KNOWLEDGE). The spirit of knowledge (*rû[a]ḥ daʿaṯ*), which was to be one endowment of the messianic descendant of Jesse (Isa. 11:2), was closely allied with wisdom and understanding, a sense which *daʿaṯ* has elsewhere (cf. Job 42:3; Ps. 119:66).

The verb *yāḏaʿ* described a process of learning by instruction (cf. Lev. 5:1) or by observation (cf. Jgs. 13:21), the recognition of an acquaintance (Gen. 29:5), the character of instinctual knowledge (Job 28:7), and the experience of a specific situation such as bereavement (Isa. 47:8) or grief in general (Isa. 53:3). In a negative sense *yāḏaʿ* was employed in Pharaoh's refusal to recognize the attainments of Joseph (Ex. 1:8). A common and important usage of "know,' "knowledge" was in a sexual context to describe coition (Gen. 4:1; 1 K. 1:4), sometimes of an immoral nature (Gen. 19:5). A wide variety of skills and professional abilities was expressed by the verb *yāḏaʿ* (cf. Gen. 25:27; 1 S. 16:16; 1 K. 9:27), as well as the idea of caring (or not caring) for someone because of knowing that person, whether referring to God (cf. Gen. 18:19; 1 S. 2:12; 2 S. 7:20; Am. 3:2) or to a person (cf. Ps. 79:6; Jer. 4:22; Hos. 5:4).

In the NT "know" is usually either *oída* or *ginṓskō,* together with some use of *epiginṓskō,* which can mean to know with clarity or completeness, but also can have the force of "recognize." The corresponding nouns are *gnṓsis* and *epígnōsis.* Still another term, *epístamai,* occurs several times (e.g., Acts 10:28), usually having the force of "understand."

It is tempting to conclude that *oída* and *ginṓskō* ought to be distinguished from one another in their force, especially when both occur in the same context, appearing to express a distinction, but this is difficult to demonstrate (cf. Jn. 21:17; 1 Jn. 5:20). A limited distinction may be noted, in that *ginṓskō* is sometimes used in the sense of "learn" (Mt. 9:30; Lk. 19:15), whereas *oída* denotes settled knowledge, whether derived from revelation or instruction (Jn. 8:55). In contrast to "opinion" (*dóxa*), *ginṓskō* embraces reality as it truly is, whether truth (*alḗtheia*) or being (*ṓn*).

Some scholars contend that *oída* signifies intuitional knowledge. The LXX uses *ginṓskō* and *epiginṓskō* three times as often as *oída,* but in Ezekiel, in contrast with more than eighty uses of the former terms, *oída* does not appear at all. Yet J. Barr rejects any suggestion that the Ezekiel source considers "the *oída* concept" distasteful; he points out that *ginṓskō* accommodated, whereas *oída* could not, the passive and future senses that Ezekiel requires (*Semantics of Biblical Language* [1961], p. 254). The term *oída* is used interchangeably with *ginṓskō* in the NT in sufficient instances to put one on guard against finding some distinctive meaning in *oída* (cf. *TDNT,* V, 116f.).

*II. OT.*–Scripture is careful to distinguish the knowledge possessed by God from that which is possible for mankind. The knowledge of the Almighty transcends time and anticipates events (Jer. 1:5). It takes cognizance of people and events alike, and nothing can be concealed from His perception (Ps. 139:1-16). He is able to declare the end from the beginning (Isa. 46:10). His knowledge of individuals (e.g., Abraham, Gen. 18:19) and of nations (e.g., Israel, Am. 3:2) sometimes involves the element of choice. He knows our frame, our physical limitations (Ps. 103:14), and our movements (Ps. 139:2), as well as the secrets of the heart (Ps. 44:21 [MT 22]) and even our thoughts (Ps. 139:2). He knows in advance what people plan to say (Ps. 139:4). This omniscience allows God to treat everyone appropriately, rewarding the believer and punishing the apostate and wicked. In particular, God knows His chosen people (Am. 3:2), who have been bound to Him by a solemn covenant. His awareness of their rebellion and idolatry, despite promises to the contrary, prompts Him to show His continuing love for them by sending prophets to warn them of the punishment that awaits the apostate (Hos. 5:3-12; Am. 2:4f.; Jer. 4:28; Ezk. 5:11), giving them ample opportunity to repent and return to Him in obedience and faith.

Human knowledge is likewise a theme of the OT. Mankind is enjoined not to glory in wisdom, might, or riches, but in the privilege of knowing God (Jer. 9:23f.). God was the supreme reality to believers of the OT era, even though at times they experienced difficulty in understanding the dispensations of His providence (Job 19:25f.). Occasionally the Almighty was pleased to reveal Himself by signs and wonders in order that those who did not belong to the covenant people might become cognizant of His power (Ex. 7:17). He resorted to similar means to strike the conscience of His backslidden people, answering the plea of Elijah when the prophet prayed that fire would come down from heaven and consume the sacrifice he had prepared, thereby assuring Israel that the Lord, not Baal, was the living and true God (1 K. 18:36-39). God's judgments on Israel were for the purpose of bringing the nation back to the realization that He alone is God (Ezk. 11:11). To know the Lord goes beyond a reaching out for Him with the mind. For example, it involves embracing His concern for the poor and needy (Jer. 22:16). Just as the key to Israel's decline was the refusal to retain God in its knowledge and in its acknowledgment (Jer. 4:22), so the key to the nation's renewal is its acknowledgment that the Lord is the nation's God and that there is no other (Joel 2:27).

*III. NT.*–The NT does not frequently allude to the knowledge possessed by God, since the strong foundation of OT teaching made this unnecessary. Jesus affirmed that God knows the state of the human heart (Lk. 16:15). Indeed, He knows everything (1 Jn. 3:20). "Before him no creature is hidden, but all are open and laid bare to the eyes of him with whom we have to do" (He. 4:13). Nothing is too trifling to escape His notice or His determining of events (Mt. 10:29). The heavenly Father knows that His children need such items as food and clothing (Mt. 6:32), but instead of making them priorities they are admonished to cease worrying and instead to seek His kingdom as a means of realizing His provision for their needs.

Much more attention is given to the knowledge possessed by the Son. As a lad of twelve, He astonished the learned men who taught in the temple (Lk. 2:46), and He continued to grow in wisdom thereafter (2:52). This was a token of His true humanity. During His ministry He was able to discern the thoughts of those who questioned Him (11:17) and to sense their hypocrisy (12:15). The penetrating insight evident during His public ministry is a matter of frequent emphasis, especially in the Fourth Gospel (2:25; 5:42; 10:14f.; 13:1, 11; 18:4; 19:28; 21:17). He was able to distinguish between true and false believers (Jn. 6:64). It is not made clear whether Jesus knew how long the infirm man had endured his affliction (Jn. 5:6) or whether He learned about it from others. When He did inquire, the reason was not ignorance but a desire to manifest interest and concern about human need.

Specific mention is made of Christ's learning obedience (to the Father) by the things He suffered (He. 5:7). One item of information was withheld from Him, namely, the specific time when He would return to earth (Mk. 13:32). Even in this case He carefully distinguished between Himself and others, whether people or angels. His voluntary admission that He did not know the time of His return has great value, in that it gives assurance that His many assertions about what He did know should be received with utmost seriousness.

During the earthly ministry, Jesus was encouraged and sustained by His unique knowledge of the Father (Jn. 8:55). This involved a clear perception of the Father's will for Him, including His sacrificial death (Lk. 22:42; He. 10:5-7). For those of the human family who desire a clear and satisfying knowledge of God, the Son is indispensable. God can be known in a personal, saving sense by knowing the Son (Jn. 14:7).

In the apostolic age, there were not only apostles, but also pastors and teachers whose task was to build up the believers in knowledge and Christian character (Eph. 4:11-13). The ministry of instruction in the local churches concentrated on the *didachḗ*, a corpus of information, oral in form, that appealed to the fact that converts to the Christian faith were called to a new life. They were summoned to put off pagan vices and put on Christ, appropriating His power to enable them to live supernaturally transformed lives. The teaching included obligations of family members to one another, responsibilities to fellow believers as well as to society and the state. These injunctions appear in the so-called practical portions of letters to churches. Writers were able to appeal to their readers' knowledge of this body of teaching. For example, in 1 Corinthians Paul repeatedly says "do you not know," chiding his readers for lack of compliance with the instruction they had received (3:16; 5:6; 6:2f., 9, 15f., 19; 9:13, 24).

In addition to human teachers, the believers had the benefit of the ministry of the Holy Spirit, enabling them to understand spiritual truths that remain inaccessible to the unsaved (1 Cor. 2:6-16).

Christian knowledge, despite its reality and richness, is limited in its scope during one's earthly life. Perfection in this area belongs to the age to come (1 Cor. 13:9f.).

***IV. Revelation and Truth.***–The fall affected the entirety of human nature. Human beings no longer, as at creation, thought God's thoughts after Him, willed to do the known will of God, or loved their Maker with their whole being. The fall, however, did not totally destroy the competence of human reason; although no universally shared system of truth and/or morality survived mankind's rebellion in Eden, human beings were still responsibly related to their Maker and were continually in revolt against light. The knowledge of God that continually penetrates the human mind and conscience even in sinful rebellion (Ps. 19:1 [MT 2]; Rom. 1:18ff.; 2:14f.) is attributed biblically to the universal revelation of God and to mankind's divine creation in the image of God. Modern evolutionary conceptions of the emergence of the categories of reason and morality from the nonmental and amoral undermine the permanent and universal significance of the rational and ethical aspects of human existence. The notion that the idea of God is simply an inference from nature or from human experience, i.e., from the not-God, plays into Ludwig Feuerbach's misconception that human beings fashion God in their own image; the soundest reply to such notions is that God Himself is the source of mankind's idea of Him.

The Bible teaches that truth has its ontological ground in God Himself (Ps. 31:5 [MT 6]; Isa. 65:16; cf. Jn. 14:6). All human knowledge is dependent upon God, who is the source and stipulator of truth. Divine revelation is identified as the truth of God, and the gospel especially is characterized as revealed truth. Apart from divine revelation all merely human affirmations about God and His purposes reduce to conjecture. Legitimate and authoritative pronouncements about God therefore presuppose God who makes Himself known.

The Hebrew and Greek conceptions of truth — both in respect to the method of knowing truth and its content — differ in important ways. But that contrast is not rooted in an essentially contradictive sense of such conceptions as truth and knowledge. Least of all did the conception of truth, either in the OT or the NT, cancel the distinction between truth and falsehood or dissolve the law of contradiction. That the God of the Bible is Himself the Truth and the source and standard of all truth, or that Jesus and the apostles stress that truth is to be done and not simply to be known, do not justify the exaggeration of Hebrew and Greek differences of usage implied by the neoorthodox emphasis on biblical truth as personal rather than propositional.

Christian knowledge does indeed carry a demand for expression in a corresponding manner of life; the practical consequences are continually implied if not actually in view (cf. Jas. 2:26, "faith apart from works is dead"). Christian learning is not an end in itself; it is the means to the love and service of God and under Him of neighbor and mankind. The believer who properly knows God forsakes his pagan vices and lives by the Spirit.

But none of these emphases discredits the importance of theological knowledge or of the cognitive aspects of faith. The researching of Scripture is enjoined by Jesus (Jn. 5:39). The Pauline statement that "knowledge puffs up, but love builds up" (1 Cor. 8:1) has in view, as the subsequent verse indicates, false opinion or misapplied truth.

Since God is the source and stipulator of truth, all human knowledge is dependent upon Him. Divine revelation is the source of truth and the human mind a created instrument for recognizing it. Human knowledge of the cosmos, as well as of other selves, rests on the ontological significance of reason. The Creator has fashioned a *Logos*-ordered and *nomos*-structured universe, one meshed to the categories of understanding implanted in mankind at creation.

Not even the direct recipients of divine revelation — i.e., the biblical prophets and apostles — "see everything from God's point of view." Human beings are and will always be finite; moreover, in their present sinful condition their rebellious disposition complicates the reception and appropriation of knowledge, the more so as knowledge is moral and spiritual in content.

In sharp contrast to the Greek view of prophecy, that mankind is endowed with a divine spark that one may fan into flame, the biblical view regards all truth as mediated by the Logos of God. Even Paul, the great apostle to the Gentiles, for all his reception of special divine revelation, emphasized that "now we know in part" and that only in the future eschatological age will we "see face to face" (1 Cor. 13:12). Yet divine revelation vouchsafes a knowledge to which human beings cannot otherwise attain, knowledge of God and of His will. This is given universally in general revelation (Rom. 1:20, 32; 2:15) and in the special redemptive disclosure conveyed to and through the Judeo-Christian prophets and apostles. The Pauline characterization of Gentiles as those who do not know God (Gal. 4:8) speaks of their culpable ignorance of Him; even the demons, as James says, "believe and tremble" (Jas. 2:19).

It is of the divinely revealed Christ that the apostle John declares: "we may be sure that we know him" (1 Jn. 2:3). Historic Christian theism acknowledges Christ as the incarnate Word of God and Scripture as the written Word of God (2 Tim. 3:16). Despite the emphasis of some theologians on the incarnate Logos as exclusively the Word of God, Jesus spoke of His own sayings (or doctrines) as *logoi* for the neglect or disbelief of which His hearers will be judged.

*See also* GNOSTICISM; TRUTH.

***Bibliography.***–R. C. Dentan, *Knowledge of God in Ancient Israel* (1968); C. H. Dodd, *Interpretation of the Fourth Gospel* (repr. 1972), pp. 151-169; *TDNT*, I, *s.v.* γινώσκω κτλ. (Bultmann); *TDOT*, V, *s.v.* "yādhaʿ" (J. Bergman, G. J. Botterweck).

C. F. H. HENRY
R. K. H.

**KOA** kō'ə [Heb. *qô(a)ʿ*]. A people named with Pekod and Shoa as enemies of Jerusalem (Ezk. 23:23). Some scholars have associated them with the Gutians, a barbaric people who inhabited areas of the Zagros Mountains, but certain identification is not possible.

**KOHATH** kō'hath; **KOHATHITES** kō'hath-īts [Heb. *qᵉhāṯ*, *qᵒhāṯî*]. Second son of Levi and ancestor of Moses and Aaron (Gen. 46:11; Ex. 6:16-20; Nu. 3:17; 1 Ch. 6:1 [MT 5:27]; etc.). The Kohathites formed one of the three divisions of the tribe of Levi; the other two were the Gershonites and the Merarites (Nu. 3:17ff.). The Kohathites consisted of four families, the Amramites, Izharites, Hebronites, and Uzzielites (3:19, 27; etc.). In the wilderness they encamped on the southern side of the tabernacle (v. 29); the males from a month old and upward numbered 8600 (v. 28). Their special charge was "the ark, the table, the lampstand, the altars, the vessels of the sanctuary with which the priests minister, and the screen; all the service pertaining to these" (v. 31; cf. 7:9). After the Conquest twenty-three cities were assigned to them by lot (Josh. 21:4-26). In David's time and after, Heman, a Kohathite, and his family had a prominent place in the service as musicians (1 Ch. 6:33-48; 16:41f.; 25:1-8). David likewise divided the Levites into courses (the Kohathites, 23:12-20; 24:20-25). The Kohathites fought at En-gedi in the reign of Jehoshaphat (2 Ch. 20:19) and helped to cleanse the temple in Hezekiah's reign (29:12, 14). J. ORR

**KOHELETH.** *See* ECCLESIASTES.

**KOLA** kō'lə [Gk. *Kōla, Chōla, Keila*]; AV COLA; NEB CHOLA. A place mentioned in Jth. 15:4, along with Betomesthaim, Bebai, Choba, "and all the frontiers of Israel," to which Uzziah sent men of Israel to tell of the flight of the Assyrian army. According to 4:6 Betomesthaim "faces Esdraelon, opposite the plain near Dothan." Bebai has not been identified; the name is missing in B and the Vulgate. Choba has sometimes been identified with el-Mekhubbi on the road from Samaria to Beth-shean. Simons (*GTTOT*, § 1606) identified it with Kāʿun, between Meḥubba and Beisan, which is in the same region as el-Mekhubbi (= Meḥubba). Abel, however, inclined to the view that this quasi-historical account of Nebuchadnezzar "king of Assyria" and Uzziah took names from other portions of the Bible, such as Gen. 14:15 (*GP*, II, 299). If the account is not historical, attempts to locate the places mentioned will be of little value. If it is, Kola can be located no more specifically than in northern Samaria.

W. S. L. S.

**KOLAIAH** kō-lā'yə, kō-lī'ə [Heb. *qôlāyâ*–'voice of Yahweh'].

**1.** A Benjaminite, son of Maaseiah (Neh. 11:7).

**2.** Father of a false prophet and lecherous man named Ahab (Jer. 29:21).

**KONA** kō'nə [Gk. *Kōna, Kōla, Keila*; A *kōmas*–'villages']; AV "the villages"; NEB CONA. A place mentioned in Jth. 4:4. The people of Judea had only recently returned from Exile and were preparing to defend the hills and the passes. Kona is mentioned with several other places after the phrase "and to every district of Samaria," suggesting that these places were not in Samaria. Attempts to identify the site have not been sucessful. W. S. L. S.

**KOR.** *See* COR; WEIGHTS AND MEASURES.

**KORAH** kō'rə [Heb. *qōraḥ*–'baldness'(?); Gk. *Kore*].

**1.** One of the three sons of Oholibamah, Esau's Hivite wife. The three were born in Canaan before Esau withdrew to the Seir mountain country. They are mentioned three times from three points of view (Gen. 36:5, 14, 18; 1 Ch. 1:35); the third mention is in the list of chiefs.

**2.** One of the sons of Eliphaz, the son of Adah, Esau's Hittite wife (Gen. 36:16). He is mentioned as one of the Edomite chiefs.

**3.** A son of Hebron (1 Ch. 2:43), the son of Mareshah, mentioned in the Caleb group of families in Judah.

**4.** The son of Izhar the son of Kohath the son of Levi (Ex. 6:16ff.; Nu. 16:1; 1 Ch. 6:18, 31-38 [MT 3, 16-23]), a younger contemporary of Moses. There may have been generations, omitted in the record, between Izhar and Korah; that is a natural way of accounting for Amminadab (1 Ch. 6:22-30 [MT 7-15]).

This Korah is best known as the man whom the opening earth is said to have swallowed up along with his associates when they were challenging the authority of Moses and Aaron in the wilderness (Nu. 16–17). Korah is presented as the central figure in the affair; the company is spoken of as his company, and those who were swallowed up as "all the men that belonged to Korah" (16:11, 32). It is under his name that the affair is mentioned (26:9; 27:3; Jude 11; AV Core). But Dathan and Abiram of the tribe of Reuben are almost as prominent as Korah. In chs. 16 and 26 they are mentioned with him and in Dt. 11:6; Ps. 106:17 are mentioned without him. Another Reubenite, On the son of Peleth, was in the conspiracy. It has been inferred that he withdrew, but there is no reason either for or against the inference. Equally baseless is the inference that Zelophehad of Manasseh joined it but withdrew (Nu. 27:3). The account implies that there were other Levites in it besides Korah (16:7-10), and it particularly mentions 250 "well-known men" (vv. 2, 17, 35) who apparently belonged to different tribes.

The malcontents argued, "All the congregation are holy, every one of them" (Nu. 16:3), so that it was a usurpation for Moses and Aaron to confine the functions of an incense-burning priest to Aaron alone. Logically, their objection lay equally against the separation of Aaron and his sons from the rest of the Levites, and against the separation of the Levites from the rest of the people. Moses arranged that Korah and the 250, along with Aaron, take their places at the doorway of the tent of meeting, with their censers and fire and incense, so that Yahweh might indicate His will in the matter. Dathan and Abiram apparently refused his proposals.

Korah, the 250 with their censers, and "all the congregation" met Moses and Aaron at the doorway of the tent of meeting (Nu. 16:19). Yahweh directed Moses to warn the congregation to leave the vicinity. Since Dathan and Abiram were not at the tent of meeting, Moses, followed by the elders of Israel, went to the two men's tents and again warned everyone to leave. Dathan, Abiram, and their households stood near their tents, and the earth opened and swallowed them and their property and all the adherents of Korah. Fire from Yahweh devoured the 250 who offered incense. Ch. 16 does not say what became of Korah or whether Korah's sons participated in the rebellion (but cf. 26:10f., "The earth opened up its mouth and swallowed them up together with Korah. . . . Notwithstanding, the sons of Korah did not die"; cf. also the comms.; G. W. Coats, *Rebellion in the Wilderness* [1968], pp. 156-184). Because the people of Israel criticized Moses and Aaron for the deaths of Korah's company, 14,700 Israelites perished in a plague (16:49 [MT 17:14]).

W. J. BEECHER

**KORAHITES** kō'rə-īts [Heb. *qorḥî*]; **SONS OF KORAH** [*b^e nê qōraḥ*]; AV also KORHITES, KORATHITES, SONS OF KORE; NEB also KORAHITE FAMILIES, LINE OF KORAH. This expression denotes Assir, Elkanah, and Abiasaph, Korah's three sons (Ex. 6:24; cf. Nu. 26:11). But it is more frequently used in the titles of Psalms.

The genealogical details concerning Korahites are rather full. In three places are lists of the seven successive generations closing with the prophet Samuel and his son Joel (1 Ch. 6:22-30, 33-38 [MT 7-15, 18-24]; 1 S. 1:1, 20; 8:2); the two in Chronicles mention most of the generations between Korah and Joel. The fragmentary lists in 1 Ch. 9, 25–26 connect the lineage with the four generations following Joel (1 Ch. 6:33 [MT 18]; 9:19-31; 26:1-11) and with two generations in the very latest Bible times (1 Ch. 9:31).

In 1 Ch. 9:31 the adjective Korahite designates an individual, but it is used collectively elsewhere (Ex. 6:24; Nu. 26:58; 1 Ch. 9:19; 12:6 [MT 7]; 26:1, 19; 2 Ch. 20:19). In these passages the families are counted in the same way as the other Levitical families. In 1 Ch. 12:6 five men designated as "the Korahites" joined David at Ziklag — Elkanah, Isshiah, Asarel, Joezer, Jashobeam. They are described as expert warriors, especially with the bow and sling, and as being of Saul's brethren of Benjamin. Some of them may plausibly be identified with men of the same name mentioned elsewhere. These Korahites may have been cousins of the Samuel family, residing near them.

The record speaks with some emphasis of a line of Korahite doorkeepers. One Mattithiah, the first born of Shallum the Korahite, was in charge of making the flat cakes (1 Ch. 9:31). Shallum was "the son of Kore, the son of Ebiasaph, the son of Korah." In this expression fifteen or more generations are omitted between Ebiasaph and Kore and perhaps as many between Kore and Shallum. The record proceeds to supply some of the omitted names between Kore and Shallum. The representative of the line in David's time was Zechariah son of Meshelemiah (v. 21). In all periods the Korahites were keepers of the thresholds of the tent. In the time of Phinehas son of Eleazar, their fathers were in charge of the camp of the Lord (vv. 19f.). Zechariah was, in his time, "gatekeeper at the entrance of the tent of meeting" (v. 21), and Shallum was still the chief of the porters (v. 17). The record for David's time supports and supplements this; the doorkeepers, according to the arrangements made by David, included a Korahite contingent. Its leading men were Meshelemiah the son of Kore of the sons of Asaph, and Meshelemiah's son Zechariah (26:1f., 9, 14). If the common conjecture that Asaph is here a variant for Ebiasaph is accepted, this chapter contains the same abridgment of the genealogical list as ch. 9.

More interesting, however, that the fighting Korahites of Benjamin or the doorkeeping Korahites who claimed succession from Moses to Nehemiah are the "sons of Korah" who were somehow connected with the service of song. The Korahites and Asaphites constituted two guilds of temple singers, and some favorite Korahite compositions are reflected by the titles of Pss. 42; 44–49; 84–85; 87–88 (*see also* PSALMS III.D). In 2 Ch. 20:19 the Kohathites are mentioned in association with the Korahites, as also in 1 Ch. 6:33 (MT 18), with the Kohathites taking precedence. Archeological discoveries in Palestine have confirmed the tradition of music and singing as an important part of culture in the early monarchy. Ugaritic texts refer to a class of temple personnel known as *šārīm*, who were analogous to the Hebrew singers of the monarchy and subsequent periods. Some of David's servants, such as Heman, Calcol, and Darda (1 K. 4:31 [MT 5:11]; 1 Ch. 2:6), had Canaanite names, and their designation as "sons of Mahol" is now known to mean "members of the orchestral guild." David's interest in sacred music is mentioned in connection with Solomon's temple, the times of Joash and Hezekiah and Josiah, and the institutions and exploits of the times after the Exile (e.g., 2 Ch. 7:6; 23:18; 29:25-30; 35:15; Ezr. 3:10; Neh. 12:36, 45f.). Asaph, Heman, and Jeduthun led the magnificent choir and orchestra at the dedication of the temple (2 Ch. 5:12). One of the sons of Asaph prophesied, and the sons of the Korahites sang at the crisis in the time of Jehoshaphat (20:14, 19). Asaph's, Heman's, and Jeduthun's sons were present, and there was instrumental music and loud singing, according to the appointment of David and his associates, at Hezekiah's Passover (29:12ff.). This singing, and Asaph, Heman, Jeduthun, and David have an important place in the record concerning Josiah. The records of the postexilic times make the singers "sons of Asaph" and make the arrangements of David as conspicuous as the law of Moses itself.

The phrases "sons of Korah," "sons of Asaph," "sons of Heman," and "sons of Jeduthun" denote in some cases merely lineal descent but in other cases aggregates of persons interested in sacred song and music — a guild, society, succession, or group — arising out of the movement that originated in David's time. See "sons of Asaph" (1 Ch. 25:1f.; 2 Ch. 20:14; cf. 20:19; 29:13; 35:15; Ezr. 2:41; 3:10; Neh. 7:44; 11:22) and "sons of Korah" in the titles of Pss. 42–49; 84; 85; 87; 88. Traces of these aggregates appear in the times of Solomon, Jehoshaphat, Joash, Hezekiah, Josiah, Zerubbabel, and Ezra and Nehemiah.

W. J. BEECHER

**KORATHITES** (Nu. 26:58, AV). *See* KORAHITES.

**KORE** kô'rə [Heb. *qôrē'*].

**1.** A Levite of David's time, descended from Kohath and Korah. (*See* KORAH **4.**) Shallum, chief doorkeeper in the latest OT times, is described as "the son of Kore, son of Ebiasaph, son of Korah" (1 Ch. 9:19). This expression omits the generations between Shallum and Kore and those between Kore and Ebiasaph, perhaps fifteen generations or more in each case. The context supplies two of the omitted names, Meshelemiah and his son Zechariah of the time of David (vv. 21f.); 1 Ch. 26:1f., 9, 14 mention these two, calling Meshelemiah the son of Kore and describing them as Korahites of the sons of Asaph. It is usual to regard this last clause as a variant for "the son of Ebiasaph," making the description identical with that in 9:19; thus "the Korahites," Kore and Meshelemiah and Zechariah, would come midway in a line of sanctuary ministrants extending continuously from Moses to Nehemiah.

**2.** "The son of Imnah the Levite, keeper of the east gate," who "was over the freewill offerings" in the time of Hezekiah (2 Ch. 31:14) and was very likely in the same line with **1.**

W. J. BEECHER

**KORHITES** (Ex. 6:24; 1 Ch. 12:6; 26:1; 2 Ch. 20:19, AV). *See* KORAHITES.

**KOZ** koz [Heb. *qôṣ*–'thorn']; AV, NEB, COZ. A man of Judah (1 Ch. 4:8), descendant of Caleb. *See* HAKKOZ.

**KUE** kōō'ə [Heb. *qᵉwēh, qᵉwē'*; Gk. *Koue*; Lat. *Coa*] (1 K. 10:28; 2 Ch. 1:16); AV "linen yarn"; NEB COA. The country from which Solomon imported horses, probably the ancient name for eastern Cilicia.

Kue was one of the small neo-Hittite states of northern Syria and southern Anatolia that formed in the wake of the destruction of the Hittite empire in the 13th cent. B.C. Kue helped Solomon supply horses and chariots to neighboring states (J. Bright, *History of Israel* [2nd ed.], p. 212). A century later it was part of the coalition that fought with Ahab of Israel and Hadadezer of Damascus against the Assyrian king Shalmaneser III at the Battle of Qarqar in 853 B.C. (*ANET,* pp. 278f.). The Zakir inscription (early 8th cent. B.C.) mentions Kue as an ally of Damascus in another war, against Zakir of HAMATH (*ANET,* pp. 655f.).

In 1946 a long inscription in Phoenician and hieroglyphic Hittite was discovered at Karatepe, Turkey, in the ancient region of Kue (*ANET,* pp. 653f.). It contains a record of the deeds of "Azitawadda," a vassal or general of "Awarka king of the Danunians" — i.e., the king of Kue. The inscription affords an important glimpse into the political and religious conditions in this area of the Near East in the 9th-8th cents. B.C.

The AV translators misinterpreted *qᵉwēh* as a form of Heb. *qāw,* "twine, line."

***Bibliography.***–W. F. Albright, *BASOR,* 120 (Dec. 1950), 22-25; J. C. Gibson, *Textbook of Syrian Semitic Inscriptions,* III (1982), 41-64; A. Goetze, *JCS,* 16 (1962), 48-58; H. Tadmor, *IEJ,* 11 (1961), 143-150.

E. M. COOK

**KUN** (1 Ch. 18:8, NEB). *See* CUN.

**KUSHAIAH** kōō-shā'yə, kōō-shī'ə [Heb. *qûšāyāhû*–'bow of Yahweh']. A Merarite Levite (1 Ch. 15:17), called KISHI in 6:44 (MT 29).

L. *See* GOSPELS, SYNOPTIC V.C, D.

**LAADAH** lā'ə-də [Heb. *laʿdâ*]. A descendant of Judah (1 Ch. 4:21).

**LAADAN** lā'ə-dən (AV, NEB, 1 Ch. 7:26; 23:7f.; etc.). *See* LADAN.

**LABAN** lā'bən [Heb. *lāḇān*–'white'; Gk. *Laban*]. Son of Bethuel, grandson of Nahor, and brother of Rebekah (Gen. 24:24, 29; 25:20; 28:5). He belonged to the branch of the family of Terah derived from Abraham's brother Nahor and niece Milcah. The genealogy of this branch (22:20-24), true to its purpose and place in Genesis, stops at Rebekah without mentioning Laban. Accordingly, the introduction of Rebekah in the narrative of ch. 24 (vv. 15, 24) calls to the reader's mind the genealogy already given. Her brother Laban must be introduced by the express announcement "Rebekah had a brother whose name was Laban" (v. 29).

Laban took a prominent part in receiving Abraham's servant and determining his sister's future. That brothers in OT times had an effective voice in the marriage of their sisters is evident not only from extrabiblical sources but also from the Bible (e.g., Cant. 8:8). In Gen. 24, however, Laban's prominence seems to deviate from the customs of the Palestinian side of the family. He usurped his father Bethuel's functions in arranging Rebekah's marriage (24:50f., 55) without actually denying Bethuel's authority. His self-interest (e.g., his showing eager hospitality after assessing the gifts brought for his sister, vv. 30-33) and his duplicity (e.g., his marrying Jacob first to Leah rather than to Rachel, 29:20-30) suggest that he may well have adapted a number of contemporary customs to his own purposes. Thus it may be unproductive to interpret his behavior according to the social modes of specific northern Mesopotamian cultural centers.

Laban was apparently old when Jacob arrived, but so energetic that even after two decades he could still exercise his role as patriarch with complete authority (Gen. 31:23-35, 43-55). He emerges as an enterprising, selfish, hardy individual, doubtless respected by his contemporaries for these qualities; beside him Jacob appears pallid and weak. He was hardly an ideal father, to judge from his daughters' complaints (vv. 14-16). Indeed, a theophany was necessary before his self-interest was curbed (v. 24).

Laban lived in Haran (*Ḫarrānu* in the cuneiform texts), the area settled by Nahor when the rest of Terah's descendants moved west to Canaan (Gen. 11:31; 12:5). Since Haran and the surrounding region where the flocks grazed belonged to the district known as PADDAN-ARAM, Laban was called "the Aramean" (25:20; 28:5; 31:20, 24; cf. Dt. 26:5), an epithet reflecting the nature of the population associated with the Haran cities and the Aramaic language spoken in the area (Gen. 31:47). The contrast between the two Semitic dialects is brought out forcibly in the MT of vv. 46f.; Laban called the pile of stones *y^egar śāh^adûṯā'* and Jacob referred to it as *galʿēḏ,* both terms meaning "the heap of witness."

Archeological discoveries at the Middle Bronze (*ca.* 2000-1550 B.C.) level of NUZI have shed light on the relationship of Jacob and Laban. Probably Laban had no male heirs when Jacob became a member of his household; after Jacob had served stipulated periods of time, Laban allowed him to marry his daughters. The memorial covenant between them required Jacob to forfeit his right of inheritance if he took additional wives (Gen. 31:50). Provisions of this kind at Nuzi were generally part of adoption contracts, and the aged Laban's demonstration of his patriarchal authority (v. 43) indicates that he was treating Jacob as a legally adopted son. But apparently during the two decades in which Jacob served Laban (v. 38), sons were born to Laban, thus depriving Jacob of any rights of primogeniture.

Some scholars have argued that in Nuzi society proof of primogeniture seems to have been possession of the household gods (*t^erāpîm*). Thus when Rachel absconded with them she would have been trying to secure for Jacob his former rights. But because the patriarch Laban still firmly controlled the entire family, Jacob and his wives would have been legally guilty in leaving the parental household without permission. Other scholars, however, have argued from a reinterpretation of the published Nuzi material that possession of the household gods did not necessarily indicate possession of inheritance rights, since the images seem to have been used only in cultic connections. In the Nuzi texts the household gods were generally bequeathed to the principal heir, and if Laban was following local tradition, the disappearance of the images was probably regarded as simple theft. More serious was the possibility of Laban's incurring the wrath of the deity or deities involved.

***Bibliography.***–M. Greenberg, *JBL,* 81 (1962), 239-248; J. van Seters, *HTR,* 62 (1969), 377-395; T. L. Thompson, *Journal for the Study of the OT,* 9 (1978), 2-34. J. O. BOYD R. K. H.

**LABAN** lā'bən [Heb. *lāḇān*–'white'; Gk. *Lobon*]. A location mentioned along with Paran, Tophel, Hazeroth, and Dizahab in Dt. 1:1, towns on the way to Mt. Seir in the

Sinai. Some scholars have identified it with Libnah, the third stopping-place of the tribes of Israel after Hazeroth (Nu. 33:20). Aharoni suggested that Raphia and Laban were towns on the southern coast of the Mediterranean Sea N of the Brook of Egypt, perhaps modern Sheikh ez-Zuweid (*LBHG*, rev. ed., p. 48) or Tel Abu Seleimeh (p. 152), stations on the Via Maris (pp. 329, 377).

J. McKENNA

**LABANA** (1 Esd. 5:29, AV, NEB). *See* LEBANAH.

**LABOR** [Heb. nouns *y$^e$gî(a)ʿ, maʿ$^a$śeh, m$^e$lā'ḵâ, ʿ$^a$ḇōḏâ, ʿāmāl, ʿeṣeḇ, p$^{eʿ}$ullâ*]; AV also SERVICE; NEB also WORK, PROPERTY (Neh. 5:13), etc.; [verbs *ʿāśâ, ʿāḇaḏ, yāgaʿ, ʿāmal, 'ûṣ*]; AV also TRAVAIL, WROUGHT, SERVE; NEB also WORK, TOIL, etc.; [Aram. hithpaal part. of *š$^e$ḏar*] (Dnl. 6:14 [MT 15]); NEB "continued his efforts"; [Gk. nouns *kópos, érgon*]; AV also WORKS; NEB also TOIL, WORK, etc.; [verbs *kopiáō, synathléō, ergázomai*]; NEB also TOIL, WORK, WORK HARD, etc.; **LABORER** [Heb. part. of *ʿāḇaḏ*] (Eccl. 5:12 [MT 11]); [Gk. *ergátēs*]; AV also WORKMAN; NEB also WORKER, MEN; [part. of *kopiáō*] (1 Cor. 16:16); **LABORIOUS** [Heb. *ʿ$^a$ḇōḏâ*]; AV SERVILE; NEB DAILY; **FORCED LABOR** [Heb. *mas, sēḇel*]; AV TRIBUTE, LEVY, etc.; NEB also FORCED LEVY, LABOUR-GANGS. For **LABOR (OF CHILDBIRTH)** *see* TRAVAIL.

*I. Terms.*–Of the many Hebrew and Greek words for "labor," most indicate service, toil, or exertion (*see also* WORK). Although the words differ in connotation and emphasis — with the emphasis variously on the activity itself, growing tired, troublesomeness, or the task — only a few distinctions need to be noted here. The NEB translation of *y$^e$gî(a)ʿ* in Neh. 5:13 as "property" correctly signifies the result of labor, i.e., acquired property. The verb *'ûṣ* in Isa. 22:4 literally means "hasten." One Greek verb for "labor," *synathléō*, literally means "struggle (in an athletic contest) along with someone"; the RSV "labored side by side with" and the NEB "shared [someone's] struggles" (Phil. 4:3) faithfully reflect this meaning. Paul used this verb to explain how early Christians joined him in proclaiming, defending, and advancing the gospel.

In the RSV the word "laborious" occurs only in Lev. 23 and Nu. 28–29. As a crucial aspect of religious feasts and festivals in the liturgical year of Israel, the law prescribed that on certain days the people must not do any "laborious work," i.e., they were to observe a kind of sabbath, a day of joyful rest.

Hebrew *mas* and *sēḇel* ("forced labor") refer to the ancient institution of the levy, by which captives of war were put to work for the state that had taken them. Moses told Israel, "When you draw near to a city to fight against it, offer terms of peace to it. And if its answer to you is peace and it opens to you, then all the people who are found in it shall do forced labor for you and shall serve you" (Dt. 20:10f.). The conquered Canaanites frequently had to endure forced labor for Israel (cf. Josh. 16:10; 17:13; Jgs. 1:28, 30, 33, 35); a military official apparently administered the levy program (cf. 2 S. 20:24; 1 K. 4:6; 11:28; 12:18; 2 Ch. 10:18). At the time of Solomon, when public works and state construction reached their greatest extent, forced labor was necessarily increased to provide the needed manpower for building the temple, the palace, cities and walls, etc. Hence Solomon for some time conscripted the remaining Amorites, Hittites, Perizzites, Hivites, and Jebusites as slave laborers ("forced levy," 1 K. 9:20f. par. 2 Ch. 8:7f.). Even among the Israelites a modified, temporary levy required them to work in quarries and in the forests of Lebanon to obtain building materials for the temple (1 K. 5:13-18 [MT 27-32]; but cf. also 9:22; 2 Ch. 8:9). *See also* LEVY; SLAVE.

M. W. MEYER

*II. Theology of Labor in the OT.*–God originally intended labor to be an integral part of human existence. Man, on God's behalf, was to master the rest of creation. Labor was something positive, since man was serving God by cooperating in His creative activity (Gen. 2:15). Rain sent by God brought forth plants from the ground that man worked (2:5).

When man fell (Gen. 3:6), he exchanged a life of pleasant tasks for one of grinding toil. Labor took on a new and ominous meaning: pain for women in childbearing (3:16), pain for men in breadwinning (v. 17).

The tilled ground would produce not only good food but also "thorns and thistles" (Gen. 3:18). Man would now be forced to depend largely on his own efforts, working by the sweat of his brow (v. 19), while God cooperated in only a minimal way. Toil became man's curse until the day of death.

Genesis 2 and 3 thus set the pattern for subsequent biblical teaching about work. Labor is a double-edged sword: at its best it cooperates with God's purposes for His people (see, e.g., Gen. 31:6-13), but at its worst it involves rebellion against His will.

Exodus describes various kinds of labor and gives seminal teaching concerning work as a whole. Slave labor, though the lesser of two evils when compared with death itself (Ex. 14:12; cf. Gen. 47:18-25), was nonetheless a particularly severe form of suffering (Ex. 1:8-14; 2:23; cf. Job 7:2f.). But Exodus does not depict nonmanual labor as infinitely better than manual labor, with all its monotony and misery; it gives examples of administrative and mental tasks that can be just as demanding and strenuous as physical toil (Ex. 18:13-18; cf. Eccl. 12:12).

Because daily work in the ancient world was exhausting and because of the human penchant for working themselves and sometimes others too hard and too long, God enjoined sabbath rest for all in Israel, including servants, sojourners, and animals. One day in seven was set aside for more leisurely activity, including especially the worship of God Himself and remembrance of His mighty acts. The rhythm between labor and rest was based on God's own example in creation and on the need for everyone to have a day off after six days of work (Ex. 20:8-11; Dt. 5:12-15). Observance of the sabbath also served as a reminder to God's people

Relief from the tomb of Ti (*ca.* 2400 B.C.) at Saqqârah showing two carpenters at work (Bildarchiv Foto Marburg)

that He had delivered them from Egyptian slavery (Dt. 5:15). The later institution of sabbatical and jubilee years was a natural extension of the original sabbath-day principle. Sabbatical years were intended to provide rest for the farmland, by letting it lie fallow, as well as freedom for indentured Hebrew slaves. Jubilee years required the remission of all debts. Such further outworking of the principle of the sabbath stressed once again that labor at its best is service to God, who is always the master of both land and time. *See also* FEASTS; SABBATH.

Although divinely ordained work is intended for mankind's benefit, its main purpose — like that of every other good gift — is to glorify the Giver. The Israelites therefore were to bring the first fruits of their labor as an offering to the Lord (Ex. 22:29f.; 23:19; Lev. 27:26; Dt. 26:1-11); a tenth of everything produced was also to be given to God (Lev. 27:30-33; Dt. 14:22-29; 26:12-15), since that tithe belonged to Him (Mal. 3:8-10).

The dual nature of labor is underscored by the Bible's observation that some work was clearly for God while other work was just as clearly against Him. For example, the tabernacle in the desert was built so that God might dwell among (Ex. 25:8) and meet with (29:43) His people. The making of idols, on the other hand, was forbidden as an affront to God's commands and nature as well as to mankind's creaturehood and dignity (Ex. 20:4-6; Dt. 4:15-18, 23; Ps. 106:19f.; Isa. 44:9-20; Jer. 10:3-5, 8f., 14f.). The attempt to build a city and tower at Babel (Gen. 11:1-9) falls into this latter category. Work for God brings His promised blessings (Isa. 65:17-25), while work against Him brings His inexorable curse (Hag. 1:5-11).

Similarly, God blessed the work of those who obeyed Him (Lev. 26:3-13; Dt. 28:1-14; Isa. 32:15-20; Am. 9:13f.; Hag. 2:15-19) and cursed the labor of those who disobeyed Him (Gen. 4:11f.; Lev. 26:14-45; Dt. 28:15-68; Isa. 5:5-7; 7:23-25; Mic. 6:15).

As people at their spiritual best always cooperate with God in labor — for human work is part of God's created order — so their work is to be done according to God's plans and commands, a principle nowhere better exemplified than in the building of the tabernacle (Ex. 25:9, 40; 26:30; 27:8; 31:1-5; etc.). Indeed, human work derives its strength and inspiration from God (Dt. 8:17f.).

Labor, though tedious and toilsome, can and should result in satisfaction and joy (Ex. 39:43; Neh. 2:18; Prov. 31:10-31). Sometimes, however, a person's wealth gained through honest labor is lost to and enjoyed by someone who has not even worked for it (Eccl. 6:1f.). Thus Ecclesiastes, like other OT writings, teaches that people's labor and its results are both good and bad because we live in a fallen world. God gives people sustenance from and joy in their work (Eccl. 2:10, 24-26; 3:12f.; 5:18-20 [MT 17-19]; 8:15; 9:7-10), but ultimately work is wasted because its results are temporary (2:11).

The exchange of wages for labor plays an important role in the OT view of work. The laborer is worthy of his hire (Lev. 19:13; Dt. 24:15; Jer. 22:13; 2 K. 12:13-15; Mal. 3:5; cf. Lk. 10:7; Jas. 5:4). Hunger can force a person to work in order to pay for food and other necessities (Prov. 16:26). Good workers can expect to better themselves by being promoted (1 K. 11:28; Prov. 22:29), while lazy workers jeopardize their future and may die prematurely (Prov. 21:25).

Although God has promised to bless His people when they are diligent and industrious, circumstances sometimes impede the successful completion of tasks (e.g., Neh. 4:10 [MT 4]). It is also evident that human labor attempted without divine help will ultimately prove unsuccessful (Job 5:8-13; Prov. 3:9f.; 10:22).

***III. Theology of Labor in the NT.***–While building on and reiterating the principles set forth in the OT, the NT has a distinctive emphasis because of the finished revelation in Jesus Christ. Like the OT, the NT shows that work is difficult and wearying (2 Cor. 6:5; 11:23, 27; cf. 1 Cor. 4:12); idleness is deplorable and to be avoided (2 Thess. 3:10-12); the worker deserves his wages (Mt. 10:10 par. Lk. 10:7; 1 Tim. 5:17f.); a man must provide for his family and relatives (1 Thess. 4:11f.; 1 Tim. 5:8). But the NT raises labor to new heights of dignity and significance. God may call people to leave their everyday work to follow Him (Mk. 1:16-20; 2:14; Lk. 5:8-11). Overemphasis on mundane tasks and their monetary benefits can stifle one's receptivity toward God's word and kingdom (Mt. 19:6-30 par. Mk. 4:19; Lk. 17:28-30; 21:34). Moreover, worry over labor and the necessities of life is contrary to God's will for His people; He has promised to provide for their legitimate needs if they seek first His kingdom and righteousness (Mt. 6:25-34). When overweening desire for money becomes the force behind working for a living, it leads to ruin. In the NT work is commendable only if the worker does not love money, trusts in God, and shows generosity (1 Tim. 6:6-10; Acts 20:33-35; Eph. 4:28).

Paul likened his and Timothy's evangelistic work to the work of soldiers, athletes, and farmers: all such responsibilities are hard and painful and require discipline and sacrifice (2 Tim. 2:4-6). But evangelists, like these other workers, do not give up, because they have a sense of obligation and recognize the importance of what they are doing for themselves and others. Those who work for Christ full time have a right to a livable wage. They may decide to relinquish that right, however, in order to serve God by not burdening others unduly (1 Cor. 9:1-18; 2 Thess. 3:6-9).

***Bibliography***–G. Agrell, *Work, Toil and Sustenance* (1976); A. T. Geoghegan, *The Attitude Towards Labor in Early Christianity and Ancient Culture* (1945). R. F. YOUNGBLOOD

**LACCUNUS** la-kōō-nəs [Gk. *Lakkounos*]; AV LACUNUS. One of the sons of Addi who returned with Ezra and had a foreign wife (1 Esd. 9:31). The name does not, as might have been expected, occur in Ezr. 10:30.

**LACE** [Heb. *pāṯîl*]. This term refers to a cord rather than to decorative openwork fabric. In Ex. 28:28; 39:21 it designates the blue cord that joined the rings of the breastplate to those of the ephod. It also fastened the engraved golden plate to the front of the high priest's turban (28:37; 39:31).

**LACEDAEMONIANS.** *See* SPARTA.

**LACHISH** lā'kish [Heb. *lāḵîš*]. One of the principal cities of Judah and a royal fortress protecting the southern Judean hill country from invasion from the southern Philistine plain. It stood midway between Jerusalem and Gaza and is identified with Tell ed-Duweir, about 8 km. (5 mi.) SW of Beit Jibrîn (modern Bet Guvrin, ancient Eleutheropolis).

The first mention of Lachish in the Bible occurs in the account of Israel's defeat of the south Canaanite coalition at Gibeon that resulted in the destruction of Lachish and the death of its king Japhia at Makkedah (Josh. 10:3ff.; 12:11). A cartouche of Ramses III, discovered in 1978 in the destruction debris of level VI associated with the city gate, indicates that Canaanite Lachish was destroyed during or following his reign (*ca.* 1182-1151 B.C.). After the conquest Lachish became a part of the territory assigned to the tribe of Judah (15:39). The destroyed site was abandoned for a long period before habitation was reestablished, perhaps in the time of David or Solomon. The

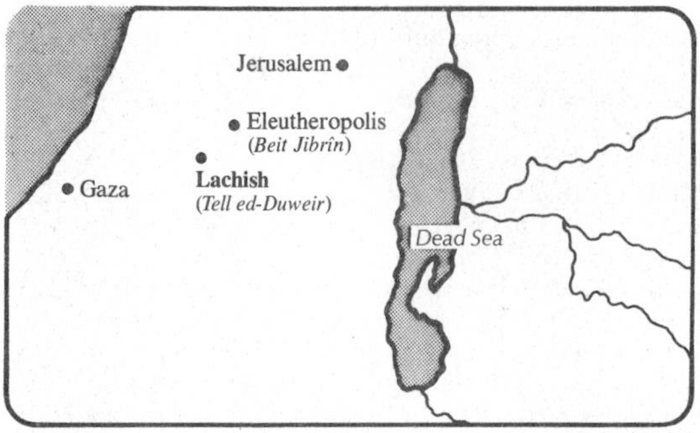


transformation of the site into a major Judean fortified city began with Rehoboam, Solomon's son, in the late 10th cent. (2 Ch. 11:9). The destruction of the early fortifications may be attributed to Pharaoh Sheshonq's (Shishak) campaign (*ca.* 925 B.C.). Amaziah of Judah fled there in a futile effort to escape assassination during a palace revolt (*ca.* 783; 2 K. 14:19; 2 Ch. 25:27). Having swept around Jerusalem in a punitive campaign against Hezekiah (cf. Mic. 1:10-15, esp. v. 13, for the southern invasion route), Sennacherib of Assyria made Lachish his field headquarters (701) and received there Hezekiah's suit for peace (2 K. 18:14, 17; 2 Ch. 32:9; Isa. 36:2). Scholars disagree on whether the Assyrian occupation of Lachish mentioned in 2 K. 19:8 refers to a second, later campaign by Sennacherib; it is more likely that he conducted a single campaign against Hezekiah's kingdom. In an impressive series of bas-reliefs adorning his palace at Nineveh, Sennacherib illustrated and described his capture of the city in 701. A sparsely populated Judean fortified city arose on the ruins of Lachish, only to be destroyed by Nebuchadrezzar of Babylon in his protracted campaign against the stubborn resistance of his rebellious regent Zedekiah (588/86; Jer. 34:7; cf. 52:3b-11). The last mention of the city in the Bible is its inclusion among the cities of southern Judah reoccupied by returnees from Babylon during Nehemiah's administration (440-428, Neh. 11:30).

The earliest extrabiblical reference to Lachish is mentioned in the Ebla commercial texts (*ca.* 2400 B.C.; cf. G. Pettinato, *Archives of Ebla* [Eng. tr. 1981], p. 226). The Amarna Letters (mid-14th cent. B.C.) contain several references to Lachish, including the role of Zimreda, prince of Lachish, in the characteristic squabbles between city-states of Palestine during the Amarna Age.

Archeological exploration of Tell ed-Duweir began with the Wellcome-Marston Research Expedition (1932-1938), directed by J. L. Starkey. His tragic murder at the hands of highwaymen brought the British investigation of the site to an end. O. Tufnell, a member of the expedition, published the four-volume final report. Y. Aharoni carried out a small-scale excavation in the area of the "solar shrine" in 1966 and 1968, a joint University of North Carolina–Hebrew University project, which was published as *Lachish V* (1976). A comprehensive excavation project was initiated at the site in 1973 by the Institute of Archaeology of Tel Aviv University and the Israel Exploration Society under the direction of D. Ussishkin. This long-term project is expected to continue into the 1990's.

The summit of the tell, impressively separated all around

Relief from the palace of Sennacherib (704-681 B.C.) at Nineveh showing the Assyrian attack on Lachish (Trustees of the British Museum)

by a valley, is 7.3 ha. (18 acres); thus it is one of the largest city mounds in Palestine (cf., e.g., Megiddo's summit of 5.3 ha., 13 acres). The well-watered region surrounding Lachish has been inhabited since Upper Paleolithic times, and there is evidence that the hill itself has been occupied since the Neolithic period (8th millennium B.C.). In the late Chalcolithic period (before 3200 B.C.), caves in the surrounding limestone hills provided shelter for the living; in the Early Bronze period (to *ca.* 2800) they became tombs. Little information about the city on the hills is available for this period. Later in the Early Bronze period the population changed (indicated by a change in burial customs from caves to single graves), and toward the end of the 3rd millennium Lachish, like other Palestinian sites, was abandoned.

The site was slowly reoccupied, and the Hyksos rulers of Egypt later made it a major fortress. Below the crest a moat, or fosse, was dug around the circumference; between it and the brick wall, whose foundations began about 30 m. (100 ft.) above the valley floor, a plaster-covered glacis was laid. Within the city a palace-citadel rose above the city walls. The fortifications of this city in the patriarchal period deteriorated after the expulsion of the Hyksos and the restoration of native rule in Egypt in the mid-16th century.

In the fosse, below the northwest corner of the wall, a small temple was built (*ca.* 1550) and twice enlarged (*ca.* 1450, 1350). It provides interesting information about pre-Mosaic Canaanite religious practices — e.g., pottery containers were placed in front of the offering table and on surrounding benches for drink offerings; pits inside and outside the rectangular temple were filled with bones of sheep and goats, especially the right foreleg (cf. Lev. 7:32) used in burnt offerings; and ovens were built outside the temple in which the fine meal for the cereal offering may have been baked (cf. Lev. 2:1-10). The large stones used in the temple were unhewn, but the altar of the last stage had three steps, proscribed by Ex. 20:24-26. The temple, whose design differed from the contemporary Canaanite temples at Hazor and the later temple of Solomon, and the city were destroyed, most likely by Joshua and the Israelites. Interestingly, this Late Bronze Age city (1550-1200 B.C.) was not surrounded by a wall at the crest of the tell, although the steep glacis from the Hyksos period provided an imposing barrier to the attackers. In the ruins of this last Canaanite city on the site, several proto-Canaanite inscriptions have been discovered, with letters reminiscent of the proto-Sinaitic inscriptions discovered early in the 20th cent. at Serābîṭ el-Khâdim in western Sinai.

Excavated Canaanite temple (*ca.* 1550-1350 B.C.) at Lachish (Israel Department of Antiquities and Museums)

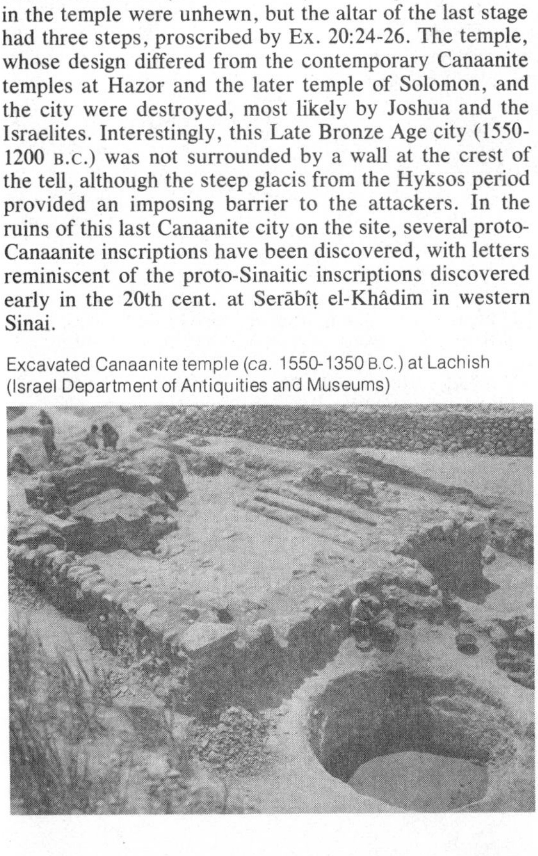

Ewer from Lachish (*ca.* 13th cent. B.C.) with drawings of several animals and an inscription, which has been variously interpreted. The script is similar to that of the Proto-Sinaitic inscriptions (Israel Department of Antiquities and Museums)

Lachish lay abandoned during the period of the judges with reoccupation beginning in the 10th cent., perhaps during the reign of David. A grave from the early monarchy has provided examples of the recently introduced iron technology: weapons and a trident (cf. 1 S. 2:13f.). The new settlement was apparently without protective walls, and little is known of it apart from a cult-room excavated in the solar shrine area. It had been destroyed by fire, an end presumably suffered by the entire settlement. Following this destruction the stump of the old Hyksos Canaanite citadel was enlarged to form a podium 32 m. (105 ft.) square. The Israelite citadel in part covered the remains of a Late Bronze temple that had been built over the ruins of the earlier Hyksos (Middle Bronze) temple. The podium (palace A) was faced with stone and filled with earth and rubble. It may be an example of a "Millo" (= filling, or terrace?), similar to that which David built in Jerusalem (2 S. 5:9). This foundation was used throughout the remaining history of Lachish, although with the major refortification of the city it was lengthened by the addition of palace B. Whether this occurred during Rehoboam's reign or later under Asa or Jehoshaphat is unclear. Before the major destruction of the city in 701 B.C., Palace C, an eastern extension of the combined Palaces A and B, was built. Further to the east was a large enclosed courtyard with a gate to the south that led to the major gateway of the city. No remains of the buildings atop the Judean palace-fortress were recovered. They had been demolished in the rebuilding of the residency in the postexilic (Persian) period, the last building to occupy the acropolis.

Abutting the palace-fortress complex to the south were the ruins of government storehouses from the Judean period, similar to structures from the same period found at Megiddo and Beer-sheba. These buildings suggest that Lachish served as an administrative center and warehouse complex in Judah. The size of the city and the immense fortifications indicate that it was second in importance only to Jerusalem in the period of the Judean kingdom.

The fortifications of Judean Lachish likely began under Rehoboam in the face of the threat of attack from the Egyptian ruler Sheshonq. A huge brick wall almost 6 m. (20 ft.) thick, with alternating salients and recesses (2 Ch. 11:5-12), was constructed. Midway down the slopes of the Middle Bronze glacis a revetment wall was built that girds the entire tell. Its purpose was to retain the glacis above it that, in turn, supported the base of the upper wall. A roadway led up the west side of the mound, through a gate protected by a massive outer bastion, where attackers were wholly exposed to missiles from the wall above them. The gate proper is similar in design to the "Solomonic" gates with their six bays, three on each side of the roadway, such as have been uncovered at Hazor, Megiddo, and Gezer; the Lachish gate, however, is greater in dimensions: about 24.4 by 25 m. (80 by 82 ft.), compared with the Megiddo gate of 18 by 20.3 m. (59 by 66.6 ft.). This defensive system served Lachish until Sennacherib breached it in 701. Sennacherib's forces penetrated the walls at two points — at the gate complex and at the southwest corner of the tell — by throwing up siege ramps against the fortifications and attacking them with battering rams and supporting fire. The archeological evidence supports the accuracy of the Assyrian artists' vivid depiction of the city's conquest in the reliefs from Sennacherib's palace. A remnant of the siege ramp at the southwest end of the tell remains in place, and a thick burn layer discovered in every area excavated atop the mound indicates that the conquerors put the city to the torch.

Perhaps in preparation for Sennacherib's assault (cf. Hezekiah's digging of the Siloam tunnel in Jerusalem; 2 Ch. 32:5f.), a water reservoir about 22 by 25 by 25 m. (70 by 80 by 80 ft.) was dug inside the southeast corner of the wall; a funnel-shaped depression of crushed chalk or rock chips was to provide drainage into this cistern, which was never completed.

After the Assyrian conquest Lachish remained a desolate and abandoned site for perhaps a half-century, while the conquerors dominated the region during the reigns of Esharhaddon and Ashurbanipal, Sennacherib's son and grandson, respectively. With the weakening of the Assyrian empire the city was reoccupied and refortified, most likely under the reign of Josiah king of Judah (639-609 B.C.). A new city wall and a new gate complex were constructed, but the population appears to have been much smaller than in the previous period. Nevertheless, Lachish once more became a major fortress in the Judean defense system. This period of resurgence was short-lived, however, ending with the conquest of the city by Nebuchadrezzar of Babylon (588-586 B.C.).

It is to the Babylon conquest that the famous "Lachish Letters" relate. Discovered by the British expedition in a room of the bastion, the outer gateway, in 1935, the ostraca are apparently copies of military communiqués. It is quite likely that the dispatches themselves were written on papyrus while the heavier ceramic copies were retained for the record. The correspondence is between Yoash, commander of the city, and Hoshiah, one of his subordinates who was in command of an outlying defensive position. The letters are a grim testimony to the inexorable advance of Nebuchadrezzar. They indicate a deteriorating military situation and a weakening morale caused by, among other things, the words of an unnamed prophet (speculation has often associated him with Jeremiah). The language of the twenty-one ostraca, where legible, is that of Jeremiah, Deuteronomy, and the Deuteronomic history. *See* LACHISH LETTERS.

For more than a century the city lay in ruins. In the mid-5th cent. a palace in the Syrian style (open court surrounded by suites of rooms approached through colonnades) was built on the ancient palace-citadel podium, perhaps as a residence for a Persian official appointed to see to Persian interests in a region controlled by Geshem the Arab (cf. Neh. 6:1) or the Edomites who had moved into the region during the previous century.

A smaller building was erected NE of the palace during the early Hellenistic period (after 330 B.C.). Though initially it was described as a "solar temple," further archeological investigation in 1966 and 1968 has resulted in its being compared in design with the preexilic shrine at Arad. Its orientation (entrance at the east end) and arrangement — an open court (*ʾûlām*) with steps leading to an inner room (the *hêḵāl*) and a small chamber beyond (the *dᵉḇîr*, "holy of holies") — are strongly reminiscent of the small Arad temple. The Lachish shrine apparently had no altar in the court like that of Arad; Arad had no steps leading up to the *hêḵāl* ("holy place"), unlike Lachish. Both had an incense altar (or altars) in the entry to the *dᵉḇîr* and additional rooms off the courtyard and temple. The Lachish structure was probably a Jewish shrine with a conventional design built by Jewish residents (perhaps returnees from the Exile; cf. Neh. 11:30). The Deuteronomic limitation of a single center of worship (at Jerusalem?) would presumably not have been violated, since this region was now under Edomite (Idumean) control (cf. the Jewish temple at Elephantine and the Oniad temple [mentioned by Josephus *BJ* vii.10.2-4 (420-436); *Ant.* xiii.3.1-3 (62-73)] at Leontopolis, both in Egypt, as well as the Samaritan temple on Mt. Gerizim and the temple of the Tobiad Hyrcanus at ʿAraq el-Amir in Transjordan).

During this period Marisa (Mareshah), 5.6 km. (3.5 mi.) northeast, replaced Lachish as the district's administrative center. During the Maccabean wars Lachish was destroyed for the last time (*ca.* 150 B.C.). Since the establishment of the state of Israel, the ancient site has been surrounded by the agricultural activities of Moshav Lachish.

***Bibliography.***–Y. Aharoni, *IEJ*, 16 (1966), 280f.; 18 (1968), 157-169, 254f.; *RB*, 75 (1968), 401f.; 76 (1969), 576ff.; *Lachish V* (1975); *ANET*, pp. 321f.; *EAEHL*, III, *s.v.* (Y. Aharoni, *et al.*); R. B. Haupert, *BA*, 1 (1938), 21-32; H. Torczyner, L. Harding, A. Lewis, and J. L. Starkey, *Lachish I (Tell ed-Duweir): The Lachish Letters* (1938); O. Tufnell, C. H. Inge, and L. Harding, *Lachish II (Tell ed-Duweir): The Fosse Temple* (1940); O. Tufnell, *Lachish III (Tell ed-Duweir): The Iron Age* (2 vols., 1953); *Lachish IV (Tell ed-Duweir): The Bronze Age* (2 vols., 1958); D. Ussishkin, *Tel Aviv*, 4 (1977), 28ff.; 5 (1978), 1-97; 10 (1983), 97ff.; *Conquest of Lachish by Sennacherib* (1982); *AOTS*, pp. 296-308; *DOTT*, pp. 212-17; G. E. Wright, *BA*, 18 (1955), 9-17.

V. R. GOLD K. N. SCHOVILLE

**LACHISH** lā'kish **LETTERS.** A corpus of twenty-one inscribed ostraca discovered at Tell ed-Duweir, which is generally identified with biblical Lachish. The first eighteen were discovered in 1935 in a small room under the gate tower, and the remaining three in 1938 in various locations. With the exceptions of nos. 1 and 19 (lists of names) and no. 20 (a docket), they all appear to be letters. Only about a third are reasonably legible. The first eighteen are dated 597-587 B.C., perhaps more narrowly to 589-588. The latter three are short, fragmentary, and of uncertain date. Four of the letters (nos. 3, 4, 6, 19) are at the Palestine Museum in Jerusalem; the remaining seventeen are in London — two (nos. 20, 21) at the Institute of Archaeology, University of London, and fifteen (nos. 1, 2, 5, 7-18) at the British Museum. The letters are of special linguistic, orthographic, and historical importance.

*I. Linguistic Importance.*–The language of the letters is identical in all essentials to the classical Hebrew prose of the OT. Some phonological characteristics of southern Hebrew (e.g., diphthongs are usually not contracted) are preserved (see Gibson, p. 36). The tetragrammaton (*YHWH*) occurs frequently (it is amply attested two centuries earlier at Kuntillet ʿAjrūd; see Z. Meshel, *Biblical Archaeology Review*, 5/2 [1979], 24-34). Also frequent are names ending in *-yāhû,* which are typical of the time of Jeremiah. Of interest are the extrabiblical occurrences (in letters 3 and 16) of the Hebrew word for prophet (*nāḇîʾ*; see below). Further, the letters are important witnesses to classical Hebrew epistolary style (see Pardee).

*II. Orthographic Importance.*–The letters are written in the Paleo-Hebrew (Canaanite) alphabet. It was gradually replaced after the Babylonian Exile by an Aramaic script, from which the later "Hebrew" alphabet derives (see J. P. Siegal, *Biblical Archaeology Review,* 5/3 [1979], 28-33). The style is basically cursive with frequent ligatures (see Gibson, p. 33). The irregular use of a space or a dot as word divider and the practice of splitting words at the ends of lines suggest how some kinds of textual errors in the Hebrew Bible may have arisen. Occasionally *w* and *y* are used as internal vowel letters. Although several scribal hands are in evidence, the script is basically the same throughout.

Lachish Letter IV, which mentions the fire-signals from Lachish (line 10) (Israel Department of Antiquities and Museums)

*III. Historical Importance.*–The letters provide firsthand documentation of the tense military and political situation in Judah shortly before the Babylonian victory of 587 B.C. In them a certain Hoshaiah (*hôšaʿyāhû*), a subordinate in charge of a garrison between Lachish and Jerusalem, writes to Yoash (*yāʾûš*), his commander in Lachish (note that both names include the divine element *ya-* ).

Most interesting are nos. 3, 4, and 6. Letter 4 attests the use of fire signals for communication: "Let my lord know that we are watching for the signals [*maśʾōṯ*] of

Lachish Letter III mentions *YHWH* (line 9) and "the prophet" (line 20), the first extrabiblical reference to a *nbʾ* to be discovered (Israel Department of Antiquities and Museums)

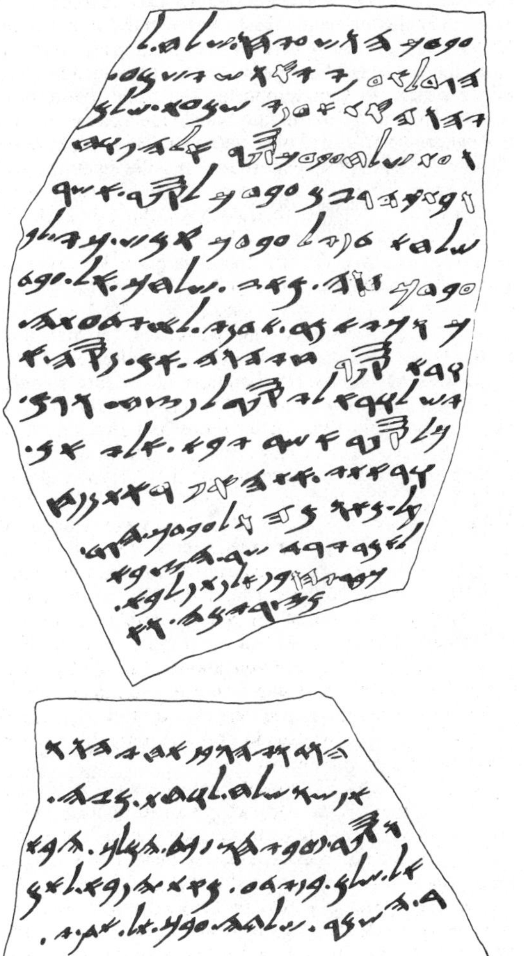

Lachish . . . we cannot see Azekah" (*ANET*, p. 322); a similar use of *maśʾēṯ* occurs in Jer. 6:1 and possibly in Jgs. 20:38, 40. Jer. 34:7 tells that Lachish and Azekah were the last of the fortified Judean cities to fall. Letter 6 refers to certain persons in Jerusalem discouraging (lit. "weakening the hands of") the soldiers (presumably). A similar accusation in the same idiom was brought against Jeremiah (38:4; cf. 27:12-16). Some scholars (e.g., Albright, *ANET*, p. 322) have attributed this discouragement to the activity of princes; others (e.g., Gibson, pp. 35f.) have attributed it to "the prophet." Unfortunately, the letter is poorly preserved, and nothing can be affirmed with certainty.

Letter 3 clearly mentions a prophet (*nāḇîʾ*) who was entrusted with delivering a letter from one of the king's servants. Letter 16 also mentions "the prophet," preceded immediately by the syllable *hû*. Some scholars have sought to identify this prophetic figure with Uriah (*ʾûrîyāhû*; Jer. 26:20-23) or even with Jeremiah (*yirmᵉyāhû*) himself. Although these suggestions are tempting, names ending with *-yāhû* were very common at this time, and the contexts are too broken; again, no firm conclusions can be drawn.

***Bibliography.***–W. F. Albright, *ANET*, pp. 321f.; *KAI*, nos. 192-99; J. Gibson, *Textbook of Syrian Semitic Inscriptions*, I (1971), 32-49; D. Pardee, *Handbook of Ancient Hebrew Letters* (1982), pp. 67-114; D. W. Thomas, *DOTT*, pp. 212-17; D. Ussishkin, *Biblical Archaeology Review*, 5/6 (1979), 16-38. M. D. GUINAN

**LACUNUS** la-ko͞o′nəs (1 Esd. 9:31, AV). *See* LACCUNUS.

**LAD** [Heb. *naʿar* (Gen. 21:12, 17-20; 22:5, 12; 37:2; 43:8; 44:22, 30-34; Jgs. 16:26; 1 S. 20:21, 35-41; 2 S. 17:18), *yeleḏ* (Gen. 37:30; 42:22); Gk. *país* (Acts 20:12) and its diminutive *paidárion* (Jn. 6:9)]. *See* CHILD.

**LADAN** lā′dən [Heb. *laʿdān*]; AV, NEB, LAADAN.

**1.** A descendant of Ephraim and ancestor of Joshua (1 Ch. 7:26).

**2.** A Levite of the family of Gershon (1 Ch. 23:7-9; 26:21).

**3.** AV rendering of Gk. *Dalan* in 1 Esd. 5:37. *See* DELAIAH **4.**

**LADDER** [Heb. *sullām* < *sālal*–'cast up, build' (Gen. 28:12)].

In the Near East ladders were made of wood, metal, and rope. In Mesopotamia, ladders were used in the 3rd millennium B.C. for constructing buildings and gaining access to the fruit on tall trees. Reliefs from Egypt and Mesopotamia illustrate the value of scaling-ladders when cities were being besieged, the earliest military use of ladders appearing in a limestone relief from Upper Egypt (24th cent. B.C.). Such ladders are not mentioned in Scripture, but are referred to in 1 Macc. 5:30.

The Hebrew term could also refer to stone steps on the exterior of a house leading to the roof and these seem to be implied in Gen. 28:12. Their appearance in Jacob's vision may have been prompted by the steplike configuration of the rocky strata which Jacob viewed at Bethel just before falling asleep. If this is true, "stairway" would be a better rendering of *sullām* than "ladder."

A similar geological structure most probably led to the designation of the narrow coastal strip some 17 km. (11 mi.) N of Ptolemais as the "LADDER OF TYRE."

*See also* SIEGE.

***Bibliography.***–Y. Yadin, *Art of Warfare in Biblical Lands* (Eng. tr. 1963), I, 146f., 228f.; II, 346, 392, 406, 434, 448f., 462.

R. K. H.

Tell Ḥalâf relief showing a man using a ladder to scale a palm tree (Trustees of the British Museum)

**LADDER OF TYRE** [Gk. *klímax Tyrou*] (1 Macc. 11:59). A landmark mentioned in the Apocrypha. Antiochus VI put his brother Simon in charge of the territory "from the Ladder of Tyre to the border of Egypt." Josephus, in commenting on this passage, located the Ladder of Tyre 100 stadia (19 km. [12 mi.]) N of Acre. He described it as the highest mountain of Galilee and Carmel, which is improbable, since Mt. Carmel is 550 m. (1800 ft.) in altitude and the highest point of the ridge overlooking the plain of Acre is only 300 m. (1000 ft.) high.

The most likely identification is with the first of the promontories at the north end of the plain of Acre, called Râs Musheirefeh. Rising sharply to a height of 90 m. (300 ft.), this ridge appears to form distinct steps down into the sea when viewed from the south. Two similar capes, likewise candidates for the historic Ladder of Tyre, are Râs en-Nakurah, only 1.6 km. (1 mi.) N of Râs Musheirefeh, and Râs el-ʿAbyadh, 10 km. (6 mi.) up the coast in the direction of Tyre. The latter cape is known to have featured man-carved steps in its steep ascent, suggesting a possible origin of the title Ladder of Tyre.

Simons attributed the name to the entire line of jutting promontories S of Tyre. "More exactly the name refers to the narrow, partly man-made passage between the sea and ğebel el-mushaqqaḥ, from rās en-nāqūrah to rās el-abjaḍ" (*GTTOT*, p. 416). A. H. LEWIS

**LADE; LADING** (Gen. 42:26; 45:17; Neh. 13:15; etc., AV); **LADEN.** *See* LOAD.

**LADY** [Heb. *śārâ* (Jgs. 5:29; Est. 1:18), *yᵉqārôṯ* (fem.)–lit. 'precious, honored (ones)' (Ps. 45:9 [MT 10]; *see also* HONOR); Gk. *kyría* (2 Jn. 1, 5)]. In 2 Jn. 1, 5, *kyría* probably denotes a local church rather than an individual (see comms. by R. Bultmann [Eng. tr. *Hermeneia*, 1973], pp. 107f.; I. H. Marshall [*NICNT*, 1978], p. 60).

*See also* ELECT LADY; JOHN, EPISTLES OF IV.

**LAEL** lā′əl [Heb. *lāʾēl*–'belonging to God']. Father of Eliasaph, the prince of the fathers' house of the Gershonites (Nu. 3:24).

**LAHAD** lā'had [Heb. *lāhad*–possibly 'slow, tardy'; cf. Arab. *lahdun* (*IP,* p. 227)]. A descendant of Judah (1 Ch. 4:2).

**LAHAI-ROI** lə-hī'roi [Heb. *lahay rō'î*]. *See* BEER-LAHAI-ROI.

**LAHMAM** lä'məm [Heb. *laḥmās,* but many MSS *laḥmām*]; NEB LAHMAS. A city of Judah, located in the Shephelah (Josh. 15:40). The LXX reads *Maches* (B) or *Lamas* (A); the Targ. reads *lḥmm* and the Vulg. *Leheman.*It has been identified with Khirbet el-Laḥm, 20 km. (13 mi.) WNW of Hebron and 4 km. (2.5 mi.) S of Beit Jibrîn. W. S. L. S.

**LAHMAS** lä'məs (Josh. 15:40, NEB). *See* LAHMAM.

**LAHMI** lä'mī [Heb. *laḥmî*]. According to 1 Ch. 20:5, the brother of Goliath of Gath. *See* EL-HANAN **1.**

**LAIR** [Heb. *'ereḇ*–'hiding place' (Job. 37:8), *mā'ôn* (Jer. 9:11 [MT 10]; 10:22), *marbēṣ*–'resting place' (Zeph. 2:15)]; AV DEN, "place to lie down"; NEB also HAUNT. The lairs of wild animals would naturally have been distant from populated areas. The jackal especially liked dry and deserted places. *See also* CAVE. G. WYPER

**LAISH** lā'ish [Heb. *layiš*]. A Benjaminite, father of the Palti or Paltiel to whom Saul gave his daughter Michal, who had been David's wife (1 S. 25:44; 2 S. 3:15).

**LAISH** lā'ish [Heb. *layiš*]. A city in the upper Jordan Valley, later called DAN (Jgs. 18:27, 29). It is called LESHEM in Josh. 19:47. Dan was situated near one of the copious springs at the base of Mt. Hermon that becomes Nahr el-Leddan, a tributary of the Jordan River.

For this name in the AV and NEB of Isa. 10:30, *see* LAISHAH. W. S. L. S.

**LAISHAH** lā'ə-shə [Heb. *layšâ*]. A village near Jerusalem mentioned in Isaiah's prophecy of the Assyrian advance on Jerusalem (Isa. 10:30). The LXX reading, *Laisa,* accounts for the AV and NEB "Laish." The context indicates a site near Anathoth (Anâtâ), 5 km. (3 mi.) NE of Jerusalem. If the tentative identification of Laishah with Khirbet el-ʿIsāwîyeh 2 km. (1.2 mi.) SW of ʿAnâtâ is correct, it is another example of the detaching of an initial *l* to form an article in the Arabic name (cf. el-ʿAzarîyeh from Lazarus, modern Bethany). Cf. *GTTOT,* § 1588, p. 482.

W. S. L. S.

**LAKE.** The OT has no specific word for lake. The Heb. *yām* is generally used of oceans and divided bodies of salt water, e.g., the Mediterranean Sea and the Red Sea. But it is also applied to inland bodies of water, e.g., the freshwater lake known as the Sea of Galilee (*yām kinnereṯ,* Nu. 34:11), and saltwater lakes like the Dead Sea (*yām hammelaḥ,* Gen. 14:3), as well as mighty rivers like the Nile (Nah. 3:8) and Euphrates (Jer. 51:36).

In the NT Gk. *thálassa* and *límnē* designate lakes (though the RSV thus renders only *límnē*). *Thálassa* is employed like Heb. *yām* to indicate the Mediterranean Sea (Acts 10:6), the Red Sea (7:36), and the Lake of Galilee (Mt. 4:18). *Límnē* (<*leíbō,* "pour, pour out") is used of the Lake of Gennesaret (Lk. 5:1, etc.) and the LAKE OF FIRE and brimstone (Rev. 19:20, etc.). S. HIGUCHI

**LAKE GENNESARET.** *See* GALILEE, SEA OF.

**LAKE OF FIRE** [Gk. *límnē toú pyrós*] (Rev. 19:20; 20:10, 14f.). The place of final torment, usually equated with GEHENNA. Here are thrown the "beast" and false prophet (Rev. 19:20) and later the devil, to "be tormented day and night for ever and ever" (20:10). After the judgment of the "great white throne" the personified Death and Hades are also thrown in, along with anyone whose "name was not found written in the book of life" (20:14f.; cf. 21:8). The lake of fire is called the second death (20:14; 21:8), apparently referring to the ultimate separation from God or spiritual death (*see* DEATH, SECOND).

The specific background of the "lake of fire" is obscure. The Egyptian lake of fire (cf., e.g., *Book of the Dead* 17:40f.; 71:18; 110:19; also J. Zandee, *Death as an Enemy* [1960], pp. 133-146) is too remote to be of direct relevance. (For other ancient Near Eastern background see *TDOT,* I, *s.v.* "'ēsh" [Krecher, Hamp].) The Apocalypse of Zephaniah mentions a lake of fire, but this is a post-Christian work no doubt influenced by the book of Revelation (*see* ZEPHANIAH, APOCALYPSE OF). The closest parallel is the "fiery abyss" of 1 En. 90:25, which according to P. Katz (*TDNT,* VI, 938 n. 51) presupposes a Greek expression very much like that of Revelation.

General background, however, is plentiful. In all the texts of Revelation that mention the lake of fire, "sulphur" (Gk. *theíon*) is added to the description, and this combination is fairly common, probably originating with the story of the destruction of Sodom and Gomorrah (Gen. 19:24; 3 Macc. 2:5; 1 Clem. 11:1; cf. Dt. 29:23 [LXX 22]; Job 18:15; Isa. 34:9). Here God rained brimstone and fire on Sodom and Gomorrah; thus the imagery of water ("rain") is joined with fire (cf. also Ps. 11 [LXX 10]:6; Ezk. 38:22). Similarly, "streams" of brimstone (and fire) are mentioned in contexts of judgment in both the OT (Isa. 30:33) and the intertestamental period (1 En. 67:7).

For a theory about the development of the meaning of the lake of fire, see R. H. Charles, comm. on Revelation (*ICC,* 1920), I, 239-242; cf. G. R. Beasley-Murray, *Revelation* (*New Century Bible Comm.,* 1974; repr. 1981), pp. 303f.

G. A. L.

**LAKKUM** lak'əm [Heb. *laqqûm*]. A town on the border of Naphtali, the last mentioned before the Jordan (Josh. 19:33). It still existed in the time of Rabbi Yosi ben Ḥaninah (*ca.* A.D. 100) and was known as Luqim (T.P. *Megillah* i.1). The site has been tentatively identified as Khirbet el-Manṣûrah, 17 km. (10.5 mi.) NW of the city of Tiberias, but this location seems too far from the Jordan.

W. S. L. S.

**LAMB** [Heb. *keḇeś* and (by metathesis) *keśeḇ*] AV also SHEEP (Gen. 30:35); NEB also RAM, YOUNG RAM, SHEEP; [*kiḇśâ* and (by metathesis) *kiśbeh*] NEB also EWE; [*śeh*] AV also SHEEP (Gen. 30:32); NEB also SHEEP, RAM, YOUNG BEAST (Gen. 22:7f.), YOUNG ANIMAL (Lev. 5:7); [*kar*] NEB also SHEEP (Ezk. 39:18); [*ṭāleh*] (1 S. 7:9; Isa. 40:11; 65:25); [*'immēr*]; [*ben-ṣō'n*] NEB YOUNG SHEEP; [*ṣō'n*] NEB SHEEP; [*pesaḥ*] AV PASSOVER; NEB also PASSOVER, PASSOVER VICTIM; [Gk. *amnós*] AV and NEB also PASSOVER (1 Cor. 5:7); [*arníon*]; [*arēn*]; [*páscha*] AV also PASSOVER; NEB also PASSOVER VICTIM.

The most frequently used Hebrew term translated "lamb" is *keḇeś* (fem. *kiḇśâ*); it is the common term used in sacrificial contexts. The RSV often distinguishes the masculine and feminine forms by translating *keḇeś* as "male lamb" (AV "he lamb," NEB "ram") and *kiḇśâ* as "ewe lamb." In sacrificial contexts male animals are usually specified. Ordinarily in other nations female animals were sacrificed to goddesses and male animals to gods. In Israel, however, male animals were more valuable for sacrifice because of Israel's male-oriented monotheism. Only rarely were female animals used (Lev. 5:6; 14:10; etc.).

The other Hebrew terms occur infrequently or are also used with other meanings. The term *śeh* refers to one of the flock, either a sheep or a goat, depending on context. Similarly, *ṣō'n* is a term for small cattle in general, either sheep or goats. The term *pesaḥ* usually means "Passover," but occasionally the RSV translates it "Passover lamb."

In ancient Israel the lamb and sheep were the principal animals of sacrifice. Thus the term "lamb" usually occurs in sacrificial contexts. A lamb was to be offered every morning and evening (Ex. 29:38-42). Two additional lambs were sacrificed every sabbath day (Nu. 28:9f.). Lambs were used for the sin offering (Lev. 4:32), for purification and cleansing (Lev. 12:6; 14:10) and for the dedication of an altar (Nu. 7:15). The lamb was also sacrificed on days of special religious significance: at the beginning of each new month (22:11), at the Feast of Pentecost (28:26ff.), the Feast of Trumpets (29:1f.), the Day of Atonement (vv. 7f.), the Feast of Tabernacles (vv. 12-16), and especially on each of the days of the Passover (28:16-19). The age of the lamb to be sacrificed is often given as one year; any animal, however, was suitable after the seventh day of its life (Lev. 22:26f.). All lambs (and other animals) to be sacrificed had to be without BLEMISH (Lev. 22:19-25).

Outside sacrificial contexts the lamb is less frequently mentioned. Lambs furnished wool for clothing (Prov. 27:26) and were required as tribute from the king of Moab (2 K. 3:4). The grazing of lambs and kids among the ruins describes the devastation of the land after the people have gone into exile (Isa. 5:17). The psalmist describes the mountains and hills skipping like rams and lambs when the extraordinary event of the Israelite exodus from Egypt occurred (Ps. 114:4, 6). More often the lamb is used to symbolize gentleness, innocence, and dependence. God is compared to the shepherd who gathers the lambs in his arms and carries them in his bosom (Isa. 40:11). After David's affair with Bathsheba, Nathan the prophet told a story of a little ewe lamb owned by a poor man who became an innocent victim of a rich man. Since by analogy Bathsheba was the lamb, the story may imply that she was the innocent victim of David's lust. The unusualness of a future age is described as a time when the wolf and lamb eat together (Isa. 65:25) or dwell together (Isa. 11:6). Jeremiah compares himself to a gentle lamb led to the slaughter in the face of plots to kill him (Jer. 11:19). In defeat Babylon will be brought down like lambs to the slaughter (Jer. 51:40). Most striking is the image of the Suffering Servant as a lamb and a sheep: "like a lamb that is led to the slaughter, and like a sheep that before its shearers is dumb, so he opened not his mouth" (Isa. 53:7b).

In the NT the terms usually refer to Christ and are always used in a figurative sense. The four occurrences of *amnós* compare Jesus to a lamb. As the lamb of God His death is efficacious (Jn. 1:29, 36), He is without blemish (1 Pet. 1:19), and He suffered patiently (Acts 8:32, where He is seen as the fulfillment of Isa. 53). (*See* LAMB OF GOD.) Jesus is referred to as the Passover lamb (*páscha*) in 1 Cor. 5:7 (cf. Mk. 14:12; Lk. 22:7). (See also *TDNT*, V, 900f.) The most frequently used term, *arníos*, occurs twenty-nine times — all but one in Revelation. The exact significance in Revelation is debated, though the term always refers to Christ and depicts Him as Redeemer and Ruler who ultimately delivers His people. In Jn. 21:15-17 the lamb represents the Christian community whom Peter is to "feed" and "tend." *Arēn* appears only in Lk. 10:3, where the seventy are sent out as "lambs in the midst of wolves." The antithesis lambs/wolves stresses the defenseless and dangerous position of the disciples.

***Bibliography***.–*TDNT*, I, *s.v.* ἀμνός κτλ. (J. Jeremias); V, *s.v.* πάσχα (J. Jeremias).

J. C. MOYER

**LAMB OF GOD** [Gk. *amnós toú theoú*] (Jn. 1:29, 36). This messianic title for Jesus appears only in John's account of the ministry of John the Baptist (in Revelation "the Lamb" is always simply *tó arníon*).

Twice John the Baptist called attention to Jesus with the words, "Behold, the Lamb of God!" (Jn. 1:29, 36, adding, in v. 29, "who takes away the sin of the world"). Because the context is so limited and the OT background a bit unclear, the passage has been variously interpreted. The most obvious place to search for the meaning of the term is in connection with the sacrifice of the paschal lamb. Jn. 19:14 emphasized that Jesus was crucified at the very hour that these lambs were being slaughtered for the Passover. In addition, Jesus was called "our passover" in 1 Cor. 5:7. But most scholars consider this background insufficient because there is no connection between the sacrifice of the paschal lambs and John the Baptist's emphasis on the forgiveness of sin. Some authorities, notably A. Schlatter (*Der Evangelist Johannes* [1960], p. 46), have attempted to link the offering of the paschal lambs and the regular Jewish sacrificial offering (Heb. *tāmîḏ*) to explain how the Lamb of God could take away the sin of the world.

C. H. Dodd explained the title "Lamb of God" in terms of the apocalyptic lamb of the book of Revelation who was sacrificed for the redemption of mankind and became the shepherd of His people (5:6-12; 7:14-17; 14:1-5; 17:14; 22:1-5). Although the book unites the redeemer and the apocalyptic leader of the people, the propriety of extending this union into the Gospel of John is questionable. The Gospel uses another related figure — that of the "Good Shepherd" — to express the role of Christ as eschatological leader of His people (Jn. 10:1-18).

Most often the solution to the problem has been found in the Suffering Servant of Isa. 53, who is likened to a lamb (v. 7) and bears the sins of many (v. 12). The only other passages where *amnós* is used in the NT refer to this passage; in Acts 8:32 Philip uses Isa. 53:7 to proclaim Jesus and 1 Pet. 1:19 echoes the terminology of Isaiah in comparing Jesus' sacrifice to that of "a lamb without spot and blemish." The patristic citations in 1 Clem. 16:7 and Barn. 5:2 show that the early Church understood the Lamb of God as the Suffering Servant.

C. J. Ball (*Expos.T.*, 21 [1909/10], 92ff.) and C. F. Burney (pp. 107f.) observed that *amnós toú theoú* might be a translation of the Aram. *talyā' dē'lāhā'*, which could mean both "Lamb of God" and "servant of God." J. Jeremias asserted that this is an example of the double meanings used by the author of the Fourth Gospel. Jeremias built his case around the Gk. *país*, which the LXX used instead of *doúlos* to designate the Suffering Servant. *País* may mean "son" or "servant." The most primitive Christologies refer to Jesus as *país* (Acts 3:13, 26; 4:27, 30). This word is used for the Suffering Servant in Mt. 12:18 in a quotation from a servant song (Isa. 42:1). The transition from one double-meaning term, *talyā'*, to another double-meaning term, *país*, was natural.

With this understanding of the Lamb of God as the servant of God, the Evangelist emphasized the messianic role of Jesus' life and ministry from the very beginning. From the time of His baptism Jesus must have been conscious of His role as the Suffering Servant of Yahweh. Thus early in his Gospel (Jn. 1:51) John contrasted Jesus' role as the Lamb of God who suffers to His role as the glorified Son of Man.

The substitutionary atonement became an important part of the role of the Lamb of God. As the Suffering

Servant of Isaiah bore the sins of many (Isa. 53:12), so the Lamb of God takes away the sin of the world (Gk. *aírōn tḗn hamartían*). O. Cullmann showed that the idea of vicarious suffering was connected with the Suffering Servant and was a common theme in Judaism. John emphasized the vicarious suffering of Jesus also in terms of the Good Shepherd who lays down his life for many (Jn. 10:15, 18). In this way the Lamb of God reestablished the covenant between His people and God.

***Bibliography.***–C. K. Barrett, *NTS*, 1 (1953/54), 210-19; C. F. Burney, *Aramaic Origin of the Fourth Gospel* (1922); O. Cullmann, *Christology of the NT* (Eng. tr., 2nd ed. 1963), pp. 51-81; C. H. Dodd, *Interpretation of the Fourth Gospel* (1953), pp. 230-38; F. Gryglewics, *NTS*, 13 (1966/67), 133-146; F. Hahn, *Titles of Jesus in Christology* (Eng. tr. 1969), pp. 54-57; *TDNT*, I, *s.v.* ἀμνός κτλ. (J. Jeremias); W. Zimmerli and J. Jeremias, *Servant of God* (Eng. tr., *SBT*, 1/20, 1957).

D. W. WEAD

**LAME** [Heb. *pissē(a)ḥ*] (Lev. 21:18; Dt. 15:21; 2 S. 5:6, 8; 9:13; 19:26 [MT 27]; Job 29:15; Prov. 26:7; Isa. 33:23; 35:6; Jer. 31:8; Mal. 1:8, 13); NEB also CRIPPLED; [niphal of *pāsaḥ*] (2 S. 4:4); [qal fem. part. of *ṣālaʿ*] (Mic. 4:6f.; Zeph. 3:19); AV HALT; NEB LOST; [Gk. *chōlós*] (Mt. 11:5; 15:30f.; 18:8; Lk. 7:22; Acts 3:2; etc.); AV also HALT; NEB also CRIPPLE, DISABLED.

The condition that prevents or impedes walking was common in biblical times. Lameness was one of the bodily imperfections that prohibited a man from becoming a priest (Lev. 21:18) and made an animal unacceptable to Yahweh as a sacrificial victim (Dt. 15:21; Mal. 1:8, 13; cf. Lev. 22:9; Nu. 6:4; Dt. 17:1; etc.).

Jonathan's son Mephibosheth (Meribbaal) became lame because his nurse dropped him (2 S. 4:4; cf. 9:13; 19:26). Knowledge about how widespread this condition was in Israel is uncertain due to lack of data, but 5:6, 8 might imply that in the early years of the monarchy some of the Jebusites who inhabited Jerusalem were blind and lame, for they boasted that even the blind and lame could successfully defend the city against its enemies.

Egyptian stele *ca.* 1200 B.C. showing a deformed right leg, perhaps due to infantile paralysis (Wellcome Institute library, London)

Job recalled his former state of blessedness in which he was praised for being as "eyes to the blind and feet to the lame" (Job 29:15). A proverb in the mouth of fools was said to be as useful as "a lame man's legs" (Prov. 26:7).

In visions of the future, the lame and outcasts are gathered with the rest of the remnant (Jer. 31:8), no longer shamed but praised in the earth (Zeph. 3:19) and subjects of the rule of the Lord (Mic. 4:6f.). The lame will illustrate how easily abundant spoils can be taken (Isa. 33:23), and their "leaping like a hart" provides a picture of the happy conditions of the new age (35:6).

The NT shows that healing the lame was a part of Jesus' therapeutic activity (Mt. 15:30f.; 21:14; Jn. 5:3). When John the Baptist's messengers asked, "Are you he who is to come?" (Mt. 11:3; Lk. 7:19), Jesus pointed to his healings of the blind, lame, and deaf to show that the kingdom of God had arrived (cf. Isa. 35:5ff.; 29:18ff.; 61:1ff.; see Cullmann, p. 194). These characteristics of His ministry are all "age-old phrases in the east for the time of salvation, when there will be no more sorrow, no more crying and no more grief. Thus in Luke 7.22f. we have an eschatological cry of joy uttered by Jesus" (Jeremias, p. 104). His kingdom is to be so desirable for His disciples that they must be willing to enter its life "maimed or lame" rather than face judgment (Mt. 18:8f.; Mk. 9:45). The "beggars" — including the lame — are brought in to enjoy God's great kingdom feast when the respectable righteous reject the invitation (Lk. 14:13, 21).

In Acts 3:2 Peter healed a man "lame from birth" at the Beautiful Gate of the temple; Philip also healed the paralyzed and lame in the city of Samaria (8:7). In He. 12:13 the author used an athletic figure of speech, urging his readers to "make straight paths for your feet, so that what is lame may not be put out of joint, but rather be healed" (cf. Prov. 4:26). Here the "lame" are those who are "spiritually lame" or "religiously weak." They would be the same group of people called the "little ones" (Mt. 10:42; 18:6, 10, 14) who might "stumble" (Buchanan, p. 215), and "who might be prevented from continuing their course if they were tripped up and permanently disabled" (Bruce, p. 363; cf. Isa. 35:3ff.). Believers should walk carefully themselves so that they do not mislead others and should "heal" the weak feet of the religiously insecure that are "out of joint" so that "the whole community may complete the course without loss" (Bruce, p. 364).

***Bibliography.***–F. F. Bruce, *Hebrews* (*NICNT*, 1964); G. W. Buchanan, *To the Hebrews* (*AB*, 1972); O. Cullmann, *Salvation in History* (Eng. tr. 1967); H. W. Hertzberg, *I & II Samuel* (Eng. tr., *OTL*, 1965); J. Jeremias, *NT Theology* (Eng. tr. 1971).

D. K. McKIM

**LAMECH** lā'mek, lä'mək [Heb. *lemeḵ*; Gk. *Lamech*].

**1.** Son of Methushael and one of the descendants of Cain (Gen. 4:18-24). He was the father of Jabel, Jubal, Tubal-cain, and Naamah. As the husband of two wives, Adah and Zillah, he furnishes the first recorded instance of polygamy.

The brief refrain in Gen. 4:23f. has been described as a "sword song" that magnifies and justifies the weapons of slaughter made by Tubal-cain because they furnish the warrior with superior strength. The poem is structurally of great interest, particularly if it can be dated in the 3rd millennium B.C., because it is an early example of Hebrew poetry in complete parallelism (S. Gevirtz, *Patterns in the Early Poetry of Israel* [1963], pp. 25-34).

**2.** Son of Methuselah and father of Noah (Gen. 5:25, 28f.; cf. 1 Ch. 1:3; Lk. 3:36). His words (Gen. 5:29) show the great difference between this descendant of Seth and Lamech the descendant of Cain. The latter was stimulated to a song of defiance by the worldly inventions of his sons; the former, in prophetic mood, expressed his sure belief in the period of comfort and rest that his son Noah would usher in, and he calmly and prayerfully awaited it.

The Genesis Apocryphon (1QapGen), in its Haggadic expansion of Gen. 5:28f., notes how Lamech father of Noah followed the spiritual traditions of Methuselah and Seth. According to this Qumrân scroll, Lamech had some doubt about the paternity of Noah but was ultimately reassured by his wife Bath-Enosh and also by Enoch (J. A. Fitzmyer, *Genesis Apocryphon of Qumran Cave 1* [rev. ed. 1971], pp. 77-98).

Adherents of the Graf-Wellhausen hypothesis regard the Cainite Lamech of Gen. 4 and the Sethite Lamech of Gen. 5 as identical, having originated from one tradition. This view seems improbable, however, since the other names in the two lists (4:18-24; 5:25-31) differ so radically as to indicate that two different families are being described. *See also* ANTEDILUVIAN PATRIARCHS II.

W. BAUR R. K. H.

**LAMED** lä'məd [ל]. The twelfth letter of the Hebrew alphabet, transliterated in this encyclopedia as *l*. It also came to be used for the number thirty. *See* WRITING.

**LAMENT; LAMENTATION** [Heb. *sāpad̲* (Gen. 50:10; 2 S. 11:26; Jer. 4:8; etc.), *mispēd̲* (Gen. 50:10; Est. 4:3; Jer. 6:26; 48:38; Mic. 1:8), *qîn* (only polel; 2. S. 1:17; 3:33; 2 Ch. 35:25; Ezk. 27:32), *qînâ* (2 S. 1:17; 2 Ch. 35:25; Jer. 7:29), *nᵉhî* (Jer. 9:20 [MT 19]; 31:15; Am. 5:16; Mic. 2:4), *nāhâ* (1 S. 7:2), *'āḇal* (Isa. 19:8; Lam. 2:8), *'āḇel* (Ps. 35:14), *bāḵâ* (Job 27:15; Ps. 78:64), *'ᵃnîyâ* (Isa. 29:2; Lam. 2:5), *zᵉʿāqâ* (Est. 9:31), *tānâ* (Jgs. 11:40), *'ānâ* (Isa. 3:26), *qād̲ar* (Jer. 14:2), *'ālâ* (Joel 1:8); Gk. *thrēnéō* (Lk. 23:27; Jn. 16:20), *thrēnos* (Mt. 2:18), *kopetós* (Acts 8:2)]; AV also WAIL, WAILING, MOURN, WEEP, SORROW (Isa. 29:2), CRY (Est. 9:31), etc.; NEB also GROAN, HOWL (Mic. 1:8), MOURN, "beat the breast," "chant a dirge," etc. In Isa 43:14 the RSV and NEB emend MT *'ᵒnîyôṯ* (lit. "ships"; cf. AV) to *'ᵃnîyôṯ*. In Nah. 2:7 (MT 8), RSV "lamenting" renders MT *mᵉnahᵃgôṯ*, the piel pl. part. of *nāhag*; the RSV, AV ("shall lead her"), and NEB ("are carried off") translations represent differing attempts to render a difficult and possibly corrupt text.

The biblical terms have various nuances. The verb *sāpad̲* originally referred to "beating the breast" as a sign of mourning (cf. KoB, p. 663). *Qād̲ar,* originally "be dark" (cf. AV), can mean "be dirty, unattended, in mourning attire" (KoB, p. 824); it refers to the somber color of mourning garb and/or to the dust and dirt gathered from rolling on the ground. *Qînâ* is a technical term for a type of musical composition, a dirge. Gk. *kopetós,* like *sāpad̲,* denotes mourning accompanied by breastbeating (Bauer, rev., p. 443); *thrēnos* signifies a dirge.

Lamentation was an integral part of ancient Semitic life. Death, calamity, devastation by war, consciousness of sin, and intense sickness brought great sorrow. People mourning over these things wore sackcloth (a coarse material) next to their skin, removed their shoes, covered their heads, and possibly veiled their faces. They did not wash or apply ointments and perfumes (2 S. 14:2). They often put earth on their heads, rolled in the dust (Mic. 1:10; cf. Jer. 14:2), and sat on a heap of ashes (Ezk. 27:30). Mourners sometimes shaved their beards and hair. Cutting and lacerating the body, however, was strictly forbidden (Lev. 19:28). Fasting also accompanied mourning; some fasted for seven days (Gen. 50:10). People lamented by loudly and bitterly weeping and beating their breast. They repeated the sharp, shrill cry "Alas! alas!" (Am. 5:16; cf. Jer. 22:18). Professional mourners heightened the atmosphere of grief (Am. 5:16); they chanted a dirge that had a special rhythm (*qînâ*).

The king led at any occasion requiring national lamentation. David mourned the death of Saul and composed a lament for him (2 S. 1:17-27). Later he lamented the death of Abner (3:33f.).

Some prophets were skilled at composing laments, the most famous of whom was Jeremiah. He composed a lament sung at the death of Josiah (2 Ch. 35:25); some scholars have attributed the book of Lamentations, mourning the destruction of Jerusalem, to him (*see* LAMENTATIONS II). Ezekiel at the outset of his ministry was to eat a book filled with dirges, laments, and woes (Ezk. 2:10, NEB); this act would indicate that he too was to prophesy devastation and destruction. When prophets proclaimed a message of destruction, they often were so certain of the fulfillment of the word of the Lord that

Lamentation scene from Memphis (*ca.* 13th cent. B.C.). Behind the widow (extreme upper right) servants prepare for the funeral. Behind the coffin (lower right) two sons are followed by Haremhab (the future king), two viziers, and other mourners (Bildarchiv Foto Marburg)

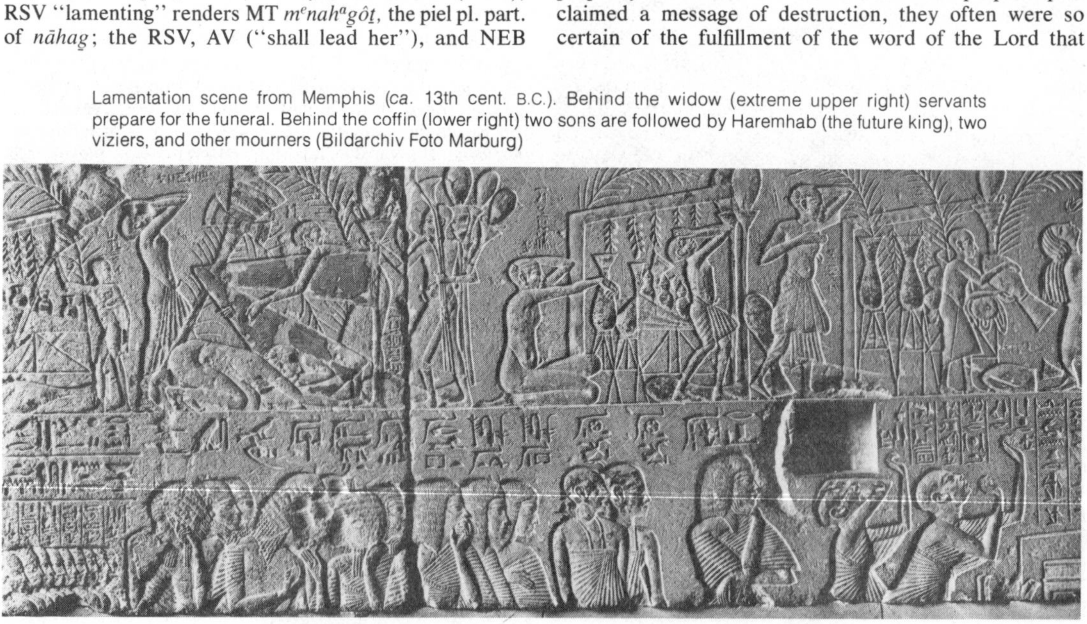

they lamented the future destruction as an integral part of their message; thus they attempted to convey the certainty and relevance of the coming horror to the people. Micah, feeling the impact of his message, cried out, "For this I will lament and wail; I will go stripped and naked; I will make lamentation like the jackals, and mourning like the ostriches" (Mic. 1:8). Am. 5 begins: "Hear this word which I take up over you in lamentation, O house of Israel." Ezekiel in similar fashion composed lamentations over the princes of Israel (Ezk. 19) and over Tyre (26:17f.; 27).

People lamented an anticipated calamity, no doubt because they dreaded its coming, but also because they hoped to move God to divert it. The Jews during the time of Queen Esther knew about the planned genocide; therefore they turned to God in fasting and lamentation (Est. 4:3). Their contrition provided a basis for God to work out their deliverance.

Both the crucifixion of Jesus and the martyrdom of Stephen produced great lamentation (Lk. 23:27; Acts 8:2). On the other hand, Jesus taught that his followers would lament while the world rejoiced, but their lamentation would be turned to joy (Jn. 16:20).

*See also* BURIAL; DIRGE.

***Bibliography.***–E. J. Young, *Isaiah,* II (1969); R. de Vaux, *Ancient Israel* (Eng. tr. 1961), I, 56-61.

J. E. HARTLEY

**LAMENTATIONS** lam'ən-tā'shənz. A relatively short book of the OT that mourns the destruction of Jerusalem, 586 B.C. In Jewish synagogues the book is read annually on the 9th of Ab (July/August) in commemoration of this event.

I. Name and Canonical Position
II. Authorship
III. Structure and Meter
IV. Literary Form
V. Theology

***I. Name and Canonical Position.***–In Hebrew Bibles the book generally bears the title *'êkâ* (translated "How!" or "Ah, how!"), the opening lament formula of chs. 1, 2, and 4. The rabbinic designation, however, was *qînôṯ,* meaning "dirges" or "laments" (T.B. *Baba Bathra* 14b; cf. also Jerome's *Prologus Galaetus*). The Greek translation of this word, *Thrēnoi,* became the title of the book in the LXX, later rendered into Latin as *Lamentationes,* from whence it was an easy step to the Eng. *Lamentations.*

In the standard twenty-four book Hebrew canon, Lamentations constitutes one of the Five Megilloth or Scrolls found in the section of the Writings. The conventional position of Lamentations within the Megilloth is third (following Canticles and Ruth), an arrangement based on the order in which the scrolls are read in the Ashkenazi (Eastern European) liturgical calendar. In some sources, however, including the Aleppo and Leningrad MSS (hence also *BH*), the Megilloth are arranged chronologically according to the presumed date of composition, whence Lamentations appears in the fourth position, following Ruth, Canticles, and Ecclesiastes. In the canon of twenty-two books referred to by Josephus (*CAp* i.8 [38]),Lamentations was probably associated with the book of Jeremiah. This connection with the book of Jeremiah is made explicit in the LXX canon, where Lamentations normally follows the books of Jeremiah and Baruch respectively; the association with Jeremiah is further strengthened in the Vulg., where the order of Baruch and Lamentations is reversed, the latter becoming practically an appendix to the text of Jeremiah. Modern Protestant Bibles normally give Lamentations independent status, but perpetuate the tradition of placing it immediately after Jeremiah.

***II. Authorship.***–The position of the book in the different OT canons relates directly to the question of authorship, for though in the Hebrew canon the book is both anonymous and placed in a section different from that of Jeremiah, in the LXX and Christian canons not only is it placed immediately next to Jeremiah but it is also explicitly attributed to the prophet. This attribution is communicated in the titles given to the book (while some Greek and Latin MSS simply have the title "Lamentations," many have the fuller title "Lamentations of Jeremiah"), but especially in the prologue to the book. In the LXX the text proper of Lamentations is introduced by the words, "And it came to pass after Israel had been taken into captivity and Jerusalem laid waste, that Jeremiah sat weeping and uttered this lament over Jerusalem and said . . ." (to which the Vulg. adds the phrase "with a bitter spirit sighing and weeping"). Since the style of this prologue is Semitic rather than Greek, it may be presumed to antedate the translation, pushing the tradition of Jeremianic authorship even further back in antiquity.

Other ancient versions such as the Tg. and the Pesh. attest to the same tradition concerning Jeremianic authorship. Thus the Tg. on Lamentations begins, "Jeremiah the prophet and chief priest, said . . ." while the Pesh. has the title, "The book of lamentations of Jeremiah the prophet." Similarly, T.B. *Baba Bathra* 15a assigns Lamentations to Jeremiah while many rabbinic passages from Lamentations are introduced by the formula "Jeremiah said." The tradition was carried forward into Christian times by Church Fathers such as Origen and Jerome and incorporated into the title of the book in English versions such as the AV, RV, ASV, and RSV.

In spite of this long tradition, the consensus of modern biblical scholarship has been to reject the Jeremianic authorship of Lamentations. This rejection typically commences with an observation regarding the anonymity of the Hebrew text and proceeds on internal grounds to argue against Jeremiah's involvement in the composition of the book. A main line of argument in this connection has been the contention that ideas expressed in Lamentations often contradict those of Jeremiah. Thus questions such as the following are often asked: (1) Would Jeremiah, who prophesied the destruction of the temple, have written about the enemies of Judah as "those whom thou didst forbid to enter thy congregation" (1:10)? (2) Would Jeremiah, who perceived the Babylonians as God's agents of judgment, call down vengeance upon them (1:21)? (3) Would Jeremiah, a prophet, write, "her prophets obtain no vision from the Lord" (2:9)? (4) Would Jeremiah, who advised against foreign alliances, have lamented, "Our eyes failed, ever watching vainly for help" (4:17)? (5) Would Jeremiah, who had no love for Zedekiah, call the king "the breath of our nostrils" and "he of whom we said, 'Under his shadow he shall live among the nations'" (4:20)? In each case, the answer to these rhetorical questions is assumed to be No.

In addition to the alleged conflicting viewpoints between the books of Jeremiah and Lamentations, it is also often maintained that the phraseology of Lamentations varies considerably from that of Jeremiah. Thus Lamentations contains a large number of words not found in Jeremiah and vice versa (for a listing see S. R. Driver, *Intro. to the Literature of the OT* [6th ed., repr. 1956], p. 463). Others find it difficult to believe that a consummate poet such as Jeremiah could possibly have restricted himself to an artificial poetic form such as the acrostic (see below).

If the case against the Jeremianic authorship is so self-evident, how then did the idea of associating Jeremiah and Lamentations originate? To this there is a simple answer: 2 Ch. 35:25 refers to Jeremiah having composed a lament over the death of Josiah that, along with the laments of the male and female singers, was preserved in the *qînôṯ*. It was mistakenly assumed that the source in question was the canonical book of Lamentations. In fact, nothing in the canonical Lamentations applies to Josiah; nonetheless — so the argument goes — in an age when it was considered important to determine the authorship of anonymous books, the connection between Jeremiah and Lamentations was easily made. This connection seemed confirmed by superficial resemblances between characteristic utterances of Jeremiah and similar passages in Lamentations (cf., e.g., Jer. 9:1 [MT 8:23] with Lam. 2:11).

The above challenges to the traditional view regarding the authorship of Lamentations must be taken seriously; yet it cannot be said that they have definitively demonstrated that the Jeremiah tradition is entirely without merit. Some of the indirect arguments against Jeremianic authorship are far from convincing. For instance, the alleged differences of viewpoint referred to above between Jeremiah and Lamentations all have alternate explanations: (1) Although Jeremiah certainly did prophesy the destruction of the temple, there is no reason to doubt that he would nonetheless have affirmed in principle the exclusion of foreigners from the temple precincts as stipulated in Dt. 23:3. (2) It is a popular, but nonetheless unfounded, notion that a prophet who speaks favorably concerning a foreign nation could not also speak of ultimate judgment on that nation. Both themes are clearly present in the book of Jeremiah. (3) Although Jeremiah was a prophet, he himself made a radical distinction between true and false prophets. The latter are no doubt in view in Lam. 2:9. (4) When the poet writes in the first person of "ever watching vainly for help" (4:17), this may simply reflect his sense of corporate identity with the people rather than document his personal faith in foreign alliances. (5) Similarly, the reference to Zedekiah as "the breath of our nostrils" can easily be understood as an expression of the popular mood rather than the author's personal opinion. As for the suggestion that Jeremiah would not likely have restricted himself to the acrostic form, that is surely an arbitrary and overly subjective judgment.

In short, it appears that the internal evidence marshaled against the Jeremianic authorship of Lamentations is far from conclusive. By the same token it has to be said that there is no positive evidence for the identification either, though parts — especially ch. 3 — are particularly consonant with Jeremiah's mood and outlook. We are brought to the conclusion, therefore, that the best policy concerning the authorship of Lamentations is to respect the anonymity of the Hebrew text, while at the same time recognizing the existence of a very ancient — and surely not entirely impossible — tradition regarding the Jeremianic authorship of the book.

With regard to the question of unity, the usual critical view is that more than one person was involved in the composition of the book. R. H. Pfeiffer's position (*Intro. to the OT* [2nd ed. 1948], pp. 722f.) may be taken as typical. Pfeiffer believed that chs. 2 and 4 could come from the same person writing in Babylon *ca.* 560 B.C. He considered the last chapter a composition by a Palestinian author writing not later than 530 B.C. Ch. 1 was composed in Jerusalem after the rebuilding of the temple (520) and before Nehemiah's reforms (444). Ch. 3 reflected the period after Nehemiah. Countering this and similar proposals one has to reckon with the sober judgment of N. K. Gottwald (*IDB*, III, 62) that "all the poems are rooted in the same historical era — i.e., the period of the Palestinian 'exile' (586-538 B.C.)" and that because of the "single mood" that pervades the collection it is likely that at least the first four, and possibly all five, poems come from the same poet.

*III. Structure and Meter.*–As indicated, Lamentations consists of five poems, each coinciding with a chapter division in our Bibles. Of these, the first four are acrostics based on the twenty-two letter Hebrew alphabet (*see* ACROSTIC), though with slight variations in the acrostic pattern from one poem to another. Chs. 1 and 2 are most alike in that each stanza of these poems consists of three lines (except 1:7 and 2:19 which have four lines), the acrostic pattern being exhibited in the first word of each stanza only. Ch. 4 is similarly constructed but has two rather than three lines per stanza. Ch. 3, on the other hand, displays the most elaborate acrostic structure of all the poems. This poem has three lines per stanza, and each of the three lines commences with the same letter of the Hebrew alphabet (thus there are three *aleph* lines, three *beth* lines, etc.; cf. Ps. 119 where each stanza has eight lines beginning with the same letter). Since every *line* in this poem is consecutively numbered (rather than every *stanza* as in the other poems), ch. 3 has the appearance of being the longest poem, with 66 rather than 22 verses as in the other chapters. In reality, chs. 1, 2, and 3 are practically of identical length. One peculiarity of the alphabetical order of chs. 2, 3, and 4 is that in these poems the letter *p* precedes the ʿ (as in the LXX version of Prov. 31 and as some would prefer to read Ps. 34), whereas ch. 1 follows the usual order of ʿ before *p*. The reason for this variation in alphabetical order in chs. 2–4 is not clear, although A. Demsky and M. Kochavi have suggested that this variation was a local Israelite tradition, reflected also in an abecedary from ʿIzbet Ṣarṭah (*Biblical Archaeology Review*, 4/3 [1978], 23-30). Ch. 5 is not an acrostic poem at all; nevertheless, it does have twenty-two verses of one line each and so is also tied to the Hebrew alphabet.

Another noteworthy feature of Lamentations is its metrical pattern. Whereas according to the traditional analysis of Hebrew verse developed by J. Ley and E. Sievers in the 19th cent. (*see also* POETRY, HEBREW), a line or bicolon of Hebrew poetry consists of two half-lines or cola of approximately equal length (represented by an accentual formula such as 3 + 3), the metrical pattern of most lines of ch. 1–4 is such that the first colon is often slightly longer than the second (e.g., 3 + 2, 4 + 3, or 4 + 2). This at least was the conclusion of K. Budde in his seminal essay on the meter of Lamentations (*ZAW*, 2 [1882], 1-52). He called this the Qinah meter (from the Hebrew word *qînâ*, meaning "lament"; cf. the rabbinic title *qînôṯ* above), since it seemed to him like the "rhythm that always dies away." He then proceeded to identify this same meter in several other biblical passages and suggested that this must have been the meter peculiar to Hebrew elegy.

Since Budde's day, however, this interpretation of the data has been modified in several ways. For example, it is now recognized that Budde overstated his case on the consistency of the Qinah meter in Lamentations. Many bicola are in fact evenly balanced (2 + 2 or 3 + 3), and some may even be of the type 2 + 3. Again, it is now clear that the typical Qinah meter is not exclusively associated with laments or funeral songs. There are passages such as Isa. 40:9 or Cant. 1:9-11 which display this meter but are manifestly not laments, just as there are other famous elegies, such as David's lament over Saul and Jonathan in 2 S. 1:17-27, which nevertheless do not employ the Qinah meter.

Further questions concerning Budde's analysis have been raised recently by D. R. Hillers. Focusing on the well-known phenomenon of parallelism in Hebrew poetry as a criterion for determining the beginning and end of a colon, Hillers notes that according to his reckoning 101 out of 244 lines in chs. 1–4 (or 41%) do not manifest traditional Hebrew poetic parallelism (to be contrasted with ch. 5 where only 3 lines out of 22 — or 14% — do not show regular parallelism). With this important criterion for delimiting a colon often missing in chs. 1–4, it becomes proportionately more difficult to determine the accentual formula of the bicola in question, and hence to say whether they are Qinah. Hillers thinks that Budde and others have simply followed a kind of intuition rather than reasoned principle when it comes to deciding the caesura in a given bicolon. In short, the presence of the Qinah meter in Lamentations cannot be affirmed with anything approaching the confidence it once was, though the appropriateness of the designation for much of the poetry in the book need not be denied altogether.

*IV. Literary Form.*–Another useful way of analyzing the poems of Lamentations is by means of the literary types or *Gattungen* identified by form criticism. Since there is much in Lamentations that is reminiscent of the Psalms, it is not surprising that literary forms discovered there have been applied to Lamentations. Much of the pioneering work in this area was done by H. Gunkel ("Klagelieder Jeremiae," *RGG,* III [2nd ed. 1929], 1049-52) and his student H. Jahnow (*Das hebräische Leichenlied im Rahmen der Völkerdichtung* [*BZAW,* 36, 1923]).

Taking the cue from Gunkel and Jahnow, scholars have generally classified chs. 1, 2, and 4 as *Leichenlieder* or funeral dirges but with national rather than personal application. Each of these poems commences with the characteristic *'êḵâ* (cf. Dt. 1:12; Isa. 1:21; 14:4, 12; Jer. 9:18; 48:17; Ezk. 26:17) and, in continuity with the typical funeral dirge elsewhere, frequently contrasts the former beauty of the deceased (in this case the personified city) with its present lowly state. Ch. 5 is normally identified as a communal complaint psalm of the type found in Pss. 44, 60, 74, 79, 80, 83, and 89.

Much more difficult to identify with regard to type is ch. 3. Is it a communal or individual lament? The matter turns on the identification of "the man" who speaks in vv. 1-24, 52-66. Is he an individual or does he represent personified Jerusalem? Some have argued for the latter, but others, impressed by the masculine word *geḇer,* "man," (rather than the fem. personification in the other poems) and by the intensely personal character of the passage, have sought a more individual interpretation. The trend in critical scholarship has been to favor a communal interpretation, but this trend may yet have to give account to the more natural reading of seeing behind these lines the testimony of a strong personality writing out of the depth of his own experience, possibly even Jeremiah himself. Some scholars (e.g., W. Rudolph) have suggested that at the very least Jeremiah is being depicted here as the people's representative sufferer.

*V. Theology.*–Although questions of authorship, structure, meter, and literary type are recognized as important in themselves, current scholarship in Lamentations has turned from a preoccupation with these more analytical matters to the broader issues relating to the message and theology of the book. One who has given significant impetus to the study of Lamentations from a theological perspective is N. K. Gottwald. In his important monograph, Gottwald advocated the thesis that "the situational key to the theology of Lamentations [is] the tension between Deuteronomic faith and historical adversity" (pp. 52f.), i.e., the tension between the nation's earnest attempt at reform under Josiah and the bitter experience of the fall of Jerusalem. How can it be, Gottwald assumes the people of Jerusalem to be asking, that at a time when the nation was most bent on reform, disaster struck? Is this not a flagrant contradiction of basic Hebrew theology — as enunciated most clearly in Deuteronomy — of divine retribution for disobedience and blessing for obedience? According to Gottwald the shipwreck of that theology on the rocks of the national catastrophe of 586 B.C. constituted "a clarion call to the entire rethinking of Hebrew religion" (p. 63).

On the above reading of the book, Lamentations is to be viewed as a major contribution to the sixth-century theological debate over the 586 B.C. debacle. In the end the answer given by Lamentations was to reaffirm the Deuteronomic message: Jerusalem had fallen because of its sin; its fate, though severe, was justly deserved. This answer is elaborated by means of various motifs, principally that of "tragic reversal," but also in the public confession of sin, the theme of Yahweh as the Divine Punisher, the Day of Yahweh, and the Great Assize of God.

In spite of Gottwald's considerable contribution to a theological study of Lamentations, his thesis has not generally met with scholarly endorsement. The fundamental weakness in the theory is the lack of positive textual support for the notion that the pressing conundrum of the day was the question, "Why does the nation suffer more than ever immediately after its earnest attempt at reform?" Were this the background, one would have expected to find at least some passage or passages affirming the people's alleged piety and reformist spirit. Instead, one encounters only passages reinforcing the nation's sin and disobedience.

Recognizing this weakness in Gottwald's argument, B. Albrektson sought to ground his interpretation of the theology of Lamentations more explicitly in the text itself. By means of a detailed analysis of Lam. 2:15c; 4:12, 20; and 5:19, Albrektson argued that the theological backdrop for the book is the tradition regarding the inviolability of Zion as enshrined in Pss. 46, 48, and 76. It was this temple tradition which produced an "unbearable contrast to the harsh historical reality after the fall of Jerusalem" (p. 223). At the same time Albrektson acknowledged that Deuteronomic allusions certainly are present in the poems as well, so that it is doubtful that one can speak of one all-inclusive "key" to the theology of the book.

Canonical criticism has sought to shift emphasis away from finding the key to the problem of the book in a tension between different OT traditions. Instead, according to B. S. Childs (*OT as Scripture* [1979]), the issue at stake in the canonical book is "the conflict between those who thought that the destruction of Jerusalem had rendered the truth of Israel's faith in God's promise meaningless, and those who confessed that in spite of the enormous rupture caused by Israel's sin, the avenue of God's renewed mercy, even if withdrawn momentarily, was still open to the faithful as it had been in the past" (p. 596).

The positions of Gottwald, Albrektson, and Childs are representative of some of the new and stimulating things being said about the theology of Lamentations. Even if modern commentators cannot agree on the precise nature of the problem addressed in Lamentations, all are agreed that the book is much more than simply an outpouring of grief over the destruction of Jerusalem; it is a profound reflection on the nature of the community's faith and identity.

***Bibliography.**–Comms.:* R. Gordis, *Song of Songs and Lamentations* (rev. ed. 1974); R. K. Harrison (*Tyndale OT Comms.,* 1973); D. R. Hillers (*AB,* 1979); G. A. F. Knight (*Torch,* 1955); H.-J. Kraus (*BKAT,* 3rd ed., 1968); M. Löhr (*Handkommentar zum AT,* 2nd ed. 1906); W. Rudolph (*KZAT,* 2nd ed., 1962); H. Wiesmann, *Die Klagelieder* (1954).

*Studies:* B. Albrektson, *Studies in the Text and Theology of the Book of Lamentations* (*Studia Theologica Lundensia,* 21, 1963);

H. Gottlieb, *A Study on the Text of Lamentations* (*Acta Jutlandica*, 48, 1978); N. K. Gottwald, *Studies in the Book of Lamentations* (*SBT*, 1/14, rev. ed. 1962); M. Löhr, *ZAW*, 14 (1894), 31-59; 24 (1904), 1-16; 25 (1905), 173-198; T. F. McDaniel, *VT*, 18 (1968), 198-209; *Bibl.*, 49 (1968), 27-53, 199-220; W. Rudolph, *ZAW*, 56 (1938), 101-122; H. Wiesmann, *Bibl.*, 7 (1926), 146-161, 412-428; 8 (1927), 339-347; 17 (1936), 71-84. S. K. SODERLUND

**LAMP** [Heb. *nēr, nîr, nir* (Prov. 21:4), *mā'ōr* (Ex. 25:6), *m^enôrâ* (2 K. 4:10); Gk. *lýchnos, lampás*]; AV also LIGHT, CANDLE, CANDLESTICK (2 K. 4:10), "plowing" (Prov. 21:4); NEB also FLAME, LIGHT, "shines" (Prov. 20:27), EMBERS, LANTERN. In Prov. 21:4 the RSV emends *nir* to read *nēr,* following the LXX Pesh., Targum, and Vulgate. Heb. *lappîḏ,* translated "lamp" in the AV, is really a torch (cf. Jgs. 7:16, 20; 15:4; Isa. 62:1; Ezk. 1:13; Nah. 2:5; etc.).

I. In the OT
II. In the NT
III. As a Symbol

*I. In the OT.*–The Bible lacks a description of a lamp, although it often mentions the uses of lamps. A few texts refer to their daily use in the tent (Job 18:6) and house (Job 21:17; Prov. 13:9; 20:20; 24:20; Jer. 25:10; Zeph. 1:12), but most references are to the lamps employed in the tabernacle (Ex. 25:37; 27:20; 30:7f.; 35:14; etc.) and the temple (1 K. 7:49; 1 Ch. 28:15; 2 Ch. 4:20f.; 13:11; 29:7). A lamp of average size held enough oil to burn throughout the night. The saying that a good wife's "lamp does not go out at night" (Prov. 31:18) may reflect the household's wealth or stability (C. H. Toy, comm. on Proverbs [*ICC,* 1899], p. 545) or the diligence of the wife (W. McKane, *Proverbs* [*OTL,* 1970], p. 668). Olive oil fueled lamps (Ex. 25:6; 27:20; Mt. 25:3f.).

Archeology has provided invaluable information on the origin, development, design, and purpose of lamps, which are among the most significant material artifacts of the

Top left: Bronze Age lamp with four spouts. Top right: Iron Age lamp with trefoil spout. Bottom left: Byzantine lamp. Bottom right: Roman lamp (R. H. Johnston)

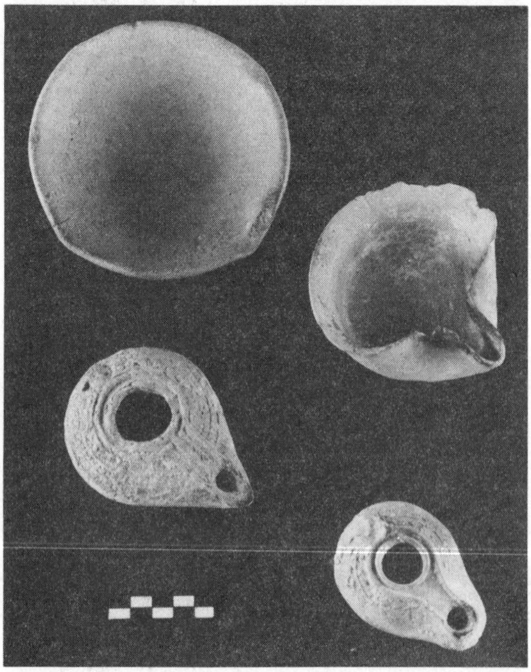

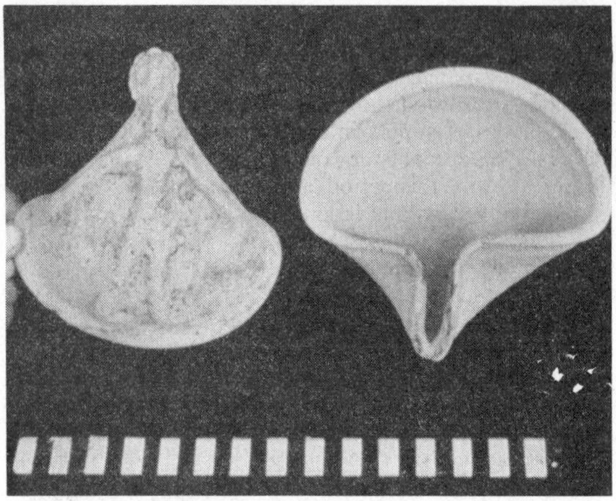

Two views of a Late Bronze pottery lamp with torso of a man on the back (left) (B. VanElderen)

ancient Near East. They first appeared in the Bronze Age and were made of clay, but in the Iron Age metal lamps also came into use. Early Bronze Age people used a fairly flat saucer with a slight lip supporting a wick as a lamp; this saucer lamp was actually a development of the common household bowl. Around the beginning of the 2nd millennium potters formed open flat-bottomed bowls with an undulating rim into lamps with four equidistant spouts (cf. Isa. 42:3). These two types served through much of the early patriarchal period and were replaced by a simpler lamp with a single little spout on one side of the saucer. The spout of the "saucer lamp" (also called "shell lamp," though it did not develop from the shell, or "cocked-hat lamp") became increasingly large and well defined during the Middle and Late Bronze ages. The term *mûṣeqeṯ,* which appears only in Zec. 4:2, should probably be translated "spout" rather than "pipe" (AV, NEB), "lip" (RSV), or "tube" (NAB).

During the Early Iron Age lamps were fitted with bases to make them more stable. At a number of Iron I and Iron II sites in Palestine specimens of "seven-spout lamps" (cf. Zec. 4:2) have been uncovered (C. Watzinger, *Tell el-Mutesellim II,* fig. 74; Smith, *BA,* 27 [1964], 14 fig. 6). The "cup-and-saucer" (also called "double-bowl") lamp (*ibid.,* p. 15 fig. 7), consisting of a saucer and an inner container, was used in sanctuaries, tombs, and homes from the 13th to 6th cents. B.C. Its fuel may have been solid rather than liquid, perhaps pitch. The "double-spout lamp" appeared in the Iron II period at Megiddo, Samaria (G. Reisner, *Samaria* [1924], fig. 187 no. 2a), and other sites. A rich coat of red slip often decorated Iron Age lamps, making them very attractive when new.

Archeologists identify the *m^enôrâ* referred to in the Elisha narrative (2 K. 4:10) as a pedestal lamp, which has a separate ceramic pedestal elevating the clay lamp to produce more light and make the lamp easier to tend. Examples include the seven-spout lamp from Tell Ta'annak and the one-spout lamps from Tell Beit Mirsim and Tell en-Naṣbeh. Some of these pedestal lamps are clearly associated with cultic activity in homes. Excavators of Palestinian cities have found a great variety of lampstands, usually made of stone, pottery, or terra cotta, but some of bronze or iron from the Iron I and II periods.

In the Persian period a new kind of broad, shallow lamp replaced the footed lamp of Judah. Examples in pottery and bronze were found at Lachish. Iron saucer lamps were found infrequently (Beth-shean and Gezer). Imported Greek lamps in which much of the oil reservoir was covered to prevent spilling appeared in significant numbers in Palestine in the latter part of the Persian period (after 450 B.C.). The new lamp forms and decorations of the Hellenistic period show the influence of Greek culture and skill. The oil supply in the spout lamp was covered, and the production of lamps on the potter's wheel reduced their size. During this period lamps began to be decorated with simple designs and later with more elaborate decorations and inscriptions. In the 2nd cent. B.C. molded lamps, some with two, three, or more spouts, appeared in Palestine; the earliest examples closely resemble wheel-made lamps.

Most ancient Near Eastern tombs contain lamps, which played an important role in burial rites. Lighting a lamp in the tomb may have symbolized rekindling the flame of life in the deceased, and the ancients buried their dead with lamps probably to provide light for them in the hereafter. Lamps were kept at the entrance to tombs (at Ugarit; cf. *Ugaritica,* III, 180) and in small wall niches similar to the niches in inhabited caves and houses.

*II. In the NT.*–The lamp with which Jesus was probably most familiar was the "Herodian" lamp, a wheel-made lamp of thin buff or light-brown clay, distinguishable from later specimens by its downward-sloping nozzle. The woman who lights a lamp to search for the lost coin in the parable (Lk. 15:8) and the virgins at the wedding party, five of whom take extra oil and five of whom foolishly do not (Mt. 25:1-12), probably use "Herodian" lamps. Since the virgins' lamps are lighted at dusk and threaten to go out at midnight, they must hold enough oil for at most four to five hours' use. The word for "lamp" in this parable is *lampás,* not the regular term *lýchnos*; *lampás* normally meant "torch" in Hellenistic times (so Jn. 18:3; Rev. 8:10) but here means "lamp," as the parallel Lk. 12:35 shows. In Acts 20:8 *lampádes* must mean "lamps" and not "torches," since they are inside a house. Rev. 4:5 may have a double meaning. Before the heavenly throne burn "seven *lampádes* of fire, which are the seven spirits of God"; the *lampádes* should be visualized as "torches" (so correctly RSV, NEB, NAB), but the reader of NT times would immediately recall the seven lamps on the lampstand in the Jerusalem temple. Jesus alludes to a lampstand, which must have been fairly common in Roman

Top row: Iron II and Persian lamps. Bottom row: Hellenistic lamps. The lamp on the left was formed on a wheel and pinched into shape, and the center and right lamps were made from a mold (L. A. Willis)

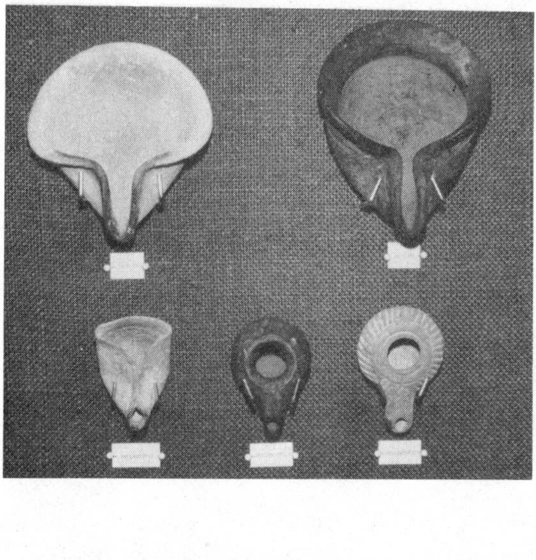

Palestine, and its importance in distributing the lamp's light in Lk. 8:16 (cf. Mt. 5:15; Mk. 4:21; Lk. 11:33).

*III. As a Symbol.*–In the OT the lamp and its light function as either a negative or a positive symbol. The "lamp of the wicked" fails because it lacks the life-giving light of God (Prov. 13:9; 21:4; cf. 20:20; 24:20; Job 18:5f.; 21:17). The lamp's going out symbolizes the destruction of the individual and community (Job 18:6; Jer. 25:10). The lamp is a positive metaphor for the continuity of the royal house of David (1 K. 11:36; 15:4; 2 K. 8:19 par. 2 Ch. 21:7; cf. Ps. 132:17) promised by God (2 S. 7; Ps. 132:12). The lamp (2 S. 22:29) and the light (*'ôr*) of the faithful (Mic. 7:8) symbolize God Himself. A Psalm written for the praise and exaltation of the law describes the word of the Lord as a lamp (*nēr*) to the feet and a light (*'ôr*) to the path (Ps. 119:105; cf. G. Vermes, *VT,* 8 [1958], 436f.) leading to life. The father's commandments are a lamp and the mother's teaching a light (Prov. 6:23). A lamp from the Lord lights up the darkest recesses of the human heart and provides the power of introspection by which people can examine their innermost parts (20:27). The lampstand (*m$^e$nôrâ*) symbolism is joined with the lamp and light symbolism in Zec. 4:1-3, 11-14.

Lamp and light symbolism also appears in the NT. John the Baptist was a lamp because he bore witness to the coming Messiah (Jn. 5:35; cf. Ps. 132:17; F. Neugebauer, *ZNW,* 52 [1961], 130). Jesus Christ the Messiah proclaimed Himself to be the light of the world (Jn. 8:12); He claimed as much for His disciples (Mt. 5:14), provided they carry on the work of their Lord and truly reflect Him before the world. The lamp symbolizes works of righteousness whose light shines far into the darkness of the world, giving glory to God (5:15f.; cf. Mk. 4:21f.; Lk. 8:16f.). The eye as the lamp of the body illuminates the inner being and radiates the brightness of the inner light (Mt. 6:22f.; Lk. 11:34-36). In 2 Pet. 1:19 the prophetic message is said to give guidance to the believer as a lamp gives light in a dark place until a new day dawns. John depicts the Lamb, Jesus Christ, as a lamp by whose light the nations shall walk in the new Jerusalem (Rev. 21:23f.). The only acknowledged source of light and life will finally be the Lord God (22:5).

On Jn. 18:3 *see* LANTERN.

***Bibliography.***–S. Krauss, *Talmudische Archäologie,* I (1911), 70; K. Galling, *ZDPV,* 46 (1923), 1-50; *Biblisches Reallexicon* (1937), *s.v.* "Lampe (und Leuchter)" (K. Galling); *DBSup.,* VIII, *s.v.* "Poterie Palestinienne" (Bonnard); F. W. Robins, *Story of the Lamp* (1939); E. R. Goodenough, *Jewish Symbols in the Greco-Roman Period* (1953-54), I, 139ff.; II, 136f.; IV, 77-98; C. Singer, *et al.,* eds., *History of Technology,* I (1954) 235-37; C. A. Kennedy, *Berytus,* 14 (1961), 67-115; R. H. Smith, *Berytus,* 14 (1961), 53-65; D. M. Bailey, *Greek and Roman Pottery Lamps* (1963); *BA,* 27 (1964), 2-31, 101-124; 29 (1966), 2-27; *TDNT,* IV, *s.v.* λάμπω κτλ. (Oepke); λύχνος, λυχνία (Michaelis); R. G. North, *Bibl.,* 51 (1970), 183-206.

G. F. HASEL

**LAMPSTAND** [Heb. *m$^e$nôrâ* (<*nûr,* "to flame, shine, give light"); Aram. *neḇr$^e$šâ* (Dnl. 5:5); Gk. *lychnía*]; AV CANDLESTICK; NEB also LAMP, STANDING LAMP. Throughout the OT period lampstands seem not to have been common household equipment; a frequent place for a lamp was a shallow wall niche. Only in 2 K. 4:10 is *m$^e$nôrâ* used of a household lampstand (by implication surmounted with a *nēr,* a clay lamp); the stand, like the bed, table, and chair that the passage mentions, was probably made of wood. Not surprisingly in view of their perishable nature, no specimens of wooden lampstands have yet been found in archeological excavations. Lampstands of bronze or iron were rare. Throughout the late Canaanite and early Israelite period terracotta lamps were occasionally manufactured in Palestine with clay pedestals attached; these may have been intended primarily for ceremonial use. Although the meaning is clear, the etymology of Aram. *nebr^eša* is debated; see J. A. Montgomery comm. on Daniel (*ICC*, 1927), p. 255; cf. F. Rosenthal, *Grammar of Biblical Aramaic* [repr. 1968], § 190).

The accounts of the wanderings of the Israelites in the wilderness describe a *m^enôrâ* used in the tabernacle (Ex. 25:31-40; 37:17-24; cf. 40:4). The lampstand is said to have been of pure — though hardly solid — gold (Ex. 31:8; 39:37; Nu. 8:4), hammered rather than cast, with its structural parts (identified as base, shaft, cups, capitals, and flowers) being all of one piece. Although the shape cannot be determined precisely and has been the subject of debate since the early rabbinic period, the lampstand is described as being a stylized tree or bush with three branches arranged bisymmetrically on each side of a sturdy central trunk. The branches are described as terminating in capitallike floral shapes, with cups shaped like almonds or almond blossoms at the top. On the trunk and branches, or perhaps only on the trunk, stood seven oil lamps, the material of which is not specified. Each lamp probably had the shape of a bowl, with one or more pinches on the rim to form wick spouts.

The lampstand is reported to have been anointed by Moses with sacred oil (Ex. 30:27) as an evidence of divine sanctification, and is said to have stood on the south side of the tabernacle (Ex. 26:35; 40:24f.). It had as its essential function the illumination of the sanctuary, and it is likely that originally the lamps may have burned only during the hours of darkness. Utensils are said to have been used in connection with the maintenance of the lamps (Ex. 35:14); these must have included storage containers for pure olive oil, a supply of wicks, needles or tongs for adjusting the wicks, and snuffers to extinguish the lamps. Exodus speaks variously of the high priest Aaron and the family of Kohath as having the care of the lampstand and its equipment, a responsibility which included ceremonial packing when the Israelites broke camp (Lev. 24:4; Nu. 3:31; 4:9f.; 8:2f.).

According to 1 K. 7:49f. the sanctuary of Solomon's temple had ten lampstands of pure gold, five on the south side of the chamber and five on the north (cf. 2 Ch. 4:7, 20). The form of the lampstands may have differed from that recorded for the tabernacle *m^enôrâ*. In his speech delivered in the northern kingdom during the reign of Jeroboam I, near the end of the 10th cent. B.C., King Abijah of Judah alludes to "the golden lampstand" as if there were only one (2 Ch. 13:10f.), but soon after the capture and sacking of Jerusalem by the Babylonians in 587 B.C. the historian refers to the captors' removal of "the lampstands" (Jer. 52:19).

1 Chronicles 28:15 mentions, along with the golden lampstands, a *m^enôrâ* of silver, the relationship of which to the other lampstands is not explained. Some differentiation of function for the various lampstands is suggested by the statement that the amount of gold and silver in the lamps was appropriate for "the use of each lampstand in the service." Nothing is known, however, about any uses of the lampstands during worship. It need not be supposed that all lampstands in the temple were in active use in the sanctuary at all times; some may have been used in other chambers or kept in reserve.

When the temple was rebuilt *ca.* 515 B.C. the sanctuary was outfitted with only one lampstand, of a form which apparently differed from that of the earlier lampstands. It was at this time, if not before, that the temple *m^enôrâ* began to be understood as having cosmic significance. Zec. 4, written near the end of the 6th cent. B.C. as the temple was beginning to be reconstructed, describes a vision in which the temple sanctuary is perceived as God's heavenly court in which there is a golden lampstand with a bowl on top and seven lamps (vv. 2, 11); the lamps are said to be the eyes of the Lord (v. 10).

Several decades before the birth of Jesus, Herod the Great rebuilt and refurbished the temple of Jerusalem. One of the benefactions that he — or possibly a Hasmonean ruler a half-century or century before him — bestowed on the temple was a new menorah, fabricated by craftsmen working under Hellenistic influence. This lampstand, which continued in use until the destruction of the temple by the Romans in A.D. 70, is presumably the one depicted on a panel in the triumphal arch set up in Rome more than a decade later in honor of the conquest of Judea by Titus.

Household lampstands may have come into more frequent use by the 1st cent. A.D., although archeological evidence for them remains scanty. The Synoptic Gospels record Jesus' analogical use of the commonsense fact that a lamp should be placed on a lampstand (*lychnía*), not under a basket (Mt. 5:15 par. Lk. 11:33; Mk. 4:21 par. Lk. 8:16). The menorahs of the tabernacle and temple are not mentioned in Jesus's teachings other than perhaps implicitly in the Johannine imagery of Jesus as the light of the world.

The cult menorah is explicitly mentioned in two NT books. He. 9:2 refers to the lampstand of the tabernacle in connection with the Old Covenant. Rev. 1:12, 20 and 2:5, standing in the tradition of prophetic imagery that has a temple setting, describe a vision of seven golden lampstands which represent seven churches (cf. Rev. 4:5, which

Lampstand from the temple in Jerusalem taken to Rome as booty after the capture of Jerusalem in A.D. 70. From the Arch of Titus (R. H. Smith)

transforms the seven lamps into torches that burn before God's throne). Rev. 11:4 draws upon the imagery of Zec. 4 when alluding to two olive trees and two lampstands as heavenly witnesses, while Rev. 1:13 associates the lampstand with the heavenly Son of man (cf. Rev. 2:1). These passages show the imagery of the lampstand moving further toward cosmic symbolism, a development which is reflected in the use of the menorah in Jewish art from the Roman period to the present day as a symbol of God's living presence and redemptive power.

***Bibliography.***–C. L. Meyers, *Tabernacle Menorah: A Synthetic Study of a Symbol from the Biblical Cult* (1976); D. Sperber, *JJS*, 16 (1965), 135-159; L. Yarden, *Tree of Light: A Study of the Menorah* (1971); P. F. Kiene, *Tabernacle of God in the Wilderness of Sinai* (1977). R. H. SMITH

**LANCE** (1 K. 18:28; cf. Jer. 50:42, AV). *See* WEAPONS OF WAR.

**LAND** [Heb. *'ereṣ*, also *'ᵃḏāmâ, śāḏeh*–'(open) field,' *gᵉḇûl*–'boundary,' 'territory' (1 S. 6:9; Ps. 78:54; Isa. 15:8; Ezk. 45:7), *ḥēleq*–'share of property' (2 K. 3:19, 25; Am. 7:4), *karmel*–'orchard' ("fruitful land," Isa. 10:18; Jer. 4:26; "fertile land," 2 Ch. 26:10), *migraš* ("pasture land," Nu. 35; Josh. 21; 1 Ch. 6; etc.), *nāweh* ("grazing land," Ezk. 34:14), *ṣᵉḇi*–'glory' ("glorious land," Dnl. 8:9; 11:16, 41; etc.), *yabbāšâ* ("dry land," Gen. 1:9f.; Neh. 9:11; Ps. 66:6; 95:5; Jonah 1:9, 13; 2:10 [MT 11]), *ḥārāḇâ* ("dry land," Gen. 7:22; Hag. 2:6), *ṣîyâ* ("dry land," Isa. 35:1), *ṣāmē'* ("thirsty land," Isa. 44:3), *ṣᵉḥîḥâ* ("parched land," Ps. 68:6 [MT 7]), *dûmâ* ("land of silence," Ps. 94:17); Gk. *gḗ, agrós, chṓra* (Lk. 12:16; Acts 27:27), *chōríon*(Acts 4:34; 5:3, 8; 28:7).]; AV, NEB, also EARTH, COUNTRY, FIELD, DRY LAND, etc.

***I. Various Meanings.***–The primary Hebrew term for "land" is *'ereṣ*, which is the fourth most frequent noun in the OT (*see also* EARTH; COUNTRY). Though generalization is difficult, a distinction can be drawn between *'ereṣ*, which denotes a geographical or political territory, and *'ᵃḏāmâ*, which refers to arable, productive earth. The LXX translates both terms by Gk. *gḗ*.

"Land" can represent the earth as the place where living things can prosper. On the third day of creation the waters are collected to one place and "dry land" (*yabbāšâ*) — called "earth" (*'ereṣ* — appears (Gen. 1:9f.). The dry land stands in antithesis to the sea, which represents the forces of chaos (cf. Job 38:8-11; Ps. 104:5-9; Rev. 10:2, 5, 8). Thus "land" is the place of safety and security (Jonah 1:9, 13; 2:10 [MT 11]; Acts 27:43f.; He. 11:29).

"Land" occasionally signifies ground or soil (*'ᵃḏāmâ*, Gen. 47:23; Dt. 11:17; Neh. 9:25; Prov. 12:11). Human life comes from the land and is inextricably tied to it (cf. Gen. 2:7; 3:19; Eccl. 12:7). "Land" sometimes designates an individual's tillable field (Heb. *śāḏeh*, Gen. 33:19; Lev. 27:16; Ruth 4:3; 1 S. 14:14; Gk. *agrós*, Mt. 19:29; Mk. 10:29f.).

"Land" (*'ereṣ*) can refer to a generalized region or political territory, as in "the land of his birth" (e.g., Gen. 11:28), "native land" (e.g., Jer. 22:10), "land of your fathers" (e.g., Gen. 31:3), "land of one's possession" (e.g., Gen. 36:43). A portion of Canaan allotted to an Israelite tribe is referred to as that tribe's land (e.g., "land of Ephraim," Dt. 34:2). The term can designate a nation-state in its socio-political as well as geographical dimensions (1 S. 13:19; 2 K. 5:2, 4; 6:23; cf. Gk. *gḗ*, Mt. 2:6, 20f.; 10:15; He. 8:9).

"Land" (*'ereṣ*) can also denote the realm of the dead, as in Jonah 2:6 (cf. "earth," Ex. 15:12; Eccl. 3:21). The place where the dead dwell can be called the "land of the shades" (Isa. 26:19) or the "land of forgetfulness" (Ps. 88:12 [MT 13]). The sense "underworld" is well attested for Akk. *erṣetu* and Ugar. *'rṣ* as well (cf. *UT*, 51:vii:7-9: "And go down into the infirmary of the underworld; you will be counted among those who go down into the land"). *See also* DEATH III.B.

***II. Land of Promise.***–In the theology of the OT the concepts of land and covenant are closely intertwined. The land is God's gift, which He guarantees by formal covenant, and it is the place where He dispenses covenant blessing. Living in the land of promise is equated with receiving God's blessings and experiencing His presence in the "land of the living" (Isa. 38:11; 53:8; Ezk. 32:23-27, 32). To belong to the Lord is to have a "portion" in His land (cf. Josh. 22:25, 27). Those who trust the Lord will live long in the land (Ps. 37:3, 9, 11, etc.). The Promised Land thus symbolizes the Lord's presence and blessing. Israel's relationship to the land is an indication of its relationship to God. Faith is required for possession of the land; unbelief results in expulsion from the land.

*A. Promise of the Land.* Land is the central feature of the Abrahamic covenant: "The Lord said to Abram, 'Go from your country [*'ereṣ*] . . . to the land that I will show you . . . to your descendants I will give this land'" (Gen. 12:1, 7; cf. 13:15; 24:7). Associated with the land promise are the covenant promises of nationhood and blessing (12:2f.). The promise is repeated to Isaac (26:3), Jacob (28:4, 13; 35:12), Joseph (48:4), and the other sons of Jacob (50:24). The patriarchs live in the land as sojourners (cf. "land of sojournings," Gen. 17:8; 28:4; 36:7; 37:1; Ex. 6:4); only in token fashion do they achieve ownership (cf. Gen. 23:1-20).

The land promise is of central importance in the Mosaic discourses of Deuteronomy — a book that forms the historical and theological bridge between the patriarchal land promise and the actual possession of the land. Deuteronomy brings together the land promise of the Abrahamic covenant and the stipulations of the Mosaic law covenant. The relationship between land and law is twofold. First, only if the statutes and ordinances are observed will the land be possessed (e.g., Dt. 6:17-19) and retained (e.g., 4:25f., 40). Second, the covenant as explicated and ratified in Deuteronomy is intended to regulate life in the promised land (e.g., 4:5, 14; 5:31); obedience to the covenant will result in prosperity in the land (28:9-11).

The land of promise is a "good land" (e.g., Dt. 1:25, 35). It is so rich, abundant and productive that it is said to "flow with milk and honey" (e.g., Ex. 3:8; Nu. 13:27; Dt. 6:3).

*B. Possession of the Land.* The so-called Deuteronomistic historical work (Joshua, Judges, Samuel, Kings) recounts Israel's history from the theological perspective of land promise, covenant breaking, and land loss. The justification for Israel's expulsion of the indigenous population is the wickedness of the Canaanites (cf. Gen. 15:16; Dt. 9:4f.). Israel's provisional possession of the land under Joshua's leadership is seen as fulfillment of the promise to the patriarchs (Josh. 21:43-45). Possession of the land brings "rest" (Dt. 12:9; 25:19; Josh. 1:13; 21:44), i.e., both freedom from foreign domination and the end of wandering.

The Lord gives the land as a gift (Dt. 5:31; 9:6; 11:17). Strictly speaking, the land never belongs absolutely to Israel but always remains the property of the Lord (Lev. 25:23). Divine ownership of the land is institutionalized in the SABBATICAL YEAR, in the Year of Jubilee (*see* JUBILEE, YEAR OF II), and in the practice of offering the FIRST FRUITS of the land to the Lord (Dt. 26:9-15; cf. also 14:22-29). The distribution of the land by lot (Nu. 26:55; Josh. 14:2; 18:1-10) is further indication that it is at the Lord's disposal (*see also* PORTION).

The boundaries of the Promised Land are variously delineated (cf. Gen. 15:18; Ex. 23:31; Nu. 34:1-10; Dt. 11:24; Josh. 1:4). While the book of Joshua suggests that full possession was achieved during Joshua's lifetime (Josh. 21:43-45), Judges indicates that the conquest was incomplete (Jgs. 1:1–2:5). Complete possession according to the larger boundaries of Ex. 23:31 takes place only in the reigns of David and Solomon (cf. 1 K. 4:25; 5:4).

*C. Exile from the Land.* Covenant breaking results in Israel's expulsion from the land (cf. Dt. 4:25f.; 28:63f.; Josh. 23:13, 15; 1 K. 9:6f.; 2 K. 17:22f.; etc.). For the Lord to dwell among His people the land must be clean, but immoral conduct (e.g., idolatry [1 K. 14:15], shedding of blood [Nu. 35:33f.], improper divorce [Dt. 24:1-4]) defiles the land and makes it unclean (*see* CLEAN AND UNCLEAN II.E). It was because the Canaanites had defiled the land through their wickedness that the land "vomited them out" (Lev. 18:24-30; 20:22-26). Likewise, the prophets specify pollution of the land as one reason for Israel's exile (cf. Jer. 12:10-12).

But Israel is not alienated from the land forever. Prophetic preaching sees beyond exile to a return to the land (e.g., Isa. 14:1f.; Jer. 16:15; 23:8; Ezk. 28:25; 36:8-15). In the age of salvation land retains an important place (Jer. 32:15; Ezk. 36:28-32; 37:25). The Lord Himself will redistribute the land in the new age (Ezk. 47:13–48:29). Prophecy is fulfilled when Cyrus issues a decree permitting a return to the land (Ezr. 1:1-4). After his return to Jerusalem, Ezra leads the people in a confession of their guilt in polluting the land, and he implores the people to cleanse the land by renouncing intermarriage (Ezr. 9:10-15).

***III. Land Promise Redefined.***–References to the promised land are sparse in the NT (He. 11:9; Acts 7:3 quotes Gen. 12:1). The central image of NT proclamation is not land but the kingdom of God and Jesus Christ as its embodiment. According to W. D. Davies (*Gospel and the Land*), the theme of land is displaced in Christianity by the person of Jesus Christ. The NT "personalizes 'holy space' in Christ, who, as a figure of History, is rooted in the land . . . but as Living Lord . . . is also free to move wherever he wills" (p. 367).

The promise of land continues to play a role in NT thought, but it takes on an eschatological dimension. It becomes a symbol of the eschatological society in time and eternity. Possession of the land is promised to the meek (Mt. 5:5; cf. Ps. 37:11). The faithful are promised rest (He. 3–4; cf. Dt. 12:9; 25:19). And the pilgrimage of faith is described in terms of land promise and fulfillment (He. 11:13-16), with the difference that the "better country" is a "heavenly one" (v. 16). *See also* ESCHATOLOGY IX.

***Bibliography.***–W. Brueggemann, *The Land* (1977); W. D. Davies, *Gospel and the Land* (1974); *Territorial Dimension of Judaism* (1982); F. W. Marquardt, *Juden und ihr Land* (1975); E. Martens, *God's Design* (1981); G. von Rad, "Promised Land and Yahweh's Land in the Hexateuch," in *Problem of the Hexateuch and Other Essays* (Eng. tr. 1966), pp. 79-93; R. Rendtorff, *Israel und sein Land* (1975); L. Rost, "Bezeichnungen für Land und Volk im AT," in *Kleine Credo und andere Studien zum AT* (1965), pp. 76-101; L. I. J. Stadelmann, *Hebrew Conception of the World* (1970); *TDNT,* I, *s.v.* γῆ (H. Sasse); *TDOT,* I, *s.v.* "ʾ$^{a}$dhāmāh" (J. G. Plöger), "ʾerets" (J. Bergman, M. Ottosson); N. J. Tromp, *Primitive Conceptions of Death and the Netherworld in the OT* (1969).

B. L. BANDSTRA

**LAND CROCODILE.** *See* LIZARD.

**LAND LAWS.** *See* AGRARIAN LAWS; INHERIT.

**LANDING** [Heb. *miprāṣ* <*pāraṣ*–'break'] (Jgs. 5:17); AV BREACH; NEB CREEK. Although *miprāṣ* occurs only here, its context and derivation indicate the meaning "harbor" (so JB; cf. Vulg. *portus,* "port, harbor, river mouth") or "landing" (i.e., a break in the coastline).

**LANDMARK** [Heb. *g*$^{e}$*ḇûl*–'boundary']. The boundary may have been marked simply by a furrow or stone (*see* picture in BORDER). The iniquity of removing a landmark is insisted on (Dt. 19:14; 27:17; Job 24:2 [Heb. *g*$^{e}$*ḇulôṯ*]; Prov. 22:28; 23:10); its removal was equivalent to theft. The rules of the brotherhood at Qumrân stigmatized any who left the community as "those who removed the landmark" (CD 5:20; 8:3; cf. Hos. 5:10).

**LANGUAGE** [Heb. *lāšôn* (Aram. *liššān*)–'tongue' (Gen. 10:5, 20, 31; Dt. 28:49; Neh. 13:24c; Est. 1:22; 3:12; 8:9; Jer. 5:15; Ezk. 3:5f.; Dnl. 1:4; 3:7, 29; 4:1 [MT 3:31]; 5:19; 6:25 [MT 26]; 7:14), *śāpâ*–'lip' (Gen. 11:1, 6f., 9; Isa. 19:18), qal part. of *lʿz*–'speak an incomprehensible foreign language' (Ps. 114:1); Gk. *diálektos* (Acts 1:19; 2:6, 8; 21:40; 22:2; 26:14), *phōnḗ*–'voice' (1 Cor. 14:10f.)]; AV also TONGUE, VOICE; NEB also SPEECH, SOUND. The term is supplied by translators for better understanding of "Hebrew," "Aramaic," etc. in 2 K. 18:26, 28 par. 2 Ch. 32:18 par. Isa. 36:11, 13; Neh. 13:24a, b. *See* TONGUE; SPEECH.

**LANGUAGES OF THE BIBLE.** *See* ARAMAIC; GREEK LANGUAGE OF THE NT; HEBREW LANGUAGE.

**LANTERN** [Gk. *phanós*]. "Lantern" is used but once in the NT, in Jn. 18:3 in the plural. There it is connected with Gk. *lampás,* which is correctly translated "torches." Accordingly, the "lanterns" in v. 3 are not torches but other sources of light carried by the mixed mob that arrested Jesus. The lantern is also to be distinguished from the normal LAMP. *Phanós* means "torch" in early Greek literature, but in the period of Koine Greek it is regularly used for "lantern." The "lanterns" referred to may be Roman types, since Roman soldiers were in the mob arresting Jesus (v. 12). Roman lanterns usually consisted of a metal frame with a surrounding cylinder of some type of translucent material, such as horn or bladder.

G. F. HASEL

**LAODICEA** lā-od-ə-sē'ə [Gk. *Laodikia,* or in most Greek literature *Laodikeia*] (Col. 2:1; 4:13-16; Rev. 1:11; 3:14-22). A city of Asia Minor.

The ancient town of Diospolis ("city of Zeus") or Rhoas was fortified as a Seleucid outpost by Antiochus II *ca.* 250 B.C. and renamed for his wife Laodice. Situated on a southern plateau more than 30 m. (100 ft.) above the valley of the Lycus River, Laodicea was flanked by two of its tributaries and protected on the south by the Salbacus and Cadmus mountains. It lay 10 km. (6 mi.) S of Hierapolis, 18 km. (11 mi.) W of Colossae, and slightly more than 160 km. (100 mi.) E of Ephesus.

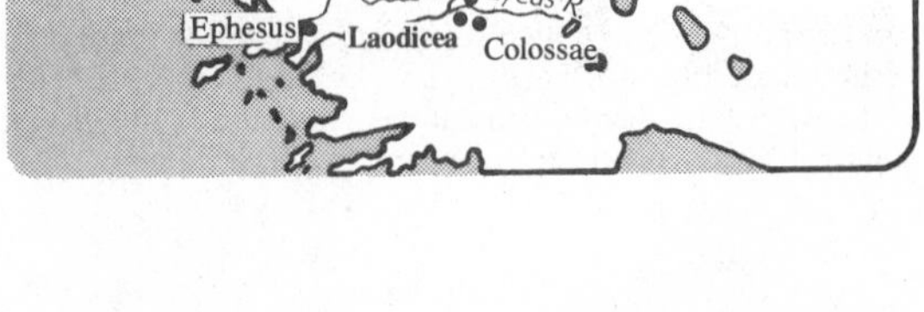

After the Syrians and the Pergamenes successively dominated the city, the Romans became its rulers in 133 B.C. They reconstructed ancient roads leading into the Anatolian hinterland, and Laodicea became the major junction for traffic west to Ephesus and the Aegean, north and west to Philadelphia, Pergamum, and Smyrna, east through southern Galatia to the Cilician Gates, and south to the Mediterranean. Although it had been a small city, it grew rapidly during Roman rule and became very wealthy (cf. Rev. 3:17). When Laodicea was destroyed by an earthquake *ca.* A.D. 60, it proudly refused imperial financial assistance in rebuilding (Tacitus *Ann.* xiv.27; cf. *RRAM,* I, 564). Among its chief exports were costly, seamless garments woven of glossy, black wool (Strabo *Geog.* xii.8.16), which Ramsay suggested may have been behind the reference to "white garments" in Rev. 3:18.

The population was cosmopolitan: Roman colonizers, the original Phrygians, and immigrant Syrian settlers, including Jews (who in 62 B.C. suffered Roman seizure of their annual contribution to Jerusalem, amounting to 20 pounds of gold; cf. Cicero *Pro Flacco* 68). The deities worshiped in Laodicea reflected this varied background. Zeus Laodicenus had some definitely Phrygian characteristics. Asclepius may have been associated with Men Karou's nearby temple, to which a famous medical school was connected. "Phrygian powder," ground locally in Laodicea, apparently was used to treat diseases of the eyes. Galen, however, regarded such medicinal preparations as magical pharmacopoeia. Nevertheless, the eye salve in Rev. 3:18 is a historically appropriate symbol for Laodicea. Mystery religions, including the cult of Isis (see below), were represented.

Paul or one of his followers (depending on the meaning of Col. 2:1) probably brought Christianity to the region. Although John judged the church there as "lukewarm" (Rev. 3:16), the city soon became the leading bishopric of Phrygia. Its bishop Sagaris was martyred *ca.* A.D. 166, and Nounechios represented this seat at Nicea in 325. The Council of Laodicea, 367, is important for its opposition to the Montanist and Quartodeciman movements as well as for its acceptance of twenty-six books in the NT canon (Revelation was not included).

The city was captured by the Seljuks (11th cent.) and retaken by the Byzantines in 1119. It became part of the Latin kingdom during the Fourth Crusade and then part of the Greek Empire. Tamerlane and the Tartars captured it in 1402, and subsequently the city fell to the Ottoman Turks. The site, known today as Eski Hissar ("old castle"), was abandoned and suffered seriously from scavengers in need of materials for building the railway and the nearby Turkish town of Denizili.

Ruins of the theater (1st or 2nd cent. A.D.) at Laodicea (Québec; Laval University excavations)

Among the distinguishable ruins are a large stadium, a gymnasium, two theaters, gates, and several churches. Also evident are the remains of a great water system. Its fine aqueduct is built from large, tightly fitted, and cemented rectangular stones, through which a circular central channel is bored. The water was transported by the aqueduct from the mountain springs and raised to a tall water-distribution tower by syphon action. Laodicea also has a magnificent nymphaeum (public fountain), near which archeologists uncovered friezes of Zeus and his captive Ganymede and of Theseus and the legendary Minotaur.

The nymphaeum at Laodicea (Québec; Laval University excavations)

Frieze of Ganymede from the nymphaeum at Laodicea (probably 3rd cent. A.D.). Zeus's eagle holds his right arm, while his dog (lower left, head missing) jumps to protect him and a lamb lies between his legs (Québec; Laval University excavations)

A large statue of Isis was also found in the dump associated with the fountain. The statue's original setting is unclear, but its later location is undoubtedly attributable to one of the postearthquake reconstruction periods during the Christian era, when such statues were destroyed or marred.

*See also* SEVEN CHURCHES.

***Bibliography.***–W. M. Ramsay, *CBP,* I, 32ff.; *LSC,* pp. 413ff.; S. E. Johnson, *BA,* 13 (1950), 1-5, 7-12; *RRAM,* I, 127, 242, etc.; J. des Gagniers, *et al., Laodicée du Lycos, Le Nymphée, Campagnes 1961-1963* (1969). G. L. BORCHERT

**LAODICEANS, EPISTLE TO THE** [Gk. *hē (epistolē) ek Laodikeías*]. The reference in Col. 4:16 to "the letter from Laodicea" has long been a puzzle. It can be taken to mean either a letter written by the Laodiceans to the Colossians or a letter written by Paul from Laodicea. The most obvious interpretation, however, supported by both the context and grammatical considerations, is that Paul wrote a letter to the church at Laodicea at the same time that he wrote the one to the church at Colossae. The problem is that no letter addressed to the Laodiceans has been preserved in the Pauline corpus.

Several attempts have been made to solve the problem. One approach was to create a new document. A pseudepigraphical Epistle to the Laodiceans has survived in a Latin translation and had some acceptance in the Western Church into the Middle Ages (*see* APOCRYPHAL EPISTLES I.B; cf. also H-S, II, 128-132).

Another approach has been to identify the letter mentioned in Col. 4:16 with one of the known Epistles. Some, apparently including Marcion, have identified it with Ephesians (*see* EPHESIANS, EPISTLE TO THE II.D), a position presented at length by J. Rutherfurd in *ISBE* (1929), III, 1836-39. Others have seen Philemon as the missing letter (*see* PHILEMON, EPISTLE TO IV). Although each identification has some plausibility, neither has gained widespread scholarly acceptance. For one reason or another (cf. the possibilities listed by R. P. Martin, *Colossians and Philemon* [*NCBC,* repr. 1981], pp. 138f.) the letter apparently has not been preserved. E. W. S.

**LAP** [Heb. (vb.) *lāqaq* (Jgs. 7:5-7), (noun) *berek̠*–'knee' (2 K. 4:20), *beged̠*–'garment' (2 K. 4:39), *ḥōṣen*–'girdle' (Neh. 5:13), *ḥêq*–'bosom' (Prov. 16:33); Gk. *kólpos*–'bosom' (Lk. 6:38)]; AV also KNEE (2 K. 4:20), BOSOM (Lk. 6:38); NEB also "skirt of a garment" (2 K. 4:39), "fold of a robe" (Neh. 5:13).

Scholars have offered various interpretations of Jgs. 7:5-7, the only passage where the RSV uses "lap" as a verb. The two key phrases are "laps the water with his tongue, as a dog laps" (v. 5), and "those that lapped, putting their hands [lit. "with their hands"] to their mouths" (v. 6). These statements seem contradictory (they are thus rearranged by, e.g., the NEB and R. Boling, *Judges* [*AB,* 1975], pp. 145f.), since a dog does not put his paw to his mouth but licks directly from the source. But possibly those who lapped scooped up handfuls of water and then licked the water like dogs (so KD; A. Cohen, *Joshua. Judges* [*Soncino,* 1950], p. 217).

The significance of this lapping is not clear. J. Myers (*IB,* II, 738) and KD interpreted it as indicating military training. Cohen, however, took it as indicating a lack of such training (cf. Josephus *Ant.* v.6.3 [216f.]) and thus enhancing God's role in the victory (note also in vv. 15-22 that these men apparently did not fight but functioned only to confuse the Midianites). Although no explanation is fully satisfactory, that of Cohen seems to handle the MT best.

The other occurrences of "lap" are less problematic. In 2 K. 4:39 one of the sons of the prophets gathers some wild gourds in his *beged̠,* probably the folds of his garment. Nehemiah's symbolic gesture of "shaking out his lap" no doubt also refers to a garment, which, according to J. Myers (*Ezra. Nehemiah* [*AB,* 1965], p. 129), was a girdle or sash whose folds served as pockets. The *ḥêq* (Prov. 16:33; LXX *kólpos*) into which the lots were cast may have been the same as the *ḥōšen,* "the breast pocket in the priestly garment where the lots lay (Ex. 28.30; Lev. 8.8)" (W. McKane, *Proverbs* [*OTL,* 1970], p. 499, following R. de Vaux, *Ancient Israel,* II [Eng. tr. 1961], 352; cf. G. André, *TDOT,* IV, 356f.). According to Bauer (rev., p. 442) *kólpos* in Lk. 6:38 means *"the fold of a garment,* formed as it falls from the chest over the girdle . . . used as a pocket." G. A. L.

**LAPIS LAZULI** la'pis laz'ə-lē [Heb. *sappîr*] (Job 28:6, 16; Cant. 5:14; Isa. 54:11; Lam. 4:7; Ezk. 1:26; 28:13); AV, RSV, SAPPHIRE; NEB also SAPPHIRE; [Gk. *sápphiros*] (Rev. 21:19); AV, RSV, SAPPHIRE. "Lapis lazuli" is the RSV marginal reading for "sapphire" in these passages. It is a precious azure stone frequently showing traces of iron pyrite, more common in Mesopotamia than in Palestine.

*See* STONES, PRECIOUS.

**LAPPIDOTH** lap'ə-doth [Heb. *lappîd̠ôt̠*–'flames, torches']; AV LAPIDOTH. The husband of Deborah (Jgs. 4:4). The name occurs only here, and since no father's name is given, the passage has been interpreted in different ways. Some scholars have preferred to translate the phrase *'ēšet̠ lappîd̠ôt̠* not as "wife of Lappidoth" but literally, as "woman of flames," i.e., a fiery, spirited woman (see A. Cohen, *Joshua. Judges* [*Soncino,* 1950], p. 186). Others (e.g., R. Boling, *Judges* [*AB,* 1975], p. 95) have taken *lappid̠ôt̠* as a nickname of Barak (whose name means "lightning"). The latter suggestion is somewhat plausible but remains conjectural. G. A. L.

**LAPWING** (AV Lev. 11:19; Dt. 14:18). *See* HOOPOE.

**LASCIVIOUSNESS.** *See* LICENTIOUSNESS.

**LASEA** lə-sē'ə [Gk. *Lasaia,* ℵ *Lassaia,* B *Lasea,* A *Laissa*]. A city on the south coast of Crete, 8 km. (5 mi.) E of FAIR HAVENS (Acts 27:8). In 1853 Captain T. A. B. Spratt found ancient ruins there, which G. Brown further examined in 1856. It is thought that ships anchored for any length of time at Fair Havens would have had to buy supplies at Lasea. F. F. Bruce (*Book of Acts* [*NICNT,* 1954], p. 504) identified Lasea with the Lasos mentioned by Pliny (*Nat. hist.* iv.12 [59]).

See T. A. B. Spratt, *Travels and Researches in Crete* (1856), II, 1-6). R. EARLE

**LASHA** la'shə [Heb. *lāšaʿ,* pausal form of *lešaʿ*]. A city mentioned only once (Gen. 10:19), in a description of the southern boundaries of Canaanite territory. Lasha's association with Sodom, Gomorrah, Admah, and Zeboiim suggests that it was located somewhere near the southeast shore of the Dead Sea, most probably in the Vale of Siddim S of the el-Lisan peninsula. Like the other cities with which it is associated, however, its actual location is unknown.

Following the tradition of the Jerusalem Targum, Jerome identified it with the hot springs at Callirhoe, the modern Zerqā Māʿîn, SW of Medeba near the eastern coast of the Dead Sea; this cannot be substantiated, however. Equally precarious is Wellhausen's suggestion (*Jahrbücher für deutsche Theologie,* 21 [1876], 403f.) that Lasha is a corruption of Heb. *lešam,* or Leshem (Dan), with Gen.

10:19 thus giving the boundary from Gaza to the Dead Sea and from there N to Dan. R. K. H.

**LASHARON** lə-shâr'ən [Heb. *laššārôn*]. A place mentioned in the list of "the kings of the land whom Joshua and the people of Israel defeated on the west side of the Jordan" (Josh. 12:7, 18). The LXX reads *basiléa Aphek tḗs Sarōn,* "a king of Aphek of Sharon." Some scholars therefore read *laššārôn* in the MT as "[which belongs] to Sharon," modifying "Aphek." The complex sentence structure makes this emendation extremely difficult, however. Since the list of kings and their city-states seems to have no geographical logic, any attempts to locate Lasharon are precarious. W. S. L. S.

**LAST DAY.** *See* DAY, LAST.

**LAST DAYS.** *See* ESCHATOLOGY; TIME, LAST.

**LAST JUDGMENT.** *See* JUDGMENT, LAST.

**LAST SUPPER.** *See* LORD'S SUPPER.

**LAST TIME.** *See* TIME, LAST.

**LASTHENES** las'thə-nēz [Gk. *Lasthenēs*]. A high official under the Seleucid king Demetrius II Nicator. He is called the king's "kinsman" (AV "cousin") and "father" (1 Macc. 11:31f.; Josephus *Ant.* xiii.4.9 [127]), but these are court titles not denoting blood relationship. According to Josephus (*Ant.* xiii.4.3 [86]) he was a native of Crete who raised an army for the king's first descent upon the coast and enabled Demetrius ultimately to wrest the throne of Syria from Alexander Balas (1 Macc. 10:67). The letter addressed to Lasthenes (11:30-37) indicates that he was probably prime minister or grand vizier of the kingdom. J. HUTCHISON

**LATCH** [Heb. *ḥōr*–'hole'] (Cant. 5:4); AV HOLE; NEB LATCH-HOLE. The Hebrew phrase in which this word occurs reads *min-haḥōr,* literally "from the hole," rendered "to the latch" by the RSV. The NEB rendering "through the latch-hole" is more likely. The beloved apparently extends his hand from the outside through the hole in the door to unlock it. Some, e.g., M. Pope (*Song of Songs* [*AB,* 1977], pp. 517-19), see in the context an erotic euphemism.

**LATCHET.** A leather thong used for tying on sandals. *See* THONG.

**LATIN** [Gk. *Rhōmaïsti*] (Jn. 19:20). The language of the Roman rulers of Palestine in NT times. The term in Jn. 19:20 is an adverb meaning "in the language of the Romans," i.e., "in Latin." It is similar to the adjective found in the marginal reading of the Lukan parallel (23:38), *Rhōmaïkos.* The Bible has no other uses of the term "Latin."

Aramaic was the native language of the Jews at that time, and Greek was the language of culture and commerce, even for Romans, in that part of the world. Latin would have been used by Roman authorities for official communications. Thus the INSCRIPTION on the cross would have been understood by virtually anyone in Jerusalem who could read. E. W. S.

**LATIN VERSION, OLD.** *See* VERSIONS I.A.

**LATRINE** [Heb. *K maḥᵃrā'ôṯ, Q môṣā'ôṯ*] (2 K. 10:27); AV DRAUGHT HOUSE; NEB PRIVY. The Israelites expressed their contempt for the temple of Baal by using it as a latrine. Cf. Ezr. 6:11. The *kethibh* is related to *ḥᵃrā'îm,* "dung," and the euphemistic *qere* (from the verb *yāṣā',* "go out") means "places of going out to" (BDB, p. 426), i.e., the outhouse or privy.

**LATTER DAYS.** *See* ESCHATOLOGY II; TIME, LAST.

**LATTER TIME.** *See* TIME, LAST.

**LATTICE.** *See* HOUSE III.D.

**LAUD** [Heb. piel of *šāḇaḥ* (Ps. 145:4); Gk. *epainéō* (Rom. 15:11, AV)]; NEB COMMEND (Ps. 145:4), PRAISE (Rom. 15:11). A synonym for PRAISE (verb).

**LAUGH; LAUGHTER** [Heb. *bûz*] (Gen. 38:23); AV BE SHAMED; NEB "get a bad name"; [*lā'ag*] (Job 22:19; Ps. 80:6 [MT 7]); AV also "laugh . . . to scorn"; NEB "make game," MOCK; [*ṣāḥaq*] (Gen. 17:17; 18:12f., 15; 21:6; Ezk. 23:32); NEB also "charged with mockery"; [*ṣᵉḥōq*] (Gen. 21:6); [*śᵉḥôq*] (Job 8:21; Ps. 126:2; Prov. 14:13; Eccl. 2:2; 3:4; 7:3, 6; 10:19); NEB also PLEASURES; [*śāḥaq*] (2 Ch. 30:10; Job 5:22; 39:18, 22; 41:29 [MT 21]; Ps. 2:4; 37:13; 52:6 [MT 8]; 59:8 [MT 9]; Prov. 1:26; 29:9; 31:25; Hab. 1:10); AV also DERIDE, MOCK, REJOICE, SCORN; NEB also DERISION, DESPISE, SCORN; [Gk. *geláō*] (Lk. 6:21, 25); [*gélōs*] (Jas. 4:9); [*katageláō*] (Mt. 9:24 par. Mk. 5:40; Lk. 8:53).

Laughter occurs often in the OT as an expression of mockery or derision. Judah fears that this will be the reaction of his neighbors to the news of Tamar's tricking him (Gen. 38:23). The people laughed at the couriers of Hezekiah who called them to celebrate the Passover in Jerusalem (2 Ch. 30:10). The fool responds with laughter to an argument he cannot counter (Prov. 29:9). The Chaldeans expressed their contempt for their enemies in such a manner (Hab. 1:10), as did the enemies of Israel (Ps. 80:6; Ezk. 23:32). But laughter is also the reaction of the righteous when the wicked reap the fruit of their ways (Job 22:19; Ps. 52:6; Prov. 1:26). Yahweh Himself laughs at the impotence of the wicked (Ps. 2:4; 37:13; 59:8).

Almost as frequently laughter occurs as an expression of joy. It may be the joy of a woman at the birth of a child (Gen. 21:6), or the relief of an accused man at his vindication (Job 8:21), or the joy of a nation when its fortunes are restored (Ps. 126:2). Such joy has its proper time (Eccl. 3:4) — the feast (10:19). Laughter is also closely related, however, to sorrow (Prov. 14:13; Eccl. 7:3), madness (Eccl. 2:2), and foolishness (7:6).

Laughter may also be an expression of disbelief, as when Abraham and Sarah laughed at the announcement of her pregnancy (Gen. 17:17; 18:12f., 15). It sometimes expressed a defiance of fear on the part of man (Job 5:22), the ostrich (39:18), the horse (v. 22), Leviathan (41:29), and the good wife (Prov. 31:25).

In the NT Jesus was the object of derisive laughter when He announced that the daughter of the ruler was not dead (Mt. 9:24 par. Mk. 5:40; Lk. 8:53). Laughter will be the reaction of those who presently weep when the time of blessing comes (Lk. 6:21), while those who now laugh will weep (v. 25). Those who would humble themselves before God should cease their joyful laughter (Jas. 4:9f.). J. R. PRICE

**LAUGHINGSTOCK** [Heb. *śᵉḥôq* (Job 12:4; Jer. 20:7; Lam. 3:14), *mᵉnôḏ-rō'š*–'a shaking of the head' (Ps. 44:14 [MT 15])]; AV MOCK (Job 12:4), DERISION (Jer. 20:7; Lam. 3:14), "shake the head" (Ps. 44:14); NEB also "shake the head." Something laughed at or ridiculed. Job felt he was a laughingstock to his friends because of his misfortune (Job 12:4); Jeremiah became a laughingstock because of his prophecies of doom (Jer. 20:7). The Israelites when defeated were mocked by other nations (Ps. 44:14; Lam. 3:14). *See also* DERIDE; MOCK.

**LAVER** [Heb. *kîyôr*; Gk. *loutrón*]; NEB usually BASIN.

***I. In the Tabernacle.***–Every priest attending the altar of Yahweh was required to wash his hands and feet before beginning his official duties (Ex. 30:19-21). Thus a laver or washstand was ordered to be made as part of the tabernacle equipment (vv. 17-21; 38:8). The laver was brass (bronze) and consisted of two parts, a bowl and its pedestal or stand (30:18). This tabernacle laver was a small one made of the recast hand mirrors of the women who ministered at the door of the tent of meeting (38:8). It was located between the altar and the TABERNACLE (40:30).

***II. In the Temple.***–In the temple of Solomon ten lavers and a "molten sea" were provided for washing parts of sacrificial carcasses (1 K. 7:23-37; 2 Ch. 4:2-6; *see* SEA, MOLTEN; TEMPLE). The "sea" was for the priests to wash in and therefore replaced the laver of the tabernacle; the ten lavers were used as baths for rinsing the portions used for burnt offerings (2 Ch. 4:6). The lavers themselves were probably cauldrons and were set on separately cast, circular stands, described in 1 K. 7:27-37. These stands were set upon a cubical base, whose four corners projected downward and were fitted with axles and wheels. Similar wheeled cauldron stands, with open-work sides closely corresponding to the "lions, oxen, and cherubim" with which the biblical stands were decorated, have been found in Cyprus and at Megiddo and seem to have been a current Phoenician type. Surviving examples, however, are much smaller than those of the temple, which were 5 cubits (3 m. [8 ft.]) high and supported cauldrons containing about 1500 l. (320 gal.) of water.

Laver and base from Solomon's temple (artist's rendering based on a reconstruction by P. L. Garber)

The idolatrous King Ahaz cut off the border of the bases and removed the lavers from the bases (2 K. 16:17). During the reign of Jehoiakim, Jeremiah foretold that the molten sea and the bases (no lavers existed then) would be carried to Babylon (Jer. 27:19-22). A few year later the bases were broken up and the brass of which they were made was carried away (52:17).

***III. In the NT.***–Greek *loutrón* occurs twice in the NT. In Eph. 5:26 Paul says that Christ gave Himself for the Church "that he might sanctify her, having cleansed her by the washing ["laver"] of water with the word; in Tit. 3:5 he says that Christians are saved "by the washing ["laver"] of regeneration and renewal in the Holy Spirit." These passages refer to the constant physical purity demanded of the Jewish priests when in attendance upon the temple. Christians are a "holy priesthood" and are cleansed not by water only but, in the former passage, "with the word" (cf. Jn. 15:3), and in the latter passage, by "renewal in the Holy Spirit" (cf. Ezk. 36:25; Jn. 3:5). The foot washing mentioned by Jesus is emblematic of this spiritual cleansing (Jn. 13:10). W. S. CALDECOTT

**LAW IN THE OT.**

I. Terms
II. Law in the Ancient Near East
III. Written Records
IV. Character and Design
  A. Decalogue
  B. Book of the Covenant
  C. Dt. 12:1–26:19
  D. Lev. 17–26
  E. Ceremonial Law
  F. Final Formation
V. Obsolescence

***I. Terms.***–The most frequently used Hebrew term for law is *tôrâ,* which occurs some 220 times in the OT. It is apparently derived from a root *yrh* used in its causative active form to mean "direction, guidance, instruction." The primary function of Hebrew law was to serve as a personal and national guide to ethical, moral, social, and spiritual living under the covenant deity. Although this law contains enactments or prohibitions that correspond to occidental concepts of codified law, it also exhibits certain fundamental differences. For example, common law in the western hemisphere is not concerned primarily with what is right or wrong but with what is permissible or not permissible. In the Hebrew enactments, by contrast, a strong and continued insistence upon ethical and moral values shows that they not merely undergird the law but in some instances form its essence. Although scholars have tended to describe Mosaic law as a code, its classification and intent are different from those of most Near Eastern legislative codes, being based more upon covenantal provisions and stipulations than upon *ad hoc* decisions. Hebrew law and Near Eastern codes have some material in common, of course, due to environmental and cultural similarities, but the distinctive ethos and intent of Hebrew law make any correspondences modest indeed.

To clarify the origin of the word *tôrâ* appeal has been made to a closely related verb *yārâ,* "cast," as with lots (Josh. 18:6). *Yārâ* is also used for the shooting of arrows (e.g., 1 S. 20:36f.), although there is no evidence that it ever describes divination by means of discharging or shaking arrows from a quiver, since a different verb is used in the OT for the casting of lots. It thus seems best to regard *tôrâ* as derived from the causative form of the verb *yārâ* and meaning "show, indicate, direct, teach," as in Ex. 24:12; 1 S. 12:23. The word for teacher (*môreh*) is derived from the same root, as in Isa. 30:20. While *tôrâ* may mean simply human direction (Prov. 1:8), it most frequently refers in the OT to divine law. The singular form can and does refer to one enactment, but it most commonly describes the general body of divinely revealed law. It conveys no information about the way that the law, in part or whole, was revealed, but indicates that its immediate purpose was to guide the covenant people in the various matters under consideration, thus leading them to a deeper knowledge of God and a more resolute commitment to fellowship with Him.

Seven other words are used as synonyms of *tôrâ*:

(1) *Miṣwâ,* "commandment, command" (Gen. 25:5; Ex. 15:26), is usually understood as a specific instruction from God that is to be obeyed rather than as a general law that is to be observed. The emphasis is therefore categorical rather than casuistic.

(2) *Mišpāṭ,* "judgment, ordinance," is a term with a variety of meanings. It is sometimes used in the singular in an abstract sense (Gen. 18:19; Dt. 34:2) and on other occasions describes the judicial decision itself (Dt. 16:18f.; 17:9; 24:17). The plural designates those enactments within the larger corpus that evidently originated in judicial decisions that were, under divine sanction, incorporated into the larger *tôrâ.* It is therefore quite permissible to translate this term "precedent."

(3) *ʿēḏûṯ,* "admonition, testimony," is a general word for God's law as it exhibits the manner of His dealings with His people Israel. Thus the ark is called the "ark of the testimony" (Ex. 25:22) because it contained the "testimony" or tablets of the law that constitute the basic covenant formulation.

(4) *Ḥuqqîm,* "statutes, oracles," is another general description of law. It apparently designates "something that is engraved" and therefore established unchangeably as a statute by a lawgiver. Such statutes when mentioned in connection with the priesthood were mandatory for worship, but when formulated by the state they had the force of royal pronouncements or decrees. The expression "ordinances and statutes" (Lev. 18:4; Dt. 4:1) describes the entire scope of Hebrew law.

(5) *Piqqûḏîm,* "orders, precepts," is used only in the Psalms (19:8 [MT 9]; 103:18; etc.), of God's orders or assignments.

(6) *Dāḇār,* "word" (Ex. 34:28; Dt. 4:13), is an important synonym for *tôrâ.* It was used early for divine oracles or revelation (Jgs. 3:20) and came to be applied in Jewish tradition especially to the Commandments or "Ten Words." Commentators have remarked frequently that this usage emphasizes the revelatory nature of the pronouncements, whereas "commandments" tends to stress their authoritarian aspect. Only in the sense that the "words" are the revelation of the divine will for the Israelites can they lay claim to the authority that must necessarily characterize a "commandment." Just as the law as a whole can be considered *tôrâ,* so the revelation of God, and especially the Sinaitic covenant, can be regarded as *dāḇār.*

(7) *Daṯ* is an Aramaic form of Old Pers. *dātam,* "royal edict, public law," and is used in this sense in Ezr. 7:26; Dnl. 2:3, 15; 6:8, 12, 15 (MT 9, 13, 16). *Daṯ* also occurs in Ezr. 7:12, 14, 21, 25f.; Dnl. 6:5 (MT 6) to describe divine law and was thus considered equivalent to *tôrâ.* In Dnl. 7:25 and probably in Ezr. 7:25 the term seems to refer to Jewish religious traditions.

The LXX generally translates *tôrâ* by *nómos,* "law," which occurs some 430 times, although only about half of these are actually matched by Hebrew words. The Greek term comes from a verb meaning "deal out, assign, apportion," referring apparently to processes that undergirded principles of legal ownership. *Nómos* occasionally translates *miṣwâ* (Prov. 6:20), *dāḇār* (LXX Ps. 118:57; MT 119:57), *mišpāṭ* (LXX Jer. 30:6; MT 49:12), and *ḥōq* (Josh. 24:25). *Nómos* occurs most frequently in the Pentateuch — about sixty times. Other Greek words include *entolḗ,* "decree, commandment," as a general rendering for *miṣwâ*; *próstagma,* "injunction," which translates *ḥōq* and *ḥuqqâ*; *dikaíōma,* "ordinance, declaration," which sometimes renders *ḥōq* and its cognate forms but more commonly translates *mišpāṭ*; *nómimos,* "conformable to law, lawful."

***II. Law in the Ancient Near East.***–The earliest formulations of law were made by the Sumerians, a very intelligent and creative people who were responsible for the world's first high culture. The Sumerians greatly emphasized law and order in society, and in the middle of the 3rd millennium B.C. they began to draw up legislation based upon what modern western lawyers would describe as a theory of social contract. By this means the freedom of individual expression was ensured as long as it did not conflict seriously with the aspirations and activities of others. But because the Sumerians were aggressive by nature, it was not long before social disputes needed to be resolved by the authoritarian pronouncements of a disinterested third party. This person was the ensi, the ruler of the individual city-state, who was responsible for the administration of justice. He appointed other citizens to serve as judges, so that court cases were presided over by two or three such officials. The oral decisions that they made constituted legal precedents, which in turn became the basis of written law when the decisions were committed to writing for purposes of reference. The Sumerian word for the record of the court proceedings was ditilla, "completed lawsuit," a term that covered other aspects of litigation as well.

A movement to reform the social abuses that had arisen in Lagash in the middle of the 3rd millennium B.C. resulted in the promulgation of regulations by a vigorous ruler named Urukagina. Coming to power *ca.* 2350 B.C., he instituted reforms to correct rampant political, economic, and social evils. Some of the more oppressive forms of taxation that had been devised by the palace bureaucracy were prohibited, including the acquisition by the ensi of property that belonged to the temple. Certain types of levies that had grown up in previous days were discontinued, and the oppression of various segments of the community was made illegal (S. N. Kramer, *The Sumerians: Their History, Culture, and Character* [1963], pp. 317-323). While there may have been even earlier attempts at the reformation of city-state life by enlightened ensis, Urukagina's regulations are the earliest surviving Sumerian ordinances of their kind. They were unparalleled until the time of Ur-Nammu (*ca.* 2070 B.C.), the Sumerian who established the celebrated Third Dynasty of Ur (*ca.* 2070-1960). To demonstrate their importance Ur-Nammu's legal promulgations may well have been engraved originally on imported stone, but all that has survived of his legislation is a fragmentary and barely legible clay tablet made several centuries after he died. A prologue to the laws contains a certain amount of cosmology, a procedure established by the Sumerians apparently to give due authority to their legal pronouncements. The remainder of the text, where legible, refers to regulations aimed at ridding society of unscrupulous merchants, correcting corrupt civic practices, and forbidding the exploitation of the poor by the wealthy (*ANET,* pp. 523-25).

By this period restitution rather than retribution seems to have been favored by the lawgivers of ancient Sumer, and this trend was continued in the social legislation of Lipit-Ishtar of Isin, *ca.* 1850 B.C. His code, inscribed originally on a stele and copied subsequently onto a single large tablet, comprised a prologue, a body of laws, and an epilogue. Although much of the text has been lost, an examination of the extant material indicates that it was

Fragment of the Lipit-Ishtar law code from Nippur dealing with boat rental, orchards, and slaves (University Museum, University of Pennsylvania)

compiled far more systematically than the enactments of Ur-Nammu. The regulations deal with boat hiring, the treatment of orchards and of uncultivated ground, the interaction of masters and slaves, inheritance and marriage, and other social issues. The epilogue invokes a blessing upon those who do not deface the original stele and a curse upon those who do. Other nations later applied this concept to the actual legislation that was being promulgated.

The most formally organized collection of laws in Mesopotamia emerged from the period of HAMMURABI of Babylon (*ca.* 1792-1750 B.C.). Apparently dependent to some extent upon Sumerian precursors, his celebrated code was devised for an urban irrigation culture. Enclosed by a prologue and an epilogue cast in poetic form, the legislative section itself contains nearly three hundred prose paragraphs governing commerce, medicine, marriage, adoption, wages, slavery, property, various crimes, etc. The cases mentioned in the legislation are grouped according to subject matter; for this and other reasons the enactments cannot be considered a code in the modern legal sense (D. J. Wiseman, *Zondervan Pictorial Encyclopedia of the Bible,* III, 24). The court cases of that day seldom if ever reflect Hammurabi's enactments, probably because his laws refer to cases that he personally judged. It is thus incorrect to imply that the laws constitute an ideal lacking in practical application, as W. J. Martin suggested (*DOTT,* p. 28). There are certain points of contact between the legislation and Moses', although it must be remembered that the latter laws were intended to meet the needs of a comparatively simple agrarian culture in Palestine.

Several closely related groups of Hittite laws have been recovered from Boghazköy and deal with the matters prominent in the Hammurabi legislation. Like the Sumerians, the Hittites seem to have based their enactments on court decisions and to have formulated them in writing about the 13th cent. B.C., although there are obvious elements from the time of the indigenous Hatti, more than half a millennium earlier.

From a somewhat later period than the Hittite laws come a group of Middle Assyrian enactments, preserved in a recension from the twelfth-century B.C. Classified or codified law does not seem to have existed as such in ancient Egypt, although various kinds of contractual documents, especially those relating to marriage, have survived from different periods.

Near Eastern legal collections often adopted the style of case law; this pattern is reflected in many Mosaic laws, particularly in those dealing with topics of a similar cultural character. Where Hebrew covenantal legislation is characterized by a prologue and an epilogue, the framework is precisely that of the laws of Lipit-Ishtar and Hammurabi. Mesopotamian prologues and epilogues name the pagan gods to whom the legislation owes its origin and from which the human administrators of the laws derive the authority to impose them. The obvious similarities between early Mesopotamian codes and ancient Hebrew law give a thoroughly historical character to the latter.

These similarities are to be expected when it is remembered that Gen. 1–11 consistently reflects a Mesopotamian culture so virile that it pervaded Near Eastern society for millennia. Traces of this culture appear in the Pentateuch, which in addition to purely legal elements has allusions to religious customs and practices from pre-Mosaic times. These include the offering of sacrifice and the use of altars (Gen. 22:13; 28:18f.; etc.), the religious use of pillars (28:18), purification for sacrifice (35:2f.), tithes (14:20; 28:22), circumcision (17:10; Ex. 4:25f.); inquiry at a sanctuary (Gen. 25:22); sacred feasts (Ex. 5:1; etc.), priests (Ex. 19:22), sacred oaths (Gen. 14:22f.), marriage customs (16:1-6; 24:1-9, 34-67; 25:6; 29:16-30), birthright (25:31-34), elders (24:2; 50:7; Ex. 3:16), homicide (Gen. 9:6), etc.

Archeological evidence from Larsa, Mari, Nuzi, Alalakh, and other sites substantiates the biblical record of Mesopotamian society in the patriarchal period. The roots of Hebrew law and tradition reach far back into the Middle Bronze Age and thus help to account for consonance between Hebrew laws and those of other Near Eastern peoples. Although some writers have attempted to disparage the value of M.B. archeological evidence for demonstrating the history of the patriarchs (e.g., T. L. Thompson, *Historicity of the Patriarchal Narratives* [*BZAW,* 133, 1974], J. van Seters, *Abraham in History and Tradition* [1975]), the validity of the elements to which the writers have objected can be shown by reference to other archeological materials antedating the 15th cent. B.C. These include legal, commercial, and personal documents from various Mesopotamian sites (see D. J. Wiseman and A. R. Millard, eds., *Essays on the Patriarchal Narratives* [1980]; for a survey of criticisms of Thompson and van Seters see E. Yamauchi, *Scriptures and Archaeology* [1980], pp. 3-6). Thus there can be no question as to the reality of the customs and traditions of the pre-Mosaic period that are reflected in books such as Genesis, and no reason to deny the genuine nature of Hebrew law as promulgated under Moses.

***III. Written Records.***–The Sumerian emphasis upon law and order commended itself to various sedentary societies of the ancient Near East, who produced their own legislation, for which, as observed above, there is significant written testimony. But the kind of regulations that governed settled urban communities did not apply in quite the same way to the Hebrew patriarchs, who were seminomadic for the greater part of their history. Thus it is hardly to be expected that they would have felt the need to devise regulations for social conduct that were significantly different from the current traditions of desert life. But certain practices of, e.g., Abraham probably show the cultural influence of his native city, Ur of the Chaldees. Following local custom, Abraham adopted his household steward as his heir when it appeared that he would not have a natural descendant (Gen. 15:2f.). An Old Babylonian contract tablet, recovered from Larsa and dated *ca.* 1800 B.C., testifies to the continuance of this provision for males without expectation of descendants. Abraham's reluctance to expel his slave-concubine Hagar and her son, despite his wife Sarai's insistence (21:10f.), is understandable in the light of Lipit-Ishtar's legislation (cf. § 24) protecting the inheritance rights of all children, including those of concubines. As the patriarchs migrated first toward Syria and then to Canaan, they must have become familiar with the customs and laws of such great cultures as Mari, Nuzi, Ebla, and Alalakh. Yet it was only near the end of Jacob's life, when sedentary settlement in Egypt had become a fact for the Hebrews, that social legislation of the Mesopotamian or Hittite pattern would have become a necessity for them.

There can be little doubt that the Hebrews formulated such legislation during their four centuries or so in Goshen to deal with specific situations and contingencies, much as other ancient Near Eastern peoples had done. Since these circumstances would have matched elements of sedentary life in pagan nations, there would obviously have been degrees of correspondence in the resultant enactments. But significant differences would also have emerged, reflecting the distinctive ethos of these early Hebrews and the revelation of the one true God that they possessed through their ancestors. The members of the Goshen community were descendants of the patriarch with whom God had entered into covenant, and their growing numbers were already in fulfillment of one aspect of that great promissory relationship (Gen. 15:5; 17:2; cf. Ex. 1:7). Even before the time of Moses the Hebrews were familiar with the concept of a covenant deity (Gen. 17:7) who promised a land (v. 8) and protection (15:13f.) in return for the keeping of the covenant stipulations (17:9-14). Still to come were the characteristic emphases upon strict monotheism and obedience to a body of enactments designed to infuse the community with moral and spiritual values as well as to order it.

The ancient Near Eastern practice of recording laws and statutes as occasion necessitated may well have been followed by the Hebrews during their sedentary life in the Goshen region, but there is certainly no independent written form of such laws extant. What is more probable is that certain relevant legislation from that period was incorporated into the laws of Israel after the revelation of the Decalogue at Mt. Sinai. Perhaps some of the material in Ex. 21–23 had its beginnings in the Goshen period and along with other sections was modified somewhat before being incorporated into the corpus of Mosaic law. A Near Eastern precedent for this procedure would have been set by Hammurabi, who included enactments from Lipit-Ishtar and the Amorite king Bilalama of Eshnunna in his code.

Whatever the precise origin of this type of enactment, the "Ten Words" were unquestionably unique to Israel. They were in written form from the beginning of Israel's history as a nation, and the existence of two "tablets" of the law (Ex. 32:15) indicates that one was a duplicate, following the pattern of Hittite international treaties. The "Ten Words" were written "in the writing of God" (v. 16), thus embodying the supreme authority of the God of Sinai, and were engraved in stone, symbolizing their permanence for mankind. Since they were meant to be binding upon every class of humanity that would enter into a spiritual relationship with God, they are just as valid in modern Christian worship as they were in ancient Israel. Modern scholars have described them as positive or categorical prohibitions and have noted that in certain instances the manner of their enforcement has not been predicated.

Certain portions of the Torah were credited specifically to Moses himself, such as the judgment against Amalek (Ex. 17:14), the Book of the Covenant (20:22–23:33), the restoration of the Covenant (34:27, referring to vv. 10-26), an itinerary (Nu. 33:1ff., relating to the source underlying vv. 3-40), and the bulk of Deuteronomy (K. Kitchen, *NBD*, p. 849). The committing of material, particularly historical or revelatory material, to writing completely accords with the ancient Near Eastern scribal practice of recording, generally in annalistic form, important events when they occurred or shortly thereafter. By uniform Hebrew tradition the Torah was always copied out on suitably prepared skins of animals, a contingency that harmonizes completely with the wilderness milieu of the leadership of Moses.

Along with the now thoroughly disproved Wellhausenian notion that writing was only invented *ca.* 1000 B.C. must be dispelled the equally misguided concept of nineteenth-century literary-critical scholars that no individual can possibly combine in himself the abilities to compose historical narrative, to write poetry, and to collate legal material. As Kitchen showed (*NBD*, p. 849), a versatile writer who lived as much as seven centuries before Moses combined the talents of poet, educator, and political propagandist and was most probably the literary stylist of *Satire of the Trades,* which was used as a text in the scribal schools. It is not necessary to suppose, of course, that attributing Mosaic authorship to pentateuchal materials means that Moses wrote out every word. Indeed, at least some of the written sources credited specifically to him could have been dictated to scribes rather than written by his own hand. Quite possibly the presence of third-person pronouns in various parts of the enactments indicates that these sections were dictated. Such sections would most probably have been transcribed by the officials mentioned in Nu. 11:16 (*šōṭᵉrîm*; cf. Akk. *šaṭāru,* "write"), whose literacy would obviously have associated them closely with judicial decisions (cf. Dt. 16:18; 1 Ch. 23:4). If portions of the law were written down as the result of discussions relating to specific social or legal issues, the materials on which the verdicts were recorded would most probably have been committed to the priests or scribes for safekeeping until they could be assembled with related enactments and incorporated into a roll.

The written record of the law should thus be seen most properly against the known background of compilatory and editing practices current in the 2nd millennium B.C. It is highly improbable that a person such as Moses, whose guiding powers touched every aspect of life in the wilderness community, would have had minimal contact with the sacred written regulations by which that community began to be governed, particularly when he was the human agent by which the "Ten Words" were transmitted to Israel. On the contrary, it is only to be expected that the educated and literate leader of the people would have devoted himself assiduously to this fundamentally important regulatory area of national life. Such a concern would have involved not merely the composing of the materials attributed in the text to Moses but also the supervision of and probable participation in some of the editing.

Even when a book was approaching its final form, an editor, whether Moses or someone else, could still have inserted additional relevant legislative or other material where two rolls, presumably of leather, were to be joined.

An example of this may be in Ex. 6, where quite possibly v. 13 marks the end of one roll and v. 28 the beginning of another. Since the genealogy of vv. 14-27 interrupts the continuity of the narrative, it may have been inserted between two rolls. The genealogy is reminiscent of Mesopotamian family trees and ends with a characteristic colophon (v. 26) attesting the scribe or owner of the source ("This is the genealogy of Moses and Aaron," poorly translated both by the RSV, "These are the Aaron and Moses," and by the NEB, "It was this Aaron, together with Moses"). In v. 27 is the scribal dating of the written record to the immediate pre-Exodus period and the concluding statement that the preceding genealogy was that of Moses and Aaron or was written by them. As with the first mention of these two individuals, the English versions confused the issue completely by mistranslation. Since the record was contemporary with Moses and Aaron his brother, Moses might well have been the redactor who inserted a genealogical section, drawn up in familiar Mesopotamian style, at what he considered to be an appropriate point in the historical narrative. That two rolls were joined at that place may be inferred from the similar nature of the material with which one ended and the other commenced, making the second roll able to be read intelligibly yet independently of the first. Such a procedure would have conformed with the literary traditions of both Babylonia and Egypt, where scribes periodically revised and added to literary, liturgical, and other documents (cf. *FSAC*, pp. 79f.). The written record of the law thus proceeds from the life-situation of Israel, not from a pastiche of purely imaginary "documentary sources" such as J, E, and P. Indeed, more than a century of intensive research has failed to uncover any Near Eastern documents, inscriptions, or annals that were compiled according to the literary-critical principles so confidently advocated by nineteenth-century pentateuchal critics.

***IV. Character and Design.***–Whatever the origin and nature of the social customs governing life among the Hebrews before Moses' time, the Exodus from Egypt and the covenant at Sinai provided the formal basis for Hebrew law, making it in effect covenant law. As such it was intended to undergird the entire life of a community chosen above all other nations to exist consciously before God as "a kingdom of priests and a holy nation" (Ex. 19:6). The Hebrews seem never to have conceived of the law as a static entity, however, but rather as a dynamic reflection of the nature and vitality of the divine revelation. Covenantal law could thus be modified and adapted to meet changing situations without serious difficulty, and even the "Ten Words" themselves were not transmitted with complete verbal consonance in the time of Moses, as the slight divergences (cf. Ex. 20:11 and Dt. 5:15; Ex. 20:17 and Dt. 5:21) in the two records indicate.

Ancient Near Eastern covenants were legally binding agreements between equals (parity treaties) or between an overlord and a vassal (suzerainty treaties). Form-critical and other studies have shown the striking parallels in structure between second-millenium-B.C. suzerainty treaties and the records of the covenant in Exodus and Deuteronomy (*see* COVENANT [OT]). These treaties furnish an excellent historical and legal background for studying the way in which the Sinai covenant was formulated and applied (cf. K. Baltzer, *Covenant Formulary* [Eng. tr. 1971], p. xii). The relationships among different types of groups as described in the Mari texts and in the Amarna correspondence support the biblical contention that the concept of covenant existed for centuries before Moses.

The Hittite suzerainty treaty resembles the biblical covenant in several significant ways. The approach to the prospective vassal is made by a victorious king, who in a preamble identifies himself by title as a powerful monarch (cf. Ex. 20:1; Dt. 1:1-5). In second-millennium-B.C. covenants this is always followed by a historical prologue, in which the great king describes his relationships with the proposed vassal's precursors and emphasizes his beneficence toward those bound to him by covenant (cf. Ex. 20:2; Dt. 1:6–3:29). This feature is noticeably absent from the small group of first-millennium-B.C. treaties that have survived, principally from Syria and Assyria, thus demonstrating the antiquity of the model upon which the Mosaic legislation was based. Not merely do first-millennium-B.C. covenants omit historical prologues but, depending upon the country from which they originate, they vary the order of the curses and stipulations and allow them to be either preceded or followed by the witnesses. Even though some of these treaties have survived only in mutilated form, there is no evidence that they once contained historical prologues like those of second-millennium-B.C. Hittite treaties. Nor are they elaborated on anything like the political scale of their precursors of the previous millennium.

After the introductory formalities are completed, the Hittite treaty continues with the basic stipulations that the vassal is required to observe (cf. Ex. 20:3-17, 22-26; Dt. 4:1–11:32). The detailed stipulations that follow explain more fully the nature of the general terms (cf. Ex. 21:1–23:33; 25:1–31:18). Hittite custom required that a copy of the treaty be deposited in the most revered place acknowledged by the vassal (cf. Ex. 25:16; Dt. 31:9, 24-26), so that it would be accessible for public reading once in a generation (cf. Dt. 31:10-13). Suzerainty treaties always include a list of gods who serve as witnesses, headed by deities that the great king reveres. Since OT monotheism precluded this practice, pagan deities were replaced by memorial stones (Ex. 24:4; Josh. 24:27), by the universe (Dt. 32:1), by the song of Moses (31:16–32:47), by the Book of the Law (31:26), and by the recipients of the covenant (Josh. 24:22). Whereas in Hittite international treaties a section of curses and blessings follows the list of witnesses, in the OT the blessings (cf. Lev. 26:3-13; Dt. 28:1-14) and curses (cf. Lev. 26:14-20; Dt. 28:15-68) precede the witnesses. In Dt. 15, as in Hittite treaties, the list of curses for disobedience is considerably longer than that of the blessings for obedience.

Other Hittite-treaty features include a feast to celebrate the ratification of the treaty (cf. Ex. 24:11) and the solemn ceremony of entering into suzerain-vassal relationship (cf. vv. 4-10) or a covenant-renewal rite (Dt. 27:9-26). Finally, there is the provision that the great king can take legal action against a vassal who refuses consistently to honor the obligations of covenant. In the OT this provision takes the form of the "controversy" pattern, by which God proposes to take His people to court for their perfidious behavior (Hos. 12:2; Mic. 6:2; see H. Huffmon, *JBL*, 78 [1959], 285-295; J. Limburg, *JBL*, 88 [1969], 291-304). The biblical use of the Hittite model indicates that it was as familiar to the Hebrews of the 2nd millennium B.C. as to other Near Eastern peoples and makes clear that the Hebrews could never convincingly plead ignorance or lack of understanding for their subsequent violation of the covenant.

Indications of internal design in Hebrew law were postulated by A. Alt, who after studying the Decalogue (Ex. 20:2-17) and the so-called Covenant Code (20:22–23:33) maintained the existence of three principal types of legislation. The first, variously named apodictic or categorical, comprises absolute commands stated positively and negatively. Such prohibitions are generally expressed in the second-person singular and in the future "tense," although the second-person plural and the imperative mood are sometimes used. The style is emphatic, rhythmic, and poetic, and apodictic material is frequently thematic in design, presumably to aid memorization and recitation. This genre is well illustrated by the Decalogue. A second type, described as casuistic or case law, resembles much of the legal material in Mesopotamian enactments. Casuistic laws in the Pentateuch normally commence with a protasis ("if" clause) in which the major issues are introduced by Heb. *kî* and subsidiary ones by *'im* (e.g., Ex. 21:2-6). When the offense has been stated, along with associated matters, the response clause or apodosis enunciates the legal pronouncement. This type of enactment has been seen as representing precedents or decisions in actual cases, whether or not from the pre-Mosaic period. A third type that Alt recognized commences with an active participial form ("a person doing . . .") and ends with the death verdict ("he shall surely be put to death," e.g., Ex. 21:12). Alt held that whereas apodictic law is entirely Israelite in origin and comes from a period when the twelve tribes were still seminomadic, casuistic law is pre-Israelite and was inherited from the Canaanites after the Israelites had conquered the land ("The Origins of Israelite Law," in *Essays on OT History and Religion*, pp. 101-171).

Subsequent investigations by other scholars (e.g., E. Gerstenberger, *Wesen und Herkunft des 'Apodiktischen Rechts'* [1965]) have enlarged the field of study and placed more emphasis on the life-setting of the Hebrew regulations. It was questioned whether the prohibitions can even be regarded as law, since no punishments are listed for violations. Some scholars have thought that apodictic law originated with the family circle, with the clan, with leaders of the community, or with tribal heads, and they have suggested that the pronouncements commencing with a participial form and carrying the death penalty derived from tribal deliberations. Other studies have shown that the design of the law includes regulations of a purely cultic character that were to be followed and taught by the priesthood. Inasmuch as these prescriptions aimed to perpetuate holiness in the community of Israel, they are at the heart of the concept of covenant law and are not to be dismissed as mere ritual.

Studies in Mesopotamian law have shown that the casuistic sections are far less likely to have been borrowed from Canaanite society than from the common traditions of the West Semitic peoples, including the Eblaites. Since Israelite law was commonly administered in the city gate, some of the precedents that the judges followed may well have been based originally on purely local issues. It is now thought improper to regard apodictic law as the product of stern desert mores with no reference to more developed cultures, since such law has been found to be consonant with certain treaties of Hittite origin (R. de Vaux, *Ancient Israel* [Eng. tr. 1961], I, 147). Indeed, the modeling of the Sinaitic covenant on the Hittite suzerainty treaty points to the influence of a contemporary high culture and indicates the suitability of the covenant formulation for desert and urban living alike.

The uniqueness of the Decalogue has already been noted, and whatever the origin of the pre-Mosaic legislative elements of the Torah, the moral and spiritual ethos of Sinai clearly imposed its distinctive imprint upon the legal elements as they were assembled. Because innovative practices were forbidden by books such as Leviticus in favor of strict obedience to the revealed will of God, those who collected and arranged the various legal components were apparently guided by the conservative traditions of the Near Eastern scribes. Any redactional presuppositions would have been strictly consonant with the theology of the Sinai revelation, and any updating or accommodating of material to changed historical or social conditions would have followed the normal practices of second-millennium-B.C. scribes. Thus the postulate that over a lengthy period of time a "school" of editors (or redactors) comprising "country Levites" or others imposed upon social legislation a distinctive theological imprint, such as a supposed Deuteronomic theology, simply cannot be substantiated by what is now known about the processes of scribal transmission in the ancient Near East. In Hebrew tradition, just as much as among the Sumerians, the scribes were guardians of what had been transmitted to them. They were not innovators, and their theology was consistently that of the tradition.

The corpus of Hebrew law contains certain rather obvious sections of legislation that scholars have frequently labeled, though not very satisfactorily, "codes." Five main units are identified by form criticism.

*A. Decalogue.* As observed above, the Ten Commandments occur twice in the Pentateuch (Ex. 20:1-17; Dt. 5:6-21), with slight transmissional variations in Deuteronomy due most probably to the material's being quoted from memory. Since Moses was involved on both occasions, the problems raised by the small differences are clearly not very significant. Much more serious has been the debate over the dating of this material, suggestions ranging from the mid-2nd millennium B.C. to the late postexilic period (cf. H. H. Rowley, *Men of God* [1963], pp. 13ff.), with some radical nineteenth-century literary critics denying any connection between the Decalogue and Moses (e.g., K. Budde, *Religion of Israel to the Exile* [Eng. tr. 1899], p. 32). But in uniform Hebrew tradition the "Ten Words" have always been associated with the work of Moses; they must have originated in the 2nd millennium B.C., since they furnished the moral and spiritual basis for the entire historic covenant relationship between God and the Israelite tribes.

If one uses Hittite suzerainty-treaty categories, the "Ten Words" represent the basic stipulations of the covenant. The fourth and fifth commandments appear as positive commands, but the remainder are strongly negative in form. Suggestions that all the commandments were stated originally in a negative manner simply cannot be substantiated. Equally uncertain is the view that every commandment was originally a very short utterance and that some were enlarged subsequently with glosses. Since monotheism and obedience are at the heart of the Sinai covenant, the second and fourth commandments in particular would have needed from the beginning to be expressed in full form. In such a case it is improper to attribute the slight divergences of the two records of the Decalogue to redactional activity at a considerably later period. It is also most precarious to assume, as some critical scholars have done, that no benefits are promised consequent upon obedience, because again there is no factual evidence that the fifth commandment (Ex. 20:12) ever existed in anything other than its present form. Hittite suzerainty treaties consistently list the blessings that will accrue to the obedient vassal, as Dt. 28:1-14 also does. Quite clearly an arbitrary truncating of the "Ten Words" raises real questions that critical scholars then attempt to solve by artificial means.

Considered as the commencement of a covenant form, the structure of the "Ten Words" is quite primitive. The preamble (Ex. 20:1) introduces God in a brief, unceremonious fashion, while the historical prologue (v. 2) is equally forthright and unpretentious. The basic stipulations (vv. 3-17) are emphatic, authoritarian, and unequivocal, as be-

LAW IN THE OT

fits the nature of apodictic pronouncements. By contrast, the covenant as presented by the book of Deuteronomy, which in itself is a covenant-renewal document, is a much more sophisticated and literary composition, even though it contains precisely the same emphases as the Exodus material. While the Ten Commandments have been interpreted as a moral or ethical code, they were in fact analogous to criminal law in their application to the life of the Israelites. Although the offenses named are predominantly against ethical or moral standards, they must still be recognized as offenses. Whether portions of certain commandments had existed in some form prior to Moses' time can only be speculated. What is certain, however, is that the commandments were given definitive form at Mt. Sinai and became fundamental for all future Israelite religious and community life.

*B. Book of the Covenant.* The Book of the Covenant, popularly regarded by scholars as comprising Ex. 20:22–23:33, corresponds to the detailed stipulations of Hittite international treaties. Quite probably, however, the "Book of the Covenant" that Moses read to the Israelites when the covenant was ratified at Mt. Sinai was only the Decalogue. The material of this book is unquestionably the oldest codified form of Hebrew law and may well have incorporated some pre-Mosaic enactments that had arisen during sedentary life in Goshen. Some may even have reflected community life at Haran in the time of Abraham, thus accounting in part for the correspondences with Mesopotamian legislation.

The life-style presupposed by the laws, while evidently sedentary, is comparatively unsophisticated. As in the Early Bronze Age, wealth was reckoned in terms of cattle and slaves (Ex. 21:20f.), relationships between master and slave were defined carefully (vv. 2-11, 20f., etc.), principles of retaliation and compensation were established (vv. 22-24, 28-32; 22:1-14), agricultural feasts were commanded (23:14-17), and social justice was stressed (22:21-27). Nothing in the legislation demands a life-setting other than the Israelites' lengthy, semisedentary sojourn near Kadesh before their entrance into Canaan. Even the prescribed altars were to be made of earth (20:24), as contrasted with the stone structures of later days.

The Book of the Covenant contains casuistic precedents and apodictic statutes. The historical situation makes it hardly surprising that the categorical prohibitions are like those of the Decalogue. Whatever common tradition of law underlies the enactments, the imprint of the Sinai ethos has very clearly been imposed upon it. Idolatry, bestiality, and unethical behavior are prohibited in favor of obedience to the revealed will of God and a concern for justice, holiness, and mutual responsibility in the community.

Since the legislation constituting the Book of the Covenant could have been amended, revised, or supplemented in very modest ways shortly after the entrance into Canaan, some scholars have dated the corpus *ca.* 1200 B.C. The character of the material, however, suggests that it would hardly have been necessary to introduce significant modifications then, since there were other, more suitable collections of rules and regulations where such changes could have been and probably were made. The Book of the Covenant was not meant to be a comprehensive compilation of laws for the guidance of the covenant community but instead a summary of the most fundamental precepts by which God's people were to live. Quite clearly the Israelites did not need to be in sedentary occupation of Canaan before such rules could be promulgated.

The content of the book has been analyzed as follows: (1) basic instructions for Israelite worship (Ex. 20:22-26); (2) civil legislation (21:1–23:13), dealing with the rights of slaves (vv. 2-11), retaliation (vv. 12-32), property (vv. 33-36), theft, dishonesty, and damage to property (22:1-15), seduction (vv. 16f.), social and religious duties (vv. 18-31), and the protection of rights (23:1-13); (3) regulations for the three major festivals (vv. 14-19); (4) the relationship of God and His covenant people (vv. 20-33).

*C. Dt. 12:1–26:19.* These passages are a comprehensive exposition of the main laws by which the Israelites were to be governed. Some scholars have seen these passages as another code of laws in whole or in part, and liberal writers have attributed them to the 1st millennium B.C. (cf. R. H. Kennett, *Deuteronomy and the Decalogue* [1920]; F. Horst, *Das Privilegrecht Jahves: Rechtsgeschichtliche Untersuchungen zum Deuteronium* [1930]; R. P. Merendino, *Das deuteronomische Gesetz* [1969]). Many thus have denied any direct Mosaic authorship of the material and have contended that Deuteronomy is a recapitulation of Israelite traditions that were compiled about the time of Josiah (640-609 B.C.). But this view is unnecessary if Deuteronomy is viewed as a covenant-renewal document. Obviously Moses wanted to explain the law to Israel at length (Dt. 1:5) because it was material that had been previously delivered to the nation and that by the end of his lifetime had probably been supplemented and modified to some degree. Perhaps 2:10-12, 20-23; 3:9-11, 13b-17 are illustrations of such additions, which are clearly minor. At a ceremonial renewal of the covenant (cf. Josh. 8:32-35; 24:2-27) such changes would have been acknowledged formally as part of the nation's covenant obligations.

Deuteronomy 12:1–26:19 deals with ethical and religious matters, and while holiness is emphasized, humanitarian concerns are also of great importance. Although this section seems to supplement earlier legislation, it also reviews the history and the ideals of the covenant nation. The material may be summarized as follows: centralization of worship (12:1-32); punishment of idolatry (13:1-18); dietary regulations (14:1-29); the poor and the enslaved (15:1-23); three yearly feasts (16:1-17); judges of the people (vv. 18-20); prohibition of pillars (vv. 21f.); penalties for idolatry (17:1-7); administration of justice (vv. 8-13); appointment of a king (vv. 14-20); priests, Levites, and prophets (18:1-22); criminal laws (19:1-21); laws regarding wars (20:1-20); laws dealing with murder, female captives, and the rights of family members (21:1-23); social and moral behavior (22:1-30); laws governing the congregation (23:1–24:22); lawbreakers' punishment, levirate marriage, and commercial rules (25:1-19); first fruits and tithes (26:1-19). It is very doubtful that this material ever circulated as an independent literary unit, if only because it is so fundamental to the structure of Deuteronomy as a whole.

*D. Lev. 17–26.* This section has been described by some writers as a "holiness code" because of its emphasis upon the ritual conditions governing the priesthood, the tabernacle, and the nation of Israel. The jubilee enactments of ch. 25 are somewhat out of harmony with the ideals of holiness expressed in this section, but nonetheless the material's antiquity should not be questioned, as many modern liberals have conceded. Since in the ancient world all priestly materials were early rather than late, the rituals and prescriptions of this section can claim their origin quite legitimately in the Mosaic period.

Some scholars (e.g., L. Horst, *Leviticus 17–26 und Hezekiel* [1881], p. 96; M. Noth, *Leviticus* [Eng. tr., *OTL*, 1965], p. 16; cf. the summary by K. W. Carley, *Ezekiel Among the Prophets* [1975], pp. 62-65) have seen an affinity between the "holiness code" and Ezekiel's writings and accordingly have assigned a postexilic date to the Leviticus material. Ezekiel, however, knew Leviticus well enough to quote it (Ezk. 20:11, 13, 21), an understandable familiarity if he had been trained as a temple priest. Leviticus, with its consistent emphasis upon holiness to the Lord, would have been ideal for his purpose of making the exiles in Babylon repentant. Thus it is rather surprising that he did not quote it even more frequently, especially if the code is an exilic or postexilic product, as liberals have maintained. Lev. 17–26 is so firmly integrated into the book as a whole that it most probably never existed as a separate literary unit but instead formed part of the God-given revelation to Moses governing worship and life in the covenant community.

The "holiness code" can be analyzed as follows: proper use of sacrificial blood (Lev. 17:1-16); religious and ethical laws and penalties (18:1–20:27); rules for priestly holiness (21:1–22:33); consecration of seasons (23:1–24:23); Sabbatical and Jubilee Years (25:1-55); blessings and punishments (26:1-46).

*E. Ceremonial Law.* The ceremonial law, an important part of Israelite life, governed the religious rituals, fasts, and feasts of the community. Because Israel was intended to be a kingdom of priests and a holy nation (Ex. 19:6), the regulations for worship and religious life were specific and exacting. The elaborate rituals governing the consecration of the priests set their own standards of communal holiness, emphasizing implicit obedience to God's commands rather than encouraging innovations, which were subject to severe punishment (cf. Lev. 10:1f.). The elaborate clothing of the priests (*see* Garments VIII; Priests and Levites) was to be worn when they ministered in the holy place (Ex. 39:41); it symbolized "glory and beauty" and is described specifically as "holy" (28:2). Thus in their service of God the priests were intended to be representative of that holiness demanded of the entire community, whether in the days of the tabernacle in the wilderness or in the later period of the temples at Jerusalem. As the spiritual head of the nation, the high priest was required to exhibit a more significant degree of religious purity than other priests (cf. Lev. 21:10-15).

The ceremonies of the offerings and sacrifices were given prominence in the written formulation of Levitical law (Lev. 1-7). The prescribed sacrifices served to gain divine favor and goodwill (1:1-17), to express thanksgiving and to secure divine blessing (2:1-16), to renew fellowship with God in public rejoicing and to secure deliverance from vows (3:1-17; 22:18-30), to purify from sin or defilement (4:1–5:13), or to relieve guilt from offenses involving holy things (5:14-19). The Day of Atonement rituals (16:3-34) were intended to cleanse the entire community annually from sins of omission or inadvertence. All these sacrifices were offered in accordance with ritual provisions, which, to maintain the community holiness that is the intent of all ceremonial law, permitted no deviation (*see* Sacrifices and Offerings in the OT).

Ceremonial law also governed such matters as the annual festivals of Passover and Unleavened Bread (Ex. 12:3-34; Lev. 23:6), Pentecost (Lev. 23:15), and Tabernacles (Ex. 23:16f.; Lev. 23:33-43), as well as the sabbath (Lev. 23:1), the New Moon Festival (Nu. 28:11-15), and periodic communal feasts (cf. Ex. 5:1; Dt. 16:14). Ceremonies such as the circumcising of male children (*see* Circumcision) and the cleansing of lepers (Lev. 14:1-32) and those with bodily discharges (15:13-30) were also the concern of ceremonial law, as were the cultic practices of priests and Levites throughout the history of Hebrew religious life (*see* Worship). The abiding principle undergirding ceremonial law was to preserve the ideal of holiness for the nation as well as to prevent national defilement through adoption of the idolatrous practices of neighboring nations.

*F. Final Formation.* Because of the political and commercial interaction of ancient Near Eastern nations, it is only to be expected that law also would manifest an international character. This has been confirmed by numerous treaty tablets. The Hittite suzerainty and parity treaties have already been mentioned. The use of the second-millennium suzerainty treaty as a model for the Sinaitic covenant indicates that the Hebrews were no strangers to international law. Indeed, they used both treaty forms themselves — the vassal treaty with the Gibeonites (Josh. 9:6-21), and the parity treaty later with the Phoenicians (1 K. 5:1-12), which proved advantageous to both participants.

Precisely how the Torah was finally compiled is open to some conjecture. During the wilderness period the *šōṭ$^{e}$rîm* would doubtless have been active with Moses in recording, collecting, and arranging laws and statutes. Once the corpus of law was in substantially its final form, they would probably have assisted the priests in instructing the Israelites in the law. They also would have maintained annals in the usual Near Eastern manner, written charters (cf. 1 S. 10:25), and attended to court correspondence. Since a significant body of evidence indicates that the Pentateuch was largely complete by Joshua's time, the *šōṭ$^{e}$rîm* would have shared with the priests the responsibility of preserving and transmitting the Torah. Ancient Near Eastern scribal traditions limited the alterations of a received tradition to the updating of grammar and syntax, the inserting of explanatory glosses, and the recording of minor changes in statutes occasioned by a modification of the original conditions for which the enactments had been intended. Wholesale redactional activity of the kind envisaged by some modern scholars was utterly foreign to the conservative training of ancient Near Eastern scribes. For the Hebrews, the formidable emphasis of divine sanction upon the Sinaitic legislation would have been sufficient to preclude any but the most modest professional changes in the content of the Torah.

Some scholarship has commonly misrepresented this situation by implying that the revelation at Sinai was at best rudimentary in its literary form and that over many centuries the material was shaped, reshaped, and edited vigorously when it came into written form at a comparatively late period, usually thought to be exilic or postexilic (cf. A. Alt, pp. 133-171; M. Noth, pp. 6-107; R. H. Pfeiffer, *Intro. to the OT* [2nd ed. 1948], pp. 210-270). So pervasive has this view become that it has even been echoed by conservative writers (e.g., F. C. Fensham, *Illustrated Bible Dictionary,* II [1980], 885). Thus it is important to remember that scribes in the ancient Near East were concerned to perpetuate received traditions with minimal changes.

Preservation of traditional laws, however, did not preclude legal reforms in OT times. Jehoshaphat of Judah (*ca.* 873-849 B.C.) suppressed much pagan worship and appointed men to teach the law of Moses (2 Ch. 17:7-9). He also reorganized the legal system and established a central appeals court in Jerusalem (19:4-11; cf. W. F. Albright, "Judicial Reform of Jehoshaphat," in *Alexander Marx Jubilee Volume* [1950], pp. 61-82). Josiah of Judah (*ca.* 640-609) similarly reformed public worship under the inspiration of an ancient law scroll discovered in the temple (2 K. 22:8-10; 2 Ch. 34:8-18). As G. E. Mendenhall pointed out, current ritual practices were doubtless purified in the effort to return to the principles and practices of ancient Israelite law (*BA,* 17 [1954], 44).

It is clearly wrong, therefore, to see Ezra the scribe, e.g., as an innovating editor, collecting and collating disparate Hebrew legal traditions that had somehow survived the onslaught of the centuries, and shaping them finally into something that could be dignified with the title "law of Moses." Ezra was a professional scribe (Neh. 8:9) and

LAW IN THE OT

thus a member of a group that composed decrees and edicts in various dialects current in Persia and also formulated official court documents in the manner of the Persian scribes (cf. Est. 9:28f.). Since he was deemed skilled in the law of Moses (Ezr. 7:6), he was obviously familiar with an ancient "received" tradition that he would have transmitted faithfully in proper accord with the traditions of his profession. When the law was promulgated in 444 B.C., it was read "clearly" (Neh. 8:8, RSV, NEB; better, "in sections"; cf. *CHAL*, p. 299) and expounded so that the people understood its import thoroughly. It seems precarious to argue from this verse, as has been done, that Ezra was proclaiming his own edition of the Torah with emendations deemed suitable for the occasion. There is no evidence whatever that Ezra instituted new legal prescriptions; on the contrary, he applied what was already known in the law to the situation in Judea, giving special attention to ensuring the purity of cultic ritual and the separation of foreign elements from the returned community. His reforms, therefore, stand very much in the tradition of those undertaken by Jehoshaphat and Josiah.

Ancient Hebrew law did not exhibit the sequential organization or formal design characteristic of modern occidental law. Sometimes the topics under consideration changed so rapidly as to defy any semblance of rationale, while at other times they dealt with spiritual matters that find no place in modern common law. Yet the loving, humane spirit pervading OT law has set a standard for other bodies of social legislation to emulate. Much of its concern, of course, arose from the nature of the covenant community itself. It was meant to function as a brotherhood in which, ideally, there were no poor (Dt. 15:4) and no exploitation of widows, waifs, or orphans. Each would care for the other, and all would be holy to the Lord as they obeyed the civil and ceremonial regulations enacted during the wilderness period. Naturally there were the usual social distinctions, e.g., "master" and "servant," but even servitude for the Hebrews was very different from the slavery elsewhere in the ancient Near East or from modern concepts of slavery. In Israel a manservant could go free after six years of service unless he chose to remain under his master (Ex. 21:2-6; Dt. 15:12-18). Women servants did not have the same liberty, partly to guard them against exploitation, and partly because it would have been virtually impossible for them to survive independently of a household. Nevertheless, their interests were also safeguarded under OT civil law (Ex. 21:7-11; Dt. 15:12).

While the Mosaic legislation ensured justice for all in Israelite society, it paid special attention to the rights and needs of the poor and underprivileged as compared with other ancient Near Eastern enactments, which tended to favor the interests of the rich. The ceremonial or religious law placed its distinctive imprint upon Israelite society by requiring the members of that community to live according to moral and ethical precepts that were foreign to the creeds of other Near Eastern peoples. The holiness of God was thus established among His covenant people both by precept and deed, making it impossible for anyone in the Mosaic period to be unaware of what was involved in the ethic of Sinai. Provision seems to have been made for every contingency in life, and all that was needed for prosperity and safety was implicit obedience to God's commands. When divine holiness was violated, a comprehensive sacrificial system was available by which atonement might be made for sins of omission or inadvertence, and fellowship renewed with God. Under the law there could be no forgiveness for sins done "with a high hand," i.e., in open defiance of known covenantal spirituality (Nu. 15:30). Prescribed feasts and celebrations, although often solemn rituals, allowed the worshiper to express the joy resulting from obeying God's will and to thank Him for the bountiful gifts that He had showered upon His people.

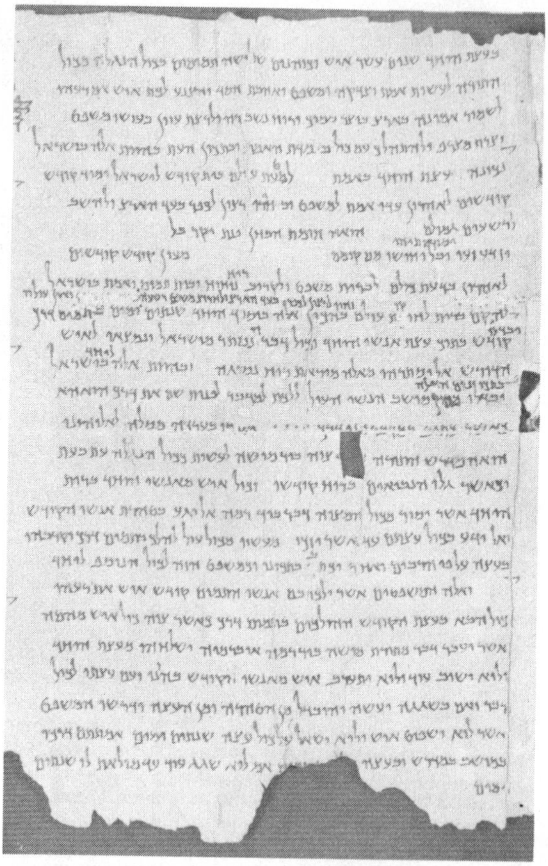

Col. 8 of the Manual of Discipline from Qumrân (1QS) referring to the importance of Torah study and penalties for transgressing the Torah (J. C. Trever)

In all these ways the law functioned supremely as *tôrâ* in the best sense, instructing and guiding the Israelites and sustaining them with the high values of the Sinai covenant. When it was neglected or ignored, the quality of community life in Israel inevitably declined. The pleas of several generations of prophets for the nation to return to the principles of covenantal life as enunciated in the law were desperate, if mostly unavailing, attempts to restore the relationship between God and Israel to the level that had existed intermittently during the wilderness wanderings and the early sedentary occupation of the Promised Land. Because the increasingly disobedient, apostate, and idolatrous nation largely ignored the prophets' pleas, God was compelled to bring upon it the curses promised under the covenant stipulations for a disobedient and disloyal vassal. Though severe, the successive destruction and exile of both Israel and Judah as nations were essentially just, inasmuch as the law had already provided for such punishment. Equally characteristic of God's mercy was that act of renewal by which exiled Judah was brought back and given a second chance to function as a religious community in postexilic Judea, obedient to the leadership of God's priesthood.

*V. Obsolescence.*–Decay is an unavoidable fact of all natural life and therefore of human culture. Most if not all "high" cultures seem to have appeared in their most advanced forms and then to have decayed in a manner consistent with the law of entropy. While periodic revivals may occur in the history of a culture, obsolescence is inevitable. Comprehensive as the Levitical sacrificial system was for dealing with infractions of covenant spirituality, e.g., it was nevertheless deficient in one important respect. As observed above, it made no provision for the forgiveness of anyone who reviled the Lord by defying covenant laws and statutes. Such a provision could have made the Levitical sacrificial tariffs perfect in every way. It would have ensured the continuance of Hebrew sacrifices for atonement and reconciliation and would consequently have made the work of Christ unnecessary.

But even in obsolescence the law was a standard of spirituality (cf. Mt. 5:18), and its abiding principles reappeared in the NT writings, prompting Paul to regard it as a "custodian until Christ came" (Gal. 3:24). The imperfect sacrificial system foreshadowed One who would make a full, perfect, and sufficient sacrifice on Calvary for human sin. The failure of the Hebrew sacrificial system was abundantly evident during the Babylonian exile, when sacrifice of any kind was impossible. The decline of the Levites (cf. Ezr. 2:36-42; 8:15-20, 24-30; Neh. 11:10-18) further indicated the law's gradual eclipse, for the attempt made under Nehemiah to revive the ancient tithing regulations (Neh. 10:38f.) was apparently abandoned at an early stage (cf. Neh. 13:10-13; Mal. 3:8-10). It is unusual that while the law was becoming obsolete the attitude toward divorce became more rigorous than the Torah's (cf. Mal. 2:16; Mt. 19:7-9), as the "Temple Scroll" from Qumrân also shows.

***Bibliography.***–A. Alt, "The Origins of Israelite Law," in *Essays on OT History and Religion* (Eng. tr. 1968), pp. 101-171; W. Beyerlin, *Origins and History of the Oldest Sinaitic Traditions* (Eng. tr. 1965); D. Daube, *Studies in Biblical Law* (1947); Z. Falk, *Hebrew Law in Biblical Times* (1964); F. C. Fensham, *JNES*, 21 (1962), 129-139; F. Horst, *EvTh*, 16 (1956), 49-75; B. S. Jackson, *Theft in Early Jewish Law* (1972); B. N. Kaye and G. J. Wenham, *Law, Morality and the Bible* (1978); M. G. Kline, *Treaty of the Great King* (1963); L. Köhler, *Hebrew Man* (Eng. tr. 1956); N. Lohfink, *Das Hauptgebot* (1963); D. J. McCarthy, *Treaty and Covenant* (rev. ed. 1978); M. Noth, *Laws in the Pentateuch and Other Studies* (Eng. tr. 1966); G. Östborn, *Tōrā in the OT* (1945); S. M. Paul, *Studies in the Book of the Covenant in the Light of Cuneiform and Biblical Law* (*SVT*, 18; 1970); G. von Rad, *Der Heilige Krieg im alten Israel* (1951); *Problem of the Hexateuch and Other Essays* (Eng. tr. 1966); *Studies in Deuteronomy* (Eng. tr., *SBT* 1/9, 1953); D. J. Wiseman, *Vox Evangelica*, 8 (1973), 5-21; comms. on the pentateuchal books.

R. K. HARRISON

## LAW IN THE NT.

- I. Law in the Gospels
  - A. Reaffirmation of OT Law
    1. Christ, the Pharisees, and the Law
    2. The Rich Young Ruler
    3. "Take My Yoke Upon You"
    4. Specific Commandments
       - a. Fourth Commandment
       - b. Fifth Commandment
       - c. Sixth Commandment
       - d. Seventh Commandment
    5. Summary
  - B. Relationship Between Law and Grace
    1. The Pharisee and the Sinful Tax Collector
    2. Law and Prophets until John
    3. "Not Far from the Kingdom"
- II. Law in the Acts of the Apostles
  - A. Jerusalem Council
  - B. Peter and Paul
- III. Law in the Epistles of Paul
  - A. Reaffirmation of the Law
    1. Establishing the Law
    2. Was Paul Antinomian?
  - B. Relationship Between Law and Grace
    1. "By the Law I Died to the Law"
    2. Paul, the Other Rich Young Ruler
    3. Paul and the Pharisees
    4. "Not under the Law"
- IV. Law in Other NT Writings
  - A. Hebrews
  - B. James

***I. Law in the Gospels.***–In the Gospels "law" always refers to the Mosaic law, although it has differing applications. Mosaic law was threefold: moral law, as summed up in the Decalogue; ceremonial law, prescribing the ritual; and civil or political law, relating to the people in their national, political life. The distinctions are not closely observed and generally the whole Mosaic law is meant, although sometimes a certain aspect is emphasized. At times "law" signifies the whole OT (Jn. 10:34; 12:34; 15:25), and at other times the Pentateuch (Lk. 24:44).

Law (Gk. *nómos*) occurs eight times in Matthew, nine in Luke, fourteen in John, and not at all in Mark. Since no certain data exist on which to determine the chronological order of Christ's sayings on *nómos,* the following discussion is topically organized.

*A. Reaffirmation of OT Law. 1. Christ, the Pharisees, and the Law.* As Bergren observed, the "Accusation portion" of the "Judgment Speeches of Amos, Micah, Isaiah, and Jeremiah reveals a correspondence in content to certain Pentateuchal laws" (p. 221), thus demonstrating the prophets' reaffirmation of the laws. So also Christ explicitly reaffirmed the OT law. He emphatically told the disciples that He had not come to abolish the law and the prophets: "For truly, I say to you, till heaven and earth pass away, not an iota, not a dot, will pass from the law until all is accomplished" (Mt. 5:18); "unless your righteousness exceeds that of the scribes and Pharisees, you will never enter the kingdom of heaven" (v. 20). The scribes and Pharisees not only taught the law and required strict conformity to it but also regarded their only hope of salvation as resting upon and resulting from their law-keeping. Christ, the preacher of grace, insisted that, unless His followers kept the law more thoroughly than the scribes and Pharisees, they could not achieve salvation. Christ was not speaking of imputative righteousness, of which the scribes and Pharisees had no notion. Rather, He taught that His disciples must surpass in the realm of moral conduct those who hope to save themselves by their conduct. This is a radical moral equivalent of His apocalyptic utterance in v. 18 that heaven and earth shall pass away before an iota or a dot pass from the law (cf. Mk. 10:18; Lk. 10:25f.).

*2. The Rich Young Ruler.* Christ told the rich young ruler (Mk. 10:17-22) that he would fulfil the law by following Him. The young man's question, however, concerned how to find eternal life. When Christ told him to sell all that he had and he found that he could not, he showed that he valued his money more than God. Thus he demonstrated that he had not even understood the first commandment (which, along with all the others, he thought that he had kept). Christ was not calling to a new way of obedience, but to the old way, which the young man thought he had been practicing all along.

How then does following Christ relate to the fulfillment of the law? Banks correctly observed that Jesus' reference to the law here "is primarily intended as an endorsement of its value as a testimony to . . . the more ethically-demanding and uniquely personal claim which follows"

(p. 164). It seems clear, however, that keeping the law and keeping Christ's commandments are synonymous. Christ said to the rich young ruler, "You know the commandments," and listed some of them as the way by which the young man would achieve his goal. The new commandments that He then gave to him — to sell all that he had, give to the poor, and follow Christ — were mere summaries of the law to love God and neighbor. Thus following Christ is keeping the commandments as a way of life. Since keeping the law of God is the way to eternal life, and keeping the law of Christ is the way to eternal life, the law of God and the law of Christ are identical.

Indeed, there is a kind of advancement on the law of God in one sense: following Christ is more personal than merely following the law of Christ. One law of Christ for the rich young ruler was to sell all and give to the poor. The second law of Christ was to follow Him; whatever He commanded should be obeyed. The law given through Moses was explicit and fixed and seemed complete in itself, although there was subsequent revelation. Christ's more open commandment, "Follow me" (presumably "Follow me and all that I may ever command you"), entails a direct personal relationship in law-keeping, perhaps a relationship implicit in the OT law of God but certainly explicit in the NT law of Christ. The law of Christ does not dispense with the old law or render the Decalogue obsolete but in a sense adds to that law by keeping the followers in constant submission to the continuing disclosure of the will of God in Christ.

*3. "Take My Yoke upon You."* Christ said, "Come to me, all who labor and are heavy laden, and I will give you rest. Take my yoke upon you, and learn from me; for I am gentle and lowly in heart, and you will find rest for your souls" (Mt. 11:28f.). It is agreed that Christ referred to persons chafing under the burdens of the law, but He neither here nor elsewhere delivered them from legal obligations. Rather, by keeping the law as He required they would find peace. Christ's commandments would fit and be suitable even though they were exacting: "For my yoke is easy, and my burden is light" (v. 30).

*4. Specific Commandments.* Christ seemed satisfied with the two-table view of the Decalogue (the first part consists of duties to God, and the second of duties to mankind). When a scribe asked, "Which commandment is the first of all?," Jesus answered, "The first is, 'Hear, O Israel: The Lord our God, the Lord is one; and you shall love the Lord your God with all your heart, and with all your soul, and with all your mind, and with all your strength.' The second is this, 'You shall love your neighbor as yourself.' There is no other commandment greater than these" (Mk. 12:28-31).

To see how Christ interpreted the law in the commandments, we shall consider samples from each table. First, as a sample of the law pertaining to God, we shall study Christ's teaching concerning the fourth commandment, the sabbath. Then, in the second table of the law, we shall consider the fifth, sixth, and seventh commandments.

*a. Fourth Commandment.* Jesus said, "The sabbath was made for man, not man for the sabbath; so the Son of man is lord even of the sabbath" (Mk. 2:27f.). Although many regard this teaching as tantamount to a rejection of the Mosaic law, Christ actually affirmed the sabbath by saying that it was made not just for the Jews, but for mankind, and was made not for one time but for all time, presumably. He observed the sabbath, worshiping and teaching in the synagogue. His conflicts with the scribes and Pharisees concerned His doing good on the sabbath, which He said did not violate the law (3:2; Lk. 13:14).

Since the sabbath was made for people and not vice versa, people cannot determine or use it as they please. It would then cease to be the sabbath and become a day that people, not God, define. Christ was alluding to what the scribes and Pharisees made of the sabbath: a day full of all sorts of regulations, which were very burdensome to conscientious followers of the law. God had not imposed those burdens. He had made the sabbath pleasant; people had made it otherwise. If people form the sabbath in their own image, it does not carry the utility and meaning that Christ attributes to the true sabbath of God. Thus, in this statement that Christians commonly take today as liberating them from sabbatical law, Christ actually bound His followers more tightly to it. It is to be remembered, of course, that God requires man to love mercy as well as do rightly and walk humbly on the Sabbath — that is the law.

*b. Fifth Commandment.* The Pharisees complained that the disciples transgressed the traditions of the elders by eating with unwashed hands. Jesus retorted, "Why do your disciples transgress the tradition of the elders?," citing their ingenious distinction of Corban that evaded and virtually broke the fifth commandment, to honor one's father and mother (Mk. 7:1-13). Again Jesus condemned and corrected the traditional interpretation while upholding the law itself.

In Mt. 8:21f., however, He told a would-be disciple (who simply stipulated, "Lord, let me go first and bury my father"), "Follow me and leave the dead to bury their own dead." Burying a parent would show the respect traditionally required by the fifth commandment. The prohibition in v. 22 would be out of keeping with filial respect unless made by God or a messenger in His name, who alone have the authority to make such a statement in perfect harmony with divine law. The first table of the law takes precedence over the second table: believers' immediate obligations to God are obviously superior to their obligations to Him via respect for fellow human beings (compare Abraham being commanded by God to sacrifice his son, Gen. 22:1-12).

A further application of the fifth commandment concerned the citizen and the state — God and Caesar. Christ's teaching (Mt. 22:17-21 par. Mk. 12:14-17; Lk. 20:22-25) was elicited by a loaded question, "Is it lawful to pay taxes to Caesar, or not?" Christ put the question to rest with a rebuke (v. 18) and an object lesson: He took a coin with Caesar's inscription and said, "Render therefore to Caesar the things that are Caesar's, and to God the things that are God's" (v. 21). Although this famous statement has been seen (by Augustine, Calvin, Erasmus, Grotius, Pufendorf, Witherspoon, Hodge, Stauffer, Shannon, Schnackenburg) as Jesus' endorsement of political authority subordinate to the all-comprehending and all-validating authority of God, others (Brandon, Kennard, Lormbrandt) question that interpretation and wonder whether (or assert that) Christ was implying that obedience and taxes should be withheld from Caesar.

The coin (denarius) that Jesus held served a double purpose: people both used it to pay taxes and worshiped the image of Caesar on it. As often happens, the teacher answered the question asked and went on to answer the unasked but implied question. People should render to Caesar what is Caesar's (cf. Eccl. 8:2, "Keep the king's command") and not render to Caesar what is not Caesar's — worship, which is one of "the things that are God's." Jesus' double purpose thus accomplished, a double rebuke is implied: of the Zealots, who would not render to Caesar what is Caesar's, and of the Herodians, who would not render to God what is God's. Christ's third and implicit rebuke is of those who suppose that Caesar's due is parallel to or independent of God's, for Christ had already informed the devil, "You shall worship the Lord your God and him only shall you serve" (Mt. 4:10).

*c. Sixth Commandment.* Christ's exposition of the sixth commandment seems to have occasioned even more difficulty than His teaching on the fifth. He said, "You have heard that it was said, 'You shall love your neighbor and hate your enemy.' But I say to you, love your enemies and pray for those who persecute you. . ." (Mt. 5:43f.), and this is often considered a reversal of the law of Moses, which supposedly required retaliation and was devoid of the principle of forgiveness and love in dealing with enemies. Jesus, however, was unaware of any such divergence. When He apparently modified Moses' law concerning divorce (Mk. 10:5), He not only frankly acknowledged the alteration but gave the reason for it. Since in Mt. 5:43f. He seemed to reverse Moses in an even sharper manner, it is more likely that modern interpreters have read something into Jesus' pronouncement than that Jesus unknowingly reversed Moses. Jesus had immediately before (according to the arrangement of Matthew) said that He did not come to abolish the law or the prophets (5:17) and made the drastic statement, "Unless your righteousness exceeds that of the scribes and Pharisees, you will never enter the kingdom of heaven" (v. 20). His subsequent statement, "Love your enemies," is cited by these interpreters as illustrating that He did come to abolish the law and His disciples (if they hoped to enter His kingdom) would have to repudiate Moses. Such interpretations are not giving Our Lord much credit for intelligence, sensitivity, or candor.

Moses, moreover, did not demand the inexorable functioning of the law of retaliation. He specifically warned the Israelites, "You shall not take vengeance or bear any grudge against the sons of your own people, but you shall love you neighbor as yourself: I am the Lord" (Lev. 19:17f.). Ex. 23:4f. states, "If you meet your enemy's ox or his ass going astray, you shall bring it back to him. If you see the ass of one who hates you lying under its burden, you shall refrain from leaving him with it, you shall help him to lift it up." Although "an eye for an eye and a tooth for a tooth" is the very principle of perfect justice, OT law was not a stranger to forbearance or unaware of the principle of returning good for evil (cf. Job 31:29; Ps. 35:12f.; Prov. 24:17), and nothing forbade the individual's foregoing some of his rights. Any momentary violence thus done to the law will be rectified by the Judge of all the earth who cannot do wrong.

Christ therefore took exception not to Moses but to what "was said to the men of old" (Mt. 5:21, 33) or simply to what "was said" (vv. 27, 38), a well-known way of referring to rabbinic traditions (in contrast to references to Scripture, introduced by "it is written"). Christ rejected those who rejected Moses, not Moses himself. He exposed the commentators who misrepresented Moses, restoring the lawgiver to his pristine position.

So far was Christ from abolishing the sixth commandment that, if anything, He intensified it. In contrast to the Pharisees and others who supposed a person to be "blameless" with regard to the law (Phil. 3:6) if he had not killed a person, Christ taught that the sixth commandment is first broken in the heart. "But I say to you that every one who is angry with his brother shall be liable to judgment; whoever insults his brother shall be liable to the council; and whoever says, 'You fool!' shall be liable to the fire of hell" (Mt. 5:22). The AV addition "without a cause" after "every one who is angry" is not supported by the best MSS, but its connotation is supported by the best interpreters, for Christ could not oppose all anger while indulging in it Himself (Mk. 3:5). The point of the text is that the law equates unjustified anger (and even more, insults and hatred) with murder.

*d. Seventh Commandment.* Christ's handling of the seventh commandment, "you shall not commit adultery," followed the same pattern as that of the sixth. Far from repealing the commandment, He intensified it: "I say to you that every one who looks at a woman lustfully has already committed adultery with her in his heart" (Mt. 5:27f.). Adultery, like murder, begins in the heart and exists there whether or not it reaches the bodily act.

In one passage, however, the pericope of the woman taken in adultery (Jn. 7:53–8:11 in some MSS), Jesus seems to some to have set aside the law of Moses completely. Although late and noncanonical, the pericope has many marks of historical authenticity. In Jesus' time persons were still put to death for adultery. Two accusers, who had caught an offender or the offenders in an act indisputably adulterous, were needed to establish the indictment. The scribes and Pharisees tested Jesus' adherence to Mosaic law by asking His judgment on this case.

What is most impressive is that Christ answered the question in a proper legal manner. Perceiving immediately that the witness had, no doubt, been stationed in a place where this suspected crime might occur, He sensed malice and not objectivity in their testimony. He no doubt also noticed the absence of a husband's concern for his erring wife. All of this was contrary to the actual OT regulations concerning such an offense and its litigation.

When Christ said, "Let him who is without sin among you be the first to throw a stone at her" (Jn. 8:7), He was appealing to the legal requirement that accusers be without fault in a matter so serious as this one. Since the legal requirements were not met, He said, "Neither do I condemn you" (v. 11). Not being a witness to the actual crime, he did not accuse the woman either.

No doubt the main reason that the Church has seriously questioned this episode is that it has usually been construed (e.g., by Augustine) as meaning that Christ disregarded the law and forgave when punishment was required. Of course the Lord of the law could have repealed the legislation, but there is no evidence here that He did so; He vitiated the biased judgment because the law was not being strictly observed. He did not Himself forgive the woman but simply refrained from condemning her. Christ's statement "Go, and do not sin again" (Jn. 8:11) contains an implied accusation but no forgiveness because no sin was confessed.

"Let him who is without sin among you be the first to throw a stone at her" (Jn. 8:7) cannot mean that Church disciplinary law requires perfection in its administrators. If Christ had meant that, He would have denied His own clear requirements. His very imperfect apostles, who were taught to pray confessing their debts (Mt. 6:12), were also to "bind" and "loose," "retain" and "forgive" sins (16:19; 18:18; Jn. 20:23), and to treat the unforgiving sinner "as a Gentile and a tax collector" (Mt. 18:17). Christ warned His disciples against trying to remove all who offend (13:36-43), since if only the sinless could discipline, all discipline would be eliminated.

Another passage is taken by many to mean that Jesus was less concessive than Moses. It seems to them that Christ's teaching on adultery in Mk. 10:11 (that those who remarry after divorcing commit adultery) rules out all divorce and thus repeals Moses' permission. The fuller statement in Mt. 5:32, however, "But I say to you that every one who divorces his wife, except on the ground of unchastity, makes her an adulteress; and whoever marries a divorced woman commits adultery," may be the general equivalent of the Mosaic law.

The fundamental OT law in Ex 20:14 states, "You shall not commit adultery." "Adultery" in law courts commonly refers to intercourse between a married person and someone who is not his or her spouse. But the OT prohibits other sexual irregularities also, which presumably the commandment would prohibit. The question, then, is whether Jesus meant by "unchastity" (*moicheía*) more than the technical term "adultery."

Moses' permission to divorce (Dt. 24:1) appears to be a divinely permissible punishment for a violation of the seventh commandment. That is, if a person committed adultery ("some indecency"), that person could be legitimately divorced by the innocent spouse. The innocent party's divorce and subsequent remarriage would not constitute adultery but would be a proper consequence of adultery and suitable punishment for the adulterous spouse.

But what of "for your hardness of heart Moses allowed you to divorce your wives" (Mt. 19:8)? Ideally (from "the beginning," i.e., of the institution of marriage) marriage should be indissoluble. Forgiveness could heal the broken bond that hardheartedness made permanent through divorce. Christ, true to OT law, stated the ideal in Mt. 19:5f. and the nonideal but legal in 5:32 ("except on the ground of unchastity") and 19:9, just as Moses stated the ideal in Gen. 2:24 and the nonideal but legal in Dt. 24:1f.

The seventh commandment seems to parallel the sixth ("You shall not kill"). The punishment for killing a person is to be killed; the second killing is legitimate and does not violate the sixth commandment. On the contrary, it is the required punishment for violation of the commandment (cf. Ex. 21:12). Analogously, if a married person destroys marriage by committing adultery, that spouse may be destroyed (with regard to marriage) by the divorce and remarriage of the innocent party. There would, properly speaking, be no stigma either on the innocent person who divorces or on the person who executes a killer. Our Lord seems to be perfectly consistent with this pattern of thought by His exceptive clause in Mt. 5:32; 19:9. (Note, too, that the exception to the law of capital punishment, the cities of refuge [Nu. 35:6f.], compares to the exception to indissolubility in marriage law.)

Christ's handling of the seventh commandment followed the same pattern as that of the sixth. Far from repealing either commandment, he intensified them, for adultery, like murder, begins in the heart and exists there whether or not it reaches the bodily act.

*5. Summary.* Christ's affirmation of the moral law was complete. Rather than setting His disciples free from the law, He tied them more tightly to it. He abrogated not one commandment but instead intensified all, as has been shown. He did not condemn the scribes and Pharisees for tithing mint and anise but for neglecting the weightier matters of the law — justice, mercy, and faith (Mt. 23:23). To be sure, they added some things that did not belong to the law to make themselves look more zealous for the law, but Christ showed that their zeal was for their own traditions, not for the law of God. Not one iota or dot did, indeed, pass away from the law until it was all fulfilled in Christ. Anyone who would come after Him could not expect the slightest diminution of legal demand: "You, therefore, must be perfect, as your heavenly Father is perfect" (5:48).

Christ fulfilled the moral law by obeying it and showing its intense spirituality, thus establishing it on a surer basis than ever as the eternal law of righteousness. He fulfilled the ceremonial and typical law not only by conforming to its requirements but by realizing its spiritual significance. He filled up the shadowy outlines of the types so that they could pass away; believers no longer must observe the Passover or slay the daily lamb, for they have the substance in Christ. He also cleared the law from the traditional excrescences that had gathered around it under the hands of the rabbis (Mt. 5:11; Mk. 7:18-23). He taught His disciples those great principles when, after His resurrection, "beginning with Moses and all the prophets, he interpreted to them in all the scriptures the things concerning himself" (Lk. 24:27) and declared, "These are my words which I spoke to you, while I was still with you, that everything written about me in the law of Moses and the prophets and the psalms must be fulfilled" (v. 44). John sums this up in the pregnant phrase, "The law was given through Moses; grace and truth came through Jesus Christ" (Jn. 1:17). Grace was in contrast to the condemnation of the moral law, and truth was the antithesis of the shadowy outlines of the types and ceremonies.

As for the relation of NT law to OT law there seems to be only a question of how much of the old is continued in the new. Christian theologians generally agree that all of the moral and none of the ceremonial laws are continued, the latter having been fulfilled. How much of the civil-political law continues is the issue. According to contemporary theonomists (Rushdoony, Bahnsen), all of it continues in force (Mt. 5:17) as to equity (essence) with appropriate casuistical modifications (railings required around flat roofs in the OT now required around backyard swimming pools). Most Christian ethicists contend only for some continuation (Murray, Henry, Kline), excommunication, for example, being the NT discipline for adultery, which was punished by death according to the OT law. The theonomic case has not yet received a sound literary refutation.

*B. Relationship Between Law and Grace. 1. The Pharisee and the Sinful Tax Collector.* Probably Christ's clearest indication of the relation between law and grace is in the parable of the Pharisee and the tax collector (Lk. 18:9-14) and in the narrative of Zacchaeus's conversion (19:1-10). Commenting on the sinful tax collector who could not even lift his eyes to heaven but could only beat his breast and ask God to be merciful to him a sinner, Christ remarked, "I tell you, this man went down to his house justified rather than the other; for every one who exalts himself will be humbled, but he who humbles himself will be exalted" (18:14). God heard the prayer of the tax collector who broke the law but not that of the Pharisee who apparently had kept it scrupulously (v. 11). Christ did not say that the Pharisee was not justified though he kept the law. The point is, rather, that the Pharisee was not, by his very spirit, keeping the law as he claimed, while the tax collector, recognizing the truth about himself and confessing it, was forgiven. The parable does not say that the tax collector began a true and spiritual keeping of the law, but in the historical incident of Zacchaeus, the tax collector was justified when he went down to his house and immediately began to return fourfold all that he had extorted in his earlier law-defying days (19:8).

*2. Law and Prophets until John.* Luke 16:15-17 is particularly significant in showing Jesus' conception of the relation between the law and His kingdom. The people of Jesus' time who were considered exemplary law-keepers (the scribes and Pharisees) actually loved money instead of God and mankind (v. 15). In the central text, v. 16, where Christ said that the law and the prophets continued until the time of John but that He introduced the kingdom of God and everyone entered it violently, He did not hint that the law would cease to exist (though the scribes and Pharisees would have considered the law to have ceased when followers of Jesus entered the kingdom). Luke used v. 15 as a preface to prevent people from jumping to that wrong conclusion from v. 16. Verse 16 contains no antithesis between the law and prophets and Christ; Christ opposed only the wrong exponents of the law, not the law itself.

But what did Christ mean by saying that the law and the prophets were until John the Baptist and that He introduced a new dispensation? The preceding verses indicate a difference of degree and not kind — a newer fulfillment of the old dispensation rather than a different dispensation. Lk. 16:17 reiterates what Christ said in His Sermon on the Mount, that not a dot shall disappear from the law until all is fulfilled, even when people violently entered the kingdom. One can see how Luke would need to assert immediately after v. 16 that the comparison of Christ's kingdom with the law and the prophets was not to be construed as an opposition to the continuance of the law.

In Lk. 16:18 Christ gave an example of what He meant by the continuation of the law: the law of divorce is tightened rather than loosened in His kingdom. Clearly a person's faith in Christ establishes his relationship with God but also involves the most rigorous kind of law-keeping. Here again Christ was obviously not abolishing the law; rather, He reaffirmed and implemented it by His own authority as Lord of the kingdom.

Although Christ represented Himself as above the law, He still observed it. Thus He told John the Baptist, "It is fitting for us to fulfil all righteousness" (Mt. 3:15). He received baptism, even though He did not need it, because the law required it. Likewise, He paid the temple tax although He did not need to do so, as He showed by paying with unearned shekels taken from a fish's mouth (17:24-27). He told those whom He healed to present themselves to the priest, in fulfillment of the legal requirements (Lk. 17:14; Mt. 8:4).

*3. "Not Far from the Kingdom."* Christ's comment to the lawyer (Mk. 12:34), that he was not far from the kingdom, is interesting in its bearing on this point. The lawyer had asked who was his neighbor and Christ had given His classic answer (the parable of the Good Samaritan). The lawyer could recognize the meaning of the law, for he accepted and approved a sound interpretation of it. Christ said, however, that he was not far — implying that he was not yet in the kingdom — apparently because the young man understood but had not committed himself to the practice of the law or, perhaps, did not apply his accurate understanding to his own situation. The experience may be parallel to John Wesley's believing that Christ was the Savior of the world before accepting Him as his personal Savior.

***II. Law in the Acts of the Apostles.***–*A. Jerusalem Council.* The Jerusalem Council is a cue to the law in the early Church. According to Acts 15:21, in the Jewish synagogues of the Diaspora there was already fellowship and worship with the uncircumcised. Similar fellowship in a mixed congregation of Jewish and gentile Christians could be defended before the Jewish world if gentile Christians accepted the conditions of the Jerusalem Council's decree. The obligation of the law was not restricted to these points for Jewish Christians, but they could engage in fellowship with Gentiles who accepted these points without giving offense to the Jews and still be consistent with the teaching of Christ. The question has been raised whether this attitude in the Church came from Jesus' teaching or whether His teachings were based on the prevalent attitude among Jews. Gutbrod has rightly argued that it derived from Jesus' teachings (*TDNT,* IV, 1069).

*B. Peter and Paul.* Peter's strict observance of the ceremonial law was shown in connection with his vision, which taught him that the grace of God may pass beyond the Jewish pale (Acts 10). Paul's preaching emphasized the fulfilling of the Scriptures, both law and prophecy, by Jesus Christ. The gist of his message, as given in his first reported sermon, is, "By him every one that believes is freed from everything from which you could not be freed by the law of Moses" (13:38f.). The conversion of the Gentiles brought up the question of their relation to the ceremonial law, specifically to circumcision. The Jerusalem Council decided that circumcision was unnecessary for Gentiles and only enjoined them to abstain from things strangled and from blood, according to the Mosaic ritual (ch. 15). The subsequent events showed that this provision was for the time of transition. Paul, though strongly opposed to the idea of imposing circumcision on the Gentiles, nevertheless, without inconsistency and as a concession to Jewish feeling, circumcised Timothy (16:3) and himself fulfilled the ceremonial enactments in connection with the taking of a vow (18:18). Following the advice of James, who wished him to conciliate the myriads of believing Jews who were zealous for the law, and to show them the falseness of the charge that he taught the Jews among the Gentiles "to forsake Moses," Paul also ceremonially purified the "four men that have a vow on them" (21:20-26). Paul's offering the required sacrifices showed that for the Jews the sacrificial system remained in force. The sequel to the transaction might raise the question whether, after all, the procedure was a wise one; it certainly did not fulfil the expectations of James. In his defense before Felix, Paul claimed that he was loyal to the Jewish faith, worshiped in the temple, and believed "everything laid down by the law or written in the prophets" (24:11-14). In his address to the Jewish leaders in Rome he declared that he had "done nothing against the people or the customs of our fathers" (28:17) and sought to persuade them concerning Jesus "both from the law of Moses and from the prophets" (v. 23).

***III. Law in the Epistles of Paul.***–The major development of the NT concept of law is found in the writings of Paul. Like Christ, he reaffirmed the law and explicated the relationship between law and grace.

*A. Reaffirmation of the Law.* Paul employed the word law (Gk. *nómos*) in various ways. He used it for the whole OT law but also (Rom. 7:7; 13:8f.) for the Decalogue. Like Christ, Paul sometimes used it for the Torah and sometimes for the Pentateuch. The law is holy, just, and good (Rom. 7:12), though it is the occasion of sin (v. 13).

*1. Establishing the Law.* Paul's basic principle was that Christ is not the negation of the law, but the fulfillment of it. Gal. 2:21 is especially significant: "If justification were through the law, then Christ died to no purpose." Paul was as emphatic as Christ in reaffirming that the law was established, not abolished, by faith. "How can we who died to sin still live in it?" he asked (Rom. 6:2; cf. 1 Cor. 6:9; Gal. 5:19-21). He showed that grace leads again to law (see III.B below). "Are we to continue in sin [violating the law] that grace may abound? By no means!" he said (Rom. 6:1f.). Not continuing in sin is not, however, the same as standing in the law and boasting of virtue (Gal. 3:10), which is what he and his fellow Jews had been doing (Phil. 3:5f.). The Christian lives in obedience to the law, not in merit from it. It was the fatal error of Paul's kinsmen after the flesh, the Jews, to think that they could establish their own righteousness (Rom. 10:1). They were mistaken not in keeping the law but in supposing that they were when in fact its meaning had not even come home to them (7:9; cf. Gal. 3:10).

Some think that Paul said that what the Jewish specialists in revealed law could not do, the pagans who knew only natural law did do (Rom. 2:14). But when Paul said, "Gentiles . . . do by nature what the law requires," he did not mean that they see God and do good (v. 14). Otherwise he could never have written in 3:10f.: "None is righteous, no, not one . . . no one seeks for God. . . . No one does good, not even one." What he meant in 2:14 was that the heathen even apart from revelation show by their actions that they are conscious of a "law written in their hearts," not that these actions successfully fulfil the moral demands of the law.

Paul's point was that the Jews were destroying the law in which they boasted while he was establishing what they accused him of destroying. They destroyed the law by misinterpreting it, thereby crediting it with doing what it cannot do and preventing it from doing in them what it was designed to do. He bore witness to their zeal in all this (Rom. 10:1) but not to their wisdom, for he once suffered from the same error (Phil. 3:3f.). The whole Christian way (not Jewish way) is "in order that the just requirement of the law might be fulfilled in us" (Rom. 8:4).

*2. Was Paul Antinomian?* Gutbrod saw Paul's end result as subtly antinomian: "No longer whatsoever is not of the Law, but whatsoever is not of faith, is sin, R. 14:23" (*TDNT,* IV, 1077). If this were so, Paul could not have exclaimed: "Do we then overthrow the law by this faith? By no means! On the contrary, we uphold the law" (Rom. 3:31). In 14:23, Paul did not replace the law with faith as the code for conduct. So far was Paul from negating the law that he would not allow Christians to act in cases where the teaching of the law seemed unclear unless they believed that the law favored their course of action, because "whatsoever is not of faith, is sin" (v. 23).

*B. Relationship Between Law and Grace. 1. "By the Law I Died to the Law."* Probably the finest NT statement of the normative use of the law is in Gal. 2:19, "I through the law died to the law" (Gk. *diá nómou nómǭ apéthanon*). Paul meant that the law became his teacher to lead him away from itself to the Savior. When he fully comprehended the law's meaning (Rom. 7:9), he realized what a violator of it he actually was and died to it as the meritorious ground of salvation. Accordingly, he asked the Galatians, "Tell me, you who desire to be under the law, do you not hear the law?" (4:21). People think they live by the law, which actually condemns them, because they do not hear it.

*2. Paul, the Other Rich Young Ruler.* There is an interesting contrast between the rich young ruler (Mt. 19:16-30) who was not converted and the rich young ruler Saul, who was converted to become the Apostle Paul. Both of them were "as to righteousness under the law" blameless (Phil. 3:6; cf. Mt. 19:20). The rich young ruler, however, seems to have had misgivings that brought him to Jesus in search of eternal life, although presumably he should have felt (as Saul apparently did) that he was on the way to securing it. The young ruler was offended by Christ's remark directing him back to the very law from which he was turning. But when Christ advised him to give up all that he had and follow Him, the rich young ruler turned away sorrowing and presumably went back to his old ways, cleaving to his fortune (which was shown to be his true god) and violating the law. In contrast, the rich young ruler Saul came to consider all that he had achieved under the law as worthless and prized only what he found in Christ (Phil. 3:8). Paul died to the law while the rich young ruler was simply troubled by it. Paul passed from serene confidence to a shattering disillusionment with the law as a scheme of salvation, whereas the rich young ruler seemed never to have had either the total confidence or the complete disillusionment; he did not die to the law, but continued to die in it.

*3. Paul and the Pharisees.* According to the Pharisees, people can do what they will and thus can keep the law. For them, the law is all that one needs for a godly life. It was the Jews' particular advantage to have such direction. But Paul realized after his encounter with Christ that the law was only pointed to salvation; Christ is the fulfillment and incorporation of the law and He alone can enable a person to fulfil it.

The mistake of the Pharisees, in Paul's opinion, was overlooking the "second use" of the law, the pedagogical. If one understands the law correctly, it becomes a tutor to bring him to Christ (second use) and Christ becomes the power to fulfil the law (third use). As Drane has seen in Gal. 3:24, "by trying to gain salvation by their own efforts at keeping the Law, men realized that it was an impossible task, and so the way was prepared for God's act of grace in Jesus Christ" (pp. 137f.). But the coming of the Savior did not liberate Paul from the law, but to the law. In fact, for the first time he was able to keep it (cf. Rom. 8:1f.). As R. Bring (p. 22) observed, the Israelites did not understand first that the law was given because of sin, and second that righteousness was to come by promise (Rom. 3:31).

The Pharisees' erroneous interpretation of the law rested on an erroneous view of mankind. They regarded the fall of Adam as simply the first example of a person deciding wrongly; people can still live correctly after the fall if guided by the law. But Paul realized that mankind is in no position to fulfil the law. Nor did faith, for him, presuppose a power to fulfil all the requirements of the law, for a believer was free from the law. In fact, faith itself is the gift of God (Eph. 2:8).

Faith justifies because it means participation in Christ who has fulfilled the law and brought righteousness (Gal. 3:11). Paul contrasted (v. 12) righteousness by the law and righteousness by faith, but believers achieve the latter by Christ's fulfillment of the law, whereas the former is the supposed righteousness of people who trust in themselves. The person who thinks that he can effect works-righteousness does not really hear the law, Paul insisted. Nevertheless, faith-righteousness does not abandon law-righteousness, which is simply placed in Christ rather than the individual. Those who are in Christ really fulfil the law (Rom. 8:4).

R. Bring sees all this very clearly. The one thing that eludes him seems to be that for Paul, Christ fulfilled the law, so that the disciples who live in Him actually fulfil the law (cf. Rom. 4:5; 8:1f.). The way of faith is the way of fulfilling the law, not a substitute for fulfilling it. Bring cited 8:1 to show that the law judges, but for those who are in Christ Jesus there is no judgment, so that the law is overcome for them (p. 28). But he did not seem to realize that the law is overcome because Christ has satisfied it and believers are victors because they actually have overcome in Christ. Believers are free from the law because they in Christ have satisfied it; they no longer stand under it but live in the Spirit.

The Pharisees believed that people by their own willing could fulfil the law; Paul entertained no such notion. But he did not deny "free will" in another sense. People "freely" accept Christ, who gives them His own righteousness, which they could never achieve by "free will." But free will is not to be confused with the ability to earn righteousness by keeping the law. Of course, earning righteousness would involve free will; but, the will can be free without having the ability to earn righteousness (which only Christ could merit). People, as Augustine taught, could be "free" to disobey and disbelieve without being "freed" to accept Christ's fulfillment of the law.

*4. "Not under the Law."* Galatians 5:18, "But if you

are led by the Spirit you are not under the law" (cf. Rom. 6:14), sets forth both of Paul's emphases: confirmation of the law and the relationship of the law to grace. In Gal. 5:17 Paul showed that the "flesh" prevents the Christian from doing "what you would"; he enumerated the "works of the flesh" (v. 19) and warned, "Those who do such things shall not inherit the kingdom of God" (v. 21). Although Christians feel the flesh's frustrating presence, they cannot be brought under it entirely to do only the "works of the flesh." The law is confirmed, therefore, because Christians bring forth some of the "fruits of the Spirit" and eschew some of the works of the flesh; their inclination to the good fruits and disinclination to the fleshly works honor the continuing law. They are not "under" the law, however, for then a single failure would destroy them totally. As Paul reminded the Galatians: "It is written, 'Cursed be every one who does not abide by all things written in the book of the law, and do them'" (3:10).

*IV. Law in Other NT Writings.*–While the remainder of the NT is not so full in its treatment, it seems to follow the pattern of teaching found in Christ and Paul.

*A. Hebrews.* The word "law" occurs fourteen times in this epistle and a great deal of attention is given to the subject, but it is generally the law in its ceremonial and typical aspect that is in question.

The ancient doubt about Paul's authorship of the epistle seems today to have become certainty that Paul did not write it, although the grounds for a conclusion are no stronger than formerly. In their desire to prove the non-Pauline authorship, scholars perhaps overemphasize the supposed un-Pauline character of the teaching. There is, after all, profound harmony between the teaching of the Pauline Epistles and the teaching of Hebrews, including harmony between their teachings on the law. Although Paul stressed the moral law in Romans, in Galatians and elsewhere he dealt with the ceremonial law in much the same way, though not so fully, as the writer to the Hebrews. Such utterances as "for Christ, our paschal lamb, has been sacrificed" (1 Cor. 5:7), "the rock was Christ" (1 Cor. 10:4), "now these things are warnings for us" (v. 6), and "these are only a shadow of what is to come; but the substance belongs to Christ" (Col. 2:17) are exactly in line with the teaching of Hebrews.

The author of Hebrews showed how the law, which was a word spoken through angels, is transcended by the gospel, which has been spoken by the Lord of the angels and so demands greater reverence (He. 2:2-4). It is the transcendent glory of the gospel dispensation introduced by Christ and ascribed to Him, that shines throughout the epistle.

The author dealt specifically in He. 7 and 8 with the law of the priesthood, showing that Christ's Priesthood, "after the order of Melchizedek," is more glorious than the Aaronic priesthood under the law and not only surpasses but supersedes it. The imperfect gives place to the perfect, the shadowy to the real, the earthly to the heavenly, the temporal to the eternal. As Paul supported his doctrine of justification apart from the deeds of the law by referring to OT teaching, so the writer of Hebrews found in the OT prediction of the New Covenant the basis for all his reasoning. His reference to the description of the New Covenant indicates that both he and Paul saw the moral law as now written on the heart and as becoming an internal power rather than an external precept.

He next dealt with the law of the sanctuary, considering the law of the sacrifices (He. 9–10). He showed that Christ's one, all-perfect, eternal sacrfice replaced the many imperfect temporary sacrifices offered under the law. At the best the law had "a shadow of the good things to come" (10:1). The shadow was useful for the time being, and the people were greatly privileged in having it, for it directed them to the great Figure who cast the shadow. The whole ceremonial system really had a system of grace at its heart. The sacrifices themselves could not take away sin, but provisional forgiveness was conveyed through them by virtue of their relation to the coming One. The great sacrifice, having been offered, secured eternal redemption, obtained perfect forgiveness, assured free access into the heavenly holy place, and provided the eternal inheritance. Christ's Spirit-taught servants now made fully known the great truth indicated by Christ Himself. Christ, who "is the end of the law, that every one who has faith may be justified" (Rom. 10:4), is also the end of the ceremonial law, the full realization of all its types and shadows.

*B. James.* In James the relationship is between faith and works, not faith and the law as in Paul (though the works are the works of the law). What has often been taken in James to be justification by works of the law versus justification by faith turns out to be a "justification" by works identical with "justification" by faith. "Show me your faith apart from your works, and I by my works will show you my faith" (Jas. 2:18). He used Abraham's willingness to sacrifice his son in obedience to God as demonstrative evidence — by works — of faith. Abraham's works justified his faith, but faith justified Abraham himself. That this is the Pauline doctrine is strikingly confirmed by their common proof-text, "Abraham believed God, and it was reckoned to him as righteousness" (Gen. 15:6), cited by James (2:23) and Paul (Rom. 4:3).

***Bibliography.***–G. Bahnsen, *Theonomy in Christian Ethics* (1977); R. Banks, *Jesus and the Law in the Synoptic Tradition* (1975); F. Baumgärtel, *Verheissung: Zur Frage des evangelischen Verständnisses des AT* (1952); K. Berger, *Die Gesetzesauslegung Jesu* (1972); R. V. Bergren, *The Prophets and the Law* (1974); R. Bring, *Christus und das Gesetz* (1969); J. D. M. Derrett, *Law in the NT* (1970); J. W. Drane, *Paul: Libertine or Legalist?* (1975); P. Fairbairn, *Revelation of Law in Scripture* (1869); C. F. H. Henry, *Christian Personal Ethics* (1957); B. Kaye and G. Wenham, eds., *Law, Morality, and the Bible: A Symposium* (1978); E. F. Kevan, *The Grace of Law* (1964); M. G. Kline, *WTJ*, 41 (1978), 172-189; J. Murray, *Principles of Conduct* (1957); R. Rushdoony, *Institutes of Biblical Law* (1973); M. J. Suggs, *Wisdom, Christology, and Law in Matthew's Gospel* (1970); *TDNT*, IV, *s.v.* νόμος (Kleinknecht, Gutbrod); W. Vischer, *Witness of the OT to Christ* (3rd ed. 1936, Eng. tr. 1949).

J. H. GERSTNER

**LAW, JUDICIAL.** The form of divine law that, under the dominion of God the supreme Judge, directed the policy of the Hebrew nation (only). The position of Yahweh as Supreme Ruler was made legally and permanently binding by formal agreement of the amphictyony of the twelve tribes (Ex. 19:3-8; 24:3-8), who clearly understood the terms involved. This covenant between Yahweh and the people was renewed annually (Josh. 8:30-35) so that there would be no question about the matter.

As G. E. Mendenhall pointed out (*Law and Covenant in Israel and the Ancient Near East* [1955]) the stipulations of this covenant seem to have some connection with the vassal treaties of the ancient Near East. The people were to acknowledge Yahweh as Founder of the nation, Sovereign, Ruler, and Judge (Ex. 20:2-6); in this capacity He was to be loved, reverently feared, worshiped, and absolutely obeyed. Breaking the covenant was regarded as high treason and, as in the case of the vassal treaties, was punishable by the strongest means (cf. Ex. 20:3-5, 7; 22:20; Lev. 24:16; Dt. 17:2-5).

The chief substitute of Yahweh was, at the early stages of Israel's history, a specially chosen person like Moses or Joshua; in the time of the judges, charismatic leaders like Gideon or Jephthah; in the monarchy, the kings and their officials; after the Babylonian Captivity, a senatorial oligarchy.

*See also* SANHEDRIN. F. E. HIRSCH F. C. FENSHAM

**LAW, ROMAN.** *See* ROMAN LAW.

**LAWFUL; LAWFULLY** [Heb. *mišpāṭ*; Aram. *šallîṭ* (Ezr. 7:24); Gk. *éxesti, nomímōs* (1 Tim. 1:8)]; NEB also JUST; PERMITTED; ALLOWED; etc. Seven times the book of Ezekiel mentions the reward of "life" belonging to those who do "what is lawful [*mišpāṭ*] and right [*ṣᵉḏāqâ*]" (18:5, 19, 21, 27; 33:14, 16, 19). This formula, adopted from the language of the law of the sanctuary (W. Eichrodt, *Ezekiel* [Eng. tr., *OTL*, 1970], pp. 237f.), refers to conduct that conforms to the commands of that law as taught by the priests. In the letter from Artaxerxes to Ezra preserved in Ezr. 7:12-26 Artaxerxes said, "it shall not be lawful" (Aram. *lā' šallîṭ*) to tax the temple personnel. *Šallîṭ*, which basically means "powerful," in this context means "possessing legal authority."

In the NT "lawful" is usually part of an expression that translates Gk. *éxesti*, "it is permissible." Frequently in NT contexts it connotes "permitted by the OT," or perhaps more specifically, "by the Torah" (Mt. 12:2, 4 par. Mk. 2:24, 26 par. Lk. 6:2, 5; Mt. 12:10; 14:4 par. Mk. 6:18; Mt. 19:3 par. Mk. 10:2; Mt. 22:17 par. Mk. 12:14 par. Lk. 20:22; Mt. 27:6; Mk. 3:4 par. Lk. 6:9; Lk. 14:3; Jn. 5:10). Occasionally it means "permissible under Roman law" (Acts 16:21; 22:25; probably also Jn. 18:31; on this passage see R. E. Brown, *Gospel According to John XIII-XXI* [*AB*, 1970], pp. 849f.). Four times in 1 Corinthians (twice in 6:12, twice in 10:23) Paul used the word in a phrase he was probably quoting from the gnostic element at Corinth (F. F. Bruce, *1 and 2 Corinthians* [*NCBC*, 1971; repr. 1980], p. 62; H. Conzelmann prefers to see its provenance in Stoicism, *1 Corinthians* [Eng. tr. *Hermeneia*, 1975], pp. 108f.); in these occurrences the word thus probably means "morally permissible." In 1 Tim. 1:8 the law (*nómos*) is said to be good if used "lawfully" (*nomímōs*); this may mean "properly," i.e., keeping in mind that the law is meant to reprove and constrain sinful persons, rather than the just, who are already motivated to behave in accordance with its precepts (v. 9; for the problems attending this passage, see the comms.). J. E. H.

**LAWGIVER** [Gk. *nomothétēs*] (Jas. 4:12). In Jas. 4:11f. James admonished his readers not to speak evil against one another, for that implied that they judged not only one another but also the law and thus usurped God's place as the lawgiver and judge. Although *nomothétēs* occurs only here in the NT, it is used similarly in Ps. 9:20 (LXX) and frequently in Philo and Josephus. Philo applied the term not only to God (e.g., *De sacrificiis Abelis et Caini* 131) but also to Moses (e.g., *De vita Mosis* i.1.1) and to all legislators in general (e.g., *De Decalogo* 176). Similarly, Josephus frequently applied the title to Moses (e.g., *Ant.* i.Proem.4 [18, 20, 22]; i.3.6 [95]) and to legislators in general (i.Proem.4 [22]). G. A. L.

**LAWLESS** [Gk. *ánomos*] (Acts 2:23; 2 Thess. 2:8; 1 Tim. 1:9; 2 Pet. 2:8); AV also WICKED, UNLAWFUL; NEB also HEATHEN, WICKED, EVIL; [*athémitos*] (1 Pet. 4:3); AV ABOMINABLE; NEB FORBIDDEN; [*áthesmos*] (2 Pet. 3:17); AV WICKED; NEB UNPRINCIPLED; "lawless one" is supplied by the RSV in 2 Thess. 2:9; **LAWLESSNESS** [Heb. *ḥāḵām*–'wise man,' emended to *ḥāmās*–'violence'; LXX *paranómon*–'law-breaking'] (Prov. 11:30); AV WISE; NEB VIOLENCE; [Gk. *anomía*] (2 Thess. 2:3, 7; He. 1:9; 1 Jn. 3:4 bis); AV SIN (based on var. reading, *hamartía*, in 2 Thess. 2:3), INIQUITY, TRANSGRESSION OF LAW; NEB WICKEDNESS, WRONG, "break God's laws."

"Lawless" can refer simply to those who do not know the law, i.e., the Gentiles. In Rom. 2:12 and 1 Cor. 9:20, e.g., those "without the law" or "outside the law" (RSV; Gk. *hoi ánomoi*), the Gentiles, are contrasted to those "under the law" (*hypó nómon*), the Jews. In Acts 2:23 "men of Israel" are accused of putting Jesus to death "by the hands of lawless men," i.e., by Gentiles. Of course, even when used in this sense the term is strongly pejorative.

Used as a term of judgment, "lawless" may refer either to the transgression of a specific law or, more generally, to any wickedness. In 1 Pet. 4:3 "lawless" describes idolatry in terms of its violation of the law against images; as such, idolatry is included in a list of "gentile" vices. On the other hand, in 1 Tim. 1:9f. the reference is not to a specific transgression of the law but to a more general state of wickedness. The latter sense also occurs in 2 Pet. 2:8 (of the "lawless deeds" of the Sodomites, contrasted with the "righteous soul" of Lot) and 3:17 (of the heretics).

Greek *anomía*, similarly, can mean either a specific violation of the law of Moses or a general state of unrighteousness and rebellion. In the passages where the RSV uses "lawlessness," however, the focus is not on the transgression of a specific precept but on hostility toward God (in Mt. 7:23; 13:41; 23:28; 24:12 [RSV "evildoers," "iniquity," "wickedness"] there may be a stronger connection to the law). Some interpret 1 Jn. 3:4 ("Every one who commits sin is guilty of lawlessness; sin is lawlessness") as a rejection of antinomianism (cf. AV, NEB); but if this were so one would expect the formulation to be "lawlessness is sin." The point seems rather that, contrary to those who hold that sin is a matter of indifference to the one who possesses *gnṓsis*, sin is rebellion against God and a mark of alienation from God (cf. vv. 6-10; so Gutbrod).

As hostility toward God *anomía* has eschatological associations, suggesting an active, personal, and malicious rebellion against God's reign. In addition to 1 Jn. 3:4, eschatological associations are clear in Mt. 24:12 (RSV "wickedness"); Did. 16:4; the Freer MS of the conclusion to Mark; and 2 Thess. 2, where the "man of lawlessness" is the very embodiment of this eschatological rebellion.

The identity of the "man of lawlessness" (2 Thess. 2:3, 8) has been the subject of much discussion. The wisest course may be to acknowledge at the outset with St. Augustine, "I frankly confess I do not know what he [Paul] means" (*Civ. Dei* xx.19). For however clear the term may have been to the Thessalonians (cf. vv. 5f.), subsequent attempts to identify this figure remain mere conjectures.

Some of the conjectures are clearly wrong. The identification of the "man of lawlessness" with the pope (e.g., the preface to the AV) was plainly inspired more by Protestant polemics than by the text. Other figures remote from Paul and the Thessalonians (e.g., Hitler, Stalin) are surely not what Paul meant or the Thessalonians "knew." Nor can the "man of lawlessness" be merely a principle of rebellion at work in the world or a general hostility toward God (J. B. Lightfoot, *Notes on Epistles of St. Paul* [1904]); for he cannot be simply identified with "the mystery of lawlessness" (v. 7). Identifying him with the Jews or a Jewish leader persecuting the Christians in Thessalonica (and the "rebellion" [*apostasía*] with the unbelief of the Jews, e.g., J. Denney, comm. on 1 and 2 Thess. in *Expos.B.* [1892]) hardly coheres with Paul's attitude toward his kinsmen in Rom. 9:1-5 or his hopes for them in 11:25-32. And to identify him with the Roman empire (B. B. Warfield, *Biblical Doctrines* [1929], p. 611) hardly fits with 13:1-7.

The more tenable conjectures can be classified as political-historical, mythological, and pastoral-catechetical. The political-historical interpretation is both ancient and persistent (*see* ANTICHRIST). According to this view the "man of lawlessness" was a historical figure of the 1st cent. B.C. Caligula and Nero are most often mentioned. Caligula did order that supplication be made to him as the supreme God and did intend to establish his statue in the Jerusalem temple. Nero persecuted the church, and a legend of his "return" (Nero *redivivus*) developed. Such behavior and such claims would surely have reminded Paul of the royal figures opposed to God in the OT (e.g., Dnl. 11:36, to which there is an evident allusion in the passage). But Caligula died before Paul visited Thessalonica, and Nero did not yet reign when the letter was written (at least if the letter is authentic). A still more telling objection to this view, moreover, is that the "man of lawlessness" is not described as a royal figure in 2 Thess. 2, although it would have been easy to capitalize on the OT passages in this way.

The mythological interpretation is of more recent origin. One representative of this type of interpretation, W. Bousset, identified the "man of lawlessness" with Beliar (cf. Sib. Or. 3:63-73) and Beliar in turn with the mythological primeval adversary in Near Eastern mythology. (Other mythological interpretations have also been proposed as the background of the "man of lawlessness.") The problems of this interpretation (although they may not be overwhelming) are that, whereas Paul distinguishes this figure, as Satan's tool, from the adversary Satan himself (2 Thess. 2:9), Beliar is not clearly distinguishable from Satan (in fact, Paul identifies them in 2 Cor. 6:15); moreover, such flights into mythological speculation seem distant from the pastoral concern that prompted the passage.

The most recent interpretation can be called pastoral-catechetical, for the focus is on Paul's pastoral concern for the Thessalonian church (cf. reference in 2 Thess. 2:5 to his earlier catechetical instruction). C. Giblin has contended that the "man of lawlessness" is part of the catechetical tradition and is representational rather than denoting a definite historical person. The figure is "entatively variable" (p. 287) — i.e., it can be shaped to address the particular situation with pastoral flexibility. Although there may be historical allusions, they need not be constant. Paul's concern in 2 Thessalonians is to meet the threat to faith presented by the claim that the parousia has already occurred (2:2). According to Giblin, Paul uses the traditional Christian teaching (entatively variable) to refer to a false prophet, the "man of lawlessness" who, as the antithesis of the "man of God" or true prophet, stands as a threat to faith and righteousness. It is the claim of the false prophet that the parousia has already occurred. Paul's pastoral response associates this claim with the Church's tradition about rebellion and then deals with the antecedent conditions for the parousia in such a way as to caution the Thessalonians against either pride or sloth, to encourage them to "stand firm" (v. 15). The time is "not yet": the "man of lawlessness" is yet to be revealed; stand firm. He will be the very embodiment of rebellion (*apostasía*); stand firm. His doom (as the "son of perdition," v. 3) is sure — but not until he has wreaked much havoc and deception; stand firm.

This description of the nature and destiny of the "man of lawlessness" is developed in vv. 4 and 8. As the culmination and embodiment of rebellion he opposes God and exalts himself — indeed, he exalts himself to the point of taking God's place, claiming to be God (v. 4). He is presently "restrained." (The identity of this restrainer — Gk. *katéchon* in v. 6, *katéchōn* in v. 7 — and its/his relation to the "man of lawlessness" is also very conjectural; *see* RESTRAIN). But the "mystery of lawlessness" is already at work (v. 7): the alienation and rebellion at work in the world are an open secret to the Thessalonians. When "the lawless one" is revealed, he will be vanquished by the Lord; his deceptions will be unveiled and his power destroyed (v. 8). "So then . . . stand firm" (v. 15).

***Bibliography.***–E. Best, *Comm. on 1 and 2 Thessalonians* (*HNTC*, 1972); W. Bousset, *The Anti-Christ Legend* (Eng. tr. 1896); C. Giblin, *The Threat to Faith: An Exegetical and Theological Re-examination of 2 Thessalonians 2* (1967); *TDNT*, IV, *s.v.* νόμος κτλ.: ἀνομία, ἄνομος (W. Gutbrod); G. Vos, *Pauline Eschatology* (repr. 1961), pp. 94-135.

A. D. VERHEY

**LAWSUIT** [Gk. *kríma*] (1 Cor. 6:7); AV, NEB, "go to law"; **SUE** [*krínomai*] (Mt. 5:40); AV "sue . . . at law." These terms refer to the process of bringing suit against another person in a court of law. The references in Mt. 5:40 (cf. Lk. 6:29) and 1 Cor. 6:1-8 indicate that the topic was a concern several times in the NT Church.

The most extensive reference is 1 Cor. 6:1-8, in which Paul condemned believers' bringing civil suits against fellow believers, on two grounds: (1) Christians ought not to have such disputes in the first place; (2) if disputes do arise, they should be settled within the Christian assembly and not by unbelievers in Roman courtrooms. Since Christians will judge angels (v. 3), the Church should have no problem settling comparatively smaller disputes.

Matthew 5:40, by describing in legal terms the taking of a debtor's coat ("if one would sue you"), reflects an awareness of rabbinic Halakah. In Jewish society from OT times, a debtor's garment could be taken as surety but had to be returned before nightfall (cf. Ex. 22:26f.; Am. 2:8; *see* PLEDGE). In NT times goods were actually collected not by one's legal opponent but by an officer of the court (cf. T.B. *Baba Metzia* 114b). Taking goods from someone unable to pay was regarded by some as inflicting injury upon him (cf. Midr. *Ex. Rabbah* xxxi.13). But both Jesus and Paul commanded a spirit of nonretaliation against legal abuse. R. J. W.

In OT studies much has been written about Heb. *rîḇ*, "lawsuit," which has come to designate a particularly important genre in prophetic literature. The verb *rîḇ*, which basically means "dispute," developed juridical connotations; hence it can be translated "conduct a lawsuit," and the noun *rîḇ* can be translated "lawsuit." According to Gemser (pp. 128f.) *rîḇ* took on a specialized meaning in the prophets: "a controversy in which Israel's God summons and accuses, threatens and decides against his chosen people." Huffmon and Harvey have emphasized the relationship between the *rîḇ* and the covenant, defining the *rîḇ* as a covenant lawsuit, which God brings against Israel for its violation of the covenant. For a convenient summary of studies on the covenantal lawsuit see W. E. March, "Prophecy," in J. H. Hayes, ed., *OT Form Criticism* (1974), pp. 155f., 166-68.

***Bibliography.***–B. Gemser, "The *ríb*- or controversy-pattern in Hebrew mentality," in M. Noth and D. W. Thomas, eds., *Wisdom in Israel and in the Ancient Near East* (*SVT*, 3; 1955), pp. 120-137; J. Harvey, *Bibl.*, 43 (1962), 172-196; H. B. Huffmon, *JBL*, 78 (1959), 285-295.

G. A. L.

**LAWYER** [Gk. *nomikós* <*nómos*–'law']. An expert in the Jewish law, specifically the law of Moses; equivalent to "scribe" (*grammateús*) or "doctor of the law" (*nomodidáskalos*). *See* SCRIBES.

The term *nomikós* is used adjectivally once in the NT (Tit. 3:9) in the context of disputes concerning the law (i.e., the OT). It is used of Zenas in Titus 3:13 probably in the normally secular sense of "lawyer" or "notary." In Luke (7:30; 10:25; 11:45f., 52; 14:3) and possibly also in Matthew (22:35, but perhaps introduced from the Lucan parallel) *nomikoí* are the Jewish leaders with the responsibility of preserving, studying, and applying the law to the situations of everyday life. In this last sense the leaders combined the function of religious teacher with that of civil magistrate or judge in Israel. It is noteworthy that Mark never used the term; if the traditional view that his Gospel was intended for a Roman audience is correct, his readers could have misconstrued *nomikós* as referring to experts in Greek or Roman civil law. "Scribe" appears in the Markan parallel (12:28) to Mt. 22:35; Lk. 10:25.

Luke's references to the *nomikoí* are all deprecatory. The lawyers steadfastly opposed Jesus, rejected the purpose of God by rejecting the message and mission of John, and placed impossible burdens on the shoulders of the common people without lifting so much as a finger to help them.

***Bibliography.***–*TDNT,* IV, *s.v.* νόμος κτλ.: νομικός (Gutbrod); J. Jeremias, *Jerusalem in the Time of Jesus* (Eng. tr. 1969), pp. 233-245.

W. W. GASQUE

**LAY.** A verb used by the English versions to render a great number of Hebrew and Greek terms. Among the OT terms frequently translated "lay" are Heb. *śîm* (lit. "put, place [something somewhere]"; e.g., Gen. 9:23; 22:6, 9), *nāṯan* (lit. "give," "set, put"; e.g., Gen. 15:10; Ex. 7:4), and *šîṯ* (lit. "put, set"; e.g., Gen. 48:14, 17; Ruth 3:15). In the NT it most frequently represents Gk. *títhēmi* (a common LXX translation of Heb. *śîm*; also used for *nāṯan* and *šîṯ*). *See also* HANDS, LAYING ON OF.

The AV uses "lay" in many obsolete or peculiar expressions that are changed by the RSV; cf., e.g., AV "laid before their faces all these words" (Ex. 19:7; RSV "set before them all these words"); AV "lay upon him usury" (Ex. 22:25 [MT 24]; RSV "exact interest from him"); AV "they laid it out to the carpenters and builders" (2 K. 12:11 [MT 12]; RSV "they paid it out . . ."); AV "the sword . . . layeth at him" (Job 41:26 [MT 18]; RSV "the sword reaches him"); AV "I have laid upon thee" (Ezk. 4:5; RSV "I assign to you"); AV "laid meat unto them" (Hos. 11:4; RSV "fed them"). N. J. O.

**LAYING ON OF HANDS.** *See* HANDS, LAYING ON OF.

**LAZARUS** [Gk. *Lazaros* < Heb. *laʿzār,* a rabbinic abbreviation of *ʾelʿāzār*–'God has helped'].

**1.** A man in a parable Jesus told (Lk. 16:19-31) to teach that people's conduct on this side of the grave determines their situations after death. This parable follows a story common in Egyptian and Jewish thought, in which the wicked rich and the pious poor have their positions reversed in the afterlife. It is told from the point of view of the rich man (often called Dives from the Latin for "rich man"), who speaks with Abraham from his place of torment.

The first part merely states the situations of both the rich man and Lazarus. Lazarus, who probably represents all the pious poor, is pictured as a beggar infested with sores who would gladly have filled himself with the leftovers from the table of the rich man.

In the second part both men die, and the rich man finds himself in torment while Lazarus resides with Abraham in a state of blessedness. Although this parable does not intend to give a topographical study of the abode of the dead, it is built upon and thus confirms common Jewish thought (*see* HADES; SHEOL). In the Jewish conception of Hades (e.g., 1 En. 22) the good and the wicked could see each other but were separated by a great impassable chasm. Across this chasm the rich man called to Abraham, begging that Lazarus be sent to comfort him. When he was assured of the impossibility of this, he begged that Lazarus be sent back to warn his brothers of their possible fate. Abraham said that if they would not believe Moses, they would not believe one returned from the dead.

The parable is not designed to teach that riches will bring destruction. Rather, it warns the rich that their possessions do not guarantee their future state. The parable was apparently directed toward Sadducean satisfaction with this life, based upon the belief that there would be no life beyond. Thus, Abraham said that even one from the dead would not convince the living to repent.

**2.** The brother of Mary and Martha. He appears only in the Gospel of John, although Luke mentions his sisters. The family lived in BETHANY on the southeast side of the Mt. of Olives, about 3 km. (1¾ mi.) from Jerusalem (15 stadia, Jn. 11:18). They were apparently well-to-do, since Lazarus had a private tomb and Mary anointed Jesus with a very expensive ointment.

When Lazarus became ill, his sisters sent a messenger to the territory on the other side of the Jordan River where Jesus and His disciples had withdrawn for their own safety (Jn. 10:40–11:3). Lazarus is described in 11:3 (Gk. *philéō*) and v. 5 (*agapáō*) as one whom Jesus loved. (From these statements and the use of *phílos* in v. 11, many have assumed that Lazarus was "the disciple whom Jesus loved" [13:23; 21:20] and thus the author of the Gospel of John; cf. J. N. Sanders and B. A. Mastin, *Comm. on the Gospel According to St. John* [*HNTC,* 1969].) After the arrival of the messenger, Jesus informed His disciples that Lazarus's sickness was "not unto death" but "for the glory of God" (11:4). His statement indicates the miracle's theological significance, which is further emphasized in His dialogue with Martha (vv. 20-27). The miracle would reveal the glory of Jesus, a glory that would point to His divine nature and role (v. 4b). Jesus delayed two days before departing for Bethany, so that when He arrived Lazarus had been dead four days (v. 17). The rabbis taught that the soul hovered near the deceased for three days after death and then returned to God (SB, II, 544); thus on the fourth day death was assured. As if to emphasize this belief, Martha told Jesus not to roll back the stone, for the body had already begun to putrefy.

Lazarus had been buried according to Jewish custom. In that warm country burial took place very soon after the time of death. Friends and sometimes hired lamenters

The resurrection of Lazarus as depicted in a fresco by Giotto di Bondone (*ca.* A.D. 1305) in the Arena Chapel in Padua, Italy (Museo Civico, Padua)

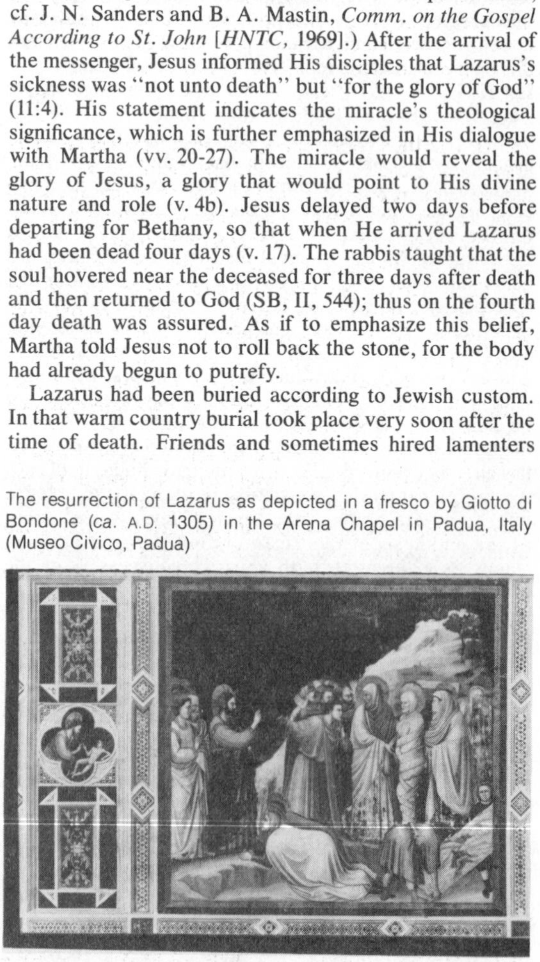

mourned, often very dramatically, after the burial, usually for thirty days. The deceased was anointed with a spiced oil and bound with a linen cloth. When Jesus came to the tomb and ordered the stone taken away, He commanded Lazarus to come forth; since he had difficulty moving, Jesus ordered him to be unbound.

The raising of Lazarus divided those Jews who had been mourning his death. Some became firm believers in Jesus; others went into the city and reported the event to the Jewish leaders, who convened the Sanhedrin and decided that Jesus should be put to death (Jn. 11:45-53). The raising of Lazarus fills an important place in the Gospel of John because it sets in motion the action of the Jewish court that culminated in Jesus' death. Here the Gospel of John carries an emphasis very different from that of the Synoptic Gospels, in which the chief causes of Jesus' death are His cleansing of the temple and His teaching during the last week of His life. They omit the raising of Lazarus altogether. The only hint of this event is the generalization in Lk. 19:37 that many went out to praise Jesus at the triumphal entry because they had seen His miracles; Jn. 12:18 relates this short statement to the raising of Lazarus.

Lazarus appears for the last time in Jn. 12:1-11 to emphasize the miracle of his resurrection and the enmity it caused among the Jewish leaders. Six days before the Passover Jesus came to a feast in Bethany where Mary, Lazarus's sister, anointed Him (vv. 1-3; but cf. Mt. 26:6-13; Mk. 14:3-9; Lk. 7:37f.). Lazarus was present at this banquet (Jn. 12:2). Vv. 9-11 relate that Lazarus's testimony to Jesus' power made so many people believe in Jesus that the high priests planned to kill him as well as Jesus.

D. W. WEAD

**LEAD; LEADEN** [Heb. *ʿôpereṯ*]. A heavy, malleable, blue-gray metal. Lead was one of the first metals to be used in its free state, probably because it was so easily extracted from its ores. In ancient times lead was found in Egypt and the Sinai peninsula. Considerable quantities were also found in northern Syria and in Asia Minor, where it was likely derived from silver production by the process of cupellation (heating in a blast of air so that the oxidized lead partly sinks into a porous shallow cup [cupel]). Tyre imported lead from Tarshish (possibly Tartessos in Spain; Ezk. 27:12). These sources no doubt furnished an important supply in biblical times, since Palestine proper has no lead ores.

Since the ancients regarded lead as the heaviest metal (cf. Sir. 22:14), it was generally used for fish lines and sounding lines (cf. Acts 27:28). All along the Mediterranean shores fishers used lead for sinkers. Pieces of Egyptian fishnets with their lead sinkers still attached, probably dating from *ca.* 1200 B.C., are preserved in the British Museum. This use of lead is reflected in the simile employed by the Song of Moses to describe the drowning of Pharaoh's hosts: "they sank as lead in the mighty waters" (Ex. 15:10). Lead was also used for plummets (*see* MEASURING LINE) and heavy covers (Zec. 5:7f.).

Ancient peoples used lead and other metals to bind stones together, as excavations in Syria have shown. The seams between stones in ancient walls and columns, once lead-filled, have been extracted by plunderers for reuse. The American University of Beirut Museum has several cast-lead sarcophagi dating from the time of Christ.

Already in the Neolithic Age lead glazes were used in ceramic manufacture. In the Late Bronze Age lead was introduced into bronze castings, as is shown by bronze crucible slags found in the Sinai that test to as much as 38 percent lead content. The addition of lead increased

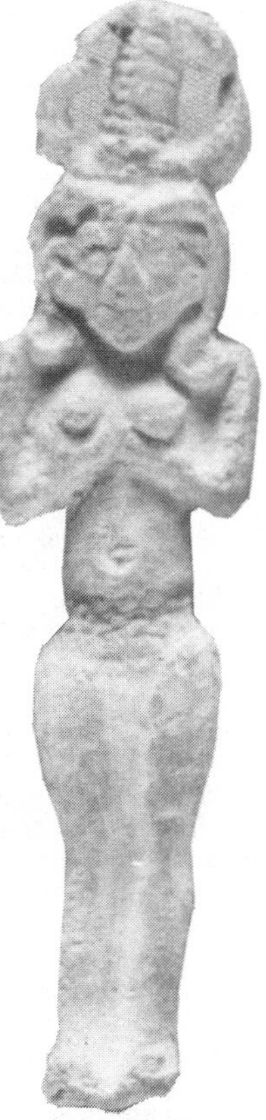

Lead figurine of the Egyptian goddess Hathor (7 cm. [2.7 in.] high) from Tell el-ʿAjjûl (Middle Bronze Age) (Israel Department of Antiquities and Museums)

the fluidity of the metal, leading to the production of finer objects and more accurate castings (Tylecote, p. 29). The Late Bronze Age also saw the production of lead objects, possibly having cultic or votive significance, in trinket moulds.

Job 19:24 mentions the use of lead in the engraving of permanent records. Of the various interpretations that have been proposed, two alternatives seem most likely: either the letters were chiseled into a rock and the incision was inlaid with lead, or the inscription was engraved with an iron tool on tablets of lead. Archeology has found examples of both types of inscriptions from ancient times (see comms.).

Lead sometimes appears in lists of metals including gold, bronze, iron, silver, and tin (Nu. 31:22; Ezk. 22:18, 20; 27:12); lead usually appears last in the list (cf. Sir. 47:18; also 22:14f.). Jer. 6:29 (cf. Ezk. 22:18-22; Mal. 3:2f.) shows that the OT writers understood the process of refining silver and gold with lead. *See* REFINE.

See R. F. Tylecote, *History of Metallurgy* (1976).

J. A. PATCH   R. A. COUGHENOUR

**LEADER** [Heb. *nāśîʾ, śar, rōʾš, nāgîḏ, ʾayil, qāṣîn, ʿattûḏ, pinnâ,* etc.; Gk. *archēgós,* part. of *hēgéomai, prōtos*; AV also CAPTAIN, PRINCE, RULER, CHIEF, MASTER, OVERSEER, etc.; NEB also CHIEF, COMMANDER, CAPTAIN, PRINCE, etc.

In the RSV OT (esp. in Numbers) "leader" is frequently the translation of Heb. *nāśî'*, which designates the leader of a tribe (e.g., Nu. 2:3, etc.; 7:18, etc.; 34:18, etc.; Josh. 9:15, etc.; 1 K. 8:1). *Śar* can denote various types of leaders, e.g., the captain of a marauding band (1 K. 11:24), a tribal leader (1 Ch. 27:22), an elder or noble (Neh. 4:16; 11:1), a military commander (Jer. 40:13; 41:11, 13, 16). *Rō'š* (lit. "head") can also be used as a general term for leader (e.g., a clan chief, 1 Ch. 4:42; 9:34; 11:42; a leader in worship, Neh. 11:17). *Nāgîḏ* often signifies a leader of Israel chosen by Yahweh (e.g., Jeroboam, 1 K. 14:7; Baasha, 16:2; Judah, 1 Ch. 28:4; David, Isa. 55:4), but it can also be used of other types of leaders (e.g., a military officer, 1 Ch. 13:1). *Qāṣîn* (e.g., Jgs. 11:6, 11; Isa. 3:6f.) is a general term for a military leader (cf. "chief," Josh. 10:24) or "ruler" (Isa. 1:10). Other terms are used metaphorically: *'ayil* (lit. "ram," representing power; e.g., a chief of Moab, Ex. 15:15; cf. "the mighty one," Ezk. 31:11), *'attûḏ* (lit. "he-goat"; e.g., Isa. 14:9; Zec. 10:3; *see* GOAT V), and *pinnâ* (lit. "cornerstone"; e.g., 1 S. 14:38; cf. Isa. 19:13; Zec. 10:4).

The participle of Gk. *hēgéomai* ("lead, guide") occurs several times as a designation of church leaders (Lk. 22:26; He. 13:7, 17, 24). *Prṓtos* means literally "first" or "foremost" (Acts 28:17; *see* PRINCIPAL). *Archēgós* can mean either "leader, prince" (cf. RSV "pioneer," He. 2:10; 12:2) or "source, author" (cf. Acts 3:15). Most scholars agree that in Acts 5:31 the term is used in the former sense or in a combination of both senses (e.g., see F. F. Bruce, *Acts of the Apostles* [2nd ed. 1953], pp. 109, 143).

*See also* CAPTAIN; CHIEF; COMMANDER; PRINCE; RULER.

R. K. H. N. J. O.

**LEAF** [Heb. *'āleh*] (Gen. 3:7; 8:11; Lev. 26:36; Neh. 8:15; Job 13:25; 30:4; Ps. 1:3; Prov. 11:28; Isa. 1:30; 34:4; 64:6; Jer. 8:13; 17:8; Ezk. 47:12); AV also BRANCH (Neh. 8:15; Prov. 11:28); BUSHES (Job 30:4); NEB also FOLIAGE (Ezk. 47:12); in Isa. 33:9 the object is not present in the MT but is supplied in translation: "Bashan and Carmel shake off [Heb. *nō'ēr*] their leaves"; AV "shake off their fruits"; NEB "are stripped bare"; [Heb. *ṭerep*] (Ezk. 17:9); [Aram. *'ᵒpî*] (Dnl. 4:12, 14, 21); [Gk. *phýlla*] (Mk. 11:13 par. Mt. 21:19; Mk. 13:28 par. Mt. 24:32 [supplied as object of Gk. *probállō* in Lk. 21:30]; Rev. 22:2); **LEAFY** [Heb. *'āḇōṯ*] (Lev. 23:40; Neh. 8:15; Ezk. 6:13; 20:28); AV THICK; **LEAFY BRANCHES** [Gk. *stibás*] (Mk. 11:8); AV BRANCHES; NEB BRUSHWOOD; the par. in Mt. 21:8 has Gk. *kládos,* "branch."

The primary Hebrew word for "leaf" is *'āleh,* which has been related etymologically to the verb *'ālâ,* "go up, spring forth." This word designates the leaf of the following trees: fig (Gen. 3:7; Neh. 8:15; cf. Mk. 11:13 par.; 13:28 par.), olive (Gen. 8:11; Neh. 8:15), wild olive (Neh. 8:15), myrtle (Neh. 8:15), palm (Neh. 8:15), oak (Isa. 1:30; Ezk. 6:13). It is also used of bushes (Job 30:4) and vines (Isa. 34:4).

The green, well-nourished leaf is a symbol of prosperity and security, especially of the righteous and godly, e.g., Prov. 11:28, "The righteous shall flourish like a leaf." In this usage "leaf" is frequently found in the vicinity of or paired with "fruit," e.g., Ps. 1:3; Jer. 17:8; Ezk. 17:9; 47:12; Dnl. 4:12, 14, 21; Mk. 11:13; Mt. 21:19.

Conversely, the withering leaf is an image of judgment and the destruction of the wicked, e.g., Isa. 64:6, "We all fade like a leaf, and our iniquities, like the wind, take us away." Separated from its source of life, the leaf withers and dies. The term *nāḇal,* "to wither, decay," is used in association with "leaf" in Ps. 1:3; Isa. 1:30; 34:4; 64:6; Jer. 8:13; Ezk. 47:12. In Ezk. 17:9 the verb is *yāḇēš,* "be dry." In Mt. 21:19 the fig tree withers after Jesus utters a curse upon it; *see* FIG, FIG TREE.

The "leafy trees" in Lev. 23:40; Neh. 8:15 refer to boughs that the Israelites carried in processions and used to make booths at the Feast of Tabernacles. The rabbis (T.B. *Sukkah* 12a; T.P. *Sukkah* iii.53d) interpreted them as MYRTLES.

In Ezekiel's temple vision, the leaves of the trees lining the river serve for healing (Ezk. 47:12). In Rev. 22:2 the river of the water of life nourishes the tree of life, whose leaves are for the healing of the nations.

At Ex. 39:3 the RSV translates Heb. *paḥê-hazzāhāḇ* (lit. "thin plates of gold"; cf. AV, NEB) by "gold leaf," which was worked into threads for the high priest's EPHOD.

*See also* BRANCH, BOUGH; FLORA.

B. L. BANDSTRA

**LEAGUE** [Heb. *bᵉrîṯ*–'covenant', *massēḵâ, nāḥâ*–'lead']. The RSV OT uses this term nine times, generally in the sense of a covenant (*bᵉrîṯ*) or military alliance of an unspecified nature or duration (1 K. 15:19 par. 2 Ch. 16:3). In 1 S. 22:8 the concept of contract is implied by the verb *kāraṯ,* "cut, engrave," which is a component of covenant terminology. In Job 5:23 *bᵉrîṯ* is used metaphorically. In vv. 17-27 Eliphaz tells Job that those whom God chastens will be blessed. Part of that blessing will entail harmony with nature; Eliphaz speaks of this harmony in terms of a "league with the stones of the field."

An unusual term, *massēḵâ,* was rendered "league" by the RSV in Isa. 30:1, but "covering" in AV and "schemes" in NEB. Those who argue for "league" base the term on a root *nsk,* which means "to pour out," and thus may refer to a libation made to seal a covenant.

The verb *nāḥâ* was used in Isa. 7:2 of the Syro-Ephraimite coalition against Judah, probably in the sense of Syria "giving leadership" in the alliance. Most English translations do not reflect this sense, however, preferring instead "in league with" (RSV), "is confederate with" (AV), or "had come to terms with" (NEB). The NEB seems to be less a translation of *nḥh* than an attempt to interpret it in the light of the known historical situation.

*See also* COVENANT (OT). R. K. H.

**LEAH** lē'ə [Heb. *lē'â*–'wild cow'; Gk. *Leia*]. Sister of Rachel and elder daughter of Laban (Gen. 29:16). The narrative about her begins (v. 17) by stating that her eyes were "weak" (Heb. *rakkôṯ*; Gk. *astheneís*), which is usually interpreted to mean that her eyes were lackluster and she was therefore unattractive (cf. Josephus *Ant.* i.19.6 [301], "she was not pleasing in appearance"). It is also possible, however, that she was afflicted with an eye disease, such as blepharitis or mucopurulent conjunctivitis. The former is an inflamed condition of the eyelids, particularly of the marginal areas (*blepharitis marginalis*); the latter is a bacillary infection of the conjunctivae that results in a discharge containing both mucus and pus. Ophthalmic disease, often disseminated by flies, was widespread in the ancient Near East (*see* DISEASE III.G). Either interpretation would mean that she was unattractive, as the contrasting description of Rachel in v. 17b suggests. Some scholars, however, translate *rakkôṯ* "tender, delicate," and explain that Leah had attractive eyes, but Rachel was more beautiful (see E. A. Speiser, *Genesis* [*AB,* 1964], p. 225; *CHAL,* p. 339).

Leah became the wife of Jacob by a ruse on the part of her father, who took advantage of the oriental custom of heavily veiling the prospective bride. When taken to task by his irate son-in-law, Laban excused himself by stating it was against the custom of his country "to give the younger before the first-born" (Gen. 29:21-26). Despite Jacob's apparently resenting her as well as her father, Leah endeavored to serve her husband with devotion and diligence. She bore him six sons — Reuben, Simeon, Levi, Judah (29:31-35), Issachar, and Zebulun (30:17-20) — and a daughter, Dinah (v. 21); three of the children may have been conceived late in her menopausal phase (cf. vv. 9, 17-21). Unlike Leah, Rachel the favorite wife had difficulty bearing children. She bore her first, Joseph, after Leah had already produced seven children, and she died in childbirth with Benjamin (35:16-18).

When Jacob decided to return to the land of his fathers, both of his wives were ready to accompany him (Gen. 31:4, 14). The meeting on the way between Jacob and his brother Esau sorely tried their courage. Although Leah was placed between the handmaids in the front and Rachel with her son Joseph in the rear, she still cannot have derived much comfort from her position. She must have felt relieved when she saw Esau and his four hundred men returning to Seir (33:2, 16).

Leah was buried at Machpelah (Gen. 49:31). According to Ruth 4:11 her conduct had become an example for successive generations to follow, as one of the two women who had "built up the house of Israel."

*See also* LABAN. W. BAUR R. K. H.

**LEANNOTH.** *See* MAHALATH (LEANNOTH).

**LEAPING.** *See* DANCE.

**LEASH.** The RSV renders Heb. *qāšar* in Job 41:5 (MT 40:29) "put . . . on leash" (AV "bind"; NEB "keep . . . on a string"). The figure is that of little girls playing with a young sparrow on a string. It illustrates God's total control over Leviathan as opposed to Job's impotence before this impressive creature.

**LEASING** [Heb. *kāzaḇ*–'lie, deceive'] (AV Ps. 4:2 [MT 3]; 5:6 [MT 7]). Archaic term for LIE.

**LEAST** [Heb. *ṣā'îr*] (Jgs. 6:15; 1 S. 9:21; Ps. 68:27 [MT 28]); [*qāṭān, qāṭōn*] (2 K. 18:24 par. Isa. 36:9; 60:22; Jer. 6:13; 8:10; 31:34; 42:1, 8; 44:12; Jonah 3:5); AV also LITTLE (Isa. 60:22); NEB also FEW, LOW (Jer. 6:13; 8:10; 31:34; etc.); [Gk. *eláchistos*] (Mt. 2:6; 5:19; 25:40, 45; 1 Cor. 15:9; Eph. 3:8); NEB HUMBLE (Mt. 25:40, 45), LOWEST (Mt. 5:19), INFERIOR (1 Cor. 15:9); [*mikrós*] (Mt. 11:11; Lk. 7:28; 9:48; Acts 8:10; He. 8:11); NEB also LOW; [*exoutheneō*] (1 Cor. 6:4); NEB "count for nothing."

"Least" is used as a translational facilitation for various Hebrew idioms (Gen. 24:55; 32:10 [MT 11]; Ex. 5:11; Nu. 11:32; Jgs. 3:2). In Jeremiah "least" occurs six times in the expression "from the least to the greatest," i.e., everyone. A theme recurring throughout the OT is that one who is politically least becomes great (cf. Jgs. 6:15; 1 S. 9:21; Isa. 60:22).

Although the rabbis and Greeks frequently disdained what was "little" and exalted what was "great," the NT reemphasized the OT theme but in more universal terms. Because the Evangelists believed that the "small" (Mt. 18:6, 10, 14), the "least" (10:42; 25:40, 45), and the "poor" (Lk. 6:20; cf. Mt. 5:3) possess the kingdom, they rejected the value system of this world. This world sees the kingdom of God itself as unimportant, but like the mustard seed the "smallest" kingdom will one day become the greatest of all (Mk. 4:31f.).

The apostle Paul did not lose sight of this understanding. As he matured in his faith, the seriousness of his past persecution of the Church increasingly disturbed him. It kept him from exulting in his achievements. In contrast to those who boasted in their greatness (2 Cor. 11–12) and saw themselves as "superlative apostles" (11:5; 12:11; cf. Gal. 2:6), he boasted in his weakness (2 Cor. 12:10). He marveled at the grace of God; he had been forgiven so much that he would always be the "least of the apostles" (1 Cor. 15:9) and "least of all saints" (Eph. 3:8). To be the "least," however, did not mean to be unimportant or insignificant, for the low and despised were those chosen by God (1 Cor. 1:28). Thus Paul rejected this world's system of values (vv. 18-31). God's grace was not given in vain to him, for he labored more than all the other apostles (15:10) and became a great example of one who, having been forgiven much, loved much (Lk. 7:47).

See *TDNT*, IV, *s.v.* μικρός (Michel). R. H. STEIN

**LEATHER** [Heb. *'ôr*] (2 K. 1:8); [*tāḥaš*] (Ezk. 16:10); AV BADGERS' SKINS; NEB STOUT HIDE; [Gk. *dermátinos*] (Mt. 3:4; Mk. 1:6); AV LEATHERN, SKIN. Skins, usually of domesticated animals (esp. sheep and goats), treated for practical uses. *See also* TANNED, TANNER; GOATSKINS; SHEEPSKIN.

The art of treating animal skins to make leather by tanning can be traced to the 4th millennium B.C. and before. The technology was highly developed in the Middle East long before the Hebrews began to write. Some leather thongs on a Chalcolithic adze handle (*ca.* 4000 B.C.) and a leather sandal dating from the time of Abraham were discovered in 1951 in Wâdī Murabba'ât Cave 2 near the Dead Sea. Biblical references to animal skins, probably tanned leather, mention garments (Gen. 3:21; Lev. 13:48-59; Nu. 31:20; He. 11:37), girdles (2 K. 1:8; Mt. 3:4; Mk. 1:6), sandals (Ezk. 16:10), coverings for the wilderness tabernacle and its utensils (Ex. 25:5; 26:14; 35:7, 23; 36:19; 39:34; Nu. 4:6-25), probably for David's "shepherd's bag" (1 S. 17:40), water- or milk-skins (Gen. 21:14; Jgs. 4:19; Job 38:37), and wineskins (1 S. 1:24; Mt. 9:17).

Leather was clearly meant by *'ôr taḥaš* ("skin of *taḥaš*") in the Exodus and Numbers passages describing the covering of the wilderness tabernacle. The confusion over the animal skins (AV "badger skin", ASV "sealskin" [mg. "porpoise skin"], RSV "goatskin" [except Nu. 4:25 "sheepskin"], NEB "porpoise-skin" [mg. "sea cow"], Jewish Publication Society translation [1962] "dolphin skin" [mg. "skins of *teḥashîm*"]) suggests the best translation be just "leather" or possibly "goatskin," the most common skins available to people wandering in the Sinai wilderness. The cognate Arabic words *tuḥas* and *duḥs* ("dolphin" or "dugong") can hardly be reconciled with the environment and customs of the biblical accounts. *See also* PORPOISE.

That leather (or PARCHMENT) was primarily used for writing in ancient Palestine has now been established by the DSS discovery. Most of the 600 MSS from the eleven Qumrân caves are leather (or parchment, if the stretching process is the only basis for distinguishing the two terms). 1QIsa[a], the oldest extant biblical MS, was copied *ca.* 100 B.C.; it has 54 cols. of Hebrew text for its 66 chapters on seventeen sheets of a coarse leather (sheepskin) sewn together with linen thread and inscribed with carbon ink, making a scroll 7.3 m. (24 ft.) long. (*See* picture in ISAIAH.) The DSS shed considerable light on the technology of leather and parchment preparation in biblical times. For articles of leather in Mishnaic times see Mish. *Kelim.*

See R. Reed, *Ancient Skins, Parchments and Leathers* (1972). J. C. TREVER

**LEAVEN** [Heb. *śe'ōr*; *ḥāmēṣ*; Gk. *zýme*; *zymóō*; Lat. *fermentum*]. Any agent added to a flour mixture or liquids to produce a state of fermentation. The ancient Hebrews always kneaded with their bread a piece of fermented dough reserved from a previous baking (cf. Mt. 13:33). The leaven may also have been softened in water in the mixing bowl before the flour was added. Other forms of leaven used in the ancient world (cf. Pliny *Nat.Hist.* xviii.26

[102-104]) were not mentioned in the Bible, whether or not the Hebrews employed them.

The Hebrew sacrificial system prohibited the use of leaven in cereal offerings and sacrifices to God (cf. Ex. 23:18; 34:25; Lev. 2:11; 6:17; etc.). It was allowed, however, in offerings that humans subsequently consumed (cf. Lev. 7:13; 23:17). It is uncertain whether the showbread was leavened, but Josephus thought that it was (*Ant.* iii.6.6 [142]; x.7 [255]). Why leaven was prohibited in offerings to God is unknown.

Unleavened bread figured prominently in a specific feast of that designation (*see* FEASTS). It commemorated the haste of the Israelites' departure from Egypt at the time of the Exodus, which left them no opportunity to use a rising agent in preparing their bread (Ex. 12:34, 39). An annual observance of this great deliverance formed part of the Passover celebrations. From the fourteenth day of Abib, the first month, the Hebrews were required to eat the "bread of affliction" (Dt. 16:3) for seven days (cf. Ex. 12:14-20; 13:3-10; 23:15; 34:18; Nu. 28:17). Anyone who ate leavened bread or cakes during that period was expelled from the company of the Israelites (cf. Ex. 12:15-20; 13:7). Fermented products other than grain were not affected by the ritual prohibitions governing the Passover celebrations.

Leaven lent itself readily to figurative use as a symbol of pervasiveness (cf. 1 Cor. 5:6-8; Gal. 5:9). Christ mentioned leaven to exemplify the penetrating or transforming power of the kingdom of heaven (Mt. 13:33; Lk. 13:21). He stigmatized the "leaven," i.e., the hypocritical teaching, of the Pharisees and Sadducees (Mt. 16:6, 11f.; Lk. 12:1; cf. Mk. 8:15). Using the Passover celebrations as an allegory, Paul urged the casting out of the leaven of malice and wickedness and the substitution of sincerity and truth as an appropriate means of keeping the feast (1 Cor. 5:6-8).

R. K. H.

**LEBANA, LEBANAH** lə-bā'nə, lə-bä'nə [Heb. *l^eḇānâ*; Gk. *Labana* (1 Esd. 5:29)]. Head of a family of returning exiles. The variant spellings in the English versions are curious, since the same person is obviously meant in all the texts. The NEB transliterations are stricter — Lebanah in the OT and Labana in 1 Esd. 5:29 — whereas the RSV uses Lebana in Neh. 7:48 and Lebanah in Ezr. 2:45; 1 Esd. 5:29. The AV agrees with the RSV in the OT but has Labana in 1 Esdras.

**LEBANON** leb'ə-non [Heb. *l^eḇānôn,* usually with definite article, "(the) very white"; Gk. *Libanos*]; AV also LIBANUS (Jth. 1:7). A forested mountain range N of Israel, and the land where that range is located. The morphology of the Hebrew, supported by Arab. *libnân* and Akk. *labnânu* (sufformative *-ân,* developing by the "Canaanite shift" to *-ôn*), is probably to be taken as an elative, "*the* white (one)," "the whitest," or "the very white."

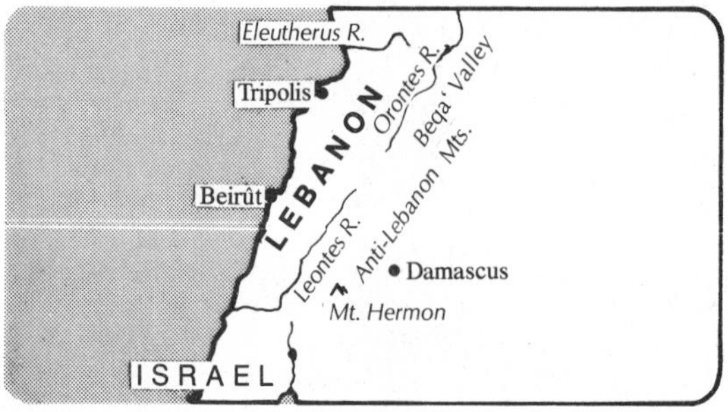


The Lebanon range, which parallels the coast, is about 160 km. (100 mi.) long, with an average elevation in the north of 2100 m. (7000 ft.) and in the south of 1650 m. (5400 ft.). It is often considered a part of a mountain range that extends from the Amanus mountains in the north to the Sinai, but the geological structure is more complex, as D. Baly showed (*GB,* 2nd ed., pp. 9-11, 29f., 191). The highest part of the Lebanon range is Qurnat es-Sawda, 3088 m. (10,131 ft.), located 30 km. (19 mi.) ESE of Tripolis (modern Ṭarâbulus). The two portions of the range are divided by a saddle, Darh el-Baidar, 1542 m. (5059 ft.), which provides an easier route from the coastal region (specifically Beirût) to the central valley and on to Damascus. The Lebanon range is cut at the northern end by Nahr el-Kebir (ancient Eleutherus, to be distinguished from another Nahr el-Kebir near Latakia), the boundary between the modern states of Lebanon and Syria, and at the southern end by the gorge of the Litani (there known as Nahr el-Qāsimiyeh). West of the range is a coastal plain, widest in the north near Tripolis, and at some points almost nonexistent because of spurs of the mountain that dip into the Mediterranean.

East of the Lebanon range is a valley, the Beqaʿ (often spelled Baqâʿa or Bakaa, *el-Biqâʿ; see* COELESYRIA). The northern portion of it is formed by the Orontes River (Nahr el-ʿÂṣi), which flows N, and the southern portion by the Leontes (Nahr el-Līṭânī, modern Litani), which flows south. The watershed of this valley is north of Baalbek at an altitude of 1149 m. (3770 ft.). The Beqaʿ separates the Lebanon from the Anti-Lebanon (Antilibanos), a parallel range that borders the Syrian desert to the east. The southern portion of the Anti-Lebanon (i.e., S of the pass near Zabdāni that provides passage for the road from Beirût to Damascus) is generally considered a separate range, Jebel esh-Sheikh, the Mt. Hermon of the Bible. *See* Plate 50.

Was the term Lebanon used also of the region adjacent to the mountain range? In Jgs. 3:3 *har hall^eḇānôn* (lit. "the mountain of the Lebanon," RSV "Mount Lebanon") has been interpreted as a possessive genitive ("Lebanon's mountain"), but it may just as well be appositional ("the mountain, i.e., Lebanon"). In Josh. 9:1 *mûl hall^eḇānôn* (lit. "in front of [RSV "toward"] the Lebanon") can be taken as the name of the region, but this interpretation is not required by the context. In 11:17 *biqʿaṯ hall^eḇānôn,* "the valley of the Lebanon," certainly refers to the Beqaʿ — but is "Lebanon" the place where the valley is located, or the mountain range that identifies this particular "valley"? Note that "Lebanon" is apparently the name of the larger region in Cant. 4:8, "come with me from Lebanon," for the same verse mentions the peaks of Amana (in the Anti-Lebanon), Senir (the northern part of Hermon), and Hermon. The cedars of Lebanon are mentioned often (Jgs. 9:15; Isa. 2:13; etc.); possibly they are intended also by "the glory of Lebanon" (Isa. 35:2), "fragrance like Lebanon" (Hos. 14:6 [MT 7]), "wood of Lebanon" (Cant. 3:9), and "Lebanon with its majestic trees" (Isa. 10:34). The "snow of Lebanon" (Jer. 18:14), according to the emendation followed by the RSV, is on the crags of Sirion (Hermon). *See* Plate 2. The "flowing streams of Lebanon" (Cant. 4:15) may indicate numerous water sources in the region, particularly those at the base of Hermon and near Merj ʿAyûn. Thus the Bible seems to use "Lebanon" for a region rather than just for the mountain range; yet the term should properly not be equated with the modern country of that name.

For the possible location of Lebo-Hamath, *see* HAMATH; cf. *GTTOT,* §§ 274, 766f., 1494f.; *LBHG,* rev. ed., pp. 72f.

*See also* PHOENICIA.

W. S. LASOR

**LEBAOTH** lə-bā'əth [Heb. *l*[e]*ḇā'ôṯ*]. A site "in the extreme South" belonging to Judah (Josh. 15:32). In 19:2-6, which duplicates much of the list of cities in 15:22-32, BETH-LEBAOTH replaces Lebaoth (cf. 15:32 and 19:6). Moreover, in 19:1 the cities are part of the lot of Simeon, "in the midst of the inheritance of the tribe of Judah." Further complicating the identification, the list in 1 Ch. 4:29-31 has BETH-BIRI instead of (Beth-)Lebaoth. The site is apparently near Sharuhen (Josh. 19:4). W. S. L. S.

**LEBBAEUS** le-bē'əs [Gk. *Lebbaios*] (Mt. 10:3, AV). Mentioned in some MSS (e.g., D C[2] L W etc.) as "Lebbaeus whose surname was Thaddaeus"; one of the twelve disciples. *See* THADDAEUS.

**LEBONAH** lə-bō'nə [Heb. *l*[e]*ḇônâ*]. A village on the road from Bethel to Shechem (Jgs. 21:19). The location of Shiloh was indicated by the phrase "north of Bethel . . . and south of Lebonah," which seems to attribute some importance to Lebonah. It is identified with the small modern village of Khan el-Lubban, just W of the main north-south road where it crosses the Valley of the Dance (the Valley of Jephthah's Daughter). This valley is the traditional dividing line between Judah and Samaria. (Bethel, which was near the southern limits of the kingdom of Israel, is S of the valley; hence the tradition must be handled critically.) The Talmud calls Lebonah Beth Laban ("house of milk"), ostensibly because of milk-white rocks in the area. It was one of five cities that provided wine for libations in the temple (E. Hoade, *Guide to the Holy Land* [1973], p. 665) and even today produces fine grapes. W. S. L. S.

The plain of Lebonah (A. D. Baly)

**LEB-QAMAI** [Heb. *lēḇ qāmāy*] (Jer. 51:1, RSV mg.). A cipher for Chaldea (*see* ATHBASH), formerly taken as a corruption of *qambullay* and identified as Gambulai (BDB, p. 525).

**LECAH** lē'kə [Heb. *lēḵâ*] (1 Ch. 4:21). A son of Er in the genealogy of Judah (so RSV, AV); some scholars, e.g., KoB, p. 482, have held that Lecah was a village founded by Er (cf. NEB).

**LECTIONARY.** *See* TEXT AND MSS OF THE NT.

**LEDGE** [Heb. *karkōḇ* (Ex. 27:5; 38:4), *ʿ*[a]*zārâ* (Ezk. 43:14, 17, 20; 45:19)]; AV also COMPASS, SETTLE; NEB also PEDESTAL, PEDESTAL-BLOCK.

The ledge described in Ex. 27:5; 38:4 was a shelflike, horizontal projection halfway down the altar of burnt offering that stood in the court of the tabernacle. Its exact purpose is not mentioned. It may have been a convenient storage apron upon which the equipment associated with sacrifice was laid. Although this suggestion is supported by the listing of such implements in the immediate context (27:3), the ledge may instead have been a purely decorative molding.

Ezekiel notes two ledges associated with the altar in the inner court of the eschatological temple (43:14, 17, 20; 45:19). This sacrificial altar is entirely different from that of the tabernacle. It stands on three superimposed stages or platforms (NEB "pedestal-block"). The bottom one is sixteen cubits square. Sitting atop it, and leaving a one-cubit border (or ledge), is a second platform fourteen cubits square. The third level, twelve cubits square, also leaves a one-cubit ledge and is the platform on which the altar actually stands.

These two ledges are thus part of a three-tiered structure, surmounted by an altar, that is vaguely reminiscent of the Babylonian ziggurat. If Ezekiel, an exile in Babylon, had so modeled this altar, then it represents the eschatological fulfillment of ancient religious aspirations as well as the final worship of the true God, in contrast with the false cultus of heathendom (W. Eichrodt, *Ezekiel* [Eng. tr., *OTL*, 1970], p. 557).

*See also* ALTAR; TEMPLE. K. H. MAAHS

**LEECH** [Heb. *ʿ*[a]*lûqâ*; Gk. *bdélla*]; AV HORSELEACH. The Hebrew word occurs once only in the OT (Prov. 30:15), and its general meaning is clear, since it is almost identical with Arab. *ʿalaqâ*, "leech." At least six species of leech flourished in Palestine and Syria in biblical times, having as their habitat pools and streams where animals drank. Once ingested, they attached themselves firmly to the interior of the mouth or pharynx and proved extremely difficult to remove. R. K. H.

Leek (*Allium porrum*)

**LEEK** [Heb. *ḥāṣîr*]. An herb of the lily family characterized by a cylindrical bulb and linear succulent leaves. Its flavor is similar to the onion's but more pungent. Although Heb. *ḥāṣîr* is almost always translated "grass," its association in Nu. 11:5 with garlic and onions has caused it, at least since the LXX, to be understood as "leek" (Gk. *práson*) in that passage. The leek, *Allium porrum* L., was widely grown and was a very popular food in ancient Egypt and Palestine. Some botanists have suggested the unrelated fenugreek (*Trigonella foenum-graecum* L.), a clover-like annual bearing aromatic seeds and used in medicine and food, but this is improbable.

See *MPB*, pp. 34f. R. K. H.

**LEES** [Heb. *šᵉmārîm*–'dregs'] (Isa. 25:6; Jer. 48:11; Zeph. 1:12); NEB also WELL-MATURED, DREGS. The DREGS or sediment that settles to the bottom of a receptacle. In biblical times WINE was often left "on the lees" to increase its strength and flavor; just before it was drunk it was strained through a cloth (cf. RSV "refined," Isa. 25:6). To prevent undesirable thickening on the lees, wine was periodically poured from vat to vat. Thus "settled (or thickening) upon one's lees" could be used as a figure for a complacent people: for Moab, who had never suffered exile (Jer. 48:11), and for the residents of Jerusalem who thought that God would not act (Zeph. 1:12). N. J. O.

**LEFT (HAND)** [Heb. usually *śᵉmō'l*, also *śᵉmā'lî*, hiphil of *śāma'l*–'go to the left'; Gk. usually *euṓnymos*, also *aristerós* (Mt. 6:3; Mk. 10:37; Lk. 23:33; 2 Cor. 6:7)]; **LEFT-HANDED** [Heb. *'iṭṭēr yaḏ yāmîn*–'impeded (on) the right hand; Gk. *amphoterodéxios*–'ambidextrous'] (Jgs. 3:15; 20:16). The terms are used primarily to indicate direction of orientation, with or without the terms for "hand." Thus Abraham says to Lot: "If you take the left hand [*śᵉmō'l*], then I will go to the right; or if you take the right hand, then I will go to the left [hiphil of *śāma'l*]" (Gen. 13:9). Frequently in Hebrew idiom the right and left hands are mentioned together to express the idea "everywhere," "anywhere," or "at all" (e.g., Gen. 24:49; Nu. 20:17; 22:26; Dt. 5:32; 17:11, 20; Josh. 1:7; 2 S. 2:19, 21; Isa. 54:3; Zec. 12:6).

Because the Jews oriented themselves by facing the rising sun (Lat. *oriens*, "east"), the left hand could represent the north (cf. Gen. 14:15; Josh. 19:27; Ezk. 16:46; AV "left hand"; RSV, NEB, "north") and the right could represent the south (cf. 2 S. 24:5, AV).

In biblical times (as in many cultures today) the respective values of the right and left hands were clearly distinguished. The right was considered the hand of power and honor; the left hand was considered weaker and less honorable. Thus Joseph was displeased when his father Israel placed his left hand on the elder son's head and his right hand on the younger son's head (Gen. 48:13-19). The left hand could also be a symbol of folly, evil, and ill fortune; cf. Eccl. 10:2: "A wise man's heart inclines him toward the right, but a fool's heart toward the left" (cf. Jonah 4:11).

Although Gk. *aristerós* could be used in a neutral sense (e.g., Lk. 23:33; 2 Cor. 6:7), in Greek literature it often had a symbolical meaning "boding ill, ominous" (LSJ, p. 240; cf. Lat. *sinister*). *Euṓnymos* (lit. "of a good name, honored, fortunate") was frequently used euphemistically in place of *aristerós* (LSJ, p. 740). In Jesus' parable of the last judgment the Son of man places the sheep (i.e., the righteous) on His right hand and the goats (i.e., the godless) on His left hand (Mt. 25:33; cf. v. 41). In Mk. 10:37, 40 both hands represent positions of honor and intimate association.

While the left hand was considered weaker than the right, it was the hand that held the bow (Ezk. 39:3). Because a warrior held his shield with his left hand, he was most vulnerable on his right side. Thus a left-handed or ambidextrous warrior could be especially deadly: e.g., Ehud the Benjaminite (Jgs. 3:15, 21), the seven hundred left-handed Benjaminites (20:16), the ambidextrous Benjaminites who assisted David (1 Ch. 12:2); cf. Joab's treacherous slaying of Amasa (2 S. 20:9f.).

*See also* HAND; RIGHT (HAND). H. L. E. LUERING N. J. O.

**LEG** [Heb. *šôq*] (Dt. 28:35; 1 S. 9:24; Ps. 147:10; Prov. 26:7; Cant. 5:15; Isa. 47:2); AV also SHOULDER, THIGH; NEB also THIGH; [*kᵉrā'ayim*] (Ex. 12:9; 29:17; Lev. 1:9, 13; 4:11; 8:21; 9:14; 11:21; Am. 3:12); NEB also SHIN, SHIN BONE; [*regel*] (Ex. 25:26; 37:13; 1 S. 17:6; Ezk. 1:7); AV also FOOT; [*margᵉlōṯ*] (Dnl. 10:6); AV, NEB, FOOT; [Aram. *šāq*] (Dnl. 2:33); [Gk. *skélos*] (Jn. 19:31-33); [*poús*] (Rev. 10:1); AV FOOT. *See also* FOOT.

*Šôq* particularly refers to a human's lower leg or shank (as distinguished from the thigh, e.g., in Jgs. 15:8: *šôq 'al-yārēḵ*; see C. F. Burney, *Book of Judges* [1920], pp. 369f.) but by extension may also signify the whole leg. Only in 1 S. 9:24 does *šôq* designate a nonhuman leg. In Dnl. 2:33, though the imagery is human, the point of reference of the Aramaic cognate *šāq* is an envisioned symbolic statue. *Šôq* appears once in the Qumrân literature (1QM 6:15), in the military idiom *battê šôqayim*, "greaves, shin-guards" (lit. "shin-receptacles"), the technical term derived from the body part covered by the armor (see Y. Yadin, *Scroll of the War of the Sons of Light Against the Sons of Darkness* [Eng. tr. 1962], pp. 122f.).

With one exception (Lev. 11:21, where the term designates the leaping legs of the locust), *kᵉrā'ayim* refers exclusively to the legs of animals, particularly in sacrificial contexts. Like *šôq*, this term specifies a particular portion of the leg, viz., the shin or lower front section, but also by extension may denote the entire leg. From this term derived the denominative verb *kāra'*, "kneel down."

*Regel*, properly "foot," occasionally by extension means "leg" (e.g., 1 S. 17:6 uses *raglayim* to indicate where Goliath wore his greaves). The Greek counterpart, *poús*, "foot," is once similarly extended in the NT (Rev. 10:1). The use of *regel* in Ezk. 1:7 and *margᵉlôṯ* in Dnl. 10:6 as apocalyptic images of power and strength prefigures the NT use of *poús* as an eschatological symbol of strength or authority (Rev. 10:1).

The NT seldom refers to legs or parts of legs; *skélos*, "(entire) leg," occurs only three times, all in Jn. 19:31-33, which relates that the legs of the two men crucified with Jesus were broken before the bodies were removed.

*See* FOOT; THIGH.

See *TDNT*, VI, *s.v.* πούς (Weiss). D. G. BURKE

**LEGEND.** Myth, saga, legend, and fairy tale are commonly considered to be the same thing. Even scholars sometimes use the terms interchangeably, and distinctions that are made are not accepted by all. One frequent distinction is that a myth is a wholly invented tale with no factual basis in history, while a legend consists of a kernel of ancient fact encased in a husk of more recent fabrication (*see* MYTH). But even this distinction is not standard.

In modern form criticism of the Bible the legend genre is most frequently confused with saga. Pioneers of OT form criticism (Gunkel, Gressmann, Sellin, Eissfeldt) spoke of myth, saga, legend, novella, fairy tale, and historical narrative, while the NT ground-breakers Dibelius and Bultmann discovered similar forms: tale, myth, legend, miracle story, and historical story (*see* CRITICISM III). When definitions are sought among these pioneers and their successors it soon becomes apparent that uniformity does not exist — indeed, confusion reigns (cf. Hals). In fact, one of the purposes of a commentary series launched in 1981 — the *Forms of the OT Literature* — is "to bring consistency to the terminology for the genres . . . of the biblical literature" (from the Editors' Foreword).

***I. Terminology.***–The English word "legend" (French *légende*) is a derivative of the Low Latin *legenda* (neuter pl.) meaning "things to be read." The classical original was *legere* ("read, gather," etc.), a cognate of Gk. *légō* ("speak," etc.). From the 12th cent. A.D. *legenda* ("something to be read or recited") referred to the stories of saints and martyrs (see H. Delehaye, *Legends of the Saints* [1962]; Jolles, pp. 23ff.). These legends tried to satisfy the need of ordinary Christians to understand the holiness of character in certain godly lives. Gradually these tales became associated with the saints' and martyrs' special days, when their memories were hallowed and their deeds recalled. In the process, popular devotion embroidered the stories with details so fanciful that the original historical facts were all but obscured. They became known as "miracle stories," though in time the term "legend" was also applied to the narratives of nonreligious heroes. Occasionally the story of one saint's life became that of someone else by the simple exchange of names and locales. Finally the *Legendarium* became a body of romantic devotions essentially devoid of biographical material of any real value to the historian.

***II. Legend as a Form-Critical Genre — the Present Confusion.***–Much modern use of the term "legend" retains the focus on notable human beings, as opposed to myth, which is oriented to the supramundane and to deities rather than mortals. In biblical study the interest is in the earthly leaders of Israel as a covenant people — the patriarchs, prophets, judges, and kings (as well as the later apostles and early Christian missionaries). The stories of the OT heroes are said to have circulated orally in Israel for so long that their eventual written forms contain little historical fact.

The study of legend as a form-critical genre has been severely retarded by the aforementioned confusion of terms and definitions. G. S. Kirk stated the case with both wit and substance: "One man's myth is another man's legend, or saga, or folktale, or oral tadition" (*Nature of Greek Myths* [1975], p. 21). Hals has clearly shown that many of the most distinguished OT scholars have been unable to express clear distinctions between legend and saga — the former often emerging as a mere type of the latter and concentrating on religious rather than secular heroes.

H. Gunkel, the father of OT form-critical study, used the Ger. *Sagen* to designate the original narrative units of the book of Genesis. Apparently he made no attempt to distinguish the oral traditions underlying chs. 1–11 from those of chs. 12–50 by designating them differently. All are *Sagen*. These sagas, originally circulating as separate, self-contained oral traditions, began to attach themselves to the history of the covenant nation. When finally collected into written groups of sagas, according to Gunkel, these stories provided the basis for the written source traditions designated by much of modern OT scholarship as Yahwistic and Elohistic (*Die Sagen der Genesis* [1901]).

Regrettably, the English translator of Gunkel's work consistently used "legend" to render Gunkel's *Sagen*. W. F. Albright, in his introduction to the English translation, noted this fact and implied that it would lead to confusion (pp. xi-xii). Unfortunately, succeeding studies of the sources of Genesis have compounded the problem. By viewing legend as a degenerate form of saga, Gunkel set the stage for further confusion. The great hero-actors of saga became the mere stand-ins of legend, wherein only God can be truly heroic. (Cf. *RGG,* V [2nd ed. 1913], 194-96.)

The Germans who followed Gunkel did little to clear up the confusion. O. Eissfeldt noted the element of the marvelous and unusual in all myths, fairy tales, sagas, and legends. The saga and legend are essentially the same form, distinguished only by the fact that legends have to do with heroes, places, and events that have "religious significance" while the subjects of saga are essentially secular (see also Weiser, pp. 61f.; cf. Fohrer, pp. 86, 90-95).

Hals demonstrated the folly of designating legend as a separate genre if it is merely a form of saga dealing with religiously significant materials. He rightly asked what constitutes the religiously insignificant material that must make up the subject matter of sagas. A. Jolles presented some hope for amelioration of this confusion. According to Jolles the legend stresses "a virtue embodied in a deed," which the readers must imitate. A similar formulation is found in *Forms of the OT Literature:* "A narrative concerned primarily with the wondrous, miraculous, and exemplary . . . aimed at edification . . . [It] belongs to the world of oral folklore and storytellers" (B. Long, *1 Kings* [*Forms of the OT Literature,* IX, 1984], p. 252). Since its purpose is edificatory, it is not bound to recount real events, though its setting is the real world.

***III. Types of Legend.***–Form critics isolate several types of "legendary" material in the Bible:

(1) Sanctuary legends, intended to inculcate awe for a holy place (e.g., Jgs. 6:11-24);

(2) Cultic legends, which encourage awe for ritual practices (e.g., 2 Macc. 1:19-22);

(3) Personal legends, which encourage respect for individuals. Personal legends may be further categorized as (a) layperson legends (e.g., Gen. 22), (b) prophetic legends (e.g., 1 K. 17–19), (c) priestly legends (e.g., Nu. 16–17), (d) court legends (e.g., Dnl. 1), and (e) martyr legends (e.g., 2 Macc. 7).

***Bibliography.***–O. Eissfeldt, *The OT: An Intro.* (Eng. tr. 1965), pp. 34ff.; G. Fohrer, *Intro. to the OT* (Eng. tr. 1968), pp. 90-93; H. Gunkel, *Legends of Genesis: the Biblical Saga and History* (Eng. tr. 1964); R. M. Hals, *CBQ,* 34 (1972), 166-176; E. Jacob, "Sagen und Legenden: Im AT," in *RGG,* V (2nd ed. 1961), 1302-1308; A. Jolles, *Einfache Formen* (2nd ed. 1958); G. S. Kirk, *Myth: Its Meaning and Function in Ancient and Other Cultures* (1970); E. V. McKnight, *What is Form Criticism?* (1969), pp. 10-13; S. Mowinckel, *IDB*, III, *s.v.*; A. Rofé, *JBL*, 89 (1970), 427-440; "Classes in the Prophetical Stories," in *Studies on Prophecy* (*SVT,* 26; 1974), pp. 143-164; J. A. Soggin, *Intro. to the OT* (Eng. tr., *OTL,* rev. ed. 1980), pp. 46-56; G. Tucker, *Form Criticism of the OT* (1971); A. Weiser, *The OT: Its Formation and Development* (Eng. tr. 1961), pp. 57ff.; J. A. Wilcoxen, "Narrative," in J. Hayes, ed., *OT Form Criticism* (1974), pp. 57-98, esp. 77-88.

R. KROEGER

**LEGION** [Gk. *legeṓn, legiṓn* < Lat. *legio*]. Literally, a military unit of six thousand soldiers in the Roman army (*see* ARMY, ROMAN I.B; *see also* JERUSALEM III.I). In the NT the term is used to symbolize the immense power and numbers of spiritual forces: both the angelic hosts of the kingdom of God (Mt. 26:53) and the demonic hosts that oppose the kingdom of God (Mk. 5:9, 15 par. Lk. 8:30). As the Son of God, Jesus has the authority to command obedience from both the heavenly and the demonic legions.

***Bibliography.***–W. L. Lane, *Gospel According to Mark* (*NICNT,* 1974), pp. 184f.; *TDNT,* IV, *s.v.* λεγιών (H. Preisker).

N. J. O.

Three pottery tiles on the Tenth Roman legion from the 1st cent. A.D. (top right) and the 3rd cent. A.D. (left and bottom right) (Israel Museum, Jerusalem)

**LEHABIM** lə-hā'bim [Heb. *l$^e$hāḇîm*; Gk. *Labieim*]; NEB LEHABITES. Descendants of the Egyptians (Mizraim), according to Gen. 10:13; 1 Ch. 1:11. They are not identifiable, but because of morphological similarity, some scholars have suggested emending the name to Lubim, i.e., Libyans. *See* LIBYA. J. McKENNA

**LEHEM** lē'həm [Heb. *lāḥem* (pausal form)] (1 Ch. 4:22). The RSV translates the AV JASHUBI-LEHEM as "returned to Lehem." No such place is known. The NEB and many commentators emend to read "returned to Bethlehem." A less drastic emendation, following the Gk. *apéstrepsen autoús,* would be Heb. *wayyāšuḇû lāhem,* "but they returned (to themselves)," an idiom attested elsewhere (cf. Dt. 5:30; 1 S. 26:12).

**LEHI** lē'hī. *See* RAMATH-LEHI.

**LEMUEL** lem'yōō-əl [Heb. *l$^e$mûʾēl, l$^e$môʾēl*–'belonging to God'; LXX Gk. *eírēntai hypó theoú*–'spoken by God,' i.e., translation rather than transliteration]. An (Arab?) king whose sayings, learned from his mother, constitute vv. 1-9 of Prov. 31. It is also possible that Lemuel was the source of the acrostic poem in Prov. 31:10-31, if the attribution in 31:1 is intended to apply to all of ch. 31.

Lemuel is called "king of Massa" (i.e., king of the Arab kingdom mentioned in Gen. 25:14?) in the RSV and NEB of v. 1. But Heb. *maśśāʾ* can also mean simply "prophecy" (so AV), a meaning it may also have in Prov. 30:1. Nothing otherwise is known of him. Lemuel and/or his mother are notable as non-Israelites through whom inspired Scripture was mediated, and Lemuel's mother as one of the female human authors of Scripture. *See* PROVERBS, BOOK OF.

D. STUART

**LEND; LENDER; LOAN** [Heb. hiphil of *lāwâ*] (Ex. 22:25 [MT 24]; Dt. 28:12, 44; Ps. 37:26; 112:5; Prov. 19:17; 22:7; Isa. 24:2); NEB also ADVANCE (Ex. 22:25); [*nāṯan (b$^e$- or bannešeḵ)*] (Lev. 25:37; Ezk. 18:8, 13); AV also "give forth (upon usury)"; NEB also ADVANCE; [hiphil of *nāšaḵ*] (Dt. 23:19f. [MT 20f.]); [hiphil of *ʿāḇaṭ*] (Dt. 15:6, 8); [*nāšāʾ*] (Dt. 24:10f.; Neh. 5:10); AV also EXACT; NEB also ADVANCE, "be a creditor"; [*š$^{e'}$ʾēlâ*] (1 S. 2:20); NEB "one (for which you asked)"; [Gk. *daneízō*] (Lk. 6:34f.); [*kíchrēmi*] (Lk. 11:5); **BORROW; BORROWER** [Heb. *lāwâ* (Dt. 28:12; Neh. 5:4; Ps. 37:21; Prov. 22:7; Isa. 24:2), *šāʾal*–'ask' (Ex. 22:14 [MT 13]; 2 K. 4:3; 6:5), *ʿāḇaṭ* (Dt. 15:6), *nāšâ* (Jer. 15:10); Gk. mid. of *daneízō* (Mt. 5:42)]; AV also "men have lent to me" (Jer. 15:10).

The OT views riches as a blessing from the Lord (e.g., Prov. 10:22) that entails responsibilities to the poor. The righteous person is characterized as being generous and lending to the poor (Ps. 112:5). One proverb says, "He who is generous to the poor lends to the Lord" (Prov. 19:17, NEB). In Israel the rich were to lend without INTEREST to their neighbors but were permitted to exact interest from a non-Israelite (Lev. 25:35-38; Dt. 23:19f. [MT 20f.]). In addition, controls were placed on a PLEDGE given as security for a loan. The rich person could not enter the borrower's house to seek out a pledge (Dt. 24:10f.). A cloak given in pledge was not to be kept overnight (Ex. 22:26f. [MT 25f.]), and anything that sustained or supported life was not to be accepted as security (Dt. 24:6). Also, a person was not to sell food for profit to a brother who had become poor (Lev. 25:35-38). An Israelite was not to serve as a slave but as a hired servant to pay off a debt, and he was to be released in the year of Jubilee (vv. 39f.).

Just as righteous persons receive the blessing of the Lord, so also does the nation Israel when it is obedient to God (Dt. 28:1-14). As a result, Israel would lend to other nations but not have to borrow (15:6; 28:12). Conversely, one of the curses for Israel's disobedience was that it would have to borrow from a stronger nation (28:44).

Jeremiah referred to the tension and hatred that can build up between a lender and a borrower when he said of the hatred he felt from the people, "I have not lent, nor have I borrowed, yet all of them curse me" (Jer. 15:10). As a result of becoming indebted to a greedy creditor, people could lose their produce, orchards, lands, house, and even their freedom. As Prov. 22:7 states, "The borrower is the slave of the lender." Such a situation existed at the time of Nehemiah, who corrected it by putting an end to lending at interest (Neh. 5:10-13; *see also* MORTGAGE).

Jesus strengthened the OT principles governing loaning. He instructed His followers to loan to everyone, even enemies, without expecting anything in return, for their source of reward is God (Lk. 6:34f.). In the same tenor, Jesus — referring to how a friend, when imposed upon, lends his neighbor bread — invited believers to ask God to satisfy their needs without fear of imposing on Him (11:5-10).

*See also* DEBT. J. E. HARTLEY

**LENTILS** [Heb. *ʿ$^a$ḏāšîm*; Gk. *phakós*] (Gen. 25:34; 2 S. 17:28; 23:11; Ezk. 4:9); AV LENTILES. An annual legume (*Lens esculenta* Moench) whose slender stalks bear pealike pods containing the lentil beans, which make a highly nutritious flour. Three or four varieties of lentils grew in the ancient Near East. Lentils were cut like wheat, threshed, and then stewed to make a soup; *ʿadas* soup is popular with Arabs. The "red pottage" of Gen. 25:34 was doubtless made from reddish-brown lentils.

When David fled from Absalom (2 S. 17:28) he was given lentils for food. Ezekiel made his bread from lentil and other flours (Ezk. 4:9). Shammah, one of David's warriors, defended a patch of lentils against marauding Philistines (2 S. 23:11f.). Some commentators have corrected the "barley" of 1 Ch. 11:13 to "lentils," since both references describe the identical place and event.

R. K. H.

**LEOPARD** [Heb. *nāmēr* (Cant. 4:8; Isa. 11:6; Jer. 5:6; etc.); Aram. *n$^e$mar* (Dnl. 7:6); Akk. *nemru*; Arab. *namir*; Gk. *párdalis* (Sir. 28:23; Rev. 13:2)]; NEB also HUNTING-LEOPARD (Hab. 1:8). A swift and ferocious member of the family Felidae, of which *F. pardus* is representative. The mature animal has a body length of about 1.5 m. (5 ft.) excluding the tail, which can add as much as 1 m. (3 ft.) to its overall dimensions. Palestinian leopards may have been somewhat smaller than their counterparts elsewhere, and apparently had paler coats than the species that inhabited forest areas. The very dark spots distributed across the leopard's body, however, were characteristic of all varieties.

In antiquity leopards were found in Africa, Asia Minor, Palestine, and south Asia. It is possible that place names such as Nimrim, Nimrah, and Beth-nimrah (Isa. 15:6; Jer. 48:34; Nu. 32:2f., 6; Josh. 13:27) reflected the original presence of leopards in the area, since the animals survived in Transjordan until the 20th century. Certainly the Wâdī en-Nuṃeirah ("valley of the small leopard"), which enters the Dead Sea S of the Arnon, perpetuates this type of tradition. Because of its predatory nature the leopard has been discouraged from breeding in Palestine, although attempts to rehabilitate the biblical flora and fauna in Israel will doubtless include one variety or other of the leopard, even if the animals have to be kept in captivity.

In the Bible "leopard" occurs mainly in figurative expressions as a large and fierce beast. The leopard is mentioned with the lion and bear (Dnl. 7:6; Hos. 13:7; Rev. 13:2); with the lion, wolf, and bear (Isa. 11:6); with the lion and wolf (Jer. 5:6); with the lion alone (Sir. 28:23); and with the wolf alone (Hab. 1:8; which also refers to its swiftness). Jer. 13:23 uses a rhetorical question — "Can . . . the leopard (change) his spots?" — to indicate human inability to do good.

In Rev. 13:2, the beast that emerged from the sea was likened to a leopard, although the animal alluded to (*párdalis*) was sometimes known by the Greeks as *pánthēr*. The composite nature of the symbolic beast reflects those of Dnl. 7, and represents the concentration of all their abominations. R. K. H.

**LEPER** lep'ər; **LEPROSY** lep'rə-sē [Heb. *ṣāraʿaṯ*; Gk. *lépra*].

A leper suffers from a specific form of mycobacterial infection that was dreaded in antiquity and that until A.D. 1960 was regarded as intractable and incurable. To reduce the psychological trauma reported by sufferers, the condition has been renamed "Hansen's disease," after G. A. Hansen, who discovered the causative organism (see III below).

I. Terminology
II. Antiquity of Leprosy
III. Symptomatology and Diagnosis
IV. Treatment
V. In the OT
VI. In the NT

***I. Terminology.***–Both ancient and modern writings show considerable confusion about the terminology for leprosy. Heb. *ṣāraʿaṯ* is of uncertain provenance and meaning, having been related variously to the roots for "strike," "become disfigured in the skin," "erupt," and "hornet." Since the ailment is given more prominence than any other in Scripture, the inability to determine the term's derivation is very unfortunate. In Lev. 13 *ṣāraʿaṯ* is evidently used in a technical sense, describing a class of pathological conditions. If related to Akk. *ṣinnītu*, "eruption," the root can describe any type of cutaneous eruptive lesion, including clinical leprosy. The comprehensive nature of *ṣāraʿaṯ* is indicated by its application not only to human pathology but also to molds, mildews, and mineral efflorescence in the walls of buildings or on fabrics.

The LXX translates *ṣāraʿaṯ* by the comprehensive term *lépra*, which for the Greeks signified an ailment that resulted in a scaly condition of the skin. *Lépra* was associated by Herodotus (i.138) and Hippocrates (who named it the "Phoenician disease") with *leúkē*, a cutaneous affliction characterized by a localized absence of pigment, probably the modern leucoderma. Galen (A.D. 130-201) and some Greek medical writers before him employed *eléphas* or *elephantíasis* for a more serious cutaneous disease that seems to have corresponded closely to modern clinical leprosy. The Romans generally preferred the Greek term *lépra* to the more cumbersome *elephantiasis Graecorum* ("of the Greeks"), and the Vulgate uses *lépra* to render Heb. *ṣāraʿaṯ*. Hence "leprosy" occurs in later English versions of the Bible.

Modern versions have difficulty rendering the obscure Hebrew terms in Lev. 13, which contains diagnostic material intended for priests of the 2nd millennium B.C. In v. 2, e.g., Heb. *śᵉʾēṯ* (Gk. *oulḗ*) is translated "rising" in the AV, "swelling" in the RSV, and "discoloration" in the NEB. For Heb. *sappaḥaṯ* (Gk. *sēmasía*) in the same verse, the AV has "scab," the RSV "eruption," and the NEB "pustule." Heb. *bahereṯ* (Gk. *tēlaúgēma*) is variously rendered "bright spot" (AV), "spot" (RSV), and "inflammation" (NEB). Particularly unfortunate is the NEB's use of "malignant skin-disease" for *ṣāraʿaṯ*, which is a comprehensive Hebrew term describing a variety of skin afflictions. Some of these were benign, and the priest could pronounce the sufferer clean. Only one form of *ṣāraʿaṯ*, a chronic, spreading affliction, was deemed malignant by the diagnostic procedure and merited the strictures of vv. 45f.

***II. Antiquity of Leprosy.***–This dreaded disease is supposed to have existed in India and China from *ca.* 4000 B.C., but this dating is very difficult to establish factually. Kinnier Wilson suggested that leprosy may have been the incurable skin condition mentioned in an Old Babylonian omen tablet, since the symptoms include loss of skin pigment, odor, and an apparent outbreak of papules (J. V. Kinnier Wilson, *Revue d'assyriologie et d'archéologie orientale*, 60 [1966], 47). Although serious skin diseases were known to both the Sumerians and the Babylonians, it is impossible to ascertain whether any of the technical terms in the various texts refer to leprosy. But probably the Mesopotamians did become familiar with leprosy during the 3rd millennium B.C.

The disease seems to have been endemic in Egypt from at least the Old Kingdom period (*ca.* 2700-2400 B.C.), and if the term *ukhedu* in the Ebers Papyrus indicates a form of clinical leprosy, then the ailment would have been familiar to the Egyptians before 1500 B.C. *Ukhedu* does seem to describe a malignant disease, but the identification with leprosy is not definite. A malformation in the upper jaw of an Egyptian mummy, *ca.* 1400 B.C., was once thought to be an instance of leprosy but is now regarded as the result of chronic gingival infection. Some writers have expressed surprise at the paucity of cases of leprosy found in Egyptian mummies, since Lucretius (99-55 B.C.) claimed that *eléphas* (leprosy) originated in Egypt. Most probably, however, leprous Egyptians died in some isolated place and were never mummified.

Leprosy was already becoming globally distributed in the 7th cent. B.C., and by *ca.* 250 B.C. it was being reported by Greek physicians. It spread slowly west across Europe, and by *ca.* 40 B.C. it had entered the British Isles.

In view of the lengthy tradition attaching to the existence of the disease, it seems ill-advised to suppose that the Hebrews became acquainted with the affliction only after they had been in sedentary occupation of Canaan for some time. Liberal writers who accept a postexilic date for Leviticus to demonstrate that *ṣāraʿaṯ* had nothing to do with clinical leprosy are actually working against their own theoretical postulates, since the later that Leviticus is dated, the more probable it is that the chronic form of *ṣāraʿaṯ* was Hansen's disease, which was unquestionably in Palestine by the 4th cent. B.C.

*III. Symptomatology and Diagnosis.*–The cause of leprosy is the minute rod-shaped organism *Mycobacterium leprae*, identified by the scientist G. A. Hansen in 1871-1873. (As his terminology indicates, Hansen thought that the infecting agent is a fungus, but it is now known to be a bacillus or bacterium.) Hansen's organism is similar to Koch's bacillus *Mycobacterium tuberculosis* (which causes tuberculosis); indeed, the two bacilli are possibly of common origin, having become different through mutation.

To speak of leprosy symptomatology is to raise some fundamental philosophical issues related to all of human pathology. In the strictest sense there are no such entities as "diseases"; a disease is actually a collection of symptoms that are given a designation for convenience. One must realize that the designation may describe only the principal symptoms, and that a person need not have all the attributed symptoms to have the disease. An equally significant observation is that the pattern, distribution, and character of some diseases have changed over the centuries. Thus Browne (p. 8) properly warned about the dangers of retrospectively diagnosing diseases mentioned in ancient literature, especially if the terminology is indeterminate.

As already noted, Heb. *ṣāraʿaṯ* in Lev. 13–14, although technical and obscure, is known to denote a variety of related conditions (cf. the broad pathological and metaphorical uses of "cancer"). The symptoms of *ṣāraʿaṯ* are detailed in Lev. 13 so that the Hebrew priest-physician could make a differential diagnosis. Since medical legislation in the Torah has a preventative nature, the priest as diagnostician functioned as a health officer more than the Babylonian or Egyptian priest-physician did. The affliction that the Hebrew priest would carefully inspect could have arisen spontaneously (vv. 2-6), or after a prodromal interval of unspecified length (vv. 7f.). It could have succeeded a furuncle, a carbuncle (vv. 18-23), or a burn (vv. 24-28), or it could have developed upon the beard, the head, or elsewhere on the body (vv. 29-44). Preliminary symptoms could include the presence of subcutaneous swellings or nodules (*śeʾēṯ*), a cuticular scab (*sappaḥaṯ*), and whitish-red spots or reddish areas of skin (*baheręṯ*).

If a person with one or more of these symptoms that had turned into a leprous disease presented himself to a priest (13:2), the priest pronounced him leprous after inspection if the local hair had turned white (*leucotrichia*) and if the affliction seemed to have penetrated the skin (v. 3). If the person did not have the last two symptoms, he was quarantined seven days, and then seven more if the symptoms showed no development (vv. 4-6); his condition was diagnosed as an eruption (Heb. *mispaḥaṯ*). *Mispaḥaṯ* appears to be a general term for the slight pustulation occurring in many of the dermatoses.

Another nonmalignant form of *ṣāraʿaṯ* covered the person from head to foot (13:13). This condition could not have been Hansen's disease, which seldom covers the entire body and never makes the skin white. The condition would probably have been psoriasis, in which round reddish patches covered with whitish scales erupt on the scalp, elbows, knees, and back. This common affliction manifests itself in several forms and is sometimes extremely resistant to treatment. Even more probably the sufferer was the victim of vitiligo (acquired leucoderma), a condition marked by white patches on the skin characterized by deficiency of pigment. The body chemistry involved has not yet been explained satisfactorily, but the affliction, like psoriasis, is neither infectious nor harmful.

If, however, the Hebrew sufferer had *bāśār ḥay* (presumably to be translated "raw flesh"), then the condition would no longer have been thought benign (13:14). Apparently ulceration was occurring, as in developed cases of nodular leprosy. If the ulceration or inflammation was local and transitory, the sufferer could be pronounced free of *ṣāraʿaṯ* and therefore would be ceremonially clean again. The extent of cuticular penetration governed the seriousness of the condition, as though the developing pathology was being viewed from inside rather than from outside the skin. This perspective would help explain the decision that any pale or reddish swelling beneath the skin was malignant. The RV translation "deeper than the skin" may thus indicate cutaneous nodules that were about to erupt and form the fetid sores seen in modern lepromatous leprosy. Persistently bright-pink patches of skin (Heb. *baheręṯ*) were a symptom of leprosy; they are sometimes seen on modern lepers.

If the site of a previous staphylococcal infection was ulcerated or inflamed (13:18f.), the symptoms of leucotrichia, cuticular penetration, and the spread of infection determined the seriousness of the condition. The swelling in question (Heb. *šeḥîn*; RSV "boil"; NEB "fester") is of uncertain nature, but it could have been a furuncle, a carbuncle, an ulcer, a keloid, or erysipelas on the site of a boil.

The mention of a burn on the skin (13:24-28) is interesting in view of the medical contention that anesthetic patches are not recorded in this chapter. Burns occur commonly among lepers when cutaneous nerve endings have been made insensitive by the disease. Infection resulting in pus formation or ulcers can have serious consequences if left untreated. Verses 24-28 seem to refer to infection of a burn, perhaps sustained because of the occurrence of maculo-anesthetic leprosy; the condition was pronounced malignant if the reddish-white area had spread and the local hair had changed color.

The seriousness of a disease of the scalp or beard (Heb. *neṯeq*; Gk. *thraúsma*) was governed by the degree of skin penetration as well as by the amount of hair lost and a change in hair color from dark to coppery (RSV "yellow," 13:29-37). These conditions, incidentally, are seen periodically in modern lepers and are attributed by some medical authorities to vitamin or protein deficiency. The condition in vv. 29-37, however, seems to be ringworm. This fungus attacks various areas of the skin and is extremely irritant in nature. It can be contracted from cattle. Hair loss accompanied by a pinkish disease spot indicates chronic leprosy, however.

Dull white spots on the body (13:38f.) were not regarded as malignant; eruption (Heb. *bōhaq*; Gk. *alphós*) was probably vitiligo. In a well-developed case of vitiligo the skin exhibits complete loss of pigment, in contrast to leprosy, the lesions of which are never white.

Leviticus 13:47-59 treats "leprous diseases" in cloth and leather garments. The expression "warp or woof" probably refers to the woven or fabricated material as a whole, which was judged diseased if it appeared greenish or reddish. Fungi, mildew, iron mold, or dampness could be the responsible or facilitating agents. Even buildings could be affected by "leprosy" (14:34-53), which was apparently dry rot or mineral efflorescence affecting stone walls.

The diagnostic principles in Leviticus were deemed sufficient both to establish the nature of the various types of *ṣāraʿaṯ* and to provide for malignant cases. Such sufficiency was very important, if only because the malignant *ṣāraʿaṯ* resembled other dermatoses in so many respects, especially in the initial stages of the ailment, just as Hansen's disease does today. Modern clinicians have similarly established cardinal signs of leprosy, namely, localized hypopigmented patches, loss of sensations particularly of temperature or touch, and the presence of *M. leprae* bacilli taken from skin lesions. If a person has more than one of these signs, he or she is deemed to be a leper. Other experts reduce these signs to two, namely, loss or impairment of cutaneous sensation regardless of the presence or absence of a skin patch, and the thickening of nerves. These basic signs indicate the two principal types of leprosy — lepromatous and nonlepromatous, the latter including tuberculoid, maculo-anesthetic, and polyneuritic varieties. In addition, an intermediate leprosy group accommodates borderline and indeterminate cases.

The prodromal symptoms include vague pains in limbs and joints, with intermittent fever. The incubation period can vary between a few months and thirty years, according to some leprologists, but when the eruptive stage occurs the disease begins to assume its special character. In the severe form, lepromatous leprosy, a hypopigmented patch of skin or numbness of skin occur first, although ulcers, nasal blockage, and other symptoms may anticipate the morbid skin changes. Lepromatous (nodular) leprosy is the most severe form, with the nodules occurring in the skin, mucous membranes, and perhaps subcutaneous tissues. Sometimes the nodules ulcerate and discharge bacilli in large quantities. Many of the peripheral nerves are affected, as are internal organs such as the spleen, liver, lymph nodes, and adrenal glands. Lesions often occur in the nasal mucosa, the larynx, and the eyes. In diffusely infiltrated lepromatous leprosy the skin of almost the entire body may thicken and redden; some hair loss commonly occurs, too. The hypopigmented lesions of macular lepromatous leprosy have smooth, reddish surfaces with little loss of sensation and poorly defined margins. By comparison, nonlepromatous leprosy is milder in character. Tuberculoid leprosy has few lesions, which may be hypopigmented or erythematous, with dry, rough surfaces generally occurring. The lesions often affect peripheral nerves, causing a loss of tactile sensation except occasionally on facial patches. Like sufferers from tuberculoid leprosy, maculo-anesthetic patients are normally noninfective but exhibit hypopigmented skin lesions that are more or less insensitive to touch. Polyneuritic leprosy only involves peripheral nerves, which thicken and sometimes necrose when nodules form and become abscesses. Frequently in advanced stages motor paralysis occurs.

The table may assist in comparing the malignant condition described in Lev. 13 with some forms of modern clinical leprosy.

| Malignant *Ṣāraʿaṯ* | Hansen's Disease |
|---|---|
| Papules or nodules on shiny or erythematous skin patch. | Typical of lepromatous leprosy. Skin patch may also exhibit edema. |
| Hypopigmentation and spreading of patch. | Seen in maculo-anesthetic leprosy, tuberculoid leprosy, and the indeterminate group of leprosy |
| Pinkish-white patches. | Diffuse cutaneous erythema. |
| Cuticular crusts. | Low-grade pustulation common. |
| Subcutaneous nodules. | Seen in nodular lepromatous leprosy. |
| Loss of scalp hair associated with a cutaneous lesion. (Scalp lesions rare?) | Seen in diffusely infiltrated lepromatous leprosy. Hair loss can occur in different areas of the body. |
| Leucotrichia. | Not reported in modern leprosy. |
| A sore on the site of a burn. | Anesthetic skin patches sometimes become infected. |
| Coppery-colored hair in a facial or scalp lesion. | Hair-color changes from black to coppery reported both in children and adults with some forms of leprosy. Scaly lesions rare. |
| Skin ulcers. | Lepromatous ulcers. |
| Disease "deeper than the skin." | Subcutaneous nodules either ready to ulcerate or erupting, seen in lepromatous leprosy. |
| "Quick raw flesh." | Ulceration or inflammation of lepromatous nodules? |
| White, spreading eruption, "no deeper than the skin." | Hypopigmented, slightly raised lesions seen in minor tuberculoid leprosy. |
| "Appearance of leprosy." | Leonine facies, indurated skin typical of diffusely infiltrated lepromatous leprosy. |

The comparison in the table suggests more correspondence between the malignant *ṣāraʿaṯ* of Lev. 13 and some forms of clinical leprosy than has been conceded by medical practitioners (e.g., Browne, p. 14; R. G. Cochrane, p. 9) and some biblical commentators. But it is true that some features of leprosy are unmentioned in Scripture, e.g., the fetid smell of gangrenous ulcers, the thickening of nerves, contractures of joints, osseous changes, and clawing of the fingers.

The fourteen-day quarantine for suspected malignant *ṣāraʿaṯ* has been quite correctly regarded as much too short for clinical leprosy to develop. But it would have allowed certain differential diagnoses, such as scabies or ringworm, to be made. Thus the quarantine would have helped to safeguard the interests of priests and patients alike, since the diagnosis of leprosy even today can be difficult in the early stages of the disease. No doubt ancient lepers, like many of their modern counterparts, usually concealed themselves when they suspected their illness. They probably would have sought a diagnosis only when the symptoms were already well advanced; note that in Lev. 13:2 the patient, his friends, or his relatives seem already to have made a tentative diagnosis. The abysmal terror associated with leprosy from ancient times was an Eastern rather than a Western phenomenon; the modern reductionists who fail to find any connection between Hansen's disease and the malign condition of Lev. 13-14 have been unable to suggest any substitute ailment that would have inspired such abject dread.

*IV. Treatment.*–In contrast to modern practice, no herbal remedies or therapeutic measures were prescribed by the Hebrew priest-physicians. Instead, the person diagnosed as having malignant *ṣāraʿaṯ* was banished from society (Lev. 13:45f.) as a hygienic precaution. He had to proclaim by his appearance and actions his social and religious uncleanness; thus he was prevented from returning and communicating the infection to members of what was meant to be a holy community. There is no record from the ancient Near East of any effort to determine whether leprosy was communicable.

Only if divine healing occurred (cf. Nu. 12:9-15) could the sufferer apply to the priest for a medical discharge. When his healing had been established, he still had to satisfy certain social and religious requirements to be pronounced clean. An appropriate ritual was provided

(14:10-32); the elaborate detail suggests that it was indeed used on occasion.

It must be noted that concepts of cleanness or uncleanness have no real bearing upon the meaning, etiology, or pathology of the term *ṣāraʿaṯ*. The covenant community of Israel was essentially a religious one (Ex. 19:6), and any form of uncleanness or defilement, including that of malignant *ṣāraʿaṯ*, was expressly prohibited. Accordingly, specific cleansing and purifying procedures were followed for mildewed or rotting garments (Lev. 13:47-58) and for buildings similarly affected (14:33-53). These rituals were mandatory when prescribed by the priests, because they carried the full sanction of the law (14:54-57).

Although the leper was regarded under the law as ceremonially unclean, in Scripture leprosy was never considered a sin. To that extent leprosy was merely one of a class of conditions that rendered a person ritually unclean, the main differences being the social abhorrence of the condition and its duration. As with all other forms of healing, the leper's restoration to health was regarded in Scripture as a token of God's grace, and thus the concept of spontaneous remission independent of divine activity had no place in biblical thought.

*V. In the OT.*–The affliction that God imposed upon Moses as a sign (Ex. 4:6) was evidently not chronic *ṣāraʿaṯ*, which, as has been noted, is never white. It may have been leucoderma or psoriasis and was possibly the same affliction as Miriam's (Nu. 12:9-16). In both texts the gloss "white as snow" (Heb. *kaššāleg*, lit. "like snow") differentiates this *ṣāraʿaṯ* from the chronic form. Naaman (2 K. 5) also does not seem to have been afflicted with Hansen's disease, since he lived and worked among his own people. After Naaman's healing the affliction was transferred to Gehazi (vv. 19-27), a gloss again occurs in the Hebrew text to show that the disease was not Hansen's disease, but perhaps scabies or vitiligo (leucoderma). In the early stages of the latter hypopigmented patches of skin develop and can easily be mistaken for lepromatous leprosy, particularly if the observer has no desire for close contact with the sufferer.

The four leprous men at the gate of Samaria most probably constituted a small "leper colony" living together for mutual support (2 K. 7:3-10); there seems no reason for doubting that they had Hansen's disease. Uzziah (2 Ch. 26:19-21) was "smitten" (Heb. *nāgaʿ*; the related noun *negaʿ* is sometimes used synonymously with *ṣāraʿaṯ*) with an ailment that the priests judged to be leprosy, and accordingly he remained in isolation until his death. Browne (p. 13) dismissed the suggestion that Uzziah had sudden hyperemia in a leprous lesion of the forehead that was otherwise inconspicuous. The perpetual quarantine strongly implies chronic *ṣāraʿaṯ*.

*Ṣāraʿaṯ* could also be invoked as a curse upon someone (cf. 2 S. 3:28f.).

*VI. In the NT.*–Although medical and other writers have doubted that OT references to *ṣāraʿaṯ* ever indicate Hansen's disease, it is clear that in Palestine during the NT period clinical leprosy was a reality. The Israelite priests still used the diagnostic criteria of Leviticus (Mt. 8:1-4; Mk. 1:40-44; etc.), and thus "cleansing" is often mentioned in connection with healings recorded in the Gospels. The Gospels' use of "leper" and "leprosy" seems less technical than that of the law, but there is little doubt even from the scanty NT descriptions of the personal and social plight of the sufferers that they were predominantly victims of Hansen's disease.

Jesus and His disciples healed persons with leprosy, but the symptoms associated with that discase are mentioned only in Luke. On their mission of witness the Twelve (cf. Mt. 10:1, 8) were to anticipate the priesthood of all believers by cleansing lepers. The account of the ten lepers (Lk. 17:11-19) uses "cleanse" and "heal" interchangeably, and the believing Samaritan appears as much under the covenant of divine grace as his Jewish companions were. This coterie was most probably a small colony of people suffering from Hansen's disease; doubtless several such groups were scattered about Palestine in NT times. The leper of Lk. 5:12-15 has been considered a victim of a dermatosis other than Hansen's disease, possibly vitiligo, but the description "full of leprosy" (Gk. *plḗrēs lépras*) seems instead to indicate a chronic condition, quite possibly clinical leprosy. Simon the leper (Mt. 26:6 par. Mk. 14:3) perhaps had only vitiligo or patches of hypopigmented macules, since he was in close contact with society.

***Bibliography.***–J. Lowe, *Leprosy Review*, 18 (1947), 54; F. C. Lendrum, *American Journal of Tropical Medicine and Hygiene*, 1 (1952), 999; R. G. Cochrane, *Biblical Leprosy: A Suggested Interpretation* (2nd ed. 1963); O. F. Skinsnes, *Leprosy Review*, 35 (1964), pp. 21, 35, 105, 115, 175; *TDNT*, IV, *s.v.* λέπρα, λεπρός (Michaelis); V. Moeller-Christensen, *History of Syphilis and Leprosy* (1969); J. Milgrom, *Encyclopedia Judaica*, XI (1971), 33-36; R. H. Thangaraj, ed., *Textbook of Leprosy* (1975); *DNTT*, II, 463-66; J. Wilkinson, *SJT*, 30 (1977), 153-169; 31 (1978), 153-166; R. David, *Mystery of the Mummies* (1978); S. G. Browne, *Leprosy in the Bible* (2nd ed. 1979); G. J. Wenham, *Leviticus* (*NICOT*, 1979); V. Moeller-Christensen, *Leprosy Changes of the Skull* (1979); R. K. Harrison, *Leviticus* (*Tyndale OT Comms.*, 1981).

R. K. HARRISON

**LESHEM** lē'shəm [Heb. *lešem*] (Josh. 19:47). A city in the upper Jordan Valley, also called LAISH (Jgs. 18:7, 27, 29). It was captured by the Danites and named DAN. The suggestion has been made (BDB, p. 546) that the name was originally **layšum*, which developed the variants *lešem* (retaining the final *m*) and *layiš* (dropping the final *m*). Lucian reads, "And the sons of Dan went and fought against Lachish [!] . . . and called its name Lesen Dan [B *Lasenndak*, A *Lesen Dan*]," i.e., Leshem-Dan (*md* > *nd*).

W. S. L. S.

**LESSAU** les'sou [Gk. *Lessaou*]; AV DESSAU, confusing uncial *delta* (Δ) with *lambda* (Λ). A village N of Jerusalem, scene of a battle between Nicanor and the Jews (2 Macc. 14:16). The location is unknown. Simons offered a detailed argument against identifying Lessau (Dessau) with Adasa (*GTTOT*, § 1143, pp. 409f.). *See* ADASA. W. S. L. S.

**LET.** Sometimes used in the AV (e.g., Rom. 1:13; 2 Thess. 2:7) in the old sense of "hinder, prevent" (Anglo-Saxon *lettan*) instead of the more common sense of "permit" (Anglo-Saxon *lǣtan*).

**LETHECH** le'thek [Heb. *leṯeḵ*] (Hos. 3:2). *See* WEIGHTS AND MEASURES.

**LETTER** [Heb. *sēper*–'writing'] (Dnl. 1:4, 17); AV LEARNING; NEB LITERATURE, BOOKS; [Gk. *grámmata*]; AV also "written" (2 Cor. 3:7), "letter"; NEB also "letter by letter" (2 Cor. 3:7). An alphabetical character; by extension, literature.

In Daniel the Eng. pl. "letters" renders the singular form, *sēper*, which can also mean "book" (cf. also LETTERS). The AV and NEB translations are suitable alternative renderings of the term in these contexts. Most commentators agree that here *sēper* refers to the Chaldean literature, which may have included works on magic, divination, and astrology written in Sumerian (contra E. J. Young, *Prophecy of Daniel* [repr. 1978], p. 41; *see* CHALDEA VI).

The letters in 2 Cor. 3:7 refer to the characters in which the law was written on the stone tablets (cf. Ex. 31:18; Dt. 5:22). In Gal 6:11 Paul refers to his own handwriting, which was distinguishable from that of the secretary who wrote the letter from his dictation or draft. Although some have thought that the "large" letters imply awkwardness in Paul's handwriting, it is more likely that they were used for emphasis. E. W. S.

**LETTERS** [Heb. *sēper*–'book,' 'writing'] (2 S. 11:14f.; 1 K. 21:8f., 11; 2 K. 5:5-7; 10:1f., 6f.; 19:14; 20:12; 2 Ch. 32:17; Est. 1:22; 3:13; 8:5, 10; 9:20, 30; Isa. 37:14; 39:1; Jer. 29:1, 25, 29); NEB also "envoy" (2 K. 20:12 par. Isa. 39:1); [*ʾiggereṯ*] (2 Ch. 30:1, 6; Neh. 2:7-9; 6:5, 17a, 19; Est. 9:26, 29); [*ništᵉwān*] (Ezr. 4:7; 7:11); [*kᵉṯāḇ*–'writing,' 'document' < *kāṯaḇ*–'to write'] (2 Ch. 2:11 [MT 10]); AV WRITING; [*miḵtāḇ* < *kāṯaḇ*] (2 Ch. 21:12); AV WRITING; [Aram. *ʾiggᵉrâ*] (Ezr. 4:8, 11; 5:6); [*ništᵉwān*] (Ezr. 4:18, 23; 5:5); [Gk. *epistolḗ, grámma*] (Acts 28:21); supplied from the context in Neh. 6:17b; Jer. 29:3 (cf. AV); Acts 15:23 (cf. v. 30); 21:25; 23:34 (cf. v. 33); Col. 4:16b. Written documents effecting communication between two or more perons who cannot communicate orally (see Pardee, p. 2).

Archeologists have discovered thousands of ancient Near Eastern letters dealing with political, military, business, and family or personal matters. Perhaps the best-known letters are the several hundred Amarna letters (*see* AMARNA TABLETS) and the several thousand MARI letters. Both these collections are political and military letters, and both are written in Akkadian cuneiform on clay tablets. The Amarna letters include correspondence between the Egyptian pharaohs Amenhotep III and IV and kings of other nations or Egyptian officials and vassals in Palestine-Syria. F. B. Knutson has given a brief overview of the style and content of some of the Amarna letters, some Râs Shamrah letters (in Akkadian), and some Neo-Babylonian letters. For English translations of some cuneiform letters, see *ANET*, pp. 482-490.

Several much smaller collections of Hebrew letters have also been found, including the LACHISH LETTERS and the ARAD letters, both written on OSTRACA, and the Bar Cochba letters from MURABBAʿÂT, written on papyrus (see Pardee for texts, translations, notes, and thorough bibliography). Similarly, several caches of Aramaic letters have been found, including from Egypt the ELEPHANTINE PAPYRI and Hermopolis Papyri, and some of the Bar Cochba correspondence from Naḥal Ḥeber (see Fitzmyer; a few are translated in *ANET*, pp. 491f.; for texts, translations, and notes, see Cowley, Driver, Kraeling, and Porten). These extrabiblical letters offer evidence for the form of letters in biblical times, evidence not available from the biblical examples, which have been modified to fit into the biblical narrative. Fitzmyer has analyzed the formulaic features of Aramaic letters, and Pardee has done the same for Hebrew letters.

The letters begin with a *praescriptio*, the address and greeting formulas (cf. Fitzmyer, p. 31, who limits the *praescriptio* to the name of the sender and the addressee). In Hebrew letters the *praescriptio* often includes the name and epithet of the recipient and only rarely the name of the sender; in Aramaic letters both recipient and sender are usually named. Greeting formulas follow, invoking a blessing (using *brk*) or wish for the welfare (*šlm*) of the recipient. The transition from the *praescriptio* to the body is marked often by *wʿt* in Hebrew pre-Christian letters (cf. *wᵉʿattâ* in 2 K. 5:6 [RSV omits]; 10:2 [RSV "now, then"]) by *š* in the Bar Cochba Hebrew letters, and by *kʿn, kʿt, wkʿn, wkʿt* (cf. *ûḵᵉʿeṯ*, "and now," Ezr. 4:17), *kʿnt* (cf. *ûḵᵉʿeneṯ*, "and now," Ezr. 4:10f.; 7:12), and *dy* (in the Bar Cochba letters) in Aramaic. Of the Hebrew letters only the Bar Cochba letters have closing formulas, comprising closing greetings and the signature. The Aramaic letters often have closing formulas, including at times the mention of a scribe or secretary and the date.

Like many of the extrabiblical letters, the OT letters are mostly political in nature. For a list of the biblical letters, *see* EPISTLE II; for texts, translations, and notes, see Pardee, pp. 169-182.

Some of the OT Hebrew and Aramaic terms for letter correspond to those used outside the OT, although no

Letter of Agathus to Aphrodite (Oxy. P. 1677). Written on papyrus (*ca.* 3rd cent. A.D.), the letter includes instructions, information, and greetings (Palestine Institute, Pacific School of Religion)

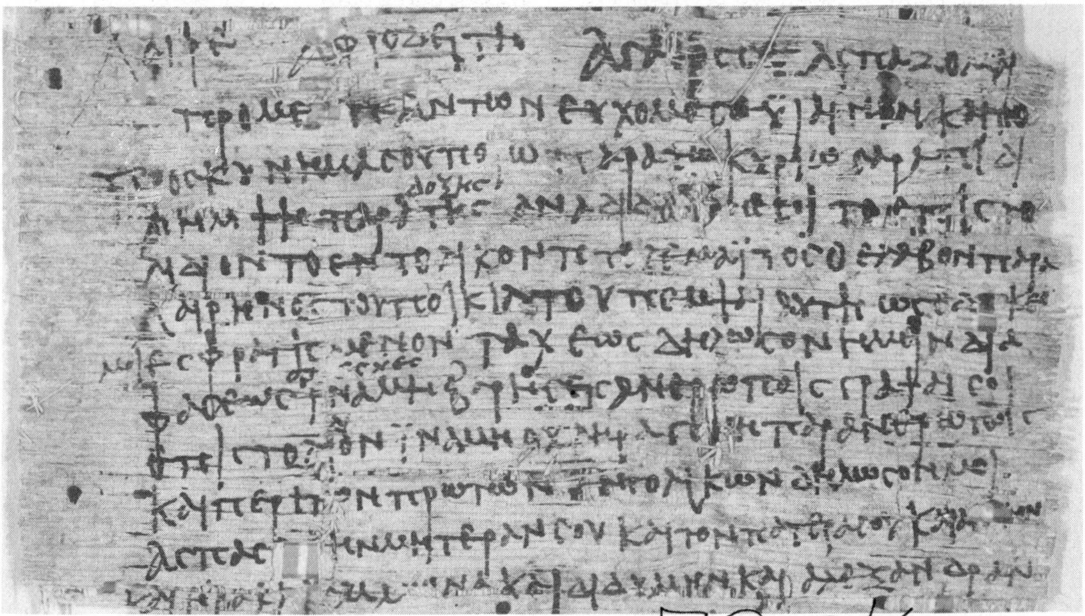

extrabiblical Hebrew letters carry a self-designation. The most common (and probably the oldest) term, both in biblical and extrabiblical letters, is *sēper*, which can refer to any kind of writing (e.g., a book, a document, a letter, an inscription), as can *keṯāḇ* and *miḵtāḇ*. The other terms, *'iggereṯ/'iggerâ* and *ništewān* (both of which occur in Hebrew and Aramaic), are loanwords from Akk. *egirtu* ("letter," "tablet") and Pers. *ništāvana* ("written order") respectively. According to Dion (p. 79), *'iggerâ* is a letter of any type, and *ništewān* can mean a letter but usually refers to an "official document, often styled as a letter" (p. 84; cf. also Fitzmyer, pp. 30f.). These distinctions do not seem to apply to biblical usage, since different terms refer to the same letter in some cases (Ezr. 4:8, 11; 5:5 — *'iggerâ*; 4:18, 23; 5:6 — *ništewān*; Est. 9:20, 30 — *sēper*; vv. 26, 29 — *'iggereṯ*).

The Gk. *grámma*, like Eng. "letter," can refer either to a letter of the alphabet or to a document. Gk. *epistolḗ* (cf. "epistle") refers only to a missive, although its use is broad enough to include both public and private letters. (On A. Deissmann's distinction between epistles and letters, the former being public documents and the latter private, *see* EPISTLE IV.) For a discussion of the NT epistles and their Greco-Roman background, *see* EPISTLE.

***Bibliography.***–A. Cowley, *Aramaic Papyri of the Fifth Century B.C.* (repr. 1967); W. Doty, *Letters in Primitive Christianity* (1973); G. R. Driver, *Aramaic Documents of the Fifth Century B.C.* (rev. ed. 1965); E. G. Kraeling, *Brooklyn Museum Aramaic Papyri* (repr. 1969); A. L. Oppenheim, *Letters from Mesopotamia* (1967); D. Pardee, *et al.*, *Handbook of Ancient Hebrew Letters* (1982); B. Porten, *Archives from Elephantine* (1968); J. L. White, ed., *Studies in Ancient Letter Writing* (Semeia, 22; 1982), which includes F. B. Knutson, "Cuneiform Letters and Social Conventions," pp. 15-23; J. A. Fitzmyer, "Aramaic Epistolography," pp. 25-57; P. E. Dion, "Aramaic Words for 'Letter'," pp. 77-88.

G. A. LEE

**LETUSHIM** lə-to͞o'shim [Heb. *leṭûšîm*] (Gen. 25:3). An obscure Arabian tribe descended from Abraham and Keturah through DEDAN.

**LEUMMIM** lə-um'im [Heb. *le'ummîm*] (Gen. 25:3). An obscure Arabian tribe listed with the Asshurim and Letushim as descendants of Abraham and Keturah through DEDAN.

**LEVI** lē'vī [Heb. *lēwî*; Gk. *Leui*]; AV Apoc. also LEVIS (1 Esd. 9:14). In 1 Esd. 9:14 the AV and NEB follow the LXX (*kaí Leuis,* "and Levi[s]"), but this reading is probably an error for *ho Leuitēs,* "the Levite" (so RSV; cf. Ezr. 10:15; Neh. 8:7).

**1.** The third son of Jacob and Leah (Gen. 29:34; cf. 35:23; Ex. 1:2; 1 Ch. 2:1) and eponymous ancestor of the tribe of Levi.

The etymology of the name Levi is suggested in Gen. 29:34. Leah says after the birth of Levi, "Now this time my husband will be joined [niphal of *lāwâ*] to me, because I have borne him three sons." The name expressed Leah's assurance that the birth of her third son would enhance the bonds of her husband's affection. A wordplay is apparent in Nu. 18:2, 4, where the tribe of Levi is directed to "join" Aaron in the ministry of the sanctuary.

Many scholars dismiss such "popular" etymologies as "pleasant examples of Biblical folklore" which have no philological support as real etymologies (Cody, pp. 29-33). While generally acknowledging that the meaning and derivation of the name are uncertain, scholars have made various suggestions. J. Wellhausen (*Prolegomena to the History of Israel* [Eng. tr. 1885], p. 145) proposed an etymology which is widely espoused today, namely, that Levi is simply a gentilic form of his mother's name Leah (*lē'â,* "wild cow"). The name has also been interpreted as adjectival, explaining Levites as those who attached themselves to and accompanied the Israelites during the Exodus from Egypt. On the basis of Minaean inscriptions from the trading colony which flourished at el-ʿUlā (biblical Dedan) in northern Arabia, W. F. Albright derived Heb. *lēwî,* "Levite," from Arab. *lawiyu,* meaning a "person pledged for a debt or vow" (*ARI,* pp. 106f., 203f. n. 42). For further discussion of proposed etymologies, see *ILC,* III-IV, 680; Cody, pp. 29-33; Meek, pp. 121-132.

Apart from those events common to all the sons of Jacob (Gen. 37; 42–45), Levi is prominent only in Gen. 34. The narrative recounts the rape of Levi's sister Dinah (Gen. 30:21) by Shechem son of Hamor the Hivite. Hamor sought a marriage alliance and the sons of Jacob set the condition of marriage, namely, the circumcision of every male (vv. 13-17). The proposal was approved by the town council and carried out. While the Shechemites were recovering, Dinah's humiliation was violently avenged by Levi and Simeon. Every male was massacred and the city was plundered (vv. 25-29). Concern for self-preservation prompted Jacob's condemnation of this treacherous slaughter (vv. 29f.). This vendetta would be remembered in Jacob's last days (Gen. 49:5-7). The tribes of Simeon and Levi were scattered, but the latter was given a blessed dispersion as the priestly element in Israel (Ex. 32:26ff.; Nu. 18:20, 23; 35:2-8).

Modern critical scholarship tends to assume that the narrative in Gen. 34, together with 49:5-7, represents a personalized history of the tribes of Simeon and Levi in their attempt to settle at Shechem (*NHI,* pp. 70f.; Rowley, pp. 122f.; cf. T. J. Meek, pp. 122ff.).

The three sons of Levi were Gershon (Gen. 46:11; Ex. 6:16; Nu. 3:17) or Gershom (1 Ch. 6:1; 6:16-20, 43, 62, 71; 15:7; 23:6), Kohath, and Merari. The family's migration to Egypt is recorded in Gen. 46:11. Jochebed, wife of Amram and mother of Aaron, Moses, and Miriam, was a daughter of Levi (Nu. 26:59; cf. Ex. 6:14-20). Levi lived to be 137 (Ex. 6:16).

In Exodus and later references Levi appears as a priestly tribe or as a tribe associated with the priesthood as ministers of the sanctuary (Nu. 1:47-54; 8:5-26; 31:30, 47; Dt. 10:8f.; 31:9, 25; 2 S. 15:24; 1 Ch. 16:4f.; 23:24-32; 2 Ch. 8:14f.; 17:7-9; 35:3; Ezr. 3:8-11; Neh. 8:7-9; 10:37-39 [MT 38-40]). For a discussion of the origins and role of the priestly tribe of Levi in Israel's history, *see* PRIESTS AND LEVITES. No further details of the personal history of this patriarch are known.

**2.** Son of Melchi and father of Matthat in Jesus' genealogy (Lk. 3:24).

**3.** Son of Simeon and father of Matthat in Jesus' genealogy (Lk. 3:29f.).

**4.** Another name for the apostle MATTHEW (Mk. 2:14 par. Lk. 5:27, 29).

***Bibliography.***–A. Cody, *History of OT Priesthood* (1969); T. J. Meek, *Hebrew Origins* (rev. ed., repr. 1960); H. H. Rowley, *From Joseph to Joshua* (1950); *TDNT,* IV, *s.v.* Λευ(ε)ί, Λευ(ε)ίς (Strathmann).

G. PRATICO

**LEVIATHAN** lə-vī'-ə-thən [Heb. *liwyāṯān*; cf. Heb. *liwyâ,* "wreath"; Arab. *lawā,* "to twist"] (Job 3:8f.; 41:1 [MT 40:25]; Ps. 74:14; 104:26; Isa. 27:1); AV also "their mourning"; NEB also WHALE. The proper name (it always occurs without the definite article) of a large aquatic animal, perhaps reflecting a mythological monster.

A widely attested theme of the pagan creation myths concerns the draconic monster that threatens the creator god, who at last overcomes the monster in the act of creation (cf. Wakeman, Heidel). But in Ps. 104:26ff. the great sea "monster" of the myths is made to be God's pet (see M. Dahood, *Psalms,* III [*AB,* 1970], 45, for this rendering so reminiscent of Job 41), who waits submissively for God's life-sustaining provision.

Lotan (or Litan, see J. Emerton, *VT,* 32 [1982], 327-331), the adversary of Baal and Anath in the Ugaritic myths, has long been recognized as the equivalent of OT Leviathan (see M. Pope, *Job* [*AB,* 3rd ed. 1973], pp. 329-331). Among the several references to Lotan in the Ugaritic literature (see *DOTT,* pp. 129-133) is one especially impressive parallel to Isa. 27:1 (*UT,* 67:I:1-3): "When you smote Lotan the fleeing serpent, you made an end of the twisting serpent, the mighty one of the seven heads" (cf. also Ps. 74:14). This parallel does not imply any challenge to the fiercely monotheistic commitment of Isaiah; as E. Smick (*WTJ,* 44 [1982], 90f.) noted, the pagan use of Leviathan exclusively in connection with nature myths is everywhere historicized in the Bible. Thus Isaiah intends it merely as a forceful poetic figure for the ultimate defeat of the power of the evil one at the end of the age (so R. Clements, *Isaiah 1–39* [*NCBC,* 1980], p. 218); cf. M. G. Kline, *Kingdom Prologue* [1981], pp. 56-59).

While Job 3:8f. involves several obscurities, Smick (*WTJ,* 40 [1978], 215) pointed out that Job's appeal to professional cursers to damn the day of his birth may find a reflex in the mythological notion that an eclipse was brought about by the chaos monster swallowing the sun (or encoiling it with its serpentine body; cf. Heidel, p. 106).

Job 41:1-34 (MT 40:25–41:26), the most extended description of Leviathan, suggests to many the crocodile (so RSVmg.). In His confrontation of Job, the Lord's point seems to be that while Job is no more a match for the power of evil than he would be for a crocodile, Yahweh is Lord of both the natural order (Job 38:1–40:2) and the moral order (40:6–41:34) — sovereign even over Satan in the figure of Leviathan, His pet crocodile. Such sovereignty provides the only adequate answer for Job in his anguish — the world is God's not man's, and Job may trust that God's inscrutable ways will not be thwarted.

For use of the Leviathan image in the apocalyptic literature (e.g., 2 Esd. 6:52; 2 Bar. 29:3-8) see O. Kaiser, *Isaiah 13–39* (Eng. tr., *OTL,* 1974), pp. 221-23; J. M. Ford, *Revelation* (*AB,* 1975), pp. 217ff.

While the NT does not explicitly mention Leviathan, the seven-headed dragon of Rev. 12:3f.; 13:1ff. may allude to him (see Ford, pp. 210, 217-221).

*See also* Dragon; Rahab.

***Bibliography.***–C. H. Gordon, "Leviathan: Symbol of Evil," in A. Altmann, ed., *Biblical Motifs* (1966) 1-9; A. Heidel, *Babylonian Genesis* (2nd ed. 1951); N. K. Kiessling, *JBL,* 89 (1970), 167-177; J. N. Oswalt, *EQ,* 49 (1977), 163-172; E. B. Smick, *JETS,* 13 (1970), 101-108; M. K. Wakeman, *God's Battle With The Monster* (1973).

G. P. HUGENBERGER

**LEVIRATE LAW.** *See* Marriage IV.A.2; Brother's Wife; Husband's Brother.

**LEVIS** (1 Esd. 9:14, AV). *See* Levi.

**LEVITES.** *See* Priests and Levites.

**LEVITICAL CITIES.** On the eve of Israel's conquest of Canaan, Moses directed that forty-eight cities, distributed proportionately among the various tribal allotments, be set aside for the use of the Levites in lieu of any unified tribal territory of their own (Nu. 35:1-8). In addition, six of these were to be established as cities of refuge (*see* Refuge, Cities of). Apart from scattered references and brief allusions to some of these cities (Josh. 14:14; 1 Ch. 13:2; 2 Ch. 11:14; 31:15, 19), three principal texts require our attention.

Leviticus 25:32-34 grants special rights to Levites within their cities, apparently to protect them from dispossession. Sale of their pasture land (adjacent to the cities, Nu. 35:1-8) is expressly prohibited. If they sell any homes within their cities they are granted an unlimited right of redemption as opposed to the usual one-year limit applicable to other tribes. Finally, all homes revert to their original owners in the Year of Jubilee.

Joshua, Eleazar the priest, and the heads of the tribal families oversaw the actual determination of the forty-eight levitical cities by lot (Josh. 21:1-42). A close parallel to this text, but with significant variations both in its framework and in the particular cities listed, is 1 Ch. 6:54-81 (MT 39-66). Further significant variants to both these lists as witnessed in the MT are to be found in the versions, especially in the Greek MSS. Some conservatives have tried to explain away these discrepancies, while many critics have interpreted them as evidence of the unhistorical character of the scheme of Levitical cities. Curiously both these approaches are inappropriately reluctant to emend the MT despite the versional evidence.

In the chart below are the Levitical clans, tribal locations, and forty-eight Levitical cities as they appear in both Josh. 21 and 1 Ch. 6 when appropriately emended according to the versional evidence (for a discussion of the text-critical issues see the articles and comms. by Albright, Auld, Boling and Wright, Mazar, and Williamson). Those marked with a question mark are of uncertain location. The six Levitical cities that are also cities of refuge are italicized.

The claim that provision of Levitical cities contradicts the more general assertion that the Priests and Levites would lack an inheritance fails to be decisive for several reasons. (1) This "inheritance" cannot be compared to that of the other tribes because these cities did not constitute a unified land area. (2) The Levites are nowhere actually granted exclusive title to these cities — what they are given is a right to their use (cf. Mazar, p. 193). This appears to be the direct implication of the repeated phrase in Nu. 35:2f. that these cities were for the Levites "to dwell in" (so M. Noth, *Numbers* [Eng. tr., *OTL,* 1968], p. 253). (3) Scripture elsewhere describes these cities as belonging to their respective tribal allotments rather than considering them the possession of a thirteenth tribe, the Levites (e.g., Josh. 21:41; Jer. 32:8).

Later biblical evidence of Levites actually living within these forty-eight cities is surprisingly limited (1 S. 6:13-15; 1 K. 2:26; Jer. 1:1; 32:7-9; 1 Ch. 26:30, 32). This may be due to the "mission station" quality of these cities (see below), or it may simply reflect the failure of practice to conform to precept, as at so many other points of Israel's experience.

Any assessment of the purpose of the arrangement of Levitical cities depends, of course, on the historical setting which is posited for this list. If the canonical context of the Conquest is granted, the purpose of the allotment of these cities was surely related to the special Levitical ministry of covenant teaching among the twelve tribes (Dt. 33:10; 2 Ch. 35:3; Neh. 8:7-9; cf. G. E. Wright, *VT,* 4 [1954], 329; E. F. Campbell, *Ruth* [*AB,* 1975], pp. 21f.; R. B. Robinson, *Studia Biblica et Theologica,* 8 [1978], 3-24; Boling and Wright, pp. 161f.).

The point of the Levitical cities would be to provide not cult shrines (with few exceptions, such places are lacking from the list) but bases of operation so that the Levites could better infiltrate each of the tribes to instruct them in Yahweh's covenant. Such bases would be most needed precisely where we find them: in those areas least accessible to the central sanctuary. Thus we cannot expect that the Levites would be confined to their cities. Rather,

### List of Levitical Cities

**Aaronic Kohathites:**

JUDAH AND SIMEON:

(1) *Hebron*/Kiriath-arba (see Mazar, pp. 196ff.; Auld, *ZAW*, 202)
(2) Libnah ?
(3) Jattir ?
(4) Eshtemoa
(5) Holon (1 Chronicles: Hilen) — unidentified
(6) Debir
(7) Ashan (Joshua: Ain) ? — unidentified
(8) Juttah (1 Chronicles omits)
(9) Beth-shemesh (see Auld, *ZAW*, 203-206)

BENJAMIN:

(10) Gibeon (1 Chronicles omits)
(11) Geba
(12) Anathoth
(13) Alemeth (Joshua: Almon)

**Other Kohathites:**

EPHRAIM:

(14) *Shechem* (see above on Hebron)
(15) Gezer
(16) Kibzaim or Jokmeam ? (Mazar, p. 198, suggested that Kibzaim was later renamed Jokmeam after the Levitical family that settled there; cf. 1 Ch. 23:19; 24:23)
(17) Beth-horon (Lower and Upper)

DAN: (This tribal name, as well as Elteke and Gibbethon, were lost in 1 Ch. 6, apparently by a scribal accident. The result of this loss is that the remaining two Danite cities are awkwardly listed as belonging to Ephraim; cf. Williamson, p. 75)

(18) Elteke (1 Chronicles omits) ?
(19) Gibbethon (1 Chronicles omits)
(20) Aijalon
(21) Gath-rimmon ?

MANASSEH:

(22) Taanach (1 Chronicles: Aner)
(23) Ibleam (Joshua: Gath-rimmon; 1 Chronicles: Bileam)

**Gershonites:**

(24) *Golan*
(25) Beeshterah or Ashtaroth

ISSACHAR:

(26) Kishon (Joshua: Kishion; 1 Chronicles: Kedesh) ?
(27) Daberath
(28) Ramoth (Joshua: Jarmuth) ?
(29) En-gannim (1 Chronicles: Anem)

ASHER:

(30) Mashal (Joshua: Mishal) ?
(31) Abdon
(32) Helkath (1 Chronicles: Hukok) ?
(33) Rehob

NAPHTALI:

(34) *Kedesh*
(35) Hammoth-dor (1 Chronicles: Hammon) ?
(36) Kartan or Kiriathaim

**Merarites:**

ZEBULUN:

(37) Jokneam (Joshua: Kartah; 1 Chronicles omits)
(38) Rimmon (Joshua: Dimnah; 1 Chronicles: Rimmono)
(39) Nahalal (1 Chronicles omits) ?
(40) Tabor (Joshua omits) ? — unidentified

REUBEN:

(41) *Bezer* ?
(42) Jahaz ?
(43) Kedemoth ?
(44) Mephaath ?

GAD:

(45) *Ramoth in Gilead*
(46) Mahanaim ?
(47) Heshbon ?
(48) Jazer ?

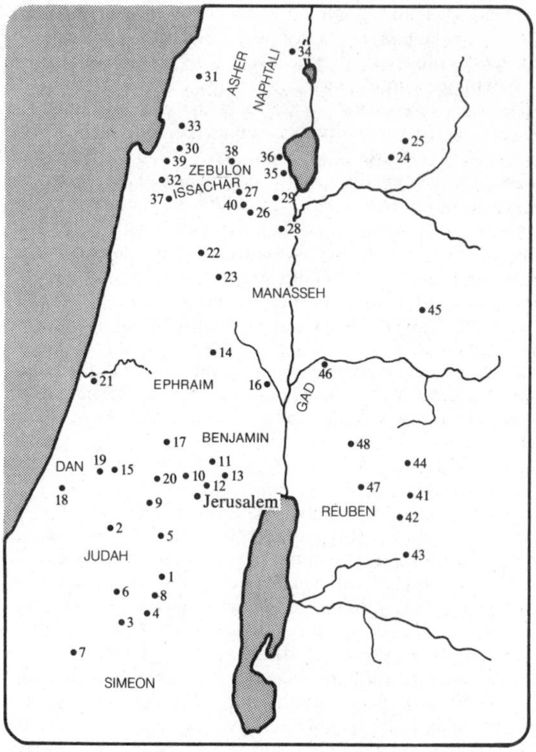


we expect exactly what is implied in the example of Abiathar, who first served at Nob, then was attached to David, and finally was dismissed by Solomon for disloyalty and returned to his assigned Levitical city, Anathoth (1 S. 21:2; 22:9-19; 1 K. 2:26).

Of course, to emphasize this teaching aspect of the Levitical ministry is not to deny other dimensions of their ministry (e.g., with respect to the ark and central sanctuary), in particular, the political dimension (cf. Mazar, *et al.*). Certainly the Levitical desire to secure Israel's loyalty to the Lord of the covenant would also imply a commitment to secure loyalty to the Lord's anointed (the king). A good example of the proper blending of political involvement and covenant teaching is 2 Ch. 17:7-9. Here the godly King Jehoshaphat sent out his princes and a number of prominent Levites to teach and further the work of reformation: "and they taught in Judah, having the book of the law of the Lord with them; they went about through all the cities of Judah and taught among the people."

***Bibliography.***–W. F. Albright, "The List of Levitic Cities," in S. Lieberman, *et al.*, eds., *Louis Ginzberg Jubilee Volume*, I (1945), 49-73; A. G. Auld, *ZAW*, 91 (1979), 194-206; "Joshua: The Hebrew and Greek Texts," in J. A. Emerton, ed., *Studies in the Historical Books of the OT* (*SVT*, 30; 1979), pp. 1-14; R. G. Boling and G. E. Wright, *Joshua* (*AB*, 1982); M. Haran, *JBL*, 80 (1961), 45-54, 156-165; *Temples and Temple Service in Ancient Israel* (Eng. tr. 1978), pp. 112-131; B. Mazar, "The Cities of the Priests and the Levites," *SVT*, 7 (1960), 193-205; H. G. M. Williamson, *1 and 2 Chronicles* (*NCBC*, 1982), pp. 68-76.

G. P. HUGENBERGER

**LEVITICUS** lə-vit'i-kəs.

I. Title and Contents
II. Structure
III. Sources
IV. Authorship and Date

V. Theology
VI. Leviticus and the Christian

*I. Title and Contents.*–The first word of the book serves as its Hebrew title, *wayyiqrā',* "and he called." The English title Leviticus is borrowed from the Latin Vulgate translation, which in turn had adapted it from the LXX. Leviticus is a fairly appropriate title for the book, for it deals largely with priestly matters, and the priests were drawn from the tribe of Levi.

Leviticus is not simply a manual for priests, however; it is equally, if not more, concerned with the part that the laity should play in worship. Most of the laws apply to all Israel: only a few sections concern the priests alone, e.g., chs. 21–22. Thus the book was relevant to every Israelite, and, as we shall see, is relevant to Christians as well.

*II. Structure.*–The material in Leviticus is for the most part clearly and logically arranged. This is immediately apparent from a summary of its contents.

I. Laws on Sacrifice (1:1–7:38)
  A. Instructions for the Laity (1:1–6:7 [MT 5:26])
    1. Burnt Offering (Ch. 1)
    2. Cereal Offering (Ch. 2)
    3. Peace Offering (Ch. 3)
    4. Purification Offering (4:1–5:13)
    5. Reparation Offering (5:14–6:7 [MT 5:26])
  B. Instructions for the Priests (6:8 [MT 6:1]–7:38)
    1. Burnt Offering (6:8-13 [MT 1-6])
    2. Cereal Offering (6:14-18 [MT 7-11])
    3. Priests' Cereal Offering (6:19-23 [MT 12-16])
    4. Purification Offering (6:24-30 [MT 17-23])
    5. Reparation Offering (7:1-10)
    6. Peace Offering (7:11-36)
    7. Summary (7:37f.)
II. Institution of the Priesthood (8:1–10:20)
  A. Ordination of Aaron and His Sons (Ch. 8)
  B. Aaron's First Sacrifices (Ch. 9)
  C. Judgment on Nadab and Abihu (Ch. 10)
III. Uncleanness and Its Treatment (11:1–16:34)
  A. Unclean Animals (Ch. 11)
  B. Uncleanness of Childbirth (Ch. 12)
  C. Unclean Diseases (Ch. 13)
  D. Cleansing of Diseases (Ch. 14)
  E. Unclean Discharges (Ch. 15)
  F. Purification of the Tabernacle from Uncleanness (Ch. 16)
IV. Prescriptions for Practical Holiness (17:1–27:34)
  A. Basic Principles about Sacrifice and Food (Ch. 17)
  B. Basic Principles of Sexual Behavior (Ch. 18)
  C. Principles of Neighborliness (Ch. 19)
  D. Capital and Other Grave Crimes (Ch. 20)
  E. Rules for Priests (Ch. 21)
  F. Rules about Eating Sacrifices (Ch. 22)
  G. Religious Festivals (Ch. 23)
  H. Rules for the Tabernacle (24:1-9)
  I. Case of Blasphemy (24:10-23)
  J. Sabbatical and Jubilee Years (Ch. 25)
  K. Exhortation to Obey the Law: Blessing and Curse (Ch. 26)
  L. Redemption of Votive Gifts (Ch. 27)

Under the Sinai covenant Israel was called to become "a kingdom of priests and a holy nation" (Ex. 19:6). Lev. 1–16 focuses almost exclusively on Israel's priestly responsibilities. By preserving its purity these laws enabled Israel to remain in contact with God and witness to His presence in the world. The closing chapters of the book focus on the demand for national holiness: "You must be holy: for I the Lord your God am holy" (Lev. 19:2). This and similar formulas are used repeatedly throughout chs. 18–26 to emphasize that Israel was redeemed to be God's holy people; they also bring together laws on a variety of subjects whose interrelationships are not always obvious. This collection of laws concludes in typical oriental fashion with blessings on the nation if it keeps the laws and threats if it does not. Chapter 27 seems to be a sort of appendix.

One striking feature of the Levitical laws is so obvious that it is easily overlooked. At the beginning of nearly every chapter, and often several times within a chapter, are the words "The Lord spoke to Moses." Thus all the laws are set within a narrative framework. According to the author they were revealed to Moses during Israel's wilderness wanderings to meet specific problems that arose at that time. This historical setting accounts for some features of the book that would seem out of place if it had been arranged in a purely logical fashion. For example, the instructions to the priests in ch. 10 are placed in their present position because they were given then, and the same motive may account for the law on blasphemy in ch. 24. The people knew that it was wrong "to take God's name in vain" (Ex. 20:7) but did not know how to punish those who did. This episode explains how God disclosed that stoning was the appropriate penalty.

The same idea underlies the arrangement of the other groups of laws. Leviticus is part of the Pentateuch and therefore cannot be looked at in isolation. The book of Exodus concludes with the erection of the tabernacle and God's appearing in glory there, a sign that He would be with them wherever they went (Ex. 40:34-38). A church building needs services and ministers as well as God's presence, so it is natural that the sequel to Exodus should begin by describing the worship in the tabernacle (Lev. 1–17). The succeeding chapters are equally apt within the historical framework of the Pentateuch. Israel's goal was Canaan, not the wilderness, and indeed until the disastrous episode of the spies (Nu. 13–14) the Israelites expected to enter the Promised Land very shortly. Guidance as to the conduct befitting a holy people was therefore welcome at this stage of their development. Many of the laws in chs. 18–27 could apply only to a sedentary agricultural community, not to wandering nomads.

*III. Sources.*–The author did not impose a uniform literary style on the book: the laws are not always cast in the same pattern. Words or turns of phrase characteristic of one section do not always appear in another section, even though both sections may deal with similar topics. In this respect Leviticus more closely resembles the laws of Eshnunna, which have variations in style between different sections, than the laws of Hammurabi, which are drafted in an artificial and uniform style. Criteria such as opening and closing formulas help to distinguish the following groups of laws.

| | |
|---|---|
| (1) Chs. 1–3 | key words: "food offerings" |
| (2) 4:1–6:7 (MT 5:26) | key words: "he will be forgiven" |
| (3) 6:8 (MT 6:1)–17:16 | opening formula: "this is (the law of)" |
| (4) Chs. 18–26 | regular formula: "I am the Lord (your God)" |
| (5) Ch. 27 | key word: "valuation" |

This analysis of the material differs from the usual analysis of Leviticus which ascribes the whole book to the priestly source (P), which in turn used earlier collections of law. Scholars generally have held that only the narrative sections (chs. 8–10, 16) come from P itself. The other sections were originally independent and have been worked over to give them a priestly slant and style. The earlier collections consisted of chs. 1–7, chs. 11–15, chs. 17–26 (the Holiness Code), and ch. 27.

The standard critical analysis just explained seems vulnerable at two points. First, it fails to recognize that the recurring opening phrase "this is" ("these are") links together chs. 6–17. Indeed, 17:2, "This is the thing which the Lord has commanded," is identical with 8:5. It is wrong to propose the existence of different sources merely on the basis that some sections are narrative, others legal. All Leviticus is law within a narrative framework. Second, it is doubtful whether ch. 17 belongs with the following chapters as part of the Holiness Code. Long ago Hoffmann (I, 469) pointed out that ch. 17 seems to belong with what precedes it, not with what follows. Much more recently R. Kilian (*Literarkritische und Formgeschichtliche Untersuchung des Heiligkeitsgesetzes* [1963], pp. 176ff.) pointed out that Lev. 17 is quite distinct from the rest of the Holiness Code.

The tentativeness of all attempts to discover sources in Leviticus must be underlined. Even if one admits their presence it does not necessarily follow that they ever circulated independently of each other. Analyses that purport to distinguish between an original source and the work of later redactors should be treated more warily still. We do not know enough about the development of Hebrew language, law, and religion to make the elaborate analyses offered in some works anything more than conjectures.

***IV. Authorship and Date.***–Leviticus claims throughout to record what God revealed to Moses; nowhere does it ever state that Moses wrote down what he heard. The book's lack of explicitness about its literary origin is one reason for the great diversity of views among modern scholars. The issue is highly complex; it really involves the question of the composition of the whole Pentateuch. Here it must suffice to set out very briefly the arguments for and against the different views as far as they concern Leviticus.

*A. The Traditional View.* This is the view that Leviticus was compiled by Moses himself or that at least the material in the book, if not its final shape, goes back to Moses.

Four main arguments are used to support this view. First, the book always presupposes that the laws were given to Moses in the wilderness. Time and again we are told, "The Lord spoke to Moses." The wilderness setting is not merely referred to in the introduction to each group of laws; it is often alluded to in the laws themselves. The sacrifices are offered in the tabernacle, not in the temple (chs. 1–17); lepers must live outside the camp, not outside the city (13:46); 17:1-9 presupposes that every Israelite is within easy reach of the tabernacle. Laws that would apply only to a settled people are generally prefaced by a statement that God is bringing Israel into the land of Canaan, where such laws will become applicable (14:34; 18:3; 23:10; 25:2).

Second, nothing in Leviticus cannot date from the Mosaic period. Elaborate rituals and sacrificial systems are attested in the ancient Near East long before the time of Moses. The normal critical view that these institutions are a late feature of Israelite religion is contrary to what is known about the religious practices in neighboring contemporary cultures.

Third, the book is unsuited to the needs of the postexilic age. For example, although Lev. 18 and 20 deal at length with the question of marriage, nothing is said about intermarriage with Canaanites, the burning issue in Ezra and Nehemiah's time (Ezr. 9–10; Neh. 13:23ff.). While Leviticus magnifies the office of high priest, the priests of Nehemiah's day seem to have been opposed to reform (Neh. 13). The tithe laws (Nu. 18:26ff.), which come from the same source as Leviticus, seem to presuppose a ratio of ten Levites to one priest, yet from Ezr. 8:15 we discover that after the Exile there was a great shortage of Levites; the lists (Ezr. 2:36ff.; Neh. 7:39ff.) suggest a ratio of twelve priests to one Levite among the returning exiles.

Finally, the book of Ezekiel quotes or alludes to Leviticus many times (cf. Lev. 10:10 with Ezk. 22:26; Lev. 18:5 with Ezk. 20:11; Lev. 26 with Ezk. 34). This does not of course prove a Mosaic date for Leviticus but merely that it was an old work whose laws were binding on Israel because they enshrined the covenant between God and His people.

*B. The Standard Critical View.* The postexilic origin of the priestly work (P) has become an axiom of biblical scholarship. J. Wellhausen's *Prolegomena to the History of Israel* (1878; repr. 1973) is the classic exposition of why P is believed to be the latest of the pentateuchal sources (cf. CRITICISM, esp. II.D).

According to Wellhausen one can trace a development in Israel's religious life and practice. In the earliest days worship was simple, free, and spontaneous. It gradually became more hidebound by law and custom, until eventually it reached a stage of rigid ritualistic legalism. With the growing emphasis on form and ritual went an increase in the power and privileges of the priesthood. P and the books of Chronicles represent the endpoint of this religious evolution.

These trends can be discerned in several different areas of religious life. First, there is the question of the place of worship. In the days of Samuel there was freedom to sacrifice wherever one chose (e.g., 1 S. 16:2). King Josiah, however, limited all sacrifice to the temple in Jerusalem (2 K. 23; cf. Dt. 12). Leviticus (e.g., 17:1-9) simply assumes that all sacrifices must be offered in the tabernacle. According to most critical scholars the tabernacle and the cult described in Leviticus are projections into the Mosaic past of the temple in Jerusalem. That Leviticus simply assumes that all sacrifice will take place in the tabernacle, i.e., the temple, shows that Josiah's centralization measures had been universally accepted, having occurred long before P would have been written.

The trend toward ritualism is obvious in the history of sacrifice. In early times sacrifice was a joyful fellowship meal (Jgs. 13:16ff.). In Leviticus sacrifice has become an elaborate priestly function whose prime purpose is the atonement of sin.

In the great national festivals the flexibility of the early period subsequently gave way to a rigid timetable. The feasts of Unleavened Bread, Weeks, and Booths were originally harvest festivals. In early times each tribe celebrated them at times that suited the state of crops in its area. Later, when all worship was centralized in Jerusalem, it was necessary to give a fixed date so that the whole nation could keep the festivals together. This is what is presupposed in Lev. 23.

Over the years the priestly hierarchy became more highly developed and richer. In early times a priest was not even necessary to offer sacrifice. By postexilic times not only were priests indispensable, but there were great differentiations within the priesthood, which had Levites, priests, and high priest. Leviticus betrays its late origin with its stress on the importance of the high priest. In early times gifts to the priests were optional, or at least unregulated. Gradually the priests extended their rights. In Leviticus they must be given tithes, first fruits, and many parts of the sacrifices. According to Wellhausen this was a late development.

One final argument in favor of a late date for P rests on the difference between the books of Chronicles and Kings. Kings, probably written *ca.* 550 B.C., says little about the worship in Jerusalem. But Chronicles, possibly written two centuries later than Kings, describes a very elaborate cult with many features akin to P. This similarity between P and Chronicles, it is claimed, proves the late date of P.

Since Wellhausen, many details of the above scheme have been modified; but the general picture has remained unaltered in most textbooks. It is, however, admitted by those who accept this general position that while P (and therefore Leviticus) was not finally edited until the late 5th cent. B.C., it does at some points reflect the practices of the preexilic temple.

*C. A Mediating Position.* A third view mediates between the traditional view and the standard critical view of Leviticus by maintaining that P is preexilic, but not Mosaic. This view owes its contemporary standing mainly to the advocacy of Y. Kaufmann (*Religion of Israel* [Eng. tr. 1960]), though it was much more common in the 19th cent. before Wellhausen's *Prolegomena* was published.

Kaufmann (p. 178) challenged the basic assumptions of the standard view: "Fixity in times and rites and absence of 'natural spontaneity' characterize the festivals of ancient Babylonia, Egypt, and all known early civilizations. . . . These elements are . . . no indication of lateness." Wellhausen assumed that Israelite society developed from a fairly secular one into one preoccupied with holiness and religion. Usually societies tend to become more secular with time, and this, it is argued, indicates that the priestly source is earlier than Deuteronomy, which is often dated to the 7th cent. B.C.

Kaufmann and his school have advanced more specific grounds for believing in the antiquity of P. Their arguments fall into three main types. First, the language, laws, and institutions of P do not fit with what else is known of the postexilic age. Chronicles, Ezra, and Nehemiah were written after the Exile, Ezekiel during the Exile. Their cultic vocabulary shares a number of terms with postbiblical Hebrew. But quite different terms are used in P. The only feasible explanation seems to be that P comes from a different, earlier period (see A. Hurvitz, *RB,* 81 [1974], 24-57). Similarly, some of the legal terminology in Leviticus was not understood in postexilic times, yet it finds parallels in second-millennium Mesopotamian law. This also points to an early date for Leviticus (see Speiser). Other sacral institutions mentioned in P, e.g., animal tithes, the anointing of the high priest, the Urim and Thummim, did not exist in the era of the second temple. This is very strange if P was composed at this time.

Second, Deuteronomy and Joshua quote Leviticus and other P passages, but not vice versa. This is understandable only if P was written before Deuteronomy.

Third, P's notions of holiness and war, and its laws on sacrifice and blood, closely resemble those mentioned in the books of Judges and Samuel. For example, Lev. 26:31 mentions a multiplicity of sanctuaries where sacrifices are offered. Lev. 17:2-9, which insists that all animals must be slaughtered in the sanctuary, could only apply to the wilderness period. If it had been intended for the settlement situation, it would have prevented most of the population from ever eating meat, unless there were scattered through the land numerous legitimate sanctuaries equivalent to the tabernacle. The ban on eating blood (Lev. 17:10ff.) is referred to in 1 S. 14:33f.

Each of three main positions has its own difficulties, and it would be rash to attempt to decide between them here. Despite the broad scholarly consensus, it does seem that a postexilic date for Leviticus is difficult to maintain in the face of the abundant quotations in Ezekiel and the linguistic evidence that P's vocabulary does not resemble that of late biblical Hebrew. A much earlier date is required by the evidence.

*V. **Theology.***–The theology of Leviticus can hardly be discussed in isolation from that of the other books of the Pentateuch. In particular, when Leviticus is read in conjunction with Exodus and Numbers, the books most closely related to it, some of its theological presuppositions stand out more clearly. For instance, Exodus describes the formation of the Sinai covenant and the erection of the tabernacle: both these institutions are fundamental to the theology of Leviticus. In an attempt to clarify some of the most important themes in the book we shall look at its theology under four main headings: the presence of God, holiness, the role of sacrifice, and the Sinai covenant.

*A. The Presence of God.* God is always present with Israel in a real way. On occasion His presence becomes both visible and tangible. This idea is expressed repeatedly in Leviticus; indeed, the enduring presence of God is one of the theological presuppositions of the book.

God is preeminently present in worship. The laws on sacrifice say repeatedly that the ceremonies take place "before the Lord" (e.g., 1:5, 11); the food offerings make "a soothing aroma for the Lord" (e.g., 1:9, 13, 17; 2:9; 3:5). In offering sacrifice the priests approach the Lord (16:1; 21:17). It is therefore of supreme importance for them to obey God's instructions strictly when performing their duties (8:9, 13, 17, 21, 29, 36, etc.). Death was a real possibility when priests acted on their own initiative (8:35; 10:2, 6f., 9; 16:2, 13). In one sense God was ever present with His people (Ex. 33:14ff.; 40:36-38), for He spoke regularly to Moses from the tabernacle (1:1; 4:1; etc.; cf. Ex. 29:42). But on special occasions the divine glory appeared in cloud and fire, so that all the people could recognize His coming. The initial lawgiving at Sinai, the erection of the tabernacle, and the ordination of the priesthood (Ex. 19; 40:34ff.; Lev. 9:23f.) were all marked in this spectacular fashion. So too were the judgments on Aaron's sons, the whole nation, and Korah and his supporters (Lev. 10:2; Nu. 14:10ff.; 16:19ff.).

God is present not only in worship but at all times, even in the mundane duties of life. The recurring refrain in the later chapters, "I am the Lord your God" (e.g., Lev. 18:2ff.; 19:3f., 10; 20:7), reminds the people of Israel that every aspect of their life — religion (chs. 21–24), sex (chs. 18 and 20), relations with neighbors (chs. 19, 25) — is of concern to their covenant redeemer. The behavior of each member of the covenant people must mirror that of God Himself (20:7). The fear of God should prompt people to undertake good deeds that they might otherwise neglect, such as help for the blind, the deaf, the elderly, and the poor. Though such people may have no redress against unfair treatment, God is aware of their plight and cares about what His people do to them (19:14, 32; 25:17, 36, 43). The people are warned that if they neglect His law, He will set His face against them. Individuals can expect to be cut off, i.e., suffer premature death (17:9f.; 18:29; 20:5f.; etc.), while the nation will endure the horrible consequences set out in 26:14-45.

For the NT Christian, God's presence was made known in the Incarnation. Alluding to the OT description of the tabernacle, John wrote, "The Word became flesh and tabernacled among us . . . ; we have beheld his glory" (Jn. 1:14). For Paul every Christian is a walking shrine, a temple for the Holy Spirit in which God is to be glorified (1 Cor. 6:19f.). Like the OT tabernacle the Christian enjoys the permanent presence of the Spirit, but just as the old shrine sometimes enjoyed a special manifestation of God's glory, so the Christian should be filled with the Spirit and display God's glory to the world (cf. Acts 6:15; 7:55f.; 2 Cor. 3; Eph. 5:18).

*B. Holiness.* "Be holy, for I am holy" (11:44f.; 19:2;

20:26) could be termed the motto of Leviticus. Certainly "holy," "clean," "unclean," and cognate words are among the most common in the book. Yet their precise significance is elusive. In this section, an attempt is made to define them more precisely. *See also* CLEAN AND UNCLEAN; HOLINESS, HOLY.

The priests were instructed "to distinguish between the holy and the common, and between the unclean and clean" (10:10). "Common" (*ḥōl*) is opposite of "holy" (*qāḏôš*), just as "profane" (*ḥillēl*) is the converse of "sanctify" (*qiddēš*), and "unclean" (*ṭāmēʾ*) the opposite of "clean" (*ṭāhôr*). In Hebrew thinking everything was either clean or unclean, holy or common. How do the different concepts relate to each other?

Everything that is not holy is common. Common things divide into two groups, the clean and the unclean. Clean things become holy when they are sanctified. But unclean objects cannot be sanctified. Clean things can be polluted and thus made unclean. Finally, holy items may be defiled and become common, even polluted, and therefore unclean.

Uncleanness may be transmitted from some unclean things by contact (e.g., 11:39f.; 14:36; 15:4ff.; etc.). Similarly, some holy objects make everything that touches them holy (Ex. 29:37; 30:29; Lev. 6:18, 27 [MT 11, 20]). But cleanness is not conveyed to other things. Cleanness is the norm, from which holiness and uncleanness are variations.

The basic meaning of cleanness is purity, as shown by the frequent use of water to purify unclean persons and things (Lev. 11:25, 28; 14:8f.; etc.). But cleanness is a broader concept than purity. It approximates our notion of normality. Many of the diagnostic tests for skin diseases in Lev. 13 conclude with the remark "he is clean" (vv. 13, 17, 39). As the passages make clear, this does not mean the person concerned was not suffering from some complaint, but merely that the complaint was thought unimportant and not to be worried about. As a modern doctor might say, "It is normal." The idea of normality underlies 21:17-23, where any priest with a physical deformity is forbidden to minister at the altar. Admittedly these priests are not said to be unclean, but the notion of normality has very wide ramifications in Levitical theology (see below).

Permanent uncleanness cannot be altered and is not contagious, so no rites are prescribed to cure it. Unclean animals do not pass on their uncleanness to others; they simply cannot be eaten. Paradoxically, temporary uncleanness is taken more seriously. Some types of this uncleanness are contagious and may be passed on to others (e.g., 15:19ff.). All types of temporary uncleanness require cleansing. Those who neglect to undergo the appropriate decontamination procedures endanger themselves and the whole community (Nu. 19:13, 20).

Different degrees of uncleanness require different cleansing rituals. For example, the slight uncleanness consequent on marital intercourse requires the couple to wash and wait till the evening for the uncleanness to clear. Menstrual discharge results in an uncleanness lasting seven days. But unnatural discharges from the sexual organs cause uncleanness that lasts for seven days after the discharge ceases and require washing and sacrifice to cleanse the person (Lev. 15). Similarly, those healed of unclean skin diseases have to wash, wait seven days, and offer sacrifice (ch. 14).

Some persistent skin diseases cause uncleanness, and the sufferer was therefore expelled from the camp for the duration of his illness (13:45f.). Theology, not hygiene, was the reason for this provision. The unclean and the holy must not meet (7:20f.; 22:3). The camp of Israel was holy, and in the middle of it stood the tabernacle, seat of God's most holy presence (cf. Nu. 5:2f.). Neglect of these purity rules polluted the tabernacle and led to the death of the offender (Nu. 19:13, 20). The Day of Atonement ceremonies were designed to cleanse the tabernacle from the uncleanness that it contracted owing to people's negligence in purifying themselves (Lev. 15:31; 16:16, 19).

This insistence on purification of the unclean is a corollary of the idea that Israel, the camp, and especially the tabernacle are holy. Contact between uncleanness and holiness is disastrous. They are utterly distinct in theory and must be kept equally distinct in practice, lest divine judgment fall.

Holiness characterizes God Himself and all that belongs to Him: "Be holy, for I am holy" (11:44f.; 19:2; 20:26). God's name, which expresses His character, is holy (20:3; 22:2, 32). His name is profaned (desanctified) by idolatry, false swearing, and other sins (18:21; 19:12; 20:3; 21:6; 22:2). God demonstrates His holiness in judging sin (10:3; Nu. 20:13). But apart from these remarks there is no explanation of what God's holiness is in itself; it is intrinsic to God's character.

Anyone or anything given to God becomes holy. For example, the priests' portions of the sacrifices are holy. The tabernacle and its equipment are holy (Ex. 40:9; 29:36; 30:29). So, too, are the sabbath and the other religious festivals (Lev. 23).

A person dedicated to the service of God is holy. Preeminently holy in this sense are the priests (Ex. 29:1; 39:30; Lev. 21:6ff.). Similarly the Levites were given wholly to the Lord in place of the firstborn Israelites who had been sanctified. This dedication involves separation from uncleanness, as the case of Nazirite makes clear (Nu. 6:6-8). In a more general sense all Israel is called out from the nations to serve God and is therefore holy (Ex. 19:5f.; cf. Lev. 20:26).

Uncleanness results from natural causes (e.g., disease) or human actions (e.g., sin), but holiness is not simply acquired by ritual action or moral behavior. Leviticus stresses that sanctification has two aspects, a divine act and human actions. God sanctifies and people also sanctify. Only those people whom God calls to be holy can become holy in reality (Nu. 16:7). The divine side to sanctification is expressed in the frequent refrain "I am the Lord your sanctifier" (Lev. 20:8; 21:8, 15, 23; 22:9, 16, 32). Sometimes both the divine and human parts in sanctification are mentioned (Ex. 20:8, 11; Lev. 21:8).

Usually, however, the main emphasis of the book is on the human contribution to sanctification, what a person must do to make something holy. In some cases, e.g., the offering of property or animals to the sanctuary, no special rituals are laid down according to Lev. 27, though sacrifice accompanied the gifts mentioned in Nu. 7. In the more important sanctifications — of the altar, the priesthood, and the tabernacle — the ritual required anointing the holy thing with oil and offering various sacrifices (Ex. 29:1-36; 40:9; cf. Lev. 8–9). When the whole nation was made holy through the covenant at Sinai, they had to cleanse themselves from uncleanness (Ex. 19:10-15), offer sacrifice, and promise to obey the law (24:3-8). Keeping the law is indeed one of the most important duties of the people of Israel if they are to demonstrate holiness (Lev. 19:2ff.; 20:7ff.; Nu. 15:39f.). To disobey God is profanity worthy of death (Ex. 31:14; Nu. 20:12).

This survey of the use of the terms for holiness, cleanness, and uncleanness has demonstrated the importance of these ideas for understanding Leviticus. Cleanness is the natural state of most creatures. Holiness is a state of grace to which people are called by God, and it is attained through obeying the law and carrying out rituals such as sacrifice. Uncleanness is a substandard condition to which people descend through bodily processes and sin. Every Israelite had a duty to seek release from uncleanness through washing and sacrifice, because uncleanness was quite incompatible with the holiness of the covenant people. (See M. Douglas, pp. 51-54, on the underlying principles that unite these concepts of holiness and cleanness. She argued that holy means more than separation to divine service. It means wholeness and completeness.)

NT theology makes full use of the idea of holiness. All Christians are holy, "saints" in most English translations. That is, they have been called by God to be His people just as ancient Israel was (Col. 1:2; 1 Pet. 1:2; 2:9f.; cf. Ex. 19:5f.). But this state of holiness must find expression in holy living (Col. 1:22; 1 Pet. 1:15). Sanctification is expressed through obedience to the standard of teaching (Rom. 6:17-19), just as in Leviticus it is expressed through obedience to the law. Peter urged his readers to make the motto of Leviticus their own: "Be holy, for I am holy" (1 Pet. 1:16). The imitation of God is a theme that unites the ethics of Old and New Testaments (cf. Mt. 5:48; 1 Cor. 11:1).

*C. The Role of Sacrifice.* "Under the law almost everything is purified with blood, and without the shedding of blood there is no forgiveness of sins" (He. 9:22). The author of Hebrews had in mind the rites described in Exodus and Numbers as well as those in Leviticus; but Leviticus is particularly concerned with sacrifice, for chs. 1–17 are devoted to explaining the occasions for sacrifice and correct procedures to be followed in it.

Various theories about the significance of OT sacrifice have been advanced, and some will be discussed below to explain the basic principles of OT sacrifice insofar as the Pentateuch makes them plain.

According to D. J. Davies (*ZAW*, 89 [1977], 387-399), Israelite sacrifice was concerned with restoring the relationships between God and Israel and between different members of the nation. The Sinai covenant had created a fellowship characterized by life and order and by harmony between God and mankind and between persons. Outside the covenant and its institutions was the realm of death and disorder from which Israel had been redeemed. Anything that disturbed this order, e.g., death, disease, or sin, was a potential threat to the whole community, and sacrifice was the principal means for remedying the disruption and restoring harmony into the community. Different types of disruptions were corrected by different kinds of sacrifice.

This analysis has much to commend it. But it only partially comes to terms with the concepts of Leviticus. In Leviticus, sacrifice, or more precisely sacrificial blood, is regularly associated with cleansing and sanctification. For example, the hallowing of the altar and the priests is effected through anointing with oil and sacrificial blood (Ex. 29:36f.; Lev. 8:11-15, 23-30). The various purification and reparation offerings detailed in chs. 4–5 are all appointed to deal with the uncleanness associated with sin. All these sacrifices reached their annual climax in the Day of Atonement ceremonies, when each part of the tabernacle was smeared with blood "to cleanse it and sanctify it from the uncleanness of the Israelites" (16:19). Thus sacrifice can undo the effects of sin and human infirmity. Sin and disease lead to profanation of the holy and pollution of the clean. Sacrifice can reverse this process.

Above it is argued that sanctification presupposes a divine call to holiness. Holiness is not acquired merely by obeying the law or undergoing some ritual (e.g., Nu. 16:5). The laws on sacrifice go further still. They assert not only that sacrifice must be in accordance with God's will for it to be effective in the first place, but that it is God Himself who gives the desired result of holiness or cleanness. Many of the laws conclude with the remark "the priest shall make atonement for him and he will be forgiven" (or "be clean") (e.g., Lev. 4:20, 26, 31; 12:7f.). The addition "he will be forgiven" ("clean") is significant. Mere performance of the rite by the priest is inadequate. God is the one who grants forgiveness and cleansing.

If uncleanness caused by sin was left unatoned for by sacrifice, deaths were liable to occur. Indeed, the Pentateuch records a number of incidents where the enormity of the sin led to instant judgment, so that it was impossible to offer a sacrifice quickly enough to avert disaster (Ex. 32:25-35; Lev. 10; Nu. 25). It may not be coincidence that on such occasions, when God's wrath was demonstrated in the death of some of the guilty, no sacrifices are mentioned to renew the holiness of the rest of the people. When a man died there was no need for animals to be sacrificed as well (Nu. 25:6-13; cf. 16:36-50 [MT 17:1-15]).

Another indication that the death of the animal in some way substituted for the death of the guilty person is provided by the verb "make atonement" (*kipper*), which regularly describes what the priest does in sacrifice. Despite its frequent occurrence, its etymology and its meaning are uncertain. One possible derivation is from the Akkadian verb *kuppuru,* "cleanse" or "wipe." This fits those contexts where the altar or the sanctuary is the direct object of the verb and the action involves smearing the altar with blood (Lev. 16:33).

Alternatively, Heb. *kipper* may derive from Heb. *kōp̱er,* "ransom price." A *kōp̱er* is the money that a man condemned to death can pay to escape the death penalty (Ex. 21:30; Prov. 6:35). *Kipper* may then be literally translated "pay a ransom (for one's life)." In certain passages where various monetary payments are said to make atonement, "pay a ransom" would seem to be a much more appropriate rendering than "cleanse" (e.g., Ex. 30:15; Nu. 31:50). Such an understanding is compatible with most of the passages that speak of sacrifice "making atonement" for someone. Through the animal's death and the subsequent rituals people are ransomed from the death that their sin and uncleanness merit.

There were at least three parties involved in every sacrifice: God, the priest, and the worshiper. We have already seen that Leviticus insists that sacrifice must be offered in response to God's call, not on one's own initiative, if it is to be effective in making people holy (cf. Lev. 10). It also points out that correct performance of the atonement rituals by the priest is not enough; God must grant forgiveness and cleansing. It makes one final point concerning the attitude of the worshiper. In the case of unintentional sin, remorse and sacrifice are sufficient for atonement. But if the sin is "high-handed," i.e., deliberate, reparation and public confession are necessary prerequisites to sacrificial atonement (5:1–6:7 [MT 5:1-26]; cf. Nu. 15:27-30).

John the Baptist, Our Lord Himself, Paul, Peter, and the writer of Hebrews are among those in the NT who make use of the idea that Christ's death was a sacrifice that atoned for sin. Unlike the sacrifices in Leviticus, the Crucifixion is unlimited in its scope and requires no repetition (1 Jn. 2:1f.; He. 9:26). But like the OT sacrifices, there must be a divine call to the individual and a response of faith and repentance if anyone is to enjoy the effects of Christ's atonement (cf. Eph. 1–2).

*D. The Sinai Covenant.* In sharp contrast to the terms for sacrifice and holiness, the covenant is mentioned rarely in Leviticus. In fact, it is mentioned only ten times altogether, of which eight occurrences are in ch. 26. But though the word for covenant (*bᵉrîṯ*) is rare, covenantal ideas pervade the whole book. Like the presence of God with Israel, the covenant is one of the fundamental presuppositions informing the theology of Leviticus.

Leviticus is the sequel to Exodus. At the heart of Exodus (chs. 19-24) is the Sinai covenant. All that follows in Exodus is a working out of the covenant. Leviticus explains how covenant worship should be conducted (chs. 1–17), then how the covenant people should behave (18–25), and closes with a section of blessings and curses, entirely appropriate to a covenant document (ch. 26). Indeed, the last verse of ch. 26 connects all that precedes with Sinai, where the covenant was concluded.

Various studies have shed much light on the form of the OT covenant (*see* COVENANT [OT]). It bears a marked resemblance to the form used in other Near Eastern texts for drawing up treaties and collections of law. This is entirely appropriate, for the Sinai covenant was at once a treaty between God and Israel and laws imposed on the nation.

The covenant-treaty background of pentateuchal law highlights three important features of the laws. First, the law was given in a context of grace. In the treaty form the stipulations came after the historical prologue. This was analogous to the historical situation: God gave His law to Israel after they had been redeemed from Egypt, not as a means for securing their redemption. God's call to Israel to be His holy people preceded the revelation of the law at Sinai, but only obedience could make holiness a living reality. In Leviticus, whenever the Exodus from Egypt is mentioned it is always as a motive for keeping the law (e.g., 11:45; 18:3; 23:43). The OT believer was to treat others as God had treated him (19:34).

Second, although Israel had been saved from Egyptian bondage and called to be God's people, they were not free to do as they pleased. The very reverse was the case. As a holy nation they had to keep themselves pure from sin and uncleanness lest God's wrath break out against them. The covenant texts express the same notion in the blessings and curses in Lev. 26 and Dt. 28. There the nation is reminded that all God's promises — of good harvests, peace, and His own presence — will be theirs if they observe His commandments. But if they forget His word and go their own way, they will experience all those things that people fear most: sickness, drought, death of children, famine, enemy occupation, and deportation to foreign lands. Leviticus stresses that if such a fate befalls Israel, it will not be in spite of the covenant but because of it. God Himself will punish His disobedient people (26:24, 28; cf. Am. 3:2).

The third point to note about the covenant is its eternity. In the covenant God pledges Himself to Israel forever, and Israel is expected to reciprocate by offering back its eternal allegiance to its sovereign redeemer. The purpose of the horrifying curses in Lev. 26 is to make Israel turn back from its evil ways and listen to God (26:18, 21, 23, 27). But the Israelites are assured that however long they take to come to their right mind and confess their sin, God will be ready to reinstate them when they do change their ways (26:40f.). Even if they do not turn back, they will not be deserted by their God, though they may suffer continued exile from their land (v. 44). The reason for God's faithfulness is His promise to the patriarchs, Abraham, Isaac, and Jacob (vv. 42, 45; cf. Ex. 32:11-14; Dt. 4:30f.; 30:1-10; Isa. 49:15; Jer. 31:36). Divine blessing depends on obedience, but disobedience will not result in total rejection, just continued divine judgment.

The prophets looked forward to a new covenant under which the law would be written in human hearts instead of on stone as the Sinai covenant had been. The NT affirms that this covenant was inaugurated by Christ's death, which saves His people from the bondage of sin. The new covenant, like the old, displays God's grace to sinful mankind and expects obedience to the law (Jn. 14:15). Finally, the new covenant also offers an assurance of God's eternal faithfulness to His people (Jn. 10:28).

*VI. Leviticus and the Christian.*–Some problems that arise in relating Leviticus to the modern Church's situation also arise for other OT books. Thus examples from other parts of the Pentateuch are included here.

Christians customarily divide the OT law into three parts: the moral, e.g., the Ten Commandments; the civil, i.e., the legislation for OT society; and the ceremonial, i.e., the sacrificial and ritual laws. Many, despite Paul's teaching that "all Scripture is inspired and profitable" (2 Tim. 3:16), assert that only the moral law binds the Christian. This position faces three main difficulties. First, the NT does not seem to distinguish among the different types of law in this way. Second, it is difficult to draw the line between moral precepts and other law. Is the sabbath a moral law or a ceremonial one? Third, much of the civil legislation is grounded on moral judgments, often expressed in the Ten Commandments. Nevertheless, even if the threefold division of the law seems arbitrary and artificial, it does provide a convenient framework for our discussion, in which a slightly different approach will be advocated.

As far as basic principles of behavior are concerned the OT and NT are in broad agreement. "You shall love the Lord your God with all your heart, and with all your soul, and with all your mind, and with all your strength. You shall love your neighbor as yourself" (Mk. 12:30f.; Dt. 6:5; Lev. 19:18). With this double quotation from Deuteronomy and Leviticus Jesus draws out the quintessence of OT law and gives it His own seal of approval. The Ten Commandments are often quoted by the NT. Peter quoted the Levitical injunction to holiness (1 Pet. 1:16). The examples could be multiplied to show that the NT advocates as high a standard of personal morality as the OT. This is to be expected, since the God of the OT is the God of the NT. The people of God are supposed to imitate God. In Leviticus God summons people to "be holy, for I am holy," just as Our Lord urges: "You, therefore, must be perfect, as your heavenly Father is perfect" (Mt. 5:48).

One may go further. The theological setting of the ethical imperatives is similar in both Testaments. In both the OT and NT, law forms part of the covenant relationship between God and His people. Although this has already been alluded to (see V.D above), it is so important that it deserves further elaboration.

Three clear parallels may be drawn between the OT view of the covenant and the NT teaching on law and grace. Although covenant terminology and structures are hard to find in the NT, the principles enshrined in the OT covenant have not disappeared. In the teaching of Jesus and Paul the covenant has come down to the level of basic presuppositions. Though as a rule they do not talk about the covenant, their assumptions about the relationship of grace and law show that their teachings are governed by the principles inherent in the OT covenant.

First and foremost the OT covenants are arrangements of divine grace. God called Abraham. He brought Israel out of Egypt. He chose David. In every case God took the initiative in saving His people and created a relationship of fellowship between Himself and them. In the NT Our Lord came to seek and to save that which was lost and to call sinners to repentance (Lk. 5:32).

Second, the covenants involve law. Abraham was told, "Walk before me and be perfect" (Gen. 17:1). The covenants create a fellowship between God and mankind; the

Davidic covenant is compared to the relationship between father and son (2 S. 7:14). Mankind is expected to respond to God's grace; proper response involves the law, which tells mankind how to imitate God. The NT insists that the law is not a means to salvation but a response to salvation. The disciple is not merely to observe the letter of the commandment; his righteousness must exceed that of the scribes and Pharisees (Mt. 5:17-48).

Finally, the covenant involves blessing and curse. Israel is told that if it obeys the law, it may expect greater and greater prosperity. If it is disobedient, its suffering will be terrible. David was warned that if his son committed iniquity, "I will chasten him with the rods of men" (2 S. 7:14). The same themes reappear in the NT. Those who seek God's kingdom and His righteousness are assured that they will not be short of food and clothing (Mt. 6:25-33). But those who refuse to forgive others will forfeit their own forgiveness (Mt. 18:23-35). Paul compared the experience of Israel in the wilderness to that of the Corinthian church. Many Israelites died in the wilderness for indulging in immorality. The same fate would befall the Corinthians if they did not repent. Indeed, some had suffered already (1 Cor. 10:1–11:32).

It seems fair to say that the NT not only accepts the moral law of the OT but reiterates the basic theology of the covenant of which the law forms a part. If the NT stresses much more strongly the grace of God, this is because Christ's incarnation and death display God's mercy more strikingly than even the Exodus from Egypt.

Besides moral laws such as "you shall love your neighbor as yourself" (19:18), Leviticus contains a number of laws that are sometimes described as civil legislation, e.g., laws about farming (vv. 9f., 19, 23-25; etc.) and rules fixing the death penalty for certain offenses (20:9-16; etc.). This type of law is quoted less frequently in the NT than the simple moral imperatives, but when quoted it is treated as equally authoritative (1 Cor. 9:9 quoting Dt. 25:4; Mk. 7:10 citing Lev. 20:9). The arbitrariness of the distinction between moral and civil law is reinforced by the arrangement of the material in Leviticus. Love of neighbor immediately precedes a prohibition on mixed breeding; the holiness motto comes just before the law on executing unruly children (Lev. 19:18f.; 20:7-9). Instead of distinguishing between moral and civil laws, it is better to say that some injunctions are generally applicable to most societies, while others are more specific and directed at the particular social problems of ancient Israel.

The moral and religious principles underlying OT legislation include the Ten Commandments, but there are other principles as well. It is the underlying principles that should bind the Christian, not the specific applications found in the OT. For example, a recurrent theme in biblical law is that the weakest members of society should be specially protected. The poor, the orphan and widow, the clergy (Levites), and the immigrant (resident alien) are often singled out for special treatment. Lev. 19:9f. says: "When you reap the harvest of your land, you shall not reap your field to its very border, neither shall you gather the gleanings after your harvest. . . . you shall leave them for the poor and for the sojourner: I am the Lord your God."

It is misguided to try to apply this law directly to our society. It does not mean that efficient combine harvesters that gather up every stalk of grain are contrary to the will of God. The aim of this law is very clear, namely, to allow the landless poor to collect some free food. Inefficient combines are of no benefit to the poor in our society, who usually live in city centers far from the harvest fields. But though this law is inapplicable literally in modern societies, the principles underlying it should still challenge Christians to devise the most effective means that can help the poor of our age. It is not the task of the commentator to say which means should be adopted, e.g., food subsidies or welfare benefits, but simply to emphasize that Christian politicians and voters have a duty to support good schemes to help the needy. The Jubilee laws in Lev. 25 also offer very relevant comment on issues of wealth and poverty.

Finally, we come to the question of the ceremonial law. Very detailed comments on the uncleanness regulations and the sacrificial rituals are to be found in the Epistle to the Hebrews. The great argument of that writer is that Christ fulfils all the ideals enshrined in the OT law. His high-priesthood is superior to Aaron's. His sacrifice is more effective in purging sin than the blood of bulls and goats. Unlike the OT rites it need never be repeated, since it has secured the forgiveness of sins once and for all. In one sense, then, the whole ceremonial law in Leviticus is obsolete for the Christian. We are interested in the sacrifice of Christ, not in animal sacrifice. But in another sense the Levitical rituals are still of immense relevance. It was in terms of these sacrifices that Jesus Himself and the early Church understood His atoning death. Leviticus provided the theological models for their understanding. If we wish to walk in Our Lord's steps and think His thoughts after Him, we must attempt to understand the sacrificial system of Leviticus. It was established by the same God who sent His Son to die for us; and in rediscovering the principles of OT worship written there, we may learn something of the way that we should approach a holy God.

***Bibliography.***–Comms. by K. Elliger (*HAT,* 1966); R. K. Harrison (*Tyndale OT Comms.,* 1980); D. Hoffmann (2 vols., 1905-1906); W. H. Gispen (*Commentaar op het OT,* 1950); KD; J. R. Porter (*CBC,* 1976); G. J. Wenham (*NICOT,* 1979).

F. M. Cross, *Canaanite Myth and Hebrew Epic* (1973), pp. 293-325; M. Douglas, *Purity and Danger* (1966); M. Haran, *Temples and Temple Service in Ancient Israel* (1978); A. Hurvitz, *RB,* 81 (1974), 24-57; B. A. Levine, *In the Presence of the Lord* (1974); D. J. McCarthy, *Treaty and Covenant* (1963); J. Milgrom, *Studies in Levitical Terminology,* I (1970); *Cult and Conscience* (1976); E. A. Speiser, "Leviticus and the Critics," in *Oriental and Biblical Studies* (1967), pp. 123-142.

G. J. WENHAM

**LEVY** [Heb. *rûm*–'raise' (Nu. 31:28), hiphil of *ʿālâ*–'cause to go up' (1 K. 9:15), *mas*]. The RSV usually translates the noun *mas* as "forced labor," but also uses "levy" (1 K. 5:13b, 14), "levy of forced labor" (1 K. 5:13a [MT 27a]), and "forced levy" (1 K. 9:21 par. 2 Ch. 8:8). When this noun is translated "levy" the verb *ʿālâ* is translated "make" or "raise." In 2 Ch. 24:6 (cf. also v. 9) the RSV supplies the verb "levy" to make a smooth translation of Heb. *maśʾaṯ mōšeh,* "tax of Moses." *See* LABOR; FORCE (5).

**LEWD; LEWDNESS** [Heb. *zimmâ* <*zāmam*–'think, plan'] (Jer. 13:27; Ezk. 16:27, 43; 22:9; 23:21, 27, 29, etc.; 24:13); NEB also OBSCENITIES (Ezk. 10:43); [*naḇlûṯ* <*nāḇal*–'act disdainfully,' 'be foolish'] (Hos. 2:10 [MT 12]). *Zimmâ* is not limited in meaning to "lewdness" but can signify any deliberate wickedness (it is translated "wickedness" in Lev. 18:17; 19:29; 20:14; "evil device" in Ps. 26:10; "evil intent" in Prov. 21:27; etc.). The RSV renders *zimmâ* "lewd(ness)" only in Jer. 13:27 and Ezekiel, where it describes the nation's idolatry in terms of adultery; cf. Ezk. 23:44, "For they have gone in to her, as men go in to a harlot. Thus they went in to Oholah and to Oholibah to commit lewdness." In Hos. 2:10 *naḇlûṯ,* "immodesty," "shamelessness," describes the shamefulness of the woman's activity and symbolically the shame of Israel's spiritual adultery.

The word "lewd" does not appear in the NT, though twice the AV translates thus in nonsexual contexts: once in the obsolete sense of "wicked" or "worthless" (Gk. *ponērós,* Acts 17:5) and once where Gk. *rhadioúrgēma* refers to criminal acts (18:14). D. J. KELLY

**LIBANUS** lib'ə-nus (Jth. 1:7, AV). *See* LEBANON.

**LIBATION** [Heb. *nesek̲* (Ex. 29:40f.; 30:9; 2 Ch. 29:35; Ps. 16:4; Jer. 44:17, 19, 25), *nāsak̲*–'pour out' ("pour out as libation," Ex. 37:16; Hos. 9:4), *m*$^{e}$*naqqît̲*–'offering bowl' (Ex. 25:29; "bowl for libation," Jer. 52:19); Gk. *spéndō* ("pour as a libation," Phil. 2:17)]; AV DRINK-OFFERING, OFFERING (Hos. 9:4), "to cover" (Ex. 25:29; 37:16), "cup" (Jer. 52:19), "be offered" (Phil. 2:17); NEB also DRINK-OFFERING, "flagon" (Jer. 52:19), "lifeblood is to crown" (Phil. 2:17). A liquid offering.

In Israel, as in the rest of the ancient Near East, libations were a secondary type of offering, i.e., they often accompanied other types of offerings (Ex. 29:40f.; 2 Ch. 29:35). Special bowls were used as containers (Ex. 25:29; 37:16; Jer. 52:19). Wine was perhaps the most common libation (Ex. 29:40f.; Hos. 9:4); according to Robertson Smith (p. 231), it was a substitute for blood. That the Israelites knew of blood offerings is clear from Ps. 16:4; 50:13 (cf. 2 S. 23:17), but these texts plainly indicate that the Israelites did not make them. Note also that these texts speak of drinking the libation, whereas normally it was poured out around the base of the altar (a distinctive characteristc of North Semitic ritual according to Robertson Smith, p. 230; cf. Jastrow, p. 666; Josephus *Ant.* iii.9.4 [234]).

On the right a worshiper pours a libation over an altar in honor of the weather-god, who rides in a chariot pulled by a lion-griffin; a goddess stands on the griffin (*ca.* 24th-23rd cent. B.C.) (Cylinder seal no. 220; The Trustees of the Pierpont Morgan Library)

Jeremiah denounced libations to the QUEEN OF HEAVEN (44:17-19, 25) as well as DRINK offerings to other gods (19:13; 32:29; cf. Zeph. 1:5). The latter were made on rooftops, a practice that is also attested in Ugaritic myths (e.g., Krt, lines 62-80, 156-172).

Paul's use of *spéndō* in Phil. 2:17 ("poured out") shows that he expected to be martyred (the only other NT occurrence of *spéndō* is in 2 Tim. 4:6, where Paul clearly anticipated his impending martyrdom).

*See also* SACRIFICES AND OFFERINGS IN THE OT.

***Bibliography.***–M. Jastrow, *Religion of Babylonia and Assyria* (1898); W. Robertson Smith, *Religion of the Semites* (rev. ed. 1907). G. A. L.

**LIBERAL; LIBERALITY; LIBERALLY** [Heb. *b*$^{e}$*rāk̲â*] (Prov. 11:25); NEB GENEROUS; [*k*$^{e}$*yad̲ hammelek̲*] ("royal liberality," Est. 2:18); AV "according to the state of the king"; NEB "worthy of the king"; [hiphil of *ʿānaq*] ("you shall furnish . . . liberally," Dt. 15:14); NEB LAVISHLY; [*ḥānan*] ("give liberally," Ps. 37:26); AV MERCIFUL; NEB GENEROUSLY; [Gk. *hadrótēs*] (2 Cor. 8:20); AV ABUNDANCE; NEB GENEROUS; [*eumetádotos*] (1 Tim. 6:18); AV "ready to distribute"; NEB "ready to give away"; [*haplótēs*] (Rom. 12:8; 2 Cor. 8:2); AV also SIMPLICITY; NEB "with all your heart," "lavishly open-handed"; [*polýs*] (Acts 10:2); AV MUCH; NEB GENEROUSLY.

The sense of "liberal giving" implicit in Heb. *bārak̲,* "bless," and the cognate substantive *b*$^{e}$*rāk̲â,* "blessing," leads naturally in the OT to using the latter to mean "gift, present" (cf. Gen. 33:11; Josh. 15:19; Jgs. 1:15; 1 S. 25:27; 30:26; 2 K. 5:15). In this sense the "person of blessing" (*nep̲eš b*$^{e}$*rāk̲â*) in Prov. 11:25 is a "person of bounty" or "liberal man" (RSV).

In Est. 2:18 King Ahasuerus is portrayed as giving gifts "according to the hand of the king" (*k*$^{e}$*yad̲ hammelek̲*). The RSV translation "with royal liberality" more felicitously approximates the idiomatic Hebrew.

The combination of the hiphil infinitive absolute *haʿ*$^{a}$*nêq* and impf. *taʿ*$^{a}$*nîq* (< *ʿānaq*) in Dt. 15:14, "make a necklace," "put around one's neck," is figurative for "liberally" or "lavishly supply." Heb. *ḥānan,* "be gracious, show favor," means "be liberal in charity" in contexts describing pious treatment of the poor, needy, etc. (cf. Ps. 37:21; 109:12; 112:5; Prov. 14:31; 19:17; 28:8).

Greek *hadrótēs,* "abundance" (lit. "stoutness, fulness"), is a hapax legomenon in the NT. The RSV renders it "liberal gift" (cf. NEB, "generous gift") in 2 Cor. 8:20, where it refers to a monetary collection. *Eumetádotos,* "bountiful, generous" (derived from *metadídōmi,* "give a share"), is also a hapax legomenon (1 Tim. 6:18). The meaning, however, is clear: the rich are admonished to be "liberal" (*eumetádotos*) and "generous" (*koinōnikós,* lit. "sharing").

The noun *haplótēs,* derived from *haploús,* "simple," thus essentially means "simplicity, plainness." A derived sense was "moderation" (in life-style), which further developed into the sense "moderation that enables one to spare something for others," i.e., "generosity" (cf. 2 Cor. 9:11, 13). It has this sense in Rom. 12:8; 2 Cor. 8:2. The use of *haplótēs* in the pseudepigraphical T. Iss. (3:1f., 8) also illustrates this nuance (see *APOT,* II, 326). Hermas frequently used *haplótēs* to refer to the simple goodness that willingly gives of itself without reserve (see Bauer, rev., p. 85). The more common sense of *haplótēs* in the NT, however, is "purity" or "singleness of heart" (cf., e.g., Eph. 6:5; Col. 3:22).

The common adjective *polýs,* "much, many," appears in Acts 10:2 in the phrase *poiōn eleēmosýnas pollás* (lit. "who did many acts of charity"; cf. AV, "who gave much alms"). To avoid woodenness the RSV translates "gave alms liberally."

*See also* GENEROSITY; GIFT; KINDNESS; PITY.

***Bibliography.***–*TDNT,* I, *s.v.* ἁπλοῦς, ἁπλότης (Bauernfeind); *RTWB,* pp. 168f.; W. J. Conybeare and J. S. Howson, *Life and Epistles of St. Paul* (new ed. 1959), pp. 54f. D. G. BURKE

**LIBERATION THEOLOGY.** *See* POVERTY II.H.

**LIBERTINES.** *See* FREEDMEN, SYNAGOGUE OF THE.

**LIBERTY** [Heb. *d*$^{e}$*rôr, r*$^{e}$*ḥāb̲â* (Ps. 119:45); Gk. *eleuthería, ánesis* (Acts 24:23), *exousía*–'authority' (1 Cor. 8:9), *apolýō* ("set at liberty," Acts 28:18), *apostéllō . . . en aphései* ("set at liberty," Lk. 4:18)]; AV also LET GO; NEB also DELIVERANCE, MANUMISSION, RELEASE, etc.; **FREE; (SET) FREE; FREED** [Heb. pual of *ḥāp̲aš*–'be freed (from slavery)' (Lev. 19:20), *ḥopšî*–'emancipated' (Ex. 21:2, 5, 26f.; Dt. 15:12f., 18; etc.), niphal of *nāqâ*–'be free from (obligation, guilt, etc.)' (Gen. 24:8, 41a; Nu. 5:19, etc.), *nāqî*–'free from (guilt, etc.)' (Gen. 24:41b; Nu. 32:22; Dt. 24:5), niphal of *nāʿar* ("shake free," Jgs. 16:20), *ʿāzaḇ* (Dt. 32:36; 1 K. 14:10; etc.), *pāṭar*–'set free from duty' (1 Ch. 9:33), *šālaḥ* ("give free rein," Ps. 50:19; piel in Ps. 44:2 [MT 3]); Isa. 32:20; 45:13; Zec. 9:11; *beḻōʾ*–'without' (Ps. 17:1), *pāḏâ*–'redeem' (69:18 [MT 19]), piel of *pāṯaḥ*–'loosen,' 'open,' 'free' (102:20 [MT 21]; 105:20), *merḥāḇ*–'open space' (118:5), hiphil of *nāṯar*–'cause to leap,' 'set free' (146:7), *ḥōr*–'freeborn' (Eccl. 10:17), *rûḏ*–'roam' (Jer. 2:31), *munnāḥ*–'open space' (Ezk. 41:9, 11), *nāśāʾ ʾeṯ-rōʾš*–'lift the head,' 'pardon' ("graciously freed," 2 K. 25:27), *ʿāḇar*–'pass by,' 'slip away' (Ps. 81:6 [MT 7]); Gk. *eleutheróō* (Jn. 8:32, 36; Rom. 6:18; etc.), *eleútheros* (Mt. 17:26; Jn. 8:33, 36; etc.), *lýō*–'loose, set free' (1 Cor. 7:27; Rev. 1:5), *apolýō*–'set free, pardon' (Lk. 13:12; Acts 26:32), *dikaióō*–'justify,' 'set free' (Acts 13:39; Rom. 6:7)]; AV also CLEAR, GUILTLESS, LEFT, LOOSE, DELIVER, JUSTIFIED, etc.; NEB also RELEASED, BREAK UP, RANSOM, UNOCCUPIED AREA, etc.; **FREEDOM** [Heb. *ḥupšâ* ("given freedom," Lev. 19:20); Gk. *eleuthería, eleútheros* (1 Cor. 7:21)]; AV also LIBERTY, FREE; NEB also LIBERTY, "to be free men." For other uses of "free," *see* ANXIETY; CHARGE; GIFT I.B; MONEY, LOVE OF; REPROACH; WILL.

I. OT
II. Intertestamental Literature
III. NT
  A. Ministry of Jesus
  B. Emancipation from Slavery
  C. Christian Freedom
  D. Freedom of Speech
  E. Liberty from Sin and Law
  F. Personal and Apostolic Liberty
  G. Defense of Liberty
  H. Consummation of Liberty

***I. OT.***–The paradigm of liberty in the OT — and to some degree in the whole Bible — is the deliverance of the Israelites from their servitude in Egypt. They had been slaves under Pharaoh; the beginning of their nationhood was marked by an act of divine liberation. As the God of their fathers had liberated them, so the liberty into which He had brought them was to be reflected in their constitution and laws (cf. Ps. 119:45). No Israelite could be deprived of liberty indefinitely. Hence the ordinance requiring that Hebrew slaves be set free in the seventh year. Only if they then made a solemn declaration, of their own choice, that they preferred to serve their master in perpetuity was their slave status to be prolonged beyond the seventh year (Ex. 21:1-6).

A later development, the year of release (Heb. *šemiṭṭâ*, lit. "remission"), provided not only for the freeing of slaves (with adequate provision for economic independence), but also for the remission of debts every seventh year (Dt. 15:1-18). It was foreseen that when the seven-year cycle was well advanced, creditors might be unwilling to lend money, and creditors were exhorted to adopt a generous outlook (vv. 7-11). (In the very different economic situation at the end of the 1st cent. B.C. Hillel instituted the *prozbul,* a provision by which the lender and the borrower agreed to declare publicly that their transaction was exempt from the requirements of the year of release.)

The same principle underlies the regulation that fields remain fallow every seventh year; even the land was to enjoy respite and protection against exploitation (Lev. 25:1-7).

The motives behind the year of release led also to the establishment of the Jubilee Year, at the end of seven sabbatical periods (i.e., every fiftieth year; Lev. 25:8-17). It may have remained an ideal in the statute book rather than an institution observed in practice. The trumpet was to be blown on New Year's Day of the fiftieth year to "proclaim liberty [*derôr*] throughout the land to all its inhabitants" (Lev. 25:10). This language recurs throughout the OT. *See* JUBILEE, YEAR OF.

During the Babylonian siege of Jerusalem (589-587 B.C.) King Zedekiah made a proclamation of liberty in the city, directing that all Hebrew slaves should be set free (Jer. 34:8f.). But shortly afterward — perhaps when the besieging army temporarily withdrew to deal with an Egyptian diversion and thus raised the Jerusalemites' vain hope that the siege was over (37:5-10) — the proclamation was rescinded and those who had been liberated were reenslaved (34:8-11). In indignation at this breach of the sacred covenant (vv. 12-16) Jeremiah proclaimed to the Jerusalemites a different and sinister liberty: "liberty [*derôr*] to the sword, to pestilence, and to famine" (34:17). By this outrage the city sealed its doom.

Ezekiel envisaged the "year of liberty" (*derôr*) as continuing into the new order after the return from Exile (Ezk. 46:17).

The return from the Babylonian Exile was viewed in some degree as a replay of the deliverance from Egypt: once again, by divine power, "the ransomed of the Lord" returned, and those who were "bowed down" found timely release (Isa. 51:11, 14). In similar idiom a prophetic voice later proclaimed a new year of release, "the year of the Lord's favor," which would bring "liberty [*derôr*] to the captives, and the opening of the prison to those who are bound" (61:1f.). These words were to play a significant part in the inauguration of the gospel age.

***II. Intertestamental Literature.***–After returning from Exile the Jews under the Persians and then under Hellenistic rulers were sufficiently comfortable for liberation movements to make little headway. But the attempt by the Seleucid king Antiochus IV Epiphanes (175-163 B.C.) to interfere with their ancestral religion provoked the determination to regain not only religious liberty but also political liberty. In 140 B.C., after a long struggle, both had been secured, and Simon the Hasmonean and his sons received public recognition for having "fought and repulsed Israel's enemies and established its freedom" (1 Macc. 14:26). Later Jason of Cyrene, in a work epitomized in 2 Maccabees, recorded how the Hasmonean family "recovered the temple . . . and freed the city and restored the laws" (2 Macc. 2:22).

But some pious groups in Israel did not equate the independence gained by the Hasmoneans with true liberty. For them true liberty involved the triumph of righteousness and the worship of God according to what they believed to be His revealed will.

One of these groups was the Qumrân community, whose members anticipated that Israel would regain its liberty when the sons of light, with heavenly aid, gave battle to the sons of darkness and annihilated them. One way that the community prepared for that consummation was by meticulously observing the sacred epochs, including the Jubilee: "at the beginning of their weeks for the season of liberty" (1QS 10:8). This practice would ensure the coming of the great jubilee at the end of the current era of wickedness. Thus 11QMelch begins by quoting the regulations for the Year of Jubilee (Lev. 25:13; cf. v. 10) and the year of release (Dt. 15:1); it interprets both in terms of the eschatological return from exile. In the tenth and last year of Jubilee, Israel will finally be gathered home. The proclamation of restoration and liberty at that time (cf. Isa. 61:1f.) is assigned to Melchizedek, "for that is the epoch of Melchizedek's 'acceptable year'" (11QMelch 1-9).

From the early phase of the Roman occupation of Judea (63 B.C. onward) comes the collection of poems called the Psalms of Solomon. The work is by a community that excoriated the Hasmoneans for "laying waste the throne of David" (Ps.Sol. 17:8) and saw in the Roman occupation divine judgment on them for their sins. The authors looked forward to being liberated from the foreign yoke when God raised up "their king, the son of David" (v. 23).

Like Anna and her friends in Luke's Nativity narrative, those pious Jews "were looking for the redemption of Jerusalem" (Lk. 2:38). Indeed, the Lukan canticles in a context other than the Nativity might be interpreted in the same vein as the Psalms of Solomon. Mary in the Magnificat welcomed the dethroning of despots and the exalting of the humble (1:52); Zechariah in the Benedictus stressed the fulfillment of the divine promise of deliverance from enemies and oppressors, but he associated this deliverance with God's forgiveness of sins and the people's serving of God in holiness and righteousness (vv. 68-79).

*III. NT.–A. Ministry of Jesus.* Jesus is described in Luke as inaugurating His Galilean ministry in the synagogue of Nazareth by reading Isa. 61:1f., which announces good news to the poor, release for captives, and the arrival of "the acceptable year of the Lord." "Today," Jesus said, "this scripture has been fulfilled in your hearing" (Lk. 4:16-21). With His exposition of the text and ensuing activity He showed that the liberation which He thus proclaimed was not the kind that many of His contemporaries were anticipating — liberation from imperial Rome. Political liberation was proclaimed in particular by the adherents of the "fourth philosophy" (as Josephus called it in *Ant.* xviii.1.1, 6 [9, 23]), i.e., the followers of Judas of Galilee, who developed in due course into the party of the Zealots. Jesus may have acknowledged the nobility of the Zealots' ideals, but He warned that their chosen way must lead to disaster.

In fact, neither in the teaching of Jesus nor in the rest of the NT does political liberty play a significant part. The incident of the tribute money (Mk. 12:13-17) shows that Jesus did not regard the payment of taxes to Caesar as an obstacle to the interests of the kingdom of God. It did not conflict with the liberty which He proclaimed. Similarly, when Peter told the collectors of the temple tax (the half-shekel) that his master habitually paid it, Jesus reminded him that kings do not exact taxes from their own children: members of the royal family are free (Mt. 17:24-27). Thus members of God's family were evidently exempt from paying Him tribute for the maintenance of His house, the temple. Nevertheless, to avoid giving offense, Jesus' followers should pay the half-shekel voluntarily, not as a religious obligation. This probably was the policy of the church of Jerusalem until its dispersal in A.D. 66.

*B. Emancipation from Slavery.* On civil liberty, as on political liberty, the NT says little. When Paul sent Onesimus back to his master Philemon, he sent him indeed "no longer as a slave but more than a slave, as a beloved brother," and he charged Philemon to give Onesimus the welcome that Paul himself would have received (Philem. 16f.). But Paul did not expressly tell Philemon to emancipate Onesimus. Onesimus, in fact, was a special case: Paul hinted that what he really wanted Philemon to do was freely and willingly to send Onesimus back, so that Onesimus might continue to be of service to Paul in his imprisonment (vv. 13f.).

The "household tables" in Colossians and Ephesians direct slaves to obey their earthly masters, because in so doing they are serving their heavenly Master (Col. 3:22-25; Eph. 6:5-8). According to 1 Tim. 6:1f. slaves must not withhold respect from their masters if the masters are Christians; they must serve them all the more faithfully. 1 Pet. 2:18-20 requires household slaves (*oikétai*) to render respectful submission not only to kind and considerate masters but even to overbearing and unreasonable ones. If the slaves suffer unjustly, they are to reflect that they are following the example of Christ, who himself suffered unjustly (vv. 21-24).

Paul's fullest statement of the principle of slavery, as distinct from the specific case of Onesimus, comes in 1 Cor. 7:20-24. Those who were slaves when they became Christians should be content to go on serving God in that status. It is not very important whether one is a slave or a free person on the earthly level; the enslaved Christian is the Lord's freedman, while the free Christian is the slave of Christ (v. 22). There is an ambiguity in v. 21b, which advises the Christian slave: "If you can gain your freedom [*eleútheros*], avail yourself of the opportunity [*mállon chrēsai*]." The RSV mg. presents the alternative rendering: "Make use of your present condition [i.e., slavery] instead." But the first reading is supported by v. 23: "Do not become slaves of men."

Masters are not told to liberate their slaves but to treat them mercifully, as their own heavenly Master treats them (Col. 4:1; Eph. 6:9). Within the fellowship of the Church, indeed, the distinction between slave and free has little relevance: "There is neither slave nor free [*eleútheros*] . . . in Christ Jesus" (Gal. 3:28; cf. Col. 3:11).

*C. Christian Freedom.* There is a counterpart to this NT teaching in Platonism and Stoicism: persons who are legally free but controlled by their vices are really slaves; those who are legally slaves but pursue goodness and truth are really free (cf. the title of Philo's treatise *Quod omnis probus liber sit, "Every good man is free"*; cf. 2 Pet. 2:19). But Christian teaching relates true freedom to the person and work of Christ: "with freedom [*eleutheríą*] Christ has set us free" (Gal. 5:1). This freedom is effected for the believer by the Spirit: "Where the Spirit of the Lord is, there is freedom [*eleuthería*]" (2 Cor. 3:17). Similar teaching (in Johannine idiom) appears in the Fourth Gospel: "The truth will make you free. . . . Every one who commits sin is a slave to sin. . . . So if the Son makes you free, you will be free indeed" (Jn. 8:32-36). The Son is the embodiment of liberating truth (cf. 14:6).

*D. Freedom of Speech.* In addition to *eleuthería,* the Greek term *parrēsía* ("freedom of speech," "free access") plays a part in NT teaching about liberty. *Parrēsía* is used of boldness in preaching the gospel (1 Thess. 2:2), of openness in disclosing the "mystery" of the divine purpose (Eph. 3:12), and of courage in the face of pagan judges, even the imperial tribunal in Rome (Phil. 1:20). It is a characteristic of Paul's ministry.

It is also a recurring note in Acts, from Peter's and John's *parrēsía* (RSV "boldness") before the Sanhedrin (Acts 4:13) to Paul's *parrēsía* as he preached the kingdom of God and told the story of Jesus to all and sundry during his two years' custody in Rome (28:31; cf. vv. 16-30; 24:23).

The term occurs only once in the Synoptic Gospels — in Mk. 8:32, where Jesus, announcing for the first time the impending suffering of the Son of man, "said this plainly [*parrēsíą*]." It is frequent in John's Gospel: Jesus claimed always to speak "openly" (*parrēsíą*), never in secret (18:20).

*E. Liberty from Sin and Law.* The gospel liberty on which Paul insisted embraced liberty from sin and from law simultaneously.

Sin is presented as a master whose slaves are unable

to escape his control except by dying or becoming the property of another. Both these ways of escape were pressed into service by Paul. Believers pass from the control of sin through their death with Christ. Those who have died to sin can no longer live in sin (Rom. 6:2-11, 15-18). But, having died with Christ, they now "walk in newness of life" (v. 5), living henceforth in the service of God and enjoying present sanctification "and its end, eternal life" (v. 22; cf. "the law of liberty," Jas. 1:25; 2:12).

Sin is also viewed as a jailer who refuses to release his prisoners. This concept is implied in Gal. 3:22, "The scripture [i.e., the written law, concentrated in such an uncompromising form as Dt. 27:26] consigned all to sin" (or "confined all under the power of sin"). The key that liberates the prisoners is the promise made to Abraham, embodied and fulfilled in Christ. Promise displaces law; sin has dominion over men and women as long as they are "under law," but that dominion is broken when they find themselves "not under law but under grace" (Rom. 6:14).

Freedom from law was a central element in Paul's experience and understanding of salvation. It is inseparably bound up with freedom from sin, although the law is not equated with sin. Rather, sin is envisioned as a force that uses the law to tempt people to disobedience so that they incur the death sentence (Rom. 7:11). In Rom. 7:1-4 the law is depicted as a husband to whom his wife (the believer) is bound as long as they both live; the husband's death frees her from that bond and enables her to marry another, namely, the risen Christ.

Galatians 3:23-25 shows that the law has a temporary custodial function in the divine purpose, until the "coming of faith." This "coming of faith" may be understood as an event both in salvation history and in the lives of individual believers. In salvation history it coincides with the appearance of Christ, in whom the parenthetic reign of law ended so that the age of faith, i.e., the age of the fulfillment of the promise to Abraham, might begin. In the lives of believers the "coming of faith" coincides with their abandonment of the attempt to establish their own righteous standing and their acceptance from God of the righteousness received through faith in Christ. The law is compared to the slave (*paidagōgós*, RSV "custodian") who accompanied the freeborn boy wherever he went and exercised a disciplinary responsibility over him until he came of age. With the dawn of faith the people of God come of age spiritually and have no further need of a custodian: they are set free from law.

Liberation from law involves redemption from the curse that the law pronounces on those who fail to keep it (Dt. 27:26). This redemption is effected by Christ's bearing the curse in His people's place (21:23), and it results in their receiving by faith the gift of the Spirit, with the liberty that He conveys (Gal. 3:10-14).

Although converts from paganism had not been under law in the same sense as converts from Judaism (like Paul himself), Paul viewed the two groups as sharing essentially the same preconversion bondage; the lives of both had been regulated by "the elemental spirits [*stoicheía*] of the universe" (Gal. 4:3, 8-10). These seem to be forces that hold in thrall the souls of people who follow their dictates, but lose their potency as soon as these souls are emancipated by the grace of God and the power of His Spirit.

*F. Personal and Apostolic Liberty.* As the servant of one Lord, Paul would not accept the dictates of anyone else nor submit to anyone else's assessment (cf. 1 Cor. 1-3). He was under an absolute obligation to preach the gospel, and that among the Gentiles, but he was allowed great liberty in the way that he fulfilled his commission. He could decide whether to live at his own expense or at the expense of those among whom he ministered; and in general he was the most adaptable of persons, living among Gentiles as a Gentile and among Jews as a Jew, so that he might convert as many as possible of both groups. "Though I am free from all men, I have made myself a slave to all, that I might win the more. . . . I have become all things to all men, that I might by all means save some. I do it all for the sake of the gospel, that I may share in its blessings" (1 Cor. 9:19, 22f.; cf. vv. 1, 18). It was these words that Luther had in mind when he opened his treatise on *The Liberty of a Christian* with two propositions: "A Christian man is a most free lord of all, subject to none. A Christian man is a most dutiful servant of all, subject to all."

Christian liberty in Paul's eyes, whether for himself or for others, is subject to only one limitation — Christian charity. But this limitation must be self-imposed. How Paul presented it may be seen in his admonition to the Corinthian Christians about eating the flesh of animals sacrificed to pagan divinities (1 Cor. 8:1-13; 10:23–11:1) and in his words to the Roman Christians about avoiding certain kinds of food or observing special days (Rom. 14:1–15:6). These were matters of utter indifference both ethically and religiously; no one had the right to restrict another's liberty with regard to them. But Christians might, and indeed should, restrict their liberty voluntarily if it were evident that by its exercise damage was likely to be done to the consciences of more scrupulous Christians who believed it wrong to eat certain kinds of food or to be lacking in respect for certain holy days. The restriction, however, must be voluntary; the scrupulous should not curb the freedom of those whose conscience was more emancipated, any more than the emancipated should force on the scrupulous a degree of liberty for which they were not yet ready.

*G. Defense of Liberty.* In his insistence on Christian liberty Paul found himself at times waging a war on two fronts. Legalism was an enemy of liberty (cf. Gal. 2:4), but so was license. This dual conflict appears clearly in the Corinthian correspondence. Some members of the church of Corinth, possibly in reaction to the moral laxity for which the city was notorious, wanted to impose a general rule of celibacy whether or not a person had that exceptional vocation (1 Cor. 7:1). Others, at the opposite extreme, believed that bodily activity of any kind was morally irrelevant. Their watchword was "all things are lawful" — including, it seems, fornication (6:12-20). Paul had to insist that freedom from law did not mean freedom to sin (e.g., Gal. 5:13; cf. 1 Pet. 2:16); that would be exchanging one form of bondage for another. Moreover, proponents of such an argument had failed to grasp the first principles of the gospel (Rom. 6:1-19).

*H. Consummation of Liberty.* The whole creation, of which the human race forms part, was created good but has been subjected by sin to frustration and futility, change and decay. Christians have been redeemed from bondage and now enjoy "the glorious liberty of the children of God," which will reach its consummation in the resurrection age (Rom. 8:19-23). It will then be shared by all creation.

It is no accident that the redemption of creation coincides with the redemption of the human body — the part of humanity that belongs to the material order. The first man, Adam, was put in charge of the "lower" creation and involved it in his fall; the "second man," Christ, through His redemptive work has broken the entail of the fall not only for humanity but also for the dependent creation. Even now human beings who, by selfish exploitation, can turn the good earth into a dustbowl, can by responsible stewardship make the earth blossom like the rose. What might a totally redeemed humanity not achieve in this realm? Paul's words imply not the annihilation of the present universe but its transformation, so that it may fulfil the purpose for which it was created.

*See also* SLAVE, SLAVERY.

***Bibliography***.–S. S. Bartchy, ΜΑΛΛΟΝ ΧΡΗΣΑΙ: *First-Century Slavery and 1 Corinthians 7:21* (1973); H. Chadwick, *NTS*, 1 (1954/55), 261ff.; M. I. Finley, ed., *Slavery in Classical Antiquity* (2nd ed. 1968); E. M. B. Green, *Jesus Spells Freedom* (1972); E. H. Hopkins, *Law of Liberty in the Spiritual Life* (1884); E. Käsemann, *Jesus Means Freedom* (Eng. tr. 1969); *Perspectives on Paul* (Eng. tr. 1975), pp. 122-137; L. De Lorenzi, ed., *Freedom and Love: The Guide for Christian Life* (1981); M. Luther, *Freedom of a Christian* (repr. 1957); *On the Bondage of the Will* (repr. 1957); S. Lyonnet, *Liberté chrétienne et loi nouvelle selon S. Paul* (1954); R. P. Martin, *Colossians: The Church's Lord and the Christian's Liberty* (1972)); F. P. Ramos, *La Libertad en la Carta a los Gálatas* (1977); P. Richardson, *Paul's Ethic of Freedom* (1979); D. W. B. Robinson, *Australian Biblical Review*, 12 (1964), 24ff.: W. C. van Unnik, *BJRL*, 44 (1961/62), 466ff.

F. F. BRUCE

**LIBNAH** lib'nə [Heb. *liḇnâ*].

**1.** A desert camp of the Israelites between Rimmon-perez and Rissah (Nu. 33:20f.), perhaps the same as Laban (Dt. 1:1; cf. BDB).

**2.** A town in the Shephelah of Judah (Josh. 15:42) that Joshua captured (10:29-31; 12:15). It also appears in the list of Levitical cities given to the descendants of Aaron (21:13; 1 Ch. 6:57 [MT 42]). Libnah joined the rebellious Edomites in a revolt against Jehoram king of Judah (2 K. 8:22), apparently due to Jehoram's evil reign (2 Ch. 21:10). Sennacherib king of Assyria besieged Libnah during Hezekiah's reign, when Judah seems to have controlled the city once again (2 K. 19:8; Isa. 37:8). The wife of King Josiah was "Hamutal the daughter of Jeremiah of Libnah"; her sons were Jehoahaz and Zedekiah (2 K. 23:31; 24:18; Jer. 52:1).

Libnah probably was a border stronghold of Judah, but its exact site is unknown. Eusebius (*Onom.*) described it, under the name Lob(a)na, as near Eleutheropolis (Beit Jibrîn). On the basis of the excavations of F. J. Bliss and R. A. S. Macalister, Libnah was associated with Tell eṣ-Ṣâfī, situated at the entrance of the valley of Elah. Contemporary scholars, however, have tended to locate Libnah at Tell Bornāt, about 8 km. (5 mi.) farther south.

K. G. JUNG

**LIBNI** lib'nī [Heb. *liḇnî*]; **LIBNITES** lib'nīts [Heb. *halliḇnî*].

**1.** Son of Gershon and eponym of the Libnites, who were one of the two divisions of Gershonite Levites (Ex. 6:17; Nu. 3:18, 21; 26:58; 1 Ch. 6:17, 20 [MT 2, 5]).

**2.** Son of Mahli and descendant of Merari, the head of another division of the Levites (1 Ch. 6:29 [MT 14]).

**LIBRARY.** A collection of writings and other artistic compositions arranged for use. Libraries in antiquity existed as temple, municipal, and private collections and, unlike modern libraries, consisted perhaps entirely of written works. In a limited but no less accurate sense, a book such as the Vedas or the Bible is a library. This article is concerned specifically with ancient libraries of works pertinent to biblical studies.

I. In the Bible
II. In the Ancient Near East
III. In Greece and the Roman Empire

***I. In the Bible.***–The English Bible does not contain the word "library" but does mention collections of writings several times. The "book of the covenant" (Ex. 24:7) may have been a collection of laws that were revealed to Moses. It is not clear whether the "book of the law" that Hilkiah found in the temple (2 K. 22:8) was the Torah, hence a collection of the five books of Moses, or a composition of the Deuteronomist. The "Book of the Wars of the Lord" (Nu. 21:14) and the "Book of Jashar" (Josh. 10:13; 2 S. 1:18) may have been collections of stories.

More certain are the official records of the kings, such as the acts of King David recorded in the "Chronicles of Samuel the seer, and in the Chronicles of Nathan the prophet, and in the Chronicles of Gad the seer" (1 Ch. 29:29). The "chronicles of King David" (27:24) may refer to the same collection. In the same category should be placed the "book of the acts of Solomon" (1 K. 11:41), the "Book of the Chronicles of the Kings of Israel" (14:19), the "Book of the Chronicles of the Kings of Judah" (v. 29), the "Book of the Kings of Israel" (1 Ch. 9:1), the "Book of the Kings of Judah and Israel" (2 Ch. 16:11), the "Book of the Kings of Israel and Judah" (27:7), the "Book of the Chronicles" (Neh. 12:23), and the "book of the records" (Ezr. 4:15; cf. "the royal archives there in Babylon," 5:17; 6:1). Esther mentions the "Book of the Chronicles" (2:23), the "book of memorable deeds, the chronicles" (6:1), and the "Book of the Chronicles of the kings of Media and Persia" (10:2).

The men appointed to describe the land to Joshua "set down in a book" their information (Josh. 18:9). Joshua wrote the words of the covenant "in the book of the law of God" (24:26). There is no indication that these were placed in a depository, although this is a reasonable assumption. The instruction to Isaiah, "Go, write it before them on a tablet, and inscribe it in a book, that it may be for the time to come as a witness for ever" (Isa. 30:8), implies that the book was preserved "for the time to come." The command to Jeremiah, "Write in a book all the words that I have spoken to you" (30:2), in context also requires that the book be preserved (cf. 45:1; 51:60, 63 [although this last reference suggests the end of that book's useful existence or perhaps is a symbolic expression of the end of the people to whom it was given]). The well-known account of the burning of Jeremiah's scroll by Jehoiakim and the subsequent command to Jeremiah to rewrite it (Jer. 36, esp. v. 28) clearly indicate that the words were of more than ephemeral value and thus would have been preserved in some kind of "library."

The *ʾᵃrôn*, "chest, ark," which was kept first in the tabernacle and later in the temple, may have served as a repository for documents. Heb. *ʾᵃrôn* is used for the ark of the covenant (e.g., Nu. 10:33) and for the ark of testimony (e.g., Ex. 25:22). It is also applied to the chest for offerings in the temple (2 K. 12:10) and to the mummy case of Joseph (Gen. 50:26). Possible support for this theory is found in the fact that Gk. *kibōtós*, "chest," renders *ʾᵃrôn* in the LXX but elsewhere also renders terms for archives (LSJ, *s.v. kibōtós*). The great sanctity of the ark and its location in the most holy place, however, make it an unlikely place for storing frequently used documents. More reasonable would be a depository set aside for this purpose in the temple. For example, the decree that gave Simon authority to be king and high priest was to be inscribed on bronze tablets, copies of which were to be kept "in the treasury" (*en tṓ gazaphylakíō*, 1 Macc. 14:49). The same basic word is found in the LXX of Ezr. 5:17 (*en oíkō tḗs gázēs*), where "royal archives" renders Aram. *bêṯ ginzayyāʾ*, "treasury."

The OT terms for types of written works are *diḇrê*, "acts/affairs of" (1 Ch. 29:29), commonly used with the meaning "words of;" *diḇrê hayyāmîm*, "daily acts," "diary, journal, chronicles" (1 K. 14:19); *sēper diḇrê*, "the book of, the acts of" (1 K. 11:41); and similar combinations with *diḇrê*. The LXX translates this word by *lógoi*, "matters, words" (1 Ch. 27:24), and by *rhēmata*, "sayings,

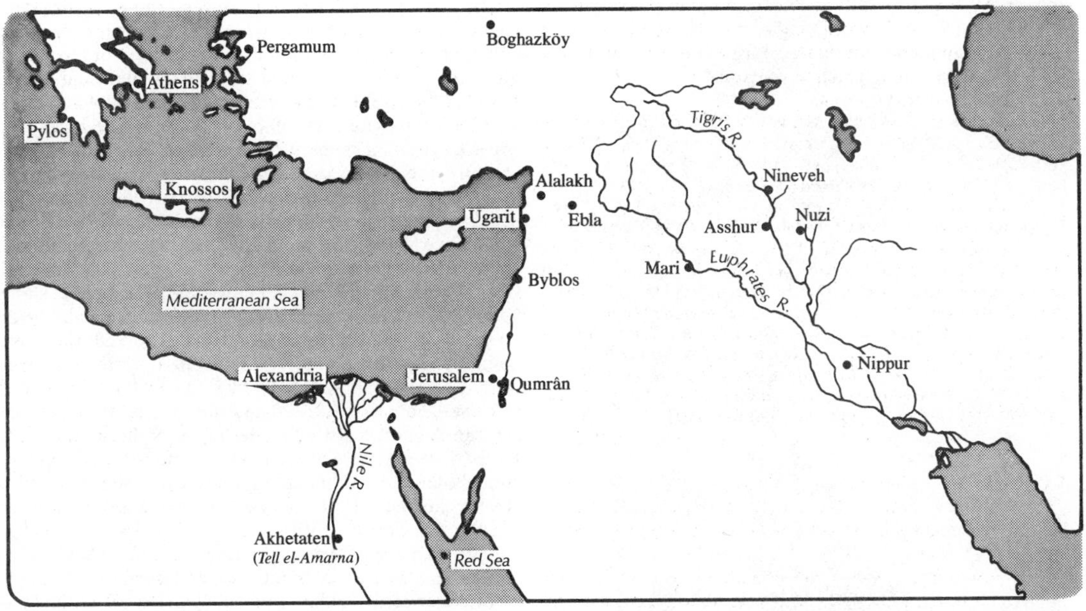


words" (1 K. 11:41); the latter does not convey the meaning of the Hebrew as fully as does *lógoi*. In the NT Gk. *práxeis*, "activities, acts," occurs in the title of Acts. *Biblía*, "books, collection of books," and *membránai*, "parchments," are found in 2 Tim. 4:13. *Ta biblía*, "the books," was the common title used for the Bible (2 Clem. 14:2), whence the English word. This usage shows that a book which is a collection of writings can be a "library."

***II. In the Ancient Near East.***–The following survey of ancient libraries helps to sustain some of the above statements concerning collections of documents and their storage as well as to present more background for biblical studies.

The libraries of Tell Mardikh (Ebla), Tell Fārah (Shuruppak), and Tell Abu Ṣalabīḫ (near Nippur), dating to the middle of the 3rd millennium B.C., have provided a wealth of material concerning collections at that early date. At TELL MARDIKH about twenty thousand tablets and fragments have provided data about administration, commercial activities, language, geography, and religion, and in addition have expanded the knowledge of libraries. The tablets were found in a room in the royal palace; their arrangement showed that they had been stacked on shelves according to categories (*see* picture in CANAAN). Lexical texts, many of them bilingual (Eblaic and Sumerian) and preserved in several copies, not only provide the meanings of many words but also exhibit an acrographic arrangement, i.e., the words, written in a cuneiform syllabary, are arranged according to the initial sign of the words.

Perhaps most important is the evidence that there were scribal schools at Tell Mardikh, Tell Fārah, and Tell Abu Ṣalabīḫ that were somehow related. Copies of the same texts written in the same hands were found at each place. Ebla and probably Tell Abu Ṣalabīḫ and Tell Fārah were cultural centers. The scribal school was headed by an *ummia*, "expert," and included the *dubzuzu*, "knower of tablets," "teacher," and *dubsar*, "scribe," "student." Student exercises and copies of translations of texts indicate that the student-scribes not only were learning their profession but also were collecting, translating, and duplicating texts. One bilingual tablet with eighteen duplicates lists nearly one thousand translated words. Another contains the names of 289 cities. Lists of animals, birds, fishes, professions, and personal names were found in the trove. Thus many of the elements of a true research library were present several centuries before Abraham in the region spanning southern Mesopotamia and northwestern Syria.

In the 2nd millennium (and possibly earlier in some instances) many places in the Near East had libraries. NIPPUR, 150 km. (90 mi.) SE of Baghdad, has given up thirty thousand to forty thousand tablets, including almost four thousand Sumerian literary works. The city, with its important "academy" (Sum. é-dubba(k), lit. "tablet house"), was Sumer's cultural center. Nippur's history can be traced to 4000 B.C. and its cultural prominence to the early 3rd millennium.

At MARI (Tell el-Ḥarîrī) on the Euphrates, 320 km. (200 mi.) NW of Baghdad, excavations have brought forth the royal archive consisting of about twenty thousand tablets, some in Hurrian, some in both Sumerian and Akkadian, but the majority in Babylonian similar to that of Hammurabi's law code. Some of the later correspondence includes letters exchanged by Zimri-Lim, who completed the building of the palace at Mari, and Hammurabi of Babylon. Mari may have been settled as early as 2600 B.C.

At Alalakh (Tell ʿAṭshânah) in northwestern Syria on the bend of the Orontes, between Aleppo and the Mediterranean, nearly five hundred tablets from the 17th to 15th cents., written in a Babylonian dialect, have been discovered. L. Woolley, the primary excavator, said that these were "only the chance survivors of a vastly greater number" (*Forgotten Kingdom* [1953], p. 64), but they have been of considerable importance for chronological studies.

Excavations at NUZI (Yoghlan [often Yorgan] Tepe, near modern Kirkûk), about 750 km. (470 mi.) to the east, have yielded approximately five thousand tablets dating from the 15th and 14th centuries. Nuzi, a province of the Mitanni, was mentioned in the Mari Texts, and in the Old Akkadian period it was known as Gasur. The Nuzi Texts include contracts of various kinds that have aided our understanding of a number of customs found in the patriarchal narratives of the OT (although not to the extent that some scholars have claimed).

Two tablets from the Alalakh library. Above is a treaty between Idrimi and Pilliya; below is a tablet in its envelope (D. J. Wiseman)

The history of the HITTITES is very complex, like their language (which is really about eight languages). The excavations at Hattusas (Boghazköy) in central Anatolia yielded about ten thousand tablets of many genres in Nesian ("Hittite"), Babylonian, and four other languages, written in Babylonian syllabic cuneiform. Since at least some of the languages often classified as Hittite are related to the Indo-European family of languages, these tablets are of major linguistic importance, especially because of their early date (mid-2nd millennium). Correspondence with other kingdoms has provided significant chronological data, and the Hittite law code has furnished OT students with additional knowledge of ancient customs and laws. Bilingual word lists provide Hittite-Babylonian equivalents. Medical texts and treaties, chiefly in Babylonian, testify to the cultural exchange in the Near East of that period.

Closely connected with the Hittite library at Boghazköy are the several hundred tablets from Tell el-Amarna in Egypt (*see* AMARNA TABLETS). Found at the capital of Amenhotep IV (Akhenaten), these tablets in cuneiform Babylonian give further proof that this dialect was the lingua franca of the period. Most of them are diplomatic correspondence between the Egyptian rulers Amenhotep III and Amenhotep IV and the allied states that bordered on or were vassals within the Asian portion of the Egyptian empire. Chronological synchronisms are thus established with Kadašman-Enlil I and Burnaburiaš II of the Kassite dynasty in Babylon, with Aššur-uballit I of Assyria, with Tušratta of Mitanni, with Šuppiluliuma of the Hittites, and with an unnamed king of Alašia (Cyprus). Details of vassal rulers in Jerusalem, Byblos, Tyre, Sidon, Qatna, Hazor, and other places in Syro-Palestine can be extracted from this correspondence. The archive was apparently a closed file, most or all of which had been brought from Karnak when Amenhotep IV (Akhenaten) relocated his capital at Akhetaten.

UGARIT (Râs Shamrah) furnished evidence of a royal library and also of a private library that was located in the house of the chief priest (*rb khnm*) in the heart of the temple quarter. Because the private library included mythological and religious texts, some in Hurrian, in addition to vocabularies, syllabaries, and school exercises, it may have been a seminary for training priestly scribes. Excavations indicate that Ugarit was occupied at various periods from *ca.* 6500 B.C. to Roman times, but the thousands of tablets of literary material discovered there date only from the 18th to 13th centuries.

These tablets have contributed immensely to our knowledge of OT language and religion (see esp. the publications of M. Dahood, e.g., *Psalms* [3 vols., *AB*, 1965-70]). Significant among them is a lexical list in four languages. Most of the texts are mythological compositions written in alphabetic cuneiform and documents in the Babylonian lingua franca written in Middle Babylonian syllabic cuneiform.

The alphabet comprised twenty-seven phonemes and the *ʾaleph-ʾileph-ʾuleph* vocalizations of *ʾaleph*. The order of the letters, as attested by several copies, is: *a, b, g, ḫ, d, h, w, z, ḥ, ṭ, y, k, š, l, m, ḏ, n, ẓ, s, ʿ, p, ṣ, q, r, ṯ, ǵ, t, i, u, s̀*. It is a reasonable assumption that the Phoenician alphabet, from which the Hebrew and Aramaic alphabets (as well as the Greek) were derived, dropped the unneeded phonemes from the alphabet represented at Ugarit.

The discovery of a library at Pylos in the Peloponnesus indicates a degree of uniformity in the "library science" of the ancient Near East. The tablets (more than twelve hundred) were written in Linear B and belong to the same general category as the four thousand found at Knossos and the limited number uncovered at Mycenae, Tiryns, and other places associated with the Minoan and Mycenaean civilization. Linear B is written in a syllabary (vowel, or consonant + vowel) of about ninety signs, fifty-nine of which were frequently used (*see* picture in GREECE). Thus it was an improvement over the considerably larger syllabary of the Akkadian language but not as advanced as the alphabet at Ugarit. Thirty different scribal hands have been identified at Pylos and perhaps seventy-five at Knossos. The language has been identified as an early form of Greek, and the system of writing was in use *ca.* 1500-1200 B.C. Apparently a "dark age" followed, for there are no literary remains, and then the Phoenician alphabet was introduced for writing Greek.

Most of the Pylos tablets were kept in an archives room, which contains the remains of shelves, hinged wooden chests, and baskets used for storing the tablets. Since the tablets were dated by month and day, but with no indication of year, it is supposed that the tablet room contained the current year's records. Tablets were found at other locations in the palace.

The link between the alphabetic cuneiform of Ugarit and the linear script of the Phoenicians is probably to be found at Byblos (Gubla, Gebal; *see* GEBAL **1**), where artifacts have shown experiments with several types of alphabet. No remains of a library have yet been discovered there, however (cf. M. Dunand, *Biblia grammata: Documents et récherches sur le développement de l'écriture en Phénicie* [1945]).

This survey of the major second-millennium libraries should not close without mention of the Kassite library of Tiglath-pileser I in the temple at Asshur. Much of its contents was taken in the sack of Babylon. For too long the Kassite period has been considered a dark age. It is now recognized that it was a time not only of collecting and arranging many literary documents but also of composing creative works. Before this period authors were anonymous and possibly reworked earlier compositions to a marked degree. C. J. Gadd wrote: "But the Kassite scribes, who begin to take on a degree of individuality, are far different characters. Shadows appear of great names, authors and scholars, whose memory was kept alive and honoured by descendants in the same professions. To such men can be attributed not merely the study, the textual fixation, and the exegesis of traditional works, but more original scholarship than can be actually identified with any other age" (*CAH,* II/2 [1975], 42).

The great library of Ashurbanipal at NINEVEH is doubtless the best known of ancient libraries. Excavated by A. H. Layard in 1845-1851, it is the oldest of the discoveries. Its "K" collection consists of more than twenty thousand tablets and portions of tablets, including nonliterary and literary texts. The nonliterary tablets include administrative texts, letters, public legal documents (e.g., law codes), and private legal documents (contracts, etc.). The literary tablets comprise religious texts, omen literature, royal inscriptions, epics and wisdom literature, and various other genres. There are lexical lists, lists in two or three languages, king lists, *limmu*-lists, annals of various kings, and lists of animals, birds, fishes, plants, stones, and place names.

At one time scholars thought that Ashurbanipal's library was the beginning of such collections, but later studies showed that it was the culmination of a long history of collecting, editing, translating, duplicating, and preserving documents. Tablets were kept on shelves, sometimes stored in baskets with clay labels (*étiquettes*). Multitablet texts had "catch-lines" at the beginnings of tablets, consisting of a few significant words from the end of the preceding tablet to facilitate arranging the tablets in order. It is very significant that Ashurbanipal had his agents search out documents already of great antiquity, so that Sumerian, early Babylonian, and other compositions were gathered, copied, and translated in a kind of seventh-century-B.C. renaissance that resembles what the Arabs did in the 9th cent. A.D.

A vast amount of literature from Egyptian libraries of the 3rd and 2nd millennia B.C. has been preserved, much of it written on the walls of buildings and tombs or on the inner sides of coffins. Egypt had scribal schools, where boys' instruction, enforced with many beatings, began when they were four and lasted twelve years. The student-scribes not only learned to write beautiful hieroglyphs on pieces of pottery or limestone but also copied extracts from the classics on papyrus. Works to be preserved were marked "to be kept in the archives of the governor" and then were given to the chief librarian of the relevant department, who placed them in jars and cataloged them (cf. A. Erman, *Life in Ancient Egypt* [1894], p. 114; for a translation of the 2nd Ger. ed. [not done in Eng.] see *La Civilisation égyptienne* [1952], p. 150 and figs. 139f.). Some scrolls have been found in temples, and a large quantity was discovered at el-Lahun (cf. H. E. Winlock, *Treasure of el Lahun* [1934]).

Extant Egyptian documents also include the Pyramid Texts of the 1st to 8th Dynasties (first half of the 3rd millennium B.C.), royal decrees of the 6th Dynasty (2600-2450), public records of the 20th Dynasty (1200-1090), and medical papyri of the 12th and later Dynasties found at Illahun (A. Gardiner, *Egyptian Grammar* [3rd ed. 1957], pp. 1-24). These texts, the great literary compositions of the Middle Kingdom (*ca.* 2000), and treatises on mathematics, architecture, and astronomy (sciences brought to an advanced state in Egypt) required some method of preserving and retrieving knowledge of previous generations. But no excavations (except at Tell el-Amarna) have produced ancient archives like those of other areas of the Near East.

Knowledge of ancient Egyptian libraries is consequently sparse. One record mentions "the land of the collected works of Khufu" (4th Dynasty). A small temple chamber at Edfu has a book catalog inscribed on a wall (H. Brugsch, *History of Egypt* [1881], I, 240). The Silsileh stele and possibly the Papyrus Harris (20th Dynasty, *ca.* 1000 B.C.) refer to libraries. Diodorus Siculus (1st cent. B.C.) described a library of Osymandyas (Ramses II, *ca.* 1304-1227) that was supposedly located at the Ramesseum in Thebes (*Library of History* i.47). The Amarna Tablets (14th cent.) mention "the place of the records of the king."

The Aramaic documents recovered at Elephantine, Egypt, date from the 4th cent. B.C. and are written on papyrus in the official Aramaic that had replaced Babylonian as the lingua franca of the Persian Empire. These documents represent only one or two genres. *See* ELEPHANTINE PAPYRI.

The extant DEAD SEA SCROLLS were found in caves near Qumrân, some of them in jars apparently made for preservation of MSS. The excavations at Khirbet Qumrân have revealed a library and scriptorium. The library, which might better be termed a reading room, is about 5 by 9 m. (16½ by 29½ ft.) and has a low clay bench around its sides and a receptacle in the wall that is believed to have held water for ritual washing of the hands after handling of the Scriptures. On the floor above the reading room was the scriptorium, attested by the remains of what seem to be large desks of clay, benches, and inkwells. In this room the scribes produced whatever scrolls were actually written at Qumrân (see R. de Vaux, *Archaeology and the Dead Sea Scrolls* [rev. Eng. tr. 1973], pp. 29-33; F. M. Cross, *Ancient Library of Qumran* [1961], pp. 66f.).

Among the Israelites religious literature was long known and passed on from generation to generation. Theories that this literature existed solely as oral tradition are being seriously challenged, particularly in view of the large number of archives antedating and contemporary with the Israelites. Later, as shown in I above, the temple was the repository of documents. It is reasonable to assume that this practice, too, had a long previous history, possibly dating back to the tabernacle (cf. Ex. 25:16, 22; Nu. 10:33).

W. S. LASOR

***III. In Greece and the Roman Empire.***–The tyrants Pisistratus of Athens and Polycrates of Samos (6th cent. B.C.) founded the first Greek public libraries, according to Gellius (*Noctium Atticarum* vii.17.1f.) and Athenaeus (*Deipnosophistae* i.3.A), but these sources are late (2nd and 3rd cents. A.D.). The book trade in Greece was well developed in the time of Pericles (5th cent. B.C.), although private libraries like those of Euripides, Plato, and Aristotle were still unusual (Hessel, p. 3). Aristotle's pupils may have consulted a library at his school (excavations show that the school could have accommodated one [Jackson, p. 7]). His student Alexander the Great, like earlier Macedonian kings, had a private library. The island of Cos, where Hippocrates lived, may have had a medical library by the early 4th cent. B.C. (Jackson, p. 9; see quotations in Platthy, pp. 146-48). Athens' libraries were so numerous by the 3rd cent. B.C. that the historian Timaeus, exiled from Syracuse, could research there for fifty years (Polybius xii.25.D-H). Libraries and the book trade depended mainly upon the labors of literate slaves, who individually copied MSS or as a group took dictation to produce multiple copies (Jackson, p. 7).

The literary center of the Hellenistic world was Alexandria. Its great library was founded, perhaps as an adjunct to the museum, by Ptolemy I Soter (d. *ca.* 283 B.C.) and Ptolemy II Philadelphus, with Demetrius of Phalerum as adviser. Ptolemy II's request that the Jews make copies of their own literature for the library (Tertullian *Apol.* xviii) led, according to the Epistle of Aristeas, to the production of the SEPTUAGINT. In the 3rd cent. B.C. a secondary library was established at the Serapeum, perhaps to hold duplicates and inferior rolls overflowing the main library. Early estimates of the library's size vary from 100,000 to 700,000 rolls (Edwards, pp. 20 n., 21).

The Ptolemies ruthlessly ensured the library's growth. Ptolemy III Euergetes (ruled 247-222) seized the books of travelers and kept those needed by the library, returning cheap papyrus copies to the owners (G. Sarton, *History of Science,* II [1959], 143f.). He gave the famine-stricken Athenians a deposit of fifteen silver talents in order to borrow the state MSS of Aeschylus, Sophocles, and Euripides; he forfeited the deposit by returning copies and keeping the originals (Galen *Comm. II in Hippocratis Epidem.* iii.239f.).

The Alexandrian collection was renowned not only for its size but also for its quality, achieved by the efforts of the scholar-librarians. These men had to identify and edit the MSS as well as to catalog and arrange them (Sarton, pp. 144f.). The standard texts produced in Alexandria made that city the center of the book trade until Caesar's time (Hessel, p. 4). Callimachus of Cyrene, a library associate, wrote the *Pinaces,* an elaborate catalog of the library's holdings that included biographical and critical information and became the model for all ancient bibliographies (Sarton, pp. 151f.; Hessel, p. 5).

Julius Caesar burned the Alexandrian library while attacking the city in 47 B.C., according to Plutarch (*Caesar* 49.3f.). Probably the damage was partial (Seneca estimated it at forty thousand volumes [*De tranquillitate animi* ix.5]); perhaps only books stored at the harborside burned (cf. Dio Cassius *Hist.* [*LCL*] xlii.38; Jackson, pp. 16f.; Savage, p. 10). But Mark Antony's reported gift to Cleopatra of the Pergamum library (41 B.C.) may indicate that replacement books were needed in Alexandria (Plutarch *Antony* 58.5–59.1; Plutarch called his source unreliable). In A.D. 272 Emperor Aurelian razed much of the Brucheion quarter of Alexandria, and with it perhaps the main library. The library of the Serapeum, thereafter the more important one, was probably destroyed in 389 on the urging of Theophilus bishop of Alexandria, who opposed pagan literature.

Alexandria's rival was the library of Pergamum in Asia Minor, founded by Attalus I (241-197 B.C.) and enlarged by his successor, Eumenes II. Pliny's report that parchment (Gk. *chárta pérgamena*) was invented because the Alexandrian kings would not export papyrus for book copying (*Nat. hist.* xiii.21 [70]) is factually inaccurate (*see* PARCHMENT). But rivalry did exist between the Ptolemies and Attalids, as shown by Eumenes' effort to hire an Alexandrian librarian and famed philologist, Aristophanes of Byzantine; Ptolemy V kept the librarian by imprisoning him (Savage, p. 13). Attempting to enlarge their collection to Alexandrian size, the Attalids seized private libraries (on the concealing of Aristotle's library from these kings, see Strabo *Geog.* xii.1.54f.). They also increased book production, at the expense of accuracy and even authenticity (Savage, p. 13; Platthy, p. 162). The Pergamum collection given to Cleopatra numbered 200,000 books (Plutarch *Antony* 58.5).

The Pergamum library was probably the model in several ways for the libraries of Rome. When Crates of Mallos, first head of the Pergamum library, lectured in Rome (*ca.* 168 B.C.), the Romans became interested in scholarly study of Greek literature, to which their Greek slave-tutors had exposed them (Savage, pp. 14f.; Suetonius *De grammaticis* 2). Moreover, Roman libraries physically resembled the one excavated at Pergamum. Usual features were proximity to a temple (at Pergamum, Athena's) and a statue of the deity in the library itself. A colonnaded portico was typically the library's study (Hessel, p. 5). In adjacent rooms the labeled papyrus rolls were stored on shelves; Roman libraries usually had separate rooms for Greek and Roman literature. Discovered at Pergamum were stones inscribed with authors' names (e.g., Homer), which have been identified as labels for portrait busts

Part of the reconstructed model of the Athena temple complex at Pergamum. The temple itself is lower right, and the library to its left (Staatliche Museen zu Berlin, DDR)

or medallions; these portraits were probably placed by the storage areas of the depicted authors' work (Jackson, pp. 22f.). *See also* PERGAMUM.

The first libraries in Rome were the spoils of war. Aemilius Paulus reportedly gathered up the books of Perseus of Macedonia after defeating him at Pydna in 168 B.C. (see Platthy, p. 140). Lucullus's library, generously open to all Greeks in Rome (Plutarch *Lucullus* 42), was taken from Mithradates of Pontus, according to Isidore of Seville (7th cent. A.D.; see Jackson, p. 8). Sulla captured Athens in 86 B.C. and with it the library of Apellicon, which originally may have been Aristotle's (Strabo *Geog.* xii.1.54f.; cf. Plutarch *Sulla* 26.1f.). Cicero, his brother Quintus, and the publisher Atticus had private libraries; such collections became so popular even among nonliterary aristocrats that Seneca commented, "Nowadays a library takes rank with a bath-room as a necessary ornament of a house" (*De tranquillitate animi* ix.4, tr. J. W. Clark). The remains of a private library were uncovered at Herculaneum in 1752.

Julius Caesar, with the help of the wealthy scholar M. Terentius Varro, planned the first public library for Rome, but not until 39 B.C., five years after Caesar's death, did C. Asinius Pollio build one (cf. Savage, p. 16, and Jackson, p. 18, with *Oxford Classical Dictionary* [1970], *s.v.* "Libraries" [F. G. Kenyon and C. H. Roberts], on the connection between Caesar's plans and Pollio's library). The Roman emperors, notably Augustus, Trajan, and Hadrian, built public libraries in imperial cities like Athens as well as in Rome (which had twenty-eight by the late 4th cent. A.D.). Antioch of Syria, Ephesus (see classical attestations in Platthy, pp. 154-57, 170-73; *see* Plate 1), and most large provincial cities had public collections, to which wealthy citizens customarily contributed funds; authors gave their own works, with benefit of publicity for themselves. Since papyrus rolls exposed to air lasted two hundred years or less, libraries had their own copying schools and also bought from dealers. New authors as well as the old masters sold well (Jackson, p. 22). In the 1st and 2nd cents. A.D. parchment codices began to be used alongside papyrus rolls and became predominant by the 5th cent. (Sarton, p. 148).

Eusebius relied upon the Christian libraries of Jerusalem (founded A.D. 212) and Caesarea (existence attested 231-386) in composing his church history. Both libraries included books by Origen and other church fathers; the one at Caesarea, unusual among Greco-Roman libraries, had law literature (Jackson, p. 29; Platthy, pp. 176f.). The early Christians organized church libraries of Scriptures, polemics, and records, which Diocletian in 303 attempted to burn. Ten years later Constantine reversed this policy by encouraging production and propagation of Christian literature; his successors maintained libraries at Constantinople (Jackson, p. 29). In the East and West, church libraries (e.g., at Nola in Italy), monasteries like Benedict's Monte Cassino and Cassiodorus's Vivarium (both founded in the 6th cent. A.D. in Italy), medieval cathedral and court schools, and Arabic translations of Greek science and philosophy (made especially in ninth- and tenth-century Spain) preserved both Christian and classical literature for later generations. K. ADAMS

***Bibliography.***–R. Biggs, *Inscriptions from Tell Abū Ṣalābikh* (1974); G. H. Bushnell, *World's Earliest Libraries* (1931); *CAH* (3rd ed. 1972), *passim*; A. Caquot, M. Szyncer, and A. Herdner, *Textes ougaritiques,* I (1974); J. Černý, *Paper and Books in Ancient Egypt* (1952); E. Edwards, *Memoirs of Libraries* (1859); *Enc.Brit.* (1911), XIV, *s.v.*; J. Friedrich, ed., *Keilschrifturkunden aus Boghazkoi* (39 vols., 1921-1963); "Zum Verwandschaftsverhältnis von Keilhethitisch, Luwisch, Paläisch und Bildhethitisch," in *Gedenkschrift P. Kretschmer* (1956); O. R. Gurney, *Hittites* (2nd ed. 1961); E. V. Hansen, *Attalids of Pergamon* (1947); A. Hessel, *History of Libraries* (Eng. tr., with supplementary material, 1955); S. L. Jackson, *Libraries and Librarianship in the West: A Brief History* (1974); F. G. Kenyon, *Books and Readers in Ancient Greece and Rome* (2nd ed. 1951); J. A. Knudtzon, *Die El-Amarna-Tafeln* (2 vols., 1915); J. Laessøe, "Literary and Oral Tradition in Ancient Mesopotamia," in *Studia Orientalia Ioanni Pedersen* (1953), pp. 205-218; A. H. Layard, *Nineveh and Its Remains* (2 vols., 2nd ed. 1850); W. von Massow, *Führer durch das Pergamon Museum* (2nd ed. 1936); F. Milkau, *Geschichte der Bibliotheken im alten Orient* (1935); F. Milkau, ed., *Handbuch des Bibliothekwissenschaft* (2nd rev. ed. 1950-57), III/1; G. Murray, *History of Ancient Greek Literature* (3rd ed. 1917); A. Parrot, *Ninive et l'AT* (1955); E. A. Parsons, *Alexandrian Library, Glory of the Hellenistic World* (1952); Pauly-Wissowa, III/I, 405-424; K. G. Pedley, *RQ,* 2 (1959), 21-41; G. Pettinato, *Catologo dei testi cuneiformi di Tell Mardikh-Ebla* (1979); J. Platthy, *Sources on the Earliest Greek Libraries* (1968); *RAC,* II (1954), *s.v.* "Bibliothek" (C. Wendel); E. C. Richardson, *Altertümer von Pergamon* (10 vols., 1885-1937); *Biblical Libraries: A Sketch of Library History from 3400 B.C. to 150 A.D.* (1914); E. A. Savage, *Story of Libraries and Book-Collecting* (n.d.); C. F. A. Schaeffer, *Ugaritica V* (1968), 545-606, 625-27, figs. 16, 16b; W. W. Tarn, *Hellenistic Civilization* (5th ed. 1952); R. C. Thompson and R. W. Hutchinson, *Century of Exploration in Nineveh* (1929); C. Virolleaud, *Le Palais royal d'Ugarit* (5 vols., 1955-1965); D. J. Wiseman, "Alalakh," in *AOTS,* pp. 119-135; *Alalakh Tablets* (1953); L. Woolley, *Forgotten Kingdom* (1953). W. S. LASOR

**LIBYA** lib'ē-ə, lib'yə [Heb. *lûḇîm* (2 Ch. 12:3; 16:8; Nah. 3:9), *luḇîm* (Dnl. 11:43); LXX Gk. *Libyes* (pl. of *Libyē;* RSV uses *Libyes* instead of Heb. *kûḇ* in Ezk. 30:5); NT Gk. *Libyē* (Acts 2:10)]; AV also LUBIM(S) (2 Ch. 12:3; 16:8; Nah. 3:9), CHUB (Ezk. 30:5). A land in northern Africa W of Egypt.

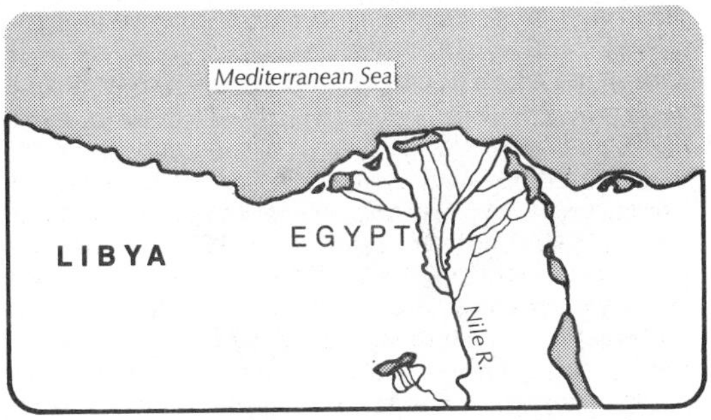


The location and significance of Libya are clear in the biblical text. A people called *rbw* occur in Egyptian texts of the 13th-12th centuries. (Since Egyptian writing had no character for *l* — *r* or *n* being used to represent the sound — *rbw* was probably pronounced "Labu.") This word apparently gave the Greeks the word *Libyē* and the Hebrews the word *lûḇîm.* Libyans raided Egypt sporadically in the 12th-10th cents., and were in the forces of Shishak ("Sheshonq" in Egyptian texts; 2 Ch. 12:3) and of Zerah (2 Ch. 14:9; 16:8). Shishak established a foreign rule over Egypt, quite possibly Libyan (cf. A. H. Gardiner, *Egypt of the Pharaohs* [1961], p. 324).

The relationship of the Lubim to the Lehabim is obscure. Put was the third son of Ham and a brother of Egypt (Gen. 10:6); Lehabim was the third son of Egypt (v. 13). But Heb. *miṣrayim* ("Egypt") and *l$^e$hāḇîm* ("Lehabim") are almost certainly gentilics, i.e., names of peoples, not of individuals (the same can be said of many other names in Gen. 10). Thus a tradition linked Lehabim, Put, and Egypt (to name just these three) with Ham, making them Hamitic peoples. "Hamitic" has generally been used to designate the people, or at least the languages, of Libya.

In the NT Simon of Cyrene was from Libya (Mt. 27:32 par.; *see* CYRENE), and people from "the parts of Libya belonging to Cyrene" were among those who witnessed the phenomena at Pentecost (Acts 2:10). W. S. LASOR

**LICE.** The AV translation of Heb. *kēn, kinnîm* in Ex. 8:16-18 (MT 12-14); Ps. 105:31; *see* GNAT. The expression "picking lice" occurs in the NEB at Cant. 1:7. The MT *ʿōṭeyâ* (from the verb *ʿāṭâ*) can be translated literally "one who is veiled" (so RSV mg.) or, following a different verb of the same spelling, "one who delouses" (cf. Jer. 43:12; RSV "cleans [his cloak] of vermin"; NEB "scours [his clothes] to rid them of lice"; *see* VERMIN). The AV and RSV, following the Syr., Vulg., and Symm., emend the MT to *ṭōʿîyâ,* "one who wanders" (so RSV).

**LICENTIOUS; LICENTIOUSNESS** [Gk. *asélgeia*]; AV LASCIVIOUSNESS, WANTONNESS (Rom. 13:13; 2 Pet. 2:18), PERNICIOUS (2:2), FILTHY (2:7); NEB also VICE, DEBAUCHERY, DISSOLUTE PRACTICES, SENSUALITY, INDECENCY, etc. Extreme indulgence in sensuality without regard for moral restraints.

The single Gospel occurrence of *asélgeia* is in Mk. 7:22, where Jesus lists it among the vices that come from the heart and defile a person. It occurs nine times in the NT Epistles, usually in the specific sense of sexual excess. Paul listed it among the "works of the flesh" (Gal. 5:19; cf. Rom. 13:13f.; *see* FLESH III.B). This vice was characteristic of pagans (Eph. 4:17-19; 1 Pet. 4:3); but the Epistles repeatedly warned that there was no place for such behavior in the Christian community (e.g., 2 Cor. 12:21; cf. Eph. 4:20-24) — a warning that was particularly urgent because "false prophets" (2 Pet. 2:1) were teaching that Christians were exempt from the demands of the moral law (cf. vv. 2, 7, 18f.; Jude 4). *See* ANTINOMIANISM; GNOSTICISM VI.C; PASSION II. N. J. O.

**LIDEBIR** lid′ə-bər [Heb. *lidebir*; LXX A *Dabir* (followed by Syr., Vulg.), B *Daibōn,* L *Debēr*]. A city in the tribal inheritance of Gad (Josh. 13:26, RSV mg.). Lidebir is generally taken to be a scribal error for LO-DEBAR (so NEB). The suggestion that the *lamed* is possessive ("[the boundary] belonging to Debir"; cf. AV, RSV) requires a definite article on *gebûl* that the MT lacks. W. S. L. S.

**LIE.** To assume, or rest in, a horizontal position. In the OT it most often represents Heb. *šāḵaḇ,* "lie down" (e.g., in sleep, Ruth 3:4, 7f., 13f.; 1 S. 3:3, 5f.; etc.; or in death, Gen. 47:30; Lam. 2:21; Ezk. 32:21, 27-30; etc.). The common phrase *šāḵaḇ ʿim* ("lie with") is a euphemism for sexual relations; deprecatory in tone, the expression is generally used to describe an illicit or inappropriate sexual act, e.g., incest (Gen. 19:32-35; Lev. 20:11f.; Dt. 27:20, 22f.), adultery (Gen. 39:7, 10, etc.; Dt. 22:22f.; 2 S. 11:4), rape (Gen. 34:2; Dt. 22:25, 28; 2 S. 13:14), homosexual relations (Lev. 18:22; 20:13), and bestiality (Ex. 22:19 [MT 18]; Dt. 27:21). *See* CRIME.

Another OT verb, Heb. *rāḇaṣ,* usually connotes a lying down to rest, or a state of repose (e.g., Gen. 29:2; Isa. 11:6f.; 14:30; Zeph. 2:7, 14; hiphil in Ps. 23:2; Ezk. 34:15). The expression "lie in wait," usually translating Heb. *ʾāraḇ* (e.g., Jgs. 9:32; 21:20; 1 S. 22:8, 13), refers to the AMBUSH as a method of warfare.

See *TWOT,* I, 68; II, 830, 921f. N. J. O.

**LIE; LYING** [Heb. *šāqar, šeqer, kāzaḇ, kāzāḇ, kāḥaš, kaḥaš, šāwʾ*–'emptiness, worthlessness' (Ps. 12:2 [MT 3]; 144:8, 11; Isa. 59:4); Aram. *kiḏbā* (Dnl. 2:9); Gk. *pseúdomai, pseúdos, apseudḗs*–'free from deceit' (Tit. 1:2, "never lies")]; AV also FALSEHOOD, FALSELY, VANITY, LEASING (Ps. 4:2; 5:6 [MT 4:3; 5:7]), GUILE (Rev. 14:5), etc.; NEB also DECEIVE, "break my word," SHAM, etc.; **LIAR** [Heb. *kāzaḇ, ʾîš kāzāḇ* (Prov. 19:22), *šeqer* (Ps. 63:11 [MT 12]; Prov. 17:4), *baḏ* (Isa. 44:25); Gk. *pseústēs* (Jn 8:44, 55; 1 Tim. 1:10; etc.), *pseudḗs* (Rev. 21:8), *pseudólogos* (1 Tim 4:2)]; AV also LIE; NEB also WRONG, FALSIFY, FALSEHOOD, etc. A statement used with the intention of deceiving or defrauding. Not only the spoken word but also an action (1 Jn. 1:6) or an idol (Am. 2:4) may be called a lie.

From the very beginning of the OT people lied and were condemmed for it. Eve accepted Satan's lie in the garden (Gen. 3). Cain killed his brother and then attempted to cover his sin with a lie (4:9). Thus lying became characteristic of humankind separated from God (e.g., Ps. 12:2 [MT 3]; 58:3 [MT 4]; 62:4 [MT 5]; cf. Jer. 9:5 [MT 4]).

From the earliest times lying was considered a breach of the moral code. The ninth commandment forbids lying, or bearing false witness (Ex. 20:16; Dt. 5:20). Both the OT and the NT consider telling the truth a religious obligation (e.g., Lev. 6:2-7 [MT 5:21-26]; 19:11; Ps. 5:6; Prov. 6:16-19; 12:19-22; Eph. 4:25; Col. 3:9). In the Sermon on the Mount Jesus stressed that a Christian's communication should be honest without the need of an oath (Mt. 5:33-37).

Many instances of lying are recorded in the OT. Some lies are motivated by fear for one's own or another's safety. Both Abraham and Isaac lied about their wives out of fear for their own lives (Gen. 12:10-20; 20:1-18; 26:6-11). By means of an elaborate deception the Gibeonites purchased their lives at the cost of the lowest form of slavery (Josh. 9). Samson lied to Delilah three times because he did not trust her (Jgs. 16:6-17). Sometimes lying is motivated by desire for personal gain or advantage. At his mother Rebekah's instigation, Jacob deceived his father Isaac in order to obtain the blessing intended for Esau (Gen. 27). Later Jacob himself was the victim of deception by his uncle Laban (29:15-30; 30:31-36). In other instances lies are used to cover up other sins. Jacob's sons used deception to conceal from their father that they had sold Joseph to Ishmaelite traders (37:26-33). In his attempt to conceal his adultery with Bathsheba, David went so far as to have her husband Uriah killed (2 S. 11).

In several instances the Scriptures appear to commend people for using deception to gain a desired end. By deception the Hebrew midwives preserved the lives of many Hebrew male babies while the Israelites were in Egypt (Ex 1:15-21). Rahab the prostitute saved the Israelite spies from certain death by hiding them and telling their pursuers that they had already left the city of Jericho; because of this act, which demonstrated her faith in Yahweh, Rahab and her family were preserved when the Israelites killed everyone else in Jericho (Josh. 2; 6:17, 22-25). Ehud deceived Eglon the king of Moab by using words that could be interpreted in two ways. After presenting tribute to Eglon, Ehud requested a private session to reveal "a message from God." The "message" was delivered in the form of a sword that Ehud thrust into Eglon's abdomen, thereby delivering the Israelites from Moabite oppression (Jgs. 3:15-30). Jael lured the exhausted Sisera into her tent with a promise of security and, after soothing him to sleep with warm milk, drove a tent peg through his head (Jgs. 4:17-22). She is praised for this act that destroyed a great enemy of Israel (5:24-27).

During the prophetic period of Israel's history, false prophets represented a significant threat to the faith and life of Israel as God's people. Isa. 9:15 (MT 14) lists them as the most despicable of all persons in Israel. Jeremiah denounced them repeatedly and cited them as the cause of the Exile (e.g., Jer. 5:31; 14:14; 23:14, 25-32; 27:9f., 14-16). These condemnations are echoed in Ezekiel (e.g., 13:1-17; 22:28), Lamentations (2:14), and Zechariah (10:2; 13:3-6).

The NT warns that false prophets are also characteristic of the end time (e.g., Mt. 7:15; 24:11; 2 Pet. 2:1; 1 Jn. 4:1). They show signs but deliver a false message about the things of God (Mt. 24:24; Mk. 13:22; cf. Rev. 16:13f.; 19:20). *See also* PROPHECY, FALSE.

The NT presents the lie as a part of the struggle in the world between the forces of good and evil. God, as the personification of all that is good, cannot lie (Tit. 1:2; cf. Nu. 23:19; He. 6:18). Satan, however, is the father of lies, and his children may be known in the world by their lying (Jn. 8:44). Jesus warned His followers that their opponents would persecute them with lies (Mt. 5:11).

This struggle between the forces of truth and falsehood also bears upon Christians' lives. Eph. 4:25 exhorts Christians to put away lying and speak the truth with their neighbors. 2 Thess. 2:9-12 warns that unbelievers, because they have closed their hearts to the truth, will receive from the Lord a "strong delusion" that will "make them believe what is false." Rom. 1:25 characterizes such persons as having "exchanged the truth about God for a lie." Thus the absolute distinction between truth and the lie distinguishes Christians from non-Christians (1 Jn. 2:21-27). Those who deny that Jesus is the Christ are liars (v. 22). The anointing by the Spirit that Christians have received teaches them what is true and frees them from lies (v. 27).

The seriousness with which the early Church viewed the sin of lying is illustrated by the story of Ananias and Sapphira, who met with sudden death after Peter confronted them with having attempted to deceive the Christian community (Acts 5:1-11). A Jewish "false prophet" named Bar-Jesus was struck with blindness after Paul denounced him as a "son of the devil... full of all deceit" (Acts 13:6-11).

The book of Revelation depicts a time when Christians will finally be free from all deceit. The 144,000 who are blessed forever are found to have no lie in their mouth (14:5). No liars will profane the new Jerusalem (21:27). The deceiving devil and the false prophet will be destroyed (19:20; 20:10), as will all those who have lived the lie (21:8; 22:15).

Paul often uses the term "lie" in a formula affirming the truthfulness of his speech and the trustworthiness of his letters (Rom. 9:1; 2 Cor. 11:31; Gal. 1:20, 1 Tim. 2:7). He emphasizes that God knows that his speech (unlike that of the FALSE APOSTLES) is true.

In the NT Gk. *pseúdos* ("false") is often combined with other terms to describe those who pervert the truth or claim to be what they are not. Most common is *pseudoprophḗtēs*, "false prophet" (see above). *Pseúdos* is also joined to *adelphós* ("brother", 2 Cor. 11:26; Gal. 2:4), *apóstolos* ("apostle," 2 Cor. 11:13), *didáskalos* ("teacher," 2 Pet. 2:1), *mártys* ("witness," Mt. 26:60; 1 Cor. 15:15), *martyría* ("testimony," Mt. 15:19; 26:59), *martyréō* ("bear witness," Mt. 19:18; Mk. 10:19; etc.), *christós* ("christ," Mt. 24:24; Mk. 13:32), and *lógos* ("word"; RSV "liar," 1 Tim. 4:2). *See also* TRUTH.

D. W. WEAD

**LIEUTENANTS** (AV Ezr. 8:36; Est. 3:12; 8:9; 9:3). *See* SATRAPS.

**LIFE.** The most basic reality common to God and mankind, native to God and imparted by Him to His creatures, first by creation, then by redemption. Angels, plants, and animals constitute other orders of created life.

Hebrew terms include *nep̱eš,* meaning "soul" (that which animates the body), "breath," and by extension a living being (*nep̱eš ḥayyâ,* Gen. 2:7), also life in general (Dt. 30:19). Sometimes *nep̱eš* is linked with blood, the life of the flesh, hence the prohibition of eating blood (Lev. 17:10-12, 14; Dt. 12:23). It can also mean livelihood (Dt. 24:6).

*Ḥayyîm* is used somewhat more frequently. The reason for the plural form is uncertain. It may be due to the fact that it is an abstract noun with more than one possible frame of reference, including the plural term Elohim, i.e., God the Almighty. *Ḥayyîm* is frequently used in connection with the span of human existence (Gen. 23:1). One's experience can affect one's evaluation of life adversely (Job 3:20) or positively (Ps. 23:6). Its full import reaches beyond the limit of human existence, for one owes one's life to God and must answer to Him.

Hebrew *ḥayyâ* occurs with the meaning "living creature" (Ezk. 1:5). The verb *ḥāyâ* ("live") expresses the process of temporal existence (Gen. 5:3), but can also denote the quality of life as successful because one seeks to honor God's will as set forth in the commandments (Ps. 119:144). The adj. *ḥay,* "living" or "alive" (1 K. 3:22), has its counterpart in the Gk. *zṓn* (Acts 1:3). Heb. *yāmîm* ("days") is used occasionally in a context indicating prolongation of life (1 K. 3:11).

Greek terms for life are principally *bíos, psychḗ,* and *zōḗ*. Of these, *bíos* is limited to the natural order. It is used of life span (Prov. 31:12, LXX) and of the financial resources essential for the sustenance of physical life (Lk. 21:4). It also involves such items as cares, riches, and pleasures (Lk. 8:14) or worldly goods (1 Jn. 3:17), and even life-style (1 Tim. 2:2). *Psychḗ* denotes self-conscious physical existence, corresponding to Heb. *nep̱eš* (Acts 20:10). *Zōḗ* can mean lifetime (Lk. 16:25). It also indicates life as the native possession of God (Jn. 5:26) and as His gift to mankind whereby people are able to feel, think, and act (Acts 17:25). In Acts 5:20 it is used as a substitute for the word "gospel." It often denotes life on the highest plane as redeemed and devoted to God (Jn. 10:10). It is the only term for life with which the adj. "eternal" is used (17:3). Occurring rather infrequently are *agōgḗ,* "manner of life" (2 Tim. 3:10); *anastrophḗ,* "way of life, conduct" (Gal. 1:13); *biōtikós,* "pertaining to ordinary life" (Lk. 21:34); *bíōsis,* "manner of life" (Acts 26:4); *zōopoiéō,* "make alive, impart life" (Rom. 4:17).

I. OT
II. Intertestamental Period
III. NT
IV. Conclusion

***I. OT.***–The opening words of Scripture presuppose the existence of God and go on to describe His activity in creation (Gen. 1:1). Although He is not described as the living God at an early point in the biblical text (Dt. 5:26 is the first such description), the delay may well indicate that there was no felt need to have this unique quality pointed out. It was a "given." God imparted life to His handiwork in all its forms, climaxed by the creation of mankind (Gen. 1:20–2:23). It is recognized that He alone has creative power (2 K. 5:7). Mankind is accountable to Him for the life He bestows. A stewardship is involved.

The folly of idolatry is increased by the fact that the images of human devising are inferior not only to the living God but even to those who fashion and worship them, for they lack the element of life. Human beings are not creators in the true sense of the word, for they are unable to impart to the objects of their craftsmanship the breath of life they themselves have received from God (Ps. 115:2-8).

In the creation account the concept of life is associated with the breath of God imparted to the form He had molded (Gen. 2:7). Another approach is presented in the prohibition of eating flesh with the blood in it, on the ground that the life is in the blood (Gen. 9:4). The entire human family can be described as "all flesh" (Gen. 6:12), which emphasizes the physical aspect of mankind and may well hint at perishability also. An additional nuance is provided by texts in which "life" seems intended to denote life-style or the conditions under which one is obliged to live (Job 10:1).

With the fall came the disclosure that the tenure of human life would be limited, marked by toil, and terminated by death (Gen. 3:17-19). Nevertheless, a distinctive feature of the account of the antediluvians is the longevity ascribed to them, reaching 969 years in the case of Methuselah (Gen. 5:27). No formal explanation is given for this phenomenon, but a hint may be provided in the following chapter, in the statement that the wickedness of man was great in the earth (Gen. 6:5). The passage of time, however lengthy, did not improve the quality of human life. The earth was filled with violence and corruption (Gen. 6:11). It seemed that the human race was incapable of producing any considerable change. The enjoyment of long life on a personal basis, however, was promised to those who would cleave to God in loving obedience (Ps. 91:16). It should be noted that throughout Israel's history God's servants were reminded that their lives were in His hand. To suffer or to be at ease, to live or to die, must depend on the divine will. In connection with long life, it may seem strange that Daniel would say to King Darius, "O king, live for ever" (Dnl. 6:21 [MT 22]), but this was the conventional language of flattery that no one, including the king, took seriously (cf. Ps. 89:48 [MT 49]).

Long life in itself is not necessarily a blessing. Generally it is extolled because the quality of life is assumed to be good, characterized by divine favor and prospering. This is made clear by Ps. 91, where the culminating favor provided by God, long life (v. 16), is for one "who abides in the shadow of the Almighty" (v. 1). To the pious Hebrew, living meant more than the continuance of bodily strength and vitality. It meant fearing God and enjoying His favor because of obedience to His will (Dt. 8:1). The purpose behind the provision of manna for Israel in the wilderness was not merely that the people might live but also that they might come to know that mankind does not live by bread alone but by every word that proceeds out of the mouth of the Lord (v. 3).

The background of the story of Job is a debate between Satan and God. Permitted to strip Job of family and fortune, Satan had to admit after his failure that Job was still loyal to God, but he insisted that deprivation of health would lead Job to renounce God (Job 2:4). Given permission to afflict Job's body, Satan tried hard but failed. Job remained loyal to his Maker, despite his misery (7:16) and the mystery of being allowed to suffer grievously with respect to possessions, family, and his own person. He continued to cling to life when it seemed no longer worthwhile to do so. By refusing to curse God and die, he refuted the claim of the evil one.

The young king Solomon, given the privilege of asking God for anything he chose (1 K. 3:5), named wisdom rather than material things. To illustrate the penetrating quality of that wisdom, the sacred historian introduced into his narrative the story of two women who came before Solomon contesting the ownership of a baby. The king called for a sword to cut the child in half so that each woman could have a portion, knowing that the true mother would not consent but would offer to let the other woman take the child, so great was the mother's love and yearning that her child might live (1 K. 3:16-28).

The word "life" is occasionally used as a synonym for health. "A tranquil mind gives life to the flesh" (Prov. 14:30). Apparently there was awareness of the influence of the state of mind on the bodily condition.

Reverence for life as the divine intention in human relations is underscored in the sixth commandment: "You shall not kill" (Ex. 20:13). The verb has no object, but human beings are clearly intended (cf. Lev. 24:17). After the Flood, permission was given to kill animals for food (Gen. 9:3f.), so they are not in view in the Decalogue, nor is death that occurs in a war that is justified (Ex. 17:8-16; Dt. 20:13-18; 1 S. 17:50). What the commandment prohibits is murder. The death penalty is biblically based (Gen. 9:5f.; Nu. 35:33) and it magnifies both the importance and sacredness of human life as made in the image of God. Far from representing an inhumane attitude by calling for the death penalty, the commandment exalts the value of human life by protecting it.

By virtue of possessing divine revelation, Israel had a loftier evaluation of human life than its neighbors. The crucial point of distinction was the heathen practice of offering up human lives as a sacrifice to the gods. Among the reasons for Israel's exile to Assyria was their resorting to this practice (2 K. 16:3; 17:17). King Manasseh in particular is cited for burning his sons as an offering (2 Ch. 33:6; cf. v. 9).

Though life is the common possession of all mankind, there is a distinctive character to each individual. Each one reflects to some extent the physical features and characteristics of the parents, yet each individual life remains unique. This uniqueness in the physical realm is doubtless intended to be a reflection of the uniqueness of each individual person in the sight of God.

In OT days people coveted the experience of enjoying a combination of long life, health, and prosperity. These were promised to those who loved and obeyed God (Dt. 30:11-16; Ps. 91:14-16). The highest plane reached by OT saints, however, was not exclusively determined by their outward circumstances, for these were not to be compared to the joy of knowing God as the greatest possible blessing (Ps. 73:23-26). When David was in the wilderness of Judah and in a potentially dangerous situation, he had opportunity for soul searching. As a result he was able to say to God, "Thy steadfast love is better than life" (Ps. 63:3 [MT 4]).

Beyond reasonable doubt, however, people in those days shrank from the prospect of death, which involved a shift from the known to the unknown. When pronouncements are made about what death involves, the reader may well be uncertain whether these are based on revelation or human speculation. Job's declaration of confidence regarding his own future state (Job 19:25-27) was possibly based on his conviction that the fellowship he had enjoyed with the Almighty was so real and personal that he refused to concede that death could terminate it. David comforted himself over the death of his child, saying, "I shall go to him, but he will not return to me" (2 S. 22:23). Such an expression of confidence seems to involve more than the prospect of sharing Sheol. It breathes hope of personal reunion. This is in line with David's word in another connection: "As for me, I shall behold thy face in righteousness; when I awake, I shall be satisfied with beholding thy form" (Ps. 17:15; see also 16:9-11). An unbroken relationship with God tended to carry with it the assurance that death could not sever the relationship. It is likely that "sleep," when used of one who has died, is intended to suggest relief from life's cares, pains, and sorrows rather than to connote lack of consciousness in the intermediate state.

It is important to keep in view the relationship between life and law. At the time of its emergence as a nation, Israel participated in an arrangement that was covenantal in nature. God chose Israel as His special people (Am. 3:2). This choice was a matter of His own initiative. It meant life and blessing for Israel (Dt. 30:15). But pursuant to this election God set before them the commandments and ordinances to test thir obedience (Lev. 18:5; Dt. 8:1). Failure on the part of Israel, especially in terms of acknowledging gods of human invention and worshiping them, would serve to curtail their enjoyment of the land of promise (Dt. 30:17-19). Such conduct would abrogate the covenant.

A special approach is found in the wisdom literature (chiefly Proverbs and Ecclesiastes), which was mainly concerned with life in this world rather than in the life to come. Basically its method was to resort to the observation of human life more than earlier Scripture had done. It tended to encourage the fostering of intellectual pursuits and achievements, focusing attention on the wise as an elite group and manifesting a somewhat condescending attitude toward the ordinary person. Yet it depended in part on the folk wisdom of the masses and on such use of earlier Scripture as would add an element of authority. Its keynote is found in the adage, "The fear of the Lord is the beginning of wisdom" (Prov. 1:7). Wisdom is described as a tree of life (3:18). The words of wisdom are life to the one who finds them (4:22).

The wisdom tradition continued into the intertestamental period, appearing especially in Sirach and the Wisdom of Solomon. It is noted that God set before Israel the covenant. "He . . . allotted to them the law of life" (Sir. 17:11) is an apparent reference to the Mosaic law. The writer of the Wisdom of Solomon asserted, "The righteous live for ever and their reward is with the Lord" (Wisd. 5:5).

The godly Israelite did not excel in excogitating his own ideas. Rather, he reflected on God's power and design in His creative handiwork and satisfied his spirit by meditating on His word, seeking to think His thoughts after Him (Ps. 92:5 [MT 6]; 139:17). He was the beneficiary of special revelation. In contrast, the typical Greek was preoccupied with the world around him and with his relationship to other individuals. He was part of a highly gregarious society, having a keen interest in politics, philosophical speculation, and scientific development. Death was an experience to be dreaded, followed by a shadowy existence, although for some, perchance, it could mean sharing the life of the gods. The Greek excelled as an inquirer, the Hebrew as a listener. It should be granted that Philo was greatly affected by Greek thought, especially that of Plato, and that he espoused the immortality of the soul rather than resurrection, but he was hardly representative of his nation in this respect. For the Hebrew, wisdom did not center in factual information about the world and what it contained, even though Solomon showed considerable interest in the natural order. The Hebrew concentrated on the life of man in relation to his Maker. Wisdom is "a fountain of life to him who has it" (Prov. 16:22). It helped one to be appreciative of nature and human life as gifts from God to be used for His glory. Next to worship, one's highest occupation was to take to heart God's word and act in accordance with its teaching.

The only clear reference in the OT to everlasting life is Dnl. 12:2, where it is linked to resurrection. The emphasis is not only on the temporal setting (the predicted time of Jacob's trouble), but even more on the quality of the resurrection life, for it is contrasted with the lot of those who will experience shame and everlasting contempt. This scanty use of "everlasting life" should not lead one to surmise that there was little expectation of a life to come. Notwithstanding its preoccupation with the present, Ecclesiastes speaks of man going to his eternal home (12:5) and of his spirit returning to God who gave it (12:7). Job also was confident that his Redeemer lived and that, when his own life was spent, he would see God (Job 19:25f.).

Isaiah 26:19 may have prepared the way for the prophetic insight expressed in Dnl. 12:2, although the life mentioned by Isaiah is not described as everlasting. The information contained in the Daniel passage is credited to superhuman (angelic) disclosure granted by Michael, the prince charged with supernatural oversight of Israel (10:21).

Several instances of resuscitation are noted in the course of Israel's history (1 K. 17:21f.; 2 K. 4:32-35; 13:20f.), but these are not properly regarded as resurrections. Closer in time and nature to Daniel's prophecy is Ezekiel's vision of the valley of dry bones in which the Spirit bestowed flesh and sinews upon them and gave them breath and life (Ezk. 37:10). It is not necessary to look to Persian sources as background for Israel's hope of resurrection. Such disclosure belongs to the ministry of the Spirit (1 Pet. 1:10f.).

***II. Intertestamental Period.***–This was a difficult time for the nation Israel, but as life in this world became more tenuous, hope became more firmly fixed on the life to come. This is illustrated by the case of seven famous brothers. When one of them was being tortured, he said to his assailant, "You dismiss us from this present life, but the King of the universe will raise us up to an everlasting renewal of life because we have died for his laws" (2 Macc. 7:9). A similar outlook characterizes the book of Enoch: "And the righteous shall be in the light of the sun, and the elect in the light of eternal life" (1 En. 58:3). In another passage the righteous are described as "those who are found to be such as loved heaven more than their life [breath] in the world" (108:10).

Under rabbinic influence Judaism tended to link a future life of bliss with rigorous adherence to the law in the present existence. D. Hill noted that the literature of the Qumrân community does not appear to make a deliberate correlation of Torah and life, yet the law was no doubt a dominant factor in showing the way to present obedience and future participation in eschatological life (p. 183). He noted further that in the passages where the terminology of eternal life occurs "the context is clearly eschatological" (p. 185).

***III. NT.***–*A. Synoptic Gospels.* With few exceptions, references to life are in the words of Jesus. He referred to life in the sense of livelihood (Gk. *bíos*) in Mk. 12:44. He used *psychḗ* with the force of soul (Mt. 22:37) as well as mortal existence (Mk. 8:35) and the means for sustaining life (Mt. 6:25 par. Lk. 12:22). His use of *zōḗ* included the concept of lifetime (Lk. 16:25), although *zōḗ* is more frequently used to denote a state that one may enter, not as a native possession but rather as a divine bestowal (Mt. 18:8f.; Lk. 18:24).

The Master warned that a person's life *(zōḗ)* does not consist in the abundance of possessions (Lk. 12:15). Similarly, He noted that life *(psychḗ)*, i.e., one's existence, is more than food that sustains it (v. 23). In one of His "hard" sayings (14:26) He declared that if one desired to become His follower he must "hate" his dear ones and even his own life *(psychḗ)*. Clearly this is a specialized use of the word "hate." The saying should be understood as calling for a renunciation of every demand that competes with Jesus' call for allegiance, no matter how valid such demands may seem to be. With keen insight the Master described the prodigal son as "dead" during his profligate days but as "alive" in view of his return to his father's house (15:24, 32). By his return the youth showed that his perception of values had radically changed. Now he was responsive to family ties.

In referring to eternal life, Jesus invariably used *zōē*, which is consistent with NT practice in general. A few problem passages merit special attention. Jesus told an inquirer that if he would enter life (*zōē*) he must keep the commandments (Mt. 19:17). He was responding to His interlocutor's question, "What good deed must I do, to have eternal life?" The Lord met the inquirer on his own ground ("What must I do?") by exposing his lack of love for his neighbor, since he was unwilling to sell his possessions and give to the poor. In Lk. 18:29f. the promise of eternal life in the age to come is not grounded on the sacrifices that one is prepared to make, for back of them is what inspired the sacrifices, namely, the faith that produces devotion and sacrificial service (cf. Mk. 10:29f.).

A crucial feature of Jesus' teaching dealt with the purpose of His mission. He declared that He "came not to be served but to serve, and to give his life [*psychē*] as a ransom for many" (Mk. 10:45). Such a statement demonstrated the incalculable worth of that life.

*B. Gospel of John.* This Gospel refers to life not only more frequently than the Synoptics but also in a definitely different way. The Synoptics present life primarily as an eschatological experience to be realized in the age to come, as in Mk. 10:30. In John, however, eternal life is characteristically a present reality, as stated most emphatically in Jn. 5:24, where Jesus asserts that one who hears His word and believes the One who sent Him has eternal life. Evidently the believer does not have to wait for eternal life until he passes from his present existence. It is the new life in Christ, mediated by the Spirit and therefore imperishable. But the futuristic aspect of life is not lacking in John, as indicated by 12:25. Yet a problem remains, for a present aspect of eternal life seems to be lacking in the Synoptics. It may be that since the kingdom of God is represented as having come in the person and work of Jesus (Mt. 12:28), the conferring of eternal life in the present is implied (Ladd, p. 76). Support for this conclusion may be found in Mk. 9:43-47, where life seems to be equated with the kingdom of God, a term that has both future and present application.

The reader of the Fourth gospel is alerted to the crucial importance of the concept of life by its early appearance (1:4), providing a broad hint that, if people are to receive this life, they must have a saving relationship with the living Word. What is here implied becomes explicit throughout the Gospel. John's statement about the purpose of his account (20:31) confirms this. In between, all references to life are credited to Jesus with the exception of Peter's confession directed to Him, "You have the words of eternal life" (6:68). The statement in 1:4 is important for the clear indication it provides that life was not imparted to the Word but was His by virtue of His participation in the Godhead. He did not gain it nor did he lose it by becoming incarnate.

Jesus referred frequently to eternal life (e.g., 10:28), distinguishing it from mortal existence. "Eternal" may refer more to the kind of life than its duration. It is the life of God shared with His people, therefore both imperishable and blessed.

The provision of life is at the very heart of the gospel message (3:16). It is a divine gift rather than a reward for human achievement (10:28). In keeping with this truth, it can be received only by faith (3:36), though John does not use the term, possibly because faith could indicate simply a concept, whereas "believe" expresses decision. Eternal life becomes one's possession not at some future time but as soon as faith is exercised. "He who believes in the Son has [here and now] eternal life" (3:36).

In the course of His teaching ministry Jesus had much to say about Himself. John has captured more of this than the Synoptists. The Lord was not content merely to assert His eternal existence as the I AM (8:58). In other sayings He added a predicate of various kinds, including "the bread of life" (6:35), "the light of life" (8:12), "the good shepherd [who] lays down his life for the sheep" (10:11), "the way and the truth and the life" (14:6), and "the resurrection and the life" (11:25). This was His chosen method of underscoring both the indispensability and the variegated nature of His person and ministry offered on behalf of humanity.

It is relatively easy for a casual reader of Scripture to magnify the public ministry of Jesus and to deplore His death. His inimitable teaching and His works of compassionate love compel admiration and gratitude, but they were not the central objective of His mission. In His own estimation the climax was reached in His self-giving at the cross (10:15). The resurrection certified that His ministry, climaxed by His redeeming death, was carried out in conformity with the will of God.

As recipients of eternal life, believers have a responsibility to ponder its meaning. It is tempting to stress its unending character, but Jesus put the emphasis elsewhere. He epitomized it as knowing God and the Son who came to reveal Him (17:3). This knowledge has its inception at conversion, its expansion during the course of Christian experience, and its consummation in the life to come.

*C. Book of Acts.* Since the Lord Jesus had conquered death, as attested by His resurrection, it was fitting that Peter should proclaim that He was not only alive but was the Author of life (3:15). The risen Lord was the guarantor of indestructible life for all who were or would be related to Him by faith (cf. 1 Cor. 15:20). Shortly thereafter the apostles, supernaturally freed from prison, were commanded to speak to the people "all the words of this Life" (Acts 5:20). The proclaimed message promised not only salvation from sin but the gift of abundant and eternal life. The new life in Christ quickly manifested its dynamic reality in two directions. Believers began to meet together, pray together, and provide for the material needs of the less fortunate among them (2:44-46; 4:32). The other development was a demonstration of fidelity and fearlessness in maintaining a testimony to the people, despite warnings from the rulers and the imprisonment of their leaders (4:18-20, 31; 5:42).

Peter's historic proclamation of the gospel to Gentiles at Caesarea brought home to the Jerusalem church the realization that God had granted to the Gentiles repentance unto life (11:18). Renunciation of their sinful past was a necessary accompaniment of the reception of new life through the Savior. This phenomenon was repeated frequently, as reported in other locations. At Pisidian Antioch, for example, "as many as were ordained to eternal life believed" (13:48). The gospel message invited them. They proved their divine ordination by their faith.

In his Areopagus address Paul said in reference to God that "he himself gives to all men life and breath and everything" (17:25). We might have expected him to use *psychē* here rather than *zōē*. But *zōē* had been used by Greek writers in this same way with reference to human existence, so Paul accommodated himself to the background of his audience. Actually, it was not a strange use of terminology, for the LXX used *zōē* of the creation of the first man (Gen. 2:7). Paul himself apparently used it elsewhere in the broad, general sense when he contrasted it with death (Rom. 8:38).

*D. Pauline Epistles.* The apostle recognized that mankind falls into two groups: the so-called natural man, who is spiritually dead (unresponsive) to God (Eph. 2:1), and the Christian, who because of his acceptance of Christ has become alive spiritually, sharing the life of the Son of God (Rom. 6:11). The former group included Paul himself in his pre-Christian period. Complacent in the possession of the law, he did not realize his true condition (Rom. 7:7-12). Though the law was holy, sin was able to provoke him to sin (vv. 8, 10). The second company includes all genuine believers. Two phases are to be noted in their spiritual pilgrimage. As long as they are in this earthly life they have to contend against indwelling sin. They are no longer lost sinners but neither are they yet entirely free from the hold of sin upon them. They have not attained to their heavenly inheritance and the complete freedom from sin that will be theirs when they reach their heavenly home. In this intermediate position between the life of sin and the life of glorious perfection, the Christian's life is hid with Christ in God (Col. 3:3). It is a hidden relationship, but spiritually dynamic. As Paul expressed it, Christ is our life (Col. 3:4), not in the sense that He extinguishes or suppresses our life, but rather in the sense that He controls and permeates our life, conforming it to His holy nature as much as we permit Him to do so. To share Christ's life in the ultimate sense promised to the Christian is the heart of the believer's hope (Tit. 1:2; 3:7).

In his use of the first Adam/last Adam tension, the apostle expounded the theme of sin leading to death and righteousness leading to spiritual life (Rom. 5). He also addressed the theme of physical death and bodily resurrection by means of the same tension (1 Cor. 15). Whereas the first Adam became a living being, the last Adam became a life-giving spirit (v. 45), the head of a new community living by Him and for Him.

Since the present situation of the Christian is that which should give him most concern, it is important to see that God has made special provision for it, namely, by making the indwelling of Christ an experiential reality. Paul expressed it most adequately by asserting that "the law of the Spirit of life in Christ Jesus has set me free from the law of sin and death" (Rom. 8:2). Two items need emphasis here. Christ Jesus was no longer on earth to assist Paul, but the Spirit is not spatially conditioned. Dwelling in the redeemed spirit of Paul (and in all believers), He was able to transmit the resources of the sinless, victorious Christ to His servant on earth. Furthermore, the effective transmission of power to maintain a transformed life, conformed to God's will, is plainly suggested by the use of the term "law." Clearly the word does not refer here to the Mosaic law, but rather points to the regularity and reliability of the Spirit's operation in the life of the believer so as to make actual the production of righteousness and true holiness. The chapter as a whole is a commentary on the effectiveness of the Spirit's activity in the experience of the child of God.

Recognition should be given also to the way in which the life of the risen Lord Jesus affected the witness of His servants. This is the theme of 2 Cor. 4:1-12. Pressure from a hostile world is heavy and there is weakness in the human vessel. Yet Paul could assert, "While we live we are always being given up to death for Jesus' sake, so that the life of Jesus may be manifested in our mortal flesh" (v. 11). The risen life of the Son of God can communicate faithfulness and fortitude to His ministering servants. Paul conceived of his God-given task as summoning him to hold forth the word of life (Phil. 2:16, AV). It was a message that promised and produced a new life in those who received it. As the apostle neared the close of his career, he naturally expressed his own hope in terms of eternal life (Tit. 3:7).

Paul is unique among NT writers in describing the Christian church as the body of Christ and believers as individual members of that body under the authority of Christ the Head (Rom. 12:5; Col. 1:18). The NT nowhere envisions an individual relationship to Christ apart from fellowship with other believers. The apostle Paul made it clear that, in addition to believers' responsibility to their sovereign Lord, they have a large area of relationship to fellow Christians. Believers are members one of another (Eph. 4:25). They have a responsibility to love one another (Rom. 13:8), to instruct one another (15:14), to encourage one another (1:12), to live in harmony with one another (12:16; 15:5), to be truthful to one another (Col. 3:9), to be subject to one another (Eph. 5:21), to be kind to one another (4:32), forbearing one another and forgiving one another (Col. 3:13), comforting one another (1 Thess. 4:18), etc. Evidently Christians are not intended to live in isolation or in neglect of fellow believers. They belong to a community of faith and life. They are expected to witness together, worship together, pray for one another, share in the sufferings and sorrows of their fellows in the faith. It all adds up to the realization that under normal conditions Christian life is a life of mutual relationship. By virtue of regeneration every believer is made a member of the one body of which Christ is the Head. Christian life is not a venture in isolationism, but rather an experience of communication and cooperation.

*E. Remainder of the NT.* Hebrews affirms the permanent nature of the priesthood of Jesus and His constant, faithful ministry on behalf of the saints. This is possible because He has an endless, indestructible life (He. 7:13, 16). Other references to life pertain to the Christian. One underscores the limited tenure of earthly life (Jas. 4:14). Another holds out the prospect of receiving the crown of life, a figurative term for recognition and reward for fidelity and endurance (1:12). In the Christian home, husbands are not to assume a superior attitude toward their wives because these women are physically weaker, but are to realize that both parties are "joint heirs of the grace of life" (1 Pet. 3:7). Husband and wife share equally in the enjoyment of spiritual life as God's gift, a life that begins on earth and reaches into eternity. We are assured of the divine sufficiency granted to us for the living of a godly Christian life (2 Pet. 1:3). Believers are bidden to recall that their spiritual life rests on divine mercy and will never end (Jude 21).

In 1 John the emphasis is on the fact that eternal life is in the Son and therefore cannot be obtained independently of Him or even simply through Him. This line of thought appears also in John's Gospel (1:4; 5:26), but it is presented more prominently in the Epistle. The Word of Jn. 1:1 is now presented as the Word of life (1 Jn. 1:1). As the Word, He is the faithful and true Witness; as the life, He is the eternal Son of God, whom death could not hold. He is risen and alive for evermore. He is even equated with eternal life (5:20). The concluding portion of the Epistle (5:13-21) is largely devoted to this theme.

In the book of Revelation the distinctive feature of the treatment of life (*zōē*) is that the word is always coordinated with some other term: breath (11:11), tree (2:7; 22:2, 14, 19), crown (2:10), book (3:5; 13:8; 17:8; 20:12, 15; 21:27), water (21:6; 22:1, 17). Nothing in the heavenly setting fails to exhibit the perfection and permanence of the living God and His operations. It is also noteworthy that the key to the unfolding picture of victory and glory throughout the book is provided in the opening chapter, where the Son of God proclaims Himself as the living one who has survived death and is alive for evermore (1:8; cf. 1 Tim. 6:16).

*IV. Conclusion.*–The writers of the NT do not offer readers a series of platitudes about life. Their message is that Jesus Christ is not only the Savior who died to provide redemption from sin, but the One who is their life, their all in all. Their relationship to Him depends on their faith, and faith will be rewarded by sight and the enjoyment of His presence throughout the ages to come.

*Bibliography*–R. Bultmann, *Theology of the NT,* I (Eng. tr. 1951), 203-210; J. C. Coetzee, *Neotestamentica,* 6 (1972), 48-67; *DNTT,* II, *s.v.* (H. -G. Link); J. B. Frey, *Bibl.,* 1 (1920), 37-58, 210-239; D. Hill, *Greek Words and Hebrew Meanings* (1967), pp. 163-201; G. E. Ladd, *Pattern of NT Truth* (1958), pp. 64-86; *TDNT,* II, *s.v.* ζάω κτλ. (G. von Rad, G. Bertram, R. Bultmann); *TDOT,* III, *s.v.* "dām" (J. Bergman, B. Kedar-Kopfstein); IV, *s.v.* "chāyāh" (H. Ringgren); H. W. Wolff, *Anthropology of the OT* (Eng. tr. 1974).

E. F. HARRISON

**LIFE, TREE OF.** *See* TREE OF KNOWLEDGE, TREE OF LIFE.

**LIFT.** A common English verb meaning to RAISE or elevate, used by the RSV to translate a great variety of Hebrew, Aramaic, and Greek terms. In the OT it most often represents Heb. *nāśā'*, a very common verb meaning "raise, lift up," "support," "carry," or "exalt." Other OT terms include Heb. *rûm* (qal, "be high," e.g., Dt. 8:14; Ps. 27:6; hiphil, "raise, exalt," e.g., Gen. 39:15; 41:44; Ex. 7:20; 14:10; Nu. 20:11), the hiphil of *qûm* ("raise up," e.g., Dt. 22:4; Eccl. 4:10), hiphil of *nûp* ("wield, swing," e.g., Dt. 27:5; Josh. 8:31), *nāṯan* ("give," e.g., Jer. 22:20), the polel of *'ûḏ* ("help up," Ps. 147:6), *gāḇah* ("be high, haughty," e.g., Ps. 131:1), Aram. *nᵉṭal* ("lift up," e.g., Dnl. 4:34 [MT 31]), etc. The most common NT term for "lift" is Gk. *epaírō* ("raise, lift," e.g., Mt. 17:8; Lk. 6:20; 16:23); other terms include *hypsóō* ("exalt, lift high," e.g., Jn. 3:14), *aírō* ("lift, carry away," Lk. 17:13; Jn. 11:41; Acts 4:24; Rev. 10:5), *egeírō* ("raise," Mk. 1:31; 9:27; Acts 10:26), *anístēmi* ("raise up," Acts 9:41), etc.

"Lift" is sometimes used literally in both the OT and NT to denote the physical lifting up of a person (e.g., Gen. 21:18; Eccl. 4:10; Mk. 1:31; 9:27; Jn. 3:14) or an animal (e.g., Dt. 22:4; Mt. 12:11). More often, however, the term is used to describe a gesture that has symbolic meaning. For example, the Lord "lifts up" — i.e., restores the rights and dignity of — the poor and the oppressed (Ps. 113:7f. par. 1 S. 2:8; Ps. 146:8; 147:6). Similarly, to "lift up" a person's HEAD or face meant to show that person favor (e.g., Gen. 40:13 [but cf. v. 19]; Ps. 3:3 [MT 4]; Jer. 52:31); but to lift one's own head demonstrated pride or rebellion (e.g., Jgs. 8:28; *see also* GESTURE V). Likewise, to have a heart that was "lifted up" was to be proud (e.g., Dt. 8:14; 17:20; 2 Ch. 25:19; Ps. 131:1; Dnl. 5:20; Hos. 13:6). *See also* EXALT.

The raising of the hand(s) could have a variety of meanings (*see* GESTURE I), e.g., rebellion (2 S. 20:21; 1 K. 11:26f.), the taking of an oath (e.g., Dt. 32:40), or the conferral of a blessing (e.g., Lev. 9:22; Lk. 24:50). The hands were also raised in prayer (e.g., Ps. 28:2; 63:4 [MT 5]; Lam. 3:41; 1 Tim. 2:8), symbolizing the internal "lifting up" of the soul — i.e., directing one's whole being — to the Lord (cf. Ps. 25:1; 86:4; 143:8). Lifting up one's horn (a symbol of strength) was a metaphor for a display of arrogance (Ps. 75:4f. [MT 5f.]), while raising a sword signified preparation for war (Isa. 2:4; Mic. 4:3) and raising a rod or staff could symbolize an intention to punish (e.g., Isa. 10:15, 24, 26).

Two very common expressions are to "lift up one's voice" and to "lift up one's eyes." The former meant to shout or cry aloud (e.g., Gen. 39:15, 18; Lk. 17:13; Acts 14:11; 22:22), whether in addressing a crowd (e.g., Isa. 42:2; 58:1; Acts 2:14) or in expressing emotions such as grief (e.g., Gen. 27:38; Ruth 1:9, 14; 2 S. 3:32) or praise and rejoicing (e.g., Isa. 24:14; 40:9; 42:11; 52:8). To "lift up one's eyes" meant simply to look up, usually in order to gaze at something in the distance (e.g., Gen. 13:10, 14; 22:4; 24:64; Dt. 3:27; 1 S. 6:13; 2 S. 18:24; Isa. 49:18; Jer. 3:2; Jn. 4:35). Lifting one's eyes to God indicated an attitude of prayer and of trust that He would provide help (e.g., Ps. 121:1; 123:1f.; cf. the prohibition against lifting one's eyes to idols, heavenly bodies, or other nations as a source of help, e.g., Dt. 4:19; Ezk. 18:6, 15; 23:27; 33:25; *see also* GESTURE V.B). Used with a human subject, to "lift up one's face" could simply mean to look up (e.g., 2 K. 9:32), or it could connote looking at someone with confidence, free of guilt and shame (2 S. 22:2; Job 22:26; cf. 10:15). But when used with God as its subject the phrase indicated favorable regard (Nu. 6:26; Ps. 4:6 [MT 7]). *See also* LOOK I.

The precise meaning of "lift [Heb. hiphil of *gāḏal*; LXX *megalýnō*; lit. "make great"] the heel against (someone)" (Ps. 41:9 [MT 10]) is disputed. Some have interpreted it as referring to a kick (cf. KD *in loc.*). G. B. Caird (*JTS,* N.S. 20 [1969], 32) translated the LXX "'has magnified his going-behind-the-back', i.e., 'has given me a grave stab in the back.'" E. F. F. Bishop claimed that to Near Eastern peoples, showing someone the sole of one's foot is considered an insult (*Expos.T.,* 70 [1958/59], 331f.). In any case the context of the psalm — as well as Jesus' application of the verse to Judas's betrayal of Him (Jn. 13:18) — points to a cruel act of treachery and contempt.

The prophets Jeremiah and Nahum used the expression "lift up the skirts" (a euphemism for a sexual attack) as a metaphor to describe the humiliation and devastation that Jerusalem (Jer. 13:22, 26) and Nineveh (Nah. 3:5) would soon suffer as punishment for their wickedness. Here "lift up" represents Heb. *gālâ,* "uncover, reveal" (niphal, Jer. 13:22; piel, Nah. 3:5), and *ḥāśap,* "strip naked" (Jer. 13:26).

Three times in John's Gospel Jesus refers to His death in terms of being "lifted up" (Gk. *hypsóō,* Jn. 3:14; 8:28; 12:32-34). As Moses' lifting up the serpent in the wilderness preserved the lives of those who looked upon it (Nu. 21:8f.), so Jesus' death on the cross gives eternal life to all who look to Him for salvation (Jn. 3:14). Some commentators have argued convincingly that Jesus' being "lifted up" refers not only to His crucifixion but also to His resurrection and ascension (cf. *hypsóō* [RSV "exalt"] in Isa. 52:13, LXX; Acts 2:33; 5:31; *hyperypsóō* in Phil. 2:9; see comms. on John, esp. R. E. Brown, I [*AB,* 1966], 145f., and L. Morris [*NICNT,* 1971], pp. 225f.).

N. J. O.

**LIGHT** [Heb. nouns: usually *'ôr* (Gen. 1:3-5, 11; etc.), also *'ûr* (Isa. 50:11), *'ôrâ* (Est. 8:16; Ps. 139:12), *mā'ôr* (Gen. 1:14-16; etc.), *nōgah* (Isa. 50:10), *nᵉhārâ* (Job 3:4); vbs.: hiphil of *'ôr* (Gen. 1:15; etc.), hiphil of *yāpa'* (Job 10:22), hiphil of *nāgah* (2 S. 22:29), etc.; Aram. *nᵉhôr* (Dnl. 2:22), *nahîrû* (Dnl. 5:11, 14); Gk. nouns: usually *phṓs* (Mt. 4:16; etc.), also *lampás* (Acts 20:8), *phéngos* (Mt. 24:29; Mk. 13:24), *phōstḗr* (Phil. 2:15; Rev. 21:11), *phōtismós* (2 Cor. 4:4, 6); vbs.: *háptō* (Lk. 8:16; 11:33), *kaíō* (Mt. 5:15), *phōtízō* (Jn. 1:9); *epiphaínō* (Lk. 1:79), *epiphaúskō* (Eph. 5:14), *lámpō* (Mt. 5:15), *astráptō* (Lk. 17:24); adjective: *phōteinós* (Mt. 6:22)].

The variety of words translated "light" show no great

difference in meaning. Generally the nouns refer to light itself or to a source of light (e.g., a lamp or a star), while the verbs mean "give light" or "kindle a light." The adjective *phōteinós* means "characterized by light."

*I. In the OT.*–Light was the first thing created. God's first words recorded in the Bible are, "Let there be light," after which light immediately appeared (Gen. 1:3). This implies that light existed before the sun (see vv. 14-18) — which was worshiped as a god by many peoples of OT times; and the light was not god or creator, for light itself was created.

The Scriptures refer to physical light many times. It may be associated with the heavenly bodies (e.g., Ps. 136:7; Jer. 4:23), lightning (Ps. 77:18 [MT 19]; 97:4), dawn (1 S. 14:36), a lamp (Ex. 27:20), or the pillar of fire that God gave the Israelites in the wilderness (13:21). But however familiar light may be, it nevertheless remains a mystery. Mankind cannot answer the questions, "Where is the way to the dwelling of light?" and "What is the way to the place where the light is distributed?" (Job 38:19, 24).

The OT constantly associates light with God. It is His garment (Ps. 104:2). It lives with Him (Dnl. 2:22). His brightness is like light (Hab. 3:4; cf. "the light of thine arrows," v. 11). The psalmist could say, "The Lord is my light" (Ps. 27:1; cf. 2 S. 22:29; Isa. 10:17). Therefore it is not surprising that darkness cannot triumph over light: God "brings deep darkness [the shadow of death] to light" (Job 12:22). In creation it is the Lord who "gives the sun for light by day and the fixed order of the moon and the stars for light by night" (Jer. 31:35).

Serving God can be described as walking in His light (Isa. 2:5). His servant is a "light" to others (42:6; 49:6; 60:3; cf. 51:4). God's word lights the path of His servant (Ps. 119:105; cf. v. 130; Prov. 6:23; Isa. 51:4). Divine favor may be expressed as lifting up "the light of [God's] countenance" (Ps. 4:6 [MT 7]; 44:3 [MT 4]; 89:15 [MT 16]; conversely, no sin can be hidden from that countenance, 90:8). The eschatological bliss of God's people may be expressed in terms of the Lord being their "everlasting light" — a light that replaces the light of sun and moon and never ceases (Isa. 60:19f.; cf. 30:26; Zec. 14:7).

"Light" is often used as a symbol of goodness, uprightness, or blessing. "Light dawns for the righteous, and joy for the upright in heart" (Ps. 97:11). Even "in the darkness" light rises for the upright because the Lord is gracious (112:4). Thus the psalmist could pray that God would send His light and truth to bring him to God's dwelling (43:3). The path of the righteous "is like the light of dawn" that continually grows brighter (Prov. 4:18). The failure to recognize the light is the most serious perversion. Those who do so "call evil good and good evil" and "put darkness for light and light for darkness" (Isa. 5:20).

Since light is linked so closely with Yahweh and with goodness, it is not surprising that it can serve as a symbol of God's blessing. This blessing may be predominantly in the "here and now," as when the warrior rejoiced: "Thou dost light my lamp; the Lord my God lightens my darkness. Yea, by thee I can crush a troop . . ." (Ps. 18:28f. [MT 29f.]; cf. Job 22:28). And this blessing can merge into "spiritual" prosperity, as when the prophet spoke of people "who walked in darkness" as having "seen a great light" (Isa. 9:2-6). Light can also be linked with mental excellence (Dnl. 5:11, 14). Life itself and light go closely together: "For with thee is the fountain of life; in thy light do we see light" (Ps. 36:9 [MT 10]; the Psalm goes on to speak of God's steadfast love and salvation; cf. 56:13 [MT 14]; Job 3:20). "To see the light" means much the same as "to be alive" (Job 3:16; 33:28, 30; Ps. 49:19 [MT 20]). Some impressive passages use this imagery to convey the importance of trusting God even when things are difficult. The prophet looked for one "who walks in darkness and has no light, yet trusts in the name of the Lord and relies upon his God" (Isa. 50:10). As he neared the end of his prophecy, Micah warned: "Rejoice not over me, O my enemy; when I fall, I shall rise; when I sit in darkness, the Lord will be a light to me. . . . He will bring me forth to the light; I shall behold his deliverance" (Mic. 7:8f.).

The absence of light is linked with disaster (Jer. 4:23; Ezk. 32:7f.). Darkness is the proper abode of the wicked. In some striking passages, sinners find "the day of the Lord" to be darkness rather than the light of blessing they anticipated (Isa. 13:9-11; Am. 5:18-20). The wicked, e.g., murderers and adulterers, operate at night (Job 24:14-17). They "do not know the light" (v. 16), but rebel against it (v. 13). The punishment of the wicked person is described as putting out his light, darkening his tent, and thrusting him from light into darkness (18:5f., 18).

*II. In the NT.*–Turning to the NT, one is impressed by the way light is constantly associated with God and with the servants of God. The NT occasionally refers to such phenomena as the light of a lamp (Mt. 5:15; Lk. 11:33, 36) or fire (Lk. 22:56), or "the light of this world" (Jn. 11:9). Some eschatological passages speak of the heavenly lights being darkened (Mt. 24:29f.; Mk. 13:24; Rev. 8:12). But for NT writers the great truth was that "God is light and in him is no darkness at all" (1 Jn. 1:5). God is said to dwell in light (1 Tim. 6:16; 1 Jn. 1:7); He is "the Father of lights" (Jas. 1:17). The seer envisioned heaven as a place that needs no sun or moon, for God is its light (Rev. 21:23f.; 22:5). Light thus forms a natural figure for God in His purity and beauty.

Again and again light is used to describe Jesus and His mission. The Gospel of John especially favors this imagery and begins to use it in the fourth verse: "In him [the Word] was life, and the life was the light of men." John continually associates life with Jesus and moves easily from the thought that life is "in" Him to the thought that this life is "the light of men," i.e., human beings owe all their life and all their light to Christ. John's Gospel proceeds, "The light shines in the darkness, and the darkness has not overcome it" (v. 5). In the conflict between good and evil, between light and darkness, the dark evil does not prevail. Notice the use of the present: light continually shines; its function is to shine precisely in the darkness.

The Gospel of John proceeds to tell how John the Baptist came to bear witness to the light (not being the light himself; Jn. 1:6-8). Then comes the great thought: the "true light," who gives light to all persons, was coming into the world (v. 9). John was not writing about a remote, holy but uncaring deity, but about One who, in addition to being light, is love (cf. 1 Jn. 4:8, 16). The God who is light shines on people for their good, i.e., He illumines them, cares for them, and lights up their way. The coming of Jesus meant the coming of the divine light to bring mankind illumination and salvation. John wrote his Gospel to convince people that Jesus is the Christ, the Son of God, so that they might enter life (Jn. 20:30f.). John did this in part by showing that Jesus is the light.

Jesus alone is "the light of the world" (Jn. 8:12; 9:5; cf. 12:46). All the illumination people have comes ultimately from Him. Anyone who follows Him "will not walk in darkness, but will have the light of life" (8:12). One's ultimate fate depends on one's reaction to the light that "has come into the world" (3:19). Sinners love darkness rather than light, and in that is their condemnation; but those who do the truth come to the light (vv. 19-21). Near the end of His public ministry Jesus challenged the crowd: "The light is with you for a little longer. . . . While you have the light, believe in the light, that you may become sons of light" (12:35f.; cf. Lk. 16:8; 1 Thess. 5:5; "children of light," Eph. 5:8). This terminology is not confined to Christianity. (It was widespread among the rabbis [see the many passages listed in SB, I, 236-38; II, 427f.; III, 656]. One of the most important Qumrân scrolls deals with the war of "the sons of light" with "the sons of darkness." Another scroll is called "The Words of the Heavenly Lights." The members of the sect frequently refer to themselves as "the sons of light.") But it has special significance in John.

Contact with the light influences conduct. It is the gospel of Christ that brings people into the light (2 Cor. 4:4). Because God commanded, "Let light shine out of darkness," and because He "has shone in our hearts," believers have received "the light of the knowledge of the glory of God in the face of Christ" (v. 6). The ascended Jesus commissioned Paul to bring the gospel to the Gentiles, "to open their eyes, that they may turn from darkness to light and from the power of Satan to God" (Acts 26:18; cf. Eph. 5:14). God has called believers "out of darkness into his marvelous light" (1 Pet. 2:9). The basic challenge of the gospel, to repent of evil and trust in Christ, is often expressed in terms of coming to the light.

The NT writers also saw light as a useful way to characterize the whole life of the Christian. To "walk in the light, as he is in the light" (1 Jn. 1:7), means to live in love. Those who claim to live in the light but hate their brothers are still in darkness (2:9); it is those who love their brothers who are really in the light (1:10). Similarly, Paul asked, "What fellowship has light with darkness?" (2 Cor. 6:14). This line of thought goes back to Christ, who taught the importance of having one's "whole body . . . full of light" (Lk. 11:34, 36; cf. Mt. 6:22) and warned, "Be careful lest the light in you be darkness" (Lk. 11:35).

Jesus called His followers "the light of the world" (Mt. 5:14). The nature of light is to shine in the darkness. It is important that those who have been illuminated become illuminators and not simply keep to themselves the light they have received. Thus Jesus said, "Let your light so shine before men, that they may see your good works and give glory to your Father who is in heaven" (Mt. 5:16). Paul described the Philippian Christians as "children of God . . . in the midst of a crooked and perverse generation, among whom you shine as lights in the world" (Phil. 2:15). Similarly, the Ephesians, who were once "darkness, but now . . . light in the Lord," are exhorted to "Walk as children of light (for the fruit of light is found in all that is good and right and true)" (Eph. 5:8f.). Paul called on the Romans to "cast off the works of darkness and put on the armor of light" (Rom. 13:12). Because this challenge was addressed to believers, it was clearly not a call to become Christians; it was rather a reminder that believers wage a continual battle with the forces of darkness, and that they can win the victory only through the light they receive from Christ. In one passage Paul spoke of the final victory as a sharing in "the inheritance of the saints in light" (Col. 1:12). But more commonly the NT writers used the imagery of light for those still in the conflict.

In both Testaments, then, light lent itself to significant spiritual imagery. Light is naturally associated with God, but the great teaching of the Bible is that God does not remain at a distance. The light came into the world to bring deliverance. And the delivered must live as those who are in the light.

*Bibliography.*–S. Aalen, *Die Begriffe "Licht" und "Finsternis" im AT, im Spätjudentum und im Rabbinismus* (1951); E. P. Dickie, *God is Light* (1954); C. H. Dodd, *The Bible and the Greeks* (1953); *Interpretation of the Fourth Gospel* (1953); M. Eliade, *The Two and the One* (1965); E. R. Goodenough, *By Light Light: The Mystic Gospel of Hellenistic Judaism* (1935); E. Lövestam, *Spiritual Wakefulness in the NT* (1963); J. Pelikan, *Light of the World* (1962); *TDNT,* IX, *s.v.* φῶς κτλ. (Conzelmann); *TDOT,* I, *s.v.* "'ôr" (Aalen).

L. MORRIS

**LIGHTNING** [Heb. *bārāq,* also *'ôr*–'light' (Job 36:30, 32; 37:3, etc.), *ḥāzîa*–'storm-cloud' (28:26), *lappîḏ* (Ex. 20:18), *'ēš*–'fire' (Ps. 105:32). Gk. *astrapḗ*]; AV also LIGHT, BRIGHT, FIRE, GLITTER(ING); NEB also THUNDERSTORM, MIST, FLAME, etc.; RSV mg., AV, "them" (Job 37:4, following MT; RSV emends *y$^e$ʿaqq$^e$ḇēm* to read *y$^e$ʿaqqēḇ b$^e$rāqîm*). The spectacular discharge of enormous amounts of electrical energy within a cloud itself or as part

Basalt relief from Arslan Tash (*ca.* 740 B.C.) of the storm-god (Hadad?) holding lightning bolts in both hands (Louvre)

of a thunderstorm. Water and ice particles in a thundercloud are thought to generate electricity as they collide because of turbulence within the cloud. Some lightning is confined to the cumulo-nimbus formation, but the tendency for electricity to ground itself leads to an explosive discharge as the lightning flashes to earth.

In the Scriptures lightning is frequently mentioned (esp. in poetic literature) as an example of the power and wisdom of God. Only God commands the forces of nature and knows its secrets: "Can you send forth lightnings. . . ?" (Job 38:35; cf. 28:26; 37:15; Ps. 18:14 [MT 15]; 77:18 [MT 19]; 97:4; 135:7; 144:6; Jer. 10:13; 51:16; etc.). Lightning was one of the signs of Yahweh's presence at Mt. Sinai that evoked awe and terror in the Israelites (Ex. 19:16; 20:18); cf. the visions of Ezekiel (Ezk. 1:13) and John (Rev. 4:5; 8:5; 11:19; 16:18).

Lightning is also used as a simile to describe something that shines brightly (Ezk. 21:10, 15, 28 [MT 15, 20, 33]; Dnl. 10:6; Mt. 28:3) or moves with great speed (Ezk. 1:14; Nah. 2:4 [MT 5]; Zec. 9:14; Lk. 10:18). In Mt. 24:27 par. Lk. 17:24 Jesus compares His parousia to the brightness and universal visibility of lighting. R. K. H. N. J. O.

**LIGN-ALOES.** *See* ALOES.

**LIGURE** lig'ər (AV Ex. 28:19; 39:12). AV for jacinth. *See* STONES, PRECIOUS.

**LIKEN** [Heb. *dāmâ*] (Isa. 40:18; 46:5; Lam. 2:13); NEB also COMPARE, etc.; **LIKENESS** [Heb. *d<sup>e</sup>mûṯ*]; AV also SIMILITUDE (Dnl. 10:16); NEB also FORM, SEMBLANCE, etc.; [*t<sup>e</sup>mûnâ*] (Ex. 20:4; Dt. 5:8); [*taḇnîṯ*] (Dt. 4:16-18); NEB probably FORM; [Gk. *eikṓn*] (Mt. 22:20 par. Mk. 12:16; Lk. 20:24; 2 Cor. 3:18; 4:4); AV IMAGE; NEB also HEAD, IMAGE; [*homoióō*] (Acts 14:11); NEB FORM; [*homoíōma*] (Rom. 8:3; Phil. 2:7); NEB also "form like that"; [*homoiótēs*] (He. 7:15); AV SIMILITUDE; NEB LIKE; [*homoíōsis*] (Jas. 3:9); AV SIMILITUDE. In Ezk. 31:3 the AV reads "Assyrian" and the NEB reads "Assyria," both following the MT (*'aššûr*); the RSV, however, apparently prefers emending to hiphil of *šāwâ*, "liken." In 41:17 the RSV conjectures "likenesses" (pl. of Heb. *d<sup>e</sup>mûṯ*), the AV has "measure," and the NEB has "figures"; the MT reads *middâ* (pl. *middôṯ*–"measures") and probably needs emendation. In Eph. 4:24 the RSV translates *katá* as "after the likeness of," while the AV uses "after" and the NEB paraphrases. The meaning of this verse, however, seems clear: the new life gained in Christ is a work of God, a creation characterized by true goodness and holiness.

The Bible teaches that people were created "in the likeness [*d<sup>e</sup>mûṯ*] of God" (Gen. 5:1; cf. 1:26; Jas. 3:9) or in the "image" (*ṣelem*, Gen. 1:26) of God: people resemble God in a significant and unique sense. Although both people and animals are part of the same natural created order, people are set apart from the animals, over which they are masters. For persons, like God, can govern, reason, will, choose, and enter into intimate relationships with others and with God. They, however, are not God but are only made in His likeness; consequently human creatures must remember their totally dependent place before their Father and Creator. Fallen humanity, whose likeness to God is distorted and darkened through sin, may be restored to the glorious image of God in Christ (cf. 2 Cor. 3:18), who Himself is the "likeness (*eikṓn*) of God" (4:4). *See* IMAGE OF GOD.

Israel, unlike many of the surrounding peoples, worshiped a God who would allow no visible representations of Himself: "You shall not make for yourself a graven image, or any likeness [*t<sup>e</sup>mûnâ*] of anything" for the purpose of worship (Ex. 20:4; Dt. 5:8; cf. also Dt. 4:16-18). Any artistic representation of God would tend to create a conception of a God limited in power and glory. Furthermore, the people of God should never bow down and serve powerless created objects, but only the powerful Creator. Finally, idolatry was associated with religious systems frequently noted for their excesses, abuses, and cultic abominations. *See* IDOL; IDOLATRY.

Three times in the NT Gk. *eikṓn* designates the portrait of the Roman emperor on a coin (Mt. 22:20; Mk. 12:16; Lk. 20:24).

Romans 8:3 and Phil. 2:7 state that Jesus came in the "likeness" (*homoíōma*) of sinful flesh and of men — i.e., although Christ was indeed true God, He was also most certainly true man, yet without sin.

***Bibliography.***–J. Barr, *BJRL*, 51 (1968), 11-26; D. Clines, *Tyndale Bulletin*, 19 (1968), 53-103; J. M. Miller, *JBL*, 91 (1972), 289-304; J. Sawyer, *JTS*, 25 (1974), 418-426. M. W. MEYER

**LIKHI** lik'hī [Heb. *liqḥî*]. Son of Shemida and descendant of Manasseh (1 Ch. 7:19).

**LILIES (ACCCORDING TO).** The RSV translation of Heb. *'al-šōšannîm* in the superscriptions to Pss. 45, 69, and 80 (AV "upon Shoshannim"; NEB omits superscriptions). "Lilies" may refer to the title or the first word of a song to the tune of which these psalms were sung. *See* EDUTH; *see also* MUSIC III.B.3.

**LILITH** lil'əth. *See* NIGHT HAG.

**LILY** [Heb. *šôšan*, *šûšan*, *šôšannâ*; Gk. *krínon*] (1 K. 7:19, 22, 26; Cant. 2:1f.; Sir. 39:14; etc.). The Hebrew term presents difficulties in botanical identification but seems related philologically to Akk. *šešanu*, a large flower such as the *Lilium candidum*, and Egyp. *ssn*, the lotus or waterlily, *Nymphaea lotus* L. The latter was probably depicted on the columns of the temple porch (1 K. 7:19), the pillars (v. 22), and the everted rim of the metal basin (v. 26).

Probably the Hebrew word was used widely of a number of flowers. The "lilies" of Cant. 5:13 may be the scarlet *Lilium chalcedonicum* L. and those of Mt. 6:28 and Lk. 12:27f. the colorful Palestinian windflowers, *Anemone coronaria* L. (cf. T. W. Manson, *Sayings of Jesus* [repr. 1979], pp. 111-13). The remaining references in Canticles (NEB omits at 4:5) may be to the garden hyacinth, *Hyacinthus orientalis* L., or the Madonna lily, *Lilium candidum* L. The "lilies" of Hos. 14:5 [MT 6]; Sir. 39:14; 50:8 are probably the yellow flag, *Iris pseudacorus* L.

Some commentators hold that names such as Susa, Shoshannim, and Shushan Eduth refer to the lily in some way (*see* LILIES, ACCORDING TO). Later Jewish literature alluded to the lily symbolically, and a lotus or lily was depicted on several Jewish coins. In ancient Ugarit the lily was a symbol of sex appeal. R. K. H.

**LILY-WORK** [Heb. *ma<sup>ʿa</sup>śēh šûšan*]. A feature of the capitals of the two pillars standing on either side of the entrance to Solomon's temple (1 K. 7:19, 22). Details in the description of the capitals are obscure, however.

The "lily-work" refers either to a curving outward at the top of the capitals in a "lily" shape (note the NEB rendering "shaped like lilies" in 7:19; and cf. 7:26), or, more probably, to an ornamentation on the sides of the capitals in the form of stylized long, narrow "leaves," the latter a common architectural ornament in the ancient Near East.

*See also* JACHIN AND BOAZ. S. WESTERHOLM

**LIME** [Heb. *śîḏ*] (Isa. 33:12; Am. 2:1); NEB ASH, WHITE-WASH. A white, alkaline substance consisting of calcium oxide obtained from limestone (calcium carbonate) in Palestine, but also from shells, by burning at temperatures above 550°C. (1022° F.) in a large roofless kiln so that the carbon dioxide could be swept away in the wind. It is

Excavated lime kiln from Heshbon (Byzantine period) (L. T. Geraty)

also called quicklime and may be used loosely to indicate slaked lime (calcium hydroxide) when water is added. It is used especially in making whitewash, mortar, and plaster for coating walls, floors, and cisterns.

It would seem that the ancients may also have burned animal bones to obtain a product similar to lime (calcium phosphate). Am. 2:1, where human bones are burned, assumes an acquaintance with the results of bone burning, but seems to suggest that the burning of human bones was remarkable (cremation does not seem to have been regularly practiced by the Semites in the ancient Near East). Isa. 33:12 is certainly talking of the same process, but it is the whole body which is reduced to "lime."

Although the use of lime in ancient technologies of the Bible lands does not seem to have flowered until the Iron Age (*ca.* 1200 B.C.), its use in processed or raw form (crushed, unburned limestone) was put to advantage relatively infrequently as early as Neolithic times (the plastered skulls from Jericho). Walls were plastered in the Chalcolithic period at Ghassul to prepare for paintings. Some form of crushed limestone was used to form water-resistant surfaces at many periods. A well-preserved lime kiln from the Byzantine period has been found at Heshbon.

*See also* PLASTER; WHITEWASH.

See M. M. Khadijah, "'Lime Kilns," *ADAJ,* 16 (1971), 107-110.

L. G. HERR

**LIMIT** [Heb. *ʿaḏ taḵlîṯ* (Job 11:7), *gāraʿ*–'withdraw' (Job 15:8), *qēṣ* (Ps. 119:96; Nah. 3:9), *ḥōq* (Prov. 8:29), *tôṣāʿōṯ* (1 Ch. 5:16); Gk. *ámetros* ("beyond limit," 2 Cor. 10:13a, 15), *tó métron tón kanónos* (2 Cor. 10:13b)]; AV END, RESTRAIN, MEASURE, etc.; NEB also "perfection," "usurp," "come to an end," etc.; **LIMITATION** [Gk. *asthenía* (Rom. 6:19)]; AV "infirmity"; NEB "weakness."

The RSV uses the noun "limit" in several different contexts. In 1 Ch. 5:16 it refers to a geographical boundary; in Nah. 3:9 the military-political might of Egypt is "without limit." In a series of rhetorical questions (Job 11:7-11), Zophar (and later Eliphaz; cf. 15:8) attacks Job for questioning God. While Zophar is correct in pointing out the finitude of man, especially vis-à-vis God's infinity, he fails to understand or sympathize with Job. This failure points up one of the dangers of dogmatism: the misapplication of a theological truth. Prov. 8:29 refers to creation, when God gave limits or orders to the sea (cf. Job 28:26; Ps. 148:6).

Although the general sense of Ps. 119:96 is clearly a contrast between the finitude of earthly things and the boundless nature of God's commands, the precise meaning of the hapax legomenon *tiḵlâ* (RSV "perfection") is uncertain. It seems to be related to *taḵlîṯ* (both < *klh,* "complete, finish," "destroy").

In Rom. 6:19 the RSV reading is unfortunate; the AV and NEB, though literal, also miss the meaning according to E. Käsemann (*Comm. on Romans* [Eng. tr. 1980], p. 182): "In Paul *asthenía* never means some kind of feebleness but the temptation . . . of Christians through the impulses of the flesh . . . not the impotence of the weak . . . but the defiance of the strong." Here Paul "envisions neither ethical [contra *TDNT,* I, 491] nor intellectual weakness [contra Bauer, rev., p. 115] nor immaturity."

In 2 Cor. 10 Paul offers a strong defense of his ministry and appears quite concerned to answer charges of boasting on his part. To that end he claims that he boasts within the limits God has set (vv. 13, 15). The NEB "proper sphere" is a suitable rendering; Paul inveighs against opponents who have invaded his sphere of ministry.

G. A. L.

**LIMP** [Heb. *ṣālaʿ*] (Gen. 32:31 [MT 32]); [*pāsaḥ*] (1 K. 18:21, 26); AV HALT; LEAP; NEB "sit on the fence"; "dance wildly." Jacob's limp, which arose from the injury incurred during his wrestling with the divine adversary at the ford of the Jabbok, is remembered in a prohibition against eating the sciatic muscle. Nowhere else in the OT is this restriction noted, but it does appear in rabbinic Judaism (T.B. *Pesahim* 22a, 83b). Today the taboo is sometimes explained symbolically as the victory of the nation Israel (Jacob) over brute force (the adversary understood as Esau's demon). See I. Grunfeld, *Jewish Dietary Laws* (1972), I, 20.

In 1 K. 18:21 Elijah asks the people, who have been vacillating between Yahweh and Baal, how long they will "go limping between two different opinions." The irony of this choice of words is evident in v. 26, when the prophets of Baal perform a limping dance as part of their ritual. This dance, involving frenzied shouts, self-laceration, and limping around the altar, is a variant of a ritual common in the ancient Near East (1 K. 18:25-29; cf. J. Gray, *I & II Kings* [*OTL,* 2nd ed. 1970], p. 396). Both religious devotees and the deities that they worshiped engaged in such dancing. In the Bible some religious dancing is approved and some not. *See* DANCE.

G. WYPER

**LINE.**

(1) Most references have to do with measuring, so that Eng. "line" represents a Hebrew word for "cord," e.g., *pāṯîl* (Ezk. 40:3), *ḥûṭ* (1 K. 7:15), *ḥeḇel* (2 S. 8:2; Ps. 16:6; Am. 7:17; Mic. 2:5; Zec. 2:1 [MT 5]), or *qāw* or *qaw* (1 K. 7:23; 2 K. 21:13; 2 Ch. 4:2; 13:3; Job 38:5; Isa. 28:17;

etc.). "Plumb line" in Am. 7:7f. represents *ʾ^a^nāḵ*, "lead." *See* MEASURING LINE.

(2) Whether the "lines" of Isa. 28:10, 13 (*qāw*) also refer to such cords or to "syllable[s] imitating prophetic speech" (*CHAL*, p. 315) has long been debated (see comms.; *see also* METE).

(3) In Nu. 34:7 "mark out a line" represents the verb *tāʾâ* ("draw a line, mark out"; so translated in vv. 8, 10), which is used in reference to boundaries.

(4) References to battle lines always represent the verb *ʿāraḵ*, "set in rows, draw up in [battle] order" (Jgs. 20:20, 22; 1 S. 4:2; 17:2; 2 Ch. 13:3; 14:10; AV usually "set in array"), or the derived substantive *maʿ^a^rāḵâ*, "row, battle line" (1 S. 4:12; 17:20, 48; AV "army," "fight").

(5) The Hebrew term for "line" in the sense of lineage (Lev. 22:4; Ps. 89:29, 36) is *zeraʿ*, "seed, descendants." The Greek equivalent is *spérma*, used in 1 Macc. 7:14. "Lineage" in the Apocrypha represents Gk. *génos* (1 Macc. 3:32) or *geneá* (Tob. 5:13 [LXX 14]; 1 Esd. 5:5, 37), each a singular noun for the descendants of a common ancestor. In Lk. 2:4 "lineage" represents Gk. *patriá*, which is related to the word for "father" (translated "family" in Tob. 5:13 and "father's house" in 1 Esd. 5:37).

(6) "Line" as a verb for covering an interior surface represents Heb. *bānâ*, "build," in 1 K. 6:15 and *ḥāpâ*, "cover" in 2 Ch. 3:5, 7 (translated "overlay" in v. 9).

K. H. MAAHS E. W. S.

**LINEAGE.** *See* LINE (5).

**LINEN; FINE LINEN; LINEN GARMENT** [Heb. *šēš* (e.g., Ex. 26–28, 35–36, 38–39), *baḏ* (e.g., Lev. 6:10 [MT 3]; 1 S. 22:18), *pištâ, pēšeṯ* (pl. *pištîm*) (e.g., Dt. 22:11), *sāḏîn* (e.g., Jgs. 14:12f.), *bûṣ* (e.g., 1 Ch. 4:21), *ʾēṭûn* (Prov. 7:16); Gk. *sindṓn* (e.g., Mt. 27:59), *býssos* (e.g., Lk. 16:19), *býssinos* (e.g., Rev. 18:16), *othónion* (e.g., Jn. 19:40), *línon* (Rev. 15:6)]; AV also SHEET (Jgs. 14:12f.), SILK (Prov. 31:22).

*I. Archeological Finds.*–Linen and wool, both locally produced, were the only two fibers generally available for clothing and other uses during most of the biblical period. Cotton (*ḥôrāy*, Isa. 19:9; *karpas*, Est. 1:6) was a foreign product, as was the *mešî* of Ezk. 16:10, 13, thought to be silk.

The earliest extant textiles from the ancient Near East were found in Neolithic Level VI (*ca.* 6000 B.C.) at Çatal Hüyük in present-day Turkey. These fragments of cloth are so badly disintegrated that analysis cannot determine whether their origin was animal or vegetable. Their thread is plyed, i.e., two spun threads have been spun together for strength and durability. (*See* SPIN.)

The dry climate of Egypt has preserved numerous examples (*ca.*5000-4000 B.C.) of linen, palm bast, and rhamie. The earliest textiles from Palestine, probably made from plant fibers, come from the Chalcolithic (*ca.* 4000-

A finely weaved linen girdle of Ramses II found on a mummy at Saqqârah (Merseyside County Museums, Liverpool)

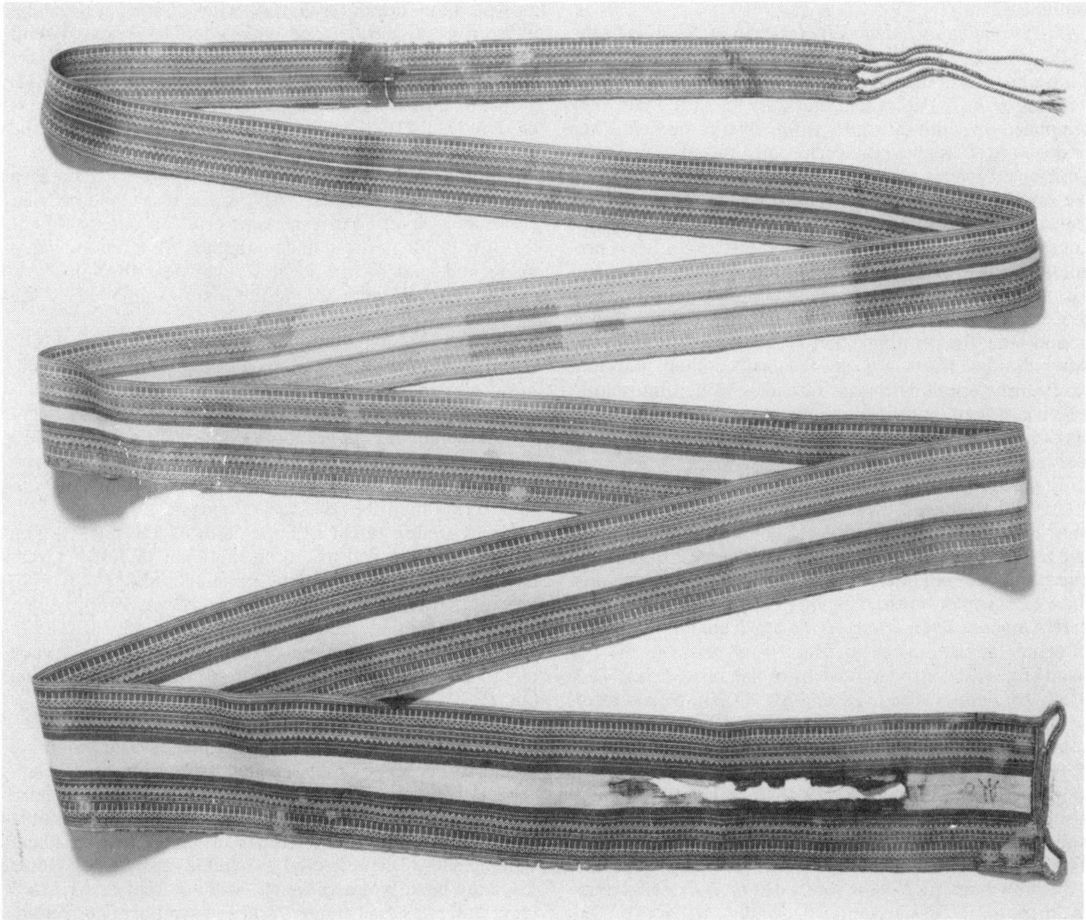

3000 B.C.) settlement at Teleilât el-Ghassûl on the east bank of the Jordan Valley. All but one of the fragments of burial garments from Jericho tombs in the Early and Middle Bronze Ages (*ca.* 3100-1700 B.C.) were made from plant fibers, either palm bast or linen. The thread is plyed, and some pieces show a selvedge. (*See* WEAVING.) The cloth has up to 45 by 50 threads per inch, similar to a fine linen handkerchief today. From the Late Bronze (*ca.* 1550-1250 B.C.) mining settlement at el-Menēʿiye (Timnaʿ) near the Gulf of Aqabah comes a relatively large find of wool and linen fabric dyed red and yellow (*see* DYE); some pieces were used as hangings and awnings for a shrine. The fabric is probably a product of Palestine.

No textile remains from the OT period proper have been found in Palestine, but textile finds from the Roman and following periods (63 B.C.) are rather numerous. Cave I at QUMRÂN contained seventy-seven fragments of linen cloth, among them wrappings for the scrolls. Some of these pieces show a selvedge as well as a woven design in blue thread dyed with indigo (cf. Nu. 15:38). Fineness ranges from 25 by 20 to 45 by 45 threads per inch. From the Cave of Letters, a shelter during the Bar Cochba Revolt (A.D. 132-135), come many well-preserved, dyed linen fragments and rolls of thread. The caves of the Wâdī Murabbaʿât have yielded a large number of garments and fragments of linen, wool, and cotton cloth (many of them dyed and embroidered), as well as mixed fabrics — cotton-wool, cotton-linen, and silk-linen. Although it is not possible to date the textiles from the last two sites with certainty, they are probably from the Roman period and later.

***II. Production of Linen.***–Linen fabric is made from the stalks of the FLAX plant (*Linum usitatissimum*; Heb. *pištâ*), whose growth is described in Ex. 9:31. When the stalks (Heb. *pištê hāʿēṣ*) are about half a meter (2 ft.) tall, they are pulled up, allowed to dry for a time in the field, then soaked (retted) for several weeks and allowed to dry again for a much longer period — about two years. After that they are beaten, scraped, and combed (hackled) to remove the outer covering and pulp, leaving the fibers. The Bible does not contain a description of the steps in linen production, but the GEZER CALENDAR (*ca.* 10th or 9th cent. B.C.) refers to the month of the agricultural year in which flax is pulled. It is probably the second, longer drying period after the "retting" that is mentioned in Josh 2:6. After the flax fibers are cleaned and combed, they are ready to be spun. The spun thread is woven into cloth, which can then be draped or sewn into GARMENTS. Lev. 19:19 prohibits the mixing of two fibers, probably wool and linen.

The many OT references to women spinning (e.g., Ex. 35:25) and to other aspects of the local linen production (Josh. 2:6; 1 Ch. 4:21; Prov. 31:13, 19), combined with the above-mentioned local finds of linen of very good quality, make unnecessary the hypothesis that fine linen must have been imported from Egypt.

***III. Biblical Terms.***–The OT and NT contain a number of terms for flax and linen. Heb. *pištâ* refers to the flax plant (Ex. 9:31) or to lamp wicks of flax or tow (Isa. 42:3; 43:17; cf. *línon* in the LXX and Mt. 12:20). *Pištim* refers to stalks of flax (*pištê hāʿēṣ*, Josh. 2:6; LXX *linokalámē*), rope made of flax (Ezk. 40:3), a supply of flax for spinning or weaving (Hos. 2:5; Prov. 31:13), or plain linen fabric in general (Lev. 13:47f., 52, 59; Dt. 22:11). The term is also used for the fabric of Jeremiah's waistcloth (Jer. 13:1) and the garments of the priests in Ezekiel's vision (Ezk. 44:17f.).

Hebrew *baḏ* (LXX *línon, býssinos, bad*) likewise refers to linen fabric for garments. It usually appears in compound expressions that specify the kind of garment, e.g., breeches (Ex. 28:42; 39:28; etc.), all priestly garments (Lev. 16:4, 23, 32; *see* GARMENTS VIII), an ephod (1 S. 2:18). In later writings the plural *bāḏîm* occurs in the expression "man clothed in linen," which in Ezekiel's vision refers to a scribe of priestly or angelic character (Ezk. 9:2f., 11; 10:2, 6f.) and in Daniel's vision refers to an angelic being (Dn. 10:5; 12:6f.).

Hebrew *šēš* (LXX *býssos, býssinos*) seems to be another linen fabric, probably of finer quality than *baḏ*, and more specific than *pištim*. It occurs in expressions indicating that it was used by rich, important, or priestly people: the pharaoh gave Joseph garments of *šēš* (Gen. 41:42); it was worn by the competent and prosperous woman in Prov. 31:22; and it occurs repeatedly in the Exodus instructions for the tabernacle and priestly vestments in the expression *šēš mošzar* (<*šāzar*, "twist"), "fine twined [or twisted] linen" (Ex. 25:4; 26:1, 31, 36; etc.). Since all linen is twisted in spinning, that expression may refer either poetically to the initial process or, more likely, to a second twisting process — i.e., the plying of two spun threads into a stronger thread, of which the textile remains from Jericho and Qumrân furnish examples.

Hebrew *bûṣ* (LXX *býssos, býssinos*) and its Greek derivatives are usually translated "fine linen." These terms can also refer, however, to fabric of linen, cotton and wool mixed, or even silk; therefore they apparently refer to the fabric's quality (i.e., its fineness and whiteness) rather than its fiber. *Bûṣ* was produced locally (cf. 1 Ch. 4:21, which refers to a family business in Beth-ashbeah) as well as in Edom (or Syria), which traded it — along with crimson, purple, and embroidered fabrics — with Tyre (Ezk. 27:16). This fine white fabric was used for royal (cf. Est. 8:15) and priestly (cf. 1 Ch. 15:27; 2 Ch. 5:12) garments and in the veil of Solomon's temple (2 Ch. 3:14; cf. 2:14 [MT 13]). Cords of *bûṣ* were used to hold up the hangings at the palace of Susa (Est. 1:6).

Hebrew *sāḏîn* (LXX *sindṓn, hyakínthinos*) denotes a large linen sheet of considerable value that could be used either as a covering of some sort or as an outer garment (cf. Jgs. 14:12f.). These linen wrappers were among items made and sold by the ideal woman described in Prov. 31:24, and they were among the luxuries enjoyed by the women of Jerusalem (Isa. 3:23).

The NT uses some of the same terms as the LXX. Gk. *býssos* and *býssinos* ("made from *býssos*"), like Heb. *bûṣ*, refer to white fabric of very fine quality. It was a luxury item worn by the rich (cf. Lk. 16:19) and bought by the inhabitants of Rome (Rev. 18:12, 16). It was also the garb of the Lamb's bride and of the armies of heaven in John's vision (Rev. 19:8, 14; cf. 15:6, which uses *línon* to describe the robes of angelic beings).

Greek *sindṓn* refers to linen cloth of fine quality. The young man who fled naked on the night of Jesus' arrest had worn only a linen tunic or sheet (Mk. 14:51f.). In preparation for His burial, Jesus' body was wrapped in a shroud of this material (Mt. 27:59; Mk. 15:46; Lk. 23:53).

Greek *othónion* (diminutive of *othónē*) refers to a linen cloth or bandage used in preparing a corpse for burial (Jn. 19:40; 20:5-7).

An allusion is probably made to linen in Eph. 5:27, although the fabric is not named. Linen is a very durable and absorbent fabric that becomes more comfortable with repeated washing. Its absorbency, while making it more comfortable in warm weather, also makes it susceptible to grease spots and other types of stains, and its fibers wrinkle badly when washed and crease easily when worn. Thus the beauty of a garment "without spot or wrinkle" (Eph. 5:27) was easily understood as a symbol of perfection.

*Bibliography*.–L. Bellinger, *BASOR*, 118 (Apr. 1950), 9-11; "Textiles," in H. D. Colt, ed., *Excavations at Nessana* (1962), pp. 92-105, plates XXIX, XXX; E. Crowfoot, "Report on Textiles," in K. Kenyon, *et al*., *Excavations at Jericho*, I (1960), 519-524, plates XXXVI, 4, 5, plates XXXVII, 1-4; "Textiles, Matting and Basketry," in K. Kenyon, *et al*., *Excavations at Jericho*, II (1965), 662-663; G. M. Crowfoot, *PEQ*, 1951, 5-31; "Linen Textiles," in *DJD*, I, 18-38, figures 4-9, plates IV-VII; G. M. and E. Crowfoot, "The Textiles and Basketry," in *DJD*, II, 51-62, figures 13-21, plates XV-XVII; R. J. Forbes, *Studies in Ancient Technology*, IV (1956), 1-80; H. Helbaeck, *Archaeology*, 16 (1963), 39-46; A. Hurvitz, *HTR*, 60 (1967), 117-121; J. Mellaart, *Çatal Huyuk, A Neolithic Town in Anatolia* (1967), 119-120, plates 116-18; B. Rothenberg, *Timna: Valley of the Biblical Copper Mines* (1972), p. 151. D. IRVIN

**LINTEL** [Heb. *mašqôp̱* (Ex. 12:7, 22f.), *ʾayil* (1 K. 6:31)]; AV also UPPER DOOR POST (Ex. 12:7); NEB also PILASTER (1 K. 6:31). *Mašqôp̱* is the wooden beam across the tops of the doorposts that ties the walls together and holds up the structure above it. At the time of the Exodus the Israelites splattered the blood of the Passover lamb on the posts and the lintel. *ʾAyil* is more difficult to translate with certainty. In Ezekiel's vision of the temple the word, used twenty-two times, is translated "vestibule" (40:14), "jambs" (v. 16, RSV), "portico" (NIV), "side pillar" (NASB), etc. BDB translates it "projecting pillar or pilaster" (p. 18). The LXX rendering in Ezekiel is *pýlē*, "gate," "door." Complicating the matter is the use of *ʾayil* in 1 K. 6:31. The MT reads *hāʾayil m*$^{e}$*zûzôṯ ḥ*$^{a}$*mišîṯ*, which the RSV translates, "The lintel and doorposts formed a pentagon." The LXX reads *kaí phliás pentaplás*, "and the lintel was fivefold." O. R. Sellers (*IDB*, III, 135f.) suggested that there was no horizontal lintel; instead, two beams met at an angle and with the doorposts formed a pentagon. This is structurally unsound. Also, the MT says nothing about two beams, while the LXX does not mention doorposts. It is impossible to translate the MT as "the lintel of the doorposts" because of the location of the definite article. The ordinal cannot be a numerical adjective because of its gender and number. The LXX allows the best translation, but caution is necessary. W. S. L. S.

**LINUS** lī′nəs [Gk. *Linos*]. One of those who joined the apostle in sending greetings, presumably from Rome, to Timothy (2 Tim. 4:21). This Christian was obviously an associate of the writer and must have been prominent in the Church, possibly an elder, but Scripture itself does not give any information about him. Irenaeus, however, in *Adv. haer*. iii.3.3, identified him with the Linus who was the immediate successor of Peter and Paul in the leadership of the Roman church. Tertullian, it is true, moved directly from the apostles to Clement (*De praescr. haer*. 32), but Eusebius (*HE* iii.2) had the same succession and made the same identification as Irenaeus. Eusebius added (iii.13) that the bishopric of Linus lasted twelve years from the death of Peter, usually calculated as A.D. 64-76. This became the established tradition in the Church, except that Jerome gave eleven years rather than twelve as the length of Linus's episcopate. Apost. Const. vii.46 contains a report, which cannot be verified, that a bishop of Rome was "Linus the son of Claudia," apparently the Claudia mentioned in 2 Tim. 4:21. The theory has been advanced that the Pudens of the same text might have been Linus's father, and that this PUDENS and CLAUDIA were the couple mentioned by the Roman author Martial (*Epigrams* iv.13). The Roman Breviary supplies the additional details, also without support, that Linus was born in Volterra, Etruria, and that he suffered martyrdom under the consul Saturninus. The latter statement is particularly doubtful, since there are no reports of persecution at that period. September 23 has been set aside as the day for the commemoration of Linus. G. W. B.

**LION** [Heb. *ʾaryēh* (Gen. 49:9; Dt. 33:22; Jgs. 14:8f.; etc.), *ʾ*$^{a}$*rî* (Nu. 23:24; 24:9; Jgs. 14:5; etc.); cf. Akk. *arū*; *k*$^{e}$*p̱îr* (Jer. 2:15; 51:38; Ezk. 32:2; etc.; "young lion," Job 4:10; Ps. 17:12; 34:10 [MT 11]; etc.), *k*$^{e}$*p̱îr ʾ*$^{a}$*rāyôṯ* ("young lions," Jgs. 14:5), *lāḇîʾ* (Dt. 33:20; Job 38:39; Isa. 5:29; etc.; "lioness," Gen. 49:9; Nu. 23:24; 24:9; etc.), *l*$^{e}$*ḇîyâ* ("lioness," Ezk. 19:2); cf. Ugar. *lbʾ*; Akk. *lābu*; *layiš* (Prov. 30:30; Isa. 30:6; "strong lion," Job 4:10); cf. Arab. *laith*; *šaḥal* (Job 10:16; 28:8; Ps. 91:13); "fierce lion," Job 4:10); Aram. *ʾaryēh* (Dnl. 6:7, 12, 16 [MT 8, 13, 17], etc.); Gk. *léōn* (2 Tim. 4:17; He. 11:33; 1 Pet. 5:8; etc.); Lat. *leo*]. Heb. *ʾaryēh* and *ʾ*$^{a}$*rî* occur most frequently; the other terms occur only as poetic variants.

The lions of ancient Palestine were the Asiatic subspecies (*Panthera leo persica* Mey) of the species *Felis leo*, and were fierce carnivores that were found also in Syria, Asia Minor, Greece, Mesopotamia, and northwest India. In Africa the lion was distributed widely, and though some had large manes, others of the species had shorter and paler manes. The population has been reduced dramatically over the centuries and now requires human assistance to ensure its survival. Lions had ceased to inhabit Greece by *ca*. A.D. 100, and apparently became extinct in Palestine with the end of the Crusades (13th cent. A.D.). They survived longer in Syria and Mesopotamia, being reported there as late as the 19th century. The last Asiatic lions in Iraq and Iran evidently disappeared in the early decades of the 20th century.

As opposed to some other carnivores, the lion lives and hunts in groups, having large animals as its prey. Lions normally attack humans only when provoked, although some develop a taste for human flesh. In antiquity the lion was a prized animal of the hunt, being particularly favored by Assyrian kings because of its strength and boldness. But apart from being hunted for sport, lions were sometimes kept in captivity, and the den of lions into which Daniel was thrown (Dnl. 6:7) was perhaps part of a royal zoo. The Assyrian king Ashurnasirpal II (*ca*. 883-859 B.C.) is reported to have maintained a breeding farm for lions at Nimrûd, while in Egypt Ramses II (*ca*. 1290-1224 B.C.) supposedly had a pet lion that he took into battle.

Such a respected animal naturally found its way into both ancient Near Eastern art and religion. When equipped with wings, presumably to augment its already formidable strength, it appeared in mythology and art as a divine cherub. Statues of winged lions were placed at the entrances of palaces and important public buildings in Assyria and Babylonia to bring the protection of magical forces to the structures and their occupants. Assyrian palaces were not infrequently decorated with bas-reliefs showing the king and his courtiers engaged in a lion hunt (*see* picture in ASHURBANIPAL). Probably the most outstanding artistic representation of a lion was seen in the glazed brick figures that decorated the Processional Street leading from the Ishtar Gate in Babylon (6th cent. B.C.; *see* Vol. I, Plate 6). The artists responsible for executing these remarkable depictions had clearly studied the musculature of the lion at first hand, and the work is a dramatic illustration of the heights to which contemporary Mesopotamian art had risen.

In Palestinian art the lion had attained a place of prominence by the end of the Amarna age, as indicated by the statue of a lion excavated from the ruins of a Canaanite shrine found in levels at Hazor that were dated to the 13th cent. B.C. (Y. Yadin, *BA*, 19 [1956], 10, figure 1).

The association of lions with temples and palaces in Mesopotamia and Canaan was followed in the construction of the Solomonic palace (1 K. 10:19f.) and the temple (1 K. 7:29, 36). This motif appeared again in Ezekiel's vision of the temple, in which the wood paneling that lined the inner room of the temple was decorated with various objects, including the face of a young lion (Ezk. 41:15-19). Other instances of Hebrew art involving lions include the ivory inlays from Samaria (9th cent. B.C.; cf. J. W. and G. M. Crowfoot, *Early Ivories from Samaria* [1938]), and the seal of Shema, Jeroboam II's steward, which depicted a lion (*see* picture in SHEMA). *See also* Plate 3.

In Mesopotamian religion the goddess Ishtar was generally represented in Assyria as the war deity, and rode upon, or was accompanied by, a lion. In Babylon, by contrast, she was associated with the mythological dragon (*mušrussu*), as on the Ishtar Gate (S. H. Hooke, *Babylonian and Assyrian Religion* [1953], p. 30). In the Assyrian form of the New Year Festival (*akîtu*), the traditional Babylonian enactment between Mardûk and the Dragon of Chaos may have been replaced by some form of contest between the king and a lion or lions, but this is uncertain. According to E. D. Van Buren the lion symbolized the militant character of most early Mesopotamian deities rather than being the emblem of a particular god (*Fauna of Ancient Mesopotamia as Represented in Art* [1939], p. 4).

In Egyptian religion the lion was less prominent than the bull (J. Černý, *Ancient Egyptian Religion* [1952], p. 24). A superbly chiseled granite lion was recovered from Tutankhamen's tomb (G. Steindorff and K. C. Seele, *When Egypt Ruled the East* [1963], p. 100 and figure 25), and bore an inscription to the effect that Tutankhamen had commissioned it in memory of his "father" Amenhotep III.

Lions are mentioned in the Bible for their strength (Jgs. 14:18), boldness (2 S. 17:10), ferocity (Ps. 7:2 [MT 3]), and stealth (Ps. 10:9; Lam. 3:10). The striking character of the millennial period is illustrated by references to fierce animals such as the lion, bear, and leopard living peaceably with other animals and children (Ps. 91:13; Isa. 11:6-8; 65:25). The roaring of the lion is often mentioned (Job 4:10; Ps. 104:21; Isa. 31:4; Jer. 51:38; Ezk. 22:25; Hos. 11:10). Judah is a "lion's whelp" (Gen. 49:9), likewise Dan (Dt. 33:22). The facial appearance of some of David's warriors was described as leonine (1 Ch. 12:8), while the wrath of the king was likened to the roaring of a lion (Prov. 19:12). David's enemy (Ps. 17:12) and the devil (1 Pet. 5:8) were curiously alike as far as their marauding, greedy ways were concerned. The violence of divine anger against Israel and Judah suggested to Hosea the threat of a predatory lion (Hos. 5:14).

Nearly all references to the lion are figurative. The only notices of the lions in narrative are of the lions slain by Samson (Jgs. 14:5), by David (1 S. 17:34f.), by Benaiah (2 S. 23:20); the prophet slain by a lion (1 K. 13:24; also 20:36); the lions sent by the Lord among the settlers in Samaria (2 K. 17:25f.); Daniel in the lions' den (Dnl. 6:16). In all these cases the word used is *'aryēh* or *'ᵃrî*, although in Jgs. 14:9-18 no fewer than three different terms (*kᵉpîr*, *'aryēh*, and *'ᵃrî*) occur. This matches the variety of usage in poetic passages such as Job 4:10f., where *'aryēh, šaḥal, kᵉpîr, layiš,* and *bᵉnê lābē'* are found.

***Bibliography.***–G. Cansdale, *Animals of Bible Lands* (1970); *TDOT*, I, *s.v.* "'ᵃrî" (Botterweck).

R. K. H.

**LIP** [Heb. *śāpâ, śᵉpāṯayim*]; NEB also MOUTH, WORDS, SPEECH, TONGUE, TALK, "(cattle from our) pens" (Hos. 14:2 [MT 3]; see comms.), etc.; [*śāpām*] (Ezk. 24:17, 22; Mic. 3:7); NEB UPPER LIP, MOUTHS; [*ḥēḵ*] (Hos. 8:1); AV MOUTH; [*peh*] (Ps. 50:16; Prov. 6:2; Jer. 7:28; Ezk. 29:21; 33:31); AV MOUTH; NEB also various paraphrases; [*mûṣāqâ*] (Zec. 4:2); AV, NEB, PIPES; [Gk. *cheílos*] (Mt. 15:8; Mk. 7:6; Rom. 3:13; 1 Cor. 14:21; He. 13:15; 1 Pet. 3:10); [*stóma*–'mouth'] (Lk. 22:71; Rom. 10:8-10; 1 Pet. 2:22); AV MOUTH; NEB also "retort"; **UPPER LIP** [Heb. *śāpām*] (Lev. 13:45).

In general, Hebraic thought regarded lips not only as physical organs but also as organs of speech. As physical organs, the lips may indeed be beautiful, "like a scarlet thread" (Cant. 4:3), and may be touched, as in Isaiah's vision (Isa. 6:7). Like the MOUTH and TONGUE in Hebraic thought, however, the lips are primarily associated with speech; as organs of speech they frequently seem to act independently. The lips may proclaim God's praises (Ps. 119:171), shout for joy (71:23), and spread knowledge (Prov. 15:7); or they may utter sinful words (Ps. 59:12 [MT 13]), speak insolently and dishonestly (31:18 [MT 19]), and talk of mischief (Prov. 24:2). The lips may function independently of the heart, in a hypocritical manner (Isa. 29:13; Mt. 15:8f. par. Mk. 7:6f.). But ultimately the heart and mind, the central and inner life of a person, direct the utterances of the lips: "The mind [AV "heart"; Heb. *lēḇ*] of the wise makes his speech judicious, and adds persuasiveness to his lips" (Prov. 16:23; also cf. 4:23; Rom. 10:8-10).

The term occurs in certain Hebrew idioms. Moses' claim to be "a man of uncircumcised lips" (Ex. 6:12, 30) meant that he was slow of speech, "a halting speaker" (NEB). In the Hebrew idioms "truthful lips" (Prov. 12:19), "righteous lips" (16:13), etc., "lips" by synecdoche may designate a person uttering a speech; thus the NEB has "truth spoken" in Prov. 12:19 and "honest speech" in 16:13. "Lip" (Heb. *śāpâ*; Gk. *cheílos*) may also mean language (Isa. 28:11; 1 Cor. 14:21; the RSV translates *śāpâ* "language" in Gen. 11:1; Isa. 19:18).

Three Hebrew terms require further explanation. *Śāpām* refers to the upper lip, moustache, or beard; according to proper Hebrew practice, a person covered his *śāpām* with his hand or his clothing to express deep grief, shame, and silent submission. Hence the unclean leper had to cover his *śāpām* and cry "Unclean, unclean" (Lev. 13:45). Ezekiel was told not to cover his *śāpām* and thus not to follow the rites for mourning when sinful Israel was to be decimated (Ezk. 24:17, 22). Micah spoke of false prophets who covered their *śāpām* in shame and confusion (Mic. 3:7). *Ḥēḵ* refers to the palate, gums, or lips, the part of the mouth (in Hos. 8:1) in contact with the trumpet. *Mûṣāqâ*, or *mûṣeqeṯ*, refers to one of the lips (or protuberances, spouts, or pipes) for oil lamps (Zec. 4:2); perhaps the wicks rested by these lips, or perhaps oil was poured through a *mûṣāqâ*. *See* LAMP I.

M. W. MEYER

**LIQUOR** (AV Ex. 22:29 [MT 28]; Nu. 6:3; Cant. 7:2 [MT 3]). The AV rendering of three hapax legomena. In Ex. 22:29, AV, "liquor" translates Heb. *dema'*, which appears to be related to *dāma'*, "shed tears" (RSV "outflow of a press" is a paraphrase based on the context). Most commentators have followed the LXX and have taken *dema'* as the product of the wine press, i.e., wine, although it could refer to olive oil, also the product of a press. In Nu. 6:3 the Nazirite is prohibited from drinking Heb. *mišrâ*, which probably indicates the "juice" (so RSV) of the grapes; cf. *šārâ*, "let loose," hence *mišrâ*, "that which is let loose." In Cant. 7:2, as in rabbinical Hebrew and Aramaic, Heb. *mezeg* probably refers to mixed or spiced wine (see also M. Pope, *Song of Songs* [*AB*, 1977], pp. 619f.).

*See also* DRINK, STRONG; WINE.

G. A. L.

**LIST** [Heb. *mispār*–'number'] (1 Ch. 25:1; 27:1); AV, NEB, NUMBER. The RSV paraphrases Heb. *mispār* in these two texts since in the context what follows is a list of names rather than a number. The AV uses "list" in the obsolete sense of "wish" to translate Gk. *thélō* (RSV "please," Mt. 17:12 par. Mk. 9:13; RSV "will," Jn. 3:8) and *boúlomai* (RSV "desire," Jas. 3:4).

**LISTEN.** Most often in the RSV OT a translation of Heb. *šāmaʿ* (AV usually "hearken") and in the RSV NT a translation of Gk. *akoúō* (AV often "hear"). Other NT terms that convey the idea of active listening, and sometimes also of understanding, responding to, or obeying, are: *eisakoúō* ("obey," 1 Cor. 14:21), *epakoúō* (2 Cor. 6:2), *epakroáomai* (Acts 16:25), *peitharchéō* (Acts 27:21), *manthánō* ("learn from someone as a teacher," 2 Tim. 3:7). "Listening" in 2 Tim. 4:4 translates the noun *akoḗ*.

*See* HEAR.

**LITERATURE, THE BIBLE AS.**

- I. General
- II. Compatibility of Hebrew and English
- III. Characteristics of Literature
  - A. Order
  - B. Unity
  - C. Wholeness, Resolution, Serenity
- IV. Literary Devices in the Bible
  - A. Parallelism
  - B. Rhythm
  - C. Imagery
  - D. Sound and Connotation
- V. Genres in the Bible
  - A. Epic Drama
  - B. History
  - C. Lyric Poetry
  - D. Story
  - E. Drama
  - F. Biography
  - G. Epistle
  - H. Apocalypse

***I. General.***–Literary scholars and general readers alike agree that the Bible is the greatest body of literature in human history. Surely it is supreme in English literature (with which this article is concerned); so much so, indeed, that great treasures in English literature from Caedmon to T. S. Eliot are incomprehensible to those ignorant of the Bible. For many generations, and certainly from the 17th cent. through most of the 19th, the only two books commonly found in simple but literate English and American homes were the Bible and the works of Shakespeare. They were sufficient to provide a liberal education and a deep grounding in the power, beauty, and wisdom of great literature. (Shakespeare himself relied partly on the Great Bible of 1539 but chiefly on the Geneva Bible of 1560, translated by English Puritans fleeing the persecutions of Mary Tudor's reign. The AV appeared only five years before Shakespeare's death in 1616, after the bulk of his work was accomplished.)

***II. Compatibility of Hebrew and English.***–When one remembers that literary style resides largely in the elements of the original language — sounds, rhythms, figures of speech, word connotations, and the like — and that it is notoriously difficult to capture in translation, one is grateful for the richness and variety of English. Our language is a river into which has flowed (in approximately chronological order) the blunt vigor of Anglo-Saxon, the rotund power of Latin words and periods, the precision of Greek, the melody and lilt of Italian, the mellifluous grace of French, and the muscularity of German. Hence, English is uniquely capable of reflecting the literary qualities of other languages, particularly those of OT Hebrew, which, though deficient in words of abstract meaning, is rich in concrete, vivid, sensuous imagery. Ernest Renan observed that this "primitive union of sensation and idea" distinguishes Semitic languages from the Aryan. When, therefore, the imagery of the Hebrew is translated literally into English (relying heavily on the Anglo-Saxon element in English), the translation captures precisely the meaning and the feeling intended by the original writer. The translatability is enhanced, too, by the universality of Hebrew imagery, drawn as it is from the forces of nature (e.g., lightning [Nah. 2:4]; rain [Ps. 72:6]; drought [Hos. 13:5]; thunder [Job 26:14]), animals (e.g., hart [Ps. 42:1]; horse [Job 39:19-25]; lion and leopard and bear [Hos. 13:7]; eagle [Ps. 103:5]; whale [Job 41:1-3]), the human body (e.g., heart [Ps. 4:7]; bones [Ezk. 32:27]; hands [Isa. 49:16]); home and shelter (Ps. 84:3f. [MT 4f.]); crops and agriculture; shepherding; food and drink; and household relationships. There is no end to the use of such imagery, and one may, literally, turn to the OT at random and find instances on every page. Such imagery, based on the most universal experiences of humankind, enhances immensely the translator's ability to transfer the literary qualities of the original to another tongue. Hundreds of such images have become a part of our language — "the sweat of his brow," "by the skin of my teeth," "a thorn in the flesh," "weighed and found wanting," "arose as one man," etc. In every case the abstract is communicated by the concrete, the idea is (in John Donne's phrase) "felt upon the pulses," the intangible is given three-dimensional tangibility. David could have written (and if he had been Greek he probably would have), "Deity manifests an interest in and a protective concern over the affairs of mankind." But he didn't. He wrote, "The Lord is my shepherd." From that point on, Ps. 23 consists of a succession of concrete images, each evocative of emotion and sensuousness, each going to our hearts as well as to our heads.

***III. Characteristics of Literature.***–"Literature" is that kind of writing which is as concerned with moving the reader as with informing him. Plain expository prose is as effective as literature, and more economical, in transmitting facts and ideas from one mind to another. (Hamlet really adds nothing to the basic idea after he has said: "To be or not to be, that is the question." The rest of the soliloquy, largely imagery, is literature.)

Literature is not, however, merely the adorning of ideas for the sake of adornment. An analogy may be found in the ark containing the tablets of the law. A simple wooden box would have served just as well for mere containment. But by God's own command, and on His own specifications, the ark was to be enriched in meaning and power by visible beauty (Ex. 25:10-22). It was God's purpose to commune with His people from above the mercy seat (Ex. 25:22). It was both fitting and necessary that His presence should show forth His beauty. How much more, then, should His written Word be invested with beauty, for in His Word He communes with His people constantly and intimately.

*A. Order.* How or why humankind is moved by beauty is ultimately a mystery. The aesthetic capability is innate in humankind, put there by God as one aspect of humankind's reflection of the Creator's image. Very near the heart of the mystery, perhaps, is fallen humanity's desperate yearning for order, the opposite of chaos. Order implies purpose, meaning, sequence, beginning-middle-ending. All works of true literature have this quality of wholeness, although the area encompassed may be small. They all (to use Milton's phrase from "Lycidas") comb the tangled locks of grief and confusion, enabling us to transcend the fragmentariness, the seeming meaninglessness and hopelessness, of random chance. The Bible, from Genesis to Revelation, gives us the ultimate order, the order determined from eternity by God for His universe.

*B. Unity.* Order implies also unity. And here, the Bible, humanly considered, presents another mystery. How can a book written over some fifteen hundred years by at least a score of authors, some learned and some not, reflecting widely divergent geographical, social, political, and intellectual environments, winnowed out over the centuries from masses of seemingly similar writings, possess unity? Embraced within the book's covers are all forms of literature — prose and poetry, narrative, history, epic and lyric verse, drama, biography, parable, debate, and many more. Here are myriad characters reflecting every human condition from the most elevated to the most debased, all presented with an economical vividness unsurpassed by Shakespeare or Dickens. Here is the rise and fall of empires, the life of the desert nomad and that of the silken courtier in great palaces. Here is every philosophy, theology, ethical system, social organization humanity has ever thought of. As Dryden said, figuratively, of Chaucer, "Here is God's plenty." The Bible is that, literally.

To the natural mind this scope and unity have no explanation. To the believer there is only one explanation: God so ordained it and brought it into being. Using the varied intellectual, spiritual, and aesthetic talents of many writers, He fashioned a verbal tapestry as intricate and exquisite as the fabric of nature, formed by His fingers.

Nor is the unifying theme far to seek, for at the center is God's revelation of Himself and of His redemptive plan. In the words of Roland Frye (*The Bible: Selections from the King James Version* [1965], p. xvi), this self-revelation is accomplished through "the interaction between individuals, societies, and God. . . . The characterization of God may indeed be said to be the central literary concern of the Bible, and it is pursued from beginning to end, for the principal character, or actor, or protagonist of the Bible is God."

It is not surprising, therefore, that the Creator of every aesthetic principle should choose (set apart, "sanctify") for His purposes those endued with literary capabilities, guiding them and preventing them from error but not overriding their individualities, to compose His Book — just as He chose cunning workmen of every craft to build and adorn His wilderness tabernacle (Ex. 26–27) and His Jerusalem temple (1 K. 6–7).

*C. Wholeness, Resolution, Serenity.* Great literature serves not only the human yearning and need for order and unity, but also the need for harmony, serenity, and fulfillment. According to Aristotle the objective of great literature is *kátharsis,* the purging or purification of the passions and the will through the participation of the reader or auditor in the sufferings of others, chiefly the hero, leading to understanding and serenity. "Calm of mind, all passion spent" is how Milton phrased it in the last line of *Samson Agonistes*. The Bible calls it "peace" (Jn. 14:27). Matthew Arnold asserted that great literature (as distinct from mere light verbal entertainment) always changes the reader's conduct and understanding of life. The greatness of the Bible measured by this criterion is transcendent.

***IV. Literary Devices in the Bible.****–A. Parallelism.* The most common device is parallelism, the repetition of an idea in parallel form for emphasis, enrichment, and memorability. Students of Hebrew poetry agree that there are three basic forms of parallelism: synonymous, antithetic, and "shadow" (or synthetic). In the first the idea is simply repeated in another or an enlarged image, e.g., "The Lord reigns; let the peoples tremble!/He sits enthroned upon the cherubim; let the earth quake!" (Ps. 99:1). In the second the basic idea is repeated from an opposite or contrasting perspective, e.g., "A wise son makes a glad father,/but a foolish son is a sorrow to his mother" (Prov. 10:1). In the third, "shadow" parallelism, the correspondence comes from a rhythmic balance between the two parts, and uses an entirely different kind of image, not a repetition of the first in positive or negative form, e.g., "As the heart longs for flowing streams,/so longs my soul for thee, O God" (Ps. 42:1). (The book of Proverbs consists almost entirely of thoughts expressed in parallel structures, and the Psalms are filled with all kinds of parallelisms.)

*B. Rhythm.* We think of poetry primarily as rhythm, with its metronomic regularity of alternation of stressed and unstressed syllables (as in Alexander Pope's "Be NOT the FIRST, by WHOM the NEW is TRIED,/Nor YET the LAST to LAY the OLD aSIDE"). But there is "another harmony of prose," as Dryden phrased it, and it can be of a subtler, richer kind than that of mechanically regular scansion. A review of the styles of the great English translations of the Bible from Wyclif (*ca.* 1382-1384) to the present shows a constant effort not only to say what the original writers meant to say but to do so with a moving and pleasing rhythm. (The RSV retains the rhythm of the AV almost intact.) Wyclif, for example, wrote, "Thei schulen no more hungre nether thirst" (Rev. 7:16). The AV addition of just two words (kept in the RSV) enhances the rhythm: "They shall hunger no more, neither thirst any more." The simple change adds the magic, with its quiet, serene (unaccented) ending. Wyclif wrote, "He is suche a man as hath good experience of sorrows and infirmities" (Isa. 53:3). The Geneva version made it, "A man of sorrows and hath experience of infirmities." With enhanced rhythmic beauty, the AV and RSV read, "A man of sorrows and acquainted with grief." (The passages must be read aloud if one is to hear the rhythmic quality sought.) Such illustrations could be multiplied almost without number. Every language has its own rhythmic capabilities (listen to the Irish, even when they are speaking English!); but when one hears Hebrew spoken well, one realizes that the rhythmic characteristics of the original tongue, like its concreteness and imagery, are eminently transferable to English.

*C. Imagery.* Another major literary device of both Hebrew and English, already referred to above in passing, is the constant use of imagery — the abstract expressed in concrete ways, figurativeness. Imagery serves many purposes, including vividness, brevity, and memorability. The most important and prevalent figure of speech in the Bible is metaphor, the expression of a correspondence between different things. We use metaphors every day — "his anger blazed up," "she's the apple of her father's eye," "he's climbed to the top of the ladder," etc. These statements are not literally true, but are "truer" by reason of their mingling of the physical with the mental, and by a deeper-than-literal correspondence. Dramatizing the variety of metaphors in the Bible, Harry Boonstra has written (*Christianity Today*, Dec. 17, 1976, p. 22): "God as a dragon, or a leopard, or lye, or a hunger, or a woman in labor. God's people as stubborn oxen, dry rot, pottery, silver, soil, dew, a bride. God's relationship with his people as that of a lover wooing his sweetheart, a ferocious bear ready to tear up his prey, a parent teaching a toddler how to walk . . ." — all metaphors.

Next to metaphor, simile is the most frequent figure

of speech in the Bible. In simile the comparison is stated with "like" or "as": "Is not my word like fire, says the Lord, and like a hammer which breaks the rock in pieces?" (Jer. 23:29); ". . . coming up like locusts for number . . ." (Jgs. 6:5); "my love is like a gazelle or a young stag" (Cant. 2:9); etc. Synecdoche, also frequent in the Bible, represents a whole by referring to a part, as in "Thou preparest a table before me . . ." (Ps. 23:5), where "table" stands for the entire feast — honor, friends, food and drink, and fitting dining room. Metonymy is that figure of speech in which the name of one object or idea is used for another to which it is related, as in "Thou hast exalted my horn . . ." (Ps. 92:10), wherein "horn" connotes power, rule, authority. Litotes is similar to irony, involving a statement recognized as conveying a literal meaning opposite to the one intended, as in Job's bitter indictment of his "friends": "No doubt you are the people and wisdom shall die with you" (Job 12:2). Hyperbole is deliberate exaggeration for dramatic effect, as in "I will surely . . . make thy seed as the sand of the sea" (Gen. 32:12). Symbolism, though technically not a figure of speech, is similar in its expansion of the meaning and implication of the truth uttered, going, indeed, far beyond the immediately understood. Ezekiel is rich in symbolism (see particularly 1:4-28), as is Revelation.

*D. Sound and Connotation.* Another literary device, and the one least translatable directly, is the use of words for their sounds and original connotations. In his splendid essay on the AV, "The Noblest Monument of English Prose" (*Essays in Appreciation* [1936]), the great Harvard professor of literature, John Livingstone Lowes, pointed out how nearly impossible it would be to translate the following lines of Shakespeare without losing the effect of their drowsy, narcotic sounds and connotations: "Not poppy nor mandragora,/Nor all the drowsy syrups of the world/Shall ever med'cine thee to that sweet sleep/Which thou owedst yesterday" (*Othello*, III, 3, lines 331f.). Onomatopoeia, the use of words that actually sound like the objects denoted, is the most difficult device to translate, and the original effect is usually lost. A notable example of both sound-connotation and onomatopoeia occurs in Isa. 28:10, 13 (*see* HUMOR IN THE BIBLE). The best that the translator can do is to search for the English word best expressive of the effect of the original.

***V. Genres in the Bible.***–*A. Epic Drama.* The term that most aptly describes the genre of the Bible as a whole is "epic drama." An epic is a long, serious, noble work expressive of the essence of a people, its history, ideals, nature, and greatness — e.g., the *Odyssey,* the *Iliad,* the *Aeneid, Beowulf, Paradise Lost.* The epic involves mighty deeds, marvelous adventures, myriad characters, the search by an entire people or nation for destiny and fulfillment, replete with victory and life, sacrifice and death, great battles — and, above all, the deeds of a hero who embodies all that is glorious. In these respects, the Bible, viewed as a single, unified whole, obviously transcends all literature. John Milton, desiring to write an epic encompassing all humanity, not just a single nation or period, inerrantly recognized that there is in human history on earth only one Hero, and in *Paradise Lost* and *Paradise Regained* the Son of God, named on earth Jesus, is He. (Some critics, understanding neither Milton nor his reliance on the Bible, have foolishly declared that Adam is the hero, and some perversely have even put Satan in that role.)

*B. History.* As a genre, history is recognized as an art. Anyone with patience can collect such facts as are available and arrange them in chronological order; but the historical portions of the Bible (a major portion of the whole) seem effortlessly to do what only the greatest historians have done. By a marvel of selectivity, a period of thousands of years is given unity, continuity, comprehensibility, and vividness. By the mingling of sharply etched moments of action, character, and dialogue with summary sweeps of long periods of time, one is held engrossed. Always the focus is maintained: the story is about God's dealing with His own people, and the working out of His redemptive plan. Great nations rise and fall, but they appear only as they affect Israel. Episodes are never inserted at random, nor extended beyond their significance. (The story of Joseph takes up the last fourteen chapters of Genesis because the spiritual lessons are central.) When we see the Bible as a whole, we discover the force of Jesus' words to the two on the Emmaus road: "And beginning with Moses and all the prophets, he interpreted to them in all the scriptures the things concerning himself" (Lk. 24:27), for He is the pervasive Hero.

*C. Lyric Poetry.* The modifier "lyric" (from "lyre") reminds us that Hebrew poetry was commonly chanted to the accompaniment of stringed instruments, not in elaborate melodies like modern arias but with rhythmic musical beats to emphasize the couplet (or distich) form of the verse. Each couplet normally contains a complete meaning, often in parallel form, and may be best seen in "wisdom" (gnomic, aphoristic) literature, as exemplified in Proverbs. Such regularity served a mnemonic as well as a rhetorical and aesthetic purpose. The greatest storehouse of lyric poetry is the book of PSALMS, an unmatched collection, which has served as the hymnbook of Jews and Christians ever since David. Even in the chiefly historical books of the OT, lyric poetry abounds — public prayers (2 Ch. 6:14-42; Neh. 9:6-37), songs of praise and thanksgiving (1 Ch. 16:5-36), elegies (2 S. 1:19-27), songs of victory (Jgs. 5:2-31), and even songs of imprecation (Gen. 9:25-27). The prophets wrote preponderantly in verse, which may be noted simply by thumbing through the RSV or any other translation that prints verse in its proper form. Canticles is a supreme example of lyric love poetry, as is Ruth, in the genre later called "pastoral romance." Ecclesiastes, though only partly in verse, is poetically lovely throughout and has influenced the poets of all ages (in our day, notably, T. S. Eliot) by its haunting images expressive of the beauty, brevity, and vanity of human life. In the NT, poetry is less commonly found, though Paul's paean to love in 1 Cor. 13 has every essential attribute of verse and is unsurpassed in secular literature.

*D. Short Story.* The Bible teaches how this genre should be handled, whether historically factual, as in such stories as those about Joseph, David and Jonathan, Jonah, etc., or parabolic, as in the story of the Prodigal Son (Lk.15:11-32).

*E. Drama.* This genre (embracing also features of "wisdom" literature) appears in Job, written in verse, and probably so early as not to have been influenced (as some critics believe) by early Greek drama. The careful threefold structure of the work indicates the conscious literary artistry applied to this account of an actual event. Overall, the work falls naturally into three parts: introduction, body, and epilogue (or conclusion). Each of Job's three friends is given three speeches, each answered by Job — with the dramatic touch of Zophar's despairing relinquishment of his third "turn" in view of Job's stubborn refusal to listen to "reason." Intellectually the work moves to its conclusion through Job's contest with his friends; Elihu's speech; and God's utterance. (The form of this drama, incidentally, is similar to that of the medieval *débat.*)

*F. Biography.* The biographical riches of the Bible are almost endless, from the smallest vignettes (e.g., the unforgettable picture of the contemptible Shimei cursing and throwing dirt and stones at the aged King David as he flees his capital, now occupied by the rebellious Absalom, with the loyal Abishai dancing along beside David, pleading, "Let me go over, I pray thee, and take off his head" [2 S. 16:5-13]) to the extended life stories of the great figures of the Bible, now woven inextricably into our cultural heritage. And transcending all, bestriding the world, forming the hinge of time before Him and after Him, the figure of Jesus Christ Himself, subject of four incomparable biographies, the Gospels, whose varying but complementary points of view give such dynamic reality to their subject that no age, no nation, no individual can ignore Him. In their brief, simple, objective narratives (only Luke shows evidence of formal rhetorical learning), stressing unerringly those events and sayings in Jesus's life crucial to our knowledge of Him, the Synoptic Gospels offer, as it were, a three-dimensional picture of the earthly scene, while the Fourth Gospel extends our gaze to the heavenly.

*G. Epistle.* Paul's literary genius is best seen in his unique mingling of the formal essay with the informal epistolary style. Immersed in disciplined learning from his boyhood, and possessed of a powerful, quick temperament, he infused his densely packed intellectual treatises with the quality of his own personality. Not only was he master of the immense Hebrew tradition of learning, but under Gamaliel he was permitted to enter into and absorb the Greek intellectual tradition as well, in a way not permitted by many of the great rabbis of the day. All Paul's intellectual power, mental quickness, spiritual understanding, and verbal resources come together in his closely reasoned Epistle to the Romans, which has been called the greatest short philosophical/theological treatise in literature.

*H. Apocalypse.* The aged John, on Patmos, his inner gaze fixed on unimaginably vast and glorious events still future, gives us the very name "apocalyptic" literature. From Dante to Blake to Dylan Thomas (to name at random), John's literary style, if not the fulness of his inspired vision, has moved beneath and inspired secular literature, emerging in visions of symbolic splendor and full-orchestrated rhythms. "After this I looked, and lo, in heaven an open door! . . . And lo, a throne stood in heaven, with one seated on the throne! And he who sat there appeared like jasper and carnelian, and round the throne was a rainbow that looked like an emerald. Round the throne were twenty-four thrones. . . . From the throne issue flashes of lightning, and voices and peals of thunder, and before the throne burn seven torches of fire, which are the seven spirits of God; and before the throne there is as it were a sea of glass, like crystal" (Rev. 4:1-6). His work is a fitting climax to the epic drama.

***Bibliography.***–R. Alter, *Art of Biblical Narrative* (1981); F. F. Bruce, *The English Bible: A History of Translation* (1961); M. E. Chase, *Life and Language in the OT* (1955); C. A. Dinsmore, *The English Bible as Literature* (1931); N. Frye, *The Great Code: The Bible as Literature* (1982); J. H. Gardner, *The Bible as English Literature* (1906); E. M. Good, *Irony in the OT* (1965); T. R. Henn, *The Bible as Literature* (1970); J. R. MacArthur, *Biblical Literature and its Background* (1936); L. Ryken, *Christianity and Literature*, 21/3 (1982), 9-29; R. G. Moulton, *Literary Study of the Bible* (1895); P. C. Sands, *Art of Biblical Narrative* (1981).

C. D. LINTON

**LITTER** [Heb. *ṣāḇ*] (Isa. 66:20); NEB WAGON; [*miṭṭâ*] (Cant. 3:7); AV BED; [Gk. *phórion*] (2 Macc. 9:8); AV HORSE-LITTER. *Miṭṭâ* is a general term for couch; in Cant. 3:7 it refers to a covered and curtained couch outfitted with shafts and used for carrying a person. King Solomon's litter is described as being quite luxurious (cf. vv. 6, 9f.; *see* PALANQUIN).

The *ṣabbîm* in Isa. 66:20 are probably covered wagons rather than litters (cf. NEB; also RSV "covered wagons" for *ʿeglôṯ ṣāḇ* in Nu. 7:3). The Gk. *phórion* of 2 Macc. 9:8 was apparently a stretcher used for carrying a sick or wounded person (cf. 3:27).

*See also* BED.

N. J. O.

**LITTLE GENESIS.** A name for the book of Jubilees. *See* APOCALYPTIC LITERATURE III.B.

**LIVE.** In the English versions the verb "live" is most often a translation of Heb. *ḥāyâ* (or one of its cognates) in the OT and of Gk. *záō* in the NT. As such, the most common meaning is "be alive, have life," as the opposite of "be dead"; cf. the expression "live and not die" (e.g., Gen. 42:2; Nu. 4:19; Dt. 33:6; 2 K. 18:32). *See* LIFE. On the expression "as I live" or "as the Lord lives," *see* OATH.

A second meaning, more common in the NT than in the OT, is "behave, conduct one's life." Gk. *záō* sometimes has this sense, especially when combined with an adverb or modifying phrase; cf. *záō eusebṓs* (RSV "live a godly life," 2 Tim. 3:12; cf. Tit. 2:12), *záō Pharisaíos* ("live as a Pharisee," Acts 26:5), *záō en pístei* ("live by faith," Gal. 2:20), *záō katá sárka* ("live according to the flesh," Rom. 8:12f.). The RSV sometimes renders "live" for *peripatéō* (lit. "walk" [so AV]; fig. "conduct oneself"), e.g., 2 Cor. 10:3; Eph. 4:17; Phil. 3:17f.; 1 Thess. 4:1 (*see* WALK).

A third meaning is "inhabit" or "dwell." In the RSV OT (and more often in the NEB OT) "live" occurs frequently as a translation of Heb. *yāšaḇ* (AV, lit., "dwell"; e.g., Gen. 21:20f.; Nu. 32:17; Dt. 1:4, 44); less often it renders *gûr* (AV, lit., "sojourn" or "dwell"; e.g., Jgs. 17:8; Jer. 42:15, 17, 22; 43:2, 5) or *šāḵan* (AV, lit., "dwell"; e.g., Job 15:28; Ob. 3). In the NT "live" in this sense usually represents Gk. *katoikéō* (AV, lit., "dwell"; e.g., Acts 7:2, 4; 9:22, 32; cf. *oikéō*, 1 Cor. 7:12f.; *synoikéō*, 1 Pet. 3:7; *enkatoikéō*, 2 Pet. 2:8). *See* DWELL.

N. J. O.

**LIVER** [Heb. *kāḇēḏ*] (Ex. 29:13, 22; Lev. 3:4, 10, 15, etc.]. As the heftiest of the internal body glands, the liver apparently came to its name quite naturally from the verbal root *kbd*, "be heavy" (cf. other Semitic cognates for liver; Ugar. *kbd*, Akk. *kabittu*, and Aram. *kaḇdā'*).

In eleven of the twelve times that *kāḇēḏ* is translated "liver" by the RSV the reference is to the "appendage [so RSV; NEB "long lobe"; AV "caul"] of the liver" (Heb. *hayyōṯereṯ ʿal-hakkāḇēḏ*), which, along with the fat on the entrails and the kidneys of a sacrificial animal, is burned upon the altar as an offering.

The twelfth occurrence of *kāḇēḏ* (Ezk. 21:21 [MT 26]) constitutes the lone biblical example of the common Mesopotamian practice of hepatoscopy (i.e., liver examination for purposes of divination). The grimly foreboding "song of the sword" in the early part of Ezk. 21 is directly followed (leaving little doubt as to whom it portends) by the ominous figure of the king of Babylon. He is on the march westward with all his irresistible military forces, and is portrayed as pausing where the fork in the highway offers a route either to Amman or to Jerusalem. Before moving in either direction the king stops to seek divine guidance, for battle was not entered into without first ascertaining the divine will (cf., e.g., 1 S. 23:9-12, where David, under threat of an attack by Saul's forces, acts only after consulting the Lord through the ephod; 23:2ff.; 2 S. 5:19, 23). In this instance the Babylonian king is said to have cast arrows, consulted the teraphim, and examined the liver, in an unparalleled threefold procedure in which "features of Israelite oracle seeking are mixed with others of a specifically Babylonian coloring" (W. Zimmerli, *Ezekiel*, I [Eng. tr. 1979], 443; see also A. Oppenheim, *Ancient Mesopotamia* [1964], p. 209, for a caution about the lack of cuneiform documentation for such an unusual combination of divination practices). This text may simply reflect a tradition known to Ezekiel that Nebuchadrezzar was very careful to use several corroborative methods of divination before proceeding into combat (rather than one unprecedented threefold combination), since he was concerned to ascertain both the favorable target and the propitiousness of action at that time. On hepatoscopy *see* DIVINATION III.E.

Beyond these twelve instances *kāḇēḏ* occurs only twice more in the entire MT (Lam. 2:11 and Prov. 7:23), in neither case translated "liver" by the RSV. Only in Lam. 2:11 does *kāḇēḏ* refer to the human liver (thus AV, but RSV has "heart" and NEB "bile"). See D. Hillers, *Lamentations* (*AB*, 1972), pp. 32, 45. It is possible that *kāḇēḏ* in Prov. 7:23 (AV "liver"; RSV "entrails"; NEB "vitals") may also refer to the human liver rather than that of a stag (cf. RSV in vv. 22b-23a, "or as a stag is caught fast till an arrow pierces its entrails"). (See the comms.)

With but fourteen occurrences in the entire MT, *kāḇēḏ* is not a common term. Even the possibility that the traditional vowel pointing has obscured further occurrences (see, e.g., KoB, p. 420, and such possible examples as Gen. 49:6; Ps. 7:5 [MT 6]; 16:9; 30:12 [MT 13]; 57:8 [MT 9]; 108:1 [MT 2]) does not diminish the rarity. Ps. 16:9 offers a striking example of ambiguous vowel pointing: *śāmaḥ libbî*, "my heart is glad," stands in parallel with *wayyāgel kᵉḇôḏî*, "my soul [RSV]/spirit [NEB] rejoices" (the LXX here has the less than enlightening *hē glṓssa mou*, "my tongue"). In the light of the parallel with "heart" and the liver's understood character as a sensitive organ and the seat of the emotions, as well as Akkadian examples of the cognate *kabittu* as that organ or internal area which "rejoices" and is associated with happiness (see *CAD*, VIII, 12ff., for examples), the possibility that "my liver" is strictly intended here merits serious consideration.

In the light of the ample Syro-Palestinian evidence for the use of clay liver models (see, e.g., H. Tadmor and B. Landsberger, *IEJ*, 14 [1964], 201-217; M. Dietrich and O. Loretz, "Beschriftete Lungen- und Lebermodelle aus Ugarit," *Ugaritica*, VI [1969], 165-179), the lexical paucity of *kāḇēḏ* in the Hebrew Bible is striking. Its minimal use may well be traceable to a polemic against the pervasive hepatoscopic practices of the pagan world, one aspect of a set of cultic policies by which Israel was determined to set itself apart from the nations (A. Caquot, p. 106). Indeed, there is no evidence that hepatoscopy was ever practiced as a part of Hebrew religion, contra the singular attempt of M. Bič to substantiate Amos as an hepatoscoper (*VT*, I [1951], 293-96; see a subsequent refutation in A. Murtonen, *VT*, 2 [1952], 170f.; cf. S. Segert, "Zur Bedeutung des Wortes *nōqēd*," in B. Hartmann, *et al.*, eds., *Hebräische Wortforschung* [*SVT*, 16; 1967], pp. 279-283). *See also* MESHA 3.

***Bibliography.***–A. Caquot, "La divination dans l'ancien Israël," in A. Caquot and M. Leibovici, eds., *La divination* (1968), I, 83-113; H. W. Wolff, *Anthropology of the OT* (Eng. tr. 1974), pp. 63-66.

D. G. BURKE

**LIVING; LIVE; LIVELY; ALIVE.** The adjectives "living" and "live" (Ex. 21:35; Lev. 16:20f.) are most often a translation of Heb. *ḥay* (cf. *ḥāyâ*, "have life, be alive") in the OT and of the participle of Gk. *záō* in the NT. *Ḥayyîm* can denote all beings that have life (cf. Gen. 2:19; 3:20; 9:15f.). "The land of the living" therefore denotes the opposite of Sheol, the abode of the dead (cf. Ps. 27:13; 116:9; Isa. 38:11; etc.); on "book of the living," *see* BOOK OF LIFE. In contrast to lifeless pagan deities, Yahweh is characterized as "the living God" (e.g., Dt. 5:26; Josh. 3:10; Jer. 10:10; Mt. 16:16; 26:63; Acts 14:15). "Living" is sometimes applied figuratively to inanimate objects: flowing water can be called "living water" because it gives life, and thus it serves also as a figure for the presence and Spirit of the Giver of life (Jer. 2:13; 17:13; cf. Jn. 4:10f.; 7:38; Rev. 7:17); cf. "living bread" (Jn. 6:51), "living oracles" (Acts 7:38), and "living stone(s)" (1 Pet. 2:4f.). *See* LIFE.

"Living creature" is usually a translation of Heb. *ḥayyâ* or Gk. *zṓon*; *see* CREATURE, LIVING.

The AV occasionally uses "lively" in its obsolete sense of "living" (Acts 7:38; 1 Pet. 1:3; 2:5). In Ps. 38:19 (MT 20) the RSV and NEB, following many scholars (e.g., *BHS*), emend MT *ḥayyîm* (AV "lively") to *ḥinnām*, "without cause," since *ḥayyîm* makes little sense in the context and *ḥinnām* occurs in two other very similar contexts (Ps. 35:19; 69:4 [MT 5]; in both, *ʾōyᵉḇay šeqer* parallels *śōnᵉʾay ḥinnām*). But A. A. Anderson (*Psalms 1–72* [*NCBC*, repr. 1981], p. 307) noted the value of M. Dahood's suggestion (*Psalms I* [*AB*, 1965], 237) that the MT be retained and translated "my mortal enemies" (lit. "my enemies of life," i.e., "the enemies of my life"). N. J. O.

"Alive" appears in the RSV over a hundred times, usually translating Heb. *ḥay* in the OT and Gk. *záō* in the NT. Related forms are Gk. *anazáō* ("live again," Lk. 15:24), *zōḗ* ("life," Rom. 8:10), *zōogonéō* ("keep alive," Acts 7:19), *zōopoiéō* ("make alive," 1 Cor. 15:22; Gal. 3:21; 1 Pet. 3:18), and *syzōopoiéō* ("make alive together with," Eph. 2:5 [whence supplied in v. 1]; Col. 2:13). "Alive" in Mt. 6:30 par. Lk. 12:28 renders Gk. *eimí*, "be"; "still alive" in 1 Cor. 15:6 renders Gk. *ménō*, "remain." "Alive" is often found in contrast to "dead" (e.g., 1 K. 3:23), as in expressions of concern for family by Joseph (Gen. 43:7) and Moses (Ex. 4:18). It is also used about Jesus by the women who reported their encounter with the angel at the tomb (Lk. 24:23; cf. Acts 1:3). Luke's account of the revivification of Eutychus contains the term (Acts 20:12). That Jesus was alive by virtue of His resurrection was an important element in Paul's preaching, an item that Jewish leaders disputed (25:19). The spirits of believers are alive because of Christ's righteousness bestowed on them (Rom. 8:10; see the comms.). In Gal. 3:21 Paul noted the inability of the law to "make alive." Conversely, God has made believers spiritually alive together with the risen Christ (Eph. 2:5). "We who are alive" in 1 Thess. 4:15 expresses a contrast with believers who have experienced physical death (v. 13). He. 9:17 observes that a will remains inoperative while the one who prepared it is still alive. "Made alive in spirit" in 1 Pet. 3:18 seems to refer to Christ's own spirit, in which He carried on the activity that occurred between His death and His resurrection (cf. v. 19). *See also* LIFE. E. F. H.

**LIZARD.** Of the eight unclean "swarming things" listed in Lev. 11:29f., perhaps as many as six may have had some reptilian form, and thus could be considered as lizards in a general sense. These are: Heb. *ṣāḇ* (AV TORTOISE, NEB THORN-TAILED LIZARD, RSV GREAT LIZARD), *ʾᵃnāqâ* (AV FERRET; NEB, RSV, GECKO), *kō(a)ḥ* (lit. "strength"; AV CHAMELEON; cf. LXX *chamailéōn*; RSV LAND CROCODILE, NEB SAND-GECKO), *lᵉṭāʾâ* (AV, RSV, LIZARD; NEB WALL-GECKO), *ḥōmeṭ* (AV SNAIL, NEB GREAT LIZARD, RSV SAND LIZARD), and *tinšemeṯ* (AV MOLE; cf. LXX *aspálax*, "mole"; RSV, NEB, CHAMELEON). In Prov. 30:28 *śᵉmāmîṯ* (AV SPIDER; RSV, NEB, LIZARD) seems also to convey the idea of a small reptile. The Hebrew terms are obscure at best, and are amenable to different interpretations (cf. G. R. Driver, *PEQ*, 87 [1955], 5-20; G. Bare, *Plants and Animals of the Bible* [1969], p. iii). It is also possible that the same terms carried different meanings in various parts of the ancient Near East, thus making for greater confusion.

The Heb. *lᵉṭā'â* appears to be a fairly certain designation of a lizard (cf. Arab. *laṭa'a*, "cling to the ground"), as does *śᵉmāmîṯ* (cf. Syr. *samāmîṯā'*, "venomous lizard"; but cf. postbiblical Heb. *śᵉmāmîṯ* [or *sᵉmāmîṯ*], "spider," whence AV). Again, the Heb. *ṣāḇ* has been compared with the Arab. *ḍubb*, a lizard sometimes used for food by the Bedouin (KoB, p. 790, suggests the *Uromastix spinipes*, a spiny-tailed lizard). Heb. *'ᵃnāqâ* may have referred to sounds made by the gecko, several species of which utter various cries (cf. *'ānaq*, "sigh, moan"). Heb. *kō(a)ḥ* probably refers to a large reptile, such as the land crocodile (also known as the land monitor), which may be 1.5 m. (4 ft.) long. Heb. *ḥōmeṭ* may refer to a skink (*CHAL*, p. 108), and may be cognate to Akk. *ḫamāṭu*, "hasten" (KoB, p. 310) or Aram. *ḥᵃmaṭ*, "kneel" (cf. BDB, p. 328); but cf. Syr. *ḥûlmāṭā'*, "chameleon." Heb. *tinšemeṯ* appears to derive from the root *nšm*, "pant, breathe," and thus would be a fitting name for the chameleon, which puffs up its body with air and hisses (cf. Pliny *Nat. hist.* viii.51).

Lizards were conspicuous members of the ancient Palestinian fauna, and whereas Tristram isolated twenty-two species, this number has now been enlarged greatly. The lizard is a member of the vertebrate suborder Sauria, comprising twenty separate families which contain some three thousand species across the world. Characteristically lizards are quadrupeds that have a cylinder-shaped body, a tail that is as long again as the body proper, and mobile lower eyelids. The animals vary in length from just over 2 cm. (1 in.) to 3 m. (10 ft.), but average about 30 cm. (1 ft.). Some have colored areas on the body, whereas others are barely distinguishable from their surroundings.

See G. S. Cansdale, *Animals of Bible Lands* (1970), esp. pp. 199-202.

R. K. H.

**LOAD** [(vb.) *'āmas* (Gen. 44:13; Neh. 13:15; Isa. 46:1), *nāśā'*–'lift' (Gen. 42:26; 45:23), *ṭā'an* (Gen. 45:17), *ṭāraḥ* (Job 37:11), hiphil of *kāḇaḏ*–'make heavy' (Hab. 2:6); Gk. *phortízō* (Lk. 11:46); (noun) Heb. *maśśā'* < *nāśā'* (2 K. 8:9); Gk. *phortíon* (Gal. 6:5)]; AV also BURDEN, "weary"; NEB also CARRY, PILE (ON), BURDEN, "enrich"; **LADEN** [Heb. *nāśā'* (Neh. 4:17 [MT 11]), *kāḇēḏ*–'weighty, heavy' (Isa. 1:4; Ezk. 27:25); Gk. *phortízō* (Mt. 11:28)]; AV also LADE "make glorious"; NEB also LOAD.

"Load" usually refers to a physical burden. Most of these texts are straightforward, but a few call for comment. Heb. *ṭā'an* occurs only in Gen. 45:17, but the context, and its later use in Aramaic leave no doubt about its meaning (on the supposed Ugaritic cognate see H. Cohen, *Biblical Hapax Legomena in the Light of Akkadian and Ugaritic* [1978], p. 127 n. 50). In Lam. 5:13 the RSV and NEB supply "load" (also implied by the AV), but the meaning of the whole verse is obscure (cf. LXX and Tg., both of which may refer to punishment by hanging). In 1 S. 16:20 the RSV and AV supply "laden"; the MT has *ḥᵃmôr leḥem* (lit. "ass of bread"), while the NEB "homer of bread" is based on the LXX, which apparently read *ḥōmer leḥem* (see comms.). The Hebrew verb *ṭāraḥ* occurs only in Job 37:11, but its meaning is clear from its cognate noun *ṭōraḥ*, "burden" (Dt. 1:12; Isa. 1:14). Although scholars have proposed various emendations for the verse, the MT makes sense and need not be emended (see L. Grabbe, *Comparative Philology and the Text of Job* [1971], pp. 114-16).

A few texts refer to various spiritual and emotional burdens. Thus Isaiah refers to Israel as "a people laden with iniquity," i.e., burdened with the weight of sin (1:4; cf. Ps. 39:4 [MT 5]; He. 12:1). In the first of a series of five woes Habakkuk warns the one who "loads himself with pledges," i.e., who exacts far more in securities than the loan was originally worth that he will be in turn plundered (2:6-8). The AV "ladeth himself with thick clay" points up the problem of translating the hapax legomenon *'aḇṭîṭ* (RSV "pledges"); the AV has apparently taken it as two words: *'aḇ*, "cloud," and *ṭîṭ*, "clay." Although the context and cognates (see Heb. *'āḇaṭ*, "borrow") support the RSV, 1QpHab offers an interpretation similar to the AV (see W. H. Brownlee, *Midrash Pesher of Habakkuk* [1979], p. 134).

In Mt. 11:28 Jesus invites His listeners: "Come to me, all who labor and are heavy laden, and I will give you rest." According to many scholars the burden here is Pharisaic legalism (see comms. by W. C. Allen [*ICC*, 1907], pp. 124f.; D. Hill [*NCBC*, repr. 1981], pp. 207f.; F. W. Beare [1981], pp. 267f.), though as R. Gundry pointed out, Jesus actually offered a stricter interpretation of the law than the Pharisees (*Matthew* [1982], pp. 218-220). Thus for Gundry the burden is the attention that the Pharisees demand, and the contrast is between the conceit of the Pharisees and the meekness of Jesus. T. H. Robinson (*Gospel of Matthew* [*MNTC*, 1928] pp. 105f.) took a broader view, including all the burdens of life, which Jesus shares and hence makes easier to bear (cf. also *TDNT*, IX, 86f.; A. Plummer, comm. on Matthew [repr. 1953], pp. 170f.).

In Lk. 11:46 Jesus delivers the first of a series of woes, accusing the lawyers of loading people with burdens hard to bear. According to T. W. Manson Jesus refers here to the burden of the law and implies that the lawyers do not help those struggling with this burden (*Sayings of Jesus* [repr. 1978], pp. 100f.). But according to other scholars (e.g., I. H. Marshall, *Gospel of Luke* [*NIGTC*, 1978], p. 500) the charge against the lawyers is that they escape the obligations of the laws that they impose on others.

Finally, the interpretation of Gal. 6:5 has also been disputed. The major problem is the relation of v. 5 to v. 2. According to some commentators, the "burdens" (Gk. *bárē*) of v. 2 differ from the "load" (Gk. *phortíon*) of v. 5, the former being "whatever oppresses man spiritually" (H. N. Ridderbos [Eng. tr. *NICNT*, 1970], pp. 213-15) or the "crushing weight" of temptation (D. Guthrie [*NCBC*, repr. 1981], pp. 144f.), while the latter is "the general load which all must carry" (Guthrie) or "the normal duty which falls upon every man" (Ridderbos). Cf. also *TDNT*, I, 555; F. F. Bruce, *NIGTC*, 1983, pp. 262f. But for E. Burton (*ICC*, 1920, pp. 333f.) and H. D. Betz (*Hermeneia*, 1979, pp. 303f.) no sharp distinction should be made between these terms: for Betz both terms refer to the general burdens of human life (pp. 299, 303f.), and for Burton both refer to the burdens of temptation and sin (pp. 329, 334). (The attempt of J. G. Strelan [*JBL*, 94 (1975), 266-276] to limit *bárē* to financial burdens is unconvincing.)

G. A. L.

**LOAF; LOAVES** [Heb. *leḥem*–'bread,' *kikkār*–'disk-shaped loaf of bread' (Ex. 29:23; Jgs. 8:5; 1 S. 2:36; 10:3; 1 Ch. 16:3; Prov. 6:26; Jer. 37:21); Gk. *ártos*–'bread']; AV also MORSEL, PIECE; NEB also ROUND LOAF. *See* BREAD.

**LO-AMMI** lō-am'mē lō-am'mī [Heb. *lō' 'ammî*–'not my people' (so RSV); LXX Gk. *ou laós mou,* translation rather than transliteration]. The AV and NEB transliteration of the name of the third child (second son) born to the prophet Hosea and his first wife Gomer, *ca.* 755 B.C. (Hos. 1:9). Hosea's three children were, at God's behest, given symbolic names indicating respectively coming military destruction (JEZREEL, v. 4), withdrawal of covenant protection (LO-RUHAMAH, v. 6, AV; cf. RSV "Not pitied"), and withdrawal of covenant relationship (Lo-ammi). Lo-ammi is parallelled in v. 9 by *lō'-'ehyeh lāḵem* ("I am not your *'hyh*"), an allusion to the initiation of the covenant by revelation of the divine name (Ex. 3:14). The negative impact of the name is reversed in 1:10 (MT 2:1) and 2:1 (MT 3), quoted in Rom. 9:25f. D. STUART

**LOCK.** *See* HAIR; LOCKS AND KEYS.

**LOCKS AND KEYS.** Devices for securing gates or doors. The earliest lock was a wooden bar or beam that fitted into sockets in the posts of the door or gate. Later clamps were added to the leaves of the gate so that the bar, clamps, and sockets formed a firm unit. Such a lock, of course, could not be opened from the outside, although it could be opened by an unauthorized person from within. The earliest known lock and key, from *ca.* 2000 B.C., was discovered at Khorsabad; it consists of a wooden beam and wooden pegs or pins that drop into holes in the beam so that it cannot be slid back from the socket in the door-post. The key is also made of wood; its pins are arranged so that they lift the pins from the bar, permitting the bar to be withdrawn from the socket. The Egyptians had a similar lock and key.

The Romans invented the metal lock and key. The lock was made with wards surrounding the keyhole, and the key had slots cut so that it would turn in these wards. A key not properly cut would not turn, and the lock could not be unlocked.

In the OT the noun *man'ûl,* "bar," "bolt," "lock" (Neh. 3:3, 6, 13-15) and the verb from which it was derived, *nā'al,* "bar," "bolt," "lock" (2 S. 13:18), are found. Other OT terms are *b^erî(a)ḥ,* "bar," "shaft" (Dt. 3:5, etc.), *baddîm* (pl. only), "poles," "bars" (Hos. 11:6; Job 17:16 [fig. of the bars of Sheol]), and *m^eṭîl,* "bar [of iron]" (Job 40:18). The word for "key" is *maptē(a)ḥ,* "that which opens," "opener," from *pāṭaḥ,* "open" (Jgs. 9:25; 1 Ch. 9:27; Isa. 22:22 [fig.]; cf. Rev. 3:7). Jgs. 3:23-25 describes the use of the lock and key.

The Greek equivalents, *kleíthron* and *mochlós,* both meaning "bar," "bolt," occur in the LXX but not in the NT. Unlike the Hebrew word for key, which comes from the verb "open," *kleís* comes from the verb *kleíō,* "close," "lock" (Acts 5:23; cf. Mt. 6:6; Rev. 3:8).

In Cant. 4:12; 5:4f., according to one interpretation, the imagery of locks and doors is used euphemistically in an erotic love song (see M. Pope, *Song of Songs* [*AB,* 1977], pp. 488, 518-525).

*See* KEY; KEYS, POWER OF THE.

***Bibliography.***–*Enc.Brit.* (1970), xiv, 186-88; V. J. M. Eras, *Locks and Keys Throughout the Ages* (Eng. tr. 1957). W. S. L. S.

Left: Roman bronze sliding key for tumble lock. Right: Roman iron sliding key. Bottom: large Roman iron key for sliding bolt (Royal Ontario Museum, Toronto)

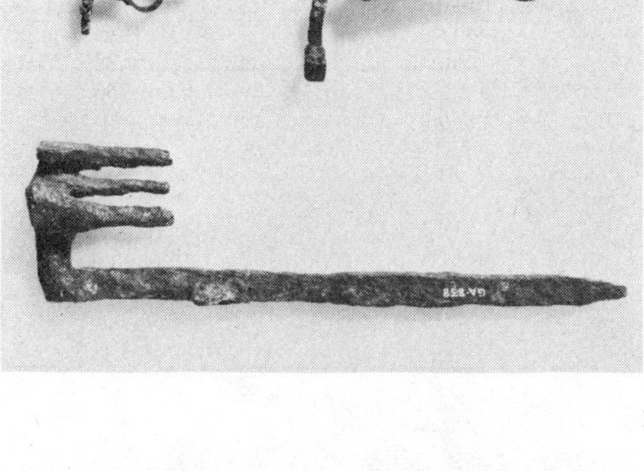

**LOCUST** [Heb. *'arbeh* < *rāḇâ*–'increase, multiply' (Ex. 10:4, 12-14, 19; Lev. 11:22a; etc.; "swarming locust," Joel 1:4; 2:25), *yeleq* (Nah. 3:15a, 16; "hopping locust," Joel 1:4; "young locust," Ps. 105:34b), *ḥāsîl* < *ḥāsal*–'devour' ("destroying locust," Joel 1:4), *gāzām* (Am. 4:9; "cutting locust," Joel 1:4), *gōḇay* (Am. 7:1; Nah. 3:17), *gôḇ* (Nah. 3:17), *gēḇ* (Isa. 33:4), *ḥāgāḇ* (2 Ch. 7:13), *sol'ām* ("bald locust," Lev. 11:22), *ṣ^elāṣal* (Dt. 28:42); Gk. *akrís* (Mt. 3:4 par. Mk. 1:6; Rev. 9:3, 7)]; AV also "palmerworm," "cankerworm," "caterpillar" (all in Joel 1:4), GRASSHOPPER (Nah. 3:17), etc.; NEB also GREAT LOCUST, LONG-HEADED LOCUST, GREEN LOCUST, DESERT LOCUST (all in Lev. 11:22), "grub" (Ps. 78:46), etc.; **GRASSHOPPER** [Heb. *ḥāgāḇ* (Lev. 11:22; Nu. 13:33; Eccl. 12:5; Isa. 40:22), *'arbeh* (Nah. 3:15, 17)]; AV also LOCUST, NEB also HOPPER, DESERT LOCUST, LOCUST. A jumping or leaping insect of the order *Orthoptera.* Although the terms grasshopper and locust are often used interchangeably, grasshoppers encompass two families (*Acridiidae* and *Tettigoniidae*), whereas locusts are only a few species of the *Acridiidae* family. Both insects can cause great devastation to plant life.

*I. Identification.*–The Heb. *'arbeh* is the most common OT word for locust; it refers to a clean species that is fully developed. Heb. *yeleq* perhaps refers to an insect at an immature stage of growth (see "young locust," Ps. 105:34b; "hopping locust," Joel 1:4). *Ḥāsîl* may also describe a locust at a particular stage of its development. *Gāzām* may indicate an underdeveloped form of locust, rather than a separate species. *Gōḇay* and *gēḇ* refer to swarms of locusts; in Nah. 3:17 many scholars delete *gôḇ* as a gloss (e.g., *BHS*; but cf. KD). *Ḥāgāḇ* is a clean species, perhaps one or more of the small grasshoppers. *Sol'ām* is also a clean species, perhaps one of the genera Truxalis or Acrida. *Ṣ^elāṣal* is an onomatopoeic word meaning "whirring," an accurate description of the sound made by a locust swarm. The LXX *erysíbē* (Vulg. *rubigo*), "rusty," suggests the reddish cricket *Gryllotalpa* (so NEB "mole-cricket"). Heb. *ḥargōl* in Lev. 11:22 (RSV "cricket") may be of the family *Tettigoniidae* (see NEB "green locust").

The most common LXX term is *akrís,* the same word used in the NT (cf. also *broúchos,* "wingless locust," Lev. 11:22; 1 K. 8:37; Nah. 3:15).

*II. Habits.*–Biblical writers were mainly concerned with the *Schistocerca gregaria,* the desert locust. This locust is responsible for periodic devastating attacks upon the vegetation of the Mediterranean region. The migratory locust (*Locusta migratoria*) and the Moroccan locust (*Dociastaurus maroccanus*) have also been reported in Palestine.

The migratory locust matures in three stages, each of which exhibits the essential characteristics of a hopping insect. The first stage, or larva, is represented by wingless locusts which hop like fleas. In the second stage, the pupa, the wings of the locust are encased in a sack. The locusts of the second stage walk like ordinary insects with only occasional jumping. The adult stage is the full-fledged

Grasshoppers and oxen heads in a ceiling pattern from the tomb of Neferhotep in Thebes (late 14th cent. B.C.) (Oriental Institute, University of Chicago)

flying insect. The locust is quite destructive at each stage of its development.

Locusts multiply rapidly, with eggs deposited by females with ovipositors containing as many as one hundred eggs each. They enable the female to deposit her eggs in holes some 26 cm. (4 in.) deep, even in the hardest of soils.

Descriptions by observers leave little question concerning the destructive potential of locusts in migration. Once such a plague begins, it is virtually impossible to control or stop, bringing tremendous destruction to affected areas. Swarms of ten billion locusts periodically enter areas in Africa, southwest Asia, and southern Europe. Areas up to 1000 sq. km. (400 sq. mi.) can be covered by locust swarms, which leave a barren, denuded landscape in their wake. It is easy to see why the locust is identified as one of biblical man's greatest calamities.

***III. Theological Significance of Locusts.***–Locusts are "clean" animals that can be used for food by the Hebrew people (Lev. 11), but they also represent an instrument of divine wrath. Thus in Rev. 9:3, 7 the locusts are used as an eschatological plague of God, and while they may be symbolic, their use is consistent with the OT concept of the plague locust.

*A. Locusts as Food.* Lev. 11:22 presents several insects that are considered "clean" and suitable as part of the diet of the Hebrew people, as do the Gospel references to John the Baptist's diet (Mt. 3:4 par. Mk. 1:6). The thorax of the locust is prepared by modern Arabs for food. The head is pulled away, bringing the viscera with it. The abdomen and legs are removed. The thoraxes may be eaten at once or dried for later use. All the insect references in Lev. 11 involve the locust family.

*B. Plague Locusts as Instruments of Divine Wrath. 1. The Egyptian Plague of Ex. 10.* The locusts of Ex. 10 (all Heb. *'arbeh*) are said to "cover the face of the land," "eat every tree," and "fill your houses" (vv. 3-6). This description is remarkably similar to descriptions of the plague of locusts that swept through Palestine in the spring of 1915.

*2. Locusts and the Day of the Lord in Joel.* Joel's controversial references to locusts form part of his message concerning the coming Day of the Lord. This event is of great eschatological significance for Israel, but its nature contradicts much of the popular tradition associated with the Day of the Lord. Whereas the prophets proclaimed judgment upon a disobedient and rebellious people, the popular tradition portrayed the Day of the Lord as a time when God would vindicate Israel in the presence of its enemies and affirm it as His covenant people, thus ignoring national sin.

Joel's locust invasion (1:4; 2:25) is a vivid description of God's judgment in action. The terrifying image of destruction is graphically represented in a way the people cannot ignore. As early as Credner (1831), an attempt was made to identify Joel's use of various locust names as representative developmental stages in the locust cycle. Whereas Credner used *'arbeh,* for one of the less significant developmental stages, subsequent research indicates that *yeleq, ḥāsîl,* and *gāzām* may describe successive stages in the developing locust.

Alternatively, the multiple use of names for locusts as rhetorical devices would serve to emphasize the complete destruction caused by the locusts. This interpretation is less complicated and is felt by many scholars to be the more credible of the two. However the use of multiple names is interpreted, the physical description of the locust invasion seems to indicate an actual plague, not a symbolic image. At the same time, use of terms like the "northerner" (2:20) may suggest directly the destructive locusts, but may also allow for the more symbolic identification with those "northern" foes who act as God's agents of judgment upon Israel in the 8th-6th cents. B.C.

*C. Locusts as Images.* Locusts (and grasshoppers) were used frequently in biblical imagery. As one might expect, most of the imagery concerns the prominent characteristics of this insect: leaping ability (Job 39:20; Isa. 33:4; Jer. 51:27), devouring appetite (Nah. 3:15f.), large numbers (Jgs. 6:5; 7:12; Jer. 46:23; etc.), and small size (Nu. 13:33; Isa. 40:22; cf. Ps. 109:23).

***Bibliography.***–L. C. Allen, *Books of Joel, Obadiah, Jonah and Micah* (*NICOT,* 1976); J. A. Bewer, comm. on Joel (*ICC,* 1911); K. A. Credner, *Der Prophet Joel* (1831); G. Hort, *ZAW,* 70 (1958), 48-59; E. Kutsch, *Theologische Zeitschrift,* 18 (1962), 81-94; O. R. Sellers, *AJSL,* 52 (1935-36), 81-85; J. A. Thompson, *JNES,* 14 (1955), 52-55; J. D. Whiting, *National Geographic Magazine,* 27 (1915), 511-550; H. W. Wolff, *Joel and Amos* (Eng. tr., *Hermeneia,* 1977).

G. L. KEOWN

**LOD** lod; **LYDDA** lid'ə [Heb. *lôḏ*; Gk. *Lydda*]. A Benjaminite town located in the picturesque plain of Sharon 18 km. (11 mi.) SE of Joppa. The name's earliest appearance is in the inscription of Thutmose III (1482-1450 B.C.) at Karnak, which lists it among the Palestinian towns held by Egypt. In 1 Ch. 8:12 the construction of the Israelite town of Lod, along with Ono, is attributed to Shemed of Benjamin. After the Babylonian Exile, families from Lod, Ono, and Hadid, numbering about 725 exiles, returned to their home towns in 521 B.C. (Ezr. 2:33; Neh. 7:37; 11:35).

Lod was located at the intersection of the highway between Babylon and Egypt with the main road between Jerusalem and Joppa. It was therefore of great military and commercial importance. In the Maccabean period it

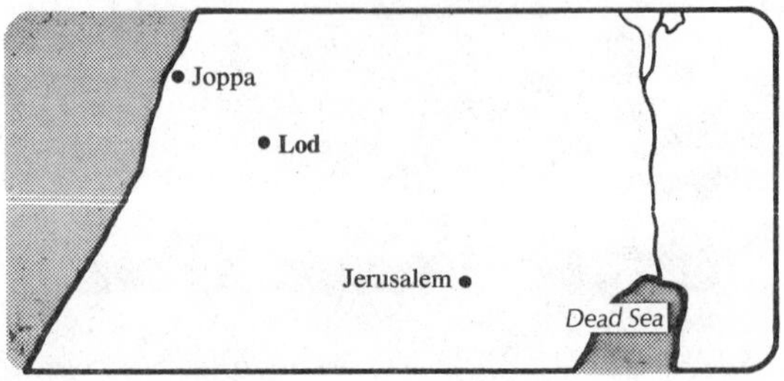

was known as Lydda. Under Syrian rule it was part of Samaria, but in 145 B.C. it was one of three Samaritan districts that were annexed to Judea by King Demetrius II at the request of Jonathan Maccabeus (1 Macc. 11:34; cf. 10:30, 38; 11:28; Josephus *Ant.* xiii.4.9 [127]). According to Josephus, Lydda presided over one of the eleven toparchies into which Judea was divided (*BJ* iii.3.5 [54-58]). Along with nearby Joppa, Lydda was granted by Julius Caesar to John Hyrcanus and the Jews (*Ant.* xiv.10.6 [205-208]). After Caesar's death, however, the inhabitants of Lydda and certain other towns were sold into slavery by Cassius for failing to pay the taxes he had demanded (*Ant.* xiv.11.2 [271-76]). Subsequently they were released by a decree of Marcus Antonius (*Ant.* xiv.12.2 [304f.]). Lydda suffered severely under Cestius Gallus, who in A.D. 66 burned the city while its inhabitants were celebrating the Feast of Tabernacles in Jerusalem (*BJ* ii.19.1 [515f.]). Along with Jamnia it surrendered in A.D. 68 to Vespasian, who populated the city with inhabitants from other places (*BJ* iv.8.1 [444]).

In NT times Lydda was the site of an early Christian community. It was during a visit to this community that Peter healed the paralyzed Aeneas (Acts 9:32-35) and was summoned to nearby Joppa upon the death of Tabitha (v. 38). After the fall of Jerusalem in A.D. 70, Lydda became noted as a seat of rabbinical learning. *Ca.* 200, however, it was made a Roman colony and renamed Diospolis. It became a center of trade in purple. Judaism virtually disappeared from the city, but Christianity survived. In the 4th cent. Diospolis had its own bishop, who attended the Council of Nicea (325). The trial of Pelagius for heresy took place at the Synod of Diospolis in 415.

Under Moslem rule Lydda was a provincial capital and boasted a magnificent mosque. During this time the city grew famous due to legends surrounding St. George, who according to tradition was martyred there in 303. The city's large Christian church was destroyed by the Moslems but captured by the Crusaders, who built a new cathedral over St. George's tomb and dedicated it to him. For a time the city itself was called St. George. The cathedral, however, was demolished by Saladin in 1191 and by the Mongols in 1271; only ruins remain. The Arabs restored the city's original name, calling it Ludd.

Modern Lod is located about 18 km. (11 mi.) E of Tel Aviv and accommodates Israel's international airport.

***Bibliography.***–*EAEHL*, III, *s.v.* "Lod" (J. Kaplan); *GB*, rev., p. 134; *HGHL*, pp. 159-162. W. EWING R. K. H.

**LO-DEBAR** lō'də-bär [Heb. *lô ḏ^e^ḇār* (2 S. 9:4f.), *lō' ḏ^e^ḇār* (17:27)–meaning uncertain]. A Transjordanian site in the region of Gilead. It was near Mahanaim, but its precise location is not certain (see *GTTOT*, §§ 300, 769, 1515).

Mephibosheth the son of Jonathan lived after Saul's death at the home of Machir the son of Ammiel at Lodebar; David brought him from there to join the royal household in Jerusalem (2 S. 9:4f.). When David fled before Absalom and arrived at Mahanaim, Machir of Lodebar was among those who brought provisions to him (17:27-29).

According to the MT of Josh. 13:26, the division of Gad extended from Mahanaim to the border or territory *lid^e^ḇir.* The AV and RSV read "of Debir" (with LXX, Syr., Vulg.; RSV mg. "Lidebir"). Many scholars and the NEB agree with F. M. Abel, who identifies it with the Lo-debar of 2 S. 17:27 and as modern Umm ed-Dabar (or Dubar), about 14 km. (9 mi.) S of the Sea of Galilee (*GP*, II, 304; cf. *WHAB*, p. 40). *See* DEBIR.

Amos 6:13 addresses those who rejoice in *lō' ḏāḇār*, apparently a reference to military successes of Jeroboam II in Transjordan. The RSV text gives the place name "Lodebar," but the margin reads "a thing of nought" (with AV; NEB "a nothing"). The expression is possibly a play on words (*see* KARNAIM). C. E. DE VRIES

**LODGE; LODGING PLACE.** *See* INN.

**LOFT** (1 K. 17:19, AV). *See* CHAMBER.

**LOFTY; LOFTILY; LOFTINESS** [Heb. *gāḇô(a)h, mārôm* (Ps. 73:8), niphal part. of *nāśā'* (Isa. 57:15), *rûm* (Isa. 2:12), *śāgaḇ* (Isa. 26:5); Gk. *hyperochē* (1 Cor. 2:1)]; AV also EMINENT, EXALT, EXCELLENCY, HAUGHTY, HIGH, LIFTED UP; NEB also EXALTED, FINE, HAUGHTY, HIGH, PROUD, SCORNFULLY, TOP.

Referring to a state of elevated height, perhaps of imposing or towering proportions. Hence, reference is made to lofty battlements (Zeph. 1:16), trees (Isa. 2:13; Ezk. 17:22; 31:14), hills (Isa. 2:14), and mountains (Isa. 30:25; 57:7; Ezk. 17:22). A further extension of the word denotes the starry abode or even the very being of God Himself (Job 22:12; Ps. 104:13; Isa. 57:15).

The "lofty places" of Ezk. 16:24-39 are elements of an allegory in which the prophet indicts the Israelites for playing the harlot (see v. 16) and being faithless to their true husband, Yahweh. In keeping with this context of spiritual adultery, "lofty places" are thinly veiled references to the "high places" of Canaanite nature religion, where sexual immorality was rampant. Symbolically, then, the religious cultus of Israel, i.e., its shrines, sacrifices, temple, and faith, had become a "lofty place," a spiritual brothel. It had polluted the land, and thus, had become like the Canaanites (cf. Lev. 18:19-28; Dt. 18:9-12). Another allegory is found in Ezk. 31:14. Here Pharaoh and his cohorts are likened to a lofty cedar (vv. 2f.) which God will strike down because of their pride.

Figuratively, the word "lofty" came to mean hubris, haughtiness, or arrogance. A statistical study of its most important Hebrew root, *gbh* (the root of *gāḇô[a]h*), indicates that this root is most frequently found in wisdom sayings. When so used it is a comment on the idolatry of the horizontal domain that exalts itself against the vertical and transcendent dominion of God. Human "loftiness" is an encroachment on that which rightfully belongs to Him alone. Thus, lofty are the eyes (Prov. 30:13) and threats (Ps. 73:8)) of the proud and arrogant (Jer. 48:29, note the amplifying synonyms). Therefore, there is a day of reckoning, on which all that is "lofty" (Isa. 2:12; cf. 10:33) will be leveled by divine judgment, a day in which "the Lord alone will be exalted" (12:17). But, further, it must also be a day of victory for all those humble of spirit, for the true "lofty one who inhabits eternity" also dwells with them (Isa. 57:15).

In 1 Cor. 2:1 Paul asserts that he did not preach to the Corinthians in "lofty words or wisdom" (the nuance of "lofty" is more appropriate than AV "excellency of speech"). The Gk. *hyperochē* means superiority; what Paul means is that he did not distinguish himself by his oratory or wisdom, for that would have detracted from the gospel (cf. v. 2). See F. Grosheide, comm. on 1 Corinthians (*NICNT*, 1953), pp. 57f.

*See also* EXALT.

See *TDOT*, II, *s.v.* "gābhah" (Hentschke).

K. H. MAAHS

**LOG** [Heb. *qôrâ*–'beam' (2 K. 6:2, 5), *'ēṣ*–'tree, timber' (Eccl. 10:9; Ezk. 24:10); Gk. *xýlon*–'wood' as construction material (1 Esd. 5:55 [LXX 53]), *dokós*–'beam' (Mt. 7:3-5 par. Lk. 6:41f.)].

Hebrew *ʿēṣ* and Gk. *xýlon* are more general terms, while Heb. *qôrâ* and Gk. *dokós* have to do with wood used in construction. The beams sought by the sons of the prophets need not have been large, only what would have been needed for the minimal shelter required in the Jericho area (J. Gray, *I & II Kings* [*OTL*, 2nd ed. 1970], p. 511). In Ezk. 24:5 the term "log" is supplied from v. 10, substituting *hāʿēṣîm* ("the logs") for *hāʿaṣāmîm* ("the bones"), which occurs in the next line of v. 5 (see RSV mg.). Gk. *dokós* is used as a striking contrast with the *kárphos*, a tiny piece of straw or wood.

For Lev. 14:10, 12, 15, 21, 24, *see* WEIGHTS AND MEASURES.

E. W. S.

**LOGIA** lō'jē-ə, lō'gē-ə.

*I. Definition.–Logia,* "sayings," is the plural of Gk. *lógion,* which is a diminutive form of *lógos,* "word." In classical texts *lógion* means an oracle, the saying of a deity. In the LXX it denotes the word of God. It is used in the NT as the "oracles" of God (Acts 7:38; Rom. 3:2; He. 5:12; 1 Pet. 4:11). Polyc. Phil. 7:1 mentions "the *logia* of the Lord."

Scholars use the word to designate sayings of Jesus, especially collections of sayings that the Gospel writers may have used. It has also been applied to the sayings of Jesus found among the Oxyrhynchus papyri, the Semitic source associated by Papias with Matthew, the so-called Q source of the Synoptic Gospels, and the sayings of Jesus in the Gospel of Thomas.

Oxy. P. 1, containing (on two sides) the Greek form of logia 26b-33 of the Gospel of Thomas. Logion 27 reads: "Jesus said, 'If you do not fast as regards the world, you will not find the Kingdom. If you do not observe the Sabbath as a Sabbath, you will not see the Father.'" (Bodleian Library, Oxford)

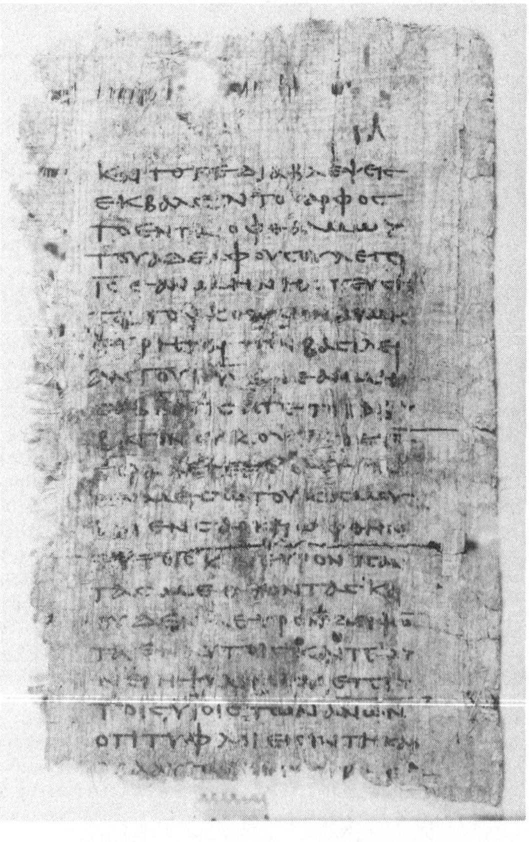

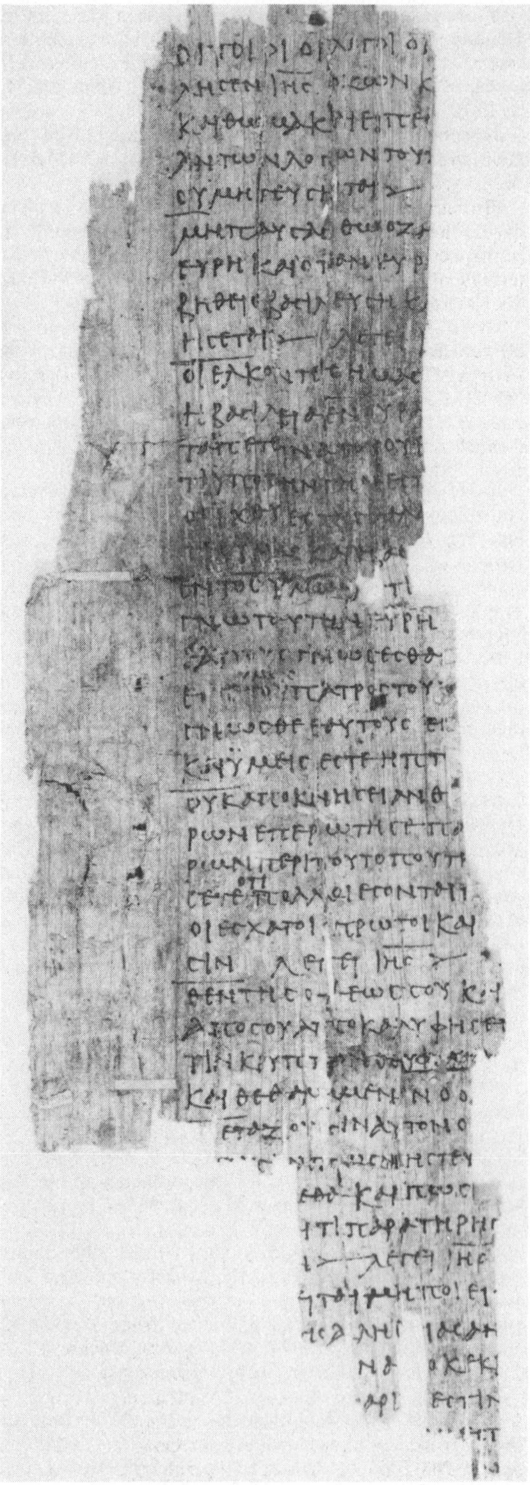

Oxy. P. 654, containing the prologue and logia 1-6 of the Gospel of Thomas (note that the ends of the lines are missing). A reconstruction of logion 2 reads: "Jesus said, 'Let him who seeks not cease seeking until he finds; and when he finds he will be amazed, and being amazed, he will rule, and ruling he will rest'" (cf. the Nag Hammadi reading: "he will marvel and he will reign over the All") (British Library)

*II. Oxyrhynchus Papyri.*–In 1897 B. P. Grenfell and A. S. Hunt discovered at Oxyrhynchus in Egypt a Greek papyrus fragment (Oxy. P. 1) containing seven noncanonical sayings attributed to Jesus (see *ISBE* [1929], III, *s.v.* [W. T. Smith]). The papyrus is dated *ca.* A.D. 200. Two other fragments (Oxy. P. 654 and 655), containing six and four additional sayings, were discovered in 1904 and dated to the 3rd cent. A.D.

In their initial publication in 1897 Grenfell and Hunt named the material *Logia Iēsou* ("Sayings of Jesus"). In retrospect, the designation was misleading. Though the term *lógoi,* "words," is found in these fragments, nowhere does the term *lógia* appear.

These discoveries caused great excitement and set off numerous speculations about the nature of these new sayings of Jesus (see the bibliography listed by Fitzmyer, pp. 420-433). A number of the APOCRYPHAL GOSPELS were considered as the source of these sayings, such as the Gospel According to the Egyptians (so A. Harnack, *Expos.* 5th ser., 6 [1897], 404-416), the Gospel According to the Hebrews (Grenfell and Hunt; P. Battifol, *RB,* 6 [1897], 501-515), and the Gospel of the Ebionites (T. Zahn, *Neue kirchliche Zeitschrift,* 16 [1905], 94-105, 165-178). Others wished to connect the sayings with the *logia* spoken of by Papias, which he claimed were used by Matthew. Not until the discovery of the Nag Hammadi Library in 1945 were the Oxyrhynchus papyri identified with certainty. They are now known to be copies of the Greek text of the Gospel of Thomas, which was recovered in a complete Coptic translation from Nag Hammadi. Oxy. P. 654 corresponds to the prologue and the first six logia of Thomas, Oxy. P. 1 matches logia 26-33, and, Oxy. P. 655 logia 36-39 of Thomas (see Fitzmyer, Till).

*III. Papias and the Gospel of Matthew.*–Papias bishop of Hierapolis (*ca.* 60-130) is an early but not always discriminating witness of the postapostolic period. According to Eusebius (*HE* iii.39) he wrote a work that has not been preserved entitled "Interpretation of the Lord's Logia." Eusebius quoted him as claiming: "Matthew compiled the oracles [*tá lógia*] in the Hebrew [i.e., Aramaic] language, and everyone translated [or "interpreted"] them as best he could."

Ever since F. Schleiermacher (*Theologische Studien und Kritiken,* 5 [1832], 735ff.) suggested that the logia mentioned by Papias should be understood not as the Gospel of Matthew but as a collection of the sayings of Jesus, their identification has been extensively discussed. Among the suggestions made are the following: (1) oracles from the OT, in particular messianic testimonia (so J. R. Harris, *Contemporary Review,* 72 [July-Dec. 1897], 341-48); (2) logia from the apocryphal Gospel According to the Hebrews (Grant); (3) the hypothetical source K (for *Koinos*) of the Synoptic Gospels (P. Parker); (4) the hypothetical source Q of the Synoptic Gospels (T. W. Manson, *Sayings of Jesus* [1957; repr. 1979], pp. 18-20; see IV below); (5) a collection of sayings and deeds of Jesus incorporated into the Gospel of Matthew (J. Munck, *HTR,* 52 [1959], 228; C. F. D. Moule, *Birth of the NT* [1962; 2nd ed. 1966], p. 89; Tasker concluded that the apostle Matthew originally compiled Papias's logia in Aramaic and later incorporated them into his Gospel; see Martin, pp. 238-243); (6) the Aramaic original of the Gospel of Matthew. Though some scholars such as Torrey, Burney, Black, and most recently Zimmermann have argued that parts of the Gospels or even entire Gospels were based on Aramaic originals, most scholars are convinced that the Gospel of Matthew was composed in Greek and not translated from Aramaic.

*IV. Quelle.*–One of the more popular suggestions for the identification of Papias's logia is the hypothetical source Q (from Ger. *Quelle,* "source"), which designates the non-Markan material common to Matthew and Luke. These two hundred or so verses include the Lord's Prayer, the Sermon on the Mount, and many other sayings of Jesus.

As early as 1838 C. H. Weisse (*Die evangelische Geschichte kritisch und philosophisch bearbeitet* [2 vols., 1838]) had discerned such a distinctive source. For a long time a two-source (Mark and Q) approach to the Synoptic Gospels was the dominant view, but it has been criticized for some years (see Martin, pp. 143-160). Because of its relatively amorphous nature some (e.g., Parker) have even questioned the existence of Q as a distinct document.

J. M. Robinson sought to isolate a new *Gattung* (literary genre) called *lógoi sophṓn*, "sayings of the sages," derived from Jewish wisdom traditions, which would include Q and the Gospel of Thomas in a gnosticizing trajectory. According to Koester, "Thus, Thomas does not use Q, but he does represent the eastern branch of the gattung, *logoi,* the western branch being represented by the synoptic *logoi* of Q, which was used in western Syria by Matthew and later by Luke" (Robinson and Koester, p. 136; cf. Devisch, Worden).

*V. Gospel of Thomas.*–The Gospel of Thomas contains 114 logia or sayings ascribed to Jesus, about half of which are related to sayings of Jesus found in the Synoptic Gospels. It is striking that there are no direct allusions to events in the life of Jesus such as His infancy, baptism, crucifixion, or resurrection.

Although some scholars, e.g., Koester, have argued for the early Palestinian origin and the independent value of the Gospel of Thomas, the Gnostic (or Encratite) cast of these logia make it extremely dubious that more than a few are genuine agrapha (cf. MacRae, Ménard, Schoedel). *See* AGRAPHA.

*VI. Form Criticism and the Logia of Jesus.*–Radical form critics such as R. Bultmann have supposed that most of the dominical logia in the Gospels are not the actual sayings of Jesus but were created in the post-Easter preaching of the early Church and originally circulated orally as separate pericopes over a considerable period of time. These critics reject as unauthentic the sayings of Jesus that: (1) accord with the teaching of the early Church; (2) accord with the contemporary teaching of Judaism; (3) presuppose a situation unthinkable at the time of Jesus; (4) contradict other, more genuine sayings; or (5) are shown when compared with the Gospels to be a development of something found in them (Calvert, p. 211; Marrow). Moderate critics have pointed out that these criteria are too narrowly based on circular arguments and presuppose an unreasonable isolation of Jesus' teachings from Judaism and from the early Church (cf. Carlston, Hooker [*NTS*], Stanton). Jesus, it is believed, customarily spoke in Aramaic, although he certainly knew Hebrew and possibly even Greek. Conservative scholars have recognized that the differences in the citations of Jesus' logia indicate that usually the Gospels do not attempt to preserve the *ipsissima verba* ("very words") of Jesus but rather His *ipsissima vox* ("very voice"). These scholars have acknowledged that the Evangelists modified the logia of Jesus but have denied that they or the early Christians created them (cf. Chilton, France, Longenecker, Maier).

*VII. Authentic Words of Jesus.*–In contrast to the skepticism of some form critics about the possibility of recovering authentic sayings of Jesus, other scholars have noted elements that give reason for optimism. J. Jeremias, for example, has identified in Jesus' sayings distinctive words, e.g., "Abba," and certain Aramaisms. H. Schürmann has shown that even on purely form-critical grounds scholars must deal with the fact that the followers of Jesus began to preserve His sayings even before Easter.

The Swedish scholars H. Riesenfeld and B. Gerhardsson have argued that Jesus like the rabbis must have taught his disciples to memorize His sayings. He transmitted them by text and commentary, terse and incisive statements, didactic and poetic devices, repetition, half-sung recitation, and written memoranda. According to Gerhardsson (*Origins of the Gospel Tradition* [1977], p. 69), Jesus' teachings were not prosaic, everyday statements: "Rather they consist of brief, laconic, well-rounded texts, of pointed statements with a clear profile, rich in content and poetic in form." This feature facilitated their accurate transmission. Gerhardsson (*Memory and Manuscript* [1961], p. 335) concluded, "They [the evangelists] worked on a basis of a fixed, distinct tradition from, and about, Jesus — a tradition which was partly memorized and partly written down in notebooks and private scrolls, but invariably isolated from the teachings of other doctrinal authorities."

The Riesenfeld-Gerhardsson thesis has been criticized (e.g., by M. Smith) on the grounds that it is uncertain that the rabbis used such methods prior to A.D. 70 and that the disciples cannot be compared to the "scholarly" disciples of the rabbis. Some scholars, such as R. Gundry and E. Ellis, have accepted the possibility that the disciples wrote down Jesus' sayings. This assumption would dispense with the long oral period presupposed by form critics and do much to insure the transmission of authentic logia of Jesus.

***Bibliography.***– D. E. Aune, *Jesus and the Synoptic Gospels* (1980); H. Biggs, *Themelios,* 6/2 (1981), 18-27; M. Black, *Aramaic Approach to the Gospels and Acts* (3rd ed. 1967); C. F. Burney, *Aramaic Origin of the Fourth Gospel* (1922); D. G. A. Calvert, *NTS,* 18 (1971/72), 209-219; C. E. Carlston, *JBL,* 99 (1980), 87-105; B. D. Chilton, *Themelios,* 3 (1978), 78-85; J. J. C. Cox, *Andrews University Seminary Studies,* 15 (1977), 97-113; 17 (1979), 1-15; 18 (1980), 17-36; B. Dehandschutter, *L'Évanglie selon Thomas: témoin d'une tradition prélucanienne?* (1973); M. Devisch, *Ephemerides Theologicae Lovanienses,* 51 (1975), 82-89; J. Dunn, *NTS,* 24 (1977), 175-198; E. E. Ellis, *Prophecy and Hermeneutic in Early Christianity* (1978), pp. 237-253; J. A. Fitzmyer, *Essays on the Semitic Background of the NT* (1971), pp. 355-433; R. T. France, "The Authenticity of the Sayings of Jesus," in C. Brown, ed., *History, Criticism and Faith* (1976), pp. 101-143; R. T. France and D. Wenham, eds., *Gospel Perspectives,* I (1980); R. H. Fuller, *St. Luke's Journal of Theology,* 23 (1980), 90-100; B. Gerhardsson, *Tradition and Transmission in Early Christianity* (1964); R. M. Grant, *ATR,* 25 (1943), 218-222; B. P. Grenfell and A. S. Hunt, *New Classical Fragments and Other Greek and Latin Papyri* (1897); R. H. Gundry, *Use of the OT in St. Matthew's Gospel* (1967); D. Guthrie, *NT Intro.,* I (1965), pp. 31-41; M. D. Hooker, *NTS,* 17 (1970/71), 480-87; *Theology,* 75 (1972), 570-581; *IDB Supp, s.v.* "Thomas, Gospel of" (J. E. Ménard); J. Jeremias, *NT Theology* (Eng. tr. 1971), pp. 3-8, *passim*; R. N. Longenecker, "Literary Criteria in Life of Jesus Research," in G. F. Hawthorne, ed., *Current Issues in Biblical and Patristic Interpretation* (1975), pp. 217-229; G. W. MacRae, *CBQ,* 22 (1960), 56-71; W. A. Maier, *Form Criticism Reexamined* (1973); S. B. Marrow, *Words of Jesus in Our Gospels* (1979); R. P. Martin, *NT Foundations I: The Four Gospels* (1975), pp. 143-150, 238-243; G. R. Osborne, *JETS,* 19 (1976), 73-85; 21 (1978), 117-130; 22 (1979), 305-322; P. Parker, *JBL,* 100 (1981), 389-413; H. Riesenfeld, *Gospel Tradition* (1970); J. M. Robinson and H. Koester, *Trajectories through Early Christianity* (1971); W. R. Schoedel, *Concordia Theological Monthly,* 43 (1972), 548-560; H. Schürmann, "Die voröstlichen Anfänge der Logientradition," in H. Ristow and K. Matthiae, eds., *Der historische Jesus und der Kerygmatische Christus* (1962), pp. 342-370; M. Smith, *JBL,* 82 (1963), 169-176; G. N. Stanton, "Form Criticism Revisited," in M. D. Hooker and C. J. A. Hickling, eds., *What about the NT?* (1975), pp. 13-27; R. H. Stein, *JETS,* 24 (1981), 127-130; R. V. G. Tasker, *Gospel According to St. Matthew* (*Tyndale NT Comms.,* 1961); R. O. P. Taylor, *Groundwork of the Gospels* (1946); H. M. Teeple, *JBL,* 89 (1970), 56-68; W. C. Till, *BJRL,* 41 (1959), 446-458; C. C. Torrey, *JBL,* 61 (1942), 71-85; J. W. Wenham, *Trinity Journal,* 7 (1978), 112-134; R. D. Worden, *JBL,* 94 (1975), 532-546; F. Zimmermann, *Aramaic Origin of the Four Gospels* (1979).

E. M. YAMAUCHI

**LOGOS.** *See* WORD.

**LOINS** [Heb. *moṯnayim*]; NEB also WAIST, BODY, LIMBS, MIGHT, etc.; [*ḥ^alāṣayim*] (Job 31:20; 38:3; 40:7; Isa. 11:5; 32:11; Jer. 30:6); AV also REINS; NEB BODY, WAISTS, SIDES, etc.; [*kesel*] (Lev. 3:4, 10, 15; 4:9; 7:4; Job 15:27; Ps. 38:7 [MT 8]); AV also FLANKS; NEB also HAUNCHES, SIDES; [Gk. *osphýs*] (Lk. 12:35; Eph. 6:14; He. 7:10); NEB also paraphrases. The RSV conjectures "loins" (Heb. *mēʿîm*–"bowels," "belly") in Isa. 48:1, while the AV has "waters" (*mayim,* with the MT), the NEB "seed" (with the Targum [*zeraʿ*]), and the LXX only "from Judah." For further discussion of this passage, see comms. (e.g., C. R. North, *Second Isaiah* [1964], p. 174).

The loins designate that general area of the body between the ribs and the thighs, the midsection between the upper and lower body that includes the hips, the small of the back, the waist, and the reproductive organs. As the place of the reproductive organs, the loins frequently denote virility and procreation: the Hebrew idiom "come forth from [someone's] loins" (cf. He. 7:10) indicates physical birth, descent, or generation. The RSV, however, tends to paraphrase this idiom: Gen. 35:11, "kings shall spring from you" (NEB "kings shall spring from your body"; AV "kings shall come out of thy loins"); 1 K. 8:19, "your son who shall be born to you" (NEB "the son who is to be born to you"; AV "thy son that shall come forth out of thy loins").

The waist or loins are naturally the place to wear a belt or girdle. Often a garment would be worn ungirded at home, and thus the act of fastening the belt and even at times tucking up the garment indicated preparation for some activity or journey. Consequently, the common Hebrew phrase "gird up the loins" (cf. 1 K. 18:46, which NEB paraphrases as "tucked up his robe"; 2 K. 4:29, NEB "hitch up your cloak"; figuratively, Eph. 6:14, NEB "fasten on the belt of truth") refers to preparation and readiness for action. Before the Exodus the people of Israel ate the Passover with their "loins girded" (NEB "belt fastened"), sandals on, and staff in hand (Ex. 12:11). Before God questioned Job He told him to "gird up [his] loins like a man" (NEB "brace yourself and stand up like a man") in readiness for God's questions (Job 38:3; cf. 40:7). Jesus told His disciples to await alertly His second coming with their loins girded (NEB "belts fastened") and lamps lit (Lk. 12:35). Clearly, then, the girding up of the loins is an idiom describing actual or symbolic dressing for action.

As the important source of procreative strength, as the place where the sword was worn (cf. 2 S. 20:8), and as the vital midsection, the loins can be seen as a center and symbol of strength and vigor (cf. Job 40:16 [Behemoth]). The good wife of Prov. 31 "girds her loins with strength and makes her arms strong" (v. 17; NEB "She sets about her duties with vigour and braces herself for the work"). Rehoboam emphasized his supreme power and harshness: "My little finger is thicker than my father's loins" (1 K. 12:10; 2 Ch. 10:10). Nahum warned the people of Nineveh, "Gird your loins; collect all your strength" (Nah. 2:1). The Lord crushes the loins (NEB "hip and thigh") of His enemies (Dt. 33:11) and ungirds "the loins [NEB "might"] of kings" (Isa. 45:1) by rendering them weaponless and powerless.

Despite their strength, the loins are prone to sickness,

pain, and fear. The loins can be "filled with burning" (Ps. 38:7) and fever, afflicted with trembling (69:23 [MT 24]), "filled with anguish" as in childbirth (Isa. 21:3; cf. Jer. 30:6), or incapacitated by grief, fear, and dread (Nah. 2:10). Such descriptions may refer to some specific abdominal disorder but frequently seem intended to depict graphically loss of strength, utter helplessness, and personal incapacitation.

Wearing sackcloth on the loins was an expression of mourning (cf. Isa. 32:11; Am. 8:10; etc.). The ceremonial law of Israel made specific statements concerning the sacrifice of certain animal parts, including the fatty parts at the loins (*kesel*) or flanks or haunches (Lev. 3:4, 10, 15; etc.). *See* SACRIFICES AND OFFERINGS IN THE OT V.

M. W. MEYER

**LOIS** lō'is [Gk. *Lōis*]. Grandmother of Timothy and probably mother of his mother Eunice, in view of the close relationship between the two women (2 Tim. 1:5). Although her name is Greek, she was a Hellenistic Jew. Apparently she helped to rear Timothy, training him especially in the OT Scriptures (cf. 3:15). Paul did not claim the two women as his converts, but probably they were brought to the Lord during his first visit to Lystra (Acts 14:6f.), for on his next visit Eunice was a believer (16:1). It is likely that Lois took a similar stand. E. F. H.

**LONELY** [Heb. *yāḥîḏ*–'only,' 'solitary,' 'isolated'] (Ps. 25:16); AV DESOLATE; [part. of *bāḏaḏ*–'be isolated, alone,' *bāḏāḏ*] (Ps. 102:7 [MT 8]; Lam. 1:1); AV ALONE, SOLITARY; NEB IN SOLITUDE, SOLITARY; [Gk. *érēmos*–'abandoned,' 'desolate,' 'solitary']; AV also SOLITARY.

In ancient times (as sometimes today) SUFFERING was often intensified by the afflicted one's isolation from human fellowship. Because adversity was regarded as divine punishment, the sufferer frequently had to endure abandonment by the human community as well as the devastating fear of having been forsaken by God (e.g., Ps. 25:16; cf. 22:1f., 6-8 [MT 2f., 7-9]). The writer of Ps. 102 compares his isolation to that of "a vulture of the wilderness . . . an owl of the waste places . . . a lonely bird on the housetop" (vv. 6f. [MT 7f.]; cf. vv. 8, 10 [9, 11]). Jerusalem's terrible loneliness (Lam. 1:1) is twofold: her people ("children") have been taken into exile (vv. 1, 4f.), and her former allies ("lovers") have turned against her (vv. 2, 5); cf. the description of the "solitary" (Heb. *bāḏāḏ*) city in Isa. 27:10.

In the NT Gk. *érēmos* occurs most often as a substantive, which the RSV usually renders "wilderness" (or, twice, "desert"); cf. also *erēmía* (RSV "desert," "wilderness"). As an adjective *érēmos* occurs nine times in the phrase *érēmos tópos* (RSV "lonely place," except in Mk. 1:45, where it unfortunately renders "country"). *Érēmos* can denote any place that is uninhabited, not necessarily a DESERT region lacking water and vegetation. Jesus retreats to a "lonely place" when He wants to escape the press of the crowds; but the crowds pursue Him, even into areas where no food is available (e.g., Mt. 14:13-15 par. Mk. 6:31-36; Lk. 9:10-12; cf. Mk. 1:45). In the "lonely place" (or WILDERNESS) one can be alone to fast and pray, to experience dependence on God and communion with Him. It is to such a place that Jesus withdraws for forty days after His baptism (Mt. 4:1f. par.). And to such places He returns when He seeks an opportunity for prayer (e.g., Mk. 1:35; cf. 6:45f. par.) or for rest with His disciples (e.g., 6:31f.).

***Bibliography***.–*DNTT*, III, 1004-08; W. Lane, *Gospel According to Mark* (*NICNT*, 1974), pp. 81, 89, 224-26; *TDNT*, II, *s.v.* ἔρημος (G. Kittel); *TDOT*, I, *s.v.* "bādhādh" (H.-J. Zobel); *TWOT*, I, 90f.

N. J. O.

**LONG (FOR)** [Heb. *tā'aḇ* (Ps. 119:40, 174), *yā'aḇ* (119:131), *kāsap* (Job 14:15; niphal, Gen. 31:30; Ps. 84:2 [MT 3]), *šā'ap*–'gasp for' (Job 7:2; 36:20 [MT 21]), piel of *kālâ*–'fail (with longing)' (2 S. 13:39), piel of *ḥākâ*–'wait for' (Job 3:21), piel of *nāśā' nepeš*–'lift up one's desire' (Jer. 22:27), *ḥāšaq*–'cling to' (Gen. 34:8), *ḥēšeq*–'pleasure' (Isa. 21:4), piel of *qāwâ*–'wait for' (Lam. 2:16), *pāqaḏ*–'miss, long for' (Ezk. 23:21), *pû(a)ḥ*–'blow' (Ps. 12:5 [MT 6]), *'āraḡ*–'pant for' (Ps. 42:1 [MT 2]); Gk. *epipothéō*–'desire' (Rom. 1:11; 2 Cor. 5:2; etc.), *échō epipothían*–'have a longing' (Rom. 15:23), *epipóthētos*–'longed for, desired' (Phil. 4:1), *epithyméō*–'desire' (Mt. 13:17; 1 Pet. 1:12; Rev. 9:6), *epithymía*–'yearning' (Rev. 18:14)]; AV also DESIRE (GREATLY/EARNESTLY), PANT (Ps. 42:1 [MT 2]), PUFF (12:5 [MT 6]), etc.; NEB also WAIT FOR, HAVE FEAR (Job 36:20), PINE, WAIT FOR, RELIVE (Ezk. 23:21), DESIRE, etc.; **LONGING** [Heb. *ta'ᵃḇâ*–'craving, longing' (Ps. 38:9 [MT 10]; 119:20), *kālâ*–'cease, fail' ("fail with longing," Dt. 28:32); Gk. *epipóthesis* (2 Cor. 7:7, 11), *apokaradokía*–'eager expectation' (Rom. 8:19)]; AV also (EARNEST/VEHEMENT) DESIRE, EARNEST EXPECTATION; NEB also LAMENT, EAGER EXPECTATION; **LONGINGLY** [Heb. hithpael of *'āwâ*–'crave'] (2 S. 23:15 par. 1 Ch. 11:17); AV LONG; NEB LONGING.

English "long, longing" are used by the RSV for a wide range of human desires and cravings. Frequently the terms denote natural human emotions that are not judged to be morally good or bad. E.g., it is natural for parents to miss their children when they are separated from them (cf. Dt. 28:32; 2 S. 13:39) and for Christians to long for one another's fellowship (e.g., Rom. 1:11; 15:23; 2 Cor. 7:7, 11; 9:14; Phil. 2:26; 4:1; 1 Thess. 3:6; 2 Tim. 1:4). Homesickness (Gen. 31:30; Jer. 22:27; cf. 2 S. 23:15 par.) and sexual desire (cf. Gen. 34:8) are likewise emotions common to mankind. Those who are oppressed long for safety (Ps. 12:5 [MT 6]), while persons suffering extreme pain may even yearn for death (Job 3:21; Rev. 9:6; cf. Paul's desire for the resurrection life, 2 Cor. 5:2).

Certain desires, however, are contrary to God's will and thus are judged to be sinful; cf. Israel's lust for illicit alliances (Ezk. 23:21) and the worldly merchants' craving for the luxuries and vices of Rome (Rev. 18:14).

By contrast, the godly Israelite longs for knowledge of God's will (Ps. 119:20, 40, 131), for God's salvation (v. 174; cf. v. 81), and for communion with God Himself (42:1 [MT 2]; 84:2 [MT 3]). 1 Pet. 2:2 instructs Christians to crave spiritual nourishment. Righteous men and prophets (Mt. 13:17) and even angels (1 Pet. 1:12) are depicted as longing to see the salvation that God has revealed in Jesus Christ, and the whole creation as anxiously awaiting its own liberation (Rom. 8:19).

*See also* DESIRE. N. J. O.

**LONG LIFE.** *See* LIFE.

**LONGEVITY.** *See* ANTEDILUVIAN PATRIARCHS III.

**LONGSUFFERING.** *See* FORBEAR; PATIENCE; on "slow to anger" *see* SLOW.

**LOOK.** The translation of a large number of Hebrew and Greek terms.

***I. In the OT.***–The most common Hebrew verb for looking is *rā'â* (usually rendered "see"). In the literal sense it simply denotes seeing with the eyes (e.g., Gen. 8:13); but it can also be used for "seeing" in a dream or vision (e.g., Ezk. 1:15; 2:9; cf. *rōʾeh,* "seer") or for God's awareness of the hearts and actions of mankind (e.g., 1 S. 16:7). Another figurative use occurs in the phrase "look one another in the face" (hithpael of *rāʾâ* + *pānîm*), which means to meet in battle (2 K. 14:8; cf. v. 11; par. 2 Ch. 25:17; cf. v. 21). *Ḥāzâ,* like *rāʾâ,* is frequently used for supernatural visions as well as natural vision (e.g., Cant. 6:13 [MT 7:1]; "gaze," Mic. 4:11; cf. *ḥōzeh,* "seer," rendered "those who gaze" in Isa. 47:13). Another common term, *pānâ* (lit. "turn the face"), generally involves turning to look in a particular direction (e.g., Ex. 2:12; 16:10). *Šāqap* (niphal or hiphil) means to look down from a high place, e.g., from a mountain (Gen. 18:16; 19:28; Nu. 21:20; 1 S. 13:18), from a window (2 K. 9:30, 32; cf. also Gen. 26:8; Jgs. 5:28; 2 S. 6:16 par. 1 Ch. 15:29; Cant. 2:9), or (of God) from heaven or a cloud (Ex. 14:24; Dt. 26:15; Ps. 14:2; 53:2 [MT 3]; 102:19 [MT 20]).

The hiphil of *nāḇaṭ* usually means to fix one's gaze on a person or thing (e.g., Gen. 19:17; Ex. 33:8; 1 S. 16:7a; cf. "gaze," Prov. 4:25; Hab. 2:15). Continually "looking to" someone (or something) indicates faith in the object of one's attention (e.g., Isa. 22:8, 11). Yahweh rewards all those who look to Him (Ps. 34:5 [MT 6]). Isaiah prophesies of a day when "men will regard [*šāʿâ,* lit. "look at with interest"] their Maker, and their eyes will look to [*rāʾâ ʾel-*] the Holy one of Israel" (17:7; cf. v. 8). The piel of *qāwâ* (lit. "wait for") can be used in a similar manner. Steadfast waiting demonstrates faith that God will act to save His people (*see also* WAIT). Isa. 64:3 praises God for performing mighty acts that Israel had not even expected. But at other times God's people express bitter disappointment that they have looked in vain for help (e.g., Job 30:26), for compassion (Ps. 69:20 [MT 21]), for justice (Isa. 59:11), for peace and healing (Jer. 8:15; 14:19); and Yahweh complains about disappointed expectations for His people (Isa. 5:2, 4, 7).

Hiding the face or eyes can signify shame, fear, or reverence, as when "Moses hid his face, for he was afraid to look [hiphil of *nāḇaṭ*] at God" (Ex. 3:6; cf. Acts 7:32; cf. also Elijah, 1 K. 19:13). But in other contexts this gesture can be a sign of indifference or rejection (e.g., Prov. 28:27; cf. the references to Yahweh hiding His face, e.g., Dt. 31:17f.; Job 13:24; Ps. 13:1 [MT 2]; 27:9; Ezk. 39:23). By contrast, looking upon persons often means turning one's attention to them in love and showing them favor (e.g., 1 S. 1:11; 2 S. 16:12; Ps. 84:9 [MT 10]; 101:6; 119:153; Lam. 1:11; cf. Am. 5:22; in the NT, cf. Mk. 10:21; Lk. 1:25, 48 ["regard"]; 9:38). God's look is imbued with great power: "[He] looks on the earth and it trembles" (Ps. 104:32). In extreme distress, God's people sometimes experience His look as hostile and pray that He will "look away from" them (*šāʿâ min,* e.g., Job 7:19; 14:6; Ps. 39:13 [MT 14]; cf. Isa. 22:4). At other times they cry out to God to look down on an evil situation and act to set it right (e.g., Isa. 63:15; Lam. 1:11; 2:20; cf. Acts 4:29), and they complain when He appears to be looking on passively (e.g., Ps. 35:17; Hab. 1:13).

In addition to functioning as an organ for sight, the eyes express many emotions. Thus a look can express envy (e.g., 1 S. 2:29, 32; Ps. 68:16 [MT 17]), pride (e.g., Ps. 101:5; Isa. 2:11; cf. AV Ps. 18:27 [MT 28]; Prov. 21:4), contempt (e.g., Gen. 16:4f.; Est. 1:17), anger (e.g., Prov. 25:23; Jer. 3:12), horror (e.g., Isa. 13:8; cf. Nah. 3:5-7), triumph (e.g., Ps. 59:10 [MT 11]; 118:7), amazement (e.g., Gen. 43:33), favor (e.g., Ps. 101:6), disgust (e.g., 119:158), dismay (e.g., Ezk. 4:17; cf. Mt. 6:16), etc. *See also* EYE; EVIL EYE; FACE.

*II. In the NT.*–The most common NT verb for seeing is Gk. *eídon* (frequently used by the LXX to render Heb. *rāʾâ*; usually rendered "see"). Like *rāʾâ,* Gk. *eídon* has a range of meanings, including literal sight with the eyes (e.g., Mk. 12:15; Lk. 18:24; 21:29) and visionary perception (Rev. 4:1; 5:11; 6:12; etc.). The demonstrative particles *idoú* and *íde* ("Look!") are used to draw attention to something (e.g., Mt. 12:2 par.; Mk. 11:21; 13:1). *Blépō* generally has a greater emphasis on the function of the eyes in seeing (cf. passages where "seeing" is contrasted with blindness, e.g., Mt. 12:22). The variety of its nuances is reflected in the RSV's renderings, which include "look" (e.g., Eph. 5:15), "look at" (e.g., Mt. 5:28), "look into" (Rev. 5:3f.), "look out for" (Phil. 3:2), and "look to" (2 Jn. 8). Among its compounds, *emblépō* is usually rendered "look at" (e.g., Mt. 6:26; 19:26 par.). The type of look that Jesus gave Peter (Lk. 22:61) is not described, but its effect was powerful: Peter "remembered . . . and he went out and wept bitterly" (vv. 61f.); cf. the maid's look in Mk. 14:67. *Anablépō* can mean either "see again" (cf. "receive one's sight," Mt. 11:5; etc.) or "look up" (e.g., Mk. 16:4; Lk. 19:5; 21:1); the term is used of Jesus' characteristic manner of looking up to heaven when He prayed (Mt. 14:19 par.; Mk. 7:34). *Periblépō* ("look around [at]") is used primarily by Mark (3:5, 34; 5:32; 9:8; etc.; cf. also Lk. 6:10). Other compounds are *epiblépō* ("look upon," Lk. 9:38; cf. 1:25 [*epeídon*]; "regard" in v. 48 [for *epiblépō*]; see I above), *apoblépō* ("look to," He. 11:26), and *diablépō* ("look intently," Mk. 8:25).

"Look for" sometimes means simply to search for a person (e.g., rendering *zētéō,* Lk. 2:48; Jn. 7:11; etc.; *anazētéō,* Acts 11:25; *see* SEEK; cf. also "look after" [*zētéō*], Phil. 2:21). But it can also mean to WAIT expectantly for the Messiah (*prosdokáō,* Mt. 11:3 par.) or for the kingdom of God (*prosdéchomai,* Mk. 15:43 par.; Lk. 2:25, 38); cf. He. 11:10: "For he looked forward to [*ekdéchomai,* lit. "wait for"] the city which has foundations. . . ."

*Atenízō* denotes the intensity of a look (e.g., "look closely at," Acts 11:6). The men on the council "gazed at" Stephen's shining face (6:15; cf. "gaze" in Lk. 22:56; Acts 1:10; 3:4; 7:55); but Moses' face shone so brightly that the Israelites could not look at it (2 Cor. 3:7). Interestingly, in three passages the term is used in connection with a miracle (Acts 3:4; 13:9; 14:9). Some rabbinic stories about healing and cursing make reference to eye contact (SB, II, 713-15), and in later Hellenistic times *atenízō* came to be used in connection with magic (*DNTT,* III, 520). The emphasis in these passages is not, however, on any kind of magical power in the glance of Peter or Paul. (See E. Haenchen, *Acts of the Apostles* [Eng. tr. 1971], pp. 199 n. 4, 400 n. 2; *see also* EVIL EYE.)

*Skopéō,* rendered "look to" three times by the RSV, can mean to inspect something critically and then hold it before oneself as a model. Paul admonishes the Corinthians (2 Cor. 4:18) to discriminate between what is eternal and what is transitory, the Galatians (6:1) to practice self-examination lest they fall into temptation, and the Philippians (2:4) to give careful consideration to the interests of others as well as themselves (cf. also "mark," 3:17; "be careful," Lk. 11:35; "take note of," Rom. 16:17).

*Theáomai* often means simply to observe something (e.g., Mt. 22:11), but it can also connote a "beholding" that includes the apprehension of a spiritual reality (cf. 1 Jn. 1:1; "behold," Jn. 1:14). *Parakýptō* can signify either a literal (Jn. 20:5, 11; cf. Lk. 24:12) or figurative (Jas. 1:25; 1 Pet. 1:12) stooping to look into something; cf. *anakýptō* (lit. "stand erect, raise oneself up"; RSV "look up," Lk. 21:28; Jn. 8:10; cf. Lk. 13:11).

*See also* SEE.

*Bibliography.*–Bauer, rev.; *DNTT,* III, 511-521; *TDNT,* V, *s.v.* ὁράω κτλ. (W. Michaelis); VII, *s.v.* σκοπός κτλ.: σκοπέω (E. Fuchs). N. J. OPPERWALL

**LOOKING GLASS** (Ex. 38:8, AV). *See* MIRROR.

**LOOM.** In Jer. 6:1 the RSV and NEB translation of the Heb. niphal of *šāqap* (lit. "look down"; cf. RSV Nu. 21:20; 1 S. 13:18; 2 S. 6:16; Ps. 85:11 [MT 12]).
*See also* WEAVING.

**LOOPS** [Heb. *lulā'ōṯ*] (Ex. 26:4f., 10f.; 36:11f., 17). Rings or folds made of blue thread along the outermost edge of each set of five curtains, so that the two sets could be coupled with gold clasps, "that the tabernacle may be one whole" (26:6). *See* TABERNACLE.

**LORD** [Heb. *YHWH* (Gen. 2:4f., 7f., etc.), *'ᵃḏōnāy* (Gen. 15:2, 8; 18:3; etc.), *yāh* (Ps. 68:18 [MT 19]; 77:11 [MT 12]; etc.), *'āḏôn* (e.g., Gen. 19:2), *ba'al*–'master' (Nu. 21:28; Isa. 16:8), *gᵉḇîr*–'lord, master' (Gen. 27:29, 37), *seren*–'prince, tyrant' (Jgs. 3:3; 16:5; etc.), *śar*–'leader, chief' (Jgs. 16:23; Ezr. 8:25), *šālîš* (2 K. 7:2, 17, 19; *see* CAPTAIN), *'addîr*–'mighty one' (Jer. 25:34-36), (verb) *šālaṭ* (Eccl. 8:9); Aram. *mārē'*–'lord, master' (Dnl. 2:47; 4:19 [MT 22]), pl. *raḇrᵉḇānîn*–'nobles, lords' (e.g., Dnl. 4:36 [MT 33]); Gk. *kýrios* (e.g., Mt. 1:22), *despótēs* (Lk. 2:29)]; AV also RULETH (Eccl. 8:9), PRINCIPAL (Jer. 25:34-36); NEB also OFFICER (Ezr. 8:25), NOBLES (Dnl. 4:36), LIEUTENANT (2 K. 7:2, 17, 19), etc. A form of the verb *kyrieúō* ("rule") is generally rendered "lords" in 1 Tim. 6:15. The AV also renders Gk. *megistán* (Mk. 6:21; RSV COURTIER) and *rhabbouní* (Mk. 10:51; Jn. 20:16; RSV MASTER, TEACHER) as "lord."

A number of the words may be applied to any person who possesses and exercises authority, from the owner of cattle (Isa. 1:3, *ba'al*) to "the Lord of all the earth" (Josh. 3:11; Ps. 97:5; Mic. 4:13, *'āḏôn*). Lordship may vary from the legitimate use of rightful authority (e.g., Lk. 20:15f.) to the arbitrary exercise of assumed power (e.g., Mk. 10:42).

I. Important OT Terms
  A. *'āḏôn*
  B. *YHWH*
  C. *'ᵃḏōnāy*
II. NT Terms
  A. *Kýrios*
  B. *Despótēs*

***I. Important OT Terms.***–*A. 'āḏôn.* Basically denoting the right to command, this honorific title (found more than 300 times) was used: (1) as a courteous form of address ("Sir," e.g., 2 S. 1:10); (2) when a subordinate addressed a person of superior rank, such as God (Ps. 97:5; Isa. 1:24), a king (Isa. 26:13), a master (Gen. 24:18), a father (31:35), or a husband (18:12). The form *'ᵃḏōnî* ("my lord") (pl. *'ᵃḏōnay*), a royal title (1 S. 29:8), is to be carefully distinguished from the divine title *'ᵃḏōnāy* ("my Lord," "Lord," or "O Lord"), used over 130 times of Yahweh, especially in the Psalms and Isaiah (see I.C below).

*B. YHWH.* These four consonants, which form the so-called tetragrammaton, are usually vocalized *Yahweh.* This form has been explained in various ways: (1) as a substantive from the root *hwh* (an old form of *hyh,* "be, become") with the preformative *y,* meaning "the self-existent One"; (2) as an archaic imperfect qal form of *hwh* (equivalent to *yihyeh*), meaning "He exists" and alluding to the divine self-existence; (3) as the imperfect hiphil of this same root, meaning either "He who brings into existence" (a reference to the creative activity of God) or "He who causes to come to pass" (a reference to the divine providence); (4) as an abbreviation of *yahweh 'ᵃšer yihweh* (cf. Ex. 3:14), "He brings into being whatever exists."

Unlike *'ᵉlōhîm,* a common or generic noun which is the general name for deity, *Yahweh* is a proper noun, the personal name of Israel's God, "the God of Abraham, the God of Isaac, and the God of Jacob" (Ex. 3:15). Ex. 6:3 implies, not that the patriarchs did not call God "Yahweh," but that, knowing Him as *'ēl šadday* (Gen. 17:1), they lacked knowledge of His character or nature as expressed by the name Yahweh.

*C. 'ᵃḏōnāy.* Like *'ᵉlōhîm,* this form is often explained as a plural of majesty, excellence, or intensity (lit. "my Lords," the special plural form distinguishing it from *'ᵃḏōnay,* "my lords"). Others interpret *'ᵃḏōnāy* as meaning "Lord of all" (e.g., Eissfeldt). In either case the form highlights the power and sovereignty of Yahweh as "Lord."

The postexilic Jewish practice of substituting *'ᵃḏōnāy* (or *'ᵉlōhîm*) for *Yahweh* in the public reading or reciting of the Scriptures may have arisen from Lev. 24:16, interpreted (erroneously) to mean that the simple utterance of the sacred tetragrammaton was a capital offense, or from the fear that to pronounce the divine name would be to reduce God to the status of a pagan deity who was addressed by a personal name.

This customary substitution of *'ᵃḏōnāy* ("Lord") for *Yahweh,* due to the reverential avoidance of the ineffable name of the God of Israel, explains: (1) why Greek-speaking Jews in the 1st cent. A.D. (and probably before) regularly used *Kýrios* ("Lord"), the Greek equivalent of *'ᵃḏōnāy,* to refer to God; (2) why the Masoretes in the 7th cent. A.D. vocalized the consonants *YHWH* with the vowels of *'ᵃḏōnāy* (which in turn produced the hybrid English form "Jehovah"); (3) why English Bibles commonly use "LORD" for *Yahweh* and Latin versions use *Dominus.* (Where the Hebrew is *'ᵃḏōnāy Yahweh* [e.g., Gen. 15:2, 8], the AV, RSV, and NEB have "Lord GOD" [the ASV has "Lord Jehovah"] to avoid the repetition of "Lord.")

*II. NT Terms.–A. Kýrios.* Originally an adjective (with the sense "having power"), *kýrios* serves only as a noun in the NT, occurring in every NT book except Titus and 1, 2, and 3 John. It means "sir," "owner," "master," "lord," or "Lord," being used of a man as an owner (Mt. 20:8), master (Lk. 13:8), father (Mt. 21:30), or one worthy of respect ("Sir," Jn. 4:11); of an angel (Acts 10:4); of Jesus, both during His ministry (Lk. 9:54) and after His resurrection (Eph. 6:5-10); and of God (Lk. 1:6; Acts 7:33; Jas. 1:7).

Although in the first-century pagan world *kýrios* was not a proper name but a title added to a deity's name (e.g., "the lord Serapis"), it became a personal name by which Christians referred to Jesus as shown by the Aramaic phrase *Māranā' ṯā* ("Our Lord, come!") in 1 Cor. 16:22. Indeed, Christians are described as "those who call upon the name of the Lord" (Acts 9:14, 21; 22:16; Rom. 10:13; 1 Cor. 1:2; 2 Tim. 2:22; cf. Joel 3:5, LXX), whether in baptism, prayer, or exorcism.

Scholars offer various explanations for the Christian application of the title *Kýrios* to Christ. (1) The pre-Pauline Hellenistic churches derived the term from the religious terminology of oriental Hellenism (cf. 1 Cor. 8:5f.); "at the very outset the un-modified expression 'the Lord' is unthinkable in Jewish usage" (R. Bultmann, *Theology of the NT,* I [Eng. tr. 1952], 51; cf. pp. 124f., following W. Bousset, pp. 119-152). (2) In the confession "Jesus (Christ) is Lord" (Rom. 10:9; Phil. 2:11), Christian worshipers registered a silent protest (cf. Jude 4) against the contemporary use of the term to refer to pagan deities or to apotheosize human rulers in the cult of the Caesar (Deiss.*LAE,* pp. 349-362). (3) Considered in the light of Christ's sharing of Yahweh's authority and functions and exercise of Yahweh's rights (note, e.g., the use of Ps. 34:8 [MT 9] in 1 Pet. 2:3, or Isa. 8:12f. in 1 Pet. 3:14f.), the LXX rendering of *YHWH* by *kýrios* may have prompted the Christians to adopt the name to designate Jesus (see Baudissin, II, 236-241; III, 697-710). Later discoveries, however, show that in the LXX the divine name *YHWH* probably was not rendered by *kýrios* but was written out in Aramaic or paleo-Hebraic letters or was transliterated into Greek letters, e.g., *IAŌ* (see G. Howard, *JBL,* 96 [1977], 63-83). (4) God's vindication of Christ by His resurrection and elevation to universal recognition and cosmic dominion as Lord, recalled in Christian worship (Phil. 2:9-11), invested the *kýrios* title with its full significance (see Cullmann, pp. 195-237).

Certainly *kýrios* is the distinctive NT title signifying the resurrected and ascended Jesus (2 Cor. 5:6, 8; 1 Thess. 4:15f.) as universal sovereign and head of the Church, although the concept of His being "Lord" doubtless arose during His earthly life as a consequence of His authoritative teaching and divine power (see Mk. 11:3; 12:35-37, citing Ps. 110:1; cf. Jn. 13:13f.). That is, the preresurrectional historical experience of the lordship of Jesus foreshadowed the postresurrectional theological confession of Jesus as Lord.

Whenever worshiping Christians repeated the Church's earliest confession of faith, "Jesus is Lord," they were: (1) implying that the Christ of faith was none other than the Jesus of history (Acts 2:34-36); (2) acknowledging the deity of Christ (Jn. 20:28; Phil. 2:6, 9-11); (3) admitting the Lord's personal rights to absolute supremacy in the universe, the Church, and individual lives (Acts 10:36; Rom. 10:12; 14:8; 1 Cor. 8:6; Jas. 4:15); (4) affirming the triumph of Christ over death and hostile cosmic powers when God raised Him from the dead (Rom. 10:9; 14:9; Eph. 1:20-22; Col. 2:10, 15), and therefore also the Christian's hope of resurrection (1 Cor. 6:14; 2 Cor. 4:14); (5) epitomizing the Christian message (*kḗrygma,* cf. Rom. 10:8f.; 2 Cor. 4:5) and defining the basis of the teaching (*didachḗ,* cf. Col. 2:6f.); (6) declaring everyone's accountability to the Lord, the righteous judge (1 Cor. 4:5; 2 Tim. 4:1, 8); (7) making a personal and public declaration of faith (Rom. 10:9), which testified to their being led by the Holy Spirit (1 Cor. 12:3); (8) repudiating their former allegiance to many pagan "lords" and reaffirming their loyalty to the one Lord through and in whom they existed (8:5f.; 1 Tim. 6:15).

*B. Despótēs.* The word is used of God the Father (Lk. 2:29; Acts 4:24; Rev. 6:10), Christ (2 Tim. 2:21; 2 Pet. 2:1; Jude 4), and human masters (e.g., 1 Pet. 2:18). See further *TDNT,* II, *s.v.* δεσπότης (K. H. Rengstorf).

*See also* GOD, NAMES OF.

***Bibliography.***–W. W. Graf von Baudissin, *Kyrios als Gottesname in Judentum* (4 vols., 1926-1929); W. Bousset, *Kyrios Christos* (Eng. tr. 1970); L. Cerfaux, *Recueil Lucien Cerfaux, I* (1954), pp. 1-88; O. Cullmann, *Christology of the NT* (Eng. tr., 2nd ed. 1963), pp. 195-237; *DBSup., s.v.* "Kyrios" (L. Cerfaux); F. Hahn, *Titles of Jesus in Christology* (Eng. tr. 1969), pp. 68-135; I. Hermann, *Kyrios und Pneuma* (1961); W. Kramer, *Christ, Lord, Son of God* (Eng. tr., *SBT,* 50, 1966), pp. 65-107; D. R. de Lacey, "'One Lord' in Pauline Christology," in H. H. Rowden, ed., *Christ the Lord* (1982), pp. 191-203; R. N. Longenecker, *Christology of Early Jewish Christianity* (*SBT,* 2/17, 1970), pp. 120-136; R. P. Martin, *Carmen Christi* (1967); V. H. Neufeld, *Earliest Christian Confessions* (1963); *TDNT,* III, *s.v.* κύριος κτλ. (Foerster, Quell); *TDOT,* I, *s.v.* "'ādhôn" (Eissfeldt); G. Vos, *Self-Disclosure of Jesus* (1954), pp. 118-140.

M. J. HARRIS

**LORD OF HOSTS.** *See* GOD, NAMES OF II.C; HOST OF HEAVEN.

**LORDLY** [Heb. *'addîr* (Jgs. 5:25), *'eḏer* (Zec. 11:13)]; AV also GOODLY (Zec. 11:13); NEB "fit for a chieftain" (Jgs. 5:25), NOBLE (Zec. 11:13). Both terms describe what befits persons of noble rank.

**LORDS OF THE PHILISTINES** [Heb. *sarnê pᵉlištîm* (Jgs. 3:3; 16:5, 8, etc.)]. The precise meaning and etymology of Heb. *seren* are unclear, although the contexts in which it occurs indicate that it refers to Philistine officials or rulers (cf. Josh. 13:3). *Seren* is probably a loanword, and scholars have appealed to various languages for its cognates. Many have assumed a relation with Gk. *týrannos.* Hence J. Soggin (*Joshua* [Eng. tr., *OTL,* 1972], p. 149) translated it "tyrannies"; although he admitted that this etymology may not be correct, he thought that the translation accurately reflected the situation of the Philistine city-states (cf. R. Boling, *Joshua* [*AB,* 1982], p. 337, who claimed the cognate is Aegean-Anatolian *tyrannos*). I. Eitan (*Revue des études juives,* 82 [1926], 223) appealed to Egyp. *śr.n.(t),* "high official of a city," which accords well with the biblical meaning. Finally, P. K. McCarter (*I Samuel* [*AB,* 1980], p. 123) noted another possibility: hieroglyphic Hittite *tarwanas,* a title of Neo-Hittite rulers.

G. A. L.

**LORD'S DAY.**

*I. NT.*–The expression "Lord's Day" (Gk. *kyriakḗ hēméra*), found only in Christian sources, first appears in Rev. 1:10 as a designation of the first day of the week. It is not to be confused with the eschatological "day of the Lord" (*hēméra toú kyríou*). The most plausible explanation of the term is that it derives from the parallel expression "Lord's Supper" (1 Cor. 11:20), since the early Christians gathered on the first day of the wek to celebrate this meal as the culmination of their corporate worship. An account of an early (late 50's) Lord's Day service is found in Acts 20:7-11, beginning with the words "on the first day of the week, when we were gathered together to break bread." Christians chose the first day of the week for worship undoubtedly because Christ rose on that day and met with the gathered disciples at the time of the evening meal. At this time He ate and drank with them (Lk. 24:41-43; cf. Acts 10:41), renewing the table fellowship that He had shared with them on the night on which He was betrayed. Hence Lord's Day worship is the Christian festival of the Resurrection, in which Christians, like the original disciples, have fellowship with one another and with the risen Christ whom they trust as Savior and worship as God.

This conclusion throws light on Paul's reference to the first day of the week when writing to the Corinthians about a collection for the Jerusalem church: "On the first day of the week, each of you is to put something aside and store it up, as he may prosper, so that contributions need not be made when I come" (1 Cor. 16:2). Paul did not choose the first day above others as peculiar to the situation of the Corinthians; he said that he gave the same instructions to the churches of Galatia (v. 1). Nor does the idea of regular saving of money imply that it must be done on the first day of the week. Hence there must have been some other reason, understood by Paul and his readers, why he expressly designated the first day. Since in a later letter (2 Cor. 9:12) he called the collection set aside on this day a *leitourgía,* i.e., a ministration of a sacred character, the choice of the day definitely points to its religious significance. Here then is further evidence that by the middle of the 1st cent. the first day of the week had unique meaning for the Christian community.

The testimony to first-day worship in the postapostolic age is in every way consonant with this view. By Justin's time (mid-2nd cent.), however, most Christians gathered on Sunday morning, evidently because the emperor Trajan's edict against seditious assemblies proscribed evening meetings. From that time to the present Christians have customarily worshiped on the morning and/or evening of the first day of the week.

Christians' worshiping on the first day not of the month but of the week indicates that the Church, as the "new Israel," accepted the sabbatical rhythm of time revealed to Israel through Moses. Some have construed the fourth commandment, "Remember the sabbath day, to keep it holy" (Ex. 20:8-11), as a mere ceremonialism, fulfilled in Christ after the analogy of the OT sacrificial ritual. Others have insisted that the Church is bound to observe the seventh day just as it is bound to refrain from idolatry, stealing, and the like. The great majority, however, have recognized that the truth lies between these two extremes.

Surely the gentile Church's universal acceptance of the weekly cycle of time indicates that it was a part of the authoritative, apostolic tradition or "pattern of teaching to which they were delivered" (Rom. 6:17). It is clear, however, that while the Christians universally observed the sabbatical rhythm of time, they did not specifically or primarily observe the sabbath (= seventh) day. Thus the apostolic Church spoke both a "yes" and a "no" to the fourth commandment. This dialectic is a specific instance of the general truth that the fulfillment of the OT in Jesus Christ is a fulfillment in principle but not yet in finality. The sabbath rest, which believers have in Christ, is not only a present reality but also a future hope; they have indeed found rest unto their souls but at the same time must give all diligence to enter into God's rest. The principle of the sabbath, then, is both an OT ceremonialism that has been fulfilled in Christ and a permanent interpretative category of redemptive history with definite eschatological implications. Christians, therefore, are free from the sabbath in that they can gather on the first day, and at the same time stand under the sign of the sabbath in that they gather every seventh day.

The unique relationship of the Jewish sabbath to the Christian Lord's Day bears on the ethical question of how Christians should observe the Lord's Day. The English Puritan tradition requires that one refrain from all labor and recreation (except "works of mercy and necessity") and spend the whole day in private and public devotion. Proponents have appealed to the OT proscription of all labor on the sabbath and traditionally have preferred the term "Sabbath Day" to designate the Christian day of worship. A less strict view, sometimes described as the "Continental Sunday," has stressed only the need for common worship on the Lord's Day, without prohibiting recreation and amusements.

Americans have traditionally observed the English Puritan sabbath. The colonists enforced observance of the day by civil legislation, now popularly called "blue laws." Many of these laws are still on the books and some are locally enforced. The constitutional separation of church and state, however, has precluded a national Sunday-closing law. Although few would advocate a return to a legally enforced observance of the Lord's Day, discerning Christian leaders are increasingly concerned that the American Sunday is being rapidly turned into a fun-day and that Christians must be taught the importance of the Lord's Day in the life of the Church and the nation. In keeping with this concern are three general principles bearing on the observance of the Lord's Day.

(1) One rightly observes the day who does so in a faith that renounces all self-confidence and trust in one's own works and rests only in God for deliverance from sin. Because believers have not yet entered the final rest of the life to come, however, they cannot say that this rest in the Lord is only a matter of the heart. An outward sign should correspond to the inner reality; they should cease their labors as a public witness of their renouncing all their works and of their trust in God's grace alone.

(2) One rightly observes the day who meets with God's people for worship. The "rest" of the Lord's Day is not idleness but a gathering in which believers have fellowship with one another and with the risen Lord. The Lord's Day is not a private day; it belongs to the Church. In fact, the Church was born as a Lord's Day assembly, whether one thinks of the original gathering of the disciples on the evening of the first Easter or of the subsequent gathering in the upper room at Pentecost when the Spirit was poured out and Christians first preached. Without such gatherings the Church cannot survive, and without the Church Christians cannot survive. Voltaire thus remarked, "If you want to kill Christianity, you must abolish Sunday."

(3) One rightly observes the day who does so with joy. The "rest" of the Lord's Day is the joyous rest of a festive day. It goes back to the original joy of the disciples when they became convinced that "the Lord is risen; he is risen indeed." Therefore Barth's rejection of Goethe's apothegm, "Bitter week, happy festival," is well taken. The joy of the Lord's Day festival illumines the remainder of the Christian week. P. K. JEWETT

*II. Early Church.*–The period immediately after the NT sheds little clear light on the Church's observance of the Lord's Day. Four apparent references, three of them by Christian writers, have been the subject of intense debate. (1) Ignatius refers to those who have "obtained new hope, no longer keeping the sabbath [lit. "sabbathing"] but living according to the Lord's Day [Gk. *kyriakḗ,* i.e, without the word for "day"] on which our life dawned through him and his death" (Magn. 9:1). *Kyriakḗ* here seems to be a shortened form of the expression used in Rev. 1:10, and this fact, along with the context, leads to use of the word "day" in translating the passage. Ignatius does not specifically mention worship in this context. (2) Did. 14:1 uses the odd expression *kyriakḗ kyríou,* "Lord's [Day] of the Lord," for the occasion of Christian worship, but does not contrast this occasion with the sabbath. (3) Similarly, Pliny, in his famous letter to Trajan (*Ep.*x.96) says that Christians meet on a fixed day to sing a hymn (or recite a form of words), but he does not specify the day. (4) Barn. 15:9 brings out the significance of the first day (called the eighth day of the old creation), but does not use the term *kyriakḗ*. Only when taken together do these passages imply that early Christians gathered for worship on the first day of the week, the day of the Resurrection.

More solid testimony comes when Justin Martyr, wanting to give a candid exposition of Christianity, offers an account of the services that were held on the day of the sun, which he identifies as the day of creation and also of the Resurrection (*Apol.* i.67). Justin obviously had in view an established practice, and although he wrote in Rome, he neither suggested that Rome had initiated the custom nor that it had only a local application. The reason he advanced for the importance of the day agrees with the thought of Barnabas (the day of the two creations) and also with the NT witness to the first day of the week as the day both of the Resurrection and of the risen Lord's meetings with His disciples.

After Justin evidence for the first day's status as the day of Christian worship accumulates rapidly. As yet, however, no suggestion was made that this day should be a day of rest. Jewish Christians already had the sabbath for this purpose, but gentile Christians enjoyed no manda-

LORD'S PRAYER

tory weekly day of rest and were thus forced to worship either early in the morning or late in the evening. Tertullian, perceiving the close relation between rest and worship, was one of the first to advise those who could do so to defer business on the Lord's Day so as to devote themselves more fully to its proper celebration (*De orat.* 23). In the 3rd cent. Cyprian of Carthage added to the arguments for the special nature of the Lord's Day the further consideration that it was the day of the covenant sign of circumcision, in which he found a prefiguring of the Resurrection (*Epistula* 64.4).

The next step came with the accession of Constantine and his recognition and favoring of the Christian Church. Hitherto the Roman empire had had no firmly established week, although Mithraism had observed the first day as the day of the sun and the seventh day had often been made a special day for feasting. In A.D. 321 Constantine, who also had some attachment to the sun-god, made the first day a regular public holiday, decreeing that all "judges, city-people, and craftsmen" should "rest on this venerable day of the sun," but allowing farmers to attend to agriculture when natural conditions made it advisable. This law naturally facilitated Christian worship, and Christians not only hailed the day as the day of the true Sun of righteousness but also claimed that its observance as a day of worship rested not on compliance with a state decision but on apostolic tradition (Eusebius *HE* v.23). Theodosius reissued the law of Constantine in A.D. 368, and testimony at this period shows increasing recognition of the Lord's Day as a day of rest as well as worship. Thus the *Apostolic Constitutions,* although focusing chiefly on worship, forbade fasting and work on both the sabbath and the Lord's Day (7.23; 8.33). Both Ambrose (*In Ps. 47*) and Chrysostom (*Hom. 10 in Gen.*) made the critical point that the fourth commandment, not an imperial enactment, forms the reason why Christians should refrain from work on the Lord's Day. The Council of Laodicea (A.D. 363) made a significant decision, illustrative of the hardening attitude toward Jewish Christians, when it condemned resting on the sabbath as Judaizing but commended resting on the Lord's Day as an obvious replacement or fulfillment.

From the end of the 4th cent. onward a trend very naturally developed toward the fuller equation of the Lord's Day with the OT sabbath, which it was now in fact to a large extent supplanting in Christian circles. The Council of Carthage in A.D. 451 forbade attendance at the games on the Lord's Day. In the 6th cent. the Council of Orleans included a rule prohibiting manual labor on the Lord's Day (canon 28). Alcuin, toward the end of the 8th cent., specifically transferred the sabbath command to the Lord's Day. Peter Alphonsus in the 12th cent. capped the whole development by describing the Lord's Day as the Christian sabbath. Voices like that of Thomas Aquinas might still be heard opposing the implied threat of legalism, and the Reformation would reopen the question of the Lord's Day and its true significance and observance in a new and challenging way; but the course was now firmly set toward the more detailed sabbath legislation of the medieval period and the Puritan sabbatarianism that succeeded it.

***Bibliography.***–S. Bacchiocchi, *From Sabbath to Sunday* (1977); H. Bettenson, *Documents of the Christian Church* (1963); P. K. Jewett, *Lord's Day* (1971); W. Rordorf, *Sunday* (Eng. tr. 1968); J. Stevenson, *A New Eusebius* (1960); *TDNT,* VII, *s.v.* σάββατον (Lohse).

G. W. BROMILEY

**LORD'S PRAYER.** The prayer that Jesus taught His disciples as a model. It occurs in two forms; one in Mt. 6:9-13, the other in Lk. 11:2-4.

I. Context
   A. Matthew
   B. Luke
II. Content
   A. Address
   B. "Thou" Petitions
   C. "We" Petitions
   D. Doxology
III. Critical Issues
   A. Text
   B. Tradition History
IV. Jewish Parallels
V. Use in the Early Church
VI. Theology

***I. Context.***–The two versions of the Lord's Prayer occur in very different contexts, where they serve distinctive purposes. It is important to study both the common core that they share and their individual contexts.

*A. Matthew.* In Matthew the prayer occurs in the SERMON ON THE MOUNT. The immediate context deals with the kind of religious activity that is pleasing to God. It is thus presented in antithesis to ostentatious and empty prayer. In this section Jesus provides three examples of popular piety: almsgiving, prayer, and fasting (Mt. 6:1-18). These activities easily lent themselves to public display, especially if they were carried on at the temple, and even more so during a time of public feasting or repentance, when there would have been large crowds and under certain circumstances a trumpet would have been sounded (Mt. 6:2; cf. Finkel in Finkel and Frizzell, pp. 132-34). The first element in the context of the Matthaean Lord's Prayer is therefore a statement concerning the *purpose* of prayer. Its purpose is not to attract attention to oneself (vv. 1, 5). Prayer that is truly directed to God alone can be done perfectly well in one's own room (v. 6).

Jesus then provides the second element, a statement about the *nature* of prayer: communication with an understanding heavenly Father (vv. 7f.). Therefore one should not babble on in an attempt to gain a hearing. Jesus' reference here to Gentiles is part of a pattern in the Sermon on the Mount in which He contrasts pagan attitudes to people (5:47), to God (6:7), and to things (6:32) with the qualitatively different attitudes of believers.

*B. Luke.* In Luke, on the other hand, the prayer is introduced as a response to the disciples' request that Jesus provide instruction in prayer, as John the Baptist (along with other ancient teachers) did (11:1). It is followed by an encouragement to pray with assurance (vv. 5-13; cf. 18:1-8). The prayer's larger context is the entire Gospel, which features prayer as a characteristic of Jesus (e.g., 3:21; 6:12; 9:18). Significantly, Luke sometimes mentions Jesus at prayer even where Matthew, in the parallel passages, does not. The crisp style of this prayer is appropriate to Luke's practical emphasis and to his gentile readership. (See further III.B below.)

It is not clear how much significance should be attached to the differing commands: "Pray then like this . . ." (Mt. 6:9), and "When you pray, say . . ." (Lk. 11:2). Matthew's concern with the manner of prayer, both its purpose and nature, makes instruction to pray "like this" especially appropriate. The implication of the differing commands is that the Lord's Prayer can be used both as a general guide without verbatim repetition (Matthew), and also as a model to be repeated exactly (Luke).

***II. Content.***–Like the Ten Commandments, the petitions of the Lord's Prayer can be divided into two parts. The first contains "you" or "thou" petitions, which pertain to God's honor and kingdom. The second contains "we" petitions, which relate to the needs of the petitioners.

*A. Address.* In Matthew's Gospel Jesus instructs the

disciples to address God as *"Our Father who art in heaven"* (Luke: "Father"). The familiar term "Father" recalls the preceding teaching in Matthew (v. 8, "your Father knows what you need") and anticipates the following encouragement in Luke (v. 13, "how much more will the heavenly Father give"). The use of "Father" in direct address to God marked an advance on common usage. Although the concept of God as a father was not absent from Hebrew thought (e.g., Dt. 32:6; Ps. 103:13; Isa. 63:16; Hos. 11:1; Mal. 2:10; T.B. *Taanith* 23b), it is difficult to establish that Jewish people before Christ approached God personally in this manner (see Jeremias, *Prayers of Jesus*, pp. 11-65, 95-98, although his position has been challenged, e.g., by Zeller, "God as Father in the Proclamation and in the Prayer of Jesus," in Finkel and Frizzell, pp. 117-125). Jesus used the term in a unique way, conscious of the special relationship of sonship that He alone bore to God, but He also taught that God was father to the believer (cf. Rom. 8:14-17; Gal. 4:6f.).

The simple form in the Lukan version ("Father") corresponds to the intimate *Abbá*, which was apparently used primarily (but not exclusively) by little children (*see* ABBA). Matthew's words "in heaven" stand in striking contrast to the familiarity of "Father"; the entire phrase thus reminds us at once both of God's immanence and of His transcendence. Apart from this prayer, Luke seldom refers to God as a heavenly Father (cf. Lk. 10:21; 11:13). The idea is frequent, however, in the Sermon on the Mount (e.g., Mt. 5:16, 45, 48) and elsewhere in Matthew's Gospel (e.g., 10:32; 12:50; 15:13; 16:17).

*B. "Thou" Petitions.* The first petition, *"Hallowed be thy name,"* is identical in both versions. In biblical times the NAME was much more closely identified with the person than it is in our culture. To glorify the name of God was to acknowledge what God was in actuality; thus to "hallow" God's name was to acknowledge that He is indeed holy. (In other contexts, *hagiázō* can mean to "make holy," but that meaning is obviously excluded here. A similar use occurs in 1 Pet. 3:15: "reverence Christ as Lord.")

The name of God was revealed in Ex. 3:13-15 (cf. Gen. 4:26) and was proclaimed by God along with a further description of His character in Ex. 34:5-7 (*see* GOD, NAMES OF I, II.C). In the OT God's people frequently expressed concern for God's name or reputation, which was maintained by His mighty saving acts (cf. Dnl. 9:19, "O Lord, give heed . . . because thy city and thy people are called by thy name"). God Himself declared, "I will vindicate the holiness of my great name" (Ezk. 36:23). The psalmist sought deliverance and forgiveness for the glory of God's name (e.g., Ps. 79:9f.). The redeemed people of God are to keep His name holy (Lev. 22:32; Isa. 29:23). It may be assumed that the hallowing of God's name is therefore the ultimate object of each of the petitions that follow.

The second petition, *"Thy kingdom come,"* has a very close association with the preceding petition. Ps. 145 combines these elements: it addresses God as "my God and King" (v. 1) and celebrates the glory of God's kingdom (vv. 11-13); it also praises God's name (vv. 1-3) and concludes with "let all flesh bless his holy name for ever and ever" (v. 21). Inherent in the idea of the kingdom is the dynamic expression of God's sovereignty, which must some day find expression throughout the whole earth. God is praised as "a great king over all the earth" to whom belong the "shields of the earth" (Ps. 47:2, 7-9 [MT 3, 8-10]). Similarly, the Jewish Kaddish prayer contains the petition, "May he let his kingdom rule in your lifetime and in your days and in the lifetime of the whole house of Israel, speedily and soon."

God's kingdom has already been introduced with the coming of Christ (cf. Mt. 12:28; Lk. 11:20), and believers have already been brought into it from the dominion of darkness (Col. 1:13). But its consummation still lies in the future. The verb in this petition (Gk. *elthétō*) is in the aorist tense, which usually signifies a simple action in contrast to a continuing one. This implies, although it does not in itself establish, that the coming of the kingdom is a particular event rather than a gradual accomplishment. That *hagiasthḗtō* in the first petition is also aorist may suggest that while God's name ought always to be hallowed, this petition will not find its ultimate fulfillment until the coming of God's kingdom.

The third petition in the Matthaean version is *"Thy will be done, on earth as it is in heaven."* The earliest MSS of the Lukan version (including $p^{75}$ and B) do not contain this petition. The aorist tense (*genēthḗtō*) once again suggests that the petition's ultimate fulfillment will coincide with the coming of God's kingdom. The "will of God" here represents not some individualized set of predetermined steps to be followed, but the revealed commands of God to be lived out in a whole range of righteous deeds as modeled by Christ, who came to do the will of God (He. 10:5-7).

*C. "We" Petitions.* The Matthaean version has as the fourth petition, *"Give us this day our daily bread."* Luke's version differs significantly at this point. Matthew has "give" in the aorist tense (*dós*, simple action), but Luke has it in the present (*dídou*, suggesting repeated or continuous action). Matthew has *sḗmeron* ("today"), but Luke has *tó kath' hēméran* ("each day"). These differences have led to the inference that whereas Matthew apparently refers to a specific time or act of giving — possibly, but not necessarily, at the consummation of the kingdom — Luke seems to refer to the supply of needs day by day.

Interpretation is complicated by the uncertain meaning of *epioúsion*, which modifies "bread." It is usually translated "daily," but it occurs only here in the NT, and the only external evidence is unclear (cf. Manson, p. 111; Metzger, pp. 52-54; Orchard, pp. 274-282; Yamauchi, p. 145). The usual approach is to understand it as a participle based on a compound verb using *epí* as a prefix with *eínai* ("to be, exist, be present") or *iénai* ("to go, come"). The latter derivation, which would give the translation "for the coming day," has received the widest acceptance (see *TDNT*, II, 591f.; Jeremias, *Prayers*, p. 100). This interpretation is supported by Jerome's statement that the lost Gospel of the Nazarenes had Aram. *maḥar*, "tomorrow" (Jerome *Comm. ad Matt.*), and by the use of *hē epioúsa* to denote "the following day" in Acts 7:26; 16:11; 20:15; 21:18 (cf. 23:11). Thus the petition could refer to the bread of the coming day (esp. if one prayed at sundown as the next day was beginning). Others, including some of the church fathers, have interpreted it eschatologically as entreating God for the "bread" (a symbol of all physical and spiritual gifts) of the future consummation, the great "Tomorrow." If, on the other hand, *epioúsion* is derived from *eimí*, then a present idea is involved. It might have a literal meaning, i.e., "for this day." It could also have a more general sense, however, such as "sufficient" or "necessary" (cf. Yamauchi, pp. 147-156). The last might be the best choice, on the basis not only of derivation but also of the context, for it would eliminate the redundancy of a double reference to time.

In any case, the basic thought is an expression of trust in God. In a culture in which workers were hired only one day at a time (Mt. 20:1-5) and bread could not be preserved as it can today, one was especially aware of the need to trust God for one's bread day by day. As a basic food, "bread" by extension represents all necessary food (cf. 2 Thess. 3:8) and the totality of one's daily needs. The eucharistic interpretation of some of the early church fathers — i.e., that the petition is a request for a "supersubstantial" bread such as Christ's coming as the "bread of life" — is not easily derived from the text itself (but cf. Brown, pp. 301-308; Jeremias, *Prayers*, pp. 100-102).

In Matthew the fifth petition reads, *"And forgive us our debts, as we also have forgiven our debtors."* Luke has "and forgive us our sins, for we ourselves forgive every one who is indebted to us." The two versions have the same meaning, for in Judaism sins were thought of as debts to God. The second clause has the present tense ("as we forgive") in Luke; Matthew has the aorist, best rendered as "have forgiven." Jesus' emphasis on the necessity of forgiving others cannot be interpreted to mean that forgiveness is earned by forgiving others, for two reasons. First, the prayer is addressed to "our Father," indicating that those who thus pray have already been reconciled to God and their guilt has already been forgiven on the basis of the cross. Daily fellowship with God is in view (cf. 1 Jn. 1:9). Second, throughout Scripture a proper approach to God is conditioned on personal qualities or attitudes, including right relationships with God and with others (*see* PRAYER VI.C). Although one does not earn the right to pray or to be forgiven, one can obstruct prayer and forgiveness by having the wrong attitude. Significantly, Jesus singles out for immediate comment this one aspect of the Lord's Prayer (Mt. 6:14f.). He emphasizes the point further in the parable of the two debtors (18:21-35), in which He shows that those who have been forgiven an immense debt to God should forgive others, whose debts to them are minuscule by comparison (cf. Lk. 17:3f.).

The sixth petition, *"And lead us not into temptation,"* has also been understood in various ways. Most interpreters agree that there is no implication that God would draw into sin someone who did not pray (see Jas. 1:13-15). The prayer is rather a request that God *prevent* those praying from falling into such temptation. It also seems clear that "temptation" (*peirasmós*) here does not have the sense of enticement to sin. Although *peirázō* does have that sense in Jas. 1:13f. and it might be inferred from Mt. 4:1, neither *peirasmós* nor *peirázō* is used in this sense in the pre-Christian literature (see Moule, pp. 69f.); rather, these terms have a neutral meaning of "test" and "testing." Testing, in the sense of external pressure, can nevertheless issue in personal failure and sin. Some scholars have read this petition as referring to the final great testing, the eschatological time of tribulation when the final battle is fought between God and Satan (see, e.g., Brown, pp. 315-17; Jeremias, *Prayers*, pp. 105f.). One would expect, however, to find a definite article with *peirasmós* if a specific time were indicated (cf. Rev. 3:10). The petition probably relates, then, to a testing that might result in defection and sin (cf. Luke's special emphasis on testing and perseverance; see S. Brown, *Apostasy and Perseverance in the Theology of Luke* [1969]).

The next question is the specific objective of the petition. It seems unlikely that Jesus would have instructed His followers to request complete freedom from testing, because elsewhere He taught that testing is an inevitable part of life in this world (cf. Lk. 22:31; Jn. 16:33; 17:15). Carmignac (pp. 268-282) suggested that the idea is not merely of entering temptation, but of going "inside" it in the sense of falling and succumbing to it. Moule (pp. 73-75) proposed, probably correctly, that the petition refers to being kept not *from* but *during* a time of testing (cf. 1 Cor. 10:13; 2 Pet. 2:9; Rev. 3:10).

*"But deliver us from evil"* occurs only in the Matthaean version. It is probably best understood as referring to the "evil one," since the preposition used is *apó* rather than *ek*, and since the definite article is used with *ponērós*, "evil" (cf. Mt. 13:19). This interpretation is also consistent with the concept, not only in the NT but also in the Qumrân literature (see R. E. Brown, p. 317), of a continuing holy war between God's people and the evil spiritual forces under the leadership of Satan.

*D. Doxology.* The doxology, *"For thine is the kingdom and the power and the glory for ever"* (cf. AV, RSV mg.), is lacking entirely in Luke and also in the earliest MSS of Matthew (see III.A below). It is generally thought to have been added later for liturgical reasons; the content is possibly based on 1 Ch. 29:10-13 (see B. M. Metzger, *Textual Comm. on the Greek NT* [1971], pp. 16f.). Although the doxology is probably not a part of the original text, it was Jewish practice to conclude prayers with a doxology, and it is highly unlikely that the prayer was ever offered in NT times without some form of doxology (see, e.g., D. Hill, *Gospel of Matthew* [*NCBC*, repr. 1981], p. 139; Jeremias, *Prayers*, pp. 106f.).

***III. Critical Issues.–A.*** *Text.* The major textual issue is the doxological conclusion to the prayer in Matthew, which most scholars hold to be a later liturgical addition. It is missing in such MSS as א, B, D, and also in early patristic commentaries; it is found in such MSS as K, L, W, and other Byzantine witnesses, as well as the Didache. (For the longer reading, see J. van Bruggen, pp. 78-87; for a defense of the shorter reading, cf. Bandstra, pp. 15-30.) Most modern translations omit the liturgical ending.

*B. Tradition History.* Scholarly opinion on the tradition history of the prayer is more diverse. At least five different views have been presented: (1) Jesus gave the prayer on two separate occasions as described in Matthew and Luke; in neither prayer has the form been modified by liturgical or other influence, either Christian or Jewish; (2) Jesus gave the prayer on two separate occasions as described in Matthew and Luke, but the actual wording may have been modified somewhat in transmission or editing (on the assumption that the Gospels contain the *ipsissima vox* of Jesus even if not the *ipsissima verba*); (3) Matthew provides the original form; Luke modified it; (4) Luke provides the original form; Matthew modified it; (5) the prayer originated elsewhere (e.g., possibly in Mark's account of the Gethsemane prayer, Mk. 14:32-42), and through form-critical and redactional analysis we can trace its development into its Matthaean and Lukan forms.

Theories (3), (4), and (5) are built on the common assumption that the development of the Gospel traditions is related to the situation of the Christian communities addressed by the individual Gospel writers (cf. J. Jeremias, *NT Theology*, I [Eng. tr. 1971], 195). The fifth position, represented by M. D. Goulder (*JTS*, 14 [1963], 32-45; *Midrash and Lection in Matthew* [1974], pp. 296-301) and S. van Tilborg, is unnecessarily speculative. With regard to positions (3) and (4), the brevity of Luke's version seems to support its priority, assuming that Christians would be unlikely to reduce a prayer taught by their Lord. Individual words and phrases in Luke (e.g., "Father") might be closer to what Jesus actually taught His disciples. Yet many scholars support Jeremias's view that, although Luke is more original with regard to length, Matthew is more original with regard to wording (Jeremias, *Prayers*, p. 93). While there seems to have been a tendency to introduce liturgical expansion, consideration of the actual words in Matthew and their probable underlying Aramaic structure speak for the integrity of the Matthaean form (pp. 89-94; see also R. E. Brown, p. 279).

Such observations can also be used to support position (2). Nothing in the texts themselves rules out the possibility of two distinct settings and prayers, except the assumed improbability that Jesus would have repeated the prayer to the same group of disciples as though they had never heard the first presentation. Other reasons for reconstructing a tradition history flow from assumptions about the composition of the Gospels rather than from within the respective texts. The belief in two distinct settings does not require, however, a denial of the probability that each prayer was adapted and edited for its own specific use in the Gospel context. If indeed the Gospels addressed the needs of different communities, there is no reason to exclude the Lord's Prayer from this function. In Matthew it can speak to those who are in danger of the meaningless repetition of formulas, and in Luke it can speak to gentile Christians, like Theophilus, who need initial instruction in prayer. This understanding in no way affects the integrity of the canonical text. View (2), therefore, has much to commend it.

*IV. Jewish Parallels.*–The phraseology of the Lord's Prayer has many parallels in Jewish literature. First, the prayer contains significant allusions to the OT (e.g., see II.B above; cf. J. Swetnam, pp. 556-563). Second, the prayer contains some theological concepts that were also held by Jewish teachers in the first several centuries of our era. Some of the terminology in the Talmud is close to the wording of Jesus' prayer. It is difficult, however, to determine the antiquity or origin of such traditions. Examples include: "Deliver us . . . from the evil impulse . . . and from the destructive Accuser" (T.B. *Berakoth* 16b; attributed to Rabbi Judah ha-Nasi, *ca.* 135-217); "do not bring me into sin, or into iniquity, or into temptation" (T.B. *Berakoth* 60b; origin uncertain); "One should never [intentionally] bring himself to the test" (T.B. *Sanhedrin* 107a; attributed through Rabbi Judah [d. 299] to Rab [d.247]); "Do Thy will in heaven above" (attributed to Rabbi Eliezer, late 1st cent. A.D.; see SB, I, 419). One earlier nonrabbinic example appears in Sir. 28:2: "Forgive your neighbor the wrong he has done, and then your sins will be pardoned when you pray"; but this concept does not seem to have been taught by the rabbis.

Third, several Jewish prayers contain terminology and petitions similar to those in the Lord's Prayer. The Kaddish reads, "Exalted and hallowed be his great name. . . . May he establish his kingdom in your lifetime. . . ." Among the Eighteen Benedictions, some of which were already in use in the 1st cent. A.D., the sixth reads, "Forgive us, Father. . . ," and "redeem us for the sake of Your Name." The Abinu Malkenu, used at New Year's services, begins, "Our Father, our King," an address attributed originally to Rabbi Akiba (late 1st to early 2nd cent.).

On these and other less clear or later parallels, see also I. Abrahams (pp. 94-108), A. Finkel ("Prayer of Jesus in Matthew," in Finkel and Frizzell, pp. 131-169), C. G. Montefiore (pp. 125-135), and the articles by J. J. Petuchowski, B. Graubard, S. Lauer, and J. Heinemann, in Petuchowski and Brocke (pp. 21-89).

*V. Use in the Early Church.*–The Lord's Prayer was apparently used extensively in the early Church. It appears in the Didache (of uncertain date, perhaps early 2nd cent.), where it is preceded by words from the Matthaean context and followed by the injunction to pray it three times daily (8:2f.). Its placement between sections on baptism and the Lord's Supper may imply its connection with one of these sacraments. Certainly it was assumed that the prayer was to be used by baptized believers only. Since it is unlikely that Christians met three times daily at that time, the prayer was apparently used privately as well as publicly. Although it is not quoted elsewhere in the earliest literature, it is mentioned by the church fathers. We may conclude that the prayer was well known and did not need to be taught in writing. In fact, since it was apparently considered so sacred that only members of the Church should repeat it, there may have been a reluctance to put it into writing, especially in the apologetic materials that were to be read by unbelievers. Both Origen and Tertullian refer to it as a model (Kistemaker, p. 327). A further connection with baptism occurs in the Apostolic Constitutions (vii.45.1), where those baptized recite it following the rite.

*VI. Theology.*–The Lord's Prayer is clearly intended to be used by believers who can call God their Father. This distinguishes it from the prayer that Jesus Himself prayed in Jn. 17 — a prayer that in essence and content reflects Jesus' unique relationship with God (cf. Jesus' distinction between "my Father and your Father" in Jn. 20:17). There is no indication in either Matthew or Luke that Jesus prayed the Lord's Prayer with His disciples. Nevertheless, these two prayers have common elements, e.g., the glorification of God (Jn. 17:1), the accomplishment of God's work on earth (v. 4), the name of God (v. 6), and being kept from evil or the evil one (v. 15). The theology of the prayer is also found throughout Paul's writings (Gal. 4:6; Phil. 2:9; 1 Cor. 15:28; Rom. 12:2; Eph. 4:32; 1 Cor. 10:13; see G. J. Brooke, *Downside Review*, 98 [1980], 306).

The Lord's Prayer expresses the repeated concern of the OT that God's name be known and glorified throughout the world. In this sense it is a missionary prayer. The order and proportion (a near balance) of "we" and "thou" petitions is also instructive. By putting the "thou" petitions first, Jesus taught that the purpose of prayer is not self-gratification. (On the petition for bread, cf. Jesus' teaching that follows in Mt. 6:25-34 par. Lk. 12:22-31.) If one's primary concern is the actualization of God's rule on earth, prayers for oneself will be made subservient to that great purpose. This recalls Jesus' promise that if we seek God's kingdom, all that we need will be ours as well (Mt. 6:33; Lk. 12:31).

It was observed above (II.C) that the petition concerning forgiveness is the only one to receive special comment at the close of the prayer. This demonstrates the strong emphasis that Jesus placed on the importance of personal relationships in connection with answers to prayer.

The closing petition regarding protection in a situation of testing and deliverance from the evil (one) reflects Jesus' teaching and miracles throughout the Gospels, in which He demonstrated the power of His kingdom against that of Satan. The final defeat of Satan will indeed mean the hallowing of God's name and the consummation of His kingdom on earth. (*See* KINGDOM OF GOD V.A.)

***Bibliography.***–I. Abrahams, *Studies in Pharisaism and the Gospels,* 2nd Series (1924), pp. 94-108; A. J. Bandstra, *Calvin Theological Journal,* 16 (1981), 15-30; R. E. Brown, *NT Essays* (repr. 1968), pp. 275-320; J. Carmignac, *Recherches sur le "Notre Père"* (1969); F. C. Fensham, *Nov.Test.,* 4 (1960), 1f.; A. Finkel and L. Frizzell, eds., *Standing Before God: Studies on Prayer in Scriptures and in Tradition* (*Festschrift* J. M. Oesterreicher; 1981); J. M. Ford, *ZNW,* 59 (1968), 127-131; R. A. Guelich, *Sermon on the Mount* (1982), pp. 283-297, 307-320; A. Hamman, *Prayer in the NT* (1971), pp. 103-145; J. Jeremias, *Expos.T.,* 71 (1960), 141-46; *Prayers of Jesus* (Eng. tr. 1978); S. Kistemaker, *JETS,* 21 (1978), 323-28; S. T. Lachs, *Nov.Test.,* 17 (1975), 6-8; R. Leaney, *Nov.Test.,* 1 (1956), 103-111; E. Lohmeyer, *Our Father* (Eng. tr. 1966); T. W. Manson, *BJRL,* 38 (1955/56), 99-113; B. M. Metzger, *Expos.T.,* 69 (1957), 52-54; C. G. Montefiore, *Rabbinic Literature and Gospel Teachings* (1930), pp. 125-136; C. F. D. Moule, *Reformed Theological Review,* 33 (1974), 65-75; B. Orchard, *Biblical Theological Bulletin,* 3 (1973), 274-282; J. J. Petuchowski and M. Brocke, eds., *Lord's Prayer and Jewish Liturgy* (1978); R. D. Richardson, *ATR,* 39 (1957), 123-130; W. Rordof, *Studia Liturgica,* 14 (1980/81), 1-19; J. Swetnam, *Bibl.,* 52 (1971), 556-563; J. van Bruggen, *Calvin*

*Theological Journal*, 17 (1982), 78-87; S. van Tilborg, *Nov.Test.*, 14 (1972), 94-105; W. O. Walker, Jr., *NTS*, 28 (1982), 237-256; G. G. Willis, *Downside Review*, 93 (1975), 281-88; E. M. Yamauchi, *WTJ*, 28 (1965/66), 145-156. W. L. LIEFELD

**LORD'S SUPPER (EUCHARIST).**

I. Fellowship Meals with Jesus and the Last Supper
II. Accounts of the Last Supper
III. Last Supper as Passover
IV. Basis of Interpretation
  A. OT Background
  B. NT Context
V. Development of Eucharistic Doctrine
VI. Development of the Liturgy
VII. Reformation of Doctrine and Liturgy
VIII. Some Essential Features in the Interpretation of the Supper

***I. Fellowship Meals with Jesus and the Last Supper.***–Throughout its history the Church has kept at the center of its life and worship not only the preaching of the Word of God but also the celebration of the Lord's Supper or eucharist. In this rite the Church follows the example and command given by Jesus Himself during His last supper with His disciples. It acts in His name and seeks His presence, believing that in the celebration Christ renews His fellowship with His people, strengthens their faith and hope, communicates to them the power of His death and resurrection, and thus enables them to present themselves afresh, within the membership of His body, as a living sacrifice devoted thus by Him more wholly to His service.

Immediately after Pentecost the Church "devoted themselves to the apostles' teaching and fellowship, to the breaking of bread and the prayers" (Acts 2:42). A glad realization of the presence of the risen Jesus in their midst seems to have marked "breaking of bread" at a common meal.

The custom of placing the eucharist at the heart of the worship and fellowship of the Church may have been inspired not only by the disciples' memory of the Last Supper with Jesus but also by the memory of their fellowship meals with Him during both His days on earth and the forty days of His risen appearances. They now realized that He had made eating and drinking with them a pledge that He, the Messiah, would renew, perfect, and make eternal such table fellowship in the fulness and glory of His kingdom, and with this belief they celebrated their eucharistic meals, awaiting His final return. Despite the memories of all their meals with Jesus before and after His resurrection, they recognized that His words and actions at the Last Supper had a deep significance of their own.

***II. Accounts of the Last Supper.***–The NT contains four accounts of what Jesus did and said at the Last Supper: Mt. 26:26-30; Mk. 14:22-25; Lk. 22:14-20; 1 Cor. 11:23-26. The common features of Luke's and Paul's accounts suggest a tradition distinct from that of Mark and Matthew. Both Luke and Paul introduce the words "This do in remembrance of me" as spoken by Jesus. Luke places this utterance at the end of the bread-saying, Paul in connection with the giving of both bread and wine. Matthew and Mark denote the cup as "my blood of the covenant which is poured out for many," whereas Luke and Paul use "the new covenant in my blood" and omit "for many." Paul alone has "for you" after the bread-saying; only Luke has "for you" after the cup-saying. Both Paul and Luke consistently use Gk. *eucharistēsas* for "having given thanks," but Matthew and Mark change this term to *eulogēsas* when referring to thanksgiving for the bread.

Some important MSS omit Lk. 22:19b-20 and alter the order of other verses, but there are good grounds for accepting the longer and more complicated account as arising from genuine traditions that were worth preserving. Luke's longer account, if accepted, may be regarded as including an extra cup not mentioned by the other traditions, or as collating two accounts, each valuable for helping the Church understand the meaning of the Supper.

The accounts all agree that the Supper took place on the night when Jesus was betrayed, that He took bread, and, when He had given thanks, He broke it and said, "This is my body." They agree that He also gave some significance to the cup. Matthew, Mark, and Luke preserve a pledge of Jesus to abstain from drinking the fruit of the vine until the kingdom comes (Mt. 26:29; Mk. 14:25; Lk. 22:16). In Matthew and Mark Jesus makes this pledge after the action with the bread and wine; in Luke it introduces the whole action. Paul's account omits this saying but contains the rubric "as often as you eat this bread and drink the cup, you proclaim the Lord's death until he comes."

Scholars disagree about which account represents the earliest tradition. Some think that Paul's statement, "I received from the Lord what I also delivered to you," is a claim that he had a special communication from the risen Lord. Others think that these words imply only that Paul was receiving and handing on a reliable church tradition. Some think that the parallelism of Mark's phraseology ("this is my body" — "this is my blood") indicates a tendency to assimilate one saying to another through usage in the Church and therefore must be later than the Pauline phraseology at these points. Others argue that Paul's repetition of "this do in remembrance of me" was molded by liturgical usage and thus indicates a late date. Some think that Luke's account shows contact with a very primitive source. The variations between Paul and Mark seem to point to access to distinct traditions. Luke certainly knew Paul's account but also had his own particular source. Matthew largely depended on Mark.

It is worthwhile to attempt to establish the most primitive facts and to show how variations could have arisen within the keen intensity of the life of the early Christian community. Even if some of these variations may seem mutually exclusive when regarded as historical accounts of the original meal, readers can thankfully accept each account as helping them to interpret and more fully understand the rite.

***III. Last Supper as Passover.***–From the precise dating of events in the Fourth Gospel, the question arises whether the supper recorded in the Synoptic Gospels can properly be regarded as a Passover feast. Jn. 18:28; 19:14, 31 indicate that Jesus died on the afternoon before the Passover lambs were slain in the temple. This sequence has given rise to the theory that the "Last Supper" was a kiddush, a simple meal of preparation either for a sabbath or for a festival at which, after religious discussion, a cup of wine mixed with water was blessed and drunk and a benediction pronounced over bread. This theory makes it easy to explain certain otherwise awkward details: why no account of the Last Supper mentions a paschal lamb, why ordinary bread was used instead of unleavened bread, and why only one cup apparently was used. The theory also accounts for how Jesus could be arrested after the Passover feast had begun, how a linen cloth could then be purchased for His burial, and how Simon of Cyrene could be found coming from work in the fields on what was apparently a holiday.

The chronology of Mark, however (cf. 14:1, 12, 16f.), apparently confirmed by Mt. 26:17; Lk. 22:15, indicates that the Last Supper took place at the regular time of the feast in the city and therefore took the form of a Passover.

Other details in the Synoptics characterize the Supper as a Passover: it was a lengthy and well-prepared meal; it took place at night; the disciples reclined at the table (Mk. 14:18) and drank wine; the whole meal closed with an act of praise (v. 26). This identification with the Passover allows for deeper and richer possibilities of interpretation.

In an effort to harmonize John's account with the Synoptics, scholars have suggested that the Sadducees and the Pharisees disputed that year over the timing of the feast and as a result fixed two different dates. A calendar found in the Qumrân community places the Passover on Tuesday evening, several days before the official Passover. Possibly Jesus Himself deliberately celebrated Passover early with His disciples.

Although certain obscurities must remain owing to the variation in the accounts, Jesus apparently interrupted the usual Passover feast at certain points with decisive words and actions. He seems to have broken and shared the bread immediately before the consumption of the lamb; His action either corresponded to the usual breaking of the cakes of unleavened bread or to the explanation by the head of the family of the deep significance of the meal in response to the traditional questions by the youngest member present about the meaning of the rite.

Jesus' offering the cup, apparently after the lamb was eaten, was connected with the blessing on the third of the four cups (1 Cor. 11:25; Lk. 22:20). His vow of abstinence and words expressing expectation and hope of the fulfillment of what was symbolized may have preceded (as in Mk. 14:24f.) the group's partaking of the fourth cup.

*IV. Basis of Interpretation.–A. OT Background.* Jesus' words and actions at the Last Supper should be considered in the light of related OT texts and ritual. The disciples would have understood the Supper in this rich and vivid context, especially after the meaning of the death and resurrection of Jesus began to dawn upon them.

It has been noted that, whether or not the Last Supper was a regular Passover meal, "the atmosphere of the Passover pervaded the whole thought and feeling of the upper room." The disciples, dwelling on the significance for the Jewish people of the Exodus from Egypt, would have interpreted Jesus' words "This do in remembrance of me" in this context; they would have remembered how He had spoken of the significance of the "exodus" He would accomplish through His death (Lk. 9:30).

The Exodus from Egypt is for the Jews an event of unique significance. It was regarded as God's once-for-all deliverance involving not only the generation that actually experienced it historically but all the succeeding generations. The celebration of the Exodus in the annual Passover feast (cf. Ex. 12) is intended not simply to evoke pious and thankful memories of the past but to bring each generation under the living power of this unique eschatological event (vv. 26f.; 13:8). Thus, in displacing the ritual of the remembrance of the Exodus by a new ritual centered on His death and resurrection, Jesus indicated that these events would uniquely affect the destiny of all generations of mankind. He deliberately instituted for His Church a means by which the power and reality of His death and resurrection could be brought to bear upon the life of each generation within the Church.

The killing of the lamb at the Passover feast, the sprinkling of its blood on the lintels and doorposts, and the partaking of its flesh (Ex. 12:7f.) signify a sacrifice that brings protection from judgment and evil powers and the favor of God. Jesus' substituting, for the lamb sacrificed in the temple and lying before them to be eaten, His own broken body and shed blood as the disciples' protection and food is thus deeply significant. This substitution signifies and pledges that His self-offering in death will be the sacrifice on which they could rely, and His blood will be their protection from the powers that hold mankind in bondage.

Jesus spoke of Himself not only as the paschal lamb, but also as a sacrifice in accordance with other OT analogies. In the sacrificial ritual, the portion of peace offering not consumed by fire, and thus not offered to God as His food (see Lev. 3:1-11; Nu. 28:2), was eaten by priest and people (Lev. 19:5f.; 1 S. 9:13) in an act of association with the altar and the sacrifice (Ex. 24:1-11; Dt. 27:7; cf. 1 Cor. 10). Jesus' giving the elements to His disciples was not only a further sign of their own fellowship and participation in His sacrificial death but also an assurance that by partaking of Him they would have fellowship with God in the reconciliation He would accomplish.

Although the traditional Jewish Passover feast may have already taken on features belonging to a meal ratifying a covenant, Jesus' words and actions were deliberately calculated to give this Passover meal a covenantal character. In the OT, after making a covenant, often by sprinkling sacrificial blood as at Sinai (cf. Ex. 24:1-8), the participants had fellowship and mutually pledged loyalty in a meal (Gen. 26:30; 31:54; 2 S. 3:20). The covenant made between God and Israel at Sinai was likewise followed by a meal in which the people "ate and drank and saw God" (Ex. 24:11). Jesus thus ratified in the Supper the new covenant (Jer. 31:1-34) between the Lord and His people.

In celebrating the Supper Jesus emphasized the messianic and eschatological significance of the Passover meal. At the Passover the Jews looked forward to a future deliverance that the Exodus foreshadowed. They set aside a cup for the Messiah in case he came that very night to deliver them and fulfil the promise of the messianic banquet (cf. Isa. 25–26; 65:13; etc.). It may have been this cup that Jesus took in the institution of the new rite, indicating that even now the Messiah was present to feast with His people.

After the Resurrection the disciples would see their frequent celebrations of the Supper (Acts 2:42-46; 20:7) as the climax of Jesus' table fellowship with publicans and sinners (Mt. 11:18f.; Lk. 15:2) and of their own daily meals with Him. They would interpret it not only as a bare prophecy but as a real foretaste of the messianic banquet and a sign of the presence of the kingdom of God in their midst in the person of Jesus (Mt. 8:11; cf. Mk. 10:35f.; Lk. 14:15-24). They would see its meaning in relation to His living presence in the Church, brought out fully in the Easter meals they had shared with Him (Lk. 24:13-35; Jn. 21:1-14; Acts 10:41). It would be a supper in the presence of the risen Lord, their Host. They would see in the messianic miracle of His feeding the multitude and in His words about Himself as the bread of life a sign of His continual hidden self-giving in the Lord's Supper.

*B. NT Context.* In 1 Cor. 10 Paul refers to Israel's being saved, revived, and nourished by miracles corresponding to the NT sacraments of baptism and the Lord's Supper. Paul asserts that Christ's presence in OT Israel was so real, and the spiritual blessing He bestowed on His people was so closely bound up with the miraculous physical help He gave them, that He could actually be identified with one of the objects He used in mediating His blessing to them — "that Rock was Christ" (v. 4).

Despite Christ's sacramental presence that generation of Israel was unfaithful, and many of them perished with a judgment that was all the more severe because they had despised His real presence so greatly. Paul uses the tragic example of this judgment to enforce his appeal to the Corinthians to shun idol worship, participation in pagan sacrificial meals, and conformity to heathen practices: "The cup of blessing which we bless, is it not a participation in the body of Christ? Because there is one loaf, we who are many are one body, for we all partake of the one bread. . . . You cannot partake of the table of the Lord and the table of demons" (1 Cor. 10:16f., 21b). In Paul's thinking the real presence of Christ, actively forming His people into one body with Himself, clearly dominates the Church's celebration of the Lord's Supper. Moreover, partaking of the Lord's Supper brings Christians into a living relationship with the power of the sacrificial death and resurrection of Christ. Paul's allusion that those who partook of the sacrifices made in heathen temples to devils entered into real and powerful communion with the devils themselves (vv. 18-21) reinforces this conclusion.

With a similar thought Paul later speaks of people's damning themselves by eating and drinking "unworthily" at the Lord's Supper through "not discerning" the Lord's body (1 Cor. 11:29). This "damnation" is not the deity's quasi-physical automatic reaction to unworthy people's eating and drinking the elements. It is rather a personal judgment incurred in a sphere where the presence of Christ is real and powerful. A casual approach to the gracious personal encounter mediated through the sacrament between Christ and His people can only spurn and profane the grace of Christ and inevitably merit judgment and rejection by Christ Himself.

Because of the NT context of the Lord's Supper, the words "this do in remembrance of me" (Gk. *eis tēn emēn anámnēsin,* 1 Cor. 11:24f.) call for careful discussion. The word "remembrance" (*anámnēsis*) echoes Ex. 12:14, which institutes the Passover as a "memorial day." The paschal feast is designed not simply to restore fading mental impressions of the past event but also to reestablish the former relationship to divine grace. The Passover "remembrance" is intended to reactualize what is remembered. In the same way, to celebrate the Lord's Supper in "remembrance" of Christ means to seek fresh communion with Him so that, as Paul says in Phil. 3:10f., "I may know him, and the power of his resurrection, and may share his sufferings, becoming like him in his death, that if possible I may attain the resurrection from the dead." In this process, however, remembering the historical events of the death and resurrection of Jesus also plays an important part.

*Anámnēsis* can also mean a memorial before God (e.g., Acts 10:4; Mk. 14:9). Thus some believe that in the Last Supper the Church recalls the sacrifice of Christ to make it again become effective. The *anámnēsis,* however, is better related to the intercession that the Church must inevitably make in its thankful response to God's grace in the sacrament. It is impossible that the Church should not pray at the Lord's table for the salvation of mankind; this intercession and Christ's own heavenly intercession (*see* INTERCESSION OF CHRIST) might be thought of as an *anámnēsis* before God.

One should similarly interpret 1 Cor. 11:26: "For as often as you eat this bread and drink the cup, you proclaim the Lord's death until he comes." Proclamation here means more than a dramatic representation of the death of Christ. Like the kerygma, it involves re-presenting in both word and action the redemptive event itself, so that participants in the eucharistic ritual relate themselves in a powerful and living way to the unique sacrifice of Christ on the cross. But all the celebrations of the Supper involve only the one sacrifice. "It is clear . . . that the bringing of the Eucharist under the rubric of proclamation excludes the idea of its being a sacrifice in itself or in its own right. Not the actual and literal offering of the sacrifice, but an action proclaiming a sacrifice once offered and eternally valid before the Father, is what the Eucharist effects" (T. F. Torrance, *Conflict and Agreement in the Church* (1959), II, 179f.).

In His discourse about the bread of life in Jn. 6, Jesus uses analogies about the spiritual hunger of people for God and its satisfaction in the Word and Wisdom of God. "The Word became flesh" (Jn. 1:14) and was offered upon the cross so that people might obtain everlasting life and be raised up at the last day (6:50-54). Through this sacrifice the eternal life of the Word is made available to all believers as their spiritual food and drink (v. 47), which alone unites them to the incarnate Word (v. 56) and enables them to have spiritual life (v. 53).

At the heart of this discourse, just as in Jn. 15, is Jesus' insistence that a real and living communion, which is the source of His people's salvation and Christian life, must exist between Him and them in every age. The institution of the Supper later gave a visible clue that enables Christians to grasp the fuller meaning of Jesus' "hard saying" (Jn. 6:60) about eating His flesh and drinking His blood. But Jn. 6 seems equally to give a clue to the interpretation of the Lord's Supper: the Supper is a means by which the Church has communion with the incarnate life that became the life of mankind. Even though Jesus has ascended to heaven, His presence in the Lord's Supper is "just as real as His physical presence was to the Apostles" (Higgins, p. 77). The Supper, however, must not be interpreted as if the mere eating and drinking of the elements had some inherently magical effect, for "it is the spirit that gives life, the flesh is of no avail" (v. 63).

***V. Development of Eucharistic Doctrine.***–The Lord's Supper was the central point in the life and worship of the early Church. Ignatius (*ca.* 35-107), Justin Martyr (*ca.* 100-165), and Irenaeus (*ca.* 130-200) referred to it in phrases deriving from a realistic interpretation of the language of Jn. 6. Ignatius, and later Irenaeus, thought of it as "the medicine of immortality, and the antidote that we should not die but that we should live in Jesus Christ forever" (Eph. 20:2). Justin said: "The food which is blessed by the prayer of His Word, and by which our blood and flesh by transmutation are nourished, is the flesh and blood of that Jesus which was made flesh" (*Apol.* i.66).

But such language is not to be understood in any crudely materialistic sense. The food is spiritual. Christians had not yet devised any theory relating the elements to the body and blood of Christ.

Similarly, late in the 1st cent. the eucharist was regarded as the Gentiles' "pure offering" referred to in Mal. 1:11. This sacrifice, however, consists especially of prayers, thanksgivings, and the offerings of gifts for the needy. The Supper was emphasized as a bond of brotherly union, and the Church as a whole was thought to make its spiritual offering to the Lord.

Christians from the 3rd cent. onward paid greater attention to the words of institution. Tertullian (*ca.* 60-220), Hippolytus (*ca.* 170-236), and Cyprian (d. 258) tended to identify the bread and wine with the body and blood of Christ and to attach the real presence of Christ to the elements. But they often clearly distinguished things spoken of at other times as identical. Tertullian called the bread the "figure" of the body. Origen (*ca.* 185-254) figuratively and allegorically referred to the Supper. Cyprian developed the idea of the eucharist as a sacrifice. Since Christ in His suffering and sacrifice is identified with His people and offers them in Himself, in a reciprocal and parallel way the Church now identified itself with Christ who is its head and thus offered a spiritual and bloodless sacrifice in the union with Christ created through the sacrament.

In the 4th and 5th cents. two tendencies are noticeable. (1) Cyril of Jerusalem (*ca.* 315-386), Gregory of Nyssa (*ca.* 330-395), Chrysostom (*ca.* 347-407), and the most influential exponent, Ambrose (*ca.* 339-397), tended to identify the bread and wine with the body and blood of Christ by alluding to a transformation of the elements themselves. Thus they used an analogy from the biblical miracle of the change of water into wine. By the Word and the Holy Spirit the bread becomes what it was not previously. These writers used realist language in an unqualified way. (2) In the same period others maintained the tradition that the elements signified things that they could not contain, but also affirmed that the elements were signs of realities actually present. Augustine (354-430), the predominant figure in this school, emphasized the distinction between the sign and the thing signified, the visible and invisible realities, of which the latter were apprehended by faith alone. He so emphasized the spiritual sense of the words bearing on the sacrament that he could say: "Believe and thou hast eaten." He also stressed the resemblance between the sign and the invisible reality, the power and place of the Word in the making of a sacrament, and the corporate nature of the mystical body in which the faithful live by word and sacrament.

Developing along with this eucharistic theology was the doctrine that the Christian shares in the divine nature through union with the incarnate Son of God. This doctrine led to the view that the incarnational union of Christ with human flesh continues in every generation of the Church through the celebration of the eucharist. The incorporation of the Christian into Christ through the sacraments was deepened (e.g., in Augustine) by the idea of the eucharist as a sacrifice. Since the Church is the body of Christ united to the Head through mystical and real union, the Church has its part in the once-for-all self-offering of the Head.

Popular superstitions and the Gallican and Roman liturgies influenced ninth-century developments of sacramental doctrine. Paschasius Radbertus (*ca.* 785-860), following Ambrose's lead, identified the eucharistic bread with the historical body of the Lord and affirmed that the real presence takes place through a change in the elements. In opposition, Ratramnus (d. 868), developing the thought of Augustine, affirmed that the bread symbolizes the mystical body of Christ, which is composed of head and members. In the 11th cent. Berengar of Tours again revived a dynamic-symbolic teaching that emphasized the spiritual aspect of the eucharist; church councils condemned his teaching. In 1215 the Fourth Lateran Council asserted that the body and blood of Christ "are truly contained in the sacrament of the altar under the forms (*sub speciebus*) of bread and wine, the bread being transubstantiated into the body and the wine into the blood by divine power, so that for the accomplishment of the mystery of unity we ourselves receive from his what he himself received from ours." With the help of Aristotle's philosophy, Aquinas (*ca.* 1225-1274) worked out this teaching in detail in a period of great development of popular eucharistic devotion.

Such teaching altered the Church's conception of grace, which came to be thought of as an impersonal substance that could be infused into the life of the Church by the sacraments, which themselves caused grace. The counter-reformational Council of Trent in 1547 decided that the sacraments confer grace *ex opere operato* (by the force of the action itself), provided no obstacle is put in the way; they do not depend on the faith of the recipient.

*VI. Development of the Liturgy.*–Immediately after Pentecost, what was essential to the Lord's Supper was removed from its Passover context and celebrated as a more ordinary Jewish community meal. Probably in one form of the

Thirteenth-century mosaic of the "Last Supper" by an anonymous artist of the Italian school (New Orleans Museum of Art, New Orleans, Louisiana, The Samuel H. Kress Collection)

earliest celebration (cf. the accounts of Paul and Luke) the bread was broken with a blessing at the start of the meal and the cup with its blessing was postponed till the end. But at an early stage the bread was given with the cup, and the two thanksgiving prayers were merged into one. The accompanying meal was dropped at an early date — already in Paul's time in Corinth it had taken on undesirable features (cf. 1 Cor. 11:20ff.). The "Supper" then became joined to the service of readings, prayers, praises, and sermon patterned after Jewish synagogue worship. Quite soon the Supper was named "eucharist."

Justin Martyr described the order of second-century Christian worship as readings (from the Prophets, Gospel, and Epistles), a sermon, intercession, the kiss of peace, offering of gifts, bringing of the elements, a thanksgiving prayer, the amen of the people, and the distribution of broken bread and wine.

In the early centuries of the Church a group of liturgical elements either consisting of phrases taken from Holy Scripture or built up from scriptural expressions (such as the *Kyrie, Sanctus, Benedictus, Pax*) took definite shape. Each element was recognized as adding a helpful or essential feature to a pattern of worship centered on both the Word and the Lord's Supper. The prayer of thanksgiving before the distribution of the elements became important; it was regarded as consecrating the bread and wine. Extempore prayer was allowed, but the authority and value of universal custom were recognized. These traditional liturgical features appear in varying order and interrelation in the important early liturgies that shaped later tradition. They are the basis of the Eastern liturgy and the Roman mass. The Reformers incorporated them into their forms of service, and they are universally used today.

In eucharistic celebrations of earlier centuries the whole congregation participated in every important aspect and could see the minister perform all the actions; the accompanying ceremonial was subordinated to the clear emergence of the meaning of the central action. Before large churches were built the vestments and accompaniments of the service were simple.

Liturgical rites became unified and fixed, mainly according to the usage in two great centers, Byzantium in the East and Rome in the West. The only variable elements allowed were ultimately those prescribed for various seasons of the church year. In the Byzantine liturgy the eucharistic elements were consecrated behind a screen and a veil; two processions, one the "little entry," in which the Word was brought in before being read, the other the "great entry," in which the elements themselves were brought in, dominated the service.

The Western Church applied the name "mass" to the eucharist. The term apparently derived from the words with which the congregation was dismissed, or blessed, at the close of the service, *ite missa est* ("Go, you are dismissed"). In the Roman liturgy the "canon" of the mass, the central core that orders the action of the actual eucharist, was gradually developed until it became fixed about the 5th century. Before long the whole service received an authoritative form.

Several influences largely deprived the eucharistic rite of its original clarity and simplicity. Especially in the East the Church's worship, coming under the emperor's patronage, developed a grandeur reflecting the secular court. Since the people could not see the central act of the mystery, they tended to center devotion on the processions, which developed features unrelated to the original institution of the Supper.

The Roman mass also became a complicated and elaborate celebration. Dramatic accompaniments added to the ritual made it resemble a spectacle that onlookers admired instead of a service that involved the congregation. The details of these accompaniments were interpreted in later centuries as a visible enactment of the life and passion of Christ. The use of Latin long after it had ceased to be a vernacular accentuated the impression that only the clergy could actively participate in the mass. The canon of the mass and the doctrine of transubstantiation led to a primarily sacrificial interpretation of the rite; moreover, the priest stood with his back to the people in front of an altar, above which he elevated the host as if offering a sacrifice to God. The development of the "low mass," an adaptation of the "high" service for more ordinary and occasional use, caused the multiplication of altars within large churches and the celebration of private masses, with the idea that each mass had its own value and could be directed by priest or church to achieve desired ends.

In the 12th cent. giving the cup to the laity was discontinued lest even a drop of the consecrated wine be spilled. The whole Christ, however, was understood to be present in the bread.

At the Council of Trent a commission was appointed to revise and purify the mass, and from 1570 until the Second Vatican Council one official form of the rite was imposed on the whole Roman Catholic Church.

***VII. Reformation of Doctrine and Liturgy.***–The Reformers denied that the mass is a sacrifice offered to God. They rejected the doctrine of transubstantiation, the philosophy that led to it, and the unnecessary miracle it implied. They insisted that the sacraments bestow their blessings only when received by a person with a personal relationship of faith in God, which is created by the Word, and that the sacraments are effective only in the sovereignty and freedom of the Holy Spirit.

The earliest writings of Martin Luther (1483-1546) emphasize the Lord's Supper as a joyful communion with Christ within the fellowship of the Church. Partaking of the one bread, Christians minister to each other in a love that is a thankful response to the love of Christ. In communion with Christ in the sacrament, they find that Christ bears all their burdens and endows them with His wealth and blessing, so that in love they can bear each other's burdens.

The early writings of Ulrich Zwingli (1484-1531) also totally reject the mass as a sacrifice. Zwingli stressed the importance of the Supper as a remembrance of the historical event of the crucifixion and a valuable means of communion with Christ.

In the controversy that broke out when differences between the German and Swiss views became more apparent, Zwingli tended to emphasize the contemplation of the cross in the Supper at the expense of the place he had earlier given to the communion aspect. He insisted on interpreting the words "This is my body" by the phrase "This signifies my body" and implied that the main effect of the sacrament was simply strengthened faith — though for him faith was itself inseparable from real communion with Christ.

Luther, in conflict with Zwingli, Oecolampadius, and others, was forced to read the early fathers; with a variety of vivid expressions that could easily be misunderstood, he insisted that in the Lord's Supper a miracle takes place comparable to the Incarnation. He emphasized that the sacrament was a gift or testament made by God that assures believers of forgiveness, not a sacrifice made to God. Under the influence of Peter d'Ailly (1350-1420) Luther denied the necessity of any inward change in the elements, but at the same time he emphasized the infallible power of the words "This is my body" to make the body of Christ objectively present in the sacrament along with the elements.

In discussing the possibility and nature of such a miracle, Luther asserted that Christ's body because of its union with deity is omnipresent. The right hand of God, to which Christ ascended in His bodily nature, can be regarded as being everywhere, since the term means God's almighty rule. Christ's body is therefore wherever God rules. But the Christian has real access to the body of Christ by faith only where the Word of God declares that body to be present, as in the sacrament. So objectively real, however, is the presence of the body of Christ in the sacrament that the wicked can damn themselves by eating it.

For Calvin (1509-1564) one of the central mysteries of the faith was the "mystical union" of Christ, the head of the Church, with the members of His body. This union is comparable to the union of the Word with human nature in the Incarnation. Paul's use of the terms "in Christ" and "Christ in us" indicates the reality and mystery of this relationship. Jesus described this union in His discourses on the bread of life in Jn. 6 and the true vine in ch. 15. But no words can sufficiently explain this mystery; God therefore gives a living picture of it in the Lord's Supper. Since God does not mock anyone, the giving and receiving of the physical bread and wine must be regarded as a reliable sign of Christ's hidden spiritual self-giving of His body and blood, or His whole humanity, to His people. In the Supper, therefore, participants' receiving Christ by their faith involves more than the mere increase and exercise of faith. Calvin thus insisted no less than the Lutherans and Romanists that Christ is truly given and received in the sacrament. He differed from them only in explaining how this mystery occurs. While he admitted that it was better, in this matter, to adore than to explain, he formulated a doctrine that won the approval of Melanchthon and brought agreement among the Swiss churches.

Calvin's doctrine asserts that the humanity of Christ remains in its integrity in heaven, which is regarded as beyond the conceivable world. By the inconceivable power of the Holy Spirit, the power and virtue belonging to the humanity of Christ are communicated to the partaker of the sacrament by faith. This faith itself is so miraculous that it can ascend to Christ to feed upon Him. Calvin thus sought to preserve a dynamic parallelism between earthly and heavenly action, which are distinct yet inseparable. His doctrine of realized eschatology, which stresses the Church's participation here and now in the resurrection of Christ, enabled him to interpret the sacrament very realistically and to speak of it as giving a foretaste of eternal life and as being a pledge of the resurrection of the body. He also stressed church members' communion with one another in the sharing of the one loaf, and the eucharistic sacrifice of thanksgiving that the Church can make by participating in the one priesthood of Christ.

While revising eucharistic doctrine through their new understanding of Scripture, the Reformers also found themselves forced to revise the liturgy. At an early date they restored communion in both kinds to the laity. The Reformers aimed "not to abolish but to cleanse"; they attempted to preserve what was essential and helpful in the traditional ritual and purge what was irreconcilable with the gospel. Andreas Karlstadt (1480-1541) and Thomas Münzer (1490-1525), who had otherwise extreme views, at early dates produced restrained and worthy liturgical forms for the celebration of the Supper.

Luther in 1523 was content to preserve most of the liturgy in Latin and just radically revised the prayer of consecration, through which he believed the mass had been turned into a sacrifice. In 1525, however, he translated the mass into German, changing the liturgy more drastically and ensuring that the uncorrupted words of the institution of the sacrament would remain the chief feature in the consecration. Luther's most valuable contributions in this field were restoring the sermon to its true place and introducing German hymns to allow the fuller participation of the people. At an early period, anxious to safeguard the rite from profanation, he included the discipline of careful self-examination or confession by the participants. He retained features that other Reformers rejected, such as the elevation of the host and traditional vestments.

Zwingli far more radically altered the traditional outward form and designed a service in which the communion was celebrated as if it were a family meal around a table. The ministers dressed soberly. There was no prayer of consecration. The elements were distributed and received in silence after the Scripture reading, the Apostles' Creed, the fencing of the tables, a prayer of humble access, and the words of institution.

In deciding the form for the celebration of the Lord's Supper in Geneva, Calvin was influenced by the form of prayers produced by William Farel (1489-1565) in 1524 and by the liturgical reform that had taken place in Strasbourg largely under the leadership of Martin Bucer (1491-1551), to whom Calvin was deeply indebted even for the wording of some prayers. Calvin's concern was to maintain the order he believed to have been prevalent in the ancient Church and to attain the ideal of a service that centered on the preaching of the Word of God and was incomplete without the celebration of the Lord's Supper. Calvin hoped that this dual celebration of Word and sacrament would take place every Sunday. He left room for freedom of prayer and sought to avoid anything that would prevent the original action at the table from being clearly expressed in its primitive simplicity.

The eucharistic doctrine expressed in the definitive (Edwardian) formulations of the Anglican Church at the Reformation is consistently Calvinistic. The Anglican liturgy took final shape when tension existed between those who wished to retain as much of the medieval practices as circumstances would allow and adherents of an incipient Puritan movement who desired more radical reconstruction after the manner of the Swiss churches. The successive prayer books reflect the influence of both points of view. Those who were more "Catholic" in their sympathies regarded the first prayer book, issued by Cranmer in 1549, as admirable and well balanced in every way. But some, supported by Martin Bucer and Peter Martyr (1500-1562), who were then in exile in England from the Continent, strongly protested this book. Its drastic revision (1552) culminated ultimately in the present prayer book of 1662. The doctrinal articles from the first version in 1553 (Forty-Two) to the definitive form in 1571 (Thirty-Nine) agree substantially with Calvin's understanding.

From the Reformation to comparatively recent times eucharistic theology has had, generally speaking, few important developments. The theology of the period of Protestant orthodoxy, the Enlightenment, and the 19th cent. was not likely to promote fresh and creative thinking on the sacraments. But the Confession of Faith and the Directory of Public Worship produced by the Westminster Assembly provided for the Presbyterian Church a worthy and rich doctrine of the presence of Christ in the sacraments. Moreover, the importance of the Lord's Supper in the devotion and experience of the common people often prevented its actual celebration from suffering too acutely from the poverty of doctrine and liturgy. Anglican theologians, like Calvin, always tended to stress the relationship of the sacrament to the Incarnation. In all the churches of the main Reformation traditions a concern has recently arisen to restore to the Church what it might have lost by neglecting its liturgical tradition. Churches are also paying fresh attention to the doctrine of the Lord's Supper, which is currently the subject of much creative thinking and writing. The Second Vatican Council made important changes in the form of the mass; it is now conducted mainly in the vernacular, and the officiating priest faces the people.

*VIII. Some Essential Features in the Interpretation of the Supper.*–From a study of the biblical background of the rite, the exegesis of Christ's own words, the traditional interpretation of the rite within the mainstream of church life, and the modern discussion, it is obvious that the Supper has never failed to present certain features that most Christians have found valuable and meaningful.

(1) Through the Lord's Supper the efficacy and power of the redemptive work of Jesus Christ in His death and resurrection are applied to His people in each generation (see IV above).

(2) Through the Supper the risen Jesus Christ is present in the midst of His people in each generation. Many commentators have agreed that the best interpretation of the words "This is my body" is "This is Myself." Others have pointed out that this sense is possibly obtained by the twofold assertion "This is my body," "This is my blood." The words were spoken to the disciples by a Christ who was leaving them (Jn. 14:2f., 28) and whose promise to come to them again (vv. 3, 28) referred not simply to a final coming in glory but to a coming through the Spirit within the continuing life of the Church. He gave the bread with these significant words to pledge that He would be with them in His risen power whenever they met to break bread in His name as He had taught them. He would make the bread signify and convey to them in part what His body had signified and conveyed when He had been with them (cf. Mt. 18:20). The table fellowship that depended on the presence and action of His earthly or resurrection body would be reconstituted around the taking of the bread and wine.

(3) In the Supper Jesus gives to all His people an irrevocable pledge of their share in His eternal destiny. At the Lord's table the disciples knew that Jesus had identified Himself with them in their need and wretched-

ness. His baptism had been a sign and the cross, to which He was now fully pledging Himself, was the climax of His ministry's self-identification with the condition and fate of sinners. But since the cross restored Him to glory, before He was crucified He deliberately gave His disciples a sign that He never willed to be without them, that henceforth they could always with complete certainty identify themselves with Him in His glorious victory and destiny. With His words "for you" and His command to all present to "take and eat," Jesus thus associated each of His disciples with Himself in all His triumphant power and heavenly greatness. In giving the bread Jesus gives Himself to the believing souls who receive it. As He gave Himself for them, so He gives Himself to them. What He did for them, He accomplishes in them (cf. Leenhardt, p. 65).

(4) Through the Lord's Supper Jesus Christ incorporates humanity into His body, as the counterpart of the completed union with all mankind effected in His incarnation, death, and resurrection. To formulate sacramental doctrine one must give due weight, as Luther, Calvin, and the early fathers did, to Jn. 6 and the realistic NT descriptions of the Church as the body of Christ and of the union of the members of the body with the Head. Through the ministry of word and sacrament, the members of Christ are incorporated into His body by faith in a union of being, which has a substantial element but is nevertheless dominated by a personal-faith relationship. This incorporation is not the "extension" of an incarnation that somehow awaits completion (as, e.g., in Gore, p. 59). The ingrafting of the branches is not necessary to complete the vine (Jn. 15:5), and basically, as Calvin pointed out, the Incarnation has already set up a relationship of flesh with all mankind as the head of all things (cf. Wallace, p. 148). Phrases such as "reenactment" or "repeated actualization" are better than "extension" or "completion" (cf. Torrance, II, 188f.).

(5) The Lord's Supper is intended to be both a representation of Christ's one sacrifice and church members' eucharistic offering of themselves to God. The Lord's Supper leads the Church to realize afresh its own involvement in the saving event of the death and resurrection of Christ and to become related in a new way to this event. In a sense, therefore, God re-presents the sacrifice of Christ to His people within the sacrament. But the sacrament presents the historical event as one in which the people did not and cannot actively take part — an event in which Christ suffered alone in their place to save them and set them free. The Church, therefore, does not reenact the sacrifice of Christ through its initiative or sacramental activity or offer afresh a sacrifice identical to the one-time sacrifice made without its cooperation.

The Church, moreover, makes a glad self-sacrifice of thanksgiving in response to Christ's sacrifice of propitiation. It is supremely in the context of the Lord's Supper that the members of the Church within the one body can present themselves in body and soul as a living sacrifice, holy and acceptable to God (Rom. 12:1).

(6) Interpretations of the Lord's Supper must take full account of its corporate nature. The Supper is a meal, which is essentially a social means of fellowship. The early Church had an actual fellowship meal between the giving of the bread and the wine. The Jewish Passover feast, which forms the background of the Lord's Supper, essentially celebrates an action in which God dealt with His people as members of one body, and individuals find themselves strengthened and built up within the revitalizing of the corporate fellowship with God. The "new covenant" is a covenant between God and His whole people before it is a covenant between God and the individual.

Christians' communion with each other within the one fellowship is, therefore, an important aspect of the Lord's Supper. Paul referred to this communion in 1 Cor. 10:17, "For we being many are one bread, and one body: for we are all partakers of that one bread." The meal strengthens, first of all, the fellowship of love and service. The Reformed custom of each member handing the elements to another, thus serving the other and encouraging the other to partake, has a deeply significant meaning.

(7) Participants in the Lord's Supper encounter in the present the actuality of what is future. The Lord's Supper, like the Passover, is the "remembrance" of a unique event, whose effect is decisive not only for those who participated in it historically but also for those in each generation who participate in it sacramentally (cf. IV.A above). But the Lord's Supper also anticipates what is to come. Instead of returning immediately in the glory of His completed kingdom, to usher in visibly the new age for mankind, Jesus Christ has held back the final full irruption and manifestation of His reign. In the lengthened interim He gives within His Church, especially in the Lord's Supper, a foretaste of the final marriage supper of the Lamb (Rev. 19:7-9) and of the powers of the age to come (He. 6:4f.).

Participants in the Supper, therefore, within a temporal form and through a transitory event confront, as far as possible while still in the "last days" (He. 1:1; 1 Pet. 1:20), what will belong to them in Christ when they see Him as He is (1 Jn. 3:2). At present they can have this confrontation only through a sacramental veil. The sacrament is thus the appointed means by which God gives participants this gracious encounter with what is to come, and it is meant to make them always look forward in hope to the glory of the final destiny of all things, even while they offer themselves, in union with the crucified Lord, to the service of His word in the life of this present world. The prayer *Maranatha,* "Lord, come!", must ever spontaneously arise from the Church in the celebration of the sacrament (cf. 1 Cor. 11:26; 16:22).

***Bibliography.***–G. Aulén, *Eucharist and Sacrifice* (Eng. tr. 1958); D. M. Baillie, *Theology of the Sacraments* (1957); Y. T. Brilioth, *Eucharistic Faith and Practice* (Eng. tr. 1953); C. Gore, *Body of Christ* (1901); A. J. B. Higgins, *Lord's Supper in the NT* (1952); J. Jeremias, *Eucharistic Words of Jesus* (Eng. tr. 1955); J. A. Jungmann, *The Mass of the Roman Rite* (Eng. tr. 1959); F. J. Leenhardt and O. Cullmann, *Essays on the Lord's Supper* (Eng. tr. 1958); H. J. Lietzmann, *Mass and the Lord's Supper* (Eng. tr. 1953ff.); I. H. Marshall, *Last Supper and Lord's Supper* (1981); W. D. Maxwell, *Outline of Christian Worship* (1936); H. Sasse, *This Is My Body* (1959); M. Thurian, *Eucharistic Memorial* (Eng. tr. 1961); R. S. Wallace, *Calvin's Doctrine of the Word and Sacrament* (1953).

R. S. WALLACE

**LO-RUHAMAH** lō-ro͞o-hä'mə [Heb. *lōʾ ruḥāmâ*–'not shown compassion' (cf. RSV "Not pitied"); LXX Gk. *Ouk ēleēmḗnē*, translation rather than transliteration]. The AV and NEB transliteration of the name of the second child (only daughter) born to the prophet Hosea and his wife Gomer, *ca.* 758 B.C. (Hos. 1:6). God commanded Hosea to give his three children symbolic names (*see* JEZREEL; LO-AMMI). The name Lo-ruhamah connoted a withdrawal of covenant protection (or "love," using ancient Near Eastern legal terminology) and thus indicated that the covenant had been abrogated and punishment was due (v. 6). Lo-ruhamah was weaned, i.e., was at least 3 years old, when Hosea's third child was born (v. 8). Nothing otherwise is known of her or the other children.

D. STUART

**LOSE; LOSS; LOST** [Heb. *ʾāḇaḏ* (e.g., Ps. 119:176; piel, Eccl. 3:6), *ʾᵃḇēḏâ* ("lost thing," e.g., Ex. 22:9[MT 8]), *šᵉḵôl–* 'loss of children' (Isa. 47:8f.), *ʾāsap̱* (Jgs. 18:25), *bôš*–'be ashamed' ("at a loss," Jgs. 3:25), niphal of *gāzar*–'be cut off' (Lam. 3:54), niphal of *dāmâ*–'be silent' (Isa. 6:5), piel of *ḥāṭā'* ("bear the loss," Gen. 31:39), *yāṣā'*–'go out' (Josh. 19:47), hiphil and niphal of *kāraṯ*–'be cut off' (e.g., Zeph. 3:7), *nāpal*–'fall' (1 K. 20:25), *šāgâ*–'stray' (Prov. 5:23), hithpael of *šāḵaḥ*–'forget' (Eccl. 9:5); Aram. *n*e*zaq* ("suffer loss," Dnl. 6:2 [MT 3]); Gk. *apóllymi* (e.g., Mt. 10:39), *zēmióō*, *zēmía* (e.g., Acts 27:10), *apobolḗ* (v. 22), *aporéō* ("be at a loss," 25:20), *eklýomai* (e.g., "lose courage," He. 12:5), *enkakéō* ("lose heart," Lk. 18:1; 2 Cor. 4:1, 16; etc.), *ekpíptō*–'fall out' (2 Pet. 3:17), *mōraínō* ("lose its taste," Mt. 5:13; Lk. 14:34), *gónomai ánomos* ("lose its saltness," Mk. 9:50)]; AV also PERISH, FAINT, DAMAGE, FORGOTTEN, UNDONE, FADE AWAY, SILENCED (Isa. 6:5), BE CUT OFF (Zeph. 3:7), GO ASTRAY (Prov. 5:23), etc.; NEB also STRAY, CLOSED, MISSING, UTTERLY FORGOTTEN (Eccl. 9:5), etc.

Because Eng. "lose" is often used idiomatically, it represents a wide variety of Hebrew and Greek words. E.g., in Gal. 6:9 the passive of Gk. *eklýō* is appropriately translated by the idiom "lose heart," while it means literally "be unloosed" or "relax." Hence, only a few of the words listed above carry the simple meaning of "lose" or "loss."

The predominant Hebrew word rendered "lose" in the nonidiomatic sense by the RSV is *'āḇaḏ*. This term occurs most often with reference to lost domestic animals that face certain doom alone in the wilds (e.g., 1 S. 9:3, 20); indeed, it always carries the sense of being on the point of destruction — a connotation that is clearer in its alternate translation as "perish" (e.g., Lev. 26:38; *see* PERISH). Because the note of urgency is lacking in Eng. "lose," which can mean merely "misplace," it is easy to miss the theological significance of the analogy of Israel to lost (*'āḇaḏ*) sheep (Jer. 50:6; Ezk. 34:4, 16; cf. Isa. 27:13). Occasionally the text suggests the sheep have wilfully wandered (Isa. 53:6), but more often the shepherds have not cared adequately for the precious but feeble flock (e.g., Ezk. 34:1-10). The significance of Yahweh as the sheep's rescuer (vv. 11-31) is grasped only in view of the urgency of their perilous and helpless predicament.

The pathos of being "lost" comes through more clearly in English when interpreted psychologically; but *'āḇaḏ* never really has this sense. Isaiah's visionary experience is sometimes considered paradigmatic of the feeling of "lostness": "Woe is me! For I am lost . . ." (Isa. 6:5). The term used here is not *'āḇaḏ* but *dāmâ* (niphal, "be silenced"), which refers to Isaiah's being struck dumb with terror.

By far the most common NT term rendered "lose" or "lost" by the RSV (esp. in the Gospels) is Gk. *apóllymi*. Used frequently by the LXX to translate Heb. *'āḇaḏ*, Gk. *apóllymi* retains the threat of imminent destruction. It occurs in the Synoptic passages that use the lost sheep analogy to describe sinners doomed to perish unless they are rescued (Mt. 10:6; 15:24; 18:11; Lk. 15:4, 6). In Lk. 15 the parable of the lost sheep is grouped with those of the lost coin and the lost son. These stories tell about the joyful reception of the infinitely precious lost sinner into the Kingdom. Jesus, who seeks the sinner, risks great loss in the process — even His life (cf. Jn. 10:11).

Other passages use *apóllymi* in the sense of sacrificing one thing to gain something more precious; these passages refer to Jesus and His followers enduring loss. Jesus exhorts His followers to be prepared to lose their lives for His sake; those who do so will save their lives (Mt. 16:25 par. Mk. 8:35; Lk. 9:24; also Mt. 10:39; Lk. 17:33; Jn. 12:25). This startling reversal evokes the image of Jesus' own life-giving death and summons His disciples to follow His example, letting go of the life of the world to gain life in the Kingdom. Similarly, Jesus' hyperbolic saying in Mt. 5:29f. teaches the need to sacrifice those things that would exclude one from the kingdom of God.

Whereas *apóllymi* is the predominant term for "lose" in the Gospels, the verb *zēmióō* and noun *zēmía* ("loss") appear more often in the Epistles (e.g., 1 Cor. 3:15; 2 Cor. 7:9). In Phil. 3:4-6 Paul tells of his former accomplishments; then in v. 7 he changes course suddenly and states that he counts all these things as loss (*zēmía*) in the light of the supreme worth of knowing Christ Jesus (cf. vv. 8-11). His loss — like the loss of life or bodily member — is not to be lightly understood. What the disciple forfeits is of some consequence, but it is small compared to what is gained in Christ.

*See also* PERDITION; SHEEP.

***Bibliography.***–*DNTT*, I, 462-64; *TDNT*, I, *s.v.* ἀπόλλυμι (A. Oepke); II, *s.v.* ζημία, ζημιόω (A. Stumpff); *TDOT*, I, *s.v.* "abhadh" (B. Otzen).

C. PINCHES

**LOT** lot [Heb. *lôṭ*; Gk. *Lōt*]. The son of Haran, grandson of Terah the father of Abram (Gen. 11:27, 31; 12:5). As Abram's nephew Lot played a significant role in the patriarchal migration from Ur to Har(r)an (Gen. 11) and on into Canaan (ch. 12) before his own move to Sodom (ch. 13). The rescue of Lot from the allied kings who had raided the plain of Jordan and captured him (ch. 14) and from the later divine destruction of Sodom, the city into which Lot married (ch. 19), both became notable for the spiritual lessons to be drawn from them.

*I. Name.*–The meaning of the name of Lot is uncertain, though it is a name of the "serial type," i.e., Lot-ben-Haran. It is usually taken to mean "covering" (< Heb. *lôṭ*, "envelop, wrap closely"), perhaps denoting the close relationship with his uncle. The name could as wel be related to Akk. *lâṭu*, "control, keep in check."

*II. Life.*–Lot's birthplace is not stated, but since he is first mentioned with his father in Ur of the Chaldeans he was probably born there. When his father died Lot joined his grandfather and Abram for the migration to Canaan via Haran (11:31). Terah died at Haran and Lot moved with the seventy-five-year-old Abram from that city to Bethel in Canaan. He was with Abram when he went down to Egypt, became increasingly prosperous there (13:1), and moved back with him to the Negeb and eventually to Bethel. Abram's growing wealth, especially in herds and flocks (including camels), led to tension between him and his nephew since pasturage was limited, and their respective employees quarreled (13:5-7).

Until this episode relations between the childless uncle and fatherless nephew were close. Lot was in a covenant relationship with Abram ("we are brothers," 13:8) and may have anticipated that he should have been Abram's *de facto* heir. To avoid strife Abram magnanimously let Lot choose the portion he wished to take of the divinely promised inheritance. Lot chose to move E of the Jordan (13:11) and pitched his tents "toward" (so AV; NEB, NIV, "near") Sodom (v. 12). The "valley" (AV "plain"; Heb. *kikkār*) of Jordan was well populated at this time. V. 12 does not suggest that Lot was necessarily a seminomad, for such groups were at this time normally associated also with urban relatives. Soon thereafter Lot appears as a householder in Sodom (19:2) and possibly a member of the local council and judiciary ("sitting in the [city] gate," 19:1; but cf. below).

*A. Rescue.* Lot's life was marked by two remarkable deliverances. First, when in Sodom he was abducted by a group of four rulers from Shinar, Ellassar, Elam, and Goiim (Heb. *gôyim*, "nations"), who, according to tradition (see 1QapGen 21:23-28), struck from the Euphrates

River to sack the prosperous region of Sodom and Gomorrah. This region had been defeated at the battle of Siddim, probably to be located some way off (14:1-12). When Abram heard this he mounted an unprecedented night attack on the coalition as it retreated through Dan to Damascus (14:15). This was a tactic also used successfully by succeeding Israelites (Jgs. 7; 1 S. 14:36). Using his own trained retainers and those of his allies Mamre, Eschol, and Aner, Abram brought back Lot, his possessions, the women, and others (Gen. 14:13-16). Lot presumably returned to Sodom following the meeting of Abram with the king of Sodom at Shaveh (v. 16). Lot may have heard his uncle decline any share of the spoils (vv. 21-24).

In Gen. 18 the Lord tells Abraham that Sodom will be destroyed. Abraham's plea for Sodom and thus for Lot's family depended on there being only ten righteous persons found there (18:32). This may have been the extent of Lot's family. Lot was considered "a righteous man" (2 Pet. 2:7f.), hospitable to strangers and vexed with the lawlessness around him (19:3, 7f.). The warning which saved his life is expressly linked with God's remembrance of Abraham (19:29). God delivers the righteous (Ezk. 14:14; 1 Pet. 3:12), whose manner of life He judges (Ps. 7:11 [MT 12]) and knows (Ps. 1:6).

When Lot received, with typical oriental hospitality, the two messengers (or angels) sent by God, the townsfolk accused Lot, an alien ("sojourner"), of wanting to act as judge (v. 9). This may imply that in receiving the messengers Lot was thought to have usurped the judicial function of the city's elders.

*B. Lot's Wife.* Lot left Sodom with his wife and daughters, fleeing overnight to Zoar. This is identified with the small town of eṣ-Ṣâfī in the Wâdī el-Ḥesā at the delta of the brook of Zered about 5 km. (3 mi.) from the southern shore of the Dead Sea. They had been warned to flee to the hills without looking back, i.e., delaying. Lot's wife held back and was apparently overcome by the sulfur cloud and eruption associated with the sudden destruction of Sodom and Gomorrah. She became a "pillar of salt" (Gen. 19:26). Tradition associates this with the salty marl at the southwest end of the Dead Sea that forms hillocks of strange shapes in the salt cliffs of Jebel Usdum. This persistent tradition was repeated in Wisd. 10:7 ("a pillar of salt [still] standing as a monument to an unbelieving soul") and by Josephus (*Ant.* i.11.4 [203]).

Salt cliffs overlooking the Dead Sea at Jebel Usdum. The knarls (pillars?) at the top of the cliff are traditionally associated with Lot's wife (W. S. LaSor)

Jesus Christ cited Lot's wife as an example of the dire consequences of disbelief in God's warnings to flee, and thus of reluctance to leave, a doomed city (Lk. 17:31f.). She had come as close as possible to the point of deliverance yet without achieving it, being overwhelmed suddenly. The episode of Lot's wife was also taken by Christ as a warning of the suddenness of the coming of the Day of the Lord, just as the unexpected immediacy of the destruction of Sodom that caught people eating and drinking, buying and selling, planting and building (Lk. 17:28f.). The deliverance of Lot thus became an example to be remembered of divine action in salvation (2 Pet. 2:7f.).

*C. Lot's End.* Lot's final disappearance was due to alcohol and the disbelieving fear that, contrary to the divine promise and action, he would be overwhelmed in the destruction. He sheltered in a cave in Moab where his daughters, fearing a lack of husband and descendants, slept with him incestuously (Gen. 19:30-38). Why they should not have been willing to intermarry with locals cannot just be explained as an instance of later Israelite insularity in relation to neighbors coloring the narrative (cf. Gen. 36:20-30; 1 S. 22:3f.; Ruth). The progeny of this incest were Moab and Ben-ammi, the fathers of the Moabites and Ammonites.

***III. Theories.***–Lot's story has been considered an etiological fiction to explain the origin of the Ammonites and Moabites; and according to some (e.g., C. Westermann, *Genesis* [*BKAT,* 2nd ed. 1975], p. 375], the metamorphosis of his wife, unique in the OT, resulted from the transgression of a magic taboo. But these remain hypotheses. Nor is there substantiated reasoning why the person of Lot should be considered unhistorical, mythological, or merely the personification of a group (*Volksname*). The proposed connection of Lot with the Seir Horite ("cave dweller") Lotan (Gen. 36:20, 22, 26) is unlikely since the latter may be the same as Egyptian *rtn* (A. Gardiner, *Ancient Egyptian Onomastica* [1947], I, 148). Lot is revered today by some Arabs as an ancestral patriarchal figure.

***Bibliography.***–D. J. Wiseman, "Abraham reassessed," in A. R. Millard and D. J. Wiseman, eds., *Essays on the Patriarchal Narratives* (1980), pp. 139-149; H. C. van Hatten, *BA,* 44 (1981), 90f.

D. J. WISEMAN

**LOTAN** lō'tan [Heb. *lôṭān*]. First son of Seir; a clan chief of the Horites (Gen. 36:20, 22, 29; 1 Ch. 1:38f.), who were the inhabitants of Edom before it was occupied by the Edomites.

Lotan was also the name of a serpent defeated by Baal in Canaanite mythology, probably the Ugaritic prototype of LEVIATHAN.

**LOTHASUBUS** loth-ə-sōō'bəs [Gk. *Lōthasoubos*]. One of those who stood at Ezra's left hand at the public reading of the law (1 Esd. 9:44); called Hashum in Neh. 8:4.

**LOTS** [Heb. *gôrāl*; LXX *klēros* (Lev. 16:8-105 Nu. 26:55; etc.)]; [Heb. *qesem*] (Ezk. 21:22 [MT 27]); NEB AUGUR'S ARROW; AV DIVINATION; [Gk. *klēros*] (Mt. 27:35; Mk. 15:24; Lk. 23:34; Jn. 19:24; Acts 1:26). Both Heb. *gôrāl* and Gk. *klēros* have two primary meanings: (1) a device used to determine the will of god or of the gods, i.e., a form of DIVINATION; (2) by extension, "share," "portion," "inheritance," i.e., that which is received by the drawing or casting of lots. For the latter meaning *see* ALLOTMENT; PORTION.

***I. Terminology.***–The Heb. *gôrāl* is derived from the Semitic root *grl,* which in Arabic is the basis for words meaning "stony," "stony ground" (KoB, p. 195) and probably referred originally to small stones or markers used for divination. Eventually a variety of small objects of stone, wood, clay, or other material were also used. Several verbs are used with *gôrāl,* all of which can mean "throw" or "cast" lots (*yārâ,* e.g., Josh. 18:6; hiphil of *šālak̠,* e.g., Josh. 18:8; hiphil of *nāpal,* e.g., Prov. 1:14; Isa. 34:17; *yād̠ad̠,* Joel 3:3 [MT 4:3]; Ob. 11; Nah. 3:10). The lots appear to have been kept in a container in which they were shaken until one was thrown or sprang out (three different verbs are used for this: *yāṣāʾ,* e.g., Nu. 33:54; Josh. 15:1; *ʿālâ,* e.g., Lev. 16:9f.; *nāpal,* e.g., Jonah 1:7). The Heb. *qesem* is the only reference in the OT to a specific type of lot, namely, arrow divination. The terms *pûr* and *pûrîm* are Hebrew transliterations or adaptations of the Akk. *pūrū,* which is used for the casting of lots for the purpose of divination (see Hallo; *see also* PURIM). The term occurs in the singular in Est. 3:7 and 9:24, 26, and in the plural in Est. 9:26, 28f., 31.

***II. In the OT.***–Although the casting or taking of lots is but one of many forms of divination, there is a wide variation in the use of lots throughout the ancient world. The central presupposition behind the use of lots in the OT and NT is clearly expressed in Prov. 16:33, "The lot is cast into the lap, but the decision is wholly from the Lord." The use of lots in making decisions, therefore, was regarded as a means of allowing God to make the choice (cf. Josh. 18:6, 8, 10).

Lots, though a form of divination, were never a forbidden practice in ancient Israel as were the other major forms of divination (cf. Dt. 18:9-14). One form of sacral lot was the URIM AND THUMMIM, which were kept in a pocket in the EPHOD worn by the high priest (Ex. 28:30). The Urim and Thummim were probably two small objects (stones, dice, small pieces of wood) that were used to secure either a yes or no answer, and were used for such sacral functions as the annual selection of goats to represent Yahweh and Azazel on the Day of Atonement (Lev. 16:7-10).

Similar to the positive or negative response expected of the Urim and Thummim, other forms of the lot were primarily used to secure a yes or no answer to a particular proposal. In the OT the lot is most frequently mentioned in connection with the apportionment of land (Nu. 26:55; 33:54; 34:13; 36:2f.; Josh. 14:2; 15:1; 17:14, 17; 18:6, 8, 10f.; 19:1, 10, 17, 24, 32, 40, 51; 21:4-6, 8, 10; 1 Ch. 6:54, 61, 65), with the result that the land so allotted expressed the divine will and thereafter became a portion or inheritance that could not be alienated.

Lots were frequently used to narrow gradually the field of choice before the final lot was cast. Thus 1 S. 10:20f. narrates how through lot the tribe of Benjamin was selected, then the family of Matrites was selected, and finally Saul was selected as God's choice of king of Israel. Similarly, the lot was probably used to determine who had caused Israel's defeat at Ai (Josh. 7:16-18); the guilty party was discovered by first narrowing the choice to the tribe of Judah, then the family of the Zerahites, then the household of Zabdi, and finally Achan was revealed as the culprit. Similarly Haman in Est. 3:7 had lots cast for each of the months of the year, and when Adar received a positive response, he determined that the Jews would be destroyed on that month.

Lots were employed in other ways as well. During the second temple period, lots were cast for the priests, Levites, and people to determine a rotation for those who would supply wood for the altar of the Lord (Neh. 10:34 [MT 35]). Lots were also cast at that time to determine who would live in Jerusalem; one man in ten was so selected (Neh. 11:1). The Chronicler also reports how the workers in the service of the first temple were organized by the casting of lots (1 Ch. 24:5, 7, 9; 26:13f.).

In three passages the rare expression *yād̠ad̠ gôrāl* occurs (Joel 3:3; Ob. 11; Nah. 3:10), apparently belonging to a tradition of the oracles against the nations. In Joel 3:3 and Nah. 3:10 the lot is cast for people, apparently referring to the distribution of the prisoners of war, a fact which emphasizes their negligible value (H. W. Wolff, *Joel and Amos* [Eng. tr., *Hermeneia,* 1977], p. 77).

***III. In the NT.***–The Gospels have four references to the casting of lots (Mt. 27:35; Mk. 15:24; Lk. 23:34; Jn. 19:24), all of which reflect the tradition that the soldiers cast lots for the garments of Jesus at the foot of the cross in fulfillment of Ps. 22:18 (MT 19). As in the OT references to the casting of lots for orphans (Job 6:27) or prisoners of war (Joel 3:3; Nah. 3:10), the utter degradation of Jesus is emphasized in this way. Acts 1:26 refers to the casting of lots to select one of two candidates, Joseph Barsabbas or Matthias, as a successor to the apostle Judas. Here, unlike the OT, there is no narrowing down of a larger field of candidates, but in conformity to Roman practice the community chooses the two candidates, though the choice between those two is made by casting lots that are an expression of the will of God.

***Bibliography.***–W. H. Hallo, *BA,* 46 (1983), 19-29; J. Lindblom, *VT,* 12 (1962), 164-178; E. Lipinski, *VT,* 20 (1970), 495f.; *TDNT,* III, *s.v.* κλῆρος κτλ.: κλῆρος (W. Foerster); *TDOT,* II, *s.v.* "gôrāl" (Dommershausen).

D. E. AUNE

**LOTS, FEAST OF.** *See* PURIM.

**LOT'S WIFE.** *See* LOT II.B.

**LOTUS** [Heb. *ṣeʾĕlîm*] (Job 40:21f.); AV "shady trees." The reference is to the *Zizyphus lotus* (L.) Lam., a species of jujube of the order *Rhamneae.* A shrub about 1½ m. (5 ft.) tall, it bears greenish flowers and small globular fruit. It has no connection with the Egyptian lotus. *See* LILY.

See also *MPB,* p. 247.

R. K. H.

**LOVE.**

I. In the OT
  A. Vocabulary
  B. Human Love
  C. Divine Love
  D. Human Love for God
II. Intertestamental Development
  A. Greek Emphasis
  B. Influence of the LXX
  C. Extrabiblical Jewish Literature
  D. Rabbinic Emphasis
III. In the NT
  A. Vocabulary
  B. Synoptic Gospels and Acts
  C. Pauline Emphasis
  D. Johannine Emphasis
  E. Related Concepts
    1. In Other Epistles
    2. Charity

With the exception of the word "life," love is the most important abstract term in the Bible. God's love, the basis for His dealing with humans in the OT, climaxes in the NT in the incarnation and death of Jesus Christ. It is the key word in the Christian summary of biblical revelation (cf. Mt. 22:37; Jn. 3:16; Rom. 13:9; Gal. 5:14; Jas. 2:8).

***I. In the OT.***–*A. Vocabulary.* The most important Hebrew term for love is *ʾāhab̠.* It has the same varied meanings as the corresponding term in English, including romantic, fraternal, and divine love. It occurs about 250 times in the OT in varied forms, the verb far more frequently than the noun. *ʾĀhab̠* describes spontaneous and outflowing love, in contrast to love arising from deliberate choice. It is used both for human and for divine-human relations.

The second most important word for love is *ḥeseḏ,* denoting a deliberate choice of affection and kindness. The AV usually translates *ḥeseḏ* as "mercy." "Kindness" frequently describes King David's attitude toward his friends (2 Samuel). (*See also* STEADFAST LOVE.) *Ḥeseḏ* is less spontaneous than *'āhaḇ* and emphasizes the idea of loyalty. The term occurs most often in Genesis (human love), Deuteronomy (divine love), Psalms, and Proverbs. Various terms — "lovingkindness," "reciprocal love" (N. Glueck), "covenant love" (N. H. Snaith), "unfailing love," and "steadfast love" (RSV) — are all good translations, for *ḥeseḏ* cannot be pressed into any one formula (cf. the various NEB renderings). The threefold meaning of kindness, mercy, and love is perhaps best conveyed in the "lovingkindness" of the AV and RV.

Another synonym is *rāḥam,* meaning "love," "be merciful," "have compassion." It appears more than twenty-six times and comes from a root meaning "born from the same womb," hence "brotherly feeling." Typical is Dt. 30:3, "God will . . . have compassion." The other synonyms for love occur less frequently and usually refer to love or affection among people (but see Dt. 7:7; 33:12; Ps. 91:14; Isa. 38:17).

*B. Human Love.* Basic to all these meanings is the love relationship between man and woman. It has sexual connotations but usually includes affection, loyalty, and admiration. Jacob's love for Rachel indicates the spontaneous nature of this love (Gen. 29:18). The sexual meaning of the term is emphasized most in Ezekiel but is also prominent in Hosea and Jeremiah (Ezk. 16:33, 36f.; 23:5, 9, 22; Jer. 2:25; Hos. 3:1; cf. Ezk. 16:8). Canticles shows sexual love in its more inclusive and wholesome aspect; the term occurs both as a noun and as a verb (1:9; 3:1). Cant. 8:6 eloquently describes this impulse's power: "Love is strong as death, jealousy is cruel as the grave" (cf. 2 S. 13:1, 4, 15).

The OT much more frequently refers to the love of one person for another, or brotherly love. This love characterizes a wide variety of person-to-person relationships: between man and man (1 S. 18:1; 2 S. 1:26; 1 K. 5:1), woman and woman (Ruth 4:15), man and woman (Gen. 29:20; 1 S. 18:20; Prov. 5:19; Eccl. 9:9), and parents and children (Gen. 22:2; 25:28; 37:3). It is difficult to see the basis for Snaith's generalization that *'āhaḇ* particularly "is used of the attitude of a superior to an inferior" (p. 169). Instances of love between persons who are equal in status include Shechem and Dinah (Gen. 34:3f.), David and Jonathan (2 S. 1:26), Isaac and Rebecca (Gen. 24:67), bride and groom (Cant. 3:4), friends (Prov. 17:17), and neighbors (Lev. 19:18).

Ivory panel from the headboard of an Ugaritic king's bed. On the right two people embrace, on the left a goddess suckles two children. From Râs Shamrah, *ca.* 1400-1350 B.C. (Direction Générale des Antiquités et des Musées, Damascus, Syria)

Although in most contexts love involves relationships between persons, human and divine, the OT does mention love of food (Gen. 27:4, 9, 14), God's law (Ps. 119:97), sleep (Prov. 20:13; Isa. 56:10), silver (Eccl. 5:20), bribes (Isa. 1:23; Hos. 9:1), and instruction (Prov. 12:1).

*C. Divine Love.* Several terms express God's love for humans. The basic one is *'āhaḇ* (Dt. 7:8; 2 S. 12:24; Prov. 3:12; Isa. 43:4; Hos. 11:1). The second synonym (*ḥeseḏ*) emphasizes the covenant relationship (Ps. 36:7 [MT 8]; Isa. 63:7; Gen. 19:19; 2 Ch. 1:8). *Rāḥam* frequently expresses God's solicitude for humans, as in Ps. 103:13, "The Lord pities those who fear him" (cf. Gen. 43:14; Ex. 33:19; Ps. 51:1 [MT 3]). Often *ḥēn* denotes God's love and favor, e.g., Prov. 8:35, "obtains favor from the Lord" (cf. Ps. 102:13 [MT 14]; 1 S. 2:26).

The noblest expression of divine love is in Hosea, whose prophecy throbs with the pathos of this love shown even to those who are unlovely, unresponsive, and antagonistic. The divine love in Isa. 43:25 may be the highest expression of grace in the OT.

*D. Human Love for God.* The Psalms most frequently express human love for God. The psalmist loved God because of gratitude for past mercies (Ps. 116:1). Israelites are exhorted to love God with their total personality in a dynamic, growing relationship (Dt. 6:5; 30:6; Ps. 31:23 [MT 24]; 145:20). This love is a reaction to the divine initiative: God manifests His love, and people either accept or reject Him.

The most distinctive element in the OT revelation of God is that His basic attitude toward people is one of love, good will, and willingness to act on their behalf. The OT God differs from the gods of other religions because He loves, seeks, and suffers for the welfare of mankind. Gradually the particularistic emphasis in OT religion widened to embrace all peoples (Isa. 60–66). Emphasis also shifted from the group to the individual (Ezk. 18).

***II. Intertestamental Development.**–A. Greek Emphasis.* The most common word for love in Classical Greek is *érōs,* which is sexual love — sensual, impulsive, spontaneous — caused in mythology by the love-god Eros. "The sexual union of gods and men narrated in mythology finds current actualization in the cultus" (Quell, p. 35). From the grosser ideas and practices of eroticism the concept arose in Plato and his successors of a purely contemplative aspiration for the divine (Plato *Symposium*). Indeed, the Platonic concept of *érōs* as the basis of human aspiration for God played an important role in the preparation of the world for Christianity (Nygren). Even the higher Platonic treatment of *érōs,* however, contrasts to love in the Bible, for in the latter God's love pursues humans, while Platonism (and paganism generally) emphasizes the human quest for God.

The derivation of *agápē* is uncertain; it was a colorless word, seldom used by the Greeks, signifying desire for someone or something. *Érōs* denoted satisfaction sought wherever it could be found, but *agápē* was selective. It often denoted the divine love specifically sought by human beings.

*B. Influence of the LXX.* Those who translated the OT into Greek ignored the common Greek term for love (*érōs*) because of its sensual associations and chose instead the obscure term *agápē* to translate Heb. *'āhaḇ* and its synonyms. *Érōs* passed from the scene as the Judeo-Christian influence became dominant; it appears only once in the LXX (Prov. 7:18), never in the NT, and only once in the early fathers (Ign. Rom. 7:2; cf. Gal. 6:14). In contrast to *érōs* with its inclusiveness, Heb. *'āhaḇ* and its Greek counterpart *agápē* stress exclusiveness, specifically God's love for His chosen people. The LXX uses *agapáō* (more than three hundred occurrences) to translate seventeen different Hebrew synonyms, but by far the greatest number of occurrences render *'āhaḇ* (HR).

Fraternal love (Gk. *philadelphía*) appears in the LXX only six times (2 Macc. 15:14; 4 Macc. 13:21, 23, 26; 14:1; 15:10). In ancient Greek it meant the love of gods for people or the love of people for each other. *Philadelphía* indicated nobility and sense of duty, in contrast to the subjectivistic nature of *érōs*. The noun *phílos* in classical Greek means "friend," "loved one," "favorite (of the gods)," "friend of the king" (sometimes when no affection is intended). The noun *philía* means "love, affection," especially for a spouse.

*C. Extrabiblical Jewish Literature.* The covenantal aspect of *agápē* is stressed in intertestamental literature as in the OT. God's love for Israel received grateful acknowledgment (Ps. Sol. 18:4). The faithful are assured of God's love and final deliverance from all adversaries (Wisd. 3:9; 4 Macc. 15:2; 16:19). The love for one's neighbor is often emphasized (T. Gad 5:2; Shep. Herm. Sim. 4:7) but lacks the universal scope of divine love found in the NT.

In the hymns of the Dead Sea Scrolls the Qumrân community frequently expressed gratitude for God's covenant love, lovingkindness, and compassion (see 1QH 5, 10, 11, 13). These hymns, like the OT, show little awareness of God's love for the world as a whole but instead emphasize gratitude for God's mercy and grace to the covenant people in contrast to the wicked. The emphasis differs from the OT in being highly personal rather than national, resembling some of the canonical Psalms. The Qumrân hymns, however, like many of the Psalms, anticipate the NT emphasis of God's grace consciously experienced. Unlike the NT, their concern is almost entirely with individual salvation rather than evangelism.

*D. Rabbinic Emphasis.* Rabbinic literature stresses God's love for humans because they are made in God's image; Israel is loved because of the covenant with the patriarchs. Love for neighbor is limited to one's countrymen. God should be loved for His own sake. The supreme expression of human love for God is being willing to die for one's faith. "By three things is the world sustained," said Simon the Just (*ca.* 220 B.C.), "by the Law, by the [Temple-] service, and by deeds of loving-kindness" (Mish. *Aboth* i.2). The rabbis were confident that the person most certain to inherit the world to come is the one known for disinterested acts of benevolence.

***III. In the NT.–A. Vocabulary.*** The word for erotic love (*érōs*) never appears in the NT and seldom in the church fathers, reflecting the LXX precedent. The noun *phílós* occurs thirty times in the NT (eighteen in Luke-Acts), usually designating a close personal friendship (e.g., Lk. 14:12; Jn. 11:11; Acts 19:31). It is the term used in the expression "friend of the bridegroom" (Jn. 3:29). The disciples are called *phíloi* of Jesus (Lk. 12:4; Jn. 15:13-15). Abraham is called "friend of God" (Jas. 2:23; cf. Jn. 8:34-40). In contrast to the LXX, the NT uses *phílos* only once in a political context, the Jews' challenge to Pilate to prove he was a *phílos* of Caesar (Jn. 19:12). In postbiblical Christian writings *phílos* (in contrast to forms of *agápē* and *agapáō*) was used infrequently.

The verb *philéō* occurs in the NT about twenty-five times. It is used for parental love (Mt. 10:37), Jesus' love for Lazarus (Jn. 11:3, 36), the disciples' love for Jesus (21:15-17; 1 Cor. 16:22), God's love for His Son (Jn. 5:50) and for His people (16:27; Rev. 3:19; but never human love for God). Once it is used for the disciple "whom Jesus loved" (Jn. 20:2); otherwise *agapáō* is the verb in this expression (13:23; 19:26; 21:7, 20). As in early Greek literature it also means "to kiss" (Mt. 26:48; Mk. 14:44; Lk. 22:47).

The main NT word for love, *agapáō,* occurs 137 times as a verb and 116 times as a noun. Both noun and verb are usually translated "love" (in the AV 29 times as "charity"). Like its Hebrew equivalent it expresses desire, leading to quest ("they loved the praise of men," Jn. 12:43), or it may mean a discriminating choice, whether of the world ("Demas, in love with this present world," 2 Tim. 4:10), of God ("You shall love the Lord your God," Mt. 22:37), or of men ("Love your enemies," 5:44). The cognate term *agapētos* — occurring 62 times — is usually translated "beloved." Besides frequent use as a designation for the Christian brethren, it also designates the Father's attitude toward the Son (Mt. 12:18; Mk. 1:11; 2 Pet. 1:17) and toward His people (e.g., Rom. 11:28).

*B. Synoptic Gospels and Acts.* Love, as set forth by Jesus, is the keynote of the new kingdom. It is also the epitome of the OT ethic. The rabbis often discussed how the Torah could be condensed and reduced to its essential elements. When a lawyer asked Him which is the law's great commandment, Jesus responded, "You shall love the Lord your God. . . . and your neighbor as yourself" (Mt. 22:37-40; cf. Lev. 19:18; Dt. 6:5). This obligation to love is really one "law" and the foundation of the entire Torah.

But Jesus went further than the OT. While love in the OT was selective and nationalistic, the Christian "Torah" is supranationalistic: the obligation to love extends not only to one's relatives (the primitive meaning of the term), not only to one's neighbor (the characteristic Hebrew emphasis), but even to one's enemies (Christ's unique contribution). The kinship of this concept with compassion, mercy, or pity, as noted in the word studies, is implicit in the Master's announcement. After stating that God the Father treats His enemies better than they deserve by sending them sunshine and rain (Mt. 5:45), Jesus declared that disciples must love even their enemies. This is more than passive resistance (Mt. 5:38-42); it is the positive reaction of love expressed in deeds (vv. 44-48; cf. Rom. 12:20). Jesus' own example on the cross — His prayer for His executioners (Lk. 23:34) — continued this emphasis. The best test of the revolutionary new ethic is Stephen's praying for his murderers, one of the noblest expressions of divine grace ever recorded (Acts 7:60). Acts shows the new dynamic of Christian love in the community of believers after the effusion of the Holy Spirit at Pentecost (2:42). As H. B. Swete has noted (*The Holy Spirit in the NT* [1910], p. 80), this dynamic fellowship (*koinōnía*) among the believers was a greater miracle than the phenomena of Pentecost. The result of the new release of love and energy was aptly termed a "new race" (A. Harnack). The new impetus to brother-love led to pioneering efforts in social responsibility. Thus gentile converts sent gifts to the poorer brethren in Judea, both as a spontaneous expression of God's love and as a fulfillment of a recognized social obligation (Acts 11:29; cf. Gal. 2:10; Rom. 15:25-27).

*C. Pauline Emphasis.* As already indicated, Paul, like his Master, placed central emphasis on the manifestation of God as love. Paul also developed the idea that God's love in giving His Son is the supreme expression of His love for mankind (Rom. 5:8; cf. Mk. 10:45; 2 Cor. 5:14). This supreme demonstration of divine love not only calls for a grateful response (2 Cor. 5:15; Rom. 10:10) but results in the divine love flowing into and through the life of the believer (Rom. 5:5). Although the source of love remains in God, believers become not only its recipients but also the channels by which it affects others. In such love is the law fulfilled, its purpose fully expressed (13:8-10).

Paul singled out love for special emphasis and, by a series of contrasts, raised it to the pinnacle of Christian graces. In addition to placing it first in the list of effects of the Spirit-filled life (Gal. 5:22), he contrasted it to the relatively inferior gifts of the Spirit such as wisdom, prophecy, and tongues (1 Cor. 12–14). After noting the supremacy of love (13:1-4) and before emphasizing its permanence (vv. 8-13) he presented the most effective analysis of its nature found in Scripture (vv. 4-8). He described love (*agápē*) as freedom from jealousy, conceit, ostentation, arrogance, self-centeredness, and resentment; love's characteristics are patience, kindness, truth, righteousness, hope, benevolence, and endurance. It even exceeds in value faith and hope, although usually it is classed with them (v. 13; cf. 1 Thess. 1:3; Gal. 5:6; Col. 1:5f.).

*D. Johannine Emphasis.* The Gospel and First Epistle of John stress love as much as or more than Paul's Epistles do. John's Gospel contains the "Golden Text of the Bible" — that God loved the world to the extent that He gave up His only Son (3:16) — and a distinctive emphasis on the love of the Father for His Son (3:35; 5:20 [*philéō*]; 10:17). This emphasis on divine love embraces believers: the same love that the Father has for the Son is given also to the disciples (17:26; 1 Jn. 3:1).

No less remarkable is the emphasis on brother-love; it is the supreme badge of discipleship (Jn. 13:35). Without it no one can pretend to be a child of God (1 Jn. 3:14). Divine love means the difference between life and death. It is expressed by word but especially by deed (vv. 17f.; cf. Jas. 2:15). The central thesis of 1 John is that since God is love, this quality characterizes His children, who by faith partake of His nature (4:7; cf. 2 Pet. 1:4).

Although *philéō* and *agapáō* appear to be used interchangeably in several passages (Prov. 8:17, LXX; Jn. 13:23; cf. 20:2; 12:25; cf. 1 Jn. 2:15; Rev. 1:5; cf. 3:19), their meanings are not necessarily identical. For example, *agapáō* never means "to kiss," but *philéō* does (Gen. 27:26, LXX; Mk. 14:44; Lk. 22:47). The Vulgate translates *agapáō* by *diligere,* a love that is discriminating and involves choice, while *philéō* is rendered *amo,* a term that, like *érōs,* means spontaneous affection. *Philéō* is linked with *phílos,* meaning a friend, and is the normal term for expressing friendship (Mt. 10:37). Origen (comm. on Lam. 1:2) concluded, "*Agapáō* is the more divine and, so to speak, the more spiritual meaning, but *phileín* is bodily and savours of men" (cited in E. A. Abbott, *Johannine Grammar* [1906], p. 431). Many scholars, however, including J. H. Bernard, J. Moffatt, C. K. Barrett, L. Morris, and G. Stählin, have doubted whether any distinction is intended in such places as Jn. 21:15-17, where Jesus used both terms while questioning Peter about his loyalty. Morris demonstrated convincingly that such variation is a consistent feature of John's style (*Studies in the Fourth Gospel* [1969], pp. 293-319).

*E. Related Concepts. 1. In Other Epistles.* In the Epistle to the Hebrews hope and faith receive greater emphasis than love. The author, however, commended the readers for their brother-love expressed in deeds (6:10; 10:24; 13:1). James emphasized that the OT law is fulfilled when one shows love to a neighbor (Jas. 2:8; cf. Jesus' statement in Mt. 22:37-40; Paul's in Rom. 13:8) and called believers in God "those who love Him" (1:12; 2:5). Christian love is presented not as a merit to be earned but as a characteristic of the new nature that results from a new birth (1 Pet. 1:23; 2:2; 3:8; 2 Pet. 1:4, 7). Love is said to be the climax of the Christian graces — "above all hold unfailing your love for one another, since love covers a multitude of sins" (1 Pet. 4:8; cf. Prov. 10:12). The relationship of the Christian to the Lord and to other Christians is best expressed in terms of love (1 Pet. 1:8, 22; 2 Pet. 1:7). Christ's love for His church and the believer's love for his Lord are voiced in the book of Revelation (1:5; 3:9, 19), but the emphasis is more upon heroic qualities of loyalty.

*2. Charity.* The English term "charity" derives from Lat. *caritas.* To translate Gk. *agápē* in the Vulgate Jerome chose *caritas,* which means "affection," "love," "esteem," with a connotation of sacrifice, and *dilectio,* which means "prize," "choice," "love," "high esteem." The difficulty of finding a Latin equivalent of *agápē* and the similarity of these terms explain Jerome's inconsistent usage. In the AV NT "charity" likewise translates *agápē* in twenty-eight of its 116 occurrences. It occurs in English versions prior to 1881 due to the Vulgate's influence; English, like Latin, lacks an exact equivalent of *agápē* as used in the NT. During the past two centuries the term "charity" has changed in meaning to connote benevolence or almsgiving ("bestowing one's goods to feed the poor"), which Paul placed in contrast to *agápē* (1 Cor. 13:3). The other contemporary meaning of tolerance of those with whom one differs also diverges considerably from the original meaning.

Due to the influence of the Vulgate, "charity" appears eighty-two times in the NT of the Douay (Douai) Version, though only thrice in the OT. The revisers wisely decided in 1881 and 1901 to drop this term in favor of "love," a precedent since followed in all English translations. "Charity" occurs only once in the RSV (Acts 9:36) and ten times in the NEB NT, in places where "alms" is the usual translation.

***Bibliography.***–*TDNT,* I, *s.v.* ἀγαπάω (G. Quell and E. Stauffer); IX, *s.v.* φιλέω κτλ. (G. Stählin); L. Morris, *Testaments of Love* (1981); J. Moffatt, *Love in the NT* (1929); A. Nygren, *Agápē and Eros* (Eng. tr. 1953); C. Spicq, *Agápē* (2 vols., 1958); N. Glueck, Ḥesed *in the Bible* (Eng. tr. 1967; repr. 1975); N. H. Snaith, *Distinctive Ideas of the OT* (1946); R. B. Girdlestone, *Synonyms of the OT* (1897; repr. 1948); R. C. Trench, *Synonyms of the NT* (1880; repr. 1978), pp. 41-44.

G. A. TURNER

**LOVE, BROTHERLY.** *See* BROTHERLY LOVE.

**LOVE-FEAST.** *See* AGAPE.

**LOVELY.** The RSV translates several Hebrew words and phrases as "lovely." Usually it denotes personal physical beauty; Rachel was *y$^{e}$paṯ mar'eh,* lit. "beautiful of appearance" (AV "well-formed"; NEB "beautiful"), and Esther was *ṭôḇaṯ mar'eh,* lit. "good of appearance" (AV "beautiful"; NEB "charming"). In a metaphor Prov. 5:19 describes a wife as a "lovely [Heb. *'$^{a}$hāḇîm;* AV "loving" is a literal translation] hind." Cant. 1:16 characterizes the beloved as "truly lovely" (Heb. *'ap̱ nā'îm*; AV and NEB "pleasant" is more literal), and in the famous description in ch. 4 the woman's mouth (or speech; see the comms.) is lovely (4:3, Heb. *nā'weh,* which the RSV translates "comely" in 1:5, 10; 2:14; 6:4).

In his lament over Saul and Jonathan David calls them "beloved and lovely" (Heb. *hanne'$^{e}$hāḇîm w$^{e}$hann$^{e}$'îmim,* 2 S. 1:23). Although *nā'îm* hardly seems to apply to Saul, especially in relation to David, it is perhaps natural that

David would remember his amiable times with Saul (1 S. 24:16-19; 26:21-25; cf. KD, *Books of Samuel*, p. 291). The RSV translation is perhaps a little misleading; although Saul is called "handsome" (Heb. *ṭôḇ*) in 1 S. 9:2, the AV "pleasant" or NEB "delightful" seems more appropriate here.

The final OT reference is Ps. 84:1 (MT 2), which describes God's dwelling place (Heb. *miškānôṯ*; the plural form probably refers to the various rooms in the sanctuary [see GKC, § 124b], or it may be a "plural of amplification" [A. A. Anderson, *Psalms 1-72* (*New Century Bible Comms.*, 1972; repr. 1981), p. 336]). This was the central sanctuary at Jerusalem that Solomon had built; it was known for its beauty (1 K. 6–7).

In Phil. 4:8 the hapax legomenon *prosphilḗs* describes one of the things about which Christians ought to think. Although F. W. Beare (*Epistle to the Philippians* [*HNTC*, 1959], p. 148) stated, "Paul here sanctifies, as it were, the generally accepted virtues of pagan morality," R. P. Martin (*Philippians* [*New Century Bible Comms.*, 1976; repr. 1980], p. 158) pointed out that *prosphilḗs* "is absent from contemporary ethical lists." In Sir. 4:7; 20:13 and Josephus *Ant.* i.18.1 (258); xvii.6.2 (149) *prosphilḗs* refers to a person and means simply "beloved."

G. A. L.

**LOVER.** In the OT "lover" usually renders the Hebrew verb *ʾāhēḇ* or its participle *ʾōhēḇ* (e.g., Ps. 88:18 [MT 19]; 99:4; Lam. 1:2, 19; Ezk. 23:5, 9, 22; Hos. 8:9). This term also often means "friend" (e.g., 1 K. 5:1, JB [AV "lover" in this sense]), which probably should be the rendering in Ps. 88:18 (RSV, AV, NEB, "lover"). Where it is translated "lover" it refers more frequently to objects of religious prostitution; the "lovers" receive Israel's and Judah's misplaced and wanton affection (Jer. 2:33; 22:20, 22; 30:14; Ezk. 16:33, 36f., etc.; Hos. 2:5, 7, etc.). Jeremiah used *rē(a)ʿ*, "friend," "companion," and *ʿāgaḇ*, "to lust," in the same way; in 3:1 the *rēʿîm* are those false gods after whom Judah chases, and in 4:30 *ʿōgᵉḇîm* (pl. part. of *ʿāgaḇ*) is derisive, denoting adulterous paramours. *See also* HARLOT. The prophet Isaiah condemned the people of Babylon for their love of luxury (*ʿᵃdînâ,* 47:8). In Cant. 5:1 *dôḏîm,* "lovers" (AV "beloved"), is used in poetic parallelism with "friends" (*rēʿîm*) in an invitation to the marriage feast.

In the NT "lover" occurs only in certain compound words that describe the object of personal affection: *philárgyros,* "lover of money" (AV "covetous," Lk. 16:14; 2 Tim. 3:2; cf. *aphilárgyros,* 1 Tim. 3:3); *philótheos,* "lover of God" (2 Tim. 3:4); *philágathos,* "lover of goodness" (Tit. 1:8; AV "lover of good men"; NEB "right-minded"; cf. *aphilágathos,* 2 Tim. 3:3); *phílautos,* "lover of self" (v. 2; NEB "arrogant"); *philḗdonos,* "lover of pleasure" (v. 4). Cf. also *philóxenos,* "hospitable" (lit. "lover of hospitality," Tit. 1:8).

D. J. KELLY

**LOVES** [Heb. *yᵉḏîḏôṯ*]. The AV's literal translation of part of the title of Ps. 45 (MT v. 1). Although the form is plural in Hebrew, it may be understood as a singular (GKC, § 124e). Hence the RSV "love song" is quite appropriate; Ps. 45 is generally recognized as an epithalamium or wedding song (see, e.g., C. H. Briggs, comm. on the Psalms, I [*ICC,* 1906], 384, and M. Dahood, *Psalms I* [*AB,* 1965], p. 270).

**LOVESICK** [Heb. *ʾᵃmulâ*] (Ezk. 16:30); AV WEAK; NEB ANGER. In the MT the clause reads *mâ ʾᵃmulâ libbāṯēḵ*. The LXX, taking *ʾᵃmulâ* as first person singular and *libbāṯēḵ* as *lᵉḇittēḵ,* translates the phrase *tí diathṓ tḗn thygatéra sou,* "how can I dispose of thy daughter?" Similarly, the Syriac version has "why should I judge thy daughter?" Symmachus rendered it *en tíni kathariṓ tḗn kardían sou,* "in what way shall I purify thy heart?" The Targum has "how strong was the wickedness of thy heart." The AV follows the tradition of the last two with the more literal "how weak is thy heart." The NEB reflects the use of the phrase in an Aramaic sense, "full of wrath against you"; the RSV interprets *ʾāmal,* literally "weak," as "lovesick" in the context of Israel's playing the harlot.

G. WYPER

**LOVINGKINDNESS.** *See* STEADFAST LOVE.

**LOW; LOWLY** [Heb. *šāpāl* (Job 5:11; Ps. 138:6; Prov. 16:19; 29:33; Ezk. 17:6; etc.), *šēpel* ("low estate," Ps. 136:23; "low place," Eccl. 10:6), *bᵉnê-ʾāḏām*–'sons of man' (Ps. 49:2 [MT 3]; "men of low estate," 62:9 [MT 10]), *qāṭān*–'small' (Est. 1:20), *šaḥ ʿênayim*–'downcast eyes' (Job 22:29), *dal* (Zeph. 3:12); Aram. *šᵉpal* (Dnl. 4:17 [MT 14]); Gk. *tapeinós* (Mt. 11:29; Lk. 1:52; Jas. 1:9), *tapeínōsis* (Phil. 3:21; "low estate," Lk. 1:48), *agenḗs* (1 Cor. 1:28)]; AV also HUMBLE, BASE, SMALL, POOR, VILE; NEB also HUMBLE, PETTY, PALTRY, POOR, "modest looks" (Job 22:29), etc.; **LOWLINESS** [Gk. *tapeinophrosýnē*] (Eph. 4:2; Col. 3:12); AV also HUMBLENESS; NEB HUMBLE; **BRING LOW; LAY LOW (etc.)** [Heb. qal and hiphil of *šāpēl* (1 S. 2:7; Prov. 29:23; Isa. 2:9, 11, 17; 5:15; 10:33; 13:11; etc.), qal and niphal of *dālal* (Jgs. 6:6; Ps. 79:8; 116:6; 142:6 [MT 7]; Isa. 17:4), *šāḥah* (Ps. 107:39; Eccl. 12:4; etc.), hiphil of *kāraʿ* (Jgs. 11:35; Ps. 78:31), hiphil of *kānaʿ* (2 Ch. 28:19; Job 40:12), *ḥālaš* (Job 14:10; Isa. 14:12), *ṣāʿar* (Job 14:21), hophal of *ṭûl* (Job 41:9 [MT 1]), *šāḵaḇ* (Isa. 14:8), hophal of *yāraḏ* (Zec. 10:11); Gk. *tapeinóō* (Lk. 3:5)]; AV also HUMBLE, CAST DOWN, BRING DOWN, WASTE AWAY, etc.; NEB also BRING TO DESTITUTION, BRING TROUBLE, BRING DOWN, REDUCE TO SUBMISSION, SINK INTO OBSCURITY, etc. Terms used by the RSV most often to denote low social or economic status, humiliation, or a spirit of humility (often contrasted with PRIDE).

*See* HUMBLE; POOR.

N. J. O.

**LOW COUNTRY; LOWLAND.** The foothill region of western Judah, between the central mountain range and the coastal plain. *See* SHEPHELAH.

W. S. L. S.

**LOYAL; LOYALTY** [Heb. *ḥeseḏ, ḥāsaḏ*–'be loyal'] (Gen. 21:23; 24:49; 47:29; 1 S. 20:14f.; 2 S. 2:5; 3:8; etc.; 1 K. 2:7; 1 Ch. 19:2; Ps. 18:25 [MT 26]; 101:1; Prov. 3:3; 14:22; etc.; Jonah 2:8); AV KINDNESS, MERCY, GOODNESS, etc.; NEB also LOYAL FRIENDSHIP, FAITH, BEFRIENDED, etc.; [Gk. *pistós*] (3 Jn. 5); AV FAITHFULLY. *Ḥeseḏ* is the trust and faithfulness that people pledge to and expect from each other in a relationship between, e.g., relatives, friends, or master and subject (*see also* KINDNESS; STEADFAST LOVE). On *pistós, see* FAITHFUL.

See N. Glueck, Ḥesed *in the Bible* (Eng. tr. 1967; repr. 1975).

**LOZON** lä-zōn' [Gk. *Lozōn*] (1 Esd. 5:33). Head of a family of Solomon's servants. The name at this point in the parallel lists (Ezr. 2:56; Neh. 7:58) is Darkon.

**LUBIM** lo͞o'bim [Heb. *lûḇîm*]. A people in northern Africa, named with Egypt, Cush, Put, and the SUKKIIM (2 Ch. 12:3; 16:8; Dnl. 11:43; Nah. 3:9). The Lubim are to be identified with LIBYA (Gk. *Libyes*), probably also with LEHABIM, and perhaps with PUT.

W. S. L. S.

**LUCAS** (Philem. 24, AV). *See* LUKE.

**LUCIAN TEXT.** *See* SEPTUAGINT III.B.5.

**LUCIFER** (Isa. 14:12, AV). *See* DAY STAR.

**LUCIUS** lōō'shəs [Gk. *Loukios* < Lat. *Lucius*– 'light, bright', *Leukios*].

**1.** A Roman CONSUL who, according to 1 Macc. 15:15-24, wrote to Ptolemy VII (145-117 B.C.) of Egypt and other Near Eastern kings notifying them of the Roman senate's support for the Jewish state. Lucius's letter (*ca.* 139 B.C.) reports that the Roman senate had accepted from the Jews a large golden shield and had renewed the alliance made with them in the time of Judas Maccabeus (cf. 8:17-32); it also warns interested parties not to harm or make war upon the Jews, nor to align themselves with the Jews' enemies.

Because only the praenomen of the consul is given, identification of Lucius is difficult. The probability seems to lie with Cnaeus (or Lucius) Calpurnius Piso, who was a consul in 139 B.C. That his praenomen sometimes appears in other sources as Cnaeus rather than Lucius is then explained by an error in transcription. An earlier consul, Lucius Caecilius Metellus, has also been suggested; but since his consulship was in 142 B.C., this proposal requires the theory that 1 Macc. 15:15-24 is out of sequence and actually belongs to ch. 14 (see Goldstein, pp. 493ff.).

Some have questioned the genuineness of the letter on several grounds, including the fact that Josephus seems to have stopped using 1 Maccabees as a historical source after 14:15. In *Ant.* xiv.8.5 (145-48) Josephus includes a document of the Roman senate that refers to a "praetor" (Gk. *stratēgós*, which rarely means "consul"; see LSJ, p. 1652; *TDNT*, VII, 704 n. 19) named Lucius Valerius. The document is strikingly similar to the letter in 1 Macc. 15:16-24, but Josephus assigns it to the time of Hyrcanus II (47 B.C.). The document's fragmentary character makes its source and date somewhat uncertain.

*Bibliography*.–J. C. Dancy, *Comm. on I Maccabees* (1954); H. W. Ettelson, *Integrity of I Maccabees* (1925); J. A. Goldstein, *I Maccabees* (*AB*, 1976); *TDNT*, VII, *s.v.* στρατεύομαι κτλ.: στρατηγός (O. Bauernfeind).

J. J. SCOTT, JR. R. K. H.

**2.** A native of Cyrene who ministered with others to the church in Syrian Antioch as a prophet (Acts 13:1).

**3.** A "kinsman" of Paul on whose behalf the apostle sent a greeting to the church at Rome (Rom. 16:21). Possibly he is to be identified with **2.** Identification with Luke is improbable, since Paul elsewhere did not refer to Luke as Lucius (cf. 2 Tim. 4:11).

E. F. H.

**LUCRE** lōō'kər. Monetary gain; used by the AV always in a pejorative sense of dishonest or unjust gain (e.g., 1 S. 8:3, Heb. *beṣaʿ*; RSV "gain"). "Filthy lucre" is used in translating Gk. *aischrós kérdos* (lit. "shameful gain," Tit. 1:11) and the compounds *aischrokerdḗs* (Tit. 1:7; 1 Tim. 3:3, 8) and *aischrokerdṓs* (1 Pet. 5:2). Greed for unjust gain was a serious threat to the early Christian community, and thus it was listed among the vices that made one unfit for the office of bishop or deacon. *See* GAIN; GREED.

**LUD** lud; **LUDIM** lōō'dim [Heb. *lûḏ, lûḏîm, lûḏîyîm* (*K*, 1 Ch. 1:11); Gk. *Loud, Loudieim*]. A people descended from Egypt and named with Put and Cush and once with Persia (Gen. 10:13, 22; 1 Ch. 1:11, 17; Isa. 66:19; Jer. 46:9; Ezk. 27:10; 30:5). Scholars have either equated the Ludim with the Lydians in Asia Minor (cf. Jer. 46:9, AV) or considered them an unidentified people of north Africa near Egypt.

In Gen. 10:13f. Egypt (*Miṣrayim*) is named as the father of "Ludim, Anamim, Lehabim, Naphtuhim, Pathrusim, Casluhim (whence came the Philistines), and Caphtorim" (= 1 Ch. 1:11). Gen. 10:22 lists Lud among the sons of Shem, along with Elam, Asshur, Arpachshad, and Aram (1 Ch. 1:17 lists these and adds the sons of Aram [Gen. 10:23] as sons of Shem). The identifiable names in 10:13 belong to northern Africa and the eastern Mediterranean, and those in v. 22 to the Mesopotamian region. Thus there is already a mixed tradition, which finds support in the population shifts of the Near East throughout much of history.

In Isa. 66:19 Lud is mentioned after Put; after a parenthetical statement Tubal and Javan are named. If Put is taken as a part of Libya (on which there is much disagreement), Lud is again linked with both northern Africa and Asia Minor (Javan is Ionia, the western coastal region of Asia Minor). Jer. 46:9 mentions Lud along with Ethiopia and Put. Ezk. 27:10 associates Persia, Lud, and Put; in 30:5 the grouping is "Ethiopia, and Put, and Lud, and all Arabia, and Libya [Heb. *kûḇ*]." In all three prophets Lud is a warrior people, described as those "who draw the bow" (Isa. 66:19) or who are "skilled in handling the bow" (Jer. 46:9). In his prophecy against Tyre Ezekiel said, "Persia and Lud and Put were in your army as your men of war" (27:10). In Jeremiah Lud is an ally of Egypt.

On biblical evidence alone the problem is seemingly insoluble. A strong case can be made for identifying Lud with Lydia, principally on the linguistic similarity, along with some later participation of Lydians in Egypt as mercenaries (cf. *IDB*, III, 179). An equally strong case can be made for a north African people, chiefly on the basis of the tradition in Gen. 10:13, which has some support in other passages (cf. *GTTOT*, §§ 150f., p. 56; BDB, p. 530). T. G. Pinches (*ISBE* [1929], III, 1935) thought that two peoples had the same name: Semitic Ludim, who lived in Lydia in Asia Minor, and Egyptian Ludim, who cannot be further identified. This solution seems a bit strained, particularly in its identification of the Lydians as a Semitic people.

W. S. LASOR

**LUHITH** lōō'hith, **ASCENT OF** [Heb. *maʿªlēh hallûḥîṯ*]. A place mentioned in Isaiah's oracle concerning Moab (Isa. 15:5). Its context includes the road to Horonaim and the waters of Nimrim. A similar oracle in Jer. 48:3-5 mentions the descent of Horonaim and Zoar. Since the definite article appears on the word in both passages, Luhith could be other than a place name; a Nabatean inscription found at Medeba contains the name Luḥitu, however. The location is to be sought in Transjordan S of the Arnon, possibly toward the southern end of the Dead Sea. Eusebius (*Onom.* 122.29) identified it with Loueitha; cf. LXX *Loueith*.

See *GTTOT*, § 125b; *GP*, II, 370.

W. S. L. S.

**LUKE** [Gk. *Loukas*]. A sometime traveling companion and co-worker of Paul, traditionally regarded as the author of the Third Gospel and the book of Acts.

***I. Associate of Paul.***–Luke's name occurs three times in the letters of Paul. Philem. 24 lists him, Mark, and Aristarchus as among Paul's "fellow workers." Col. 4:10-14, presumably written about the same time, mentions this same trio along with Jesus "who is called Justus" and Epaphras; here Luke is given the epithet "the [possibly "my"] beloved physician" and is distinguished from the first three colleagues, who are called "men of the circumcision." 2 Tim. 4:11 finds him as the faithful companion of Paul in Rome, shortly before the apostle's martyrdom.

***II. Hypothetical Identifications.***–As early as Origen (*ca.* 185-254; *Comm. on Romans*) Luke was identified with the otherwise unknown Lucius (Gk. *Loukios*), whom Paul referred to as his "kinsman" (Gk. *syngenḗs*, "relative" or "fellow countryman") in Rom. 16:21. Ephrem Syrus (*ca.* 306-373; *Comm. on Acts*) suggested that he was Lucius of Cyrene, the Christian prophet and teacher at Antioch (Acts 13:1). Although various modern scholars (e.g., Deissmann [*LAE*, pp. 435-38] and Reicke [pp. 12-16]) have identified Luke with one or both of these men, the most that can be said for these suggestions is that probably the two names are equivalent, Luke being the more familiar form (though some have equated the name Luke with Lucanus or argued that it was originally an Aramaic name totally independent of the Greek Lucius), and that a strong early tradition connects Luke with Antioch (i.e., the so-called anti-Marcionite prologue to Luke, *ca.* 170, and the Western text of Acts 11:28). Ramsay combined the Antiochene tradition with the suggestion that Luke was a member of the tribe of Makedones, who settled in Antioch, and thus gave Luke an additional link with Philippi, a city in which the Evangelist also showed special interest (cf. Acts 16:12). Thus Ramsay (*Luke the Physician* [1908], pp. 35ff.) thought that Luke could be the "man of Macedonia" who appeared to Paul in a vision (Acts 16:9). He further speculated that Luke was also the brother of Titus, which explains the absence of both names from the narrative of Acts. Others have proposed an identification with "the brother who is famous among all the churches for his preaching of the gospel" (2 Cor. 8:18; note that 2 Corinthians was written from Macedonia). All these suggestions are possible, but unprovable.

*III. His Ministry and Special Interests.*–If the tradition connecting Luke with the Third Gospel and Acts is reliable — and there are very good reasons to think so — one can know more about his life, ministry, and personal interests and convictions as a Christian leader and thinker. His sharing in Paul's missionary endeavor is indicated by the "we" sections of Acts, where the author introduced his presence by the use of the 1st person plural (Acts 16:10-17; 20:5–21:18; 27:1–28:16). The suggestions that the "we" is introduced for dramatic effect (so Haenchen [*Journal for Theology and the Church,* 1 (1965), 65-99] and Conzelmann) or represents an itinerary source (so nineteenth-century German exegetes and, more recently, Dibelius [*passim*] and Trocmé [pp. 121-153]) have proved unconvincing. Luke shared in Paul's missionary work only for a few years (namely, during the initial mission in Greece, *ca.* 57/58; on the voyage as a prisoner to Rome, *ca.* 59/60; and at the time of his final Roman imprisonment 65/66). Luke may have used the period of Paul's imprisonment in Caesarea to collect data for his two-volume account of Christian origins. In the preface to his first volume (Lk. 1:1-4, probably to be understood as the preface to Luke-Acts as a whole), he distinguished himself from the first generation of Christian leaders, who were "from the beginning eyewitnesses and ministers of the word," and identified himself with the recipients of their tradition, though he had been part of the Christian movement for some time and therefore had become well informed (so Cadbury, *et al.*). His writings indicate that he was an educated person, whose Greek was the most literary in the NT (along with that in Hebrews); a church member, profoundly interested in both the mission and unity of the Church; a historian, showing interest in the life and times of Jesus and the early Church and using common techniques of Greco-Roman historiography (thus justifying Dibelius's appellation of "the first Christian historian"); an apologist, seeking to promote the faith by both explaining its main tenets and answering the criticism that the followers of "the Way" menaced imperial law and order; an evangelist, preaching the gospel as he understood Jesus and the early apostles to have preached it; and a theologian, whose version of the story of Jesus and the early Church brought out his own theological concerns. He had a special interest in the poor and down-trodden of the world, prophecy and prophets, women, the ministry of the Holy Spirit, prayer, the relationship between Jews and Gentiles, and the special mission of Paul. He was a physician (according to the witness of Col. 4:14; but, contrary to Hobart, Ramsay, and Harnack, his writings do not evince a special medical vocabulary: see, e.g., H. J. Cadbury, *Style and Literary Method of Luke* [1919-20]).

*IV. Jew or Gentile?*–Luke may have been a Gentile (cf. Col. 4:11), though some scholars have challenged this view (e.g., Ellis, who argued that "men of the circumcision" referred to a particular type of Jewish Christian, namely, those who strictly observed the rituals of Judaism, followed a Greek life-style and took a more relaxed approach to ritual observance). The chief argument for the view that Luke was a Jewish Christian rather than a gentile Christian is the author's intimate knowledge of the OT. A gentile Christian, however, particularly if he had been a "God-fearer" before his conversion, could have been as interested in the OT and attained as intimate a knowledge of its contents as a Jewish Christian, as subsequent history has demonstrated. Arguments supporting the traditional view, still held by most scholars, that Luke was a Gentile, are that the author of Acts refers to "the Jews" as a group distinct from the early Christians and that Greek elements (as distinct from Roman and Jewish) seem to permeate his writings more than other NT writings (cf. Cadbury, *Book of Acts in History* [1955], ch. 2). For example, Acts 28:2, where Luke speaks of "the foreigners" (Gk. *bárbaroi*) who "showed us extraordinary kindness," is characteristically Greek, as is also his habit of looking at the world in terms of the city rather than other geographical or political units. Although the author possibly was a Hellenistically oriented Jew or proselyte, the Gentile alternative seems at least plausible if not more probable.

*V. Author of Luke-Acts?*–Some scholars, primarily on the basis of alleged differences between the theologies of Paul and the author of Luke-Acts, have strongly denied that Luke or any other missionary companion of Paul could have written Luke-Acts (e.g., Vielhauer ["On the 'Paulinism' of Acts," in Keck and Martyn, eds., *Studies in Luke-Acts,* pp. 33-50], Haenchen, pp. 112-16, and Conzelmann). In particular, the Paul portrayed in Acts seems to have had a radically different perspective from the Paul known through the Epistles. Paul in Acts stresses the resurrection rather than the cross and sounds strikingly like Peter in the earlier chapters; he also frequents synagogues and keeps Jewish customs. Could this be the Paul who wrote Romans and Galatians? Contemporary critics are divided on the answer. While recognizing that Lukan theology is quite distinct from Pauline — this distinction is the major achievement of more recent scholarship — many believe that the contemporary German scholars' portrayal of the "Paul of the Epistles" is influenced more by the writings of Martin Luther and F. C. Baur than by balanced exegesis of Paul's letters. Luke was not an intimate associate of Paul over a long period of time, and even if he had been, perhaps, as Harnack quipped many years ago, Paul allowed more diversity of opinion among his followers than some professors of theology allow among theirs! Thus most contemporary scholars do not regard the obvious differences between the theology of Luke-Acts and that of Paul as ruling out the traditional Lukan authorship. If Luke did not write the Third Gospel and Acts, it is difficult to explain how the tradition connecting his name with these documents ever arose, since he is otherwise an insignificant figure in the early Church.

*Bibliography.*–W. K. Hobart, *Medical Language of St. Luke* (1882; repr. 1954); H. J. Cadbury, *Making of Luke-Acts* (1927; repr. 1955); M. Dibelius, *Studies in the Acts of the Apostles* (Eng. tr. 1956; repr. 1973), esp. ch. 8; E. Trocmé, *Le "Livre des Actes" et l'histoire* (1957); B. Reicke, *Gospel of Luke* (Eng. tr. 1965); L. E. Keck and J. L. Martyn, eds., *Studies in Luke-Acts* (1966); I. H. Marshall, *Luke: Historian and Theologian* (1970); E. E. Ellis, *Gospel of Luke* (*NCBC,* rev. ed. 1974; repr. 1980); E. Haenchen, *Acts of the Apostles* (Eng. tr. 1971); W. W. Gasque, *History of the Criticism of the Acts of the Apostles* (1975); I. H. Marshall, *Gospel of Luke* (*New International Greek Testament Commentary*, 1978).

W. W. GASQUE

## LUKE, GOSPEL ACCORDING TO.

- I. Background of the Research
  - A. Early Tradition
  - B. Beginnings of Modern Research
- II. Trends in the 20th Century
  - A. Literary Style
  - B. Text
  - C. History and Theology
  - D. Purpose
  - E. Date of Composition
- III. Formation and Structure
  - A. Sources
  - B. Structure and Theme
  - C. Special Lukan Interests
- IV. Authorship
  - A. Case for Lukan Authorship
  - B. Mid-Century Objections
  - C. The Underlying "Hegelian Factor"

***I. Background of the Research.***–*A. Early Tradition. 1. Author.* The author of the Third Gospel is first mentioned in the latter half of the 2nd century. In *ca.* 180 Irenaeus (*Adv. haer.* iii.1.1; 3.3; 14.1) attributed the Gospel to Luke the physician and "follower" of Paul. Somewhat earlier, perhaps, is the similar witness of the Muratorian Canon. The "anti-Marcionite" prologue to the Gospel gives a more detailed description. At least in its earliest form this prologue may also have originated during the late 2nd cent. (cf. Ellis, *Gospel of Luke,* p. 41).

The Gospel of the heretic Marcion, dating from *ca.* 150, also indirectly supports Lukan authorship. As reconstructed from quotations and detailed references in Tertullian and Epiphanius, it represents an abbreviated form of Luke (so Harnack, *TU,* 45 [1921], 231; see I.B.2 below).

The title "according to Luke" appears in the best MSS of the Gospel. The Church created it to distinguish Luke from other known Gospels. The presence of similar titles on the Gnostic Gospels "according to" (*katá*) Philip and Thomas suggests that the practice goes back at least to the middle of the 2nd century.

The name of Luke, however, probably was attached to the Gospel at the beginning. In the ancient Orient, a book was identified by title. "The most significant contribution which the Greeks made to [book] cataloging was the use of the author of a work for its entry" (R. F. Strout, *Toward a Better Cataloguing Code* [1956], p. 7). "If the *titulus* was lacking, the roll would be tagged with the name of the author when it was placed in a library, for after going to the general subject . . . [the reader] was accustomed to look next for the author — title was secondary" (*ibid.*). Private libraries had become very common among the rich, and a copy of Luke's volumes, properly tagged, was in all likelihood placed in the library of his patron, Theophilus. (Cf. M. Hadas, *Ancilla to Classical Reading* [1954], p. 25; Seneca *De tranquillitate animi* 9.4ff.; Suetonius *De gram.* 6; Aurelius *Ad Frontonem* 4.5.)

*2. Authority.* The authority of the Gospel, i.e., its canonical status in (many areas of) the Church, is explicitly

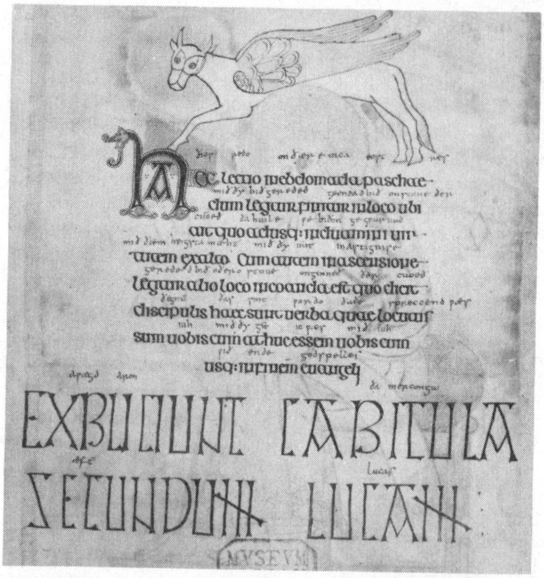

Vellum Vulgate of the illuminated Lindisfarne Gospels (*ca.* A.D. 700) showing the end of the index of contents that precedes Luke's Gospel. The Anglo-Saxon interlinear glosses were added by Aldred in the 10th cent. (Trustees of the British Museum)

affirmed from the time of Irenaeus. Indirectly, it may be traced back to the first half of the 2nd century. (1) Marcion (or his teacher Cerdo) used Luke in constructing his own "Gospel" (see above). (2) Before 140 it probably was cited as Scripture in 2 Clem. 13:4 ("says God") and, a little later, alluded to by the Gospel of Truth (33:15) and the Gospel of Philip (126:7). (3) About mid-century Justin used the Gospel or a harmony based on it (cf. *Apol.* i.34.2; *Dial.* 51.3; 76.6; Lk. 2:2; 16:16; 10:19; 2:1-5; B. F. Westcott, *Canon of the NT* [1881], pp. 100-173). (4) Valentinus derived his chronology from it (Irenaeus *Adv. haer.* ii.22.4; Lk. 3:23; cf. 4:19; cf. J. B. Lightfoot, *Biblical Essays* [1904], pp. 56f.), and his disciple Heracleon apparently wrote a commentary on it (Clement *Misc.* iv.9). (5) It is a part of the second-century tradition of the "fourfold" Gospel (see 3 below).

Apparently the status accorded to the Gospel had a twofold basis: the association of Luke with Paul's apostolic authority, and the conviction that Luke himself was a prophet. Irenaeus, Tertullian (*Adv. Marc.* iv.5), and perhaps even Justin Martyr (*Dial.* 103.8) pointed to Luke's relation to Paul. Like the Muratorian Canon and the prologue mentioned above, however, Origen (*Homily on Luke 1*) included Luke among Evangelists who "wrote from the Holy Spirit" (cf. Ellis, *Gospel of Luke,* pp. 38-41).

*3. Relationship to Other Gospels.* The relationship of Luke and the other Gospels is mentioned most frequently in connection with their chronological sequence. According to Eusebius (*HE* vi.14.5ff.), Clement believed that the Gospels containing genealogies, i.e., Matthew and Luke, were written first. Tertullian (*Adv. Marc.* iv.2) placed Luke and Mark after John and Matthew. Although there are other such variations, most of the canonical lists and other statements refer to the Gospels in the order in which they now appear in the NT.

*B. Beginnings of Modern Research.* In the post-Reformation period, the historical analysis of biblical writings raised again the patristic issues and initiated new questions. Before the end of the 17th cent., R. Simon concluded that Luke's title, like those of the other Gospels, was not original (cf. Kümmel, *Problems,* p. 44). A century later J. D. Michaelis (*Intro. to the NT* [Eng. tr. 1793-1801], I, 87-97) questioned Luke's inspired authority and canonical status since it, like Mark, was not written by an apostle. Going further, his pupil J. G. Eichhorn (cited in Kümmel, *Problems,* p. 88; cf. S. Davidson, *Intro. to the NT* [1848-51], I, 184f.) rejected the second-century view that Luke wrote under Paul's oversight as a mistaken inference designed to place the Gospel under an apostolic umbrella. These departures from the tradition were not in themselves critical of the historical accuracy or authenticity of the Gospel, nor was Lukan authorship seriously questioned.

A challenge to Lukan authorship was implicit, however, in J. S. Semler's suggestion (in 1776) that both Luke and Marcion's Gospel were offshoots of a common original. J. G. Eichhorn (*Einleitung in das NT* [5 vols., 1804-1827], I, 43-84) and others virtually regarded the Marcionite Gospel as the original Gospel of Luke (cf. J. Knox, *Marcion and the NT* [1942], p. 78).

This novel hypothesis, which turned the patristic testimony upside down, rested on rather slight historical evidence: (1) some readings in the Marcionite Gospel were more primitive than Tertullian's canonical text; and (2) the earliest second-century citations of Luke may have been from the "original" Gospel. Scholars generally rejected the hypothesis (cf. F. Bleek, *Intro. to the NT* [Eng. tr. 1873-74], I, 143-45; Davidson, I, 202f.). It gained new support, however, from F. C. Baur (*Evangelien,* p. 424), who found it congenial to his views of early Christian history. J. Knox (cf. p. 139) revived it with variations in the present century but had little success. The early witness to the fourfold Gospel, the tendentious character of Marcion's Gospel, the stylistic unity of Luke-Acts, and the lack of telltale marks of a second-century composition have confirmed the priority of the canonical Gospel in the minds of almost all contemporary students.

In this period the relationships of what now were termed the "Synoptic" Gospels, particularly their origin and sequence, were intensively investigated. Scholars maintained the Augustinian view of the literary interdependence of the Gospels but suggested various opinions as to their chronological order (cf. Marsh, pp. 5-18). Most influential, perhaps, was the sequence advocated by H. Owen and, in more detail, by J. J. Griesbach: Matthew, Luke, Mark. G. E. Lessing ("New Hypothesis Concerning the Evangelists Considered as merely Human Historians," in H. Chadwick, ed., *Theological Writings* [Eng. tr. 1956], pp. 65-81) suggested that the Gospels were independently derived from an original Aramaic Gospel written in narrative form, were based on apostolic tradition, and were developed in variant recensions (cf. Farmer, pp. 3-11; Kümmel, *Problems,* pp. 74-79).

H. Marsh (pp. 196-211), following the suggestion of Lessing (in *Theological Writings,* p. 77 § 45), argued that the title of this Gospel actually appeared in the preface of Luke (1:1f.): "A narrative of the things that have been fulfilled among us just as they, who from the beginning were eyewitnesses and ministers of the Word, delivered to us." Elaborating the views of Michaelis and Eichhorn, he suggested further that this "narrative of *facts*" (א) formed the basis of (Aramaic) Matthew, Luke, and Mark and was supplemented by "a *collection of precepts, parables, and discourses*" (ב) that was used, in different copies, "only by St. Matthew and St. Luke" (p. 202). In distinguishing a "narrative" and a "sayings" document and in combining theories of literary interdependence (of Greek Matthew on Mark and Luke) with theories of precanonical written sources, Marsh contributed to later research more than has usually been recognized.

Both J. G. Herder (pp. 174ff., 210-232) and B. F. Westcott much later (*Intro. to the Study of the Gospels* [1860], pp. 165-212) rejected written sources, posited an original oral Gospel reflecting the apostolic preaching and containing narratives and teachings, and gave to Mark chronological priority — Mark, Luke, Greek Matthew. Herder (pp. 174-77) anticipated later research and issues of contemporary debate in a number of ways. (1) Rejecting the hypothesis that the oldest Gospel arose out of hearsay, he identified the locus of the tradition's transmission as a school (cf. B. Gerhardsson, *Memory and MS* [1961], pp. 324-335). (2) He connected the writing of Gospels with the baptismal instruction of converts (cf. Schürmann, I, 383). (3) He advocated the priority of Mark and thus of the *narrative* Gospel-form and recognized a two-document source for Luke and Greek Matthew. (4) He anticipated the problems of form criticism and of the historical Jesus, i.e., that in the Gospels one must look for the work and teaching of Jesus (Kümmel, *Problems,* pp. 82f.). (5) He posited an oral narrative delivered by the apostles to "ministers of the Word" who put it into written form (cf. G. Klein, "Lukas 1,1-4 als theologisches Programm," in E. Dinkler, ed., *Zeit und Geschichte* [1964], pp. 200, 205; contra Haenchen, pp. 126f.).

Like Marsh, F. Schleiermacher (pp. 366-69, 382ff.) also postulated a "sayings" document and a collection of "words and deeds of Christ" (p. 387), identifying them respectively with Papias's Matthaean *logia* and his "Mark" (Eusebius *HE* iii.39.15f.). K. Lachmann and others developed this idea into the two-document hypothesis, which became the dominant theory explaining the relationship of the Synoptic Gospels (cf. Kümmel, *Problems,* pp. 146-155; S. Neill, *Interpretation of the NT* [1964], pp. 108-112; Farmer, pp. 22-25, 36-47).

F. C. Baur, influenced by the dialectical process theory of G. W. F. Hegel, reconstructed the history of early Christianity in terms of its postulates. Earliest Jewish Christianity (Hegel's "thesis"), with its continuing commitment to the Mosaic rituals, encountered an "antithesis" in Paul's emphasis on freedom from the law and salvation through faith. The "tendency" of later Christianity was to achieve a compromise between the conflicting attitudes (e.g., Baur, *Church History,* I, 99-116, 180-83).

For Baur the book of Acts represents such a compromise or "synthesis" and cannot, therefore, be the work of Luke the companion of Paul, "at least in the form . . . in which we possess the work" (*Paul,* I, 12). To support this, Baur argued (*ibid.,* I, 103f., 129-137) that the presentation of the death of Christ (Acts 13:26-41), the philosophical ideas of the Areopagus speech (ch. 17), and the general attitude toward the law conflicted with the Paul of the letters. Like Acts, the canonical Luke (and Mark) shows the same conciliating "tendency" (Baur, *Markus,* pp. 211-226). Only Matthew, reflecting Jewish (i.e., Judaizing) Christianity, is relatively free from it. Baur's dialectical approach led him, therefore, to support the view that Luke represents a second-century reaction to Marcion and to champion the order of the Gospels given by Griesbach and earlier by Clement of Alexandria: Matthew, Luke, Mark, John (so also Farmer, p. 200).

Baur made a decisive impact on NT — and especially Lukan — studies. (1) By tying literary-historical analysis to an imaginative philosophical framework, he initiated a new and comprehensive approach, which still has appeal, to the reconstruction of early Christian history (see IV.C below; cf. Haenchen, p. 17). (2) With both good and ill effect his dialectic laid the foundation of later "tendency criticism" and of "adversary theology," i.e., the interpretation of a document or an age in terms of the (supposed) opposition that it addresses (see II.D below). (3) He made the first consistent effort to explain the origin and development of Christianity in accordance with principles of historical criticism.

Nevertheless, Baur's views reflected an unjustified skepticism toward the patristic testimony and weighted the historical probabilities in the interest of a largely theoretical reconstruction of Christian origins. Also, there is truth in the charge that Baur was more a systematic theologian (*Systematiker*) than a critical historian (E. Barnikol, *F. C. Baur als rationalistisch-kirchlicher Theologe* [1970], pp. 38f.). For his reconstruction of early Christian history was decisively shaped by his a priori acceptance of Hegelian dialectic and philosophical rationalism. Thus Baur, like nineteenth-century "scientific historians" generally (cf. J. S. Lawton, *Miracles and Revelation* [1959], pp. 93-105), considered "miraculous claims clearly *incompatible* with historical considerations" (P. C. Hodgson, *Formation of Historical Theology* [1966], p. 192; cf. Baur, *Church History,* I, 1f.). Viewing historical reality as a closed continuum of natural causes and effects, Baur, like R. Bultmann (e.g., in *Kerygma and Myth,* ed. H. W. Bartsch [1960], p. 7) in the 20th cent., axiomatically excluded miracle from historical inquiry (cf. A. Richardson, *History, Sacred and Profane* [1947], p. 121). Baur's world view allowed him to give only psychological or mythological explanations of reported miracles, e.g., Paul's conversion (cf. *Paul,* I, 65-77). He freed NT exegesis from the domination of traditional dogma only to make it the servant of contemporary philosophy. Although his historical reconstructions did not last, the philosophical commitments he popularized significantly influence current NT studies (cf. Ellis, "Gospels Criticism"; B. Rigaux, *St. Paul and His Letters* [1966], pp. 10-16).

***II. Trends in the 20th Century.***–Lukan studies from the later 19th cent. until the present largely follow trends set by earlier scholarship. Some of these earlier issues remain in the forefront of contemporary discussion; some have moved toward a consensus or have quietly been left to die. In the last category is the short-lived hypothesis that Luke used Josephus (cf. Zahn, III, 94-100).

*A. Literary Style.* Since the stylistic analysis of J. C. Hawkins (*Horae Synopticae* [1909], pp. 174-193) and others, there has been a virtual consensus that Luke-Acts is a literary unity. Luke's style, rightly described as that of "a gentleman of ability and breadth of interest," is characterized by sensitivity and variety (cf. Cadbury, *Making,* pp. 213-238). Generally written in a more polished Greek than Mark, it at times removes Mark's Hebraisms (cf. Mark 11:9; 14:36) or substitutes Greek equivalents (Lk. 3:12; 6:15; 23:33). But some Hebraic idioms, e.g., "it came to pass that," are common in Luke; several (L) sections seem to reflect Semitic sources: Lk. 1:5–2:40; 5:1-11; 7:11-17, 36-50; 8:1-3; 9:51-56; 11:27f.; 13:10-17; 14:1-6; 17:11-19; 19:1-10; 23:50–24:53 (E. Schweizer, *TZ,* 6 [1950], 183). Less probable is the view, e.g., of H. J. Cadbury, that such idioms represent a Lukan imitation of LXX Greek (cf. Ellis, *Gospel of Luke,* pp. 3, 28).

*B. Text.* In the last century studies in textual criticism called attention to the variations between the Western and Alexandrian textual families. To solve the problem, F. Blass (pp. 138-164; cf. Zahn, III, 8-25) developed the thesis that Luke wrote the Gospel first in Palestine at the time of Paul's Caesarean imprisonment and issued a second, "Western" draft later from Rome. His thesis was not generally accepted, although a Caesarean origin may be reconsidered if the Qumrân fragment 7Q5 (? = Mk. 6:52f.) does, in fact, prove that Mark's Gospel was then present in Palestine. But this identification of the fragment appears

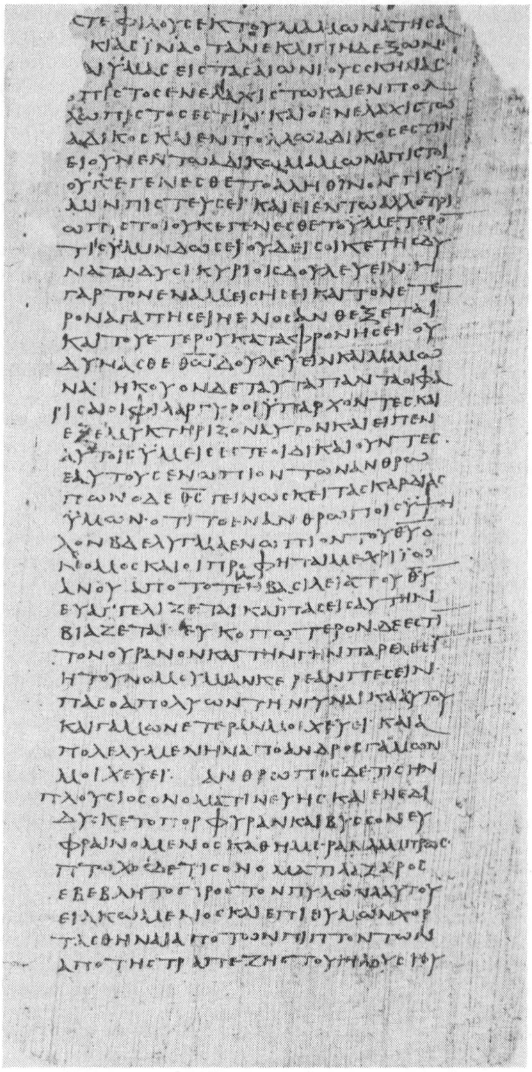

Luke 16:9-21 in Bodmer Papyrus XIV, the earliest known copy of Luke's Gospel (**$p^{75}$**; *ca.* A.D. 175-225) (Bodmer Library, Geneva)

doubtful. The solution of Westcott and Hort, that only the "non-interpolations" in the Western text are original, also is unsatisfactory. Today the evaluation of the individual reading rather than of its family plays a more decisive role in determining the original text of Luke. Among the important variants the following passages have Western readings absent or different from the Alexandrian text: Lk. 3:22; 6:5; 9:55; 11:2-4; 22:43f. The following have Alexandrian readings absent from the Western text: Lk. 14:5; 20:36; 22:19f.; 24:51f.

*C. History and Theology.* The Evangelist's secular-historical and geographical notices express not only his literary technique but also his concern to relate the history of Jesus and the Church to general history. Synchronisms with world history occur at Lk. 2:1f.; 3:1f., and similar geographical notices appear to be a regular feature in Luke-Acts: "Capernaum, a city of Galilee," "Emmaus, about seven miles from Jerusalem," "Perga in Pamphylia," "Antioch by Pisidia," "Phoenix, a harbor of Crete looking northeast and southeast," "Manaen, a member of the

LUKE, GOSPEL ACCORDING TO

court of Herod, the tetrarch" (cf. Cadbury, *Making,* pp. 239-253). Note also the suitably vague *hēgemonías* (Lk. 3:1) referring to an office whose precise title varied during the 1st cent.: an inscription found in Caesarea in 1961 (*L'Année epigraphique* [1963], p. 26, no. 104) reads, "[PON]TIUS PILATUS [PRAE]FECTUS JUDAE[AE]" (*see* picture in CAESAREA).

The remarkable accuracy of such references, confirmed by his own observations and archeological finds in Asia Minor, caused W. M. Ramsay (cf. *Pauline and Other Studies* [1906], pp. 199f.) to withdraw his earlier sympathy for the reconstructions of F. C. Baur and to become a convinced advocate of Luke's historical reliability. Contemporary Roman historians have concurred (cf. A. N. Sherwin-White, *Roman Society and Roman Law in the NT* [1963], pp. 188f.). Ramsay (*SPT*, p. 20), however, recognized that Luke "could not stand with the same confidence on the soil of Syria and Palestine as on that of Asia and Greece." H. Conzelmann (pp. 18-94; cf. Ellis, *Gospel of Luke,* p. 209; see III.B below) pursued this question further. The judgment of Ramsay and, e.g., E. Meyer (*Ursprung und Anfänge des Christentums* [1921-23], I, 2f.; III, 167f.) brought a renewed emphasis on "Luke the historian" (cf. H. J. Cadbury in *BC,* II, 7-29; IV, 405-407; Bruce, pp. 15-18).

But scholars began to realize that they could not ignore the theological character of Luke. In contrast to a popular nineteenth-century view, "historian" meant more than Schleiermacher's "collector and arranger." M. Dibelius (pp. 123-185) contributed importantly to this trend: Luke is "an historian who expounds the meaning of an event by striking description; we see him also in his capacity as *herald* and *evangelist,* a role which he fulfills completely in his first book and wishes ultimately to fulfil also in Acts" (pp. 134f.). Dibelius may at times have drawn too sharp a dichotomy between history and interpretation in Luke, as subsequent writers certainly did. For, in the words of C. K. Barrett (pp. 39f.), "Luke was well equipped to write history, and the form his history took arose not out of his imagination but out of the historical event itself." Within this context Luke's conscious interpretative orientation and his subordination of other interests to his theological concerns do not in themselves detract from his reputation as a historian (cf. Stonehouse, p. 67; Marshall, *Luke: Historian and Theologian,* pp. 18-20). But these factors increasingly led researchers to consider "Luke the theologian" and tempted them to fall back into the "tendency" interpretation of the Baur School (see IV.C below; J. Rohde, *Rediscovering the Teaching of the Evangelists* [1968], pp. 153-239). All in all, the resulting "composition criticism" has fostered a new appreciation for the contribution of the Gospel of Luke to the theology of the NT.

*D. Purpose.* Some scholars have identified the Lukan writings as an apologetic intended to defend Christianity before Roman officialdom (e.g., H. Sahlin, *Der Messias und das Gottesvolk* [1945], pp. 44ff.) or to present its claims to the Roman public (e.g., Streeter, p. 535; Bruce, pp. 30f.; O'Neill, pp. 180-83). Others have thought that Luke meant to confirm believers in their faith (cf. Lk. 1:3f.) by writing a careful history of Christian origins (Plummer, p. xxxvi) within the context of a "salvation" motif (Marshall, *Luke: Historian and Theologian,* p. 9) or by offering (in the Gospel) an extensive post-baptismal instruction for Christian converts (Schürmann, I, 179-183, 258f.). Somewhat similar is E. Haenchen's (pp. 100-103) view: Luke intended to show the continuity of the mission to the Gentiles, carried out apart from the law, with the salvation history of Israel. A third group of scholars has seen Luke-Acts as an expression of "adversary theology": Luke wrote to counter gnosticizing influences in the Church (C. H. Talbert, *Luke and the Gnostics* [1966]) or to respond to attacks of Judaizers on Paul (Trocmé, p. 67).

The content and emphases in Luke-Acts show that its message was directed primarily to the Church and to issues important for the Church. Within this context probably no exclusive purpose should be singled out, but at least three significant motifs may be discerned. (1) Luke emphasized Jesus' virgin conception and physical resurrection (Lk. 1:35; 3:23; 24:39) and the identity of the suffering Jesus with the ascended/returning Christ (9:51; 24:26; Acts 1:11) apparently to counter docetic/gnosticizing aberrations in the Church (cf. Schürmann, I, 11, 259; C. H. Talbert, *NTS,* 14 [1967-68], 259-271). (2) The "delay" motif in Luke's eschatology (e.g., Lk. 17:22-25; 19:11; 21:8f.; 20:24; Acts 1:7f.) probably is a calculated response to those who view the kingdom of God solely in terms of an immediate (and/or secret) return of Jesus. (3) The most pervasive theme, which echoes the concern of Paul in Rom. 9–11, is the problem of the Jewish rejection of the Messiah (e.g., Lk. 2:34f.; 4:16-30; Acts 28:25-28). Luke approached each of these matters in terms of the instruction of believers, rather than of direct apologetic, and within the framework of a comprehensive theology of salvation history. (Cf. Conzelmann; O. Cullmann, *Salvation in History* [1967], pp. 239-268; Ellis, *Gospel of Luke,* pp. 58f.; P. Borgen, *CBQ,* 31 [1969], 168-182.)

*E. Date of Composition.* The last two motifs apparently reflect a time of apocalyptic fever and of crisis in the relationship of Judaism and the Church. Luke's sixfold repetition of Jesus' judgments against Jerusalem (11:49-52; 13:1-9, 34f.; 19:41-44; 21:20-24; 23:28-31; cf. 20:16) and simultaneous stress on the Church's abiding relationship to that city (2:38; 9:31; 20:24; 24:47; Acts 1:8) support this view. These and other factors suggest a date for Luke-Acts of *ca.* 70 (cf. T. W. Manson, *Studies in the Gospels and Epistles* [1962], p. 67), although such concerns may have arisen in 60-65 (A. Harnack, *Date of the Acts and of the Synoptic Gospels* [1911], pp. 116-125; Bruce, pp. 10-14; cf. Blass, pp. 33f.) or 70-90 (Kümmel, *Intro.,* pp. 150f.). But see Ellis, *Gospel of Luke,* pp. 55-58. In fact, Luke-Acts depicts Christianity as a sect within Judaism, a situation that changed drastically with the Neronian persecution in 65-68, and displays no knowledge of any events after the mid to late 60's, neither the deaths of James or Peter or (perhaps) of Paul nor the fall of Jerusalem, which is described (Lk. 21:20-24) "*entirely* from the language of the Old Testament" and in some respects at odds with the A.D. 70 destruction (C. H. Dodd, "The Fall of Jerusalem and 'The Abomination of Desolation,'" in *More NT Studies* [1968], p. 79). Second-century dates suggested by J. C. O'Neill (pp. 17-21) and A. Loisy (*L'Évangile selon Luc* [1924], pp. 44-63) have little to commend them (cf. V. Taylor, *NT Essays* [1970], pp. 72-82).

***III. Formation and Structure.***–*A. Sources. 1. Two-Document Hypothesis.* In the present century the two-document hypothesis, popularized in Germany by H. J. Holtzmann (see I.B above), became dominant in British and American scholarship as well. It postulated that Matthew and Luke depended on two primary documents, Mark and Q, the latter inferred from non-Markan passages common to Matthew and Luke. B. H. Streeter (pp. 223-270) proposed special Lukan (L) and Matthaean (M) sources and developed a four-document hypothesis:

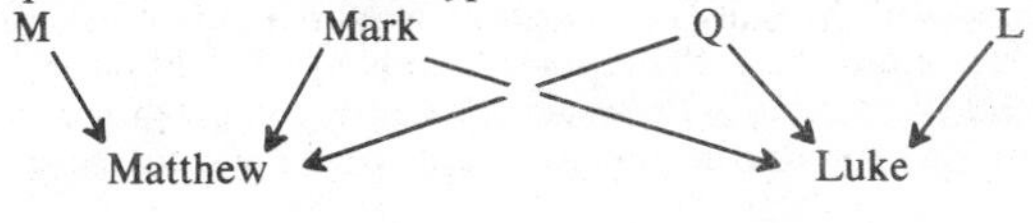

This reconstruction, however, has not settled the matter. (1) A number of scholars have raised important objections to the priority of Mark (cf. Farmer, pp. 118-176), and at least one writer (R. L. Lindsey, *A Hebrew Translation of the Gospel of Mark* [1969], pp. 12-31) has argued, partly on the basis of Luke's Hebraic idioms and word structure, that the Third Gospel is the earliest. (2) With due respect to Kümmel (*Intro.*, pp. 63-76), neither the common sequence in Mark and Luke of *some* Q episodes nor any other criterion has demonstrated that Q is one document.

But some scholars, e.g., A. Farrer ("On Dispensing with Q," in D. E. Nineham, ed., *Studies in the Gospels,* [1955]), who favor in Q passages a simple dependence of Luke on Matthew, also cannot be followed. Several considerations require a hypothesis that Luke used, in non-Markan passages paralleled in Matthew, a source or sources on which Matthew also depended (further, cf. Kümmel, *Intro.*, pp. 64-67). (1) A few non-Matthaean settings (e.g., Lk. 11:1) and textual variations (e.g., 7:1; 11:49) do not appear to be Lukan editorial. (2) Some repetitious phraseology (e.g., 7:19f.; 11:47f.), an un-Lukan characteristic (cf. Cadbury, *Style,* pp. 83ff.), also is not in Matthew. (3) Some Matthaean sayings presuppose a non-Markan source that appears in Luke (e.g., 12:38, *phylakḗ*; cf. Mt. 24:43). Probably Q is best understood as several independent tracts existing in varied textual forms on which Matthew and Luke drew (so W. L. Knox, *Sources of the Synoptic Gospels,* II [1957], 4f., 45-47; cf. Ellis, *Gospel of Luke,* pp. 21-24).

*2. Proto-Luke.* Posing a more fundamental alteration in the two-document hypothesis, B. H. Streeter (pp. 201-222; cf. P. Feine, *Eine vorkanonische Überlieferung des Lukas* [1891], pp. 124f.) and others suggested that Q + L (less Lk. 1–2) were joined to form a "proto-Luke" into which Markan material was inserted. This theory encounters a number of objections. (1) There is no evidence for the contention of F. Rehkopf (*Die lukanische Sonderquelle* [1959], pp. 86-90) and V. Taylor (*Behind the Third Gospel* [1926], pp. 68f., 172f.) that these Lukan passages were once a unified document. (2) The non-Markan sections of Luke presuppose the context and order of the canonical Gospel and are better understood as separate pieces that Luke fitted to his present format (cf. Conzelmann, pp. 32f., 60f.). (3) The presence in Luke of Markan "blocks" and the development of the central division of Luke on the structure of the journey in Mk. 10 indicate that Mark provided the scaffold or "form" into which Q and L materials were incorporated. But Luke also omitted parts of Mark and enriched his Markan passages with parallel materials from other sources (cf. T. Schramm, *Der Markus Stoff bei Lukas* [1971], pp. 185f.); i.e., the Evangelist subordinated Mark no less than the Q and L traditions to his own purposes.

*3. Classification of Q and L Elements.* Many scholars have attempted to classify elements of the Q and L materials used in Luke. The Mary/Martha stories, the Satanic possession of Judas, the prominence given to Samaria, and other items found only in Luke and John suggest a source or sources common to these two Gospels (cf. J. Schniewind, *Die Parallelperikopen bei Lukas und Johannes* [1914]). A number of episodes contain a similar "Hebraizing" style (see II.A above). Others may reflect a special Lukan (L) Passion narrative and a Jerusalem source incorporating prophetic oracles on a given theme (e.g., Lk. 11:49-51; 13:34f.; 21:20-24). As is the case for Q, however, the unity of those segments of tradition has not been established. Perhaps the sixfold cycle of prophecies and visions in 1:5–2:40 makes the strongest case for derivation from one document — at least the visions, which present a similar and non-Lukan structure (cf. Ellis, *Gospel of Luke,* p. 65). Luke's use of his sources shows that no one of them is the foundation of his Gospel. All are building blocks quarried and shaped to fit an edifice that is, in its specific form and content, Luke's own creative achievement.

*B. Structure and Theme.* According to H. Schürmann (I, 258f.) Mark originated the Gospel pattern by placing traditions about "the way of Jesus" between two pre-Markan traditions, a "narrative of beginnings" and a "Passion narrative." To this pattern Luke prefixed a "narrative of origins" (Lk. 1–2). Schürmann's view accords with the general division of Luke's Gospel into four sections reflecting both a chronological and a geographical sequence: (1) the Jerusalem infancy narratives (1–2), (2) the Galilean mission (3:1–9:50), (3) the journey to Jerusalem (9:51–19:44), and (4) the Jerusalem ministry, death, and resurrection of Jesus (19:45–24:53).

The transition points in the theme and sources further define the structure. An initial source (Lk. 1:5–2:40) precedes six non-Markan "witnesses to Messiah" (2:41–4:30), including the baptism (3:21f.), which Luke treats independently by placing it after the Baptist's witness (3:20). Mark is the basis of the following six stories (except one: 5:1-11) illustrating "the authority of Messiah" over various areas of life (4:31–6:11), and of the final twelve "messianic acts" of the Galilean mission (8:1–9:50). Inserted between these sections are six non-Markan episodes that emphasize certain "characteristics of the messianic kingdom" (6:12–7:50). The structure develops the theme; throughout and within the individual episodes the acts of the Messiah implicitly direct the reader to His teachings.

A journey provides the framework for the central division (e.g., 13:22; 17:11), although actual movement toward Jerusalem, begun in 9:51f., resumes only with the return to the Markan episodes at 18:15. The division's primary concern is not geography but "the teaching of Messiah" (cf. Ellis, *Gospel of Luke,* pp. 146-49). It oscillates between the instruction of disciples and discussion with opponents and culminates in the movement via Jericho to Jerusalem (18:15–19:44).

The concluding division, "the consummation of Messiah's mission" (19:45–24:53), uses Mark only in a few episodes and then only in a supplementary fashion. Characteristically the structure serves a thematic interest: "Messiah and the temple" (19:45–21:38) and "the meaning of Messiah's death" (22:1–23:25). The last six episodes set forth "the glorification of Messiah" (23:26–24:53) in terms of the fulfillment of prophecy, the theme with which Luke's story began (cf. P. Schubert, in W. Eltester, ed., *Neutestamentliche Studien für Rudolf Bultmann* [1954], pp. 178f.).

*C. Special Lukan Interests.* Luke's emphasis on particular themes and editorial alteration, supplementation, and arrangement of material display his special theological concerns. Among them is the role of the Holy Spirit, which he stressed more than the other Evangelists. By the Spirit Jesus was conceived (Lk. 1:35) and confirmed (3:22), proclaimed His message (4:14; 10:21), and healed (4:10; 11:20; cf. 5:17). After His resurrection He mediated the Spirit to His followers (3:16; 24:49; cf. Acts 2:33). Similarly, contemporary prophecy is prominent in the Infancy narratives. The Holy Spirit is none other than the OT "Spirit of the Lord" (cf. 4:18). But He appears now in a new role, which brings into being the new creation, the kingdom of God (11:13, 20; cf. 9:27).

The kingdom of God is, of course, a central motif in all the Synoptic Gospels, but Luke distinctively underscores and develops it. Unlike Matthew (3:2), Luke began the proclamation of the kingdom with the mission of Jesus

(4:43). In accord with Jesus' teaching Luke presented the kingdom of God as both a future and a present reality (11:2, 20) but tended to set the two aspects in explicit contrast (16:16, 19-31; 17:21, 22-37; cf. 3:16f.; 9:26f.; 23:42f.). These practices show an affinity with the Gospel of John (Jn 5:25, 28f.; 6:54; 11:24f.; 14:3, 18; cf. Maddox, pp. 100-157, 182f.).

Luke defined the ministry of Jesus not only in connection with the Spirit and the kingdom but also in connection with Jerusalem. He began and ended his Gospel in the Holy City: the Infancy narratives are written from the perspective of "the redemption of Jerusalem" (Lk. 2:38), and all of the resurrection appearances in ch. 24 are located there. Jesus "set his face to go to Jerusalem" (9:51), for it was not fitting for Him to meet His death elsewhere (13:33). Consequently, as a judgment motif, Luke more than any other Gospel draws attention to prophecies of the destruction of Jerusalem (those in 13:1-9; 19:41-44; 23:28-31 occur only in Luke).

The importance of the temple in Luke's presentation (1:13; 2:27, 49; 4:9; 21:6; Acts 6:13f.) is also related to the theological significance of Jerusalem. Our Lord's act of judgment in cleansing the temple (19:47) was the prelude to His ejection as the "rejected stone" (20:17). Jesus would become the "cornerstone" not of the temple in Jerusalem but of a new temple of God "not made with hands" (Acts 7:48). With such traditional imagery Luke made clear that the locus of God's presence and the identification of God's people no longer were to be found in the house or city of national Judaism.

***IV. Authorship.**–A. Case for Lukan Authorship.* Scholars in the early 20th cent. reaffirmed Lukan authorship — even those who, like Harnack and Dibelius, found important historical and theological differences between the Paul of Acts and the Paul of the Epistles (cf. Dibelius, pp. 77, 88-90, 192 n.; A. Harnack, *Luke the Physician* [1907], pp. 139-145; Streeter, pp. 540-562; Zahn, III, 142-165). Several reasons account for this affirmative verdict. (1) Differences are to be expected since Luke was only an occasional companion, not a disciple, of Paul, and (as a good historian) made his own interpretations. (2) Although the "medical language" in Luke-Acts cannot prove that the author was a physician (rightly, Cadbury, *Style,* pp. 39-72), as W. K. Hobart (*Medical Language of St. Luke* [1882]) and Harnack contended, it significantly corroborates the patristic witness. (3) The "we" passages in Acts 16; 20–21; 27–28, like the "I" in Luke 1:3; Acts 1:1, are most reasonably explained as a reference to the author. The use of such "travel reports" agrees with ancient practice (e.g., Ammianus Marcellinus xviii.6.5) and, in the judgment of A. D. Nock (*Essays on Religion* [2 vols., 1972], II, 827f.), there is little if any evidence for a writer in antiquity to use another's notes in this fashion (cf. J. Dupont, *Sources of Acts* [Eng. tr. 1964], pp. 126-132, 129 n.). (4) The accuracy of Luke-Acts, both in the historical-geographical notices and in the depiction of Paul's missionary practice, suggests a writer not far removed from the events (see II.C above; *TDNT,* VI, 744 [H. W. Kuhn]). (5) The Gospel was identified from the beginning with the name "Luke," implying that its first recipient tagged it with the author's name (Streeter, p. 588; Dibelius, p. 89; see I.A.1 above).

*B. Mid-Century Objections.* While most scholars continued to affirm Lukan authorship, some German writers in the mid-20th cent. again raised objections (cf. Kümmel, *Intro.,* pp. 147-150; Ellis, *Gospel of Luke,* pp. 42-52). They pointed to theological emphases and historical descriptions in Luke-Acts that differ fundamentally from those in Paul's letters. Their objections rested in part on exegetical judgments, e.g., a philosophical interpretation of the Areopagus speech, the general attitude toward the law in Acts, and the traditional identification of Gal. 2 with the conference in Acts 15. They also presupposed the second-century tradition that Luke was a disciple of Paul and would therefore have reflected his theology. In each instance the conclusions are questionable, if not doubtful; in some they are only a return to the views of F. C. Baur.

More serious are the differences between the portrait of Paul in Acts and the impression one receives of him in the Epistles. But these differences have sometimes been exaggerated. For example, is the Paul of Acts, as opposed to his opponents' estimate in 2 Cor. 10:10; 11:6, really presented as "an *outstanding orator,*" as E. Haenchen thought (p. 114), when he could not hold his audience (Acts 22:22; 23:1f.), impressed some listeners as absurd or mad (17:32; 26:24), and frightened his friends with a proposal to speak to a hostile crowd (19:30f.)? In any case, the differences do not exceed the variation that might be expected between a sometime colleague's impressions of a man and the man's own letters that the colleague did not take into account (cf. Trocmé, pp. 143-47).

*C. The Underlying "Hegelian Factor."* The rejection of Lukan authorship did not arise primarily from individual historical or theological problems, however, but from a conviction about Luke's place in the development of early Christianity. A certain preconception about this development was implicit in the work, e.g., of H. Conzelmann (pp. 131-36), E. Haenchen (pp. 95f., 100-103, 115f.), E. Käsemann (*Essays on NT Themes* [Eng. tr., *SBT,* 1/41, 1964], pp. 28f.), and P. Vielhauer (cf. Keck, pp. 47, 290f., 302, 306f.). Like Baur in the 19th cent., these scholars also read history in the framework of Hegelian dialectic (see I.B above). Although a number of themes, including Baur's specific concerns, reflect this framework, it is perhaps most evident in the area of eschatology: the imminent expectation of the Parousia in the earliest Church ("thesis") encounters the problem of its delay ("antithesis") and is resolved, in the case of Luke-Acts, with a theology of salvation history ("synthesis"). These scholars followed Baur by placing Luke-Acts in the third stage of the dialectic, decisively separated from Paul; they concluded that Paul's colleague could not have written it and that it cannot accurately represent that period of the Church's life (cf. Ellis, *Eschatology,* pp. 17f.; *NTS,* 26 [1979/80], 499f.).

This approach to the history of early Christianity has a number of weaknesses, many of which were observable in Baur. (1) It equates theological difference with chronological distance and assumes, in the words of E. R. Goodenough, that Christianity advanced from stage to stage as a block (cf. Keck, p. 57). (2) It tends toward an exaggerated "adversary theology." (3) Most seriously, in an inordinate and indeed rather arbitrary manner it allows an abstract philosophical theory about history to shape the selection and interpretation of historical data.

While the scholars mentioned above offered many valuable insights, their general reconstruction and concomitant conclusion about the authorship of Luke-Acts were untenable. Recent work (e.g., of Fitzmyer, Hengel, and Marshall) has tended to confirm the tradition of Lukan authorship, which is, on the whole, consistent with the literary and historical character of the documents and can be accepted with reasonable certainty.

***Bibliography.***–C. K. Barrett, *Luke the Historian in Recent Study* (1961); F. C. Baur, *Kritische Untersuchungen über die kanonischen Evangelien* (1847); *Das Markusevangelium* (1851); *Church History of the First Three Centuries* (Eng. tr. 1966); *Paul* (Eng. tr. 1876); F. Blass, *Philology of the Gospels* (1898); F. Bovon, *Luc le théologien* (1978); F. F. Bruce, *Acts of the Apostles* (1951); H. J. Cadbury, *Making of Luke-Acts* (1927); *Style and Literary Method* *of Luke* (1920); H. Conzelmann, *Theology of St. Luke* (Eng. tr. 1960); J. M. Creed, *Gospel According to St. Luke* (1930); M. Dibelius, *Studies in the Acts of the Apostles* (Eng. tr. 1956); E. E. Ellis, *Gospel of Luke* (*New Century Bible Comm.*, 1966); *Eschatology in Luke* (1972); "Gospels Criticism: a Perspective on the State of the Art," in P. Stuhlmacher, ed., *Das Evangelium und die Evangelien* (1983); W. R. Farmer, *Synoptic Problem* (1964); J. A. Fitzmyer, *Gospel According to Luke I-IX* (*AB*, 1981); J. J. Griesbach, in J. P. Gabler, ed., *Opuscula Academica* (1825), II, 358-425; E. Haenchen, *Acts of the Apostles* (Eng. tr. 1971); M. Hengel, *Acts and the History of Earliest Christianity* (Eng. tr. 1979); J. G. Herder, *Von Gottes Sohn* (1797); L. E. Keck, ed., *Studies in Luke-Acts* (1966); W. G. Kümmel, *Intro. to the NT* (Eng. tr. 1975); *The NT: The History of the Investigation of Its Problems* (Eng. tr. 1972); R. Maddox, *Purpose of Luke-Acts* (1982); H. Marsh, "Origin and Composition of Our Three First Canonical Gospels," in J. D. Michaelis, *Intro. to the NT* (Eng. tr. 1793-1801), IV, Appendix; I. H. Marshall, *Gospel of Luke* (*New International Greek Testament Comm.*, 1978); *Luke: Historian and Theologian* (1970); F. Neirynck, ed., *L'Évangile de Luc* (1973); J. C. O'Neill, *Theology of Acts in Its Historical Setting* (2nd rev. ed. 1970); H. Owen, *Observations on the Four Gospels* (1764); A. Plummer, *Gospel According to St. Luke* (*ICC*, 5th ed. 1922); F. Schleiermacher, *Werke*, I, 2 (1836), 1-220, 361-392; H. Schürmann, *Das Lukasevangelium: Erster Teil* (1969); N. B. Stonehouse, *Witness of Luke to Christ* (1953); B. H. Streeter, *The Four Gospels* (1927); C. H. Talbert, ed., *Perspectives on Luke-Acts* (1978); E. Trocmé, *Le 'Livre des Actes' et l'histoire* (1957); T. Zahn, *Intro. to the NT*, I-III (Eng. tr. 1909).

E. E. ELLIS

**LULLUBI** loo'lə-bē; **LULLU** lo͞o'loo [Akk. *lu-lu-bu-(um), l/nu-ul-lu(me)*]. An ancient people who inhabited the mountain region of modern Iraq around Sulaimaniya and the Shahrazur Valley. Their origins are unknown, although they can be associated with the neighboring Gutians and Elamites on linguistic grounds.

In the 3rd millennium B.C. they came into conflict with the expanding empires of the Akkad and Ur III dynasties of Babylonia and were conquered several times. Naram-Sin of Akkad celebrated his victory over King Satuni of Lullubi by carving a rock relief at Darband-i-Gawr. Sculptures on cliffs near Sar-i-Pul bearing inscriptions of Anubaninu and another Lullubi monarch, however, evince a period of local power. These texts are written in Akkadian, invoke Akkadian deities, and accompany reliefs in a provincial Akkadian style. Their date can be given only approximately as late 3rd millennium B.C.

A later Babylonian legend describes a war between Naram-Sin and 360,000 ferocious raven-faced soldiers led by an Anubaninu, probably the king of the Sar-i-Pul inscriptions or a descendant. Even if this legend exaggerates, it illustrates the mental image the city-dwelling Babylonians had of their alien neighbors. Similarly, Lullubi is named as a hated enemy to be defeated in the Irra Epic, written at the end of the 2nd millennium B.C. when Babylon had suffered from raids by the mountain tribes. These hardy mountain people, however, made tough slaves for work in the cities, as the archives of Nuzi frequently attest (to this day the porters of Baghdad are drawn from the same area). Hittite texts list Lullubi with Habiru, perhaps as two sources of cheap labor. According to the Hittites and lists compiled for Egyptian kings of the 15th cent. B.C. and shortly after, the Lullu land was the eastern extremity of the world.

Assyrian kings fought against Lullume with varying success from Adadnirari I (*ca.* 1307-1275 B.C.) onward until Ashurnasirpal conquered the region *ca.* 880 B.C. and annexed it as the province of Zamua. Lullubi was not then an organized state, and perhaps various ethnic groups had settled there in previous centuries, although the term Lullu lingered as a regional and linguistic marker.

*See also* GUTI.

Stele commemorating Naram-Sin's victory over the Lullubi (early 23rd cent. B.C.) (Louvre)

*Bibliography*.–H. Klengel, *Mitteilungen des Institut für Orientforschung*, 11 (1966), 349-371; E. A. Speiser, *AASOR*, 8 (1928), 1-42, for geography.

A. R. MILLARD

**LUNATICK** (AV Mt. 4:24; 17:15). *See* EPILEPSY.

**LURK** [Heb. *'āraḇ*] (Ps. 10:9); AV LIE IN WAIT; NEB CROUCH; [*šûr*–'regard, gaze on'] (Jer. 5:26; Hos. 13:7); AV LAY WAIT, OBSERVE; NEB LAY SNARES, PROWL; [*yāšaḇ*–'sit, crouch'] (Ps. 17:12); NEB CROUCH; [hiphil of *ṣāp̱an*–'hide'] (Ps. 56:6 [MT 7]); AV HIDE THEMSELVES; NEB WATCH; [*maḥᵃḇō'îm*] ("lurking places," 1 S. 23:23); NEB HIDING-PLACES. To lie in wait in a concealed place with the intention to do harm, as a predatory animal crouches in readiness to spring on its prey (*see also* AMBUSH). This image is usually applied to evildoers, but Hos. 13:7 applies it to God.

**LUST** [Heb. *hawwâ*] (Prov. 11:6); AV NAUGHTINESS; NEB GREED; [niphal part. of *ḥāmam*] ("you who burn with lust," Isa. 57:5); AV "enflaming yourselves"; [*ta'ᵃnâ*] (Jer. 2:24); AV "occasion"; NEB HEAT; [*taznûṯ*] (Ezk. 23:8, 17); AV WHOREDOM; NEB FORNICATION; [Gk. *epithymía*] (Rom. 1:24; Eph. 4:22; 1 Thess. 4:5; 2 Pet. 2:10; 1 Jn. 2:16f.); AV also CONCUPISCENCE; NEB also VILENESS, "pander to," "entice," ALLUREMENTS;

[*sárx*] (Jude 7); AV FLESH; **LUSTFUL** [Heb. *giḏlê ḇāśār*] (Ezk. 16:26); AV "great of flesh"; NEB GROSS; **LUSTFULLY** [Gk. *epithyméō*] (Mt. 5:28); AV "to lust after"; NEB "with a lustful eye." In Ps. 68:30 (MT 31) the RSV renders the MT *raṣṣê-ḵāsep* "those who lust after tribute," apparently taking *raṣṣê* as a participle of *rāṣâ*, "be pleased with." The AV understands *raṣṣê* as a noun meaning "pieces," and the NEB conjectures "precious stones."

Though contemporary English uses "lust" only in a negative way, the word originally meant "craving, strong desire" and was morally neutral. Passages in which the original words mean "desire" and only the AV (reflecting earlier English usage) has "lust" include: the hithpael of Heb. *'āwâ* ("crave") in Nu. 11:34 (RSV "craving"; NEB "be greedy") and the piel in Dt. 14:26 (RSV, NEB, "desire"); *ḥāmaḏ* ("covet") in Prov. 6:25 (RSV, NEB, "desire"); *nepeš* ("soul," "desire") in Ex. 15:9 (RSV "desire"; NEB "appetite"); Ps. 78:18 (RSV "craved"; NEB "hunger").

Meanings of the frequently used Gk. *epithymía* include: "[any] strong desire" (Mk. 4:19; Rev. 18:14), "pure desire" (LXX Gen. 31:30; LXX Prov. 10:24; Lk. 22:15; Phil. 1:23; 1 Thess. 2:17), "evil desire for something forbidden" (LXX Wisd. 4:12; Rom. 7:7; 2 Pet. 1:4). "sexual passion or obsession" (Eph. 2:3; 1 Thess. 4:5). Most frequently the term has negative connotations (although the Bible does not deprecate the natural use of sex). Among the passages in which *epithymía* or *epithyméō* refer to strong desire, and accordingly the AV has "lust" or "lust after," are Mk. 4:19; Jn. 8:44; Rom. 6:12; 7:7; 13:14; Gal. 5:16, 24; Eph. 2:3. The NEB uses "lust" only in the bad sense, e.g., for Gk. *porneía* in 1 Cor. 6:13 (RSV "immorality"; AV "fornication") and for *páthos* in Col. 3:5 (RSV "passion"; AV "inordinate affection").

If a biblical term has two or more meanings, its context usually provides the key to meaning and translation. Accordingly, although *páthos* means "emotion" for Philo, "bad impulses" sixty-three times in the LXX of 4 Maccabees, and "sickness" in Prov. 25:20, in Col. 3:5 a list of four closely related concepts makes clear that *páthos* here means "erotic passions." Similarly, the verb *orégō* (lit. "reach, stretch out") carries the commendable meaning of "aspire to" or "strive for" in 1 Tim. 3:1; He. 11:16, but the context indicates the unfavorable meaning "sexual desire" for the noun *oréxis* in Rom. 1:27 (cf. Josephus *Ant.* vii.8.1 [169]). A third term, *hēdonḗ* (cf. *hēdýs*, "sweet, pleasant, delightful"), carries a noble meaning in classical Greek philosophy; later, however, in popular philosophy influenced by the Cynics and Stoics, it designates a vice. In the NT *hēdonḗ* "represents one of the many forces which belong to the world of unsanctified carnality, which strive against the work of God and His Spirit and which drag man back again into the kingdom of evil" (*TDNT,* II, 909). Since simple pleasure as such is not contrary to God's will, *hēdonḗ* in the NT designates "evil pleasure" or "enslaving desire," much like the "evil impulse" of Judaism (Heb. *yēṣer hārā'*; see SB, IV, 469f.).

*See also* COVET; DESIRE; SEX.

***Bibliography.***–G. Cole, *Sex and Love in the Bible* (1959); B. S. Easton, *Pastoral Epistles* (1948), pp. 186-88; O. A. Piper, *Biblical View of Sex and Marriage* (1959); *TDNT,* II, *s.v.* ἡδονή, φιλήδονος (Stählin); III, *s.v.* θυμός κτλ. (Büchsel); V, *s.v.* ὀρέγομαι, ὄρεξις (Heidland); πάσχω κτλ. (Michaelis).

J. G. GIBBS

**LUSTY** [Heb. *maškîm*] (Jer. 5:8); AV "in the morning." *Maškîm,* perhaps a hiphil participle of **šāḵâ*, "roam at large(?)," may alternatively be an abbreviated form of *ma'ašîḵîm* (denominative < *'ešeḵ*, "testicle" [Lev. 21:20]), "having (strong) testicles"; cf. BDB (p. 1013) and KoB (p. 968). The LXX translates it *thelymaneís*, "mad after females." Aquila and Theodotion have *hélkontes*, "drawing, attracting." The context seems to support the RSV and NEB over the AV, which apparently bases its translation on the Hebrew verb *šāḵam*, "rise early."

**LUTE.** *See* MUSIC II.B.

**LUXURIANT** [Heb. *bôqēq*] (Hos. 10:1); AV "empty"; NEB RANK. Hebrew *bôqēq* is apparently a participle modifying "vine" (Heb. *gepen*; the difference in gender [*gepen* is fem.; *bôqēq* masc.] is explained by *bôqēq*'s proximity to [masc.] "Israel") in a metaphor about Israel (cf. Ps. 80:8-16 [MT 9-17]; Isa. 5:1-7; 27:2-6; Ezk. 17:5-10; 19:10-14). But *bqq* elsewhere means "empty" (hence AV), a meaning that does not seem appropriate in the context; thus the RSV and NEB follow the LXX *euklēmatoúsa*, "growing luxuriantly." In accordance with the LXX reading, various scholars have posited either another Hebrew root *bqq* (e.g., BDB, p. 132) or a root *bwq* (F. I. Andersen and D. N. Freedman, *Hosea* [*AB,* 1980], pp. 549f.). Support for such roots comes from Arab. *baqqa*, "branch off, split, spread" (H. W. Wolff, *Hosea* [Eng. tr., *Hermeneia,* 1974], p. 170). Perhaps equally plausible is KD's explanation, that the "primary meaning" of *bqq* is "pour out, overflow," and hence "run luxuriantly" in Hos. 10:1.

G. A. L.

**LUXURY** [Heb. *ta'anûg*] (Prov. 19:10); AV DELICATE LIVING; NEB "at the helm"; [*šāmēn ḥelqô*] (Hab. 1:16); AV "his portion is fat"; NEB SUMPTUOUSLY; [Gk. *tryphḗ*] (Lk. 7:25); AV DELICATELY; [*trypháō*] (Jas. 5:5); AV DELICATELY; NEB WANTON LUXURY. Rich surroundings and life-style. The term has evaluative connotations in Scripture. Prov. 19:10, "It is not fitting for a fool to live in luxury," e.g., neither simply condemns the "newly rich" nor confirms that "a fool and his money are soon parted." It rather advises that both luxury and power (v. 10b), though not wrong, can easily tempt to wrong and become wrong themselves if not handled with wisdom. In Hab. 1:16 luxury tempts people to idolatry; the prophet's answer condemns unjust gain (2:7-13) and idolatry (2:18f.).

In Lk. 7:25 Jesus referred to luxury in His rhetorical questions concerning the people's expectations of John the Baptist. Matthew (11:8) only mentioned soft clothing. This peculiarity of Luke is one instance of his advocacy of the poor. To say that Luke had an "Ebionite tendency," i.e., that he regarded poverty itself as pleasing to God and promised the poor compensation in the future aeon (cf. E. Percy, *Die Botschaft Jesu* [1953], pp. 89-106), is an exaggeration. But Luke undeniably was an advocate for the poor and a prosecutor of the wealthy. He was sensitive to the temptations of luxury, e.g., idolatry and avarice, and to the opportunity in poverty of a remarkable freedom to serve God. Lk. 7:25 rejects luxury as a criterion of value. It is not an Ebionite rejection, which keeps luxury as a criterion but with a contrary formulation, moving from "luxury is good" to "luxury is evil"; it is rather a total dismissal of luxury as a standard. The service of God, responsibility to the Lord, is the standard by which John the Baptist and "the least in the Kingdom" are discerned to be good.

James inveighed fiercely against the unjust exploiter who, living in "luxury," delights in the excess of his field, table, and savings while his conscience is insensitive to the dignity of his laborers (Jas. 5:5).

The Bible does not, however, prohibit surplus or adornment beyond the mere necessities of life. It would seem impossible to deny people the "luxury" that gives quality to life — e.g., play and decoration — and still affirm their humanity. The question is therefore posed: when does the enjoyment of excess become idolatry and injustice? This difficult question has steep slopes to error on both sides: the dangers of legalism and irresponsibility. Calvin, for one, recognized these dangers and cautioned against legalism: "If a man begins to doubt whether he may use linen for sheets . . . he will afterward be uncertain also about hemp; finally doubt will even arise over tow" (*Inst.* iii.19.7; on irresponsibility cf. iv.10).

As well as warning against idolatry and injustice, the Scripture forbids identification of luxury and virtue. Luxury is not a moral criterion; rather, it must be subject to a moral criterion — responsibility to the Lord (Lk. 7:25), which is given concrete significance as responsibility for one's fellow men (Jas. 5:5). Luxury is proscribed when the dignity of others is injured. Luxury without responsibility to God is idolatry; luxury without responsibility for the needs of one's neighbors is injustice. Luxury can serve joy — but only where it also serves the love of God and neighbor.

***Bibliography.***–D. L. Munby, *God and the Rich Society* (1961); O. Piper, *Christian Meaning of Money* (1965); H. van Oyen, *Affluence and the Christian* (1966). A. D. VERHEY

**LUZ** luz [Heb. *lûz*].

**1.** A Canaanite city, renamed Bethel by Jacob (Gen. 28:19). This tradition is also preserved in Gen. 35:6; Josh. 18:13; Jgs. 1:23; Jub. 27:19, 26. However, Josh. 16:2 reads "then going from Bethel to Luz," suggesting that these are two places. The MT has *mibbêṯ-'ēl lûzāh* (with *hê* directive), "from Beth-el toward Luz." The LXX supports this reading with *Louza* but appears to make Bethel-Louza a single place by using one preposition, *eis,* "to," before the two words. Scholars have therefore been divided, some holding to the identification of Luz with Bethel, others considering the two as different places and the passages that support Gen. 28:19 as containing glosses (cf. *GTTOT,* p. 164). *See* BETHEL **1.**

**2.** A city in the land of the Hittites built by a man who had escaped from Canaanite Luz after betraying it to "the house of Joseph" (Jgs. 1:26). It could be anywhere in the region now known as Syria and Lebanon, which the Hittites occupied. Simon (*GTTOT,* p. 283) suggested that Luweizeh, halfway between Sidon (Saida) and Ḥasbeiyeh, may preserve the ancient name. W. S. L. S.

**LYCAONIA** lik-ā-ō'nē-ə, lī-kə-ō'nē-ə [Gk. *Lykaonia*]. A region in the southern part of the Anatolian plateau (Acts 14:6). Anatolia (Asia Minor) is divided into three geographical regions: the Armenian highlands in the east, the Anatolian plateau in the center, and the mountainous region, cut by valleys that provide access between the Aegean coastal region and the plateau, forming the western part of Asia Minor. The Anatolian plateau, which has an average elevation of about 1000 m. (3300 ft.), is bordered on the north by the Pontus range and on the south by the Taurus range, both mountain systems extending from the Armenian highlands. In Roman times most of the plateau was the province of Galatia, but Lycaonia still retained some of its more ancient character (the term "Galatic Lycaonia" is sometimes used, and the people spoke the Lycaonian dialect [Acts 14:11]). Using the older divisions, we may therefore describe Lycaonia as bordered on the north by Galatia, on the east by Cappadocia, on the south by Cilicia Tracheia, on the southwest by Pamphylia, and on the west by Pisidia and Phrygia. The boundary between Lycaonia and Pisidia probably lay between Iconium and Antioch of

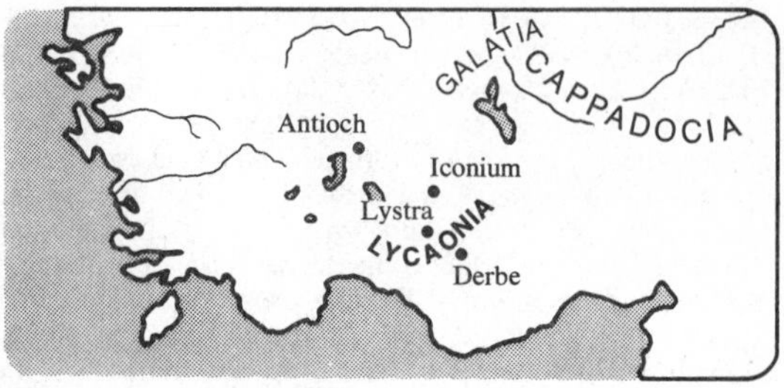


Pisidia, although Strabo called it "Antioch toward Pisidia" (*Geog.* xii.8.14). The boundary between Lycaonia and Phrygia is even more indefinite, for the inhabitants of Iconium considered themselves to be Phrygian, which may have influenced Luke's language in Acts 14:6. According to Strabo, however, Iconium at that time was an important city of Lycaonia (*Geog.* xii.6.1). Lystra and Derbe, visited by Paul, were also in Lycaonia; Strabo said that Derbe was almost at its border with Cappadocia, an obvious mental lapse for Cilicia (*Geog.* xii.6.3). Lycaonia is a flat, dry, and almost treeless plain, extremely dusty at the end of summer, and inhospitably cold in winter. Near Karaman (and also Derbe) the plain is broken by the volcanic mountain group known today as Kara Dağ ("Black Mountain"), which rises to 2272 m. (7454 ft.).

The early history of Lycaonia is unclear. It was long believed that there were no early inhabitants in the Anatolian plateau, but archeological discoveries have disproved this theory. The *lu-* element indicates that Lycaonia, and perhaps also Lystra, were connected with the Luwian peoples, ancestors of the Hittites. Although a main road from Ephesus to the Cilician Gates passed through a part of Lycaonia, the region seems to have maintained relative independence in the Persian period. Lycaonia came under control of Alexander the Great and, after him, the Seleucids. When Antiochus the Great was defeated by the Romans at Magnesia in 190 B.C. Lycaonia was given to Pergamum. Later it was parceled up among Galatia, Cappadocia, and Cilicia. In 36 B.C. it was given to Amyntas when he became king of Galatia. When he died (25 B.C.) the Romans made his kingdom into the province of Galatia. There were Jewish communities in Antioch and Iconium, probably from the Seleucid era. Lycaonia was Christianized early, as a result of Paul's work and his oversight of the churches there. By the 4th cent. A.D. the Church was well organized, spreading over most of Galatia.

Paul visited Lycaonia at least three times. On his "first journey" he and Barnabas traveled from Pisidian Antioch to Iconium (Acts 13:51), Lystra, and Derbe (14:6). The apostles returned from Derbe by the same route. On his "second journey" Paul took Silas and journeyed from Cilicia to Derbe and Lystra (16:1) and certainly Iconium. Timothy joined the evangelistic team either at Derbe or at Lystra (16:1; that Timothy was "well spoken of by the brethren at Lystra and Iconium" lends some support to the view that he came from Derbe). Paul also visited this region when he "went from place to place through the region of Galatia and Phrygia" on his "third journey" (18:23; the RSV does not accurately represent the Greek, "the Galatic region and Phrygia"). It is generally believed today, according to the "South Galatian theory" (*see* GALATIANS, EPISTLE TO THE III), that Paul's letter to the Galatians was written to the churches of the southern part of Galatia, which would include Lycaonia.

***Bibliography.***–W. M. Ramsay, comm. on Galatians (1900), pp. 180-232; *Cities of St. Paul* (1907), pp. 247-419; *Pauline and Other Studies* (1906), pp. 273-298; A. H. M. Jones, *CERP,* ch. 5; Strabo *Geog.* xii *passim.* W. S. LASOR

Central Anatolian plain and volcanic cones near Iconium (A. D. Baly)

**LYCIA** lish'yə [Gk. *Lykia*]. A region on the western part of the southern coast of Asia Minor, bounded on the west by Caria, on the east by Pamphylia, and on the north by Pisidia (1 Macc. 15:23; Acts 27:5). Lycia is a rugged, mountainous region, the only level portions being the alluvial plains formed by the Xanthus (modern Koca [kō-ja]) and the Limyrus rivers. The mountains are actually spurs developed from the Taurus range, some of them rising to considerable heights (two above 3000 m. [10,000 ft.] and at least three others above 2300 m. [7600 ft.]). Each of the highest mountains bears the local name of Ak Dağ, "White Mountain," the higher (3086 m. [10,125 ft.]) being the ancient Massicytus. Solyma (2375 m. [7792 ft.]), in the extreme eastern part, slopes into the Gulf of Antalya, making direct passage from Lycia to Pamphylia impossible. The mountainous topography accounts for the inhospitable coastline, the rivers providing the few good harbors: Patara (Acts 21:1) at the mouth of the Xanthus (now useless because of silting); Myra (Acts 27:5; modern Demre) at the entrance to the Andriacus valley (also silted up); and Limyra, near the modern Fenike (Phoenicus) at the mouth of the Limyrus. Telmessus (modern Fethiye) on the Gulf of Fethiye is still a good harbor.

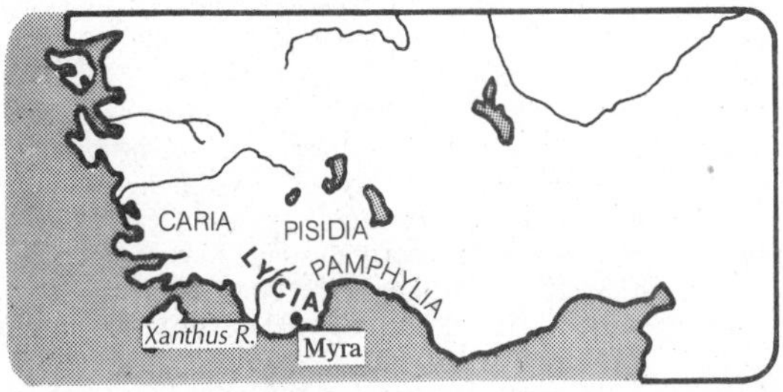


The history of Lycia is still not known to a satisfactory degree. The early inhabitants, an Anatolian people related to the Hittites, can be traced back to the Bronze Age. The *lu-* element in the names Lycia, Lycaonia, Lydia, Lulahhi, and Luwian indicates some common background. Linguistic remains from Lycia give satisfactory evidence that it is a dialect of the Luwian language, and Luwian deities can be identified in personal names. Archeological discoveries at Elmalı point to a settlement there in the Early Bronze Age (M. J. Mellink, *American Journal of Archaeology,* 68 [1964], 269-278). According to tradition, the cyclopean walls of Tiryns were built by Cyclops, who had been sent by the king of Lycia, along with an army, to make Tiryns secure for his daughter. In an Amarna Letter the king of Alashiya wrote the king of Egypt, complaining, "Year by year the people of Lukki have taken a small city from my land" (Am.Tab. 38:11f.). A king of Ugarit appealed to the king of Alashiya for help, saying, "My forces and chariots are stationed in Khatti Land, and all my ships are in Lukka Land" (*CAH,* II/2, 369). In the battle between Ramses II and the Hittite Muwatallish, at Qadesh on the Orontes (*ca.* 1300 B.C.), an Egyptian scribe listed the *Rk* (=*Lk*) among the Hittite allies. These are sometimes identified as the Lukka. The Lukka lands are mentioned in Hittite records as a turbulent area (*CAH,* II/2, 361). Merneptah boasted that he had won a victory in Libya in his fifth year against an alliance that included *Lk* (Lukka). According to the Iliad, the Lycians, led by Sarpedon, were allies of Troy (*Il.* ii.876; v.479). Hephaestus, god of fire and husband of Aphrodite, was probably a Lycian god whose cult moved westward to the islands and to Lemnos.

Neither the Phyrgians nor the Lydians were able to conquer Lycia, but after Croesus was defeated (*ca.* 546 B.C.) Lycian cities were conquered by Harpagus, one of Cyrus's generals. Lycia was incorporated into the kingdom of Alexander the Great. Its location afforded a large degree of independence, however, even into Roman times. In 188 B.C. it was given by the Romans to Rhodes but was free twenty years later, as attested by the letters of Lucius the Roman consul written to Ptolemy and the heads of a number of other countries, including Lycia, on behalf of the Jewish populations in those lands (1 Macc. 15:16-24). The Romans made Lycia a province in A.D. 43, and Vespasian united it with Pamphylia in A.D. 74, but it became a separate province again in the 4th century.

In the Iron Age the principal cities of Lycia were Xanthus (near modern Kınık), Myra, Pinara, Phellus (modern Suaret), and Antiphellus (modern Kaş). Artemidorus (*ca.* 100 B.C.) reported that twenty-three towns made up the Lycian league. Pliny stated that Lycia at one time possessed seventy towns, but that only twenty-six of these remained at the time of his writing.

The apostle Paul, on his journey from Miletus to Palestine, came to Patara from Rhodes and then caught a ship to Phoenicia (Acts 21:1). On his journey to Rome, he landed at Myra, where he boarded a ship for Italy (27:5). Myra is noted in church history as the seat of Nikolas bishop of Myra, who was martyred under Diocletian. Saint Nicholas, as he has come to be known, endeared himself by giving many gifts. He is the patron saint of sailors and children; through Dutch tradition, he became the Santa Claus of western Christendom.

*Bibliography.–Enc. Brit.* (1970), XIV, 461f.; *CAH,* II/2 (3rd ed. 1975), 360-371, 438-442. W. S. LASOR

**LYDDA** lid'ə. *See* LOD.

**LYDIA** lid'ē-ə [Gk. *Lydia*]. A woman residing in Philippi who apparently was Paul's first convert in Europe (Acts 16:14f., 40). Lydia may have been not her given name but rather a means of identifying her as originally from Lydia, a section of western Asia Minor. Her native city was Thyatira, famous for its purple dye. Whether unmarried or widowed, she had a commodious house in Philippi where she sold purple goods.

While living in Thyatira she had become attracted to the Jewish faith but was a God-fearer (*see* DISPERSION V.C) rather than a proselyte (16:14). Faithful to this commitment, she frequented the "place of prayer" outside the city of Philippi, where she heard Paul's presentation of the gospel. The Lord opened her heart to the truth and she accepted baptism. Her "household," whether employees, children, or both, followed her in baptism. She showed her gratitude by urging the missionary party to be her guests.

Rather strangely, her name does not appear in Paul's letter to the Philippian church. Some have conjectured that her real name was either Euodia or Syntyche (Phil. 4:2), but these women's tendency to disputation hardly fits the portrayal of Lydia in Acts 16. It is likely, however, that the prominence of women in Paul's letter reflects Lydia's continuing influence in the church, even as this congregation's generosity toward Paul, attested by the letter, reflects her initial care for his welfare.

E. F. H.

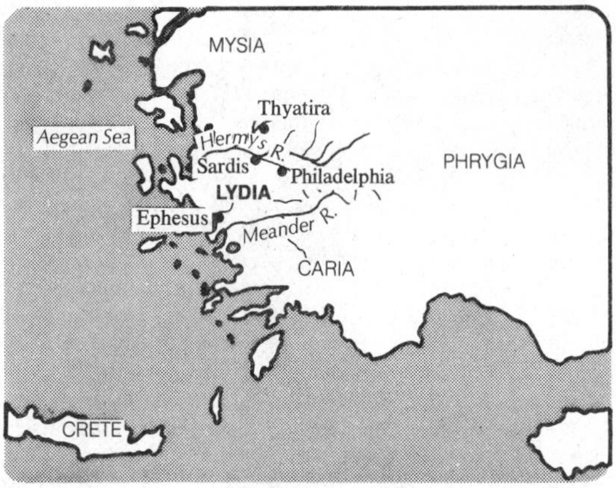


**LYDIA** lid'ē-ə [Gk. *Lydia*]. A region in the western part of Asia Minor, bounded on the north by Mysia, on the east by Phrygia, on the south by Caria, and on the west by the Aegean Sea. The western third of Asia Minor (W of 31 degrees East Longitude) is a mountainous region cut by numerous river valleys. Historically, these valleys have provided the trade routes as well as the settlements of peoples. Lydia lay between the valley of the Hermus (modern Gediz) in the north and that of the Meander (modern Büyük Menderes, "Big Meander," to distinguish it from the Küçük Menderes, "Little Meander," which we know better as the Caÿster), in the south. It included the valley of the Caÿster. The border with Mysia was somewhat N of the Hermus; that with Phrygia was disputed throughout much of Lydia's history. The Meander formed the boundary between Lydia and Caria (Strabo *Geog.* xii.8.15). The western portion of Lydia was often occupied by Greeks. Important cities of Lydia included Sardis (the capital), Ephesus, Thyatira, Philadelphia, Colophon, Lebedos (Ptolemais), Clazomenas, Teos, and Phocaea. Although the place name Lydia does not occur in the Bible, the region is of great importance under the name of ASIA, which came into existence as a Roman province after 133 B.C. and included Lydia, Caria, Mysia, and part of Phrygia.

The early history of Lydia is obscure. The *lu-* element in the name suggests Luwian (early Hattic or Proto-Hittite) origin. Hittite records have no mention of Lydia, but it is possible that Aššuwa (from which probably comes the name Asia) was the term by which the region was then known. Luwian was written in Hittite hieroglyphs (*CAH,* II/2, 435), and a bas relief of a warrior or god located near Karabel bears an inscription in this system of writing (cf. Herodotus ii.106). Homer recorded that the region under Mt. Tmolus (Boz Dağ) and around the Gygean Lake (Marmara Gölü) was assigned to the Meonians (*Il.* ii.864-66). Herodotus thought these were the Lydians (i.7), but Strabo recorded differing opinions (*Geog.* xiii.4.5). The invasion of the Phrygians (probably from Thrace) in the 12th cent. B.C. isolated the Luwians of western Anatolia and was instrumental in pushing the Hittites east from the Halys region toward Syria. Troy fell *ca.* 1200 B.C.; Troy VIIb, built after the city was destroyed by fire, had a new population using pottery of a coarse material. About this same time the sea-peoples, probably as a result of this same population movement, were attempting invasions of Egypt; some landed on the coast of Palestine. According to Lydian tradition, the Philistines were from Lydia (Xanthus, contemporary of Herodotus, was a Lydian historian; cf. C. and T. Muller, eds., *Fragmenta Historicum Graecorum,* I [1841]). The word Philistine has been related to Pelastikon = Pelasgikon, the "spear-brandishing Pelasgians" of Homer (*Il.* ii.840; cf. *CAH*, II/2, 512f.). The Hebrew word *seren*, "tyrant, lord," is a loanword from the Philistine *seranim*, which was also taken over by the Greeks as *týrannos* (Acts 5:39, D). If this complex theory can be established, it may support some of the references to Lud in the OT (cf. Jer. 46:9; *see* LUD). Another tradition speaks of famine for eighteen years that led the king finally to divide the people into two groups and draw lots. One group, under his son Tyrrhenus, emigrated to Umbria in Italy, founding Tyrrhenia, better known as Etruria, home of the Etruscans (Herodotus i.94). If this legend is historically based, the event must have taken place before 1000 B.C. According to Gen. 10:2 the sons of Japheth included Tiras (the Tyrsenoi or Tyrrhenians), Tubal and Meshech, both of whom are often identified with peoples in Asia Minor, and Javan (Ionia), who settled the Ionian coastal region of Lydia.

The Heraclid (Tylonid) dynasty (the Mermnadae) ended with Candaules (Myrsilus), *ca.* 700 B.C., after reigning for 505 years. This would put the start of that dynasty, under Agron the first king of Sardis, *ca.* 1205 B.C. Before Agron the kings were descended from Lydus son of Atys, from whom the Lydians took their name (Herodotus i.7). Candaules was slain by Gyges (Herodotus i.13), with whom Lydia comes into history. Gyges (reigned 685-652 B.C.) attacked Greek cities on the coast; then the Cimmerians invaded Asia Minor, and he turned to Ashurbanipal to form an alliance, *ca.* 668 B.C. (Rassam Cylinder, *ARAB*, II, §§ 784, 849, 909, where he is called Guggu, considered by some to be the Gog of Ezk. 39:1). After the defeat of the Cimmerians, Gyges sought an alliance with Psamtik I of Egypt, and sent troops to help liberate Egypt from Assyria (*ca.* 654 B.C.). The Cimmerians, however, ransacked Lydia and Gyges died. He was succeeded by his son Ardys (652-615), who restored good relations with Assyria and was followed by Sadyattes (*ca.* 615-605).

The next king, Alyattes (*ca.* 605-560), finally expelled the Cimmerians, but Indo-European migrations brought Scythians and Medes into Asia Minor. Alyattes waged a war with the Median ruler Cyaxares, which can be dated by the eclipse of the sun that occurred in its sixth year (on May 28, 585). The war ended with a peace treaty that set the Halys River (KIZIL) as the boundary between the Lydian and Median kingdoms. Alyattes' daughter was married to Astyages son of Cyaxares. According to Herodotus (i.15-108, *passim*; but cf. denial by Ctesias *Persica* exc. 2) their daughter Mandane was married to Cambyses, and from this union was born Cyrus the Great.

Alyattes' son Croesus, who reigned 560-546, was the last king of Lydia. He gained lasting fame because of his wealth, obtained from the gold-filled sandy bed of the Pactolus River flowing from Mt. Tmolus. Croesus made lavish gifts to the oracle at Delphi and to the rebuilding of the archaic temple of Artemis at Ephesus.

Cyrus captured Sardis in 546, overthrew Croesus, and made Lydia a Persian satrapy separate from the Ionian satrapy. Lydia came under the rule of Alexander the Great when he defeated the Persians at the battle of Granicus in 334. It was subsequently ruled by the Seleucids until the defeat of Antiochus III at Magnesia in 190, when it was given to Pergamum (1 Macc. 8:8). On the death of Attalus III in 133 B.C., by the terms of his will, the region passed to the Romans; the proconsular province of Asia was formed subsequently.

Lydians were famed as horsemen, warriors, merchants, and bankers. During the famine that led to the Tyrrhenian emigration they are supposed to have invented games, "dice and knuckle-bones and ball" (Herodotus i.94). The daughters of the commoners became prostitutes in order to collect dowries and get husbands (Herodotus i.93). (These statements by Herodotus are disputable.) The Lydians were also well known for textiles, carpets, a Roman guild of woolworkers and dyers (cf. Lydia of Thyatira, Acts 16:14), and perfumes put up in containers of a shape known as Lydion. Most important, the Lydians were the first (mid-7th cent. B.C.) to coin gold and electrum into stamped ingots that could not be unnoticeably reduced in weight. Through trade, and particularly through the Persian empire, coinage became the accepted medium of exchange.

Kybele (Cybele, Artemis; the Luwian Kubaba [Herodotus, v.102]) was the great mother-goddess of Lydia, with traces of her worship going back to Neolithic times. At Sardis (Sart) the remains of a temple dedicated to her can still be seen. The great temple at Ephesus, however, was destroyed by the Goths (A.D. 262), and columns were later taken to adorn the basilicas of Hagia Sophia at Istanbul and St. John at Aysaluk (modern Ephesus). The cult of Bacchus (Dionysus) was imported from the Lydian region to Greece (*CAH*, II/2, 887). The adoration of a triad consisting of the mother-goddess, a male god later equated with Zeus, and the equestrian moon-god Mēn has been posited (*CAH*, II/2, 439). (It may be more than a coincidence that the *theotókos* ["Mother of God"] dogma came into Christendom by the Council of Ephesus [A.D. 431].) Antiochus III was responsible for settling two thousand Jews from Babylon in Lydia and Phrygia (Josephus *Ant.* xii.3.4 [§§ 147-153]). Paul the apostle, with unerring instinct, early set his sights on proconsular Asia (Acts 16:6) and later put that vision into reality with a work in Ephesus that resulted in the evangelization of much of Asia (19:10). The Seven Churches of Asia (Rev. 2–3) doubtless originated from that work, as did churches at Colossae and Hierapolis (Col. 4:13), Miletus, Magnesia, Tralles, and other places known from early church history.

***Bibliography.***–Herodotus i.6-56, 67-94, 154-56, *et passim*; vii.30-32; *CAH*, II/2 (3rd ed. 1975), 349-364, 418-439, 788-790; M. C. Astour, *Hellenosemitica* (1965); *RRAM*, pp. 45-50; *SPT*, pp. 262-282.

W. S. LASOR

**LYDIAN** lid'ē-ən (Jer. 46:9, AV). *See* LUD, LUDIM.

**LYE** [Heb. *bōr*] (Job 9:30; Isa. 1:25); AV "clean," "purely"; NEB also POTASH; [*neṯer*] (Jer. 2:22); AV NITRE; NEB SODA. A strongly alkaline substance used in cleaning and making soap.

It is difficult to know precisely how the two Hebrew terms translated "lye" differ. *Bōr* may have been potassium carbonate leached from wood ash or other vegetation. It would have been readily available in Palestine, and when combined with oil it could have been used like modern soap. In Job 9:30 it is not strong enough, however, to take away Job's guilt. It is elsewhere translated "cleanness" (e.g., 2 S. 22:21; Job 22:30), which may have influenced the AV translation here (cf. also Syr.). The RSV and NEB "lye" is preferable, however (note the parallelism). Isa. 1:25 refers to the ancient practice of adding lye or another alkali during smelting in order to accelerate the process (so KD).

*Neṯer*, together with its Semitic cognates, reflects the origin of Eng. "natron" and "nitre"; in antiquity it seems to have been saltpeter (nitre). In Jer. 2:22 it is very clearly a cleansing agent. In Prov. 25:20 *neṯer* is translated "wound" following the LXX, but "lye" would make sense in the context just as well, because vinegar added to lye (an alkali) makes it useless. Suggestions that it was sodium carbonate, obtainable from Egypt and Armenia, probably are not correct, since vinegar would effervesce with it, thus rendering Prov. 25:20 meaningless. Moreover, to have imported sodium carbonate when other good cleansing agents were locally available is not reasonable. Cf. W. McKane, *Proverbs* (*OTL*, 1970), pp. 588f.

*See also* SOAP. L. G. HERR

**LYING.** *See* LIE.

**LYRE.** *See* MUSIC II.B.

**LYSANIAS** lə-sā'nē-əs [Gk. *Lysanias*]. Tetrarch of ABILENE when John the Baptist began his ministry (Lk. 3:1). As can be seen from this passage, a tetrarch ruled a minor area as compared with a governor's jurisdiction.

No further information about Lysanias is provided in the NT; however, the name occurs several times in the writings of Josephus. Some scholars have concluded that Luke must have depended on the Jewish historian for the name Lysanias and assigned him a role in history *ca.* A.D. 28, whereas the Lysanias introduced by Josephus died in 36 B.C. For a historian of Luke's caliber to have made such a mistake in chronology is antecedently improbable, however (cf. Lk. 1:3). Moreover, certain evidence suggests that two men named Lysanias ruled in the same general area but at different times. The earlier Lysanias is mentioned by Josephus (*Ant.* xix.5.1 [274f.]; *BJ* ii.11.5 [215f.]), who states that Gaius gave to Agrippa I not only the territory that had been governed by Agrippa's grandfather Herod but also Abila, which had been ruled by Lysanias.

It is worth noting that earlier references in Josephus mention Lysanias's father, a certain Ptolemy (*Ant.* xiv.13.3 [330-33]; xv.4.1 [92]; *BJ* i.13.1 [248]). Other passages dealing with Lysanias, which from their contents must refer to a later time, do not refer to the father. Nor does Luke mention Ptolemy.

In his first reference to a Lysanias, Josephus designated him a ruler of Chalcis in Lebanon (*Ant.* xiv.13.3 [330-33]). Since Chalcis was a larger territory than Abilene, the two districts were probably ruled by different men named Lysanias. Further substantiation of Luke's chronology in 3:1 is an inscription found near Abila datable no later than A.D. 14; it claims to be the work of Nymphaeus, a freedman of Lysanias (Easton, p. 35).

It appears reasonably clear that Josephus noted two men by the name of Lysanias, whereas Luke mentioned only the later one. Thus the confusion probably has been caused by Josephus's failure to distinguish the men clearly, rather than by a lapse on the part of Luke. Still, some readers of Luke may wonder why he, in giving the setting for the entrance of John the Baptist on the stage of history, mentioned a relatively obscure ruler of a minor section of the Roman empire. But nine of Josephus's eleven references to Lysanias concern persons or situations in Palestine, so his territory must have been closely related to Palestine.

***Bibliography.***–Comms. on Luke by J. M. Creed (1950), pp. 307-309; B. S. Easton (1926), pp. 34f.; *HJP* II/2, 337-39.

E. F. HARRISON

**LYSIAS** lis'i-əs [Gk. *Lysias*].

**1.** A Seleucid nobleman whom Antiochus IV Epiphanes appointed regent of Syria and guardian of his son while he attacked Persia (the Parthians) in 166-165 B.C. (1 Macc. 3:32f.; cf. 2 Macc. 10:10f.; Josephus *Ant.* xii.7.2 [295-97]). His charge from Antiochus included waging a punitive war against Judas Maccabeus (1 Macc. 3:34-37). Lysias sent Ptolemy, Nicanor, and Gorgias with a large army against Judas, but the Jews soundly defeated them near Emmaus (3:38–4:25; *Ant.* xii.7.3f. [298-312]). The following year Lysias personally led an invasion of Judea and encamped at Beth-zur (1 Macc. 4:26-29; 2 Macc. 11:1-5; *Ant.* xii.7.5 [313]). Although discrepancies exist between the accounts of 1 and 2 Maccabees, it appears that Judas defeated Lysias (1 Macc. 4:34f.; cf. 2 Macc. 11:6-12; *Ant.* xii.7.5 [314f.]) and that this victory occasioned the cleansing and rededication of the Jerusalem temple in 164 B.C. (1 Macc. 4:36-59; *Ant.* xii.7.6f. [316-325]; cf. 2 Macc. 10:1-8), which has been celebrated ever since in the Feast of Lights (also called the Feast of Dedication, or Hanukkah).

Upon his deathbed Antiochus Epiphanes appointed PHILIP (4) regent and guardian of his son in place of Lysias. But when Lysias learned of Antiochus's death, he set up the king's son, ANTIOCHUS V EUPATOR, as king of Syria (1 Macc. 6:14-17; *Ant.* xii.9.2 [360f.]) and continued to function as his guardian. Lysias and Eupator invaded Judea with troops and elephants, defeated Judas at Beth-zechariah in a battle in which Judas's brother Eleazar was killed, and besieged Jerusalem. Philip's arrival in Antioch and attempt to take control of the government forced Lysias and Eupator to withdraw and to make peace with the Jews (which Eupator immediately violated by breaking down walls in Jerusalem). Lysias defeated Philip at Antioch but was later killed by another claimant to the Seleucid throne, Demetrius. (See 1 Macc. 6:27–7:4; cf. 2 Macc. 13:1–14:2; *Ant.* xii.9.3–10.1 [366-390].)

*See also* MACCABEES II.C.

**2.** *See* CLAUDIUS LYSIAS. J. J. SCOTT, JR.

**LYSIMACHUS** lī-sim'ə-kəs [Gk. *Lysimachos*].

**1.** Son of Ptolemy; a Jerusalem Jew who is said by Ad. Est. 11:1 to have translated the book of Esther into Greek.

**2.** Brother of the unscrupulous Menelaus who outbid Jason for the high priesthood during the reign of Antiochus IV Epiphanes (175-163 B.C.). When forced to appear before the king for failing to continue payments for his office, Menelaus appointed Lysimachus as his deputy in the high priesthood (2 Macc. 4:29). Lysimachus, with the connivance of his brother, stole some of the gold vessels of the temple and committed other acts of sacrilege. When the Jews learned of this they became incensed, and a crowd assembled to protest these actions. Lysimachus attempted to disperse the crowd with an armed force, but the crowd counterattacked by throwing stones, blocks of wood, and ashes. Lysimachus's men were put to flight, and he himself was killed (4:32-42). J. J. SCOTT, JR.

**LYSTRA** lis'trə [Gk. *Lystra*; occurs also as neut. pl. dative *Lystrois*]. A city of south-central Asia Minor that Paul evangelized on his first missionary journey and where he nearly lost his life from stoning (Acts 14:8-21); he revisited it on his second (16:1) and probably his third (18:23) missionary journeys.

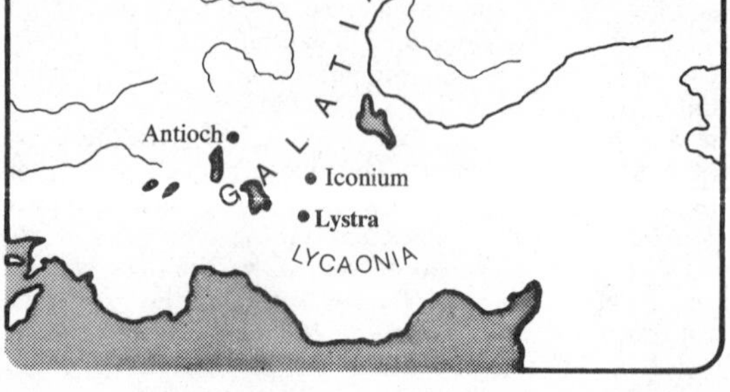

*I. Topography and Character.*–Little is known of the early history of Lystra (the name is apparently from the Lycaonian language). J. R. S. Sterrett in 1885 established its location beyond doubt as the large mound just N of the Turkish village of Hatun Sarai ("Lady's Mansion"), thus 29 km. (18 mi.) SSW of Iconium in the region of Lycaonia. The site is exceptionally attractive, in a secluded valley at the junction of two broad streams, and was probably inhabited from prehistoric times. (No systematic archeological excavation has been undertaken.) But since Lystra did not lie along the course of the main roads, it was not destined to become a great city. It was able, therefore, to preserve its primitive, local character more than cities such as Iconium; Hellenism (during the hundred-year rule of the Seleucids), for example, apparently made little impact on Lystra.

The site of Lystra (W. S. LaSor)

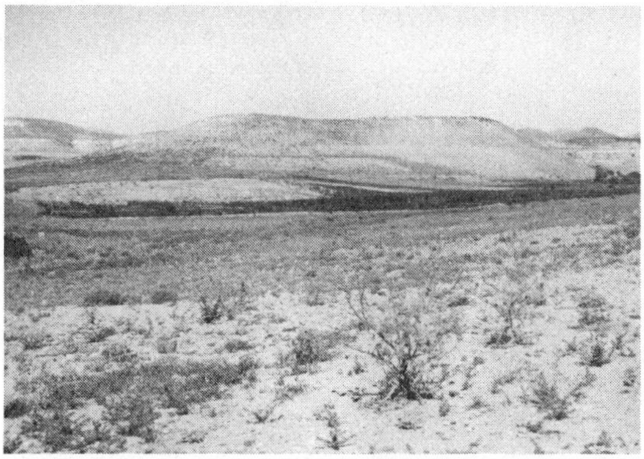

Despite these drawbacks, Augustus designated Lystra, with Antioch of Pisidia, a Roman colony in A.D. 6, thereby necessitating a Roman road ("the Imperial Road") to be built between the two cities. The Romans had ruled Lystra for some time previously, following the reigns of the Seleucids and Attalids. Amyntas of Galatia had willed the city to the Romans at his death (25 B.C.). Augustus's generals regarded Lystra as a suitable place for the Roman garrison charged to defend the province of Galatia, primarily from the mountain tribes to the west and south. This decision was obviously important to the development of Lystra (although the threat of the mountain tribes soon diminished remarkably); the official Roman presence, which must have contrasted strongly with the native Lycaonian populace and culture, brought the city prestige. Colonial coins of Lystra and a statue of Concord sent by Lystra toward the end of the 2nd cent. to its sister colony Antioch have been recovered. The later history of Lystra is not well known. The foundations of a Byzantine church have been found at the eastern slope of the tell.

*II. Paul and Barnabas.*–Ramsay has argued that Lystra was probably not significant enough to have been on Paul's original itinerary. Paul and Barnabas were driven there from Iconium by hostile opponents, and thus Lystra functioned as a relatively unimportant city of refuge, as did Berea later when Paul and Silas fled the wrath of the Thessalonians (Acts 17:10).

In Lystra, identified along with Derbe by the author of Acts as "cities of Lycaonia" (in contrast to Iconium), Paul and Barnabas healed a man crippled from birth (Acts 14:8-18). This miracle caused the greatest astonishment among the inhabitants of the city, who immediately concluded in their own language, "The gods have come down to us in the likeness of men!" (v. 11). Their use of Lycaonian, an ancient language of the region, rather than Greek, supports the conclusion that Lystra more than other cities retained its own local culture against Hellenism. (The language continued to be spoken as late as the 6th century A.D.) It also indicates that the crowds were natives rather than Roman colonists, who would have spoken Latin.

Paul and Barnabas apparently did not understand, until they saw the preparations for sacrifice, that they were being hailed as gods — namely Zeus (Barnabas) and Hermes his messenger (Paul the spokesman). Lystra had a temple of Zeus just before the gates of the city, although the religion represented was probably a local Lycaonian type with only a Greek veneer. Inscriptions from the middle of the 3rd cent. A.D. discovered by W. M. Calder in the vicinity of Lystra refer to "priests of Zeus" and a statue of Hermes dedicated to Zeus, thus confirming the historical probability of the Acts account. An altar dedicated to the "Hearer of Prayer" (Zeus) and Hermes has also been found. Moreover, in a popular tale of Ovid, Philemon and Baucis unknowingly entertained Jupiter and Mercury, the Roman counterparts of Zeus and Hermes (*Metamorphoses* viii.626ff.). Conceivably the native populace regarded such a spectacular occurrence as a theophany (cf. Acts 28:6). Paul and Barnabas reacted by rending their garments, a Jewish practice in the presence of blasphemy.

Paul's remarks were the first address to a pagan audience in Acts (the other occasion was at Athens, 17:22-31). In this telescoped sermon he alluded to good news and announced the truth of one living God who is the source of all good things experienced by human beings and who is sovereign over their lives. As at Athens, Paul began with a point of common knowledge to draw his listeners into the truth of the gospel.

Converts were made at Lystra (Acts 14:21-22), but the fickle majority allowed themselves to be carried away by Jews from Antioch and nearby Iconium into supporting an abrupt attempt on Paul's life. Although Lystra was a Roman colony, the account contains no hint of the Roman order or justice one might expect. At the end of his career Paul referred to the persecution he experienced at Lystra (2 Tim. 3:11). Earlier, when he explicitly referred to having been once stoned (2 Cor. 11:25), he had in mind the episode at Lystra. It is also possible, if not probable, that he alluded to this experience in the letter to the Galatians, sent poignantly to Lystra among other churches of Galatia: "I bear on my body the marks of Jesus" (6:17).

*III. Timothy.*–On his second missionary journey Paul met Timothy at Lystra (Acts 16:1-5). Timothy, who may have been converted as the result of Paul's first visit to Lystra, was highly regarded by the brethren at Lystra and Iconium. His Jewish mother had become a believer (with his grandmother, 2 Tim. 1:5); his father is described as a Greek (Acts 16:1) and thus would have belonged to the small elite class of Lystra who had been educated in Greek language and culture.

***Bibliography.***–B. Levick, *Roman Colonies in Southern Asia Minor* (1967); W. M. Ramsay, *CRE; SPT; Cities of St. Paul* (1907); F. F. Bruce, *Acts of the Apostles* (1951).

D. A. HAGNER

**M.** *See* GOSPELS, SYNOPTIC V.D.

**MAACAH** mā'ə-kə [Heb. *maʿ$^a$ḵâ*–'stupid, foolish'(?)]; AV usually MAACHAH.

**1.** Son of Abraham's brother Nahor by his concubine Reumah (Gen. 22:24).

**2.** Wife of David; daughter of Talmai king of Geshur; mother of Absalom (2 S. 3:3; 1 Ch. 3:2).

**3.** Father of Achish king of Gath (1 K. 2:39); probably the same as MAOCH in 1 S. 27:2.

**4.** Granddaughter of Abishalom (Absalom); favorite wife of Rehoboam (2 Ch. 11:21); mother of Abijam (1 K. 15:2; 2 Ch. 11:20, 22); grandmother of Abijam's son King Asa. According to 1 K. 15:2; 2 Ch. 11:20f. she was the daughter of Absalom, but Tamar was Absalom's only daughter (2 S. 14:27), and Maacah was probably the daughter of Tamar and Uriel of Gibeah (cf. 2 Ch. 13:2; *see* MICAIAH **1**). In 1 K. 15:10, 13; 2 Ch. 15:16 Maacah is called the mother of Asa; this may be because she held the position of queen mother until he deposed her on account of her idolatrous practices.

**5.** Concubine of Caleb son of Hezron, and mother of Sheber, Tirhanah, Shaaph, and Sheva (1 Ch. 2:48f.).

**6.** Wife of Machir the Manassite (1 Ch. 7:16); but apparently called his sister in v. 15. The text is corrupt.

**7.** Wife of Jeiel from Gibeon; an ancestor of King Saul (1 Ch. 8:29; 9:35).

**8.** Father or ancestor of Hanan, one of David's mighty men (1 Ch. 11:43).

**9.** Father or ancestor of Shephatiah, chief officer of the Simeonites under King David (1 Ch. 27:16). N. J. O.

**MAACAH** mā'ə-kə [Heb. *maʿ$^a$ḵâ*; Gk. *Maacha, Mōcha*]; AV also MAACHAH (1 Ch. 19:7); **MAACATH** mā'ə-kath [Heb. *maʿ$^a$ḵāṯ*] (Josh. 13:13); AV MAACHATHITES; NEB MAACATHITES. A small Syrian kingdom in the Golan Heights S of Mt. Hermon, N of Gilead, and W of Bashan. The kingdom of Geshur, which is mentioned frequently with Maacah, adjoined it to the south. The name ABEL-BETH-MAACAH indicates that this city once belonged to Maacah.

In Dt. 3:14 the border of the MAACATHITES (the inhabitants of Maacah) and Geshurites defines the limits of the territory in Bashan conquered by Jair the Manassite (cf. Josh. 12:5). Josh. 13:11, 13 lists the land of the Maacathites and the Geshurites as part of the territory in Transjordan given to the half-tribe of Manasseh, the Reubenites, and the Gadites. The region's inhabitants, who were among the native peoples that Israel failed to expel, were Arameans. Consequently the name of the country is given as Aram-maacah in 1 Ch. 19:6, RSV (simply "Aram" in 2:23), and Maacah is the name of one of the sons of Nahor (Gen. 22:24).

Apparently this little kingdom had regained its independence by the time of David, for the mercenaries hired by the Ammonites for their encounter with David included a thousand soldiers from Maacah. Joab completely routed these Maacathites (2 S. 10:6-14). The kingdom became a vassal of Israel and may ultimately have been absorbed into the kingdom of Damascus.

See B. Mazar, *JBL*, 80 [1961], 16-28.

D. H. MADVIG

**MAACATHITES** mā-ak'ə-thīts [Heb. *hammaʿ$^a$ḵāṯî*; Gk. B *ho Machatei*, A *Machathi*]; AV MAACHATHITES, also MAACHATHI (Dt. 3:14); NEB also BETH-MAACA. The inhabitants of MAACAH. Maacathites mentioned by name are Ahasbai (2 S. 23:24; but cf. 1 Ch. 11:36; *see* MECHERATHITE), Jaazaniah (2 K. 25:23), Eshtemoa (1 Ch. 4:19), and Jezaniah (Jer. 40:8).

**MAADAI** mā'ə-dī [Heb. *maʿ$^a$ḏay*; Gk. *Moodi*, Apoc. *Momdios*]; AV Apoc., NEB Apoc., MOMDIS. One of the Israelites who divorced their foreign wives; a son of Bani (Ezr. 10:34; 1 Esd. 9:34).

**MAADIAH** mā-ə-dī'ə [Heb. *maʿaḏyâ* <*yhwh*–'Yahweh' + *māʿaḏ*–'shakes' or possibly Old South Arabic *mʿd*–'promises']. A priest who returned from the Babylonian Exile with Zerubbabel (Neh. 12:5); cf. the names Moadiah in 12:17 and Maaziah in 10:8, either of which may refer to this person.

**MAAI** mā'ī [Heb. *māʿay*]. A musician who took part in the procession at the dedication of the walls of Jerusalem (Neh. 12:36).

**MAALEH-ACRABBIM** mā-ə-le-ə-krab'im (Josh. 15:3, AV). *See* AKRABBIM, ASCENT OF.

**MAANI** mā'ə-nī.

**1.** (1 Esd. 5:31, NEB). *See* MEUNIM.

**2.** (1 Esd. 9:34, AV). *See* BANI **5**.

**MAARATH** mā'ə-rath [Heb. *maʿ$^a$raṯ*; Gk. B *Magarōth*, A *Marōth*]. A city in the hill country of Judah, mentioned between Gedor and Beth-anoth and along with Halhul, Beth-zur, and Eltekon (Josh. 15:59). The reading in B with *gamma* suggests an original *ghain* (cf. Lucian *Maarōth*), but A reads as though the *ʿayin* had already become silent. The identification of Maarath with Maroth (Mic. 1:12) is, according to Simons, "very questionable" (*GTTOT*, § 1534). He (§ 319, D-4) and Abel (*GP*, II, 91) identified Maaroth with Beit-Ummar (-Immar), about 10.5 km. (6.5 mi.) N of Hebron and 1.2 km. (¾ mi.) W of the Bethlehem-Hebron highway. W. S. L. S.

**MAAREH-GEBA** mā'ə-rē-gē-bə [Heb. *(mim)maʿᵃrē-gāḇaʿ*; Gk. A *(apó) dysmṓn tḗs Gabaa*–'from the west of Geba'; B *(apó) Maaragabe*]; RSV "place west of Geba"; AV "out of the meadows of Gibeah"; NEB "neighborhood of Gibeah." A place where Israelites lay in ambush against the Benjaminites (Jgs. 20:33, RV). Because of the reading in A the RSV and many scholars have emended the Hebrew to read *min-maʿᵃraḇ*, "from the west of"; B, however, supports the Hebrew text. Simons suggested that the unemended text might be read "from the vicinity of Geba" (*GTTOT*, § 637; cf. NEB), but BDB translates "from the bare (open) space of Gebaʿ (*si vera l.* ['if properly read'])" (p. 789).

A second problem is the possible identification of GEBA with Gibeah. Because of the textual problems, particularly the ambivalence of the Greek, it may be specious to insist on emending the text. A location in Benjamin near Baal-tamar is certainly indicated, but this site is also unknown. W. S. L. S.

**MAASAI** mā'ə-sī [Heb. *maʿśay*–'work (of Yahweh)']; AV MAASIAI. A priest who returned from the Babylonian Exile (1 Ch. 9:12). In Neh. 11:13 the corresponding name is Amashsai.

**MAASEIAH** mā-ə-sē'ə, mā-ə-sī'ə [Heb. *maʿᵃśēyâ, maʿᵃśēyāhû*–'Yahweh's work'; Gk. usually *Maasaia*, also *Masaia, Maasia, Maasēa, Masēa* (for Gk. Apoc. see below)].

**1.** A Levite musician of the second order, among those appointed by David to make music when the ark was brought up to Jerusalem (1 Ch. 15:18, 20).

**2.** A Levite military commander who aided Jehoiada in overthrowing Queen Athaliah and putting Joash on the throne (2 Ch. 23:1).

**3.** A military officer under King Uzziah who helped to number the army under the direction of Hananiah (2 Ch. 26:11).

**4.** Son of King Ahaz of Judah; he was slain by Zichri of Ephraim in a war between Israel and Judah (2 Ch. 28:7).

**5.** The governor of Jerusalem during the reign of King Josiah; he assisted in repairing the temple (2 Ch. 34:8).

**6.** [Gk. Apoc. *Mathēlas*, Lucian *Maasias*]; AV MATTHELAS; NEB MATHELAS. A priest from the family of Jeshua who was required to divorce his foreign wife (Ezr. 10:18; 1 Esd. 9:19).

**7.** [Gk. Apoc. *Manēs*, Lucian *Maasias*]; AV EANES; NEB MANES. A priest from the family of Harim who was required to divorce his foreign wife (Ezr. 10:21; 1 Esd. 9:21). *See* MANES.

**8.** [Gk. Apoc. *Massias*]; AV, NEB, MASSIAS. A priest from the family of Pashhur who was required to divorce his foreign wife (Ezr. 10:22; 1 Esd. 9:22).

**9.** A layman from the family of Pahath-moab who was required to divorce his foreign wife (Ezr. 10:30; cf. "Moosias" in 1 Esd. 9:31, whose father is listed as Addi); possibly the same as **11** or **13.**

**10.** Father of the Azariah who helped to rebuild the wall of Jerusalem (Neh. 3:23).

**11.** One of those who stood at Ezra's right hand during the reading of the law (Neh. 8:4; cf. 1 Esd. 9:43, where the name is Baalsamus); possibly the same as **9** or **13.**

**12.** [Gk. Apoc. *Maiannas*]; AV MAIANEAS; NEB MAEANNAS; RSV mg. MAIANNAS. One of the Levites who interpreted the law to the people after Ezra's reading of it (Neh. 8:7; 1 Esd. 9:48).

**13.** One of the "chiefs of the people" who sealed the covenant with Nehemiah (Neh. 10:25 [MT 26]); possibly the same as **9** or **11.**

**14.** A Shilonite who lived in Jerusalem after returning from the Exile (Neh. 11:5; called Asaiah in 1 Ch. 9:5).

**15.** A Benjaminite ancestor of Sallu, who lived in Jerusalem after returning from the Exile (Neh. 11:7; not listed in 1 Ch. 9:7f.).

**16, 17.** Two priests who took part in the music at the dedication of the wall of Jerusalem (Neh. 12:41f.); either may be the same as **6, 7,** or **8.**

**18.** Father of Zephaniah the priest, who lived during the reign of King Zedekiah and the ministry of Jeremiah (Jer. 21:1; 29:25; 37:3).

**19.** Father of the false prophet Zedekiah (Jer. 29:21).

**20.** Son of Shallum; a doorkeeper in the temple during the reign of King Jehoiakim (Jer. 35:4).

**21.** (Jer. 32:12; 51:59, AV). *See* MAHSEIAH. N. J. O.

**MAASIAI** mā-as'ē-ī (Ch. 9:12, AV). *See* MAASAI.

**MAASIAS** mā-ə-sī'əs (Bar. 1:1, AV). *See* MAHSEIAH.

**MAASMAS** mā-as'məs [Gk. *Maasmas*]; AV MASMAN. One of the leading men sent by Ezra to obtain Levites, after it was discovered that the latter were not represented in the group returning to Jerusalem (1 Esd. 8:43).

**MAATH** mā'əth [Gk. *Maath*]. An ancestor of Jesus in Luke's genealogy (Lk. 3:26).

**MAAZ** mā'əz [Heb. *maʿaṣ*]. A descendant of Judah (1 Ch. 2:27).

**MAAZIAH** mā-ə-zī'ə.

**1.** [Heb. *maʿazyāhû*]. One of David's priests and the leader of the twenty-fourth course (1 Ch. 24:18).

**2.** [Heb. *maʿazyâ*]. A priest who took part in sealing the covenant of Ezra (Neh. 10:8 [MT 9]), possibly representing the family of priests who traced their lineage back to Maaziah **1.**

**MABDAI** mab'dī (1 Esd. 9:34, AV). *See* MAMDAI.

**MACALON** mak'ə-lon (AV, NEB, 1 Esd. 5:21). Gk. *Makalōn* here corresponds to *Machmas* in Ezr. 2:27. *See* MICHMAS, MICHMASH.

**MACCABEES** mak'ə-bēz [Gk. *Makkabaioi*]. Maccabeus is the name given to Judas son of Mattathias (*Ioudas ho káloumenos Makkabaios*; 1 Macc. 2:4; 3:1; cf. Josephus *Ant.* xii.6.1 [266]), who defended the rights and traditions of the Jews in the 2nd cent. B.C. By extension his family and party were called Maccabees.

The name Maccabee has a rather obscure derivation. It may mean "extinguisher" or "quencher" of Hellenism (Heb. *mᵉḵabbî* < *kāḇâ*, "be extinguished, quenched"), or, more likely, it means "hammer," in reference either to Judas's crushing military feats or to the mallet or hammer shape of his head (cf. Mish. *Bekhoroth* vii.1; *maqqāḇî* < *maqqeḇeṯ*, "hammer"). "Hammerhead" is the most preferred explanation because commonly in the Hellenistic

MACCABEES

world, and apparently in Judas's family (1 Macc. 2:2-4), people were named for their physical characteristics.

Judas's family is designated as the HASMONEANS in the rabbinic literature (Mish. *Middoth* i.6) and in Josephus (*Ant.* xi.4.8 [111]; xii.6.1 [265]; xiv.16.4 [490f.]; xv.11.4 [403]; xvi.7.1 [187]; xvii.7.3 [162]; xx.8.11 [190]; 10.3 [238]; 10.5 [247, 249]; *BJ* i.proem 7 [19]: 1.3 [36]; *Vita* 1 [2, 4]). This name derives from the great-great grandfather of Judas, Hashman (Josephus *Ant.* xii.6.1 [265]).

- I. Historical Background
  - A. Alexander the Great (356-323 B.C.)
  - B. Ptolemaic Rule (323-198 B.C.)
  - C. Seleucidian Rule (198-63 B.C.)
- II. Maccabean Revolt
  - A. Antiochus's Revenge (168-166 B.C.)
  - B. Mattathias (166 B.C.)
  - C. Judas Maccabeus (166-160 B.C.)
    - 1. Rededication of the Temple (166-164 B.C.)
    - 2. Religious Freedom Gained (163 B.C.)
    - 3. Political Freedom Attempted (162-160 B.C.)
  - D. Jonathan (160-143 B.C.)

***I. Historical Background.***–A survey of the historical background will clarify the reason for the Maccabean revolt.

*A. Alexander the Great* (356-323 B.C.). While the Persian empire was rapidly disintegrating, Philip II of Macedon was consolidating his forces and preparing to destroy it (Diodorus xvi.91.2f.; 92.3f.; Plutarch *Alexander* viii.5). He wanted to see Grecian control of the whole world. But in 336 B.C. he was murdered by his bodyguard Pausanius (Diodorus xvi.94.1-4; Plutarch *Alexander* x.4).

Philip's son Alexander III, the Great, was only twenty years old when he took the throne. Aristotle had tutored him since he was thirteen, and he was convinced that the Greek way of life was superior; consequently his dream was to continue his father's conquest of the world in order to hellenize it. His first two years of rule involved the consolidation of the Hellenic League (Arrian i.1.1–10.6; Plutarch *Alexander* xi-xiv; Diodorus xvii.1.1–16.4). In 334 he crossed the Hellespont and soundly defeated the Persian army at the foot of Mt. Ida by the river Granicus (the Troy area). This opened Asia Minor to Alexander, and in little more than a year he was at Issus. In the fall of 333 he defeated Darius III at Issus and marched southward, conquering Tyre and Gaza (Plutarch *Alexander* xi-xxv; Diodorus xvii.17.1–48.7; Curtius Rufus iv.6.7-30). While in Palestine (though it is difficult to know the chronological sequence) Alexander went to the temple in Jerusalem and offered sacrifices to God under the direction of the high priest Jaddua (Josephus *Ant.* xi.8.4f. [326-339]; cf. also T.B. *Yoma* 69a). Alexander was shown from the book of Daniel that he was the one predicted to destroy the Persian empire (cf. Dnl. 8:5-7, 20f.). He accepted this interpretation, and being favorably disposed, he granted the Jews' request that in Palestine, Babylonia, and Media they might live according to their ancestral laws and might be exempt from tribute every sabbatical year. Although the historicity of this account has been greatly disputed among scholars, it does show that the relationship between Alexander and the Jews was amicable, and history gives no reason to doubt this.

Alexander then proceeded to Egypt, conquered it without trouble, and spent the winter there. In the spring of 331 he marched east and by July, 330, he had defeated Darius and become king over Persia (Arrian iii.1-22; Plutarch *Alexander* xxvi-xliii; Diodorus xviii.49-73). He moved eastward as far as the Lower Indus and died in Babylon in 323 as a world conqueror when he was only four months short of age thirty-three (Arrian vii.28.1).

*B. Ptolemaic Rule* (323-198 B.C.). Alexander's death caused great strife among his generals as they attempted to gain control of portions of his kingdom. By 311 B.C. Seleucus was recognized as the ruler of Babylonia; this marked the commencement of the Seleucid dynasty/era (Appian *Syr.* 54). Between 323 and 301 Palestine was the battlefield in the strife among the generals. For eight years it was controlled by the Ptolemies, but in 315 it was taken by Antigonus (ruler of Asia Minor and northern Syria). Ptolemy recaptured it in 312, only soon to lose it again to Antigonus. In 301, however, Antigonus was killed in a decisive battle at Ipsus in Phrygia. An agreement had been made (in 303) that upon Antigonus's defeat Coelesyria should be given to Ptolemy. Since Ptolemy had not taken part in the battle as had been planned, Seleucus felt that he (Seleucus) should receive Coelesyria, but Ptolemy forestalled him and took the land. This action was the bone of contention between the Seleucidian and Ptolemaic houses for decades to come. Palestine remained under the control of the Ptolemies until won by the Seleucids led by Antiochus III (the Great) at the Battle of Panias (Caesarea Philippi of the NT) in 198. (Josephus *Ant.* xii.3.3 [132-37]; Polybius xvi.18f.; xxviii.1; Dnl. 11:13-16). Thus the Seleucids finally acquired the land that they considered rightly theirs.

*C. Seleucidian Rule* (198-63 B.C.). The rule of the Seleucids over Palestine lasted until Pompey made it a Roman province in 63 B.C. This article discusses the period only from 198, when Palestine came under Seleucid control, until 143, when Israel gained its independence (for the later development, *see* HASMONEANS II, III). Upon the victory over the Ptolemies, Antiochus III allowed the Jews to worship according to their laws and to complete and maintain the temple. He exempted the council of elders, priests, and the scribes of the temple from taxes; the citizens of Jerusalem enjoyed this exemption for three years and after that period were exempted from a third part of their taxes. Antiochus also released the prisoners (Josephus *Ant.* xii.3.3f. [138-153]). The Jews enjoyed a brief period of tranquillity under the Seleucids because of these privileges and also because their rulers were concentrating their efforts in the West.

Rome had defeated both Hannibal at Zama (near Carthage) in 202 and the Macedonian monarch in 197. Because of the new threat, the Seleucids made a peace treaty with Egypt (Polybius xxviii.20; Appian *Syr.* 5; Josephus *Ant.* xii.4.1 [154]; Dnl. 11:17). Antiochus then invaded Thrace in 196, and with the persuasion of Hannibal he invaded Greece (which the Romans had evacuated) in 194. The Romans retaliated, however, and defeated Antiochus at Thermopylae in 191 and at Magnesia in Asia Minor in 190. At Apamea in 189 a peace treaty was signed; Antiochus agreed to give up Asia Minor N and W of the Tarsus Mountains and much of his military force and to pay a heavy indemnity over a twelve-year period. To guarantee the payment of the indemnity, the Romans took twenty hostages to Rome, among them Antiochus's son Antiochus IV Epiphanes (Appian *Syr.* 36-39; Polybius xx-xxi; Livy xxxvi-xxxvii; Dnl. 11:18f.; 1 Macc. 1:10; 8:6-8; Josephus *Ant.* xii.10.6 [414]).

Antiochus III was succeeded by his second son Seleucus IV Philopater in 187. In 175, however, Heliodorus assassinated Seleucus to seize the throne. Antiochus's third son, Antiochus IV Epiphanes, had just been released from Rome as a hostage, and with the help of Eumenes II king of Pergamum he ousted Heliodorus and made himself king. Because his newly acquired kingdom lacked political and financial stability, Antiochus IV attempted to unify it by a vigorous hellenization program (Tacitus *Hist.* v.8). One of the unifying factors was religion; he encouraged the people (*ca.* 169) to worship his own person in the form of the Olympian Zeus (Dnl. 11:21-24). Although his name *Theos Epiphanēs* means "the manifest god," his enemies called him *Epimanēs* (a change of only one letter in Greek), which means "madman" or "insane" (Polybius xxvi.10).

Soon after Antiochus had acquired the throne, he had to settle a dispute between the high priest Onias III, who was pro-Ptolemaic, and Onias's brother Jason (the Greek name that he preferred over Jesus for his Hebrew name Joshua), who was pro-Seleucid. By offering a larger payment of money to Antiochus and by pledging his wholehearted support in the hellenization of the Jerusalemites, Jason secured the high priesthood in 174 (1 Macc. 1:10-15; 2 Macc. 4:7-17; Josephus *Ant.* xii.5.1 [237-241]). In 171 Menelaus, a friend of Jason, obtained the high priesthood by offering three hundred more talents than Jason and by promising a vigorous hellenization program. Antiochus gladly accepted this offer because he was in desperate need of funds and because a high priest outside the Aaronic line (according to 2 Macc. 4:23; 3:4 Menelaus was a Benjaminite) destroyed a great unifying force among the Jews. The nomination also deprived the Jews of the privilege of selecting their own high priest. Jason went into hiding in the Ammonite country.

The next year, in 170, Ptolemy VI Philometor, who was a minor, was advised to avenge Panias by recovering Coelesyria from the Seleucids. Antiochus, hearing of their plans, with a large army invaded Egypt in 170/169 and defeated Ptolemy VI. He proclaimed himself king of Egypt and allowed rivalry to exist there by making Ptolemy VI Philometor king of Memphis and his brother Ptolemy VIII Euergetes king of Alexandria (Dnl. 11:25-27). Upon returning from Egypt, Antiochus heard that the inhabitants of Jerusalem, with the help of Jason (who had come out of hiding in the Ammonite territory), had had to take refuge in the Acra. In fact, Menelaus had plundered the temple and the people had begun to riot. Furthermore, it had been rumored that Antiochus had died in Egypt. This had emboldened Jason to come out of hiding and help the Jerusalemites avenge Menelaus's plunder of the temple. Upon hearing this Antiochus felt that this was a rebellion against himself and thus decided to subdue Jerusalem (2 Macc. 5:11-17). On returning to Jerusalem Antiochus, with Menelaus, desecrated and plundered the temple of its treasures and left the city under the rule of one of his commanders, Philip, a Phrygian (1 Macc. 1:20-29; 2 Macc. 5:18-22; Josephus *Ant.* xii.5.3 [246f.]). (On the chronological problems of these events see *HJP*², I, 149-154, esp. nn. 32, 37.)

***II. Maccabean Revolt.***–*A. Antiochus's Revenge* (168-166 B.C.). In the winter of 169/168, the rival brothers Ptolemy VI and Ptolemy VIII agreed to end their dispute and united against their uncle Antiochus IV. Thus, in the spring of 168 Antiochus IV invaded Egypt a second time. He captured Memphis, but when he attempted to subdue Eleusis, a suburb of Alexandria, the Roman general Popillius Laenas gave him an ultimatum from the senate to withdraw immediately from Egypt (cf. Polybius xxix.2.1-4; 27.1-8; Livy xlv.12.1-6; Diodorus xxxi.2; Velleius Paterculus i.10.1f.; Appian *Syr.* 66; Justinus xxxiv.3; Dnl. 11:28-30). Antiochus immediately retreated, having learned of Rome's power as its hostage for fourteen years.

Embittered, Antiochus decided to establish Palestine as a buffer state between him and the Roman encroachment (Polybius xxix.27.9; Dnl. 11:30). He destroyed the walls of Jerusalem and refortified the old Davidic city making it the pagan stronghold (Acra). Considering himself Zeus Epiphanes, he ordered a vigorous hellenization program that would exterminate the Jewish religion. He forbade the Jews to celebrate the sabbath and feasts, to offer the traditional sacrifices, and to perform circumcision, and he ordered the destruction of the copies of the Torah.

The Jews were ordered to offer up unclean sacrifices on idolatrous altars and to eat swine's flesh (2 Macc. 6:18). The climactic act was on 25 Chislev (Dec. 16) 167, when the temple of Jerusalem became the place of worship of the Olympian Zeus. The altar of Zeus was erected on the altar of burnt offering, and swine's flesh was offered on it (Dnl. 11:31f.; 1 Macc. 1:41-64; 2 Macc. 6:1-11).

*B. Mattathias* (166 B.C.). In every village of Palestine sacrifice was to be offered to the heathen gods under the supervision of imperial representatives. In the village of Modein (27 km., 17 mi., NW of Jerusalem) an aged priest named Mattathias defied the command of Antiochus IV's legate to offer the sacrifice on the heathen altar. When another Jew was about to comply, Mattathias killed him and the legate and destroyed the altar, saying, "Let everyone who is zealous for the law and supports the covenant come out with me" (1 Macc. 2:15-27; Josephus *Ant.* xii.6.1f. [265-272]; cf. Dnl. 11:32-35). Mattathias, his five sons (John, Simon, Judas, Eleazar, and Jonathan) and many other Jews fled to the mountains; this marked the beginning of the Maccabean revolt.

Mattathias and his followers exhorted Jews everywhere to join their struggle against hellenization. They gained the support of the Hasidim, those who were faithful to the Torah. They tore down heathen altars and circumcised children who had been left uncircumcised. After a long life, Mattathias died in 166. He exhorted his sons to continue the struggle and appointed his third son Judas as the commander of the war (1 Macc. 2:42-70; Josephus *Ant.* xii.6.2-4 [273-286]).

*C. Judas Maccabeus* (166-160 B.C.). *1. Rededication of the Temple* (166-164 B.C.). The selection of Judas to carry on the struggle was the right one, for he proved to be a very capable leader in defeating the Seleucids. In his first year he defeated the Syrian governors Apollonius and Seron (1 Macc. 3:10-26; Josephus *Ant.* xii.7.1 [287-292]).

Part of Antiochus's inability to put down the Maccabees was caused by the trouble he had in the East, which prevented him from being involved in Judea himself. Instead, he ordered Lysias, regent of the western part of the empire (Syria), to stop the rebellion and to destroy the Jewish race (1 Macc. 3:32-36; Josephus *Ant.* xii.7.2 [295f.]). Lysias sent a large army under the leadership of Ptolemy, Nicanor, and Gorgias. So confident they were of victory that traders went along to purchase Jewish slaves (1 Macc. 3:38-41). But Judas decisively defeated Gorgias at Emmaus, causing the Syrian soldiers to flee (1 Macc. 4:1-27; Josephus *Ant.* xii.7.4 [305-312]).

In 164 Lysias made one last attempt against the Jews by personally leading a larger army to attack Jerusalem from the south. Judas, however, completely defeated him in Beth-zur (24 km., 15 mi., S of Jerusalem). Lysias retreated, and Judas marched to Jerusalem and regained all of Jerusalem except the Acra. Having captured the temple mount, he destroyed the altar of the Olympian Zeus, built a new altar, rebuilt the temple, and selected a priest who had remained faithful to Yahweh. Thus on 25 Chislev (Dec. 14) 164, exactly three years after its desecration, the temple was rededicated and the daily sacrifices were restored (1 Macc. 4:36-59; 2 Macc. 10:1-8; Josephus *Ant.* xii.7.6f. [316-326]). This event marked the beginning of the Jewish Feast of Dedication or Lights (Hanukkah). Judas then fortified the Jerusalem walls and the city of Beth-zur. This completed the first phase of the Maccabean struggle. The Maccabees could rejoice, for they had not experienced defeat.

*2. Religious Freedom Gained* (163 B.C.). Judas's victories made Judah reasonably secure. Two things, however, needed to be accomplished. First, although Judah was reasonably secure, it was felt that all the Jews of Palestine had to be independent from Antiochus's rule. After several campaigns this freedom was won.

Second, the Maccabees wanted to end Syrian control of the Acra in Jerusalem. The Syrian presence was a constant reminder of Antiochus's hellenization program intended to exterminate the Jewish religion. When Judas laid siege to the Acra in the spring or summer of 163, some Syrian soldiers and Hellenistic Jews escaped and went to Antioch for help (1 Macc. 6:18-27).

Antiochus IV died in 163 (Polybius xxxi.9.3f.; Josephus *Ant.* xii.9.1 [356-59]) and was succeeded by his nine-year-old son Antiochus V Eupator. Just before his death, Antiochus IV had appointed his friend Philip as the regent and guardian over Antiochus V. But Lysias claimed that these privileges had been given to him at an earlier date, and so he crowned Antiochus V (both he and Philip were in Antioch when Antiochus IV died). Because of the troubles in Jerusalem, Lysias with the boy-king went south and defeated Judas at Beth-zechariah (18 km., 11 mi., SW of Jerusalem). There Judas's youngest brother Eleazar was killed.

Lysias then laid siege to Jerusalem (1 Macc. 6:28-54). Judas faced severe food shortages (because it was the sabbatical year) and was about to be defeated. Lysias, however, received the news that Philip was marching from Persia to Syria to claim the boy-king Antiochus V and the kingdom; thus he was anxious to make a peace treaty with Judas. Judas agreed to tear down the walls of Jerusalem, and Lysias guaranteed religious freedom to the Jews (1 Macc. 6:55-63). The Jews, however, were still under the Seleucidian rule.

*3. Political Freedom Attempted* (162-160 B.C.). Having obtained religious freedom, Judas now wanted political freedom. To counteract his drive, the Seleucids strengthened the Hellenistic elements among the Jews. Lysias, it seems, appointed the high priest Alcimus (Jakim or Jehoakim) who, although of Aaronic descent, was ideologically a Hellenist (cf. 1 Macc. 7:14; 2 Macc. 14:3-7; Josephus *Ant.* xii.9.7 [384-88]; xx.10.3 [235]) and thus unacceptable to Judas.

Meanwhile in Syria, Demetrius I Soter, nephew of Antiochus IV and cousin of Antiochus V, escaped from Rome (where he had gone as a hostage when Antiochus IV had been released), killed both Lysias and Antiochus V, and assumed the throne. He confirmed Alcimus as high priest (162) of Israel and sent him with an army to Judea under his general Bacchides. The Hasidim accepted Alcimus as the high priest probably, it can be conjectured, because he was of Aaronic descent and because the Syrians (or Seleucids) had guaranteed them freedom of worship. Thus the Hasidim broke from Judas's ranks, but they quickly returned when Alcimus, disregarding his promise not to harm them, slew sixty of them (1 Macc. 7:15-20; Josephus *Ant.* xii.10.2 [393-97]). Hence Alcimus asked Demetrius for more military help against Judas and his followers, called the HASIDEANS (2 Macc. 14:6). Demetrius sent NICANOR, but he was defeated and killed at Adasa (6 km., 4 mi., N of Jerusalem) on 13 Adar (Mar. 9) 161, (which the Jews celebrate annually as Nicanor's Day); the army fled to Gazara (32 km., 20 mi., W of Adasa) and was destroyed. Alcimus fled to Syria (1 Macc. 7:26-50; Josephus *Ant.* xii.10.3-5 [398-412]).

Judas sent for help from Rome, but before any could arrive, Demetrius sent Bacchides with Alcimus to avenge Nicanor's death. Because of the might of the Syrian army, many deserted Judas, and in the Battle of Elasa (about 16 km., 10 mi., N of Jerusalem) he was slain (160). His brothers Jonathan and Simon took his body to be buried at Modein (1 Macc. 8:1–9:22; Josephus *Ant.* xii.10.6–11.2 [413-434]).

*D. Jonathan* (160-143 B.C.). Judas's death was a great blow to morale. The Hellenists were temporarily in control while Jonathan and his followers were in the wilderness of Tekoa, waging only guerrilla warfare. Bacchides fortified Jerusalem and other Judean cities against possible Maccabean attacks. In May, 159 B.C., Alcimus died, and no successor was chosen. Soon after, Bacchides left his command in Judah and returned to Antioch (157); he went back to Jerusalem at the request of the Hellenists but was defeated at Beth-basi (10 km., 6 mi., S of Jerusalem). He made a peace treaty with Jonathan and then returned to Antioch.

This treaty weakened the Hellenists' position. Jonathan made Michmash (14 km., 9 mi., S of Jerusalem) his headquarters, where he judged the people, punishing the hellenizers (1 Macc. 9:23-27; Josephus *Ant.* xiii.1.1-6 [1-34]). During the next five years his power increased. In 152 he was further helped by internal struggles for power in Syria. A pretender, Alexander Balas, who claimed to be the son of Antiochus Epiphanes, challenged Demetrius I. Both desired Jonathan's support. Fortunately, Jonathan sided with Alexander Balas, for in 150 Demetrius was slain in a battle against Alexander. Alexander made Jonathan a general, governor, and high priest of Judah and considered him one of his chief friends (1 Macc. 10:22-66; Josephus *Ant.* xiii.2.3f. [46-61]; 4.1f. [80-85]). This was certainly a strange alliance, i.e., Alexander Balas, professed son of Antiochus Epiphanes, in league with a Maccabean!

New troubles came in Syria. Demetrius's son, Demetrius II Nicator, challenged Alexander Balas in 147 and finally defeated him in 145. Since Demetrius II was only sixteen and inexperienced, Jonathan took the opportunity to attack the Acra in Jerusalem, where the Hellenistic Jews were still in control. Although Demetrius II opposed the attack, he later conceded to Jonathan by confirming his high-priesthood and granting his request for three districts in southern Samaria. Jonathan was not able to conquer the Acra, however.

In 143 Demetrius II's army rebelled, and Diodotus Trypho (a general of Alexander Balas) claimed the Syrian throne (becoming its first non-Seleucid king) in the name of Alexander Balas's son Antiochus VI. Jonathan took advantage of the situation and sided with Trypho, who in turn made him civil and religious head of the Jews and his brother Simon head of the military. Trypho, however, fearful of Jonathan's success, deceived him, arranged a meeting with him, and subsequently killed him. Jonathan was buried at Modein (1 Macc. 10:67–13:30; Josephus *Ant.* xiii.4.3–6.6 [86-212]).

Jonathan was succeeded by Simon, the only remaining son of Mattathias. A new phase of the Maccabean rule had emerged. Although generally speaking one does apply the term "Hasmonean" to the whole of the Maccabean family, it is more specifically applied to the high-priestly house from the time of Simon to Rome's intervention in 63 because in that period the Maccabean dream had finally come true, namely, the Israelites had become an independent nation. Hence the political and religious life was headed by one family or dynasty — the Hasmoneans.

*See* Vol. I, Maps XIV, XV.

***Bibliography.***–E. R. Bevan, *House of Seleucus* (2 vols., 1902); *Jerusalem under the High-Priests* (1904), pp. 69-108; *CAH,* VIII (1930), 495-533; E. Bickerman, *From Ezra to the Last of the Maccabees* (Eng. tr. 1947), pp. 93-145; S. Tedesche and S. Zeitlin, *First Book of Maccabees* (1950); J. C. Dancy, *Comm. on I Maccabees* (1954); W. R. Farmer, *Maccabees, Zealots, and Josephus* (1956), pp. 47-158; R. A. Parker and W. H. Dubberstein, *Bab-*

*ylonian Chronology 626 B.C.-A.D. 75* (2nd ed. 1956), pp. 40f.; V. Tcherikover, *Hellenistic Civilization and the Jews* (1959), pp. 117-239; S. K. Eddy, *The King Is Dead* (1961), pp. 183-238; S. Zeitlin, *Rise and Fall of the Judaean State*, I (1962), 37-140; O. Mørkholm, *Antiochus IV of Syria* (1966); D. S. Russell, *The Jews from Alexander to Herod* (*New Clarendon Bible*, 1967), pp. 1-57; B. Reicke, *NT Era* (1968), pp. 42-62; Y. Aharoni and M. Avi-Yonah, *Macmillan Bible Atlas* (1968), pp. 110-128; J. R. Bartlett, *First and Second Books of the Maccabees* (*CBC*, 1973); E. Schürer, *HJP*$^2$, I, 125-188; M. Hengel, *Judaism and Hellenism* (Eng. tr., 2 vols., 1974); *Jews, Greeks and Barbarians* (Eng. tr. 1980).

H. W. HOEHNER

**MACCABEES, BOOKS OF.** Books of the OT Apocrypha (1 and 2 Maccabees) and Pseudepigrapha (3, 4, and 5 Maccabees). Since the history of the Maccabean period is nowhere better delineated than in 1 and 2 Maccabees, this article concentrates on the exposition of those books, treating other topics synoptically. Outside the Protestant canon of Scripture, few documents are of greater importance for the history and theology of the faith.

- I. Historical Introduction
- II. First Maccabees
  - A. Literary Introduction
  - B. Historical Prologue, Ch. 1
  - C. Career of Mattathias, 2:1-70
  - D. Career of Judas Maccabeus, 3:1–9:22
  - E. Career of Jonathan, 9:23–12:53
  - F. Career of Simon, Chs. 13–16
  - G. Conclusion
- III. Second Maccabees
  - A. Literary Introduction
  - B. Chs. 1–2
  - C. Historic Roots of the Maccabean Revolt, Chs. 3–7
  - D. Career of Judas Maccabeus, Chs. 8–15
- IV. Third, Fourth, and Fifth Maccabees

*I. **Historical Introduction**.*–Alexander the Great defeated the Persians at the Battle of Issus in 333 B.C., and after further whirlwind victories and unexampled triumphs, he died an untimely death ten years later. His rapidly gained empire passed to his generals, and thus Greeks came to occupy Asiatic thrones. Palestine survived precariously and sometimes turbulently between the rival power blocs of Egypt and Syria. In 198 Antiochus III finally conquered Syria, which became part of the Seleucid empire begun in Babylonia in 312. (Seleucid chronology is discussed in *ORHI*, II, 23f. Round dates are sufficient here.) The Jews, some already Hellenistic in tendency and unfaithful at heart to the strict religion of the OT, accepted Antiochus III favorably enough, and the zealous observers of the law were left at peace. The whole structure and being of Judaism was threatened, however, after Antiochus IV Epiphanes came to the Syrian throne in 175.

Antiochus IV, a typical oriental despot, saw an outward Judaism that Moses would have failed to recognize, for it was rotten to the core. Moreover, its worst enemies were within its own ranks. Small wonder that the tyrant failed to make sufficient allowance for the sacredness of the high priest's office and treated it as something to sell for profit — there were Jews by blood far more blameworthy than himself. He determined further to abolish all Mosaic ceremonial and observance and compel the Jews to conform to a unified Greek culture. The extremity of these measures saved the historic faith by arousing a frenzy of religious zeal in the family of the Maccabees, who prevailed against fantastic odds and saved the Jewish nation, albeit in a bloodbath.

Mattathias sparked the Maccabean rebellion and led it from 168 until 166 B.C. Of his sons, Judas Maccabeus exercised command until 161, Jonathan to 143, and Simon until 135. Fortunately for the Jews, a period of plot and counterplot followed Antiochus's death in 164. His young son Antiochus V Eupator had a brief nominal reign but with his regent was assassinated by the treachery of Demetrius I Soter (162-150), who was ousted in turn by the upstart Alexander Balas (150-145). Revolts punctuated the reign of Demetrius II Nicator (145-138); his successor, Antiochus VII Sidetes (138-128), was the last Syrian monarch to reign within the main Maccabean period.

For a map of Palestine under the Maccabees, *see* Vol. I, Map XV.

*II. First Maccabees.–A. Literary Introduction.* The testimony of Origen and Jerome, reinforced by internal textual evidence, points to a Hebrew original for 1 Maccabees that perished at an early date, leaving the Greek text as the primary extant witness. Swete (*OTG*, III, 594-661) covers all the uncial evidence. Two Latin and two Syriac recensions of the Greek exist.

The author, an unknown but burning patriot, avoids the name of God and does not ostensibly preach. His religion seems implicit rather than explicit, Sadducean rather than Pharisaic, natural rather than supernatural; yet he possesses a religious sincerity of his own. The events of the narrative, accurately presented, range from 175 to 135 B.C. The date of writing may be given roundly as 100 B.C., with editorial opinions swinging in both directions.

The etymology of "Maccabee" is an unsolved problem. The name is a nickname adapted from a Hebrew or Aramaic word subsequently transliterated as Gk. *makkabaios*. The process of development from the original root to the nickname and thence to the Greek transliteration provided ample opportunity for changes in the vocalization and spelling of the original word (Goldstein, pp. 230f.). Jerome (*Prologus Galeatus*) states that 1 Maccabees was written in Hebrew, and Origen (Eusebius *HE* vi.25) gives the title as Gk. *sarbēthsabanaiel* (*LCL* ed. II, 74) or *sarbēth sarbane ēl* (H. Valesius, *Eusebius Pamphili Ecclesiasticae Historiae* [1720]), another enigmatic transliteration from a Semitic original, variously construed as "history of the house of the warriors" (J. Oulton and H. J. Lawlor, *HE* [*LCL*], II, 74f.), "the Book of the House of the Princes of God" (W. Brownlee, *IDB*, III, 203), etc. Though Origen's title has no direct relationship in meaning to *makkabaoi*, it does reflect knowledge of a Hebrew (or Aramaic) version of the book. The name "Maccabees" does not appear in the Talmud or midrash; there the equivalent term is "Hasmoneans" (cf. Mish. *Middoth* i.6; 1 Macc. 4:46).

The most widely accepted solution for *makkabaios* is that found in G. Dalman, *Grammatik des jüdisch-palästinischen Aramäisch und aramäische Dialektproblem* (2nd ed. 1905), who postulated an original *maqq*$^e$*ḇ'* or *maqq*$^e$*bay*, both similar to Heb. *maqqeḇeṯ*, "hammer, mallet." Thus, "Maccabee" could mean "hammer," i.e., the one who hammers or strikes the enemy, but Dalman also suggested the translation "(he whose head is shaped like) a hammer" on the basis of *maqq*$^e$*bān* (p. 178 n. 3; cf. Mish. *Bekoroth* vii.1; T.J. *Bekoroth* 43b). Other suggestions include "general," from Arab. *manqab*; "(a man with unusual) nostrils," from Syr. *mqb' dnḥyr'* (lit. "hole of the nose, nostril"; F. Perles, *JQR*, 17 [1926/27], 403-406); "designated by the Lord," from Heb. *nāqaḇ*, "name, designate" (A. A. Bevan, *JTS*, 30 [1929], 191f.); "(source of) hope" from Heb. *miqweh*, etc. (see *HJP*$^2$, I, 158; *Jew.Enc.*, VIII, 238).

*B. Historical Prologue, Ch. 1. Summary.* The prologue is a lightning sketch, partially inaccurate, of Alexander's last ten years, which marked the inception of Greek influence in the East. The writer then leaped straight to the far-off consequence of Alexander's campaigns, the accession to the Syrian throne in 175 of Antiochus IV Epiphanes, the pagan villain of all that is to follow (vv.1-10). The apostate, hellenizing, Torah-breaking party within Judaism, however, not Antiochus, was the real root of all the trouble (vv. 11-15). Antiochus made a successful military campaign against Egypt (vv. 16-19) and a first raid on the temple to pillage its wealth (vv. 20-28), followed by a dastardly sabbath attack on Jerusalem itself (vv. 29-40). Finally he attempted to exterminate the Jewish faith but only made martyrs (vv. 41-64).

*Notes. 1:10.* Greek *Epiphanḗs,* "manifest, renowned, etc." — an honorific title of pagan deities self-claimed by Antiochus, speedily turned to the mocking assonance *Epimanḗs,* "madman." Gk. *rhíza,* Heb. *šōreš,* "root" — better, as Antiochus was an end product, "sprout" or "shoot." For the root metaphor with good implications, cf. Isa. 11:1; Rev. 5:5; with bad connotations, Dt. 29:18; 1 Tim. 6:10. He. 12:15 is more complex than Dt. 29:18 and seems to mix both metaphors. See further *TDNT,* VI, *s.v.* ῥίζα (Maurer).

*1:15.* Greek *akrobystía* here means not uncircumcision, but epispasm, surgical manipulation of the prepuce to conceal evidence of circumcision — the extremity of apostasy. Many Jews wished to exercise naked with their Greek friends in the new gymnasium and avoid being ridiculed because of their race. Nakedness in public was abhorrent enough to their orthodox brethren. See Celsus *De medecina* vii.25. The Greek technical verb is *epispáō,* used in the middle; see 1 Cor. 7:18. The Talmud uses *mšk ʿrlh,* "stretch the prepuce" (e.g., *Sanhedrin* 38b, etc.). For copious references see Winer, *Biblisches Realwörterbuch,* I (1847), *s.v. "Beschneidung,"* esp. pp. 160f. Cf. also Bauer, rev., p. 299; SB, IV, 33f.; *TDNT,* VI, *s.v.* περιτέμνω (Meyer).

*1:34.* "Sinful people" — cf. "strangers," v. 38 — probably means apostate Jews rather than the heathen garrison.

*1:36.* "Adversary" — Gk. *diábolos,* Heb. *śāṭān* — is an interesting collective personification. The stone building and all the men inside formed a fused entity in the writer's mind.

*1:45-49, 56f.* With devilish insight the very pillars of Judaism are attacked — temple, sabbath, law, circumcision, abstinence from pork, etc. Jewish horror of the pig went far beyond the pentateuchal food prohibitions in Lev. 11:7; Dt. 14:8 — cf. modern Islam. Frequently the Talmud will not give the animal its name, *ḥᵃzîr,* but employs the circumlocution of abhorrence, *dbr ʾḥr,* lit. "another thing." Cf. further Prov. 11:22; Isa. 65:4; 66:3, 17; Mt. 7:16; etc. The barbarity of Antiochus's extremes fanned the flames of martyr zeal.

*1:54.* The *bdélygma erēmṓseōs,* the abomination of desolation, Heb. *šiqqûṣ šōmēm* and cognates, the "desolating sacrilege" is here specifically the small idol altar superimposed on the altar of burnt offering (cf. v. 59), the crowning insult to Judaism's temple and God. Cf. Dnl. 9:27; 11:31; 12:11, Greek and Hebrew. Mk. 13:14 may point symbolically to the antichrist; cf. Mt. 24:15. *See* Desolating Sacrilege; see further *s.v.* "Abomination of Desolation" in *HDB; Jew.Enc.;* cf. SB, I, 951; *TDNT,* I, *s.v.* βδέλυγμα (Foerster).

*C. Career of Mattathias, 2:1-70. Summary.* Mattathias defied the king's edict to offer heathen sacrifice, slew lawfully an apostate Jew on the detested heathen altar, and declared open war by slaying the king's officer and summoning others to his revolt (vv. 15-30). A thousand Jews who had not sided with Mattathias were attacked on the sabbath and died without resistance rather than break the law. But Mattathias elected to resist if necessary. Sympathetic compatriot elements joined him (vv. 31-48). The dying charges of old Mattathias included a briefer and more law-oriented version of He. 11 and the appointment of Judas Maccabeus as his successor (vv. 49-70).

*Notes: 2:6.* Blasphemy is by derivation spoken and invisible; sacrilegious deeds are included only figuratively. Cf. 2 Macc. 8:4, etc.; *TDNT,* I, *s.v.* βλησφημέω (Beyer).

*2:19f.* Cf. Peter in Mt. 26:33. Mattathias emerges better.

*2:41.* A difficult decision for Jews who loved precedent. The proscription of sabbath attack is still a heavy military disadvantage.

*2:42.* The aloof Hasidim, spiritual ancestors of the Pharisees, were stricter in observance but joined Mattathias through pressure of circumstance.

*2:44ff.* The boldness of the Jews against the Seleucids is due to shining courage, Palestinian topography, and guerrilla potential.

*2:57.* Wace, *in loc.*: "The continuance of the temporal kingdom was conditional (Ps. 132:12) and . . . forfeited. But the spiritual kingdom remains in the line of David for ever and ever through the eternity of the kingdom of Christ."

*D. Career of Judas Maccabeus, 3:1–9:22. Summary.* The incredible military successes of Judas stretched in an almost unbroken chain till his death on the field of battle. A bold initiative in attack was his guiding principle. Against frightening odds he regained Jewish religious independence and rededicated the profaned temple. His lifetime witnessed also the death of Antiochus and the alliance with Rome. See *HNTT,* pp. 464-68. In the poetic panegyric in his praise (3:2-9) he is aptly likened to giant and lion. Selfless, a man of deeds and not words, he fought fanatically and singlemindedly for the faith of his fathers. Like the Homeric Agamemnon, he was a "king of men."

*Notes. 3:45ff.* A scene of infinite drama and pathos. Within sight of Jerusalem, occupied but soon to be regained, Judas and his followers accurately and expectantly enacted the sacred ritual. They then went forth in frenzy to a holy war. Before such men an Antiochus may well tremble.

*4:1-61.* The reader gasps at the defeats of the stronger Gorgias and Lysias and then at the bold reappropriation of the temple for God, literally under fire. The stones of the abomination of desolation were ejected with loathing (v. 43), but the altar of burnt offering posed a casuistic problem (vv. 44f.): which weighed more, the recent desecration or the former consecration? Because the matter could not be settled without a prophet and there had been none since Malachi, the stones were dismantled but carefully preserved for a later decision (Mish. *Middoth* i.6).

*5:5.* Greek *anathematízō* and Heb. *ḥāram* mean "devote to extermination" — as enemies of religion. Cf. Saul's orders to wipe out the Amalekites (1 S. 15) and his disobedience.

*5:16.* Greek *ekklēsía* signifies (1) a summoned pagan assembly; (2) the called Jewish theocracy; (3) the called Christian Church.

*5:19.* Disobedience brought dire consequences; see vv. 55-62.

*6:8.* The king's psychological ailment was plausibly attributed to remorse for sacrilege, which Josephus (*Ant.* xii.9.1 [357-59]), against Polybius, connected with the Jerusalem temple.

*6:37.* Probably two or three warriors rode each elephant, not thirty-two; see *APOT* and Wace. "Tower" doubtless meant a glorified saddle with protective canopy. Habituating the elephants to smaller accompanying animals (v. 36) and inciting them with fermented fruit liquors (v. 34) sound graphic and accurate. Eleazar, youngest brother of Judas, was crushed as he killed an elephant he thought carried Antiochus V Eupator (vv. 43-46).

*6:39.* Prose burst into Homeric poetry, in exquisite description.

*6:47-54.* The admission of Jewish defeat establishes the honesty of the writer. Note how the personal ambition of Lysias saved the Jews (v. 55), how the unscrupulous Lysias broke the treaty (v. 62), and how Syrian rivalry and intrigue for the throne saved Judas once again (7:4).

*7:5ff.* Cf. vv. 21ff. The contemptible apostate compatriots whom Judas had roughly treated hated him.

*7:8-20.* The sneaking treachery and inept, futile murderings of Bacchides brought no military advantage. He beguiled certain trusting Hasideans with the bait of a high priest Alcimus, of the right family though otherwise unworthy, but was rightly spurned by the sturdy, perceptive Judas. Judas and the Hasideans doubtless made uneasy bedfellows; cf. 2:42.

*7:26.* The relationships of Judas and Nicanor are very differently portrayed in 2 Macc. 14. Change of heart or treachery with a time interval might reconcile some of the statements, but probably the tradition itself contains a discrepancy.

*7:33.* Given religious freedom, the Jews did not mind praying for a secular overlord.

*8:1-32.* The Jewish approach to Rome aimed at freedom from the Syrian yoke — and Rome loved to curb larger powers by temporary magnanimity toward smaller ones. Cordial in its inception, tragic in its final outcome, this move of Judas is of profound significance in the history of religion. The writer's assessment of the Romans, secondhand and too laudatory (cf. v. 16) and also inaccurate in minor particulars (vv. 8, 15, etc.), is yet amazingly shrewd and balanced in essentials. But v. 13 has ominous undertones, perhaps imperfectly understood. Judas seemed, humanly speaking, to make a good policy move (v. 17), but it came too late to serve the immediate crisis and led to the ultimate downfall of his nation. His fatal misjudgment, often repeated in history, was that because the friendship of the larger power was prompt, it would also be disinterested.

*9:10-18.* The Jews' breathtaking courage and hours of stubborn resistance against a larger host resulted in final defeat and the fall of one of the greatest battle heroes of all ages — but defeat in a blaze of imperishable glory!

*E. Career of Jonathan, 9:23–12:53. Summary. 9:23-73.* The death of Judas left the patriots discomfited and leaderless. Famine and apostate reprisals encouraged by Bacchides caused much suffering, and Jonathan was pressed into command. Although Jonathan lacked the admirable selflessness and piety of Judas, his more earthy cunning and ruthlessness made him a skillful leader and brought him to pinnacles of worldly glory unconceived by Judas. Bacchides, endeavoring to crush him, found his efforts strangely thwarted.

*10:1-89.* Balas, probably a low-born pretender, styled himself Alexander son of Antiochus Epiphanes and challenged Demetrius for the Syrian crown (*see* ALEXANDER BALAS). His incredible rise was furthered by Demetrius's being obnoxious to Rome and hated by his own subjects for drunkenness and misrule. Demetrius, proud potentate at heart, offered Jonathan inadequate concessions; Jonathan cleverly profited but entirely ignored the other side of the bargain (vv. 10f.). Balas, knowing his man, bid higher for Jonathan's favor, recognizing his sovereignty and conceding him the high-priesthood (v. 20). Probably Jonathan neither knew nor cared whether his patron's blood was royal, desiring merely the best bargain. Demetrius, now maddened by lost opportunity, tried in magnificent style to outbid Balas (vv. 25-45), but the Jews distrusted him and threw in their lot with the pretender. Two years later, in 150, Demetrius fell in battle, and Balas triumphed (v. 50). The upstart, seeking to consolidate his prestige, married the daughter of Ptolemy VI Philometor, and his friend Jonathan rose with him — though the pomp of both men smacked somewhat of nouveau riche. In 148 a second Demetrius, son of the slain king, advanced his claims against Balas. He scornfully challenged Jonathan (vv. 70f.), but the Maccabean, more at home on the battlefield than in the royal purple, gained a resounding victory, which led him to further honors.

*11:1-74.* Ptolemy guilefully and slanderously turned against his new son-in-law Balas, minded to gain Syria for himself. He offered hypocritical support and his already married daughter to Demetrius. Balas was slain in battle, but Ptolemy himself died within days. The new Syrian monarch (*ca.* 144) was Demetrius II, but Trypho produced another claimant: young Antiochus son of Balas. Jonathan rode the rough seas of rival dynasties with remarkable skill but learned that Demetrius was not to be trusted.

*12:1-53.* Jonathan by embassy renewed covenant with Rome and forged friendship with Sparta. Both the Jews and Spartans believed that they had descended from Abraham. These foreign prestige alliances did not materially affect Jonathan's immediate problems in Palestine. Jonathan had a further brief period of military success, discomfiting the forces of Demetrius II. Trypho, ostensibly championing Antiochus, but with purely personal ambitions, desired to eliminate the formidable Jonathan, who was not really his enemy. With perfidious gestures of friendship he lured him, with a thousand men, into Ptolemais, only to massacre his men and take him prisoner. Jonathan, who was executed a little later in *ca.* 144, may have been an opportunist, but the Jews lost in him another leader of astonishing courage and skill.

*Notes. 9:23.* After Judas's death, the apostates, for whom the reader's dislike steadily grows, "peep out," as a snail from its shell — a literal translation of the vivid Gk. *ekkýptō*.

*9:40.* The murder of Jonathan's brother John was a dubious excuse for an ugly vendetta that might fall on the innocent. The incident is not to Jonathan's credit.

*9:43.* Contrast 2:31-38. Bacchides' hopes that Jonathan would show an equal sabbath strictness were disappointed.

*9:54-56.* High priest Alcimus, detestable above most apostates, more hostile than Bacchides, tried to pull down the wall of the inner court of the temple to obliterate the Jew-Gentile distinction. He died of a stroke, naturally interpreted as a divine judgment.

*9:58-73.* The patriot cause prospered in two years of respite; the apostates finally recalled Bacchides to hostilities. Jonathan had high morale and the verbal support of Rome. Bacchides failed dismally and then exacted deserved penalties from his own apostate friends (v. 69). Jonathan governed peaceably from 156 to 152.

*10:25-45.* The bait was tempting, and the fiscal details are historically important. Demetrius probably tried to bargain with the people against Jonathan. Ptolemais (v. 39), now held by Balas, was a reward requiring proximate support and ultimate victory for its realization.

*10:50.* 150 B.C.

*10:61.* "Pestilent men" — Gk. *ándres loimoí,* Vulg. *viri pestilentes* — was an admirable description from the Maccabean viewpoint. Cf. 15:21.

*11:10.* Balas was ill fitted for royal status, as Ptolemy knew, but the postulated intention of assassination was probably a fictitious pretext for treachery. The account of Josephus is discrepant (*Ant.* xiii.4.1 [80-82]).

*11:34.* The exemptions were for the orthodox patriots, not the hellenizers.

*11:53.* Demetrius II, enormously helped by the Jews

and Jonathan, perfidiously and to his own loss preferred greedy exaction to loyal and valuable friendship.

*12:9.* The tone shows the arrogance of a "chosen people."

*12:21.* The ethnic kinship probably rested on the gratuitous postulate of a nonexistent document — a diplomatic fiction convenient for the moment to both parties (cf. 14:20ff.).

*F. Career of Simon, Chs. 13–16. Summary. 13:1-53.* Simon had already distinguished himself in subordinate command (11:59; 12:35f.). In this fresh crisis, believing his brother dead, he stepped forward as leader with loyal acclaim. But Trypho really held Jonathan captive, offering his release for 100 talents of silver and two of his sons. Simon, realistically skeptical of Trypho's good faith but fearing compatriot misunderstanding, fulfilled these terms to the letter; Trypho then callously executed Jonathan. Simon buried his brother and erected magnificent family memorials at Modein. In 142 Trypho murdered young Antiochus and styled himself king in opposition to Demetrius II. Simon made friends with Demetrius, gained virtual political independence for Israel, and inaugurated what to some was a new Jewish calendar. Simon made himself master of Gaza (or Gazara, see note on v. 43) and Jerusalem.

*14:1-49.* Demetrius failed to prevail against Trypho and was captured. Simon was confirmed as high priest and ruler in an Israel temporarily peaceful; he demonstrated abilities not exclusively military. Friendship with the Spartans and Romans was reaffirmed. The Jews memorialized the deeds of Simon on tables of brass to be erected on Mt. Zion.

*15:1-41.* Antiochus VII Sidetes, son of Demetrius I and brother of Demetrius II, anxious to overthrow the usurper Trypho, sought Jewish friendship and right of passage. The Romans were cordial. Antiochus proved as dastardly as Trypho, and the clouds of war returned.

*16:1-24.* Simon, too old to fight, appointed his sons Judas and John. Unfortunately, through betrayed trust and the pleasures of wine, the father and two of the sons were trapped and killed just as Jonathan was; John Hyrcanus, however, escaped. The year 135 closed a forty-year family record of almost unparalleled contest between the Maccabees and their enemies.

*Notes. 13:43.* Gaza is probably an error for Gazara (so Josephus), an apostate city practicing idolatry. The (Gk.) *elépolis* was probably a wooden tower on wheels, brought close to the walls for attack.

*14:4.* The tranquillity lasted three or four years, not throughout Simon's career. The poetic praise of vv. 6-15 contains further exaggerations.

*14:14.* John the Baptist fulfilled Mal. 4:5. An earlier acknowledged realization would have superseded any hereditary monarchy.

*14:18f.* The munificent gift to Rome (cf. 14:24) was not wasted.

*16:13.* Ptolemy son of Abubus plotted to succeed the Maccabeans in Jewish sovereignty and made his victims drunk in order to murder them (v. 16). The escape of John Hyrcanus foiled his plan, but three good men succumbed to him.

*G. Conclusion.* 1 Maccabees is an unvarnished historical record of gripping sincerity, in which shining heroism and despicable treachery sharply contrast. The reader quickly and rather justly detests the apostate Jews, quislings, and renegades. The book, though basically honest, is a partisan document, and this reaction is precisely the one that the writer intended. 1 Maccabees says little of God or religion in specific terms, but it does show the patriotic and observant side of Judaism at its highest. For the historian, it provides one source of reliable information for the period between the prophet Malachi and the prophet John.

*III. Second Maccabees.–A. Literary Introduction.* 2 Maccabees was originally written in Greek, though certain limited quoted documents may be translations from Hebrew. Swete (*OTG*, III, 662-708) prints the A-text in full, with the variants from V and several minuscules. Versions in Syriac and Latin also exist. See further *HNTT*, pp. 499-506.

2 Maccabees was almost certainly put together by an Alexandrian Jew, who professedly epitomizes, from ch. 3 onward, a larger work in five books by the otherwise unknown Jason of Cyrene. It has been argued that the redactor was a poor hack and contrariwise that he transformed an unreadable treatise into a fine and popular book. The arguments for dismissing Jason as a figment of the writer's imagination seem insufficient: the Jason-redactor pattern may be accepted in outline, with frank admission that the work of the two men is intertangled beyond the resources of confident analysis. The question of dating is complicated and double-barreled. A round mediating figure might be 100 B.C. for Jason's work, 80 B.C. for that of the redactor, but other arguable options exist.

The second book is Pharisaic rather than Sadducean, cultic rather than military, theological rather than accurately historical, supernatural rather than objective. In fact, this is not Pharisaism at its best, and for once the better job seems to have emanated from the Sadducean school of thought. The Roman Church insists on the canonicity of the second book because it seems to support dogmas such as prayer for the dead, intercession of saints, and treasury of merits. Apart from this special interest, the second book is largely a variant presentation of the first, supplementing it particularly in the period just before and after Antiochus Epiphanes. The subjoined notes, presupposing the first book, will stress matters of fresh interest.

*B. Chs. 1–2.* The writer quotes two letters professedly from Jews of Palestine to Jews of Egypt, (1:1–2:18) and adds his own preface to the book (2:19-32). It has been widely suspected that the writer, honest perhaps in intention, was duped by worthless forgeries, and that these chapters should have been omitted. The ostensible purpose of the second letter is to persuade the Egyptian Jews to join their Palestinian coreligionists in celebrating two new anniversaries, the Festival of Lights or Hanukkah, memorializing Judas Maccabeus's rededication of the temple exactly three years after Antiochus Epiphanes had defiled it, and Nicanor's Day, celebrating the Jewish victory over the enemy general. With Hanukkah is associated the story of the miraculous preservation of sacred fire from the days of the first temple and the elaboration of the account into the days of Jeremiah.

Two of the writer's key themes make their first appearance in these chapters: the doctrine of reconciliation, 1:5, and his marked propensity to invoke the miraculous, 2:21.

*C. Historic Roots of the Maccabean Revolt, Chs. 3–7. Summary.* These chapters are a valuable supplement to 1 Maccabees. The first two show apostate Jews shamefully bartering their own sacred high-priesthood; the last three record the persecutions of heathendom.

*3:1-40.* Onias III was lawfully and peacefully serving as high priest *ca.* 187 when a jealous colleague Simon caused Apollonius to incite the greed of Seleucus IV king of Syria for the temple treasure. To the horror of all the pious, the king ordered Heliodorus to raid and appropriate. The officer, however, was circumvented in the temple itself by an apparition of horse and rider, scourged by two men in wondrous apparel, carried out as though dead, and revived by Onias.

*4:1-50.* Simon still attempted to overthrow Onias, but Jason, the high priest's own brother, supplanted him in office by bribing the new Syrian king Antiochus IV Epiphanes. Onias had served from 198 until 175. A thorough Hellenist, despising his ancestral religion and its most sacred office, Jason built a Greek gymnasium in Jerusalem itself. Three years later Menelaus, brother of Simon, offered Antiochus larger payment and ousted Jason from office. Pressed to meet his rash commitments, he robbed and sold temple vessels and had the protesting Onias murdered. An angry mob killed Lysimachus, a temple freebooter in league with Menelaus.

*5:1-27.* While Antiochus was in Egypt, Jerusalem witnessed prodigious celestial signs. Jason, falsely informed that the king had died, attempted to wrest back the high-priesthood from Menelaus, slaying many compatriots, but utterly failed. Antiochus returned in fury, punished Jerusalem, and, aided by Menelaus, plundered the temple. Judas Maccabeus retired with a few companions. (The second book never mentions Mattathias.)

*6:1-9.* The temple was heathenized, and death penalties for observing the Jewish faith were instituted.

*6:10–7:42.* This gruesome martyrology reflects on retribution as chastisement.

*Notes. 3:4.* This verse foreshadows the split between orthodox patriots and hellenizing apostates.

*3:24-34.* Cf. 2:21. The comments of 3:32 and 4:1 increase suspicion in the "miracle." The trick may be historical, but the horseman and angelic attendants were almost certainly temple attendants exercising their histrionic skill.

*4:7.* Jason, typically, had hellenized his true name of Joshua; v. 13 aptly describes his character.

*4:37.* If this is historical, it is a pleasing and unusual slant on Antiochus.

*5:2-4.* The "miracle," whether physical product of refraction and reflection, optical illusion, or genuine prodigy, had impressed the writer. Before "forty," a round and sacred number, the qualifying preposition *schedón* "almost," reads strangely.

*5:6.* Usurper Jason, unlike Menelaus, had been at least a high priest "of the blood," although his shameful conduct entirely negated this qualification. Note the theology of retribution, vv. 7-10.

*5:11-21.* Antiochus, greedy for temple treasure, found a feeble pretext in the crushed Jason. He, however, could not have succeeded in his impious purpose, the writer insisted, if the temple servants had been lawful and holy, for God would have blasted him in wrath. Note the doctrine of reconciliation in v. 20; cf. 1:5; 7:33; etc.

*5:25.* Cf. 1 Macc. 2:31-38; 2 Macc. 6:11; etc.

*5:27.* The silence concerning Mattathias is one of the puzzling discrepancies with the first book.

*6:1-9.* This account of the "abomination of desolation" occurring in 168 differs from 1 Maccabees.

*6:12-17.* This profound theological reflection on the purifying power and final mercy of God's judgment, has special reference to apostates.

*6:18-31.* The resistance under torture of Eleazar, innocent, distinguished nonagenarian, is deeply moving. To him the eating of pork was equivalent to the Christian denial of Christ. His positive eschatology, which gives glow and volition to his dying, comes out in v. 26. Cf. He. 11:35.

*7:1-42.* Seven brothers and their mother were martyred under like circumstances. Cf. 4 Macc. 8–18 for a longer account. Critics may speak of "detailed ghastliness," "poor rhetoric," or "an anguish that was once real and quivering" (*APOT,* I, 130f.), but if martyrdom means anything at all, these were noble exemplars. The developed theological and eschatological ideas of the chapter include creation *ex nihilo* (v. 28), the potential of gaining (v. 9) and losing (v. 29) eternal life, corporeal resurrection (v. 11) and its parallelism with conception (vv. 22f.), and the denial of resurrection for the wicked (v. 14).

*D. Career of Judas Maccabeus, Chs. 8–15. Summary.* The writer recounted in his own way, with exaggerations, distortions, and valuable additions, the story of 1 Macc. 3:1–9:22.

*Notes. 9:5.* The epithet applied to God, Gk. *panepóptēs,* really means all-observing, with the implication of action following observation.

*9:6.* This value judgment may contain elements both of theological interpretation and wishful thinking.

*9:13.* This further theological interpretation, sin beyond repentance, is not strictly relevant. Prov. 1:24-31; He. 10:26f.; 12:17; etc. refer to apostates, not heathens. Antiochus's intent to become a proselyte (v. 17) probably existed only in the writer's imagination. The king's letter to the Jews (vv. 19-27) is a nonsensical forgery.

*10:10.* The picture is misleading. Antiochus Eupator the new king is a mere child, Lysias the regent and real ruler.

*10:17-23.* Gross numerical hyperbole, with obvious discrepancy between v. 18 and v. 23. Susceptibility to bribery (v. 20) is here sharply punished.

*10:25-31.* The power of prayer is sufficient, without the celestial co-warriors. Cf. 11:8.

*11:1ff.* This campaign really belongs to the reign of Antiochus IV Epiphanes — so 1 Maccabees. There are numerous additional errors.

*11:13.* The Jews had profoundly impressed Lysias regardless of whether he acknowledged the power of their God to the extent claimed.

*12:15.* For Gk. *dynástēs,* well translated "potentate," see HR, p. 355; *TDNT,* II, *s.v.* (Grundmann). The NT applies the word both to human beings (Lk. 1:52; Acts 8:27) and to God (1 Tim. 6:15). The emphasis is on the power, not the person.

*12:16.* This verse contains another of the hyperboles that blemish the book.

*12:24, 40.* The Greek names (v. 24) and the heathen amulets concealed on the persons of unsuspected Jews (v. 40) show the permeation of Hellenism.

*12:43-45.* Neither canonical Scripture nor early Jewish literature outside the present passage contains injunctions to offer sacrifice or prayer for the dead. The mourner's kaddish of the Jewish liturgy (cf. J. H. Hertz, *Authorized Daily Prayer Book with Comm.* [1947], pp. 212f.) is used in memorial for the dead, not in intercession. The usual rabbinic approach (cf. T.B. *Zebahim* 9b) is *'yn kprh lmtym* — no atonement is to be made for the dead. Judaism seems to give no clearly documented support for the doctrine. Evangelical theology treats the doctrine of the second chance with considerable reserve. The Roman Catholic Church uses this passage to support the doctrines of purgatory and the communion of saints. The two sides are well stated in the *Catholic Encyclopedia,* IV, 653-58, and the *Protestant Dictionary* (1933), pp. 166-68. The *Dictionary* argues that Judas may merely have made a sin offering for his living soldiers, textual corruption suggesting the wrong interpretation, or, alternatively, that the epitomizer was a schismatic Egyptian Jew whose teaching cannot be accepted as orthodox. The second hypothesis seems more plausible. Cf. the LXX and Vulg. texts.

*13:4.* Gk. *basileús tṓn basiléōn* is a title of earthly kings now advanced to divine service. Cf. Rev. 17:14; 19:16; etc. Cf. also *TDNT,* I, *s.v.* (Kleinknecht, Schmidt).

*13:23.* Cf. 1 Macc. 6. Syrian throne rivalries, humanly speaking, saved Judaism from utter annihilation.

*14:24f.* Some hyperbole may be suspected. Cf. note on 1 Macc. 7:26.

*14:37-46.* The suicide of Razis, shorn of its unedifying and physiologically impossible conclusion, probably rests on fact. The author's apparent approval of suicide in certain circumstances is a further rebuttal of the canonicity of the book.

*15:1ff.* Inconsistent with 1 Macc. 2:41. The incident subjoined is probably unhistorical.

*15:12-16.* The doctrine of the treasury of merits, familiar in rabbinic and Catholic theology, is presupposed. Cf. notes on 12:43-45 above.

*15:30ff.* The punishment of Nicanor's exceptional sin (14:33) took an exceptional form, normally foreign to Judaism. His defeat inaugurated Nicanor's Day.

*15:37-39.* The author's epilogue.

*IV. Third, Fourth, and Fifth Maccabees.*–These books have never been part of either the Roman Catholic or Protestant canon. Their reputation for historical exactitude stands somewhat low, although a substratum of truth may be present. The professed events of 3 Maccabees are dated *ca.* 217 B.C., whatever the date of composition may be, and have no real connection with the Maccabees. Ptolemy IV Philopator visited the Jerusalem temple and insolently determined to enter the holy of holies, but he became divinely smitten with temporary paralysis. Infuriated, he schemed bitter revenge on his Jewish subjects in Egypt, but intoxicated elephants expected to trample them to death turned instead on their Egyptian masters, and Ptolemy was forced to respect the chosen people. The propaganda motive is obvious. *See* PSEUDEPIGRAPHA III.

4 Maccabees is a Jewish interpretation of Stoic philosophy, designed to prove reason stronger than passion and choosing Maccabean heroes as exemplars. *See* PSEUDEPIGRAPHA IV.

Recent study suggests that 5 Maccabees may be a composite of several first-century documents, some of which were possibly written originally in Hebrew. *See* PSEUDEPIGRAPHA V. The oldest surviving version is in Arabic.

*Bibliography.*–*Comms. and Intros.: APOT*; J. Bartlett, *First and Second Books of Maccabees* (*CBC*, 1973); E. Bickerman, *God of the Maccabees* (Eng. tr. 1979); J. Dancy, *Comm. on I Maccabees* (1954); W. A. Farmer, *Maccabees, Zealots and Josephus* (1956); J. A. Goldstein, *I Maccabees* (*AB*, 1976); M. Hengel, *Judaism and Hellenism* (2 vols., Eng. tr. 1974; repr. in one-vol. 1981), pp. 267-309; *HJP*², I, 125-233; *HNTT*, pp. 9-24, 461-522; W. S. McCullough, *History and Literature of the Palestinian Jews from Cyrus to Herod* (1975), pp. 105-142, 207-214; Pauly-Wissowa, XIV/1, 779-805; M. Pearlman, *The Maccabees* (1973); *RGG*, *s.v.* "Makkabäerbücher" (V. Luck);S. Tedesche and S. Zeitlin, *First Book of Maccabees* (1950); *Second Book of Maccabees* (1954).

*Specialized Studies:* F. M. Abel, *Livres des Maccabees (EtB*, 1949); H. Bénerot, *Beider Makkabäerbücher (Schrift des AT*, IV/4, 1931); R. L. Bensley, *Fourth Book of Maccabees and Kindred Documents in Syriac* (1895); J. G. Bunge, *Journal for the Study of Judaism*, 6 (1975), 1-46; 10 (1979), 166-178; H. Burgmann, *Journal for the Study of Judaism*, 9 (1978), 153-191; J. M. Geller, *JJS*, 32 (1979), 202-211; J. A. Goldstein, *HTR*, 68 (1975), 53-58; R. S. Hanson, *BASOR*, 216 (Dec. 1974), 21-23; F. Millar, *JJS*, 29 (1978), 1-21; K.-D. Schunk, *Quellen des I. und II. Makkabäerbuches* (1954); B. Z. Wacholder, *HUCA*, 49 (1978), 89-133; W. Wirgin, *PEQ*, 101 (1969), 15-20; 104 (1972), 104-110; 106 (1974), 141-46.

R. A. STEWART

**MACCABEUS.** *See* MACCABEES.

**MACEDONIA** mas-ə-dōn'ē-ə [Gk. *Makedonia*]; **MACEDONIAN** [Gk. *Makedōn*].

I. Land and Climate
II. Ethnic Identity of the Peoples
III. History
  A. Prehistory
  B. Bronze Age
  C. Historical Developments, 1125-550 B.C.
  D. Rise of the Macedonian State, 550-358 B.C.
  E. Philip II, 358-336 B.C.
  F. Alexander the Great, 336-323 B.C.
  G. Macedonia from 323 to 276 B.C.
  H. Antigonus II Gonatas and Decline, 276-148 B.C.
  I. Roman Rule, 148 B.C.-A.D. 44
  J. Macedonia after A.D. 44

*I. Land and Climate.*–Ancient Macedonia lay on the Balkan peninsula N of Greece, S of Illyria and Thrace, and E of Epirus. Its territory included the Haliacmon and Axius rivers and their tributaries, which flow SE to the Thermaic Gulf of the Aegean Sea. Most of the country is mountainous, cut by great river valleys, and remote from the sea. Unlike peninsular Greece, its climate is much more eastern European than Mediterranean, with summer and winter rains, severe winters, and very hot summers; this makes it suitable for most horses, cattle, sheep, cereals, and European fruits, but not for olives or figs.

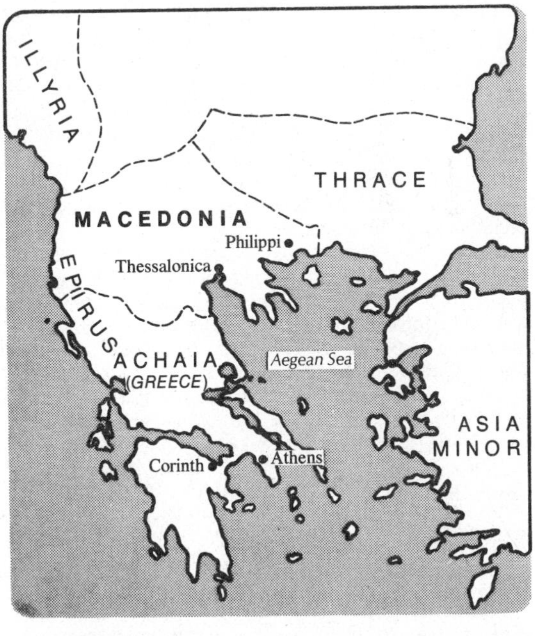


*II. Ethnic Identity of the Peoples.*–The Neolithic peoples in Macedonia were evidently related to similar groups in the Danube basin. Early in the Bronze Age (*ca.* 2800 B.C.) new immigrants from Anatolia brought copper-smithing skills. The cultural clash produced a vigorous ethnic mix that had contacts as far west as Hungary. During the Early Helladic period (*ca.* 2800-1900) the first Kurgan peoples entered Macedonia, evidently from the north and east. The Middle Helladic period (*ca.* 1900-1600) saw the first invasion, from the north, of Greek-speaking peoples. Some settled in Macedonia while others occupied Greece.

*III. History.*–*A. Prehistory.* The early Neolithic settlers of Macedonia were of various cultures. The southern settlers had well-developed architectural and artistic abilities; their artifacts include human clay figurines, chipped axes of serpentine, woolen garments, and beautiful serpentine figurines of frogs. The people of this period (*ca.* 6000-3000 B.C.) were clearly dependent upon the horse.

*B. Bronze Age.* The period from *ca.* 3000 to *ca.* 1125 B.C. chronicles the gradual formation of the cultures known collectively as "Greek." Greek dialects gradually displaced the old Illyrian and other languages, and the general culture remained tribal. Pottery, jewelry, and metalworking developed toward classical Greek forms but remained distinctly Macedonian; e.g., chiefs were usually buried in a tumulus tomb. Archeological evidence from about the Middle Helladic period points to an ethnic distinction between the preexisting local population and a ruling class of invading Indo-Europeans. This period had passed its zenith in material culture when contacts with Mycenaean civilization to the south (*ca.* 1350 B.C.) brought a new infusion of ideas in warfare, art, and technology.

*C. Historical Developments, 1125-550 B.C.* Around 1125 B.C. a major technological breakthrough occurred throughout Greece and Macedonia: the making of iron. Iron was used first for making knives, later for swords, then for other weapons and tools such as plow points. This metallurgical advance — which may have come with the Phrygian invaders — coincided with the emergence of a vigorous culture and burgeoning literacy throughout the entire Middle East. But it was also a time of great cultural dislocations, immigrations, and incessant wars. Thus the Dorians, evidently speakers of Western Greek, invaded southwestern Thessaly during the 12th cent. B.C., possibly due to displacement by the Phrygians (Appian *Bella Civilia Romana* ii.39) who now occupied Macedonia. Later, *ca.* 700 B.C., an invasion by the Cimmerians from Anatolia shattered an Illyrian dominance that had begun *ca.* 800 B.C. Within this instability, sometime after 650 B.C., the Macedonian monarchy was founded by Perdiccas I (Herodotus viii.139). The Macedones controlled most of the mountains and the coastal plain.

*D. Rise of the Macedonian State, 550-359 B.C.* The Macedones did not long maintain their dominance. The Paeonian tribes of the interior immediately gained power and broke through to the coast. They remained in power until Darius invaded Scythia *ca.* 513 B.C. Persian control directed Macedonian trade — and therefore its culture — eastward. Macedonian silver and timber were in demand by both Persians and Greeks. During the Persian advances of 483-480 only Macedonia evaded Persian suspicions, partially because the Persian triremes were built of Macedonian timber. After the withdrawal of Xerxes in 480 the Persians allowed Alexander I, seventh king of the Macedonians, to expand his territory. Alexander also cultivated relations with Greek city-states, but he was killed before Xerxes' assassination in 466 B.C. Free from Persian interference, Perdiccas II, son of Alexander, made his way to power by deception. By 434 he was at war with Athens, but almost immediately he turned about to ally with Athens against his Macedonian neighbors. His erratic relationship with Athens persisted until his death at the hands of the Illyrians in 359.

*E. Philip II, 358-337 B.C.* At the death of Perdiccas II in 359 B.C. Macedonia was thrown into disarray. The army came together (a Macedonian custom) and acclaimed Philip II their new ruler. He immediately set out to neutralize the threat of the Paeonians, Thracians, and Illyrians. Philip was successful in both war and diplomacy. By 357 he had brilliantly defeated his enemies and contracted the first two of at least six political marriages. By his third wife, Olympias the daughter of King Arybbas of Epirus, he fathered Alexander, later called "the Great." Philip campaigned throughout Greece, Thessaly, Epirus, and as far east as Byzantium. In addition, he functioned as a judge (cf. Plutarch *Moralia* 178A-179C) and appointed judges at his court at Pella in eastern Macedonia. He developed the Macedonian institution of the "Companions" (or retinue) of the king, selecting Greeks as well as Macedonians to serve as his advisors, confidants, and deputies. (This group later became Alexander's formal Council.)

Krater with bacchic scene. From Derveni, 2nd half of the 4th cent. B.C. (Archaeological Museum of Thessalonike, Republic of Greece)

A man of culture, Philip successfully persuaded Aristotle to become Alexander's tutor. Philip's assassination in 336 by a Macedonian noble was described by Aristotle as murder for personal revenge (*Pol.* v.1311b). *See also* PHILIP **1.**

Recent archeological excavations at Vergina have shed further light on this period of history. Vergina is almost certainly ancient Aegeae, the burial place of all the Macedonian kings except Alexander the Great. In 1949 archeologists began a systematic excavation of the Great Tumulus at Vergina, which was so imposing (12.5 m. [41 ft.] high and 110 m. [360 ft.] in diameter) that scholars believed it to be the burial place of Macedonian royalty. In 1977 excavators discovered an older, smaller tumulus beneath the southwest edge of the Great Tumulus. Within this smaller tumulus was a masonry tomb (3.50 by 2.09 m. [11.5 by 6.9 ft.]) that had been one of three: two built beneath the ground and one above, but all covered by the Great Tumulus. The first tomb, clearly of the 4th cent. B.C. and decorated with magnificent frescoes, had been robbed in antiquity. The second, equally beautifully decorated,

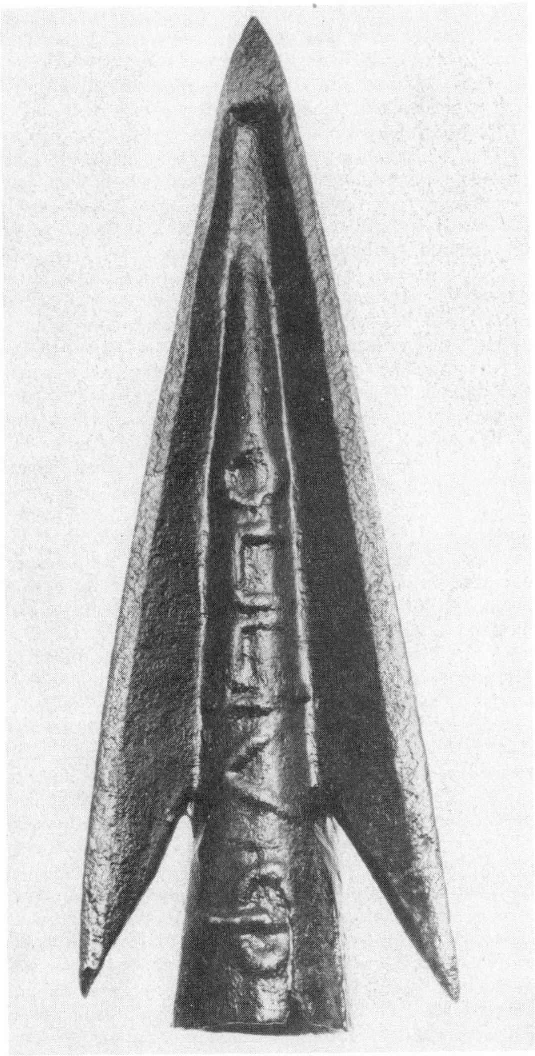

Bronze arrowhead inscribed *Philippo,* "of Philip," from Olynthos (Archaeological Museum of Thessalonike, Republic of Greece)

was unexpectedly intact. Its inner chamber measured 4.46 by 4.46 m. (14.6 by 14.6 ft.) and was separated from its antechamber by a marble door. The finds from this inner chamber included bronze and silver vessels, remains of a richly decorated shield, an iron helmet, a sword, a cuirass with a gold plaque of the head of Athena in relief, and remains of a diadem and a scepter — all dated *ca.* 350-325 B.C., pointing almost certainly to Philip II as the Macedonian king buried here. Within the marble sarcophagus was found a footed, gold larnax or box, measuring 40 by 33.5 by 17 cm. high (15.7 by 13.2 by 6.7 in.) and containing bones and ash. A series of small ivory heads (remnants of statuettes) included two that resembled well-known portraits of Philip and Alexander and also one identified by the excavator as Olympias. Within the antechamber was another marble sarcophagus with a gold box containing bones and a woman's diadem. M. Andronikos, the excavator, believed that the woman was Cleopatra, Philip's last wife; it is also possible, however, that she was the Scythian King Atheas's daughter (Justinus ix.2.1-6).

*F. Alexander the Great, 336-323 B.C.* ALEXANDER THE GREAT (mentioned in 1 Macc. 1:1 and 6:2 as "the son of Philip the Macedonian") spent the greater part of his short but energetic reign outside Macedonia. Antipater, Philip's trusted general and ambassador, now served as the young king's deputy in Macedonia. There he quelled rebellions and dispatched relief troops to Alexander. Alexander in turn sent back prodigious sums he had gained through conquest, enabling him to avoid taxing the Macedonians. Although he ruled ably, Antipater had trouble with Olympias, who apparently warned her son that Antipater's powerful position might threaten Alexander's own place. Alexander sent the Macedonian troops home in 324 under Craterus, who was to replace Antipater upon arrival. But the replacement never occurred, because Alexander died in Babylon on June 10, 323 B.C., at the age of thirty-two, master of Greece, Macedonia, Asia, Egypt, and the Fertile Crescent as far as India.

*G. Macedonia from 323 to 276 B.C.* Upon Alexander's death a tremendous power struggle broke out among his generals, who divided up the satrapies and attempted to take control of the whole empire. By 321 war had erupted among the "Successors" (Diodochi) of Alexander. The rule of Macedonia proper (and control of Greece) fell to Antipater. He formed a coalition with Antigonus of Phrygia and Ptolemy I of Egypt against Perdiccas of the house of Orestis, who had taken control of Asia. After Perdiccas's defeat and death, the united Macedonian armies proclaimed Antipater regent, an office he held until his death in 319. He was succeeded by the ineffectual Polyperchon. By 316, however, Antipater's son Cassander had seized control of Macedonia and Greece (Diodorus xix.52). His death in 298 resulted in civil war. Demetrius took control in 294, but in 288 he failed to prevent Thrace and Epirus from partitioning Macedonia. Lysimachus of Thrace ruled Macedonia from 285, in addition to Thessaly and part of Asia, until his death in battle in 281. Invading Gauls killed King Ceraunus in 279 B.C. Into this state of anarchy and chaos stepped Antigonus II Gonatus, son of Demetrius, who had just defeated the Gauls in Thrace. In 276 he was accepted by the army as king (Polybius ii.45; ix.29).

*H. Antigonus II Gonatus and Decline, 276-148 B.C.* Antigonus and the Antigonid dynasty ruled until the Roman invasion of 168 B.C. Antigonus represented a return to some of the older Macedonian values. He cultivated the Stoic philosophers Menedemus and Zeno, reestablished Pella as his capital, and earned his subjects' gratitude by his moderate policies. He won the Chremonidean War against Athens and its allies in 262 B.C. and restored Macedonia proper to its fullest historical boundaries. Together with Antiochus II of Syria he won a naval victory over Ptolemy II Philadelphus, thus gaining control of the Aegean Sea. But in 243 he lost Corinth, a key city, through revolt. He died *ca.* 239 B.C. without regaining Corinth and left his son Demetrius II a defensive war with the Aetolian and Achaean Leagues.

This melancholy decline continued largely unabated until the accession of Philip V in 221. By 215 Philip had joined with Hannibal of Carthage in an attempt to drive Rome from Illyria. Despite Rome's alliance with Aetolia in the First Macedonian War (212-205), Philip was victorious. But Roman military might was now looming large, and Macedonian forces were exhausted by generations of war. The Romans finally defeated Philip at the close of the Second Macedonian War (197 B.C.). The rest of the period to 148 B.C. saw a rapid decline in Macedonia's independence. The crowning blow came in 168 B.C., when Philip's son Perseus (cf. 1 Macc. 8:5) was utterly defeated at Pydna by the Roman consul Paulus at the end of the Fourth Macedonian War (Polybius xxix.17-21; Plutarch

Alexander the Great in Heliopolitan costume, reflecting his belief that he was the son of Amon-Re, the Egyptian sun-god whose main temple was at Heliopolis (Louvre)

*Aemilius Paulus* xvi-xxii). Rome now turned vengeful, dividing Macedonia into four republics (Pella, Thessalonica, Amphipolis, and Pelagonia) and elevating the old leagues to a position of power equal with Macedonia (Livy xlv.17f., 29f.). Macedonia played almost no role in world politics until it was made a Roman province twenty years later.

*I. Roman Rule, 148 B.C.-A.D. 44.* For two decades after the battle of Pydna Macedonia continued to decline. Then in 149 a certain Andriscus arose, claiming to be Philip the son of Perseus. This false "Philip" scored a victory over a small Roman force in Thessaly in 148, but later that same year he was defeated by the Roman praetor Metellus and sent to Rome for execution. Rome solved the problem of administering this troubled area by making it a province. Thus when the old Achaean League declared war on Sparta in 148, Rome intervened from Macedonia. Metellus razed Athens, massacred the male citizens, and sold the women and children as slaves. Rome dissolved the Achaean League and made Greece a Roman protectorate administered from Macedonia. Interestingly, the apocryphal Additions to Esther, dating from this time, include a false accusation by Artaxerxes that Hamman was a Macedonian bent upon overthrowing the Persian empire (Ad. Est. 16:10, 14). Without an Athens or Corinth to attract peripatetic philosophers, Macedonia sank slowly into obscurity. When Mithridates Eupator of Pontus in Asia rose against Rome in 88 B.C., many Macedonians joined him, but Rome seemed not to notice Macedonian complicity. This was fortunate, for the Romans razed rebellious Greek cities to the ground, in some cases so thoroughly that they virtually disappeared from history.

In 27 B.C. Augustus perceived the political and cultural differences between Macedonia and Greece and separated them into the two provinces of Macedonia and Achaia. While the Greeks held to a democratic ideal, the Macedonians remained monarchic. The Caesars saw to it that the Via Egnatia, the existing major west-east route through Macedonia, was paved, maintained, and elevated to imperial status. This highway led from Apollonia in the west to Thessalonica (which Augustus had allowed to remain a free city) in the east. Economically the province prospered, but politically it remained submissive. Macedonians, unlike Greeks, were sought for military conscription, especially for the imperial guard. No significant changes occurred until A.D. 44, when Claudius made Macedonia again a senatorial province. The spirit of Philip II had died out in Macedonia.

*J. Macedonia after A.D. 44.* The political fortunes of Macedonia did not improve after Tiberius. Yet this politically depressed province figured prominently in Paul's second and third missionary journeys. During Paul's second journey he and Silas sailed from Asia to Thrace, then walked or rode by way of the Via Egnatia to Philippi (Acts 15:36–16:40). After their escape from the Philippian prison they traveled through Amphipolis and Apollonia to Thessalonica (17:1-9), again on the Via Egnatia, but then moved SW to Beroea of Macedonia (vv. 10-13). On his third journey he sent Timothy and Erastus to an unnamed locality in Macedonia (19:22) while he stayed in Asia. Later, Paul traveled again to Macedonia but continued on to Greece (20:1f.). He returned to Troas of Asia via Macedonia (v. 3), this time accompanied by — among others — Macedonian believers (v. 4). In his correspondence Paul spoke of the Macedonian Christians or of the province at least sixteen times in six letters (Romans, 1 and 2 Corinthians, Philippians, 1 Thessalonians, 1 Timothy). He addressed three letters to Macedonian congregations (Philippians, 1 and 2 Thessalonians). "Macedonia and Achaia" are mentioned together three times by Paul (Rom. 15:26; 1 Thess. 1:7f.) and once by Luke (Acts 19:21); this reflects the order of Paul's reception in Europe but also the political reality of the two provinces of Greece that contained Pauline churches. On Paul's final trip to Rome, he and Luke were accompanied by "Aristarchus, a Macedonian from Thessalonica" (Acts 27:2), who is surely the same companion mentioned in 20:4.

Apart from the Pauline references, we know about Macedonia at this period only from the action of Emperor Nero (A.D. 54-68), who proclaimed "the freedom of Greece." This actually meant that Achaia was again split off from Macedonia. Trajan (96-117) heavily taxed the upper classes to support his wars in Dacia and Parthia. The later wars with Parthia (161-165) resulted in a plague that devastated the population not only in Macedonia but throughout the empire. A century later Macedonia had to absorb the invading Goths. Yet in this unhappy atmosphere Christianity took root and flourished. As early as the reign of Diocletian (A.D. 284-305) there were sufficient numbers of Christians in this area to warrant a diocese

Site of Herod's fortress overlooking the Dead Sea from the east. In the background is the plateau of Judah (A. D. Baly)

of Moesia, which included Achaia and Macedonia. In 383 the Christian emperor Theodosius condemned "Macedonianism," a heresy that insisted on the created nature of the Holy Spirit. Archeological evidence for churches is extensive and continues to witness to the "Christianization" of this province.

*See also* GREECE.

***Bibliography.***–M. Andronikos, *Archaeology,* 31 (1978), 33-41; A. E. R. Boak, *History of Rome to 565 A.D.* (4th ed. 1955); S. Casson, *Macedonia, Thrace, and Illyria: Their Relations to Greece from the Earliest Times down to the Time of Philip Son of Amyntas* (1926); J. R. Hamilton, *Alexander the Great* (1973); N. G. L. Hammond, *History of Macedonia* (2 vols., 1972, 1979); *Greek, Roman, and Byzantine Studies,* 19 (1978), 331-350; F. Hooper, *Roman Realities* (1979); P. W. Lehmann, *American Journal of Archaeology,* 84 (1980), 527-531; G. H. Macurdy, *Hellenistic Queens* (1932); T. Mommsen, *History of Rome* (5 vols., Eng. tr. 1957); *History of Rome: The Provinces from Caesar to Diocletian* (Eng. tr. 1887); H. H. Scullard, *From the Gracchi to Nero* (3rd ed. 1970).

J. F. STRANGE

**MACHAERUS** ma-kē'rəs [Gk. *Machairous*]. A mountain fortress, second in strength to Jerusalem, identified with the modern Mukâwer, overlooking the eastern shore of the Dead Sea. It was fortified first by Alexander Janneus (*BJ* vii.6.2 [171-77]) and then demolished by Gabinius (*BJ* i.8.5 [167f.]; *Ant.* xiv.5.4 [90]). Herod the Great established a residence on the site and refortified it (*BJ* vii.6.1f. [163-177]). On his death the citadel was assigned to Herod Antipas, and following the rule of Antipas it became a Roman garrison until the Jewish uprising in A.D. 66, when the Jews captured it. The Romans under Lucilius Bassus recaptured and destroyed it in 72.

Josephus stated that the Nabatean wife of Herod Antipas asked to be sent there when she became aware of her husband's infidelity, because the region was allegedly subject to her father Aretas (*Ant.* xviii.5.1 [111f.]). It seems more likely, however, that Machaerus served as a prison for Antipas's wife. Josephus also suggested that John the Baptist was imprisoned and beheaded there (xviii.5.2[119]). Descriptions of the palace, which was situated on the slope of the mountain (elevation 720 m., 2360 ft.), suggest that Antipas probably lived there in the summer to escape the heat of Tiberias and hence could have housed John there. The beheading related in Mk. 6:14-29, however, may well have occurred in a prison farther north.

The ruins in the area have not yet been excavated.

See C. Kopp, *Holy Places of the Gospels* (1963), pp. 141f.

G. L. BORCHERT

**MACHBANNAI** mak'ba-nī [Heb. *makbannay*]; AV, NEB, MACHBANAI. One of the mighty warriors from the tribe of Gad who joined David at Ziklag and were appointed officers of his troops (1 Ch. 12:13 [MT 14]).

**MACHBENAH** mak-bē'nə [Heb. *makbēnâ*; Gk. *Machabēna*]. A name recorded in the genealogy of Judah in 1 Ch. 2:49. It is considered to have been a settlement of the sons of Caleb in the Judean hills S of Beth-zur and Hebron (*LBHG,* rev. ed., p. 248; cf. NEB). BDB, p. 460, suggests identifying Cabbon (Josh. 15:40) with Machbenah (both names may be from the same Hebrew root, *kbn*), but this is speculative.

J. McKENNA

**MACHI** mā'kī [Heb. *mākî*]. A man from the tribe of Gad whose son Geuel was chosen as one of the twelve spies (Nu. 13:15).

**MACHIR** mā'kər [Heb. *mākîr*]; **MACHIRITES** mā'kər-īts [Heb. *mākîrî*]; NEB also MACHIRITE FAMILY.

**1.** The firstborn son of Manasseh (Gen. 50:23; Josh. 17:1); the father of Gilead (Nu. 26:29; 27:1; 36:1; Josh. 17:3; 1 Ch. 2:21, 23; etc.). The genealogy of 1 Ch. 7:14-19, which appears to have undergone significant textual disruption, lists Manasseh's Aramean concubine as Machir's mother (v. 14); it names Maacah first as Machir's sister (v. 15) and later as his wife (v. 16).

In the distribution of the land in the Transjordan under Moses, the family of Machir was given the region of Bashan and Gilead (Nu. 32:40; Dt. 3:15; Josh. 13:29-31; *see* Vol. I, Map VI), apparently because Machir and his sons had fought for and conquered the area (Nu. 32:39; cf. Josh. 17:1). Machir's military exploits must have been memorable, for he is one of the select few designated by name as a "man of war" (Josh. 17:1; cf. David, 2 S. 17:8; Goliath, 1 S. 17:23; Yahweh, Ex. 15:3).

The relationship between the tribal names Manasseh and Machir is problematic. According to Nu. 32:33, 39f.; Josh. 13:29-31; etc., Machir is identified with the half-tribe of Manasseh (or at least the main part of it) that settled E of the Jordan (see Boling and Wright). But the Song of Deborah, one of the oldest passages in the OT, names Machir (instead of the western half-tribe of Manasseh) among the tribes W of the Jordan that went out to do battle against the Canaanites (Jgs. 5:14). These passages suggest that at one time the name Machir could refer to the whole tribe of Manasseh. This problem has also been explained by various theories about the migrations of the Machirite clan (see, e.g., Aharoni and Avi-Yonah, Noth, and Soggin).

**2.** A namesake of the earlier Machir from the half-tribe of Manasseh in the Transjordan; son of Ammiel. He was a wealthy man who lived in Lo-debar in the region of Gilead. After the death of Saul and Jonathan, Machir sheltered Jonathan's son Mephibosheth until David brought Mephibosheth to Jerusalem and restored his princely status (2 S. 9:4f.; cf. Josephus *Ant.* vii.5.5 [113-16]). During the revolt of Absalom, Machir aided David and his troops at Mahanaim by supplying them with beds, vessels, and foodstuffs (2 S. 17:27-29; cf. *Ant.* vii.9.8 [230f.]).

***Bibliography.***–Y. Aharoni and M. Avi-Yonah, *Macmillan Bible Atlas* (rev. ed. 1977), p. 48; R. G. Boling and G. E. Wright, *Joshua* (*AB*, 1982), pp. 333, 347; M. Noth, *History of Israel* (Eng. tr. rev. ed. 1960), pp. 61f., 73 n. 1; J. A. Soggin, *Joshua* (Eng. tr., *OTL*, 1972), pp. 159, 181; M. H. Woudstra, *Book of Joshua* (*NICOT*, 1981), pp. 223f., 263.

D. H. ENGELHARD N. J. O.

**MACHMAS** mak'məs (1 Macc. 9:73, AV). *See* MICHMASH.

**MACHNADEBAI** mak-nad'ə-bī [Heb. *maḵnaḏᵉḇay*] (Ezr. 10:40); NEB MAKNADEBAI. A son of Binnui; one of the Israelites who were required to divorce their foreign wives. Machnadebai is unusual as a Hebrew name form, and the text may be corrupt. Some have conjectured, on the basis of the LXX of the parallel name list in 1 Esd. 9:34, that the text originally read "of the sons of Ezora" (Heb. *mibbᵉnê-ʿazzûr*). In 1 Esd. 9:34 the RSV renders "Machnadebai" for LXX *Mamnitanaimos* (AV Mamnitanaimus; NEB Mamnitanaemus) in an attempt to reconcile the two lists of names. This rendering, however, is quite unlikely, since the names that precede and follow "Machnadebai" on the two lists do not match.

See comms., especially L. H. Brockington, *Ezra, Nehemiah and Esther* (*NCBC*, repr. 1977); J. M. Myers, *I and II Esdras* (*AB*, 1974).

N. J. O.

**MACHPELAH** mak-pē'lä [Heb. *maḵpēlâ*–prob. 'double'; Gk. *tó diploún*]. A field E of Mamre, with trees and an adjacent cave, in the western part of what was later Hebron. The name (with the article; cf. the LXX) may somehow describe the form of the cave. Abraham bought Machpelah from Ephron the Hittite for 400 shekels of silver and buried his wife Sarah there (Gen. 23:8-16). Later he (25:9), Isaac, Rebekah, Leah (49:31), Jacob (50:13), and possibly others were buried there.

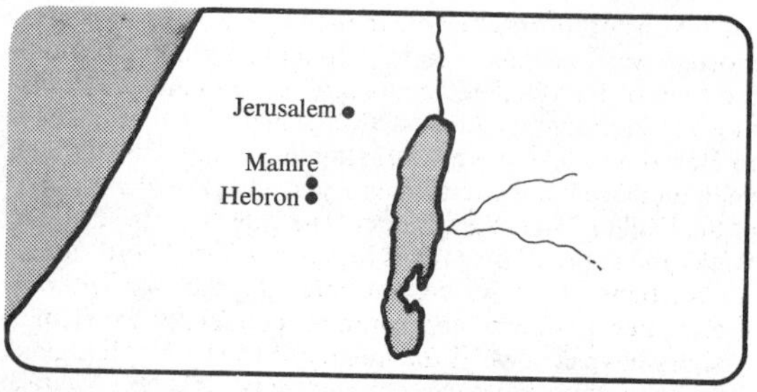


Modern research, comparing Abraham's transaction with ancient Assyrian and Hittite laws, lends verisimilitude to Gen. 23. The trees growing in the field, the bargaining of Abraham and Ephron, the weighing of the silver used for payment, and the witnesses who sat at the city gate, where the sale was made, all accord with Hittite laws, forgotten at the dissolution of the Hittite kingdom *ca.* 1200 B.C. Ephron's desire to sell the entire field, although Abraham asked for just "the cave of Machpelah . . . which is in the end of his field" (v. 9), is connected with the law and feudal practice of the period. According to the Hittite collection of laws found in Boghazköy, the buyer was to submit to certain feudal duties (taxation and other hardships) if he bought all the property of the seller. If just part of the property was sold, these duties remained with the seller. Ephron probably demanded that Abraham buy the entire field (v. 11) so that the latter would become a vassal responsible for the whole field. *See also* HITTITES III.

Josephus (*BJ* iv.9.7 [530f.]) mentioned that a monument of the patriarchs stood in Hebron in the days of Jesus. A pilgrim in A.D. 333 told of the extraordinary beauty of the cave tombs. Today the cave tomb lies at the southern end of a mosque, Ḥarâm el-Khalîl (Abraham's mosque). A massive stone wall (its area 61 m. by 34 m. [197 ft. by 111 ft.]) surrounds the cave, above which is, among other things, Sarah's memorial tomb. The area has not been excavated.

Mosque built over the patriarchal tomb in the cave of Machpelah (J. Finegan)

Certain authorities believe that on the site of the present mosque was once an important building dating as early as the time of Herod. The square wall surrounding the cave mosque is probably the best extant masonry dating back to Herod and may even antedate him. In any case, it has been found to belong to the same period as the lower parts of the Wailing Wall of Jerusalem. The wall is 2.6 m. (8.5 ft.) thick, and some of the stones are over 7.3 m. (24 ft.) long.

Christians and Jews cannot enter the mosque without special permission of the supreme council of Moslems. Visitors have described the memorial tombs of Abraham, Isaac, and their wives as covered with richly decorated cloths. The actual cave tomb lies under the monument. A memorial tomb W of the Mosque of Women at Machpelah marks the traditional site of Joseph's grave, but according to Josh. 24:32 Joseph was buried in Shechem.

A. A. SAARISALO

**MACRON** mā'kron [Gk. *Makrōn*]. Ptolemy Macron, who had been appointed governer of Cyprus by Ptolemy VI Philometor king of Egypt but deserted to Antiochus IV Epiphanes king of Syria (2 Macc. 10:12f.). Under the rule of Antiochus V Eupator, successor of Antiochus IV Epiphanes, Macron espoused pro-Jewish policies, was accused of treason by the king's supporters, and consequently poisoned himself and died.

Opinions differ whether Ptolemy Macron is to be identified as Ptolemy son of Dorymenes, whose attitude toward the Jews was different. According to 1 Macc. 3:38–4:25, when Antiochus IV was in Persia, LYSIAS (1) chose Ptolemy son of Dorymenes along with two others to lead in battle against Judas Maccabeus, who defeated their army of 47,000 men.

The account in 2 Macc. 8:8f. that identifies Ptolemy son of Dorymenes as governor of Coelesyria and Phoenicia, one of the seventy-two satrapies of Antiochus IV's kingdom, is perhaps more accurate than the parallel in 1 Macc. 3:38ff. Ptolemy son of Dorymenes was bribed by Menelaus (2 Macc. 4:45-47) and then pursuaded Antiochus IV to clear Menelaus of the accusations made against him by the Jews. 2 Macc. 6:8 further reveals this Ptolemy's hostility toward the Jews by stating that he issued the order for Jews to conform with Greek customs and sacrifices (cf. Goldstein, *II Maccabees*, pp. 268, 276-78).

***Bibliography***.–J. A. Goldstein, *I Maccabees* (*AB*, 1976); *II Maccabees* (*AB*, 1983); S. Tedesche and S. Zeitlin, *II Maccabees* (1954), pp. 142-191.

R. L. OMANSON

**MAD; MADNESS; MADMAN** [Heb. pual and hithpael of *šāga'* (Dt. 28:34; 1 S. 21:14 [MT 15]; 2 K. 9:11; Hos. 9:7; pual and hithpael part., 1 S. 21:15 [MT 16]; Jer. 29:26), *šiggā'ôn* (Dt. 28:28; Zec. 12:4), poel part. and hithpoel of *hālal* (1 S. 21:13 [MT 14]; Eccl. 2:2; Jer. 50:38; 51:7), *hôlēlôṯ* (Eccl. 1:17; 2:12; 7:25; 9:3), *hôlēlûṯ* (Eccl. 10:13), hithpalpel part. of *lāhah* (Prov. 26:18); Gk. *maínomai* (Jn. 10:20; Acts 12:15; 26:24f.; 1 Cor. 14:23), *manía* (Acts 26:24), *paraphronéō* (2 Cor. 11:23), *paraphronía* (2 Pet. 2:16)]; AV also BESIDE ONESELF (Acts 26:24), FOOL (2 Cor. 11:23); NEB also CRAZY, RAVING, etc. In all cases the English words refer to exceptional mental states and intense inward excitement. It would be a mistake, however, to assume that the biblical terms they translate all have the same meaning or that they can be understood in any modern, clinical sense.

The verb *hālal* and cognate nouns *hôlēlôṯ* and *hôlēlûṯ* denote foolish, irrational behavior. The author of Ecclesiastes usually links these terms with *siḵlûṯ*/*śiḵlûṯ* ("foolishness, folly"; e.g., 2:12; 10:13). H. Cazelles suggested that the root meaning is "nothingness, powerlessness," and that the terms therefore refer to worthless activity (*TDOT*, III, 412f.; cf. Eccl. 2:2, 12). The verb seems to connote insanity in 1 S. 21:13, however, which states: "So he [David] changed his behavior before them, and feigned himself mad in their hands, and made marks on the doors of the gate, and let his spittle run down his beard." (The verb *šāga'* is used in vv. 14f.) *Hālal* is used to describe the senselessness of idolatry in Jer. 50:38 and drunken behavior in 51:7.

Less benign are the verb *šāga'* and its derivative noun *šiggā'ôn*, which refer to being driven to despair or wildness. Madness here means panic or lack of control, with the implication that some stress has provoked extreme anxiety and an inability to cope. In Dt. 28:34 Moses warns the Israelites that the horrifying curses that will befall them if they disobey God's commandments will be too much to bear: "you shall be driven mad by the sight which your eyes shall see." Zec. 12:4 promises that God will strike panic in the hearts of Judah's enemies. Prophets were sometimes accused of being madmen, perhaps because they foresaw the events about which they prophesied and were frightened by the future (cf. 2 K. 9:11; Jer. 29:26; Hos. 9:7). The prophets' strange behavior resulting from their ecstatic experiences may also have contributed to their reputation for madness (*see also* PROPHECY III.D).

In Prov. 26:18 "a madman" is used to translate the hithpalpel part. of *lāhah* ("startle," "amaze," "stupefy"). The emphasis here is on the wild and dangerous behavior of the madman.

Like the OT prophets, Jesus and His followers are sometimes accused of being "mad." The Greek verb *maínomai* ("rave, be crazed, be out of one's mind") is applied several times to those who bring an incredible message. In Acts 12:15 the disciples call Rhoda "mad" when she announces Peter's miraculous deliverance from prison. Similarly, Festus, having heard Paul's testimony, says to him, "Paul, you are mad; your great learning is turning you mad" (26:24). Here much learning is compared with strong drink's capacity to rob a person of his better judgment; thus Paul defends himself by saying that he is "sober" (v. 25). In 1 Cor. 14:23 Paul admonishes the early Christians that visitors who witness the whole congregation speaking in tongues might think them mad. An important use of this term occurs in Jn. 10:20, where the unbelieving Jews react to Jesus' message by saying, "He has a demon, and he is mad; why listen to him?" The two accusations mean the same thing for in first-century Palestine insanity was thought to be the result of demonic possession. While those who believed Jesus' words recognized them as coming from God, to unbelievers they were madness.

Both the verb *paraphronéō* and its cognate noun *paraphronía* refer to thinking that occurs outside of or beside the mind. In 2 Cor. 11:23 Paul applies the verb to himself in order to indicate his awareness that the boasting in which he is engaging is irrational behavior for an apostle. He implies that what he is saying comes from outside his normal mind and is different from his customary way of thinking. The writer of 2 Pet. 2:16 describes the "prophet" Baalam, "who loved gain from wrong doing" (v. 15), as having been "out of his mind" until he was restrained by an ass speaking with a human voice.

The Apocrypha uses "mad" or "madness" to translate several other Greek terms. Gk. *ánoia* (2 Macc. 14:5) basically means "unreason." The same term is rendered "fury" (in the sense of an irrational rage) in Lk. 6:11 and "folly" in 2 Tim. 3:9. The cognate term *apónoia* (2 Macc. 6:29) refers to an even more intense loss of all sense. On the other hand, the verb *agrióō* (3 Macc. 5:2) implies wildness and savagery.

In OT times people pitied and were in awe of both prophets and the insane, because both were thought inspired or possessed by God. The people's reaction to King Saul at the time of his ecstasy was, "Is Saul also among the prophets?" (1 S. 10:11). Since his insanity was thought to be divinely inspired, no one interfered with him.

In some cases in the OT insanity was meted out by God as punishment. Nebuchadrezzar was possessed by an evil spirit as God's punishment for his pride. He thought he was an animal and ate grass like an ox (cf. Dnl. 4:28-33). The Israelites who disobeyed God were threatened with "madness and blindness and confusion of mind" (Dt. 28:28; cf. Jer. 25:16; Zec. 12:4; see above).

In the NT two changes occur. First, it is not kings and nations but common folk who are afflicted with madness (e.g., Mt. 17:14-18; Lk. 8:26-33). Second, the insane are no longer considered possessed by God. Instead, reflecting the changes that occurred in Jewish demonology during the exilic and postexilic periods, mental illness is now thought to result from demonic possession. The insane are not protected or held in awe (cf. the treatment of the epileptic boy [Mt. 17:14f.] and the demoniac [Lk. 8:27, 29]). Rather, the evil spirits are considered alien to the Spirit of God; they must be driven out to effect a cure. (*See* DEMON.)

*See also* DISEASE III.D; IV.H,I.

***Bibliography.***–W. Alexander, *Demonic Possession in the NT* (1980); *The Churchman,* 94/3 (1980); *DNTT,* I, 526-530; *TDNT,* IV, μαίνομαι (H. Preisker); *TDOT,* III, *s.v.* "hll III" (H. Cazelles); *TWOT,* I, 218f.; II, 905; L. D. Weatherhead, *Psychology, Religion and Healing* (n.d.).

H. N. MALONY N. J. O.

**MADAI** mā'dī [Heb. *māḏay*] (Gen. 10:2; 1 Ch. 1:5). One of the sons of Japheth, whose descendants lived in Media. *See* MEDES; TABLE OF NATIONS.

**MADEBA (MAP).** *See* MEDEBA.

**MADIABUN** mə-dī'ə-bun (1 Esd. 5:58, AV). *See* EMADABUN.

**MADIAN** mā'dē-ən (AV Acts 7:29; Jth. 2:26). *See* MIDIAN.

**MADMANNAH** mad-man'ə [Heb. *maḏmannâ*; Gk. B *Machareim,* A *Bedebēna* (Josh. 15:31), B *Marmēna,* A *Madmēna* (1 Ch. 2:49)]. A town in the Negeb of Judah, listed after Ziklag. In a comparable list (Josh. 19:5) the replacement of Madmannah with Beth-marcaboth suggests that the one location had two names. Since Beth-marcaboth means "house of chariots," it may have been an alternate name from the time of Solomon (who was famous for his chariots). The various Greek translations suggest some confusion over the name. In Neh. 11:28 the name Meconah follows Ziklag. 1 Ch. 2:49 calls Shaaph the father of Madmannah and then names Sheva as the father of two cities, Machbenah and Gibea. Simons (*GTTOT,* § 322, p. 155) suggested that Machbenah is another name for Madmannah. If all these suggestions are accepted, Madmannah = Beth-marcaboth = Machbenah = Meconah. Madmannah has been identified with Khirbet Umm Deimneh, 6 km. (4 mi.) E of Ziklag and about 19 km. (12 mi.) NE of Beer-sheba, but Y. Aharoni (*LBHG,* 2nd ed., 1979, p. 353) and others have prefered Khirbet Tatrît, a nearby site with Iron Age (and later) remains. W. S. L. S.

**MADMEN** mad'men [Heb. *maḏmēn*]. A place mentioned by Jeremiah in his oracle against Moab (Jer. 48:2). The name is generally emended to Dimon (= DIBON) and identified with Khirbet Dimneh, about 13 km. (8 mi.) from the Dead Sea E of Masada. Some scholars have suggested that Heb. *mê dîmôn,* "waters of Dimon," in Isa. 15:9 may refer to a place by that name, but there is no objective support for this theory. The LXX *kaí paúsin paúsetai* (Jer. 48:2 [LXX 31:2]), "she shall be completely still," suggests that Jeremiah was making a play on words that is lost to modern readers. One possibility is an original **maḏmēm,* from the root *dmm,* which is also the root of the following verb, thus reading, "Silencer, you shall be silenced." Aharoni, however, took the name as descriptive of the soil (*LBHG,* 2nd ed., 1979, p. 109). W. S. L. S.

**MADMENAH** mad-mē'nə [Heb. *maḏmēnâ*–'dunghill' (Isa. 10:31; cf. 25:10)]. A place mentioned in Isaiah's prophecy of the Assyrian invasion of Jerusalem, after Anathoth and before Gebim and Nob; therefore it was probably close to the northern limits of Jerusalem. L. Grollenberg (*GAB,* p. 156) suggested that Madmenah was Shuʿfat, but no identification is certain.

**MADON** mā'dən [Heb. *māḏôn*; Gk. B *Marrōn,* A *Madōn* (Josh. 11:1), B *Mamrōth,* A *Marōn* (Josh. 12:19 [LXX 20])]. A Canaanite city in Galilee whose king sided with the surrounding rulers against Joshua (Josh. 11:1). It is probably identical with the Maron of 12:19, where the common confusion of Heb. ר for ד has likely occurred. The site is uncertain, but it is probably to be identified with modern Qarn Ḥaṭṭîn about 8 km. (5 mi.) NW of Tiberias.

**MAEANNAS** mī-an'əs (1 Esd. 9:48, NEB). *See* MAASEIAH **12.**

**MAELUS** mā-ē'ləs (AV, NEB, 1 Esd. 9:26); LXX A *Maēlos,* B *Milēlos.* The RSV renders "Mijamin" to reconcile this name with the parallel in Ezr. 10:25. *See* MIJAMIN **2.**

**MAGADAN** mag'ə-dan [Gk. *Magadan*]; AV MAGDALA. A place visited by Jesus after the feeding of the four thousand (Mt. 15:39). The parallel passage (Mk. 8:10) has "Dalmanutha" instead of "Magadan." Both passages have a number of variant readings. In Codex Koridethi both read "Magdala," but the late date of this codex (9th cent.) and lack of other significant support do not commend this reading. Some late MSS of Mark read "Magadan," but this seems to be harmonistic.

Magadan and Dalmanutha are often considered to be contiguous locations on the eastern shore of the Sea of Galilee, but a number of scholars have placed Magadan on the western shore, possibly near the plain of Gennesaret. The general progression in Mark is not conclusive. Since Jesus and the disciples had come from the region of Tyre through Sidon and the region of the Decapolis to the Sea of Galilee (Mk. 7:31), they apparently approached Galilee from the east. The crossing of the sea (8:13), then, would have been from east to west. The insertion of "in those days" (8:1), however, suggests that Mark had begun a new part of his story; thus no geographical connection with the end of ch. 7 is required. "Bethsaida" (8:22) is likewise of no help, for there were possibly two places of this name (the word means "place of fish[ing]"), one on the northwestern shore near Capernaum (possibly ʿAin eṭ-Ṭâbghah), and one near the entrance of the Upper Jordan into the Sea of Galilee. *See* BETHSAIDA. W. S. LASOR

**MAGBISH** mag'bish [Heb. *magbîš*; Gk. *Magebōs*; Apoc. *Niphis;* A *Phineis*]; RSV Apoc. mg. NIPHIS; AV Apoc. NEPHIS; NEB Apoc. PHINIS. A place settled by 156 persons who returned from exile with Zerubbabel (Ezr.

2:30; cf. 1 Esd. 5:21, where the RSV renders LXX *Niphis* by "Magbish," probably to harmonize the list with Ezr. 2:30). The parallel account (Neh. 7:33) omits Magbish (Lucian, however, has *Magbeis*). Abel (*GP,* II, 373) located it at Khirbet el-Makhbiyeh, 5 km. (3 mi.) SW of Adullam and 8 km. (5 mi.) ENE of Beit Jibrîn (Beth Guvrin, Eleutheropolis) in the Shephelah. Simons (*GTTOT,* p. 380) said that Khirbet Qanân Mugheimis, 2 km. (1.2 mi.) W of ʿElam, is "considerably more probable," basing his statement on the proximity of ʿElam in the text of Ezra. However, there seems to be no geographical arrangement of the places mentioned in Ezr. 2:21-35. Further complicating the problem is the probability that some of the names are of persons rather than places. W. S. L. S.

**MAGDALA** mag'də-lə. *See* MAGADAN.

**MAGDALENE** mag'də-lēn, mag-də-lē'nə. *See* MARY **1.**

**MAGDIEL** mag'dē-əl [Heb. *magdîʾēl*] (Gen. 36:43; 1 Ch. 1:54). One of the chiefs of Edom.

**MAGED** mā'gəd. *See* MAKED.

**MAGI.** *See* MELCHIOR; WISE MEN.

**MAGI, STAR OF THE.** *See* STAR OF THE WISE MEN.

**MAGIC; MAGICIAN.** The English cognates are derived from Gk. *mageía* ("magic"), *mageúō* ("practice magic"), and *mágos* ("a Magus, magician"), all found in the NT and all taken from the Iranian noun *magus* (etymology unknown), which was the name of a Median tribe with priestly specializations. In Latin the term *magus* was used both of a class of Persian priests and diviners (Cicero *De legibus* ii.26; *De divinatione* i.90; Vitruvius viii.1; Pliny *Nat. hist.* xvi.249; xxv.13) and also in a pejorative sense of sorcerers or magicians (Horace *Carmina* i.27.22; Ovid *Metamorphoses* vii.195; Quintillian *Institutio Oratoria* ii.10.5); the cognate noun *magia* ("magic," "sorcery") and adjective *magicus* ("concerned with magic," "magical") were frequently used in a pejorative manner (Ovid *Fasti* ii.426; Pliny *Nat. hist.* xxvii.57; Apuleius *Metamorphosis* iii.16; vi.26), though in Apuleius *Apologia* 2 *magia* is used of the religion of the Persian Magi. Similarly, the Greek noun *mágos* was used to refer to members of the Median tribe of that name (Herodotus i.101) as well as to astrologers, interpreters of dreams, and fortune tellers from the East (Herodotus vii.37; Josephus *Ant.* xx.7.2 [142]; Dnl. 2:2 [LXX]; 1:20 [Theod.]). Many different terms are used for magic and magicians in biblical Greek, Hebrew, and Aramaic. A consideration of the more important terms will precede the discussion of the OT and NT evidence.



*I. Definition.*–Developments in the religious history of the Western world since the 16th cent. have made it difficult to investigate and understand the phenomenon of magic, particularly with regard to religion. In the ancient Mediterranean world, terms corresponding to such modern words as "magic," "witchcraft," and "sorcery" were used in a primarily pejorative manner because the phenomena that they described were considered illegal or antisocial. Magic was not regarded as a distinct institution with its own specialized characteristics but rather as a set of beliefs and practices that were deviant in character. It was not until after the Reformation in the 16th cent. that the concept of magic became associated with ritual words and actions that function *ex opere operato* (i.e., have their desired effect merely by being performed or spoken).

As a result of the Protestant reaction to Roman Catholic sacramentalism, magic came to be understood to have as one of its essential features the automatic efficacy of ritual words (incantations) and procedures (magical operations). On this basis magic and religion were further differentiated in terms of two very different fundamental relationships between humankind and the gods (or God). Magic (primarily because of its supposed *ex opere operato* character) was said to be manipulative and coercive, while religion (viewed from the Reformation emphasis on faith) was said to be based on the attitudes of supplication and veneration.

This dichotomy is inherently problematic, however, for many religions (e.g., ancient Egyptian and ancient Roman religion) exhibit a stronger emphasis on the manipulative than on the supplicative aspect. Even the obsolete distinction between "white" and "black" magic (the former regarded as socially benevolent, the latter as socially malevolent) reveals an ambivalent attitude toward magic, yet clings to the term itself because of its supposed *ex opere operato* character over against religion. Since field anthropology, from its beginnings in the 19th cent. until well into the 20th cent., was closely related to Protestant missionary activity, it was natural that the conceptual framework used to understand the cultures of small societies was based in part on the post-Reformation dichotomy between manipulative magic and supplicative religion. Magic even came to be regarded as a rudimentary form of religion that characterized human culture in earlier stages of development. Yet the religions of many third-world societies seem to be constituted of both manipulative and supplicative elements; and because of the difficulty of separating these elements, twentieth-century anthropologists began to speak more cautiously of "magical-religious phenomena." Similarly, a leading historian of ancient Near Eastern religions, Helmer Ringgren, has concluded that "religion" and "magic" are almost inseparable in Sumerian, Babylonian, and West Semitic religion (pp. 34f., 90f., 168f.).

W. J. Goode, a leading American anthropologist, recognized the difficulties in rigidly distinguishing magic from religion and proposed seven "nondichotomous" empirical differences between them (*Religion,* pp. 50-55): (1) Magic tends to adopt a manipulative, religion a supplicative, attitude toward extra-ordinary reality. (2) Magical activities tend to be used instrumentally to achieve particular goals, while religious activities tend to be regarded as ends in themselves. (3) Magic tends to focus on individual goals, religion on group goals. (4) Magical activities tend to be private and individual, while religious activities tend to occur in groups. (5) Magic tends to develop professional-client relationships, while religion tends to emphasize the "shepherd-follower" relationship. (6) In cases of failure, magic tends to introduce substitute techniques, while substitution is less characteristic of religion. (7) Magic tends to act impersonally, with minimal emphasis on emotion, while religion tends to make greater use of emotion and to evoke attitudes of awe and worship.

While Goode's description of the "nondichotomous" differences between magic and religion is carefully formulated and represents the tendency in modern anthropology to avoid rigid distinctions between magic and religion, it does not take into account the one universal characteristic of magic, namely, its perceived illegal or antisocial character. This ancient perception of magic again became influential in modern times through the work of the French sociological school represented by Emile Durkheim and Marcel Mauss. Mauss emphasized the illegal or deviant character of magic: "A magical rite is any rite which does not play a part in organized cults — it is private, secret, mysterious and approaches the limit of a prohibited rite" (p. 24). Once magic is viewed in terms of its religiously, and hence socially, deviant character, it can be seen that many of Goode's distinctions between magic and religion (particularly nos. 2, 3, and 4) are correlatives of the deviant social setting within which magicians operate.

A definition of magic may best take into account its illegal and antisocial character by using the theoretical framework of the sociology of deviance, i.e., by understanding magic as a form of deviant behavior. This leads to a two-stage definition. First, magic is that form of religious deviance in which individual or social goals are sought by means not normally sanctioned by the dominant religious institutions. Second, such religious deviance is magical only when the goals sought are considered virtually guaranteed through the management of supernatural powers. Probably any social institution that functions to improve or rectify human existence will have deviant counterparts that pretend to provide benefits more effectively, concretely, and rapidly than the dominant institution; thus legal systems have their deviant counterparts in kangaroo courts and lynch law, medical institutions in quackery, and religion in magic. If the central characteristic of magic is religious deviance, then what is magic depends upon the judgment of those who represent dominant social norms and values, rather than upon any universal beliefs and practices attributed to magic and magicians. Thus, as indicated below, even though Jesus and the early Christians were not infrequently charged by both Jews and pagans with practicing magic, they certainly viewed their own beliefs and practices in a totally different way. The distinction between "magic" and "miracle," then, is primarily based on perspective. Early Christian "miracles" were regarded as "magic" by Jewish and pagan opponents, while pagan "miracles" were labeled "magic" by the early Christians.

Modern anthropologists have also found it useful to distinguish between witchcraft and sorcery, based on distinctions found in the languages of some, though certainly not all, modern small-scale societies in the third world (cf. E. E. Evans-Pritchard). Among anthropologists "witch" is widely used as a technical designation of a person with innate supernatural powers (e.g., the evil eye), while "sorcerer" denotes a specialist who has learned from a master practitioner the craft of controlling or using supernatural powers. The former is feared but usually tolerated, while the latter is feared and subjected to various penalties from persecution or ostracism to death.

***II. OT.*–*A. Terminology.*** (1) The regular Hebrew term for "magic" is derived from the stem *kšp*. The verb in the piel (*kiššēp̱*) means "practice magic," "enchant" (2 Ch. 33:6, RSV "practice sorcery"). The piel participle (*m$^{e}$ḵaššēp̱*) is used to refer to magicians or sorcerers (RSV "sorcerer," Ex. 7:11; Dt. 18:10; Dnl. 2:2; Mal. 3:5; fem. *m$^{e}$ḵaššēp̱â*, RSV "sorceress," Ex. 22:18 [MT 17]), as is the term *kaššāp̱* in Jer. 27:9 (RSV "sorcerer"). The noun *kešep̱*, meaning "magical art, magic," is used only in the plural and is consistently translated "sorceries" by the RSV (2 K. 9:22; Isa. 47:9, 12; Mic. 5:12 [MT 11]; Nah. 3:4), with the exception of Nah. 3:4 (RSV "charms"). *K$^{e}$šāp̱îm* is paired with *ḥ$^{a}$ḇārîm* ("enchantments") in Isa. 47:9, 12, and with *m$^{e}$ʿôn$^{e}$nîm* ("soothsayers") in Mic. 5:12 (MT 11).

The stem *kšp* corresponds to Akk. *kašāpu* ("enchant," "bewitch") and nominal forms *kišpu* ("magic," "sorcery") and *kaššāpu* ("sorcerer," "magician"). Thus Heb. *k$^{e}$šāp̱îm* appears to be one of the more general terms for "magic" and "sorcery," perhaps along with *ḥereš*, a term found in the OT only once, in the phrase *ḥ$^{a}$ḵam ḥ$^{a}$rāšîm* (RSV "skilful magician," Isa. 3:3; AV "cunning artificer"). While not attested in Akkadian or Arabic, *ḥrš* does occur with the connotation "practice magic" in Ugaritic, Aramaic, Ethiopic, and Syriac (*TWAT*, III, 237f.; KoB, 3rd ed., p. 344).

(2) The Hebrew and Aramaic term *ḥarṭōm* (never used with a magical connotation in the Talmud or midrashim) occurs in the OT only in the plural (except in Dnl. 2:10) and is consistently translated "magicians" in the RSV (Gen. 41:8, 24; Ex. 7:11, 22; 8:7, 18f. [MT 3, 14f.]; 9:11; Dnl. 1:20; 2:2, 10, 27; 4:7, 9 [MT 4, 6]; 5:11). Derived from Demotic Egyp. *ḥr-tp* ("recitation-priest," "magician-priest"), the term is used of Egyptian dream interpreters in Gen. 41 and of Babylonian dream interpreters in the Daniel stories (which appear to be modeled after those in Genesis). In Ex. 7-9 it is used of Pharaoh's wonder-workers. The LXX translates *ḥarṭōm* by Gk. *exēgētḗs* ("interpreter") in Gen. 41:8, 24, but uses *epaoidós* ("singer of spells," "enchanter") or *sophós* ("wise") in the Exodus and Daniel passages. The interpretation of the Daniel texts is complicated by the lists of three or four kinds of magicians or diviners that occur in every passage except 1:20 and 4:9. It is clear, however, that the task of all these specialists was to interpret the king's dreams (2:2, 27f.; 4:4-9).

All three passages in which this term appears deal with struggles between sages whose mantic wisdom is given by God (Joseph, Moses, and Daniel) and various types of magicians and diviners whose powers (though not inconsiderable, according to Ex. 7–9) are no match for those of the God-fearing contestants (cf. Gen. 41:8; Dnl. 2:10, 27). Similar contests are described in the NT and in later Christian literature (e.g., the *Clementine Homilies* vii.1-12; *Recognitions* ii.5-72; iii.52-65), confirming the idea that the distinction between magic and miracle is primarily one of theological perspective.

(3) The OT uses two terms from the stem *ḥbr*. They are probably derived from the Semitic stem *ḫbr*, "sound," "noise," rather than *ḥbr*, "tie," "bind" (cf. Finkelstein, p. 331). In Isa. 47:9, 12 the noun *ḥeḇer* occurs in the plural (RSV "enchantments"). The substantival participle *ḥōḇēr* is twice used with the noun in the phrase *ḥōḇēr ḥeḇer*, obviously referring to some type of magic or sorcery (RSV "charmer," Dt. 18:11; "enchanter," Ps. 58:5 [MT 6]). Finkelstein concluded that the magical activity referred to was neither knot-tying nor "weaving words together" (common older views; cf. BDB, pp. 287f.); rather, he proposed that *ḥōḇēr ḥeḇer* denoted a charmer or enchanter in the sense of "one who mutters sounds," "a mutterer" (cf. LXX *epaeídōn epaoidḗn*, "one who sings enchantments," in Dt. 18:11). The connection of *ḥōḇēr* with snake charming is evident from Sir. 12:13.

(4) The stem *lḥš* ("whisper") occurs in Ps. 58:5 (MT 6) as a plural substantival participle *m$^{e}$laḥ$^{a}$šîm* (RSV "charmers"; cf. LXX *epᾳdóntōn*, "those who sing charms"), in what

is probably a synonymous parallelism with *hôḇēr ḥᵃḇārîm*. The nominal form *laḥaš* ("a whispering," "charming") clearly refers to snake charming in Jer. 8:17 and Eccl. 10:11.

(5) The poel of *ʿānan* (apparently derived from a stem meaning "appear," "present oneself"; cf. KoB, p. 721b), means "practice soothsaying." It occurs ten times in the OT and is usually translated "soothsayer" or "practice soothsaying" by the RSV (Lev. 19:26 [RSV "witchcraft"]; Dt. 18:10, 14; Jgs. 9:37 [RSV "Diviner's (Oak)"]; 2 K. 21:6 par. 2 Ch. 33:6; Isa. 2:6; 57:3 [RSV "sorceress"]; Jer. 27:9; Mic. 5:12 [MT 11]). The LXX often translates these terms with the Gk. *klēdon-* stem, which connotes divination of some type. The practice is condemned in Lev. 19:26; Dt. 18:10, 14; 2 K. 21:6 par. 2 Ch. 33:6 and mentioned negatively in Mic. 5:12.

(6) The stem *nḥš* in its nominal form means "divination" or "enchantment" (RSV "enchantment," Nu. 23:23; "omens," 24:1), while the piel of *nāḥaš* means "practice divination," "observe signs" (cf. RSV "divine" [using a cup], Gen. 44:5, 15; "watch for an omen," 1 K. 20:33). The practice is condemned in Lev. 19:26 and Dt. 18:10 (RSV "augury," "augur"); it is listed in 2 K. 21:6 par. 2 Ch. 33:6 (RSV "augury") as one of the sins of Manasseh and in 2 K. 17:17 (RSV "use sorcery") as a sin of Israel. In Gen. 30:27 the RSV renders the niphal form as "learn by divination." It is noteworthy that several passages (e.g., Gen. 30:27; 44:5, 15; 1 K. 20:33) neither explicitly condemn nor approve of the practice.

Cippus (amulet) of Horus with a hieroglyphic inscription used magically to heal those attacked by scorpions, snakes, and other animals. 24th-25th Dynasties (*ca.* 700 B.C.) (Oriental Institute, University of Chicago)

(7) The enigmatic "magic bands" (*kᵉsāṯôṯ*) of Ezk. 13:18, 20 (AV "pillows") are apparently magical amulets intended to bring about untimely deaths, expressed as "hunting for souls [i.e., lives]." The "veils" (*mispāḥôṯ*) mentioned in the same context apparently complement the magic bands, perhaps in a "binding/loosening" pattern (W. Zimmerli, *Ezekiel*, I [Eng. tr., *Hermeneia*, 1979], 297).

*B. Lists of Terms.* Since most of the terms discussed above occur in the OT only in lists of prohibited professions and practices and are never described more specifically, it is often very difficult to define precisely the kinds of professions and practices they refer to. The most comprehensive list is in Dt. 18:10f., which has the juridical intention of prohibiting all forms of sorcery and divination with the single exception of prophecy. Similar though less extensive lists of prohibited practices and professions occur in 2 K. 21:6 par. 2 Ch. 33:6 (the latter adds *kiššēp*, "practice sorcery," to the list of 2 Kings); Jer. 27:9; Lev. 19:26, 31; 20:6, 27; and Ex. 22:18, where the death penalty is prescribed for a sorceress. In addition, lists of various types of divination and sorcery appear in contexts that express strong disapproval (2 K. 9:22; 17:17; 23:24; Isa. 2:6; 8:19; 47:9, 12; Mic. 5:12 [MT 11]). These texts clearly show that the various named types of magic can appropriately be viewed from the perspective of their illegality or social deviance. Since many of the terms are derived from the languages of surrounding nations (primarily Babylonia, Assyria, and Egypt), the corresponding practices are both alien and unacceptable to the OT (Dt. 18:14). Though in many lists in Daniel the various types of Babylonian diviners and sorcerers are mentioned without express disapproval (Dnl. 1:20; 2:2, 10, 27; 4:7 [MT 4]; 5:11), the entire context makes it clear that such arts are no match for one who depends upon God for wisdom (Dn. 2:27; cf. 2:10).

The lists of prohibited professions and practices contain two basic types of magical art: DIVINATION and sorcery. While divination is an attempt to understand and interpret messages from the gods (often received in coded form), sorcery is basically concerned with influencing people and events for personal reasons or for clients. (Witchcraft, i.e., the possession of innate supernatural powers [e.g., the *ʿayin hārāʿ*, or "evil eye," mentioned in 1 S. 18:9; Prov. 28:22, RSV "miserly"], so prevalent in later rabbinical literature, is remarkably rare in the OT.) Yet sorcery and divination cannot be neatly distinguished, not only because sorcery is often concerned with revelation, but also because Canaanite and Israelite prophets often attempted to influence the outcome of the events they predicted (cf. the symbolic or magical actions of the Israelite prophet Zedekiah ben Chenaanah in 1 K. 22:11) by "creating" the fulfillment of their prophecies.

*C. Forms of Magic.* Aside from the various forms of magical DIVINATION referred to in the OT, and such specializations as snake charming (Jer. 8:17; Eccl. 10:11), very little is known about the specific practices that characterized magic in ancient Israel. Certainly the reiterated prohibitions of various magical practices throughout the various strata of OT literature suggest that the religious establishment in ancient Israel saw such practices as constituting a widespread and persistent problem. Magic was also associated with other forms of social deviance, e.g., prostitution (Lev. 19:26-29, 31; 2 K. 9:22; Isa. 57:3; Nah. 3:4).

Many of the Hebrew terms for magical practioners suggest that the chanting of ritual incantations was one of the characteristic features of their activities. In spite of Urbach's claim that "there is no adjuration by God's name" in the OT (I, 124), the opposite is suggested by 2 K. 2:23f., which presents Elisha as cursing some boys "in the name of the Lord," with the result that they were attacked by bears and many of them killed. Further, the third commandment (Ex. 20:7 par. Dt. 5:11), "You shall not take the name of the Lord your God in vain [*laššaw'*]," may well reflect the negative, hence evil, use of God's name for magical purposes (M. Noth, *Exodus* [Eng. tr., *OTL*, 1962], p. 163). The stem *šāw'* ("evil," "emptiness") also appears to have magical connotations elsewhere in the OT (cf. Isa. 5:18; Ps. 41: 6 [MT 7]; Job 11:11; 31:5; Ps. 24:4; 26:4; see M. Klopfenstein, pp. 315f.). S. Mowinckel (*Psalmenstudien*, I, 50-57) has maintained the use of the same stem with magical connotations in many other biblical Psalms (12:2 [MT 3]; 26:4; 119:37; 144:8; etc.; but cf. *Psalms in Israel's Worship* [Eng. tr. 1962], I, 182 n. 195; II, 25 n. 64). It was perhaps due to the magical misuse of the divine name that the tetragrammaton (now commonly vocalized "Yahweh") was so rarely pronounced that its original pronunciation was forgotten. The use of the name of the God of Israel in magical adjurations appears to have become more popular during the second temple period. In 1 En. 69:13 Kasbeel, the chief of oaths (his name is probably related to the stem *kšp*, from which the regular Hebrew terms for magic are derived), asks Michael to show him the hidden name, that he might use it in the oath "so that those might quake before that name and oath who revealed all that was in secret to the children of men." In Jub. 36:7 Isaac makes his children swear a great oath "by the name glorious and honoured and great and splendid and wonderful and mighty." The Mishnah (*Taanith* iii.8) quotes Honi the Circle-Drawer, an enigmatic Jewish sage who apparently dabbled in magic. Honi made it rain by drawing a circle (a magical diagram), standing within it, and pronouncing, "I swear by thy great name that I will not stir hence until thou have pity on thy children."

The malevolent use of magic may also be reflected in the Psalms. Mowinckel has proposed that the expression *pō'alê 'āwen* ("workers of iniquity"), which occurs some sixteen times in the Psalms, refers to those who used sorcery to bring illness and destruction upon the psalmist; cf. esp. Pss. 38 and 41 (S. Mowinckel, *Offersang og Sang-offer* [1951], pp. 254-56).

In sum, the evidence shows that the practice of magic in various forms in ancient Israel was probably widespread. But the censorship exercised by various authors and redactors has not permitted a more intimate acquaintance with the exact forms and settings of such magical activities. More light may be shed by postbiblical Jewish sources, yet the extent to which they illuminate on earlier periods is questionable.

***III. Postbiblical Judaism.***–*A. Rabbinic Judaism*. Rabbinic literature (extending from the final redaction of the Mishnah by Rabbi Judah the Prince toward the end of the 2nd cent. A.D. to the completion of the Jerusalem and Babylonian Talmuds four centuries or more later) does not exhibit a unified perspective on magic. While the rabbinic sages were well acquainted with the prohibitions against the various forms of divination and sorcery in the Torah, they were also well acquainted with magical practices. Some even practiced the art themselves. There are several reasons for this tension between theory and practice. The rabbis, like other ancients, made no clear distinction between science and magic, particularly in the areas of diagnosis and curing (cf. T.B. *Shabbath* 33a, where three causes of dropsy are proposed [sin, hunger, or magic], based on the nature of the specific symptoms). What appear to be magical healing remedies are discussed extensively in rabbinic literature (cf. T.B. *Shabbath* 66b-67a),

Execration text written in hieratic on a clay figurine, which was broken to effect the curse. From Saqqârah, *ca.* 18th cent. B.C. (Brussels, Musées Royaux d'Art et d'Histoire, inv. E. 7442. *Copyright A. C. L., Bruxelles*)

including even the prescription of *voces magicae* (i.e., magical gibberish), such as those quoted in T.B. *Shabbath* 67a: "Bazak, bazik, bibazik, mismasik, kamun kamik." Similarly, the nature and function of amulets receive extensive discussion (cf. 61a-62a), and the sages appear to have been fully aware of the legal and theological problems involved. Thus 61a says: "Our Rabbis taught: What is an approved amulet? One that has healed (once), a second time and a third time; whether it is an amulet in writing or an amulet of roots, whether it is for an invalid whose life is endangered or for an invalid whose life is not endangered." Furthermore, the rabbis could deviate from the biblical prohibitions for the purpose of studying and familiarizing themselves with magical arts. Finally, it appears that they were able to harmonize the biblical prohibitions with the practice of some forms of magic by redefining both. Nevertheless, the rabbis' opposition to the prohibited practices is clear from this representative saying of Rabbi Simeon ben Eleazar (Mish. *Sotah* ix.13): "Fornication and sorceries have made an end of everything." The strong antifeminist tendencies in rabbinic literature (probably originating in the effect of relationships between men and women on ritual purity) found expression in the rabbinic view that many, if not all, women engage in witchcraft (T.B. *Sanhedrin* 67a; *Berakoth* 53a; *Erubin* 64b), for "the best of women is a sorceress."

*B. Sepher ha-Razim.* The *Sepher ha-Razim,* "Book of Mysteries," is a carefully constructed Jewish magical handbook, compiled rather late (6th to 7th cents. A.D.) but probably reflecting material contemporaneous with the earlier talmudic period (3rd-4th cents. A.D.). According to the *Sepher ha-Razim* itself, the book (with many similar books) was revealed to Noah by the angel Raziel before the flood, and then passed down with other such literature to Solomon, who was associated with traditions of magic and healing and was regarded as the patron of Jewish exorcists (SB, IV, 510-12, 533f.; L. Ginzberg, *Legends of the Jews* [repr. 1956], IV, 149-154; VI, 291-93). The handbook deals with three kinds of magic: magical healing, magical revelation, and magical procedures for gaining power over enemies. The primary agents for the magician are angelic beings, whose proper names must be called out or written down so that they can be sent on their missions. The book has a cosmological structure, being divided into seven parts corresponding to the seven heavens, with various classes of angels located in each of the heavens.

The book is remarkable for several reasons. First, it was apparently compiled by an educated Jew (though many of the practices were doubtless popular) in spite of the numerous and clear biblical prohibitions of nearly all forms of divination and sorcery. Second, a number of features are strikingly pagan: the inclusion of a procedure for consulting the dead, the sacrifice of a white rooster and the offering of incense to the moon and stars, and a prayer to Helios, the sun. On the other hand, the *voces magicae* (magical gibberish) found typically in the Greek magical papyri are totally absent, and the spiritual forces relied upon are of course not gods and daimons, but angels organized into complex groups. The *Sepher ha-Razim* constitutes one more piece of a growing body of evidence that Judaism of late antiquity exhibited a more heterodox character than was previously supposed.

*C. Judaism and the Greek Magical Papyri.* The importance and popularity of Jewish magic in the Greco-Roman world can be partially gauged by the influence that it apparently exerted on pagan magical practices. One of the more striking examples of this influence is seen in the popularity of the Jewish names for God used in pagan magical procedures. Such names as Iao, Sabaoth, Adonai, and Eloe occur frequently (Preisendanz [hereafter *PGM*], IV, 1577; V, 481; VII, 400; XXXVI, 42; XLIII, 13), often in combination (Iao, Sabaoth, Adonai, Eloai, and Abrasax are found together in *PGM,* XXXVI, 42; Adonai, Eloai, Abraam in V, 481; Sabaoth, Adonai, Eloai, in XLIII, 13). Furthermore, biblical names appear, e.g., Adam (*PGM,* III, 146), Abraham (VII, 315, 481), and Moses (XIII, 970; VII, 619); so also do the names of angels from Jewish tradition (Michael in *PGM,* I, 301; III, 148; VII, 609; Gabriel in XLIII, 23; VII, 1018; Raphael in XXXV, 3; III, 212; and others). Moreover, a number of magical names and words end in *-oth,* a typical Semitic ending.

Several magical papyri exhibit a particularly striking Jewish influence. *PGM,* XIII, e.g., is a complex composition entitled "Eighth Book of Moses," embodying several earlier documents and traditions. It includes the "Key of Moses" (XIII, 21) and another section that begins with the description, "The sacred secret book of Moses called the eighth or holy" (XIII, 343f.). The *subscriptio* of the composition appears in line 730 as "The Eighth Hidden Book of Moses," but the author has supplied an alternate title as well: "In another copy it was written, 'The Hidden Book of Moses on the Great Name, that for Everything, in which is the Name of the One Who Rules All." At the conclusion of the papyrus (lines 1077f.) is another *subscriptio,* "The Tenth Hidden Book of Moses." These varied titles indicate that the document has had a very long and complex literary history. The content is predominantly pagan, despite a veneer of Jewish magical and religious traditions. Another, much shorter, document is called "From the Diadem of Moses" (*PGM,* VII, 619-627). It is apparently an excerpt from a much larger collection and contains formulas for invisibility and for attracting the love of women. The divine names Iao, Sabaoth, and Adonai are part of the incantation (lines 626f.). Yet another magical composition, called the "Prayer of Jacob" (*PGM,* XXIIb), appears to be thoroughly Jewish with scarcely a trace of pagan elements. The closing lines clearly exhibit its Jewish character:

I invoke you who gives power of the Abyss
  to those above, to those below, and
    to those under the earth.
Hear the one who has this prayer,
  Lord God of the Hebrews Epangaēl alamn
of whom is the eternal power, Elōēl, Souēl.
  Maintain the one who possesses this prayer,
who is from the stock of Israel and from those
  who have been favored by you.

Thus the Greek magical papyri provide evidence both that Jewish magic was influential upon its pagan counterpart, and that (as in the OT), pagan magic had a profound impact upon Jewish magical practices as well.

*D. Aramaic Incantation Bowls.* One important source of knowledge about Jewish magical practices is the nearly eighty extant incantation bowls made by Jews in Babylonia during the Sassanian period (A.D. 226-636). Such bowls have been found primarily at Nippur, but also at Khuzestan, Hamadân, and Nehavand. They are made of clay and contain magical texts written in spirals beginning at the center of the bowl. Though the exact use of the bowls is disputed, their function is clearly apotropaic in that they are meant to ward off the evil effects of a number of malevolent supernatural beings and influences, e.g., the evil eye, Lilith, and Bagdana. These evil effects are often associated with witchcraft rather than sorcery and are thought to be activated by jealousy. Children are particularly susceptible. Lilith (Heb. *līlîṯ,* occurring in the OT only in Isa. 34:14 [RSV "night hag"]), regarded as a demonic creature of the night, was depicted by the rabbis as a being with wings and long flowing hair. As a female succubus Lilith was thought to be capable of taking on the likeness of a man's wife and luring him into sexual relations. As a male incubus (Aram. *lyly*) Lilith could similarly impersonate a husband in order to have sexual relations with his wife, perhaps producing children. (*See also* NIGHT HAG.) Bagdana, regarded as a high-ranking demon, was called "king and ruler" of the liliths, demons, and devils, and "great ruler of the liliths."

The bowls used quotations from the OT for their apotropaic powers. Zec. 3:2 occurs most frequently: "And the Lord said to Satan, 'The Lord rebuke you, O Satan! The Lord who has chosen Jerusalem rebuke you! Is not this a brand plucked from the fire?'" One name that occurs several times on the bowls is that of an apparently famous rabbi, Joshua ben Peraḥiah, who was also a magician. In one text in which Lilith is exorcised with divorce termi-

Incantation bowl with spiral inscription in Jewish Aramaic for protection of the household of Babai (Royal Ontario Museum, Toronto)

nology, the text concludes "I bind and I seal with the seal of El Shaddai and with the seal of Joshua b. Peraḥia the healer" (Neusner, pp. 335f.). Joshua ben Peraḥiah is placed, in rabbinic legend, in relation to Jesus of Nazareth, whom he reportedly excommunicated (T.B. *Sanhedrin* 109b; *Sotah* 47a). The Aramaic incantation bowls, despite the many problems involved in their proper interpretation, again suggest that Judaism of late antiquity exhibited a great deal of magic.

*IV. NT.–A. Terminology.* In the NT the Greek noun *mageía* (RSV, NEB, "magic"; AV "sorceries") is used only in Acts 8:11, while the verb *mageúō* (RSV "practice magic"; AV "use sorcery"; NEB "magical arts") is also used but once, in the same context (8:9). The noun *mágos* (RSV "magician"; AV, NEB, "sorcerer") is found only twice in the NT with a pejorative meaning (Acts 13:6, 8); it also occurs four times in the Matthaean infancy narrative (Mt. 2:1, 7, 16) with its more original nonpejorative meaning of "wise man" (RSV, AV; cf. NEB "astrologer"). Gk. *phármakos* ("sorcerer") occurs twice in the NT (Rev. 21:8; 22:15), while *pharmakeía* (always "sorcery" in RSV) is found three times (Gal. 5:20 [AV "witchcraft"]; Rev. 9:21; 18:23; cf. *érga pharmakeiōn,* Wisd. 12:4). Furthermore, the term *períergos* (with the vb. *prássō,* "do," "practice") occurs once in the NT with the meaning "magical arts" (RSV, Acts 19:19; AV "curious arts"; NEB "magic"; but cf. its use in the sense of "busybody" in 1 Tim. 5:13). The noun *práxis* is used in Acts 19:18 as a technical term meaning "magical practice" or "magical procedure"; it is translated "practice" by the RSV, "deed" by the AV, but more appropriately "magical spell" by the NEB.

Several general observations can be made on the basis of this relatively meager terminological evidence. First, aside from the single reference in Gal. 5:20, the technical terminology for magic occurs only in Revelation and Acts. Each of these writings exhibits an opposition to current magical practices, which suggests that magic posed a serious threat to these authors and the communities in which they wrote. Second, the author of Luke-Acts is particularly familiar with the technical terminology of magic. Third, as in the OT, some of the terms for magic or its practitioners occur in lists of vices or offenders with which they were apparently closely associated. Thus in Gal. 5:19-21 sorcery appears in a list of "works of the flesh" that also includes fornication, impurity, licentiousness, idolatry, enmity, strife, jealousy, anger, selfishness, dissension, party spirit, envy, drunkenness, and carousing. In Rev. 21:8 the list of those excluded from the Holy City includes the cowardly, faithless, polluted, murderers, fornicators, idolaters, and liars, in addition to sorcerers. A similar list in 22:15 includes "dogs and sorcerers and fornicators and murderers and idolaters, and every one who loves and practices falsehood." As in the OT, the mere mention of magical practices in a list of vices does not offer much information about what these practices involved. It is clear, however, that, in spite of the relatively few uses of magical terminology in the NT, ancient magic had a profound impact on early Christianity, both as an external enemy and as an internal threat.

*B. Magic in the World of the NT.* The Greco-Roman world within which Christianity originated and began to expand was a world in which various religions and philosophies from both East and West competed with one another. Because most of these religions focused on myths and rituals rather than theology, leaving them open to influences from other religions, the period was characterized by syncretism. Various magical traditions from the East moved into the West and became, often because of a nostalgia for the ancient and mysterious, part of a growing body of international magical lore. From Assyria and Babylonia came an interest in astrology. From Egypt came an emphasis on the power inherent in the spoken or written word, especially the secret name. From Persia came an emphasis on demons, both as causes of illness and human problems and also as agents that could be enlisted to carry out the wishes of the magical practitioner. From Israel came a repertoire of divine and angelic names that were considered particularly effective in magical incantations. Greco-Roman magic was thoroughly utilitarian, and particular magicians, incantations, and amulets were judged primarily by their rates of success. This is one reason why many of the procedures preserved in the Greek magical papyri conclude with a statement such as "this one really works," or "this spell is guaranteed to produce the desired results."

Greco-Roman magic can be divided into four major categories according to purpose: (1) protective or apotropaic magic (particularly against dreaded illnesses), (2) aggressive and malevolent magic, (3) love magic and magic aimed at the acquisition of power over others, and (4) magical divination or revelation. Along with erotic magic, magical revelation was one of the more popular and widespread types of magical practice. The Elymas of Acts 13:6 was both a magician and a false prophet.

*C. Antimagical Polemic.* Jesus and the earliest Christians were persistently charged, by both Jews and pagans, with practicing the magical arts. The controversy centered on the performance of miracles of healing and exorcism. Jesus and the early Christians claimed that they were agents of God, while their opponents charged that they were rather agents of evil spiritual forces. These charges were serious enough to require refutation. Consequently, a vigorous antimagical polemic permeates the four Gospels and Acts, and traces of it can be found in the remainder of the NT as well.

In the Synoptic Gospels this antimagical polemic is clearly reflected in the Beelzebul pericope (Mk. 3:22 par. Mt. 12:24; Lk. 11:15f.). BEELZEBUL is apparently a name for Satan, and the phrase "by the prince of demons"

(Matthew and Luke have "by Beelzebul") must be understood as a contraction of "in the name of the prince of demons," or "in the name of Beelzebul." Jesus, then, is here charged with practicing magic, for His opponents accuse Him of having performed His healings and exorcisms by the power of Beelzebul, who is supposedly indwelling Jesus and being controlled by Him. Mt. 10:25 suggests that Jesus' opponents may have actually nicknamed Him "Beelzebul." This charge and all that it implies are refuted in the following pericope (Mk. 3:23-30 par.). In the Fourth Gospel Jesus is three times accused of having a demon (Jn. 7:20; 8:48-52; 10:20f.), which is an abbreviated way of charging Him with being a fake prophet and a charlatan whose powers to perform miracles come from Satan. Similarly, the accusation that Jesus was an impostor or deceiver (e.g., Mt. 27:63; Jn. 7:12, 47) must be understood in relation to the charge that He practiced magic, for false prophets and magicians were subject to the death penalty according to the Deuteronomic code (Dt. 13:5; 18:20). Jesus' Jewish opponents may have used these ancient laws to justify His execution.

The Gospel accounts of the temptation of Jesus (Mt. 4:1-11 par. Lk. 4:1-13; cf. Mk. 1:12f.) also express an antimagical polemic. Only Satan's offer of the kingdoms of the world can be considered a "messianic" temptation. The accounts of the other two temptations should be understood as depicting Jesus' rejection of conventional magical means to attain His goals. Such feats as turning stones to bread and flying through the air are commonly claimed by magicians.

The charge that Jesus practiced magic is reflected in Mark's account of the various rumors that King Herod heard about Jesus' miraculous deeds (6:14-16). According to one rumor, "John the baptizer has been raised from the dead; that is why these powers are at work in him" (v. 14). Those who died violent deaths were thought particularly susceptible to postmortem control by magical practitioners (cf. Lucian *Philopsendes* 29; Tertullian *Apol.* 23; *PGM*, IV, 333, 1914, 1950; LVII, 6); thus Jesus is here accused of performing wonders by gaining control of the restless spirit of John the Baptist.

These representative examples reveal the widespread nature of the antimagical polemic in the Gospels. The charge that Jesus was a magician has also been preserved outside the NT in both pagan and Jewish traditions (Jewish sources: T.B. *Sanhedrin* 43a; cf. Klausner, pp. 18-47; pagan traditions: Origen *Contra Celsum* i.6, 38, 68; Koran 5:113).

Antimagical polemic also occupies a prominent place in the Acts of the Apostles, and the author of Luke-Acts appears to have been exceptionally well informed regarding the techniques and technical terms of Greco-Roman magic. This is most evident in three important passages: Acts 8:9-24; 13:4-12; and 19:11-20. The first describes how the infamous Simon Magus, who has a great reputation as a powerful magician (and in later Christian literature is the arch-magician and father of Christian heresies), is drawn to the Christian faith by the superior power exhibited by Christians through the Holy Spirit. Acts 13:6-12 describes a contest between Paul and Elymas or Bar-Jesus, the false prophet and magician, in the court of the Roman proconsul Sergius Paulus. Paul's power proves superior to that of Elymas, who is struck blind by a judicial miracle performed by Paul. In 19:11-20 seven Jewish exorcists or magicians attempt to use the name of Jesus in their exorcisms, only to be overpowered by the demoniac whom they are attempting to cure. The story ends with many in Ephesus confessing their magical practices and burning their magical handbooks. All of these passages describe contests between Christians with miraculous powers and magicians whose powers are derived from incantations and the control of malevolent supernatural forces. The author of Acts carefully demonstrates the superiority of Christianity in each of these encounters.

*V. After the NT.*–In the 2nd cent. A.D. and later, Greco-Roman magic continued to pose a formidable threat to Christianity, and some deviant forms of Christianity (e.g., the Gnostic groups) developed a complex magical lore of their own. Christians continued to be accused by both Jews and pagans of practicing magic, and they hurled back the charge with equal vigor. Celsus, a second-century critic of Christianity, charged that Christians got their power by pronouncing the names of certain demons and using incantations (Origen *Contra Celsum* i.6). Origen, a firm believer in the efficacy if not the legitimacy of magical practices, responded that Christians received power by pronouncing the name of Jesus and reciting narratives concerning Him. Justin Martyr also contrasted the successful Christian exorcists, who used the name of Jesus, with others (presumably pagans) who relied on incantations and drugs. Ignatius of Antioch (d. *ca.* A.D. 115) noted that one significant effect of Jesus' incarnation was the dissolution of the powers of magic (Ign. Eph. 19:3). Three vice lists in the Apostolic Fathers (Barn. 20:1; Did. 2:2; 5:1) pair the terms *pharmakeía* ("sorcery") and *mageía* ("magic"), or *pharmakeúō* ("practice sorcery") and *mageúō* ("practice magic"). Such lists clearly indicate that magical practices were categorized as deviant and inconsistent with the Christian faith.

*See also* CHARM; ENCHANT; EXORCISM.

***Bibliography.***–D. E. Aune, "Magic in Early Christianity," in H. Temporini and W. Haase, eds., *Aufstieg und Niedergang der römischen Welt,* II/23 (1980), 1507-57; L. Blau, *Das altjüdische Zauberwesen* (2nd ed. 1914); E. E. Evans-Pritchard, *Witchcraft, Oracles and Magic among the Azande* (1937); J. J. Finkelstein, *JBL,* 75 (1956), 328-331; M. J. Geller, *JSS,* 25 (1980), 181-192; W. J. Goode, *Religion among the Primitives* (1951); I. Gruenwald, *Apocalyptic and Merkavah Mysticism* (1980); H. A. Hoffner, *JBL,* 86 (1967), 385-401; T. Hopfner, *Griechisch-ägyptischer Offenbarungszauber* (2 vols., 1921-1924); J. M. Hull, *Hellenistic Magic and the Synoptic Tradition* (1974); C. D. Isbell, *Corpus of the Aramaic Incantation Bowls* (1975); A. R. Johnson, *Cultic Prophet in Ancient Israel* (2nd ed. 1962); J. Klausner, *Jesus of Nazareth* (Eng. tr. 1925); M. A. Klopfenstein, *Die Lüge nach dem AT* (1964); C. H. Kraeling, *JBL,* 59 (1940), 147-157; J. Levy, *Wörterbuch über die Talmudim und Midraschim* (4 vols., 1963); E. MacLauren and B. Colin, *VT,* 25 (1975), 27-45; M. Mauss, *General Theory of Magic* (1972); M. A. Morgan, *Sepher Ha-Razim: The Book of Mysteries* (1983); S. Mowinckel, *Psalmenstudien* (4 vols., 1921-1924); *Religion og Kultus* (1950); J. Neusner and J. Z. Smith, "Archaeology and Babylonian Jewry," in J. A. Sanders, ed., *Near Eastern Archaeology in the Twentieth Century* (*Festschrift* N. Glueck, 1970), pp. 331-347; K. Preisendanz, ed., *Papyri graecae magicae* (2nd ed., 2 vols., 1973-74); H. Ringgren, *Religions of the Ancient Near East* (Eng. tr. 1973); P. Samain, *Ephemerides theologicae lovanienses,* 15 (1938), 449-490; J. B. Segal, *JJS,* 1 (1976), 1-22; M. Smith, *Jesus the Magician* (1978); *TWAT,* IV, *s.v.* "כָּשַׁף" (G. André); E. E. Urbach, *The Sages: Their concepts and Beliefs* (2 vols., 1979); E. M. Yamauchi, *Tyndale Bulletin,* 14 (1983), 169-200.

D. E. AUNE

**MAGISTRATE** [Aram. *šāpēṭ*] (Ezr. 7:25); NEB ARBITRATORS; [pl. of *tiptāy*] (Dnl. 3:2f.); AV SHERIFFS; NEB CHIEF CONSTABLES; [Gk. *árchōn*] (Lk. 12:58); NEB COURT; [pl. of *stratēgós*] (Acts 16:20, 22, 35f., 38). The term is used for a variety of officials whose functions, while not precisely known, are generally judicial. In the expression "magistrates and judges" (Ezr. 7:25) the terms are practically synonymous, since the former (not found elsewhere in Aramaic) is a loanword from Heb. *šāpaṭ,* "judge"; however, the LXX reading, "scribes" (Gk.

*grammateís* = Aram. *sap<sup>e</sup>rîn*), is often preferred. In the lists of Persian titles for officials in Dnl. 3:2f. "magistrate" translates a term whose meaning is unknown, but is probably a loanword from Persian *tāyu-pātā*, "police chief"(?). Gk. *árchōn* may denote any of a wide variety of authorities (see Delling, *TDNT*, I, 488f.); e.g., the same author uses it in Acts 16:19 ("rulers"), as a synonym for the *stratēgoí* of v. 20. The latter were the leading officials of the Roman colony of Philippi, the *duumviri*. E. W. S.

**MAGNIFICAL.** An old form retained by the AV from the Genevan Version at 1 Ch. 22:5, translating the Heb. hiphil of *gāḏal* (lit. "make great"; RSV, NEB, "magnificent").

**MAGNIFICAT, THE** mag-nif'i-kat. Luke 1:46-55, the song of praise attributed to Mary the Lord's mother; she offered it in response to Elizabeth's blessing (vv. 41-45). The name comes from the first word of this passage in the Vulg.: *Magnificat anima mea Dominum* ("My soul magnifies the Lord"). The passage forms one of several Lukan canticles (Lat. *canticulum*, "little song") and has liturgical significance as a song used in Christian worship that was not from the OT Psalter.

Scholarship has attained a consensus that this is a poetic speech (possibly of the genre known as "Hymns of Praise," Heb. *hodāyôṯ*, from the Dead Sea Scroll 1QH). It is definitely Hebraic in its meter, with the use of couplets (*parallelismus membrorum*), and in its use of OT idioms. There is less certainty whether it is based on a Semitic original (as suggested by H. Gunkel, who has been supported by Aytoun, D. R. Jones, Laurentin, and P. Winter), perhaps even going back directly to an Aramaic poem sung by Mary in her Galilean dialect (J. G. Machen, *Virgin Birth of Christ* [1930], pp. 95-98).

But a Hebrew or Aramaic *Vorlage* for the Magnificat is a minority position, although several scholars have lent support to it (see Marshall, p. 47). When this view is linked with the notion of the Lukan canticles (the Magnificat of Mary, the Benedictus of Zechariah [1:68-79], and the Nunc Dimittis of Simeon [2:29-32]) as directly emanating from a local tradition associated with the holy family at Nazareth, it is summarily dismissed. In fact, the modern debate has sought a more complex origin for the Magnificat, as indicated below.

***I. Who Spoke the Magnificat?***–The textual witnesses in Lk. 1:46 present an interesting problem. Almost all the Greek MSS, ancient versions, and patristic citations read "Mary" (*Mariam*, but *Maria* in MSS C* D), but three copies of the Old Latin version have "Elizabeth" (with variant spellings). Elizabeth was taken to be the speaker by Irenaeus (*Adv. haer.* iv.7.1), in Jerome's translation of Origen *In Luc. Hom.* 7, and by Bishop Niceta(s) of Remesiana (*ca.* A.D. 400). See R. E. Brown, pp. 334-336, for a full discussion turning on the variant textual data, which are of doubtful worth and chiefly from Latin sources.

The textual evidence for an attribution to Elizabeth is so slender that if it alone counted none would entertain its value. But other factors have entered the picture (listed by S. Benko, *JBL*, 86 [1967], 263-275, and discussed in detail by R. Laurentin). The chief argument is that of *lectio difficilior* ("a more difficult reading"); i.e., one can understand a later scribe changing Elizabeth to Mary but not the other way around. Other arguments in favor of Elizabeth as the speaker are (1) the evidence of her being "filled with the Holy Spirit" (Lk. 1:41) and so gifted to prophesy; (2) the parallel of the speaker's condition with that of Hannah (1 S. 2:1-10), which suggests that Elizabeth's praise would have been occasioned by her bearing a child when her physical condition rendered motherhood unlikely; (3) the speaker's reference in v. 48 to her own "low estate" (*tapeínōsis*, lit. "humiliation"), which fits Elizabeth's barrenness (vv. 7, 25) more than Mary's modesty; (4) the parallelism that would be secured between the two speeches assigned to two parents of John (Elizabeth in the Magnificat and Zechariah in the Benedictus); (5) the awkward mention of Mary in v. 56, since she has already been introduced as the speaker in v. 46. This double allusion to Mary's name in the MSS led A. von Harnack to conjecture that the original text lacked a name altogether and read simply *kaí eípen*, "and she said." R. Laurentin, on the basis of his theory of a Hebrew original, tried to support this theory by arguing that the verb "magnifies" (*megalýnei*) translates the Hebrew part. *m<sup>e</sup>rîmâ* (<*rûm*), "raises on high, exalts"; thus it plays on Mary's Hebrew name *miryām*, which would have been added by dittography (*Bibl.*, 38 [1957], 1-23). But this argument requires a Semitic *Vorlage*, which is doubtful. See also W. Wink, *John the Baptist in the Gospel Tradition* (1968), pp. 64f.

None of the above suggestions carries much weight, and there are counterbalancing arguments for each (see Marshall, p. 78; Fitzmyer, p. 366; Brown, pp. 335f.; J. McHugh, *Mother of Jesus in the NT* [1975], p. 445, with additional bibliography). (1) Much of the Magnificat fits neither woman, but the macarism (blessing) of Lk. 1:48b matches the macarism applied to Mary in v. 45a. (2) The song fits Elizabeth on the model of Hannah (in 1 S. 2:1-10), but Mary's presenting her child and meeting Simeon also parallel Hannah (in 1 S. 1:21-28; 2:19f.). (3) If Elizabeth's name did stand in Lk. 1:46, then it is as repetitious as Mary's name (in vv. 46, 56), since v. 41 mentions Elizabeth twice. (4) What scribe would have altered "Mary" to "Elizabeth" or inserted Elizabeth's name *de novo* in the light of the encomium of v. 48b: "all generations will call me blessed"? (5) There is a powerful symmetry in having Mary and Zechariah as authors of hymns of praise, since both persons are recipients of angelic annunciations.

***II. Composition of the Magnificat.***–Even with the majority opinion settling for Mary as the name in the text and the one to whom the canticle is assigned, it is by no means agreed that she composed the Magnificat. Marshall (p. 79), who considered the song appropriately attributed to Mary, conceded that of all the canticles "the hymns . . . are unlikely to have been spontaneous compositions" (p. 46).

Various compositional possibilities present themselves. (1) The Magnificat was a Lukan creation, composed by him *ad hoc* as he was writing his Gospel. The chief difficulty is that all the canticles fit only loosely into the narrative framework and can be easily removed. (2) The song of Mary along with the other canticles was composed by Luke and added to an already existing narrative (a pre-Lukan source or birth-cycle has been postulated by several scholars; see Marshall, pp. 47-49). (3) The most persuasive view, stated by Brown (pp. 346-357), is that the Lukan birth hymns are pre-Lukan and were added by the Evangelist to an existing narrative frame. The lines of argument are literary (their OT and Qumranic character but stylized composition), form-critical (involving Luke's method of composition in both Gospel and Acts, where the speeches appear to be kerygmatic pieces inserted in appropriate places), and especially topical (i.e., related to content).

The warlike character (as some interpreters have judged) of such lines as Lk. 1:52f. has suggested a setting in the battle hymns of the Maccabean times (so Winter). Moreover, the past tenses in the canticle suggest that in its original form the hymn celebrated God's providential deliverance as already in the past; it would have combined personal thanksgiving and praise to God for His eschatological deeds (so H. Schürmann, p. 71, who found this "mixed form" acceptable).

The scholarly consensus is that the Magnificat originated in Jewish-Christian circles rather than in a strictly Jewish milieu. As Brown asked pertinently (p. 350), what Jewish setting would explain the tremendous sense of accomplished salvation through the house of David? And the fulfillment of the covenant with Abraham (Lk. 1:55) seems clearly to reflect Jewish-Christian convictions, which are also mirrored in the early chapters of Acts. Brown took this line further and postulated the *Sitz im Leben* of the Lukan canticles in the Anawim (whose presence he found in Acts 2:43-47; 4:32-37), a group of Jewish messianic pietists who were centered in Jerusalem and treasured these expressions of faith. The way that Luke associated the hymns with John's origins and the holy family is entirely fitting.

***III. The Picture of Mary.***–The song attributed to Mary is in keeping with Luke's characterization of Jesus' mother throughout the Third Gospel. The notes of joy voiced by Elizabeth (Lk. 1:41, 44) and Mary (v. 47) recur in the body of the Evangelist's work, where Gk. *agallíasis* indicates eschatological joy caused by God's intervention in salvation-history (see R. Bultmann, *TDNT,* I, 19-21).

Mary is accordingly set forth as a model believer and a spokesperson for Christian discipleship. The "blessedness" that she is given (Lk. 1:48b) is, to be sure, unique to her as the mother of the Lord, but it is a joy that, on its human side, hinges on her obedient acceptance of a divine vocation (vv. 38, 45). Mary is a prototypical believer, in Luke's picture of Christian existence, and a founding member of the eschatological family around Jesus (8:21). Indeed, some would highlight her role as the first "Pentecostal" Christian (see J. M. Ford, *Six Pentecosts* [1976], pp. 7-14). Luke evidently wished to portray Mary as having a pivotal role in salvation-history, as the most illustrious representative of the group in early Christianity upon whom the Spirit came at Pentecost (Acts 1:14; 2:1ff.) and whose life-style as the "poor" (Lk. 6:20-22) was specially favored by God.

***IV. Meaning of the Magnificat.***–The stately couplets that form this song of Mary have been suggestively arranged into (1) an introduction (Lk. 1:46b-47), (2) strophe 1 (vv. 48-50), (3) strophe 2 (vv. 51-53), and (4) a conclusion (vv. 54f.). See Brown (pp. 357-365), who demonstrated how the canticle is made up of a *cento* of OT passages arranged in a series of couplets (see also J. M. Creed, *Gospel According to St. Luke* [1930; repr. 1942], pp. 303f.). V. 48 is best treated, as by many recent commentators, as a sign of Luke's editorial adaptation of a precomposed Jewish-Christian hymn of praise in order to make the hymn applicable to Mary's situation; the verse — "Because he has looked favorably on the lowly condition of his servant. From now on all generations will call me blessed" — is rich in Lukan expressions and recalls the descriptions of Mary's own character in vv. 38, 45a.

Strophe 1 emphasizes a personal reaction to God's holiness and His mercy shown to the pious who trust in Him (the Anawim). The community that speaks this language recognizes in the crucified and risen Jesus precisely these traits of the divine character (Acts 3:14; 4:27, 30), but on human lips the praise of an individual (Mary) who speaks for the group.

Strophe 2 is less individualistic. The six verbs, all in the past tense, express the community's praise for God's redeeming acts in the Messiah and celebrate His covenant faithfulness (Heb. *ḥeseḏ*) in the new age of messianic salvation (a theme in Acts 2–4). The strophe also contains a claim to self-identity, as this group sees how Jesus' own teaching on eschatological "reversal" (*Umwertung*), especially in the Lukan Beatitudes (Lk. 6:20-26) and the parables (12:16-21; 14:7-11; 16:19-31), has been understood in the group's own situation and in retrospect in the life and service of its "patron," Mary. She found true blessedness and joy in accepting her lowly situation and was raised to high privilege by becoming the vehicle of God's saving purpose. Thus the community's praise is rightly placed on her lips, since she speaks for it and for all Christians who believe in God, whose nature and grace are revealed in the incarnation and exaltation of His Son (Phil. 2:6-11; 2 Cor. 8:9).

***Bibliography.***–The journal articles cited above are only a selection of the main contributions. See further references in the following: H. Schürmann, *Das Lukasevangelium,* I (*HTK,* 1969); R. E. Brown, *Birth of the Messiah* (1977); I. H. Marshall, *Gospel of Luke* (*NIGTC,* 1978); R. E. Brown, *et al., Mary in the NT* (1978); J. A. Fitzmyer, *Gospel According to Luke I-IX* (*AB,* 1981).

R. P. MARTIN

**MAGNIFICENCE** [Gk. *megaleiótēs*–'greatness'] (Acts 19:27); NEB DIVINE PRE-EMINENCE. The Greek term is rendered "majesty" by the RSV when used of God (Lk. 9:43) or Christ (2 Pet. 1:16). *See* MAJESTY.

**MAGNIFY; MAGNIFICENT** [Heb. *gāḏal*–'become great,' 'consider great' (hiphil, 1 Ch. 22:5; Job 19:5; etc.; qal, 2 S. 7:26; 1 Ch. 17:24; piel, Ps. 34:3 [MT 4]; 69:30 [MT 31]; hithpael, Isa. 10:15; Dnl. 11:36f.), *rāḇâ*–'become great, numerous' (Dnl. 11:39); Gk. *megalýnō*–'make large' (Lk. 1:46), *doxázō* (Rom. 11:13)]; AV also MAGNIFICAL, BOAST, BECOME GREAT, WAX GREAT, INCREASE; NEB also BE GREAT, DEFY, GLORIFY, etc. To cause someone to be held in higher esteem.

While the Hebrew and Greek roots (esp. *gdl*) have widely varied usage, the translation "magnify" is used by the RSV primarily to denote human exaltation of God or human self-exaltation — the latter usually being depicted as presumptuous. The AV also uses "magnify" several times to denote God's exaltation of a person (e.g., Josh. 4:14). In seven of the RSV occurrences, God is exalted (e.g., Ps. 34:3: "O magnify the Lord with me, and let us exalt his name together"), while in eleven occurrences men magnify themselves. In the latter category the royal interloper of Dnl. 11:21-39 is especially notable: he will "magnify himself above every god, and shall speak astonishing things against the God of gods" (v. 36). He will also magnify those who recognize him (v. 39). Isa. 10:15 uses a rhetorical question and a metaphor to describe the absurdity of the Assyrian king's claim to have conquered by his own might: "Shall . . . the saw magnify itself against him who wields it?" Job complains that his "friends" have wronged him by magnifying themselves at his expense (19:5).

In one instance the exaltation of one's own work is not cast in negative light. In Rom. 11:13 Paul says that he magnifies (i.e., "boasts of," "makes much of") his ministry to the Gentiles in the hope of thereby effecting the salvation of Jews.

Perhaps the most sublime and familiar use of "magnify" is found in Mary's hymn of praise to God in Lk. 1:46-55, the Latin version of which begins with the words "*Magnificat anima mea Dominum*" (*see* MAGNIFICAT, THE).

See *TDOT,* II, *s.v.* "gādhal" (Bergman-Ringgren, Mosis).

S. S. STUART

**MAGOG** mā'gog [Heb. *māgôg*; Gk. *Magōg*]. Named as a son (or descendant) of Japheth in a list that includes Gomer, Tubal, and Meshech (Gen. 10:2; 1 Ch. 1:5). In Ezekiel's prophecy Magog is the kingdom of Gog, the chief prince of Meshech and Tubal (Ezk. 38:2; 39:6) and an invader of Israel. Josephus identified the Magogites with the Scythians, who were a sinister military power in the 6th cent. B.C. (*Ant.* i.6.1 [123]). A resemblance between the names Gog and Gyges (Gugu) king of Lydia (*ca.* 600 B.C.) has led to the suggestion by some scholars that Magog is Lydia; others, however, urge that Magog is probably only a variant of Gog (cf. Assyr. *māt gugu,* "land of Gog"). The LXX understands Magog as a people, not a country; and if the identification with either the Scythians or the inhabitants of Lydia is tenable, it is difficult to see Magog as simply an eschatological figure for challengers of the divine supremacy over mankind (cf. D. S. Russell, *Method and Message of Jewish Apocalyptic* [*OTL,* 1964], pp. 190-93).

In the book of Revelation Gog and Magog represent all the heathen opponents of the Messiah (20:8). In this sense these names recur frequently in Jewish apocalyptic literature (e.g., Jub. 7:19; 9:8; see R. H. Charles, comm. on Revelation [*ICC,* 1920], II, 188f., for other references to Gog and Magog).

*See* Gog **2, 3.**

See *TDOT,* II, *s.v.* "gôgh" (Otzen).

J. A. LEES R. K. H.

**MAGOR-MISSABIB** mä-gōr' mis-ə-bib' [Heb. *māgôr missāḇîḇ*–'terror all around' (cf. RSV "Terror on every side"); LXX Gk. *Metoikon*–'exile', reading *māgôr* II and omitting *missāḇîḇ*]. The AV and NEB transliteration of a symbolic name given to Pashhur son of Immer, the governor of the temple, who had ordered Jeremiah beaten and held in stocks (Jer. 20:3). The name signified the coming terrors of war via the Babylonian invasion as punishment for Judah. The same expression is found, though not as a name, in a variety of other passages (Ps. 31:13 [MT 14]; Jer. 6:25; 20:10; 46:5; 49:29; Lam. 2:22). Since the LXX and Syr. do not witness to the second part of the compound (*missāḇîḇ*) in Jer. 20:3 it is possible that the name in the original text was simply *Magor* ("terror").

***Bibliography.***–A. M. Honeyman, *VT,* 4 (1954), 424-26; J. A. Thompson, *Book of Jeremiah* (*NICOT,* 1980), p. 455.

D. STUART

**MAGPIASH** mag'pē-ash [Heb. *magpîʿāš*]. One of the "chiefs of the people" who signed the covenant of Ezra (Neh. 10:20 [MT 21]).

**MAGUS, SIMON.** *See* Simon Magus.

**MAHALAB** mā'ə-lab [Heb. *mēḥeḇel*] (Josh. 19:29); AV "from the coast"; NEB MEHALBEH. A term traditionally understood as a town, but better taken as "district, area."

Mahalab has been proposed as a site in Asherite territory on the assumption that it was the Ahlab of Jgs. 1:31, and that the compiler's understanding of Helbah as a separate settlement resulted from confusion or misreading. On such a view Ahlab-Helbah would be one coastal city named Meheleb, conveniently identified by Y. Aharoni (*LBHG,* rev., p. 235) and others with Khirbet el-Maḥâlib, about 6 km. (4 mi.) NE of Tyre. While it probably preserves the ancient name Ahlab, it does not do the same for Helbah.

The MT of Josh. 19:21 reads "from Hebel"; thus the conjectured place name involves a transposition of the last two Hebrew consonants. Such a change might be explained by metathesis, as some have argued from the LXX, which interpreted the MT *mēḥeḇel* as a town or district named Leb.

Judges 1:31, however, furnishes no textual warrant either in the MT or the LXX for assuming that Ahlab and Helbah were different names for a site named Mahalab. Consequently the translation of MT *mēḥeḇel* by "Mahalab" seems purely conjectural, and it appears more satisfactory to regard *ḥeḇel* as a common noun meaning "district, area of land" (cf. Dt. 3:4; 1 K. 4:13) than as a place name. Josh. 19:29 would thus read preferably ". . . at the sea by the region of Achzib," as in the New King James Version.

See M. H. Woudstra, *Joshua* (*NICOT,* 1981), pp. 289f.

R. K. H.

**MAHALAH** mā'hə-lä (AV, NEB, 1 Ch. 7:18). *See* Mahlah.

**MAHALALEEL** mə-hal'ə-lēl [Gk. *Maleleēl*] (Lk. 3:37); AV MALELEEL; **MAHALALEL** mə-hal'ə-lel [Heb. *mahᵃlal'ēl* –'God flashes forth,' 'praise of God'; AV MAHALALEEL.

**1.** Son of Kenan in the line of Seth; father of Jared; ancestor of Joseph the father ("as was supposed," Lk. 3:23) of Jesus (Gen. 5:12f., 15-17; 1 Ch. 1:2; Lk. 3:37). Some (e.g., *IDB, s.v.* "Mehujael") think this is the Sethite variant of Mehujael in the Cainite genealogy (5:12f.), though others (e.g., KD) maintain that these genealogies are distinct.

**2.** Son of Perez; father of Shephatiah; a Judahite whose descendants lived in Jerusalem after the Exile (Neh. 11:4).

**MAHALATH** mā'hə-lath [Heb. *maḥᵃlaṯ, māḥᵃlaṯ*].

**1.** The daughter of Ishmael and sister of Nebaioth whom Esau married because his father Isaac was displeased with his Canaanite wives (Gen. 28:9). *See also* Basemath **1.**

**2.** One of the eighteen wives of Rehoboam and a granddaughter of David (2 Ch. 11:18).

**MAHALATH (LEANNOTH)** mā'hə-lath (lə-an'ôth) [Heb. *māḥᵃlaṯ (leʿannôṯ)*]. Technical terms of uncertain meaning. *Māḥᵃlaṯ* occurs in the superscriptions to Pss. 53 and 88 (MT 53:1; 88:1), in the latter instance followed by *leʿannôṯ*. Several interpretations have been suggested. (1) Some have read *ʿal-māḥᵃlaṯ* as "for the round dance," derived from *ḥwl*; cf. M. Dahood, who then derived *leʿannôṯ* from *ʿny,* "sing an antiphonal song" (*Psalms,* II [*AB,* 2nd ed., 1973], 302). (2) Others have noted that the somber tone of these Psalms renders the dance interpretation unlikely. S. Mowinckel read *ʿal-māḥᵃlaṯ* as "in connection with illness" and *leʿannôṯ* as "to humiliate [one's soul]," thus indicating a psalm of penitence, possibly as part of a ritual of purification from illness (*Psalms in Israel's Worship* [Eng. tr. 1962], II, 211f.). (3) Still others have suggested that this phrase represents "the opening words of a well-known song, to the tune of which the Psalm was to be performed" (A. A. Anderson, *Psalms (1–72)* [*NCBC,* repr. 1981], p. 47; cf. C. A. Briggs and E. G. Briggs, comm. on Psalms, I [*ICC,* 1906], lxxv-lxxvi).

*See also* Psalms II.C; Music III.B.2. N. J. O.

**MAHALI** mā'hə-lī (Ex. 6:19, AV). *See* Mahli.

**MAHANAIM** ma'hə-nā-əm [Heb. *maḥᵃnayim*–'two camps']. A fortified city in Gilead that was Ishbosheth's headquarters after Saul's death and David's refuge during Absalom's coup (Gen. 32:2 [MT 3]; 2 S. 2:8; 17:24).

*I. **Location.***–The OT locates Mahanaim E of the Jordan in Gilead. It was a town of Gad (Josh. 21:38; 1 Ch. 6:80 [MT 65]) on the border between the territories of that tribe and the half-tribe of Manasseh (13:30). Gen. 32 implies that Mahanaim was slightly N of the Jabbok (v. 22), possibly on its north bank across from Peniel (v. 30).

After his truce with Joab, Abner crossed the Jordan, marched "the whole forenoon" (*habbiṯrôn*), and arrived at Mahanaim (2 S. 2:29). This half-day journey would locate Mahanaim some distance from the Jordan. But *biṯrôn* can also mean "cleft, ravine" (*BDB*, p. 144; W. Arnold, *AJSL*, 28 [1911], 274ff.), in which case Mahanaim would probably be situated on the side of a wadi.

Because he "ran by the way of the [Jordan] plain" (2 S. 18:23) and not across the hills, Ahimaaz preceded the Cushite in bringing the news of Absalom's death to David, who was waiting at Mahanaim. If Mahanaim was on the north bank of the Jabbok or any other "ravine," then Ahimaaz took the longer but smoother route down the Jordan plain and up the wadi. That the watchman saw the two runners coming also implies that Mahanaim was on high ground.

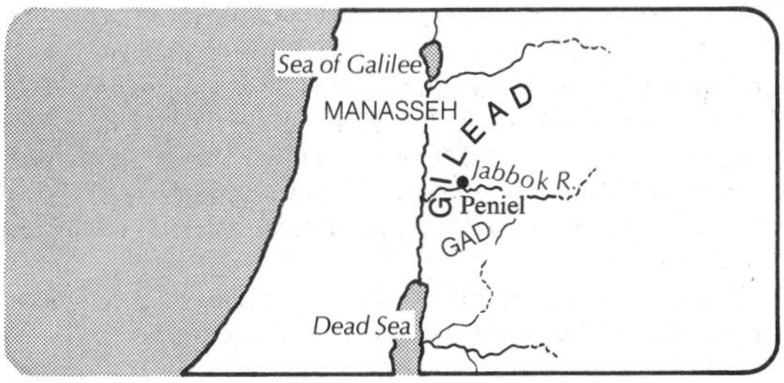


Beyond this, the precise location of Mahanaim cannot be confirmed, although suggestions are many (cf. Bartlett). Tulûl edh-Dhahab was once considered a possible site, but it is probably Peniel instead (cf. Glueck). Merrill suggested Khirbet Saleikhat, which is about 5 km. (3 mi.) E of the Jordan and about 6 km. (4 mi.) N of Wâdī Ajun. It is about 100 m. (300 ft.) above the plain and would afford David's watchman a high vantage point from which he could see Ahimaaz and the Cushite running (2 S. 18:24ff.). Others (e.g., *WHAB*) have suggested Khirbet Maḥneh, about 14 km. (9 mi.) E of the Jordan and 20 km. (12½ mi.) N of the Jabbok near ʿAjlûn. This is the only place that may preserve the ancient name. ʿAjlûn has been suggested, but both it and Khirbet Maḥneh are farther from the Jordan than Jacob's comment about "this Jordan" (Gen. 32:10) may imply, and are too far north. De Vaux (*Vivre et penser*, 1 [1941], 16ff., 31), followed by Simons, suggested Tell Ḥajjāj, which is S of Tulûl edh-Dhahab and the Jabbok. Aharoni thought that it is Tell edh-Dhahab el-Gharbi, since he identified Tell edh-Dhahab esh-Sherqiyeh as Peniel (*LBHG* [2nd ed. 1979], p. 34). According to Ottoson (*Gilead* [1969], p. 127) it is Tell Ḥeggāg, but this is S of the Jabbok.

*II. Name.*–On his return to Canaan Jacob met the angels of God, exclaimed, "This is God's army," and named the place Mahanaim, which means "two camps," i.e., God's and Jacob's (Gen. 32:1f. [MT 31:55–32:1]). Jacob mentioned "two companies" in Gen. 32:10 (MT 11) because the previous night he had divided all he had into two companies (v. 7 [MT 8]); thus this verse is not necessarily a second explanation of the name Mahanaim. S. Cohen (*IDB*, III, *s.v.*) commented that originally the form might have been "'Mahaneh' ('encampment'), lengthened by mimation to 'Mahanem,' which in turn became 'Mahanaim' (cf. *yerûshālēm* and *yerûshālayim* for 'Jerusalem')." But other explanations are also possible (cf. P. Joüon, *Grammaire de l'hébreu biblique* [1923], § 91h; on the form of Jerusalem *see* JERUSALEM I.A).

*III. History.*–Mahanaim is first mentioned as the place where Jacob rested the night before his reconciliation with Esau (Gen. 32:2). It was a Levitical (Merarite) city (Josh. 21:38; 1 Ch. 6:80 [MT 65]) within the inheritance of the Gadites (Josh. 13:26, 30). After Saul's death Abner took Ishbosheth to Mahanaim to make him king (2 S. 2:8, 12), and Abner returned there after his defeat at Gibeon (v. 29). It was probably also at Mahanaim that Ishbosheth was murdered (4:1-8).

David chose Mahanaim as his refuge from Absalom (2 S. 17:24, 27; 19:32 [MT 33]; cf. 1 K. 2:8). From here he fought Absalom, and here he wept over his son's death (2 S. 18:33).

Mahanaim was the seat of Solomon's seventh district; each district provided the king's food for one month (1 K. 4:14). The only other time Mahanaim may be mentioned in the OT is Cant. 6:13 (MT 7:1), which can be translated either "the dance of Mahanaim" (NIV) or "a dance before two companies" (RSV).

In *ca.* 925 B.C. Mahanaim was overrun by Shishak of Egypt in his raid on Palestine (cf. J. Simons, *Egyptian Topographical Lists Relating to Western Asia* [1938], pp. 89-101, 178-186).

***Bibliography.***–S. Merrill, *East of the Jordan* (1881), pp. 433f.; N. Glueck, *AASOR*, 18-19 (1937-39), 232 n. 607, 234; J. Simons, *GTTOT*, §§ 229-232; K.-D. Schunk, *Zeitschrift der deutschen morgenländischen Gesellschaft*, 113 (1963), 34-40; J. R. Bartlett, "Moabites and Edomites," in D. J. Wiseman, ed., *Peoples of OT Times* (1973), p. 252 n. 47.

W. D. MOUNCE

**MAHANEH-DAN** mā'hə-nə-dan [Heb. *maḥ^anēh-ḏān*– 'the camp of Dan']; AV also "the camp of Dan" (Jgs. 13:25). A place where "the Spirit of the Lord began to stir" Samson (Jgs. 13:25) and where six hundred Danites camped before migrating northward (18:12). According to 13:25, it was between Zorah and Eshtaol, which were only a mile apart. Jgs. 18:12, however, states that the Danites came from Zorah and Eshtaol and pitched camp in Judah "behind" (i.e., W of) Kiriath-jearim. A camp between Zorah and Eshtaol would not be in Judah and could hardly be said to be "behind" Kiriath-jearim regardless of whether Kiriath-jearim is identified with Kiryat-el-enab or with Tell el-Azhar. Since the site was only a camp, one need not look for ruins, but the event was so memorable that long afterward the place was still called "the camp of Dan." Suggested solutions for the discrepancy in location are that a temporary camp might shift about or be only vaguely defined, or that the mention of Zorah and Eshtaol immediately before Mahaneh-dan in Jgs. 18:12 may have prompted a copyist to insert the name in 13:25 also.

In his excavation of Tell Dan, A. Biran found that the stratum believed to have been occupied by the Danite forces who conquered Laish was a level platform with no house foundations, only a few pits used for grain storage. This suggests that the site remained a mere tent camp for some time after the Danite settlement.

***Bibliography***–*GTTOT*, § 606, p. 301; A. Biran, *BA*, 43 (1980), 173f.

F. WEDDLE

**MAHARAI** mā'hə-rī [Heb. *mah^aray*–'servant of Yahweh'(?)]. One of the thirty chief men in David's army, who were renowned for their heroic deeds (2 S. 23:28; 1 Ch. 11:30). He came from Netophah in Judah, from the clan of the Zerahites, and was commander of the tenth division of the army (1 Ch. 27:13). Cf. the common Punic name *mhrbʿl*, "servant of Baal"(?) (or perhaps "soldier of Baal"; on Ugar. *mhr*, cf. A. F. Rainey, *JNES*, 24 [1965], 24). See F. L. Benz, *Personal Names in the Phoenician and Punic Inscriptions* (1972), pp. 340f.

**MAHATH** mā'həth [Heb. *maḥaṯ*].

**1.** Son of Amasai, a Levite of the Kohathite family (1 Ch. 6:35).

**2.** A Kohathite Levite, son of Amasai, who assisted in cleansing the temple (2 Ch. 29:12) and overseeing the offerings brought into the temple (31:13) during the reign of Hezekiah.

**MAHAVITE** mā'hə-vīt [Heb. *maḥ^a^wîm*; Gk. *Mawi*; Vulg. *Mahumites*]. A name used to describe Eliel, one of David's thirty chief men (1 Ch. 11:46). The MT is obscure here, and some scholars have suggested emending it to *maḥ^a^naymî*, "of Mahanaim" (see *BHS*; KD; and other comms.).

**MAHAZIOTH** mə-hā'zē-əth [Heb. *maḥ^a^zî'ôṯ*–'visions']. One of the sons of Heman, appointed by David as a musician in the temple (1 Ch. 25:4, 30). *See also* JOSHBEKASHAH.

**MAHER-SHALAL-HASH-BAZ** mā'hər-shal'əl-hash'baz [Heb. *mahēr šālāl ḥāš baz*–'the spoil speeds, the prey hastes' (RSV mg.)] (Isa. 8:1, 3). A symbolic name given to Isaiah's third son (cf. SHEARJASHUB; IMMANUEL). The name was first recorded on a tablet in the presence of legal witnesses before the child was even conceived, so that later, when Isaiah's prediction of the destruction of Syria and Ephraim was fulfilled, the tablet would bear witness to the truth of the prophet's message and Ahaz's culpability in refusing to trust that message.

**MAHLAH** mä'lə [Heb. *maḥlâ*–'sickness' or 'weakness'(?)]; AV, NEB, also MAHALAH (1 Ch. 7:18).

**1.** The oldest of the five daughters of Zelophehad of the tribe of Manasseh (Nu. 26:33; 27:1; 36:11; Josh. 17:3). Because their father had no sons, they petitioned Moses that they be allowed to claim the family inheritance (Nu. 27:1-4). Their request was granted, on the condition that they marry within their father's tribe (36:1-9). They met this condition by marrying their cousins (vv. 10-12).

**2.** A descendant of Manasseh, possibly male (1 Ch. 7:18).

**MAHLI** mä'lī [Heb. *maḥlî*–'weak one'(?); Gk. *Mooli*]; AV also MAHALI, AV Apoc. MOLI; NEB Apoc. MOOLI.

**1.** Son of Merari and brother of Mushi; head of the Levitical family of MAHLITES (Ex. 6:19; Nu. 3:20, 33; 26:58; 1 Ch. 6:19, 29 [MT 6:4, 14]; 23:21; 24:26, 28; Ezr. 8:18; 1 Esd. 8:47).

**2.** Grandson of Merari and son of Mushi (1 Ch. 6:47 [MT 42]; 23:23; 24:30).

**MAHLITES** mä'līts [Heb. *maḥlî*–'weak ones'(?); Gk. *Mooli*]. A Levitical family; descendants of MAHLI (**1**) the son of Merari (Nu. 3:33; 26:58). They appear to have followed the example of the daughters of Zelophehad (*see* MAHLAH **1**): because Eleazar had no sons, his daughters married the sons of his brother Kish (1 Ch. 23:21f.).

**MAHLON** mä'lōn [Heb. *maḥlôn*–'weakness'(?)]. Son of Elimelech and Naomi; first husband of Ruth the Moabitess (Ruth 1:2, 5). He died in Moab without any children, and thus, to perpetuate his name in his inheritance, his widow Ruth married his kinsman Boaz (4:9f.).

**MAHOL** mā'hōl [Heb. *māḥôl*–'dance,' 'place of dancing,' 'orchestra']. Most versions render *b^e^nê māḥôl* as "sons of Mahol" (AV, RSV, NEB, 1 K. 4:31 [MT 5:11]); thus, Mahol would be the proper name of the father of the four wise men whom Solomon surpassed in wisdom. Scholars have demonstrated, however, that the phrase is more correctly translated "members of the orchestral guild" (Albright) or "choristers" (de Vaux). In the ancient Orient wisdom and poetry were considered to be inspired by the same spirit, and thus it is not surprising that these men were renowned for their wisdom as well as their psalmody (cf. superscriptions to Pss. 88, 89).

*Bibliography.*–W. F. Albright, *ARI* (5th ed. 1968), pp. 122f., 210 n. 96; J. Gray, *I & II Kings* (*OTL*, 2nd ed. 1970), p. 147; S. Mowinckel, *Psalms in Israel's Worship* (Eng. tr. 1962), II, 96f.; R. de Vaux, *Ancient Israel* (Eng. tr. 1961), II, 382.

N. J. O.

**MAHSEIAH** mä-sē'yə [Heb. *maḥsēyâ*–'Yahweh is a refuge'; Gk. *Maasaias*]; AV MAASEIAH, Apoc. MAASIAS. Grandfather of Baruch (Jer. 32:12 [LXX 39:12]; Bar. 1:1) and of Seraiah (51:59 [LXX 28:59]).

**MAIANEAS** mā-ən-ē'əs (1 Esd. 9:48, AV). *See* MAASEIAH **12.**

**MAID; MAIDEN** [Heb. *šipḥâ* (Gen. 16:1ff.; 25:12; 29:24, 29; 30:4ff.; 32:22 [MT 23]; 33:1f., 6; 35:25f.; Ps. 123:2; Prov. 30:23; Isa. 24:2), *'āmâ* (Gen. 30:3; Ex. 2:5; 2 S. 6:20, 22; Nah. 2:7 [MT 8]), *na'^a^râ* (Gen. 34:3, 12; 1 S. 9:11; 1 K. 1:3f.; Job 41:5 [MT 40:29]; Prov. 27:27; Am. 2:7; etc.), *b^e^ṯûlâ* (1 K. 1:2; Ps. 78:63; 148:12; Jer. 2:32; 31:13; 51:22; Lam. 1:4, 18; 2:10, 21; Ezk. 9:6; Zec. 9:17), *baṯ* (Cant. 2:2; 6:9; 7:1 [MT 2]; Lam. 3:51), *'almâ* (Ps. 68:25 [MT 26]; Prov. 30:19; Cant. 1:3; 6:8), *yaldâ* (Gen. 34:4), *raḥam* (Jgs. 5:30); Gk. *paidískē* (Mt. 26:69; Mk. 14:66, 69; Lk. 22:56; Jn. 18:17; Acts 12:13), *parthénos* (Mt. 25:1, 7, 11)]; AV also HANDMAID, DAMSEL, DAUGHTER, VIRGIN, etc.; NEB also SLAVE-GIRL, VIRGIN, DAUGHTER, GIRL, etc.; **MAIDSERVANT** [Heb. *šipḥâ* (Gen. 12:16; 24:35; 30:43; 32:5 [MT 6]; Ex. 11:5; 1 S. 8:16; 2 S. 17:17; 2 K. 5:26; Joel 2:29; etc.), *'āmâ* (Gen. 31:33; Ex. 20:10, 17; Dt. 5:14, 21; Jgs. 9:18; 19:19; 1 K. 1:13, 17; Job 19:15; 31:13; etc.); Gk. *paidískē* (Lk. 12:45), *doúlē* (Acts 2:18)]; AV also HANDMAIDEN, etc.; NEB also FEMALE SLAVE, SLAVE-GIRL, etc.

These terms have two different meanings: (1) an unmarried girl or woman, and (2) a female slave. According to strict English usage, "maiden" denotes an unmarried girl or woman, "maidservant" denotes a female slave, and "maid" can be used with either meaning.

*I. Unmarried Young Woman.*–Hebrew *na'^a^râ* has the primary meaning of a marriageable but unmarried young woman (e.g., Gen. 24:14, 16, etc.; Est. 2:4, 7ff.; cf. also Ruth 2:5f.; 4:12, where the widow Ruth is called a *na'^a^râ*). In some instances, however, the term can signify a female attendant or maid (e.g., Gen. 24:61; Ex. 2:5; 1 S. 25:42; 2 K. 5:2, 4; Est. 4:4, 16; Prov. 9:3; 31:15; cf. also Ruth 2:8, 22f.; 3:2), parallel to the use of *na'ar* ("lad, youth") to signify a male attendant (e.g., Gen. 22:3; Nu. 22:22).

*B^e^ṯûlâ* is usually translated "virgin" (e.g., KoB, p. 160), but some scholars have contested this interpretation (e.g., G. J. Wenham, M. Tsevat). Probably the term originally denoted a marriageable young woman (who was normally a virgin) but later developed the narrower meaning "virgin" (cf. the same development in Gk. *parthénos* and Ger. *Jungfrau*).

Other OT terms rendered "maiden" are *baṯ* (lit. "daughter" but also "girl, young woman"), *'almâ* ("girl at the age of puberty," "marriageable young woman"), *yaldâ* ("girl, young woman"; cf. *yeleḏ*, "boy, young man"), and *raḥam* (lit. "womb," used contemptuously in Jgs. 5:30).

Greek *parthénos* is the usual LXX translation of Heb. *b^e^ṯûlâ*, and its meaning appears to have evolved in the same way (see above). In Mt. 25:1-12 the *parthénoi* are virgins.

*See also* GIRL; MARRIAGE; VIRGIN.

*II. Female Slave.*–In the OT Heb. *šipḥâ* and *'āmâ* appear to be virtually synonymous designations for "female slave" (a common RSV translation in the Pentateuch). Both can also be used figuratively by a woman to express humility or submission when she speaks to a man or to God (e.g.,

*ʾāmâ* in Ruth 3:9; 1 S. 1:11, 16; 2 S. 20:17; 1 K. 3:20; *šip̱ḥâ* in Ruth 2:13; 1 S. 1:18; 2 K. 4:2, 16). Although no distinction between *šip̱ḥâ* and *ʾāmâ* is apparent, possibly the *šip̱ḥâ* was originally more closely associated with the family (*mišpāḥâ*). Another term that sometimes denotes a female servant is *naʿᵃrâ* (see I above).

In the NT Gk. *paidískē* (cognate of *país,* "child") and *doúlē* (cognate of *doúlos,* "servant") always designate a female slave (cf. RSV "slave" for *paidískē* in Gal. 4:22f., 30f.; "slave girl" in Acts 16:16).

*See also* HANDMAID; SERVANT; SLAVE.

***Bibliography.***–*DNTT,* III, 1071-73 (O. Becker, C. Brown); *TDNT,* V, *s.v.* παρθένος (G. Delling); *TDOT,* II, *s.v.* "bᵉthûlāh" (M. Tsevat); *TWOT,* I, 49f., 137f.; II, 946f.; G. J. Wenham, *VT,* 22 (1972), 326-348.

N. J. O.

**MAIL.** *See* WEAPONS OF WAR.

**MAIMED** [Heb. niphal of *šāḇar*] (Zec. 11:16); AV "that that is broken"; NEB INJURED; [Gk. *kyllós*] (Mt. 15:30f.; 18:8; Mk. 9:43); AV also HALT; NEB also CRIPPLED; [*anápēros*] (Lk. 14:13, 21); NEB CRIPPLED.

The niphal part. *nišbār*/*nišbereṯ,* "maimed, crippled," in its few applications specifically denotes the "breaking of a limb," as its verbal root (*šāḇar,* "break") suggests. In Zec. 11:16 *nišbereṯ* refers to a maimed or injured sheep that the incompetent shepherd fails to heal; it also is applied to injured animals in Ex. 22:10, 14; Ezk. 34:4, 16. *See* CRIPPLE; HURT; LAME. This term is used of people only in Isa. 8:15; 28:13, where it describes those who have figuratively stumbled over the law.

*Kyllós* specifically denotes a human limb that is abnormal or incapacitated, whether by congenital defect or injury. It is thus used substantively to designate those who are "deformed," "crippled," or "maimed." Twice (Mt. 15:30f.) it delineates a special subclass of the disadvantaged society, "the cripples." In the remaining two occurrences the sense of "disabling injury" or "maiming" is pronounced. Gk. *anápēros,* appearing only twice in the NT, is also used substantively to denote the same societal subclass.

D. G. BURKE

**MAINSAIL.** *See* SHIPS.

**MAJESTY; MAJESTIC** [Heb. *gāʾôn*] (Ex. 15:17; Job 37:4; 40:10; Isa. 2:10, 19, 21; 24:14; 60:15; Mic. 5:4); AV also EXCELLENCY; NEB also TRIUMPH, PRIDE; [*gaʾᵃwâ*] (Dt. 33:26; Ps. 68:34 [MT 35]); AV EXCELLENCY; NEB GLORY, PRIDE; [*gᵉʾûṯ*] (Ps. 93:1; Isa. 26:10); [*hāḏār*] (1 Ch. 16:27; Ps. 21:5 [MT 6]; 29:4; 45:3f. [MT 4f.]; 96:6; 104:1; 111:3; Isa. 35:2); AV also HONOUR, GLORIOUS, EXCELLENCY; NEB also SPLENDOUR, HONOUR; [*hôḏ*] (1 Ch. 29:11, 25; JOB 37:22; 39:20; Ps. 145:5; Isa. 30:30); AV also GLORY, GLORIOUS; NEB also "shrill"; [*ʾaddîr*] (Ps. 8:1, 9 [MT 2, 10]; 76:4 [MT 5]; Isa. 10:34; 33:21; Ezk. 32:18); AV GLORIOUS, EXCELLENT, MIGHTY, FAMOUS; NEB GLORIOUS, MIGHTY, NOBLE; [niphal of *ʾāḏar*] (Ex. 15:11); AV GLORIOUS; [*gᵉdûlâ*] (Est. 1:4); [*śᵉʾēṯ*] (Job 13:11; 31:23); AV EXCELLENCY, HIGHNESS; [Aram. *hᵃḏar*] (Dnl. 4:30 [MT 27]); [*rᵉḇû*] (Dnl. 4:36 [MT 33]; 5:18); [Gk. *megaleiótēs*] (Lk. 9:43; 2 Pet. 1:16); AV also MIGHTY POWER; [*megalōsýnē*] (He. 1:3; 8:1; Jude 25); [*megaloprepḗs*] (2 Pet. 1:17); AV EXCELLENT; NEB SUBLIME. When one generation commends to another generation the mighty acts of Yahweh, they speak of His majesty (Ps. 145:4f.), which is associated with His greatness, power, glory, victory, and kingship over the heavens and the earth (1 Ch. 29:11f.). Creation bears witness to it (Ps. 104:1-4). His acts of redemption and judgment proclaim it (Ex. 15:1, 7, 11, 21). Although God's majesty is in the skies (Ps. 68:34) and on the earth (Isa. 35:2), the wicked cannot now perceive it (Isa. 26:10). But on the Day of Yahweh it will be something from which they will wish to hide (Isa. 2:10, 19, 21). For the upright, in contrast, God's majesty is the reason for wholehearted praise (Ps. 111:1-3).

Man himself is crowned with majesty (RSV "honor") by this One whose very name is majestic (Ps. 8:1, 5, 9). The king especially is the recipient of that divine gift (Ps. 21:5). But the glory given to the creature is not identical with that possessed by the Lord Himself; only if one were to clothe himself in the divine majesty would he be able to exercise divine power (Job 40:10-14).

In the NT God's majesty is closely associated with Jesus Christ. Christ's exorcising a demon from a child is viewed as an expression of it (Lk. 9:42f.). At the transfiguration the apostles heard the voice of the Father borne by the Majestic Glory while they were eyewitnesses of the glory of the Lord Jesus (2 Pet. 1:16-18). In He. 1:3; 8:1 "majesty" is a synonym for God Himself; it is at the right hand of the Majesty on high that Christ has seated Himself after having made purification for sin.

G. WYPER

**MAKAZ** māʹkaz [Heb. *māqaṣ*–'cutting-off place, end'(?); Gk. *Machemas, Machmas, Magchas*]. A city under Ben-deker in the second administrative district of Solomon (1 K. 4:9). Other cities in the district were Shaalbim, Beth-shemesh, and Elon-beth-hanan; hence this district was in the Shephelah on the western border of Dan (cf. Josh. 19:40-46). Since the LXX readings suggest a Hebrew original with *ḫ* instead of *q,* Makaz has tentatively been identified with Khirbet el-Mukheizin, about 6 km. (4 mi.) S of Ekron (*GAB,* Map 17). This site accords with the general location indicated by the other cities, but no positive identification has been made.

W. S. L. S.

**MAKE; MAKER.** Some of the most common terms rendered by these words are Heb. *ʿāśâ, nāṯan, śîm śûm, šîṯ,* and Gk. *poiéō.* God is repeatedly acknowledged as the maker of heaven and earth (e.g., Gen. 14:19, 22). Since humans are made in the image of God, they can fashion the raw materials of creation into articles useful for their existence (1:26-28). Here lies the God-given potential — as well as justification — for the arts and crafts of human society. The potential can be used for good, as when the tabernacle was built with meticulous attention to precise specifications so that the finished product would reflect the glory of God and the proper approach to Him in worship (Ex. 25:40). It can also be used for evil, as in the making of idols (20:4).

The manifold nuances of "make" include: engage in some form of activity, e.g., war (1 Ch. 5:10); prepare something, e.g., a feast (Est. 1:3); write a book (Eccl. 12:12; Acts 1:1); publish a decree (Ezr. 5:13); voice a prayer (Lk. 5:33); win followers to a cause (Mt. 28:19, NEB); accord a certain status to a person (Acts 2:36); misrepresent someone (1 Jn. 1:10); pervert by misuse (Jn. 2:16); make claims about oneself that others consider false (5:18; 19:12).

Especially significant is the promise of Jesus to make certain prospective disciples "fishers of men" (Mk. 1:17). His example, teaching, and mighty works were needed to achieve the promised result.

The verb in "was made flesh" in Jn. 1:14, AV, expressing transition from one state or mode of existence to another, renders Gk. *gínomai,* which is usually translated "became" (RSV, NEB, etc.).

*See also* CREATION; CREATOR.

E. F. H.

**MAKEBATES** māk'bāts (AV mg. 2 Tim. 3:3; Tit. 2:3). Archaic term for one who stirs up strife, translating Gk. *diáboloi* (cf. AV "false accusers"; RSV "slanderers"). *See* SLANDER.

**MAKED** mā'kəd [Gk. ℵ *Maked* A *Makeb*]; AV also Maged (1 Macc. 5:36). A "strong and large" city in Gilead (1 Macc. 5:26, 36). Judas Maccabeus and his brother Jonathan "crossed the Jordan and went three days into the wilderness" (v. 24) to rescue Jews captured "by the Gentiles in Gilead" (v. 9) and "shut up" in five cities, including Maked (v. 26). Judas and his army captured those cities, slaughtering many (vv. 28-36).

Thutmose III in his roster of Canaanite towns lists *m-q-t* between Ashtaroth and Laish; see *LBHG,* rev., p. 160. *GAB* identifies Maked with Tell Miqdâd (p. 156), but this is open to question. W. S. L. S.

**MAKER.** *See* MAKE.

**MAKHELOTH** mak-hē'loth [Heb. *maqhēlōṯ*–'places of assembling'(?)]. One of Israelites' stopping-places in their journey from Sinai to Kadesh-barnea (Nu. 33:25). It was located between Haredah (v. 24) and Tahath (v. 26), but none of these sites has been positively identified. Because of the similarity of the terms Makheloth and Kehelathah (v. 22), some scholars have equated them and suggested a location at modern Kuntillet Jerâya (*GAB,* p. 156; *GP,* II, 214, gives the name as "*Kuntilet Qrayé,* also called *'Aǵrûd*"). However, this site breaks the sequence of the stations as given in vv. 16-37 and has no textual support. The LXX distinguishes *Makellath* (v. 22) and *Makēlōth* (v. 25). W. S. L. S.

**MAKKEDAH** mə-kē'də [Heb. *maqqēḏâ*; Gk. *Makēda*] (Josh. 10; 12:16; 15:41). A royal Canaanite enclave in the southern Shephelah that became part of the inheritance of Judah (15:41). Josh. 10 tells the story of Joshua's victory over five "Amorite" kings. During a battle the kings hid in "the cave" at Makkedah; Joshua closed them in with great stones while the Israelites routed their troops. Then the kings were brought out, put to death, hung on trees, and finally thrown back into the cave (vv. 10-29). 12:16 includes the king of Makkedah in the catalog of kings conquered by Joshua.

The site has not been identified with certainty. Aharoni was content to locate it "somewhere in the Lachish region" (*LBHG,* rev., p. 278 n. 73). Simons said, "None of the proposed identifications . . . is quite satisfactory" (*GTTOT,* § 318, p. 147; § 492, p. 273). Eusebius located it 8 Roman mi. (12 km., 7.3 mi.) E of Eleutheropolis (Beit Jibrîn). Some scholars have placed it N of Beit Jibrîn, possibly at Tell eṣ-Ṣâfī. W. S. L. S.

**MAKNADEBAI** mak-nad'ə-bī (Ezr. 10:40, NEB). *See* MACHNADEBAI.

**MAKTESH, THE.** *See* MORTAR, THE.

**MALACHI** mal'ə-kī [Heb.*mal'āḵî*–'my messenger, angel']. The title associated with the last of the twelve Minor Prophets.

I. Author
II. The Book
  A. Outline of the Message
  B. Composition of the Prophecy
  C. Theological Significance

*I. Author.*–Malachi is traditionally thought to have written the book of that name on the basis of the superscription in 1:1, but early textual variants cast some doubt on this position. The LXX, instead of giving a name, rendered "his messenger, angel" (*angéllou autoú*; but cf. Aq., Symm., Th., *malachion,* "of Malachi") as if the word in question was a common noun. The Targum of Jonathan ben Uzziel explicitly stated that Ezra the scribe was "my messenger" in Mal. 1:1. Jerome and Calvin, in the prefaces to their comms. on Malachi, also supported this view. Rashi and T.B. *Megillah* 15a recorded a similar view, but Rabbi Naḥman said that Malachi was really Mordecai (Est. 10:3). The Ezra tradition can hardly be trusted, for it seems to be based purely on a few similarities between the books (Mal. 2:11 and Ezr. 10:2). Later scholars objected to the construction of the prophet's name (most preferred *mal'āḵîāh,* "messenger of Yahweh") and credited the present superscription to an editor who arranged the three anonymous "burdens" in Zec. 9:1; 12:1; Mal. 1:1. "My messenger" was the name given to the final collection of oracles on the basis of its use in Mal. 3:1. G. Wallis believed that the messenger was an "interpreting angel" ("Wesen und Struktur der Botschaft Maleachis," in F. Maass, ed., *Das ferne und nahe Wort* [*BZAW,* 105, 1967], pp. 229-231).

In spite of the scarcity of evidence concerning the authorship of this prophecy, there are good reasons to believe that Malachi is the name of the author. The word *mal'āḵî* is comparable to other Hebrew names that end in *î,* such as Beeri, "my well" (Gen. 26:34; Hos. 1:1) or Ethni, "my gift" (1 Ch. 6:41), and it is placed where one would expect to find the name of the author. The similarities of Zec. 9:1; 12:1; Mal. 1:1 are superficial (Zec. 9:1; 12:1 do not function as superscriptions; cf. B. Childs, *Intro. to the OT as Scripture* [1979], pp. 491f.). Finally, the anonymity theory heavily depends on the nearly impossible editorial blunder of interpreting the messenger in Mal. 3:1 as the author of the book.

The book itself provides very little information about the prophet. Presumably he lived in or near Jerusalem and had an intimate knowledge of worship practices in the temple (1:6–2:9). Pseudo-Epiphanius recorded the view that he was a Levite from the tribe of Zebulun. His message demonstrates his concern for proper spiritual leadership (2:1-9) as well as popular morality (vv. 10-16; 3:5). He was traditional in his application of the Torah to life and forthright in his demands for holiness and performance of duty.

*II. The Book.*–Since the date of the book is not given, it must be determined from internal evidence. A summary of the prophet's message will provide a general introduction to the book's setting and to discussions of its date, structure, unity, and theological significance.

*A. Outline of the Message.* A general analysis of the contents of the book leads to a division of these oracles into six units (see II.B.3 below). The six oracles concentrate on present problems within the community caused by a misunderstanding of the nature and character of God. The book begins with a superscription (1:1) and ends with a conclusion (4:4-6 [MT 3:22-24]); both are outside the dialogue pattern of the rest of the book.

*1. "I have loved you" (1:2-5).* Malachi countered the Israelites' skepticism by reminding them of God's love for them. Although Deuteronomy emphasizes this teaching (4:37; 7:7f.; 10:15), the prophet chose to contrast God's election of Jacob with His rejection of Esau because God had verified his anger toward Edom in recent historical events. God's anger that caused Edom's destruction would prevent all attempts to rebuild that nation (Mal. 1:3f.). Earlier prophets had told that God's hatred for Edom was due to the Edomites' sins against Israel (Obadiah; Ezk. 35:1-15). God's anger is proof of His greatness (Mal. 1:5) and love for His people.

*2. "Where is my honor?" (1:6–2:9).* Such love and greatness requires a response of fear and love (Dt. 5:10; 6:5; 11:1, 13; 30:15, 19f.), but the priests despised God and did not even give Him the honor due a father or master (Mal. 1:6f.). They could not expect God to be gracious to them if they continued to offer sick and lame sacrifices (vv. 8f.). It would have been better not to sacrifice at all (v. 10) than to go through the motions with an unworthy offering (vv. 12f.). God is the King feared among the nations (vv. 11, 14), but where was His honor in Israel? These accusations are followed by a threat: God would curse the priests if they did not glorify Him (2:1-3). The warning was given so that the priests would honor and fear God (v. 5), be true messengers of His law (vv. 6-9), and continue His covenant with Levi (vv. 4f.; cf. Ex. 33:26-29; Nu. 25:11-13; Jer. 33:12).

*3. "Why are we faithless to one another?" (2:10-16).* Faithlessness was contrary to the natural and spiritual unity (by creation and the covenant) between God and Israel and among the individual Israelites. Marriages with heathen women (vv. 11f.) and divorce (vv. 13-15) were faithless acts that destroyed this unity; God could not accept the offerings from disunified homes.

*4. "Where is the God of justice?" (2:17–3:5).* In spite of God's love and the people's unfaithfulness, some accused Him of injustice because He did not judge the wicked (2:17). God assured the nation that He would judge the wicked priests (3:3f.) as well as those who mistreated others (v. 5). These people would learn to fear and please God when the "coming one" appeared to purify the nation (vv. 1-4) and establish justice.

*5. "Return to me and I will return to you" (3:6-12).* The famine (3:11) that had already struck the nation illustrated the justice of God. Because He is consistent in His judgment, He could not change (3:6) until the nation turned to Him and tithed (Nu. 18:21; Lev. 27:30) what He had given to them (Mal. 3:8f.). When they turned to God, He would turn to them, and all would see how His blessings filled the land to overflowing (vv. 10b-12).

*6. "I will distinguish between the righteous and the wicked" (3:13–4:3 [MT 3:13-21]).* The prosperity of the wicked, who do not serve God, caused some to wonder about the value of serving God (3:13-15), but those who truly feared God encouraged one another with His promises (v. 16). God will remember their righteousness and treat them as persons very special and dearly loved (vv. 17f.). On the day of judgment, He will distinguish the wicked from the righteous (v. 18); the wicked will be destroyed, but the righteous ones who fear God will enjoy His blessings forever (4:1-3).

The final three verses (4:4-6 [MT 3:22-24]) summarize the book and present two challenges. The first encourages the people to follow God's word through Moses (4:4), and the second reminds them to put their lives in order before the appearing of Elijah on the great day of the Lord.

*B. Composition of the Prophecy. 1. Date.* The references to sacrifice (1:7-14) and the doors (v. 10) point to a period of Jewish history when the temple was standing. The reference to the governor (Heb. *peḥâ*) in v. 8 (Hag. 1:1; Neh. 5:14; 12:26) indicates that Malachi lived in the Persian period after the completion of the second temple in 515 B.C. (Ezr. 6:14f.). The laxity with which the priest fulfilled his duties (Mal. 1:8-13) and the failure of the people to pay their tithe (3:8-10) suggest a date when religious fervor had begun to wane, well after 515 B.C. Ezra and Nehemiah also faced the problems of tithing (Neh. 10:32-39 [MT 33-40]; 13:10-13), mixed marriages (Mal. 2:10f.; Ezr. 9:1f.; Neh. 13:1-3, 23-27), and oppression of the poor (Mal. 3:5; Neh. 5:1-5). The exact relationship of Ezra and Nehemiah to Malachi is not given in the text. Scholars argue three main possibilities.

*a. Before Ezra.* The majority of scholars, including Marti, von Bulmerincq, Dentan, and Baldwin, have placed Malachi *ca.* 460 B.C., before the time of Ezra. The two main supports for this view are that Malachi must be before Ezra and Nehemiah, since Malachi never mentioned their work in his book, and that Malachi's tithing (Dt. 14:22-29) and offering laws (Dt. 15:1; 17:1) and use of Levites and priests as synonyms (Dt. 21:5) indicate that he relied on Deuteronomy and preceded the "priestly writings." Von Bulmerincq supposed that Malachi was Ezra's assistant, but others attributed the success of Ezra's preaching to the earlier work of Malachi. Mason questioned both of these main criteria and dated the book on the basis of style, tone, and eschatology to an earlier period just after Haggai.

*b. Around the Time of Nehemiah's Second Visit to Jerusalem.* Other scholars, e.g., Perowne and J. M. P. Smith, have placed Malachi between, during, or shortly after Nehemiah's visit to Jerusalem *ca.* 432 B.C. (Neh. 13). The backbone of proof is the existence of identical abuses in Nehemiah and Malachi (tithes in Mal. 3:8-10 and Neh. 13:10-14; mixed marriages in Mal. 2:11 and Neh. 13:23; social ills in Mal. 3:5 and Neh. 5:1-13). Additional support for this view includes, first, Malachi's and Nehemiah's presupposition that the law was in force (thus after Ezra), and, second, the need for temple funds, which does not fit the period of Ezra when the cost of the temple was met from the royal treasury (Ezr. 6:15-17, 20-24).

*c. Long after Nehemiah.* O. Kaiser (*Intro. to the OT* [Eng. tr. 1975], pp. 285f.) dated Malachi *ca.* 400-350 B.C., while O. Holtzmann (*Archiv für Religionswissenschaft,* 39 [1931], 1-21) put the book in the first half of the 3rd cent. because he identified the "company of the Hasideans" in 1 Macc. 2:42 with the covenant of those who feared God in Mal. 3:6.

*d. Conclusions.* A date around the second visit of Nehemiah is most likely. The absence of any reference to Malachi in Ezra or Nehemiah or to Ezra and Nehemiah in Malachi is a double-edged sword that in the end cannot determine the order of the books. An early date for Malachi cannot be based on his use of Deuteronomy and disuse of a later "priestly writing," for Malachi's tithe formula is closer to the "priestly" guideline in Nu. 18:21 than to Dt. 14:22-29. The relationship of the priests and Levites in Mal. 2:4-9 is also an inadequate criterion for dating the book, for these groups are not synonymous in the official list of those returning from exile *ca.* 536 B.C. (Ezr. 2:36-42) or in other postexilic writings (Ezr. 6:18; 8:15; 10:18, 23; Neh. 11:10, 15). One apparently cannot date Malachi on the basis of its pentateuchal sources. A date *ca.* 420 B.C. is preferable, since it is far enough away from Nehemiah's reform to explain the failure of the two to mention one another. A considerable amount of time between Malachi and Nehemiah allows one to take Nehemiah's reform seriously and provides time for its effects to have worn thin. There is also a distinction between the marriage problems in Neh. 13 and Mal. 2:10-16. "I hate divorce" (Mal. 2:16) addresses a later problem that developed among Israelite couples because Ezra's and Nehemiah's permission to divorce foreign women was later extended to all marriages. The problem of the tithe in Malachi is also later than Nehemiah. In Neh. 13:4-9 Tobiah prevented the bringing of the tithes, thus causing the Levites to forsake the temple and go to work (vv. 10-14), but in Malachi the Levites were back teaching and sacrificing in the temple (1:6–2:9), and famine was the reason that the "full tithe" was not brought (2:11).

*2. Unity.* Most scholars have maintained the essential unity of Malachi although questioning a few short verses. Elliger rejected Mal. 1:11-14, Marti questioned 2:7, and Mason believed that 3:1b-4 are secondary, but the major problems are 2:11f. and 4:4-6 (MT 3:22-24). Mal. 2:11f. is frequently assigned to a later editorial stage because it introduces the extraneous topic of foreign wives into the discussion of divorce in vv. 10-16, uses third-person verbs instead of first person (cf. vv. 10, 13), and makes a distinction between Israel and Judah. These peculiarities, however, indicate only the complexity of the socio-religious issue with which the author dealt and the difficulty of the Hebrew text (esp. v. 12), not the secondary nature of the verses.

Malachi 4:4-6 (MT 3:22-24) is clearly outside the regular dialogue pattern of the rest of the book. While some have regarded these verses as completely foreign to Malachi, others have seen them as a fitting conclusion to the prophetic canon as a whole (cf. Rudolph, pp. 291-93). The former view (cf. J. M. P. Smith, pp. 81-85) is that v. 4 is a later addition by a strict legalist who used terminology from Deuteronomy ("remember," "servant," "statutes," "all Israel," "law of Moses," and "Horeb") that is foreign to the rest of Malachi. Childs (*Intro. to the OT as Scripture*, p. 495) argued against both views and integrated vv. 4-6 into the context of Malachi itself. Verses 5f. develop 3:1 by explaining the role of the future Elijah by analogy to the first Elijah.

*3. Structure and Style.* The dialogue style of Malachi determines the structure within the paragraphs. Each paragraph is structured around (a) an initial statement; (b) an objection to the statement; and (c) a detailed substantiation of the statement that ends with a promise, threat, or encouragement. This framework enables one to identify six main paragraphs within the book. The overall structure of the book is difficult to perceive. Sellin transposed 3:6-12 and 2:10-16 after 1:2-5 to create a more natural progression: oracles of repentance to the people, to the priests, and to the doubters. Wallis attempted to arrange the material on the basis of the audience and nature of the message: rebuke, threat, salvation message. The parallel development of the justice of God in 2:17–3:5; 3:13-21 and the connection of the intervening paragraph (3:6-13) with the earlier section on worship make the material look unorganized. The difficulty of arranging the book on the basis of the audience, topic, or type of message suggests that the book is arranged around the theological statements at the beginning of each section. The flow of the message is: "I love you [1:2] but you do not honor me [v. 6] and are not faithful to me [2:10]; therefore I will show my justice [v. 17]. If you return to me, I will return to you and bless you [3:7], for I will distinguish between the wicked and the righteous who serve me [vv. 14, 18]."

The style of the book resembles "prophetic disputations" (cf. C. Westermann, *Basic Forms of Prophetic Speech* [Eng. tr. 1967], p. 201) and the dialogue style of Haggai. These short and direct challenges put in the mouth of the people are rhetorical literary devices used to focus attention on underlying theological issues that motivate behavior. The book is prose with a limited use of figurative language.

*C. Theological Significance.* If the preceding analysis is correct, Malachi was not a shallow legalistic scribe with no prophetic insight (cf. Neil, *IDB*, III, p. 231). The book lacks any reference to widespread discouragement among the people because the glories of the messianic age had not come (cf. Dentan, p. 1118; J. M. P. Smith, p. 11). Two very common problems faced the community: economic depression (3:10f.), and a lack of sound theological teaching (2:6-8). Since the people had no theological foundation, the economic conditions led to a misunderstanding of God's character and thus to a perversion of morality and worship. Malachi provided the instructions they needed by emphasizing the lordship of God. God is like a father and master (1:6), a great king (v. 16) and creator (2:10, 15); He loves those who fear and serve Him and judges the wicked (3:17). Because the priests failed to instruct the nation, the basis for morality, worship, and service did not exist, and many people did not fear or honor God. In Malachi God assured the people of His blessings on those who returned to Him, reminded them of His love, and promised that the "coming one," who would be preceded by Elijah, would refine the nation through judgment.

Among the many important theological themes within the book, the universalism of Mal. 1:11 is one of the most problematic. Elliger denied the authenticity of the verse, but many others (cf., e.g., Torrey, Marti, Dentan, and Mason) held that Malachi was teaching that God accepts the universal worship of other gods as true worship of Himself. In light of the condemnation of the heathen gods in the rest of the OT and Malachi's teaching concerning God's hatred of Edom (1:2-5) and His rejection of mixed marriages (2:11f.), this view must be rejected. The Targum, Rashi, von Orelli, and J. M. P. Smith believed that the verse refers only to the worship of Jews still in exile or possibly Jewish proselytes. A few scholars have thought that the prophet was just making a nontheological exaggeration to prove a point. But the particularism of "my name" and "pure offering" can only be fully integrated into the universalism of "every place, from the rising of the sun to the setting of it" if the verse has a future reference. This traditional interpretation does not deny the present "greatness of God's name beyond the borders of Israel" (1:5, 14) through His acts of grace and judgment, but neither does it mean that all nations now worship Him in purity and truth (v. 11).

Of particular significance to the NT is the prophecy of the messenger who "prepares the way" before the coming of the Lord in 3:1. This phraseology is picked up from Isa. 40:3 and applied to a new Elijah in Mal. 4:5 (MT 3:23). In the NT an angel connected this idea with the birth of a child to Zechariah and Elizabeth (Lk. 1:17), and later Jesus identified John the Baptist as this Elijah (Mt. 11:10, 14; Mk. 9:11-13).

***Bibliography.***–*Comms.:* T. T. Perowne (*CBSC*, 1890); C. von Orelli (1893); G. A. Smith (*Expos.B.*, 1898); J. Wellhausen (3rd ed. 1898); K. Marti (*Kurzer Hand-Commentar zum AT*, 1904); J. M. P. Smith (*ICC*, 1912); E. Sellin (*KZAT*, 1930); A. von Bulmerincq (1926-32); R. C. Dentan (*IB*, 1956); F. Horst (*HAT*, 3rd ed. 1964); K. Elliger (*ATD*, 6th ed. 1967); P. A. Verhoef (*Commentar op het Oude Testament*, 1972); J. G. Baldwin (*Tyndale OT Comms.*, 1972); W. Rudolph (*KZAT*, 1977); R. A. Mason (*CBC*, 1977). The standard dictionaries, encyclopedias, and introductions also give a survey of opinions on Malachi.

*Articles:* C. C. Torrey, *JBL*, 17 (1898), 1-15; G. R. Driver, *JTS*, 39 (1938), 393-405; H. J. Boecker, *ZAW*, 78 (1966), 78-80; L. Kruse-Blinkenberg, *ST*, 20 (1966), 95-119; 21 (1967), 62-82; J. Fisher, *CBQ*, 34 (1972), 315-320; F. Kuehner, "Emphases in Malachi and Modern Thought," in J. H. Skilton, ed., *The Law and the Prophets* (1974), pp. 482-493; N. Waldman, *JBL*, 93 (1974), 543-49; T. Vriezen, "How to Understand Malachi 1:11," in J. Cook, ed., *Grace upon Grace* (1975), pp. 128-136; W. Dumbrell, *Reformed Theological Review*, 35 (1976), 42-52; R. Althann, *Bibl.*, 58 (1977), 418-421; R. L. Braun, *Currents in Theology and Missions*, 4 (1977), 297-303; S. Schrenen, *ZAW*, 91 (1979), 207-228; W. Rudolph, *ZAW*, 93 (1981), 85-90.

G. V. SMITH

**MALACHY** mal'ə-kī (2 Esd. 1:40, AV). Another form of the name of the prophet MALACHI.

**MALCAM** mal'kam [Heb. *malkām*].

**1.** AV, NEB, MALCHAM. Head of a Benjaminite family; son of Shaharaim and Hodesh (1 Ch. 8:9).

**2.** (RV Jer. 49:1, 3; Zeph. 1:5; cf. RSV, NEB, "Milcom";

AV "their king," "Malcham"). The national deity of Ammon, usually called MOLECH or Milcom.

**MALCHIAH** mal-kī'ə. Alternate form of MALCHIJAH.

**MALCHIEL** mal'kē-əl [Heb. *malkî'ēl*–'God is king']. Descendant of Asher (Gen. 46:17; Nu. 26:45; 1 Ch. 7:31).

**MALCHIELITES** mal'ki-əl-īts [Heb. *malkî'ēlî*]. Descendants of Malchiel (Nu. 26:45).

**MALCHIJAH** mal-kī'jə; **MALCHIAH** mal-kī'ə; **MELCHIAS** mel-kī'əs [Heb. *malkîyâ, malkîyāhû* (Jer. 38:6)–'Yahweh is king'; Gk. Apoc. *Melchias*]; AV also MELCHIAH; NEB omits in Jer. 38:6.

**1.** A Gershomite Levite; father of Baaseiah and ancestor of Asaph, one of the leading temple musicians in David's time (1 Ch. 6:40 [MT 25]).

**2.** Son of Parosh; a layman who divorced his foreign wife (Ezr. 10:25a; 1 Esd. 9:26).

**3.** (Ezr. 10:25b, AV, NEB). *See* HASHABIAH **12.** The RSV follows the LXX (*Asabia*; cf. also Asibias in par. 1 Esd. 9:26), while the AV and NEB follow the MT.

**4.** Son of Harim; a layman who divorced his foreign wife (Ezr. 10:31; cf. 1 Esd. 9:32, where he is called a son of Annan); probably the same man who helped to rebuild the wall of Jerusalem under Nehemiah (Neh. 3:11).

**5.** A descendant of Aaron and head of the Levitical family assigned by David to the fifth division of temple service (1 Ch. 24:9). Adaiah, a descendant of this family, was one of the first priests to settle in Jerusalem after the Exile (1 Ch. 9:12; Neh. 11:12).

**6.** Son of Rechab; one who helped to rebuild the Dung Gate in the time of Nehemiah (Neh. 3:14).

**7.** A goldsmith who helped to rebuild the wall of Jerusalem (Neh. 3:31).

**8.** One of those who stood at Ezra's left hand when he read the law to the people (Neh. 8:4; cf. 1 Esd. 9:44); possibly the same as **2, 4, 6,** or **7** above.

**9.** A priest who signed the covenant with Nehemiah (Neh. 10:3 [MT 4]).

**10.** A priest who sang in the choir at the dedication of the rebuilt wall of Jerusalem (Neh. 12:42); possibly the same as **9.**

**11.** Son of King Zedekiah and owner of the cistern in which Jeremiah was imprisoned (Jer. 38:6); possibly the same as **12.**

**12.** The father of Pashhur, an officer of King Zedekiah and persecutor of Jeremiah (Jer. 21:1; 38:1); possibly the same as **11,** but to be distinguished from **5.** N. J. O.

**MALCHIRAM** mal-kī'rəm [Heb. *malkîrām*–'my king is uplifted']. Son of Jeconiah (Jehoiachin), descendant of David (1 Ch. 3:18).

**MALCHISHUA** mal-kə-shōō'ə [Heb. *malkîšûa*ʿ–'my king saves']; AV also MELCHISHUA. One of the sons of Saul (1 S. 14:49; 31:2; 1 Ch. 8:33; 9:39). He was slain with his father and brother by the Philistines in the battle on Mt. Gilboa (1 Ch. 10:2; 1 S. 31:2).

**MALCHUS** mal'kəs [Gk. *Malchos*]. The servant of the high priest, whose right ear was cut off by Peter when Jesus was arrested (Jn. 18:10). The Gospel of John alone names the assailant and the victim (cf. Mk. 14:47; Mt. 26:51; Lk. 22:50). All four Gospels report that the victim was a servant or slave (*doúlos*) of the high priest (probably Caiaphas; cf. Jn. 18:13) and therefore not one of the officers or attendants (*hypērétai*, Jn. 18:3, 18). Both Luke and John report that it was the right ear that was wounded. Only Luke records that Jesus healed the ear (Lk. 22:51). Only John's Gospel reports that one of Peter's challengers when he denied his Lord was another of the high priest's servants who had seen him in the garden and who was a relative of Malchus (Jn. 18:26). These details in John perhaps derive from the author's personal acquaintance with the high priest (Jn. 18:15).

The name Malchus is the Grecized form derived from the Semitic root for king (*mlk*). It also appears in Greek as *Malichos* and *Malchaios*. The name was particularly common among the Nabatean Arabs (two Nabatean kings bore the name, Malchus I, 50-28 B.C., and Malchus II, A.D. 40-71). It is also prominent among the Palmyrene inscriptions. It has been suggested from this that Malchus was an Arab slave (cf. Josephus *Ant.* xiii.5.1 [131]; 1 Macc. 11:39).

Why was Malchus struck? Was it an act of defense or defiance? The high priest's servants were noted for their high-handed violence (cf. Tosefta *Menahoth* xiii.21; Josephus *Ant.* xx.8.8, 9.2 [181, 206]). Peter may have lashed out to defend Jesus in the spirit expressed in Jn. 13:37. On the other hand, it is quite possible that this was a symbolic act of defiance deliberately directed against the servant of the high priest who was present as his representative. An insult could be directed against the master by contemptuously striking his surrogate (cf. 2 S. 10:4; Mt. 21:35). Wounding the ear was a particularly suggestive form of violence against one associated with the high priest (see Daube; cf. Josephus *Ant.* xiv.13.10 [366]; Tosefta *Parah* iii.8). The particular manner in which Malchus was wounded would not have disqualified the high priest, but it would have been taken as a patently contemptuous act. If this were an act of defiance, the right ear may have been the one struck because the right organ was considered the most valuable according to the indemnity laws of the time. It need not mean that the servant dodged the blow or was struck from behind, nor that Peter was left-handed.

***Bibliography.***–J. Jeremias, *Jerusalem in the Time of Jesus* (Eng. tr. 1969), p. 346; M. Rostovtzeff, *ZNW*, 33 (1937), 196-99; D. Daube, *JTS*, 11 (1960), 59-61.

D. E. GARLAND

**MALE** [Heb. *zāḵār*]; AV also MAN CHILD (Gen. 17:10, 12, 14; etc.), MANKIND (Lev. 18:22; 20:13); NEB also HE-GOAT, etc.; [*'îš*] (Gen. 7:2); [*maštîn b<sup>e</sup>qîr*] (1 S. 25:22, 34; 1 K. 14:10; 16:11; 21:21; 2 K. 9:8); AV "(one) that pisseth against the wall"; NEB "mother's son"; [Gk. *ársēn*] (Mt. 19:4; Mk. 10:6; Lk. 2:23; Gal. 3:28); **MALE CHILD** [Heb. *yeleḏ*] (Ex. 1:17f.); AV MAN CHILD; NEB BOY; [Gk. *país*] (Mt. 2:16); AV, NEB, CHILD; [*ársēn*] (Rev. 12:5, 13); AV MAN CHILD; **MALE SLAVE** [Heb. *'eḇeḏ*] (Gen. 20:14; Ex. 21:7, 27, 32; Lev. 25:44; etc.); AV SERVANT, MAN-SERVANT, BONDMAN; NEB also SLAVE; **MALE MEMBER** [*šop<sup>e</sup>ḵâ*] (Dt. 23:1 [MT 2]); AV PRIVY MEMBER; NEB TESTICLES; **MALE LAMB** [*keḇeś*] (Lev. 14:10, 12, 21; 23:12, 19; Nu. 6:12; etc.); AV LAMB, HE LAMB; NEB EWE, RAM, SHEEP; **MALE GOAT** [*śā'îr*]; AV KID; NEB HE-GOAT; [*'attûḏ*]; AV, NEB, HE-GOAT; **MALE (CULT) PROSTITUTE** [*qāḏēš*] (1 K. 14:24; 15:12; 22:46); AV SODOMITE.

Hebrew *zāḵār* (Akk. *zikru, zikaru*), though common in the OT, is of unknown etymology. It designates the male of the species, as in Gen. 6:19; Lev. 3:1; Nu. 1:2, in contrast to the female (*n<sup>e</sup>qēḇâ*). Heb. *'îš*, more commonly rendered "man," describes a man as the counterpart of a woman (Gen. 2:24; Lev. 15:19; etc.), or a male animal as opposed to a female animal (Gen. 7:2). The two terms may be used indiscriminately of animals and men, e.g., "Take with you seven pairs of all clean animals, the male [*'îš*] and his mate . . . and seven pairs of the birds of the air also, male [*zākār*] and female" (Gen. 7:2f.; but note that Sam. Pent. and the versions presuppose *zākār* instead of *'îš*; see *BHS*). The Hebrew phrase *maštîn b$^e$qîr*, translated literally by the AV, expresses maleness by a circumlocution. It is apparently from *šîn*, "urinate" (cf. Ugar. *tyn*); *CHAL*, p. 367, suggests calling the anomalous form a "hiftil," although BDB, p. 1010, prefers to designate it a secondary verb, *štn* (<*šyn*), in the hiphil. This expression is always used of those male members of a family who are to be executed. Thus the AV's slightly vulgar translation may accurately convey the nuance of this Hebrew expression.

Hebrew parents generally preferred male children to female, as shown by the desire for male progeny (1 S. 1:8-18) and the ransom paid to Yahweh for firstborn sons (Ex. 13:12; Lk. 2:23). It was the Christian faith that proclaimed the equality of the sexes, as it does of the races and condition of humans. The NT speaks clearly on the matter, e.g., "There is neither Jew nor Greek, there is neither bond nor free, there is neither male nor female; for you are all one in Christ Jesus" (Gal. 3:28).

One of the prevalent practices among ancient peoples was the sexual relationship of male with male. Heb. *qādēš* refers to the male devotee of lascivious idolatry (cf. Dt. 23:17; 1 K. 14:24; 15:12; 22:46; 2 K. 23:7; Job 36:14 [RSV mg.]). The Greek word is a compound noun, *arsenokoítes*, which means literally "he who lies with man." Scripture regards this unnatural vice as an abomination and frequently warns God's people against it (1 Cor. 6:9).

*See also* SERVANT; SLAVE.

***Bibliography.***–*TDOT*, I, *s.v.* "'îsh" (N. P. Bratsiosis); IV, *s.v.* "zākhār" (Clements).

H. L. E. LUERING L. HUNT

**MALEFACTOR** mal'ə-fak-tər (Jn. 18:30, AV). *See* EVILDOING; EVILDOER.

**MALELEEL** mal'ə-lēl (Lk. 3:37, AV). *See* MAHALALEL **1.**

**MALICE** [Heb. *ra'* (Ps. 41:5 [MT 6]; 73:8, *š$^e$'āṭ* (Ezk. 25:6, 15); Gk. *ponēría* (Mt. 22:11), *kakía* (Rom. 1:29; 1 Cor. 5:8; Eph. 4:31; Col. 3:8; Tit. 3:3; 1 Pet. 2:1)]; AV also EVIL, WICKEDLY, WICKEDNESS, DESPITE(FUL); NEB also "desperate" (Ps. 41:5), SCORN, MALICIOUS, CORRUPTION, BAD FEELING; **MALICIOUS** [ Heb. *ḥāmās*] (Ex. 23:1; Dt. 19:16; Ps. 35:11); AV UNRIGHTEOUS, FALSE; **MALICIOUSLY** [Heb. *m$^e$zimmâ* (Ps. 139:20)]; AV WICKEDLY; NEB DELIBERATE EVIL; [Aram. *q$^e$raṣ* (Dnl. 3:8)]; AV WICKEDLY, "accused"; NEB VICIOUS, "brought a charge"; **MALIGNANT** [hiphil fem. part. of Heb. *mā'ar* (Lev. 13:51f.; 14:44)]; AV FRETTING; NEB ROTTING, CORROSIVE; **MALIGNITY** [Gk. *kakoḗtheia*] (Rom. 1:29); NEB MALEVOLENCE. The RSV supplies "malign" in Mt. 10:25, where the Greek verb of the previous clause (*epikaléō*) is understood.

The RSV translates five OT terms as "malice," "malicious," or "maliciously." *Ra'* appears over five hundred times with the usual translation of "evil"; only twice is the word rendered "malice." Heb. *š$^e$'āṭ*, "contempt," describes the vengeful attitude of Israel's enemies toward it. *Ḥāmās* carries the sense of "violent wrong," so that the AV "unrighteous/false witness" (*'ēḏ-ḥāmās*) is weak; the RSV and NEB rendering, "malicious," more accurately shows that the witnesses are guilty of hateful intent. *M$^e$zimmâ*, translated "wicked deeds" in Jer. 11:15, is rendered "maliciously" in Ps. 139:20 in reference to the disposition of those who defy God. The RSV "maliciously accused" in Dnl. 3:8 translates the Aramaic idiom *'$^a$kal qarṣîn*, lit. "eat the pieces of," thus "gnaw at" or "denounce."

The RSV uses "malignant" only to describe leprosy; most commentators point out that "persistent" (cf. LXX) is a better translation of *mam'ereṯ*, whose meaning is uncertain (cf. G. Wenham, *Book of Leviticus* [*NICOT*, 1979], p. 202; N. Snaith, *Leviticus and Numbers* [*NCBC*, repr. 1977], p. 72). *See also* LEPER, LEPROSY.

In the NT two Greek words are rendered "malice" and one "malignity." In Hellenistic thought *kakós* represented the principle of evil, a concept that lost its significance for NT writers. *Kakía*, sometimes designating a special moral depravity, is the quality, or working out of the quality, of *kakós* (*TDNT*, III, 482). It is usually rendered "malice" and denotes a particular evil disposition of the person unreconciled to God. Like *kakía*, *ponērós* is a LXX translation of Heb. *ra'*; in the NT it occurs over seventy times and is usually translated "evil." *Kakoḗtheia* occurs in the NT only at Rom. 1:29 in the list of vices, where it denotes "conscious and intentional wickedness" (*TDNT*, III, 485).

See *TDNT*, III, *s.v.* κακός (Grundmann).

D. J. KELLY

**MALLET** [Heb. *halmûṯ*] (Jgs. 5:26); AV, NEB, HAMMER. A workman's tool, normally used to drive tent pegs, used by Jael to kill the Canaanite commander Sisera (cf. 4:21). *See also* HAMMER.

**MALLOS** mal'əs (2 Macc. 4:30, AV). *See* MALLUS.

**MALLOTHI** mal'ə-thī [Heb. *mallôṯî*]. Son of Heman, head of the nineteenth division of temple musicians (1 Ch. 25:4, 26). *See also* JOSHBEKASHAH.

**MALLOW** [Heb. *mallû(a)h*; Gk. *halimón*] (Job 30:4); AV MALLOWS; NEB SALTWORT; in Job 24:24 the RSV ("mallow") and NEB ("mallow-flower") follow the LXX (Gk. *molóchē*) rather than the MT (Heb. *kōl*). Because the Hebrew root implies saltiness, botanists have assumed that species of the saltwort plant (*Atriplex*) are indicated. Gk. *halimón* is the sea orach (*A. halimus* L.), a shrub related to the spinach. Any one of the twenty-one kinds of saltwort in Palestine, however, would suit the biblical requirements of being short-lived and edible in times of privation.

Some authorities think the reference is to some kind of "mallow," an herb of the genus *Malva* that starving people could eat. The marsh mallow (*M. sylvestris* L.) and dwarf mallow (*M. rotundifolia* L.) grow wild in Palestine, but how often they were used as food in antiquity is uncertain.

R. K. H.

**MALLUCH** mal'ək [Heb. *mallûḵ*].

**1.** A Levite of the Merari branch, ancestor of Ethan the temple musician (1 Ch. 6:44 [MT 29]).

**2.** [Gk. Apoc. *Mamouchos*]; AV, NEB, MAMUCHUS. Son of Bani; a layman who divorced his foreign wife (Ezr. 10:29; 1 Esd. 9:30).

**3.** Son of Harim; a layman who divorced his foreign wife (Ezr. 10:32).

**4.** A priest who signed the covenant with Nehemiah (Neh. 10:4 [MT 5]).

**5.** A "chief of the people" who signed the covenant with Nehemiah (Neh. 10:27 [MT 28]); possibly the same as **2** or **3** above.

**6.** A priest who returned from the Exile with Zerubbabel (Neh. 12:2); probably the same as "Malluchi" (NEB Malluch) in v. 14; possibly the same as **4** above.

N. J. O.

**MALLUCHI** mal'oo-kī [Heb. *mallûḵî*; Gk. *Malouch*]; AV MELICU; NEB MALLUCH. The head of a family of priests in the time of Joiakim (Neh. 12:14); probably the same as MALLUCH **6.**

**MALLUS** mal'əs [Gk. *Mallos*]; AV MALLOS. A city in Cilicia, Asia Minor, inhabited by the *Mallōtai* (2 Macc. 4:30). The RSV translates "the people of . . . Mallus." Its inhabitants and those of nearby Tarsus revolted because Antiochus IV Epiphanes had given the cities to his concubine Antiochis. W. Ramsay (*Cities of St. Paul* [1907], pp. 161f.) said that Persian kings had begun this practice of giving the taxes from a city to favorites.

According to Strabo (*Geog.* xv.16), Mallus, located on a height above the Pyramus (Ceyhan) River, was founded by Amphilochus and Mopsus (after the Trojan War) and was the birthplace of Crates the grammarian. Modern discoveries indicate that the area was settled at least as early as the time of the Hittites.

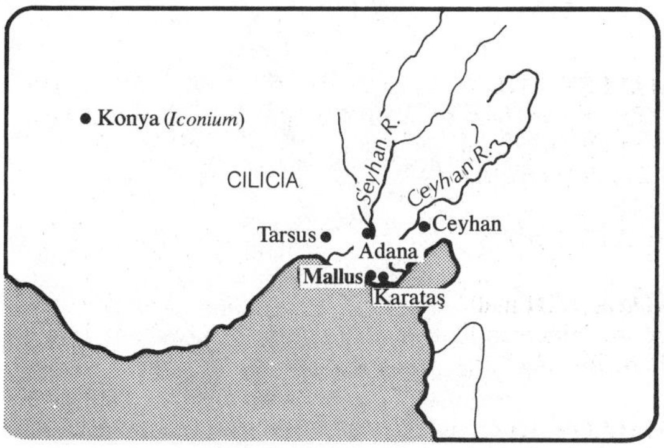


The modern highway from Adana to Osmaniyeh crosses the Ceyhan at the village of Ceyhan. The route followed by Alexander the Great went from Konya (Iconium), through the Taurus range by the Cilician Gates, and then through Tarsus and Mallus to Issus (*CAH*, VI [1953], Map 9). Adana (Seyhan) — the most important modern city in the area — is 36 km. (22 mi.) from Tarsus and 48 km. (29 mi.) from Ceyhan. The region S of this route is today largely an alluvial plain formed by the deposits of the Seyhan (Sarus) and Ceyhan (Pyramus) rivers. The only road goes from Adana to the seaport of Karataş (49 km., 30 mi.). The site of Mallus is a short distance W of Karataş, where inscriptions of Antiocheia and Mallus were found. Antiocheia (one of many cities of the same name) was possibly Magarsus, which may have been the port of Mallus. Doubtless the silting-up of the Cilician plain and the navigability of the Sarus to Tarsus led to the decreasing importance of Mallus. The remaining sixteen arches of a Roman bridge across the Seyhan at Adana indicate that the route had shifted by Roman times.

W. S. L. S.

**MALOBATHRON** mal-ə-bath'rən [Heb. *hārê ḇāṯer* (pausal form of *beṯer*); Gk. *órē koilōmátōn*] (Cant. 2:17, RV mg.); AV "mountains of Bether"; RSV "rugged mountains"; NEB "hills where cinnamon grows." Cant. 2:17 is followed closely by Cant. 8:14, except that the last phrase reads *hārê ḇeśāmîm* (RSV "mountains of spices"; NEB "spice-bearing mountains") and clearly alludes to rugged elevations.

The spice malobathron, derived from the *Cassia cinnamomum*, is not native to Palestine, being thought to have been imported from Ceylon, and thus it probably did not given its name to a mountain or a range in Israelite territory. The spice could, however, have been associated with BETHER, a site in the uplands of Judah near Jerusalem that perhaps served as a staging point for spice caravans from the east in the Solomonic period. It thus appears preferable to retain Bether as a proper name in Cant. 2:17 and "mountains of spices" as a general poetic description in 8:14.

R. K. H.

**MALTA** mal'tə [Gk. *Melitē* (Acts 28:1)]; AV MELITA. The island where Paul was shipwrecked. Though some have identified Malta with Meleda on the east coast of the Adriatic Sea, the African Melita (Malta) is most likely the correct identification. The Romans called the island and principal town Melita.

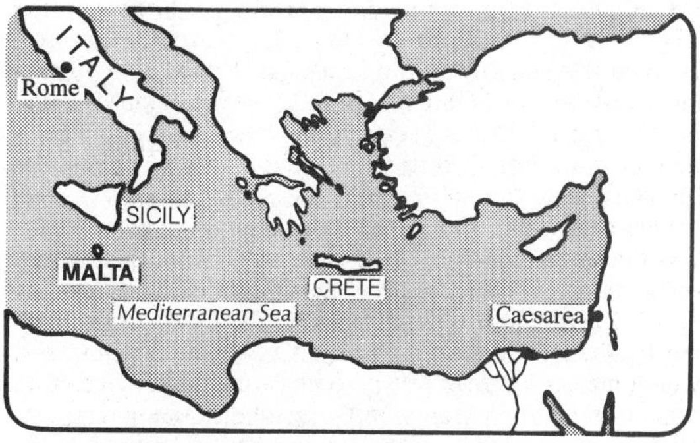


Malta is a rocky islet 93 km. (58 mi.) S of Sicily, 240 km. (149 mi.) S of the Italian mainland, and 290 km. (180 mi.) N of Cape Bon in Tunisia. A little over 27 km. (17 mi.) long, 14 km. (9 mi.) wide, and with a shoreline of 137 km. (85 mi.), it is the chief island of the Maltese group — which includes Gozo and Comino islands.

Though Malta lacks significant natural resources, it has often had strategic importance as a base from which to control the Mediterranean narrows. Its excellent harbor can accommodate a considerable fleet.

Phoenicians occupied Malta in Paul's day. Luke's calling the people *bárbaroi* (not Greco-Roman; Acts 28:2) agrees with the testimony of Diodorus (v. 12) that they were Phoenicians, neither hellenized nor romanized. The date of the Phoenician arrival is uncertain, but Carthage dominated Malta after the 6th cent. B.C. and Rome captured the Maltese islands from Carthage in 218 B.C.

On his voyage to Rome, Paul was shipwrecked on the island (Acts 27:43) and stayed there three months until favorable sailing weather (28:11). The traditional site of Paul's shipwreck is 13 km. (8 mi.) NW of the present capital of Valletta at a place now called St. Paul's Bay. The location is reasonably certain. W. Ramsay (*SPT*) and J. Smith (*Voyage and Shipwreck of St. Paul* [1880]) have exhaustively treated the topographical question.

Two points about the incident of Paul and the snake (Acts 28:3-6) need mention. First, as F. F. Bruce (comm. on Acts [*NICNT*, 1954], pp. 521f.) and others have pointed out, there are now no snakes on Maltá, but there may have been in Paul's day. Second, in the natives' initial reaction to the incident, "Though he has escaped from the sea, justice [Gk. *díkē*] has not allowed him to live," Gk. *díkē* is probably Luke's hellenizing of a Punic deity (see E. Haenchen, comm on Acts [Eng. tr. 1971], p. 713 n. 5). Thus Bauer, rev., p. 198, defined *díkē* here as "*Justice* personified as a goddess" (cf. NEB "divine justice"; NASB, NIV, Justice).

H. F. VOS.

**MAMAIAS** mə-mā'əs (1 Esd. 8:44, AV). *See* SHEMAIAH **19.**

**MAMDAI** mam'dī [Gk. B *Mamdai,* A *Mandai*]; AV MABDAI; NEB MANDAE. An Israelite who divorced his foreign wife at Ezra's order (1 Esd. 9:34). The parallel in Ezr. 10:35 is BENAIAH **11.**

**MAMMON** mam'ən [Gk. *mamōnás*]; NEB also MONEY (Mt. 6:24); WEALTH (Lk. 16:9, 11). The Greek transliteration of the common Aramaic term *māmônā'* (the emphatic state of the noun *māmôn*), meaning wealth of any kind.

The etymology of the term is disputed. One possibility is that it derives from *'mn* ("trust") to refer to that in which one trusts because it appears to provide security. The meaning, however, is clear; it refers to wealth, property, anything of value. The word appears frequently in the Targums and rabbinic literature. It also occurs in Sirach (e.g., 31:8), 1 Enoch (e.g., 63:10), and the Dead Sea Scrolls. Although the word could be applied to something gained dishonestly, it had no bad connotation in Jewish usage (cf. *TDNT,* IV, 389). It referred simply to property in general (cf. Mish. *Sanhedrin* i.1; *Aboth* ii.12). This makes Jesus' statements about mammon all the more arresting, because He always used it in a derogatory sense.

In Mt. 6:24 (par. Lk. 16:13) Jesus said that one cannot serve God and mammon. The Aramaic term was retained here because it was personified and stood in antithetic parallelism to God. The context refers to a slave who becomes the property of two owners and finds that divided loyalties are impossible. Similarly, one cannot devote oneself to making money and to serving God at the same time (cf. Lk. 14:33).

In the conclusion to the parable of the unjust steward the term "unrighteous mammon" is used (Lk. 16:9, 11), perhaps as a reference to money or property acquired dishonestly. But does the command "make friends for yourselves of unrighteous mammon" simply mean that money gained wrongfully should be given away? It seems more likely that for Jesus, "All money, however acquired, is tainted unless it is used in God's service" (G. B. Caird, *Saint Luke* [*Pelican,* 1963], p. 189). The steward recognized his crisis and acted boldly, using what was not his, to ensure his security in this world. So disciples should use their worldly possessions, which are only on temporary loan from God, in deeds of mercy to store up treasures for themselves in heaven (cf. Mt. 6:19-21; 19:21).

*Bibliography.–DCG,* II, *s.v.* (J. Moffatt); *TDNT,* IV, *s.v.* Μαμωνᾶς (F. Hauck); H. P. Rüger, *ZNW,* 64 (1973), 127-131.

D. E. GARLAND

**MAMNITANEMUS** mam-nə-tə-nē'məs [Gk. A *Mamnitanaimos,* B *Mamtitanaimos*] (1 Esd. 9:34, RSV mg.); AV MAMNITANAIMUS; NEB MAMNITANAEMUS. An Israelite who consented to divorce his foreign wife. *See* MACHNADEBAI.

**MAMRE** mam'rə [Heb. *mamrē'*]. One of the three Amorite brothers who fought with Abraham against Chedorlaomer king of Elam and three other kings to rescue Abraham's nephew Lot and the other captives from Sodom and Gomorrah (Gen. 14:13). Abraham refused the recovered goods that the king of Sodom offered him but asked that Mamre and his brothers receive their share (v. 24).

**MAMRE** mam'rə [Heb. *mamrē'*]. The oak grove where Abraham dwelt and built his altar (Gen. 13:18), traditionally identified with Râmet el-Khalîl ("friend's [Abraham's] hill"), a hill 3 km. (2 mi.) N of what is now Hebron. The Lord appeared to Abraham at his tent by the oaks (Josephus *BJ* iv.9.7 [530-33] and NEB "terebinths") in Mamre and promised him and Sarah a son (18:1-15). From there Abraham saw the smoke of the destruction of Sodom and Gomorrah (19:27f.). East of Mamre were the field and cave of Machpelah, which Abraham bought from Ephron the Hittite for the burying place of Sarah (23:17-19). Later Abraham's son Isaac lived in Mamre (35:27).

Herodian ruins at Râmet el-Khalîl (J. C. Trever)

Because of Abraham Mamre was very early a holy place for the Jews. The paving there dates from the 9th or 8th cent. B.C. In the 4th cent. A.D. Constantine had a basilica built next to the oak at Râmet el-Khalîl. New churches replaced those destroyed in wars; the present ruins are thought to be in the same place as Constantine's basilica and to have the same ground plan. Part of the surrounding wall dates back to Herod and part to Hadrian.

See *EAEHL,* III, *s.v.* (S. Appelbaum).

A. A. SAARISALO

**MAMUCHUS** mə-mo͞o'kəs [Gk. *Mamouchos*] (RSV mg., AV, NEB, 1 Esd. 9:30). One who consented to divorce his foreign wife. The RSV renders MALLUCH (2) because of the parallel in Ezr. 10:29.

**MAN.** *See* ANTHROPOLOGY.

**MAN, NATURAL.** *See* SPIRITUAL MAN.

**MAN, NEW.** *See* NEW MAN.

**MAN OF LAWLESSNESS** [Gk. *ho ánthrōpos tḗs anomías*] (2 Thess. 2:3); AV MAN OF SIN; NEB "wickedness . . . in human form." *See* LAWLESS.

**MAN OF SIN.** The AV translation of Gk. *ho ánthrōpos tḗs hamartías* in 2 Thess. 2:3. The RSV ("man of lawlessness") follows earlier MSS (B, א) that read *anomías* instead of *hamartías.* *See* LAWLESS.

**MAN, OLD.** *See* OLD NATURE; NEW MAN.

**MAN, OUTWARD.** *See* INNER MAN; NEW MAN I.

**MAN, SON OF.** *See* SON OF MAN.

**MANACH** man'ək [Gk. *Manochō*]. A town of Judah listed only in Josh. 15:59, NEB, following the LXX (v. 59a), which adds eleven names apparently making up the Bethlehem district (*LBHG,* rev., p. 355). These names may have been accidentally omitted from the MT (see comms.).

**MANAEN** man'ə-en [Gk. *Manaēn*; Greek form of the Hebrew name Menahem–'comforter,' 'consoler'; cf. LXX *Manaēm* (2 K. 15:14)]. One of five "prophets and teachers," including Barnabas and Saul, of the church at Antioch (Acts 13:1). He is described as *sýntrophos* of Herod (Antipas) the tetrarch. The precise meaning of *sýntrophos* (lit. "fed/reared with") here is debated. The term was often applied to children of the same age as royal or noble children, with whom they were brought up. According to F. F. Bruce, the translation "foster brother" is more appropriate here than "courtier" or "intimate friend" (*Book of the Acts* [*NICNT,* 1954], pp. 260ff.).

This mention of Manaen implies that he was a person of some influence, because of his connection with Herod Antipas. He was probably one of those who "laid their hands" on Barnabas and Saul (Acts 13:3) and may have been one of the "others" who represented the Antioch church at the Council of Jerusalem (15:2).

Josephus mentions an older Manaen, associated with Herod the Great (*Ant.* xv.10.5 [373-79]). According to Bruce this Manaen may have been the grandfather of the NT Manaen. Both Bruce and I. H. Marshall (*Acts of the Apostles* [*Tyndale,* 1980], p. 215) suggested that Manaen was Luke's source of information about the Herodian dynasty. E. WALHOUT

**MANAHATH** man'ə-hath [Heb. *mānaḥaṯ*]. The second son of Shobal and grandson of Seir the Horite (Gen. 36:23; 1 Ch. 1:40); the ancestor of an Edomite clan.

**MANAHATH** man'ə-hath [Heb. *mānaḥaṯ*]. A place to which certain Benjaminites from Geba, victims apparently of intratribal jealousy, were carried captive (1 Ch. 8:6). It is mentioned in the Amarna Letters (Am.Tab. 292:30) and is often identified with Manocho, which the LXX adds to the list of towns in Judah (Josh. 15:59; NEB Manach). The modern town is Mâlḥā, about 5 km. (3 mi.) SW of Jerusalem. D. J. WIEAND

**MANAHATHITES** man'ə-hath'īts [Heb. *mānaḥtî*]; AV, NEB, MANAHETHITES. A clan that descended from CALEB (**2, 3**). Half of the clan were descendants of Salma (1 Ch. 2:54); the other half are probably to be identified with the half of the MENUHOTH (so RSV; cf. AV, NEB, "Manahethites") who descended from Shobal (v. 52). They apparently resided in the vicinity of MANAHATH. (See KD.)

**MANAHETHITES** man'ə-heth'īts (AV, NEB, 1 Ch. 2:52, 54). *See* MANAHATHITES; MENUHOTH.

**MANASSEAS** man-ə-sē'əs [Gk. *Manassēas*]. A layman who had married a foreign woman (1 Esd. 9:31).

**MANASSEH** mə-na'sə [Heb. *m^enaššeh*–'(God) has made (me) forget,' *m^enaššî*; Gk. *Mannassēs*]; AV Apoc. and NT MANASSES; NEB Apoc. MANASSES.

**1.** The firstborn son of Joseph, and a tribe and territory of Israel. His mother was Asenath the daughter of Potiphera priest of On (Gen. 41:50). Joseph named his firstborn son Manasseh ("causing to forget") because, he said, "God has made me forget all my hardship and all my father's house" (v. 51). When Jacob was near death, Joseph brought his two sons to his father, who blessed them. Because Jacob was a younger son who had received the blessing of the firstborn, he preferred Ephraim, the second son of Joseph, to Manasseh the elder brother, thus indicating the relative positions of their descendants (Gen. 48). Before Joseph died he saw the children of Machir, son of Manasseh (50:23) by his Aramean concubine (1 Ch. 7:14). Scripture records no details of Manasseh's personal life. According to Jewish tradition he became steward of his father's house and acted as interpreter between Joseph and his brethren. The tribe of Manasseh subsequently traced its ancestry to Machir (1 Ch. 7:14).

At the beginning of the desert march Manasseh's men of war numbered 32,200 (Nu. 1:34f.). At the second census they had increased to 62,700 (26:34). Their position in the wilderness was with the tribe of Benjamin, by the standard of the tribe of Ephraim W of the tabernacle. At Sinai the prince of the tribe was Gamaliel son of Pedahzur (2:20). Gaddi son of Susi represented the tribe among the spies (cf. 13:11, where "tribe of Joseph" seems to be used as an alternative). At the census in the plains of Moab, Manasseh is named before Ephraim and appears as much the stronger tribe (26:28ff.). Manassites performed the main military exploits in the conquest of eastern Palestine. Machir son of Manasseh conquered the Amorites and Gilead (32:39). Jair son of Manasseh took all the region of Argob, containing sixty cities, and called them by his own name, "Havvoth-jair" (32:41; Dt. 3:4, 14). Nobah captured Kenath and its villages (Nu. 32:42; Josh. 17:1, 5). The warriors of this half-tribe passed over with those of Reuben and Gad before the host of Israel, and took their share in the conquest of western Palestine (Josh. 22). They helped to raise the great altar in the Jordan Valley, which so nearly led to disastrous consequences (vv. 10ff.).

Only a general outline can be given of the territory of Manasseh, principally because the extent of the tribe's holdings varied from time to time. Their territory straddled the Jordan in central Canaan, with the west section of the tribe having its S border at the Wâdī Kanah, but also including on the southeast an extent of territory stretching from Shechem to Jericho. To the north the tribe was allotted holdings up to the foot of Mt. Carmel (cf. Josh. 17:15), close to where Issachar and Zebulun had their territory. Manasseh experienced great difficulty in uprooting the Canaanites in Beth-shean, Dor, Ibleam, and Megiddo (Jgs. 1:27), and may not have controlled the coast in the northwestern part of its holdings. During the wars with the Canaanites Issachar suffered more than all the other tribes and was forced to retreat from areas that were its patrimony, which Manasseh then occupied (Josh. 17:11-13). Gideon of the tribe of Manasseh fought the Midianites at the foot of the hill of More in the Valley of Esdraelon in the center of Issachar's territory. Y. Aharoni suggested identifying Ophrah, Gideon's home, with the village eṭ-Ṭaiyibeh NE of the hill of More. Thus Manasseh's expansion northward took land from the tribes in Galilee, Issachar, and perhaps Asher. The Valley of Esdraelon (with the cities Beth-shean, Ibleam, Dor, Endor, Taanach, and Megiddo) was not actually conquered in the beginning (Jgs. 1:27f.) but came under Manasseh's influence; probably part of the valley fell into Manasseh's hands after Deborah's war and the rest at the time of the monarchy.

The half-tribe of Manasseh located E of the Jordan (Josh. 13:29-31) occupied territory S of the Sea of Galilee close to Syrian holdings. It included the villages of Jair (NEB Havvoth-jair) in Bashan, half of Gilead, as well as Ashtaroth and Edrei. By this means the former kingdom of Og, ruler of Bashan, was kept in subjection. The southern border was most probably the river Jabbok, but in any event it ran close to Mahanaim, an important city of Gilead in Gadite territory. The northern and eastern boundaries of Transjordanian Manasseh are impossible to establish with certainty, as is the degree of control which the tribe exerted over its holdings. Biblical tradition (1 Ch. 5:23) included Mt. Hermon as the northern limit of Manasseh's eastern holdings, but the reference may be to the maximum extent of the kingdom in the Davidic period rather than to the tribal holdings in the time of Joshua.

Some problems have arisen with respect to the genealogies of Manasseh as a tribe in Nu. 26:26-34; Josh. 17:1-3; 1 Ch. 2:21-23; 7:14-19. Part of the difficulty may be topographical in nature, especially where Manasseh is mentioned in connection with neighboring Ephraim on the one hand (cf. Josh. 21:5) and Reuben and Gad on the other (cf. Josh. 21:27), where both halves of the tribe of Manasseh are being considered. More serious is the genealogical problem presented by comparing Nu. 26:29-34 and 1 Ch. 7:14-19, especially the insertion of Huppim in 1 Ch. 7:15. The text may well have preserved the name as a variant form of Hupham, one of Benjamin's sons (Nu. 26:39), since he is not mentioned elsewhere by the name Huppim. Similarly Shuppim is probably a postexilic contracted form of Shephupham (cf. Nu. 26:39), also a Benjaminite, and the incidence of the names in Chronicles is probably the result of an accidental gloss from the preceding Benjaminite genealogy.

Ten cities W of the Jordan, in the portion of Manasseh, were given to the Levites, and thirteen in the eastern portion (Josh. 2:5f.). Manasseh took part in the conflict with the host of Sisera (Jgs. 5:14). Two famous judges, Gideon and Jephthah, belonged to this tribe. The men of the half-tribe E of the Jordan were noted for skill and valor as warriors (1 Ch. 5:18, 23f.). Some men of Manasseh had joined David before the battle of Gilboa (12:20). Others, all mighty men and captains in the host, joined him on the way to Ziklag and helped him against the band of rovers (vv. 21ff.). From the half-tribe W of the Jordan 18,000 men were expressly summoned to Hebron to make David king (v. 31). Those who came from the east numbered, along with the men of Reuben and Gad, 120,000 (v. 37). David organized the eastern tribes under 2700 overseers for "everything pertaining to God and for the affairs of the king" (26:32). The rulers of Manasseh were Joel son of Pedaiah in the west and Iddo son of Zechariah in the east (27:20f.). Many belonging to Manasseh humbled themselves and came to Jerusalem at the invitation of Hezekiah to celebrate the Passover (2 Ch. 30:11). Although not cleansed according to the purification of the sanctuary, they ate the Passover. The king successfully sought pardon for them, because they set their hearts to seek God (vv. 18ff.).

The eastern half-tribe "played the harlot after the gods of the peoples of the land" and in consequence were overwhelmed and expatriated by Tiglath-pileser king of Assyria (1 Ch. 5:25f.). 2 Ch. 31:1; 34:6 refer to the idolatries of the western half-tribe.

Ezekiel's ideal picture provides a portion for Manasseh (48:4), and the tribe appears in a list in Rev. 7:6.

***Bibliography.***–W. J. Phythian Adams, *PEQ*, 61 (1929), 228-241; K. Elliger, *ZDPV*, 53 (1930), 265-309; *JPOS*, 18 (1938), 7-16; W. F. Albright, *JPOS*, 11 (1931), 241-251; A. Bergmann, *JPOS*, 16 (1936), 224-254; M. Noth, *PJ*, 37 (1941), 50-101; J. Mauchline, *VT*, 6 (1956), 19-33; E Danielius, *PEF*, 89 (1957), 55-67; 90 (1958), 122-144; E. Jenni, *ZDPV*, 74 (1958), 35-40; *GTTOT*, §§ 123-25; 158-169; J. Myers, *I Chronicles* (*AB*, 1965); *II Chronicles* (*AB*, 1965).

A. A. SAARISALO
R. K. H.

**2.** The son of Hezekiah and successor to the Davidic throne in Jerusalem (2 K. 21:1-18; 2 Ch. 33:1-20; Mt. 1:10).

Manasseh's reign was the longest in the Davidic line. Including a decade of co-regency with his father, Manasseh reigned fifty-five years (696-642 B.C.). Apparently he was made king in 696/695 at the age of twelve when he became a "son of the law," but he probably had little cpportunity to assert himself while Hezekiah was living.

There are two accounts of Manasseh's reign (2 K. 21:1-18 and 2 Ch. 33:1-20) that diverge to a significant degree. Unmentioned in the Chronicles account are the name of his mother (2 K. 21:1), the comparison of his idolatry with that of Ahab, especially the Asherah idol (v. 3), the divine prophecy of doom upon Judah (vv. 10-15), and Manasseh's shedding of innocent blood (v. 16). Whereas in the Kings narrative Manasseh burned "his son," in the Chronicles account he burned "his sons." Absent from the Kings description but mentioned in 2 Ch. 33:1-20 are Manasseh's Assyrian captivity, his repentance (vv. 11-13), and his rebuilding activities in Jerusalem, accompanied by the destruction of pagan shrines (vv. 14-17). The source for the Kings narrative is the Book of the Chronicles of the Kings of Judah, while the Chronicler drew upon two works, the Chronicles of the Kings of Israel and the Chronicles of the Seers.

The life of Manasseh is thus attested in no fewer than three annalistic sources, though to what extent they were quoted verbatim is unknown. Where verbal correspondences occur in the two biblical descriptions the Chronicler may have had the Kings narrative as his source, or else had access to the tradition upon which the author of Kings drew. His use of such material, however, was obviously limited by the special approach which he adopted in interpreting preexilic history. It seems probable that the Chronicler's mention of Manasseh's disobedience, punishment, and repentance was a deliberate attempt to emphasize to the nation the fundamental need for covenantal obedience and holiness to characterize the theocracy, which because of the return from exile had a new opportunity to manifest the ethos of the Sinai agreement. Whatever the sources of the divergent narratives it must be apparent that if the cited material underlying the Kings account is taken as genuine, those on which the Chronicler based his account must be accorded the same recognition also.

Manasseh plunged his nation into gross idolatry unequaled in Palestine since the days of Ahab and Jezebel. His reign was the antithesis of his father's, which was marked by godly zeal and piety. Worship of stars and planets was instituted as part of the religious rites and ceremonies. In the Hinnom Valley outside the city wall of Jerusalem the Hebrew king sacrificed children to the Ammonite deity Moloch. This was one of the most abominable rites of Canaanite paganism; Ps. 106:36f. associates it with demon worship. Manasseh also allowed divination, occultism, and astrology. Altars in the temple courts used for worshiping the host of heaven and graven images of Asherah the wife of Baal in the temple itself represented open defiance of God. Moreover, Manasseh shed much innocent blood; protesters against these abominable practices were likely silenced by death (cf. 2 K. 21:16). Although the last king associated with Isaiah in the historical record is Hezekiah, the tradition attributing the martyrdom of Isaiah to King Manasseh seems reasonable. Since the moral and spiritual conditions in Judah were worse than those of the nations that the Israelites were commanded to exterminate under the leadership of Joshua, Isaiah doubtless thought that the judgment he had announced upon Judah and Jerusalem was inevitable.

Scripture does not indicate how much Assyria influenced Manasseh in his idolatrous practices. Under Esarhaddon and Ashurbanipal the Assyrian kingdom reached its pinnacle of wealth and prestige. In all likelihood Manasseh curried the favor of Esarhaddon in subservient vassalage when the Assyrian king subjugated Tyre in 678 and extended his control down into Egypt, occupying Memphis is 673 and capturing Tirhaka a few years later. In his list of twenty-two kings from the Hittite country, Esarhaddon mentions Manasseh king of Judah among those who made a compulsory visit to Nineveh in 678. Although Babylon perhaps was rebuilt by then, Unger's assertion that Manasseh was taken to Babylon at this time may be incorrect (cf. M. F. Unger, *Archaeology and the OT* [1954], pp. 280f.).

Ashurbanipal (669-633) extended Assyrian control about 800 km. (500 mi.) along the Nile with the capture of Thebes in 663. A bloody civil war in Babylon in 652 shook the Assyrian empire; although it was suppressed in four years, other rebellions erupted in Syria and Palestine. Judah may have joined Edom and Moab, which are named in the Assyrian inscriptions. Since Moab's autonomy was terminated at that time, Judah's king Manasseh probably was taken as a captive to Babylon then and released later (2 Ch. 33:10-13).

The biblical record seems to substantiate a late date for Manasseh's captivity. Although he repented and was returned to this throne, the conditions that existed when Josiah assumed the kingship after Amon's short reign do not indicate much of a change from Manasseh's earlier evil influence. In all likelihood Manasseh was not able to turn the idolatrous tide in Judah after his return, and it is probable that his own reforms were short-lived.

*See also* MANASSEH, PRAYER OF. S. J. SCHULTZ
R. K. H.

**3.** A layman who divorced his foreign wife in the time of Ezra (Ezr. 10:30); called Manasseas in 1 Esd. 9:31.

**4.** Another layman who divorced his foreign wife; son of Hashum (Ezr. 10:33 par. 1 Esd. 9:33).

**5.** Judith's wealthy husband, who died of sunstroke during the barley harvest (Jth. 8:2f., 7; 10:3; 16:22-24).

**6.** The Manasseh of Jgs. 18:30f. (AV, NASB) is evidently a deliberate attempt to avoid the suggestion that the esteemed Moses (a name read by RSV, NIV, NEB, following some MSS) had an idolatrous descendant. A small *n* has been inserted in the Hebrew text above and between the first and second consonants in the word Moses, which also happened to be the name of the priest officiating at the idolatrous shrine of Dan. The scribal insertion, probably added some centuries after Judges was written, effectively changed "Moses" into "Manasseh," thereby removing any possible stigma from the Hebrew lawgiver's name and reminding subsequent generations of a notorious royal idolator in Judah.

**MANASSEH** mə-nas'sə, **PRAYER OF.** This piece of devotional literature is an anonymous composition which exhibits elegance of construction, correctness of liturgical form, and the finest traditions of historic Jewish piety. Its scant fifteen verses make it the shortest book of the Apocrypha.

***I. Title.***–In Codex Alexandrinus (5th cent. A.D.) it was entitled "A Prayer of Manasseh" and included in a collection of Odes (Ode 8, following Isa. 38:9-20). In the Vulg. it was known as "A Prayer of Manasses, king of Judah, when he was held captive in Babylon," a title which the AV and RV followed.

***II. Canonicity and Text.***–Doubtless on the authority of Codex Alexandrinus, which has preserved the LXX textual tradition better than any of the comparable codices, the Greek church has always included the Prayer in its canonical Scriptures. Yet it does not seem to have been part of the original LXX; it appeared first in the 3rd cent. A.D. in Syriac in the *Didascalia* (ii.21), a manual of church order. The Prayer formed part of a midrash, and the Syriac balanced the reference to confession in v. 9 by a statement concerning punishment in a way characteristic of Hebrew poetic parallelism. The enlargement may have filled a gap in the Greek text, but this is uncertain.

In the 4th cent. it was incorporated into the *Apostolic Constitutions,* a situation which led some scholars to assign a very late date to the Prayer. Apparently the composition was unknown to Jerome also, since it was not included in his Vulg., a revised form of the Old Latin version. Its presence in some medieval Latin MSS led to the inclusion of the Prayer in the Stephanus (1540) edition of the Vulg., but it was excluded from the Vulg. of Sixtus V (1590). It reappeared, however, in the edition of Pope Clement VIII (1592), but only in the Appendix. Its position varies in MSS, versions, and printed editions of the LXX. It is most frequently found among the odes or canticles following the Psalter (as in A T; see Rahlfs' ed., II, 180f.). In Swete's LXX the Psalms of Solomon, followed by the odes (of which the Prayer is the eighth), appear as an Appendix after 4 Maccabees. It was placed after 2 Chronicles in the original Vulg., but in the Romanist Vulg. it stands first, followed by 3 and 4 (1 and 2) Esdras in the apocryphal appendix. It is found in all MSS of the Armenian Bible, where, as in Swete's LXX, it is one of many odes. Though not included in Coverdale's Bible or the Geneva version, it was retained (at the close of the Apocrypha) in Luther's translation, in Matthew's Bible, and in the Bishops' Bible, whence it passed into our English versions. The text has been preserved very well, and no significant problems seem to have arisen during its transmission. The Prayer is omitted from several modern editions of the LXX.

***III. Background.***–The composition purports to contain what Manasseh said as he prayed for divine mercy during his incarceration in Babylon. While the ascription of the work to the cruel and idolatrous Hebrew monarch is unhistorical, the tradition of Manasseh's captivity in Babylonia (2 Ch. 33:11) should not be casually dismissed. Manasseh's reign was notorious for its idolatry (2 K. 21:1-18), and the Chronicler regarded the Assyrian invasion of Jerusalem and Manasseh's exile as a divine punishment for national sin (2 Ch. 33:1-20). Archeological sources have not confirmed Manasseh's presence in Babylon, although Assyrian records mention a visit by him to Nineveh at the command of Esarhaddon (*ARAB,* II, 690). The name "Manasseh king of Judah" appeared on the prisms of both Esarhaddon and Ashurbanipal (*ANET,* p. 294), the latter attesting to his status as a vassal. Manasseh's exile may have occurred as a consequence of a revolt against Assyria in support of the viceroy of Babylon, Šamaš-šum-ukīn (cf. *ANET,* p. 298), probably *ca.* 650 B.C. The Chronicler evidently preserved an otherwise unrecorded tradition about Manasseh's captivity and release, a parallel to which can be observed in Ashurbanipal's treatment of Pharaoh Neco I, as recorded on the Rassam Cylinder. (*ANET,* p. 295).

The Chronicler indicated that Manasseh repented of his evil ways, and also made two references to his prayer to God (2 Ch. 33:18f.). Whether this prayer was some formal dedication at the time of his succession (cf. 1 K. 8:23-53) or an expression of penitence toward the end of his rule is uncertain. Whatever its nature, the prayer was preserved in the Chronicles of the Kings of Israel, and also independently in the Sayings of Hozai (New King James Version; RSV and NEB have "the seers," following one LXX MS, with other MSS reading "my seers"). None of this material is extant, however, and it is thus impossible to be certain of the prayer's form, or of any correspondence to the Prayer of Manasseh. The latter may have been composed by a pious scribe as a theodicy, attempting to show that God tolerated Manasseh's iniquitous reign because He knew that repentance would occur ultimately.

***IV. Original Language, Authorship, and Date.***–In such a short document it is difficult to determine whether the composition was first written in Hebrew or Greek. The formulation of the Prayer and its syntax would suggest Hebrew or Aramaic as the original language, but nothing precludes its composition in Greek, due to its flexibility of style and simple religious vocabulary. Hebrew thought and structure go hand in hand with reflections of LXX language, and while most modern scholars have suggested a Greek original, it is equally possible that the Prayer was translated into Greek from a Hebrew source that is no longer extant. The Prayer is strictly anonymous, and speculation about authorship is thus largely unproductive, other than that the author was a Jew. He may have composed the Prayer between *ca.* 250 and 150 B.C., and he could have been Palestinian or Alexandrian in origin. Perhaps the Maccabean period, with its great evils, inspired the composition of the Prayer. As such it may have been related, as one product of pietistic activity, to the fragmentary Prayer of Nabonidus recovered from Qumrân cave 4 and dated to the same period.

***V. Content and Theology.***–The Prayer opens with an invocation to the Lord as God of the patriarchs, the God who orders the entire creation by His power and mercy. God is extolled as One who has promised forgiveness to the penitent sinner, and on this basis the supplicant implores pardon for his manifold iniquities. He confesses them in the confidence that he will be pardoned through divine mercy, and ends his petition on a note of continuous praise. The composition contains the appropriate liturgical elements of adoration (vv. 1-7), confession (vv. 8-10, 12), petition (vv. 11, 13f.), and praise (v. 15).

The Prayer is a noteworthy manifestation of postexilic Jewish piety, but as a confession of sin it is quite general in character and content. As such it could be employed on a variety of occasions in public worship, quite apart from being used profitably in private devotion. Had the Prayer reflected the situation of Manasseh to any great degree, it would certainly have made more specific reference to the apostasy and human sacrifice of which he was guilty. By contrast, only the most general transgressions are confessed. A discordant theological note is struck by the attribution of sinlessness to the patriarchs (v. 8). This claim is unscriptural, and would have been untenable in any other than a late postexilic period of Jewish theology (cf. R. A. Stewart, *Rabbinic Theology* [1961], pp. 127-131). The terms "God of the righteous" and "God of those who repent" are characteristic of postexilic Judaism, as is the reference to the "glorious name" and its associated power, but the main emphasis upon God's mercy to the penitent sinner is thoroughly orthodox.

*See also* MANASSEH **2**.

***Bibliography.***–*APOT,* I, 612-624; B. M. Metzger, *Intro. to the Apocrypha* (1957), pp. 123-28; R. K. Harrison, *Intro. to the OT* (1969), pp. 1255-58.

R. K. HARRISON

**MANASSES** mə-na'sēz.

**1.** (AV Mt. 1:10; Rev. 7:6; AV, NEB, 1 Esd. 9:33; Jth. 8:2f., 7; etc.). *See* MANASSEH.

**2.** A person mentioned in the AV of Tob. 14:10, following Gk. B and A (*Manassēs epoíēsen eleēmosýnēn,* "Manasses gave alms"). The NEB follows א (*en tǭ poiēsai me eleēmosýnēn,* "Because I gave alms"). The RSV also follows א but deletes *me* and understands *Achiacharos* as the subject ("Ahikar gave alms"). The RSV and NEB readings make more sense than the AV reading, but no satisfactory explanation has yet been offered for the insertion of *Manassēs* in the text of B and A. N. J. O.

**MANASSITES** mə-na'sīts [Heb. *m^enaššî, b^enê-m^enaššeh*] (Dt. 4:43; 29:8 [MT 7]; Josh. 13:29; etc.); AV also CHILDREN OF MANASSEH, etc.; NEB also MANASSEH, (MANASSEH'S) SONS. Members of the tribe of MANASSEH (**1**).

**MAN-CHILD.** The AV and RSV translation of Heb. *geḇer* ("vigorous young man") in Job 3:3, where Job curses the night of his conception (MT; but according to the LXX, his birth). The AV also renders "man child" five times for *zāḵār,* "male" (Gen. 17:10, 12, 14; Lev. 12:2; Isa. 66:7).

**MANDAE** man'dī (1 Esd. 9:34, NEB). *See* MAMDAI.

**MANDAISM** man-dē'izm. An ancient Gnostic religion that began in the 2nd cent. A.D. or earlier. Its adherents, known as Mandeans, assert that the original group came from Palestine; they now inhabit areas close to the marshy swamps of southern Mesopotamia (modern Iraq and Iran). Because John the Baptist is extolled as one of their prophets, travelers of the 17th cent. named them "St. John's Christians." The Mandeans are highly critical of orthodox Christianity and virulently anti-Jewish. Their sect is the only form of ancient GNOSTICISM that has survived into modern times. They consider themselves descendants of the Egyptians who were saved from drowning in the Red Sea, with Pharaoh functioning as their first high priest and king.

Mandean mythology populates the universe with an enormous number of spiritual and astrological beings, both good and evil. The myths are obscure and sometimes contradictory. The major savior figure is Manda d-Hayye (Knowledge of Life). Man was formed in the image of a beneficent male deity, while woman was made in the form of Ruha, an evil female demon whose misdemeanors were in part responsible for the creation of the material universe. The physical body is a tomb that holds the soul as in a prison. Ritual purity is effected through rites, taboos, and strict conformity to the prescribed rules. Purification of body and soul through continual baptisms is an essential practice. At death the pure soul ascends past the hostile demons of the planets to the presence of the Great Life, the Supreme Entity of the Universe.

The religion makes a sharp distinction between the relatively ignorant laity, who are known as Mandeans or Gnostics, and the priests, who are divided into three ranks: the *asganda* or apprentice, who must have an unblemished pedigree in a priestly family; the *tarmida* or ordinary priest, to whom the fundamental mysteries are revealed; and the *nasoreans* (disciples), who have reached the highest stage of knowledge and purity. The head priest is known as the *ganzibra* or treasurer. Qualifications for the priesthood are extremely rigorous, and the group faces extinction because of a lack of eligible priests. Chaste marriage and the procreation of large families are considered the highest duties of the nasoreans.

The sect has numerous sacraments and ritual meals, including a feast for the dead. Cult huts, ritual garments, and sacred handclasps all figure in elaborate ceremonies. Running water is especially reverenced. Incantations, astrology, and magic are widely practiced.

Mandaic literature has been available to the western world since the 19th cent., especially through E. S. Drower's efforts. The texts, some of quite early composition, are written in an Eastern Aramaic similar to that used in the Babylonian Talmud. Gnostic, Jewish, Iranian, Platonic, astrological, and ancient Egyptian and Babylonian influences are all evident. Certain Manichaean Psalms (*see* MANICHAEISM) of the late 3rd cent. appear to be adaptations of earlier Mandean writings. Earlier speculation that the writer of the Fourth Gospel used Mandean literary sources now appears doubtful, since the highly dualistic nature of Mandaism stands in stark contrast to the monotheism of John.

*Bibliography*.–E. S. Drower, *Secret Adam* (1960); *Mandaeans of Iraq and Iran: Their Cults, Customs, Magic, Legends, and Folklore* (1962); E. M. Yamauchi, *JNES*, 25 (1966), 88-96; *Mandaic Incantation Texts* (1967); *Gnostic Ethics and Mandaean Origins* (1970). R. C. AND C. C. KROEGER

**MANDRAKES** man'drāks [Heb. *dûḏā'îm*; Gk. *mandragóras*] (Gen. 30:14-16; Cant. 7:13 [MT 14]). The mandrake (*Mandragora officinarum* L.) is a member of the *Solanaceae* or potato order and is closely allied to the nightshade and tomato. Commonly found in Palestine, it ripens during the wheat harvest (Gen. 30:14). The mandrake bears a rosette of lanceolate green leaves, with purple flowers and yellowish globular fruit. The root was venerated superstitiously in antiquity (cf. Josephus *BJ* vii.6.3 [178-189]) and was considered an aphrodisiac (cf. Cant. 7:13). But the suggested rendering "love apples" (Gen. 39:14, RV mg.) incorrectly associates Heb. *dûḏā'îm* with *dôḏîm*, "love," unless the dual form is an oblique, erotic designation of the female breasts. Even the most vivid imagination would be hard pressed to see in the shape of the mandrake root anything approaching that of an apple, regardless of the reputed aphrodisiac qualities of the plant.

Possibly Ugar. *ddym*, occurring occasionally in the Anath cycle, is related to the Hebrew for "mandrakes" (cf. J. C. L. Gibson, *Canaanite Myths and Legends* [rev. ed. 1978], pp. 49, 51, 144). The reference in ʿnt IV:53 to setting mandrakes in the dust (C. H. Gordon, *Ugaritic Literature* [1949], p. 20) has been interpreted, although not uniformly, in an erotic sense. But if the translation "mandrakes" is correct, the allusion is almost certainly poetic, not a factual reference to the planting of mandrakes (cf. M. H. Pope, *Song of Songs* [*AB*, 1977], p. 600). R. K. H.

**MANEH** mä'nä. *See* MINA.

**MANES** mā'nēz (1 Esd. 9:21, NEB). One of those who divorced their foreign wives. The parallel in Ezr. 10:21 (LXX) reads Gk. *Masaia kaí Elia* in place of *Manēs*. Thus, in 1 Esd. 9:21 the RSV reads MAASEIAH (7) instead of Manes in an attempt to reconcile the two name lists. The AV has Eanes, apparently mistaking *M* for *H* in the Greek text.

**MANGER** mān'jər [Gk. *phátnē*]; AV also STALL (Lk. 13:15). A term in the NT used only in Lk. 2:7, 12, 16; 13:15 and usually understood to mean a feeding trough for cattle, although the usage is ambiguous. In Lk. 2 *phátnē* could be the stable, in contrast to the inn proper where the people were lodged, or a feeding trough in an open field. But on the basis of contemporary Arab practice, K. Bailey (*Theological Review*, 2 [1979], 33-44) has suggested that the manger was actually in the house, which was divided into an upper level for the people and a lower level for the animals. In Lk. 13:15 the reference is to a "stall" or "pen" for animals.

In the LXX *phátnē* translates four Hebrew words that range in meaning from "manger" or "crib" (Job 39:9; Prov. 14:4; Isa. 1:3) to "stall" or "cattle pen" (2 Ch. 32:28; Hab. 3:17) and even "fodder" (Job 6:5). In classical Greek the term usually means "manger" or "crib."

Several sites where barns or inns were built near or over caves used as stables have been uncovered. The early Church believed that Jesus was born in a cave (Justin Martyr *Dial*. 78.5, *ca*. A.D. 150), and in 330 Constantine erected a basilica, to which Justinian later added, over the traditional grotto in Bethlehem. It is known today as the Church of the Nativity.

The excavations at Megiddo have uncovered mangers hewn out of solid blocks of limestone, and stone feeding troughs were found at Lachish. This archeological evidence and the scarcity of wood in Palestine lend some credence to Jerome's statement that the manger was made of mud or clay (*Homily 88, On the Navity of the Lord*).

The manger serves to emphasize the humble birth of the Son of God, who came not as a mighty king or general on a horse, but, in fulfillment of Zec. 9:9, humble and riding on an ass. He came not to be served but to serve and to give his life as a ransom for many (Mt. 20:28).

W. W. BUEHLER

**MANI.**

**1.** mā'nē (AV, NEB RSV mg., 1 Esd. 9:30). Head of a family whose sons had married foreign wives. The RSV renders BANI **4** (cf. Gk. *Mani*) because that form appears in the parallel Ezr. 10:29.

**2.** ma'nē. Founder of MANICHAEISM, also known as Manes or Manicheus.

**MANICHAEISM** ma-nə-kē'izm, man'ə-kē-izm. A syncretistic religion that flourished in the 3rd-14th centuries. Mani, the founder of Manichaeism, was born to an aristocratic Parthian family in Babylonia *ca*. A.D. 216. Shortly thereafter his father, Pattik, became involved in a baptistic sect, probably of Elkesaite origin, in southern Mesopotamia. Mani also joined the group, but broke with it at the age of twenty-four, after two encounters with an angel who was identified as his "twin companion." Mani began to preach a new religion derived from his revelatory experiences and soon gained adherents. Shapur, the Parthian king, supported his message, although there was serious hostility from other regimes.

Both Mani and his followers traveled widely as they propagated the new faith, which spread within his own lifetime as far as Egypt, China, and India. Drawing heavily upon Christian, Jewish, Persian, Gnostic, and perhaps Babylonian and Buddhist traditions, Mani himself wrote extensively and encouraged the faithful to translate and reproduce the texts. He viewed himself as the Paraclete promised by Jesus and as the ultimate prophet after Adam, Abraham, and Jesus.

Despite his claim of seeking to integrate the old Persian wisdom with Christianity, Mani met fierce opposition from representatives of Persian religious traditions, including Zoroastrianism, and was crucified by them in A.D. 276. The cult, perpetuated and augmented by Mani's disciples, developed an extensive following among a variety of peoples from North Africa to China. It survived until at least the 14th century. In Europe, Manichaeism influenced the thought of the Bogomils, Albigensians, and Paulicians.

Manichaean theology may be described as a consistent Gnostic dualism. It posits two opposing forces in the universe, which were originally separate and totally antagonistic to one another both essentially and existentially. Mani called these two governing principles God and Hyle (matter) and thought them to be expressed in the universe by darkness and light. The boundaries between the realms of darkness and light were breached, however, with the result that the whole world, including all humanity, became filled with a mingling of the two principles. For Manichaeism the goal of history is to achieve an ultimate reseparation of the two forces, which would render evil harmless and never again able to merge with good. An elaborate mythology embodies these theological tenets.

Humanity might be delivered from evil by a recognition

of the forces of good and evil and by adherence to precepts gained through recognition of this universal dualism. Human beings have the special responsibility of preventing further harm to the light. They are also to release from admixture with darkness the particle of light that lies within themselves. At the death of an elect Manichee, the light-particle trapped within the body might pass again to the realm of light. If the light does not thus escape from its union with evil, it must pass again into another human body.

Manichaean devotees were divided into two classifications, the "elect" and the "hearers." The elect were monks and nuns who had been initiated into the complete mysteries of Manichaeism and were forbidden normal activities and occupations in the world, including all sexual activity and the consumption of meat. The hearers, commissioned with providing support for the elect, lived in the world but avoided killing, idolatry, sorcery, and sexual immorality. A hearer might hope to return to this life as one of the elect. Before his conversion to Christianity, Augustine was a Manichaean hearer for nine years.

Mani held orthodox Christianity to be a grievous error. Three different figures of Jesus appear in Manichaeism, but none is congruent with the biblical picture of Him. In consequence, Manichaeism met with vehement opposition and condemnation by Christians, among whom Augustine became a leading proponent.

A considerable amount of Manichaean literature has been preserved, including a recently published account of Mani's life (see Henrichs). Manichaean homilies, psalms, and theological writings are also extant. Most are beautifully copied translations from the original Eastern Aramaic dialect in which Mani wrote. In the 19th cent. significant new texts were discovered, principally in Egypt and Chinese Turkestan. More recently the Cologne Mani Codex and some personal letters attributed to Mani have been published.

***Bibliography.***–F. C. Burkitt, *Religion of the Manichees* (1925); H.-C. Puech, *Le Manichéisme* (1949); H. Jonas, *Gnostic Religion* (rev. ed. 1963), pp. 206-237; G. Widengren, *Mani and Manichaeism* (1965); A. Henrichs, *Harvard Studies in Classical Philology*, 90 (1979), 339-367.

R. C. AND C. C. KROEGER

**MANIFEST** [Heb. *rā'â*] (Ps. 90:16); AV APPEAR; NEB SHOW; [hophal of *yāḏa'*] (Ps. 77:14 [MT 15]); AV DECLARED; NEB SHOWN; [Gk. *phanerós*] (Lk. 8:17; Acts 4:16; 1 Cor. 3:13); NEB DISCLOSED, PUBLIC, etc.; [*phaneróō*] (Mk. 4:22; Jn. 2:11; 9:3; Rom. 3:21; Col. 1:26; Tit. 1:3; etc.); AV also APPEAR; NEB also DISPLAYED, SHOWN, REVEALED, etc.; [*emphanízō*] (Jn. 14:21f.); NEB DISCLOSE; [*epiphanḗs*] (Acts 2:20); AV NOTABLE; NEB RESPLENDENT; [*emphanḗs*] (Acts 10:40); AV SHEWED; NEB APPEAR; [*deiknýō*] (1 Tim. 6:15); AV SHEW; NEB APPEARANCE; **MANIFESTATION** [Gk. *anádeixis*] (Lk. 1:80); AV SHEWING; NEB APPEARED; [*phanérōsis*] (1 Cor. 12:7); NEB MANIFESTED; [*pneumátōn*] ("manifestation of the Spirit," 1 Cor. 14:12); AV, NEB, GIFTS. The RSV and NEB follow the LXX in emending the MT of Isa. 24:23 to read *yikkāḇēḏ* (niphal of *kāḇēḏ*) instead of *kāḇôḏ*. In Ezk. 20:41; 28:22, 25, the RSV employs "manifest" in rendering the niphal form of the verbs *qāḏaš* ("show oneself holy") and *kāḇēḏ* ("show one's glory").

In both the OT and NT "manifest" describes God's revelation of Himself or His purposes to the world. Characteristically, God and His purposes are "hidden" from the understanding of sinful humans until He chooses to make Himself known through word or act (*see* HIDE; REVELATION). His saving and redeeming of His covenant people are celebrated throughout the OT and led the psalmist to praise the God who works wonders, who manifests His might among the peoples (Ps. 77:14 [MT 15]; cf. 92:5 [MT 6]). Moses prayed that God's gracious will and work might be shown to His servants and their children (Ps. 90:16). God's being the One who "shows his holiness" that the peoples might know Him is a favorite theme in Ezekiel (20:41; 28:22, 25).

The NT uses the Greek verb *phaneróō* and related words to portray God's activity of revelation as His disclosure and "display" of His purposes. Jesus reveals His glory in His first miracle at Cana (Jn. 2:11). The man born blind is healed "that the works of God might be made manifest [displayed] in him" (9:3). To those to whom God has given Him, to those who keep His commandments and love Him (14:21f.), Jesus has made known His Father's name (17:6). God's purpose in His Kingdom, though hidden from His disciples, will not always be so, for there is "nothing hidden which is not bound to become known" (Lk. 8:17; *Expos. G.T.*, I, 521) and to come to the light for all to see plainly (Mk. 4:22).

Yet, too, for the early Church the "mystery hidden for ages and generations" (Col. 1:26) has already come into the open through Jesus Christ's appearing in the flesh (1 Tim. 3:16; 1 Jn. 1:2; 1 Pet. 1:20). In Him the secret divine purpose for salvation has now been revealed to the world in culmination of the "hope of eternal life which God . . . promised ages ago" (Tit. 1:2f.; 2 Tim. 1:9f.). This incarnate Christ now brings to light the "righteousness of God" (Rom. 3:21) through His act of redemption, by which comes salvation by grace as God's free gift (v. 24).

The final disclosure of God will take place when the chief Shepherd appears (1 Pet. 5:4; cf. Col. 3:4; 1 Jn. 3:2) at the "proper time" set by God (1 Tim. 6:15; cf. 1 Clem. 5:5). Before Him in that Day of Judgment "each man's work" will become visible and be tested (1 Cor. 3:13). The "day of the Lord" is "splendid" or "glorious" (Acts 2:20). In this life, though, Christians are united with Christ in suffering, so that the world might see the life of Jesus lived in their lives (2 Cor. 4:10f.).

In 1 Cor. 12:7 the "revelation of the Spirit" may mean either that the Spirit is being revealed or that the Spirit is revealing something, perhaps the gifts as an "announcement" (Bauer, rev., p. 853) of His presence. Paul stated that the people of Corinth were "zealous for spirits" (14:12), meaning that they were fascinated with and desired to obtain the gifts given to the Church. (The Greek plural referring to the "Spirit of God" probably describes the varieties of spiritual gifts bestowed by the Spirit, hence the RSV's "manifestations of the Spirit.")

D. K. MCKIM

**MANIFOLD** [Heb. *kep̄el*–'double' (Job 11:6), *rāḇaḇ*–'be numerous' (Ps. 104:24); Gk. *pollaplasíōn*–'many times as much' ("manifold more," Lk. 18:30), *polypoíkilos*–'most varied' (Eph. 3:10)]; AV also DOUBLE (Job 11:6); NEB WONDERFUL, COUNTLESS, "many times over," "in all its varied forms." Great in number or in variety.

The meaning of Job 11:6 is obscure. The dual form *kip̄layim* literally means "double" (cf. AV). According to the RSV interpretation, Zophar reminds Job that God's wisdom is greater in its dimensions than Job thinks. Several commentators have suggested deleting the *k* as dittography and reading *pᵉlā'îm*, "marvelous, wonderful" (cf. NEB; see Rowley, p. 88). M. Pope, on the other hand, has taken *kip̄layim* to mean "duplex, two-sided": "For there are two sides to wisdom" (pp. 83-85). Ps. 104:24 also refers to God's great wisdom. The psalmist marvels at the tremendous number and variety of things that God has created (cf. vv. 1-23). In Eph. 3:10 Paul states that the wisdom of God, which "has shown itself in Christ to be varied beyond measure and in a way which surpasses all previous knowledge thereof" (*TDNT,* VI, 485), is now being made known to the principalities and powers through the Church.

Jesus assured His followers that those who gave up families and possessions for the sake of God's kingdom would receive such blessings in far greater numbers in the present life through their entry into the kingdom of God (Lk. 18:30); i.e., His followers would become members of a far greater family and would share in its common property (cf. Acts 4:32, 34f.).

***Bibliography.***–M. Pope, *Job* (*AB,* 3rd ed. 1973); H. H. Rowley, *Job* (*NCBC,* rev. ed. repr. 1980); *TDNT,* VI, *s.v.* ποικίλος, πολυποίκιλος (H. Seesemann). P. L. BREMER

**MANIUS, TITUS** man'i-əs, tī'təs [Gk. *Titos Manios*] (2 Macc. 11:34); AV TITUS MANLIUS (cf. Vulg. *Titus Manilius*). A Roman ambassador (Gk. *presbýtai*) who with Quintus Memmius, sent a letter to the Jews (addressed as a political body; see Abel, p. 430) verifying certain agreements with the Syrian Lysias, the guardian and relative of King Antiochus.

Since there are no other references to these two legates, their identification is difficult. Some have identified Manius with Manius Sergius, a Roman envoy (with C. Sulpicius) to Syria before the death of Antiochus IV (Polybius xxxi.9.6; see Abel, p. 430). This identification requires the spelling "Manios" (as in A V Syr.) which is less likely than "Manilius." The dates also pose problems. (Cf. Goldstein, pp. 423f.) Others have identified Titus Manius with Titus Manlius Torquatus, noted by Livy (xliii.11) as ambassador in Egypt (not Syria!) in 164 B.C., but this identification also has its difficulties.

The historicity of the letters in 2 Macc. 11 is also questionable, especially because of differences between 2 Maccabees and 1 Maccabees, which is generally regarded as the more reliable of the two. 1 Macc. 4:26-35, e.g., describes Lysias's campaign in 165 B.C. as taking place before the death of Antiochus IV and the rededication of the temple, and it makes no mention of negotiation with the Jews. According to 1 Macc. 6:28-63 a second expedition took place three years later; the letter of 2 Macc. 11 may be confusing the two campaigns. That the date of Titus Manius's letter (2 Macc. 11:38) is exactly the same as that of the preceding letter (v. 33) also makes its reliability suspect. Furthermore, only fifteen days are allowed between the writing of the letter and the final date of the amnesty. According to 1 Macc. 8 it was not until 162 B.C., after the arrival of Demetrius I and Nicanor's defeat, that Judas Maccabeus first communicated with the Romans.

On the other hand, some chronological differences between 1 Maccabees and 2 Maccabees are easily reconciled when it is noted that 1 Maccabees uses the calendar of Judea in the Seleucid era beginning in the autumn of 313 B.C., whereas 2 Maccabees uses that of the Seleucid empire, beginning in the autumn of 312 B.C. (Zeitlin, pp. 57ff.). Differences in the sequence of historical events are more difficult to explain. For an attempt at reconstructing the order of events, see Zeitlin, pp. 65ff.

***Bibliography.***–F.-M. Abel, *Les Livres des Maccabées* (1949); J. R. Bartlett, *First and Second Books of Maccabees* (*CBC,* 1973); J. A. Goldstein, *II Maccabees* (*AB,* 1983); S. Zeitlin, ed., *Second Book of Maccabees* (Eng. tr. 1954). W. MOULDER

**MANKIND** [Heb. *'āḏām* (Isa. 13:12; Jer. 32:20; Zeph. 1:3), *b*ᵉ*śar-'îš* (Job 12:10); Gk. *ánthrōpos* (Rev. 9:4, 15, 18, 20; 14:4), *hoí loipoí*–'the others' (Eph. 2:3)]; AV usually MEN, OTHERS (Eph. 2:13); NEB also MEN, HUMAN KIND, THE REST (Eph. 2:3). The human race, including males and females. Heb. *'āḏām* and Gk. *ánthrōpos* both designate "human being" or, collectively, the "human race" (cf. Heb. *'îš* and Gk. *anḗr,* usually "man" as distinguished from "woman"). The RSV, like the AV and most other versions, usually translates *'āḏām* and *ánthrōpos* "man" (in the generic sense); in the above passages, however, it uses "mankind" to emphasize the totality of the human race. In Lev. 18:22; 20:13 the AV renders "mankind" for Heb. *zāḵār,* "a male" (cf. RSV). N. J. O.

**MANLIUS** man'lē-əs, **TITUS** tī'təs. *See* MANIUS, TITUS.

**MANNA** man'ə [Heb. *mān* (Ex. 16:31, 33, 35; Nu. 11:6f., 9; Dt. 8:3, 16; Josh. 5:12; Neh. 9:20; Ps. 78:24); Gk. *mánna* (Jn. 6:31, 49; He. 9:4; Rev. 2:17)]. The breadlike food miraculously supplied for Israel during their forty years in the wilderness. Ex. 16:15 explains the etymology of the Hebrew term: When the Israelites saw (the manna), they said to one another, *mān hû'* (RSV, NEB, "What is it?"; AV, incorrectly, "It is manna"), because they did not know "what it was" (*mah-hû'*). Gk. *mánna* was used in Greek literature from the time of Hippocrates (5th cent. B.C.) to denote grains, crumbs, or morsels of food. It was used by the LXX to render Heb. *mān* (except in Ex. 16, where the LXX simply transliterates the Hebrew), possibly because of the similarity in sound.

The word "manna" first appears in Ex. 16. In the second month after their exodus from Egypt, as they were journeying through the wilderness of Sin, the Israelites complained about the lack of food (vv. 1-3). God responded to this complaint by providing quails in the evening (vv. 8, 12f.) and "bread from heaven" in the morning (v. 4; cf. v. 12). In response to the question "What is it?" Moses said: "It is the bread which the Lord has given you to eat" (v. 15). In spite of the people's frequent complaints and general ingratitude, the daily provision of the "bread from heaven" continued for forty years (Ex. 16:35; Josh. 5:12).

This *mān,* as the Israelites named it, appeared on the ground with the morning dew. It is described in Ex. 16:14, 31 and in Nu. 11:7-9. It consisted of small, flake-like particles similar to frost (Ex. 16:14) or coriander seed (v. 31; Nu. 11:7; i.e., about 3-4 mm. or ⅛ in. in diameter) and was white (Ex. 16:31) or pale amber in color. It looked like BDELLIUM (Nu. 11:7), and its taste was like honey-wafers (Ex. 16:31) or "like cakes baked with oil" (Nu. 11:8; NEB "butter-cakes").

Manna could be ground into flour in mills or mortars (Nu. 11:8) and baked into cakes or boiled into a sort of porridge (Ex. 16:23). It probably could also be eaten raw.

Ever since ancient times many attempts have been made to identify the OT manna with some natural edible substance found in the Sinai desert. Josephus, e.g., claimed that "to this very day all that region is watered by a rain like to that which then, as a favour to Moses, the Deity sent down for men's sustenance" (*Ant.* iii.1.6 [33]). One common theory postulates some sort of lichen or fungus, but there is little evidence for any such identification. The most widely held theory, which has received support from scientific investigations, links manna with a secretion of the tamarisk tree (*Tamarix gallica*) that forms small, yellowish-white balls that are very sweet. The substance melts in the heat of the sun. F. S. Bodenheimer has argued that these are actually excretions of insects that penetrate the tender bark of the twigs, rather than a product of the tree itself. In either case, this phenomenon normally occurs for only a few weeks beginning in June. The OT reports that the manna began "on the fifteenth day of the second month" (Ex. 16:1) — i.e., no later than early May — and continued for forty years on a regular six-day cycle; this demands a more-than-natural explanation. One possible explanation is that the Israelites, familiar with this natural "manna," were surprised at seeing something so similar in appearance in such quantity and so early in the season. They may have simply carried the name over to their new food.

Every Israelite man was instructed to gather each morning "as much as he can eat . . . an omer [about 2.2 liters, or slightly more than 2 dry quarts] apiece, according to the number of persons whom each . . . has in his tent" (Ex. 16:16). The manna could not be kept for more than one day or it would spoil and breed maggots (vv. 19f.). On the sixth day, however, a double portion was collected, and the unused portion was kept, unspoiled, for the sabbath (vv. 22-30). This miraculous provision continued until the entrance into Canaan at Gilgal (Josh. 5:12).

While the Exodus account emphasizes the relationship between the provision of manna and the sabbath, and the Numbers account the appearance and preparation of the manna, the other OT references focus on manna as a sign of God's continuing provision for the needs of His people. An omer of manna was later placed in a jar and kept in the tabernacle as a physical reminder of that provision (Ex. 16:33f.; cf. He. 9:4). The leaders of the community also reminded the people of that provision. Moses spoke of the pedagogical purpose of manna: it was to remind the people of their total dependence on God. "And he . . . fed you with manna . . . that he might make you know that man does not live by bread alone, but . . . by everything that proceeds out of the mouth of the Lord" (Dt. 8:3, 16; cf. Mt. 4:4; Lk. 4:4). Ps. 105:40 praises God for supplying His people with "bread from heaven in abundance."

Psalm 78 refers to manna in the context of God's judgment upon the Israelites (vv. 17-31; cf. Nu. 11); the psalmist sharply contrasts the people's ingratitude and rebelliousness with God's faithful provision of the "grain of heaven" (Heb. *d$^e$g̲an š$^e$mayim,* v. 24). In v. 25 most versions and biblical scholars render Heb. *leḥem 'abbîrîm* "bread of the angels," following the LXX (Gk. *ártos angélōn*; see, e.g., RSV, NEB; cf. Wisd. 16:20; see *TDOT,* I, *s.v.* "'ābhîr, 'abbîr" [A. Baumann]). But since there is no other instance in the OT where *'abbîrîm* means "angels," a better translation might be "bread of the mighty" (so AV); the plural form might represent a poetic plural for God (i.e., "the mighty One"), giving the translation "bread from God."

In his public confession, Ezra linked God's provision of the manna with the giving of His Spirit to instruct the people (Neh. 9:20). This reflects the sequence of events in Nu. 11, where the manna episode precedes the giving of the Spirit to the seventy elders (cf. 11:16f., 24f.).

The motif of manna played an important role in later Jewish literature. Philo, e.g., interpreted the OT references to manna as a type of the divine *lógos* (*Legum allegoria* iii.56-61 [162-176]). Apocalyptic and haggadic literature (written texts all date from post-NT times) provide evidence of a popular expectation that in the time of the messianic kingdom God would again provide manna for the faithful (e.g., 2 Bar. 29:8; Sib. Or. Fragment 3:46-49; for rabbinic literature, see SB, II, 479-484; *TDNT,* IV, 463f.; Brown, pp. 265f.). The "latter redeemer" would "cause manna to descend" in the same way that Moses, the "first redeemer," had caused bread to rain from heaven (Midr. *Eccl. Rabbah* i.9).

Although the later date of these written documents makes it difficult to be certain about how important a place the manna motif had in the oral tradition of NT times, haggadic traditions do appear to lie behind the references to "manna" and "bread from heaven" in Jn. 6 (see Borgen; Childs, pp. 293-297). The Jews' response to the "sign" of Jesus' multiplication of the loaves was to see Him as the expected Prophet like Moses (v. 14; cf. Dt. 8:15f.; see Brown, pp. 234, 265). In this light, it is strange that on the next day the Jews demanded that Jesus give them a sign such as Moses' giving of the manna (vv. 30f., which includes a conflation of Ex. 16:4, 15; Ps. 78:24; Wisd. 16:20). Some commentators (e.g., L. Morris, *Gospel According to John* [*NICNT,* 1971], pp. 362f.) have suggested that they were demanding a greater sign, e.g., manna that could supply the whole nation with food for forty years (cf. v. 34). In any case, Jesus responded that He Himself was the true "bread from heaven" (vv. 32-51), for in contrast to the wilderness manna, the "living bread which came down from heaven" confers eternal life to all who eat of it (vv. 47-51). Thus, using the symbolism of bread for the divine *lógos* (cf. Philo), Jesus identified Himself as the incarnation of the divine wisdom and revelation (see Brown).

Manna is also referred to in He. 9:4. Based on a scribal deduction from Ex. 16:33f. (cf. T.B. *Yoma* 3, 7; see *TDNT,* IV, 464, 466), the "golden urn holding the manna" was included in the ark of the covenant along with the tables of the law (cf. 1 K. 8:9 par. 2 Ch. 5:10, which states that the ark contained nothing but the two tables of stone). This idea may also underlie the statement in Rev. 2:17 that "to him who conquers I will give some of the hidden manna." According to Jewish tradition the ark and its contents were hidden by Jeremiah in a cave of Mt. Nebo (2 Macc. 2:4-7). This passage probably also reflects the tradition that the manna will appear again in the messianic kingdom (see above).

***Bibliography.***–F. S. Bodenheimer, *BA,* 10 (1947), 2-6 (repr. in G. E. Wright and D. N. Freedman, eds., *BA Reader,* I [1961], 76-80); P. Borgen, *Bread from Heaven* (*Nov. Test., Supp.* X, 1965); R. E. Brown, *Gospel According to John,* I (*AB,* 1966), 260-294; B. S. Childs, *Book of Exodus* (*OTL,* 1974), pp. 270-304; *DNTT,* I, 252f.; SB, II, 479-484; *TDNT,* I, *s.v.* ἄρτος (J. Behm); IV, *s.v.* Μάννα (R. Meyer).

G. L. CARR

**MANNER** [Heb. *'ōraḥ*] (Gen. 18:11); NEB AGE; [*dereḵ*] (Gen. 19:31; Ezk. 20:30; Am. 4:10); NEB WAY, LIKE; [*kāḵâ*] (Ex. 12:11; Jer. 27:12); AV "thus," "according to"; NEB WAY; [*dāḇār*] (Dt. 15:2; Neh. 6:4); NEB "how"; [*mišpāṭ*] (Josh. 6:15; Jgs. 13:12; 18:7; 2 K. 17:33f., 40); AV ORDER; NEB WAY, FORM, CUSTOM, PRACTICES, etc.; [*zan*] (Ps. 144:13); [*kāzō'ṯ*] ("after this manner," 1 K. 7:37); NEB "this is how"; [Gk. *homoíōs*] (Mk. 4:16; Lk. 16:25; Jude 8); AV "likewise"; NEB "same," "so too"; [*akríbeia*] ("strict manner," Acts 22:3); AV PERFECT; NEB "in every point"; [*bíōsis*] ("manner of life," Acts 26:4); NEB LIFE; [*pás*] ("all manner," Rom. 1:29); AV "all"; NEB KIND; [*anáxiōs*] ("manner of life," Eph. 4:22); AV CONVERSATION; NEB WAY OF LIFE; [*politeúomai*] ("manner of life," Phil. 1:27); AV CONVERSATION; NEB CONDUCT. In Ruth 4:7 the AV and RSV supply "manner" and the NEB "custom," following the LXX, Syriac, and Targum, which apparently read *mišpāṭ,* a term not occurring in the MT of this passage.

"Manner" in the OT is generally equivalent to "way," "custom," "habit," etc. Sometimes it refers to the habit or mode of life of a people, e.g., the Sidonians (Jgs. 18:7), the pagan foreigners who inhabited Samaria after the fall of Israel (2 K. 17:33f., 40; cf. Ezk. 20:30), or the Israelites, who customarily confirmed a transaction by removing a sandal and giving it to the other party (Ruth 4:7). In Gen. 18:11 "after the manner of women" denotes menstruation (cf. 31:35); thus Sarah was past the age of child-bearing (cf. NEB). When Lot's daughter feared that "there is not a man on earth to come to us after the manner of all the earth" (19:31), she meant that no men would marry them and produce offspring.

The term sometimes expresses a particular way of doing something, e.g., eating the Passover (Ex. 12:11), releasing debtors from their debts (Dt. 15:2), marching around the walls of Jericho (Josh. 6:15), or making the stands of bronze for Solomon's temple (1 K. 7:37). Heb. *mišpāṭ* is the word for the "orderly government or training" (Gray, p. 345) or "manner of life" that Samson was to receive as a Nazirite (Jgs. 13:12). "Manner" refers to a way of speaking in Nehemiah's four-time refusal to stop work on the temple (Neh. 6:4) and in Jeremiah's speech to King Zedekiah (Jer. 27:12). The *dereḵ* of Am. 4:10 describes the coming pestilence as "after the manner of Egypt" but does not specify the similarities (see W. R. Harper, *Amos and Hosea* [*ICC*, 1905], p. 100).

*Zan* means "kind" rather than "way." It is thought to be a Persian loan word, literally meaning "from kind to kind" (Anderson, p. 935). It expresses the "every kind" of earthly blessing gleaned from the rich harvest in Ps. 144:13 (cf. Ps. 72:16).

The NT renders a number of Greek terms "manner." The adverb *homoíōs*, meaning "likewise," "so," or "in the same way," is found in the parable of the Sower (Mk. 4:16), in the description of the rich man and Lazarus (Lk. 16:23), and in a warning against false teachers (Jude 8). Paul's training "in the manner of the law of our fathers" (Acts 22:3) means "according to careful observance of the law given to the fathers" (Haenchen, p. 625), i.e., with exact strictness (Bauer, rev., p. 33). His phrase "my manner [way] of life" (*bíōsis*, Acts 26:4) similarly implies that he grew up as a strict Jew.

Paul affirmed that one's old nature which belongs to a former "manner of life" is to be put off like a change of clothes (Eph. 4:22). He used *politeúomai* in his injunction, "Let your manner of life be worthy of the gospel of Christ" (Phil. 1:27). This term signifies "conduct relative to some law of life — political, moral, social, or religious" (Brewer, p. 80). Paul chose it to instruct the people about their public duties both as citizens under the Roman empire and as members of the community of Philippi. They had to reject all patriotic pressures to give to the state more than its due, however; their conduct had to be "worthy of the gospel of Christ," who is lord over the state.

In Rom. 1:29 Paul used "manner" (RSV) in the sense of "everything belonging to a certain class" — in this case the vices of the pagans (see Bauer, rev., p. 631). A textual variant in Lk. 9:55 is similarly rendered, "You do not know what manner of spirit you are of."

***Bibliography.***–A. A. Anderson, *Psalms* (*NCBC*, repr. 1981); R. R. Brewer, *JBL*, 75 (1956), 76-83; J. Gray, *Joshua, Judges, Ruth* (*NCBC*, 1967); E. Haenchen, *Acts of the Apostles* (Eng. tr. 1971).

D. K. McKIM

**MANOAH** mə-nō'ə [Heb. *mānô(a)ḥ*–'rest,' 'resting place']. A member of the tribe of Dan and a resident of Zorah, 23 km. (14 mi.) W of Jerusalem across the valley from Beth-shemesh. Manoah was the father of Samson. His unnamed wife, like Sarah (Gen. 15–16) and Elizabeth (Lk. 1), was barren (Jgs. 13:2). An angel of the Lord revealed to her that she would conceive and bear a child; he would be a Nazirite who would deliver Israel from the Philistines (vv. 3-5). Manoah's piety is shown by his praying for the angel to return and instruct his wife in the proper care of the coming child (v. 8). The request was granted (vv. 9-13). The angel rejected Manoah's hospitality and instead commanded a sacrifice to Yahweh. When Manoah placed the sacrifice on the altar, the angel disappeared in the flame (vv. 15-21). In due time the child was born and named Samson. The parents accompanied Samson when he asked for the hand of the Philistine woman of Timnah in marriage; they also attended the wedding. When Samson died, his brothers brought his body from Gaza to bury beside Manoah in the family tomb near Zorah (16:31).

D. W. DEERE

**MANSERVANT** [Heb. *ʿeḇeḏ*] (Ex. 20:10, 17; Dt. 5:14, 21; 12:18; 16:11, 14; Job 31:13); NEB SLAVE, MALE SLAVE. A male slave; usually coupled with "maidservant." *See* SERVANT; SLAVE.

**MANSION.** A term used by the AV in the archaic sense of "dwelling, abode," to render Gk. *monḗ* (Jn. 14:2; RSV "room"; NEB "dwelling-place"). A cognate of the verb *ménō* ("remain, abide"; cf. 15:4-10), *monḗ* expresses the permanence of the believer's dwelling in the Father's house after death. In 14:23 *monḗ* is used similarly to describe Jesus' and the Father's dwelling in the believer (AV "abode"; RSV "home"; NEB "dwelling").

***Bibliography.***–R. E. Brown, *Gospel According to John XIII–XXI* (*AB*, 1970), pp. 618f., 625-27; *TDNT*, IV, *s.v.* μένω κτλ.: μονή (F. Hauck).

N. J. O.

**MANSLAYER** [Heb. *rōṣē(a)ḥ* (Nu. 35:6, 11, etc.), *hammakkeh* (Nu. 35:24)]; AV also SLAYER; NEB also HOMICIDE, STRIKER; [Gk. *androphónos* (1 Tim. 1:9)]; NEB MURDERERS.

Of the eighteen occurrences of Heb. *rōṣē(a)ḥ* in Nu. 35, the RSV translates seven as "manslayer" (vv. 6, 11f., 25-28) and eleven as "murderer" (vv. 16-19, 21, 30f.). "Manslayer" distinguishes one who accidentally commits homicide (v. 11) from one who premeditatedly murders and is thus "guilty of death" (vv. 20, 31). The NEB makes a similar distinction here by using the terms homicide and murderer (cf. the AV "slayer," "manslayer," and "murderer").

Numbers 35:11 provides for cities of refuge, to which "the manslayer who kills any person without intent" (Heb. *rōṣē[a]ḥ makkēh-nepeš bišᵉgāgâ*) could flee. In these cities the manslayer was legally protected from the avenger of blood, so that he "may not die until he stands before the congregation for judgment" (v. 12). In cases of killing without enmity (vv. 22-24) the congregation (Heb. *hāʿēḏâ*) had as its responsibility to "judge between the manslayer [Heb. *hammakkeh*] and the avenger of blood [Heb. *gō'ēl haddām*] in accordance with these ordinances" (v. 24) and to "rescue the manslayer from the hand of the avenger of blood" (v. 25). When the manslayer was restored to his city of refuge after his trial, he had to be content to remain within its bounds; if he ventured beyond them, the avenger of blood had the right to kill him (vv. 25-27). After the death of the incumbent high priest the accidental homicide could return to his original landholdings (v. 28).

The RSV also translates Heb. *rōṣē(a)ḥ* "manslayer" in Josh. 20:3 and in Dt. 4:42; 19:3f., 6 (cf. AV "slayer," NEB "homicide"). Each passage designates cities of refuge (in Dt. 4:42, Bezer, Ramoth-gilead, and Golan, chosen by Moses) for the manslayer (Heb. *rōṣē[a]ḥ*) "who kills [Heb. *yirṣaḥ*] his neighbor unintentionally [Heb. *biḇlî-ḏaʿaṯ*], without being at enmity with him in time past" (4:42; 19:4). One city was located in each third of the land (19:3), so that the manslayer who kills without enmity (e.g., one whose loose axe-head slays another, v. 5) would not be overtaken by the avenger because the distance to refuge was excessive (v. 6).

Greek *androphónos*, "murderer," appears only once in the NT, in the plural in 1 Tim. 1:9. The RSV translates "manslayers" (cf. NEB "murderers"). This rare Greek term also appears in 2 Macc. 9:28, applied to Antiochus IV Epiphanes, the Seleucid monarch. *See also* MURDER; KILL; CITIES OF REFUGE.

D. G. BURKE

**MANSTEALING.** *See* CRIME, *s.v.* "Kidnapping."

**MANTELET** mant'lət [Heb. *sōk̲ēk̲*] (Nah. 2:5 [MT 6]); AV DEFENCE. A portable protective shelter used by besiegers when attacking a city. Because it appears only once in the MT, the precise meaning of *sōk̲ēk̲* is uncertain. "Mantelet" does, however, seem to be the best translation for this piece of protective equipment used by the attackers of Nineveh, assuming that it is a cognate of *sāk̲ak̲*, "block an advance," "cover," "protect"; cf. LXX *prophylakḗ*, "advanced guard." *See* SIEGE.

**MANTLE** [Heb. *'adderet̲*] (Gen. 25:25; Josh. 7:21, 24; 1 K. 19:13, 19; 2 K. 2:8, 13f.; Zec. 13:4); AV also GARMENT; NEB also CLOAK; [*śimlâ, śalmâ*] (Ex. 12:34; 22:27; Isa. 3:6f.); AV RAIMENT, CLOTHING, CLOTHES; NEB CLOAK; [*miṭpaḥat̲*] (Ruth 3:15); AV VAIL; NEB CLOAK; [*me'îl*] (Ezr. 9:3, 5; Ps. 109:29; Isa. 59:17); AV, NEB, also CLOAK; [*tak̲rîk̲*] (Est. 8:15); AV GARMENT; NEB CLOAK; [*r^edîd̲*] (Cant. 5:7); AV VEIL; NEB CLOAK; [*ma'^aṭeh*] (Isa. 61:3); AV, NEB, GARMENT; [*ma'^aṭāpâ*] (Isa. 3:22); [Aram. *sarbāl*] (Dnl. 3:21, 27); AV COATS; NEB TROUSERS; [Gk. *himátion*] (Mt. 24:18; Mk. 10:50; 13:16; Lk. 22:36; Acts 12:8); AV CLOTHES, GARMENT; NEB COAT, CLOAK; [*chitṓn*] (Mk. 14:63); AV CLOTHES; NEB ROBES; [*peribólaion*] (He. 1:12); AV VESTURE; NEB CLOAK.

"Mantle" in the RSV designates several types of clothing. The *'adderet̲* was a cloak that could be made of animal hair (Gen. 25:25), could be quite beautiful and costly (Josh. 7:21, 24), and could be worn by prophets like Elijah (1 K. 19:13, 19; etc.). The common *śimlâ* was used not only as a basic outer garment but also as a blanket (Ex. 22:27) and cloth basket (12:34). Other cloaks or robes included the *tak̲rîk̲*, the *me'îl* (used figuratively in Ps. 109:29; Isa. 59:17), the *ma'^aṭeh* (cf. "the mantle of praise" in Isa. 61:3), and the *ma'^aṭāpâ*. Ruth carried her barley in her *miṭpaḥat̲*, a wrapper, mantle, or headcloth for women. The *r^edîd̲* (Cant. 5:7) could have been some kind of wide wrapper, veil, or stole; in its other occurrence in the OT (Isa. 3:23), the RSV translates it as "veils" (AV "vails"; NEB "flowing veils"). What precisely the *sarbāl* was remains quite uncertain. Suggestions include trousers, cloak, or shoes. According to K. Kitchen ("The Aramaic of Daniel," in D. J. Wiseman, *et al., Notes on Some Problems in the Book of Daniel* [1965], p. 35 n. 24), the common designation of *sarbāl* as a loanword from Persian is unlikely.

The *himátion* was an outer robe and the *chitṓn* an undertunic, although a more general meaning for *chitṓn* may be preferable in Mk. 14:63, particularly since the plural is used. The *peribólaion*, used in a figure of speech in He. 1:12, was some sort of wrap.

*See also* CLOAK; COAT; GARMENTS; ROBE.

M. W. MEYER

**MANUSCRIPT.** In the broadest sense, any handwritten document. In a narrower sense a MS is a handwritten codex, roll, or folded document, as distinguished from a printed book or an inscription. The Hebrew and Greek MSS of the OT and NT, respectively, are the primary sources used in the attempt to determine the text or original words of the authors. MSS play the same part in the attempt to determine the original text of subordinate sources such as versions, writings of the church fathers, and quotations from other ancient writers who referred to biblical matters.

*See* TEXT AND MSS OF THE OT; TEXT AND MSS OF THE NT; VERSIONS; WRITING.

**MANUSCRIPTS OF THE OT.** *See* TEXT AND MSS OF THE OT.

**MANUSCRIPTS OF THE NT.** *See* TEXT AND MSS OF THE NT.

**MANY WATERS** [Heb. *mayim rabbîm*] (Nu. 24:7; 2 S. 22:17; Ps. 18:16 [MT 17]; 29:3; 93:4; 107:23; 144:7; Cant. 8:7; Isa. 17:13; 23:2; Jer. 51:13, 55; Ezk. 1:24; 32:13; 43:2; Hab. 3:15); AV also GREAT WATERS; NEB also GREAT WATERS, MIGHTY WATERS, GREAT TORRENT, MIGHTY TORRENT; [Gk. *hydáta pollá*] (Rev. 1:15; 14:2; 19:6); NEB RUSHING WATER. The imagery of many waters is used in a variety of contexts. It can refer to the fruitful blessing of God on Israel (Nu. 24:7) or to the enemy from whom the psalmist is rescued (2 S. 22:17f. par. Ps. 18:16f.). It may describe marine trading routes (Isa. 23:2; "great waters," Ps. 107:23) or the location of the capital of an empire (Jer. 51:13, 55). Ezk. 1:24; 43:2 associate the sound of many waters with the vision of the glory of Yahweh, and Rev. 1:15 compares it with the voice of the glorified Christ.

Because of the Ugaritic myth in which Baal contends with the sea, cosmic overtones have been discerned in at least some of the occurrences of *mayim rabbîm* (see H. G. May, *JBL*, 74 [1955], 9-21). Yahweh's victory over Pharaoh's army at the Sea of Reeds is pictured as a defeat of Rahab the chaos monster (Isa. 51:9f.). Although *mayim rabbîm* is not explicitly mentioned in Isa. 51, the parallel in Hab. 3:13-15 does include the term. Ps. 89:9f., moreover, understands the defeat of Rahab and the stilling of the waters as the scattering of Yahweh's enemies, a prominent motif in the Song of Moses in Ex. 15. However, Ex. 15 describes Yahweh as using the might of the waters as His weapon in destroying just such enemies. The cosmic metaphor, then, is biblically relevant but is not to be seen in all occurrences of *mayim rabbîm*.

G. WYPER

**MAOCH** mā'ok [Heb. *mā'ôk̲*]. King of Gath; father of Achish, with whom David and his men took refuge while fleeing from Saul (1 S. 27:2). He is probably the same as MAACAH **3**.

**MAON** mā'on [Heb. *mā'ôn*–'abode,' 'dwelling']. The son of Shammai, of the family of Caleb and tribe of Judah. He was the "father" (ancestor) of the inhabitants of the city of BETH-ZUR (1 Ch. 2:45), a fortress city important in Maccabean times.

**MAON** mā'on [Heb. *mā'ôn*–'abode,' 'dwelling']. An important town (modern Tell Ma'în) named along with Carmel and Ziph (Josh. 15:55), situated upon a high isolated hilltop in southern Judah W of the Dead Sea. It was about 11 km. (7 mi.) S of Hebron, where David and his men hid from Saul (1 S. 23:24f.). An urgent message about a Philistine raid relieved David of the pressure of Saul's pursuit and allowed him to flee south into the Wilderness of Ziph.

It was also the home of NABAL, a churlish property owner and great flock master. He denied to David and his outlaw band the customary felicitations accorded men who "protect" one's property (1 S. 25:2). The hasty but wise counsel of Nabal's wife Abigail averted David's plan to kill the family of Nabal. After hearing of these events, at a feast, Nabal was fatally stricken. David married the widowed Abigail and they had one son, Chileab.

F. E. YOUNG

**MAONITES.** *See* MEUNIM **1**.

**MAR** [Heb. hiphil of *šāḥaṯ*–'destroy, disfigure'] (Lev. 19:27); NEB SHAVE; **MARRED** [*mišḥāṯ*–'destruction, disfigurement'] (Isa. 52:14); NEB DISFIGURED (transposed to 53:2). The Torah forbade the Israelites to engage in pagan Semitic rites that included cutting HAIR (II, IV) from the head or BEARD (Lev. 19:27; cf. 21:5; Dt. 14:1). Nevertheless, this custom apparently persisted in Israel as a sign of mourning throughout OT times (cf. Job 1:20; Isa. 22:12; Jer. 16:6; etc.; *see also* BALDNESS). The same verb form is rendered "mar" by the AV in Ruth 4:6 (RSV "impair"); 1 S. 6:5 (RSV "ravage"); Jer. 13:9 (RSV "spoil"); cf. the piel in Nah. 2:2 (MT 3; RSV "ruin").

Isaiah describes the Suffering Servant as being so disfigured by his suffering that he no longer looks like a man (52:14). Because of its apparent connection with 53:2f., many commentators have transposed this verse to the end of 53:2 (cf. NEB). N. J. O.

**MARA** mä'rə [Heb. *mārâ*–'bitter']. A name NAOMI applied to herself on her return from Moab to her native country. The name Bitter seemed more appropriate than Naomi ("pleasant"), "for the Almighty has dealt very bitterly with me" (Ruth 1:20).

**MARAH** mar'ə, mar'a, mä'rə [Heb. *mārâ*, 'bitter']. The first stopping-place of the Israelites after they crossed the Red Sea (Ex. 15:23). It was reached by a three-day journey into the Wilderness of Shur (v. 22; "the Wilderness of Etham," Nu. 33:8). The Israelites, thirsty from the journey, complained because they could not drink the bitter water; at the Lord's direction Moses threw a tree into the water "and the water became sweet" (Ex. 15:25). Some scholars have regarded the account as an etiological explanation of the name. One suggested site is ʿAin Hawâra, about 11 km. (7 mi.) E of the Red Sea (*GAB*, p. 156).
W. S. L. S.

**MARALAH** mar'ə-lə [Heb. *marʿ<sup></sup>*^a^*lâ*; Gk. B *Maragella*, A *Marila*]. A place on the western border of Zebulun (Josh. 19:11), possibly in the plain of the Kishon, modern Tell Ghalta. The RSV reads MAREAL, taking the ending as *hê* directive, as is the case on the preceding word, but neither the MT pointing nor the versions support this reading. Moreover, if Abel's suggestion that Heb. *ʿayin* was an original *ghain* is followed (Gk. *Maragella* also suggests this) and if *Ghalta* is accepted as the modern form, the *t* seems to require an original *ṭ* (> *h* in Hebrew).
W. S. L. S.

**MARANATHA** mar-ənath'ə [Gk. *maranathá* < Aram. *māranā' ṯā'* or *māran ʾ<sup></sup>ĕṯā'*–'Our Lord, come!' or *māran ʾaṯā'*–'Our Lord has come']. An ancient Palestinian Aramaic expression recorded in transliterated Aramaic in 1 Cor. 16:22 and in Greek translation (*érchou, kýrie Iēsou*) in Rev. 22:20. Scholars differ on (1) whether to divide the transliterated Aramaic as *māran ʾaṯā'* or *māranā' ṯā'*, (2) whether "Our Lord" could have been either *māran* or *māranā'* (in Aramaic), and (3) whether "come" could have been *ʾaṯā'* or *ṯā'*. The problem is complex.

If the word is divided as *māran ʾaṯā'* (see AV "Maranatha"), it is best understood as a perfect indicative assertion meaning "Our Lord has come." If it is divided as *māranā' ṯā'*, it is best interpreted as an imperatival prayer, "Our Lord, come!" (so RSV; cf. NEB "Marana tha — Come O Lord"). Understood as an indicative, *māran ʾaṯā'* can refer to either Christ's incarnational presence in the historical past or His spiritual presence in the Eucharist. If the imperatival *māranā' ṯā'* is correct, however, it is a plea either for Christ's parousia or for His presence at the Eucharistic celebration.

As Fitzmyer and others have shown, the underlying Aramaic was probably an imperatival *māranā' ṯā'*, "Our Lord, come!" This interpretation is supported by the unambiguous translation of *maranathá* in Rev. 22:20 as a Greek imperative. Furthermore, Conzelmann argued that 1 Cor. 11:26 ("until he comes") is probably an allusion to the (*maranathá*) formula and so confirms an imperatival-eschatological interpretation of 1 Cor. 16:22.

The sudden occurrence of such an untranslated Aramaic expression in Paul's letter to the Greek-speaking church at Corinth suggests a widely accepted liturgical use of this phrase (much like "Amen" and "Hosanna"). This use would have originated among the Jewish Christians in Jerusalem. Thus, "Lord" should be interpreted in terms of a Jewish understanding of Yahweh rather than a Hellenistic conception of the gods of the mystery religions. The presence of *maranathá* in Did. 10:6 (*ca.* A.D. 100) — at the end of a discussion on the Eucharist — is further evidence that it had acquired quasi-official liturgical status in early Christian worship.

But as Moule has rightly shown, 1 Cor. 16:22 has no "eucharistic context." The verse is not a plea for Christ to be present at the Lord's Supper but a plea for the parousia of Christ in judgment on those who do not love the Lord. The context is one of cursing and judgment. Let those who have no love for the Lord be *anáthema*, Paul said (1 Cor. 16:22a), then added, *maranathá* — "Our Lord, come!" (1 Cor. 16:22b). *Maranathá* reinforces the *anáthema* formula without itself being limited to use in curses. *See* ANATHEMA. Similarly, "Come, Lord Jesus!" in Rev. 22:20 seems to be a plea for the parousia of Christ in judgment.

Because it is early, widespread, liturgical, and Palestinian, *maranathá* reflects the early Church's high Christology: Jesus is Lord. As such, He is worthy to receive the worship and praise once reserved exclusively for Yahweh. And as Lord, He will return in judgment.

***Bibliography***.–H. Conzelmann, *1 Corinthians* (Eng. tr., *Hermeneia*, 1975), pp. 300f.; G. H. Dalman, *Jesus-Jeshua* (Eng. tr. 1929), p. 13; J. A. Fitzmyer, "Semitic Background of the NT *Kyrios*-Title," in *Wandering Aramean* (1979), pp. 115-142; C. F. D. Moule, *NTS*, 6 (1959-60), 307-310; *DNTT*, II, *s.v.* (Mundle, Brown); *TDNT*, IV, *s.v.* μαρανaθά (Kuhn). J. J. HUGHES

**MARAUDER; MARAUDING BAND** [Heb. *g^e^ḏûḏ*] (1 K. 11:24; 2 K. 13:21; Jer. 18:22); AV TROOP, BAND; NEB RAIDERS, FREEBOOTERS. The Hebrew term may refer to a band of men in pursuit of plunder, though the contexts of 1 K. 11:24 and Jer. 18:22 point instead to another possible meaning, "troop, army."

**MARBLE** mär'bəl [Heb. *šayiš* (1 Ch. 29:2), *šēš* (Est. 1:6); Gk. *mármaros*–'brilliant,' 'sparkling' (Rev. 18:12)]; NEB also ALABASTER. Petrologically, marble is limestone or dolostone that has metamorphosed to form a recrystallized mosaic of calcite or dolomite grains. Crystal size and coloration vary from quarry to quarry and even within a given rock mass. Small amounts of iron, manganese, carbon, and silicates introduce color patterns in the material, which is sometimes quarried for effects. Aegean and North African sources are especially known for colorful varieties. The soft brilliance of white marble, chosen for sculpture and architecture (from Paros, Pentelicus, and Carrara), occurs as a result of the internal reflectivity of the mineral's rhombohedral cleavage planes and crystal faces. Historically, the term marble seems also to have included carbonate rocks of the Levant capable of taking a polish, such as that used for the Solomonic and Herodian temples (cf. Josephus *Ant.* viii.3.2 [64], white stones, quarried in Lebanon; also, the golden and pink Judean limestone formation was quarried by Herod's workmen for the temple closure walls). Known and valued sources for marble in the biblical world were the Aegean islands with the Greek and the Anatolian (Carian and Phrygian) mainlands, Apuan Alpine (Carrara), North African (e.g., Chemtou), and Persian quarries. Est. 1:6 describes the palace of Xerxes (Ahasuerus) at Susa (Shushan) as having pillars of marble (cf. Cant. 5:15) and a patterned flooring, *opus sectile,* of white marble, oriental alabaster, and lithics of other colors.

In Rev. 18:12 marble is part of Babylon's cargo that no one buys any more. R. G. BULLARD

**MARCH.** *See* WAR.

**MARCION** mär'shən, **GOSPEL OF.** *See* APOCRYPHAL GOSPELS V.A; CANON OF THE NT III.B.1.

**MARCUS** mär'kəs. The AV reading for Mark in Col. 4:10; Philem. 24. *See* MARK, JOHN.

**MARDOCHEUS; MARDOCHAEUS** mär-də-kē'əs.

**1.** (AV, NEB, 1 Esd. 5:8). *See* MORDECAI **1.**

**2.** (AV, NEB, Ad. Est. 10:4; 11:2, 12; etc.). *See* MORDECAI **2.**

**MARDUK** mär'dook; **MERODACH** mer'ə-dak [Heb. *m^e rôḏāḵ*] (Jer. 50:2). Chief god of the Babylonian pantheon, whose name in Sumerograms is ᵈAMAR.UTU, "calf of the sun," but is attested syllabically as ᵈ*Ma-ru-du-uk-ku* (A. Deimel, *Šumerisches Lexikon,* II [1928-1933], 841). Upon the political ascendancy of Hammurabi of Babylon (*ca.* 1750 B.C.), Marduk the god of Babylon became supreme among the older Sumerian gods as creator and ruler — a position formerly enjoyed by Enlil but affirmed for Marduk in the Code of Hammurabi (*ANET,* pp. 163-180) and the Creation Epic (*ANET,* pp. 60-72) and retained until the end of indigenous Mesopotamian religion (*ca.* A.D. 100-200). Jeremiah prophesied that Marduk, also called *Bêl,* "lord," would be put to shame (Jer. 50:2).

The divine name Marduk can be seen in the royal names Merodach-baladan (2 K. 20:12 par. Isa. 39:1; cf. Akk. *Marduk-apal-iddin,* "Marduk has given a son") and Evil-merodach (2 K. 25:27 par. Jer. 52:31; cf. Akk. *amel-Marduk,* "man of Marduk"), and possibly in the name Mordecai. *See* RELIGIONS OF THE BIBLICAL WORLD: ASSYRIA AND BABYLONIA.

Glazed tile of the dragon of Marduk, a creature with a serpent's head, a lion's body, and an eagle's claws for hind feet. From the Ishtar Gate, which guarded the Procession Way to the temple of Marduk in Babylon (*ca.* 600 B.C.) (Founders Society Purchase, courtesy of the Detroit Institute of Arts)

*Bibliography.–New Larousse Encyclopedia of Mythology* (Eng. tr. 1968), pp. 56f. (F. Guirand); T. Jacobsen, *Treasures of Darkness: A History of Mesopotamian Religion* (1976).

P. W. GAEBELEIN, JR.

**MARE** [Heb. *sûsâ*] (Cant. 1:9); AV COMPANY OF HORSES; NEB HORSES. *See* HORSE.

**MAREAL** mā're-əl [Heb. *mar'ᵃlāh*; Gk. B *Maragella,* A *Marila*]. A place on the western border of Zebulun (Josh. 19:11). The RSV Mareal appears to be derived from a misreading of the final *hê* as *hê* directive. *See* MARALAH.

W. S. L. S.

**MARESHAH** mə-rē'shə [Heb. *mārēšâ, mêšā'* (1 Ch. 2:42a)]; AV, NEB, RSV mg., also MESHA (2:42a).

**1.** The first son of Caleb; the father of Ziph and Hebron (1 Ch. 2:42). The AV and NEB follow the MT, in which Caleb's son is first called *mêša'* (v. 42a) and later *mārēšâ* (v. 42b). The RSV follows the LXX, which has *Marisa* in both places.

**2.** A Judahite, son of Laadah (1 Ch. 4:21).

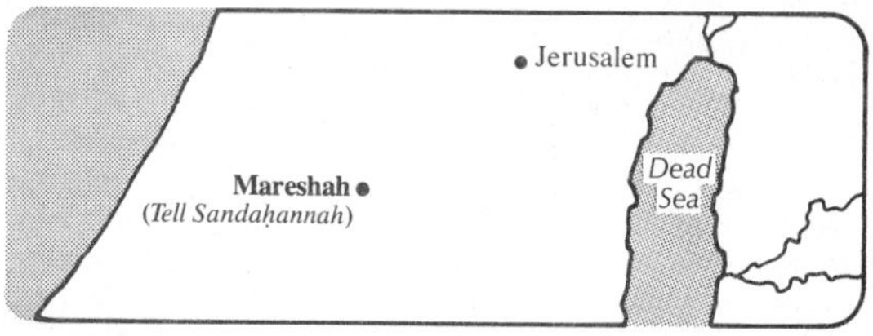


**MARESHAH** mä-rē'shə [Heb. *mārēšâ*; Gk. *Marēsa*]; Apoc. **MARISA** [Gk. *Marisa*]; AV, RV, also "Samaria" (1 Macc. 5:66). A Palestinian town in the Shephelah. It is represented today by Tell Sandaḥannah, which also is the site of Hellenistic Marisa, 1.6 km. (1 mi.) S of Beit Jibrîn (Eleutheropolis). F. J. Bliss excavated the site in 1900; in 1902 interesting painted tombs were discovered.

Interior of a tomb at Mareshah (Israel Department of Antiquities and Museums)

Aerial view of the excavations at Mari (Institut Francais d'Archéologie du Proche-Orient, Beirut)

Mareshah first appears in the Bible in Josh. 15:44, in a grouping of nine cities of Judah. It was one of the cities fortified by Rehoboam after the division of the kingdom (2 Ch. 11:8). Asa's troops decisively defeated an army of Ethiopians in a battle that began in the Valley of Zephathah near Mareshah (14:9-14). Eliezer the son of Dodavahu of Mareshah prophesied against King Jehoshaphat for joining Ahaziah of Israel in a shipping enterprise (20:37). In prophecies of Micah concerning an Assyrian invasion Mareshah is mentioned with Achzib and Moresheth-gath (Mic. 1:14f.).

In Hellenistic times Marisa was a leading town of the Idumeans and figured often in the wars of the Maccabees. Judas Maccabeus captured and burned Marisa after defeating the Idumeans and before conquering Philistia (Josephus *Ant.* xii.8.6 [353]; 1 Macc. 5:66). In a battle between Jonathan's forces and the Idumeans, Gorgias the governor of Idumea was nearly taken captive, but a Thracian horseman rescued him, and he escaped to Marisa. His army was routed (2 Macc. 12:35). After the death of Antiochus Epiphanes, John Hyrcanus captured Marisa but allowed the Idumeans to remain there after they agreed to be circumcised and observe the Jewish law (*Ant.* xiii.9.1 [257]). John Hyrcanus completely destroyed Samaria because of injuries the people of that city had done to Marisa, "a colony of the Jews and confederate with them" (*Ant.* xiii.10.2 [275]). The Jews possessed Marisa in the time of Alexander Janneus (*Ant.* xiii.15.4 [396]).

In 63 B.C. the Romans under Pompey restored Marisa to its people and gave it independence (*Ant.* xiv.4.4 [75]). The actual rebuilding of the city is attributed to Gabinius (*Ant.* xiv.5.3 [88]). Antigonus secured Parthian aid against Herod, who made Marisa a stronghold; the Parthians destroyed the city in 40 B.C. (*Ant.* xiv.13.9 [364]).

For plan of Marissa *see* CITY.

See *EAEHL*, III, *s.v.* (M. Avi-Yonah and A. Kloner).

C. E. DE VRIES

**MARI** mä'rē. An ancient city in eastern Syria, identified with modern Tell el-Ḥarîrī near the west bank of the Euphrates River, about 25 km. (15 mi.) from the border of Iraq. Mari is not mentioned in the Bible, but heightened recognition of the importance of Syria since the discoveries at Tell Mardikh (Ebla) enhances the significance of information from Mari about West Semitic civilization and the pastoral nomadic background of Israel.

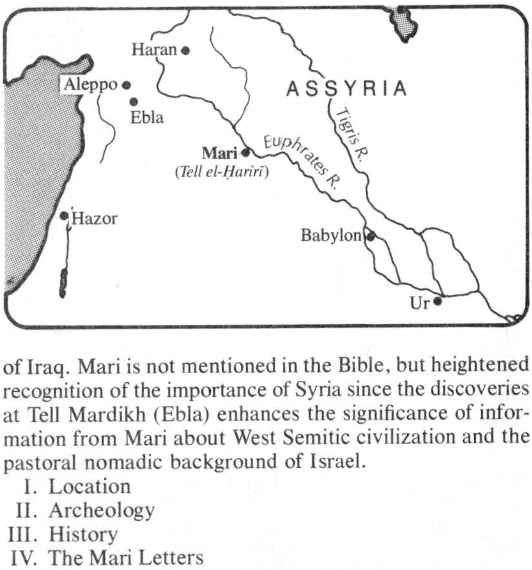


I. Location
II. Archeology
III. History
IV. The Mari Letters
V. The Letters' Relationship to the Bible

*I. Location.*–In the 3rd and early 2nd millennia B.C. the metropolis of Mari, like nearby Dura Europos in Roman times, probably owed its importance to its location. The fertile Euphrates valley was the main trade route from Ur and Babylon to western Syria and the Haran area. Mari stood midway between Babylon and the Syrian cities of Aleppo and Ebla. Moreover, it was a terminus of a caravan road that led via Tadmor (Palmyra) to Qatna in the Orontes valley and thence to Damascus and Hazor.

*II. Archeology.*–Mari was already well known from Mesopotamian sources in 1925 when W. F. Albright observed a large mound with abundant Bronze Age pottery. In 1933 bedouin found a broken statue, and identification of the site was soon confirmed. Excavations were begun at once by A. Parrot for the Louvre and were still in progress in 1981.

MARI

Although its population may always have been ethnically West Semitic, the kingdom was a flourishing outpost of Sumerian culture in the Early Dynastic Period from *ca.* 3000 B.C. until Sargon's conquest of the city, *ca.* 2300 B.C. Two palaces, one superimposed on the other, have been recovered, along with temples of Šamaš the sun-god, Ishtar (biblical Ashtoreth, Gk. Astarte), and Dagan (biblical Dagon), the principal deity of the region. Dagan's main sanctuary was at Terqa, about 50 km. (30 mi.) upstream on the Euphrates. Abundant artifacts from this period include votive images and statues of the kings.

A second era of prosperity in the Isin-Larsa and Old Babylonian periods, *ca.* 2000 to 1750 B.C., furnishes a contemporary background for the patriarchal narratives of Genesis. An enormous palace complex, the showplace of the ancient Near East, was built above the remains of its earlier counterparts. A single, heavily fortified block of buildings, now partially eroded, it must have covered an area well in excess of 2.5 ha. (6.3 acres). More than three hundred rooms and spacious courtyards, whose walls are preserved to a height of 5.0 m. (16.5 ft.), lie just beneath the surface of the mound. The palace was elaborately decorated with sculpture, fountains, and the earliest wall paintings in Mesopotamia. One delicately colored panel, about 2.5 by 2.0 m. (8.3 by 6.6 ft.), now in the Louvre, has a spiral border clearly related to Minoan art and depicts the investiture of the king in a mythological scene with trees and streams of water reminiscent of the garden of Eden.

Also uncovered at Mari were a school for scribes and an archive of more than twenty thousand cuneiform tablets comparable in importance to the Amarna Tablets, to the texts from Ugarit, and to finds at Tell Mardikh (Ebla).

***III. History.***–According to the Sumerian King List, Mari was the tenth royal city after the Flood. Oblique attestations to its status in the Early Dynastic Period are a claim of victory by a Sumerian ruler, Eannatum of Lagash, and tentative evidence from Tell Mardikh (Ebla) that King Iblul-Il of Mari submitted and paid tribute to that city. Sargon made Mari a part of the first Semitic empire *ca.* 2300 B.C., and the city remained subject to Mesopotamian rulers of Agade and Ur until Ishbi-Erra, a "man of Mari," overthrew the Sumerian Third Dynasty of Ur (Malamat, p. 2). In the 19th and 18th cents. B.C. Mari was ruled by a powerful but ill-starred West Semitic dynasty. King

Statue of the steward Ebih-Il with inscription to Ishtar (mid-3rd millennium B.C.) (Louvre)

Shell fragments of human figures, including a soldier (left) facing a standard-bearer, who is followed by four dignitaries. From Mari, mid-3rd millennium B.C. (Louvre)

Yaḫdun-Lim led his armies to the Mediterranean Sea but did not long enjoy his victories. The murder of Yaḫdun-Lim in his palace was almost certainly arranged by the formidable King Šamši-Adad of Assyria, who installed his son, Yasmaḫ-Adad, as viceroy at Mari. Yaḫdun-Lim's son Zimri-Lim, a tragic figure, took refuge at Aleppo, capital of the Syrian state of Yamḫad, where he married Shibtu daughter of the king. When Šamši-Adad died, Zimri-Lim regained his throne and ruled an extensive domain for about two decades until overwhelmed by new danger. HAMMURABI of Babylon conquered his city and burned the splendid palace, which was never rebuilt. Buried in the rubble were records that shed a brilliant light on the history and society of the period.

*IV. The Mari Letters.*–Most of the tablets contain administrative records, and there are texts from earlier periods, some in Sumerian and Hurrian. But of primary interest to historians and biblical scholars is a large archive of correspondence from the reigns of Yasmaḫ-Adad and Zimri-Lim. By 1981 well over 1000 letters of kings of Mari, Assyria, Babylon, Aleppo, and Qatna, of ambassadors, officials, and members of the royal household, including 179 letters to or from women, had been published with meticulous care by a distinguished team of French Assyriologists (*ARM*). Although Amorite, a language known to scholars only through personal names, may have been spoken in the city, the Mari Letters are in Akkadian, the *lingua franca* of the ancient Near East, with only minimal traces of West Semitic influence on the Old Babylonian dialect of Akkadian that was normative of that time. This royal archive deals with such topics as troop movements, state affairs, military victories, the lighting of signal fires by the nomads, the repair of dikes, and the procurement of locusts for the king's table and of lions for the royal hunt.

From their tone the letters seem to have been dictated personally rather than issued in the name of the king from a royal chancery: "To Yasmaḫ-Adad speak: thus Šamši-Adad your father. . . . How long must we continue to direct you? You are young. Don't you have a beard on your chin? . . . . Will you not look at your brother who commands great armies?" (*ARM*, I, no. 73). The king of Qatna, paid with tin instead of silver for two horses that had been sent across five hundred miles of desert via Tadmor and Mari, wrote to Išme-Dagan of Assyria: "If you had not sent anything at all, I would not have been angry. But you sent tin. . . . Any one who hears of it will talk about us. . . . You are not a great king. Why have you done this? (But) this house is (still) your house" (*ARM*, V, no. 20). The final expression of allegiance is still current among the Arabs of Iraq, and, through the Moors, may have come to us in the Spanish response: *Esta es su casa*. The king of Aleppo wrote to a recalcitrant vassal that his city "would have been windblown dust, like chaff" (*Syria*, 33 [1956], 63-69; cf. Ps. 1:4; Isa. 40:24).

About twenty-five letters report brief ecstatic utterances in the name of a god. Šibtu the queen wrote to Zimri-Lim: "In the temple of Annunitum [probably an epithet of Ishtar] Selibum went into a trance: 'Thus says Annunitum: "O Zimri-Lim, they will test you in a revolt. Take care of yourself. Set up around you trustworthy servants whom you love. Station them and let them guard you. Do not go walking about by yourself. As for the men who are testing you, I will hand over these men to you"'" (*ARM*, X, no. 7).

Above all, the letters vividly portray the tribes of pastoral nomads, often called Amorites by modern scholars. Roaming vast grasslands from southern Mesopotamia to Syria and Lebanon, but most numerous in the central area around Haran, they tended their flocks, took part in raids, served in the armies of the king, and founded new dynasties of their own.

*V. The Letters' Relationship to the Bible.*–The prophetic letters are unique in portent-ridden Mesopotamia, where professional divination from omens was the standard practice. Ecstatic utterance of a divine message could well be a West Semitic phenomenon related to biblical prophecy, especially to the oracles of Balaam, who may have come from eastern Syria (Nu. 22:5). But the prophecies' obvious relevance to biblical study should not divert attention from their brevity (none is much longer than the one quoted above) or from their stark contrast to the superb poetry and ethical monotheism of the Hebrew prophets.

Some suggested parallels appear problematical. The so-called Benjaminites (TUR$^{\text{MEŠ}}$ *Ia-mi-na*) are now simply designated Yaminites, "people [lit. "sons"] of the South" (TUR$^{\text{MEŠ}}$ means "sons"). In the personal name Yawi-Ila, the element *Yawi*, followed by *Ila*, "god," seems to be not the name Yahweh but rather a verb, "be, become," as attested with familiar gods in the common theophoric names Yawi-Adad and Yawi-Dagan (cf. H. Huffmon, "Yahweh and Mari," in H. Goedicke, ed., *Near Eastern Studies in Honor of William Foxwell Albright* [1971], pp. 283-89).

Nonetheless, the letters may provide early confirmation of certain biblical traditions. (1) Hazor, which is described in Josh. 11:10 as "*formerly* the head of all those kingdoms," is the only Palestinian city often mentioned in the Mari Letters. (2) There is a reference to Laish (*La-yi-si-im*$^{\text{KI}}$, *ARM*, XVI/1, 21), the former name of Tell Dan (Jgs. 18:7). (3) There are attestations of *šāpiṭum*, "judge" (*ARM*, XV, 205), which make "untenable . . . the widely accepted opinion that the concept *šōfēt* in the Book of Judges represents a later editorial (the so-called Deuteronomic) stage" (Malamat, p. 46 n. 3). (4) Naḫur (biblical Nahor) and Haran (Ḫarran), related to Ur as a second sanctuary of the moon-god Sin, furnish obvious links to the patriarchal traditions.

While other affinities, admirably set forth by Malamat, might be cited, the general contribution of the Mari texts far exceeds in significance any specific parallel. The world of the 2nd millennium is well known from many cuneiform sources, but these are complementary to the Mari texts, and strong overtones from Mari reverberate throughout the cuneiform sources. Led by W. F. Albright (e.g., *FSAC*, pp. 236-39) and R. de Vaux (e.g., *Early History of Israel* [Eng. tr. 1978], pp. 229-233), many scholars have placed the patriarchal traditions of the Bible firmly in the early 2nd millennium, although particular items of evidence, e.g., the "Benjaminites," adduced in support of this consensus have recently been called into question, notably by T. L. Thompson (*Historicity of the Patriarchal Narratives* [1974]). Controversy may continue, but the general picture of the pastoral nomads remains valid, and the probability that there actually was a desert sheikh named Abram who resembled the ancestors of Šamši-Adad and Zimri-Lim cannot easily be set aside.

***Bibliography.***–*ARM*, I-XIX (1950-1976), XX in preparation; A. Finet, *L'Accadien des Lettres de Mari* (1956); A. Parrot, *Mission Archeologique de Mari* (4 vols., 1958-1968); *Mari, Capitale Fabuleuse* (1974); J.-R. Kupper, *Les Nomades en Mésopotamie au Temps des Rois de Mari* (1957); V. H. Matthews, *Pastoral Nomadism in the Mari Kingdom (ca. 1830-1760 B.C.)* (1978); *BA*, 44 (1981), 215-18; A. Malamat, *Mari and the Bible: A Collection of Studies* (1975); H. B. Huffmon, "Prophecy in the Mari Letters," in E. F. Campbell, Jr., and D. N. Freedman, eds., *Biblical Archaeologist Reader*, III (1970), 199-224 (repr. of *BA*, 31 [Dec. 1968], 101-124); *Amorite Personal Names in the Mari Texts* (1965); A. Marzal, *Gleanings from the Wisdom of Mari* (1976); P. W. Gaebelein, Jr., "Graphemic Analysis of Old Babylonian Letters from Mari" (Ph.D. diss., University of California, Los Angeles, 1976); B. J. Beitzel, "From Ḫarran to Imar along the Old Babylonian Itinerary," in G. A. Tuttle, ed., *Biblical and Near Eastern Studies* (*Festschrift* W. S. LaSor; 1978), pp. 209-219.

P. W. GAEBELEIN, JR.

**MARIMOTH** mar'ə-moth (AV, NEB, 2 Esd. 1:2). *See* MERAIOTH.

**MARINER** [Heb. *mallāḥ*] (Ezk. 27:9, 27, 29; Jonah 1:5); NEB SAILOR. According to BDB, p. 572, Heb. *mallāḥ* is a loanword from Akk. *malaḫu,* "sailor"; the Akkadian word is in turn a loanword from Sum. ma-laḫu, "boat builder." Cognates are also found in Phoenician, Aramaic, and Arabic.

The infrequent use of this term in the OT reflects Israel's lack of interest in the sea, no doubt due in part to Phoenicia's hold on the seacoast. The references in Ezk. 27 are in the context of a lament over Tyre, the most important coastal city in Phoenicia. Jonah went to Joppa on the Palestinian coast in his effort to flee from the Lord; the mariners on his ship were non-Israelite, probably Phoenician.

G. A. L.

**MARISA** mar'i-sə. *See* MARESHAH.

**MARISH** mar'ish (Ezk. 47:11, AV). An archaic form of MARSH.

**MARITAL RIGHTS** [Heb. *ʿōnâ*] (Ex. 21:10); AV "duty of marriage"; NEB CONJUGAL RIGHTS; **CONJUGAL RIGHTS** [Gk. *opheilḗ*] (1 Cor. 7:3); AV DUE BENEVOLENCE; NEB DUE.

The meaning of Heb. *ʿōnâ* is uncertain. Traditionally scholars have taken it to refer to conjugal rights on the basis of the context. But other interpretations are also possible. U. Cassuto (*Comm. on the Book of Exodus* [Eng. tr. 1967], p. 269) suggested "the condition of her abode" (cf. *māʿôn,* "dwelling"); thus the master shall provide her basic needs of food, clothing, and shelter. According to S. M. Paul (*Studies on the Book of the Covenant in the Light of Cuneiform and Biblical Law* [*SVT,* 18; 1970], pp. 55-61; *JNES,* 28 [1969], 48-53) *ʿōnâ* means "oil, ointment"; he deduced this on the basis of parallels from cuneiform texts in which provision for food, clothing, and oil is made (e.g., Code of Lipit-Ishtar, § 27; *ANET,* p. 160).

The Gk. *opheilḗ* is a more general term for "obligation," used in 1 Cor. 7:3 as a euphemism for the marital obligation of cohabitation (cf. *TDNT,* V, *s.v.* ὀφείλω κτλ.: ὀφειλή [Hauck]).

G. A. L.

**MARK** nouns: [Heb. *'ôṯ, qaʿᵃqaʿ, tāw, mipgāʿ, maṭṭārâ, maṭṭārā'*; Gk. *cháragma, stígma, sēmeíon, týpos* (Jn. 20:25)]; AV also TOKEN, PRINT; NEB also SIGN, TARGET; verbs: [Heb. *šāmar, śîm, śîm lēḇ(lᵉ)* ("mark well"), *rā'â, yāḏaʿ, bîn,* hiphil of *nāḵar,* piel of *tā'ar,* piel of *tāwâ* ("make marks," 1 S. 21:13); Gk. *skopéō, epéchō*]; AV also DISCERN, CONSIDER, SCRABBLE, APPOINT; NEB also RECOGNIZE, WATCH, LOOK AT, TRACE OUT, etc.; **MARK OUT** [Heb. piel of *tā'â,* piel of *tā'ar, ḥāqaq*]; AV also POINT OUT, APPOINT; NEB also DRAW, MEASURE; **MARK OFF** [Heb. *nāṭâ,* piel of *tāḵan*]; AV STRETCH OUT, METE OUT; NEB TAKE MEASURE, SET LIMITS; **MISS THE MARK** [Gk. *astochéo*] (1 Tim. 6:21); AV ERR; NEB SHOT FAR WIDE; **REMOVE THE MARKS OF CIRCUMCISION** [Gk. *epispáomai*] (1 Cor. 7:18); AV BECOME UNCIRCUMCIZED.

*I. As a Noun.*–The use of religious tattoos or markings on the hand or FOREHEAD to symbolize one's devotion to the deity and desire for protection was widespread in the ancient world. This may be the background of the protective mark (Heb. *'ôṯ*) that Yahweh gave to Cain (Gen. 4:15), which was possibly some form of TATTOO that later became the tribal mark of the Kenites (see G. von Rad, *Genesis* [Eng. tr., *OTL,* 1972], pp. 107-109). The Israelites were forbidden to deface their bodies with the tattoos used in the pagan cults (*qaʿᵃqaʿ,* Lev. 19:28; *see also* CUTTINGS IN THE FLESH). As an analogy to this practice, however, they were commanded to demonstrate their consecration to Yahweh by keeping the feast of unleavened bread and circumcising the first born "as a mark [*'ôṯ,* "sign"] on your head or frontlets between your eyes" (Ex. 13:16; cf. v. 9; Dt. 6:4-9; 11:18-21). This command was later interpreted literally and is still fulfilled by wearing phylacteries on the hand and forehead (*see* PHYLACTERY).

In Ezekiel's vision (9:4, 6) all the faithful who grieved over the wickedness of Jerusalem were to have written on their foreheads the Hebrew letter *tāw* (X in ancient Canaanite script), a protective mark that early Christians interpreted as a symbol of Christ. Reminiscent of this is the SEAL (Gk. *sphrágis*) of ownership and protection with which God's servants are marked in John's apocalyptic vision (Rev. 7:2-8; 14:1); by contrast, those who worship the beast have the numbers of his name stamped on their foreheads (*cháragma,* 13:16f.; 14:9, 11; 16:2; 19:20; 20:4). In Gal. 6:17 Paul apparently alluded to the custom of branding slaves when he called his scars from beatings and stonings the *stígmata* of Jesus."

In 1 Cor. 7:18 Gk. *epispáomai* is a medical term for removing the marks of circumcision. Some Hellenistic Jews underwent this operation so that they could pass for Greeks (cf. 1 Macc. 1:15).

In several passages "mark" denotes a target for arrows (e.g., 1 S. 20:20, Heb. *maṭṭārâ*). In Lam. 3:12 the poet complains that Yahweh has made him His target (*maṭṭārā'*); similarly, Job complains that he has become the object of God's attack (*mipgāʿ,* 7:20; cf. 36:32). In 1 Tim. 6:21 "miss the mark" is a literal translation of Gk. *astochéō* (cf. 1:6, "swerve"); in 6:11f. Timothy is instructed about the targets at which he should aim (see J. N. D. Kelly, *Pastoral Epistles* [*HNTC,* 1963], pp. 47f., 152).

As was the custom, Paul concluded his letters in his own handwriting as a sign (*sēmeíon*) of their genuineness (2 Thess. 3:17).

*II. As a Verb.*–Most often the verb "mark" denotes a mental attitude of watching, discerning, or paying close attention to something being said or done (e.g., Heb. *bîn,* Ps. 50:22; hiphil of *nāḵar,* Gen. 38:25; *yāḏaʿ,* 1 K. 20:7; *rā'â,* 2 S. 13:28; *śîm lēḇ(lᵉ),* Ezk. 44:5; Gk. *epéchō,* Lk. 14:7; *skopéō,* Phil. 3:17). Heb. *šāmar* is sometimes used in this sense (Ps. 37:37), but in Job 10:14 it has the hostile sense of guarding a prisoner (cf. also Ps. 130:3). *See also* LOOK II; NOTE, TAKE NOTE OF.

In other passages "mark" denotes a physical action. In contexts (often metaphorical) about surveying, constructing a building, or carpentering, it means to draw or measure (usually with a tightly stretched line): e.g., Lam. 2:8 (*nāṭâ*); Nu. 34:7f., 10 (piel of *tā'â*); Prov. 8:29 (*ḥāqaq*); Isa. 40:12 (piel of *tāḵan*); 44:13 (piel of *tā'ar*). In Ezk. 21:19f. (MT 24f.) the prophet is told to mark out (*śîm*) with a signpost a route for the enemy.

N. J. OPPERWALL

**MARK, GOSPEL ACCORDING TO.**

IV. Genre and Structure
  A. Markan Hypothesis
  B. Form-Critical Assessment
  C. Vincent Taylor's View
  D. Liturgical Theories
  E. Gottfried Schille's View
  F. Ernst Lohmeyer's View
V. Authorship
VI. Date
  A. External Evidence
  B. Internal Evidence
VII. Origin and Destination
VIII. Special Problems
  A. Opening
  B. Ending
IX. Markan Theology
  A. Kingdom of God
  B. Person of Jesus Christ

***I. Mark's Gospel in the Early Church.***–The Gospel according to Mark has had a checkered history since the time of its publication. A number of facts show that the first Christians accepted it enthusiastically and acknowledged its authoritative witness to the life of the Lord. The other Synoptic Evangelists used this Gospel (*see* GOSPELS, SYNOPTIC). It was evidently known to the Johannine Evangelist (see B. H. Streeter, *The Four Gospels* [1924], pp. 397ff.) and the author of the *Gospel of Peter* (a second-century "Passion gospel"; cf. L. Vaganay, *L'Évangile de Pierre* [1930]).

Later attestation in early Christian literature includes Shepherd of Hermas (*ca.* 130) in Mand. 4:2 (cf. Mk. 6:52; 8:17) and Tatian, who compiled a Harmony of the Gospels (the *Diatessaron*) *ca.* 170 and used Mark as one of his sources. Irenaeus (180) regarded it as one of the canonical documents, adding the testimony: "After their departure [i.e., Peter's and Paul's death], Mark the disciple and interpreter of Peter, did also hand down to us in writing what had been preached by Peter." Clement of Alexandria, in the next decade, endorsed this statement, "Mark wrote his Gospel from matter preached by Peter."

For direct citation of the text of the Gospel, however, there is little evidence from the early centuries. That the Gospel of Mark was known and highly regarded is clear; but it is a singular fact that the Apostolic Fathers and Apologists (in the 2nd cent.) seldom cited it (cf. P. N. Harrison, *Polycarp's Two Epistles to the Philippians* [1926], pp. 285-88, for Polycarp's knowledge of the Gospel). Moreover, although the Gospel found a place in the canon, its position in the order of the Gospels is unsettled. It is never placed first, and in some lists (e.g., the Old Latin, and the Greek MSS D and W) it is last. Irenaeus, in his celebrated description of the Gospel writers that likens them to the four cherubim of Ezk. 1 and the four living creatures of Rev. 4, reflected the confusion over the place and office of the Gospel of Mark. The father in successive parts of his writing depicted Mark as an eagle, a lion, a man, and a calf, apparently unable to decide which characterization fitted the Evangelist best.

No commentary on the Gospel of Mark was written before that of Victor of Antioch in the 5th century. There is evidence that the Gospel was neglected, mainly on the ground that the larger Gospels of Matthew and Luke embodied most of its contents and were much smoother than Mark's rugged and unstylistic account. Moreover, the theory that Matthew's Gospel was the first to be written and that Mark was "one who followed Matthew's footsteps and shortened his Gospel" (*pedisequus et breviator Matthaei*), as Augustine put it, was commonly held until the rise of modern criticism.

Thus the facts of the early dissemination and recognition of Mark point to two conclusions. First, it was immediately received on its publication as a fundamental witness to the life of Christ; and its prestige in the Church was greatest just after it was written (Rawlinson, p. xxv). These features led Rawlinson to believe that the Gospel was circulated with the backing of some important church; he found that the double tradition that this church was the one at Rome and that Peter's authority assured to the Gospel a ready reception in the churches throughout the Christian world most adequately explained its initial acceptance. Second, after Mark was incorporated into the later evangelical records, its popularity waned, and it was seldom quoted in the following centuries. As a consequence of the modern assessment of Mark as the earliest Gospel to be written and the claim that it objectively records Jesus' historical life — two suppositions deriving from H. J. Holtzmann's *Die synoptischen Evangelien* (1863) — the Gospel of Mark has come into its own once again. The last century of biblical scholarship has witnessed a resurgence of interest in this Gospel and its writer — "The saint who first found grace to pen/The life which was the Life of men" (L. Housman).

***II. Outline.***–The Gospel opens with a summary of the mission of John the Baptist (1:1-13) as a frontispiece to the narratives of the baptism and temptation of Jesus. These events lead into the public ministry of Jesus, which is depicted in two large sections: the Galilean ministry (1:14–9:50) and the Judean ministry (chs. 10–13). The former is further divided into a summary of Jesus' work in eastern Galilee (1:14–7:23), with His headquarters at Capernaum, and His later ministry in northern Galilee (7:24–9:50). He returned to Capernaum and journeyed farther south into Judea (chs. 10–13); this section concludes with His triumphal entry into Jerusalem (11:1-27), His controversies with the Jerusalem religious authorities (11:27–12:44), and His apocalyptic discourse (13:1-37). The remainder of the book is a full, graphic depiction of His arrest, trial, crucifixion, and burial (14:1–15:47). Mark abruptly ends with the account of how three women arriving at the tomb found His grave empty and heard an angel bidding them to return with the disciples to Galilee (16:1-8).

***III. Features.***–*A. Linguistic Style.* Vincent Taylor (chs. 5–6) has the fullest modern discussion, in which the important studies of Swete and C. H. Turner are used. Interest has centered upon Mark's supposed Semitic style, about which Taylor concluded: "We have good reason to speak of an Aramaic background to the Greek of the Gospel; there are grounds for suspecting the existence of Aramaic sources, which may, however, be oral; and we can speak of the Evangelist's use of a tradition which ultimately is Aramaic; but to say more is speculation" (p. 56).

The most evident features of a Semitic style are: the way the sentences are joined by the paratactic *kaí* in preference to the use of subordinate clauses; the use of *ḗrxato,* "he began," before the verb; the introduction of direct speech by the participle *légōn,* "saying" — a common OT feature; the very common genitival pronoun; the habit of using *pollá,* "many," with adverbial force (see Moulton, *Grammar,* II, 446); and the arrangement of pericopes in groups of two or usually three (a Semitic trait to which E. Lohmeyer and W. Grundmann called attention in their comms.).

A second trait of Markan style is his predilection for Latin terms and expressions. The most obvious are in verses in which the Greek thinly disguises the underlying Latin word or words: *modius* (4:21), *legio* (5:9, 15), *speculator* (6:27), *denarius* (6:37), *sextarius* (7:4), *census* (12:14), *quadrans* (12:42), *flagellare* (15:15), *praetorium* (15:16), *centurio* (15:39, 44f.). Some of these are direct loanwords (i.e., Latin words written in Greek characters). It is also significant that in the case of *centurio*, the parallel verses in Matthew and Luke (which do not use this word) read the Gk. *hekatontárchēs* in place of Mark's *kentyríōn*. The term *Hērōdianoi* in a section (3:6) that contains another Latinism is particularly striking (see the comms. on the phrase *symboúlion edídoun*, "they held a council"). Other Latinisms include *verberibus eum acceperunt* ("they received him with blows," 14:65); *satisfacere* ("satisfy," 15:15); *genua ponere* ("kneel," 15:19). Mark retained the names of Simon's sons — Alexander and Rufus (15:21) — which recur in Rom. 16:13 as the names of church members at Rome, where presumably Latin was the language used. Mark's Latinisms directly bear on the question of the recipients of the Gospel (so Grundmann, p. 19).

*B. Distinctive Presentation*. The vivid way in which the stories are told impresses all careful readers. The narratives are full of intimate details, unimportant in themselves, yet such as an eyewitness would have been likely to recall later when he related the mighty works and words of Jesus and the decisive reactions of those present. For instance, Mark reported the attitudes, the expression, and even the gestures of Jesus (see 7:34; 9:36; 10:16) with special emphasis upon His observation (5:32) and His attitude toward those who came under His scrutiny (1:41, where the reading *orgistheís*, "being angry," is to be preferred to the TR; 3:5, 34; 10:21, 23; 11:11). Similarly, he noted snatches of conversation between the disciples and the remarks of the onlookers and the crowd; the unusual wealth of detail in 9:14-29 convinced even the form critic K. L. Schmidt (*RGJ*, p. 227) that the story "can only go back to good tradition." The story of the rich young man (10:17-22) in the parallel version in Luke (18:18-27) lacks the details that an eyewitness might have supplied. Luke does not tell that the young man ran and knelt, that Jesus looked upon him and loved him, or that when faced with the Lord's challenge, his countenance fell. In Mk. 10:32, Jesus walked alone on the last journey to Jerusalem, and as the disciples followed Him, fear gripped them. B. K. Rattey commented, "Mark alone tells us all this; but who told Mark? It could only have been one of the Twelve" (*Making of the Synoptic Gospels* [1942], p. 32). This deduction has been severely criticized, however, by form critics and redaction critics; see Martin, *Mark: Evangelist and Theologian*, pp. 55-61 for details.

J. Weiss noticed that some stories are told more from the standpoint of those who see Jesus than from the standpoint of Jesus Himself, especially the story of the call of the Galilean fishermen (1:16-20, cited by V. Taylor, *The Gospels* [5th ed. 1945], p. 53 n.). This observation again indicates that Mark depended upon an eyewitness tradition, notably that of Peter himself.

Another distinguishing feature of the Gospel is its attitude toward Peter. B. W. Bacon pointed out that Peter was shown as disgraced or rebuked in most Markan references to him (see, e.g., 8:27ff.; 9:5f.; 10:28ff.; 14:29ff., 66-72). Rawlinson (p. xxix) deduced from these candid criticisms of Peter that when the Gospel was published, Peter was already revered as a martyr and no stain drawn from the record of this earthly life could dishonor him. Rawlinson's explanation is plausible but lacks proof. A second explanation is that Peter's own confessions of failure and disgrace account for the report of these episodes; his name is significantly attached to certain parts of the record where the other Gospels give only a vague reference to "they" or "one of the disciples" (1:36; 11:21; 16:7). If Mark had desired to glorify Peter, he would not have omitted the encomium of Mt. 16:17-19; only the humbled apostle who willingly related in such detail his denial of the Lord would have left out the words of the Lord's blessing upon him. Further, 11:21 ("And Peter remembered and said") must have come to the Evangelist directly from Peter himself.

A further confirmation that Mark depended directly on Peter for these details is that he spared no detail when reporting the failures and misunderstandings of the Twelve. The clearest instance of this feature is 4:38 — "Teacher, do you not care if we perish?" — a curt reproof on the lips of the disciples in the boat, which the corresponding accounts in Matthew (8:25) and Luke (8:24) soften.

The prominence given to the cross is a marked trait of this Gospel, whose *Leitmotiv* may be said to be suffering and martyrdom. Almost a third of Mark is the Passion story, and the shadow of the cross falls across the page as early as 2:20 and 3:6. The book explicitly predicts the Passion three times (8:31; 9:31; and 10:33f.) and contains allusions, sometimes veiled (9:12), sometimes not (10:45), to the way in which Jesus expected His ministry to end. (On these Passion prophecies, see the important study of R. H. Fuller, *Mission and Achievement of Jesus* [1954], pp. 55-64.) Interwoven with the thought that the Lord would die a sacrificial death for sinners is the teaching that His followers must expect to suffer for His sake (8:34ff.; 10:38f.). Rawlinson (p. xvii) proposed that this interest shows that the Gospel was first addressed to a church that was being persecuted at Rome and faced the very real possibility of martyrdom.

The emphases on the cross and on the teaching of the disciples' dying for Christ's sake are the two most important supports for the theory, put out by G. Volkmar in 1857 and maintained since by B. W. Bacon, that the entire Gospel was a narrative in the form of an allegory written to undergird the distinctive tenets of Paulinism. (For the other features of Mark that are supposedly Pauline see V. Taylor, *The Gospels*, pp. 56f.) The theory has met with little acceptance (cf. J. Moffatt, *Intro. to the Literature of the NT* [1911], pp. 235f.; Rawlinson, pp. xliii ff.; and esp. M. Werner, whose book *Der Einfluss paulinischer Theologie im Markusevangelium* [1923] was written expressly to refute this notion). A later trend in Markan interpretation, however, was to see Mark as a Pauline theologian of the cross (cf. E. Schweizer; essays by W. L. Lane and R. P. Martin in *Southwestern Journal of Theology*, 21 [1978]).

***IV. Genre and Structure.***–It is an axiom of modern Gospel criticism that Mark (like the other Evangelists) did not present a biography of Jesus, in the popular sense of that term (see J. M. Robinson, ch. 1, on the influence of modern historiographical views on the understanding of the nature of the Gospels). The exordium in 1:1 makes it clear that Mark intended to write a *gospel*, i.e., a record of the good news that came with Jesus Christ (cf. 1:14f.; 14:9; the appendix, 16:15). Christ's coming into the world constituted the content of this good news; His proclamation of the gospel made Him its author. Mark was not concerned, however, to describe fully the Lord's personality. His focusing attention upon the events of the ministry explains his obvious omissions (e.g., the Birth narratives, accounts of Jesus' boyhood, influences on His thought and career, an estimate of His personal appearance, the impact of His personality on others [although there *are* certain hints of this feature, as already shown], and a day-to-day diary of events in chronological and orderly sequence). Mark himself is hidden; he made no attempt to pass a personal judgment on the story he narrated. Likewise all the persons who appear on the stage are mentioned not for their own sake but for the Lord's.

*A. Markan Hypothesis.* Even if Mark's Gospel was not intended to be a biography of the historical Jesus after the style of Boswell's *Life of Johnson,* it may present an intended sequence of events, set in a true historical framework, of Jesus' public ministry and activity. This theory, known as the "Markan hypothesis," was the basis of the once-popular "Lives of Jesus." The two best-known titles were J. Stalker's *Life of Jesus Christ* (2nd ed. 1891) and A. C. Headlam's *Life and Teaching of Jesus Christ* (1923). C. E. Raven and E. Raven in 1933 wrote *Life and Teaching of Jesus Christ* and in an engaging style offered (in ch. 3) what they called "An Outline of the Ministry," which traced the historical and psychological development in three phases: the public ministry in Galilee, the training of the disciples, and the crisis in Jerusalem. The authors held that Jesus' public and private teaching corresponded to the different phases of development.

The rise of form criticism has caused this theory to be seriously attacked. The first effects of opposition to the Markan hypothesis are seen in A. E. J. Rawlinson's commentary, which starts from the premise that "such attempts to treat the Marcan arrangement of the Gospel materials as supplying an outline, in chronological order, of the course of events are profoundly mistaken" (p. xx). He recorded the ways in which the Markan hypothesis "in recent years has been riddled with criticisms of the most damaging kind." The most fundamental difficulty, he said, is the intrinsic improbability that a chronological outline of Jesus' ministry or an itinerary of His movements would be preserved for a generation as oral tradition by a Church not primarily interested in such matters. On this view, the Gospel writers themselves provided the framework and arranged the materials, which were derived from the tradition. This assumption may be said to be the guiding principle of the form-critical approach to the Gospels and to Mark in particular. The form critics developed their approach as a denial of the Markan hypothesis. C. H. Dodd, in an important article (*Expos.T,* 43 [1932], 396-400; repr. in *NT Studies* [1951] as "Framework of Gospel Narrative," pp. 1-11), argued that the Markan framework conforms to the pattern of the Acts kerygma (especially in Peter's speech in Acts 10:34ff.) and that Mark's "generalizing summaries," when placed together, form a continuous piece of narrative. This proposal has bolstered the Markan hypothesis by showing that the author evidently did intend some historical progression in his relating of the movements of Jesus. Dodd's article, however, was critically scrutinized by D. E. Nineham ("The Order of Events in St. Mark's Gospel — an Examination of Dr. Dodd's Hypothesis," in *Studies in the Gospels* [1955], pp. 223-239), who held that the order of events was of no significance in the apostolic preaching. But Dodd's thesis has proved very influential, especially in Britain, and has checked any large-scale capitulation to the conclusions of the form critics, for his conclusion runs counter to theirs: "Marcan order does represent a genuine succession of events, within which movement and development can be traced."

*B. Form-Critical Assessment.* A view at the opposite end of the scale from Dodd's was that of the German form critics Dibelius and Bultmann. Their argument, popularized by R. H. Lightfoot (*History and Interpretation in the Gospels* [1934]) and F. C. Grant (*The Earliest Gospel* [1943]), was that the Markan material forms an accidental collection of disconnected stories and sayings. K. L. Schmidt made an even more devastating attack on Mark's order of events: "As a whole, there is no life of Jesus in the sense of an evolving biography, no chronological sketch of the story of Jesus, but only single stories, sections (*pericopae*), which are put into a framework" (*RGJ,* p. 317). V. Taylor (*The Gospels,* p. 59) mentioned the points of interest that emerged from this treatment but said, "Schmidt's views have every appearance of a reaction which has been carried too far." The tide in scholarly circles has been running against this negative assessment, and most later commentators (Anderson, Schmid, Schweizer, Pesch — but not Lane) treat the Markan material as a loose collection of individual pericopes (or paragraphs) put together by the Evangelist for his own purposes.

Other theories of the way that Mark's Gospel is built up may be tabulated.

*C. Vincent Taylor's View.* Taylor started from the supposition that the Evangelist used a series of "complexes" (after Dodd, p. 10), which he regarded as small groups of narratives or sayings that belong together (see his comm., pp. 90-104). Mark, according to Taylor, took over these complexes (which had an independent existence), added his own comments, and connected them with some simple literary ligatures. On this view Mark's role is strictly that of editor and compiler.

A modification of this idea is found in the attractively presented work of H. A. Guy, who discerned in Mark a *Grundschrift,* which consisted of the papyrus leaves on which were written stories of Jesus and which would have proved of inestimable value to the early preachers. An unknown editor brought these sheets together and added teaching material but did not arrange them into any coherent pattern. John Mark, who was held in high esteem in the churches on account of his association with Peter, undertook the task of "compiler."

Taylor (ch. 7) described older views of Markan sources that scholars have postulated. Of special note are the elaborate attempt at source-criticism by W. L. Knox (*Sources of the Synoptic Gospels,* I [1953], especially his isolation of the "Twelve-source" showing Jesus' dealings with the disciples and a Passion story); B. S. Easton's work on the controversy stories of Mk. 2–3, 12 ("A Primitive Tradition in Mark," in S. J. Case, ed., *Studies in Early Christianity* [1928], pp. 85-101), according to which 2:13–3:6 and 12:13-27 were originally a unit that "was formed in pre-Markan times and belonged to the tradition of the Palestinian Christian community" (p. 92); and T. W. Manson's development of the views of C. H. Turner, who sought to isolate certain passages as "Petrine." Manson (*BJRL,* 28 [1944], 119-136; repr. in his *Studies in the Gospels and Epistles* [1962], pp. 28-45) sought to enlarge the scope of this Petrine material and to classify it (pp. 41ff.). He added that other sources of considerable antiquity and consequent worth were at Mark's disposal, such as the "Passion of John" (6:17-29), which "has all the appearance of being a piece of Palestinian (originally Aramaic) tradition" (p. 43). The tendency that Manson's work represents led to an increased confidence in the Gospel record and away from the form-critical idea that the sections of the Gospel were "manufactured" by preachers in the Hellenistic Church. On the other hand, P. J. Achtemeier's contributions on the theme of "Pre-Markan Miracle Catenae" (*JBL,* 89 [1970], 265-291; 91 [1972], 198-221) have given the Evangelist a more creative role in incorporating collections of miracle stories, and E. J. Pryke, *Redactional Style in the Marcan Gospel* (1978) offers a systematic stylistic analysis of Mark in the hope of separating out a corpus of Markan source material (S) from redactional elements (R). This exercise has produced little that is conclusive, however.

*D. Liturgical Theories.* Some scholars have maintained that Mark's structure is governed by considerations arising from the liturgical and cultic needs of the early churches. The best-known views are those of P. Carrington and

A. Farrer. Carrington in *The Primitive Christian Calendar* (1952, with later studies in *Expos.T.*, 67 [1956]; and *According to Mark* [1961]) began with the assumption that the Church took over a lectionary scheme from Jewish synagogue worship; the sections of Mark follow the order of festivals in the Jewish festal lectionary. This novel theory has met with little favor (see the criticisms by R. P. Casey, *Theology*, 55 [1952], 362ff.; and in great detail by W. D. Davies in his contribution to the *Dodd Festschrift* ["Reflections on Archbishop Carrington's *The Primitive Christian Calendar*," in W. D. Davies and D. Daube, eds., *The Background of the NT and Its Eschatology* (1954), pp. 124-152], repr. in his *Christian Origins and Judaism* [1962], pp. 67-95). Its weakness is its implication, *ex hypothesi*, that the Gospel material was altered to conform to a supposed liturgical pattern and that some verses do not fit in and therefore need to be ironed out. The transmission of the gospel via the worshiping life of the early churches is nonetheless a presupposition for which recent study has produced some important evidence.

Austin Farrer, in a series of erudite volumes, supported the view that the governing principle of Mark's composition is conformity to OT typology and prefigurations. On this theory, even the simplest Gospel story becomes invested with cryptic significance and esoteric meaning, especially if it employs numbers. The elaborateness of such a construction does not argue for its cogency, and its oversubtlety is its weakness. Farrer himself revised its construction (cf. his modification of the earlier *Study in St. Mark* [1952] in *St. Matthew and St. Mark* [1954]). Helen Gardner, in a penetrating survey of Farrer's ideas ("The Poetry of St. Mark," *Limits of Literary Criticism* [1956]), placed her finger upon the real point: "I find it hard . . . to believe that the first readers of St. Mark would have been as ingenious in picking up symbolic references as is suggested [by Farrer]" (p. 34). The same negative judgment must be passed on the latest attempt to find symbolism in Mark, F. Kermode's *Genesis of Secrecy* (1979), ch. 3. J. M. Robinson found fault with the methodological assumptions of both Carrington and Farrer, whose "argument is not built upon what Mark clearly and repeatedly has to say, but upon inferences as to the basis of the Marcan order, a subject upon which Mark is silent" (p. 12). If the Markan order is uncertain, then Carrington and Farrer have lost their cases.

*E. Gottfried Schille's View.* Schille considered the catechetical needs of the early Christians the decisive issue in Mark's structure (*NTS*, 4 [1957/58], 1-24). Schille maintained that the entire composition of the Gospel elaborately paralleled the life of the Lord and the experience of catechumens who came into the Church through the gateway of baptism, instruction, the holy supper, and the prospect of martyrdom. Other parts of early Christian literature (esp. He. 6:1ff. and Didache) also reflect this sequence.

*F. Ernst Lohmeyer's View.* Lohmeyer based his elaborate thesis (*Galiläa und Jerusalem* [1936]) on the geographical data of the Gospel. His advocacy of the idea that there were two main centers of early Christianity, quite distinct from each other and located in Galilee and Jerusalem, has been examined sympathetically by R. H. Lightfoot, *Locality and Doctrine in the Gospels* (1938), F. C. Grant, *The Earliest Gospel* (1943), amd Marxsen, *Mark the Evangelist*. The dominant motif in Mark, according to Lohmeyer, is the importance of Galilee as the locus of divine revelation and the place to which the apocalyptic Son of man will return as a prelude to the Parousia (see 14:28; 16:7, on which Lohmeyer built much of his theory). Lohmeyer detected that Markan material is grouped into threes (see pp. 6f. for this triadic structure of the entire Gospel), but his rigid literary analysis made his proof unconvincing.

*V. Authorship.*–The earliest witnesses to the Gospel (Papias, Irenaeus, Clement of Alexandria, Origen, Jerome, and probably the Muratorian Canon if the usually allowed textual conjecture is accepted; see Rawlinson, p. xxvii) associated the author of the Gospel with Mark and equally linked him with Peter. Vincent Taylor (pp. 1-7) dealt with the original texts in the church fathers. The Papias tradition (related in Eusebius *HE* iii.39) has pride of place in the patristic tradition: "The Elder said this also; Mark who had been Peter's interpreter, wrote down carefully as much as he remembered, recording both sayings and doings of Christ, not however in order. For he was not a hearer of the Lord, nor a follower, but later a follower of Peter, as I said. And he [Peter or Mark] adapted his teachings to the needs of his hearers (not as arranging them) as one who is engaged in making a compendium of the Lord's precepts." (Cf. H. E. W. Turner, *Expos.T.*, 71 [1960], 260-63.) Modern discussion has raised many objections to the validity of this ancient *testimonium*, but none is decisive (cf. A. C. Perumalil, "Are Not Papias and Irenaeus Competent to Report on the Gospels?" *Expos.T.*, 91 [1980], 332-37; that the matter is not so simple is shown by Martin, *Mark: Evangelist and Theologian*, pp. 80-83). The important argument attacks the traditional connection between the author of the Gospel and the apostle Peter. The lack of a strict chronological outline and Mark's dependence upon traditional material make it hard to explain the somewhat ambiguous statement that he adapted Peter's teaching to the needs of the hearers of the moment. But one should also observe the qualifying remark that follows, as well as the preceding comment of the Elder that Mark wrote of the "sayings and doings" of Christ but not, however, "in order." (For the different uses of the term "order" [Gk. *táxis*] — chronological, rhetorical, and calendrical — see H. A. Guy, ch. 2.)

This testimony does make three positive points. First, it traces one of Mark's sources back to Peter's teaching. Second, it remarks that Mark himself had no firsthand knowledge of the sayings and deeds of the Lord but depended upon eyewitnesses. Third, Mark picked up his information in his work as Peter's *hermēneutḗs*, a term meaning something like "private secretary" and aide-de-camp (so T. W. Manson, *The Teaching of Jesus* [1935], p. 23 n.). The anti-Marcionite prologue to the Gospel similarly describes the Evangelist as Peter's *interpres* (see W. F. Howard, *Expos.T.*, 47 [1936], 534-38). The same document declares that Mark composed his Gospel in Italy after Peter's "departure" (*post excessionem*). Although problems are connected with this statement, T. W. Manson's assessment seems reasonable (*Studies in the Gospels and Epistles* [1962], p. 40): "If Peter had paid a visit to Rome some time between 55 and 60; if Mark had been his interpreter then; if after Peter's departure from the city Mark had taken in hand — at the request of the Roman hearers — a written record of what Peter had said; then all the essential points in the evidence would be satisfied."

John Mark is known from references in Acts (12:12, 25; 13:5, 13; 15:37, 39) and the Epistles (Col. 4:10; 2 Tim. 4:11; Philem. 24; 1 Pet. 5:13). These texts clearly indicate his close association with apostolic testimony. Both his home and his family connections played an important part in early Christian history. His mother (of sufficient importance to be named) was a member of the Jerusalem church; to her home, a regular place of Christian assembly, Peter came after his escape from prison. Subsequently Mark had intimate contact with Paul and his party, associated

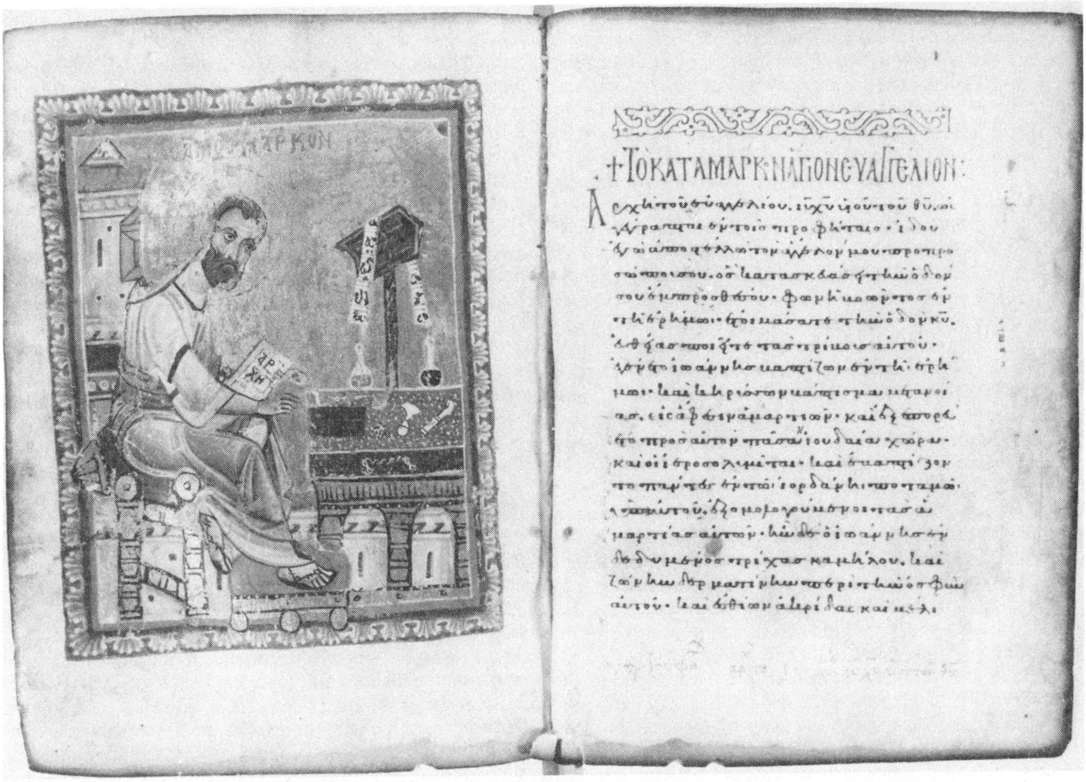

Miniature of Mark, who is writing the first word of his Gospel, and the first page of his Gospel. Michigan MS 22 (11th cent. A.D.) (Department of Rare Books and Special Collections, The University of Michigan Library)

with his own cousin Barnabas, and went on the mission to Cyprus. About twelve years later (according to the Captivity Epistles) Mark was reconciled to Paul, who commended him to the church at Colossae. Paul asked Timothy to bring Mark to him at Rome, saying, "He is useful to me for ministering." At last Mark rejoined Peter, who referred to him as "my son" in a letter written from Rome (so 1 Pet. 5:13, apparently; see Papias in Eusebius *HE* ii.25; E. G. Selwyn, *First Epistle of St. Peter* [1947], pp. 60-62). *See* MARK, JOHN for a possible link between Mark (and his Gospel) and Paul.

These varied allusions to Mark's acquaintance with early Christian leaders confirm the judgment of T. W. Manson that "Mark had considerable opportunities of gathering knowledge of the kind that would later be useful in the composition of the Gospel" (*Studies,* p. 37). Furthermore, Mark's close contact with Peter, both in Jerusalem and in Rome, greatly helps to explain the phenomenon to which C. H. Turner has drawn attention, that Mark's account of many incidents stands in direct contrast to Matthew's and Luke's. Mark's version "may be called autobiographical. They [Matthew and Luke] write Lives of Christ, he records the experience of an eye-witness and companion" (*New Comm. on Holy Scripture,* ed. Gore, *et al.*, pt. 3 [1928], p. 48). Turner perceptively noted that changing the 3rd person plurals in Mark to 1st person plurals would make his narration vivid and forceful. He applied this principle to Mk. 1:29 and read: "We came into our house with James and John; and my wife's mother was ill in bed with a fever, and at once we tell him about her." Mark's 3rd person may be understood as representing a 1st person plural of Peter's discourse; the same process may be detected elsewhere in the Gospel (at 1:21; 5:1, 38; 6:53f.; 8:22; 9:14, 30, 33; 10:32, 46; 11:1, 12, 15, 20, 27; 14:18, 22, 26, 32). Turner's observations are one of the most cogent proofs of the apostolic testimony (Peter's) behind the Second Gospel, written by John Mark.

*VI. Date.–A. External Evidence.* The external data speak with no decisive voice. Irenaeus (*Adv. haer.* iii.1.2) wrote, "After their deaths [Peter's and Paul's] Mark, the disciple and interpreter of Peter, himself also handed down to us in writing the things which Peter had proclaimed." On the other hand, Clement of Alexandria said that Peter instructed Mark to write what he had said, and that this literary effort was published later, but in Peter's lifetime, for Peter's comment on the composition is recorded (in Eusebius *HE* vi.14). A view discounting this interpretation suggests that Irenaeus intended not to give chronological information but simply to state the continuity of Mark's writing and Peter's preaching. This deduction (which Taylor granted, *The Gospels,* p. 51) is far from obvious, although the accuracy of Irenaeus may be impugned because of his earlier remark that Matthew was produced while Peter and Paul were still preaching — a statement that would be difficult to maintain historically. The external evidence is thus divided, and no certain dating is possible from this source.

*B. Internal Evidence.* The references to persecutions (8:34-38; 9:31; 10:33f., 45; 13:8, 10; see Rawlinson, pp. xvi f.) and to the controversies that surrounded the issue of gentile freedom (7:17-23, 26f.; 13:10) have been taken to mean that the Gospel belongs to the decade 60-70 (so Taylor, comm., p. 31).

The cryptic allusion to the profanation of the Jerusalem temple in 13:14, "But when you see the desolating sacrilege [Gk. *to bdélygma tḗs erēmṓseōs*] set up where it ought not to be (let the reader understand), then let those that are in Judea flee to the mountains," has been used to suggest that Mark must have been written within a few years of the siege of the Holy City in A.D. 66-70. On this verse see G. R. Beasley-Murray, *Jesus and the Future* (1954), pp. 255ff.; *Southwestern Journal of Theology*, 21 (1978), 37-53; *Comm. on Mk. 13* (1957), pp. 59-72.

As an alternative proposal, C. C. Torrey (*Our Translated Gospels* [1936], p. 262) and T. W. Manson (*Sayings of Jesus* [1949; repr. 1979], p. 329) sought to relate the text to Caligula's attempt to set up his statue in the temple in A.D. 40. For some scholars (e.g., B. W. Bacon, *Gospel of Mark* [1925], p. 93) the reference to the desolating scourge is a prophecy *post eventum* and therefore has a different bearing on the question of the Gospel's dating. Against this view is the objective fact that certain verses (13:1ff.) imply that the temple was still standing when the Evangelist wrote.

A date in the decade 60-70 seems certain, despite some notable attempts to champion an early dating, e.g., Harnack (*Date of the Acts and Synoptic Gospels* [1911], p. 126-133, before A.D. 60) and W. C. Allen (before 50). Rawlinson (pp. xxix f.), Blunt (pp. 69-76), and Taylor (comm., p. 32) offered a more precise dating: 65-67, chiefly because the vague and imprecise references in ch. 13 do not show that the Jewish War had begun. On the other hand, S. E. Johnson (p. 20) thought that the Gospel may have been written after the destruction of the temple (which seems to be hinted at, he said, in certain premonitory signs of ch. 13, esp. vv. 19-22) but before the hostilities in Palestine ended in April, 73; thus the writing of the Gospel may have occurred within a larger period of time. Marxsen has argued that ch. 13 indicates that Mark wrote between A.D. 67 and 69 to urge the church to leave Jerusalem and resettle in Pella. S. G. F. Brandon, in *Jesus and the Gospels* (1967), ch. 5, placed the publication date of Mark at the opposite end of the historical continuum, A.D. 66-72, and made Mark an apologist for the Church in the years after the Flavian triumph of A.D. 71-72. The sociological setting of Mark is the theme of H. C. Kee's *Community of the New Age: Studies in Mark's Gospel*. Kee placed the Markan community in rural Syria and thought it had suffered persecution in the early years of the war of A.D. 66-70.

***VII. Origin and Destination.***–No final answers are possible to the queries where and to whom the Gospel was written, but external and internal evidence imply that Mark wrote in Rome and for a gentile constituency.

A statement in Irenaeus, endorsed by the otherwise divergent testimony of Clement, is that Mark was in Rome when the Gospel was published. The anti-Marcionite prologue preserves the same tradition: "After the departure of Peter himself he [Mark] wrote down this same Gospel in the regions of Italy [*in partibus Italiae*]." (Cf. also R. M. Grant, *ATR*, 23 [1941], 231ff.)

This evidence tallies with Papias's witness that Mark was Peter's interpreter and the knowledge that Peter was martyred at Rome. (Cf. O. Cullmann's full treatment in *Peter* [Eng. tr., 2nd ed. 1962], pt. 1, ch. 3.) 2 Tim. 4:11 and 1 Pet. 5:13 locate Mark in Rome, if one assumes (with most commentators) that in the latter text "Babylon" is a cryptogram for the capital city of the empire.

The earliest attestation of the use of the Gospel comes from 1 Clem. 15:2 and Shep. Herm. Sim. 5:2, which are both associated with Rome. (On the latter text, see Johnson, p. 7.) 1 Clement quotes Isa. 29:3 in the form in which it is used in Mk. 7:6 (cf. H. Köster, *Synoptische Überlieferung bei den apostolischen Vätern* [*TU*, 65, 1957], pp. 21f.; cf. pp. 105f. on 2 Clem. 7:6 (= 1 Clem. 17:5), which cites Isa. 66:24b in the same way as Mk. 9:48 does).

A Roman place of origin is consonant with the references in Mk. 8:34-38; 10:38f.; 13:9-13 to persecutions and martyrdom. The claim that these texts are best understood in the light of Nero's treatment of Christians in Rome in the 60's is not conclusive, despite Rawlinson's attractive case for it (pp. xxi f.). (Cf. Streeter, *The Four Gospels*, pp. 495ff.; W. L. Lane, comm., pp. 12-17.)

This consentient witness to the Roman origin of the Gospel is contradicted by Chrysostom's report that the Gospel originated in Egypt (*Hom. 1 in Mt.* 7). This statement, as Johnson said (p. 15), is probably based on a misunderstanding of Eusebius (*HE* ii.16.1): "They say that Mark set out for Egypt and was first to preach there the Gospel which he had composed" (cf. also Eusebius *HE* ii.24 on Mark's association with the church at Alexandria). An Alexandrian connection with Mark should not be lightly dismissed (see Manson, *Studies*, pp. 38f.), but the evidence seems weighted in favor of Rome.

The arguments of some modern scholars (e.g., J. V. Bartlet, comm. [1922], pp. 36f., following G. C. Storr of Tübingen), that Antioch was the place of origin, are more speculative than substantial. Storr, for instance, claimed that Mk. 15:21 referred to the father of Alexander and Rufus because his sons went to Antioch in the gentile mission of Acts 11:19f., but this is sheer hypothesis. Nor is W. C. Allen's theory any more convincing. He believed (following Blass and C. C. Torrey) that the Gospel was first written in Aramaic in Jerusalem and later translated into Greek at Antioch, a bilingual center of early Christianity of which G. Dix (*Jew and Greek* [1953], p. 33) wrote: "It was a bastion of Hellenism in the Syriac lands . . . the inevitable meeting point of the two worlds." More recently, W. Marxsen (pp. 64-66) sought to uphold the view that the Gospel was first published in Galilee.

The internal evidence of the Gospel almost conclusively proves that Mark wrote for gentile readers. The Evangelist explained Jewish customs and practices that may have been unfamiliar to his non-Palestinian readers (e.g., 7:3f.). Aramaic expressions that remain in the text in a Grecized form are interpreted, e.g., *Abba* (14:36), which receives the same interpretative addition in Rom. 8:15; Gal. 4:6. But the addition is only approximately correct, as Johnson noted (pp. 15f.). In other places, however, Mark incorporated a block of teaching in its Aramaic form, woodenly turning it into Greek (esp. in 14:22ff., the Semitic background of which has been demonstrated by J. Jeremias, *Eucharistic Words of Jesus* [Eng. tr. 1966], pp. 173-184). A series of Latinisms (see III.A above) betrays both the author's gentile milieu and a gentile audience for whom these expressions would have been meaningful. Some scholars (e.g., Johnson, pp. 15, 18f.) have claimed that Mark was unacquainted with Palestine because his references to place names (such as Dalmanutha, 8:10; Gerasa, 5:1; Bethsaida, 7:26), the Herodian family (6:17), and Jewish divorce laws (10:12) show no firsthand knowledge of Palestinian topography and life. The allegation of inaccuracy is unnecessary if Mark was simply following the tradition he received. He normally wrote as if more concerned to relate the gospel tradition than to interject his personal reminiscences.

***VIII. Special Problems.***–*A. Opening*. The abrupt opening of the Gospel (1:1), "The beginning of the Gospel of Jesus Christ, the Son of God," has often called forth comment. The usual view is that this sentence is the title of the whole book (e.g., Marxsen, p. 125), but it may be simply the heading of the first paragraphs (to 1:8 or 1:13, as R. H. Lightfoot thought, *Gospel Message of St. Mark*, pp. 15ff.; cf. also N. B. Stonehouse, ch. 1). The textual problem, involving the omitting of "Son of God," is well considered

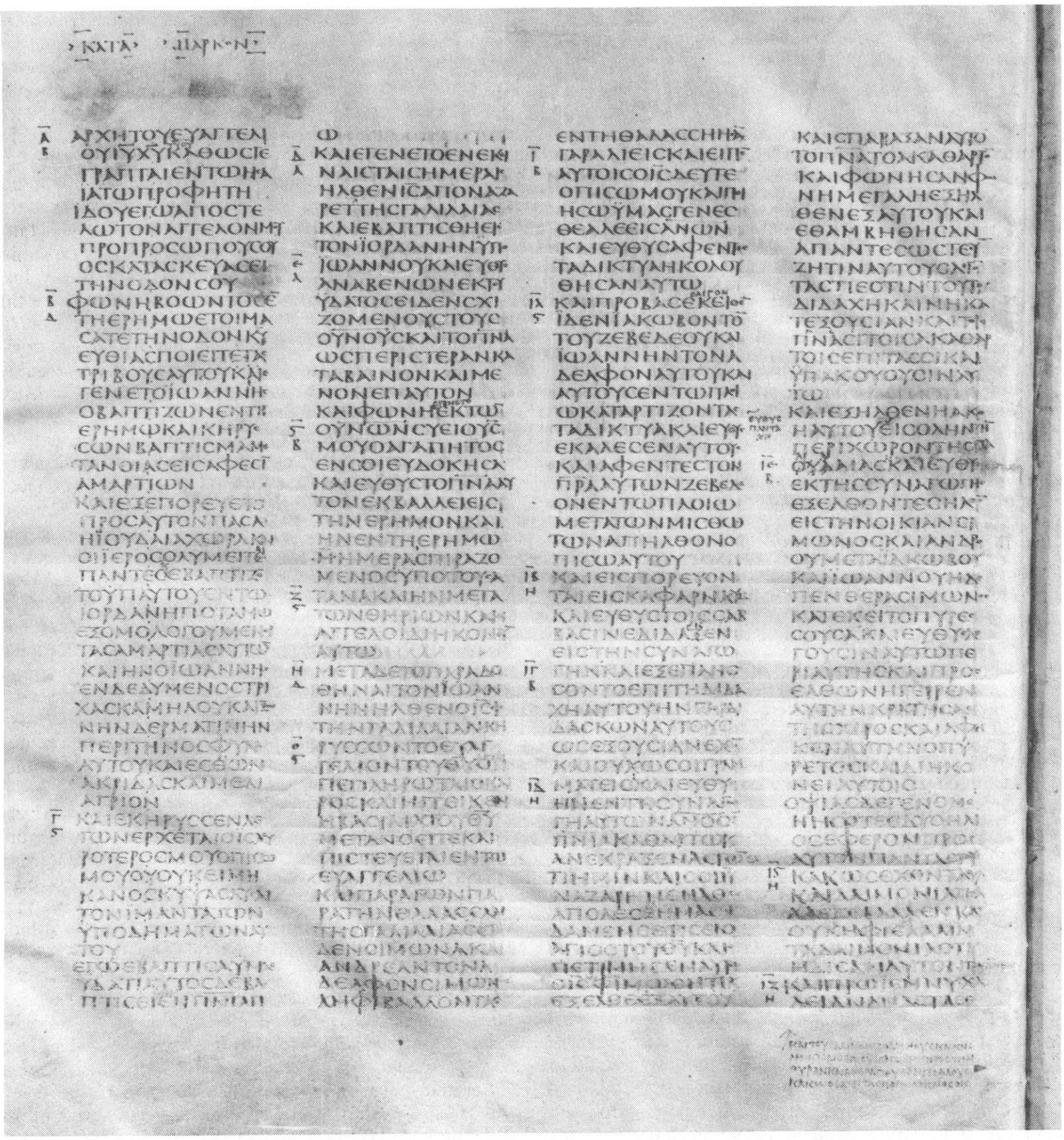

Beginning of Mark's Gospel in Codex Sinaiticus (4th cent. A.D.), which does not have the later reading "son of God" in v. 1 (Trustees of the British Museum)

by Cranfield, comm., p. 38, with reasons given for its (non-significant) omission from patristic and some textual authorities.

Allied with the theory that the first verse introduces only the opening sections of the Gospel are two other suggestions. The first is that the verse is syntactically related to what follows in v. 4. Verses 2f. are thus a parenthesis of the OT *pēšer* type, citing Malachi and Isaiah as prophetic witnesses to the advent of Christ. If this OT section is omitted, the text reads smoothly: "The beginning of the Gospel of Jesus Christ . . . was [Gk. *egéneto*] John, who baptized in the wilderness."

T. W. Manson (*Studies,* pp. 31ff.), following Spitta, argued that Mark's beginning is defective because it fails to follow the "normal order . . . that first the fact is stated, and then the relevant [OT proof] text . . . cited with the formula *kathṓs gégraptai* or the like." Manson's explanation was that the first page of Mark's Gospel became mutilated or missing (he assumed that the Gospel was written in codex form). This explanation was criticized by H. A. Guy (pp. 155ff.) on the ground that if the page was lost through "fair wear and tear" (as Manson claimed), it is difficult to imagine that the autograph became mutilated in this particular way. (Guy's argument bears on the related question of the so-called Lost Ending of Mark.) Also, Manson's statement that Christian practice was first to give the event and then to add the OT corroboration holds for only a certain usage; many instances of Christian apologetic in Acts begin with the OT texts and then show how Jesus fulfilled them.

Explanations of the opening verses, therefore, need not have recourse to the idea of a lost page. If the OT texts are a parenthesis, the subject of v. 1 is picked up at v. 4; this pattern accords with the early Christian kerygma of Acts, in which John the Baptist is made the *terminus a quo* (Acts 1:22; 10:37; 13:24f.) of the Gospel story.

*B. Ending.* The last twelve verses (16:9-20) are something of a cause célèbre of textual criticism. (Cf. esp. Rawlinson, pp. 267ff.; F. F. Bruce, *EQ*, 17 [1945], 169ff.; also N. B. Stonehouse, ch. 4, pp. 86ff.; W. R. Farmer, *Last Twelve Verses of Mark* [1974].)

The facts are that (1) the verses are omitted by ℵ, B, Sinaitic Syr., and most MSS of the Armenian versions; and Eusebius is a witness that the best MSS in his day ended at v. 8a; (2) a "shorter ending" (printed in the RSV and NEB) is attested along with TR in L, Ψ, 579, Sah., Eth., Harclean Syr., and the earliest Boh. MS, while in k the shorter text stands alone; (3) a third ending is given by W, which adds, in addition to vv. 9-20, an extra interpolation after v. 14; (4) a tenth-century Armenian version ascribing vv. 9-20 to "the presbyter Ariston" is too late to be of any value, although F. C. Conybeare professed great respect for this attribution (*Expos.* [4th ser. 1893], pp. 241-254; [1896], pp. 401ff.). C. S. C. Williams (*Alterations to the Text of the Synoptic Gospels and Acts* [1951], p. 41) regarded this attribution as possibly no more than a guess based on the Armenian version of the well-known passage in Eusebius *HE* iii.39, which refers to the presbyters Aristion and John (notice the spelling in Armenian E 299: *"Ariston* [*sic*] *eritzu"*).

The "longer ending" (which is printed in the AV) was apparently known to Tatian (*ca.* 170) and occurs in a preponderant number of MSS (C, L, Sah., Boh., A, W, D, Old Lat. — except k, which represents the African Latin). Von Soden (*Schriften des NT* [1902-1913], I, 1621ff.) suggested that Justin (*ca.* 140) wrote this longer recension (but contra see E. R. Buckley, *JTS*, 36 [1935], 176). Whether or not this attribution is correct, it is clear that the longer ending was written in the first half of the 2nd cent. (so Williams, p. 42). But it is equally clear that Mark did not write it (clearly shown by J. K. Elliott [*Theologische Zeitschrift*, 27 (1971), 255-262], who demonstrated non-Markan linguistic elements in 16:9-20). Several minuscules marked it with an asterisk to show that it was suspect. Moreover, both the vocabulary and the style of the verses differ noticeably from the rest of the Gospel (against Farmer, who seeks to show Markan authorship of 16:9-20). The description of Mary in 16:9, e.g., apparently overlooks the earlier reference to her in v. 1. Verses 9-20, which seem to consist of material taken from the other Gospels, also endorse the supposition that the longer ending was added (as were the "shorter" and the "third" ending) by a later scribe or editor who thought that "they were afraid" (16:8) should not close the chapter and the Gospel. See Lane's full note in his comm., pp. 601-605.

The question now emerges whether Mark intended to finish here. Was it accidental that he did so? Was he prevented from completing his task? Or was the ending deliberately suppressed because it was believed to contradict the Resurrection accounts in the other Gospels, as K. Lake (*The Resurrection of Jesus Christ* [1907], pp. 70f., 88ff., 143ff., 224ff.) and R. Bultmann (*HST*) believed? See also Williams, pp. 44f., for further motives for suppressing the original ending.

Many scholars following the initial discussion of Wellhausen (*Das Evangelium Marci* [1903], p. 146) argued that Mark intended his work to finish with the cryptic *ephoboúnto gár,* "for they were afraid." J. M. Creed (*JTS*, 30 [1930], 175ff.), R. R. Ottley (*JTS*, 27 [1926], 407ff.), Lohmeyer (pp. 356-360), and especially R. H. Lightfoot (*Locality and Doctrine in the Gospels* [1938], chs. 1–2; *Gospel Message of St. Mark,* pp. 80-97, 106-116), A. Farrer (*A Study in St. Mark* [1952], pp. 172-181), and N. B. Stonehouse (pp. 101ff.) all espoused this theory on the ground that the unusual ending is not impossible and has certain precedents (given in Lightfoot, *Locality,* pp. 10-18, to answer the charge of W. L. Knox, *HTR*, 35 [1942], 13ff., that such an abrupt ending would violate all the canons of ancient story-telling). Furthermore, the conclusion accords with the note of mystery and the "numinous" that some think pervades the Gospel as a whole (cf. Dibelius's dictum that Mark is a book of "secret epiphanies").

The major difficulty with this view is conceiving a situation in which the Evangelist would break off in what seems to be the middle of a sentence and leave the women in great fear. Some interpreters, therefore, have proposed that the words "they were afraid" (*ephoboúnto*) should be taken to mean "reverential awe or fear" (so Stonehouse, p. 107) rather than terrified uncertainty. On this view, the Gospel ends on the climactic note of the human response to the solemn announcement (in vv. 6f.) that Jesus of Nazareth is risen and will await His followers in Galilee. "The chief impact of the verse [i.e., v. 8] is simply to describe the indescribable. . . . The amazement of the women turns into trembling, astonishment, fear, flight, silence. All of these are considered in the Bible to be appropriate and normal human responses to an appearance of God, to a message from God, to an event in which God's power is released" (P. S. Minear, p. 136). Moreover, it accords with the theology of the Gospel as a whole that the note of mystery in the revelation of the hidden Son of man should be preserved up to the last verse.

This reconstruction has not persuaded all scholars. Perhaps most are content to believe that Mark's abrupt ending may be explained in one of a number of coincidental ways. The termination of the Gospel may have resulted from accidental or deliberate damage; the difficulty with this view is the corollary that "this damaged copy should be the sole legitimate ancestor of all existing manuscripts" (Taylor, *The Gospels,* p. 50).

The remaining possibility is that the original author never completed the Gospel, for reasons that cannot be ascertained (Rawlinson, p. 270; Zahn, *Intro. to the NT* [Eng. tr. 1909], II, 930ff.).

***IX. Markan Theology.***–If we interpret the term "theology" strictly, we must be content with the simple observation that Mark's Gospel assumes as a fundamental postulate the Jewish belief in one holy and righteous God whose will is revealed in His law. To the question of which commandment is most important, Jesus replied, in the orthodox Jewish fashion, "The most important is . . . ," and quoted Dt. 6:4-9 (the first word of which, Heb. *šᵉmaʿ*, formed the Jewish credo, along with Dt. 11:13-21; Nu. 15:37-41). This great statement of Hebrew monotheism underlies also Mk. 2:7; 10:18. To confess the Shema (see the rubrics for this in Mish. *Berakoth* i-iii) was tantamount to professing Judaism, taking upon oneself the yoke of the kingdom. The binding authority of God's holy law forms the basis of the controversy story in Mk. 7:1-23.

With a wider understanding of the word "theology" there are two main themes in the Gospel — the kingdom of God and the Christological presentation of Jesus. (For a wider setting of the Evangelist's theology see R. P. Martin, *Southwestern Journal of Theology,* 21 [1978], 23-36.) But these themes cannot be considered in isolation from each other. This Gospel illustrates more than any other book in the NT the famous dictum of Origen (comm. on Mt. 18:23) that Christ Himself is the kingdom (*autobasileía*). Moreover, Jesus did not herald and explicate the reign of God as though He were but its announcer, as Bultmann

MARK, GOSPEL ACCORDING TO

argued (*Jesus and the Word* [Eng. tr., 2nd ed. 1958]; see the perceptive criticism of this evaluation in G. Lundström, *Kingdom of God in the Teaching of Jesus* [Eng. tr. 1963], pp. 146-155). Rather, the kingdom brought Him, as R. Otto showed in *The Kingdom of God and the Son of Man* (Eng. tr., 2nd ed. 1943), p. 103.

*A. Kingdom of God.* C. E. B. Cranfield's commentary (pp. 63-68) contains a lucid account of the meaning of this term in the Gospels. The kingdom of God is God's rule in human life. It is an axiom of the modern study of biblical language that the Greek phrase *hē basileía toú theoú (tōn ouranōn)* goes back to Heb. *malkûṯ šāmayim* (Aram. *malkûṯāʾ dišmayāʾ*), which can denote only the kingly rule of God, the activity of God in His sovereignty and rulership. One aspect of this kingly rule is the personal allegiance of the pious Jews, who are said by the rabbis to take upon themselves "the yoke of the kingdom" (e.g., T.P. *Berakoth* 4a, 7b; so Dalman, *Words of Jesus* [Eng. tr. 1902], pp. 96ff.). It has also been maintained, however, that the immediate background of Jesus' use of the term "kingdom of God" is to be sought not in rabbinic Judaism but in the apocalyptic literature. N. Perrin (*Kingdom of God in the Teaching of Jesus* [1963], pp. 168ff.) cited and discussed the most germane texts: Ps. Sol. 17:3; Sib. Or. 3:46f.; Asm. M. 10:1; 1QM 6:6; 12:7. In these five references the key term, the kingdom of God, expresses the expectation that God will act decisively and openly and bring about the inauguration of a new age in which He will manifest His sovereignty over all His foes (and foes of Israel or a remnant within Israel). A synagogue prayer (in the Kaddish) voices the same earnest hope: "May He [God] establish His sovereignty in your lifetime and in your days and in the lifetime of all the house of Israel even speedily and at a near time."

The Gospels show that the coming of Jesus and His teaching in Galilee signaled that this expectation was being realized. Mk. 1:15 contains the important announcement that with the coming of Christ the kingdom is present: "The time is fulfilled; the rule of God is at hand; repent and put your trust in the good news." In Mark this fact is attested in four ways.

(1) The parables, such as 4:26-29 (found only in Mark) and Jesus' illustrations of His work in 2:18-22, assume that a new order has appeared.

(2) The binding of the "strong man" in 3:27 is to be understood in the light of the expectation that Satan would be bound in the last days (Asm. M. 10:1). W. G. Kümmel (p. 109) commented: "It is the meaning of the mission of Jesus, when announcing the *approach* of the Kingdom of God, to make this future at the same time already now a present reality." The Qumrân texts have shown the added importance of this claim that the devil is bound, for the men of Qumrân confessed that the powers of evil ("the dominion of Belial") were strong against them (e.g., 1QM 13) and yearned for an eschatological deliverance when Satan would be cursed and checked. The community's expectation of a new, eschatological Torah (see esp. CD 12:23; 14:19) elucidates Jesus' claim to supersede the law of Moses in its rabbinized form (cf. Mk. 10:2-10).

(3) Many of the acts of Jesus can make sense only if they are seen as His tacit announcement that the kingdom is on the scene. The outstanding events in Mark are (a) the conflict with the demons (Mt. 12:28 par. Lk. 11:20; cf. the important discussion of Kümmel, p. 105, and the extended comment of J. M. Robinson, pp. 33-42); (b) the entry into the Holy City (Mk. 11:1-10) and the cleansing of the temple (11:15-17), both of which are His claim to realize the present hour as the Savior who was expected at the end time; and (c) His offering bread and wine at the Last Supper (14:17-25), which allowed "the disciples to share the messianic salvation in present experience" (Kümmel, p. 121).

(4) Finally, His claim to build a new temple (reported in 14:57f.) was an overt admission that He had come to establish in the present a new order to replace the old Judaic one. Such an expectation was cherished by the apocalyptists (1 En. 90–91; Jub. 1) and the Qumrân covenanters (see B. Gärtner, *The Temple and the Community in Qumran and the NT* [1965]).

It seems indisputable, then, that the Jesus of Mark claimed to embody the present kingdom in His own person and acts. But this is not the whole story, or else the school of "realized eschatology" would have carried the day. Side by side with the teaching "the kingdom of God is in your midst" (Lk. 17:21) is the idea that the kingdom is an object of future hope. In Mark the clearest references are: 9:1 — the coming of the kingdom "with power" lies in the future (i.e., some time after the announcement of the Passion); 13:26 — the Son of man will come in apocalyptic glory, at an unspecified time (v. 32). This prospect is held out at the trial scene (14:62), since it had formed the future orientation of the Lord's thought and the disciples' hope at the Last Supper (v. 25).

These apocalyptic pronouncements should not be dismissed as spurious or as misunderstood by the early Church. The attempts of T. F. Glasson (*Second Advent* [3rd ed. 1963]) and J. A. T. Robinson (*Jesus and His Coming* [1957]) to do so have not carried conviction, mainly because verses like Mk. 13:26 and 14:62 do not demand any other interpretation than the most straightforward one, that Jesus envisaged a visible coming to earth and that advent explains the Parousia hope of the later Church (cf. J. E. Fison, *The Christian Hope* [1955]; G. R. Beasley-Murray, *Jesus and the Future* [1954], pp. 90f.). See D. Wenham, *Theological Student Fellowship Bulletin,* 71 (1974), 6-15; 72 (1975), 1-9.

It is scarcely possible to survey the modern attempts to hold together the twin ideas of a kingdom that came with the announcement of Jesus in Galilee (1:15) and the futurist hope of 13:26, 30; 14:62. Kümmel supplied what may be the Ariadne's thread out of the maze of solutions. He wrote: "The inseparable union of hope and present experience demonstrate the fact that the true meaning of Jesus' eschatological message is to be found in its reference to God's action in Jesus himself, that the essential content of Jesus' preaching about the Kingdom of God is the news of the divine authority of Jesus, who has appeared on earth and is awaited in the last days as the one who effects the divine purpose of mercy" (p. 155). In more precise form, the issue of the kingdom is a christological one; the thought that binds together the kingdom's present manifestation and its future glory is the ambiguous character of the kingdom of God itself.

The kingdom came in Christ. This strand of teaching is shown clearly in Mt. 11:2-6 par. Lk. 7:18-23; Mt. 12:28; 13:16f. par. Lk. 10:23f.; Lk. 10:18; 16:16; and probably in Mt. 11:12f. But Jesus revealed the kingdom "not in such a way as to make assent unavoidable, but in a way that still left room for men to make a personal decision" (Cranfield, p. 67). Mark's account of Jesus' teaching makes this plain. The Lord announced to His disciples "the secret [Gk. *mystḗrion*] of the kingdom of God" (4:11), which is the truth that the rule of God was personally present in His advent as the Son and Messiah of God. But the incarnate Lord shunned all that would give the impression of earthly splendor and worldly power. He taught indirectly by parables to avoid inflaming the people and leading them to expect a messianic war against the Roman power (Ps. Sol. 17–18 had, a few decades earlier than the time of the public ministry, hinted that this war would be the true work of the Lord's anointed). Jesus tried to conceal His identity (see Cranfield, p. 157). Yet the kingdom is a divine reality no less real because it is hidden and because its presence is unattended by signs and portents that would unmistakably declare its power (cf. A. M. Ambrozic, *The Hidden Kingdom: A Redaction-Critical Study of the References to the Kingdom of God in Mark's Gospel* [1972]). But to those who by faith penetrate the Lord's humanity and His claims to allegiance and discipleship, the truth is given that He is the divine Son and the King of glory whose ultimate destiny is a universal dominion (8:38–9:1; 13:26; 14:62).

This is the significance of Peter's confession at Caesarea Philippi and the subsequent disclosure in the Transfiguration. But the disciples had still to learn that the way to lordship is the way of the cross and that His title to universal sovereignty was in a ministry of service and obedience to death (10:35-45). Jesus taught the mystery of the kingdom to disabuse their wrong notions of the kingdom (they [vv. 35ff.] and the crowd [11:10] thought of it in terms of political influence and worldly fame) and to show that the kingdom involves lowly service on behalf of others. The greatest object lesson was His self-sacrifice on the cross; only by His death and resurrection could the kingdom come.

*B. Person of Jesus Christ.* Just as the kingdom was veiled throughout Jesus' earthly ministry with the promise that one day it would be openly displayed, so nothing in Jesus of Nazareth compelled belief that in Him God was personally present and active in saving power. Jesus' own townspeople recognized Him as "the carpenter" (6:3), who belonged to an ordinary family, and were scandalized. Not less affronted were the religious authorities, who sought to explain His exorcisms by insinuating that He was a fake "holy man" in league with the devil (3:22f.). Moreover, there is some justification for fastening upon His human traits in Mark's Gospel. Particularly in the Passion narrative the stark reality of His sufferings comes out — at Gethsemane (14:33f.) and on the cross (15:34). Mark more than the other Gospels reveals the grim realism and unspeakable horror of His Passion (Hans-Ruedi Weber, *The Cross: Tradition and Interpretation* [Eng. tr. 1979], pp. 103-110).

Yet the darkness of the Lord's humiliation and suffering is relieved and shot through with shafts of light. For all his preoccupation with the persecuted Church to which he addressed his Gospel, Mark did not picture the Lord as a martyr. The Evangelist made the frontispiece of the entire Gospel the full post-Easter confession — that Jesus Christ is the Son of God (*si vera lectio*). The citation of OT prophecy (1:3 quoting Isa. 40:3) indicates that "in the Prologue he [Mark] is pointing to the truth . . . that the One whose ministry he is about to record is the One whom the church acknowledges as 'the Lord'" (Cranfield, *IDB*, III, 273).

Throughout His public ministry the Lord deliberately made no overt claims to His divine nature and status. The "hiddenness" of Mark's christological portrait is an outstanding feature. He recorded that Jesus refused to offer a sign (8:11f.), silenced demons who knew Him (1:25, 34; 3:12), shunned all publicity after performing miracles (1:44; 5:43; 7:36; 8:26), commanded the disciples not to publish the news of His messiahship (8:30; 9:9), and taught by the indirect method of parables (4:33f.).

Yet some confessed His true stature; they were forthwith bidden to secrecy. The demons were the first (1:24, 34; 3:11f.), followed by various classes of folk who witnessed His miracles (1:45; 5:43; 7:36f.; 8:26; 10:52). The disciples confessed Him as the Messiah and were similarly enjoined to secrecy (8:30; 9:9). The Roman soldier admitted His more-than-human character (15:39), and the women at the tomb were confronted with the news of His victory over death, which they greeted with a stunned silence (16:8).

W. Wrede used this body of evidence (in his influential *Das Messiasgeheimnis in den Evangelien* [1901]) to support the theory of the "messianic secret" in Mark. (See V. Taylor, *Expos.T.*, 59 [1947/48], 146-151; 65 [1953/54], 246-250.) On Wrede's view, Jesus never claimed to be the Messiah in His earthly life; the Church created this status after the Resurrection and read it back into the Gospel story as a piece of dogmatic belief superimposed upon the evidence. Rawlinson (pp. 258ff.) showed the weakness of this hypothesis but noted that Mark *does* contain a messianic secret, bound up with Jesus' claim to be the Messiah (cf. J. D. G. Dunn, *Tyndale Bulletin,* 21 [1970], 92-117; Martin, *Mark,* pp. 91-97).

This leads to a consideration of the chief christological titles in Mark: Messiah, Son of man, Son of God.

*1. Messiah.* First-century Palestinian Judaism had two definite strands of messianic expectation (although it must be conceded that the sources do not always yield consistent pictures, and the evidence from Qumrân shows that such expectation could acquire features differing from normative, rabbinic Judaism). The Messiah was viewed as both a political warrior-king (as in Ps. Sol. 17–18, although cf. *TDNT,* IX, *s.v.* χρίω κτλ. [Grundmann, Hesse, de Jonge, van der Woude] in relation to this assumption) and as a celestial, quasi-divine figure who executes a universal judgment (as in the Enoch literature, although the dating of 1 Enoch is disputed and the Similitudes of Enoch significantly have not been found in the Qumrân caves). Despite the ambiguity of the texts depicting the messianic salvation for which the pious Jews yearned, it seems clear from the data of the Gospels themselves that both the disciples and the people associated the Messiah with national glory and supremacy. The temptation narrative of Mt. 4:1-11 par. Lk. 4:1-13 provides the best insight into dominant messianic expectations. Miraculous manna, worldly dominion, and preternatural signs — these were the hopes of a people subject to the Roman *imperium* who groaned because of economic taxation and spiritual frustration.

On the assumption that messiahship conjured up a picture of a messianic war with Rome and Israel's worldwide victory and glory, we can understand why Jesus at every point turned away from the popular ideal. When the crowd followed Him seeking food or healing, He retired lest His mission be misunderstood (Mk. 1:36-38; cf. Jn. 6:15, 26). When the disciples asked for thrones or defended Him with force, He rebuked them (Mk. 10:35-45; Lk. 22:49-51). He preemptorily refused to provide a sign as a credential of His ministry (Mk. 8:11-13; cf. Lk. 11:29f.).

It is not surprising, then, that in Mark's witness to Him, Jesus adopted an attitude of distinct reserve to the actual title "Messiah." Three texts in particular merit attention: Mk. 8:27ff.; 14:61f.; and 15:2ff. O. Cullmann's convincing treatment (*Christology of the NT* [Eng. tr., 2nd ed. 1963], pp. 117ff.) demonstrated that (1) Jesus showed extreme reserve toward the title "Messiah" and, as it was connected with popular ideas of earthly power, saw in it Satanic temptations; (2) in decisive passages He substituted for Messiah the title "Son of man"; and (3) over against the Jewish political conceptions He set the picture of His mission as the suffering Servant of the Lord in Isaiah.

*2. Son of Man.* This enigmatic title (found esp. in Mark at 2:28; 8:31ff.; 10:45; 14:62) was peculiarly suited to Jesus' purposes, for it could easily carry the overtones of His characteristic and distinctive teaching. For Him the person of the Messiah blended a present humiliation and obedience unto death with a future glory. (Phil. 2:6-11 may well be the "text" of which Mark's Gospel is the extended commentary.) He spoke, therefore, about the Son of man who is rejected and killed (cf. the predictions of the Passion) but who is vindicated by God and enters upon His kingdom and dominion. This theme of humiliation-exaltation is common in much early Christian literature (see the evidence of early hymns and confessions in R. P. Martin, "Some Reflections on NT Hymns," in H. H. Rowdon, ed., *Essays in Christology Presented to Donald Guthrie* [1982]; "NT Hymns: Background and Development," *Expos.T.*, 93 [1982]). In the Markan Christology, Jesus is the true Servant-Son who offered to God a perfect obedience and is honored by Him in His future triumph.

*3. Son of God.* The title "Son of God" is frequent, whether explicitly or implicitly, in this Gospel (1:1[?], 11; 3:11; 8:38; 9:7; 12:6; 13:32; 14:36, 61; 15:39). The OT background seems to be that of Pss. 2:7 and 89:27 (MT 28), but the texts that speak of Israel as God's son (Ex. 4:22f.; Hos. 11:1; etc.) should not be overlooked. Certain scholars (e.g., Bultmann, *Theology of the NT* [Eng. tr. 1952], I, 128ff.) have argued that this title was applied to Jesus in the Hellenistic Church on the supposed analogy between Jesus and Greek "divine men" who exercised a peripatetic ministry in the ancient world (like Apollonius of Tyana). But a careful examination of the Gospel data shows that the picture of Jesus as Son of God in Mark especially is "completely un-Greek" (see J. Bieneck, *Sohn Gottes als Christusbezeichnung der Synoptiker* [1951]; J. D. G. Dunn, *Christology in the Making* [1980], ch. 2). The most direct antecedents of the title are Jewish.

No evidence, however, clearly shows that "Son of God" was ever applied to the Messiah in rabbinic Judaism (see W. Manson, *Jesus the Messiah* [1942], pp. 103ff.). (Evidence from Qumrân, in 4QPs Dan A[a], has been taken to mean that "son of God *was just coming into use* as a Messianic title in pre-Christian Judaism" [R. H. Fuller, *Foundations of NT Christology* (1965), p. 32]. Earlier references in the DSS are in 4QFlor, citing 2 S. 7:14, and 1Q*28a*, which seems to refer Ps. 2:7 to God's begetting the Messiah.) Thus the title apparently derives from the Lord's unique, personal relationship to God, from His awareness of His destiny, which "had its support, if not its origin, in something which . . . can only be called the filial quality of his spirit in relation to God" (Manson, p. 107). Verses in Mark such as 1:11; 9:7; 12:6; 13:32; 14:36 are a window through which Christian eyes may see the mystery of the unique filial relationship of Jesus to God the Father. The superscription of 1:1 is congruous with the presentation of the Lord in the Gospel, for the following record tells of the Father's Beloved, whose real and filial nature is His secret, disclosed only to favored persons (4:11), who trod a pathway of lowly obedience and suffering to His death, yet who, after the pattern of Isaac (see A. Richardson, *Intro. to the Theology of the NT* [1958], pp. 228f., for Isaac-Christology), came again from the place of sacrifice, truly "raised up" and vindicated. The Christology of Mark upon close examination turns out to be as high as that of John (I. H. Marshall, *Origins of NT Christology* [1976], ch. 7).

***Bibliography.***–Comms. by W. C. Allen (1915); H. Anderson (*New Century Bible Comm.*, 1976; repr. 1981 — the most useful comm. for the English-speaking student who knows no Greek); B. W. Bacon (1909); A. W. F. Blunt (1929); B. H. Branscomb (*MNTC*, 1937); R. A. Cole (*Tyndale*, 1961); C. E. B. Cranfield (*CGT*, 1959); F. C. Grant (1953); W. Grundmann (*ThHK*, 1962); A. M. Hunter (*Torch*, 1948); S. E. Johnson (1960); E. Klostermann (*HNT*, 4th ed. 1950); M. J. Lagrange (1947); W. L. Lane (*NICNT*, 1974); E. Lohmeyer (*KEK*, 15th ed. 1959); P. S. Minear (*Layman's Bible Comm.*, 1963); C. F. D. Moule (*CBC*, 1965); A. E. J. Rawlinson (*WC*, 1925); J. Schniewind (*NTD*, 1937); E. Schweizer, *Good News According to Mark* (1970); H. B. Swete (1909); V. Taylor (1952).

C. Beach, *Gospel of Mark* (1959); H. J. Ebeling, *Das Messiasgeheimnis und die Botschaft des Marcus-Evangelisten* (1939); H. A. Guy, *Origin of the Gospel of Mark* (1954); W. G. Kümmel, *Promise and Fulfilment* (Eng. tr., 2nd ed., *SBT*, 1/23, 1957); R. H. Lightfoot, *Gospel Message of St. Mark* (1952); R. P. Martin, *Mark* (*Knox Preaching Guides*, 1981); *Mark: Evangelist and Theologian* (1972); W. Marxsen, *Mark the Evangelist* (Eng. tr. 1969); A. Menzies, *Earliest Gospel* (1901); D. E. Nineham, *St. Mark* (1963); R. Pesch, *Markusevangelium* (2 vols., 1976-1977); J. M. Robinson, *Problem of History in Mark* (1957); J. Schmid, *Gospel According to Mark* (1968); N. B. Stonehouse, *Witness of Matthew and Mark to Christ* (1944).

R. P. MARTIN

**MARK, JOHN.** A person known variously as "John whose other name was Mark," "John called Mark," and simply "John" or "Mark" (Acts 12:12, 25; 13:5, 13; 15:37, 39; Col. 4:10; 2 Tim. 4:11; Philem. 24; 1 Pet. 5:13; AV also Marcus [Col. 4:10; Phlm. 24]). These texts indicate his close association with the first apostles, especially Paul and Peter, and family connection to his "cousin" Barnabas (Col. 4:10). Both his home and family played an important part in early Christian history. His mother Mary was a member of the Jerusalem church. Christians regularly met in her home (Acts 12:12), and Peter came there after his release from prison.

Mark's first days as a believer are unknown. Zahn's fanciful suggestion that the "young man" of Mk. 4:51f. should be identified with John Mark lacks substance. The first solid evidence about him is that he joined the missionary party sent out from Antioch in Syria (Acts 13).

*I. Mark and Paul.*–From the time of Acts 13:5 John Mark traveled with Paul and Barnabas, possibly in the role of catechist (so W. Barclay, "A Comparison of Paul's Preaching," in W. W. Gasque and R. P. Martin, eds., *Apostolic History and the Gospel* [1970], pp. 169ff.). But Mark's decision (for reasons not supplied in the NT) to leave the apostolic group as it pressed beyond the Taurus mountains of Asia Minor (v. 13) caused some bitterness later when Barnabas wanted to take him on the second journey (15:39). The result was that Barnabas, out of loyalty to his kinsman Mark, left Paul and went off with Mark to Cyprus.

Some years later (exactly how long depends on a dating of the letter to the Colossians) Mark was restored to Paul's favor (Col. 4:10), although the wording of the appeal — "If he comes to you, receive him" — has suggested to commentators (see R. P. Martin, *Colossians* [1972], pp. 142f.) that Mark was perhaps only slowly winning back his reputation in the Pauline mission churches. Thus he would have needed Paul's special plea, "receive him," i.e., without censure or suspicion, especially since Mark does not seem to have been widely known at this period and had to be identified as Barnabas's cousin. An even more moving display of reconciliation comes in 2 Tim. 4:11, where Mark is unhesitatingly commended as a faithful Christian worker. His restoration was apparently complete and, if the letter to Timothy was written while Paul was a prisoner in Rome, the summons to bring Mark to Rome would mean that he was at Paul's side during the apostle's final days.

*II. Mark and Peter.*–1 Peter 5:13 also suggests that John Mark was in Rome. Greetings are sent from the church "at Babylon" and from "my son Mark." "Babylon" is usually regarded here as a sobriquet for Rome, as in Rev. 14:8; 17:5 (Eusebius *HE* ii.25.5-8; *see also* PETER, FIRST EPISTLE OF).

The first link between Mark and Peter is found in 1 Peter. This reading of the evidence, however, has been challenged on two grounds. The first, set forth by D. E. Nineham, is that "Mark (Marcus) was the commonest Latin name in the Roman Empire and that the early Church must have contained innumerable Marks" (*St. Mark* [1963], p. 39). The inference is that the tradition associating Mark with Peter and with the writing of the second Gospel is probably mistaken, since many persons with the same name may have lived in Rome. No one can know how many people in Christian circles were named Mark. Nineham's many examples of Romans whose *praenomen* (first name) was Marcus are inconclusive, because Marcus was the *cognomen* (family name) of John Mark. What can be maintained with some plausibility (as by W. Michaelis, *Einleitung in das NT* [2nd ed. 1965], pp. 53-55) is that the several allusions to "John whose other name was Mark" in the NT form a consistent picture and that no other Mark is recognized as a candidate for the office of evangelist or companion of Paul and Peter in patristic times.

The second ground on which the theory is challenged is that 1 Peter is a later, nonapostolic composition. Thus, alleged F. W. Beare (comm. on 1 Peter [3rd ed. 1970], *in loc.*), the collection of names in 5:12-14 is a literary device to recall the distant apostolic age, and "it required no great effort of the imagination to place Marcus and Silvanus in the entourage of Peter at Rome." But the hypothesis that 1 Peter is a postapostolic document is far from proved and, when tested by the objective evidence of its historical allusions to persecution and the type of Christianity it describes, can hardly support other conclusions drawn from it (see J. N. D. Kelly, *Comm. on the Epistles of Peter and Jude* [*HNTC*, 1969], pp. 26ff., 33ff., as well as his observations on 5:13, p. 220).

***III. Mark and the Second Gospel.***–The *testimonium* of Papius (recorded in Eusebius *HE* xxxix) that situates Mark at Rome with Peter ascribes a close relationship to Mark and Peter. It thus confirms the authenticity of Mark's authorship of his Gospel, since authenticity depends upon his intimate association with Peter, whose teaching he purportedly related. The key term describing Mark's relationship to Peter, *hermēneutḗs,* has several possible meanings. The most likely are: "translator," as Mark turned Peter's Aramaic or Greek into a more acceptable form; or "interpreter," as Mark acted as teacher and applied the *didachḗ* as a follow-up to Peter's preaching of the *kḗrygma*. W. C. van Unnik (*ZNW,* 54 [1963], 276f.) has made the positive suggestion that, whatever the nuance of this Greek word, the content of Mark's interpretation is more important than the way that he performed his role as interpreter. The implication is that Mark became Peter's *hermēneutḗs* by publishing a Gospel in which he recorded Peter's teaching — or as much of it as he remembered, modified by his knowledge of Paul's gospel and of that gospel's effect on the life of the mission churches in the Greco-Roman world.

This last statement raises the question of Papias's purpose in closely connecting Mark's Gospel and Peter's teaching. Recent discussion of the Papias text (see R. P. Martin, *Mark: Evangelist and Theologian* [1972], pp. 80-83) shows that this church father probably defended Mark's Gospel to refute Marcion's gnostic use of Luke's Gospel. Papias's evident interest in binding Mark as an interpreter of the apostolic gospel as closely as possible to an apostolic source would explain his insistence on Mark's strong link to Peter. Once that link is seen to be no more than an inference from the NT data, it becomes possible to submit that Mark's closer ties are with Paul. Mark should then be given his due as the evangelist who records, in the newly created literary *Gattung* of Gospel, the essential message of the Pauline *kḗrygma,* namely, the two-beat rhythm of the rejection and death of the Son of God and His vindication, set within the framework of the story of a fully human life (for an elaboration of this thesis see R. P. Martin, *Expos.T.,* 80 [1969], pp. 361-64; *Mark: Evangelist and Theologian* [1972]).

*See* MARK, GOSPEL ACCORDING TO V.

R. P. MARTIN

**MARKET; MARKET PLACE** [Heb. *reḥôḇ*] (Ps. 55:11 [MT 12]; Prov. 1:20; 7:12); AV STREETS; NEB PUBLIC SQUARE, PUBLIC PLACES; [*seḥōrâ*] (Ezk. 27:15); AV MERCHANDISE; NEB SOURCE OF COMMERCE; [Gk. *agorá*] (Mt. 11:16; 20:3; 23:7; Mk. 6:56; 7:4; 12:38; Lk. 7:32; 11:43; 20:46; Acts 16:19; 17:17); AV also STREETS; NEB also STREET, MAIN SQUARE, CITY SQUARE; **MEAT MARKET** [Gk. *mákellon*] (1 Cor. 10:25); AV SHAMBLES.

Hebrew *reḥôḇ* usually seems to designate a broad, open place near the city gate or gates. This plaza was the site of formal and informal assemblies and meetings; of speeches, proclamations (Prov. 1:20), celebrations, and military displays; of public lamentations; of playing, sitting, shopping, socializing (Prov. 7:12), judging (Ps. 55:11), and even sleeping if no lodging was available (Gen. 19:2, RSV "street"). *See also* STREET.

Heb. *seḥōrâ* occurs only in Ezk. 27:15, where it apparently means "merchandise," "source of trade," "territorial market," or "commercial client." The text may require minor emendation.

The well-known *agorá* or public square, frequently characterized by busy crowds, functioned as the center of public life in NT times. There children danced and played (Mt. 11:16; Lk. 7:32) and the unemployed wandered about and perhaps eventually obtained a job (Mt. 20:3). The haughty scribes and Pharisees strutted in the market place in search of honor and adulation (Mt. 23:7; Mk. 12:38; Lk. 11:43; 20:46). Sick people were brought there for the compassionate Jesus to heal (Mk. 6:56). At the *agorá* in Philippi Paul and Silas were given a hearing in the public law courts before the magistrates (Acts 16:19). At the *agorá* in Athens, Paul discussed and debated the Christian religion with all sorts of interested passersby, even some Epicurean and Stoic philosophers (17:17).

The precise background and significance of Gk. *mákellon* (1 Cor. 10:25; RSV "meat market") are uncertain. Both J. Schneider (*TDNT,* IV, 370) and MM (p. 336) noted a possible connection with Heb. *miḵlâ,* "enclosure"; Bauer (rev., p. 487) and H. Conzelmann (*1 Corinthians* [Eng. tr., *Hermeneia,* 1975], p. 176) agreed with Schneider that Gk. *mákellon* is not a loanword from Lat. *macellum* (contra F. F. Bruce, *1 and 2 Corinthians* [*New Century Bible Comm.,* 1971; repr. 1981], p. 98). At Corinth H. J. Cadbury (*JBL,* 53 [1934], 134-141) found a fragmentary Latin inscription (1st cent. A.D.) that mentions the *macellum.* Some evidence suggests that this *macellum* was a general marketplace selling fish, fruit, and bread as well as meat; thus the NAB's "market" is perhaps a more accurate translation of Gk. *mákellon.* This rendering does not change the point that Paul made (1 Cor. 10:25), as Conzelmann noted, "since the principle of freedom is upheld."

*See also* CITY.

M. W. MEYER
G. A. L.

**MARKET, SHEEP.** *See* SHEEP MARKET.

**MARMATHI** mär'mə-thī (1 Esd. 8:62, NEB); **MARMOTH** mär'məth (AV). *See* MEREMOTH **3.**

**MAROTH** mâr'oth [Heb. *mārôṯ*]. A town mentioned in Mic. 1:12 and otherwise not identified. The LXX reads *katoikoúsę̄ odýnas*, "who is dwelling in sorrows," rendering *mārôṯ* as a common noun. Some scholars have suggested that Maroth is equivalent to MAARATH (Heb. *maʿ^a^rāṯ*), but this possibility is highly unlikely, since it does not explain the LXX translation, and since the *ʿayin* could hardly have been so easily lost. It should be noted that the places mentioned in vv. 10-16 seem to suggest the points that the prophet wishes to make (cf. NIV mg.); possibly he alterred some of the names to make the play on words more apparent. W. S. L. S.

**MARRIAGE; MARRY.**

- I. Terms
- II. Nature of Marriage
  - A. Definition
  - B. Marriage and the Church
- III. In the Ancient Near East
- IV. In the OT
  - A. Patriarchal Structure
    1. Polygyny
    2. Levirate Marriage
  - B. Mate Selection
    1. General Procedure
    2. Betrothal
    3. Limitations
  - C. Rituals
  - D. Status of the Hebrew Wife
- V. In the NT
  - A. Jesus' Teaching
  - B. Paul's Teaching
- VI. Symbolism
  - A. Interpretations
  - B. Ethical Implications
- VII. Sex

***I. Terms.***–The RSV terms for "marry" include Heb. *lāqaḥ*, lit. "take" (Gen. 19:14; 28:1; Lev. 21:7f.; AV "take a wife"), *nāṯan lᵉʾiššâ*, lit. "give for a wife" (RSV "give . . . in marriage"; AV "give . . . to wife"; Gen. 34:8; 41:45; Jgs. 21:1; 1 K. 11:19), *hāyâ lᵉnāšîm*, lit. "be for wives" (Nu. 36:3, 6, 11f.), hiphil of *yāšaḇ*, lit. "make a resident" (Ezr. 10:2, 10, 17f.; Neh. 13:27; AV "take"), *nāśāʾ*, lit. "carry away, take" (1 Ch. 23:22; Ezr. 10:44; AV "take"), *bāʿal*, "marry," "rule over" (Dt. 24:1; Isa. 54:1; 62:4f.), and the hithpael of *ḥāṯan*, lit. "make oneself a daughter's husband" (1 K. 3:1; 2 Ch. 18:1; AV "make/join affinity").

Throughout the OT Heb. *kallâ* is rendered "bride" by the RSV (AV "spouse" in Cant. 4:8-12; 5:1). This term generally refers to a woman before marriage (e.g., Isa. 49:18; 61:10; Jer. 2:32) but may also refer to her after marriage (Hos. 4:13f.). Heb. *ḥāṯān* (RSV "bridegroom," Ex. 4:25f.; AV "husband") is "one who becomes related to another family by marriage" (*CHAL*, p. 120). "Bride" and "bridegroom" occur together in Isa. 62:5; Jer. 7:34; 25:10; and Rev. 18:23; where they depict the joy and happiness that accompany the marriage celebration.

"Wife" usually represents Heb. *ʾiššâ* (AV "woman" in Prov. 12:4; 31:10) and "wives" *nāšîm* (Gen. 4:19, 23). Abraham's wife Sarah is referred to in Gen. 20:3 as a *bᵉʿulāṯ bāʿal* (NEB "married woman"), a phrase that connotes her husband's ownership. The OT terms for "husband" include *ʾîš*, "man" (Gen. 3:6, 16), *baʿal*, "owner, lord" (Ex. 21:22; Dt. 24:4), *ʾāḏôn*, "lord" (Gen. 18:12; Am. 4:1), *rē(a)ʿ*, "friend, companion, fellow" (Jer. 3:20), and *ʾᵉnôš*, "man, mankind" (Ruth 1:11; Jer. 44:19; AV "man").

In the NT Gk. *gaméō* is the most common verb for "marry." Another term, *gamízō*, is used in both the active sense ("give in marriage," Mt. 24:38) and passive sense ("be given in marriage," Mt. 22:30; Mk. 12:25; Lk. 17:27; 20:35; cf. *gamískomai*, v. 34). The use of Gk. *epigambreúō* (lit. "marry as next of kin") in Mt. 22:24 probably reflects the LXX of Gen. 38:8 (cf. the levirate law in Dt. 25:5).

The cognate noun *gámos*, a word commonly used in the LXX for Heb. *mišteh* ("drinking," "feast"; cf. Gen. 19:3; Est. 2:18), refers either to a marriage celebration (Mt. 22:2-14; Jn. 2:1f.) or banquet (Lk. 12:36; 14:8), or to the institution of marriage (He. 13:4). In Rev. 19:7, 9 *gámos* is a figure for the joy of the messianic kingdom.

The NT terms for "bride" and "bridegroom" are Gk. *nýmphē* ("daughter-in-law" in Mt. 10:35; Lk. 12:53) and *nymphíos* respectively. "Bride" also translates *parthénos* in 2 Cor. 11:2 (AV, NEB, "virgin") and *gynḗ* in Rev. 19:7 (AV "wife"). *Gynḗ* is most commonly rendered "wife" (e.g., 1 Cor. 7; Eph. 5:22; etc.), although it may refer simply to a woman as a female person (e.g., Mt. 5:28; Jn. 4:7, 9, etc.), or to one who is betrothed (RSV "wife," Mt. 1:20, 24; cf. Dt. 22:24, LXX). The translation of *skeúos* in 1 Thess. 4:4 presents various difficulties. While there is evidence to support the translation "wife" (RSV), there is also strong support for *skeúos* referring to a man's own body (cf. AV "vessel"; NEB, NIV, "body"). For a fuller discussion see I. H. Marshall, *1 and 2 Thessalonians* (*NCBC*, repr. 1983), pp. 107f.

Greek *anḗr* is the usual term for "husband" in the NT (AV "man" in 1 Cor. 7:16; 11:3). An exception is the use of the hapax legomenon *phílandros* (lit. "loving her husband") in Tit. 2:4.

***II. Nature of Marriage.***–*A. Definition.* Marriage may be defined as that lifelong and exclusive state in which a man and a woman are wholly commited to live with each other in sexual relationship under conditions normally approved and witnessed to by their social group or society. Although Christian opinion is divided on the necessity of coitus for validating marriage, Paul plainly taught that it is the specific act by which man and woman become one flesh (Bailey, *Sexual Relation in Christian Thought*, p. 119). True marriage, therefore, must not be confused with a wedding ceremony, which only solemnizes and symbolizes a couple's total commitment.

Although cultural forces influence marriage as an institution, its essential core is determined primarily by the orders of creation (Thielicke, p. 104). Thus today monogamy is generally accepted from both a natural point of view (e.g., conjugation takes place between two persons, and children are produced by two parents) and a biblical one ("the two shall become one," Mt. 19:5; Eph. 5:31), despite the varied and complex social customs that have allowed for polyandry, polygyny, and other marital arrangements.

Marriage has been described as a biological act, as a legal contract, and as an economic arrangement. Personal, social, property, and inheritance rights for the partners as well as for any progeny have been concerns in all such views. A theological view of marriage does not exclude such considerations but goes beyond them in affirming the involvement of a divine element in all true marriages ("what therefore God has joined together . . . " Mt. 19:6).

*B. Marriage and the Church.* Historically, weddings were family or community events; not until after the 10th cent. A.D. were they performed in the church. Nevertheless, wedding ceremonies in both the OT and NT periods had a distinctly religious dimension because religion was woven into the daily life of the Hebrew family. The Church's recognition of civil weddings — which perhaps lack the religious symbolism of a church ceremony —

acknowledges the right of the state to regulate marriage as it does other social institutions. In accordance with Rom. 13, the Church expects couples who desire marriage to seek civil approval before the performance of any church ceremony.

*III. In the Ancient Near East.*–In the ancient Near East the primary purpose of marriage was procreation rather than companionship or mutual support. At a very early period marriages began to be arranged by parents, and this resulted in greater social solidarity, since mergers of families were involved. While marriage frequently had a mercenary aspect, genuine love and even some surreptitious degree of intimacy were by no means unknown.

The engagement of a man and a woman was sealed when the prospective bridegroom gave a gift to the bride's father. To describe this as a "bride price" may be confusing, since the wife was not purchased as a slave was, but it could well be considered some compensation to the bride's father for the loss of her services to his household. The marriage itself was probably conducted in some area of the local temple, and the couple was united by a priest who administered oaths. A tablet containing contractual material was inscribed by both parties and remained the official record of the marriage, after which the bride and groom were legally entitled to recognition as a married couple (cf. S. N. Kramer, *Sumerians* [1963], pp. 78, 250-57).

Amarna Tablet discussing the marriage of a Kassite princess to Pharaoh and the gifts exchanged (horses and lapis lazuli) (Trustees of the British Museum)

Marriage contracts were used widely in subsequent times. At Ugarit the contract generally spelled out the terms of the union, which by agreement could be either temporary or permanent and indissoluble. Of the many tablets recovered from Nuzi, one specified that if a wife remained childless for any reason, she was obligated to provide a concubine for her husband, so that children might be born into the family (C. H. Gordon, *BA*, 3 [1940], 3). The Middle Assyrian *erēbu*-legislation provided for the husband to reside with his wife's family rather than his own, which seems to have been intended to protect the marriage of a woman with a foreign man in her homeland (cf. C. H. Gordon, *Common Background of Greek and Hebrew Civilizations* [rev. ed. 1965], pp. 249f.).

While Egyptian women were normally discouraged from marrying foreigners, especially when Egypt was strong militarily, the *erēbu*-marriage was not unknown even there. Egyptian sources have preserved records of international marriages, instituted for political reasons, such as that between Amenhotep III and the Mitannian princess Tadu-ḫepa, for whom the pharaoh was compelled to pay an enormous bride price (G. Steindorff and K. C. Seele, *When Egypt Ruled the East* [1962], pp. 108f.). Marriage between native Egyptians was celebrated on a much smaller scale, but involved betrothals, dowries, legal settlements, and general marriage festivities common to all cultures. Marriage contracts seem to have come into use gradually among the middle and upper classes in Egypt, and by the Saitic period (26th Dynasty) were fairly common. An Aramaic wedding contract (5th cent. B.C.) from Elephantine stated the terms of the marriage, made provision for alimony in the event of a divorce, and settled the disposition of the family property should the husband Ananiah or his wife Tamut die. A woman named Mibtahiah who contracted three marriages, the second of which was liquidated in a settlement of claim by oath (*ANET*, p. 491), left two contracts, duly witnessed, attesting to her nuptial endeavors (*ANET*, pp. 222ff.).

*IV. In the OT.–A. Patriarchal Structure.* In Hebrew culture, society was built on the family, and the family in turn on the institution of marriage. Within the marital framework, patriarchal supremacy was the unquestioned pattern. A man could have more than one wife; he could divorce her but she could not divorce him. The law required a bridal sum (Heb. *mōhar*) to be given to the family of the bride (Gen. 34:11f.; Ex. 22:16 [MT 15]; Dt. 22:29). The woman, however, had no part in this transaction as an independent individual under the law.

Because property and inheritance were primarily concerned with the males in the family, it was almost imperative that a man have a son who could continue the family line and to whom he could leave his estate. This need for a male successor is critical to the understanding of Hebrew marriage practice in the OT.

*1. Polygyny.* Hebrew marriage was from the beginning essentially monogamous (Mace, p. 262), but since a man needed a male heir he could take another woman if his first wife was barren. Polygyny (the practice of having multiple wives) was largely confined to the ruling and upper classes. It was practiced by Abraham (Gen. 16), Jacob (Gen. 30:1-8), Gideon (Jgs. 8:30), King David (1 S. 25:39f.; 2 S. 3:2f.; 5:13), Solomon (1 K. 9:16; 11:3; Cant. 6:8), and Rehoboam (2 Ch. 11:21).

Concubinage existed along with polygyny (the OT offers no clear evidence of polyandry) and was a legalized form of cohabitation. A wife held much higher status than a concubine because of her birth and family's support. Children born to concubines could receive gifts as a form of inheritance (Gen. 25:6), and some were known to rise to

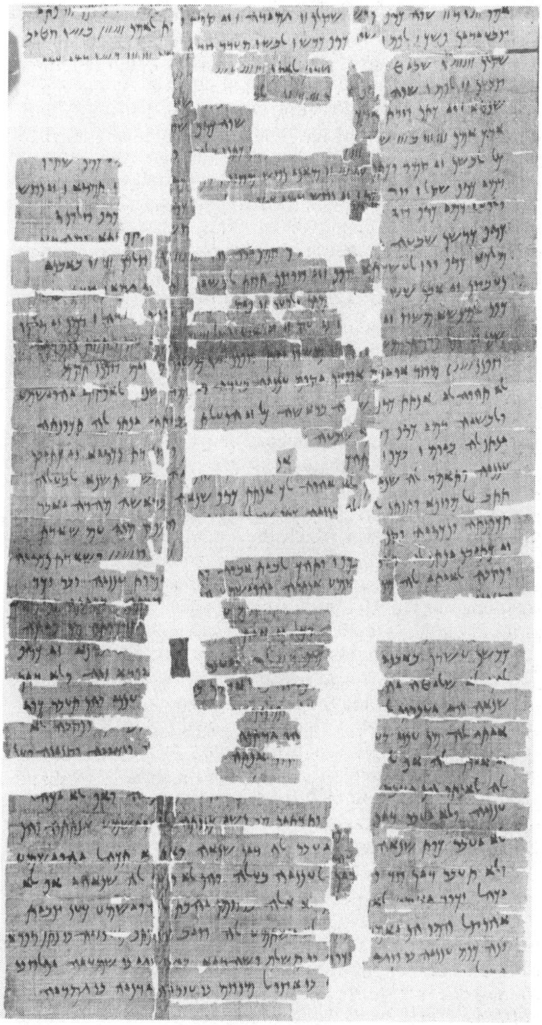

Aramaic marriage contract (from Elephantine) listing gifts for groom and bride and the bride's possessions, as well as the conditions for divorce (Brooklyn Museum)

positions of power (Jgs. 8:31–9:22), but their rights were obviously less protected than those of children born to wives. Both concubinage and polygyny created problems in Hebrew married life: cf. Abraham's and Hagar's unhappiness (Gen. 21:8-16), Rachel's bitterness (Gen. 30:15), the death of Gideon's offspring (Jgs. 9), Hannah's anger (1 S. 1:6f.), David's complicity in the death of Bathsheba's husband (2 S. 11), and Solomon's idolatry (1 K. 11:1-8). Hebrew kings were especially warned against multiplying wives because their hearts might be turned away from God (Dt. 17:17). *See* POLYGAMY.

2. *Levirate Marriage.* This form of marriage (named from Lat. *levir,* "husband's brother") allowed a man to receive his deceased brother's property and manage it for the widow, thereby keeping the family property and possessions intact. If the deceased brother left no male children, then the surviving brother was expected to take the deceased's wife. Any son born of this relationship to the widow would be counted as the dead brother's heir, who would then be expected to continue the family line (Dt. 25:5-10). It was apparently the infraction of levirate law (although a male relative was not without option in this regard) that brought judgment upon Onan, not his effort of contraception itself (Gen. 38:8-10). Levirate practice extended beyond immediate brothers to other relatives; e.g., Boaz took Ruth as his wife after a closer kinsman waived his right to her (Ruth 4:5f.). *See also* HUSBAND'S BROTHER; BROTHER'S WIFE.

B. *Mate Selection.* Hebrews usually chose wives from their own nation (e.g., Gen. 24:2-4; 28:1f.; Neh. 13:25), but occasionally wives were purchased as slaves (Ex. 21:7-11) or taken as prizes of war (Dt. 21:10-13).

1. *General Procedure.* The selection of a bride or groom was usually left to the families, but customs varied widely. Sarah's maid Hagar chose a wife for her son Ishmael (Gen. 21:21) and Judah for his son Er (38:6). Reuel gave his daughter Zipporah to Moses (Ex. 2:21). Caleb offered the hand of his daughter Achsah to "whoever smites Kiriath-sepher" (Josh. 15:16), and Saul offered his daughter Merab to David (1 S. 18:17). Sometimes the woman's family chose the mate, as with Naomi (Ruth 3:1f.) and Saul, whose daughter Michal loved David (1 S. 18:20-22). At other times the groom made the selection and then prevailed upon his family to work out the necessary arrangements with the woman's family, as in the cases of Shechem (Gen. 34:4, 8) and Samson, who told his reluctant parents to "get her for me as my wife" (Jgs. 14:2). Apparently a family sometimes sought the consent of a daughter: Rebekah was asked, "Will you go with this man?" (Gen. 24:58), and Abraham had instructed his servant that if the woman was "not willing," the servant was released from his promise to find a wife for Isaac (v.8).

The importance of romantic attraction in mate selection was not entirely unknown. Jacob's love for Rachel led him to remain with his father-in-law for an additional seven years to earn her as his wife (Gen. 29:20). Shechem loved Jacob's daughter Dinah (34:3), and Michal, Saul's daughter, loved David (1 S. 18:20).

2. *Betrothal.* The usual Hebrew word for "betroth" (e.g., Ex. 22:16 [MT 15]; Dt. 22:23, etc.; 28:30) is *'āraś* (NEB also "pledge"), though Lev. 19:20 uses the niphal of *ḥārap* (NEB "assign"). The AV also uses "betroth" (RSV "designate") for the Heb. *yāʿaḏ* (lit. "appoint") in Ex. 21:8f.

The NT renders several words "betroth" or "(be) betrothed": the pass. of *mnēsteúō* in Mt. 1:18; Lk. 1:27; 2:5 (AV "espoused"); *parthénos* in 1 Cor. 7:36f. (AV "virgin"; NEB "partner"); *harmózomai* in 2 Cor. 11:2 (AV "espoused"; *see also* BETROTH).

Betrothal in the Bible differs considerably from modern engagements. As an act preliminary to marriage, betrothal implied a commitment almost as binding as marriage itself; its dissolution involved at least a formal divorce (Mt. 1:19). The betrothed persons were referred to as "husband and wife" (Gen. 29:21; Mt. 1:18, 20) and were to be completely faithful to each other. Any violation of the betrothed state was treated as adultery and could result in death for the offender (Dt. 22:23-25). The permanency and faithfulness within the betrothal bond are pictured in God's relation to Israel: "I will betroth you to me forever . . . I will betroth you to me in faithfulness" (Hos. 2:19f.). Miscellaneous Jewish traditional laws concerning betrothals are found in Mish. *Kiddushin.*

a. *Kinds.* At the time of Mary and Joseph betrothal called for a solemn oral commitment in the presence of witnesses with an added pledge of a piece of money or a written pledge *(šeṭārê 'ērûsîn)* that would conclude with a benediction. Another kind of betrothal, cohabitation, was strongly disapproved by the rabbis (see T. B. *Yebamoth* 118b; cf. Mish. *Ketuboth* iv.4; *LTJM,* I, 149).

b. *Gifts in Betrothal.* Of the three types of gifts connected with bethrothal, the *mōhar* (only in Gen. 34:12; Ex. 22:16f.; 1 S. 18:25) or "marriage present" (RSV), given by the bridegroom to the bride's family, was probably the most important. Although the bridal sum was originally thought to be a purchase price, M. Burrows and others have noted that the father of the bride gave his daughter a dowry and did not merely exchange value for value, as was the case in purchase of a concubine. Instead, the payment of the *mōhar* was a form of compensation and constituted a betrothal because it sealed the covenant between the two families (Burrows, p. 13; Mace, pp. 169, 172). The payment or gift may have been in the form of money, service (such as Jacob provided, Gen. 29), or other consideration (1 S. 18:25; cf. Josh. 15:16).

The dowry was a gift presented usually by the bride's father to his daughter or to the groom. It may have consisted of servants (Gen. 24:59-61; 29:24, 29), valued possessions, or land (Jgs. 1:14f.), though the case of Solomon's marriage to Pharaoh's daughter (1 K. 9:16) perhaps reflects Egyptian custom (de Vaux, p. 28). The bridegroom apparently had a gift for the bride, also, such as the jewelry and clothes presented to Rebekah (Gen. 24:51-53).

The interval between betrothal and marriage under normal circumstances did not exceed twelve months (*LTJM*, I, 353f.).

*3. Limitations*. Restrictions on the choice of spouses were usually enacted to assure the continuation of the Hebrews as a nation.

*a. Intermarriage*. Marriages with foreigners were strictly opposed (Dt. 7:3; Josh. 23:12; Ezr. 9:2f.; Neh. 13:23ff.; Tob. 4:12f.). Esau married two Hittite women, making life "bitter" for the parents (Gen. 26:34f.), and Moses married a Cushite woman, causing his siblings, Miriam and Aaron, to speak against him (Nu. 12:1). Solomon intermarried and had his heart turned away "after other gods" (1 K. 11:1-4). Forced dissolution of intermarriages occurred rarely, however, and was usually a drastic effort to preserve the Hebrews as a people (Ezr. 10).

*b. Intrafamilial Marriage*. Danger lay not simply in intermarriage with those too distant from the Hebrews. Mates too closely related also threatened the psychological and social stability of the family. The code on female consanguinity (also females associated by affinity, e.g., marriage) that was the foundation of the Hebrew law on this subject appears to have included all the females whose relationship to a male were not more distant than two successive steps by blood and one by marriage (cf. Lev. 18:6-18; 20:10-21). Thus, as determined by Mace, the forbidden consanguinous and affinity relationships are: (a) mother, sister, daughter (assumed); (b) father's wife, brother's wife, son's wife; (c) grandmother, mother's sister, father's sister, sister's daughter, brother's daughter, daughter's daughter, son's daughter; (d) grandfather's wife, mother's brother's wife, father's brother's wife, sister's son's wife, brother's son's wife, daughter's son's wife, son's son's wife; (e) wife's mother, wife's sister (in lifetime of wife), wife's daughter; and (f) wife's grandmother, wife's mother's sister, wife's father's sister, wife's sister's daughter, wife's brother's daughter, wife's daughter's daughter, and wife's son's daughter (pp. 154-56).

These regulations on marriage provided societal and familial stability and preserved property within the family (Nu. 36). Patai observed that in the patriarchal family of Abraham and his descendants marriage between first-degree relatives did occur. Although the limited biblical evidence does not indicate its frequency, there can be no doubt that it was legal but fell into disuse by the end of the period of the Hebrew monarchy (p. 26).

*C. Rituals*. Occasionally a marriage ceremony was marked by certain unusual procedures, such as Solomon being crowned by his mother, rather than by a high priest, on his wedding day (Cant. 3:11). But under normal conditions the activities connected with marriage (preceded by betrothal) were: (1) the transfer of the bride to the bridegroom's home, (2) the marriage feast, and (3) the consummation. The transfer of the bride was probably a joyful procession (Jer. 7:34; 16:9; 25:10). The wedding feast took place in the evening, as suggested by the parable of the ten virgins (Mt. 25:1-13) and the servants who with their lamps burning waited for their master to return from the marriage feast (Lk. 12:35-38). Riddles (Jgs. 14:12-14), love songs (Ps. 78:63; Isa. 5:1; Ezk. 33:32), and a joyous spirit marked the feast (cf. Mt. 9:15; Mk. 2:19; Lk. 5:34) which might have been as long as a week (Jgs. 14:12-17), or even two weeks (Tob. 8:20–9:2; 10:7). A high point in the feast was the custom of spreading the cloak or skirt over the bride to indicate the marital commitment. Ruth 3:9 and Ezk. 16:8 (God speaking symbolically to Israel: "I spread my skirt over you . . . I plighted my troth to you and entered into a covenant with you . . . and you became mine") seem to refer to this custom. The couple entered the nuptial chamber *(ḥeḏer),* in which the bridal bed stood with its canopy, to show that the marriage would be consummated. The final act, the proving of the bride's virginity, was the responsibility of the bride's parents (Dt. 22:13-21).

*D. Status of the Hebrew Wife*. The wife in the Hebrew home was restricted but was highly respected. Though the man was called the lord *(ba'al)* and the woman was called property *(bᵉ'ûlâ)* and the seduction of a virgin was a violation of property rather than of personal rights (Ex. 22:15f.; Dt. 22:28f.), a wife was not property in the usual sense. Wives were not classified along with concubines (e.g., Jgs. 8:30f.). A wife may have been under her husband's authority, but she was a free woman, not bound or owned by him, as were many concubines. A wife shared with her husband not only the functions of sex and parenthood but also comradeship, in which she ranked as his equal. Although this principle may have been abused, it was nonetheless the basis of the Hebrew marriage relation (Mace, p. xiv).

Any review of the practice of marriage in the OT will reveal departures at many points from the original intentions of the Creator. Gen. 2:24; Canticles; Ezk. 16; and Hos. 1–3, however, provided descriptions of true marriages that at different times influenced individual lives and the people as a whole.

***V. In the NT.–A.*** *Jesus' Teaching*. Our Lord's instruction about marriage is found primarily in the Synoptic Gospels (Mt. 5:31f.; 19:3-12; Mk. 10:2-12; Lk. 16:18). Instead of disputing with the Pharisees (Mt. 19:3; Mk. 10:2) about OT practices in marriage and divorce, He directed them to the true nature of marriage as found in Gen. 2:24. Man and woman were created to become "one flesh," i.e., a unity effected by God Himself so that a permanent union would result (Mt. 19:5f.). "Flesh" in Hebrew thought represents the entire person: thus marriage involves a unity of soul and body, of sympathy, interest, and purpose: a husband and wife are no longer two, but one flesh, one spirit, one person (A. B. Bruce, "Synoptic Gospels," in *Expos. G. T.,* I, 246). Thus Jesus recalled the original order of creation, assuring the elementary unity and inviolability of marriage (*TDNT,* I, 649f.). Jesus pointed people to the true nature of marriage so that they would abandon the imperfect and move steadily toward a marriage that reflected God's revealed purpose.

Jesus' teaching contains certain reservations about the married state, however. He said that marriage is an institution for this life only (Mk. 12:25). Not all people necessarily marry, nor are all given the gift of celibacy (Mt. 19:11). Celibacy, therefore, is not a higher state for which one strives but a gift from God which one may or may not receive.

Divine involvement in true marriage implies that wedlock is good, holy, and honorable (He. 13:4). Our Lord's presence at the wedding in Cana of Galilee (Jn. 2) also suggests this, as does Paul's use of the union of man and woman as one flesh to signify the relationship of Christ with His Church (Eph. 5:31f.).

*B. Paul's Teaching.* In his treatment of marriage, Paul tied together the body, the self, and the flesh (Eph. 5:28-31), quoting Gen. 2:24 ("[the two] shall become one flesh"; cf. also 1 Cor. 6:16), the same Genesis passage that Jesus quoted (Sampley, p. 143). Sexual union involves a physical and also a metaphysical factor (*TDNT,* I, 651), the latter undoubtedly including spiritual and psychological elements.

Paul dealt with the subject of love in terms of Christ's love for the Church and its implications for marriage: husbands should love their wives as they do themselves and as Christ loved the Church (Eph. 5:25). Paul added that wives should submit to their husbands as the Church submits to Christ's authority (vv. 22-24); this "is fitting in the Lord" (Col. 3:18). But it comes within mutual subjection (Eph. 5:21).

***VI. Symbolism.****–A. Interpretations.* In analyzing the institution of marriage in the Bible, one finds that figurative language is highly important. Marriage is a symbol for God's covenant with His people (*TDNT,* I, 654). The unity, sacrificial love, and interdependence usually associated with marriage enable the individual to comprehend, in part, the unity, love, and interdependent features of God's relationship with His people under the symbols of God's covenant with Israel and the Church as bride and body of Christ. The focus is on the individual's understanding of the relationship between God and His people. Spiritual realities are made clearer by comparison with earthly experiences. The NT "bride image," e.g., emphasizes certain basic truths: (1) the Church-bride is elected to God's purpose but is free to make a choice (Eph. 4:1); (2) Christ in love gives Himself to establish a covenant relationship with His *one* bride; (3) Christ's atonement is a "betrothal gift"; (4) Christ's love cleanses and makes the bride worthy of Him; (5) the bride looks to the future wedding day (Parousia) (Batey, pp. 29f.). *See* BRIDE OF CHRIST.

An equally important interpretative approach is viewing the intimate relationship between God and His people (God and Israel, Christ and His Church) as a paradigm (Sampley, p. 152) or christological analogy of the husband-wife relationship in its earthly existence (Batey, pp. 31f.).

*B. Ethical Implications.* Covenantal and Church-bride imagery suggest that certain qualities are essential to marriage from a biblical perspective. Marriages should be characterized by (a) intentions of a permanent relationship (Hos. 2:19; Mt. 19:6), (b) overriding, sacrificial love of the husband for the wife (Hos. 2:19; Eph. 5:25), and (c) a unity by which the two become one, physically and spiritually.

Means for achieving a unity of husband and wife appear to include primarily sexual intercourse (1 Cor. 6:16), and secondarily mutual subjection out of reverence for Christ (Eph. 5:21) and submission of the wife to the husband as the "head" of the marriage (vv. 22, 24; 1 Cor. 11:3).

In respect to a wife's submission, some scholars (e.g., K. Stendahl) dispute the general universality of the biblical model of marriage and hold that Near Eastern thought patterns may or may not be relevant to contemporary movements or needs (pp. 22-37). Passages quoted by Stendahl and others stress the interdependence and reciprocal nature of marriage as found in Gal. 3:28 ("there is neither male nor female . . . in Christ Jesus"), 1 Cor. 7:3f. ("the wife does not rule over her own body, but the husband does; likewise the husband does not rule over his own body, but the wife does"), and 1 Pet. 3:7b ("you are joint heirs of the grace of life").

The traditional view holds that the interdependent factor is important to the marital relationship and that the husband's headship in the marriage has been God's directive for married couples since the fall (Gen. 3:16). The doctrine of subordination declares that neither man nor woman is different in status before God (Gal. 3:28), especially since marriage does not exist in the aeon beyond this one (Mk. 12:25). In the present age, however, some hierarchical organization appears to be necessary for marriage as for churches and other institutions. It is not a hierarchy dictated by coercion but rather one adopted out of devotion to Christ (Eph. 5:21f.). It is a practical hierarchy of function in which the wife and husband have equal standing before God and complementary relationships with each other. The husband's headship does not rule out all decision making by the wife; one gathers, e.g., that Priscilla had a strong role to play in her joint activities with her husband Aquila (Acts 18:18, 26; Rom. 16:3f.; 2 Tim. 4:19; cf. 1 Cor. 16:19). It should be stressed that subordination does not mean inferiority.

***VII. Sex.***–Sexuality is an expression of one's being. It testifies to the fact that mankind was created male and female (Gen. 1:27) with natural attraction between the sexes. It points up the human need for fellowship and personal fulfillment; it is good and honorable, though sin or misunderstanding may distort its goodness (He. 13:4). The use of the sexual relationship as a symbol of the unity of Christ with His church (Eph. 5:22f.) indicates that God approves the act when rightly used. It is the means of procreation, which the Hebrews of the OT saw as a gift of God to be received with gratitude (Mace, p. 262). A man and a woman find in sexual relationship a source of joy and freedom, as pictured in Canticles. Paul declared (without referring to a need for procreation) that husbands and wives are entitled to conjugal rights, which are essential to the marriage relationship (1 Cor. 7:3-5).

Without the definite intention of establishing a marriage relationship, both OT and NT disapprove of premarital and extramarital relations. Paul warned that even a sexual liaison with a prostitute makes the two persons "one flesh" (1 Cor. 6:16). Theological and psychological evidence suggests that varying degrees of attachment result from acts of sexual intercourse, however casual they may seem initially. In the OT period if an unmarried, unbetrothed couple were discovered in the act of sexual relations, the young man was forced to take the woman as his wife and make a payment of money to her father (Dt. 22:29), unless the father (in line with patriarchal prerogative) refused to enforce this regulation (Ex. 22:17). Betrothal was considered such an intimate relationship that, if a betrothed woman voluntarily engaged in sexual relations with a man to whom she was not betrothed, both were condemned to death (Dt. 22:22), although this penalty was apparently modified at a later period to permit divorce (Mt. 1:19; cf. Mish. *Sotah* i.5).

Gen. 2:24 stresses that man "cleaves" to his wife, signifying an underlying sense of "belongingness" or commitment (cf. *TDOT,* IV, *s.v.* "dābhaq" [Wallis]). Commitment is essential, therefore, to any true marriage as described in the Scriptures and requires more than a voluntary physical experience (contra Piper pp. 138f.). A scriptural view cautions against sexual relations without the intention of a permanent relationship and also against a concept of marriage that stresses a physical relationship with no lifelong commitment.

*See also* SEX.

***Bibliography.***–S. Bailey, *Sexual Ethics* (1963); *Sexual Relation in Christian Thought* (1959); R. A. Batey, *NT Nuptial Imagery* (1971); G. W. Bromiley, *God and Marriage* (1980); M. Burrows, *Basis of Israelite Marriage* (1938); P. Jewett, *Man as Male and Female* (1975); D. R. Mace, *Hebrew Marriage* (1953); E. Neufeld, *Ancient Hebrew Marriage Laws* (1944); R. Patai, *Sex and Family in the Bible and Middle East* (1959); O. A. Piper, *Biblical View of Sex and Marriage* (1960); J. P. Sampley, *And the Two Shall Become One Flesh* (1971); K. Stendahl, *Bible and the Role of Women* (Eng. tr. 1966); *TDNT,* I, *s.v.* γαμέω (Stauffer); *TDOT,* I, *s.v.* "'îsh" (N. P. Bratsiotis); H. Thielicke, *Ethics of Sex* (Eng. tr. 1964); R. deVaux, *Ancient Israel* (Eng. tr. 1961).

R. K. BOWER
G. L. KNAPP

**MARRIAGE ALLIANCE** [Heb. hithpael of *ḥāṯan*–'marry'] (1 K. 3:1; 2 Ch. 18:1); AV AFFINITY; NEB ALLIED . . . BY MARRYING. Literally, the hiphil of *ḥāṯan* means "become somebody's son-in-law." In biblical times marriage was viewed as a covenant between two families, and thus marriages often served the political function of cementing a treaty between two families or nations. INTERMARRIAGE with pagan nations was opposed by the prophets because it would lead to the worship of other gods, as it did with Solomon (1 K. 11:1-8).

**MARROW** [Heb. *mō(a)ḥ* (Job 21:24), *ḥēleḇ*–'fat' (Ps. 63:5 [MT 6]), pual part. of *māḥâ*–'fatty dishes' (Isa. 25:6); Gk. *myelós* (He. 4:12)]; NEB also RICH. Because the marrow nourishes and strengthens the bones, moist bones are a figure of health (Job 21:24; cf. Prov. 3:8). In Ps. 63:5 (MT 6) and Isa. 25:6 "marrow" denotes the fatty foods served at a sacrificial feast or messianic banquet (see C. A. Briggs and E. G. Briggs, Comm. on Psalms, II [*ICC,* 1907], 73); figuratively, these foods represent the satisfaction of one's total needs, spiritual as well as physical. The author of the Epistle to the Hebrews speaks of the divine revelation as penetrating and laying bare the innermost core of a person's being (4:12).

On the use of "bones" and "marrow" to represent the whole personality, see A. R. Johnson, *Vitality of the Individual in the Thought of Ancient Israel* (1964), pp. 67-69.

N. J. O.

**MARS' HILL** (Acts 17:22, AV). *See* AREOPAGUS.

**MARSENA** mär-sē'nə [Heb. *marsᵉnā'*]. One of the "seven princes of Persia and Media" under Ahasuerus (Est. 1:14). *See* PRINCES, THE SEVEN.

**MARSH** [Heb. *biṣṣâ*] (Job 8:11; 40:21); AV MIRE, FENS; [*geḇe'*–'cistern,' 'pool'] (Ezk. 47:11); AV MARISH; NEB POOL. The climate in Palestine is dry and the terrain is generally rocky; thus marshes are almost unknown except along the shore of the Dead Sea, especially at its south end. The marshes referred to in Job are probably in Egypt's Nile Delta, where papyrus grows in the extensive marshes. In Ezekiel's vision the salty waters of the Dead Sea are purified by the river of fresh water issuing from under the threshold of the temple; but the "swamps and marshes" (Heb. *biṣṣâ* and *geḇe'*) will remain salty so that the industry of collecting salt can be maintained.

**MARSHAL** [Heb. *sōpēr*–'scribe'] (Jgs. 5:14); AV WRITER; NEB MUSTERER; [*ṭipsār* < Akk. *ṭupšarru*–'tablet writer'] (Jer. 51:27); AV CAPTAIN; NEB COMMANDER-IN-CHIEF. A high-ranking military officer. The context of Jgs. 5:14 indicates that *sōpēr* must refer to an officer who mustered the troops. In later military organization this duty was assigned to a specific officer (cf. 2 K. 25:19; 2 Ch. 26:11; 1 Macc. 5:42), but in this text it is probably the general military leader of the clan. The same function appears to have been performed by the *ṭipsār,* a term that occurs also in Nah. 3:17 (RSV "scribes"; but RSV mg., more appropriately, "marshals") parallel to "princes" (Heb. *minnᵉzārîm* < Akk. *manzazu,* "courtier").

N. J. O.

**MART.** *See* MERCHANT.

**MARTHA** mär'thə [Gk. *Martha* < Aram. *mārtā'*–'lady' or 'mistress (of the house)']. A friend of Jesus; the sister of Mary and Lazarus, who lived in Bethany (Lk. 10:38-39; Jn. 11:1f., 18f., 39; 12:2). Although Luke may appear to locate Martha's house in southern Galilee, the central section of his Gospel (9:51–19:27) shows little concern for chronological or geographical order; also, the indefinite phrase *kṓmēn tiná,* "a village," indicates his deliberate lack of precision (10:38). Luke's account may reflect one of Jesus' journeys to Jerusalem during the last six months of His ministry, when He frequently lodged in Bethany (cf., e.g., Mt. 21:17; 26:6).

Martha, the older sister, was mistress of the house (Jn. 11:5, 19; Lk. 10:38). When Jesus visited them Martha bore the responsibility of meeting, welcoming, and serving Him (Lk. 10:38, 40; Jn. 11:20; 12:2). Because she served dinner at Simon the leper's home in Bethany when Mary anointed Jesus, some have surmised that Martha was Simon's wife, widow, or daughter (Mk. 14:3 par. Jn. 12:1-3). But the relation of Martha and Simon is never stated. (The anointing in Lk. 7:36-50 happened in the house of Simon a Pharisee.)

Martha was less famous than her brother, whom Jesus raised from the dead (Jn. 11:38-44), and her sister, who anointed Jesus' feet (Jn. 11:2; 12:3; cf. Mt. 26:6f. par.), but John records that "Jesus loved Martha and her sister and Lazarus" (11:5). It was Martha who met and conversed with Jesus as He approached Bethany after Lazarus's death. On that occasion she was the first to declare openly her faith in Jesus' power to heal and in His identity as the Son of God and the Messiah (Jn. 11:21f., 27).

Luke and John deliberately contrast Mary's and Martha's responses to Christ. Martha's impatient preoccupation with showing hospitality to Jesus precluded paying adequate attention to Him and His teaching (Lk. 10:39-42) and thus differs from Mary's humility and abandonment in her devotion to the Lord (Lk. 10:39, 42; Jn. 12:3). Jesus reprimanded Martha for being "anxious and troubled about many things," whereas "only one thing is needful" (Lk. 10:41f.). Mary had "chosen the good portion, which shall not be taken away" (Lk. 10:42). Although no less devoted to Jesus than Mary, Martha was engrossed in the details of the meal and so failed to discern what would please Jesus most.

Jesus' reference to "the good portion, which shall not be taken away" is a wordplay that associates the ideas of spiritual nourishment and food. True and everlasting nourishment is found only in devotion to Christ. This was Mary's spiritual insight, reflected in her devout contemplation of the Lord as she sat listening at His feet, that Jesus commended to Martha (Lk. 10:39-42). The proper way to serve and honor Him, Mary had discerned, is to heed His words. Interestingly, the Mishnah exhibits a similar concern in the exhortation "Let thy house be a meeting-house for the Sages and sit amid the dust of their feet and drink in their words with thirst" (*Aboth* i.4).

*Bibliography.*–A. Baker, *CBQ*, 27 (1965), 127-137; F. Godet, comm. on Luke (2nd ed. 1878), II, 42-46; E. Laland, *ST*, 13 (1959), 70-85; J. B. Lightfoot, *Biblical Essays* (1893), pp. 37-39; I. H. Marshall, *Gospel of Luke* (*NIGTC*, 1978), pp. 450-54; L. Morris, *Gospel According to John* (*NICNT*, 1971), pp. 532-577; A. Plummer, comm. on Luke (*ICC*, 4th ed. 1913), pp. 289-293; J. N. Sanders, *NTS*, 1 (1954/55), 29-41.

J. J. HUGHES

**MARTYR** [Gk. *mártys*–'witness'] (Rev. 17:6). The word appears in the AV also in Acts 22:20 and Rev. 2:13, where the RSV translates "witness," the primary sense of *mártys*. In its developed ecclesiastical usage, found indisputably for the first time in the late 2nd cent. A.D. (M. Polyc. 17:3; cf. Eusebius *HE* v.2.3 for usage in Lyons in A.D. 177), "martyr" denotes a believer who voluntarily died for his confession of Christ.

Various answers have been given to the problem of the semantic transition from the active sense of the word "witness" to the passive sense of "martyr." Similarities between the attitudes and circumstances of the martyrs and of non-Christian people of conviction shed some light on the history of rhetorical writing but are not particularly relevant to the semantic concern. Elijah (1 K. 19:10) and Uriah (Jer. 26:20-23) were indeed persecuted, but the former did not die a martyr's death, and the latter attempted to escape from his persecutors. The sufferings of Israel encouraged heroic adherence to the faith (cf. 1 Macc. 2:50), but in the exhortation of 1 Macc. 2 the witnessing of Caleb (v. 56) is only one of many displays of heroism. Socrates (cf. Plato *Apologia* 39c) and the Stoics (cf. Epictetus i.19.8) offered models for calmness in the face of death (cf. Asc.Isa. 5:14; Martyrdom of Polycarp; 4 Maccabees) and lack of vindictiveness (cf. Lk. 23:34), but even Epictetus's statement about the witness called by God (i.29.46f.) does not explain the later reservation of the word "martyr" for those who die for their religious convictions. A more probable connection is with Rev. 17:6 and 2:13, but even in these passages the primary sense of witness still appears to be dominant. Gk. *mártyres* in Rev. 17:6 must mean "witnesses," since a reference to "martyrs" would be inexplicable after a clear reference in the same passage to the saints who sacrificed their lives for the faith. Antipas is similarly called *ho mártys mou* ("my witness," Rev. 2:13); the use of the possessive pronoun parallels Acts 22:20, where Stephen is a witness of Christ (cf. Acts 7:54-56). Both the addition of the phrase "who was killed among you" (Rev. 2:13) and the parallel expression *martyría* in Acts 22:18 point to the meaning "witness." That others who remained faithful to death are not called *mártys* (Rev. 6:9-11; 13:15; 20:4), despite testimony to Christ (6:9; 20:4), suggests, however, that *mártys* in Acts 22:20; Rev. 2:13; 17:6 is associated with a special type of witnessing (cf. 1 Clem. 5:3-7). These latter passages, then, represent a transitional stage in the history of the word *mártys*; it is erroneous to read them as though the transition had already taken place or as though other factors did not condition the semantic development.

One of these factors is the heavy accent placed by the writers of the NT on the continuity of the history of salvation. NT terms for witness associate the apostolic mission with that of earlier Israel. David is called a witness to the people (Isa. 55:4); Israel will call to the nations (vv. 5f.). According to Isa. 43:10, 12; 44:8, the people of Israel are God's witnesses. The twelve apostles assume jurisdiction over Israel (cf. Lk. 22:30), and Jesus sent them forth as witnesses of God's beneficence (24:48; Acts 1:8). Since Jesus and His work constituted the message of the eyewitness, any member of this Israel who proclaimed that message even without having seen Jesus could also be called a witness (e.g., Stephen, Acts 22:20; *martýrion* and *euangélion* are in fact interchangeable; cf. Mk. 13:9f.; Lk. 21:13). Jesus, as the true remnant in Israel (cf. Lk. 3:22; Isa. 42:1), would be the *mártys kat' exochḗn* ("par excellence"; cf. the use of the verb in Jn. 3:11; 4:44; 18:37), greater than Moses (cf. Jn. 1:17; on Moses as a witness see Jub. 6:30). Jesus as the Lord is the "faithful" witness (Rev. 1:5; 3:14; cf. Jer. 42:5). That He is said to have made a good confession before Pontius Pilate (1 Tim. 6:13), which culminated in His death, undoubtedly encouraged the use of the word "martyr" as a description of confessors faithful to death. Jesus' expressions about the hazards of association with Him (cf. Mk. 8:34-38; Jn. 15:20; 16:2) and an observation like Paul's in 1 Thess. 2:14f. are also probable factors in the semantic development of *mártys*. When the term becomes technical in the sense of one who seals his witness in death, the expression *homologḗtēs* is applied to those confessors who have not yet resisted to blood (cf. Eusebius *Onom.* 5.2).

*Bibliography.*–See bibliography in Bauer, rev., p. 494; *TDNT*, IV, *s.v.* μάρτυς κτλ. (Strathmann). See also R. P. Casey, in *BC*, V (1933), 30-37; F. W. Danker, *Benefactor* (1982), pp. 442-47; E. Günther, *ZNW*, 47 (1956), 145-161; F. Kattenbusch, *ZNW*, 4 (1903), 111-127; J. Leipoldt, *Der Tod bei Griechen und Juden* (1942), esp. pp. 63-84; E. Lohse, *Märtyrer und Gottesknecht* (1955).

F. W. DANKER

**MARVEL** [Heb. *pālā'*, *pele'*] (Ex. 34:10; Ps. 78:12); AV also MARVELOUS; NEB MIRACLE, WONDER; [Gk. *thaumázō*] (Mt. 8:10, 27; 9:33; 21:20; 22:22; Mk. 5:20; 6:6; Lk. 1:63; 2:33; 7:9; 8:25; 9:43; 11:14; 20:26; Jn. 3:10; 4:27; 5:20, 28; 7:15, 21; 2 Thess. 1:10; Rev. 17:6-8); AV also WONDER, ADMIRE; NEB ASTONISHED, TAKEN ABACK, AMAZED, ADMIRE, etc.; [*thaumastós*] (Jn. 9:30); NEB EXTRAORDINARY THING; **MARVELOUS** [Heb. *pālā'*] (1 Ch. 16:24; Job 5:9; 9:10; Ps. 96:3; 98:1; 118:23; 131:1; Isa. 29:14; Mic. 7:15; Zec. 8:6); AV also WONDER, HIGH; NEB also MIRACLE, IMPOSSIBLE, etc.; [Gk. *thaumastós*] (Mt. 21:42; Mk. 12:11; 1 Pet. 2:9); NEB also WONDERFUL; **MARVELOUSLY** [Heb. *pālā'*] (2 Ch. 26:15); NEB WONDERFULLY.

"Marvel" in the RSV expresses a sense of wonder and astonishment linked with an act of God's revelation or an object or experience that seems to "transcend all human possibilities" (*TDNT*, III, 29). The miracle is that He who is "hidden" (*see* HIDE) should now reveal Himself and allow people to experience His presence.

In the OT, Israel's faith in Yahweh as the Lord who shapes history and controls the powers of nature according to His sovereign will is affirmed in the remembrance of His "marvelous works" (1 Ch. 16:24; Ps. 96:3; cf. Ps. 9:1 [MT 2]; 78:11; etc.). Yahweh's extraordinary works of creation, saving actions toward His covenant people (Ps. 78:12; 98:1), and "unbroken rule" in their nation stun one's power of comprehension (Ps. 131:1; 118:23; Job 5:9; 9:10). Human wisdom, pride, and hypocrisy "perish" in the face of Yahweh's "wonderful and marvelous" deeds (Isa. 29:14; Zec. 8:6), which are "miraculous help" to His people (2 Ch. 26:15). The prophet desired Yahweh to "do marvels" as He had promised before (Ex. 34:10) in order to humiliate Israel's enemies (Mic. 7:15).

In the Synoptics *thaumázō* (also translated "wonder," Mt. 15:31; 27:14; Mk. 15:5; Lk. 24:41; etc.) is used in connection with miracle stories to show the miracles' effect on the spectators. The disciples expressed their astonishment at Christ's stilling the storm and asked, "What sort of man is this?" (Mt. 8:27; Lk. 8:25). Their amazement after seeing the barren fig tree that Jesus had cursed showed in their question, "How did the fig tree wither at once?" (Mt. 21:20). When Jesus cast the demons out of the dumb man, the crowd's exclamation was, "Never was anything like this seen in Israel" (9:33; cf. also Mk. 5:20; Lk. 9:43; 11:14).

The teachings of Jesus, e.g., about taxes (Mt. 22:22; cf. Mk. 12:17; Lk. 20:26), promoted wonder and surprise. The "divine wisdom with which he saw through and refuted his enemies" (*TDNT,* III, 38) astonished His opponents, according to early exegesis. In keeping with Jewish messianic expectation, Jesus applied Ps. 118:22ff. to Himself in the parable of the Wicked Husbandman (Mt. 21:42; Mk. 12:11).

"Marveling" occurs twice in Lukan Infancy stories (cf. Lk. 1:21 and 2:18 for *thaumázō* as "wondering"). People marveled at the miraculous concurrence of Zechariah and Elizabeth in naming John the Baptist (1:63). The prophecy of Simeon in the temple astonished Joseph and Mary (2:33). The other Synoptic uses of "marveling" refer to Jesus Himself: He expressed astonishment at the faith of the Roman centurion (Mt. 8:10; Lk. 7:9) and at the unbelief among His people in Nazareth (Mk. 6:6).

In the Gospel of John expressions of amazement and surprise are not related to individual miracles. Rather, "marvel" describes the "impact made by the works of Jesus" (*TDNT,* III, 40), as in 5:20, where He spoke with unbelieving opponents in mind, and in 7:21 (cf. Sir. 11:21), where He intended to surprise and shock (Brown, pp. 214, 312). Knowing the Jewish and rabbinic warnings against speaking with women in public (cf. Sir. 9:1-9; *Expos.G.T.*, I, 729), the disciples were "shocked" to see Jesus conversing with a Samaritan woman (Jn. 4:27). His learning caused wonderment among the Jews (7:14); in another context the blind man whom He healed taunted the Pharisees, "That's strange! Here you don't even know where he comes from; yet he opened my eyes" (9:30; Brown, p. 370). Yet Jesus' admonition in the story of Nicodemus (3:7) and in the saying concerning the hour of revelation (5:28; cf. 1 Jn. 3:13) is "Do not be surprised" (cf. the rabbinic phrase *'al tiṯmah,* "do not wonder," e.g., Mish. *Pesahim* vi.2).

In the rest of the NT uses of "marvel," the eschatological tones are strong. Peter reminded his readers that as God's own people they had been called out of the "darkness" of their former heathen lives to new life in God's "marvelous light" (1 Pet. 2:9; cf. 1 Clem. 36:2). In 2 Thess. 1:10 the verb is in the passive and refers to the manifestation of the Lord Jesus in His glory among the saints and believers.

A more literal translation of Rev. 17:6b is: "And seeing her I was amazed with great amazement." John's astonishment may have been mystification regarding the significance of the sight (17:6f.), or it may have been human wonderment at the sight of such an antigodly being (*TDNT,* III, 41). In the latter case the angel's question may be seen as a warning to prevent astonishment from leading to prostration before the beast and whore.

***Bibliography.***–R. E. Brown, *Gospel According to John I-XIII* (*AB,* 1966); *Expos.G.T., in loc.*; *TDNT,* III, *s.v.* θαῦμα (G. Bertram).

D. K. McKim

**MARY** [Gk. *Maria, Mariam* < Heb. *miryām*–'fat one'?].

**1.** Mary Magdalene. The name Magdalene was derived from Magdala, a town on the western shore of the Sea of Galilee. The only mention of her outside the Crucifixion and Resurrection narratives is in Lk. 8:2. (She is not to be identified, as she frequently used to be, with the woman of Lk. 7, "who was a sinner.") Jesus had cast several demons out of her, and this helps to explain the devotion to Him that she showed by the following actions. (1) Together with other formerly demon-possessed women, she followed Jesus and His disciples from town to town, helping to support them from her own means (Lk. 8:1-3). (2) She followed Him to Jerusalem to care for His needs (Mt. 27:55), and even when His disciples fled, she followed Him to the cross (Mk. 15:40). (3) She watched to see where He would be buried (Mk. 15:47). (4) On the day of the Resurrection she was among the first who went to the tomb to bring spices for Jesus' body (Mt. 28:1; Mk. 16:1). On seeing that the tomb was empty, she ran and told Peter and John (Jn. 20:2) and then returned to the tomb. There she met Jesus and wanted to cling to Him. But He told her not to hold on to Him, for He wanted her to realize that His former way of living among the disciples was to be changed, since He was to ascend to heaven. He commanded her to go and tell the disciples that He would ascend into heaven (Jn. 20:17); she obediently went and reported, "I have seen the Lord."

**2.** Mary the sister of Martha and Lazarus, who all lived in Bethany. Two striking characteristics of her are set forth in the Gospels. (1) She had a contemplative nature. Luke reports that on one occasion when Jesus stopped at their home, Mary sat at His feet listening to Jesus while Martha was busy as a hostess (10:38-42). Jesus complimented Mary on choosing the "good portion." John reports that a year later at the death of Lazarus, Mary stayed home while Martha went out to meet Jesus (11:20). When Jesus subsequently visited Bethany, Martha again served Him, while Mary expressed her devotion to Him by anointing Him with perfume (Jn. 12:1-8).

(2) She was deeply devoted to Jesus. Mt. 26:6-13, Mk. 14:3-9, and Jn. 12:1-8 all tell of an incident in Bethany at the home of Simon the leper, where Mary lavished nard (perfume) on Jesus. Judas—and even the other disciples—objected to such extravagance as a waste, but Jesus defended her action as a "beautiful thing" (Mt. 26:10), stating that it would be remembered wherever the gospel was preached. (This incident should not be confused with a similar anointing of Jesus by a woman "who was a sinner" in Lk. 7:36-50.)

**3.** Mary the mother of James and Joseph (sometimes called Joses). She was probably the wife of Clopas (Jn. 19:25; cf. Mk. 15:40), but this depends on two suppositions: (1) that "Mary of Clopas" is not in apposition to "his mother's sister" (this seems likely, since there would hardly be two Marys in one family); and (2) that the literal "Mary the of Clopas" means "Mary the wife of Clopas" (it seems unlikely that it means "Mary the daughter of Clopas," since she seems to have had grown-up sons and would more likely have been known by her relation to her husband than to her father; see the comms.).

This Mary's devotion to Jesus can be seen by the following data. (1) With other women, she followed Jesus in Galilee and to Jerusalem, taking care of His needs (Mt. 27:55; Mk. 15:40f.; cf. Lk. 8:3; 23:49). (2) In spite of danger, she stayed close to Him at the cross (Mt. 27:55; Mk. 15:40; Jn. 19:25). (3) She watched His burial (Mt. 27:61; Mk. 15:47; cf. Lk. 23:55). (4) She was with the first group at the empty tomb, bringing spices (Mt. 28:1; Mk. 16:1; cf. Lk. 23:56). (5) She reported His resurrection to the disciples (Lk. 24:10).

**4.** Mary the mother of John Mark. Several facts about her can be gathered from Acts 12:12, the only place where she is mentioned in Scripture. (1) She was the mother of John Mark, who helped Paul and Barnabas and probably wrote the Gospel of Mark. (2) She was wealthy, for her home was large enough for many to gather there for prayer, and she had at least one maidservant. (3) Her house was a prominent center for the local church, since Peter went directly to it after his release from prison, and the church was praying there. (4) She was probably a widow, since there is no mention of her husband. (5) She was the aunt of the missionary Barnabas (Col. 4:10).

**5.** Mary of Rome. All that is known about her is that she was one of the twenty-four people whom Paul greeted at the end of his letter to the Romans (16:6), and that she worked hard for the church at Rome. These data suggest that she was one of its earliest members.

E. H. PALMER

**6.** Mary the mother of Jesus.

I. Ancestry
II. The Virgin Birth
III. Marital Relations
IV. Character
V. Separation from Her Son
VI. Mariology

***I. Ancestry.***–Just as Joseph was descended from David (Mt. 1:1-16), so also was Mary. This cannot be proved conclusively from the genealogy of Lk. 3:23-38; otherwise there would never have been the long and indecisive controversy as to whether "of the house of David" goes with "virgin" or "Joseph" in Lk. 1:27. The former seems more probable. But v. 32 does point in the direction of Mary's Davidic ancestry when it says, "The Lord God will give to him the throne of his father David," for Mary was engaged but not yet married to Joseph. It is evident that Mary realized that Joseph was excluded when she said, "How shall this be, since I have no husband?"

Similarly, in Acts 2:30 the expression Luke used of Jesus' ancestry, "one of his [i.e., David's] descendants," can hardly refer to an ancestry through a purely legal relationship, via Joseph. It implies a flesh-and-blood relationship, through Mary (cf. Rom. 1:3; 2 Tim. 2:8). *See* GENEALOGY OF JESUS.

***II. The Virgin Birth.***–The VIRGIN BIRTH, or, more accurately, the virgin conception, is attested in many ways in Matthew and Luke. (1) The sharp contrast between the long series of verses that use "begot" and the statement that Joseph was "the husband of Mary, of whom Jesus was born" (Mt. 1:16) clearly implies that a man was not involved in the procreation of Jesus. (2) Mt. 1:18 states, "Before they came together she was found to be with child of the Holy Spirit." (3) Joseph's desire to divorce her quietly presupposes that he had had no sexual relations with her (Mt. 1:19). (4) The angel said "That which is conceived in her is of the Holy Spirit" (Mt. 1:20). (5) In citing Isa. 7:14, Matthew called Mary a virgin (1:23). (6) Joseph "knew her not until she had borne a son" (Mt. 1:25). (7) Twice Luke called her a virgin and said that she was betrothed, which, although almost tantamount to marriage, was not marriage in the fullest sense (1:27). (8) Mary was amazed at the angel's announcement that she would conceive, since, as she said, "I know not a man" (Lk. 1:34, ASV). (9) Luke said delicately but explicitly that the Holy Spirit, and not Joseph, would be the cause of the conception (1:35).

Thus Joseph was completely excluded from the procreation of Jesus. This fact, along with Mary's completely passive role, points to God's sovereignty in the Virgin Birth. Mary responded to the angel's announcement with "Behold, I am the handmaid of the Lord" (Lk. 1:38), but she was not first asked permission. Rather, she was simply told by Gabriel that she would conceive and bear a son. She responded in faith and obedience to that sovereign act of God.

***III. Marital Relations.***–The Roman Catholic Church teaches that Mary was a virgin *ante partum, in partu, et post partum*. The *ante partum* is substantiated in the comments above on the virgin conception. The *in partu* concept (of virginity during birth) is based on highly speculative deductions. The *post partum* or perpetual-virginity concept is held by some Protestants and was held by many Reformers (e.g., Calvin in his sermon on Mt. 1:22-25), but the Scriptures probably do not substantiate it.

The evidence points to normal marital relations between Mary and Joseph after the birth of Jesus. (1) The negative *ouk* plus *héōs,* "until" ("knew her not until she had borne a son"), does not automatically mean that the negative action is replaced by a positive one, i.e., that Joseph did "know" her after Jesus' birth (Mt. 1:25). But it often does imply a reversal of action. And if Mary and Joseph did not have normal marital relationships after the birth of Jesus, then the "until" clause has little meaning.

(2) The term "first-born son" (Lk. 2:7) does not always signify that other children follow this birth. If Mary had died in childbirth, Jesus would still have been called her firstborn. But the term usually signifies that other children followed and, in the light of the previous and following two comments, it is significant.

(3) Several passages speak of the brothers and sisters of Jesus and even name some of them (Mt. 12:46f.; Mk. 3:31f.; 6:3; Lk. 8:19f.; Jn. 2:12; 7:3, 5, 10; Acts 1:14). Although the Greek word can be taken in a wider sense than uterine brothers, the natural usage would be in the uterine sense.

(4) Much of Roman Catholic argumentation for the *semper virgo* concept stems from the thought that sexual abstinence or celibacy is more holy than sexual activity. But there is no basis for that idea in either the OT or the NT.

The natural reading of these several passages is that Mary and Joseph had normal marital relations.

***IV. Character.***–The intent of Scripture is not to portray Mary, but Jesus (Jn. 20:31). Matthew sets the tone for the entire NT with its opening words: "The book of the genealogy of Jesus Christ" (cf. also the openings of the other three Gospels). Yet in the course of the telling of the good news, a small glimpse of Mary's character is given. One dominant trait stands out: her faith in God. It evidences itself in her humility, obedience, praise, and familiarity with the OT.

When Gabriel announced to her that she would have the awesome task of carrying in her womb and then nurturing the Messiah, the son of God, and that this baby would not be from Joseph but from the Spirit of God, instead of weighing her unworthiness and insufficiency, or expressing disbelief as Zechariah did (Lk. 1:18), after the initial question she simply declared in humble, faithful obedience, "I am the Lord's servant; as you have spoken, so be it" (NEB). When Mary did not understand a message from an angel or her Son, she believingly pondered its meaning (Lk. 2:19, 51).

Mary's response to Elizabeth was steeped in praise of God. This is seen not only in the express statements, "My soul magnifies the Lord" and "my spirit rejoices in God my Savior," but also in the recitation of all the good things God has done (Lk. 1:46-56). In addition to praise, the Magnificat abounds in true humility before God, which is the foundation of her obedience.

That she was at home with the OT is seen in her allusions and phraseology in the Magnificat and in her faithful adherence to the OT regulations about circumcision (Lk. 2:21), purification and presentation in the temple (vv. 22-28), and the Passover (v. 41).

***V. Separation from Her Son.***–Mary's prime task in life was to bear the Savior of the world and bring Him up. But once that work was accomplished, and even while she was doing it, she had to begin to separate herself from her son. Although she was His mother, she was subservient to Him. He was her Lord and Savior. She needed to ask Him for the forgiveness of her sins. This fact of necessary separation and subservience must be kept in mind in order to understand the post-Infancy narratives where Mary appears.

*A. The Boy Jesus at the Temple (Lk. 2:41-51).* Although the conclusion of this episode is that Jesus went home "and was obedient" to His parents, there is already a hint of the separation between Jesus and His parents that had to come. For the first time He intimated His messianic work, when He asked them, "Did you not know that I must be in my Father's house?" (2:49).

*B. Wedding at Cana (Jn. 2:1-12).* Although Jesus was still obedient to Mary at the temple, the separation was clearly evidenced at the wedding in Cana. The story begins with "the mother of Jesus" (2:1-11) but ends with the disciples. Mary knew of John the Baptist's pointing to the Lamb of God and of the calling of Andrew, John, Peter, and Philip. She recalled the miraculous birth thirty years earlier and the appearance of the angels and the star. And now at the wedding, as His mother, she was suggesting that He assert His authority. Surely His hour had come.

But Jesus, in order to draw more sharply the Lord-servant, Savior-saved relationship between Himself and His mother, said to her: "O woman, what have you to do with me? My hour has not yet come" (2:4). He used "woman" instead of "mother" not out of disrespect but as a polite form of address to show that He was no longer under His mother. The separation was now definite. Mother must no longer dominate. He was the Messiah. John caught this import by beginning with Jesus' mother but ending the episode by narrating that this was the first of the signs Jesus did and that His disciples put their faith in Him.

*C. Jesus' Mother and Brothers (Mt. 12:46-50; Mk. 3:31-35; Lk. 8:19-21).* It is only by understanding this spirit of independence from His mother that Jesus' reply to His mother and brothers can be understood. When they tried to see Him, it was not out of discourtesy that He pointed to His disciples and said, "Here are my mother and my brothers!" Rather, He wanted to impress on His mother and brothers that they must become His spiritual daughter and sons.

*D. Mary at the Cross (Jn. 19:25-27).* At the cross the separation was made definite. The close mother-son relationship now had to be severed by death and replaced by a John-Mary, son-mother relationship. But more importantly, Mary had to learn that the woman-Lord relationship had to replace that of the mother-son. In this tender moment Jesus brought this out clearly and kindly by addressing her as "woman."

*E. Mary and the Apostles.* This separation of Mary from her son found its fulfillment in her spiritual union with Him. Luke provided this final glimpse when he stated that after the Ascension Mary joined in continual prayer with the apostles (Acts 1:14). Nothing more is recorded of her, even though, in the judgment of many, Luke's Infancy narrative indicates that he had received this information from her and therefore had been close to her. Mary had fulfilled her task of bearing the Messiah. Once her work was done, she had to join other believers and be like them. When Luke recorded Peter's Pentecostal speech or Paul's work, he made no reference to Mary. Her place was in the Church, not in heaven as the Dispensatrix of all grace.

John's treatment of her in his Gospel proclaims the same truth. Jn. 19:27 reports that from the time of the crucifixion John took her into his home. If any apostle could have told a great deal about Mary, it was John. Yet he mentioned her only twice (at the wedding of Cana and at the cross), and on both occasions instead of exalting her he brought out that she was subservient to her son. This fits in perfectly with the purpose of his Gospel (Jn. 20:31), which is to point to Christ. E. H. PALMER

*VI. **Mariology.**–A. Mary in Scripture. 1. Dignity of Mary.* It is not to be questioned that Mary occupies a place of peculiar honor and dignity in Scripture. To be chosen as the human mother of the Messiah, the incarnate Word, is indeed to be the recipient of the high favor or grace of God (Lk. 1:28). There is thus every reason for the Magnificat as Mary's song of praise for the exaltation of His humble servant, and for the greeting of Elizabeth in v. 42: "And why is this granted me, that the mother of my Lord should come to me?"

Nor is Mary to be honored only for this exaltation. We must also respect her humble but obedient faith manifested in response to the divine decision and communication. What she was told was undoubtedly difficult to credit (Lk. 1:29, 34). Yet in spite of her initial questioning and astonishment, Mary made a quick response of faith (Lk. 1:38). Again, what was asked exposed her to particular difficulties in spite of its intrinsic dignity. Yet while she must have had many fears, her "Let it be to me" is in its way a model of unassuming yet resolute obedience to the divine call and commission — an obedience that she no doubt continued to manifest in the comparative obscurity of her later church membership (Acts 1:14).

That her motherhood involved a unique exercise of miraculous power is a further reason to approach this servant of God with due respect. We can easily do her disservice at this point by excessively exalting Mary in virtue of the miracle. We can also do her disservice, however, by rejecting the miracle. Neither mistake should be allowed to obscure the singular dignity of her service as the virgin mother.

*2. Fallibility of Mary.* Nevertheless, when these points have been made, it is still to be recognized that Mary did nothing of herself even in this supreme moment of her life. She was passive in the great miracle of the conception of Christ. She simply offered herself as a handmaid of the Lord. Neither in herself nor as a representative of the race did she contribute positively to the great work of reconciliation. Rightly in the Magnificat she turned her thoughts to God as her Savior. So little did she participate in the final act of reconciliation that Jesus on the cross could not merely make provision for her but as it were transferred the filial relationship, in order that He might truly die alone and in order that the motherhood might not be misunderstood in relation to His resurrection, ascension, and session.

Moreover, as Mary contributed nothing of herself to the great work of God, she gave evidence that in herself she was only an errant and sinful mortal like all others. She did not even grasp the wonder of what took place at Bethlehem (Lk. 2:19). She was bewildered by the action of the Lord Jesus as a boy in the temple (Lk. 2:48-50). With the brethren, she even tried to interrupt the public ministry of the Lord (Mk. 3:31ff.). Although she was faithful at the cross and the tomb, learning the aptness of her name and experiencing to the full the piercing prophesied by Simeon, she was no quicker than others to see through the tragedy to the triumph.

We are not to censure Mary for her human fallibility or to dwell upon it in a spirit of superiority. She is not worse than others in her lack of understanding at these early stages. She won through to a place among the first believers when what was dark was made plain. But the point is that, if she is not to be blamed or scorned, she is also not to be exalted as a supernatural being full of all graces and wisdom and exempt from all human frailty. We honor Mary best by giving her the dignity that is hers in Scripture and not by indulging in speculative glorification.

*B. Early Church. 1. Virgin Birth.* A first stage in thinking about Mary was the legitimate defense of the Virgin Birth against the unbelief of the Jews and the scoffing of pagans. The Apologists in particular were exercised about this question. Justin Martyr, for example, devoted much attention to the fulfillment of Isa. 7:14, both in his *Apology* and in the *Dialogue with Trypho*; in the *Apology* he also took into account the corrupt parallels in pagan mythology, which he ascribed to Satanic imitation. The miracle of the Virgin Birth is naturally linked with the chastity of Mary herself, so that some of these defenses perhaps tend to shift the emphasis at some points to the moral character of the Virgin. In some writers the parallel of Christ with Adam and the fulfillment in the Virgin Birth of the prophecy of Gen. 3:15 also suggest an understanding of Mary as the new Eve. But one hardly sees more than the possibilities of later Mariology in these first postapostolic statements.

*2. Perpetual Virginity.* From the later 2nd cent., the growing emphasis on the ascetic life, and particularly on celibacy, as a supposedly superior form of Christian practice combined with the emphasis on the chastity of Mary to produce the very different conception of her perpetual virginity. To the monastic mind, influenced to some degree by dualistic considerations, all sexual intercourse, even in lawful wedlock, carried with it at least a suggestion of sin, and therefore it was inconceivable that after the birth of Jesus Mary should have lived a normal married life and had children in the usual way. To be sure, there are references in the Bible to the brethren of Jesus, but it could be argued that the Greek term does not necessarily denote true brothers and sisters, that it might be used for cousins or for the children of Joseph by a previous marriage, and that in any case the word cannot be applied too strictly, since even children of Joseph and Mary would not be full brothers and sisters of Jesus. By the end of the 4th cent. the great Jerome could thus condemn as a shocking error the idea of Mary as a normal wife and mother, and Bishop Siricius wrote to Anysius (392): "For the Lord Jesus would not have chosen to be born of a virgin if he had judged that she would be so incontinent as to taint the birthplace of the body of the Lord, the home of the eternal king, with the seed of human intercourse." One detects a certain strain of Docetism, as well as of Gnostic dualism, in this pontifical utterance. Also apparent are a common Mariological phenomenon, namely, the appeal to the glory of the son as a ground for exalting the mother, and a refusal plainly to face up to the biblical data.

*3. Theotókos.* The christological debates of the 4th, 5th, and 6th cents. added a new element to the developing Mariology of the period. As we have seen, the exaltation of the Son naturally seemed to many to carry with it the exaltation of His mother. Thus the struggle for the true deity of Christ in His incarnation demanded literal acceptance of the statement in Lk. 1:35 and therefore of the implied fact that Mary is the one who bears God (*theotókos*), i.e., the mother of God . In the Nestorian controversy of the early 5th cent. *theotókos* became indeed a catchword of christological orthodoxy. To reject it was to reject the true deity of Christ, to see an illegitimate distinction between the divine nature and the human, and therefore to overthrow the unity of the person. Now from the christological angle and in a christological context the term is in fact unobjectionable and has been accepted by all orthodox theologians. Yet it is not a biblical term, and is perhaps better avoided in view of its dangerous Mariological implications when isolated from Christology and applied more strictly to Mary herself. We are certainly not surprised to find that insistence on the term carried with it a spread of false notions concerning Mary, both in relation to salvation as the new Eve and in relation to the Godhead as the mother, which helped to distort later theology and to prepare the way for the further elevation of Mary.

*C. Middle Ages. 1. Theological Considerations.* Several forces combined to foster Mariological development during the Middle Ages, especially, although not exclusively, in the Western church. Among the more directly theological factors we may mention the whole conception of sacramental grace, the consequent false dilemma of postbaptismal sin, the idea of a compensating treasury of merit and the efficacy of the intercession of saints, and the associated sense of the need of a special intercessor between the Lord and His people after the analogy of Cana of Galilee, where the Son is approached through the mother. In relation to the person of Mary there is no great development during this period apart from the growing tendency to postulate her freedom from original sin. But there is a marked growth of emphasis on the mediatorial or intercessory office and work of Mary and therefore a growing cult of the Virgin that found expression even in the prayers of so great a theologian as Anselm.

*2. Intercession of Mary.* The theological root of this emphasis, and of the related cult, is the postulate that nothing but severity can be expected from Jesus once we have spoiled His work and spurned His sacrifice by postbaptismal sin. To be sure, salvation from hell still finally depends on the atoning work of Christ. But how can we approach Him again when we have failed so miserably? Can we expect at His hands anything but the prolonged if purifying torments of purgatory? It is here that the intercession of saints, and more particularly of Mary, can help us, even as the pleas of confessors helped those who lapsed in days of persecution. The mother, it is argued, will plead our cause with the Son; her gentleness will mitigate His severity. As the mother of God, and therefore as Lady even in the courts of heaven, already exalted in virtue of her sanctity, she is in a position of influence to open again the fountain of divine mercy. Hence penitent sinners may turn the more naturally to her than to the Lord.

*3. Veneration of Mary.* They do so, however, with a full sense of her exaltation, as suppliants enlisting the aid of one who has power and authority. Hence there is required an adoration of Mary in her greatness and goodness. Mary's intercession is naturally accompanied by veneration of Mary. In strict theological definition, of course, careful distinctions are made at this point. The Lord Himself is still true God and the true fountain of grace, even though an approach is made to Him through the mother. The Virgin is mother of God and Lady of heaven, but she obviously cannot be described as herself God. The worship or veneration rendered to her cannot be the same as that accorded to God. In terms of the distinctions here made, the term Mariolatry is not strictly correct for the devotion rendered to Mary. *Latria* (true worship) is proper to God alone. *Hyperdulia* (extreme honor) is proper to Mary, and *dulia* (honor) to the saints. It can hardly be contested, however, that in relation to both the forms and the language of veneration these theological distinctions are of little practical significance. The same forms both of speech and action are used in relation to Mary as to God Himself. Indeed, some of the prayers and hymns to Mary achieve a magnificence and extravagance of adulation nowhere surpassed in addresses either to the trinity or to any one of the three persons. Mariolatry may not correspond to the verbal definitions; it is certainly in keeping with the attested practice.

Certain nontheological factors probably contributed quite heavily to this development. The notion of a female deity is widespread in paganism, and in Mariology there is a modified though perhaps unconscious counterpart filling a gap in popular religion. The medieval development of chivalry, with its ideal of the lady's honor and knightly devotion to it, both derived from and yet also influenced thinking about Mary. The rough-and-ready justice of the age, occasionally tempered by the gentler feelings and pleas of women, provided something of a model for the imagined procedure in the court of heaven. Without the basic theological misunderstanding it is doubtful whether these factors could have played any great part. But in the circumstances they could make a strong and distinctive contribution, especially at the popular level.

*D. Modern Period. 1. Trent.* Rather strangely, the Council of Trent made no great addition to Mariological development in spite of the decisive Reformation criticism and the insistence of the Reformers on the sole mediatorship of Christ. The most that can be said is that no ground was yielded to the Reformers, e.g., in relation to the intercession or veneration of Mary, and that the statement on original sin left the way open for the later dogma of the Immaculate Conception: "It is not its intent to include in this decree on original sin the blessed and immaculate Virgin Mary, Mother of God." As yet, however, there was no positive definition of this dogma.

*2. The Mary Cult.* The Roman Catholic revival of the 19th cent. seems to have brought a tremendous development of popular Mariology continuing far into the 20th century. Congregations of Mary were formed, and, incongruous though it might seem, an age affected by romantic ideas of love almost seemed to find a place for a quasi-erotic element, calling young men especially to dedicate to the Virgin the devotion that young women might more easily give to Jesus. The part played by this element in the whole development of the Mary cult is, of course, difficult to assess. One may suspect that it is present even in an early celibate like Jerome. It is certainly a factor in the medieval period. It is an irrefutable element in the pagan intrusion. It seems almost to have been sanctioned in the 19th century. We certainly go astray if we isolate this element and make it a guiding principle in our whole understanding. On the other hand, one of the surprising features of Mariology is the part played by popular instincts and pressures, so that in the later period at least the theological definition seems to be a product of popular demand rather than the contrary.

*3. The Immaculate Conception.* The Mary cult of the 19th cent. was quickly accompanied by the promulgation of the Immaculate Conception by Pius IX in the bull *Ineffabilis Deus* (1854). The statement is: "We declare, pronounce and define: the doctrine that maintains that the most Blessed Virgin Mary in the first instant of her conception, by a unique grace and privilege of the omnipotent God, and in consideration of the merits of Christ Jesus the Savior of the human race, was preserved free from all stain of original sin, is a doctrine revealed by God, and therefore must be firmly and constantly held by all the faithful." It should be noted that the pope took the initiative in this definition, thus making an early practical experiment in the direction of papal infallibility in a field where he could rely on strong popular support. The status of Jesus Christ is carefully safeguarded in the decree, since the Virgin's freedom from original sin is not by nature but only in virtue of His merits. Yet the uniqueness of the Virgin is also asserted, since a completely sinless life is now postulated, whether in respect of original sin or actual. The claim to divine revelation is odd in view of the silence of Scripture and the late promulgation of the doctrine in Christian history. Incidentally, the Immaculate Conception is not to be confused with the purity of Mary in respect of the Virgin Birth.

*4. The Assumption.* It has often been noted that popes whose ex cathedra pronouncements are now claimed to be infallible are very sparing in such pronouncements. Nor is it less significant that Mariology again suggested itself as a safe and proper sphere for the exercise of this alleged infallibility. The next stage was reached in the *Munificentissimus Deus* of Pius XII (1950), which defined as an article of divinely revealed faith, necessary to be believed on pain of damnation, that the Blessed Virgin Mary, having completed her earthly life, was in body and soul assumed into heavenly glory. This strange belief seems to come originally from some apocryphal fourth-century writings (*The Passing of Mary,* etc.), which Gelasius had condemned as spurious, but the point of which was adopted by writers like Gregory of Tours. John of Damascus described the assumption as an ancient catholic tradition, and from his age it passed into the Middle Ages as a pious opinion. Nevertheless, as late as 1740 Benedict XIV could say that the tradition is not of such a kind as to warrant the elevation of the belief to the rank of a doctrine of faith. The twentieth-century decision, however, is more in keeping with Mariological development. For if it is inconceivable that she should have been guilty of any form of sin, it is surely no less inconceivable that she should be subject to the ordinary processes of mortality and corruption. In other words, if Mary is to be removed from the ordinary ranks of human nature in virtue of the one unique and special action of the birth of Jesus, she might just as well be removed at every point.

*5. Coredemptrix.* Recent Mariological development has been related more to the person of Mary than to her work, although the two aspects are plainly linked. Emphasis on the intercessory role of the Virgin has increased rather than diminished, and the intensified Mary cult is obviously related to her assumed mediatorial role. Hence many circles believed for a time that the strands would be pulled together at an even higher level by her official recognition as mediatrix or coredemptrix, which would further elevate her person and exalt the conception of her work, both in its original stage as the mother of the Lord and in its later stages as the one who mercifully pleads for sinners. But more recent developments in Roman Catholicism have halted this process and have raised serious and yet unanswered questions regarding the status of Mary.

*E. Significance of Mariology.* In view of the slender basis on which it is built, Mariology is in some sense a mystifying structure. What is the secret of its power? What is the driving religious impulse behind it? How are we to explain and therefore to meet it?

*1. Heresy.* A first answer is that it takes up and perpetuates various heretical but persistent conceptions that appeal to the natural mind. The strain of Docetism has already called for notice. But most important in this regard is probably the element of Gnostic or semi-Gnostic dualism, especially in its interrelation with the high estimation of virginity. A failure to understand and accept the normative authority of Scripture removed the most powerful restraining factor and allowed fanciful traditions unduly to influence later thinking and action.

*2. Paganism.* Yet Mariology can hardly be explained merely in terms of such factors, and we may therefore suggest the second answer, that it derives much of its power from its enshrining many of the conceptions and impulses of pagan religion. The quasi-erotic factor may be recalled in this respect. Also relevant are the belief in female as well as male deities, the whole conception of deity in terms of supernatural humanity, and the ease with which pagan festivals can often be adapted to the Mary cult.

*3. Anthropocentricity.* Again, however, we cannot come to the simple conclusion that Mariology is merely a badly baptized paganism. We are thus led to a third and final answer, which in a very real sense underlies the first two, that Mariology corresponds in a Christianized form and context to our constant urge and need to fashion our own religion, to achieve our own salvation, to be our own god. In Mariology, of course, there is a twofold reservation, which can also serve as a twofold disguise. The movement here takes place within the saving work and revelation of God Himself in grace, and it is related to the idealized figure of Mary rather than to humanity in general. Yet a little reflection shows that in this idealized figure we may indeed cooperate in our salvation, attain almost to the title of deity, and enjoy an autonomous apotheosis. To see this heart of Mariology is to understand why it could so readily incorporate heretical and pagan features. It is also to see why it could arise so easily at a time when the evangelical doctrines were increasingly obscured. It is to grasp why it can flourish most readily in the Roman synergism worked out in the Middle Ages and formally sanctioned from the Tridentine period. It is to perceive the perennial appeal to the human mind and heart either of Mariology or of its more rationalistic substitute in Liberal Protestantism. And it is finally to see the antidote in an exclusive committal to, and proclamation of, Jesus Christ Himself as our only and all-sufficient Savior both in life and in death.

***Bibliography.***–H. Denziger, *Enchiridion Symbolorum* (rev. ed. 1973); Pohle-Preuss, *Dogmatic Theology* (1911-17), VI; G. Miegge, *The Virgin Mary: The Roman Catholic Marian Doctrine* (Eng. tr. 1956); K. Barth, *CD*, I/2, pp. 139ff.; *Catholic Encyclopedia* (15 vols., 1907-1914).

G. W. BROMILEY

**MARY, PASSING OF.** *See* APOCRYPHAL GOSPELS II.F.

**MASADA** mə-sä′də [Heb. *m^e ṣāḏâ*–'mountain fortress'; Gk. *Masada*]. A rocky plateau rising from the western shore of the Dead Sea, used as a fortress by Herod the Great and then by the Zealots, and given lasting memory by Josephus. Although it is not mentioned by name in the Bible, this subject should be included in a Bible dictionary for several reasons. (1) It allows further insight into the almost psychoneurotic character of Herod the Great. (2) It sheds light on the next-to-final chapter of the Jewish revolt against Rome. (3) The manuscript fragments discovered there include canonical as well as deuterocanonical writings that are indisputably related to those found at Qumrân.

I. Physical Description
II. Historical Outline
III. Herodian Constructions
IV. Zealot Occupation

***I. Physical Description.***–Masada (es-Sebbe) is well described by Josephus: "A rock of no slight circumference and lofty from end to end is abruptly terminated on every side by deep ravines, the precipices rising sheer from an invisible base and being inaccessible to the foot of any living creature, save in two places where the rock permits no easy ascent" (*BJ* vii.8.3 [280], *LCL*). It is an isolated rock bluff or table mountain 16 km. (10 mi.) S of En-gedi on the western shore of the Dead Sea, opposite el-Lisan ("the tongue") peninsula. The rock is separated from the cliffs that border the western shore of the Dead Sea by deep wadis on the west and south. According to D. Baly, Masada is at the northeastern end of the Dimona ridge (*GB*, 2nd ed., pp. 35f.). The top is 59 m. (193 ft.) above sea level, and the surface of the Dead Sea is 399 m. (1309 ft.) below sea level (1976 survey; still lower at the time of this writing). Masada rises to a height of about 400 m. (1300 ft.) above the surrounding land, but because of the accumulation of detritus at its base, its eastern face is 250 m. (820 ft.) high, and its western face 180 m. (600 ft.). Masada is about 580 m. (1900 ft.) from north to south and 200 m. (650 ft.) from east to west, pointed at each end, with almost sheer sides. The top, with an area of about 8 ha. (20 acres), is flat, somewhat lower at the southern end, so that to a traveler approaching from the north it resembles a huge ship.

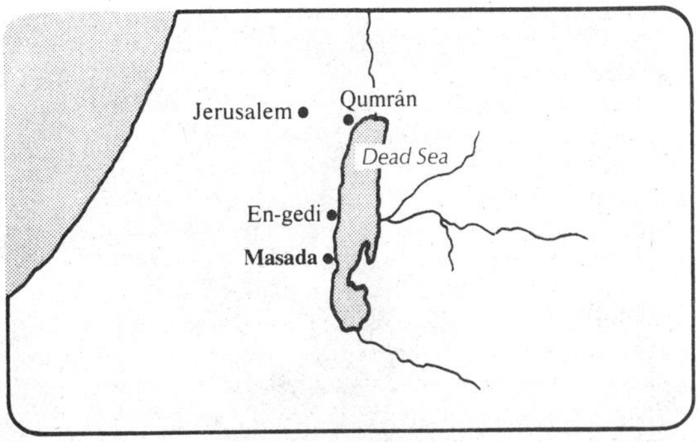


There are only two approaches to the top of Masada. One is the famous "snake path" (cf. Josephus *BJ* vii.8.3 [282]), a tortuous trail that winds up the eastern side and takes a person in excellent condition fifty minutes to climb. The other is a ramp built by the Romans during the siege of Masada that in effect connects the insular rock with the cliffs from which it had originally been severed. Josephus mentioned a second "track" on the western side "by which the approach is easier" (281), which "Herod barred at its narrowest point by a great tower" (293). This track was probably covered by the Roman ramp. A gate in the western wall suggests an earlier access at that point.

***II. Historical Outline.***–According to Y. Yadin remains (discovered 1963-1965) in caves in the Masada cliffs revealed Chalcolithic occupation in the 4th millennium. Scattered sherds from the time of the first temple (10th-7th cents. B.C.) have been found, but there are no indications of buildings or other evidence of occupation. Coins of Alexander Janneus (104-78 B.C.) indicate that Josephus may have been correct in attributing the first defenses on Masada to the Hasmonean period (specifically to the high priest Jonathan [161-143]; cf. *BJ* vii.8.3 [285]). Yadin, however, considered any buildings and cisterns constructed on the site before the Herodian period the work of the king Alexander Janneus (*Masada*, p. 203).

In 42 B.C. Helix, who opposed Herod and his brother Phasael, occupied Masada while Herod was in Syria. Recognizing the military value of the place, Herod recaptured it and located his family there while he went to Rome to claim his kingdom (40-39 B.C.; *BJ* i.12.1f. [236-39]; i.13.7f. [263-67]; i.15.1 [286f.]; *Ant.* xiv.13.8f. [355-364]; xiv.14.6 [390-93]). Upon his return from Rome Herod forced Antigonus to lift the siege of Masada, thus freeing the members of his family (*BJ* i.15.3f. [290-94]; i.16.1 [303]; *Ant.* xiv.15.1f. [394-405]).

The major period of building at Masada was during the reign of Herod the Great (37-4 B.C.) and evidently occurred in two stages. Some of the earlier construction, which Yadin was inclined to attribute to Herod rather than to

Aerial view of Masada showing Herod's three-tiered palace (W. Braun)

Jonathan or Janneus, was altered by later operations (see III below).

The Romans had a garrison in Masada from *ca*. A.D. 6 until the summer of 66, the first year of the Jewish Revolt, when the soldiers were slain by Jews (*BJ* ii.17.1 [208]). The Jews — called "Sicarii" by Josephus and "Zealots" by Yadin — then took over the site, modifying buildings, constructing dwellings, a synagogue, and ritual baths (*miqwîm* or *miqwā'ôṯ*) and altering the place in other ways. The revolt ended in 73 (see IV below). There are indications of the presence of a Roman garrison at Masada in 73-111. During the Byzantine era (5th-6th cents. A.D.) a chapel and monks' cells were built. Of these periods only the Herodian and the Zealot are of concern in this article.

***III. Herodian Constructions.***–There were two large Herodian palaces, the northern and the western, and a few smaller palaces. The northern palace was a private villa (hence Yadin's term "palace-villa"), built in three tiers at the northern end of the rock and on its cliff. The uppermost level consisted of a large semicircular porch and ornately decorated living quarters (only four rooms, indicating that it was a family villa rather than a royal palace). The middle level, 20 m. (66 ft.) below, had a circular pavilion and a colonnade whose columns and capitals suggest that it had been roofed over; to the south were the living quarters, described by Yadin as "a place where one could sit, eat, relax and look at the view" (*Masada,* p. 59). The lowest level, 15 m. (50 ft.) below the second, consisted of buildings on a platform 17 by 17 m. (57 by 57 ft.) that was raised at the narrowest point of the rock and therefore required elaborately engineered retaining walls. Mosaic floors, beautiful frescoes, and columns and panels simulated in plaster (some veined to resemble marble), provided lavish decoration throughout the villa. For a description with numerous illustrations (monochrome and color) see Yadin, *Masada,* pp. 41-86.

The western palace was the largest (3340 sq. m., 36,000 sq. ft.) and was the administrative center. It was divided into four blocks: the southeastern containing living quarters and the throne room; the northwestern, the administrative wing; the northeastern, service and work rooms; and the southwestern, store rooms, one very long (70 m., 230 ft.) and three smaller. The palace's main entrance was on its north side, and the western gate was just N of the palace itself. (Cf. Yadin, *Masada* 117-140.) The smaller palaces were for members of the king's family and for the court functionaries.

South of the palace-villa was an elaborate bath, very well preserved, built in Roman fashion with warm, tepid, and cold rooms. Alongside, to the east and to the south, were large storerooms, five long rooms measuring 20 by 3.7 m. (66 by 12 ft.) in the northern block, and eleven even longer rooms measuring 27 by 4 m. (88 by 13 ft.) in the southern block. An administrative building completed the building complex at the northern end (the highest part of the rock, and the most easily defended).

Other buildings included an "apartment" or garrison building that housed the top administrators, a swimming pool S of the western palace, and a columbarium, 7.5 m. (25 ft.) in diameter, designed to hold the ashes of non-Jewish members of the Herodian garrison, toward the southern end of the rock. For descriptions see Yadin, *Masada,* pp. 75-110.

A large casemate wall surrounded the entire area except for the palace-villa area. Josephus described it as follows: "First he [Herod] enclosed the entire summit, a circuit measuring seven furlongs [Gk. *stádia*], with a wall of white stone, twelve cubits high and eight broad; on it stood thirty-seven towers, fifty cubits high, from which access was obtained to apartments constructed round the whole interior of the wall" (*BJ* vii.8.3 [286], *LCL*). Seven stadia (1295 m., 4250 ft.) is quite close to the measurement given by Yadin (4200 ft.). The description of "apartments round the whole interior" fits the discovery that the wall was casemate, i.e., a double wall, with rooms between the walls, actually 110 rooms, varying in size from 5.5 m. (18 ft.) to 35 m. (114 ft.) in length, and 4.1 m. (13.5 ft.) in width (i.e., the width between the walls). It appears that Josephus's figure of the breadth of the wall (8 cubits, approximately 3.6 m., 12 ft.), takes into account only the space between the two walls. Yadin found thirty towers (cf. Josephus's 38), and he challenged Josephus's figures on the height of the wall (12 cubits = 5.5 m., 18 ft.) and of the towers (50 cubits = 23 m., 75 ft.). The wall was entirely constructed of dolomite, which was obtainable on the site. According to Yadin, Josephus described the color as white because the wall was covered with plaster, remains of which were found by the excavators. The rooms in the wall contained many personal items from the Zealot occupation, including hundreds of coins from Years 1-5 of the Jewish revolt. See Yadin, *Masada,* pp. 141-163.

The northwest gate, located at the northern end of the western wall, provided access to the upper row of cisterns on the western cliffs. The southern (cistern) gate, NE of the southern end of the wall, gave access to the cistern on the southeastern cliff. The western gate, mentioned above, guarded the western path, and the gate on the eastern wall, near the northern complex of buildings, guarded the access by the snake path to the plateau.

An elaborate system of water collection and storage was essential to life on Masada, and the remains of some of it can be seen today. Rain water was collected from the surface of the plateau and particularly from dams that had been built in the wadis N and S of the rock, and stored in cisterns. In the rainy season, water flowed by gravity from the dammed-up areas to huge cisterns built on the northwestern cliffs of Masada. The visitor who ventures over the Roman ramp and looks back at the rock can see two rows of cisterns, eight in the upper row and two in the lower, each having a capacity of 3900 cu. m. (140,000 cu. ft.), for a total of nearly 40,000 cu. m. (1,400,000 cu. ft., approximately 10.5 million U.S. gallons). The wadi at the southern end of Masada fed the upper row of cisterns, while that at the northern end fed the lower row. Other cisterns at the top of Masada were filled during the rainy season by surface water but during most of the year by persons who carried the water from the cisterns on the flanks of the rock. See Yadin, *Masada,* pp. 21-34.

The reason for the extensive fortification of this impregnable rock is given by Josephus: "For it is said that Herod furnished this fortress as a refuge for himself, suspecting a twofold danger: peril on the one hand from the Jewish people, lest they should depose him and restore their former dynasty to power; the greater and more serious from Cleopatra, queen of Egypt" (*BJ* vii.8.4 [300 f.], *LCL*). The same fear led Herod to build fortresses at Machaerus in Transjordan and at the Herodium in Cisjordan.

***IV. Zealot Occupation.***–In the summer of A.D. 66, according to Josephus, "some of the more ardent promoters of hostilities banded together and made an assault on a fortress called Masada; and having gained possession of it by strategem, they slew the Roman guards and put a garrison of their own in their place" (*BJ* ii.17.2 [408], *LCL*). Some of the weapons from Herod's armory were used in the revolt in Jerusalem (ii.17.8 [433f.]). When Jerusalem fell (A.D. 70) and pockets of Jewish resistance were wiped out, only Masada remained; it was finally taken by Silva in 73.

During this period some changes were made in the Herodian structures. Private dwellings were built toward the southern part of the eastern wall. The rooms in the casemate wall were modified. Columns and capitals from the Herodian buildings were used in this construction, not only causing great damage to those buildings but also scattering the parts, thus making the task of the archeologists more difficult. The palace-villa was modified to become the military headquarters, as attested by quantities of arrows and other weapons. The western palace was the administrative center, which became the main target of the Roman attack via the ramp and the breaching of the wall. Quantities of burnt arrows and coins from the days of the revolt were found there. The smaller palaces were divided with interior walls to provide additional private housing. *See* Plate 44.

Ritual baths (*miqwîm*) were installed. When discovered the first *miqweh* drew great interest from the orthodox religious Jews, for it was the earliest known, and they were concerned to see whether it had been built in accordance with the detailed regulations preserved in the Talmud. It had been: it contained "forty measures." Because of the shortage of "pure" water, the provision had been made to admit a very small amount of "pure" water, which was supposed to purify the rest — a practice that not only violates physical law but even seems to oppose the principle set forth in Hag. 2:12f. An almost identical *miqweh* was discovered on the opposite side of the plateau. See Yadin, *Masada,* pp. 164-67.

A long room in Palace XIII had been converted to what apparently was a religious study house. Benches were found along three sides of the room, and in the center was a table (*EAEHL,* III, 809).

There was also a synagogue 12.5 by 10.4 m. (41.0 by 34.1 ft.) on the western wall, opposite the administrative building at the northern end. It faced west (i.e., toward

Jerusalem) and had four tiers of benches along three of its walls. According to Yadin the building existed in two stages. The earlier building (which likely also served as a synagogue) was constructed in the Herodian period by removing the inner wall and extending the casemate. There is clear evidence that the second-stage building was from the Zealot occupation. (See Yadin, *Masada,* pp. 181-191.) This synagogue is of great significance, since it is the earliest and the only one from the second temple period discovered to date.

The story of the siege of Masada, including the stubborn resistance of the Jewish inhabitants that ended in self-imposed death, has been brilliantly described by Josephus (*BJ* vii.8.1 [252f.]; vii.8.2–9.2 [275-406]) and illustrated by the excavations. Silva built a circumvallation around the base of Masada and located Roman camps at several points. The remains can be clearly seen from the top of the rock. The Zealots had a supply of food from the Herodian period, some of it from the time of Cleopatra, according to Josephus (vii.8.4 [297]). Huge stones weighing 45.5 kg. (100 lbs.), ostensibly used to roll down onto the heads of invaders, as well as stores of arrows, were found. Silva ordered slaves to build a ramp from a projection of rock called Leuke ("white") to the western side of Masada. The ramp, according to Josephus, was 200 cubits high (91.4 m., 300 ft.). (Visitors today who arrive via Arad can cross this ramp, scale a flight of steps, and enter the fortified area atop Masada.)

When it became apparent that the Romans would breach the wall, in spite of valiant defense efforts, Eleazar, the leader of the Zealots, made a speech (reconstructed by Josephus *BJ* vii.8.6f. [323-388]) urging the 960 inhabitants to die rather than submit to slavery. The men killed their wives and children and then were slain by ten who had been chosen by lot for the deed. Finally one, chosen also by lot, slew the nine and then killed himself. The Zealots had burned everything that could be of use to the Romans, preserving only a small store of food to show that they had died willingly while life was still possible. There were seven survivors, women and children, who it seems had hidden to escape the death pact and then surrendered to the invaders. The story of that pact is probably to be traced to their accounts. According to Josephus the end came on the 15th of Xanthicus, or May 2, A.D. 73 (or, according to another calculation, the year was 72; cf. Josephus *BJ* vii.9.1 [401], with note in *LCL*).

Among the archeological discoveries were 700 ostraca, most inscribed in Hebrew or Aramaic but some in Greek or Latin, which Yadin suggested were ration chits. Some had a single name and one the name Ben Ya'ir, quite possibly Eleazar ben-Ya'ir the commander of Masada (cf. Josephus *BJ* ii.17.9 [447]). Yadin suggested that these ostraca bore the names drawn by lot and were mute evidence of the gruesome pact. In the palace-villa Yadin discovered remains of a youth, a female, and a male; he asked the poignant question, "Could it be that we had discovered the bones of that very fighter and of his kith?" (*Masada,* p. 58, referring to Josephus *BJ* vii.9.1 [397]). See Yadin, *Masada,* pp. 193-99.

Also among the discoveries were quantities of pottery, leather, glass, stone, bronze ware, remains of food, and coins. Most important are the manuscript finds. Those from various parts of the plateau include fragments of the Psalms, notably 81–85 and 150; small fragments of Leviticus; and of the Songs of the Sabbath Sacrifice (fragments of which were also found at Qumrân; the texts from both sites are clearly Essenic or sectarian); and fragments in Hebrew of the Wisdom of Ben Sira and of Jubilees. In the synagogue were found portions of fourteen scrolls, and in a genizah under the floor of the synagogue parts of Ezk. 37 and the two final chapters of Deuteronomy.

***Bibliography.***–M. Avi-Yonah, *et al., IEJ,* 7 (1957), 1; *Masada* (Eng. tr. 1957); *HJP,* II/1, 251-53; Josephus *BJ* vii.8.1–9.2 [252-406]; A. Schulten, *ZDPV,* 56 (1933), 1-185; Y. Yadin, *IEJ,* 15 (1965), 1-120; *Masada* (1966); *EAEHL,* III, *s.v.* (Y. Yadin).

W. S. LASOR

**MASALOTH** mas'ə-loth (1 Macc. 9:2, AV). *See* MESALOTH.

**MASCHIL** mas'kil. *See* MASKIL.

**MASH** mash [Heb. *maš*; Gk. *Mosoch*]. Named as a son of Aram (Gen. 10:23). The name is given as Meshech in 1 Ch. 1:17; cf. LXX *Mosoch* in both passages. Meshech, however, is a Japhetic name (Gen. 10:2 par. 1 Ch. 1:5), and Mash may be the correct Shemite name. It is possible that Mash is to be identified with a mountain, perhaps the Mons Masius of classical writers (e.g., Strabo, *Geog.* xi.14.2) on the northern boundary of Mesopotamia.

**MASHAL** mā'shäl [Heb. *māšāl*] (1 Ch. 6:74 [MT 59]). A town in Asher given to the Levites; called MISHAL in Josh. 19:26; 21:30.

**MASIAH** mə-sī'ə [Gk. A *Masias,* B *Meisaias*]; AV, NEB, MASIAS. Head of a family of Solomon's servants who returned from the Exile with Zerubbabel (1 Esd. 5:34); the name is not listed in the parallel accounts in Ezr. 2:57; Neh. 7:59.

**MASKIL** mas'kil [Heb. *maśkîl*]; AV MASCHIL; NEB omits all Psalm titles. A technical term in the titles to Pss. 32, 42, 44, 45, 52–55, 74, 78, 88, 89, and 142. It designates a type of psalm, but its meaning is uncertain. It is derived from the hiphil of *śāḵal,* "have insight," "have success." According to S. Mowinckel, "the verb *hiśkîl* means to know how to reach one's aims and succeed in reaching them, and thus be justified as a wise man" (*Psalms in Israel's Worship* [Eng. tr. 1962], II, 209). He suggested the translation "efficacious song." Others have suggested "didactic poem," "meditative poem" (e.g., C. A. Briggs and E. G. Briggs, comm. on Psalms, I [*ICC,* 1906], lxi), "sense-giving harmony" (M. Dahood, *Psalms,* I [*AB,* 1965], 194), etc. *Maśkîl* occurs once within the body of a Psalm (Ps. 47:7 [MT 8]), where it is variously rendered "psalm" (RSV), "understanding" (AV), "all your art" (NEB), "skillful song" (*AB*), etc.

*See also* PSALMS. N. J. O.

**MASMAN** mas'mən (1 Esd. 8:43, AV). *See* MAASMAS.

**MASON** [part. of *gāḏar* (2 K. 12:12 [MT 13]; 22:6), part. of *ḥāṣaḇ* (2 Ch. 24:12; Ezr. 3:7), *ḥārāš qîr* (1 Ch. 14:1), *ḥārāš 'eḇen* (1 Ch. 22:15), *ḥārāš 'eḇen qîr* (2 S. 5:11)]; AV also WORKER OF STONE; NEB also SCULPTOR, STONE-MASON; **MASONRY** [supplied by the context] (Ezk. 46:23); AV "building"; NEB "stones." A (usually skilled) worker who cuts, forms, and lays stone or brick for construction purposes.

The verb *gāḏar* (part. *gōḏēr*) seems to refer specifically to the building of a wall; the term may thus refer to a person who lays stones (or bricks) into wall formation; in 2 K. 12:12 he is separated from the "stonecutter," who is called a *ḥōṣēḇ* (part. of *ḥāṣaḇ*), qualified by the word for "stone." The latter term thus refers to the skilled workmen who prepared the stones for placement in the wall by the *gōḏēr.* The *ḥārāš 'eḇen qîr* of 2 S. 5:11 was probably identical to the *ḥōṣēḇ,* because the phrase, literally translated, means "cutter of the stone of the city (or wall)"; it could refer to quarriers, however. 1 Ch. 14:1, *ḥārāš qîr,* is repeating 2 S. 5:11 minus the word *'eḇen* (note 1 Ch. 22:15, *ḥāraš 'eḇen,* perhaps another variant of the fuller expression). Although bricks were used frequently for superstructures in Palestine, the Bible does not seem to mention brick masons.

Stone masonry has been used from earliest times, when it was largely done with unhewn stones. During the 18th and 17th cents. B.C. extremely large stones were used for fortifications in a style named after the Greek Cyclops (cf. Gezer, Hazor, Megiddo, etc.). During the period of the monarchy, very finely-hewn stones (ashlars) were used in a header-stretcher fashion for governmental constructions. The largest stones, up to 7.5 m. (24.6 ft.) long, were used by Herod the Great for his construction of the Jerusalem temple. It was to these that the disciples alluded in Mt. 24:2. The stones for most common houses were only slightly hewn.

*See also* STONECUTTER.

***Bibliography.***–*EAEHL,* II, *s.v.* "Gezer" (W. G. Dever); "Hazor" (Y. Yadin); "Jerusalem" (B. Mazar, *et al.*); "Ramat Raḥel" (Y. Aharoni); "Samaria" (N. Avigad); Y. Shiloh, *The Proto-Aeolic Capital and Israelite Ashlar Masonry* (1979).

L. G. HERR

**MASORETIC** mas'ə-ret-ik **TEXT.** *See* TEXT AND MSS OF THE OT.

**MASPHA** mas'fə.

**1.** (1 Macc. 3:46, AV). *See* MIZPAH. **3.**

**2.** (1 Macc. 5:35, AV). *See* ALEMA.

**MASREKAH** mas'rə-kə, mas-rē'kə [Heb. *maśrēqâ*–'place of choice vines'; Gk. *Masekka*]. A place in Edom, probably a royal city (Gen. 36:36; 1 Ch. 1:47). "Samlah of Masrekah" is named as the successor of Hadad but is not called that king's son. Eusebius (*Onom.* 125.16) located Masrekah in the Gebalene in the northern part of Edom. Because of the similarity of names modern scholars have suggested that it was near Jebel el-Mushraq, 32 km. (20 mi.) SSW of Ma'an, near the Nabatean site of et-Telajeh. Cf. *AASOR,* 15 (1935), 62; *GP,* II, 380f.

W. S. L. S.

**MASSA** mas'sə [Heb. *maśśā'*–'load, burden,' 'oracle']. Name of the seventh of the twelve sons of Ishmael (Gen. 25:14; 1 Ch. 1:30); evidently eponymous head of a tribe of the same name. Since other sons of Ishmael, e.g., Dumah, Tema, etc., seem to be associated with northeast Arabia, it is probable that the descendants of Massa settled in this area as well. An inscription of Tiglath-pileser III (745-727 B.C.) indicates that tribes from the area of north Arabia, including the "inhabitants of Mas'a [and] of Tema . . . ," brought him tribute (*ANET,* p. 283). From the Jebel Ghunayn region a text of the 6th cent. B.C. indicates the presence of the tribe (*Massā'*) in the region between al-Jauf and Taymā' (Tema) (Winnett, pp. 90f., 101f.). The tribe of Massa is possibly connected with the *Masanoi* of the Arabian desert, mentioned by Ptolemy (*Geog.* v.18.2).

In Prov. 30:1 and 31:1 the RSV and NEB indicate Massa as the name of a country or tribe from which Agur and Lemuel came. The AV translates *maśśā'* as "prophecy," partially supported by the LXX. *Maśśā'* as an oracle, however, usually conveys the sense of doom or judgment, which does not fit the context. The former interpretation is more probable, for the personal names are non-Hebrew, appearing in Minaean and other south Arabian inscriptions (Hitti, p. 43). The construct configuration in 31:1, "the king of Massa," favors this interpretation. The suggestion of wise men being from this region agrees with the later note that "the sons of Hagar [= Ishmaelites or north Arabians] . . . see for understanding on the earth" (Bar. 3:23).

***Bibliography.***–P. K. Hitti, *History of the Arabs* (1951); F. W. Winnett, *et al., Ancient Records from North Arabia* (1970).

C. G. RASMUSSEN

**MASSACRE OF THE INNOCENTS.** *See* INNOCENTS, MASSACRE OF THE.

**MASSAH AND MERIBAH** mas'ə, mer'ə-bə [Heb. *massâ ûm^e rîḇâ*–'proving and strife'; Gk. *peirasmós kaí loidórēsis*]. These names occur together to indicate a single place only in Ex. 17, although according to some (e.g., M. Noth, *Exodus* [Eng. tr. *OTL,* 1962], pp. 139f.) this passage conflates two traditions: "Meribah and Massah were two different places, each with its own special local tradition." This conflation, it is thought, was due to these two places being paralleled in Ps. 95:8 and Dt. 33:8 (see Noth, p. 139). Outside Ex. 17 the two names clearly apply to two separate places. Although many scholars also assert that the accounts in Ex. 17:1-7 and Nu. 20:1-13 are variants of one tradition (see the discussion of B. Childs, *Book of Exodus* [*OTL,* 1974], pp. 305-309), others hold that these are two separate but quite similar stories (e.g., KD). Thus Massah in Ex. 17:7 refers to the incident near the outset of the journey of Israel, and Meribah in Ex. 17:7 and Nu. 20:13 to the incident at Kadesh just before the people entered the Promised Land. Each incident had elements of strife, but in Ex. 17 the element of "proving" is uppermost.

(1) Exodus 17:1 records that at REPHIDIM, near the beginning of the desert wanderings, the people murmured and complained because they lacked water. Moses, appealing to God, was told to take with him the elders of Israel and smite with his rod the rock on which Yahweh stood in Horeb. Water gushed forth, and the people drank. Moses alone was God's agent and did nothing blameworthy in this account. He called the place Massah (<*nāsâ,* "test") and Meribah (<*rîḇ,* "strive") because the children of Israel caused strife and tempted the Lord (note the wordplay in vv. 2, 7: "find fault," *rîḇ,* "put to the proof," *nāsâ*). In some way not indicated, here and at Meribah, God tested the Levites (Dt. 33:8; cf. Ps. 95:8f.).

(2) The second narrative, Nu. 20:1-13, describes an episode at Kadesh (i.e., Kadesh-barnea) when the desert wanderings had nearly ended. The flow of water from the famous spring for some reason had ceased. In their distress the people became impatient and petulant. At the door of the tent of meeting Moses and Aaron received Yahweh's instructions; but instead of speaking to the rock as commanded, Moses struck it twice with his rod. The flow of water was at once restored, but Moses and Aaron were severely punished because they did not uphold God's holiness in the eyes of the people. The waters of Meribah was the name given to the scene of this strife.

M. A. MACLEOD

**MASSEBAH** mə-sē'bə. Transcription of Heb. *maṣṣēḇâ,* "pillar," "stone set up as a memorial"; a technical term in archeology for a sacred pillar. *See* PILLAR.

**MASSIAS** mə-sī'əs [Gk. A *Massias,* B *Asseias*] (AV, NEB, 1 Esd. 9:22). *See* MAASEIAH **8.**

**MAST** [Heb. *tōren*] (Isa. 33:23; Ezk. 27:5); [*ḥibbēl*] (Prov. 23:34); NEB RIGGING. A long pole rising from the keel or deck of a ship and supporting the sails. Heb. *ḥibbēl* is a hapax legomenon for which various translations have been suggested; the NEB understands it as an intensive form of *ḥeḇel,* "rope." Following the proposal of P. Calderone (*CBQ,* 24 [1962], 412f. n. 5), M. Dahood (*Proverbs and Northwest Semitic Philology* [1963], pp. 49f.) suggested that *ḥbl* be translated "mountain" as the cognate of Ugar. *ḫlb* and Akk. *ḫalbu.* But this proposal is not only semantically improbable, since Akk. *ḫalbu* means "forest" (*CAD,* VI, 40f.; note, however, that Ugar. *ḫlb* is often rendered "forested height"), but also contextually inappropriate, since it moves the image from sea to land. See the discussion in W. McKane, *Proverbs* (*OTL,* 1970), pp. 395f.

G. A. L.

**MASTER** [Heb. *māšal*] (Gen. 4:7); AV RULE; [*šālaṭ*] (Eccl. 2:19); AV RULE; [*bāʿal*] ("be master," Jer. 3:14); AV "be married"; NEB "be patient"; [*ʾāḏôn*]; AV also LORD; NEB also KING, etc.; [*baʿal*] (Jgs. 19:22f.; Isa. 1:3); NEB also OWNER, etc.; [*ʾommān*] (Cant. 7:1 [MT 7:2]); AV CUNNING WORKMAN; NEB SKILLED CRAFTSMAN; [Gk. *katakyrieúō*] (Acts 19:16); AV OVERCOME; NEB OVERPOWER; [*kýrios*]; AV also LORD, GOD (Rom. 14:4); NEB also EMPLOYER; [*kathēgētḗs*] (Mt. 23:10); NEB TEACHER; [*rhabbí*] (Mt. 26:25, 49; Mk. 9:5; 11:21; 14:45); NEB RABBI; [*rhabbouní*] (Mk. 10:51); AV LORD; [*epistátēs*] (Lk. 5:5; 8:24, 45; 9:33, 49; 17:13); [*despótēs*] (1 Tim. 6:1f.; Tit. 2:9; 1 Pet. 2:18; 2 Pet. 2:1; Jude 4); AV also LORD; **MASTER BUILDER** [Gk. *architéktōn*] (1 Cor. 3:10); **MASTER OF THE HOUSE** [Gk. *despótēs*] (2 Tim. 2:21); AV MASTER; [*oikodespótēs*] (Mt. 10:25); NEB MASTER; **MASTERY** [Heb. *šālaṭ*] ("get the mastery," Est. 9:1); AV "have power," "had rule"; NEB "gain the upper hand." For Prov. 8:30, the RSV reads "master workman" (Heb. *ʾāmôn* or even *ʾommān*), though the margin suggests another reading: "little child" (*ʾāmûn*); the AV reads "one brought up with him," while the NEB has "darling." (See R. B. Y. Scott, *Proverbs* [*AB,* 1965], p. 72 for a discussion of the possibilities.) In Rom. 14:4 the AV does not follow *kýrios* but rather an inferior reading, *theós,* "God." In Tit. 1:8 the RSV paraphrases *sṓphrōn* as "master of himself" (AV lit. "sober"; NEB lit. "temperate").

Hebrew *ʾāḏôn* refers to the possessor of servants or slaves (Gen. 24; 39; Ex. 21; etc.); a husband of a concubine (Jgs. 19:26f.); a prophet with a young helper-apprentice, servants, or the "sons of the prophets" (2 K. 2; 5; 6; etc.); a king with administrators and servants under him (2 K. 5; 9; 10; etc.); and other authority figures (see *TDOT,* I, *s.v.* "ʾādhôn" [Eissfeldt]). God, too, is termed a "master" (Mal. 1:6; for *ʾaḏōnāy,* "my Lord," as a divine name, *see* LORD). *Baʿal* as "master" denotes the owner of a house (Jgs. 19:22f.) or of an animal (Isa. 1:3); for *baʿal* as the name of the Canaanite god, *see* BAAL I.

The Gk. *kýrios,* frequently translated "lord" in the NT, refers particularly to God or Jesus but also to certain human "masters": the possessor of servants or stewards (Mt. 10:24f.; 25:19-26; etc.), the owner of a household (Mk. 13:35), or the owner of an animal (Mt. 15:27). Masters of slaves are urged to treat their slaves kindly, justly, and fairly: both masters and slaves "have the same Master [*kýrios*] in heaven, and he has no favourites" (Eph. 6:9, NEB; cf. also Col. 4:1). Jesus frequently mentioned masters in parables and warned that believers cannot be slaves of "two masters," God and money (Mt. 6:24; Lk. 16:13). See *TDNT,* III, *s.v.* κύριος κτλ. (Quell, Foerster).

*Kathēgētḗs,* used twice in Mt. 23:10 (and only in this passage), designates a teacher. *Rhabbí* and the heightened form *rhabbouní* in the Greek NT are transliterations of Heb. *rabbî,* meaning "my master" or, as the NT indicates, "my teacher" (cf. Jn. 1:38; 20:16; *TDNT,* VI, *s.v.* ῥαββί, ῥαββουνί [Lohse]). *Rhabbí* and *rhabbouní* were thus respectful and honorary titles used for addressing people like John the Baptist (Jn. 3:26, RSV "rabbi"), teachers like the scribes and Pharisees (Mt. 23:7, RSV "rabbi"), and Jesus (RSV "master," "rabbi," or "rabboni"). *See also* RABBI. *Epistátēs* is used only in Luke, as a title given to Jesus (see *TDNT,* II, *s.v.* ἐπιστάτης [Oepke]).

As a translation of *despótēs,* "master" usually refers to humans (1 Tim. 6:1f.; 2 Tim. 2:21; Tit. 2:9; 1 Pet. 2:18), though twice it refers to Christ (2 Pet. 2:1; Jude 4; cf. *oikodespótēs* in Mt. 10:25; cf. also *despótēs,* translated "Sovereign Lord" in Acts 4:24; Rev. 6:10, and "Lord" in Lk. 2:29). See *TDNT,* II, *s.v.* δεσπότης κτλ. (Rengstorf).

Finally, *architéktōn* is a hapax legomenon in the NT (1 Cor. 3:10), though it occurs a few times in the LXX and elsewhere in Greek literature and was even a loanword in rabbinic Hebrew (*ʾarᵉḵîṭîqṭôn*).

*See also* SERVANT; SLAVE; TEACHER.

M. W. MEYER

**MASTIC** [Gk. *schínos*] (Sus. 54); AV MASTICK; NEB CLOVE (to preserve original pun). The lentisk or mastic tree (*Pistacia lentiscus* L.) is a shrub that grows in thickets in Mediterranean lands, attaining a maximum height of 3½ m. (12 ft.). From incisions in the bark it exudes a fragrant terebinthine sap ("mastic" or "mastich"), which has been a commercial article from earliest times. Even today it is used as a masticatory to preserve the teeth and gums.

It is thought that the "balm" of Gen. 43:11 was actually mastic gum, since the substance sent by Jacob to Joseph must have been native to Palestine and unknown in Egypt. It could not have been either *Commiphora opobalsamum* or *Commiphora myrrha,* the true myrrh, since neither is indigenous to Palestine. R. K. H.

**MATHANIAS** math-ə-nī'əs (1 Esd. 9:31, AV). *See* MATTANIAH **12.**

**MATHELAS** ma-thē'ləs (1 Esd. 9:19, NEB). *See* MAASEIAH **6.**

**MATHUSALA** mə-thōō'sə-lə (Lk. 3:37, AV). *See* METHUSELAH.

**MATRED** mā'trəd [Heb. *maṭrēḏ*] (Gen. 36:39; 1 Ch. 1:50). The mother or father of Mehetabel, the wife of Hadad ("Hadar," Gen. 36:39) king of Edom. According to the MT, Matred was the "daughter" (*baṯ*) of Mezahab, but the LXX and Syr. read "son" (*ben*). The same problem occurs in vv. 2, 14 (see RSV mg.; *BHS*).

**MATRI** mā'trī (AV, NEB, 1 S. 10:21). *See* MATRITES.

**MATRITES** mā'trīts [Heb. *hammaṭrî*]; AV, NEB, MATRI. A family of the tribe of Benjamin to which King Saul belonged (1 S. 10:21).

**MATTAN** mat'ən [Heb. *mattān*–'gift'].

**1.** A priest of Baal, slain before Baal's altar by the followers of Jehoiada (2 K. 11:18; 2 Ch. 23:17).

**2.** The father of Shephatiah, a prince of Judah under King Zedekiah during the time of Jeremiah (Jer. 38:1).

**MATTANAH** mat'ə-nə [Heb. *mattānâ*–'gift'; Gk. B *Manthanaein,* A *Manthanein*]. An encampment of the Israelites on their journey north from the river Arnon toward Pisgah and the territory of Sihon king of the Amorites (Nu. 21:18f.). Mattanah was between Beer and Nahaliel (vv. 16, 18f.). Eusebius located it 19 km. (12 mi.) SE of Medeba. Possibly the site is modern Khirbet el-Medeiyineh, about 18 km. (11 mi.) NE of Dibon (*GTTOT,* § 441, p. 262; cf. N. Glueck, *AASOR,* 14 [1934], 13-27). If *miṯnî* is gentilic (1 Ch. 11:34; < **mitt^e^nî*) it may refer to Mattanah (*GTTOT,* § 844, p. 344).

**MATTANIAH** mat-ə-nī'ə [Heb. *mattanyâ, mattanyāhû*–'gift of Yahweh'; Gk. *Maththanias, Mathania, Manthanias, Matthanias,* etc.]; NEB also MATTANAIAH.

**1.** The original name of ZEDEKIAH king of Judah, changed by Nebuchadrezzar king of Babylon when he made Mattaniah king in place of his nephew Jehoiachin (2 K. 24:17).

**2.** An Asaphite Levite, son of Mica; one of the first to live in Jerusalem after the Exile (1 Ch. 9:15) and a leader in the temple choir (Neh. 11:17; 12:8).

**3.** Son of Heman; a musician in the temple choir in the time of King David (1 Ch. 25:4, 16).

**4.** An Asaphite Levite; ancestor of the Jahaziel who prophesied in the time of King Jehoshaphat of Judah (2 Ch. 20:14).

**5.** An Asaphite Levite who assisted in cleansing the temple during the reign of King Hezekiah (2 Ch. 29:13).

**6.** An Asaphite Levite, son of Mica, father of Hashabiah, and great-grandfather of the Uzzi who was overseer of the Levites in postexilic Jerusalem (Neh. 11:22); possibly the same as **2.**

**7.** A Levite who guarded the storehouses of the gates of Jerusalem in the time of Joiakim, Nehemiah, and Ezra (Neh. 12:25).

**8.** An Asaphite Levite, son of Micaiah, father of Shemaiah, and great-grandfather of the Zechariah who played the trumpet at the dedication of the rebuilt walls of Jerusalem (Neh. 12:35).

**9.** Father of Zaccur and grandfather of Hanan, the assistant to the treasurer of the Levitical storehouse in the time of Nehemiah (Neh. 13:13).

**10.** [Gk. Apoc. B *Matanias,* A *Matthanias*]; AV Apoc., NEB Apoc., MATTHANIAS. Son of Elam; a layman who divorced his foreign wife as directed by Ezra (Ezr. 10:26; 1 Esd. 9:27).

**11.** Son of Zattu; another layman who divorced his foreign wife (Ezr. 10:27); called Othoniah in 1 Esd. 9:28.

**12.** Son of Pahath-moab; another layman who divorced his foreign wife (Ezr. 10:30). In 1 Esd. 9:31 the AV (Mathanias) and NEB (Matthanias) follow Gk. A *Matthanias*; but the RSV (Bescaspasmys) follows Gk. B *Beskaspasmys.*

**13.** Son of Bani; another layman who divorced his foreign wife (Ezr. 10:37). In 1 Esd. 9:34 the text may be corrupted by the blending of "Matthaniah" with "Mattenai," resulting in Gk. *Mamnitanaimos* (cf. AV, NEB, RSV mg). incorrectly rendered MACHNADEBAI by the RSV.

N. J. O.

**MATTATHA** mat'ə-thə [Gk. *Mattatha*]. Son of Nathan the son of David; an ancestor of Jesus (Lk. 3:31).

**MATTATHAH** mat'ə-thə (Ezr. 10:33, AV). *See* MATTATTAH

**MATTATHIAH** mat-ə-thī'ə [Gk. *Mattathias*] (1 Esd. 9:43); AV, NEB, MATTATHIAS. One of those who stood at Ezra's right hand during the public reading of the law; called MATTITHIAH (4) in Neh. 8:4.

**MATTATHIAS** mat-ə-thī'əs [Gk. *Mattathias*].

**1.** (1 Esd. 9:33, NEB). *See* MATTATTAH.

**2.** (1 Esd. 9:43, AV, NEB). *See* MATTATHIAH.

**3.** A pious priest of the family of Jehoiarib (cf. 1 Ch. 24:7) who moved from Jerusalem to MODEIN, evidently because of the hellenizing activities of Antiochus Epiphanes (1 Macc. 2:1; Josephus *Ant.* xii.6.1 [265]). When the Seleucids insisted on pagan sacrifice in Modein, the refusal of Mattathias and his five sons precipitated the rebellion that eventually led to the cleansing of the temple (*ca.* 164 B.C.) and Jewish independence (*ca.* 142 B.C.). Thus, Mattathias is the "father" of the Maccabean (from the name of his son, Judas Maccabeus) or Hasmonean (from his great-grandfather, Hashman) period of Hebrew history, which extended until the Roman conquest in 63 B.C. (*See also* HASMONEANS I; MACCABEES II.B.)

In spite of his great age, Mattathias fled to the wilderness, gathered loyal Jews, and personally led the resistance movement for one year (1 Macc. 2:27-70; *Ant.* xii.6.2-4 [271-285]). Following his death (in his 146th year) and burial in Modein, leadership passed to his sons, of whom Judas Maccabeus, Jonathan, and Simon were the most prominent. Mattathias's cry, "Let everyone who is zealous for the law and supports the covenant come out with me!" became a slogan for the movement. He established the principle that the Jewish fighters would engage in defensive actions on the sabbath (1 Macc. 2:41; *Ant.* xii.6.2 [276]). According to Josephus, his belief in the resurrection of the dead helped to embolden his followers (*Ant.* xii.6.3 [282]).

In the Talmud (*Meg.* 11a) Mattathias is memorialized in Hanukkah prayers. Some have suggested that he is represented by the mysterious "Taxo" figure in Asm. M. 9:1 (*see* APOCALYPTIC LITERATURE III.E).

See E. Schürer, *History of the Jewish People in the Age of Jesus Christ,* I (rev. ed. 1973), 155-58.

**4.** Son of Absalom; a commander of the Jewish army under Jonathan the Hasmonean (1 Macc. 11:70). In combat in Galilee with the Seleucid Demetrius, Jonathan's forces were ambushed. All of Jonathan's army fled except for Mattathias and another comander, Judas. The example of these two seems to have given to Jonathan and the rest of the army the courage necessary to defeat the enemy.

**5.** Third son of Simon and grandson of Mattathias **3.** 1 Macc. 16:11-17 relates that Simon and two of his sons, Mattathias and Judas, were murdered by Ptolemy, governor of Jericho and a son-in-law of Simon, while they were in a drunken condition at a banquet in that city. Josephus (*Ant.* XIII.7.4 [228]) does not mention this Mattathias.

**6.** An envoy sent by Nicanor to make a treaty with Judas Maccabeus, according to the account in 2 Macc. 14:19.

**7.** Son of Amos; an ancestor of Joseph the father of Jesus (Lk. 3:25).

**8.** Son of Semein; another ancestor of Joseph the father of Jesus (Lk. 3:26). J. J. SCOTT, JR.

**MATTATTAH** mat'ə-tə [Heb. *mattattâ*–'gift'; Gk. *Mathatha,* Apoc. *Mattathias*] (Ezr. 10:33; 1 Esd. 9:33); AV MATTATHAH, Apoc. MATTHIAS; NEB Apoc. MATTATHIAS. A son of Hashum; one of the returned exiles who divorced their foreign wives.

**MATTENAI** mat'ə-nī [Heb. *matt^e^nay*–'gift'; Gk. Apoc. A *Altannaios,* B *Maltannaios*]; AV Apoc. ALTANEUS; NEB Apoc. ALTANNAEUS.

**1.** A son of Hashum; one of the returned exiles who divorced their foreign wives (Ezr. 10:33; 1 Esd. 9:33).

**2.** A son of Bani; another of the returned exiles who divorced their foreign wives (Ezr. 10:37; not listed in par. 1 Esd. 9:34).

**3.** A priest representing the family of Joiarib in the time of Joiakim the high priest (Neh. 12:19).

**MATTHAN** math'an [Gk. *Matthan*; cf. Heb. *mattān* (*see* MATTAN)]. An ancestor of Jesus; grandfather of Joseph the husband of Mary (Mt. 1:15); given as MATTHAT in Luke's genealogy.

**MATTHANIAS** math-ə-nī'əs.

**1.** (AV, NEB, 1 Esd. 9:27). *See* MATTANIAH **10.**

**2.** (1 Esd. 9:31, NEB). The RSV, following LXX B, reads "Bescaspasmys." *See* MATTANIAH 12.

**MATTHAT** math'ət [Gk. *Matthat, Maththath, Maththat, Mattath*].

**1.** An ancestor of Jesus; grandfather of Joseph the husband of Mary (Lk. 3:24); given as MATTHAN in Matthew's genealogy.

**2.** Another ancestor of Jesus in Luke's genealogy (3:29).

**MATTHELAS** ma-thē'ləs (1 Esd. 9:19, AV). *See* MAASEIAH 6.

**MATTHEW** math'ū [Gk. *Matthaios*]. One of the twelve apostles.

Greek *Matthaios* is an approximate transliteration of the Aramaic (or Hebrew) *matta'y* or *mattᵉyā'*, abbreviations of *mattanyāh* or *mattiṯyāh*. The name derives from the noun *mattān*, "gift" (<*nāṯan*, "give") combined with the name *Yāh*, so it means "gift of Yahweh."

Beyond its regular appearance in the four lists of the twelve apostles (Mt. 10:3; Mk. 3:18; Lk. 6:15; Acts 1:13), the name occurs only once in the NT — in Mt. 9:9 the tax collector who follows Jesus is called Matthew, whereas the parallel accounts (Mk. 2:14; Lk. 5:27, 29) identify him as Levi. It is virtually certain that the Gospel of Matthew is dependent upon Mark in this passage. Mark and Luke, had they been dependent upon Matthew, would hardly have felt free to substitute the name of an otherwise unknown person, Levi, for the name of an apostle. It is thus very probable that the author of the Gospel of Matthew changed the name Levi to Matthew in this passage. Also, as though to alert readers to the intended equation of the two names, when in the next chapter (10:3) the Evangelist lists the Twelve, he alone adds "the tax collector" to Matthew's name. But why did the Evangelist change the name Levi to Matthew? The most natural conclusion is that the tax collector Levi came to be called Matthew (a name so appropriate to the situation) after his conversion, and that this new name, now the name of an apostle, was significant to the author of the Gospel — a Gospel that, according to tradition, derived from that very Matthew.

We know very little about Matthew beyond the fact that he was one of the Twelve. He was the son of Alphaeus (Mk. 2:14), but we have no evidence that this Alphaeus is to be identified with the father of the Apostle James (Mk. 3:18). We do know that Matthew was a tax collector, who, upon his call and decision to follow Jesus, gave a "great banquet" (Lk. 5:29) for Jesus in his house, together with a "large company of tax collectors" and "sinners." As a tax collector Matthew probably lived in or near Capernaum and collected tolls for Herod Antipas on the commercial traffic using the major road between Damascus and cities of Palestine. We may infer that he had become relatively wealthy and that to become a disciple of Jesus meant a dramatically new style of life. Beyond this the NT is silent about Matthew, as it is about most of the Twelve.

By far the most widely attested tradition concerning Matthew in the early Church concerns his association with the Gospel that bears his name. Early in the 2nd cent. Papias referred to Matthew as the collector of the "oracles" of Jesus; shortly thereafter the Gospel as a whole was attributed to Matthew (*see* full discussion under MATTHEW, GOSPEL ACCORDING TO I.A). Later traditions about Matthew are mixed and unreliable. Eusebius said only that Matthew first preached to "the Hebrews" and then to "others" (*HE* iii.24.6), the latter being amplified in later sources to include residents of such places as Ethiopia, Persia, Parthia, Macedonia, and Syria. Clement of Alexandria provided the interesting note that "the apostle Matthew partook of seeds, and nuts, and vegetables, without flesh" (*Paed.* ii.1). The traditions about Matthew's death are contradictory. According to some, Matthew was a martyr for his faith, although the place and means of his martyrdom vary considerably in different reports. Part of the confusion in these later traditions may be due to the similarity of the names Matthew and Matthias. Probably more reliable is the conclusion that Matthew died a normal death, as implied by Heracleon (recorded by Clement of Alexandria in *Stromata* iv.9).

***Bibliography.***–E. J. Goodspeed, *Matthew, Apostle and Evangelist* (1959); for a representative account of Matthew's martyrdom, see *ANT,* pp. 460-62; for a tabulation of the traditions concerning Matthew, see H-S, II, 60f., 64.

D. A. HAGNER

**MATTHEW, GOSPEL ACCORDING TO.**

The Gospel of Matthew dominated the attention of the early Church, at least so far as the Synoptic Gospels are concerned, to the extent that it all but eclipsed the others. The church fathers cited Matthew far more than either of the other Synoptics (cf. E. Massaux, *Influence de l'Évangile de saint Matthieu sur la littérature chrétienne avant saint Irénée* [1950]), and Matthew was much more prominent in the liturgies of the early Church. Only in the 19th cent., with the hypothesis of the priority of Mark and the resulting new importance of that Gospel, did this situation change. In the 20th cent. the discovery and use of new methods of study have made Matthew the subject of renewed interest. The Gospel remains enigmatic at many points, however, and continues to challenge interpreters.

I. Sources
- A. Tradition about Matthew
- B. Problems with the Tradition
- C. Two-Source Hypothesis

II. Structure
- A. Five Discourses
- B. Two Major Turning Points
- C. Other Structural Elements

III. Genre
- A. Gospel
- B. Midrash
- C. Lectionary
- D. Catechesis or Catechetical Manual
- E. Church Correctives
- F. Missionary Propaganda
- G. Polemic Against the Rabbis

IV. Theological Emphases
- A. Fulfillment: The Kingdom of Heaven
- B. Use of the OT
- C. Christology
- D. Discipleship and Righteousness
- E. Community (Church)
- F. Eschatology
- G. Salvation-History

V. Theological Tensions
- A. Particularism and Universalism
- B. Israel and the Church
- C. Law and Grace

VI. Intended Readers and Purpose

VII. Date and Provenance

VIII. Authorship

*I. Sources.*–The Gospel of Matthew itself says nothing about its sources. Information must be gained from comparative study of the other Synoptics and what can be learned from available traditional materials.

*A. Tradition about Matthew.* The earliest information comes from Papias, bishop of Hierapolis in Asia Minor, who in the first quarter of the 2nd cent. wrote (according to the fourth-century church historian Eusebius): "Matthew composed the logia [Gk. *tá lógia*] in the Hebrew tongue and everyone interpreted them as he was able" (*HE* iii.39.16). The interpretation of this passage turns on the meaning of the word *lógia*. Traditionally, and in accord with the priority of Matthew in the corpus of the four Gospels, it has been understood to mean the Gospel of Matthew itself. Those who "interpreted" in this case may be the other Evangelists, who supposedly made use of Matthew's *lógia* in drawing up their own accounts. According to this view, Matthew is the earliest of the Gospels and nothing is known of the sources Matthew may have used. It is questionable, however, whether Papias is to be interpreted in this way and, even if so, whether Papias can be trusted regarding this information. The word *lógia*, literally "oracles," is an unusual word to use in referring to the Gospel, and there are several other more natural options for the meaning of the word.

So far as *lógia* itself is concerned, the most natural meaning is "words of the OT" (which were called "oracles" by the early fathers), in this case perhaps a collection of OT prophecies or prooftexts (Lat. *testimonia*) concerning the Messiah or messianic fulfillment. This would agree well with the fact that Matthew contains some interesting quotations from the OT (see below) and these could indeed raise the problem of interpretation. A second possibility is that the word refers to a collection of the sayings of Jesus, perhaps Q (or something like Q), the sayings source used in the Gospels of Matthew and Luke (although in this case one would expect the word *lógoi* rather than *lógia*). In favor of accepting the word *lógia* as referring to the Gospel itself, however, is the fact that a few lines earlier Eusebius (*HE* iii.39.15) quotes Papias as mentioning "the Lord's oracles" (*tá kyriaká lógia*) in reference to the Gospel of Mark, a Gospel hardly known for its record of the sayings of Jesus. Papias himself had written a five-volume commentary entitled *Exegesis of the Oracles of the Lord* (*exḗgēsis logíōn kyriakṓn* [*HE* iii.39.1]). Was this a commentary on both the deeds and words of Jesus as contained in one or more of the Gospels, or are we to understand "oracles" as referring only to the sayings of Jesus? The latter is more probable, as can be seen from Papias's specific interest in "the commandments from the Lord" (*HE* iii.39.3), and Eusebius's reference to Papias's inclusion of "some strange parables and teachings of the Savior" and "other interpretations of the words of the Lord" (*hoi toú kyríou lógoi, HE* iii.39.14). True, Eusebius also refers to Papias's inclusion of "certain marvels [*parádoxá tina*] and other details" (*HE* iii.39.8).

Probably the explanation is that by *lógia* ("oracles") Papias meant in the first instance the words of Jesus. As early as the 2nd cent. these came to be treasured as the supreme authority in the early Church. Indeed, already by the time of Clement of Rome the words of Jesus were put alongside the OT in authority, and even came to supersede them in authority (cf. esp. 1 Clem. 13). Papias could easily have used the word "oracles" to refer to the words of Jesus, for Jesus was the divine revelation of God and His words thus ranked in authority with those of the OT. For Papias, then, because the words of Jesus were supremely authoritative, *lógia* or "oracles" became synonymous with the term "Gospel." Thus Papias could refer both to the words of Jesus as *lógia* and to the written Gospels as collections of the *lógia* of Jesus, alongside, of course, His deeds. When Papias wrote, therefore, that "Matthew collected the oracles of Jesus," he could have referred either to what we know as the Gospel of Matthew or to a collection of the sayings of Jesus. The reasons for preferring the latter interpretation will emerge below.

*B. Problems with the Tradition.* Two main problems with the Papias tradition as it is understood by some scholars are: (1) our Greek Gospel of Matthew is not the translation of a Hebrew or Aramaic original; (2) modern study of the Synoptics for the most part does not support the priority of Matthew and the consequent dependence of Mark and Luke upon Matthew. Almost all scholars agree that our Gospel of Matthew was originally written in Greek and is not a translated document. Matthew's Greek reveals none of the telltale marks of a translation. Furthermore, Matthew's OT quotations are derived from the LXX rather than the Hebrew text (see below), although of course they could be derived from a different Hebrew text or could later have been made to conform to the LXX text. The assessment that Matthew was originally written in Greek has caused advocates of the priority of Matthew to set forth a complicated hypothesis wherein the present Gospel of Matthew is said to be dependent upon the Greek of Mark's Gospel while being simultaneously the perpetuator of Matthew's Aramaic tradition. Thus the Aramaic Gospel supposedly referred to by Papias can at best be a Proto-Matthew, which somehow became incorporated or transformed into the present Gospel of Matthew other than by direct translation, while at the same time being influenced by the Greek of Mark.

On the question of dependence, it must be acknowledged that a growing number of scholars question the hypothesis of Markan priority. Advocates of Matthaean priority, led by W. R. Farmer (*Synoptic Problem* [1964]), include B. Orchard (*Matthew, Luke and Mark* [1976]) and H. H. Stoldt (*History and Criticism of the Markan Hypothesis* [Eng. tr. 1980]). They follow in the steps of such earlier proponents of Matthaean priority as J. Chapman (*Matthew, Mark, Luke: A Study in the Order and Interrelation of the Synoptic Gospels* [1937]), B. C. Butler (*Originality of St. Matthew* [1957]) and L. Vaganay (*Le problème synoptique* [1954]). J. M. Rist (*On the Independence of Matthew and Mark* [1978]) has argued the independence of Matthew and Mark, explaining the common material on the basis of a common oral tradition. Although this ferment serves as an important and useful reminder that Markan priority is only a hypothesis and can never be assumed in an absolute way or without further thought, the majority of NT scholars remain convinced that Markan priority is a superior hypothesis.

In the face of these problems it must be concluded either that Papias was wrong in what he said or, giving him the benefit of the doubt, that he has been misunderstood, perhaps by the early church fathers (e.g., Irenaeus, Pantaenus, Origen, who seem dependent upon him for their view of the priority of Matthew), and certainly by scholarship until the 19th cent. Although the evidence allows only speculation, it may well be that what Papias referred to was a collection of sayings of Jesus in Aramaic that ultimately, in Greek, became the core of Matthew's Gospel, and that the whole then took the name of the part—"the oracles of the Lord." Papias was misunderstood not only because of the ambiguity of the word *lógia*, but also because several Jewish Christian Gospels apparently existed in the 2nd cent. (e.g., the Gospels of the Nazarenes, of the Ebionites, and of the Hebrews; *see* APOCRYPHAL GOSPELS IV), and it was easy enough to suppose that one or all of them originated in the *lógia* referred to by Papias. Even the great Jerome at first identified one of these Gospels, which he examined in Syria, with the work of Matthew, only later to withdraw this conclusion (cf. *De vir. ill.* 3; *Adv. Pelag.* iii.2; Comm. on Mt. 12:13).

*C. Two-Source Hypothesis.* (*See* GOSPELS, SYNOPTIC.) The arguments for the priority of Mark and Matthew's dependence upon Mark are too strong to be overthrown by the testimony of Papias, which as we have seen is difficult to interpret. Matthew reproduces some 90 percent of Mark, much of it verbatim. In single pericopes drawn from Mark, Matthew's version is generally more terse; Matthew pares away redundancies. Matthew furthermore improves the Greek of Mark at many points. The Markan sequence of events, moreover, seems normative for the Synoptics in that Matthew and Luke never agree against the order of Mark: where Matthew departs from the Markan order, Luke follows it; where Luke departs from the Markan order, Matthew follows it. These facts, combined with Mark's directness and freshness, which itself makes it very unlikely that Mark is simply an abbreviation of Matthew and Luke, suggest Markan priority and Matthew's dependence on Mark as highly probable. That there was no need for an abridgment of Matthew, as some regard Mark, is clear from the neglect of Mark in the Church once Matthew became available. Thus, despite the reopening of the question by advocates of Matthaean priority, it is best to accept the priority of Mark as a working hypothesis.

Because of the unlikelihood that the author of Matthew knew the Gospel of Luke or vice versa (the differences are too great to accept dependence either way), a second source is needed to explain the many agreements of Matthew and Luke when Mark is not the source. For convenience this source is called Q. It is possible — even probable — that Q is to be understood as oral tradition(s) rather than a written source. Oral tradition could equally explain the so-called minor agreements between Matthew and Luke against Mark in "triple tradition" passages, a point often used against Markan priority. We may, then, with a fair degree of confidence assume that the author of Matthew had two major sources available, Q and the Gospel of Mark. Indeed, if our understanding of Papias is correct, then Matthew himself had collected the sayings of Jesus in Aramaic, possibly into something similar to Q; indeed, Q may well have been Matthew's *lógia* in Greek translation(s). A third source sometimes mentioned in discussions of Matthew is that from which the author derived his special material, usually designated M. It is particularly difficult, however, to isolate this material from that which may derive from the Evangelist himself, and therefore M is not a very helpful classification.

*II.* **Structure.**–*A. Five Discourses.* The most conspicuous structural element in the Gospel is the phrase repeated with slight modifications at the end of each of the five major discourses: "When Jesus finished all these sayings . . ." (7:28; 11:1; 13:53; 19:1; 26:1). B. W. Bacon argued that the Evangelist intended this fivefold structure to correspond to the five books of the Pentateuch, with Jesus represented as a new Moses who brings a new law. Although this may indeed be possible, W. D. Davies has pointed out that Matthew does very little with the implicit Moses typology in the Gospel. A fivefold structure, moreover, is found in other Jewish writings (e.g., the five books of Psalms; the five Scrolls) and need not point to the Pentateuch. In a way similar to the Fourth Gospel, the author alternates his blocks of the teaching of Jesus with narratives describing the mighty deeds of Jesus; unlike John, however, he makes little attempt to relate the deeds to the content of the discourses. The discourses, which appear to have been artistically constructed by the Evangelist rather than delivered by Jesus as they stand, seem to have decidedly catechetical interests: (1) the Sermon on the Mount, chs. 5–7; (2) mission directives to the Twelve, ch. 10; (3) parables of the Kingdom, ch. 13; (4) discipleship and discipline, ch. 18; (5) eschatology, chs. 24–25. Although this fivefold structure may be meant to include a section of narrative preceding each discourse (chs. 3–4; 8–9; 11–12; 14–17; 19–22), it seems hardly adequate to be regarded as the basic plan of the Gospel. Certain parts of the Gospel do not fit into the structure at all. Thus ch. 23 (the criticism of the Pharisees) is not a part of the eschatological discourse that follows, and ch. 11 contains a number of sayings of Jesus outside the structure of the five teaching discourses. A more serious point is that the fivefold structure excludes the Infancy narrative and the Passion narratives, with the result that these two important passages must be regarded as prologue and epilogue. The narrative of the death of Jesus, however, is the goal and climax of the story, and thus any analysis of Matthew's structure must include it as a major element. Accordingly, the fivefold discourse structure should be recognized as a subsidiary structure rather than the primary one. For the latter we are better advised to look to the major divisions of the Gospel.

*B. Two Major Turning Points.* Two pivotal points in the Gospel are noted with the phrase "From that time Jesus began" (4:17; 16:21). J. D. Kingsbury (*Matthew: Structure, Christology, Kingdom,* pp. 1-39) understands these phrases as indicating the basic structure of the Gospel, which he then describes under the following three headings: The Person of Jesus Messiah (1:1–4:16); The Proclamation of Jesus Messiah (4:17-16:20); The Suffering, Death, and Resurrection of Jesus Messiah (16:21–28:20). Because these are such critical junctures in the narrative, we can probably do no better in defining the basic structure of Matthew. The five discourses may then be regarded as an additional structural element, to be taken as important but subordinate to the more basic threefold structure.

*C. Other Structural Elements.* In addition to the two major structural frameworks mentioned above, other more minor elements of structure deserve mention. Matthew repeatedly gives capsule summaries of the ministry of Jesus, some of which are at the conclusion of narrative and teaching sections (e.g., 4:23-25; 9:35; 11:1; 14:35f.; 15:29-31; 19:1f.; 21:14). Within smaller sections of the Gospel the author displays his literary artistry in grouping certain items. As examples, note his grouping of ten "mighty deeds" of Jesus in chs. 8–9, but particularly his groupings of sevens (e.g., the seven petitions of the Lord's prayer, 6:9-13; the seven parables in ch. 13; the seven woes in ch. 23; the double sevens of the genealogy) and of threes (e.g., the three divisions of the genealogy, 1:1-17; the three kinds of piety, 6:1-18). It is not the numbers themselves that are significant but the Evangelist's practice of grouping (cf. the six antitheses, 5:21-48; the nine benedictions, 5:3-11).

The Evangelist also apparently has a tendency to double items drawn from his sources, as in the two demoniacs of 8:28-34 (cf. Mk. 5:1-20), the two blind men of 20:29-34 (cf. Mk. 10:46-52), and the probable doublet of 20:29-34 in 9:27-31. This, like some of the threes in the Gospel, may well be due to the concern to have the two or three witnesses required by the Law (18:16; cf. 26:60). The author uses other stylistic devices in his Gospel, such as chiasm (e.g., 13:15; 8:14f.) and poetry (see Goulder, pp. 70-94). The twelve formula quotations from the OT, the preponderance of which occur in the first two chapters, are not significant structural elements for the Gospel as a whole, although they do occasionally have structural significance for smaller portions in which they occur.

Matthew shows careful, if complex, organization. The author has used a variety of stylistic devices with considerable artistry. The result is an alternating presentation of deeds and words of Jesus, which have been collected and arranged topically for the sake of their impact on the reader. Apart from the larger, fixed points in the life of Christ, chronology is not a concern of the author.

***III. Genre.***–The genre, or literary character and form, of a document is vitally related to the purposes of its author. How can the Gospel of Matthew be described so as to account for its unique emphases and its peculiar formal elements? Several answers must be considered.

*A. Gospel.* Matthew is of course preeminently a Gospel, an account of the life of Jesus, though not a biography in the modern sense. Matthew, like the other Gospels, is an expansion of the kerygma concerning the fulfillment brought through Jesus, especially in His death and resurrection. Fundamentally a Gospel proclaims the good news concerning the saving activity of God. Without question Matthew does this in a most powerful way. In addition, however, its special characteristics have raised the question of whether Matthew may also be seen to possess the traits of a more specific genre. The categories listed below are not necessarily parallel and by no means mutually exclusive, but are grouped in this way for convenience.

*B. Midrash.* This word is used with various meanings by scholars who have applied it to Matthew. "Midrash" is a noun derived from the Hebrew verb *dāraš,* which means "investigate" or "inquire into." In Jewish literature it came to mean interpretation of biblical texts. In its broader meaning, when applied to Matthew, it refers to the setting forth of an edifying, theological interpretation of Jesus in, or under the form of, historical narrative. In its more restricted meaning, midrash refers to such "historicizing" done in connection with specific OT quotations. Many scholars argue that Matthew contains much midrash, in both the narrower and the wider sense of the word. According to M. D. Goulder, Matthew is a midrashic (or "interpretative") expansion of the Gospel of Mark, to be compared to the Chronicler's treatment of Kings. R. H. Gundry argues for the midrashic character of much of Matthew and maintains that Matthew's readers would have had no trouble in distinguishing the midrashic material from straightforward historical narrative or in accepting it for what it was. It cannot be denied that the Evangelist works midrashically with some of his OT quotations, but it does not follow from this that whatever appears as historical narrative in Matthew is without any historical basis. Matthew contains narratives (e.g., the Infancy narrative) that make much use of OT quotations, and these indeed appear to have had their effect on the wording of the narratives. But this does not mean that the author created historical narratives at will for his own convenience.

*C. Lectionary.* Following G. D. Kilpatrick and P. Carrington (*The Primitive Christian Calendar* [1952]), M. D. Goulder has argued not merely that the composition of the Gospel of Matthew was determined by the lectionary year, but also that it was in fact written to be used liturgically, by supplying consecutive readings based on the Jewish festal year (pp. 171-198). For Goulder the genre of Gospel is liturgical rather than strictly literary.

*D. Catechesis or Catechetical Manual.* The collection of the sayings of Jesus into the five discourses, one of the most obvious characteristics of Matthew, has led many scholars to conclude that it should be thought of as a catechetical document for the upbuilding of Christian discipleship. It is clear that in the early Church the sayings of Jesus were supremely authoritative, and that they played a great role in the instruction of new converts as well as older members of the Church. The view of the Gospel as catechesis is in keeping with the importance of teaching throughout the Gospel (see esp. 28:20). K. Stendahl extended this view of Matthew as catechesis to the hypothesis of a Matthaean School, modeled on the rabbinic schools, that produced in the Gospel a kind of teacher's manual, a Christian equivalent to the Qumrân community's Manual of Discipline. Particular evidence of the school's work, according to Stendahl, is seen in the use of the OT quotations throughout the Gospel.

*E. Church Correctives.* Some have seen Matthew as providing correctives to a community facing serious difficulties, and find in the negative material a clue to the purpose of the Gospel. W. G. Thompson, in a study of 17:22–18:35, argued that Matthew's community was seriously divided and that scandal was commonplace. It is of course possible to argue that behind every positive instruction of the Gospel lies a corresponding vice in the community. Kingsbury (*Parables of Jesus in Matthew 13*) found indications in ch. 13 that Matthew's community was troubled not only by internal strife but also by a spiritual malaise that manifested itself in materialism, secularism, and a disregard for the law. Others (e.g., Minear and Trilling) detected a special concern for the leaders of Matthew's community who were in danger of becoming false prophets or falling into hypocrisy. Still others (e.g., E. Schweizer) have called attention to the polemic in Matthew against false prophets and certain charismatics in the community who did not keep the law (7:15-23). Although the Evangelist accepts the place of prophecy and charismatic healings in the Church, he has no tolerance for the exercise of these gifts apart from the other Christian virtues that are exemplified preeminently in the keeping of the law.

*F. Missionary Propaganda.* Since one of the main intentions of the Gospel is to demonstrate that Jesus is the Messiah, it is possible to see the Gospel as primarily a tool to be used in the Church's mission to the Jews. B. Gärtner and R. S. McConnell have explained the unique OT quotations in Matthew as derived from the missionary preaching directed to the Jews. The great stress on fulfillment throughout the Gospel can be taken as support for this hypothesis.

*G. Polemic Against the Rabbis.* That Jesus debates and criticizes the Pharisees so frequently through the course of the Gospel (see esp. ch. 23) leads naturally to the conclusion that the author and his readers faced a continuing problem in their defense of the gospel against the claims of the synagogue. The debate concerned the question of who possessed the true interpretation of the Torah. Thus the Gospel draws on the traditions about Jesus and the Pharisees and uses this material in the struggle with the Pharisaic Judaism of a later time.

This variety of options concerning the genre of Matthew indicates its multifaceted character. Several of these explanations may well be equally true. The Evangelist could have had several purposes. It is at least clear that Matthew is a "community book," written for the immediate needs of the Evangelist's church during the interim period between the historical events narrated and the return of Christ. The author wrote above all for the Church, in order to interpret the Christ-event, but also to instruct and edify the Christians of his own and future generations.

***IV. Theological Emphases.***–Although Matthew contains much material in common with Mark and Luke, it has some distinctive theological emphases. These are evident

MATTHEW, GOSPEL ACCORDING TO

both from the Gospel's unique material and from the Evangelist's handling of his sources.

*A. Fulfillment: The Kingdom of Heaven.* Without question the theme of fulfillment is a favorite of Matthew. Indeed, the central emphasis of the book is found in "the gospel of the kingdom" (4:23; 9:35; 24:14; cf. 26:13), the good news that the reign or rule of God is now realized in history through the presence of Jesus Christ. Matthew is practically a demonstration of the reality of this kingdom through the words and deeds of Jesus. The Evangelist prefers the Jewish expression the "kingdom of heaven" (lit. "the heavens"), a circumlocution for "kingdom of God" (which, however, does occur in Matthew in 12:28; 19:24; 21:31, 43). The importance of the kingdom for him is obvious from the fact that Matthew uses the word much more frequently than does any of the other Gospels, nearly three times as often as Mark. The message of Jesus (like that of John the Baptist, 3:2) is the coming of the kingdom (4:17) and this in turn becomes the message of the disciples (10:7). Everything in the Gospel relates in one way or another to this controlling theme. To be sure, the kingdom of God has come as a mystery, in an unexpected way, as we learn especially from the parables of ch. 13. In particular, the kind of fulfillment brought by Jesus involves a delay in the judgment of the wicked (13:36-42, 47-50). Nevertheless, the excitement of what has come is not to be missed: "Blessed are your eyes, for they see, and your ears, for they hear. Truly I say to you, many prophets and righteous men longed to see what you see, and to hear what you hear, and did not hear it" (13:16f.). Matthew's special interest in the theme of fulfillment, however, is most clearly evident in the frequent quotations from the OT, particularly the so-called fulfillment quotations.

*B. Use of the OT.* Matthew contains over sixty explicit or substantial quotations (not including far more numerous allusions) from the OT, more than twice as many as any other Gospel. Among these quotations twelve stand out because of the emphasis on fulfillment in the introductory formulae, e.g., "This happened to fulfil what was spoken by the prophet." Ten of these employ the verb "fulfil" (*plēróō*): 1:23 (Isa. 7:14); 2:15 (Hos. 11:1); 2:17f. (Jer. 31:15); 2:23 (Isa. 11:1?); 4:14-16 (Isa. 9:1f.); 8:17 (Isa. 53:4); 12:17-21 (Isa. 42:1-4); 13:35 (Ps. 78:2); 21:4f. (Isa. 62:11; Zec. 9:9); 27:9f. (Zec. 11:12; Jer. 18:2ff.). In 13:14f. a compound form of "fulfil" (*anaplēróō*) occurs (Isa. 6:9f.), and 2:6 (Mic. 5:2) is often ranked alongside these quotations, although it lacks any form of "fulfil" in the formula ("for so it is written by the prophet," words spoken by Herod's chief priests and scribes). These quotations are unique to Matthew among the Gospels except for the quotations of Zec. 9:9 in Jn. 12:15 and Isa. 6:9f. in Mk. 4:12. Matthew's interest in the fulfillment of the OT in relation to the Passion narrative may also be seen in 25:56: "But all this has taken place that the scriptures of the prophets might be fulfilled" (cf. 26:54).

These quotations (except for 13:14f.) are distinctive in that, unlike those taken over from Mark and Q (the text of which is consistently dependent upon the LXX), they exhibit a mixed text, i.e., a text reflecting dependence upon the Hebrew (Masoretic) text of the OT but also influenced by the LXX and other contemporary text forms (see Gundry, *Use of the OT*). The explanation of this and the answer to the related question concerning the source of these special quotations have been much debated. Earlier speculation about Matthew's dependence upon a written *testimonia* source or a fixed oral tradition for the quotations has given way to more specialized theories. K. Stendahl proposed the interesting hypothesis of a Matthaean school, wherein exegesis of OT texts was undertaken using principles similar to the *pesher* hermeneutic (i.e., arguing "this is that") practiced by the Qumrân community. According to Stendahl, this school is responsible for producing the distinctive formula quotations. B. Gärtner has argued against this hypothesis, denying the similarity of Matthew's quotations to the quotations used by the Qumrân community. Gärtner (like Rothfuchs) prefers to understand the formula quotations as derived from the missionary preaching of the early Church, possibly directed against Jewish opponents. Opinion remains divided, however, about whether the formula quotations came to the Evangelist from some form of tradition or whether they were his own formulations. Because they reflect the Evangelist's theology, with its strong emphasis on fulfillment, it is clear that he at least made the quotations his own in his portrayal of Jesus as the Messiah. The argument of the quotations often depends not upon the historico-grammatical meaning of the OT texts, but upon their *sensus plenior* (i.e., a fuller or deeper sense, of which the original authors were unaware at the time they wrote), particularly patterns of typological correspondence. That is, a deeper meaning of these texts is seen by the Evangelist in retrospect and in the light of Christ as the *télos* (the ultimate goal) of the OT expectation.

*C. Christology.* Matthew's doctrine of Christ is fundamentally important to every theological emphasis in the Gospel, for it is the identity of Jesus that determines such things as fulfillment, authoritative exposition of the law, discipleship, ecclesiology, and eschatology. Matthew heightens the Christology of the material drawn from Mark, making it more explicit (e.g., Mk. 8:29, "You are the Christ," becomes in Mt. 16:16, "You are the Christ, the Son of the living God"; cf. Mt. 19:17 with Mk. 10:18; Mt. 9:3 with Mk. 2:7). However, it is in Matthew's unique material that the Evangelist's emphasis on Christology is most apparent.

According to Kingsbury (*Matthew: Structure, Christology, Kingdom*, pp. 40-83) the key christological title in Matthew is "Son of God." This emerges not only where the title actually occurs (e.g., 8:29; 14:33; 16:16; cf. 3:17 and 17:5) but also in such passages as 1:23, "his name shall be called Emmanuel (which means, God with us)"; 14:27, "it is I" (Gk. *egṓ eimi*; cf. Ex. 3:14); and the passages promising the future presence of Jesus with His disciples (18:20 and 28:20). Matthew also stresses the sonship of Jesus by having Him refer to God as His Father some twenty-three times, fifteen of which are unique to Matthew (eight in original material, seven in redactional alteration). For Matthew the most exalted confession, which alone expresses the mystery of Jesus' identity, is that He is the Son of God (16:16). This confession is made only by believers (except where it is blasphemy), and only by revelation (16:17; 11:27; cf. 13:11). The second major title, Son of man, is regularly used by Jesus and thus serves as the public counterpart to the confessional title. In references to the Parousia and the eschatological judgment, it tends to coincide with Son of God. Kingsbury finds no material difference between the titles. J. P. Meier (*The Vision of Matthew*) has argued the equal importance of the two titles.

The important title "Lord" (Gk. *kýrios*) is analogous to Son of God, being found almost exclusively on the lips of the disciples. Messiah (Gk. *Christos*) and Son of David, being closely linked with the stress on fulfillment, are also very important in Matthew. Kingsbury, however, is probably correct in arguing that these titles support the title Son of God. The same is true of such lesser titles or categories as Son of Abraham, The Coming One, Teacher

MATTHEW, GOSPEL ACCORDING TO

(Rabbi), Shepherd, and Servant. Some scholars (esp. M. J. Suggs; cf. J. M. Gibbs, "The Son of God as the Torah Incarnate in Matthew," *SE,* IV [1968], 38-46; R. G. Hamerton-Kelly, *Pre-Existence, Wisdom and the Son of Man* [1973], pp. 67-83) have found the key to Matthew's Christology in the concept of Jesus as the incarnation of Wisdom (e.g., 11:19, 25-27; 23:34-39) and Torah (e.g., 11:28-30). These analyses are consistent with Matthew's emphasis on a Son of God Christology, i.e., "God with us."

*D. Discipleship and Righteousness.* The Evangelist emphasizes the importance of discipleship. The noun "disciple" (*mathētḗs*) occurs much more often in Matthew (seventy-three times) than in the other Synoptic Gospels, and the verb "disciple" (*mathētéuō*) occurs only in Matthew among all four Gospels (13:52; 27:57; 28:19). Disciples are called "sons of God" (5:9, 45), but more frequently by terms meant to emphasize humility, e.g., "brothers" (esp. 12:49f.; 18:15, 21, 35; 23:8; 25:40; 28:10) and, most distinctively, "little ones" (*mikroí,* 10:42; 18:6, 10, 14). Discipleship involves following in the steps of the Lord, which entails self-denial and taking up one's cross (10:38f.; 16:24-26), the suffering of persecution (5:10-12; 10:16-25; 24:9-13), and the humility of a servant (20:26f.; 23:11f.) or child (18:1-4).

Discipleship for this author is inseparable from "righteousness" (*dikaiosýnē*), a word that occurs only in Matthew among the Synoptic Gospels (except for Lk. 1:75). Some of the references have what may be described as a salvation-history orientation (3:15; 5:6, 10; 21:32), but others refer to an unmistakable call to personal righteousness associated with discipleship (5:20; 6:1, 33). The cognate word *díkaios* (usually translated "just") occurs seventeen times, more than all the references in the other three Gospels. This righteousness finds its definition and standard in the law, especially as authoritatively interpreted by Jesus. B. Przybylski properly noted, however, that righteousness in Matthew should not be regarded as the key to discipleship, since the word tends to be limited to the demand of God upon mankind and thus necessarily falls short of describing the good news that Matthew proclaims in Jesus. It is at least a better or higher righteousness to which Jesus calls His disciples. It is a call to the doing of the will of the Father (7:21; 12:50; 21:31).

*E. Community (Church).* The Greek word for "church" (*ekklēsía*) occurs among the Gospels only in Matthew (16:18; 18:17 twice). In ch. 16, at Peter's confession that Jesus is "the Christ, the Son of the living God," Jesus promises to build His community (as the underlying Aramaic would have to be translated) upon Peter. The authority bestowed on Peter in 16:19 (singular verbs) is extended to the Church in a disciplinary context in 18:18 (plural verbs). Here Matthew's church receives its commission to exercise discipline over believers in the full knowledge that it is being led by the Lord (see esp. 18:19, "if two of you agree on earth about anything they ask, it will be done for them by my Father in heaven"). Matthew can appropriately be called an "ecclesiastical" Gospel for other reasons as well. We have already noted that the Evangelist, in his collecting of sayings of Jesus into major discourses, writes particularly for the instruction and edification of the Church. The disciples and their experiences serve as models for the Evangelist's contemporaries; Peter is a prototype of Christian leadership.

It is clear that the Evangelist addresses some urgent matters in his Gospel. His community was probably experiencing division, lawlessness, and even apostasy. He accordingly stresses that the Church is a mixed community that includes both true and false disciples (e.g., 13:29f., 47-50; 22:11-14). He gives severe warnings concerning "false prophets," that is, charismatic enthusiasts who prophesy, cast out demons, and heal — all in the name of Jesus — who come "in sheep's clothing but inwardly are ravenous wolves" (7:15-23). The fault in these false prophets is that they are "evildoers" who bear "evil fruit"; they do not observe the law (cf. E. Schweizer, *NTS,* 16 [1969/70], 213-230). Elsewhere (10:41) the author can encourage hospitality to the itinerant prophet. He urges leaders to avoid the pride and hypocrisy of the Pharisees (23:8-12), who also fail to keep the law. He repeatedly uses the words of Jesus to address the needs of his own church.

*F. Eschatology.* The special interest in eschatology can be seen simply from the length of the apocalyptic discourse compared with that of Mk. 13. Not only is ch. 24 longer than its Markan source (including the warning pericopes 24:37-51, drawn from Q), but the author adds a whole chapter of material not found in Mark, centering on the reality of eschatological judgment. (The parables of the ten virgins [25:1-13] and the last judgment [25:31-46] are unique to Matthew.) Other unique eschatological material in Matthew is found in 13:24-30, 36-43; 20:1-16; and 22:1-14. The technical word *parousía,* which refers to the eschatological return of Christ, is found only in Matthew (24:3, 27, 37, 39) among the Gospels. G. Bornkamm has furthermore shown ("End-Expectation and Church in Matthew," in *Tradition and Interpretation in Matthew,* pp. 15-51) that the Evangelist's eschatology is vitally important to his ecclesiology, Christology, and view of the law. As is true throughout the NT, the primary purpose of eschatology for Matthew is not so much to provide information concerning the future as to motivate the Church to conduct that is appropriate in the light of imminent judgment. Thus in Matthew eschatology is important not only to theology but also to discipleship. The promise of future judgment and deliverance make perseverance in the present a possibility as well as a necessity.

*G. Salvation-History.* Much debate has centered on the structure of Matthew's salvation-history perspective — that is, does the author conceive of three epochs (Israel, Jesus, and the Church) or two (Israel and Jesus, with the Church an extension of the latter)? Kingsbury (*Matthew: Structure, Christology, Kingdom,* pp. 25-37) has argued in favor of two because of the greater importance of Christology than ecclesiology in the Gospel. The threefold analysis, however, may be held without concluding that ecclesiology is the dominant theme of the Gospel. A threefold analysis can give proper emphasis to Christology and the schema of promise and fulfillment while at the same time finding a place for the obvious importance of the transition from Israel to the Church, the limitations of the time of Jesus (cf. the restriction of the mission to Israel), and the determinative significance of the cross and Resurrection for Matthew (cf. J. P. Meier, *The Vision of Matthew,* pp. 26-39).

***V. Theological Tensions.***–On some very important issues Matthew holds perspectives that seem antithetical. These have presented to interpreters some of their largest challenges. The conclusions drawn concerning these issues can affect many other important questions.

*A. Particularism and Universalism.* The particularist emphasis in Matthew is at first shocking. Jesus limits the mission of the Twelve by forbidding them to go to either the Gentiles or the Samaritans (10:5f.), and when entreated by a gentile woman He responds, "I was sent only to the lost sheep of the house of Israel" (15:24). This attitude is so contradictory to the attitude of the author's day, when the Gentile mission was an undeniable reality, that even the most radical scholars accept these sayings as originating from the historical Jesus. This emphasis fits well the basic Jewish orientation of Matthew. Alongside this particularism, however, a universalism is implicit throughout the Gospel (e.g., the Magi from the East, 2:1-12; the Roman centurion, 8:5-13; the Canaanite woman, 15:21-28; the parable of the tenants, 21:33-43; the parable of the marriage feast, 22:1-10; the prophecy in 24:14) that finally becomes explicit in the climactic commission in 28:18-20. It seems logical to conclude from this pattern that particularism was appropriate before the death and resurrection of Christ, but that once this salvific goal had been reached the particularism necessarily gave way to the universal proclamation of the good news. The author, unlike the other Evangelists, retains the record of this particularism during the ministry of Jesus for the sake of his Jewish-Christian congregation. The effect of this motif is to stress to these Jewish-Christian readers the actuality of the fulfillment of the promises to Israel, the continuity of God's purpose for His covenant people. In the face of an increasingly gentile church, which must have given its Jewish opponents the embarrassing ability to argue that Christianity was an alien religion, the readers were able to realize that they, unlike the Gentiles, had a place in the ministry of Jesus from the beginning. They were thus important in the fulfillment of God's plan as a righteous remnant attesting the faithfulness of God to His covenant promises.

*B. Israel and the Church.* This tension, closely related to the preceding one, grows out of the apparently antithetical attitudes toward Israel in Matthew. Alongside the positive orientation to the Jews already noted (see also 2:6; 15:31), as well as the thoroughly Jewish character of the Gospel, Matthew contains a polemic against the Jews. This is most conspicuous in the passages that refer to a transference of the kingdom from Israel to those who believe (the Church): "the sons of the kingdom will be thrown into the outer darkness" (8:12; cf. 21:41, 43). The judgment of unbelieving Israel is found also in such passages as 11:20-24; 12:45 ("this evil generation"); 13:10-15 (the citation of the judgment oracle of Isa. 6:9f.); 22:1-10 ("those invited were not worthy"); and 23:37f. ("your house is forsaken and desolate"). This Gospel emphasizes this motif more than do the other Synoptic Gospels, and only Matthew includes the bitter words "His blood be upon us and on our children" (27:25). This material raises the difficult question of the relation between the Church and Israel or, more concretely, between the author's congregation and the synagogue. He can write "their synagogues" (9:35), "your synagogues" (23:34), and "the Jews to this day" (28:15). Throughout the book the Pharisees are Jesus' main antagonists (cf. "their scribes," 7:29), and the author speaks of Jewish persecution of the Church (23:34; cf. 10:23).

Several divergent conclusions have been drawn from these negative data. Some have argued that the Evangelist's church was gentile rather than Jewish, others that it was Jewish but that the split between synagogue and church (*ca.* A.D. 85) had already taken place (see below). If the latter is not true, the author's Jewish-Christian congregation had at least begun to think of itself as separate from, and over against, unbelieving Judaism — a righteous remnant against the rabbinic Judaism represented in the Gospel by the Pharisees. The transference of the kingdom brought about by Jewish unbelief produced the Church as a "true" Israel, which inherits the promises and within which believing Jews find their rightful place. Against D. R. A. Hare, it is probably the case, moreover, that the author of Matthew had not abandoned the mission to the Jews. The whole thrust of the Gospel argues against such an abandonment, as does the "Great Commission," which should not be understood as excluding Jews (cf. also 23:39). The polemics against, and the distance from, "the Jews" reflected in Matthew are by no means unthinkable within a Jewish-Christian context, but may be akin to intramural criticism of Israel in the prophetic tradition, and are indeed what was naturally to be expected, given the circumstances.

*C. Law and Grace.* Matthew is well known for its emphasis upon Jesus' faithfulness to the law, particularly as expressed in 5:17f.: "Think not that I have come to abolish the law and the prophets; I have not come to abolish them but to fulfil them. For truly, I say to you, till heaven and earth pass away, not an iota, not a dot, will pass from the law until all is accomplished." Jesus' teaching about righteousness and the doing of the will of the Father (7:21; 12:50; 21:31) is understood throughout the Gospel as nothing other than the explication of the true meaning of the law. For the sake of his Jewish-Christian readers the Evangelist portrays Jesus as less radical toward the law than does Mark (against Mk. 7:1-23 compare 15:1-20, where Matthew avoids the conclusion that Jesus "declared all foods clean," and emphasizes only the issue of hand-washing). Jesus is, moreover, shown to agree in principle with the Pharisees (23:2f.), that is, to the extent that they truly expound the meaning of the Mosaic law. Even in Matthew, however, Jesus transcends not only the teachings of the Pharisees (see 9:10-17; 15:1-20) but also the letter of the law while penetrating to its inner spirit (see 5:31-42; 12:1-14; 15:11; 19:3-9). This uniquely authoritative interpretation of the law is possible only because of who Jesus is (the Messiah) and what He has brought (the kingdom). The Pharisees are accordingly no match for Jesus in their interpretation of the law, and at the same time the author's Jewish-Christian church and not the synagogue is shown to be in true succession to Moses. The emphasis upon the law in Matthew is thus much more probably due to the Jewish-Christian orientation of the Gospel than to a direct attempt to counteract a "Pauline" antinomianism, as some have thought.

The law as expounded by Jesus is not a "new" law (note Matthew's omission of Mark's reference to "a new teaching" [1:27]) but the "true" or intended meaning of the Mosaic law. Matthew's stress on the law, however, occurs in the context of the good news of the presence of the kingdom. The announcement of grace is antecedent to the call to live out the righteousness of the law (e.g., the Beatitudes precede the exposition of the law in the Sermon on the Mount). Thus, alongside the stern calls to righteousness (e.g., 5:19f.; 7:21-27; 25:31-46) is also an emphasis upon grace (e.g., 5:3-12; 9:12f.; 10:7f.; 11:28-30; 18:23-35; 20:1-16; 22:1-10; 26:26-28). The grace of the kingdom and the demands of the law as interpreted by the messianic King stand in dynamic tension throughout the Gospel.

***VI. Intended Readers and Purpose.***–What has been said above indicates the high probability that Matthew was written to a Jewish-Christian community. It is not impossible that Matthew was written to a mixed community or even to a gentile community, but the data of the Gospel are again and again explained most satisfactorily on the hypothesis that the first readers were Jewish-Christians. Among the key items to be mentioned here are: the stress throughout the Gospel on fulfillment, especially the formula quotations pointing to Jesus as Messiah and the dawning of the messianic age; the importance of Jesus' fidelity to the law; and the limiting of Jesus' ministry to Israel. Also to be noted is the apologetic motif of the Infancy narrative (against Jewish claims of the illegitimacy of Jesus' birth) and the Resurrection narrative (against the Jewish claim that the body was stolen, 28:12-15), as well as Matthew's omission of Mark's explanation of Jewish customs (cf. esp. Mk. 7:3f. with Mt. 15:2).

A further probability is that the readers were Hellenistic Jews. This is implied by the fact that Matthew was written in Greek. Thus the readers were probably Diaspora rather than Palestinian Jews. The Gospel seems to presuppose the proximity of both unbelieving Jews and Christian Gentiles. This required context, together with the fact that the earliest clear knowledge of Matthew comes probably from Ignatius (*ca.* A.D. 110), bishop of Antioch, has led many scholars to favor Antioch of Syria as the location of the readers. This remains, however, only one possibility among many, and it is worth emphasizing that the nature of the data allows us only to speculate where Matthew's community was located.

From the content of the Gospel and the probable identity of the readers, it is possible to draw the following conclusions about the author's purpose. The Gospel was written to confirm Jewish believers in the truth of Christianity as the fulfillment of the promises to Israel, hence the argument that Jesus is the Messiah, that He was loyal to the law, and that He came to the Jews. The argumentation is designed, on the one hand, to enable the readers to become conscious of and to maintain their identity over against the gentile church with whom they are undeniably in relationship, but, on the other hand, and more importantly, to provide a defense against the charges made by the readers' unbelieving brethren in the synagogue. Matthew's community was thus in need of an account of the story of Jesus that would enable them to relate both to gentile Christians and to unbelieving Jews. The increasing success of the gentile mission and the failure of the mission to Israel raised questions not only in the readers' minds, but also among their Jewish opponents.

The author wrote primarily to strengthen the faith and spiritual life of his congregation. This he did through the teaching and exhortation in the Gospel as well as through the polemic against the Pharisees. What he produced, however, could also have been particularly useful in the mission to unbelieving Jews, which, though increasingly difficult, had not ceased.

*VII. Date and Provenance.*–Two key questions that pertain to the dating of Matthew are whether the Gospel reflects a knowledge of the fall of Jerusalem (A.D. 70) and whether the relationship between church and synagogue indicates that the final break, usually dated to 85 or 90, had already occurred when the Gospel was written. Both questions are difficult to answer. Matthew does allude to the destruction of Jerusalem in 24:2 (cf. 24:15-28), but this can be naturally explained as a record of the prophecy of Jesus, unless the possibility of foretelling the future is ruled out *a priori*. The reference in 22:7 to the king who, being angry because those invited to the marriage feast did not come, "sent his troops and destroyed those murderers and burned their city" is more problematic. The reference to "troops" who "burned the city," unnecessary and alien to the context, seems to point to the destruction of Jerusalem. Even if it does, however, the possibility remains that Jesus prophesied the event through the parable or that the words were added to the Gospel after the event had occurred. Thus 22:7 cannot itself be proof that Matthew as a whole is to be dated after A.D. 70.

It is often thought that a crucial turning point in the relationship of church and synagogue was reached at Jamnia toward the end of the 80's, when liturgical alterations were enacted that forced covert Christians out of the synagogues. But this was in reality only the final development in a hostility and estrangement that had long characterized relations between Christian and non-Christian Jews. From the data in Matthew alone it is impossible to conclude whether the Gospel was written before or after the decisions made at Jamnia. Alienation, competition, and hostility, were not unusual before the break, and the mission to the Jews did not cease after the break.

One further important point in dating Matthew is the probable dependence upon Mark. If Mark was written in the 60's, then Matthew may have been written in the 70's. Some have found encouragement for accepting a later date (80-100) in the developed ecclesiology (16:18f.; 18:15-20) and doctrine of the Gospel (e.g., 28:19). Yet the letters of Paul have similar perspectives several years before the destruction of Jerusalem. It may further be asked why, if Matthew was written after 70, no attempt is made (as in Lk. 21) to disentangle the references to the fall of Jerusalem and the end of the age in Jesus' apocalyptic discourse (ch. 24).

Although the majority of scholars date Matthew after 70 (the 80's appearing most popular), it must be admitted that the evidence is short of compelling, and a pre-70 date remains a possibility. (See the arguments of Gundry, comm., pp. 599-609, in favor of an early date — which, however, also fall short of demonstration.)

With no evidence to the contrary, either from the Gospel or tradition, it is fair to conclude that the author of Matthew wrote as a member, and in the locale, of the community for which he composed the Gospel (see discussion of intended readers, above).

*VIII. Authorship.*–Matthew, like the other three Gospels, is an anonymous document. The title *katá Matthaion* ("according to Matthew") was affixed to the Gospel sometime in the 2nd century. From early in the 2nd. cent. the unanimous tradition of the Church supports Matthew as the author (e.g., Papias, who received the tradition from the Elder [Apostle?] John, Pantaenus, Irenaeus, Origen, Eusebius, Jerome). The only clues within the text of the Gospel itself are the substitution of the name Matthew (9:9) for Levi in the calling of the tax-collector to be a disciple (Mk. 2:13; cf. Lk. 5:27), and the addition of the words "the tax collector" to the name Matthew in the listing of the Twelve in Mt. 10:3 (cf. Mk. 3:18; Lk. 6:15). For some reason the Evangelist wants to show that Levi is the Matthew listed among the Twelve. Is this because he believes that Levi was or should have been one of the Twelve, or is it perhaps because in writing of himself he preferred the name Matthew to his own preconversion name, Levi?

The real question is the reliability of the tradition about the authorship of the Gospel. It is possible, although uncertain, that the whole tradition derives from, and is thus dependent upon, the testimony of only one man, Papias (as recorded in Eusebius *HE* iii.39.16). In any event, the tradition appears to have been unchallenged. It is difficult to believe that the Gospel would have been attributed to Matthew without good reason, since, so far as we can tell from the available data, Matthew was not otherwise a leading figure among the apostles or in the early Church (his name is mentioned only once outside the Gospels, Acts 1:13). A key objection, it should be noted, has often been set against the traditional ascription of the Gospel to Matthew. Can one of the Twelve, an eyewitness of the events, have depended so much upon the account of Mark, a nonparticipant in the events narrated? According to the tradition handed on by Papias (Eusebius *HE* iii.39.15), however, Mark is essentially the preaching of Peter, and it is not at all inconceivable that Matthew might depend upon the Petrine account.

But can Matthew the apostle have written the Greek document that goes by his name, a document apparently addressed to Hellenistic Jews of the Diaspora, a document that contains such developed and "late" perspectives? Here it is more difficult to be confident. The tradition about Matthaean authorship may be compatible with a conclusion that the Gospel contains traditions stemming from the apostle (who as a former tax-collector may well have kept records of Jesus' ministry), perhaps now recognizable particularly in the Gospel's special material, e.g., in the formula quotations or the five discourses. A disciple (or disciples) of Matthew may later have translated and adapted these materials, combined them with the Markan and Q traditions, and reworked the whole to produce the present Gospel. Such a hypothesis, speculative though it must be, would account for problems (e.g., putting the Pharisees and Sadducees together; the possible misunderstanding of Zec. 9:9 in 21:1-9 to involve two animals rather than one) that have caused a number of scholars (see J. P. Meier, *The Vision of Matthew*, pp. 17-25) to go so far as to conclude that the author was a Gentile rather than a Jew.

Matthew the apostle is thus probably the source of major portions of the Gospel, in particular the sayings of Jesus. One or more disciples in succession to Matthew may then have put these materials into the form of the Gospel we have today. The final editing probably was done by Hellenistic Jewish Christians, who in transmitting the tradition addressed Jewish brethren who, like themselves, had come to believe in Jesus as Messiah. If all this is so, then in this Gospel the words of Jesus preserved by the apostle, and sometimes regarded as an autobiographical allusion, found their fulfillment: "Therefore every scribe who has been trained for the kingdom of heaven is like householder who brings out of his treasure what is new and what is old" (13:52).

***Bibliography.–Comms.:*** W. F. Albright and C. S. Mann (*AB*, 1971); W. C. Allen (*ICC*, 3rd ed. 1912); A. W. Argyle (*CBC*, 1963); F. W. Beare (1981); P. Bonnard (*Comm. du NT*, 2nd ed. 1970); J. C. Fenton (*Pelican NT Comms.*, 1963); F. V. Filson (*HNTC*, 1960); P. Gaechter (1963); H. B. Green (*New Clarendon Bible*, 1975); W. Grundmann (*ThHK*, 1967); R. A. Guelich, *Sermon on the Mount* (1982); R. H. Gundry (1982); D. Hill (*NCBC*, repr. 1981); E. Klostermann (*HNT*, 4th ed. 1971); M. J. Lagrange (*Études bibliques*, 7th ed. 1948); E. Lohmeyer and W. Schmauch (*KEK*, 4th ed. 1967); J. P. Meier (*NT Message*, 1980); W. Michaelis (*Züricher Bibelkommentare*, 2 vols., 1948-1949); A. H. McNeile (1938); A. Plummer (5th ed. 1920); A. Schlatter (6th ed. 1963); J. Schmid (*Regensburger NT*, 1959); J. Schniewind (*NTD*, 12th ed. 1968); E. Schweizer (*NTD*, 1973; Eng. tr. 1975); R. V. G. Tasker (*Tyndale*, 1961); T. Zahn (*KZNT*, 4th ed. 1922).

*Other works:* E. L. Abel, *NTS*, 17 (1970/71), 138-52; B. W. Bacon, *Studies in Matthew* (1930); E. P. Blair, *Jesus in the Gospel of Matthew* (1960); G. Bornkamm, G. Barth, and H. J. Held, *Tradition and Interpretation in Matthew* (Eng. tr. 1963); K. W. Clark, *JBL*, 66 (1947), 165-172; O. L. Cope, *Matthew: A Scribe Trained for the Kingdom of Heaven* (1976); W. D. Davies, *Setting of the Sermon on the Mount* (1963); M. Didier, ed., *L'Évangile selon Matthieu* (1972); P. F. Ellis, *Matthew: His Mind and Message* (1974); H. Frankemölle, *Jahwebund und Kirche Christi* (1974); P. Gaechter, *Literarische Kunst im Matthäus-Evangelium* (1966); B. Gärtner, *ST*, 8 (1954), 1-24; B. Gerhardsson, *Mighty Acts of Jesus According to Matthew* (1979); T. F. Glasson, *JQR*, 51 (1960/61) 316-20; E. J. Goodspeed, *Matthew, Apostle and Evangelist* (1959); M. D. Goulder, *Midrash and Lection in Matthew* (1974); R. H. Gundry, *Use of the OT in St. Matthew's Gospel* (*Society for NT Studies Supp.*, 18, 1967); D. R. A. Hare, *Theme of Jewish Persecution of Christians in the Gospel According to Matthew* (*Society for NT Studies Monograph*, 6, 1967); D. J. Harrington, *Heythrop Journal*, 16 (1975), 375-388; D. Hill, *Irish Biblical Studies*, 1 (1979), 139-149; R. Hummel, *Auseinandersetzung zwischen Kirche und Judentum im Matthäusevangelium* (1963); G. D. Kilpatrick, *Origins of the Gospel according to St. Matthew* (1946); J. D. Kingsbury, *Matthew* (1977); *Matthew: Structure, Christology, Kingdom* (1975); *Parables of Jesus in Matthew 13* (2nd ed. 1976); G. Künzel, *Studien zum Gemeindeverständnis des Matthäus-Evangeliums* (1978); R. S. McConnell, *Law and Prophecy in Matthew's Gospel* (1969); J. P. Meier, *Law and History in Matthew's Gospel* (1976); *The Vision of Matthew* (1979); P. S. Minear, *Matthew: The Teacher's Gospel* (1982); P. Nepper-Christensen, *Matthäusevangelium: ein juden-christliches Evangelium?* (1958); J. J. O'Rourke, *CBQ*, 24 (1962), 394-403; B. Przybylski, *Righteousness in Matthew and his Word of Thought* (*Society for NT Studies Monograph*, 41, 1980); W. Rothfuchs, *Erfüllungszitate des Matthäus-Evangeliums* (1969); G. Schille, *NTS*, 4 (1957/58), 101-114; E. Schweizer, *Matthäus und seine Gemeinde* (1974); G. M. Soares Prabhu, *Formula Quotations in the Infancy Narrative of Matthew* (1976); K. Stendahl, *School of St. Matthew and Its Use of the OT* (2nd ed. 1968); G. Strecker, *Weg der Gerechtigkeit* (1962); M. J. Suggs, *Wisdom, Christology, and Law in Matthew's Gospel* (1970); K. Tagawa, *NTS*, 16 (1969/70), 149-162; W. G. Thompson, *Matthew's Advice to a Divided Community* (1970); W. Trilling, *Das wahre Israel* (1959); S. Van Tilborg, *Jewish Leaders in Matthew* (1972); R. Walker, *Heilsgeschichte im ersten Evangelium* (1967).

D. A. HAGNER

**MATTHEW'S BIBLE.** *See* ENGLISH VERSIONS III.E.

**MATTHIAS** ma-thī'əs [Gk. *Matthias* or *Maththias* (a shortened form of *Mattathias*)].

**1.** The man chosen to take the place of Judas among the Twelve (Acts 1:23, 26). Matthias is the contracted form of the name Mattathias, which derives from Heb. *mattiṯyâ*, "the gift of Yahweh." Eusebius (*HE* i.12.3) believed that Matthias was one of the seventy sent out by Jesus (Lk. 10:1). Clement of Alexandria (*Misc.* iv.6.23) suggested that Zacchaeus was the proper identification. Church tradition says that Matthias's body was sent by Constantine to Trier, where it was lost, miraculously recovered, and reburied (cf. J. Jeremias, *Heiligengräber in Jesu Umwelt* [1958], p. 88). Acts 1:21-26 is the only scriptural information.

When Peter addressed the assembly of Christians regarding the fall of Judas and the need to fill his place, he gave the qualifications for the apostolate, as it was understood by Luke. An apostle was to be a man who had been with Jesus throughout His ministry, from His baptism to His resurrection. Two men were put forward, Joseph Barsabbas and Matthias. Peter led what seems to be the first corporate prayer mentioned in the NT, praying that the choice not be that of men but that of God. Then, following the OT practice for discovering God's choice (Prov. 16:33), lots were cast. Matthias was chosen. Casting lots probably involved writing the name of each man on a stone and putting the stones into a vessel. The vessel was then shaken until one stone came out; the man whose name was on that stone was chosen.

In the patristic era Matthias was identified with Gnosticism. Origen (*Hom. I on Luke*) referred to a Gospel of Matthias known in his time. Clement of Alexandria (*Misc.* ii.9.45; iii.4.26; vii.13.82) possibly referred to the same work as the Traditions of Matthias. Gnostics, chiefly those associated with Basilides, claimed Matthias the apostle as the origin of their teaching in this writing.

**2.** (1 Esd. 9:33, AV). *See* MATTATTAH.

D. W. WEAD

**3.** Son of Margalus. He and Judas the son of Saripheus were well-known interpreters and teachers of the law during the last days of Herod the Great. Contrary to Jewish law, Herod had placed a large golden eagle over the gate of the temple. Thinking that Herod was at the point of death, Matthias and Judas instigated their students to dismantle the offending object. Herod rallied, however, and the two teachers and forty of their students were brought before him and condemned to be burned alive (Josephus *BJ* i.33.2-4 [648-655]; *Ant.* xvii.6.2-4 [149-167]). Josephus records that a lunar eclipse occurred on that night (*Ant.* xvii.6.4 [167]). This is the only reference to a lunar eclipse in Josephus's writings, and this phenomenon (4 B.C.) is of great importance in dating the death of Herod and the birth of Jesus.

**4.** Son of Theophilus; a native of Jerusalem who was elevated to the high priesthood by Herod the Great during the intrigues that immediately preceded that king's death (*Ant.* xvii.4.2 [78]). Shortly after his appointment Matthias became ceremonially unclean on the Day of Atonement, with the result that Josephus the son of Ellemus became high priest for that day alone. Herod removed Matthias from the high-priestly office during the disruptions that resulted in the death of Matthias son of Margalus (*Ant.* xvii.6.4 [164-67]).

**5.** Son of Ananus (the Annas of Lk. 3:2; Jn. 18:13, 24; Acts 4:6); high priest from A.D. 42-43. After deposing Simon Cantheras from office, Agrippa I had determined to reappoint Jonathan high priest, but Agrippa complied with Jonathan's request that the honor be given instead to his brother Matthias (*Ant.* xix.6.4 [313-16]).

**6.** Son of Theophilus (*Ant.* xx.9.7 [223]; but called the son of Boethus in *BJ* v.13.1 [527]); appointed high priest by Agrippa II shortly after the completion of the temple (*ca.* A.D. 65). Matthias was high priest at the start of the war with the Romans (*Ant.* xx.9.7 [223]). He opened Jerusalem to Simon the son of Giora (*BJ* iv.9.11 [574]); but later Simon accused him of complicity with the Romans and executed him and three of his sons (*BJ* v.13.1 [527-531]).

**7.** Son of Simon Psellus; ancestor of Josephus. He married a daughter of Jonathan the Hasmonean (Josephus *Vita* 1 [4]).

**8.** Son of Matthias (7); great-grandfather of Josephus (*Vita* 1 [5]).

**9.** Father of Josephus; described by his son as a man of eminence because of his noble birth and personal righteousness (*Vita* 1f. [5, 7]).

10. Brother of Josephus (*Vita* 1 [8]).

J. J. SCOTT, JR.

**MATTITHIAH** mat-ə-thī'ə [Heb. *mattiṯyâ, mattiṯyāhû*–'gift of Yahweh'].

**1.** Son of Jeduthun (1 Ch. 25:3); a Levitical temple musician appointed in David's time to play the lyre before the ark (15:18, 21; 16:5; 25:21).

**2.** First son of Shallum; a Korahite Levite in charge of making flat cakes for the temple service after the return from the Babylonian Exile (1 Ch. 9:31).

**3.** [Gk. Apoc. *Mazitias*]; AV, NEB, RSV mg., MAZITIAS. Son of Nebo; a layman who had married a foreign woman (Ezr. 10:43; 1 Esd. 9:35).

**4.** One of those who stood at Ezra's right hand during the public reading of the law (Neh. 8:4); called Mattathiah in 1 Esd. 9:43.

**MATTOCK** [Heb. *'ēṯ*] (1 S. 13:20f.); AV COULTER. An agricultural tool with a pick or narrow blade at one end and a broader blade at the other, used for grubbing or digging. The metal blade quickly became worn from constant use in the vineyards on the rocky hillside terraces of Palestine. The RSV renders "plowshare" for *'ēṯ* in Isa. 2:4; Joel 3:10 (MT 4:10); Mic. 4:3 (but cf. NEB "mattock"). The AV renders "mattock" for *maḥ^a^rēšâ* in 1 S. 13:20f. (RSV, NEB, "sickle," "plowshare" [v. 21]). Both the mattock and the plowshare were in common use by the time of David.

The various translations of *'ēṯ* by the RSV and AV reflect various scholarly opinions of its meaning. Heb. *'ēṯ* is often related to Akk. *ittu,* but according to B. Landsberger (*JNES,* 17 [1958], 56 n. 4), Akk. *ittu* is the "seed funnel (of seeder plow)," not a plowshare (cf. *CAD,* VII, 312). S. Byington (*JBL,* 68 [1949], 49-54) argued that Heb. *'ēṯ* was a spade or heavy hoe rather than a plowshare, since the former could more appropriately be forged from a sword (Isa. 2:4; Mic. 4:3; vice versa in Joel 3:10).

*See also* IRON I.D; PLOW. N. J. O. G. A. L.

**MATURE** [Gk. *téleios*–'complete, perfect'] (1 Cor. 2:6; 14:20; Eph. 4:13; Phil. 3:15; Col. 1:28; 4:12; He. 5:14); AV PERFECT, FULL AGE, MEN, PERFECTION; NEB also RIPE, GROWN UP, GROWN MEN; [*telesphoréō*–'bear fruit to maturity'] (Lk. 8:14); AV PERFECTION; **MATURITY** [*téleios*] (He. 6:1); AV PERFECTION. *See also* PERFECT.

Maturity results from a full knowledge of the apostolic teaching about Christ and salvation and from correct application of this teaching to everyday life. Thus maturity is the Church's goal for its members.

Although the concept of Christian maturity occurs mainly in the Epistles, Luke contains an important illustration — the parable of the Sower (8:14). Here Jesus tells of optimum spiritual growth, from initial reception of the gospel to steadfast discipleship, and warns that those who become overly concerned with their material goods and other affairs of this present age will not bear mature "fruit," i.e., a life of righteous behavior and Christian endeavor.

A child-adult metaphor is the basis of Paul's exhortations to mature conduct in 1 Cor. 2:6; 3:1-3 and in 14:20. These passages must be understood in relation to the various problems in the Corinthian church.

In 2:6, 10-12 Paul speaks of Christian wisdom, i.e., the mystery of salvation, formerly hidden but now revealed to the Christian community by the Spirit of God. This wisdom is from God and is not the worldly rhetoric popular among the Corinthians (1:20; 3:18). The "mature" of 2:6 are those who competently discern the doctrinal and spiritual matters of the Christian life. The "mature" and the "spiritual" person (2:15) are counterparts.

Because some of the church members are divisive, Paul addresses the Corinthians as "people of the flesh" (*sárkinoi*) as opposed to "spiritual people" (*pneumatikoí*) in 3:1. The actions of the Corinthians are typical of "babes" (*nḗpioi*) in Christ. They are no longer "natural" people (RSV mg., 2:14), for they have believed in Christ and have been incorporated into His body. But neither are they "spiritual" people, for they are squabbling about leadership in their church (1:12; 3:1-4). Hence they are immature, and Paul addresses them as such. The implication of his argument is that mature Christians will not glory in various teachers such as Paul and Apollos but instead will discern that church growth ultimately comes from God (3:6) and that the Church is built by Him (v. 9).

The child-adult metaphor in 1 Cor. 14:20 also concerns proper conduct. The Corinthians' preoccupation with unintelligible ecstatic speech had resulted in confusion in church worship. Paul repeatedly points out the value of speech that is understood (14:3-5, 9, 12, 15, etc.), offering several simple analogies to illustrate his reasoning (vv. 7f., 10f., 23). The direct appeal for maturity (v. 20) calls for agreement with these simple truths. The Corinthians are not immature in the sense that they lack Christian knowledge. Rather, their practical application of the knowledge they possess is defective. Behavior that is immature by the standards of apostolic doctrine is the usual target of Paul's argument. This is made clear by his statement, "When I was a child, I spoke like a child, I thought like a child, I reasoned like a child; when I became a man, I gave up childish ways" (13:11). Similar is his closing exhortation in 16:13 to "be manly" (*andrízesthe*; RSV "be courageous"; NEB "be valiant"; cf. Shep. Herm. Vis. i.4.3).

In similar fashion the author of Hebrews chides his readers for being immature children, still living on milk. In contrast, those who eat "solid food" are the mature, who are described as able "to distinguish good from evil" (He. 5:12-14).

Paul speaks of those who have attained maturity (1 Cor. 2:6; Phil. 3:15) and describes his effort to attain conformity with Christ in his ministry (Phil. 3:11-15). But an absolute state of maturity is not possible in this present evil age, and maturity nowhere in the NT implies sinless perfection (cf. 1 Jn. 1:8-10).

In Colossians Paul makes clear that his objective and that of those who minister with him is to bring every member of the believing community to maturity (1:28). This is to be brought about by the proclamation of Christ, by admonition, and by teaching all that Christian salvation involves. This active, thorough instruction intends to instill in every Christian an "assured understanding" of Christ, God's mystery (2:2). The doctrinal knowledge necessary for maturity is not like the intellectual mastery of esoteric formulas that Gnosticism proclaimed as the way to salvation. Rather, this knowledge is a developing of the believer's understanding of Christian truth and is thoroughly christocentric (2:3, 6, 9f.), because the believer matures "in Christ" (1:28). Christian knowledge is not only intellectual but also experiential and personal. The believer "walks" in Christ and is "rooted" and "built up" in Him (2:6f.). Paul certainly has in mind an ongoing process of growth through daily Christian experience and assimilation of teaching. Maturity will prevent deception by erroneous teachers who promise spiritual maturity and perfection through philosophical and other worldly means (vv. 8-23).

Ephesians, too, presents maturity as an antidote to the popular religious speculation that threatened to undermine the teaching of the apostles. Mature Christians will not be like children, who are easily deceived and swayed by new ideas (4:14). As in Philippians, maturity is a goal desired for the body of Christ and is realized through those who teach and proclaim Him. This cooperative ministering will result in the "perfecting" (*katartismós*) of the saints, the development of yet more ministerial activity, and the building up of the body of Christ (v. 12). The Church will then be unified in faith and mature in "the knowledge of the Son of God" (v. 13). Essential to Paul's concept of growth here is Christian love (*agápē*, vv. 15f.). As in Col. 2:6f., spiritual growth is not exclusively intellectual but also results from the personal experience of being in Christ.

It is significant that in the NT the idea of growth into maturity is in each instance related to obedience to the apostolic teaching. The concept of maturity is communicated in both parabolic and analogic fashion to Christians of the early Church; those who have not moved toward this goal are reproved (He. 5:11–6:1; 1 Cor. 14:20). Christian maturity is a result of acquiring a comprehensive knowledge of Christ and His salvation. Such knowledge prevents deception by erroneous doctrine and enables the believer with discernment and competence to apply the apostolic teaching to everyday life (He. 5:14). Thus the life of the mature Christian, both in thought and in action, is in accordance with NT teaching.

***Bibliography.***–C. K. Barrett, comm. on 1 Corinthians (*HNTC*, 1968); *TDNT*, VIII, *s.v.* τέλος κτλ.: τέλειος (Delling).

R. J. WYATT

**MAUL.** The AV translation of Heb. *mappēṣ* in Prov. 25:18 (RSV "war club"). *See* CLUB; WEAPONS OF WAR.

**MAW.** *See* STOMACH.

**MAXIMS** [Heb. *zikkārôn*] (Job 13:12); AV REMEMBRANCES; NEB POMPOUS TALK. The Hebrew term is related to the verb *zāḵar*, "mention" or "remember." Thus it may mean "remembrances of the aged," "wise sayings," or simply "the things (you) mention" (cf. E. Dhorme, *Book of Job* [Eng. tr. 1967], pp. 185f.).

**MAZITIAS** maz-ə-tī'əs (AV, NEB, RSV mg., 1 Esd. 9:35). *See* MATTITHIAH **3.**

**MAZZAROTH** maz'zə-roth [Heb. *mazzerôṯ*] (Job 38:32); NEB SIGNS OF THE ZODIAC. The RSV and AV transliterate the Hebrew term, which occurs only in this list of constellations in Job 38:31f. The NEB rendering equates *mazzerôṯ* with *mazzelôṯ* ("constellations," 2 K. 23:5), a term only slightly less obscure because of its use in rabbinical Hebrew, where it can refer generally to the signs of the zodiac, planets, or constellations (see Jastrow, I, 755; cf. also M. Pope, *Job* [*AB*, 1973], p.301). E. Dhorme (comm. on Job [Eng. tr. 1967], pp. 589f.) rejected the equation with *mazzelôṯ*, claiming instead that it referred to the Corona Borealis (deriving *mazzerôṯ* as a plural of majesty from *nēzer*, "crown"). As R. Gordis stated, the identification remains enigmatic (*Book of Job* [1978], p. 450).

G. A. L.

**MEADOW** [Heb. *kar*] (Ps. 65:13 [MT 14]; Zeph. 2:6); AV PASTURE, "cottage"; NEB also KERETH. The plural of Heb. *kar* can apparently be either masculine (Heb. *kārîm*, Ps. 65:13) or feminine (Heb. *kārôṯ*, Zeph. 2:6). Cf. GKC, § 87 n–o for other biforms. As M. Dahood (*Psalms*, I [*AB*, 1965], 230) pointed out, both the etymology (<*kārâ*, "dig, hollow out") and the context (note the parallel to *ʿēmeq*, "valley") suggest the translation "hollows" for *kārîm* (cf. J. Kselman, *CBQ*, 32 [1970], 581 n. 13). While this translation is also possible in Zeph. 2:6, the parallelism favors the AV "cottage" or RSV "meadow." The NEB translation points out a textual problem: the LXX apparently renders Heb. *krt* as *Krētē*, "Crete," the supposed home of the Philistines (*see* CAPHTOR; CRETE). This translation does fit the general context (cf. Chereth in v. 5), but the LXX may be corrupt, since it omits some words that are in the MT (the NEB has to reorder the text for its translation). Thus the RSV is perhaps preferable, since its only emendation is to repoint MT *newôṯ* (pl. construct of *nāwâ*) as *nāwôṯ* (as it stands, the MT reads lit. "pasture of meadows of shepherds").

G. A. L.

**MEAH** mē'ə (AV Neh. 3:1; 12:39). *See* HUNDRED, TOWER OF THE; JERUSALEM III.F.2.x.

**MEAL** [Heb. *qemaḥ* (Nu. 5:15; 1 K. 4:22 [MT 5:2]; 17:12 14, 16; 2 K. 4:41; 1 Ch. 12:40 [MT 41]; Isa. 47:2; Hos. 8:7); Gk. *áleuron* (Mt. 13:33 par. Lk. 13:21)]; AV also FLOUR; NEB also FLOUR, GRAIN; **COARSE MEAL** [Heb. *ʿarîsâ* (Nu. 15:20f.; Neh. 10:37 [MT 38]; Ezk. 44:30)]; AV DOUGH; NEB FIRST KNEADING (or LUMP) OF DOUGH; **FINE MEAL** [Heb. *qemaḥ sōleṯ* (Gen. 18:6), *sōleṯ* (2 K. 7:1, 16, 18)]; AV also FINE FLOUR; NEB FLOUR; **MEAL OFFERING** [Heb. *minḥâ*] (Ezk. 46:15); NEB GRAIN-OFFERING.

Meal is the food product that results from the grinding of the whole kernels and the bran of the grains of cereal plants, but it is not the grains themselves (Isa. 47:2; Hos. 8:7; 2 S. 17:28). It was the staple flour of the common folk, e.g., it was used by the widow of Zarephath to make cakes (1 K. 17:12ff.). This common meal (*qemaḥ*) was not normally used for sacrificial purposes as was fine flour (*sōleṯ*;

see below but cf. Nu. 5:15; Jgs. 6:19). Meal was part of the foodstuffs brought to Hebron for the celebration of the kingship of David (1 Ch. 12:40), and it was used in the preparation of food in Solomon's court (1 K. 4:22 [MT 5:2]). Elisha also threw meal into the "poisoned pottage" (2 K. 4:41), probably a prophetic act (so W. S. LaSor, *NBC* [rev. ed. 1970], p. 351) rather than a magical charm (cf. J. Gray, *I & II Kings* [*OTL*, rev. ed. 1970], p. 500).

Meal was normally made from wheat, but on occasion could be made from barley. A coarse barley meal was used in the rite pertaining to the adjudication of the accused wife (Nu. 5:15). Some rabbinic authorities (e.g., T.B. *Sotah* 14a) suggested that this barley meal was food for beasts; it was presented in this ceremony because she was accused of a "beastly thing" (see N. H. Snaith, *Leviticus and Numbers* [*NCBC*, 1969], p. 31). Note the usage of barley by the poorer classes in Ruth 2:17; Jn. 6:9ff.; cf. Jgs. 7:13.

Fine flour (*sōleṯ*; 1 K. 4:22) was a more luxurious food than meal, probably made from the inner kernels of wheat (*TWOT*, II, 628). In one instance *sōleṯ* describes the special type of meal (*qemaḥ*) that was used to prepare cakes for honored guests (Gen. 18:6; cf. J. Skinner, comm. on Genesis [*ICC*, 1910], p. 300, who considers *sōleṯ* a gloss). Fine flour was used in the king's palace (1 K. 4:22) and was also the flour which was normally used for sacrificial purposes. During the period of the divided monarchy it was twice as expensive as barley (2 K. 7:1ff.).

The first portion of coarse meal (Heb. *ʿarîsâ*) was presented to the priests as an act of worship (Nu. 15:20f.; Neh. 10:37; Ezk. 44:30; *see also* SACRIFICES AND OFFERINGS OF THE OT V.E). The LXX *sítos*, "grain," supports the RSV's translation, but certain early Jewish traditions considered it to be some type of pasty substance (see G. B. Gray, comm. on Numbers [*ICC*, 1903], p. 177; L. W. Batten, comm. on Ezra-Nehemiah [*ICC*, 1913], p. 378 for references).

In the NT "meal" occurs only in Jesus' parable of the leaven: He likened the kingdom of God to the little bit of leaven that produces such a dramatic change in measures of meal (of flour, Gk. *áleuron*, Mt. 13:33 par. Lk. 13:21).

C. G. RASMUSSEN

**MEALS.** A meal (Heb. *ʾōḵel, ʾoḵlâ, ʾaruḥâ*) denoted the portion of food eaten at a given time, whether alone or in company, as well as the occasion of eating, described more fully as *ʿēṯ hāʾōḵel*, "mealtime" (Ruth 2:14).

I. Daily Meals
II. The Royal Commissary
III. Treatment of Guests
IV. Ritual and Symbolic Meals

*I. Daily Meals.*–Generally speaking, many people in the ancient Near East ate only one light and one substantial meal each day, while the poor were fortunate if they ate modestly once daily. In OT times there was no such formal repast as breakfast, although pangs of hunger experienced on awaking might be satisfied by eating a small piece of bread or some fruit, such as grapes, olives, or figs. Those who worked as fishermen, laborers, or craftsmen might take a small amount of food in a fold of their garments to eat while they walked to their place of work, but that procedure could hardly be dignified by the term breakfast. Nor is it really comparable to the "breaking of fast" mentioned in Jn. 21:12, 15, although the nature of the Greek *áriston* is uncertain in any event. In late Greek it was regarded as the equivalent of the classical *deípnon* or dinner, as described in Mt. 22:24; Lk. 11:38; 14:12, but the incident described in John does not appear to involve a proper meal.

Relief showing a man and a woman eating a ceremonial meal (Zenjirli, 9th-8th cent. B.C.) (University Museum, University of Pennsylvania)

According to an old custom, the laborers worked all morning with little or no food, and then had their first meal of the day about noon (cf. Gen. 43:16; Ruth 2:14), although the time varied according to the occupation and circumstances of the eater. This meal normally consisted of pieces of bread, roasted grain, olives, figs, or other fruit in season, and was generally light in character so as not to interfere with the afternoon's work. Eating a heavy meal in the morning was considered a sign of decadence (cf. Eccl. 10:16), since it was inevitably accompanied by drinking (cf. Acts 2:15). Those who had abstained from the noon meal were considered to be "fasting" (cf. Jgs. 20:26; 1 S. 14:24).

The main meal of the day, equivalent to "dinner" (Gk. *deípnon*), occurred about sunset, when the day's labors were finished (cf. Lk. 17:7; 24:29f.). The entire family was present for the occasion, and it was a time of fellowship and general conversation. The food, which normally consisted of a soup or stew augmented by vegetables or herbs, was served in a common dish. Each person took a small piece of bread and dipped it into the bowl (cf. Mt. 26:23; Mk. 14:20) in order to scoop up a little of the contents.

The poor would have to be satisfied with bread and water, and perhaps some olives or other fruits in season, and would seldom taste meat unless they hunted. A lamb was roasted annually at the Passover, with a single animal sometimes being shared between several poor families. This festival, instituted at the time of the Exodus (Ex. 12:3), was celebrated by rich and poor alike. The flesh of goats was also eaten at mealtime, and fish was plentiful in maritime areas. Tasteless meals, or those of inferior quality, were made more appetizing by being flavored with a range of condiments and spices. Children drank milk, but adults normally partook of wine or some similar alcoholic beverage, which was sometimes diluted.

In a nomadic environment the eaters would sit or squat on the ground, but in urban society chairs, seats, and benches would be grouped around a low table for the benefit of the diners (cf. 1 S. 20:25; 1 K. 10:5). The luxurious living conditions against which Amos protested saw the use of elaborate couches and cushions (Am. 3:12; 6:4), while Ezekiel described elegant furniture (Ezk. 23:41; cf. Est. 1:6) as though it was in normal use among all except the very poor.

By the NT period the Syrian custom of reclining on couches had been adopted by the Greeks and Romans. While women and children sat upright, the men leaned on the left elbow (Sir. 41:19) and ate with the right hand. In the time of Jesus the sabbath was celebrated by means of elaborate banquets (cf. Lk. 7:36; 11:37; 14:7-14; Jn. 12:2). Jesus made use of such occasions to instruct His hearers in charitable and religious duties, even rebuking His host at times because he was manifesting a disparaging attitude (cf. Lk. 7:39; 11:38, 45f.; cf. Jn. 12:7f.).

*II. The Royal Commissary.*–In the ancient Near East, kings' households were noted for their lavish banquets. This was due partly to the number of retainers, officials, and soldiers that needed to be supported, but also to the practice of entertaining many relatives and guests (cf. 1 S. 20:29; 2 S. 9:7, 13), sometimes including defeated enemies of the king (2 K. 25:29). Solomon in particular followed the expensive tastes of Near Eastern royalty in setting up his household (cf. 1 K. 10:5), and members of his court feasted daily on oxen, sheep, roebucks, deer, and plump fowl (1 K. 4:22f.). Even if some of these foodstuffs came in the form of tribute from lands outside Palestine, life in the royal court was lived in a culinary fashion that could scarcely be imagined by the poor people of the land.

To all this was added the services of such royal officials as bakers, butlers, and wine-tasters, with their own groups of servants. Musicians and dancers frequently performed during large banquets, which often continued for many days. In the Persian period Ahasuerus gave a banquet for his court and state officials that continued for 180 days (Est. 1:4). To maintain royal courts in their traditional opulence was very costly, and all the more inequitable because the great mass of the population struggled to eke out a bare existence year by year.

*III. Treatment of Guests.*–Traditional Near Eastern hospitality particularly emphasized the proper treatment of guests, who were accorded positions of honor in the households where they were staying. They were under the protection of the host (cf. Gen. 19:8; Jgs. 19:23f.), and on their arrival they were usually extended such courtesies as water with which to wash their feet (cf. Gen. 19:2; Jgs. 19:21; Mk. 7:2; etc.). By NT times the guest was even welcomed ceremonially by means of a kiss (Lk. 7:45), which differed in its intent from the false friendliness of Joab toward Amasa (2 S. 20:9f.) or Judas toward Jesus (Mt. 26:48; Mk. 14:44; Lk. 22:47f.). If the guests did not already possess a change of clothing (cf. Eccl. 9:8), the host would provide whatever was needed, and occasionally placed ceremonial wreaths on their heads (Isa. 28:1). A special honor was bestowed on a guest when the host, or one of his attendants, anointed him with a sweet-smelling ointment (cf. Am. 6:6; Lk. 7:38; Jn. 12:3; etc.).

To sit at a royal table was a special mark of favor, as was the place of honor beside the host at less important gatherings. Guests were normally seated close to the door through which the servants brought the food, so that those who were being honored could partake of it while it was still reasonably hot. In large households servants washed the guests' hands before the eating actually commenced, but in family gatherings the women and children of the household attended to the needs of guests. By NT times it was customary for a formal grace to be said before eating a meal (cf. Mt. 14:19; Mk. 14:22f.; Acts 27:35; etc.), and this was the responsibility of the host. All guests were treated with the greatest courtesy, and Near Eastern traditions required that only the finest that the host had to offer was to be made available for the guest.

*IV. Ritual and Symbolic Meals.*–Ancient Near Eastern sacrificial rituals involved the offering of food to gods as part of the worship, in the belief that a meal would appease them in some manner. While the burnt offerings of the Levitical sacrificial system were not construed in terms of presenting food to a hungry deity, they were executed carefully so as to achieve the effect of being "a pleasing odor to the Lord" (Lev. 1:17; cf. R. K. Harrison, *Leviticus* [*Tyndale OT Comms.*, 1980], p. 47). The idea of restoring or maintaining fellowship with God in the context of a meal was further stressed in the peace offerings (*zeḇaḥ šᵉlāmîm*). For these sacrifices to take place, the occasion had to be one of gratitude to God, whether of a private or public nature; these sacrifices indicated a desire for continued fellowship, which was expressed as priests and worshipers joined in eating the sacrificial animal (except for the fat, which was burned as God's portion).

The Feast of Passover assumed a quasi-sacramental character from the very beginning, since it commemorated God's saving acts within the context of a ceremonial meal (Ex. 12:3-20). As early as the time of Isaiah (25:6) the Hebrews began consciously to expect the messianic kingdom to be ushered in with a banquet and feasting, perhaps analagous to the way in which the ceremony of the Sinai covenant had been celebrated (Ex. 24:11). Such a belief was also prevalent at Qumrân, where a Davidic and a priestly Messiah were expected, and was a firm part of the eschatology popular in Christ's time (Lk. 13:29). The ritual meal instituted by Jesus just prior to His death, and known as the Lord's Supper, was based upon the Passover celebration. Jesus prescribed it for His followers as a sacramental ordinance that commemorated His vicarious atonement for sinful humanity (cf. 1 Cor. 11:23-26).

*See also* BANQUET; EAT; FEASTS; FOOD.

***Bibliography.***–A. C. Bouquet, *Everyday Life in NT Times* (1953); E. W. Heaton, *Everyday Life in OT Times* (1956); R. de Vaux, *Ancient Israel*, II (Eng. tr. 1961), 468-577.

R. K. HARRISON

**MEAN; MEANING.** *I. Adjective.*–"Mean" is used by the AV, RSV, and NEB as an adjective meaning "obscure, insignificant," in Acts 21:39, where Paul describes Tarsus, the capital of Cilicia, as "no mean city" (Gk. *ásēmos*, lit. "without mark"). The AV also uses "mean" to denote "common" in the phrases "mean men" (Heb. *ḥᵃšukkîm*, Prov. 22:29; RSV "obscure men"; NEB "common men") and "mean man" (*'āḏām*, Isa. 2:9; 5:15; 31:8; RSV "man"). The parallelism in the Isaiah passages suggests that the AV's treatment of *'āḏām* here may be incorrect (contra E. J. Young, *Book of Isaiah*, I [*NICOT*, 1965], 120; cf. RSV, NEB).

*II. Verb and Noun.*–In the RSV the verb "mean" is used in two different senses: "intend" and "signify." It also appears in idiomatic expressions in which one sense is not clearly present to the exclusion of the other. The noun "meaning" in the RSV generally denotes "signification," i.e., the idea that is conveyed by a particular word, action, symbol, etc.

*A. OT.* The RSV OT uses "mean" in the sense of "intend" to translate several Hebrew verbs: *ḥāšaḇ* (lit. "plan"; Gen. 50:20), *'āmar* (lit. "say"; Ex. 2:14), *zāmam* (lit. "think, plan"; Dt. 19:19), *ḥāp̄ēṣ* (lit. "desire, wish to"; Jgs. 13:32), and the piel of *dāmâ* (lit. "think, plan, intend"; Jgs. 20:5).

Where "mean" is used in the sense of "signify," it does

not represent a verb. Sometimes it is simply supplied by the translators (e.g., Gen. 41:32; Dt. 30:20). In 1 K. 1:41 the question "What does this mean?" represents Heb. *maddû(a)ʿ* (lit. "wherefore?"; so AV). Elsewhere "mean" is used in idiomatic translations of the interrogative pronoun *mâ* (lit. "what?"; e.g., Dt. 29:24; Josh. 4:21; 1 S. 4:6; cf. also "meaning," Gen. 21:29; Dt. 6:20), usually in phrases such as *mah-lᵉkâ* (lit. "what [is it] to you?"; RSV "What do you mean?" Ex. 12:26; Josh. 4:6; cf. *mî-lᵉkā*, Gen. 33:8), *mah-zōʾṯ* (lit. "what is this?"; Ex. 13:14) or *mah-ʾēlleh* (lit. "what are these?"; Ezk. 17:12; 24:29; 37:18). Frequently these questions (usually translated "What do you mean [by or that]...?)" are used not to seek an answer but to express amazement or outrage (cf. *mallāḵem*, Isa. 3:15; *mah-lᵉkā*, Isa. 22:1; Ezk. 18:2; Jonah 1:6; *mah-taʿᵃśî* [lit. "what are you doing?"], Jer. 4:30; *mah-ʾēlleh*, Ezk. 17:12).

"Meaning" occurs twice in the narratives of Joseph's interpretations of dreams in Egypt (Gen. 40:5; 41:11). In both instances it translates Heb. *piṯrôn* (lit. "interpretations [of a dream]"; cf. RSV "interpretation," 40:8, 12, 18), a noun derived from the verb *pāṯar* (RSV "interpret," 40:8, 16, 22, 41:8, etc.). On the interpretation of dreams, *see* DIVINATION III.A; DREAM III.

*B. NT.* The RSV NT uses "mean" in the sense of "intend" in only three passages: in Mk. 6:48 "mean" represents Gk. *thélō* (lit. "wish"); in Rom. 2:4 and 1 Cor. 6:13 (twice) it is supplied by the translators.

Elsewhere in the NT "mean" is used in the sense of "signify." Gk. *légō* (lit. "say") can sometimes be used and translated in this sense (e.g., Mt. 26:70 par. Mk. 14:68; Jn. 16:18a [in v. 18b "mean" represents *laléō*, and in v. 19 the RSV supplies "mean" in a rather free translation]; 1 Cor. 10:29; Gal. 4:1). In Jn. 11:13 "mean" represents *légō perí* (lit. "tell about"); similar expressions using *toúto* ("this") occur in 1 Cor. 1:12; 7:29 (which uses *phēmi* instead of *légō*); and Gal. 3:17. The cognate noun *lógos* (lit. "word," "speech," "message") is rendered "mean" by the RSV in a paraphrase of Jn. 7:36 (Gk. *tis estin ho lógos hoútos hón eípen*, lit. "What is this word that he is saying?"; RSV "What does he mean by saying?").

The phrase "which means" is used to translate a variety of formulas employed by the Greek NT to introduce Greek translations of Aramaic and Hebrew names and expressions. These formulas include Gk. *hó estin ... legómenos* (mid. part. of *légō;* Mt. 27:33), *hó légetai* (Jn. 20:16), *hó hermēneúetai* (pass. of *hermēneúō*, "interpret, translate"; Jn. 1:42; 9:7), *hó estin methermēneuómenon* (pass. part. of *methermēneúō*, "translate"; Mt. 1:23; Mk. 5:41; 15:22, 34; Jn. 1:41; Acts 4:36), *hó légetai methermēneuómenon* (Jn. 1:38), and *hḗ diermēneuoménē légetai* (pass. of *diermēneúō*, "translate"; Acts 9:36). In Acts 13:8 the RSV uses "be the meaning of" to render the passive of *methermēneúō*.

In contexts dealing with the interpretation of sayings (esp. of Jesus) and events, the RSV often uses "mean" to translate Gk. *eimí* (lit. "be," thus "be a representation of"; see Bauer, rev., pp. 223f.), e.g., Mt. 9:13; 12:7; 13:38; Mk. 9:10; Rom. 9:8; Eph. 4:9. The optative form (lit. "would be") appears in the Lukan writings at Lk. 8:9; 15:26; 18:36; Acts 10:17. Similar in meaning is the expression *thélō eínai* (lit. "wish to be") in Acts 2:12; 17:20. Following acceptable Greek practice, a form of *eimí* is sometimes assumed; thus the translators supply "mean" in Rom. 11:12, 15; Phil. 1:22. "Mean" is also supplied in 1 Cor. 5:10; 2 Cor. 8:13.

In 1 Cor. 15:29 "mean" represents Gk. *poiéō* (lit. "do"). The RSV paraphrases the Gk. *tí poiḗsousin hoi baptizómenoi hypér tṓn nekrṓn* (lit. "what will they do who are baptized on behalf of the dead?"; cf. AV) with "what do people mean who are baptized on behalf of the dead?" The interpretation of this verse is difficult and has been the focus of much scholarly dispute (see comms.).

The noun "meaning" occurs twice in Paul's discussion of problems that arise in public worship when worshipers exercise the gift of tongue-speaking without the concomitant gift of interpreting tongues (1 Cor. 14:10f). In v. 10b "without meaning" represents Gk. *áphōnos* (lit. "silent," "void of language"), playing on *phōnḗ* (lit. "sound," "voice," "language") in v.10a (RSV "language"). In v. 11 "meaning" represents *dýnamis* (lit. "power" [of the *phōnḗ*, "language"]). *See* SPIRITUAL GIFTS.

*See also* INTERPRET. N. J. O.

**MEANI** mə-ā'nī (1 Esd. 5:31, AV). *See* MEUNIM.

**MEANS.** A plural noun used by the RSV to translate a variety of terms and expressions. Often it is used to denote "resources": e.g., "[he] who devises means" (Heb. *maḥᵃšeḇeṯ*, "invention," 2 S. 14:14); "finds sufficient means" (*day*, "sufficiency," Lev. 25:26; cf. v. 28); "provided for them out of their means" (Gk. *hypárchonta*, Lk. 8:3; AV "substance"; NEB "resources"); "gave according to their means" (Gk. *dýnamis*, "ability," 2 Cor. 8:3; AV "power"; NEB "limit of their resources").

The RSV also uses "means" in various phrases to express agency. For example, "by means of" translates the Greek prepositions *ek* (Lk. 16:9), *diá* (Jn. 11:4; 2 Pet. 3:5), and *en* (Rev. 9:19), and "by what means (?)" renders Heb. *bammeh* (Jgs. 16:5; 1 K. 22:22 [MT 21] par. 2 Ch. 18:20) and Gk. *en tíni* (Acts 4:9). The RSV sometimes employs the phrases "by any means," "by all means," and "by no means" to show the emphasis conveyed by the common Hebrew construction of an infinitive absolute with a finite verb from the same root; e.g., "if by any means he be missing" (Heb. *ʾim-hippāqēḏ yippāqēḏ*, 1 K. 20:39), "by all means return" (*hāšēḇ tāšîḇû*, 1 S. 6:3), "by all means pass over" (*gam ʿāḇôr taʿᵃḇôr*, 2 S. 17:16), "by no means slay" (*hāmēṯ ʾal-tᵉmîṯûhû*, 1 K. 3:26f.), "by no means clear" or "by no means leave ... unpunished" (*naqqēh lōʾ yᵉnaqqeh*, Ex. 34:7; Nu. 14:18; Jer. 30:11; 46:28; Nah. 1:3).

The phrase "By no means!" occurs ten times in the RSV of Romans (3:4, 6, 31; 6:2, 15; 7:7, 13; 9:14; 11:1, 11) as a translation of Gk. *mḗ génoito* (lit. "May it not be"; cf. AV "God forbid"; NEB "Certainly not!" etc.). Paul uses this phrase as a strong negation following a rhetorical question, indicating his abhorrence of such a suggestion. *See* FORBID.

"By their means" is the AV rendering of Heb. *bᵉyāḏām* (lit. "by their hand") in 1 K. 10:29 par. 2 Ch. 1:17 (cf. AV use of "means" for *yāḏ* also in Jer. 5:31; Mal. 1:9); the RSV and NEB offer paraphrases. In the NT the AV frequently renders "if by any means" for Gk. *eí pōs* (lit. "if somehow," Acts 27:12; Rom. 1:10; 11:14; 1 Cor. 8:9; 9:27; etc.; RSV "on the chance that," "somehow," "in order to," etc.). N. J. O.

**MEARAH** mē-âr'ə [*mᵉʿārâ*]. A Sidonian city or region that is named among the numerous territories remaining for Israel to possess (Josh. 13:4). Because of the difficulties of the text, the identification and location have been much disputed. The LXX reads *enantíon* (or *apó*) *Gazēs*, "before (from) Gaza," which suggests the reading *mēʿāzâ* (with *mêm* representing the preposition, and *zayin* replacing *rêš*). But Gaza can hardly be described as belonging to the Sidonians. Other interpreters have identified the Aphek of v. 4 with Râs el-ʿAin, which is not far from Lod (*see* APHEK; ANTIPATRIS). If so, then the Hebrew word might be emended to *mēʿārâ*, "from ʿAra," and ʿAra could be located along the Wâdī ʿAra, which leads from the Sharon plain to the plain of Jezreel alongside Megiddo. Simons (*GTTOT*, §§ 239, 295) accepted this location in general, arguing that "Sidonians" is equivalent to "Phoenicians," which in turn equals "Canaanites"; however, he emended *meʿārâ* to *mēʿārîm*, "from the cities." Simons thought that the structure of the clause, which ends with "to Aphek," requires "from [place-name]" at its beginning (*GTTOT*, p. 110). But his main argument seems somewhat forced, and even if his identification of "Sidonians" with "Canaanites" is accepted, the suggested emendation is not entirely necessary, for *ʿÊn ʿIrôn*, a site NE of Hadera on Nahal ʿIrôn (Wâdī ʿAra), would be the equivalent of *Mê ʿAra*, "the spring (waters) of ʿAra" (cf. *GAB*, Map 12; "Israel Touring Map" [Survey of Israel], 1:250,000, Northern Sheet, G-10).

Scholars who would locate the land of the Sidonians farther north (near Sidon) have suggested that Mearah is Mughar Jezzin, E of Sidon (*IDB*, III, 318), or the *Moġeiryié* of Conder (cf. *GP*, II, 381), 9 km. (6 mi.) NE of Sidon. Following this suggestion, Abel (*GP*, II, 247) identified the Aphek of Josh. 13:4 with Afqā, located at the source of Nahr Ibrahim, which courses SE of Byblos near the southern limit of the land of the Amurru (Amorites, also mentioned in v. 4).

Aharoni, who also believed that the sentence structure requires a *terminus a quo* and that this is hidden in the word *meʿārâ*, regarded attempts to identify the name as "purely conjectural" (*LBHG* [2nd ed.], p. 237).

W. S. LASOR

**MEASURE.** The RSV translation of a variety of Hebrew and Greek verbs, nouns, and expressions.

***I. The Verb.***–As a verb "measure" means to ascertain or set a length or quantity. In the OT it usually represents the Hebrew verb *māḏaḏ*. Most often *māḏaḏ* is used for measuring length, e.g., the boundaries of pasture lands (Nu. 35:5), distances to cities (Dt. 21:2), the dimensions of Jerusalem (Zec. 2:2 [MT 6]) or of the heavens (niphal, Jer. 31:37); it occurs frequently in Ezekiel's description of the dimensions of the new temple that is to be built in the time of restoration (Ezk. 40–42). In several passages *māḏaḏ* refers to measuring a quantity, e.g., of manna (Ex. 16:18; AV "mete") or barley (Ruth 3:15). Yahweh's greatness is displayed in His ability to measure what no human can measure: He "has measured the waters in the hollow of his hand . . . enclosed the dust of the earth in a measure" (Isa. 40:12; cf. Job 28:25). Moreover, He will create a people who are as measureless as the sand of the sea (Jer. 33:22; Hos. 1:10 [MT 2:1]). On the other hand, the figure of measuring out payment into the fold of one's garment (used as a pocket by the Jews; cf. Ps. 79:12; Lk. 6:38) can depict God's justice (Isa. 65:7). Other OT terms for measuring are *sāpar* (lit. "count, number"; cf. AV), which in Gen. 41:49 describes Joseph's inability to keep records of the vast quantities of grain stored during the seven plenteous years, and *sāḇaḇ* (lit. "go round about"; cf. AV, NEB), which the RSV renders "measure its circumference" in 1 K. 7:15, 23; 2 Ch. 4:2.

In the NT the verb always represents Gk. *metréō*. In a vision that recalls Ezk. 40–42, John is commanded to measure the temple as a symbolic promise of its preservation (Rev. 11:1f.); later he observes an angel measuring the vast and perfectly symmetrical dimensions of the new Jerusalem (21:15-17; see comms.). In 2 Cor. 10:12 Paul criticizes the false apostles who measure their success by one another instead of by God's standard.

***II. The Noun.***–As a noun "measure" denotes the spatial dimensions, quantity, or capacity of something. The terms thus rendered by the RSV include Heb. *middâ* (Ex. 26:2, 8; Job 28:25), *meśûrâ* (1 Ch. 23:29), *tōḵēn* and *maṯkōneṯ* (Ezk. 45:11); Gk. *métron* (Mt. 7:2 par.; 23:32; Jn. 3:34; Rom. 12:3; Eph. 4:7, 13; Rev. 21:17) and *tosoútos* (lit. "so much"; RSV "a like measure," Rev. 18:7). In some instances the RSV translates a specific unit of volume by "measure": Heb. *ʾêpâ* ("ephah," Dt. 25:14f.; Mic. 6:10; *ʾêpâ weʾêpâ*, RSV "diverse measures," Prov. 20:10), *seʾâ* ("seah," Gen. 18:6; 1 S. 25:18; 1 K. 18:32; 2 K. 7:1, 16, 18), *kōr* ("cor," 1 K. 4:22); Aram. *kōr* (Ezr. 7:22); Gk. *bátos* ("bath," Lk. 16:6), *kóros* ("cor," v. 7), *sáton* ("seah," Mt. 13:33 par. Lk. 13:21). Elsewhere "measure" is supplied where the Hebrew text gives only the numerical unit: Heb. *šēš* ("six," Ruth 3:15, 17; the Tgs. interpreted these to be six seahs — a very heavy load), *ʿeśrîm* ("twenty") and *ḥamiššîm* ("fifty," Hag. 2:16), *ʿiśśārôn* ("tenth," possibly a tenth of an ephah; Ex. 29:40), and *šālîš* ("third," probably a third of an ephah, which would be equivalent to a seah; Isa. 40:12; "full measure," Ps. 80:5 [MT 6]). *See* WEIGHTS AND MEASURES.

One of the most common forms of injustice in biblical times was the use of unjust measures. The OT continually reminds God's people that their use of measures must reflect God's standard of justice (e.g., Lev. 19:35f.; Ezk. 45:10f.). "Diverse measures" (NEB "a double standard in . . . measures") are "an abomination to the Lord" (Prov. 20:10), and the "scant measure" is "accursed" (Mic. 6:10).

Several figurative uses occur in the NT. The concern for just measures provides background for Lk. 6:38 (cf. par. Mt. 7:2; Mk. 4:24), where Jesus depicts God's generosity as "good measure, pressed down, shaken together, running over," and assures His followers that "the measure you give will be the measure you get back" — i.e., human generosity will be rewarded by divine generosity. In Jn. 3:34; Rom. 12:3; Eph. 4:7, 13 "measure" is used in connection with gifts of the Spirit. Jn. 3:34 describes God's gift of the Spirit to Christ as being without limit: "for it is not by measure that he gives the Spirit" (cf. vv. 31-35; for differing interpretations of this verse, see comms.). On the other hand, each Christian is assigned by God a (limited) "measure of faith" (Rom. 12:3; cf. v. 6) or "measure of Christ's gift" (Eph. 4:7). All members are enjoined to use their own spiritual gift to build up the body of Christ; in this way the whole body will attain to the (full) "measure of the stature of the fulness of Christ" (v. 13; cf. vv. 15f.).

***III. Special Expressions.***–Several Hebrew and Greek terms or phrases are translated by English expressions using "measure."

(1) "Beyond measure" is used to describe realities that go beyond the norm — e.g., Solomon's wisdom (1 K. 4:29 [MT 5:9]; Heb. *harbēh meʾōḏ*, lit. "exceedingly greatly"), the blind optimism of Israel's leaders (Isa. 56:12; *yeṯer meʾōḏ*, lit. "exceedingly abundantly"), astonishment at Jesus' healings (Mk. 7:37; Gk. *hyperperissṓs*), and human sinfulness (Rom. 7:13; *kath' hyperbolḗn*, "to excess") — or that are limitless: God's understanding (Ps. 147:5; Heb. *ʾên mispār*, "without number") and the appetite of Sheol (Isa. 5:14; *liḇlî ḥōq*, "without limit"). (Cf. Gk. *ámetros* [RSV "beyond limit"] in 2 Cor. 10:13, 15; *see* LIMIT.)

(2) "Full measure" emphasizes completeness, as in references to total misery (Ps. 80:5 [MT 6]; Heb. *šālîš*), judgment (Isa. 47:9; *tōm*, "completeness"), and manifestation of evil (Dnl. 8:23; hiphil of *tāmam*, "complete"; cf. "fill up the measure," 1 Thess. 2:16; Gk. *anaplēróō*, "fill up").

(3) "Just measure" represents Heb. *mišpāṭ*, "justice," in Jer. 10:24; 30:11; 46:28, where corrective punishment

is contrasted with the judgment that destroys completely. A "just measure" of divine chastisement shows restraint because of human weakness but does not leave sin unpunished.

*IV. Difficult Usages.*–The meaning of Heb. *sa'ss$^{e}$'â* (or *sass$^{e}$'â*) in Isa. 27:8 is uncertain. The AV ("in measure") and RSV ("measure by measure") understand it as a reduplication of *s$^{e}$'â* (see KD); but other scholars have interpreted it as denoting "shouts to stir sheep and goats" (KoB, p. 646), thus "scaring" or "driving out."

In Acts 27:17 Gk. *boḗtheia* (AV, lit., "helps"; RSV "measures"; NEB "tackle") denotes some form of nautical equipment, the precise nature of which is not known. For a brief summary of the four main conjectures, see E. Haenchen, *Acts of the Apostles* (Eng. tr. 1971), p. 703 n. 1.

K. H. MAAHS N. J. O.

**MEASURING LINE** [Heb. *qāw, qāweh* (2 K. 21:13; Zec. 1:16), *q$^{e}$wēh hammiddâ* (Jer. 31:39), *ḥeḇel hammiddâ* (Zec. 2:1 [MT 5])]; AV also LINE; NEB also PLUMB-LINE; **MEASURING REED** [Heb. *q$^{e}$nēh hammiddâ*] (Ezk. 40:3, 5; 42:1619); NEB (MEASURING-) ROD; **MEASURING ROD** [Gk. *kálamos* (Rev. 11:1), *métron kálamos* (21:15)]; AV REED; **PLUMB LINE** [Heb. *'$^{a}$nāḵ*] (Am. 7:7f.); **PLUMMET** [Heb. *mišqōleṯ* (2 K. 21:13), *mišqeleṯ* (Isa. 28:17), pl. of *'eḇen*–'stones' (Isa. 34:11), *'eḇen habb$^{e}$ḏîl*–'stone of tin' (?) (Zec. 4:10)]; AV, NEB, also STONE(S); *see also* LINE. Implements used in taking measurements.

The measuring line (usually *qāw* or *ḥeḇel; see* LINE) was an important tool used by builders and carpenters (e.g., 1 K. 7:23; Isa. 44:13); but most often it is mentioned as a tool of surveyors (e.g., Jer. 31:39; Zec. 1:16; 2:1f. [MT 5f.]), frequently in connection with the apportionment of land (e.g., Ps. 16:6; Am. 7:17; Mic. 2:4f.). Such lines were often used in conjunction with plummets (cf. 2 K. 21:13; Isa. 28:17) and measuring reeds (Ezk. 40:3). They were probably made of various materials, FLAX being one of the more durable varieties (Ezk. 40:3). Sometimes the exact length of the line is given, e.g., twelve cubits (1 K. 7:15), thirty cubits (v. 23 par. 2 Ch. 4:2).

The measuring reed is mentioned primarily in Ezk. 40–42, where it is used to describe the dimensions of the eschatological temple. These measuring sticks were derived from tall, stalky grasses that grow in marshy areas (Heb. *qāneh*). The reeds referred to are most likely the *Arundo donax* and the *Phragmites communis*. The latter, very common along the rivers of Palestine, grows from 1¼ to 3 m. (4 to 10 ft.) in height, with a bamboo-like stalk 1¼ to 2½ cm. (½ to 1 in.) in diameter. In time, no doubt, reed measures came to be made of many materials. The *kálamos* of Rev. 21:15 (RSV "rod," but usually "reed" in NT; cf. Mt. 11:7; 12:20; Mk. 15:19, 36), e.g., is made of gold. It is apparent, therefore, that the terms for "reed" came to designate a standardized measurement. Thus, Ezekiel's reed was six long cubits or about 3 m. (10 ft.) in length (40:5; 41:8). *See also* REED.

A plummet is a weight made of stone (cf. AV, NEB, Isa. 34:11) or metal which, when suspended by a cord, produces a plumb line. The plumb line is used to measure a straight vertical plane.

These tools are used figuratively in several passages to describe God's judgment upon His people. In Lam. 2:8 God stretches out a plumb line to discover defects in Zion (see *IB*, VI, 18). Similarly, in Am. 7:7f. God tests the vertical dimension of Israel, here symbolized by a wall. Israel had originally been built with vertical rectitude but had failed to maintain this standard. Such a wall is unstable and fit only to be toppled (cf. v. 9). (The "plummet" of Zec. 4:10, however, is quite possibly a mistranslation; for a defense of the NEB ["stone called Separation"], see Baldwin, pp. 122f.) In 2 K. 21:13 God announces that Judah and Jerusalem will be judged by the "line of Samaria, and the plummet . . . of Ahab" — i.e., they will receive the same judgment of total destruction.

Job 38:5 pictures God using these tools to construct the cosmos out of chaos. Conversely, however, with a clear reference to Gen. 1:2 (where the precreational chaos is described as "without form [Heb. *tōhû*] and void [*bōhû*]"), Isaiah prophesies that God will use "the line of confusion [*tōhû*] . . . and the plummet of chaos [*bōhû*]" as instruments of vengeance against a people who oppose His purposes (Isa. 34:11).

***Bibliography.***–J. Baldwin, *Haggai, Zechariah, Malachi* (*Tyndale OT Comms.*, 1972); *TDOT*, IV, *s.v.* "ḥbl" (H.-J. Fabry).

K. H. MAAHS

**MEASURING REED; MEASURING ROD.** *See* MEASURING LINE.

**MEAT** [Heb. *bāśār*] (Nu. 11:4, 13, 18, 21, 33; Jgs. 6:19-21; 1 S. 2:13, 15; 1 K. 17:6; etc.); AV FLESH; NEB also FLESH, FLESHPOTS, etc.; [*ṭiḇḥâ*] (1 S. 25:11); AV FLESH; [*š$^{e}$'ēr*] (Ps. 78:20); AV FLESH; [*'ešpār*] (2 S. 6:19; 1 Ch. 16:3); AV FLESH; [Gk. *kréas*] (Rom. 14:21; 1 Cor. 8:13); AV FLESH. In Mic. 3:3 the RSV has "meat" and the NEB "flesh," both following the *sárx* of the LXX, while the AV has "as," following the MT *'$^{a}$šer,* which could be emended to read *š$^{e}$'ēr* (see the comms.). On "meat market" (1 Cor. 10:25), *see* MARKET.

In general, Heb. *bāśār, ṭiḇḥâ* (slaughtered meat), *š$^{e}$'ēr,* and Gk. *kréas* designate the meat or flesh of animals, used particularly for food and for sacrifice. Thus these terms describe the quails sent for food for the complaining Israelites (Nu. 11), the young goat offered as a sacrifice by Gideon (Jgs. 6), the offered meat greedily snatched up by Eli's sons (1 S. 2), the food sent to Elijah (1 K. 17:6), etc. Addressing the problem of eating food sacrificed to idols, even if sold in a meat market (1 Cor. 10:25), Paul advised love and care for the sake of the weaker brother: "Therefore, if food is a cause of my brother's falling, I will never eat meat, lest I cause my brother to fall" (8:13).

A precise identification of *'ešpār* is impossible. Conjectures include meat (NAB), date cake (JB, NIV), or wine (KD).

M. W. MEYER

**MEAT OFFERING.** *See* SACRIFICES AND OFFERINGS IN THE OT.

**MEBUNNAI** mə-bun'ī [Heb. *m$^{e}$ḇunnay*]. Listed in 2 S. 23:27 as one of David's thirty mighty men who were renowned for their heroic deeds. In the par. 1 Ch. 11:29 (cf. also 27:11; 20:4 par. 2 S. 21:18) his name is given as SIBBECAI. Scribal error and some similarity of the two forms in Hebrew account for the difference in spelling.

**MECHERATHITE** mə-ker'ə-thīt [Heb. *m$^{e}$ḵērāṯî*]; NEB FROM MECHERAH. Patronymic of Hepher, one of the mighty men of David's army (1 Ch. 11:36); but cf. par. 2 S. 23:34, where "of Maacah" is given without the name "Hepher." It is possible that both passages are corrupt and should be read, "Hepher the Maacathite." *See* MAACATHITES.

**MECONAH** mə-kō'nə [Heb. *m$^{e}$ḵōnâ*–'foundation'; Gk. *Machna*]; AV MEKONAH. A place in the Shephelah settled by Jews who returned from the Exile (Neh. 11:28). From the context it was probably near Ziklag; thus Simons (*GTTOT*, § 317, p. 145) proposed Khirbet umm ed-Deimineh, about 23 km. (14 mi.) NNE of Beer-sheba. He also identified it with Madmannah (Josh. 15:31) and with Machbenah (1 Ch. 2:49). See *GTTOT,* §§ 322, 1076, pp. 155, 389.

W. S. L. S.

**MEDABA** med'ə-bə (AV, NEB, 1 Macc. 9:36). *See* MEDEBA.

**MEDAD** mē'dad [Heb. *mêḏāḏ*–'affectionate' (?)]. One of the seventy elders chosen to share with Moses the burden of leadership. Medad and Eldad were not in the tent of meeting when the Spirit of the Lord descended on the rest of the seventy, equipping them for their office; but they received the same Spirit and prophesied in the camp (Nu. 11:24-30).

**MEDAN** mē'dan [Heb. *m^eḏān*]. Third son of Abraham by Keturah (Gen. 25:2; 1 Ch. 1:32), and like the other sons, e.g., Midian, Dedan, etc., probably eponymous head of an Arabian tribe. Since Dedan and Midian settled in north Arabia, probably the tribe of Medan did as well. The suggested connections with the Badana conquered by Tiglath-pileser III (*ca.* 732 B.C.; cf. *ANET,* p. 283) and the Arabian personal name Abd al-Madan are not certain.

The name also appears in the MT of Gen. 37:36 (*ham-m^eḏānîm*), but the RSV, NEB, AV, and NASB, following most ancient versions and the context (see v. 28), translate "Midianites." Although *hamm^eḏānîm* does seem to be a corruption of Midian, it is not necessary to consider Medan as a corrupt doublet for Midian in Gen. 25:2 or 1 Ch. 1:32.

C. G. RASMUSSEN

**MEDEBA** med'ə-bə [Heb. *mêḏ^eḇā'*; Gk. *Maidaba,* Apoc. *Mēdaba*]; AV Apoc., NEB Apoc., MEDABA. A town about 32 km. (20 mi.) S of Rabbath-ammon (modern Amman, Jordan) on the King's Highway between Heshbon and Dibon. The modern town, named Madaba, is located upon the ruins of the earlier cities.

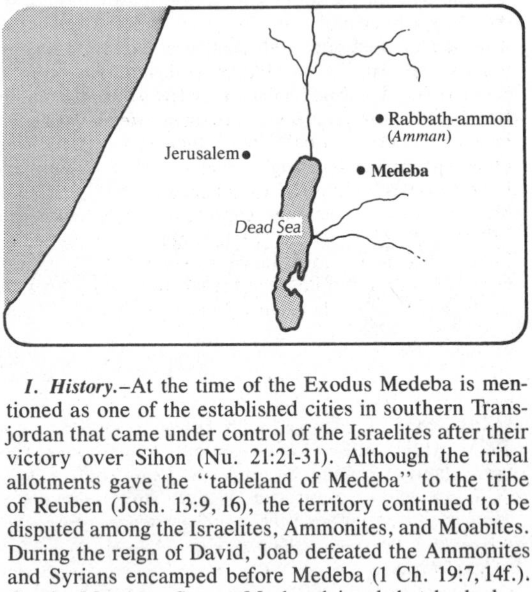


*I. History.*–At the time of the Exodus Medeba is mentioned as one of the established cities in southern Transjordan that came under control of the Israelites after their victory over Sihon (Nu. 21:21-31). Although the tribal allotments gave the "tableland of Medeba" to the tribe of Reuben (Josh. 13:9, 16), the territory continued to be disputed among the Israelites, Ammonites, and Moabites. During the reign of David, Joab defeated the Ammonites and Syrians encamped before Medeba (1 Ch. 19:7, 14f.). On the MOABITE STONE Mesha claimed that he had recovered Medeba from the Israelites who had occupied it under Omri. Isa. 15:2 foretells its destruction as a Moabite city. During the Maccabean period John the son of Mattathias was killed by the Jambri, a brigand tribe from Medeba (1 Macc. 9:35-42; Josephus *Ant.* xiii.1.2 [10f.]). John Hyrcanus captured Medeba from the Syrians after a six-month siege (*Ant.* xiii.9.1 [254f.]). Much later, to gain the help of the Nabateans, Hyrcanus II offered Medeba and some other towns to their king (*Ant.* xiv.1.4 [18]).

Medeba was a flourishing city during the Nabatean and Roman periods. It is listed in the *Onomasticon* of Eusebius, and its bishop was present at the Council of Chalcedon in A.D. 451. Medeba no doubt suffered under the Persian invasion in the early 7th cent., but the demise of Christianity and subsequent abandonment of the city apparently occurred a few centuries later.

The modern resettlement of Medeba occurred in 1880, when bedouin Christian nomads from Kerak obtained permission to occupy the ruins. The Christian character of the modern town has been qualified by the arrival of Palestinian refugees in the late 1940's. This modern resettlement has restricted archeological work, which has concentrated on the Byzantine period, especially the churches.

*II. Mosaics.*–Medeba has become famous for its many and beautiful mosaics, some of the Roman period but most in the churches of the Byzantine period.

The "Medeba Map," the best-known mosaic floor, is from the 6th cent., making it the oldest extant map of Palestine. Originally about 23 m. by 6 m. (77 ft. by 20 ft.), this unusual mosaic depicted the eastern Mediterranean coast from Lebanon to the Delta in Egypt and inland as far as Amman, Kerak, and Petra (i.e., Transjordan). Unfortunately, more than two-thirds of it was destroyed by the construction of St. George's Orthodox Church (1896). The remaining portion shows the Delta area, the Sinai desert, and south-central Palestine (including the Dead Sea, Jerusalem, and part of the Jordan River). *See* Plate 42.

Like other mosaics from this period, this floor is made of stone cubes averaging about 1 cm. (½ in.) on a side in a variety of natural colors — black, white, yellow, gray, brown, and several shades of red and blue-green. The cubes (numbering about 2,300,000) were tightly fitted together and laid in a cement bed with no lateral mortar, demonstrating the skilled craftsmanship in this art during the late Roman and Byzantine periods.

This map has been very helpful for the study of topography and the identification of sites in Palestine during the biblical and Byzantine periods. Some sites are not merely named but also given brief descriptions of their significance during a given period. The many churches of the Byzantine period are depicted with red roofs. Of central significance is the plan of Jerusalem, showing its streets, walls, gates, and churches — with the Church of the Holy Sepulchre in direct perspective to give it prominence. Archeological work has sometimes been guided by this map and has sometimes confirmed its details. It will continue to contribute to the study of the art, architecture, liturgy, topography, flora, and fauna of ancient Palestine.

Although not as spectacular as the map, the mosaic floors in the other churches of Medeba reveal the same high level of craftsmanship and contribute significantly to the study of early Christianity. The remains of these sixth- and seventh-century churches allow the following observations.

(1) Medeba was a large Christian community, which had to be affluent to build and maintain these edifices (at least fourteen in the 6th cent.). In this respect, Medeba was typical of many cities in Transjordan and Cisjordan — e.g., Jerash, Umm el-Jimal, Rihab, Amman, Ma'an — reflecting the extent and wealth of Christianity during this period.

(2) The scenes depicted in these floors are taken from everyday experiences and activities — hunting, fishing, harvesting of grapes and wine making, pastoral life, various flora and fauna. In none of these is it possible to identify

positively a biblical scene or theological motif, although such scenes and motifs were prevalent in contemporary church art in other parts of the Byzantine Empire (as in Italy and Greece). At times even pagan motifs were incorporated into the mosaics. In the nave of the Apostles Church (dated A.D. 578/579), a large medallion contains the figure of a woman whose upper torso emerges from a body of water containing various forms of marine life. She is identified as *Thalassa* ("Sea"), a well-known goddess in the pagan pantheon. The Medallion is surrounded by a Greek inscription containing an OT citation. These phenomena suggest that the development of Christian art as a distinct modality was very complex.

(3) The evidence of iconoclasm in some of these sixth-century churches indicates that this negative reaction to pictorial representations of living beings (animals, birds, humans) in the churches arose much earlier than has traditionally been maintained.

(4) The three Greek inscriptions addressed to Mary in the mosaic floor of the Chapel of the Virgin Mary reflect the veneration of Mary in this community. The central inscription is a fine hexameter verse calling the worshiper to sanctification by "looking to the Virgin Mary, the mother of God [Gk. *theomḗtōr*], and Christ. . . ."

(5) The date of another inscription in the Chapel of the Virgin Mary indicates that the chapel was constructed in A.D. 662/663 — about thirty years after the Moslem conquest of this area. This and other evidences from seventh- and eighth-century churches indicate a much more tolerant attitude to Christianity in early Islam than has often been thought.

A picture emerges of early Christianity very much in the world and enjoying its experiences and delights and of a church and community in relationship to and sometimes in conflict with its environment. Clearly, early Christianity was a far more complex, varied, and richer institution than commonly supposed.

***Bibliography.***–M. Avi-Yonah, *Medeba Mosaic Map* (1954); *EAEHL*, III, *s.v.* "Medeba" (M. Avi-Yonah); V. R. Gold, *BA*, 3 (1958), 50-70; H. Leclerq, *Dictionnaire d'archéologie chrétienne et de liturgie*, X/1, *s.v.* "Madaba"; U. Luf, *ZDPV*, 84 (1968), 130-142.

B. VANELDEREN

**MEDES** mēdz; **MEDIA** mē′dē-ə [Heb. *māḏî, māḏay*; Aram. *māḏay*; Assyr. *Madai*; Old Pers. *Māda*; Gk. *Mēdoi, Mēdia*]; AV also MEDIAN (Dnl. 5:31 [MT 6:1]). An ancient people and land SW of the Caspian Sea, between the Zagros Mountains and the Salt Desert (Dasht-i-Kavir), including Azerbaijan in the north (Media Atropatene). Most of this area is mountainous, with fertile valleys and some broad plains where horses were raised.

*I. **Culture and Religion.***–So little excavation has been done in the Median homeland that there is only scattered material evidence for cultural and religious history. The Medes were Aryans (cf. Gen. 10:2), closely akin to the Persians, and entered Iran as nomads *ca.* 1000 B.C. Their religion may have begun as a form of nature worship with animal sacrifices, the Magi tribe having a privileged role. Before the rise of Cyrus this faith had been altered by assimilation of the teachings of Zoroaster (7th cent.?). Zoroaster conceived of two gods — a good power, Ahuramazda, and an evil power, Ahriman — and propagated a nonsacrificial cult that involved the sacred fire and lacked images. (*See* RELIGIONS OF THE BIBLICAL WORLD: PERSIA.) Details of Median beliefs remain hypothetical in the absence of early documentation.

That the Medes had knowledge of writing is unquestionable, but the nature of their script, if any, is uncertain. It could have been a complicated cuneiform script like

Babylonian, a simple form like Urartian, Old Persian, or Elamite, or a hieroglyphic script. Consequently the Median language can be only incompletely reconstructed from philological research in related tongues and from occasional quotations and loanwords.

Sculptures of the Persian period give hints of Median appearance, and a few objects unearthed in Persia can be called Median by comparison with these sculptures (e.g., a golden dagger sheath from the Oxus Treasure, now in the British Museum). Some rock-cut tombs in the Zagros Mountains were probably made for Median nobles of the Achaemenian court.

*II. **History.***–From the 9th cent. B.C., Assyrian inscriptions record attacks on Median settlements in northern Iran (*ARAB*, I, § 581, Shalmaneser III; § 739, Adadnirari III). At that time there was no single Median state but instead numerous tribal groups that often fought each other and raided the neighboring states of Mannai and Urartu. Tiglath-pileser III established control over some Median territory, claiming capture of 65,000 men, *ca.* 740 B.C. (*ARAB*, I, §§ 784, 795); Sargon II fought against Medes, Manneans, and Urartians, with numbers of chieftains submitting to him. One leader, Dayaukku, was deported to Syria, and Israelite citizens were settled in Media (*ARAB*, II, § 56; 2 K. 17:6; 18:11).

Apparently Media posed little threat to Assyria for the next two decades. Cimmerian and Scythian invasions, however, ousted Assyria from Mannai and pressed upon Media so hard that three Median chiefs sought Assyrian aid *ca.* 676 B.C. Having lost his supply of valuable horses from Mannai, Esarhaddon of Assyria was ready to take them from more distant Media. His troops penetrated as far as the Salt Desert near Tehran, and various cities were subjugated (R. Borger, *Die Inschriften Asarhaddons* [*AfO*, Beiheft 9, 1956], pp. 34, 54f.). Vassal treaties were imposed upon the principal Median rulers in 672 B.C., binding them to Assyria and its kings. The number of chieftains mentioned shows that Media was still a collection of separate principalities.

Little is known of the course of Median history through the subsequent decades. Ashurbanipal claimed conquest

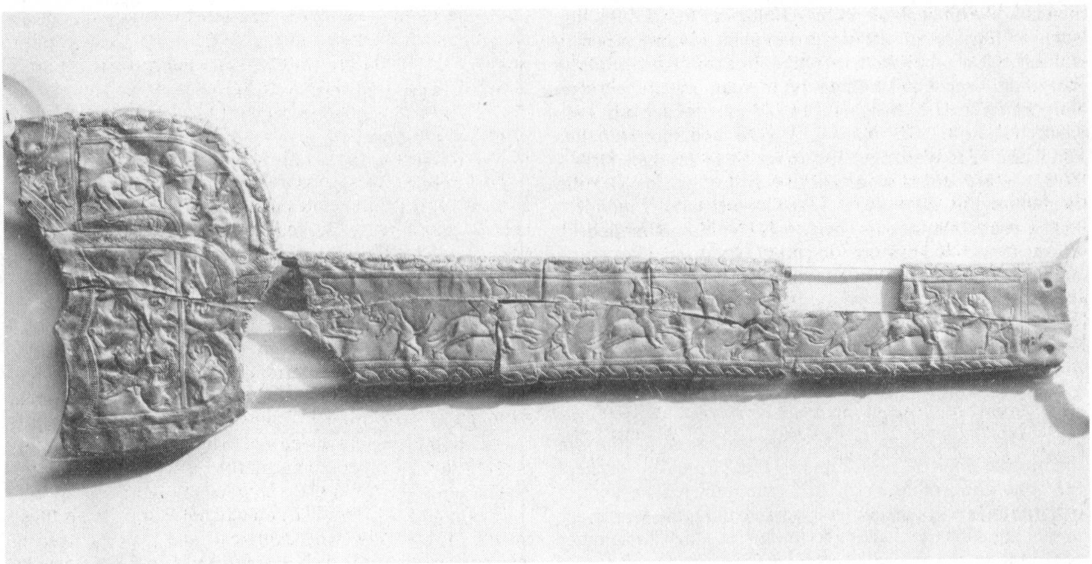

Golden dagger sheath from the Oxus Treasure (Trustees of the British Museum)

of one chieftain and several Median settlements in the course of his campaign against the Mannai, *ca.* 660 B.C. (*ARAB*, II, § 854). The cuneiform records mention nothing more about Media until 615 B.C. This gap may be partly filled from Herodotus's account of the rise of Media (i.97ff.), although it is open to varying interpretations, only one of which is given here. He named four kings of Media: Deioces, Phraortes, Cyaxares, Astyages. The first may be the Dayaukku whom Sargon exiled or another prince of the same name (a second Cyaxares is attested, in Sargon's time, *ARAB*, II, § 147). Unification of the six Median tribes is credited to Deioces, while his son Phraortes subjected the adjacent Persian tribe, conquered Asia (Armenia and Anatolia), and died in an attack on Assyria. Phraortes is commonly identified with Kashtaritu, a chieftain who troubled Esarhaddon *ca.* 670 B.C., but the tenuous argument for this equation should most probably be discounted (R. Labat, *Journal asiatique*, 249 [1961], 1-12) and his reign dated between 650 and 625 B.C.

With Cyaxares more information becomes available through the combination of Greek and Babylonian sources. His first years were clouded by Scythian dominance, brought about by a continued Median attack on Assyria, who summoned these barbarian allies. By 616 B.C. Cyaxares had regained Median independence, enabling him to launch a new assault on Assyria. After Median troops had sacked the ancient capital of Asshur, Cyaxares made alliance with Babylon, and one of his princesses married the crown prince Nebuchadrezzar (who built the "Hanging Gardens" of Babylon to counter her pining for the Median hills, according to Berossus, *apud* Josephus *CAp* i.19 [141]). Cyaxares destroyed Nineveh, in conjunction with Babylonian forces, in 612 B.C. and the last remnants of Assyrian power at Haran in 610 B.C. While Babylon established its sway over Syria and Palestine, Cyaxares extended Median rule across Anatolia to the kingdom of Lydia. After an inconclusive war, Media and Lydia concluded a peace treaty through the mediation of their respective allies, Babylon and Cilicia (585 B.C.; Herodotus i.74).

Cyaxares died about that time, and the throne passed to his son Astyages, whose daughter Mandane was mother of CYRUS, ruler of the related subject nation of Persia. Cyrus built up his strength, overthrew his grandfather in 549 B.C. with the help of disaffected Median generals, and inaugurated the Persian (Achaemenian) Empire. Only in this period does Media figure in the OT; Jeremiah saw her drinking the cup of wrath (25:25) and soon afterward participating in the fall of Babylon (539 B.C.; Jer. 51:11, 28; Isa. 13:17; 21:2).

Media's loss of power did not involve loss of identity or influence, however. A Mede attempted to assert independence at the beginning of Darius's reign, claiming royal lineage, and was crushed with difficulty. Cyrus made the Median capital Ecbatana (modern Hamadân) his capital, a position it retained beside Persepolis and Susa until Alexander's conquest (cf. Ezr. 6:2). Moreover, he adopted the system of government set up by Median kings and

Median guards from the relief on the eastern stairway of the Apadana in Persepolis (*ca.* 485 B.C.) (L. A. Willis)

retained Medes in high office. It is significant that the term "satrap" (governor of a province) is Median in origin and that the word for king is written in Median form in Old Persian texts. The predominating Median influence is also shown by the word order in the phrase "Medes and Persians" (cf. Dnl. 5:28; 6:8, 12, 15; 8:20; *see also* DANIEL, BOOK OF VIII.B) during the early decades, and Greek writers spoke of the great Persian War as "the war with the Medes" in some cases (Thucydides i.14). Later the names were reversed (cf. Est. 1:3, 14, 18f.), although an official chronicle kept the old usage (10:2).

1 Maccabees mentions Media under Syrian rule (6:56) and under the Parthians (14:1-3; cf. Josephus *Ant.* xx.3.1-4 [54-74]). Among the Pentecost crowd (Acts 2:9) were Medes, most likely from Media Atropatene, a state allied with Rome against the Parthians.

***Bibliography.***–R. N. Frye, *Heritage of Persia* (1962); E. Porada, *Art of Ancient Iran* (Art of the World Series, rev. ed. 1969), pp. 143-46; G. Widengren, "The Persians," in D. J. Wiseman, ed., *Peoples of OT Times* (1973), pp. 312-357. A. R. MILLARD

**MEDIAN** mēd'ē-ən (Dnl. 5:31, AV). *See* MEDES, MEDIA.

**MEDIATE** [Heb. *pālal* (1 S. 2:25); Gk. *mesítēs* (He. 8:6)]; AV also JUDGE (1 S. 2:25); NEB also INTERVENE (1 S. 2:25); **MEDIATOR** [Heb. *mēlîṣ* (Job 33:23; Isa. 43:27); Gk. *mesítēs* (1 Tim. 2:5; He. 9:15; 12:24)]; AV also INTERPRETER (Job 33:23), TEACHER (Isa. 43:27); NEB also SPOKESMAN (Isa. 43:27).

Scholars disagree about the meanings of Heb. *pālal* and *mēlîṣ*. KoB (p. 263) and *CHAL* (pp. 292f.) list two roots for *pll*, one meaning "arbitrate," "intercede" (only in the piel), and the other meaning "pray" (only in the hithpael). But BDB (p. 813) is probably correct in seeing here only one root, which perhaps originally meant "break" or "cut off" and developed to mean "divide," "put on one side," "compare with one another," "distinguish," "discriminate," "pass judgment," "mediate" (so D. R. Ap-Thomas, *VT*, 6 [1956], 230-39; cf. E. A. Speiser, *JBL*, 82 [1963], 301-306). The meaning "pray" for the hithpael probably arose from the sense of making oneself a mediator, interposing oneself, between man and God (cf. KD, *Isaiah*, p. 94; *see also* INTERCESSION). Thus 1 S. 2:25 may be translated: "If a man sins against a man, God will mediate [piel of *pālal*] for him; but if a man sins against Yahweh, who will make himself a mediator [hithpael of *pālal*] for him?" Although this question seems to rule out the possibility of a mediator between man and God, it probably only reflects the absence of spiritual leadership at that time (cf. vv. 12-17, 27-36, and esp. 3:1, which implies a lack of prophets, who served a mediatorial function; see R. R. Wilson, *Prophecy and Society in Ancient Israel* [1980]).

The Heb. *mēlîṣ* is a hiphil participle from *lîṣ*, which means "boast" in the qal and "mock," "ridicule" in the hiphil (hence the more common meaning of *mēlîṣ*, "mocker," "scorner"). Although it is at first difficult to see how *mēlîṣ* could mean both "mediator" and "mocker," M. A. Canney (*AJSL*, 40 [1924], 137) suggested that the basic meaning of *lîṣ* was "talk freely," and that this meaning developed in two directions. Negatively, it came to mean "babble," "boast" (i.e., talk freely about oneself) or "ridicule," "mock" (i.e., talk freely [in a negative way] about others). Positively, *lîṣ* may mean "be articulate," hence in the hiphil "cause to be articulate," "interpret," and the participle "interpreter," "spokesman," "intermediary" (cf. R. Gordis, *Book of Job* [1978], p. 377). H. N. Richardson (*VT*, 5 [1955], 167-69, 434-36) preferred to avoid the idea of "interpreter." He translated *mēlîṣ* "intermediary," even in Gen. 42:23, since this meaning fits all the contexts well. Certainly in Isa. 43:27 *mēlîṣ* means "intermediary," "mediator," rather than "interpreter"; it probably refers to the priests (cf. "princes of the sanctuary" in v. 28, a term used of priests in 1 Ch. 24:5), although the prophets may also be in view (R. N. Whybray, *Isaiah 40–66* [*New Century Bible Comm.*, 1975; repr. 1981], p. 93), for both groups served as mediators (*see* MEDIATION).

In Job 33:23 Elihu states that one of the functions of an angelic mediator is "to declare to man what is right" (Heb. *yošrô*, lit. "his uprightness," which E. Dhorme, *Comm. on the Book of Job* [Eng. tr. 1969], p. 501, translated "his duty," i.e., what one must do to be upright). M. Pope (*Job* [*AB*, 3rd ed. 1973], p. 251) related this idea to the "Mesopotamian belief in a personal god who looked after the interest of his mortal client." In intertestamental times the similar notion of guardian angels developed, although in most of the OT angels function as messengers who communicate the divine will to mankind (*see* ANGEL).

*Mēlîṣ* occurs several times in the Qumrân Thanksgiving Hymns. M. Burrows (*More Light on the Dead Sea Scrolls* [1958; repr. 1978], pp. 286f.) concluded that *mēlîṣ* in these hymns means "one who declares" and may be used in reference to an angel, as it is in Job 33:23. While an angelic spokesman seems to be in view in 1QH 6:13f., a human spokesman is clearly referred to in 1QH 2:13 ("a spokesman of knowledge"); he is contrasted with a "spokesman of lies" in 2:14, 31 (cf. 4:7, 9).

Bauer (rev., pp. 506f.) defined Gk. *mesítēs* as "one who mediates between two parties to remove disagreement or reach a common goal." Thus Christ is the "one mediator between God and men" (1 Tim. 2:5), the only one who can reconcile the world to God (2 Cor. 5:18f.; Eph. 2:12-16; Col. 1:20). In Hebrews Christ's mediatorial role is always linked to the new covenant (M. Dibelius and H. Conzelmann, *Pastoral Epistles* [Eng. tr., *Hermeneia*, 1972], p. 42, saw this same link presupposed, though not stated, in 1 Tim. 2:25). The stated superiority of the new covenant to the old implies a similar superiority of the mediator of the new covenant to the mediator of the old, i.e., Moses, whom Philo (*De vita Mosis* ii.166) and Paul (Gal. 3:19) called the *mesítēs* of the old covenant (see F. F. Bruce, *Epistle to the Hebrews* [*NICNT*, 1964], pp. 167f.; J. N. D. Kelly, *Comm. on the Pastoral Epistles* [*HNTC*, 1963], p. 63; but cf. *TDNT*, IV, 618f.). O. Becker (*DNTT*, I, 374f.) and A. Oepke (*TDNT*, IV, 619f.) stressed that this link with the covenant gives *mesítēs* a legal connotation in Hebrews: one who procures and guarantees "the right instituted by God through Christ for liberation from death and sin." Hence in Hebrews *mesítēs* means "guarantor (of the covenant)." G. A. LEE

**MEDIATION.**

F. Christ as Prophet
G. Christ as Servant

*I. General Concept.*–When God reveals Himself to mankind or brings His authority, power, and love to bear on the life of His people, Scripture describes Him as acting through some intermediate figure. An intermediary was sometimes an angel, sometimes one member of the community responding to a special call from God to act between Him and the people. More often, however, the mediator was an official figure within the life of the people, a prophet, priest, or king, fulfilling a traditional office to which he or she had been called and appointed, sometimes by anointing. Such mediating figures also led and directed the approach of people to God in response to His power and love.

In the NT the mediation, leadership, and inspiration of Jesus Christ dominate the approach of God to mankind and the response of mankind to God. "There is one God, and one mediator between God and men, the man Christ Jesus" (1 Tim. 2:5).

It is true that many passages in Scripture severely criticize official mediation, especially that of the priests in the temple worship (Isa. 1:10-16; Hos. 6:6; cf. Am. 7:10). Such criticism, however, is leveled not at the office of the mediating priesthood but at superstitious trust in the automatic efficacy of the mere paraphernalia of mediation. It is also true that many passages in Scripture seem to record an individual's bypassing a mediator to approach God directly (Gen. 12:1; Ps. 32:5). All such passages, however, should be interpreted as occurring within the context of a life and worship inalienably based on mediation. It is frequently insisted that without some form of mediation, God does not bless or receive mankind (cf. He. 9:22).

Greek *mesítēs,* "mediator," is used six times in the NT (Gal. 3:19f.; 1 Tim. 2:5; He. 8:6; 9:15; 12:24). In Hellenistic Greek it has the sense of umpire, arbitrator, or negotiator for peace. It can also refer to the security or guarantee for an agreement. (See *TDNT,* IV, 599-601.)

*II. Mediation and the Covenant.*–In the Bible, beginning with creation, all intercourse between God and mankind occurs within the framework of the COVENANT. Mankind is created and elected to express love and obedience always within the definite form of a covenant established by God's grace that calls for a response of love and trust. The covenant is the context of the office of mediator.

The OT constantly reveals humans as hopelessly unable to fulfil their part in the covenant relationship within which they are meant to find true health and destiny. God never breaks the covenant, but in the history of Israel the people constantly repudiated it and called it into question. Thus God called and authorized mediators to restore the broken covenant in His name and by His grace, so that the people could again enter into relationship with Him, claim the covenant promises, seek afresh to keep the commandments given with the covenant, and fulfil their calling as the chosen people of the covenant.

The task of mediation fell at times on certain outstanding individuals, such as Moses or the "servant" described in Isaiah, who seemed to belong to no distinct office or class. But more often the mediators were the prophets, priests, and kings of Israel, whose role was routinely fulfilling an office rather than personally responding to a crisis. "To conclude this covenant and maintain it, God willed to make use of the ministry of men. Moses was mediator of the covenant of Sinai. But through all the course of Israel's history, men are called, anointed and sent to continue to make known this Covenant, to seal it freshly, and to affirm that in virtue of this Covenant God reigns over the people whom He has chosen and called into communion with Himself" (Bosc, pp. 17f.).

The covenant has a universal goal. Although its history is recounted within the particular sphere of the life of Israel, its framework reveals it as the basis of God's whole creative activity and of His relationship with all nations (Gen. 1–11; 12:1-13; Isa. 2:1-5; 56:1-8). God's people, in fulfilling the covenant, are meant to fulfil a role of mediation so that all mankind will receive the blessings of the one covenant.

The NT places the mediating work of Jesus Christ in the context of fulfilling the covenant. Hebrews especially describes Christ as the mediator of the "new or better covenant" (He. 8:6; 9:15; 12:24). In Christ the universal nature of mediation is brought clearly to light.

*III. Mediation in the OT.–A. Prophet.* The prophets' task was to "stand in the counsel" of God to cause His people to hear His words (cf. Jer. 23:18, 22). Since the prophets' relationship to God had a directness and closeness that marked them off from those to whom they spoke, they were inevitably mediators. They not only received a message to deliver in the name of God, as if God were speaking through them (cf. Hos. 12:10; Isa. 55:11), but they were given insight into the meaning and direction of historical events, especially as these were affected by the Word of God (Am. 3:7f.; Nu. 24:3). In the eyes of the people the true prophet was the man of God whose word had all the truth and reliability of the Word of God (1 K. 17:24). Köhler observed: "Prophet and seer are not merely media of God's Word, they are also the prototype and foreshadowing of that which really ought to be. Man's remoteness from God is thrown into relief by the directness of their relation to Him" (p. 163).

Prophets witnessed the word of God to the people not only by their speeches but also by their lives, attitudes, and other signs. They were forced to adopt an attitude and behavior that made them noticeable (Isa. 8:11f.). They were involved in outward conflict and intense inward suffering (Jer. 20; Am. 7:10). Like watchmen without relief in the midst of danger, they bore a burden of responsibility and anxiety (Ezk. 3:17ff.; 33), especially in the face of the destruction and judgment that they saw advancing. Their task therefore became praying for those to whom they were called to speak (Jer. 42:2ff.; 27:18; Gen. 20:7). Although the prophets' ministry acquired this Godward aspect, its primary direction was from God toward man.

There were at times schools of the prophets (2 K. 2:3; 6:1-7). The prophet was thus, as much as the priest or the king, an institution in the life of Israel (cf., e.g., Isa. 28:7; Mic. 3:11; Jer. 29:1). Prophets came to have a relationship with the court as well as with the temple (cf., e.g., 1 K. 22). Prophets sometimes criticized the cult and priesthood (cf. Am. 7:10; Isa. 1:10ff.) because their task was "to maintain that standard which must decide the life of the nation, alike in its conduct and in its worship" (A. C. Welch, *Prophet and Priest in Old Israel* [1936], p. 34).

*B. Priest.* The priest was, generally speaking, appointed to a hereditary office of mediation between the people and God within the cultic activity of Israel. Though the sin of Israel called into question the validity of the covenant and their election to be a holy nation, God provided them a "Law which clearly set forth His Will, and an order of worship and sacrifice in the Cult which supplied His people in their weakness with a covenanted way of response to His Will" (T. F. Torrance, Intro. to Calvin's *Tracts and Treatises* [repr. 1958], p. xxii). The cult was meant constantly to reestablish and purify the covenant relationship, which cannot permanently be broken. The cult not only brought back the people into a true outward relationship to God but also gave them a new inward communion with Him.

Chiefly through sacrificial atonement the priest fulfilled his mediating office within the life of the people of God

Relief on a stone tablet depicting Nabû-apla-iddina (middle left) being presented to the sun-god Šamaš (right) by a goddess (far left) and a third figure (a priest?). From Abû Habbah, mid-9th cent. B.C. (Trustees of the British Museum)

(Lev. 17:11). "In the atoning sacrifice, and also in the other sacrifices to which the idea of atonement has been transferred, the essential theme is that the gulf between the angry God and the human sinner can only be bridged by the interposition of an act of reparation; and in that it is God himself who establishes the way in which such an atoning substitute can be offered, he shows himself by this very act the covenant God, who is concerned for the maintenance of the covenant despite all the sin of man" (Eichrodt, I, 170).

As in giving the covenant, so in establishing and fulfilling the priests' ritual of the cult, the initiative is entirely with God. The sacrifices and the manner of the offering are minutely prescribed. The priest is called to his office or is the member of a family or tribe set apart by God for this service. The meaning of the ritual must be understood primarily as a gracious approach from God to mankind, a gracious provision by which sinners can find forgiveness and restoration. The people's approach to the altar with their sacrifice is a response to this grace, with confession, fear, confidence, and thankfulness.

The priest represented the congregation before God chiefly in this response within the cult. He was called to "stand before the Lord" (Dt. 10:8) for the people. The worshipers who brought the sacrifices were asked only to lay their hand upon the head of the animal offered. They were asked to lay their hand upon the head of the animal offered and to kill it. They then remained passive while the priest manipulated the blood on their behalf (Lev. 3–4). Although in earlier times individuals built their own altars and offered their own sacrifices (Gen. 12:7), and the heads of families had this responsibility for their own kin (Jgs. 17f.), the tribe of Levi came to be regarded as peculiarly fitted to represent the people in the offering of their sacrifices, being substitutes for the firstborn (Nu. 3:12f., 41; 8:16f.). The representative capacity of the Levitical priesthood was itself a covenant within the covenant (Jer. 33:15ff.; Mal. 2:4).

As the cult developed, however, the central functions of the priesthood became more narrowly specialized, and the Aaronic priesthood (Nu. 4:19ff.; cf. 16:1-11) attained a special status. The representative mediatory function of the priesthood was most vividly embodied and illustrated in the high priest, who when entering the holy of holies wore the breastplate with twelve stones on which the names of the twelve tribes were engraved (Ex. 39:6-14). The ceremony of "filling the hand," performed not simply in the consecration of the Aaronic priesthood but in that of the whole priesthood (Lev. 16:32; Ex. 29:24; Jgs. 17:5, 12), may have signified the endowment with this representative capacity.

In this Godward aspect of his mediatory work the inward attitude of both priest and people was of deep importance, as the warnings of the prophets against trusting in mere outward ritual show (cf. Isa. 1:11ff.; Joel 2:13). The priests were solemnly reminded that their office was to "bear the iniquity" of those whom they represented before God (cf. Lev. 10:17; Nu. 18:1). Intercession is not explicitly stressed as the duty of the priest, though the prophets referred to it as something that priests neglected (Joel 2:17; Mal. 1:9). But the history of Moses shows a close connection between sacrifice and intercession.

In the work of mediation the priests also represented God before the people. They blessed the people (Dt. 10:8; Nu. 6:22ff.) and were custodians of the Urim and Thummim (Ex. 28:30; Dt. 33:8; Lev. 8:8), through which God's will might be known (1 S. 28:6). They manipulated the lot (1 S. 14:36-41). As Moses fulfilled the priestly office, the Lord spoke to him in a way that had obvious relevance for the people who sought his teaching (Ex. 33:7-11). The priests read the law at the feasts and expounded it (Dt. 31:9ff.; Neh. 8), for it was their duty to enable the people to understand the cult so that they could discern between the holy and the profane, the clean and the unclean (Ezk. 22:26; 44:23). But priests were meant to teach the widest and deepest implications of the whole law (Dt. 33:10; Mal. 2:7; cf. Hos. 4–6), in full cooperation with the messages of the prophets (Jer. 18:18; Hag. 2:10f.; Zeph. 3:4). In Dt. 33:8ff. the office of teaching seems to have priority over that of sacrificing.

One must assume that the Israelite community found the ministry of the priests sacramentally efficacious — a "means of grace." Through the services of the temple people attained God's forgiveness and blessing. Thus the Psalms, which stress the cleanness and rightness of the heart, and reality rather than ritual (cf. Pss. 40, 50, 51), were used in temple worship. In performing their sacramental actions, the priests guaranteed communion with God. Köhler said: "The priest is, to those in the midst of whom he lives, a reminder of God's holiness expressed in quite definite habits of life, and demanding a constantly renewed effort to reach that condition in which one may draw near to God. The priest is what all will one day be (Ex. 19:6). The priesthood of the OT is the prototype of the priesthood of all believers" (p. 164; cf. also Isa. 61:6).

*C. King.* The king, like the priest, stood before God as

the representative of the people (1 K. 8:22-53). He was anointed by the whole people (2 S. 2:4). He approached God for the people with a heart engaged by God for this purpose (Jer. 30:21). God dealt with him on behalf of the whole nation and made with him an "everlasting covenant, ordered in all things and sure" (2 S. 23:5; 7:5-17; cf. Ps. 89:19-37 [MT 20-38]; 132:11f.). God's blessing on the king was a blessing on the whole nation. God's gifts to the king — judgment, righteousness, and mercy — ultimately flowed to the people, bringing aid to the poor, needy, and oppressed (Ps. 72:1-13) and safety and prosperity to the whole commonwealth (cf. Jer. 23:5f.; 33:15f.). The king was the "light of Israel" (2 S. 21:17) because through his rule prosperity could spread throughout the land (2 S. 23:3f.). Without him the nation languished (Lam. 4:20). To him people ascribed the power of healing (2 K. 5:7).

God exalted the king before the people as a sign and symbol of the majesty and rule He desired to exercise within the covenant relationship. God is called King (Ps. 84:3 [MT 4]; 145:1) and is to be regarded as ruler of the nation's life and affairs (Dt. 33:5). The exalted throne of the king points to that of "the Lord high and lifted up" (Isa. 6:5). The court of the king could be a symbol for the court of heaven itself (1 K. 22:19). The presence of the king signified the presence of God in Israel (Nu. 23:21). The king is called "son of God" (2 S. 7:14; Ps. 2:7; cf. Ps. 89:26) and "Lord" (Ps. 110:1; Jer. 22:18; 34:5; cf. Gen. 40:1). Divine attributes are ascribed to kings (Ex. 15:18). As a symbol and sign of God Himself, the king's person was inviolable (1 S. 24:10; 26:9; 2 S. 1:14, 16) and had to be protected (21:17).

Because of his exalted position the king had a heavy responsibility. It was his duty to lead and protect the people in danger and war (1 S. 31:2; 1 K. 22:29; 2 K. 9:15ff.). He was the final court of appeal for justice (2 S. 15:2; 1 K. 3:16-28). He had to plead for his people before God (2 S. 24:17; 1 Ch. 21:17; 2 Ch. 6:21-42; 14:11; 20:5-12; Isa. 37:14-20). But the king also had to be conscious of his limitations. He depended on the prayers of his subjects (Ps. 72:15) and had to study the law (Dt. 17:20) and remember that God alone is King.

*D. Servant of God.* Mediation in the OT often arose from an urgent human situation. Abigail, for example, mediated between David and her foolish husband (1 S. 25). Esther interceded with the king on behalf of her people (Est. 4).

The activity of Moses at times seems typical of the official prophet or priest. Like a prophet he stood in the presence of God to hear His word (Ex. 19:3, 9) and then went down to speak it (v. 21) to a people who acknowledged that apart from him they could not bear to confront a God who speaks (Ex. 20:19; Dt. 5:24-27). Moses' shining face signified the reality and efficacy of his mediation (Ex. 34:29). Like a priest, he represented the people before God (Ex. 34:2) to receive and give the cultic law (Lev. 1:2a). He established the covenant with the sprinkling of the blood of sacrifice (Ex. 24:8) and made intercession (Nu. 21:7).

But the mediatory task to which Moses was called cannot ultimately be fitted into any official category. Israel's need could be met not by the performance of a traditional role but only by the personal involvement of a lonely leader who bore a permanent and often crushing burden of responsibility and suffering (cf. Dt. 9:25). His prayers have an urgency and a spontaneity that liturgical forms cannot contain or express (Ex. 32:11-14, 30-32). His separateness was due more to the tension he felt as the bearer of the word of God to a people hostile to its claim than to any official consecration (15:24; 17:1-3; 32:1; etc.). His "bearing the sin" of his people (cf. above) took place in heart and life rather than in the sacrificial ritual at the altar and arose out of his intense self-identification with the people he was bound to serve despite their antagonism (32:32; 34:8f.). The denial of his wish to live long enough to lead the people into the Promised Land shows the suffering his role required (Dt. 3:24-27).

Although official forms of mediation should therefore not be despised, merely holding an office and performing a routine task will not restore a true relationship between God and His people. The prophecy that the Lord will raise up another prophet like Moses (Dt. 18:15, 18), whose ministry will also have a unique significance, should be understood in the light of this aspect of Moses' ministry.

Other prophet-priest figures in the OT were deeply involved, like Moses, in a ministry that demanded much more than fulfilling an official role. Jeremiah, too, felt seized by a word that isolated him as it dominated him (Jer. 15:16f.). He was elected to peculiar suffering (12:1f.) and gave a remarkable account of the inward tension and agony of His surrender to this call (8:18; 20:7-18). Ezekiel, too, witnessed that a true prophet is one who must stand "in the breach" in a critical situation (Ezk. 13:5; 22:30).

The "servant" passages in Isa. 40–50 give preliminary intimations of one whose career is to exemplify, more fully than Moses or Jeremiah, such a ministry of mediation. He is described as one who will bring forth judgment and make people know the law (42:4). He is to be a covenant to the peoples and a light to the Gentiles (v. 6), a witness and servant that all nations might believe (43:10). He is to suffer discouragement and scorn but be constrained and upheld by great promises (49:1-12; 50:4-9). Since these passages frequently use an autobiographical way of speaking, it is difficult to decide whether this is the soliloquy of a particular individual or whether the nation Israel is being imagined in its ideal form, in order to embody and express deep and true insights about how it should mediate salvation to all mankind. In 52:13–53:12, however, the autobiographical way of speaking is replaced by the realistic description of an individual undergoing the most intense suffering and shame. He perfectly submits to God's will in fulfilling a work of priestly and sacrificial mediation (53:6f., 10) that is to bring peace and healing to all people before God (v. 5). His death and obedience are an offering to God by which the sin of all people is borne (vv. 4, 11), and he prevails in his unceasing intercession (v. 12).

*E. Other Forms of Mediation.* In both the OT and NT, God communicates with humans through angelic intermediaries (cf. Nu. 22:35; Josh. 5:13-15; Jgs. 14:3; Zec. 1:9; Dnl. 8:15-18; 9:20-23; Mt. 1:20; 2:13; 28:2-5; Acts 8:26). Angels also helped people understand the significance of visions and signs (Ezk. 40:4; Zec. 4:1-7). When the "angel of the Lord" is identified with the Lord Himself (Gen. 16:7-11; Ex. 13:21; 14:19), one must assume that God was making an angelic form the sign of His presence among mankind. Otherwise, angels seem to be created beings (cf. Zec. 1:9, 12-14) who, belonging to the heavens, serve God's purposes on earth and are guardians and ambassadors to mankind (cf. Ex. 32:12; Nu. 20:16; Ps. 91:11f.; Mt. 4:11; 26:53; He. 1:14). Angels reported to God the doings of mankind (Job 1:6; Zec. 1:11) and presented people's prayers to God (Rev. 8:3f.) but did not have any significant role as mediators.

Some OT passages depict the mediating agent between God and the world as proceeding directly from God. In Prov. 8:22-31, Wisdom is an individual energy, God's companion and master workman in creation, whose chief delight is the children of men. Some think that Wisdom here is simply the personification of a divine attribute. But if this passage is linked with Prov. 1:20ff. and 8:1ff. and interpreted as the efficient expression of God's thought and the medium of His activity (Isa. 55:11; Ps. 33:6; 107:20), it undoubtedly indicates an important aspect of the mediatory activity of Jesus Christ in the NT.

*IV. Mediation in the NT.–A. Jesus Christ as Mediator. 1. In the Mystery of His Person.* The NT discusses mediation on the basis of the fulfillment of the covenant in the person and work of Jesus Christ. "The covenant broken by Israel and the whole of humanity, but never repudiated and destroyed by God, is maintained in the life and act of this one man. He does that which is demanded and expected in the covenant as the act of human faithfulness corresponding to the faithfulness of God" (Barth, *CD*, IV/2, 166f.). Gal. 3:16 describes Jesus as the true seed of Abraham, who is the true object of the covenant promises and grace. His fulfillment of the covenant is based on the sheer grace of God to One elected to be God's rightful partner within it. As Augustine said, God "made righteous this man of the seed of David, never to be unrighteous, without any merit of His will preceding" (*De bono perseverantia* xxiv.67, quoted in Calvin *Inst.* ii.17.1). This is the miracle of grace that brings about the possibility of mediation. Thus in Jesus Christ, God pardons man and calls him into communion with Himself, and man also "looks to his Creator, turns towards Him, receives all things from Him, and submits to His will" (Bosc, p. 14).

Jesus Christ the mediator is true God (1 Tim. 3:16; 1 Cor. 8:5f.; 2 Cor. 3:14) and true man (1 Tim. 2:5; Gal. 4:4; Jn. 1:14). The NT stresses the significance of the humanity in which Jesus Christ fulfils the covenant of grace and thus takes upon Himself the mediatorship of the covenant. It acknowledges the individual and Jewish character of His humanity (cf. Rom. 1:3; 9:5), but it also affirms of the same humanity that it has a universal characteristic, which gives its career and destiny a significance for all people. Christ is the Second Adam, the archetype and representative man (Rom. 5:15-21; 1 Cor. 15:22, 45). The title "Son of man" includes the concept of an individual in whose person and glorious destiny His people are also involved (Mk. 14:62; Mt. 19:28; 24:27; Dnl. 7:9-22). The idea of the recapitulation and inherence of "all things" in Christ (Eph. 1:10; Col. 1:17) as the head of the new humanity (Eph. 1:22; 4:13-16; Col. 1:18; 2:19; 3:10f.) also witnesses to the universal significance of His human nature and work.

In Jesus Christ, therefore, God deals with humanity as a whole (cf. Brunner, pp. 502ff.), and the representative of humanity as a whole deals with God. The incarnate Son of God dwelt not simply in a selected and special man but *in us* (cf. Hooker, *Ecclesiastical Polity* [1594-1662], II, 52f.). Moberly rightly insisted that because Jesus' humanity is the humanity of deity, it can stand in this wide, inclusive, consummating relationship to the humanity of all other people (p. 90). The humanity of Jesus is human nature in its full spirit-body essentiality and individuality, whose personal subsistence, however, is found only in the Logos (cf. Heppe, pp. 414ff., 466; cf. also Barth, *CD*, IV/2, 269ff.).

*2. In the Fulfillment of His Work.* In this discussion of the whole work of mediation, the words of Calvin (*Inst.* iii.1.1) should be remembered: "We must understand that as long as Christ remains outside of us, and we are separated from him, all that he has suffered and done for the salvation of the human race remains useless and of no value for us. Therefore, to share with us what he has received from the Father, he had to become ours and to dwell within us. For this reason, he is called 'our Head' [Eph. 4:15], and 'the first-born among many brethren' [Rom. 8:29]. We also, in turn, are said to be 'engrafted into him' [Rom. 11:7], and to 'put on Christ' [Gal. 3:27]; for, as I have said, all that he possesses is nothing to us until we grow into one body with him. It is true that we obtain this by faith." Christ's mediatory work is therefore made effective and strengthened for people united to Him by faith through the word and sacraments (cf. Jn. 15). To effect this union is the work of the Holy Spirit.

The work of Jesus Christ is simply the manifestation of His person. The covenant maintained and fulfilled in His history is perfectly embodied within the mystery of His personal life (cf. Bosc, pp. 14f.). Precisely because Christ Himself is to some extent "the place where God willed and worked the salvation of men" (A. Wikenhauser, *Pauline Mysticism* [Eng. tr. 1960], p. 25), Paul used the phrase "in Christ" where at times one would expect "by Christ." "In Christ" is the expression in action of the deep inward reality that constitutes the mystery of His person. This expression is consummated in the cross, which seals forever, through His blood, the mediating union between God and man. His resurrection and ascension fully manifest the exaltation of mankind accomplished in His work (Col. 1:18; 1 Cor. 15:20; Rom. 8:29) but already real in Himself even during the days of His humiliation.

*B. The Threefold Office of Christ.* The NT describes in various terms Christ's place and role in accomplishing the work of mediation (cf. Rev. 1:5; Jn. 14:6; 1 Cor. 1:30). An examination of these terms has led the Church to depict the person and work of Christ as the fulfillment of the mediatory offices of prophet, priest, and king. It is taken as significant that in the OT holders of these offices were anointed (cf. Lev. 8:12; 1 S. 15:17; 16:13; 1 K. 19:16). The reality signified by anointing was finally fulfilled at the baptism of Jesus in the Jordan, when the Spirit descended upon Him, and He entered His active ministry as Messiah, Christ, Anointed One.

The early Church tended to emphasize the royal Priesthood of Christ, although the three offices were not entirely forgotten. Aquinas summarized the work of Christ under the threefold formula (*Summa Theol.* iii.22.1-3). But it was Calvin who first sought systematically to develop the threefold office in dealing with Christ's person and work (*Inst.* ii.15.1). Calvin did not develop the doctrine as fully as he had proposed, but later Reformed theology thoroughly explored the way he had opened (cf. Bosc, pp. 5f.; also J. F. Jansen, *Calvin's Doctrine of the Work of Christ* [1956]). Schleiermacher also followed Calvin's lead, and Karl Barth in his doctrine of reconciliation (as outlined in *CD*, IV/1-3) found that the three offices give "three 'christological' aspects of the being of Jesus Christ — aspects of His active person and personal work, which broaden out into three perspectives for an understanding of the whole event of the atonement" (IV/1, 128; cf. also T. F. Torrance, *School of Faith* [1959], pp. lxxxviii ff.).

Since Christ is always, in everything He does and at the same time, Prophet, Priest, and King, no one aspect of His work can be fully explained under one heading. Even in OT times the functions of prophet, priest, and king overlapped. The prophets were often associated with the cult. The priests taught and gave oracles and took over the ruling function. Kings acted as both prophets and priests. Certain prominent figures in the OT, such as Moses and the Servant of the Lord, do not easily fit into one class.

*C. The Two Natures of Christ.* The mediating work of Christ must be interpreted in the light of the unity of the divine and human in His person. Mediation in all its aspects is a work common to both natures and shared by both. Although one must regard each nature as accomplishing a work peculiarly its own, one must seek to discern in all the activity of the God-man the divine within the human rather than alongside of and not fully cooperating with the human. One must deal with God *in, for,* and *as* man. The humanity is a real reflection and utterance of the deity, and the work of the humanity is always a work of God Himself, acting and suffering and triumphing as man (cf. Moberly, pp. 94-97; Torrance, *School of Faith,* p. lxxvii).

*D. Christ as Priest.* The NT constantly teaches that Christ perfectly embodies and fulfils all the mediatory functions signified in the person and work of the priest in the cultic ritual of Israel. Hebrews especially gives this witness: "Therefore he had to be made like his brethren in every respect, so that he might become a merciful and faithful high priest in the service of God, to make expiation for the sins of the people" (2:17).

Hebrews sketches throughout a pattern characteristic of true priesthood. The priest shares the common frailty of the people but stands apart from them; he is separate but identified with them (He. 5:1-4). His function, especially as high priest, is to offer sacrifices (8:3) in a ritual that climaxes on the Day of Atonement, in the entry of the high priest with his offering, alone, into the inner sanctuary, the holy of holies (9:1-10), cleansing all things with the shedding and sprinkling of blood (v. 22).

As this pattern is unfolded, it is shown that Christ fulfils it. He is a great High Priest who has passed into the heavens (4:14f.). He is identified with sinners, sympathetic with their needs and frailties, but separate from them (2:10, 17f.; 4:15; 5:5-9). He fulfils the role of both priest and victim by offering Himself "through the eternal Spirit" (7:27; 9:11-14, 28; 10:10).

Hebrews dwells on the utter superiority of Christ's ministry. Since He is the Son of God, His mediatorship is bound to rank far above that of Aaron (5:1-10). The unique and majestic priesthood of Melchizedek is used to illustrate this superiority (5:6, 10; 7:1-21; Gen. 14:18-20; Ps. 110:4), which makes Christ the mediator of a new and better covenant (He. 8:6; 9:15-20; 12:24). The mediatorship of the Levitical priests took place only in an earthly tabernacle, patterned after the form of the heavenly reality as seen by Moses (Ex. 25:40; He. 8:5; 9:23; 10:1) but nevertheless always remaining shadowy and waiting to be replaced by the true reality to which it pointed. In the OT cult all the offerings required constant repetition (7:27) and were efficacious only for sins done in ignorance (5:2; cf. Lev. 4:2; 5:15). They were never felt to be fully satisfying (He. 9:9; 10:11), nor were they ever meant to be finally effective (7:11, 19). The effect they had was superficial (9:13). But Christ's mediatory work, accomplished once for all, stands forever (7:27; 9:24–28; 10:10; 13:12). It is effective in the immediate presence of God, of which the inner sanctuary is a sign (8:2; 9:3, 8, 24). It removes all that hinders the approach of sinners into the near presence of the Most High (4:16; 7:19, 25; 8:2; 9:24; 10:19f.). It cleanses the conscience and inspires true and living worship and service (9:14).

Many features in the Synoptic Gospels lead to the same analogy in interpreting the work of Christ. Jesus' identification with sinners at His baptism (Mt. 3:13 par.) found deepening expression throughout His ministry (8:15; Lk. 7:37-39; 15:1-10; 19:1-10) and was finally completed in the cross (Lk. 12:50; 23:39-44; Mt. 27:39-45). But He remained separate from all other people (Mt. 14:23; Lk. 11:1; Mk. 9:1-10; Mt. 17:17), consecrating Himself to the task that He had to fulfil alone (Mt. 26:31, 36-45), conscious that His death would be the focal point and consummation of His life (Mk. 9:12-31; 10:32-34; 12:8; 14:8). In His priestly ministry He acted as one who had a right to bestow forgiveness and gave signs of the reality of its bestowal (Mk. 2:1-12; Lk. 7:47-50).

His teaching about the meaning of His death as a sacrifice confirms this interpretation. Two sayings especially are relevant. (1) Mk. 10:45 reads, "For the Son of man also came not to be served but to serve, and to give his life as a ransom for many." If the word for "ransom," Gk. *lýtron,* denotes the purchase price for the emancipation of a slave, the dominant thought is of Jesus as a kingly deliverer or redeemer, though in the form of a humble servant. But more likely *lýtron* should be understood as a propitiatory gift offered in satisfaction for a life forfeit in the sacrificial ritual. (2) Mk. 14:24 (cf. Mt. 26:28; 1 Cor. 11:25) reads, "This is my blood of the covenant, which is poured out for many." Jesus here linked the new covenant, which offers forgiveness of sins (Jer. 31:34), with the ratification of the covenant of Sinai by sacrificial blood (Ex. 24:8). He thus implied that His sacrificial death on the cross, in establishing the new covenant, would mediate forgiveness to "many." This saying, no doubt, refers to the "righteous servant" (Isa. 53:11) who "justifies many," and the Passover background further stresses that His death was a sacrifice.

In the Gospel of John Jesus is the "Lamb of God" (1:29, 36). The reference is possibly to the ram provided for Abraham in substitution for Isaac (Gen. 22:13), or to the lamb of the Passover feast (Ex. 12:3), or to the lamb of Isa. 53:7. Throughout the Gospel, Jesus is shown as the one who freely "[laid] down His life" (Jn. 10:11, 18) as He faced His sacrificial death. In His high-priestly prayer in ch. 17 He consecrated Himself as and for this offering. His benediction of "peace" as He showed the disciples His hands and side (20:19-21) fits into the same "priestly" pattern and confirms the impression that John was designed to testify to this aspect of Jesus' ministry.

Romans 3:25 is to be understood in the context of Christ's work as priest: "whom God put forward as an expiation [Gk. *hilastḗrion*] by his blood, to be received by faith." *Hilastḗrion* could refer to appeasing the anger of God and thus changing His attitude. But it seems more directly to refer to the removal of sin in an expiation and cleansing that depend primarily on the mercy of God, in the context of the OT cult, where *hilastḗrion* corresponds to the "mercy seat" of the ark or to the place of expiation on the day of atonement (Heb. *kappōreṯ*). In 2 Cor. 5:14-21, the appeal to become "reconciled to God" (v. 20) is possible because in Christ the whole world (v. 19; cf. also v. 14) has already been fully reconciled. This reconciliation seems to involve some objective spontaneous act by which God created through love and costly suffering the conditions that enable people to return to Him. The identification of Christ with the sin of mankind (v. 19), corresponding to the nonimputation of sin to people (v. 21), and the phrase "one died for all" (vv. 14f.) suggest the transfer of the sin of the worshiper to the sacrificed victim in the sacrificial ritual. Paul also used sacrificial language in 1 Cor. 5:7; Eph. 5:2. 1 Pet. 1:18f. and 3:18 may refer to the same idea.

*E. Christ as King.* The witness of the NT is that Jesus Christ is Lord and King (Rom. 10:9; 14:8f.; Phil. 2:6-11). He is the King of the Jews (Mt. 2:2; 21:5; 27:11; Lk. 23:2; Jn. 12:13; Acts 17:7). The Lord will give Him the throne of David (Lk. 1:32), of whom He is the seed (Jn. 7:42; Rom. 1:3; 2 Tim. 2:8), the root and offspring (Rev. 5:5). He was witnessed to as the Son of David (Mt. 1:1), especially by those who implored His help (Mt. 9:27; 15:22; 20:30f.; Mk. 10:47f.; Lk. 18:38), and He was finally acclaimed as such by the multitude (Mt. 12:23; 21:9, 15).

Signs were given that He is King, e.g., the manner of His entry into Jerusalem (Mk. 11:1ff.) and the superscription upon the cross (15:26). The establishment of His kingdom in the midst of human life was shown by His regal bearing and His facing the cross not as one driven to it by overwhelming circumstances but as the Lord who laid down His life of His own free will (Jn. 10:17f.; Mt. 16:21) and who took the initiative over all His enemies (cf. Jn. 13:27; Mt. 13:24-30). In His death on the cross He was glorified (Jn. 12:23). As He submitted to its shame and weakness He could majestically decree people's destinies (Lk. 23:43) and utter a final word of triumph (Jn. 19:30). He proclaimed Himself as one who brings "deliverance to the captives" (Lk. 4:18). His miracles were signs that the kingdom of God was at work in the midst of mankind, and that the powers of death, destruction, and decay were being overcome by His Word, which sows, spreads, and nurtures the kingdom in the midst of human life and history (Mt. 13). As people are inevitably drawn to Him, the "prince of this world" is being "cast out" (Jn. 12:31f.).

In the early speeches in Acts, Jesus is "Lord" (Acts 2:36; 3:13-15). In Him the promise of Ps. 110:1 has been fulfilled (2:34f.). Similar and more elaborate confessions punctuate the Epistles (Rom. 14:8f.; Phil. 2:6-11). His liberating power from sin and the law (Rom. 7:23-25) and from the powers of evil and death (Rom. 8:37-39; 2 Tim. 1:10; Rev. 1:18) is stressed. He is King of kings and Lord of lords (Rev. 17:14; 19:16).

In accordance with this witness to His kingship, His mediating work is referred to as "redemption." Texts like Mk. 10:45 and 1 Pet. 1:18f. link the thought of redemption with sacrificial language. But many places in the Epistles more clearly express the thought of redemption (*apolýtrōsis*) as release from bondage, either by overcoming a captor or by paying a ransom or debt (*lýtron*; cf. Rom. 3:24; 1 Cor. 1:30; Eph. 1:7; Col. 1:14; 1 Tim. 2:6). Gal. 3:13; 4:5; 1 Cor. 6:20; 7:23 (cf. 1 Pet. 1:18f.) emphasize the costliness of this liberation. Col. 2:14f. describes the whole work of Christ in redemption as the "spoiling" of principalities and powers.

*F. Christ as Prophet*. In the synagogue at Nazareth, Jesus claimed to have come to fulfil a unique ministry in which good news is preached and deliverance proclaimed (Lk. 4:18-21; cf. Isa. 61:1-3). He referred to Himself as a prophet (Mt. 13:57; Lk. 13:33), and many characteristics of His bearing and teaching forced people to refer to Him as such (Mt. 21:11; Mk. 6:15; Jn. 4:19; 9:17). This implication sometimes is that He is the Prophet expected in fulfillment of Dt. 18:15-18 (Jn. 1:21; 6:14; 7:40), and to this ministry the voice at the Transfiguration witnessed (Mk. 9:7). But Jesus is greater than the prophets (Mk. 8:27-36; Mt. 12:41; 11:2-11). He contrasted the content of the prophets' teaching with His own (Mt. 5:21-28). Moreover, His word is the Word of God simply because He uttered it as His will and decision, whereas the prophets could derive the Word only from a source and authority other than themselves.

In His teaching Jesus took up the themes that were the burden of the preaching of the prophets, but He fulfilled His prophetic ministry especially in revealing God and proclaiming God's love, righteousness, and lordship. He did this not only in His teaching, but in His personal bearing and activity (Jn. 14:6, 9). "His death preeminently as illuminated by the resurrection mediated the full disclosure of God" (H. R. Mackintosh). But His death can be seen in this light only by the witness and illumination of His own teaching, e.g., in Mk. 10:45; 14:24 (see IV.B above).

The NT elsewhere refers directly to Jesus as *the* prophet (Acts 3:22; 7:37). The prophetic aspect of His mediatory work in His death is brought out in Rom. 3:21-25, which emphasizes the cross as manifesting or declaring the righteousness of God, and in 5:8: "But God shows his love for us in that while we were yet sinners Christ died for us." Paul also referred to Christ in His person and work as the "image of God" (2 Cor. 4:4; Col. 1:15).

*G. Christ as Servant*. The Gospels do not use "servant" as a title for Jesus, but there are several references to His fulfilling the servant prophecies in certain aspects of His life (cf. Mt. 8:17; 12:17-21; Lk. 22:37; Mk. 10:45; 14:24). The voice that came from heaven at His baptism (Mk. 1:11), when He was "numbered with the transgressors" (Isa. 53:12), likely refers to Isa. 42:1. (Cf. also Lk. 24:26; Mk. 8:31; 9:31; 10:33.)

In the early preaching in Acts, Jesus is frequently called "servant" (Acts 3:13, 26; 4:30; cf. 8:30-35). In 4:26f. Jesus is confessed both as the king of Ps. 2 and as the servant of Isa. 53. 1 Pet. 2:18-25 tells servants to be willing to suffer by reminding them of the example of Jesus, the Suffering Servant who identified Himself with human beings in their sin, punishment, and death so that they might be identified with Him in His exaltation. Thus, through His entry into the human condition, the straying are now found, the dead now live, the wounded are now healed.

***Bibliography.***–J. Bosc, *Kingly Office of the Lord Jesus Christ* (Eng. tr. 1959); E. Brunner, *The Mediator* (Eng. tr. 1947); O. Cullmann, *Christology of the NT* (Eng. tr. 1959); J. Denney, *Death of Christ* (1902, 1951); W. Eichrodt, *Theology of the OT* (2 vols., Eng. tr. 1961-67); H. Heppe, *Reformed Dogmatics* (Eng. tr. 1950); E. Jacob, *Theology of the OT* (Eng. tr. 1958); L. H. Köhler, *OT Theology* (Eng. tr. 1957); R. C. Moberly, *Atonement and Personality* (1910); S. Mowinckel, *He That Cometh* (Eng. tr. 1956); T. C. Vriezen, *Outline of OT Theology* (Eng. tr., rev. ed. 1968); *TDNT*, I, *s.v.* βασιλεύς κτλ. (Kleinknecht, von Rad, Kuhn, K. L. Schmidt); III, *s.v.* ἱερός κτλ. (Schrenk); IV, *s.v.* μεσίτης, μεσιτεύω (Oepke); VI, *s.v.* προφήτης κτλ. (Krämer, Rendtorff, Meyer, Friedrich).

R. S. WALLACE

**MEDICINE** [Heb. *gēhâ*] (Prov. 17:22); NEB "countenance"; [Heb. *r^epû'â*] (Jer. 30:13; 46:11) NEB REMEDY. Words designating medicines are rather rare in the OT. In addition to those listed above there are more general words for "health," "healing," "remedy," etc. *See* HEAL.

Unless the NEB reading is correct (cf. W. McKane, *Proverbs* [*OTL*, 1970], p. 506), Prov. 17:22 is one of many OT passages that call attention to the importance of emotional states in physical and mental well-being. The lack of "healing medicines" (Jer. 30:13) was held figuratively to have caused Israelite backsliding. Subsequently (46:11) the prophet compared Israel to a dying woman going to Gilead to take balm as a medicine without resultant benefit. In Ezk. 47:12, the leaves of the envisioned tree of life are said (AV) to be for medicine. The RV and RSV read "healing," thus assimilating the language to that of Rev. 22:2.

R. K. H.

**MEDITATE** [Heb. *śî(a)ḥ, śû(a)ḥ*] (Gen. 24:63; Ps. 77:3, 6 [MT 4, 7]; 119:15, 23, 27, 48, 78, 148; 145:5); AV also COMPLAIN, "commune with mine own heart" (Ps. 77:6), TALK OF, SPEAK OF; NEB also "hoping to meet" (Gen. 24:63), "lay thinking" (Ps. 77:3, 6), STUDY, "my theme shall be" (Ps. 145:5); [*hāgâ*] (Josh. 1:8; Ps. 1:2; 38:12 [MT 13]; 63:6 [MT 7]; 77:12 [MT 13]; 143:5); AV also IMAGINE; NEB also "keep in mind" (Josh. 1:8), MUTTER, "think on," MEMORY; [Gk. *promeletáō*] (Lk. 21:14); NEB "prepare beforehand"; **MEDITATION** [Heb. *śî(a)ḥ*] (Ps. 104:34); [*śîḥâ*] (Job 15:4; Ps. 119:97, 99); AV also PRAYER; NEB SPEAK, STUDY; [*higgāyôn*] (Ps. 19:14 [MT 15]); NEB "all that I . . . think"; [*hāgûṯ*] (Ps. 49:3 [MT 4]); NEB "thoughtful."

In the biblical world meditation was not a silent practice. *Hāgâ* means "growl," "utter," or "moan" (cf. BDB, p. 211) as well as "meditate" or "muse." No doubt meditation involved a muttering sound from reading half aloud or conversing with oneself (cf. Ps. 77:6). Consequently, translations can vary: e.g., in Job 15:4 "meditation" (RSV) is rendered "prayer" by the AV and "to speak" by the NEB; in the AV Ps. 5:1 (MT 2) has, "O Lord, consider my meditation", but the RSV has "give heed to my groaning" and the NEB "consider my inmost thought."

Meditation takes place any time of the day or night (Josh. 1:8; Ps. 1:2). It produces inward strength and joy (Ps. 63:5f.). The object of meditation is particularly the law with its precepts (119:15), statutes (v. 48), testimonies (v. 99), and promises (v. 148). The glorious splendor of God's majesty, along with His wondrous works or miracles, is also the content of meditation (143:5; 145:5). Meditation takes place in the heart, the seat of the emotional and rational life. Therefore, the psalmist prays that the meditation of his heart will be acceptable in God's sight (19:14; 104:34), i.e., he wants his inner thoughts to approach the standard God approves. Thus the righteous, when they encounter the plots of the wicked, maintain a pure mind by meditating on God's law (119:23).

Jesus instructed His followers not to waste their time meditating their anticipated defense before their persecutors. Such confrontations are so versatile and unpredictable that undue preoccupation with them only increases one's anxiety and reduces one's effectiveness in the task at hand. To meet such a crisis Jesus promised special wisdom in speech from the Holy Spirit (Lk. 21:14f.). Conversely, as Paul taught Timothy, the mind is to be occupied with spiritual matters to increase spiritual growth (1 Tim. 4:15, using Gk. *meletáō,* RSV "practice," AV "mediate").

See *TDOT,* III, *s.v.* "hāghāh" (Negoiță, Ringgren).

*See also* COMMUNE; MUSE; STUDY. J. E. HARTLEY

**MEDITERRANEAN SEA** med'ə-tə-rā-nē-ən. The body of water bounded by north Africa on the south, the Levant on the east, Turkey (Asia Minor) and southern Europe on the north, with the western end being constricted by Morocco and Spain. The Mediterranean is connected to the Atlantic Ocean by the Straits of Gibraltar.

The English name derives from a Latin designation ("inland") that appeared in the 7th cent. A.D. In antiquity the names for the Mediterranean varied considerably, usually depending on a nation's geographic relationship to the sea. Geographically, Israel was a maritime nation, but its people were not known as sailors like the Minoans of Crete or the neighboring Phoenicians. When Solomon wanted to establish a Red Sea fleet he used Phoenician sailors sent by Hiram king of Tyre because they "were familiar with the sea" (1 K. 9:26-28; 2 Ch. 8:18). The Hebrews were not mariners like the Phoenicians because of the lack of natural harbors along Israel's coast. Thus they early on became dependent on the Phoenicians to transport trade goods.

Frequently in the OT the Mediterranean is called simply "the sea" (Heb. *hayyām*). When describing the ethnic composition of Canaan at the time of the Conquest, Nu. 13:29 states that "the Canaanites dwell by the sea" (cf. Josh. 5:1). References to Sidon (Isa. 23:2) and Tyre (Ezk. 27:3f., 9, etc.) being situated by "the sea" leave no doubt that *hayyām* may be used for the Mediterranean Sea, although *yām* is also applied to the Re(e)d Sea (Ex. 14:2, 16, 22), the Gulf of Aqabah/Red Sea (1 K. 10:22), the Dead Sea (Josh. 12:3), and the Sea of Galilee (Josh. 13:27). *Hayyām* may be a shortened form for one of several longer expressions for the same body of water. For example, since the Mediterranean was the largest body of water known to the Hebrews, they sometimes called it *hayyām haggādôl,* "the great sea" (Nu. 34:6f.; Josh. 1:4; 15:12, 47; 23:4; Ezk. 47:15, 19f.).

Another OT expression for the Mediterranean Sea is *hayyām hā'ahªrôn* (lit. "the sea behind"), "the western sea" (RSV) or "the uttermost sea" (AV). Since the Hebrews oriented the cardinal points by facing the rising sun in the east (*qeḏem,* lit. "in front," BDB, p. 869), what is behind would be the west. The name "western sea" is not restricted to the OT (cf. Dt. 11:24; 34:2; Joel 2:20; Zec. 14:8), but is found in Egyptian and Babylonian inscriptions (cf. "Upper sea," "Great Sea," "Western Sea," *ANET,* pp. 267-69, 275-281; note that from the mid-2nd millennium on, Assyrian texts include "west" or Amurru [i.e., Syrian] as part of the name).

The common Egyptian expression for both the Mediterranean and Red seas is *w3ḏ wr,* "great green" (A. Erman and H. Grapow, *Wörterbuch der ägyptischen Sprache*, I [1926], 269); this was questioned by A. Nibbi in *Sea Peoples and Egypt* (1975), but her thesis was amply refuted by K. Kitchen (*JEA*, 64 [1978], 169-171).

As a loanword, *yām* is attested in Egyptian texts as early as the middle of the 15th cent. B.C. (*Wörterbuch der ägyptischen Sprache,* I, 78.11). In the Story of Wenamun (11th cent. B.C.) the Mediterranean is called *P3 y3m ʿ3 n ḫ3rw,* "the Great Sea of Syria" (*ANET,* p. 26).

Ezra 3:7 refers to cedar for the building of the second temple being floated down the Phoenician coast *'el-yām yāpô'*. The LXX, followed by AV, understood this to mean "to the sea of Joppa." The RSV and other more recent translations properly render this "to the sea, to Joppa," because *yām* is in its absolute form and so is not bound to Joppa. Also, the final *aleph,* which is not a part of the normal spelling of the word (cf. Jonah 1:3), appears to function like the directive *-â,* thus meaning "to Joppa." Therefore it is doubtful that the Mediterranean was ever called "sea of Joppa." Similarly the grammatical construction *ʿaḏ yām pᵉlištîm* in Ex. 23:31 should be rendered "to the sea, Philistia" (contra LXX, RSV, AV, *et al.*).

Therefore it can be concluded that in the OT there were essentially three expressions for the Mediterranean Sea: the sea, the great sea, and the western sea. All three of these, and the combination "the great western sea," are attested in Near Eastern literature.

The NT has little to say specifically about the Mediterranean. Most references are found in Acts. Simon the tanner, with whom Simon Peter stayed, lived in Joppa in a house "by the seaside" (Gk. *thálassa,* Acts 10:32). In Paul's journeys he travels by sea, which is clearly the Mediterranean (17:14; 27:30, 38; 28:4). Acts 27:5 uses the term *pélagos* for Paul's sailing off the coast of Cilicia. This term usually means "open sea" or "high sea" (LSJ, p. 1356) and therefore is a technical term, not a proper name. Before the shipwreck on Malta, the ship that carried Paul was swept across the Adriatic (Sea) (Gk. *Adria,* 27:27). The name "Adriatic" is known as early as Strabo (1st cent. B.C.) and usually refers to the extension of the Mediterranean along Italy's eastern coast, but in the 1st cent. A.D. this included the area from Crete to Malta (*see* ADRIA).

*See also* Plate 53. J. K. HOFFMEIER

**MEDIUM** [Heb. *'ôḇ*] (Lev. 19:31; 20:6, 27; Dt. 18:11; 1 S. 28:3, 7, 9; 2 K. 21:6; 23:24; 1 Ch. 10:13; 2 Ch. 33:6; Isa. 8:19; 19:3); AV "(one who has a) familiar spirit"; NEB "(one who traffics with, calls up, etc.) ghost(s)," "(one who has a) familiar spirit" (1 S. 8:7); **NECROMANCER** [Heb. *dōrēš 'el-hammēṯîm*–'one who consults the dead'] (Dt. 18:11); **WIZARD** [Heb. *yiddᵉʿōnî*] (Lev. 19:31; 20:6; etc.); NEB "(one who traffics with, etc.) spirit(s)." A human agent who facilitates communication with the dead for the purpose of learning the future. *See* DIVINATION III.G.

Because the terms *'ôḇ* and *yiddᵉʿōnî* are almost always paired (*yiddᵉʿōnî* appears only with *'ôḇ*; *'ôḇ* appears alone only in 1 S. 28 and 1 Ch. 10:13), they are best considered together. Most scholars agree that *yiddᵉʿōnî* (RSV "wizard") is derived from the verb *yāḏaʿ* ("know") and means "knowing one," referring either to the knowledge possessed by the spirits of the underworld or to the knowledge or skill of the practitioners; thus the two main alternatives for translation are "familiar spirit" and "soothsayer" (KoB, p. 367).

There is much less agreement about the derivation of *'ôḇ* (RSV "medium"). According to one view it is the same word that means a "bottle made out of skins" ("wineskin," Job 32:19). The term would then refer to the technique of ventriloquism or, more accurately, "belly-talking" (cf. LXX *engastrímythos*), i.e., to the mediums' ability to produce a deep, husky voice, apparently not their own, which represented the spirit of the dead person speaking through, or from within, them. According to a second view *'ôḇ* is derived from the Arabic root *'wb* ("return") and means a "revenant," i.e., the ghost of the deceased who is called back by the medium (e.g., see W. Eichrodt, *Theology of the OT,* II [Eng. tr. 1967], 215). J. Lust has argued for a derivation from *'āḇ* ("father, ancestor"). According to this view the *'ōḇôṯ* were the ghosts of the deceased fathers living in the netherworld (and possibly also images representing them).

Perhaps the most satisfactory explanation of *'ôḇ* thus far is the one propounded by H. A. Hoffner. According to Hoffner *'ôḇ* is a "non-Semitic migratory word" that appears in Sumerian (*ab*), Hurro-Hittite (*a-a-bi*), Akkadian (*aptu,* Neo-Assyr. *apu*), and Ugaritic (*'ēb* < *'ayb*), always with the meaning "sacrificial pit" (*TDOT,* I, 131), i.e., a ritual pit dug in the ground for the purpose of sacrificing to chthonic deities and calling up the spirits of the deceased. The meaning of *'ôḇ* shifted from "pit" to "spirit(s) of the pit" to "necromancer who calls forth the spirits through the use of a ritual pit." Prophets apparently mocked the use of such ritual pits; cf. Isa. 29:4: "Then deep from the earth you shall speak, from low in the dust your words shall come; your voice shall come from the ground like the voice of a ghost, and your speech shall whisper [piel of *ṣāpap*] out of the dust." In 8:19 the prophet clearly applies both *'ōḇôṯ* and *yiddeʿōnîm* to the practice of necromancy (here the RSV translates Heb. *dāraš 'el-hammēṯîm* "consult the dead," whereas in Dt. 18:11 it renders the participle form "necromancer") and suggests that the practitioners used unnatural voices: "the mediums and wizards who chirp [pilpel part. of *ṣāpap*; cf. Isa. 29:4; used of birds in 10:14; 38:14] and mutter."

1 Samuel 28 provides a description of the practice of necromancy in ancient Israel. After Saul had exhausted all legitimate means of seeking advice (dreams, Urim, prophets) and the Lord had not answered him (v. 6), he sought out a medium (*baʿalaṯ-'ôḇ,* lit. "mistress of the pit," v. 7). It is probable, though not specifically stated in the text, that the disguised Saul visited the medium of Endor at her ritual pit and that some kind of sacrifices or offerings preceded the "bringing up" of the deceased Samuel (cf. vv. 11-15; in v. 13 the medium describes Samuel's ghost as an *'elōhîm,* "supernatural being" [RSV "god"]). Saul was apparently not able to see Samuel himself (vv. 13f.), and it is probable that the interview between Saul and Samuel was mediated by the woman.

The terms *'ôḇ* and *yiddeʿōnî* occur repeatedly in lists of practices that were prohibited or condemned (e.g., Lev. 19:31). In Isa. 19:3 the practice of consulting *'ōḇôṯ* and *yiddeʿōnîm* is associated with the consultation of idols and *'iṭṭîm* (prob. < Akk. *eṭimmu,* "ghost of a dead person" [KoB, p. 34]; RSV "sorcerers"); cf. the association of necromancy with various forms of idolatry and magic in 2 K. 21:6 par. 2 Ch. 33:6; 2 K. 23:24. While Lev. 20:27 prescribes the death penalty for those who practice necromancy, the normal penalty was apparently banishment (1 S. 28:3, 9; 2 K. 23:24).

***Bibliography.***–H. A. Hoffner, *JBL,* 86 (1967), 385-401; J. Lust, "On Wizards and Prophets," in G. W. Anderson, *et al.,* eds., *Studies on Prophecy* (*SVT,* 26; 1974), pp. 133-142; *TDOT,* I, *s.v.* "'ôbh" (H. A. Hoffner).

D. E. AUNE
N. J. O.

**MEEDA** mə-ē'də (1 Esd. 5:32, AV); **MEEDDA** mə-ē'də (1 Esd. 5:32, NEB). *See* MEHIDA.

**MEEK; MEEKNESS** [Heb. *ʿānāw*] (Nu. 12:3; Ps. 10:17; 37:11; Isa. 11:4; 29:19); AV also HUMBLE (Ps. 10:17); NEB "of great humility" (Nu. 12:3), HUMBLE, LOWLY (Isa. 29:19); [Gk. *praýs*] (Mt. 5:5); NEB "of a gentle spirit"; [*praýtēs* (var. *praótēs*)] (2 Cor. 10:1; Eph. 4:2; Col. 3:12; Jas. 1:21; 3:13); NEB GENTLE(NESS), QUIETLY (Jas. 1:21), MODESTY (Jas. 3:13).

In each of the five OT occurrences of "meek" the Hebrew term is *ʿānāw,* usually rendered "poor" or "needy" (*see* POOR). Originally *ʿānāw* meant "a person in subjection," but later it referred more often to a person who viewed his own role in relation to God as that of a servant and who thus quietly and gently subjected himself to God's will.

In Isa. 11:4 (paralleling the *dal,* "poor") and 29:19 (paralleling the *'eḇyôn,* "needy") the meek are the poor of Israel (i.e., the powerless) oppressed by their rich and powerful compatriots for personal advantage. The context is generally similar in Ps. 10:17 and 37:11 — it is the meek and lowly who, despite appearances, bear the divine promise. Thus *ʿānāw* came rather naturally to characterize the truly pious or faithful person in Israel — one who completely depended on God and was humble and gentle toward others. Moses is characterized as a "meek" man (probably as a result of later piety; see *TDNT,* VI, 647) in Nu. 12:3 because he refused to elevate his own importance over that of God, and his authority was exercised within the perspective of humility.

The OT concept of meekness, then, is rooted in God and the eschatological hope that He will judge in justice and give the land to the lowly (cf. Ps. 37:11; Mt. 5:5). From another point of view meekness is the opposite of PRIDE, for pride is the arrogant reliance on self alone rather than on God (hence pride is the essence of sin). It is significant that the cognate substantive *ʿanāwâ,* "meekness, humility," appears prominently in the Qumrân *Manual of Discipline* (1QS 2:24; 3:8; etc.) as a requisite quality in communal life of the "sons of light."

Meekness also enjoys a high standing among the virtues stressed in the NT (cf. *praýtēs* in Eph. 4:2; Col. 3:12), particularly in the living example and teachings of Jesus. *Praýtēs* was considered an essential Christian virtue by the time of the postapostolic fathers, who in exhorting the Church to meekness strangely do not cite the example of Jesus in support.

The NT term's relationship to the OT is best exemplified by the use of *praýs* (the usual LXX equivalent for *ʿānāw*) in Mt. 5:5 (only Matthew, of the three Synoptists, uses the term). This beatitude, "Blessed are the meek, for they shall inherit the earth" (the only beatitude that is a quotation), is drawn from Ps. 37:11. Mt. 5:5 stresses the future promise. The oppressed and lowly (*praeís*) who can still affirm in their adversity the good and gracious will of God instead of their own will find the tables turned to their advantage in the *eschaton.* The two occurrences of *praýtēs* in Jas. 1:21 and 3:13 also manifest a carry-over from the OT conception, particularly the latter in its emphasis upon the relationship between meekness and divine wisdom.

The truly righteous are humble and receptive to the Word of God.

In 2 Cor. 10:1 Paul brought the "meekness [*praÿtēs*] and gentleness [*epieíkeia*] of Christ" to bear against the wilfulness and recalcitrance of the Corinthians. He realized that the meek and gentle approach could easily appear as weakness to those unfamiliar with Jesus' example. (In secular Greek *praÿtēs* meant "mild and gentle friendliness" and, although valued by classical writers as a social virtue, it was nevertheless suspect because of this tendency for meekness to appear as weakness. See *TDNT,* VI, 646.)

In general the NT distinguishes meekness and gentleness; the former is an internal attitude, and the latter refers to external behavior (cf. "the meekness and gentleness of Christ" in 2 Cor. 10:1). The RSV also makes this distinction in translating *praÿtēs*: "meekness" describes an internal attitude and "gentleness" a social or interpersonal behavior.

True "meekness" is then ultimately always measured by the meekness of Jesus. His humility, patience, and total submission of His own will to the will of His Father exemplify superlatively "meek" persons, who possess a balanced perspective on themselves, in their relationships both to God and to others.

*See also* GENTLE; HUMBLE; LOW.

***Bibliography*.**–*TDNT,* VI, *s.v.* πραΰς, πραΰτης (Hauck, Schulz); R. de Vaux, *Ancient Israel* (Eng. tr. 1961), I, 72-74; *RTWB,* p. 176.

D. G. BURKE

**MEET** [Heb. *qārā'* (Gen. 14:17; 18:2; 19:1; etc.), piel of *qāḏam* (e.g., Dt. 23:4 [MT 5]), *pāga'* (Gen. 32:1 [MT 2]; Ex. 5:20; etc.), *māṣā'*–'find' (1 S. 10:3; 1 K. 13:24; etc.), niphal of *yā'aḏ*–'appear,' 'meet by appointment' (Ex. 25:22; 29:42; etc.), *pāgaš* (e.g., Gen. 32:17 [MT 18]; niphal in Ps. 85:10 [MT 11]; Prov. 22:2; 29:13), *lipnê*–'to the face of' (e.g., 1 Ch. 12:17; 2 Ch. 15:2), etc.]; AV also FIND, PREVENT, etc.; NEB also COME UPON, FIND, etc.; [Gk. *hypantáō* (e.g., Lk. 14:31; Jn. 11:20, 30; 12:18; Acts 16:16), *hypántēsis* (Mt. 8:34; 25:1; Jn. 12:13), *apantáō* (Mk. 14:13; Lk. 17:12), *apántēsis* (e.g., Mt. 25:6), *synantáō* (Lk. 9:37; 22:10; Acts 10:25; He. 7:1, 10), *synérchomai*–'come together' (Acts 22:30; 1 Cor. 11:20), pass. of *synágō*–'bring together' (Jn. 18:2; Acts 11:26), *episynagōgḗ*–'gathering together' (2 Thess. 2:1; He. 10:25), *peripíptō*–'fall in with,' 'encounter' (Jas. 1:2), *symbállō*–'converse,' 'fall in with' (Acts 17:18; 20:14), *synkeránnymi*–'mix, blend, unite' (He. 4:2), *adókimos*–'not standing the test,' 'unqualified' ("fail to meet the test," 2 Cor. 13:5), etc.]; AV also COME TOGETHER, ASSEMBLING, etc.; NEB also ASSEMBLE, GATHERING, FACE, etc.

The normal course of human life provides the context for most occurrences of "meet" in the Scriptures. Several main categories of biblical usage can be discerned.

Most often it refers to people encountering one another; e.g., Melchizedek and Abraham (He. 7:1, 10), Esau and Jacob (Gen. 33:4), Aaron and Moses (Ex. 4:27), Saul and David (2 S. 6:20), Ahab and Elijah (1 K. 18:16), Isaiah and Ahaz (Isa. 7:3), Jael and Sisera (Jgs. 4:18), Samson and the Philistines (15:14), Amasa and Joab (2 S. 20:8), Abigail and David (25:20), Ahaziah and Joram (2 Ch. 22:7). Often someone meets an anonymous party, e.g., "runners" and "messengers" (Jer. 51:31), a "fugitive" (Isa. 21:14), an angel (Zec. 2:3 [MT 7]), a man carrying a jar of water (Mk. 14:13). The parties may meet in opposition (king against king, Lk. 14:31), or they may find unity through a shared dependence on one Creator: rich and poor (Prov. 22:2), poor and oppressor (29:13).

God also encounters or meets people in the course of their lives. Thus Moses brings the Israelites out of their camp in the wilderness "to meet God" (Ex. 19:17). On the way to the Promised Land their worship centers on the "tent of meeting" (see Ex. 25:22). There the people of Israel "meet God" and are in His presence (29:42f.; 30:36; Nu. 17:4 [MT 19]). The initiative in these experiences, however, lies with God, who summons His people to meet Him, directs their worship, and through this encounter reveals Himself to them. The prophet Amos warns Israel of coming punishment in words reminiscent of Sinai: "Prepare to meet [*qārā'*] your God" (Am. 4:12; cf. Ex. 19:11, 15).

Similarly, individuals such as Balaam (Nu. 23:15; cf. 23:3), Jacob (Hos. 12:4 [MT 5]), and the psalmist (Ps. 59:10 [MT 11]) "meet God." God meets the person who "joyfully works righteousness" (Isa. 64:5 [MT 4]); He meets with "goodly blessings" the king who rejoices in the strength of the Lord (Ps. 21:1, 3 [MT 2, 4]). Individuals encounter God in His various attributes. Thus God meets His people as a faithful friend "in his steadfast love [Heb. *ḥeseḏ*]," (Ps. 59:10 [MT 11]; by contrast, cf. the Ammonites and Moabites, who shunned the fugitive Israelites, refusing to "meet [them] with bread and with water on the way" [Dt. 23:4 (MT 5); cf. Isa. 21:14]). God meets in His "compassion" (*raḥ*ᵃ*mîm*) those who are brought low (Ps. 79:8). In Ps. 85:10 (MT 11) the divine attributes "steadfast love" and "faithfulness" are personified as God's servants or messengers who "meet" in the fullness of salvation.

In the NT "meet" may indicate a gathering together (e.g., the chief priests and council, Acts 22:30; the church, 1 Cor. 11:20). More often, however, "meet" denotes an act of welcoming someone (e.g., *hypantáō,* Mt. 8:28; 28:9; Mk. 5:2; Lk. 8:27; Jn. 4:51; etc.). As Paul approached Rome, one group of Christians met him at the "Three Taverns" (a stopping place on the Appian Way some 53 km. [33 mi.] from Rome), while another group went out as far as the market town of Appii Forum (10.5 km. [6.5 mi.] farther from the city) in order to escort him into Rome (Acts 28:15). The term used here (*apántēsis*) is "almost a technical term for the official welcome of a visiting dignitary by a deputation which went out from the city to greet him and escort him for the last part of his journey" (Bruce, p. 527 n. 26). The term is also used in Jesus' parable of the bridegroom (Mt. 25:6; in v. 1 the earliest MSS have *hypántēsis,* which the NT uses interchangeably with *apántēsis*) and in 1 Thess. 4:17, which envisions living believers as caught up "to meet the Lord in the air," i.e., to welcome Christ and acclaim Him as Lord (see *TDNT,* I, 380f.).

Greek *episynagōgḗ* refers to both an assembly of believers and the action of meeting together. In the NT it carries strong eschatological coloring (cf. Mk. 13:27, *episynágō*). The Church awaits the day when it will assemble to meet Christ at His parousia (2 Thess. 2:1). In the meantime, believers must not neglect their regular assembly (He. 10:25). The prefix *epi-* points to the definite center to which the gathering is directed, namely, to Jesus Christ (see Westcott, p. 325).

Figuratively, one can speak of "meeting" a challenge or test. In 2 Cor. 13:5 Paul exhorts the Corinthian Christians to examine whether they are holding to their faith, reminding them that Jesus Christ is in them unless they "fail to meet the test" (*adókimos*; Lat. *reprobus*; AV "reprobate"). Similarly, He. 4:2 warns that some do not benefit from hearing the good news because the message "did not meet with faith in the hearers"; this indicates that the gospel in itself does not save until the believer responds with faith. Jas. 1:2 states that believers are tested when they "meet various trials" (*peripíptō*); yet they are to "count it all joy," for this testing (*dokímion*) produces steadfastness and perfection (vv. 3f.).

*Bibliography.*–F. F. Bruce, *Acts* (*NICNT,* repr. 1971); *TDNT,* I, *s.v.* 'απάντησις (E. Peterson); VII, *s.v.* ἐπισυναγωγή (W. Schrage); B. F. Westcott, *Epistle to the Hebrews* (repr. 1970); H. W. Wolff, *Joel and Amos* (Eng. tr., *Hermeneia*, 1977).

D. K. McKIM

**MEETING PLACES OF GOD** [Heb. *môʿadê ʾēl*] (Ps. 74:8); AV SYNAGOGUES OF GOD; NEB GOD'S HOLY PLACES. The term refers to places of assembly for the worship of the Lord. The AV rendering is unlikely (but cf. Aq. *synagōgás*), since synagogues did not appear until after the Exile (see R. de Vaux, *Ancient Israel* [Eng. tr. 1961], II, 343f.). The plural form has caused much debate (see the comms.), but as A. A. Anderson noted, it may be a plural of extension or amplification (*Psalms,* II [*NCBC,* repr. 1981], 541).

**MEGIDDO** mə-gid'ō [Heb. *meg̱iddô, meg̱iddôn*]; AV also MEGIDDON mə-gid'ən. A royal Canaanite city in north-central Israel overlooking the Valley of Jezreel. It passed into the hands of the Israelites and became a major administrative center. Eshtori Haparhi (14th cent. A.D.) deduced that Megiddo should be located at Khan el-Lejjûn. In late Roman times the town had been called Legio after the Sixth Legion stationed there; its Jewish name was Cephar ʿOtnai. E. Robinson made the same deduction independently. Archeology has shown that the general vicinity was correct, but the actual site of the Bronze and Iron Age town was Tell el-Mutesellim, beside Lejjûn.

*I. History.*–The site of Tell el-Mutesellim was occupied as early as the Chalcolithic Age (4th millennium B.C.); it was a mighty urban center in the Early Bronze Age (3rd millennium) but was destroyed, like most great cities in the country. For perhaps a century or so prior to 2000 B.C. it must have been only a crude village settlement (M.B. I, the "Intermediate Bronze Age") of which few traces remain.

*A. Middle Bronze* (M.B. II, *ca.* 2000-1550 B.C.). The new city that rose on the ruins of Megiddo enjoyed close relations with the rulers of the 12th Dynasty of Egypt, as shown by the presence of a statue base of Thuthotep, a high official in Egypt, along with two other stelae. The Execration Texts contain curses on many other towns in

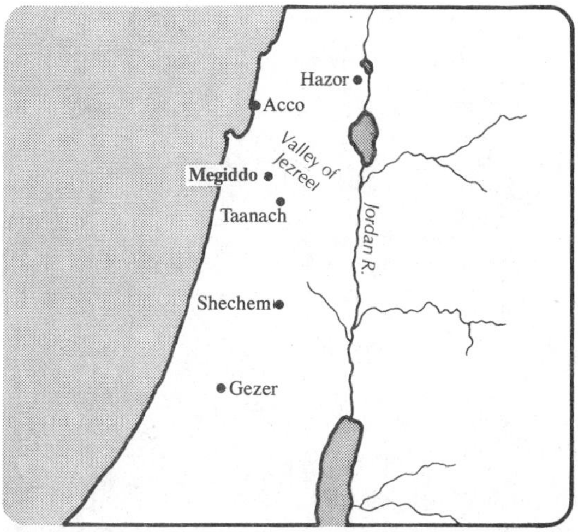


the region, indicating that they were at enmity with the pharaohs, but do not mention Megiddo. The city may have represented the Egyptian interests in the area during this period (M.B. II.A, *ca.* 2000-1800 B.C.). In the so-called Hyksos Age (M.B. II.B, *ca.* 1800-1630 B.C.), a mighty rampart of beaten earth surrounded Megiddo; its settlement was not only on the impressive citadel but also in a "lower city," a "step" on the north side of the mound (where the museum presently stands). No extant inscriptions illuminate the history of Megiddo in this period when the great "Amorite" dynasties were ruling Mesopotamia and the Levant.

*B. Late Bronze Age* (*ca.* 1550-1200 B.C.). When the West Semitic and Hurrian "rulers of foreign lands" were expelled from Egypt, the new 18th Dynasty began to campaign earnestly in Canaan and sought to spread its hegemony over the entire area. The Levantine rulers under the leadership of Kadesh on the Orontes and Megiddo resisted this effort. They took their stand in the Valley of Jezreel expecting the Egyptians to come from the Sharon

Aerial view of the excavations at Megiddo (W. Braun)

Ivory plaque showing the prince of Megiddo (left, seated on a throne) receiving tribute and prisoners (*ca.* 1350-1150 B.C.) (Oriental Institute, University of Chicago)

plain via the Valley of Dothan. Two other passes were available, however, one coming out NW of Megiddo (beside Jokneam) and the other, Wâdī ʿÂra (= Nahal ʿIron), by Megiddo itself. The attacking pharaoh, Thutmose III, claimed to have surprised the defenders by advancing through the central pass and taking a stand near Megiddo. The ensuing battle resulted in an Egyptian victory, but the Canaanite allies fled for refuge into Megiddo and capitulated only after a lengthy siege (seven months). Thutmose's annals of the campaign stress the great agricultural wealth of the area (*ANET,* pp. 234-38). Henceforth Megiddo resumed its former role as a base for Egyptian power. A certain Amenhotep, probably the crown prince under Thutmose III, commanded the ruler of Taanach to send a contingent of troops and auxiliaries to Megiddo. This may have been during Amenhotep II's campaign to Takhsi in Lebanon; on his return to Egypt, Amenhotep found that his father had died, leaving him the throne. As pharaoh, Amenhotep encamped at Megiddo after a campaign to quell rebellions at Anaharath to the northeast and Geba-suman to the northwest. Papyrus Leningrad No. 1116a records the presence of an ambassador from Megiddo at the Egyptian court under the 18th Dynasty.

During the mid-14th cent. Megiddo was ruled by Biridiya (or Birdiya), a prince of apparent Indo-Aryan descent whose letters to Pharaoh were found in the Amarna archive. He complained that Egyptian officers were abusing him though he was obedient in all things and had even provided them with thirty head of cattle (Am.Tab. 243). The Egyptian garrison had been removed, and from Biridiya was hard pressed to protect his sheepshearers from ʿApiru raids (Am.Tab. 243). Lab'ayu prince of Shechem had extended his influence northward by force and was threatening Megiddo (Am.Tab. 250). Biridiya begged for one hundred archers to protect the city (Am.Tab. 244). When Pharaoh ordered the troublemaker from Shechem apprehended, Biridiya and his colleagues from the neighboring towns acted in concert to carry out the arrest; however, the culprit apparently bribed the ruler of Acco and thus gained his release while being transported via Hannathon. Biridiya reported that he and a political exile residing with him heard of the escape and rushed to the spot where the prisoner's enemies had recaptured him (apparently in the land of Gina, SE of Megiddo at Jenîn), but he was too late — the suspect had already been put to death (Am.Tab. 250). One result of Shechem's aggression had been the destruction of Shunem, which made the princes in the Jezreel Valley responsible for cultivating the fields of Shunem. Biridiya contended that he alone was faithful to this charge, exerting his influence in the region to bring corvée workers from Japhia on the opposite side of the valley as well as from Megiddo and elsewhere (Am.Tab. 365). Megiddo continued to have its troubles, both with the new rulers of Shechem (Am.Tab. 246) and with the successor at Acco (Am.Tab. 234).

Little is known about the history of Megiddo under the pharaohs of the 19th Dynasty. Megiddo may be mentioned in Seti I's topographical records, but the reading is uncertain. Papyrus Anastasi I, dating from about the reign of Ramses II, stresses Megiddo's strategic position on the highway leading to Beth-shean and illustrates dramatically the dangers to be encountered by a lone charioteer when traversing the Megiddo pass (i.e., Wâdī ʿÂra).

*C. Iron Age.* The king of Megiddo appears in the list of rulers conquered by Joshua (Josh. 12:21). The Manasseh tribe was to inherit the town and its territory, but they failed to occupy it or the neighboring towns (Josh. 17:11; Jgs. 1:27; cf. also 1 Ch. 7:29). During Barak's victory over Sisera the fighting extended as far as the "waters of Megiddo" near Taanach (Jgs. 5:19), evidently the streams draining the southwest corner of the valley. Excavations at Taanach have shown that its occupation during the transition period between the Late Bronze and Iron Ages was contemporary with that at Megiddo. Thus Albright's suggestion that the two towns were occupied alternately at this time should be rejected. The population of Megiddo was subjected to forced labor, a status they had formerly imposed on others, when the Israelites became strong enough to dominate the cities in the Jezreel Valley (Jgs. 1:28). Since forced labor was possible only under the monarchy, it would seem obvious that Megiddo first came under Israelite control during David's reign (the Philistine presence had curtailed Saul's power in this region; cf. 1 S. 28:4). In converting the city into an Israelite administrative center, David may have built the two sturdy "palaces," one on the north and the other on the south.

Solomon refortified Megiddo, along with Hazor and Gezer (1 K. 9:15). The contemporary gates at each of these sites have been excavated; they show variations in construction methods, but their basic ground plan is strikingly similar. On the other hand, casemate walls were built at Hazor and Gezer, but a heavy wall of the salient-and-recess type surrounded Megiddo. Large storehouses and related structures served the garrison stationed there.

During the fifth year of King Rehoboam (*ca.* 920 B.C.), Pharaoh Shishak marched victoriously through the northern kingdom of Jeroboam I. He listed Megiddo as one of his conquered towns (no. 27), and a stele of his was actually found in the excavations there.

After Jehu's revolt Ahaziah of Judah fled to Megiddo, where he died from his wounds (2 K. 9:27; cf. 2 Ch. 22:9). Megiddo fell under the Assyrian yoke *ca.* 732 B.C. and evidently became the capital of the Galilee province named for it. During his short-lived period of expansion after the Assyrian collapse, Josiah of Judah also extended his own authority over Megiddo, where he chose to confront Pharaoh Neco. His efforts, however, were no more successful than those of the Canaanites many centuries earlier, and he lost his own life (2 K. 23:29; 2 Ch. 35:23). Sometime during the subsequent period the ritual mourning for Hadadrimmon occurred (Zec. 12:11).

In NT times the settlement had moved to nearby Cephar ʿOtnai, but the ancient mound with its history of wars and tumults was not forgotten. The book of Revelation placed "the battle on the great day of God the Almighty" at ARMAGEDDON (Gk. *Harmagedōn,* Rev. 16:14-16), meaning "the hill of Megiddo" (Heb. **har-m^e^giddôn*). (But cf. W. S. LaSor, *Truth about Armageddon* [1982], pp. 135-147.)

***II. Excavation.***–Tell el-Mutesellim was first examined archeologically by G. Schumacher (1903-1905). The Oriental Institute of the University of Chicago resumed work there; their excavation was one of the most important ever carried out in Palestine (1925-1939). Y. Yadin and J. Dunayevski of the Hebrew University of Jerusalem later conducted minor investigations of certain problems.

The important remains still preserved include the entryway and part of the Solomonic gate (*see* picture in FORTIFICATION); gates from the Middle and Late Bronze Ages; parts of the foundation for Solomon's salient-and-recess wall (remains of the Davidic [?] palace appear beneath this wall on the north edge of the tell); a sacred area having three temples and a circular "high place," which, it is now clear, date to the Early Bronze Age (*see* picture in ALTAR); a section of the E.B. city wall; some Iron Age houses; parts of the main storehouse complex; a grain silo; and, most impressive of all, the great shaft and water tunnel.

Two major finds of the Chicago expedition have been debated. The expedition's interpretation of the large public complexes of stratum V as stables was clearly wrong. No artifacts pertaining to horses or chariotry were found. The cobblestone floors would be detrimental to hooves, and the holes supposedly for tethering face the center aisles, not the sides where animals would have stood. Most conclusively, there was only one door through which to lead the fifteen horses in any one hallway. Identical structures found recently at Beer-sheba were full of storage and other vessels. Thus, the Megiddo buildings were storehouses, like similar structures found at numerous other sites in Israel.

Yadin and others later claimed that the salient-and-recess wall associated with these storehouses dates to the reign of Ahab, not to that of Solomon. This wall, however, is the only one attached to the "Solomonic gate" (like those at Hazor and Gezer). Structures found by Yadin under the salient-and-recess wall hardly constitute a casemate wall as he assumed. Some are the outermost rooms of poorly built dwellings; others are the courtyard rooms of an impressive palace. Yadin may have found the palace of David (not Solomon) under the storehouses of Solomon, though exact historical dating of these strata is a precarious undertaking.

***Bibliography.***–Y. Aharoni, *JNES,* 31 (1972), 302-311; W. F. Albright, *BASOR,* 94 (Apr. 1944), 12-27; W. G. Dever, *BA,* 32 (1969), 71-78; *EAEHL,* III, *s.v.* (Y. Aharoni and Y. Yadin); R. M. Engberg and W. F. Albright, *BASOR,* 78 (Apr. 1940), 4-9; R. M. Engberg, *BA,* 3 (1940), 41-50; 4 (1941), 11-16; C. Epstein, *IEJ,* 15 (1965), 39f.; R. O. Faulkner, *JEA,* 28 (1942), 2-15; K. M. Kenyon, *Bulletin of the Institute of Archaeology, University of London,* 4 (1964), 143-156; *Levant,* 1 (1969), 25-60; R. Lamon, *Megiddo Water System* (1935); R. S. Lamon and G. M. Shipton, *Megiddo I* (1939); G. Loud, *Megiddo II* (1948); H. May, *Material Remains of the Megiddo Cult* (1935); B. Mazar, "The Campaign of Pharaoh Shishak to Palestine," in *SVT,* 4 (1957), 57-66; A. F. Rainey, *Journal of the American Research Center in Egypt,* 10 (1973), 71-75; J. N. Schofield, "Megiddo," in *AOTS,* pp. 309-328; G. Schumacher, *Tell el Mutesellim,* I (1908); T. L. Thompson, *ZDPV,* 86 (1970), 38-49; C. Watzinger, *Tell el Mutesellim,* II (1929); Y. Yadin, *BA,* 23 (1960), 62-68; *IEJ,* 16 (1966), 278-280; *IEJ,* 17 (1967), 119-121; *BA,* 33 (1970), 66-96; *Hazor* (1972), pp. 147-164.

A. F. RAINEY

**MEGILLOTH** mə-gil-lōth′, mə-gil′əth [Heb. *m^e^gillôṯ*–'scrolls']. Plural noun (sing. *m^e^gillâ,* "scroll," Jer. 36:28f.; Ezk. 2:9; etc.) derived from the verb *gālal,* "roll," hence meaning that which is rolled up, i.e., a SCROLL. The five Megilloth, grouped in the following order in the MT, are the books of Ruth, Canticles, Ecclesiastes, Lamentations, and Esther, each of which was read at a festival (respectively, Pentecost, Passover, Tabernacles, the ninth of Ab [anniversary of the destruction of Jerusalem], and Purim). The mishnaic tractate *Megillah* deals with the reading of Scripture at these festivals, especially the reading of Esther at Purim. G. A. L.

**MEHETABEL** mə-het′ə-bəl [Heb. *m^e^hêṭaḇ'ēl*–'God is doing good']; AV also MEHETABEEL (Neh. 6:10).

**1.** Daughter of Matred; wife of Hadad (or Hadar), one of the kings of Edom (Gen. 36:39; 1 Ch. 1:50).

**2.** Grandfather of Shemaiah, the false prophet hired by Tobiah and Sanballat to tempt Nehemiah to commit sacrilege (Neh. 6:10).

**MEHIDA** mə-hī′də [Heb. *m^e^ḥîḏā'*; Gk. *Maouda* (Ezr. 2:52), *Meida* (Neh. 7:54), *Meedda* (1 Esd. 5:32)]; AV Apoc. MEEDA; NEB Apoc. MEEDDA. Ancestor and patronymic of a family of temple servants (Nethinim) who returned from Babylon with Zerubbabel.

**MEHIR** mē′hər [Heb. *m^e^ḥîr*]. Son of Chelub; father of Eshton; descendant of Judah (1 Ch. 4:11).

**MEHOLATHITE** mə-hō′lə-thīt [Heb. *m^e^ḥôlāṯî*]; NEB OF MEHOLAH. A description applied to Adriel, son of Barzillai, who married Saul's daughter Merab (1 S. 18:19; also 2 S. 21:8, where "Michal" is apparently a copyist's error). It indicates that Barzillai and Adriel came from ABEL-MEHOLAH, and suggests that Saul's motive for giving Merab to Adriel rather than David was to form a marriage alliance with a powerful family (cf. 1 S. 18:17f.).

**MEHUJAEL** mə-hōō′jə-el [Heb. *m^e^ḥûyā'ēl, m^e^ḥîyā'ēl*]. Descendant of Cain through Enoch and Irad; father of Methushael (Gen. 4:18). The slight difference between the Hebrew words may reflect the common confusion between Heb. *w* and *y*, which (in writing) were almost indistinguishable by the time of the Dead Sea Scrolls. But U. Cassuto (comm. on Genesis, I [Eng. tr. 1961], 232f.) pointed out the improbability of a scribal error in the same word occurring twice in succession. He suggested that the different forms were intentional, reflecting the common ancient Near Eastern practice of preserving variant traditions as "a mark of literary elegance."

According to some scholars (e.g., G. von Rad, *Genesis* [Eng. tr., rev. ed., *OTL,* 1972], p. 71), Mehujael and the other names in the Cainite genealogy of Gen. 4 are variants of the Sethite genealogy in ch. 5. Thus Mahalalel (5:12f., 15-17) is identified with Mehujael (see *IDB, s.v.*). Other scholars, however, noting the differences between the lists, have kept the genealogies distinct (*see* ANTEDILUVIAN PATRIARCHS II). G. A. L.

**MEHUMAN** mə-hōō'mən [Heb. *m^ehûmān*]. One of seven eunuchs who served as chamberlains for King Ahasuerus (Est. 1:10).

**MEHUNIM** mə-hōō'nim (AV 2 Ch. 26:7; Ezr. 2:50; Neh. 7:52). *See* MEUNIM.

**ME-JARKON** mē-jär'kon [Heb. *mê hayyarqôn*–'the waters of the Yarkon']. A place in the northwestern part of the territory of Dan, before Dan relocated in the upper Jordan Valley (Josh. 19:46). There is a textual problem, however. The MT reads *ûmê hayyarqôn w^ehāraqqôn,* "and the waters of the Yarkon and the Raqqon." Because of a grammatical rule (see GKC, § 128a) "the waters of" cannot modify also Raqqon; hence this is another place. But the LXX has *kaí apó thalássēs Ierakōn,* "and from the sea Hieracon" (i.e., at the western limit, seemingly from a Hebrew text reading something like *yammâ hayyarqôn*). This suggests that the reading *Raqqon* is the result of dittography with some transposition, and thus scholars have been divided on the identification of the site(s). Israelis consider *mê hayyarqôn* to be the Wâdī el-ʿAujā N of Tel Aviv, on "no sufficient grounds," according to Simons (*GTTOT,* § 336, p. 201). Abel, *et al.,* took Me-jarkon to be Tell ej-Jerîsheh just S of the Wâdī el-ʿAujā (*GP,* II, 53; see his discussion in I, 472f.). Others have identified Me-jarkon with Tell el-Qasîleh on the north side of the Yarkon almost opposite Tell ej-Jerîsheh. Raqqon (Rakkon) has been identified with Tell er-Reqqeit on the coast N of the Yarkon. W. S. LASOR

**MEKONAH** mə-kō'nə (Neh. 11:28, AV). *See* MECONAH.

**MELATIAH** mel-ə-tī'ə [Heb. *m^elaṭyâ*–'Yahweh has delivered']. A Gibeonite who assisted in rebuilding the wall of Jerusalem in the time of Nehemiah (Neh. 3:7).

**MELCHI** mel'kī [Gk. *Melchi, Melchei* < Heb. *malkî*–'my king']. The name of two ancestors of Jesus in Luke's genealogy (Lk. 3:24, 28).

**MELCHIAH** mel-kī'ə. *See* MALCHIJAH.

**MELCHIAS** mel-kī'əs. *See* MALCHIJAH.

**MELCHIEL** mel'ki-əl [Gk. *Melchiēl*]. The father of Charmis, one of the magistrates of Bethulia (Jth. 6:15).

**MELCHIOR** mel'ki-ôr [Lat. *Melchior;* prob. < Heb. *meleḵ 'ôr*–'king of light'] **MELKON** mel'kon [Lat. *Melchon*]. According to late Western tradition, one of the three Magi who came to Bethlehem to worship the infant Christ. The NT account (Mt. 2:1-12) says nothing about the number, names, or country of origin of the WISE MEN, but these and many other details have been supplied by fanciful legends that have arisen throughout the centuries. Although their number varies in other traditions (in Syria they usually were twelve in number), in the West they came to be represented as three kings. The earliest reference to their names appears in a sixth-century chronicle, the *Excerpta Latina Barbari,* which calls them Bithisarea, Melchior, and Gathaspa. The traditional spellings of their names appear in later artistic and literary works (e.g., *Excerpta et Collectanea,* wrongly attributed to Bede), which also provide details of their origin and appearance. Bede (*ca.* 673-735) interpreted them as representing the three divisions of the human race (Asia, Africa, and Europe) that had descended from the three sons of Noah (*In Matthaei Evangelium Expositio* i.2). The fourteenth-century Armenian Infancy Gospel cites a tradition identifying the Magi as Melkon king of Persia, GASPAR king of India, and BALTHASAR king of Arabia. Another legend depicted them as being found by Thomas in Parthia, receiving baptism from him, and becoming evangelists.

In the Middle Ages the three came to be venerated as saints, their feast day being January 6 in the Western Church. Their relics were supposedly discovered in the East in the 4th cent. and moved first to Constantinople and then, in the 5th cent., to Milan. In 1162 Frederick Barbarossa transferred them to Cologne, where they remain enshrined.

***Bibliography.***–S. Baring-Gould, *Lives of the Saints* (3rd ed. 1914), I, 82-85; B. M. Metzger, "Names for the Nameless in the NT," in P. Granfield and J. A. Jungmann, eds., *KYRIAKON: Festschrift Johannes Quasten,* I (1970), 79-85; MSt, V, *s.v.* "Magi"; *New Catholic Encyclopedia* (1967), IX, *s.v.* "Magi (in the Bible)" (E. J. Joyce); *ODCC, s.v.* "Magi." N. J. O.

**MELCHISHUA** mel-kə-shōō'ə (AV 1 S. 14:49; 31:2). *See* MALCHISHUA.

**MELCHIZEDEK** mel-kiz'ə-dek [Heb. *malkî-ṣeḏeq*] (Gen. 14:18; Ps. 110:4); [Gk. *Melchisedek*] (He. 5:6, 10; 6:20; 7:1, 10f., 15, 17); AV NT MELCHISEDEC. The king of Salem and priest of God Most High who blessed Abram and received tithes from him following the patriarch's victory over Chedorlaomer and his allies.

***I. Historical Account*** (Gen. 14:17-20).–As Abram returned from his victory over the kings who had captured Lot, the priest-king of Salem met him. This Canaanite dignitary manifested his friendship toward Abram by serving him bread and wine and blessing him in the name of God Most High. In recognition of Melchizedek's priesthood, Abram gave him a tithe of the goods taken in the battle against the kings.

"Melchizedek" appears to have been a Canaanite royal name. It is very similar to "Adonizedek" (Josh. 10:1), a later king of Jerusalem who was slain by Joshua. "Melchizedek" is composed of the words *meleḵ,* "king," and *ṣeḏeq,* "righteousness." Although each of these terms was frequently used in West Semitic names (see H. Huffmon, *Amorite Personal Names in the Mari Texts* [1965], pp. 230f., 256f.; *IP,* pp. 114f., 118f., 161f.), only here are they found together. The Amarna Tablets (*ca.* 1400 B.C.) give evidence of the use of the word *ṣeḏeq* in Jerusalem (Johnson, pp. 34f.) and the use of *meleḵ* in the formation of proper names (e.g., *Ilu(-i)-milku* and *Abi-milki*; Johnson, pp. 39f.). The Râs Shamrah literature contains similar personal names.

The author of Hebrews declares the meaning of "Melchizedek" to be "king of righteousness" (7:2). Philo's explanation that it means "the righteous king" confirms that this was the first-century understanding of the term (*Legum allegoriae* iii.79). The Amarna and Râs Shamrah parallels suggest, however, that the original meaning was "my (the) king is righteous," "my (the) king is Zedek" (a deity), or "Milki (a deity) is righteous." See Delcor, pp. 115f.

That "Salem" was a designation for Jerusalem is confirmed by its use in Ps. 76:2 (MT 3) in synonymous parallelism with "Zion." The Genesis Apocryphon and the Targums on Gen. 14 also identify Salem as Jerusalem. The Amarna letters of Abdu-Ḫeba to the king of Egypt reveal that as early as 1400 B.C. *Urusalim* was an important Canaanite city-state.

The historicity of the Melchizedek account is further confirmed by the appearance of the terms 'El ("God") and 'Elyon ("Most High") in Ugaritic and Phoenician literature as names of deities. The two terms also occur together in an Aramaic inscription from Sujin (M. H. Pope, *El in the Ugaritic Texts* [*SVT*, 2; 1955], pp. 55-58).

***II. Messianic Application*** (Ps. 110:4).– Although commentators do not agree about the messianic character of Ps. 110, the NT writers did not doubt this identification. Christ interpreted the Psalm as messianic while debating with the Pharisees (Mt. 22:44 par.), and it may be assumed from the silence of the religious leaders that they also accepted the messianic interpretation. Peter likewise treated the passage as messianic (Acts 2:34), as did the writer of Hebrews (1:13). The psalmist's distinguishing himself from the exalted person described in vv. 1-4 indicates that its application extends beyond David.

The greatness of Melchizedek puzzled Jewish scholars. Abraham's paying tithes to Melchizedek and being blessed by him suggested that his importance exceeded even that of the patriarch. In explanation some Jews identified Melchizedek with Shem, who was thought to have lived until Abraham's time (Targum Neofiti I). Although the psalmist did not adopt this identification of Melchizedek, he did recognize the greatness of the priest-king, viewing him instead as a representation of the Messiah. It may be conjectured that the messianic identification was based on two factors: (1) the greatness of Melchizedek and (2) his unending priesthood (inferred from the silence of the Genesis account about his death).

***III. Typological Significance*** (He. 7).–The author of Hebrews built his argument for the superiority of Christ's priesthood on Ps. 110:4, obviously viewing that Psalm as messianic. He cited the psalmist's declaration three times (He. 5:6, 10; 6:20) to justify the messianic application of Gen. 14:17-20. But his treatment of the Genesis account (He. 7) is not allegorical like Philo's (*Legum allegoriae* iii.79, 82). Instead he saw Melchizedek as a type of Christ. The argument of He. 7 is similar to the rabbinic argument from silence, which assumed that nothing exists unless Scripture mentions it. Since Genesis says nothing of Melchizedek's parents, genealogy, birth, or death, he serves as a type representing the eternal Son of God (v. 3).

"Melchizedek" and "Salem" also are seen as having messianic significance (v. 2). "Melchizedek" is interpreted as meaning "king of righteousness" and "Salem" as "peace," explanations previously advanced by Philo (*Legum allegoriae* iii.79).

Some have thought that Melchizedek was a Christophany rather than a historical character and thus understood vv. 2b-3 literally rather than typologically. A major objection to such an interpretation is the statement that Melchizedek resembled (Gk. *aphōmoiōménos*) the Son of God (v. 3). The verb *aphomoióō* always assumes two distinct and separate identities, one of which is a copy of the other. Thus Melchizedek and the Son of God are represented as two separate persons, the first of which resembled the second.

Having established a relationship between Melchizedek and Christ, the author of Hebrews then showed that Christ is a greater priest than the Levitical priests because in the person of Abraham, Levi paid tithes to Melchizedek and was blessed by him (vv. 4-10). Furthermore, long after the establishment of the Levitical priesthood, David spoke of another priest who was not a descendant of Levi. This statement is taken as proof that the Levitical priesthood was replaced by a priest like Melchizedek, namely Christ (vv. 11-19).

***IV. Qumrân Identification of Melchizedek***.–In 1956 thirteen fragments of a first-century manuscript were found in Qumrân Cave 11 (11QMelch). The text is an eschatological midrash built on the concept of the Jubilee Year (Lev. 25) and weaving in a number of eschatological passages (Dt. 15:2; Isa. 61:1; Ps. 82:1f.; 7:8f. [MT 9f.]; Isa. 52:7). A. S. van der Woude, the original publisher of 11QMelch, saw Melchizedek as playing a significant role, standing in the assembly of God among the angelic beings. There he is depicted as executing divine judgment, which is somehow related to the Jubilee Year. He also seems to be involved either as the one who atones for the sins of the people or as the priest who mediates atonement to them.

A few students of Qumrân literature identify the Melchizedek of 11QMelch as an earthly person who met Abraham (Gen. 14) and whose likeness will be reproduced in the coming Messiah. Most Qumrân scholars, however, view the Qumrân Melchizedek as a high angelic being who was thought to have appeared to Abraham. This tradition, preserved at Qumrân, may provide the background for the use of the Melchizedek figure in He. 7:1ff. to emphasize the superiority of Christ over the Levitical priesthood.

***Bibliography***.–F. F. Bruce, *Epistle to the Hebrews* (*NICNT*, 1964); M. Delcor, *Journal for the Study of Judaism*, 2 (1971), 115-135; J. A. Fitzmyer, *CBQ*, 25 (1963), 305-321; *JBL*, 86 (1967), 25-41 (repr. in *Essays on the Semitic Background of the NT* [1971], pp. 221-267); F. Horton, *Melchizedek Tradition* (1976); A. R. Johnson, *Sacral Kingship in Ancient Israel* (2nd ed. 1967); C. Spicq, *L'Épître aux Hébreux* (2 vols., 1952-53); *TDNT*, IV, *s.v.* Μελχισεδέκ (O. Michel); A. S. van der Woude, *Oudtestamentische Studiën*, 14 (1965), 354-373; R. Williamson, *Philo and the Epistle to the Hebrews* (1970).

D. W. BURDICK

**MELEA** mē'lē-ə [Gk. *Melea*]. An ancestor of Jesus in Luke's genealogy (Lk. 3:31).

**MELECH** mel'ək [Heb. *meleḵ*–'king']. Grandson of Meribaal the grandson of Saul, from the tribe of Benjamin (1 Ch. 8:35; 9:41).

**MELICU** mel'ə-ko͞o (Neh. 12:14, AV). *See* MALLUCHI.

**MELITA** mə-lē'tə (Acts 28:1, AV). *See* MALTA.

**MELKON** mel'kon. *See* MELCHIOR.

**MELODY** [Heb. *higgāyôn* (Ps. 92:3 [MT 4]), *zimrâ* (Ps. 98:5; Am. 5:23)]; **MAKE MELODY** [Heb. *zmr* (only in the piel, *zimmēr*; Jgs. 5:3; Ps. 27:6; 33:2; 57:7 [MT 8]; 147:7; 149:3), piel of *nāgan* (Isa. 23:16); Gk. *psállō* (Eph. 5:19)]; AV also SOLEMN SOUND (Ps. 92:3 [MT 4]), PSALM (Ps. 98:5), SING (or GIVE) PRAISE(S), etc.; NEB SOUNDING CHORDS (Ps. 92:3 [MT 4]), PSAL-

TERY (Ps. 98:5), MUSIC (Am. 5:23), TOUCH THE STRINGS (Isa. 23:16), SING (or RAISE) A PSALM, etc.

The most common of these words, *zimmēr,* has cognates in most Semitic languages, ranging in meaning from strictly singing (Akkadian) to singing with instrumental accompaniment (Akkadian, Syriac) to strictly playing of instruments (Aramaic, Arabic). The music could be either secular or religious, depending on context and purpose. In the OT the word refers exclusively to joyful singing of praises to God, often accompanied by stringed instruments of various types (the RSV most commonly renders it as "sing" or "sing praises"). The root *ngn* refers to playing of strings (as a verb), or to music or songs accompanied by strings (as a noun). It can be used in either a secular or religious sense (cf., e.g., the use in 7 Psalm superscriptions with Isa. 23:16, which describes a harlot's sweet melody making, or Lam. 3:14, 63, or Job 30:9, which refer to taunt songs). *Psállō* originally meant to play a stringed instrument; in the LXX it generally translates *zimmēr* and *ngn.* In the NT it refers to singing God's praises (not necessarily accompanied by strings).

*See also* MUSIC; PSALMS; SONG.

***Bibliography.***–*DNTT,* III, *s.v.* "Song" (K. H. Bartels); *TDNT,* VIII, *s.v.* ὕμνος, ὑμνέω, ψάλλω, ψαλμός (G. Delling); *TDOT,* IV, *s.v.* "zmr" (C. Barth). D. M. HOWARD, JR.

**MELONS** [pl. of Heb. *ʾaḇaṭṭî(a)ḥ*; cf. Arab. *baṭîḫ*]; NEB WATERMELON. The melons of Nu. 11:5 probably included two delicious indigenous melons, the common Egyptian *Citrullus vulgaris* (watermelon), and the *Cucumis melo* L. (musk melon). Both have been cultivated in Egypt from early times and grow to a considerable size. Melons formed an inexpensive part of the food eaten by the Israelites during their captivity in Egypt, and were recalled with longing by the parched Hebrews when wandering in the Sinai Peninsula. R. K. H.

**MELT** [Heb. hiphil of *māsâ* (Dt. 1:28; Josh. 2:9; Mic. 1:4; etc.), *śûś*–'rejoice' (Isa. 8:6), *mûg* (Isa. 14:31; Jer. 49:23; Ezk. 21:15 [MT 20]; etc.), niphal of *māsas*–'dissolve' (Ezk. 21:7 [MT 12]), hiphil of *nāṯaḵ* (Ezk. 22:20); Gk. *lýō* (2 Pet. 3:12)]; AV also "discourage," "faint," "be dissolved," etc.; NEB also "discourage," "dissolve," "be troubled," etc. The various biblical terms express the "dissolving" or "melting" of elements and often metaphorically describe cowardice ("our hearts melt," Dt. 1:28; Josh. 14:8; etc.). The references to mountains melting in God's presence (Ps. 97:5; Mic. 1:4; Nah. 1:5) occur in connection with God avenging Himself upon His enemies. The allusions do not seem to be merely metaphorical, but would encompass the kind of volcanic activity that occurred periodically in Palestine. Cf. 2 Pet. 3:12, which describes apocalyptically the fiery termination of the earth. Ezk. 22:20 uses a metallurgical term for the reduction of ores prior to the manufacture of an alloy. R. K. H.

**MELZAR** mel'zär. The AV translation of Heb. *hammelṣar* in Dnl. 1:11, 16. The AV follows the LXX, Syr., and Vulg. in regarding the term as a proper name. In the MT, however, it is clearly a title, as the definite article proves (hence RSV "steward"; NEB "guard"). The word is probably derived from Akk. *maṣṣaru,* "guard" (see J. A. Montgomery, comm. on Daniel [*ICC,* 1927], pp. 131, 134). *See* STEWARD.

**MEM** mem [מ, ם]. The thirteenth letter of the Hebrew alphabet, in *ISBE* transliterated as *m.* It also came to represent the number forty. *See* WRITING.

**MEMBER** [Heb. *ʿēqer*–'offspring,' *šāpᵉḵâ*–'penis,' *nepeš*–'breath,' *bēn*–'son,' *yᵉṣurîm, bāśār*–'flesh'; Gk. *mélos, bouleutḗs*–'council,' *sýntrophos*–'brought up together with,' *oikeios*–'belonging to the house' (Eph. 2:19), *sýssōmos*–'belonging to the same body' (Eph. 3:6)]; AV also STOCK, PRIVY MEMBER, COUNSELLOR, PERSON, CHILDREN, FLESH, etc.; NEB also ORGANS, LIMBS AND ORGANS, PART(S), BODILY PARTS, etc.

"Member" may refer to parts of the body (Job 17:7), e.g., the tongue (Jas. 3:5f.; cf. 4:1), or the male sexual organ (Dt. 23:1; Ezk. 23:20).

"Member" also denotes one who belongs to a group, e.g., a family (Lev. 25:47), a tribe (1 Ch. 5:23), or a council (Mk. 15:43). In two texts the RSV supplies "member," although the Greek text has no separate word for it (Rom. 11:1; 1 Cor. 6:5; cf. AV, NEB).

The occurrences of the Gk. *mélos* have great theological significance. Paul uses *mélos* in various ways. In Rom. 6 he instructs his readers not to allow their members (bodily parts) to be servants of sin but to use them as instruments of righteousness (v. 13). Christians are under an obligation to serve God in their entire being. In 7:5 Paul asserts that sin can exert its power over the members of a person's body (see the comms. on the issue of whether he is describing a regenerate or unregenerate person).

More specifically, Paul also uses *mélos* to warn that sexual intercourse is not a casual relationship (1 Cor. 6). If a Christian engages in a relation with a prostitute, the Christian has taken his body, which is a member of Christ (belonging and devoted to Christ), and has made it a member of a prostitute.

In Rom. 12:4f. and 1 Cor. 12:12-26 Paul uses the image of a body and its parts or members to describe the character of the Church. Just as a body is a unity and has a variety of members, so a church must recognize that it is a unified body and yet allow for a variety of members. Neither the unity nor the diversity may be overlooked.

In Ephesians Paul uses the metaphors of both the body (3:6; 4:25) and a household (2:19) to describe the Christian's situation (cf. 4:25). Participation in the Church involves a relation to Christ, who is the cornerstone, and to fellow Christians (both Jew and Gentile), since they are members of the same body. P. L. BREMER

**MEMMIUS, QUINTUS** mem'i-əs, kwin'təs [Gk. *Kointos Memmios*]. A Roman legate sent along with Titus Manius to the Jews after they had defeated the Syrian troops of Lysias at Beth-zur in 165 B.C. (2 Macc. 11:34). In the letter they bore, the Romans offered to negotiate with Antiochus Epiphanes on behalf of the Jews. However, it was not until 161 B.C. and renewed pressure from Demetrius I of Syria that a formal treaty with Rome was concluded (1 Macc. 8:20-32). As no record exists of either legate, many have voiced doubts over the letter's authenticity. Nonetheless, while the date of the letter may be incorrectly stated (it probably should follow that of Lysias, 2 Macc. 11:16-21), there remains little reason to doubt the historical authenticity of the letter.

See V. Tcherikover, *Hellenistic Civilization and the Jews* (1959), pp. 213-220. R. L. OMANSON

**MEMORABLE DEEDS, BOOK OF** [Heb. *sēper hazziḵrōnôṯ (diḇrê hayyāmîm)*] (Est. 6:1); AV BOOK OF RECORDS; NEB CHRONICLE. Royal archives. Est. 2:20-23 relates that Mordecai saved the life of King Ahasuerus and that this deed was recorded in the official annals of the court (in v. 23 abbreviated to *sēper diḇrê hayyāmîm,* lit. "book of the events of the days," i.e., "chronicles"). Similar expressions occur in Mal. 3:16, "BOOK OF REMEMBRANCE"

(Heb. *sēper zikkārôn*), a book kept in heaven, and Ezr. 4:15, "book of the records" (Aram. *sᵉpar-doḵrānayyā'* [Aram. *dkr* = Heb. *zkr*]), apparently Persian and Babylonian historical documents. G. A. L.

**MEMORIAL** [Heb. *zikkārôn*] (Ex. 12:14; 13:9; 17:14; Lev. 23:24; Nu. 31:54; Josh. 4:7; Neh. 2:20); NEB REMEMBRANCE, REMINDER, TRADITIONAL RIGHT, etc.; [*'azkārâ*] (Lev. 2:2, 9, 16; 5:12; 6:15; 24:7; Nu. 5:26); NEB TOKEN; [*zēḵer*] (Isa. 26:8); AV REMEMBRANCE; NEB MEMORY; [*šēm*] (Isa. 55:13); AV NAME; NEB GREAT NAME; [*zāḵar*] ("make a memorial offering," Isa. 66:3); AV "burn"; NEB "burn as a token"; [Gk. *mnēmósynon*] (Acts 10:4); NEB "to speak for you"; **MEMORY** [Heb. *zēḵer*] (Job 18:17; Ps. 9:6 [MT 7]; 109:15; Prov. 10:7; Eccl. 9:5); AV also REMEMBRANCE; NEB also NAME, etc.; [Gk. *mnēmósynon*] (Mt. 26:13; Mk. 14:9); NEB MEMORIAL.

Part of the identity of the people of God comes from remembering God's great acts and faithfulness and the origins of His people. Remembrance leads to gratitude and praise for the present and hope and security for the future. Appointed feast days and rites of celebration (Ex. 12:14; 13:9; Lev. 23:24), written records (Ex. 17:14), stored booty (Nu. 31:54), and a stone monument (Josh. 4:7) could all function as "memorials" to remind Israel of what God had done for them. The stone MONUMENT was to be a memorial for Israel for ever, so that when children asked about the meaning, the parents could tell how God brought Israel across the Jordan. Such things as the written records and the stored booty could also function as a memorial for Israel before God, a reminder to God of His great deeds and promises for this people: Nu. 31:54, NEB, tells that Moses and Eleazar brought the booty "to the Tent of the Presence that the Lord might remember Israel." *See also* REMEMBER.

According to Childs (pp. 66-70) *zikkārôn* has two broad categories of meaning. In an active sense *zikkārôn* is a memorial "which calls something else to remembrance," almost always in cultic contexts. In a passive sense *zikkārôn* is a memorandum, "a thing worthy itself of remembrance," usually used in noncultic contexts. Both meanings developed independently from the basic meaning of *zkr*. Cf. *TDOT*, IV, 77-79.

The ceremonial regulations pertaining to certain offerings specify several times the "memorial portion," or *'azkārâ*. The *'azkārâ* may have been an offered portion reminding the worshiper of his God or an appeased God of the worshiper (as the RSV seems to suggest), or it may have been a part functioning and substituting for the whole (as the NEB seems to suggest with "token"; cf. *TDOT*, IV, 79f.). *See also* SACRIFICES AND OFFERINGS IN THE OT.

The LXX uses *mnēmósynon* for *'azkārâ* in Lev. 2:2, 9, 16, etc. In Acts 10:4 the sacrificial significance also seems to be included in "memorial": the angel said to Cornelius, "Your prayers and your alms have ascended as a memorial before God." Similarly, in Tob. 12:12 the angel Raphael offers a "memorial" (*mnēmósynon*) of the prayers before God; the NEB, however, paraphrases this verse and consequently has Raphael say to Tobit, "When you and Sarah prayed, it was I who brought your prayers into the glorious presence of the Lord; and so too whenever you buried the dead." In Mt. 26:13 par. Mk. 14:9 Jesus states that "wherever the gospel is preached in the whole world" the woman's anointing Him with expensive ointment would be told "in memory of her." As W. Lane (*Gospel of Mark* [*NICNT*, 1974], pp. 494f.) points out, the inclusion of this incident in the Gospels "already marks a fulfilment of Jesus' promise." Cf. H. Anderson, *Gospel of Mark* (*New Century Bible Comm.*, repr. 1981), p. 306.

In Isa. 55:13 the RSV translates the Hebrew word for "name" (*šēm*) as "memorial." This translation is quite accurate: as a name remembered and thus living on and on, *šēm* can denote reputation and fame (cf. *TDOT*, IV, 76f.) *See* FAME; NAME. Cutting off the memory of wicked men (Job 18:17; Ps. 9:6 [MT 7]; 109:15) is a curse of death. Prov. 10:7 states (note the poetic parallelism), "The memory [*zēḵer*] of the righteous is a blessing, but the name [*šēm*] of the wicked will rot."

For a thorough discussion of the role of memory and oral tradition in Judaism and early Christianity see Gerhardsson.

*Bibliography.*–B. Childs, *Memory and Tradition in Israel* (*SBT*, 1/37, 1962); *DNTT*, III, 230-247; B. Gerhardsson, *Memory and Manuscript* (Eng. tr. 1961); *TDNT*, IV, *s.v.* μιμνῄσκομαι κτλ. (Michel); *TDOT*, IV, *s.v.* "zāchar" (Eising).

M. W. MEYER
G. A. L.

**MEMPHIS** mem'fis [Heb. *nōp̄* (Isa. 19:13; Jer. 2:16; 44:1; 46:14, 19; Ezk. 30:13), *mōp̄* (Hos. 9:6); Gk. *Memphis* (Jth. 1:10)]; AV, NEB, also NOPH. A northern capital of ancient Egypt.

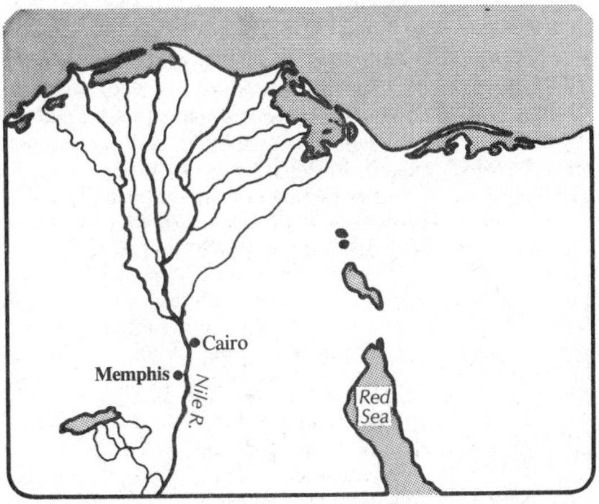


*I. Name.*–The Greek, Latin, and English name Memphis, Heb. *mōp̄* and *nōp̄*, Assyr. *Me-im-pi*, and Arab. *Manf* are all derived from an Egyptian name for the city, *mn-nfr*, probably meaning "the goodness (of Pepi I) endures." The Egyptian religious name of the city was *Ḥt-k3-ptḥ*, "the abode of the spirit of Ptah," which appears in the Akkadian transcription of the Amarna Letters as *Hi-ku-up-taḫ*. From this name for the city came the name for the whole country, Gk. *Aigyptos* and Eng. Egypt.

*II. Scripture References.*–Hosea 9:6 warns that Memphis will bury exiles from Israel, perhaps an allusion to the extensive cemeteries of this city. Isa. 19:13 denounces the princes of Memphis as deluded. Jer. 2:16 says that the men of Memphis have broken Israel's head, perhaps referring to Pharaoh Neco's conquering and slaying King Josiah. According to 44:1, after the fall of Jerusalem in 587 B.C. some exiles from Judah settled in Memphis, but the LXX lacks this city name. 46:14 includes Memphis among the cities of Egypt to be warned of Nebuchadrezzar's attack, and v. 19 predicts the devastation of Memphis. Ezk. 30:13 foretells the destruction of the idols and images of Memphis. In v. 15 the LXX says that the people of Memphis (instead of No or THEBES, as in the MT) will be cut off, and v. 16 (MT) predicts that Memphis will be attacked by adversaries (AV "Noph shall have distresses daily"; but cf. RSV "its walls [shall be] broken down," based on an unsupported emendation; NEB "flood-waters shall burst into it," based on the LXX).

The Apocrypha lists Memphis among the chief cities of Egypt in the time of Nebuchadrezzar (Jth. 1:10). The enthronement of Ptolemy VI Philometor mentioned in 2 Macc. 4:21 was doubtless celebrated in both Memphis and Alexandria.

Among the Pseudepigrapha the Sibylline Oracles refer to Memphis several times: as yielding to Augustus (5:16f.), as once the mistress of the earth but to become miserable (vv. 60-72), as to be afflicted so that her very pyramids would groan (vv. 180f.). The Testaments of the Twelve Patriarchs call the wife of Potiphar (here named Pentephris) a woman of Memphis (T. Jos. 3:6) or the Memphian woman (12:1; 14:1, 5 [variant]; 16:1).

Some Moslem traditions localize incidents in the lives of Joseph and of Moses in Memphis (yāqūt *Muʿjam al-buldān, s.v. Manf,* and al-Bayḍāwī on the Koran, 18:13, 15).

***III. Topography and Archeology.***–The ruins of Memphis are on the western bank of the Nile between the villages of Badrashayn on the east and Mīt Rahīnah on the west, about 19 km. (12 mi.) S of Cairo, the modern capital of Egypt. Memphis thus shared with Cairo a strategic location near the apex of the delta. It was called "the place in which the Two Lands [Upper and Lower Egypt] are united" (an Egyptian inscription sometimes called the *Theology of Memphis,* line 4). Since most of the remains of the ancient city are destroyed or underground, its limits are hard to determine; Diodorus (i.50) said its original circumference was 150 stadia (28 km., 17 mi.).

The heart of the city was evidently near Mīt Rahīnah, where archeological expeditions have found, from north to south: (1) a temple of the goddess Neith(?); (2) a palace of Apries (biblical Hophra, of the 26th Dynasty); E of this (3) a fort and (4) a camp, where doubtless Egyptian and later invading troops, like the Persians and the Greeks, were quartered; (5) the great temple of Ptah, to which many pharaohs added for three thousand years; in the southwest corner of the enclosure of the temple of Ptah (6) the embalming house of the Apis bulls; near the south propylon of the temple of Ptah (7) a colossal limestone statue, now recumbent, of Ramses II of the 19th Dynasty; near which is (8) an alabaster sphinx, perhaps representing Ramses II; also nearby lay until recently (9) a pink granite colossus of Ramses II, now restored and erected in the station square (Bāb al-Ḥadīd) in Cairo; (10) an approach to the east pylon of the temple of Ptah, constructed by Ptolemy IV; on Kōm al-Qalʿah, SE of the temple of Ptah, (11) a temple constructed by Merneptah of the 19th Dynasty; S of the temple of Ptah (12) a temple built by Siamon of the 21st Dynasty and (13) a temple of Apis; and (14) many terra-cotta heads made by Greek artists and representing Egyptians and other nationalities resident in Memphis during the 5th cent. B.C., including Persians, Greeks, and Ethiopians.

Alabaster sphinx at Memphis from the time of Ramses II (W. S. LaSor)

Memphis contained many other temples, according to Egyptian inscriptions and Greek literary sources, especially Herodotus, Diodorus, and Strabo. In addition to the great temple of Ptah, there were two other temples to this god and also temples to Amon, Apis, Aton, Bastet, Imhotep, Isis, Khnum, Osiris, Sekhmet, Sobek, Sokar, Thoth, and the children of Ptah (called Cabeiri by Herodotus [iii.37]). The most important of these structures were dedicated to Ptah and Apis. Ptah, according to the *Theology of Memphis,* created all things, including the other gods, by his word. He is usually represented as a mummy with the head exposed and the hands grasping a scepter. Apis, a god of fertility and of the dead, later associated with Osiris and called Serapis, was worshiped in the form of a bull with special markings. Beginning perhaps in the Hyksos period, temples were built to the Canaanite gods Baal and Baal-zaphon and goddesses Qedesh, Baalat, and Astarte. Astarte may have been the QUEEN OF HEAVEN whose worship by the Jewish exiles in Egypt Jeremiah condemned (Jer. 44:17-19, 25).

Connected with the city of Memphis were cemeteries unrivaled in extent, length of use, and grandeur of their monuments. Immediately W of the heart of the city, on the edge of the desert, was the pyramid field of Saqqârah, containing the mortuary temple and step pyramid of Djoser of the 3rd Dynasty (*see* picture in EGYPT), the Serapeum in which the embalmed Apis bulls were buried, nobles' tombs elaborately decorated with reliefs depicting the life of the Old Kingdom, and the pyramid of Unis of the 5th Dynasty, with its Pyramid Texts, among the most ancient interpretations of the afterlife. The cemetery of Memphis extended 24 km. (15 mi.) N of Saqqârah along the edge of the desert, including the pyramids and mastabas of Abusir, Zawiyat al-ʿAryan, Gîzeh (whose pyramid of Khufu, or Cheops, of the 4th Dynasty was a wonder of the ancient world; *see* picture in EGYPT), and Abu Ruwash. Also within the cemetery S of Saqqârah were the pyramids of Dahshur from the Old and Middle Kingdoms.

***IV. History.***–The priests of Memphis told Herodotus (ii.99) that the city and the great temple of Ptah were founded by Menes (*ca.* 3100 B.C.), the uniter of Upper and Lower Egypt and the first king of the 1st Dynasty. The earliest name for the city, *inb-hd,* "white wall," continued as the name of the nome, or province, and of the military citadel of Memphis (Herodotus iii.91; Thucydides i.104). During the Old Kingdom Memphis remained the capital, and *mn-nfr,* the name of the pyramid of the pharaoh Pepi I (6th Dynasty), was transferred from the cemetery of Saqqârah to the neighboring city of the living.

In the Middle Kingdom the capital was moved to Heracleopolis and then to Thebes, which surpassed Memphis in grandeur under the 18th Dynasty. Memphis, however, remained an important religious and cultural center. The Hyksos captured it in the 18th cent. B.C., and according to Josephus (*CAp* i.14 [75-82]), one of their kings, Salatis, lived there as well as at Avaris. The Nubian Pi-ankhi captured Memphis *ca.* 720 B.C. Esarhaddon the Assyrian conquered the city in 675 B.C. and took as booty crowns, antimony, linen, copper, tin, and utensils of gold, silver, and ivory; his captives included physicians, diviners, goldsmiths, and cabinetmakers (his Dog River stele). In 525 Cambyses took the city and later shocked the Egyptians by killing the Apis bull (Herodotus iii.13, 28). Alexander the Great entered Memphis without opposition in 332 to be acknowledged as successor to the pharaohs; he offered sacrifices to Apis and other gods (Arrian *Anabasis* iii.1). The Ptolemies continued to be enthroned in Memphis at least till Ptolemy VII Euergetes II Physkon (Diodorus xxxiii.13). By 7 B.C. (Strabo *Geog.* xvii.1.32) Alexandria had replaced Memphis as the largest city in Egypt. The Arab general ʿAmr ibn-al-ʿĀs captured Memphis in A.D. 638 and moved the seat of government to al-Fusṭāṭ. An Arab physician of Baghdad, Abdallatif, visited Memphis *ca.* A.D. 1200 and saw marvelous and extensive ruins covered with reliefs and many statues, most of which have since disappeared.

*See also* ARCHEOLOGY OF EGYPT; EGYPT.

***Bibliography.***–Pauly-Wissowa, XV/1, 660-688; *ANET*; J. Capart and M. Werbrouck, *Memphis à l'ombre des pyramides* (1938); H. Hermann, *Führer durch die Altertümer von Memphis und Sakkara* (1938); W. M. F. Petrie, *Memphis I* (1909) and subsequent volumes on Memphis II-VI (1909-1915); B. Porter and R. L. B. Moss, *Topographical Bibliography of Ancient Egyptian Hieroglyphic Texts, Reliefs, and Paintings, III: Memphis* (1931).

JOHN ALEXANDER THOMPSON

**MEMUCAN** mə-mōō'kən [Heb. *m^emûḵān*] (Est. 1:14, 16, 21). One of "the seven princes of Persia and Media, who saw the king's face, and sat first in the kingdom." Because of their legal knowledge (v. 13), King Ahasuerus consulted them concerning the proper treatment of the rebellious Queen Vashti. Memucan was the group's spokesman (vv. 16-20), and his advice was adopted by the king (vv. 21f.). *See* PRINCES, THE SEVEN.

**MENAHEM** men'ə-hem [Heb. *m^enaḥēm*–'comforter']. The 17th king (including Tibni) of the northern kingdom of Israel who ruled for ten years (2 K. 15:17). His father's name of Gadi suggests that he probably came from the tribe of Gad. He was not in line for succession to the throne but came to it by assassinating Shallum (v. 14), who in turn had assassinated Zechariah, the son and heir of Jeroboam II (v. 10). Menahem's reason for overthrowing Shallum is unclear. It could have stemmed from a sense of loyalty to the dynasty of Jeroboam, or it could have resulted simply from military adventurism. That Menahem came from Tirzah when he overthrew Shallum has reasonably been taken as indicating that he probably was commander of the troops of the army stationed there.

Not all of the northern kingdom accepted his rule readily. He crushed some of the holdouts at Tipsah (= Khirbet Tafsah?) by executing its population after he conquered it (v. 16). Since there is no other mention of such an Israelite place in the Bible this name is sometimes taken, with the Lucianic version of the LXX, as a reference to Tappuah that became corrupted in the course of textual transmission. The cruelty Menahem exercised here seems to have ended further resistance to his rule.

Having established himself as king, Menahem ruled over a country which had been prosperous and victorious since the days of Jeroboam (2 K. 14:28; Am. 6:4-6, 13). This picture soon changed, however, for the slumbering colossus of Assyria awoke and renewed its expansionistic policies in pursuit of an empire. Through the first half of the 8th cent. B.C. the army had seen little action in foreign fields because Assyria was ruled by a series of weak kings (from Shalmaneser IV to Aššur-nirari V) who were more concerned with internal affairs than external conquests. With the accession of Tiglath-pileser III in 745 this picture changed, for he campaigned against the Medes to the east, against Babylon to the south, and against allies of Urartu to the north and west.

Following up these victories in the west the Assyrians penetrated into Syro-Palestine, where they eventually encountered Israel and Judah. On two different occasions during his reign Tiglath-pileser devoted a series of annual campaigns to the west, from 743 to 738 and again from 734 to 732. These campaigns brought him into contact with two kings of Israel, Menahem and Hoshea, and Ahaz of Judah. His contacts with the king of Judah and Hoshea of Israel occurred during his later campaigns to the west, but those with Menahem came during the first series of these campaigns. This contact is referred to both in the Assyrian king's annals, where Menahem is listed as one of the western kings who paid tribute to him, and in 2 K. 15:19-20, where some of the circumstances surrounding that payment are related.

The amount of tribute that Tiglath-pileser demanded, one thousand talents of silver according to 2 K. 15:19, was a very high price to pay (cf. the 30 talents of gold and 800 [300?] talents of silver Sennacherib of Assyria demanded of Hezekiah of Judah, 2 K. 18:14; *ANET,* p. 288). While Hezekiah paid off his debt by stripping the temple of its precious metals, Menahem paid off his Assyrian oppressor by raising the funds through a tax of fifty shekels of silver levied upon each of the mighty or wealthy men of the realm. That fifty shekels was the price of a slave in Assyria in the 7th cent. B.C. provides an indicator of the relative value of this amount of silver. From the amount of money raised in this way it has been calculated that sixty thousand men were taxed. This large a class of wealthy persons may indicate that a fairly high level of prosperity in Israel continued into the reign of Menahem. The payment of tribute by Menahem was effective in preserving peace in Israel for a time, but this turn of events presaged more dire consequences that were soon to follow. That this is the main event narrated for the reign of Menahem emphasizes how important a turning point it was.

The name of the Assyrian king collecting this tribute is given in the biblical narrative dealing with Menahem only as Pul, not as Tiglath-pileser (2 K. 15:19). The Assyrian king is only named as Tiglath-pileser when the record deals with later events (v. 29; 16:7, 10). The use of the name Pul here reveals an awareness of events that transpired in Mesopotamia when Tiglath-pileser conquered Babylon in 729. After that conquest he installed himself upon the throne of Babylon, taking the name of Pulu as king there according to a Babylonian king list (*ANET,* p. 272). While this historical detail in the biblical record is accurate, this throne-name has been used in a proleptic way, referring to actions of Tiglath-pileser in the past, *ca.* 740, by a title he took up later, in 729. There is no evidence that Pul was his personal name prior to the time he took the Assyrian throne-name of Tiglath-pileser. The correct translation of 1 Ch. 5:26 points out an awareness that these two names referred to the same person by referring to "the spirit of Pul king of Assyria, even the spirit of Tiglath-pilneser king of Assyria" (so NASB; see NIV, NEB; on the variant spelling *see* TIGLATH-PILESER).

The date when Menahem paid this tribute is disputed because the Assyrian royal annals lack precision in dating events of this period. Three positions have been advocated: (1) that Menahem paid tribute in 743, the first year of Tiglath-pileser's western campaigns, (2) that Menahem paid tribute in 740 when other western kings paid tribute at Arpad in Syria, and (3) that Menahem paid tribute in 738, the last year of the first series of western campaigns.

The first alternative seems too early strategically for the Assyrians to have penetrated as far south as Israel. The last alternative rests upon the weak argument of identifying two different tribute lists in the annals as referring to tribute taken on only one occasion. The most likely of these three alternatives, therefore, appears to be that Menahem paid tribute in 740. A stela of Tiglath-pileser discovered in Iran in 1967 lends some support to this view.

It is even more difficult to date the end of Menahem's reign. Through the contact of Hoshea with Tiglath-pileser the death of Pekah can be dated in 732 B.C. (*ANET,* p. 284). It should be a simple task to work backward from that point to Menahem. It is not, however, because of the twenty years assigned to Pekah (2 K. 15:27). Presumably this figure includes his rule in Gilead as a rival to Menahem. Thus there is an overlap here of an inexactly known number of years. The other way to approach the dates for Menahem is to work down to him through the kings of Israel starting with Jehu in 841 B.C. When this is done the best calculations currently available date Menahem's ten-year reign from 747 to 737 B.C.

Aside from this king the name Menahem was well known in the ancient Near East. It was used for an Asiatic in an Egyptian papyrus from the 13th Dynasty (*ca.* 1730 B.C.), it appears on ancient Hebrew seals, and it also is found on an Aramaic ostracon found at Nimrûd in Assyria. There was a king of another western territory, a contemporary of Hoshea of Israel, who was also attacked by Tiglath-pileser of Assyria, but this was not Menahem of Israel (*ANET,* p. 283). It has been advocated that the Samaria Ostraca should be dated in his reign, but more recent information available indicates they should be dated earlier in the 8th cent. B.C.

The reign of Menahem was evaluated as evil from a religious perspective (2 K. 15:18). The evils of this time were those to which the prophets Amos and Hosea addressed themselves. Of the six last kings of Israel it is significant that he appears to have been the only one to have died a natural death (v. 22). This is further testimony to the religious and political difficulties that had developed in the northern kingdom by his time. These difficulties went on to bear their final harvest in the fall of Samaria to the Assyrians less than a quarter of a century after Menahem's death.

***Bibliography.***–I. T. Kaufman, *BA,* 45 (1982), 229-239; L. D. Levine, *Two Neo-Assyrian Stelae from Iran* (1972), pp. 11-24; B. Oded, *ZDPV,* 90 (1974), 42; W. H. Shea, *JNES,* 37 (1978), 43-49; H. Tadmor, "Asriyau of Yaudi," *Scripta Hierosolymitana,* 8 (1961), 252-58; E. R. Thiele, *MNHK* (3rd ed. 1982).

W. H. SHEA

**MENAN** mē'nən (Lk. 3:31, AV). *See* MENNA.

**MENE, MENE, TEKEL, AND PARSIN** mē'nē, tek'əl, pär'sin [Aram. *m$^{e}$nē' m$^{e}$nē' t$^{e}$qēl ûparsîn*]; AV, RV, UPHARSIN; NEB U-PHARSIN. The words that according to Dnl. 5:25 appeared on the wall during Belshazzar's feast. The *u-* attached to *parsîn,* the Aramaic conjunction "and," softens the following "p"-sound to "ph," pronounced "f." The words can thus be written as in the RSV, "MENE, MENE, TEKEL, and PARSIN."

***I. Language of the Handwriting.***–Although there can be no certainty here, probably the Aramaic of Dnl. 5 is also the language used for the handwriting. It has come to be called Official Aramaic and is known to have been used from 700-200 B.C. as a lingua franca in the chancelleries of the Near East. Officials of Sennacherib used it in 701 B.C. (2 K. 18:13-37). Since the form of the characters remained relatively stable over a long period, an idea of the appearance of the handwriting can be gained from the sketch below, which the writer has abstracted from a number of Aramaic papyri of the 5th cent. B.C.

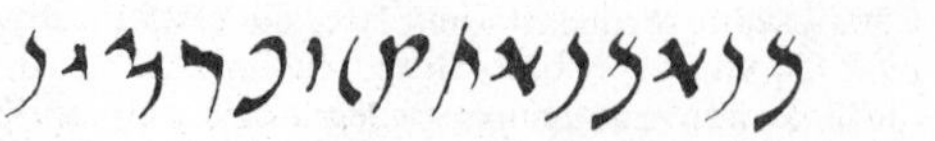

***II. Wording.***–In the interpretation of the inscription (Dnl. 5:26-28), only three words are used, and the last, Peres, is singular rather than plural. Thus many scholars have conjectured that the original form was "Mene, tekel, pares." Support for this view was thought to be found in the ancient versions (see III below).

The confusion of the LXX text in this place and its looseness of translation weaken its testimony. Moreover, Theodotion contradicted its word order. The agreement of Jerome's text with Theodotion may be due to the former's known preference for that Greek text. The supposition that the LXX, Theodotion, and Vulgate represent an attempt at harmonization with vv. 26-28 may account for their divergence from the MT. The support of the MT by the Peshitta cannot be overlooked. The intrinsic probability favors the MT reading. Here J. A. Bengel's critical canon seems to apply: *difficilior lectio potior* ("the more difficult reading is more likely").

***III. Meaning.***–The following are the various interpretations of this enigmatic phrase: MT: "Mene, God has *numbered* the days of your kingdom and brought it to an end; Tekel, you have been *weighed* in the balances and found wanting; Peres, your kingdom is *divided* and given to the Medes and Persians."

Syriac Peshitta: "Mene, God has *numbered* your kingdom and brought it to an end; Tekel, you are *weighed* in the balances and found wanting; Peres, your kingdom is *divided* and given to the Medes and Persians."

Josephus (*Ant.* x.11.3 [243f.]): "*Manē* . . . would in the Greek tongue signify 'number'; that is to say, God has numbered the time of your life and reign. . . . *Thekel*: this means 'weight'; for God has weighed the time of your kingship and shows that it is already declining. *Phares*: this means 'a break' in the Greek tongue; accordingly He will break up your kingdom and divide it between the Medes and the Persians."

Theodotion: "Mane, God has *measured* your kingdom and fulfilled it; Thekel, *weighed* in the balance and found wanting; Phares, your kingdom is *divided* and given to the Medes and Persians."

Vulgate: "Mane, God has *numbered* your kingdom and He has fulfilled it; Thecal, thou art *weighed* in the balance and found wanting; Phares, your kingdom is *divided* and is given to the Medes and Persians."

LXX summary: "Mane, *Numbered*; Phares, *carried away*; Thekel, *weighed.*"

LXX text: *"Numbered; reckoned up; carried away."*

"The time of your kingdom is *numbered*; your kingdom is *rejected*; your kingdom has been *cut short* and completed and given to the Medes and Persians."

The meaning given by the MT is fully supported by the Peshitta and confirmed by Josephus; the LXX text is farthest from the MT. Although there is no clear reason for not accepting the meaning of the handwriting given in Dnl. 5:26-28 or the words of the inscription given in v. 25, their vocalization is not equally reliable, since the pointing of the text took place many centuries after it was written. The punctuation of the words of the handwriting is presently as obscure as their message was to the wise men of Babylon. The words *TQL* and *PRSYN* are both pointed irregularly, perhaps intentionally.

The interpretation appears to find double meanings in each of the components of the inscription. The primary meaning of the three parts of the handwriting (the duplication of the first word is probably for emphasis, as elsewhere in the OT) is then *NUMBERED, WEIGHED, DIVIDED*; the secondary meaning is *ENDED, WANTING, PERSIANS*.

All the above meanings are legitimately abstracted from the given Aramaic words on the principle of assonance so common in the OT.

The affinity with commercial symbols, as noted by C. S. Clermont-Ganneau (*Journal Asiatique*, 8 [July/Aug. 1886], 36-67) and T. Nöldeke (*Zeitschrift für Assyriologie*, I [1886], 414-18), was probably intended: Mene = Maneh (cf. Ezk. 45:12); Tekel = Thekel-Shekel of the Aramaic papyri of the 5th cent.; Parsin = half-shekels (O. Eissfeldt, *ZAW*, 63 [1951], 109-114). Thus a second view of the words is reached, "A minah, a shekel, and half-shekels."

Some scholars find in these names of weights a reference to individuals in the Daniel story, e.g., Nebuchadrezzar, Belshazzar, and the Medes and Persians. But the many different combinations favored by commentators leave this interpretation inconclusive and doubtful.

***Bibliography***.–Comms. on Daniel; H. L. Ginsburg, *Studies in Daniel* (1948), pp. 24ff.; D. N. Freedman, *BASOR*, 145 (Feb. 1957), 31f.

R. J. A. SHERIFFS

**MENELAUS** mēn'ə-lā'əs [Gk. *Menelaos*]. Brother of Simon, the captain of the temple, from the tribe of Benjamin. He unscrupulously bought the office of high priest from Antiochus Epiphanes, the king of Syria, and through bribes and cunning behavior retained his position for nearly a decade. Josephus probably incorrectly identifies Menelaus as a brother of Jason and Onias III (*Ant.* xii.5.1 [237f.]; xv.3.1 [41]).

According to Josephus (*Ant.* xii.5.1 [237-39]), Antiochus Epiphanes was angry with the high priest Jason and gave the office to Menelaus. According to 2 Macc. 4:23-26, in 171 B.C. Jason sent Menelaus to Antiochus to pay the tributes, and Menelaus used the occasion to purchase the high priesthood for himself by paying three hundred talents of silver more than Jason had paid.

Jason fled into the land of Ammon, and Menelaus returned to Jerusalem "possessing no qualification for the high priesthood, but having the hot temper of a cruel tyrant and the rage of a savage wild beast" (2 Macc. 4:25). When Menelaus failed to make the promised payment to Antiochus, he was summoned to Antioch to apppear before the king. Menelaus left his brother Lysimachus as deputy in the high priesthood (vv. 26-29). Meanwhile, Antiochus had suddenly left Antioch and had appointed Andronicus as his deputy. Menelaus now bribed Andronicus with several gold vessels stolen from the temple and persuaded him to murder the ex-high priest Onias III before this legitimate high priest could undermine Menelaus's position by further exposing his sacrilege. When Antiochus returned to Antioch he executed Andronicus in response to the outcry of both Jews and Greeks, but Menelaus went free (2 Macc. 4:30-38).

Back in Jerusalem the general populace finally rebelled against the plundering of the temple by Lysimachus. In the ensuing battle the troops of Lysimachus were defeated, and he himself was killed. The Jews sent a delegation to Antiochus at Tyre with charges against Menelaus; but once again he bribed his way free, this time paying a substantial sum to Ptolemy son of Dorymenes, who persuaded the king to acquit Menelaus and sentence to death the three men sent as witnesses against Menelaus (2 Macc. 4:39-50).

At this time the false rumor arose that Antiochus had been killed in Egypt, so the deposed Jason led a vigorous attack against Menelaus, forcing him to flee. Antiochus, hearing of the events in Judea, returned from Egypt with his troops, murdered large numbers of citizens, and along with Menelaus, who was restored to power, plundered the temple (2 Macc. 5:1-23).

Menelaus appears once more in 162 B.C. during the reign of Antiochus Eupator. Lysias, the king's chancellor, denounced him to the king as the cause of all the troubles in Judea, whereupon Eupator had him taken to Beroea and killed by being thrown from the top of a high tower into the ashes that filled the tower (2 Macc. 13:3-7). "And this was eminently just; because he had committed many sins against the altar whose fire and ashes were holy" (2 Macc. 13:8).

***Bibliography***.–*HNTT*, pp. 11-16; V. Tcherikover, *Hellenistic Civilization and the Jews* (1959), pp. 170-74.

R. L. OMANSON

**MENESTHEUS** mə-nes'thē-əs [Gk. *Menestheus*] (2 Macc. 4:4, 21); AV omits in v. 4. Father of Apollonius the governor of Coelesyria and Phoenicia around the time of Antiochus Epiphanes' ascension to the Seleucid throne (175 B.C.). In v. 4 the Greek text is uncertain (cf. AV), and the RSV and NEB follow a Latin version.

**MENI** mə-nē' [Heb. *m^eni*] (Isa. 65:11). A pagan deity, rendered "destiny" by the RSV, "fortune" by the NEB, and "that number" by the AV. *See* DESTINY; FORTUNE.

**MENNA** men'ə [Gk. *Menna, Mainan*]; AV MENAN. An ancestor of Jesus in Luke's genealogy (Lk. 3:31).

**MEN-PLEASERS** [Gk. *anthrōpáreskos*] (Eph. 6:6; Col. 3:22); NEB "to curry favor with men."

This word, found within the admonitions to slaves in the NT, evidently functioned also in broader contexts in early Christian literature. In 2 Clem. 13:1 it occurs in the context of an appeal to all the brethren to repent. The letter of Clement tells its readers to be neither men-pleasers nor pleasers of self (Gk. *heautṓi aréskein*), but rather to practice what they preach, namely, love for enemies. "Men-pleasers" is thus contrasted to a certain integrity with the Christian confession (cf. Ign. Rom. 2:1).

Twice Paul defended himself from the charge of pleasing men rather than serving God (Gal.1:10; 1 Thess. 2:4, Gk. *anthrṓpois aréskein*). He argued that he had not surrendered any principle entailed by the gospel in either his preaching or his practice.

This contrast to integrity with the confession is also important within the context of admonitions to slaves. The parallel passages of Colossians and Ephesians exhort slaves to obey their "according-to-the-flesh masters" (Gk. *toís katá sárka kyríois*), not as men-pleasers but as slaves of Christ the Lord (Gk. *kyríos*), doing the will of God *ek psychḗs* ("from the heart"). Evidently participation in the institution of slavery was not considered a surrender of gospel principles. But it is equally evident, as Théo Preis makes clear, that tension was felt between master-slave relationships and integrity with the confession. The roles of master and slave stood under the criticizing and transforming norm of obedience to the Master of all, in whom there is no partiality (cf. Eph 6:9; Col. 4:1).

See T. Preis, *Life in Christ* (1954), ch. 2.

A. D. VERHEY

**MENSTRUATION** [Heb. *niddaṯ dāwâ*] (Lev. 12:2); AV "separation for her infirmity"; NEB "impurity through menstruation"; [*niddâ*] (Lev. 12:5); AV "separation"; **MENSTRUAL UNCLEANNESS** [Heb. *niddaṯ ṭum'â*] (Lev. 18:19); AV "put apart for uncleanness"; NEB PERIOD

OF MENSTRUATION. The period of menstruation rendered an Israelite woman ceremonially unclean for seven days and therefore excluded her from worship in the sanctuary and from fellowship with other Israelites (Lev. 15:19-24). The similarity between menstruation and childbirth (i.e., the discharge of blood) no doubt accounts for the comparison in Lev. 12:2, 5.

Leviticus offers what appears to be conflicting legislation regarding intercourse with a menstruating woman. 15:24 states simply that the man, like the woman, "should be unclean for seven days." Thus the result of such intercourse seems to be only temporary uncleanness. In 18:19, however, such intercourse is strictly forbidden, and 20:18 adds a punishment — both man and woman "shall be cut off from any among their people" (*see* CUT, CUT OFF; cf. G. Wenham, *Book of Leviticus* [*NICOT,* 1979], pp. 241-43). Some, e.g., N. Micklem (*IB,* II, 76), have appealed to the documentary hypothesis to explain the discrepancy: 15:24, assigned to the priestly writer, "may represent a later mitigation of an earlier law" (i.e., chs. 17–26, which are usually assigned to the Holiness Code; *see* CRITICISM II.D.5). Others, e.g., Wenham (p. 220), have seen no conflict in these passages; "rather they approach the same topic from different angles," ch. 15 being devoted to rules of impurity, ch. 18 to categorical prohibitions, and ch. 20 to punishments of various sins.

For the rabbinical development of the OT law see Mish. *Niddah.*

*See also* CLEAN AND UNCLEAN; for the hemorrhaging woman healed by Jesus *see* HEMORRHAGE.

G. A. L.

**MENUHAH** mə-nōō'hə. The AV mg. translation of Heb. *m^enûḥâ* in Jgs. 20:43. Translated literally, the term means "resting-place" (so RSV mg.; cf. AV "with ease"; NEB "without respite"). The RSV and NEB mg. read "from Nohah," following LXX B (*apó Noua*), which reads the Hebrew text as *minnôḥâ. See also* NOHAH.

**MENUHOTH** mə-nōō'hoth [Heb. *m^enuḥôṯ*–'resting places']; AV, NEB, MANAHETHITES. A clan that descended from Caleb. Half of the clan were descendants of Shobal (1 Ch. 2:52). Heb. *mānaḥtî* (RSV "Manahathites") in v. 54 comes from the same root as *m^enuḥôṯ* and probably refers to another segment of the same clan (cf. AV and NEB, which render "Manahethites" in both passages). *See* MANAHATHITES.

**MEONENIM** mē-on'ə-nim, **PLAIN OF** (Jgs. 9:37, AV). *See* DIVINER'S OAK.

**MEONOTHAI** mē-on'ə-thī [Heb. *m^eʿônōṯay*–'my dwellings']. Son of Othniel and father of Ophrah (1 Ch. 4:13f.). The AV omits "and Meonothai" in v. 13, following the MT. The RSV and NEB reading is probably correct, following the Vulgate and the Lucian recension of the LXX.

**MEPHAATH** mef'i-ath, mə-fā'əth [Heb. *mēp̱aʿaṯ, mêpaʿaṯ,* also *môpaʿaṯ*]. A city of the Amorites in the territory given to Reuben (Josh. 13:18) and assigned to the Merarites (21:37; 1 Ch. 6:79). It is later named among the cities of Moab against which Jeremiah pronounced judgment (Jer. 48:21).

Eusebius (*Onom.* 128.22) identified it as the location of a Roman military post, which is the modern Khirbet Nefaʿa, NW of Ḥesbân (Heshbon) and 10 km. (6 mi.) S of Amman. Alt located the Amorite city at Tell Jâwah, which is near Khirbet Nefaʿa. Cf. *AASOR,* 14 (1934), 4; *GAB,* Maps 11, 17.

W. S. L. S.

**MEPHIBOSHETH** mē-fib'ō-sheth [Heb. *m^epîḇōšeṯ*–'utterance of shame,' i.e., of Baal, or 'idol-breaker'; Gk. *Memphibosthe*].

**1.** Son of Saul by his concubine Rizpah, daughter of Aiah (2 S. 21:8). David gave him, his brother Armoni, and five grandsons of Saul to the Gibeonites to expiate the "bloodguilt" incurred by Saul's house (cf. v. 3) for Saul's violation of the ancient covenant with the Gibeonites (Josh. 9). To alleviate the three-years' famine caused by this "bloodguilt" (2 S. 21:1), David gave these seven relatives of Saul to the Gibeonites, who "hanged them on the mountain before the Lord" (v. 9).

**2.** Grandson of Saul, son of Jonathan, nephew of Mephibosheth (**1.**) and father of Mica(h), who had numerous progeny (2 S. 4:4; 1 Ch. 8:34ff.).

He was five years old when Saul and Jonathan were slain. The news of these deaths caused his nurse to flee with him from Gibeah; as she hurried, Mephibosheth fell and became permanently lame in both legs (2 S. 4:4). He was carried to Lodebar and put in the charge of Machir, a man of great wealth (9:4; cf. 17:27; Josephus *Ant.* vii.5.5 [113]), and there Mephibosheth married.

When the affairs of the kingdom had settled down David felt compelled to fulfil his oath to Jonathan (1 S. 20:15) by showing favor to a member of his friend's house. Ziba, who was probably managing Saul's estate for David, told him about the crippled prince, and David sent for him. Mephibosheth approached in great fear, for eastern peoples customarily exterminated all the kindred of a previous dynasty. David handed over Saul's estate to Mephibosheth and commanded Ziba to manage it. The king also invited Mephibosheth to eat daily at his table and thus to live according to his royal position (2 S. 9).

Seventeen years later, during Absalom's revolt, David fled from Jerusalem and met Ziba, who provided him with food and wine. David understandably inquired for Mephibosheth. Ziba replied that his master had remained behind in Jerusalem for his own ends, hoping to take the kingdom. Although support still existed for the house of Saul, this was probably a blatant deception; but David was excited enough to believe Ziba and rewarded him by granting him his master's property (2 S. 16:1-4). Later Mephibosheth had the opportunity of giving his version of the story. He approached the king at Gilgal in deep mourning; he had neither washed his clothes nor trimmed his beard since David's departure. He told the king of Ziba's deception and left his fate with David, who spoke, he said, "as an angel of God." Whatever he decided would be right. Most likely David accepted the prince's explanation, although it is strange that he decided to share the property between the two of them; perhaps David suspected both of duplicity. Mephibosheth, anxious to have the king's friendship, declared that he would be willing to forego all (19:24-30).

The last reference to this unfortunate man is the sparing of his life when other members of Saul's household were slain. David was true to his oath to the very end (2 S. 21:7).

In the Chronicler's genealogy (1 Ch. 8:34; 9:40) he is called MERIB-BAAL; no doubt the name *bōšeṯ,* "shame," was a later substitution for the false god.

J. A. BALCHIN

**MERAB** mē'rab [Heb. *mēraḇ*–'increase']. The eldest daughter of Saul (1 S. 14:49), promised to the man who would kill Goliath (17:25). Although David fulfilled the requirement, no marriage followed. Some time later (18:17) David was again promised her hand if he again defeated the Philistines, though the promise was merely a ruse to have David killed by the Philistines. By this time Saul's jealousy constituted a neurotic condition. Again the promise was not fulfilled, but Michal's love for David may have been the retarding factor from the first. At the time of betrothal Merab was given to Adriel the Meholathite instead (18:19).

The passage in 2 S. 21:8 probably contains a textual error and "Merab" should be read for "Michal" (following Lucian and Pesh.), although the LXX and Josephus endorse the MT. It is possible that Merab died comparatively young and that her children were left in the care of Michal, who had none. Thus a Targum explanation reads: "The five sons of Merab (which Michal, Saul's daughter brought up) which she bare," etc. The simplest explanation, however, is to assume a scribal error, especially since Heb. *yālaḏ,* "bear (a child)," which is used of Merab in v. 8, cannot mean "bring up." J. A. BALCHIN

**MERAIAH** mə-rā'yə [Heb. *m^erāyâ*]. Head of the priestly house of Seraiah in the time of Joiakim the high priest (Neh. 12:12).

**MERAIOTH** mə-rī'oth [Heb. *m^erāyôṯ*; Gk. *Mariēl, Mariōth, Marerōth* (Ezr. 7:3), etc.; Lat. *Marimoth* (2 Esd. 1:2)]; AV Apoc., NEB Apoc., MARIMOTH.

**1.** A Levitical descendant of Aaron and ancestor of Ezra; listed in 1 Ch. 6:6f., 52 (MT 5:32f.; 6:37); Ezr. 7:3 as a son of Zerahiah and father of Amariah (Azariah in Ezr. 7:3). 2 Esd. 1:2 probably refers to the same person, but lists him as the son of Arna. The same person may be named in 1 Esd. 8:2, where the RSV omits Gk. *Marerōth* and two other names, following LXX B (cf. AV Meremoth; NEB Mareroth).

**2.** Another priest in the same family, listed as the son of Ahitub and father of Zadok (1 Ch. 9:11; Neh. 11:11).

**3.** A priestly family, of which Helkai was the head, in the postexilic period (Neh. 12:15; but cf. v. 3, where the name is given as MEREMOTH).

**MERAN** mer'an (Bar. 3:23, AV). *See* MERRAN.

**MERARI** mə-rär'ī [Heb. *m^erārî*–'bitterness'? (cf. *mārar*–'be bitter'; cf. also Egyp. *mrr*–'beloved'); Gk. *Merari, Merarei*]; **MERARITES** mə-rä'rīts [Heb. *m^erārî* (Nu. 26:57), *b^enê m^erārî*–'sons of Merari' (Josh. 21:7, 34, 40; 1 Ch. 6:63, 77 [MT 48, 62])].

**1.** The third son of Levi; younger brother of Gershon and Kohath (Gen. 46:11; Ex. 6:16; Nu. 3:17; 1 Ch. 6:1, 16 [MT 5:27; 6:1]; 23:6). He was among the seventy who went down to Egypt with Jacob (Gen. 46:8, 11). He was head of one of the three chief Levitical families, the Merarites. They were subdivided through Merari's two sons Mahli and Mushi into the Mahlites and Mushites (Ex. 6:19; Nu. 3:20, 33; 26:58; 1 Ch. 6:19 [MT 4]).

At Sinai the Merarites were set apart, with the other Levitical families, to serve at the tabernacle (Nu. 3:33-37; 4:29-33, 42-45; 7:8; 10:17). Their leader was Zuriel son of Abihail (3:35), but together with the Gershonites their service at the tabernacle was under the direction of Aaron's son Ithamar (4:28, 33; 7:8). They were assigned a place of encampment on the north side of the tabernacle (3:35), the Gershonites being on the west, the Kohathites on the south, and Moses and the Aaronites on the east (3:23, 29, 38). Their duties were the care, servicing and transportation of the frames of the tabernacle, with its crossbars, pillars, bases, and accessories, as well as of the pillars of the surrounding courtyard, with their bases, pegs, and cords (3:36f.; 4:31-33).

According to the command of Moses in the plains of Moab, the Merarites were assigned cities to dwell in, along with the surrounding pasture lands for grazing their livestock (Nu. 35:1ff.; Josh. 21:1-3). They received twelve cities in all, four in each of the territories of Zebulun, Reuben, and Gad (Josh. 21:7, 34-40; 1 Ch. 6:63, 77-81 [MT 48, 62-66]), which included Ramoth in Gilead, a city of refuge (Josh. 21:38; 1 Ch. 6:80 [MT 65]).

After the defeat of the Philistines, 120 Merarites under their leader Asaiah (1 Ch. 15:6) participated in carrying the ark from the house of Obed-edom (2 S. 6:10-15; 1 Ch. 15:25) to the tent sanctuary David had prepared for it in Jerusalem (1 Ch. 15:1-15). In his reorganization of the worship of the sanctuary, David divided the Levites into the Gershonites, the Kohathites, and the Merarites (1 Ch. 23:6). The Merarites were charged with "the work for the service of the house of the Lord" (1 Ch. 23:4, 24, 28, 32; cf. 24:26-30); some may have been officers and judges, some were gatekeepers, and some were involved in music and song (1 Ch. 16:42; 23:4f.; 26:1-19, esp. 10f., 16-19). They may also have assisted the Aaronite priests in their priestly duties (1 Ch. 23:28f.). Those appointed to share in the organization of music and song were the Merarite sons of Ethan (or Jeduthun), along with the Kohathite sons of Heman and the Gershonite sons of Asaph (1 Ch. 6:31-48 [MT 16-33]; 15:16-24; 16:41f.; 25:1-31).

In Hezekiah's time two Merarites, Kish and Azariah, participated in the cleansing of the temple (2 Ch. 29:12). In the reign of Josiah two Merarites, Jahath and Obadiah, were among the overseers of the workmen repairing the temple (2 Ch. 34:12). Merarites were also among those who returned to Judah from Babylon and served under Ezra (Ez. 8:18f.) and Nehemiah (1 Ch. 9:14; cf. Neh. 11:15).

See R. de Vaux, *Ancient Israel* (Eng. tr. 1961), 390-94.

**2.** The father of Judith (Jth. 8:1; 16:7).

M. J. HORSNELL

**MERATHAIM** mer'ə-thā-əm [Heb. *m^erāṯayim*–'two rebellions']. A name used for "Babylon" in Jer. 50:21. It is believed to be a wordplay on Bab. *nâr marratu,* "bitter river" (i.e., the Persian Gulf), since the root of both words is *mrr,* "bitter." The name Pekod, used similarly in the same verse, may be a wordplay on *Puqudu,* an Aramean tribe in the same region. Cf. *GTTOT,* § 1397-8.

W. S. L. S.

**MERCHANDISE** [Heb. *saḥar, sāḥār*] (Prov. 31:18; Isa. 23:18; 45:14); NEB BUSINESS, TRADING, MERCHANTS; [*r^eḵullâ*] (Ezk. 26:12); [*ma'^arāḇ*] (Ezk. 27:13, 17, 19, 25, 27, 33f.); AV also MARKET; NEB IMPORTS, MERCHANTS (Ezk. 27:27), WARES.

The RSV uses "merchandise" only in the OT. *Saḥar* refers basically to the goods sold, but can be extended to mean "trade" (Ezk. 28:16, NEB "commerce") or "business" (Prov. 31:18, NEB). *Ma'^arāḇ* is a collective term denoting "articles for exchange," translated "wares" in Ezk. 27:9. The term occurs only in Ezk. 27 in a description of the extensive commercial relationships of Tyre.

*See also* BUSINESS; COMMERCE; MARKET; MERCHANT; TRADE; TRAFFIC. J. E. HARTLEY

**MERCHANT** [Heb. *sôḥēr*] (Gen. 23:16; 2 Ch. 9:14; Prov. 31:14; Isa. 23:2f., 8; Ezk. 27:36; 38:13); AV also MART; NEB also TRADER, MERCHANDISE, TRADE; [*rôḵēl*] (1 K. 10:15; Neh. 3:31f.; 13:20; Cant. 3:6; Ezk. 17:4; 27:3; Nah. 3:16); NEB also TRADE, "foreign trade," SPY; [*k^ena'anî*] (Job 41:6 [MT 40:30]; Prov. 31:24); [Gk. *émporos*] (Mt. 13:45; Rev. 18:3, 11, 15, 23); NEB also TRADER.

Hebrew *sôḥēr* is the active participle of the verb *sāḥar,* "go about, go to and fro, go in" (KoB, p. 655). In Isa. 23:3 the RSV apparently takes the construct *s^eḥar* as a participle; the AV ("mart") and NEB ("trade") take it as the noun *saḥar.* The verb *rāḵal,* "go about," occurs in the Hebrew Bible only in the part. *rōḵēl,* "trader, trafficker" (KoB, p. 892). *K^ena'anî* comes from *k^ena'an,* "Canaan"; originally it referred to the Phoenicians, who were traders of red-purple wool. Gk. *émporos* denotes a "wholesale dealer" (Bauer, rev., p. 257).

Merchants constantly crossed Palestine or Canaan, the land bridge between Asia, Africa, and Europe. As the basic roots imply, they were always on the move, from house to house or from village to village. In particular, the Phoenicians had numerous colonies as trading bases along the Mediterranean; Tyre and Sidon were the most famous in Lebanon. They were seamen and traders who monopolized much of the Mediterranean market during the Israelite occupation of Palestine. As a result, "Canaanite" and "merchant" came to be synonymous terms. Thus most OT references to merchants are to the Phoenicians (cf. Ezk. 27–28). Ezekiel called Tyre the "merchant of the peoples on many coastlands" (27:3).

Thanks to the merchants, palaces and homes enjoyed exotic wares and were enriched with unique objects from distant lands (Ezk. 27:33). Spices and fragrant perfumes were valued highly (Can. 3:6). The reign of Solomon in particular brought much international commerce to Jerusalem (1 K. 10:11-29). The traders then included royal merchants (v. 28, NEB). Solomon was in league with the Phoenicians; together they financed long expeditions from Ezion-geber to Africa, bringing back gold, silver, ivory, apes, and peacocks (v. 22).

The merchants had their own standard weights (Gen. 23:16). There was no National Bureau of Standards at that time; however, governments and temples established standard measures to control their revenues (cf. Dt. 25:14).

In quest of greater profits the merchant frequently cut corners or cheated the buyer outright. The merchants in northern Israel around the time of Jeroboam II sought to "make the ephah small and the shekel great, and [to] deal deceitfully with false balances" (Am. 8:5). They gave less goods and exacted more money. Hosea recorded a proverb from the same period: "False scales are in merchants' hands, and they love to cheat" (Hos. 12:7, NEB). For these false practices the merchants were warned that they would experience the judgment of God. When the Day of the Lord comes, "it [will be] all over with the merchants" (Zeph. 1:11, NEB). Ezekiel also delivered strong oracles of judgment against the Phoenicians of Tyre (chs. 27–28). With pride and self-exaltation they vaunted their increased wealth. Because of such a bearing they came under God's condemnation. Rev. 18 picks up a similar motif in the lamentation against Babylon, the obstinate enemy of God. The merchants had grown wealthy from Babylon's extreme extravagance (v. 3). Now that she was gone, so was their source of wealth (v. 11). Thus they became mourners at her departure (vv. 11-20), but they wept at a distance, fearing that her torment would become theirs (v. 15). Babylon's merchants were a significant means by which her false ideology and religion reached distant places and held peoples bound (v. 23), and consequently they participated fully in her judgment.

Scripture does not consider merchants *per se* evil; they are condemned only when their practices violate God's moral standards. A righteous merchant enjoys the blessing of God (Dt. 25:15; Prov. 11:1). In the same tenor, the proper role of a merchant provided the setting for one of Christ's parables about the kingdom of Heaven: "A merchant looking out for fine pearls found one of very special value; so he went and sold everything he had, and bought it" (Mt. 13:45f., NEB). Thus the people of God need to possess some basic business sense in seeking God's kingdom.

*See also* COMMERCE; DEALER; MERCHANDISE.

J. E. HARTLEY

**MERCURIUS** mər-kyoo'rē-əs (Acts 14:12, AV); **MERCURY** mer'kyə-rē (NEB). The Latin name of the Greek god HERMES (1).

**MERCY; MERCIFUL** [Heb. *rāḥam* (Ex. 33:19; Ps. 116:5; Prov. 28:13; etc.), *raḥ^amîm* (Gen. 43:14; Dt. 13:17; 2 S. 24:14; etc.), *raḥûm* (Ex. 34:6; Dt. 4:31; 2 Ch. 30:9; etc.), *ḥānan* (Dt. 7:2; Job 9:15; Ps. 51:1 [MT 3]; 57:1 [MT 2]; 123:2f.; Prov. 21:10), *t^eḥinnâ* (Josh. 11:20), *ḥeseḏ* (1 K. 20:31; Ps. 23:6), *ḥasîḏ* (Jer. 3:12), *ḥāmal* (Lam. 2:2, 21), *ḥemlâ* (Gen. 19:16); Aram. *raḥ^amîn* (Dnl. 2:18); Gk. *eleéō* (Mt. 5:7; 9:27; 15:22; etc.), *éleos* (Mt. 9:13; 12:7; 23:23; etc.), *eleḗmōn* (Mt. 5:7; He. 2:17), *híleōs* (He. 8:12), *hiláskomai* (Lk. 18:13), *oiktirmós* (Rom. 12:1; 2 Cor. 1:3; He. 10:28), *oiktírmōn* (Lk. 6:36; Jas. 5:11)]; AV also PITY, COMPASSION, MAKE SUPPLICATION (Job 9:15), FIND FAVOUR (Prov. 21:10), etc.; NEB also TENDERNESS (Jer. 31:20), AFFECTION (Ezk. 39:25), KINDNESS (Neh. 1:11), HEART (Prov. 12:10), SPARE (Dt. 7:2; Gen. 19:16), etc.

*I. OT.*–The Heb. *rāḥam* (cf. *reḥem,* "bowels") referred to the seat of compassion (cf. Gen. 43:30; 1 K. 3:26 [RSV "heart"]). It was used for the deep, tender feeling of compassion that was awakened by the trouble, weakness, suffering, or vulnerability of another in need of help. It was particularly applicable in cases where a familial tie would arouse compassion for one in a pitiable condition, e.g., a father's love for a son (Jer. 31:20), a mother's love for her nursing infant (Isa. 49:15 [RSV "compassion"]), a man's love for his betrothed (Isa. 54:7 [RSV "compassion"]).

The OT affirms that mercy was a basic characteristic of God. The psalmist declared, "our God is merciful" (Ps. 116:5; cf. Prov. 12:10). Israel's earliest experience of God was that of One who was merciful, gracious, and slow to anger (Ex. 34:6). Thus the OT is rich in words that express the concept of mercy. Since mercy was part of God's nature, it would never fail (Dt. 4:31; Lam. 3:22), even when Israel proved unworthy (Neh. 9:17, 19, 27f., 31). God's compassion was something the enemies of Israel totally lacked (Isa. 13:18; 47:6; Jer. 6:23; 50:42). Therefore, David preferred the mercy of God, even if it should bring pestilence, rather than be left to the hands of men (2 S. 24:14; 1 Ch. 21:13).

The mercy of God is integrally related to His steadfast love (*ḥeseḏ*), the loving demonstration of God's covenant faithfulness to His chosen people. The Psalms frequently link God's mercy and steadfast love. They are of old (Ps. 25:6); they preserve and help those in distress (Ps. 40:11 [MT 12]; 69:16 [MT 17]); they redeem from the pit and provide the basis for God's willingness to forgive, heal (Ps. 103:4), and give life (Ps. 119:77, 156; cf. Ps. 51:1 [MT 3]; 86:15; 103:8; 145:8; Isa. 63:7; Jer. 16:5; Joel 2:13; Jonah 4:2).

Because of God's mercy toward the helpless and His forbearance of human frailty, sinners are able to appeal to Him in hope. Daniel appealed to God on the ground of His great mercy, not on the ground of his own righteousness (Dnl. 9:8f.). Sinners who confess and forsake sin may boldly appeal for and find mercy (Ps. 51:1; Prov. 28:13). While mercy can be expected because of God's nature and historical actions, it can never be demanded or earned; God freely bestows it. As God said to Moses, "I will be gracious to whom I will be gracious, and will show mercy on whom I will show mercy" (Ex. 33:19).

Finally, it must be noted that the mercy of God is not simply an emotion; it is always manifested historically in personal actions. He has mercy on His people and multiplies them (Dt. 13:17), restores their fortunes (Jer. 33:26; Ezk. 39:25), and delivers them from their enemies (Jer. 42:12).

*II. NT.–A. God's Mercy.* The OT record of God's mercy forms the context for its manifestation in the NT. His steadfast, covenantal, electing love (*ḥeseḏ*) for Israel is conspicuously reflected in the Lukan infancy canticles. The birth of the Messiah reveals God's covenantal mercy and faithfulness to save His unworthy people (Lk. 1:50, 54, 72, 78; cf. Ps. 103:17).

In the OT, God's steadfast love (*ḥeseḏ*) was focused on His covenant people, Israel. Thus Rom. 9–11 (where the key word is mercy) is striking, for there Paul argued that God's mercy was for *all* peoples. In Rom. 9:15, Paul cited Ex. 33:19 to affirm the freedom of God's mercy. No one has a claim on it. He has mercy on whomever He wills and hardens whomever He wills (Rom. 9:18); He has vessels of wrath and vessels of mercy (9:23). The hardening that has come upon Israel (11:25) has resulted in riches for the Gentiles (11:12). God shut up Jew and Gentile to disobedience that He might have mercy on all (vv. 30-32). Therefore, Gentiles in particular may glorify God for His mercy (15:9). That same line of thought is expressed in the quote from Hos. 2:23 in 1 Pet. 2:10: the no-people are now God's people; the ones who formerly were outside God's mercy have now received mercy. The Church, therefore, lives by God's mercy alone. That assumption provides the basis in Rom. 12:1 for Paul's subsequent exhortations; his "therefore" is grounded in the mercies of God.

God's mercy is the foundation of mankind's salvation. It is God's unmerited response to human need: "He saved us, not because of deeds done by us in righteousness, but in virtue of his own mercy" (Tit. 3:5). Mercifully, God made those dead in trespasses alive together with Christ (Eph. 2:4f.). By His great mercy He caused Christians to be born anew to a living hope (1 Pet. 1:3); He will be merciful (*híleōs*) toward their iniquities (He. 8:12).

God's mercy is displayed in many other ways. When Elizabeth was advanced in years, He gave her a son (Lk. 1:58). He saved Epaphroditus from death (Phil. 2:27). By God's mercy Paul, the blasphemer and persecutor of the Church, became an apostle of Christ (2 Cor. 4:1; 1 Tim. 1:13, 16) and was made trustworthy (1 Cor. 7:25).

God is compassionate and merciful (Jas. 5:11); He is the Father of mercies (2 Cor. 1:3). God's mercy was so prominent that "mercy" was added to the usual greeting "grace and peace" in some NT epistles (1 Tim. 1:2; 2 Tim. 1:2; 2 Jn. 3; Jude 2) and to the conclusion of Galatians (6:16).

*B. The Mercy of Jesus Christ.* The healing ministry of Jesus revealed the breaking in of divine mercy and compassion on the helpless and weak. Jesus told the Gerasene demoniac to proclaim what the Lord had done, how He had mercy on him (Mk. 5:19). Trench's famous distinction between grace (*cháris*) and mercy (*éleos*) applies: ". . . the *cháris* of God, his free grace and gift, displayed in the forgiveness of sins, is extended to men, as they are *guilty,* his *éleos,* as they are *miserable*" (Trench, p. 170). Jesus was consistently confronted with and responded to appeals for help from those in misery. Blind men (Mt. 9:27; 20:30f. par. Mk. 10:47f.; Lk. 18:38f.), a Canaanite mother (Mt. 15:22), the father of an epileptic (Mt. 17:15), and ten lepers (Lk. 17:13) all pleaded for and received mercy from Jesus.

Hebrews interprets Jesus' compassion in terms of its significance for salvation. He became a merciful and faithful high priest to make expiation for the sins of the people (He. 2:17). Because of Him, they can draw near to the throne of grace to receive mercy and find help in time of need (4:16).

*C. Mercy Required of Humans.* Because God has been merciful, He expects His people to be merciful. The merciful shall receive mercy as their reward (Mt. 5:7). This is not a matter of *quid pro quo.* That which renders one incapable of being merciful to others also renders one incapable of receiving mercy. In the parable of the unmerciful servant (Mt. 18:23-25), the king compassionately forgave the enormous debt; but the servant dealt harshly with his fellow servant who owed him only a token amount. The ruthless servant was punished because mercy requires mercy (Mt. 18:33). James states the corollary: "judgment is without mercy to one who has shown no mercy" (Jas. 2:13). The requirement to show mercy is clearly expressed in Luke's Gospel. Disciples are to be merciful, as their Father in heaven is merciful (Lk. 6:36). By showing mercy, the Samaritan proved to be the neighbor of the man who fell among robbers; Jesus commanded the inquiring lawyer to go and do likewise (Lk. 10:37). The tormented rich man cried out to Abraham for mercy but received none since he had not shown mercy to Lazarus (Lk. 16:19-25).

The Jewish leaders in Matthew's Gospel failed to grasp the fundamental requirement of being merciful. Because of their relentless legalism, Jesus instructed them to learn Hos. 6:6, "I desire mercy, and not sacrifice" (Mt. 9:13). Failing to learn that, they remained intolerant (Mt. 12:7). Therefore, Jesus condemned them for their pettiness, the scrupulous tithing of garden herbs, while ignoring the weightier matters of justice, mercy, and faith (Mt. 23:23).

Mercilessness (*aneleḗmōn*) is a result of deliberately rejecting the knowledge of God (Rom. 1:28, 31). Finally, mercy also appears in lists of Christian virtues (Rom. 12:8; Jas. 3:17).

*See also* PITY.

***Bibliography.***–N. Glueck, *Ḥesed in the Bible* (Eng. tr. repr. 1967); W. F. Lofthouse, *ZAW,* 51 (1933), 29-35; N. H. Snaith, *Distinctive Ideas of the OT* (repr. 1975); W. L. Reed, *JBL,* 73 (1954), 35-41; *TDNT,* II, *s.v.* ἔλεος κτλ. (R. Bultmann); V, *s.v.* οἰκτίρω κτλ. (R. Bultmann); R. C. Trench, *Synonyms of the NT* (1880).

D. E. GARLAND

**MERCY SEAT** [Heb. *kappōreṯ*; LXX usually *hilastḗrion* (as in He. 9:5; cf. "expiation," Rom. 3:5)]; NEB COVER. A rectangular slab, 2½ cubits by 1½ cubits, of an unspecified thickness, which Bezalel fashioned of solid, refined gold under Moses' direction (Ex. 25:17ff.; 37:6ff.). This slab covered the ARK OF THE COVENANT, and also supported the two gold CHERUBIM figures.

The importance of the mercy seat is twofold: it is the place of the Lord's revelation of His Word to Moses from the cloud of His presence between the cherubim figures (Ex. 25:22; Nu. 7:89) and the place where blood was sprinkled on the Day of Atonement (Lev. 16). Appropriately, the mercy seat was to be obscured from view at all times, either by the inner veil (Ex. 26:31ff. — also used when moving the ark, Nu. 4:5) or by a cloud of incense on the Day of Atonement (Lev. 16:13).

Though compatible with the imagery of God's throne (cf. Ps. 99:1, 5; 132:7) Heb. *kappōreṯ* in no way suggests a seat. Most modern translations render *kappōreṯ* "cover" (so NEB) or "lid," in part on the basis of the position of the slab on top of the ark. Also, one possible etymology for Heb. *kpr* relates this term to Arab. *kafara,* "to cover." It is then suggested that the usual meaning of Heb. *kpr,* "propitiate" or "make atonement," derives from the more original concept "to cover (sin)." This etymology is by no means certain, however (cf. Driver; Görg; Wenham), and in biblical usage *kpr* no longer bears its alleged etymological meaning. Rather, it is used exclusively in contexts appropriate to the ideas of propitiation (including bribery) and atonement.

Thus the LXX *hilastḗrion* and the Vulg. *propitiatorium,* "a place of propitiation" or "a propitiatory," admirably suit the context of the use of this object on the Day of Atonement, and comport well with the preeminence and distinctiveness of the propitiatory from the ark below (cf. *TDNT,* III, 318f.).

*See also* ATONEMENT, DAY OF.

***Bibliography.***–G. R. Driver, *JTS,* 34 (1933), 34-38; M. Görg, *ZAW,* 89 (1977), 115-18; *Biblische Notizen,* 5 (1978), 12; M. Haran, *Temples and Temple Service in Ancient Israel* (Eng. tr. 1978); L. Morris, *Apostolic Preaching of the Cross* (3rd ed. 1965), pp. 161-174, 184-202; R. Nicole, *WTJ,* 17 (1955), 117-157; G. Wenham, *Leviticus* (*NICOT,* 1979), pp. 59ff., 229.

G. P. HUGENBERGER

**MERED** mē'red [Heb. *mereḏ*–'rebellion']. Son of Ezra; a Judahite who married two wives: one an Egyptian ("Bithiah, the daughter of Pharaoh") and the other a Jewess (1 Ch. 4:17f.). His sons founded (cf. NEB "founder" in place of RSV [lit.] "father") the towns of Eshtemoa, Gedor, Soco, and Zanoah. The MT of vv. 17f. is confused (cf. AV, which follows the MT), and the RSV and NEB are probably correct in transposing the last clause of v. 18 to v. 17 (see KD). *See also* BITHIAH.

**MEREMOTH** mer'ə-moth [Heb. *m^e^rēmôṯ*–'heights'(?); Gk. *Mereimōth*].

**1.** AV, NEB, also MERAIOTH (Neh. 12:15). One of the twenty-two priestly leaders who returned to Palestine from the Babylonian Exile with Zerubbabel in 537 B.C. (Neh. 12:3, 7). At Neh. 12:15 the Hebrew MSS read *m^e^rāyôṯ,* i.e., MERAIOTH, but this is probably an error for Meremoth (see LXX, Syr.).

**2.** One of the descendants of Bani who put away his foreign wife at Ezra's insistence (Ezr. 10:36).

**3.** AV Apoc. MARMOTH; NEB Apoc. MARMATHI. A priest, the son of Uriah; he was one of those entrusted by Ezra with the weighing of the silver and gold brought from Mesopotamia (Ezr. 8:33; 1 Esd. 8:62).

**4.** The son of Uriah, the son of Hakkoz; he repaired two sections of the Jerusalem wall under Nehemiah in 445 B.C. (Neh. 3:4, 21). This is no doubt the same individual who signed the covenant under Nehemiah (Neh. 10:5 [MT 6]).

Since both **3** and **4** have the same patronymic, many scholars identify them as one individual. Advocates of the "reverse order," which places Nehemiah in 445 and Ezra later in 398, argue that it is more likely that Meremoth worked on the wall in his youth under Nehemiah and then served as a treasurer some forty-seven years later under Ezra (see Brockington, p. 88). Those who follow this interpretation must assume that the difficulty that the descendants of Hakkoz had in establishing their lineage (Ezr. 2:61-63) was later resolved.

Supporters of the traditional order, which has Ezra returning in 458 before Nehemiah, suggest that despite similar patronymics we have two different individuals — Meremoth **3**, a priest, and Meremoth **4**, a layman.

**5.** (1 Esd. 8:2, AV); NEB MAREROTH. *See* MERAIOTH **1.**

***Bibliography.***–U. Kellermann, *ZAW,* 80 (1968), 69; L. H. Brockington, *Ezra, Nehemiah and Esther* (*NCBC,* 1969), p. 135; K. Koch, *JSS,* 19 (1974), 190; E. Yamauchi, *Themelios,* 5/3 (1980), 9f.

E. M. YAMAUCHI

**MERES** mer'əz [Heb. *meres*] (Est. 1:14). One of the seven princes who ranked next after King Ahasuerus in the Medo-Persian kingdom. *See* PRINCES, THE SEVEN.

**MERIBAH** mer'ə-bə [Heb. *m^e^rîḇâ*–'strife']. The name of two different places at which the Israelites stopped on their journey through the wilderness: (1) at Rephidim (Ex. 17:1-7; referred to also in Dt. 33:8; Ps. 95:8; probably also 81:7 [MT 8]); (2) at Kadesh-barnea (Nu. 20:1-13; referred to also in Dt. 32:51; Ps. 106:32; Ezk. 47:19; 48:28). At both places the Israelites complained because they had no water (hence the name Meribah), and the Lord gave them water from a rock. Other passages allude to one or both of these occasions as examples of God's power and providence (e.g., Dt. 8:15; Ps. 78:15-20; 105:41; 114:8; Isa. 48:21).

According to some scholars these were not two different places but two different traditions (JE in Ex. 17; P in Nu. 20) about one place. *See* MASSA AND MERIBAH.

N. J. O.

**MERIBATH-KADESH** mer'ə-bəth-kā'dəsh [Heb. *m^e^rîḇaṯ-qāḏēš*–'strife of Kadesh'] (Dt. 32:51; Ezk. 47:19; 48:28); AV MERIBAH-KADESH, STRIFE IN KADESH; NEB MERIBAH-BY-KADESH. The southern border of the restored land of Israel in Ezekiel's vision. *See* MERIBAH; KADESH **1.**

In Dt. 33:2 some scholars have emended the MT slightly so that it reads *mimriḇaṯ qāḏēš,* "from Meribath-Kadesh" (so NAB; *BHS*) rather than *mēriḇ^e^ḇōṯ qōḏeš,* "from the ten thousands of holy ones." On this difficult text see A. D. H. Mayes, *Deuteronomy* (*NCBC,* repr. 1981), pp. 398f.; S. R. Driver, comm. on Deuteronomy (*ICC,* 3rd ed., repr. 1973), pp. 392f.; P. D. Miller, *Divine Warrior in Early Israel* (1973), pp. 75-81.

G. A. L.

**MERIB-BAAL** mer-ə-bā'əl [Heb. *m^e^rîḇ-ba'al* (1 Ch. 8:34; 9:40), *m^e^rî-ḇa'al* (9:40)]. The original name of MEPHIBOSHETH (**2**) the grandson of Saul. The name appears in two forms in 9:40. Some commentators have conjectured that *m^e^rî-ḇa'al* ("hero of Baal") was the original form, later changed to *m^e^rîḇ ba'al* ("Baal contends" or "contender with Baal"). The substitution of *bōšeṯ* ("shame") for *ba'al* ("lord") in the later form "Mephibosheth" reflects a reluctance to use a name by which a Canaanite deity was honored. For other examples of this substitution, cf. Jer. 3:24; Hos. 9:10; *see also* ISHBOSHETH; JERUBBESHETH.

N. J. O.

**MERNEPTAH** mer-nep'tə [Egyp. *mr-n-ptḥ*–'the beloved of Ptaḥ']. A pharaoh of the 19th Dynasty (*ca.* 1224-1214 B.C.); thirteenth son and successor of Ramses II (*ca.* 1290-1224). Merneptah inscribed a series of victory hymns on a black granite stele, the so-called Israel Stele (first published by W. M. F. Petrie, *Six Temples at Thebes* [1897], plates XIII-XIV; see also *ANET,* pp. 376-78; *DOTT,* pp. 137-141). The monument was discovered by Petrie in 1895 in the ruins of Merneptah's mortuary temple at Thebes. A fragmentary duplicate also exists in the temple of Karnak.

Among Merneptah's conquests in Syria-Palestine is *Ysr'r* (Egyptian for *Yśr'l*), clearly recognizable as "Israel." *See* ARCHEOLOGY OF EGYPT IV.D; ISRAEL II. Thus the Israel Stele provides a *terminus ad quem* for the presence of the Israelites in Palestine (*ca.* 1220 B.C.). (On the efforts of some scholars to deny a Palestinian campaign to Merneptah, see K. Kitchen, *Ancient Orient and OT* [1966], pp. 59f.) Neither Merneptah nor this event is mentioned in the OT.

A few scholars have viewed the Israel Stele as bearing

Granite statue of Merneptah wearing the royal *nemes* headdress. From Thebes (Cairo Museum; picture courtesy of The Metropolitan Museum of Art)

witness to the Exodus event. Merneptah is thus considered to be the pharaoh of the Exodus and Ramses II, his father, is identified as the pharaoh of the oppression (P. Montet, *Le Drame d'Avaris* [1940], p. 149; H. H. Rowley, *From Joseph to Joshua* [1950], p. 137ff.). But *see* EXODUS, DATE OF THE.

*See also* EGYPT VIII.G. G. PRATICO

**MERODACH** mer'ə-däk. *See* MARDUK, MERODACH; MERODACH-BALADAN.

**MERODACH-BALADAN** mer'ə-dak-bal'ə-dən [Heb. *m*$^e$*rō-ḏaḵ bal'*$^a$*ḏān* (Isa. 39:1), *b*$^e$*rō'ḏaḵ bal'*$^a$*ḏān* (2 K. 20:12); Gk. *Marōdachbaladan*]; AV also Berodach-baladan (2 K. 20:12). The king of Babylon who sent envoys to congratulate Hezekiah on his recovery from illness. Hezekiah "welcomed them," showing them all the assets of his kingdom (Isa. 39:2), for which he earned a stinging rebuke from Isaiah, together with a prophecy that the wealth and even some of the king's sons would be carried off to Babylon (vv. 6f.).

Merodach-baladan II, whose name in Assyrian is written Marduk-apla-iddina, "Marduk has given an heir," claimed descent from Erība-Marduk, a king of the 8th Babylonian dynasty; Sargon called him "seed of a murderer" (*ARAB*, II, § 66), suggesting that he had descended from one who had gained the throne by assassinating the legitimate king. The biblical texts call him "son of Baladan," a name that obviously lacks the divine element. Merodach-baladan's patronymic, according to Sargon, was "son of Yakini," most likely meaning that he was a member of the Yakin tribe. He is also called "King of Kaldu" (*ARAB*, II, § 31). The Kaldu (Chaldeans) were a people that occupied the "Sea-Land" region, i.e., lower Babylonia, and were divided into five tribal groups: Bīt-Dakkūri, who were located along the Euphrates S of Borsippa; Bīt-Sa'alli, their neighbors; Bīt-Amukkani, who occupied the southernmost part of the country; Bīt-Šilani, who by the time of Sargon had been assimilated by the Bīt-Amukkani; and Bīt-Yakin, who lived along the Tigris and were bordered on the north and east by Aramean tribes. The largest tribes were Bīt-Dakkūri and Bīt-Amukkani, which were composed of subtribes, Bīt-Adini belonging to Bīt-Amukkani.

Tiglath-pileser III (747-727 B.C.) in the Nimrud Tablet recorded that when he invaded Babylonia in his seventeenth year (731), Merodach-baladan, who had previously not submitted to Assyrian kings, "came to the city of Sapia, into my presence, and kissed my feet." The Assyrian king also recorded the huge tribute paid by Merodach-baladan (*ARAB*, I, § 794). The silence of the records suggests that Merodach-baladan was permitted to maintain only a limited kingship over his people during the reign of Shalmaneser V (727-722). When Sargon II (722-705) acceded to the Assyrian throne, however, Merodach-baladan apparently seized the throne of Babylon, where he reigned for the next twelve years. Various references to his allies allow the situation to be reconstructed as follows: Merodach-baladan gradually won the loyalty of the other tribes of the Kaldu; next he gained the support of the Aramean tribes; finally he made an alliance with Ḫumbanigaš king of Elam. He "took the hands of Bel," symbolizing his claim to Babylon, at the New Year Festival in 721.

Sargon engaged Merodach-baladan's allies in battle near the city of Dēr in 720 (*ARAB*, II, § 55), but the Chaldean arrived late, when the Elamites and the Assyrians were well spent. All parties claimed victory, but the Chaldean king continued to reign (cf. G. Roux, *Ancient Iraq* [1964], p. 258). In 717 Ḫumbanigaš I died and was succeeded by his son Šutur-nuḫundu. In his twelfth year (710) Sargon marched on the tribes in the lower parts of Babylonia, and Merodach-baladan fled to the marshes of the Persian Gulf. Sargon conquered Dūr-Yakin, the royal city, and brought all of Bīt-Yakin under his sway (*ARAB*, II, § 69). Then he entered Babylon and grasped the hands of Marduk, making the pilgrimage to "the House of the New Year's Feast" (II, § 70). Sargon seems to have allowed Merodach-baladan to continue as a tribal sheikh in Bīt-Yakin.

Upon the death of Sargon, Merodach-baladan again asserted his desire to rule Babylon. It was most likely during the turmoil, which was usual at any change of rulers, that Merodach-baladan managed to get envoys through to Jerusalem (2 K. 20:12). There is little doubt that he also attempted to incite his former allies to rebel against Assyria. A complication occurred, however, when the people of Babylon installed Marduk-zākir-šumi II as king (703). Sennacherib (705-681) acted swiftly, reporting that in his first campaign (702) he "accomplished the defeat of Merodach-baladan, king of Babylonia, together with the army of Elam, his ally, in the plain of Kish" (*ARAB*, II, § 234). The Chaldean saved his life but lost everything else.

Sennacherib placed Bēl-ibni on the throne of Babylon, but his claim of total victory over the entire region seems to have been somewhat exaggerated, for in his fourth campaign (701) he again moved against Bīt-Yakin. Bēl-ibni had revolted, and Merodach-baladan probably had a hand in this event. Sennacherib conquered the region and placed Aššur-nadin-šumi on the throne in Babylon. According to Sennacherib's account Merodach-baladan "gathered together the gods of his whole land in their shrines, and loaded them into ships and fled like a bird to the city of Nagite-riqqi, which is in the midst of the sea" (II, § 242)—actually in Elam—"and in that place he died" (II, § 345).

The peoples of lower Mesopotamia continued to give Assyria trouble, and Sennacherib at last mounted a sea invasion of coastal regions (693). Since various inscriptions name sons of Merodach-baladan but not the father, we conclude that he died prior to this campaign. Of his son Nabû-šum-iškun Sennacherib said, "My hands took [him] alive" (II, § 338). Another son, Nabû-zēr-kitti-līšir, trusted in the king of Elam but "failed to save himself" (II, § 534). A third son, Nā'id-Marduk, seeing what happened to the others, fled and "came to Nineveh," where he kissed Sennacherib's feet in submission (II, § 534). Another son (?) is mentioned, Adinu "son of the wife of Merodach-baladan" (II, § 259). Esarhaddon named a grandson of Merodach-baladan, Nabû-bēl-šumāti, and also his "twin brother" (?), Nabû-kātā-sabat (II, § 815).

The annals of Sargon and Sennacherib, with their many references to Merodach-baladan and boasts of conquests over him, his city, his people, and his allies, give the impression that he was indeed a very powerful king. We can well understand how Hezekiah could have been greatly impressed by stories that Merodach-baladan's emissaries must have told.

***Bibliography.***–*CAH,* III (1925), 32-87; *ARAB,* II, *passim*; J. A. Brinkman, "Merodach-Baladan II," in *Studies Presented to A. L. Oppenheim* (1964), pp. 6-53.

W. S. LASOR

**MEROM, WATERS OF** mir'əm [Heb. *mê mērôm*–'waters of Merom'; LXX *epí toú hýdatos Marrōn* (Josh. 11:5), *epí tó hýdōr Marrōn* (v. 7)]. The location of the alliance of kings with Jabin of Hazor and the subsequent battle with Joshua (Josh. 11:1-9). Since the Middle Ages the waters of Merom have been identified with Lake Huleh (*Baḥret el-Ḥûleh*), a small lake about 22.5 km. (14 mi.) N of the Sea of Galilee (cf. *GP,* I, 493). Prior to the middle of the 20th cent. this region was a swamp, which was drained by the State of Israel and is now known as the Huleh basin. But careful study of the passage in Joshua makes this location unlikely. (1) The alliance had "very many horses and chariots" (11:4), and the Huleh basin was probably too marshy for such troops. (2) More important, the scattered forces, suffering defeat by Joshua, seem to have gone in two directions: some to "Great Sidon and Misrephoth-maim," which is westward toward the coastal plain and then northward toward Sidon; and others "eastward as far as the valley of Mizpeh" (v. 8), which is "under Hermon" (v. 3), possibly in the vicinity of Bâniyâs (Caesarea Philippi). These data suggest a location between the Huleh basin and the coast rather than in the Huleh basin, so that the forces of Joshua, most likely coming from the south (cf. 10:43), split the allied armies, driving some to the east and some to the west.

Although he recognized that the Huleh location was not without difficulties and furthermore identified Merom with Meirôn at the foot of Jebel Jarmāq (*GP,* II, 285), Abel hinted that the Huleh basin may be the intended gathering point of waters from the heights of Kadesh, Marûn er-Râs, and Meirôn (*GP,* I, 494), and he described Joshua's campaign in this region in some detail (*RB,* 56 [1949], 335ff.). The argument sometimes suggested (cf. *HDB,* III, 348) that Jonathan was basing his campaign against Demetrius on Joshua's example (1 Macc. 11:67) has little if any worth, for "the waters of Gennesaret" can hardly be equated with "the waters of Merom."

Rejecting Huleh as the possible site, some scholars have proffered other suggestions. On the basis of the occurrence of *m-r-m-ì-m* in the list of Thutmose III (*LBHG,* rev., p. 181; *ANET,* p. 243 no. 85), *m-r-m* in a list of Ramses II (*ANET,* p. 256), and *marum* in an inscription of Tiglath-pileser III (*ARAB,* I, § 779 [p. 280]), attempts have been made to locate Merom, generally at Meirôn (Har Mêrôn, see below), but with no certain consensus. Garstang gave a vivid picture of the battle and rout of the allies of Jabin, preferring the location at Jebel Marûn (elevation 930 m. [3050 ft.]) and the village of Marûn er-Râs (*Joshua-Judges,* pp. 183-198, esp. 193f.). Simons accepted this identification (*GTTOT,* § 505), pointing out that it has an abundant water supply. Aharoni agreed that the location is more suitable to the account in Joshua and that the name has probably been preserved in these sites (*LBHG,* rev., p. 225); he was inclined, however, to locate Merom at Tell el-Khirbeh, "one of the large Canaanite tells" in Upper Galilee (p. 226). Jebel Marûm and Marûn er-Râs are located 2 km. (1¼ mi.) N of the modern frontier between Israel and Lebanon, 11 km. (6 mi.) S of Tibnine, 16 km. (10 mi.) NNW of Safed (Ṣfat), and about the same distance W of the Huleh basin.

Noth, however, preferred Meirôn (Meirun) on the slopes of Jebel Jarmāq (Har Mêrôn, elevation 1208 m. [3962 ft.]), located 6 km. (4 mi.) WNW of Safed (*Das Buch Josua* [2nd ed., *HAT,* 1953], p. 67; *OT World* [Eng. tr. 1966], p. 54). This location, which is about 19 km. (11 mi.) SW of the Huleh basin, has been accepted by many other scholars (cf. *Macmillan Bible Atlas* [rev. ed. 1977], Map 62), although the terrain is less well suited to horses and chariots than the region around Marûn er-Râs. It is true that the region around Meirôn would have fitted with Joshua's tactics, but one must question why the Canaanite kings, who arrived first at the scene (vv. 5-7), would have let Joshua trap their cavalry in such a difficult situation. On the other hand, Meirôn is located near the junction of a road from the south with a main east-west road that would allow for the surprise attack of Joshua and the flight of the defeated armies as described in 11:8.

There are other, less likely suggestions. Conder and Kitchener (*SWP,* I, 251ff.) proposed Wâdī el-Melek (Shimron-merom [cf. Josh. 12:20], modern Šammûmiye, 8 km. [5 mi.] W of Nazareth); this identification depends on the equation of Shimron (11:1) with Shimʿôn (cf. LXX *Symoōn,* 12:20) and with Shimron-merom (12:20; cf. *LBHG,* rev., p. 118). The location seems to be too far south to fit the account (cf. 11:10), and depends in part for support on attempts to conflate the records in Josh. 11 and Jgs. 5. Madon (Khirbet Madîn, 1 km. [2/3 mi.] S of the Horns of Ḥattin) depends on efforts to equate Madon with Maron (MT *Māḏôn,* Josh. 11:1; 12:19; LXX B *Marrōn* but A *Madōn* in 11:1) and the similarity in sound of Madon and Madîn. The same objection based on location applies equally to Šammûniye and Khirbet Madîn. Quite impossible is the location of the site of the conflict in the vicinity of Dothan, 12 Roman m. (18 km., 11 mi.) from Sebaste in Samaria (*Onom.* p. 129, Latin text *apud* Abel, *GP,* I, 494 n. 2).

In an account that seems to be largely imaginary and certainly without biblical basis, Josephus has Joshua making a five-day forced march against the coalition that numbered 300,000 men-at-arms, 10,000 horsemen, and 20,000 chariots. He engaged them at Berothē, "a city of Upper Galilee, not far from Kedese" (*Ant.* v.1.18 [63]). Kedese is Kedesh in Naphtali (Jgs. 4:6), identified with Tell Qades, about 10 km. (6 mi.) NW of the Huleh basin, which would be an acceptable location but without support since there is no indication of Josephus's source.

Positive identification of the site is not possible.

W. S. LASOR

**MERONOTHITE** mə-ron'ə-thīt [Heb. *mērōnōṯî*]. The designation of two persons in the OT: Jehdeiah, who was in charge of King David's asses (1 Ch. 27:30), and Jadon, who was among those who repaired the wall under Nehemiah (Neh. 3:7). Meronoth seems to have been near Gibeah, but its precise location is unknown.

**MEROZ** mē'roz, mer'əz [Heb. *mērôz*]. A village placed under a curse in the Song of Deborah (Jgs. 5:23) for failing to aid the armies of the Lord in the battle against Jabin king of Canaan. The poet used the reprehensible inactivity of this people to set the heroic intervention of Jael in bold relief. It is generally supposed that the forces of Jabin fled past Meroz, an Israelite village, and that the inhabitants, who were in a position to block his path of retreat, were prevented by cowardice. Alt, however, presents the theory that the inhabitants were Canaanites, one of the many non-Israelite peoples who were incorporated into the tribe of Manasseh. In this conflict they remained neutral because their sympathies were with the enemy, and as a consequence their relationship with Israel was severed by the curse (A. Alt, *ZAW*, 58 [1940/41], 244-47).

No attempt to locate the site has been conclusive, but many favor the suggestion of Abel (*GP*, II, 385) that Meroz is to be identified with Khirbet Mārûs a few kilometers SW of Lake Huleh. D. H. MADVIG

**MERRAN** mer'ən [Gk. *Merran*] (Bar. 3:23); AV MERAN. A place name that seems unidentifiable as it stands. Probably the name is the result of a transcription error in the Hebrew original by which ד (*d*) was read as ר (*r*). If so, the correct reading would be *Meddan*, probably meaning MIDIAN (cf. Gen. 37:36). See *APOT*, I, 589.

**MERRY** [Heb. *ṭôḇ*–'good' (adjective), *yāṭaḇ* (vb.)] (Jgs. 16:25; 19:6, 9, 22; Ruth 3:7; 1 S. 25:36; 2 S. 13:28; Est. 1:10; Eccl. 9:7); NEB also ENJOY YOURSELF, "feel at peace with the world" (Ruth 3:7), CHEERFUL; **MAKE MERRY** [Heb. piel of *śāḥaq*–'dance,' 'play'] (1 S. 18:7; 2 S. 6:5, 21; 1 Ch. 13:8; 15:29; Jer. 30:19); AV also PLAY; NEB also DANCE; [*šāḵar*–'become drunk'] (Gen. 43:34); [*śāmaḥ*–'rejoice'] (Jer. 31:13); NEB REJOICE; [Gk. *euphraínomai*–'be glad'] (Lk. 12:19; 15:23f., 29, 32; Rev. 11:10); NEB also ENJOY, CELEBRATE, FESTIVITIES, FEAST; **MERRY-HEARTED** [Heb. *śāmē(a)ḥ lēḇ*] (Isa. 24:7); NEB REVELLERS; **MERRYMAKERS** [Heb. piel of *śāḥaq*] (Jer. 15:17; 31:4); AV also MOCKERS; NEB ROISTERERS; MERRY THRONG.

In the RSV "merry," "make merry," etc. are used most often in contexts of eating and drinking. WINE was an important part of any festive occasion; although the lightheartedness it induces was not viewed as evil in itself (Eccl. 9:7; cf. Gen. 43:34; Jgs. 19:6, 9, 22; Ruth 3:7; Lk. 15:23-32), the dangerous consequences of excessive drinking were well known: imprudent behavior (e.g., Est. 1:10-12) and blindness to danger, resulting sometimes in death (e.g., Jgs. 16:25-30; 1 S. 25:36-38; 2 S. 13:28f.; cf. Lk. 12:16-20). *See also* DRUNKENNESS.

Where it renders the piel of *śāḥaq*, "make merry" is associated not so much with drinking as with the dancing that was also an important part of festive occasions, especially victory celebrations. In times of estrangement from Yahweh conviviality was not appropriate; thus Jeremiah could not participate in the merrymaking of his time (Jer. 15:17), but he prophesied a day of victory when it would be appropriate again (31:4; cf. Eccl. 3:4).

*See also* MIRTH. N. J. O.

**MERUTH** mer'əth (1 Esd. 5:24, AV). *See* IMMER **1.**

**MESALOTH** mes'ə-loth [Gk. *Maisalōth, Messalōth*]; AV MASALOTH; NEB MESSALOTH. A place where the army led by Bacchides and Alcimus encamped on the march to Judah (1 Macc. 9:2). The passage includes the words "by the road which leads to Gilgal," which may be somewhat misleading. Mesaloth is "in Arbela" (*see* ARBELA **2**), which has been identified with Khirbet Irbid on the Wâdī el-Hamam in Galilee, 4 km. (2.5 mi.) W of the Sea of Galilee. Simons suggested that "Gilgal" is a scribal error for "Galilee" (*GTTOT*, §§ 1127f.), a reading that accords with Josephus (*Ant.* xii.11.1 [421]). "Gilgal" and "Galilee" are apparently confused in Josh. 12:23, where the MT reads *gilgāl* and the LXX *Galilaias*, and in 22:10, where the MT reads *gᵉlîlôṯ* and the LXX *Galgala*. Simons, however, further suggested that the LXX *Massaloth* is a transcription of Heb. *mᵉsillôṯ*, "highways, raised roads," and refers to the raised banks of the Wâdī el-Hamam (*GTTOT*, §§ 1147f.). But the spellings of the Greek word in both cases do not confirm this theory. W. S. L. S.

**MESECH** mē'sək. *See* MESHECH.

**MESHA** mē'shə.

**1.** [Heb. *mêšā'*] (1 Ch. 8:9). A Benjaminite, son of Shaharaim by his wife Hodesh, born in the country of Moab (v. 8).

**2.** (AV, NEB, RSV mg., 1 Ch. 2:42). *See* MARESHAH **1.**

**3.** [Heb. *mêšâ*–'salvation'(?); Gk. *Mōsa*]. A king of Moab and son of Chemosh-melek. All the biblical information regarding this monarch is contained in 2 K. 3, which describes him as a contemporary of Ahab, Ahaziah, and Jehoram. As Moab was at this time under Israelite control, Mesha was tributary to Israel. His annual contribution probably comprised the wool sheared from 100,000 lambs and 100,000 rams. The breed of animals that he raised was renowned for the superior quality of its fleece. Some have regarded the description of Mesha as a *nōqēḏ* ("sheep breeder," v. 4) with suspicion. Thus M. Bič (*VT*, 1 [1951], 293-96), followed by J. Gray (*I & II Kings* [*OTL*, rev. ed. 1970], pp. 484f.), translated *nōqēḏ* as "hepatoscoper," i.e., one who reads livers to get omens. But A. Murtonen (*VT*, 2 [1952], 170f.) and S. Segert ("Zur Bedeutung des Wortes *nōqēḏ*," in B. Hartmann, *et al.*, eds., *Hebräische Wortforschung* [*SVT*, 16; 1967], pp. 279-283) pointed out the weaknesses of this theory and reasserted the traditional meaning of sheep breeder (cf. also P. Craigie, *Studies in Religion*, 11 [1982], 29-33; *Ugarit and the OT* [1983], pp. 71-74, 108).

After the death of Ahab, Mesha asserted his independence. The kings of Judah (Jehoshaphat) and Edom joined forces with Jehoram king of Israel in an attempt to quell the rebellion. Together they marched through the wilderness of Edom to approach Moab from the south. When they were about to perish of thirst, water was miraculously provided through Elisha. Mesha came out against them, but his attack was repulsed with heavy slaughter and he was pursued by the allies to the great fortress of Kir-hareseth. Thwarted in his attempt to escape the besieged city, Mesha in desperation offered his eldest son as a sacrifice to Chemosh upon the city wall (see A. Green, *Role of Human Sacrifice in the Ancient Near East* [1975], pp. 169-171; *see also* SACRIFICE, HUMAN). This act apparently terrified the Israelites (so W. F. Albright, *ARI*, p. 158), and they withdrew, leaving their conquest incomplete.

Mesha's description of his rebellion is preserved on the MOABITE STONE, an inscription in which he names the places he captured and fortified during the reign of Omri's "son" after forty years of Israelite subjugation. Not surprisingly, Mesha's inscription does not mention his reverses at the hands of Jehoram of Israel and his allies. The date of the rebellion is uncertain. If it began forty years after the vigorous Israelite king Omri (*ca.* 884-873 B.C.) subjugated Moabite territory, it would have occurred in the reign of Omri's grandson Ahaziah (*ca.* 853-852 B.C.) or great-grandson Jehoram (*ca.* 852-841 B.C.). Understanding *bnh* ("his son") to mean "his grandson" or "his descendant" is in complete accord with Semitic usage. It was evidently interpreted in this way by Josephus, who placed Mesha's uprising in the second year of Ahaziah (*Ant.* ix.2.1 [18-19]).

*Bibliography.*–N. Glueck, *Explorations in Eastern Palestine* (*AASOR,* 14, 1933/34), 82; A. D. Tushingham, *BASOR,* 133 (Feb. 1954), 25. W. EWING R. K. H.

**MESHA** mē'shə [Heb. *mēšā'*; Gk. *Massē*]. A boundary town of the land occupied by the sons of Joktan, a son of Shem, a son of Noah; it is listed in the TABLE OF NATIONS with SEPHAR (Gen. 10:30). The sons of Joktan were tribes of south Arabia, hence Mesha is probably not to be identified with MASSA in north Arabia (Gen. 25:14; 1 Ch. 1:30). According to one view the ethnic and geographical information in the Table was from the period of the Israelite monarchy and reflects conditions of that time (*LBHG,* rev. ed., p. 8). J. McKENNA

**MESHACH** mē'shak [Heb. *mêšak*]. The Babylonian name given to Daniel's companion in captivity, Mishael, by Nebuchadrezzar's chief official (Dnl. 1:7). Each of Daniel's three associates received a new name corresponding roughly to his Hebrew name. Mishael in Hebrew (*mîšā'ēl*) probably meant "Who is what God is?". Meshach appears to reflect an attested Babylonian name, *Mišaaku,* which probably meant "Who is what (the god) Aku is?".

Daniel's three associates, Shadrach, Meshach, and Abednego, are always mentioned together in the book of Daniel, and always in the same order (Dnl. 1:7; 2:49; 3:12-30). They, like Daniel, were young, attractive, noble-born, well-educated captives from Judah, taken prisoner in the first deportation (605 B.C.) and assigned to be trained to serve the Babylonian court (1:1-7). They showed loyalty to Israel's God Yahweh by such actions of faith as keeping the Mosaic food laws (vv. 8-16) and refusing to engage in idolatry (3:12-27), and thus won praise for their God as well as honor for themselves (3:28-30). D. STUART

**MESHECH** mē'shek [Heb. *mešek*; Gk. *Mosoch*]; AV also MESECH.

**1.** One of the sons (or descendants) of Japheth, named along with Gomer, Javan, Tubal, etc. (Gen. 10:2; 1 Ch. 1:5; *see* TABLE OF NATIONS). He founded a small but formidable kingdom in Asia Minor. Its people, who appear in classical Greek authors as the *Moschoi* and in Assyrian annals as the Muški, belonged to the Indo-European group of nations. They were associated with Javan and Tubal as trading partners with Tyre in bronze vessels and slaves (Ezk. 27:13). Excavations at Gordion in 1950 produced evidence that the Muški also traded extensively with Syria and Urartu as well as with Cilicia.

Perhaps because of trading opportunities with the Assyrians, or possibly as the result of aggression from their neighbors, the Muški migrated to an area of Armenia SE of the Black Sea, where from their mountain strongholds they engaged in sporadic battles with the Assyrians. The Muški suffered their first recorded defeat *ca.* 1100 B.C., when Tiglath-pileser I overcame five of their kings in Kutmuhi territory E of the Euphrates. Despite the tendency of Assyrian records to exaggerate victories, it appears that the Muški fared poorly on that occasion.

The Muški engaged in numerous battles with Assyria over the next three centuries, including skirmishes with Tukulti-Ninurta II and Ashurnasirpal II. The most important occurred during the reign of Sargon II (727-705 B.C.), who decided to conquer the Muški allies one by one. In 717 B.C. he subjugated Pisiris king of Carchemish and made him tributary. Two years later Sargon captured some cities of Cilicia (known as Que to the Assyrians) that had been held by Mita, a Muški ruler in Asia Minor. Then he began to consolidate and reinforce Assyrian power in the area, finally subjugating Mita in 709 B.C. Mita is probably the legendary King Midas of Greek tradition, who died *ca.* 695 B.C. While Midas was known to the Greeks as a Phrygian king, his cosmopolitan empire would undoubtedly have embraced the warlike Muški.

In Scripture Meshech is described as a barbaric and remote people (cf. Ps. 120:5-7). Ezekiel includes Meshech and Tubal among the peoples destined for the underworld (32:26). They are also associated with GOG (**2**), the ruler of MAGOG and leader of the northern hordes who are to fight a final battle against Israel in the messianic age (38:2f.; 39:1).

*Bibliography.*–*ARAB,* I, §§ 221, 276, 318; II, §§ 25-27, 42f., 96f.; S. Parpola, *Neo-Assyrian Toponyms* (1970), pp. 252f.; J. N. Postgate, *Iraq,* 35 (1973), 21-34. R. K. HARRISON

**2.** A son of Shem and founder of an Aramean people (1 Ch. 1:17). The name appears as MASH in Gen. 10:23.

**MESHELEMIAH** mə-shel-ə-mī'ə [Heb. *mᵉšelemyâ* (1 Ch. 9:21), *mᵉšelemyāhû* (26:1f., 9)–'Yahweh repays']. Son of Kore, a Korahite; a gatekeeper at the temple. The names Shelemiah (26:14), Shallum (9:17, 19, 31), and Meshullam (Neh. 12:25) may refer to the same person.

**MESHEZABEL** mə-shez'ə-bel [Heb. *mᵉšêzēbᵉ'ēl*–'God delivers']; AV MESHEZABEEL.

**1.** An ancestor of Meshullam, who helped to repair the wall of Jerusalem (Neh. 3:4).

**2.** One of the "chiefs of the people" who signed the covenant with Nehemiah (10:21).

**3.** A descendant of Judah through Zerah; father of Pethahiah (Neh. 11:24).

**MESHILLEMITH** mə-shil'ə-mith [Heb. *mᵉšillēmîṯ*] (1 Ch. 9:12); **MESHILLEMOTH** mə-shil'ə-moth [Heb. *mᵉšillēmôṯ*] (2 Ch. 28:12; Neh. 11:13).

**1.** A priest, son of Immer (1 Ch. 9:12; Neh. 11:13).

**2.** An Ephraimite ancestor of Berechiah, who was a chief of the tribe in the reign of Pekah (2 Ch. 28:12).

**MESHOBAB** mə-shō'bab [Heb. *mᵉšôḇāḇ*] (1 Ch. 4:34). A Simeonite "prince" whose clan settled in rich pasture land near Gerar (LXX; MT Gedor) after driving out its former inhabitants (vv. 39-41).

**MESHULLAM** mə-shoo͞'ləm [Heb. *mᵉšullām*–'restitution' (for a child who died); Gk. *Mesollam, Mosollam(os), Mesoulam, Masallam* (1 Ch. 9:8), *Ōlamos* (1 Esd. 9:30)]; AV Apoc. MOSOLLAMON, MOSOLLAM, OLAMUS; NEB Apoc. MOSOLLAMUS, OLAMUS.

**1.** Grandfather of Shaphan the secretary of King Josiah (2 K. 22:3).

**2.** A son of Zerubbabel (1 Ch. 3:19).

**3.** The head of a Gadite family that lived in Bashan (1 Ch. 5:13).

**4.** Son of Elpaal, a Benjaminite (1 Ch. 8:17).

**5.** Father of the Sallu who was one of the first Benjaminites to live in Jerusalem after the Exile (1 Ch. 9:7; Neh. 11:7).

**6.** Son of Shephatiah and one of the first Benjaminites to live in Jerusalem after the Exile (1 Ch. 9:8).

**7.** A priest, son of Zadok and father of Hilkiah (1 Ch. 9:11; Neh. 11:11).

**8.** Another priest, son of Meshillemith and father of Jahzerah (1 Ch. 9:12; the name is omitted in Neh. 11:13).

**9.** A Kohathite appointed by King Josiah as one of the overseers to direct the repairs of the temple (2 Ch. 34:12).

**10.** One of the "leading men" sent by Ezra to procure Levites to serve in the temple at Jerusalem (Ezr. 8:16; 1 Esd. 8:44).

**11.** A layman or Levite (some MSS read "the Levites") who opposed either Ezra's policy regarding the divorcing of foreign wives or the procedural change requested by the people (Ezr. 10:15; cf. 1 Esd. 9:14); possibly the same as **10** and **12.**

**12.** Son of Bani; a layman who had married a foreign wife and was required to divorce her (Ezr. 10:29; 1 Esd. 9:30); possibly the same as **10** and **11.**

**13.** Son of Berechiah; one who helped to repair the wall of Jerusalem (Neh. 3:4, 30). His daughter was married to Jehohanan the son of Tobiah the Ammonite (6:18).

**14.** Son of Besodeiah; one who helped to repair the Old Gate of Jerusalem after the Exile (Neh. 3:6).

**15.** One who stood at Ezra's left hand during the reading of the law (Neh. 8:4; omitted in 1 Esd. 9:44); possibly the same as one or more persons mentioned above.

**16.** A priest who signed the covenant with Nehemiah (Neh. 10:7 [MT 8]).

**17.** A "chief of the people" who signed the covenant with Nehemiah (10:20 [MT 21]).

**18, 19.** The heads of two priestly families in the time of Joiakim the high priest (Neh. 12:13, 16).

**20.** A gatekeeper at the storehouses of the gates in the time of Joiakim, Nehemiah, and Ezra (Neh. 12:25). *See also* MESHELEMIAH.

**21.** One of those who took part in the procession at the dedication of the rebuilt walls of Jerusalem (Neh. 12:33); possibly the same as one or more persons mentioned above.

See *IP,* p. 174. J. A. LEES N. J. O.

**MESHULLEMETH** mə-sho͞o'lə-meth [Heb. *m^e^šullemeṯ*–'restitution' (fem. of Meshullam)] (2 K. 21:19). Wife of King Manasseh; mother of Amon; daughter of Haruz of Jotbah.

**MESOBAITE** mə-sō'bə-īt (1 Ch. 11:47, AV). *See* MEZOBAITE.

**MESOPOTAMIA** mes-ə-pə-tā'mē-ə. The Greek equivalent (lit. "between the rivers") of the Heb. *'^a^ram nah^a^rayim* ("Aram of two rivers"). The Greek historian Polybius (2nd cent. B.C.) and the geographer Strabo (1st cent. A.D.) used the term to define the area enclosed between the Euphrates and the Tigris rigers. This agrees with its use in the LXX in Gen. 24:10, which includes the city of Haran, and Dt. 23:4 (MT, LXX, 5), which mentions Pethor, the home of Balaam son of Beor. The AV and RSV use Mesopotamia also in Jgs. 3:8, 10 to designate the land ruled by Cushanrishathaim, and in 1 Ch. 19:6 for the area from which the Ammonites hired mercenaries to fight against Israel. Many modern texts (e.g., NAB, NEB, and NIV) transliterate the Hebrew as Aram-naharaim in Gen. 24:10; Dt. 23:4 (NAB 5); Jgs. 3:8, 10; and 1 Ch. 19:6. All the English translations use Aram-naharaim in the title of Ps. 60 (except NEB, which omits all titles).

Mesopotamia is used in Acts 7:2 to designate the home of Abraham before he lived in Haran. The inclusion of "the residents from Mesopotamia" with Parthians, Medes, and Elamites (Acts 2:9) probably indicates the Jews of the Diaspora from Babylonia. If so, this would extend the use of Mesopotamia to include the whole Tigris-Euphrates valley, i.e., from the Persian Gulf to the eastern part of modern Turkey. This would conform to its use by Greek and Roman authors after the 4th cent. B.C.

The term Mesopotamia is ambiguous. To some it means the "region between and around the Euphrates and Tigris from the Persian Gulf to Mosul; to others, at home in the classics, it implies an area at the north-west end of this" (Saggs, p. 3). The OT use seems to be the latter. If the original home of Abraham was Ur of Sumer, then Mesopotamia would include Sumer and Akkad (*see* ASSYRIA; BABYLONIA; SUMER; SYRIAN).

***Bibliography.***–J. J. Finkelstein, *JNES,* 21 (1962), 73-92; M. A. Beek, *Atlas of Mesopotamia* (1962); H. W. F. Saggs, *The Greatness that was Babylon* (1962); J. Oates, *Babylon* (1979).

R. E. HAYDEN

**MESSALOTH** mes'ə-loth. *See* MESALOTH.

**MESSENGER** [Heb. *mal'āḵ*]; AV also ANGEL (Ps. 104:4; Eccl. 5:6 [MT 5]); NEB also MAN, ANGEL OF GOD (Eccl. 5:6), ENVOYS, DEPUTATION, MISSION, MESSAGE, SERVANTS, PARTY, EMBASSY, etc.; [part. of *nāgaḏ*] (2 S. 15:13; Jer. 51:31); NEB also NEWS; [*ṣîr*] (Prov. 25:13; Jer. 49:14; Ob. 1:1); AV also AMBASSADOR; NEB also HERALD; [*rāgal*] ("secret messengers," 2 S. 15:10); AV SPIES; NEB RUNNERS; [Gk. *ángelos*] (Mt. 11:10; Mk. 1:2; Lk. 7:24, 27; 9:52; 2 Cor. 12:7; Jas. 2:25); NEB also HERALD; [*apóstolos*] (Phil. 2:25; 2 Cor. 8:23); NEB DELEGATES, etc.

In 1 S. 31:9 (and par. 1 Ch. 10:9) the RSV and the NEB supply "messengers," although the AV does not; in these difficult passages the head or armor of Saul could also have been sent among the Philistines (cf. the *autá* used in the LXX of 1 S. 31:9; see S. R. Driver, *Notes on the Hebrew Text and Topography of the Books of Samuel* [2nd ed. 1913], pp. 229f.). In Isa. 23:2 the RSV uses "messengers" and the NEB "agents" (both reading *mal'āḵāw* for MT *mil'ûḵ*; cf. 1 QIs[a], *mal'āḵayiḵ*) in an attempt to correct and clarify a difficult passage; the AV follows the MT literally. In Nah. 2:13 (MT 14) both the RSV and AV read "messengers" for *mal'āḵ,* following the MT, while the NEB suggests as a correction "feeding" (*ma'^a^ḵōlēḵ*). In Eccl.

5:6 the AV translates *mal'āk̲* as "angel" (NEB "angel of God"; cf. the Targ.); the LXX (followed by Pesh.) reads *theós*, "God" (on the tasks of the angels serving God, cf. Tob. 12:12-22; Acts 10:4). As noted above, the RSV twice renders *apóstolos* as "messenger," i.e., a delegate sent out for some service (*see also* APOSTLE).

Runners and messengers of various sorts were crucial to ancient Near Eastern societies, for they provided a vital link between parties wishing to communicate. Runners carried messages from Jacob to Esau (Gen. 32:3-5); from Moses to the king of Edom (Nu. 20:14-17); from Gideon to Ephraim, to gather soldiers (Jgs. 7:24); between Jephthah and the king of the Ammonites (Jgs. 11:12-28); between David and Joab (2 S. 11:18-25); from Queen Jezebel to Elijah (1 K. 19:2); between King Benhadad and King Ahab (1 K. 20:1-12); from King Sennacherib to King Hezekiah (2 K. 19:9-14; Isa. 37:9-14); to Job with words of the calamities (Job 1:13-19); etc. Furthermore, Heb. *mal'āk̲*, by far the most common term translated as "messenger," also denotes those who spied and explored for Joshua (Josh. 6:17, 25; cf. Jas. 2:25), retrieved Achan's booty (Josh. 7:22), watched and attempted to capture David for Saul (1 S. 19:11-21), functioned as an embassy from King Hiram to King David (2 S. 5:11; 1 Ch. 14:1), and consulted Baalzebul god of Ekron for King Ahaziah (2 K. 1), etc.

Prophets, too, are messengers of God, sent from God with a divine word for humanity (cf. Isa. 44:26 and particularly Hag. 1:13, where the prophet is termed "the messenger of the Lord"; cf. also 2 Ch. 36:15f. for a summation of how God sent His prophetic messengers and His words and was angry when the people rejected them). Mal. 2:7 calls the priest "the messenger of the Lord of hosts," and 3:1 promises God's coming messenger, later to be identified with John the Baptist (cf. Mt. 11:10; Mk. 1:2; Lk. 7:27). (*See* MALACHI.)

Angels are heavenly messengers. In Ps. 104:4 the AV translates *mal'āk̲* (LXX *ángelos*) as "angels," though it seems more likely that winds are here being described as the cosmic "messengers" of God (cf. the RSV and NEB). Again, though the RSV, AV, and NEB all translate *ángelos* in 2 Cor. 12:7 as "messenger," thus terming Paul's thorn in the flesh "a messenger of Satan," this "messenger of Satan" may denote a real or symbolic angel. Thus, both *mal'āk̲* and *ángelos* can designate either an earthly or a heavenly messenger (i.e., an angel).

*See also* ANGEL. M. W. MEYER

**MESSIAH.**

I. Usage of the Term
II. OT
  A. Anointing
  B. Oriental Kingship Ideology
  C. Eschatology
III. Intertestamental Literature
IV. NT
  A. Messianic Titles
  B. Jesus' Self-understanding
  C. Experience of the Early Church
  D. Proof from Scripture

***I. Usage of the Term.***–"Messiah" is the current English equivalent of Lat. *messias*, derived from Gk. *messías*. In the NT that term is found only in Jn. 1:41; 4:25. It is the transliteration of Heb. *māšî(a)ḥ* and the corresponding Aram. *mašîḥā'*. Both terms are verbal adjectives or nouns derived from the root *mšḥ*, which means "touch lightly" or "rub with oil" and hence "anoint." In the OT *māšî(a)ḥ* is an honorific title given particularly to the high priest and the king. Occasionally, however, it refers to the patriarchs (Ps. 105:15), to a prophet (1 K. 19:15), to the Servant of the Lord (Isa. 61:1), or to the cherub appointed for the protection of Israel (Ezk. 28:14). In Hab. 3:13 the term probably applies to the chosen people.

Rabbinic literature uses the expression as a proper name and hence without article, as also in Jn. 4:25, whereas in English usage the articular form is common. The LXX and NT do not as a rule transliterate the Semitic term but rather prefer the Greek translation *ho christós*. In the few places where the Vulgate preserved the transliteration, Wyclif and the other early Protestant translators of the Bible adopted the Latin form *messias*. The Geneva Bible (1557-1560) introduced the transliteration *Messiah*, and the popularity of that version accounts for English writers preferring the form. The AV somewhat inconsistently adopted the form "Messias" in John and "Messiah" in Dnl. 9:25f. The RV and all subsequent English translations espoused the form "messiah" in John, reflecting the common theological usage, but translated Heb. *māšî(a)ḥ* in the OT, including Daniel, as "anointed."

***II. OT.–A. Anointing.*** From early antiquity the use of olive oil was common in the eastern Mediterranean area. The OT reports two of its applications, one practical and the other ritual. The practical use was mainly cosmetic: people anointed their faces and hair when going to a feast (e.g., Ruth 3:3; 2 Ch. 28:15), and hosts anointed their guests as a sign of welcome (e.g., Ps. 23:5).

Equally common in the Near East was ritual unction with oil, a practice based upon the belief that oil of olives has special properties of healing and preservation. Ritual unction was thought to extend the oil's efficacy both to objects and to persons. Thus the tabernacle (Ex. 40:9) and the altar (29:36; cf. v. 29; 40:10) were anointed to make them fit for religious purposes. In order to officiate validly, the priests, too, had to be anointed (e.g., Lev. 4:3, 5, 16; 6:15, 20; Nu. 3:3). Underlying this rite was the belief that ordinary things and persons lack "power" to serve the ends of the deity and are unfit to render its presence effective.

Ritual anointing, unlike cosmetic anointing, had to be done by a person endowed with special authority in order for the "power" to be conferred to objects or persons. Thus Moses was commissioned to anoint Aaron as high priest (Ex. 28:41; 29:7; 30:30; 40:13); Aaron in turn was to anoint his successor as well as the "lower" priesthood. Similarly, when Israel adopted the monarchic system, those with political authority would anoint the incumbent of the throne; for instance, the "men of Judah" (2 S. 2:4) and the elders of the tribes (5:1-3) anointed David. The mention of Samuel as well (1 S. 16:13) indicates differing views concerning the seat of political authority in ancient Israel.

The designation "the anointed one" originated from the anointing of the king. Appellations like "Yahweh's anointed one" or "my anointed one" in preexilic Psalms (e.g., Ps. 2:2; 18:50 [MT 51]; 20:6 [MT 7]; 28:8; 45:7 [MT 8]; 84:9 [MT 10]; 105:15) show that the title went back to the days of the monarchy and cannot be considered a late Jewish reinterpretation of the royal office. It is true, however, that exilic and postexilic use of the term "messiah" is generally metaphorical. When in Isa. 61:1 the prophet calls himself anointed, when in a vision Zechariah saw Zerubbabel as God's anointed one (Zec. 4:1-14), or when in the Dead Sea Scrolls prophets are designated as anointed ones (1QM 11:7; CD 2:12), the title no longer refers to the original rite. The term's metamorphosis cannot be understood as a historical change in the interpretation of the religious rite of anointing. Its explanation must be found in two new factors: Israel's adoption of the oriental kingship ideology, and the rise of eschatological hopes. Among many others, Volz, Engnell, A. Bentzen, S. Mowinckel, and S. H. Hooke, have greatly contributed to the elucidation of that development.

*B. Oriental Kingship Ideology*. The so-called royal Psalms (esp. Pss. 2, 18, 20–22, 89, 101, 139) entertain the view that the king's authority derives from God Himself rather than from those who appointed him. In the light of Ugaritic and Mesopotamian documents there is considerable evidence that those Psalms were connected with the New Year Festival, which commemorated God's rejuvenating not only nature but also His people. By manifesting His renewing power God was, as it were, reascending to His throne after defeating the forces of destruction (e.g., Tiâmat, Behemoth, or Leviathan). In this connection, the king would be regarded as God's representative on earth, whom God Himself anointed. Even if this kingship ideology is rooted in a myth of primeval man, as Reitzenstein, Schaeder, and Bentzen contended, the Israelites would not adopt it in its primitive form but rather as a political myth. God's power manifests itself through the political institution, and thus it would be as the temporary incumbent of the institution, rather than as a particular individual, that the king was God's delegate. The institution of kingship did not merely symbolize God's reign, however; it was in the political field, through the king of Israel, that God actually wielded His power over the world.

In this view Israel's king was the "Son of God" (Ps. 2:7) whom Yahweh "engendered" as he ascended to the throne. Divine sonship did not result from procreation, in which divine substance is joined with a human being, as Greek mythology held, nor was it a purely legal fiction by an act of adoption. Rather, it resulted from God's power that effectively operates through His chosen agent. As such the king shared God's privileges, in particular those of legislator, judge, and lord over his subjects' life and property. Moreover, God endowed him with wisdom and justice, which enabled him to convey divine blessings (cf. Ps. 72:4, 12-14, etc.) to the people. Although rightly called the "Son of God," the king of Israel, unlike rulers in the rest of the Fertile Crescent, was never addressed or worshiped as God. Though he never ceased to be human and a creature, he was, nevertheless, the legitimate owner of his country and people, and whoever challenged him opposed God Himself. In turn, the actual rule of Israel's king was considered evidence of God's care and concern for His people (e.g., 2 S. 7:14).

The language of the royal hymns of the OT has often been considered unrealistic and typical of oriental exaggeration. Yet one must remember that in the person of the sovereign it was the institution that was extolled. An unending reign and life was ascribed to the king as representative of the institution (Ps. 72:5). In him as anointed by God the nation enjoyed unending prosperity (72:6f., 15-17; Isa. 9:7) and would triumph over all its enemies (Ps. 2:1-9; 18:44-48 [MT 45-49]; 72:8-11), for in the king's rule God's power was revealed (45:7). Since he was the "Son" of God, the king's person is sacrosanct and inviolable; God alone had a right to punish him (1 S. 26). Sellin and other scholars held that 2 S. 7:14 describes David himself as savior. But the next verse shows that God acts as the savior of His people by conferring certain privileges on David and his descendants.

A comparison of Israel's kingship ideology with that of its neighbors shows not only that the Israelites had dropped all features incompatible with their view of God as Creator but also that they had no use for such ceremonies as the king's dying and rising again. Rather, the king was reminded of his moral task. God had chosen Israel as His property (Ex. 6:7) and through a covenant destined it to be holy (Lev. 11:44f.). To work to attain this goal was the king's obligation (Mic. 5:3f.).By anointing Zerubbabel and Joshua as political and spiritual heads of Israel, God indicated that He had not lost sight of the goal for which He had chosen Israel as His people (Zec. 4).

In Israel the kingship ideology was apparently coupled from an early period with the promise of the permanent rule of David and his successors (cf. 2 S. 7:11-16; 1 K. 2:3f.; Ps. 18:50 [MT 51]; 28:9; 89:4, 29-38). Among the prophets, Isaiah especially emphasized the providential role of David and his house (Isa. 4:2; 9:6; 11:1; 16:5; 55:3f.). Isaiah was followed by Micah (5:2-4), Jeremiah (17:25; 23:5; 30:9; 33:17), Ezekiel (34:22f.; 37:24f.), and Zechariah (3:8; 6:12). Most scholars also regard Am. 9:11 as preexilic. The references to the house and descendants of David have often been interpreted in a genealogical sense. In the light of 1 K. 2:3f. it seems more probable, however, that the term "house of David," like "Son of God," meant David's spiritual successors who "walked like him in the ways of God."

*C. Eschatology*. Quite apart from its nonmythical character, the OT idea of the Messiah differs from the oriental kingship ideology by its eschatological character. The ancient Near East understood time as determined by the cosmic law of change. Each deity had his or her own limited period of rule and would be succeeded by another deity. As Creator, however, the God of the Bible controls everything in this world, including time. Furthermore, His character lifts Him high above mere nature. His is a reasonable will, by which He pursues a comprehensive goal for the whole universe. This teleological element in God was originally understood as His asserting His holy will by means of the law He had given to His people; that idea was eventually supplemented by the notion of a transformation of the structure of this world. By coupling the latter view with the belief in a divinely appointed kingship, the prophets endowed Israel with a new idea: the Messiah. The political institution of kingship was no longer understood as an end in itself, but rather as the foretaste of the rule of a perfect king by whom peace and justice would be realized forever.

Until the time of Isaiah, Israel's hope was confined to the restoration of the splendor of David's kingdom, whose glory increased in proportion to the deterioration of Israel's political and social conditions. Isaiah in particular castigated these expectations as the wishful thinking of a people in search of happiness. Yet he also offered a genuine hope, which rested upon God's work in the past. In God's acts the prophet saw the evidence of His purposiveness. As Creator, God was concerned not exclusively with the Hebrew people, but rather with all mankind. Out of the combination of the kingship ideology and this new perspective, the belief in the advent of the Messiah as divinely appointed Savior of the world was born.

The eschatological outlook did not necessarily include the kingship ideology. The description in Ezk. 40–48 of the final age, for instance, mentions no mediator of the divine blessings. The term "messianic age," although invariably implying the expectation of an age of bliss, should be confined to the type of eschatology that looks forward to the appearance of a personal savior. A strict division of prophetic eschatology into a messianic and a nonmessianic type is not feasible, however, because in either instance the language of both the creation story and the kingship ideology is used. The absence of direct references to a personal, divinely appointed savior does not necessarily mean that a prophet did not believe in one. The cryptic language with which the prophets refer to the final age makes one think that the eschatological hopes were treated as top secrets. Some scholars make a possibly helpful distinction between a "historical" and an "eschatological" Messiah. Haggai and Zechariah as well as rabbinic Judaism understood the Messiah as an ordinary human being, although one "anointed" by God and thus endowed with extraordinary capacities. The Messiah was to inherit all the promises given to David, Israel's first anointed king, and like David was to be a political ruler. This view seems to contrast with views of the Messiah as a heavenly gift to Israel. But references to the raising of David (Ezk. 34:23f.; cf. 2 Esd. 13; 2 Bar. 29; 72) and in particular the characterization of the age to come as something entirely new (Heb. *ḥāḏāš*, Isa. 50:6-8; 63:4; 65:25; Jer. 31:31-34; 34:16; Ezk. 37:24; 48:35; Hos. 3:5) clearly indicate that even rabbinic messianic literature conceives of the coming of the eschatological future as a creative act of God by which this world is remade rather than as a mere restoration or reform of the nation's political or social life.

Notwithstanding their common origin in Israel's religion and history, the two kinds of messianic hope differ fundamentally. Like the kingship ideology, the expectation of a "historical" Messiah presupposed a sense of security and adequate power. The institution of kingship was held to be firmly rooted in the covenant, even though no king may have been available. This outlook explains the Jews' wavering reception of Jesus: was He the legitimate representative of the institution? The expectation of the "eschatological" Messiah, on the contrary, was held against the background of impending disaster and ruin, the "messianic woes" (e.g., Mic. 5:3; cf. Ezk. 21:27), from which God alone could save. Although the conflicts were usually described in terms of the ancient creation myth, God's fight and triumph were nevertheless spiritualized as the conflict of belief and unbelief (cf., e.g., Isa. 11:9; Zec. 9:10). The eschatological hope remained closely related, nevertheless, to the fate of Israel, the Lord's chosen people. God's victory would entail prosperity for the Jewish people as well as international order. The prophets pointed out, furthermore, that God's "coming" was not to be understood as an automatic process. God challenges His nation; by a kind of second exodus Israel would be tested and sifted (Isa. 40:3-5, 10f.; 44:24-28; 51:4-6; 52:8-10). The final goal of Yahweh's saving work is the establishment of His holy will on earth.

As with all His works, God carries out that of savior-king through His agents. Agents are implied in all references to God's salvation, even though they may not specifically mention a mediator. The centrality of His saving plan is indicated, for instance, in that the prophet who proclaims the news of salvation considers himself God's anointed (Isa. 61:1-3; cf. Zec. 2:9-13 [MT 13-17]). As messenger of God's final salvation, the "Servant of the Lord" (Isa. 42:1-7; 49:1-9; 50:4-9; 52:12–53:12) himself ushers in the new age (ch. 53; cf. Mal. 3:1). Mal. 4:5 (MT 3:23) emphasizes the messenger's spiritual function: the prophet Elijah rather than King David will make the final announcement. Dnl. 7 describes the agent of God's salvation as "one like a son of man," who after the brutal and wicked reign of the four earthly kingdoms, symbolized by the wild beasts, will consummate God's rule as His viceregent. The Danielic vision shows the principal difference between the kingship ideology and the messianic idea. The term "messiah," originally a generic noun, is in the eschatological context transformed into a proper name or personal title. While many officebearers in Israel may be anointed, it is through His Messiah that God completes His plans with mankind and the universe, whereas the kingship ideology is inevitably tied up with the well-being of the Jewish people. Because of the finality implied in the idea of Messiah, his work is capable of an ever deepened and widening interpretation.

The very idea of a divinely appointed yet earthly agent through whom God's comprehensive purpose is carried out is apt to perplex the modern reader. Although the expression "one like a son of a man who was brought before the Ancient of Days" in Dnl. 7:13 is meant to symbolize true humanity as contrasted with the beasts designating the preceding empires or periods of history, v. 18 states that the saints of the Most High shall possess the divine kingdom. Thus the symbol stands for the divine commission of the faithful members of Israel. The same event is described as a heavenly as well as an earthly reality.

It is obvious that the new prophetic idea of the Anointed One, though heavily indebted to the kingship ideology, has been detached from the rite of anointment. While in constitutional life the actual rite was required in order to confer God's approval on the ruler, the prophets use the term metaphorically. It is meant primarily to designate the divine mission and commission of the Messiah and the finality of his ministry.

***III. Intertestamental Literature.***–The prophetic literature of the preexilic and exilic age describes the coming of the Messiah and the nature of the final age in various ways. As growing emphasis was laid upon instruction and theoretical understanding, a tendency to systematize eschatology and messianic hope characterized the rich Jewish literature of the intertestamental period. All the diverse prophetic visions of the future age of bliss are presumed to refer to the same event. Likewise, the various agents of God's salvation are fused into one savior. Thus 2 Esdras holds that the "anointed one" is of David's lineage (12:32); he is a mortal like Israel's past kings (7:28), yet he is also the "Son of God" (13:32ff.). Similarly, the Tannaim interpreted all eschatological and messianic passages of the OT according to a preestablished pattern. Along with the idea of a canonical Scripture, Israel developed the belief in the canon's intrinsic unity. Divine promises that originally referred to historical events (e.g., Gen. 13:16; Ps. 72:17; Zec. 8:13) were then presumed to refer to the Messiah or the age to come. Likewise, references to the anointing of the king, especially in the royal Psalms, were applied to the Messiah. Such exegesis was not altogether arbitrary. Through searching for the intrinsic oneness of the Scriptures Israel learned to think of God as one who pursued a saving purpose throughout the ages. Historical events could thus be interpreted as indicating the ongoing work of salvation; Jesus and His followers interpreted their Bible in this sense. The extent of this process of reinterpretation can be seen in the LXX espousal of translations with eschatological connotations, even in cases where such meaning is not obvious in the Hebrew text. The best-known instance is Isa. 7:14, where Heb. *ʿalmâ*, "young woman," is rendered *parthénos*, "virgin," whereby the historical promise is transformed into a hope based upon supernatural eschatology.

In spite of those exegetical tendencies the Jewish Messiah never evaporated completely into a purely mythical or supernatural being, nor was he thought of as a deity. He had been promised to Israel and thus remained closely related to the fate of the Jewish people and their political history. He was thought of as a ruler who would be thoroughly familiar with the law and whose faithful observance of it would set an example to the whole nation. Thus he would be worthy to be the king and judge of God's chosen people. But despite all harmonizing and systematizing attempts, the Jewish people never succeeded in forming a generally accepted view of the Messiah and his work. In the light of Dnl. 7:18, Ezekiel, Amos, Obadiah, and certain

Psalms, some Jewish exegetes identified the Messiah with the faithful remnant of the people of Israel, while others conceived of him as an individual. The apocalyptic and devotional literature of intertestamental Judaism has given free rein to imagination in depicting the manner in which God would accomplish His saving work. According to the Apocalypse of Moses, for instance, an angel of the Lord will eventually overcome Satan (ch. 10). In the Psalms of Solomon it is the "anointed of the Lord" (18:3-9) who comes to Israel's rescue. Similarly, 2 Baruch and 1 Enoch distinguish the "days of the Messiah," which have limited duration, from the never-ending "age to come." Whereas 1 Enoch says that the Messiah will live forever, the rabbis discussed the limits of his reign. Messiah ben Joseph was thought of as a suffering Messiah who would be killed in battle.

Moreover, it is not clear whether the Messiah was to establish God's kingdom or only to prepare its advent (2 Esd. 7:28; 12:34; 2 Bar. 40:3). The great diversity of titles used for the saving agent of God — Messiah is by far the least frequent one — should warn against the modern fashion of building views of intertestamental soteriology on those names and titles as though each of them had a clearly circumscribed and different meaning. As a rule, the intertestamental literature considers God rather than the Messiah the one who ushers in the cosmic transformation and salvation (1 En. 90:37f.; 2 Esd. 7:28f.; 2 Bar. 72:1-5). In Ps. Sol. 18:7-9 God installs the Messiah as the ideal judge and ruler. The whole Jewish literature agrees on only one feature of the Messiah: he will be a political ruler and national hero. His saving power requires that he deliver Israel from its oppressors and restore the authority of the law.

The excessive Jewish nationalism that characterizes the intertestamental period resulted in transferring OT features of Yahweh the warrior and conqueror to the Messiah (Sib.Or. 5:108f., 414-431; 2 Bar. 70:9; 73; 1 En. 38:2f.; 90:38; Jub. 23:30; 2 Esd. 13:10f.). It is not surprising, therefore, that the idea of the Messiah as rebel and political deliverer appeared in the Maccabean age. Since God will appoint the Messiah, no one, not even the Messiah Himself, will foreknow his election and dignity (e.g., Justin Martyr *Dial.* 8.4). Did postexilic Judaism believe in the preexistence of the Messiah? Dnl. 7:13 speaks of the Messiah as though he belonged to the retinue of God (cf. also 2 Esd. 7:26; Apoc. Abr. 31), but that is not the preexistence later ascribed by Christian theology to Christ. Some scribes postulated for the Messiah an ideal existence in God's mind. The notion of a Messiah residing in heaven (*Pesikta Rabbathi,* 7th cent. A.D. but based on earlier traditions) shows clearly the influence of Christian speculation.

In postexilic Judaism anointing designated a status directly below God rather than a specific task or function. In Ps. Sol. 17:21-40, for instance, all the kings allied with Israel will be anointed. This view of anointing is particularly obvious in the coexistence of two messiahs, one from the house of David and one from the house of Aaron or Levi (e.g., T. Jud. 21:2-5; 24; T. Levi 18; Jub. 31:12-20; 1 QS 9:11; CD 12:23; 14:19; 19:10; 20:1). The idea of dual messiahship goes back to Zec. 4:14. It may be rooted in the primitive office of a priest-king, of which traces still linger in the NT (e.g., 1 Pet. 2:9f.; Rev. 1:6). A late rabbinical distinction was made between Messiah ben Joseph, a belligerent and suffering Messiah who would eventually be killed, and Messiah ben David, who would succeed him and reign forever. Though the rabbis identified this Joseph with the patriarch, the distinction of these two messiahs is an attempt to reconcile the Jewish and Christian messianic ideas. Apart from this instance, Judaism has never known a suffering Messiah. Although the Qumrân community identified itself with the Servant of the Lord in Isaiah and understood its mission in a messianic sense, the Dead Sea writings never refer to the sufferings of the Messiah.

This survey of the intertestamental period has shown that Judaism had never reached agreement on what to expect of the future, except that all believed that God would eventually vindicate His people. In turn, none of the eschatological and messianic views claimed exclusive authority; thus divergent views could easily coexist. Modern attempts to reduce this multiplicity to one system do violence to the evidence. Above all, the relationship of the Jewish ideas of the Messiah and the Christian idea should not be thought of as an evolution from a primitive to an articulate view. While the early Church adopted most of the representational material of the Jewish view of the Messiah, it rejected the underlying understanding of time. According to postexilic Judaism the world necessarily moves according to the Creator's will (cf., e.g., the three times and a half time in Dnl. 7:25). The coming of the Messiah is the sign that the final period has begun or that the goal has been reached. The early Christians were aware of a divine purpose realizing itself in and through creatures of this world. The final goal is seen in God's manifesting His mercy in sending a savior-messiah to this earth.

*IV. NT.–A. Messianic Titles.* In the NT the designation *christós* occurs with great frequency as a title of Jesus. 1 Jn. 2:20, 27 refer to the anointing (*chrísma*) of believers but do not call them *christoí.* By giving Jesus alone the title "Christ," the Greek-speaking congregations of the first generation obviously followed the LXX. The use of this title is an indication that the idea of God's Anointed One was deeply embedded in the religious thinking of the apostles. In Christian usage *christós* lost a number of its OT and Jewish connotations. In fact, by forming an integral part of the Christian message, it was fraught from the beginning with features alien to its Jewish antecedents. *Christós* is not the only title given to Jesus by the early Church. Paul in particular used *kýrios,* "lord," in many instances, either alone or combined with "Jesus" or "Jesus Christ." In most of its NT uses "Christ" had become part of Jesus' name, and "Lord" was the title then given to Jesus. The use of the appellation *kýrios* probably originated in the Greek-speaking Jewish-Christian churches and was considered the full equivalent of Messiah. Since the Hellenistic world was not familiar with the ritual practice of anointing, the title "anointed one" as a religious designation would not have been meaningful to people not familiar with its Jewish connotation. According to the Synoptic Gospels Jesus never designated Himself by the title "Messiah." He was sometimes acclaimed as Christ (e.g., Mk. 10:47 par.; 15:18; Mt. 9:27) but never encouraged the use of this appellation. After Peter's confession, for instance, the tradition has Jesus foretelling the sufferings of the "Son of man" rather than of the Messiah (Mk. 8:27–9:1 par.); He also spoke of Himself as "master" or "shepherd." Most appropriate in Jesus' opinion, however, was the self-designation "Son" or "Son of God" (e.g., Mt. 11:27 par. Lk. 10:22; Mt. 24:36 par. Mk. 13:32) or the indirect reference to His Sonship implied in the phrase "my (the) Father" (e.g., Mt. 7:24; 10:33; Mk. 8:38 par.; Lk. 22:29).

The evidence preserved in the Gospels points to the following facts. Jesus was reluctant to use or claim the title "Messiah" for Himself, probably because of its political connotations in contemporary Judaism. The various agents through whom, according to the OT, God took care of this world (e.g., Servant, Son of man, Son of David) were for Jesus integrated in the title "Son of God." The "Son" is God's redemptive presence (e.g., Lk. 4:21). On the basis of Jesus' understanding of His ministry, the early Church could acclaim and proclaim Jesus as Messiah in an entirely new way, which transcended both the OT understanding and the intertestamental development of the title.

*B. Jesus' Self-understanding.* Even scholars who, like the representatives of form criticism or the school of *Traditionsgeschichte,* assign most of the teachings found in the Gospels to the literary activity of the early Church must admit that the position the Evangelists ascribe to Jesus would be inexplicable without Jesus' awareness of His divinely assigned mission. Two factors cooperated to form His self-consciousness: His experience of a unique relationship with God His "Father," and the assurance that He had been commissioned to start the final phase of the redemptive history whose beginnings were recorded in the OT. To understand Jesus' self-consciousness it is therefore wrong to start from the titles ascribed to Him in the NT.

The Evangelists formed their portraits of Jesus by describing how He dealt with all kinds of people. Although their portrayals of Jesus differ according to their vantage points, these writers had one feature in common: they all characterized Jesus as a man who in His actions was certain that He played a central role in the advent of God's kingdom and the execution of His redemptive plan (e.g., Mk. 8:38 par.; 9:14-29 par.; Mt. 13:16; Lk. 10:23f.). Jesus appears in the Gospels as one who has dedicated His whole life to the task set before Him irrespective of the cost. This awareness gives Him the right to demand unreserved allegiance to His person (e.g., Mk. 1:16-20 par.; Mt. 19:21 par.). It also explains the paradox of Jesus' mission. His place was within the framework of Jewish history and national life. Nevertheless, on account of His special relation to God, His ministry would benefit the whole of mankind. This self-consciousness enabled Him to use traditional titles in a new and sovereign way, interpreting and transforming them in the light of God's will as it shone in Him. He was certain that such obedience would imply suffering. Unlike most of Judaism, He saw in the Suffering Servant of Isa. 53 a type of the final savior. The Jews were confounded and irritated by Jesus' humility and meekness, which contradicted their idea of a national liberator who would appear in royal splendor and power. From their viewpoint they were bound to reject Jesus. But to Him this very rejection was proof of His divine mission, for God had predicted it long ago (Mk. 4:11f. par.). The close connection that Jesus felt with God can be seen in His giving commandments that practically upset Jewish law and His foretelling the way in which God's reign would be established without feeling the need to indicate the source of such knowledge.

Like his contemporaries, Jesus thought of the messianic age as an eschatological event. But whereas for them it was the future fulfillment of certain prophetic predictions and divine promises, for Jesus it was the realization of a divine dynamic working in and through Him. He viewed the eschatological events as a process of which His earthly ministry was but an intermediate phase; it was, however, the decisive phase (Mk. 8:38 par.; Lk. 12:8f.). This conviction explains the sense of finality with which Jesus spoke and acted as well as His assurance that His mission would not be terminated until His Parousia. Thus Jesus' eschatological outlook was not purely futuristic, as held by Bultmann and others, according to whom Jesus had announced the imminent arrival of a Messiah not identical with Himself. Also, He did not conceive of Himself as merely designated to become the Messiah at a later date (e.g., B. Weiss). The NT books do not bear out, either, the view of C. H. Dodd and others that Jesus saw all the promises of God already fulfilled in His earthly ministry ("realized eschatology"). Jesus was painfully aware of the power of Satan and the forces of evil over this world. Nevertheless, since He saw God as the Father of all creatures, He interpreted the Lord's redemptive plan for Him as embracing the whole world.

In 1 Cor. 15:20-28 Paul lucidly interpreted Jesus' eschatological outlook. The progressive character of Jesus' eschatological work, of which the apostle was aware, explains the bewildering way in which Jesus referred to His "coming." He could say that He had come (Mt. 11:19 par. Lk. 7:33f.; Mt. 10:34; Mk. 10:45; Lk. 12:49) and also that He was the coming one (e.g., Mt. 16:28; Mk. 8:38; Mt. 25:31; Mt. 26:64 par. Mk. 14:62, where the present participle *erchómenos* is used with a future meaning). The assurance with which Jesus announced His Parousia has no parallel in Jewish messianism. The Parousia is not a return but rather His self-manifestation in glory.

Another feature in the Gospels that points back to Jesus' experience is what W. Wrede called the "messianic secret." It is strange indeed and without parallel in Judaism that at no occasion did Jesus proclaim Himself as Messiah. His references to the "Son of man," which unquestionably have a messianic meaning, are invariably enigmatic and indirect. But according to Wrede this "messianic secret" is a secondary feature in the Gospels, invented by Mark to explain the otherwise scandalous fact that one whom His followers proclaimed as the Messiah had been killed by those to whom He had been sent.

Wrede's ingenious hypothesis rests on a precarious foundation, however. Quite apart from the psychological problems that would be involved in such a literary fraud, Wrede implies that Jesus had in fact proclaimed Himself as Messiah. To make His historical fiction plausible Mark would have had to suppress all references to Jesus' messiahship. One wonders how Mark's Gospel would ever have won acceptance if it so blatantly contradicted the original tradition of the Church. Much more plausible is the assumption that Jesus was reluctant to use messianic titles for His mission because He was afraid of popular misunderstandings. The political connotation of the title "Messiah" might have pushed His work in the wrong direction; for instance, He might have been proclaimed leader in a popular uprising (cf. Jn. 6:15). While eager to see people recognize the nature and effects of His ministry, Jesus did not care for specific titles. Thus He stated unambiguously that a person's salvation would not depend on the title by which he addresed Jesus but rather on his following the man of Nazareth and His example because He was the true man according to God's will (e.g., Mt. 8:22; 10:38; 19:16-22; cf. Jn. 1:9; 15:1; 1 Jn. 2:8; 5:20). By following Him, people would learn from experience that He was the Son of God. Thus Jesus liked to speak of Himself, His work and destiny, in parables (Mt. 13:34; Mk. 4:34), not in order to keep certain people out of God's kingdom but rather in order to induce people first to receive the "mystery of the kingdom" (Mk. 4:11 par.). The "mystery" was that God was establishing His reign on earth through the man Jesus and His followers. Jesus intimated His dignity in a veiled way only, by referring, e.g., to the Son of man in the 3rd person.

The Gospel portrait of the man Jesus is difficult to reconcile with the dogma of the two natures of the incarnate Christ. Often in the traditional presentation of the hypostatic union either the deity of Christ is lost or His manhood is suppressed. To do justice to the Gospel portrait of Jesus, Thomasius, von Hoffmann, and many other nineteenth-century Lutheran theologians advocated the kenotic hypothesis. They thought that the work of the Messiah consisted of two successive stages, namely, His humiliation during His earthly ministry and His exaltation in His resurrection and heavenly reign. Although already divine on earth, the Logos would not have used His divine attributes and thus would have appeared as mere man. According to the Synoptic records, however, Jesus was fully aware of God's redemptive power as it operated in His ministry. That presence manifested itself in Jesus' ability to cast out Satan and the demons (Mt. 12:28; Lk. 11:20), in His lordly use of the divinely instituted sabbath (Mk. 2:28 par.) and in His sharing the divine prerogative to forgive sins (Mk. 2:10 par.). Similarly, Jesus could state confidently that, however His adversaries might harm Him, God would vindicate Him in His resurrection (Mk. 8:31 par.; 9:30-32 par.; 10:32-34 par.). Thus the Synoptic Gospels depict Jesus as a man who is aware of His being God's instrument and servant in the execution of His redemptive work and who plainly states that fact.

On account of the NT evidence, some scholars abandoned the ontological explanation of Jesus' ministry and attempted a psychological approach. Ever since Albert Schweitzer's *Quest of the Historical Jesus*, however, theologians have contended that seeking a psychological explanation of the "messianic self-consciousness" of Jesus has a serious methodological fault because it leads to an insuperable dilemma. When Jesus' consciousness was interpreted in analogy with an ordinary man's mind, the result was a portrait of Jesus that despite its attractiveness failed to explain how such a man could ever be proclaimed the Savior of mankind. The alternative is the assumption that Jesus suffered from paranoia or schizophrenia, because no healthy-minded man would make for himself the claims that Jesus made. According to Schweitzer, the solution to that dilemma is recognizing that Jesus considered Himself the servant of God and that His messiahship consisted in His willingness to be used by God as an obedient instrument for the execution of God's saving will.

J. Weiss and numerous other theologians suggested another way to come to terms with the historical record. Jesus, they held, never thought of Himself as occupying the central place in God's plan. He was a mere teacher or at the best a prophet who announced the coming of God's sovereign rule. Belief in His messiahship resulted from some strange experience that His disciples had at Easter. In the early years of the 20th cent. that "Easter faith" was conceived of as having an extra-subjective basis, but Bultmann and his followers interpreted it in terms of existential experience, regarding the gospel story as a myth never meant to be understood as history. The first-century presentation of the gospel, however, in no way bears out this ingenious hypothesis. Far from relating a myth of a dying and rising savior or a "redeemed redeemer," the NT documents refer to a man whose place in history is unmistakably circumscribed. Saying that the early Church invented the materials found in the Gospels is tantamount to asserting that it committed one of the biggest frauds in the history of religion.

*C. Experience of the Early Church.* Although Jesus did not leave a single written line, it is absurd to postulate complete discontinuity between the ministry of Jesus and the worship of Christ. If during his lifetime Jesus had never intimated that He was the Son of God, it would be very strange that His followers worshiped Him in that capacity after His death. In lieu of the books of the NT, they might have left writings that combined the teachings of Jesus with Jewish apocalypticism. Nothing in Jewish tradition would lead them to the worship of Christ. One can agree with the form critics' contention that at the bottom of the new religion is a powerful spiritual experience that permeated the whole life and thinking of the early Church. Yet, difficult as it may be to produce a scientific explanation of the Resurrection, the fact is incontestable that the Church was built upon the disciples' witness that their faith was occasioned by a miraculous event outside of their minds, which concerned the man Jesus with whom they had associated during His earthly ministry.

The Synoptic Gospels are the early Church's witness to the power of God as manifested in Jesus' life and ministry. The disciples had been able to discern a divine plan in the healings and exorcisms, the miracles and heavenly manifestations, the singular fellowship of Jesus and His followers, the faith of those who were considered religious outcasts, and the rejection of Jesus by the official representatives of the Jewish religion. Jesus' resurrection had confirmed the paramount significance of these events. Hence His first associates proclaimed Him as Messiah or Christ, as the early speeches in Acts show. The importance of that proclamation is best indicated by the early Church's confession or *homología* that Jesus was the Messiah or *christós* (e.g., 1 Jn. 4:2f.; Jn. 20:31) or the heavenly Lord *kýrios*, e.g., Rom. 10:9; 1 Cor. 12:3; Phil. 2:11). By assuming the grammatical form of a nominal sentence, the *homología* expresses the substantial identity of name and title. The confessional statement does not mean that Jesus happened to be a messiah or a lord, but rather that it was His very nature to be such. "Confessing Christ" meant that a Christian was willing to make a public stand for the messianic dignity of Jesus, regardless of hostile reactions.

Literary criticism indicates that the sayings of Jesus found in the Gospels probably were rarely preserved in their original form. For teaching purposes the apostles and leaders of the early Church would have altered the original tradition concerning Jesus to bring out His significance for them. In particular they would have insisted that in His resurrected life Jesus had manifested His full identity. As a result, certain sayings of Jesus and narratives about Jesus' deeds might have been styled to make their mysterious intimations obvious; the procedure of the Fourth Evangelist is especially illuminating. John was anxious to show that although God Himself was speaking through Jesus' teachings, God's sublime meaning was hidden by Jesus' veiled or metaphorical language. Similarly, John intended to bring to light the revelatory meaning of Jesus' miraculous deeds. Such editorial activity of the early Church has been grossly misrepresented, however, by those who contend that the early Church fabricated the Gospel material.

The tradition about Jesus' self-consciousness was also influenced by the varied spiritual experiences of the early Church leaders, which caused them to interpret Jesus' messianic role in various ways. For instance, the materials forming the original tradition of the Church were not placed side by side at random, as K. L. Schmidt surmised. Rather, apart from the general frame that all Gospels have in common, each Gospel was arranged in agreement with a specific messianology. For that purpose some of the NT writers adopted traditional patterns. Matthew describes the work of Jesus more or less in accordance with the kingship ideology of the OT; Jesus' dignity and claim as the Son of David are frequently underscored (e.g., Mt. 1:1, 6, 17, 20; 9:27; 15:22; 20:30; 21:9, 15). The authors of Mark and Revelation obviously had in mind the apocalyptic image of the Son of man. Both books describe Jesus as winning His kingdom by fighting with Satan, the ruler of this world, and finally overcoming Satan's opposition (e.g., Mk. 1:13; 3:22, 26; 4:5; 8:33; Rev. 2:9, 13, 24; 3:9; 12:9; 20:2, 7). Luke finally seeks to adjust the record to the pattern of the Suffering Servant of Isa. 53, who takes upon himself the burden of God's people. The book of Hebrews, which depicts Jesus both as the Son of God appearing on earth and as the heavenly high priest, seems to follow a sacerdotal tradition of which few traces have been preserved elsewhere (e.g., Testament of the Twelve Patriarchs and the Qumrân Scrolls).

Paul and John made an entirely new departure. Their interpretations of Jesus' person and work indicate the shift that Christian thinking underwent from the Hebraic categories of Palestine to the Hellenistic perspective of the Dispersion. These writers were familiar with the Church's original proclamation and evangelistic tradition but seem anxious to overcome the particularism that for a Hellenistic mind were still inherent in the traditional patterns. On the basis of the radical transformation that the encounter with the risen Jesus had called forth in their lives, Paul as well as the Fourth Evangelist felt touched by God Himself. Both described Jesus as the preexistent Son of God who had participated in the work of creation and prepared the whole world for its final salvation. In the historical life of Jesus, the redemptive plan that God envisaged for mankind had entered into a new and final stage (e.g., Jn. 3:16; Rom. 11; Eph. 1–2). In this process the followers of Jesus were held to be united in and with Him organically (Jn. 15:1-7; Eph. 4:12-16). That view led to the realization that, as the Messiah, Jesus had given His life as a sacrifice by which a sinful mankind had been reconciled with God (e.g., Rom. 3:25f.; 5:6-8; Jn. 1:29; 10:11; 1 Jn. 2:2; 3:16) or as a ransom by which believers had been freed from slavery to sin and death (e.g., Mk. 10:45; Mt. 20:28; Rom. 6; Gal. 4:8; Eph. 2:1f.; 1 Tim. 2:6).

This shift of emphasis from rulership to remission of sins and newness of life indicates the transition from the traditional Jewish messianic ideology to a new understanding of Jesus' achievement. Guided by such spiritual experience, the apostles could then apply to the ministry of Jesus all kinds of OT metaphors. There is, however, one remarkable fact. As in the Synoptic Gospels, in the Pauline and Johannine writings mythical language may be used; yet it is never coupled with mythological representations or speculations. Rather, such figurative terminology is determined and restricted by the conviction that the risen Lord is identical with the man Jesus of Nazareth. Hence such expressions as "ascending to heaven," "absence," "coming of the Lord," "first and second man," "light of the world," "heavenly city," "Satan the prince of this world," and "hell" must be interpreted metaphorically.

Seen in the light of this new experience, the ministry of Jesus the Christ forms the turning point of history. It takes place at the "fulness of time" (Gal. 4:4; cf. Mk. 1:15). Yet Jesus' coming is a blessing only to those who join Him and acknowledge the divine origin of His mission. Through His redemptive work He becomes Lord, the ruler of believers, for He wields power over their consciences (e.g., Rom. 12:1-21; Eph. 5:22–6:9) as well as over their destinies. Hence His coming results in doom for those who reject Him (e.g., Jn. 5:22; 8:16; 12:47; Rom. 8:3, 34), because apart from Him there is no effective help against the hostility of the cosmic forces (e.g., Jn. 6:68; Acts 4:12; Gal. 4:6-9; Col. 2:8, 15).

Protestant exegesis has often stressed the atonement as the only objective of Christ's ministry and the exclusive basis of His messianic dignity. To the early Church, however, both the miracles and the resurrection of Jesus were conclusive evidences of His messiahship because they revealed Him as the Lord of the universe (e.g., Rom. 8:18-23, 31-39; cf. Col. 1:15-20). In turn, however, the NT has no Christology that confines the messianic office of Jesus to His fight with and triumph over the evil forces of the universe, as Aulén contended (*Christus Victor* [Eng. tr. 1937]).

Having experienced the power of the risen Christ over their lives, believers like Paul and John concluded that in contrast to the transitory and corruptible natural life, they had been endowed with a never-ending and divine life (e.g., Jn. 3:15; 20:31; Rom. 5:17; 6:23; 2 Cor. 4:10). Christ's lordship would manifest itself in that in and through Him the believers were used as the instruments through whom God transformed this world into His kingdom (e.g., Jn. 6:5; Rom. 5:17; Col. 3:4; Rev. 5:10). The weaknesses and shortcomings of believers were no obstacle to the full deployment of God's saving power.

Although the Synoptic description of Jesus' messiahship might have seemed strange to the apostles' contemporaries, it was nevertheless rooted in the OT and thus compatible with orthodox Judaism. John and Paul, however, proclaimed an entirely novel Messiah. The reason is to be found in their specific experience. Their encounters with the risen Lord had caused a powerful change in their self-consciousness that they could not account for as a merely mental process. They were reborn (Jn. 3:3) or created afresh (2 Cor. 5:17). As they proclaimed Christ, unexpected and extraordinary results became manifest in the lives of the people addressed. So radical was the transformation that they were constrained to ascribe it to the operation of Jesus' divine power in them.

Unlike the Jewish Messiah, who was thought of as an extraordinary human being who acted at God's behest, Jesus appeared to His disciples as the direct manifestation of God's redemptive will. John underlined this by making Jesus frequently use the formula "I am," which in the light of Ex. 3:14 was understood as authenticating the deity's presence on earth. In Paul's writing the title "Lord" (*kýrios*) had the same function. Regardless of the origin of the appellation *kýrios* in the early Church, Paul obviously understood the title as the LXX did, namely, as designating the divine power by which this world was being transformed toward its divinely appointed goal (e.g., Rom. 10:8f.; 1 Cor. 1:8; 10:22).

Although such a view of Jesus' messianic work transcended the understanding of the title "Son of God" as found in the Synoptic Gospels, it did not imply, as the Jewish critics contended, that Paul and John introduced a second deity in the manner of pagan Hellenism. Similarly, the Nativity narratives in Matthew and Luke do not describe the birth of a new god but are rather intended to make clear that in the person of Jesus, the Son of God has identified Himself with the historical predicament of mankind. Thus these apostles emphasized that whatever the Son has was given Him by the Father (Jn. 3:35; Col. 1:15f.) and that the Son's authority rested upon His having been "sent" by the Father (Jn. 5:23f.; Acts 3:26; Rom. 8:3). Though Christ participated in the work of creation, the world was not made by Him. Rather, through Him (*diá* with gen.) as mediator all things were related to each other (Jn. 1:3; 1 Cor. 8:6; Eph. 4:12-16), i.e., through Him they received their meaning and value, because through Christ's work God accomplished the harmony of all things (*eis autón,* Col. 1:16). In contrast to the Father's invisible power of creation stands Christ's redemptive manifestation in this world.

*D. Proof from Scripture.* The messianic titles given to Jesus did not exclusively depend on the experience of the apostolic generation. In addition to the hints given by Jesus Himself, the early Church also turned to the OT.

A Messiah whose life and work would not be in agreement with God's promises to His people could not be accepted as God's appointed agent. The first Christians were strengthened in their belief in Jesus' messiahship by the fact that His ministry and its outcome proved to be the fulfillment of the Scriptures. This feature is most conspicuously expressed in 1 Cor. 15:3f., where Paul, quoting oral tradition, twice added "in accordance with the Scriptures." The scribes and rabbis also took an active interest in Scripture but emphasized the correct interpretation of the Law much more than the predictions found in the Prophets. They believed in the inspiration of the Scriptures but did not infer from them a system of messianic thought. They were satisfied with quoting a few OT statements about birthplace, family, and work of the coming Messiah in order to check the rank growth of popular expectations and apocalypticism.

Scriptural exegesis differed in Christian circles. To rebut the Jewish rejection of the messianic claim made for Jesus, the early Church deemed it necessary to prove that theirs was not a self-styled Messiah, let alone that He had been raised to messianic dignity by the acclaim of His followers. The Church argued that the Scriptures offered proof that Jesus had been sent by God, since His ministry fulfilled God's requirements for His Savior. The NT refers, e.g., to the scriptural character of His birth in Bethlehem (Mt. 2:1-6; Lk. 2:4), to His descent from David (Rom. 1:3), and to His mission to the Jewish people (Gal. 4:4f.). Only people who considered the OT a divinely inspired book, i.e., the Jews, found the proof from Scripture meaningful and valid. It is therefore arbitrary and gratuitous to contend that the early Church used the OT to invent stories about Jesus and then presented those "facts" as fulfillment of OT promises and predictions. Quite apart from the absurdity of establishing faith on self-fabricated legends, this hypothesis makes no sense historically, for Palestinian Jews would have easily refuted such fictions. Extant Jewish literature shows on the contrary that the Jews of the 1st cent. A.D. accepted the Gospel record in principle. Judaism questioned only the Christian contentions that Jesus was the Messiah and that God had been directly at work in the ministry of Jesus.

A novel exegetical feature introduced into Scripture exposition by the early Church was typology. It consisted in the parallel arrangement of certain OT features and the person and ministry of Jesus, e.g., Adam and Christ (Rom. 5:12-21; 1 Cor. 15:45f.), the mission of Moses in the wilderness and that of Christ (1 Cor. 10:1-6), and Moses and Christ as legislators (Jn. 1:17; 6:32-35). The underlying idea is that since God does not change, neither does the goal He set for this world. Specific characteristics of the manner in which God moves this world can therefore be recognized in the similarity of types. Yet since in all His doings God aims at a future objective, the final realization is infinitely greater and more marvelous than all the preceding phases. Typology was another way of showing that the providential role and heavenly dignity that the disciples ascribed to Jesus was more than a subjective evaluation even though based upon their experience, for that experience was confirmed by God's own Word. The Bible showed that as the fulfiller of the OT Jesus occupied the supreme and final place in holy history. The similarities proved that Jesus' ministry fulfilled and surpassed what the OT had predicted of the Messiah. This "much more" of the final stage (e.g., Rom. 5:9f., 15, 17) denies the contention that the disciples applied contemporary Jewish messianic expectations to Jesus. It is obvious that already in the Synoptic Gospels the portrait of Jesus by far surpassed that of a Jewish Messiah.

Closely related to typology was the spiritualization of the OT. This device was used, e.g., in interpreting the effect of Jesus' messianic power as an atoning sacrifice (e.g., Lk. 24:20; Jn. 1:29; Rom. 3:25; Eph. 5:2; Col. 1:20; He. 2:15; 1 Pet. 1:18; Rev. 5:6). In God's dealing with His chosen people, Jesus occupies the place that under the old covenant was assigned to the cultic sacrifices. This spiritualization had nothing in common with the apocalyptic extolling of the Messiah in popular Jewish expectation nor with Philo's allegorical interpretation of the OT sacrifices. Jewish apocalypticism had formed an idea of the Messiah that grossly and fantastically magnified Jewish kingship ideology. Philo, in turn, had attempted to rationalize the OT institutions, treating them as allegories of mankind's spiritual powers. Quite differently, the Christian exegetes recognized the redemptive purpose of God imparting meaning to the OT sacrifices. They contended, however, that the institution had a limited and provisional significance. The history of God's revelation had demonstrated that the personal approach to Him must take precedence over the institutional approach (Mt. 9:13; Acts 7:45-50; Rom. 12:1; 1 Pet. 2:5). The early Church saw in the death of the Messiah the disclosure of the profoundest mystery of God's redemptive purpose, which Jesus had intimated to the Twelve in the Last Supper (Mk. 14:24 par.). That in spite of this spiritualizing tendency the Christians nevertheless should have called Jesus by the Jewish title "Messiah" or "Christ" was due to the spiritualization that the concept had already undergone in exilic and postexilic times, and also to Jesus' determination to interpret His ministry in agreement with the spiritual purpose of God's past works.

Quite apart from typology and spiritualization, the early Christians' searching of Scripture made them adopt a new perspective in their exegesis. Jesus had taught His disciples that what made Jewish history worth remembering was that in it God's redemptive will was being disclosed. The future of the Jewish nation, though closely connected with that process, was nevertheless not its final goal. Consequently, the early Christians attempted to learn from the OT how God, in sacred history, had prepared trends that the Messiah would bring to completion (e.g., Jn. 1:45; 12:38; 1 Cor. 2:9; Gal. 3:8). The Gospel of Matthew is particularly fond of such perspectival or "christocentric" interpretation of the OT, probably because in addressing a Jewish audience it would support the Church's proclamation that Jesus was the Christ. The proof from Scripture meant more than that OT predictions had come true in Jesus' ministry; the events of Jesus' life were thereby shown to carry finality. Judaism had never been quite certain about the function of the "age of the Messiah." (Would the period of final bliss foretold by God coincide with the reign of the Messiah, or would the blessings of the "age to come" surpass those of His reign?)

The early Church had no doubt about the finality of Jesus' work. Since Judaism had never completely cast off the circular view of history inherited from Babylon, sacred history was identified with the restoration of earlier conditions, e.g., the reign of David or the bliss of Adam's Paradise. The apostolic congregation, however, adopted their Master's teleological eschatology. They consequently saw Jesus' messianic work as infinitely greater than the whole past of Israel and Jesus as surpassing in dignity all of Israel's outstanding men, whether Adam (e.g., Rom. 5:15), Moses (Lk. 11:31; Jn. 1:17; 7:22), or David (Mt. 13:3; Mk. 12:35 par,; Acts 2:29-36). Everything in the OT was understood as merely provisional, a promise, seed, or sign of the definitive redemption ushered in by Christ. Hence, in exegeting the OT the NT writers looked for the hidden teleology of teachings and events. In 1 Cor. 9:9, for instance, Paul pointed out that the commandment not to muzzle the threshing ox (Dt. 25:4) implies a principle applicable to all who work for the benefit of others, including the messengers of the Christ. No circular reasoning is implied in this kind of exegesis. It was based upon two premises: first, that the work of Jesus had offered deliverance from all evils and thus would never be surpassed; second, that through Jesus the very purpose of the OT had been revealed to His disciples (e.g., Lk. 24:32; Jn. 5:46f.; 1 Cor. 1:24, 30; Col. 2:3). The very existence of the OT was for the followers of Jesus the evidence of God's willingness to make Himself known to mankind. As a result human beings not only can transcend their natural limitations but also can avail themselves of God's power to free themselves from the bondage of cosmic forces.

The OT's role in the early history of Christology has recently been interpreted as though the followers of Jesus had arbitrarily and recklessly read their ideologies into the OT text. It is not surprising that this impression was formed. The Messiah whose picture the primitive Church found preformed in the OT was indeed different from what Jewish exegesis and positivistic Christian scholarship discover in the OT. But the exegetical differences do not result from an unscientific and dogmatic approach to the OT as contrasted with a scholarly and unprejudiced one, but rather from different underlying views of history. Jewish and later Christian exegetes regarded history as the self-explanatory, gradual deployment of an initial urge or the constant modification of its substance, whereas the NT writers held that apart from an absolute goal history remains ambiguous and perplexing. The ministry of Jesus indicated to the apostles that by the will of God the world process was drawing to its goal. As God's own work, the coming of Jesus was an eschatological event, namely, the apex of history (Gk. *syntéleia toú aiṓnos,* He. 9:26; cf. Mt. 13:39f.; 24:3). Like Jesus, His apostles were convinced that Judaism had become the slave of the letter of the OT law (e.g., Jn. 5:46; Rom. 7:6; 2 Cor. 3:6; cf. Mt. 11:10; Mk. 14:27; Lk. 10:27-37) and thus had failed to realize that Jesus was nothing less than the mighty agent and final revelation of God's redemptive purpose. Conversely, Jesus was for His followers the Lord of Scripture, to whose redemptive power all subsequent revelation would bear witness (e.g., Rom. 16:25-27; Eph. 3:20; Col. 2:3).

***Bibliography.***–*DBSup.*, V; *ERE,* VIII; *HDB,* III; A. Bentzen, *King and Messiah* (Eng. tr. 1955); J. Bonsirven, *Palestinian Judaism in the Time of Jesus Christ* (Eng. tr. 1964); J. J. Brierre-Narbonne, *Le Messie souffrant dans la littérature rabbinique* (1940); F. Delitzsch, *Messianic Prophecies in Historical Succession* (Eng. tr. 1891); J. Drummond, *Jewish Messiah* (1877); H. Gressmann, *Der Messias, FRLANT,* N.F. 26 (1929); S. H. Hooke, ed., *Myth, Ritual, and Kingship* (1958); A. R. Johnson, *Sacral Kingship in Ancient Israel* (1955); J. Klausner, *Messianic Idea in Israel* (Eng. tr. 1955); R. Koch, *Geist und Messias* (1950); S. Mowinckel, *He That Cometh* (Eng. tr. 1956); *NHI*; H. Ringgren, *Messiah in the OT* (*SBT,* I/18, 1956).

L. Cerfaux, *et al., L'Attente du Messie* (1954); *Christ in the Theology of St. Paul* (Eng. tr. 1959); O. Cullmann, *Christology of the NT* (Eng. tr., 2nd ed. 1963); H. J. Ebeling, *Das Messiasgeheimnis und die Botschaft des Markusevangeliums* (1939); T. W. Manson, *Servant Messiah* (1953); W. Manson, *Jesus the Messiah* (1943); E. Massaux, *et al., La Venue du Messie* (1962); W. Marxsen, *Anfangsprobleme der Christologie* (1960); H. Sahlin, *Der Messias und des Gottesvolk* (1945); W. Wrede, *Das Messiasgeheimnis in den Evangelien* (1901).

O. A. PIPER

**METAL** [Heb. *massēḵâ*] (Hab. 2:18); AV MOLTEN; NEB "image"; **METALLURGY.**

I. Terminology
II. Metals in Ancient Palestine
III. Description and Definition of Metallurgy
IV. Metallurgical Language in the Bible
V. Metallurgical Discoveries from Ancient Palestine

***I. Terminology.***–In its only occurrence in the RSV (Hab. 2:18) "metal" is an adjective describing an idol shaped by human hands. The term it represents, Heb. *massēḵâ* (<*nsk,* "pour out"; cf. Isa. 40:19; 44:10), is usually translated "molten" (so AV; see RSV Ex. 32:4, 8; 34:17; Lev. 19:4; Nu. 33:52; Dt. 9:16; Neh. 9:18; Isa. 30:22) although twice, on the basis of context, the RSV translates it "molten image" (2 K. 17:16; Ps. 106:19). A noun (*nesek*) from the same root is used of a molten image in Isa. 41:29; 48:5; Jer. 10:14; 51:17. Two other Hebrew words, *mûṣāq* and *mûṣāqâ*, are used for castings of metal (1 K. 7:16-27; 2 Ch. 4:3). These passages refer to capitals of molten bronze for the tops of pillars and for other accoutrements in the Solomonic temple. The use of *mûṣāq* is more obscure in Job 38:38, which refers to dust clodding into a "mass" as a result of rains, perhaps like a bloom of metal gathering in a refining FURNACE.

***II. Metals in Ancient Palestine.***–Ancient Palestine was never known for its variety or quantity of mineral resources. The one exception is stone, of which there is an abundant supply for construction purposes, including limestone, sandstones, granites, and basalt. Metal-bearing ores, however, are present sparsely and only in portions of the country. Transjordan has ancient sources of iron ore, especially in the Gilead (ʿAjlûn) region N of the Jabbok (Zerqā) River and in the Wâdī Feinan region E and S of the Dead Sea. Copper ores are found both E and W of the Arabah between the Dead Sea and the Gulf of Aqabah. Dt. 8:9 recognizes the presence of these ores in describing Canaan as "a land whose stones are iron, and out of whose hills you can dig copper" (*see* MINE).

Despite the paucity of ancient resources, biblical references to metals are rather frequent. They are allusive, however, and a few passages refer to the processes by which metals are produced (see REFINE; SMITH; SMELTING).

The significance of metals for Palestinian antiquity is demonstrated by the fact that researchers designated the cultural shifts from age to age by means of the principal metal in use; e.g., the Chalcolithic (copper-stone Age, *ca.* 4000-3150 B.C.; the Early Bronze Age, *ca.* 3150-2200; the Middle Bronze Age, *ca.* 2200-1500; the Late Bronze Age, *ca.* 1550-1200; the Iron Age, *ca.* 1200-300. (For the period after *ca.* 300 B.C. historians and archeologists use historical/cultural designations, e.g., Hellenistic, Roman, Byzantine, Islamic.) This practice of dividing world history according to metals is probably of Iranian origin, but it is found biblically in Dnl. 2:31-45, where successive ages are designated gold, silver, bronze, and iron (so also in the Avesta, Buddhist doctrine, Hesiod, and even in Plato's *Republic*).

Recent textual and object evidences for metals have come from Tell Mardikh (Ebla), dating from as early as 3200 B.C. The excavated objects include a ceremonial hammer of gold and silver, and pictures in bas-relief attached to wooden frames by means of copper pegs; some of the wood frames are overlaid with gold. A burial site named "Tomb of the Lord of Goats" shows evidence of a goldsmith's art.

The Ebla texts seem to indicate the existence of a guild or caste of smiths. They also mention tin, which was probably brought overland from northeast Iran, and quite specific quantities of precious metals brought to Ebla or stored at Ebla (e.g., bronze, 77 bars; gold, 100 bars; silver, 840 bars). There are a few not-yet-clarified references to the metallurgy of bronze. The letters also mention the use of silver for payments to state officials and judges and for

Reconstruction of an Egyptian wall mural of metalworkers who (from right to left) weigh out metal, smelt and hammer copper, and chisel a golden sphinx (Royal Ontario Museum, Toronto)

demonstrating the value of cattle. The Kingdom of Mari apparently paid tribute to Ebla in quite large quantities of silver and lesser quantities of gold.

For metals mentioned in biblical texts, *see* BRASS; BRONZE; COPPER; GOLD; IRON; LEAD; SILVER; TIN.

***III. Description and Definition of Metallurgy.***–Metallurgy is the art or science of separating metals from their ores, of making or compounding alloys, and of working or heat-treating metals to give them certain desired shapes or properties. "Today, metallurgy would be described as the science of metals, but up to the 18th century, it was only concerned with the practice of metallurgy, which consists of the traditional methods of smelting, melting, and working of metals" (Tylecote, p. ix). The stages in the development of metallurgy are characterized by many processes and methods, a complex of discoveries and inventions. Forbes describes four stages in this development. (1) Native metals e.g., copper, gold, silver, and meteoric iron were simply collected as stones and used as they were found. (2) The native metal stage came when it was realized that these "strange stones" had individual properties, that they could be reshaped by heating, and that they held their shape when cooled. There arose a complex of treatments including hammering, tempering, cutting, and grinding. (3) The ore stage came when it was discovered that ores could be reduced and the resultant metal could be melted and cast. The methods associated with this stage are casting, welding, and soldering. The manufacturing of alloys is placed in this stage. (4) The iron stage, roughly corresponding to the Iron Age, is described in terms of its methods of treatment: tempering, quenching, and annealing (Forbes, VIII, 8f.).

***IV. Metallurgical Language in the Bible.***–*A. Persons.* Tubal-cain (Gen. 4:22) is known as the prototype of all smiths and as the father of metallurgy. The "cain" (Heb. *qayin*) portion of the name is probably a personification of the KENITE tribe. Since Arab. *qayn* means "smith", it is likely that the name Kenite comes from the tribe's use of copper and iron ore in the Arabah. Moses' marriage to the daughter of Hobah the Kenite (Nu. 10:29; Jgs. 4:11) suggests a connection of Israelites with the craft of bronze metallurgy.

The name of Barzillai the Gileadite (2 S. 17:27) is obviously related to Heb. *barzel*, "iron." His importance to David might be associated with the Davidic exploitation of the Gilead iron mines and smelting sites. Solomon brought Hiram from Tyre to do the bronze work for the temple (1 K. 7:13-47). Hiram's father (1 K. 7:14) is also called a "worker in bronze."

The Bible employs general terms for metalworkers of various sorts, e.g. artisans (Jer. 52:15), or craftsmen and smiths (2 K. 24:14, 16; Jer. 24:1; 29:2). The Bible also mentions silversmiths (Jgs. 17:4; Acts 19:24), goldsmiths (Isa. 40:19), a goldsmith's guild (Neh. 3:8, 31f.), and an ironsmith (Isa. 44:12).

*B. Processes and Techniques.* The Bible alludes to a large number of metallurgical processes and techniques. Many of these must be inferred from the adjectives describing particular products, e.g., "hammered" gold or "molten" idols, or from verbs demonstrating activities such as refining, smelting, melting, overlaying. In addition to refining (*see* REFINE), SMELTING (and melting), and SOLDERING, the Bible knows of forging (*see* FORGE), casting, beating (or hammering), overlaying, burnishing (or polishing), whetting, and cutting. Other known techniques for the handling of metals are not mentioned at all, e.g., tempering, welding, quenching, annealing, and grinding (the verb is often used but never in connection with ores or metals).

The forming of molten metal into particular shapes by pouring it into molds must have been well known in Palestine as early as the 10th century B.C., judging from the numerous references to images, idols, and gods. Many passages refer to casting with gold (e.g., Ex. 25:12; 37:13), silver (e.g., 36:36; 38:27), and bronze (e.g., 26:37; 38:5); but none of these describes the process.

Beaten (i.e., hammered) silver or gold is mentioned in many passages (e.g., 1 K. 10:16f. par. 2 Ch. 9:15f.; Jer. 10:9). References to swords being beaten into plowshares (Isa. 2:4; Mic. 4:13) and plowshares into swords (Joel 3:10 [MT 4:10]) imply that there were those who could accomplish the task. Of the passages that mention hammering as a method (cf. Ex. 25:18, 31, 36; 37:7, 17, 22; Nu. 8:4; 16:38) Ex. 39:3 is especially important, for it describes how gold sheets were hammered out thin enough to be cut into threads to be woven into Aaron's linen ephod. Two of the three Hebrew nouns for "hammer," *maqqāḇâ* (Isa. 44:12) and *paṭṭîš* (41:7), are used in shaping metals. The plural form in 44:12 suggests that several hammers were used for various stages of the process.

Another technique, overlaying objects with precious metals, is indicated some forty-seven times in the OT by the intensive form (piel) of *ṣāpâ* (e.g., 1 K. 6:20, 35; 2 K. 18:10; 2 Ch. 3:10; Ex. 24:11; 26:19, 32; 38:5, 27). Most likely the process involved hammering out the metal and then fastening it with pegs or nails to various forms — frames, idols, and occasionally even walls and doors.

Burnishing to smoothness is a technique well known in

Gold cups from Ur (*ca.* 2700 B.C.). From left to right: long fluted cup, chalice, fluted cup with spout (University Museum, University of Pennsylvania)

both ceramics and metallurgy. The polishing of metal objects by friction was known as early as the Bronze Age and continued into the later biblical periods (cf. "burnished," niphal part. of *māraṭ*, 1 K. 7:45; pass. part. of *māraq*, 2 Ch. 4:16; *qālāl* Ezk. 1:17; Dnl. 10:6; "burnished bronze," Gk. *chalklíbanon*, Rev. 1:15; 2:18).

The whetting or sharpening of metal weapons and implements is referred to several times. To "whet" (Heb. pilpel of *qālal*) an iron implement requires wisdom as well as strength (Eccl. 10:10). Two other terms are used for sharpening. 1 S. 13:19-21 says that the Israelites did not possess the metallurgical technology even to sharpen (*lāṭaš*) plow points, axes, and mattocks (cf. Ps. 7:12 [MT 13]. Other passages use the verb *šānan* for sharpening a sword (Dt. 32:41), arrows (Isa 5:28), and (metaphorically) the tongue (Ps. 64:3 [MT 4]). In none of these passages, however, is the technique described.

The only passages referring to the cutting of metal are Ex. 39:3 (the cutting of hammered gold sheets) and 2 K. 24:13 (the cutting of vessels already formed and in use). The implement used (probably shears or saw) is never named.

*C. Objects*. The Bible mentions various tools and utensils used in the manufacturing or shaping of metal, including the BELLOWS, FORGE, FURNACE, CRUCIBLE, HAMMER, ANVIL, and TONGS. Tongs made of gold are mentioned in 1 K. 7:49 par. 2 Ch. 4:21, and tongs of unspecified manufacture and use are well known from Isaiah's call/vision (Isa. 6:6).

A great variety of metal objects receives mention in the Bible. Such objects were used, e.g., in temple and architectural materials, as weaponry, as idols, for ornaments, and for agricultural implements.

*D. Figurative Use*. In all sections of the Hebrew Bible and at all periods of biblical history, metals and metallurgical processes are referred to figuratively. The smith at work illustrates diligence and skill (Sir. 38:28; cf. Isa. 44:12). Mining for hidden ore is compared to the search for inacessible widsom (Job 28:1). GOLD and SILVER were symbols of wealth (e.g., Job 3:15; 22:25; 27:16; 28:15, 17; 31:24f.; Isa. 60:17; Zec. 9:3). Refined silver symbolized the purity of God's promises (Ps. 12:6 [MT 7]). The corrosive deterioration of silver and other metals into dross is a metaphor for a people's unfaithfulness and impurity (Isa. 1:22; Jer. 6:29f.; Ezk. 22:18-20), while the refining process (esp. for silver or gold) is a metaphor for the testing and purifying of God's people (Ps. 66:10; Isa. 48:10; Jer. 9:7 [MT 6]; Zec. 13:9; Mal. 3:7f.; cf. Prov. 17:3; 27:21; 1 Cor. 3:12f.; 1 Pet. 1:6f.). IRON can be used as a simile because of its hard and unyielding property (e.g., Lev. 26:19), proverbially, "iron sharpens iron and one man sharpens another" (Prov. 27:17). Alternately iron may be a symbol of strength (e.g., Jer. 1:18) or oppression (28:13).

***V. Metallurgical Discoveries from Ancient Palestine*.–*A. The Chalcolithic Period*.** Several excavated sites from this period yield information on metallurgical processes and products. The sites are Teleilât el-Ghassûl in southeast Jordan across the valley from Jericho (first half of the 4th millennium B.C.), Abū Matar near Beer-sheba (*ca.* 3500 B.C.), Beer-sheba and Kefar Monash (*ca.* 3300 B.C.), Jericho (*ca.* 3200 B.C.), and Timnaʿ in the southern Negeb (near the end of the 4th millennium B.C.).

Timnaʿ's site 39 disclosed a rock-hewn bowl-type smelting furnace 50 cm. (20 in.) across by 40 cm. (16 in.) deep with the air probably blown by a bellows. Most likely the slag was broken up after removal from the furnace in order to recover copper pellets still embedded in it. The copper recovered from this furnace was found to be impure, low in arsenic, and typical of the oxide ore deposits of the region. A crucible furnace was also found at Timnaʿ constructed of square stone boxes within which four stone slabs had been set into the ground.

The earliest known crucible furnace is located at Abū Matar near Beer-sheba. This type of circular furnace had a diameter of 30-40 cm. (12-16 in.) with vertical walls 3 cm. (1 in.) thick and about 12-15 cm. (5-6 in.) high. Crucibles made of gray clay mixed with straw are oval shaped with rounded bottoms 11 by 8 cm. (4 by 3 in.) outside and about 7 cm. (3 in.) deep inside. Abū Matar also produced the first known copper workshop. Archeologists uncovered malachite ores, flint anvils for breaking the ore, fireplaces with metal slag and vessels for pouring and casting the copper, in addition to axes, chisels, awls, and mace-heads (Aharoni, p. 42).

Other artifacts from this period include a cache of objects found in "The Treasure Cave" at Mishmar about 10

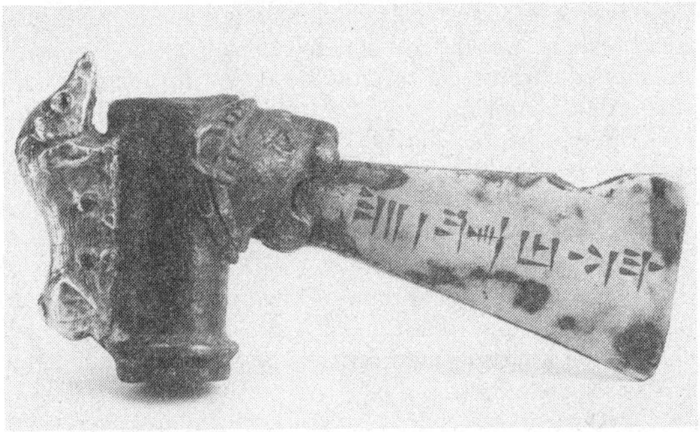

Bronze and electrum axe inscribed with the name of the Elamite king Untaš-Ḫumban (*ca.* 1285-1206 B.C.) (Louvre; picture M. Chuzeville)

km. (6 mi.) SW of En-gedi on the west side of the Dead Sea. Of the 429 objects uncovered, most were copper cultic artifacts, including mace-heads, tubes, and crowns (Aharoni, p. 45); these were composed mainly of arsenical coppers (1.92-12.0% As) with strong traces of antimony and silver (Tylecote, p. 9). Other objects included a staff-head from Beer-sheba, axes, a chisel, and a saw from Kefar Monash, and awls and axes from Ghassul. Thus the earliest Palestinian copper objects were mainly cultic in use and date from *ca.* 3200 B.C.

*B. Bronze Age.* Bronze Age sites in Palestine are too numerous to cite all the findings. Generally, while copper continued to be used, bronze in abundance replaced copper and new types of weapons, vessels, and ornaments appeared. The Egyptian inflence on bronze metallurgy is well attested.

For details of furnace technology the sites in the Negeb are most productive. Dating from the 14th-12th cents. B.C., the Timnaʿ furnaces have furnished much information about metallurgy in this period. Dug into the sandy soil, they are roughly cylindrical in shape, about 60 cm. by 60 cm. (24 by 24 in.). Ground was cut away in front to give access for the tapping of slag. The furnace was blown through inclined tuyeres of unusual form. Tuyeres (i.e., ceramic tubes, often flanged to admit a bellow's nozzle, through which air was forced into the furnace) were found with holes about 2 cm. (0.8 in.) in diameter. Discovered near the furnaces were slag discs (about 50 kg., 110 lbs.) with a central hole. The bowl is lined with a limey cement (Tylecote, pp. 30f.). The presence of this copper smelter in Bronze Age Timnaʿ demonstrates clearly that copper continued to be used during this period and serves as a reminder that all archeological terminology is general and schematic (Aharoni, p. 35).

Among the other significant sites is Hazor. Here a workshop for bronze was uncovered, in which was found a ritual standard of bronze covered with gold. Documents at Hazor include a receipt for large quantities of tin for use in the manufacture of bronze (Aharoni, p. 101). Beth-shemesh (Stratum III), about 19 km. (12 mi.) W of Jerusalem, had bronze ovens and furnaces. Archeologists found at Tell Harashim a room that served as a copper and bronze workshop, containing a kiln, ovens, benches, and vessels (Aharoni, p. 160). Wâdī Feinan in south Jordan, yet to be excavated, shows remains dating probably to 2000 B.C. At Metsamor two types of smelting furnaces dating to the 2nd millennium B.C. were found by Russian archeologists in 1956-1965.

Some of the artifacts from the Bronze Age deserve mention: from Timnaʿ a copper snake in the L.B. Egyptian temple (sometimes called the Hathor temple; Hathor was the Egyptian goddess of mining); from Nahariyah, a town near the Israel-Lebanon border, a mold for bronze figurines from M.B. II.B; from Shechem, a bronze Egyptian sickle sword; from Meggido, a cache of bronze implements and ornaments from tombs in Strata VII A and VI: from Kefar Monash, metal weapons and tools; from Ma'borot, a fenestrated bronze axe; from Tell Beit Mirsim, an adze-head and a mace-head.

*C. Iron Age.* It is generally believed that the Iron Age began in Asia Minor *ca.* 2000 B.C. The Hittites held a monopoly on iron in the 14th-13th cents., after which the products and technology were disseminated throughout the ancient Near East. Iron materials began to be used in Palestine in the 12th and 11th cents., but iron findings are much more rare than previously thought (see Dothan, pp. 91f.). Iron was first used as jewelry and then for daggers, knives, and other implements. A table of the distribution of iron from twenty-one sites in Palestine shows few thirteenth-century findings and far greater volume in the 11th cent. B.C. (Y. Baumgarten in Dothan, p. 92). Probably too much has been made of the Philistine monopoly on iron that David broke when he came to power: too little is known about the industry in the Davidic period to be conclusive.

Iron Age metallurgical centers include the Timnaʿ mining and smelting camps and four other ARABAH sites: Meneʿiyyeh, Khirbet en-Nahas, Khirbet el-Gheweibeh, and Khirbet el-Jariyeh. A building at Tell el-Kheleifeh was originally interpreted by N. Glueck to be a large copper smelter of the Solomonic era, making this site the "Pittsburgh of ancient Palestine." It is now known, however, that the building was not a copper smelter. The ruins date as early as Chalcolithic and as late as Roman; the site was used in the 13th cent. and first half of the 12th cent., but not in the Solomonic period. Iron workshops have been found at Tel Zeror in the plain of Sharon and at Tell Jemmeh, 10 km. (6 mi.) S of Gaza. At Tell Jemmeh a number of smithing furnaces dating between the 12th cent. and 870 B.C. have been found. Metal-working forges have been found in the Jordan Valley at Tell Deir-ʿallā (biblical Succoth) and at a site just a few kilometers farther south. Tell el-Mazâr, ʿAin Shems, et-Tell (Ai), and Tell el-Qasîleh also had furnaces. Artifacts of iron have been uncovered at Tell el-Fârʿah, at Tell el-Fûl, and in large quantities in ninth- and eighth-century Ashdod. An iron mine with an associated smelting operation was found at Mughâret el-Wardeh in Gilead (ʿAjlûn), but the evidence is mainly medieval (A.D. 1185-1450). Iron artifacts found at this site include knives, sickles, an iron plow blade, bracelets, rings, toggle-pins, arrowheads, lance heads, spearheads, swords, axes, chisels, pins, hooks, nails, needles, and tweezers.

***Bibliography.***–Y. Aharoni, *Archaeology of the Land of Israel* (Eng. tr. 1982); J. Bimson, *Tyndale Bulletin,* 32 (1981), 123-149; T. Dothan, *The Philistines and Their Material Culture* (1982); R. J. Forbes, *Studies in Ancient Technology,* VII-IX (rev. ed. 1971); J. L. Kelso, *BASOR,* 122 (Apr. 1951), 26-28; A. D. Merriman, *Concise Encyclopedia of Metallurgy* (1965); J. D. Muhly, *IEJ,* 30 (1980), 148-161; *Biblical Archaeology Review,* 8/6 (1982), 42-54; O. Negbi, *Canaanite Gods in Metal* (1976); B. Rothenberg, *PEQ* (1962), 5-71; R. F. Tylecote, *History of Metallurgy* (1976); J. Waldbaum, *From Bronze to Iron* (1978); T. A. Wertime, *Science,* 146 (Dec. 4, 1964), 1257-1267; *Science,* 1982 (Nov. 30, 1973), 857-887; T. S. Wheeler and R. Maddin, "Metallurgy and Ancient Man", in J. A. Wertime and J. D. Muhly, eds., *Coming of the Iron Age* (1980).

R. A. COUGHENOUR

**METE.** To measure, either with a utensil of dry measure (e.g., AV Ex. 16:18; Lk. 6:38 par.) or with a measure of length (e.g., AV Ps. 60:6 [MT 8]; 108:7 [MT 8]; Isa. 40:12).

The RSV uses "mete out" only in Job 28:25 (AV "weigh"; NEB "measure out") to render the Heb. piel of *tāḵan*, which here means "determine the measure of" (*CHAL*, p. 390). *See* MEASURE; PORTION.

In Isa. 18:2, 7 the AV renders "meted out" for Heb. *qaw-qāw*, based on the usual meaning of *qāw* ("measuring line"; cf. *qaw lāqāw*, 28:10, 13; AV, RSV, "line upon line"). The meaning of the Hebrew is obscure. Some scholars have understood it as a cognate of Arab. *qūwa* ("strength"; cf. RSV "mighty"; NEB "strong"). KD suggested the translation "command upon command," i.e., "a commanding nation." In any case, the context indicates that the prophet is describing a powerful nation that subdues other nations — not one that is "meted out and trampled down" (AV; see comms.). N. J. O.

**METERUS** mə-tē'rəs (1 Esd. 5:17, AV). *See* BAITERUS.

**METEYARD** mēt'yärd. Archaic for "measuring rod" in Lev. 19:35, AV, translating Heb. *middâ*, "measure, measurement" (RSV "measures of length").

**METHEG-AMMAH** me-theg-am'ə, meth-eg-am'ə [Heb. *meṯeg hāʾammâ*–'bridle of the mother-city'; Gk. *hē aphōrisménē*]; NEB METHEG-HA-AMMAH; cf. RV "the bridle of the mother city." Apparently a place taken from the Philistines by David (2 S. 8:1), although no such site is known. The parallel passage (1 Ch. 18:1) reads differently: "David . . . took Gath and her daughters [i.e., her surrounding towns]." To "take the bridle" in Eastern idiom means to "take control of"; the meaning then would be that David took control of Gath and its metropolitan area. The Philistines, however, had no single metropolis; Gath was but one of five chief cities. The text is difficult, and the JB (as the NEB) leaves the expression untranslated, with the comment that it is unintelligible. See S. R. Driver, *Notes on the Hebrew Text and Topography of the Books of Samuel* (2nd ed. 1913), pp. 279f.

F. WEDDLE

**METHUSAEL** mə-thōō'sə-el (Gen. 4:18, AV). *See* METHUSHAEL.

**METHUSELAH** mə-thōō'sə-lə [Heb. *m$^e$ṯûšelaḥ*; Gk. *Mathousala*]; AV also MATHUSALA (Lk. 3:37). Son of Enoch and father of Lamech (Gen. 5:21-27; cf. 1 Ch. 1:3; Lk. 3:37).

The meaning of "Methuselah" is debated. If one assumes a Semitic background for the name, the first element, *m$^e$ṯû*, should mean "man (of)" (cf. Akk. *mutu*, Ugar. *mt*, Egyp. *mt*, and Heb. *m$^e$ṯîm* [a pl. form]; proper names with this element are common in Amorite as well; see H. Huffmon, *Amorite Personal Names in the Mari Texts* [1965], pp. 119f., 134f.).

But scholars disagree about the etymology of the second element, *šelaḥ*.

(1) The traditional view, still held by many, understands *šelaḥ* as the Hebrew word for "javelin," hence "javelin man" (i.e., referring to the inventor of, or expert with, the javelin).

(2) Others relate *šelaḥ* to the general meaning of the root, "send," hence, "man of sending," or "a sent man." Such an interpretation comports well with the prophetic cast of Gen. 5 (see below).

(3) According to some (e.g., *CHAL*, p. 372), *šelaḥ* can also mean "canal." On this view, a person would have been so named because he came from such a place, or possibly invented or improved this form of irrigation.

(4) A. van Selms divided *šelaḥ* into *š$^e$*, a relative particle meaning "who," and *laḥ*, which he takes as the name of a Semitic deity. But the use of *š$^e$* in such a name is elsewhere unattested (Tromp, p. 149), and it is by no means clear that a deity named *laḥ* existed (as Fensham admits).

(5) Similarly, M. Tsevat took *šelaḥ* as the name of a deity associated with a canal or river of judgment in the netherworld — hence "man of *šlḥ*" (cf. the Ugaritic and Amarna name *mtbʿl*, "man of Baal"; cf. also the Phoenician name *ʾbšlḥ*). But *šlḥ* is nowhere directly attested as a divine name; thus this proposal must remain conjectural.

Various attempts have been made to account for the astounding longevity and fertility of Methuselah and the other early Sethites (*see*, e.g., ANTEDILUVIAN PATRIARCHS). M. G. Kline suggested that the governing interest in Gen. 5 is a contrast between Sethites selected for their prophetic witness and the apostate Cainites in Gen. 4:17-24 and 6:1-8. Evidence for this prophetic cast is most obvious in the prophetic ministry of Noah as the climactic descendant, but apparent also in the prophetic imagery implied in the description of Enoch as one who "walked with God" (cf. Kline, *NBC*, p. 87; *Images*, p. 102). Anticipating the later prophet Elijah, Enoch too was translated, and so was supernaturally spared from death. In the context of Gen. 5 the unusual longevity of Methuselah and the other Sethites perhaps conveys miraculous interventions suited to the prophetic ministry of these individuals, who would have been concerned to address the self-made immortality of the Cainites (Gen. 4:17, 23; 6:4).

On the selective nature of the genealogy, *see* GENEALOGY II.

*See also* METHUSHAEL.

***Bibliography.***–M. G. Kline, "Genesis," *NBC* (3rd ed. 1970); *Images of The Spirit* (1980); N. J. Tromp, *Primitive Conceptions of Death and the Nether World in the OT* (1969); M. Tsevat, *VT*, 4 (1954), 41-49; *IDBS*, *s.v.* "Shalah (God)"; A. van Selms, "A Forgotten God: *Laḥ*," in *Studia Biblica et Semitica* (*Festschrift* for T. C. Vriezen, 1966), pp. 318-326.

G. P. HUGENBERGER

**METHUSHAEL** mə-thōō'shə-el [Heb. *m$^e$ṯûšāʾēl*–'man of God'(?); Gk. *Mathousala*]; AV METHUSAEL. A descendant of Cain and ancestor of Lamech in the Cainite genealogy (Gen. 4:18). Some scholars (e.g., E. A. Speiser, *Genesis* [*AB*, 1964], pp. 35f.) assign the Cainite genealogy to one source or tradition (J) and the Sethite genealogy (Gen. 5) to another source (P), both stemming from one original tradition, and thus identify Methushael and Methuselah. Others (e.g., KD), however, note the differences in the genealogies and regard them as distinct (*see* ANTEDILUVIAN PATRIARCHS II). G. A. L.

**MEUNIM** mə-ū'nim; **MEUNITES** mə-ū'nīts.

**1.** [Heb. *m$^{e}$ʿûnîm*, *m$^{e}$ʿînîm* (1 Ch. 4:41 *K*); Gk. *Minaioi*]; AV also MEHUNIM(S) (2 Ch. 26:7); "habitations" (1 Ch. 4:41); [Heb. *ʿammônîm*; Gk. *Minaioi*] (2 Ch. 20:1); AV "Ammonites"; **MAONITES** mā'ə-nīts [Heb. *māʿôn*; Gk. *Madiam*] (Jgs. 10:12); NEB "Midianites." A hostile people, linked with the Amalekites and Zidonians, who at some unknown time oppressed Israel (Jgs. 10:12); also, a pastoral people attacked by Hezekiah (1 Ch. 4:41) and Uzziah (2 Ch. 26:7). They may have come from Maʿan, about 35 km. (22 mi.) SE of Petra on the ancient caravan route that led from Damascus to Mecca. The Alexandrian (LXX) translators seem to identify the Meunim with the Minaeans, Arabian tribes in southern Arabia (Hadramaut) that dealt in spices and incense. See *GTTOT*, § 164.

In 2 Ch. 20:1 the RSV, following the LXX, makes better sense than the MT (followed by AV), which seems to be redundant (see KD).

**2.** [Heb. *b^enê-m^e'ûnîm*; Gk. *Maōnim, Meinōm*] (Ezr. 2:50; Neh. 7:52); AV also MEHUNIM (Ezra); [Gk. *hyioí Maani*] (1 Esd. 5:31); AV MEANI; NEB MAANI. A people mentioned in the official list of those who returned from exile (Ezr. 2:50; Neh. 7:52). They may be the descendants of prisoners taken in the wars of Jehoshaphat and Uzziah, who were given menial tasks in the service of the temple (*see* NETHINIM).Today Tell Ma'în (Maon) is a small heap of ruins S of Hebron, and as in ancient times the surrounding territory is widely used as pasture for numerous flocks. F. E. YOUNG

**MEUZAL** mə-o͞o'zəl (Ezk. 27:19, AV mg.). *See* UZAL.

**MEZAHAB** mez'ə-hab [Heb. *mê zāhab̲*–'waters of gold']. According to most versions, the father of Matred and grandfather of Mehetabel the wife of Hadar, one of the kings of Edom (AV, RSV, Gen. 36:39; 1 Ch. 1:50). The name may, however, denote a place (cf. NEB); some scholars have suggested that it may be identical with Dizahab (Dt. 1:1).

**MEZARIM** mez'ə-rim [Heb. *m^ezārîm*]. *See* ASTRONOMY II.C.

**MEZOBAITE** mə-zō'bə-īt [Heb. *hamm^eṣōb̲āyâ*]; AV MESOBAITE. The designation of Jaasiel, one of the "mighty men" in David's army (1 Ch. 11:47). The meaning is unknown. Possibly the MT should be emended to *miṣṣōb̲â*, "from Zobah."

**MIAMIN** mī'ə-min (AV Ezr. 10:25; Neh. 12:5). *See* MIJAMIN.

**MIBHAR** mib'här [Heb. *mib̲ḥār*]. According to 1 Ch. 11:38, the name of one of the "mighty men" of David's army. No such name, however, appears in the par. 2 S. 23:36, which reads "of Zobah, Bani the Gadite" in place of "Mibhar the son of Hagri." The 2 S. 23:36 reading is probably the original, with *mib̲ḥār* being a corruption of *miṣṣōb̲â* and *ben-hagrî* a corruption of *bānî haggāḏî*.

**MIBSAM** mib'sam [Heb. *mib̲śām*].

**1.** A son of Ishmael (Gen. 25:13; 1 Ch. 1:29), and the name of an Arabian tribe (cf. Gen. 25:16, 18).

**2.** A descendant of Simeon; the father of Mishma (1 Ch. 4:25).

**MIBZAR** mib'zär [Heb. *mib̲ṣār*–'fortress']. An Edomite clan chief (Gen. 36:42; 1 Ch. 1:53). Eusebius identified Mibzar with *Mabsara*, a village subject to Petra in Northern Edom. Others have suggested Bozrah (v. 33; so *GTTOT*, § 393) or Petra itself.

**MICA** mī'kə [Heb. *mîḵā'*]; AV MICHA, MICAH; NEB also MICAH. A contracted form of MICAIAH.

**1.** A son of Mephibosheth and grandson of Jonathan the son of Saul (2 S. 9:12); called Micah in 1 Ch. 8:34f.; 9:40f.; *see* MICAH (**3**).

**2.** An Asaphite, son of Zichri (1 Ch. 9:15; Zabdi in Neh. 11:17; MICAIAH [5] son of Zaccur in 12:35); father of Mattaniah (11:17, 22) and ancestor of Uzzi, an overseer of the Levites in Jerusalem (v. 22), and Zechariah, a trumpeter at the dedication of the wall of Jerusalem in the time of Nehemiah (12:35).

**3.** A Levite who sealed the covenant with Nehemiah (Neh. 10:11 [MT 12]).

**MICAH** mī'kə [Heb. *mîḵâ*–abbreviated form of *mîḵāyāhû*, "who is like Yahweh?"; LXX *Michaias*; Vulg. *Michaeas*].

**1.** An Ephraimite and the central character of an episode given as an appendix to the book of Judges (Jgs. 17–18). Micah stole one thousand one hundred pieces of silver from his mother, but later confessed and returned the silver because of a curse she had pronounced on the thief. In gratitude she blessed Micah and gave two-hundred pieces of silver to have a graven and molten image crafted for him. Micah established a domestic shrine and appointed one of his sons priest, and his worship accessories included an ephod and teraphim. A Levite (Jonathan son of Gershom, son of Moses), from Bethlehem-Judah, soon replaced Micah's son as priest in exchange for room, board, clothing, and wages. The Levite gave a favorable oracle to five Danites who were seeking a new home; they later returned with an army of six hundred, confiscated the ephod and teraphim, and enlisted the Levite as their priest in Laish. Micah protested and pursued the Danites, but was helpless in the face of their superior strength, and he returned home empty-handed. Micah's graven image thus became the focus of the well-known cultic center in Dan.

While scholars agree that the account in Judges is an ancient record of the traditions behind the origin of the Danite shrine and has great value historiographically and for the study of early Israelite worship, the exact nature and purpose of the narrative remain topics of debate. The story certainly has etiological significance, since it seeks to explain the origin of the Danite cult and priesthood, and attempts to legitimize that shrine by making it contemporary with Shiloh and by tracing its priesthood to Moses himself. More importantly, the account further illustrates the purpose of the compiler of Judges in that it graphically portrays the political and religious anarchy of the day. This breach of covenant led to idolatry, immorality, political and religious syncretism, and finally Israel's destruction (Jgs. 2:1-6, 11-15; cf. 2 K. 17:7-23; 24:1-7).

**2.** A son of Shimei, a descendant of Reuben, and an ancestor of the Beerah who was carried into captivity by Tiglathpileser III (1 Ch. 5:5f.).

**3.** A son of Meribaal (Mephibosheth) and grandson of Jonathan; the father of four sons (1 Ch. 8:34f.; 9:40f.; called Mica in 2 S. 9:12; *see* MICA **1.**).

**4.** AV MICHAH. A Levite, head of the chief family of the Uzziel branch of the Kohathite Levites, who lived during the last days of David's reign (1 Ch. 23:20; 24:24f.).

**5.** The father of Abdon and a contemporary of Josiah (2 Ch. 34:20; called Micaiah in 2 K. 22:12).

**6.** Micah of Moresheth, a prophet of God (Jer. 26:18; Mic. 1:1; 2 Esd. 1:39 [AV MICHEAS]). *See* MICAH, BOOK OF.

**7.** A Simeonite, father of Ozias, and one of the three rulers of Bethulia in the days of Judith (Jth. 6:15; cf. 9:2).

***Bibliography.***–J. D. Martin, *Judges* (*CBC*, 1975); M. Noth, "The Background of Judges 17–18," in B. W. Anderson and W. Harrelson, eds., *Israel's Prophetic Heritage* (*Festschrift* for J. Muilenburg; 1962), pp. 68-85. A. E. HILL

**MICAH, BOOK OF.** The sixth book of the Minor Prophets.

I. Date
II. Historical Background
III. Author
IV. Literary Structure
V. Literary Value
VI. Theological Value
VII. Relevance

***I. Date.***–The superscription to the prophecy of Micah places the book in the 8th cent. B.C., during the reigns of Jotham (*ca.* 740-732), Ahaz (*ca.* 732-716), and Hezekiah (*ca.* 716-687), kings of Judah. The consonance of the prophet's message with the contemporary historical situation supports the chronological parameters of the superscription.

According to 1:6, the destruction of Samaria, the capital of the northern kingdom, was still in the future. Thus Micah's prophetic ministry would have begun some time before that event, which occurred in 722 B.C. Probably this prophecy about Samaria was proclaimed during the reign of Jotham. The discourses in chs. 2–5, which do not mention Samaria, probably came from the time of Ahaz and the early period of Hezekiah.

Certainly the strong denunciation of paganism in the oracles of Micah is in keeping with the syncretistic tendencies of Ahaz's reign (2 K. 16:3f., 10-18). The specific mention of Ahaz's use of the high places (*bāmôṯ*) in 2 K. 16:4 indicates that Micah's condemnation of the high places in 1:5 is appropriate for the religious climate during the reign of Ahaz, and the prereformation period of Hezekiah's reign.

K. Elliger (*ZDPV,* 57 [1934], 81-83) thought that ch. 1 reflected Micah's personal involvement in the siege of Jerusalem by the Assyrians in 701 B.C., but this cannot be demonstrated. Chapters 4 and 5 were denied to Micah by numerous nineteenth-century OT scholars and attributed mostly to later unknown authors. But such conservative writers as G. Wildeboer affirmed that there was no one element in the prophecy that was inconsistent with Micah's authorship and a date in the 8th cent. B.C. (*De Profeet Micha* [1884], p. 57). Part of the difficulty lies in the messianic oracles, as well as in the promises of restoration in 4:6f. and 5:6-9. The sections concerning restoration, however, reflect the language of Isaiah (2:2-4, 6-8), while the promise of a Messiah in 5:2 constitutes a forthright and genuine element of prediction in a section of the prophecy that is free from any suspicion of textual corruption. While the passage may be assigned to a later date on a priori grounds such as the impossibility of a futuristic element in Hebrew prophetism, such grounds would be tendentious rather than historical. Comparative study of the text shows distinct consonance with the thought of Amos, Hosea, and Isaiah in such matters as the mention of Canaanite idolatry (cf. Isa. 2:6-8; Am. 5:26; 8:14), the Messiah (cf. Isa. 9:1-7; 11:1-9), and the defeat of the pagan assault upon Zion (cf. Isa. 10:24-34; 17:12-14; 29:1). There is thus little reason to question the chronological span of time established by the superscription.

***II. Historical Background.***–The halcyon days of prosperity and relative peace achieved under Uzziah king of Judah (792-740 B.C.), and Jeroboam II king of Israel (793-753 B.C.) were on the wane in the time of Micah. A new era was dawning in which the political situation in the ancient Near East began to change. The major force in this change was the nation of Assyria. After a long period of quiescence, Assryia again became a potent political force. The kings of Israel and Judah were forced to regard that nation as an important factor in their political considerations.

The prosperity enjoyed by Israel and Judah in the first part of the 8th cent. B.C. was more apparent than real. It was actually the result of a lack of military pressure upon the northern kingdom by the Syrians, who had been forced to defend their eastern frontier against attacks by the resurgent Assyrians. While trade and commerce flourished, they did so largely at the expense of the small landowners and the peasants, who steadily lost whatever land they had possessed because of the greed of the wealthy classes. Perhaps emboldened by Ahab's example (1 K. 21:1-16), rich landowners bribed the judges to look favorably upon improper land acquisitions (cf. 2:1f.; 3:11), and the result was the rapid disappearance of the small farmer. Those who were dispossessed drifted from the countryside to the city, and for the first time in Hebrew history the larger centers of population experienced overcrowding. Micah was outspoken in his condemnation of corrupt judges, who were supposed to be upholding covenant law, and he castigated venal priests and prophets, who would condone the perversion of justice for the poor as long as they continued to receive money for doing so.

Micah's utterances, like those of the other eighth-century prophets, reflect the extent to which the Sinaitic covenantal stipulations had been abandoned in favor of the grossly licentious Baal-worship that was practiced in Israel and had also influenced religious and social life in Judah. Under the so-called controversy (*rîḇ*) provisions of the covenant, God was proposing to summon His people to court to make them formally answerable for their misdeeds (6:1f.). The high moral and ethical values of the Sinai covenant (6:8) had been replaced by Canaanite idolatry and sensual worship at the shrines. Samaria, the leader in such apostasy, would pay the ultimate penalty of destruction for such blatant disobedience of the covenant stipulations. Unless Israel rejected the example of Ahab's house and returned to its God in penitence and faith, its current prosperity would be short-lived. Although Micah sorrowed over the fact that the provisions of the covenant had been violated for so long, he believed that true repentance would result in God's forgiveness and a consequent restoration of the whole nation to spiritual fellowship with Himself. Despite his faith in God's mercy, however, Micah held out no hope for the future of Israel and Judah. Their doom was absolute (1:6; 3:12). However, a remnant was to be delivered under the aegis of a king who would provide security for his people (5:2-4 [MT 1-3]).

***III. Author.***–Little is known about the prophet Micah. The superscription identifies him with the town of Moresheth (1:1), probably MORESHETH-GATH, a town in Judah.

Micah appears to have been as individualistic as his other eighth-century counterparts in his prophetic ministry. Whatever prophetic guilds existed at that time did not include him in their membership, since in 3:5-8 he drew a sharp distinction between their activities and his own spirit-filled prophetic ministry.

The prophecy of Micah portrays him as a man of deep religious sensitivity. His prophetic statements are bold and forthright, yet tempered with a deep concern for his nation.

The influence of Micah is attested in Jer. 26:18, where a prophecy of his (Mic. 3:12) was cited by certain elders in the time of Jeremiah. They argued that Micah, who prophesied earlier, had not been put to death by Hezekiah, even though he also had predicted the destruction of Jerusalem. Thus this passage implies that Hezekiah's reforms were due in part to the influence of Micah: "Did Hezekiah, king of Judah, and all Judah put him to death? Did he [Hezekiah] not fear the Lord and entreat the favor of the Lord, and did not the Lord repent of the evil which he had pronounced against them?" One may wonder why the reference to Micah is immediately followed by the account of Hezekiah's return to the Lord if there was no substantive connection between them. On the other hand, the message of Micah had so much in common with that of his senior contemporary Isaiah that the supposed influence of Micah upon Hezekiah's spiritual life could well be coincidental though correlative. Micah apparently had no access to the royal court, unlike Isaiah, and his advice was never sought by the officials of Jotham, Ahaz, or Hezekiah.

Micah's prophecy bears a close resemblance both in

form and content to certain portions of Isaiah, e.g., Mic. 4:1-3 and Isa. 2:2-4. Conjectures to the contrary, it is not possible to state with certainty who the original author was, or whether the material was adapted from the utterances of some earlier prophet whose work has not otherwise survived. Mic. 4:4f. is an addition to the parallel material in Isaiah; thus Micah's oracle was a specific prediction of peace in the nation and points to a time when the people will be walking in the name of their covenant Lord. To that extent, therefore, Micah places his own prophetic imprint upon the saying, regardless of whether Isaiah or some other person was the original author. Mic. 1:10-16 is reminiscent of Isa. 10:27-32, while Mic. 2:1f. reflects Isa. 5:8, but in both instances Micah is clearly the author of his own oracles.

*IV. Literary Structure.*–Three literary units are apparent in the book. Each is based on a structure that begins with a summons to hear followed by statements of doom, and each concludes with a statement of hope. These units are 1:2–2:13; 3:1–5:15; 6:1–7:20.

It is possible that these oracles were given by Micah at various times in the course of his prophetic career. The first oracle may be assumed to be the earliest because of its prediction of the doom of Samaria. Since the second concerns only Jerusalem, the northern kingdom may have already fallen. In Jer. 26:18f. a portion of this oracle (Mic. 3:12) is placed in the time of Hezekiah. The third oracle is difficult to place historically.

Several portions of the book are commonly regarded as late redactive intrusions. Perhaps the most celebrated of these is 5:7f. (MT 8f.), which apparently indicates an ideological conflict with respect to the way in which the remnant effects its mission in the world. In v. 7 the remnant seems to be portrayed in pacifistic terms, whereas the portrayal of v. 8 is militaristic in nature. This conflict seems to support the presence of several "hands" in the construction of the final form of the book.

But the point of v. 7 is the inexorability of the progress of the remnant. The "dew" and "showers" "tarry not for men." That is, the remnant will not achieve its destiny because of human effort. The same concept of the inexorable progress of the remnant is set forth in v. 8 as well. Thus the two verses have no clear ideological conflict.

The unity of literary style that pervades the book and the closely knit structure of the religious concerns within it give strong support to the possibility that the work is a literary production of the eighth-century prophet whose name it bears.

*V. Literary Value.*–The most distinctive literary characteristic of the prophecy of Micah is its use of paronomasia. This device, which plays on the sounds of words for literary effect, may be found in a number of places in the book. The most outstanding example of paronomasia is in 1:10-15, where the prophet effects a consonance between his statements of doom and the names of towns that will experience that doom in the impending exile. Thus in 1:10 the inhabitants of Beth-le-aphrah ("house of dust") are told "roll yourselves in the dust." In 1:14 the prophet says that "the houses of Achzib [Heb. *'akzîḇ*] shalt be a deceitful [Heb. *'akzāḇ*] thing."

Another example of paronomasia may be found in the double reference assigned to the word *bāmôṯ* ("high places") in 1:3-5. In 1:3 it refers to mountains, but in 1:5 it occurs in a parallel structure as the counterpart of "sin" (*peša'*). This latter usage evidently requires the connotation of pagan sanctuaries. This deft use of the pun thus serves to picture Yahweh treading across the mountains as the pagan sanctuaries are crushed beneath His feet.

Like other prophets, Micah made use of bold anthropomorphism. The first oracle begins with a depiction of Yahweh treading upon the mountains, which melt beneath His feet (1:4). This theophanic motif elicits within the mind of the reader images of the majestic grandeur of Yahweh, as well as His awesome power to judge within the sphere of human events.

*VI. Theological Value.*–One of the most important theological concepts of the prophecy of Micah is the immanence of God in history. The theophanic imagery of 1:2-4 does not represent a literal appearance of God. It is a depiction of His intervention in history to bring about the destruction of Samaria, the capital of the northern kingdom (1:6). This cataclysm was actually brought about by the Assyrians, but Micah saw it as the direct result of Yahweh's response to the disobedience of His people.

The immanence of God is a concept shared by other Israelite prophets, but in the prophecy of Micah it develops into a theology of the nations that is depicted by him in a way unique to his prophecy. Yahweh's intervention in history to effect the destruction of Samaria (1:6) and Jerusalem (3:12) was seen by Micah as a witness against the nations (1:2). The destruction of the vaunted capitals of God's own people had a direct relevance to the nations. It witnessed to the fact that God punishes sin even in His own people. In that way the charred remains of the two cities were a portent of doom for the nations, whose wickedness would spell their doom as well.

The doom spelled out for Israel and Judah was not absolute. Therein lay the theology of hope of the prophet Micah. In the oracle in 4:11-13 the prophet envisions Israel in the sphere of the nations. The nations are pictured as gloating over the destruction of Israel and Judah. But they are unaware that God has a purpose for them (4:12). God's people will be made into a powerful force that will ultimately triumph over the nations (4:13).

The people of God are portrayed as a REMNANT (*šᵉ'ērîṯ*) by Micah. This concept is a theme that appears in several prophetic books. Micah adds an important perspective to that concept. Above we observed that the remnant of God's people will make inexorable progress throughout the course of history toward the achievement of God's purposes for them (5:7f.). This affirms that God's promise to His people of future blessing will never be vitiated.

This emphasis on the remnant as a powerful force in history is set forth by the prophet in 4:6f. as well: "and the lame I will make the remnant; and those who were cast off, a strong nation." Micah envisioned the remnant not simply as a residue of people, as the term "remnant" may imply, but as a strong nation. The lame are to be made into (*śîm lᵉ*) a remnant. They do not automatically constitute the remnant.

In 2:12f. the ultimate restoration of the remnant is accomplished in association with one whom Micah calls "the breaker" (*happōrēṣ*; RSV "he who opens the breach"). The people of God are pictured as a milling flock of sheep penned up in a fold, but "the breaker" will open a breach in the enclosure and will lead them out, with the Lord marching triumphantly at their head. This figure is evidently one of the people, and his close association with Yahweh warrants his identification as the messianic figure cited in 5:2-4 (MT 3-5). This future restoration of the people of God effects their vindication and establishes the continuing validation of God's promises to His people.

Thus Micah's contribution to the theological concept of the people of God is to be found in his doctrine of the remnant. The people of God are a strong force in the world, a force that moves inexorably forward toward the ultimate goal of the manifestation of God's kingdom in history (4:7b).

In Micah's theology Yahweh is no mere tribal god. His universality is too apparent for that. He intervenes in history, yet He is in constant control of the forces of history that move toward the manifestation of His absolute rule.

The concept of covenant is also an essential element in Micah's theology. He makes no direct reference to the Mosaic covenant as such, but it is evident that its stipulations and curses are very much in his mind. In 2:2 he speaks of those who covet (*ḥāmaḏ*) fields and who oppress their fellow man. Both are clear violations of the covenantal stipulations (e.g., Dt. 5:21; Lev. 19:13).

His denunciation of the oppression of the less fortunate is particularly vehement. Some of his harshest and most vivid language is used to condemn that violation of the spirit of the Mosaic law. He pictures the oppressing classes as treating the people like an enemy (Mic. 2:8). They eat the flesh of the people, flay their skin, and break their bones in pieces (3:3).

The covenant pronounced curses on those who violated its commands. Micah is quick to note that those curses must surely be realized. One of the curses cited in the Deuteronomic expression of the covenant is dispersion among the nations (Dt. 28:64-68). Micah envisioned a future exile of the people in 4:10 and a dispersion of the people in 4:6 (note that those who have been driven away will be regathered). The curses of Deuteronomy also involved Israel's destruction at the hands of its enemies (Dt. 28:25f.). This was fulfilled in the destruction of the capital cities so vividly described by Micah in 1:6 and 3:12.

Micah's God is clearly the God of the Sinaitic covenant. The power, righteousness, and high morality that motivated God's approach to the Israelite tribes at Mt. Sinai were at the forefront of his prophetic message. He saw clearly that the covenant stipulations required implicit obedience on the part of God's people to His revealed will, as one means of protecting them from idolatry. But despite the Israelites' strict commitment to monotheism, they became conformed to Canaanite idolatrous ways after settling in the Promised Land. Despite periodic revivals of covenantal faith, the general trend, especially in the northern kingdom, was to espouse the worship of false gods, and it was this act of apostasy that called down the wrath of the Hebrew prophets. Micah was particularly aware that the northern kingdom would not be able to withstand the attacks of the Assyrians once they commenced. He regarded Israel's impending doom as appropriate punishment under the covenant stipulations (cf. 6:13-16) for the nation's infidelity and defiant espousal of a totally false system of worship. More than that, Micah strove energetically in elegant poetic utterances to convince the people of Judah that they should learn a lesson from the forthcoming destruction of Samaria and return in repentance and faith to the religion of the Sinai covenant. See, e.g., 6:8:

"He has showed you, O man, what is good;
  and what does the LORD require of you
but to do justice, and to love kindness,
  and to walk humbly with your God?"

The theology of hope in the prophecy of Micah is centered in a messianic figure who is associated with Bethlehem, the city of David. This obvious Davidic motif is typical of other prophets (Isa. 9:7; Ezk. 34:23f.; 37:24f.; Hos. 3:5; Am. 9:11), but no other prophet cites his birthplace. The Davidic king will provide his people with security in a kingdom that will extend his power to "the ends of the earth" (5:4).

*VII. Relevance.*–The prophecy of Micah extends the sphere of God's control beyond the confines and interests of the people of Israel to the nations of the world. The prophet warns that sin must ultimately come under God's judging hand, whether that sin is found among His chosen people or other peoples.

His description of the nature of God's forgiving love in 7:18-20 is one of the classic OT passages. He sees God as a vital, living power, in implied contrast to the deities of wood and stone that the apostate Israelites had been venerating. This God is a moral Being, who is well aware that transgressions of covenant holiness have been taking place in Israel. Yet although He is holy and just, and could therefore quite legitimately bring upon His apostate people the curses promised in the covenant (Dt. 28:15-68), He is also a God whose mercy is over all His works. Because of His covenant love toward Israel, He is both anxious and ready to pardon the penitent transgressor and renew the bond of covenant spirituality that had been severed. Micah affirms that God is faithful to His promises and will remove His people's sins far from them (7:19).

The prophetic vision of a future king, to be born in Bethlehem, is one of the most distinctive and apposite Messianic utterances in the entire OT. Coming nearly seven centuries before the event itself, this prediction (5:2 [MT 1]) is a dramatic illustration of one facet of prophetic activity. The reference occurs as part of a straightforward oracle, and is the more remarkable because there is no evidence of textual corruption or interpolation of any kind. So firmly rooted did this tradition of the Messiah's birthplace become that, when Herod inquired of his priests and scribes about the locale where the newborn "king of the Jews" could be found, they promptly cited Bethlehem on the authority of the verse from Micah (Mt. 2:5f.).

The prophet's urgent call to obedience should not be relegated only to the era of the old covenant in which Micah lived. It reflects God's continuing concern for the allegiance of His people and the ethical response of His people which is echoed so clearly by the NT writers.

Micah's vision of an era of peace in which nations would cease to learn war (4:3) is the expression of an optimistic philosophy of history. In conjunction with the other eighth-century prophets, Micah regarded the God of Sinai as Lord of human history. All nations were under His supreme control and could be raised up or thrown down as He desired. The rebellious would be pounded like sheaves on the threshing floor (4:12), but the obedient, by contrast, would be nourished and tended like sheep under the care of a loving shepherd (5:4 [MT 3]).

The basis of Micah's optimism is not to be found in a humanistic philosophy nor in a shallow view of history. It is found in his faith in God. Even though he lived in a society that was desperately corrupt and bent on its own ruin (7:1-6), he could say, "But as for me, I will look to the Lord, I will wait for the God of my salvation; my God will hear me" (7:7). The prophet expected God to act on behalf of His people. Micah could triumph over the wrongs so evident about him because his was the triumph of faith.

***Bibliography.***–*Commentaries:* L. C. Allen (*NICOT,* 1976); KD; P. Kleinert (Eng. tr. 1960); H. McKeating (*CBC,* 1971); J. Marsh (*Torch,* 1959); J. L. Mays (*OTL,* 1976); C. von Orelli (Eng. tr. 1897); J. M. P. Smith (*ICC,* 1911); B. Vawter (OT Message VII, 1981); H. W. Wolff (Eng. tr. 1981).

*Articles:* J. L. Crenshaw, *CBQ,* 34 (1972), 39-53; M. Collen, *VT,* 21 (1971), 281-297; J. Knudd, *JSOT,* 8 (1978), 3-32; J. T. Willis, *Bibl.* 48 (1967), 534-541; *ZAW,* 80 (1968), 50-54; *ZAW,* 81 (1969), 191-214, 353-368; *VT,* 18 (1968), 372-79; 529-547; "A Reapplied Prophetic Hope Oracle," in *Studies in Prophecy* (*SVT,* 26; 1974), pp. 64-76.

T. E. MCCOMISKEY

**MICAIAH** mī-kā'yə, mī-kī'ə [Heb. *mîḵāyāhû*–'who is like Yahweh?'; Gk. *Meichaias, Michaias*]; AV usually MICHAIAH. A frequently occurring OT name occasionally contracted to MICA or MICAH.

**1.** NEB MAACAH. The mother of Abijah (2 Ch. 13:2). The parallel passage (1 K. 15:2; cf. 2 Ch. 11:20) indicates that Michaiah here is a corruption of MAACAH (so LXX, NEB).

**2.** The father of Achbor (2 K. 22:12). *See* MICAH **5.**

**3.** A prince of Judah sent by Jehoshaphat to teach in the cities of Judah (2 Ch. 17:7).

**4.** The son of Gemariah (Jer. 36:11, 13) who heard Baruch reading the roll of Jeremiah to the people and informed the nobles. As a result of his report the roll was read to the nobles and then to the king. He may have been the same as **3.**

**5.** The son of Zaccur and ancestor of Zechariah, a priestly trumpeter and processionist at the dedication of the wall (Neh. 12:35); probably the same as MICA **2.**

**6.** A priestly trumpeter and processionist at the dedication of the wall (Neh. 12:41).

**7.** Eng. versions MICAH. The Morashthite in Jer. 26:18, the same as the canonical prophet MICAH.

**8.** The son of Imlah, a prophet contemporary with Elijah who appears only in 1 K. 22:4-28 par. 2 Ch. 18:3-27, although he had made previous prophecies (1 K. 22:8).

The one incident in which he appears is significant for the understanding of the nature of OT prophecy. Jehoshaphat was on a visit to Ahab, who suggested that they join in a campaign to take Ramoth-gilead from the Syrians. Jehoshaphat agreed but asked that first the mind of Yahweh be ascertained. Ahab readily consented and inquired of the four hundred prophets attached to the court, who, realizing that the king desired the expedition, gave a unanimous and encouraging prophecy. Jehoshaphat, however, detected their obsequious conformity to their master's wishes and asked if there were not another prophet of Yahweh from whom they might inquire. Ahab reluctantly called for Micaiah but warned Jehoshaphat that this man had never prophesied anything but evil for him. At first Micaiah agreed with the other four hundred prophets, but Ahab recognized the note of irony in his agreement, and adjured him to tell the truth. Micaiah therefore prophesied in solemn and majestic language a disastrous outcome to the expedition. Ahab tried to detract from the prophecy by declaring that it was only in line with Micaiah's usual unfavorable predictions. In reply the prophet related a vision he had had of a scene in the heavenly court in which Yahweh sent a lying spirit to deceive the false prophets and bring about Ahab's downfall. Zedekiah, the spokesman for the four hundred, struck Micaiah, not denying the allegation but asserting that Micaiah too had been deceived. In the spirit of true prophecy (Dt. 18:22) Micaiah appealed to the fulfillment of his prediction to show its truth; the death of Ahab in the battle (1 K. 22:37f.) did prove his claim.

Thus true and false prophecy existed side by side in Israel. Any attempt to understand OT prophecy or to compare it with prophecy in other parts of the ancient Near East (e.g., Mari) must acknowledge this distinction. Particular care must be taken not to compare things that differ in origin, expression, and result.

M. A. MACLEOD

**MICE.** *See* MOUSE.

**MICHA** mī'kə (AV 2 S. 9:12; Neh. 10:11; 11:11, 22). *See* MICA.

**MICHAEL** mī'kəl [Heb. *mîḵā'ēl*–'who is like God?'; Gk. *Michaēl*].

**1.** An Asherite, the father of Sethur who scouted the promised land for the Israelites (Nu. 13:13).

**2.** A Gadite clan patriarch, otherwise unknown (1 Ch. 5:13).

**3.** Another Gadite clan patriarch, also otherwise unknown (1 Ch. 5:14).

**4.** A temple musician, great-grandfather of the temple singer and psalm writer Asaph (1 Ch. 6:40 [MT 25]).

**5.** An Issacharite clan chieftain and warrior, one of the sons of the Issacharite clan patriarch Izrahiah (1 Ch. 7:3).

**6.** A Benjaminite, son of Beriah, otherwise unknown (1 Ch. 8:16).

**7.** A Manassite military commander who defected from Saul to David at Ziklag. He was appointed a commander in David's army (1 Ch. 12:20f.).

**8.** The father of the Issacharite tribal military leader Omri (1 Ch. 27:18).

**9.** A son of King Jehoshaphat of Judah. He was killed and his land holdings were confiscated by his brother Jehoram once Jehoram had firmly established his grip on the kingship (1 Ch. 21:1-4).

**10.** A descendant of Shephatiah and father of Zebadiah, the latter being a family leader who returned with Ezra from Babylonia to Judah *ca.* 458 B.C. (Ezr. 8:8).

**11.** The archangel, guardian of Israel. Michael is called "official" or "prince" (Heb. *śar*) over Israel in Dnl. 10:21. He was one of the "chief princes" (10:13), i.e., archangels, involved in the angelic warfare against the demonic powers that influenced the national leadership in Persia and Greece (v. 20) during and after the Israelite Exile. Michael is the only archangel identified as such in the Bible, though GABRIEL (Dnl. 8:16; 9:21; Lk. 1:19, 26) appears to function as an archangel.

In Jewish apocalyptic tradition as reflected in 1 En. 20:1-7 and Tob. 12:15 there were seven archangels, four of whom stood in God's presence (1 En. 9:1; 40:9). These were Michael, Gabriel, RAPHAEL, and URIEL (sometimes called Phanuel). Rev. 8:2 mentions "the seven angels who stand before God," but the Bible otherwise neither names archangels nor describes specifically their duties. Nevertheless it may be presumed that they, on the analogy of generals in an army, stand directly under the supreme authority of God, and command other angels, though never independently of God's will. The Bible clearly implies that the events of nations can be influenced by both God's angels and by fallen angels (Ex. 23:20-23; Ps. 78:49; 82:1-8; Isa. 63:9; Mt. 4:8f.) and seems to imply also that archangels may be assigned individually to given nations (e.g., Dnl. 10:13, 21; 11:1; 12:1).

In the rather baroque angelology of noncanonical Jewish and Christian apocalyptic, Michael's character and role are elaborated far beyond the biblical evidence. He is called "merciful and long-suffering" (1 En. 40:9; 68:2f.), "mediator and intercessor" (Asc. Isa. 9:23 [Latin]; T. Levi 5; T. Dan 6). He is the angel who records the names of those deserving eternal life in Asc. Isa. 9:22f. (Latin) and the intermediary for the giving of the Law from God to Moses in the (Greek) Apocalypse of Moses; Jub. 1:27; 2:1; Shep. Herm. Sim. 8:3:3, etc. In 1 En. 60:12 he is depicted as the angel who guards the incantations by which the heavens and the earth are sustained. The apocalyptic Book of Elijah portrays Michael as the intermediary for information about the future revealed to Elijah (*see* ELIJAH, APOCALYPSE OF [HEBREW]). Among the Dead Sea Scrolls is a fragmentary Aramaic apocalypse beginning: "Words of the book which Michael repeated to the [other] angels . . .", thus presumably demonstrating his status as a commander of a host of angels. Michael is the gatekeeper to paradise in the Ethiopian Bar. 9:5 and the one who reveals Mary's body in the clouds in the Syriac History of the Blessed Virgin. He serves as guardian of the souls of the righteous in the Testament of Abraham, ch. 19. Michael's role as an angelic warrior is developed in 2 En. 22:6 and 33:10, and his name is written on the shields of one division of the divine army listed in the Dead Sea War Scroll (1QM 9:14-16). All of these noncanonical characterizations of Michael appear to be imaginative embellishments of the few details which can be gleaned about him from the biblical accounts.

Michael is specifically the heavenly defender and patron of Israel who supports God's people against their foes, both human and demonic. Some scholars have attempted to identify Michael with the preincarnate Christ on the basis of Dnl. 10, though this has not been widely accepted. The unnamed "man dressed in linen" (Dnl. 10:5) who speaks to Daniel at length about angelic warfare and the related future of several nations is more probably Gabriel, Michael's co-archangel.

Michael is mentioned twice by name in the NT. In connection with teaching about blasphemy Jude 9 relates that Michael disputed with Satan over the body of Moses and yet held back from attacking Satan verbally, leaving Satan's judgment to God. The background of this allusion is not clear. Perhaps the devil sought to deny Moses a proper burial (cf. Dt. 34:6). Origen (*De prin.* iii.2.1) claimed that Jude's words reflect the pseudepigraphic Assumption of Moses, though nothing similar is found in the extant text. Rev. 12:7-9 identifies Michael as the leader of the righteous angels in the battle that caused Satan to fall from heaven.

***Bibliography.***–S. Grill, *Bibel und Liturgie,* 21 (1953/54), 10-13, 41f., 137-143; U. Holzmeister, *Verbum Domini,* 23 (1943), 176-186; G. L. Lawlor, *Translation and Exposition of the Epistle of Jude* (1972), pp. 77-80; J. P. Schultz, *JQR,* 61 (1970-71), 282-307.

D. STUART

**MICHAH** mī'kə. *See* MICAH **4**.

**MICHAIAH** mī-kā'yə, mī-kī'ə. *See* MICAIAH.

**MICHAL** mī'kəl, mē'kal [Heb. *mîk̲al,* prob. a contraction of *mîk̲āʾēl*–'who is like God?'; cf. Phoen., Ugar., *mkl*; Gk. *Melchol,* as if from *mlkl* (?); cf. Syr. *mlky'l* < *malkîʾēl*–'God is my king']. The younger daughter of Saul; David's first wife (1 S. 14:49; 18:20ff.).

Saul saw in Michal's love for David an opportunity to have David killed: he set the brideprice for Michal at one hundred Philistine foreskins (1 S. 18:20-30; cf. David's similar design against Uriah, 2 S. 11). This plan failed, so Saul set an ambush, but Michal helped David to escape. When Saul confronted her she lied, saying that David had threatened her. This lie sharply contrasts Michal with her brother Jonathan, who defended David against Saul even at the risk of his own life (1 S. 20:32f.; cf. 19:4f.).

Apparently Michal's false testimony implied David's repudiation of the marriage, and so Saul gave her to Palti(el) (1 S. 25:44). However, because David and Michal had not been legally divorced, fourteen years later David demanded his wife back (2 S. 3:14ff.) — without violating Dt. 24:1-4. While one should not rule out a motive of love (1 S. 18:20ff.; 2 S. 6:20a), David's renewed marriage to Michal would legitimate his succession to the throne (cf. Tsevat and Levenson-Halpern).

Michal rebuked David for his unseemly self-degradation (at least in her eyes) when he danced before the Lord as the ark was brought up to Jerusalem (2 S. 6). The transfer and housing of the ark in Jerusalem, David's royal city, implied peace and the promise of dynastic succession (cf. Ulshoefer). David detected in Michal's rebuke an underlying bitterness that God had so established a dynasty for David rather than her father (v. 21). For her rejection of God's purpose toward David, Michal was cursed with barrenness (2 S. 6:22f.; so Hertzberg, p. 281).

The mention of Michal's name in 2 S. 21:8 (AV, following MT) is based on a corrupt reading and ought to be corrected to Merab (Michal's elder sister), with the LXX (so RSV, NEB).

***Bibliography.***–Z. Ben-Barak, "The legal background to the restoration of Michal to David," in J. A. Emerton, ed., *Studies in the Historical Books of the OT* (*SVT,* 30; 1979), pp. 15-29; H. W. Hertzberg, *I & II Samuel* (Eng. tr., *OTL,* 1964); P. K. McCarter, Jr., *I Samuel* (*AB,* 1980); J. D. Levenson and B. Halpern, *JBL,* 99 (1980), 507-518; M. Tsevat, *JSS,* 3 (1958), 237-243; H. Ulshoefer, "Nathan's Opposition to David's Intention to Build a Temple" (Diss., Boston University, 1977).

G. P. HUGENBERGER

**MICHEAS** mī'kē-əs (2 Esd. 1:39, AV). *See* MICAH **6**.

**MICHMAS** mik'mas [Heb. *mik̲mās* < *kāmas*–'store up'; Gk. *Machmas, Machemas*] (Ezr. 2:27; Neh. 7:31); [Gk. Apoc. *Makalōn*] (1 Esd. 5:21); AV, NEB, MACALON; **MICHMASH** mik'mash [Heb. *mik̲māś* (*BHS*), other MSS *mik̲māš, mak̲māś*; Gk. *Machamas, Machemas, Machmas*] (1 S. 13:2; Neh. 11:31; etc.); AV also MACHMAS (1 Macc. 9:73). A village in Benjamin, the modern Mukhmâs, 12 km. (7.5 mi.) N of Jerusalem. In NT times it was called Machmas.

No archeological research has been done in the village; K. Baedeker mentioned a grotto with columbaria (*Palestine and Syria* [1912], p. 98). Cf. Josephus *Ant.* vi.6.2 (103-114).

Saul occupied Michmash and the hill country of Bethel (1 S. 13:2) but left it to gather more troops at Gilgal near Jericho, which he reached by way of Wâdī Ṣuweinit and its prolongation Wâdī Qelt, a distance of about 26 km. (16 mi.). The Philistines occupied Michmash, cutting off the way from Gilgal to the area around Bethel (vv. 5, 11).

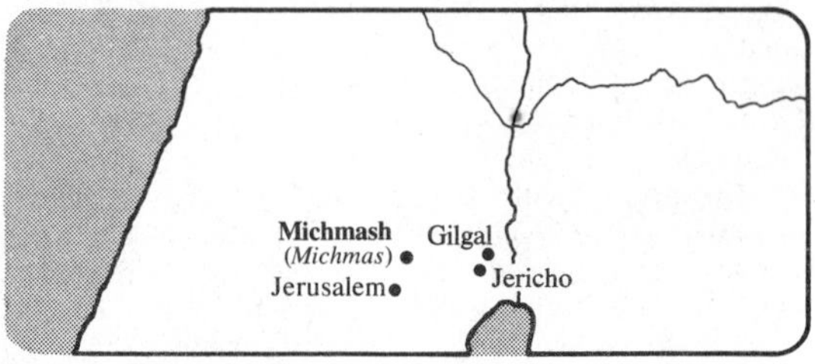


With the few men left to him Saul encamped at Geba 3 km. (2 mi.) S of Michmash (v. 16). By sending a detachment to the pass of Michmash the Philistines protected their eastern flank (v. 23). Jonathan attacked this detachment (14:1-15), while Saul stayed at Migron, Tell Miriam, 1.6 km. (1 mi.) SW of Michmash (v. 2). After Jonathan's initial success Saul went into battle against the Philistines and drove them past Beth-aven (Bethel or a locality in its immediate neighborhood). Thus a two-pronged attack from the southeast and southwest resulted in the flight of the enemy to the northwest. Michmash seems to have remained an open village.

The next time its name occurs is in Isa. 10:28, the description of the impending attack by the Assyrians. Here the prophet alluded to the etymology of the name ("to the storehouse he confides his baggage"). After the Exile a small Israelite population came to Michmash (Ezr. 2:27; Neh. 7:31); they were Benjaminites (Neh. 11:31).

Michmash became newly important during the time of the Maccabees. Jonathan chose it for his armed camp (158-152 B.C.; 1 Macc. 9:73; Josephus *Ant.* xiii.1.6 [34]) "because he could not easily be taken by surprise there" (S. Zeitlin, *First Book of Maccabees* [1950], p. 167). The gorge of Wâdī Ṣuweinît protected it from Jerusalem on the south. After the Maccabean period Michmash sank to insignificance again, though the Mishnah (*Menahoth* viii.1) praises the quality of its grain.

*Bibliography.*–G. Dalman, *Hundert deutsche Fliegerbilder aus Palästina* (1925), plate 28; *GAB*, plates 188f.; A. Alt, *PJ*, 23 (1927), 17-20. A. VAN SELMS

**MICHMETHATH** mik'mə-thath [Heb. *hammiḵmᵉṯâ*]; AV MICHMETHAH. A place named in defining the territory of Ephraim and Manasseh (Josh. 16:6; 17:7). It is said to lie "before," i.e., E of, Shechem. The meaning of the name is obscure, and the presence of the article suggests that it may be a description rather than a proper name. Most commentators identify Michmethah with Khirbet Juleijil, E of Shechem. Another site has been suggested at Khirbet Makhneh el-Fôqā, about 8 km. (5 mi.) SE of Shechem (*LBHG*, rev., p. 257). R. P. DUGAN

**MICHRI** mik'rī [Heb. *miḵrî*]; NEB MICRI. A Benjaminite, ancestor of Elah (1 Ch. 9:8).

**MICHTAM** mik'təm. *See* MIKTAM.

**MIDDAY.** *See* NOON.

**MIDDIN** mid'ən [Heb. *middîn*]. One of a group of six cities in the wilderness of Judah (Josh. 15:61) that constituted part of the inheritance of the tribe of Judah. The LXX B reads *Ainōn*, "springs," but A reads *Madōn*. If the six cities in the MT are to be read from north to south (cf. *GTTOT*, § 320), the last two being City of Salt, identified with Khirbet Qumrân, and En-gedi on the west side of the Dead Sea, then the others are to be located N of Qumrân. Middin has been tentatively identified with Khirbet Abū Ṭabaq in the Buqeiʿah (Valley of Achor) (cf. F. M. Cross and J. T. Milik, *BASOR*, 142 [Apr. 1956], 5-17). Abel's suggestion of Qumrân (*GP*, II, 92) is now generally rejected. Aharoni maintained that sites between ʿAin Feshkha (Qumrân) and En-gedi are candidates for these cities (*LBHG*, rev., p. 356); these sites do not accord with the N-S interpretation of the list, but this is not a serious objection. The reading *Ainōn* seems to support a location near springs, such as those by ʿAin Feshkha and En-gedi. The locations of Middin and the other cities, except En-gedi and probably City of Salt, remain doubtful.

W. S. L. S.

**MIDDLE WALL OF PARTITION** (Eph. 2:14, AV). *See* HOSTILITY, DIVIDING WALL OF.

**MIDIAN** mid'i-ən, **MIDIANITES** [Heb. *miḏyān, miḏyānî, miḏyānîm*]. The biblical materials regard the Midianites as the descendants of the union between Abraham and Keturah (Gen. 25:2). References to the Midianites and the land of Midian are scattered throughout the OT, but are more frequent prior to the establishment of the monarchy under Saul (*ca.* 1020 B.C.). The ancestors of Israel and the Midianites sustained a curious relationship, ranging from close, cordial ties with Moses (Ex. 2:15-18) to an attempt by Israel to exterminate the males of Midian (Nu. 31:1-9). Defining the nature of this relationship is difficult since little is known of the Midianites outside the biblical references.

In the Bible the Midianites first appear in connection with the sale of Joseph (Gen. 37:25-36). Some confusion exists since this narrative identifies those responsible for the sale both as "Midianites" and as "Ishmaelites." Perhaps Ishmaelite is a more inclusive term subsuming the Midianites (cf. Jgs. 8:22-24; *see also* ISHMAELITES). Interestingly, in

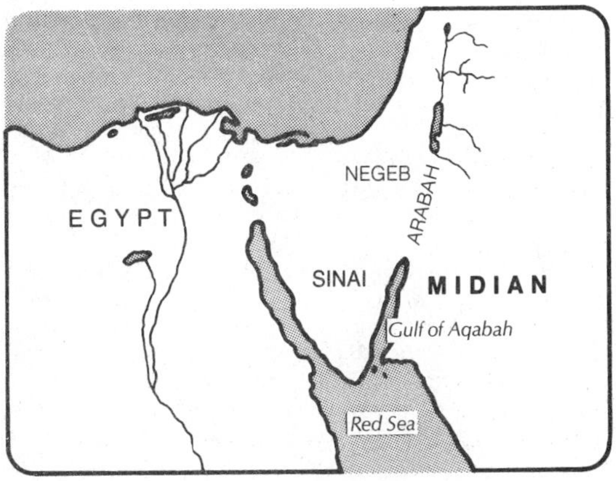


the Joseph story the Midianites are called "traders" while elsewhere they appear as shepherds (Ex. 2:17).

Midianites are next mentioned in connection with Moses. After Moses was forced to leave Egypt he traveled to the "land of Midian," where he encountered Jethro, a Midianite priest, and subsequently married his daughter (Ex. 2:15-21). Later at Mt. Sinai Jethro aided Moses in certain organizational tasks and participated in cultic ceremonies before Yahweh (Ex. 18). Moses' close relationship with a priest of Midian has led some scholars to speculate that Jethro mediated the worship of Yahweh to Moses and Israel. Elsewhere the father-in-law of Moses is termed a Kenite (Jgs. 1:16; 4:11). These links form the basis of the so-called Kenite hypothesis, in which the origins of Yahwism are sought among the nomadic or seminomadic Kenites, perhaps a wandering group of metalsmiths, who in turn are considered to be related to the Midianites. This hypothesis has received some support from the excavation at Arad, a site in a region said to be settled by the Kenites (Jgs. 1:16), where an early Israelite temple and an altar built according to early biblical specifications (Ex. 20:24-26; 27:1) have been found. All such speculations are based on circumstantial evidence, however, and may be said to read much more into the biblical text than what in fairness may be said to be there. It is doubtful that the Midianites played any part in mediating Yahwism to Moses.

The Midianites appear next in connection with Israel's attempt to penetrate the Transjordan region after the wilderness wanderings. The elders of Midian and the Moabites conspired against Israel and secured the services of BALAAM to curse Israel (Nu. 22:4-7). Apparently Midianite women were also involved in an attempt to lead Israel into apostasy (Nu. 25:1-9). Although the attempt failed, the Midianites were linked firmly with the paganism of Baal-peor; consequently the Midianites were considered the enemy of both Israel and Yahweh. Israel took vengeance on the Midianites through warfare. Five kings of Midian were killed along with their men, and the women were taken captive (Nu. 31). Henceforth the Midianites consistently appear in an adversary relationship to Israel.

The Midianites, along with the Amalekites and the "people of the East," periodically harassed certain tribes of Israel during the period of the Judges. Since Palestine at this time was particularly vulnerable due to the collapse of the Canaanite city-states and the decline of Egyptian influence, groups from the fringe areas could penetrate deeply into otherwise secure areas. Moving from the Transjordan region into the Jezreel Valley and beyond, the Midianites preyed upon Israel, apparently during the harvest times (Jgs. 6:1-6). The Israelites had difficulty dealing with the Midianites, who used the camel to make long raids and retreat quickly. Under the leadership of Gideon the Hebrews routed the Midianites in the eastern Jezreel Valley and pursued them across the Jordan (Jgs. 7–8). This victory over Midian was long remembered and served as a source of confidence in Yahweh's ability to deliver (Isa. 9:4; 10:26; Ps. 83:9 [MT 10]).

The Moses narrative raises the problem of the location of the land of Midian. The biblical materials reflect a significant diversity with regard to the geographical distribution of the Midianites. Most references imply that the Midianites were found in and along the southern fringes of Transjordan, where they are associated with the Amorites (Josh. 13:21) and the Moabites (Nu. 22:4-7; 1 Ch. 1:46). After Gideon's victory the Midianites fled across the Jordan southward (Jgs. 8), implying that their home lay in southern Transjordan. 1 K. 11:18 suggests that Midian was E of Paran and W of Edom. Since Paran refers to an area near Kadesh-barnea, i.e., some part of the northeast Sinai or southwest Negeb, Midian would seem to be restricted to the Arabah in this description. Further, some passages indicate that the Midianites had contacts as far south as Egypt (Gen. 37:25) and possibly as far north as the Euphrates ("the River," Nu. 22:4f.).

Classical sources are unanimous in locating the land of Midian in northwest Arabia. Josephus located a city of Mediane on the Red Sea in Arabia (Josephus *Ant.* ii.11.1 [257]). Ptolemy described two cities in Arabia, a certain Modiane and Madiane, the former apparently located on the Red Sea coast and the latter further inland (Ptolemy *Geog.* vi.7.27). Eusebius likewise mentioned a town of Madian located in Arabia (Eusebius *Onom.* 124). All these references place the land of Midian E of the Gulf of Aqabah in northwest Arabia. Indeed, on the basis of the traditional location of the land of Midian in northwest Arabia and because Moses was so closely associated with the land of Midian, some scholars have proposed that Mt. Sinai should be located in northwest Arabia.

Although many scholars have agreed with the classical authors in locating the land of Midian in northwest Arabia, some caution regarding this equation is necessary. As indicated above the biblical evidence suggests that the Midianites ranged over a large area, including northwest Arabia, southern Transjordan, the Arabah, portions of the Negeb, and possibly northern Sinai. Although northwest Arabia eventually became associated with the land of Midian, probably the range of the Midianites at one time was much larger. This would be particularly true if, as B. Mazar believes, the Midianites were involved in the spice and incense trade between southern Arabia and western Asia. Further, some research has raised the possibility that Midian refers not to a land but to an amorphous league of tribes (see Dumbrell). This league dominated the people and areas of the southern Transjordan, Negeb, and portions of Arabia from the Late Bronze Age until approximately the 11th cent. B.C., when other people gradually supplanted the league. If this hypothesis is true, then the "land of Midian" should be understood less in purely geographical terms and more in geopolitical terms.

Biblical references contain clues to the political organization of the Midianites that strongly imply some sort of tribal structure. Five "kings" of Midian are mentioned in Nu. 31:8; these same persons were termed "leaders" elsewhere (Josh. 13:21). Zur, one of these kings, seems to have been a tribal chieftain (Nu. 25:15). Oreb and Zeeb are referred to as two "princes" of Midian (Jgs. 7:25). All these terms suggest a tribal organization in which smaller groups were headed by local chieftains. The association of the Midianites with other known nomadic and seminomadic groups, e.g., the Amalekites and "the people of the East" (Jgs. 6:3), suggests that the Midianites shared a similar mode of existence.

Archeological research has shed some light on the Midianites through the recovery of a distinctive pottery

The Wâdī Rām region of Midian (A. D. Baly)

Typical Midianite juglet with bichrome decorations representing an ostrich (14th-mid-12th cent. B.C.) (Institute of Mining and Metals in the Biblical World, Arabah Expedition)

with bichrome decorations in surveys conducted in the northern Hejaz, E of the Gulf of Aqabah. The pottery, dating from the 13th-12th cents., was found in the region classically associated with Midian and has been designated "Midianite." The same type of pottery appeared in the excavation at Timnaʿ, a copper-mining and smelting site located in the southern Arabah a few miles N of the Gulf of Aqabah. In addition, a small shrine found at Timnaʿ has been attributed to the Midianites. The shrine, in its initial phases an Egyptian temple built during the reign of Seti I and dedicated to Hathor, was repaired after its destruction by an earthquake. New features included the defacing of all Egyptian sculpture, the erection of a row of standing stones (*maṣṣēḇôṯ*), and possibly a tent that covered parts or all of the structure. The last is particularly interesting in the light of Israel's tent-shrine (*'ōhel mōʿēḏ*) of its desert days.

See *EAEHL,* IV, *s.v.* "Timnaʿ" (B. Rothenberg), for a full report on the excavations.

***Bibliography.***–W. F. Albright, "Midianite Donkey Caravans" in H. T. Frank and W. L Reed, eds., *Translating and Understanding the OT* (*Festschrift* H. G. May, 1970), pp. 197-205; W. J. Dumbrell, *VT,* 25 (1975), 323-337; O. Eissfeldt, *JBL,* 87 (1967), 383-393; P. J. Parr, G. L. Harding, and J. E. Dayton, *Bulletin of the Institute of Archaeology,* 8-9 (1970), 193-242; B. Rothenberg, *Were These King Solomon's Mines? Excavations in the Timna Valley* (1972); R. de Vaux, *The Early History of Israel* (Eng. tr. 1978), pp. 330-38; 569f.

T. V. BRISCO

**MIDIANITISH** mid'ē-ən-ī'tish **WOMAN** (AV Nu. 25:6, 14f.). *See* MIDIAN.

**MIDNIGHT** [Heb. *ḥᵃṣôṯ laylâ*–'middle of the night' (Ex. 11:4; Job 34:20; Ps. 119:62), *ḥᵃṣî hallaylâ*–'the half of the night' (Ex. 12:29; Jgs. 16:3; Ruth 3:8), *tôḵ hallaylâ*–'the division of the night' and hence the middle point (1 K. 3:20); Gk. *mésēs nyktós* (Mt. 25:6), or *méson tēs nyktós*–'the middle of the night' (Acts 27:27), *mesonýktios*–'midnight'; WH, *mesonýktion* (Acts 16:25; etc.)]. Before the Exile midnight does not seem to have been very accurately determined. The night was divided into three watches, the middle one including midnight. In NT times the four-watch division was used, and midnight must have been more accurately determined. *See* TIME; WATCH.

N. GREEN

**MIDRASH** mid'rash [Heb. *miḏrāš* < *dāraš*–'to seek, examine, investigate']. This term, which is evidently postexilic in usage if not in origin, occurs only in the MT of 2 Ch. 13:22 (RSV, AV, NEB, "story") and 24:27 (RSV "commentary"; AV, NEB, "story"); both JB and NAB have "midrash." The New King James Version renders the word on both occasions by "annals," which brings out clearly the implication that the materials involving Abijah and the records of Joash's reign were official court documents, and not writings analogous to the later rabbinic commentaries on scriptural passages, for which *miḏrāš* came to be used after the return from exile.

Ezra seems to have practiced the use of *miḏrāš,* having as his objective in life to study and apply the Torah, as well as to instruct the nation in the ordinances and statutes of the Law (Ezr. 7:10). The necessity for interpreting these precepts for the life of the postexilic theocracy prompted the rise of two varieties of midrash, the *haggadah* or "narration," which interpreted nonlegal materials in an ethical and expository manner, and the *halakah,* which applied the general principles of OT laws to more specific situations.

Midrashic material was preserved orally from its inception for a considerable period, and only in the 2nd cent. A.D. were the halakic midrashim written down. The most important of these were the *Mekilta* (treatise) to Exodus and the *Sifra* (book) on Leviticus, Numbers, and Deuteronomy. The earliest written haggadah was the midrash on Genesis, going back to the 3rd cent. A.D., and this was followed by the midrashim on the rest of the Pentateuch and the Five Scrolls (Megilloth). These commentaries became known as the Midrash *Rabbah,* and with later compositions were much favored by the rabbis for homiletical purposes.

*See also* COMMENTARIES, HEBREW III.

***Bibliography.***–*DBSup.,* V, 1263-81 (R. Bloch); R. Le Déaut, *Interp.,* 25 (1971), 259-282; H. L. Strack, *Intro. to the Talmud and Midrash* (Eng. tr. 1931); A. G. Wright, *The Literary Genre Midrash* (1967).

R. K. H.

**MIDWIFE** [piel part. of *yālaḏ*–'to bear, bring forth'; thus, 'one who causes or helps to bring forth']. Midwives are mentioned briefly in Gen. 35:17, where the midwife assures Rachel that her son would be born safely, and in 38:27-30, where, to determine the firstborn, the midwives tie a scarlet cord on the hand that comes out first.

The most notable account of midwives in the OT is in the story of the Egyptian oppression (Ex. 1:15-20). Here Pharaoh instructs the midwives attending the Hebrew women to kill all the male babies, but the midwives refuse because of their fear of God. This account has several problems. First, scholars disagree whether Shiphrah and Puah were Hebrew midwives (so MT) or non-Hebrew midwives who took care of the Hebrew women (cf. LXX, Vulg.). Second, it is uncertain whether they were the only midwives for the Hebrews; perhaps they were in charge of the midwives or were the only two remembered. Third, a theological problem arises in that God appears to bless these midwives for lying (vv. 19f.), although some scholars argue that God rewarded them because they feared Him, not because they deceived Pharaoh. See B. Childs, *Book of Exodus* (*OTL,* 1974), pp. 16f., 22-24, for a good discussion of these problems.

Ezekiel 16:4 may reveal some of the standard practices of Hebrew midwives: they cut the navel cord, cleansed

Clay statuette of a midwife assisting a birth (*ca.* 8th cent. B.C.) (published by permission of the Director of Antiquities and the Cyprus Museum)

the baby, rubbed it down with salt (although no biological purpose is known), and wrapped it in strips of cloth.

*See also* BIRTH. R. B. ALLEN

**MIGDAL-EDER.** *See* EDER, TOWER OF.

**MIGDAL-EL** mig'dal-el [Heb. *migdal-'ēl*]. The name, which means "fortified tower of Ēl," appears between Yiron (AV, NEB, Iron) and Horem (Josh. 19:38) in the list of fortified towns in the territory of Naphtali. The site is unknown, but the context seems to place it in Upper Galilee (cf. M. Woudstra, *Book of Joshua* [*NICOT,* 1981], pp. 292f., who mentions the possible identification with Mejdel-Islim, about 26 km. [16 mi.] ESE of Tyre). It is thought by some to be the Magadan of Mt. 15:39.

D. PECOTA

**MIGDAL-GAD** mig'dəl-gad [Heb. *migdal-gaḏ*–'tower of Gad']. One of sixteen cities named along with other groups of cities in the Shephelah (Lowlands) as part of the inheritance of the tribe of Judah (Josh. 15:37; cf. vv. 33-36; 42-47). Migdal-gad is named between Hadashah and Dilean in a group that includes Lachish and Eglon; therefore it is to be located near those four cities. Since the name appears to be preserved in Khirbet el-Mejdeleh ("ruins of the tower"), this identification has been widely accepted. Khirbet el-Mejdeleh is 1.8 km. (1.1 mi.) E of ed-Dawaniyah (Harûs), 6 km. (3.7 mi.) ESE of Tell ed-Duweir, 8 km. (5 mi.) SSE of Beit Jibrîn (Beth Guvrin, Eleutheropolis). W. S. L. S.

**MIGDOL** mig'dol, mig'dōl [Heb. *migdôl*; Gk. *Magdōlon*]. The term is of West Semitic, probably Canaanite, origin, meaning "fortress" or "tower" (Ugar. *mgdl*). In this sense it appears as a loanword in Egyptian and also as the proper name of various military stations on the northeast frontier of Egypt. In Am.Tab. 234:29 the name $^{alu}$*ma-ag-da-lí*$^{ki}$ *ina* $^{mātu}$*mi-iṣ-ri* occurs as the designation of an Egyptian city, but the context unfortunately furnishes no hint as to its precise location. The OT mentions Migdol as a town or city in Lower Egypt in three different contexts.

**1.** A place along the route of the Exodus, adjoining PI-HAHIROTH, BAAL-ZEPHON, and the sea (Ex. 14:2; Nu. 33:7). Identification is difficult, depending partly upon the route of the Exodus and partly upon the location of Pi-hahiroth and Baal-zephon, neither of which can be placed precisely. Advocates of a northern route for the Exodus identify Baal-zephon variously with Râs Qasrun on the Mediterranean coast (Greco-Roman Casium) or Tahpanhes. Pi-hahiroth, which according to Nu. 33:7 lay E of Baal-zephon, has been seen as the Hebrew equivalent of *Pr-Ḥtḥr,* "the house of Hathor." Egyptian papyri, however, make clear that the Hebrew location was not the well-known *Pr-Ḥtḥr* of the west delta region. Several Egyptian cities bore this name, but in its present form Pi-hahiroth cannot be identified with any *Pr-Ḥtḥr* or another known town or city in the east delta region. Albright proposed a broadly southern route for the Exodus, locating Baal-zephon at later Tahpanhes (Tell Defneh) and placing Migdol at Tell el-Her, just S of Pelusium, near his site for the *yām sûp* or "Reed Sea." The name "Baal-zephon" or "Baal of the North" suggests the presence of a notable Canaanite sanctuary in the east delta area, probably dating from the early Amarna period. In any event, the Migdol of the Exodus can be placed with certainty in the east delta region. The papyrus sources mention a Migdol of Seti I near Tjeku; if this site can be identified with Succoth (modern Tell el-Maskhûṭah), it is likely the Migdol of the Exodus.

*See also* EXODUS, ROUTE OF THE.

**2.** A residence of Egyptian Jews, along with Memphis and Tahpanhes (Jer. 44:1; 46:14).

**3.** A north Egyptian site, contrasted with Syene in the south (Ezk. 29:10; 30:6). This northern Migdol is probably the Magdolum (perhaps Tell el-Ḥeir) of *Itinerarium Antonii,* 12 Roman mi. (18 km., 11 mi.) from Pelusium.

***Bibliography.***–W. F. Albright, "Baal-Zephon," in W. Baumgartner, *et al.*, eds., *Festschrift Alfred Bertholet* (1950), pp. 1-14; P. Montet, *Géographie de l'Égypte ancienne,* I (1957); *Égypte et la Bible* (1959); C. de Wit, *Date and Route of the Exodus* (1960).

R. K. H.

**MIGHT; MIGHTY.** *See* POWER.

**MIGHTY MEN** [Heb. *gibbôrîm*]; NEB HEROES, FIGHTING MEN, SOLDIERS, BODYGUARD, etc. Warriors who were stronger and more agile in combat than ordinary men. Physical strength was probably combined with an inner strength or courage to make them stand out as powerful people of their times. While "mighty men" are frequently referred to in groups, sometimes an individual was identified as "a mighty man" (*gibbôr*), e.g., Nimrod (Gen. 10:8), Gideon (Jgs. 6:12), David (2 S. 17:10; cf. 1 S. 16:18), and Naaman (2 K. 5:1). Nimrod was remembered as a mighty hunter (Gen. 10:9) as well as a great city builder (vv. 10-12). But more frequently the *gibbôrîm* were remembered for their military exploits.

David's "mighty men" were a group of warriors, at first numbering four hundred (1 S. 22:2) and later six hundred (27:2), who through their loyalty and adeptness in battle helped him to secure the kingdom after Saul's death (1 Ch. 11:10). Sometimes David divided them into two or three units, with four hundred doing the fighting and two hundred protecting the camp and weapons (1 S. 25:13; 30:9f., 21-25). In the succession dispute between Adonijah and Solomon these warriors supported Solomon (1 K. 1:8, 10; 1 Ch. 29:4).

Some of the best of David's "mighty men" were known as "the thirty," and among these were three whose heroic deeds were especially notable. Josheb-bas-shebeth, the chief of "the three," killed eight hundred men with his spear in one encounter (2 S. 23:8; cf. 1 Ch. 11:11); Eleazar the son of Dodo struck down the Philistines single-handedly after the rest of the Israelite troops retreated (2 S. 23:9f.; cf. 1 Ch. 11:12); and through Shammah the son of Agee the Hararite the Lord brought a great victory against the Philistines after the other Israelite troops had fled (2 S. 23:11f.; cf. 1 Ch. 11:13f. "The three" once fulfilled David's longing for a drink of water from the Philistine-held well in Bethlehem by an act of bravery that so overwhelmed David that he was unable to drink the water they brought him (2 S. 23:13-17 par. 1 Ch. 11:15-19).

While information about "the thirty" is limited, this special unit of troops probably served as a commanding council for the remaining warriors and for the army that David later assembled (2 S. 23:24-39 par. 1 Ch. 11:26-47). The position of chief of "the thirty" must have changed hands, because more than one person is identified as holding this title: Ishmaiah (1 Ch. 12:4), Amasai (v. 18), Jashobeam (according to 1 Ch. 11:11 *K;* cf. RSV mg.), and Abishai (according to the Syr. and two Hebrew MSS of 2 S. 23:18, and also the Syr. of 1 Ch. 11:20; the MT of both passages reads "the three"; cf. also RSV mg. of 1 Ch. 11:11, where the MT reads "the thirty").

Among David's *gibbôrîm* were also a group of mercenaries (including CHERETHITES and PELETHITES) who formed his bodyguard after he had become king (cf. 2 S. 23:23; cf. 15:18; 16:6; 1 K. 1:8, 10, 38, 44).

*Bibliography.*–B. Mazar, *VT,* 13 (1963), 310-320; *TDOT,* II, *s.v.* "gābhar" (H. Kosmala); Y. Yadin, *Art of Warfare in Biblical Lands* (1963), II, 275-77. D. H. ENGELHARD

**MIGRATE** [Heb. *nāsa'*–'pull out'] (Gen. 11:2); AV, NEB, JOURNEY. The verb *nāsa'* perhaps developed in meaning from "pull out (a tent peg)" (see Isa. 33:20) to "journey" (so BDB, p. 652; KoB, p. 620). According to G. von Rad (*Genesis* [Eng. tr., rev. ed., *OTL,* 1972], p. 148) Gen. 11 here "betrays an acute historical observation: nationalities tend to emerge from great migrations." *See also* NOMADISM.

**MIGRON** mig'ron, mig'rən [Heb. *migrôn*; Gk. *Magōn*]. A place in Benjamin, on or near Wâdī Ṣuweinît (1 S. 14:2; Isa. 10:28). 1 S. 14:2 states, "Saul was staying in the outskirts of Gibeah under the pomegranate tree which is at Migron." It is generally accepted that "Gibeah" here must be Geba (*Jeba'*), which is across the valley from Michmash (cf. *GP,* II, 387). Wâdī Ṣuweinît is an eastward-deepening ravine that joins Wâdī Farah to form Wâdī Qelt, the spectacular ravine emptying into the Jordan Ghor near Jericho. According to v. 5 Michmash (Mukhmâs) was on the north and Geba on the south. Migron has been provisionally identified with Tell Miriam, which lies on the northern edge of the wadi where the crossing is less difficult, 7.5 km. (4.5 mi.) SE of Ramleh, and 1 km. (0.6 mi.) SW of Mukhmâs.

In Isaiah's vision of the Assyrian invasion (Isa. 10:28-34), however, Migron appears to be N of Michmash. It is possible, of course, to follow Alt's suggestion (abstracted in *GP,* II, 387) and assume that the invader sent the baggage to Michmash while the troops took the less difficult route through Migron. But it should be recognized that Isaiah was recounting a vision, not lecturing on geography. Albright's proposed emendation (*AASOR,* 4 [1924], 37, 135-38) — the transposition of the positions of Michmash and Geba in vv. 28f. — is likewise not necessary if the passage is accepted as a vision whose purpose was to portray the frightening advance of the enemy.

See also *GTTOT,* § 1588. W. S. LASOR

**MIJAMIN** mij'ə-min [Heb. *mîyāmîn, mîyāmin* (contraction of *minyāmîn*–'from the right hand,' i.e., 'fortunate'); Gk. *Meamin, Miamin, Meimin,* Apoc. *Maēlos*]; AV also MIAMIN, Apoc. MAELUS; NEB Apoc. MAELUS.

**1.** A priest, descendant of Aaron, in David's time, who was assigned to the sixth division of the temple service (1 Ch. 24:9).

**2.** A son of Parosh who was among those required to divorce their foreign wives (Ezr. 10:25 par. 1 Esd. 9:26).

**3.** A priest who participated in sealing the covenant with Nehemiah (Neh. 10:7 [MT 8]).

**4.** A priest who returned from the Exile with Zerubbabel (Neh. 12:5).

**MIKLOTH** mik'loth [Heb. *miqlôṯ*].

**1.** A Benjaminite, descendant of Jeiel, who lived at Gibeon; the father of Shimeah (1 Ch. 8:32; 9:37f.). A comparison of the two passages and support from LXX B, Vulg., Syr., and Arab. shows that the name Mikloth has been dropped by haplography at 8:31 and should be restored (cf. NEB; *BHS*).

**2.** According to the RSV mg. of 1 Ch. 27:4, a chief officer under Dodai the Ahohite during the reign of David. The RSV omits "and his division and Mikloth the chief officer," based on the LXX, but the AV includes it, based on the MT. The MT is corrupt here, and the clause should probably be deleted.

**MIKNEIAH** mik-nē'yə [Heb. *miqnēyāhû*–'Yahweh possesses']. A Levite of the second order in David's time, appointed as one of the leaders on the lyre in the procession at the return of the ark (1 Ch. 15:18, 21). His name is omitted in the similar list in 16:5.

**MIKTAM** mik'təm [Heb. *miḵtām*]; AV MICHTAM. A technical term of uncertain meaning in the superscriptions (= MT v. 1 in each case) to Pss. 16, 56–60 (and possibly in Isa. 38:9, if *miḵtāḇ* is emended to *miḵtām*). Several interpretations have been suggested. (1) An early rabbinic interpretation derived it from *keṯem,* "gold," and some modern interpreters have followed this theory (e.g., Luther, "a gold jewel"; C. A. Briggs, "a choice piece"; see Briggs, comm. on Psalms, I [*ICC,* 1906], lx). (2) Combining this derivation with the LXX translation *stēlographía,* "inscription," J. D. Michaelis understood it as a gold-lettered inscription (cf. M. Dahood, *Psalms I (1-50)* [*AB,* 1966], 87; P. D. Miller "Psalms and Inscriptions," in *SVT,* 32 [1981], 311-332, esp. pp. 312-14). (3) S. Mowinckel, on the other hand, derived *miḵtām* from Akk. *katāmu,* "cover" (i.e., "atone for"); thus he took it to mean a "Psalm of Atonement" (*Psalms in Israel's Worship* [Eng. tr. 1962], II, 209). N. J. O.

**MIKVAH** mik-vä' or **MIKVEH** mik've [Heb. *miqwâ,* plur. *miqwā'ôṯ*. An immersion pool used for ritual washing (not used in this sense in the MT). The word *miqwâ* is translated "ditch" (AV), "reservoir" (RSV, NASB), or "cistern" (NEB) in Isa. 22:11. The word *miqweh,* "collection, gathering, mass," is used of water (Gen. 1:10; Ex. 7:19; Lev. 11:36).

The religious Jew was required to cleanse him- or herself from ceremonial uncleanness by immersion in a mikveh. Vessels or other objects that were required to be ceremonially clean could be immersed in a mikveh. According to the Mishnah, flowing water or, even better, water from a spring of any amount is valid for ritual purification (*Mikwaoth* i.6-8). An immersion pool (mikvah) is valid only if it contains 40 seahs (approximately 75 U.S. gals., 270 l.) of water and is deep enough for total immersion while standing (*Encyclopedia Judaica* [1971], XI, 1536 f.). Making a play on a similar word, *miqweh,* "gathering" (Gen. 1:10), the rabbis declared that all seas are valid as an immersion pool (*Mikwaoth* v.4; *Parah* viii.8). With a similar

Mikvah in the south wall of the temple mount in Jerusalem (W. S. LaSor)

play on the word *miqweh,* "hope," God is the one who cleanses Israel (*Yoma* viii.9, using Jer. 17:13 and Ezk. 36:25). Immersion was self-administered (see n. 4 to *Mikwaoth* iii.4 in Danby's edition), with a witness to ascertain that the entire body (including the hair) was immersed. Even if a finger was held by someone, or a girl had ribbons on her head, the immersion was invalid since it was not total (cf. *Mikwaoth* viii.5; ix.1 and n. 5 to ix.1 in Danby's edition).

The discovery of a number of *miqwā'ōṯ* in Israel, notably at Masada and in connection with the great staircase at the south wall of the temple mount as well as at Qumrân and several excavated synagogues, has increased interest in the immersion pools. By way of contrast, G. F. Moore, for example, seems to deal only with baptism of proselytes (*Judaism,* I [1927], 332ff.) and pagan slaves (*Judaism,* II [1927], 18, 136). He states, "In the whole ritual there is no suggestion that baptism was a real or symbolic purification . . . It is essentially an initiatory rite, with a forward and a backward look" (I, 334). I do not find in his work a single reference to the tractate *Mikwaoth.* Similarly, there is only one reference to *miqweh* in C. G. Montefiore and H. Loewe, *Rabbinic Anthology* (repr. 1974), and this concerns the play on the word for "hope" (p. 152).

In view of the practice of self-immersion, the relationship of John the Baptist to baptism probably needs further study. The expression "repent and be baptized," in some contexts at least, could as well be translated "repent and immerse yourself." Gk. *ho baptízōn* as the reflex of Heb. *hammaṭbîl* could have the meaning "the one causing someone to immerse him/herself" (cf. 1 Cor. 10:2 — Moses obviously did not perform the act of baptizing Israel in the Red Sea).

The presence of a fairly large number of immersion pools by the staircase leading to the temple beyond doubt indicates provision for a multitude of ritual immersions as worshipers approached the temple mount. Some scholars have suggested that this would be the most feasible place for the baptism of the three thousand to have taken place on the day of Pentecost (Acts 2:41). W. S. LASOR

**MILALAI** mil'ə-lī [Heb. *milᵃlay*]. A Levitical musician who took part in the dedication of the rebuilt wall of Jerusalem (Neh. 12:36). The name is omitted in the LXX and may have entered the MT through a scribal error (note the similarity with the following name, Gilalai).

**MILCAH** mil'kə [Heb. *milkâ*–'queen'].

**1.** Daughter of Haran the brother of Abraham; wife of Nahor, another brother of Abraham; mother of eight sons; grandmother of Rebekah (Gen. 11:29; 22:20-23; 24:15, 24, 47).

**2.** One of the five daughters of Zelophehad (Nu. 26:33; 27:1; 36:11; Josh. 17:3); *see* MAHLAH **1.** It appears that the names of Zelophehad's daughters represented towns; Milcah may be an abbreviated form of Beth-milcah.

**MILCOM** mil'kəm. *See* MOLECH.

**MILDEW** [Heb. *yērāqôn*; Gk. generally *íkteros*–'jaundice']; NEB RED BLIGHT. A condition associated with "blasting" (Heb. *šiddāpôn*) in Dt. 28:22; 1 K. 8:37 par. 2 Ch. 6:28; Am. 4:9; Hag. 2:17. In Jer. 30:6 *yērāqôn* is translated "paleness" (AV) or "pale" (RSV, NEB) in reference to people, indicating either a jaundiced condition or loss of color due to fear. (The LXX interpreted 1 K. 8:37; 2 Ch. 6:28; Jer. 30:6; Am. 4:9 as referring to humans and thus used *íkteros*.) Arab. *yarqān,* related philologically, means "jaundice" or "blight." The mildew of grain may have been the fungus *Erysiphe graminis,* though many other fungi were designated "mildew." R. K. H.

**MILE** [Gk. *mílion*] (Mt. 5:41). Literally, "a thousand paces" (cf. Lat. *mille passuum*). The Roman mile was equal to about 1,479 m. (1,618 Eng. yds.) and thus was slightly shorter than the Eng. mile. In Lk. 24:13; Jn. 6:19; 11:18 the RSV and NEB translate the Gk. *stádia* (equal to about 185 m. or 607 ft.) into Eng. miles (the AV uses "furlongs"). *See* WEIGHTS AND MEASURES.

**MILETUS** mī-lē'təs [Gk. *Milētos*]. The most illustrious Ionian seaport on the west coast of Asia Minor, situated on the south promontory of a gulf into which the Meander River once emptied. It lies in ruins today, but the small town of Palatia occupies part of the ancient site.

Although the identification of the ancient Hittite settlement of Millawanda with Miletus is not certain, the region was inhabited by Hittites before Minoan traders moved into the area. The discovery of Minoan artifacts of probable Cretan origin in the western segment of the city suggests a Minoan settlement, perhaps as early as the 16th or 15th cent. B.C. The area was certainly colonized by Mycenaean settlers, who fortified the city in the 13th cent. B.C. The fortifications were destroyed about a century later, but the importance of Miletus assured its rebuilding. If Homer is correct (*Il.* ii.868f.), the Carians controlled the city during the Trojan War. During the Ionian period this seaport was a leading city, a jewel for which Persians and Greeks regularly fought from the 6th to the 4th cents. B.C. In Roman times Miletus experienced significant prosperity, but during the Byzantine period it declined because the

silt from the river gradually closed the harbor and left the city about 8 km. (5 mi.) from the coast. Ephesus now lies overland less than 65 km. (40 mi.) N of Miletus, but in NT times the overland traveler had to go about 50 km. (30 mi.) farther, around the large Gulf of Priene. Today this gulf is an inland lake, and the island of Lade, which once sheltered the harbor, has become a hill surrounded by a swampy alluvial plain.

Paul was eager to reach Jerusalem by Pentecost on the return segment of his third missionary journey and did not wish to take the time necessary to stop at Ephesus. Accordingly, he summoned the Ephesian elders to meet him at the major seaport city of Miletus in order to give them his final charge (Acts 20:15–21:1). The last biblical reference to Miletus is 2 Tim. 4:30, which seems to indicate that Paul visited the city after his imprisonment in Rome.

German archeologists have worked the site several times in the 20th cent., and an extensive plan of the Roman city has been reconstructed. The seaport encompassed four harbors, the most sheltered being in the north. Near this inlet, where Paul may have landed, were the Delphinion (sanctuary of Apollo) and the northern agora (market). To the south were the town hall, a large agora, and a Serapeum (temple of the Egyptian god Serapis). Immediately to the west was a magnificent nymphaeum (bath) apparently dedicated to Queen Faustina, who visited the city *ca.* A.D. 164. It had both hot and cold rooms adorned with beautiful marble statues and friezes such as those of Apollo and the nine Muses, now in a museum in Istanbul. Along the coast to the northwest was a large theater, and on a small western peninsula was a temple to Athena. Although Apollo was the chief god of the Roman city, Athena had been worshiped there at least since the 7th cent. B.C.

A worshiper at the Apollo sanctuary of Miletus could pass through the sacred gate built in the time of Emperor Claudius (A.D. 41-54) and journey 18 km. (11 mi.) south along the sacred way to the magnificent Milesian temple of Apollo at Didyma (Branchidae), famed for its oracles. Construction of this temple began in the time of Alexander and continued through the Roman period, but it was never finished.

Not only was the city economically prosperous, architecturally beautiful, and religiously significant, but during the 7th and 6th cents. B.C. it also produced some of that period's most important Greek minds, including the great philosopher-scientist Thales and the early evolutionist Anaximander.

In the Christian period a Byzantine church was built within the environs of the great temple, but before Constantine few Christian memorials seem to have been erected at Miletus, probably because of the close imperial surveillance kept on this strategic seaport. During the 5th cent., however, it became an independent archbishopric.

***Bibliography.***–*SPT,* pp. 292ff.; *RRAM,* pp. 73f.; G. Kleiner, *Das Römische Milet* (1970). G. L. BORCHERT

**MILK** [Heb. *ḥālāḇ, hemʾâ* (Job 29:6, emending MT *ḥēmâ,* "anger," with some MSS; see *BHS,* comms.); Gk. *gála*]; AV also BUTTER (Job 29:6); NEB also MILKY WATER (Cant. 5:12). Humanity's oldest food is a white or creamy fluid secreted by the mammary glands of female mammals for the nourishing of their young. In Scripture the term is used both of human secretions (Isa. 28.9) and those of animals (Ex. 23:19).

As a food milk ranked next in importance to bread (Sir. 39:26). Palestine is frequently described as a land "flowing with milk and honey" (e.g., Ex. 3:8, 17; Nu. 13:27; Dt. 6:3; Josh. 5:6; Jer. 11:5; Ezk. 20:6, 15; cf. Sir. 46:8; Bar. 1:20). Milk was among the first things set before the weary traveler (Gen. 18:8). In fact, it was considered a luxury (Jgs. 5:25; Cant. 5:1). The people used the milk of cattle and also that of sheep (Dt. 32:14), and especially that of goats (Prov. 27:27). It was received in pails and kept in leather bottles (Jgs. 4:19), where it turned sour quickly in the warm climate of Palestine before being poured out thickly like a melting substance (cf. Job 10:10). Cheese of various kinds was made from it; or the curds were eaten with bread, and possibly also made into butter by churning (Prov. 30:33). *See* FOOD III.

From the references in Ex. 23:19; 34:26; Dt. 14:21 the Israelites appear to have been prohibited from cooking a young goat in its mother's milk, and by a very general understanding of these passages Jews have come to abstain from consuming mixtures of meat and milk. Support of this tradition was thought to be furnished by a damaged text from Ugarit (*UT,* 52:14), which was interpreted in this way by C. Virolleaud (*Syria,* 14 [1933], 128-151) and followed by H. L. Ginsberg (*Journal of the Royal Asiatic Society* [1935], pp. 45-72). Closer examination shows, however, that the Ugaritic text says nothing about any physical relationship between the kid and the source of the milk in which it was supposedly cooked. Furthermore, the term that Virolleaud rendered "cook" (*ṭbḫ*) actually seems to mean "slaughter" (cf. Heb. *ṭbḥ,* "slaughter"), thus removing the proposed support completely. Ugaritic studies therefore do not explain Dt. 14:21, and the most that can be said about the verse is that it prohibits something that was abhorrent in Canaanite religion, though for what reason is unknown. See P. C. Craigie, *Ugarit and the OT* (1983), pp. 74-76.

Figuratively the word is used of abundance (Gen. 49:12; Isa. 7:21f.); of a loved one's charms (Cant. 4:11); of blessings (Isa. 55:1; 60:16; Joel 3:18 [MT 4:18]); of the (spiritual) food of immature people (1 Cor. 3:2; He. 5:12f.; cf. 2 Esd. 8:10f.); of purity (1 Pet. 2:2; cf. Lam. 4:7). R. K. H.

**MILL; MILLSTONE** [Heb. *rēḥayim* (Ex. 11:5; Nu. 11:8; Dt. 24:6; Isa. 47:2; Jer. 25:10), *reḵeḇ* ("upper millstone," Dt. 24:6), *pelaḥ reḵeḇ* ("upper millstone," Jgs. 9:53; 2 S. 11:21), *pelaḥ taḥtîṯ* ("nether millstone," Job 41:24 [MT 16]), *ṭāḥan* ("grind at the mill," Jgs. 16:21), *ṭᵉḥôn* (Lam. 5:13); Gk. *mýlos onikós*–'donkey millstone' ("great millstone," Mt. 18:6; Lk. 17:2), *mýlinos mégas* ("great millstone," Rev. 18:21), *mýlos* (Mt. 24:41; Rev. 18:22), *líthos mylikós* ("great millstone," Mk. 9:42)]; NEB also HANDMILL, "to grind corn" (Lam. 5:13).

In biblical times mills were used to GRIND grain and — during the journey through the wilderness — manna (Nu. 11:8). Primarily one basic type of handmill was used in Israel during the whole of the OT period. These mills, consisting of two carved stones (note the dual ending on *rēḥayim*), were made of basalt, a rough black volcanic rock whose hardness was proverbial (Job 41:24). Although the sizes of the mills varied, a typical bottom stone (*pelaḥ taḥtîṯ*) was rectangular in shape and had a flat or slightly concave surface. The miller knelt at one end of this semistationary stone, which sloped downward about 15° away from the miller (see *ANEP,* no. 149, for a picture of an Egyptian model, *ca.* 2700-2200 B.C.). The upper stone (*reḵeḇ* or *pelaḥ reḵeḇ*) was smaller in size and fitted into the hand of the worker. After placing the grain on the lower stone, the miller rubbed the upper stone against the lower in a back-and-forth motion, applying downward pressure on the upper stone. The ground grain fell off the far end of the mill, forming a small heap.

Scattered archeological finds indicate that small rotary handmills may have been in use in the Levant from 1200 B.C., but their usage was very limited. They may have been primarily employed to grind pigments (see Forbes, pp. 148f.). Rotary handmills were not in common use until the Hellenistic period (*ca.* 330 B.C. to 63 B.C.; Forbes, p. 146; Moritz, p. 105).

Grinding grain was a daily task usually performed by women or their female slaves (Ex. 11:5). Isa. 47:2 (cf. Ex. 11:5) indicates that this was considered humble work. Occasionally male captives such as Samson were humiliated by being forced to grind at the mill (Jgs. 16:21; Lam. 5:13). For poor families the mill was a valuable piece of equipment. To lose the mill, or even just the upper millstone, would deprive the family of the means of making bread, the basic element of their diet; thus the Israelites were forbidden to take such an essential household tool as a pledge against a loan (Dt. 24:6). The grinding of the millstones was a common sound in the small Israelite villages; its absence indicated that catastrophe had befallen the community (Jer. 25:10; Rev. 18:22). A woman of Thebez once used a millstone as a deadly weapon. Standing on the top of the city wall she dropped an upper millstone on the head of "King" Abimelech, who besieging the city had approached its wall too closely (Jgs. 9:53; 2 S. 11:21).

Some time during the 2nd or 1st cent. B.C. donkey-mills were introduced. These mills were also composed of two parts but were much larger than the handmills used in OT times. Usually made of basalt, the lower portion (Lat. *meta*) was a solid bell-shaped stationary piece, typically measuring about 75 cm. (2.5 ft.) in diameter at the base and 60 cm. (2 ft.) in height. Placed on top of this was a large basalt stone carved in the shape of a hollowed-out hour glass (Lat. *catillus*). Its outer diameter was approximately 70 cm. (28 in.), while at the narrow "waist" its inner diameter was only about 18 cm. (7 in.). A donkey was yoked to this upper "hopper," which was filled with grain. As the donkey walked in a circle, the grain was ground between the rotating upper hopper and the lower, stationary stone. In this way large amounts of grain could be processed for commercial purposes. Many such mills have been found at Roman sites such as Pompeii and Ostia, and a few have been discovered in Israel also. Since this type of mill was not introduced until the late Hellenistic or early Roman period, it could not have been the type of mill that Samson operated.

Small grain mill from Beth-shean. The upper circular stone was rotated by a lever inserted in the hole on the side (Jamie Simson/Das Photo)

Large grist mill from Alaça Hüyük (D. H. Condit)

Jesus referred to the upper stone of a donkey mill when He said that those who cause "little ones" to sin would be better off to have a "great millstone" fastened about their necks and be cast into the sea (Mt. 18:6 par. Mk. 9:42; Lk. 17:2). A similar image is used in Rev. 18:21, which depicts the violent downfall of Babylon (= Rome) as a great millstone being hurled into the sea by a mighty angel. A sign of the city's desolation will be the cessation of "the sound of the millstone" (v. 22). In His Olivet Discourse Jesus used the image of two women at their daily task of grinding grain (Mt. 24:41; cf. Lk. 17:35). The TR here reads *mýlōn* ("mill, millhouse"), but the earliest texts read *mýlos;* the phrase is probably best rendered "grinding with the handmill" (Bauer, rev., p. 529).

*Bibliography.*–L. A. Moritz, *Grain-mills and Flour in Classical Antiquity* (1958); R. J. Forbes, *Studies in Ancient Technology,* III (1965).

C. G. RASMUSSEN

**MILLENNIUM** mə-len'ē-əm [Lat. *mille*–'thousand' plus *annus*–'year']. A time of penultimate divine triumph over the forces of evil on earth before God's final conquest of all His enemies and the establishment of everlasting righteousness. The corresponding Greek expression in Rev. 20:4-7, *chília étē,* gives rise to the term "chiliasm," properly a synonym for "millennialism" but sometimes used in a pejorative sense to designate especially gross and sensual conceptions of bliss on earth.

I. In Ancient Religious Literature
  A. Canonical Picture
  B. Apocrypha and Pseudepigrapha
  C. Question of Persian Origin
II. In Church History
  A. Patristic Period
  B. Middle Ages and Reformation
  C. Modern Times
  D. Utopian Dream

III. Contrasting Millennialisms
 A. Amillennial Allegory
 B. Postmillennial Progress
 C. Premillennial Philosophy of History

***I. In Ancient Religious Literature.***–*A. Canonical Picture.* Much stress is placed in the canonical OT on a future condition of earthly blessedness for the Jewish nation (Isa. 9:6; 11:1–12:6; 40:9-11; 52:7-12; Jer. 33:17-22; Ezk. 37:25; Hos. 3:4f.; Joel 3:20 [MT 4:20]; Am. 9:14f.; Zec. 9:9f.; etc.). But this period is not temporally limited and so, though compatible with a time of millennial bliss, does not expressly require it. The eternity of the messianic kingdom as delineated in such key prophetic books of the OT as Daniel (2:44; 7:27) leads millennial interpreters to extend the history of Israel's restoration across the millennial age into the ultimate eschaton when "God shall be all in all" (cf. Culver; W. M. Smith, *World Crisis and the Prophetic Scriptures* [1951], pp. 179-237; *Israeli/Arab Conflict and the Bible* [1967]; Saarnivaara, pp. 24-37). Thus, in spite of attempts, represented by W. E. Biederwolf's *Millennium Bible* (1924), to find chiliastic teaching clearly set forth in the OT, the biblical foundation of the doctrine cannot be located there.

As for the NT, 1 Cor. 15:22ff. is regarded, even by those who oppose millennial views, as providing through its "doctrine of a limited reign of Christ . . . a foothold in the Church for chiliastic expectations" (E. Bratke, in Sch.-Herz. [repr. 1950], VII, 375). Other NT passages to which millennial interpreters occasionally appeal are Mt. 19:28; 25:31-46; Lk. 14:14; 1 Thess. 4:13-18. But it is almost universally admitted, by both opponents and advocates of millennialism, that the case for the doctrine rests squarely on the exegesis of Rev. 20. According to this text, after Messiah's victory over the beast, the false prophet, and all their followers, Satan will be confined in a bottomless pit for one thousand years. During this period Christ will reign with His martyred saints, who have been brought to life in the "first resurrection" at the outset of the millennial period. At the end of the thousand years Satan will be loosed for a little time, the ultimate battle between God and His adversaries will occur, and the last judgment will take place, followed by "second death" of all evil forces and the establishment of everlasting righteousness. The disputed questions relative to this passage are whether the text is to be taken literally (millennialism) or figuratively (amillennialism) and, assuming a millennial interpretation, whether the second coming of the Lord is to precede (premillennialism) or follow (postmillennialism) the time of chiliastic victory. To these questions we shall return later (see III below).

*B. Apocrypha and Pseudepigrapha.* Noncanonical Jewish literature of the biblical era offers several instances of temporally delimited periods of divine rule. The four most important examples, in chronological order, are: (1) 1 En. 91:12-17 and ch. 93; (2) 2 En. 32:3–33:1; (3) 2 Esd. 5:1–7:35; and (4) 2 Baruch.

(1) The 1 Enoch passages are in the section known as the "Apocalypse of Weeks," considered by R. H. Charles (*Book of Enoch* [1917], p. xiv) "the oldest pre-Maccabaean" portion of the book. The seer has Enoch predict the future in terms of ten unequal "weeks." During the final three apocalyptic weeks judgment will take place against oppressors (eighth week), the whole godless earth (ninth week), and the evil angels (tenth week). Although only at the end of time, following the tenth week, does perfection come about ("the first heaven shall depart and pass away, and a new heaven shall appear, . . . and all shall be in goodness and righteousness, and sin shall no more be mentioned for ever"), the eighth week constitutes a kind of millennial interlude, since "at its close they [the righteous] shall acquire houses through their righteousness, and a house [the temple] shall be built for the Great King in glory for evermore, and all mankind shall look to the path of uprightness" (Charles, pp. 132-34). No personal Messiah, however, plays a role in these predictions.

(2) An analogous picture is offered by 2 En. 32:3–33:1. In this apocalypse, "written by an Alexandrian Jew during the first fifty years of our era" (R. H. Pfeiffer), the world exists for a total of seven days of a thousand years each, and the Lord decrees that the seventh constitutes a penultimate sabbath, to be followed by the endless eighth day of eternal bliss. No Messiah is integrated into this millennial picture, but the implicit use of the canonical theme that "a thousand years in thy sight are but as yesterday" (Ps. 90:4; 2 Pet. 3:8), with the consequent specification of a future era of explicitly millennial dimensions, is noteworthy.

(3) 2 Esd. 5:1–7:35 presents a vision of the end time almost certainly written before the end of the 1st cent. A.D. "The details include the promise that God's Messiah will reign in his kingdom four hundred years; after this he and all humankind will die, and primeval silence will prevail for seven days; finally will come the Resurrection and the Day of Judgment" (B. M. Metzger, *Intro. to the Apocrypha* [1957], p. 26). The sharp contrasts between this prediction and canonical teaching should be noted — contrasts in no way blunted by the reference to "Jesus" in 7:28, which derives from the Latin text only and "is due to a Christian corrector" (Oesterley). The four-hundred-year figure is explained in the Talmud (T.B. *Sanhedrin* 99a; Midr. *Tanhuma, Ekeb* 7) as deriving from Israel's period of captivity in Egypt (cf. Gen. 15:13; Ps. 90:15; Mic. 7:15). Other talmudic estimates of the length of Messiah's kingdom were 40 years (equaling the period in the wilderness), 70 years, 100 years, 365 years, 600 years, 1000 years, 2000 years, and 7000 years. The logic behind such figures was often the assumption of symmetry (history consisted of 2000 years before the giving of the Law and 2000 years under it, so Messiah's reign would be of this same length) or the symbolism of joy contained in the numbers 1000 and 7000 (see F. Weber, *Jüdische Theologie auf Grund des Talmud* [1897], pp. 371-73).

(4) 2 Baruch, "written about the same time as II (IV) Esdras (*ca.* A.D. 90)" (Pfeiffer, *HNTT*, p. 86), portrays a messianic kingdom as the successor to four world kingdoms, the last of which is Rome (chs. 39–40). In chs. 29 and 73 the messianic reign is depicted in terms quite obviously recapitulating the Edenic paradise and annulling the curse placed upon our first parents: childbearing will occur painlessly (cf. Gen. 3:16), and the soil will become so fertile (cf. Gen. 3:17-19) that each vine will have a thousand branches, each branch a thousand clusters, each cluster a thousand grapes! Papias later applied this description to the Christian millennium.

What is the bearing of these pseudepigraphical and apocryphal millennialisms on the NT conception as set out in Rev. 20? If any influence exists at all, it is of the most indirect kind, not extending beyond the general idea of a future divine interregnum. Neither 1 Enoch nor 2 Enoch connects a personal Messiah with penultimate bliss; the Messiah of 2 Esdras reigns only four hundred years and then dies; and the technicolor portrait of chiliastic blessings in 2 Baruch (almost certainly composed too late to have influenced Revelation in any case) has no parallel in the NT. Even the thousand-year span of time in Rev. 20 need not be derived from 2 Enoch, since the apostle John was able to rely, no less than the author of 2 Enoch, on Ps. 90:4 for the 1 day = 1000 years formula.

*C. Question of Persian Origin.* Some have made efforts

to locate in ancient Persian religious literature an extra-canonical source for the Bible's millennial teaching. Zoroastrianism conceived of the last times as consisting of three millennia, each with its particular savior. "The later Parsi legends distinguish three great prophets who will appear before the end of the world.... They will be commissioned to check the influence of the devil, which increases at the time when this world is verging toward its end" (M. Haug, *Essays on the Sacred Language, Writings, and Religion of the Parsis* [1878], p. 314). Only with the appearance of the third and greatest savior — Sosyosh, a supernatural offspring of Zoroaster himself — will the world be permanently transformed; then "the devil will disappear" and "all the world will remain for eternity in a state of righteousness" (Yt. 19:89f.; quoted in Haug, p. 217). We are told that "these ideas exerted strong influence upon the apocalyptic expectations of late Judaism" (*Encyclopedia of the Lutheran Church,* II [1965], *s.v.* [K. Hutten]), and this opinion is supported by F. Cumont (*RHR* [1931], 29-96) and M. Eliade (*Myth of the Eternal Return* [1954], pp. 124-27). On the other hand, W. Adams Brown warned, "Our sources for the Persian eschatology are so late (the Bundahis, in their present form, dating not earlier than the 7th cent. A.D....) that we must use great caution in drawing conclusions" (*HDB,* III, *s.v.*). Factors such as the lateness of the Mazdean sources and the radical difference between their trimillennial view and the unitary messianic kingdom in the Judeo-Christian tradition have led to a rejection of the Persian-influence theory by N. Söderblom (*La Vie future d'après le mazdéisme* [1901], pp. 270-320), and, more recently, P. Vulliaud (p. 33); and with this judgment we concur. One must be especially careful, even when some genuine similarities exist between two religious positions, not to assume that one must have influenced the other. The unique characteristics of the millennial eschatology in Rev. 20 warrant the closest examination on their own ground.

***II. In Church History.–A.*** *Patristic Period.* Those who regard millennialism as an alien import into the Christian faith have been much embarrassed by its early and widespread acceptance in the patristic Church. Salmond, for example, who considered millennial conceptions totally foreign to Christ's teachings, had to admit that "the dogma of a Millennium... took possession of Christian thought at so early a date and with so strong a grasp that it has sometimes been reckoned an integral part of the primitive Christian faith" (p. 312).

Papias, who had personal contact with those taught by Christ and His apostles and may well have been a disciple of the apostle John, asserted that "the Lord used to teach concerning those [end] times" that "there will be a period of a thousand years after the resurrection of the dead and the kingdom of Christ will be set up in material form on this very earth" (cited in Eusebius *HE* iii.39.12; Irenaeus *Adv. haer.* v.33.3f.). Though Papias fleshed out his millennial reference with details from 2 Baruch (see above), his account is a weighty testimony to primitive Christian eschatological beliefs.

The author of the Epistle of Barnabas (no later than A.D. 138) "is a follower of chiliasm. The six days of creation mean a period of six thousand years because a thousand years are like one day in the eyes of God. In six days, that is in six thousand years, everything will be completed, after which the present evil time will be destroyed and the Son of God will come again and judge the godless and change the sun and the moon and the stars and he will truly rest on the seventh day. Then will dawn the sabbath of the millennial kingdom (15, 1-9)" (Quasten, I, 89).

Justin Martyr, "the most important of the Greek apologists of the second century" (Quasten, I, 196), while granting that "many who belong to the pure and pious faith and are true Christians think otherwise" than he on the millennial issue, explicitly declared: "I and others are right-minded Christians in all points and are assured that there will be a resurrection of the dead and a thousand years in Jerusalem, which will then be built, adorned and enlarged" (*Dial.* 80f.; cf. J. Daniélou, *VC,* 2 [1948], 1-16).

Other important patristic millennialists were Irenaeus (see below, the final quotation in this article); Hippolytus of Rome and Julius "Africanus" (see Froom, I, 268-282, and note his helpful tabular summary of patristic views, pp. 458f.); Victorinus of Pettau, the chiliasm of whose commentary on Revelation was edited out by amillennialist Jerome (see Quasten, II, 411-13; Froom, I, 337-344); and the Africans Tertullian (*Adv. Marc.* iii.24; *Apol.* 48; cf. Quasten, II, 318, 339f.), Cyprian (see Froom, I, 331-36), and Lactantius (whose detailed picture of millennial bliss in *Divine Institutes* vii.14, 24, 26 by no means presupposes Zoroastrian influence — Eliade notwithstanding). In taking a millennial viewpoint, these fathers ranged themselves on the side of orthodoxy in two particulars: they supported the apostolicity and canonicity of Revelation (against those who combined a denial of its authenticity with amillennialism, e.g., Dionysius of Alexandria, as cited in Eusebius *HE* vii.14.1-3; 24.6-8); and they opposed both the Gnostics, whose dualistic spiritualizing of Christian doctrine completely wiped out eschatological hope, and Christian Platonists such as Origen (*De prin.* ii.11.2), whose rejection of a literal millennium stemmed from an idealistic depreciation of matter and a highly dangerous allegorical hermeneutic (A. C. McGiffert, *History of Christian Thought,* I [1932], 227f.).

It is a moot point whether the Clementine epistles, the Shepherd of Hermas, the Didache, the Apocalypse of Peter, Melito of Sardis, the letters of the Lyons martyrs, Methodius of Tyre, and Commodian show traces of millennialism. Polycarp of Smyrna and Ignatius of Antioch certainly do not — but little can be derived one way or the other from arguments from silence. Active opposition to chiliastic views arose (1) as a result of Origen's influence (thus Eusebius's later shift to amillennialism, *HE* iii.39, with his false attribution of chiliastic origins to the heretic Cerinthus, *HE* iii.28); (2) in reaction to Montanist excesses, e.g., their prophetess's claim that "Christ came to me in the form of a woman... and revealed to me that this place [the insignificant village of Pepuza] is holy and that here Jerusalem will come down from heaven" (Epiphanius xlix.1; cf. McGiffert, I, 171); and (3) as a defense against attempts to calculate the end time (a practice that has consistently brought discredit, through guilt-by-association, to millennialism in every age: e.g., cf. Vulliaud, pp. 75-85; Toulmin and Goodfield, *Discovery of Time* [1965], pp. 55-73; H. J. Forman, *Story of Prophecy* [1940]; R. Lewinsohn, *Science, Prophecy and Prediction* [1961]; L. Festinger, *et al., When Prophecy Fails* [1956]; T. C. Graebner, *Prophecy and the War* [1918]; *War in the Light of Prophecy* [1941]; and finally, as an especially gross modern example, O. J. Smith, *Is the Antichrist at Hand? What of Mussolini* [1927]).

*B. Middle Ages and Reformation.* No theologian of the ancient Church had a greater influence on its history during the medieval period than Augustine. Once a chiliast himself but driven away from that position by the "immoderate, carnal" extremism of some of its advocates (*Civ. Dei* xx.7), he followed the symbolical-mystical hermeneutic system of the fourth-century donatist Tyconius in arguing that the thousand years of Rev. 20 actually designated the interval "from the first coming of Christ to the end of the world, when He shall come the second time" (xx.8). Thus was "a new era in prophetic interpretation" introduced, wherein Augustine's conception of the millennium as "spiritualized into a present politico-religious fact, fastens itself upon the church for about thirteen long centuries" (Froom, I, 479, with tabular summary of medieval views, 896f.; see also R. C. Petry, *Christian Eschatology and Social Thought: A Historical Essay on the Social Implications of Some Selected Aspects in Christian Eschatology to A.D. 1500* [1956], pp. 312-336). Millennialism did not die, but under the pressure of the "medieval synthesis" it tended to assume aberrational forms, particularly after the year 1000 when the Augustinian chronology (if literalized) ran out. Thus, as is frequently the case, polar extremes developed: mystical, spiritualistic chiliasms presupposing the end of the church-age, as represented by Joachim of Fiore's "third age of the Spirit," and by Cathari, Spiritual Franciscans, and Waldenses; and grossly materialistic chiliasms bound up with the crusading enterprise, as illustrated by Urban II's speech at Clermont: "As the times of Antichrist are approaching and as the East, and especially Jerusalem, will be the central point of attack, there must be Christians there to resist." (On both varieties of medieval chiliasm, see J. J. von Döllinger *The Prophetic Spirit and the Prophecies of the Christian Era,* published with his *Fables Respecting the Popes* [1872]; A. Vasilev, *Byzantion* [1942/43], pp. 462-502; R. A. Knox, *Enthusiasm* [1950], pp. 110-13; and esp. N. Cohn, *Pursuit of the Millennium . . . in Europe from the 11th to the 16th Century* [1961].)

Though both Renaissance and Reformation stood against the world view of medieval scholasticism, they did not oppose the accepted Augustinian amillennialism. The Renaissance was too favorable toward Neoplatonic modes of thought to be chiliastic, and the Reformers were so (legitimately) preoccupied with correcting the Church's soteriological errors that they could not give high priority to eschatology. But from the pre-Reformers Wyclif and Hus to Luther, Calvin, and the doctrinal affirmations of Protestant Orthodoxy, the papacy was identified with the antichrist. This conviction led many Reformation Protestants to believe that the end of the world was at hand (T. F. Torrance, *SJT,* Occasional Papers 2, pp. 36-62; Vulliaud, pp. 127f.). Had it not been for the outbreak of chiliasm in a particularly offensive form at Münster (1534), early Church teaching on the millennium might have been recovered along with other doctrines obscured in the medieval synthesis. The speculations of radicals, however, as concretized in Münzer's "Zion," were so offensive to all that this was rendered impossible. The Augsburg Confession, art. 17 (Lutheran) and the Helvetic Confession, art. 11 (Reformed) expressly rejected such "Jewish opinions" (but, let it be noted, did not reject millennialism per se — cf. Peters, *Theocratic Kingdom,* I, 531-34; M. Reu, *Lutheran Dogmatics* [1951], pp. 483-87; and Saarnivaara, pp. 94f.).

Virtually all the Reformation commentators on Rev. 20 followed the Augustinian line, even when other aspects of their eschatology seemed to cry out for a millennial interpretation of the passage (cf. tabulation of views in Froom, II [1948], 530f.). The same was true even of Anabaptists: "except for Melchior Hofmann, only a few fringe figures of the Anabaptist movement were chiliastic" (*Mennonite Encyclopedia,* I, 557). The oft-heard claim that theosophical mystic Jacob Boehme was a millennialist is repudiated by his own writings (cf. J. J. Stoudt, *Sunrise to Eternity* [1957], pp. 127f.). In contrast, many of the seventeenth-century divines of the Westminster Assembly, e.g., Thomas Goodwin, were decidedly premillennial in their theology (cf. P. Schaff, *Creeds of Christendom,* I, 727-746); and "Cambridge Platonist" Henry More believed in a chiliastic future when "all the goodly Inventions of nice Theologers shall cease . . . and the Gospel shall be exalted" (see A. Lichtenstein, *Henry More* [1962], pp. 101f.).

*C. Modern Times.* New England Puritanism, continental Pietism, and the evangelical revivals of the 18th cent. came long enough after the events of the Reformation that perspective on the Reformers' limitations became possible. Among the results were increased missionary outreach and more careful eschatological study. Chiliasm revived, and it was generally of the premillennial variety (cf. the tabular summary of seventeenth- and eighteenth-century interpretations of Rev. 20 in Froom, II, 786f.). Except for Jonathan Edwards, who was postmillennial (J. P. Martin, *The Last Judgment . . . from Orthodoxy to Ritschl* [1963], pp. 71f.), virtually all the Christian leaders of colonial America maintained premillennialism: John Davenport; Samuel, Increase, and Cotton Mather; Samuel Sewall; Timothy Dwight (tabulation of views in Froom, III, 252f.; see also G. H. Williams, *Wilderness and Paradise in Christian Thought* [1962]). Spener, Halle Pietist and hymnwriter Joachim Lange, and distinguished NT scholar J. A. Bengel held millennial views. John Wesley's hymns attest his early premillennarian belief, though later he embraced Bengel's concept of a future double millennium (first on earth, with Satan bound; second in heaven, representing the saints' rule with Christ).

In sum, it can hardly be maintained, as is commonly alleged, that chiliastic belief did not have serious influence in Christendom before the rise of Adventist sects and J. N. Darby's Plymouth Brethren in the 19th cent., and the appearance of the Scofield Reference Bible and the Fundamentalist movement early in the 20th cent. (cf. W. H. Rutgers, *Premillennialism in America* [1930]; L. Gaspar, *The Fundamentalist Movement* [1963], pp. 7f., 53f., 157). Certainly Darby and the Scofield editors introduced the Church to dispensationalism (at least as a formal theology), and premillennialism was an essential element in that hermeneutical schema; but a premillennarian view of Rev. 20 did not logically require dispensational commitment and had in fact existed independently of it since the early days of the Church.

*D. Utopian Dream.* Secular utopianism is a theme in the history of ideas correlative with the millennial hope, and it is instructive to note that where Christian millennial expectation has been absent or downplayed its utopian counterpart has entered the breach. Greco-Roman civilization conceived of history cyclically, with the "golden age" as a future hope (cf. Vergil's 4th Eclogue). During the amillennial Middle Ages the legend of an idealistic kingdom in the East, under the rule of Christian "Prester John," captured the imagination and directly influenced the mythology of exploration (Ponce de Leon's search for the fountain of youth, Pizarro's quest for a city of gold). The Renaissance, similarly unsympathetic to chiliasm, marked the beginning of literary utopianism wth the work of Thomas More. The rise of the modern secular era during the deistic "Enlightenment" offered a secular alternative to the Christian millennium in what Carl Becker perceptively termed "the heavenly city of the 18th-century philosophers." The Marxist goal of a "classless society," the Nazi dream of the "thousand-year Reich," and aspects of the capitalist-materialist "American way of life" are inversions of the millennial hope. E. Voegelin (*Order and History* [1956]) has rightly seen them as illustrations of "metastatic gnosis," the idolatrous effort of man to create a millennial kingdom for himself without God. It would appear that the loss of theocentric chiliasm leaves a vacuum into which rush the monstrosities of anthropocentric utopianism. At the same time, perennial utopian dreams (and extrabiblical religious chiliasms, as in the Parsi faith — see I.C above) can be viewed as the groping of the human soul, individual and collective, for the truth embodied in Christian eschatology. (See, e.g., S. Baring-Gould, *Curious Myths of the Middle Ages* [1866-1868]; K. Mannheim, *Ideology and Utopia* [1936]; E. Sanceau, *The Land of Prester John* [1944]; F. R. White, ed., *Famous Utopias of the Renaissance* [1946]; K. Amis, *New Maps of Hell* [1960]; S. B. Liljegren, *Studies on the Origin and Early Tradition of English Utopian Fiction* [1961]; J. P. Roux, *Les Explorateurs au moyen âge* [1961]; R. Thévenin, *Les Pays légendaires* [1961]; C. Walsh, *From Utopia to Nightmare* [1962]; G. Kateb, *Utopia and Its Enemies* [1963]; *Daedalus*, Spring, 1965; L. Gallagher, *More's "Utopia" and Its Critics* [1964]; E. L. Tuveson, *Millennium and Utopia* [1964]; H. B. Franklin, *Future Perfect* [1966]; M. R. Hillegas, *The Future as Nightmare* [1967]; T. Molnar, *Utopia, the Perennial Heresy* [1972]; J. W. Montgomery, *Where Is History Going?* [1969].)

***III. Contrasting Millennialisms.–A.*** *Amillennial Allegory.* Since chiliasm is bound directly to the interpretation of Rev. 20, consideration must be given to the diverse ways in which this passage has been exegeted. Amillennialists are unconvinced that the chapter should compel belief in a literal period of penultimate divine triumph, either before or after the Parousia. Liberal theology takes this viewpoint because of its objection to the miraculous character of predictive prophecy and because of its reductionistic approach to biblical inspiration; the book of Revelation loses force because of its alleged disunity, lack of authenticity, or factual unreliability (see, e.g., A. Harnack, *Enc.Brit.* [11th ed. 1910-1911], XVIII, 461-63; R. H. Charles, *Studies in the Apocalypse* [1913]; comm. on Revelation [2 vols., *ICC*, 1920]; *Lectures on the Apocalypse* [1922]; G. R. Berry, *Premillennialism and OT Prediction* [1929]; and R. W. McEwen's "Factors in the Modern Survival of Millennialism" [Diss., University of Chicago, 1933]). "Conservative" amillennialism holds to a symbolical interpretation of Rev. 20, either in the Augustinian manner or along the lines of W. W. Milligan (*Expos.B.*): "The saints reign for a thousand years; that is, they are introduced into a state of perfect and glorious victory." Important orthodox proponents of amillennialism include G. Vos, *Teaching of Jesus Concerning the Kingdom of God and the Church* (1903; repr. 1951); W. Masselink, *Why Thousand Years?* (1930); F. E. Hamilton, *Basis of Millennial Faith* (1942); P. Mauro, *The Seventy Weeks* (1944); O. T. Allis, *Prophecy and the Church* (1945); G. L. Murray, *Millennial Studies* (1948); A. Pieters, *Seed of Abraham* (1950); L. Berkhof, *Kingdom of God* (1951); *Second Coming of Christ* (1953); J. Wilmot, *Inspired Principles of Prophetic Interpretation* (1967). The difficulty all amillennialisms face is the textual weight of Rev. 20. The admission of liberal amillennialist Salmond concerning this passage is noteworthy: "The figurative interpretation, it must be owned, cannot be made exegetically good even in its most plausible applications.... This remarkable paragraph in John's Apocalypse speaks of a real millennial reign of Christ on earth together with certain of His saints, which comes in between a first resurrection and the final judgment" (pp. 441f.).

*B. Postmillennial Progress.* Postmillennialism of both a "conservative" and a "liberal" type is likewise to be found in the Church. Orthodox advocates of this position (among the best: P. Fairbairn, *Interpretation of Prophecy* [1865]; Hodge, Shedd, and Strong, in their systematic theologies; B. B. Warfield, *Biblical Doctrines* [1929]; J. M. Kik, *Revelation Twenty* [1955]; L. Boettner, *The Millennium* [1958]) interpret Rev. 20 less symbolically than do the amillennialists (a period of divinely ordained blessedness will in fact precede the end), but nonliteral force is given to the details of the chapter (no de facto resurrection of martyrs or physical presence of Christ on earth is anticipated during the millennial period). Rather, God's immanent power will be more fully manifest over His enemies as the time of Christ's return draws closer. Boettner argues, "We do not understand how anyone can take a long range view of history and deny that across the centuries there has been and continues to be great progress, and that the trend is definitely toward a better world" (p. 136).

This is precisely the opinion of "liberal" postmillennialists — but their confidence stems from a different quarter: the eighteenth-century optimistic view of man as basically good and the nineteenth-century "myth of progress." Thus the old modernism found premillennialism abhorrent because "the world is found to be growing constantly better" (S. J. Case, *The Millennial Hope* [1918], p. 238) and "the clear vision of present-day prophets... in religion, in philosophy, and in business, revels in a growing future of blessedness for mankind" (G. P. Mains, *Premillennialism* [1920], p. 107). Unchastened by two world wars, the new secular theology endeavors to revivify nineteenth-century motifs along much the same lines, e.g., with its view of an immanent Christ more and more fully manifested in the social movements of our day. (For critique see J. W. Montgomery, *Suicide of Christian Theology* [1970].) Protestant "process theology" (J. B. Cobb, Jr., S. Ogden, N. Pittenger) sees man dynamically growing into God. Roman Catholic evolutionary theologian Teilhard de Chardin glimpses God "up ahead" where human history will be fully divinized at a Christic "Omega point" (cf. Schillebeeckx, *God the Future of Man* [1968]; J. W. Montgomery, *Ecumenicity, Evangelicals and Rome* [1969]). Moltmann's "theology of hope," in part dependent on Ernst Bloch's dialectic humanism, has similar affinities with postmillennial confidence in the future of the human drama.

Critics of postmillennialism, whether of the conservative or of the liberal variety, argue that neither the Bible nor human history offers ground for assuming that the human situation is in process of continual amelioration; indeed, because of humanity's sinful condition, the reverse would appear to be the case. And "if world history is not a movement of progress but rather tends to an increasing concentration of anti-christian power, then the second advent of Jesus for which the Church is praying is not a direct continuation and completion of world history but an event that comes from an entirely different dimension, that suddenly breaks off the preceding development and throws the whole constitution of the present world off its hinges" (K. Heim, *Jesus the World's Perfecter* [1961], p. 189).

*C. Premillennial Philosophy of History.* Premillennialism endeavors to offer as literal an interpretation of Rev. 20 as possible (Christ will physically return to a world under the sway of the antichrist, defeat him, and with the resurrected saints rule on earth a thousand years; the ultimate destruction of Satanic power will then occur and "God shall be all in all"). Naturally, such an eschatology is anathema to the liberal theological community, so premillennialism is a phenomenon to be observed today only among those holding a strong doctrine of biblical inspiration. The major differences among contemporary premillennialists do not touch the above points, but have to do with whether the millennium ought to be integrated into a dispensational view of Scripture, and whether the "lifting up" of the Church spoken of in 1 Thess. 4:17 occurs before, during, or after the great antichristic tribulation ("pretribulation rapture," as supported by E. S. English, *Re-Thinking the Rapture* [1954], *v.* "midtribulation rapture," as argued by N. B. Harrison, *The End* [1941], *v.* "posttribulation rapture," as maintained by N. S. McPherson, *Triumph Through Tribulation* [1944]). Without any attempt to classify according to these differences, we can list the most important modern supporters of the premillennial position: Alf.; F. Godet, *Studies on the NT* (1873); E. R. Craven, comm. on Revelation (Lange, 1874); N. West, *The Thousand Years* (1880); Peters; S. P. Tregelles, *Hope of Christ's Second Coming* (1886); J. A. Seiss, *The Last Times* (1878); *Lectures on the Apocalypse* (1900); W. E. Blackstone, *Jesus is Coming* (1908); A. Reese, *Approaching Advent of Christ* (1917); T. Zahn, *Intro. to the NT* (1909); comm. on Revelation (*KEK,* 1926); A. C. Gaebelein, *Return of the Lord* (1925); H. A. Ironside, *Lamp of Prophecy* (1940); L. S. Chafer, *Systematic Theology* (1948); G. E. Ladd, *Crucial Questions about the Kingdom of God* (1952); *The Blessed Hope* (1956); C. C. Ryrie, *Basis of Premillennial Faith* (1953); Culver; C. L. Feinberg, *Premillennialism or Amillennialism?* (1954); J. D. Pentecost, *Things to Come* (1958); J. F. Walvoord, *Millennial Kingdom* (1959): M. C. Tenney, "Importance and Exegesis of Rev. 20:1-8," in J. F. Walvoord, ed., *Truth for Today* (1963.

The arguments for premillennialism are generally of two types: exegetical and doctrinal. Exegetically, the claim is made that only a literal interpretation of Rev. 20 fulfills the basic hermeneutic rule that a passage of Scripture must be taken in its natural sense unless contextual considerations force a nonliteral rendering. (The burden of proof thus falls upon the opponent of premillennialism to show that such considerations do in fact exist.) Doctrinally, the premillennialist argues that the vindication of God's ways to humanity entails Christ's victory and reign in the very sphere in which Satanic power has so long been manifest. For God's will to be done "on earth as it is in heaven" demands what T. A. Kantonen has so effectively termed "the harvest of history" (*The Christian Hope* [1954], pp. 65-70; cf. Peters, III, 427-442; and A. J. McClain, *Greatness of the Kingdom* [1959], pp. 527-531). A. Saphir asked, "Is earth simply a failure, abandoned by God to the power of the enemy, the scene of divine judgment, and not the scene of the vindication and triumph of righteousness?" (*Lectures on the Lord's Prayer* [1870]). Perhaps the best statement of the case remains that of Irenaeus (*Adv. haer.* v.32.1) at the end of the 2nd cent.: "It behooves the righteous first to receive the promise of the inheritance which God promised to the fathers, and to reign in it when they rise again to behold God in this creation which is renovated, and that the judgment should take place afterwards. For it is just that in that very creation in which they toiled or were afflicted, being proved in every way by suffering, they should receive the reward of their suffering; and that in the creation in which they were slain because of their love to God, in that they should be revived again; and that in the creation in which they endured servitude, in that they should reign. For God is rich in all things and all things are his. It is fitting, therefore, that the creation itself, being restored to its primeval condition, should be without restraint under the dominion of the righteous" (*ANF* translation).

*See also* PAROUSIA.

***Bibliography***.–Two encyclopedic general works are H. Corrodi, *Kritische Geschichte des Chiliasmus* (4 vols., 1794); L. F. Froom, *Prophetic Faith of our Fathers* (4 vols., 1946-1954). Bibliographical sources are best represented by A. D. Ehlert, *Bibliographic History of Dispensationalism* (1965); for utopianism, G. Negley, ed., catalog of the Utopia Collection of Duke University Library (1965). Other significant works and those cited twice or more in the article are: R. D. Culver, *Daniel and the Latter Days*; W. S. LaSor, *The Truth about Armageddon* (1982); J. B. Payne, *Encyclopedia of Biblical Prophecy* (1980); G. N. H. Peters, *Theocratic Kingdom* (3 vols., 1884; repr. 1952); J. Quasten, *Patrology* (3 vols., 1950); U. Saarnivaara, *Armageddon* (1966); S. D. F. Salmond, *Christian Doctrine of Immortality* (2nd ed. 1896); P. Vulliaud, *La Fin du monde* (1952).

J. W. MONTGOMERY

**MILLET** [Heb. *dōḥan*; Gk. *kénchros*]. One ingredient of the prophet's bread (Ezk. 4:9) when he was symbolically acting out the role of the besieged. The European millet (*Panicum miliaceum* L.) is one of the oldest cultivated grains. An annual that seldom exceeds 1 m. (3 ft.) in height, it bears an enormous number of tiny seeds in each panicle. It has been used continuously as both animal fodder and a staple item in human diet. The seeds were commonly ground to flour, which was then mixed with other cereals to make bread. Very often impoverished peasants ate the seeds uncooked. Millet, durra (*Sorghum vulgare*), and Italian millet (*Panicum italicum* L.) were cultivated in the ancient Near East; *dōḥan* refers to millet but could include all three.

R. K. H.

**MILLO** mil'ō [Heb. *millô'*–'filled,' 'mound,' 'rampart,' hence interpreted as 'fortress,' 'tower,' or something that fills a gap or hole; or, with both meanings, as a tower of solid stone standing on a terrace or raised platform 'filling' the defense gap of a depression or gully; cf. LXX Gk. *ákra*–'citadel,' 'acropolis,' *Maallōn* (Jgs. 9:6, 20)].

**1.** (Jgs. 9:6, 20, AV). *See* BETH-MILLO.

**2.** An element of the circumvallation of Jerusalem, especially constructed for the defense of a naturally vulnerable spot and known well enough in Solomon's time to be recognized by its name alone. In 2 S. 5:9; 1 Ch. 11:8, it is named in connection with David's activities in fortifying or refortifying the city. The references identify a place where the Millo stood in a later time or possibly suggest that, beginning with the Jebusite Millo, David reinforced the Canaanite city walls.

In 1 K. 9:15, 24; 11:27 Solomon is credited with having "built" the Millo; the verb here, as above, may mean "rebuild," "repair," or "remodel." The extent of Solomon's activities made them noteworthy. They would be understandable if structural weakness in the Millo had been suddenly disclosed or if new developments in the techniques and potential of offensive warfare had alarmed the defense officers.

According to 2 K. 12:20, the assassination of Joash took place in "the house of Millo," probably indicating, following **1** above, the precinct in which Millo was located (cf. J. Gray, *I & II Kings* [*OTL,* 2nd ed. 1970], pp. 590f.).

In response to Sennacherib's threat to invade Jerusalem, Hezekiah reinforced the Millo (2 Ch. 32:5).

That the Millo was located on the southeast hill of Jerusalem, S of the temple hill and on the northern border of the Jebusite city, is uncertain but plausible, since only the north side of the city lacked formidable natural defenses. The precise nature of the Millo has so far not been demonstrated, though many suggestions have been made. K. Galling (*Biblisches Reallexikon* [1937], col. 300) thought that Millo was the name for the entire area where Solomon built the palace, temple, and government buildings. W. R. Arnold (*Ephod and Ark* [1917]), followed by G. E. Wright, more plausibly speculated that the Millo was a broad, solid-fill, raised platform built by Solomon as a causeway over a steep gully that had previously isolated the temple area from the Jebusite stronghold. J. Simons moderately urged that present information permits a description for Millo no more specific than "a special feature of the defense works of the City of David" (*Jerusalem in the OT* [1952]).

*See also* JERUSALEM III.C.1.c. P. L. GARBER

**MILLSTONE.** *See* MILL.

**MINA** mī'nə [Heb. *māneh*; Gk. *mná*] (Ezk. 45:12); AV MANEH mä'nā. A unit of measure elsewhere translated "pound" or "shekel." The science of metrology was not highly developed among the Israelites, and the standard of weights and measures varied from city to city. Abraham is said to have "weighed to Ephron . . . four hundred shekels of silver, current with the merchant" (Gen. 23:16); consequently the *māneh,* which was the equivalent of 60 shekels, varied in value also. If the shekel is taken as 16.7 gm. (0.6 oz.) then the ordinary or heavy *māneh* would be about 1 kg. (2.2 lbs.). The light *māneh* was only half that value. These two values explain the difference between the parallel passages in 1 K. 10:17 and 2 Ch. 9:16. *See* WEIGHTS AND MEASURES. M. A. MACLEOD

Weight of one (Babylonian) mina (about 60 shekels). The inscription states that it is an exact copy of a weight made by Nebuchadrezzar II (605-562 B.C.) after the standard fixed by Shulgi (king of the 3rd Dynasty of Ur, *ca.* 2000 B.C.) (Trustees of the British Museum)

**MINAEANS** min-ē'ənz. The people of a kingdom in the southwestern Arabian peninsula (northern Yemen; *see* ARABIA X, bibliography); they are not mentioned in the Bible. The south Arabic name, *mʿn,* pl. *mʿnyn* and *'mʿnn* (K. Conti Rossini, *Chrestomathia Arabica Meridionalis* [1931], pp. 179f.), has sometimes led to identification of the Minaeans with the biblical MEUNIM (*K mᵉʿînîm,* 1 Ch. 4:41), an Arab people who lived near Maʿan, SE of Petra. This identification is unlikely, for the south Arabian kingdom, which has been historically and geographically established, was far from the city of Maʿan. Possibly Minaean caravaneers settled in or near Maʿan, thereby giving it its name, but the Meunim of the Bible (9th-8th cents. B.C.) predated the period of Minaean supremacy (4th cent. B.C.). W. S. L. S.

**MINCING** [Heb. *ṭāp̄ap̄*–'go like a child' (cf. *ṭap̄*–'small child'), i.e., 'trip along,' 'take small steps']. An affected manner of walking or acting, descriptive of the haughty women of Jerusalem (Isa. 3:16).

**MIND** [Heb. often *lēḇ* or *lēḇāḇ*–'heart,' also *šāmar*–'keep' (e.g., "keep in mind," Gen. 37:11), *nep̄eš*–'soul' (e.g., 2 K. 9:15; Eccl. 7:28), *rû(a)ḥ*– 'spirit, breath' (e.g. 1 Ch. 28:12; Ezk. 11:5; 20:32), *zāḵar*–''remember' (e.g., "keep in mind," Ps. 78:42), *yēṣer*–'form,' 'purpose' (e.g., Isa. 26:3), niphal of *nāḥam*–'regret' (e.g., "change [one's] mind," Ps. 110:4), etc.; Aram. *lēḇ* (Dnl. 7:28), *lᵉḇaḇ* (e.g., Dnl. 2:30), *bāl*–'heart' (Dnl. 6:14 [MT 15]); Gk. often *noús,* also *diánoia*–'understanding,' *phronéō*–'think, set one's mind on,' *sōphronéō*–'be in one's right mind' (e.g., 2 Cor. 5:13), *phrónēma*–'thought,' *nóēma*–'mind,' 'thought,' *kardía*–'heart'; (e.g., Lk. 21:14), *psychḗ*–'self, soul' (Acts 14:2; 15:24; Phil. 1:27), *pneúma*–'breath, spirit' (2 Cor. 2:13; 7:13), *dialogízō*–("consider in [one's] mind," Lk. 1:29), *meteōrízō*–'worry' ("be of anxious mind," Lk. 12:29), *mélei*–'care' (1 Cor. 7:21), *metamélomai*–'regret' ("change one's mind," He. 7:21), *eknéphō*–'become sober' ("come to one's mind," 1 Cor. 15:34), *prássō*–'do' (1 Thess. 4:11), *nephrós*–'kidney' (Rev. 2:23), *metabállō*–'change' ("change one's mind," Acts 28:6), *krínō*–'judge' ("make up [one's] mind," 2 Cor. 2:1)]; AV also HEART, SPIRIT, SOUL, RESPECT, REMEMBER, UNDERSTANDING, AFFECTION, etc.; NEB also HEART, SKILL, UNDERSTANDING, THOUGHT, DESIGN, REASON, etc.; **(BE) MINDFUL** [Heb. *zāḵar*–'remember' (e.g., Ps. 8:4 [MT 5]), *pāqaḏ*–'visit' (Zeph. 2:7); Gk. *mimnḗskomai*–'remember' (He. 2:6), *syneídēsis*–'consciousness' (1 Pet. 2:19)]; AV also REMEMBER, VISIT, CONSCIENCE; NEB also CALL TO MIND, REMEMBER, TURN TO, etc. *See also* DOUBLE MIND; HUMBLE II.B.

***I. In the OT.***–The Hebrew OT does not have one term that refers to "mind" in the modern sense of brain or organ of cognition. Most instances of "mind" are a translation of *lēḇ*/*lēḇāḇ,* "heart," a comprehensive term for the integrative center of a person's emotional, volitional, and intellectual life. (*See* HEART.) The translation "mind" is used in passages that focus on the heart as the seat of remembrance, reason, or direction. The LXX reflects this nuance by translating *lēḇ*/*lēḇāḇ* with Gk. *noús,* "mind", rather than *kardía,* "heart," in Ex. 7:23; Josh. 14:7; Job 7:17; Isa. 10:7, 12; 41:22.

*A. Memory.* The mind of the faithful Israelite harbors knowledge of the Lord's past redemptive deeds (Isa. 46:8; 65:17; Jer. 3:16; Lam. 3:21). God promised that if His people "call to mind" the blessing and the curse and return to Him, He will return their prosperity (Dt. 30:1-3). "Mind" is also used idiomatically to reproduce verbs of remembering, as in Ps. 77:11 (MT 12): "I will call to mind [*zāḵar*] the deeds of the Lord." God too remembers. He is "mindful"(*zāḵar*) especially of His covenant (1 Ch. 16:15; Neh. 9:17; Ps. 25:6; 105:8; 111:5) and also of His people (Ps. 9:12 [MT 13]; 115:12). But He remembers in judgment when He calls to mind Israel's evil deeds (Jer. 44:21).

*B. Reason.* The mind is the seat of reason and comprehension. This sense is evidenced extensively in wisdom contexts. Solomon is given a "wise and discerning mind" (1 K. 3:12) that enables him to distinguish between right and wrong. He is given the power of judgment and perception, literally a "hearing mind" (*lēḇ šōmē[a]ʿ*, v. 9). Mind (comprehension) and ear (perception) are contextually associated also in Prov. 18:15; 22:17; 23:12; both are necessary for the acquisition of knowledge. Eyes, ears, and mind are linked in Dt. 29:4; Isa. 32:3f.; Ezk. 40:4.

The mind possesses knowledge and wisdom (Prov. 18:15; 22:17; 23:12; Eccl. 1:13, 17; 7:25; 8:16). The innermost thoughts and secrets are found in the mind (Jgs. 16:17f.). Some things, however, are beyond comprehension. According to Eccl. 3:11 God put a yearning for ultimate meaning into the human mind, but the mind, being finite, cannot discover that meaning. "Mind" can denote a practical understanding as well as cognition. The tabernacle craftsman who has technical skills and abilities has an "able mind" (lit. "wise spirit," *rû[a]ḥ ḥoḵmâ*, Ex. 28:3; cf. also 36:2).

*C. Direction.* The mind is the seat of intention and direction as well as disposition, attitude, and inclination. It is the faculty that makes choices and is responsible for a person's course in life. The mind plans, but ultimately God determines the way (Prov. 16:9; 19:21). The mind reflects a person's true being (Prov. 27:19). The directing core of an individual's life is sometimes called the "heart and mind," (*lēḇ/lēḇāḇ* and *nep̱eš*, 1 S. 2:35; 1 K. 8:48; 1 Ch. 22:19; 28:9; 2 Ch. 6:38; cf. *k$^e$lāyôṯ* and *lēḇ*, Ps. 26:2; *qereḇ* and *lēḇ*, 64:6 [MT 7]). This expression does not refer to two bodily organs or even to emotion and reason respectively, but to the seat of a person's direction. The heart is deep within, but God is able to search it out and see what lies at the base of one's life (*k$^e$lāyôṯ* and *lēḇ*, "heart" and "mind," Jer. 11:20; 17:10; 20:12). Once a course of action has been chosen, one sets one's mind (*lēḇ/lēḇāḇ*) upon it (Ex. 14:5; Dt. 5:29; 1 Ch. 12:38 [MT 39]; Neh. 4:6 [MT 3:38]), i.e., intends to realize it. God also sets about to accomplish "the intents of his mind" (Jer. 23:20; 30:24).

Persons of perverse mind despise the way of the Lord (Prov. 11:20; 12:8; 17:20; 23:33). They do not perceive the way that leads to righteousness, but choose the way of wickedness. But the nation whose mind (*yēṣer*, lit. "inclination") is fixed on God is kept in peace (Isa. 26:3).

***II. In the NT.***–The RSV NT uses "mind" to translate terms for the cognitive, reasoning, and purposive parts of human personhood. Mk. 12:30 par. ("heart ... soul ... mind [Gk. *diánoia*] ... strength") shows a unified, but not rigid, concept of personhood, one that allows for both a physical and a spiritual nature (cf. also the hendiadys "body and mind" in Eph. 2:3 [*diánoia*], and "hearts" and "minds" in Phil. 4:7 [*nóēma*]; He. 10:16 [*diánoia*]). The mind can and should be fixed upon God (Rom. 7:25 [*noús*]; 8:6 [*phrónēma*]) and Christ (Col. 3:2 [*phronéō*]); it should be under one's control (2 Thess. 2:2 [*noús*]; 1 Pet. 1:13 [*diánoia*]). But it has been corrupted (Rom. 1:21 [*kardía*], 28 [*noús*]; 2 Tim. 3:8 [*noús*]) by earthly things (Phil. 3:19 [*phronéō*]) and is now depraved (1 Tim. 6:5 [*noús*]), following its own desires (Eph. 2:3 [*diánoia*]). The Gentiles are futile in their minds (Eph. 4:17 [*noús*]), and even the Jews are hardened in mind by a Christless law (2 Cor. 3:14f. [*nóēma, kardía*]). Unless the mind is set on the Spirit there can be no life (Rom. 8:5-7 [*phronéō, phrónēma*]). Therefore the mind needs renewal (Rom. 12:2 [*noús*]), which brings transformation of character, an integration of personality, and submission to the will of God.

As the center of intellectual undestanding and perception (cf. Lk. 24:45 [*noús*]), the mind can be seriously altered both by demonic possession (Mk. 5:15; Lk. 8:35 [pass. part. *sōphronéō*]) and by ecstatic experience, which in public worship is less desirable than full use of the mind (1 Cor. 14:14-19 [*noús*]). Indeed, people should strive to submit their minds in obedience to God (1 Cor. 15:34 [*eknḗphō*]; Phil. 2:5 [*phronéō*]; 1 Pet. 1:13 [*diánoia*]), and then by the leading of the Spirit they will do the will of God and have the mind of God (1 Cor. 2:16 [*noús*]; Rom. 8:5 [*phronéō*]). Where minds are set on the will of God, there will be unity (Phil. 2:2, 5 [*phronéō*]; 1 Cor. 1:10 [*noús*]).

Several NT occurrences of "mind" merit special comment. Mt. 22:37 ("heart ... soul ... mind [*diánoia*] ") has sometimes been used to support a trichotomous theory of human nature. By this reckoning, however, since the parallels in Mk. 12:30 and Lk. 10:27 add "strength" (*ischýs*), one might argue for a quadripartite nature. But in Dt. 6:5 ("heart [Heb. *lēḇāḇ*] ... soul [*nep̱eš*] ... might [*m$^e$'ōḏ*]"), the text upon which the NT passages are based, "mind" is conspicuously absent. Total commitment is the concern here, not the dissection of human nature.

Romans 12:2 speaks of the renewing (Gk. *anakainóō*) of the mind (*noús*). In discussing the need for repentance (*metánoia*) in Christian faith, Paul appears to move beyond the initial change of mind to a continual yielding of the mind to the will of God ("be transformed," present pass. imperative of *metamorphóō*). (Cf. the thanksgiving of Col. 1, where, after acknowledging the faith, love and hope of the Colossians, Paul says that he prays continuously that they might know God's will [v. 9].)

Philippians 2:5 presents a special problem. It is not clear whether the present imperative of *phronéō* exhorts readers to have the same mind as Christ (i.e., to have Christ's mind; so AV) or to have the same mind or attitude toward one another as they do *toward* Christ (so RSV). Perhaps it is best to accommodate both positions. As stated in 1 Cor. 2:16, the Spirit of God helps Christians to know the mind (*noús*) of Christ. As believers conform to His will, they have the mind of Christ. Thus they will treat others as they treat Christ, and they will be in harmony with one another, which is Paul's main concern (cf. Phil. 1:27; 2:2).

*See also* PSYCHOLOGY.

***Bibliography.***–R. Bultmann, *Theology of the NT,* I (Eng. tr. 1952), 211-227; *DNTT,* II, 180-84, 616-620; R. Dentan, *Knowledge of God in Ancient Israel* (1968); W. Eichrodt, *Theology of the OT,* II (Eng. tr. *OTL*, 1967), 142-45; A. R. Johnson, *Vitality of the Individual in the Thought of Ancient Israel* (2nd ed. 1964); *TDNT,* III, *s.v.* καρδία (F. Baumgärtel, J. Behm); IV, *s.v.* νοέω κτλ.: νοῦς, νόημα, διάνοια (J. Behm); IX, *s.v.* φρήν κτλ. (G. Bertram); ψυχή κτλ., B.4 (E. Jacob); H. W. Wolff, *Anthropology of the OT* (Eng. tr. 1974).

B. BANDSTRA S. S. STUART

**MINE** [Heb. *môṣā'*] (Job 28:1); AV VEIN; **MINING**. A pit for extracting minerals from the earth; the process of working mines. The absence of a technical vocabulary for mining in the Bible may demonstrate the ancient Hebrews' unfamiliarity with the science. Heb. *môṣā'*, the only word translated "mine" by the RSV, is a general term meaning "source," derived from the verb *yāṣā'* ("go out, come out"). Dt. 8:9 uses the verb *ḥāṣaḇ* (RSV, lit., "dig") for the mining of copper.

The only OT description of mining occurs in Job 28, a passage showing the inaccessibility of wisdom. The author recognizes there is a "source" (*môṣā'*) for silver and a "place" (*māqôm*) for gold (v. 1); that iron is "taken" (pual of *lāqaḥ*) out of the earth and copper is "poured out" (pass. part. of *yāṣaq*; RSV "smelted") from the "stone" (*'eḇen*; RSV "ore," v. 2); that "they" (RSV "men") search underground for "stone" (RSV "ore," v. 3); that they open a "stream bed" (RSV "shafts") in uninhabited valleys (v. 4); that man puts his hand to flinty rock, overturns mountains (v. 9), and cuts "channels" (*y$^e$'ōrîm*) in the rocks (v. 10). In none of this descriptive language can one find a technical term connected with the mining industry.

Archeological and geological explorations have shown that, apart from various formations of stone adequate for construction purposes, mineral resources in Palestine are generally scarce. The Arabah, however, possesses rich

Mining sanctuary of Hathor at Timna' in its Midianite phase. The pillars are from the original Egyptian sanctuary; they were reused in the Midianite phase after the destruction of the Hathor shrine (Institute of Mining and Metals in the Biblical World, Arabah Expedition)

deposits of copper. Copper mines dating as early as the end of the 4th millennium B.C. have been found on both sides of the Arabah between the Dead Sea and the Gulf of Aqabah (Elath), notably at Timna' in Israel and at PUNON (Feihân) in Jordan. The largest iron mine in Palestine is found at Mughâret el-Wardeh in the 'Ajlûn Mountains of Gilead, but as yet there has been no definite evidence linking the mining activity there to a time earlier than the 1st cent. A.D. For specific information on these and other centers of mining *see* ARABAH III, V; METAL, METALLURGY; IRON I.D.

The Israelites most likely learned mining from the KENITES, who inhabited the areas in which copper deposits have been found. Desire to control the mines of the Arabah was probably an important factor in the frequent wars between Judah and Edom.

See R. J. Forbes, *Studies in Ancient Technology,* VII (1966), 104-245. R. A. COUGHENOUR

**MINERALS.** *See* METAL; STONES, PRECIOUS.

**MINGLED PEOPLES.** *See* MIXED MULTITUDE.

**MINIAMIN** min'yə-min [Heb. *minyāmîn*–'from the right hand,' i.e., 'fortunate'; *see also* MIJAMIN].

**1.** A priest who assisted Kore the Levite in distributing the freewill offering in the time of King Hezekiah (2 Ch. 31:15).

**2.** A priestly family in the time of Joiakim the high priest (Neh. 12:17).

**3.** One of the priests who played the trumpet at the dedication of the rebuilt wall of Jerusalem (Neh. 12:41).

**MINISH.** Archaic for "diminish" in the AV of Ex. 5:19; Ps. 107:39.

**MINISTER** [Heb. piel of *šārat̲*–'serve, wait upon,' piel of *kāhan*–'act as priest' (Dt. 10:6), *'āḇad̲ et̲-'ᵃḇōd̲â*–'perform the service' (Nu. 3:7f.), *'āmad̲*–'stand' (Jgs. 20:28; Neh. 12:44), *ṣāḇā'* –'serve' (Ex. 38:8)]; AV also SERVICE, STAND, WAIT, ASSEMBLE, etc.; NEB also ASSIST, ATTEND, SERVE, "on duty" (Ex. 38:8), etc.; [Gk. *diakonéō*–'serve,' *diákonos*–'servant,' *dynástēs*–'court official' (Acts 8:27), *leitourgós*–'servant' (Rom. 13:6; 15:16; Phil. 2:25; He. 8:2), *leitourgikós*–'serving' (He. 1:14), *hypēretéō*–'help, assist' (Acts 20:34), *hypērétēs*–'helper' (Lk. 1:2)]; AV also "of great authority" (Acts 8:27); NEB also "come to (one's) help," ATTENDANT, WAIT ON, DISPENSE (2 Cor. 3:6), HELPER, WORKER, etc.; **MINISTRY** [Heb. *yād̲*–'hand' (2 Ch. 7:6), piel inf. of *šārat̲* (2 Ch. 8:14); Gk. *diakonía*–'service,' *leitourgía*–'service' (He. 8:6)]; NEB also TASK, COMMISSION, etc.

***I. In the OT.***–In the RSV OT the noun "minister" always represents Heb. *mᵉšārēt̲* (piel part. of *šārat̲*); the verb usually translates *šēret̲* (piel of *šārat̲,* "serve"), with the exceptions noted above. In contrast to *'āḇad̲* and *'eḇed̲,* which often refer to menial service, *šēret̲* and *mᵉšārēt̲* (sometimes rendered "attend," "attendant," or "servant" by the RSV) generally describe personal service rendered by someone who stands in a special relationship to a superior.

Sometimes these terms are used of one human being rendering service to another. Joseph "attended" *(šēret̲)* Potiphar as a highly trusted servant whom Potiphar put in charge of his entire household (Gen. 39:4). Joshua served as Moses' personal attendant and deputy before succeeding his master as leader of the Israelites (Nu. 11:28; Josh. 1:1; RSV "servant," Ex. 24:13; 33:11). Similarly, Elisha rendered personal service to Elijah before succeeding him (1 K. 19:21). Elisha also had a personal servant who was designated a *mᵉšārēt̲* (RSV "servant," 2 K. 4:43; 6:15). The term is also applied to royal servants of various kinds, e.g., Abishag the Shunammite, who ministered to the aged King David (1 K. 1:4, 15); the personal servants of King Solomon (2 Ch. 9:4); the nephews of King Ahaziah, who served as his attendants (22:8); and the courtiers of King Ahasuerus (Est. 2:2; 6:3).

Far more frequent, however, is the use of *šēret̲* and *mᵉšārēt̲* to designate Yahweh's personal attendants. The angelic hosts (Ps. 103:2) and "fire and flame" (104:4) can be described as Yahweh's "ministers" because of their devoted service to His will. Samuel, an Ephraimite (1 S. 1:1), from his boyhood ministered to Yahweh in the temple under Eli's supervision (2:11, 18; 3:1). Most commonly, however, these terms are used to designate the priests and Levites.

All the Levites were set apart for special service to Yahweh in the tabernacle and later in the temple (cf. Nu. 16:9; 2 Ch. 29:11). Among the Levites, some (Aaron and his sons, Nu. 3:3; cf. v. 10; the Zadokites, Ezk. 40:46; 44:15f.) were ordained as priests, and it was especially they who were designated as Yahweh's "ministers" (cf. Jer. 33:21; Joel 1:9, 13; 2:17). The priests had the weighty responsibility of representing the people before God, and a very important part of their ministry involved offering sacrifices to Yahweh on behalf of the people (e.g., Ezk. 43:19). The holiness of their ministry required that they wear special garments when they entered the holy place to perform their priestly service (e.g., Ex. 28:40-43; 29:29f.; 39:1, 41; Ezk. 42:14; 44:17-19). Their ministry also included burning incense, blessing the people, and settling legal disputes (Dt. 17:12; 21:5; 1 Ch. 23:13; cf. Nu. 6:23; Ezk. 44:24). The rest of the Levites were appointed to minister to the priests and to attend to cultic duties in the tabernacle and temple (Nu. 3:6-9; 18:2-4; Ezr. 8:17). These duties included the care of the furniture of the tabernacle (Nu. 3:31), carrying the ark (Dt. 10:8; 1 Ch. 15:2; 16:37), and, from the time of David, a ministry of music and praise (1 Ch. 6:32; 2 Ch. 7:6; 8:14; cf. 31:2). (*See also* PRIESTS AND LEVITES.)

Isaiah (56:6f.) prophesies a messianic age when even

foreigners will worship Yahweh and "minister" *(šēreṯ)* to Him. They will minister to the Israelites by rebuilding their cities (60:10) and by offering their animals as sacrificial victims (v. 7). At this time the distinctions between priests and laity will break down, and all Israelites will be called "the priests of the Lord" and "the ministers of our God" (61:6).

Exodus 38:8 refers to "the mirrors of the ministering [part. of *ṣāḇā'*] women who ministered [*ṣāḇā'*] at the door of the tent of meeting." These women are mentioned elsewhere only in 1 S. 2:22, which states that the sons of Eli "lay with the women who served [part. of *ṣāḇā'*] at the entrance to the tent of meeting." The use of *ṣāḇā'* (which most often denotes military service but refers to the cultic service of the Levites in Nu. 4:3, 23, 30, etc.) suggests some kind of organized service, but the precise function performed by these women is not known. Some commentators have suggested a service of cleaning and repairing the tabernacle, others of singing and dancing, others of doorkeeping. Still others have suggested a parallel to the Canaanite practice of temple prostitution, based on 1 S. 2:22; but the fact that the behavior of Eli's sons is condemned argues against this interpretation (see comms.).

*II. In the NT.*–In the RSV NT "minister" and "ministry" most often represent the *diakon-* word group. The verb *diakonéō* originally means "wait at table" (e.g., Acts 6:2; cf. RSV "serve," Mt. 8:15 par.; Lk. 12:37; 17:8; Jn. 12:2). More often, however, the term is used in the wider sense of "render a service." The noun *diakonía* denotes the activity of *diakonéō*, i.e., "service at table, provision of food" (e.g., Lk. 10:40; cf. RSV "distribution," Acts 6:1), or, in a wider sense,"service" of any sort. Likewise, the noun *diákonos* denotes a "waiter at a meal" (cf. RSV "servant," Jn. 2:5, 9; "attendant," Mt. 22:13) or, in general, a "servant"; in a few instances it designates a specific ecclesiastical office (*see* DEACON).

The angels' ministry to Jesus following His temptation in the wilderness probably involved the provision of nourishment (Mt. 4:11 par. Mk. 1:13; cf. 1 K. 19:5-7). A group of Galilean women accompanied Jesus and His disciples on their travels and provided them with food and other forms of material support (Mt. 27:55 par. Mk. 15:41; cf. RSV "provide" [*diakonéō*], Lk. 8:3).

Jesus Himself provides the model for ministry in the NT. He defined His own mission in terms of serving others (*diakonéō*, Mt. 20:21 par. Mk. 10:45) by giving His life for them. Likewise, His true disciples are those who minister to the needs of others (Mt. 20:26f. par. Mk. 10:43f.; cf. Mt. 25:44).

In Acts and the Epistles *diakonía* can denote any form of loving service performed by members of the Christian community (Eph. 4:12). More specifically, it is often used as a technical term for the work of proclaiming the gospel, a ministry especially entrusted to the apostles and their coworkers (Acts 1:17, 25; 6:4; 20:24; 21:19; Rom. 11:13; 2 Cor. 4:1; 5:18; 6:3; Col. 4:17; 2 Tim. 4:5). Thus the apostles and other office-bearers in the Church who are entrusted with this task can be referred to as *diákonoi* (Eph. 6:21; Col. 1:25; 4:7; of the gospel, Eph. 3:7; Col. 1:23; of Christ, Col. 1:7; 1 Tim. 4:6; of the new covenant, 2 Cor. 3:6). (*See also* MINISTRY.)

Another general term for "servant" or "assistant" is Gk. *hypērétēs*. Lk. 1:2 uses the phrase *hypērétai toú lógou* (RSV " ministers of the world"; cf. Acts 6:4) to describe those who served the cause of Christ by passing on the tradition of His teaching (see J. A. Fitzmyer, pp. 294f.). Acts 20:34 records Paul's use of the verb *hypēretéō* in stating that he had supported himself and his companions through his own labor.

In four passages the RSV NT uses "minister" to render Gk. *leitourgós*. Unlike the verb *leitourgéō*, which the LXX employs to render only the cultic uses of Heb. *šēreṯ*, *leitourgós* is employed by the LXX primarily for the noncultic uses of Heb. *m^e šārēṯ*. *Leitourgós* refers to the priestly ministry in Rom. 15:16 and He. 8:2; similarly, in 8:6 the noun *leitourgía* denotes Christ's priestly ministry, which far surpasses that of the old covenant. In Rom. 13:6 and Phil. 2:25, however, *leitourgós* simply means "servant" and is basically synonymous with *diákonos*. The use of *leitourgikós* in He. 1:14 to describe the angels is likewise non-cultic.

The term *dynástēs* differs from the preceding terms in that its primary idea is one of ruling power rather than of servanthood (cf. *dýnamis* ["power"], *dynatéō* ["be strong"], etc.). In Acts 8:27 the term designates an official in the court of the queen of Ethiopia.

***Bibliography***.–*DNTT*, III, 544-553; J. A. Fitzmyer, *Gospel According to Luke I-IX* (*AB*, 2nd ed. 1983); *TDNT*, II, *s.v.* διακονέω κτλ. (H. W. Beyer); IV, *s.v.* λειτουργέω κτλ. (H. Strathmann, R. Meyer); VIII, *s.v.* ὑπηρέτης κτλ. (K. H. Rengstorf); *TWOT*, II, 958.

N. J. OPPERWALL

**MINISTRY** [Heb. *yāḏ*–'hand,' *šārēṯ*, *ʿᵃḇôḏâ*; Gk. *diakonía*, *leitourgía*].

I. Distinctions of Ministry
II. Apostolic Ministry
  A. Apostles
  B. Prophets
  C. Teachers
  D. Evangelists
III. Local Ministry
  A. Deacons
  B. Elders
  C. Bishops
IV. Threefold Ministry
  A. Emergence
  B. Enforcement
  C. Development

NT cognates to Gk. *diakonía* include *diákonos, ho diakonōn,* and *diakonein*. All these words can be used very generally. Even when applied to Christian service they have such varied meanings as (1) discipleship in general (Jn. 12:26); (2) service as a spiritual gift (Rom. 12:7; 1 Cor. 12:5) and therefore service of all kinds (Acts 6:2; Mt. 20:26); (3) the ministry of the word (Eph. 4:12) and most frequently the apostleship (Acts 1:17; 20:24; 21:19; Rom. 11:13; etc.); (4) charitable service such as feeding the poor (Acts 6:1; 11:29; 12:25) or organizing and providing the great collection for the poor at Jerusalem (Rom. 12:25; 2 Cor. 8:4, 19; etc.); and (5) such services as those of Stephanas (1 Cor. 16:15), Archippus (Col. 4:17), Tychicus (Eph. 6:21; Col. 4:7).

The present article is concerned with the Christian usage and more particularly with its application to the regular ministry of word and property in the Church. The very existence of the Church implies not only a general ministry but also the more specific ministry demanded by orderly life of both inward and outward mission. The specific ministry is not to be divorced from the more general, nor is it to be understood or fashioned in categories other than those of ministry, e.g., hierarchical. No matter how correct in other respects, ministry loses its very essence if it is not true service impelled and oriented by the spirit of service. Many problems of the specific ministry take on a new aspect, and many related tensions or conflicts are resolved when these simple but basic truths are perceived, maintained, and practiced.

***I. Distinctions of Ministry.***–The first specific ministry in the Church is obviously that of the apostles chosen and commissioned by Christ Himself. In important respects it was a unique ministry. Therefore there can be no apostolic succession in the full and strict sense. But secondarily the apostles exercised a ministry that has permanent validity and with which others are particularly associated, namely, the ministries of prophets, teachers, and evangelists, and also in a slightly different sense of bishops, elders, and deacons. Apostolic ministry must be understood primarily as a ministry of prayer and preaching rather than of practical administration. But in contrast to that of bishops or elders, it may also be regarded as a universal and extraordinary ministry primarily adapted to missionary and evangelistic activity rather than a local and settled ministry of edification and direction.

The distinction between the ministries of Word and administration is clear enough in the NT and seems to have been carried through locally in the form of elders or bishops on the one side and deacons on the other. Even here, however, we are to see a difference of function rather than of office. Thus the Seven appointed to serve tables also exercised a powerful ministry of Word (at least in the case of Stephen and Philip), and the apostles could not escape some involvement in practical concerns (cf. Paul's organizing of the great collection). In later historical practice bishops often were leading administrators, and deacons had their place in the administration of word and sacrament.

Behind this distinction of functions is the larger distinction between extraordinary and ordinary ministry, to use two inadequate and rather question-begging terms. Thus in the missionary and evangelistic situation of the early Church, which perhaps is or ought to be the true norm of every church situation, the "missionaries" on the one side exercised an itinerant ministry of evangelism, exhortation, and instruction, and the local pastors on the other were instituted to fulfil the regular demands of spiritual and practical ministry in the newly established churches. This is the distinction that has given rise to most of the misconceptions, difficulties, and tensions in later discussion and practice.

On the one side, the relationship has been wrongly conceived. Thus it has sometimes been identified with the basic distinction between a ministry of word and a ministry of organization, as though the local ministry were of the latter category. This view is shattered by the twofold fact that the apostles are also elders (1 Pet. 5:1) and that bishops must be able to teach (1 Tim. 3:2). When apostles or prophets were present, the local ministers no doubt gave them precedence in the ministry of the word, but in their absence the ministers themselves had to see to the ongoing ministry of word and sacrament.

Again, the distinction has often been stated in terms of a charismatic ministry on the one side and a noncharismatic on the other. What is meant is that there is a specific moving of the Spirit in the one case and a more institutional form in the other. But one cannot presuppose too easily that there is no gift of the Spirit where there is no extraordinary call or task. Although the Holy Spirit cannot be institutionalized, He can be assumed to work through the regular order, even if in less spectacular fashion. Nor should one assume too easily that in the NT any person might become a wandering evangelist or prophet without some form of authorization. To put the distinction in this form is to introduce confusing factors and misleading assumptions.

It is surely another misconception to think that the extraordinary ministry was only for a limited period and then came to be invested solely in the ordinary ministry of presbyter-bishops. The data available from the first centuries contradict this. In the Didache, Justin Martyr, Barnabas, and Hermas are traces of a prophetic ministry different from that of the local bishops and elders. The continuing evidence of history also contradicts this idea. In spite of the concentration of ministry and ministerial power in the regular ministry, there have always been special figures who in evangelism, edification, or missionary endeavor have transcended the ordinary limits and channels and exercised a ministry of apostolic range, power, and authority, at least in a secondary sense. Indeed, many missionaries, themselves elders or bishops, have often reflected the apostolate even in the institution and supervison of a new regular and local ministry. Finally, it runs counter to the obvious needs and tasks of ministry, which can never consist merely of the shepherding of settled congregations but always involves at some level the ongoing task of evangelism and mission. Even the terms "extraordinary" and "ordinary" do not properly express the distinction, since the evangelistic and missionary and wider edificatory ministry is as much a part of the ordinary ministry as the local fulfillment. It can be argued that the failure to see this and the resulting treatment of the NT situation as unusual rather than normative are responsible for most of the difficulties in the conception of the ministry and of the weaknesses in its exercise.

Accompanying misconception of the relationship has been failure to achieve a right attitude to the varying ministries. Thus the more local ministry has sometimes been disdained, and the wider ministry has been the object of subjugation and even attempted elimination. The proper relationship of the ministries, however, is not competitive but complementary. There is a local exercise of the ministry of the word but also an ongoing task of mission, edification, and theology that cannot be fulfilled in the local setting and creates a constant need for wider ministry in the Church. The pastoral claim and task are legitimate but they are not the totality. Indeed, it may be doubted whether they can or should be described as the primary claim and task. Alongside them in every age and situation exists the urgent missionary, evangelistic, and theological need that can be met only by apostles, prophets, and teachers, who may also, of course, be local elders or bishops. This does not mean that a twofold structure of ministry is required or that a larger hierarchical ranking is demanded, for these are distinctions of function or discharge rather than of office. What it does mean is that the one ministry is fulfilled in different modes according to divergent callings, needs, and tasks, and therefore that the order necessary for the ministry must not enforce a rigid pattern or seek to compress all the expressions of ministry into a single form. Order must be based upon a comprehensive understanding of what the ministry is for, what it is summoned to do, and how it may best fulfil its total task according to the NT norm. Practical difficulties arise if this understanding is achieved not at all or only partially, or if an exclusive claim is thus lodged at some point to inheritance of apostolic calling and prerogative.

A working integration of the forms or functions of ministry is possible to attain, however. A missionary, evangelist, or theologian may very well be a bishop, presbyter, deacon, or recognized minister at some level; it is reasonable that they be allowed responsibly to exercise their ministry across, above, or beyond the regular parochial framework. On the other hand, the special minister can and should aim at strengthening the local ministry, and even at instituting it in a pioneer missionary situation, so that a ministry of the word continues, and calling, endowment, or authority is not centralized in the minister's person. Problems naturally arise in the detailed outworking of these arrangements, but they are by no means insoluble once the underlying antithesis is seen to be more apparent than real. Indeed, the exigencies of real situations have often led to reasonably harmonious solutions, e.g., in the relations of theological teachers to their churches or of missionaries to the local ministries they have established.

Perhaps one of the most helpful considerations is that neither the local nor the special ministry inherits the actual ministry of the apostles in the full sense. Each may make a certain claim. The first bishops, elders, and deacons were apostolically appointed in order that the ministry might continue in the new congregations. The apostolic function thus devolves in some measure upon them. Yet they are obviously secondary and derivative in this ministry and perform it only in the local and predominantly pastoral sphere. Special ministers and particularly missionaries come closer to what the apostles actually did, moving out to new peoples, establishing new churches, and supervising the formation of new local ministries. Yet they, too, are ultimately derivative. Although they are the first preachers in a given place, they are not the first in the absolute sense of the apostles. Although they are normative for those who learn the gospel through them, they are themselves under the apostolic norm. Similarly, theologians may guide the thought and therefore the preaching and instruction of their generation, but in a responsible fulfillment of their office can never aspire to apostolic authority. Properly conceived, the apostolic element thus unites rather than divides, for in different ways the ministers in both forms are fulfilling the same task, ministering the same word, and acknowledging the same unique authority of the first apostles. Once it is seen that the apostolic function may be variously discharged in its secondary form, that there are varying needs and tasks which constantly demand this varying discharge, and that the apostolate in its primary form is unique, normative, and nontransmissible, there is no further room for the rivalry and even conflict of ministry and the consequent arrogance of rule or divisiveness of individualism that have so often created havoc in the Church and prevented the effective fulfillment of the commissioned task.

*II. Apostolic Ministry.*–In the NT the wider or special ministry is fulfilled by three or possibly four main groups or by three or four main functions. These functions, however, merge into one another, and the use of terms is quite fluid. The decisive point is that this nonlocal ministry, which is primarily that of the apostles, was fulfilled by a special ministry of evangelism, edification, and instruction both outside and inside the churches. The groups mentioned in relation to this ministry are the apostles, prophets, teachers, and evangelists. The apostles engaged in both evangelism and edification, the prophets and teachers primarily in the latter, the evangelists in the former.

*A. Apostles.* In the NT the word "apostles" has both a narrower and a wider sense. It can be used of the Twelve (and later the Eleven) who had been called by Jesus and who had shared His incarnate ministry at the most intimate level (cf. Mk. 3:14). In place of Judas, Matthias was added to this group as one who had also known the Lord during the span of His earthly ministry (Acts 1:25). Paul, too, was granted a special, direct knowledge that qualified him for inclusion in the narrower circle of apostles on equal terms with the rest (Rom. 1:1ff.; Gal. 2:7-9). Barnabas can be called an apostle, was almost certainly an eyewitness, and seems to have ranked with the Twelve (Acts 14:14; Gal. 2:7-9), but in his case with some transition to a wider usage. In the wider sense, though probably with the implication of eyewitness, the term was also applied to others like Andronicus and Junias (whom Chrysostom took to be a woman, Rom. 16:7), Silvanus and Timothy (1 Thess. 1:6), and possibly Apollos (2 Cor. 8:23) and Epaphroditus (Phil. 2:25), though in the latter case the term seems differently used. The NT already recognized the possibility of false apostles (2 Cor. 11:13; Rev. 2:2), so that demarcation was demanded.

Certain leading characteristics of the apostolate may be briefly mentioned. Apostles had a direct calling, knowledge, and authority by association with the Lord. They were the pioneers of the Christian mission. Their primary task was prayer and the ministry of the word; they were thus evangelists and teachers. Though they may have settled for shorter or longer periods in specific places, they exercised an itinerant and ecumenical ministry. They had a final responsibility for the nurture and instruction of Christians, the purity of doctrine, and the continuation of the ministry on a more local scale. As noted already, the first apostles are unique. No others can enjoy the same normativeness as sources of information and understanding. Nevertheless, there may have been a secondary exercise of their ministry. Wherever missionary outreach or even doctrinal and spiritual reformation was needed, people of special calling and endowment may have been elected who were charged with a wider ministry. But this field in particular needed to differentiate between people of true calling and false or pretended apostles, the ultimate tests being faithfulness to the apostolic norm and conformity to the mind and commission of Christ.

*B. Prophets.* A resurgence of OT prophecy also marked the NT period. In the earliest stages John the Baptist (Mt. 11:9), Simeon (Lk. 2:25-35), Anna (Lk. 2:36), perhaps Zacharias, and even Mary herself gave evidence of the prophetic gift. Many regarded Jesus as a prophet (Jn. 4:19), and He certainly promised the coming of prophets (Mt. 10:41; 23:34; Lk. 11:49). After Pentecost, this promise found swift fulfillment; prophets were at Caesarea, Antioch, and the various Pauline communities (Acts 11:27; 15:32; 21:9f.; Rom. 12:6f.; 1 Cor. 14:32, 36f.; 1 Thess. 5:20; Gal. 3:3-5). Some of these prophets are named, e.g., Agabus (Acts 11:28; 21:10), Symeon (13:1), Judas and Silas (15:32). The reference to the daughters of Philip shows that there might still have been prophetesses, as in the OT (21:9; cf. also Anna). Paul not only mentioned prophets next to the apostles but also expected to find the gift of prophecy in the Church and urged all members to cultivate it (1 Cor. 14:1, 5; 1 Thess. 5:20; Rom. 12:6). At the same time he warned against a false use of the gift.

The exact nature of NT prophecy is not easy to determine. It might have carried an element of foretelling, as in the OT. It might also have involved enacted illustration (cf. Acts 21:11). In the main, however, it seems more likely to have consisted of edifying utterance and exhortation distinguished from simple exposition or instruction by a more direct inspiration and even sometimes by ecstatic or visionary elements or aspects. Like the apostolate, it was a special ministry probably exercised by itinerants, though it must also have been found within the local congregations, and there is no reason why elders should not also have been prophets. The possibility of false prophets was no less real than in the OT, and therefore the tests of apostolic conformity and appropriate conduct were to be applied. Thus no one speaking in the Spirit could contradict the basic elements of the faith (1 Jn. 4:1ff.), nor could a true prophet demand things for himself in the name of the Spirit (Did. 11–13). The Didache seems to assume not merely that the prophets could use extemporaneous forms of prayer (ch. 10) but also that they could take precedence in church affairs, though the reference seems to be to itinerant rather than local prophets.

Prophecy fell into some disrepute after the excesses of the Montanists at the end of the 2nd century. Although the phenomenon of prophecy has never regained its former recognition, church history confirms that either within the congregation or over a wider sphere the Holy Spirit does constantly give special gifts to meet special needs of edification, instruction, admonition, or warning, especially in days of decadence, corruption, or secularization. The important point is that prophecy should not be suspected or viewed as a threat to the settled ministry but welcomed and allowed for as a special gift of God to His people (cf. Moses in Nu. 11). The difficulty is that this type of ministry cannot be brought under formal rules or organization. A ministry of prophecy cannot be instituted, trained, and supervised, but the basic test of apostolicity and conformity of life may still be made. Thus it is possible to steer the delicate course between flexibility and gullibility that is necessary if this ministry is to be effectively pursued without schism on the one side or scandal on the other.

*C. Teachers.* Alongside the apostles and prophets, teachers exercised a special ministry in the NT and postapostolic Church. Paul gave them a definite place in the local meeting (1 Cor. 14:26) and on the wider scene described himself as a teacher as well as an apostle or a prophet (cf. also Apollos). Teaching differs from the apostolate in that it is primarily devoted to edification rather than evangelism. It differs from prophecy by demanding greater regularity of form and content than does prophecy with its freer exhortation. Thus teachers might be itinerant ministers but usually need to settle in a particular center for longer periods, although they can exercise a more than local ministry. There is thus a greater tendency for teachers to be incorporated into the local ministry or for teaching to pass more fully into the sphere of the bishops and later of the elders, who might well be among the great teachers of the Church at large. Calvin could rightly argue that teaching is an integral part of the local ministry and thus plead for a "doctor" as well as a pastor in each congregation (cf. the lectureships set up by many Puritans in England and the modern ministers of education in many American churches). On the other hand, Dominic in the Middle Ages saw the need, at least in certain circumstances, for a wider order of teaching missionaries, and the medieval universities saw the need for teachers of the whole Church, the doctors of theology, as well as teachers in the local congregations. The modern tendency for theologians to be academic specialists isolated to some degree from the pastoral work of the Church is an evil fruit of failure to maintain a comprehensive view of the ministry and more specifically of the teaching office. Teaching is necessarily more exacting and systematic and therefore less spectacular than certain other functions, e.g., prophecy. Yet in addition to its obvious importance in the NT, there is evidence that it lingered much longer than prophecy in the early Church and that no age has been able to dispense with a ministry of teaching supplementary to that of the regular local ministers.

*D. Evangelists.* Paul mentioned evangelists as a separate group, but little is said about them or their work. They might perhaps be defined as people who, like the apostles, declared the gospel but without the particular qualifications of the apostolate: i.e., without necessarily being firsthand witnesses or having a firsthand commission. Thus Philip the evangelist initiated preaching the gospel to Samaria, so that in a more extended sense he might be called the apostle to Samaria. Yet he was not strictly an apostle, and the apostles themselves followed up his work, adding the seal of their authority and confirming the believers as members of the Church of Christ and not just of a sect. If the apostles were evangelists, they were more than evangelists, playing a role that has since been played by their writings, as the authoritative norm of all Christian witness. The evangelists fulfilled an apostolic role in the work of preaching but could not claim direct apostolic authority. The need of evangelists quickly manifested itself both for the assistance of the apostles in pioneer operations and for the extension of the Church from established centers to surrounding areas. Perhaps the closest modern parallel is the mission field, where exists the normative situation from the NT standpoint. Evangelists are associates of the missionaries, who are also evangelists but have a wider role analogous to that of the first apostles. On the other hand, Christianity can never be taken for granted in any place or generation, and therefore the modern use of the word evangelist for special preachers of the gospel in Christianized lands seems to be a legitimate extension with many historical examples to support it. More churches might do well to find a place for some special order of evangelists to fulfil this special function, preferably within the organized ministry.

***III. Local Ministry.***–The local ministry raises many problems of great historical difficulty. How was it instituted? On what patterns or precedents was it fashioned? How was it related to the apostles on the one side and the congregations on the other? How far did it derive from a fixed policy, and how far did it arise simply as a response to given situations that might have varied in different places?

*A. Deacons.* The appointment of the Seven in Acts 6 forms an obvious starting point. Their appointment was to meet a practical situation; they supervised the daily ministration, thus relieving the apostles for prayer and the ministration of the word. The work of Stephen and Philip shows, of course, that they might also have fulfilled other tasks in addition to the primary administrative duty. The congregation obviously selected the Seven according to certain specified qualifications. The number was possibly suggested by the common Jewish practice of committing the rule of a village to seven wise men, though others find a closer general parallel in the synagogue deacons.

Whether the Seven were the first deacons is a much disputed question. Some writers argue that they were in fact the elders later referred to in connection with the Jerusalem church. On the other hand, even if they are not called deacons, their primary function was more readily associated with the diaconate. *See* SEVEN, THE.

Although Acts does not tell of the appointment of deacons in the apostolic churches, Philippians refers to deacons, and the Pastorals stipulate that deacons are to be appointed and indicate the necessary qualifications (1 Tim. 3:8ff.). Little light is shed, however, either on the mode of appointment or on the exact nature of the duties.

*B. Elders.* The NT gives no information about the origin of elders. Acts 11 mentions elders in relation to the Jerusalem church, but their identities, functions, method of appointment, supervisors, and relations with the apostles and deacons are unknown. In favor of a more congregational polity it is sometimes argued that the Church could call to account even the apostles (Acts 11:1), but Peter did not so much render an account to the whole body as meet the charges of a Judaistic group (11:2f.), and the apostles and elders certainly took the lead in the conference in Acts 15 (v. 6, though cf. vv. 22f.). Paul's and Barnabas's ordination of elders in the communities they founded shows that the Jerusalem elders were not simply a local phenomenon (14:23; cf. 20:17). For more detailed information, *see* ELDER (IN THE NT); PRESBYTER.

Various explanations of this form of local ministry have been given. Some argue that the apostles instituted it in accordance with a special commission from the Lord, but in the absence of information this is mere conjecture.

Others see a parallel to the confraternities of the gentile world (guilds, burial clubs, unions, etc.), but despite possible similarities, it is hard to think that the first Christians, with their strong OT background, found it either right or necessary to follow a gentile pattern. The most natural explanation still seems to be the best, namely, that the system of administration by elders was taken over from Judaism, especially from the Jewish synagogues with their archons. Two main arguments have been brought against this: first, that there were differences in function, and second, that Epiphanius saw this model followed by Jewish (Judaizing) Christians in contrast to the gentile churches. On the other hand, the first converts in many Pauline churches came from the synagogues, where some had held office (Acts 18:8). The varied development does not of itself refute a common origin, and Epiphanius may well have been referring to the detailed system or even to titles rather than to the general structure in its initial stages.

The relationship of the elders to the congregation is another problem. The importance of the congregation is apparent in the NT; the Church is in no sense an organization of hierarchs. One may also assume that the various communities had no little say in the selection of elders and that some account of their stewardship would have been expected. Certainly, the NT never suggests autocratic or oligarchical rule. Nevertheless, the presbytery apparently ordained elders, and we have no grounds for thinking that elders could have been easily deposed or even subjected to attack (cf. 1 Tim. 5:19). Indeed, the instruction to elders not to be lords over God's heritage (1 Pet. 5:3) is counterbalanced by the admonition to submit to the elder (v. 5) and to obey the leaders (He. 13:17).

*C. Bishops*. As noted in other articles (*see* BISHOP; PRESBYTER), a distinction between the original elders and bishops is hardly possible unless one assumes that only some elders are bishops. Yet even in the NT certain forces contributed, perhaps by a process of assimilation, to the later emergence of a single bishop supported by presbyters in each church. Thus James, possibly by a unique right of kinship, obviously assumed a position of leadership, or at least presidency, in the Jerusalem church, though he could hardly have been called a bishop in the later sense (cf. Acts 15:13; 21:18). The supervisory functions of Timothy and Titus, while apparently temporary, suggest the need for some oversight by an individual at least in certain areas. Again, the synagogue pattern provides for an *archisynágōgos* (Acts 18:8); if this pattern was followed at all, it undoubtedly contributed to the final development of a presiding elder to whom the title of bishop was gradually appropriated even though the presbytery in concert exercised the function of oversight. Although the matter is indefinite, this was perhaps the most important single factor in the slow emergence of monepiscopacy. The examples of James, Timothy, and Titus probably contributed. The model of the Lord and His apostles may also have had some influence, e.g., on the later Benedictine conceptions of the abbots and monks. Neither the NT nor early Church history shows transmission of apostolic authority to bishops alone, since the critical passage in 1 Clement 40ff. is ambiguous and the statements in Ignatius (e.g., Smyrn. 8) presuppose an integrated ministry and cannot be proved to have a universal reference.

***IV. Threefold Ministry.–A.*** *Emergence*. Although the NT provides no clear evidence of a threefold structure of ministry, the germs are already present both in the threefold functions of diaconate, spiritual ministration, and rule, and also in the existence of the three groups of deacons, elders, and presiding elders (or outstanding figures like James, Timothy, and Titus). Postapostolic literature has further traces of the gradual, or possibly sporadic, emergence of this system. Thus the Didache seems to encourage prophets or apostles to settle as local leaders (13:1), and Justin told of the president and deacons (*Apol.* i.65). History mentions bishops in particular churches, e.g., Polycarp in Smyrna, Papias in Hierapolis, and Irenaeus in South Gaul (cf. the Roman lists). Finally, Ignatius presented a more developed form of the structure in his advice to the Ephesians, Magnesians, Trallians, and others to avoid heresy and schism by loyal adherence to the bishop, elders, and deacons and by attendance at only their ministrations.

One can hardly presume that this had become the general rule by the time of Ignatius. Perhaps many presbyteries still had temporary presidents and therefore a plurality of bishops, if any distinction was made. One cannot even say that the bishops of Ignatius were permanent, although this seems likely. Concerted action and loyalty are certainly emphasized. The bishoprics, if one may use such a term, were still much smaller than the feudal episcopate of a later period. Nevertheless, the pressure of the 2nd cent. is evidently toward a form of episcopacy and therefore a threefold structure. The threats posed by heresy and persecution probably accelerated the process.

*B. Enforcement*. By the 3rd cent., definite instructions were being given to all local Christian groups, however small, to organize a threefold ministry. One bishop and at least two elders and three deacons were to be appointed, with perhaps a reader if the bishop was illiterate and deaconesses to minister more specifically to women. No great financial burden was thereby imposed, since the ministers were unremunerated and the churches at first had little property except copies of the Scriptures, records, and a place of burial. The deacons were primarily administrators of charitable relief, the elders supervised the orderly life of the church, and the bishop led in worship and exhortation. Discipline lay in the hands of the whole church, but the bishops and elders could take the initiative.

The Apostolic Canons contain rules for the appointment of bishops. The congregation has a right of election, although not of ordination or consecration. In a very small church, neighboring larger churches were to be invited to send three men to assist. Some historians see here the origin of the later and more general custom of insisting on the presence of at least three bishops at an episcopal ordination, though the Council of Arles seems to have appointed the practice largely to prevent irregular or purely factional consecrations (canon 20).

Four features of primitive episcopacy demand attention. First, it was on a small scale, the bishop being for the most part the local pastor. Second, it had no external grandeur. The evils of prelacy were hardly possible in the 3rd cent., though we do perhaps see trends in this direction in the larger and wealthier sees. Third, there was no autocracy; both the elders and the whole congregation had an important voice. Fourth, the exact relations of bishops and elders in the work of ministry are uncertain. In small churches, the bishops naturally took the lead in pastoral functions. In the larger, which might have included many congregations, the presbyters shared the work and were later allocated to specific charges. The idea that they were simply delegates of the bishop, however, is probably an inversion of the real truth that the bishop himself is a representative of the presbytery in the personal discharge of his function. This is not a decision for Presbyterianism but a decision for the unity of bishop and presbytery that makes the Presbyterian-Episcopalian alternative both unnecessary and misleading.

*C. Development*. The problem arises of how the simple

organization of the early centuries could culminate in the more elaborate hierarchy of a later time. Two separate though related questions are involved: that of the emergence of an ecclesiastical order, and that of the extension of diocesan or provincial control. In both cases one probably must account for the influence of both the political and the religious organization of the contemporary world. But inner factors should not be underestimated.

As concerns the ecclesiastical order of the clergy, the decisive words *ordo* and *clerus* may well have been suggested by current usage, *ordo* denoting the municipality or the committee in charge of a confraternity and *clerus* signifying rank or class. In the 3rd cent. the bishops and elders constituted the ecclesiastical order or class, but before long others were added, especially the deacons. Probably the very mundane factor of the introduction of stipends did more than anything else to accentuate the ideas of ecclesiastical persons distinct from others, for all recipients of church funds, including even widows and orphans, might be regarded as members of the *ordo*. Thus minor assistants appointed and paid to attend to the lesser duties, either in answer to practical needs or partly by assimilation to pagan usages, soon constituted the minor orders of readers, acolytes, exorcists, singers, subdeacons, or doorkeepers.

Organization was extended through a similar natural development, with perhaps some assimilation to secular or pagan structures. The numerical growth in larger centers obviously created a need for more elaborate organization of the Church in these cities, and when surrounding areas were evangelized, often in accordance with geographical or political groupings, the new communities naturally looked to the central churches for guidance and often preferred to attach themselves to them if they were reasonably near rather than forming new churches (Justin *Apol.* i.67). The existence of a supporting presbytery enabled the bishop to minister to several congregations at the same time, and it is interesting to note that the NT model was taken to be an autonomy of the one Church in the one place rather than of the individual congregation. Even new bishoprics founded in smaller towns and villages could have enhanced the position of the bishop in the original larger center, partly through his role in appointments and consecrations and partly through his authority at the synods or local councils, which were not unnaturally convened on matters of mutual concern and at which the more prominent bishops very quickly came to preside. Outstanding cities like Rome, Carthage, Alexandria, Antioch, and later Constantinople almost inevitably came to have even greater spheres of influence commensurate with their size, political and economic importance, and centrality in such varied Christian enterprises as evangelism and theology. Hence, even though one may deplore the tendency toward a hierarchy of metropolitans and patriarchs, one must see that it corresponded to certain needs and realities, however influenced in form by extraneous factors. Indeed, modern experience teaches that the Church in its interrelationships will always be influenced by geographical, national, and linguistic groupings, is always pressed toward a wider confederacy by outgoing missionary enterprise, and will always follow, more perhaps than it realizes, the contemporary forms of political and economic organization (cf. the growth of bureaucracy in so many modern churches irrespective of the professed polity).

In spite of the dangers inherent in this type of development, the ministry might have been spared the worst evils of medieval prelacy and papacy had it not been for the virtual establishment of Christianity as the religion of the empire and of the resultant Western European states. This enabled the bishops to take over the civil precedence and prerogatives of the higher priests of the imperial cult and thus completed the process of secularization against which the NT, and especially Our Lord Himself, plainly warned. One need hardly be surprised at the consequences for the ministry, whether in the form of tyranny, ambition, and avarice on the one side or of pastoral neglect, theological and practical aberration, and missionary sterility on the other. Nor need one wonder that the more vital work of the Church had often to be done through the special ministrations of monks, friars, reformers, and even supposed heretics outside the established structure.

***Bibliography.***–*TDNT*, II, *s.v.* διακονέω κτλ. (Beyer); IV, *s.v.* λειτουργέω κτλ. (Strathmann, Meyer); K. Barth, *CD*, IV/3, § 72; H. von Campenhausen, *Ecclesiastical Authority* (1969); H. G. Goodykoontz, *Minister in the Reformed Tradition* (1963); K. E. Kirk, ed., *Apostolic Ministry* (2nd ed. 1957); T. W. Manson, *Church's Ministry* (1948); S. Neill, ed., *Ministry of the Church* (1947); H. R. Niebuhr, *Purpose of the Church and Its Ministry* (1956); R. S. Paul, *Ministry* (1965); J. K. S. Reid, *Biblical Doctrine of the Ministry* (1955).

G. W. BROMILEY

**MINNI** min'ī [Heb. *minnî*]. A kingdom mentioned only in Jer. 51:27.

Jeremiah summoned the kingdoms of Minni, Ararat (Urartu), and Ashkenaz (the Scythians), as subjects of the Medes, to crush Babylon. This association points to the identity of Minni with the Mannai of Akkadian sources, a people who occupied the Persian highlands S of Lake Urmia. They were perhaps non-Indo-Europeans, akin to the Elamites. Assyrian and Urartian inscriptions reveal names of some Mannean kings from *ca.* 840 B.C. onward, but no native records are known. Assyria and Urartu held sway over different parts of Mannean territory during the 8th cent.; Mannai's importance especially as a horse-breeding land drew the Assyrians' interest. The Mannai helped the king of Assyria crush Urartu in 714. In the early decades of the 7th cent. Mannai gained strength, revolting with the Scythians and Medes against Assyria *ca.* 673, only to be subjugated again *ca.* 660. Scythian invaders took control of Mannai soon afterward and held it until the Medes broke their yoke some time after 625. Mannia may have enjoyed a brief independence then; at least a Mannean contingent aided the Assyrians against the Chaldean attackers from Babylon in 616. By the end of the century, however, the Medes had conquered all of Mannai, and it passed from them under Persian rule.

Electrum bracelet decorated with lions. From Kurdistan, early 1st millennium B.C. (Louvre)

Fulfillment of Jeremiah's words may be found in the Persian conquest of Babylon in 539, when troops from Mannai no doubt comprised a part of the army of Cyrus.

Excavations at Hasanlu, just S of Lake Urmia, and discovery of a rich treasure at Ziwiye further S near Saqqiz reveal something of the Mannean culture. The people were skilled in metalworking, adapting and copying the styles of their more advanced neighbors. One silver bowl from Ziwiye bears a row of hieroglyphs that may show that there was a native script, most probably inspired by the Urartian. Nothing definite is known of Mannean religious beliefs.

*Bibliography*.–R. M. Boehmer, *Baghdader Mitteilungen*, 3 (1964), 11-24; R. H. Dyson, *JNES*, 24 (1965), 193-217.

A. R. MILLARD

**MINNITH** min'ith [Heb. *minnîṯ*; Gk. A *Semōith*, B *áchris Arnōn*]. A city in the region of the Ammonites mentioned in connection with Jephthah's military campaign against the "twenty cities" (Jgs. 11:33). A possibly corrupt second text (Ezk. 27:17) names Minnith (so AV, NEB; RSV "olives") as the source of wheat exported from Judah in commerce with Tyre. Eusebius (*Onom.*) equates it with a village known to him in the Greek as *Maanith*, and located 4 Roman miles NE of Heshbon on the way to Philadelphia. While several contemporary sites have been suggested, none is yet confirmed.

See A. Alt, *PJ*, 29 (1933), 27f. G. H. WILSON

**MINOAN** mə-nō'ən **CULTURE.** *See* GREECE III.B.

**MINT** [Gk. *hēdýosmon*] (Mt. 23:23; Lk. 11:42). An herb mentioned by Jesus as one of the small things tithed by the Pharisees. Of the various species of mint that grow in Palestine, either the peppermint (*Mentha piperita*) or, more likely, the perennial horse mint (*Mentha longifolia*) would suit the Gospel references. The Greek name *hēdýosmon* (lit. "sweet-smelling") refers to the plant's fragrance, which results from its aromatic oils. Mint was a very popular condiment in the ancient Near East. Jesus' mention of this and other herbs was not a depreciation of tithing but a criticism of the Pharisees' legalistic scrupulosity in small matters while they neglected such moral issues as justice, mercy, and faith.

Although not mentioned by name, mint was traditionally one of the "bitter herbs" eaten at the Passover meal (cf. Ex. 12:8; Nu. 9:11). R. K. H.

**MINUSCULE.** *See* TEXT AND MSS OF THE NT.

**MIPHKAD** mif'kad. *See* MUSTER GATE; JERUSALEM III.F.2.v.

**MIRACLE.**

- I. The Concept of Miracle
  - A. Biblical Terminology and Its Use
    - 1. OT Terms
    - 2. NT Terms
  - B. Later Definitions
- II. Miracles in the Bible
  - A. OT
  - B. Synoptic Gospels
  - C. Gospel of John
  - D. Book of Acts
  - E. Other NT Writings
- III. Miracles in the Jewish and Hellenistic Worlds
  - A. The Jewish World
  - B. The Hellenistic World
- IV. Miracles in Philosophy and Christian Apologetics
  - A. Miracles and Apologetics
  - B. Skepticism
  - C. Reassessment

***I. The Concept of Miracle.**–A. Biblical Terminology and Its Use. 1. OT Terms.* Two Hebrew words are commonly used in the OT to denote what we loosely call a miracle. They are *'ôṯ*, "sign, pledge, token," and *môp̄ēṯ*, "wonder, sign, portent." They occur together in the warning of Dt. 13:1-3, which was decisive for Jewish attitudes to miracles: "If a prophet arises among you, or a dreamer of dreams, and gives you a sign or a wonder, and the sign or wonder which he tells you comes to pass, and if he says, 'Let us go after other gods,' which you have not known, 'and let us serve them,' you shall not listen to the words of that prophet or to that dreamer of dreams; for the Lord your God is testing you, to know whether you love the Lord your God with all your heart and with all your soul." Not only should such signs and wonders be disregarded. The prophet or dreamer should be put to death, so that evil would be purged out of the midst of the people (vv. 5-11). Signs and wonders, however, are not necessarily the work of false prophets. They are also performed by Yahweh Himself, notably in bringing His people out of Egypt (Ex. 7:3; Dt. 4:34; 6:22; 7:19; 26:8; 29:3; 34:11; Ps. 78:43; 105:27; 135:9; Jer. 32:20f.; Neh. 9:10). The decisive factor is the relationship of the sign or wonder to Yahweh, and this is recognized in the light of previous teaching, the previous acts of Yahweh, and continuing knowledge of Him.

The Heb. *'ôṯ* and *môp̄ēṯ* are usually translated by *sēmeíon* and *téras* in the LXX, and by *signum* and *portentum* in the Vulgate. Heb. *'ôṯ* does not necessarily denote violations of nature. A sign points beyond itself and indicates Yahweh's ordering and overriding of nature and history. It is used in Gen. 1:14 of the sun and the moon; in Gen. 17:10 of circumcision; in Ex. 12:13 of the blood of the Passover lamb; in Isa. 7:11, 14 of Immanuel; and in Isa. 38:7 of Ahaz's sun dial. A sign may confirm faith that Yahweh will do what He has undertaken (cf. Ex. 4:1-10), or embody and exemplify His saving action (cf. Ex. 7:1-17). Heb. *môp̄ēṯ* often carries with it the suggestion of a divine threat or warning, as a discouragement to wrongdoing (Ex. 11:9; Dt. 28:46). It, too, does not necessarily imply a violation of the natural order. At the same time it indicates an ordering and a significance beyond the natural (cf. Ps. 71:7; 105:5; Isa. 8:18; 20:3; Zec. 3:8).

Other terms that occur in the OT are *pele'*, "wonder, marvel" (Ex. 15:11; Ps. 77:11, 14 [MT 12, 15]; 78:12; 88:10, 12 [MT 11, 13]; 89:5 [MT 6]; Isa. 25:1), and its cognate *niplā'ôṯ*, "wonderful deeds" (Ex. 3:20; Jgs. 6:13; Ps. 9:1 [MT 2]; 26:7; etc.). Meditation on Yahweh's great and terrible acts, which include the signs and wonders of the Exodus, is a cause for praise and encouragement (2 S. 7:23; 1 Ch. 17:19; Ps. 105:5; 145:5f.).

*2. NT Terms.* The OT expression "signs and wonders" occurs frequently in the NT (*sēmeía kaí térata* Mt. 24:24 par. Mk. 13:22; Acts 2:19 [citing Joel 2:30 (MT 3:3)], 22, 43; 4:30; 5:12; 6:8; 7:36; 15:12; Rom. 15:19; 2 Cor. 12:12; 2 Thess. 2:9; He. 2:4). Signs and wonders are wrought by God as a testimony, but they also may be performed by false prophets who seek to deceive. The apocalyptic, though not necessarily miraculous, sense of a sign is evident in Mt. 24:3 par. Mk. 13:4; Lk. 21:11, 25f. The demand for conclusive signs is deprecated (Mt. 12:39; 16:4; cf. Lk. 11:16, 29; Jn. 4:48; 1 Cor. 1:22). Such a demand is indicative of a refusal to respond to what has been already revealed.

The Gk. *téras* occurs only in the plural and in conjunction with *sēmeía*. However, *sēmeíon* is found on its own in addition to the phrase "signs and wonders." It occurs in connection with the request to Jesus for a sign and His saying about the sign of Jonah (Mt. 12:38f. par. Lk. 11:29f.; cf. Mt. 16:1, 3f.; Lk. 11:16), the sign of the parousia (Mt. 24:3 par. Mk. 13:4; Lk. 21:7; cf. Mt. 24:30; Lk. 21:11, 25), the attendant signs in the longer ending of Mark (Mk. 16:17, 20). Luke also mentions signs in his birth narratives (Lk. 2:12, 34), and observes that Herod hoped to see Jesus perform a sign (Lk. 23:8).

The word *sēmeíon* is characteristic of the Fourth Gospel (Jn. 2:11, 18, 23; 3:2; 4:54; 6:2; 7:31; 9:16; 10:41; 11:47; 12:18, 37; 20:30). The signs of Jesus are grounds for belief. At the same time John also describes Jesus' miracles and other actions as "work" (*érgon*) or "works" (*érga*) which are also the Father's "work" or "works" (Jn. 4:34; 5:20, 36; 7:3, 21; 9:3f.; 10:25, 32f., 37f.; 14:10-12; 15:24; 17:4; cf. also Mt. 11:2, 19; Lk. 24:19). The vb. *ergázomai* is similarly used to describe Jesus' work (Jn. 3:21; 5:17; 6:27f., 30; 9:4).

The word *dýnamis*, "power," is also used of a deed of power, a mighty work, mostly in the pl. *dýnameis* (Mt. 7:22; 11:20f., 23; 13:54, 58; Mk. 6:5; Lk. 10:13; 19:37; Acts 2:22). The mighty works of Jesus are presented as grounds for response. Failure to respond is culpable. Mighty works wrought by Christians in the NT Church are attributed to the Spirit (1 Cor. 12:10, 28f.; Gal. 3:5; He. 2:4; 6:5). They belong to the signs of an apostle (2 Cor. 12:12).

*B. Later Definitions.* The English word "miracle" derives from the Lat. *miraculum*, "a wonder, a wonderful thing." Both the Latin noun and the cognate vb. *miror*, "wonder, be astonished," draw attention to the subjective response to the event rather than to speculation as to whether the event breaks the laws of nature. Augustine gave an open-ended definition of a miracle as "whatever appears that is difficult or unusual above the hope and power of them who wonder" (*De utilitate credendi* xxxiv). He preferred to think of a miracle as "contrary to what we know of nature," for God never acts against Himself and the ultimate order that He has created (*Contra Faustum Manichaeum* xxvi.3). Aquinas followed Augustine but stressed the incapacity of nature to produce miracles. "The more it exceeds nature's capability, the greater any miracle is said to be" (*Summa Theol.* i.105.8).

With the advent of modern science and its increasing stress on laws, miracles came to be defined increasingly in terms of violations of the laws of nature. This led Spinoza to seek natural explanations for the biblical miracles (*Tractatus Theologico-politicus*, § 6) and Hume to claim that the whole idea of miracles was self-refuting (*Essay Concerning Human Understanding*, § 10).

R. F. Holland is representative of thinkers who have sought to draw a distinction between the violation and contingency or coincidence concept of miracle. In the latter case it is possible to discern, at least in principle, natural causes and factors which brought about the event (e.g., the strong east wind which caused the waters to part for the Exodus, Ex. 14:21). In such a case the miracle consists in the divine ordering of events. In the case of the violation concept of miracle two conditions must be fulfilled. On the one hand, the event must involve a violation of the laws of nature. Otherwise, it is an ordinary event or a case of the contingency concept. On the other hand, the event must be empirically certain. Otherwise, doubt may be entertained as to whether it occurred at all.

C. S. Lewis represented a return to a more Augustinian position with his definition of a miracle as "an interference with Nature by supernatural power" (*Miracles*, p. 15). This leaves open the question as to how nature has been interfered with. It gives recognition to the fact that God's working is ultimately a mystery. It allows for the fact that miracles are never seen directly. What is observed is a state of affairs before and after the event. Recognition of an event as a miracle is bound up with the wider view that one takes of reality, just as rejection of miracles is bound up with one's beliefs about the uniformities of nature.

***II. Miracles in the Bible.**–A. OT.* Miracles are not uniformly distributed throughout the OT. This has led some scholars to conclude that the miracles occur only at special times of crisis and redemptive history. They are mentioned in connection with the Exodus from Egypt under Moses, the life-and-death struggle with Baal-worship under Elijah and Elisha, and the trials of Daniel.

Miracles serve to legitimate the mission of Moses before the people (Ex. 4:1-9) and Pharaoh (Ex. 7:8-13). In the latter case Pharaoh's magicians duplicated Aaron's act of casting down his rod, so that it became a serpent. But Aaron's rod swallowed their rods. Later tradition identified the magicians as Jannes and Jambres (2 Tim. 3:8).

Through the "plagues" of Egypt (Ex. 9:14) both Israel and Pharaoh learn who the Lord is. The magicians are compelled to recognize the limits of their magic and tell Pharaoh, "This is the finger of God" (Ex. 8:19). Although Pharaoh hardens his heart at the first nine plagues, he finally allows Israel to leave Egypt (Ex. 7:8–13:16). The first nine plagues are narrated in a continuous series, but the literary structure suggests their grouping into three sets of three: (1) water turned into "blood"; frogs; the land filled with mosquitoes or gnats; (2) flies; cattle plague; boils; (3) hail destroying the crops; locusts devouring what is left; darkness. The tenth and final plague destroys the firstborn. The sources of the stories have been variously assigned to J, E, and P by some scholars, though only the first and the last miracles are thought to be reported in all three sources. The plagues have been interpreted as a series of natural disasters, beginning with the washing down of red earth from the Abyssinian and Ethiopian plateau together with reddish microorganisms called flagellates (cf. G. Hort, *ZAW*, 69 [1957], 84-103, and 70 [1958], 48-59). Decomposing fish caused the frogs to leave the Nile and spread the diseases described in the second set of plagues. The third set begins with hail and thunderstorms typical of the time of year which produced the earlier sequences. The hail would destroy flax and barley, but would leave wheat and spelt for the locusts. The darkness was an unusually strong Khamsin, or desert sandstorm, of the kind which strikes Egypt from the south in late February or early March. Although natural explanations are to hand, Yahweh is shown to be the one who controls nature and history for His purposes.

Yahweh's subsequent provision for His people in leading them through the Red Sea and providing food and drink also exhibits Yahweh's control of nature. When Moses stretched out his hand over the sea, "The Lord drove the sea back by a strong east wind all night, and made the sea dry land, and the waters were divided" (Ex. 14:21; cf. vv. 26f.). The quails were brought by "a wind from the Lord" (Nu. 11:31). It is known that eating quails which have fed on poisonous plants may cause illness and death. The manna described in Ex. 16:14, 31 and Nu. 11:7-9 resembles the excretion of two scale-insects which feed on the twigs of the tamarisk tree. The discovery of water (Ex. 17:1-6; Nu. 20:2-13) appears to be related to the known geological phenomenon of water which lies below the limestone surface in the Sinai desert and may be found through striking the rock. Such considerations have led many scholars, including W. Eichrodt (*Theology of the OT*, II [Eng. tr. 1967], 162-67), to see the characteristic

OT emphasis to fall on Yahweh's control of nature in miracles. They are not violations of the natural order but evidence of His control of it.

The book of Joshua presents the conquest of Canaan as divine work rather than a purely military achievement. The long day of Josh. 10:13 has been variously explained as a supernaturally induced thunderstorm, an abnormal refraction of light, and poetic imagery (cf. Homer *Od.* xxiii.243-46).

A series of miracles is associated with Elijah and Elisha. Against the background of a time of drought in the reign of Ahab, the cycle begins with three stories which show Yahweh to be the Lord and giver of life. Elijah is fed by the ravens at the brook Cherith (1 K. 17:1-7). The jar of meal and cruse of oil of the widow of Zarephath sustain Elijah, the widow, and her son (1 K. 17:8-16). Elijah restores the boy to life by lying on the boy and crying to the Lord (1 K. 17:17-24). As a consequence the woman recognizes that the prophet is a man of God, and that the word of the Lord in his mouth is truth. The contest with the prophets of Baal issues in fire from heaven that vindicates Elijah and his God and ends the drought (1 K. 18). Nevertheless, Elijah is forced to flee for his life.

The ascension of Elijah introduces the Elisha cycle. Elisha has already been appointed Elijah's successor. Like the eldest son, he receives a "double portion" of his inheritance, Elijah's "spirit" (2 K. 2:9, 15; cf. Dt. 21:17). This is recognized by the sons of the prophets from Elisha's act of striking the Jordan with Elijah's mantle and crossing the parted waters (2 K. 2:13-15). The act is followed by miracles greater and more numerous than those performed by Elijah. Elisha purifies the water of Jericho by throwing in salt (2 K. 2:19-22), an act interpreted by some scholars as a fertility rite. This is followed by the incident of the bears (2 K. 2:23-25). 2 K. 4 parallels the Elijah miracles in the account of the provision for the widow's household (vv. 1-7) and the restoration of the Shunammite woman's son (vv. 8-37). Elisha purifies a poisoned pot (2 K. 4:38-41) and feeds a hundred men with twenty loaves (2 K. 4:42-44). Naaman, the commander of the army of the king of Syria, is cleansed of his leprosy after bathing seven times in the Jordan (2 K. 5). Like the story of Elijah at Carmel, this story shows the superiority of Yahweh over other gods. Whereas some take the recovery of the iron axe head (2 K. 6:1-7) to be an outright miracle defying the laws of gravity, others see the locating of the axe head as a result of Elisha probing in the water and report the story more as an account of the prophet's insight and Yahweh's providential care. The story of the chariots of fire at Dothan (2 K. 6:8-23) illustrates Yahweh's saving care, comparable with His care and provision for Elijah. The relief of Samaria fulfils Elisha's prophecy (2 K. 7).

The Immanuel sign of Isa. 7:14 has been the subject of much discussion, not least over whether the young woman was a virgin. The point of the sign in Isaiah, however, is not to describe a miraculous conception, but to give a token that "God is with us." In the time that it takes for the child to be conceived, born, and weaned, the danger will be over. In Mt. 1:23 the Immanuel sign of Isaiah is seen as typology which points prophetically to the greater fulfillment by Jesus.

The sun dial of Ahaz was probably a series of steps (2 K. 20:8-11; Isa. 38:7f.; cf. Josephus *Ant.* x.2.1 [24-29]). Attempts to explain the phenomenon of the changed position of the shadow include the suggestion that it was some kind of mirage, and the possibility that the light was a manifestation of the Shekinah glory.

The view that one takes of Jonah and the great fish (Jonah 1:17–2:10), of Shadrach, Meshach, and Abednego in the fiery furnace (Dnl. 3), and of Daniel in the lions' den (Dnl. 6) is bound up with the view that one takes of the literary genre of the books in question. Traditionally these stories have been regarded as historical miraculous events, not least because Jesus' allusion to "the sign of the prophet Jonah" (Mt. 12:39; cf. 16:4; Lk. 11:29) has been taken to be an endorsement of the historicity of an event which provides a historical type for the death and resurrection of Jesus. Critical study, however, has raised the question of whether Jesus' reference to Jonah was intended to be taken in this way, and whether the book of Jonah is not itself intended to be an allegory or parable concerning Jewish exclusivism.

The fiery furnace in Dnl. 3 has been thought to be a kiln for baking bricks or smelting metal. The fire which killed the guards has been attributed to a sudden gust of flame or an explosion. Execution by being cast into a furnace is attested by documentary evidence from Babylonian times (cf. J. B. Alexander, *JBL,* 69 [1950], 375f.). In the case of the lions a spiritual presence may have inhibited them from attacking Daniel (Dnl. 6:22 [MT 23]). If, however, the book of Daniel is an apocalyptic pseudepigraph, written *ca.* 164 B.C. to encourage Jewish resistance to Antiochus Epiphanes, the stories may have an intended allegorical character.

*B. Synoptic Gospels.* For an outline of Jesus' miracles in all four Gospels see the accompanying table of Miracle Stories in the Gospels. *See also* VIRGIN BIRTH OF JESUS CHRIST, TRANSFIGURATION, and RESURRECTION for further discussion of these subjects. Form-critical studies dealing with possible motives in the handling of the miracle stories by the respective evangelists are noted in the bibliography. Comment here is restricted to the place of miracles in the Gospels and to remarks on some of their features.

The Gospels themselves draw no sharp distinction between Jesus' acts of healing, His exorcisms, and the nature miracles. Luke, especially, speaks of healing in terms of casting out evil spirits or Satan (e.g., Lk. 4:38f.; 13:16). John, on the other hand, omits all mention of exorcism. In their descriptions of Jesus' exorcisms, healings, and nature miracles the Gospels present the events either explicitly or implicitly as following His pronouncement of the word of God in the power of the Holy Spirit. Jesus acts and speaks with the authority of Yahweh Himself.

The tendency to treat the miracles of Jesus apart from His teaching and the course of His life has been encouraged by Christian piety, apologetic interests, and critical study. Piety has found encouragement and inspiration from reflection on individual miracles. Apologetics has tended to focus on the Gospel miracles as supernatural attestation of the divinity of Christ. Critical study has tended to prefer the teaching of Jesus to the miracles, and form criticism has seen the miracle stories as products of pious belief, produced by churches anxious to invest Jesus with the credentials of a divine man.

The miracles of Jesus cannot, however, be detached from His teaching, the course of His ministry, or indeed the reason why the Pharisees and others sought to kill Him. At a very early stage Jesus was perceived by His opponents as a blasphemous false teacher, who was possessed by Satan and who must be eliminated. Underlying this attitude was the conviction that action must be taken in accordance with the teaching laid down in Dt. 13. Jesus' attitude to the sabbath and the current interpretation of the law and His presumption in pronouncing forgiveness of sins (Mk. 2:7, 18, 23 par.) were perceived as the work of a blasphemous false prophet who used signs and wonders in order to accredit Himself. The healing of the

## Miracle Stories in the Gospels
### I. Particular Events

| Events | Matthew | Mark | Luke | John |
|---|---|---|---|---|
| Virginal Conception and Birth of Jesus | 1:18-25 | | 1:26–2:20 | |
| Descent of the Spirit and the Voice from Heaven | 3:16f. | 1:10f. | 3:22 | (1:33) |
| Exorcism in the Synagogue at Capernaum | | 1:21-28 | 4:31-37 | |
| Fever of Peter's (Mt.)/Simon's (Mk., Lk.) Mother-in-Law | 8:14f. | 1:29-31 | 4:38f. | |
| Catch of Fish | | | 5:1-11 | (21:1-14) |
| Water into Wine at Cana | | | | 2:1-11 |
| Cleansing of the Leper | 8:1-4 | 1:40-45 | 5:12-16 | |
| Centurion's Servant | 8:5-13 | | 7:1-10 | |
| Nobleman's Son at Capernaum | | | | 4:46-54 |
| Stilling of the Storm | 8:23-27 | 4:35-41 | 8:22-25 | |
| Gerasene Demoniac (Mk., Lk.); Two Demoniacs (Mt.) | 8:28-34 | 5:1-20 | 8:26-39 | |
| Paralytic Whose Sins Jesus Forgave | 9:1-8 | 2:1-12 | 5:17-26 | |
| Lame Man by the Pool of Beth-zatha | | | | 5:1-18 |
| Jairus's Daughter and the Woman with a Hemorrhage | 9:18-26 | 5:21-43 | 8:40-56 | |
| Two Blind Men | 9:27-31 | | | |
| Dumb Demoniac | 9:32-34 | | 11:14 | |
| Man with a Withered Hand | 12:9-14 | 3:1-6 | 6:6-11 | |
| Raising of the Widow's Son at Nain | | | 7:11-17 | |
| Blind and Dumb Demoniac | 12:22-24 | | | |
| Feeding of the Five Thousand | 14:13-21 | 6:30-44 | 9:10-17 | 6:1-15 |
| Jesus Walks on the Sea | 14:22-33 | 6:45-52 | | 6:16-21 |
| Canaanite (Mt.), Syrophoenician Woman's Daughter (Mk.) | 15:21-28 | 7:24-30 | | |
| Deaf Mute | | 7:31-37 | | |
| Feeding of the Four Thousand | 15:32-39 | 8:1-10 | | |
| Blind Man at Bethsaida | | 8:22-26 | | |
| Transfiguration of Jesus | 17:1-8 | 9:2-8 | 9:28-36 | |
| Epileptic Boy with a Demon | 17:14-21 | 9:14-29 | 9:37-43 | |
| Woman Bent for Eighteen Years | | | 13:10-17 | |
| Man with Dropsy | | | 14:1-6 | |
| Ten Lepers | | | 17:11-19 | |
| Two Blind Men (Mt.), Bartimaeus (Mk.), Blind Man (Lk.) at Jericho | 20:29-34 | 10:46-52 | 18:35-43 | |
| Man Born Blind | | | | 9:1-41 |
| Raising of Lazarus | | | | 11:1-44 |
| Cursing of the Fig Tree | 21:18-22 | 11:12-14, 20-25 | | |
| High Priest's Servant's Ear | | | 22:50f. | |
| Darkness and Rending of the Temple Curtain | 27:45, 51 | 15:33, 38 | 23:44f. | |
| Appearance of the Dead and Earthquake | 27:52-56 | | | |
| Earthquake (Mt.) and Angelic Appearances | 28:1-7 | 16:5-7 | 24:4-7 | (20:12f.) |
| Resurrection Appearances of Jesus and Ascension (Lk.) | 28:9-20 | (16:9-20) | 24:13-53 | 20:14-29; 21:4-23 |

man with a withered hand on the sabbath led to the Pharisees taking counsel with the Herodians to destroy Jesus (Mk. 3:6 par.).

The result was the charge that Jesus was possessed by Beelzebul, i.e., Satan (Mk. 3:22f. par. Mt. 12:24; Lk. 11:15). Conviction on such a charge, as the Pharisees and their colleagues well knew, carried a sentence of death. Jesus' rebuttal of the charge drew attention to the patent self-contradiction involved in it, and led Him to make the counter-charge of blasphemy against the Holy Spirit. By attributing Jesus' works to Satan, when they were in fact the work of the Spirit of God, Jesus' opponents were themselves guilty of blasphemy (Mk. 3:29f. par. Mt. 12:32; Lk. 12:10).

Both the charge of being possessed by Beelzebul in the performance of His works and Jesus' response should be read in the light of Jesus' anointing by the Spirit at His baptism and His identification as the anointed Son of God by the voice from heaven (Mk. 1:11 par.; cf. Ps. 2:7; Isa. 42:1). John the Baptist identified Jesus with the one who would baptize with the Holy Spirit (Mk. 1:8 par.). This identification is further brought out in connection with Jesus' works by Mt. 12:18-21 (citing Isa. 42:1-4). Luke's account of Jesus' reading of Isa. 61:1f. in the synagogue at Capernaum (Lk. 4:18f.) presents Jesus as one who understood Himself to be anointed by the Spirit of the Lord in order to fulfil His preaching, healing, and saving work. Jesus' casting out of demons by the Spirit of God is evidence of the presence of the kingdom of God (Mt. 12:28; cf. Lk. 11:20; 17:21).

Jesus' refusal to perform a sign and His allusion to the sign of Jonah (Mt. 12:38-42; 16:4; Lk. 11:16, 29-32; cf. Mk.

## Miracle Stories in the Gospels

### II. SUMMARIES AND ALLUSIONS

| Events | Matthew | Mark | Luke | John |
|---|---|---|---|---|
| The Spirit's Anointing and Jesus' Mission | (12:15-21) | | 4:18f. | |
| Sick and Possessed on the Sabbath Evening | 8:16f. | 1:32-34 | 4:40f. | |
| Jesus' Early Tours of Galilee | 4:23-25; 9:35 | 1:39 | 5:15 | 6:2, 26 |
| Claims of Evildoers Rejected | 7:22f. | | | |
| Women Followers of Jesus Healed/Exorcised | | (16:9) | 8:2f. | |
| Sending of the Twelve with Authority | 10:1, 8 | 3:15; 6:7 | 9:1f. | |
| Exorcist Who Was Not One of the Twelve | | 9:38-41 | 9:49f. | |
| Sending of the Seventy (-Two) and Their Report | | | 10:1-20 | |
| John the Baptist's Question and Jesus' Answer | 11:2-6 | | 7:18-23 | |
| Jesus' Continued Healings and Exorcisms | 12:15-21 | 3:7-12 | 6:17-19 | |
| The Charge That Jesus' Actions Were Attributable to Beelzebul (Mt., Mk., Lk.) or a Demon (Jn.), and Jesus' Attribution of Them to the Spirit as Signs of the Kingdom of God (Mt., Mk., Lk.) | 12:22-30<br>9:34 | 3:22-30 | 11:14-23<br>(17:20f.) | 7:20; 8:48, 52; 10:20f. |
| Jesus' Refusal to Perform a Sign and the Sign of Jonah (Mt., Lk.) | 12:38-42<br>16:1-4 | 8:11f. | 11:16, 29-32 | 2:18; 6:30 |
| Not Many Mighty Works Done in His Own Country Because of Unbelief | 13:53-58 | 6:1-6 | (4:16-30) | |
| Opinion of Herod Antipas | 14:1f. | 6:14-16 | 9:7-9; 23:8 | |
| Healings at Gennesaret | 14:34-36 | 6:53-56 | | |
| Healings in the Hills of Galilee | 15:29-31 | | | |
| Opinions of the People and Peter's Confession of Jesus as the Christ | 16:13-20 | 8:27-30 | 9:18-21 | |
| Jesus Foretells His Resurrection | 16:21<br>17:23<br>20:19<br>(28:6) | 8:31<br>9:31<br>10:34<br>(16:7) | 9:22<br><br>18:33<br>(24:7, 46) | (2:18-22; 10:18; 14:28) |
| Jesus' Reply to Herod | | | 13:32 | |
| Healings in Judea Beyond the Jordan | 19:1f. | | | |
| Blind and Lame in the Temple | 21:14 | | | |
| Signs and Wonders of False Christs and Prophets | 24:24 | 13:22 | | |
| Jesus' Reply to the High Priest | 26:64 | 14:62 | 22:69 | |
| Opinion of Nicodemus | | | | 3:2 |
| Jesus' Works as Works of the Father | (11:2, 19) | | (24:19) | 4:34; 5:17, 20, 36; 6:27-30; 7:3, 21; 9:3f.; 10:25, 32f., 37f.; 14:10-12; 15:24; 17:4 |
| Signs of the Christ, the Son of God | | | | 20:30f.; cf. 2:11, 18, 23; 3:2; 4:54; 6:2, 14, 26; 7:31; 9:16f.; 10:41; 11:47; 12:18, 37 |

8:11f.) were not simply the result of His reluctance to perform a sign on demand. For those who had eyes to see His works bore eloquent testimony. However, Jesus' reply needs to be seen in the light of the consistent attitude of the Pharisees and their understanding of Dt. 13:1-11 and 18:15-22. No amount of signs could legitimate a false prophet, whose teaching should be evaluated by the word of God. (Indeed, according to Mk. 13:22 par. Mt. 24:24, this was also Jesus' own attitude to the deceptive character of signs and wonders.) A sign would be at best neutral and at worst positively damning. Given their preconceived attitude to Jesus, the Pharisees viewed Jesus as a blasphemous subverter of the law. Any sign that He might perform would only incriminate Him further.

The motivation behind the request for a sign was the desire to "test" Jesus (Mk. 8:11). In Mark the request comes immediately after the feeding of the four thousand. Having failed in their attempt to convict Jesus of being possessed by Beelzebul, and having only hearsay evidence of a nature miracle to go on, the Pharisees evidently hoped to get Jesus to perform a sign before competent witnesses, viz., themselves. If Jesus had performed such a sign, it would have been impeccable evidence of their contention that He was in league with Satan. They could then have proceeded with His conviction and execution. Such signs were the subject of the temptations described in Mt. 4:1-11 and Lk. 4:1-13.

The sign of Jonah was not a sign performed by the prophet to accredit himself. His fate of being cast into the sea was a judgment on the prophet by the crew of the ship in order to save themselves from shipwreck. The fish was the means of Jonah's rescue and reinstatement. The story of Jonah is thus used as an ironic parable, commenting on the actions of Jesus' opponents, who seek to do away with Him in order to avoid national shipwreck. The resurrection of Jesus will reverse their verdict.

For those who had eyes to see, Jesus' actions were such as fulfilled the prophecies of the coming one, and this was sufficient (Mt. 8:17; cf. Isa. 53:4; Mt. 11:5 par. Lk. 7:22; cf. Isa. 35:5f.; 61:1). The signs of Jesus were in the tradition of prophetic signs. These were not, in the first instance, performed to accredit the prophet. They were part of his message, and were in fact the embodiment of it. Jesus enacted numerous such signs. The act of taking children in His arms, His washing of the disciples' feet, His entry into Jerusalem, the rite of baptism, and the Last Supper were all in the prophetic tradition of signs which embodied and actualized the message. In the same way the miracles of Jesus were enactments of His message.

The cursing of the fig tree was a symbolic, prophetic act of judgment. The words and actions of Jesus embody the words and actions of God Himself. Like Yahweh, Jesus stills the roaring of the seas (Ps. 65:7 [MT 8]; 89:9 [MT 10]) and even tramples it (Job 9:8; Hab. 3:15). The saving acts of Yahweh described in Ps. 107 are mirrored by many of the events in the synoptic accounts of the miracles of Jesus. The feeding of the multitudes takes up the theme of God's provision for His people in the wilderness and also that of the eschatological banquet. The miracles of Jesus show God the Creator, Sustainer, and Redeemer at work in the end time.

*C. Gospel of John.* The Fourth Gospel makes no mention of exorcism, and focuses attention on seven signs. For the location of the signs see the table of Miracle Stories in the Gospels. For John's use of the terms "sign" and "work," see I.A.2 above. The choice of seven may reflect the idea of the perfect number, completeness, the days of creation, or the restoration of creation. The signs have been seen as reflecting Jesus' lordship over quality (water into wine), space (the healing of the nobleman's son at a distance), time (the healing of the man who had been lame for 38 years), quantity (the feeding of the five thousand), nature (walking on the sea), misfortune (the healing of the man born blind), and death (the raising of Lazarus). At the same time the signs are parabolic and function like prophetic signs which illustrate and embody the message of Jesus. Thus the feeding of the five thousand leads to the discourse on the bread of life (Jn. 6:35-65). The healing of the lame man and the blind man and the raising of Lazarus are parabolic of the saving work of Jesus, who restores the spiritually lame and blind, and gives life to the dead.

The miracle at Cana has been interpreted as a Christian borrowing from the cult of Dionysus, who was credited with turning water into wine (C. K. Barrett, *Gospel According to John* [1955], p. 157). It is questionable, however, whether John's Jewish readers would have appreciated such a comparison. J. D. M. Derrett has suggested that the incident be understood against the background of obligations incumbent upon wedding guests in the Jewish community, and the problems created by Jesus' appearance at the wedding in the company of His disciples (*Law in the NT,* pp. 228-246).

Whereas in the Synoptics Jesus' actions are attributed to Beelzebul, in John Jesus is said to be a Samaritan and to have a demon (Jn. 8:48; cf. 7:20; 10:20). The accusation was evidently bound up with Jesus' attitude to official Judaism, His associations with Samaritans (cf. Jn. 4), and the identification of Samaria with a deviant religion and magical practices (cf. Acts 8:14-24). The charges of demon possession and blasphemy were linked with attempts to kill Jesus on the grounds that He was leading the people astray (Jn. 7:12, 20, 25; 8:59; 10:33, 36). Jesus' death was justified by Caiaphas as the ultimate act of expediency that would avert the national disaster which would come about through the people being led astray by following Jesus' signs (Jn. 11:47-53). Nicodemus, on the other hand, recognized Jesus as "a teacher come from God; for no one can do these signs that you do, unless God is with him" (Jn. 3:2).

The signs of Jesus, like His teaching, provoke both belief (Jn. 2:11, 23; 4:50, 53; 5:9; 6:14, 21; 9:11, 17, 33, 38; 11:27, 45; 12:11) and unbelief (Jn. 5:18; 6:66; 9:16, 24, 29, 40f.; 11:53). Rejection of the signs on the basis of pretended claims to know the truth is culpable. The signs are the work of the Father, revealing the Father in Jesus (Jn. 10:37f.; cf. 5:20-27, 30-47; 7:27-29; 8:28f.; 9:3f.; 14:10f.; 15:24; 17:2-4, 21). As such, they reveal the glory of God and bring glory to God (Jn. 6:41-47; cf. 1:14; 2:11; 5:41, 44; 7:18; 8:50; 9:24; 11:4, 40; 12:41, 43; 17:5, 22, 24). They are reported, so that those who have not seen, and who are not in a position to prove by examining for themselves, may believe that Jesus is the Christ, the Son of God, and that believing they may have life in His name (Jn. 20:30f.; cf. vv. 20-29).

*D. Book of Acts.* The preaching of Peter at Pentecost describes Jesus of Nazareth as "a man attested to you by God with mighty works and wonders and signs which God did through him in your midst" (Acts 2:22). Peter describes to Cornelius "how God anointed Jesus of Nazareth with the Holy Spirit and with power; how he went about doing good and healing all that were oppressed by the devil, for God was with him" (Acts 10:38). In the preaching of Acts the resurrection of Jesus is proclaimed as His vindication and reinstatement, which reverses the verdict and the action of the lawless, wicked men who killed Him. He who was anointed by the Spirit is the one who pours out the Holy Spirit (Acts 2:33; cf. 1:5; 11:16).

The new situation calls for repentance and dissociation from the crooked generation which condemned Jesus (Acts 2:37-40). The disciples are to receive the Holy Spirit and be witnesses to Jesus "in Jerusalem and in all Judea and Samaria and to the end of the earth" (Acts 1:8). In the context of this mission Acts describes a number of healing miracles and exorcisms, wrought by the apostles and their associates. The use of the expression "signs and wonders" is a deliberate echo of OT language. Its use by Stephen draws attention to the fact that they are a counterpart to "signs and wonders" wrought in connection with the Exodus (Acts 7:36). At Pentecost Peter declares them to belong to the eschatological outpouring of the Spirit (Acts 2:19, 22; cf. Joel 2:28-32 [MT 3:1-5]). They are wrought by the apostles at Jerusalem (Acts 2:43; 4:30; 5:12), by Stephen (Acts 6:8), and by Paul and Barnabas at Iconium (Acts 14:3) and on their missionary journey (Acts 15:12). The word "sign" is used on its own to describe Peter's healing of the lame man in the temple (Acts 4:16, 22; cf. 3:1-10) and Philip's healings and exorcisms in Samaria (Acts 8:6, 13).

Acts 5:12-16 describes the many healings and exorcisms

performed by the apostles and the great response. Some even sought to have Peter's shadow fall on them. The healings by Peter are counterbalanced by those of Paul, who healed a lame man at Lystra (Acts 14:8), cast out a spirit from a slave girl with the gift of divination at Philippi (Acts 16:16-18), and performed such extraordinary miracles at Ephesus that handkerchiefs or aprons were carried from his body for the healing and exorcism of the sick (Acts 19:11f.). At Troas, Eutychus survived a fall that everyone except Paul deemed fatal (Acts 20:9-12).

As in the Gospels the healings and exorcisms produced a mixed reaction. They led to the imprisonment of both Peter and Paul, and in both cases the apostles were given an opportunity to escape (Acts 5:17-20; 16:19-27). In both cases, too, healings and exorcisms provided opportunity to proclaim the word of God. Whereas the actions of Peter and the apostles in Jerusalem were questioned, but could not be gainsaid (Acts 4:13-22; 5:33-40), those of Paul in the gentile world were attributed to his being a god (Acts 14:11; 28:6). In Samaria Simon Magus deemed the gift of the Spirit to be a form of superior magic and sought to purchase it from Peter and John (Acts 8:14-24). At Ephesus itinerant Jewish exorcists undertook to practice in the name of Jesus, but failed (Acts 19:11-20). The episode led to wholesale abandonment of magic and the opposition of those with vested interests.

*E. Other NT Writings.* The ambivalent character of signs is also evident in Paul's writings. He could describe his ministry among the Gentiles in terms of winning their obedience "by word and deed, by power of signs and wonders, by the power of the Holy Spirit" (Rom. 15:18f.). He rejected sign seeking by the Jews and wisdom seeking by the Gentiles (1 Cor. 1:22) and, in a manner comparable with the sign of Jonah, proclaimed Christ crucified as the power and wisdom of God (vv. 23-25). At the same time Paul could point to "the demonstration of the Spirit and power" (1 Cor. 2:4). Healing and miracle working are among the gifts of the Spirit in the body of Christ, but such gifts are given only to some (1 Cor. 12:28-30). They have their place only in relation to the other gifts. A faith which could move mountains is nothing without love (1 Cor. 13:2). Miracle working in the Church is again related to the Spirit in Gal. 3:5, where it also related to faith.

Although Paul wrought "the signs of a true apostle . . . in all patience, with signs and wonders and mighty works" (2 Cor. 12:12), his thorn in the flesh was not removed. In response to his earnest petitions he received the reply, "My grace is sufficient for you, for my power is made perfect in weakness" (2 Cor. 12:9).

Signs, wonders, and the gifts of the Spirit are a witness which God gives (He. 2:4). On the other hand, "The coming of the lawless one by the activity of Satan will be with all power and with pretended signs and wonders" (2 Thess. 2:9). The visions of Rev. 12:1 and 15:1 describe various signs in heaven. But Satan, the beast, and demonic spirits also perform signs that deceive (Rev. 13:13f.; 16:14; 19:20).

In Jas. 5:13-18 prayer, the anointing of the sick by the elders of the Church, and confession of sin are encouraged for the healing of the sick. Such healing is not treated as a sign or wonder. It is not advocated for apologetic purposes in order to convince the heathen. It belongs to the context of prayer, for which Elijah provides a role model in his intercession for rain (cf. 1 K. 18:42).

***III. Miracles in the Jewish and Hellenistic Worlds.***–*A. The Jewish World.* Rabbinic thought recognized miracles in the Jewish canonical Scriptures and also in subsequent times. Miracles, however, were not regarded as a test of truth. The Torah was more decisive than either miracles or a voice from heaven, as Rabbi Eliezer found to his cost in his debate with Rabbi Joshua (T.B. *Baba Metzia* 59b). Having reportedly moved a carob tree, caused water to flow backward and the walls of a house to bend inward, and having received endorsement by a voice from heaven, Rabbi Eliezer was told by Rabbi Joshua and Rabbi Jeremiah that the Torah was not in heaven but on the earth, and that the Torah provided for judgments to be made in accordance with majority decisions. (For this and other rabbinic teaching see C. G. Montefiore and H. Loewe, *Rabbinic Anthology* [repr. 1974], pp. 339-341, 690-93.)

Rabbinic literature contains many fanciful tales of miracles. Some scholars think that Galilee was more prone to superstition, credulity, and charismatic phenomena than Judea. Rabbinic discussion of miracles tended to stress the miracle of creation (Midr. *Ex. Rabbah* 24:1; the thanksgiving prayer Modim in the daily Amidah). Some rabbis explained the biblical miracles as having been implanted in the created order at the beginning of the creation (Midr. *Gen. Rabbah* 5:45; Midr. *Ex. Rabbah* 21:6; Mish. *Aboth* v.6).

In the 1st cent. B.C. Honi (Onias) the Circle Drawer was regarded as a saint and miracle worker (Josephus *Ant.* xiv.2.1 [22]; Mish. *Taanith* iii.8; T.B. *Taanith* 23a; T.J. *Taanith* iii.10-12, 66d). His nickname derives from the occasion when he drew a circle, stood in it, and successfully interceded for rain. The incident is more illustrative of God's grace in answering prayer, however, than of a sign or wonder.

Similarly Hanina ben Dosa (1st cent. A.D.) appears to have been a pious charismatic, known as a prayerful intercessor for the sick and troubled (T.B. *Berakoth* 34b; *Yebamoth* 121b). He is also said to have caused vinegar to burn in lieu of oil in the sabbath light, and to have performed numerous miracles (T.B. *Taanith* 25a).

A decisive difference between these miracles and those of Jesus lies in the fact that these miracles were not associated with particular teaching or messianic claims. Jesus' miracles, on the other hand, were associated with His distinctive teaching and practices. Moreover, they are presented in the NT as the work of the Spirit-anointed Christ.

*B. The Hellenistic World.* In Greece Asclepius was revered as the god of healing. Cures were reported at shrines dedicated to him, notably at Epidaurus and Pergamum, which were centers of healing. In the East Asclepius was supplanted by Serapis, whose cult originated in Egypt. Tacitus reports how at Alexandria the Emperor Vespasian was induced (albeit reluctantly) to put spittle on the eyes of a blind man and allow his foot to be touched by a man with an ailing hand (*Hist.* iv.81). Both sufferers had received instructions from Serapis, and both were healed to the surprise of the Emperor. Thereafter Vespasian became interested in the cult of Serapis.

Charges that Jesus was really a magician, who had acquired His arts from the magi and His sojourn in Egypt, were made by Celsus in his comprehensive polemic against Christianity, the *True Word* (*ca.* 178-180). They were preserved and rebutted by Origen in *Contra Celsum* (*ca.* 249; cf. 1.28, 68).

Through the centuries critics of Christianity have repeatedly drawn attention to what they conceived to be parallels between Jesus and Apollonius of Tyana, a Neo-Pythagorean sage and wandering ascetic who lived in the first century and was credited with exorcistic and miraculous powers. Philostratus was commissioned by the Empress, Julia Domna, who was the wife of Septimius Severus, to write a *Life of Apollonius*. The circumstances and contents of the book have prompted the suggestion that Apollonius and his cult were fostered as a rival alternative to Christianity. The most striking parallel occurs in the comparison of Lk. 7:11-17 and the *Life of Apollonius* iv.45, which tells how Apollonius encountered the funeral procession in Rome of a bride who had died in the hour of her marriage. Apollonius restored her, but Philostratus leaves open the question of whether the ascetic "detected some spark of life in her . . . or whether life was really extinct."

In the 19th and 20th cents. the History of Religions School sought to demonstrate parallels between the Gospel miracles and miracle stories from the Hellenistic world. In *Kyrios Christos* (1913; Eng. tr. 1970) W. Bousset tried to trace Jesus' Lordship and the miracle stories to the influence of Hellenistic religion on the Church. His sources were largely post-Christian, however, and some of them were patently suspect of being anti-Christian polemic. Other scholars who sought to investigate parallels include R. Reitzenstein, O. Weinreich, and P. Fiebig. Their work deeply influenced R. Bultmann in his program of demythologization.

L. Bieler's thesis that the Hellenistic world provided the Church with a role model of the "divine man" also found some following (cf. Bieler, *Theios Anēr,* I-II [1935-36]). Apollonius was seen as an instance of such a "divine man." The term is found in the Hellenistic Jewish writers Josephus, Philo, and Artapanus. Further investigation, however, has not confirmed the suggestion that "divine man" was a technical term denoting a distinctive category of divinized men in antiquity. Contrary to assumptions, it was not associated, in the sources where it occurs, with miracle working. It was capable of a variety of senses, suggesting an inspired man, a man somehow related to God, or simply an extraordinary man. The term does not occur in the NT, and in view of its broad range of meaning and the fact that it was not associated with miracle working, it does not seem to have been used in any way as a model for NT christology.

J. M. Hull attempted to show possible connections between magic and the Gospels' picture of Jesus in *Hellenistic Magic and the Synoptic Tradition* (1974). His sources date from the 3rd and 4th cents. A.D., however, and few scholars appear to have found his case convincing. Whereas Hull stopped short of attributing magical practices to Jesus Himself, M. Smith contended that Jesus practiced magical arts (*Jesus the Magician* [1978]). Smith argued that the NT writers and the early Church tried to cover this up. His case turns on radical reinterpretation of incidents and sayings on the supposition that their present form is a deliberate, but not altogether successful, attempt to remove all suggestions of magic. Smith regarded the Lord's Supper as "the clearest evidence of Jesus' knowledge and use of magic" (p. 152). It may be noted that his reconstruction (like Hull's) leans heavily on Egyptian magical papyri of the 3rd and 4th cents. A.D. and other artifacts that are not earlier than the 2nd century. These themselves are patently products of a syncretism which sought to combine Christianity with magic. Smith's contentions bear a marked resemblance to the views of Celsus and to those of the opponents of Jesus in the Gospels. Smith himself, however, gives no credence to magic.

***IV. Miracles in Philosophy and Christian Apologetics.***–*A. Miracles and Apologetics.* From the 2nd cent. onward Christian apologists have appealed to miracles as evidence of divine attestation in support of the truth claims of Christianity (e.g., Justin Martyr *Dial.* 39, 69; Origen *Contra Celsum,* i.2, 46; Athanasius *De Incarnatione Verbi Dei* xviii; Augustine *Civ. Dei* xxi, xxii). At the same time the fathers were aware that a simple appeal to miracles was not without difficulty. There were skeptics in the ancient world just as there are today. In ancient times people were well aware of the uniformities of nature and judged reports of alleged happenings in the light of their understanding of the way things are. In other words, long before E. Troeltsch developed his doctrine of analogy in the 19th cent., people were applying it in practice.

In reply to the anticipated objection that miracles no longer occur, and hence reports of miracles in the Bible should be dismissed, Origen, Augustine, and others appealed to continued miracles in the Church which were supported by reliable testimony. The fathers tended to lay greater stress on fulfilled prophecy than on miracles as accreditation of their faith. Whereas reports of miracles were open to question, clear fulfillment of a prophecy made hundreds of years beforehand could not readily be gainsaid. Augustine, in particular, wrestled with the philosophical questions raised by miracles, and argued, as noted, that miracles were not necessarily contrary to nature, but only to what we know of nature. Miracles are the result of the higher, divine ordering of nature (*Contra Faustum Manichaeum* xxvi.3). Augustine suggested that miracles were like the fruit of seeds long dormant (*De trin.* iii.9.16).

Aquinas, on the other hand, tended to shun such speculation and stressed the incapacity of the created order to produce miracles on its own (*Summa Theol.* i.105; *Summa Contra Gentiles* iii.102-106). The Reformers were, in general, skeptical of postbiblical miracles. Calvin, in particular, repudiated the claim that continued miracles in the Church accredited the teaching of the Church. He denounced such works as "sheer delusions of Satan" that drew people away from God and that should be repudiated in accordance with the teaching of Dt. 13; Mt. 24:24; and 2 Thess. 2:9 (*Inst.,* Prefatory Address; cf. also i.8.5-7; i.13.13; i.14.18; iv.19.6, 18). The miracles of Scripture accredit the biblical revelation, which Calvin insisted was the test of all truth in religion. Miracles which draw people away from this do not bring glory to God in the way that the biblical miracles do. Hence they must be rejected. The miracles of Christ show His divinity. They serve as sacramental signs, embodying in nature what God promises and does in His Word.

Following the Reformation, the Roman Catholic Church continued to appeal to miracles in the Church as divine accreditation of its position, whereas Reformed theology, in line with Calvin, insisted that miracles ceased with the apostolic age. From the Catholic side J. H. Newman offered a notable defense in *Two Essays on Biblical and Ecclesiastical Miracles* (1870). The First Vatican Council (1869-70) pronounced that since miracles and prophecies "so excellently display God's omnipotence and limitless knowledge, they constitute the surest signs of divine revelation, signs that are suitable to everyone's understanding" (*Dogmatic Constitution on the Catholic Faith,* ch. 3). Subsequent Modernist questioning of miracles was condemned. The Second Vatican Council held that "the miracles of Jesus also demonstrate that the kingdom of God has already come on earth" (*Lumen Gentium* [1964], ch. 1, § 5). But it went on to say that the kingdom is principally revealed in the person of Christ Himself.

A classic statement of the Protestant appeal to the miracles of Jesus as divine authentication of His teaching was given by Locke in *Discourse of Miracles* (1702). The Deistic controversy in the late 17th and first half of the 18th cents. further served to confirm Protestants in their defense of miracles as objective events in history which accredited Christian beliefs. In Britain J. B. Mozley's Bampton Lectures on *Miracles* (1865) made a strong statement of the evidentialist case. In America A. Alexander's

*Evidences* (1825), which clearly focused on the Deistic question, reiterated the Reformed position in the light of philosophical objections. In doing this, it laid down the lines followed by subsequent Reformed apologists. The position of C. Hodge and B. B. Warfield is not materially different from that of Alexander. Warfield's *Counterfeit Miracles* (1918; reissued as *Miracles: Yesterday and Today, True and False* [1954]) was a catalog and critique of post-biblical miracles. It thus developed and strengthened the Reformed Protestant belief that miracles ceased with the apostolic age.

*B. Skepticism.* Skepticism concerning the Gospel miracles dates from NT times. But with the rise of modern science and history skepticism became increasingly articulate. Spinoza rejected miracles on the grounds that they were precluded by "the universal laws of science" which were decreed by God (*Tractatus Theologico-politicus* [1670], § 6). Spinoza used the language of Calvinistic orthodoxy to express a rationalistic pantheism, which admitted no interventions in the universal, rational order. The British Deists sought to detract from the Gospel miracles by appealing to those of Apollonius of Tyana and the miracles of other religions. Advocating the religion of reason and nature, they made it their aim to undermine the Christian appeal to miracles and fulfilled prophecy. T. Woolston's six *Discourses on the Miracles of Our Saviour* (1727-29) pronounced the Gospel miracles to be fraudulent and the Resurrection a Robinson Crusoe romance. Woolston was condemned for blasphemy. His attack on the Resurrection led to T. Sherlock's classic *Tryal of the Witnesses of the Resurrection* (1729).

By the time that Hume published his celebrated attack on miracles in *An Inquiry Concerning Human Understanding* (1748), § 10, the British debate concerning the historicity of miracles and their evidential value had been going on for over half a century. In the first part of his essay Hume rejected miracles as impossible on the grounds that they violated the laws of nature and that "a firm and unalterable experience has established these laws." In the second part of the essay Hume argued that the actual testimony to miracles was weak and inconclusive, originating in obscure parts of the world from ignorant, obscure men. When account is taken of human propensity to exaggerate and of miracles in other religions which cancel out those of Christianity, miracles are devoid of apologetic value. Instead of providing reasons for faith, they cannot be believed in without faith.

Hume's essay came to be regarded as the classic attack on miracles. Subsequent skepticism has only modified details. Hume studiously avoided mention of the Gospel miracles, but it was evident to all that Hume was attacking the apologetic appeal to the miraculous as divine accreditation of the Christian revelation. His thoughts were further prompted by discussions that he had in France and by reports of continued miracles connected with the tomb of François de Pâris, who had died in 1727. Such miracles, like the earlier Jansenist miracles which had confirmed the faith of Pascal, were appealed to as acts of divine attestation.

It is now widely recognized that Hume did not disprove the possibility of miracles. His argument was essentially defensive. It was more concerned with demonstrating the impossibility of appealing to miracles as proof of a religious belief system, than with showing outright that miracles could not happen, although at times Hume spoke as if he had shown that miracles were impossible. Hume acknowledged that scientific laws are based on statistical observation. On this basis laws may be said to describe the observed regularities of nature. This may lead us to call in question the veracity of testimony to the miraculous and invite consideration whether such testimony might be mistaken. At the same time testimony to the unusual, if well founded, may call in question our understanding of the laws of nature and the extent of their applicability. Only on the basis of an absolute knowledge of nature could it be argued that this or that miracle would be impossible.

This consideration has led contemporary philosophers in Hume's tradition to modify his argument. Instead of trying to show the impossibility of miracles as violations of the laws of nature, and therefore that any given miracle could not have happened, such skeptics argue that an event which was previously thought to have been a violation must be regarded as an instance of a law which is not yet understood. The historicity of the event is acknowledged at the price of its character as a miracle (if a miracle be indeed a violation of natural law).

In his own day Hume's argument was overshadowed by C. Middleton's *Free Inquiry into the Miraculous Powers which are Supposed to have Subsisted in the Christian Church* (1748). Like Hume, Middleton refrained from questioning the Gospel miracles. His aim was to criticize testimony to miracles in the early Church. Although his work found endorsement from B. B. Warfield, whose views on miracle stories in the early centuries were substantially similar to Middleton's, J. Wesley believed that Middleton had contrived to "overthrow the whole Christian system" (*Journal*, Jan. 28, 1749).

The Deistic approach to religion and miracles found expression in America among such founding fathers as Jefferson and in Europe among such leaders of the Enlightenment as Voltaire, Lessing, Reimarus, and Kant. In the 19th cent. D. F. Strauss scorned the explanations of the rationalists who proffered psychological and natural accounts of the miracles. His *Life of Jesus* (1835-36; Eng. tr. 1846) saw the Gospel miracles as the product of the myth-making mind which invested Jesus with supernatural characteristics drawn from the OT. L. Feuerbach explained miracles as projections of deep-seated wishes. The History of Religions School ascribed the Gospel miracles to the alien influence of pagan religion (see III.B above).

Underlying these objections to miracles was the common conviction that the world is a closed system of natural causes which does not admit of supernatural interventions. Bound up with this is the doctrine of analogy, enunciated by E. Troeltsch, which maintains that all historical judgments must be made in the light of our contemporary understanding of the world. Hence, that which bears no analogy to our present experience and understanding is rejected.

Such convictions underlie Bultmann's demythologizing program. Bultmann differed from Strauss, however, in that he ascribed what he considered to be the mythical elements of the NT world view to the influence of Gnosticism, Jewish apocalyptic, and Hellenistic religion.

*C. Reassessment.* That acceptance and rejection of miracle stories is bound up with one's wider view of reality has become increasingly recognized by Christian apologists. If miracles are thought of as violations of the laws of nature, and if such laws cannot be violated, no amount of historical testimony to any alleged miracle will suffice to qualify it as a miracle. It will always be explained away as myth, pious fabrication, deception, or an event which was only *thought* to be miraculous. For this reason, Christian apologists like A. E. Taylor and C. S. Lewis attempted to establish a prior theistic world view which would allow them to interpret miracles as the action of a personal God in nature and history.

Given a personal Creator who is free to use powers beyond man's imagination, as and when His own purposes require, miracles are feasible. Much of C. S. Lewis's influential study of miracles was devoted to showing the inadequacy of materialism and determinism, and the superiority of Christian theism as an explanation of the world, as a prior step to presenting the feasibility of the NT miracle stories within the context of Christian theism. Similar approaches had, in fact, long been adopted by apologists who are generally regarded as evidentialists. Paley, Alexander, Hodge, and Warfield all appealed to theological considerations concerning God and His purposes in arguing for the historicity of the NT miracles. In doing this they were in fact agreeing that prior beliefs played an important part in their judgment that the Gospel miracles were historical events.

If apologists posit certain attributes and purposes of God, which belong to the Christian revelation, as the condition for grasping the feasibility of the miracle stories, it must be recognized that they have shifted the traditional apologetic appeal to miracles. Miracles no longer function as an objective, external guarantee of the Christian belief system, for their historicity is dependent upon the truth of that system. This is particularly evident in writers like C. S. Lewis who urge that individual miracle stories be seen in the context of "the grand miracle" of the Incarnation. For in this case belief in the Incarnation has become the necessary ground for determining the intelligibility and historicity of the miracle stories.

This view enables the believer to grasp the feasibility of miracles, but it raises the question of whether the NT miracle stories were ever intended to provide the objective, evidential attestation that they were deemed to have in some apologetic systems. In this connection several observations may be made. In Scripture the miracle stories never have the function of proving the existence of God. They come within the context of belief in God, and within that context serve as signs. But a sign is not the same as a proof. It is a pointer, an indication, and a revelation. As such it calls for a response. But both true and false signs have themselves to be identified and evaluated in the light of prior revelation. The signs of a false prophet are to be rejected, not on account of lack of empirical evidence but because they conflict with prior revelation (Dt. 13:1-6). The signs of Jesus are identified, according to the Synoptic Gospels, because they are those works which fulfil messianic prophecy. In the Fourth Gospel they are identifiable, because they can be recognized to be the work of the Father. In the Gospels miracles and fulfilled prophecy do not function as two parallel tracks of objective attestation to Jesus as the Christ. It is because the miracles of Jesus fit what is known through previous revelation that they can be recognized as the work of God.

Thus miracles in the NT are part of the revelation itself. They reveal God in Christ. In the NT the resurrection of Jesus is presented as a historical event, corroborated by testimony, by experience of the power of the risen Christ, and by the existence of the Church. The thought is not (as in some modern writers) that, if God could raise Jesus from the dead, then all the other miracles would be relatively easy for Him to perform. Rather, the Resurrection vindicates Jesus as the Lord's anointed and the one in whom God had been active all along. This point has added significance in view of the repeated charge leveled against Jesus that He was possessed by Satan, the charge of blasphemy for which He was ultimately condemned, and the charge that His death on the cross was self-evidently a sign of God's curse (Mk. 14:64 par.; Gal. 3:13; cf. Dt. 21:23). That Jesus was perceived by His Jewish opponents as a false prophet, who wrought signs and wonders in order to accredit Himself, shows incidentally that His miracles belong to the thought world of Judaism, rather than to the Hellenistic world. The point is corroborated by the apostolic preaching in Acts. Stress on miracles belongs to preaching to the Jews rather than to the Gentiles.

In response to Hume's charge that miracles of rival religions cancel each other out, two observations may be made. On the one hand, the charge would hold, if rival religions had duplicate miracles which functioned to validate diametrically opposed truth claims (e.g., if a rival religion could claim the resurrection of a messiah). On the other hand, claims to miracles are susceptible of various interpretations. They may be false claims or works of a false prophet. Just as God sends His sun and rain upon the just and the unjust (Mt. 5:45), His providential acts are not necessarily the monopoly of the Church. Moreover, it is possible for people to place a wrong construction on such acts, just as people in Paul's day attributed his actions to a pagan deity (Acts 14:11-13; 28:6).

The decisive factor from the biblical standpoint is not the stupendous character of the miracle per se but the way in which it relates to the self-revelation of God. Signs and wonders may or may not involve suspension of ordinary, natural causes. Where natural causes are present in biblical signs and wonders (e.g., the plagues and the Exodus miracles), they are identified as such. Unlike some apologists, the Bible never suggests that miracles are simply accelerated natural processes. Regardless of whether natural factors are identifiable, biblical miracles are signs of the intervention of God and His ordering of events. Such divine ordering is presented against the background of the normal, observed regularities of nature and human life.

The resurrection of Jesus especially is seen as the breaking of the resurrection order into our world of time and space. Jesus Himself with His resurrection body is the first fruits (1 Cor. 15:20-56; Col. 1:18). As such, the Resurrection is not a pure anomaly. It represents the incursion of a higher order into the present world. Some events, like the Transfiguration, may also be thought of as anticipations of the eschatological glory in the present world. Other miracles, like the healings and exorcisms, are sacramental signs embodying and exemplifying the redemptive love and power of the Creator in the person and actions of Jesus Christ.

***Bibliography.***–P. J. Achtemeier, *JBL,* 89 (1970), 265-291; 91 (1972), 198-221; 94 (1975), 447-462, repr. in C. H. Talbert, ed., *Perspectives on Luke-Acts* (1978), pp. 153-167; G. Bornkamm, G. Barth, and H. J. Held, *Tradition and Interpretation in Matthew* (1963), pp. 52-57, 165-299; C. Brown, *Miracles and the Critical Mind* (1984); R. E. Brown, "The Gospel Miracles," in *NT Essays* (1965), pp. 168-191; *Gospel According to John,* I (*AB,* 1967), 525-532; A. B. Bruce, *Miraculous Elements in the Gospels* (1886); R. M. Burns, *Great Debate on Miracles: From Joseph Glanvill to David Hume* (1981); D. Cairns, *Faith that Rebels* (3rd ed. 1929); J. D. M. Derrett, "Water into Wine" and "Peter's Penny," in *Law in the NT* (1970), pp. 228-246, 247-265; "Legend and Event: The Gerasene Demoniac: An Inquest into History and Liturgical Projection," in *Studia Biblica 1978,* II (1980), 63-73; P. Edwards, ed., *Encyclopedia of Philosophy* (repr. 1973), V, *s.v.* (A. Flew); H. H. Farmer, *World and God* (1936); E. S. Fiorenza, ed., *Aspects of Religious Propaganda in Judaism and Early Christianity* (1976); A. Flew, *Hume's Philosophy of Belief* (1961); R. T. Fortna, *Gospel of Signs: A Reconstruction of the Narrative Source Underlying the Fourth Gospel* (*Society for NT Studies Monograph,* 11; 1970); A. Fridrichsen, *Problem of Miracle in Primitive Christianity* (1972); R. H. Fuller, *Interpreting the Miracles* (1963); E. V. Gallagher, *Divine Man or Magician: Celsus and Origen on Jesus* (1982); N. L. Geisler, *Miracles and Modern Thought* (1982); B. Gerhardsson, *Mighty Acts of Jesus According to Matthew* (1979); L. Goppelt, *Theology of the NT,* I (Eng. tr. 1981), pp. 139-155; R. M. Grant, *Miracle and Natural Law in Graeco-Roman and Early Christian Thought* (1952); A. Harvey, *Jesus and the Constraints of History* (1982), pp. 98-119; J. P. Heil, *Jesus Walking on the Sea* (1981); C. H. Holladay, *Theios Aner in Hellenistic Judaism: A Critique* *of the Use of this Category in NT Christology* (1977); R. F. Holland, *American Philosophical Quarterly*, 2 (1965), 43-51, repr. in D. Z. Phillips, ed., *Religion and Understanding* (1967), pp. 155-170; D. Hume, "Of Miracles," § 10 of his *Inquiry Concerning Human Understanding* (1748), repr. in *Hume's Enquiries*, ed. L. A. Selby-Bigge, rev. P. H. Nidditch (1975), pp. 109-131; J. Kallas, *Significance of the Synoptic Miracles* (1961); E. and M.-L. Keller, *Miracles in Dispute: A Continuing Debate* (1969); J. S. Lawton, *Miracles and Revelation* (1959); C. S. Lewis, *Miracles: A Preliminary Study* (rev. ed. 1960); H. van der Loos, *Miracles of Jesus* (1965); L. Monden, *Signs and Wonders: A Study of the Miraculous Element in Religion* (1966); L. Morris, *Gospel According to John* (*NICNT*, 1971), pp. 684-691; C. F. D. Moule, ed., *Miracles: Cambridge Studies in Their Philosophy and History* (1965); W. Nicol, *Sēmeia in the Fourth Gospel: Tradition and Redaction* (*Nov.Test. Supp.*, 32; 1972); I. T. Ramsey, *et al.*, *Miracles and the Resurrection* (1964); H. Remus, *JBL*, 101 (1982), 531-551; A. Richardson, *Miracle-Stories of the Gospels* (1941); L. Sabourin, *Divine Miracles Discussed and Defended* (1977); W. Schaaffs, *Theology, Physics, and Miracles* (1974); R. Swinburne, *Concept of Miracle* (1970); A. E. Taylor, "David Hume and the Miraculous," *Philosophical Studies* (1934), pp. 330-365; *The Faith of a Moralist*, II (1937), 150-196; F. R. Tennant, *Miracle and Its Philosophical Presuppositions* (1925); G. Theissen, *Miracle Stories of the Early Christian Tradition* (1982); D. L. Tiede, *Charismatic Figure as Miracle Worker* (1972); R. C. Trench, *Notes on the Miracles of Our Lord* (1846); B. B. Warfield, "The Question of Miracle," *Selected Shorter Writings*, ed. J. E. Meeter, II (1973), 167-204; *Counterfeit Miracles* (1918), repr. as *Miracles: Yesterday and Today, True and False* (1954).

C. BROWN

**MIRACLES, GIFT OF.** *See* SPIRITUAL GIFTS; MIRACLE.

**MIRD** mird; **KHIRBET EL-MIRD** [Arab.] A ruin in the Wilderness of Judea where some of the Dead Sea Scrolls were found.

In the desert of Judah, 3 km. (2 mi.) NE of the present monastery of Mar Saba, rose the Hasmonean fortress Hyrcania, razed by Gabinius in 57 B.C., and rebuilt by Herod the Great. He had his son Antipater executed and buried there (Josephus *Ant.* xiv.5.4 [89]; xv.10.4 [366]; xvii.7.1 [187]; *BJ* i.8.2 [161], 5 [167]; 19.1 [364]; 33.7 [664]).

In A.D. 492 St. Saba passed the Lenten season at this place, called *Marda* ("fortress") in Aramaic and *Kastellion* in Greek. He had the ruins rebuilt for a monastic community. John Moschos mentioned it in several places in *Pré Spirituel* (end of the 6th cent.), and it still existed in 1355.

In 1925 some monks of Mar Saba attempted to establish themselves at this site, but within a few years they were obliged to withdraw because of the harassment by the bedouin, who *ca.* 1939 completed the demolition of the monks' modest accommodations.

In 1952 the bedouin discovered a considerable number of documents in Greek, Christian-Palestinian Aramaic, and Arabic, which the Palestinian Archeological Museum of Jerusalem (now the Rockefeller Museum) acquired.

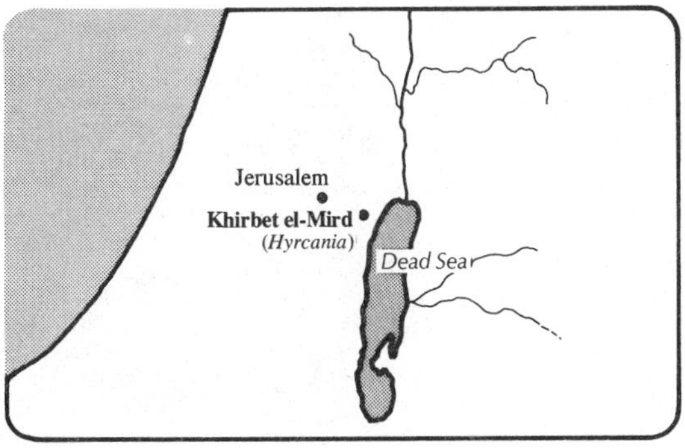


From February 10 to April 16, 1953, Monsignor Robert De Langhe, professor at the University of Louvain, guided by Ibrahim Shaourieh, systematically excavated a cave-cistern belonging to the ruins and recovered about six hundred fragments of parchment or papyrus, of which nearly a quarter contained written characters. These remains proved beyond doubt that the documents sold by the bedouin had indeed come from Khirbet el-Mird. The excavations are described by De Langhe (*Onze Alma Mater* [in Flemish], 7/4 [1953], 14-19; 8/1 [1954], 3-5; 8/3 [1954], 1-6), G. Leclercq (*Bulletin de la société Belge de géologie*, 64 [1956], 414-431), and J. Coppens (*Ephemerides theologicae Lovanienses*, 40 [1964], 104-125 and esp. pp. 111-16).

In April 1960 a new expedition comprising J. M. Allegro, De Langhe, G. R. H. Wright, and four other scholars continued the archeological investigations but could not complete them in an exhaustive manner. For the Herodian period they studied: (1) the fortress itself with its central court and the living quarters constructed on vaulted basements provided with cisterns; (2) an aqueduct of beautiful dressed stone; (3) a mysterious monument situated 300 m. (1000 ft.) SE; (4) two dug stepped tunnels 300 m. (1000 ft.) N; (5) some tombs, 500 m. (550 yds.) E, which contained various objects of pottery. For the monastic period they yielded especially the remains of the church constructed in the northern part of the ancient fortress and an adjacent building (*diakonikón*) decorated with a mosaic of the finest workmanship. Wright described these results in *Bibl.*, 42 (1961), 1-21; in the same issue J. T. Milik traced the history of the monastery (pp. 21-27).

The Greek documents from Khirbet el-Mird relate to both the OT and the NT and contain some verses of Euripides.

Documents in Christian-Palestinian Aramaic, constituting the oldest extant documents in this language, include: Josh. 22:6f., 9f.; Mt. 21:30-34; Lk. 3:1, 3f.; Col. 1:16-18, 20f.; sixteen minuscule fragments of parchment of which six are palimpsests, six small fragments of papyrus, and remnants of an inscription on plaster. The first texts to have been edited are (1) a letter published by J. T. Milik in *RB*, 60 (1953), 526-39, with some corrections in *Bibl.*, 42 (1961), 21-27; (2) a passage from Acts 10:28f., 32-41, published by Perrot in *RB*, 70 (1963), 506-555, which seems to be from the 6th century.

The documents in Arabic, mainly of the first two centuries after the Hegira (i.e., *ca.* A.D. 700-800), have been edited and studied by Adolf Grohmann, *Arabic Papyri from Ḫirbet el-Mird* (Bibliothèque du Muséon, 52; 1963), with a review by B. Couroyer in *RB*, 62 (1965), 1467f.

In addition, a small notebook bought for De Langhe in 1953 by Shaourieh came from a cave in the region. M. Baillet published it (*Le Muséon*, 76 [1963], 375-401).

See also *EAEHL*, III, *s.v.* "Monasteries," 882f. (R. Cohen).

J. CARMIGNAC
tr. W. S. L. S.

**MIRE** [Heb. *ṭîṭ*–'mud, wet clay' (2 S. 22:43; Job 41:30 [MT 22]; Ps. 18:42 [MT 43]; 69:14 [MT 15]; Jer. 38:6; Mic. 7:10), *ḥōmer*–'clayish mud' (Job 30:19; Isa. 10:6), *yāwēn*–'mud' (Ps. 69:2 [MT 3]), *repeš*–'slime' (Isa. 57:20), *bōṣ*–'silt' (Jer. 38:22); Gk. *bórboros*–'mud, slime' (2 Pet. 2:22)]; **MIRY** [Heb. *yāwēn* (Ps. 40:2 [MT 3]); Aram. *ṭîn* (Dnl. 2:41, 43; cf. Heb. *ṭîṭ*)]; AV also DIRT (Ps. 18:42); NEB also MUD, MUDDY DEPTHS, etc. Heavy, deep mud; wet, spongy earth, as in a bog.

To be trampled "like the mire of the streets" (2 S. 22:43; Ps. 18:42; Isa. 10:6; Mic. 7:10) is a simile for total defeat and humiliation. The mud of the unpaved streets would have contained debris, since these areas were often used as refuse dumps (Frick, p. 85).

In Hebrew poetry the place of the dead is often pictured as a miry pit (*bôr*) or watery abyss into which one sinks as in quicksand (cf. Ps. 69:1f., 14f.). When critically ill or in great danger, the afflicted poet pictures himself as already sinking into the miry depths of the underworld. God is the only one who can draw him up and set his feet on solid ground again (cf. Ps. 40:2). Job, in his extreme distress, complains that God is killing him (i.e., has cast him into the mire, 30:19). The prophet Jeremiah was literally thrown into a miry pit (*bôr*) to die, but he was rescued before he suffocated in the mud (Jer. 38:1-13). Later he prophesied that King Zedekiah would suffer this fate (figuratively) but would have no one to rescue him (v. 22).

*See also* CLAY; PIT.

***Bibliography***.–A. A. Anderson, *Book of Psalms*, I (*NCBC*, repr. 1981), 165, 315; F. S. Frick, *The City in Ancient Israel* (1977), p. 85; L. I. J. Stadelmann, *Hebrew Conception of the World* (1970), pp. 169f.; J. A. Thompson, *Book of Jeremiah* (*NICOT*, 1980); N. J. Tromp, *Primitive Conceptions of Death and the Nether World in the OT* (1969), pp. 54-69.

N. J. O.

**MIRIAM** mir'ē-əm [Heb. *miryam*; Gk. *Mariam*, the name rendered MARY in the NT]. The name Miriam is difficult etymologically. It may mean "loved," from Egyp. *mr*; "loved of Yahweh" (*mr* + *yw*/*m*); "plump," from Heb. *mr*ʾ III; "bitter(ness)," from Heb. *mr*ʾ I/*mrh*/*mrr* (cf. Ruth 1:20); or some other option. Jerome interpreted it to mean *stella maris* ("star of the sea"); in some rabbinic texts it is related to Heb. *mrh*, as above.

**1.** Sister of Moses and Aaron, prophetess and influential member of the Exodus leadership. As the only known daughter of Amram and Jochebed, Miriam was probably the sister who stood watch over the ark of bulrushes which bore the fugitive baby Moses on the Nile (Ex. 2:4). Her quick thinking upon the discovery of the baby by Pharaoh's daughter allowed Jochebed to help raise her own son (2:7-10). After the crossing of the Red Sea where Pharaoh's pursuing troops were drowned, Miriam led the Israelite women in music and dancing and sang the "Song of the Sea" (Ex. 15:20f.), in the composition of which she may even have had a part. That she is called a "prophetess" (Heb. *nᵉḇîʾâ*) in 15:20 may indicate not only that she composed what is now part of Scripture but also that God spoke to the Israelites through Miriam as well as through her brothers (Nu. 12:2).

Miriam and Aaron came to oppose the leadership of Moses, using his probably unpopular interracial marriage to a Cushite (Nubian) woman as their occasion. In ironic punishment for their opposition to God's leadership through Moses and their antiblack racism, God turned them completely white, i.e., leprous. As a result of Moses' intercessory prayer they were healed; but Miriam was confined outside the Israelite camp for seven days (Nu. 12). No further mention is made of Miriam until Nu. 20:1, where her death and burial at Kadesh are recorded. The Law uses Miriam as a warning to the people of Israel about the importance of strict adherence to the leprosy regulations (Dt. 24:9). Miriam's part in the Exodus triumvirate leadership is remembered in Mic. 6:4.

**2.** A descendant of Ezrah (1 Ch. 4:17). The text of v. 17 is extremely difficult to reconstruct in both the MT and LXX. Miriam may be a son or daughter of Ezrah, or a grandson or granddaughter. The AV, following MT, lists neither father nor mother. The RSV and NEB, following LXX in part, take Miriam to be a daughter of Mered and Bithiah.

***Bibliography***.–O. Bardenhewer, *Der Name Maria* (1895); B. Childs, *Book of Exodus* (*OTL*, 1974), pp. 246-48; F. M. Cross, Jr. and D. N. Freedman, *JNES*, 14 (1955), 237-250; A. H. Gardiner, *JAOS*, 56 (1936), 194f.; I. Hösl, "Zur Orientalistische Namenkunde: Maria — Moses — Aaron," in H. J. Kissling and A. Schmaus, eds., *Serta Monacensia* (1952), pp. 80-85; G. Wenham, *Numbers* (*Tyndale OT Comms.*, 1981), pp. 110-14; F. Zorell, *Zeitschrift für katholische Theologie*, 30 (1906), 356-360.

D. STUART

**MIRMAH** mûr'mə [Heb. *mirmâ*]. A Benjaminite; son of Shaharaim by his wife Hodesh (1 Ch. 8:10).

**MIRROR** [Heb. *marʾâ* (Ex. 38:8), *rᵉʾî* (Job 37:18); Gk. *ésoptron* (1 Cor. 13:12; Jas. 1:23)]; AV GLASS; LOOKING GLASS. Mirrors in antiquity consisted of a metal surface, made usually of copper, silver, gold, electrum, or, especially in Palestine during the postexilic period, of bronze. Some are simply round surfaces; others have handles, often shaped in the form of a female figure; others have pedestals and can be placed on furniture. The unpolished face was usually bare. The Amarna correspondence suggests a heavy production of mirrors in Egypt, since Ikhnaton sent thirty-two mirrors of polished bronze as a gift to Burnaburiaš; the Kassite king gave in return a silver mirror.

Bronze mirror with handle in the form of a girl supporting a papyrus flower (Egypt, 18th Dynasty, 16th-14th cents. B.C.) (Royal Ontario Museum, Toronto)

In Ex. 38:8 women who rendered menial service at the tabernacle supplied bronze mirrors for a laver. Job 37:18 compares the vault of heaven to a mirror (cf. Dt. 28:23). The "glasses" of Isa. 3:23 (AV) may be articles of women's apparel (the RSV follows the suggestion of the LXX, "garments of gauze"; NEB "scarves of gauze"; *see* GAUZE, GARMENTS OF); in any event, if glass is meant, the reference is more likely to beads than to mirrors, which were made of metal. In the Apocrypha, wisdom is called an "unspotted mirror [Gk. *ésoptron*] of the power of God" (Wisd. 7:26); Sir. 12:11 warns not to trust an enemy, for his wickedness is like the rust that clings to a mirror (Heb. *rᵉʾî*) after it has been wiped.

In Jas. 1:23-25 the author compared the thoughtless hearer of the Word to a man who looks in a mirror and immediately forgets what he has seen, making no personal improvement. The use of the word in 1 Cor. 13:12 in connection with Gk. *aínigma* (lit. "a riddle") is more difficult. Most versions and commentaries suggest that Paul saw a deficiency in the reflecting quality of the mirror, but a number of ancient writers, including Plato (*Timaeus* 71b, 72c), illustrated spiritual purity and mental clarity by referring to mirrors (some of the mirrors found by archeologists still possess a remarkable luster). Nor was it Paul's habit to imply that he had received an indistinct impression of God's revelation in Christ (cf. Rom. 8:38f.). More probably he contrasted the personal encounter in the beatific vision ("face to face") with the reflected image received in the present time. The reflection need not be indistinct to be less satisfactory than the possession of the thing reflected. The possibility that very early a scribe who misunderstood Paul's meaning added *en ainígmati* as a gloss cannot be dismissed. 2 Cor. 3:18, which uses *katoptrízō* to describe looking in a mirror (see Bauer, rev., p. 424), probably refers to a similar secondhand view of the glory of the Lord.

***Bibliography.***–K. Galling, *Biblisches Reallexikon* (1937), cols. 493f.; A. G. Barrois, *Manuel d'archéologie biblique*, I (1939), 393f.; N. Hugedé, *La Métaphore du miroir dans les Epîtres de Saint Paul aux Corinthiens* (1957); H. Conzelmann, *I Corinthians* (Eng. tr., *Hermeneia*, 1975), pp. 226-29; *TDNT*, I, *s.v.* αἴνιγμα (Kittel).

F. W. DANKER

**MIRTH** [Heb. *śimḥâ* (Gen. 31:27; Ps. 137:3; Eccl. 7:4), *māśôś* (Isa. 24:8; Hos. 2:11 [MT 13]), *śāśôn* (Jer. 7:34; 16:9; 25:10; 33:11), (vb.) *śûś* (Ezk. 21:10 [MT 15])]; AV also JOY; NEB also SONGS, MERRY, JOY, etc. All the terms rendered by "mirth" denote both the emotion of joy and its outward expression in singing and merrymaking.

From earliest times the Israelites observed certain FEASTS to celebrate Yahweh's goodness to them. They were constantly tempted, however, to attribute to Baal the fruitfulness of the land and to turn their harvest festivals into fertility rites. Because of Israel's unfaithfulness Hosea prophesied that Yahweh would end all such festivities by withdrawing His blessing on the land (Hos. 2:8-13). Similarly, Isaiah and Jeremiah spoke of the lack of festivals (vintage festivals, Isa. 24:4-13; wedding feasts, Jer. 7:34; 16:9; 25:10) as a picture of the total devastation of the land. Jeremiah was commanded to refrain from marriage and all festive meals as a sign that Yahweh had withdrawn His *šālôm* from the land (16:1-9); he prophesied, however, of a time when there would again be occasion for rejoicing (33:11). Ps. 137 expresses the psalmist's inability to be joyful because of the destruction of Jerusalem.

*See* JOY I-II; *see also* MERRY.

N. J. O.

**MISAEL** mis'ə-el (AV, NEB, 1 Esd. 9:44; AV Song Three 66; 1 Macc. 2:59). *See* MISHAEL.

**MISCARRIAGE** [Heb. *yāṣᵉʾû yᵉlāḏeyhā*–'her children came out'] (Ex. 21:22); AV "her fruit depart"; [piel fem. part. of Heb. *šāḵal*] (2 K. 2:21); AV "barren land"; **MISCARRY** [piel of Heb. *šāḵal*] (Gen. 31:38); AV "cast (their) young"; [hiphil part. of Heb. *šāḵal*] (Hos. 9:14). The premature ejection of a fetus was an especially disturbing event to ancient peoples, and laws were made to punish those who caused miscarriages. Both the Babylonian and Hittite laws imposed fines on one who caused a miscarriage resulting in the fetus's death. For the Babylonians the amount of the fine depended on the status (class) of the mother (Code of Hammurabi, §§ 209-214; see *ANET*, p. 175; G. R. Driver and J. C. Miles, *Babylonian Laws*, I [1952], 413-16), while the Hittites added distinctions based on the age of the fetus (see E. Neufeld, *Hittite Laws* [1951], p. 5). The Middle Assyrian laws, however, appear to stipulate a life-for-life retribution or *talion* (Middle Assyrian Laws, §§ 21, 50-53; see G. Cardascia, *Les lois Assyriennes* [1969], pp. 136-38, 239-247; *ANET*, pp. 181, 184f.), although some scholars (e.g., Jackson) interpret the Assyrian laws as calling for substitution rather than *talion*.

The interpretation of Ex. 21:22f. is debated. The meaning and referent of Heb. *ʾāsôn* ("harm") are unclear. According to BDB (p. 62) it means "mischief, evil, harm," but *CHAL* (p. 23) defines it as "mortal accident" (cf. Childs, pp. 471f.; Tg. Onk. translates it *môṯāʾ*, "death"). The only other OT occurrences of *ʾāsôn* (Gen. 42:4; 44:29) seem to refer to mortal harm (see JB), though other interpretations cannot be ruled out (cf. LXX *malakía*, "sickness," in Gen. 42:4; 44:29; and *mḗ exeikonízō*, "not fully shaped," in Ex. 21:22). The referent of *ʾāsôn* could be the woman (so JB, NEB, Moff., Hyatt), the fetus (Jackson; cf. Kline), or perhaps both (as implied in the ambiguous translations of RSV, NIV, NAB, etc.; see Kline, Cassuto). See the comms., especially Childs, Cassuto, and KD.

In Gen. 31:38 Jacob indicates his good work to Laban by pointing out the lack of miscarriages among the animals under his care. In 2 K. 2:21 Elisha's first miracle is the healing of some poisonous water so that "neither death nor miscarriage" results. In Hos. 9:14 the prophet asks God to curse the fertility worshipers with lack of fertility.

***Bibliography.***–Comms. on Exodus by U. Cassuto (Eng. tr. 1967); B. Childs (*OTL*, 1974); J. Hyatt (*NCBC*, repr. 1980); articles by B. Jackson, *VT*, 23 (1973), 273-304; M. G. Kline, *JETS*, 20 (1977), 193-201.

G. A. L.

**MISCHIEF** [Heb. *rāʿâ*–'evil,' 'misery' (Jgs. 15:3; 1 K. 11:25; Ps. 28:3; 52:1 [MT 3]), hiphil part. of *rāʿâ*–'do evil' ("bent on mischief," Dnl. 11:27), *ʿāmāl*–'trouble,' 'labor, toil' (Job 15:35; Ps. 7:14, 16 [MT 15,17]; 10:7; 94:20; 140:9; Prov. 24:2; Isa. 59:4), *ʾāwen*–'trouble,' 'sorrow,' 'wickedness' (Ps. 36:3f. [MT 4f.]; 41:6 [MT 7]; 55:10 [MT 11]), *mᵉzimmâ*–'[evil] plot' (Ps. 21:11 [MT 12])]; AV also INIQUITY, DISPLEASURE; NEB also HARM, MALICE, BAD NEWS, WICKEDNESS, CONSPIRACY; **MISCHIEF-MAKER** [Heb. *baʿal mᵉzimmôṯ*– 'master of [evil] plots' (Prov. 24:8); Gk. *allotriepískopos* (1 Pet. 4:15)]; AV MISCHIEVOUS PERSON, BUSYBODY IN OTHER MEN'S MATTERS; NEB INTRIGUE, INFRINGING THE RIGHTS OF OTHERS; **MISCHIEVOUS** [Heb. *ʾāwen*] (Prov. 17:4); AV NAUGHTY; NEB SLANDER.

"Mischief" has serious connotations in the Bible. It translates Hebrew terms that often refer to evil or wickedness, and it is usually associated with evildoers. Thus "mischief" parallels "evil" (*ʾāwen*, Job 15:35; Ps. 7:14; *rāʿâ*, 21:11; hiphil of *rāʿâ*, Prov. 24:8), "violence" (Ps. 7:16; Prov. 24:2), "iniquity" (*ʾāwen*, Ps. 10:7; Isa. 59:4), "deceit" (Job 15:35; Ps. 36:3), "trouble" (*ʿāmāl*, Ps. 55:10); note the interchange among the Hebrew terms.

Samson's mischief was the burning of Philistine fields and orchards (Jgs. 15:3-5). Other mischievous acts include slander (Ps. 10:7; cf. 41:6; 52:1-4; 140:9-11; Prov. 17:4), and fighting or war (1 K. 11:25; Ps. 21:11f.; 55:9-11; Prov. 24:2). Wicked rulers, those who legislate "mischief," cannot be allied with God (Ps. 94:20; cf. Isa 59:4; Dnl. 11:27).

The meaning of *allotriepískopos* (lit. "those who watch over another's things") in 1 Pet. 4:15 is uncertain (Bauer, rev., p. 10). Some scholars argue that it must refer to a criminal offense, since the other offenses are criminal (so Beyer, *TDNT,* II, 62f.), while others disagree (e.g., according to E. G. Selwyn, *First Epistle of St. Peter* [2nd ed. repr. 1981], p. 225, the repetition and position of *hōs* ["as"] indicate that the author is moving from a legal category to a social one; but cf. *TDNT,* II, 62). J. H. Elliott rightly pointed out that the context must determine the meaning. He concluded that *allotriepískopos* means "a type of person . . . who transgresses the boundaries of the household of God, . . . one who meddles or interferes in the affairs of others to whom he does not belong" (*Home for the Homeless* [1981], p. 141). G. A. L.

**MISGAB** mis'gab. The AV and NEB translation of Heb. *hammiśgāḇ* (lit. "the high spot," "the refuge"; Gk. A *tó krataíōma,* B *Amath*) in Jer. 48:1. No such place name has been found in Moab, and the RSV may be correct in rendering it "the fortress." *See* FORTIFICATION I.B; IV.A.

**MISHAEL** mish'ə-el [Heb. *mîšā'ēl*–'who is what God is?'(?); Gk. Apoc. *Misaēl*]; AV, NEB, also MISAEL.

**1.** A Levite in the line of Kohath; son of Uzziel and cousin of Aaron (Ex. 6:22). He and his brother Elzaphan carried out Moses' order to remove from the camp the bodies of Nadab and Abihu (Lev. 10:4f.).

**2.** One who stood beside Ezra at the public reading of the Law (Neh. 8:4; 1 Esd. 9:44).

**3.** The Hebrew name of one of Daniel's three companions (Dnl. 1:6f., 11, 19; 2:17; Song Three 66; 1 Macc. 2:59). The Babylonians named him MESHACH.

**MISHAL** mī'shəl mish'al [Heb. *miš'āl* (Josh. 19:26; 21:30)]; AV also MISHAEL; **MASHAL** mā'shal [Heb. *māšāl* (1 Ch. 6:74 [MT 59])]. A Gershonite Levitical town in the territory of Asher (Josh. 21:30). It is thirty-ninth in a list of towns conquered by Thutmose III; it also appears in an Execration Text (19th-18th cents. B.C.) and in a papyrus mentioning the *maryannu* (military élite); see *LBHG,* rev., pp. 144, 165. The exact location is unknown, although Aharoni (*LBHG,* rev., p. 439) suggests Tell Keisân, which others (e.g., *WHAB*) identify with ACHSHAPH.

D. B. PECOTA

**MISHAM** mī'sham [Heb. *miš'ām*]. A Benjaminite; second son of Elpaal who built Ono and Lod (1 Ch. 8:12).

**MISHEAL** mish'i-əl (Josh. 19:26, AV). *See* MISHAL.

**MISHMA** mish'mə [Heb. *mišmā'*].

**1.** A son of Ishmael and founder of an Arabian tribe (Gen. 25:14; 1 Ch. 1:30).

**2.** A Simeonite, son of Mibsam and father of Hammuel (1 Ch. 4:25f.). The fact that the names Mibsam and Mishma appear together in this list as well as the Ishmaelite genealogies of Gen. 25:14 and 1 Ch. 1:30 has led to speculation that these may have been two Arabian tribes that later became affiliated with the Simeonites.

**MISHMANNAH** mish-man'ə [Heb. *mišmannâ*]. A famous Gadite warrior who joined David at Ziklag and became an officer in his army (1 Ch. 12:10 [MT 11]; cf. v. 14 [MT 15]).

**MISHNAH** mish'nə [Heb. *mišnâ*–'repetition']. The body of Jewish oral law that was written down by the end of the 2nd cent. A.D. *See* TALMUD.

**MISHNEH** mish'nə. The district of Jerusalem in which the prophetess Huldah lived was called Heb. *mišneh* (2 K. 22:14; 2 Ch. 34:22; Zeph. 1:10; AV "college," "second"; RSV, NEB, "second quarter"). *See* SECOND QUARTER.

**MISHRAITES** mish'rə-īts [Heb. *mišrā'î*]. One of the families of Kiriath-jearim, from whom came the Zorathites and the Eshtaolites (1 Ch. 2:53).

**MISMATED** [Gk. part. of *heterozygéō*–'draw unequally,' 'be unequally yoked'] (2 Cor. 6:14); AV UNEQUALLY YOKED; NEB UNITE. *See* YOKE.

**MISPAR** mis'pär [Heb. *mispār*; Gk. Apoc. *Aspharasos*]; AV MIZPAR, Apoc. ASPHARASUS; NEB Apoc. ASPHARASUS. One of those who returned from the Exile with Zerubbabel (Ezr. 2:2; 1 Esd. 5:8 [RSV mg. "Aspharasus"]). In the par. Neh. 7:7 the name is given in the feminine, "Mispereth."

**MISPERETH** mis'pə-reth [Heb. *mispereṯ*] (Neh. 7:7). *See* MISPAR.

**MISREPHOTH-MAIM** miz'rə-fōth mā'əm [Heb. *miśrᵉpôṯ mayim* < *śārap*–'burn'; perhaps 'lime burning at the water']. A place on the Phoenician coast 48 km. (30 mi.) S of Sidon and 19 km. (12 mi.) N of Acco. It has been identified by some with Khirbet el-Musheirefeh (*WHAB; GAB*) and with 'Ain Mesherfi by others. Nearby warm springs favor the latter identification. With a surprise attack Joshua routed the forces commanded by Jabin king of Hazor near the waters of Merom. The defeated armies of Jabin and his allies fled to Great Sidon, Misrephoth-maim, and the Valley of Mizpeh, where Joshua pursued and annihilated them (Josh. 11:8). The inhabitants of the hill country extending from Lebanon to Misrephoth-maim are called Sidonians in 13:6, indicating that the Sidonians controlled that area. God promised this territory to Israel and promised to expel the native population. Joshua was to include it in the land allotted to the Israelites.

D. H. MADVIG

**MISSION.** A noun derived from Lat. *mittō* ("send"), denoting a task that a person or group has been assigned (usually by God or God's representatives) and sent out to perform. In the RSV OT the term occurs only in 1 S. 15:18, 20 as a translation of Heb. *dereḵ* (lit. "way"; AV "way," "journey"; NEB paraphrases). Here it refers to King Saul's God-given assignment to destroy the Amalekites.

In the NT the RSV uses "mission" more specifically with reference to the ministry of the GOSPEL, both in word and in deed. In Acts 12:25 "mission" translates Gk. *diakonía* (lit. "service, ministry"; AV "ministry"; NEB "task"), referring to the famine-relief expedition upon which the church in Antioch sent Barnabas and Saul (Paul) (cf. 11:29; RSV "relief"). In Gal. 2:8 the RSV appropriately uses "mission" to render Gk. *apostolḗ* (lit. "apostleship" [so AV]; NEB "apostle"; cf. *apostéllō,* "send out"), which here refers to Peter's commission to PREACH the gospel to the Jews. In 2 Cor. 11:12 the RSV supplies "mission" and the NEB supplies "apostleship" in rendering the obscure Greek phrase *en hǭ kauchṓntai* (lit. "in which they boast"; cf. AV "wherein they glory"). The passage is difficult to interpret, since the exact situation that Paul faced in Corinth is not known today, but Paul appears to be referring to the claims to apostleship made by some who opposed him (cf. v. 13; see comms.).

For discussions of missions in NT times, *see* APOSTLE; APOSTOLIC AGE; PROSELYTE; SEND. N. J. O.

**MIST** [Heb. *'ēḏ* (Gen. 2:6; Job 36:27), pl. of *nāśî'* (Jer. 10:13; 51:16), *'ānān* (Isa. 44:22; Hos. 13:3), *śeḵwî* (Job 38:36); Gk. *achlýs* (Acts 13:11), *atmís* (Jas. 4:14), *homíchlē* (2 Pet. 2:17)]; AV also VAPOUR(S), CLOUD, "heart" (Job 38:36); NEB also FLOOD (Gen. 2:6), "secrecy" (Job 38:36). Water vapor that causes the air to be only partially transparent, differing from a CLOUD in that it is near the ground.

Hebrew *'ēḏ* is an obscure term occurring only in Gen. 2:6 and Job 36:27. In Gen. 2:6 it seems to refer to water that came from below the earth and preceded the first stages of plant life (cf. v. 5). The RSV renders it "mist," but other contemporary versions have translated it "flood" (NEB, JB; cf. also RSV mg.) or "stream(s)" (NIV, NAB). The translation "flood" is supported by a possible derivation from Akk. *edû*, "high flooding of a river" (see *CAD*, IV, 35f.; Speiser; Kidner; cf. also Gen. 1:2), although Albright proposed an alternative derivation from Akk. *id*, "fresh-water stream" (the river-god Id was one of the chief deities of the Middle Euphrates region). The context suggests that the earth was uninhabitable and unproductive in its watery state prior to the special creative care given to it by Yahweh. The term may also denote subterranean waters in Job 36:27 (see Pope, p. 273; most versions, however, use "mist"), a passage that describes Yahweh's control over the watering sources of the universe (cf. vv. 28-33).

The meaning of *śeḵwî* in Job 38:36 is even more difficult (as is *ṭuḥôṯ* [RSV "clouds"], the parallel term in the preceding line), and numerous conjectures have been proposed (cf. AV, NEB). Several commentators have followed Jewish tradition in rendering *śeḵwî* "cock" (see KoB, p. 921; KD *in loc.*; cf. Tg.; Vulg.); others have connected it with the Coptic name of the planet Mercury (see Pope, p. 302). The RSV apparently understands the term as a passive noun derived from the root *śkh*, "look at" (thus "something seen," "celestial phenomenon"; see comms.). Although the translation "mist" lacks strong philological support, it does fit well with the context.

Yahweh's sovereignty over meteorological forces is also described in Jer. 10:13; 51:16: it is He (and not the other gods) who causes the "mist" (*n^eśî'îm*; cf. RSV "clouds" in Ps. 135:7; Prov. 25:14) to rise from the earth and releases the rain.

All other RSV uses of "mist" are figurative. The rapid evaporation of mist in the sunshine is used as a simile for the removal of sins (Isa. 44:22), the swiftness of judgment (Hos. 13:3), and the transitoriness of life (Jas. 4:14; cf. Wisd. 2:4). Unlike rainfall, mist lacks real substance and provides no refreshment; thus 2 Pet. 2:17 uses the metaphor of "mists driven by a storm" to describe false teachers. Gk. *achlýs* is a medical term denoting an inflammation that causes a clouding of the eyes (Acts 13:11).

*Bibliography.*–W. F. Albright, *JBL*, 58 (1939), 102f. n. 25; *CAD*, IV, *s.v.* "edû"; D. Kidner, *Tyndale Bulletin*, 17 (1966), 109-114; M. Pope, *Job* (*AB*, 3rd ed. 1973); E. Speiser, *BASOR*, 140 (Dec. 1955), 9-11.
D. H. ENGELHARD N. J. O.

**MISTRESS** [Heb. *g^eḇîrâ* or *g^eḇereṯ* < *gāḇar*–'excel,' 'be strong' (Gen. 16:4, 8f.; 2 K. 5:3; Ps. 123:2; Prov. 30:23; Isa. 24:2; 47:5, 7), *ba'^alâ* < *ba'al*–'lord, master, owner' (1 K. 17:17), *huṣṣaḇ* (Nah. 2:7 [MT 8])]; AV also LADY (Isa. 47:5, 7), HUZZAB (Nah. 2:7); NEB also QUEEN (Isa. 47:5, 7), "train of captives" (Nah. 2:7). A term usually referring to a noblewoman, especially as she relates to her (female) servant. For example, Sarah was Hagar's mistress (Gen. 16), and the wife of the Syrian commander Naaman was mistress of an Israelite maid (2 K. 5:1-3). The context of Isa. 47:5, 7 seems to point to a more exalted personage (see NEB), while 1 K. 17:17 seems to refer only to a woman who owns a house (see NIV).

The psalmist parallels the servant-master and maid-mistress relationships with the believer's relationship to God (Ps. 123:2f.). Similar parallels are used in Isa. 24:2 to express the totality of Yahweh's judgment.

Scholars disagree about the interpretation of Prov. 30:21-23, which lists several reversals of fortune, including a "maid" who becomes a "mistress." According to some (e.g., KD) these reversals cause societal upheaval, but others (e.g., W. McKane, *Proverbs* [*OTL*, 1970], pp. 659f.) interpret these as satirical examples of people who become insufferable when their situations change radically for the better.

The difficult text of Nah. 2:7 (MT 8) has given rise to a number of interpretations. The crux of the problem is the meaning of *huṣṣaḇ*. The AV transliterates as a proper name, Huzzab, who was supposedly a Babylonian queen. But no such queen is known, and the form of the name is unparalleled. KD also tried to make sense of the MT, analyzing *huṣṣaḇ* as the hophal of *nāṣaḇ*, hence "it is determined, established (by God)" (see NASB), but this does not fit the context well. The RSV rendering is conjecture based on the context; "mistress" probably refers to (a statue of) Ishtar, the Assyrian war-goddess who was of primary importance in Nineveh. (It was common ancient Near Eastern practice to carry off the idols of a captured city.) For a convenient summary of various emendations, some of which result in interpretations similar to the RSV, see K. Cathcart, *Nahum in the Light of Northwest Semitic* (1973), pp. 96-98; cf. *BHS*. G. A. L.

**MITANNI** mə-tä'nē. A political term referring to a state or empire in northwest Mesopotamia that played an important role in the history of the area from a little before 1500 to shortly after 1340 B.C. The population of Mitanni was predominantly Hurrian, and the state's establishment and duration are intimately connected with the penetration of the Hurrians into northwest Mesopotamia and Syria in ever-increasing numbers during the 16th cent. B.C. The scarce written evidence from the area for the 17th and 16th cents. tells the names of several of its early kings but almost nothing else about the foundation and development of the state.

Surprisingly, none of the known kings of Mitanni bears a Hurrian name. On the contrary, their names are generally explained as Indo-Aryan, especially since one of their last kings invoked Indo-Aryan gods in a treaty with the

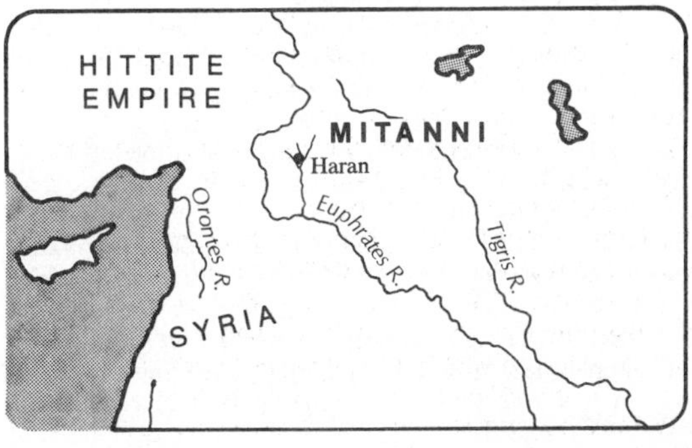

Hittites. Consequently, the formation of Mitanni is usually linked with the arrival of the Indo-Aryans in the Near East. They formed a very small ruling aristocracy at the head of the Mitannian state, and their presence has been detected in numerous other sites that fell under Hurrian influence after 1500. Their contribution to the Mitannian civilization has at times been exaggerated, however; their influence was mainly political. It is quite improper to speak of a Hurro-Indo-Aryan "symbiosis," as has sometimes been done.

Although it appears unlikely that the Indo-Aryans introduced the horse and chariot to the ancient world, they probably developed them as weapons of war and pioneered in the breeding of horses. The Mitanni-Hurrians and their Indo-Aryan aristocracy also seem to have introduced the composite bow and the defense for it, a type of scaled armor used on men, horses, and chariots, the Hurrian name (*šaryani*) of which appears in Egyptian, Akkadian, Hittite, Ugaritic, and Hebrew (*širyôn*; see E. A. Speiser, *JAOS*, 70 [1950], 47-49). These new weapons revolutionized warfare and became decisive in battle beginning in the 15th century.

At the height of its power, under Saustatar in the latter half of the 15th cent., Mitanni controlled territory from the Mediterranean Sea in the west to beyond the Tigris River in the east. In the north it controlled Kizzuwatna (modern Cilicia in southeast Asia Minor), and states as far south as Hamath on the middle Orontes River in southern Syria were tributary to it. Its hegemony, however, was brief. Its Syrian territories fell to the early pharaohs of the Egyptian 18th Dynasty in the last decades of the 15th cent., and the Hittites under Šuppiluliuma finally destroyed it shortly after 1350 and made it a vassal state.

The term Mitanni does not appear in the OT, but the flood of Hurrians (with their Indo-Aryan ruling aristocracy) that created Mitanni also widely influenced the Near East. By the 14th cent. their presence was attested in Palestine itself, where, however, they represented nothing more than a ruling class imposed in feudal style on the city-state system. Probably the OT ethnic term "Horite" was related to this presence, although that relationship is obscure (*see* HORITES).

The patriarchal homeland, the region of Haran, is situated in the heart of what was to become the state of Mitanni proper, an area where Hurrian presence is attested from late Akkadian times (*ca.* 2250 B.C.). It is thus not surprising that numerous parallels have been suggested between Hurrian customs, particularly family law, and some of the puzzling aspects of the patriarchal narratives (*see* NUZI). F. W. BUSH

**MITE.** The smallest copper or bronze coin current among the Jews of Jesus' time (Gk. *leptón*; AV Mk. 12:42; Lk. 12:59; 21:2). *See* MONEY.

**MITHKAH** mith'kə [Heb. *miṯqâ*]; AV, NEB, MITHCAH. An Israelite encampment during the wilderness wanderings, between Terah and Hashmonah (Nu. 33:28f.). The location is unknown. *See* WANDERINGS OF ISRAEL.

**MITHNITE** mith'nīt [Heb. *miṯnî*]. Designation of Joshaphat, one of David's officers (1 Ch. 11:43).

**MITHRADATES** mith-rə-dā'tēz (1 Esd. 2:11, 16, NEB). *See* MITHREDATH.

**MITHREDATH** mith'rə-dath [Heb. *miṯrᵉdāṯ* < Pers. 'gift of Mithra'] (Ezr. 1:8; 4:7); **MITHRIDATES** mith-rə-dā'tēz [Gk. A *Mithradatēs*, B *Mithridatēs*] (1 Esd. 2:11, 16); NEB MITHRADATES.

**1.** The treasurer of Cyrus king of Persia who delivered to Sheshbazzar the temple vessels that were to be brought back to Jerusalem by the returning exiles (Ezr. 1:8; 1 Esd. 2:11).

**2.** An official, probably the Persian consul at Samaria, who was among those who wrote a letter to Artaxerxes I persuading him to order a cessation of the rebuilding of Jerusalem (Ezr. 4:7; 1 Esd. 2:16).

**MITRE.** *See* TURBAN.

**MITYLENE** mit-ə-lē'nē [Gk. *Mitylēnē*] (Acts 20:14). A town on the island of Lesbos, located off the northwest coast of Asia Minor about 100 km. (60 mi.) S of Troy. At the end of his third missionary journey, Paul stopped briefly at Mitylene as he traveled from Philippi down the western side of Asia Minor to Jerusalem.

Aeolians settled Mitylene before 1000 B.C.; they colonized a small nearby island and in time spread to Lesbos proper. Eventually they linked the two parts of their city by bridges. Mitylene's position near the old trade route between the Hellespont and ports south and east made it an important center. In the 7th cent. B.C. its commercial power and cultural development were considerable.

Mitylene became a member of the Athenian Empire. For revolting against Athens in 428, it lost its fleet and fortifications and was brought to the verge of destruction. Membership in the Second Athenian Confederacy in 377 was amicable, however. Under Rome's rule the island became a favorite resort for Roman aristocrats. From the middle of the 1st cent. B.C., Mitylene was a free city within the province of Asia. An earthquake destroyed the city of NT times in A.D. 151. H. F. VOS

**MIXED MULTITUDE; FOREIGN FOLK.** The RSV uses various expressions to translate Heb. *ʿēreḇ* ("mixture," "mixed company"). The "mixed multitude" (*ʿēreḇ raḇ*, Ex. 12:38; NEB "large company of every kind") that left Egypt with the Hebrews was probably a conglomeration of slaves from a variety of tribal backgrounds (cf. Nu. 11:4; *see* RABBLE; see also *BHI*, pp. 131-37). After the Exile, INTERMARRIAGE with "those of foreign descent" was viewed as a threat to the Jewish community (Neh. 13:3; AV "mixed multitude"; NEB "all who were of mixed blood"). *See also* FOREIGNER.

Sometimes *ʿēreḇ* refers to foreign populations living in other countries: Egypt (Jer. 25:20; RSV "foreign folk"; AV "mingled people"; NEB "rabble"), Arabia (25:24; RSV "mixed tribes"; AV "mingled people"; NEB omits, apparently assuming a dittography with *ʿᵃrāḇ*, "Arabia"), and Babylon (50:37; RSV "foreign troops"; AV "mingled people"; NEB "rabble").

Some scholars have emended *ʿēreḇ* to *ʿᵃrāḇ* in Ex. 12:38; Neh. 13:3; Jer. 25:20 (cf. KoB, p. 733). N. J. O.

**MIZAR** mi'zar, **MOUNT** [Heb. *har miṣʿār*; Gk. *óros mikrós*–'little mountain']; AV, NEB, HILL (OF) MIZAR. The name of a mountain found only in Ps. 42:6 (MT 7), apparently in the region of Mt. Hermon and the Jordan River: "I remember thee from the land of Jordan and of Hermon, from Mount Mizar." *Miṣʿār*, however, may be taken as an adjective meaning "little," and the phrase may be understood as meaning "from the little (or humble) mountain" — i.e., the little mountain of Zion — which is contrasted with the lofty Mt. Hermon. Some scholars have thought that the *m* in *mēhar* may have arisen from dittography and have read instead, "From the land of Jordan, and the Hermons, O thou little mountain (of Zion)." Modern scholars have been unable to identify the site, although the name may be an allusion to *za'ūrā* or Khirbet Mazârā near the source of the Jordan (cf. *HGHL,* p. 476 n. 1).

W. W. BUEHLER

**MIZPAH** miz'pä; **MIZPEH** miz'pə. The Hebrew word in both these forms (fem. and masc., respectively) means "lookout" or "watch tower" and is a place name or place-name element. It is appropriate for towns occupying high, commanding positions.

**1.** Mizpah in northern Gilead [Heb. *hammiṣpâ* (Gen. 31:49; Jgs. 10:17; 11:11, 34), *miṣpâ* (Hos. 5:1); Gk. *Massēpha,* etc.]; AV Apoc. Maspha. A city of Gilead mentioned in Jgs. 10–11 in connection with Jephthah's conflict with the Ammonites. At Mizpah, Jephthah's residence (11:34), the Israelites assembled for battle against the Ammonites encamped in Gilead. Verse 11 implies that the town served as a cult center in Transjordan as its namesake did in Benjamin (1 S. 7:5). The description of the covenant between Jacob and Laban in Mt. Gilead intimates the sanctity of this site (Gen. 31:44-50). Hosea may have intended this Mizpah (5:1), and 1 Macc. 5:35 (AV) mentions it (the AV Maspha has no textual support; it may have been interpolated on the basis of 3:46; cf. J. Goldstein, *I Maccabees* [*AB,* 1976], p. 302).

The above references do not specifically indicate the site's location. Its identification depends upon: (1) the location of the original Gilead, N of the Jabbok near 'Ajlûn, or S in the Jebel Jel'ad (if the latter suggestion is correct, then Mizpah was located either near Mt. Gilead [Gen. 31:23], or on the mountain opposite Gilead [Gen. 31:25; Jgs. 10:17]); (2) the relationship among the names Mizpah, Mizpah of Gilead, RAMATH-MIZPEH, and RAMOTH-GILEAD.

Jacob's crossing the Jabbok only after making his covenant with Laban (Gen. 32:23) favors the northern location. Though some scholars look for Mizpah S of the Jabbok, Gen. 31 and the allusion in 1 Macc. 5:35 (AV; NEB mg. Maapha) seem to demand that it be to the north. Jacob probably entered Transjordan by the principal route from Mesopotamia to Tadmor and Damascus, whence he continued on the "King's Highway." The events pertaining to Jephthah do not require that Mizpah should be S of the Jabbok.

It would not be surprising if the Ammonites had crossed the Jabbok northward. Furthermore, Jephthah did not cross the Ammonite boundary from Mizpah but from Mizpah of Gilead (Jgs. 11:29), which is probably to be located in southern Gilead (see **2** below).

**2.** Mizpah (AV, NEB, Mizpeh) of Gilead [Heb. *miṣpēh gil'āḏ*]. In Jgs. 11:29 Jephthah is said to have passed Mizpah-gilead on his way to battle with the Ammonites. This place is usually identified with the Mizpah discussed above, whose location seems almost certainly to be in northern Gilead. The LXX distinguishes this present site from the other by calling it *skopián Galaad,* "the lookout point in Gilead" (cf. Isa. 21:8; 2 Ch. 20:24). Jephthah passed through Gilead and Manasseh, but these are only general indications. Perhaps Jgs. 11:33, "And he smote them from Aroer to the neighborhood of Minnith, twenty cities, and as far as Abel-keramim," provides a more adequate clue to the southern orientation of the passage as a whole. The generally accepted identifications for these latter places point to the southern region of Gilead, between Rabbath-ammon and Heshbon. Thus it is difficult to equate Mizpah-gilead with Mizpah, which was most likely in the north. According to Josh. 13:26 it is possible to identify it with Ramath-mizpeh, listed as a town in the inheritance of Gad between Heshbon and Betonim.

**3.** In Benjamin [Heb. *hammiṣpâ*; Gk. *Massēpha, Maspha, Masphe,* or (due to Heb. directive suffix) *Massēphath,* and once translated *skopiá* (1 K. 15:22)]. A city in the northern part of the Benjaminite territory. It appears in the list of Benjamin's towns (Josh. 18:26), but the order is not sufficiently clear to determine its location.

Mizpah is mentioned in the account of the concubine who was raped and murdered at Gibeah (Jgs. 20–21). The entire Israelite congregation gathered at Mizpah before opening hostilities against Benjamin; it was also important as a place of sacred assemblies during the judgeship of Samuel (1 S. 7:5-12). The town was one of his main centers of activity (vv. 16f.). With the division of the monarchy Mizpah began to assume special importance as a border fortress between Judah and Israel. After Abijah's occupation of Mt. Ephraim and the collapse of Jeroboam's dynasty, Baasha came to the throne and pushed his boundary with Judah S to Ramah, thus posing a threat to Jerusalem's communication with the coastal plain via the Beth-horon road. Asa called on the Arameans from the north; when this diversion caused Baasha's withdrawal, the Judeans dismantled the fortification at Ramah and moved the border back northward as far as Mizpah and Geba (1 K. 15:17-22; 2 Ch. 16:1-6).

Toward the end of the preexilic period Mizpah assumed special importance as the residence of Gedaliah, whom the Babylonians appointed governor over Judea after the destruction of Jerusalem (2 K. 25:22-25; Jer. 40–41). During the postexilic period Mizpah became a district capital in the province of Jehud (Neh. 3:15). The town reappears as an assembly point during the intertestamental period; Judas Maccabeus gathered his forces at Mizpah "opposite Jerusalem" in preparation for a battle with Gorgias (1 Macc. 3:46). Neither Josephus nor Eusebius provided any precise details about its location.

The principal suggestions for the site of Mizpah are Nebī Ṣamwîl and Tell en-Naṣbeh. The main passages that must be considered in making any identification are 1 K. 15:22, Asa's fortification of Mizpah; Jer. 40–41, Ishmael's murder at Mizpah of pilgrims from Shechem, Shiloh, and Samaria who were going to Jerusalem; and 1 Macc. 3:46.

Those who equate Mizpah with Nebī Ṣamwîl argue that the expression "opposite Jerusalem" (1 Macc. 3:46) suits this site and that the name Mizpah is appropriate for the highest topographical point in the region. In the opinion of these scholars, Asa was not extending the border of his territory but was making a purely defensive measure along the line Nebī Ṣamwîl — Tell el-Fûl (Gibeah of Saul). To maintain this suggestion it is necessary to emend Geba to Gibeah.

The position of Mizpah in the war between Asa and Baasha, its importance as an urban center in all periods, and archeological excavations there favor the identification with Tell en-Naṣbeh. Nebī Ṣamwîl is not of such great strategic importance and hardly represents a town that enjoyed such administrative significance. No ancient source requires an association with Nebī Ṣamwîl, not even 1 Macc. 3:46. That Ishmael, while fleeing to Ammon, met Jochanan beside Gibeon (Jer. 41:12) tells nothing about the location of Mizpah, since neither the direction from which Jochanan and his men came nor the route taken by Ishmael is known. Neither can anything be inferred concerning the return of the prophet Jeremiah from Ramah to Gedaliah (40:5f.). On the other hand, 41:5 suggests the equation with Tell en-Naṣbeh. The men who came from the land of Samaria probably were on their way to the ruins in Jerusalem when Ishmael came forth to meet them from Mizpah, which was on their route, in order to lure them into the town. Ishmael's action would have been unnecessary if these men had intended to go to the temple at Mizpah (off the main road, i.e., at Nebī Ṣamwîl).

Tell en-Naṣbeh is in the northern part of the Benjaminite

City gate at Tell en-Naṣbeh (Mizpah?) (Iron Age) (Israel Department of Antiquities and Museums)

territory near the ascent to the hill country around Bethel and beside the main road that follows the watershed from north to south. It commands the whole district, especially the narrow pass through Wâdī Jilyân. According to the excavations, the settlement was founded at the beginning of the Iron Age (there had also been an Early Bronze settlement) and was occupied until the Hellenistic period. Signs of destruction by the Chaldeans in 587 B.C., so typical of Judean sites further south, are remarkably absent here. The archeological finds, especially the solid fortification wall from the monarchial period and its geographical position, indicate that a very important urban center had been located on this site. Tell en-Naṣbeh is by far the most likely candidate for the identification of Mizpah.

Placing Mizpah at this site helps to elucidate the account of the war between Asa and Baasha. Only this identification and that of Geba with Jebaʿ permit discerning how Asa extended the northern boundary of Judah to a reasonable and safe distance from Jerusalem without going too far, as his father had done (thus provoking the ire of Baasha).

***Bibliography.***–C. C. McCown and J. C. Wampler, *Excavations at Tell En-Nasbeh* (2 vols., 1947); G. E. Wright, *BA,* 10 (1947), 66-77; *EAEHL,* III, *s.v.* "Naṣbeh, Tell en-" (M. Broshi); *LBHG.*

**4.** In Judah [Heb. *hammiṣpâ*; Gk. *Maspha*]. A town in the second precinct of the Shephelah (Josh. 15:38) associated with Lachish and Makkedah. Eusebius apparently referred to this site when he mentioned another Mizpah (Gk. *Massēba*) on the northern border of the Eleutheropolis district (*Onom.* 130.2f.) and in the same context a Mizpah on the road to Jerusalem. The latter, however, must be sought NE of Beit Jibrîn (Beth-guvrin, ancient Eleutheropolis) and is too far E for identification with the Shephelah town. In any case the Mizpah of the Shephelah must be near Lachish; therefore the old suggestion to locate it on Tell eṣ-Ṣâfī must be abandoned (the latter is probably ancient Gath).

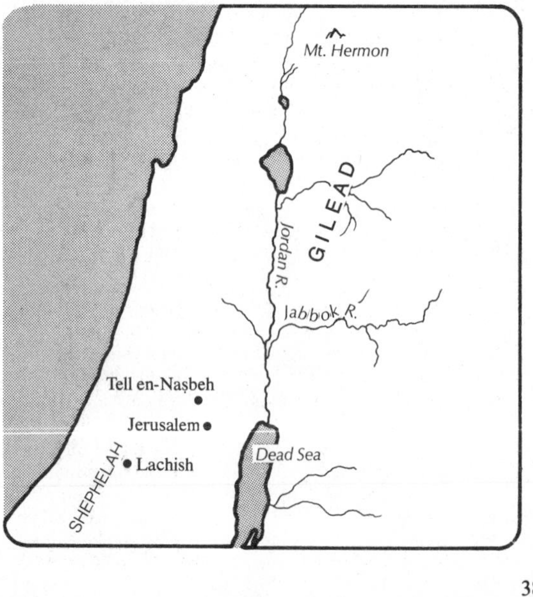


**5.** Land of Mizpah (Upper Galilee). A region at the foot of Mt. Hermon occupied by Hivites (Josh. 11:3). It is called both "the land of Mizpah" (Heb. *ʾereṣ hammiṣpâ*; Gk. *gēn Massēpha* [v. 3]) and "the valley of Mizpeh" (Heb. *biqʿaṯ miṣpeh*; Gk. *tōn pedíōn Massēpha* [v. 8]). It is evidently to be equated with the Merj ʿAyyûn.

***Bibliography.***–*LBHG* (Eng. tr., rev. ed. 1979), pp. 32, 239; B. Maisler, *Untersuchungen zur alten Geschichte Syriens und Palaestinas* (1930), p. 75.

**6.** Mizpeh of Moab [Heb. *miṣpēh môʾāḇ*; Gk. *Massēpha tḗs Mōab*]. The place where David sought refuge for his family with the king of Moab (1 S. 22:3). Since David was being pursued by King Saul, he most likely reached Moab via the southern end of the Dead Sea (cf. the route taken by the kings of Israel and Judah, 2 K. 3). None of the suggested identifications is particularly convincing. Mizpeh-moab has even been proposed as another designation for KIR OF MOAB.

***Bibliography.***–N. Glueck, *AASOR,* 18-19 (1939), 60-63, 82-88; *GP,* II, 391; A. Musil, *Arabia Petraea,* I (1907), 270, 274; A. H. van Zyl, *Moabites* (1960), pp. 88, 134 n. 2. A. F. RAINEY

**MIZPAR** miz'pär. *See* MISPAR.

**MIZRAIM** miz'rā-əm [Heb. *miṣrayim,* a dual form perhaps referring to Upper and Lower Egypt; Gk. *Mesraim*]. Except for the RSV (and Moff.), the major English versions transliterate Heb. *miṣrayim* when it is used for the son of Ham (Gen. 10:6; 1 Ch. 1:8). Egyptians are thus classified as Hamites. In Gen. 10:13; 1 Ch. 1:11 Mizraim "begot" the Ludim and six other peoples. This expression may simply mean that these peoples had some connection with Egypt (cf. RSV), and in other cases *miṣrayim* is translated "Egypt" in all the versions. Some scholars think that in a few passages referring to horses (1 K. 10:28; 2 K. 7:6; 2 Ch. 1:16f.; 9:28) the word should be emended to Muṣri or Muṣur, a land in Asia Minor (cf. Moff. Muzri).

***Bibliography.***–*DBSup.,* V, cols. 1468-1474; *GTTOT,* §§ 69, 835, 913. JOHN ALEXANDER THOMPSON

**MIZZAH** miz'ə [Heb. *mizzâ*]. Son of Renel and grandson of Esau; an Edomite clan chief (Gen. 36:13, 17; 1 Ch. 1:37).

**MNASON** nā'sən [Gk. *Mnasōn*]. A Cypriot Christian who lived in Jerusalem (Acts 21:16). As a Hellenist he made an ideal host for Paul and his gentile companions when they came with the collection at the end of the third missionary journey (A.D. 57). The designation "early disciple" probably refers to a founding member of the Jerusalem Church, one of the original 120 on whom the Spirit came at Pentecost (Acts 1:15). As such, Mnason may have provided Luke with valuable information about the early Church.

The Western text places Mnason's residence in a village on the way from Caesarea to Jerusalem. The AV, RV, and NEB have Caesarean disciples bringing Mnason, while the RSV, NIV, JB, and NASB have Paul's party being brought to the house of Mnason. While either understanding is possible from the difficult syntax of this passage, the latter is probably correct since it is difficult to understand why the disciples would bring the prospective host.

***Bibliography.***–F. F. Bruce, *Comm. on the Book of the Acts* (*NICNT,* 1954), pp. 426f.; H. J. Cadbury, "Some Semitic Personal

Names in Luke-Acts," in H. G. Wood, ed., *Amicitae Corolla* (1933), pp. 51-53; W. M. Ramsay, *Bearing of Recent Discovery on the Trustworthiness of the NT* (1915), p. 309; *BC*, IV, 270.

J. J. HUGHES

**MOAB** mō'ab [Heb. *mô'āḇ*]. Nation and state in Transjordan. Moab was also a territorial name for the land occupied by the Moabites, who were known to the ancient Israelites as kinsmen, clients, vassals, and enemies.

- I. Name
- II. Geography
  - A. Terrain
  - B. Climate
  - C. Vegetation
  - D. Way of Life
- III. Prehistory
- IV. Formation of Urban Culture
- V. Decline of Population
- VI. Moabite Kingdom
- VII. Israel and Moab (*ca.* 1400-1000 B.C.)
  - A. The Exodus
  - B. Israel, Moab, and Midian
  - C. Period of the Judges
  - D. Kingdoms of Moab and Israel
- VIII. Decline of Moab (*ca.* 735-500 B.C.)
  - A. Assyria, Judah, and Moab (*ca.* 735-609 B.C.)
  - B. Moab in the Babylonian and Persian Empires (*ca.* 605-500 B.C.)
- IX. Later History
- X. Language
- XI. Religion

***I. Name.***–The name appears in Akkadian sources as *ma'aba, ma'ab,* or *mu'aba,* in an Egyptian text as *m-'i-b,* in the LXX as *Mōab,* and in Josephus as *Mōabos.* According to Gen. 19:37 Lot's older daughter named her son Moab, a name explained in the LXX as "from my father" (= Heb. *mē'āḇî*). Thus to the Israelites the name may have been a derogatory pun reminding them of Moab's incestuous origins.

***II. Geography.***–Moab proper is a high plateau between the valleys of the Arnon (Wâdī el-Môjib) and the Zered (Wâdī el-Ḥesā) and between the scarps of the Dead Sea rift and the gorge of the north-flowing Arnon. Bounded by desert to the east and the rift-valley to the west, it covered only about 2100 sq. km. (800 sq. mi.).

Territory N of the Arnon fell under Moabite control in at least two periods, when the nation included the plains (the *belqā* or *mîšôr*) from the Arnon to N of Heshbon and the plain in the Jordan Valley E of Jericho. At its greatest extent Moab covered an area of about 3600 sq. km. (1400 sq. mi.). Within these borders conditions suitable for agriculture and permanent settlements were found in a narrow band about 19 km. (12 mi.) wide.

*A. Terrain.* Jebel Shīḥān (about 1070 m., 3500 ft.), an extinct volcano in the north, and Jebel Khinzira (about 1240 m., 4060 ft.) in the south dominate the Moabite plateau. Thick layers of rich, brown Mediterranean soil cover the undulating plains that slope away from these peaks, especially along the western rim of the plateau. Outcroppings of limestone and basalt are found throughout Moab.

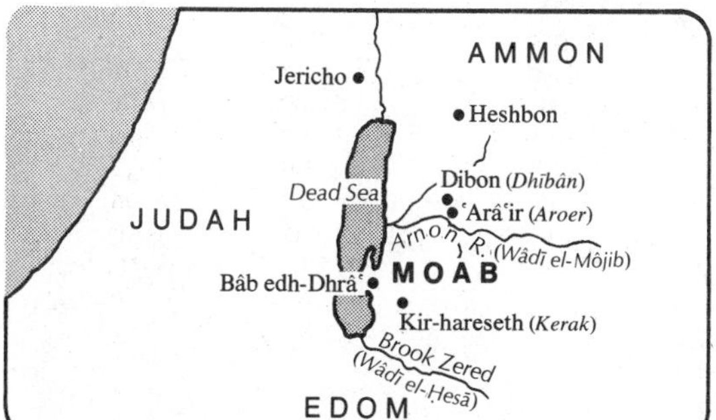


Deep gorges cut the plateau's perimeters into segments and reduce the areas useful for agriculture. Within the wadis freshwater springs form small pools or seep onto natural terraces. Bālū', a large site occupied in most periods since the Early Bronze Age (*ca.* 2700 B.C.), sits on a rocky bluff above such a spring.

Mt. Nebo, projecting westward from the plateau, rises to 802 m. (2631 ft.) and overlooks the *mîšôr,* a tableland flatter than the plateau of Moab proper to the south. The agricultural potential of the *mîšôr* was superior to that of the plateau; consequently its cities, e.g., Heshbon, Elealeh, Dibon, and Jalul, grew larger than those S of the Arnon. Yet its gentle terrain provided no natural boundaries, and Amorites, Ammonites, Midianites, Gad, Reuben, and Israel contested with Moab for its control.

The Arnon presents a formidable barrier to traffic between these two regions of Moab. It flows from a source near Lejjun north through a gorge 24 km. (15 mi.) long, that divides the arable plateau from the eastern desert; the wadi then turns west and descends sharply to the Dead Sea. The gorge at its widest point has rims about 5 km. (3 mi.) apart that tower about 700 m. (2300 ft.) above the stream bed.

*B. Climate.* Up to 33 cm. (13 in.) of rain normally fall annually on the *mîšôr* and along the western rim of the plateau. The shores of the Dead Sea receive a mere 5 to 7½ cm. (2 to 3 in.) annually, and only 20 cm. (8 in.) fall near the southern reaches of the Arnon. Variations in annual rainfall are important to life in such an area. Kerak has received as much as 67 cm. (26.25 in.) and as little as 9.4 cm. (3.7 in.) in a single year. Ancient peoples' migrations into and out of Moab were probably stimulated by similar fluctuations. Ruth 1:1-6 suggests that in some years the plateau was better watered than were the hills of Bethlehem, and that in such times migrations occurred across the rift-valley.

*C. Vegetation.* Deforestation, overgrazing, and erosion have reduced Moab's topsoil. Few trees survive there; grain crops or winter grasses cover most of the land. A definitive statement on the ancient vegetation of Moab awaits adequate excavation of its archeological deposits.

From Isa. 15–16 and Jer. 48, however, one can conclude that in the 8th and 7th cents. the wadis of the *mîšôr* and around Kir-hareseth (Kerak) were noted for their vineyards. But use of land for wine production depends on relatively stable military conditions, since crops must be cultivated over several years. During most of their history Moabites planted light grains.

*D. Way of Life.* Since the soil and rainfall needs of settled, agrarian people are met only on the western edges of the plateau, most Moabite settlements were located in the western 16 km. (10 mi.) of the plateau. The valleys, including the Dead Sea ghors, are generally lost to agricultural subsistence.

Herders of sheep, goats, and cattle found the entire land useful, however, and formed an important aspect of its economy. Pastoralists move toward the drier zones — which in Moab are E of the Arnon and on the slopes of the rift-valley — in the rainy season and bring their flocks to the wetter regions in the rainless summer. In so doing they establish various social, economic, and military ties with the sedentary peoples.

In return for allowing the sheep and goats to graze on their wheat and barley stubble, farmers receive organic fertilizer, wool, and meat from the flocks. Townspeople provide needed craft products and food stuffs for the nomads. Often the settled folk are kin to the nomads. Wealthy pastoralists may buy land (or take it by force) when their flocks exceed the resources of their pastures and wells, and unfortunate shepherds may be forced to a sedentary life when they lose their flocks.

Such interaction of pastoral and agricultural peoples began in Moab by the end of the Early Bronze Age at the latest. By the Israelite monarchy it was basic to the Moabite economy and culture. 2 K. 3:4 recalls Mesha's reputation as a sheep baron. The "King of Moab" in the narratives of the Exodus need not have been a monarch over an entirely settled population. Only an occasional merchant settlement was needed to provide a background for Dt. 2:9-11 (see VII.A below).

At no point did large cities develop in Moab. Walled towns of over 4 ha. (10 acres) were infrequent. Small villages and in some periods isolated farmsteads and campsites seem to have served as the seats of Moab's culture.

A mixed economy of grain farming, herding, and trading provided the population's livelihood. As climatic and political conditions varied the peoples of Moab correspondingly increased or decreased their dependence on one or another of these elements.

*III. Prehistory.*–Biblical references to a prehistoric population in Moab (Dt. 2:10f.) offer no clues about the actual nature or precise date of such peoples. Consequently, it is unknown whether the Emim were E.B. sedentarists, hunters and gatherers of earlier periods, or L.B. invaders.

A scattering of stone tools at Khirbet el-Mahāriʿam on the east-central plateau suggests sporadic but recurrent camping from the late Lower Paleolithic period (*ca.* 78,000 B.C.) through the Upper Paleolithic (*ca.* 10,000 B.C.). Although no Mesolithic or Neolithic remains have been reported, their absence may merely indicate that the peoples of such prehistoric cultures inhabited zones that have not been explored.

Chalcolithic settlements fairly covered the Jordan rift-valley, especially in the area later called the "plains of Moab" and near Bâb edh-Dhrâʿ by the south end of the Dead Sea. Only a few sherds from this period appear in campsites on the plateau.

With the appearance *ca.* 3000 B.C. of the E.B. cultures came a way of life that has persisted into modern times. People settled in hamlets near the heads of small wadis. One extended family probably made up the population of most settlements. Women tended grain crops in the upland plateaus and in the valleys near the Dead Sea, while men and boys herded small flocks in areas less suited to agriculture. Herders' camps might be found dozens of kilometers from the village in the moist winter months but merged with the base settlements in the summer.

No large cities dominated E.B. I Moab. Bâb edh-Dhrâʿ, which grew into a major walled town, was a small, unwalled village of stone and brick huts. ʿArâʿir on the north edge of the Arnon seems to have been only a campsite.

The villagers of Bâb edh-Dhrâʿ were former nomads who had made earlier periodic visits to the location to tend crops and to bury in laboriously cut tombs the bodies of those who had died during the migratory circuit. They experimented with agriculture and *ca.* 3000 B.C. (E.B. IB) began building more permanent structures. Whether the E.B. IA nomads had immigrated or had developed from earlier local peoples is subject to question.

The E.B. I pottery is widely scattered on the plateau in regions favorable to both agricultural and pastoralist use.

*IV. Formation of Urban Culture.*–Some of these settlements began to outstrip their neighbors in size and importance with the rise of the E.B. II culture (*ca.* 2900 B.C.). Twenty-seven sites on the plateau and several from the less adequately surveyed northern area are known. Of these only Ader, Arjum, Rujm umm el-Quleib, Khirbet umm es-Sedeirah, and Khirbet Iskander exceed 5 ha. (12 acres), and most are smaller than 2½ ha. (6 acres). No walled city from E.B. II-III is known on the plateau, although several ruins show surface clues that may indicate walls from E.B. II-III. Bâb edh-Dhrâʿ may have been walled during E.B. II and certainly was so by 2500 (E.B. III).

Moab in E.B. II and III seems to have been mainly agricultural, although pastoral pursuits no doubt continued. All but three of the known E.B. II-III settlements are in the area that receives enough rain for farming. Lejjun, Khaif, and Bâb edh-Dhrâʿ, the exceptions, are near perennial springs and may have used irrigation. Carbonized grain in a pit in Level 6B at ʿArâʿir suggests agriculture there. Glueck thought that the terraces around Khirbet umm es-Sedeirah, on the north slope of the Wâdī el-Ḥesā, were built in this period, but his suggestion has not been tested by excavation.

Villages in Moab at this time probably housed craftsmen, including metallurgists, and participated in trade. Some scholars have suggested that Moab traded stone — basalt and hematite — to western Palestine, where it was used for maceheads, vessels, palettes, and grinding stones. Transit across the el-Lisan area of the Dead Sea, known from the historical period, would have made Moab a trade partner of Arad, Ai, and other southwest Palestine cities.

Evidence of worship includes the menhirs of Lejjun, Ader, Arjum, and Iskander, where ceremonies were probably enacted to bind scattered regional populations in political and religious alliances. Fertility figurines found at Bâb edh-Dhrâʿ suggest the importance of the divine gift of life to these people.

By 2200 B.C. Moab, like much of Transjordan, had taken on a new appearance. Villages appeared more frequently, including five towns large enough to house over one thousand persons. Indeed, two town sites in the Bālūʿ area could have been inhabited by over two thousand, and Lejjun's population is estimated at two thousand to four thousand in E.B. IV.

Curiously, this explosion of settlements occurred when the cities of western Palestine had fallen to unknown forces. Some suggest that immigrants from the west had spread themselves over the agricultural land in Transjordan in an attempt to survive the dissolution of the E.B. III-IV urban culture. New elements from the north brought some stylistic innovations, but the basic population continued from the native stock. Bâb edh-Dhrâʿ remained settled, and the vast cemetery continued to grow. But burial styles changed once more, and the E.B. III town was abandoned for areas N, E, and S of its decaying walls.

Ader, a town of about five hundred persons, had a small sanctuary building. One broad room, entered on its long side unlike the later Canaanite and Israelite temples, contained an altar table. Nearby were menhirs not unlike the Israelite *maṣṣēḇôṯ* ("standing stones"). The date of this complex and the form and object of any ceremonies performed there are, unfortunately, uncertain.

Nomads also ranged into Moab during this time, if the DOLMENS found in the northern Moab area are taken as artifacts of a nomadic culture. Dolmens are rectangular structures of massive stone slabs that once were covered by earth heaps. Recent excavation shows that dolmens housed burials from the E.B.-M.B. transitional period. Since most dolmens are located away from settlement sites and since they contain secondary burials, it has been suggested that nomads built them. The stylistic attributes

Pottery and bones from a tomb at Bâb edh-Dhrâʿ (*ca.* 2000 B.C.) (B. VanElderen)

of artifacts from dolmens indicate that the dolmen builders before migrating to Transjordan may have had contact with Syrians.

Was E.B. the time of the Emim? Although the biblical and archeological references are too fragmentary to allow certainty, this period of expansion provides an attractive hypothetical matrix.

*V. Decline of Population.*–Although remarkably few artifacts from the M.B. and L.B. have turned up in archeological surveys and excavations in Moab, the plateau and northern Moab were not necessarily abandoned during most of the second millennium. Jālûl, Dhībân (Dibon), ʿArâʿir, el-Miṣnaʿ, and Bālūʿ are among the sites that have yielded M.B. and L.B. sherds. A tomb at Medeba contained bronze weapons and jewelry along with scarabs of the 19th and 20th Egyptian Dynasties and poorly made pottery.

Egyptian records seem silent about Transjordan at least until the late 13th century. Egyptians were aware, however, of a group called the Shasu as early as Amenhotep II (1436-1410). These seemingly nomadic inhabitants of southern Transjordan may be the ancestors of the Edomites and Moabites.

Did the decline in settled population in southern Transjordan result from the attack of the armies of the Elamite king Chedorlaomer (Gen. 14:5-7)? Some have held that he demolished city-states there sometime in the late E.B. IV-M.B. I period, leaving the area decimated. This reconstruction rests on no biblical or extrabiblical evidence, however. Gen. 14 is notoriously difficult to fit into a chronological context. Archeological evidence allows the event to be dated at any time from the early second millennium, when the names of the kings fit well enough but the cities of Moab and Edom did not exist, into the Iron Age, when the narratives probably were written down.

Genesis 14 cannot explain the near absence of settled population in Moab for one thousand years because the chapter cannot be precisely dated and because an invasion does not account for a lengthy population decline. Perhaps Moab lost its settled population as a result of the political disturbances in the power centers of the eastern Mediterranean, especially in the Palestine-Lebanon area. As Egyptian commercial and military interests increased in the 19th cent., cities built massive defenses, apparently against one another. In the wake of Egypt's expulsion of the Hyksos these cities fell. Fifteenth-century pharaohs plundered and subjugated the Canaanites, and in the 14th cent. ʿApiru disrupted domestic tranquillity. As petty kings warred and tyrannized, border areas such as Moab became refuges. Settled agricultural peoples became nomads, thus avoiding taxation and military conscription. This explanation fits the evidence of M.B. II-L.B. II Moab. Hadad son of Bedan and king of Edom, who thwarted a Midianite incursion into his tribe's pasturage, was likely chief of a small group during this kind of period in Moab.

The *ʾêlîm* (Ex. 15:15) may be such tribal leaders. *ʾÊlîm* means "rams," but the term parallels references in adjacent lines to the leaders of Edom and the inhabitants of Philistia and Canaan. Thus Israelite tradition, recalling the pastoralist foundation of Moabite economy, nicknamed Moab's leaders "rams."

*VI. Moabite Kingdom.*–As Egypt's sovereignty waned in the late 13th cent. and as small settlements appeared in the hills of Palestine, an incipient kingdom of Moab emerged. This nation-state did not spring suddenly from the desert. L.B. pottery from sites on the Moabite plateau suggests that the area became settled in the 13th cent. or even earlier.

Three lines of evidence may point to increased political organization on the plateau in the 13th century. First, the Luxor inscription of Rameses II may portray a fortified town that Egypt plundered in Moab (*ca.* 1285 B.C.). Second, a stele found at Bālūʿ in 1930 shows three figures, two presumably divinities and the third a king. The Egyptian style of art and attire is often interpreted as indicating royalty in Moab and relations with Egypt. Third, an apparent line of fortresses, dated by Glueck from *ca.* 1200 B.C. (*Other Side of the Jordan,* pp. 169-171), further suggests national organization. It should be noted, however, that the Luxor inscription is not clearly legible, the Bālūʿ stele was not found in stratified context and has not been translated, and Glueck's fortresses have not been excavated and therefore are not dated. A developing monarchy in thirteenth-century Moab is as yet an untested hypothesis.

By 1100 B.C., however — and probably as early as 1200 — many villages and fortified sites punctuated the Moabite landscape. In central Moab these appeared along the fertile central area as well as around the edge of the plateau. Probably Bālūʿ, Rabbah, Miṣnaʿ, Imraʿ, and others covered over 0.4 ha. (1 acre) and were unwalled. Farmsteads or hamlets like Abū Zārūra, in the eastern farmland of the plateau, covered barely 900 sq. m. (10,000 sq. ft.).

Walled towns or fortresses are found around the southern and eastern edges of Moab. Typical are two nearly identical sites in central Moab now called by the frequently used Arabic name Medeiyineh ("little city"). These Medeiyinehs stand on flat-topped hills on the eastern edge of the plateau. Fortifiers cut dry moats into the ridge connecting them with the plateau, thus isolating oval areas of about 17,300 sq. m. (186,000 sq. ft.), and further strengthened them by erecting stone towers beside the moats. Walls of flat blocks cut from the fortress site dominate the steep slopes, and thick gate towers protect the only entrance. Buildings one and two stories high were constructed of limestone blocks and slabs. At the southern Medeiyineh stairway treads and lintels of stone remain undisturbed. The pottery and house styles suggest a date of 1200-1000 B.C. for these fortresses.

Similar strongholds stand at Medinet er-Ras, Mahaiy, and Khirbet Medeiyineh on the Wâdī Themed. Other bastions feature blockhouses, some preserved to 6 m. (20 ft.) in height. Qaṣr el-ʿAl on Moab's northeast border is a structure of large blocks laid in header-and-stretcher manner that measures over 12 by 18 m. (40 by 60 ft.) Qaṣr Abū el-Kharaq, el-Maḥri, and Khirbet Remeil, equally remote and agriculturally unlikely areas, also have blockhouses. Since none of the blockhouses has been excavated, their precise date and function are not known. All seem to have been constructed between 1200 and 1100, however, and their locations suggest that they guarded the border of an agricultural kingdom.

Well-formed pottery head of a Semitic king or god from Khirbet Medeiyineh (*ca.* 900-600 B.C.) (E. K. Vogel; picture N. Glueck)

The population of this kingdom probably was largely descended from the Bronze Age folk. Some evidence suggests that an external stimulant provoked the formation of the town culture of the Iron Age. The script on the Bālūʿ stele is similar to Linear B, used in the second-millennium Minoan civilization. This resemblance, the discovery of Mycenaean imported pottery in a thirteenth-century tomb near Medeba, and the Cypro-Phoenician decorative style of Moabite pottery (12th-6th cents.) may indicate that the leaders of Moab entered from the west. An alternative hypothesis is that the catalyst of Moabite political growth and unification was the establishment of a trade network from Syria southward to Arabia that crossed Moab. The presence of anthropoid clay coffins — associated with Egypt and/or the Philistines — in Transjordan (including a ninth-century context at Dibon [Dhībân]) adds to the evidence, as yet inconclusive, for Moab's associations with the west.

Moabite tribes and towns quite likely united under a single leader in response to external pressures from north and west and exploited their location on the trade route. Connections of some sort with Egypt seem certain, as the Bālūʿ stele suggests.

***VII. Israel and Moab*** (*ca.* 1400-1000 B.C.).–*A. The Exodus*. When did Israel first encounter Moab? Nu. 21 portrays Sihon as Israel's enemy N of the Arnon and indicates that he had earlier overthrown Moab's first king (if *riʾšôn* in v. 26 is translated "first" [JB] rather than "former" [RSV]). This situation would harmonize nicely with a reconstruction that sees Moab established as a state in the 13th cent. and Israel dealing with it shortly thereafter.

According to this scenario Israel petitioned the king of Moab, who controlled only from the Arnon to the Zered, for permission to pass through his area. Permission having been denied, Moses led his cohorts around Moab, through the eastern desert, and then into the *mîšôr,* where the tribes defeated Sihon at Jahaz. Sihon had recently taken the region from the Moabites, so his defeat did not transgress the brotherhood of Israel and Moab. Weakened by his wars with Moab, he was vulnerable to Israel's assaults and fell to its armies.

Problems beset this reconstruction, however. First, the biblical episodes could fit several periods in Moab, and archeological evidence does not demand a thirteenth-century date for the Israel-Moab encounter. Enough sedentary life to form a setting for the biblical events existed in L.B. Moab. Approximately 25 percent of the largest sites surveyed in central Moab, including the ruins of Bālūʿ, Rabbah, and Imraʿ, yielded L.B. surface sherds. ʿAráʿir on the north rim of the Arnon also showed signs of L.B. use. Without excavation and careful pottery analysis it would be wrong to claim that some city-states did not appear on the plateau earlier than the 13th century.

Is it necessary that the Moabites of the Exodus were city-dwellers, however? Nomads have chiefs who could be called "kings." Such peoples normally guard jealously the very rights at issue in Israel's communications (Nu. 20:14-21; Dt. 2:26-37; Jgs. 11:15-20): land passage and water.

Whether or not the Exodus events in Transjordan require a sedentary Moab, they could have occurred as early as the 15th or as late as the 12th century.

Archeological evidence for a placement of the Sihon event is limited. If ancient Heshbon was identical with modern Ḥesbân, it left no ruins for excavators. Unless Sihon's city was located in another nearby site (the ruin at Jālûl has been suggested), it did not exist as early as the 13th century.

A second challenge to the popular harmonization of archeological and biblical evidence emerges when the varied biblical references to Israel's routes and to its contacts with Moab are examined. Nu. 33:44f. seems to indicate passage through Moabite territory, as do the references to the favorable treatment "by the men of Ar" (Dt. 2:29; cf. vv. 9, 18) and to Israel's passage over the Arnon to Sihon's territory (v. 24). Nu. 21:10-13 and Jgs. 11:18, however, show Israel's avoidance of Moabite lands. Also geographically difficult is the order of events in Nu. 21:18-23. Regardless of Jahaz's location — most have placed it SE of Heshbon — it is unclear why Sihon challenged Israel there if the latter had already encamped "by the top of Pisgah which looks down upon the desert" (v. 20), a site W of Heshbon.

The Sihon texts are themselves difficult. Since the song of Nu. 21:27-30 also occurs (slightly modified) in Jer. 48:45f. but there lacks the name Sihon, and since the line "to an Amorite king, Sihon" (Nu. 21:29) disrupts the assumed meter of the poem, it has been suggested that the song in its original form had nothing to do with Sihon or his victory over Moab. If this is so, Israel did not encounter Sihon in its move from Kadesh-barnea to Canaan. Rather, the account was added to show that Israel legitimately owned territory later claimed by Moab, since it was commanded to take no land from Moab (Dt. 2:9).

Since the biblical and archeological evidence is uncertain, scholars have proposed several ways of treating the historical encounter of early Israel and Moab. Some have suggested that two or more groups moved across Transjordan to settle in Canaan and become Israel. One crossed Moab in the 14th cent., before a dense and well-organized kingdom appeared there. The other, traveling in the 13th cent., was forced to circumvent Moab's newly formed state but could not avoid conflict with Heshbon. Later Israelite historians merged the two episodes but never smoothed out the details. Hence the Bible contains seemingly inconsistent narratives.

An alternative to such a reconstruction is that there was no actual unified movement by all of Israel, but that individual tribal groups conquered and settled the land. No one has successfully identified the origins of these tribes, but it should be noted that Nu. 32:33-38 suggests that Reuben and Gad occupied their land peacefully, building sheepfolds and towns.

Other scholars have said that actual events may underlie

the narratives but cannot be precisely known because of editorial transformations made centuries later. Each editor thought of the Transjordan of his day and used the older traditions to support his own political position. This explanation accounts for some differences in the various passages but is so speculative that it is difficult to test.

*B. Israel, Moab, and Midian.* In the earliest period of Moabite statehood the nation seems to have been allied with the fully nomadic Midianites who ranged into Canaan from south Arabia. The episodes in Num 22–32 show a conflict between the Israelites (or at least the tribes of Reuben and Gad) and the pastoralist Midianites allied with the Moabite king Balak. When Israel was camped in the plains of Moab across the Jordan from Jericho, it was confronted by Balak and his hired seer Balaam. This encounter, in which the foreign holy man blessed rather than cursed Israel, stands as the first of Yahweh's several victories over the political-religious establishments of the land's owners. Another "first" incident at the same campsite — Israel's participation in the worship of Baal of Peor — began the apostasy that plagued Israel for the rest of its time in the land.

Moses gave his final instructions to Israel while in this area (Dt. 1:5) and was buried near the Moabite-Midianite shrine at Beth-peor (32:48-52; 34:1-8).

*C. Period of the Judges.* Moab must have regained territory N of the Arnon soon after these events, for according to Jgs. 3 Eglon, a rotund king of Moab, had expanded his nation to include the Jordan ford near Gilgal and Jericho. Gad and Reuben, not yet ensconced in their territory, would have been cut off from their allies on the west bank of the Jordan, and Benjamin also would have been threatened.

Some references (Jgs. 3:19,26) confuse one's understanding of the geography, but Eglon most likely resided at Jericho ("city of palms") and was there assassinated by Ehud. Ehud then led the Ephraimites in retaking the fords of the Jordan. Moab's eighteen-year domination of east-west trade was thus broken.

The events in Ruth reflect a more peaceful relationship between Moab and Israel when, as probably had been customary since the E.B., the passage of peoples between the two sides of the rift-valley permitted survival when periodic climatic fluctuation or political unrest made life difficult on the west bank. The ease of communication and social involvement of the two peoples underscores the archeological evidence of similar pottery, house styles, scripts, and languages. Kinship ties such as those of Ruth and Elimelech maintained a necessary potential for the survival of many common folk.

*D. Kingdoms of Moab and Israel. 1. Israelite Domination* (*ca.* 1050-922 B.C.). By the time of Saul Moab had matched its western neighbors in building towns and fortresses (see VI above). Dibon, later the capital of Moab, was at least a small town, and the building of the Moabite fortress system had neared completion.

Efforts at fortification were likely a part of a military upsurge in the Transjordan. Both Saul and David entered the area (1 S. 14:47; 2 S. 8:2), and David severely retaliated against Moab, killing two-thirds of its warriors and confiscating a significant spoil of silver and gold. The unparalleled harsh treatment of this nation raises the question of what had happened to the personal relationship of David and Moab, since it was in Mizpeh of Moab that David had found refuge from Saul (1 S. 22:3-5). Perhaps Moab had joined its neighbors against Israel once too often and was punished for disregarding a former treaty of brotherhood. Mass execution of Moabite males left the state powerless and allowed Israel to dominate the increasingly valuable trade route, thus advancing its sovereignty over Syria (2 S. 10:15-19; 1 K. 8:65). Solomon maintained this domination but seemingly by his ritual alliance system, since 1 K. 11 recounts that he loved a Moabite woman (v. 1) and built a high place for Chemosh, the Moabite god, on a mountain E of Jerusalem (vv. 7, 33).

*2. Moabite Resurgence and Omride Sovereignty* (922-735 B.C.). Israelite dominion was short-lived. Moab seemingly took advantage of the disunity that followed Solomon's death and asserted its independence. The Moabite Stone's report that Omri subjugated Moab suggests that Israel's dominion had not continued unbroken from Solomon. Dibon and other areas N of the Arnon came under Moabite control.

Omri's reassertion of sovereignty over Moab — which Moabite religion interpreted as divine punishment of Moab — was probably no more than the establishment of a garrison at Jahaz (Moabite Stone, lines 19f.) and the imposition of tribute in wool and meat (2 K. 3:4). Israel was thereby able to control the trade route and to protect Gadites dwelling in the *mîšôr* at Ataroth and Nebo.

According to both the Moabite Stone and 2 K. 3, Mesha successfully overthrew the Israelite yoke late in the Omride dynasty. The chronology and the identity of the Israelite personalities involved in these events are not clear, however.

Israel had dominated Moab for forty years, according to the Moabite Stone. This dominion lasted through half of the reign of Omri's son. Since the reigns of Omri and his son Ahab total only thirty-four years, and since the account in 2 Kings states that the revolt occurred after Ahab's death (3:5f.), scholars (e.g., Murphy, Miller) have sought to clarify the chronology.

First, regarding the "forty-year" sovereignty of Israel, scholars have suggested that Omri overcame Moab before his reign began, i.e., while he was a general in Baasha's army (J. Morgenstern, cited by Murphy, p. 412). Most have thought this solution unlikely, however, and have preferred to take the "forty years" as a round number. The available information on Omri and Baasha indicates that Omri was more likely to have reached across the Jordan to control trade there and thus to enhance his relations with the Phoenician merchants.

As for the claim of Mesha that Chemosh released him from Israel midway through the reign of Omri's son, one solution is that Mesha reckoned his victories beginning with early skirmishes against Ahab. Ahab was quite strong at that point, however, and not likely to allow a petty vassal to disrupt a valuable area of his trade empire. Other historians have read "grandson" (i.e., Joram) for "son" in Mesha's inscription, thus lengthening Israel's years of sovereignty nearer the forty years that Mesha claims and harmonizing with 2 K. 3:5.

If Mesha was not referring to a particular victory but to the results of his total reign, however, the discrepancies evaporate. The turning point in Chemosh's favor of Moab was not a victory but the god's gift of the throne to Mesha during the reign of Omri's son, although actual reconquest from Israel did not begin until the turmoil following Ahab's death.

*3. Mesha's Kingdom.* Mesha cleared Israelite garrisons and settlements from the *mîšôr,* established a Moabite population in the Israelite fortress at Jahaz, connected the two sides of the Arnon with a highway, secured his own forts, and built Dibon into a self-sufficient city.

Israel responded with an attack through the southern wilderness (2 K. 3:5-27). Since the northern approaches were blocked by Mesha's fortresses, Joram allied with Jehoshaphat of Judah and the king of Edom, Jehoshaphat's vassal, to strike at Moab's southern border. Both Judah and Edom stood to lose if Moab controlled the trade route from Elath to Damascus. The armies circled SE of Moab's fortresses on the Wâdī el-Ḥesā. Their initial encounter resulted in a rout of the Moabite garrison (perhaps Mahaiy) when its defenders, mistaking the sunlit pools of water in the wadi for blood, rushed the invaders' camp in quest of booty. Joram led his troops to the walls of Kir-hareseth and put the fortress under seige. The allies' victory seemed only a matter of time. Mesha tried to break through with a troop of swordsmen who directed their attack at the Edomite cohorts, thinking perhaps that these were the inferior army. The failure of this thrust left Mesha with the desperation tactic of bringing his firstborn son to the city's wall to sacrifice him. Distressed by this extreme act, the invaders retreated. Perhaps superstition motivated their flight. On the other hand, it has been suggested (Herzog and Gichon, p. 125) that Mesha offered his son to placate the god because a plague had broken out in the city. Israel may have retreated due to the fear of contagion.

Another confrontation of Moab with its western neighbors is reported in 2 Ch. 20. Moab, with Ammon and "the men of Mt. Seir" (Edom), seems to have crossed the ford of the Dead Sea at the Lisan and aimed an attack at the area S of Bethlehem. After Ammon and Moab turned on Edom and then on each other, however, Jehoshaphat led his men in looting the dead invaders' camp. The passage vaguely resembles 2 K. 3 and may be a prophetic version of that account. As it stands, the 2 Chronicles account cannot be fitted into the Mesha-Joram chronology.

Mesha's successes should be measured in terms of his liberation of the Moabites' economy as well as his securing of the borders. Rather than devoting their energies to producing sheep and wool for Israel, the Moabites were free to set their own priorities and to trade on their own terms. More of the plateau could be used for agriculture, and a larger portion of the people could settle and unify under the monarch. Mesha's boasting about settling and modernizing towns (Moabite Stone, lines 9, 23-32) reflects this aspect of his policy. Chemosh gained adherents as tribesmen relinquished tribal and ancestral deities. Conversely,the god served to unify the once politically divided nomads.

Isaiah 15–16 and Jer. 48 reflect the success claimed by Mesha; Heshbon, Elealeh, Sibmah, and Jaazer — all in the *mîšôr* — are known as Moab's. Furthermore, these same prophets refer to Moab's strength in terms of agricultural produce rather than pastoral wealth.

Sherds collected from Moabite ruins demonstrate that Moab had links with the north and possibly with trading interests in Phoenicia. Yet it developed its own distinctive artistic style. I.A. II decorated pottery is polished and banded in red or brown. While similar to Cypro-Phoenician and Edomite wares of the same period, it is clearly distinct from the foreign products of both Syria and Edom.

Walled cities have been excavated at ʿArâʿir and Dhībân. At the former an eighth-century fortress of over 2000 sq. m. (2500 sq. yds.) was constructed of roughly hewn stones laid in header-and-stretcher style. A citadel, perhaps Mesha's capitol, stood on the crest of Dhībân's mound.

***VIII. Decline of Moab*** (*ca.* 735-500 B.C.).–*A. Assyria Judah, and Moab* (*ca.* 735-609 B.C.). After Mesha's death Moab lost control of some territory but still made forays outside its base between the Arnon and Zered. Israel and Aram vied for control over the towns N of the Arnon (2 K. 10:32f.), but Moabites during this period were able to raid the area of Elisha's tomb, perhaps in Gilead (13:20f.).

Jeroboam II seems to have reasserted Israel's control over all Transjordan or at least to have restricted Moab's sovereignty to the Arnon (2 K. 14:25-28). Uzziah's subjugation of Ammon (2 Ch. 26:8) probably shifted the rule of much of Transjordan to Judahite hands, facilitated Jerusalem's control over the eastern routes to the newly reopened part of Elath (2 K. 14:22), and provided additional grazing herds that complemented Uzziah's expanded agricultural enterprises (2 Ch. 26:10).

Assyria's ambitions, which first intruded into Transjordan *ca.* 800 B.C. (*ANET,* pp. 281f.), guaranteed that Israel and Judah would not long control Moab. Though Adadnirari III's dominion (*ca.* 810-783) was short-lived, Tiglath-pileser III in 733 took captives from Gad, Reuben, and Manasseh and received tribute from Transjordanian and Arabian chiefs, including Salamanu of Moab (*ANET,* pp. 282-84). Between the reigns of Sargon II (722-704) and Esarhaddon (681-669) Moab paid one mina of gold to Assyria. Moab's relative poverty during this period is indicated by Ammon's payment of twice this amount.

Tribute was not paid without protest. Moab was invited to join the Ashdod rebellion along with Judah and Edom (*ANET,* p. 287). Somehow it was spared Sargon II's reprisals (711) and participated in the rebellion that Merodach-baladan of Babylon provoked against Sennacherib. The latter's military response against Judah is well known from 2 K. 18–19 as well as from Assyrian texts. Moab escaped destruction by paying tribute (*ANET,* p. 287).

Decimated by decades of warfare and costly vassalhood, Moab was overrun by Arabian tribes. Although the Moabite king Kamashaltu, a vassal of Ashurbanipal, sent an Arabian chieftain bound in chains to Nineveh (*ANET,* p. 298), the nation soon became a sparsely settled pastureland for Arabian herds. Town sites with late I.A. pottery are rare, although the larger cities of Dibon, Heshbon, and possibly Bālūʿ and Kir-hareseth survived. The battered stone wall at Dhībân, built *ca.* 600 B.C., may well represent Dibon's final refortification in the face of the desert hordes; the dirges in Isa. 15–16 and Jer. 48 may reflect destructions by these bands, although many scholars (e.g., Bartlett, pp. 242f.) have read them as referring to Nebuchadrezzar's invasion. The abundant references in these texts to cities N of the Arnon reinforces the impression left by archeology that few large towns remained in central and southern Moab.

Zephaniah's oracle against Moab (Zeph. 2:8-11; *ca.* 630 B.C.) responded to Moab's recent taunts against Judah in a time that Assyria dominated both lands. Shortly thereafter Josiah defiled an altar of Chemosh that had presumably stood since Solomon's apostasy (2 K. 23:13). While Moab was then in no position to retaliate, it joined bands of Syrians, Ammonites, and Chaldeans to strike Judah after Jehoiakim's rebellion against Nebuchadrezzar (24:2).

*B. Moab in the Babylonian and Persian Empires* (*ca.* 605-500 B.C.). Moab was by no means solidly in Babylonia's camp, however. Jer. 27:3-11 indicates that it plotted a rebellion in 594, and Josephus (*Ant.* x.9.7 [181f.]) implied that Nebuchadrezzar struck Ammon and Moab in 582, doubtless a punitive action. Ruined cities at Ḥesbân, Dhībân, and ʿArâʿir probably testify to this attack.

In their mutual adversity Moab and Judah seem temporarily to have rediscovered their earlier kinship. Jews found refuge in Moab (Jer. 40:11) between the fall of Jerusalem (598) and Gedaliah's restoration (*ca.* 586). Following the Babylonian Exile Moabites intermarried with Judahites (Ezr. 9:1f.; Neh. 13:23). Moabites also suffered a somewhat similar dispersion, if the presence of seemingly Moabite names in Neo-Babylonian and Persian inscriptions is indicative. Nevertheless, by the mid-5th cent. leaders of Judah and Moab were at odds, probably due to competition within the Persian satrapy (Neh. 13:1-3, 23-27; Josephus *Ant.* xi.2 [19-30]).

***IX. Later History.***–No town life appeared in Moab until the arrival of Nabatean organization. The NABATEANS had probably been among the Arabian raiders of the mid-7th cent. (*ANET,* p. 298). They may have originated in the merging of desert tribes with native Edomite and Moabite populations, but not until the mid-2nd cent. did they extend political sovereignty north toward ancient Ammon. Nabatean temples at Qaṣr and Khirbet et-Tannur demonstrate their presence in Moab, as do dozens of settlements in agricultural areas.

When Emperor Trajan finally brought the Nabateans under Roman control he linked their domains with Damascus by a new highway, still marked by numerous mile posts and roadbed remnants. Roman and Byzantine road networks cover Moab.

*X. Language.*–While knowledge of the Moabite language is limited primarily to the Moabite Stone and a few seals, it is clear that Moabite is a dialect of Northwest Semitic and is closely related to Hebrew, Phoenician, Ugaritic, and Aramaic. Moabite script is similar to the old Aramaic and Phoenician scripts.

A three-consonant verbal root is basic. Gender, number, and tense are indicated by afformatives and preformatives, and the causative by the *h-* preformative. The perfect denotes completed actions, events, and states; the imperfect indicates acts yet to be accomplished or completed.

Moabite differs from Hebrew in its use of the *iphteal* form of the verb and from Judahite Hebrew in its contraction of the *ay* and *aw* diphthongs to *ê* and *ô,* respectively.

As in northern (Israelite) Hebrew the final *t* indicates a feminine noun, but the Moabite plural and dual masculine use the final *n,* as in Aramaic. Other similarities to Hebrew include the use of pronominal suffixes, independent first and second personal pronouns, *waw* consecutives, the accusative particle *ʾt,* the relative *ʾšr,* and the *h-* preformative demonstrative pronoun.

Seal inscriptions indicate that Aramaic had become dominant in Moab at least in the sphere of business and government by the 6th century.

*XI. Religion.*–The Moabites of the kingdom period worshiped Chemosh, whom they believed provided national security. The Moabite Stone, biblical statements, and nonverbal artifacts provide fragments of information about the history and nature of the Moabite cult.

Moab's and its neighbors' religions had several features in common. Animals were sacrificed on hilltop altars (Nu. 22:40; 23:1, 14, 29), and standing stones (menhirs or *maṣṣēḇôṯ*) marked holy sites. Sexuality was openly admitted into worship and the pantheon, astral symbolism appeared, gods were thought to bring military victory, and kings led priestly functions.

The Moabites knew at least two deities. Chemosh led the pantheon of the kingdom. God of war and judgment, he may be pictured with astral symbolism in the Bālūʿ stele and represented on horseback on a clay figurine discovered at el-Medeiyineh in the *mîšôr.* Since no inscriptions verify the identity of these figures, however, scholars should remain cautious on this point. Mesha recognized Chemosh as a deity involved with the history of his nation just as the eighth-century Israelite prophets claimed Yahweh as active in their history. Chemosh had chastened Moab by giving it into the power of Omri and later had made Mesha his champion to restore Moab's good fortune. Furthermore, Chemosh called for devotion of war spoils, as did Yahweh.

Names compounded with the divine name Chemosh appear on inscriptions as late as the Persian period. Whether they always refer to the Moabite deity cannot be said, however, since there may be evidence of a general Semitic divinity by that name from as early as the Ebla documents (*ca.* 2400 B.C.).

Aštar, a female consort of Chemosh, seems to have received Moabite devotion as well (Moabite Stone, line 17; but cf. J. Gray, *JNES,* 8 [1949], 77f.). She was presumably the goddess of fertility and may be represented in the figurines discovered in several Moabite ruins. These images show a female clutching an object — perhaps a bread loaf — to her breast in earth-mother fashion. *See* ASHTORETH.

Perhaps the Bālūʿ stele shows a meeting of Chemosh, Aštar, and a Moabite king. But the Egyptian motifs on this relief suggest that these figures may not be local deities at all. Since the inscription accompanying the scene has not been translated, scholars cannot be certain.

Baal also appears in connection with Moabite history (Nu. 25:3; Moabite Stone, lines 9, 30). "Baal" need not be always a name, however; it can denote a "lord" or master of a location or power. Other possible divine names associated with Moab that are known from Semitic religion include Peor, Meon, Nabu (Nebo), and Horon (Horanan of the Moabite Stone; Horonaim of Isa. 15:5). *See also* MOABITE STONE.

***Bibliography.***–N. Avigad, "Ammonite and Moabite Seals," in J. Sanders, ed., *Near Eastern Archaeology in the 20th Century* (1970), pp. 284-295; J. R. Bartlett, "Moabites and Edomites," in D. J. Wiseman, ed., *Peoples of OT Times* (1973), pp. 229-258; *PEQ,* 101 (1969), 94-100; *BHI* (2nd ed. 1972); W. G. Dever, "The 'Middle Bronze I' Period in Syria and Palestine," in J. Sanders, ed., *Near Eastern Archaeology in the 20th Century* (1970), pp. 132-163; *GB,*

Bālūʿ stele showing the Moabite king (center) submitting to a god (Chemosh?) on the left. Above the relief is a faint inscription, as yet undeciphered, perhaps dating to the 3rd millennium B.C. The relief is probably from the 13th-12th cent. B.C. (Jordanian Museum in Amman)

pp. 235-39; N. Glueck, *AASOR*, 14 (1933/34), 1-82; 15 (1935), 104-111; 18-19 (1939), 60-113, 251-269; *Other Side of the Jordan* (rev. ed. 1970), esp. pp. 139-179; L. Harding, *Antiquities of Jordan* (1967), pp. 26-51, 108-114; J. H. Hayes and J. M. Miller, eds., *Israelite and Judaean History* (*OTL*, 1977); C. Herzog and M. Gichon, *Battles of the Bible* (1978), pp. 123-25; J. R. Kautz, *BA*, 44 (1981), 27-35; K. A. Kitchen, *JEA*, 50 (1964), 47-70; *LBHG* (Eng. tr., rev. ed. 1979); G. L. Mattingly, *Reconstruction of E. B. Age Cultural Patterns in Central Moab* (1980); J. M. Miller, *BASOR*, 234 (Spring 1979), 43-52; *PEQ*, 106 (1974), 9-18; R. E. Murphy, *CBQ*, 15 (1953), 409-417; *NHI*; A. D. Tushingham, *AASOR*, 40 (1972); J. Van Seters, *JBL*, 91 (1972), 182-197; A. H. van Zyl, *Moabites* (1960); R. de Vaux, *Early History of Israel* (Eng. tr. 1978); M. Weippert, "Israelite 'Conquest' and the Evidence from Transjordan," in F. M. Cross, ed., *Symposia* (1979), pp. 15-34.

J. R. KAUTZ, III

**MOABITE STONE.** A stele of black basalt found at modern Dhībân (OT Dibon) in the Transjordan, containing an inscription of about thirty-four lines commemorating various military and building activities of Mesha king of Moab in the 9th cent. B.C. The following translation is the author's.

1) I am Meshaʿ, son of Chemosh[-yat], king of Moab, the Di-
2) bonite. My father ruled over Moab thirty years, and I became
3) king after my father./ I made this high place for Chemosh in Qarḥoh/as a high [place of de]liverance
4) because he delivered me from all assailants (?) and caused me to triumph over all my enemies./ Omri,
5) the king of Israel, had oppressed Moab many days because Chemosh was angry with his land./
6) His son succeeded him, and he too said, "I will oppress Moab."/ In my time he spoke thus,
7) but I triumphed over him and his house./ Israel has utterly perished forever. Now Omri had occupied al[l the lan]d
8) of Medeba./ He had dwelled in it his days and half the days of his son, forty years. But Chemosh
9) restored it in my days. I built Baʿal-meʿon and made in it the reservoir; and I built
10) Qiryaten./ Now the people of Gad had dwelled in the land of ʿAtarot from of old, and the king of Israel had built for himself
11) ʿAtarot./ But I fought against the city and took it./ I killed all the people of
12) the city as satiation for Chemosh and for Moab. I brought back from there ʾArʾel (?), its DWD, and I
13) dragged it before Chemosh into Qiryat./ I settled in it people of Sharon and people
14) of Maḥarit./ Then Chemosh said to me, "Go, seize Nebo from Israel." So I
15) went by night and fought against it from the break of dawn until noon./ I
16) seized it. I killed all of them, seven thousand men and male aliens,/ women, and female aliens
17) and female slaves; for I had devoted them to destruction to ʿAshtar-Chemosh./ I took from there the
18) [ves]sels of Yahweh and dragged them before Chemosh./ The king of Israel had built
19) Yahaṣ and lived in it when he fought against me./ But Chemosh drove him out before me, and
20) I took from Moab one hundred men, all its chiefs (?),/ and set them against Yahaṣ and seized it
21) to add on to Dibon./ It was I who built Qarḥoh, the wall of the forests and the wall of
22) the citadel./ I am the one who built its gates. I built its towers./ I
23) built the royal palace. And I am the one who made the pair of reservoirs (?) [for the spr]ing in the midst
24) of the city./ But there was no cistern in the midst of the town at Qarḥoh. So I said to all the people, "Each of
25) you make for yourselves a cistern in his house."/ And it was I who cut the beams(?) for Qarḥoh with Israelite
26) prisoners./ I am the one who built ʿAroʿer and made the highway in the Arnon (valley)./
27) It was I who built Bet-bamot, for it was destroyed./ I built Beṣer — for it was in ruins —
28) with fifty men(?) of Dibon, because all Dibon is subject (to me)./ And I ruled over
29) [ ] hundreds in the towns which I added to the land./ It was I who built
30) Medeba and Bet-diblaten/ and Bet-baʿalmeʿon; and I brought there
31) [ ] the flock of the land./ And as for Ḥauronen, there dwelled in it [ ]
32) [And] Chemosh said to me, "Go down, fight against Ḥauronen."/ And I went down [ ]
33) [and fought against the town and seized it]; and Chemosh [dwelled] in it in my days . . .
34) . . .

*I. Discovery and Authenticity.*–F. A. Klein, a German missionary, discovered the stone in 1868. While negotiations for its purchase were underway Arabs broke up the stone, but not before the French scholar C. S. Clermont-Ganneau had made an imprint of the inscription. Most of the pieces were recovered and are in the Louvre. The fragments and the imprint have allowed the stone and its important inscription to be restored and reconstructed. Although the authenticity of the inscription was long disputed, it is no longer in doubt. The form of the letters is consistent with other inscriptions of the 9th cent. B.C. and could not have been known when the stone was discovered. Certain linguistic peculiarities have since found parallels in other epigraphic discoveries.

*II. Linguistic Characteristics.*–The inscription is the primary evidence for the Moabite language, a Canaanite dialect in the group of Northwest Semitic languages. It is closely related to Hebrew in grammar and vocabulary but has affinities with Ugaritic (the infixed *-t* verbal form, which is found sporadically in Hebrew), Phoenician (the nominal feminine singular ending *-t*), and Aramaic (orthography and the nominal masculine plural ending *-n*). The similarity between the language of the inscription and Hebrew is best seen in the following characteristics: use of the *waw* consecutive; the relative *ʾšr*; the infinitive absolute in connection with the finite verb; *ʾt* as the sign of the direct object; and such vocabulary and forms as *hwšyʿ*, *yrš*, *grš*, *hrg*, *hḥrym*, *lpny*, *bqrb*, *wʾʿś*. The syntax closely resembles that of Hebrew.

*III. Stylistic Characteristics.*– Mesha's inscription is comparable to numerous monumental inscriptions set up by ancient Near Eastern kings. It is essentially a victory stele celebrating Mesha's victory over Israel and the dynasty of Omri and acknowledging the help of the Moabite national deity Chemosh, who figures significantly in the text. The inscription also catalogs various building activities of Mesha, some of which resulted from his military accomplishments. The first twenty lines deal primarily with military matters and the last thirteen or fourteen with construction, although the subject matter sometimes overlaps. Despite a basic consistency in the language of the inscription, two distinct styles of writing are discernible in the two sections (see F. I. Andersen for details). The style of the war section resembles classical Hebrew narrative prose; that of the building section is similar to various Phoenician and Aramaic monumental inscriptions.

*Plate 1.* The library of Celsus at Ephesus (W. S. LaSor)

*Plate 3.* Mosaic of a lion from the synagogue at Tiberias (Roman period) (A. D. Baly)

*Plate 2.* One of the famous cedars of Lebanon on the snow-covered slopes of the Lebanon Mountains (W. S. LaSor)

W. S. LaSor photographed the following coins from the collection of G. L. Archer.

*Plate 4.* Persian gold daric (*ca.* 400 B.C.)

*Plate 5.* Silver decadrachma from Syracuse (*ca.* 480 B.C.)

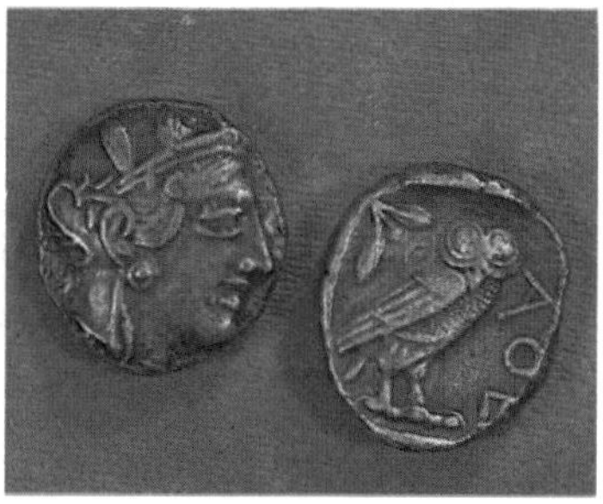

*Plate 6.* Athenian tetradrachma. Obv.: Athena. Rev.: owl (*ca.* 490-430 B.C.)

*Plate 7.* Silver tetradrachma, rev.: Athena Promachos (*ca.* 300 B.C.)

*Plate 8.* Bronze coin, rev.: date palm (A.D. 133-134)

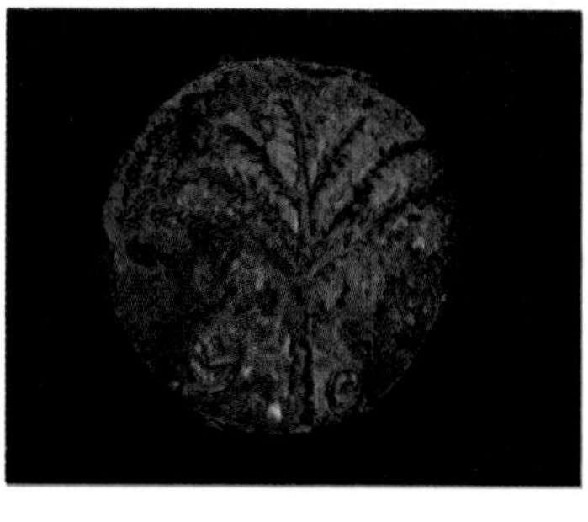

*Plate 9.* Gold aureus of Domitian (obv.; see Plate 37 for rev.) (A.D. 81-96)

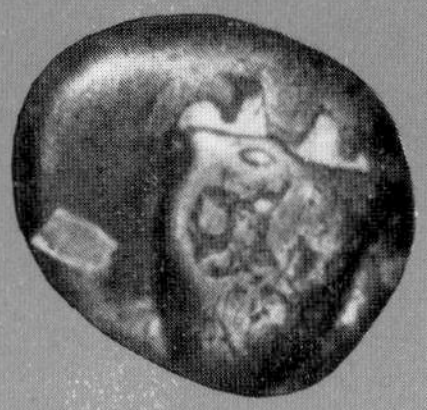

*Plate 10.* Aegina stater (obv.), the earliest silver coinage known (650 B.C.)

*Plate 11.* Rev.: mill incuse (punch mark)

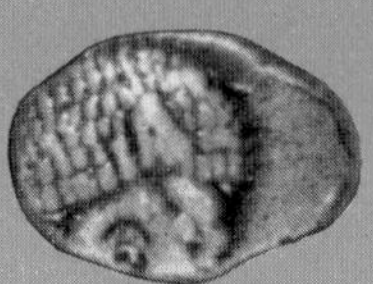

*Plate 12.* Coin from Miletus (obv.), *ca.* 500 B.C.

*Plate 13.* Corinthian drachma, obv.: Aphrodite (*ca.* 400-388 B.C.)

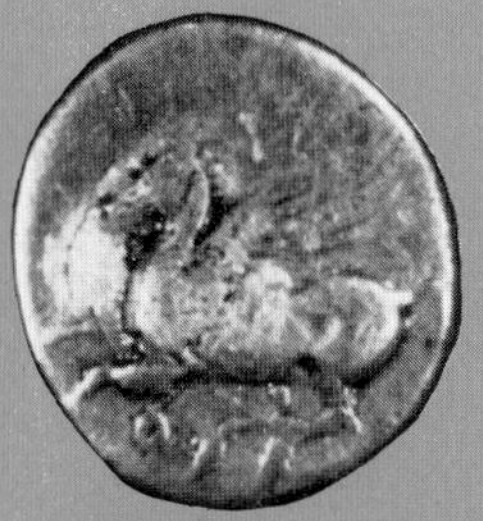

*Plate 14.* Corinthian drachma, rev: Pegasus

*Plate 15.* Corinthian stater, obv.: Athena (*ca.* 350 B.C.)

*Plate 16.* Rev.: Pegasus

*Plate 17.* Athenian tetradrachma, obv.: Athena Parthenos (*ca.* 163 B.C.)

*Plate 18.* Athenian tetradrachma, rev: owl with inscription

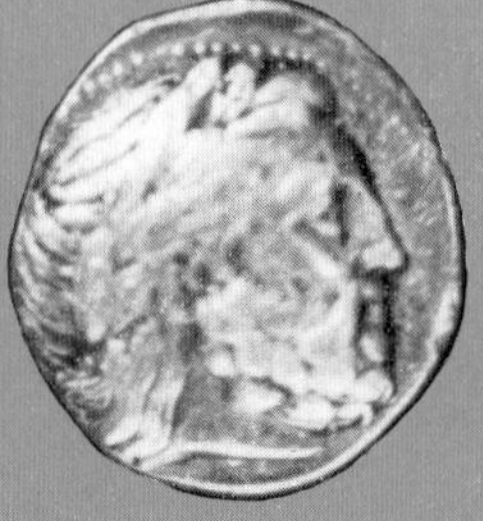

*Plate 19.* Silver tetradrachma of Philip of Macedon. Obv.: Zeus (*ca.* 359-336 B.C.)

*Plate 20.* Rev.: horse and rider

*Plate 21.* Silver tetradrachma of Alexander the Great. Rev.: seated Zeus

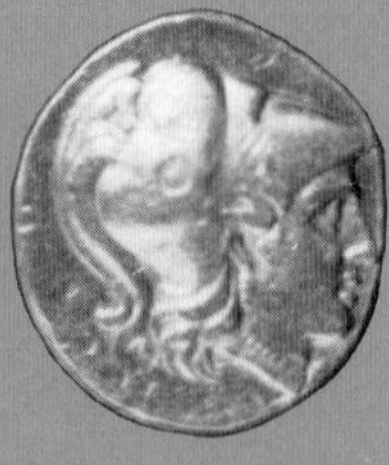

*Plate 22.* Gold stater of Alexander the Great. Obv.: Athena

*Plate 23.* Macedonian gold stater of Alexander the Great. Rev.: Nike

*Plate 24.* Tetradrachma of Lysimachus of Thrace. Rev.: Athena (*ca.* 300 B.C.)

*Plate 25.* Coin of Ptolemy I, obv.: head of Ptolemy (*ca.* 323-285 B.C.)

*Plate 26.* Coin of Ptolemy I, rev: eagle

*Plate 27.* Shekel of Seleucus I, rev.: lion of Babylonia (*ca.* 300 B.C.)

*Plate 28.* Roman silver denarii. Left: Aretas beside camel (*ca.* 58 B.C.). Right: Pompey the Great (*ca.* 40 B.C.)

*Plate 29.* Rev. of Roman denarii shown in Plate 28

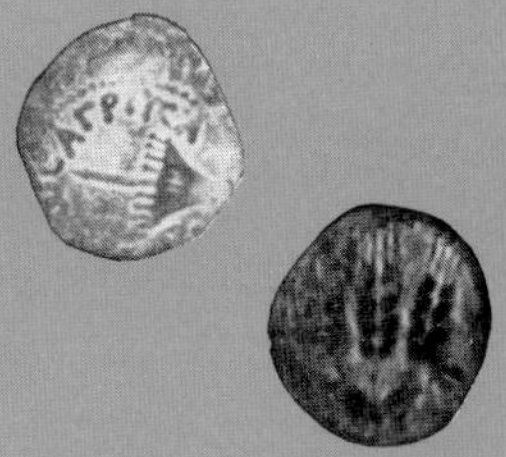

*Plate 30.* Bronze lepton of Herod Agrippa (*ca.* A.D. 41-44)

*Plate 31.* Denarius, obv.: head of Claudius Caesar (*ca.* A.D. 45)

*Plate 32.* Rev.: Pax with caduceus

*Plate 33.* Denarius, obv.: head of Nero (*ca.* A.D. 60)

*Plate 34.* Bronze lepton from the First Jewish Revolt (*ca.* A.D. 68)

*Plate 35.* Silver denarius, obv.: head of Tiberius (*ca.* A.D. 14-37)

*Plate 36.* Rev.: seated vestal priestess

*Plate 37.* Gold aureus of Domitian (rev. of Plate 9)

*Plate 38.* Paphos tetradrachma, obv.: head of Vespasian (A.D. 68-79)

*Plate 39.* Rev.: temple of Aphrodite

*Plate 40.* Denarius, obv.: head of Domitian (A.D. 92)

*Plate 41.* Rev.: Minerva

*Plate 42.* Part of the Medeba Map showing Jerusalem and environs (J. C. Trever)

*Plate 43.* The Wâdī el-Môjib (Arnon River), which divided Moab and Ammon (B. VanElderen)

*Plate 44.* The Byzantine church (foreground) and Herod's main palace (background) at Masada (Jamie Simson, Das Photo)

*Plate 45.* Irrigated field in the Nile Delta near Tanis (W. S. LaSor)

The Moabite Stone (Oriental Institute, University of Chicago)

If, as Andersen has suggested, the inscription is "a mixture of conventional models" (p. 119), a mixed style may characterize other royal inscriptions.

*IV. Historical Significance.*–The inscription is of primary importance as extrabiblical testimony to the relationship between Israel and Moab in the 9th century. It is a valuable supplement to the account of Mesha's revolt against Israel in 2 K. 3:4-27 but also apparently conflicts with the biblical data. The chief issue is the meaning of the chronological data in lines 7-9 and the identification of the king of Israel against whom Mesha rebelled. The inscription says that Israel conquered and maintained control of the land of Medeba during Omri's reign and half of his son's, i.e., forty years. Mesha's revolt would therefore have occurred during the latter part of Ahab's reign, presumably while Ahab, who was fighting the Arameans and involved in the coalition against Shalmaneser III of Assyria, could not have put it down.

This interpretation, accepted by the majority of scholars, may well be correct. It is faced with two problems, however: (1) the "forty years," if taken literally, would extend considerably beyond Ahab's death; and (2) the account of 2 Kings twice states explicitly that Mesha rebelled after the death of Ahab (1:1; 3:5). The usual answers are that "forty years" is only a round number referring to a generation or two, and that the biblical report is somewhat inaccurate. These assumptions are questionable and do not remove the difficulty in correlating this interpretation with Mesha's implication that he triumphed completely over the house of Omri. That suggests a time for the revolt — as well as the inscription — toward the end of the Omride dynasty. It is possible, therefore, that Mesha revolted against Joram, the last of the house of Omri to sit on the throne of Israel. This view, which accords with the account in 2 Kings, necessitates understanding "his son" *bnh*) in line 8 as "his grandson," a solution that is not entirely satisfactory although *bēn* can mean grandchild or descendant as well as son. Still another possibility is that the revolt took place after the end of the Omride dynasty, i.e., against Jehu, but neither the inscription nor the biblical text suggests that.

The question when the revolt began remains, therefore, unresolved. It may have started shortly before Ahab's death but reached its full force only during the reign of Joram. In any event, the inscriptional and biblical accounts combine to give a fairly detailed picture of the ensuing conflict between Israel and Moab during the 9th century.

Under Omri Israel had conquered Moab and established citizens and garrisons in various Moabite cities, particularly in the northern plateau country. The inscription alludes to certain building operations by the king of Israel during this period. When Mesha revolted, he moved north from his capital in Dibon to capture the four main districts of the northern plateau: the land of Medeba (lines 8f.), the land of Ataroth (lines 10f.), Nebo (lines 14-18), and Yahaṣ (lines 18-21) — possibly in that order. The time span of these military operations is unknown. They may have been individual campaigns over a long time that are summarized in order on the stele. But more likely that they were particular engagements of a single, well-devised campaign.

Mesha also described his extensive construction of new towns and rebuilding of others previously destroyed. He apparently used Israelite captives in these endeavors (lines 25f.).

The broken conclusion to the inscription tells of a campaign against Ḥauronen (or Horonaim). The exact location of this city is uncertain, but it was in the southern part of Moab, where Joram of Israel in alliance with the kings of Judah and Edom sought to put down Mesha's revolt (2 K. 3:4-27). Apparently to avoid confronting Mesha's fortified cities in the north, Joram took a circuitous route to the south through Judah and Edom. Although the coalition armies initially captured a number of southern cities, their siege of Kir-hareseth failed and they were forced to withdraw, leaving Moab under Mesha's control.

*V. Religious Significance.*–The worship of Chemosh in Moab as reflected in the inscription resembles in several ways the worship of Yahweh in Israel. The roles of the deities in military activities are especially comparable. Like Yahweh, Chemosh was regarded as the source of victory or defeat. The Israelite conquest of Moab was attributed to the anger of Chemosh at his land (lines 5f.). Chemosh, however, also saved Mesha or Moab (line 4) and gave victory to the king.

Chemosh directed the military activities of Moab. His responses to the important pre-battle inquiry of the deity ("Then Chemosh said to me, 'Go, seize Nebo from Israel'" [line 14]; "[And] Chemosh said to me, 'Go down, fight against Ḥauronen'" [line 32]) resemble the oracular divine responses prior to battle in the OT (e.g., Jgs. 10:23, 28; 1 S. 23:2, 4). The expression in line 19, "But Chemosh drove him out [*wygršh*] before me," is used in the OT for Yahweh's expulsion of the people of Canaan before Israel in the Conquest (Ex. 23:29f.; Dt. 33:27; Josh. 24:18).

The most significant characteristic from a religious point of view is the mention in line 17 of the *ḥērem* or ban as an element of war. This is the only clearly attested example outside the OT; it reveals the similarity between the sacral war practices of Israel and those of Moab. The *ḥērem* was a strongly religious activity involving a vow or promise to give the spoils of war to the deity who had commanded the attack (line 14) and insured victory. The phrase "for I had devoted them to destruction [*hḥrmth*] to ʿAshtar-Chemosh" indicates that the *ḥērem* had been vowed to Chemosh prior to battle. The following sentence, "I took from there the [ . . . ] of Yahweh and dragged them before Chemosh," has an unfortunate break; the missing word would give further insight into the practice of *ḥērem*. The most plausible reconstruction for this word is "vessels" (*kly*), which allows a comparison with the Israelites' taking of silver, gold, and vessels (*kᵉlê*) of bronze and iron from Jericho for the treasury of Yahweh (Josh. 6:19). Lines 11f. may contribute further to the understanding of *ḥērem*; they appear to say that Mesha killed all the people of Ataroth as satiation (*ryt*) for Chemosh and for Moab. This episode may be likened to the apocalyptic war scene of Isa. 34:5-7, which describes the bloodthirstiness of the sword of Yahweh.

Finally, the inscription contains the oldest extant extra-biblical occurrence of Yahweh as the name of the God of Israel. It also suggests that shrine or cultic implements involved in the worship of Yahweh were in the town of Nebo while it was under Israelite control (lines 17f.); perhaps the presence of a Yahweh sanctuary is indicated.

***Bibliography.–LBHG***, pp. 305-309; F. I. Andersen, *Orientalia*, 35 (1966), 81-120; P. Auffret, "Essai sur la structure littéraire de la stèle de Mesha," *Ugarit-Forschungen*, 12 (1980), 109-124; F. M. Cross and D. N. Freedman, *Early Hebrew Orthography* (1952), pp. 35-44; *KAI*, I, 33; II, 168-179; J. C. L. Gibson, *Textbook of Syrian Semitic Inscriptions*, I (1971), 71-83: J. Liver, *PEQ*, 99 (1967), 14-31; J. M. Miller, *PEQ*, 106 (1974), 9-18; S. Segert, *Archiv Orientální*, 29 (1961), 197-267; A. H. van Zyl, *The Moabites* (1960).

P. D. MILLER, JR.

**MOABITESS** mō-ə-bī'təs [Heb. *môʾᵃḇîyâ*]; NEB also MOABITE WOMAN (2 Ch. 24:26). A woman from MOAB. The term is applied to Ruth (1:22; 2:2, 21; 4:5, 10) and to Shimrith, whose son was one of the conspirators who murdered King Joash (2 Ch. 24:26). Some of Solomon's wives also came from Moab (1 K. 11:11).

**MOADIAH** mō-ə-dī'ə [Heb. *môʿaḏyâ*–'Yahweh shakes' or 'Yahweh promises']. A priestly family in the time of Joiakim (Neh. 12:7). *See* MAADIAH.

**MOAT** [Heb. *ḥārûṣ*] (Dnl. 9:25); AV WALL; NEB CONDUITS. The Hebrew term, a hapax legomenon, is based on the verb *ḥāraṣ*, "cut," and thus probably refers to a protective trench surrounding the walls of the restored Jerusalem. Cf. *ḥrṣ* in the early (8th cent. B.C.) Aramaic inscription of Zakkur (formerly called Zakir). Here the context is one of a siege against Zakkur's city Ḥatarikka; Zakkur's enemies built a higher wall and deeper moat (*ḥrṣ*) than those of Ḥatarikka (for the text, translation, and discussion see *KAI*, I, 37 [Text 202 A]; II, 204-209; cf. *ANET*, pp. 655f.). The cognate *ḥārîṣ* also occurs in postbiblical Hebrew (e.g., T.B. *Shabbath* 22a) with the meaning "furrow, trench," as well as in postbiblical Aramaic, where *ḥᵃrîṣâ* can denote a channel or trench (Tg. to Job 38:25).

G. A. L.

**MOCHMUR** mok'mər [Gk. *Mochmour*] (Jth. 7:18). A wadi (seasonal brook) near Acraba where a contingent of Edomites, Ammonites, and Assyrians attempted to surround the Israelites, cutting off their water supply (vv. 7:16-19). The town of Chusi (Quza) was located on the banks of the wadi, and Acraba was nearby. Acraba has been tentatively identified with ʿAqrabeh, 12.8 km. (7.7 mi.) SE of Nablus and 8.8 km. (5.5 mi.) E of Quza, and Mochmus with Wâdī Maḫfuriyeh S of Acraba. Another suggested site is Wâdī Aḥmar, but it is farther east and does not support the identification of Chusi with Quza.

W. S. L. S.

**MOCK** [Heb. hiphil of *tālal* (Jgs. 16:10, 13, 15), *hāṯal* (1 K. 18:27), piel of *ḥārap* (2 K. 19:4, 16, 22f. par. Isa. 37:4, 17, 23f.; Ps. 89:51 [MT 52]), *lîṣ* (Prov. 19:28; 20:1), hiphil part. of *lāʿaḇ* (2 Ch. 36:16), *lāʿag* (2 Ch. 30:10; Job 9:23; 11:3; 21:3; Ps. 22:7 [MT 8]; 79:4; Prov. 1:26; 17:5; 30:17; Jer. 20:7), *lāʿēg* (Ps. 35:16), hithpael of *qālas* (Ezk. 22:5), *qallāsâ* (Ezk. 22:4), *śāḥaq* (Lam. 1:7), pilpel part. of *tāʿaʿ* (Gen. 27:12); Gk. *diachleuázō* (Acts 2:13), *chleuázō* (17:32), *empaigmós* (He. 11:36), *empaízō* (Mt. 20:19; 27:29, 31, 41; Mk. 10:34; 15:20, 31; Lk. 14:29; 18:32; 22:63; 23:11, 36), *myktērízō* (Gal. 6:7)]; AV also REPROACH, SCORN, LAUGH, LAUGH TO SCORN; NEB also TAUNT, DERIDE, RIDICULE, JEER, etc.; **MOCKER** [Heb. *hᵃṯulîm* (Job 17:2), qal part. of *lîṣ* (Hos. 7:5)]; AV also SCORNER; NEB MEN TAUNT, ARROGANT MEN.

The Hebrew words translated "mock" have a wide variety of meanings: reproach, scorn, scoff, deceive, jest, and laugh. Sennacherib king of Assyria high-handedly taunted the living God (2 K. 19:4, 16, 22f. par. Isa. 37:4, 11, 23f.; cf. 2 K. 18:33-35). The Israelites mocked Hezekiah's messengers, who urged repentance and the keeping of Passover (2 Ch. 30:1-10). This mocking of God's messengers persisted and brought God's judgment (36:16f.). In his role as a prophet of doom Jeremiah was also mocked (Jer. 20:7; cf. 2 K. 2:23f., where Elisha is also mocked). The righteous sufferer is often mocked by enemies surrounding him (Ps. 22:7; 35:16; 89:51; cf. Job 17:2; 21:3), a circumstance that influenced the martyr piety of Judaism (see *TDNT*, V, 633).

But the situation can be reversed. Thus with biting sarcasm Elijah mocked the prophets of Baal on Mt. Carmel (1 K. 18:27; cf. God's scorn for impious rulers, Ps. 2:4).

Mocking could also refer to the playful deception of lovers. Delilah complained that Samson mocked her by withholding the secret of his strength (Jgs. 16:10, 13, 15).

Proverbs warns against (1) mocking the poor and rejoicing over calamities (17:5), (2) making a mockery of justice (19:28), and (3) scorning obedience to parents (30:17). Drunkenness, too, is associated with mockery (Prov. 20:1; Hos. 7:5). God also warns that when the people are disobedient, He will subject them to the mockery of neighbors (Ps. 79:4; Lam. 1:7; Ezk. 22:4f.; Prov. 1:26).

In the NT *chleuázō* and the related *diachleuázō* each occur twice. They are related to *chleúē*, which means joke or jest, and suggest a flippant kind of mockery. At Pentecost the disciples were mockingly accused of being filled with new wine (Acts 2:13). At the Areopagus Paul spoke of the resurrection of the dead, and some (presumably the Epicureans) mocked (Acts 17:32). In the parable of the tower builder, Jesus said that a wise man counts the cost to see if he has enough to complete the project. Otherwise, he is subject to ridicule (*empaízō*) for laying an incomplete foundation that serves as a monument to failure (Lk. 14:29).

Like the OT prophets and righteous sufferers, Jesus was severely mocked, especially during the Passion. He had predicted that He would be mocked by the Gentiles (Mt. 20:19 par. Mk. 10:34; Lk. 18:32). According to Luke, those who had arrested Jesus mocked Him and buffeted Him about (Lk. 22:63). Luke also reported that Jesus' silence provoked the frustrated Herod and his soldiers to treat Him with contempt and to mock Him. They arrayed Him in "gorgeous apparel" and transferred Him back to Pilate (Lk. 23:11). Possibly the fine clothing was the white

The *Mocking of Christ*, a fresco by Giotto di Bondone (*ca.* A.D. 1305) in the Arena Chapel, Padua, Italy (Museo Civico, Padua)

*toga candida* worn by the candidate for office; if so, the soldiers were mocking Jesus' claim to royalty (cf. Acts 12:21). Or, since Luke used that phrase in Acts 10:30 to describe the appearance of an angel (cf. Rev. 15:6; 19:8), "gorgeous apparel" perhaps mocked His claim to be God's messenger.

After the sentence of death, Matthew and Mark report that the Roman soldiers mocked Jesus for His messianic claims (Mt. 27:27-31 par. Mk. 15:16-20). They gave Him a red cloak, which footsoldiers wore (Mt. 27:28; Mk. 15:17 has a purple cloak, suggesting the emperor's cloak; see comms.), a plaited crown of thorns, and a reed as a mock sceptre (Mt. 27:23), and then saluted and knelt in feigned homage. The crown of thorns was not expressly said to be a form of torture; it may have been simply a mock radiate crown. The greeting, "Hail, King of the Jews," was a parody of *Ave Caesar, victor, imperator.* This perverted humor was combined with violence.

Finally, Jesus was taunted by the chief priests, scribes, elders (Mt. 27:41 par. Mk. 15:31), and soldiers (Lk. 23:36) at His crucifixion. All the mocking scenes in the passion narratives make sport of the claims of Jesus: that He was a prophet (Lk. 22:63f.), that He was king of the Jews (Mk. 15:18), and that He could save others (Mt. 27:42 par. Mk. 15:31). The mocking of Jesus also accords well with the martyr theology of Judaism; righteous martyrs had to expect mockery (He. 11:36).

The word *myktērízō* occurs in Gal. 6:7: "God is not mocked." Literally it means "to turn up the nose at" and hence to treat with contempt. The context does not suggest blatant ridicule of God, but an attempt to outwit Him by evading the responsibilities of His laws and reaping a harvest different from what was sown (E. D. Burton, comm. on Galatians [*ICC*, 1920], pp. 340f.; cf. H. D. Betz, *Galatians* [*Hermeneia*, 1979], pp. 306f.).

*See also* DERIDE; SCOFF.

***Bibliography.***–*TDNT*, IV, *s.v.* μυκτηρίζω (H. Preisker; G. Bertram); V, *s.v.* παίζω (G. Bertram); H. D. Preuss, *Verspottung fremder Religionen im Alten Testament* (*Beiträge zur Wissenschaft vom Alten und Neuen Testament*, 92; 1971).

D. E. GARLAND

**MODAD, BOOK OF ELDAD AND.** *See* ELDAD AND MEDAD, BOOK OF.

**MODEIN** mō'din, mō'dēn [Gk. *Mōdeein, Mōdein, Mōdeeim*, etc.; Talm. *môḏî'îm* and *môḏî'îṯ* are reflected in the caption of the Madeba Map, *Mōdeeim hē nýn Mōditha*, "Modein which is now Moditha" (Avi-Yonah, no. 58)]; AV, NEB, MODIN. A town on the plain near Lod (Lydda); the ancestral home and burial place of the Maccabee family.

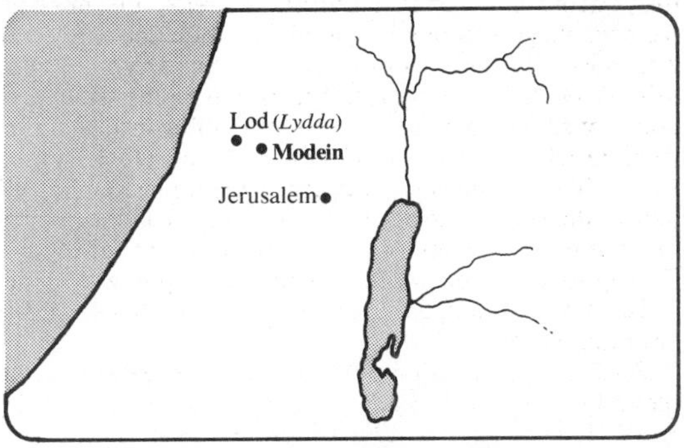


Mattathias, a priest of the sons of Joarib, had sought seclusion at Modein from the campaign of blasphemy and defilement instigated by Antiochus IV Epiphanes. But when a Jew went forward to make a heathen sacrifice in response to a Seleucid officer who offered royal beneficence in order to seduce the people to idolatry, Mattathias became enraged. He slew on the altar both the offerer and the official. Thus began the Maccabean revolt (1 Macc. 2; Josephus *Ant.* xii.6.1-4 [263-286]; *BJ* i.1.3 [36f.]). Mattathias, his wife, and his sons were all buried in Modein (1 Macc. 2:70; 9:19; 13:25-30; *Ant.* xii.6.4 [285]; 11.2 [431f.]).

It was near Modein that Judas Maccabeus pitched his camp, in the face of a new Seleucid threat. He went forth by night under the slogan "To God be the victory" and by a surprise attack overwhelmed the army of Antiochus V Eupator (2 Macc. 13:14). Judah and John, the sons of Simon Maccabeus, rested at Modein before the battle in which they defeated Cendebeus (1 Macc. 16:4).

Over the tombs of his ancestors Simon Maccabeus erected a magnificent monument consisting of seven pyrmids standing on pillars and bearing the designs of all their weapons; it was capped by models of ships facing the sea (1 Macc. 12:29). Eusebius remarked that their tombs were still shown in his own day (*Onom.* 132.16).

The Talmud (T.B. *Pesahim* 36) gives the distance from Modein to Jerusalem as 15 Roman miles (about 22 km., 14 mi.). The modern site has been confidently located at el-Arba'în beside el-Midieh, where remains of ancient buildings and especially tombs carved in the rock are visible. About ½ km. (¼ mi.) W of el-Midieh is a special group of tombs formerly known as Qubûr el-Yehûd, the most important being that of Sheikh el-Gharbâwī. The monument erected by Simon may have been situated here.

***Bibliography.***–M. Avi-Yonah, *Madaba Mosaic Map* (1954); C. S. Clermont-Ganneau, *Archaeological Researches in Palestine*, II (1899), 353-379; *GP*, II, 391; *HGHL*, p. 150 n. 8; A. Neubauer, *La Géographie du Talmud* (1868), p. 99.

A. F. RAINEY

**MODERATELY.** The AV translation of Heb. *liṣᵉḏāqâ* in Joel 2:23. The translation of this term has been in much dispute. Its literal meaning, "according to righteousness," has been interpreted in basically three ways: (1) "in just measure" (ASV; cf. AV "moderately"; NEB "in due measure"; BDB [p. 842] "for prosperity"); (2) "according to [God's covenant] righteousness," with the derived meaning, "for your vindication" (RSV); and finally (3) the whole expression *hammôreh liṣᵉḏāqâ* has been translated "teacher for [or of] righteousness" (cf. NIV, NAB). According to some scholars (e.g., A. Dupont-Sommer, *Essene Writings from Qumran* [Eng. tr. 1961], p. 228 n. 1), this expression and the similar one in Hos. 10:12 were the basis for the title "Teacher of Righteousness" at Qumrân. H. Wolff (*Joel and Amos* [Eng. tr., *Hermeneia*, 1977], pp. 63f.), however, pointed out that no Qumrân texts relate these verses to that title. Cf. also L. Allen, *Books of Joel, Obadiah, Jonah, and Micah* [*NICOT*, 1976), pp. 92f. n. 26. On the theme of rain as a sign of God's covenant righteousness, cf. Lev. 26:3f.; Dt. 11:13-15. (See comms.; *see also* VINDICATE.) N. J. O. G. A. L.

**MODERATION.** The AV rendering of Gk. *epieikés* in Phil. 4:5. *See* FORBEAR.

**MODESTY** [Gk. *euschēmosýnē*] (1 Cor. 12:23); AV COMELINESS; NEB SEEMLINESS; [*sōphrosýnē*] (1 Tim. 2:15); AV SOBRIETY; NEB "with a sober mind"; **MODESTLY** [Gk. *aidṓs*] (1 Tim. 2:9); AV SHAMEFASTNESS.

The RSV's translation of *euschēmosýnē* as "modesty" in 1 Cor. 12:23 obscures its connection with words of the same group in that passage (*aschḗmona, euschḗmona*) and hides Paul's intended contrast. The unity of the body of believers is shown by Paul's statements that the "weaker" members are really indispensable, the "dishonorable" members are treated with special honor, and the "unpresentable" members (Gk. *aschḗmona*) are given a special quality of presentability (Gk. *euschēmosýnē*). The "presentable" members (Gk. *euschḗmona*) do not require special treatment. The NEB attempts to retain this contrast: "To our unseemly parts is given a more than ordinary seemliness, whereas our seemly parts need no adorning." If the translation "modesty" is retained, then it must be remembered that it does not refer to a virtue but to the honor accorded the "unpresentable" members of the body.

The Gk. *sōphrosýnē* of 1 Tim. 2:15 gives quite a different meaning to "modesty." *Sōphrosýnē* and its cognates were among the most important in the vocabulary of Greek ethics. The term refers to a basic disposition that makes possible and demands certain modes of conduct. Its broadest meanings include rationality, prudence, temperance (cf. AV, NEB). It took on special narrower meanings when recommended for various roles. *Sōphrosýnē*, meaning restraint of sexual desire, i.e., chastity, was frequently recommended for women (e.g., Plutarch *Coniugalia praecepta*, 9f. [139c]).

In the NT *sōphrosýnē* and its cognates appear only infrequently; most occurrences are in the Pastoral Epistles. There seems to have been a gradual acceptance of the Greek ethical tradition in the early Christian tradition, culminating in the Pastorals (*see* GODLINESS, on Gk. *eusébeia*). One should not too summarily disparage this acceptance as accommodation. It provided a defense against dualistic misunderstandings of the faith and, as a consequence, against both ascetic and libertinistic misunderstandings of the Christian ethic. According to the Pastorals moderation and contentedness mark life in this world as a life in God's presence. In this context the *sōphrosýnē* required especially of women must find its referent. Thus in 1 Tim. 2:15 "modesty" means a disposition toward sexuality including both moderation and contentedness, excluding both asceticism and libertinism. Similarly, v. 9 (where *sōphrosýnē* also occurs but is translated "sensibly" by the RSV while *aidṓs* is translated "modestly," the two terms being virtually synonymous) demands that women show restraint and contentedness in all things, as is suitable to godliness (Gk. *theosébeia*). Cf. 2 Macc. 15:12, where *aidḗmōn* (RSV, NEB, "modest"; AV "reverend") occurs in a description of Onias the high priest.

*Bibliography.*–*TDNT*, I, *s.v.* αἰδώς (R. Bultmann); VII, *s.v.* σώφρων (U. Luck). A. D. VERHEY

**MOETH** mō'eth [Gk. *Mōeth*]. Son of Binnui (RSV; but cf. Gk. *Sabannos*; RSV mg., NEB, Sabannus); one of the Levites to whom the returned exiles handed over the temple treasures they had carried from Babylon (1 Esd. 8:63); probably the same as NOADIAH in Ezr. 8:33.

**MOLADAH** mō'lə-də [Heb. *môlāḏâ*, perhaps < *môleḏeṯ*–'offspring,' 'parentage'; Gk. *Mōlada*]. A place in the Negeb, the southern desert of Palestine. According to Josh. 19:2 it belonged to the tribe of Simeon (cf. 1 Ch. 4:28). Josh. 15:26, however, assigns it to the territory of Judah in a list that reflects conditions under Joshua, when the tribe of Simeon no longer formed a separate entity. Neh. 11:26 mentions it in a list of places where "some of the people of Judah lived"; this does not mean that it was part of the postexilic province of Judah but rather that it was a place outside the province that Jews peacefully penetrated and settled in the 4th cent. B.C.

Moladah cannot be identified with any certainty. Scholars point to Malatha, where Agrippa in his penury retreated and considered suicide (Josephus *Ant.* xviii.6.2 [147-150]); it was later a fortress of the *limes* in southern Palestine, mentioned in Eusebius (*Onom.* 14.3) and in the form Moleatha in the *Notitia Dignitatum* (74.45). Malatha may be confidently identified with present-day Tell el-Milḥ, 24 km. (15 mi.) E of Beer-sheba, called Malḥ$^{a}$tā on the Israeli topographical map. The objection that Malatha is described in the *Onomastikon* as "near Iattir," whereas Tell el-Milḥ lies nearly 16 km. (10 mi.) S of that village, is not valid. In that desolate region few places are in immediate proximity to each other, and moreover the same name (Malathis oppidum) is given to a civil settlement a few kilometers NE, only 11 km. (7 mi.) from Iattir (*Onom.* 15.2). Perhaps ancient Moladah should be identified with the latter settlement, present-day el-Quseife. It is clear, however, that the two names Moladah and Malatha are unrelated; thus the identification remains uncertain.

*Bibliography.*–W. F. Albright, *JPOS*, 4 (1924), 149ff.; M. Avi-Yonah, *Quarterly of the Department of Antiquities in Palestine*, 5 (1936), 177; *Holy Land From the Persian to the Arab Conquests* (1966), pp. 120, 163; *GP*, II, 391; *EAEHL*, III, *s.v.* "Malḥata, Tel" (M. Kochavi). A. VAN SELMS

**MOLDING** [Heb. *zēr*–'circlet, border']; AV CROWN; NEB BAND. Evidently a decorative ridge made of gold, attached to and surrounding each of the following pieces of tabernacle furniture: the ark of the covenant (Ex. 25:11; 37:2), the table for the show bread (25:24f.; 37:11f.), and the incense altar (30:3f.; 37:26f.). For examples of moldings on an altar and on an incense stand, see *ANEP*, nos. 575, 583. C. G. RASMUSSEN

**MOLE.** This term appears in the RSV only in Isa. 2:20, where *laḥpōr pērôṯ* has for long been emended conjecturally to *ḥ$^{a}$parpārôṯ*, "moles, rats." Apparently these animals were worshiped in Egypt (see KoB, p. 322). In Lev. 11:30 *tinšemeṯ* was rendered "mole" by the AV but "chameleon" by the RSV. Precisely what was signified by the term *tinšemeṯ* is uncertain (*see* LIZARD), and the RSV rendering has no greater intrinsic probability of correctness than that of any other version. That the Vulg. used the word *talpa*, "mole," could imply that the animal was thought to have been a member of the genus *Talpa*, but this is purely coincidental since the Vulg. appears to have been translating the LXX *aspálax*, "mole," into Latin. In actuality small insectivore Talpidae mammals have not been observed in Palestine.

The Isaiah emendation may indicate the activity of mole-rats (*Spalax typhlus*), which belong to the *Rodentia*. They are larger than moles, varying from about 13 to 23 cm. (5-9 in.) in length, and have adapted to an almost completely subterranean existence. Their teeth are similar to those of a rat or squirrel, and they are herbivorous rather than insectivorous. Though blind like moles, the mole-rats dig with their noses, whereas the true moles excavate their tunnels and nests by means of large incisor teeth and powerful, peculiarly shaped front feet. The activity of mole-rats is marked by little mounds of fresh soil pushed to the surface as the rodents search for roots and other edible material. For "mole-rat" in Lev. 11:29, NEB *see* WEASEL. R. K. H.

**MOLECH** mō'lek [Heb. *mōlek̲* (Lev. 18:21; 20:2-5; 1 K. 11:7; 2 K. 23:10; Jer. 32:35), *melek̲* (Isa. 57:9)]; AV also "king" (Isa. 57:9); NEB also "tresses" (Isa. 57:9); **MILCOM** mil'kom [Heb. *milkōm* (1 K. 11:5, 33; 2 K. 23:13), *malkām* (Jer. 49:1, 3; Zeph. 1:5)]; AV MALCHAM (Zeph. 1:5), "their king" (Jer. 49:1, 3); **MOLOCH** mō'lok [Gk. *Moloch*] (Acts 7:43).

All OT references allude to an individual deity identified in specific instances with the Ammonite god Molech (cf. 1 K. 11:7), for whom Solomon built a shrine in Jerusalem. Elsewhere the Ammonite national deity was known as Milcom (1 K. 11:33), but it is incorrect to identify them uniformly since they were worshiped individually (cf. 1 K. 11:5, 33; 2 K. 23:13). Some scholars have thought that Molech was a combination of the consonants for "king" (*m-l-k*) and the vowels of the word "shame" (*ō-e*), since the title of king not infrequently forms part of the names of deities in Phoenician and Hebrew. *See also* ASHTORETH.

This association of kings and gods was not unusual in the Near East, because the king was regarded as the earthly representative of the national deity. He was also accorded certain quasidivine attributes by virtue of having supposedly been nursed in infancy by a goddess (cf. C. H. Gordon, *Ugaritic Literature* [1949], p. 122; T. H. Gaster, *Thespis* [1950], p. 179). Such a situation would account in part for the usage whereby a pagan god was called "king." (Cf. Jer. 49:1, 3, where the RSV reads "Milcom," and Am. 5:26, where the RSV has "their king," but AV Moloch.) The LXX rendering of "ruler" (*árchonti*, e.g., Lev. 18:21) or "king" (*basileús*, e.g., 1 K. 11:5) in some instances may also reflect this understanding. It should be noted that the designation also occurs in lists of names from Mari (*ca.* 1800 B.C.) in the forms *malik* and *muluk*, probably the Adrammelech and Anammelech of 2 K. 17:31.

Supporting the concept of Moloch as a deity is the occurrence of Milkom with Baal in a list of gods recovered from Ugarit (C. H. Gordon, *Ugaritic Literature*, p. 108; *UT*, p. 434). J. Gray (*IDB*, III, 422) argued from the Mesha inscription, where the Moabite deity was described as Athtar (ʿAshtar)-Chemosh, that Chemosh, regarded by Jephthah (Jgs. 11:26) as Moab's national god, was in fact an astral deity Athtar, with Chemosh and Milcom constituting local titles. Alternatively, the reference in the Moabite Stone might well represent the fusion of two gods, following such notable combinations as Amon-Re of Egypt, or Kothar-and-Hasis from Ugarit.

There is also the possibility that Molech may not allude to a deity at all, but instead may designate some type of sacrifice, perhaps votive in nature. O. Eissfeldt and others have pointed to Punic inscriptions (Phoenician-Carthaginian) from *ca.* 400-150 B.C. in which the term *mlk* occurs alone or in the compound expressions *mlk'mr* and *mlk'dm*. Their argument that *mlk* may mean "votive offering" is based on Latin inscriptions from Carthage dated *ca.* A.D. 200 in which the Punic *mlk'mr* was vocalized as *malchomor*.

An even earlier inscription containing *mlk'mr* was found by Dussaud on a stele from Malta dated between the 7th and 6th cents. B.C. (R. Dussaud, *Comptes-rendus de l'Académie des Inscriptions et Belles-Lettres*, I [1946], 376f.). No Phoenician inscription employing *mlk* in a sacrificial context has yet been recovered, but traditions ascribed to Sanchuniathon stated that the Phoenicians sacrificed children. *Mlk* occurs in Ugaritic texts, and has been interpreted by Gordon as a kind of sacrifice (C. H. Gordon, *Ugaritic Handbook*, [1947], p. 246, no. 1183; but cf. *UT*, pp. 433f., no. 1484, where Gordon did not cite any instances of *mlk* as a sacrifice — rather it is the divine name). A text discovered in 1956 contained the plural form *mlkm*, which was associated with cultic activities, but the nature of these activities is uncertain.

In speaking of Molech the OT clearly referred to a specific deity (cf. Am. 5:26 AV; quoted in Acts 7:43) whose cult flourished among the Ammonites (1 K. 11:7, 33). His regnal position may well be indicated by the appellative form in the MT of Lev. 18:21; 20:2-5; 2 K. 23:10; Jer. 32:35. In the last of these references Baal also appears with the definite article as an appellative, and is associated with the fire rituals in the valley of the son of Hinnom. Molech-worship was prohibited to the Israelites, partly because it was pagan but also because its abhorrent rites involved offering children to Moloch (cf. Lev. 18:21; 20:2-5). Scholars have frequently inferred that instances of child sacrifice mentioned in the OT (cf. 2 K. 17:17; 21:6; Ps. 106:38; Ezk. 16:21; etc.) involved Molech-worship. Ahaz offered his children by fire (2 Ch. 28:3), and this example was followed by Manasseh (2 K. 21:6). Although Josiah destroyed the shrines of Molech in Judah (2 K. 23:10, 13), the memory of this detestable ritual was still alive in the 6th cent. B.C. (cf. Ezk. 16:20f.; 20:26, 31; 23:37).

Precisely how Molech-worship was conducted is uncertain. It is usually assumed that children were thrown into a furnace or fire as part of a ceremony, though whether they were killed or made insensitive is unknown. Among the Canaanites, Baal Melkart was offered human sacrifice at Tyre, a tradition that was also evident in Judah during the 7th cent. B.C. (cf. Jer. 19:5). The name Topheth most probably comes from a root meaning "fireplace, incinerator," and Jer. 7:31 makes it clear that Molech cult-worship involved the cremation of human victims rather than the presentation and subsequent withdrawal of live child offerings.

A divergent view suggesting that children were dedicated to Molech prostitution instead of being sacrificed by fire was based on the inclusion of a reference to the Molech cult (Lev. 18:21) in a section that otherwise dealt with sexual morality (cf. Snaith; cf. also Jub. 30:10). This opinion has the disadvantage of presupposing a late date for the Leviticus material, while at the same time introducing the concept of cultic prostitution, which was entirely foreign to Israelite life at the period when the Levitical material was promulgated by Moses. Furthermore, the antiquity and pervasiveness of Molech-worship was already well known long before the Mosaic period, and there is nothing inherently impossible about Moses being familiar with Ammonite cultic depravity.

The rabbinic writers described a bronze statue, human in form but with an ox's head, hollow within and heated from below. Children were placed inside this structure and immolated while drums drowned out their cries. Cf. also Diodorus xx.14 for a similar description.

***Bibliography.***–O. Eissfeldt, *Molk als Opferbegriff im Punischen* *und Hebräischen und das Ende des Gottes Moloch* (*Beiträge zur Religionsgeschichte des Altertums*, III; 1935); J. Gray, *JNES*, 8 (1949), 72-83; W. F. Albright, *ARI* (5th ed. 1969), pp. 156-59; *Yahweh and the Gods of Canaan* (1968), pp. 235-242; E. Dhorme, *Anatolian Studies*, 6 (1956), 57; R. de Vaux, *Studies in OT Sacrifice* (Eng. tr. 1964), pp. 73-90; *Ancient Israel* (Eng. tr. 1961), pp. 444-46; N. H. Snaith, *VT*, 16 (1966), 123f.

R. K. HARRISON

**MOLI** mō'lī (1 Esd. 8:47, AV). *See* MAHLI **1**.

**MOLID** mō'lid [Heb. *môlîḏ*]. A descendant of Judah; son of Abishur and Abihail (1 Ch. 2:29).

**MOLLIFY.** Used by the AV in Isa. 1:6 (RSV "soften"); Wisd. 16:12 (RSV "poultice" for AV "mollifying plaister") for "soften" in the literal sense.

**MOLOCH** mō'lok [Heb. *malkᵉḵem*–'your king'; cf. LXX *Moloch*] (Am. 5:26, AV); [Gk. *Moloch*] (Acts 7:43). A variant form of MOLECH, thought by some to be an Ammonite or Canaanite deity, although O. Eissfeldt suggested that Heb. *mōleḵ* was a sacrificial term for the royal (cf. *mlk*) sacrifice (*Molk als Opferbegriff im Punischen und Hebräischen und das Ende des Gottes Moloch* [1935]; cf. W. F. Albright, *Yahweh and the Gods of Canaan* [1968], pp. 236-242). In Am. 5:26 the RSV and NEB follow the MT for the most part, but the AV follows the LXX. On this difficult text see H. W. Wolff, *Joel and Amos* (Eng. tr., *Hermeneia*, 1977), pp. 260, 265-68; S. R. Driver, *Joel and Amos* (*CBSC*, 2nd ed. 1915), pp. 192f.

The passage in Acts is also problematic. Here Stephen quotes from the LXX of Am. 5:26f., and as E. Haenchen pointed out, it is difficult to believe that Stephen would have tried "to persuade the High Council with a LXX text which diverges widely from the Hebrew" (*Acts of the Apostles* [Eng. tr. 1971], p. 289). Thus he concluded that this was a Lukan addition to Stephen's speech. Although I. H. Marshall agreed that Luke's hand may be seen here, he also noted that Stephen's point could have been made equally well from either the LXX or the MT (*Acts of the Apostles* [*Tyndale*, 1980], p. 145; cf. F. F. Bruce, *Acts of the Apostles* [*NICNT*, 1954], pp. 153-56).

G. A. L.

**MOLTEN IMAGE.** *See* IDOL.

**MOLTEN SEA.** *See* SEA, MOLTEN.

**MOMDIS** mom'dis (1 Esd. 9:34, AV, NEB). *See* MAADAI.

**MOMENT** [Heb. *regaʿ*] (Ex. 33:5; Nu. 16:21, 45; Job 7:18; Isa. 27:3; etc.); AV also SPACE (Ezr. 9:8), SUDDENLY (Ps. 6:10 [MT 11]); NEB also INSTANT, SUDDEN, etc.; [hiphil of *rāgaʿ*] (Prov. 12:19); [piel of *bālaʿ*] (Nu. 4:20); AV "covered"; NEB "passing"; [*peṯaʿ*] (Prov. 6:15); AV, NEB, SUDDENLY; [*mᵉʿaṭ*] (Ruth 2:7); AV "a little"; [*paʿam*] (Isa. 66:8); AV "at once"; [Gk. *hṓra*] (Mt. 8:13; Gal. 2:5); AV HOUR; [*apó tóte*] (Mt. 26:16); AV TIME; [*stigmḗ*] (Lk. 4:5); NEB "in a flash"; [*exautḗs*] (Acts 11:11); AV IMMEDIATELY; [*átomos*] (1 Cor. 15:52); NEB "in a flash"; [*páreimi*] (He. 12:11); AV PRESENT; NEB TIME; **MOMENTARY** [Gk. *parautíka*] (2 Cor. 4:17); NEB SHORT-LIVED.

In Ps. 30:5 (MT 6), a difficult passage, the NEB has "in his anger is disquiet, in his favour there is life" for RSV "for his anger is but for a moment, and his favor is for a lifetime." Since the Hebrew verb *rāgaʿ* can mean "stir, disturb" in some OT passages (cf. BDB, pp. 920f.), the NEB reading has much to commend it (for a similar approach cf. M. Dahood, *Psalms I* [*AB*, 1965], 182f.). Comparable considerations led the NEB to translate Jer. 4:20b as "my tents are thrown down, their coverings torn to shreds" rather than the RSV's "suddenly my tents are destroyed, my curtains in a moment." Here, however, the NEB reading is hardly correct, since it entirely omits *piṯʾōm*, "suddenly," in the first clause, which parallels *regaʿ* in the second clause.

An examination of the above sampling of passages in their contexts will reveal that stress on the moment often signalizes the momentous in the Bible. In such cases point in time rather than duration of time is emphasized (cf. esp. D. Daube, *The Sudden in the Scriptures* [1964]).

*See* TIME.

R. F. YOUNGBLOOD

**MONEY.** A "medium of exchange," a commonly recognized item of value that usually can be stored and transported more easily than items for which it is exchanged. In ancient times there was no money in the common modern sense of objects used only for this purpose, i.e., coins and paper money (see I.C. below).

Since silver came to be the most common medium of exchange in early OT times, "money" in the RSV usually represents the word for silver in Hebrew (*kesep̱*) or Greek (*argýrion*). These became the usual terms for money in those languages.

Of the four exceptions in the OT, three involve the RSV's use of "piece of money" (Gen. 33:19; Josh. 24:32; Job 42:11) to translate Heb. *qᵉśîṭâ* which actually represents a unit of weight (amount unknown). In Lev. 25:52 "money" is supplied by the translators to clarify the meaning of this use of *gᵉʾullâ* the Hebrew word for redemption."

In the NT "money" twice represents Gk. *chalkós*, lit. "copper, bronze" (Mk. 6:8; 12:41), and three times *chrḗma*, "wealth, means" (sing. as a definite amount in Acts 4:37; pl. in 8:18, 20; 24:26). In Mt. 22:19 "money" represents Gk. *nómisma* (cf. Eng. "numismatic"), a term for money that is put into use legally (cf. "legal tender") and is therefore an acceptable coin. In 27:6 Gk. *argýria* is translated in its original sense, "(pieces of) silver," and "blood money" represents Gk. *timḗ haímatos*, "price [or reward] of blood." For the expression "love(r) of money" (Lk. 16:14; 1 Tim. 3:3; 6:10; 2 Tim. 3:2; He. 13:15), *see* MONEY, LOVE OF. For Gk. *glōssókomon* in Jn. 12:6; 13:29, *see* MONEY BOX.

I. Before Coinage
   A. Bartering and Payment in Kind
   B. Silver and Gold as Money
   C. Anachronistic Terms for Money
II. Quality and Weight Standards
III. Early Coinage
   A. Lydian, Greek, and Persian
   B. Under Philip of Macedon and Alexander the Great
   C. Ptolemaic and Seleucid
   D. Hasmonean
IV. Coinage in NT Times
   A. Roman
   B. Herodian
   C. Under Judah's Procurators
   D. Qumrân Excavations
   E. NT References to Money

***I. Before Coinage.***–*A. Bartering and Payment in Kind.* Money was developed as a suitable and convenient medium of exchange to supplement the system of barter and to facilitate commercial transactions. It was not intended to replace barter, which is still evident in modern times in the exchange of skills and commodities. In OT times wealth was determined by possessions, particularly cattle but also rare metals, e.g., gold and silver. Gen. 13:2 describes Abraham as "very rich in cattle, in silver, and gold"; he was therefore quite able to pay what seems to have been an exorbitant price for the cave of Machpelah as a burial place for his wife Sarah (23:16).

In the ancient nomadic or seminomadic societies wealth was determined predominantly by the number of cattle that a person possessed, and as a result the animals themselves became a readily acceptable medium of exchange. The degree to which cattle were recognized as the normal standard for evaluating wealth is reflected in the Latin term for money, *pecunia*, which is derived from *pecus*, "cattle." In the ancient Near East dues were frequently paid in cattle, and the priests readily bartered surplus animals for things needed to maintain the temple, its sacrificial system, and its personnel.

Perishable goods, especially food, were less acceptable as a medium of exchange than animals or weighed amounts of gold or silver, although timber, wine, and honey were used frequently instead of money in commercial dealings (1 S. 8:15; 2 K. 3:4; Ezk. 45:13-16). Taxes, tribute, and debts were paid in any acceptable form of exchange, as illustrated by the international transaction between Solomon and Hiram king of Tyre (1 K. 5:11), in which Solomon exchanged wheat and olive oil for the Tyrian king's assistance in constructing the Jerusalem temple. Jars of wine and olive oil were frequently substituted for gold or silver when citizens paid their taxes to the state in the 8th cent. B.C. This practice was verified archeologically in 1910, when the Harvard University expedition to Samaria uncovered sixty-three inscribed potsherds in ruins lying just W of the royal palace. One potsherd records the name of the treasury official who had received the wine as well as the names of the peasants who had paid their taxes in this manner. The clarified wine and refined oil shipped to Samaria typified the demands of the luxury-loving royal court and provoked a characteristic reaction from Amos (Am. 6:6). Mesha king of Moab paid his annual tribute to Ahab king of Israel in commodities — 100,000 lambs and the wool of the same number of rams (2 K. 3:4)

*B. Silver and Gold as Money*. The most common precious metal available in the ancient Near East was silver; it is the metal most frequently mentioned in Scripture as used in exchanges by weight (Heb. *šeqel*, "shekel"). Later it became the preferred metal for coins. When Abraham purchased the field and cave of Machpelah (Gen. 23:13-16), Ephron the Hittite apparently would accept only pieces of silver as payment. As was customary, Abraham's four hundred shekels of silver were weighed out before witnesses according to the weights current among the merchants (cf. Jer. 32:9f.). Since Abraham's transaction took place early in the 2nd millennium B.C., the term "shekel" would have represented a weighed amount of silver (perhaps 11.5 gm.; 0.4 oz.), and not a coin. Joseph's brothers sold him as a slave to the merchants for twenty shekels of silver (Gen. 37:28). So frequently was silver used as a medium of exchange in antiquity that the word itself was not mentioned in transactions but simply understood from the context. Solomon, for example, purchased chariots and horses for 600 and 150 (shekels) respectively (1 K. 10:29). Smaller amounts were the BEKA (Heb. *beqa'*), half a shekel (Ex. 38:26, cf. 30:13, 15; Gen. 24:22); the PIM (Heb. *pîm*, 1 S. 13:21) perhaps two-thirds of a shekel; and the GERAH (Heb. *gērâ*), one twentieth of a shekel (Ex. 30:13; Lev. 27:25; Nu. 3:47; 18:16; Ezk. 45:12). Gen. 33:19; Josh. 24:32; and Job 42:11 mention a different unit of weight for metal — the *qᵉśîṭâ*, which may have represented a value approximating that of a lamb. Its worth is uncertain, however, since the value of a lamb could vary also.

The talent, a basic weight of gold or silver, was the largest measure in use before the introduction of coins. Even after that development, money continued to be weighed out on occasions. Thus John Hyrcanus sent three thousand talents of silver to Antiochus VIII Sidetes in 133 B.C. as a ransom for the city of Jerusalem. The talents were part of a nine-hundred-year-old hoard from the sepulcher of King David. The treasure that the Romans took from the temple in A.D. 66 amounted to seventeen talents.

Business dealings, general trade, and the payment of tribute required the transportation of vast quantities of gold and silver. 2 K. 5:5 records that *ca.* 895 B.C. Naaman's servant departed for Israel to give Elisha ten talents of silver, which would have weighed well over six hundred pounds, and six thousand shekels of gold, about two hundred pounds. Although biblical weights are neither precise nor uniform and thus the load could have been considerably heavier, it is noteworthy that the two talents stolen by a servant (vv. 23-27) required two servants to carry them.

Metals used as a medium of exchange increasingly were formed into standardized shapes. Egyptian bas-reliefs show piles or bundles of silver. According to Gen. 42:35 the sons of Jacob tied their silver in bundles when traveling to Egypt to purchase grain; Dt. 14:25 also implies the use of strips of silver bundled together. By *ca.* 1500 B.C. metal bars, ingot, tongues, and animal heads, in addition to flat discs and then rings made of gold, were used for commercial transactions.

Metal jewelry has always been a popular medium of exchange. Gold chains, bracelets, signet rings, and earrings (Nu. 31:50) were listed among the booty captured by the Israelites in their war against Midian. Although there is no direct evidence for this supposition, it is possible that by Moses' time bracelets and rings were made in a fairly standardized weight and used as currency. It is noteworthy, however, that the gifts sent to Rebekah by her fiancé Isaac were recorded in terms of weight: "a gold ring weighing half a shekel, and two bracelets for her arms weighing ten gold shekels" (Gen. 24:22). The value of gold at that time has been estimated as thirteen to sixteen times that of silver. Thus Rebekah's engagement gifts represented a sum far in excess of the twenty pieces of silver paid *ca.* 1700 B.C. by the merchants for Joseph.

To define ancient monetary values in terms of modern currency tends to be meaningless, and therefore it is more appropriate to relate values to purchasing power. While the cost of sacrificial animals is not stated, fifty shekels would buy four bushels of barley (Lev. 27:16). In the middle of the 9th cent. B.C. one shekel purchased one-fifth of a bushel of fine flour or two-fifths of a bushel of barley at the end of a siege (2 K. 7:16; *see* WEIGHTS AND MEASURES). Comparative values for types of food and animals would probably have remained constant, despite the fluctuations of the economy and the effects of climate.

*C. Anachronistic Terms for Money*. Since coins apparently were not known in Palestine before the Exile, biblical references to money in the preexilic period are to the weight of metal. Occasionally an author writing about an earlier event used a monetary term familiar to his readers rather than the word for the money of the earlier period. This procedure may explain the term "daric" in 1 Ch. 29:7.

Later translators used English terms like "farthing" (AV Mt. 5:26; 10:29 par. Lk. 12:6; Mk. 12:42) to familiarize readers with the minuscule value of the widow's mite. Similarly, "penny" was used for the Roman denarius (e.g. AV Mt. 20:2, 9f., 13), and as a result the English abbreviation for penny became *d*, which remained in use until the introduction of decimal coinage in the early 1970's.

*II. Quality and Weight Standards*.–Although goods or

pieces of metal used as a medium of exchange could all be measured or counted, their size and quality were often surprisingly variable. These variations provoked attempts to institute standards based on an item's intrinsic value or purchasing power. A uniformly high level of quality was demanded of those who brought sacrificial offerings to the tabernacle or temple in Israel (Lev. 1:3; 3:1, 6; etc.), but in certain periods in Israelite history some people attempted to avoid such stringent requirements (Mal. 1:7f.). No standard weights and measures existed, however, in any period of ancient Near Eastern history. The age of David and Solomon came closest to establishing a uniform measure of weight for the Hebrews. This "king's weight" (2 S. 14:26) was used for goods received at the royal court, but there is no evidence that it was imposed on the country as a whole or even accepted voluntarily. The same was true for the "sanctuary shekel" (Ex. 30:13; Lev. 5:15; etc.), a standard of weight favored by the Hebrew priests.

Estimating the quantity of ancient currency by observation alone was often inaccurate, and determining quality was yet more difficult. Even the weighing and close examination of metal did little to hinder those determined to cheat. Because of the lack of uniform standards, the weighing process was frequently long, elaborate, and inaccurate. Sometimes the pieces of iron, bronze, or dressed stone employed by merchants were labeled or engraved with the purported weight, but still there was considerable disparity. Coins show evidence of having been clipped over many centuries until they represented a far lower weight of silver or gold than was originally intended. Indeed, this practice continued to some degree until the invention of milling for the edges of coins in the late 18th cent. A.D.

In the postexilic period the metal used as currency, whether a disc, strip, ring, or bar, began to carry a stamp, and in this way pieces of silver began to be recognized as monetary units valid for trading. In the Greek and Roman periods the city of origin was sometimes stamped on gold to indicate its purity. Silver from Tyre was renowned in the ancient world for its purity and the tetradrachmas produced by the mint at Tyre were accepted gladly everywhere. Coins were sometimes slashed to prove that they were solid gold or silver, not merely bronze coated in the precious metal. The idea that a coin's face value could be greater than the value of the metal of which it was made was slow to develop.

***III. Early Coinage.**–A. Lydian, Greek, and Persian.* The earliest coins were probably minted somewhat before 700 B.C. in Lydia and displayed a lion's head. Called staters by the Greeks, they were made of electrum, a natural or artificial alloy of gold and silver; in the ancient world natural electrum occurred most plentifully in the Pactolus River area of Lydia. The first electrum coins were actually irregularly shaped ingots and bore the stamp of King Gyges of Lydia as a guarantee that the bars could be negotiated at a specific value. About this time silver coins of irregular shape and thickness and bearing a turtle design were in use on the Greek island of Aegina. *See* Plates 10-11.

One of the earliest designs on Lydian gold coins — a lion confronting a bull — came from the reign of King Croesus (560-546 B.C.). The reverse side of the coin simply has a punch mark or indentation that is common to the earliest coins from Lydia, Aegina, and Persia. The Lydians and subsequently the Persians produced silver coins in this design; one has been found that dates from the reign of Alyattes (617-560), the father of King Croesus of Lydia. It is very unlikely, however, that these coins were familiar to the Hebrews.

After Lydia came under the control of Persia in 546 B.C., a new style of coin was developed, probably during the reign of Darius I (522-485). The gold coin, called a daric, shows the king poised on one knee holding a bow and spear. Coins of similar design in gold and silver were circulated widely for the next two centuries and were probably among the first coins encountered by the Hebrews. *See* Plate 4. Two coins of the 6th cent. B.C. have been discovered in Palestine, one originating from Thrace and found at Shechem, and the other originating from Athens and found at Jerusalem.

When the Persians under Cyrus the Great overthrew Babylon in 538 B.C., it was natural that the area became flooded with the new Persian coinage, much of it minted in Lydia. As the Hebrew people were released from their Babylonian captivity and returned to Palestine, they took with them vast quantities of the new coins (Ezr. 2:68f.). Very soon thereafter values began to be mentioned in terms of new coinage as well as in terms of shekels and talents (8:27; Neh. 7:70-72).

During the 6th and 5th cents. B.C. the influence of Hellenism spread far beyond the city-states of Greece itself. Traders established settlements in southern Europe and the Middle East, and Greek coins, including the stater and didrachma, circulated along with the Persian darics. *See* Plates 5, 12. The Greek coins were distinctive with their clear designs on the reverse which sometimes had a definite pattern and sometimes an animal or bird. When the heads of gods or goddesses began to appear on coinage, they were usually on the obverse. A silver coin that bears the winged Pegasus on the obverse and the goddess Athena on the reverse, found at Corinth and dated about 4 B.C., was unusual. Much more common were coins like the Athenian tetradrachma with Athena on the obverse and an owl on the reverse. This style of coin circulated from *ca.* 500 B.C. Respected because it always contained the same weight of fine silver, it became the standard monetary unit in Greece, Asia Minor, and Phoenicia because of the extensive trading among these areas and has been found in coin hoards in sites from the Black Sea to Israel. In 230 B.C. it was replaced by a tetradrachma with a helmeted Athena on the obverse and the owl standing on an upturned amphora on the reverse. *See* Plates 6, 13-18.

During the latter part of the Persian period, between 350 and 332 B.C., small coins were minted in Judah with a

Silver hemiobol struck in Jerusalem *ca.* 350 B.C. (Israel Museum, Jerusalem)

design similar to designs of the Athenian coins but with the inscription "Yehud" (Judah) in ancient Hebrew script. These tiny silver coins were probably minted with the permission of the Persian authorities at a time when the Jews had a little more autonomy. Had the Jewish people been in a position to authorize the general minting of coins, they would have made coins of larger size, greater value, and more impressive appearance than these minute ones.

Another coin, perhaps found in Gaza, is inscribed with Aramaic script and was probably made by the Persian authority in Judah; it has been dated to the 4th cent. B.C. A mint in Judah would account for its greater size and worth. On the obverse is the helmeted head of a god and on the reverse a seated figure, presumably a deity holding a falcon. Unusual among these coins bearing the provincial name Yehud is one with a lilylike flower on the reverse instead of the owl, and a bird similar to the falcon on the obverse. This beautiful lily was found commonly throughout the area, and the frequent reference to it in the Talmud indicate its special significance for the Hebrews. Several other coins with a lily design were minted in Jerusalem in the late Hasmonean period.

The Greek monetary system was based, like others, on a concept of weight, in this case the Babylonian silver *mina*. In Greek coinage seventy *drachmas* equaled one mina, and four drachmas equaled one *tetradrachma*. Many of the tetradrachmas minted by smaller city-states are smaller than the tetradrachmas from which they were copied; and in fact they greatly resemble the Greek *didrachma*, which was worth only half as much. Unscrupulous merchants and others could use such differences to their own advantage. The Greek coins popularized a design that showed Athena, the patron deity of Athens, but sometimes they displayed other gods and goddesses. The coins also depicted creatures of land, sea, and air, the products of the land, and familiar objects such as wine jugs and shields. It has been suggested that many of the designs constituted a subtle form of advertising. The Arkagos didrachma used a design incorporating its famous crabs; the turtle on the coins of Aegina indicated that island's maritime economy.

*B. Under Philip of Macedon and Alexander the Great.* As Philip of Macedon obtained control of Greece in 338 B.C., his silver stater bearing the portrait of the god Zeus and gold stater with the head of Apollo became the accepted units of monetary exchange in Greek trading areas. Philip's love of horses was evident in the prancing hoofs and two-horse chariot on the reverse of the gold stater, and the noble horse and jockey on the reverse of the silver stater. The king's portrait was not shown on coins for fear of incurring the wrath of the gods, whose privileges would have been usurped. *See* Plates 19, 20.

After Philip died his son Alexander the Great began minting coins representing figures from Greek mythology. The tetradrachma bears the portrait of Heracles, a deity popular with the Romans as Hercules. The legend of the invulnerable lion's skin associated with Heracles particularly appealed to Alexander, who may have thought that it reflected the stability of his monetary system. The reverse of the coin shows a seated figure of the all-powerful Zeus. Alexander's gold stater from the same period shows the helmeted head of Athena on the obverse and the standing winged goddess of victory, Nike, on the reverse. *See* Plates 21-23.

Alexander's army defeated the Persians under Darius III in 331 B.C. Not only the entire area of Asia Minor, northern Syria, and Assyria but also Afghanistan and the Indus Valley fell under his sway. In Egypt Alexander was hailed as the son of a god, and being thus deified he could join all the other gods and have his own portrait on coins. He did not venture to place this kind of personal stamp on the monetary system himself, probably because of a superstitious fear of reprisal by the other gods. After his death, however, his portrait appeared on coins, e.g., the tetradrachma of Lysimachus of Thrace, which has the portrait of Alexander as Zeus on the obverse and a seated Athena with Nike on the reverse. The gold stater and the silver tetradrachma became the standard coins of his rule. *See* Plate 24.

*C. Ptolemaic and Seleucid.* After the untimely death of Alexander in Babylon in 323 B.C., the empire was divided among four of his generals. In Greece and Macedon the power-hungry and bloodthirsty Cassander retained the use of the gold and silver coinage of his predecessor. Lysimachus of Thrace continued to mint the beautiful, unique, gold and silver coins showing Alexander as the son of Zeus-Amon. It is not surprising that Ptolemy I of Egypt issued coins bearing the head of Athena, goddess of wisdom, since he turned his attention increasingly away from war toward founding the great center of learning at Alexandria with its world-renowned library. More successful in military campaigns was the fourth general, Seleucus of Syria. His early coins strongly resemble those of the former period, showing Heracles and the lion's-skin headdress, with Zeus and Nike on the reverse. As his lust for power increased, he followed Ptolemy I in minting coins with his portrait on the obverse, sometimes wearing a horn as a symbol of strength. *See* Plates 7, 25-27. During this time Palestine was part of the empire of Ptolemy I and in consequence used Egyptian coins extensively. Ptolemy II, who subsequently married his sister, issued a beautiful gold tetradrachma showing in profile the sensitive Grecian features of the brother and sister side by side.

As the names of the kings and the cities in which the coins were minted were gradually incorporated into the design of the coins, inscriptions lengthened and became propaganda. An example is the silver tetradrachma of Antiochus IV Epiphanes (175-164 B.C.), which is inscribed ΒΑΣΙΛΕΩΣ ΑΝΤΙΟΧΟΥ ΘΕΟΥ ΕΠΙΦΑΝΟΥΣ ΝΙΚΗΦΟΡΟΥ *(BASILEŌS ANTIOCHOU THEOU EPIPHANOUS NIKĒPHOROU)*, "King Antiochus, magnificent god [or god who manifests himself], bringer of victory."

In 198 B.C. Antiochus III captured Jerusalem from Egypt and made the Jews part of the Syrian empire. The peaceful tolerance and gradual process of hellenization that had existed under Egyptian rule abruptly halted when Seleucus IV succeeded to the Syrian throne in 187.

*D. Hasmonean.* The rebellion of the MACCABEES, whose descendants are known as the HASMONEANS, against the intense hellenizing policies of Antiochus IV Epiphanes (175-164 B.C.), gave the Jewish people about a century of relative independence from direct Syrian rule, the Hasmonean era. Sometime in this period the first Jewish coins were minted, but just when is a matter of disagreement among numismatists.

The strong city of Tyre began minting its own shekels in the latter part of the 2nd cent. B.C. but Gaza and Ashkelon, cities similar in importance to Jerusalem, did not begin their own minting until almost the end of the century, 104 B.C. It is therefore unlikely that Jewish coins were minted in Jerusalem before that date. According to 1 Macc. 15:6, Simon Maccabeus, as high priest and governor (143-135 B.C.), received a letter from Antiochus VII (139-129 B.C.) granting permission to mint his own money. This permission, however, was probably either withdrawn or not acted upon at the time. Coins bearing the Hebrew inscription *šmʿwn* were once thought to have been minted by Simon Maccabeus, but now they are dated to the period of the Second Revolt (B.C. 132-135) under Simon Bar Cochba. F. Banks, however, dated the first Jewish coins, the small bronze lepta, to 139 B.C., the period of Simon Maccabeus.

According to G. L. Archer, Simon's son and successor John Hyrcanus I (135-105 B.C.) was the first Hasmonean ruler to strike Jewish coins (*Zondervan Pictorial Encyclopedia of the Bible* [1975], I, 906). If this is true, the minting of coins probably occurred in conjunction with a declaration of independence from Syria at the death of Antiochus VII in 129 B.C. The coins that some attribute to Hyrcanus are inscribed "Yehohanan the High Priest and the Community [*ḥeḇer*] of the Jews," which reflects Hyrcanus's opinion that he was foremost a priest and only secondly a prince. Other coins bear the name Yehudah, the Hebrew name of Hyrcanus's son and successor Aristobulus.

Other scholars (e.g., Y. Meshorer) have argued that since Yehohanan and Yehudah were common names during the Hasmonean era, these names could just as easily refer to two later Hasmoneans. After the one-year reign and death of Aristobulus, his three brothers, whom he had imprisoned, were released. The eldest, Alexander Janneus (Hebrew name Yehonathan) eventually won control. His sons were Aristobulus II (Hebrew name Yehudah) and Hyrcanus II (Hebrew name Yehohanan). Meshorer has contended that the title inscribed on the freshly minted coins in the Beth Sahur hoard, "head of the community [*ḥeḇer*] of the Jews," probably did not come into use until 47 B.C. The late date of this hoard and the ambiguous evidence of the names (stated above) have led him to conclude that it is not certain that Jewish coins were minted during the reign of Hyrcanus I.

It is certain, however, that coins were minted in the time of Alexander Janneus (103-76 B.C.), for two hoards of them have been found, at Jaffa (Joppa) and at Gideon. One indication that these may have been the first Jewish coins is that they follow very closely the designs on the coins of the former Syrian masters of Judea. If Alexander's Hasmonean predecessors had minted their own coins, he probably would have copied a more Jewish style.

Throughout the reign of Alexander Janneus bronze coins featuring the double cornucopia and a pomegranate were minted. These designs were frequently struck over the previous flower-and-anchor design. Because of his military victories, on some coins Janneus used the title "king" in bilingual inscriptions — "Yehonathan the King — King Alexander" — in Hebrew and Greek. Others were inscribed "Yehonathan [or "Yonathan"] the High Priest and the Community of the Jews"

The quality of these early Jewish coins varies considerably. Some are large, thick, and well shaped, but coins of the more turbulent years later in Janneus's reign are thin and small, possibly reflecting a shortage of metal. These coins are of low denomination, and large quantities of the smallest, the lepton, were minted. These lepta remained in circulation for more than a century and were still plentiful in the time of Jesus. The tiny lepton is the coin commonly known as the widow's mite, mentioned by Jesus in Mk. 12:41-44 (cf. Lk. 21:2; 12:59). It was made of bronze or copper of such inferior quality that the coin deteriorated readily; obtaining clear specimens has thus been very difficult. The radiant sun, typifying the sun of righteousness (Mal. 4:2 [MT 3:20]), and the ship's anchor, signifying the reliability of God's promises, are common motifs on these coins.

Bronze coin of Hyrcanus II. Obverse (right): Hebrew inscription, "Yehohanan the high priest and the community of the Jews." Reverse (left): double cornucopiae (Israel Museum, Jerusalem)

Any semblance of independent Hasmonean rule came to an end within fifteen years after the death of Alexander Janneus in 76 B.C. His widow, Salome Alexandra, ruled for nine years. At her death Janneus's younger son Aristobulus II seized power and ruled for four years, not without opposition from the supporters of the elder son, Hyrcanus II. Both sides appealed to the Roman Pompey to arbitrate the dispute. Pompey settled the matter in his own way by taking over Judea in 63 B.C., making it a Roman province.

Pompey had also destroyed the once-powerful Seleucid dynasty by conquering Syria. The last Seleucid king, Philip II Philadelphus (*ca.* 93-82 B.C.), minted a traditional silver tetradrachma with his own portrait on the obverse and Zeus with Nike on the reverse. Throughout the Hasmonean period the silver coins of the Seleucid empire had continued to be the main coinage in Palestine. The tetradrachma, which had been the principal unit of monetary exchange for several centuries, at first existed along with the Roman denarius but eventually gave way to the denarius as the inscriptions were changed from Greek to Latin.

Another Hasmonean, Antigonus II (Greek for Mattathias), a son of Aristobulus II, gained power briefly through the aid of the Parthians in the early 30's B.C. Some of his coins read "Mattathias the High Priest and the Community of the Jews" on the obverse in Hebrew and "King Antigonus" on the reverse in Greek. Antigonus was the first to inscribe the seven-branched lampstand on coins. He was defeated by Herod the Great, who had been appointed King of Judea by Rome, and was beheaded in 37 B.C.

***IV. Coinage in NT Times.*–*A. Roman.*** Roman coinage had developed gradually from the 4th cent. B.C. The as, originally a measurement of weight (the Roman pound, about 340 gm., 12 ozs.), was at first oblong and later round. The quadrans is one of several coins bearing a ship design to signify the importance of Rome as a maritime power. Because of the idea that the metal in the coin must have a value equivalent to that represented by the coin, these early coins, made of bronze, are thick, heavy, and cumbersome. Merchants who traded abroad found that peoples who normally dealt in silver or gold would not accept bronze coins.

In the 3rd cent. B.C. the Romans began to mint silver drachmas, which almost immediately were reduced in size. By the Second Punic War (218-201) the coins weighed only 28 gm. (1 oz.), and by 89 B.C. they were half that size. From 180 B.C. the drachma gave way to the denarius, a coin of similar value that was the established day-laborer's wage in NT times and also the Roman soldier's daily wage. The AV translates denarius as "penny" (Mt. 20:2-10). Several denarii were minted to commemorate the capture of Judea. One of these, struck *ca.* 40 B.C.,

Menorah (lampstand) on bronze coin (reverse) of Antigonus II. A Greek inscription (mostly broken off) read "King Antigonus" (Israel Museum, Jerusalem)

shows the head of Pompey, who had been murdered in 48, and bears the inscription MAG(NUS) PIUS I(MPERATOR) ("great holy conqueror"). *See* Plates 28, 29. Another denarius, minted *ca*. 58, carries a design of King Aretas, who had allied himself with Hyrcanus II, in supplicant position beside his camel; it is inscribed REX ARETAS, "King Aretas." Julius Caesar was the first living Roman to be immortalized on a coin; his head is drawn on the obverse of the denarius and Venus appears on the reverse. The inscription reads CAESAR DICT(ATOR) PERPET(UUS) ("Caesar, perpetual dictator").

Circulating at the same time were the silver quinarius, worth half a denarius, and a sestertius, worth one-fourth of a denarius. The latter, originally a small silver coin, was later replaced by a large bronze coin of the same name. The shekel and half-shekel, previously known as a weight rather than a coin, were minted for two centuries at the great silver mint at Tyre. It is likely that such Tyrian shekels or tetradrachmas, rather than Roman coins, were those paid to Judas Iscariot (Mt. 26:15; 27:3-5). These and other coins minted at Tyre remained among the most readily accepted in the Roman world because of the purity of the silver.

*B. Herodian.* Herod the Great, who had chosen sides wisely, became vassal king of Judea and continued to mint Jewish coins of small denominations. In 37 B.C., when he returned in triumph with his new title of king, he began minting lepta. These lepta are easily recognizable because they are dated, an innovative feature for Jewish coins. The inscriptions on Herod's coins are in Greek, unlike his predecessors' inscriptions, which are either entirely in Hebrew or on later coins, in both Greek and Hebrew. The symbols on his coins show foreign influences and thus are not necessarily Jewish. Many have a noncommital design that could be interpreted as either a local or a foreign symbol; e.g., the tripod on a lepton could be seen as a Jewish symbol of worship or as a familiar Greek object. Some coins, however, show undeniably non-Jewish objects, e.g., the small caduceus in the double cornucopiae and the eagle, the latter a symbol of Roman strength.

Jewish coins struck in the reign of Herod's son Archelaus (4 B.C.-A.D. 6) are small and made of bronze. Archelaus continued the tradition of using symbols that were inoffensive to the Jews. The coins he minted have traditional designs, such as the helmet and cornucopiae, but they also frequently have maritime symbols and a new design of grapes, a characteristic Jewish symbol in view of the quantity of grapes grown in Judea. The name and title ΗΡΩΔΗΣ ΕΘΝΑΡΧΗΣ or ΗΡΩΔΟΥ ΕΘΝΑΡΧΟΥ (Gk. *HĒRŌDĒS ETHNARCHĒS* or *HĒRŌDOU ETHNARCHOU,* "[of] Herod, ethnarch") form the only inscription on these bronzes; these coins are thus readily identified, for Archelaus was the sole ruler of his dynasty to bear the title of ethnarch rather than king. Since the kingdom of Herod the Great was divided among his three sons, it is not surprising that the coins of Archelaus had limited circulation and have been unearthed only in a relatively small area, ranging from Caesarea in the north of Jerusalem and Jericho in the south. A few have also been found in excavations of Herod the Great's fortress at Masada about 48 km. (30 mi.) SE of Jerusalem on the western shore of the Dead Sea.

Bronze lepton of Herod the Great. Obverse: tripod with bowl; Greek inscription, "King Herod"; the date is just to the left of the tripod (year 3). Reverse: incense altar between two palm branches (Trustees of the British Museum)

Herod's second son, Herod Antipas, minted thick, heavy coins that are clearly dated, although for some unknown reason he did not begin minting coins until the twenty-fourth year of his reign. His bronzes are Jewish in design and depict the familiar local palm trees, particularly the date palm. The earliest bronzes of his reign, dated A.D. 19/20, bear the design of a reed, a symbol of the city newly founded by Herod Antipas and named ΤΙΒΕΡΙΑΣ (*Tiberias*) in the inscription. Excavations indicate that the coins of this reign, minted at Tiberias, circulated solely in the region of northern Israel controlled by Herod Antipas.

The third son of Herod the Great, Philip II, ruled a population far less Jewish in character. As a result, the coins struck at Caesarea Philippi (Paneas) completely lack Jewish symbolism and have a distinctly Roman style — the head of the emperor and a temple — showing strong allegiance to the overlords. This was the first time a Jewish coin was minted that disregarded the second commandment. The few extant coins from this reign usually have the head of Augustus with the title ΚΑΙΣΑΡ ΣΕΒΑΣΤ (*KAISAR SEBAST*, "revered Caesar") on the obverse and the name and title of Philip surrounding the temple design on the reverse. One coin, however, shows on the obverse the head of Augustus surrounded by (ΦΙΛΙΠΠ)ΟΥ ΤΕΤΡΑ(ΡΧΟΥ) (*PHILIPPOU TETRA[RCHOU]*, "Philip, tetrarch"). The coins of Philip's reign have mostly been found in the area that he controlled, although one has been unearthed as far away as Cyprus. Philip's successor, Herod Agrippa I, first used his predecessor's mint at Paneas; but when he succeeded to all the lands of his grandfather Herod the Great, he transferred his minting operations to Caesarea and Jerusalem. The few large coins from his reign show confusing designs that are difficult to interpret, but it is noteworthy that Agrippa I was the first Jewish king to mint a coin showing his own head. His small bronzes issued for use in Judea show a canopy as a symbol of monarchy, rather than the head of Agrippa or the emperor; the latter symbols would have offended the Jews, and thus, they appeared on coins circulated in mostly non-Jewish areas. *See* Plate 30; *see also* pictures in HEROD.

The last ruler of the Herodian dynasty was Agrippa II. Educated in Rome and having sympathies that lay more with his Roman masters than with his Jewish ancestors, he reigned during, and survived, a turbulent period of Jewish history. Coins of his reign present severe dating problems, since many carry two dates separated by a five-year gap. H. Seyrig has plausibly suggested that the two dates derive from two eras in the reign of Agrippa II, one beginning in A.D. 56 and the other in 61. The earlier coins have Greek inscriptions and styles, while those with later dates have Latin inscriptions. Most belong to the earlier era, but those bearing the double dates and Latin inscriptions show changes in style and composition; the artistry is undoubtedly superior, and the coins are thinner and have a higher copper content. The head of Nero appears on coins once thought to have been undated but later dated by Meshorer to A.D. 61. Meshorer has suggested that the refounding of Caesarea Philippi (Paneas) as Neronias in 61, in honor of the emperor who had come to power in 54, was such an important event in the reign of Agrippa II of Chalcis (the last of the Herodian line) that he issued commemorative coins and regarded 61 as the start of his second era. *See* Plate 33.

*C. Under Judah's Procurators.* Most of the Roman procurators sent to Judea minted small coins. Some, like those of Pontius Pilate, are undeniably Roman in style, but others, like those of Antonius Felix (A.D. 52-60), bear symbols that would have been more acceptable to the Jews. Most of the procurators adhered to the practice of not overtly offending Jews with their coinage. Even though Felix married the sister of Agrippa II, the Jews never quite trusted him, and his coins reflect his dual sympathies. Although some show Jewish symbols of palm trees and branches, others with designs incorporating Roman weapons reconfirm the overbearing presence of Rome.

Porcius Festus became procurator in A.D. 60 and two years later was succeeded by increasingly career-oriented procurators who managed to inflame once more the latent nationalism of the Jewish people. The rebellion against Rome began in 66 and continued for four years; during that time the Jews again began to mint coins, some of them "dated" by the words "Year One of the Liberation of Zion" ( = A.D. 66). Some of these coins were silver, the minting of which was itself an act of rebellion. At the beginning of the revolt they minted shekels (*see* Vol. II, Plate 41) and half-shekels, which supplanted the foreign silver currency (Tyre's shekel and Antioch's tetradrachma).These coins reflected the ideology behind the rebellion, having inscriptions such as "Jerusalem is Holy," "Freedom of Zion," and "Of the Redemption of Zion." Later in the revolt half-, quarter-, and eighth-shekels were made of bronze, as were the small lepta, perhaps because the supply of silver in the treasury was depleted. Many of the coins show the libation cup with pearls on the rim that was used in Jewish sacrifices. Vine-leaf designs, pomegranates, and date palms are also stamped on the coins. *See* Plate 34.

The second revolt in A.D. 132 again included the minting of coins as a proclamation of independence. The Jews minted silver and bronze coins, but, evidently because they had no raw materials, they overstruck other coins with their own design and inscriptions. These coins have sayings such as "Year One of the Redemption of Israel," "Simeon Prince of Israel," and "Eleazar the Priest." Probably the coins formerly dated to the time of Simon

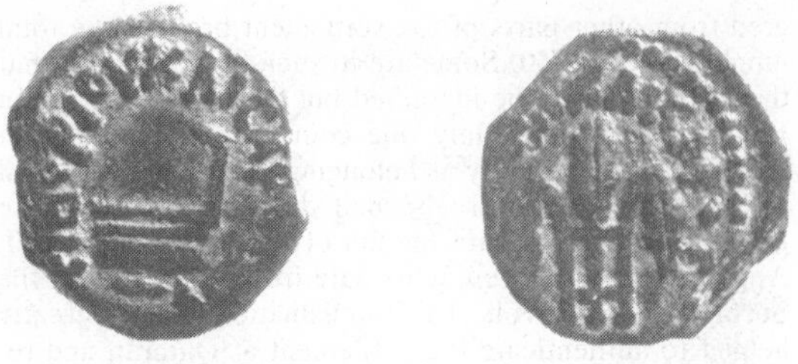

Bronze coin of Pontius Pilate. Obverse: simpulum (ladle) with Greek inscription, "Tiberius Caesar." Reverse: three ears of corn with inscription, "Julia Caesar" (Trustees of the British Museum)

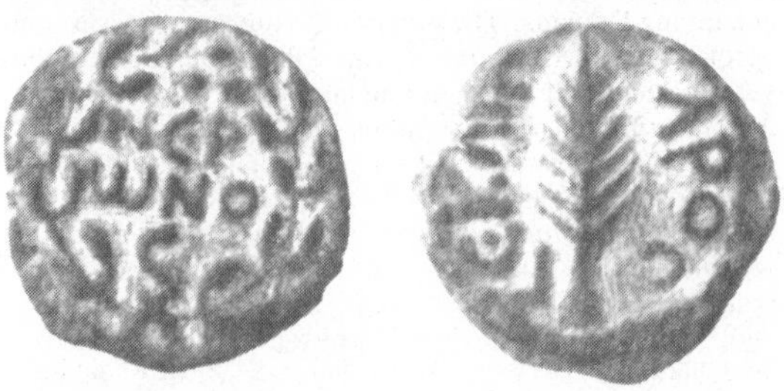

Bronze coin of the procurator Porcius Festus struck in Judea in A.D. 59. Obverse: Greek inscription within wreath, "Of Nero." Reverse: palm branch with Greek inscription, "Year 5 of the emperor" (Israel Museum, Jerusalem)

Silver shekel from the First Jewish Revolt. Obverse: chalice with Hebrew inscription, "shekel of Israel." Reverse: stem with three flowers and Hebrew inscription, "Jerusalem is Holy" (Trustees of the British Museum)

Silver tetradrachma of Bar Cochba. Obverse: temple with shrine containing scroll. Reverse: palm branch and ethrog with Hebrew inscription, "Deliverance of Jerusalem" (Trustees of the British Museum)

Maccabeus come from this period (see III.D above). *See* Plate 8.

*D. Qumrân Excavations.* Excavations in the area of the community center at Qumrân uncovered a number of coins dating from the Hasmonean period to the second Jewish revolt. Almost 250 coins were found in the ruins of the community center itself, while caches of coins recovered from other parts of the settlement brought the total number to over 750. Some are in such bad condition that they cannot easily be identified but clearly belong to the Hasmonean period. Only one coin, however, has been identified with certainty as belonging to the time of Herod the Great. Others were isssued during the rule of the Roman procurators until the fall of Jerusalem in A.D. 70. Approximately a dozen coins date from the period of the Second Jewish Revolt. This numismatic evidence greatly helped to authenticate the settlement at Qumrân and relate the occupational activity of the site to the contents of the Qumrân caves.

*E. NT References to Money.* In the time of Christ, locally minted Jewish coins circulated along with those of the occupying Romans. The portrait of Augustus Caesar, emperor at the birth of Jesus (Lk. 2:1), dominates the obverse of the silver denarius and later the bronze sestertius, with inscriptions attesting to his divine status. The Roman Senate had bestowed divinity on Augustus, partly in recognition of his being the adopted son of Julius Caesar. The "coin" (Gk. *dēnárion*) used for tribute and requested by Jesus when the Pharisees asked him whether paying tribute to Caesar was lawful (Mt. 22:19 par.) would have been the silver denarius of the succeeding emperor, Tiberius (14-37). This coin displays a portrait of Tiberius on the obverse and a seated female figure on the reverse. *See* Plates 35, 36. The Good Samaritan of Jesus' parable left two denarii with the innkeeper to pay for food and care for the man attacked by robbers (Lk. 10:35); this sum was two days' wages (Mt. 20:2, 9f., 13). In Jn. 6:7 Philip estimated that supplies of food worth two hundred denarii would be insufficient to feed the multitude that was assembled to hear Jesus (cf. Mk. 6:37). The "silver coin" of Lk. 15:8f. represents the drachma (Gk. *drachmá*), a Greek coin of about the same value as the Roman denarius.

The "thirty pieces of silver" (Gk. *triákonta argýria*, "thirty silver [coins]") given to Judas for the betrayal of Christ (Mt. 26:15; 27:3, 5f., 9; cf. the sing. *argýrion*, "money," in Mk. 14:11; Lk. 22:5) were probably Tyrian shekels or tetradrachmas; these also may well have been the form of the "sum of money" (Gk. *argýria hikaná*, "much money") given by the chief priests and elders to the Roman guards to misrepresent the circumstances of the Resurrection (Mt. 28:12f.) Abbreviations on these coins included DIV ("divine"), AUG (*Augustus*), PON (*Pontifex Maximus*, "highest priest" or "religious ruler") and PM (*Pontifex Maximus*), COS ("consulship"), TRP (*Tribunica Potestate*, "tribune authority," "civil head of state"), and IMP (*Imperator,* "emperor"). *See* Plates 9, 31, 37-41.

"Penny" is used in the RSV for Gk. *assárion* ( = Lat. *as*), worth about one-sixteenth of a denarius, in Mt. 10:29 par. Lk. 12:6. The quadrans (Gk. *kodrántēs*), one-fourth of an as, is mentioned twice in the Gospels (Mt. 5:26; Mk. 12:42) and rendered "farthing" by the AV but "penny" by the RSV. For the "copper coin" (Gk. *leptón*) of Mk.12:42; Lk. 12:59; 21:2 (AV "mite") see III.D above.

Silver denarius of Tiberius. Obverse: head of Tiberius with Latin inscription, "Tiberius Caesar son of the divine Augustus." Reverse: Livia holding branch and scepter; Latin inscription, "high priest" (Trustees of the British Museum)

The shekel (Gk. *statḗr*) found in the fish's mouth by Peter (Mt. 17:27) would have paid the dues of two persons, since the temple tax was half a shekel. Jewish tradition used the shekel, either as a weight or as a coin, for the temple tax, the poll tax, and redemption from the priesthood (cf. Ex. 13:13; 30:11-16; Nu. 3:44-51). If three thousand shekels equaled one talent of silver, the ten thousand talents owned by the unmerciful servant was indeed an enormous debt (Mt. 18:23-25). The RSV "pound" (Lk. 19:13) is the rendering of the old weight known as *mina* or *maneh* (Gk. *mna*), equivalent to fifty shekels in Hebrew weight and one hundred drachmas in Greek money; thus the parable values highly the activities of those who work for the coming of Christ's kingdom.

*See also* BANK; BUYING; DARIC; DENARIUS; HALF A SHEKEL; MONEY, CURRENT.

*Bibliography.*–F. Banks, *Coins of Bible Days* (1955); *HJP*², I, 602-606; L. Kadman, ed., *Corpus Nummorum Palaestinensium*, III (1960), 106-108; L. Kadman, *et al.*, *Dating and Meaning of Ancient Jewish Coins* (1958); B. Kanael, *BA*, 26 (1963), 38-62; *IEJ*, 1 (1950/51), 170-75; A. Kindler, *IEJ*, 4 (1954), 170-185; 6 (1956), 54-57; F. W. Madden, *History of Jewish Coinage and of Money in the Old and New Testments* (1864, repr. 1967); *Coins of the Jews* (1881); Y. Meshorer, *Jewish Coins of the Second Temple Period* (1967); M. Narkis, *Coins of the Jews* (1939); R. Oster, *JBL*, 101 (1982), 195-223; A. Reifenberg, *Ancient Jewish Coins* (2nd ed. 1947); *Israel's History in Coins from the Maccabees to the Roman Conquest* (1953); P. Romanoff, *Jewish Symbols on Ancient Jewish Coins* (1944).

H. W. PERKIN

**MONEY BOX** [Gk. *glōssókomon*] (Jn. 12:6; 13:29); AV BAG; NEB COMMON PURSE. Originally a container for holding mouthpieces of wind instruments (*glṓttai*) but more generally a container for varied purposes.

According to Jn. 12:6; 13:29 this container was used for storing money (cf. 2 Ch. 24:8, 10 par.) held in common by the disciples. From this common purse, replenished by the friends of Jesus (Lk. 8:3), the necessities of life were supplied for the group (cf. Mk. 6:37; Jn. 4:8; 6:5; 13:29) and for the poor (Jn. 13:29). Jn. 12:6 describes the character of JUDAS ISCARIOT, the treasurer of the group; his betrayal of Jesus for thirty pieces of silver was in perfect accord with his being a thief during the ministry of Jesus.

R. H. STEIN

**MONEY, CURRENT** [Heb. *kesep̱ ʿōḇēr*–'money passing (along)'] (Gen. 23:16, AV). Abraham paid Ephron 400 shekels "current money with the merchant" (AV) for the field and its cave, in which he buried Sarah. ("Shekel" at that time was not a coin but a weight; *see* MONEY; WEIGHTS AND MEASURES.) The RSV translates "according to the weights current among the merchants," while the NEB translates "of the standard recognized by merchants." There are four different interpretations of the phrase.

(1) Coinage was not yet in use. In order to assure that, for example, a bar of silver had as much silver as the owner claimed, the bar would be weighed against other weights, which the merchant knew were accurate. Ephron was thus assured that he had received a full 400 shekels. "Current money" would refer to the weights currently in use in checking the weight of silver ingots. See E. Speiser, *Genesis* (*AB*, 1964), p. 171.

(2) Some think that "current money" refers to the fact that Abraham paid a price that was current for the value of the field. The price of 400 shekels, however, seems to be abnormally high.

(3) Others think "current money" indicates that the

silver with which Abraham paid the price was an acceptable medium of payment. S. R. Driver cites the Targum of Pseudo-Jonathan as saying "good silver, passing at every (banker's) table, and receivable in all transactions" (*Book of Genesis* [*WC*, 1913], p. 227).

(4) On the basis of the occurrence of the same Hebrew verb in 2 K. 12:4 (MT 5), some would interpret "current money" as a poll tax paid in addition to the price of the field. W. D. MOUNCE

**MONEY, LOVE OF** [Gk. *philargyría*] (1 Tim. 6:10). The dangers of the "love of money" was a popular theme in the ethical literature of both paganism (e.g., Democritus and others, who described *philargyría* as the mother city [*mētrópolis*] of all evil; see Diogenes vi.50) and Judaism (e.g., T. Jud. 17–19). Jesus also warned that striving after material WEALTH brings alienation from God and neighbors (e.g., Mt. 6:24; Lk. 16:19-31). The Pharisees scoffed at Jesus' teaching because they were "lovers of money" (pl. of *philárgyros*; AV "covetous;" cf. 2 Tim. 3:2). 1 Tim. 3:3 instructs that a bishop must be "no lover of money" (*aphilárgyros*; AV "not covetous"), while He. 13:5 warns all its readers to keep themselves "free from the love of money" (*aphilárgyros*; AV "covetousness"; cf. NEB "do not live for money").

*See also* MAMMON; RICHES. N. J. O.

**MONEY-CHANGER** [Gk. *kollybistḗs*] (Mt. 21:12 par. Mk. 11:15; Jn. 2:15); AV also CHANGER; [*kermatistḗs*] (Jn. 2:14); AV CHANGER OF MONEY. *See* BANK III.

**MONGREL PEOPLE** [Heb. *mamzēr*] (Zec. 9:6); AV BASTARD; NEB HALF-BREEDS. The Hebrew term apparently denotes one born of a prohibited union, in this case probably the offspring of intermarriage with another people (cf. "bastard," Dt. 23:2, the only other occurrence of *mamzēr*; cf. also P. Craigie, *Book of Deuteronomy* [*NICOT*, 1976], p. 297). KD saw the fulfillment of Zec. 9:5f. in Arrian's later description of how Alexander the Great conquered Gaza, put the male citizens to death, sold the women and children into slavery, and populated the city with neighboring tribesmen (Arrian *Anabasis* ii.27).

**MONSTER; SEA MONSTER** [Heb. *tannîn*] (Gen. 1:21; Job 7:12; Ps. 148:7; Jer. 51:34); AV WHALE, DRAGON; NEB also SEA-SERPENT, WATER-SPOUT, DRAGON. *See* DRAGON.

**MONTH.** *See* CALENDAR II.A.2, B.1.

**MONTHLY PROGNOSTICATORS** (Isa. 47:13, AV). *See* ASTROLOGY IV.

**MONUMENT** [Heb. *yāḏ*–'hand'] (1 S. 15:12; 2 S. 18:18; 1 Ch. 18:3; Isa. 56:5); AV PLACE, DOMINION; NEB also MEMORIAL; [*ṣîyûn*] (2 K. 23:17); AV "title"; [Gk. *mnēmeíon*–'token of remembrance'] (Mt. 23:29); AV SEPULCHRE. A landmark such as a cairn or gravestone made from one stone or a pile of stones.

The very common Hebrew word *yāḏ*, which basically means hand, in a few instances means monument, a reflection of the hand's function of pointing. In most of these occurrences it refers to a gravestone or a more elaborate memorial to mark a burial. This may be what Saul made for himself (1 S. 15:12). Clearly that is the case with Absalom in 2 S. 18:18, with the anonymous Judean prophet in 2 K. 23:17, and in the one NT reference (Mt. 23:29), where Jesus spoke of the tombstones of the righteous. Isaiah used the term figuratively when he spoke of godly eunuchs who would be remembered by something better than a gravestone (56:5).

The reference in 1 Ch. 18:3 (par. 2 S. 8:3) is doubly ambiguous. (1) Heb. *yāḏ* may mean "power" (see 2 S. 8:3, RSV), "dominion" (so AV; *CHAL*, p. 243; J. Myers, *I Chronicles* [*AB*, 1965], pp. 131, 135) or "monument (of victory)" (so RSV; NEB; BDB, p. 662). (2) The subject of "set up" (hiphil of *nāṣaḇ*) may be David (see M. Unger, *Israel and the Aramaeans of Damascus* [repr. 1980], pp. 50, 139 n. 15) or Hadadezer (so NEB; KD; S. R. Driver, *Notes on the Hebrew Text and Topography of the Books of Samuel* [2nd ed. 1913], p. 281). R. L. ALDEN

**MOOLI** mōō'lī (1 Esd. 8:47, NEB). *See* MAHLI **1**.

**MOON** [Heb. usually *yārē(a)ḥ*, also *lᵉḇānâ*; Gk. *selḗnē*]; **FULL MOON** [Heb. *kese'* (Prov. 7:20), *kēseh* (Ps. 81:3 [MT 4])]; AV DAY (TIME) APPOINTED; in Job 26:9 the RSV and NEB emend MT *kissēh* (AV, lit., "throne") to read *keseh*. *See also* NEW MOON.

According to the creation account in Gen. 1, God made two lights — the greater light (the sun) to rule the day and the lesser light (the moon) to rule the night (vv. 16-18; cf. Jer. 31:35; Ps. 104:19; 136:9; 2 Esd. 6:45). God set these light-giving bodies in the heavens along with the stars as signs for days, seasons, and years (Gen. 1:14). Appearing in multiple phases, the moon (*yārē[a]ḥ*) measured time in months (cf. *yeraḥ*, "month"; *see* CALENDAR II.A.2) and set the times for festivals (cf. Sir. 43:6-8). The great festivals of Passover in the spring and the Feast of Booths in the fall began at full moon. Furthermore, the "new moon" (*ḥōḏeš*, also rendered "month") was celebrated each month in a manner similar to a sabbath but with a little more festivity (cf. Nu. 28:11-15).

The term "moon" usually occurs in combination with "sun" and "stars." All three times that "moon" represents Heb. *lᵉḇānâ* (lit. "white lady") it is paralleled by *ḥammâ* (lit. "hot one," i.e., "sun"; Cant. 6:10; Isa. 24:23; 30:26). "Moon" occurs with "stars" in Job 25:5; Ps. 8:3 (MT 4); Jer. 31:35.

Ancient Near Eastern peoples believed the moon to be a powerful force. They thought it could strike a person by night, producing mental illness (cf. Ps. 121:6). Such an idea may lie behind Gk. *selēniázomai* (lit. "be moonstruck"; cf. Eng. "lunatic"), which in Mt. 4:24; 17:15 may be describing a case of epilepsy.

Like the sun, the moon is a common symbol of permanence (Ps. 72:5; 89:37 [MT 38]; cf. Jer. 31:35f.), although its changing phases can also be a simile for the instability of a fool (Sir. 27:11). The moon's brilliant whiteness symbolizes beauty (Cant. 6:10), and as one of the heavenly bodies it represents regal glory (cf. 1 Cor. 15:41); thus the woman in Rev. 12:1, who most likely represents the true Israel, is pictured as "clothed with the sun, with the moon under her feet, and on her head a crown of twelve stars."

The ancient Near Eastern peoples were fascinated by the heavenly bodies and worshiped them with great devotion (cf. 2 K. 23:5; Jer. 8:1f.). The prominent deity of Ur and Haran, two Mesopotamian cities closely associated with Abraham, was the moon-god Sin (Sum. Nanna). This deity appears in the name of the Assyrian king Sennacherib ("Sin has replaced the [lost] brothers"), who set siege to Jerusalem during the reign of Hezekiah. Ugaritic texts refer to a moon-deity called *yrḫ*. Thoth, the Egyptian moon-god, was the god of knowledge; order and wisdom were his special powers. Moon-worship probably lies behind the name Jericho (*yᵉrîḥô*). The crescent was a beloved symbol associated with the moon and its worship (*see* CRESCENTS). The ancients believed that careful observa-

Boundary stone of Meli-shipak (12th cent. B.C.) from Susa. The text on the back of this stone is a grant to King Marduk-apla-iddina; gods, whose symbols are pictured here (note the crescent, top left, the sign of the moon-god), are invoked to curse anyone who violates the terms of the grant (Louvre)

tion of the moon, particularly in its relationship to the sun, could offer insight into the course of affairs on earth. In Mesopotamia, e.g., an eclipse was feared as a bad omen, and special rituals were performed to ward off the portended dangers.

The OT presents a strong polemic against the worship of heavenly bodies (Dt. 4:19; cf. 17:2-5; Job 31:26-28; Isa. 47:13; *see also* ASTROLOGY IV). They are not worthy of human devotion, for they have their origin solely in Yahweh and He continually directs their courses (cf. Ep. Jer. 6:60). As one of God's creatures, the moon renders Him praise (Ps. 148:3; cf. Song Three 40). Because their movements are fully subject to God, Joshua was able to command both the moon and the sun to stand still (Heb. *dāmam,* lit. "be silent, be motionless") during a critical battle (Josh. 10:12f.).

Certain passages speak of great disturbances occurring throughout nature in the last days. The prophet Joel spoke of the moon being darkened (2:10; 3:15 [MT 4:15]; but cf. 2 Esd. 5:4) or turned to blood (Joel 2:31 [MT 3:4], quoted in Acts 2:20; cf. Rev. 6:12; 8:12). According to Isaiah (13:10; cf. Ezk. 32:7; Mt. 24:29; Mk. 13:24; Lk. 21:25), the moon will not give its light on the day of the Lord; but in the new age when God, the eternal light, will reign supreme, there will be no need for the light of either the sun or the moon (Isa. 60:19; Rev. 21:23; cf. 2 Esd. 7:39).

Deuteronomy 33:14 contains the unusual expression *gereš y$^{e}$rāḥîm* (lit. "yield of moons," parallel to *t$^{e}$ḇû'ōṯ šāmeš,* "fruits of the sun"). The RSV renders it "the rich yield of the months." Although *y$^{e}$rāḥîm* sometimes means "months," the parallel to "sun" indicates that the meaning "moons" is prominent here. No doubt the ancients thought that the moon played a critical role in the crops' coming to harvest; at least several moons must pass before the fields ripen. Unfortunately this play on the meaning of *y$^{e}$rāḥîm* cannot be captured in English.

*See also* ASTRONOMY.

***Bibliography.***–*TDOT,* IV, *s.v.* "chādhāsh, chōdesh" (R. North), esp. pp. 230f.; *TWOT,* I, 406f., 468. J. E. HARTLEY

**MOON, NEW.** *See* NEW MOON.

**MOOSSIAS** mō-ə-sī'əs [Gk. *Mooseias*]; AV MOOSIAS. One of those who had married a foreign wife and was obliged to divorce her (1 Esd. 9:31); possibly the same as MAASEIAH (9) in Ezr. 10:30.

**MORALITY.** *See* ETHICS.

**MORALS** [Gk. pl. of *ḗthos*–'habit, custom,' 'character (as the result of habit)'] (1 Cor. 15:33); AV MANNERS; NEB CHARACTER. The term occurs only here in the RSV. "Bad company ruins good morals" is a proverbial saying that occurs in Menander's comedy *Thais*. The same idea is expressed by other Greek authors (cf. Bauer, rev., p. 344). Paul's quotation of the proverb need not imply that he is familiar with Menander's play. He uses the saying to warn the Corinthian Christians against cultivating friendships with those libertines who, lacking hope in the resurrection, reject moral restraints in their pursuit of pleasure (cf. v. 32; 5:9-13). N. J. O.

**MORASTHITE** môr-as'thīt (AV Jer. 26:18; Mic. 1:1). *See* MORESHETH, OF.

**MORDECAI** mor'-də-kī [Heb. *mord$^{o}$ḵay, mord$^{e}$ḵay;* Gk. *Mardochaios*]; AV Apoc. MARDOCHEUS; NEB Apoc. MARDOCHAEUS.

**1.** A man who returned with Zerubbabel from exile (Ezr. 2:2; Neh. 7:7; 1 Esd. 5:8).

**2.** One of the two central characters in the book of Esther.

***I. Role in Esther.***–Mordecai is identified as a Jew, resident in the Persian capital of Susa, who had raised Hadassah (Esther), his orphaned cousin (Est. 2:7). When Esther was chosen by Ahasuerus to be his queen, Mordecai ingratiated himself with the king by revealing, through Esther's auspices, a plot against the king's life (ch. 2). Haman, the king's chief minister, stung by Mordecai's refusal to do obeisance to him, devised a stratagem to destroy all the Jews in the Persian empire (ch. 3). When this intended pogrom became publicly known, Mordecai instructed Esther to go to the king and inform him (chs. 4–5). While Esther was thus engaged in unmasking Haman, Mordecai's previous good deed for the king was remembered and suitably rewarded (ch. 6). Immediately thereafter Esther told Ahasuerus of Haman's plot to annihilate the Jews, Haman was executed, and Mordecai succeeded to Haman's place as the second in rank in the kingdom. Mordecai then mobilized the Jews to defend themselves and procured the assistance of Persian officials throughout the empire to this end. As a result the Jews were delivered, and all those who attacked them were put to death (chs. 7–9). Mordecai then wrote to the Jews throughout the empire to establish the festival of Purim to commemorate this event (ch. 9), and he subsequently achieved a position of honor and repute in the kingdom and among his people (ch. 10).

***II. Name.***–There is now no doubt that the name Mordecai is genuine; it is the Hebrew form of a Babylonian name based on the divine name Marduk. It occurs as *mrdk* in an Aramaic letter of the 5th cent. B.C., as *mardukkâ* in the Persepolis Treasury Tablets, and as the theophoric element in the name *mardukkannaṣir.* (For documentation see C. A. Moore, *Esther* [*AB,* 1971], p. L.) Much more important, because of date and provenance, is the appearance of *Mardukâ* (possibly *Mardukaya*) in a text apparently from Borsippa that mentions Persian dignitaries from Susa. Note that the LXX form of the name, *Mardochaios,* is closer to the Babylonian original than the Hebrew is.

***III. Date and Historicity.***–The date of the story hinges on the identification of Ahasuerus, since no other person mentioned is known from extrabiblical documents. Few today doubt that Ahasuerus is to be identified with Xerxes I, 486-465 B.C., although the matter is complicated somewhat by the consistent LXX rendering Artaxerxes (*see* AHASUERUS **1**). A fact favoring the identification with Xerxes I is that his Greek campaign can explain the chronological gap of four years between 1:3 and 2:16 (*see* ESTHER, BOOK OF VI; see W. Shea, *Andrews University Seminary Studies,* 14 [1976], 227ff.).

Mordecai cannot with certainty be identified with any

extrabiblical individual, but this may well be due to the extreme paucity of extant texts from the period and the limited historical pertinence of those that do exist (see Yamauchi, pp. 102f.). The major historical difficulty concerning Mordecai is the statement in 2:6, which seems to read that he was taken into exile with Jeconiah (Jehoiachin) in 597 B.C.; thus he would have been well over one hundred by the time of Xerxes. But possibly the pronoun "who" in 2:6 refers not to Mordecai but to Kish, the preceding final name in his patronymic. It has been suggested that the genealogies in 2 Ch. 22:9 and Ezr. 2:61 use similar syntax (see J. S. Wright, p. 38). However, the parallels are not exact, particularly since the phrase "a Benjaminite," which stands between the name Kish and the pronoun "who," much more likely describes Mordecai than his great-grandfather Kish. At any rate, such a chronological mistake would not in itself impugn the historicity of Mordecai himself.

A much more important piece of evidence may be the discovery of the cuneiform text mentioned in II above (see A. Ungnad, *ZAW,* 17 [1940/41], 243f.). It lists payments of silver to Persian dignitaries and their agents, who were apparently at Borsippa on an inspection trip from Susa. Although the tablet itself is undated, its contents allow a date either late in the reign of Darius I or early in that of Xerxes (see Ungnad, *AfO,* 19 [1959/60], 79-81). The tablet twice mentions a certain *Mardukâ,* identified as a *sipir* ("accountant" or "privy councillor") of *Uštannu* of Babylon, who is well known from other texts as a satrap of Persia. According to Ungnad, it is improbable that two high officials named Mardukâ would have served in Susa at the same time.

It is also important to note the implication in Est. 2 that Mordecai already occupied a position of some importance in Susa; women from the common ranks of society would hardly have been considered as eligible for the queenship. Moreover, Mordecai is often described as "sitting at the king's gate" (2:19, 21; 5:9, 13; 6:10). Since the gate (and the square before it) was where business was conducted (Ruth 4:1-12) and legal tribunals were held (Dt. 21:18-21; 22:13-21, 23f.; etc.; *see* GATE), this phrase very likely refers to an official position. R. Gordis (pp. 47f.) interpreted the phrase to mean that Mordecai was a magistrate or judge. In addition, Greek sources indicate that royal officials in Persia had to stay at the gate of the royal palace (see C. A. Moore, *BA,* 38 [1975], 74). Thus the Borsippa inscription may well contain, as Ungnad suggested, the only extrabiblical mention of Mordecai. Yet one must reserve judgment, for nothing makes the identity certain. For example, there is no evidence for determining how common the name Mardukâ/Mordecai was in Susa in Achaemenian times (so C. A. Moore, *BA,* 38 [1975], 73f.; but cf. Horn, p. 22 n. 45).

***Bibliography.***–R. Gordis, *JBL,* 95 (1976), 47-53; S. H. Horn, *Biblical Research,* 9 (1964), 14-25; A. Ungnad, *ZAW,* 17 (1940/41), 240-44; 18 (1942/43), 219; *AfO,* 19 (1959/60), 79-81; J. S. Wright, "The Historicity of the Book of Esther," in J. B. Payne, ed., *New Perspectives on the OT* (1970), pp. 37-47, esp. 44-46; E. Yamauchi, *Bibliotheca Sacra,* 137 (1980), 106-108.

F. W. BUSH

**MOREH, HILL OF** mōr'ə [Heb. *giḇʿaṯ hammôreh*–'hill of the teacher (or archer)'; Gk. B *Gabaath Amōra,* A *toú bounoú toú Abōr*]. A hill mentioned in Jgs. 7:1 to locate the Midianite camp that Gideon was preparing to attack. It is probably the modern Jebel Daḥi, located between Mt. Gilboa and Mt. Tabor on the north side of the Valley of Jezreel, about 5 km. (3 mi.) N of the spring of Harod by which Gideon was camped. Jezreel is about 6½ km. (4 mi.) SSW of Moreh; Shunem is at the southwest edge of the hill, Endor about 1½ km. (1 mi.) N, and NT Nain at the northern base.

R. J. HUGHES, III

**MOREH, OAK OF** mōr'ə [Heb. *'ēlôn môreh*–'terebinth of the teacher'; Gk. *tḗn drýn tḗn hypsēlḗn*]; AV incorrectly PLAIN OF MOREH; NEB TEREBINTH-TREE OF MOREH. A place where Abraham built an altar (Gen. 12:6); probably where Jacob hid the teraphim (35:4), and where Joshua set up a memorial stone (Josh. 24:26). It is undoubtedly the place mentioned in Dt. 11:30; Jgs. 9:37 (*see* DIVINERS' OAK). The location cannot be identified today. The name of the tree or wood may indicate that it was a place to consult a teacher or a Canaanite abode of ancestral spirits; or perhaps the name refers to the theophany that occurred there.

R. P. DUGAN

**MORESHETH** môr'ə-sheth, **OF** [Heb. *môraštî*]; AV MORASTHITE. Designation of the prophet Micah, indicating his home town (Jer. 26:18; Mic. 1:1), which was otherwise known as MORESHETH-GATH.

**MORESHETH-GATH** môr'ə-sheth-gath; mō-resh'eth-gath [Heb. *môreṣeṯ gaṯ*–'possession of Gath'; LXX Gk. *klēronomías Geth*–'inheritance of Gath']. A town in the Shephelah of Judah, mentioned by its full name only in Mic. 1:14. It was near Mareshah (v. 15) and is identified as Tell ej-Judeideh, about 2½ km. (1½ mi.) NNE of Beit Jibrîn.

The Palestinian Exploration Fund excavated Tell ej-Judeideh in 1899-1900 under the direction of F. J. Bliss (cf. *PEQ* [1900], pp. 87-101, 199-222; Bliss and Macalister, *Excavations in Palestine, 1898-1900* [1902]). Many jar handles with royal stamps were found (with the inscription *lmlk,* 'to the king," followed by the name of a city), as well as handles with private stamps giving some personal names known in the OT.

Moresheth was the home town of the prophet Micah, who is called "Micah of Moresheth" (Mic. 1:1; Jer. 26:18; AV "the Morasthite").

The compound name Moresheth-gath indicates not only a relationship to the city of Gath, one of the five leading cities of the Philistines (1 S. 6:17), but also some degree of domination exercised by a larger and more powerful city over smaller towns in its area. Verse 18 mentions

Stamped jar handle from Moresheth-gath. The inscription reads *lnḥm ʿbdy,* "to Nahum, Abdi" (Israel Department of Antiquities and Museums)

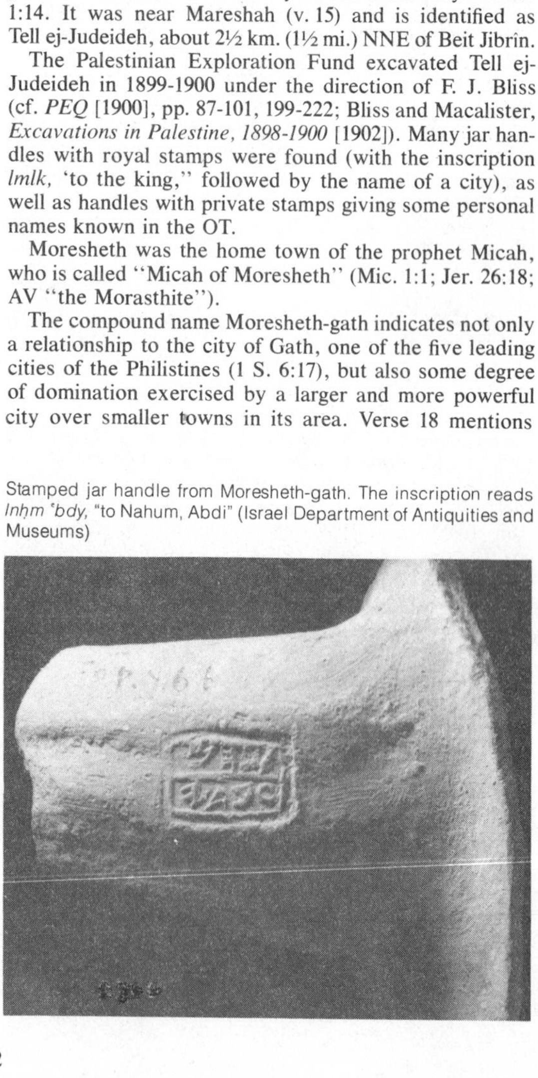

both fortified cities and country villages controlled by the Philistine Pentapolis (cf. 7:25).

Micah 1:15 names Moresheth-gath as one of the cities of the Shephelah that would figure in an invasion of Palestine by the Assyrians.

See *EAEHL*, III, *s.v.* "Judeideh, Tell" (M. Broshi).

C. E. DE VRIES

**MORIAH** mō-rī′ə.

**1.** [Heb. *har hammôrîyâ*]. The prominent hill of Jerusalem upon which Solomon's temple was built. 2 S. 24:16-25 describes the site as "the threshing floor of Araunah the Jebusite" and implies ("go up") that it was on high ground, as threshing floors often were. 1 Ch. 21:16-26 names "Orman the Jebusite" as owner of the threshing floor to which "David should go up." Only 2 Ch. 3:1 refers to the temple site as "Mount Moriah" (also called ZION; cf. Ps. 65:1 [MT 2]; Jer. 31:6), thus reflecting a theological tradition that was to develop later. See below and the comms. by P. Ackroyd (*Torch*, 1973), pp. 106f., and H. Williamson (*NCBC*, 1982), pp. 203-205.

**2.** [Heb. *'ereṣ hammôrîyâ*]. "The land of Moriah" (Gen. 22:2), a hill territory that was a three-day journey from Beer-sheba. The topographical requirements could be met by some hilltop sanctuary in the Hebron district, possibly the Râmet el-Khalîl (MAMRE). In some texts, as well as in Samaritan claims, "Moriah" (Gen. 22:2) reflects the Moreh ("sight," "vision") of Gen. 12:6, a place near Shechem where a sacred oak grew (Jgs. 9:6; *see* MOREH, OAK OF). 2 Ch. 3:1 probably intends to associate the temple mount with the theophanies of both 2 S. 24 and Gen. 22:14. Josephus (*Ant.* i.13.1f. [222-27]; vii.13.4 [329-334]), Jub. 18:13, rabbinic literature, and Islamic folklore concerning the Dome of the Rock made this connection explicit.

*See also* JERUSALEM I.F.

P. L. GARBER

**MORNING** [Heb. *bōqer*–'daybreak, morning' (e.g., Gen. 1:5; Ex. 7:15), *šaḥar*–'reddish light before dawn' (e.g., Gen. 19:15; Ps. 139:9), *mišḥar*–'light before dawn' (Ps. 110:3), *'ôr*–'light,' 'daybreak' (Neh. 8:3), *šāḵam*–'rise early' (Jgs. 6:38; 19:9; 2 K. 6:15); Gk. *prōí* ("in the morning," Mt. 16:3; 20:1; 21:18; etc.), *prōḯa* (Mt. 27:1), *prōïnós* (Rev. 2:28; 22:16), *órthros* ("early in the morning," Jn. 8:2), *orthrinós* ("early in the morning," Lk. 24:22), *orthrízō* ("early in the morning . . . came," Lk. 21:38)]; AV also DAY, EARLY, MORROW, "dawning of the day," etc.; NEB also DAWN, DAYBREAK, DAYLIGHT, EARLY, etc.; **MORNING STAR** [Gk. *phōsphóros*–'bringing light'] (2 Pet. 1:19); AV DAY STAR.

The Hebrews reckoned a day as a unit of time lasting from evening to evening (cf. Gen. 1:5, 8, 13, 19, 23, 31). Morning was the beginning of the light part of the day and the second component of their threefold division of the day (evening, morning, and noon; cf. Ps. 55:17 [MT 18]). Postexilic and NT times saw a twelve-hour day measured from sunrise to sunset (or dawn to dusk, Jn. 11:9; cf. Mt. 20:1-12). Morning sunrise marked the end of the third night watch in OT times (Ex. 14:24; Jgs. 7:19) and the end of the fourth night watch in Roman times (Mt. 14:25 par. Mk. 6:48). Morning began at sunrise, usually calculated at 6:00 A.M. The first hour was therefore 7:00 A.M. and the sixth hour was noon (cf. Mt. 20:5).

The most common OT word for "morning" is Heb. *bōqer,* which is derived from a root meaning "to split" or "to break"; hence morning is the splitting of darkness by daylight. *Bōqer* can refer to a period of time (e.g., Gen. 19:27) or to the precise moment when light begins to overrule darkness (e.g., Jgs. 16:2).

"Morning" (*bōqer*) is first mentioned in the creation account of Gen. 1; it began when God separated the light from the darkness (v. 5; also vv. 8, 13, 19, 23, 31; cf. Job 38:12). In the OT morning was a time for travel (Gen. 24:54; Jgs. 19:8f.; cf. Gen. 19:15), for waging war (Josh. 8:10; 1 S. 11:11), and for decisive action (Gen. 28:18; Josh. 7:16; 2 S. 11:14). It was also the time of day when God provided manna for Israel in the wilderness (Ex. 16:7-24). Occasionally revelation was received from God in the morning (Nu. 16:5; Jgs. 6:38).

More importantly, morning was a time of prayer (Ps. 5:3 [MT 4]; 88:13 [MT 14]), sacrifice (Lev. 6:12 [MT 5]; 9:17), and worship (1 S. 1:19). The morning was a time of rejoicing (Ps. 30:5 [MT 6]) and was eagerly awaited (130:6) because it symbolized God's faithful love, mercy, and justice for His people (cf. 90:14; 92:2; Isa. 33:2). As each dawn brings a new day, so the morning reminded Israel of the freshness, reliability, and vastness of God's care for His people (cf. Lam. 3:23; Zeph. 3:5).

In the NT the early morning was the time when Jesus prayed (Mk. 1:35), taught in the temple during His passion week (Lk. 21:38), was tried by the Jews and delivered to Pilate (Mt. 27:1; Mk. 15:1); it was also the time when the women arrived at Jesus' tomb (Lk. 24:22).

Jesus Christ is described as the "morning star" in 2 Pet. 1:19 (*phōsphorós*) and in Rev. 2:28 (*astḗr prōïnós*), and He identifies Himself as "the bright morning star" (*ho astḗr ho lamprós ho prōïnós*) in Rev. 22:16. This apocalyptic motif reflects OT and intertestamental teaching on the "celestial" nature of Messiah and His advent (cf. "star of Jacob," Nu. 24:17; "sun of righteousness," Mal. 4:2 [MT 3:20]; T. Levi 18:3; T. Jud. 24:1). "Morning star" actually refers to the planet Venus, which appears in the eastern sky just before sunrise and the beginning of the new day. Jesus Christ is the "Venus star," that first light which marks the dawn of the new age (cf. Mt. 24:29-31). The words also connote the brightness of His second coming (already portended in the Transfiguration; cf. 2 Pet. 1:16-19). Believers in Thyatira who conquered and kept Christ's works until the end were promised the "morning star" (Rev. 2:28), i.e., possession of Jesus Christ and the blessed hope of life everlasting (cf. 22:16). *See also* LIGHT.

*See also* DAWN; DAY; DAY AND NIGHT; EARLY; TOMORROW.

***Bibliography.***–*DNTT,* II, 490-96; *TDNT,* IX, *s.v.* φῶς: φωσφόρος (H. Conzelmann); *TDOT,* I, *s.v.* "'ôr" (S. Aalen); II, *s.v.* "bōqer" (J. Bergman, H. Ringgren, C. Barth).

A. E. HILL

**MORNING WATCH** [Heb. *'ašmōreṯ habbōqer* (Ex. 14:24; 1 S. 11:11); Gk. *heōthinḗ phylakḗ* (Jth. 12:5)]. The last division of the night. *See* DAY II; DAY AND NIGHT; WATCH.

**MORNING, WINGS OF THE** [Heb. *kanpê-šāḥar*] (Ps. 139:9); NEB FLIGHT TO THE FRONTIERS OF THE MORNING. The psalmist seems to be picturing a flight from the extreme East (the place where the dawn breaks) to the extreme West ("the uttermost parts of the sea"). *See* ASTRONOMY II.B.

**MORROW.** *See* TOMORROW.

**MORROW AFTER THE SABBATH.** *See* SABBATH.

**MORSEL** [Heb. *paṯ* (e.g., Jgs. 19:5; 1 S. 28:22), *kikkār* (2 S. 2:36), hithpael part. of *lāham*–'swallow greedily' ("delicious morsels," Prov. 18:8; 26:22); Gk. *psōmíon*]; AV also MEAT, SOP, "wound"; NEB also LITTLE FOOD, SOMETHING TO EAT, BREAD, CRUST, DISH,

PIECE. A bit of bread that is used for food. As a gracious host, Abraham modestly offered a "morsel of bread" to his three visitors (Gen. 18:5) — and then served them a lavish meal (vv. 6-8; cf. Jgs. 19:5; 1 S. 28:22; *see also* ENTERTAIN). Boaz invited Ruth to eat some bread and dip her morsel in wine (Ruth 2:14). Job maintained that he was not guilty of eating his morsel alone — a figurative way of saying that he shared his food with the poor (Job 31:17). In Prov. 18:8; 26:22 the words of a slanderer are compared to delicious morsels, probably a reference to the "appetite for evil gossip and the relish with which it is . . . devoured" (W. McKane, *Proverbs* [*OTL*, 1970], pp. 519f.; similarly KD). The AV rendering "wounds" is based on LXX *malakoí*. Ps. 147:17 figuratively describes hailstones as morsels of bread that God scatters on the earth.

In the NT "morsel" occurs only in Jn. 13:26-30. In an action that most of the disciples did not understand, Jesus, acting as the host at the Last Supper, dipped a bit of food (probably — but not necessarily — bread) into a sauce and gave it to Judas, who accepted it and left the room to betray Him.

The AV uses the term also in He. 12:16, where it renders Gk. *brṓsis* by "morsel of meat" (RSV, NEB, "meal").

P. L. BREMER

**MORTAL; MORTALLY** [Heb. *'$^{e}$nôš* ("mortal man," Job 4:17), *b$^{e}$nê 'āḏām*–'children of man' ("mortal men," Ezk. 31:14), hiphil of *nāḵâ*–'strike' (+*nep̱eš*–'life') ("wound mortally," Dt. 19:6, 11), *ḥālāl*–'pierced' ("mortally wounded," Ezk. 30:24); Gk. *phthartós*–'perishable' (Rom. 1:23), part. of *apothnḗskō*–'die' (He. 7:8), *(prós) thánaton*–'(unto) death' (1 Jn. 5:16f.; Rev. 13:3, 12), *thnētós*–'mortal, subject to death' (Rom. 6:12; 8:11; 1 Cor. 15:53f.; 2 Cor. 4:11; 5:4)]; AV also "children of men" (Ezk. 31:14), DEADLY, SLAY, UNTO DEATH, THAT DIE, CORRUPTIBLE; NEB also "common doom" (Ezk. 31:14), "take a life," "strike a blow," DEADLY, etc. Related to death, usually in one of two ways: (1) subject to death or (2) causing death.

In most passages "mortal" bears the meaning "subject to death." Subjection to decay and death is the common lot of all mankind (cf. Ezk. 31:14), and the fleetingness of human life is a pervasive theme in the OT (e.g., Job 4:17-21; Ps. 39:4-6 [MT 5-7]; 90:3-12; 103:15f.; *see also* DEATH II). The biblical concept of human mortality, however, refers to more than mankind's natural vulnerability to death and decay: it also points to the moral condition of the human race. The biblical writers perceived an intimate connection between human mortality and human sinfulness (cf. Gen. 2:17; 3:19). This theme was developed especially by Paul (cf. Rom. 6:23: "For the wages of sin is death . . ."; cf. also 5:12-14). And just as sin is not produced by and confined to the body but is produced by the whole person that allows sin to rule the body (cf. 6:12), so also mortality applies to the whole of human nature and not simply to the body (in contrast to the Platonic idea of the immortality of the soul; *see* IMMORTAL I.A; V). The whole person (described as Heb. *'$^{e}$nôš* and *geḇer* in Job 4:17; *see* ANTHROPOLOGY III.A) is unable to measure up to the righteousness and purity of God, who alone is inherently immortal (1 Tim. 6:16; cf. Rom. 1:23: the folly and perversity of idol-worshipers is that they worship "a copy of an image of mortal [*phthartós*] man" and other creatures in place of "the glory of the immortal [*áphthartos*] God"). It is only through the divine gift of life in Jesus Christ that mortal human nature can "put on immortality" (1 Cor. 15:53f.; cf. Rom. 8:11; 2 Cor. 4:11) or — to use another metaphor — that everything in human nature that is presently inclined toward death and decay "may be swallowed up by life" (5:4). *See* IMMORTAL; *see also* DEATH V.

In a few passages "mortal" means "deadly" or "leading to death." Severe wounds are mentioned as a cause of death in Dt. 19:6, 11; Ezk. 30:24; Rev. 13:3, 12. The meaning of "mortal sin" in 1 Jn. 5:16f. has been the subject of much debate. John recommends intercessory prayer for fellow Christians who commit "what is not a mortal sin" but not for those who commit "sin which is mortal" (Gk. *hamartía prós thánaton*; AV, lit., "sin unto death"; NEB "deadly sin") — although he does not in fact forbid prayer for such persons. Some scholars have suggested that "mortal sin" is sin that leads to the immediate physical death of the sinner (cf. Acts 5:1-11; 1 Cor. 5:5; see Bruce, pp. 124f.); but most have understood it as sin that results in eternal death. Perhaps the soundest interpretation is that offered by I. H. Marshall (p. 248): "Sin that leads to death is the deliberate refusal to believe in Jesus Christ, to follow God's commands, and to love one's brothers. It leads to death because it includes a deliberate refusal to believe in the One who alone can give life, Jesus Christ the Son of God." *See also* SIN XI.

***Bibliography***.–Comms. on 1 John, esp. those by F. F. Bruce (1970) and I. H. Marshall (*NICNT*, 1978), pp. 245-251; also *DNTT*, I, 435-37; 467-470; *TDNT*, III, *s.v.* θάνατος (R. Bultmann).

N. J. O.

**MORTAL SIN.** *See* MORTAL.

**MORTAR.**

**1.** [Heb. *m$^{e}$ḏōḵâ*] (Nu. 11:8); [*maḵtēš*] (Prov. 27:22; Zeph. 1:11). A vessel in which items are pounded or ground with a pestle.

It is likely that *m$^{e}$ḏōḵâ* is the typical mortar found frequently on almost all archeological excavations. Usually made of basalt or related magmatic stone because of its hardness and abrasiveness, mortars were used to crush grain into flour, herbs into seasonings and medicines, and various materials into pigments, dyes, and cosmetics. In Roman and Byzantine times, according to the Mishnah, large mortars could be embedded into the floors of houses. Small mortars could be carved very delicately for use as cosmetic palettes. But the most frequent forms are medium in size (15 to 25 cm. [6-9 in.] in diameter) and shaped like

Tripod mortar of medium size, from Jericho (Israel Department of Antiquities and Museums)

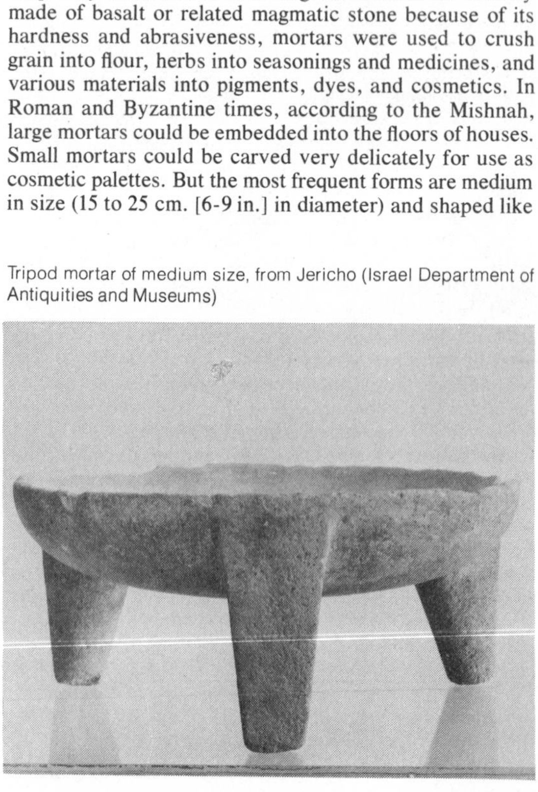

a thick bowl. Finer examples were made with three feet. Copper mortars are known from rabbinic literature, and Herod's temple was furnished with mortars of gold. According to Nu. 11:8 a *meḏōḵâ* was used to grind manna into flour to be used in making cakes. The Akkadian cognate (*daku*) of the verbal root from which *meḏōḵâ* is derived means "kill," indicating the violent, beating nature of the activity associated with this item.

The second word translated "mortar," *maḵtēš*, probably should be understood as a geographical or geological formation, a HOLLOW place as the RSV translates the word in Jgs. 15:19. Prov. 27:22 can certainly be understood in this fashion, as can Zeph. 1:11. Modern Hebrew uses the word as a geographical descriptor in names such as Maktesh Ramon in the central Negeb. The use of the term "pestle" in Prov. 27:22 would be a logical part of a metaphor to be used with such a mortarlike natural depression.

**2.** [Heb. *ḥōmer*] (Gen. 11:3; Ex. 1:14; Isa. 41:25; Nah. 3:14); NEB also CLAY, MUD; [*meleṭ*; cf. Syr. *mlṭ*] (Jer. 43:9); AV CLAY; NEB CEMENT. An initially plastic material, which may harden when dry; used to bind bricks or stones together in construction.

The common mortar of ancient Palestine (*ḥōmer*) was made of clay or soil sometimes mixed with straw for binder and lime for hardener. Isa. 41:25 and Nah. 3:14 seem to indicate large, open vats of mortar mixed at one time. Clay dries so slowly that when covered a single batch could last for several days. After the ingredients had been placed together workers entered and mixed the materials by treading on them. Ex. 1:14 makes it clear that this was very hard work. In Mesopotamia BITUMEN could be used for mortar, because it was readily available (Gen. 11:3).

The hapax legomenon *meleṭ* in Jer. 43:9 is problematic, because it would seem difficult to hide large stones in the mortar-filled interstices of a flagstone pavement as the text seems to suggest. The word probably means cracks or open spaces which, in more modern parlance, could indicate potholes.

The best masons needed no mortar because they used stones which were very finely cut to fit tightly. Ordinary houses also used no mortar. For these reasons mortar is a relatively infrequent find on archeological excavations. All brick constructions, of course, used mortar, but it is very difficult at times to separate the bricks from the mortar, which was essentially undried brick material.

L. G. HERR

**MORTAR, THE** [Heb. *hammaḵtēš*]; AV MAKTESH; NEB LOWER TOWN. A part of the city of Jerusalem, apparently near the Mishneh (second quarter) and the Fish Gate (Zeph. 1:11). Heb. *maḵtēš* occurs three times in the OT: Prov.27:22, where "mortar" and "pestle" are used literally (*see* MORTAR); Jgs. 15:19, translated "a hollow place" near Lehi; Zeph. 1:11, which intends a portion of Jerusalem. In all three passages the Greek translators appear to have had difficulty with the word, translating it "hollow" only in the B text of Jgs. 15:19. In Zeph. 1:11 the LXX translates "the [city that has] completely fallen" (*katakekommenēn*). The shape of a mortar determines the location in Jerusalem; it is quite likely at the confluence of the cross valley and the Central Valley but possibly somewhat farther north in the Central Valley. *See* JERUSALEM II.B; III.D.5.e.

See J. Simons, *Jerusalem in the OT* (1952), pp. 52f. n. 2.

W. S. L. S.

**MORTGAGE.** Used by the RSV, AV, and NEB in Neh. 5:3 to translate the Hebrew verb *'āraḇ*, "give (or become)

surety." In this passage it refers to putting up real estate as security on a loan. Some poverty-stricken Jews were forced to put up their property as a PLEDGE in order to secure loans for buying food. Vv. 5, 11 show that the creditors had already taken over these lands, thus depriving their fellow Jews of a means of income and making it impossible for them to redeem their sons and daughters sold into slavery. This was a violation of Israelite law, which was designed to protect the poor from oppression by the rich, and it provoked Nehemiah's righteous indignation (vv. 6-11). *See* DEBT; INTEREST; LEND; OPPRESS III.

N. J. O.

**MORTIFY.** A term used by the AV in the obsolete sense of "put to death" (cf. RSV, NEB), which is a literal translation of Gk. *thanatóō* (Rom. 8:13) and *nekróō* (Col. 3:5). In both passages Paul calls his readers' attention to the ethical implications of their union with Christ. If they have died and been raised with Christ, then their lives must show that they have died to the rule of sin and are now governed by the new principle of life in the Spirit. *See* DEATH V; OLD NATURE.

**MOSERAH** mō'sə-rä [Heb. *môserâ*–'bond'] (Dt. 10:6); AV MOSERA; **MOSEROTH** mō'sə-roth [Heb. *môserôṯ*– 'bonds'] (Nu. 33:30f.). An Israelite encampment during the wilderness journey, between Hashmonah and Bene-jaakan (Nu. 33:30f.). According to Dt. 10:6, however, the people traveled from Beeroth Bene-jaakan (= Bene-jaakan) to Moserah, where Aaron died. This tradition thus seems also to conflict with that of Nu. 33:38, which states that Aaron died on Mt. Hor (but *see* HOR). The location of Moserah is unknown.

*See also* WANDERINGS OF ISRAEL.

**MOSES** mō'zəs [Heb. *mōšeh*; Gk. *Mōysēs*]. The liberator and lawgiver of Israel, the most important person in the OT. While Abraham may be regarded as the founder of Israel's faith, Moses is the founder of Israel's religion.

I. Historicity and Date
II. Life
    A. Early Years
        1. Birth
        2. Name
    B. Refuge in Midian and Call
    C. Before Pharaoh
    D. Exodus
    E. From Egypt to Sinai
    F. Theophany
    G. From Sinai to Moab
    H. Conquest of Transjordan
    I. Deuteronomic Legislation
III. Work and Ministry
    A. Leader
    B. Lawgiver
    C. Prophet
    D. Author
IV. Outside the Pentateuch
    A. OT
    B. Intertestamental Literature
    C. NT

*I. Historicity and Date.*–Many who have affirmed the historicity of Moses have often questioned certain elements of the traditions embodied in the pentateuchal narratives (or regarded them as embellishments; cf. Auerbach, Bimson, Horn, Herrmann, *Israel in Egypt*, p. 61). After observing that many of the key figures of the Exodus narrative are unnamed (e.g., Pharaoh and his daughter; Moses' mother, father, and sister — in ch. 3, that is), Herrmann said, "Thus we are left ultimately with only the mighty figure of Moses, which cannot be put aside as invention or interpolation, but which is constitutive for the whole account" (*Israel in Egypt,* pp. 41f.).

One of the vexing problems relating to Moses is the dating of the Exodus (*see* EXODUS, DATE OF THE). The Merneptah stele (*ca.* 1233 B.C.) seems to indicate that the Hebrews had already arrived in Canaan; thus it provides a *terminus ad quem.* The so-called biblical date is based on 1 K. 6:1, which places the Exodus 480 years before Solomon's fourth year (967 B.C.). This would date the Exodus *ca.* 1447, during the reign of Amenhotep II. Since concrete information on the sojourn and Exodus was not evident in Egypt, biblical scholars naturally looked to Palestine for data to determine when the Conquest took place. Then they could reckon back forty years to find the date of the Exodus. Initially this approach appeared successful when Garstang's work at Jericho produced a destruction level that he dated *ca.* 1400 B.C. Subsequently, however, K. Kenyon's work showed that Garstang's conclusions were erroneous.

The work of Albright, Wright, and others uncovered destruction in levels from the 13th cent. in many sites in Palestine, thus opening the way for widespread acceptance of the thirteenth-century date. This squared nicely with the appearance of Raamses in Ex. 1:11 as the name of one of the store-cities built by Hebrew forced labor. Thus it was concluded that the Exodus occurred in the first third of Ramses II's reign, (i.e., *ca.* 1304-1275). Many scholars followed this dating scheme, even those of a more conservative position (e.g., Kitchen, Harrison); some, however, continued to hold to the traditional dating (S. Schultz, *OT Speaks* [3rd ed. 1980], p. 48; M. Unger, *Archaeology and the OT* [1954], p. 148; J. Rea, pp. 58f.). Others advocated a date as late as the 20th Dynasty (1200-1085; cf. M. B. Rowton, *PEQ,* 85 [1953], 46-60).

In a most thorough review of how scholarship has dealt with the dating of the Exodus, Bimson argued quite convincingly for a mid-fifteenth-century date. Basing his conclusions on an exhaustive reassessment of the Palestinian sites traditionally associated with Joshua's conquest, he suggested that the termination of the M.B. II culture, usually attributed to the Hyksos and the kings of the early 18th Dynasty, should be lowered to *ca.* 1430 B.C. and credited to the Israelites.

Thus some have returned to a fifteenth-century date, or at least recognized its possibility (cf. S. Horn, p. 23, who chided those who criticize the earlier date but uncritically accept the thirteenth-century date). But this is by no means the position of the majority. The issue is far from settled; perhaps future excavations will provide new evidence.

*II. Life.–A. Early Years.* The period from Moses' birth until his flight from Pharaoh is perhaps the most intriguing part of his life, and yet one that is most obscure. According to later tradition Moses was forty years old when he left for Midian (Acts 7:23), but the OT is silent on this. Ex. 7:7 reports that he was eighty when he returned to Egypt, and Dt. 34:7 says he was one hundred twenty when he died. Although these figures may be approximate, they suggest a stylized division of his life into three forty-year periods: the first, in the Egyptian courts; the second, in Midian; and the third, during the Exodus and the period of wandering.

*1. Birth.* The narrative dealing with the birth of Moses and his placement in the "ark of rushes" by his mother to save his life (Ex. 2:1-10) has been likened to the tales surrounding the birth of Sargon the Great, king of Akkad (Gressmann; Redford, *Numen*). The story of the humble beginnings of a child who achieves hero status is thought to be a borrowing from the well-known motif found in Near Eastern, Classical, and Indian literature, and is often relegated to a later strand of the Exodus traditions (Childs, *Exodus,* pp. 11f.). In the more than thirty stories that deal with the birth of a child who is then abandoned (for his own safety), many include a prophetic statement that the child will grow up to be a king. This usually leads the reigning monarch to try to kill the baby or all babies (Redford, *Numen*; his category II contains thirteen such examples). Gressmann wanted to fit the birth of Moses into this classification. As Childs (*JBL,* pp. 109f.) has pointed out, however, this element about the prophecy is missing in Ex. 2. Moses' leadership was never a threat to Pharaoh's crown. Therefore, Pharaoh's edict had nothing to do with the birth of Moses.

Others think the purpose of the Sargon tale was to legitimate his kingship, since his birth would have been under very special circumstances and his pedigree clearly royal. This interpretation has been challenged by H. Güterbock (*Zeitschrift für Assyriologie,* 42 [1934], 62-64), who believed that the function of the Sargon tale was oracular, and its purpose was to consolidate the future by tying it to the past. Other Near Eastern kings whose legitimacy was questioned (e.g., Amenemhet I, Hatshepsut, Ḫattusilis) used apologetic literature showing divine favor to help legitimate their kingship. This would have been true of Sargon, a Semite who had usurped the throne of the Sumerian king Ur-Zabbaba. The narrative about the birth of Moses appears to have no apologetic intent. Moses does not need this so-called rags-to-riches tale to legitimate his leadership. His position comes by the divine appointment of Ex. 3, not from the birth narrative.

Since the setting of Ex. 2 is Egypt, one might expect any borrowing of the abandoned-child motif to reflect Egyptian tradition. But similar Egyptian stories are not true parallels (Redford, *Numen,* p. 219). These are regarded as purely etiological, which Childs claims is not the case with the Moses story. Redford favored a Levantine or Mesopotamian origin for the motif that would have been known in the 2nd millennium B.C. Since the majority of the tales come from Greek, Anatolian, and Indian traditions, the origin of the motif might be Indo-European. This would explain why the motif is not found in Egypt until Ptolemaic times, when it would have been imported by the Greeks. The Moses story, therefore, may well have had a completely independent origin.

Many scholars (e.g., Beegle, p. 52; cf. Childs, *Exodus,* p. 18) believe that Ex. 2:1 makes it appear that Moses was the firstborn, a mistake due to the "lateness" of the birth narrative. But it is hard to believe that the author (or subsequent redactor[s]) would create the impression in v. 1 that Moses was the firstborn and then so naturally tell about his elder sister in v. 4 (cf. 7:7, which states that Aaron was three years older than Moses). The birth of Moses was simply the first birth to this family after the king's edict, making Moses the endangered child. There was no need to mention the birth of Miriam and Aaron since they were not subject to the edict.

Ironically the daughter of the king is the one responsible for saving the child's life. (There is no way to be certain that she was the reigning monarch's daughter; her father could just as well have been the preceding king.) Attempts to identify this princess must be viewed with skepticism, since a king who reigned for a substantial period could have had many daughters. Ramses II, it has been reckoned, may have had around one hundred daughters!

Some who favor the fifteenth-century date of the Exodus have suggested Hatshepsut as a possible candidate for this unnamed princess (*see* EXODUS, DATE OF THE III.B.2).

This creates the problem that she could then have been the ruler from whom Moses fled for fear of being killed (2:15). It seems unlikely that the same woman who had sympathy on Moses the baby would not have compassion on her adopted son in this case of involuntary manslaughter.

The discovery of the tomb of a daughter of Seti I (and sister of Ramses II) at Saqqârah (G. T. Martin, *JEA*, 69 [1983], 25-29) raised another possibility for the unnamed princess. The name of Seti's daughter is Tia, and a connection between this woman and "Bithiah the daughter of Pharaoh" in 1 Ch. 4:17 has been put forward. It has been suggested that Bithiah is a corruption or an abbreviation for *bat̠ (melek̠) tîyâ*, "the daughter (of the king), Tia." The appearance of this Egyptian princess in the genealogy of Judah is puzzling. Her position in the list seems to be too late to fit the thirteenth-century Tia.

Regardless of the date of the events in Ex. 2 and the identity of the princess, she was responsible for Moses' being brought up in the court along with the royal children. Albright (p. 123) saw no reason to doubt this tradition. Because of Moses' connections with the court he would have received the education of a prince that later traditions ascribe to him (Acts 7:22; Josephus *Ant.* ii.9.7–10.2 [236-253]). Life in the royal harem for the prince was a very good one that included learning to read, training in weapons and horsemanship, etc. (cf. *NBD*, 843f.).

2. *Name.* The etymology of Moses has long been associated with the Egyptian root *msi* ("to bear") and would probably fit nicely into the popular name formulas of the New Kingdom (e.g., Ahmose, Thutmose, Amenmose, Ramose; the second *s* in Moses reflects the LXX writing of the name). But this poses a linguistic problem, for when the name Rameses appears in Gen. 47:11 and Ex. 12:37; Nu. 33:3, 5 (cf. Raamses in Ex. 1:11), the Hebrew letter *s* is used, whereas in the name of Moses Hebrew *š* is used. These two sibilants are quite different phonetically and therefore cast doubt on associating the two words. The best discussion of this problem still is that of J. G. Griffiths. Griffiths pointed out that there are essentially two types of loanwords: those of a temporary nature (e.g., a place-name) and those that find a permanent place in the language of the borrower (esp. personal names). Thus, e.g., in Phoenician inscriptions the Egyptian goddess Isis is written with *s* when *ś* is expected. More interesting is the mixed name *ʿana(t)moš(e)* (9th cent., found at Samaria), which incorporates the name of the Canaanite goddess Anath with the Egyptian root *msi,* written with *š* rather than *s*. Therefore Canaanite or Hebrew *š* can equal Egyptian *s*, and the name Moses may well find its root in Egyp. *msi.*

Herrmann believed that Moses' Egyptian name could have come from his servitude (or that of his parents) to some member of the royal family. From the Middle Kingdom, lists of servants on papyri show that many of these had Semitic names while their children had Egyptian names (*ANET,* pp. 553f.). Sometimes they actually bore the name of their master or mistress.

The name of Moses, then, may have been part of a theophoric name (i.e., divine name + *mōse*). (The name *mōse* [with no divine name], meaning "son" [Cassuto, pp. 20f.], cannot be ruled out, however.) Once aware of his Hebrew, monotheistic tradition, Moses may have dropped the pagan deity's name, leaving only the verb stem. Since many date the birth of Moses to the Ramesside period (though such a date is still debated), the name Raʿmose(s) is frequently suggested, sometimes with great certainty (e.g., *ISBE,* III, 2084). The abbreviation Mose for the longer theophoric names is attested in the New Kingdom (*ca.* 1570-1085; see Griffiths, pp. 226f.).

After Moses grew (and perhaps was weaned) he was brought to the princess and then named "Moses" (Ex. 2:10). Part of the problem surrounding the naming is that the meaning of "Moses" is said to be "draw out," which argues that Jochebed named him, not the princess as many assume. The statement, "She called [*wattiqrā'*] his name Moses, for she said [*watt'ōmer*]" could apply grammatically to either woman, the mother or the princess. Kitchen (*NBD,* p. 845) and Cassuto (pp. 20f.) favored the mother as the speaker. Noth (*Exodus,* p. 26) recognized that the nature of the woman's statement requires the use of Hebrew. Some have falsely assumed that the Hebrew writer imposed the Hebrew language on the princess here as in 2:6f. It is far more likely that the Hebrews were bilingual (cf. the Joseph story, where it is clear that in just over ten years in Egypt Joseph had mastered the Egyptian language, e.g., Gen. 42:23).

It might be expected that Moses' name would appear in the passive form since he was "drawn out" of the water. In fact it is written in the active voice (*mōšeh*), no doubt a deliberate wordplay: written in this fashion it lent itself to the Egyptian word *mōse* (meaning "son") or divine name + *mōse,* which is undoubtedly how the princess understood the name. Both the Egyptians and the Hebrews enjoyed wordplays and this is clearly a bilingual one. Symbolic wordplays between Egyptian and Hebrew words and concepts are known elsewhere (cf. J. K. Hoffmeier, *Journal of the Society of the Study of Egyptian Antiquities,* 11 [1981], 167f.).

*B. Refuge in Midian and Call.* The enslavement of the Hebrew people had begun before the birth of Moses (Ex. 1:11-14). In the years between 2:10 and 2:11 Moses had grown to manhood and the oppression had continued. Although thoroughly Egyptian in language, dress, and culture, Moses had not forgotten his Hebrew roots. One day as he toured the work sites (perhaps in some official capacity) he observed a Hebrew being beaten (apparently to death — hiphil part. of *nāk̠â*) by an Egyptian taskmaster (2:11-15). This angered Moses, who in turn struck (hiphil of *nāk̠â*) the Egyptian dead when he thought no one was watching. But word of this incident reached Pharaoh, who was enraged and sought to kill Moses. This led him to flee across the Sinai to Midian (located on the eastern side of the Gulf of Aqabah; certain Midianite tribes may have been located in southeastern Sinai). He there met the nomadic peoples of the area when he helped the daughters of Reuel/Jethro the priest of Midian (*see* JETHRO for discussion of the interchange of these names). Moses and Jethro established a good relationship, and Jethro married his daughter Zipporah to Moses.

A literary parallel between this section of Moses' life and the Egyptian "Tale of Sinuhe" has been recognized (Herrmann, *Israel in Egypt,* pp. 45f.; Beegle, 56f.; tr. in *ANET,* pp. 18-22; M. Lichtheim, *Ancient Egyptian Literature,* I [1973], 222-233). Both stories reflect well the hospitality shown by bedouin to their guests. In both cases the chief marries his daughter to "the Egyptian" (as Moses appears to the daughters of Jethro, Ex. 2:19) who was escaping the wrath of Pharaoh. Both return to Egypt to appear before Pharaoh, albeit under different circumstances.

Moses' stay in Midian proved to be valuable in several ways. It has been suggested that Jethro, the "Midianite priest" (Ex. 2:16), was a worshiper of Yahweh (18:10-12 bears this out) and that Moses was introduced to Yahwism by Jethro. The Midianites, it must be recalled, were the descendants of Abraham's and Keturah's son Midian (Gen. 25:1). The Keturah tribes apparently were linked in a tribal confederacy with the Ishmaelites (note the close association between the Midianites and Ishmaelites, Gen. 37:25-28; Josh. 8:22-24) as well as with the Medanites (so MT, Gen. 37:36; *see* MEDAN). Such tribal confederacies were well known in Syria-Palestine during the 2nd millennium B.C. For example, Abraham was an ally (*b^erîṯ*) of Mamre, Eshcol, and Aner (Gen. 14:13), who joined him in fighting the coalition of Mesopotamian kings to free Lot (v. 24). Likewise, while living in Syria (Retjenu) Sinuhe could speak of his tribal confederates.

Since the Ishmaelite-Midianite(-Medanite) confederacy was made up of descendants of Abraham, it is not inconceivable that they knew "the God of Abraham." The name of Yahweh is thought to appear in Egyptian monuments as early as the time of Amenhotep III (1416-1379). The writing *ya-h-wa* is appended to the name Shasu (bedouin), who were primarily located in northern Sinai and Edom (see M. Astour, "Yahweh in Egyptian Topographic Lists," in M. Görg, ed., *Elmar Edel Festschrift* [1979], pp. 17-33). Therefore Moses may well have been introduced to Yahweh, "the God of Abraham," while in Midian. His introduction to Yahweh was necessary since he had been raised in the Egyptian court and may not have known his Hebrew religious heritage.

Also, by staying in the area of Sinai-Midian Moses became familiar with the terrain and would have gained valuable experience in wilderness survival, which would prove valuable to the future leader of the Israelites in that same area. And by living in Midian and marrying into Jethro's family, he became the brother-in-law of Hobab, who would act as a guide for Moses and the Israelites in their trek from Sinai to Moab (Nu. 10:29-32).

The greatest and most important experience of Moses in his exile from Egypt was his call by God at the mount of God, Sinai (Ex. 3:1–4:17). The call of Moses is also one of the thornier problems in the Pentateuch. Literary critics see this unit as a blending of J, E, and P traditions, largely because of the use of the divine names (Beegle, pp. 59-63; Clements, pp. 19-21; Childs, *Exodus*, pp. 52-56; Noth, *Exodus*, pp. 38-40). Scholars still disagree, however, about how the unit is to be divided into the different sources. The use of the divine names as a criterion for determining sources is extremely unreliable (cf. W. J. Martin, *Stylistic Criteria and the Analysis of the Pentateuch* [1955]; Kitchen, *Ancient Orient*, pp. 112-125; *see also* PENTATEUCH). The wide range of the conclusions by literary critics shows that this methodology should be subordinated to a more objective approach.

According to Ex. 3:1-3 Moses discovered the theophany. The principle of discovery is consistent with records of theophanies in other religious traditions (M. Eliade, *The Sacred and the Profane* [Eng. tr. 1959], pp. 20-24). Furthermore, mountains are often associated with such manifestations, not because the gods are thought to dwell there but because the mountain marks the meeting place of heaven and earth (Eliade, pp. 40-42.)

The precise location of the call of Moses is disputed. The traditional location is Jebel Mûsā in southern Sinai, although nearby Jebel Serbal has also been suggested. A location in northeastern Sinai, closer to Kadesh-barnea, has been proposed. According to 17:1ff. the Israelites moved toward Mt. Sinai and stopped at Rephidim for a while. Verses 1-6 suggest that Rephidim was in Horeb, but that the Israelites had not quite reached the mountain (cf. 19:1f.). Since a Wâdī Refâyid (which is cognate with Rephidim) is located near Serābîṭ el-Khâdim (an Egyptian mining center often identified with Dophkah, an early stop on the Israelites' journey; cf. Nu. 33:12-16), a southern location seems preferable to the northern one. Furthermore, Dt. 1:2 states that it is an eleven-day journey from Horeb, by way of Edom, to Kadesh-barnea. This, too, seems to argue in favor of a more southern location. The problem of the designations Sinai and Horeb for this area is discussed below (II.E). *See also* SINAI.

When the theophany appeared in the bush, Moses saw "the angel of Yahweh." As Moses approached the "fiery bush" God called to him by name. The presence of the "angel of Yahweh" and 'Elohim's speaking have been cited as evidence of the blending of the J and E traditions (Beegle, pp. 59-61). But this pattern of the appearance of an angel followed by a speech of 'Elohim (or Yahweh) is consistent with other OT theophanies (e.g., Gen. 18:1-10 records that three men appear to Abraham; one turns out to be Yahweh [18:10-33] and the other two were angels [19:1]; similarly, see Josh. 5:13–6:2 and Jgs. 13:3-8, where angels are seen before Yahweh speaks). It could be that the angel appears and then speaks Yahweh's word without Yahweh actually appearing. Alternatively, perhaps the angel precedes the theophany as the guardian of the divine presence (Gen. 18:1-10 supports this). In any event, the encounter of Moses with God fits a well-established pattern and need not be seen as a conflation of traditions.

Yahweh introduced Himself as "the God of Abraham, Isaac, and Jacob" who had seen the suffering of His people, Israel. His plan was to "come down" and deliver the Israelites and bring them back to Canaan. Cassuto (p. 34) noted that the expression "come down" (Heb. *yāraḏ*) is well known in Canaanite literature to describe "divine intervention in human affairs." In this case deliverance was the purpose, while elsewhere in the Pentateuch *yāraḏ* occurs in contexts of judgment ("go down," Gen. 11:7; 18:21).

God told Moses that He would send him to Pharaoh (Ex. 3:10) to help secure Israel's release. Moses' response is to be expected: "who am I that I should go to Pharaoh . . .?" (3:11). God assured Moses that He would be with him.

The dialogue continues in 3:13ff. with Moses asking God the name by which He should be introduced to the Israelites. What follows is the disclosure of the divine name *YHWH* (Yahweh), which is derived from the verb *hāyâ*, "be." Inherent in this name and the description is the unchanging character of "the Lord God Almighty who was and is and is to come" (Rev. 4:8b). (For additional information on the divine name and titles of God *see* GOD, NAMES OF.) Buber (p. 48) argued that this emphasis on the character of Yahweh, not simply the name, was the purpose behind Moses' question. In 3:13 Moses posed the question "what is your name" with the interrogative *mah*; normally *mî* is used to inquire about one's name (Buber, p. 48; J. Motyer, *Revelation of the Divine Name* [1959], pp. 18f.). Therefore, Motyer argued, Moses did know the name Yahweh; it was something more of the character of Yahweh that he wanted to know in order to communicate it to the Israelites.

Literary critics have seen this passage (J-E) as a parallel account to Ex. 6:2ff. (P; Clements, pp. 23, 37; Beegle, pp. 90-92). The contexts of the two are different, however, and other differences have been recognized by form critics (e.g., Childs, *Exodus*, p. 111). Ex. 6:2ff. appears to be a further word to Moses to assure him that despite the initial rebuff from Pharaoh, Yahweh would fulfil His covenant (apparently that of Gen. 15 and 17, which promised Canaan as Israel's possession after a four-hundred-year period of enslavement in another land). The declaration "I am Yahweh" is completely different in form from the introduction of the divine name in 3:14f. The formula "I am god (or king) X" is well known in ancient Near Eastern texts as "an elevated style of address which asserts the authority of the speaker of the name" (Childs, *Exodus*, p. 113). Noth believed that the affinities between the two are so close that 6:2ff. was a literary expansion on Ex. 3. This explains why there was no need to discuss the etymology and meaning of the name Yahweh in 6:2ff.

What is extremely perplexing is God's statement in 6:3 that He had appeared to the patriarchs as God Almighty (*'ēl šaddāy*), "but by my name Yahweh I did not make myself known to them." This statement was the *locus classicus* for nineteenth-century scholars who argued that the religion of Israel had evolved (in accordance with current evolutionary theory). While the evolutionary model has been abandoned by most historians of religion, some OT scholars still maintain that a new name for God was given at this point (e.g., Childs, *Exodus*, p. 113). This view is questionable for two reasons. (1) It assumes that the use of Yahweh earlier in the Pentateuch (e.g., Gen. 22:14) is anachronistic. (2) It dismisses some possible extrabiblical occurrences of Yahweh in the 2nd millennium, e.g., fifteenth-century Egyptian inscriptions that appear to use Yahweh's name in connection with the Shasu bedouin and the occurrence of the name *Yahwi-el* at Mari (Beegle, p. 70). Most scholars explain the former as a geographic designation and the latter as a verb form (see, e.g., F. M. Cross, *Canaanite Myth and Hebrew Epic* [1973], pp. 60-75; de Vaux, pp. 334, 337-348; *TDOT*, V, *s.v.* "yhwh" [Freedman, O'Connor]).

It appears that more than a literal reference to knowledge of the divine name is behind God's statement "by my name Yahweh I did not *make myself known* [*nôḏa'tî*, niphal of *yāḏa'*] *to them*." Both Cassuto and Motyer argued that the use of the niphal form is not the normal way of referring to such disclosures (cf. Ezk. 20:9, which refers to the Exodus as the way God made Himself known [*nôḏa'tî*] to the nations). Motyer argued that the meaning was thus *revelation* (p. 13).

The word *yāḏa'* can mean more than simply to know a fact. It also means to experience and to know in a sexual sense (and therefore it means to know intimately). As the prophets looked back on the Sinai experience, they regarded it as the marriage ceremony of Yahweh and Israel (e.g., Hos. 13:5; Hosea uses this term throughout his book in the sense of intimate and sexual knowledge). Ezekiel also discussed the wilderness experience in 16:1-14. Here clearly the marriage motif is used. Even though this passage is allegorical, it does refer back to the Sinai event. God speaks of finding Israel as an abandoned baby (16:4-6) whom He cared for and nourished. After she had matured He "spread his skirt" over her, a way of claiming her for marriage (Ruth 3:9); this claim is followed by the promise of marriage or betrothal. In Near Eastern marriage customs a written or unwritten covenant agreement preceded the actual marriage. The marriage was consummated on the wedding night (e.g., Gen. 29:21-23).

It may be that Ezekiel looked back in history and saw the Abrahamic covenant as the betrothal (cf. Ex. 6:4) and the revelation at Sinai as the consummation of the marriage. The choice of *yāḏa'* in Ex. 6:3, as in Hos. 13:5 and Ezk. 20:9, bears out the sexual intimacy of the union that was about to take place. The Sinai revelation and covenant were unique, and therefore God could say that in this sense (i.e., marriage covenant) He had not been *known* to the patriarchs.

*C. Before Pharaoh.* Moses returned to Egypt after his commission by Yahweh with the assurance that God would be with him and that his staff would be a vehicle for God to show His power over Egypt (4:1-17). Additionally, Moses had been informed that "all the men" who were seeking his life were now dead (v. 19). This is an interesting statement, for it could mean that the king (from whom Moses had fled) and his co-regent were dead. The length of time that Moses was in Midian is described as "many days."

At God's instruction, Aaron joined Moses at "the mountain of God," where Moses informed his brother of the mission to which they had been called. When they returned to Egypt Moses and Aaron approached the Israelite elders believing that God had seen the affliction of His people and that He would liberate them (vv. 29-31).

The situation of the Israelite bondage had not changed. Moses requested that the Hebrew people be excused from work in order to go into the wilderness to celebrate a feast to Yahweh (5:1-3). This request may have had a precedent. Egyptian work rosters from Deir el-Medinah occasionally mention a person being absent from work for some religious observance. The king's response is an emphatic "no," with the addition of increased quotas. The Egyptians were very conscious of quotas. This applied to a quarrying expedition to Sinai or even to brick making (Kitchen, *Ancient Orient*, pp. 56f.). In the latter, even the Egyptians fell far behind the daily quotas (Kitchen, *Tyndale Bulletin*, 27 [1976], 140-42).

Moses was understandably distressed by this turn of events, and so God encouraged him that He was about to fulfil the promise made to Abraham (6:2-9; see II.B. above for discussion of this passage).

With Aaron at his side Moses approached the king once more, and the contest between Yahweh and Pharaoh began (7:8-15). Perhaps Moses' earlier connections with the court gave him the opportunity to approach Pharaoh. The story of Aaron's staff turning into a serpent and this act being matched by the Egyptian magicians has been called "fanciful" by some (e.g., Beegle, p. 96). But the writer has seen present-day snake charmers handle a cobra that remained as stiff as a stick one moment and then at a command began to move freely. Apparently the charmers use some sort of hypnosis or by massaging create a temporary paralysis. See *Biblical Archaeology Review*, 9/3 (1983), 72f.

When this initial show of strength proved fruitless, the plagues began in earnest (*see* PLAGUES OF EGYPT). The accounts of the ten plagues (7:20–12:22) are regarded by source critics as an excellent illustration of the blending of the sources J, E, and P (*IDB*, III, 822-24; Beegle, pp. 92-96; Childs, *Exodus*, pp. 130-142). Some who subscribe to this literary analysis of the plague cycle admit, however, that the results of separating the traditions are "rather unsatisfactory" (Auerbach, p. 50). Other scholars have argued that the ten plagues have a literary unity, which Childs maintained is simply due to final redaction (*Exodus*, pp. 130f.). Cassuto suggested that the plague stories were originally an epic poem, traces of which can still be seen in the use of parallelism and rhythm (pp. 92ff.). This may account for the complex literary quality of this section.

The historicity of the plagues is generally accepted even by more liberal scholars. G. Hort's thorough study (*ZAW*, 69 [1957], 84-103; 70 [1958], 48-59) has been instrumental in demonstrating that the first nine plagues can all be linked to natural occurrences, the first seven arising out of an especially high Nile. The Nile being turned to blood (or the appearance of blood) echoes a statement in the "Admonitions of Ipuwer" (a late 12th-Dynasty work): "Lo, the river is blood."

After the first nine plagues the Egyptians greatly feared Moses and the Israelites (11:3) and no doubt were only too happy to see the Hebrews leave (v. 2). But one more decisive plague was needed to persuade the stubborn monarch that liberating the Israelites was in his best interest.

God instructed Moses that the final plague would affect everyone in Egypt, including Israelites (who had been exempt from the previous plagues [Ex. 9:4, 26]), unless they responded in faith to what God was about to do. The tenth plague would be the death of all the firstborn in Egypt, including the crown prince (11:5). The Israelites would be spared if they sacrificed an unblemished, year-old lamb and sprinkled the blood on the doorposts and lintels of their houses (12:5-7). This was to take place on the evening of the 14th of Abib (Nisan). As God Himself traveled through the length of the land, every house would be struck with the plague unless the blood was seen on the doorway. For those who had so responded, God would pass over (*pesaḥ*; vv. 12f.). For this reason, PASSOVER was to be celebrated as an annual memorial of God's deliverance from Egypt (v. 14).

*D. Exodus.* The results of this plague (which cannot be explained by natural causes) evoked an immediate response from Pharaoh; Moses and his people were free to leave (12:31f.). The group started from Rameses and headed for Succoth to pick up other Israelites along the way. Added to this number were other peoples, called "a mixed multitude" (*'ēreḇ*). Perhaps these were other Semites and Ḫabiru who had been pressed into forced labor. The number of people leaving Egypt with Moses is debated. The text reads six hundred *'elep̄* (usually translated 600,000) men, as well as women and children (12:37). If one assumes at least an equal number of women and of children, the total could easily approach two million. This figure presents several problems when consideration is given to the terrain in Sinai through which this large group would have to pass. Furthermore, in the initial attempt to conquer Ai in Josh. 7:2-5, the Israelites suffered a grave setback in which thirty-six were killed. This number is hardly a serious loss to an army that would have exceeded 600,000 (Nu. 1:45f.)! The problem lies not with the text of Ex. 12:37 but with the interpretation of *'elep̄*. While *'elep̄* does mean one thousand, it also means a tribal unit or clan (*CHAL*, p. 18). Therefore, six hundred *'elep̄* could refer to the number of units. Following this interpretation one could read the figures for each tribe as, e.g., Nu. 1:21 (Reuben's fighting men), forty-six *'elep̄* totalling 500 rather than 46,500). Counting through the twelve tribes, one arrives at a total of 598 *'elep̄* or 5,500 men (see Beegle, p. 141). In the light of the figures from the census in Nu. 1, which was to determine the size of Israel's fighting force (made up of men twenty years old and upward, Nu. 1:3), the six hundred *'elep̄* could be a round figure. The grand total, including the tribe of Levi (not counted in the census), along with women, children, and elderly men, may have been between fifteen and twenty thousand.

The Israelites were humanly led out of Egypt by Moses, but divinely guided by a pillar of cloud by day and a pillar of fire at night (Ex. 13:21). The normal route to Canaan was along the northern coast of Sinai and then north via Gaza. But for two reasons the Israelites did not go that way. First, God had indicated to Moses that the people were to assemble before him at "the mountain of God" (3:12). Second, 13:17 relates that the Israelites were not led "by the way of the land of the Philistines [known in Egyptian as the way of Horus] although that was near, for God said, 'Lest the people repent when they see war, and return to Egypt.'" For many years it has been known that a network of forts with garrisons protected Egypt's northern frontier. It was also known from pictorial and inscriptional material from Ramesside times that such forts were located periodically along this well-traveled route to guarantee Egyptian control. One of these forts, uncovered at Deir el-Balaḥ (near Gaza), has prompted the excavator T. Dothan to suggest that the Egyptian military presence was what the Israelites feared (report at the International Congress of Egyptology in Toronto, Ontario, Sept. 1982). Moses may well have known about these forts from his earlier flight from Egypt.

The precise movements of the Israelites from this point are difficult to reconstruct since many of the place-names are not known with certainty (*see also* EXODUS, ROUTE OF THE). Ex. 12:37 suggests that Moses led the people from Rameses, which could be the city of 1:11 or the name for the area (Gen. 47:11; also known as Goshen in Gen. 47:6). Probably Hebrews lived in Succoth; this would account for the Israelites' going there first. If Succoth is to be identified with Tell el-Maskhûṭah then it is located at the east end of the Wâdī Ṭumilât, an important route of travel to northern Sinai. This is probably why military outposts were in the area (cf. E. Bleiberg, "The Location of Pithom and Succoth," in J. K. Hoffmeier and E. S. Meltzer, eds., *Egyptological Miscellanies* [*Ancient World*], 6 [1983], pp. 21-27). Papyri Anastasi V and VI (cf. *ANET*, p. 259) make clear that a number of military installations, forts, and "walls" were in the east end of the Wâdī Ṭumilât. In one of the letters in Anastasi V (*ANET*, p. 259) an officer of one of these outposts during the 19th Dynasty reported that he had not seen the two runaway slaves that he had been sent to hunt down, but he had seen their footprints. A second letter (Anastasi VI, *ANET*, p. 259) mentions the monitoring of the Edomite bedouin who were passing the fort. These communications illustrate that the Egyptians were very concerned to maintain control of their borders. Thus the Israelites moved north to avoid contact with these forts. Ex. 14:2 suggests that the Israelites were in the general vicinity of Baalzephon (perhaps Tell Defneh) and Migdol (Egyptian Sile). Migdol, as the Hebrew name bears out, was also a fortified installation on the northern frontier of Egypt (A. Gardiner, *Ancient Egyptian Onomastica* [1947], II, 202f.). Its Egyptian name was *ḫtm ṯ3rw*, "the fortress of Tjelu." No doubt the Israelites wanted to avoid this location.

While they were between Baal-zephon and Migdol, near Pi-hahiroth (14:2, 9), the identification of which is still unknown, Pharaoh decided to pursue his runaway slaves (14:1-7). He believed the Hebrews to be "entangled in the land; the wilderness has shut them in" (v. 3b). This may allude to the difficulty the Israelites were having in trying to escape Egypt; the forts and impassable desert areas had impaired their exodus. The chariot corps was dispatched to round up and return the escapees.

God had forewarned Moses of the coming of the Egyptian force (14:1-4). When the Israelites saw the approaching chariots, they were understandably fearful and began to complain to Moses and blame him for their plight (vv. 10-12). Here Moses' faith and strong leadership emerged. He was convinced that God would deliver Israel from the charging Egyptian army and the "sea of reeds" against which they were pinned. Throughout the narrative it is clear that God wanted to show Pharaoh, once and for all, that He is supreme (vv. 4, 17). At God's bidding, Moses commanded the people to move forward toward the sea; he raised his staff and the waters were divided, providing a way of escape. The text explains that a "strong east wind" was used to part the waters (v. 21). When the Egyptian chariotry pursued the Israelites their wheels became clogged and hampered movement (vv. 24f.). After the Israelites had gone through, Moses stretched out the staff once again, and the waters returned to their place, thus inundating the Egyptian army (vv. 26-31). This great triumph for Yahweh and His people is echoed in the so-called Song of the Sea or Song of Moses (ch. 15; *see* MOSES, SONG OF).

For a discussion of the Re(e)d Sea problem, *see* RED SEA.

*E. From Egypt to Sinai.* The deliverance of the Israelites was a test of Moses' leadership, but the testing did not end when the Egyptians were left behind. From this point on the people continually murmured against Moses and the plan of seeking freedom. The pattern is that the people complain to Moses, who in turn calls on God. Ex. 15:23-25 records a problem with water, a real concern for anyone traveling in the Sinai. The water found at Marah (which in Hebrew means "bitter") was bitter and therefore undrinkable. When Moses cried to God, He told him to throw a tree in the water, and the water became sweet. In Ex. 16:2-8 the people murmur about the lack of food. In this situation God provided MANNA from heaven (vv. 14-16) and QUAIL, which "covered the camp" (v. 13). While the quail appear to have been available for a short period, the manna was available throughout the wilderness wanderings (v. 35).

During their stay at Rephidim, the Israelites again murmured against Moses because of the lack of water (17:1-4). Moses was instructed to strike "the rock at Horeb" with his staff and water would spring forth. By following God's command the water was produced. But Moses was clearly angered by his people; thus he called the place "Massah" (proof) and "Meribah" (contention) "because of the faultfinding of the children of Israel, and because they put the Lord to the proof by saying 'Is the Lord among us or not'" (v. 7).

Also while at Rephidim the Israelites encountered their first military opposition (vv. 8-13) — the Amalekites, descendants of Edom-Esau (Gen. 36:12). Apparently they were a seminomadic people whose movements took them as far north as the southern Negeb (1 S. 30:1-10); they were fearful that the presence of the Israelites in their territory could deplete their grazing land, food, and water sources (Beegle, p. 186).

Moses took his position on a nearby hill, with his associates Aaron and Hur, who upheld Moses' hands until Israel triumphed. The gesture of holding up hands is associated with prayer (cf. 1 K. 8:22f.; Ps. 63:4 [MT 5]). While Moses was apparently engaged in the spiritual end of the battle, JOSHUA (whose name appears here for the first time) was in the valley below leading the army in the fighting (Ex. 17:9, 13).

Apparently only a short distance from Rephidim was the mountain of God where the revelation of Yahweh and the giving of the law was to take place (Ex. 19:1f.). Ch. 18 records the arrival of Jethro, ZIPPORAH, and her children to meet Moses. Apparently Moses had sent his wife and children back to her father when he feared for their safety in Egypt (18:2f.). The activities described in ch. 18 appear to take place after the arrival at Sinai. Therefore many have speculated about its placement before ch. 19, which speaks of the arrival at "the mountain," but no convincing answers have been put forward (Childs, *Exodus,* pp. 321f.).

The Israelites had come to this location because they were to "serve" God at the same spot where He had appeared to Moses (Ex. 3:12). This statement comes in the context of Moses' call to liberate the enslaved Hebrews (3:1–4:17). The theophany takes place at "the mountain of God." Some think that this mountain had a history of theophanies, but that Moses was simply not aware of this (Buber, p. 39). Cassuto (p. 30) is probably correct in saying that "mountain of God" is used "proleptically," i.e., "the mountain that was destined to become God's mountain" by virtue of the revelation that was to take place (Ex. 19ff.).

Exodus 3:1 may provide crucial information on locating the mountain of God: "Now Moses was keeping the flock of his father-in-law, Jethro, the priest of Midian; and he led his flock to the west side of the wilderness, and came to Horeb, the mountain of God." The translation of *'aḥar* (lit. "behind") as "west" is possible and is supported by some commentators (Cole, p. 62; cf. Childs, p. 49). Since Midian, which was E of the Gulf of Aqabah, would have been the starting point of Moses, his point of reference would have been the east (or Midian) and thus *'aḥar* would refer to the Sinai Peninsula. (Although this seems far from his home base, shepherds are forced to move where pasture is available [cf. Gen. 37; 46:1].)

The use of Horeb (*ḥōrēḇ*) rather than Sinai (*sînay*) in 3:2 has provoked much discussion. Literary critics observe that Horeb is the name of the sacred mountain in the E and D traditions, while Sinai is preferred by J and P (*IDB,* IV, 376; Clements, p. 19; Noth, *Exodus,* pp. 31-35). While it is generally true that the name Yahweh appears when Mt. Sinai is mentioned in the Pentateuch, in Ex. 31:18 it is on Mt. Sinai that Moses receives the two tablets of stone that God (*'ᵉlōhîm*) had written with His finger. After being in the presence of Yahweh for forty days and nights, Moses descended Mt. Sinai after talking with God ('Elohim, 34:28f.). So there are two occasions where God ('Elohim) is mentioned in connection with Mt. Sinai. (Mt. Sinai is mentioned sixteen times in the Pentateuch.) In Deuteronomy (1:6, 19; 4:10; 5:2; 9:8; 18:16; 29:1) when Horeb is mentioned "Yahweh your (or our) God ['Elohim]" is used. Only in Dt. 4:15 does the name Yahweh appear alone. So the use of divine names in connection with Horeb or Sinai is not consistent and therefore simply cannot be used as a criterion for sources or authorship. Also, it seems unlikely that the name of the place where God made His covenant with Israel would have been confused and thus give rise to different traditions since the Sinai theophany was the most important event in the history of Israel. OT scholars generally agree, regardless of the critical approach used, that Horeb and Sinai refer to the same place and that the terms are used synonymously. *See also* SINAI.

*F. Theophany.* The high point in the career of Moses is the intercessory role he played on the mountain of God. The people were informed that in three days they were to stand before the mountain, where the revelation would take place (Ex. 19:10-15). In the meantime the people were to sanctify themselves, including washing their clothes (19:10). The mountain was to be cordoned off and thus segregated from the profane, and no one was to pass the markers (19:12f.; for a discussion of segregation of a holy spot from a phenomenological perspective with numerous examples from Egypt see J. K. Hoffmeier, *"Sacred" in the Vocabulary of Ancient Egypt* [1985]).

On the third day, Yahweh descended onto the mountain, which was wrapped in smoke and fire (19:16-20). What followed was the ceremony in which the covenant was made (chs. 20–24). The form of this ceremony fits into the six-point structure of Hittite suzerainty-vassal treaties of the period 1600-1200 B.C. (Kitchen, *Bible in Its World,* pp. 79-85; *see* COVENANT [OT]). The ceremony on the mountain culminated with a fellowship meal attended by Moses, other leaders, and the seventy elders (24:9-11). The leaders witnessed God (apparently shrouded) and they were unharmed because they had been properly initiated (24:5f., 8). Following the ceremony of the verbal declaration of the law, Moses received instructions concerning the building of the tabernacle, the ark of the covenant, priestly regalia, and cultic paraphernalia (chs. 25–31). Most of the material contained in this section is attributed to the priestly writer and dated late (see Haran; Childs, *Exodus,* 529f.). Some of the material, however, is considered early (Childs, *Exodus,* 531f.). The questions about the date of the material arise partly from the differences in terminology for the structure(s). The tabernacle (*miškān*) would house the ark and be located in the center of the camp while the tent of meeting (*'ōhel mō'ēḏ*) was pitched outside the camp and was named by Moses (33:7). The functions of the two were different. The *miškān* appears to be the residence of God (as the root *škn* implies), while the "meeting" is where He would appear at appointed times (Haran, p. 58). In other words, the *miškān* was both the palace and place of Yahweh's appearing. The *'ōhel mō'ēḏ* was a place where people could go to seek God (33:7-10) and worship. The function of the tabernacle was more cultic, the tent of meeting more a place of prophetic utterance (Nu. 11:24f.), where Moses would converse with God (Ex. 33:11). The importance of this tent increased when the mountain was no longer available as a place from which one could call on God.

Because Moses could communicate with God in this unique way, he asked God if he could see His glory (Ex. 33:18). This suggests that in the theophanies in Ex. 19–32 God's glory was veiled by the smoke; thus Moses wanted to see God unveiled. The nature of God made such a request impossible, but God did reveal more of His glory, allowing Moses to see His back (33:20-23). The nature of Moses' relationship to God is unique in the OT, a point acknowledged by God (Nu. 12:6-8).

The material contained in the covenant of Ex. 20–24 was presented to Israel orally by God. Now the time had come for the covenant with the stipulations (or laws) to be recorded. So Moses was summoned to the mountain to receive the tablets of stone on which God had inscribed the laws (31:18). During Moses' stay on the mount, the Israelites under Aaron's leadership made the golden calf and worshiped it (32:16). When he descended and saw what was taking place, Moses threw down the tablets, shattering them (v. 19). The Israelites had violated the first and second commandments, or two of the covenant stipulations. By destroying the inscribed tablets Moses may have been trying to nullify the covenant in order that Israel might not immediately be destroyed by God.

Through this incident Moses emerges again as the intercessor for his people (32:30-34). He was willing to receive the punishment due the people rather than let them be destroyed.

At God's command, Moses made replacements of the original tablets (34:1f.) and the laws were rewritten on them (vv. 27f.). This time when Moses descended the mountain he was met by people who witnessed an unusual phenomenon: "Moses did not know that the skin of his face shone because he had been talking with God" (v. 29). The Hebrew verb rendered "shone" is *qāran,* which may literally mean "have horns" (as in Ps. 69:31 [MT 32]; cf. *qeren,* "horn"; the Vulgate translated this as "horns" and is thus the source for some medieval representations of Moses with horns). As the commentators point out (e.g., Cassuto, pp. 448f.; Childs, *Exodus,* p. 604) the word is used here metaphorically and may be related to the common depiction in ancient Near Eastern iconography of horns or rays as symbols of power on crowns of divinities. The LXX understood the word metaphorically, and Paul explained it in the same way (2 Cor. 3:7f., 12f.).

*G. From Sinai to Moab.* After a stay in the vicinity of Mt. Sinai for nearly a year (Nu. 10:11) the Israelites moved on "at the command of the Lord by Moses" (Nu. 10:13). Nu. 1–10 describe a census taken by Moses at God's directive (1:1-3; 4:1-3). The purpose was twofold: to determine the size of Israel's fighting force (1:3), and to find out the number of Kohathites available to serve in the "tent of meeting" (4:3).

This segment of the wilderness period was most difficult in every way. Moses received the complaints of the people on many occasions and had to intervene when God's wrath was released on them (e.g., 11:1-3, 4-15; 20:2-7; 21:4-9). His leadership was challenged by Aaron and Miriam (12:1-8) and also by some of the priests headed by Korah (16:1ff.). In both cases God vindicated Moses.

God's intention in leading Israel to Mt. Sinai was to make the covenant. From there the plan was for Israel to move to Canaan via the Negeb. From Kadesh-barnea, in the wilderness of Paran, Moses dispatched the twelve spies (one representing each tribe) to determine the best route for invasion (13:1-16). After forty days of spying they returned, but only Joshua and Caleb gave a promising report concerning the feasibility of conquest (14:6-10). The people accepted the report of the other ten and were prepared to return to Egypt (14:1-3).

This display of unbelief angered God, who was ready to destroy the people (14:10b-12), but Moses pleaded the cause of Israel, arguing that should God do this, it would be a victory for Egypt and Israel's enemies. Above all, God could not then fulfil His promise to give Israel the Promised Land (14:13-19). This act of rebellion marked the tenth occasion that Israel had broken faith with God (14:20-22). Therefore God would not allow that generation, except Joshua and Caleb, to enter Canaan; rather, they would remain in the wilderness forty years and die (14:26-35).

The forty-year length of the wandering cannot be doubted, since Dt. 2:14 mentions that it was thirty-eight years from the departure from Kadesh until the crossing of the brook Zered in Moab. The number forty is used so often in the OT that it appears to have a symbolic meaning for a period of judgment, purging, purification, or rest (e.g., Gen. 7:17; Jgs. 3:11; 5:8; 8:28; Jonah 3:4). No doubt the forty years of the wilderness gave rise to the later symbolic use.

The most tragic event in the life of Moses took place at Kadesh when he did not follow God's instructions (Nu. 20:1-13). The parallels between this story and that of Ex. 17 are so numerous that many scholars assign Nu. 20 to P and Ex. 17 to JE (Beegle, p. 299). The most troubling point is that the spot is named Meribah in both stories (Ex. 17:7; Nu. 20:13). Apart from this, the differences between the two are so great that they appear to be independent traditions. In Nu. 20:8 Moses is told to take the rod with him, but to speak to the rock in order to produce water. But he struck the rock twice (Nu. 20:11). In Ex. 17:6 Moses is instructed to strike the rock. It has been pointed out that in disobeying God's directive, Moses was rebelling against God, since in the OT these two concepts are related and associated with unbelief (Nu. 20:12; see Wenham, *Numbers [Tyndale OT Comms.,* 1981], p. 150). Just as the unbelief of the nation in Nu. 14 prevented them from entering the Promised Land, so Moses' rebellion barred him from this privilege.

The association of Nu. 20 with P is questionable. Dt. 32:48-52 recalls the incident and gives it as the reason for Moses being denied entrance to Canaan. It is thought that P simply looked back at this and expanded the story to explain why Moses did not enter Canaan (Beegle, p. 300). But some studies on P from grammatical, linguistic, and socioreligious perspectives raise very serious questions on the lateness of the priestly material (see, e.g., G. Rendsburg, *Journal of the Ancient Near Eastern Society of Columbia University,* 12 [1980], 65-80; A. Horvitz, *RB,* 81 [1974], 24-56; *A Linguistic Study of the Relationship Between the Priestly Source and the Book of Exodus* [1982]; Z. Zevit, *ZAW,* 94 [1982], 481-511).

After Israel's unsuccessful attempt to enter Canaan from the Negeb (Nu. 14:39-45), the Canaanite king of Arad felt confident that he could destroy Israel (21:1), and he enjoyed initial success. But Israel rallied, and with God's help conquered some of the cities of the Negeb (vv. 2f.).

*H. Conquest of Transjordan.* The conquest of Transjordan was the first step in taking possession of the Promised Land since this area was to be allotted to the tribes of Reuben, Gad, and Manasseh (Nu. 32). Transjordan was controlled by the Edomites in the south, the Moabites in the area E of the Dead Sea, and the Ammonites E of the Jordan River and N of Moab. The accounts of the conquest of this region are recorded in Nu. 20–24 and Dt. 2. The key figures who confronted Moses and the Israelites were Sihon king of Heshbon, Og king of Bashan, and Balak king of Moab. Sihon and Og were the Amorite overlords of the area, while Balak was a Moabite. Israel's policy was simply to pass through this region without fighting Edom, Moab, and Ammon, because they were all distantly related (cf. Gen. 19:36-38; Dt. 2:4-6, 9, 19), but they met opposition (Nu. 20:14-21) and so had to detour to the east of this area (21:4, 10-13). Even against the Amorite kings the Israelites had no desire for conflict, only to pass through (v. 21). When passage was denied, battle ensued and Israel defeated these kings. The details are incomplete but the event was well remembered (vv. 27-30; cf. Dt. 2:26-37; Josh. 24:12; Ps. 135:11).

The historicity of these events has been called into question due to the complexities and apparent tension between the traditions of Deuteronomy and Numbers (cf. J. Van Seters, *JBL,* 91 [1972], 182-197; M. Weippert, "Israelite 'Conquest' and the Evidence from Transjordan," in F. M. Cross, ed., *Symposia* [1979], pp. 15-34). While such investigations raise important critical questions, the solutions proposed are not especially convincing.

The archeological evidence for the Conquest has been problematic. From his survey of sites in Transjordan N. Glueck concluded that there was a hiatus in settled occupation of Transjordan from 1900 B.C. to the beginning of the Iron Age (*Explorations in Eastern Palestine* [*AASOR,* 15, 1935]). This evidence lent support to the thirteenth-century date of the Conquest, when Moab would have been reestablishing fortified cities. Subsequently Glueck modified his conclusions, and more Middle and Late Bronze material has come to light (Bimson, pp. 61-68; Weippert, pp. 25f.). Excavations at Heshbon, however, have revealed no material from before 1200 B.C. Problems surrounding the Israelite conquest of Transjordan thus remain. The Israelite presence at an early date (pre-monarchy) cannot be denied. Jephthah (Jgs. 11:12-26) argued with the Ammonites that the Israelites' right to the territory went back three hundred years when they took it, not from the Ammonites and Moabites, but from the Amorite Sihon. Furthermore, the Moabite stone (*ca.* 830 B.C.) mentions that the men of Gad had been living in Ataroth from time immemorial (*mʿlm*).

*I. Deuteronomic Legislation.* While camped in the plains of Moab and waiting for the command to enter Canaan, the Israelites received the Deuteronomic legislation. As early as the beginning of the 19th cent., de Wette had thought that Deuteronomy was written during Josiah's reign (7th cent. B.C.) to provide the apologetic needed for his reforms (2 K. 22:3-13). This interpretation of the origins of Deuteronomy is certainly the most widely accepted by source critics (*see* DEUTERONOMY).

The book itself claims to be Moses' interpretation or explanation (*bēʾēr,* "explain," Dt. 1:5) of the law. The form of the book fits into the Hittite covenant treaty formula and appears to be a covenant renewal (Kitchen, *Bible in Its World,* pp. 80-85). The fourth section of the Hittite treaty called for the periodic reading of the treaty by the vassal. Ex. 24 does not specify how often this should take place, but since the wilderness tradition has no record of such a renewal earlier, it appears that it was to take place during each generation. Josh. 24 contains such a renewal at the end of Joshua's life, perhaps for the next generation. In Dt. 31:10f. Moses informed the people that on the sabbatical year the law was to be read publicly.

Moses not only took the lead in this ceremony, but he also established the tradition that the role of the scribes was to teach and interpret the law (e.g., Ezr. 7:10). Since Moses was "explaining" the law, he digressed in certain areas and expanded in others. But throughout, the passion of a preacher who is concerned with his flock is very evident. He regarded commitment to the covenant and its stipulations as an actual encounter with God at Horeb just as had happened at the initial revelation (Dt. 5:2-5). In other words, the faith of Israel involved a dynamic, ongoing theophany.

Moses finished writing a copy of "this law" (Dt. 31:9, 24), and it was given to the Levites to place in the ark along with the tablets of stone (vv. 24-26). Moses then addressed a song to the people reminding them of God's past faithfulness and of his future provision (Dt. 31:30–32:1-43). Shortly before his death Moses gave one last blessing to the people (Dt. 33). In form it is very much like Jacob's blessing (Gen. 49:1-27), in which each tribe is mentioned by name and is given an appropriate blessing.

At the age of 120 (Dt. 34:7) Moses died, after seeing the Promised Land from the top of Pisgah on Mt. Nebo, and was secretly buried by God (34:6). Thus Moses, the servant of God, completed his course, liberating his people from Egypt, being the medium of receiving God's law, and bringing Israel to the land of their inheritance.

***III. Work and Ministry.***–In the Pentateuch Moses has many different roles. He was the divinely appointed leader of Israel and thus had both civil and religious duties. Some scholars are disturbed by Moses having so many qualities; they see him as larger than life and therefore regard some of these attributes as embellishments. But Moses was indeed an outstanding figure, and later tradition must have had its basis in reality. His special encounters with God at Sinai are reason enough to elevate him to such a position in biblical and postbiblical traditions.

*A. Leader.* Without a doubt Moses was Israel's greatest leader, though he was a reluctant one (Ex. 3:11) who was aware of his limitations (4:10). For this reason, God provided Aaron to be his spokesman (4:14-16; 7:1). Throughout the period of the plagues Moses emerged as a strong individual who was willing to confront Pharaoh. Under the extreme pressure of the situation at the sea of reeds (14:13-18) Moses showed great confidence in God: "Fear not, stand firm, and see the salvation of the Lord . . ." (v. 13). In his exuberant response to God's saving act, he led the nation in a song of triumph (ch. 15).

One of Moses' responsibilities was to judge. The task was enormous (18:13-16), and Jethro suggested that he appoint other judges to lighten the load (vv. 17-23). Moses responded positively to this suggestion (vv. 24-26), thus illustrating that he did not cling to his responsibilities but was willing to delegate work. We are told that Moses was very meek (Nu. 12:3). Thus when Miriam and Aaron contested his authority (v. 2), he did not try to justify himself. Then God rebuked Aaron and Miriam (vv. 4-8), pointing out that there was no one with whom He communicated like Moses. Miriam, who apparently was the instigator of this incident, was made leprous because of God's anger toward her (vv. 9f.). But Moses could not accept this judgment on his sister; he interceded for her (v. 13), and after seven days she was cleansed.

When Korah led what appeared to be a rebellion against Moses (Nu. 16), once again Moses did not retaliate but said that God would declare which of the two was right.

God clearly responded in favor of Moses (vv. 31-33). Moses apparently felt that, since he had been called by God to lead this people, he did not need to defend himself. Despite these attacks he remained absolutely committed to his people and to God. In so doing he was the prototype for future leaders of Israel.

*B. Lawgiver.* Moses is best remembered as being the "lawgiver" par excellence. The Pentateuch depicts Moses as the recipient of God's laws, which he in turn passed on to the people after recording them (Ex. 24:4). Ex. 24:12 maintains, however, that some laws were given to Moses in written form by God on the "tables of stone." Those apparently contained the Ten Commandments (Ex. 34:27f.). In the Pentateuch both covenant stipulations and codified laws are present for the theocratic nation. When Moses appeared in history, whether in the 15th or the 13th cent., codified laws had existed in Mesopotamia for a millennium. This is not true of Egypt, since Egypt was ruled by the religio-philosophical concept of *ma'at,* which comprises right, order, justice, truth, etc.

Mesopotamian law codes were actually collections of common laws and legal precedents that could be consulted in legal cases (see J. J. Finkelstein, *JCS,* 15 [1967], 91-103). In the Pentateuch certain legal and religious precedents were established in patriarchal times, e.g., tithing (Gen. 14:20; Nu. 18:24-28) and circumcision on the eighth day (Gen. 17:11-12; Lev. 12:3).

The laws given at Mt. Sinai were not the only legal material to be placed in the Pentateuch. In certain cases laws were subsequently introduced to address particular problems. A good example is the petition of the daughters of Zelophehad that they be able to inherit their father's possessions since he had no son (Nu. 27:1-4). Moses took this case to God, who then declared that women should inherit their father's estate if there were no sons (Nu. 27:5-11).

*See also* Law in the OT.

*C. Prophet.* Not only was Moses a prophet, he was the standard by which subsequent prophets were measured. In Dt. 18:15-18 God announced that He would raise up prophets after Moses who would be like him — they would be God's spokesmen. The prophet in Israel was one who constantly called the people back to the covenantal obligations. The meaning of the root of *nābî'* (prophet) is "call" (BDB, p. 611). Not only does the prophet call the people's attention to the law, he also receives a "call" from God. The call of Moses in Ex. 3 has been seen as a prophetic call like that of Samuel (1 S. 3:1-14), Isaiah (Isa. 6:1-13), Jeremiah (Jer. 1:4-19), and Ezekiel (Ezk. 1:1ff.) (see Childs, *Exodus,* pp. 67f.).

Prophets were usually intercessors, not in the cultic and sacrificial sense of the priest, but in prayer. Moses so regularly interceded on behalf of sinful Israel (e.g., Ex. 33:12-16; Nu. 11:1f.; 12:13; 14:10b-19; 21:4-9) that he gained the reputation of being effective in turning God's heart from anger (see Jer. 15:1).

Moses also prophesied ecstatically, which is not reported of others until Nu. 11. When God's Spirit rested on others, Joshua wanted Moses to stop them from prophesying, perhaps because Joshua thought this activity was solely the prerogative of Moses. Moses rebuked him (Nu. 11:25-29), again demonstrating his willingness to share his responsibilities.

*See also* Prophecy.

*D. Author.* OT, rabbinic, and NT traditions credit Moses with the authorship of the Pentateuch. Early in the Christian era Gnostics began to raise questions concerning Mosaic authorship of the Pentateuch, and Jewish and Moslem scholars continued raising questions into medieval times (see R. K. Harrison, *Intro. to the OT* [1969], pp. 3-7). From the 17th cent. onward much of the quest of OT scholarship was to determine the sources used by Moses or subsequent writers. This was especially true for Genesis since the period it covers is pre-Mosaic. Scholars of the 18th and early 19th cents. raised the legitimate question concerning the ability to write during the 15th cent. B.C. By the end of the 19th cent., however, the cuneiform scripts of Mesopotamia and the hieroglyphic and hieratic writings of Egypt had been deciphered and were being actively studied. The Proto-Sinaitic inscriptions attest an alphabetic script in the 15th cent. (*see* Inscriptions I.A.3). Not only was writing at a sophisticated level during the 15th cent. B.C., but writing of lengthy literary works could be traced back a millennium earlier. It is now very clear that one cannot use the question of writing for denying a priori that Moses could have been an author.

Since Moses was reared in the royal court (Ex. 2:10) he undoubtedly learned to read and write along with the other princes. The Pentateuch makes several references to Moses recording the events of the wilderness period (Ex. 17:14-16; Nu. 33:2), the covenant (Ex. 24:4, 7), and covenant renewal (Dt. 31:9, 22). That Moses had a central role in the writing and forming of the Pentateuch cannot be denied. However, such statements as "Now the man Moses was very meek, more than all men that were on the face of the earth" (Nu. 12:3) appear to be the words of an editor, not Moses, if the statement is taken at face value. But this description does seem to have come from someone who intimately knew Moses. The questions concerning subsequent editorial work and just when the books appeared in final form are perhaps impossible to answer.

***IV. Outside the Pentateuch.**–A. OT.* In the remainder of the OT Moses is mentioned frequently, mostly in connection with his law, commands, or instructions. The book of Joshua contains more references to Moses than any other book. The approximately fifty occurrences deal mostly with Joshua and the Israelites doing this or that "as Moses had commanded (or directed)" (e.g., Josh. 4:10, 12; 8:33), "according to what is written in the Book of the Law of Moses" (Josh. 23:6), etc. The book of Joshua contains the history of the Conquest after the death of Moses and the allotting of the tribal territories. Moses had given specific directions about these matters (Josh. 11:12; 13:8; 14:3, etc.), so the writer is making it clear that Israel and its leaders were faithful in executing this command. No doubt the great respect the people had for Moses (Josh. 4:14), who had recently departed from them, accounts for the frequency of these references.

The "law of Moses" is mentioned by David (1 K. 2:3) and in connection with Joash (2 K. 21:8) and Josiah (2 K. 23:25). The stone tablets of Moses were apparently in the ark at the dedication of the temple by Solomon (1 K. 8:9).

Moses is remembered as the miracle worker who delivered Israel from the servitude of Egypt (1 S. 12:6-8; Ps. 105:26-37; Isa. 63:11f.; Mic. 6:4). Other events surrounding the wilderness experience are also recalled (Ps. 106:23, 32). Ps. 90 was called "a prayer of Moses." The prophets do not refer to Moses by name as frequently as might be expected, but their messages are couched in covenant terminology with frequent quotations from, and general references to, the Law (e.g., Isa. 1:2; 5:24; 24:5; Jer. 2:8; 9:13; Hos. 4:6; Am. 2:4). Mic. 6:1-8 and Jer. 2:9ff. use the *rîḇ* pattern (a legal letter form charging the covenanted vassal with violation of stipulations and warning that reprisals will follow if the stipulations are not kept). This of course presupposes the covenant of Ex. 20–24.

The postexilic writings continue to refer to the book or law of Moses (Ezr. 6:18; Neh. 1:7f.; 8:1, 3; 9:3; 13:1).

Moses and the Pentateuch play a vital part throughout the OT. It is fitting that Malachi, the last prophetic book (last book of the OT in the LXX and English versions), in the closing chapter should say, "Remember the law of my servant Moses, the statutes and ordinances that I commanded him at Horeb for all Israel" (Mal. 4:4 [MT 3:22]).

*B. Intertestamental Literature.* As one might expect, this literature not only continues the OT traditions about Moses but also embellishes them. The Apocrypha frequently refers to "the law of Moses" (e.g., 1 Esd. 8:3; 9:39; Tob. 6:12; Bar. 2:2; cf. T. Zeb. 3:4) and "the book of Moses" (e.g., 1 Esd. 1:11; 5:49; 7:6, 9), and 2 Macc. 7:6 refers to the Song of Moses (cf. 4 Macc. 18:18). Several texts recount events of Moses' life, either summarily (e.g., IV Ezra 14:3-6) or with many embellishments (e.g., Sib. Or. 3:253-260; Jubilees; cf. 1 Enoch 89:16-40, which uses the image of Moses as a sheep). 2 Esd. 14:3 refers to the burning bush episode, 7:106 to his intercessory role, and 2 Bar. 17:4 to his death at the age of 120. In his praise of famous men, Sirach says Moses "was beloved by God and man" (Sir. 45:1; cf. vv. 2-6). On the pseudepigraphic Assumption of Moses, *see* APOCALYPTIC LITERATURE III.E.

Moses was also important to the Qumrân community. This community was organized according to the Mosaic law (see F. M. Cross, *Ancient Library of Qumran and Modern Biblical Studies* [rev. ed. repr. 1980], p. 78 n. 36a). Each member took an oath to "return to the Torah of Moses" (1QS 5:8), and anyone who "transgressed a word of the Torah of Moses" would be banished (1QS 8:20-22). Because of their eschatological orientation, they naturally focused more on the prophetic and apocalyptic OT texts, but even here they stressed the "prophet like Moses" and appealed to Moses as the authority for this emphasis (4QTestim 1-8, quoting Dt. 5:28f.; 18:81f.).

Josephus and Philo also have many references to Moses, including extensive accounts of his life (see esp. Josephus *Ant.* ii.9.1 [201]–iv. 7.49 [331]; Philo *De vita Mosis*).

See also *TDNT,* IV, 848-864.

*C. NT.* Moses' importance extended through NT times as well. Throughout the Gospels, the law of Moses is seen as the absolute standard for faith and conduct among the Jews. Therefore references to the "law," "teaching," and "customs" of Moses abound. There is no question in the NT that the Pentateuch came from the hand of Moses. In fact, "Moses" is used synonymously with "the law" (Lk. 24:27). The Jews believed that God had spoken to him (Jn. 9:29), and therefore they were his disciples (Jn. 9:28).

In His teaching, Jesus Christ regarded the writings of Moses (or the Law) and the Prophets as ultimately pointing to Himself (Lk. 24:27, 44). As an endorsement of this view, the Synoptics all mention that Moses and Elijah appeared to Jesus on the mount of transfiguration (Mt. 17:4; Mk. 9:4; Lk. 9:30).

Since the early Church was mostly Jewish, Moses and the law continued to have a place of importance in its life and teaching. Peter's sermons frequently included quotations of or allusions to the law (Acts 3:22f., 25). Stephen's sermon before the Sanhedrin included nine citations of the name of Moses (Acts 7:20-44). The Epistles have several quotations from Moses, as well as more allegorical interpretations of the life of Moses or events from his lifetime (1 Cor. 10:2; 2 Cor. 3:7, 13, 15; see esp. He. 3:2f., 5, 16; 7:14; 8:5; 9:19; 10:28; 12:21). Moses is upheld in He. 11:23-29 as an example of a man who lived by faith. Finally, in heaven the saints will sing "the song of Moses" (Rev. 15:3), apparently a reference to Ex. 15. Thus Moses is connected with the Bible in some way from Genesis to Revelation.

***Bibliography.***–W. F. Albright, "Moses in Historical and Theological Perspective," in F. M. Cross, *et al.*, eds., *Magnalia Dei: The Mighty Acts of God* (*Festschrift* for G. E. Wright; 1976); E. Auerbach, *Moses* (Eng. tr. 1975); D. M. Beegle, *Moses, the Servant of Yahweh* (1972); J. Bimson, *Redating the Exodus and Conquest* (1981); J. Bright, *BHI* (3rd ed. 1981); M. Buber, *Moses* (1946); U. Cassuto, *Comm. on the Book of Exodus* (Eng. tr. repr. 1974); B. S. Childs, *JBL,* 84 (1965), 109-122; *Book of Exodus* (*OTL,* 1974); R. E. Clements, *Exodus* (*CBC,* 1972); G. W. Coats, *VT,* 18 (1968), 450-57; *Rebellion in the Wilderness* (1968); R. A. Cole, *Exodus* (*Tyndale OT Comms.,* 1973); H. Gressmann, *Mose und seine Zeit* (1913); J. G. Griffiths, *JNES,* 12 (1953), 225-231; M. Haran, *JSS,* 5 (1960), 50-65; L. S. Hay, *JBL,* 83 (1964), 397-403; W. Helck, *VT,* 15 (1965), 35-48; S. Herrmann, *History of Israel in OT Times* (Eng. tr., 2nd ed. 1981); *Israel in Egypt* (Eng. tr., *SBT* 2/27, 1973); S. H. Horn, *Biblical Archaeology Review,* 3/2 (1977), 22-31; K. Kitchen, *Ancient Orient and OT* (1963); *Bible in Its World* (1978); B. Mazar, *JNES,* 24 (1965), 297-303; D. J. McCarthy, *JBL,* 85 (1966), 137-158; *NBD, s.v.* (K. Kitchen); C. Nims, *BA,* 13 (1950), 22-28; M. Noth, *Exodus* (Eng. tr. *OTL,* 1962); *History of Pentateuchal Traditions* (Eng. tr. 1972); J. Rea, *Bulletin of the Evangelical Theological Society,* 3 (1960), 38-69; D. B. Redford, *VT,* 13 (1963), 401-418; *Numen,* 14 (1967), 209-228; N. H. Snaith, *VT,* 15 (1965), 395-398; *TDNT,* IV, *s.v.* Μωυσῆς (J. Jeremias); R. de Vaux, *Early History of Israel* (Eng. tr. 1978).

J. K. HOFFMEIER

**MOSES, ASSUMPTION OF.** *See* APOCALYPTIC LITERATURE III.E.

**MOSES' SEAT** [Gk. *tḗs Mōuseōs kathédras*]; NEB CHAIR OF MOSES. In Mt. 23:2, Jesus said, "The scribes and the Pharisees sit on Moses' seat." Many claim that Jesus was referring to a familiar piece of furniture in ancient synagogues and identify the stone chairs excavated from synagogues in Hammath by Tiberias and in Chorazin as the Moses' seat (see Sukenik). With their backs toward Jerusalem the elders of the synagogue sat facing the people. The most prominent elder sat in the stone seat on a raised platform next to the ark containing the OT scrolls. From here, it is supposed, teachers expounded the Mosaic law. This seat symbolized their authority as interpreters of the law in unbroken succession from Moses. The earliest reference to Moses' seat in rabbinic literature appears in *Pesikta de Rab Kahana* 7b where Rabbi Aḥa (*ca.* A.D. 320) referred to a seat of special shape, like the throne of Solomon (1 K. 10:19), that was reserved for the president of the Sanhedrin.

While a conspicuous seat may have been situated at the head of the congregation in the synagogue, Jesus was not referring simply to a physical chair. That "scribes" and "Pharisees" are plural and "Moses' seat" is singular and that in Mt. 23:6 Jesus denounced their love for the first *seats* of the synagogue strongly suggest that He was not referring to a physical sitting but to the collective symbol of their legal authority. The imperatives in 23:3 ("do and keep") are based on the authority implied in v. 2. Mt. 23:2f. is the prelude to the denunciation of the scribes and Pharisees and presents the claims of the Pharisaic scribes to be the ordained guardians and interpreters of the Mosaic law.

***Bibliography.***–E. L. Sukenik, *Ancient Synagogues in Palestine and Greece* (1934); I. Renov, *IEJ,* 5 (1955), 262-67; D. E. Garland, *The Intention of Matthew 23* (*Nov.Test. Supp.,* 52; 1979).

D. E. GARLAND

**MOSES, SONG OF** [Gk. *hē ǭdḗ Mōyséōs*]. The name given to the song that John heard the saved singing (Rev. 15:3). Scholars disagree about the identity of this song, since two poetic passages in the Pentateuch are often designated the Song of Moses: Ex. 15:1-18 extols Yahweh's deliverance in the Exodus, and Dt. 32:1-43 recites His faithfulness despite the waywardness of the Israelite nation.

Exodus 15:1-18 is the better known and liked of the two Songs of Moses (it is also called the Song of the Sea [cf., e.g., Cross, *Canaanite Myth*] and the Song of Miriam [cf. Cross and Freedman, *JNES*]). It is quite positive, celebrating the victory of Yahweh at the Red Sea and His miraculous deliverance of His people from the oppressive hand of Pharaoh.

The song does not immediately lend itself to an outline. There are, however, two foci both given in v. 1: God the miracle-working deliverer (esp. vv. 11-17), and the actual defeat of the Egyptian army by drowning (vv. 1, 4f., 10, 12). In vv. 1-3 God is spoken of in the 3rd person almost as if Moses were addressing the people. Beginning with v. 6 he speaks to God, and this continues through v. 17. V. 18 is a kind of doxology. The whole episode appears in a capsule prose form in v. 19.

Another theme dominates the last third of the poem. It is the testimony that such a deliverance will have on the neighboring nations. The miracles were, after all, not merely designed to benefit Israel but proofs to both believers and unbelievers that the Lord did exist, had power to save, and did choose to bless His people.

The other Song of Moses, Dt. 32:1-43, has a different focus. This longer one is more negative in its underscoring the faithlessness of the nation (vv. 5f., 15-18, 21) in contrast to the faithfulness of God (vv. 3f., 7-14). In addition there is the theme of God's discipline or retribution both on His own people (vv. 19-35) and on their enemies (vv. 40-43).

***Bibliography.***–B. Childs, *Book of Exodus* (*OTL*, 1974), pp. 240-253; P. C. Craigie, *Book of Deuteronomy* (*NICOT*, 1976), pp. 373-389; F. M. Cross, *Canaanite Myth and Hebrew Epic* (1973), pp. 112-144; F. M. Cross and D. N. Freedman, *JNES*, 14 (1955), 237-250; *Studies in Ancient Yahwistic Poetry* (1975), pp. 45-65; P. Miller, *Divine Warrior in Early Israel* (1973), pp. 113-17.

R. L. ALDEN

**MOSOLLAM** mō-sol'əm (1 Esd. 9:14, AV); **MOSOLLAMON** mō-sol'ə-mən (1 Esd. 8:44, AV); **MOSOLLAMUS** (1 Esd. 8:44; 9:14, NEB). *See* MESHULLAM 10, 11.

**MOST HIGH.** *See* GOD, NAMES OF II.B.2.

**MOST HOLY PLACE** [Heb. *qōḏeš haqq*[o]*ḏāšîm*] (Ex. 26:33); NEB HOLY OF HOLIES; [*d*[e]*ḇîr*] (1 K. 6:16); AV ORACLE; RSV INNER SANCTUARY; NEB INNER SHRINE; [Gk. *hágia hagíōn*] (He. 9:3); AV HOLIEST OF ALL; RSV HOLY OF HOLIES. The innermost compartment of the several biblical sanctuaries. *See* HOLY PLACE; TABERNACLE; TEMPLE.

The generally accepted view is that the most holy place in the tabernacle was a room of ten cubits (approximately 4½ m., 15 ft.) on a side. This supposition is strengthened by the cubic form of the inner sanctuaries in both Solomon's and Ezekiel's temples. The only furniture in the most holy place was the ark of the covenant, which held the two tablets of the law (Ex. 25:10-16). The mercy seat, a slab of pure gold surmounted by two golden cherubim, rested on top of the ark (vv. 17-22). Dividing the most holy place from the holy place (the outer chamber) was a curtain ornamented with figures of cherubim (26:31-33). Access to the inner shrine, whether in tabernacle or temple, was forbidden to all but the high priest who, on the annual Day of Atonement, was allowed to enter bearing sacrificial blood (Lev. 16; He. 9:7).

The most holy place in Solomon's temple was a room of twenty cubits (approximately 9 m., 30 ft.; see 1 K. 6:20) on a side. Flanking the ark were two cherubim made of olivewood and overlaid with gold (1 K. 6:23, 28); these faced the entrance of the most holy place (2 Ch. 3:13). In his temple plans Ezekiel retained the dimensions of the Solomonic inner sanctuary (Ezk. 41:4), and the same probably holds for the second temple founded by Zerubbabel (Ezr. 3). Since the ark was lost when the Babylonians destroyed Jerusalem in 587 B.C., the most holy place in the rebuilt temple had no furniture at all. There is no representation of the ark on the Arch of Titus, erected in Rome to commemorate the Romans' destruction of Jerusalem in A.D. 70; only furniture from the holy place is depicted.

The writer of Hebrews expounded the death of Christ to show that the barrier between God and mankind, symbolized by the partition of the OT sanctuaries, had been removed, making access to the presence of God the prerogative of every Christian (He. 10:19-22).

R. P. GORDON

**MOTE.** *See* SPECK.

**MOTH** [Heb. *ʿāš*–'waster,' 'consumer'; Gk. *sḗs* (Mt. 6:19f.; Lk. 12:33), *sētóbrōtos*–'moth-eaten' (Jas. 5:2)]. The clothes moth, of the insect order *Lepidoptera*. In Palestine the common form is the *tineola biselliella*. Moths lay eggs especially in wool, the most common clothing fabric of biblical times, and the larvae mutilate garments as they feed on their fabric. Thus moths are associated often with destruction, decay, frailty, etc. in the Bible (Job 4:19 [NEB "bird"]; 13:28; Ps. 39:11 [MT 12; NEB "festers"]; Isa. 50:9; 51:8; Hos. 5:12 [NEB "festering sore"]; Mt. 6:19f.; Lk. 12:33; Jas. 5:2). The MT of Job 27:18 ("moth") is usually corrected with the LXX and Syr. to "spider" (see comms.).

D. STUART

**MOTHER** [Heb. *'ēm* (cf. Akk. *ummu;* Ugar. *um*); Gk. *mḗtēr*]; AV also DAM; NEB also GRANDMOTHER; PARENT; etc.

***I. Meaning of Heb.* 'ēm.**–Hebrew *'ēm* is probably related to the root *'mm,* "be wide, roomy," although some see *'ēm* as a *Lallwort* (KoB, p. 58), i.e., the lisping of an infant. Both derivations easily associate the term with children. Along with the usual, biological meaning of "mother" (e.g., Gen. 2:24; Ex. 2:8; Ps. 113:9), *'ēm* can also mean "grandmother" (e.g., 1 K. 15:10; cf. NEB or "ancestress" (e.g., Gen. 3:20; Ezk. 16:3); pejoratively, it can denote undesirable origins (Job 17:14; Ezk. 16:45). Some passages use *'ēm* in a less literal sense to designate the nation as the "mother" of the people (e.g., Hos. 2:2,5 [MT 4,7]; Isa. 50:1), either unfavorably (e.g., Babylon as the "mother" of her inhabitants, Jer. 50:12) or as a term of honor (e.g., Deborah as a "mother" in Israel, Jgs. 5:7). In combination with Heb. *'āḇ,* ("father") the meaning is "parents" (so occasionally, NEB). Usually the order is "father and mother," but in Lev. 19:3; 21:2; Ezk. 16:45 the order is inverted. Heb. *'ēm* is also used for nonhuman species (e.g., Lev. 22:27; Dt. 22:6f.), in which cases the AV usually translates it "dam." In Ezk. 21:21 (MT 26) *'ēm* means "parting of the way;" that it is coupled with the *rō'š* ("head") suggests that *'ēm* can connote "origin" in somewhat the same way as *'āḇ*.

***II. Function of the Mother in the Family.***– Biblical society was clearly a male-centered world with the family structured along patriarchal lines. Some have claimed to find traces of a matriarchate in Israel (cf. R. de Vaux, *Ancient Israel* [ Eng. tr. 1961], I, 19f.; see esp. *Real-Encyclopädie für Protestantische Theologie und Kirche,* V [1898], 739f. (I. Benzinger); E. B. Cross, *Hebrew Family* [1927], pp. 31, 39). The evidence is not sufficient, however, to prove that matriarchy existed in Israel; at best there is evidence of metronymy (tracing the genealogy through the mother).

The mother's primary role in the Israelite family was to bear and nurture children, a function that began often as early as sixteen years of age (cf. L. Koehler, *Hebrew Man* [Eng. tr. 1961], p. 53). Motherhood was honored and coveted, and painful was the lot of the Israelite woman who was BARREN (e.g., 1 S. 1:4-11; cf. Ps. 113:9; Isa. 54:1). The Israelites' high regard for faithful motherhood is indicated by the biblical writers' utilization of the word or concept to express the idea of deepest loving attachment (e.g., Ps. 131:2; Isa. 49:15), of self-giving love (e.g., Isa. 66:13), and of profound sorrow when bereaved (e.g., Jer. 31:15). Consequently children were expected to obey and honor their mothers (Ex. 20:12; Lev. 19:3; Dt. 5:16; Prov. 1:8; 10:1; 15:20; 19:26; 20:20; 23:22, 25; 28:24; 29:15; 30:17). It was not uncommon for the mother to take the initiative in directing the affairs of the family. Sarah insisted on the expulsion of Hagar despite Abraham's misgivings (Gen. 21:10); Rebekah instigated the shift of the blessing from Esau to Jacob (Gen. 27:5-17); Abigail interceded on behalf of her household (1 S. 25:14-35); Bathsheba intervened on behalf of her son Solomon (1 K. 1:11-31). It appears that the primary responsibility for instructing the children lay with the father (e.g., Dt. 6:20-25), but it is noteworthy how frequently the book of Proverbs speaks of the mother's instruction (1:8; 6:20; 30:17; 31:1). Timothy was apparently instructed in the faith by his mother Eunice, who was taught by her mother Lois (2 Tim. 1:5).

*III. Mother as Imagery for God, Israel, and the Church.*– Nowhere does the Bible apply "mother" metaphorically to God as it does "father." The Bible's hesitation to introduce a feminine element into its concept of God can, no doubt, be explained partially by its polemic against the fertility cult in which the mother-goddess played such a prominent role. It is more significant that Yahweh is nonsexual; unlike pagan deities, He has no consort other than Israel, which is figuratively called His bride. Since a gender had to be chosen to refer to Yahweh as a personal God, it is not surprising that the masculine was preferred. Several factors may have been active in this choice; e.g., there is solid evidence that in the ancient world the mother was considered less the parent than the father. Aeschylus in *Eumenides* (658-661) has Apollo defend Orestes, the murderer of his own mother, by saying, "To be called mother is no wise to be Parent, but rather nurse of seed new-sown. The male begets: she's host to her small guest; preserves the plant, except it please God to blight it." That the biblical authors chose masculine rather than feminine metaphors to refer to God is to be attributed to the role of the sexes in that society rather than to the nature of God Himself.

It should not be overlooked, however, that the Bible does at times employs figurative language that is maternal in character to speak of God. "As one whom his mother comforts, so will I comfort you" (Isa. 66:13). The eagle of Dt. 32:11 can be considered maternal (so AV, ASV) or neuter (so RSV, NEB, and NIV; this, of course, is biologically impossible). Clearly maternal is the imagery of Isa. 49:15; "Can a woman forget her sucking child . . . ?" But here one should not infer too much from the feminine aspect of the figure, since its purpose is to show that the Lord's compassion transcends even that of a mother: "Even these may forget, yet I will not forget you." 2 Esdras freely combines masculine and feminine similes; "Thus says the Lord Almighty: Have I not entreated you as a father entreats his sons or a mother her daughters or a nurse her children, that you should be my people and I should be your God, and that you should be my sons and I should be your father? I gathered you as a hen gathers her brood under her wings . . . " (2 Esd. 1:28-30). Jesus' simile concerning Jerusalem (Mt. 23:37) is nearly identical.

In the NT "mother" takes on a new dynamic with the VIRGIN BIRTH. While the Roman Catholic theology may have exaggerated the role of MARY, her role as "mother of Our Lord" has received scanty attention in Protestant theology. Especially noteworthy are Jesus' submission to His parents (Lk. 2:51) and His deep concern for His mother even during the crucifixion (Jn. 19:26f.). Nevertheless, Mary's significance must be seen in the light of Jesus' statement that His relationship with believers transcends that of maternal affection (Mt. 12:46-50 par.).

The OT frequently alludes to Israel as a mother, but often with negative overtones. Isa. 50:1 challenges the Israelities to produce their mother's bill of divorce in order to justify their disbelief in the Lord's saving power (cf. vv. 2f.). Ezekiel ironically portrays Israel as a mother lioness who raises her cubs (i.e., kings) only to have them captured and put in cages — first by Egypt (Ezk. 19:1-4) and then by Babylon (vv. 5-9). Hosea's wife Gomer also represents Israel as a faithless wife and mother (Hos. 2:2, 5 [MT 4,7]; 4:5; cf. 1:2f.).

By contrast, the NT refers to the Church as "the mother of us all" (Gal. 4:26). This term, says J. Calvin, "is a title of wonderful and highest honor," and "he who refuses to be a son of the church desires in vain to have God as his Father" (comm. on Galatians, *in loc.*). Negatively, Rev. 17:5 describes "Babylon the great"(probably representing Greco-Roman culture) as the "mother of harlots;" this imagery, no doubt echoes that of Jer. 50:11-15 (cf. Rev. 18).

***Bibliography***.–D. G. Bloesch, *Is the Bible Sexist?* (1982); V. R. Mollenkott, *Women, Men and the Bible* (1977); *TDNT*, IV, *s.v.* μήτηρ (W. Michaelis); P. Trible, *God and the Rhetoric of Sexuality* (1978); *TWOT*, I, 50f.; R. de Vaux, *Ancient Israel* (Eng. tr. 1961).

C. J. VOS

**MOTHER-IN-LAW.** *See* RELATIONSHIPS, FAMILY.

**MOTHER-OF-PEARL** [Heb. *dar*] (Est. 1:6); AV WHITE (MARBLE). "Mother-of-pearl" was perhaps part of the costly material in the mosaic pavement of the royal palace's garden at Susa. Since *dar* occurs only here its meaning is uncertain, but the LXX *pínninos*, "mother-of-pearl," supports the RSV's translation (cf. also Arab. *durr*, "pearl").

**MOTION** [Gk. *kataseíō* (Acts 12:17; 13:16; 19:33; 21:40), *neúō* (24:10)]; AV BECKON; NEB also "with a movement . . . signed," "made a gesture," etc. *See* GESTURE I.

In Rom. 7:5 the AV renders "motions of sin" for Gk. *pathḗmata tṓn hamartiṓn*; the RSV and NEB offer a more accurate translation, "sinful passions" (cf. Bauer, rev., p. 602).

**MOTTLED** [Heb. *bārōḏ*] (Gen. 31:10, 12); AV GRISLED; NEB DAPPLED. The Hebrew term may be related to *bārāḏ*, "hail," in which case it would mean "spotted as with hail." Zec. 6:3, 6 apply the same term to horses. *See* DAPPLED.

**MOUND** [Heb. *tēl*] (Josh. 11:13; Jer. 30:18; 49:2); AV "in their strength" (Josh. 11:13), HEAP; NEB RUINED MOUNDS, MOUND OF RUINS. In the OT Heb. *tēl* sometimes refers to the mound formed by centuries of building, destruction, and rebuilding on the same site. Arab. *tell* and Heb. *tel* in many Near Eastern place names (e.g., Tell Mardikh, Tel Aviv) attest to this practice.

The AV reading in Josh. 11:13 is apparently an interpretative rendering, inferring strength from the idea of a large mound.

*See also* ARCHEOLOGY V; for the other references to mounds, *see* SIEGE. G. A. L.

**MOUNT; MOUNTAIN.** *See* HILL.

**MOUNT EBAL.** *See* EBAL, MOUNT.

**MOUNT EPHRAIM** [Heb. *har 'eprayim*] (Jer. 4:15). Elsewhere the RSV and NEB translate this expression "hill country of Ephraim" (AV consistently Mount Ephraim); no reason for this exception is apparent. *See* EPHRAIM, HILL COUNTRY OF.

**MOUNT GERIZIM.** *See* GERIZIM, MOUNT.

**MOUNT OF CONGREGATION.** *See* ASSEMBLY, MOUNT OF.

**MOUNT OF CORRUPTION.** *See* CORRUPTION, MOUNT OF.

**MOUNT OF OLIVES.** *See* OLIVES, MOUNT OF.

**MOUNT OF THE AMALEKITES.** The AV rendering of Heb. *har hā'ᵃmālēqî* in Jgs. 12:15 (RSV "hill country of the Amalekites"; NEB "hill of the Amalekite"). The Amalekites were a nomadic tribe generally associated with the valleys (cf. Nu. 14:25) and hill country (vv. 40-45) of the Negeb (13:29). From this passage, however, it appears that for a time they had penetrated as far north as the hill country of Ephraim. *See* AMALEK; EPHRAIM, HILL COUNTRY OF.

**MOUNT OF THE AMORITES.** The AV translation of Heb. *har hā'ᵉmōrî* in Dt. 1:7, 19f. (RSV, NEB, "hill country of the Amorites"; cf. vv. 24, 44; Nu. 13:29; Josh. 10:6; etc.). The reference is probably to the central mountainous regions later assigned to Judah and Ephraim; but some commentators take it to mean all the hill country of both eastern and western Palestine (see comms.). *See* AMORITES; PALESTINE IV.

**MOUNTAIN-SHEEP** [Heb. *zemer*]; AV CHAMOIS; NEB ROCK-GOAT.

The Heb. *zemer* is used only in Dt. 14:5; context indicates it is a wild animal useful for food, though exact identification is difficult. It cannot be the chamois, since this goat-like antelope did not inhabit the Palestinian region. Most likely it is a type of mountain-sheep. The best possibility is a type of mouflon standing about 66 cm. (26 in.) high and dark reddish brown. It is thought to be an ancestor of the domesticated sheep. A less likely possibility is the barbary sheep (aoudad) standing about 1 m. (40 in.) high. It is attested in Africa, including Egypt, where it has been found mummified. It probably never inhabited the Palestinian area, however.

See G. S. Cansdale, *All the Animals of Bible Lands* (1970), pp. 86f. J. C. MOYER

**MOURN.** *See* BURIAL II.C; III.D; DEATH III.A; DIRGE; GRIEF; LAMENT.

**MOUSE; MICE** [Heb. *'akbār*; Gk. *mýs*]; NEB also JERBOA (Lev. 11:29), RATS (1 S. 6:4f., 11, 18).

Of infrequent occurrence in Scripture, the term could refer to any one of numerous species of Palestinian rodents, of which Tristram identified twenty-three varieties near the end of the 19th century. If the true mouse or rat was actually being described, the animals concerned would be species of the genus *Mus*. The Arab. *'akbar* is used of the male jerboa, hence the NEB rendering and the identification of *CHAL* (p. 272) with the species *Jaculus jaculus*. In Lev. 11:29 the prohibition seems to cover a wide range of small rodents that were deemed unclean for food while living, and defiling to the touch when dead. The concern of the legislation was evidently a hygenic one, since infectious disease could be spread by contaminated containers or polluted food.

In 1 S. 6 Philistine priests advise the Philistine lords to return the ark of the Lord to Israel with a "guilt offering" — five golden tumors and five golden mice — to rid the land of the devastating disease (cf. the Israelite practice of a scapegoat, Lev. 16). Presumably the tumors represented the effects of the disease, the mice represented the transmitters of the disease, and the number five corresponded to the number of chief Philistine cities. The ailment in question was bubonic plague, which occurred suddenly and spread rapidly along lines of human communication (*see* DISEASE III.H). Both plague buboes (1 S. 5:12) and dead rodents (1 S. 6:5) were mentioned, the latter acting as host to the rat flea (*Pulex Cheopis*), that infects human beings. The black rat, which has now spread worldwide, is the main transmitter of bubonic plague.

The rodent mentioned as part of the diet of those indulging in idolatrous cultic rites (Isa. 66:17) was probably a small animal, perhaps the size of a hamster. In ancient Egyptian therapeutics, a freshly killed, skinned mouse was sometimes forced down the throat of a moribund person in an attempt to prolong life. R. K. H.

**MOUTH** [Heb. usually *peh*, also *ḥēḵ*–'palate' (e.g., Ps. 137:6; Ezk. 3:26), *miḏbār* (Cant. 4:3), *mišbār* (Hos. 13:13), *śāpâ* (Ps. 22:7 [MT 8]; Isa. 37:29); Aram. *pum* (Dnl. 7:5, 8, 20); Gk. usually *stóma*, also *lógos* ("word of mouth," Acts 15:27; 2 Thess. 2:15), *aphrízō* ("foam at the mouth," Mk. 9:20)]; AV also LIPS, SPEECH, "uttermost part," "breaking forth," END, etc.; NEB also BEAK, FACE, GREED, JAWS, LIPS, etc.

*I. As the Organ of Speech.*–In the Bible the mouth is most typically the organ of speech. As the organ that gives intelligible expression to what is seen or heard, the mouth distinguishes humans from all other living creatures. It stands, therefore, quite near to mankind's essential being. No other human organ has so many distinct activities predicated of it (see Wolff, pp. 77f.; *see also* LIP; TONGUE).

The Semitic formula "to open the mouth and speak" is sometimes used to call attention to something especially significant that is said (cf. Jgs. 11:35f.; Dnl. 10:16; Mt. 5:2; Acts 8:35; cf. Job 3:1; Ps. 119:131). The prudent person guards his mouth (Prov. 13:3; Mic. 7:5; cf. Ps. 39:1 [MT 2]; 141:3). One of the highest functions of the mouth is to testify concerning the saving deeds of God (Ps. 89:1 [MT 2]; Lk. 21:13-15; cf. Rom. 10:8-10, where the RSV translates Gk. *stóma* by "lips").

The mouth reveals much about a person's disposition: laughter (Ps. 126:2), derision (Ps. 35:21; Isa. 57:4), flattery (Prov. 26:28), exultation (1 S. 2:1), arrogance (2:3; Ps. 17:10), thankfulness (Ps. 63:5 [MT 6]; 109:30), bluster (Job 8:2), cursing (Rom. 3:14; cf. Prov. 11:9, 11), and blasphemy (Rev. 13:6) all proceed from the human mouth (cf. Jas. 3:10), "for out of the abundance of the heart the mouth speaks" (Mt. 12:34). By their mouths the wicked reveal themselves (cf. Ps. 36:3 [MT 4]; 50:19; 59:12 [MT 13]; Prov. 15:28; 18:6f.; Col. 3:8; Jude 16; etc.) and the righteous manifest their true being (cf. Ex. 13:9; Josh. 1:8; Ps. 34:1 [MT 2]; 37:30; 40:3 [MT 4]; 119:43; Prov. 8:7f.; 10:11, 31; etc.). Hypocrisy can be described as a lack of agreement between the heart and the mouth (Ps. 62:4 [MT 5]; Jer. 12:2; cf. Ezk. 33:31, where the RSV translates Heb. *peh* by "lips"); it inevitably results in judgment (Isa. 29:13f.). The mouth's importance as a reflection of the inner essence of a person explains the apostles' repeated calls for purity of speech (Eph. 4:29; 1 Pet. 3:10; cf. Jas. 3:10; Rev. 14:5).

As its Creator (Ex. 4:11), Yahweh can use the human

mouth as a means of revelation by putting His words into it (v. 12; Nu. 22:38; 23:5, 12, 16; Isa. 51:16; Jer. 1:9; cf. 1 K. 17:24; 2 Ch. 36:21). Thus the prophet becomes the mouth of the Lord (Jer. 15:19); cf. the same process at the human level when one becomes the messenger of another (Ex. 4:15f.; 2 S. 14:3). When a human mouth is used by God, however, it must first be purified at the altar of His holiness (Isa. 6:7; Jer. 1:9). If it is taught to the people, the word of God can even live on in the mouths of succeeding generations (Dt. 31:19, 21f.; Isa. 59:21).

By way of anthropomorphism the Bible also speaks of the "mouth of God" as an organ of speech by which He reveals Himself (Dt. 8:3; Jer. 9:12 [MT 11]; cf. Mt. 4:4), e.g., in judgment (Isa. 1:20), in blessing (34:16), and in commandments (cf. Ps. 119:13, 72, 88). Idols also have mouths (Jer. 51:44) but no word of power (Ps. 115:5; 135:16f.). From Yahweh's mouth, however, issues the power of righteousness (Isa. 45:23), the power to create (Ps. 33:6) and to destroy (18:8 [MT 9] par. 2 S. 22:9; cf. the mouth of Jesus' witnesses, Lk. 21:15; Rev. 11:5).

The authority and majesty of Jesus' words are sometimes highlighted by reference to His mouth (Mt. 5:2; Lk. 4:22). Moreover, from the mouth of the resurrected Lord issues an eschatological sword of judgment (Rev. 1:16; 2:16; 19:15, 21) reminiscent of the prophecy of Isa. 11:4; 49:2.

***II. As the Organ for Eating and Drinking.***–In many contexts the Bible refers to the mouth as the organ for eating and drinking (e.g., Ps. 78:30; Dnl. 10:3). Ezekiel is invited to eat a scroll (Ezk. 2:8) and finds that in his mouth it is "sweet as honey" (3:3; cf. Ps. 119:103). The mouth is the place where either clean or unclean foods enter the body (Acts 11:8; cf. Mt. 15:17) and where liquids are either taken in (Jgs. 7:6) or spewed forth (Rev. 3:16). When thirst is great the tongue may cleave to the roof of the mouth (Lam. 4:4; cf. the reference to Jesus' thirst in Jn. 19:28f.). The mouths of animals are similarly referred to in Ps. 22:21 (MT 22); Dnl. 6:22 (MT 23); 7:5; Am. 3:12.

***III. As the Organ for Kissing.***–The erotic use of the mouth in kissing is noted in Cant. 1:2 (cf. 4:3). The Kiss was also an ancient form of adoration. Kissing the hand in Job 31:27 probably refers to the idolatrous act of throwing kisses to the moon, a practice known elsewhere in the ancient Near East (see comms.). A similar kind of idolatry involving Baal is evidenced in 1 K. 19:18 (cf. Hos. 13:2).

***IV. Other Entrances or Openings.***–"Mouth" occurs in figurative descriptions of the earth soaking up blood (Gen. 4:11) or "swallowing" persons or a river in an earthquake (Nu. 16:30, 32; Rev. 12:16); similarly, Sheol is described as swallowing people (Ps. 141:7; Isa. 5:14; cf. Ps. 69:15 [MT 16]). Other objects described as having a mouth are caves (Josh. 10:22), lions' dens (Dnl. 6:17 [MT 18]), wells (Gen. 29:2f., 8, 10; 2 S. 17:19), rivers (Josh. 15:5), a gorge (Jer. 48:28), sacks (Gen. 42:27f.; 43:12, 21; 44:1f., 8) and the womb (Hos. 13:13). The "mouth" of a sword is its "edge" (*see* Edge).

***V. Idiomatic Usages.***–To speak "mouth to mouth" (Heb. *peh 'el-peh,* Nu. 12:8) means to speak directly or "face to face" with someone (cf. AV, RSV, Jer. 32:4; cf. Gk. *stóma prós stóma,* 2 Jn. 12). To be of "one mouth" (*peh 'eḥāḏ*) means to be unified (AV 1 K. 22:13; cf. AV, RSV, "with one accord," Josh. 9:2).

***VI. Gestures.***–The Hebrew genius for expressing abstract ideas through concrete language is shown in the use of gestures to describe various emotions or attitudes. Laying the hand on the mouth is a gesture of awed silence or shame (Job 21:5; 29:9; 40:4; Mic. 7:16). Putting one's mouth in the dust is a sign of self-abasement (Lam. 3:29). *See also* Gesture V.C.

***Bibliography.***–*TDNT,* VII, *s.v.* στόμα (K. Weiss); *THAT,* II, *s.v.* פֶּה (C. J. Labuschagne); H. W. Wolff, *Anthropology of the OT* (Eng. tr. 1975).

K. H. MAAHS

**MOWING; MOWN GRASS** [Heb. *gēz*] (Ps. 72:6; Am. 7:1); NEB EARLY CROP. Heb. *gēz* denotes something that is shorn (e.g., fleece of sheep, Dt. 18:4; etc.) or cut (cf. the verb *gāzaz,* "cut"). "The king's mowings" (Am. 7:1) refers to the first cutting of grain, claimed by the kings of Israel as tribute for the support of their military establishment (cf. 1 S. 8:15; 1 K. 18:5). In Ps. 72:6 *gēz* might better be rendered "grass about to be mown" (see Anderson, pp. 521f.; Briggs, p. 134); cf. 2 S. 23:4, which likens a just king to rain that causes grass to grow (cf. also Dt. 32:2). The process of mowing grain is described in Ps. 129:7 (AV, NEB, "mower"; RSV "reaper"). In Jas. 5:4 "mow" represents Gk. *amáō.* The withholding of wages from laborers was a common form of oppression in biblical times (see Adamson, pp. 185f.; Davids, pp. 177f.; *see also* Oppress).

*See also* Agriculture III.A.2; Harvest.

***Bibliography.***–Comms. on Amos by J. L. Mays (*OTL,* 1969); on Psalms by A. A. Anderson (*NCBC,* I, repr. 1981) and C. A. Briggs and E. G. Briggs (*ICC,* II, 1907); on James by J. Adamson (*NICNT,* 1976) and P. Davids (*NIGTC,* 1982).

N. J. O.

**MOZA** mō'zə [Heb. *môṣā'*].

**1.** Son of Caleb and his concubine Ephah (1 Ch. 2:46).

**2.** A descendant of Saul; son of Zimri and father of Binea (1 Ch. 8:36f.; 9:42f.).

**MOZAH** mō'zə [Heb. *(ham)môṣâ*; Gk. A *Amōkē,* B *Amosa*]. A town of the tribe of Benjamin in Judah (Josh. 18:26). It was an ancient settlement absorbed by the Israelite tribes, possibly to be identified with modern Qâlunyah, (<Lat. *Colonia?*) an Arab village 6½ km. (4 mi.) NW of Jerusalem on the road to Tel Aviv (*LBHG,* rev. ed., p. 356). It is mentioned in the Babylonian Talmud (*Sukkah* iv.5) and is said by Josephus (*BJ* vii.6.6. [217]) to have been settled by eight hundred troops of Vespasian, who called the town Emmaus; it is possibly the town mentioned in Lk. 24:13 (*see* Emmaus). Its name is stamped on the handles of royal pottery of the Roman Empire excavated at Jericho and Tell en-Naṣbeh. The name may survive in Khirbet Beit Mizzah, somewhat N of Qâlunyah and has been adopted by the Jewish colony of Moṣah W of Qâlunyah (*GTTOT,* § 327, pp. 176f.).

J. McKENNA

**MUFFLERS.** The AV translation of Heb. *$r^{e}$ʿālôṯ* in Isa. 3:19 (cf. RSV "scarfs"; NEB "coronets"). *See* Garments IX (and chart).

**MUGHÂRAH** moo-gär'ə, **WÂDĪ EL-** wä'dē el [Arab. *wâdī el-muġârah*–'valley of the cave']. A valley on the south-

Wâdī el-Mughârah caves (B. VanElderen)

western slope of Mt. Carmel with four caves, three of which contained important archeological remains of several successive Stone Age cultures.

Excavated 1929-1934 by the Joint Expedition of the British School of Archaeology in Jerusalem and the American School of Prehistorical Research under the direction of D. A. E. Garrod, the caves have provided the key to the relative sequence of cultures for a large segment of the Stone Age in that region. Although individual cultural industries had been previously identified from isolated sites, the relationship between industries was only imperfectly known from evidence of incomplete series of occupations. Garrod's correlation of stratigraphy from the Wâdī el-Mughârah caves (Mughâret el-Wâd, eṭ-Ṭābūn, and Mughâret es-Skhûl) demonstrated successive occupation of the site beginning with the Tayacian and extending through the Acheulean, Yabrudian, Levalloiso-Mousterian, Aurignacian, Atlitian, and Natufian cultures. The data indicate that Stone Age Palestine was more closely tied with Eurasia than with Egypt and Africa, and they further suggest that the Aurignacian culture, known in central and western Europe, spread there from Palestine, where it originated.

D. M. A. Bate's analysis of faunal remains has revealed that Palestine was a bridge for successive mammalian migrations from Asia to the African continent. Bate also tried to deduce from the relative frequency of certain types of fossil remains the fluctuation of wet and dry periods during this segment of the Stone Age. It proved difficult (if not impossible), however, to make satisfactory connections between these wet-dry oppositions and the various glacial stages of the Pleistocene period.

Human fossil remains from the Wâdī el-Mughârah caves show extremely broad variation in their physical characteristics, ranging from Paleoanthropic, Neanderthal-like individuals (eṭ-Ṭābūn) to those more nearly associated with the Neanthropic Cromagnon man (es-Skhûl). This variation led T. D. McCown and A. Keith (1939) to believe that Wâdī el-Mughârah was the scene of evolutionary change from Paleoanthropic to Neanthropic man. By 1962, however, Garrod concluded that the two types represented at Wâdī el-Mughârah are most likely distinct races, widely separated in time.

*Bibliography.*–D. A. E. Garrod and D. M. A. Bate, *Stone Age of Mount Carmel*, I: *Excavations at the Wadi El-Mugharah* (1937); T. D. McCown and A. Keith, *Stone Age of Mount Carmel*, II: *The Fossil Human Remains From the Levalloiso-Mousterian* (1939); D. A. E. Garrod, *Journal of the Royal Anthropological Institute of Great Britain and Ireland*, 92 (1962), 232-251; E. Anati, *Palestine before the Hebrews* (Eng. tr. 1963), pp. 47-135; *CAH* (3rd ed.), I/1, 75-86; *EAEHL*, *s.v.* "Carmel Caves" (T. Noy).

G. H. WILSON

**MULBERRY** [Gk. *móron*]. The black mulberry, *Morus nigra* L., native to northern Persia, whose juice was used to incite the elephants of Antiochus to battle (1 Macc. 6:34).

On 2 S. 5:23f.; 1 Ch. 14:14f., AV "mulberry trees," *see* BALSAM TREES.

On Ps. 84:6 *see* BACA, VALLEY OF.

On Lk. 17:6 *see* SYCAMINE TREE. R. K. H.

**MULE** [Heb. *pereḏ* (2 S. 13:29; 18:9; Ps. 32:9; etc.); fem. *pirdâ* (1 K. 1:33, 38, 44)]. The offspring of a mare bred by a donkey. The mule is a hybrid animal that is strong, patient, and surefooted. It is a more vigorous species than the reverse cross between a stallion and a donkey mare, which produces an animal known technically as a hinny. Because the Torah specifically prohibited the crossbreeding of animals (Lev. 19:19), it was necessary for the Israelites to import mules at some expense, either from Phoenicia, or from more distant places such as Beth-togarmah, which sold horses and mules in Palestine (Ezk. 27:14). Mules appeared in Israel in the early monarchy, and they seem to have been used for riding only by royalty (2 S. 13:29; 18:9; 1 K. 1:33, 38, 44; cf. Isa. 66:20). They were also used as pack animals (2 K. 5:17; 1 Ch. 12:40; cf. Zec. 14:15). That they were presented to Solomon as gifts indicates their high value (1 K. 10:25 par. 2 Ch. 9:24; cf. 1 K. 18:5; Ezr. 2:66).

In a wisdom saying the psalmist urges his listeners to be sensitive to his teaching, and not like the horse and mule, who can be guided only by physical means since they lack understanding (Ps. 32:9).

N. Davies's reconstruction of a New Kingdom tomb painting. Harvest scene with unique Egyptian representation of mules (Oriental Institute, University of Chicago)

In Neh. 7:68 the MT omits mention of the horses and mules; the English versions supply these references on the basis of the parallel Ezr. 2:66. R. K. H.

**MULTITUDE** [Heb. *hāmôn, rōḇ, raḇ*–'numerous, many' (e.g., Ex. 12:38), hiphil of *rāḇâ* (Jer. 46:16), *m$^{e}$lō'*–'abundance' (e.g., Gen. 48:19), *marbîṯ*–'majority, multitude' (2 Ch. 30:18), *šip'â*–'mass' (Isa. 60:6), *qāhāl*–'assembly' (2 Ch. 31:18)]; AV also MANY, COMPANY, CONGREGATION; NEB also HOST, GREAT PEOPLE, LARGE COMPANY, MAJORITY, MOB, HORDE, etc.; [Gk. *óchlos, plḗthos*]; AV also PEOPLE, COMPANY; NEB also PEOPLE, CROWD, GREAT NUMBERS, WHOLE BODY, VAST THRONG, etc.

In the OT "multitude" usually represents Heb. *rōḇ* (*rôḇ*) or *hāmôn*. *Rōḇ* simply means a "great number" or "abundance." Often it denotes a number too great to count, e.g., the descendants promised to Hagar (Gen. 16:10) and to Abraham (32:12 [MT 13]), the Israelites at the time of their entry into Canaan (Dt. 1:10; 10:22; 28:62) and during Solomon's reign (1 K. 3:8), and the enemies (and their camels) who opposed Gideon (Jgs. 7:12). The term is also used to describe the vast number of Israel's idols (Ezk. 14:4) and transgressions (Lam. 1:5), of Tyre's iniquities (28:18), of Jerusalem's inhabitants in Zechariah's vision (Zec. 2:4 [MT 8]), etc. Covenant law warned against perverting justice in order to find favor with the masses (*rabbîm*, Ex. 23:2), and the prophets warned Israel against seeking security in the "multitude" (*rōḇ*) of its warriors (Hos. 10:13) or sacrifices (Isa. 1:11).

In some passages *hāmôn*, like *rōḇ*, seems to denote simply a very great number, i.e., "any large aggregate whose individual components are discernible" (*TDOT*, III, 416; see, e.g., Gen. 17:4f.; 2 S. 6:19; Job 31:34; Isa. 5:13f.). But overtones of the term's primary meaning of "confusion, uproar, tumult" (cf. vb. *hāmâ*, "make an uproar") are present in most of its uses (cf. 1 S. 14:16; 2 K. 7:13; Ps. 42:4 [MT 5]; Ezk. 7:12-14; 23:42; Dnl. 10:6). The term is frequently applied to the assaulting armies of enemy nations, which in their attack upon Yahweh's people represent the forces of chaos in revolt against God (1 K. 20:13, 28; 2 Ch. 13:8; 14:11 [MT 10]; 20:2, 12, 15, 24; Isa. 16:14; 29:5, 7f.; Ezk. 30:15; 31:2, 18; Dnl. 11:10-13, etc.; see *TDOT*, III, 416f.).

The LXX primarily uses Gk. *plḗthos* ("large number," "crowd") to render Heb. *rōḇ*; both *plḗthos* and *óchlos* ("crowd, throng, populace") are among its translations of Heb. *hāmôn*. In the Apocrypha "multitude" occasionally represents *óchlos* (e.g., Wisd. 8:10; 1 Macc. 9:35; 1 Esd. 2:30; 5:65); most often, however, it translates *plḗthos*, which is variously used to describe a crowd that cannot be numbered (Jth. 2:20; 5:10), the vast army of an enemy (7:2, 18; 16:4; 1 Macc. 3:17; 6:41), the assembled people of Israel (1 Esd. 8:91; 9:2, 4, 6, etc.), etc. Like the OT prophets, Sirach warns against trusting in a multitude of sacrifices as an atonement for sin (Sir. 7:9; 34:19; cf. 5:6).

In the NT the RSV uses "multitude" interchangeably with "crowd" to translate Gk. *óchlos* (the AV consistently uses "multitude"). Apart from Rev. 7:9; 17:15; 19:1, 6, *óchlos* occurs only in the Gospels and Acts. Usually it refers to the disorganized crowd of people who followed Jesus (e.g., Lk. 7:9; Jn. 6:2, 5) and heard His teaching (e.g., Lk. 5:15; 12:54; 14:25) or, similarly, to the crowds that gathered to hear the preaching of the apostles (Acts 8:6; 13:45; 14:14). Sometimes the *óchlos* is contrasted with the religious leaders, whose actions were influenced by their fear of popular opinion (Mt. 21:26, 46 par.). *Plḗthos* also occurs predominantly in the Gospels and Acts. In the Gospels it is sometimes used to highlight the large number of people who followed Jesus and witnessed His ministry and crucifixion (e.g., Mk. 3:7f.; Lk. 6:17; 23:27). Similarly, in Acts 5:14 it calls attention to the great masses of men and women who responded to the apostles' ministry, forming a large community of believers (6:5; cf. 4:32 [RSV "company"]; 6:2 [RSV "body"]; see Haenchen, p. 230 n. 1; Bauer, rev., p. 668). In 2:6 it refers to the large crowd of Diaspora Jews assembled at Jerusalem for Pentecost. *Plḗthos* also occurs in Jas. 5:20 and 1 Pet. 4:8, which speak of the power of mutual discipline and love to cover "a multitude of sins" (cf. Prov. 10:12).

*See also* CROWD; PEOPLE II.

***Bibliography.***–*DNTT*, I, 731-33; II, 800f.; E. Haenchen, *Acts of the Apostles* (Eng. tr. 1971); *TDNT*, V, *s.v.* ὄχλος (R. Meyer, P. Katz); VI, πλῆθος (G. Delling); *TDOT*, III, *s.v.* "hāmāh" (A. Baumann). N. J. O.

**MUNITION.** Archaic term meaning "rampart" or "defense," used by the AV to render Heb. *m$^{e}$ṣôḏâ* in Isa. 29:7 (RSV "stronghold"; NEB "siege-works"), *m$^{e}$ṣāḏ* in 33:16 (RSV "fortresses"; NEB "fastness"), and *m$^{e}$ṣûrâ* in Nah. 2:1 (RSV "ramparts"; NEB "siege"). *See* FORTIFICATION; SIEGE.

**MUPPIM** mup'im [Heb. *muppîm*]. A son of Benjamin (Gen. 46:21), elsewhere called SHUPPIM (1 Ch. 7:12, 15), SHEPHUPHAM (Nu. 26:39), and SHEPHUPHAN (1 Ch. 8:5).

**MURABBA'ÂT** mōō'rab-ba-at [Arab.]. A wadi in the Wilderness of Judea where caves that contained some of the Dead Sea Scrolls are located.

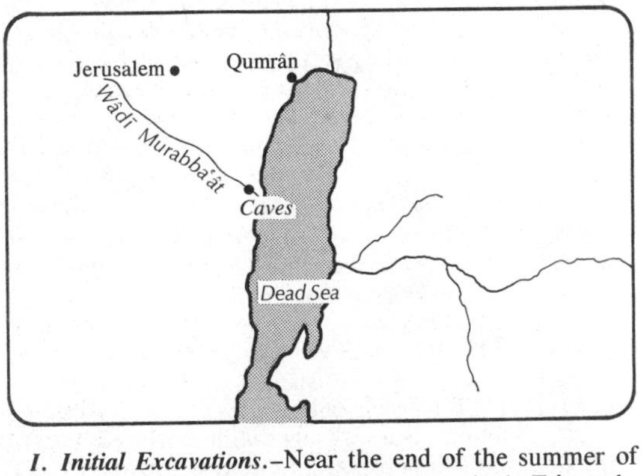


***I. Initial Excavations.***–Near the end of the summer of 1951, in the gorges of a wadi called successively Ta'amrah, Marshash, Murabba'ât, and Daradjeh, 26 km. (16 mi.) SE of Jerusalem, 18 km. (11 mi.) S of Qumrân, and 4.8 km. (3 mi.) W of the Dead Sea, bedouin explored four nearly inaccessible caves. They discovered documents and brought them to Jerusalem to sell. R. de Vaux and G. L. Harding bought the documents for the Palestine Archeological Museum and then organized a scientific expedition that completely excavated the caves under extremely difficult conditions from Jan. 21 to Mar. 3, 1952.

Numerous remains showed that Caves 1 and 2, very narrow but about 50 m. (165 ft.) deep, and Caves 3 and 4, somewhat smaller, had been inhabited at different periods. In the Chalcolithic era (4000-3000 B.C.) nomads left objects of bone, wood, flint, and ceramic. In the Middle Bronze Age (2000-1600 B.C.) a refugee left a scarab, a comb, and an alabaster cruse, imported from Egypt. To Iron II, *ca.* 850-700 B.C., belong some knives, lamps, different kinds of pottery, and most importantly a papyrus palimpsest. During the First Jewish Revolt (A.D. 66-73) and particularly during the Second Revolt (132-135) Jewish warriors accom-

MURABBAʿÂT

panied by their families sought refuge at Murabbaʿât. They left much pottery, various utensils, domestic items, cloth, arms, coins, and numerous parchments and papyri. The Romans finally exterminated these refugees and established there a military post, as evidenced by later coins, documents, a Roman javelin, and a seal in the name of "Gargiliu(s), of the H(undred) of Annaeus." A coin of the Omayyads and some papers written in Arabic indicate that the caves again served as a temporary shelter.

For these excavations and their results see the preliminary reports by G. L. Harding, *PEQ*, 1952, pp. 104-109; R. de Vaux, *RB*, 60 (1953), 245-275. The official edition is *Discoveries in the Judaean Desert II: Les Grottes de Murabbaʿât*, by P. Benoit, J. T. Milik, and R. de Vaux, with contributions by G. M. Crowfoot, E. Crowfoot, and A. Grohmann, vol. I text, vol. II plates (1961).

***II. Recovered Artifacts.–A. Principal Documents. 1. Hebrew.*** The papyrus palimpsest (no. 17 of the official edition) of the 8th cent. B.C., which is the oldest known papyrus in Hebrew, contains first a private letter and then a list of proper names. See F. M. Cross, *BASOR*, 165 (Feb. 1962), 34-46.

Biblical fragments (nos. 1-3), conforming to the MT, contain Gen. 32:4f., 30, 33; 33:1; 34:5-7, 30f.; 35:1, 4-7; Ex. 4:28-31; 5:3; 6:5-11; Nu. 34:10; 36:7-11; Dt. 10:1-3; 11:2f.; 12:25f.; 15:1 or 2; Isa. 1:4-14.

A phylactery (no. 4), well preserved, contains Ex. 13:1-10, 11-16; Dt. 11:13-21; 6:4-9. Another document (no. 5) is in such bad condition that no one has determined whether it is a phylactery or a mezuzah. See H. Stegemann and J. Becker, *RQ*, 3/3 (1961), 443-48.

A badly damaged fragment (no. 6) juxtaposes biblical quotations to form a poem resembling that of 1QM 12:7-16.

Three deeds of sale of land (nos. 22, 29, and 30) are dated in Year 1, Year 2, and Year 4 of the Liberation of Israel (A.D. 132, 133, and 135).

A series of rent contracts (no. 24) are all dated in Year 2 (A.D. 133).

A letter of the administrative officers of Beth-Mashiko to Joshua the son of Galgula (no. 42), concerning the sale of a cow, states, "The nations [the Romans] are approaching us." For this letter and for the following, the official edition supplies a bibliography up to 1956.

A letter of Simon son of Kosbah (Simon Bar Cochba, the head of the Jewish Resistance) to the same Joshua (no. 43) says: "I call heaven to witness against me that if any one of the Galileans who are with you is mistreated I will put your feet in irons as I did to Ben Aphlul."

Another letter of Bar Cochba to the same Joshua (no. 44) concerns the ration of wheat (see the important interpretation by M. R. Lehmann in *RQ*, 4/1 [1963], 68-70).

A partly mutilated letter (no. 45) reveals moving details about the Jewish resistance: ". . . until the wheat supply is finished . . . they can no longer exist . . . at Meṣad Ḥasidin [Qumrân or Masada?] and I shall remain . . . some among them have perished by the sword . . . only my brother. . . ."

Another letter (no. 46), sent from En-gedi, recommends a person who, among others, "will take up the dead."

*2. Aramaic.* Among the Aramaic documents are several tax receipts (nos. 8, 9, 10a); a statement of indebtedness (no. 18, dated the Year 2 of Nero); an act of repudiation (no. 19) written perhaps A.D. 111; two marriage contracts (no. 20, written A.D. 117, and no. 21); and four deeds of sale (nos. 23, 25, 26, 27, the first two dated in Year 1 and Year 2 of the Liberation of Jerusalem [A.D. 132 and 133]).

*3. Greek.* Identifiable documents include two marriage contracts (no. 115, dated in Year 7 of Hadrian [A.D. 124], and no. 116); an admission of indebtedness (no. 114, perhaps A.D. 171); two extracts of official laws (no. 117) that mention the emperor Commodius, A.D. 180-192; and a prayer of St. Basil, transcribed about the 11th or 12th cent. (no. 156). Two leaves of Greek shorthand have not been deciphered (no. 164).

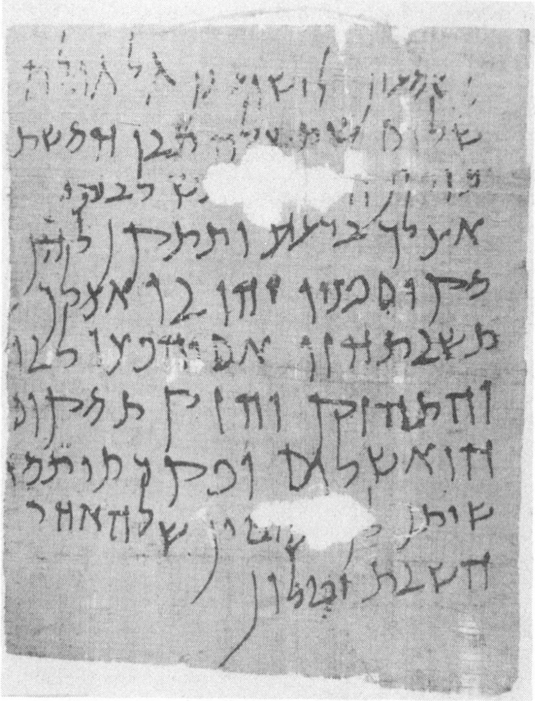

Letter of Simon Bar Cochba to Joshua concerning wheat ration. In Hebrew, on papyrus (Israel Museum, Jerusalem)

*4. Latin.* Some badly damaged papyri have been recovered.

*5. Arabic.* Arabic documents comprise a receipt of the year 327 of the Hegira (i.e., A.D. 948-949); a fragment of a contract from the 9th or 10th cent.; two magical texts in bad condition (10th cent.); and a large amulet fairly well preserved (10th cent.).

*B. Coins and Cloth.* The coins from the Murabbaʿât caves that can be identified with some certainty are described in the introduction of the official edition (I, 44-47), but the photographs are not reproduced. These coins are distributed as follows:

Antigonus Mattathias (40-37 B.C.)
Agrippa I (A.D. 42-43)
The Procurators under Nero (A.D. 58-59), three coins
Year 4 of the First Revolt (A.D. 69-70)
Ashkelon, under Trajan (A.D. 113-114)
Tiberiades, under Hadrian (A.D. 119-120)
Year 1 of the Second Revolt (A.D. 132), two coins
Year 2 of the Second Revolt (A.D. 133), two coins
Second Revolt (A.D. 132-135), five coins
Two Roman coins with a double surcharge of the Tenth Legion
A Roman coin not identified
A coin of the Omayyads

Cloth or clothing found in the Murabbaʿât caves comprises sixty-nine articles in wool that seem to date approximately from the Second Jewish Revolt (A.D. 132-135), forty articles in linen that are difficult to date, and thirty-two articles in linen, cotton, or silk that are certainly medieval, one even bearing an Arabic inscription in Kufic. G. M. and E. Crowfoot have technically studied all of these articles in the official edition (I, 51-63; II, plates XV-XVIII).

*III. Subsequent Excavations and Studies.*–The four caves were completely excavated, and treasures that according to reliable "information" also had come from Wâdī Murabbaʿât were offered for sale in Jerusalem in 1952. Recovered pieces comprised 119 or 120 Nabatean denarii (of Aretas IV, Maliku II, or Rabbel II), fifty-one Roman denarii (from the time of C. Allius Bala, *ca.* A.D. 96, to Hadrian), fourteen tetradrachmas of Antioch (from Nero to Trajan), forty-three coins from Caesarea in Cappadocia (all under Trajan) (see J. T. Milik and H. Seyrig, *Revue Numismatique,* 6th ser., 1 [1958], 11-26).

In March 1955 a bedouin discovered another cave 300 m. (1000 ft.) upstream from the first caves and retrieved from it a MS of the Twelve Prophets, which once consisted of forty columns and still contains twenty-one, more or less complete. The passages preserved (no. 88 of the official edition) are Joel 2:20; 2:26–4:16 (Eng. 3:16); Am. 1:5–2:1; 7:3–8:7; 8:11–9:15; Obadiah and Jonah complete; Micah complete except 6:8-10; Nahum complete; Hab. 1:3–2:11; 2:18 to the end; Zeph. 1:1; 1:11–3:6; 3:8 to the end; Haggai complete except 2:11; Zec. 1:1-4. The text is remarkably similar to the MT, and its few variant readings are unimportant for the general meaning.

Since the publication of the official edition, several authors have contributed articles clarifying certain problems posed by these documents. S. Segert studied the philological side in *Archiv Orientální,* 31 (1963), 122-137. The legal side was discussed by R. Yaron, *JJS,* 11 (1960), 157-171; E. Koffmann, *RQ,* 4/3 (1963), 421-27. The historical side was discussed by Y. Yadin, *IEJ,* 11 (1961), 51f.; J. A. Fitzmyer, "Bar Cochba Period," in *Bible in Current Catholic Thought: Gruenthaner Memorial Volume* (1962), pp. 133-168 (repr. in J. A. Fitzmyer, *Essays on the Semitic Background of the NT* [1971], pp. 305-354); E. M. Laperrousaz, *Syria,* 41 (1964), 347-358.

Explorations carried out farther south by Israeli scholars, particularly in 1960, resulted in the discovery of important documents that complement the information furnished by the Murabbaʿât documents (see the official edition, or *IEJ,* 11 [1961], 2-72).

J. CARMIGNAC
tr. W. S. L. S.

**MURATORIAN** mūr-ə-tōr'i-ən **FRAGMENT.** A list of NT books preserved in medieval Latin MSS that provides valuable evidence about the formation of the NT canon. L. A. Muratori discovered the list in an eighth-century MS that was in the Ambrosian Library, Milan, but originally belonged to Columban's Monastery, Bobbio. Muratori published the text in 1740. Four fragments of the same list were later found in Latin MSS of the 11th or 12th cent. at Monte Cassino. The poor Latin of the Fragment makes exact interpretation of the text difficult and indicates that it was copied from an earlier text. Most scholars believe that it was written originally in Greek, but some have suggested a Latin original.

Comprising eighty-five lines, the eighth-century document is mutilated at the beginning and end. Luke is the first book named, but it is described as the third Gospel; thus references to Matthew and Mark likely had appeared at the beginning. The list also cites as acceptable to the Church the Gospel of John, 1 John, the Acts of the Apostles, and thirteen Pauline Epistles: 1 and 2 Corinthians, Ephesians, Philippians, Colossians, Galatians, 1 and 2 Thessalonians, Romans, Philemon, Titus, and 1 and 2 Timothy. It rejects as forgeries the Epistles to the Laodiceans and the Alexandrians that are attributed to Paul. Also listed as accepted are Jude, two (additional?) Epistles of John, the apocryphal Wisdom of Solomon, the Revelation of John, and the Revelation of Peter, although the last work is said to be rejected by some. Shepherd of Hermas is excluded from public reading in church but is recommended for private use. More emphatically rejected are the writings of various figures apparently regarded as heretics (Arsinous, Valentinus, Miltiades, Marcion, and Basilides). In the light of the later development of the canon, James, 1 and 2 Peter, and Hebrews are conspicuously absent.

The exact importance of the list depends upon its date and origin, and these matters are disputed. The dominant view has been that the list was composed in the Western Church *ca.* A.D. 200 (Tregelles, Harnack, Beare); this position is still stoutly defended (von Campenhausen, Grant, Kümmel). Sundberg's 1973 article, however, is a strong case for a fourth-century date and an Eastern origin (see also *IDB Supp.*). But he has not settled the issue, for the absence of Hebrews from the list may reflect an origin in the West, where that book took longer to be accepted. Moreover, the heresies mentioned in the Fragment are 2nd cent. and thus suggest a date *ca.* A.D. 200 or a little later. Other evidence for this date may be the categorization of Christian writings — as recognized, disputed, or spurious — found in Eusebius (*HE* iii.25; 3rd-4th cent.); this categorization seems more developed than that in the Muratorian list. But the list is difficult to interpret with full confidence, and conclusions about it both affect and are affected by one's understanding of the early history of the NT canon. Von Campenhausen has given the most complete recent treatment of this subject (but cf. Groh, Dungan).

Not only the list's date but also its purpose and occasion remain problematic. Suggestions about authorship are only speculative. The lengthy description of the origin of John's Gospel may be a reply to the Alogoi (late 2nd cent.), who rejected both the Gospel and the Revelation of John. The emphasis upon the symbolic significance of Paul's letters to seven churches may be a response to Marcionism. The rejection of works believed to be forgeries in Paul's name reflects some stress upon authorship as a basis for the Church's acceptance of writings. The rejection of Shepherd of Hermas because of its late date indicates the idea that normative revelation was given for a limited time; this idea perhaps countered Montanist claims of ongoing inspiration. But the list's dominant criterion for acceptance of writings seems to have been simply their widespread use in church services.

Whatever the conclusion about the date, purpose, and origin of the Muratorian Fragment, it remains an important witness to the complex process of NT canonization. *See also* CANON OF THE NT.

***Bibliography.–Text:*** S. P. Tregelles, *Canon Muratorianus* (1867); H. Lietzmann, *Das Muratorische Fragment,* (*Kleine Texte,* 1, 1908).

*English Translation:* H-S, I, 42-45.

*Studies:* F. W. Beare, *IDB,* I, 527-29; J. Beumer, *Theologie und Philosophie,* 48 (1973), 534-550; H. Burkhardt, *Theologische Zeitschrift,* 30 (1974), 207-211; H. von Campenhausen, *Formation of the Christian Bible* (Eng. tr. 1972); N. A. Dahl, *ZNW,* 52 (1961), 39-53; D. L. Dungan, *Interp.,* 29 (1975), 339-351; A. Ehrhardt, *Framework of the NT Stories* (1964), pp. 11-36; R. M. Grant, *Formation of the NT* (1965), pp. 156-59; "The NT Canon," in P. R. Ackroyd and C. F. Evans, eds., *Cambridge History of the Bible,* I (1970), 284-308; D. Groh, *Interp.,* 28 (1974), 331-343; A. Harnack, *Zeitschrift für Kirchengeschichte,* 3 (1879), 358-408, 595-98; *IDB Supp., s.v.* (A. C. Sundberg); W. G. Kümmel, *Intro.*

*to the NT* (Eng. tr., rev. ed. 1975), pp. 475-510; J. Quasten, *Patrology*, II (1964), 207-210; K. Stendahl, "The Apocalypse of John and the Epistles of Paul in the Muratorian Fragment," in W. Klassen and G. F. Snyder, eds., *Current Issues in NT Interpretation* (1962), pp. 239-245; A. C. Sundberg, *HTR*, 66 (1973), 1-41; *Interp.*, 29 (1975), 352-371.

L. W. HURTADO

**MURDER; MURDERER** [Heb. *rāṣaḥ* (Nu. 35:16-31; Jgs. 20:4; Dt. 22:26; 2 K. 6:32; Job 24:14; Ps. 94:6; Isa. 1:21; Jer. 7:9; Hos. 6:9), *hārag* (1 K. 2:5; 2 K. 9:31; Ps. 10:8; Jer. 4:31), hiphil of *mûṯ* (Jer. 41:4), hiphil of *nāḵâ* (2 K. 14:6), pl. of *dām*–'blood' (Hos. 4:2); AV also SLAY, KILLING; NEB also KILL, DO TO DEATH, HOMICIDE, SLAUGHTER; [Gk. *phónos* (Mt. 15:19 par. Mk. 7:21; 15:7; Lk. 23:19, 25; Acts 9:1; Rom. 1:29; Rev. 9:21), *phoneús* (Mt. 22:7; Acts 3:14; 7:52; 28:4; 1 Pet. 4:15; Rev. 21:8; 22:15), *phoneúō* (Mt. 23:31, 35), *spházō* (1 Jn. 3:12), *anthrōpoktónos* (Jn. 8:44; 1 Jn. 3:15), *patrolǭas* ("murderer of fathers," 1 Tim. 1:9), *mētrolǭas* ("murderer of mothers," 1 Tim. 1:9)]; NEB also "murderous threats," PARICIDES, MATRICIDES.

*I. In the OT.*–Homicide is a person's killing of another person, and murder is a homicide done unlawfully and with malice aforethought. Israelite law functioned within the overarching framework of the covenant to safeguard the covenant relationship. It was therefore never lax in prescribing punishment for offenses against God and for the crimes that diminished the holiness of His people. In contrast to earlier codes, the Deuteronomic code exhibits a markedly increased disposition (through the influence of the prophets according to the documentary hypothesis) to protect those who tend to slip between the societal cracks — the widows, orphans, sojourners, poor, and needy (cf. Dt. 23–24). The *lex talionis* was in force but apparently was not followed to the letter. Rather, it served to enforce the principle of proportional compensation (i.e., it kept compensation or punishment from exceeding the crime). Indeed, the context of Ex. 21:23 (the earliest expression of *lex talionis*) is a list of compensations for specific injuries. The development of the *lex talionis* was an important breakthrough in the ancient Near East in that it gave equal legal standing to the poor and curbed the callousness of the nobility toward them. The only crime for which compensation in money or kind was not allowed was murder. The murderer had to forfeit his life, because the blood that he had shed unlawfully was understood to defile the holiness of the land (Nu. 35:31-34).

The very infrequency of Heb. *rāṣaḥ* in the MT (forty-six occurrences; other Hebrew verbs for taking life occur three or four times as often) suggests its specialized meaning. The RSV usually translates the verb as "murder" and the participle as "murderer," but in both the Exodus and the Deuteronomic versions of the Ten Commandments it renders "kill" in the sixth commandment (Ex. 20:13; Dt. 5:17).

Numbers 35 constitutes the most significant context for defining *rāṣaḥ*. There *rōṣē(a)ḥ*, the participle of *rāṣaḥ*, occurs eighteen times (seven times rendered "manslayer," eleven times "murderer"). In vv. 16-18 certain crimes are defined as *rāṣaḥ* by the formula *rōṣē(a)ḥ hû'*, "He is a murderer": (a) killing with an iron weapon (*keli barzel*), (b) killing with a throwing stone (*'eḇen yāḏ*), and (c) killing with a wooden hand weapon (*keli 'ēṣ-yāḏ*). In each case the penalty for the murder is defined by the formula *môṯ yûmaṯ hārōṣē(a)ḥ*, "The murderer shall be put to death." This penalty was carried out by the "avenger of blood" (*gō'ēl haddām*), usually a relative of the deceased (vv. 17-21).

In its earliest usage *rāṣaḥ* has a certain neutrality or objectivity, so that it can be used both for the acts of murder by weapon in Nu. 35:16-18 and for the act of blood revenge by the *gō'ēl haddām* in v. 27. Yet in the later usage reflected in vv. 20f. (see B. S. Childs, *Book of Exodus*, pp. 419-421) *rāṣaḥ* loses that neutrality and takes on sharper definition as a malicious act (i.e., murder as distinguished from homicide). The proofs of malicious intent to deprive of life listed in vv. 20f. are the sort that a court would seek to demonstrate: hatred for the victim, and ambush (cf. Ex. 21:13). The sense of "murder," then, ultimately characterizes *rāṣaḥ* as it is used in the sixth commandment. (*See also* KILL.)

When a homicide was demonstrably accidental the killer could flee to a designated city of refuge, where he would be safe by law from the avenger of blood (cf. Nu. 35:9-15; Ex. 21:13; Dt. 19:1-10; *see also* AVENGER; REFUGE, CITIES OF). When a homicide was demonstrably malicious, the Hebrew view of the utter sanctity and inviolability of human life made the killer's death at the hands of the avenger of blood the just and requisite punishment. The rationale was not simply to punish, however, but, as stated in Dt. 19:13, to "purge the guilt of innocent blood from Israel, so that it may be well with you." To determine justice in cases of alleged malicious intent there were two very important procedural regulations: "If any one kills a person, the murderer shall be put to death on the evidence of witnesses," and "No person shall be put to death on the testimony of one witness" (Nu. 35:30; cf. Dt. 19:15-19 for the requirement of more than one witness and the problem of false witnesses).

Although it was common custom to offer and to accept compensation for bodily injury, despite the principle of the *lex talionis*, compensation was never allowed in cases of murder. Nu. 35:31, in contrast with some other ancient Near Eastern law codes, prohibits the payment of ransom for the life of a *rōṣē(a)ḥ* "who is guilty of death," for it would have made life far too cheap and would have allowed the wealthy to run roughshod over the poor.

Even though the RSV translates *rāṣaḥ* "kill" in the two primary texts of the sixth commandment (Ex. 20:13; Dt. 5:17), it has "murder" in Jeremiah's prophetic echo of the sixth commandment (Jer. 7:9). This is Jeremiah's famous temple speech, in which the people are said to "steal, murder, commit adultery, swear falsely, . . . and go after other gods," convinced in their self-delusion that the temple (and thus the city itself) was inviolate. Jeremiah counseled instead that they "execute justice" and "not oppress the alien, the fatherless or the widow, or shed innocent blood" (vv. 5f.). Cf. Hos. 4:2 (RSV "killing"), where similarly the callous breaking of the commandments (the dark side of the thriving economy under Jeroboam II) violates the covenant relationship in that each cited transgression is against the neighbor and has no place in the life of God's covenant people. In Ps. 94:6 it is the ignominy of the "wicked" that they stoop even to "slay [Heb. *hārag*] the widow and the sojourner, and murder [piel of *rāṣaḥ*] the fatherless." Hosea observed (6:9) that even bands of priests were like robbers waiting to murder (piel of *rāṣaḥ*) on the road to the old refuge city of Shechem (cf. Josh. 20:7). Isa. 1:21 laments how in the erstwhile justice-cherishing Jerusalem "righteousness [once] lodged . . . but now murderers [Heb. *meraṣṣeḥîm*]." Hos. 9:9 likens Israel to the lawless premonarchial Gibeah, where the especially vicious and wanton murder of the Levite's concubine occurred (Jgs. 20:4f.).

The RSV translates Heb. *hārag* "murder(er)" four times: 1 K. 2:5 (Joab's revenge against Amasa and Abner); 2 K. 9:31 (Jezebel's accusation of Jehu); Ps. 10:8 (the work of the wicked); Jer. 4:31 (Zion's gasping cry of woe).

The RSV renders the hiphil of the Hebrew verb *mûṯ* "murder" (noun) only in regard to the assassination of

Gedaliah in Jer. 41:4. The RSV once translates the plural participle of Heb. *nāḵâ* (hiphil) "murderers" (2 K. 14:6), in reference to Amaziah's "servants who had slain the king his father" (v. 5).

In Hos. 4:2 the RSV translates Heb. *weḏāmîm beḏāmîm nāḡā'û* "and murder follows murder" (cf. AV "and blood toucheth blood," NEB "one deed of blood after another"). The phrase characterizes the preceding list of societal crimes as unrelenting (and unaddressed) offenses that merit only the death penalty (see H. W. Wolff, *Hosea* [Eng. tr., *Hermeneia,* 1974], pp. 67f.). The same term *dāmîm* is translated "bloodguilt [incurred by a murderer]" in Ex. 22:2 (MT 1). *See* BLOODGUILTINESS.

***II. In the NT.***–Greek *phoneús,* "murderer," occurs seven times in the NT and is always translated "murderer(s)" or "murdered." In Matthew's highly allegorized version of the parable of the marriage feast (Mt. 22:1-10) the invited guests who had not only refused their invitations but also killed the messengers so outraged the king that (v. 7) "he sent his troops and destroyed those murderers [Gk. *phoneís*] and burned their city" (an action thought by some commentators, e.g., D. Hill [*NCBC,* 1972], p. 302, to allude to the destruction of Jerusalem in A.D. 70; this violence is peculiar to Matthew — cf. Lk. 14:16-24).

*Phoneús* appears three times in Acts (though never in Luke): in Peter's mention of Barabbas the "murderer" (3:14), who ironically was released while the "Author of life" was "killed" (Gk. *apokteínō,* v. 15); in Stephen's climactic reference to the Righteous One's being "betrayed and murdered" (7:52); and in the Maltese people's initial assessment of Paul, who had survived shipwreck only to be bitten by a viper (28:4). *Phoneús* also appears in a list of criminal activities in 1 Pet. 4:15 and twice in lists of vices (Rev. 21:8; 22:15; cf. Barn. 20:2; Did. 5:2).

Greek *phónos,* "murder, killing," has nine occurrences in the NT, of which eight are translated "murder(s)" by the RSV. The term appears in Mt. 15:19, where Matthew reduced Mark's parallel list (Mk. 7:21f.) of evil things that proceed out of the human heart from thirteen to seven and ordered them so that the final six correspond to the sixth ("murder") through the ninth commandments. In three places *phónos* is associated with Barabbas, "who had committed murder [Gk. *phónos* + *poiéō*] in the insurrection" (Mk. 15:7 par. Lk. 23:19, 25). It occurs twice in lists of crimes and vices (Rom. 1:29; Rev. 9:21) and is applied to Saul of Tarsus when, "breathing threats and murder," he was zealously persecuting the disciples of Jesus (Acts 9:1; cf. NEB "murderous threats").

The idiom *en phónǭ machaírēs apothaneín* (lit. "be killed in murder by sword," RSV "be killed with the sword") appears once in He. 11:37 (cf. the same idiom in the LXX of Ex. 17:13; Dt. 13:15 [MT 16]; 20:13, representing Heb. *lepî ḥāreḇ,* "with the edge of the sword"). *Phónos* also represents Heb. *rāṣaḥ* in Hos. 4:2, LXX (RSV "killing"). In 2 Macc. 4:3 the plural form *phónous* refers to "murders" by agents of the treacherous temple captain Simon.

The RSV translates the cognate Greek verb *phoneúō* "murder" in only two of its ten NT occurrences. One of Matthew's woes against the scribes and Pharisees (Mt. 23:31, 35) uses *phoneúō* twice in reference to the killing of the prophets (cf. v. 37, where the same act is expressed with *apokteínō* [NEB "murders"]). The RSV has "kill" for the other eight occurrences of *phoneúō,* six of which cite the sixth commandment (e.g., Mt. 5:21; 19:18 par.; the NEB usually has "murder").

Greek *anthrōpoktónos,* "murderer," occurs only three times in the NT. Jn. 8:44 says that the devil has been "a murderer from the beginning" (according to his traditional role in leading Adam and Eve into sin; cf. Wisd. 2:24). The term occurs twice in 1 Jn. 3:15, where the person who hates his brother is considered a "murderer."

Greek *spházō* is usually translated "slay" (e.g., Rev. 5:6, 12; 6:4; 13:8), but in 1 Jn. 3:12 it twice refers to Cain's "murder" of his brother (although the LXX in Gen. 4:8 uses *apokteínō,* "kill," for the original narration of Cain's deed).

In 1 Tim. 1:9 plural forms of *patrolǭas,* "murderer of one's father," and *mētrolǭas,* "murderer of one's mother," appear in a list of criminals. The two terms are followed immediately by the plural of Gk. *androphónos,* "manslayers" (NEB "murderers").

*See also* KILL; MANSLAYER.

***Bibliography.***–J. J. Stamm and M. E. Andrew, *Ten Commandments in Recent Research* (*SBT,* 2/2, 1967), pp. 98f.; *TDOT,* III, *s.v.* "hāragh" (Fuhs).

D. G. BURKE

**MURMUR** [Heb. *lûn* (Ex. 15:24; 16:2, 7f.; 17:3; Nu. 14:2, 27, 29, 36; 16:11, 41 [MT 17:6]; 17:5 [MT 20]; Josh. 9:18), *rāgan* (Dt. 1:27; Ps. 106:25; Isa. 29:24); Gk. *gongýzō* (Lk. 5:30; Jn. 6:41, 43, 61), *diagongýzō* (Lk. 15:2; 19:7), *gongysmós* (Acts 6:1)]; AV also MURMURING (Acts 6:1); NEB also COMPLAIN, "make complaint," "raise an outcry" (Ex. 17:3), "be indignant" (Josh. 9:18), GRUMBLE, etc.; **MURMURINGS** [Heb. *telunnôṯ*] (Ex. 16:7ff.; Nu. 14:27; 17:5, 10 [MT 20, 25]); NEB COMPLAINTS; **GRUMBLE** [Gk. *gongýzō* (Mt. 20:11; 1 Cor. 10:10), *stenázō* (Jas. 5:9)]; AV MURMUR, GRUDGE; NEB also BLAME; **GRUMBLER** [*gongystḗs*] (Jude 16); AV MURMURER; **GRUMBLING** [*gongysmós*] (Phil. 2:14); AV MURMURING; NEB COMPLAINT; **MUTTER** [Heb. *hāgâ* (Isa. 59:3), hiphil part. of *hāgâ* (8:19); Gk. *gongýzō* (Jn. 7:32)]; AV also MURMUR; NEB also GIBBER, UTTER; **MUTTERING** [*gongysmós*] (Jn. 7:12); AV MURMURING; NEB WHISPERING.

Murmuring is an outward expression of deep inward discontent and rejection of one's lot. During the wilderness journey from Egypt to Sinai the Israelites frequently complained against Moses. They became thirsty (Ex. 15:24), hungry (16:2f.), and distressed (Nu. 14:2f.). The memory of their better moments in Egypt caused them to ask why they had ever left. Although they murmured against Moses and at times against Aaron, their real complaint was against God. God heard their complaining and took action against it, generally by eliminating the area of complaint and punishing a portion of the congregation. For the congregation of God, murmuring signifies unbelief and may result in death (Nu. 17:10). Dt. 13 requires one who deliberately turns the people away from God to be killed immediately.

When the Israelites first approached Palestine to occupy it, the spies brought back an evil report and caused the congregation to murmur against God and His chosen leaders, Moses and Aaron. God answered the people's complaint, "Would that we had died in this wilderness!" (Nu. 14:2), by allowing no one to enter the land. The spies who incited the congregation to complain died by plague (vv. 1-37).

Afterward Korah and his company rebelled against Moses and Aaron for assuming too much of the leadership of the nation (Nu. 16:1-35). A test was made between Korah and the house of Aaron. The Lord accepted Aaron's censer but rejected Korah's, who thus was subject to immediate death. After Korah's punishment the rods of all twelve tribes along with Aaron's were presented before the Lord (17:6f.). Aaron's rod budded; thereby God reconfirmed visibly that the household of priests was to come from the family of Aaron (v. 8). This visual test was undertaken to end the murmuring among the people (v. 5).

Murmuring in the OT is concentrated in these incidents

in the wilderness. A complaining congregation is a divided congregation that can accomplish little. To achieve His purpose for Israel God had to rid the people of their persistent murmurings. Thus Isa. 29:24 speaks of a time when "those who murmur will accept instruction."

In the NT the words and acts of Jesus caused a great deal of murmuring. The Pharisees and scribes particularly were offended at Jesus' practice of eating with tax collectors and sinners (Lk. 5:30; 15:2; 19:7). Jesus' teaching at Capernaum, "I am the bread which came down from heaven," caused not only the crowds but also the disciples to murmur (Jn. 6:41-71). Jesus quickly perceived this and asked them, "Do you take offense at this?" In compassion He wished to destroy the seeds of their unbelief. The Twelve began to separate from Jesus, but Peter confessed the deity of Jesus and thereby held the Twelve together. Judas, however, persisted in unbelief; perhaps he was the one who murmured against the woman who anointed Jesus (Mk. 14:3ff., AV; cf. Jn. 12:3-8).

The NT Church experienced the murmuring of the Hellenists against the Hebrews "because their widows were neglected in the daily distribution" (Acts 6:1). The disciples, realizing the detrimental force of discontent, moved quickly to end its cause.

Paul exhorted the Corinthians not to murmur as the Hebrews had done in the wilderness; they had been destroyed (1 Cor. 10:10). The worst portrait of the complainer appears in Jude 16: "These are grumblers [AV "murmurers"], malcontents, following their own passions, loud-mouthed boasters, flattering people to gain advantage." Murmurings oppose faith and will soon destroy it. Therefore, in regard to achieving salvation, Paul exhorted the Philippians: "Do all things without murmurings and disputing" (Phil. 2:14, AV). Faith eliminates murmurings.

*See also* COMPLAIN; GRUDGE. J. E. HARTLEY

**MURRAIN** mûr'ən [Heb. *deber*; Gk. *thánatos*] (Ex. 9:3, AV); RSV PLAGUE; NEB PESTILENCE. A medieval term describing diseases of high morbidity affecting people or animals. The fifth Egyptian plague involved a plague of flies; it was probably epizootic in nature and conveyed by insects. Many writers have reported the incidence of severe cattle plagues in Egypt.

The disease may have been rinderpest, an affliction that can be transmitted by flies and quickly attain destructive proportions. Human contact with putrefying carcasses sometimes results in staphylococcal infection, which produces boils. An alternative diagnosis is anthrax, an infectious disease of the herbivora characterized by the presence of *Bacillus anthracis* in the bloodstream. Severe losses often occur among animals, and the disease can be transmitted to people. R. K. H.

**MUSE** [Heb. qal and polel of *śî(a)ḥ*] (Ps. 77:12 [MT 13]; 143:5); AV also TALK; NEB also "fill my mind"; [*hāgâ*] (Isa. 33:18); AV MEDITATE; NEB "call to mind"; [*hāgîg*] (Ps. 39:3 [MT 4]); NEB "mind wandered." To be absorbed in thought, repeated turning something over in the mind.

*Śî(a)ḥ* and *hāgâ* are used in synonymous parallelism (Ps. 77:12 [MT 13]; 143:5) to express the idea of being completely absorbed in thought about God. In times of distress the psalmists found hope in meditating on God's saving deeds in the past. In 39:3 (MT 4), however, the psalmist is ruminating on his own miserable condition. He chose to brood in silence, in order not to give the wicked occasion for gloating (vv. 1f.), but this only intensified the excruciating feelings that raged inside of him; he found relief only when he expressed his anguish to God. In Isa. 33:18 the prophet foretells a time when the terror of defeat and captivity will be merely a painful memory.

In Lk. 3:15, AV, "muse" renders Gk. *dialogízomai*, "ponder," "discuss" (RSV "question"); *see* QUESTION; DISCUSSION.

*See also* MEDITATE. N. J. O.

**MUSHI** mo͞o'shī [Heb. *mûšî, mušî*]; **MUSHITES** mo͞o'shīts [Heb. *hammûšî*]; NEB also FAMILY OF MUSHI. The second son of Merari and the patronymic of one of the two families of Levites descended from Merari (Ex. 6:19; Nu. 3:20, 33; 26:58; 1 Ch. 6:19, 47 [MT 4, 32]; 23:21, 23; 24:26, 30).

**MUSIC** [Heb. *neḡînâ*] (Lam. 5:14); AV MUSICK; NEB STRINGS; [*maśśā'*–'burden'] (1 Ch. 15:22, 27); AV MUSICK; NEB also SONG; [pl. hiphil part. of *šāma'*–'cause to hear'] (1 Ch. 16:42); AV "those that should make a sound"; NEB "players"; [*šîr*–'sing'] (1 Ch. 25:6); AV SONG; NEB SINGING; [*hamôn*–'noise'] (Ezk. 26:13); AV "noise"; NEB "clamour"; [Aram. *zemārā'*] (Dnl. 3:5, 7, 10, 15); AV MUSICK; NEB SINGING; [Gk. *symphōnía*] (Lk. 15:25). The RSV paraphrases two prepositional phrases: [Heb. *'alê-'āśôr wa 'alê-nāḇel*] (Ps. 92:3 [MT 4]) — "to the music of the lute and the harp"; AV "upon an instrument of ten strings and upon the psaltery"; NEB "to the music of a ten-stringed lute, to the sounding chords of the harp"; [*bekinnôr*] (Ps. 49:4 [MT 5] — "to the music of the lyre"; AV "upon the harp"; NEB "on the harp"; **MAKE MUSIC** [hiphil part. of *šāma'*] (1 Ch. 15:28); AV "make a noise"; NEB "play"; **MUSICAL INSTRUMENTS, INSTRUMENTS OF MUSIC, INSTRUMENTS FOR MUSIC, INSTRUMENTS** [Heb. *kelê šîr*] (1 Ch. 15:16; 16:42; 2 Ch. 5:13; 7:6; 23:13; 34:12; Neh. 12:36; Am. 5:6); AV also INSTRUMENTS OF MUSICK; NEB also MUSICIANS (2 Ch. 34:12); [*šālîšîm*–'three'] (1 S. 18:6); NEB "dancing"; **STRINGED INSTRUMENTS** [pl. of *neḡînâ*] (Isa. 38:20; titles of Pss. 4, 6, 54, 55, 61, 67, 76 [all MT v. 1]); AV also NEGINOTH (in Psalms); NEB "music of praise" (NEB omits all Psalm titles); [pl. of *mēn*] (Ps. 45:8 [MT 9]); AV "whereby"; NEB MUSIC OF STRINGS.

- I. Ancient Near Eastern Music
  - A. Mesopotamia and Egypt
  - B. OT
- II. Musical Instruments
  - A. Horn and Trumpet
  - B. Strings
  - C. Woodwinds
  - D. Percussion Instruments
  - E. Collective Terms
  - F. Uncertain Terms
  - G. Instruments in Daniel
  - H. NT Instruments
- III. Musical Performance
  - A. Mesopotamian Music Theory
  - B. Psalm Superscriptions

***I. Ancient Near Eastern Music.**–A. Mesopotamia and Egypt*. The history of ancient Near Eastern music begins at approximately the same time in both Mesopotamia and Egypt.

On clay tablets found at Uruk, dating to the turn of the 4th millennium B.C., there appears the earliest form of the cuneiform sign *balaĝ*, clearly showing the rounded contours and diagonal strings of the typical Sumerian arched or boat-shaped harp. From several centuries later, two harpers figure on a fragment of a stone vase from ancient Adab (Bismaya). From the Royal Cemetery at Ur, the traditional home of Abraham, come the actual remains of nine richly ornamented lyres, one arched harp with gold-capped tuning pegs, and a set of pipes, found among the funerary furnishing of Queen Pu-Abi and her retinue (*ca.* 2650 B.C.). One panel of a plaque of shell inlay that once decorated one of the Ur lyres shows a fanciful animal orchestra: a donkey plays a lyre, a bear claps and sings, and a jackal beats time with a percussion instrument and a sistrum (*see* picture in BEAR). The so-called Standard of Ur mosaic depicts a leisurely banquet scene, the entertainment provided by a male lyre player and singer. This and other iconographic evidence from Mesopotamia throughout the 3rd millennium witness to the prominent place of music in the secular life of ancient Sumerian culture.

As the cuneiform writing system matured to the point that ideas as well as objects could be represented, textual evidence begins to appear. From the early second half of the 3rd millennium comes the first mention of the *kinnāru,* the West Semitic lyre (Heb. *kinnôr*), in lexical lists from the ancient Syrian kingdom of Ebla. The Mesopotamian hymnic tradition begins at about the same time, at Tell Abu Ṣalabīḫ, with a collection of divine hymns of praise and a fragment of a hymn to the temple-city of Kish. The poetess Enheduanna, daughter of Sargon of Akkad (*ca.* 2350 B.C.) and high priestess of the moon-god at Ur, is credited with the composition of several powerful and finely crafted hymns to the goddess of love and war, Inanna/Ishtar, and of a long, litany-like collection of hymns to the principal temples and deities of Sumer and Akkad — all known from versions preserved in later scribal schools. At the end of the 3rd millennium, texts commemorating temple construction at Lagash and numerous hymns to and for the kings of the 3rd Dynasty of Ur — replete with musical terminology — attest to a rich and well-developed musical tradition in the last days of Sumerian civilization.

Resources for the history of Assyro-Babylonian music in the 2nd and 1st millennia are even more extensive. Iconographic evidence from both the heartland of Mesopotamia and neighboring countries within the Mesopotamian cultural area increases substantially. New instruments make their appearance, particularly the long-necked lute sometime before the beginning of the 2nd millennium. First-millennium Assyrian reliefs depict a number of common musical instruments, often in great detail, including several varieties of harps and lyres, hand drums, pipes, and cymbals. Lexical lists from the scribal schools and other sources have preserved the Sumerian and Akkadian names of many different instruments and varieties of instruments, although — as in the case of the biblical instruments — identification, beyond general type or character, is usually difficult, as is the exact matching of names with graphic illustrations.

While little is known about Mesopotamian secular song, the use of song in religious ritual is well attested. An extensive repertory of divine hymns, lamentations, and liturgical litanies is preserved, albeit often in fragmentary form, and catalogs of hymn titles mention many further examples not yet recovered. Many hymns still composed in Sumerian from the first half of the 2nd millennium feature performance indications. The *tigi* and *adab* hymns, for example, both named after types of drums, were generally composed of two sections of approximately the same length, the *sag̃ara,* "set(?) strings," and the *sagida,* "plucked(?) strings"; the *adab* ended with a coda-like doxology, its *uru,* "high/loud-part(?)." Each of the major sections could be further divided and subdivided into subsections all identified by descriptive technical terms, all of which suggests formalized and complicated choral or instrumental performance. Other Sumero-Akkadian hymn-types named after (accompanying?) instruments include the *zami* (lyre) hymn of divine praise, and the *balag̃* (harp) and *eršema* (drum-wail) liturgical hymns of penitential petition.

Mesopotamian sacred and courtly music was primarily the province of families of musicians. The *nâru* was an ordinary musician,probably providing secular entertainment as well as assisting in temple performances. The *kalû* had a more specialized profession, performing harp music and laments at private funerals and officiating in the lengthy, involved, penitential liturgies particularly associated with the later stages of Assyro-Babylonian religion. Descriptions of rituals from Mari (18th cent. B.C.) and Uruk (4th cent. B.C.) give details of some of the *kalû*'s activities, and late Babylonian calendars list the names and orders of different temple liturgies to be performed by him on specific days of the year. Professional musicians were necessarily literate, trained in the temple schools, and such musician-scribes were probably responsible for the cuneiform tablets from *ca.* 1800 to *ca.* 500 B.C. that set forth the Mesopotamian theory of musical intervals and scales whose details have gradually come to light over the past several decades (see III.A below).

Egyptian musical practice also has a long and well-documented history. Among the earliest iconographic evidence is a depiction of a fox playing an end-blown flute, accompanied by a dancing giraffe and ibex, found on a ceremonial palette from Hierakonpolis (*ca.* 3000 B.C.). Depiction of end-blown flutes, single and double clarinets, harps, and trumpets appear in tombs of the Old Kingdom (*ca.* 2686-2040 B.C.), alongside singers and, often, dancers. By the New Kingdom (*ca.* 1558-1085 B.C.) soloists and ensembles illustrate a variety of new instruments, including the lute (a Mesopotamian import), several types of lyres and harps, the double oboe, and various sorts of drums, tambourines, clappers, and sistra.

Many of these instruments still exist. Among preserved percussion instruments are animal-headed clappers from

Musicians on a mural from the tomb of Nakht (18th Dynasty), playing a double flute (left), lute (center), and harp (right) (Oriental Institute, University of Chicago)

the 1st Dynasty (*ca.* 3100-2890 B.C.), other sorts of wooden clappers, bronze cymbals of varying size and shape, bells, jingles, rattles, decorated metal and faience sistra, and an array of hand drums. Extant wind instruments include a bronze and copper trumpet from the tomb of Tutankhamen (1347-1338 B.C.), a number of end-blown true flutes, a much larger number of pipes, double clarinets (Old Kingdom) and double oboes (New Kingdom), and terra-cotta rhyton-shaped wind instruments from the Greco-Roman period. Strings include symmetrical and asymmetrical lyres, both angular and arched or bow-type harps, which show great variety in size and number of strings, and two sizes of two or three-stringed lutes. The well-preserved state of many of these instruments has permitted experimentation on the spacing of flute finger holes and lute frets, and reconstructions of lyre and harp stringing, in attempts to determine the musical intervals in use at the times of their construction. The attempts have met with some small success, but as no written music exists, nothing is known about the actual sound of ancient Egyptian music. Music was apparently of great importance to the Egyptians. Many of their greatest deities, including Hathor, Isis, and Osiris, had musical associations. The iconographic evidence is extensive, and the literature of Egypt is replete with musical references. Remarks concerning Egyptian music and musical traditions are common in the works of the classical authors (see *New Grove Dictionary of Music and Musicians* [1980], VI, *s.v.* "Egypt I" [R. Anderson]).

*B. OT.* Biblical references to music open with the ascription of its origin to one of Cain's descendants, the legendary Jubal, who was "the father of all those who play the lyre and pipe" (Gen. 4:21). His name is related to Heb. *yôḇēl,* "ram," from whose horns the primitive *šôpār*-horn was made, easily perceived as a most ancient instrument indeed. While Enki/Ea, the god of wisdom, magic, and crafts, was the proper Sumero-Akkadian patron of music, Jubal's counterpart in the Mesopotamian king-sage tradition may have been the first postdiluvian sage Nungal-piriĝgal, who is associated with the introduction of musical instruments.

References to the popular uses of music are common in the early times of biblical history. It was always a vital part of secular celebrations. Laban chides Jacob for denying him the opportunity to hold a farewell party, complete with "mirth and songs, with tambourine and lyre" (Gen. 31:27); Jephthah's daughter showed her happiness at her father's return by greeting him "with timbrels and with dances" (Jgs. 11:34). Isaiah condemns the idle rich who wile away their days with "lyre and harp, timbrel and flute and wine at their feasts" (Isa. 5:12); and Job complains of the happy lives of the wicked, whose children dance, and who "sing to the tambourine and the lyre, and rejoice to the sound of the pipe" (Job 21:11f.). In more mundane circumstances the welcome arrival at an oasis could occasion a work song by the well diggers (Nu. 21:17f.); and singing enlivened the labors of the watchman (Isa. 21:12), the vineyard keeper (Isa. 27:2-5), or the wine pressers (Jer. 25:30; 48:33).

The first biblical song depicts Lamech's vengeance (Gen. 4:23), and warfare, particularly during the nomadic period and the time of the Conquest, gave rise to many songs or song quotations. Such heroic songs were probably the subject matter of the lost Book of the Wars of the Lord (Nu. 21:14) and the Book of Jashar (Josh. 10:13; 2 S. 1:18), and no doubt formed a good part of the repertory of the early OT minstrels and bards (cf. Nu. 21:27-30).

Victory in battle was an especially heady theme. Miriam sang of the victory over Pharaoh while "all the women went out after her with timbrels and dancing" (Ex. 15:20f.); and Deborah's song celebrating the defeat of the Canaanite king Jabin is a brilliant and artful celebration of Israel's triumph (Jgs. 5). Samson exults over his defeat of the Philistines with a rhythmic couplet (Jgs. 15:16): "With the jawbone of an ass,/heaps upon heaps,/With the jawbone of an ass/have I slain a thousand men," a chant doubtless taken up and repeated by the men of Judah, like that which the women sang to one another at Saul's homecoming (1 S. 18:6f.): "Saul has slain his thousands,/And David his ten thousands."

Not every battle was won, however, and songs mourning the deaths of heroes were also recorded. The earliest example is David's moving lament for Saul and Jonathan, a citation from the lost Book of Jashar (2 S. 1:19-27); cf. also David's lamentation for Abner (2 S. 3:33f.).

Apart from the use of the trumpet as a signaling instrument (cf. Nu. 10:1-10), music seems to have played a rather minor role in the national religion of the nomadic period and during the Conquest. The arrival of the monarchy, however, and with it the first temple, saw the beginnings of professional musicianship at the court (cf. 1 K. 1:34, 39f.; 10:2; Eccl. 2:8) and in religious ritual. David served as Saul's private musician (1 S. 19:9), and by tradition David was a skillful lyre player (1 S. 16:16-18), an inventor of instruments (Am. 6:5), and also a dancer (2 S. 6:14f.). King David's prowess in music was foreshadowed only by that of the Sumerian King Shulgi of Ur (2093-2045 B.C.), who boasted of his remarkable talents in music as well as in athletics and statesmanship. Whether the establishment of liturgical music in Israel truly began only with David, as described in detail in 1 Ch. 15, cannot be easily ascertained; it was probably less elaborate in Solomonic times.

Apart from trumpet flourishes (Nu. 10:10; Ps. 98:6), the music of the temple probably consisted essentially of the singing of religious lyrics to the accompaniment of primarily stringed instruments (cf. Am. 5:23) following the offering of the sacrifices (2 Ch. 29:20-30). Since much of the Psalter may be a postexilic creation or recasting, it is a better guide to the nature of the liturgy of the second temple. But praise, thanksgiving, and penitential petition are common themes in religious expression, and the psalms that feature them may give some idea of the form and content of the earlier liturgy.

After the Exile and the reestablishment of the temple the responsibility for the vocal and instrumental music of the shrine was reassumed by the descendants of the original Levitical musicians (cf. Ezr. 2:41), and the influence of these guilds of musicians is reflected in the Levitical ascriptions in the headings of the Psalter (see III.B below). Some idea of liturgical performance techniques may be gained from the structures of many psalms. The appearance of refrains and recurrent acclamations (e.g., "Hallelujah"), the strophic construction of many psalms, and above all the common device of poetic parallelism frequently suggest varieties of responsorial or antiphonal presentation.

***II. Musical Instruments.***–Identification of the sixteen or more distinct biblical musical instruments must rely primarily on literary evidence: the Bible itself and its early translations, the reports and explanations of the rabbinic and patristic literature, and descriptions and observations of Greek and Roman authors. In recent years the Qumrân discoveries and the recovery of the Ugaritic literature have added somewhat to the discussion, as has the increasing availability of Sumero-Akkadian materials. The newly discovered written remains of ancient Ebla are now also beginning to make their impact. Each resource, however, has its own weaknesses. Many of the biblical names occur only once or twice, and descriptive or explanatory information is extremely rare. The translations frequently provide the only hints as to the exact nature of an instrument, but they are often inconsistent or contradictory, as are many of the rabbinic and patristic explanations; the problem of anachronisms is always present, and motivation and point of view must also be taken into account. Parallels drawn from the languages of neighboring countries or linguistic areas are often valuable but must be utilized with care; many secondary sources for Sumerian and Akkadian references, for example, are now completely out of date and misleading, and the names of instruments change over time, as do the instruments themselves.

Much additional evidence has been obtained from archeological discoveries. Excavations in Israel, Syria, and Asia Minor have produced a surprising number of fragmentary instruments, mostly of metal, bone, or clay, since the climate of the eastern Mediterranean does not favor the preservation of wooden remains. Many Egyptian instruments have survived intact, however, including those made of wood and reed, and a number of Mesopotamian instruments have also been found.

More significant, perhaps, are the abundant pictorial representations on reliefs, sherds, and coins, also in the form of figurines, that have been found throughout the entire Near Eastern and Mediterranean world. Based upon such data, reliable generalizations concerning the existence and development of instrument types and the wandering of instrument styles across cultures are beginning to be possible.

Despite the help provided by both recent archeology and new literary and linguistic resources, however, the matching of a biblical name with a specific instrument or variety of instrument must still, in most cases, represent merely the best guess possible at the present stage of research.

*A. Horn and Trumpet.* The Bible distinguishes between two types of horns: one made of natural animal horn and the other a trumpet of metal.

*1. Qeren* is the ordinary Hebrew term for "(animal) horn"; this basic meaning may be seen, e.g., in Gen. 22:13 (of a ram) or Ps. 22:21 ([MT 22] of oxen). As a musical instrument it appears only in Josh. 6:5 (*qeren hayyôḇēl,* "horn of a ram") as a synonym for *šôp̱ār* (see next entry). The Aramaic form *qarnā'* also occurs in Dnl. 3:5, 7, etc. (see II.G.1 below).

*2.* The *šôp̱ār* "horn," the most frequently named instrument in the OT, is the only ancient instrument to have survived in Hebrew ritual, where it is used to announce the New Year and the Day of Atonement.

The origin of the word is uncertain. It may have a borrowing from Akk. *šappāru,* itself considered a loan from Sum. *šeğbar,* "ibex" or "wild goat." If so, the *šôp̱ār* was named from the material from which it was made, usually the horn of a ram (cf. *šôpᵉrôṯ [hay]yôḇᵉlîm* in Josh. 6:4ff.), but also that of a wild goat, especially in the time of the second temple (Mish. *Rosh ha-shanah* iii.3-5). *Qeren yôḇēl,* "ram's horn," and *šôp̱ār* are exact synonyms in Josh. 6:5, and *yôḇēl* is used alone with the same meaning in Ex. 19:13 (cf. *šôp̱ār* in 19:16). The *yôḇēl* lent its name to the Jubilee (*hayyôḇēl,* Lev. 25:13, etc.), which was inaugurated by the blowing of the ram's horn (Lev. 25:9); it may also be the source of the name Jubal, the legendary "inventor" of musical instruments (Gen. 4:21).

Both modern and ancient translations fail to distinguish consistently between the (animal) horn and the (metal) trumpet. The RSV, NEB, and AV usually give "trumpet," but use "horn" (AV "cornet") where the *šôp̱ār* and the trumpet (*ḥᵃṣōṣᵉrâ*) co-occur (1 Ch. 15:28; 2 Ch. 15:14; Hos. 5:8 [the NEB reverses the terms!]; Ps. 8:6 [MT 7]); the NEB also uses "horn" in other scattered occurrences (Job 39:24f.; Ps. 81:3 [MT 4]; Zec. 9:14). In the LXX *keratínē* translates only *šôp̱ār,* while *sálpinx* translates several terms; the Vulg. translates both *buccina* and *tuba,* but once also *tuba cornae,* "horn trumpet," to mark the contrast in Ps. 81:3.

The *šôp̱ār* could be embellished with carved ornamentations and inscriptions. The natural horn could also be softened in hot water and straightened or shaped. Even when provided with a mouthpiece, however, it could still produce only a few notes, the first one or two harmonic overtones of its fundamental, and these only approximately. Its sound was more threatening or frightening than musical, especially when used in concert, and its ability to inspire fear and awe helps explain its role in the fall of Jericho (Josh. 6:6-20) and at the giving of the Law at Mt. Sinai (Ex. 19:13ff.; 20:18).

The *šôp̱ār* was fundamentally a signaling instrument, especially in times of war. It signaled a call to arms (Jgs. 3:27; 6:34; Neh. 4:18-20), a warning of impending war (Jer. 6:1; Ezk. 33:3-6; Hos. 5:8), a retreat (2 S. 18:16), the proclaiming of victory (1 S. 13:3), and the disbanding of forces (2 S. 20:1, 22). Its voice alarmed the enemy (Jgs. 7:8, 16-22) and was a fearful symbol of war itself (Jer. 4:19-21). It would herald the destruction on the Day of Judgment (Zeph. 1:16) and the ultimate return to Zion (Isa. 28:13). The stilling of its voice was synonymous with peace (Jer. 42:14).

In ritual use it heralded David's transfer of the ark (2 S. 6:15; 1 Ch. 15:28) and King Asa's repentance and renewal of the covenant (2 Ch. 15:14). It accompanied the coronations of Absalom (2 S. 15:10) and Jehu (2 K. 9:13) and the anointing of Solomon (1 K. 1:34). A signal horn (*šôp̱ār tᵉrûʿâ*) was sent about the land on the tenth day of the seventh month to proclaim the Day of Atonement (Lev. 25:9); it also announced the new and full moons (Ps. 81:3). Its "joyful voice" could be heard in the psalms of praise (Ps. 98:6; 150:3).

*3.* The *ḥᵃṣōṣᵉrâ,* "trumpet" (NEB also "horn" in Hos. 5:8, reversing the two instruments), was very likely a short, straight instrument with a mouthpiece and a conical or bell-shaped end. As described it must have possessed a fairly shrill, clarion tone, with a range probably limited to the first three or four harmonic overtones. Unlike the horn it was made of metal, usually bronze, but beaten silver in the case of the temple instruments. Thus the LXX and Vulg. use only *sálpinx* and *tuba,* respectively, never *keratínē* or *buccina;* where trumpet and horn contrast, in Ps. 98:6, they both paraphrase: *en sálpinxin elataís kaí phōnḗ sálpingos keratínēs / in tuba ductilis et voce tubae cornae,* "with hammered-metal trumpets and the sound of trumpets [made] of horn."

The first mention of the trumpet, as well as a good summary of its main uses, can be found in Nu. 10:2-10. Moses was commanded to make two trumpets of hammered silver, to be blown to summon the congregation or its leaders to the tent of meeting, to break camp, and above all to sound the alarm in times of war. But they were to be sounded also on "days of gladness" (cf. 1 Ch. 13:8; Ps. 98:6), on holidays; at the beginning of each new moon (cf. *šôp̱ār,* above); and over burnt offerings and sacrifices (cf. 2 Ch. 29:26), as a reminder of God's presence among His people. Moreover, the sounding of the trumpets was to be the duty and privilege of the Aaronite priests (v. 8), who exercised it both in war (2 Ch. 13:12; Nu. 31:6) and in sacred ceremonies: at the bringing of the ark to Jerusalem (1 Ch. 15:24; 16:6, 42), at the dedication of Solomon's temple (2 Ch. 5:12; 7:6), and at the dedications of the second temple (Ezr. 3:10) and the wall of Jerusalem (Neh. 12:35, 41).

As the quintessential priestly instrument the trumpet was included among the gold and silver vessels of the temple in 2 K. 12:14 (cf. Nu. 31:6); thus it may be two temple trumpets that are depicted among the spoils of Israel on the Roman arch erected by Titus to commemorate his victory over the Jews (*see* picture in LAMPSTAND). If so, they appear to be somewhat longer than the example described by Josephus, who compares it to the Roman military trumpet: "(Moses) also invented a type of silver trumpet... whose length was a little less than a cubit; it was a narrow tube slightly wider than an *aulós* [pipe]... ending in a bell like [Roman] trumpets" (*Ant.* iii.12.6 [291]). The rough representations of the pair of temple trumpets found on Bar Cochba silver denarii do not permit an accurate assessment of their length.

In twenty-eight of its twenty-nine occurrences *ḥᵃṣōṣᵉrâ* appears in the plural, and it can be assumed that trumpets were sounded in pairs or in larger ensembles, both to magnify their effect and to fulfil the command of Nu. 10:2. Large choirs could also be amassed: at the magnificent dedication of Solomon's temple 120 priestly trumpeters joined the Levitical singers "in unison in praise and thanksgiving" (2 Ch. 5:12f.).

Two terms describe the trumpet's blast: *tᵉqîʿâ*, elsewhere describing a "thrust" or "clap," and *tᵉrûʿâ*, referring to a (shouted) alarm. The technical meanings of each remain unclear. According to some rabbinic interpretations *tᵉqîʿâ* refers to a long, sustained tone, while *tᵉrûʿâ* designates a kind of tremolo (see Sendrey, p. 347). Both terms occur in Nu. 10:7: "blow" and "sound an alarm," respectively (NEB "sound a trumpet," "raise a shout").

*4.* For NT *sálpinx*, see II.H.3 below.

*B. Strings.* The commonest term for "musical instruments" in general was *kᵉlê šîr*, lit. "instruments of/for song," virtually always referring to the strings, which provided the chief accompaniment to singing. Despite their relative prominence, however, and the relative richness of comparative information that now exists concerning ancient Near Eastern stringed instruments, the exact identification of at least one of the principal biblical terms still remains problematic. Three fundamentally different classes of instrument invariably come into question.

The lyre had a quadrilateral shape with a framework consisting of a sound box and two uprights, often of unequal length, topped by a yoke or crosspiece. The strings passed over a bridge and were attached either to the base of the sound box or to the bridge itself. The strings were roughly of the same length.

The harp consisted of a sound box from one end of which a neck protruded at a right or oblique angle; the resonator and the neck often appear to be of one piece, frequently curved. A set of strings of unequal lengths stretched from the top of the resonator to the neck.

The ancient lute generally had a relatively small, rounded or quadrilateral sound box, joined to a long, narrow straight neck. Two or three strings were attached to the base of the resonator, passed over a bridge, and ran parallel to the neck. The instrument was often fretted, like the modern guitar.

*1.* The *kinnôr* is the most often mentioned OT stringed instrument, and the term itself was used widely throughout the ancient Near East. This is David's "harp," although it is now generally considered to a type of lyre.

The RSV translates "lyre" in nearly all occurrences, but "harp" in Ps. 150:3 and Isa. 23:16, (NEB and AV usually "harp"; AV also "psaltery" in Ps. 33:3). The LXX usually either borrows from the Hebrew *(kinýra)* in Samuel, Kings, Chronicles, and Nehemiah, or identifies *kinnôr* with the Greek *kithára*-lyre; the LXX also uses *psaltḗrion* (Gen. 4:21; Ps. 49:5; 83:3; 149:3) and *órganon* "instrument" (Ps. 137:2). The Vulg. has mostly *cithara* but also *lyra* (1 Ch. 15:16; 16:5), *psalterium* (Ps. 49:5; 149:3), and *organum* (Ps. 137:2), following the LXX.

The word's origin is uncertain. It has been connected etymologically with the Persian-Arabic word for lotus-wood *(kunar)*, from whose wood other ancient instruments are known to have been constructed. Its first attestation is in Ebla cuneiform lexical lists (G. Pettinato, *Materiali epigrafici di Ebla*, 4 [1982], 264, no. 572), spelled *gi-na-ru₁₂-um, gi-na-lum, gi-na-rúm*, and equated there with Sum. balaĝ, normally "harp" but perhaps also, by extension, "resonating object." It reappears much later as Akk. *kinnāru* (with wood determinative) in Mari texts dated to the reign of Zimri-Lim (*ca.* 1775 B.C.), whose diplomatic missions included all the princely courts of Syria. One text (*ARM*, XIII [1964], 20) records the shipment of two of five *kinnāru* ordered by the king. In another text (*ARM*, XXI [1983], 298) hides of an exotic animal *(šinuntum)* are issued for the fabrication of temple and palace furnishings, including a variety of "musicians' instruments": 3 *kinnāru*, a "Dilmun-instrument," and a *šepītum*-instrument (elsewhere equated with Sum. ĝiš.balaĝ.tur, "small harp"). It is often attested in Ugaritic as *knr* (once equated with a divinized Akk. *kinnāru* in a bilingual list of gods). It occurs in the Hurrian term LÚ.*kinnaruhuli*, "lyre player/maker" (D. J. Wiseman, *Alalakh Tablets* [1953], no. 172, line 7); in LÚ.*kinirtalla-*, a Hittite term for a kind of musician; and in Ramesside Egypt as *kn-ỉnỉw-rw*.

A good number of illustrations of the West Semitic lyre exist for the biblical period, including the well-known, early nineteenth-century fresco in an Egyptian tomb at Beni-hasan depicting a lyre-player among "Amorite" nomads entering Egypt (*see* picture in BELLOWS); lyre-players on an ivory panel (*see* picture in MEGIDDO) and a "Philistine" jug from Megiddo (12th and 11th cents.); lyre-players among prisoners from Lachish on an Assyrian relief depicting Sennacherib's conquests in Israel (early 7th cent.); and the two types of lyres on Bar Cochba coins (A.D. 132-135) that are thought to represent temple instruments. A seal (*ca.* 7th cent. B.C.) published in 1978 features an elegantly curved twelve-stringed lyre accompanied by the Hebrew inscription, "Belonging to Maʿadanah, the king's daughter" (see N. Avigad, *IEJ*, 28 [1978], 148, for a summary of lyre illustrations).

The illustrations mostly depict a portable, rectangular or trapezoidal instrument, held out from the body at an angle of forty-five to ninety degrees, often with asymmetrical arms, the upper being longer and sometimes curved, and with an average of eight to nine strings. The chief exceptions are the two instruments on the Bar Cochba coins, one of which closely resembles the rounded Greek *kithára*. If the two instruments are truly meant to commemorate sacred instruments in use in the late days of the second temple, then the LXX's treatment of the *kinnôr* may reflect a memory of changes in the shape of temple lyres: an older instrument in use in the time of the historical books, for which the original term was retained *(kinýra)*, and later instruments, more Hellenic in style, for which the translation *kithára* was more accurate. The term has come into English both as "guitar" and "zither," and an early type of guitar *(guitare,* or *gittern/cittern/cithern)* is shown in the hands of David or others of his musicians in medieval Psalteries or on architectural reliefs

Musicians at a banquet. From left to right: harp player (singing), lute player (singing) with plectrum, double-pipe player. From the tomb of Amenemhet, 15th cent. B.C. (Oriental Institute, University of Chicago)

(see M. Remnant and R. Marks, "A Medieval 'Gittern,'" in T. C. Mitchell, ed., *Music and Civilization* [1980], pp. 83-134).

According to Josephus the *kinnôr* had ten strings and was played with a plectrum (*Ant*. vii.12.3 [306]); but David played his lyre "with his hand" when comforting Saul (1 S. 16:23), which suggests that the *kinnôr* was also plucked in order to produce a softer, more soothing sound. The pictorial remains show lyre players with and without plectra, and the Gk. *kithára* was played both ways.

The *kinnôr* was played alone, or with other instruments, particularly the *nēḇel* (see next section). Its sound was "sweet" (Ps. 81:3), and it was usually an instrument of joy and celebration, though it was capable of more somber tones (Job 30:31; Isa. 16:11). It was employed at secular festivities (Gen. 31:27; Job 21:12; Isa. 5:11), and it accompanied songs of praise and thanksgiving (Ps. 33:2; 43:4; 92:3; etc.), as well as the ecstasies of itinerant prophets (1 S. 10:5). Its invention is ascribed to Jubal (Gen. 4:21). David is said to have introduced it to the temple service (1 Ch. 15:16), and it was regularly played as part of the Levitical orchestra (2 Ch. 5:12; 9:11; 29:25; Neh. 12:37). With grim irony Isaiah fortells that Assyria's downfall will be accomplished "to the sound of timbrels and lyres" (30:32), and that Tyre will be forgotten like an aged harlot, remembering happier days, who wanders the city making bittersweet music on her lyre (23:16). In the end the joyful sound of the lyre will never again be heard either in Assyria or in Tyre (Isa. 24:8; Ezk. 26:13).

*2*. The identification of the *nēḇel* (also *neḇel; k*$^{e}$*lî-neḇel*), the second commonest OT stringed instrument, remains problematic. It was most likely a variety of lyre or harp (hence RSV "harp," also "lute" [Ps. 150:3]; cf. NEB "lute"; AV "psaltery," also "viol" [Isa. 5:12; 14:11; Am. 5:23; 6:5]). The LXX treats *nēḇel* much as it does *kinnôr*. In the historical books (Samuel, Kings, Chronicles) the original term was retained as *nábla;* other, newer terms appear elsewhere: *psaltḗrion* (in Nehemiah, Psalms, Isaiah), *órganon* (Am. 5:23; 6:5), and *kithára* (Ps. 81:2). The Vulg. gives *nablium* in 1 Ch. 15:16; 16:5; 20:28, but otherwise mostly *psalterium;* also *lyra* (2 S. 6:5; 1 K. 10:2; Isa. 5:12; Am. 5:23) and *cithara* with the LXX in Ps. 81:2. Both the LXX and Vulg. paraphrase or misunderstand Ps. 71:22 and Isa. 14:11.

In extramusical use *nēḇel* signifies a clay or skin storage vessel for liquids or cereals, from whose shape the musical instrument may have gotten its name; this, in fact, may be the implication behind the unique expression *k*$^{e}$*lî-neḇel*, "*neḇel*-instrument," of Ps. 71:22 (contrast *k*$^{e}$*lê han-n*$^{e}$*ḇālîm*, "*neḇel*-vessels," in Isa. 22:24). In its musical sense both it and Gk. *nábla* may also have been borrowings from a third language. Sopater (*ca*. 300 B.C.), quoted by Athenaeus (*Deipnosophistai* iv.175b), mentions the "Sidonian *nabla*," suggesting the possibility of a Phoenician origin. According to Eusebius (cf. Sendrey, p. 278) it came from Assyria via the Cappadocians, although no such term is as yet attested in Akkadian.

In early usage Gk. *psaltḗrion* was a general term for harplike instruments that were plucked *(psállein)* rather than played with a plectrum (H. Roberts, "Technique of Playing Ancient Greek Instruments of the Lyre Type," in T. C. Mitchell, ed., *Music and Civilization* [1980], p. 44); *órganon* signified any "instrument." Sopater (*op. cit.*, 175c) describes the *nábla* as an inelegant instrument, with lotus wood fixed in its ribs causing it to give forth "breathy music." In Bayer's view (*Yuval*, pp. 114f.) the LXX, continuing the "conservative" policy adopted for the *kinnôr*, retained the term in the historical books, but in view of the *nábla*'s poor contemporary reputation, substituted more neutral terms elsewhere.

The *nēḇel* is virtually always mentioned together with the *kinnôr*-lyre, and must have had a similar or at least complementary character. Comparing the two, the Mishnah states that the strings of the *nēḇel* were made of a sheep's large intestine, those of the *kinnôr* of its small intestine (*Kinnim* iii.6). Having thicker strings, the instrument's register was therefore presumably lower and its sound possibly louder than that of the *kinnôr,* the latter confirmed by T.B. *Arakhin* 13b. Moreover, since it was louder, the *nēḇel* had to be matched with additional lyres when played in ensembles: "no fewer than two *n*ᵉ*ḇālîm* and no more than six," but "never fewer than six *kinnôrôṯ*, and more may be added" (Mish. *Arakhin* ii.2, 5). A *nēḇel ʿāśôr,* "ten(-stringed) *nēḇel,*" appears in Ps. 33:2; 144:9 (and, personified, in 1QM 4:4f.), while Ps. 92:3 (MT 4) has *ʿ*ᵃ*lê-ʿāśôr waʿ*ᵃ*lê-nāḇel,* "upon the 10 (-stringed instrument) and upon the *nēḇel,*" suggesting that the *nēḇel* usually had other than ten strings. According to Josephus the *kinnôr* had ten strings and was played with a plectrum, while the *nēḇel* had twelve tones *(phthóngous)* and was played with the fingers (*Ant.* vii.12.3 [306]); T.J. *Sukkah* 5:6 states merely that the *nēḇel* had more strings than the *kinnôr*.

Somewhat more useful is the general agreement among the early Church fathers that the *psalterium (nēḇel)* had its resonator "on the upper part," the *cithara (kinnôr)* "on the lower part" (Jerome, Augustine, Isidorus), and that the *psalterium* sounded or was played "from above," not "from below" like the *cithara*. While several explanations have been advanced, this description could fit the vertical angular harp, whose resonator extends above the player's head and whose strings descend diagonally to a neck jutting out from the body at an approximate right angle. This sort of harp, played without plectrum, was in common use in Mesopotamia after the beginning of the 2nd millennium, alongside a horizontal variety that was played with a long rodlike plectrum; it also existed in Egypt.

Bayer (*Yuval,* pp. 130f.) has offered a more intriguing solution. One of the two lyres depicted on the Bar Cochba coins is a three-stringed, rounded, Greco-Roman *kithára,* presumably representing a late style of sacred *kinnôr*. The second lyre is somewhat larger and of an unusual design. The arms, which curve outward and resemble animal horns, protrude from a sausage-shaped sack. Three to six strings end at a kind of elliptical holder located *above* the pouchlike body, rather than at a conventional bridge or at the bottom of the instrument. The second Bar Cochba lyre thus demonstrates all of the known main features of the *nēḇel:* it resembles the *kinnôr-kithára* but is somewhat larger; it has a (symbolically) larger number of strings that appear to be attached above the resonator, like those of a harp; and like some varieties of harps and lyres its resonator is covered with leather and resembles a *nēḇel*-"waterskin." Kilmer (*Reallexikon,* VI, 574) compared the Akk. *tungallu*-instrument (< Sum. tùn-gal, "large sack/container" [with wood determinative!]).

As the *nēḇel* is usually found together with the *kinnôr,* the occasions for its use were similar: secular celebrations, the rendering of joyful praise and thanksgiving, and temple ritual.

*3.* The term *ʿāśôr,* lit. "ten," appears only in Psalms, twice describing the *nēḇel* (33:2; 144:9). The RSV translates it as "ten-stringed harp"; the NEB, "ten-stringed lute"; and the AV, "instrument of ten strings." Once *ʿāśôr* occurs together with *nēḇel* (Ps. 92:3; RSV "lute": NEB and AV as above). If it is indeed a separate, distinct instrument in Ps. 92, it is probably best regarded as a ten-stringed variety of *nēḇel;* there is no substantive evidence for "lute" or "zither" (the latter proposed by C. Sachs, *History of Musical Instruments* [1940], p. 117). *Nēḇel ʿāśôr* also occurs in 1QM 4:4f., personified as a group of ten men.

*4.* For the Aram. *qayṯ*ᵉ*rōs, ś/sabb*ᵉ*ḵā',* and *psanṯ/ṭērîn* of Dnl. 3:5, 7, etc., see II.G.3-5 below.

*C. Woodwinds.* Two classes of woodwind were known throughout the ancient Near East: the vertical end-blown flute, and the single- or double-reed shawm, ancestors of the modern clarinet and oboe, which were usually played in pairs. The true flute, usually made of reed, was a pastoral instrument, with a soft, breathy voice. The louder, more penetrating shawms, made of reed, wood, or metal, were better able to hold their own in orchestral ensembles.

*1.* The *ḥālîl* was a variety of *aulós,* either a double clarinet or a double oboe. It appears in 1 S. 10:5; 1 K. 1:40; Isa. 5:12; 30:29; and Jer. 48:36. The RSV renders it "flute," also "pipe"; the NEB, "(reed-)pipe," also "fife"; and the AV "pipe." The LXX translates it as *aulós* (except 1 K. 1:40, *echóreuon en choroís,* "dancing dances"), and the Vulg. as *tibia*.

The word may originally have referred to the buzzing sound of a reed instrument. It is commonly derived from Heb. *ḥll,* "to pierce, wound." Compare, however, Akk. *halālu,* which describes not only the sound of an Akk.

Flute player. Fragment of an alabaster relief from Nineveh (*ca.* 650 B.C.) (Staatliche Museen zu Berlin, DDR)

*malīlu*-shawm, but also the wheezing or whistling of ailing lungs, the cooing of doves, and the bubbling of a spring.

The double clarinet or double oboe was in widespread use throughout the ancient Near East.

A marble statuette of a double pipe player found on the island of Keros (2200-2000 B.C.) provides the first illustration of an Aegean *aulós* (B. Aign, *Die Geschichte der Musikinstrumente des ägäischen Raumes bis um 700 vor Christus* [1963], p. 34). The classic Greek instrument consisted of two separate pipes, usually of equal length, originally of reed or bone but later of wood or ivory. At the end of each pipe was a bulbous mouthpiece that held a single or, less commonly, a double reed. The pipes usually had three to five finger holes (more in later Roman examples) and were played simultaneously, held at an acute angle, often with the help of a band *(phorbeía)* that encircled the player's neck and compressed his lips and cheeks. Opinions differ as to whether the pipes were played in unison or one served as a drone; polyphony is usually ruled out.

At least three double clarinets and nearly seventy oboe pipes have been found in Egyptian excavations (L. Manniche, *Ancient Egyptian Musical Instruments* [1975], pp. 18ff.).

The double clarinet *(mmt)* was constructed of two parallel pipes of equal length (average 28 cm. [11 in.]) joined together with cloth and resin. Each tube had its own mouthpiece containing a single reed. The extant examples show four or six finger holes placed directly opposite each other, with sufficient differences as to produce slightly different scales. One finger covered two holes simultaneously, to produce, in Manniche's view, intentionally slightly discordant unison tones.

The double oboe (*wdnî*[?]) also consisted of two reed pipes, slightly thinner and frequently longer than those of the clarinet: each mouthpiece held a double reed. Like the Gk. *aulós,* the pipes were not joined together but were played as separate integral instruments, held either at an angle or almost parallel. Finger holes number from three to eleven, and some pipes show as many as three thumb holes on the back. Resinous paste was used to fill certain holes, either to change a pipe's intonation or, possibly to produce a tuneable drone. Perforated metal bands rotated by small knobs served the same function on Roman instruments.

Representations of the Egyptian double clarinet are limited to the period of the Old Kingdom (*ca.* 2686-2160 B.C.); the double oboe appears at the beginning of the New Kingdom (*ca.* 1558 B.C.) and continues until the time of Augustus. The double clarinet was apparently played only by men, while the double oboe was played mainly by women; both were common in orchestral ensembles.

Two thin silver pipes, one with four finger holes, the other with only one (a variable drone?), were found in the royal graves at Ur (*ca.* 2650 B.C.); otherwise, Mesopotamian representations of double pipes first begin with a late 3rd millennium Akkadian cylinder seal, and continue into the 1st millennium B.C.

Palestinian illustrations include a *ḥālîl* player together with a dancing girl on a late thirteenth-century ivory box from Tell el-Fâr'ah (Sharuhen), and a female *ḥālîl* player on a bronze lamp from Megiddo (9th cent. ?).

The *ḥālîl* was primarily a secular instrument. After the sounding of the sacred *šôpār* at Solomon's coronation, "all the people went up after him, playing on *ḥ$^a$lilîm,* and rejoicing with great joy" (1 K. 1:39f.). It accompanied drunken revelry (Isa. 5:12), the beginning of a joyous pilgrimage (Isa. 30:29), and the ecstasies of wandering prophets (1 S. 10:5). Children dance to the piping of the *aulós* in Mt. 11:7 (par. Lk. 7:32). The plaintive, nasal tone of the *ḥālîl* also made it a fitting instrument for lamentation. Jeremiah's heart moaned for Moab like *ḥ$^a$lilîm* (48:36), and *aulós* players accompanied the mourning in Mt. 9:23.

The *ḥālîl* was not a regular temple instrument, but according to the Mishnah it was played before the altar twelve days in the year: at the Passover sacrifices, on the first day of Passover, at Pentecost, and on the eight days of the Feast of Tabernacles. A reed, rather than bronze, pipe *('abbûḇ)* was used because its sound was sweeter; and the music ended with only a single pipe playing to produce a nicer effect (Mish. *Arakhin* ii.3). The *ḥālîl* was also employed at the Water Drawing Festival (T.J. *Sukkah* 5:1) and during the harvest procession to Jerusalem (Mish. *Bikkurim* iii.3f.).

Like a modern oboist, the pipe player must have carried a supply of extra reeds with him. The money box in which Judas Iscariot kept the disciples' funds was a *glōssókonon,* originally a small case for a piper's spare reeds (Jn. 12:6; 13:29).

*2.* The nature of the *'ûgāḇ* is still unclear. Some evidence favors a stringed instrument, but it is mostly considered a type of pipe, perhaps a true end-blown flute, for which no other term is known. It occurs only four times (Gen. 4:21; Job 21:12; 30:31; Ps. 150:4). The RSV translates it as "pipe"; the NEB,"flute," and the AV, "organ" (< LXX and Vulg.), but both AV and NEB also "pipe" in Genesis.

The Targums consistently translated *'ûgāḇ* by *'abbûḇā'*. According to Mish. *Arakhin* ii.3 the *'ûgāḇ* was one of the instruments played in the first temple; but as it was too delicate for constant use it was later replaced by the sturdier *'abbûḇ*. The latter was also apparently used in a technical sense to refer to one of the two tubes of the *ḥālîl* (Bayer, *Encyclopedia Mikra'it,* V, 771). If so, the *'ûgāḇ* might have been a single-tube clarinet or oboe. Compare the Syr. *'abôbā'*, presumably a double pipe, and the female prostitutes who played it *(ambubaiae)* described by Horace (*Satires* i.2) and Suetonius (*Nero* 27). Akk. *ebbūbu*/*embūbu* ( = Sum. GI.GÍD, "long reed," GI.DI.DA, either "single reed" or "reed to be played") was apparently a single-tube pipe or flute; cf. its secondary meaning, "trachea" or "windpipe."

The LXX, on the other hand, seems to have considered the *'ûgāḇ* a stringed instrument. It translates *kithára,* "lyre," in Genesis, *órganon* in Psalms, and *psalmós* in Job, closely paralleled by Pesh. *kinorā',* "lyre," *minē ḥalyāṯā',* "sweet-sounding strings," and *z$^e$mārā',* "(string-) music," respectively. *Órganon* elsewhere translates *k$^e$lê šîr,* "instruments of song" (generally strings), as well as *kinnôr* (Ps. 137:2) and *nēḇel* (Am. 5:23; 6:5); and *psalmós* (< *psállein,* "to pluck"), particularly outside Psalms, always refers directly or indirectly to string music (cf. 1 S. 16:18; 2 S. 23:1; Am. 5:23; etc.). The Vulg. offers only *organum,* "instrument."

Jubal was the father of all who handled *(tōpēś)* the *kinnôr* and *'ûgāḇ* (Gen. 4:21), and the psalmist praises with *minnim,* "strings," and *'ûgāḇ*. The *'ûgāḇ* always occurs together with a stringed instrument, and most have preferred to see a contrast between two fundamentally different classes of instrument. Bayer (*Encyclopedia Mikra'it,* V, 771), however, has followed the lead of LXX, citing the Qumrân version of the apocryphal Ps. 151: "My hands have made the *'ûgāḇ,* my fingers the *kinnôr*" (11QPsAp$^a$151:2), for which the LXX has *órganon* and *psaltērion* respectively, both of which elsewhere translate *kinnôr* and *nēḇel.* Since the text is attributed to David, who is never mentioned in connection with wind instruments, Bayer concluded that the *'ûgāḇ* was a stringed instrument different from the lyre, probably a lute.

*3.* For the Aram. *mašrôqîṯā'* of Dnl. 3:5, 7, etc., see II.G.2 below.

*D. Percussion Instruments. 1.* The *tōp* (onomatopoeic; cf. Ugar. *tp*) was a shallow, round hand drum, consisting of a wooden frame about 25 cm. (10 in.) in diameter covered on one side with a parchment membrane. "Tambourine" is an accurate translation but misleading to the modern reader since, to judge from preserved illustrations, the *tōp* was never provided with the metal jingles found on the modern instrument. The RSV has "timbrel" or "tambourine"; the NEB also "tabor," "drum," and "jingles" (Jer. 31:4); the AV also "tabret."

In Mesopotamia and Egypt the hand drum was a feminine instrument. In Israel, too, the *tōp* seems to have been played mainly by women, despite several instances that might be construed otherwise (2 S. 6:5; 1 Ch. 13:8; etc.). The instrument provided rhythmic accompaniment to singing, dancing, and instrumental music. The prophetess Miriam seized a tambourine and sang of Pharaoh's final defeat, while "all the women went out after her with timbrels and dancing" (Ex. 15:20); Jephthah's daughter greeted his return with "timbrels and dancing" (Jgs. 11:35); and the women of Israel came out to greet Saul singing, dancing, and playing tambourines (1 S. 18:6f.). The *tōp* was played at banquets and other joyous occasions (Isa. 5:12; Jer. 31:4) and, while it was not used in the temple, it could also accompany religious ecstasy (1 S. 10:15) and songs of divine praise (Ps. 81:3; 149:3; 150:4).

Several examples of both round and rectangular Egyptian tambourines are preserved; no such remains have as yet been found in Palestine or Mesopotamia. Sure illustrations of the frame drum begin in Mesopotamia at the beginning of the 2nd millennium B.C., and by *ca.* 700 B.C. the instrument is well represented throughout the entire ancient Near East. Neither the Egyptian barrel-shaped drum nor the Akkadian kettledrum *(lilissu)* had any apparent counterparts in Israel.

*2.* Two synonymous terms for the cymbals were derived from the onomatopoeic root *ṣll,* "to ring, tremble."

*M$^e$ṣiltayim,* the more common term, is a dual: "pair of cymbals." The word also occurs in Ugaritic sources, e.g., Râs Shamrah text 24.254:3f.: *dyšr wyḏmr bknr wṯlb* [cf. Akk. *šulpu,* "reed"] *btp wmṣltm,* "who sings and plays on the lyre and the flute, on the tambourine and cymbals" (J. Nougayrol, *et al., Ugaritica,* V [1968], 552).

*Ṣelṣ$^e$lîm* is a plural, and occurs only in 2 S. 6:5 and Ps. 150:5.

Preserved examples of cymbals have been found at Ugarit, in Egypt, and at numerous sites in Israel dating from the 14th to the 8th cent. B.C. Generally found in pairs, they take the form of round flat plates, 10-15 cm. (4-6 in.) in diameter, with central bowl-like depressions (cf. Gk. *kýmbalon* < *kýmbē* or *kýmbos,* "cup, basin"). They were made of bronze (cf. 1 Ch. 15:19) and were fitted with (iron) finger rings. A terra-cotta female figurine from a Phoenician tomb in Achzib (8th cent.?) shows them held horizontally, presumably played with an up-and-down motion, like the well-known conical Assyrian cymbals.

In Ps. 150:5 the phrases *ṣilṣ$^e$lê-šāma',* "cymbals of (pleasing?) sound," and *ṣilṣ$^e$lê t$^e$rû'â,* "cymbals of alarm" (RSV "sounding cymbals" and "loud clashing cymbals"; NEB and AV vary slightly), are thought to refer to a difference in size or manner of playing. A difference in loudness or of relative pleasantness is certainly implied by the early translations: LXX *kýmbala euḗcha* vs. *alalagmoú,* Vulg. *cymbala bene sonanta* vs. *jubilationis.* Compare Paul's "noisy gong" and "clanging cymbal" in 1 Cor. 13:1 *(chalkós ēchōn . . . kýmbalon alalázon).* Bayer, however, stressed that the size of the cymbals excavated in Palestine remains unchanged over a considerable period of time, even though, by Josephus's time, they may have become larger (*Encyclopedia Mikra'it,* V, 768; cf. *Ant.* vii.12.3 [306]).

Nubian drummer on a wall painting from a Theban tomb (18th Dynasty) (Oriental Institute, University of Chicago)

Cymbals make their first appearance in the Bible in the time of David (1 Ch. 13:8; 2 S. 6:5), who introduced them to the temple (1 Ch. 15:16), assigning responsibility for their use to Asaph and his descendants (1 Ch. 16:5; Ezr. 3:10). Thereafter they remained a Levitical instrument (2 Ch. 5:12f.; 29:25; Neh. 12:27).

*3. M$^e$na'an'îm* (pl. only; < *nw',* "to quiver, shake") were a kind of noisemaker: clappers, rattle, or sistrum. The RSV and NEB have "castanets"; the AV, "cornets." The word occurs only in 2 S. 6:5, among (folk) instruments played at the transfer of the ark to Jerusalem; it was omitted from the second report (1 Ch. 13:8). The LXX, in a confused version of the passage apparently based on an obsolete text, translates *kýmbala.* The Vulg. has *sistra* (< Gk. *seistrón,* "that which is shaken"), which is followed by a number of modern versions. The sistrum originated in Africa and was well known in Egypt and Mesopotamia; but apart from an Egyptian Hathor-headed handle found at Bethel dated to pre-Israelite times (16th or 15th cent. B.C.), no example has been found in Israel.

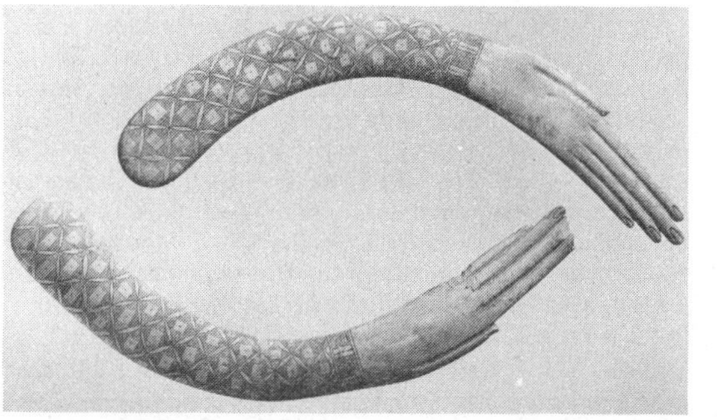

Egyptian (Middle Kingdom) ivory castanets carved into the shape of human arms (Louvre)

On the other hand, fifty-two pottery rattles, averaging 7 cm. (2.7 in.) in length and containing two or three clay balls, have been discovered, dating from the beginning of the 3rd millennium to the 7th cent. B.C. They first appear in temples, later in burial deposits; by the Israelite period they are found in private dwellings and were presumably toys. Their disappearance coincides roughly with the appearance of metal bells, especially in connection with burials (Bayer, *Relics,* pp. 8-14; *Encyclopedia Mikra'it,* V, 766). Bayer suggested that these represent *m^ena^can^cîm,* since in Samuel's time the rattle had not yet apparently become a toy.

*4.* Two kinds of bells or, better, "metal jingles" (true bells with clappers are unknown before the 9th cent. B.C.) are mentioned in the OT. They were not considered musical instruments in the proper sense, but had, instead, an apotropaic, protective function.

*a.* The *pa^camôn* (LXX *kṓdōn;* Vulg. *tintinnabulum*) occurs only in Ex. 28:33f.; 39:25f. Golden bells, alternating with blue, purple, and red cloth pomegranates, were fastened to the bottom of the high priest's robe, which he was always to wear "when he goes into the holy place before the Lord, and when he comes out, lest he die" (Ex. 28:35). The description matches Josephus's later report: "On the fringes hung golden bells alternating with pomegranates, the bells symbolizing thunder and the pomegranates lighting" (*BJ* v.5.7. [231]). Compare the statue of a priest found at Hierapolis/Bambycé in northwest Syria (*ca.* 1st cent. B.C.), wearing a row of bells near the hem of his garment (Bayer, *Relics,* p. 11).

*b.* The *m^eṣillôṯ* (< *ṣll,* "to ring") of Zec. 14:20 were attached to the reins or bridles of horses, whence the LXX *chalinós,* Vulg. *frenum.* They were very likely larger than *pa^camônîm* since they had to carry an inscription, and were probably similar to the bell-shaped jingles on horses in Assyrian reliefs (*see* pictures in BIT; HORSE).

*5.* For the *chalkós ēchṓn* "loud gong," of 1 Cor. 13:1 see II.H.4 below.

*E. Collective Terms. 1.* The generic OT term for "musical instrument" is *k^elî,* "vessel, implement, instrument" (LXX *órganon,* Vulg. *organum);* cf. the parallel use of Akk. *enūtu,* "implement, utensil," in *ARM,* 21 (1983), 298:4, *e-nu-ut* LU.NAR!?. M[EŠ], "musicians' instruments." The term refers in practice to the stringed instruments, the "instruments of David" or "instruments of music" (*k^elê šîr,* "instruments of song"), which frequently stand in contrast to the other sacred instruments, especially the trumpets and cymbals (cf. 1 Ch. 16:42; 2 Ch. 5:13; 7:6; Neh. 12:36; Am. 6:5).

*2.* The term *minnîm* (LXX *chórdai;* Vulg. *chordae*) "strings" (AV also "stringed instruments"), occurs in Ps. 150:4 and, possibly, in Ps. 45:8 (*šel minnî* emended to *k^elê minnîm,* the latter also in Sir. 39:15), "stringed instruments" (cf. NEB "music of strings"; AV omits). The interpretation of *minnîm* (sing. **mēn*) is based upon the LXX and Syr. *minā,* "hair," "cord"; cf. Akk. *manānu,* "sinews." Bayer (*Encyclopedia Mikra'it,* V, 766) suggested "lute" instead, since in Ps. 150:3f. the two chief OT strings are already mentioned, and the lute was not entirely unknown in ancient Israel. But other terms for the lute existed (cf. Akk. *inu;* Arab. *^cūd,* Ugar. *^cd* [?] < Sum. gudi [?]; Arab. *al-^cūd* > Span./Port. *[a]laude,* Ger. *Laute,* Eng. lute?). See Kilmer, *Reallexikon,* VI, 33; D. Collon and A. Kilmer, "The Lute in Ancient Mesopotamia," in T. C. Mitchell, ed., *Music and Civilization* (1980), pp. 15-17.

*F. Uncertain Terms. 1.* The word *šālîšîm* appears only in 1 S. 18:6: "the women came out of all the cities of Israel, singing and dancing, to meet King Saul, with timbrels, with songs of joy, and with instruments of music." The RSV mg. offers "triangles" or "three-stringed instruments." Other suggestions incorporating the meaning of the Hebrew root for "three" *(šlš)* include: three-stringed lute, a triangular harp, castanets held by the thumb and two fingers, and a dance-name (cf. Lat. *tripudium*), whence NEB "dancing." The Vulg. translates *sistra,* and mention has been made of the frequent examples of sistra with three horizontal rods. O. Sellers (*BA,* 4 [1941], 46) noted that there are three beats in each half line of the victory chant sung by the women in the next verse. But the LXX, Pesh., and Tg. all translate "cymbals," and therefore Bayer connected it with Ugar. *ṯlṯ*-metal, suggesting "cymbals or struck-metal bowls" (*Encyclopedia Mikra'it,* V, 775).

*2.* The superscriptions of some psalms include a number of obscure words that have been thought to represent musical instruments, e.g., *gittîṯ, n^egînôṯ, š^emînîṯ.* According to more recent interpretations, however, they are instead technical terms referring to performance styles or other musical categories (see III.B below).

*G. Instruments in Daniel.* In Dnl. 3:5, 7, 10, 15 there appears a list of instruments reportedly used in the court of the Babylonian king Nebuchadrezzar (604-562 B.C.). The first two terms are Aramaic; the remainder are Aramaized versions of Greek words. None of the terms has any known counterpart in Akkadian.

*1. Qarnā'* is the Aramaic form of Heb. *qeren* (see II.A.1 above), "(animal) horn," correctly reflected by the RSV and NEB "horn" and AV "cornet." The LXX and Vulg. (incorrectly) translate (respectively), *sálpinx* and *tuba,* "trumpet." The straight trumpet with mouthpiece is relatively rare in Mesopotamia, seen only on Assyrian reliefs from Nineveh; it was probably an Egyptian import. Depictions of curved horns, however, have been found at Mari (early 2nd millennium), at Alaça Hüyük in Asia Minor, and at Carchemish (early 1st millennium). No musical use is as yet attested for Akk. *qarnu.*

*2.* The *mašrôqîṯā'* (RSV, NEB "pipe"; AV "flute") was possibly a simple reed pipe of the type played by shepherds, whence Vulg. *fietula.* The root (*šrq,* "to whistle, hiss") is also seen in Heb. *š^eriqôṯ ^cadārîm,* "the piping of the flocks," in Jgs. 5:16. The LXX, however, translates *sýrinx,* also a well-known pastoral instrument (cf. Homer, *Il.* x.13; xviii.256). The panpipe may have originated in eastern Europe. An actual set was found in a burial near Mariupol in the south Ukraine (*ca.* 2000 B.C.); the instrument is popular in Rumanian folk orchestras to this day. The syrinx reappears in Aegean representations after the 6th cent. B.C., and in Mesopotamia in the 3rd or 2nd cent. B.C. Thus it is not impossible that the *mašrôqîṯā'* was a variety of multiple flute, particularly if, as has been suggested, the Greek term was originally a Semitic borrowing.

*3.* The *qayṯ^e^rōs* (*Q qîṯārōs* or *qîṯ^e^rōs*) was a type of lyre (so RSV; NEB "zither"; AV "harp"). The word is presumably a borrowing from some phonetic variant of Gk. *kithára* (so LXX; Vulg. *cithara;* see II.B.1 above); cf. Homeric *kítharis* (*Il.* xiii.731; *Od.* i.153), unless both words are derived from some third source. Since the rounded *kithára*-lyre is not attested in Mesopotamia proper, if Daniel's is an accurate report the *qayṯ^e^rōs* may refer to one of the two types of lyre commonly seen on Assyrian reliefs, one rectangular in form, the other asymmetrical.

*4. Ś/sabb^e^ḵā'* is a loan from Gk. *sambýkē* (so LXX; Vulg. *sambuca*), an instrument introduced into Greece in the late 5th cent. B.C., but described as more ancient. Several Greek authors identified it with the *trígōnon,* a small triangular harp with very few strings and a high, bright tone (thus RSV "trigon"; NEB "triangle" [the literal meaning of *trígōnon*]). The AV "sackbut" (a medieval trombone) was evidently chosen based on its slight phonetic resemblance to *śabb^e^ḵā'*. A Greek nautical siege-engine was named after the musical instrument, and from written descriptions of it attempts have been made to reconstruct the shape of the musical instrument. In the majority view the *sambýkē* was a small, arched or boat-shaped harp, with a few short strings and a high pitch. The harp in general was foreign to Greece and considered a somewhat decadent instrument. The *trígōnon* and *sambýkē* in particular were ridiculed and condemned as instruments of debauchery. The boat-shaped harp was at home in Egypt and in early Mesopotamia, but the instrument most resembling it in first-millennium Assyrian sources was the horizontal angular harp played with a plectrum.

*5. Psant/ṭērîn* is a loan from Gk. *psaltērion,* originally signifying the comparatively rare (angular) harp that was plucked *(psállein),* unlike the lyre that was played with a plectrum. Via Lat. *psalterium* it is the source of the medieval psaltery, properly a rectangular or trapezoidal zither, either plucked or played with plectra. The same Greek word, possibly via Aram. *psanterîn,* became the Pers. *santur* and its variants (*santīr, santari,* etc.) a trapezoidal dulcimer played with hammers. Thus the *psanṭērîn* has been described as a boxlike lyre. The varied English translations reflect the long and confusing history of the related terms: RSV "harp"; NEB "dulcimer"; AV "psaltery."

*6.* The last term, *sûmpōn^e^yâ* (*K sîppōn^e^yâ, Q sûppōn^e^yâ* in v. 10; omitted in v. 7), may not be an instrument at all. The LXX gives *symphōnía,* lit. "sounding together," which has been interpreted in two different ways.

Some have assumed that it referred to an instrument that was capable of sounding two notes simultaneously; cf. RSV "bagpipes"' AV "dulcimer." In the late Middle Ages a corruption of the term yielded Ital. *zampogna,* Span. *zampoña,* "bagpipes"; but that instrument is not mentioned in Greece before the 4th cent. B.C.and then not by that name. There is, moreover, no evidence for bagpipes in Mesopotamia at any time.

Others have assumed that the term referred to the sound of several instruments playing at the same time, whence NEB "music." This translation gains contextual support from the single NT occurrence of *symphōnía,* Lk. 15:26: "and as he came and drew near to the house he heard *music* and dancing." It is also in accord with the earliest meaning of the term: "consonance" of sound, specifically of two different tones at intervals of a fourth, fifth, or an octave. If this is the correct interpretation, then *sûmpōn^e^yâ* and the last phrase in the line, "all kinds of (string) playing" *(kōl z^e^nê z^e^mārā'),* are equivalent expressions, and one of them may be a gloss.

On the other hand, it has been suggested that *sûmpōn^e^yâ* may instead be a translation of a dialectal form of Gk. *týmpanon,* "drum" (T. C. Mitchell and R. Joyce, "Musical Instruments in Nebuchadrezzar's Orchestra," in D. J. Wiseman, *et al., Notes on Some Problems in the Book of Daniel* [1965], p. 26). The drum is a particularly characteristic Mesopotamian instrument, and it is otherwise conspicuously absent from Daniel's list. Moreover, the instruments would then follow a neat sequence of classes: a horn, a wind instrument, several strings, ending with a percussion instrument.

*H. NT Instruments.* Only four or perhaps five different instruments are mentioned in the NT: the double pipe, the lyre, the trumpet, the cymbals, and possibly a gong.

*1.* For a description of the Gk. *aulós* (RSV, NEB "flute"; AV "pipe") see II.C.1 above. The instrument occurs only in 1 Cor. 14:7, but "flute players" (AV also "piper" and "minstrels") appear in Mt. 9:23 and Rev. 18:22, and the verb "pipe" (RSV, NEB also "to play") in Mt. 11:17; 1 Cor. 14:7. The playing of the *aulós* is associated both with dancing (Mt. 11:17; 1 Cor. 14:7) and with mourning (Mt. 9:23).

*2.* For a description of the Gk. *kithára,* see II.B.1 above. It appears four times (1 Cor. 14:7; Rev. 5:8; 14:2; 15:2). While there is now no doubt that the *kithára* was a type of lyre, the versions maintain the traditional translation "harp" (NEB once also "lyre" in 1 Corinthians), also for the associated verb and *nomen professionis* (1 Cor. 14:7; Rev. 14:2; 18:22).

*3.* The LXX used Gk. *sálpinx* to translate both Heb. "trumpet," and *šôpār,* "(ram's) horn" (see II.A.1,2 above). In the NT there is no direct evidence favoring one over the other. The instrument itself appears eleven times (Mt. 24:31; 1 Cor. 14:8; 15:52; 1 Thess. 4:16; He. 12:19; Rev. 1:10; etc.); the RSV translates it as "trumpet," also "bugle" (1 Cor. 14:8); the AV also has "trump." The verb and *nomen professionis* appear only in Revelation, Mt. 6:2; 1 Cor. 15:52.

*4.* Cymbals are mentioned only in Paul's musical metaphor in 1 Cor. 13:1: "clanging cymbal" (*kýmbalon alalázon;* cf. AV "tinkling cymbal"). The first member of the comparison *(chalkós ēchōn)* is also usually taken as another type of musical instrument (hence RSV "noisy gong"; NEB "sounding gong"; the AV translates more literally: "sounding brass"). The two phrases might represent a modified quotation of Ps. 150:5 (see II.D.2 above). According to a more recent interpretation, however, *chalkós ēchōn* refers to the brass sounding vases, about 1 m. (3 ft.) tall, tuned musically to roughly the range of an octave, that were placed in niches at the rear of Greek amphitheaters. They resonated sympathetically to various pitches of the actors' voices, providing a primitive but effective acoustic amplification system (see W. Harris, *Biblical Archaeology Review,* 8/1 [1982], 38-41).

***III. Musical Performance.*–*A. Mesopotamian Music Theory.*** Assyriological research since 1960 has led to the discovery of six Akkadian texts that, from a variety of different standpoints, describe Mesopotamian music theory and practice from *ca.* 1800 B.C. to *ca.* 500 B.C. The texts, from different places and times, have shown that the musical scales in general use in ancient Mesopotamia were heptatonic and diatonic, thus providing evidence for the antiquity of Western music some 1400 years before the earliest Greek sources.

Fourteen Akkadian terms, used in the tuning procedures for the lyre, are known to be names of musical intervals — seven for intervals of fifths and fourths, and seven for thirds and sixths.

| String Designations | Fifths and Fourths | |
|---|---|---|
| 1-5 | *nīš gabarî* | "rise of the duplicate" |
| 2-6 | *išartu* | "normal" |
| 3-7 | *embūbu* | "reed-pipe" |
| 4-1 | *nīd qabli* | "fall of the middle" |
| 5-2 | *qablītu* | "middle" |
| 6-3 | *kitmu* | "closed" |
| 7-4 | *pītu* | "open" |
| | **Thirds and Sixths** | |
| 7-5 | *šēru* | "song" |
| 1-6 | *šalšatu* | "third" |
| 2-7 | *rebūtu* | "fourth" |
| 1-3 | *isqu* | "throwstick/lot" |
| 2-4 | *titur qablītu* | "bridge of the middle" |
| 3-5 | *titur išartu* | "bridge of the normal" |
| 4-6 | *serdû* | "lamentation" |

These terms do not indicate differences between major or minor thirds, perfect or augmented fourths, etc.; i.e., they do not reflect the positions of semitones in the scale. These positions depend on the tuning. The seven tunings are:

| | | | | | | | | | Corresponding Greek Octave-Species* |
|---|---|---|---|---|---|---|---|---|---|
| *išartu* | "normal" | E | F | G | A | B | C | D | Dorian |
| *kitmu* | "closed" | E | F♯ | G | A | B | C | D | Hypodorian |
| *embūbu* | "reed-pipe" | E | F♯ | G | A | B | C♯ | D | Phrygian |
| *pītu* | "open" | E | F♯ | G♯ | A | B | C♯ | D | Hypophrygian |
| *nīd qabli* "fall of the middle" | | E | F♯ | G♯ | A | B | C♯ | D♯ | Lydian (= our major scale) |
| *nīš gabari* "rise of the duplicate" | | E | F♯ | G♯ | A♯ | B♯ | C♯ | D♯ | Hypolydian |
| *qablītu* | "middle" | E♯ | F♯ | G♯ | A♯ | B♯ | C♯ | D♯ | Mixolydian |

(*Contrast R. Vitale's different interpretation, "La Musique suméro-akkadienne — Gamme et Notation musicale," *Ugarit-Forschungen,* 14 [1982], 241-263.)

Tuning of the lyre was accomplished by a progressive series of fifths and fourths, which produced a diatonic scale in Pythagorean tuning. Each tuning or scale was named for the fifth or fourth that began the series; in each tuning the tritone was located in a different place, which also altered the locations of the semitones.

One complete piece of music, a syllabic cuneiform Hurrian cult hymn to the moon-goddess Nikkal dating to *ca.* 1400 B.C., has been found at ancient Ugarit. Its Akkadian colophon identifies it as follows: "This is a song of the Fall-of-the-Middle (scale), a hymn(?) of the gods, from Urhiya; copied by Ammurapi." This piece, written in the *nīd qabli* ( = major) scale, uses a notational system based on the Akkadian terminology discussed above. No directions for rhythm or tempo are given. The Hurrian lyrics are provided separately, followed by the notation, which consists of interval names followed by numerals. There are several differing interpretations of this notation; see A. Kilmer, *et al., Sounds from Silence: Recent Discoveries in Ancient Near Eastern Music* (1976), p. 14, for an explanation of the basic differences in existing interpretations; cf. M. Duchesne-Guillemin, *Revue d'Assyriologie, 69* (1975), 159-173; R. Vitale, *Ugarit-Forschungen,* 14 (1982), 255-263.

It is of interest to note that a Middle Assyrian song catalog from Asshur (E. Ebeling, *Keilschrifttexte aus Assur Religiösen Inhalts* [1923], no. 158; *ca.* 1100 B.C.), one of the six cuneiform texts that utilize the Akkadian technical musicological terms, lists more than 360 Sumerian and Akkadian song titles, which are divided into thirty-one different song types, ranging from divine and royal hymns to work and love songs. Two of these song types are further divided according to tunings, which is to say that the catalog groups some songs according to the scale or mode in which they were played. This Mesopotamian practice, also exemplified in the colophon of the Hurrian hymn, may have some bearing on the meaning of some of the obscure technical terms in the psalm superscriptions (see next section).

In the Neo-Babylonian period (mid-1st millennium B.C.) a different but related system of notation appears. These notations are placed next to or within the lines of lyrics and apparently signify abbreviated directions (see W. Lambert, "Converse Tablet: A Litany with Musical Instructions," in H. Goedicke, ed., *Near Eastern Studies in Honor of W. F. Albright* [1971], pp. 335-353). This late system is not yet understood.

*B. Psalm Superscriptions.* While it offers nothing so extensive as the full repertory of Sumero-Akkadian technical musical terms, the OT provides good evidence for a developed or developing musical performance terminology. Much of this evidence is to be found in the Psalm superscriptions. (*See also* PSALMS II.C.)

Two-thirds of the Psalms include personal ascriptions in their headings. The majority of the references are to David, the traditional author of the Psalter. The remainder, apart from three Psalms ascribed to Moses or Solomon, mention members of the Levitical families to which David entrusted the responsibility for vocal performances within the temple ritual: the singers Asaph, Heman, and Ethan, and the sons of Korah. Most of the remaining, more properly musical, terms found in the superscriptions may be divided into three categories.

*1. Titles.* These are types, characterizations, or remarks concerning the uses of the compositions:

*Tᵉhillâ,* "song of praise," is applied only to Ps. 145, although it is common in the psalmodic text itself and elsewhere.

*Tᵉpillâ,* the common term for "prayer," is found with four Psalms (17, 90, 102, and 142), also with the "misplaced" psalm in Hab. 3. In the postscript to Ps. 72:20 that and all preceding Psalms are also so identified.

*Mizmôr,* "psalm" (< LXX *psalmós,* "song to the accompaniment of plucked [*psállein*] instruments") is the title of fifty-seven Psalms. The root meaning is "to play (an instrument)" or "to sing (with instrumental accompaniment)"; cf. Akk. *zamāru,* "to sing (with or without instrumental accompaniment)," also a type of song. Note that the colophon of the Hurrian cult hymn from Ugarit (discussed above) employs this term: *annû zammarum,* "this (is) a *zammaru*-song."

*Šîr,* "song," is thought to be derived from Sum. šìr, "song; to sing," either directly or via Akk. *šēru,* "song"; cf. Ugar. *šr.* The term appears alone in Pss. 46 and 18 (var. *šîrâ*), otherwise coupled with *mizmôr* — five times preceding it, four times following it; no distinctions are discernible. The RSV gives "song" in all three cases; the AV translates the linked terms separately. One might compare the Middle Assyrian song catalog mentioned above (see III.A), which lists *šēru*-songs *(zamār šēri)* as a distinct category.

*Šîr hammaʿᵃlôṯ* occurs in Pss. 120–134. The translation "Song of Ascents" (AV "Song of Degrees") relies on the root meaning (*ʿlh,* "to rise, ascend") and on the LXX and Vulg. (respectively, *ōdḗ tṓn anabathmṓn, canticum graduum,* "song of steps"). The term has been thought to refer to songs sung by pilgrims ascending the high city of Jerusalem at the three great agricultural festivals (cf. Ex. 23:17; Dt. 16:16). This set of Psalms is also characterized by an "ascending" structure, in which a verse repeats an element from the preceding verse. Compare the *elēlū sad-*

*rūtu,* "ordered *elēlu*-songs" (i.e., following in a row), another song type from the Middle Assyrian catalog.

*Maśkîl* ( < *śkl,* "to have insight, act with insight") occurs in thirteen Psalms. The meaning remains uncertain; the RSV and AV transliterate rather than translate. The LXX offers *synéseōs* or *eis sýnesin,* "on insight, understanding"; the Vulg., *intellectus* or *intelligentia.* The term also occurs in Ps. 47, where the RSV has "psalm," the NEB "art," and the AV "understanding." (*See also* MASKIL.)

*Miḵtām* (Pss. 16, 56–60) is also obscure, and is left untranslated by the RSV and AV. The LXX has *stēlographía,* "inscription"; the Vulg., *tituli inscriptio.* The term is generally derived from the root *ktm,* "to conceal, secrete." Compare the cognate Akkadian musicological term *kitmu,* "closed," which is known to refer to hymns to be played or sung in a particular tuning or scale (see III.A above). (*see also* MIKTAM.)

*L^e^lammēḏ,* "for instruction" (AV "to teach"), occurs only in the heading of Ps. 60. The implications of the expression are unclear.

*L^e^hazkîr,* lit. "to cause to remember," may be a request for divine remembrance on the part of the psalmist, or a reference to a certain sacrificial ceremony. It occurs only in Pss. 38 and 70 (RSV "for the memorial offering"; AV "to bring to remembrance").

*Šiggāyôn* in Ps. 7 is thought to be related to Akk. *šigû,* a cry of woe or lamentation, also a type of prayer (cf. LXX *psalmós;* Vulg. *psalmus*). The term also appears in the heading of Hab. 3: "upon, or in the manner of (?), laments" (*ʿal šigyōnôṯ;* LXX *metá ōdḗs,* "with a song"). The RSV and AV simply transliterate.

*Šîr ḥ^a^nukkaṯ habbayiṯ,* "song at the dedication of the house" (Ps. 30), and *šîr y^e^ḏîḏôṯ,* "love song" (Ps. 45), may refer to psalms recited at special occasions: dedications or rededications of the temple, and, perhaps weddings.

2. *Performance Indications.* Some enigmatic terms bear directly on musical practice and may well have been relatively obscure even at the time of the LXX.

*Lamm^e^naṣṣē(a)ḥ,* "to the choirmaster" (AV "chief musician"), occurs in the Psalm heading fifty-five times, and again in the subscript of Hab. 3. The piel of *nṣḥ* has the significance "to act as overseer, director" (e.g., 1 Ch. 23:4; Ezr. 3:8f.), and in a musical context it occurs in 1 Ch. 15:21, where Mattithiah and five other Levitical musicians are directed by David "to lead with lyres." The office seems to be described in 1 Ch. 15:27, where the Levite Chenaniah is called "leader of the music of the singers" (*haśśar hammaśśāʾ ham^e^šōr^e^rîm;* NEB "precentor"; AV "master of the song with the singers"); he was David's choice (v. 22) to "direct the music [*yāśōr bammaśśāʾ*], for he understood it." *Lamm^e^naṣṣē(a)ḥ* may well refer to solo performance by the director himself.

*N^e^gînôṯ* (*n^e^gînaṯ* in Ps. 61), "(with) stringed instruments" (AV "[upon] Neginoth"), as a technical term in the superscriptions is not entirely clear. "Stringed instrument" is one meaning of the term ( < *ngn,* "to play on a stringed instrument"), but elsewhere it can also refer to music or songs (Isa. 38:20; Lam. 5:14), including a mocking song (Job 30:9) and a drunkard's song (Ps. 69:12 [MT 13]). Its use in the psalm headings is reminiscent of that of the Sumerian hymnic subscript zà-mí, "lyre," also "praise," a label for songs of divine praise which lack any special formal structure. It is unknown whether the hymns so labeled were actually performed to the accompaniment of the lyre; the same might be said for *n^e^gînôṯ* (*see* NEGINAH). Cf. Akk. *nigûtu,* "music" ( < *nagû,* "to sing joyously").

*ʿ^a^lāmôṯ* (Ps. 46) and *š^e^mînîṯ* (Pss. 6 and 12) may possibly refer to instrumental tunings or pitches. The terms occur in 1 Ch. 15:20f. David designated one group of string players "to play harps according to Alamoth" (*ʿal-ʿ^a^lāmôṯ*) and another "to lead with lyres according to the Sheminith" (*ʿal-haššᵉmînîṯ l^e^naṣṣē[a]ḥ*). *ʿ^a^lāmôṯ* has been connected with *ʿalmâ,* "young woman," and the expression interpreted as "in the style of young female voices," perhaps referring to a soprano register. *Š^e^mînîṯ* (lit. "eighth") has been taken as an eight-stringed instrument or the "eighth mode." Since the heptatonic scale is now known to have been in common use both in Mesopotamia and in Ugarit (see III.A above), the older interpretation "eighth tone" or "octave" is now less unlikely. *ʿAl-ʿ^a^lāmôṯ* may thus refer to a particular harp tuning, and *ʿal-haššᵉmînîṯ* to a punctuating of the melody line an octave higher on the smaller lyres. The RSV and AV transliterate. (*See also* SHEMINITH.)

*ʾEl-māḥ^a^laṯ* (Pss. 53 and 88) is obscure. If related to *māḥôl,* "round dance," it may represent either a characteristic rhythmic or melodic pattern, or even a choreographic direction. In Ps. 88 it is followed by *l^e^ʿannôṯ,* which has been connected either with *ʿnh,* "to sing, wail," therefore "to be sung (in some particular way)"; or with *ʿnh,* "to humble, oppress," therefore, perhaps, "to perform with a reduced sound, 'piano'." The RSV and AV (also LXX and Vulg.) again transliterate. *See also* MAHALATH (LEANNOTH).

*N^e^ḥîlôṯ* (Ps. 5) is usually connected with *ḥālîl,* "double pipe" (see II.C.1 above), and therefore thought to refer to a piped accompaniment: hence RSV "for the flutes" (AV transliterates). The term, however, is still unclear (*see* NEHILOTH). Cf. LXX *hypér tēs klēronomoúsēs,* "on behalf of the heirs." Note, for the sake of comparison, the Akkadian technical term *embūbu,* "reed pipe," used to describe a tuning/scale/mode of certain songs (see III.A above).

*Gittîṯ* (Pss. 8, 81, and 84) is often linked with the city of Gath (*gaṯ*); the heading *ʿal-haggittîṯ* would thus signify "in the style of Gath," or "upon the instrument-of-Gath," since place names are not infrequently associated with musical instruments. Another possible source of the term is *gaṯ,* "wine-press," followed by LXX *hypér tṓn lēnṓn* and Vulg. *pro torcularibus,* "for the pressers/treaders of wine." The RSV and AV again transliterate. It is probably not productive to compare the Akkadian term occurring in the Middle Assyrian song catalog (see above) describing a special song type: *gangiṭṭu,* possibly derived in part from Sum. gíd-da ( > Akk. *giṭṭu,* "long"); or to connect it with ancient Egyp. *gngnti,* "lute"(?).

3. *Song Cues.* A number of superscripts represent *incipits* of favorite older songs, to whose tunes new lyrics were sung — a practice common to hymnology up to the present day. These include:

*ʿAl-mûṯ labbēn* (Ps. 9); obscure, perhaps for *ʿal-ʿ^a^lāmôṯ labbēn,* "upon maidens; to the son." Cf. LXX *hypēr tṓn kryphíōn toú hyioú;* Vulg. *pro occultis filii,* "for the son's secret." *See* MUTH-LABBEN.

*ʿAl-ʾayyeleṯ haššaḥar* (Ps. 22), "upon hind of the dawn." *See* HIND OF THE DAWN, THE.

*ʿAl-yônaṯ ʾēlem r^e^ḥōqîm* (Ps. 56), "upon dove on far-off terebinths."

*ʿAl-šōšannîm* (Pss. 45, 69, and 80), "upon lilies." *See* LILIES (ACCORDING TO).

*ʿAl-šûšan ʿēḏûṯ* (Ps. 60), "upon lily of the testimony(?)." Cf. Ps. 85, *ʾel-šōšannîm ʿēḏûṯ l^e^ʾāsāp,* "upon lilies; testimony(?) to Asaph." Ps. 60 may consequently represent an abbreviation; the RSV and AV transliterate. *See* EDUTH.

*ʾAl tašḥēṯ* (Pss. 57–59, 75), "do not destroy" — thought to refer to a category of penitential prayer for divine clemency; cf. Moses' prayer in Dt. 9:26. *See* AL-TASCHITH.

The term *selâ* (RSV, AV "Selah") occurs seventy-four times in the psalter and in Hab. 3, not as a superscription but at points within the texts (70 times) and at the ends (4 times). It probably indicates a pause in the singing (cf. LXX *diápsalma;* Vulg. omits), possibly signaled by the sounding of cymbals. The pauses may mark points at which differing groups take up the song, or possibly occasions for musical interludes. In Ps. 9:16 (MT 17) *selâ* is preceded by the term *higgāyôn,* perhaps signifying a kind of low "murmuring" (*hgh*) on the strings. Cf. Ps. 92:3, *ʿ$^a$lê higgāyôn b$^e$ḵinnôr;* RSV "to the melody of the lyre"; NEB "to the sounding chords of the lyre"; AV "upon the harp with a solemn sound."

***Bibliography.***–H. Avenary, *Encounters of East and West in Music — Selected Writings* (1979); R. D. Barnett, *Iraq,* 31 (1969), 96-103; B. Bayer, *Material Relics of Music in Ancient Palestine and its Environs* (1963); *Biblical Archaeology Review,* 8/1 (1982), 20-33; *Yuval,* 1 (1968), 89-131; *DBSup.,* V (1956), *s.v.* "Musique de la bible" (E. Gerson-Kiwi); L. Delekat, *ZAW,* 76 (1964), 280-297; F. Ellermeier, "Beiträge zur Frühgeschichte altorientalischer Saiteninstrumente," in A. Kuschke and E. Kutsch, eds., *Archäologie und AT* (*Festschrift* K. Galling; 1970), pp. 75-90; *Encyclopedia Judaica* (1972), XII, *s.v.* (H. Avenary and B. Bayer); *Encyclopedia Mikra'it,* V (1967), *s.v.* (B. Bayer); S. B. Finesinger, *HUCA,* 3 (1926), 21-77; 8-9 (1931/32), 193-228; E. Gerson-Kiwi, *Studia Musicologica,* 7 (1965), 61-70; P. Grelot, *VT,* 29 (1979), 23-38; H. Gressman, *Musik und Musikinstrumente im AT* (1903); S. Haik Vantoura, *La Musique de la Bible Révélée* (1976); H. Hartmann, *Die Musik der sumerischen Kultur* (1960); E. Kolari, *Musikinstrumente und ihre Verwendung im AT* (1947); J. C. Landels, *Journal of Hellenic Studies,* 86 (1966), 69-77; *Lexikon der Ägyptologie,* IV (1982), *s.v.* "Musik," "Musiker," "Musikinstrumente," "Musikleben," "Musik, Militär-" (E. Hickmann); J. W. McKinnon, *Music in the Ancient World* (1971); T. C. Mitchell, "An Assyrian Stringed Instrument," in *Music and Civilization* (1980), pp. 33-42; *New Grove Dictionary of Music and Musicians* (1980), I, *s.v.* "Aulos"; IV, *s.v.* "Christian Church, Music of the Early"; IX, *s.v.* "Jewish Music I"; XI, *s.v.* "Lyre"; XV, *s.v.* "Psaltery"; XVI, *s.v.* "Sambuca"; XIX, *s.v.* "Trigonon"; *New Oxford History of Music* (1957), I, *s.v.* "Music in the Bible" (C. H. Kraeling and L. Mowry); R. North, *JBL,* 83 (1964), 372-389; *Reallexikon der Assyriologie,* IV (1973), *s.v.* "Harfe" (W. Stauder); VI (1983), *s.v.* "Laute. A. Philologisch" (A. D. Kilmer); "Leier. A. Philologisch" (A. D. Kilmer); "Laute. B. Archäologisch" (D. Collon); "Leier. B. Archäologisch" (D. Collon); *RGG,* IV (1960), *s.v.* "Instrumentale Musik, Gesang und Dichtung in Israel" (C. Westermann); J. Rimmer, *Ancient Musical Instruments of Western Asia in the British Museum* (1969); A. M. Rothmeuller, *Music of the Jews* (1967); H. H. Rowley, "Psalmody and Music," in *Worship in Ancient Israel* (1967), pp. 176-212; C. Schmidt-Colinet, *Die Musikinstrumente in der Kunst des alten Orients* (1981); H. Seidel, *VT,* 33 (1983), 503-509; A. Sendrey *Music in Ancient Israel* (1969); J. A. Smith, *Music and Letters,* 65 (1984), 1-16; W. S. Smith, *Musical Aspects of the NT* (1962); J. A. Soggin, *VT,* 14 (1964), 374-77; A. Spycket, *Journal des Savants* (1972), 153-209; W. Stauder, *Die Harfen und Leiern der Sumerer* (1957); *Die Harfen und Leier Vorderasiens in babylonischer und assyrischer Zeit* (1961); *TDNT,* V, *s.v.* σάλπιγξ κτλ. (G. Friedrich); *THAT,* II, *s.v.* שיר (R. Ficker); L. Vorreiter, *Die schönsten Musikinstrumente des Altertums* (1983); E. Werner, *Musical Quarterly,* 43 (1957), 21-37; *Sacred Bridge* (1959); D. Wohlenberg, *Kultmusik in Israel. Eine Forschungsgeschichtliche Untersuchung* (1967); D. Wulstan, *Studies in Eastern Chant,* II (1971), 5-20; *Galpin Society Journal,* 26 (1973), 29-46.

*Mesopotamian Musical Theory:* M. Bielitz, *Orientalia,* 39 (1970), 152-56; R. Crocker, *Orientalia,* 47 (1978), 99-104; R. Crocker and A. D. Kilmer, *Iraq,* 46 (1984), 81-85; M. Duchesne-Guillemin, "Note complémentaire sur la Découverte de la Gamme babylonienne," in *Studies in Honor of Benno Landsberger* (1965), pp. 268-272; *Revue de Musicologie,* 49 (1963), 3-17; 52 (1966), 147-162; 55 (1969), 3-11; O. Gurney, *Iraq,* 30 (1968), 229-233; H. G. Güterbock, *Revue d'Assyriologie,* 64 (1970), 45-52; A. D. Kilmer, "The Strings of Musical Instruments: Their Names, Numbers, and Significance," in H. G. Güterbock and T. Jacobsen, eds., *Studies in Honor of Benno Landsberger* (1965), pp. 261-68; *Proceedings of the American Philosophical Society,* 115 (1971), 131-149; *Revue d'Assyriologie,* 68 (1974), 69-82; *Iraq,* 46 (1984), 69-80; H. M. Kümmel, *Orientalia,* 29 (1970), 252-263; H. Shanks, ed., *Biblical Archaelology Review,* 6/5 (1980), 14-25; A. Shaffer, *Iraq,* 43 (1963), 39-50; D. Wulstan, *Iraq,* 30 (1968), 215-228; *Music and Letters,* 52 (1971), 365-382; *Revue d'Assyriologie,* 68 (1974), 125-28.

D. A. FOXVOG A. D. KILMER

**MUSICAL INSTRUMENTS.** The AV translation of Heb. *šiddâ w$^e$šiddôṯ* in Eccl. 2:8. The meaning of the Hebrew phrase is uncertain; the NEB omits it (cf. mg.), while the RSV renders "many concubines" (but cf. mg.; *CHAL,* p. 361, supports RSV with "lady [concubine][?]"). For discussions of the various possibilities, see KD and R. Gordis, *Koheleth — The Man and His World* (3rd ed. 1968), pp. 218f.

For the RSV references to "musical instruments" (1 Ch. 15:16; 2 Ch. 5:13; 23:13; Neh. 12:36) and "instruments of music" (1 S. 18:6; 2 Ch. 34:12; Am. 6:5; etc.), *see* MUSIC.

**MUSICIAN, CHIEF.** *See* ASAPH **2**; HEMAN 1; JEDUTHUN **1** MUSIC III.B.2; PSALMS III.D.

**MUSTARD** [Gk. *sínapi*]. The smallness of the mustard seed is mentioned in Mt. 13:31f.; 17:20; Mk. 4:31; Lk. 13:19; 17:6. The rabbis used a "grain of mustard" to characterize something very minute. The mustard plant, however, can be described as a "tree" (Mt. 13:32; cf. Lk. 13:19) and as putting out "great branches" (Mk. 4:32). Of several varieties of mustard, the references seem to be to *Sinapis nigra* L., cultivated black mustard. Normally attaining a maximum height of 1.2 m. (4 ft.), some species can grow to 4.6 m. (15 ft.) under favorable conditions. *Sinapis nigra, S. alba, S. orientalis,* and others were grown for their aromatic seeds. Birds came to the trees to eat these seeds (Mt. 13:32, etc.), not to build their nests (cf. NEB and RSV). The spindly appearance of the mature shrub might convey the impression of a large tree when compared with the minuteness of the seed, but in any event the contrast is a deliberate exaggeration. The mustard seed was the smallest of its kind in the ancient Near East, and in such an environment it germinated and grew quickly. Birds could then lodge in its branches. It is not necessary to suppose that the large *Salvadora Persica* Garrin is the plant referred to by the Gk. *sínapi.* R. K. H.

**MUSTER.** Used by the RSV to translate several verbs, always in the context of assembling troops for battle. Most often it translates a form of Heb. *pāqaḏ* (AV usually, RSV often, "number"), which has various nuances of meaning, e.g., "call up" (for military service) or "enroll" (in the army) (e.g., piel in Isa. 13:4; niphal in Ezk. 38:8; qal in 2 S. 18:1; 1 K. 20:15, 26f.), "count" or "call the roll" (e.g., hithpael in Jgs. 20:15, 17; 21:9), "hold a military inspection" (e.g., qal in Josh. 8:10), etc. Other verbs rendered "muster" by the RSV are *qāḇaṣ* (lit. "assemble," 2 K. 6:24; AV "gather"; NEB "call up"), *mānâ* (lit. "count," 1 K. 20:25; AV "number"; NEB "raise"), the niphal of *ʾāsap* (lit. "gather," 1 S. 13:5, 11; 1 Ch. 19:7; AV "gather together"), and the hiphil of *ṣāḇaʾ* (lit. "conscript," 2 K. 25:19; Jer. 52:25). In Nah. 2:3 (MT 4) the RSV renders "mustered in array" for MT *h$^a$ḵînô,* the hiphil infinitive of *kûn* (lit. "make ready, prepare"; AV "his preparation"; NEB "the line is formed"; cf. Jer. 46:14; Ezk. 7:14; 38:7, where the hiphil of *kûn* denotes preparing an army for battle).

The noun *p$^e$quddâ,* a cognate of *pāqaḏ,* occurs in 2 Ch. 17:14; 26:11, denoting a CENSUS.

*See* ARMY. N. J. O.

**MUSTER GATE** [Heb. *šaʿar hammipqāḏ*–'muster gate,' 'inspection gate'; Gk. *pýlē toú Maphekad*] (Neh. 3:31); AV GATE MIPHKAD; NEB MUSTERING GATE. One of the gates of Jerusalem or of the temple precinct. It probably was near the northeast corner of the temple area. *See* JERUSALEM III.F.2.v. D. J. WIEAND

**MUTH-LABBEN** mo͞oth-lab'ən [Heb. *(ʿal)mûṯ labbēn*]. A technical term of uncertain meaning in the superscription to Ps. 9 (MT v. 1). It has traditionally been interpreted as meaning "for the occasion of the death of the son" (cf. Anderson) or as the first two words of a popular song to the tune of which the psalm was to be sung (e.g., "Die for the son" [Weiser]; "Dying [is] to the son" [KD]). More likely, however, is the theory that *ʿalmûṯ* is a scribal error for *ʿal ʿalāmôṯ,* a reading that has the support of some ancient versions (e.g., Aq.). It may then mean "in the manner of young women, for a son" (i.e., falsetto voice) (see Briggs).

***Bibliography.***–A. A. Anderson, *Psalms,* I (*NCBC,* repr. 1981), p. 50; C. A. Briggs and E. G. Briggs, comm. on Psalms, I (*ICC,* 1906), lxxvi-lxxvii; KD, in loc.; S. Mowinckel, *Psalms in Israel's Worship* (Eng. tr. 1962), II, 216f.; A. Weiser, *Psalms* (Eng. tr. *OTL,* 1962), pp. 146, 148. N. J. O.

**MUTILATE** [Heb. *ḥārum* ("mutilated face," Lev. 21:18), *ḥārûṣ* (Lev. 22:22); Gk. *apokóptō* (Gal. 5:12), *katatomḗ* (Phil. 3:2)]; AV also "flat nose," MAIMED, CONCISION; NEB also "stunted"; **MUTILATION** [Heb. *mûm*] (Lev. 22:25); AV BLEMISH; NEB PERMANENT DEFECT. Scripture countenances CIRCUMCISION, but any other kind of mutilation, such as the self-imposed cuts of the Baal priests (1 K. 18:28), is forbidden (cf. Jer. 47:5; Hos. 7:14). The mutilated face of Lev. 21:18 could describe incisions of the kind practiced in pagan Baal worship (1 K. 18:28), or possibly disfigurements of a genetic origin (cf. LXX *kolobórin,* lit. "flat nose"; cf. also Heb. *ḥrm,* "split"; *CHAL,* p. 117). Mutilated animals (Lev. 22:22) would include those that had been maimed, hurt, or gouged through fighting, or had survived encounters with wild beasts. Human mutilation of animals, as distinct from the sacrificing of animals according to ritual procedure, was not favored by the Hebrews because of the belief that wild and domestic creatures alike belonged to God (Ps. 50:10). The mutilation referred to in Lev. 22:25 was castration (see v. 24), a procedure that made any such animal, whether imported or domestic, unsuitable for a sacrificial offering. Castration rendered the animal somewhat less than perfect physically, and as such the creature could not reflect divine perfection and holiness adequately.

The allusion in Gal. 5:12 employs the middle voice of *apokóptō* to mean "mutilate oneself," "have oneself mutilated." The reference can hardly be to circumcision, since Paul's opponents would already be circumcised; possibly the apostle was referring to the kind of sacral castration practiced in the cults of Attis and Cybele. Phil. 3:2 contrasts those who mutilated the flesh with the Judaizing Christians who practiced true circumcision. The LXX uses *katatémnō* for forbidden mutilations mentioned in Lev. 21:5 and elsewhere.

*See also* CUTTINGS IN THE FLESH. R. K. H.

**MUTTER.** *See* MURMUR; DIVINATION III.G.

**MUZZLE** [Heb. *ḥāsam*; Gk. *phimóō*]. The prohibition against muzzling an ox while it was treading out grain (Dt. 25:4) was interpreted by rabbinic commentators to mean that animals were not to be deprived of sustenance while they were working. Most modern scholars agree that "the law affords another example of the humanity which is characteristic of Dt., and which is to be exercised even towards animals" (S. R. Driver, comm. on Deuteronomy [*ICC,* 1895], p. 280). Paul, however, interpreted it allegorically to illustrate the principle that Christian preachers (1 Cor. 9:9) and elders (1 Tim. 5:18) should receive financial remuneration from the community they serve.

The author of Ps. 39 figuratively put a "muzzle" (Heb. *maḥsôm,* RSV mg., NEB) on his own mouth to restrain himself from complaining aloud about God's apparent injustice (v. 1 [MT 2]). *See* BIT. N. J. O.

**MYCENAEAN** mī-sə-nē'ən **CULTURE.** *See* GREECE III. C.

**MYNDOS** min'dəs [Gk. *Myndos*]; AV MYNDUS. A city on the coast of Caria, the southwest portion of Asia Minor, famous for its silver mines. It is also called Mindos.

About 139 B.C. the Roman consul Lucius sent letters to Myndos and other important cities in Asia Minor on behalf of the Jews (1 Macc. 15:23). This action implies that Myndos possessed a measure of independence and was the home of a considerable Jewish colony. The modern location is Gumushli, which takes its name from the silver mines located in its vicinity. W. W. GASQUE

**MYRA** mī'rə [Gk. *Myra*]. An old Lycian-speaking city that became one of the leaders of the Lycian confederacy of Greek and Roman times, having the maximum of three seats in the federal assembly (*see* PATARA). It lay on the southern coast of Asia Minor on a lofty hill a few kilometers from the sea, being served by its port of Andriace. At Myra Paul and his escort, after making the crossing from Sidon, boarded an Alexandrian vessel bound for Rome (Acts 27:5f.). In spite of its prominence, still attested by the remains, and its large territory, very little is known of ancient Myra.

See Pauly-Wissowa, XVI, 1083-89. E. A. JUDGE

**MYRRH** mûr.

**1.** [Heb. *mōr*; Akk. *murru*; Ugar. *mr*; Arab. *murr*; Gk. *smýrna* (Mt. 2:11; Jn. 19:39), *smyrnízō* ("mingled with myrrh," Mk. 15:23), *mýron* (Rev. 18:13)]; AV also OINTMENT; NEB also "drugged wine," PERFUME. This substance is mentioned as valuable for its perfume (Ps. 45:8 [MT 9]; Prov. 7:17; Cant. 3:6; 4:14), and as one constituent of the anointing oil (Ex. 30:23; see also Cant. 4:6; 5:1, 5, 13). Several shrubs produce a perfumed resinous substance described as "myrrh," but the one compounded in the anointing oil was most probably from the *Commiphora myrrha* Nees, a low thorny tree which is distributed across south Arabia and Ethiopia. The exudate from the branches is pleasantly scented and dries quite readily into a solid resin. Myrrh was capable of being diluted to form a liquid cosmetic product (Ex. 30:23 [but AV "pure"; NEB "sticks of"]; Cant. 5:5, 13 [AV "sweet-smelling"]), and this was probably the "oil of myrrh" (RSV; NEB "oil and myrrh") mentioned in Est. 2:12. Such a liquid was known to the Canaanites in the 2nd millennium B.C. (C. H. Gordon, *Ugaritic Literature* [1949], p. 130), and according to Herodotus ii.86 seems to have been used by the Egyptians in embalming. A reflection of this is seen in the use of myrrh in connection with Jesus' burial (Jn. 19:39). The specific mention of myrrh in this context, as opposed to the more general "spices" of Mark (16:1) and Luke (24:1), suggests an eyewitness report. As the end of Christ's life was associated with myrrh (Mk. 15:23), so was its beginning, since this aromatic substance was one of the gifts tendered by the Magi (Mt. 2:11).

Myrrh was also used as a medicine (cf. Am.Tab. 268), for perfuming clothes (Ps. 45:8 [MT 9]) and harlots' beds

(Prov. 7:17), as well as for general deodorant purposes. Myrrh was a familiar symbol in Hebrew poetry (cf. Cant. 4:6, 14; 5:1, 13; Sir. 24:15).

The *mýron* of Rev. 18:13 was the "ointment" of Mt. 26:7, 12; Mk. 14:3-5; Lk. 7:37-46; Jn. 11:2; 12:3, 5, and should be rendered in that manner, since it occurs in the LXX principally as a translation of the Heb. *šemen*, "oil," "butter," "fat."

**2.** [Heb. *lōṭ*; Gk. *staktḗ*] (Gen. 37:25; 43:11). The fragrant resin obtained from some species of cistus and called in Arab. *lādham*, in Lat. *ladanum*. The cistus or "rock rose" was once common all over the mountains of Palestine (*see* FLORA IV.A), the usual varieties being the *C. villosus* with pink petals, and the *C. salviaefolius* with white petals. Quite probably the "bag of myrrh" (Cant. 1:13) used as a perfume and deodorant consisted of dried pellets of the gum, since there is some doubt as to whether Solomon would have imported *C. myrrha*, or a related species *C. kataf*, for his gardens.

**3.** [Heb. *nēšeq*; Gk. *staktḗ*] (1 K. 10:25; 2 Ch. 9:24); AV "armour," "harness"; NEB PERFUMES. The Heb. *nēšeq* usually refers to armor or some kind of weapon (cf. Ugar. *nṯq*), but that hardly fits the context, which is a list of tribute brought to Solomon. The LXX *staktḗ* and the next item in the list, "spices" (Heb. *b^eśāmîm*), provide the basis for the RSV and NEB readings.

*Bibliography.*–M. Zohary, *Arboreal Flora of Israel and Transjordan* (1951); *MPB*, pp. 77, 82-84. R. K. H.

**MYRTLE** mûr'təl [Heb. *h^adās*; Gk. *myrsínē*] (Isa. 41:19; 55:13; Neh. 8:15; Zec. 1:8, 10f.); also the name "Hadassah" (a transliteration of the fem. form *h^adassâ* in Est. 2:7), the Jewish form of Esther. A native of western Asia, the myrtle (*Myrtis communis* L.) is commonly found in Palestine. In suitable locations it can attain a height of 9 m. (30 ft.) and bears dark green leaves, beautiful white flowers, and scented berries. It yields a fragrant oil. Sacred in antiquity to Astarte, it was one of the choice plants of the land (Isa. 41:19; 55:13). It was used at the Feast of Tabernacles (Neh. 8:15; cf. T.P. *Sukkah* iii.4) and is popular today when procurable. For references to the myrtle in Jewish writings see *Jew.Enc.*, IX, 137.

In Greek religion the myrtle plant was venerated by the cult of Aphrodite in ceremonies held at Athens, Corinth, Argos, and other Aegean sites. In postexilic Judaism the myrtle was a symbol of justice and peace. R. K. H.

**MYSIA** mish'yə, mizh'yə [Gk. *Mysia*] (Acts 16:7f.). A region in northwestern Asia Minor. As Strabo noted (*Geog.* xii.4.10), the precise boundaries of Mysia are not defined, but it may be described as bounded on the north by the Propontis, on the east by Bithynia and Phrygia, on the south by Lydia, and on the west by the Aegean Sea. Mysia was never a separate state but rather part of various states. In 133 B.C. it was incorporated into the Roman Empire as part of Hellespontus. Cities of Mysia included Adramyttium (Acts 27:2), Alexandria Troas (16:8, 11; etc.), Assos (20:13f.), and Pergamum (Rev. 1:11; 2:12).

According to Acts 16:6-10, Paul, Silas, and Timothy, on Paul's second journey, were forbidden "by the Holy Spirit" to preach in proconsular Asia. Thus they passed through Phrygia and Galatia and were "opposite" (i.e., E of) Mysia. They were kept from entering Bithynia by the Spirit of Jesus, and (according to the RSV) "passing by Mysia, they went down to Troas" (v. 8). But Troas was in Mysia, and their route, since it was not through the principal portion of Asia (which included Phrygia, Lycia, Caria, Lydia, and probably part of Mysia) or Bithynia, had to pass through Mysia. Therefore the expression "passing by" must mean that they traversed the region but did not evangelize it, instead continuing to Troas and thence to Macedonia (see F. F. Bruce, *Book of Acts* [*NICNT*, 1954], pp. 325-28, esp. p. 327 n. 20).

Paul passed through Mysia on his third journey, probably on his way north from Ephesus (20:1), and certainly on his return journey (vv. 6-14).

*see* Vol. I, Map XIX. W. S. LASOR

**MYSTERY.**

I. Etymology
II. Meaning
III. Use
 A. Synoptic Gospels
 B. Pauline Literature
 C. Book of Revelation
IV. Sources of the Pauline Idea of Mystery
 A. Mystery as a Phenomenon in the OT
 B. Apocryphal and Pseudepigraphical Literature
 C. Qumrân Literature

***I. Etymology.***–Although the word occurs in the OT in Daniel (see the LXX of 2:18f., 27-30, 47; 4:6) its chief importance as a biblical term depends on its use in the NT. Here it translates Gk. *tó mystḗrion*, which appears in the Synoptics once, in the Pauline literature twenty or twenty-one times, and in Revelation four times.

The etymology is uncertain, but the word appears to derive from Gk. *mýō*, "to close or shut" (see esp. H. Frist, *Griechisches Etymologisches Wörterbuch*, II [1963], 279f.; cf. also *TDNT*, IV, *s.v.* μυστήριον, μυέω [G. Bornkamm]). Although *mýō* may mean to shut the mouth or any other aperature of the body, its chief reference is to shutting the eyes. From *mýō*, therefore, appears to derive *ho mýstēs*, one who shuts his eyes, hence one who is initiated in the mysteries. Probably this use accounts for the rise of *myéō*, which in the active means "to initiate" and in the passive "to be initiated into the mysteries."

It is within the context of religious terminology, therefore, that *tó mystḗrion* and its more usual plural form *tá mystḗria* occur in nonbiblical Greek. The term is applied mostly to the mysteries, a religious phenomenon of ancient Greece that thrived *ca.* 700 B.C.-A.D. 400.

Paul's frequent use of this word and of other key terms in the mystery religions was once taken as proof that he either belonged to such a cult or at least was strongly influenced by one. More careful examination has shown, however, that such a supposition is entirely unnecessary, since much of the language of the mysteries was common to Greek culture in general. Moreover, Paul's practices and beliefs move in such a completely different direction that direct borrowing cannot be maintained. It is well known that Paul selected certain words out of the general flow of language, knowing something of their backgrounds, and used them for his own purposes. Thus he could communicate the gospel in terms and concepts with which non-Jews were already familiar. That *mystḗrion* was such a word, however, is certain (see A.D. Nock, *JBL*, 52 [1933], 139).

***II. Meaning.***–Although the meaning of *mystḗrion* in the Scriptures can be determined only by a careful examination of each occurrence, one important preliminary observation can be made. *Mystḗrion* is by no means an exact equivalent of the English word "mystery." In contemporary usage mystery refers to something unexplainable, e.g., the disappearance of a painting, a peculiar phenomenon in the sky, or the actions of an individual for which no one can account. In each instance, once the riddle is solved the mystery disappears.

The Greek term, however, refers to a mystery of divine

nature that remains hidden from human beings because their normal powers of comprehension are insufficient. Nonetheless, these mysteries are intended for human beings and when known prove profitable to them. Not only do they heal people's afflictions and provide successes in their life endeavors, but they also assure them of a blessed immortality.

To gain access to these mysteries it was necessary to depend on specially appointed persons (e.g., priests) who had in turn received their knowledge from divine messengers or the deity itself. After special rites of initiation that prepared candidates safely to possess the information, they were instructed in the secret teachings and granted possession of the sacred words belonging to the mystery. Possession of these secrets, however, in no way lessened their mysterious character. Because candidates had been joined to the deity, the element of mystery was enhanced, not diminished. *See also* RELIGIONS OF THE BIBLICAL WORLD: GRECO-ROMAN II.D.

In the NT *mystērion* as a religious term has an even more precise meaning. In its fullest expression it refers to the secret thoughts, plans, and dispensations of God, which, though hidden from human reason, are being disclosed by God's revealing act to those for whom such knowledge is intended. Here also, disclosure does not mean that the mysterious nature of what has been revealed has been diminished. On the contrary, because the disclosure is of God and pertains to divine things, it continues always as "mystery." Although the word of this mystery can be proclaimed in human terms, apart from God's act it remains forever enigmatic and incomprehensible.

The Hellenistic mysteries and the Christian mystery differ significantly. The content of the Hellenistic mystery had to be carefully hidden lest it fall into unworthy hands. In the Christian mystery the revelation is freely proclaimed to the whole world, for even where it is most openly displayed it remains unknown apart from the grace of God.

*III. Use.–A. Synoptic Gospels.* Mark 4:11 (par. Mt. 13:10f.; Lk. 8:9f.) states: "Those who were about him with the twelve asked him concerning the parables. And he said to them, 'To you has been given the secret [*mystērion*] of the kingdom of God, but for those outside everything is in parables; so that they may indeed see but not perceive, and may indeed hear but not understand; lest they should turn again, and be forgiven.'"

In this text two questions are raised: the relationship between mystery and Jesus' parabolic utterances, and the meaning of mystery insofar as it relates to the kingdom of which the text speaks. With reference to the parables three observations can be made. First, it becomes quite clear in the tradition that Jesus' practice was to speak the Word (i.e., the word of the gospel or, as in this context, the mystery of the kingdom) in parables. Mark preserves the statement "He did not speak to them without a parable" (4:34). Certainly this cannot mean that all Jesus' utterances originally consisted of parables. The Gospels record that Jesus taught the multitudes many things apart from parables. What is meant, therefore, is that what was most characteristic of Jesus' teaching was its parabolic (i.e., enigmatic) character. Although He taught the people many things about God, righteousness, sin, and judgment in the plainest of terms, all His teachings had a mysterious side that they did not understand. Uncertainty about exactly what Jesus was saying and what he wanted them to believe is present in the Baptist's questions, "Are you he who is to come, or shall we look for another?" (Lk. 7:20); in the disciples' complaint about what the parables really mean; and in a statement of his enemies, "If you are the Christ, tell us plainly" (Jn. 10:24). The crowds, the enemies of Jesus, and the disciples were aware of a certain hidden element in Jesus' utterances.

Second, Jesus did not speak in this way because He was anxious to conceal from His hearers the Word that He spoke, but rather because He desired to preserve for them a genuine possibility to hear in His words the Word of grace, i.e., the Word of mystery. The hearing of this Word depended not on His skill as a teacher nor on the plainness of His utterance, but first on their own desire to be addressed by God's Word and second, upon the gracious act of God by which their blind eyes and deaf ears were opened to it. That is why Jesus says, "I thank thee, Father, Lord of heaven and earth, that thou hast hidden these things from the wise and understanding and revealed them to babes; yea, Father, for such was thy gracious will" (Mt. 11:25f.).

Third, there is the question of the force of Mk. 4:12, which says that Jesus spoke in parables lest those outside should turn again and be forgiven. There seems little doubt that in the Synoptic tradition Jesus' parabolic utterance was seen, at least in part, as symbolic of Israel's hardening and rejection. But since Mk. 4:12 is a quotation of Isa. 6:9f., Jesus most likely meant that uttering parables was necessary to protect hearers from a faulty seeing and distorted hearing of His words. Many were anxious to hear in Jesus' words and see in His actions the Word of God as they conceived it. Therefore some wanted to hear from Him the words of a new prophet. Others wished to see Him as Elijah come from the dead. Most wished to find in Him a Messiah who would deliver Israel from the hand of its enemies. Thus Jesus' words not only had to reveal the Word of God, but also had to conceal it. If His hearers had concluded that He was the Messiah on a basis other than hearing in His words the Word of the Father, then they would have inevitably been led to repentance, but the repentance offered and the forgiveness gained would not have been of God — in which instance, as in the parables, the Word would have had no effect. Either Satan would have come and stolen it, or it would have developed no proper root, or it would have been strangled by the world (Mk. 4:15f.). Jesus, therefore, spoke the Word only in parables "as they were able to hear it" (v. 33).

The last question is the meaning of the "mystery" of the kingdom. Mystery might have referred to individual elements of the gospel that are either hidden or disclosed within Jesus' parables if Mark had used the plural form (*tá mystēria;* cf. Matthew and Luke). Since Mark used the singular, however, it seems clear that he was regarding the mystery of the kingdom of God (i.e., of the gospel) in its most singular aspect. He is concerned for that to which all the parables, acts, and words of Jesus bear witness (cf. Mk. 4:17). On this basis the secret or mystery of the kingdom could be nothing other than Jesus Himself, who as God's own Son is the Messiah, the one in whom God's reign is both revealed and concealed. In His person God's kingdom has broken into human history in its ultimate expression. The kingdom is where the Messiah is, and the Word of the kingdom is His utterance.

If, then, Jesus is the secret of the kingdom, it is easier to understand why there must always be a "mystery" to His actions and His word, and why He must conceal His identity (cf. Mk. 1:24f., 43f.; 9:30). As *mystērion* He cannot on human terms bear witness to Himself. Only the Father knows Him for who He is (Mt. 11:27), and therefore only the Father can reveal Him. If He is known apart from the Father (i.e., apart from grace), then He will become part of people's activity on their own behalf. He will be made king, Messiah, and Savior, but His kingdom will be of this world and will belong to Satan, and not God.

Therefore Jesus said of Peter's confession ("You are the Christ, the Son of the living God," Mt. 16:17) that flesh and blood were not sufficient to reveal this to him, but only his Father in heaven. Peter may indeed have known that Jesus is the Christ, and for this reason he was "blessed," but he knew because of God's grace ("To you it has been given to know," 13:11) and through God's grace ("no one knows the Son except the Father," 11:27).

At this point of the revelation of the mystery one can discover what distinguishes the Christian mystery from all others. In the Hellenistic mysteries revelation took place through special rites and ecstasies. In the apocalyptic literature the mysteries of God are revealed by visions or angelic beings. But in the NT the disciples meet the revelation or mystery of God in a historical event, in Jesus who is the Christ.

*B. Pauline Literature.* In the Pauline literature *mystḗrion* occurs more frequently, more deliberately, and more pointedly than in any other group of writings. It appears already in 2 Thess. 2:7, twice in Romans (11:25; 16:25), six times in 1 Corinthians (2:[1], 7; 4:1; 13:2; 14:2; 15:51), and twice in 1 Timothy (3:9, 16). But the word attains its most significant development in Ephesians and Colossians, where it is used no less than ten times. Although the idea represented by the term is usually limited to those passages where *mystḗrion* occurs, in a few instances elements of the concept appear independently of the word (i.e., 2 Cor. 12:4; Gal. 1:3). Its use undeniably progresses from a rather simple application to what, by the time of the Captivity Epistles, must be termed a highly sophisticated application.

*1. 1 Cor. 4:1; 13:2; 14:2.* The simplest usages have to do with its appearance in plural forms *(tá mystḗria).* Since these are limited to three passages in 1 Corinthians, it seems likely that Paul was using the term in these contexts polemically against certain developments within the Christian assembly. In none of these instances did he attempt to develop or define the term conceptually.

In 1 Cor. 4:1 Paul required that he be acknowledged as a servant of Christ and a steward of the mysteries of God. *Tá mystḗria* appears to be equivalent to the revelation of God of which he was an apostle. The plural form might indicate the breadth of Christian teaching and therefore have a more general scope than the great mystery of salvation mentioned elsewhere by Paul (so Deden, *Ephemerides Theologicae Lovanienses,* 13 [1936], 410: R. E. Brown, *Bibl.,* 39 [1958], 440).

In 13:2 ("if I understand all mysteries") Paul employed the terminology of those who considered themselves superior in their understanding of Christian teaching in order to rebuke them. The mysteries are not different from the mystery but rather are its essential ingredients. He might have said, "If I were acquainted with the sum of knowledge possible through divine revelations."

It is even more difficult to determine the force of "mysteries" in 14:25 "For one who speaks in a tongue speaks not to men but to God; for no one understands him, but he utters mysteries in the Spirit." Paul apparently meant that with tongues one may speak the hidden truths of God in the Spirit, but unless these mysteries are interpreted (i.e., reduced to specifics) so that they become intelligible, they accomplish little.

*2. 1 Cor. 2:7.* Paul's own use of the term is in its singular form. Although "mystery" occurred in a negative sense as early as 2 Thess. 2:7, not until Paul's letter to the Corinthians did the basic structure of the idea begin to be clarified.

The context of its occurrence is as follows: "...that your faith might not rest in the wisdom of men but in the power of God. Yet among the mature we do impart wisdom, although it is not a wisdom of this age or of the rulers of this age, who are doomed to pass away. But we impart a secret and hidden wisdom [*sophían en mystḗrioi*] of God, which God decreed before the ages for our glorification. None of the rulers of this age understood this; for if they had, they would not have crucified the Lord of glory. But, as it is written, 'What no eye has seen, nor ear heard, nor the heart of man conceived, what God has prepared for those who love him,' God has revealed to us through the Spirit. For the Spirit searches everything, even the depths of God" (1 Cor. 2:5-10).

Paul obviously used *mystḗrion* here in an early attempt to subsume the divine plan under a single comprehensive term or phrase (so Brown, p. 437). He did not repeat the expression "the wisdom of God in mystery." Perhaps the wisdom enthusiasts in Corinth and the forerunners to Gnosticism elsewhere doomed its usefulness. Although Paul continued the conjunction of wisdom (or knowledge) with mystery (i.e., Col. 1:28; 2:2; Eph. 1:8f.; 2:9f.), he reversed the order, and the mystery became the dominant term. Undoubtedly it proved to be a happier choice, since mystery suggested in a far more definitive way Paul's twofold understanding of the gospel as divine disclosure and power (see K. Prümm, *Bibl.,* 37 [1956], 146f.). Even in this early attempt by Paul occur some of the emphases that characterize later developments.

(1) The mystery is intended not for everyone, but only for the mature *(téleioi)* (1 Cor. 2:6; cf. Col. 1:28). The *téleioi* mentioned here are not the *téleioi* ("initiates") of the Hellenistic mysteries, who became qualified through sacred rites, but rather those mature by the Spirit (1 Cor. 2:13f.). In later contexts Paul designated those for whom the mystery is intended simply as saints (cf. Col. 1:26; Eph. 3:5).

(2) The mystery that is imparted is not new; God decreed it before the ages (1 Cor. 2:7; cf. Eph. 1:9, 11; Col. 1:26). Therefore it is more than knowledge. It is nothing less than the salvation that God ordained through the cross of Jesus Christ. The choice of the cross as the means for human salvation is possible because it already belonged to God's original and eternal purpose.

(3) The mystery has been hidden from human view till this present moment (cf. Col. 1:26; Eph. 3:9; Rom. 16:25). It has been hidden from the prophets and saints in the past, from the Jews, and most of all from those who are perishing (cf. 2 Cor. 4:3-6). Moreover, it has been kept hidden from the dark rulers and powers of this world; even if they had knowledge of Jesus and the cross, they could not understand it, for God concealed the true meaning from their eyes (1 Cor. 2:8).

(4) The mystery is now being revealed by God through His Spirit (1 Cor. 2:10; cf. 14:2; Eph. 3:5). The chief point of reference to God's revealing act is the historic event of Jesus' death upon the cross. This event by no means exhausts the meaning, however, for even where it is known it remains hidden or foolish apart from the Spirit. Moreover, what is revealed at the cross is never fully comprehended even by those for whom it is intended. Because it belongs to the depths of God, only the Spirit of God can unveil it. Therefore only those willing to be taught and matured by the Spirit can really apprehend these depths of God.

*3. Rom. 16:25f.* Although Paul made no attempt in Romans to set forth his concept of mystery, he nonetheless used the term twice, and each time with some significance. The more important use occurs in Rom. 16:25f. in the context of doxology. Although circumstances did not let Paul elaborate, his words are important as a transition between his early use of mystery and the use that develops in Ephesians and Colossians. The two especially noteworthy facets are (1) the identification made between the mystery and Jesus (see Sanday and Headlam, comm. on Romans [*ICC*, 1901], p. 434), and (2) the connection between mystery and the salvation of the Gentiles; it is interesting to note that the term's only other occurrence in Romans is a reference to the other side of the mystery, the salvation of the Jews (11:25).

*4. Col. 1:26f.; 2:2; 4:3.* All of the traditional elements of mystery previously mentioned are present here. Among the new elements is Paul's word that the grandeur of the divine plan can be recognized only where Christ Himself is recognized as present in His people (cf. Col. 1:27, "the glory of this mystery, which is Christ in you, the hope of glory"). Since Christ is the one who is supreme over all things (1:15-18) and the one in whom the fulness of God is present (1:19), Christ's presence gives to the Colossians their hope of glory (see R. E. Brown, *Bibl.*, 40 [1959], 71). Therefore Paul strove for the Colossians that they might have knowledge of God's mystery, namely Christ, in whom are hid all the treasures of wisdom and knowledge (2:2).

In Col. 4:3 Paul again referred to the mystery of Christ, but this time in the context of proclamation (cf. Eph. 6:19f.). Whereas apostles of other mysteries were required to conceal their word, Paul was obliged to declare his. This connection of proclamation with mystery can be traced to the earliest statements of Paul — 1 Cor. 2:1f. as well as Rom. 16:26. In the latter instance Paul said that the mystery was made known according to the command of the eternal God, who had established the basis for the proclamation through the prophetic writings.

*5. Ephesians.* Ephesians has been called "the Epistle of the mystery." Six times Paul employed the term; moreover, 3:2-11 set forth the most elaborate NT expression of the idea. All the familiar expressions occur, along with many of the key words ordinarily associated with *mystērion*.

Two new concepts add to the overall picture. Eph. 1:10 states that God's plan is to unite in Christ all things in heaven and on earth. The context of the first chapter, especially vv. 22f., is the work of subduing all things — not only earthly creatures but also heavenly powers — and placing them under the feet of Christ. Every principality and power that has dominion shall become subject to Him. Here is the picture of the final stage of the divine plan. From God's point of view the mystery of subjection to Christ already exists, for Christ has come and evil is vanquished; from the temporal point of view, however, the forces of evil are now engaged in a mighty conflict against the headship of Christ (Brown, *Bibl.*,40 [1959], 77). Nonetheless, in the fulness of time all things shall become united under Him.

Along with this statement belongs Eph. 3:10, "that through the church the manifold wisdom of God might now be made known to the principalities and powers in the heavenly places." The very existence of the Church and Christ's headship over it bears witness not only to the earthly powers but also to angelic powers that their authority is ended. Within the *koinōnía* of the Church, where every barrier is broken down and every alienation overcome, is already manifest the mystery of the headship of Christ. Whereas Colossians emphasizes the essence of the mystery, which is Christ present in and with the believer, Ephesians emphasizes the realization of the mystery, which is Christ present in and over the Church.

In Eph. 3:3 Paul mentioned that particular element of the mystery over which he observed stewardship, the salvation of the Gentiles. Although Paul had made other references to this event (cf. Col. 4:3), here he stated it most precisely. The mystery included more than that Gentiles could be saved; to Paul had been revealed that the Gentiles were destined also to be fellow heirs, members of the same body, and partakers of the same promises as Israel (Eph. 3:6). It was this development, the reconciliation of Jew and Gentile in one body, that revealed the unsearchable riches of Christ and demonstrated the manifold wisdom of God (vv. 8, 10). It also provided the "earnest" for the future expectation — God's ultimate demonstration to mankind and angels of the reconciling power of the blood of Christ.

*6. Other Usages in the Pauline Literature.* In 1 Thess. 2:7 Paul spoke of the mystery of lawlessness. What he likely meant is the mystery of Satan's rule and the kingdom of evil. Since they are supernatural and beyond human understanding, Paul had no difficulty referring to them in a negative sense as mystery.

In 1 Cor. 15:51 Paul mentioned the Resurrection as mystery. This use is consistent with his overall use of mystery as something hidden but now revealed. Here, however, application is limited to one facet of the great mystery.

In the context of a homily on marriage, Eph. 5:32b, Paul concluded, "This is a great mystery, and I take it to mean Christ and the church." The "secret mystery" appears to be the symbolic reference to the union of Christ and the Church, whose meaning, like that of the marital union described in Gen. 2:24, is hidden. Paul's use of the term mystery here is quite different from his use elsewhere; its closest parellel is the symbolic visions of Revelation.

The final Pauline use of "mystery" is in 1 Timothy, where the mysteries of faith (3:9) and of religion (v. 16) are mentioned. The mystery of faith is what is believed, i.e. true doctrine. The mystery of religion is further defined by a hymn of praise to Christ, which makes clear that the center of the Christian religion, the supreme mystery, is Christ Himself.

*C. Book of Revelation.* The use of mystery in Revelation is generally of a different order from that found in Paul. Its employment is less deliberate and its meaning less precise. In addition, since Revelation is an apocalypse, the use resembles that of Daniel and apocalyptic literature more than that of the rest of the NT. Thus mystery has special reference to the supernatural form (visions, symbols, etc.) in which communication from God takes place.

Mystery in Rev. 1:20 designates the nature and source of the revelation, while the context makes clear that the subject involved is in the historical incidence of the Church and its particular fate in history. The material is parenetic and practical, not theological. Rev. 10:7 refers to the day of the trumpet call by the seventh angel, when there will be no more delay (cf. 10:6) but the mysterious plan of God will be finished. Mystery here means the secret counsel of God (cf. Am. 3:7), which finds its ultimate and final expression in the eschatological acts of God. In 17:5, 7 mystery again designates the particular form of the communication as well as its symbolic meaning. Since the disclosure is from God it is necessary that its meaning be somewhat hidden, but it is to be assumed that the name Babylon was meant to convey a specific reference to the reader.

***IV. Sources of the Pauline Idea of Mystery.***–Attempts to designate sources from which Paul supposedly developed his ideas are a modernization of history of the worst order. Whatever ideas influenced Paul, they passed through the crucible of his own particular understanding of Christian faith in such a way that they appear always with a unique form and meaning. It is equally strange to try to separate Paul from the stream of life from which he emerged as if there had never been any connection between it and his faith. One must look not for the source of his ideas but for the stream of life from which they emerge. Here will be found the way of approach, the kind of thinking and feeling, the type of discussion and questioning that prompted his own contribution. As has been already indicated, no matter how much Paul may have been at home in the Roman world, the stream of of life from which he emerged was not that of Greek religion or philosophy. The work expended in this area, particularly as it relates to his use of *mystērion,* has proved to have only negative value. Far more profitable has been the quest within Hebrew culture.

*A. Mystery as a Phenomenon in the OT.* Although mystery as a term appears only in Daniel, the idea of a secret council (Heb. *sôḏ*) and a heavenly assembly are present elsewhere (cf. Pss. 82, 89; Job 2:1f.; see also H. W. Robinson, *JTS,* 45 [1944], 151f.). It is also clear that the prophets were those who had access to this hidden council of God and authority to declare it (so Jer. 23:18; Am. 3:7). In Daniel God is further revealed as the one who makes known secrets (Aram. *rāz),* i.e., grants visions that unveil particularly the course of future events as He has determined them.

*B. Apocryphal and Pseudepigraphical Literature.* This literature emphasizes the council of God as consisting of secrets hidden from mankind, (e.g., Sir. 11:4; 3:21f.) and connects mystery with wisdom (Sir. 4:18; Wisd. 6:22). *Mystērion* occurs in Tob. 12:7, 11; Jth. 2:2; 2 Macc. 13:21 but usually with a profane meaning. In Enoch, 2 and 3 Baruch, and 2 Esdras mysteries become an ever greater matter of concern. Important discourses revolve around cosmic mysteries (1 En. 41:3f.; 60:11f.; 3 Bar. 1:8), and mysteries having to do with evil (1 En. 6–11), human destiny (41:1), God and His providential acts (63:3), and eschatology (38:3; 69:14; 2 Bar. 76–86; 2 Esd. 14:5).

*C. Qumrân Literature.* This literature extensively treats the mysteries of divine providence (1QM 14:14; 1QpHab 2:1f.; 1QS 11:3f.), mysteries only for the elect (1QS 11:5-8), and cosmic and evil mysteries.

When all this diverse Hebrew literature is examined (and the materials are far too many to receive more than a cursory treatment here), it becomes very clear that (1) mystery was used in a great variety of situations and with many different meanings, (2) the terminology was exceedingly prevalent and demonstrates the wide range of interest the Jews had in the subject, (3) Hellenistic words and concepts had already penetrated Jewish thought before NT times. It is difficult to point to any one facet of Paul's use of mystery, including facets that are apparently most Hellenistic, that he could not have found in Judaistic thought. This does not mean that the Hellenistic world contributed nothing to Paul's thought, but only that the kind of penetration it made took place largely within the framework of Judaism, not outside of it.

***Bibliography.***–*TDNT,* IV. *s.v.* μυστήριον, μυέω (G. Bornkamm); C. K. Barrett, *NT Background* (1958), pp. 91-104; R. E. Brown, *CBQ,* 20 (1958), 417-443; E. Jüngel, *God as the Mystery of the World* (Eng. tr. 1983); H. A. A. Kennedy, *St. Paul and the Mystery Religions* (1913); P. Pokorny, *ZNW,* 53 (1962), 160-194; H. Rahner, "The Christian Mystery and the Pagan Mysteries," in J. Campbell, ed., *The Mysteries* (1955), pp. 337-404, repr. in *Pagan and Christian Mysteries* (1963), pp. 146-210; J. A. Robinson, comm. on Ephesians (1907), Appendix.

G. W. BARKER

**MYTH, MYTHOLOGY.** Since the terms "myth, mythology, mythical, and mythological" have often been used in biblical studies to characterize biblical narratives or aspects of the biblical story, it is necessary to discuss the appropriateness and accuracy of using such terminology. This discussion will consider the ancient Near Eastern and Greek contexts and survey representative scholarly positions.

I. Terminology
   A. Classical Greek
   B. LXX
   C. NT
II. Ancient Near Eastern Myth
   A. Mythopoeic Thought
   B. Characteristics of Ancient Near Eastern Myth
III. Greek Myth
   A. Rise and Development
   B. Greek Myth vis-à-vis Ancient Near Eastern Myth
IV. The OT and Mythology
V. Myth and Ritual
VI. Modern Redefinition of Myth
VII. The NT and Mythology
VIII. Mythology in Biblical Interpretation

***I. Terminology.***–The terms "myth" and "mythology" are related to the Greek words *mýthos* and *mythológos* (and the related verbs *mythologeúō* and *mythologéō*). *Mýthos* occurs five times in the NT (1 Tim. 1:4; 4:7; 2 Tim. 4:4; Tit. 1:14; 2 Pet. 1:16) and once in the LXX (Sir. 20:19). *Mythológos* occurs once in the LXX (Bar. 3:23). The two verbs do not occur in the LXX or the NT. *Mýthos* is thus the most important word of the group for our purposes.

*A. Classical Greek. Mýthos* originally meant "thought" (*TDNT,* IV, 766), either unexpressed ("intention," "purpose," "opinion," "idea") or expressed ("word," "saying," "statement," and "speech"). As expressed thought *mýthos* can be either an "account of facts," i.e., a true story, or an "(unauthenticated) story" or "rumor" such as "primitive history," "saga," "legend," "fairy story," "fable," i.e., an invented story or fiction (*TDNT,* IV, 766f.). *Mýthos* could, therefore, come to mean "a story dealing with gods and demigods" that is by nature unverifiable.

*Mýthos* has a semantic range similar to that of *lógos.* The distinction between true and false is not any better developed for *lógos* than for *mýthos. Lógos,* however, did eventually come to be used for a "true story" in contrast to *mýthos,* a "false story," although this distinction in meanings was never absolute; it was a later, but dominant, development (*TDNT,* IV, 770), which shows up in the negative connotation given *mýthos* in the NT.

*Mythológos* as a substantive means "teller of legends," "romancer," and as an adjective, "mythological." The related verbs are *mythologeúō,* meaning "tell word for word," "relate," and *mythologéō,* meaning "tell mythic [or legendary] tales," "tell stories," "converse," "relate [with exaggeration]." (See LSJ, p. 1151.)

*B. LXX. Mýthos* and *mythológos* occur once each in the LXX, only in the Apocrypha. *Mýthos* occurs in Sir. 20:19: "An ungracious man is like an ill-timed story [*mýthos*]." Here the context (vv. 18-20), which deals with inappropriate speech, allows for a pejorative sense. *Mythológos* occurs in Bar. 3:23: ". . . the story tellers [*mythológoi*] and the seekers for understanding have not learned the way to wisdom, nor given thought to her paths." Again the context allows a pejorative sense; if the story-tellers (*mythológoi*) have not learned the way to wisdom, the implication is that their stories (*mýthoi*) are false.

*C. NT.* Of the word-group, only *mýthos* appears in the NT and only with a pejorative sense. In 1 Tim. 1:4 teachers are not to occupy themselves with myths which "promote speculations" and are opposed to the divine order or economy, for such myths teach spurious doctrine (cf. v. 3) and are not conducive to "love," a "pure heart," a "good conscience," and "sincere faith" (cf. v. 5). In 1 Tim. 4:7 myths are said to be "godless and silly" and are set in contrast to "the words of the faith and of the good doctrine" (cf. v. 6). 2 Tim. 4:4 refers to myths into which listeners with "itching ears" allow themselves to be beguiled by false teachers (cf. v. 3). Such myths are contrary to "sound teaching" (v. 3) and are contrasted with the "truth" (*alḗtheia*). Tit. 1:14 says that to give heed to "Jewish myths" is to give heed to "commands of men who reject the truth [*alḗtheia*]" and is not conducive to being "sound in the faith" (cf. v. 13). 2 Pet. 1:16 refers to "cleverly devised myths," i.e., apparently imaginative speculations not rooted in historical facts in contrast to the eyewitness testimony that bases the making known of "the power and coming of our Lord Jesus Christ" on historical events.

In the above contexts the term *mýthos* does not mean "myth" in the modern technical sense nor in the ancient Greek or Near Eastern senses (see II, III, VI below). It would best be translated as "untrue story" or "fiction," referring to a mixture of Jewish and Christian Gnostic speculations (cf. *TDNT,* IV, 781-84).

***II. Ancient Near Eastern Myth.***–*A. Mythopoeic Thought. 1. Lucien Lévy-Bruhl* regarded myth as the product of the prelogical thought of ancients and primitives. Such thought is mystical; primitives feel surrounded by unseen but real and directly apprehended powers. Thus they experience a "mystical participation" with the objects of thought in contrast to the modern separation of subject and object in the context of scientific, logical thinking.

Primitives apprehend what Lévy-Bruhl calls "collective representations" or "group ideas and sentiments" that are "common to the members of a given social group" and are "transmitted from one generation to another within it" (*Primitive Mentality,* pp. 5-13). Their overwhelming tendency is to avoid "discursive operations of thought" such as logical or reflective thought, which is abstract. This is not because the primitive mind has an inherent incapacity for such thought but because it has not differentiated logical and reflective thought in the modern way. Instead, it thinks with ideas that are more concrete than abstract.

The weaknesses of Lévy-Bruhl's position are: (1) that one should not simply equate the thought processes of ancients and contemporary primitives; (2) one should not so strongly contrast the prelogical, mystic thought of antiquity and the logical, reflective thought of today. The ancients could think logically and reflectively, though not to the same extent as moderns, and moderns often think prelogically and mystically.

*2. H. and H. A. Frankfort* believed that Lévy-Bruhl had overemphasized the difference between modern thought and mythopoeic thought (*Kingship and the Gods,* p. 362 n. 4). The Frankforts distinguished three kinds of thought (*Before Philosophy,* pp. 11-19): (1) scientific, logical thought, which involves a disciplined reasoning that clearly separates subject and objects and which predominates in modern society; (2) speculative thought, which, although not ignoring reality, is intuitive; which transcends experience by seeking order, coherence, and meaning from the "chaos of experience"; and which is today informed and limited by scientific, logical thought; but which in antiquity "found unlimited possibilities for development" since "it was not restricted by a scientific (that is, a disciplined) search for truth" (*Before Philosophy,* pp. 11f.); (3) mythopoeic thought, in which the ancient persons as subject experienced the world as personal subject, having an I-Thou relationship with the world; it viewed man as embedded in nature, which as a whole constituted a living organism that was apprehended from within in the form of subject apprehending subject.

Mythopoeic thought apprehends the world intuitively through mystical participation. This direct apprehension of transcendent ontological realities is not open to experience through the ordinary physiological senses. It expresses its apprehension in myths, which in narrative form portray transcendent reality in imaginative and concrete symbols of gods and goddesses, and of their interrelationships with each other and humanity.

Ancient mythopoeic thought was influenced by speculative thought, but without the restrictions of scientific, logical thought, so that in the resultant myths we can detect a clear attempt to order and organize the direct mystical experience of transcendent reality. What we perceive as inanimate the ancients perceived as animate. They experienced natural forces as personal and also as transcendent, suprahuman powers. They thus conceptualized them pictorially through imagination as having personal existence and concrete form as gods, goddesses, and other supernatural beings. They imaginatively conceived of the interaction of these forces with each other and with humanity as mythical events.

For further discussion see Rogerson, pp. 85-100.

*B. Characteristics of Ancient Near Eastern Myth. 1.* It is *tied to nature and the cosmos* (and thus to reality), since it grew out of a direct experience of them. The imaginative, personalized symbols used to represent this experience seldom gain a personality independent of the forces and entities experienced.

*2.* It expresses an experience of *nature and the cosmos as personal* and animate. Cosmic powers and entities are therefore conceptualized imaginatively as having personal form. Their interrelationships are conceptualized as events in which personal beings interact with each other. This was not personification, which implies that what is represented as animate and personal is consciously known to be inanimate and impersonal.

*3.* It is *dynamic* by virtue of being tied to nature and natural forces, which are all experienced as personal and pulsating with life.

*4.* It also expresses the ancient Near Eastern *experience of transcendence,* of transcendent ontological realities. Mythopoeic thought began with a direct experience of nature and the cosmos but moved beyond it, experiencing the personal forces and entities in the universe, as well as their interrelationships, as in some way beyond human comprehension and empirical experience, i.e., as transcendent and mysterious. Cosmic forces and entities were experienced as more than merely empirical, natural, and inanimate.

The content of the myths illustrates this transcendent awareness. The mythical events portrayed take place in an "otherworldly" time and space, beyond ordinary matter and history. Myths deal with primordial events — with the origins and organization of the cosmos, humanity, and the origins of earthly institutions. Myths may deal with ends, with eschatological events, although this is not prominent in ancient Near Eastern myths. Myths may also deal with humanity's continuing quest for meaning.

*5.* It was *prescientific and prelogical.* Scientific and logical thought was not foreign to the ancient Near East but it was not paramount in attempts to comprehend cosmic and human existence.

*6.* It *used imagination in producing symbols* to represent the natural and cosmic powers and entities. Such symbols had personal, animate form, e.g., gods, goddesses, and other superhuman beings. The interrelationships of natural and cosmic powers and entities were conceived of as events in which the personalized, animate symbols interacted with each other as living beings. Mythopoeic thought, although imaginative, was not fantasy. Whereas fantasy loses contact with reality, ancient Near Eastern myth maintains that contact.

*7.* It expressed itself in *narrative form* as myth. Because of the imaginative and personalized symbols used, this narrative form is pictorial, dramatic, and storylike.

*8.* It is *intuitive and revelatory.* The universe as personal revealed itself through a direct, mystical, and intuitive encounter of subject with subject.

*9.* It *conveys truth authoritatively.* Myth, through its imaginative symbols, established direct contact with truth concerning ontological realities. It conveyed this truth with an authority difficult for the modern scientific, logical, and critical mind to comprehend.

*10.* It *evidences reflective thought.* Mythopoeic thought, which dominates, is combined with reflective thought. The reflective aspect of ancient Near Eastern myth shows up in the tendency to order, organize, and explain natural and cosmic powers and entities.

*11.* It is *polytheistic.* The various natural and cosmic powers and entities are symbolized as diverse divine and superhuman beings. Even when one god is supreme a hierarchy of lesser gods remains.

***III. Greek Myth.***–Greece created a rich world of mythology that has been most influential on Western civilization. Modern popular concepts of myth have been conditioned by an understanding of Greek mythology rather than of ancient Near Eastern mythology, from which Greek mythology differs noticeably.

*A. Rise and Development.* Greek mythology arose largely as a native phenomenon, with only a few instances of borrowing from the ancient Near East. We may suppose that in archaic times, prior to Homer, it originated from mythopoeic thought as an unconscious but natural process. The rise of Greek critical thought in the 5th cent. B.C., challenged what was sacred and traditional. Homer (8th cent. B.C.?) could laugh at the gods in his humorous depictions of them. Euripides (485-406 B.C.), deeply critical of traditional religious and social beliefs, was "the destroyer of myths" (*TDNT,* IV, 771). Socrates (469-399 B.C.), a constant and strong critic of the inherited standards and values of society, pointed up their inconsistencies; he was "cool towards myth" (*TDNT,* IV, 773). The Sophists undermined myth by developing logic and strongly criticized communal loyalty to the gods.

Many myths were reformulated so that their origin in mythopoeic thought became less clear, and other myths came into being through a conscious desire to entertain or to instruct. In the 4th cent. Plato (427-347 B.C.) revived myth in his dialogues, as a means of conveying in symbols the final vision of the otherworldly reality which was accessible only to faith, not logic. He no longer believed in myths and their world of gods per se. He either created new myths from traditional materials or made completely new ones as tools for instruction. Built into his myths is the allegorical method of interpretation. Consequently, he was aware of the differentiation between symbol and reality.

After Plato "myth falls from its high place" (*TDNT,* IV, 775). Plato's pupil, Aristotle (384-322 B.C.), is renowned for his work in logical thought and his use of the scientific method. These made him critical of myth and of the allegorical interpretation of traditional Greek myth. Stoicism, founded by Zeno (335-263), strongly advanced this method of interpretation. It viewed the world as divinely governed on rational principles and defined the wise as those who live their lives in conformity to the rational divine plan. It interpreted traditional Greek mythology allegorically in an attempt to safeguard myth against attacks on its irrationality and immorality. The use of this method, however, implied the untruth of myth when interpreted literally. Stoicism's monotheistic concept of divine power was also incompatible with the polytheism of traditional Greek myth. Epicurus (342-271 B.C.) adopted the atomic theory to show that the universe was made up of atoms, although these atoms had a measure of free will to move on their own. Epicurus also adopted and emphasized the principle of the reality of sensation. The blessed life was the life that was able to secure pleasure as the most desirable end. The gods played no active role in this materialistic scheme. Epicureanism was naturally critical of traditional Greek myth and also of its allegorical interpretation.

The intellectual world of Greece had an ambivalent attitude toward myth. It never totally rejected it but it openly criticized and sometimes derided the traditional understanding of myth and its deities as deficient in truth and morality and nonsensical and childish (cf. *TDNT,* IV, 779). Throughout the Hellenistic world mythology continued to play a strong role in poetry, although in an increasingly figurative way, and in religion. Christianity, as documented in the NT and early Christian writers, finally rejected myth on religious grounds (*TDNT,* IV, 779). The antithesis that developed between *mýthos,* "myth," and *alḗtheia,* "truth," in the Greek world never emerged in its full profundity and radicalness until the rise of Christianity. In the NT *mýthos* is diametrically opposed to the truth of the gospel. (See *TDNT,* IV, 784.)

*B. Greek Myth vis-à-vis Ancient Near Eastern Myth.* *1.* Greek mythology in the form it has been handed on is *not closely tied to nature and reality* as is ancient Near Eastern myth. It early lost its contact with the forces of nature. The independence of Greek myth from nature and reality led to a number of consequences: (a) The actors in Greek mythology exhibit *highly personified and individualized forms,* which are independent of the forces of nature. (b) Greek mythology often moves in the realm of *fantasy* in its development of actors and plots. (c) Greek mythology often functions to *entertain.* (d) As a result of (b) and (c) Greek mythology is often *fictitious* in content. (e) Greek mythology is *static* in contrast to ancient Near Eastern mythology. Perhaps it arose under the influence of a more dynamic view of nature but it early lost that contact. (f) Greek mythology *does not exhibit the same consciousness of transcendence* as ancient Near Eastern mythology. In Greek mythology the divine actors are more human; they are depicted as subdivine rather than as fully divine. The Greeks tended to make their gods in their own image.

*2.* Greek mythology, as transmitted to us, is *no longer prescientific and prelogical.* Greek logical and scientific thought affected the form in which myth was handed down, and became more and more critical of myth.

*3.* The Greek understanding of myth came to imply an *implicit untruth* to myth in contrast to the truth of philosophical and logical thought and the scientific method. The awareness of the untruth value of myth produced the allegorical method of interpretation in an attempt to try to salvage its truth value. The term *mýthos* itself came to mean "untrue story" or "invented story" in contrast to *alḗtheia,* "truth." Greek mythology is thus no longer revelatory or authoritative in the same way as ancient Near Eastern myth. The educated Greek had a growing awareness of the differentiation between symbol and reality, which were held together in ancient Near Eastern mythological thinking.

*4. Reflective thought is less obvious* in Greek mythology than in ancient Near Eastern mythology. In the latter, reflective thought shows itself in its attempt to order and organize the personal powers of nature. In Greek mythology such an attempt is overshadowed by the tendency to fantasize and entertain, which in turn is due to loss of contact with the forces of nature. In ancient Greece speculative thought made its main impact in philosophical theorizing about the structure, order, and meaning of the universe.

Greek mythology has some similarities to ancient Near Eastern mythology. Both take narrative form. Both are polytheistic. Both may trace their origins to a conception of nature and the cosmos as pulsating with life. Only ancient Near Eastern mythology, however, retained this view. In the final analysis the differences between the two mythologies are greater than the similarities.

*IV. The OT and Mythology.*–The narrative forms of myth that existed in the ancient Near East and in ancient Greek culture do not exist in the Bible. Comparative studies may show the influence of the ancient mythological world, but the dissimilarity of the biblical narratives from ancient mythological thought overshadows any similarities. Influences of ancient mythological thought can readily be adduced, but any conceptual borrowings have been profoundly modified by ancient Israelite and early Christian thought.

Only the latest parts of the OT could have been influenced by Greek thought by way of Hellenistic culture. But Greek influence on the Hebrew canon is minimal and no influence of Greek mythology is detectable. Ancient Near Eastern culture, which provided the OT life-setting, is thus the only potential source of mythological influence on the OT. As R. K. Harrison has stated: "It seems difficult to imagine on purely rational grounds that the OT writings could remain completely untouched by mythological tendencies in the ancient Near East" (*Intro. to the OT* [1969], p. 451). From a human perspective, the OT was conditioned by a culture that included mythopoeic thought. Though sharing basic patterns of thought as those with the rest of the ancient Near East, Israelite thought had distinctive aspects.

T. H. Gaster has offered a useful and concise presentation of the ways in which scholars have found an influence of ancient Near Eastern mythopoeic thought on the OT (*IDB*, III, 481-87). Gaster categorized such supposed influence as figurative expressions, allusions, and direct parallels.

Examples of figurative expressions are: (1) the voice of God as thunder (2 S. 22:14); (2) the wind as winged (2 S. 22:11; Ps. 104:3; Hos. 4:19), which reflects the ancient Near Eastern idea that storms were caused by the flapping of the wings of a large bird; (3) the sun as winged (Mal. 4:2 [MT 3:20]), which reflects the idea of the winged solar disk; (4) references to a mountain in the north (Isa. 14:13; Ps. 48:2 [MT 3]) where the gods assembled; (5) the Promised Land as a land "flowing with milk and honey" borrows from ancient Near Eastern mythological concepts of paradise; (6) the idea of a Book of Fate, which recorded a person's days even before birth (Ps. 139:15f.); (7) references to *lîlîṯ*, "night hag" (Isa. 34:14); *rešep*, "Canaanite god of pestilence" (Hab. 3:5); and the latter's sons, *b*^e^*nê rešep* (Job 5:7), all of whom reflect divine beings in ancient Near Eastern mythology. All the above ideas are readily explicable as borrowed mythological ideas that the OT has used in a purely figurative way without any commitment to the underlying theology.

The allusions are:

(1) The idea of a primordial revolt of the gods in heaven. In Ps. 82:6f. Yahweh metes out judgment upon certain "gods," and in Isa. 14:12-15 the king of Babylon arrogantly aspires to divinity and heavenly enthronement (Canaanite mythology is reflected in *hêlāl*, "day star," and *šāḥar*, "dawn," which are names of gods, and in the reference to "the mount of assembly," i.e., the mountain in the north [see above] where the council of the gods convened). Again, however, there is no evidence that the biblical writers accepted the underlying theology. They made figurative use of a borrowed mythological idea in order to demonstrate Yahweh's supremacy over nature and created beings.

(2) Mythological and astrological ideas. Job 38:31f. refers to "the chains of the Pleiades," "the cords of Orion," and "the Bear with its children," but once again there is no evidence that the underlying theology of these mythological and astrological ideas is accepted; in their present use they emphasize the power and sovereign rule of Yahweh.

(3) The wondrous child motif (Isa. 7:14; 9:6f.), which, Gaster said, reflects ancient myths "familiar especially from the Iranian lore of the Saoshyant (Savior) and from Vergil's Fourth Eclogue — of the virgin-born hero and of the Miraculous Child who is to usher in the New Age" (*IDB*, III, 483). Isa. 7:14, however, seems in context (7:1-17) to refer to an actual historical child. The ideals of government in Isa. 9:6f. are best seen as a development of, and a projection into the future of, the ideals inherent in the Davidic covenant (2 S. 7). Any perceived influence of ancient mythology on these two Isaianic passages rests on supposed evidence that is weak and tangential. The poem of Vergil (70-19 B.C.) is too late to have had any influence.

(4) Traces of ancient Hebrew hero myths. But references to Enoch, who "walked with God; and he was not, for God took him" (Gen. 5:24), and to Nimrod, who was "a mighty man [*gibbōr*] . . . a mighty [*gibbôr*] hunter before the Lord" (Gen. 10:8f.; Gaster took *gibbōr* to mean "giant"), provide no evidence that we are dealing with mythological ideas.

Gaster also referred to the "use of the name David to denote the future messianic king" (Jer. 30:9; Ezk. 34:23f.; 37:24; Hos. 3:5) as reflecting "a version of the widespread myth that great national heroes . . . do not die, but will return to their peoples in the hour of need." There is no evidence that such mythological ideas existed contemporary with the biblical passages cited; Gaster adduced only Arthur of Britain and Friedrich Barbarossa. Furthermore, it is doubtful that the idea that David was to be the future ideal ruler should be treated as myth in the ancient Near Eastern and Greek senses. What is more likely is that the name "David" is used with poetic license to refer to the heir of the Davidic dynasty who was expected to reign in the New Age; and the passages in which this idea is expressed project into the future an ideal already inherent in the Davidic covenant rather than reflecting the influence of any ancient mythology.

Gaster accepted the untenability of the assertion of some scholars that an ancient sun myth may have influenced the biblical statement that Enoch lived 365 years (Gen. 5:23) and the story of Samson, whose name (*šimšôn*) is compared with the Hebrew for "sun" (*šemeš*).

(5) The annual dying and reviving of the deity, who died or slept in the nether world during the dry summer and revived with the return of vegetation in the autumn. Associated with this idea is the myth and ritual of "sacred marriage" of a god and a goddess, through the instrumentality of a priest/king and a priestess, to ensure fertility. Some scholars find these ideas reflected in the OT, in such passages as Isa. 53 (the Suffering Servant), several Psalms in which the psalmists call on Yahweh to "wake" (Ps. 35:23; 44:23 [MT 24]; 59:4 [MT 5]), Canticles, and Hosea's imagery of Yahweh's marriage to Israel. The arguments adduced for this view are weak, and better

interpretations of the supposed biblical evidence are available (see *IDB,* III, 483).

Three major examples of "direct parallels" between ancient Near Eastern mythology and the OT are:

(1) The story of Yahweh's battle with a dragonlike creature. This does not occur as a complete narrative in the OT, but a number of passages allude to various aspects and variant traditions of the story and can be used as a basis for reconstructing the general outline. The monster against which Yahweh is said to have fought is variously called Leviathan (*liwyāṯān* — Job 3:8; 41:1 [MT 40:25]; Ps. 74:14; Isa. 27:1; 2 Esd. 6:49, 52), Rahab (Heb. *rahaḇ* — Job 9:13; 26:12; Ps. 89:10 [MT 11]; Isa. 30:7; 51:9), Tannin (*tannîn*), i.e., "dragon" or "sea monster" (Job 7:12; Ps. 74:13; Isa. 27:1; 51:9), Yam (*yām*), i.e., "sea" (Job 7:12; Ps. 74:13; Isa. 51:10; Hab. 3:8), Nahar (*nāhār*), i.e., "river, stream" (Ps. 93:3; Hab. 3:8), and Nahash (*nāḥāš*), i.e., "serpent" (Job 26:13; Isa. 27:1). It had several heads (Ps. 74:13f.) and had apparently made the gods afraid (Job 41:25 [MT 17]). Yahweh subdued and killed it (Isa. 27:1) by smiting it (Job 26:12), by cutting it to pieces (Isa. 51:9), by piercing it (Job 26:13; Isa. 51:9), by crushing it (Ps. 89:10 [MT 11]), and by bludgeoning its heads (Ps. 74:13f.). Yahweh also defeated the monster's allies (Job 9:13; Ps. 89:10 [MT 11]). A variant tradition presents Yahweh as merely restraining the monster (Job 7:12). To this tradition probably belongs the idea that the monster would break loose at the end of the world to engage in a renewed but unsuccessful fight against Yahweh (Job 3:8; Isa. 27:1; 2 Esd. 6:52). This story resembles the Ugaritic "Myth of Baal" (in which Baal wages a victorious fight with Yam, the god of sea and rivers) and the victorious fight of Marduk against the monster Tiâmat in the Mesopotamian creation epic. The story occurs elsewhere in variant forms in Sumerian, Egyptian, and Phoenician mythology. (See M. Wakeman, *God's Battle with the Monster* [1973].)

That the OT uses traditional mythological concepts in the above passages cannot be denied, but there is no evidence of a commitment to the underlying theology. The purpose for which these scattered mythological concepts are used is the crucial issue. The OT uses them to demonstrate the power and supremacy of Yahweh over nature. Their occurrence no more indicates a commitment to the underlying pagan theology than does the use of similar mythological concepts in Milton's *Paradise Lost.* As R. K. Harrison said: "Where the language of myth was countenanced in the OT writings, it carried with it a very different meaning for the Hebrews than for the pagan nations of the Near East" (*Intro. to the OT,* pp. 452f.).

(2) The stories of Creation and Paradise. These reflect ancient Near Eastern mythology in a number of ways.

(a) The Creation story (Gen. 1:1–2:4a). In ancient Near Eastern creation myths the idea of a primeval watery mass from which the gods created the universe is a common motif. The Egyptian "Theology of Memphis" describes the god Ptah as conceiving the various parts of the universe in his mind ("heart") and bringing them into being through his divine speech ("tongue"), after which he was "satisfied" or "rested" (lines 53-59; see *ANET,* pp. 4f.; W. Beyerlin, *Near Eastern Religious Texts,* pp. 4f.). God's speech in the first person plural, "Let *us* make man in *our* image, after *our* likeness" (Gen. 1:26, italics mine), may reflect the ancient Near Eastern idea of a divine assembly of heavenly beings (cf. Job 1:6; 2:1).

The closest parallel to the Genesis Creation story is the Mesopotamian creation myth, *Enuma Elish* (*ANET,* pp. 60-72; Beyerlin, *Near Eastern Religious Texts,* pp. 80-84). Both narratives describe a primordial watery mass (*Enuma Elish,* I:1-4; Gen. 1:1f.) out of which the universe was created. In Genesis this watery mass is called *tᵉhôm.* In the *Enuma Elish* it is made up of a comingling of *Apsû* (fresh waters) and *Tiâmat* (salt waters). Hebrew *tᵉhôm* is etymologically related to Akk. *Tiâmat,* although *tᵉhôm* in Genesis has lost the mythological force of its antecedent. In both accounts light, and also day and night, are present before the luminaries are created (*Enuma Elish,* I:38, 68, 102-104; Gen. 1:3-5). Heaven and earth are created from the primeval waters (*Enuma Elish,* I:55-77; IV:137-45; Gen. 1:6-10). The creation of humankind is the final and climactic act (*Enuma Elish,* VI:1-34; Gen. 1:26-30). At the end of all the creative activity there is a divine rest (*Enuma Elish,* VI:45-70; Gen. 2:2f.). The order of creative events is similar.

(b) The Paradise story (Gen. 2:4b-25). The forming of man from dust or clay (Gen. 2:7; cf. Job 33:6) is reflected in a Babylonian myth concerning the creation of humankind from clay mixed with the flesh and blood of a god (*ANET,* pp. 99f.) and in the Sumerian myth *Enki and Ninmah* in which man is fashioned from clay (Beyerlin, *Near Eastern Religious Texts,* pp. 76f.). Ancient Near Eastern mythology conveys the idea of a tree of life or of a life-giving plant. In Egypt the gods are represented as sitting in a large tree, from the eating of which they gain life and immortality. Mesopotamian cylinder seals often show scenes with a sacred tree from which a king draws life by touching it. The tree or plant of life is for humankind a potential source of immortality, which, however, it fails to attain. Thus in the *Epic of Gilgamesh* the hero Gilgamesh gets a plant of life from the bottom of the sea, but a serpent steals it from him. Gilgamesh sits down and weeps because he has lost the chance to become immortal. There is no ancient Near Eastern parallel to the tree of knowledge. An Assyrian myth quoted by Gaster (*IDB,* III, 482) described mankind as created to care for the soil and plants (*Keilschrifttexte aus Assur religiösen Inhalts,* I, no. 4; cf. Gen. 2:15). An Old Babylonian myth declares that "the *burden* [?] of creation man shall bear" (*ANET,* p. 99). Ancient Mesopotamian mythology also contains the idea of an original place of paradise in primeval times (cf. *ANET,* pp. 34ff.; Beyerlin, *Near Eastern Religious Texts,* pp. 85f.).

(3) The biblical story of the Deluge (Gen. 6:5–9:29). This has counterparts throughout the ancient world. The most important parallels are the Sumerian *Deluge Myth,* the Akkadian *Gilgamesh Epic* (tablet XI), and the Akkadian *Myth of Atra-ḫasis* (*ANET,* pp. 42-44, 104-106, 93-97; Beyerlin, *Near Eastern Religious Texts,* pp. 89-97), which are dependent on each other in the order listed above. Of the three accounts, tablet XI of the *Gilgamesh Epic* bears the closest affinity to the Genesis Deluge narrative. For a summary of these myths and their relation to the biblical story *see* BABYLONIA IX.A; FLOOD (GENESIS) VI.

That there is a relationship between the Genesis and Mesopotamian accounts of Creation, Paradise, and Deluge is clear. The precise nature of the relationship is not so clear. The basic questions explored by scholars are: (1) is there a dependence of one set of narratives on the other; if so (2), in which direction does that dependence function; and if not (3), do both derive from a common original narrative, or should we conceive of both sets of narratives as arising out of a general cultural milieu? The most likely answer probably lies in a combination of some sort of dependence and the derivation of both sets of narratives from common thoughts and ideas.

If we have so far emphasized the similarities between the Genesis and the Mesopotamian accounts of Creation, Paradise, and Deluge, it is the differences that are most important and that clearly set them apart. The Mesopotamian accounts are clear examples of ancient Near Eastern mythology. The Genesis accounts are not. The purpose and theology of the two sets of narratives are quite different. The Genesis narratives have used the ancient mythological ideas to support the radically different theology of Yahwistic faith: (1) The OT narratives have been historicized. They are part of the prologue, i.e., the "Primeval History" (Gen. 1–11), of a more extensive narrative that describes Yahweh's redemptive actions in history. (2) The OT narratives have a high view of deity. (a) There is a strong monotheistic tendency in contrast to the polytheism of the myths. (b) God is transcendent. He is not tied to the forces of nature, which in Genesis are inanimate and impersonal; only Yahweh is personal, and mankind whom He made in His own image. Yahweh has sovereign power over natural forces and entities. (c) Yahweh is a moral God who requires obedience to His will and judges disobedience and wickedness. His judgment in the Flood is not arbitrary nor due to a mere capricious dissatisfaction with the tumult of multiplying mankind. His judgment is just; it is due to the magnitude of human wickedness and rebellion. (d) Throughout, Yahweh is demonstrated to be a God of grace who acts with a view to human redemption and reconciliation. (3) Ancient Israelite Yahwistic faith maintained a strong antimythological tendency in its condemnation of polytheistic religion and its rejection of any representation of Yahweh in natural forms.

*V. Myth and Ritual.*–The expression "myth and ritual" refers to studies of the relation of myth to ritual. Jane Harrison in her work on ancient Greek religion (*Themis* [1912]) described the *mýthos* ("the tale told, the action recounted") as the spoken correlative of the *drṓmenon* ("the acted rite, the thing done"). The *mýthos* and the *drṓmenon* were two complementary ingredients of a sacred ceremony or drama (pp. 327-331).

In OT studies the relation of myth and ritual was pursued by Scandinavian scholars, such as S. Mowinckel, and by the British "myth and ritual" school led by S. H. Hooke. Mowinckel (*Psalmenstudien, II: Das Thronbesteigungsfest Yahwäs* [1922]; *Psalms in Israel's Worship,* I [Eng. tr. 1962], 106-192) concluded, on the basis of comparative studies, that the autumn Festival of Tabernacles/Ingathering in ancient Israel included a New Year Enthronement Festival patterned after a festival of divine kingship in Canaan and Babylonia. In this festival Yahweh was reenthroned seasonally as universal king. He believed that the festal myths and ritual activities of the Enthronement Festival were reflected in, and could be reconstructed from, many of the Psalms, especially Enthronement Psalms, as well as other Scriptures.

In Britain S. H. Hooke and his followers argued for a "cultic patternism," namely, that throughout the ancient Near East there was a single cultic pattern of rituals and myths (Hooke, ed., *Myth and Ritual* [1933]; *Labyrinth* [1935]). This pattern, which was central to a New Year Festival, included: (a) a dramatic representation of the death and resurrection of the deity, (b) a recitation of the myth of creation, (c) a ritual combat in which the deity triumphed over his enemies, (d) a sacred marriage, and (e) a triumphal procession. The king had a central role, as source of community well-being; he played the part of the deity. Hooke and his followers argued that this pattern influenced the early religion of the Hebrews, e.g., in myths and rituals concerning sacral kingship and the enthronement rite, which were considered central to the main Hebrew festivals, especially the autumn Festival of Tabernacles.

Both Scandinavian and British scholars have been criticized for subjectivity. Parallels between the Babylonian *akītu* festival and a reconstructed Hebrew New Year Feast of Ingathering are weak and conjectural. The existence of a New Year Enthronement Festival among the ancient Hebrews has not been proven. Furthermore, the ancient Hebrew festivals did not fit the supposed ancient Near Eastern pattern. Hooke's use of the OT to support ideas of divine kingship and of the king acting as Yahweh's cultic substitute lacks any sound basis. Both the historical emphasis and the antifertility emphasis of ancient Hebrew religion argue against the possibility that the ancient Hebrews shared in a common ritual and mythical pattern of the ancient Near East.

T. H. Gaster (*Thespis* [1950]) continued to argue for a primitive and seasonal pattern of myth and ritual, survivals of which are reflected in the ancient literature of the Canaanites, Hittites, Egyptians, and Hebrews. Gaster conceded, however, "that most of the texts in question now stand a long way from the primitive form and have been subjected to considerable literary and artistic development" (p. 18). The latter is true of the OT. Any survivals there of the seasonal pattern of myth and ritual are just that, survivals. They do not indicate a commitment to the underlying theology or attitude to nature and the gods of the ancient Near Eastern seasonal pattern. In the OT such survivals have been theologized, historicized, and adapted to Yahwism.

See Rogerson, pp. 66-84; *see also* NEW YEAR.

*VI. Modern Redefinition of Myth.*–In modern times the idea of myth has been redefined and broadened, as a transcultural and transhistorical phenomenon, to include much more than would fit into our previous descriptions of ancient Near Eastern and Greek mythology. This redefinition has occurred in response to the influence and growth of scholarly investigations in anthropology, sociology, psychology, linguistics, and history of religions. A modern approach would, generally speaking, view myth as a technical term for the symbolical expression, using picturesque terms and concepts familiar to ordinary human experience, of transcendent ontological realities, intuited emotively, which surpass ordinary human comprehension, and which concern the origins, ends, and meaning of human existence.

This broadened definition stands in contrast to the older scholarly view, which understood myth to be both religious and polytheistic per se, as was ancient Near Eastern and Greek mythology, and which understood myth to entail a way of thinking superceded by modern logical, scientific thought. The new redefinition sees myth as neither religious nor secular per se. It considers mythological thinking to be integral to being human and basic to all human thought and expression. Mythological thinking is as real today as in ancient times. When human knowledge reaches the limits of what can be logically and scientifically explained, it faces the unknown or transcendent, which, if an attempt is made to express it in human language, can be expressed only in terms of the known or ordinary. Creative imagination steps in to provide order and meaning to the unintelligible, transcendent realities by speaking in picturesque symbols. This, according to much modern scholarship, is to think mythologically.

The transcultural and transhistorical redefinition of myth needs to be evaluated both positively and negatively. On the positive side we might readily agree with the main point made in the redefinition. If myth is "the picturesque and symbolic expression of transcendent reality," it is a fundamental aspect of human nature and characteristic of all culture.

On the negative side the following considerations are important:

(1) In the popular mind the term "myth" continues to

bear the later Greek connotation, namely, that which is false, untrue, contrary to reality, and therefore unbelievable.

(2) According to its modern redefinition, myth is often used to describe what is consciously understood not to accord with reality. Raphael Patai pointed to George Sorel's "myth of the general strike" (*Myth and Modern Man,* pp. 91f.), and Ernst Cassirer to the "myth of German Social Nationalism" (in Verene, ed., *Symbol, Myth and Culture,* pp. 234-39). These so-called myths convey only an apparent truth. They have lost contact with reality. The myth of the general strike shields the striker from the truth, i.e., the "uselessness of the general strike"; the term "mythical" describes that which does not accord with actual reality. Cassirer allowed that modern myths are no longer spontaneous, but artificially and consciously tailored for planned, political ends due to the influence of logical and scientific thought.

(3) The modern redefinition of myth, with its emphasis upon the possibility of purely secular myths, tends to lose sight of the truly transcendent aspect of reality and to deal instead with that aspect of the immanent, physical universe that is not yet comprehended by intellect. Since the aspect of reality that is beyond intellectual comprehension has something of the sacredness of the transcendent, some scholars, working with a modern redefinition, define myth in religious terms. Mircea Eliade said: "Myth narrates sacred history; it relates an event that took place in primordial Time, the fabled time of the 'beginnings'" (*Myth and Reality,* p. 5). Elsewhere he said: "Myths reveal that the world, man, and life have a supernatural origin and history, and that this history is significant, precious, and exemplary" (*Enc.Brit.,* XV, 1133). G. Henton Davies said: "Mythology is a way of thinking and imagining about the divine rather than a thinking or imagining about a number of gods" (as quoted by J. L. McKenzie, *Dictionary of the Bible* [1965], p. 599).

(4) The above three considerations point to the conclusion that the redefined concept of myth differs essentially from that of ancient Near Eastern myth. The latter wedded symbol and reality together. With Greek logical and scientific thinking human thought began to become conscious of the differentiation between symbol and reality. Modern logical and scientific thought, the heir of ancient Greek thought, has the tools available to see the differentiation more clearly. Modern thought made it possible to opt for a logically, scientifically, and phenomenologically accurate description of more and more of reality. Thus Eliade could say, "at least apparently, the modern world is not rich in myths" (*Myths, Dreams and Mysteries,* p. 25; cf. pp. 24-38).

(5) In the light of the above considerations, the validity and usefulness of the continued use of the terms "myth," "mythology," "mythical," and "mythological" is open to question. The transcendent and sacred aspects of reality remain, however, and humanity continues to respond intuitively and emotively, expressing its experience of the transcendent in symbolic language. Rather than speak of this as mythological thought (which implies falsehood) we might better speak of intuitive thought (which implies neither truth nor falsehood). Instead of myth we might speak of "story" (Fackre, *Christian Story*), "religious drama" (R. K. Harrison, *Intro. to the OT,* p. 451), "parable" (A. Richardson, *Genesis 1-11* [*Torch,* 1953], pp. 27-32), "narrative drama" (M. Horsnell), or even coin a new term.

***VII. The NT and Mythology.***–We saw previously that the OT has been influenced by ancient Near Eastern mythology. The NT, through its use of the OT as Scripture, has, therefore, been indirectly influenced as well. Although the NT might also have been influenced by ancient Greek mythology, nothing comparable to Greek mythology occurs in the NT. In fact, the NT uses the term "myth" (*mýthos*) pejoratively to mean "untrue story" or "fiction." "Myths" in the NT most probably refer to a mixture of Jewish and Christian Gnostic speculations that are to be rejected because they are contrary to the gospel. The negative meaning of the NT term "myth" is comparable to the later meaning that the ancient Greeks developed for it when they became critical of their own myths, and came to see *mýthos* as the opposite of "truth" (*alḗtheia*), as that which was not in accord with reality. It is natural, then, that the NT would not use Greek mythology as the OT does ancient Near Eastern mythology.

The English term "myth" entered into the arena of modern theological and biblical debate primarily through the work of D. F. Strauss, who provided a mythological interpretation of the life of Christ (for the following survey of Strauss's position see P. C. Hodgson, "Editor's Intro.," in Strauss, *The Life of Jesus Critically Examined,* pp. xv-l). He maintained that the Gospels are composed of myths, legends, materials deriving from the authors' literary activity, and a residue of historical materials. Myth, for Strauss, is the narrative expression of an idea. By "idea" Strauss meant "religious imagery" in contrast to the Gospels' essential content of truth and historical facts. For Strauss the following narratives are largely mythical and therefore unhistorical: the Birth, Infancy, and Childhood narratives; the narratives dealing with the relations between Jesus and John the Baptist; the miracle stories; the Transfiguration account; the description of the entrance into Jerusalem; predictions of the Passion; the Passion story; and the Resurrection and Ascension narratives.

Inevitably, the result of Strauss's study were negative, for (1) his approach was atomistic; Strauss emphasized the individual stories, the smallest units of tradition, apart from their function in the Gospel as a whole; (2) he was also not overly concerned with the historical and theological context of the Gospels in their final form.

Part of Strauss's lasting impact on biblical studies was his broad understanding of myth. To quote from Hodgson's estimate of Strauss: "Religion is by definition *imaginative* . . . and therefore *mythical* . . . , for myths are expressions in storylike form of temporally conditioned religious ideas. This definition has the effect of greatly enlarging the role of myth, for where true religion is found so also is myth, as its proper mode of expression" (p. xxvi).

A scholar who was influenced by Strauss and who has profoundly affected the modern understanding of the NT is Rudolf Bultmann (see *Kerygma and Myth; Jesus Christ and Mythology*). In 1941 Bultmann initiated a debate concerning the demythologizing of the NT in a paper entitled "NT und Mythologie." The initial debate that ensued is reflected in a series of essays, including Bultmann's original paper, which was published in two volumes entitled *Kerygma und Mythos* (Eng. tr. *Kerygma and Myth*). Bultmann believed the NT to be heavily laden with mythical ideas, conditioned by a prelogical and prescientific world view. Under the influence of Strauss, he treated myth as a narrative dealing with the "other side" (i.e., a narrative concerning transcendent religious realities) expressed in terms of "this side" (i.e., in time-bound terms derived from ordinary human language and experience) (see *Jesus Christ and Mythology,* pp. 18f.). Bultmann claimed that the NT presents a "mythical view of the world" (i.e., a three-storied universe) and a "mythical view of redemption" (see *Kerygma and Myth,* I, 1f.). "It proclaims in the language of mythology that the last time has now come. 'In the fulness of time' God sent forth his Son, a pre-existent divine Being, who appears on earth as a man. He dies the death of a sinner on the cross and makes atonement for the sins of men. His resurrection marks the beginning of the cosmic catastrophe. Death, the consequence of Adam's sin, is abolished, and the daemonic forces are deprived of their power. The risen Christ is exalted to the right hand of God in heaven and made 'Lord' and 'King'. He will come again on the clouds of heaven to complete the work of redemption, and the resurrection and judgement of men will follow. Sin, suffering and death will then be finally abolished. All this is to happen very soon; indeed, St. Paul thinks that he himself will live to see it. . . . All this is the language of mythology. . . . To this extent *the kerygma is incredible to modern man, for he is convinced that the mythical view of the world is obsolete*. . . . Theology must undertake the task of stripping the Kerygma from its mythical framework, of 'demythologizing' it" (pp. 2f.). Demythologizing was necessary because the NT embodies "a truth which is quite independent of its mythical setting?" (p. 3).

Bultmann's approach was a twofold program of demythologizing and existential interpretation. The biblical interpreter must demythologize to distinguish the mythological, time-bound language that constituted the "setting" or "framework" within which a real truth was conveyed. That truth could be detected by existential interpretation. Bultmann used the existential philosophy of Martin Heidegger as a tool to arrive at the truth of the NT kerygma. This truth lay in what it conveyed concerning one's self-understanding within the world and concerning one's existence before God. By responding to the truth of the kerygma one comes to faith and experiences authentic human existence in freedom from insecurity, in independence of the tangible and transitory sphere of this world, and in loving fellowship with others (pp. 17-22).

The kerygma was all-important for Bultmann. He saw no continuity between the Jesus of history and the Christ of faith, i.e., the Christ of the kerygma. The Jesus of history was a Jewish apocalyptist. Proclaiming a Word of God in view of the imminent end of the world, He called for decision. He finally died a tragic death. The Jesus of history occasioned the kerygma but the Christ of the kerygma is a mythical reinterpretation of the historical Jesus by the post-Easter Church. Jesus was reinterpreted, under the influence of Jewish apocalyptic and Gnostic redemption mythology, as having risen bodily from the dead, as "Son of Man" who would return as judge, as "begotten of the Holy Spirit," as "born of a virgin," and as "the Son of God in a metaphysical sense, a great, preexistent heavenly being who became man"(*Jesus Christ and Mythology*, pp. 16f.). His resurrection, for Bultmann, meant His rising into the kerygma to become the kerygmatic Christ. In the process the Christ of the kerygma has been separated from history, for Jesus of Nazareth was not what the kerygma claimed Him to be. Here lies the profound weakness in Bultmann's program. Without a continuity between the kerygmatic Christ and the historical Jesus, faith is faith in a mythical construction. In order for faith in the kerygmatic Christ to be grounded in reality the Christ of the kerygma must also be continuous with the Jesus of history. It is not enough to reply that Bultmann emphasized the historical event of Jesus and therefore did not abandon the historical basis of the kerygma; the gulf between the historical Jesus and the kerygmatic Christ remains too great.

Much of what Bultmann called myth should be seen as factual event or metaphysical reality (either past, present and continuing, or yet to be), e.g., the Incarnation, the supernatural activity of God and of Satan in human history, miracles, the death of Jesus as atonement, the bodily resurrection of Jesus, the resurrection of the dead, and final judgment.

Some of Bultmann's students and followers have seen the inherent weakness of his radical discontinuity between the historical Jesus and the kerygmatic Christ, and have initiated a new quest for the historical Jesus, in which Jesus' words and deeds are seen as part of the kerygma. God is manifested in the "language-event" of the historical Jesus, not merely in the Christ of the kerygma. Thus, continuity is re-established. (Cf. Bornkamm, Robinson, and Conzelmann.)

Bultmann has been criticized on other grounds too. His argument for the influence of Gnostic redeemer mythology on the NT kerygma has been strongly contested in the light of recent Gnostic research. He has also been censured for working with an outdated concept of myth as a prescientific way of representing transcendent otherworldly reality in this-worldly terms, a concept that has not taken contemporary redefinitions into account.

Later interpreters have taken a literary and linguistic approach to the problem of the NT and mythology. The structuralists, using theories of Claude Lévi-Strauss and Ferdinand de Saussure, seek to move beyond the surface structures of a text to the deep structures, which correspond to universal and transhistorical structures of human life and thought, that are present in the human unconscious. Myths, or mythological texts, manifest a mythical structure as one of these deep structures. The mythical structure reflects real, absolute oppositions that are characteristic of human experience, such as Life-Death, Nature-Culture, Heaven-Earth, God-Man. (Cf. D. Patte, *What is Structural Exegesis?* [1976], esp. pp. 53ff.; Rogerson, pp. 101-127.) Structural exegesis has been applied in NT studies by scholars such as Daniel Patte, John Crossan, and Dan Via, and to OT studies by Robert Culley and Robert Polzin, *et al.*

Other interpreters who take a literary approach focus on the biblical text as it confronts the reader. Amos Wilder (*Jesus' Parables and the War of Myths*) believes in the validity of the historical and theological study of the text. Ultimately, however, the text must be read and heard so that its imagery, symbolism, and mythology have an immediate impact. For Wilder, both figurative discourse (poetry, imagery, symbolism, and myth) and discursive discourse are grounded in truth and reality. In them "the 'word' has been wedded to 'reality'" (p. 16), to create a "language-world' (p. 19). Language reflects a particular understanding of reality that is time-bound and conditioned by the social and historical dimensions of human existence. There is also, in spite of many differences, a basic continuity in human nature and experience. The task of the interpreter is to enter into the frame of mind, the experience of human existence, conveyed by the biblical text and its imaginative language. The interpreter can relate the text to the present by discovering the continuity between the text and today. Because myth is part of a unified "language-world," the interpreter cannot, following Bultmann, engage in "demythologizing." (See also Wilder, *Theopoetic*.)

In contrast to Bultmann, the merit of structural exegesis and of Wilder's literary approach is that they work with an understanding of myth that is compatible with the modern scientific view of reality. Their understanding of myth has been so broadened and attenuated, however, that the term "myth" has clearly moved in the direction of equation with metaphor, imagery, and symbol, and has thus become rather meaningless and confusing. Hence the question arises whether the use of such terms as "myth," "mythology," "mythological," and "mythical" to characterize biblical literature is not ill-advised.

***VIII. Mythology in Biblical Interpretation.***–By way of summary, a number of principles, helpful as guides to a correct interpretation of Scripture, can be drawn from the preceding discussion.

*A. The Bible Is Culturally Conditioned.* Mythopoeic thought was an integral part of the ancient Near Eastern "setting in life" out of which the OT arose. It was impossible for the ancient Hebrews to remain unaffected by such thought. Communication always occurs in contemporary categories. Thus, OT thought shares in much of what constitutes mythopoeic thought.

*B. Biblical Transformation of Culture.* Mythopoeic thought has been transformed and adapted in the OT by the following forces stemming from Yahwistic faith: (1) ancient Hebrew religion was not tied to nature but to a reality that transcended nature, namely, Yahweh; (2) nature was not experienced as personal; (3) a high view of deity was maintained with a strong monotheistic and anti-polytheistic tendency, which opposed fertility religion and entailed a high ethical demand for obedience; (4) a strong antimythological tendency, inherent in its condemnation of the polytheistic and fertility religion that was the matrix of ancient Near Eastern mythology, was present in Yahwistic faith; (5) there was a strong tendency to historicize ancient Hebrew religious traditions.

The NT, which is firmly rooted in the OT, is even further removed from true mythopoeic thought. In the NT the OT's antimythological tendency is raised to a higher level and, under the influence of the Greek world's negative critique of its own *mýthoi,* the NT came to view *mýthos* pejoratively.

*C. The Bible Is Not Mythological but Uses Mythological Ideas.* Biblical thought should not be called "mythopoeic," neither should any of the resultant biblical narratives be termed "myth." The OT uses ancient Near Eastern mythological ideas figuratively and symbolically without any commitment to the underlying theology of the mythological world from which they have been borrowed. Biblical narratives, such as those of Creation (Gen. 1:1–2:3), Paradise (2:4-25), Fall (3:1-24), and Flood (6:5–9:17), may appear to be of the same type as ancient Near Eastern myths, but are different due to the impact of the transforming forces of Yahwistic faith.

*D. Picturesque Symbolism Is a Biblical Phenomenon.* The picturesque, symbolic narrative expression of an emotive intuition of the transcendent and sacred does occur in the Bible. Examples are the Creation, Paradise, Fall, and Flood narratives in Genesis as well as apocalyptic eschatology and parables in the NT. The use of picturesque symbolism does not mean that historical or factual reality did not occasion such narratives. Scholars may differ over the extent to which factual reality is represented in them, but in the above examples that factual reality includes the following: God's primordial creative action in bringing the universe, living creatures, and human beings into being; human nature as fallen in primeval time; the occurrence of a primeval flood interpreted as divine judgment on human sin; and the occurrence of an end and consummation to this age of human history.

*E. Validity of Distinguishing Symbol and Reality.* Ancient Near Eastern mythopoeic thought held symbol and reality together as an undifferentiated whole. Since the ancient Hebrews shared in much (but not all) of mythopoeic thought, we find in the OT a similar holding together of symbol and reality. The rise of Greek scientific and logical thought placed a wedge between them and eventually led the Greeks to a negative assessment of their own mythology. This negative connotation of *mýthos* was taken over into the NT. In the NT the tendency to hold symbol and reality together is still present, but perhaps not as strongly as in the OT.

Modern scientific, logical, and reflective thought, the heir of ancient Greek thought, can differentiate symbol and reality more readily. OT and NT thought was *sui generis* unable to think in precisely this same way. Modern interpreters can and ought so to think. The responsible interpretation and application of Scripture today demands that they attempt to differentiate symbol and reality. This is not always an easy task and may at times seem to be impossible, for often transcendent reality can be expressed only in picturesque symbols.

***Bibliography.****–Terminology: TDNT,* IV, *s.v.* μῦθος (G. Stählin).

*Ancient Mythology: ANET*; W. Beyerlin, ed., *Near Eastern Religious Texts Relating to the OT* (Eng. tr., *OTL,* 1978); H. Frankfort, *Kingship and the Gods: A Study of Ancient Near Eastern Religion as the Integration of Society and Nature* (repr. 1978); H. and H. A. Frankfort, J. A. Wilson, and T. Jacobsen, *Before Philosophy: The Intellectual Adventure of Ancient Man* (repr. 1973); G. S. Kirk, *Myth: Its Meaning and Function in Ancient and Other Cultures* (1970); S. N. Kramer, *Mythologies of the Ancient World* (1961); L. Lévy-Bruhl, *Primitive Mentality* (1923); *How Natives Think* (1926); H. J. Rose, *Gods and Heroes of the Greeks* (1958).

*OT and Mythology:* B. S. Childs, *Myth and Reality in the OT* (*SBT,* 1/27, 1960); F. M. Cross, *Canaanite Myth and Hebrew Epic* (1973); *IDB,* III, *s.v.* (T. H. Gaster); D. Irvin, *Mytharion* (1978); F. R. McCurley, *Ancient Myths and Biblical Faith* (1983); B. Otzen, H. Gottlieb, and K. Jeppesen, *Myths in the OT* (1980); J. W. Rogerson, *Myth in OT Interpretation* (*BZAW,* 134, 1974).

*Myth and Ritual:* T. H. Gaster, *Thespis: Ritual, Myth, and Drama in the Ancient Near East* (rev. ed. 1961); J. E. Harrison, *Themis: A Study of the Social Origins of Greek Religion* (1912); S. H. Hooke, ed., *Myth and Ritual: Essays on the Myth and Ritual of the Hebrews in Relation to the Culture Pattern of the Ancient East* (1933); *The Labyrinth: Further Studies in the Relation Between Myth and Ritual in the Ancient World* (1935); *Myth, Ritual, and Kingship: Essays on the Theory and Practice of Kingship in the Ancient Near East and in Israel* (1958); A. R. Johnson, *Sacral Kingship in Ancient Israel* (1967); S. Mowinckel, *Psalmenstudien, II, Das Thronbesteigungsfest Yahwäs* (1922); *Psalms in Israel's Worship,* I (Eng. tr. 1962), 106-192.

*Modern Redefinition:* K. W. Bolle, *The Freedom of Man in Myth* (1968); E. Cassirer, *Language and Myth* (Eng. tr. 1946); M. Eliade, *Myth of the Eternal Return* (1954); *Myth and Reality* (1963); *Myths, Dreams and Mysteries* (1960), *Enc.Brit.,* XII (1974, repr. 1982), *s.v.* (K. W. Bolle); XV (1970), *s.v.* (M. Eliade); H. A. Murray, ed., *Myth and Mythmaking* (1960); R. Patai, *Myth and Modern Man* (1972); T. A. Sebeok, ed., *Myth: A Symposium* (repr. 1965); D. P. Verene, ed., *Symbol, Myth, and Culture: Essays and Lectures of Ernst Cassirer 1935-1945* (1979).

*NT and Mythology:* R. Bultmann, *et al., Kerygma and Myth: A Theological Debate* (Eng. tr., 2 vols., 1953, 1962); G. Bornkamm, *Jesus of Nazareth* (Eng. tr. 1960); R. Bultmann, *Jesus Christ and Mythology* (Eng. tr. 1958); H. Conzelmann, *Outline of the Theology of the NT* (Eng. tr. 1969); J. D. G. Dunn, "Demythologizing: The Problem of Myth in the NT," in I. H. Marshall, ed., *NT Interpretation* (1977), pp. 285-307; J. Hick, ed., *Myth of God Incarnate* (1977); K. Jaspers and R. Bultmann, *Myth and Christianity* (Eng. tr. 1958); N. Perrin, *The NT: An Intro.* (1974), pp. 21-34; J. M. Robinson, *New Quest of the Historical Jesus* (1959); D. F. Strauss, *The Life of Jesus Critically Examined* (Eng. tr. repr. 1972); A. N. Wilder, *Jesus' Parables and the War of Myths* (1982); *Theopoetic: Theology and the Religious Imagination* (1976).

*The Bible and Mythology:* G. Fackre, *The Christian Story* (2nd ed. 1984); N. Frye, *The Great Code: The Bible and Literature* (1982).

M. J. A. HORSNELL

# n

**NAAM** nā'əm [Heb. *naʿam*]. A son of Caleb (1 Ch. 4:15).

**NAAMAH** nā'ə-mə [Heb. *naʿᵃmâ*–'pleasant'; Gk. *Noema*].

**1.** Daughter of Lamech and Zillah, and sister of Tubal-cain (Gen. 4:22; cf. Josephus *Ant.* i.2.2 [65]).

**2.** Ammonite wife of Solomon and mother of Rehoboam (1 K. 14:21; 2 Ch. 12:13). According to an addition in the LXX following 1 K. 12:24, "her name was Naaman, the daughter of Ana (Hanun) son of Nahash, king of the sons of Ammon" (see I. Benzinger, *Die Bücher der Könige* [1899], *in loc.*).

**NAAMAH** nā'ə-mə [Heb. *naʿᵃmâ*–'delightful'; Gk. *nōman, nōma,* suggesting that the LXX translators read a short *o* vowel in the first syllable, possibly by analogy to the name Naomi (Heb. *noʿᵒmî*)]. A city in the Philistine plain assigned to the tribe of Judah (Josh. 15:41). It is one of sixteen listed in vv. 37-41, where it is named between Beth-dagon and Makkedah. The name, it is said, is preserved in ʿArâq Naʿaman, but the location has been identified with nearby Khirbet Fered (*GP,* II, 89), 3 km. (2 mi.) S of the railroad station of Nahal Soreq (*GP,* II, 393). Since the list in vv. 37-41 includes Lachish, Eglon, and Migdal-gad, however, it may be more reasonable to look for Naamah in the region nearer to Lachish, about 25 km. (15 mi.) farther S, than to place confidence in the supposed similarity of the names.

In Job, Zophar is called "the NAAMATHITE," the Hebrew word being a gentilic (name of a people) formed on *naʿᵃmâ* (apparently a different place). W. S. L. S.

**NAAMAN** nā'mən [Heb. *naʿᵃmān*–'pleasantness']. Similar names, or names containing this element, are found in the Ugaritic texts and in the Mari texts (see Gray, p. 504, and H. Huffmon, *Amorite Personal Names in the Mari Texts* [1965], pp. 53f., 237-39, for references).

**1.** A descendant of Benjamin who entered Egypt (Gen. 46:21). He is further described as a son of Bela and eponymous ancestor of the "Naamites" (Nu. 26:40; 1 Ch. 8:4, 7).

**2.** The commander of the Syrian army who was cured of "leprosy" by Elisha (2 K. 5). The Syrian king mentioned in the story is probably Ben-hadad II (cf. 2 K. 8:7); although the name of the Israelite king is not given, the event probably took place during the reign of Jehoram (852-841 B.C.). Naaman, to whom the Lord had given victories (5:1), was a leper. His wife's Israelite servant girl suggested that the prophet in Samaria would be able to cure him. Following her advice, Naaman traveled to Samaria with gifts and a letter from his king demanding that Naaman be cured (see Montgomery, p. 374, for ancient Near Eastern parallels). When the Israelite king read the letter he believed that the king of Syria was attempting to provoke war. Hearing of the king's distress, Elisha sent a messenger to request that Naaman come to him. When Naaman arrived, however, Elisha did not even go out to meet him, but through an intermediary told him to wash in the Jordan seven times. Following the promptings of his servants, Naaman obeyed the prophet's command and was indeed cured. Returning to thank the prophet, Naaman confessed, "I know that there is no God in all the earth but in Israel" (5:15). In addition, in proof of his sincerity, he took "two mules' burden of earth" back with him to Syria to use in the construction of a sacrificial altar (5:17). This probably reflects the traditional Near Eastern attitude that a deity was god over a specific land. Naaman even requested that the Lord would pardon him when, for the sake of expediency, he entered the temple of Rimmon, the storm-god of Damascus, with his master. Instead of rebuking him for such a request, Elisha told him to "go in peace" (5:19; see Ellul, pp. 35-40). After Naaman's departure, Elisha's servant Gehazi pursued Naaman and lied in order to receive a portion of the gifts that his master Elisha had refused. His scheme having been exposed upon his return to Elisha, Gehazi and his descendants were cursed with leprosy (Heb. *ṣāraʿaṯ,* 5:27).

It cannot be ascertained with certainty what type of disease Naaman had, for the term "leprosy" (Heb. *ṣāraʿaṯ*) includes more illnesses than Hansen's disease (*see* LEPER V). It must not have been the most severe type, for his case did not require isolation (Lev. 13:45f.). Possibly he had what Herodotus (i.138) called *leúkē* as distinct from *lépra* (J. Gray, p. 504).

In Lk. 4:27 Jesus uses Naaman to illustrate God's freedom — God chose to heal Naaman, an enemy of Israel, but no Israelites. This scandal of God's grace so provoked Jesus' listeners that they attempted to kill Him (vv. 28f.), thus dramatically illustrating Jesus' point that "no prophet is acceptable in his own country" (v. 24).

***Bibliography.***–J. Ellul, *Politics of God and the Politics of Man* (Eng. tr. 1972), pp. 23-40; J. Gray, *I & II Kings* (*OTL,* rev. ed. 1970); J. Montgomery, comm. on Kings (*ICC,* 1951).

C. G. RASMUSSEN

**NAAMATHITE** nā'ə-mə-thīt [Heb. *naʿᵃmāṯî* (Job 2:11; 11:1; 20:1; 42:9); Gk. *ho Minaiōn basileús*–'the king of the Mineans' (2:11), *ho Minaios*–'the Minean' (11:1; 20:1; 42:9)].

A person of or from Naamah; Zophar in the book of Job is the only person so described. In view of the location of the book of Job, a site in Edom or northwestern Arabia has been proposed, possibly in the vicinity of Jebel el-Na‘ameh (*IB*, III, 923). The Greek, if it is to be taken seriously, locates the site in southern Arabia. Except for Naamah in Josh. 15:41 no other place of this name is mentioned in the Bible. W. S. L. S.

**NAAMITE** nā'ə-mīt [Heb. *na‘$^a$mî*]. A family that traced its descent from Naaman (Nu. 26:40). *See* Naaman **2.**

**NAARAH** nā'ə-rə [Heb. *na‘$^a$râ*–'a girl']. One of the two wives of Ashhur father of Tekoa (1 Ch. 4:5f.).

**NAARAH** nā'ə-rə [Heb. *na‘$^a$râ*; Gk. B *hai kṓmai autṓn*, A *Naaratha*] (Josh. 16:7); AV, NEB, NAARATH nā'ə-rath; **NAARAN** nā'ə-ran [Heb. *na‘$^a$rān*; Gk. B *Naarnan*, A *Naaran*] (1 Ch. 7:28). A town in the territory of Ephraim, not far N of Jericho (Josh. 16:7). Eusebius (*Onom.*) places it 5 Roman mi. (about 7½ km., 4½ mi.) from Jericho. Naarah has been considered to be near ‘Ain Dûq (see *EAEHL*, III, *s.v.* "Na‘aran" [M. Avi-Yonah]), but since that site has no early archeological evidence, N. Glueck suggested Khirbet el-‘Ayâsh near the Wâdī el-‘Aujā. In NT times the name was Noarah (cf. Neara in Josephus *Ant.* xvii.13.1 [340]).
R. P. DUGAN, JR.

**NAARAI** nā'ə-rī [Heb. *na‘$^a$ray*]. Son of Ezbai, and one of David's mighty men (1 Ch. 11:37). In the parallel list in 2 S. 23:35 he is called Paarai the Arbite.

**NAARAN** nā'ə-ran [Heb. *na‘$^a$rān*] (1 Ch. 7:28); **NAARATH** nā'ə-rath (AV, NEB, Josh. 16:7). *See* Naarah.

**NAASHON** nā'ə-shon (Ex. 6:23, AV); **NAASSON** nā'ə-son (Mt. 1:4; Lk. 3:32, AV). *See* Nahshon.

**NAATHUS** nā'ə-thəs [Gk. A *Naathos*, B *Lathos*]. A son of Addi; one of those who had married a foreign wife and was required to divorce her (1 Esd. 9:31); possibly the same as Adna in the parallel list in Ezr. 10:30.

**NABAL** nā'bəl [Heb. *nāḇāl*–'fool']. A wealthy Calebite who lived in Maon and pastured his large flocks of sheep and goats in Carmel near Hebron (1 S. 25). The account of Nabal's folly and demise forms an episode in the story of David's progress toward the throne.

Nabal's name portrays his character before his actions and behavior are reported. Heb. *nāḇāl* denotes a "fool" in a spiritual and moral sense, i.e., one who is impious and ignoble (*see* Fool I); cf. Abigail's description of Nabal: "for as his name is, so is he; Nabal is his name, and folly [*n$^e$ḇālâ*] is with him" (v. 25).

Nabal's folly is manifested in the magnificent banquet he prepared for himself and his friends when he knew that David and his men were going hungry nearby. It is demonstrated further in his callous rejection of David's request for food (vv. 5-11) in compensation for the protection David and his men had provided for Nabal's shepherds (v. 7; cf. vv. 14-16). Nabal was like the fool described in Isa. 32:6: "For the fool [*nāḇāl*] speaks folly, and his mind plots iniquity . . . to leave the craving of the hungry unsatisfied, and to deprive the thirsty of drink." When David was told about Nabal's churlish denial of his request, he prepared to take vengeance (vv. 12f., 21f.). David and his men were intercepted, however, by Nabal's wise and beautiful wife Abigail, who, having heard about her husband's insolent behavior, went out to meet David with a generous gift of food and persuaded him to desist from taking vengeance into his own hands (vv. 18-35). Nabal's drunkenness prevented Abigail from relating to him what she had done to save him and the family. But when he was sober the following morning she told him these things, "and his heart died within him, and he became as a stone. And about ten days later the Lord smote Nabal; and he died" (vv. 37f.; *see* Disease III.B). Ironically, Nabal lived his last ten days as he had the rest, i.e., with a heart like stone, unresponsive to the needs of others.

The author presents Nabal as emblematic of the fool who rejects God (cf. Ps. 14:1) and His anointed. Nabal's feigned ignorance of David (1 S. 25:10) is strange, since David's military exploits were well known (17:50; 18:7, 13-16, 30) and he was widely recognized as Israel's future king, e.g., by Jonathan (20:14f.), by the servants of Achish (21:11 [MT 12]), by Abigail (25:30), and even by Saul himself (24:20f. [MT 21f.]). Except for Yahweh's intervention by Abigail, David might well have damaged his own reputation and future by responding violently to Nabal's rebuff (cf. vv. 26, 30-34, 39).

***Bibliography.***–J. D. Levenson, "I Samuel 25 as Literature and History," in K. R. Louis, ed., *Literary Interpretations of Biblical Narrative*, II (1982), 220-242; P. K. McCarter, Jr., *I Samuel* (*AB*, 1980), pp. 389-402.
D. H. ENGELHARD

**NABARIAH** nab-ə-rī'ə [Gk. *Nabarias*] (1 Esd. 9:44); AV, NEB, NABARIAS. One of those who stood at Ezra's left hand as he read the law to the people. The name is lacking in the parallel list in Neh. 8:4.

**NABARIAS** nab-ə-rī'əs (AV, NEB, 1 Esd. 9:44). *See* Nabariah.

**NABATEANS** nab-ə-tē'ənz [Gk. *Nabataioi*] (1 Macc. 5:25; 9:35); AV NABATHITES. An originally South Semitic tribe that emerged in history and inhabited Petra in southeast Transjordan sometime in the 4th cent. B.C. By the 1st cent. B.C.–A.D. they controlled the land caravan routes from China, India, southern Arabia, and Egypt to the west. By the time of Josephus their kingdom was called Nabatene (*Ant.* i.12.4 [220f.]) and was of major commer-

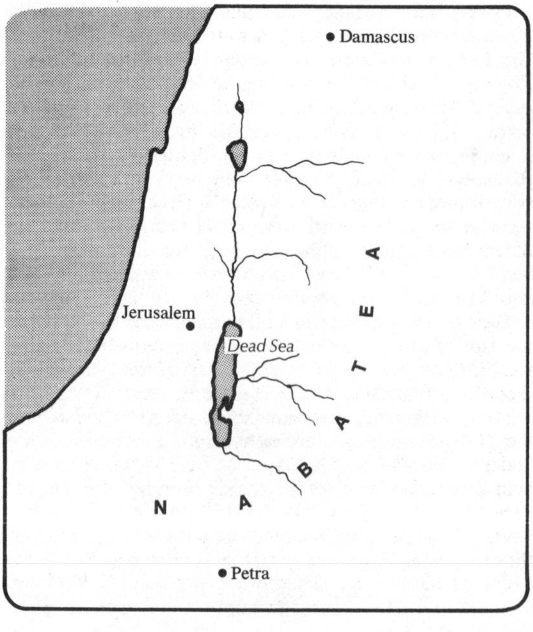

Sculpture of the goddess Tyche encircled by eleven signs of the zodiac. From Khirbet et-Tannûr, 1st-2nd cent. B.C. (Israel Department of Antiquities and Museums)

cial significance in the Near East. Early identifications of this group with the Ishmaelite tribe of Nebaioth, the Nebayat of the Assyrian chronicles, or other similar-sounding tribal names are no longer accepted.

Although of Arabic origin, the Nabateans apparently had given up their own language by at least the 4th cent. B.C. and had adopted the Aramaic script and language used by the rest of the Persian empire. This is indicated both by Diodorus's account of their letter to Antigonus (312 B.C.) and by the earliest recorded inscriptions.

Inscriptional materials (largely short inscriptions and graffiti) in the cursive greatly ligatured script evolved by the Nabateans are abundant, but their content is extremely sketchy. Few long, connected inscriptions exist (one of the exceptions is the Turkmaniyeh Tomb inscription at Petra), and most epigraphic remains are the caravaners' terse greetings found along the trade routes, especially in the Sinai Peninsula.

The prehistory of the Nabateans is unknown aside from allusions to Red Sea piracy thwarted by the Egyptians. The first historical note of the group is Diodorus's description (xix. 94-97) of an abortive campaign by the Greek general Antigonus I, who dispatched Athenaeus against Petra in 312 B.C. The action was little more than a raid, but it surprised the inhabitants of the Petra area during the absence of most of the male population and netted the victors considerable booty. While the Greeks were returning northward, however, word of the pillage reached the absent warriors of Petra, who regained the spoil in an ambush. A second expedition by the Greeks in the same year was foiled, and no record of further attempts is extant.

Thus by the 4th cent. B.C. the Nabateans had secured the site of Petra and had begun to amass considerable wealth through caravan trade. After 312 B.C. nothing is recorded about them until 2 Macc. 5:8, which notes their relations with the Hasmoneans in *ca.* 169 B.C. By that time the Nabateans had consolidated into a political body under a "tyrant" or king, Aretas I. It was this ruler who held Jason, the Jewish high priest, prisoner after his escape from the Greek-appointed high priest Menelaus. Aretas I was probably followed by an unknown king and then by Aretas II, known as Erotimus, who opposed Alexander Janneus at Gaza (Josephus *Ant.* xiii.13.3 [360]) in 96 B.C. and expanded Nabatean territory during the internal disorder that weakened Seleucid power. Obodas I became king *ca.* 95 B.C. and continued his predecessor's skirmishes with Janneus (*Ant.* xiii.13.5 [375]; *BJ* i.4.4 [90]) and territorial expansions.

Antiochus XII led an expedition against the Nabateans but was defeated and slain at Kana (*Ant.* xiii.15.1 [387-391]; *BJ* i.4.7 [99-102]), possibly by Rabbel I (88-86 B.C.). Aretas III Philhellene was able to extend his kingdom somewhat farther, apparently with the help of the people of Damascus, and to defeat Janneus at Adida in 85 B.C. (*Ant.* xiii.15.2 [392]). No mention is made of Nabatean influence at Damascus until long after the Armenian conquest of the city (70 B.C.) and its occupation by the Romans (66 B.C.). Aretas espoused the cause of Hyrcanus against Aristobulus, at the instigation of Antipater. He helped to defend Jerusalem during the siege and thus incurred the displeasure of Pompey. The Roman general Scaurus was sent against the Nabateans but soon withdrew after receiving three hundred talents as tribute (*Ant.* xiv.2.3 [29-33]; *BJ* i.6.3 [128-130]). In 55 B.C. Gabinius defeated a Nabatean force, but the victory was not decisive.

Malichus I, the successor of Aretas, emerged in history only as an ally of Caesar in the Egyptian War and as an opponent of Herod. Although Herod was part Nabatean through his mother Kypros, Malichus refused to grant him sanctuary and aid in his flight to Rome *ca.* 40 B.C. to escape the Parthian puppet Antigonus II Mattathias. Thus

One of the many inscriptions of Nabatean king Aretas IV (B. VanElderen)

began anew a period of Nabatean-Jewish clashes, which culminated in 31 in an almost disastrous defeat of the Nabateans in a pitched battle with Herod over taxes. Anthony had "granted" Nabatean lands to Cleopatra, with Herod as the guarantor. Only Roman entanglement in the Egyptian civil war precluded Roman support of Herod in the field and probably reduction of all of Nabatene.

Obodas II (30-9 B.C.) inherited the quarrel and let relations between the two states further degenerate under the influence of his prime minister Syllaeus, whose career was one of continual intrigue, abetted by the weakness of his monarch. It was Syllaeus who led the forces of Augustus in circles through the southern desert until Gallus their commander, in sheer desperation, gave up searching for trade routes. This action did not escape the notice of Augustus, however, and relations with Rome became even more strained. In addition, Syllaeus became enamored of Salome, the sister of Herod, and after being spurned by Herod began a period of active harassment of the Jews.

The death of Obodas brought to the throne Aretas IV (9 B.C.–A.D. 40), the most powerful ruler that Nabatene ever had. After a period of estrangement from both Caesar and Herod, Aretas began a consolidation of strength and an ultimate expansion of territory. Under Aretas the Nabatean kingdom reached its zenith culturally and artistically as well as commercially. Its relationship to Rome is unclear, although the Romans obviously considered it a subject state.

Domestic problems weakened Roman control in Syro-Palestine as well as Jewish strength in the north; Aretas used both factors for commerical and territorial gains. He reexerted some influence over Damascus, as Paul's report indicates (2 Cor. 11:32).

Malichus II (A.D. 40-70) is known chiefly from coins and inscriptions. During his apparently uneventful reign the kingdom weakened politically and in other ways. Malichus II was the king cited by Josephus (*BJ* iii.4.2 [68]) who assisted the Romans during the First Jewish Revolt, but this identification is problematic.

In the reign of Rabbel II (A.D. 70-106), the last king of the Nabateans, Nabatean holdings and power completely declined. In A.D. 106 the army of Trajan occupied Petra, and Nabatene ceased to exist as a separate kingdom. Cornelius Palma, governor of Syria, made the area part of the province of Arabia with Petra as its capital.

Thus the Nabateans, who had risen to great commercial heights, political power, and national awareness, became once again an indistinct Transjordanian tribe. Culturally they rose from nomadic simplicity to hellenized sophistication and then returned to nomadic obscurity.

*See also* NEGEB III.A.

***Bibliography.***–J. Cantineau, *Le nabatéen* (2 vols., 1930-32); N. Glueck, *Deities and Dolphins* (1965); P. C. Hammond, *BA*, 23 (1960), 29-32; *The Nabataeans — Their History, Culture and Archaeology* (1973); J. Kammerer, *Pétra et la Nabatène* (2 vols., 1929-30); J. Starcky, *BA*, 18 (1955), 84-106.

P. C. HAMMOND

**NABATHITES** nab'ə-thīts (1 Macc. 5:25; 9:35, AV). *See* NABATEANS.

**NABONIDUS** nab-ə-nī'dəs [Akk. *Nabû-na'id*–'Nabû is exalted'; Gk. *Labynētos*]. The last Neo-Babylonian king (556-539 B.C.). Although he is not mentioned in the OT, his son BELSHAZZAR is depicted in the book of Daniel as king of Babylon when it fell to Cyrus in 539.

I. Parents
II. Pre-accession Years
III. Accession and Early Years
IV. Religious Convictions

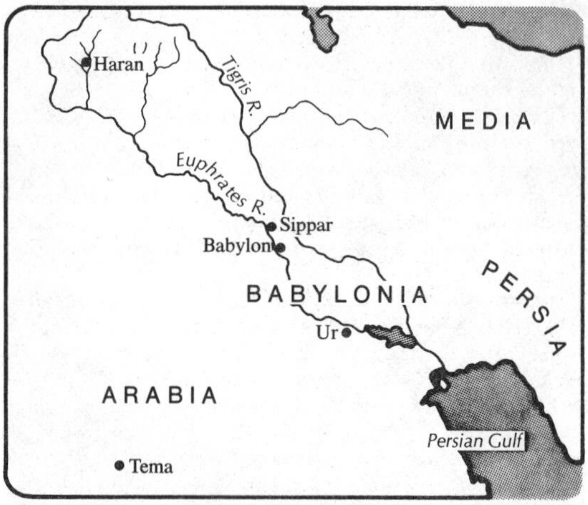


V. Sojourn in Arabia
VI. Belshazzar and Daniel
VII. Final Years
VIII. Text from Qumrân

***I. Parents.***–We know relatively little about Nabonidus's father, Nabû-balātsu-iqbi. He may have been an Assyrian governor of Aramean origins. Thanks to several stelae from Haran (see *ANET*, pp. 311f.; 562f.) we know a great deal about his mother, one of the most long-lived women in antiquity. Adad-guppi was born in the twentieth year of Ashurbanipal (650). Whether or not she was a priestess at Haran (as suggested by É. Dhorme, *Revue d'assyriologie*, 41 [1947], 1-21; but denied by B. Landsberger, *Halil Edhem hâtira kitabi*, 1 [1947], 115-151 [cited by W. Röllig, p. 236] and J. Lewy, *HUCA*, 19 [1945-46], 405-489), she was extraordinarily devoted to the moon-god Sin, to whom she dedicated her only son. Nabonidus was most likely born before 610, when the family probably left Haran due to the invasion of the Medes and Chaldeans; they were perhaps transferred to the court at Babylon.

Adad-guppi was ninety-five years old when she saw her son crowned king, and then lived on to the ninth year of her son's reign (547). Her memorial stelae claim that she was still clear-sighted at the time of her death and could number descendants to the fourth generation (*ANET*, pp. 312).

***II. Pre-Accession Years.***–Adad-guppi boasted that she introduced her son into the service of Nebuchadnezzar. Since Belshazzar is described in Dnl. 5:2 as a "son" (or descendant) of Nebuchadnezzar, it is quite plausible that Nabonidus married a daughter of Nebuchadnezzar (perhaps the queen mentioned in Dnl. 5:10); see Dougherty, *Nabonidus and Belshazzar*; D. J. Wiseman, *NBD*, p. 139; J. C. Baldwin, *Daniel* (1978), p. 122.

Herodotus has three passages (i.74, 77, and 188-191) which refer to a Labynetus, but whether they refer to the same individual is debated (cf. R. Dougherty, *Nabonidus and Belshazzar*, pp. 193f.; H. Lewy, *Archiv Orientální*, 17 [1949], 28-109). It is certainly possible to regard the Labynetus (Herodotus i.74) who mediated a peace between the Medes and the Lydians in 585 as Nabonidus in the service of Nebuchadnezzar. He demonstrated in this case the political skill which qualified him to be chosen eventually as a candidate for the throne.

***III. Accession and Early Years.***–Nabonidus came to the throne in 556, which in the Babylonian postdating system would be his accession year (*see* CHRONOLOGY OF THE OT V.A). His first regnal year would have begun with the New Year on March 31, 555. According to Berossus, Nabonidus received the throne as the result of a conspiracy. According to his own basalt stele, Nabonidus was elevated by the order of Marduk even though he was "one who did not know Marduk."

In his first three years he campaigned in Syria, Cilicia, and northern Arabia.

*IV. Religious Convictions.*–Because of Nabonidus's concern to restore ancient temples, earlier scholars characterized him as an "antiquarian." But this zeal to rediscover the ancient roots characterized all the Neo-Babylonian kings. Some of Nabonidus's texts refer to the discoveries of foundations of Sargon and Naram-Sin, who lived 1700 years before.

Inscriptions speak of the king's concern for the temples of the sun-god Shamash. The king restored his temple at Sippar after discovering the original foundations buried deep underground. He also restored the Shamash temple at Larsa and the temples of Ishtar at Agade, Babylon, and Sippar.

But it was above all the moon-god Sin which commanded Nabonidus's devotion. He restored the ziggurat at UR, a notable center of the moon cult. In his second year Nabonidus dedicated his only daughter to the lunar temple in Ur. The exaltation of Sin over all the other gods and even the suggestion of converting the Esagila, the temple of Marduk in Babylon, into a temple of Sin, naturally offended the Babylonians. Moreover, the king's insistence in interpreting divinatory signs himself must have alienated the priestly interpreters (see the Haran inscription, *ANET,* p. 562).

In a dream Marduk commanded Nabonidus to restore the temple of Sin at Haran, which had been destroyed by the Medes in 610. The god reassured the king that within three years CYRUS (the Persian king, see VII below) would defeat the Umman-manda (Medes) who had occupied the site. Following indications in the Persian Verse Account (*ANET,* pp. 312-15), most scholars have placed Cyrus's uprising against the Medes in Nabonidus's third year (553/552) and have placed Nabonidus's rebuilding of the temple soon thereafter. But H. Tadmor noted that the Chronicle places Cyrus's victory over his Median grandfather Astyages in Nabonidus's sixth year (550), soon after which Nabonidus retired to Arabia (see V below). He has therefore argued that Nabonidus was not able to complete the rebuilding until his return from Arabia toward the end of his reign. According to Tadmor, Nabonidus's devotion to Sin was intensified by his sojourn at the center of a moon cult in Arabia. The Haran texts, written after his sojourn there, are replete with exaggerated praise for Sin (*ANET,* pp. 562f.).

*V. Sojourn in Arabia.*–In an unprecedented move Nabonidus shifted his capital into the middle of the Arabian peninsula some 800 km. (500 mi.) from Babylonia. We learn from the Haran texts that he was away for a total of ten years. From the fragmentary entries in the Nabonidus Chronicle (*ANET,* pp. 305-307) we are certain that he was away at least from the seventh to the eleventh year. We also know that the king returned to Babylon in time to participate in the New Year's festival in 539. His stay must therefore have begun at the earliest in his fourth year, since we know his activities for the first three years (see III above). He must also have returned not later than 540. His sojourn in Arabia therefore lasted either from 552 to 542, or from 550 to 540.

The reasons for Nabonidus's self-imposed exile have been much debated. Some suggested that Nabonidus went for reasons of health; he had become ill early in his reign. Others have suggested that he wanted to control the lucrative Arabian trade or obtain allies against the rising power of Persia.

According to the Haran texts Nabonidus chose to occupy a string of six oases about 160 km. (100 mi.) inland from the coast in northwestern Arabia, with his capital at Tema (Teimā). Tema was strategically situated halfway between Babylonia and Egypt, and between Damascus and Mecca. According to the Verse Account Nabonidus beautified Tema and built a palace there like his palace in Babylon. The famous Tema Stone, an inscription in Aramaic that scholars have dated to the 5th cent. B.C., may actually date from Nabonidus's reign in view of the close iconographic parallels with the Haran stelae. The image of Ṣalm on the stone may represent the deified Nabonidus (see Winnett). Other oases were Dedan, Padakku, Ḫibrâ, Yadiḫu, and Yatribu (Medina).

*VI. Belshazzar and Daniel.*–Nabonidus associated his son Belshazzar with him in oaths and inscriptions. Though he did not abdicate, Nabonidus did entrust kingship to his son as he left for Arabia. In view of Nabonidus's long absence, Belshazzar served as the de facto king of Babylon as far as the Jews there were concerned. This explains why Daniel mentions Belshazzar but not Nabonidus, and also why Daniel was exalted to the "third" position in the kingdom (Dnl. 5:7, 16, 29). As G. Hasel (*Andrews University Seminary Studies,* 15 [1977], 153-168) pointed out, Belshazzar's first year (Dnl. 7:1) would correspond to the first year of Nabonidus's ten-year stay at Tema. W. H. Shea has suggested that the feast of Dnl. 5 was held to celebrate the coronation of Belshazzar after the defeat of Nabonidus at Sippar two days earlier.

*VII. Final Years.*–As the Persian threat on the eastern frontier became acute, Nabonidus hastened home to organize resistance some time between 542 and 540. But it was too late. His attempt to collect the gods of the cities to the north of Babylon failed, because the images of the gods of Borsippa, Cutha, and Sippar were not sent. Indeed, morale was so low that many of the Babylonians welcomed Cyrus, who honored Marduk more than their own king, according to the Cyrus Cylinder (*ANET,* pp. 315f.).

According to the Chronicle, in September, 539, Cyrus "did battle at Opis on the Tigris against the army of Akkad." By October 10 the Persians were able to capture Sippar "without a battle." The Chronicle indicates that Gubaru, Cyrus's general, and his troops entered Babylon "without a battle" on October 12 (cf. Dnl. 5; Herodotus i.191; Xenophon *Cyropaedia* vii.5.15). Cyrus himself entered the city on October 29, greeted as a liberator by the inhabitants, who spread green branches before him.

We do not hear of the fate of Belshazzar. According to the Chronicle Nabonidus was captured in Babylon. Berossus (preserved in Josephus *CAp* i.20 [153]) maintains that Cyrus spared Nabonidus and gave him a residence in Carmania in south central Persia. But according to Xenophon (*Cyropedia* vii.5.30) two of Cyrus's nobles killed the king in the palace. In view of the tradition that Cyrus also spared Croesus, Berossus was probably correct. The fragmentary line in the Chaldean Chronicle, which has been interpreted to contradict Cyrus's clemency to Croesus, is too broken to inspire confidence (see M. Mallowan, *Iran,* 10 [1972], 1-17; J. Cargill, *American Journal of Ancient History,* 2 [1977], 97-117).

*VIII. Text from Qumrân.*–Many scholars since H. de Genouillac (*Revue d'assyriologie,* 22 [1925], 71-83) and W. von Soden (*ZAW,* 53 [1935], 81-89) have assumed that the madness of Nebuchadnezzar in Dnl. 4 is actually the story of Nabonidus's irrational behavior in Arabia. For many that conviction has been strengthened by the discovery of "The Prayer of Nabonidus" in Cave 4 of Qumrân in 1955. The Aramaic text of four fragments (4QPrNab) contains thirteen lines with many lacunae. It is dated to the second half of the 1st cent. B.C.

The text relates the prayer said in *Teman,* by King *Nabunai,* who had been afflicted with a sickness for seven years. Evidently after repenting of his worship of idols, the king is healed through the intervention of a Jewish diviner (*gzr*, lit. "divider"; cf. Dnl. 2:27). Some scholars restore line 3 to read, "so I became like the animals," but this is gratuitous.

Because of the broad parallels and similar vocabulary many scholars who hold to a Maccabean date for the composition of Daniel believe that the Prayer of Nabonidus may have influenced the composition of Daniel. There are, however, some major differences between Dnl. 4 and the Prayer of Nabonidus:

(1) Dnl. 4 speaks of Nebuchadnezzar, the Qumrân fragment of Nabonidus.

(2) Nebuchadnezzar was in Babylon, Nabonidus in Tema.

(3) Nebuchadnezzar suffered from boanthropy; according to the Qumrân text Nabonidus suffered from *šᵉḥîn* (cf. Job 2:7), a skin inflammation.

(4) Nebuchadnezzar was restored through Daniel, Nabonidus by an unnamed Jewish diviner.

(5) Nebuchadnezzar was insane for seven seasons (*ʿiddānîn*; Dnl. 4:13, 22, 29), which may not necessarily have been seven years. The Haran texts now indicate that Nabonidus was in Tema for ten years.

(6) The earlier identification of Nabonidus with Nebuchadnezzar was based in part on S. Smith's rendering of a line in the Verse Account, "an evil demon [*šedu*] had altered him," i.e., made him mad (*Babylonian Historical Texts*, p. 87). But Oppenheim rendered this line, "(his) protective deity became hostile to him" (*ANET*, p. 313). Another phrase in the Verse Account, "the king is mad" (*ANET*, p. 314), does not mean that Nabonidus was "insane," but that he was "angry" (Akk. *a-gu-ug šarru*).

***Bibliography***.–R. Dougherty, *JAOS*, 42 (1922), 305-316; S. Smith, *Babylonian Historical Texts* (1924), pp. 82-97, 106-123; R. Dougherty, *Nabonidus and Belshazzar* (1929); *American Journal of Archaeology*, 34 (1930), 296-312; *Mizraim*, 1 (1933), 140-43; M. Gruenthaner, *CBQ*, 11 (1949), 406-27; K. Galling, *ZDPV*, 69 (1953), 42-64; B. Segall, *American Journal of Archaeology*, 59 (1955), 315-18; J. Milik, *RB*, 63 (1956), 407-415; C. J. Gadd, *Anatolian Studies*, 8 (1958), 35-92; W. Moran, *Orientalia*, N.S. 28 (1959), 130-140; P. Garelli, *DBSup.*, VI (1960), 269-286; R. Meyer, *Das Gebet des Nabonid* (1962); K. Galling, "Jesaia 21 im Lichte der neuen Nabonid Text," in A. Weiser, ed., *Tradition und Situation* (1963), pp. 49-62; W. Dommershausen, *Nabonid im Buche Daniel* (1964); W. Röllig, *Zeitschrift für Assyriologie*, 56 (1964), 218-260; H. Tadmor, "The Inscriptions of Nabunaid: Historical Arrangement," in H. Güterbock and T. Jacobsen, eds., *Studies in Honor of Benno Landsberger* (1965), pp. 351-363; E. Yamauchi, *Greece and Babylon* (1967), pp. 67-72; W. G. Lambert, *AfO*, 22 (1968-69), 1-8; M. McNamara, *Irish Theological Quarterly*, 37 (1970), 131-149; F. W. Winnett and W. L. Reed, *Ancient Records from North Arabia* (1970); D. Baltzer, *Die Welt des Orients*, 7 (1973), 86-95; D. B. Weisberg, "Royal Women of the Neo-Babylonian Period," in P. Garelli, ed., *Le Palais et la royauté* (1974), pp. 447-454; A. K. Grayson, *Assyrian and Babylonian Chronicles* (1975), pp. 104-111; W. L. Reed, *Lexington Theological Quarterly*, 12 (1977), 23-30; P. Grelot, *RQ*, 9 (1978), 483-496; A. S. van der Woude, "Bemerkungen zum Gebet des Nabonid," in M. Delcor, ed., *Qumran: sa piété, sa théologie et son milieu* (1978), pp. 121-29; W. H. Shea, *Andrews University Seminary Studies*, 20 (1982), 133-149.

E. M. YAMAUCHI

**NABOPOLASSAR** [Akk. *Nabû-apal-uṣur*–'may Nabû protect the son']. The ruler of a small southern Babylonian state who became king of Babylon (626-605 B.C.) after rebelling against Sin-šar-iškun, the son and successor of Ashurbanipal, in 626 B.C. Of professedly lowly origins, Nabopolassar was the founder of the Chaldean dynasty, which his illustrious son Nebuchadrezzar II continued in the Neo-Babylonian period.

Sensing that the Assyrian empire would collapse with the demise of Ashurbanipal and the resultant threat of

Scythian invasion from the north, Nabopolassar endeavored to reduce the Assyrian garrisons of Nippur and Uruk. His initial attempts were unsuccessful, but once he had consolidated his political and military position in Babylon he seized Uruk in 623 B.C. and occupied Nippur the following year. For the next few years he marshalled his armies in the north along the Euphrates, avoiding costly battles with Assyrian forces but ensuring that the enemy moved steadily out of Babylonia and into the more northerly areas of Asshur, Nineveh, and Haran.

About 616 B.C. Nabopolassar made an alliance with Cyaxares king of the Medes and both the Babylonians and the Medes prepared to attack Asshur. The city ultimately fell to the Medes in 614 B.C., but Nabopolassar gained some of the spoils. As a result of the political alliance, which was apparently made more binding by the marriage of Nebuchadrezzar and Cyaxares' daughter Amytis (for whom the celebrated "hanging gardens" of Babylon were reportedly constructed), Nabopolassar's eastern front was secured. He inherited what remained of the Assyrian empire, and the Medes occupied themselves with preparations for reducing Nineveh. Nabopolassar made Assyria's vassals in Syria, Palestine, and Cilicia pay tribute to him, and in 612 B.C. he joined the Medes in victory over Nineveh. The remaining Assyrian forces fled to Haran, which then came under attack by Nabopolassar, and in 610 B.C. the city fell, thus terminating the mighty Assyrian empire and fulfilling the predictions of Zephaniah (2:13-15) and Nahum (3:1-19).

The warlike tribes of the Zagros mountains were a potential threat to the security of the Babylonians after the Assyrian empire fell, and this, coupled with the control which Pharaoh Neco II held over Carchemish, prompted Nabopolassar to regroup his forces in the north Euphrates area. He became ill at this period, however, and it was left to his son Nebuchadrezzar to defeat the Egyptians at Carchemish and Hamath (cf. Jer. 46:2) and expedite their withdrawal from Palestine. Meanwhile, Nabopolassar journeyed back to Babylon and died there in August, 605 B.C., leaving his son to continue the task of making the Neo-Babylonian empire one of the most splendid in the Near East.

***Bibliography***.–*CCK*, pp. 5-21; A. Malamat, *IEJ*, 6 (1965), 246-256; G. Roux, *Ancient Iraq* (1964), pp. 312-14. R. K. H.

**NABOTH** nā'both [Heb. *nāḇôṯ*–'sprouts'(?), 'elevation'; Gk. *Nabouthai*]. The owner of a vineyard adjacent to the palace of King Ahab in Jezreel (1 K. 21:1-29). Ahab desired to extend his property by purchasing the vineyard or by offering Naboth a better one in its place. Naboth justifiably refused the offer of the king on the valid ground that the vineyard was his family inheritance. Since his land was a gift from God, Naboth would have been transgressing God's law as well as being unfaithful to his descendants by selling it (Lev. 25:23-28; Nu. 36:7-9). When Ahab gave up his attempt, Jezebel ruthlessly secured the vineyard for him by hiring false witnesses who accused Naboth of blaspheming both God and king. Naboth and apparently his sons as well (2 K. 9:26) were executed. This cruel plan of Jezebel gave Ahab access to the vineyard, but when he came to take possession of it, the prophet Elijah met him and condemned him for the crime. A temporary respite was given to Ahab because of his repentance (1 K. 21:27-29). Later, however, dogs licked his blood at the pool of Samaria where his dead body had been returned from the battle at Ramoth Gilead (1 K. 22:38). Jehu, remembering Elijah's curse, brought it to complete fulfillment when he killed Jehoram, Ahab's second son, and dumped his body on the vineyard of Naboth (2 K. 9:24f.). In addition, Jehu was responsible for the death of Jezebel (2 K. 9:33) and the execution of seventy other sons of Ahab (1 K. 10:1-11).

G. KROEZE

**NABUCHODONOSOR** nab-ə-kə-don'ə-sôr. The AV Apoc. form of NEBUCHADREZZAR, rendering LXX *Nabouchodonosor* (e.g., 1 Esd. 1:40f., 45, 48; Ad. Est. 11:4; Bar. 1:9, 11f.).

**NACHON** nā'kon (2 S. 6:6, AV). *See* NACON.

**NACHOR** nā'kôr (Josh. 24:2; Lk. 3:34, AV). *See* NAHOR.

**NACON** nā'kon [Heb. *nāḵôn*–'correct'; Gk. B *Nōdab*, A *Nachon*] (2 S. 6:6); AV NACHON; NEB "a certain." A proper name of either a person or a place. At the threshing floor of Nacon (CHIDON in 1 Ch. 13:9), Uzzah "put out his hand" to steady the ark of God and was struck dead. The place was thereafter called Perez-uzzah ("the breaking forth upon Uzzah"); it was probably located near Baale-judah (2 S. 6:2) or Baalah, which is Kiriath-jearim (1 Ch. 13:6).

Hebrew *nāḵôn* occurs in 1 S. 23:23; 26:4 but is translated, respectively, "with sure information" and "of a certainty" (see the comms.). In modern Hebrew *nāḵôn* means "right!, correct."

W. S. L. S.

**NADAB** nā'dab [Heb. *nāḏāḇ*–'generous, noble'; LXX *Nadab, Nabat,* and *Nabath*].

**1.** The eldest son of Aaron. He is always associated in the Bible with his brother ABIHU, although he also had two other brothers, Eleazar and Ithamar (Ex. 6:23). Nadab and Abihu accompanied Moses, Aaron, and the seventy elders on Mt. Sinai when they saw the God of Israel (although at some distance from Moses and the Lord Himself, 24:1, 9-11). With his father and his brothers Nadab was consecrated a priest before the Lord and was arrayed in holy garments (28:1-4).

Leviticus 10:1f. describes only briefly the event for which we remember Nadab and Abihu — their offering of "unholy fire" (Heb. *'ēš zārâ*) before Yahweh. Immediately a fire of judgment (lightning? but cf. Laughlin, pp. 561f.) fell on them. This occurred on the very first day that Aaron served as high priest. What should have been Aaron's finest hour was indelibly marred by the grief he suffered with the loss of his sons (10:2). Despite their grief, Moses forbade Aaron and his two remaining sons to mourn the deaths of Nadab and Abihu, although the rest of the Israelites were permitted to mourn (v. 6; cf. Wenham, p. 157, who has suggested that Aaron and his sons were forbidden to mourn in order "to identify themselves entirely with God's viewpoint"). Aaron and his sons were instead to confront in a new and drastic way the holiness of Yahweh (see vv. 3, 7; cf. the story of Uzzah, 2 S. 6:6f.).

The precise meaning of the phrase "unholy fire" has long confounded scholars. Some Jewish interpreters (e.g., Rashi) have suggested that the young priests had approached their duties in a drunken state (see Lev. 10:8-11), or that they were filled with pride (see, e.g., *Encyclopedia Judaica,* XII, 750f.). Others have wondered if they had taken the coals from the wrong location (cf. Lev. 16:12) or had offered the sacrifice at the wrong time of day (see KD *in loc.*; cf. Ex. 30:7f.). Wenham offers perhaps the most cogent explanation: Nadab and Abihu offered fire that God had not commanded (p. 155).

Both Nadab and Abihu died childless (Nu. 3:4). Thus not only did they die abruptly at God's judgment; their lines were ended as well.

Israel remembered the sad end of Nadab and Abihu; all but one (1 Ch. 6:3) of the subsequent notices of these brothers point back to this event (Nu. 3:1-4; 26:60f.; 1 Ch. 24:1f.).

***Bibliography.***–J. C. H. Laughlin, *JBL,* 95 (1976), 559-565; G. J. Wenham, *Book of Leviticus* (*NICOT,* 1979), pp. 152-160.

**2.** The son and successor of Jeroboam I. He ruled for parts of two years (1 K. 14:20; 15:25-32). The wickedness of his father became a model for his own reign (v. 26) and a pattern for the kings that followed in the northern kingdom (thus fulfilling 14:10f.). The only notable thing about the reign of Nadab was his assassination at the hands of Baasha while he was besieging Gibbethon, a city in Dan under Philistine control.

**3.** One of the descendants of Jerahmeel. He was one of the two sons of Shammai and is mentioned with his brother Abishur (1 Ch. 2:28) and his sons Seled and Appaim (v. 30).

**4.** A son of Gibeon and an ancestor of King Saul. He was the sixth of Gibeon's ten sons (1 Ch. 9:35-37; cf. 8:30).

**5.** AV NASBAS (Tob. 11:18), AMAN (Tob. 14:10). The nephew of AHIKAR who attended the marriage ceremony of Tobias (Tob. 11:17f.). In 14:10 Tobit briefly recounts Nadab's fate, which is described in detail in the book of Ahikar: after trying to have his uncle Ahikar killed, Nadab was caught and punished, dying in chains (see *APOT,* II, 768-776). *See also* AHIKAR, BOOK OF.

The AV variants result from the AV's following different MS traditions. "Aman" may indicate some confusion with Haman, a similar character in the book of Esther. The extant MSS of the book of Ahikar include several other variants for Nadab (e.g., Nadin, Nabas, Nabal, etc.).

R. B. ALLEN

**NADABATH** nad'ə-bath [Gk. *Nadabath*] (1 Macc. 9:37); AV NADABATHA na-dab'ə-thə. A city in Transjordan from which the sons of Jambri were conducting a bride when Jonathan and Simon attacked to avenge the murder of their brother John (1 Macc. 9:37ff.). If this is the Nadabatha mentioned by Josephus (*Ant.* xiii.1.4 [18-21]; Loeb ed. reads Nabatha), it was near Medeba (although another reading in Josephus is Gabatha; the story is otherwise the same as the account in 1 Maccabees).

It has been identified with en-Nebâ, the ancient Nebo, NW of Medeba, and with Khirbet et-Teim, 2 km. (1¼ mi.) S of Medeba. Cf. N. Glueck, *AASOR,* 14 (1934), 33.

W. S. L. S.

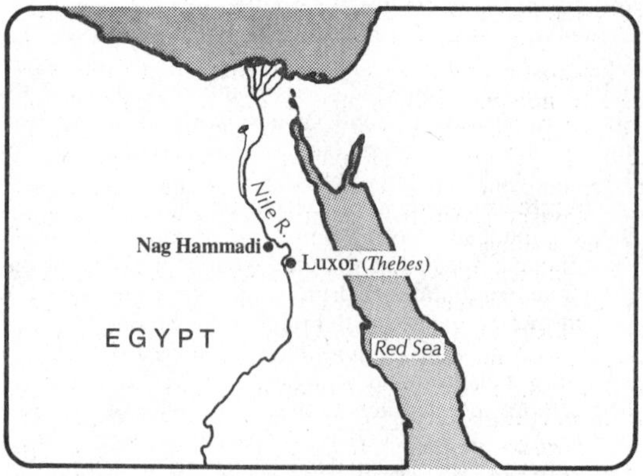


**NAG HAMMADI** näg hə-mä'dē **LITERATURE.** A collection of documents found in the area of Nag Hammadi, Egypt.

I. Discovery
II. Publication of Texts and Translations
III. Contents of the Thirteen Codices
IV. Literary and Religious Relationships
V. Evaluation

***I. Discovery.***–In 1945 peasants from Hamra Doum, a village about 10 km. (6 mi.) NE and across the Nile from Nag Hammadi, found a large jar containing thirteen Coptic codices (or, more exactly, twelve plus some sections of a thirteenth). The site of the discovery is about 80 km. (50 mi.) downstream from Luxor, in the area of the Nile Valley sometimes called the "great bend." The exact site is believed to be at the foot of cliffs that are honeycombed with tombs of kings of the 6th Dynasty.

Coptic codices were found under the boulder (lower right) at the foot of Jabal al-Tārif in Upper (southern) Egypt (by courtesy of the Institute for Antiquity and Christianity, Claremont, California)

Nag Hammadi codex in its cover (photograph by J. Doresse by courtesy of the Institute for Antiquity and Christianity, Claremont, California)

The codices were offered for sale surreptitiously. G. Page finally purchased one codex (I) on May 10, 1952, and presented it to the famous Swiss psychologist C. G. Jung of the Jung Institute in Zurich. Part of this codex was missing. The missing material was subsequently identified with certain pages published in a photographic edition along with the first half of Codex II. (P. Labib, *Coptic Gnostic Papyri in the Coptic Museum at Old Cairo,* I [1956]). The Coptic Museum in Cairo purchased Codex III in 1948. After much haggling, on June 9, 1952, the Egyptian government took possession of all the remaining codices. The unstable political situation in Egypt delayed study of Codices II-XIII until 1956. Complete details of the discovery and subsequent vicissitudes of the codices are given in J. M. Robinson's introduction to the *Facsimile Edition of the Nag Hammadi Codices*. John Dart's *Laughing Savior* (1976) is a popular report basically dependent on Robinson and Doresse.

***II. Publication of Texts and Translations.***–Inevitably, in the long delays before all the codices were acquired and properly preserved, some pages were lost and small fragments were torn from some pages. P. Labib, director of the Coptic Museum, began the actual work of preservation in 1957. Later (1959-1961) M. Krause worked on the preservation of Codices IV-XIII, taking inventory and assigning numbers to the pages as they were sealed in plexiglass. A UNESCO team was charged in 1961 with the publication of the Coptic texts, translations, critical notes, and indices, but because of delays they did not complete their photographing of the texts until the summer of 1966. In response to an appeal by the International Colloquium on the origins of Gnosticism (held at Messina, Italy, in April, 1966) to undergird the restoration of the texts and publish a facsimile photographic edition of the MSS, UNESCO negotiated a new contract with the Egyptian government, and a team of international experts set to work on the texts. The international editorial board has completed the twelve-volume *Facsimile Edition of the Nag Hammadi Codices* (1977ff.), which includes all the codices and also an introductory volume by J. M. Robinson, director of the Institute for Antiquity and Christianity at Claremont Graduate School.

In addition, under Robinson's leadership, a group of international scholars undertook preparation of text editions and translations of all the texts, to appear as the Coptic Gnostic Library, a series within the *Nag Hammadi Studies*. The original plan of the Institute to publish text editions for Codices VII–XIII was expanded to include Codices I–VI, Codex Berolinensis 8502, Codex Askew, and Codex Bruce.The following is a list of the text editions already published (with dates) and some that are still in preparation.

*Nag Hammadi Codex I*, ed. H. Attridge;

*Nag Hammadi Codex II, 1, III, 1 and IV, 1 with Papyrus Berolinensis 8502, 2: The Apocryphon of John*, ed. F. Wisse;

*Nag Hammadi Codex II, 2-7*, ed. B. Layton;

*Nag Hammadi Codices III, 2 and IV, 2: The Gospel of the Egyptians*, ed. A. Böhlig and F. Wisse in co-operation with P. Labib (1975);

*Nag Hammadi Codices III, 3-4 and V, 1 with Papyrus Berolinensis 8502, 3: Eugnostos the Blessed and the Wisdom (Sophia) of Jesus Christ*, ed. D. Parrott;

*Nag Hammadi Codex III, 5: The Dialogue of the Savior*, ed. S. Emmel (1984);

*Nag Hammadi Codices V, 2-5 and VI with Papyrus Berolinensis 8502, 1 and 4*, ed. D. Parrott (1979);

*Nag Hammadi Codex VII*, ed. F. Wisse;

*Nag Hammadi Codex VIII*, ed. B. Layton;

*Nag Hammadi Codices IX and X*, ed. B. Pearson (1981);

*Nag Hammadi Codices XI, XII, and XIII*, ed. C. Hedrick;

*Nag Hammadi Codices: Greek and Coptic Papyri from the cartonage of the Covers*, ed. J. Barns, G. Browne, and J. Shelton (1981);

*Pistis Sophia*, text ed. Carl Schmidt, and notes by V. MacDermot, vol. ed. R. Wilson (1978);

*The Books of Jeu and the untitled text in the Bruce Codex*, ed. C. Schmidt, tr. and notes by V. MacDermot, vol. ed. R. Wilson (1978).

A one-volume English translation of the Nag Hammadi texts along with the *Gospel of Mary* and the *Acts of Peter* from BG 8502 has been published as *The Nag Hammadi Library in English* (ed. J. M. Robinson, 1977). (BG 8502 is a MS found late in the 19th cent. and first mentioned in scholarly works by C. Schmidt in 1896. After a series of unfortunate events, the texts were finally published by W. Till, *Die gnostischen Schriften des koptischen Papyrus Berolinensis 8502* [*TU*, 60, 1955]. This work also contains versions of the *Apocryphon of John* and *Sophia of Jesus Christ* that are duplicates of works in the Nag Hammadi library.)

As a corollary to these endeavors, E. J. Brill (Leiden) is publishing a monograph series, *Nag Hammadi Studies (NHS)*, which contains some text editions. The volumes published include D. Scholer, *Nag Hammadi Bibliography, 1948-1969* (1971); A. Böhlig and F. Wisse, *Nag Hammadi Codices III, 2 and IV, 2 (The Gospel of the Egyptians)* (1975); M. Krause, ed., *Gnosis and Gnosticism* (1978); *Pistis Sophia*, ed. C. Schmidt, tr. and notes by V. MacDermot (1978); D. Parrott, ed., *Nag Hammadi Codices V, 2-5 and VI with Papyrus Berolinensis 8502, 1 and 4* (1979); C. Schmidt and V. MacDermot, *The Books of Jeu and the Untitled Text in the Bruce Codex* (1978); R. Wilson, ed., *Nag Hammadi and Gnosis* (1978); B. Pearson and S. Giversen, *Nag Hammadi Codices IX and X* (1981); J. Barns, G. Browne, and J. Shelton, *Nag Hammadi Codices, Greek and Coptic Papyri from the Cartonnage of the Covers* (1981).

***III. Contents of the Thirteen Codices.***–Although the most common name for these MSS is "Nag Hammadi Gnostic Texts," not all of the tractates are Gnostic. Some are semi-gnostic (e.g., *Gospel of Thomas*) and others are clearly non-gnostic (e.g., *Sentences of Sextus*, Plato's *Republic*). There are duplicate texts in the corpus (e.g., *Gospel of Truth, Apocryphon of John*). All of this is understandable only if the codices are considered a library of a Gnostic group that included semi-gnostic and non-gnostic writings.

In technical terms the find consisted of twelve codices (some very fragmentary) and a folio of Codex XIII. The cover of Codex XIII is missing and eight of its folios were found inside the front cover of Codex VI (see J. M. Robinson, "Inside the Front Cover of Codex VI," in M. Krause, ed., *Essays on the Nag Hammadi Texts in Honor of Alexander Böhling* [*NHS*, 3, 1972], pp. 74-87). The MSS restored and inventoried number 1261 pages, plus some fragments not yet identified.

It seems likely that most of the tractates are translations from Greek or (possibly in a few cases) Aramaic. The dialects of Coptic into which they were translated are Sahidic, Akhmimic, and sub-Akhmimic. The spellings in Codex II seem to indicate a date *ca.* A.D. 340 for the translation (or final copying), which has been verified by the discovery of some backing sheets dated *ca.* 340. Most of the other codices seem to date from that time to about seventy years later. The original composition of the various treatises seems to have occurred *ca.* A.D. 150–250. The Coptic language, the final stage of ancient Egyptian, possibly became a written language when the NT was translated into it, beginning *ca.* A.D. 200.

The following list of codices and tractates is the one officially adopted for the *Facsimile Edition*, replacing several lists used earlier. In scholarly works the codices are referred to by the abbreviation CG (Cairensis Gnosticus) for the corpus, Roman number for the specific codex, and Arabic number for the tractate in the codex; e.g., CG V, 1 is Codex V, Tractate 1: *Eugnostos the Blessed*.

Codex I (Jung Codex)

Tractate 1, *Apocryphon of James*
Tractate 2, *Gospel of Truth*
Tractate 3, *Treatise on the Resurrection*
Tractate 4, *Tripartite Tractate*
Tractate 5, *Prayer of the Apostle Paul*

Codex II

Tractate 1, *Apocryphon of John*
Tractate 2, *Gospel of Thomas*
Tractate 3, *Gospel of Philip*
Tractate 4, *Hypostasis of the Archons*
Tractate 5, *On the Origin of the World*
Tractate 6, *Exegesis on the Soul*
Tractate 7, *Book of Thomas the Contender*

Codex III

Tractate 1, *Apocryphon of John*
Tractate 2, *Gospel of the Egyptians*
Tractate 3, *Eugnostos the Blessed*
Tractate 4, *Sophia of Jesus Christ*
Tractate 5, *Dialogue of the Savior*

Codex IV

Tractate 2, *Apocryphon of John*
Tractate 3, *Gospel of the Egyptians*

Codex V

Tractate 1, *Eugnostos the Blessed*
Tractate 2, *Apocalypse of Paul*
Tractate 3, *First Apocalypse of James*
Tractate 4, *Second Apocalypse of James*
Tractate 5, *Apocalypse of Adam*

Codex VI
Tractate 1, *Acts of Peter and the Twelve Apostles*
Tractate 2, *Thunder, Perfect Mind*
Tractate 3, *Authoritative Teaching*
Tractate 4, *Concept of Our Great Power*
Tractate 5, Plato *Republic* 588B-589B
Tractate 6, *Discourse on the Eighth and the Ninth*
Tractate 7, *Prayer of Thanksgiving*
Tractate 8, *Asclepius 21-29*
Codex VII
Tractate 1, *Paraphrase of Shem*
Tractate 2, *Second Treatise of the Great Seth*
Tractate 3, *Apocalypse of Peter*
Tractate 4, *Teaching of Silvanus*
Tractate 5, *Three Steles of Seth*
Codex VIII
Tractate 1, *Zostrianos*
Tractate 2, *Letter of Peter to Philip*
Codex IX
Tractate 1, *Melchizedek*
Tractate 2, *Thought of Norea*
Tractate 3, *Testimony of Truth*
Codex X
Tractate 1, *Marsanes*
Codex XI
Tractate 1, *Interpretation of Knowledge*
Tractate 2, *A Valentinian Exposition*
Tractate 2a, *On the Anointing*
Tractate 2b, *On Baptism A*
Tractate 2c, *On Baptism B*
Tractate 2d, *On the Eucharist A*
Tractate 2e, *On the Eucharist B*
Tractate 3, *Allogenes*
Tractate 4, *Hypsiphrone*
Codex XII
Tractate 1, *Sentences of Sextus*
Tractate 2, *Gospel of Truth*
Tractate 3, Fragments
Codex XIII
Tractate 1, *Trimorphic Protennoia*
Tractate 2, *On the Origin of the World*

*IV. **Literary and Religious Relationships.***–Literary genres of the tractates in the Nag Hammadi corpus include the following: apocryphons (hidden, secret books, often using revelational dialogue), epistles, gospels, prayers, apocalypses, acts of apostles. Until scholars have studied all the tractates it is premature to draw final conclusions about their contents, but it is possible to indicate certain features that stand out in the materials already published.

(1) The documents tend to validate the church fathers, who have often been accused of overrating the influence of Gnosticism. The first part of the *Apocryphon of John,* e.g., is almost identical to a section of Irenaeus's *Adv. haer.* xxix that deals with the Barbelo-gnostic beliefs.

(2) The find includes materials that are plainly Valentinian (e.g., *Gospel of Truth*), but more of the documents are Sethian or Barbelo-gnostic in their contents. Scholars will be studying these documents for evidence of the priority of either the Sethian or Barbelo-gnosticism or the Valentinian; i.e., they will be trying to discover which form of Gnosticism developed first, the philosophical or the mythological.

(3) The codices contain some Hermetic tractates that were already known, but they also include Hermetic literature not previously published.

(4) The unresolved question of the source and scope of the collection has important bearing on the interpretation of the various documents. At first the collection was called by a title such as "The Nag Hammadi Gnostic Texts"; but the discovery that the documents include everything from the vague Gnostic ideas in the *Gospel of Thomas* to a section from Plato's *Republic* and *The Sentences of Sextus* has raised questions about the nature of the collection. Some have called it a Gnostic library, others have suggested that it was a collection made by an unknown heresiologist (Pachomius's monastery was nearby), while A. K. Helmhold has suggested that it was simply a collection of works made by a Gnostic individual or community that accepted works not strictly Gnostic in character (*JBL,* 87 [1968], 69f.).

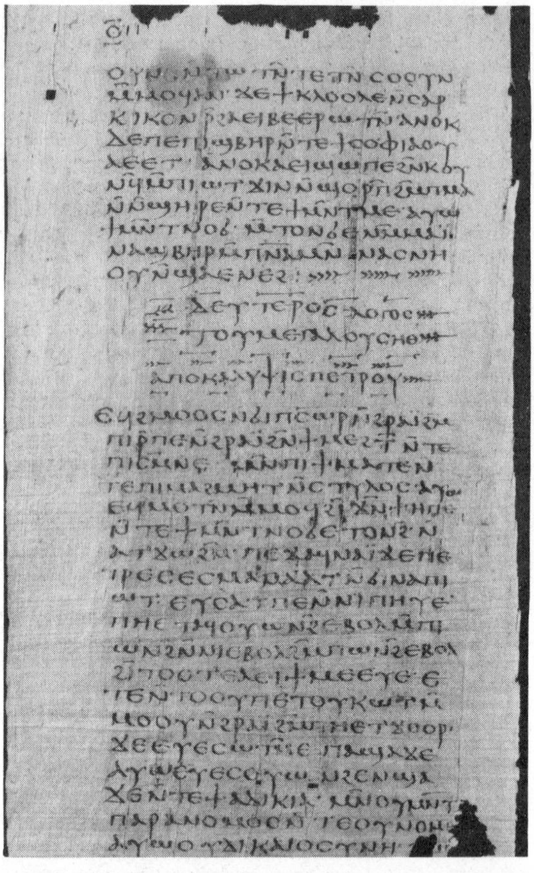

Nag Hammadi Codex VII, p. 70. It contains the Second Treatise of the Great Seth 2:55, 14-56, 19, an account of the Crucifixion, and the beginning of the Apocalypse of Peter, a pseudonymous Gnostic work about a vision seen by Peter and explained by Jesus. The titles of both works are in Greek and the texts in Coptic (by courtesy of the Institute for Antiquity and Christianity, Claremont, California)

(5) Comparisons and contrasts of the Nag Hammadi texts with writings of other groups, e.g., the Mandean and Manichaean communities, may settle the question whether the Mandeans and Manichaeans should be called Gnostic. The texts may also help scholars determine the priority and source of these and similar movements (cf. Yamauchi's books dealing with these issues).

*V. **Evaluation.***–Some scholars have called the Nag Hammadi texts the most important MS find of the century. In part this is because these texts provide prolific sources from which scholars can trace the philosphical-theological ideas in Gnosticism and its influence upon other religious movements. The Nag Hammadi texts (like the Dead Sea Scrolls) not only give the scholar insights into the character of the group producing them: they also contribute to textual criticism. Furthermore they offer new resources for studying the nature and development of the languages in which they were written or translated. Obviously, it will take scholars many years to exhaust the mine of information contained in these codices. Some of the more important (but no means exhaustive) results or by-products of research in these texts are given below.

(1) The finds at Nag Hammadi have already given much information in those writings that are definitely Gnostic about what Gnosticism taught and practiced. E.g., the *Gospel of Philip* has a list of Gnostic sacraments. Most Gnostic documents say much about the doctrine or philosophy taught by a particular Gnostic sect, but references to Gnostic rites and worship are much less known or documented.

(2) While the essence of Gnosticism has been known since the days of the early church fathers, the Nag Hammadi texts enable scholars to delineate more precisely the distinctions between various Gnostic groups and the relation of the Gnostic movement as a whole to Christianity. Scholars can more accurately assess the Gnostic impact on Christianity that compelled it to define the doctrine of the Church, the canon of Holy Scripture, and the governmental structure of the Church.

(3) With all the texts edited and translated, scholars can give a complete listing of biblical parallels, which will be useful in understanding how the Gnostics used the Scriptures. Since most scholars date the Nag Hammadi texts to A.D. 150-200, any reference by these texts to a biblical book tends to support a date for that book earlier than the 2nd cent. A.D.

(4) As study progresses, the source (or sources) of Gnosticism may be conclusively determined. Some scholars have suggested that the movement was a Jewish heresy (so R. Grant, *Gnosticism and Early Christianity* p. 34), others that it originated in Jewish-Christian circles, and still others that it was originally Hellenistic or Babylonian.

(5) The Nag Hammadi texts contain some quotations from the so-called Western text of NT. This factor could prove profitable for pinpointing the source(s) of Gnosticism.

(6) Finally, and most importantly, these texts should shed clearer light on the Reitzenstein-Bultmann thesis that early Christianity freely borrowed existing Gnostic terms and beliefs. G. Quispel ("Jewish Gnosis and Mandaean Gnosticism," in J. É. Ménard, ed., *Les Textes de Nag Hammadi* [*NHS*, 7, 1976] pp. 82-122) theorized that *Thunder* (VI, 2) was a piece of Jewish wisdom literature from the 1st cent. B.C. Other scholars have looked elsewhere for the origins of Gnosticism, while still others have attempted to demonstrate that Christianity was a Gnostic sect created by the interaction of Gnostic beliefs with the life and work of Jesus.

Was Christianity, indeed, a mythologization of earlier Gnostic concepts, especially concepts about a "redeemed redeemer"? Is the Gnostic "primal man" an archetype of the Christian savior? To understand the question, one must go back to W. Bousset, who argued (*Hauptproblem der Gnosis* [1907]) that the Gnostic redeemer was originally a pagan concept and that Gnosticism was a pre-Christian movement. Bousset cited Philo, the *Hermetica*, and the *Chaldean Oracles*, but especially emphasized the Babylonian and Persian sources. He was followed by R. Reitzenstein, who contended (*Poimandres* [1904]), on the basis of the Naasene sermon found in Hippolytus *Ref.* (rejecting its Christian element) and the Hermetic work published by Bousset, that the myth of a primal man (*ánthrōpos*) was pre-Christian. He argued that belief in a primal man who descended into the world, was given a revelation and reascended to heaven, was borrowed from the Parthian *Avesta's* teaching about Gayomart. This Gnostic redeemer myth was developed, he argued, in the Son of man motif in the Gospels. When Reitzenstein discovered that the Parthian texts he used had been found in Chinese Turkestan and were Manichaean, he concluded that these texts must reflect a pre-Christian Iranian source. When the Mandean texts became available Reitzenstein concluded, on the basis of the *Right Ginza*, that the Mandean messenger from heaven was the prototype of the NT Son of man motif.

R. Bultmann, convinced that Reitzenstein had demonstrated the existence of the redeemer myth long before the 1st cent. A.D., tried to prove (*ZNW*, 24 [1925], 100-146) that this redeemer myth was basic in the Gospel of John. He cited as proof Mandean and Manichaean texts, the Odes of Solomon (2nd cent. A.D.), and the apocryphal acts of the apostles — all writings later than John's Gospel. But he considered much of the Gospel to have been derived originally from writings about John the Baptist (cf. his 1941 comm., *Gospel of John* [Eng. tr. 1971]). Many of Bultmann's students not only held his views of the Gospel of John but also applied his theories about pre-Christian origins to other parts of the NT. (Cf. details in E. Yamauchi, *Pre-Christian Gnosticism*; "Some Alleged Evidence for Pre-Christian Gnosticism," in R. Longenecker and M. Tenney, eds., *New Dimensions in NT Study* [1974], pp. 46-70.)

Reitzenstein's reconstruction of the redeemer myth has been assailed by scholars such as C. Colpe (*Die religionsgeschichtliche Schule* [1961]). The leading scholars of the *Hermetica* believe that the extant texts of this work date from the 2nd to 4th cents. A.D.; this is also true of the Manichaean texts, both those from Turfan and those found in Egypt in 1931. The Mandean texts are much later, but may contain ideas that go back to the postapostolic times. The only way that one can set forth these documents as the source of the redeemer myth is by assuming that the doctrines and motifs contained in them (2nd cent. and later) had their origin in the pre-Christian era.

Numerous attempts have been made to relate Gnostic and gnosticizing literature to portions of the NT. C. Talbert (*Luke and the Gnostics* [1966]) viewed Luke and Acts as written to refute Gnostic tendencies. W. Schmithals contended that Gnosticism was the source of the licentiousness depicted in 1 and 2 Thessalonians and that the words "the day of the Lord is here" (cf. 2 Thess. 2:1f.) reflect a Gnostic saying that spiritualized the return of Christ. He also thought that the Gnostic problem was faced in the Corinthian Epistles, Philippians, and Galatians (*Gnosticism in Corinth* [Eng. tr. 1971]).

Some scholars have seen Gnostic influence and reinterpretation in Philippians. J. B. Lightfoot (*St. Paul's Epistle to the Colossians and to Philemon* [1897]) described the Colossians heresy as "incipient Gnosticism." Others have seen certain ideas in Ephesians as being originally Gnostic motifs. Bultmann found an expression of a Gnostic redeemer myth in 1 Tim. 3:16 (cf. A. K. Helmbold, "Redeemer Hymns — Gnostic and Christian," in R. Longenecker and M. Tenney, eds., *New Dimensions in NT Study* [1974], pp. 71-78). Many passages in the Pastorals about false teaching and portions of Hebrews have affinities to Gnostic doctrine, but frequently these affinities and parallels are tenuous. Bultmann and Käsemann attributed ideas in 1 and 2 Peter to borrowings from the Gnostics. Bultmann's thesis that 1 John had a pre-Christian Gnostic source has been widely followed.

John's apology for Christianity probably was a polemic against Gnosticism (cf. A. Wikenhauser, *NT Intro.* [Eng. tr. repr. 1967]). Suggestions of Gnostic parallels in the book of Revelation have not been generally accepted.

***Bibliography.–General:*** U. Bianchi, ed., *The Origins of Gnosticism* (Colloquium of Messina 13-18 April 1966; Texts and Discussions; 1967); J. Doresse, *Secret Books of the Egyptian Gnostics* (Eng. tr. 1960; repr. 1977); R. M. Grant, *Gnosticism and Early Christianity* (1959); *Gnosticism: A Source Book of Heretical Writings* (1961); A. K. Helmbold, *Nag Hammadi Gnostic Texts and the Bible* (1967); H. Jonas, *Gnostic Religion* (2nd ed. 1963); H. -C. Puech, G. Quispel, and W. C. van Unnik, *The Jung Codex* (1955); J. M. Robinson, *NTS,* 14 (1967/68), 356-401; *NTS,* 16 (1969/70), 178-195; *Nov.Test.,* 12 (1970), 81-85 (repr. in *Essays on the Coptic Gnostic Library* [1970], pp. 81-85); K. Rudolph, *Gnosis* (1983), esp. pp. 34-52; R. M. Wilson, *The Gnostic Problem* (1958); *Gnosis and the NT* (1968); E. Yamauchi, *Gnostic Ethics and Mandaean Origins* (1970); *Pre-Christian Gnosticism* (1973).

*Exhaustive Bibliography:* D. M. Scholer, *Nag Hammadi Bibliography, 1948-1969* (*NHS,* 1, 1971), updated as *"Bibliographica Gnostica; Supplementum": Nov.Test.,* 13 (1971), 322-336; 14 (1972), 312-331; 15 (1973), 327-345; 16 (1974), 316-336; 17 (1975), 305-336; 19 (1977), 293-336; 20 (1978), 300-331; 21 (1979), 357-382; 22 (1980), 352-384; 23 (1981), 361-380; 24 (1982), 340-368; 25 (1983), 356-381; 26 (1984), 341-373.

A. K. HELMBOLD

**NAGGAI** nag'ī [Gk. *Naggai*]; AV NAGGE. Son of Maath and father of Esli; an ancestor of Jesus (Lk. 3:25).

**NAHALAL** nā'hə-lal; **NAHALOL** nā'hə-lol [Heb. *nahᵃlāl* (Josh. 19:15; 21:35), *nahᵃlōl* (Jgs. 1:30)–possibly 'pasture, watering place'; Gk. *Naalōl, Nabaal, Domana,* A *Enamman,* L *Amman, Analōth, Alōm*]; AV also NAHALLAL (Josh. 19:15). A Levitical city in Zebulun. The site was formerly identified with Tell en-Naḥl N of the Kishon River at the southern end of the Plain of Acco, but two arguments can be raised against this suggestion. (1) The word is always written with *hê,* not *ḥēṯ* (*pace* Abel). (2) There is no conclusive evidence that Zebulun's territory extended so far west at that period. Simons believed that the ancient name is preserved in Maʿlûl, a village 4 km. (2½ mi.) NE of the modern Nahalal. The Talmud (T. B. *Megillah* 77a) identifies *mahlûl* with Nahalal, but the equivalence of *mahlûl* and *maʿlûl* is difficult to accept. Hence Simons' observation (p. 182) may be challenged on this point. He observed, moreover, that Maʿlûl is not sufficiently ancient and suggested that the ancient site may be Tell el-Beiḍā S of the modern village of Nahalal. The parallel passage in 1 Ch. 6:77 (MT 62) reads "Tabor," which seems highly improbable. The numerous and very different readings in Greek versions further complicate the problem.

***Bibliography.***–F.-M. Abel, *GP,* II, 63, 74; Simons, *GTTOT,* §§ 329, 337, 525.

W. S. L. S.

**NAHALIEL** nə-hā'lē-əl [Heb. *naḥᵃlîʾēl*–'wadi of 'El'; Gk. B *Naaliēl,* A *Manaēl*]. One of the last stopping places in the march from Sinai to the Promised Land, between the Arnon gorge and Jericho (Nu. 21:19). Eusebius (*Onom.*) placed it near the Arnon, and its name suggests that it was a wadi rather than a town.

It has been identified with Wâdī Wāleh, a tributary of the Arnon, and with Wâdī Zerqā Māʿîn, which flows through a gorge into the Dead Sea 18 km. (11 mi.) N of the Arnon. *WHAB,* plate IX, adopts the latter. W. S. L. S.

**NAHALLAL** nā'hə-lal (Josh. 19:15, AV); **NAHALOL.** *See* NAHALAL.

**NAHAM** nā'ham [Heb. *naḥam*–'comfort']. The brother-in-law of Hodiah (1 Ch. 4:19). The AV and NEB read "his wife Hodiah (the) sister of Naham," making Hodiah, rather than Hodiah's wife, the sister of Naham; but HODIAH is elsewhere a masculine name, and the RSV reading ("the wife of Hodiah, the sister of Naham") has stronger MS support (but cf. *BHS*). The text is difficult (see comms.).

**NAHAMANI** nā-hə-mā'nī [Heb. *naḥᵃmānî,* an abbreviated form of *nᵉḥemyâ*–'Yahweh has comforted'; Gk. *Naemani*]. One who returned from the Exile with Zerubbabel (Neh. 7:7). In Ezr. 2:2 the name is omitted; in 1 Esd. 5:8 it is replaced by Gk. *Enēnios,* rendered "Bigvai" by the RSV, without any MS support, in an attempt to reconcile this list with the two parallel lists.

See *IP,* pp. 39, 175.

**NAHARAI** nā'hə-rī [Heb. *naḥᵃray*]; AV also NAHARI (2 S. 23:37). One of David's thirty mighty men, Joab's armor-bearer, from the city of Beeroth (2 S. 23:37; 1 Ch. 11:39).

**NAHASH** nā'hash [Heb. *nāḥāš*–'serpent'].

**1.** King of the Ammonites during the reigns of Saul and David. His military incursions were part of the reason that the Israelites sought a king of their own (1 S. 12:12), and Nahash's attack upon Jabesh-gilead and Saul's subsequent victory over him was the event that cemented Saul's kingship in Israel (11:12-15). Nahash was not content with a "peaceful" victory over Jabesh-gilead (i.e., by way of a treaty, 11:1), but insisted on a more violent victory. He apparently wished to disgrace Israel more than he wanted to conquer it (11:2). Thus he allowed the inhabitants of Jabesh-gilead seven days to secure more troops to deliver them — the more Israelites defeated and disgraced the better. This was his undoing, however, since Saul mustered an army large enough to scatter Nahash's troops and deliver Jabesh-gilead (11:11).

Later in Saul's reign or early in David's the relationship with Nahash must have improved. When Nahash died, David pledged loyalty to his son Hanun (2 S. 10:2). Furthermore, Nahash's son Shobi later helped David during the time of Absalom's uprising (17:27). Some suggest this relationship between David and Nahash's family is due to their both having a common enemy (i.e., Saul). While this may be true, it may also be that David and Nahash were related through David's (step-)sisters Abigail and Zeruiah (17:25).

**2.** The father (or mother?) of Abigail (2 S. 17:25). While it is remotely possible that Nahash is a woman's name, it is more likely that here it refers to the father of Abigail. Jesse is not said to be the father of Abigail (although cf. variant in some LXX and Lat. MSS of 17:25), but she is referred to as the sister of David (1 Ch. 2:16). When and under what circumstances Nahash became the father of Abigail is not recorded. If this is the same Nahash as above, then David's loyalty to his family would be for familial as well as political reasons.

D. H. ENGELHARD

**NAHATH** nā'hath [Heb. *naḥaṯ*–'clear, pure'(?); cf. Arab. *naḥtun*].

**1.** Grandson of Esau (Gen. 36:13; 1 Ch. 1:37); an Edomite clan chief (Gen. 36:17).

**2.** A Kohathite Levite, son of Zophai and ancestor of Samuel (1 Ch. 6:26 [MT 11]); probably the same as Toah (v. 34 [MT 19]) and Tohu (1 S. 1:1).

**3.** A Levite appointed by King Hezekiah to assist in overseeing the collection of offerings (2 Ch. 31:13).

See *IP,* p. 228.

**NAHBI** nā'bī [Heb. *naḥbî*]. Representative of the tribe of Naphtali among the twelve spies (Nu. 13:14).

**NAHOR** nā'hōr [Heb. *nāḥôr*; Gk. *Nachōr*]; AV also NACHOR (Josh. 24:2; Lk. 3:34). Terah's father and Terah's son, brother of Abraham.

**1.** The most elementary facts about the older of the two Nahors appear in Gen. 11:22-25. His father was Serug, the seventh recorded generation from Noah. Nahor's father was 30 years old when Nahor was born, and lived for 200 more years. Nahor himself was 29 when he fathered Terah, the father of Abraham. Nahor died at 148 years of age; thus he lived well into the life of Abraham. The two genealogies where his name appears later offer no additional information (1 Ch. 1:26; Lk. 3:34).

**2.** The younger Nahor, a grandson of **1**, also appears in Gen. 11, but always in the shadow of his more famous brother Abraham. We cannot be certain that Abraham was the oldest of the three brothers mentioned in v. 27. Nahor married Milcah, the daughter of Haran, Nahor's other brother (v. 29). Gen. 22:20-24 provides the names of Nahor's twelve children — eight by Milcah his wife (his son Kemuel is called the father of Aram; this familial relationship accounts for the close relation between the Arameans and the Hebrews) and four by Reumah his concubine. The purpose of these details is to point out that Rebekah, who later became Abraham's daughter-in-law, was a granddaughter of Nahor.

Genesis 24 records the episode of Abraham's servant's discovery of Rebekah as a wife for Isaac. It happened in "the city of Nahor" (v. 10). A city Naḫur, or Nakhur, on the Habor (Ḫābûr) River, appears in both the Mari and Ebla texts. This may indicate that the city of Gen. 24:10 is not merely Haran, an even more frequently mentioned city, or simply the city where Nahor lived, but a city actually named Nahor, perhaps after either of the two Nahors (cf. de Vaux, pp. 195f.).

Rebekah is identified twice as Nahor's granddaughter in response to the demand of Abraham that Isaac wed someone from his own relatives. Although Nahor was alive at this time, Laban his son and hence Rebekah's brother played the major role in the negotiations for the wedding. Laban's important role here has led some to posit that the society in which he lived was fratriarchal, or at least had fratriarchal elements (see C. H. Gordon, *JBL*, 54 [1935], 223-231; E. A. Speiser, *Genesis* [*AB*, 1964], pp. 92, 184f.; N. Sarna, *Understanding Genesis* [repr. 1978], pp. 174f.; but cf. de Vaux, pp. 234f., 246). In the Rachel-Leah episode a generation later, Laban was again identified by his grandfather Nahor (Gen. 29:5).

Although Gen. 31:53 might appear to imply that Nahor was also a Yahwist (thus B. Vawter, *On Genesis: A New Reading* [1977], p. 343, suggests that J thought the gods were identical) most scholars distinguish Nahor's pagan god from Yahweh (see the comms.).

See R. de Vaux, *Early History of Israel* (Eng. tr. 1978).

R. L. ALDEN

**NAHSHON** nä'shon [Heb. *naḥšôn*–'snake'(?)]; AV also NAASHON, NAASSON. Son of Amminadab and brother of Elisheba, who married Aaron the high priest (Ex. 6:23). He was the leader of the tribe of Judah at the time of the first census in the wilderness (Nu. 1:7; 2:3), and as the leader he brought the tribal gifts and offerings at the time of the dedication of the tabernacle (7:12, 17). In addition, he led his tribe as they set out on their march from Sinai (10:14). He also appears in the genealogical lists of David and Jesus (1 Ch. 2:10f.; Mt. 1:4; Lk. 3:32).

C. G. RASMUSSEN

**NAHUM** nā'həm [Heb. *naḥûm*–'comfort'; LXX *Naoum*]. This title appears at the beginning of the seventh book within the collection of the Twelve Minor Prophets and is the name of the author of the "vision" within the book.

I. Author
II. Book
  A. Survey of the Message
  B. Composition of the Prophecy
  C. Theological Significance

*I. Author.*–The prophet Nahum cannot be identified with Naham (1 Ch. 4:19), Nehemiah (Neh. 1:1), or Nahamani (Neh. 7:7); thus knowledge of him must be derived from evidence within the book. Haldar questioned whether he was an individual and regarded the reference to "comfort" (Heb. *naḥûm* in 1:1; 3:7) as an allusion to the purpose of the book. "Nahum of Elkosh" in 1:1, however, implies that Nahum was a person who was born or who lived in a certain city (cf. Mic. 1:1, Micah of Moresheth). ELKOSH has been identified with (1) the Galilean cities of Capernaum ("the city of Nahum") and Helkesei, modern el-Qauze (Jerome); (2) el-Qôsh, a town about 50 km. (30 mi.) N of modern Mosul in Iraq; (3) Eleutheropolis (modern Beit Jibrîn) in southwestern Judah (pseudo-Epiphanius), Kessijah, a city near Beit Jibrîn (G. Nestle, *PEQ* [1879], pp. 136-38), and Umm Lagish, which is also near Beit Jibrîn (U. Cassuto, *Giornale della Società Asiatica Italiana,* 26 [1914], 291-302). The Assyrian location is unacceptable, since the book makes no allusions to the life of Israelites exiled from Samaria. A Galilean location is also unlikely unless the prophet had moved from Galilee to Judah (KD), for the northern nation of Israel was in exile at this time. Most believe that the book was written with a Judean audience in mind, since 1:15 mentions Judah and temple worship. Those who take the book to be a liturgical text (e.g., Humbert, Sellin) think that Nahum was a cultic prophet, but these conclusions are unwarranted. Nahum was neither a narrow-minded nationalist from the country nor a false prophet (J. M. P. Smith, Marti), but a man well acquainted with international affairs and possessing a clear concept of God's sovereignty over the nations.

*II. Book.*–A summary of the book will introduce the message of the prophet and provide a perspective for discussion of the book's date, unity, structure, and theological significance.

*A. Survey of the Message.* A general analysis of the prophecy indicates that the message can be divided into five paragraphs (see II.B.2 below), which present a message of comfort for Judah. The Assyrians had afflicted Judah, but now God would destroy Nineveh and restore Judah.

*1. God's Powerful Wrath and Goodness (1:2-8).* Although God is not quick to judge, His great power will take vengeance on His enemies (1:2-3a). When He appears in majesty, nature shrinks before His presence, for all the world is under His control (vv. 3b-6). His indignation destroys everything, but His strength protects those who trust in Him (vv. 7f.).

*2. God Would Destroy Those Who Afflicted Judah (1:9–2:2 [MT 3]).* Judah had suffered distress and affliction (1:12f., 15; 2:2) and might have doubted the goodness of God (1:9a), but God promised to restore its peace (v. 15; 2:2) and not to afflict it again (1:9, 12, 15). He would make a complete end of its enemies (vv. 9, 11, 15), decree that their graves be dug, and send an army to destroy them (v. 14; 2:1).

*3. Fall of Nineveh (2:3-13 [MT 4–14]).* Troops and chariots attacked the city (2:3f.), and the defenders raced to the wall (v. 5), but in the end the city was entered and its leadership removed (v. 6). Some mourned and others fled (2:7f.), but the enemy plundered the city and turned it into a desolate place (vv. 9f.). This paragraph ends with lion imagery and a mocking question concerning the former greatness of Nineveh (vv. 11f.); a final divine answer interprets this defeat as an act of God (v. 13).

*4. Nineveh Would Be Destroyed Because of Its Sin (3:1-7).*

Nineveh's sins included murder, robbery, a thirst for war, bloodshed, and deceptive policies (3:1-4). Because of these sins, God would shame Nineveh. When the nations saw it destroyed, they would laugh (vv. 5-7).

*5. Nineveh's End, Like No-amon's, Was Inevitable (3:8-19).* No-amon, the Egyptian capital of Thebes, had good defenses and many allies, but it was captured and the people were killed (3:8-10). In like manner, Nineveh's walls and troops would be nothing (vv. 11-13), and all efforts to withstand the enemies' siege would be useless (vv. 14-15a). Nineveh's swarming masses and its army would disappear (vv. 15b-17), its leaders would perish, and its people would run for the hills, for the city's fate was sealed (vv. 18-19a). The nations that Assyria had once humbled would rejoice at this news (3:19b).

*B. Composition of the Prophecy. 1. Date.* The reference to the fall of Thebes (No-amon) in 3:8 indicates that Nahum proclaimed his message after 663 B.C. Since Nineveh's defeat was yet to come, this prophecy must be dated before 612. Three possible dates within this period have been proposed. A few scholars have suggested a date after the fall of Nineveh.

*a. Soon After the Fall of Thebes.* Von Orelli, Maier, Christensen, and van der Woude placed the prophecy *ca.* 654-648 B.C. because 1:12f., 15; 2:1 presuppose that Judah was suffering under Assyrian rule (Judah was suppressed by Esarhaddon and Ashurbanipal from 687 to 642, during the reign of Manasseh, and by Sennacherib in 701, during the reign of Hezekiah). The reference to the fall of Thebes is more fitting if Nahum wrote soon after the event and before Egypt recovered the city (654).

*b. Around the Time of Ashurbanipal's Death.* Some scholars, e.g., van Hoonacker, Eybers, Keller, and Rudolph, chose a date near the death of Ashurbanipal (632-626 B.C.). Nineveh was strong (3:1) but under attack (2:3-12; 3:2f., 13) and about to be defeated. Most of these scholars preferred a date *ca.* 627 B.C., but Eybers and Rudolph suggested a slightly earlier date (632-630 B.C.) when Assyria was stronger and not yet under direct attack.

*c. Just Before the Fall of Nineveh.* Most scholars, including Davidson, Marti, J. M. P. Smith, Haldar, Mihelic, Horst, Taylor, van Selms, and Watts, dated Nahum *ca.* 614-612 B.C. because the fall of the city was imminent and Judah was pictured in a positive light (implying a date after the reform of Josiah in 621 B.C.).

*d. Shortly After the Fall of Assyria.* Humbert and Sellin interpreted Nahum as a liturgy celebrating the defeat of all Assyrian forces. H. Schulz derived most of the book from a postexilic setting.

*e. Maccabean Date.* Happel and Haupt believed that the foe in Nahum was actually the Greeks, not the Assyrians, and therefore dated the book *ca.* 175-165 B.C.

*f. Conclusion.* The Maccabean date is out of the question because of the discovery of the Nahum Pesher at Qumrân and Sir. 49:10-12 (cf. H. H. Rowley, *JBL,* 75 [1956], 188-193; Y. Yadin, *IEJ,* 21 [1971], 1-12). A date after the fall of Nineveh or very soon after the defeat of Thebes is contrary to the threatened disaster for Nineveh that lay in the near future. A date *ca.* 614-612 B.C. places the book in a period when Judah was not afflicted, for after 621 Josiah was free from Assyria, Judah was enjoying its feast (1:15), and God had already restored it (2:2). A date around the death of Ashurbanipal (628) seems preferable. Assyria still was powerful but was under tremendous pressure from the Medes and Babylonians. Assyrian domination during the reigns of Manasseh and Amon had just ended for Judah. Nahum was a message of comfort to Josiah and Judah (2 Ch. 34:3 mentions a reform in 628).

*2. Unity and Structure.* Since the work of Gunkel in 1893 many have questioned the authenticity of the acrostic poem in 1:2-8/10 and the contrasting promises and threats in 1:9/11–2:2. J. M. P. Smith, Taylor, and Schulz believed that the negative statements (1:11, 14; 2:1) are from Nahum but the initial poem (1:2-8/10) and the positive portions (1:12f., 15; 2:2) are from another source. Smith concluded that the poem and positive sections presuppose the fall of Nineveh, and Taylor followed Arnold in positing a third-century origin for this material. Horst, van Selms, and Childs (*Intro.*), however, believed that Nahum had found an earlier poem and adapted it to his message. Nothing in the poem requires a third-century date, and the positive sections,which picture Judah under oppression and looking forward to release, are before the fall of Nineveh. Van Selms thought that a recasting of an earlier acrostic poem might explain the imperfect acrostic form of the present text. Smith also dated 3:18f. after the fall, but this date overlooks the verses' canonical function of confirming the certainty of the prophecy (Childs, *Intro. to the OT as Scripture* [1979], p. 445).

The structure is marked by changes in the form of literature and the introduction of new themes. The initial poem magnifies the power of God (1:2-8) and is followed by a series of positive and negative statements that contrast the power of God's goodness and His wrath (1:9–2:2). The vision of the fall of Nineveh in 2:3-14 is very descriptive and ends with a mocking question (vv. 11f.) and a prose divine answer (v. 13). 3:1-7 is a woe speech. The final paragraph (vv. 8-19) contains a lengthy comparison and also ends with a mocking encouragement for the people of Nineveh (vv. 14-17) and with a divine answer that removes all hope (vv. 18f.). Allis defined many of the subtle stylistic features of Nahum.

*3. Problems of Interpretation.* Humbert, Sellin, and Mihelic believed that Nahum is a liturgy composed for reading at the New Year Festival to celebrate the sovereignty of God over Nineveh. Horst, von Rad (*OT Theology,* II [Eng. tr. 1965], 189), de Vries, and Watts supported a more general cultic use of Nahum. The works of Elliger and Rudolph reject this approach. Haldar also rejected this interpretation and developed Mowinckel's radical suggestion (*Jesaja-disiplene* [1926], p. 58; *Psalmenstudien* [repr. 1961], II, 57) that Nahum uses the basic themes of the Babylonian enthronement festival in the *Enuma Elish.* Judah employed this myth-ritual battle between God and His foes (the mythical sea or Assyria) for political propaganda. H. Schulz found an eschatological emphasis in the prophecy. J. Jeremias (*Kult prophetie und Gerischtsverkundigung* [1970]) approached the book from a completely different angle and concluded that the threats of destruction were originally against Judah. Rudolph made all of 1:11–2:3 an oracle of salvation for Judah; J. M. P. Smith, Taylor, and Schulz derived the positive and negative portions from sources from different time periods. None of these interpretations seems to solve the complex problems of the book adequately. The liturgical, cultic, and mythical connections remain unproven and improbable; the highly complex contrasts in 1:9–2:2 cannot be weakened or destroyed without eroding the thrust of the prophet's message.

*C. Theological Significance.* Judah faced two problems: oppression from Assyria and discouragement within. The prophet addressed these issues by reminding the people of God's character and promises. The initial poem (1:2-8) reaffirms God's awesome power over the earth. He is living and active, administering justice with vengeance (v. 2) as well as loving care (v. 7). This perspective establishes a foundation for the application of God's sovereignty over the nations. His universal control of history is demonstrated by His wrath toward those who plot against Him and afflict Judah (1:9–2:2). Those who trust Him will be delivered from bondage and receive peace and restoration (1:15; 2:2). Nineveh's defeat was envisaged because God was against it (2:13; 3:5) and because of its violence, bloodshed, and deceptive political policies (3:1-4). God's promises to destroy Assyria (Isa. 10:5-27; 31:6-9) are repeated using eschatological imagery (cf. Isa. 33) to assure Judah of God's comfort. The Qumrân community saw these theological issues and took comfort because they believed that God would destroy their enemies.

***Bibliography.****–Comms.:* KD; C. von Orelli (1893); A. B. Davidson (*CBSC,* 1896); G. A. Smith (*Expos.B.,* 1898); J. Happel (1902); K. Marti (*Kurzer Hand-Commentar zum AT,* 1904); A. van Hoonacker (*EtB,* 1908); J. M. P. Smith (*ICC,* 1911); E. Sellin (*KZAT,* 1930); C. L. Taylor (*IB,* 1956); W. A. Maier (1959); F. Horst (*HAT,* 3rd ed. 1964); K. Elliger (*ATD,* 6th ed. 1967); C. A. Keller (*Commentaire de l'AT,* 1971); H. Shulz (1973); J. D. W. Watts (*CBC,* 1975); W. Rudolph (*KZAT,* 2nd ed. 1975). The standard Bible dictionaries, encyclopedias, and OT introductions give a brief survey of opinions on Nahum.

*Articles:* H. Gunkel, *ZAW,* 13 (1893), 223-244; W. R. Arnold, *ZAW,* 21 (1901), 225-265; P. Haupt, *JBL,* 26 (1907), 1-53, 151-164; P. Humbert, *ZAW,* 44 (1926), 226-280; *Revue d'histoire et de philosophie religieuses,* 12 (1932), 1-15; W. A. Maier, *Concordia Theological Monthly,* 7 (1936), 692-98; A. Halder, *Studies in the Book of Nahum* (1947); J. L. Mihelic, *Interp.,* 2 (1948), 199-208; O. Allis, "Nahum, Nineveh, Elkosh," *EQ,* 27 (1955), 67-80; R. Weiss, *RQ,* 4 (1963/64), 433-39; S. J. de Vries, *VT,* 16 (1966), 476-481; I. Eybers, "Note Concerning the Date of Nahum's Prophecy," in A. H. van Zyl, ed., *Biblical Essays (Ou-Testamentiese Werkgemeenskap in Suid-Afrika,* 1969), pp. 9-12; A. van Selms, "Alphabetic Hymn in Nahum 1," in A. H. van Zyl, ed., *Biblical Essays* (1969), pp. 33-45; W. van Wyk, "Allusions to 'Prehistory' and History in the Book of Nahum," I. H. Eybers, *et al.,* eds., *De Fructu Oris Sui* (1971), pp. 222-232; K. Cathcart, *Nahum in the Light of Northwest Semitic* (1973); D. L. Christensen, *ZAW,* 87 (1975), 17-30; A. S. van der Woude, "The Book of Nahum: A Letter Written in Exile," *Oudtestamentische Studiën,* 20 (1977), 108-126.

G. V. SMITH

**NAIDUS** nā'ə-dəs [Gk. A *Naeidos,* B *Naaidos*]. Son of Addi; a layman who had married a foreign wife (1 Esd. 9:31); called Benaiah in par. Ezr. 10:30.

**NAIL.** (1) In biblical times carpenter's nails (Heb. *masmēr* and *maśmēr* [Eccl. 12:11]; Gk. *hḗlos*) were first made out of bronze and then out of iron. The range of sizes was similar to nails used in modern times, i.e., 2.5-23 cm. (1-9 in.) in length. Ancient nails were usually hand forged, having squared tapered shanks with either squared flat or domed heads.

Bronze nail (Late Bronze Age, *ca.* 1500-1200 B.C.) from Megiddo and two iron nails (right) (late 5th cent. A.D.). All are shown about three-fourths actual size (Israel Department of Antiquities and Museums)

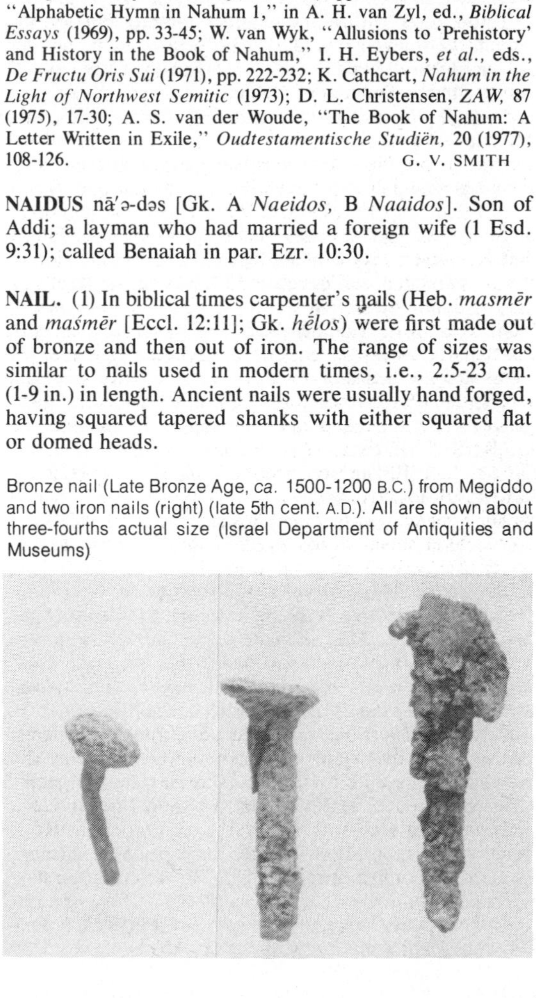

Bronze nail, Iron II (*ca.* 900-539 B.C.), from Tell el-Kheleifeh in the Negeb. It is about 23 cm. (9 in.) long (Israel Department of Antiquities and Museums)

Iron nails, shown about three-fourths actual size (3rd-4th cents. A.D.) (Israel Department of Antiquities and Museums)

David stored iron from which nails were forged for the construction of the doors of the temple gates (1 Ch. 22:3). In addition, Solomon used golden (headed? plated?) nails in the construction of the inner sanctuary of the temple (2 Ch. 3:9). The prophets mocked the worshipers of idols by noting that their statues had to be secured with nails in order to remain upright (Isa. 41:7; Jer. 10:4). In Ecclesiastes the sayings of the wise were compared to the permanence of firmly fixed nails (12:11).

John 20:25 indicates that the Romans nailed Jesus to the cross. This method of execution in Roman Palestine has now received archeological confirmation. The bones of a man who had been crucified were found in an ossuary that was discovered in a tomb located on the outskirts of Jerusalem. The two heel bones were pierced by an iron spike almost 18 cm. (7 in.) long. The spike still had a piece of olive wood attached to it (N. Haas, *IEJ,* 20 [1970], 38-59; *see* CROSS VI). Col. 2:14 states that God nailed (*prosēlóō*) to the cross the "bond which stood against us"; this is probably a reference to the work of Christ on the cross rather than to alleged customs such as canceling bonds by "crossing" them out or by driving nails through them (see F. F. Bruce, comm. on Colossians [*NICNT,* 1957], p. 238 n. 64).

The AV also translated Heb. *yāṯēḏ* as "nail" (e.g., Jgs. 4:21f.; 5:26). But *yāṯēḏ* usually means "peg, tent peg" (so RSV; see KoB, p. 415).

(2) Fingernails, toenails, and claws receive scant mention in Scripture. A captive woman who was going to be taken by an Israelite man for his wife had to shave her head, pare her nails (Heb. *ṣippōren*), change her clothes, and mourn the loss of her parents for a month. After this period she could become the wife of an Israelite (Dt. 21:10-13). This rite seems to mark the transfer of the woman from her pagan community to the Israelite one (see A. D. H. Mayes, *Deuteronomy* [*NCBC,* repr. 1981], p. 303).

The Aramaic word for nails ($t^epar$) is used in the description of Nebuchadnezzar's beastlike behavior and appearance. His nails are said to have been like "birds' claws" (lit., "like birds," Dnl. 4:33 [MT 30]). Later in the book, in the vision of the four beasts, the fourth beast is depicted as having "teeth of iron" and "claws [*t$^e$par*] of bronze" (Dnl. 7:19).

C. G. RASMUSSEN

**NAIN** nān [Gk. *Nain* < Heb. *nāʿîm*–'pleasant' (so *SSW*, p. 191)]. A town mentioned in Scripture only in connection with Jesus' visit and miracle of raising the widow's son from the dead (Lk. 7:11). It is identified with the modern Arab village of Nein (about two hundred inhabitants), which lies on the northern slope of Jebel ed-Dahi. This hill, with an elevation of 515 m. (1690 ft.), may be the OT "hill of Moreh" (Jgs. 7:1). Since the Middle Ages it has been known as Little Hermon. Josephus (*BJ* iv.9.4 [509-513]) mentioned a town called Nain, but it was E of the Jordan and thus is not to be confused with the Nain of the Gospel narrative.

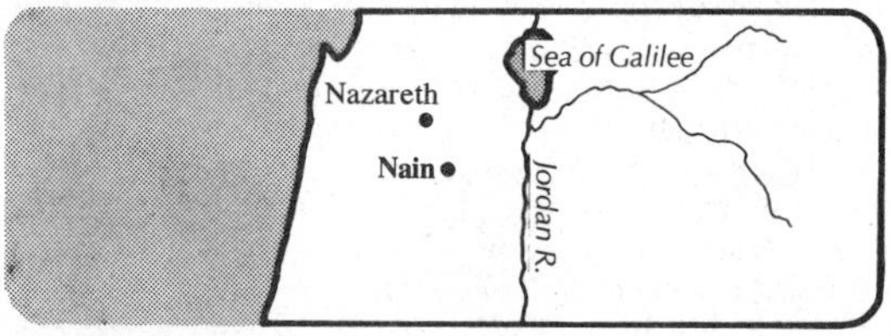


The town of Jesus' day may have stood higher on the hill than the present village. It probably was named for the pleasant view that the site affords across the plain of Esdraelon. To the west one can see Mt. Carmel, and to the north the hills behind Nazareth stand out, about 9½ km. (6 mi.) away. To the northeast one can look past nearby Tabor (3 km. [2 mi.] away) to snowcapped Mt. Hermon in the distance. Southward lies Mt. Gilboa.

The reference to a city gate (Lk. 7:12) has caused some discussion, since the evidence indicates that Nain was never enclosed by a wall. "Gate" probably refers to the entrance into the village between houses. H. B. Tristram (*Eastern Customs in Bible Lands* [2nd ed. 1894], pp. 100f.) thought that he had found traces of an ancient city wall, but apparently he was mistaken.

East of Nain are rock-cut tombs of an ancient cemetery, which Jesus had probably just passed when He saw the funeral procession coming out of the city. A small sanctuary N of the village is called "place of our Lord Jesus." A spring W of the town furnishes water for the olive and fig groves that help to make it a "pleasant" place.

R. EARLE

**NAIOTH** nā'oth [Heb. *Q nāyôṯ, nāywôṯ*–'dwellings(?)' or 'pasture lands'; Gk. B *Auath*, A *Nauiōth*]. A region, possibly a dwelling or a compound in Ramah belonging to Samuel (1 S. 19:18f., 22f.; 20:1). Something like a "school of the prophets" was located at Naioth under the leadership of Samuel (19:20). David fled there apparently for refuge, and Saul sent messengers three times to capture him. On each occasion the messengers came under the influence of the Spirit and "prophesied." Finally Saul himself went to Naioth; the Spirit of God also came upon him, and he "prophesied," which gave rise to the saying, "Is Saul also among the prophets?" (v. 24). Because of the *kethibh* (which has support of LXX A), some would emend to *nāwôṯ*, "pastures," but this hardly fits the picture as set forth in this passage (cf. P. K. McCarter, *I Samuel* [*AB*, 1980], pp. 327f.).

W. S. L. S.

**NAKED** [Heb. *ʿārôm, ʿêrōm, ʿeryâ, maʿ$^a$rōm*; Gk. *gymnós*]; AV also NAKEDNESS (RSV "naked flesh," Ex. 28:42); NEB also EXPOSED (RSV "made naked," Lev. 20:18f.), EXPOSURE, BARE, STRIPPED, PRIVATE PARTS; **NAKEDNESS** [Heb. *ʿerwâ, maʿar* (Nah. 3:5), *ʿêrōm* (Dt. 28:48); *yāḏ* (Isa. 57:8); Gk. *gymnótēs* (Rom. 8:35; Rev. 3:18)]; AV also NAKED (Mic. 1:11); NEB also LUST, NAKED, NAKED BODY, PRIVATE PARTS, HAVE INTERCOURSE, RAVISH, BRING SHAME UPON (previous three for "uncover the nakedness"), DISHONOR (1 S. 20:30).

Occasionally "nakedness" is a euphemism for sexual organs. Thus the laws of Ex. 20:26 and 28:42 prohibit the exposure of priests' "nakedness" because it would be cultically defiling. "Uncover the nakedness" in Lev. 18 and 20 refers to incest. In these chapters the same expression also denotes the result of incest, i.e., the bringing of shame upon the aggrieved party (the NEB correctly conveys both meanings).

Shame is also generally associated with nakedness and is seen as originating in the garden of Eden (Gen. 2:25). When the man and woman became aware that they were naked, they were ashamed. The presupposition is that prior to the disobedience nakedness was natural, as it continued to be for animals.

Nakedness can also symbolize lack of possessions. It is the condition of the newborn and the dead (Job 1:21; Eccl. 5:15; cf. Ezk. 16:7, 22, where Israel is likened to an abandoned infant). It can be a synonym for "poor," as Job 22:6 clearly shows: "You strip off the garments of the naked," i.e., oppress the poor (cf. also Job 24:7; Isa. 58:7; Ezk. 18:7, 16; Mt. 25:36f.).

To be naked can refer to the condition of prisoners or victims of war (Ezk. 16:39; 23:29). Thus Isaiah was told to walk about naked in order to symbolize what would happen to the Egyptians and Ethiopians (Isa. 20:2-4). An individual may also be stripped of everything as a divine punishment (Hos. 2:3; Am. 2:16; Rev. 17:16).

In some instances nakedness was part of mourning customs. Micah stated that he would go naked in mourning over the fall of Samaria (Mic. 1:8).

According to 1 S. 19:24 Saul prophesied in a state of nakedness. This is undoubtedly a reflection of the ecstatic nature of such prophecy. Acts 19:16 illustrates the results of possession by an evil spirit.

In 2 Cor. 5:1f., Paul employed the figure of an "earthly tent" for the body. At death the believer's earthly tent will be destroyed, and he will put on a "heavenly dwelling," so that he "may not be found naked." Here to be naked is to have no place in heaven, i.e., to be damned; cf. C. K. Barrett, comm. on 2 Corinthians (*HNTC*, 1973), pp. 153-56; P. E. Hughes, comm. on 2 Corinthians (*NICNT*, 1963), pp. 169-173.

The practice of sleeping unclothed is attested in Rev. 16:15, where being awake and clothed is contrasted with being asleep and naked.

See *TDNT*, I, *s.v.* γυμνός κτλ. (Oepke).

F. B. KNUTSON

**NAME** [Heb. *šēm*; Aram. *šum*; Lat. *nomen*; Gk. *ónoma*]. In the Bible "name" is that title, label, designation by which a person, place, or thing can be known or marked out as distinguishable from another. More fundamentally, however, "name" is that which (1) reveals the true nature of its bearer (1 S. 25:25), so that to know the name is to know the person (Ps. 9:10 [MT 11]), or (2) designates the relationship that exists between entities, especially between God and His people (2 Ch. 7:14; Isa. 43:6f.).

I. OT
  A. Etymology
  B. Significance
  C. The Divine Name

II. NT
  A. Etymology
  B. Significance
  C. Conclusion

*I. OT.–A. Etymology.* The most common OT word for "name" is Heb. *šēm.* It is a very old word. Some have related it to the root *wšm,* "sign" or "token," or to the verb *šmh,* "be high," from which are derived such ideas as "monument" (Isa. 55:13) or "memorial" (Isa. 56:5). In this connection note that "name" also translates Heb. *zēḵer* (lit. "remembrance," "memorial") in Ps. 30:4 (MT 5); 97:12; 102:12 (MT 13); Hos. 12:5 (MT 6), and that *šēm* and *zēḵer* parallel each other in Ex. 3:15; Job 18:17; Ps. 135:13; Prov. 1:7; Isa. 26:8.

*B. Significance.* In many places throughout the OT *šēm* serves no greater purpose than to identify some person, place, or thing, and to distinguish this one from other persons, places, or things. But it would be quite incorrect to say that in the OT a name was just an identity tag and no more. There, as in other ancient literature, the name of a person sometimes revealed his character, his personality, even his destiny. In fact, a person's name was often considered to be but an expression, indeed a revelation, of his true nature, as the many popular etymological explanations of names given to people in the OT makes clear. These explanations may be correct or fanciful, but they bear witness to the widespread belief that name and nature should correspond. For example, Esau can say of Jacob: "Is he not rightly named Jacob? For he has supplanted me these two times" (Gen. 27:36; cf. Hos. 12:2-4 [MT 3-5]). And Abigail can say of her churlish husband: "As his name is, so is he; Nabal [= "fool"] is his name, and folly is with him" (1 S. 25:25; cf. also Gen. 3:20; 11:9; 21:3, 6; 1 S. 4:21; Isa. 7:3; etc.). That "name" on occasion is synonymous with "person" (Nu. 1:2; 26:53) and that to speak or act in the name of another is to speak or act as that person (Ex. 5:23; 1 S. 17:45; 1 K. 21:8; etc.) also indicate the close association between name and essence.

But a person does not need to remain what he has been, nor is his nature forever determined by the name first given to him. This can be seen in those several OT references to a change in one's name, and with it a concomitant change in character and conduct. The new name signifies a new beginning, a new opportunity, a new position, a new person. For example, Jacob, "the crafty one, the overreacher," is renamed Israel and thus becomes the one who has "striven with God and . . . prevailed" (Gen. 32:27f.). Abram is renamed Abraham (17:5), Sarai is renamed Sarah (17:15), Joseph is renamed Zaphenath-paneah (41:45), and Jerusalem, purged of injustice, is renamed "the city of righteousness" (Isa. 1:26), or "Yahweh is there" (Ezk. 48:38; see also Isa. 62:2; 65:15; Dnl. 1:7).

Because a person's name is so closely related to what he is, *šēm* comes also to mean "fame," "renown," "reputation." For one's reputation, the name one makes for oneself, is but an extension of what that person is. The Nephilim, for example, were mighty men of old, whose deeds were told far and wide. Thus they gained the title of "the men of renown" (lit. "the men of the name," Gen. 6:4). So also the people of Shinar attempted to build a tower with its top in the heavens to make a name for themselves, to gain a reputation, and thus to establish themselves in the earth (Gen. 11:3f.; see also 1 S. 18:30; 2 S. 8:13). Hence, *šēm* by itself, without any modifiers, can mean "a *good* name" and is so translated in Prov. 22:1 and Eccl. 7:1, while senseless, disreputable people are literally people "without a name" (Job 30:8, NASB).

In one sense name and existence come extraordinarily close together in Hebrew thought. Perhaps it is going too far to say that the Hebrews believed that nothing existed unless it had a name (cf. Eccl. 6:10a). But certainly they believed that one's name lived on in one's descendants (Gen. 48:16), and that without male heirs one would be left with "neither name nor remnant upon the face of the earth" (2 S. 14:7; cf. Dt. 25:5-10). Thus, on the one hand, expressions like "to blot out their name from under heaven" mean in essence "to destroy, to put an end to, to put out of existence" (Dt. 7:24; 9:14; 20:20; Josh. 7:9; 1 S. 24:21; 2 K. 14:27; Ps. 109:13; etc.), whereas, on the other hand, God's promise to give His people "an everlasting name which shall not be cut off" (Isa. 56:5) is a promise that they will exist forever.

It is widely held that the giving of a name was an OT way of declaring one's power over the person or object named. That is to say, Adam names all the animals (Gen. 2:19f.) and thus exercises his dominion over them. He names his wife, "Eve," and thereby asserts his authority over her (Gen. 3:20). But this is a dubious interpretation of these passages. Notice that when David takes a city and establishes his right of possession over it, he does so not simply by naming it, but by giving to it *his* name (2 S. 12:28; cf. 49:11). Further, in times of national distress, when the male population has been decimated by war, seven women will take hold of one man and seek to become his possession by being called by *his* name (Isa. 4:1). And Yahweh lays claim to Israel, the temple, the ark, and Jerusalem, not by naming them but by calling out *His* name over them (2 Ch. 7:14; Jer. 7:10f.; 2 S. 6:2; Dnl. 9:18). Thus, God's bringing the beasts of the field and the birds of the air (Gen. 2:19f.) and even the woman (2:21-23; 3:20) to Adam to see what he would name them was not to establish Adam's dominion over them by the act of naming (cf. Gen. 1:26f.), but through that act to discover what impression these would make upon him and how he would regard them in relation to himself.

It becomes clear, therefore, that "to call [*qārā'*] one's name over" a people or a place is an idiom that does not mean that these will henceforth bear the name of the person whose name was "called over" them. Rather it declares that they now belong to him. They are now under his authority and protection (2 S. 12:28; Ps. 49:11 [MT 12]; Isa. 4:1). This idiom is especially significant when used to describe the relationship of Yahweh to the people of Israel. They are His peculiar possession, subject to His rule and under His protection and care (2 Ch. 7:14; Isa. 63:19; Jer. 14:9; 15:16; Dnl. 9:19).

On customs and practices involving names, *see* NAMES, PROPER.

*C. The Divine Name.* For the various names of God and their relation to His nature, *see* GOD, NAMES OF. Here we will discuss aspects of the divine name not treated in that article.

God, who delights to reveal Himself to His people by His name or names, on occasion withholds His name. Jacob, for instance, while wrestling with "God" asks, "What is your name?" but he receives no reply (Gen. 32:24-30). Many say that the reason for such silence springs from the conviction that to know the name of a deity was to possess the secret of his character and therefore to have access to the power which the deity possesses, i.e., to know the name of the god is to prevail over the god. Hence, God here keeps His name to Himself. Such an explanation, while taking note of a primitive and popular belief, fails to take into account the theological significance of the Jacob story — that although one must triumph over personal weakness by perseverance, it is God who is ultimately responsible for this triumph, for God Himself in fact contended with Jacob, forcing him to fight until he won spiritual blessing and became a new man with a new name (Gen. 32:30).

God sent people to speak "in his name" (Jer. 11:21; 14:14f.; etc.). This sharing of His name with others meant that the message they spoke was spoken under inspiration, with authority, by divine appointment, and thus was to be heard as the word of the Lord and responded to accordingly.

"To blaspheme the name of Yahweh" does not mean that someone uses the divine name in a thoughtless oath or expletive. Rather it means that the proud and arrogant and strong intentionally abuse the people of God, those people who bear His name (Ps. 74:10, 18; Isa. 52:5; Jas. 2:7). It means, therefore, that whenever persons revile the people of God, they revile the name of God, and thus revile God Himself (cf. Mt. 25:40).

It is also possible for the people of God themselves to blaspheme the name of God by living in a way contrary to the nature of God, whose name they bear. If the name of God is the revelation of the nature of God, and if the nature of God is characterized by compassion, grace, forgiveness, lovingkindness, truth, justice, etc. (cf. Ex. 34:6f.), and if those who carry that name live in a way opposite to that name, to the nature of God, then that name is reviled by the scandal of inconsistency (Ezk. 36:20; Rom. 2:24).

*II. NT.–A. Etymology.* In the NT *ónoma* has some meanings that overlap with, and other meanings that are foreign to, classical usage. The latter meanings are due, no doubt, to the influence of the OT upon the NT.

*B. Significance.* In the NT *ónoma* simply may be that title which distinguishes one person, place, or thing from another. For example, the Roman soldiers seized a certain man whose name was Simon to carry Jesus' crossbar (Mt. 27:32; cf. Mk. 14:32; Lk. 1:5; 3 Jn. 14).

It is also clear that as in the OT so in the NT one's name was at times considered to be a revelation of who the person was or what he would do. Hence, the angel gave strict instructions to Joseph to call Mary's son "Jesus, for he will save his people from their sins" (Mt. 1:21; "Jesus" = "Savior"); and Zechariah said emphatically that his child was not to be named after him, but, contrary to contemporary custom, his name was to be called "John" ("favored of Yahweh"; Lk. 1:63).

A change in name signals a change in character or conduct. Jesus placed a new name on Simon — the name *Petros,* "rock" (Jn. 1:42; cf. Mk. 3:17) — and with this new name came the promise of what he could and would become.

In this connection it is important to notice the references to "a new name" in the Apocalypse. Through the Spirit the risen Christ promises: "To him who overcomes I will give . . . a new name . . . which no one knows but he who receives it" (Rev. 2:17). And again: "He who overcomes . . . I will write upon him the name of my God, and the name of the city of my God, the new Jerusalem [cf. Isa. 62:2] . . . and my new name" (Rev. 3:12). In the first instance, the name which no one knows but the person to whom it is given, it is possible to hear an echo of the Jacob story. The new name is the name of the victor himself, who through perseverance wins the victory. For no one else but the overcomer can know the personal transforming power of fidelity to Christ in the struggle to be true to the faith and to the Savior. In the second instance, the "new name" is Christ's own new name — not that of the overcomer. It symbolizes the full revelation of Christ's character that awaits the second advent (cf. Rev. 19:12; see R. Mounce, *Book of Revelation* [*NICNT,* 1977], p. 121). Like the new commandment, which is really an old commandment newly understood (1 Jn. 2:7f.), so Christ's new name is in reality His former name(s) newly understood in the light of the freshness of His resurrection and return.

*Ónoma* is so closely identified with what a person is, i.e., name and existence are so nearly one and the same thing, that expressions such as "your names are written in heaven" (Lk. 10:20), "whose names are in the book of life" (Phil. 4:3), "whose name has not been written . . . in the book of life" (Rev. 13:8), and "I will not blot his name out of the book of life" (Rev. 3:5), crop up several times within the NT. The figure is taken from the OT (cf. Isa. 4:3; Ezk. 13:9; Dnl. 12:1), or from the secular world where a criminal's name was removed from the civic register to take from him all rights of citizenship. But now it is endued with a higher meaning. If one could argue from these statements that all names have been recorded in the book of life, thereby assuring existence for each person, and if one might also argue that for some reason, e.g., wilful disobedience to God's commands, deliberate refusal to accept Christ as Savior and Lord, etc., one's name could be removed from this divine register, "blotted out," then one might argue that that person would cease to exist, for his name would no longer exist.

"Name" and that which a person is are so close together in meaning that on occasion "name" by itself simply means "person(s)" (Acts 1:15; Rev. 3:4). Furthermore, because a person's name is so closely linked with the person himself, with what he is and does, it is not surprising to discover that "name" and "reputation" are again used synonymously (Mk. 6:14; Lk. 6:22; Phil. 2:9; Rev. 3:1). This close association of name and person is also seen in the fact that the expression "the Name" becomes a metonym for Jesus (Acts 5:40f.; 3 Jn. 7), just as "the Name" had been a metonym for Yahweh in the OT.

Statements made about God in the OT are now made about Christ in the NT (cf. He. 1:7-12). The most frequent name for God in the OT, Yahweh (LXX *Kyrios,* "Lord"), now becomes the Church's favorite name for Christ. The Church's earliest confession of faith in Christ was in all likelihood "Jesus is Lord" (cf. Rom. 10:9; Phil. 2:9-11). Hence, all that can be said about the name of Yahweh — that prophets prophesy in that name (Jer. 20:9), the righteous trust in that name (Isa. 50:10), people call upon that name (Ps. 105:1), etc. — can be and is said about the name of Jesus Christ (Acts 4:17f.; Jn. 14:1; 1 Cor. 1:2).

Jesus' disciples prophesied "in his name" (Mt. 7:22), cast out demons "in his name" (Lk. 10:17), performed miracles "in his name" (Mk. 9:39), etc. With the use of this expression it becomes evident that the disciples spoke and acted like Jesus, in His place and with His authority, as did the prophets of Yahweh in the OT (see Acts 4:7-10). Similarly, the gospel is to be preached in all the world "in his name," i.e., by His authority, and thus be made effectual to save people (Lk. 24:47), justify sinners (Acts 10:43), and forgive people their sins (1 Jn. 2:12).

The expression "to believe in the name of Jesus" is found only in the Johannine writings (Jn. 1:12; 2:23; 3:18; 1 Jn. 3:23; 5:13). Since it alternates with the phrase "to believe in him/me," i.e., Jesus (Jn. 2:11; 5:38; 6:35; etc.), it is clear that belief in the name of Jesus is not different from belief in Jesus. The former expression, however, "brings out clearly that to believe in Jesus one must believe that he bears the divine name given him by God" (Jn. 17:11f., 26; R. E. Brown, *Gospel According to John,* I [*AB,* 1966], 11; cf. Phil. 2:9-11). Thus it is that John's Gospel presents the christological interpretation of the OT statements about the name of Yahweh. That is to say, "the Fourth Gospel . . . picks up and follows through the lines of the ancient biblical tradition, that God's revelation is bound to a personal name" — here to the name of Jesus

(H. Bietenhard, *DNTT,* II, 653; cf. Mt. 11:27; 28:18 with Jn. 3:35; 5:21; 13:3; 7:29; 10:15; 17:25).

The most common baptismal formulas in the NT are "in the name of Jesus Christ" (Acts 2:38; 10:48), and "in the name of the Lord Jesus" (8:16; 19:5). The constructions used in these phrases involve the Greek prepositions *en* ("in"), *eis* ("into"), and *epi* ("upon"). From each use of these formulas, irrespective of the prepositions used, one gets the picture that the persons baptized invoke the name of Jesus as Messiah, and that the baptizer names the name of Christ over them as they are being baptized. This is made especially clear from Jas. 2:7, where the writer speaks of men who, by evil acts against the people of God, blaspheme "the honorable name which was invoked over" them. Thus, in the baptismal formula there appears a Christian formula modeled after a very similar Jewish one. Just as the name of Yahweh was named over Israel with the result that Israel became His people, His special possession (see I.B above), so the name of Jesus has replaced the name of Yahweh, with the result that the Church becomes His peculiar treasure, His very own people. And when it is said that Christians bear the name of Jesus, or that the name of Jesus is pronounced over them, this is more than a metaphor. For in baptism the name of Jesus is named over those who are baptized as a sign that they are now the possession of Jesus (M. Dibelius and H. Greeven, *James* [Eng. tr., *Hermeneia,* 1976], p. 141; W. Heitmüller, *Im Namen Jesu* [*FRLANT,* 2, 1903], pp. 88-91, 115-17).

The significance of the name of Jesus in relation to prayer deserves special notice. To pray in the name of Jesus, to ask anything in His name (Jn. 14:13; cf. v. 14; 15:16; 16:23f.; etc.), is not merely to add to one's prayers a meaningless formula, but it is to ask something from God as Christ's representatives on earth, in His mission and stead, in His spirit, and with His aim. Such a phrase, correctly understood, cannot help but govern the kind and quality of the prayers Christians pray.

*C. Conclusion.* The importance of a name to the biblical writers cannot be overstated. Their fondness for names and their understanding of the significance of names is everywhere observable — from their noting that God knows Moses by name (Ex. 33:17) and calls Cyrus by name (Isa. 45:3) to simply filling whole pages with names (see Gen. 5; Nu. 1–3; Mt. 1:1-17; Lk. 3:23-37; etc.). These writers thus articulate in a quiet but emphatic way what has been called "the personalism of the Bible." The Bible presents people not as a mass, nor as a fraction of a mass, or as cases to be studied, but as persons. The proper name in the Bible is the symbol of the person, and to address a person by name is to give to that person significance, meaning, dignity, and worth.

*See also* GOD, NAMES OF; NAMES, PROPER.

***Bibliography.***–B. S. Childs, *Memory and Tradition in Israel* (*SBT,* 1/37; 1962), pp. 9-30; A. Deissmann, *Bible Studies* (1901), pp. 196f.; *DNTT,* II, *s.v.* (H. Bietenhard, F. F. Bruce); *TDNT,* V, *s.v.* ὄνομα κτλ. (Bietenhard); T. H. Gaster, *Myth, Legend and Custom in the OT* (1969), I, 205-212; G. B. Gray, *Studies in Hebrew Proper Names* (1896); *ILC,* I-II, 245-259; B. Jacob, *Im Namen Gottes* (1903); A. F. Key, *JBL,* 83 (1964), 55-59; L. Lévy-Bruhl, *Die Seele der Primitiven* (1930), pp. 205, 216-220, 335-39; E. Norden, *Agnostos Theos* (1913); M. Noth, *Die israelitischen Personennamen* (1928); *RGG,* IV, *s.v.* (H. Schmidt, E. Wissmann); G. van der Leeuw, *Religion in Its Essence and Manifestation* (Eng. tr., 2nd ed. 1964).

G. F. HAWTHORNE

**NAMES OF GOD.** *See* GOD, NAMES OF.

**NAMES, PROPER.**

- I. OT Proper Names
  - A. Place Names
    - 1. Hebrew
      - a. Pre-Israelite
      - b. Derived from Flora and Fauna
      - c. Derived from Geographical Characteristics
      - d. Miscellaneous
    - 2. Non-Hebrew
  - B. Names of Persons
    - 1. Hebrew
      - a. The Practice and Significance of Naming
      - b. Morphology and Semantics
      - c. The Divine Element
      - d. Derived from Flora and Fauna
      - e. Derived from Geographical Characteristics
      - f. Derived from Circumstances
      - g. Volitive Names
      - h. Kinship Names
      - i. Prophetic Names
      - j. Significance of Name Changes
      - k. Name Styles in Various Eras
    - 2. Non-Hebrew
- II. NT Proper Names
  - A. Place Names
  - B. Names of Persons

*I. **OT Proper Names.***–Names provide a means of indicating specific identity, and as such are essential to efficient communication about times and circumstances involving individual people and places. Proper names are therefore found most frequently in the historical portions of the OT, less frequently in the Prophets, and least frequently in the purely poetic, wisdom, and legal portions. In general, the more any portion of the OT is concerned with specific past events, the more likely it is to contain proper names.

*A. Place Names.* Events described in the OT cover a wide field geographically. Place names of various sorts and of various language groups from parts of Asia, Europe, and Africa are recorded in the OT in connection with the peoples and activities chronicled.

*1. Hebrew.* The vast majority of place names in the OT are Hebrew/Canaanite in form. As Hebrew is a dialect of Canaanite, it is not always possible to determine whether a given geographical name has its origin with the Israelites or with their Canaanite predecessors in Palestine. Virtually no Hebrew place names are mentioned in the Bible outside of Palestine, however.

*a. Pre-Israelite.* This group includes the names of Palestinian sites already in existence and presumably already fixedly named by the time of the Israelite conquest (15th cent. B.C.?), as well as other sites in the OT world likely extant and named by that time. For example, Jericho, which means something like "(city of the) moon (-god)," was settled already by 7000 B.C. according to carbon-14 dating. Jerusalem, "foundation of (the god?) peace," was settled in 4000 B.C.

Several early sites bear names compounded with *beth,* meaning "place of" or "location of" (less accurately "house of"): Beth-shean/Beth-shan, "location of security" (Josh. 17:11), Beth-shemesh, "location of the sun (-god?)" (Josh. 15:10), Beth-peor, "location of the open area" (Dt. 3:29), and Beth-horon, "location of hollow ground" (Josh. 10:10).

Other major pre-Israelite sites mentioned in the OT include, in northern Canaan: Megiddo (meaning uncertain; Josh. 12:21), Hazor, "enclosed" (Josh. 11:1), Tirzah, "delight" (Josh. 12:24); Kedesh, "holy" (Josh. 20:7), and Dothan, "two feasts/decrees" (Gen. 37:17); in central and southern Canaan: Gezer, "precipice" (Josh. 10:33), Gibeon, "hill" (Josh. 9:3), Lachish (meaning uncertain; Josh. 10:3), and Beer-sheba, "southern well"/"well of the oath" (Gen. 21:14). Where their meaning is clear these names indicate that a variety of name types was already in evidence prior to the Israelite conquest, and that the Israelites did not invent *de novo* most of the naming techniques they used.

*b. Derived from Flora and Fauna.* A substantial number of sites were named after plants and animals, in a fashion analogous to the modern practice (Appleton, Moose Lake, Palm Springs, etc.). Names derived from plants include Tamar, "palm" (Ezk. 47:19); Baal-tamar, "lord of the palm" (Jgs. 20:33); Luz, "almond (tree)" (Gen. 28:19); Shittim, "acacia (trees)" (Nu. 25:1); Tappuah, "apple tree" (Josh. 12:17); and En-tappuah, "apple tree spring" (Josh. 17:7).

Several dozen place names derive primarily from animals, in many cases probably because the animals they were named after frequented the local area. Included in this group are the pass of the Akrabbim, "scorpions" (Nu. 34:4); Arad, "wild ass" (Josh. 12:14); Aijalon, "hart" (1 S. 14:31); Laish, "lion" (Jgs. 18:7); Humtah, "lizard" (Josh. 15:54); Zorah, "wasp" (Jgs. 13:2); as well as names deriving from domesticated animals: Eglon "young bull" (Josh. 10:3); En-gedi, "kid spring" (Josh. 15:62); En-eglaim, "pair of young bulls spring" (Ezk. 47:10); Hazar-susah, "horse enclosure/village" (Josh. 19:5); Parah, "cow" (Josh. 18:23); Telaim, "lambs" (1 S. 15:4).

*c. Derived from Geographical Characteristics.* Just as modern place names are often based upon local physical characteristics (Butte, Portsmouth, Hot Springs, Twin Forks, etc.) ancient sites were frequently so named. The brine of its waters led to the naming of the "Salt Sea" (Gen. 14:3), the modern Dead Sea. The rough resemblance of the Sea of Galilee to a harp produced its ancient name, Chinnereth, "harp" (Nu. 34:11). The Sidonians saw in Mt. Hermon the likeness of a soldier's torso armor, and thus they originally called the mountain Sirion, "breastplate" (Dt. 3:9). Carmel, "garden land" (1 K. 18:27); Lebanon, "white" (Dt. 1:7); Bashan, "fruitful" (Nu. 21:33); and Argob, "mound(s)" (Dt. 3:4), all represent regions named after local geographical features.

Many cities were likewise named, including Adam, "soil" (Josh. 3:16); Abel, "meadow" (2 S. 20:14); Beer, "well" (Nu. 21:16); Beeroth, "wells" (Dt. 10:6); Beth-emek, "location of the valley" (Josh. 19:27); Bezer, "fortification" (Dt. 4:43); Bethlehem, "location of bread" (Gen. 35:19); Gath, "wine press" (1 S. 5:8); Gibeah, "hill" (Jgs. 19:12); Jabesh, "dry place" (1 S. 11:1); Rabbah, "big" (Dt. 3:11); Ramah, "height" (1 S. 1:19); Ramoth, "heights" (1 S. 30:27); Ziz, "shining" (2 Ch. 20:16); and Zoar, "small" (Gen. 13:10).

*d. Miscellaneous.* Several other criteria apparently played a role in the naming of regions and towns. Historical events sometimes resulted in the naming or renaming of a place. Examples of the results of this practice include: the valley of Achor, "trouble," in connection with the sin of Achan/Achar (Josh. 7:26); Peniel, "God's face," named by Jacob after his wrestling with an angel (Gen. 32:30); Beer-lahai-roi, "well of the Living One who sees me," named by Hagar on the occasion of her encounter with God's angel in the wilderness (Gen. 16:14); Witness, the altar area named to remind Reubenites and Gadites of their covenant obligations (Josh. 22:34); Bochim, "weepers," a town named for the response of the Israelites to God's hard warning (Jgs. 2:5); Ramath-lehi, "jawbone height" (Jgs. 15:17) and En-hakkore, "the caller's spring" (Jgs. 15:19), both named by Samson in connection with God's aid in his exploits; and Perez-uzzah, "Uzzah's breaking," named by David after God punished Uzzah for defiling the ark in transport (1 Ch. 13:11).

Religion also played a prominent role in the process of naming places. Many sites bear titles which reflect the religious practices associated with them, or the god or goddess worshiped at a prominent sanctuary. The Canaanites worshiped especially the god Baal ("lord") and the goddess Asherah ("blessed woman"), as well as Asherah's syncretistic alter-egos Anat and Ashtoret/Ashtaroth. Asherah, being Baal's consort, was also known as Baalat ("lady"). These deities figure in the names of towns which continued in Israel after the Conquest. Among such sites are: Baal-hamon, "Baal of the multitude" (Cant. 8:11); Baal-hermon, "Baal of Mt. Hermon" (Jgs. 3:3); Baal-meon, "Baal of the dwelling" (Nu. 32:38), also called Beth-baal-meon, "location of Baal of the dwelling" (Josh. 13:17) and shortened to Beth-meon in Jer. 48:23; Baal-tamar, "Baal of the palm" (Jgs. 20:33); Baal-zephon, "Baal of the north" (Ex. 14:2); Baalah, "lady" (Josh. 15:9); Baalath-beer, "lady of the well" (Josh. 19:8); Ashteroth (simply the name of the goddess, 1 Ch. 6:71); Ashteroth-karnaim, "Ashteroth of the two horns" (Gen. 14:5); and Anathoth, "the Anats [another Canaanite goddess]" (Josh. 21:18).

The Israelites also assigned names to places on the basis of religious associations, or took nonoffensive names over from their predecessors. Such names include: Yahweh-shalom (RSV "The Lord is peace"), an altar area at Ophrah built by Gideon and used by the Israelites thereafter (Jgs. 6:24); Yahweh-nissi (RSV "The Lord is my banner"), an altar erected by Moses (Ex. 17:15); Yahweh-yireh (RSV "The Lord will provide"), a part of Jerusalem named by Abraham (Gen. 21:14); El-bethel, "God of Bethel," named by Jacob as the place God appeared to him (Gen. 35:7); El-tolad, "God is begetter" (Josh. 15:30); and Elon-beth-hanan, "oak of the place of grace" (1 K. 4:9). It should be noted that the Israelites founded relatively few new cities after the Conquest, but tended rather to occupy cities already named by their previous Canaanite inhabitants. Moreover, orthodox Israelite worship was limited to a single sanctuary (Dt. 12:5ff.) while Baal-Asherah worship was dispersed among countless small "high places" (Dt. 12:2; cf. 1 K. 14:23f.). As a result, many more Israelite towns bore "Baal" names than "Yahweh" names.

Many sites were named on the basis of a wish or attitude about a location, sometimes in connection with its beauty or pleasant environs. The names of such places were presumably intended simply to inspire the heart or to bring positive associations to mind (cf. modern Philadelphia, Concord, Buena Vista, Mount Pleasant, etc.). Among such names are Salem, "peace" (Gen. 14:18); Tirzah, "delight" (Josh. 12:24); Timnah, "allotment" (Josh. 15:10); Joppa, "beauty" (2 Ch. 2:16); and Janoah, "rest" (2 K. 15:29).

A few names represent associations with important personages as in "Gibeah of Saul" (1 S. 15:34), a convenience in distinguishing it from other Gibeahs once Saul's fame was manifest; Samaria, "Shemer's place" (1 K. 16:24), named after its original owner; or the City of David (1 Ch. 11:7).

*2. Non-Hebrew.* Of the many non-Hebrew/Canaanite language families extant in OT times, the Egyptian, Akkadian, and Aramaic language groups had the greatest representation among OT names. Such non-Hebrew names appear, as expected, most frequently where events connected with the nations where these languages were spoken are described.

The meanings of several of the Egyptian place names found in the OT are understood: "Egypt" translates Heb. *miṣrayim,* meaning "the two red mud lands," i.e., Upper and Lower Egypt, the traditional divisions of the two-part united nation. The meaning of No (Jer. 46:25), the Hebrew rendering of the Egyptian name for Thebes, is simply "the city" (Egyp. *nỉw*). Noph (Isa. 19:13) is Hebrew for the Egyptian name of Memphis, *mn-nfr,* "fire platform," which is a shortened form of the name of the temenos of the pyramid of the pharaoh Pepi. Rameses (Nu. 33:3; cf. Raamses in Ex. 1:11) was presumably named after the great pharaoh Rameses II. Tahpanhes (Jer. 2:16) probably means "mansion of the Nubian." The meaning of Egyptian names such as Zoan (Isa. 19:11) or the Palestinian city of Sharuhen (Josh. 19:6) is not clear.

A significant number of Babylonian-Assyrian names are found in the OT, including some which incorporate Sumerian elements, such as Ir-nahash, "snake city" (1 Ch. 4:12), and Shinar (Gen. 10:10), probably lower Mesopotamia, a transliteration of Sum. *Kengir.* Babylon, Heb. *bāḇel,* represents the Akk. *bāb-ili,* "gate of the gods." Assyria is named for its chief god, Ashur.

Aramaic place names in the OT whose meanings are understood include: Berothai, "cypresses" (2 S. 8:8); Tibhath, "slaughtering place" (1 Ch. 18:8); Hamath, "fortress/citadel" (2 S. 8:9f.); Betah, "trust" (2 S. 8:8); Riblah, "bare place" (2 K. 23:23); Kadesh, "holy" (Ps. 29:8); and Hazar-enon, "enclosure of the two fountains" (Ezk. 48:1).

*B. Names of Persons.* Personal names in the OT are of special interest for what they tell of the religious and philosophical views of the ancient Israelites. The naming of persons in OT times obviously went beyond a concern for a convenient means of providing individual designation. Naming intended to capture in some way the essence of an individual, expressing actual identity rather than merely identification (*see* NAME).

*1. Hebrew.* The vast majority of personal names in the OT as well as many in the NT are of Hebrew origin. Because of a concern for genealogical data in several OT books (e.g., 1 Chronicles) as well as a tendency to provide listings of names such as important forebears (Gen. 10), kings (Josh. 12), or famous soldiers (2 S. 23:8ff.), the OT contains more personal names, even proportionally, than the NT. The great majority of the Hebrew names have discernible meanings, and the range of meanings is quite large. From the hundreds available for study, groupings and classifications are possible that help provide an understanding of the naming process itself.

*a. The Practice and Significance of Naming.* During the OT era, children were usually named at the time of their birth, rather than before. In other words, no tentative selection of names was normally undertaken prior to a child's birth, and virtually none prior to conception. Because so much importance was attached to a name, people in the ancient Near East had a strong desire to associate a child properly with its name, and vice versa, so that the name would accurately and valuably reflect the individual's character or even destiny. Events or remarks which occurred during the time the mother was in labor were apparently considered especially auspicious for the naming process. Though this can be inferred from the OT evidence, it is explicit in some Mesopotamian texts. The Sumerian mother goddess, variously called Ninḫursag, Nintur, and Aruru, among other titles, plays the role of the divine midwife in several myths. She says of herself, "I am the good midwife of the gods. I say only that which is wise at the time of birth." Jacobsen (*Treasures,* p. 108) comments: "at the moment of birth . . . an incautious word may saddle the child with any manner of unpropitious fate. Therefore Aruru is [called] the 'Lady of Silence'. . . ."

The Israelites, likewise, took very seriously anything which was said or which happened in connection with a child's birth, and often based a name thereupon. It was not necessary for the name actually to have a meaning directly related to the event or saying in question; all that was required was some sort of connection. Frequently, a name already well known as a part of the general stock of names in the culture was chosen by the parent(s) simply because it sounded roughly like something significant which surrounded the birth event. An example using a modern name illustrates this process of nonhomologous homophone naming: Suppose that during a birth process, word was received that workers had completed digging a new well in the village. If a male child were born, the mother (or father; see below) might name the child Doug. That etymologically "Doug" has nothing to do with digging would be considered unimportant. The important consideration would be that the child's birth coincided with something that suggested the name Doug, and the mother or father would take this as an indication of what the child's name should be. In some developing nations in our own day, names such as Hospital, Doctor, Nurse, Ambulance, and even Needle are represented among the names of children because birth-event naming is still practiced. This practice, then, requires three things especially: a sufficiently high view of the significance of a name that parents seek special, circumstantial guidance in the naming process; a reluctance to choose children's names prior to their birth; a willingness to select from a stock of possible names, or sometimes to create new names, according to various kinds of suggestion, the most prominent being homophony.

In the OT the principle of homophony naming without regard for technical etymology is overtly evidenced most often in Genesis. For example, the name Cain (Gen. 4:1) sounds like but is not apparently etymologically derived from the Hebrew for "bring forth" (*qānâ*), a word Eve used at the time of Cain's birth. Jacob, a name attested more than once in pre-Israelite texts, was selected by his parents for the boy who was born grasping his twin's heel since the consonants for "heel" (*ʿqb*) appear in the Hebrew form of Jacob (*yaʿaqōḇ*). Reuben, which actually means "Behold the/a son," sounds something like "he has seen my misery," and it therefore was a fitting name for Leah's firstborn in the light of one of her birth-event remarks (Gen. 29:32). Issachar sounds like the Hebrew word for "reward" (*śāḵār*). Because Leah used the term at his birth, the name Issachar was then suggested to her (Gen. 30:18).

Many names given on the basis of homophony are indeed connected etymologically to something in the vocabulary quoted as used at the time of birth. In Genesis, names like Peleg, "division" (10:25); Seth, "provide" (4:25); Esau, "hairy" (25:25); Edom, "reddish" (25:30); Judah, "praise" (29:35); Dan, "judge" (30:6); Naphtali, "my struggle" (30:8); Zebulun, "honor" (30:20); Joseph, "add" (30:24); and Simeon, "hear" (29:33) are, etymologically, technically correct. But this is probably not due to a concern for linguistic precision on the part of the parents who gave the name. Rather, a large stock of names and name patterns was readily available to these parents as a result of their normal social interconnections in a society where naming was taken so seriously. Thus it was virtually guaranteed that many names would happen to coincide etymologically with birth-event vocabulary.

Additionally, however, it must be admitted that since the vast majority of OT names are positive names — giving children ugly or unpleasant names was certainly avoided except in special circumstances — people must have done their best to speak wisely and precisely during a woman's labor and delivery, just as Ninḫursag (see above) claimed. It is possible that parents and other relatives had names in mind when they chose their words during the birth event, and thus helped predispose the choices. Some choices of names may even have been foregone conclusions (other than names revealed prior to birth; see below). But there was apparently a careful avoidance of any discussion of names prior to the birth. So if the parent(s) or relatives did have a name in mind prior to a child's birth, and one can hardly imagine their not thinking at least idly about the matter, they nevertheless did not say anything to predispose the naming until after the birth. Then, and only then, were names actually given by the parents.

God, however, was free to assign a name prior even to conception. In some instances where a child would grow into a position specially ordained for him or her in relation to God's plan for Israel, a name was revealed well in advance; partly, perhaps, to preempt any tendency on the part of the parents to follow the usual practice of letting events or statements influence their decision. Because a name could relate to a person's character or even destiny, a divinely appointed name could function as a sort of promise of the role he or she would play upon reaching maturity.

Examples of such proleptically divinely revealed names are few, however. Isaac, "he laughs," is a name relating not simply to the fact that Abraham (Gen. 17:17) and Sarah (18:12-15) laughed at the thought they could have a child, but probably also indicating that Isaac would represent the delightful, joyful, originally unpredictable fulfillment of God's promise (21:6f.). Ishmael, "God listened/listens," was a name divinely revealed to Hagar in reference to her plight (16:11). The name probably indicated not only that God had "heard of" Hagar's cruel treatment at the hand of Sarah, but that Ishmael was destined to represent God's response of faithfulness to Arabs, of whom Ishmael was the ancestor. The name Samuel, "name of God(?)," may have been divinely revealed to Hannah, depending on how one interprets 1 S. 1:23, "may the Lord establish his word." Divinely revealed names were also mediated through the prophets (see I.B.1.i below).

It was the parents' prerogative to name. Even a divinely ordained name still had to be given *after* the birth by the parents (Gen. 21:3; 16:5; 1 S. 1:20; cf. Lk. 1:60-63; Mt. 1:25). Either parent could give the name, though more often the mothers are reported as naming their children than the fathers, in those few instances where any mention is made of who gave a name. In one recorded instance, the parents disagreed on a name: Rachel, dying in childbirth, named her last son Ben-oni, "son of my trouble." She undoubtedly felt it to be her right and duty to assign the name. But after her death, Jacob named the child Benjamin, "son of the right hand," a more positive name, and one still probably reflecting the birth-event circumstances (the child would be a support to his father now that his mother was dead). Jacob's intervention in this way was apparently unusual, but nevertheless reasonable, and it may well have been the case that when a mother died in childbirth a renaming was in order. The modern practice of renaming upon adoption may be analogous to this practice.

In later periods patronymy (naming a male child after his father; cf. Lk. 1:59-61) and papponymy (naming a male child after his grandfather) were not uncommon. The practice came into vogue during the Persian period, and may account for the popular identification of Darius with Cyrus (if this is the intent) in Dnl. 6:28 (MT 29).

*b. Morphology and Semantics.* Semitic names reflected a variety of structures, virtually all of which are represented in the OT. The three basic categories are: single-element names, phrase names, and sentence names. The single-element and phrase names may in many instances have represented shortened forms of sentence names, but this cannot be proved generally to be the case. Virtually any multisyllable name could be abbreviated; an abbreviated form of a name attested in a longer form is called a hypocoristicon.

Single-element names were often common nouns, such as Barak, "lightning" (Jgs. 4:6); Achsah, "anklet" (Josh. 15:16); Deborah, "honey bee" (Jgs. 4:4); or abstract nouns such as Uzzah, "strength" (2 S. 6:3); Hannah, "grace" (1 S. 1:2); Manoah, "rest" (Jgs. 13:2); Shimeah, "fame" (2 S. 13:3); Judith, "(female) Judean" (Gen. 26:34). Single-element names may be participial in form, such as Saul, "asked" (1 S. 9:2); Menahem, "comforting (one)" (2 K. 15:14); Shammua, "heard" (Nu. 13:4); or adjectival in form, such as Ikkesh, "tricky" (2 S. 23:26); Maharai, "quick" (2 S. 23:28); Shallum, "recompensed" (2 K. 15:10).

A single-element name cannot, however, technically be composed of a perfect or imperfect verb form, since such verb forms in Hebrew always contain a morphological element indicating subject, and thus are two-element sentences in themselves. Moreover, such single "verb" names were probably thought of as shortened forms of longer sentence names (e.g., Ahaz from Jehoahaz or Ahaziah, both meaning "Yahweh has taken"). Examples of such single verb names are Shillem, "he has paid back" (Gen. 46:24), and Zarah, "he has sprouted" (Gen. 38:30).

Phrase names are occasionally prepositional, as in Besodeiah, "in Yahweh's council" (Neh. 3:6), but most often are based on the Hebrew construct (possessive) pattern, as in: Penuel, "God's face" (1 Ch. 4:4); Jedidiah, "Yahweh's beloved" (Neh. 11:10); Obadiah, "Yahweh's servant" (1 K. 18:3).

Sentence names follow virtually any of the normal Hebrew patterns for simple sentences, tending especially to compound a divine element with a finite verb. Sentence names with the implicit verb "be" are common: Abijah, "Yahweh is (my) father" (2 Ch. 13:1); Tobiah, "Yahweh is (my) good" (2 Ch. 17:8); Elimelech, "My God is King" (Ruth 1:2). Participial forms also appear in such names, e.g., Obed-edom, "Edom is serving" (2 S. 6:10). Perfect verb forms very commonly occur, some with the divine subject element prefixed: Jonathan, "Yahweh has given" (1 S. 13:2); Jehoshaphat, "Yahweh has given justice" (1 K. 15:24); Eleazar, "God has helped" (Ex. 6:23); Elkanah, "God has created" (1 S. 1:1); and some with the divine element affixed: Benaiah, "Yahweh has built" (2 S. 8:18); Shephatiah, "Yahweh has given justice" (2 S. 3:4); Asahel, "God has made" (2 S. 2:18).

The divine element may precede imperfect verb forms, as in Eliahba, "God conceals/has concealed" (2 S. 23:32; on the problem of translating imperfects as past/present/future in tense, see below). Or it may follow them, as in Ishmael, "God hears/has heard/will hear" (Gen. 16:11); Jezreel, "God sows/has sown/will sow" (1 Ch. 4:3).

In construct phrase names, especially if the first element is a segholate noun or ends in a consonantal cluster, an *î* is commonly found conjoining the two elements (as in Melchizedek or Amminadab). This *î* must be considered anaptyptic, and not the 1st common singular possessive suffix. Thus Melchizedek means "king of righteousness" and not "my king is righteousness." Names from the Amarna period such as Abdi-ḫepa make this apparent, since "my servant is Ḫepa" is nonsensical, Ḫepa being a deity. "Servant of Ḫepa," however, makes perfect sense for the name, the *i* being anaptyctic and probably representing a neutral sound similar to shewa (cf. W. von Soden, *Grundriss der Akkadischen Grammatik* [repr. 1969], pp. 82-86).

A number of hypocoristic elements are found at the end of short or shortened names, the most common of these being *î* and *ay*. These correspond to *y* and *ie* in English, as in Joey and Edd*ie*. The *on* ending may express endearment, but more likely indicates "the one who" or the like, as in Abdon, "the one who serves" (Jgs. 12:13).

It is impossible to be certain of the precise meaning of names that contain imperfect verb forms. Early Canaanite contained *yaqṭul preterite* forms, and the association of the imperfect with past action is preserved in the so-called converted imperfect forms of Hebrew, and the past *durative* sense of the imperfect is well attested. Thus to the usual present/future semantic value of the imperfect we must add the past tense value as well. Names such as Jehoiakim (2 K. 23:34) may therefore have meant any or all of the following: "Yahweh has established"; "Yahweh establishes"; "Yahweh will establish." As in Hebrew poetry, no article need be present for nominal sentence elements to be definite: e.g., Adoni-bezek, "the Lord of the lightning" (Jgs. 1:5).

*c. The Divine Element.* The religious character of the OT era is reflected in the frequency of names which mention God or a god. The most common divine element is Yahweh, which has four hypocoristica: *yāhû* (from *yahw*) and *yâ*, both of which are terminal elements; and *y^ehô* and *yô* (both from *yahw* by slightly different phonetic processes), which occur as initial elements. Yahweh, in some form, appears in over 10 percent of Israelite names.

'El, "God," is slightly less common as a divine element in names. It occurs both initially and terminally. Baal, "lord," was the name of the Canaanite deity of fertility and the elements. Because the majority of Israelites were so frequently heterodox, false religion found its way, predictably enough, into names. For example, Saul, evidently not always a thoroughgoing Yahwist, named one of his sons Ishbaal, "man of Baal" (1 Ch. 8:33), and Jonathan similarly named his son Mephibaal, "from the mouth of Baal." The Baal element in such names was later changed to *bosheth*, "shame," by pious copyists (Ish-bosheth, 2 S. 2:8; Mephi-bosheth, 2 S. 4:4) in the MS of Samuel-Kings. Baal names are attested with frequency extrabiblically in the eighth-century Samaria ostraca (*ANET*, p. 321), though there, as well as in eighth-century OT names, they are outnumbered by names compounded with Yahweh.

Other divine elements include Shaddai (lit. "the mountain one"), usually translated "Almighty," as in Zuri-shaddai, "the Almighty is my rock" (Nu. 1:6); *melek*, "king," as in Abimelech, "my father is (the) king" (Jgs. 8:31); *'adon*, "lord," as in Adoniram, "my Lord is high" (1 K. 4:6). Some scholars have considered other terms, such as *ṣûr*, "rock," and *ṭôḇ*, "good," to be divine elements, but the evidence is inconclusive.

*d. Derived from Flora and Fauna.* Plants and animals figure occasionally in OT personal names. Examples of plant-derived names include Elon, "large tree/oak" (Gen. 26:34); Hadassah, "myrtle" (Est. 2:7); Rimmon, "pomegranate" (2 S. 4:2). Animal-derived names include Caleb, "dog" (Nu. 13:6); Aiah, "vulture" (2 S. 3:7); Eglah, "heifer" (2 S. 3:5); Jonah, "dove" (Jonah 1:1); Hamor, "ass" (Gen. 34:4); Nahash, "snake" (2 S. 17:25); Rachel, "ewe" (Gen. 29:6); Zibiah, "gazelle" (1 Ch. 8:9); Zimri, "mountain sheep" (1 K. 16:9). The widespread use of plant and animal names in the ancient Near East would seem to militate against the once popular notion that some sort of totemistic religious impulse was behind such names.

*e. Derived from Geographical Characteristics.* In a few instances words denoting natural objects or regions were employed in personal names, as with Gibea, "hill" (1 Ch. 2:49); Gilead, "rocky" (Nu. 26:29); Peninnah, "coral" (1 S. 1:2); and Seir, "wooded" (Gen. 36:30).

*f. Derived from Circumstances.* Situations or conditions prevailing at the time of a child's birth, or which came to mind at that time, undoubtedly influenced the giving of personal names in many instances. Solomon, "peaceable" (2 S. 12:25); Baruch, "blessed" (Jer. 32:12); Kareah, "bald" (Jer. 40:8); and Japhia, "gleaming" (2 S. 5:15), fit this category.

*g. Volitive Names.* Some names express a wish or a hope, either generally, i.e., unfocused, or specifically on behalf of a child. Examples are: Jeberechiah, "may Yahweh bless" (Isa. 8:2); Iphedeiah, "may Yahweh redeem" (1 Ch. 8:25); Ishmaiah, "may Yahweh hear" (1 Ch. 27:19); Ephraim, "double fruitfulness" (Gen. 41:52); Manasseh, "causing to forget" (Gen. 41:51); Adonijah, "Yahweh be my lord" (2 S. 3:4).

*h. Kinship Names.* A number of personal names employ terms for relatives (father, brother, kinsman). At least two factors may have been operative in the assignment of such names. In some instances, the kinship terms appear to have been used in reference to God. Additionally, children were sometimes valued symbolically as replacements for beloved relatives now dead. Some names of this type are: Abialbon, "father of strength" (2 S. 23:31); Abiasaph, "my father has gathered" (Ex. 6:24); Abiathar, "father of overabundance" (1 S. 22:20); Abidan, "my father judges" (Nu. 1:11); Ahikam, "my brother has arisen" (2 K. 22:12); Ahilud, "a brother is born" (2 S. 8:16); Ahimelech, "my brother is king" (1 S. 21:1); Ahitub, "good brother" (1 S. 14:3); Ammiel, "my kinsman is God" (Nu. 13:12); Ammishaddai, "my kinsman is the Almighty" (Nu. 1:12).

*i. Prophetic Names.* In a number of instances, names were given with a conscious prophetic significance attached to them. For example, at God's behest Isaiah named his son Maher-shalal-hashbaz, "hurry prey, hasten plunder" (Isa. 8:1-4), as a sign of the coming Assyrian conquest of Syria and northern Israel (733 B.C.). He had named his first son Shear-jashub, "a remnant will return" (Isa. 7:3), suggesting only a partial escape from the coming destruction (cf. Dt. 4:27-30). The messianic names Immanuel, "God with us" (Isa. 7:14), and "Wonderful Counselor [lit. "miracle counselor"], Mighty God, Everlasting Father, Prince of Peace" (9:6) also convey predictions of coming events. Hosea was instructed by God to name his three children Jezreel, "God sows," the site of a massacre (Hos. 1:4), Lo-ruhamah, "not shown compassion" (1:6), and Lo-ammi, "not my people" (1:9), to symbolize Israel's coming loss of both kingship and covenant protections. Jeremiah renamed Pashhur the priest Magor-missabib, "terror all around," as a prediction of coming miseries (Jer. 20:3-6). Through Ezekiel God gave Samaria the symbolic name Oholah, "dwelling place," and Jerusalem the symbolic name Oholibah, "my dwelling place is in it," as part of an allegory of judgment (Ezk. 23).

*j. Significance of Name Changes.* Since names were considered to represent something of the essence of a person, a major change in circumstances could lead to a renaming of or by an individual. The change of name signified a new status or relationship. Abram, "lofty father," was renamed by God Abraham, "multitudinous father" (Gen. 17:5), in the light of his election to the headship of a nation. Jacob became Israel, "let God prevail" (Gen. 32:28), in the light of his success with men and God. Sarai became Sarah (both names meaning approximately "princess") when her role as ancestress of a nation was announced (Gen. 17:15). It is the mere fact of a change, rather than what a name was changed to, that is important here. Naomi, "sweet," suggested that her name be reversed to Marah, "bitter," when circumstances had become hard for her (Ruth 1:20). In Hos. 1:9 God even symbolically changes His own name from *'ehyeh*, "I am" (as revealed in Ex. 3:14) to *lō'-'ehyeh-l^eḵā*, "I am not your I am," as an indication of the temporary withdrawal of His protection and blessing from Israel.

*k. Name Styles in Various Eras.* Where an office was inherited, as in the case of the kingship and the priesthood, there was a tendency for personal names to be reused frequently through successive generations. Moreover, after the time of the Judean exile, names were probably not based very often on birth-event statements, judging especially from the relative popularity of patronymy and papponymy (see I.B.1.a above), these being incompatible with the earlier emphasis on the relationship between name and essence or destiny. Some variation in popularity over the centuries of Israel's history is also observable among different name types (single-element *v.* multiple-element names; names with perfect verb forms *v.* names with imperfect verb forms) though the patterns of variation are complex. One constant during OT times was that feminine names only rarely contained divine elements, probably because the role of women in the religion of Israel was less prominent than that of men.

*2. Non-Hebrew.* At any stage of Israel's history, some Hebrew individuals bore foreign names. This fact reminds us that in many instances, intercultural influences must have played as important a role in the naming process as did purely religious influences. Foreign names tend to be found according to the eras in which Israelites had substantial contact with foreign groups. For example, in the Exodus and post-Exodus generations, several Egyptian names are attested, such as Moses, which sounds something like "pulled out" in Hebrew (Ex. 2:10), Phinehas (Ex. 6:25), and Hophni (1 S. 1:3). In the Neo-Babylonian period, during and after the Judean exile, Babylonian names were common. Shadrach, Meshach, and Abednego were simply the new Babylonian names of Hananiah, Mishael, and Azariah (Dnl. 1:6f.). Mordecai is Babylonian for "the one of (the god) Marduk" (Est. 2:5). Sheshbazzar, "(the moon-god) Sin guard the father" (Ezr. 1:8), and Zerubbabel, "prince of Babylon" (Ezr. 3:2), are also Babylonian names. Esther is a Persian name, meaning probably "star" or the like. Of course, persons identified in the OT as non-Israelites normally bore non-Israelite names.

***II. NT Proper Names.***–Many of the observations made about OT names apply to NT names as well. Indeed, the names of many persons and places mentioned in the NT text have Hebrew origins. A large number are of Greek or Latin origin, however.

*A. Place Names.* For the most part, Hebrew place names (especially of Palestinian places) continued from OT times to NT times, though their transliteration into Greek from Hebrew/Canaanite in some instances resulted in slight sound changes. In other instances a Greek term replaced the Hebrew. For example, Chinnereth, the OT Hebrew name for the Sea of Galilee, was replaced by Tiberias, named after the emperor Tiberias (Jn. 6:1). Crete, a Greek name, replaced Caphtor, a Semitic name. Syria was the Greek equivalent of Hebrew Aram; Babylon of Hebrew Babel. Where Greek or Roman influence established a site, that site tended to be known by its Greek name: e.g., Caesarea (Acts 8:40), Caesarea Philippi (Mt. 16:13), or the Decapolis, "the ten cities" (Mk. 5:20).

A very wide range of place names reflects Greek and Roman influence, since most of the places mentioned in the NT had been under the control of Greek-speaking regimes since their conquest by Alexander the Great, *ca.* 333 B.C. This influence is reflected historically, for example, in the fact that Alexandria (Acts 6:9) was named after Alexander, just as Ptolemais (Acts 21:7) was named after Ptolemy, one of Alexander's successors. Likewise, Philip II named Philippi (Acts 16:12) after himself. Greek mythology is reflected in some names, e.g., Areopagus, "hill of Ares" (Acts 17:19), and Euroclydon, "east wind-northeast wind" (Acts 27:14). Physical characteristics or circumstances influenced the naming of such sites as Trachonitis, "stony district" (Lk. 3:1), Puteoli, "sulfurous" (Acts 28:13), and Neapolis, "new city" (Acts 16:11). A name like Philadelphia, "brotherly love" (Rev. 1:11), is essentially volitive in character.

*B. Names of Persons.* In general, the practices and reasons for naming places and people in NT times were analogous to those in OT times, with the important exception that homophonic naming appears to have largely been abandoned. Personal names were given more on the basis of family tradition (Lk. 1:59) and desirability to the ear, and less on the basis of semantic value, much as in modern Western practice. The official naming of males awaited the circumcision ceremony in the case of orthodox Jews (Lk. 2:21).

Many NT personal names are Greek versions of Hebrew or Aramaic names, the meanings of which reflect the range of possibilities known from OT names. Examples include: Ananias, "Yahweh has shown mercy" (Acts 5:1); Barnabas, "son of consolation" (Acts 4:36); Martha, "lady" (Jn. 11:1); Jason, "Yahweh saves" (Acts 17:5); Barachias, "blessed of Yahweh" (Mt. 23:35); Lazarus, "God has helped" (Lk. 16:19); Zaccheus, "pure" (Lk. 19:2); Zebedee, "Yahweh has granted" (Mt. 4:21).

Other personal names reflect native Greek vocabulary, as in Aretas, "pleasing" (2 Cor. 11:32); Onesimus, "useful" (Philem. 10); Paul, "little" (Acts 13:9); Timothy, "one who honors God" (1 Thess. 3:2); Archelaus, "people's chief" (Mt. 2:22); Eunice, "good victory" (2 Tim. 1:5); Trophimus, "nutritious" (Acts 20:4f.); Aristarchus, "best ruler" (Acts 19:29); Eutychus, "lucky" (Acts 20:9); Tryphaena, "dainty," and Tryphosa, "delicate," who were probably sisters (Rom. 16:12); Aristobulus, "best counselor" (Rom. 16:10); and Philetus, "beloved" (2 Tim. 2:17).

The rapid spread of the gospel through various ethnic groups can be seen in the variety of names borne by believers mentioned in the NT. A list of Christians in a single church reveals a typically variegated mix of Jewish and pagan names of many types, both masculine and feminine (Rom. 16:3-16).

*See also* GOD, NAMES OF; NAME.

***Bibliography.***–T. Bauer, *Die Ostkanaanäer* (1926); M. Coogan, *West Semitic Names in the Murašû Documents* (1975); G. B. Gray, *Studies in Hebrew Proper Names* (1896); M. von Grunwald, *Die Eigennamen des AT* (1895); H. Huffmon, *Amorite Personal Names in the Mari Texts* (1965); T. Jacobsen, *Treasures of Darkness* (1976), pp. 93-164; A. MacRae, *Semitic Personal Names from Nuzi* (1943); W. Moran, "The Hebrew Language in its Northwest Semitic Background," in *BANE*, pp. 54-72; E. Nestle, *Die israelitische Eigennamen nach ihrer religionsgeschichtlichen Bedeutung* (1876); M. Noth, *Die israelitischen Personennamen* (1928); J. Stamm, "Hebräische Ersatznamen," in H. Güterbock and T. Jacobsen, eds., *Studies in Honor of Benno Landsberger* (*Assyriological Studies,* 16; 1965), pp. 413-424; "Hebräische Frauennamen," in B. Hartmann, *et al.*, eds., *Hebräische Wortforschung* (*Festschrift* for W. Baumgartner; *SVT,* 16; 1967), pp. 301-339.

D. STUART

**NANEA** na-nē'ə [Gk. *Nanaia*] (2 Macc. 1:13, 15); NEB NANAEA. A Syrian goddess who was also one of the early Sumerian deities, Inanna, the goddess of love, later identified with Ishtar. The Phoenicians identified her with Ashtoreth (Astarte), the Persians with Anahita, the Greeks with Aphrodite, and the Romans with Venus. Her cult was centered in Uruk for centuries, until the end of the Assyrian empire (*APOT,* I, 87).

According to 2 Macc. 1:13-17 Antiochus IV Epiphanes was killed in the temple of Nanea in Persia while attempting to seize its treasure. Under pretext of marrying the goddess and obtaining the treasure as a dowry, the king and a few of his men had entered the sacred precinct. The priests closed the temple door to prevent them from escaping and opened a secret door in the ceiling through which they threw stones, killing and dismembering the entire royal party. As a further indignity the heads were thrown to the people outside.

1 Maccabees 6:1-17, however, connects the death of

Antiochus IV with his attempt to plunder a temple in Elymais in Persia. This temple was described to the king as being exceedingly rich, containing among its treasures the golden shields, breastplates, and other weapons left there by Alexander the Great. The people of the city learned of Antiochus's plan to plunder the temple and defeated his army in battle. This defeat and the simultaneous report of a defeat of his army in the land of Judah caused the king to take to his bed in discouragement and hastened his death.

The account of Antiochus's death in 1 Maccabees is considered the more reliable of the two. The temple that he was prevented from looting, however, may actually have been the temple of Nanea mentioned in 2 Maccabees. Possibly the reference to the temple at Elymais is taken from the story of the death of Antiochus III, who was killed while robbing a temple of Belus in the hills near Elymais (Strabo *Geog.* xvi.1.18). H. E. FAGAL

**NAOMI** nā-ō'mē, nə-ō'mē, nā-ō'mī [Heb. *no*ʿ*°mî*-'Sweetie' or the like, possibly a fem. form of the name Naaman; the *î* of the name is more likely a hypocoristic ending than the 1st common sing. possessive suffix]. The mother-in-law of RUTH and one of the three leading figures in the book of Ruth. Naomi makes several significant decisions in the story, and shows in each case a deep faith in God, even in the midst of bitter bereavement ("call me Mara" [i.e., "bitter" — a play on the meaning of her name; cf. RSV mg.], 1:21).

During the time of the Judges, specifically in the late 12th cent. B.C., Naomi, her husband Elimelech, and their two sons left Bethlehem in Judah during a famine to seek a better living in Moab. There the sons married. Later Elimelech and both sons died, leaving Naomi widowed and bereaved. She decided to return to Bethlehem and urged her daughters-in-law to stay in Moab and remarry. Orpah agreed, but Ruth insisted on accompanying Naomi to Bethlehem in spite of the dangers and financial strictures two single women faced in that era. Ruth's promise to Naomi, "Your God [will be] my God" (1:16), is a commitment to conversion, influenced undoubtedly by Naomi's faithfulness to Yahweh in spite of many trials.

In Bethlehem Ruth was befriended by a close relative of Naomi's, Boaz, whose responsible, consistent actions Naomi predicted in advising Ruth (ch. 2). As Naomi suggested, Boaz was willing to act as next of kin (ch. 3) and married her, thereby preserving the inheritance rights of Elimelech's succession (*see* KIN I.C; MARRIAGE IV.A.2). Obed, born to Ruth and Boaz, was considered virtually a compensatory son to Naomi. His grandson was David, king of Israel (ch. 4). D. STUART

**NAPHATH** nā'fəth [Heb. *nāpeṯ*] (Josh. 17:11); AV COUNTRIES; NEB "the district (of Dor)." This term (perhaps meaning "heights") appears to refer to DOR, the third city mentioned in this verse. The designation is apparently used to distinguish it from En-dor. Cf. NAPHATH-DOR in Josh. 11:2; 12:23; 1 K. 4:11. G. WYPER

**NAPHATH-DOR** nā'fəth dôr [Heb. *nāpaṯ dôr* (Josh. 2:23), *nāpaṯ dō'r* (1 K. 4:11)]; AV "coast of Dor," "region of Dor"; NEB "district of Dor." A region in the vicinity of, or identical to, the city of DOR.

**NAPHISH** nā'fish [Heb. *nāpîš*] (Gen. 25:15; 1 Ch. 1:31; 5:19); AV, NEB, also NEPHISH; **NEPHISIM** nə-fī'sim [Heb. *K n*ᵉ*pîsîm, Q n*ᵉ*pûsîm*; Gk. Apoc. *Naphisi*] (Ezr. 2:50; 1 Esd. 5:31); AV, NEB, NEPHUSIM, Apoc. NAPHISI; **NEPHUSHESIM** nə-fo͞o'shə-sim [Heb. *K n*ᵉ*pûš*ᵉ*sîm, Q n*ᵉ*pîš*ᵉ*sîm*] (Neh. 7:52); AV, NEB, NEPHISHESIM. The eleventh son of Ishmael (Gen. 25:15; 1 Ch. 1:31), and the chief (Heb. *n*ᵉ*śî'*; RSV "prince") of the Arabian tribe that descended from him (Gen. 25:16). The tribe was defeated by the Transjordan Israelite tribes, and their surviving men were taken captive (1 Ch. 5:19; cf. v. 21). Some of them apparently became temple slaves (*see* NETHINIM); they are listed among the families that returned from the Exile (Ezr. 2:50; Neh. 7:52; 1 Esd. 5:31).

**NAPHISI** naf'ə-sī (AV, NEB, 1 Esd. 5:31). *See* NAPHISH.

**NAPHOTH-DOR** nā'fəth dôr [Heb. *nāpôṯ dôr*] (Josh. 11:2); AV "borders of Dor"; NEB "district of Dor." A region in the vicinity of, or identical to, the city of DOR.

**NAPHTALI** naf'tə-lī [Heb. *naptālî*–'wrestling'; Gk. *Nephthali, Nephthalim*]; AV Apoc. NEPHTHALI; NT NEPHTHALIM. The fifth son of Jacob — the second born to him by Rachel's handmaid Bilhah — and the tribe named for him. He was a full brother of Dan (Gen. 30:6-8). At his birth Rachel is said to have exclaimed, *naptûlê *ᵉ*lōhîm niptaltî*, "Mighty wrestlings have I wrestled." Her sister's fruitfulness had been a sore trial to the barren Rachel. Since the offspring of her maid ranked as her own, by artifice her reproach of childlessness was removed. The name Naphtali given to this son was a monument of her victory. She had won the favor and blessing of God as made manifest in the way yearned for by the oriental heart, i.e., the birth of sons.

Scripture has no personal details about the patriarch Naphtali, and the traditions say little about him. According to Tg. Pseudo-Jonathan he was a swift runner and was one of the five brothers that Joseph chose to represent the family of Jacob in the presence of Pharaoh. He is said to have been 130 years old at his death (T. Naph. 1:1). When Jacob and his family moved to Egypt, Naphtali had four sons (Gen. 46:24). In Egypt he died and was buried (cf. Ex. 1:1-6; T. Naph. 9:1-3).

*I. The Tribe.*–When the first census was taken in the wilderness, the tribe numbered 53,400 fighting men (Nu. 1:43; 2:30), but at the second census the number had shrunk to 45,400 (26:48-50). The position of Naphtali in the desert was N of the tabernacle with the standard of the camp of Dan, along with the tribe of Asher (2:25-29); when the host was on the march, this camp came in the rear (v. 31). The prince of the tribe at Sinai was Ahira son of Enan (2:29). The tribe was represented among the spies by Nahbi son of Vophsi (13:14). Prince Pedahel son of Ammihud was chosen from Naphtali to assist in the division of the land (34:28). Toward the end of David's reign the ruler of the tribe was Jeremoth son of Azriel (1 Ch. 27:19). Hiram the Tyrian artificer is described as "the son of a widow of the tribe of Naphtali" (1 K. 7:14; 2 Ch. 2:14, however, calls him "the son of a woman of the daughters of Dan"). Jgs. 5:15 does not definitely associate Barak with the tribe of Issachar; since he resided at Kedesh (Jgs. 4:6), he possibly belonged to the tribe of Naphtali.

*II. The Territory.*–In the allocation of the land the lot of Naphtali was the next to last to be drawn (Josh. 19:32-39). In the description of the territory of Naphtali the borders and the list of towns are given separately. Although the list of towns is comparatively complete, the description of the border is shortened and depends on that of the Asher and Zebulun tribes. It is difficult to reconstruct the original lists from which the description of the territory was made. According to Alt, the compilers used a system of shortening with regard to the territory of the tribes in Galilee to avoid repeating names of towns mentioned previously both in the list of towns and in that of the borders. Noth, on the other hand, believed that the original consisted of a list of the borders that was worked upon by an editor whose knowledge of the geography of the north was insufficient.

Joshua 19:33f. describes the border, and vv. 35-38 lists the fortified towns. Most scholars agree with Aharoni (*LBHG*, rev., p. 259) that the first passage gives the southern part of Naphtali. In his view v. 33 describes the line from Mt. Tabor to the Jordan, which line runs along the brook of Jabneel; all the places in v. 33 should be in the vicinity. The most likely identification is that Adami-nekeb is Khirbet Dâmiyeh, where traces of Canaanite and Israelite settlements have been found. The city's original name was apparently Adamim, as found in the list of Thutmose III (no. 36) and in Papyrus Anastasi I. The name Nekeb probably refers to the Wâdī el-Malâq, through which the caravans used to travel. Nekeb is connected with the quarrying in that area. Other probable identifications (based on Saarisalo's archeological survey) are: Jabneel with Tell en-Nâʿam; Heleph and Aznoth-tabor with two sites of the Israelite period; Khirbet Arbâtah and Khirbet Um Jubeil; and Lakkum with Khirbet el-Manṣûrah. For Za-anannim no satisfactory identification has yet been suggested.

The continuation of the southern and western border of Naphtali is not given; the Bible refers only to the border of Zebulun and Asher. In any case, Khirbet Jumjuma may be the border town separating Asher, Naphtali, and Zebulun. During a survey carried out by Aharoni sherds of the Israelite period were found there. The river Jordan is mentioned as the eastern border of Naphtali, but no northern border is given. Aharoni believed that the first seven names in the list of towns in Naphtali are arranged in geographical order from south to north. The territory of the tribe of Naphtali lay between the area of Mt. Tabor in the south and the river Litani in the north; in the east it reached the river Jordan and thus covered almost the whole of Galilee.

***III. History of the Tribe.***–The tribe never lacked ready and able warriors; its history afforded ample opportunity for the development of their skills. In the struggle with Sisera, Naphtali was found on the high places of the field (Jgs. 5:18). To David's forces at Hebron Naphtali contributed "a thousand commanders with whom were thirty-seven thousand men armed with shield and spear" (1 Ch. 12:34). Their position exposed them to the first brunt of attack by enemies from the north. They had an important part in the wars of the kings (1 K. 15:20; 2 K. 12:18; 13:22) and were the first living W of the Jordan to be carried away captive (2 K. 15:29).

Jesus spent a great part of His public life in the land of Naphtali. Gennesaret, Bethsaida, Capernaum, and Chorazin all lay within its boundaries (cf. Mt. 3:15).

***Bibliography.***–W. F. Albright, *AASOR*, 6 (1924/25), 24-26; *BASOR*, 29 (Feb. 1928), 6; 35 (Oct. 1929), 9f.; A. Alt, *Palästinajahrbuch*, 23 (1927), 43; *ZAW*, 45 (1927), 59-81; G. Dalman, *Palästinajahrbuch*, 10 (1914), 41f.; J. Garstang, *Joshua, Judges* (1931), pp. 101f.; M. Noth, *ZDPV*, 58 (1935), 215-230; A. A. Saarisalo, *Boundary Between Issachar and Naphtali* (1927); R. de Vaux, *Bulletin of the Israel Exploration Society*, II (1954), 33f.

A. A. SAARISALO

**NAPHTALI, MOUNT** [Heb. *har naptālî*] (Josh. 20:7, AV); RSV, NEB, "hill country of Naphtali." This was the most northerly of the three parts into which the western range of Palestine was divided, the other two being "Mt." Judah and "Mt." Ephraim, named after the tribe that mainly occupied them. D. PECOTA

**NAPHTHA** naf'thə [Gk. *náphtha*] (Song Three 23; 2 Macc. 1:36); AV ROSIN, NEPHI. In Song Three 23 the term refers to an inflammable material, rock oil. 2 Macc. 1:36, however, interprets it as "purification." *See* NEPHTHAR.

**NAPHTHAR** (2 Macc. 1:36, AV). *See* NEPHTHAR.

**NAPHTUHIM** naf'tə-him [Heb. *naptuḥîm*]. One of a series of peoples of which Egypt was the "father" (Gen. 10:13; 1 Ch. 1:11). The identification and location of this people is not certain, but they are usually associated with the delta region of Egypt. Spiegelberg suggested that the Hebrew name reflects the Egyp. *na-patoḥ*, "the people of the delta," while Erman emended the MT and suggested a relationship with *p-t-maḥi*, "the northland" = Lower Egypt. Kitchen has suggested the possibility of a relationship with Egyp. *nʾ(-n-)/nʾ(yw-) pʾidḥw*, "they of the Delta" (lit. marshland) or with *nʾ(-n-)/nʾ(yw-)pʾ tʾ wḥʾ(t)* = "they of the oasis land" = oases west of the Nile(?). The location of the Naphtuhim in the delta would fit well with the identifications of the Lehabim as Lybians and the Pathrusim with the inhabitants of Upper Egypt.

***Bibliography.***–A. Erman, *ZAW*, X (1890), 118f.; W. Spiegelberg, *Orientalistische Literaturzeitung*, IX (1906), 276-79; K. Kitchen, *NBD*, *s.v.* C. G. RASMUSSEN

**NAPKIN** [Gk. *soudárion*] (Lk. 19:20; Jn. 20:7); NEB also HANDKERCHIEF. The Greek term is a loanword from Lat. *sudarium*, a cloth used to wipe off perspiration (cf. Lat. *sudāre*, "to perspire"), similar to a handkerchief or small towel. Storing money in a napkin, as the unfaithful servant in Jesus' parable did (Lk. 19:20), was viewed by rabbinic writers as an unsafe practice (cf. SB, I, 970f.; II, 252). The *soudárion* is also mentioned as an item in the burial garb of Lazarus (Jn. 11:44; RSV "cloth") and of Jesus (20:7). It was probably tied under the chin to keep the jaw in place (see comms.). In Acts 19:12 the same term refers to Paul's "handerkerchiefs" (AV, RSV, NEB), which were used in miraculous healings. N. J. O.

**NARCISSUS** när-sis'əs [Gk. *Narkissos*] (Rom. 16:11). Among others, in Rom. 16 Paul greeted "those in the Lord who belong to the family of Narcissus." Although Narcissus was a common name among slaves and freedmen in the Roman empire, it occurs only here in the Bible. This Narcissus may have been a Christian absent from Rome at the time Romans was written (cf. Ambrosiaster in *PL*, XVII, cols. 179f.), a pagan (since only the Christians of his household are addressed), or a deceased Christian (since he is not addressed). If deceased he could have been the famous freedman Tiberius Claudius Narcissus. (If Rom. 16:1-23 was originally part of Romans, this identification is likely.) This Narcissus, a freedman of the Emperor Tiberius and a person of proverbial wealth, exercised virtually unlimited influence under the Emperor Claudius. After Agrippina poisoned Claudius in A.D. 54, and shortly after Nero's consecration as emperor, she forced Narcissus to commit suicide (only a few years before Romans was written). In accordance with tradition, his household slaves would have become Nero's, but they would have retained the name of their former master and thus been called *Narcissiani*. So Paul may have been referring to a group of Christians among the *Narcissiani* then living in the imperial household (cf. Phil. 4:22).

J. J. HUGHES

**NARD** [Heb. *nērd*, *nᵉrādîm*; Gk. *nárdos*, *nárdoi*] (Cant. 1:12; 4:13f.; Mk. 14:3; Jn. 12:3); AV SPIKENARD; NEB also SPIKENARD. Spikenard (*Nardostachys jatamansi* Wall.), was native to northern India and was a favorite perfume in antiquity. The prefix "spike-" refers to the shape of the plant from which the oily perfume was obtained. The best spikenard was imported from India in sealed alabaster boxes, which were opened only on very special occasions. Pliny (*Nat. hist.* xii.24-26 [41-46]) commented on the expensive nature of Indian nard.

The NT adjective *pistikḗ* (RSV "pure," Mk. 14:3; Jn. 12:3) may mean "genuine, pure" or may be derived from *piçta,* the Sanskrit term for spikenard. See Bauer, rev., p. 662; B. Lindars, *Gospel of John* (*New Century Bible Comm.*; repr. 1981), p. 416. R. K. H.

**NASBAS** nas'bəs (Tob. 11:18, AV). *See* NADAB **5**.

**NASITH** nā'səth (AV, NEB, 1 Esd. 5:32). *See* NEZIAH.

**NASOR** nā'sôr (1 Macc. 11:67, AV). *See* HAZOR **1**.

**NATHAN** nā'thən [Heb. *nāṯan*–'gift'; Gk. *Nathan*].

**1.** The prophet in the period of David and Solomon who figures prominently in three narratives: God's promise to David of the continuation of his dynasty (2 S. 7); the announcement of God's punishment of David for his theft of Bathsheba (2 S. 12); Solomon's succession to the throne (1 K. 1).

In the first narrative Nathan simply appears in David's company, with nothing told of his background. To David's query about building a temple Nathan responds that David should do as he wishes, since Yahweh is with him (2 S. 7:3). That night, however, Nathan receives "the word of Yahweh" to the effect that David should not build a temple (vv. 4-8). The message continues with the divine promise of the continuance of a Davidic dynasty (vv. 9-16). Nathan fulfils the command (v. 5) to relay the message to David (v. 17).

Nathan next appears before David in 2 S. 12. Chapter 11 has reported the success of David's plan to have Uriah the Hittite killed, his subsequent marriage to Bathsheba, and the birth of their son. Nathan appears at Yahweh's command (12:1) and tells David the story of a rich man who took a poor man's only lamb (vv. 1-5). The story has the desired effect: David condemns himself. In vv. 7-13 Nathan pronounces Yahweh's judgment upon David for his actions: his wives will be given to another, and the child born of the sinful union will die. (The heading for Ps. 51 presupposes this story.) In v. 25 Nathan figures in the etiological narrative explaining Solomon's other name, Jedidiah ("beloved of the Lord") — although Nathan's role here is unclear.

In 1 Kings 1 Nathan is pivotal in the events that result in Solomon's obtaining the throne. He is among those supporting Solomon, so when Adonijah attempts to gain the throne during David's final illness Nathan alerts Bathsheba (vv. 11f.), who brings it to David's attention. Nathan himself then appears before David (vv. 22f.) and is commanded (with Zadok the priest) to anoint Solomon (v. 34). This is done, ensuring Solomon's succession.

The Chronicler twice mentions "the words" (RSV "Chronicles," "history") of Nathan the prophet, which contain stories of David (1 Ch. 29:29) and Solomon (2 Ch. 9:29). At least part of these "words" are probably represented in 2 S. 12 and 1 K. 1. The Chronicler omitted traditions that were antithetical to his theology, but he did refer to them. Thus in 2 Ch. 9, though he did not relate the selection of Jeroboam as king in the North, his mention of the "prophecy of Ahijah the Shilonite" is an obvious reference to 1 K. 11:26ff. According to 2 Ch. 29:25 the role of the Levites in the temple as musicians came from Yahweh, through David, Gad, and Nathan. Nathan is mentioned in Zec. 12:12 as the head of a "house" (family) in Jerusalem in David's time.

***Bibliography.***–H. W. Hertzberg, *I & II Samuel* (Eng. tr., *OTL,* 1964), pp. 283-88, 312-15; J. Gray, *I & II Kings* (*OTL,* rev. ed. 1970), pp. 78-97.

**2.** A son of David, born in Jerusalem (2 S. 5:14; 1 Ch. 3:5; 14:4).

**3.** Nathan of Zobah, the father of Igal, one of David's warriors (2 S. 23:36). This may be the same man mentioned in the Chronicler's list of David's warriors. There Igal is missing, but listed in his place is Joel the brother of Nathan (1 Ch. 11:38).

**4.** The son of Attai and the father of Zabad, in the genealogy of Judah (1 Ch. 2:36). According to this genealogy both this Nathan and David are descended from Hezron. There are nine generations from Hezron to David, and eleven from Hezron to Nathan.

**5.** The name occurs twice in 1 K. 4:5: "Azariah the son of Nathan was over the officers [Solomon's]; Zabud the son of Nathan was priest and king's friend." This Zabud may be identical to Zabad, a son of Nathan (**4**). If so, then perhaps 1 K. 4:5 refers to two different Nathans. On the other hand, there is textual evidence against equating Zabud with Zabad, for thirteen MSS have Zakur in 1 K. 4:5; cf. Zachour for Zabouth in some LXX MSS of 1 K. 4:5; also 2:46h.

**6.** One of a group that returned to Jerusalem with Ezra (Ezr. 8:16; 1 Esd. 8:44), who may be identical with one of the sons of Binnui who agreed to divorce his wife (Ezr. 10:39; 1 Esd. 9:34). F. B. KNUTSON

**NATHANAEL** nə-than'ē-əl [Gk. *Nathanaēl* < Heb. *n*e*ṯan'ēl* –'God has given'].

**1.** (AV, NEB, 1 Esd. 1:9). *See* NETHANEL **7**.

**2.** Son of Pashhur; a priest who had married a foreign wife and was required to divorce her (1 Esd. 9:22; cf. NETHANEL [**8**] in Ezr. 10:22).

**3.** An ancestor of Judith (Jth. 8:1).

**4.** An Israelite from Cana of Galilee whose name is found in the Gospel of John. Although John does not explicitly say so, Nathanael appears to have been one of the apostles. At the beginning of Jesus' ministry he becomes a disciple in the same context as Andrew, Peter, and Philip (Jn. 1:45-49). He is mentioned also as being with Peter, Thomas the Twin, the sons of Zebedee, and two other disciples when Jesus appears to this group (21:2); thus Nathanael is a witness to the Resurrection.

Nathanael is not mentioned in the Synoptic lists of the Twelve. But since all the other disciples associated with Nathanael in Jn. 1 and 21:2 became apostles, many have attempted throughout church history to identify Nathanael with one of the apostles listed in the Synoptics. Because Matthew means "gift of Yahweh," some have identified him with Nathanael. Since the 9th cent., however, the most popular theory equates Nathanael with the Synoptic Bartholomew. The evidence for this view is as follows: (1) There is no Johannine mention of Bartholomew; (2) Bartholomew is coupled with Philip in the apostolic lists in all three Synoptic Gospels (Mk. 3:18 par. Mt. 10:3; Lk. 6:14) — the only place that Bartholomew appears in the Synoptics; (3) Bartholomew is listed immediately after Thomas (and Philip) in Acts 1:13 (cf. Jn. 21:2); (4) Bartholomew is a patronymic meaning "son of Tolmai," and the person so called would undoubtedly have another name. Thus, if Nathanael is to be identified with one of the Twelve, it should probably be Bartholomew. But this identification is certainly not necessary, and it may be best to see Nathanael as a disciple of Jesus standing outside the twelve apostles. This view finds patristic support (e.g., Chrysostom, Augustine). In the final analysis the question must be left open.

Some have even held that Nathanael is to be understood allegorically as a representative of the ideal disciple; but there is no evidence that Nathanael was a purely symbolic figure who did not actually exist.

Nathanael's encounter with Jesus in Jn. 1:45-51 is very interesting. Jesus commented that Nathanael was "a true Israelite in whom there is no guile." Jesus was apparently affirming that Nathanael was a model Jew — an Israelite of integrity and openness to the working of God. Jesus demonstrated supernatural knowledge (cf. 2:24f.; 5:42) by referring to an experience Nathanael had had under a fig tree. Many have speculated about what Nathanael experienced under the fig tree, but the contemporary reader cannot determine this with any certainty. What is known, however, is that Jesus' knowledge of this event caused Nathanael to voice an amazing confession of faith: "Rabbi, you are the Son of God! You are the King of Israel!" (a confession very much in line with John's high Christology, especially in the opening sections of his Gospel). In a Gospel that puts great emphasis on believing (cf. 1:7, 12; 20:31), Nathanael has the distinction of being the first person who is said "to believe" (1:50; this statement may be either indicative or interrogative). Finally, Jesus promised Nathanael a marvelous vision of the Son of man (v. 51; cf. Gen. 28:12; see comms., esp. R. E. Brown, I [*AB*, 1966], 88-91). Nathanael stands as an example of how a true Israelite responds to Jesus.

V. R. GORDON

**NATHANIAS** nath-ə-nī'əs (AV, NEB, 1 Esd. 9:34). *See* NETHANIAH **5.**

**NATHAN-MELECH** nā'thən mel'ək [Heb. *n*<sup></sup>*ṯan-meleḵ*–'the king has given']. A court official who had a room in the temple during the reign of King Josiah of Judah (2 K. 23:11). He is called a *sārîs,* usually translated "eunuch" (cf. NEB; AV, RSV, "chamberlain"), but most likely the term occurs here in its general sense to designate a high political or military officer (see R. de Vaux, *Ancient Israel* [Eng. tr. 1961], I, 121; *see also* EUNUCH II.B.1).

**NATIONS.** Ancient perceptions of nationality were diverse and often quite different from modern notions, in which political considerations predominate.

I. OT
- A. Terminology
- B. Factors in Ancient Perceptions of Nationhood
- C. The Nation Israel
- D. Foreign Nations

II. NT
- A. Terminology
- B. NT Perspectives

*I. OT.–A. Terminology.* The Hebrews used four expressions to denote "nation," each contributing its distinctive nuance.

The RSV usually renders the singular *ʿam* as "people," the plural as "nations." Heb. *ʿam* is the most frequent term for "nation," and it has cognates in all Semitic languages. The semantic evolution of the expression may be reconstructed as follows: (a) In proto-Semitic *ʿm* appears to have been a kinship term (along with *ʾāḇ,* "father," and *ʾāḥ,* "brother"; cf. the Hebrew personal names ʾAbinadab, ʾAhinadab, and ʿAmminadab; also expressions like "cut off from one's people [*ʿam*]," and "gathered to one's people [*ʿam*]"); it signified "paternal uncle." (b) It became a collective term for all male relatives. (c) It encompassed all male members of the clan, tribe, or settlement. (d) It was applied to all citizens or members of the community. (e) It denoted the entire nation, including women and children. The entire range of usage is found in the OT. *See* PEOPLE. Heb. *ʿam* was a warm and personal relational term (reflected in the frequent application of pronominal suffixes ("my, his, your people," etc.). Not only did the term imply internal blood relationship, but it was used also when a nation was stated to belong to its deity (e.g., "people of Yahweh," "people of Chemosh"), ruler, or private citizen.

The RSV renders *gôy* as "nations," except in Ps. 79:1 ("heathen"). The AV sometimes translates *gôy* as "gentiles," more often as "heathen," but usually as "nation." *Gôy* seems to have been a uniquely West Semitic term, being attested only in Hebrew, although a cognate has surfaced in the Mari Texts, *gāʾum/gāwum,* "group, gang (of workmen)" (*CAD,* V, 59), or perhaps "tribe, *Volk*" (cf. W. von Soden, *Akkadisches Handwörterbuch,* I [1959], 284; R. de Vaux, *Early History of Israel* [Eng. tr. 1978], p. 239; P. Fronzaroli, *Archivio glottologico Italiano,* 45 [1960], 47-49). This gentilic sense may be hinted at in the table of nations, Gen. 10. Usually, however, the term bears distinct political overtones, being commonly paired with *meleḵ/maml*<sup></sup>*ḵâ,* "king/kingdom." *Gôy* is applied to a variety of entities, including the pre-Israelite Canaanite tribes (Dt. 7:1), bedouin-type desert tribes (Isa. 60:5ff.), city-states (2 K. 19:13), nation-states (Israel), and large imperial states (Egypt, Babylon, Jer. 25:17ff.). This was a rather cold and objective term, not given to much variation in form. Only in exceptional cases were pronominal suffixes applied (Gen. 10:5, 20, 31, 32; Ezk. 36:13-15; Zeph. 2:9; Ps. 106:5).

The Heb. *l*<sup></sup>*ʾōm* is an archaic term, not used in everyday speech. The word occurs thirty-five times, always in poetry. Two-thirds of these uses are in Isaiah and Psalms. *L*<sup></sup>*ʾōm* rarely appears without a correlative (always *ʿam* or *gôy* or a term paired elsewhere with these words). Morphologically the expression seems to have fossilized into a standardized plural form, the singular appearing only in Gen. 25:23; Isa. 51:4; Prov. 11:26; 14:28. Only in Isa. 51:4 does it have a suffix. The usage betrays few signs of vitality and creativity characteristic of ordinary speech. Its formality is reminiscent of *gôy,* but the singular form in the Proverbs texts requires the translation "population," a sense closer to *ʿam.* The only Northwest Semitic cognate is Ugar. *limm,* "peoples"; cf. *li-ʾ-mu,* "family, clan," a shadowy concept in Akkadian lexical texts (cf. A. D. Kilmer, *JAOS,* 83 [1963], 427ff.; *CAD,* IX, *s.v.* "*līmu* C").

The Heb. *ʾummâ* has the sense "nation" only in Ps. 117:1 (where it parallels *gôyim*; cf. "clan," Gen. 25:16; Nu. 25:15). The Aramaic cognate appears in Dnl. 3:4, 7, etc., in association with *ʿam* and *lāšôn,* "tongue," and in Ezr. 4:10. A probable derivation from **ʾmm,* "mother," suggests that the gentilic usage implies descent from a common mother; cf. A. Malamat, *Ugarit-Forschungen,* 11 (1979), 528ff. It is cognate to Ugar. *umt* and Akk. *ummatu.*

Although each of these words bore its own distinctive nuances (contra G. Bertram, *TDNT,* II, 364ff., the distinctions are inherent in the words; they do not develop only in the course of history), the ease with which they could be synonymously paralleled and interchanged indicates a common semantic range which may be illustrated as in Diagram 1.

*B. Factors in Ancient Perceptions of Nationhood.* In the development of national self-consciousness the ancient Semites viewed several factors to be operative.

*1. Ethnicity.* The importance of this factor varied. In northern Syria (encompassing the Phoenicians and Arameans) this element appears to have been superseded by others. In the "national states" farther south (cf. G. Buccellati, pp. 13f., for the distinction between "national" and "territorial" states) it was crucial. The He-

**DIAGRAM 1**
**THE SEMANTIC RELATIONSHIPS AMONG THE OT DESIGNATIONS FOR "NATION"**

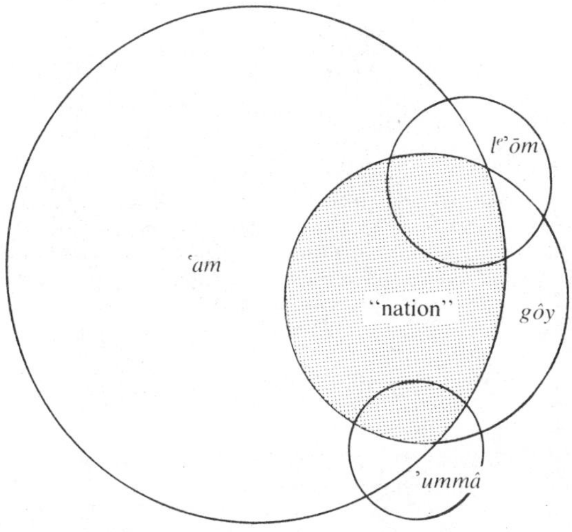


brews' keen sense of descent from a common ancestor is demonstrated by (a) the use of the eponym Israel as the national name; (b) the designation of the nation as "sons of Israel," "house of Israel/Jacob," and "seed of Israel"; (c) their national and tribal genealogies; (d) preserved traditions of the patriarchal ancestors. This does not mean that such nations were ethnically or racially pure. Extraneous elements were introduced through intermarriage (cf. Gen. 34:15f., "We will give our daughters to you, and we will take your daughters to ourselves, and we will dwell with you and become one people [*ʿam*]"; also Ruth 1:16, "Your *ʿam* shall be my *ʿam*"), foreigners' identification with Israel in its worship of Yahweh (Ex. 12:48), the incorporation of native Canaanites (cf. the Gibeonites, Josh. 9), dynastic marriages, which brought with them large retinues of attendants from the princess' native land (cf. Jezebel, 1 K. 16:31), and the engagement of foreigners in royal service (cf. David's staff, 2 S. 15:18ff.; 1 Ch. 27:30f.). Caleb ben Jephunneh, the Kenizzite of Edomite descent, represents the clearest example of total integration (cf. Nu. 13:6; 14; 26:65; Josh. 14:8). However, the core of the population was perceived to be ethnically united. The Hebrews viewed the Edomites, Ammonites, and Moabites similarly (cf. Gen. 19:37f.; 36:1ff.). Whether these nations perceived themselves this way cannot at present be determined.

2. *Territory.* The geographical limits of nation-states tended to be coterminous with the area inhabited by the ethnic group. This contrasts sharply with the northern territorial states where a single ethnic group (*ʿam*) could be divided into a series of states (*gôyim*), each with its own capital city (from which the state usually received its name) and reigning monarch. The difference may be illustrated as in Diagram 2. The boundaries of the territorial states fluctuated, depending upon the ability of the king to control his region or incorporate more land. The territory played a critical role in national development. It was more than a place of residence; it provided the context in which fulness of life (Dt. 4:40; etc.), prosperity (cf. expressions like "a land flowing with milk and honey," Ex. 3:8, 17; Dt. 8:7-10; 11:9-12; 2 K. 18:31f.; also Azitawadda's comment, *ANET*, p. 654, "May this city possess plenty to eat and wine [to drink]! May they have many children, may they be strong numerically . . . by virtue of Baʿl and the Gods [*El*]"), and security (note the emphasis on the land as a resting place [*mᵉnûḥâ*, Dt. 12:9], and the people living securely [*lᵉḇeṭaḥ*, Lev. 25:18; etc.]) could be found. For this reason the promise of land to Abraham represented a natural corollary to the promise that his descendants would become a great nation (*gôy gāḏôl*). Cf. C. Westermann, *Promises to the Fathers* (Eng. tr. 1980), pp. 143-49. This perception of the role of territory in national self-consciousness underlies the ancient practice of deporting entire populations from conquered lands. Cf. B. Obed, *Mass Deportations in the Neo-Assyrian Empire* (1979).

3. *Theology.* Among the Semites, people as groups commonly identified themselves with a patron deity in a special way. Thus the Ammonites were known as "the people of Malkam" (Jer. 49:1), the Moabites as "the people of Chemosh" (*ʿam kᵉmôš*, Nu. 21:29; Jer. 48:46), and the Israelites as "the people of Yahweh" (*ʿam yhwh*; cf. N. Lohfink, "Beobachtungen zur Geschichte des Ausdrucks *ʿm Yhwh*," in H. W. Wolff, ed., *Probleme biblischer Theologie* [*Festschrift* G. von Rad, 1971], pp. 275-

**DIAGRAM 2**
**THE RELATIONSHIP BETWEEN ETHNIC AND GEO-POLITICAL BOUNDARIES IN ANCIENT SYRIA**

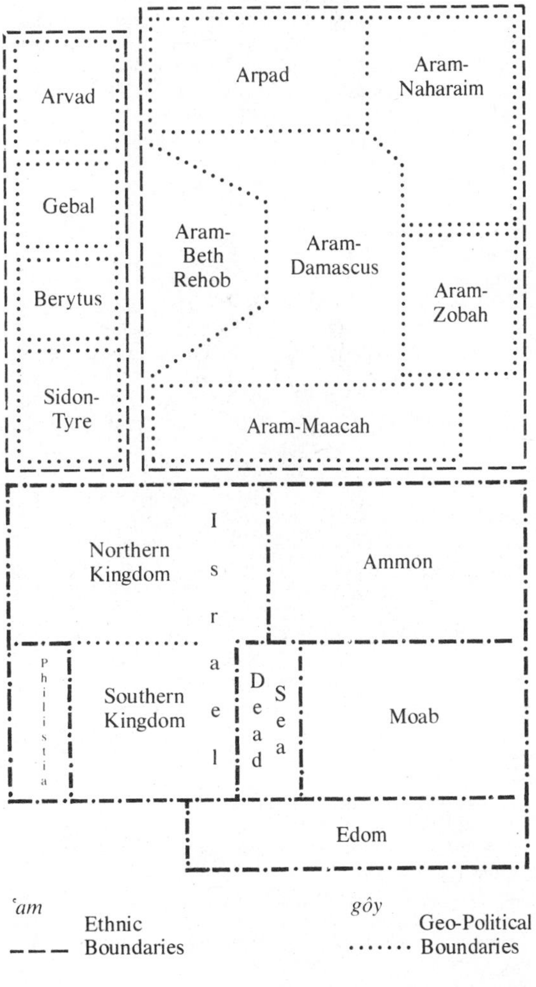

305). The Phoenicians and Arameans, like the Mesopotamians, perceived a people to be related to a specific god by virtue of residence in that god's land. The Hebrews by contrast, viewed their association with Yahweh as primary; the land of Canaan represented His grant to them. Indeed, Yahweh was acknowledged as the source of territorial claims of the other nations as well (Dt. 32:8; cf. 2:5, Edom; 2:9, Moab; 2:19, Ammon). The divine patron's function was to maintain the welfare of the people by making them prosper and defending them against foreign aggression. The people, for their part, were charged with maintaining the cult of the god and abiding by his moral expectations. Failure to comply would result in the departure of the deity (cf. R. Borger, *Asarhaddon* [1956], pp. 10ff.; L. Cagni, *Poem of Erra* [1979], pp. 21ff.; Ezk. 8–10) or the expulsion of the people from the land. Uniquely in Israel, the deity-nation association was established prior to the people's presence in the land and maintained even after their departure.

The notion of national deities was not absolute. The gods of the nations outside Israel tolerated the worship of other divinities by their subjects. But to the orthodox in Israel, Yahweh's position was unchallenged and His intolerance of rivals total (Ex. 20:1ff.; Dt. 6:4ff.). Yahweh welcomed veneration by non-Israelites, however. Although He had established a special relationship with Israel as His people, and declared Himself to be their god (Lev. 26:12; etc.), the prophets also proclaimed Him to be the universal God (Isa. 54:5; Jer. 32:27).

*4. Politics.* In theory the monarchical institution should have promoted national self-consciousness insofar as kings were expected (a) to provide leadership in the conduct of war, the administration of justice (1 S. 8:5f., 19f.), and the support of the national cult; (b) to model the highest standards of courage, dignity, justice, and piety, thus serving as an ideal for the citizens; and (c) to embody the collective aspirations of the people. In practice, however, the exercise of leadership was frequently motivated by ambition and the protection of vested interests. In northern Israel especially, leadership in the cult was replaced by leadership in apostasy and impiety (cf. 1 K. 14:7ff.; 16:30ff.; 2 K. 17). Far from modelling the highest ideals, the kings became known for their inhumanity, treachery, opportunism, and injustice. Instead of embodying the collective aspirations of the nation, they became the focus of collective mistrust and hatred, a cause of shame to the nation (cf. 1 K. 11:26; 12:1ff.). On balance, in view of the disparity between the theory and the exercise of the royal office, the influence of the kings of ancient Syria on the development of national self-consciousness was much less than it might have been. *See also* KING.

*5. Linguistic.* The "shibboleth" affair in Jgs. 12:1-7 serves as a grim reminder, not only of the linguistic fragmentation occurring in Israel during the era of the judges (*see* JUDGES, PERIOD OF), but also the nation's political disintegration. The account seems to imply a close relationship between language and national self-consciousness. This is supported by the conjoining of "language," *lāšôn,* with *ʿam* and *ʾummâ* in the Aramaic parts of Daniel (e.g., 3:4, 7, etc.), the identification of specific languages on the basis of national names (e.g., *ʾarāmîṯ,* Dnl. 2:4; Ezr. 4:7; *yehûḏîṯ,* 2 K. 18:26; cf. *ʾašdôḏîṯ,* Neh. 13:24), bound expressions like "the language of the people" (Est. 1:22), in Esther also associated with a national script (cf. 8:9), the appearance of "tongues" in the table of nations (Gen. 10) as one of the organizing features alongside "families" (*mišpāḥôṯ*), "lands" (*ʾarāṣôṯ*), and "nations" (*gôyim*), and references to foreigners as those who speak a strange language (Dt. 28:49; Isa. 33:19; Jer. 5:15; Ezk. 3:5f.; Ps. 81:5 [MT 6]; 114:1). The importance of language in modern nationalist movements, however, should not be read into the ancient Semitic records. Designations for "language" (*lāšôn, śāpâ*) occur only thirty-six times in the OT; never, according to the present state of knowledge, in other Northwest Semitic texts. This suggests that the relationship between language and nationality may not have been the subject of much reflection. Gen. 11:1-9 represents an attempt unique in the ancient world to explain the origin of linguistic diversity. A few references to language appear in contemporary Mesopotamian (cf. *CAD,* IX, *s.v. "lišānu"*; A. Borst, *Der Turmbau von Babel* [1952], I, 74-89) and Egyptian (Borst, pp. 32-42) texts. However, given the royal nature of most of the inscriptions, and their preoccupation with territory and power, one may conclude that linguistic realities were of little consequence. Interestingly (contra I. J. Gelb, *Hurrians and Subarians* [1944], pp. v-vi), all of the nations of southern Syria (the Philistines, Edom, Moab, Ammon, Israel) gave up their native tongues in favor of the Canaanite dialect without any loss of national self-consciousness. This seems to have occurred before the turn of the millennium; cf. Samson's ability to converse freely with the Philistines (Jgs. 13–16). The concern of Neh. 13:24 with the loss of *yehûḏîṯ* has a religious, rather than nationalistic, basis.

*C. The Nation Israel.* This variegated ancient Near Eastern perception of nationhood has important implications for an understanding of Israel's history. According to the patriarchal promise, the achievement of *gôy* status for Israel was a divinely ordained objective. The narratives speak proleptically of a numerous population (Gen. 17:2, 6, etc.), a national deity (17:7f.), a territorial homeland (17:8; 35:12), and even a king (17:16). It appears that the royal institution was commonly perceived as a prerequisite for nationhood status (cf. 1 S. 8:5, 19f.). It is clear from Dt. 26:5ff., however, that the formative period in Israel's evolution toward nationhood transpired in Egypt, independent of a homeland and in the absence of a king. The establishment of the monarchy in the 11th cent. did not mark the emergence of Israel as a *gôy*; it merely brought Israel into conformity with the neighboring nations. The monarchic aspect is also minimized in the rest of the OT. After the arrival of the kingship, Israel is never referred to as a *gôy* in the historical narratives. In the prophets, Jer. 18:6-9 speaks quite naturally of the destruction and rebuilding of a nation or kingdom, but Mic. 4:7 refers to the sick becoming a *gôy* over which Yahweh will function as king (*meleḵ*). This notion of a divine king is also common in the enthronement psalms (e.g., Pss. 93, 95, 96).

On the other hand, the point of Jeroboam's policies at the time of the northern secession now becomes apparent. By establishing a separate national religion, complete with its own shrines, priesthood, and religious calendar (1 K. 12:25ff.), he added the religious dimension to the existing tribal, territorial, and political foundations of the new kingdom. He desired not only a separate state, but a nation, completely divorced from Judah to the south.

The multifaceted nature of the eschatological visions of many of the prophets (in the face of the Assyrian and Babylonian conquests in 722 and 586 B.C.) gains new significance when the complex oriental understanding of nationality is recognized. If the restoration of Israel was to be complete, it had to be described in terms of (a) a return to the land of Canaan; (b) a spiritual renewal of relationship with Yahweh, the patron deity; (c) the involvement of the entire house of Jacob; (d) the restoration of an indigenous (messianic) monarchy (e.g., Hos. 2:1ff.; Jer. 23:3ff.; 30:8-11, 18-22; 33:4-25; Ezk. 37:18-28). Without any one of these elements the restoration would have been interpreted as aborted.

In many contexts the identification of Judah/Israel as

a *gôy* bears overtones of reprimand for the nation's infidelity to Yahweh and its characteristically negative moral qualities. But this usage is not as consistent as A. Cody (*VT,* 14 [1964], 1-6) suggests. Note Isa. 26:2, "Open the gates that the righteous *gôy* which keeps faith may enter in." Cf. also Jer. 31:36, which describes, not the rejection of a faithless *gôy,* but the opposite: Yahweh's commitment to the preservation of Israel as a *gôy* before Him. Cf. also Ps. 33:12; 106:5. On the other hand note also Hag. 2:14 and Mal. 3:9. In the former the tone of reprimand is expressed, not so much in the use of *gôy* (*ʿam* appears as a correlative), as in the use of the demonstrative "this." Cf. J. Boehmer, *JBL,* 45 (1926), 124-148. Furthermore, even after allowances have been made for the negative connotations which the term assumes in later times, the identification of the postexilic community as a *gôy,* even though it consisted of only a limited population and possessed no king, testifies to the great flexibility of usage.

*D. Foreign Nations.* The Hebrew explanation for the origins of the nations is summarized poetically in Dt. 32:8,

> When the Most High gave to the nations their
> inheritance, when he separated the sons of men,
> he fixed the bounds of the peoples
> according to the number of the sons of God.

(So RSV, following the LXX and 4Q. Cf. AV "children of Israel," following MT.) According to the MT, the existence of the separate nations is attributed to an act of Yahweh whereby He divided the population of the earth into nations on the basis of the tally of the sons of Israel. Tg. Yerushalmi I associates the number of nations with the number of the tribes of Israel, i.e., twelve. But an expanded paraphrase of this Targum identifies the nations as seventy, thus conflating ideas derived from the table of nations, the tower of Babel account (Gen. 11), and the seventy sons who accompany Jacob to Egypt (Gen. 46:27; Ex. 1:5). Cf. D. Barthélemy, "Les tiqquné sopherim et la critique textuelle de l'AT," *SVT,* 9 (1963), 300f.; R. Meyer, "Die Bedeutung von Dt. 32:8f., 43 (4Q) für die Auslegung des Mosesliedes," in A. Kuschke, ed., *Verbannung und Heimkehr* (*Festschrift* W. Rudolph; 1961), p. 206. The LXX and a fragment from 4Q may, however, preserve the original reading, suggesting that the nations were divided on the basis of the number of angelic patrons available (cf. Dt. 4:19f.; 29:24-28; Dnl. 10:13; Sir. 17:17). To these nations Yahweh then allocated their respective territories. The special status of Israel is reflected in Yahweh's reserving it for Himself; no mediating patron is needed (but cf. later references to Michael, Dnl. 12:1f.). This understanding contrasts with the apparently prevailing perception by the surrounding peoples that the territories had been allocated to the respective patron deities by the highest god, either by lot or as rewards for services rendered. Cf. Block, pp. 415ff.

But Yahweh's authority over the nations was not restricted to this original occasion; He continued to control their boundaries (Isa. 10:13; cf. 2 K. 10:32) and guide the migrations of entire national groups to new lands (Am. 9:7; cf. Acts 17:26). In the apocalyptic writings of Daniel Yahweh's sovereignty over all the nations serves as a dominant motif (e.g., 2:36ff.; 4:31-35 [MT 28-32]; etc.).

The TABLE OF NATIONS (Gen. 10) represents the only extant ancient Near Eastern attempt to explain, on a level approaching the theoretical, the existence of the nations and their relationships to one another from a human perspective. The primary concern of this document is to trace the history of the Noachian family, and to show how its growth and segmentation are reflected in the association of the various groups of descendants with specific territories (*ʾᵃrāṣôṯ*), languages (*lᵉšōnôṯ*), kinship groups (*mišpāḥôṯ*), and political entities (*gôyim*). Cf. vv. 5, 20, 31f. This interpretation helps to account for the variety of forms entered; the names consist of a mixture of eponyms, tribal names, gentilics, and toponyms. Within its broader context the Table also recognizes the fulfillment of the Noachian mandate to fill the earth (9:6), and it places the election of Abraham (and the origins of Israel) firmly in the line of universal history. Thus the text goes beyond the patriarchal narratives, in which the origins of Israel are tied genealogically to those of Edom, Moab and Ammon, by treating all the nations as members of one large family.

Although the OT is primarily concerned with the Hebrew nation, a universalistic thread is evident throughout. To Abraham it was announced that he would become an agent of universal blessing (Gen. 12:3, etc.). When Yahweh established His covenant with Israel, He declared it to be "a kingdom of priests and a holy nation," indicative of the nation's mediatorial spiritual role among the "peoples" (*ʿammîm*) of the world (Ex. 19:5f.). This mission was to be served even by the temple in Jerusalem (1 K. 8:41-43). Many prophetic texts call attention to the universal recognition of Yahweh in general terms (e.g., Isa. 2:1-4; Mic. 4:1-3; Isa. 66:18ff.; Joel 2:28ff. [MT 3:1ff.]; Zec. 2:11; 8:20ff.; 14:16f.). In Isa. 19:22ff. Yahweh speaks specifically of Egypt as "my people" (*ʿammî*) and Assyria as "the work of my hand," while in the same breath referring to Israel as "my inheritance." Perhaps this universalism is displayed most clearly in the Servant Songs in Isaiah. The Servant brings justice to the nations (42:1; cf. 51:4f.); He is a covenant to the people, a "light to the nations," a mission fulfilled by opening blind eyes and releasing prisoners from dungeons (42:6f.; cf. 49:8ff.; 61:1f.). On Israel's universal mission see R. Martin-Achard, *Light to the Nations* (Eng. tr. 1962).

If on the one hand the nations are subject to Yahweh's control and their salvation is His ultimate goal, on the other they represent the antithesis to His chosen people. Israel must be delivered from the nation Egypt (Dt. 4:34ff.; cf. Ex. 15:21). The Canaanite nations must be obliterated in a holy war lest they lead Israel into apostasy (Dt. 7:1ff.). When apostate Israel fails to comply with this injunction, the nations serve as agents of Yahweh's judgment (Jgs. 2:11ff.; 3:1ff.). Later Israel's doom is sealed when it is scattered among the nations or lands of its enemies (Ezk. 11:16, *et passim*; Ps. 106:27; cf. Lev. 26:38). Naturally, then, its restoration will involve a regathering from the nations and the lands (e.g., Ezk. 36:24). It is not surprising that in the Psalms the nations are perceived as the embodiment of evil. Note the paralleling of *gôyim* with "the wicked" (Ps. 9:5 [MT 6]), the treacherous plotters of evil (59:5 [MT 6]), Israel's enemies (106:41). Cf. also 2:1-3; 9:3-6; 17:18; etc. It should be observed, however, that at this stage the negative overtones are not yet inherent in the term *gôy*; *ʿam* is used similarly (cf. Ps. 7:7f. [MT 8f.]; 33:10; 56:7 [MT 8]; 68:30 [MT 31]; 89:50 [MT 51]; 96:5). The connotation of "heathen" derives from the contexts.

Although the nations were often perceived as agents of divine wrath, this did not excuse them for their barbarous and inhumane treatment of their victims. Even if they were not party to Yahweh's covenant, they were still accountable to Him for their conduct. Thus the oracles against the nations proclaim God's judgment on them for their arrogance and violence (Am. 1:3–2:4; Isa. 13–24; Jer. 46–51; Ezk. 25–32). In the eschatological visions of the prophets the conflict between Israel and the nations becomes a battle with Yahweh Himself. It is Yahweh who summons them to Zion and delivers the final blow (Isa. 24–27; Ezk. 38–39; Joel 3 [MT 4]; Zec. 9–14). In the postexilic period the polarization of Israel and the nations becomes complete. Ezra commands the people of the new commonwealth to put away the foreign wives because "the holy race has mixed itself with the peoples of the lands" (9:2).

*II. NT.–A. Terminology.* The LXX generally translates *gôy* as *éthnos,* especially when the nations, excluding Israel, are in view. But this pattern is broken occasionally. *Laós* is used of these nations in Isa. 55:5; 60:5; Ezk. 20:41; 28:25. In Ex. 19:6 *gôy qāḏôš* is rendered *éthnos hágion.* In seven texts in which *gôy* is understood to refer to Israel *laós* is used (Josh. 3:17; 4:1; Isa. 9:2; 26:2; 58:2; Jer. 9:8; 40:9). Cf. *TDNT,* IV, 32ff. The Greek translation of *ʿam* is more varied, reflecting the wider semantic range of the Hebrew term. Usually, however, when the foreign nations are in view *éthnos* is used; when *ʿam* refers to Israel *laós* is preferred. Cf. *TDNT,* II, 364ff.

In the main the NT follows the LXX. The "nations" are usually designated by *éthnos,* whether they are referred to in general, without qualification (e.g., Mt. 24:9, 14), or the Jewish nation in particular (cf. Lk. 7:5; 23:2; Jn. 11:48, 50-52; 18:35; Acts 10:22; 24:2, 10, 17; 26:4; 28:19; 1 Pet. 2:9). The RSV translates *éthnos* as "gentiles" when the reference is to non-Jewish nations in contrast to the Jews (Lk. 21:24; Acts 9:15; 1 Cor. 1:23; etc.) or Christians (Mt. 6:7, 32; 10:5; 20:19; Eph. 2:11f.). "Nations" includes the Jews (Mt. 24:9, 14; etc.). "People" is preferred for *éthnos* in Acts 13:19.

*Laós* occurs 141 times in the NT (including Jn. 8:2), usually to designate "people, population." A national sense is clear when *laós* applies to Israel (e.g., Lk. 2:32). See further *TDNT,* IV, 52ff. The plural *laoí* is found only eight times, but in each instance the characteristically Semitic pairing of words is apparent. *Laoí* is paralleled with *éthnē* in three poems: Lk. 2:31; Acts 4:25 (cf. the coordinate pair in v. 27); Rom. 15:11. The quadruplets in Rev. 7:9 (*éthnos, phylaí, laoí, glṓssai*), 10:11 (*laoí, éthnē, glṓssai, basileíai*), 11:9 (*laoí, phylaí, glṓssai, éthnē*), and 17:15 (*laoí, óchloi, éthnē, glṓssai*) are reminiscent of Dnl. 3:4, 7, etc. (cf. also Gen. 10).

*B. NT Perspectives.* By NT times, as a result of the successive Assyrian, Babylonian, Persian, Greek, and Roman empires, the populations and cultures of the ancient Near East had undergone considerable mixing. The dominance of the imperial presence served to weaken national activities in many ways. That the Jews retained a sense of nationhood is to be attributed to their strong religious traditions. For religious reasons they continued to hold non-Jews in contempt (Jn. 4:9), viewing them as unclean (cf. Acts 10:11f.). Although Jesus initially instructed His disciples to go only to the house of Israel (Mt. 10:5f.), after the nation's rejection of His messianic status He began to break new trails by (1) identifying with the Servant of the Lord of Isa. 42:2ff. in His mission to the Gentiles (Mt. 12:18ff.; cf. Simeon's response to the birth of Jesus, Lk. 2:29ff.; also Jesus' inaugural speech, Lk. 4:17ff.); (2) ministering to non-Jews personally (Mt. 15:21ff.; Mk. 7:24ff. [the Syro-Phoenician woman]; Jn. 4:1ff. [the Samaritan woman]) on the basis of the principle stated in Jn. 10:16; (3) predicting the eventual spread of the gospel to all nations (Mt. 24:14; 25:31ff.; cf. Jn. 12:32); (4) commissioning His disciples to take the gospel to all nations (Mt. 28:19f.; Mk. 16:15; Lk. 24:47; Acts 1:8).

Whereas the activity of the Church was initially concentrated in the Jewish mission, Peter's visit to Cornelius (Acts 10) and the conversion of Paul (Acts 9) signalled a revolution in Christian thought. Fundamental to Paul's message was the good news of access for all to God's grace, irrespective of nationality, social status, or sex (Gal. 3:28; Rom. 10:12). In Rom. 9–11 he describes in detail how the Jewish rejection of Christ had turned out for the benefit of the Gentiles. However, he appears to hold out the prospect of an eventual national return of Israel to God (Rom. 11:25ff.).

The Apocalypse of John displays considerable interest in the salvation of the nations. According to Rev. 5:9-10 the ransomed of God will include "men from every tribe and tongue and people and nation"; these will constitute the kingdom of God and exercise dominion over the earth (cf. 2:26f.; 20:6; also Rom. 15:12). In general the book describes the universal triumph of God and His sovereignty over the nations in terms reminiscent of earlier apocalyptic. The establishment of the kingdom of the Lamb through suffering, however, is new (Rev. 5:9ff.).

***Bibliography.***–*TDNT,* II, *s.v.* ἔθνος (Bertram, K. L. Schmidt); IV, *s.v.* λαός (Strathmann); *TDOT,* II, *s.v.* "gôy" (Clements); D. I. Block, "The Foundations of National Identity: A Study in Ancient Northwest Semitic Perspectives" (Diss., Liverpool, 1981); G. Buccellati, *Cities and Nations of Ancient Syria* (1967); W. Eichrodt, "Gottesvolk und die Völker," *Evangelische Missionsmagazin*, 8615(1942), 129-145; L. Rost, "Bezeichnungen für Land und Volk im AT," in *Kleine Credo und andere Studien zum AT* (1965), pp. 76-101; E. A. Speiser, *JBL,* 79 (1960), 157-163; H. Wildberger, *Jahwes Eigentumsvolk* (1960); D. J. Wiseman, ed., *Peoples of OT Times* (1973).

D. I. BLOCK

**NATIVITY OF MARY, GOSPEL OF THE.** *See* APOCRYPHAL GOSPELS II.D.

**NATURAL, NATURE** [Heb. *lē(a)ḥ*] ("natural force," Dt. 34:7); NEB "vigour"; [Gk. *génesis* (Jas. 1:23; 3:6)];NEB also "existence"; [*psychikós*] (1 Cor. 2:14; see also "physical body," 1 Cor. 15:44, 46); NEB "unspiritual"; [*phýsis* (Rom. 2:14; 11:21, 24; 1 Cor. 11:14; Gal. 4:8; Eph. 2:3; 2 Pet. 1:4)]; NEB also NATIVE, BEING; [*physikós*] (Rom. 1:26f.); [*ánthrōpos* (2 Cor. 4:16; Eph. 4:22, 24; Col. 3:9)]; AV "(outward) man"; NEB also "humanity"; [*sárx*] (Rom. 6:19); AV "flesh"; NEB "weakness"; [*hypóstasis*] (He. 1:3); AV "person"; NEB BEING; [*spérma*] (1 Jn. 3:9); AV, NEB, "seed"; [*ídios*] ("own nature," Jn. 8:44); AV "own"; NEB "own language"; [*homoiopathḗs* (Acts 14:15; Jas. 5:17)]; AV "passions"; NEB "mortal," "frailty"; [*phthartós* ("perishable nature," 1 Cor. 15:53a), *thnētós* ("mortal nature," v. 53b), *néos* ("new nature," Col. 3:10), *autós* ("same nature," He. 2:14)]; AV omits except for "new man" (Col. 3:10); NEB also "perishable being," "what is mortal."

The terms "natural" and "nature" must be examined carefully. Several factors underline the problem of translation and use: (1) A variety of Greek roots lies behind this rendering in the modern translations. (2) The word "nature" is contaminated by nonbiblical concepts from Greek thought onward, especially concepts lacking the foundational biblical confession of God as Creator. (3) The term's ambiguity (for whatever reasons) allows a spectrum of usage ranging from the abstract and universal to the subjective, sensate life of a person. The present article will focus primarily on the words "natural, nature" in the RSV, with particular attention to *phýsis* and *physikós,* the words most frequently so translated.

The Heb. *lē(a)ḥ* occurs only in Dt. 34:7, but its meaning is suggested by the related adjective *laḥ,* "moist, fresh." W. F. Albright (*BASOR,* 94 [Apr. 1944], 32-35) attempted to relate Ugar. *lḥḥ* to Heb. *lē(a)ḥ,* both relating to sexual potency, but most scholars have rejected his proposal. Moses' "natural force," i.e., the native vigor of youth, was not abated to the time of his death.

Of minor interest in the NT, the Gk. *génesis* stems from a root indicating "birth," "coming into being." The NT canon begins in Matthew with the declaration "The book of the genealogy [*génesis*; AV "generations"] of Jesus Christ." Here the genealogy is kindred to the ideas of "source," "commencement," "origin," otherwise embodied in *phýsis* and its cognates. The noun *génesis* in Jas. 1:23 and 3:6 carries the thought of a natural but God-ordained order of things — man's "natural face in a mirror" and the larger "cycle of nature," both being subject to the order of evanescence and decay. Philo also made prominent a similar contrast between the eternal stability of God the Creator and *génesis,* i.e., the changing world scene (see *DNTT,* II, 658f.).

The Greek terms *phýsis* and *physikós* appear 17 times in the NT. As suggested earlier, the term "nature" does not appear in the OT; on the other hand, the idea of nature, embodied in the term *phýsis,* became a key concept in early Greek thought and remained prominent in Hellenistic thought, including that sector most closely related to the NT writers. The word "nature" has various connotations in the NT. (1) Birth or physical origin (Rom. 2:27; Gal. 2:15) — the notion of a line of descent governing one's condition. (2) The essential characteristics of a species or person, whether human (Jas. 3:7) or divine (2 Pet. 1:4). Jas. 3:7 twice uses *phýsis* in the sense of "kind," i.e., according with the regular order of nature. 2 Pet. 1:4 may be compared with Paul's teaching on the new creation (*see* NEW NATURE); the thought is that true humanity can be effected only through the work of God Himself, mediated by the knowledge of Jesus Christ (v. 3). (3) An inherited or acquired condition (Eph. 2:3). Whereas the person apart from Christ is, as a sinner, a child of wrath by nature, the grace of God has established the person in Christ in a new order of grace and mercy (Eph. 2:4-10). (4) An inborn perspective of propriety or morality (1 Cor. 11:14; Rom. 2:14). Here "nature itself" teaches one about proper adornment and the just requirement of the law. (5) The forces or laws which govern the world and its inhabitants (Rom. 1:26; 11:21, 24; Gal. 4:8). The natural relationship between the sexes is established in the regular order of nature (Rom. 1:26). The pagan is indicted for the violation of this *phýsis.* In Rom. 11 Paul points to the laws which determine the culture of the olive tree as a parable of the relationship between Jew and Gentile.

All the aforementioned nuances of *phýsis* show the utilization of Greek concepts by early Christian thought, but also the distance between the world view of Hellenism and Christian faith in its NT expression.

The contrast between *psychikós* and *pneumatikós* in 1 Cor. 15:44-46 is especially interesting and instructive, and may be viewed as paradigmatic of the biblical teaching on the concept "natural." The adjective *psychikós* in the NT refers to that which belongs to the *psychḗ,* i.e., sensate, emotive and intelligent life not in covenant with God. The natural body is derived from the first Adam, who perished; all human life bounded by its origins in Adam is subject to death and decay. But there is a new, spiritual life (*pneumatikós*) issuing from union by faith with Christ, the second Adam from above. Flesh and blood, i.e., those determined by descent from the first Adam cannot inherit the kingdom of God (1 Cor. 15:20). Those who are of the new order, the *pneumatikoí,* already have experienced new life in Christ, and in keeping with this new order of existence, will be raised imperishable in the great resurrection of the dead in Christ (1 Cor. 15:35ff.). This is the "natural" outcome of the new life by faith in Christ, whom God has already raised from the dead to a new order of existence.

***Bibliography.***–G. Bornkamm, "The Revelation of God's Wrath (Romans 1–3)," *Early Christian Experience* (Eng. tr. 1969), pp. 47-70; R. G. Collingwood, *The Idea of Nature* (1945); *TDNT,* IX, *s.v.* φύσις (Köster); *RGG,* IV, 1326ff. (Trillhaas); *DNTT,* II, 656-662.

R. P. MEYE

**NATURAL FEATURES.** The purpose and limits of this article are to define certain terms used in the Bible with reference to natural features. Terms that have several meanings or that are ambiguous to the modern mind need to be understood as the biblical writers intended them in the contexts in which they are used.

I. Universe
II. Heaven
III. Earth, World
IV. Time
V. Seas, Waterways
VI. Land Features
VII. Climate, Weather
VIII. Directions

***I. Universe.***–No single term, in either Hebrew or Greek, conveys this idea. In Hebrew "the heavens and the earth," as in Gen. 1:1, is usually understood to mean the universe, but the context is limited to EARTH and the heavens as seen from earth. The sun and moon are the principal bodies ("great lights," 1:16), and the stars, with no distinction between stars and planets, are added almost as incidental. This is not to deny that God created the entire universe (cf. He. 1:3, where "universe" is used to translate Gk. *tá pánta,* "all things"), but rather to understand that the ancients, particularly the Hebrew people, did not have the concept of "universe" that modern scientists have.

***II. Heaven.***–The Heb. *šāmayim,* "heaven(s)," in general conveys the idea of that which is extraterrestrial or "non-earth." It denotes the heavens that are seen from earth (Gen. 15:5) and which, taken together with earth, constitute the "creation." The term can also be used in a spiritual sense as the dwelling place of God (Dt. 26:15; Isa. 66:1). The statement has sometimes been made that the Hebrew conceived of three (or seven) heavens, and Gen. 1:6-8, 14-17 have been understood to mean that a "firmament" divides earth's atmosphere from outer space. But it is better to consider the passages phenomenological, i.e., they describe heaven as it appears from earth. There are three "heavens" that can be distinguished visually, as the ancients did: the heaven where birds fly and across which clouds move; the heaven where sun, moon, and planets (cf. Jude 13, Gk. *planḗtēs*) move against the background of the fixed stars; and the heaven of the fixed stars. The Gk. *ouranós* as used in the Bible has approximately the same meanings as the Heb. *šāmayim* (cf. Bauer, rev., pp. 593-95). Paul's use of the expressions "third heaven" (2 Cor. 12:2) and "far above all the heavens" (Eph. 4:10) should not be pressed to formulate doctrines where other scriptural support is lacking and a figurative meaning is not unsatisfactory. *See* ASTRONOMY; FIRMAMENT; HEAVEN.

***III. Earth, World.***–The Hebrew and Greek words variously translated "earth," "world," etc., lack precision as much as the English words. Heb. *tēḇēl,* "world" (BDB, p. 385), is often used in parallel structures with *'ereṣ,* "earth," and refers generally to the planet Earth (1 S. 2:8; Ps. 89:11 [MT 12]). Heb. *'ereṣ,* on the other hand, can mean the entire earth (Gen. 18:18), a country or region (Gen. 21:21), a tribal territory (Dt. 34:2), or just a small piece of ground (Gen. 23:15). Likewise, Heb. *'ᵃḏāmâ,* "ground," has approximately the same range of meanings as *'ereṣ* (BDB, pp. 9f.). Heb. *'ôlām,* "age," is sometimes translated "world" (Ps. 73:12; Isa. 64:4, AV), but refers rathers to the age or world-system. Gk. *kósmos,* "world," has meanings that range from the universe (Rom. 1:20) to the planet (Jn. 11:9) or the inhabited portion (1 Cor. 5:10), from the world that is opposed to God (Jn. 15:19) to the redeemable world that God's Son came to save (Jn. 3:16), as well as spiritual connotations (1 Cor. 1:20f.) similar to

Heb. *ʿôlām,* "age, world-system." Gk. *oikouménē,* "inhabited earth, world," may mean the earth where mankind dwells (Acts 17:31), or a smaller portion, perhaps the Roman empire (Lk. 2:1), or even that part inhabited by Jews (Acts 24:5).

*IV. **Time.***–The ancients depended largely on natural phenomena for indications of time. The basic unit was the day, which at first was marked from sunset to sunset. The month was based on the moon, each month beginning with the first appearance of the new moon. Heb. *yārē(a)ḥ,* "moon, month," however, gave place to *ḥōḏeš,* "newness (of moon)." Likewise Gk. *mēn,* "month," is related to *mēnē,* "moon." The year consisted of twelve months (the lunar year of 354 days), but this quickly got out of phase with the seasons, hence an intercalary month was necessary. The Egyptians, from their need to plan for the annual flooding of the Nile, developed a modified solar year of 365 days, which also needed a slight correction. This was done by observations of the Dog Star Sothis. *See* ASTRONOMY I; EGYPT VI.A.

Smaller divisions of time also depended on natural phenomena. The Sumerians marked a "double hour" (Sum. kaskal.gíd or da.na; Akk. *bêrum)* as a measure of distance; it is relatively simple to distinguish the sun-angle as one-third or two-thirds of the way to zenith or from zenith. The hour was unknown in OT times. Aram. *šāʿâ,* "moment, short time," in Dnl. 3:6, etc., has been translated "hour," leading to questionable interpretations. The sundial appeared in Egypt by the 8th cent. B.C., with six divisions for the day (i.e., double hours). This was improved by Berossus (*ca.* 300 B.C.), who divided the day into twelve equal parts. The twelve-hour day was used by Greeks and Romans, and is found in the NT (Jn. 11:9; Mt. 20:2-7). *See also* HOUR.

Longer periods of time were based on the elements developed from nature, such as the sabbatical year (7th year), the year of the Jubilee (50th year), and the generation. The length of a generation is often figured at forty years, but this is without convincing support. Heb. *dôr,* Aram. *dār,* "generation," are clearly related to Akk. *dârum,* which formerly was defined as 50 years, but now "may tentatively be established as 70 years" (*CAD,* III, 115). It would be unwise to press mathematical precision into the biblical statements concerning generations.

*See also* CALENDAR.

*V. **Seas, Waterways.***–The Heb. *yām,* "sea," has a wider variety of meanings than the English word sea. It is used of the Mediterranean (Nu. 13:29, also called "the great sea," 34:6), of the Red Sea (Reed Sea, Ex. 13:18), of the Dead Sea ("sea of salt," Gen. 14:3), of the Sea of Galilee (*yam kinnereṯ,* Nu. 34:11), of the sea in contrast to the land (Gen. 1:26), and even of a river such as the Nile (Isa. 19:5) or the Euphrates (Isa. 21:1). That the Mediterranean was the common meaning is indicated by the use of *yammâ,* "seaward," to mean "west" (Gen. 13:14). Heb. *nāhār,* "stream, river," indicated a river that normally had flowing water, as opposed to *naḥal,* "torrent-valley, wadi." The former is used of the Nile (Isa. 19:5), the Euphrates (Mic. 7:12; Gen. 15:18), the Tigris (Dnl. 10:4), and of other rivers (e.g., Zeph. 3:10). It may be used of canals (cf. Ezk. 1:1; Ezr. 8:21; Ex. 7:19) and may have referred to underground waters (Job 28:11; cf. BDB, p. 625). The *naḥal,* on the other hand, was a seasonal river, a rushing torrent after a heavy rain (Jgs. 5:21), but dry or nearly so in the dry season. ("Torrent" is often a misleading translation.) Heb. *ʿayin,* "spring (of water)," was a source of water bubbling from the ground (Jgs. 7:1). A synonym is *māqôr,* "source, spring, fountain" (Jer. 2:13; cf. BDB, p. 881). On the other hand, the pit or dug well was *bᵉʾēr* (Gen. 21:25) or *bôr* (*Q,* 2 S. 23:15; *K bôʾr*). Dt. 8:7 speaks of "brooks" (*naḥᵃlê mayim*), "fountains" (*ʿᵃyānôṯ*), and "springs" (*tᵉhômôṯ*). This last term, *tᵉhôm,* has a wide range of meanings, but in general refers to underground waters (Gen. 7:11; Prov. 8:23); it may be related to Akk. *tiâmat* etymologically, but mythological identification is highly questionable (cf. DEEP).

The Greek words are not always equivalents. Gk. *thálassa,* "sea," is used of sea as distinguished from land (Mt. 23:15), of the Mediterranean (Acts 10:6), the Red Sea (7:36), and other seas, and of the lake (sea) of Galilee (Mt. 4:18) or Tiberias (Jn. 21:1). Gk. *límnē,* "lake," is used of Galilee by Luke (Lk. 5:1). The word *potamós,* "river," is used as the equivalent of Heb. *nāhār* (Mk. 3:6), but it is also used to refer to a seasonal torrent (= Heb. *naḥal*) in Mt. 7:25. The more precise term for the seasonal river or wadi is Gk. *cheimárros* (Jn. 18:1). Gk. *pēgḗ,* "spring, fountain," is used chiefly for sources of water issuing from the ground (Jn. 4:14), but it is also used of a dug well (Jn. 4:6). For the "deep," Gk. *ábyssos,* "abyss," is generally joined with *pēgḗ* (cf. Gen. 7:11, LXX; lit. "fountains of the deep").

*See also* RIVER.

*VI. **Land Features.***–The land to which the Israelites were directed (Dt. 1:7) is described as "the hill country of the Amorites, . . . their neighbors in the Arabah, in the hill country and in the lowland, and in the Negeb, and by the seacoast." "Hill country" (lit. "mountain," Heb. *har*) can be used as a general description of the mountain range (Dt. 1:7) or of specific mountains (Sinai, Ex. 19:23) or hilly regions (Bashan, Ps. 68:15 [MT 16]; *see also* HILL). The "lowland" (Heb. *šᵉp̄ēlâ*) was the region of foothills lying between the mountain range and the sea. The name was obviously given to it by those who lived above it. The "seacoast" (Heb. *ḥōp̄ hayyām,* "shore of the sea") was also called in Heb. *śᵉp̄aṯ hayyām,* "the lip of the sea" (Gen. 22:17). The coastal plain was Heb. *ʿēmeq,* "deep place, valley" (Philistine plain, Jgs. 1:19). This word, however, was generally applied to a valley (Mic. 1:4), although it was also used of a broad plain (Ezk. 37:1). The Negeb (Heb. *negeḇ,* "dry region, southland") was the term applied to the region S of Judah (Josh. 15:21ff.), although the region is not clearly defined (cf. Gen. 20:1). The word was commonly used also to mean "south" (Nu. 34:4). The Arabah (Heb. *ʿᵃrāḇâ,* "steppe, desert-plain") was an imprecise name that could be applied to the Jordan Valley (Josh. 11:2, Arab. el-Ghôr), a region W of the Dead Sea (1 S. 23:24), a plain E of the Jordan (Dt. 1:1; 3:17), the region S of the Dead Sea (Dt. 2:8, Arab. Wâdī el-ʿArabah), the plain of Moab (Nu. 22:1), the northern part of the Arabian desert (Isa. 40:3), or the steppe in general (Jer. 17:5, parallel with *miḏbār*). *See* PALESTINE.

In addition to the words used in Dt. 1:7 other terms are used. The "slopes" (Josh. 10:40) were the detritus at the foot of the mountains that appeared to be the foundation of the mountain (Heb. *ʾᵃšēḏâ,* "foundation, mountain slope"; BDB, p. 78). For "valley" or "plain" Heb. *biqʿâ,* "cleft, valley, plain" occurs (of Jericho [Dt. 34:3], Lebanon [Josh. 11:17], etc.; cf. Dt. 11:11). Heb. *mîšôr* is also imprecise, being used in parallel with *ʿēmeq* (Jer. 21:13), referring to a level place (1 K. 20:23), and particularly referring to the high plateau between the Arnon and Heshbon (Dt. 3:10; cf. BDB, p. 449). The LXX translates the word variously: by Gk. *koiládos,* "deep valley" (LSJ, p. 966) in 3 K. 21:23 (MT 1 K. 20:23); by *tríbos,* "well-worn path," in Ps. 26:11 (MT 27:11); and as a proper noun *Misor* in Dt. 1:7. Heb. *miḏbār,* "wilderness, steppe," is often translated "desert," giving an erroneous impression. The Midbar was land with marginal rainfall: in dry years it was barren, but with a slight amount of precipitation it yielded greenness (Joel 2:22). It could be uninhabited (Job 38:26), or it might contain cities (Josh. 15:61; Isa. 42:11).

*VII. Climate, Weather.*–The annual seasons are mentioned in Gen. 8:22. Summer, the dry season (May-Oct.), is Heb. *qayiṣ*, Gk. *théros* (Mt. 24:36), "summer, summer fruit." This is also Heb. *zeraʿ*, "seed(time)," and *ḥōm*, "heat." The latter can be used of the heat of the day, regardless of season (Gen. 18:1; cf. Gk. *kaúma*, Rev. 7:16). Winter, the wet season (Dec.-Mar.), is Heb. *ḥōrep̱*, Gk. *cheimṓn* (2 Tim. 4:21). This is also Heb. *qōr*, "cold" (Gen. 8:22, cf. Gk. *psýchos*, Acts 28:2) and *qāṣîr* (Gen. 8:22), Gk. *therismós* (Mt. 13:30), "harvest, harvest time." For the remaining months, see "early" and "latter" rains, below.

Because of the importance of rain, the Hebrew vocabulary has various terms that are more or less specific. Heb. *māṭār* (Gen. 2:5), Gk. *brochḗ* (Mt. 7:25), "rain, watering," are the general terms referring to the seasonal rainfall, often conveying the idea of heavy rain. Heb. *gešem* (Gen. 7:12) "rain, showers," Gk. *huetós* (Acts 14:17), are also general terms. Other words are Heb. *zerem*, "downpour, storm" (Isa. 4:6); *śaʿar*, "storm" (Isa. 28:18); *śeʿîrîm*, "rain drops," and *reḇîḇîm*, "copious showers" (Dt. 32:2). The "former rains" (Heb. *yôrê*, Dt. 11:14; *môrê*, Joel 2:23) are the early showers that precede the rainy season, preparing the ground for cultivation. Likewise the "latter rains" (Heb. *malqôš*) are showers that extend the rainy season, maturing the crops (cf. *leqeš* "spring crop," Am. 7:1). The LXX of Dt. 11:14 uses a paraphrase to express both these terms. DEW was also of great importance; the word is Heb. *ṭal*, Aram. *ṭal*. Words for "cloud" are Heb. *ʿāḇ* (with or without *māṭār*) (Jgs. 5:4; Prov. 16:15), *ʿānān* (Ex. 19:9) and *ʿanānâ* (Job 3:5), Gk. *nephélē* (Lk. 12:54). "Rainbow" is Heb. *qešeṯ*, "bow" (Gen. 9:13), Gk. *íris* (Rev. 4:3).

"Thunder" is Heb. *qōl*, *qōlôṯ*, "voice(s)" (Job 37:2, 4; Am. 1:2), *raʿam*, "thunder" (Isa. 29:6), Gk. *brontḗ* (Mt. 10:27). "Lightning" is Heb. *bārāq* (Ezk. 1:13), *bāzāq* (1:14, unless *z* was erroneously written for *r*), *ḥazîz*, "thunderbolt, lightning flash" (Job 28:26; Zec. 10:1), *ʾôr*, "light" (Job 36:32), Gk. *astrapḗ* (Mt. 24:27). "Hail" is Heb. *bārāḏ* (Josh. 10:11), *ʾelgāḇîš* (Ezk. 13:11), *ʾeḇen*, "stone" (with and without *bārāḏ*, Josh. 10:11), Gk. *chálaza* (Rev. 8:7). "Wind" is Heb. *rû(a)ḥ*, "wind, spirit" (Gen. 8:1), Aram. *rûḥâ* (Dnl. 2:35), Gk. *ánemos* (Mt. 11:7). For heavy winds, Heb. *sûpâ* (Isa. 21:1), *śeʿārâ* (Zec. 9:14), hithpael of *śāʿar* ("rush like a whirlwind," Dnl. 11:40) convey the idea of "whirlwind"; similar in meaning are Gk. *kataigís*, "sudden blast" (Isa. 28:18, LXX); and *eurakýlōn*, "northeast wind," or *euroklýdōn*, "south-southeast wind" (Acts 27:14; *see* NORTHEASTER). Heb. *rû(a)ḥ śeʿārâ* (Ps. 107:25) is "storm wind." Winds that bring the *ḥamsîn* are Heb. *rû(a)ḥ qāḏîm*, "east wind" (Jonah 4:8), *rû(a)ḥ ṣaḥ*, "hot wind" (Jer. 4:11), Gk. *nótos*, "south" (Lk. 12:55; *kaúsōn*, "scorching heat," describes the *ḥamsîn*).

*VIII. Directions.*–"Sunrise" is Heb. *môṣāʾ haššemeš*, "the going forth of the sun" (Ps. 19:7), and "sunset" is *meḇôʾ haššemeš*, "the entering of the sun." Heb. *mizrāḥ* (Nu. 21:1), Gk. *anatolḗ*, "east," is the direction toward the sunrise (or the rising stars, Mt. 2:2). The NT uses paraphrases with *anatéllō*, "rise" (Mt. 5:45) and *dýnō*, "set" (Lk. 4:40). Since the people of the Bible world "oriented" themselves to the east, Heb. *qeḏem* (Gen. 25:6), *qāḏîm* (Gen. 41:6), and other formations from the root meaning "before, in front of" were used for "east." It follows that *yāmîn*, "right (hand)" would mean "south" (Ps. 89:13) and *śemōʾl*, "left (hand)," would mean "north" (Gen. 14:15). Other words for "south" are *negeḇ*, "dry (region)" (Gen. 13:14), *dārôm*, "south" (Ezk. 42:18, chiefly in poetic passages), *têmān*, "south" (Dt. 3:27, derived from the root meaning "right [hand]"), while *ṣāpôn* also is used for "north" (Ps. 89:12 [MT 13]). "West" is *ʾaḥarôn*, "behind, after" (Dt. 11:24), *ʿereḇ*, "evening, sunset" (Gen. 8:11), *maʿaraḇ*, "west" (Isa. 45:6, from the root *ʿrb*, "to enter"; cf. Akk. *ereb šamši*, "going in of the sun, sunset"), and *yammâ*, "toward the sea" (Gen. 13:14). The four directions are mentioned in Gen. 13:14; Ezk. 42:16-20, and in Greek in Lk. 13:29. (*See also* NORTH; NORTHEAST; ORIENTATION.) W. S. LASOR

**NATURAL HISTORY.** *See* BIRDS; FISH; FLORA; ZOOLOGY.

**NATURAL MAN, THE.** *See* SPIRITUAL MAN.

**NATURE.** *See* NATURAL.

**NAUGHT; NAUGHTY; NAUGHTINESS.** Used by the AV in the sense of "bad, worthless, worthlessness," translating Heb. *raʿ* (RSV "bad," 2 K. 2:19; Prov. 20:14; Jer. 24:2), *rō(a)ʿ* (RSV "evil," 1 S. 17:28), *hawwâ* (RSV "lust," Prov. 11:6; "mischievous," 17:4), *ʾāḏām beliyaʿal* (lit. "man of Belial"; RSV "worthless person," Prov. 6:12), and Gk. *kakía* (RSV "wickedness," Jas. 1:21). In Wisd. 12:10, AV, "naughty generation" translates Gk. *ponērá hē génesis autṓn* (RSV "their origin was evil"). J. ORR

**NAUM** nā'əm (Lk. 3:25, AV). *See* NAHUM.

**NAVE.** *See* TEMPLE. On 1 K. 7:33, AV, *see* SEA, MOLTEN.

**NAVE** nā'və (Sir. 46:1, AV). *See* NUN.

**NAVEL; NAVEL STRING** [Heb. *šōr*]. Hebrew *šōr* is probably a cognate of Arab. *šurr*, which denotes first the umbilical cord and then the scar or navel.

In Ezk. 16:4 Israel is likened to a newborn infant who is abandoned shortly after birth without the care necessary to preserve life. Even her umbilical cord was not cut and tied, with the result that the infant's blood would flow out through the placenta until she died. The verse describes the normal midwifery procedures still practiced by Arab peasants in Palestine, which include cutting the umbilical cord, bathing to remove the fatty substance covering the infant's skin as well as any blood or meconium, rubbing with salt and oil, and wrapping for seven days in tight bindings known as "swaddling clothes." (See E. W. G. Masterman, *PEQ*, 1918, p. 118.)

Most modern versions read "navel" in Cant. 7:2 (MT 3) (but for a different interpretation, see M. Pope, *Song of Songs* [*AB*, 1977], pp. 617f.). The AV and RSV mg. read "navel" in Prov. 3:8; but the RSV ("flesh"; cf. NEB "health") apparently follows the LXX, which has Gk. *sṓma* ("body, flesh"), suggesting that the translator read Heb. *šeʾēr* (cf. Akk. *šīru*, "flesh") or *bāśār* in place of MT *šōr*. If *šōr* is correct, the "navel" by synecdoche implies the entire person. In Job 40:16 the AV reads "navel" for *šārîr*. The RSV and NEB more correctly render "muscles." R. K. H.

**NAVY.** The AV translation of Heb. *ʾonî* in 1 K. 9:26f.; 10:11, 22 (RSV, NEB, "fleet [of ships]"). *See* SHIPS I.

**NAZARENE** naz'ə-rēn, **OF NAZARETH** naz'ə-reth [Gk. *Nazōraios, Nazarēnos*]. An appellation or adjective that occurs nineteen times in the NT, all in the Gospels and Acts. It was applied first to Jesus Christ because He spent His boyhood in the Galilean town of Nazareth, then by extension to His followers. It is probably to be understood as a Semitic equivalent to the later Greek term "Christian."

Difficulty arises over the word because of its two forms in the NT. Four times in Matthew and twice in Luke the word is spelled *Nazarēnos*; the remaining instances are spelled *Nazōraios*, the form used exclusively in Acts, twice in Matthew, once in Luke, and three times in John. Thus Mark uses only the form *Nazarēnos*, Matthew, John, and Acts use *Nazōraios*, and Luke employs both spellings. This requires some explanation.

The form *Nazarēnos* is simple to trace, for it plainly points to someone from Nazareth, and in the case of the NT, to Jesus Christ. However, the form *Nazōraios* is more complex because of the use of the Gk. *ōmega*, a vowel that may correspond to a weak vowel in the Semitic original of the name; indeed, variations existed in Hebrew and Aramaic spellings of the name Nazareth. But this still does not answer the question posed by the two forms of the word in the NT, and in Luke the problem is intensified in that both forms appear in the one document.

Matthew 2:23, which uses *Nazōraios*, may explain this form, for it relates that Jesus' family settled in Nazareth so that the prophetic utterance might be fulfilled: "He shall be called a Nazarene." The prophecy that was fulfilled may be Isa. 11:1 or Zec. 6:12. If so, Matthew would be making a wordplay on Heb. *nēṣer*, which occurs in Isa. 11:1 as "branch."

Another proposal is that *Nazōraios* derives from the Hebrew proper name *Nesar, from which the name Gennesaret, "vale of Nesar," is taken. Or it may be connected with an earlier Hebrew name *Nazara, which refers not to the town of Nazareth but to the entire district, with the result that *Nazōraios* means "Galilean."

It is indisputable that the two forms of the word are interchangeable and equal in the Gospels, and in several passages the English versions render these adjectives by the words "of Nazareth." In Acts 24:5, however, the form *Nazōraios* presents a difficulty, for it speaks of a *sect* of *Nazōraioi*. Tertullus at Jerusalem accused Paul of being "a ringleader of the sect of the Nazarenes," clearly alluding to those called Christians. Thus the term seems to be a derogatory Jewish term for Christians.

But did the term "Nazarene" (*Nazōraioi*) have a history before Jesus Christ? At Paul's time the Christians were held by the Sanhedrin to be a Jewish sectarian party, in this case subversive and schismatic. Epiphanius (4th cent.) distinguished between Nasareans and Nazoreans; the Nasareans were Jewish heretics (*Haer.* 1.18), and the Nazoreans were Jewish-Christian heretics who had separated from the main body of the Church (*Haer.* 29.7, 9). But since Epiphanius was not a reliable historian, his distinctions may be valueless in this inquiry. It is conjectured that in pre-Christian times a Nazorean party of Jewish sectaries was known for close observance of ascetic rules of conduct (from the Heb. *nṣr*). Perhaps this party was taunted with the name *Nazōraioi* by orthodox Jews, who by Christian times applied the term of disrespect, knowingly or ignorantly, to the new Christian sect.

The end of the matter is that no certain explanation of these two forms of the word Nazarene is at hand. It may be that by NT times, whatever the history of the two words in pre-Christian Judaism, the two forms of the word were completely convertible, having no special meaning attached to them beyond the historical and geographical reference to Nazareth.

*See also* NAZARETH.

***Bibliography***.–*TDNT*, IV, *s.v.* Ναζαρηνός, Ναζωραῖος (Schaeder); M. Black, *Aramaic Approach to the Gospels and Acts* (3rd ed. 1967); G. F. Moore, "Nazarene and Nazareth," in *BC*, I; *DNTT*, II, 332-34 (K. H. Rengstorf). D. H. WALLACE

**NAZARETH** naz'ə-reth [Gk. *Nazara(th), Nazaret(h)* (etymology uncertain; see below)]. A city of Lower Galilee in the hill area just N of the great plain of Esdraelon. The top of the hill behind Nazareth commands a magnificent panorama, with the Sea of Galilee about 24 km. (15 mi.) to the east and the blue Mediterranean 32 km. (20 mi.) due west. Mt. Tabor rises 8 km. (5 mi.) to the east, and snow-capped Mt. Hermon stands as a sentinel about 100 km. (60 mi.) to the northeast. The modern city of Nazareth (en-Nâṣirah) lies in a high secluded valley open only to the west. The ancient village seems to have been located higher on the eastern slope of the hill to the northwest. Rock tombs have been located in the area.

Many scholars have regarded the Nazareth of Jesus' time as an unimportant village. This evaluation is based upon its location off the international trade routes, the lack of any mention in the OT, Apocrypha, or Josephus, and Nathanael's rather uncomplimentary "Can anything good come out of Nazareth?" However, it is always designated a *pólis* (city) and never a *kṓmē* (village). A. S. Geden observed that Nathanael's disdain may have been that of a "polished town-dweller for the uncultivated rural population" (*DCG*, II, 236) and need not represent a widely held opinion of the specific town.

The derivation of the name Nazareth is not certain. Some connect Mt. 2:23 ("He went and dwelt in a city called Nazareth [*Nazaret*] that what was spoken by the prophets might be fulfilled, 'He shall be called a Nazarene' [*Nazōraios*]") with Isa. 11:1, which says that a branch (*nēṣer*) would grow out of the roots of Jesse. In this case Nazareth would mean "sprout, shoot." Others relate the name to Heb. *nāṣar*, "watch," and understand it to mean "watchtower" or "guard place." This would imply that the original town was perched upon or near the brow of the hill, an idea that may be supported by Lk. 4:16-30, where Jesus is rejected by His townspeople and "led . . . to the brow of the hill on which their city was built, that they might throw him down headlong." If the same verb is taken in a passive sense, Nazareth could mean "preserved, protected" and the reference would be to the town's secluded setting.

In the NT Nazareth is best known as the boyhood home of Jesus. There Gabriel told Mary of the child she was to bear (Lk. 1:26-38). After the birth in Bethlehem it was to Nazareth that Joseph, Mary, and the Christ-child returned (2:39). Upon beginning His Galilean ministry Jesus left Nazareth to dwell in Capernaum by the sea (Mt. 4:13). He once returned to announce "the acceptable year of the Lord" and was rejected by His own townspeople (Lk. 4:16-30). The Lord was often identified as "Jesus of Nazareth" (Mk. 1:24; 10:47; Jn. 18:5, 7; etc.), and in Acts 24:5 His followers were called the "sect of the Nazarenes."

It is significant that Jesus spent His early manhood in

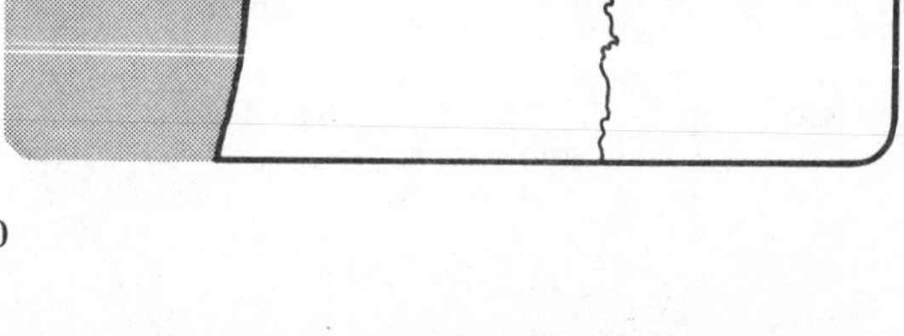

Greek Orthodox church built over the original Fountain of the Virgin in Nazareth (J. C. Trever)

a city free from the dominance of a parochial regime that would hold a strong aversion to anything foreign. "Galilee of the Gentiles" (Mt. 4:15) lent its impact to the growth of a religion destined to be universal in scope. Secluded, yet not isolated, Nazareth cradled the origin of the Christian faith.

Of the many sacred sites established by the Franciscans in Nazareth, only the Fountain of the Virgin can claim some credibility. However, many feel that this spring, situated in the center of modern Nazareth, is too remote from the ancient settlement to have served in Jesus' day. Nazareth enjoys a moderate climate and sufficient rainfall for vegetation. It began to be populated by Christians in the time of Constantine and in modern times has thousands of inhabitants, many of them Arab Christians.

*See also* NAZARENE.

***Bibliography.***–*DNTT,* II, 332-34 (K. H. Rengstorf); *EAEHL,* III, 919-922 (B. Bagatti); W. F. Albright, *JBL,* 65 (1946), 397-401; C. Kopp, *Holy Places of the Gospels* (1963), pp. 49-87.

R. H. MOUNCE

**NAZARETH DECREE.** An inscription said to have come from Nazareth, brought to Paris in 1878. Its "Ordinance of Caesar" proclaims capital punishment for violation of a grave. Since this is an unusual provision of Roman law at that time, some have taken it as an official response to reports of the resurrection of Jesus (cf. Mt. 28:13), thus as indirect evidence for His resurrection. Even assuming that the inscription is genuine, that it did come from Nazareth, and that it should be dated no later than the middle of the 1st cent., the most that can reasonably be inferred from the proclamation of such a law is evidence for a climate of opinion that would make it highly improbable that the disciples stole Jesus' body.

See *LAP,* pp. 299f. E. W. S.

**NAZIRITE** naz'ə-rīt [Heb. *nāzîr*–'consecrated one,' < *nāzar,* 'to consecrate'; cf. also *nāḏar*–'to vow'; Gk. *nazeiraíos,* plus various words indicating "holiness" or "devotion." In Nu. 6:21b, c the RSV supplies "Nazirite" (cf. AV, NEB)]; AV NAZARITE. The basic meaning of the different Hebrew and Greek terms is that of "one consecrated, a devotee."

I. Origin and Nature
II. Regulations
III. Nazirites in Scripture
IV. Later Developments

***I. Origin and Nature.***–The Nazirites were an ancient order of persons consecrated to God by means of a vow. This order was the Israelite counterpart of the votive persons commonly found in ancient Near Eastern religions. Precisely when the institution originated is unknown, but when the regulations governing the Nazirites were laid down in the time of Moses (Nu. 6:1-21) it seems possible that they were intended to normalize a tradition that was already of some antiquity, and bring it firmly within the life of the covenant community.

The role of Nazirite was that of a votary, a sacred person who was consecrated to divine service for a specific period of time as the result of a vow and as an expression of special commitment to God. The nature of this relationship was given formal legal expression in Nu. 6, and was distinctive in character on several counts. A Nazirite could be one whose vow was made for him without his knowledge or approval, as with Samuel, who was offered to God in a vow made by his mother (1 S. 1:11). It is conceivable that Hannah herself was a Nazirite, since she was familiar with the general prescriptions, but the narrative does not mention her in such a capacity. Another involuntary Nazirite was Samson (Jgs. 13:3-5), who was proclaimed a person consecrated to God according to Nazirite tradition in an annunciation.

But the Nazirite could also enter into a relationship with God in full awareness of what would be involved. Some scholars (e.g., G. B. Gray, comm. on Numbers [*ICC,* 1903], pp. 57-61) have thought of an "early" Nazirite tradition, in which an individual such as Samson or Saul was pledged or pledged himself in a lifelong charismatic dedication, as contrasted with a "late" tradition, represented for them by the Numbers regulations, where the commitment was of a temporary nature. Others (e.g., Eichrodt; cf. de Vaux) have developed the idea of different traditions by positing an early Nazirite tradition not only of lifelong service but also of dedication to holy war. Thus the Samson narratives do not mention the prohibition about contact with corpses, and Samson had a great deal of such contact in his exploits. Those who assign an early date to the enactments in Numbers find the distinction between "early" and "late" Nazirite traditions unsupported by the text. The nature of the Nazirite vocation was consistently that of a distinctive, holy person who had dedicated himself to divine service and in return received certain spiritual endowments. Some scholars have related the separateness (*n^ezîr*) of Joseph (Gen. 49:26; Dt. 33:16, AV) to the office of a prince (cf. Dt. 33:16; cf. also Gen. 49:26, NEB) as one eminent among his brethren (cf. Lam. 4:7, AV, NEB mg.). But aside from the fact of separation by virtue of position the other distinctive characteristics of the Nazirite are lacking. Finally, God "raised up" the Nazirites in a way that was not true of Israelite nobility or princes (Am. 2:11f.; note that here the Nazirites parallel the prophets, thus indicating the importance of the Nazirites to Israelite religion).

***II. Regulations.***–Basic to the Nazirite's status was the vow, which when made voluntarily was probably marked by a ceremony of dedication that included a consecrated offering (cf. Nu. 6:2, New King James Version). This marked the point of separation, which itself had two aspects, one "to the Lord," implying a definite spiritual relationship that may not have been particularly observable in others, while the second separated the Nazirite from certain contemporary customs and attitudes. He was to abstain from the fruit of the vine in any form, a prohibition that worked some hardship in a land where clean water was scarce and fermented drinks were the normal adult beverage. Yet this regulation alone made for distinctiveness in a cultural environment where alcoholism was an extremely serious social problem, and could leave no doubt as to the status of the Nazirite. It also recaptured the stern life-style followed by the desert nomads of the wilderness period, and contrasted it forcibly with the far less rigorous sedentary life in Canaan, with its attendant moral temptations.

Equally distinctive was the prohibition against shaving or cutting the hair during the period of the vow (Nu. 6:5). The Nazirite's life was to be analagous to that of the unpruned vine (*nāzîr*) of Lev. 25:11; the vine was deliberately left untended for the first few years of its life so that thereafter its fruit would be mature. The Nazirite's entire body, including the hair, belonged to God, and if the hair remained untrimmed it would serve as a witness against any who shaved the head in the service of pagan deities.

The priestly nature of the Nazirite's witness was indicated by regulations forbidding consumption of unclean food (Jgs. 13:7) and contact with a corpse (Nu. 6:6f.), because of its defiling nature. Such a prohibition also applied to Aaron and his descendants (Lev. 21:1), except that they were excused when the deceased was a close relative. The Nazirite, like the high priest of Israel, was to be consecrated to God and serve as an example of a strict, obedient life of the kind demanded by the Sinai covenant. If the Nazirite became accidentally defiled by a dead person, he had to shave his hair off and make an offering to God to remove the defilement. Then if he so desired he could undertake an entirely fresh vow of consecration and separation.

When the period of a voluntary vow had ended, the Nazirite brought an offering to the door of the tabernacle and the sacrifice was performed by the priest. At that time the Nazirite's hair was shorn and burned, signifying publicly the termination of the vow (Nu. 6:13-20).

*III. Nazirites in Scripture.*–In the OT the only lifelong Nazirites mentioned were Samson and Samuel. Whereas the former was especially designated in this way by an angel from God (Jgs. 13:7), a commitment that was subsequently acknowledged by Samson himself (Jgs. 16:17), Samuel was nowhere mentioned in the MT as a Nazirite. In a fragmentary recension of 1 Samuel recovered from 4Q, the phrase "he shall be a *nāzîr* for ever" had been omitted from the Hebrew of 1 S. 1:22, due to haplography (F. M. Cross, *BASOR,* 132 [Dec. 1953], 15ff.). In the Hebrew recension of Sir. 46:13, discovered in the Ezra synagogue in Cairo in 1897, Samuel was described as a "Nazirite of God."

In the NT John the Baptist was the most outstanding example of a Nazirite, and may well have begun a fashion that other ascetic Christians emulated. While Jesus was a Nazarean (i.e., from Nazareth, Mt. 2:23) He was not a Nazirite, and as such He contrasted Himself to John (Mt. 11:18f.). Paul had evidently taken a Nazirite's vow which he began to terminate at Cenchreae by cutting off his hair (Acts 18:18), and which was completed formally in Jerusalem with other Christians under Nazirite vows (Acts 21:23f.).

*IV. Later Developments.*–By the NT period the Nazirite tradition was probably being encouraged in some areas of Essene life. According to Eusebius (*HE* ii.23.3) James the brother of Christ seemed to belong to a Nazirite group, as did a certain Bannus, tutor of Josephus, who was probably the Buni mentioned in T.B. *Sanhedrin* 43a as a disciple of Jesus. The vow taken by the immoral Bernice, the sister-wife of Herod Agrippa II (Acts 25:13), was apparently Nazirite in character (cf. Josephus *BJ* ii.15.1 [313f.]). Josephus also recorded that on his return from Rome Agrippa was a benefactor to some Nazirites seeking release from their vows (*Ant.* xix.6.1 [294]). In the Mishnah the burning of the hair was recognized as an offering to God (*Nazir* iv.7; this entire tractate deals with the Nazirite vow).

*Bibliography.*–W. Eichrodt, *Theology of the OT,* I (Eng. tr. 1961), 303-306; R. de Vaux, *Ancient Israel* (Eng. tr. 1961), pp. 466f.

R. K. HARRISON

**NEAH** nē'ə [Heb. *nē'â*]. A city on the boundary of the territory in Lower Galilee that Joshua allotted to the tribe of Zebulun (Josh. 19:13). It is listed between Rimmon and Hannathon. The exact location has not been established, but modern Tell el-Wâwiyât and Nimrin have been suggested.

D. H. MADVIG

**NEAPOLIS** nē-ap'ō-lis [Gk. *Nea pólis* or *Neapolis*] (Acts 16:11). The seaport of the city of Philippi on the north coast of the Aegean Sea.

From Neapolis Paul launched his second missionary journey to Europe after he had a vision of a man from Macedonia (Acts 16:11). He probably passed through the town again on his third missionary journey (20:1) and certainly embarked there on his last voyage to Troas (v. 6).

The harbor area at Kavalla (ancient Neapolis), with sailing vessels drawn up on the sands and the Roman aqueduct in the background (W. S. LaSor)

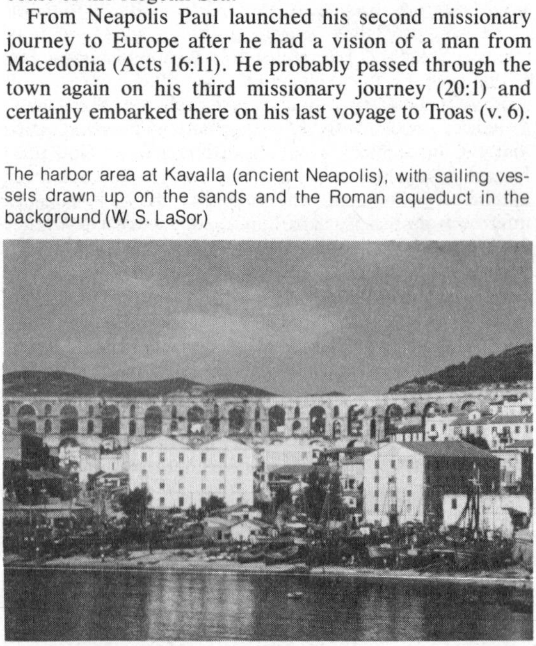

Neapolis was about 16 km. (10 mi.) SE of Philippi and was beautifully situated on a promontory that stretched out into the north Aegean. It had a harbor on either side; at the better one on the west the galleys of Brutus and Cassius were moored during the battle of Philippi in 42 B.C. Although its location was once in doubt, Neapolis is now quite conclusively known to be covered by the modern town of Kavalla (see J. Finegan, *Archeology of the NT: The Mediterranean World of the Early Christian Apostles* [1981], pp. 100f.).

A member state of both the Athenian Empire (5th cent. B.C.) and the Second Athenian Confederacy (4th cent.), Neapolis later passed under the control of Macedonia and at the time of Paul was part of the Roman province of Macedonia. As a result of the success of the gospel in the area, the town was known as "Christopolis" in the early centuries of the Christian era. The only significant ruin at Kavalla that dates back to Roman times is an aqueduct. *See* Plate 62. H. F. VOS

**NEAR.** A term used by the English versions (AV often "nigh") to denote closeness or proximity of various kinds.

In the OT "near" as an adverb usually translates Heb. *qārôḇ*. Frequently it denotes spatial proximity; e.g., the angel of the Lord tells Lot that a city is "near enough to flee to" (Gen. 19:20). It can also signify temporal imminence; e.g., the prophets (Isa. 13:6; Ezk. 30:3; Joel 1:15; 2:1; 3:14 [MT 4:14]; Ob. 15; Zeph. 1:14) proclaimed that "the day of the Lord is near" (see also below). Sometimes it denotes closeness in a kinship relationship (e.g., Lev. 21:3; cf. "nearer," Ruth 3:12). A close blood relationship can also be signified by *šᵉʾēr* (lit. "flesh, body"; e.g., *šᵉʾēr bᵉśārô,* "near of kin," Lev. 18:6; cf. 18:12f.; 20:19; 25:45). In Ruth 3:12 "near kinsman" renders *gōʾēl* (lit. "redeemer"). (*See also* KIN.)

The expression "draw near" (or "come near") is usually the translation of Heb. *qāraḇ* or the virtually synonymous *nāgaš*. Both verbs are used frequently of approaching a person or object, e.g., coming close enough to speak to (*nāgaš,* Gen. 18:23) or even to touch (27:21f.; *qāraḇ,* Lev. 10:4f.) someone. In military contexts to "draw near" can signify approaching or entering into battle with an enemy (e.g., *qāraḇ,* Dt. 2:37; 20:2f.; *nāgaš,* 1 S. 7:10; 17:40f., 48). To "come near" (*qāraḇ,* Dt. 22:14; cf. "go near," *nāgaš,* Ex. 19:15) can also be a euphemism for sexual relations.

Of more significance is the way these verbs are used in relation to God. Because of God's HOLINESS and mankind's sin there is a great distance between God and humanity. To a human being, therefore, it is an awesome thing to "draw near" to God (cf. Ex. 3:5). At Sinai only Moses was able to ascend the mountain to meet God; the people of Israel "stood afar off" (Ex. 20:21; cf. 24:2). Only the consecrated priests could go near the altar (e.g., 28:43; 30:20; Lev. 9:7; cf. Nu. 3:10, 38; etc.). Yet the OT saints also confess that God draws near to His people (e.g., Ps. 119:151; 145:18; cf. 34:18 [MT 19]; 69:18 [MT 19]; 73:28; Isa. 50:8; 55:6; Lam. 3:57; cf. also in the NT the teaching of Jas. 4:8, which shows both dimensions: "Draw near to God and he will draw near to you").

The NT uses "near" in much the same way as the OT. The most common adverb, Gk. *engýs* (the usual LXX translation of Heb. *qārôḇ*), can denote either spatial proximity (e.g., Lk. 19:11; Jn. 11:38) or temporal imminence (e.g., Mt. 24:32 par.). "Draw near" is used to translate the verbs *engízō* (e.g., Mt. 21:1, 34) and *prosérchomai* (Acts 7:31; He. 4:16; etc.).

The NT presents the work of Christ against the background of the OT's teaching about mankind's alienation from God. Through Christ's blood Gentiles as well as Jews have been brought near to God (*engýs,* Eph. 2:13; cf. vv. 17f.). Therefore, because Jesus through His sacrifice has broken down the barrier between God and mankind, and because as high priest He intercedes for His people, believers can now draw near to God with confidence (*prosérchomai,* He. 4:16; 7:25; 10:22).

In some NT passages *engýs* and *engízō* are used in an eschatological sense to point to the imminence of the day of judgment and salvation promised through the OT prophets (see above; cf. also Isa. 51:5; Ezk. 7:7, 12). In the coming of Jesus, God's kingdom was already present; thus Jesus instructed His disciples to announce that "the kingdom of God has come near" (Lk. 10:9, 11). But the consummation of the kingdom still lies in the future, and the imminence of that day provides the basis for exhortations to a life of readiness and hope (e.g., Rom. 13:11; He. 10:25; Rev. 1:3; 22:10).

*See also* KINGDOM OF GOD V; PAROUSIA III.C, D; PRESENCE OF GOD.

*Bibliography.*–*DNTT,* II, 53-55; *TDNT,* II, *s.v.* ἐγγύς κτλ. (H. Preisker); *TWOT,* II, 553f., 811f.

P. L. BREMER N. J. O.

**NEARIAH** nē-ər-ī'ə [Heb. *nᵉʿaryâ*–'squire (or servant) of Yahweh'].

**1.** Son of Shemaiah; a descendant of David (1 Ch. 3:22f.).

**2.** Son of Ishi; a Simeonite who led in defeating the Amalekites in the time of King Hezekiah (1 Ch. 4:42).

**NEBAI** nē'bī [Heb. *K nôḇāy, Q nêḇāy*] (Neh. 10:19 [MT 20]). One of the "chiefs of the people" who signed the covenant with Nehemiah.

**NEBAIOTH** nə-bā'yoth, nə-bī'yoth [Heb. *nᵉḇāyōṯ, nᵉḇāyôṯ*; Gk. *Nabaiōth*]; AV also NEBAJOTH. The first-born son of Ishmael, and the chief of an Arabic tribe named after him (Gen. 25:13; 28:9; 36:3; 1 Ch. 1:29). The tribes of Nebaioth and his brother KEDAR were apparently renowned for sheep-raising in the time of Isaiah (Isa. 60:7). Nebaioth and Kedar are often mentioned together in Assyrian inscriptions (e.g., cf. "Nabaiati" and "Qedar" in *ANET,* pp. 298-300). They were apparently two of the most prominent tribes in northwest Arabia. Many scholars formerly identified Nebaioth with the NABATEANS; but the fact that the former is spelled with a Heb. *t* and the latter with a *ṭ* makes this theory unacceptable.

A. S. FULTON N. J. O.

**NEBALLAT** nə-bal'ət [Heb. *nᵉḇallaṭ* (Neh. 11:34); possibly from Akk. *Nabu-uballiṭ,* considered to be an Assyrian governor of Samaria in the 7th cent. B.C. (*IDB,* III, 528)]. A town of postexilic Benjamin in the northern Shephelah, named in a list (Neh. 11:31-35) just before Lod. It has been identified with Beit Nabala (Khirbet Nevallat), 7 km. (4 mi.) NE of Lod (*GTTOT,* §§ 1090, 1095 [p. 395]).

W. S. L. S.

**NEBAT** nē'bat [Heb. *nᵉḇāṭ*]. The father of Jeroboam (1 K. 11:26, and frequently elsewhere in 1 Kings, 2 Kings, and 2 Chronicles). The name occurs only in the phrase "Jeroboam the son of Nebat," and is evidently intended to distinguish Jeroboam I from the later son of Joash.

**NEBO** nē'bō [Heb. *nᵉḇô* < Akk. *Nabû*].

**1.** One of the two principal gods of the later Babylonian pantheon, mentioned with Marduk (Bel) in Isa. 46:1: "Bel bows down, Nebo stoops, their idols are on beasts and cattle," an ironic allusion to the New Year (*Akitu*) procession in which the image of Nabu was brought to Babylon from his temple, Ezida, in Borsippa. Considered the son of Marduk, keeper of the tablets of the gods, and a patron of learning and the scribal art, Nabu began in the 2nd millennium (e.g., with Nebuchadrezzar I, 1125 B.C.) to supersede older Sumerian gods in many theophoric names, including the names of three of the six rulers of the Neo-Babylonian Empire (625-539 B.C.), Nabopolassar, Nebuchadrezzar, and Nabonidus. Cited in the Bible are NEBUCHADREZZAR and his officers NEBUZARADAN and NEBUSHAZBAN. ABEDNEGO may well be an altered name meaning "servant of Nabu." The Neo-Babylonian kings described themselves as "beloved of Marduk and Nabu," an encomium also affirmed by Cyrus when he entered Babylon in 539 B.C.

*Bibliography.*–H. W. F. Saggs, *The Greatness that was Babylon* (1962), pp. 342, 385-87; *ANET,* pp. 315f., 331-34.

P. W. GAEBELEIN, JR.

**2.** [Heb. *nᵉḇô* (Ezr. 10:43); Gk. *Nabou, Nooma* (1 Esd. 9:35)]; AV also ETHMA (1 Esd. 9:35); NEB also NOOMA (1 Esd. 9:35). One of the faithful Jews who put away their foreign wives.

**NEBO** nē'bō [Heb. *nᵉḇô*].

**1.** A town in Moab assigned to the tribe of Reuben (Nu. 32:3) and occupied by Bela (1 Ch. 5:8). Nu. 32:3 lists it between Sebam and Beon (taken by some to be Baal-meon) and in 32:38 after Heshbon and Elealeh. Isa. 15:2 names it with Medeba. Jeremiah joins it with Kiriathaim (Jer. 48:2) and mentions it between Dibon and Beth-diblathaim (v. 22). Mesha king of Moab claimed that he captured it, killed its inhabitants, and dedicated it to Ashtar-Chemosh (Moabite Stone, lines 14-18). Jerome said that it was the site of an idol of Chemosh (comm. on Isa. 15:2).

Eusebius (*Onom.* 136.12) located Nebo 8 Roman mi. (about 11 km. [7 mi.]) S of Heshbon, but modern scholars tend to identify it with Khirbet el-Mekhaiyeṭ, about 8 km. (5 mi.) SW of Ḥesbân (Heshbon). Cf. *AASOR,* 15 (1935), 110f.

*Bibliography.*–M. Piccirillo, *Liber Annuus,* 23 (1973), 332-358; S. Saller, *Liber Annuus,* 16 (1966), 164-298; 17 (1967), 5-64; S. Saller and B. Bagatti, *The Town of Nebo (Khirbet el-Mekhayyat)* (1949).

**2.** A place in Judah mentioned after Bethel and Ai in the account of the return of the exiles (Ezr. 2:29 par. Neh. 7:33). Grollenberg (*GAB*) identified it with Nûbā NW of Bethzur. *WHAB* locates it near Aijalon, which fits the context better. Abel, following Conder, argued that a site near Khirbet Qilā (Keilah), i.e., NW of Beth-zur, fits the context, but he attempted to identify Elam, Harim, and Magbish as places, whereas the text identifies them as persons (*GP,* II, 398). W. S. L. S.

**NEBO, MOUNT** [Heb. *har-nᵉḇô*]. The mountain from which Moses saw the Promised Land and where he died.

In the Bible this name occurs twice (Dt. 32:49; 34:1). In the first passage Mt. Nebo is said to be in the Abarim mountains; in the second it is called the headland of PISGAH. Today Mt. Nebo is identified with a headland called Râs es-Siâghah, 10 km. (6 mi.) NW of the town of Mâdebā (Medeba) in East Jordan. This headland forms the western extremity of a ridge that is an extension of the plateau more to the east. The ridge could represent Pisgah; it and the neighboring ridges could represent the Abarim Mountains. Dolmens and menhirs, along with flint tools, attest that the ridges wre inhabited in remote antiquity. Two tombs of the Early Bronze Age III (3rd millennium B.C.) and one of the Middle Bronze II (2nd millennium B.C.) have been found in the vicinity. Near the foot of the northern slope of the ridge are several springs that supply

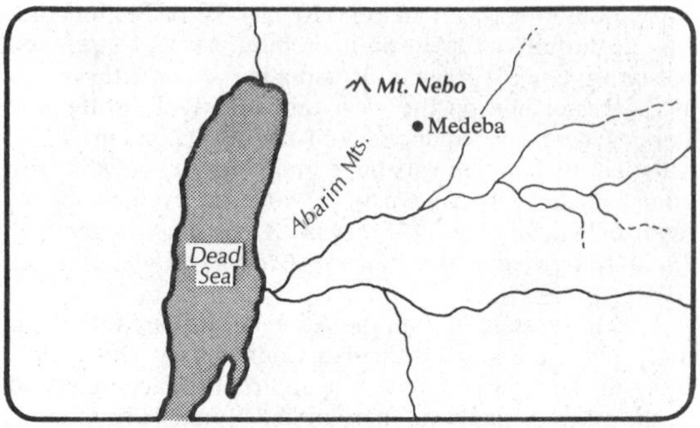


water not only to the fields to the west but also to the town of Mâdebā to the southeast. These springs are called ʿAyun Mûsā, the springs of Moses; the name of Moses is applied also to the wadi on the west, a ruin on the north, and the ridge and headland with its ruin on the south. They thus serve to keep alive the memory of Moses.

The chief events in Moses' career commemorated there were his view of the Promised Land, his death, and his burial. The vision of Moses is described in Dt. 34:1-4 and his death is reported in v. 5. His burial is described in v. 6 as follows: "He was buried in a valley in Moab opposite Beth-peor, but to this day no one knows his burial place" (NEB). Beth-peor, according to O. Henke (*ZDPV,* 75 [1959], 155-163), must be identified with Khirbet ʿAyun Mûsā, the only site in the region that can satisfy the requirements of the biblical text. In this case the "valley" would be Wâdī ʿAyun Mûsā. Thus the approximate location of the burial place of Moses was known but not its precise position.

In Byzantine times, however, the tomb was pointed out to pilgrims. Noteworthy among those pilgrims was Etheria (or Egeria), an abbess, and Peter the Iberian, a bishop. Egeria visited this region toward the end of the 4th cent. A.D. The hermits of ʿAyun Mûsā conducted her to a small church on the top of Mt. Nebo. Near the pulpit of the church a monument, which was a little higher than the pulpit, attracted her attention. When she asked what that monument was, she was told that it was the tomb of Moses. When she protested that according to the Bible no one knew where that tomb was, she was told that the hermits had this information from their forebears. Outside the church the hermits pointed out all the places that were visible from there.

Peter the Iberian visited Mt. Nebo twice in the 5th cent. A.D. He and his companions were informed that the large church that they saw stood over the cave in which Moses was buried. This fact had been revealed to a shepherd from the nearby town of Nebo. He reported his vision to his fellow citizens, who believed the story and on that account erected the church there. Around the church the pilgrims saw extensive monastic buildings. These remained in use until about the 8th cent., when they were abandoned and fell into ruins.

Mt. Nebo with its ruins was acquired by the Custody of the Holy Land in 1932. In 1933, 1935, and 1937 the ruins were thoroughly explored by the archeologists of the Franciscan Biblical Institute under the direction of Fr. Sylvester Saller. The excavations brought to light an extensive Byzantine monastic complex, which had developed around a sanctuary constructed on the highest point of the eastern summit of Siâghah. The archeologists focused their attention on this sanctuary so as to gain a more comprehensive view of its history. Their excavations clarified the last period of the sanctuary as well as of the

General view (looking east) of the basilica, showing the Presbytery (center rear), baptistery (right rear), Theotokos chapel (right front), and diakonikon-baptistery (left) (M. Piccirillo)

Mosaic floor of the baptistery chapel (6th-7th cent. A.D.) (M. Piccirillo)

Mosaic floor of the Theotokos chapel (6th-7th cent. A.D.)
(M. Piccirillo)

monastery. The inscriptions of the mosaic floors, which still remained in the presbytery and in the side chapels, constituted a source of primary importance for the history of the Medeba bishopric and of the Medeba School of mosaics. Likewise, the pottery found in the monastery proved particularly useful for the knowledge of Byzantine pottery in Jordan. A platform found near the pulpit, on the eastern end of the southern aisle, was identified as part of the memorial of Moses seen by the pilgrims.

New data on the history of the sanctuary were added during the 1960's when the Superiors of the Custody of the Holy Land decided to cover the ruins of the basilica in order to begin the restoration of the mosaic floors. Fr. V. Corbo removed the mosaics of the Presbytery (area I), southern aisle (area II), baptistery (area III), and Theotokos chapel (area IV), and then excavated and examined the area down to bedrock.

In 1976-1978 the removal of the mosaics in the northern aisle (area V) and in the northern hall (area VI-VII-VIII) enabled Fr. M. Piccirillo to find the ancient diakonikon of the sanctuary, which served also as a baptistery, decorated in A.D. 531 by Soelos, Kayomos, and Elia with a splendid mosaic floor.

At the conclusion of archeological research in the basilica in 1978, the following tentative reconstruction of the history of the monument was made. In Phase I, around the first half of the 4th cent. A.D., a three-apsed monument, a *cella trichora* (possibly a mausoleum) was built on the highest spot of Siâghah. It was used for funeral purposes, if not originally then at least at a later time, perhaps after its violent destruction. In Phase II Christian monks readapted the cella trichora into a church with adjoined synthronon in the central apse, while reusing the two lateral apses as sacristies. To this reconstruction are to be connected the atrium and two funeral chapels on either side. It was in this church that the monks showed the "tomb of Moses" to Egeria. In Phase IIa a diakonikon-baptistery was added on the northern slope of the mountain. In August A.D. 531 the restoration and beautification of the diakonikon took place. On the southern slope, the funeral chapel was changed into a new room, itself decorated with a new mosaic floor. In Phase III, from the middle of the 6th cent. to the first years of the 7th, the sanctuary under went complete reconstruction. The atrium of the 4th century church was destroyed and the new three-nave basilica was built with its atrium extending toward the west. Subsequently the rooms and chapels to the north and south were dismantled and their floor raised to the floor level of the basilica. A long diakonikon was erected to the north, while to the south a baptistery chapel and a Theotokos chapel were the last features added to the basilica in 587/588 and in the first years of the 7th century.

***Bibliography.***–B. Bagatti, *EAEHL,* III, *s.v.;* V. Corbo, *Liber Annuus,* 17 (1967), 241-258; 20 (1970), 272-297; M. Piccirillo, *Liber Annuus,* 26 (1976), 281-318; S. Saller, *The Memorial of Moses on Mount Nebo,* Part I: The Text, Part II: The Plates (1941); H. Schneider, *The Memorial of Moses on Mount Nebo,* Part III: The Pottery (1950); S. Yonick, *Liber Annuus,* 17 (1967), 162-221.

S. J. SALLER M. PICCIRILLO

**NEBUCHADREZZAR** neb-ə-kə-drez'ər, neb-yo͞o-kə-drez'ər; **NEBUCHADNEZZAR** neb-ə-kəd-nez'ər, neb-yo͞o-kəd-nez'ər [Heb. *n$^e$ḇûḵaḏre'ṣṣar, n$^e$ḇûḵaḏne'ṣṣar* < Akk. *nabû-kudurri-uṣur*–'Nabu has guarded my boundary-stone' or 'May Nabu protect . . .' or '. . . the accession-rights'; Gk. *Nabouchodonosor*]. King of Babylon (605-562 B.C.) and conqueror of Jerusalem.

I. Forms of the Name
II. Historical Sketch
III. Biblical Significance
  A. Historical
  B. Apocalyptic

***I. Forms of the Name.***–The form *n$^e$ḇûḵaḏre'ṣṣar* (and its variants), with an *r,* occurs thirty-three times in the OT — twenty-nine times in Jeremiah, four times in Ezekiel. The form *n$^e$ḇûḵaḏne'ṣṣar* (and its variants), with an *n,* occurs fifty-eight times — thirty-two times in Daniel and otherwise in Kings, Chronicles, Ezra, Nehemiah, Esther, and Jeremiah. On the basis of the Akkadian, the form with *r* is generally preferred. The theory that the form with *n* comes from Aramaic is perhaps to be rejected, since the illustration usually given (Ben/Bar Hadad) has *r* in the Aramaic form. Another theory, that "Nebuchadnezzar" arises from an Aramaic word that translates Akk. *kudurri,* is specious. The LXX supports the form with *n* and is followed by the Vulgate; these versions are late, however, and do not provide evidence contemporary with the prophets. The form used by Josephus is that of the LXX. Possibly the *n/r* shift is dialectal, but this explanation is made questionable by occurrences of both forms in one book, Jeremiah (chs. 27–29 only). Since Jeremiah and Ezekiel are unquestionably from the time of the king, their evidence may be stronger — but the evidence of Daniel and of Jer. 27–29 is not to be brushed aside lightly.

***II. Historical Sketch.***–Nebuchadrezzar, frequently called "king of Babylon" in the OT, was the son of Nabopolassar (a usurper of the throne). His sons were Awîl-Marduk

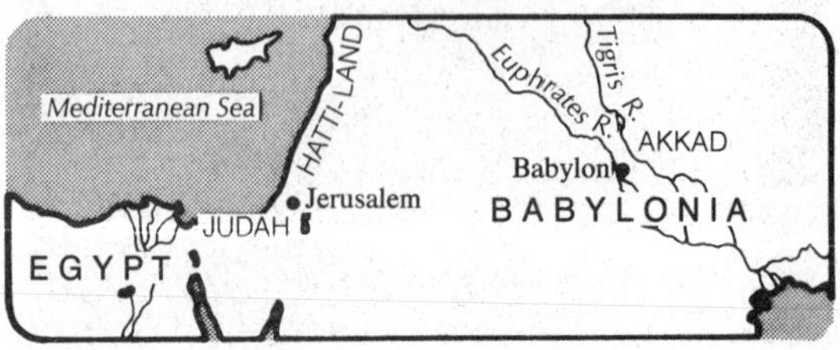

(Evil-merodach; the later spelling Amēl-Marduk is orthographic, not phonetic, as the Hebrew form indicates), Marduk-šum-uṣur, and Marduk-nadin-aḫi, and his wife was Amytis, the daughter of Astyages king of Media. Knowledge about Nebuchadrezzar comes from a number of sources: about five hundred contracts dated variously to forty-three years of his reign, about thirty inscriptions, the biblical books mentioned above, and the authors Berossus, Menander of Ephesus, Megasthenes, Abydenus, and Alexander Polyhistor, who are known mostly from citations in Josephus and Eusebius. Most important for chronology, however, are the tablets published in *CCK*. Records from the eleventh to forty-third years of the reign of Nebuchadrezzar are almost entirely lacking, however, except for fragments of an inscription dated in the thirty-seventh year.

Nebuchadrezzar II — so designated to distinguish him from Nebuchadrezzar I (1112-1103) and from the pretenders Nebuchadrezzar III (Nidintu-Bēl, who reigned three months in 522) and Nebuchadrezzar IV (Arakha, who reigned from Aug. to Nov., 521) — acceded to the throne when his father died in 605. In Nabopolassar's nineteenth regnal year (607) in the month of Siwanu he and the crown prince had led an expedition against mountain tribes (*CCK*, pp. 64-67). The father in his twenty-first year (605) remained in Babylon, probably because of failing health, and the army under Nebuchadrezzar engaged the Egyptians at Carchemish. The Egyptians were badly beaten, and Nebuchadrezzar proceeded to conquer Ḫatti-land (Syria and Palestine; *CCK*, pp. 66-75; cf. Josephus *Ant*. x.6.1 [84-86]). On 8 Abu (Aug. 15) Nabopolassar died, and when Nebuchadrezzar received the news, he hurried back to secure his claim, ascending the throne on 1 Elul (Sept. 7), 605. Following the custom of his predecessors he counted this his "accession year" (MU.SAG; *CCK*, pp. 68f.); the first year of his reign commenced when he "took the hands" of the gods Bel and Bel's son on 1 Nisanu (Apr. 2, 604; lines 14f.). According to lines 13f. Nebuchadrezzar returned to Ḫatti-land in his accession year "until the month of Shabatu" (Feb. 2–Mar. 2, 604) and took "heavy tribute."

In his first year Nebuchadrezzar again invaded Ḫatti-land in Siwanu (May-June), receiving heavy tribute from "all the kings" and sacking Ashkelon in Kisliwu (Nov.-Dec.). According to his chronicle he "turned the city into a mound and heaps of ruins" and returned to Babylon in Shabatu (Jan. 23–Feb. 20, 603). In his second, third, and fourth years Nebuchadrezzar conducted campaigns in Ḫatti-land. The significance of these data for biblical studies will be mentioned below.

Foundations of the Hanging Gardens. According to classical sources, Nebuchadrezzar II designed the gardens as a series of terraces supported by arches to remind his bride Amyitis of her former home in mountainous Media (J. Finegan)

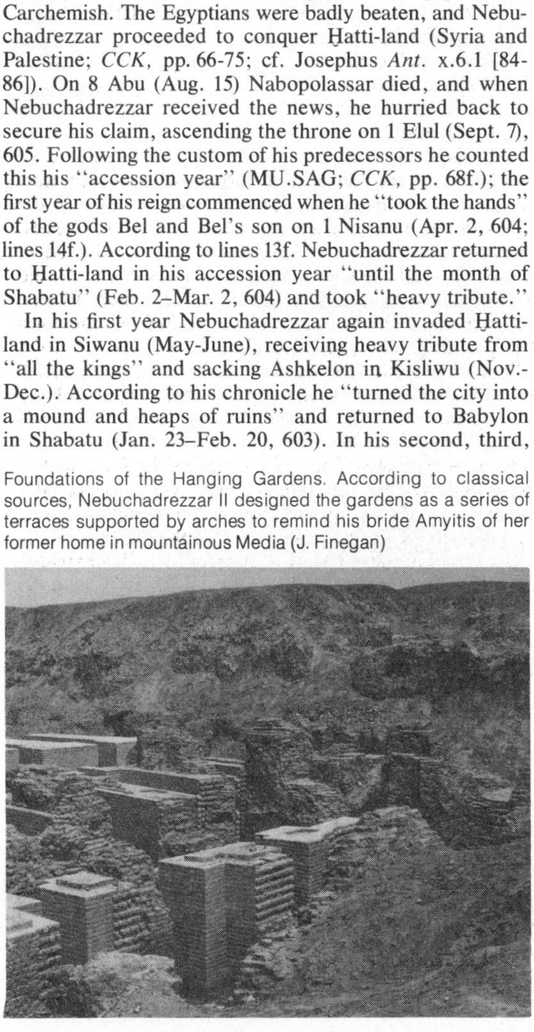

The campaign in the fourth year (Kisliwu, early Dec., 601) brought a confrontation with the Egyptian forces. The chronicle reports that they "inflicted great havoc on each other" (reverse, line 7), and as a result Nebuchadrezzar spent his fifth year at home rebuilding his army (reverse, line 8). Jehoiakim had been placed on the throne of Judah by Pharaoh Neco in 608. 2 K. 24:1 states: "Nebuchadnezzar . . . came up, and Jehoiakim became his servant three years; then he turned and rebelled against him." It is reasonable to assume that this revolt took place soon after the battle with Egypt (cf. Josephus *Ant*. x.6.2 [88]). In his sixth year Nebuchadrezzar was in Ḫatti-land from Kisliwu (Nov.–Dec., 599) until Addaru (Feb.–Mar., 598), during which time he "took much plunder from the Arabs" (reverse, line 10; cf. Jer. 49:28).

In the seventh year in the month of Kisliwu (Dec., 598–Jan., 597) the king marched his troops to Ḫatti-land and "encamped against the city of Judah." After a siege of three months he took the city and captured the king (cf. 2 K. 24:10-16). He dated this event "the second day of Addaru," i.e., Mar. 15/16, 597 (not 598, as sometimes given; the author of 2 Kings, using a Tishri-Tishri year, calculated that this was Nebuchadrezzar's eighth regnal year — the first would have commenced in Tishri, 605, the beginning of Jehoiakim's fourth regnal year). Nebuchadrezzar put on the throne of Judah "a king of his heart," namely, the puppet Zedekiah (v. 17). Jehoiachin, who had succeeded his father Jehoiakim, was taken to Babylon (v. 12; 2 Ch. 36 10; Ezk. 40:1).

In his ninth year the Babylonian king seems to have had a confrontation with Akkad and Elam (reverse, lines 16-20, broken text). In the tenth year (595-594) and again in the eleventh he put down a rebellion in Akkad and also had reason to march into Ḫatti-land (reverse, lines 21-25). The Babylonian Chronicles break off at this point and do not resume until the third year of Neriglissar, 556. Nebuchadrezzar was succeeded by his son Awîl-Marduk (Evil-merodach) in early October, 562. This date is deduced from two bits of evidence: the last date formula based on the reign of Nebuchadrezzar, 26 Ululu of his forty-third year, which is found on a tablet from Uruk (modern Warka, biblical Erech); and the first date formula based on the reign of Awîl-Marduk, 26 Ululu of his accession year, found on a tablet perhaps from Sippar. Nebuchadrezzar could not have died much earlier than the latter date, i.e., Oct. 8, 562 (cf. R. A. Parker and W. H. Dubberstein, *Babylonian Chronology* [2nd ed. 1956], p. 12).

Between Nebuchadrezzar's eleventh and forty-third years a number of events must be placed. According to Josephus there was a thirteen-year siege of Tyre beginning in Nebuchadrezzar's seventh year (*CAp* i.21 [156, 159], an account probably from Menander of Ephesus; cf. Ezk. 29:18). A text published in 1882 by T. G. Pinches (*Transactions of the Society of Biblical Archaeology*, 7 [1882], 210-225) records Nebuchadrezzar's march in the thirty-seventh year of his reign against Amasis king of Egypt. According to Pinches this was an expedition to quell the revolt of Amasis (Ahmoses), who had been placed on the Egyptian throne as a Babylonian puppet after the defeat of Apries (Hophra) in 572. The many building projects in Babylon, some of which have left inscriptions, must be placed in this period (cf. Dnl. 4:30; *see* BABYLON IV). And, of course, the siege and destruction of Jerusalem occurred in this period (*see* JERUSALEM III.E).

***III. Biblical Significance.***–Since Nebuchadrezzar is named about ninety times in the OT, his importance is to be carefully evaluated. It falls biblically into two categories, the historical and the apocalyptic.

*A. Historical.* Nebuchadrezzar was the king who brought the Davidic dynasty to an end. He besieged Jerusalem, captured it, and finally destroyed it completely. He carried its last legitimate king (Jehoiachin) captive to Babylon, recognizing his royal status by providing daily rations and thus preserving his seed.

According to Dnl. 1:1-6 the Babylonian king came to Jerusalem in the third year of Jehoiakim (*see* DANIEL, BOOK OF VIII.B), besieged it, and carried off not only treasures but also members of the royal family and nobility, among whom was Daniel. It is not known what chronological system Daniel used. According to that used in 2 Kings Jehoiakim's first regnal year began in Tishri (Sept. 10), 608, and he reigned eleven years (23:36), or until 597. His third year, according to this reckoning, would have begun in Tishri, 606, and extended to Tishri, 605. It is clear that Nebuchadrezzar was still crown prince until he ascended the throne in September, 605, and it is hardly likely that he would have taken time to collect people and goods from Jerusalem when he was rushing back to Babylon to secure his throne. More reasonable, it seems, is the view that the "siege" of Jerusalem to which Daniel refers took place in 604, when the Babylonian king destroyed Ashkelon and made Jehoiakim his tributary (2 K. 24:1; cf. Jer. 47:5). Jehoiakim revolted in the third year, which coincides with the terrible beating that the Babylonians took at the hands of Egypt in Nebuchadrezzar's fourth year (Josephus *Ant.* x.6.2 [88]).

The siege to which the author of 2 Kings referred (24:10) occurred in the eighth year of Nebuchadrezzar's reign (v. 12). As pointed out above, Nebuchadrezzar's eighth regnal year by his reckoning did not begin until 1 Nisan (Apr. 13) 597, whereas according to the Tishri-Tishri year it had already begun the preceding October, which was also the start of Jehoiakim's eleventh year. Jehoiakim died and was succeeded by his son Jehoiachin (Coniah), who reigned but three months (v. 8; 2 Ch. 36:9). According to the Babylonian Chronicle, Jerusalem was taken on 2 Adar (Mar. 16); hence Jehoiachin's accession to the throne can be calculated as at the end of 598 (specifically Dec. 9, 598, if the "three months and ten days" of 2 Ch. 36:9 are taken literally). Mattaniah, son of Josiah and uncle of Jehoiachin, was put on the throne as a puppet and given the throne-name of Zedekiah (2 K. 24:17). Zedekiah's first regnal year was counted from 1 Tishri (Oct. 9) 597.

Because of Zedekiah's revolt against Babylon, in the ninth year of his reign, on the tenth day of the tenth month (Jan. 15), 588, the armies of Nebuchadrezzar laid siege to Jerusalem (2 K. 25:1; Jer. 52:4; Ezk. 24:1f.). The Egyptians apparently attempted to come to the aid of Judah (cf. Jer. 37:4f.). Ezekiel's prophecy against Pharaoh (Ezk. 29:1ff., dated Jan. 7, 587) and Jeremiah's attempt to go to the land of Benjamin (Jer. 37:11f.) are to be related to this event. On 9 Tammuz (July 18) 586 there was severe famine in Jerusalem (2 K. 25:3; Jer. 39:2). A breach was made in the walls; the Judean king and his warriors attempted to flee but were overtaken "in the plains of Jericho" (2 K. 25:5). Zedekiah was taken prisoner to Riblah (near Hamath on the Orontes), where the Babylonian king had his headquarters, and punishment was meted out (vv. 6f.; Jer. 39:4-8; 52:6-11). On 7 Ab (Aug. 12; cf. 2 K. 25:8) or 10 Ab (Aug. 15; cf. Jer. 52:12) in the nineteenth year of Nebuchadrezzar Jerusalem was burned, the walls were destroyed, and many of the people were taken captive (Jer. 52:13ff.). Gedaliah was appointed governor with his headquarters at Mizpeh (2 K. 25:22f.). He was killed by what appears to have been some of the pro-Egypt Judeans (v. 25; Jer. 41:2; cf. 40:1–43:13). Jehoiachin, the last surviving king of the Davidic dynasty, was released from prison on 27 Adar (Apr. 2) 561, "in the year that he [Evil-merodach] began to reign" (i.e., in his accession year; cf. 2 K. 25:27-30; Jer. 52:31 dates the release two days earlier).

According to Dnl. 2:1 Nebuchadrezzar's dreams occurred in his second regnal year. He built a colossal image of gold and set it up on the plain of Dura (3:1); Daniel's companions refused to worship it. The king's tree dream was fulfilled by a curious disease (sometimes identified as lycanthropy, but more accurately boanthropy) that lasted for "seven times," generally interpreted to mean seven years. Whether these data are to be taken as a record of historical events or as figures used in an apocalyptic prophecy is debatable. The disease in particular has led some scholars to conclude that the author has mistakenly identified Nabonidus, Babylon's last king and often characterized as insane, with Nebuchadrezzar.

*B. Apocalyptic.* Beyond question, Daniel is an apocalyptic work, for its stated purpose is to reveal what is to take place "in the latter days" (10:14; cf. 2:45). A characteristic of apocalypses is the use of historical and geographical names symbolically to set forth a revelation. Thus "Babylon" in Rev. 17–18 is generally interpreted to mean "Rome," but more likely it was meant to symbolize any tyrannical and satanic anti-God system. "Nebuchadrezzar" can be similarly interpreted as the splendid head of a great world kingdom that was given several opportunities to recognize the kingdom of God (and appeared to do so — but repeatedly, indicating a lack of true repentance; cf. Dnl. 2:29; 4:34-37 [MT 31-34]; likewise Darius, 6:26-28 [MT 27-29]). This interpretation is not a rejection of the historicity of Daniel; it is rather a recognition that the author's dreams and visions were God-given revelations, in the form of apocalyptic, of what would take place concerning the people of God, and in particular the establishment of the kingdom of God (cf. W. S. LaSor, D. A. Hubbard, and F. W. Bush, *OT Survey* [1982], ch. 51). In the days of the great king Nebuchadrezzar, who is portrayed as the head of gold (2:38), was foretold the end of man-made governments and the advent of the kingdom that God will establish and that will never be destroyed (v. 44).

***Bibliography.***–D. J. Wiseman, *CCK; Assyria and Babylonia, ca. 1200-1000 B.C.* (1965), pp. 14-17; Josephus *Ant.* x.6.1–11.1 (84-228); *CAp* i.19-21 (131-160).

W. S. LASOR

**NEBUSHAZBAN** neb-ə-shaz'ban [Heb. *nᵉḇûšazbān*; Akk. *Nabû-šûzibanni*–'Nabû, deliver me']; AV NEBUSHASBAN. A high Babylonian military or diplomatic officer (the RABSARIS) who, with other chief officers of King Nebuchadrezzar, was appointed to protect Jeremiah after the taking of Jerusalem (Jer. 39:13).

**NEBUZARADAN** neb'ə-zär-ā'dən, -zär'ə-dan [Heb. *nᵉḇûzarʾᵃḏān*; Akk. *Nabû-zēr-iddin*–'Nabû has given offspring']. A senior officer of Nebuchadrezzar's army, who destroyed Jerusalem after the siege of 586 B.C. (2 K. 25:8-10; Jer. 52:12-14) and carried out his orders concerning the deportation of exiles (2 K. 25:11f., 18-21; Jer. 39:9f.; 52:15f., 24-27; cf. 41:10; 43:6) and the safety of Jeremiah (39:11-14; 40:1-5). He returned to Jerusalem some four years later (52:30) to deport a further 745 Judeans to Babylonia. His title, *raḇ ṭabbāḥîm* (RSV "captain of the guard"), perhaps means "chief executioner" (cf. *ṭāḇah*, "slaughter [for sacrifice]"; *tabbāḥ*, "cook," "butcher"); it was comparable to that bestowed on high court officials in Egypt (Gen. 37:36) and Babylonia (Dnl. 2:14); *see also* CAPTAIN; GUARD.

R. K. H.

**NECHO; NECHOH.** *See* NECO.

**NECK** [Heb. *ṣawwā'r, 'ōrep̱, 'ārap, gārôn* (Isa. 3:16; Ezk. 16:11), *gargārōṯ* (Prov. 1:9; 3:3, 22; 6:21), *mapreqeṯ* (1 S. 4:18); Aram. *ṣawwa'r* (Dnl. 5:7, 16, 29); Gk. *tráchēlos*]; NEB also STUBBORN, OBSTINATE. The Hebrews' choice of word for "neck" apparently depended upon which of its physical aspects they wished to emphasize. *Mapreqeṯ* (<*pāraq,* "break off, split," perhaps denoting the neck as what separates or splits the head from the body trunk) seems to describe the upper spinal column, which if fractured, can cause sudden death (1 S. 4:18). The verb *'ārap* means "break the neck" and is used in sacrificial connections (Ex. 13:13; 34:20; Dt. 21:4; Isa. 66:3). The related noun *'ōrep̱,* "neck," apparently refers to the neck's rigid, skeletal structure (which can be broken; see Lev. 5:8; Job 16:12; cf. Prov. 29:1). *'Ōrep̱* is used in eight of its twelve occurrences in the metaphor "stiffened his neck" (i.e., refused to obey), which the NEB translates "be stubborn, obstinate" (cf. 2 Ch. 36:13; Neh. 9:16f., 29; Prov. 29:1; Isa. 48:4; Jer. 7:26; 17:23; 19:15). *Gārôn,* "throat" usually refers to the organs of swallowing or speaking (cf. Ps. 5:9 [MT 10]; 69:3 [MT 4]; 115:7; 149:6; Isa. 58:1; Jer. 2:25) and apparently also to the front of the neck. One pictures the daughters of Zion (Isa. 3:16) with heads not only lifted but haughtily tilted back, exposing the throat. Perhaps more appropriate for the external neck is the related *gargārōṯ,* used only in Prov. 1:9; 3:3, 22; 6:21, which liken certain virtues to ornaments hung around the neck.

The common word for neck is *ṣawwā'r,* which means "the back of the neck" (BDB, p. 848), and has a number of associations. It is used of an embrace — "he fell on his neck (and wept)" — especially in Genesis (33:4; 45:14; 46:29). It suggests strength, beauty (Job 39:19; 41:22; Cant. 4:4; 7:4), or resolve (Neh. 3:5). The *ṣawwā'r* is adorned with jewels, collars, and chains (Gen. 41:42; Jgs. 5:30; 8:21, 26; Cant. 1:10; cf. Aram. *ṣawwa'r* in Dnl. 5:7, 16, 29). It dramatizes vulnerability to the sword (Ezk. 21:29) and to drowning (e.g., Isa. 8:8, "[the waters] will overflow and pass on, reaching even to the neck" [cf. 30:28; Ps. 69:1, where *nep̱eš,* "soul," is translated "neck"]). In Mt. 18:6 par. Jesus said that it is better to be drowned with a millstone around one's neck than to make children sin. Military victory is demonstrated by a foot on the enemy's neck (Josh. 10:24), and servitude and oppression by a yoke around the neck (Gen. 27:40; Dt. 28:48; Isa. 10:27; 52:2; Jer. 27:2–28:14; 30:8; Lam. 1:14; 5:5; Mic. 2:3; cf. Acts 15:10; the NT frequently uses the image without mentioning the neck [e.g., Mt. 11:29]). The "yoke around the neck" is probably the dominant image that uses the neck. The most complete use of the image is in Jer. 27:2–28:14; here the Lord instructs Jeremiah to wear "thongs and yoke-bars" as symbols of submission to Nebuchadrezzar.

Certain animals that were not allowed as food (e.g., the firstborn that were not redeemed) were to be killed by having their necks broken (Ex. 13:13; 34:20); the turtledoves and young pigeons, which were sacrificed as sin offerings or burnt offerings, had their necks wrung (Lev. 5:8).

Finally, Paul praised the devotion of Prisca and Aquila, who had "risked their necks" for him (Rom. 16:4).

H. VAN BROEKHOVEN, JR.

**NECKLACE.** Several varieties of neck ornaments were popular in the ancient Near East. Gold chains were worn about the neck not only as ornamentation (cf. Heb. *rāḇîḏ,* "chain," Ezk. 16:11) but also as symbols of high rank and royal favor (cf. Gen. 41:42; Dnl. 5:7, 16, 29; *see* CHAIN). Ps. 73:6 (Heb. *'ānaq,* lit. "put on as a necklace"; cf. AV

Early Natufian necklace of dentalia and bone, found with a group burial in one of the Carmel caves, Wâdī el-Mughârah (Israel Department of Antiquities and Museums)

Bead or shell necklaces decorated with gold pendants. From Ur, *ca.* 19th cent. B.C. (Trustees of the British Museum)

"compass about as a chain") probably refers to such a chain worn as a status symbol. This form of necklace is also referred to in 2 Ch. 3:16, where most commentators (with the RSV and NEB) emend the MT *badd$^e$ḇîr* (lit. "in the inner sanctuary" [so RSV mg.]; cf. AV "in the oracle") to read *k$^e$rāḇîḏ* (RSV, NEB, "like a necklace"). (For one conjectural explanation of the process by which the Hebrew text may have changed see H. G. M. Williamson, *1 and 2 Chronicles* [*NCBC,* 1982], p. 210.)

Another style of necklace, a string of beads or jewels (cf. *ḥ$^a$rûzîm,* Cant. 1:10), is apparently referred to in Cant. 4:9. Although the precise meaning of *ṣaww$^e$rôn* (cf. *ṣawwā'r,* "neck") is uncertain, the context supports the RSV and NEB rendering of the phrase *b$^e$'aḥaḏ '$^a$nāq miṣṣaww$^e$rōnāyiḵ* by "with one jewel of your necklace" (cf. AV "with one chain of your neck"; see M. Pope,

*Song of Songs* [*AB*, 1977], p. 482). *See also* Stones, Precious.

Another variety of necklace was made of plaited wire to which pendants might be attached (cf. RSV "pendants," *ʿᵃnāqîm,* Prov. 1:9).

*See also* pictures in Garments; Ornament.

N. J. O.

**NECO** nē'kō [Heb. *nᵉḵōh,* also *nᵉḵô*; Gk. *Nechaō*]; AV NECHO, NECOH; NEB NECHO. Neco II, who reigned fifteen years (610-595 B.C.), the second king of the 26th Dynasty in Egypt and son of its founder Psamtik I (664-610; on these dates, see R. A. Parker, *Mitteilungen des deutschen archäologischen Instituts, Kairo,* 15 [1957], 208-212).

Neco inherited a strong and reunited Egypt from his shrewd father. At home he continued his father's main policies, including fostering Egyptian prosperity, strengthening the central government, and granting trade facilities to Greek merchants. He began a canal from the Nile to the Red Sea, which was either completed or reconditioned by Darius I of Persia a century later, and he sent out a Phoenician expedition that actually circumnavigated Africa (Herodotus iv.42, with unjustified skepticism; but cf. J. A. B. Lloyd, *JEA*, 63 [1977], 142). Again like his father, in foreign affairs Neco supported the failing strength of Assyria against the rising powers of Babylon and Media, probably to maintain a balance of powers in west Asia.

Thus in 609 B.C. Neco marched through Syria to help the last Assyrian king, Aššur-uballiṭ II, against the Babylonians (so the Babylonian Chronicle and 2 K. 23:29, RSV, NIV, and esp. NEB; contra AV, "Pharaoh-nechoh . . . went up against the king of Assyria"; for a discussion of the textual and political problems, see J. Gray, *I & II Kings* [*OTL,* 2nd ed. 1970], pp. 747f.). But in Palestine Josiah of Judah forced Neco to do battle and lost his life in the process (2 K. 23:29; 2 Ch. 35:20-24). This delay in Neco's march N to Assyria left unaided Assyria to be destroyed by Babylon. Perhaps this was what Josiah had intended — without foreseeing that Babylon would thereafter menace his country. Returning to Egypt, Neco replaced Josiah's son Jehoahaz with another son, Jehoiakim, and required tribute of him (2 K. 23:31-35; 2 Ch. 36:1-4). Egypt thus laid claim to Palestine after Assyria's demise, but at the battle of Carchemish in the summer of 605 Nebuchadrezzar of Babylon, just prior to his accession, captured Carchemish and chased the Egyptian forces home to Egypt (cf. Jer. 46). Judah then passed under Babylonian overlordship (2 K. 24:1, 7).

Egypt did not immediately interfere further in Syro-Palestinian affairs. But the Babylonian Chronicle records that in 601 Nebuchadrezzar II of Babylon marched against Egypt; in the ensuing battle (location not specified), both sides sustained heavy losses, and the Babylonian army had to refit for eighteen months. This Babylonian setback may have tempted Jehoiakim of Judah to rebel against Babylon (2 K. 24:1). Egypt under Neco, now neutral, sent him no aid.

Very few Egyptian historical records from Neco's reign are known. The OT and the Babylonian chronicles are the main sources for his Syrian campaigns; Herodotus added further data.

***Bibliography.***–Detailed study of Neco's reign by J. Yoyotte, *DBSup.*, VI (1960), cols. 363-393. See also A. H. Gardiner, *Egypt of the Pharaohs* (1961), pp. 357-59, 383; É. Drioton and J. Vandier, *L'Égypte* (4th ed. 1962), pp. 592-94, 618, 678; *CCK*; H. De Meulenaere, *Herodotus over de 26te Dynastie* (1951); M. F. Gyles, *Pharaonic Policies and Administration, 663 to 323 B.C.* (1959).

K. A. KITCHEN

**NECODAN** nə-kō'dən (AV, NEB, 1 Esd. 5:37). *See* Nekoda **2.**

**NECROMANCER** nek'rō-man-sər [Heb. *dōrēš 'el-hammēṯîm*–'inquirer of the dead'] (Dt. 18:11). *See* Divination III.G; Medium II.

**NECTAR** [Heb. *nōpeṯ*] (Cant. 4:11); AV HONEYCOMB; NEB SWEETNESS. *Nōpeṯ* literally means "liquid honey" (from the comb); cf. Ps. 19:10 (MT 11), where the RSV renders *nōpeṯ ṣûpîm* "drippings of the honeycomb."

**NEDABIAH** ned-ə-bī'ə [Heb. *nᵉḏaḇyâ*–'Yahweh has freely given'] (1 Ch. 3:18). A descendant of David and son of Jeconiah (Jehoiachin).

**NEEDLE** [Gk. *hraphís* (Mt. 19:24; Mk. 10:25), *belónē* (Lk. 18:25)]. A word occurring only in the Synoptic accounts of Jesus' saying about the eye of the needle. Reflecting his medical background, Luke used *belónē,* which refers to a needle regularly used for surgical purposes.

Jesus' saying in the Synoptics is both eschatological and proverbial. It is used to illustrate (from a human perspective) the impossibility and cost of entering the kingdom of God. In Palestine the camel was the largest animal and the eye of the needle the smallest opening (cf. Mt. 23:24), hence the appropriateness of the proverb for Jesus' point. The rich man in the saying is someone who trusts in and identifies himself with his wealth. For such a person to expect a share in God's kingdom is absurd since trust in the Messiah (Mt. 16:13-20), identification with the kingdom and its priorities (6:33), and obedience to its law are the conditions for eternal life (cf. 19:16). Thus Jesus' command to the rich man to sell his possessions, give to the poor, and follow Him in order to have treasure in heaven (19:21) tested him at the point of his resistance to God and His kingdom. So understood, Jesus' words are neither a universal command for all disciples nor a critique of wealth per se, but a warning about the spiritual danger wealth poses to the hearts of the rich and the implications of this for membership in the kingdom.

Other interpretations of "the eye of the needle" have been suggested in order to make Jesus' words less harsh. (1) It was a narrow gorge. (2) It was one of the gates in the walls of Jerusalem. Both views lack supporting evidence. (3) *Kámēlos,* "camel," has been changed to *kámilos,* "cable, rope," in some late MSS.

The proverbial nature of Jesus' saying is reflected in two later talmudic passages (T.B. *Baba Metzia* 38b; *Berakoth* 55b; cf. also Midrash *Cant.* 5:2; Koran 7:38).

J. J. HUGHES

Bronze needle, Middle Bronze Age (*ca.* 2000-1500 B.C.) from Tell el-ʿAjjûl (Israel Department of Antiquities and Museums)

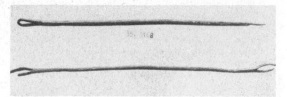

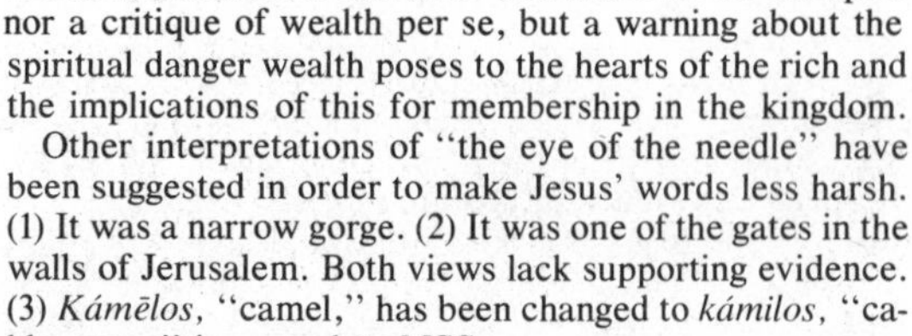

**NEEDLEWORK.** *See* Embroidery.

**NEEDY** [Heb. *'eḇyôn,* also *dal* (Isa. 10:2; 26:6), *ʿanî* (Ps. 68:10 [MT 11]); Gk. *endeḗs*–'poor, impoverished' (Acts 4:34)]. *See* Poor; Poverty.

**NEEMIAS** nē-ə-mī'əs (AV Sir. 49:13; 2 Macc. 1:18-36). *See* Nehemiah.

**NEESING.** *See* Sneeze.

**NEGEB** neg′eb, neg′ev [Heb. *negeḇ*; LXX usually *lips* or *notos*– 'south'; sometimes *Nageb*]. The southernmost district of Judah (Dt. 1:7; 34:3; Josh. 10:40; 11:16; 12:8; "South," 15:21; Jgs. 1:9).

*I. Name.*–Because of the verbs derived from the root *ngb*, it is generally thought that *negeḇ* means "dry"; cf. T.B. *Temurah* 16a; Rashi on T.B. *Babba Kamma* 81b. But the LXX renderings and the parallelism with *têmān*/ *têmānâ* (Ex. 26:18; 27:9; 36:23; 38:9; Josh. 15:1; Ezk. 47:19) suggest that the original meaning was "south." *Negeḇ* is probably cognate with Arab. *janûb*, "south (wind)," and *janb*, "beside."

***II. Location and Topography.***–In the Bible the term Negeb is applied to the district E and W of Beer-sheba and N of Kadesh-barnea (Nu. 13:17, 22). Kadesh was not in the Negeb, but in the Wilderness of Paran (vv. 3, 26) or Wilderness of Zin (v. 21; 20:1; 27:14), which was the southernmost district of Canaan (34:3; Josh. 15:1). The "wilderness of Beer-sheba" was S of Beer-sheba but N of Zin (Gen. 21:14; 1 K. 19:3f.). Thus the Negeb was not the triangle extending to Elath that is now called by the name.

The biblical Negeb corresponds to today's Beer-sheba Valley and the Besor region, sometimes called the northern Negeb. It is an hourglass-shaped, east-west zone. The eastern loop is a tectonically sunken area separating the Judean hills from the "wilderness of (Beer-sheba)," now called the Negeb highlands. On the north this loop is divided into two "bays" by a ridge running SW, an extension of the Hebron uplift. The Eocene hills from the Shephelah on the north (Givʿot Lahav = Khasm el-Buteiyir) nearly close with those on the south (Givʿat Hablanim = Râs Ḥablein), forming a bottleneck near Beer-sheba.

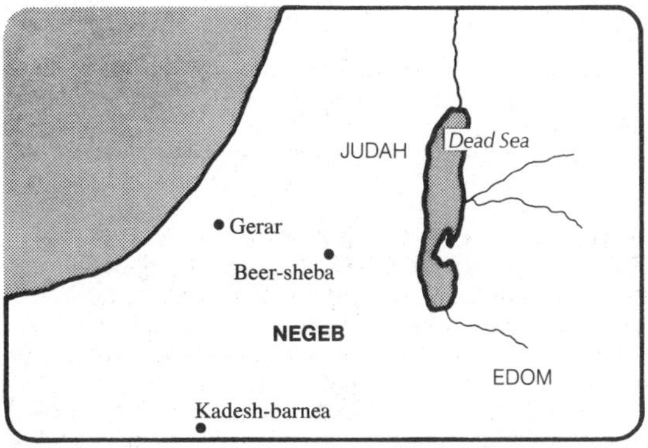


The valley is drained westward by the Beer-sheba wadi system, which includes Nahal Malhata (Wâdī el-Milḥ) and Nahal Aroer (Wâdī ʿArʿarah) from the south. The Beer-sheba system joins Nahal Hebron (Wâdī el-Khalîl) in the center and then flows in a wide arc westward. The eastern loop is encompassed by Nahal Besor (Wâdī el-Khalaṣah) as it curves north and then west (Nahal ʿAzza = Wâdī el-Ghazzeh). It collects Nahal Gerar (Wâdī Sherîʿah), the main streambed of an extensive system.

The entire region is covered by a layer of loess soil, a silt rich in quartz in the west and carbonates in the east. It is wind deposited; with the first rain it forms a crust that makes subsequent rains run off in deep gully erosion. The rainfall is marginal, averaging 20 cm. (8 in.) per year.

***III. Pre-Israelite History.***–*A. Chalcolithic* (4300-3200 B.C.).

Tell Abū Hureirah in the Negeb (A. F. Rainey)

Lining the streambeds are remains of numerous communal settlements, built by groups of pastoralists who possibly stayed only seasonally. The settlements are found in the east, center, and west; examples were excavated at Beer-sheba.

*B. Early Bronze* (3200-2000 B.C.). A major E.B. I and II city developed at Arad, and an Egyptian trading post was found at ʿEn ha-Besor (ʿAin esh-Shellâl). No traces of E.B. III or IV are found.

*C. Middle Bronze* (2000-1550 B.C.). No Negeb settlements remain from the pastoralists of M.B. I, a nomadic culture once thought to reflect the patriarchal narratives. Two M.B. II sites are known in each of the "loops": Tel Malḥata (Tel el-Milḥ) and Tel Masos (Tell el-Meshâsh) in the east, and Tel Haror (Tell Abū Hureirah) and Tell el-Fârʿah (S) in the west.

*D. Late Bronze* (1550-1200 B.C.). Not a trace of L.B. settlement appears in the eastern Negeb, but the west has some major sites: Tel Haror, Tel Seraʿ (Tell esh-Sherîʿah), Tel Gamma (Tell Jemmeh), Tel Ḥalif (Tell el-Khuweilfeh), and Tell el-Farʿah (S). Egyptian inscriptions (particularly those of Thutmose III) refer to some of these towns. Seti I encountered Shasu (pastoral nomads, often of a warlike character) when he marched across the north Sinai route toward Gaza. The area S of Beer-sheba, the Negeb highlands of today, was often called Edom and Seir; texts from the reigns of Ramses II and Ramses III speak of Shasu in the land of Edom/Seir (cf. *ANET,* p. 243; called Bedouin on p. 262). The biblical Amalekites and other ethnic groups (see below) were probably part of this nomadic society.

*IV. Israelite History.–A. Patriarchs.* The patriarchs spent much time in the Negeb (Gen. 12:9; 13:1; 24:62), mainly at Beer-sheba and Gerar. They also lived for a time "between Kadesh and Shur" (20:1) and traveled to Egypt by the "way to Shur" (16:7), the inland route to the delta across Sinai (Ex. 15:22). The Shasu were known to roam there (*ANET,* p. 259a), seeking pasturage in Egypt.

*B. Southern Invasion.* When the Israelites were at Kadesh-barnea, the Amalekites were in the Negeb (Nu. 13:29); thus the Israelites had to "go up" by the "way of the spies" (LXX interpretation of Atharim) during their abortive attempt to invade Canaan from the south (21:1). They were opposed by the Amalekites and Canaanites (13:29; 14:45; 21:1; 33:40) under the mysterious "king of Arad." The Israelites were routed and pursued from the hill country as far as Hormah (14:45). Their revenge, predicted in 21:1-3, is realized in Jgs. 1:17, but the theory that Simeon (mentioned with Judah in v. 17) penetrated the Negeb from the south has no support.

*C. Tribal Groups.* In addition to the Amalekites, other groups settled in the Negeb and later were absorbed into Judah. The tribal group of Caleb played a leading role in the conquest of the southern hill country (Josh. 15:13-19; Jgs. 1:10-15). There was also a "Negeb of Caleb" (1 S. 30:14), and one Calebite town, Madmannah, was assigned to the Negeb (Josh. 15:30; cf. 1 Ch. 2:49). The Negeb of Caleb was thus in the northern zone above Beer-sheba and also comprised the southern hill-country district (Josh. 15:48-51; cf. v. 19; Jgs. 1:15).

The "Negeb of the Kenites" (1 S. 27:10) must be sought in the eastern basin around Arad (Jgs. 1:16). Using the LXX (see *BHS*), one may deduce that the Kenites, the sons of Moses' father-in-law Hobab, entered via the wilderness "on the descent of Arad, which is in the Negeb, and they dwelled with the Amalakites" (see also the comms.).

There is also a "Negeb of the Jerahmeelites" (1 S. 27:10), and "the cities of the Jerahmeelites" appear alongside "the cities of the Kenites" (30:29). Like the Calebites, the Jerahmeelites appear in the family tree of Judah (1 Ch. 2:9, 25-33), but no geographical names are listed. The victory list of Sheshonq mentions two Arads, the second being "Arad of Beth-*yrḥm,*" which may be a shortened form of Jerahmeel.

The "Negeb of the Cherethites" (1 S. 30:14) was in the western "loop," with GERAR as the chief town. The Cherethites are probably the Caphtorim of Dt. 2:23 (see also Am. 9:7; Jer. 47:4), since the Philistines came from Caphtor and are parallel to the Cherethites in Ezk. 25:16; Zeph. 2:5.

The Bible mentions a "Negeb of Judah" (1 S. 27:10; 30:14) but no "Negeb of Simeon." These tribes' joint conquest of Hormah is recorded in Jgs. 1:17. Judah may have begun to settle there after that victory or perhaps when Saul launched his campaign against the Amalekites (1 S. 14:48; 15:1-9). Simeon is known to have settled in a few places in addition to Hormah (Jgs. 1:17). Some were in the southern Shephelah and others in the northern fringe of the Negeb, namely, "Etam, En-rimmon, Tochen, Ether, and Ashan" (1 Ch. 4:31f.; Josh. 19:7). These were Simeon's towns until the reign of David (1 Ch. 4:31b-32).

*D. Early Monarchy.* Saul campaigned to drive the Amalekites out of the Negeb (1 S. 15:1-9, 32f.). While at Ziklag, David used his forces to carry the fight into the southern deserts "as far as Shur, to the land of Egypt" (27:8). When he became king in Hebron, David must have encouraged Simeon to occupy towns in the Negeb (Josh. 19:1-9; 1 Ch. 4:28-31); he had won the allegiance of the Negeb communities (e.g., 1 S. 30:26-31). Beer-sheba was evidently the capital of the Negeb of Judah under the united monarchy, as shown by David's census (2 S. 24:7).

*E. Later Monarchy.* The main Israelite settlements are listed in Josh. 15:21-32, probably in E-W geographical order with Beer-sheba in the center (read Arad for Eder in v. 21, and Aroer for Adadah in v. 22). Very few towns are firmly identified, although many ancient sites are in the area. Most Hebrew place names are not preserved in the Arabic toponymy.

The Negeb was Judah's main link in the trade route from Arabia to the Mediterranean coast (Philistia); because of its strong presence in the Negeb, Judah was able to fortify and control the route to Elath (via Qadesh and the forts in the wilderness of Beer-sheba and Zin/Paran). Solomon could thus launch his fleet to Ophir (1 K. 9:26-28; 2 Ch. 8:17). But in the fifth year of Rehoboam (926 B.C.) Sheshonq destroyed the Judean towns and forts, including two named Arad. Only during the first ten years of Asa's reign (911-901 B.C.; 2 Ch. 14:1, 6 [MT 13:23, 14:5]) could Judah refortify itself; some strongholds in the Negeb were probably built then. Asa's fifteenth year (896) saw a great Judean victory in the western Negeb around Gerar (14:8-14 [MT 7-13]; 15:10f.).

Judah's position was strengthened even more after 870 by Jehoshaphat, who not only increased the Judean armed forces (2 Ch. 17:1f.) but so controlled the caravan routes that the Philistines and Arabs paid him heavy tribute (vv. 10-13). To maintain his forces and stock provisions for sale to the caravans, he built many forts and store-cities. He not only controlled the Negeb as far as Beer-sheba (19:4), but also ruled Edom through a commissioner and dominated the route to Ezion-geber, although his maritime venture from there was unsuccessful (1 K. 22:47f.; 2 Ch. 20:35-37).

Judean hegemony was lost in the reign of Jehoram (849-841) when Edom revolted and set up its own king (2 K. 8:20-22 par. 2 Ch. 21:8-10), and the Philistines and Arabs invaded Judah and even Jerusalem (2 Ch. 21:16f.).

In the 8th century Judah was rejuvenated. Amaziah

reconquered Edom (793), and after his death (767) his son Azariah (Uzziah) rebuilt Elath (2 K. 14:22 par. 2 Ch. 26:2) and dominated the southern and western expanses (2 Ch. 26:7f.), receiving tribute from the Ammonites. But in 734 Rezin king of Syria aided the Edomites in regaining Elath (2 K. 16:5f.); the Edomites in turn joined the Philistines in attacking Judah as part of the Syro-Ephraimite war against Ahaz (2 Ch. 28:17f.; cf. vv. 5-15; 2 K. 16:5f.).

This situation prevailed until Hezekiah restored Judean control over the western Negeb in preparation for the war with Sennacherib. He sent his forces, mainly Simeonites, against the territory of Gaza in the west and against Mt. Seir (the Wilderness of Zin/Paran?) in the south (2 K. 18:8; 1 Ch. 4:39-43, reading Gerar for Gedor, with LXX). But Hezekiah's control of these territories was short lived; in 701 Sennacherib conquered all of Judah except Jerusalem (2 K. 18:13; 2 Ch. 32:1) and gave all the western plain to the loyal king of Gaza (*ANET*, p. 288a).

Judah was thus denied access to the border zones throughout the reigns of Manasseh and Amon, but by 722 could carry out administrative reforms even in Beer-sheba (2 K. 23:8). Judean settlements flourished in the Negeb in the late 7th cent. (Jer. 17:26). But while Nebuchadrezzar was refurbishing his army for an attack on Judah, the neighboring peoples began to raid and plunder (2 K. 24:1f.). As young King Jehoiachin and his mother awaited the Babylonian onslaught (597), the towns of the Negeb were besieged (Jer. 13:18f.). The Edomites supported Babylon and seized the Negeb and southern Judah (Ob. 8-10, 14; Ps. 137:7), as illustrated dramatically by the ostracon found at Arad urging the reinforcement of Ramath-negeb, "lest Edom should come there."

*F. Postexilic Period.* Some Judean communities must have survived in the Negeb, because Nehemiah recognized them as legitimate even though they were not within his small province of Jehud (Neh. 11:25-30; 444 B.C.).

The Negeb remained part of Idumea throughout the Persian and Hellenistic periods (Josephus *Ant.* v.1.22 [82]). John Hyrcanus conquered it in 125 B.C. and required the inhabitants to convert to Judaism or leave (Josephus *Ant.* xiii.9.1 [257f.]; *BJ* i.2.6 [63]). In the Herodian (early Roman) period a line of forts guarded the frontier.

***Bibliography.***–Y. Aharoni, *IEJ*, 8 (1958), 26-38; "The Negeb," *AOTS*, pp. 384-403; *Arad Inscriptions* (1981); D. Alon and T. E. Levy, *IEJ*, 30 (1980), 140-47; R. Amiran, *et al.*, *Levant*, 12 (1980), 22-29; J. Barth, *Etymologische Studien* (1893); *Wurzeluntersuchungen* (1902); W. Dever, *BASOR*, 237 (Winter 1980), 35-64; D. Ginzburg and D. H. Yaalon, *Israel Journal of Earth Sciences*, 12 (1963), 68-70; R. Giveon, *Les Bédouins Shosou* (1971); R. Gophna, *Tel Aviv*, 3 (1976), 31-37; N. Na'aman, *ZDPV*, 96 (1980), 136-152; L. Picard and P. Solomonica, *JPOS*, 16 (1936), 180-222; A. F. Rainey, *Tel Aviv*, 7 (1980), 194-202; "Early Historical Geography of the Negeb," in Z. Herzog, ed., *Beer-sheba II* (1984), pp. 88-104.

A. F. RAINEY

**NEGINAH** nə-gē'nə; **NEGINOTH** nə-gē'nōth. A technical musical term indicating the use of stringed instruments, such as the lyre and harp; the AV transliteration of Heb. *n<sup>e</sup>gînâ* (sing.) and *n<sup>e</sup>gînôṯ* (pl.) in the superscriptions to Pss. 4; 6; 54; 55; 61; 67; 76 (MT v. 1 in each case; RSV "with stringed instruments"). The Hebrew term is derived from the verb *nāgan*, which in the piel means "touch" or "strike," indicating the manner in which a musical instrument is played (cf. 1 S. 16:16; 18:10; 2 K. 3:15; cf. also part. *nōg<sup>e</sup>nîm*, "string-players," Ps. 68:25 [MT 26]).

*See also* MUSIC III.B.2.

***Bibliography.***–Comms. on Psalms; S. Mowinckel, *Psalms in Israel's Worship* (Eng. tr. repr. 1979), II, 210; A. Sendrey, *Music in Ancient Israel* (1969), pp. 118-120. N. J. O.

**NEHELAM** nə-hel'əm, **OF** [Heb. *hanneḥ<sup>ĕ</sup>lāmî*]; AV, NEB, THE NEHELAMITE. The designation of Shemaiah, a false prophet who opposed Jeremiah (Jer. 29:24, 31f.). The RSV interprets it as referring to the place from which he came, but no such place-name has been found. Another possibility is that it may be a family name. Its similarity to the verb *ḥālam* ("dream") has led to the unlikely conjecture that it means "dreamer" (cf. Jer. 23:25, 32), an interpretation favored by L. Yaure, *JBL*, 79 (1960), 306-309.

**NEHEMIAH** nē-ə-mī'ə [Heb. *n<sup>e</sup>ḥemyâ*–'Yahweh comforts'; Gk. *Neemia*]; AV Apoc. NEHEMIAS (1 Esd. 5:8), NEEMIAS (2 Macc. 1:18-36; 2:13; Sir. 49:13).

**1.** A postexilic governor of Judah and writer of the memoirs in the book called by his name. All that is known from contemporary sources about this Jewish patriot is found in this book. He was the son of Hacaliah (Neh. 1:1), and one of his brothers, Hanani (v. 2; 7:2), was a man of sufficient character and importance to have been made a ruler of Jerusalem. Some have inferred from 10:1-8 (MT 2-9) that Nehemiah was a priest, since he comes first in the list of names ending with the phrase "these were the priests." This view is supported by the Syr. and Arab. versions of 10:1 and by the Vulgate of 2 Macc. 1:21, which all refer to him as a priest. 2 Macc. 1:18 also refers to sacrificial activity on his part.

The argument based on Neh. 10:1-8 disappears if the pointing of *ś<sup>e</sup>rāyâ*, "Seraiah" (v. 2) is changed to *śārāyw* and the verse reads "its princes," referring to the princes of 9:38 (MT 10:1). In this case, Nehemiah and Zedekiah would be the princes; then would come the priests, followed by the Levites.

Since Nehemiah was so grieved at the desolation of the city and sepulchres of his fathers and so zealous for the laws of the God of Judah, one can justly infer that he was brought up by pious parents who instructed him in the history and law of the Jewish people. The prevalence of names with the element Yah(weh) throughout the family reinforces this impression.

Doubtless because of his probity and ability he was apparently at an early age appointed by Artaxerxes king of Persia (Artaxerxes I Longimanus) to the responsible position of cupbearer. The office was "one of no trifling honor" (Herodotus iii.34). One of his chief duties was to taste the wine for the king to see that it was not poisoned, and he was even admitted to the king while the queen was present (Neh. 2:6). As cupbearer his responsibilities most probably included some palace administration, since this office in most royal courts seems to have been of a senior nature. Such personages were often eunuchs whether or not they had administrative duties connected with the female quarter of the palace. Perhaps the fact that Nehemiah was able to be present while the king and queen were together would imply that he was in fact a eunuch, though whether the term *sārîs* is the equivalent of a "castrate" or merely describes the office that Nehemiah held is uncertain. Some eunuchs at least seem to have been married (Gen. 39:1, where in different versions Potiphar is described as an officer, captain, or chamberlain), which leaves the traditional understanding of the term open to some question (cf. W. Rudolph, *Esra und Nehemia* [*HAT*, 1949], p. 103; J. M. Myers, *Ezra. Nehemiah* [*AB*, 1965], p. 96). This position close to the king enabled Nehemiah to obtain his commission as governor of Judea, along with the letters and edicts that enabled him to restore the walls of Jerusalem.

The occasion of Nehemiah's commission was as follows. Hanani brother of Nehemiah and other men of Judah came to visit him while he was in Susa (the Persian winter capital) in the ninth month of the twentieth year of Artaxerxes (Neh. 1:1; probably Nov./Dec., 445 B.C.). They reported that the Jews in Jerusalem were in great affliction and that the wall was broken down and its gates burned with fire. Nehemiah then grieved and fasted and prayed to God that he might be granted favor by the king. Appearing again before the king in the month Nisan (Mar./Apr.) of the twentieth year (Neh. 2:1, probably 444), he was granted permission to go to Jerusalem to build the city where his fathers were buried. He was given letters to the governors of Syria and Palestine and especially to Asaph, keeper of the king's forest, who was ordered to supply timber for the wall, fortress, and temple. To afford him the proper degree of authority he was appointed royal commissioner (*tiršāṯāʾ*) of that Persian province ("Beyond the River") of which Jerusalem was the capital.

Armed with these credentials and powers he traveled to Jerusalem and immediately began the restoration of the walls. He was hindered by Sanballat governor of Samaria and others, among them part of the much more assimilated Jewish community that had lived in Jerusalem through the Exile. He nonetheless succeeded in these external renovations, including the provision of gates for the various entrances to the city.

Nehemiah then instituted a number of social reforms. He appointed the officers necessary for better government, caused the people to be instructed in the Law by public readings and expositions, celebrated the Feast of Booths, and observed a national fast at which the sins of the people were confessed and a new covenant with Yahweh was solemnly confirmed. The people agreed to avoid marriages with the heathen, to keep the sabbath, and to contribute to the support of the temple. To provide for the safety and prosperity of the city, one out of every ten persons living outside Jerusalem was compelled to settle in the rebuilt city. In all of these reforms Nehemiah was assisted by Ezra, who arrived in Jerusalem before Nehemiah. In 444 B.C. Ezra dealt firmly with the problem of marriages between Jews and people who stood outside the covenant (Ezr. 9:1–10:44) when he was organizing the life of the theocratic community, although he encountered some opposition to his plans for purifying the national stock. For Ezra, the difficulty was that foreign wives presented a grave threat to the spiritual integrity of the covenantal faith because of their general unwillingness to repudiate their national deities when they married Jews. To a large extent it was the women who perpetuated the religious traditions of the time, and trained their children to follow their ways. This situation continues to exist in some oriental countries, where the women are still regarded as responsible for maintaining the integrity of the religious and social traditions of the particular culture involved. The religious reforms that Ezra instituted regarding mixed marriages caused a considerable amount of social and personal upheaval. Necessary though it was for the spiritual stability of the theocracy, it could only have been carried to completion by the authoritative backing of Nehemiah, who evidently remained in office as governor until 433 B.C., when he visited Persia for a year.

On his return he discovered that Tobiah, one of his principal Ammonite opponents, had been granted accommodation in the temple courts by Eliashib the high priest, with whom Tobiah was evidently on friendly terms (Neh. 13:4-7). Nehemiah ejected Tobiah summarily and restored the accommodation to its former use. He was equally forthright with those Jews who had married women of Ashdod, Ammon, and Moab, beating, cursing, and abusing them for laying again the foundations of those processes of apostasy that had ultimately destroyed the Hebrew monarchy (Neh. 13:23-27). One of the sons of Joiada, the son of Eliashib the high priest, had married a daughter of Sanballat the Horonite, and he too was expelled.

Tobiah seems to have been an important Persian official bearing the title "servant" (Neh. 2:10), who obviously had influential friends in Judea (Neh. 6:18f.; 13:4f.). He may have had some jurisdiction over Ammonite territory (cf. W. F. Albright, "Dedan," in *Geschichte und AT* [A. Alt *Festschrift*; 1953], pp. 4, 6). The connection between this Tobiah and the Tobiad family which governed Ammonite territory from ʿArâq el-Amir is difficult to determine (cf. C. C. McCown, *BA*, 20 [1957], 63-76; P. W. Lapp, *BASOR*, 171 [Oct. 1963], 8-39). An inscription on the family shrine in their capital city mentioning Tobiah was once thought to refer to the enemy of Nehemiah, but it has been assigned subsequently to the period of Antiochus IV Epiphanes (*ca.* 175 B.C.).

Another influential opponent of Nehemiah's named Geshem (Neh. 2:19; 6:1f.; most probably the MT Gashmu of 6:6), was named on a silver bowl recovered from a pagan shrine in the east Delta region of Egypt (I. Rabinowitz, *JNES*, 15 [1956], 2-9 and plates 6-7). Another inscription in ancient Dedan (el-ʿUlā) was dated "in the days of Jasm [Geshem]," indicating his prominence in Arabia (K. A. Kitchen, *Illustrated Bible Dictionary* [1980], I, 554).

The overall aim of the activities of Nehemiah was to purify the nation so that it would constitute a true theocracy grounded on the ethos of the Sinai covenant. By removing the stigma of foreign marital connections from the priesthood, Nehemiah was in effect restoring the temple personnel to their characteristically representative position in the nation as the ceremonially pure guardians and exemplars of the Law.

At least once during his governorship Nehemiah returned to Persia or Babylon (Neh. 13:6). Nothing is known about when or where he died. It is certain, however, that he was no longer governor in 407, for at that time, according to the Elephantine correspondence to the priests of Jerusalem, Bagoas occupied the position. Josephus (*Ant.* xi.5.8 [182f.]) reported only that Nehemiah died at an advanced age.

*See also* EZRA, BOOK OF.

**2.** Son of Abzuk and a district governor of Beth-zur (Neh. 3:16); he helped Nehemiah to rebuild the wall around Jerusalem.

**2.** A man who returned with Sheshbazzar from Babylonia *ca.* 533 B.C. (Ezr. 2:2; Neh. 7:7; 1 Esd. 5:8).

***Bibliography.***–The only early extrabiblical data concerning Nehemiah and the Judea of his time are to be found in the Aramaic papyri of Elephantine in Egypt (A. E. Cowley, *Aramaic Papyri of the 5th Cent. B.C.* [1923] and *ANET*, pp. 491f.); Josephus *Ant.* xi.5.6-8 [159-183]; Sir. 49:13; 2 Macc. 1:18-36; 2:13. For additional secondary literature, *see* NEHEMIAH, BOOK OF.

C. E. ARMERDING R. K. H.

## NEHEMIAH, BOOK OF.

***I. Name.***–The book of Nehemiah, like its companion Ezra, is called by the name of its principal subject; more than half the book consists of Nehemiah's personal memoirs. In the LXX Ezra-Nehemiah is called Esdras B, while in English versions of the Apocrypha Nehemiah is usually called 2 Ezra.

***II. Purpose.***–Nehemiah carries the themes and narrative of Ezra to their conclusion, picking up the story with Nehemiah's concern for the problems facing the community that returned in the days of Artaxerxes I (464-424 B.C.). The account presupposes a remnant already in Jerusalem (Neh. 1:3) and the troubles faced in the work of Zerubbabel and Joshua if not of Ezra as well. Concern for building the wall dominates Nehemiah, as concern for the temple does Ezra. Completion of the temple in Ezra leads to a great spring festival (Passover and the Feast of Unleavened Bread, Ezr. 6:19, 22) while Nehemiah's wall building culminates in the autumn Feast of Booths (Neh. 8:12-18).

In both books the divine service is restored, but Nehemiah carries the worship to a higher climax of its development ("not since the days of Joshua," 8:17).

*III. Sources.*–Most of Nehemiah consists of personal memoirs. Neh. 1:1–7:4; 13:4-31, possibly augmented by some temple lists (e.g., ch. 3; 7:5-73a), are of the most personal kind of writing in Scripture. Although the final redaction is no doubt the work of someone other than Nehemiah (many find the hand of the Chronicler here), few would question the authenticity of the Nehemiah source.

The rest of Nehemiah consists of various lists (10:1-27 [MT 2-28]; 11:3-32; 12:1-26) and the narrative sections that link them. Of special interest is ch. 8, a narrative in which Ezra and Nehemiah are seen to be contemporaries. The lists in Nehemiah come from various periods, but all are probably taken from temple records. The list of wall builders (ch. 3) would naturally fit into a governor's report. The source of ch. 7 (cf. Ezr. 2) is identified in its heading (v. 5) as the genealogical record of the earliest returnees; Nehemiah himself probably appended it to his memoirs. Neh. 10:1-27 lists the "leaders, Levites, and priests" who signed the covenant of ch. 9. It is certainly to be connected with the source for the Ezra-Nehemiah section. Neh. 11, although it begins like a general census list, is clearly a temple roster, as is 12:1-26 with its genealogy of priests and Levites. The latter list may well have been kept open until the days of Darius II (423-404) or later; it terminates with one Jaddua, whose date is still a matter of dispute.

*IV. Style.*– For the literary style of Nehemiah, *see* EZRA, BOOK OF IV.

*V. Special Problems.*–Nehemiah is, compared to Ezra, relatively free from historical difficulties. The major problem remains that of fitting Ezra and Nehemiah together, which for Nehemiah involves dating the legal reforms of ch. 8.

Of considerable interest in dating the final form of the book is the attempt to correlate royal and sacerdotal figures in Nehemiah to references in other historical sources. In addition to the references to Eliashib and Jehohanan in Ezr. 10:6, Neh. 12:10f. traces the priestly line through six generations: Jeshua, Joiakim, Eliashib, Joiada, Jonathan (or Jehohanan), and Jaddua. The problem is not only to harmonize Neh. 12:10 with Ezr. 10:6 but to determine the date and identity of such figures as Jaddua the priest and Darius the king (called "Darius the Persian" in Neh. 12:22).

External sources affecting the discussion include the Elephantine papyri from Egypt (late 5th cent. B.C.), the much later *Antiquities* of Josephus, and the Samaria papyri (latter half of the 4th cent. B.C.). According to the Elephantine papyrus (Cowley, no. 30; cf. *ANET,* pp. 491f.), in *ca.* 408/7 B.C. one Bagoas was governor of Judah, King Darius was enthroned in Persia (Darius II Nothus, 423-404), and Jehohanan was the high priest. So far correlation is simple. The first priest to return, Jeshua (Ezr. 2:2; 3:2; 5:2; Hag. 1:1; etc.), was known to have been in office in both 539 and 520. His son Joiakim is identified with "the days of Nehemiah . . . and of Ezra" (Neh. 12:26). The third generation, Eliashib, appears frequently in the sacred text, being identified with Nehemiah's wall-building effort (444; see Neh. 3:1) in the days of Artaxerxes I (464-424). The same figure incurred Nehemiah's wrath by making a marriage alliance with the Ammonite Tobiah (13:4-6) sometime after Artaxerxes' thirty-second year (433).

Of the fourth incumbent less is known, but it is not unreasonable to find an identification between the fifth (Jonathan or Jehohanan) and the priest of the same name in the Elephantine papyri. (For the related problem of the Jehohanan of Ezr. 10:6 *see* EZRA, BOOK OF VI.F.) If this Jehohanan was high priest in 408/7 B.C. (and the Darius of Neh. 12:22 was Darius II Nothus), then the Jaddua of Neh. 12:11 would have been in office close to 400, thus providing a proper *terminus ad quem* for the book's historical lists.

The problem arises with Josephus. Joiakim is confirmed as roughly contemporary with Ezra (*Ant.* xi.5.5 [157f.]), and his son Eliashib is said to have succeeded him. There the easy correlation stops. A later section (xi.8.2 [306-308]), dated by Josephus to the times of Alexander of Macedon (who ruled 336-323), refers to Jaddua (Jaddus) as high priest, Darius as king (clearly Darius III Codomannus, 336/5-331), and Sanballat as the treacherous and double-dealing satrap of Darius (*Ant.* xi.7.2 [302f.]), whose daughter was married to a brother of Jaddua, Manasseh. The entrance of Sanballat as father-in-law of a priest raises a further question in the light of Neh. 13:28, where "one of the sons of Joiada [i.e., a brother of Jehohanan, not of Jaddua] was son-in-law to Sanballat."

One may assume that either Nehemiah or Josephus or both are hopelessly confused, and adherents of each position have not been wanting (see Rowley, "Sanballat," p. 250 n. 1). Evidence from the Samaria papyri, uncovered in 1962 (F. M. Cross, *BA,* 26 [1963], 110-121), has helped unravel at least a part of the mystery. From the data at hand F. M. Cross posited a succession of Sanballats: Sanballat I, who was governor of Samaria when Nehemiah arrived in Jerusalem (*ca.* 445/4); his grandson Sanballat II, the figure mentioned in the papyri (early 4th cent.); and the latter's grandson, Sanballat III, the governor mentioned by Josephus. Evidence for the reappearance of a name in alternate generations (papponymy) has strengthened the argument for more than one Jaddua as well, with the result that Nehemiah's reference to that figure need no longer be seen as equally problematical. Josephus has obviously telescoped certain events and people; Nehemiah, on the other hand, carries the picture down to only the beginning of the 4th cent. B.C.

The nature and activities of one of Nehemiah's opponents, Shemaiah the son of Delaiah, have presented perennial problems to translators. The MT of Neh. 6:10 characterized him as an *ʿāṣûr,* which from such passages as Jer. 33:1; 36:5 was interpreted in terms of restraint (AV, RSV, "who was shut up"; NEB "confined to his house"; NIV "shut in at his home"). These interpretations understood the verb *ʿṣr* to mean "withhold, retain," but encountered the immediate difficulty of explaining how Shemaiah could at once be confined to his home (whether through a vow or for ceremonial uncleanness, so BDB, p. 783), and at the same time be free to meet Nehemiah in the temple. The sense of the passage, however, makes it clear that *ʿāṣûr* is being employed in a special sense to describe a hidden or secret informer (so New King James Version) who had been hired by Tobiah and Sanballat to report on the activities and plans of Nehemiah.

Many scholars have experienced difficulties in interpreting the sections dealing with the topography of Nehemiah's walls. Ch. 3 described the course of the walls, beginning at the northeast with the Sheep Gate, continuing W and then S to the Kidron Valley, E to the Dung and Fountain Gates, and then N past Ophel and the East Gate to the Corner and back to the Sheep Gate (*see* JERUSALEM III.F.2). While there are difficulties in locating all the points on the city's perimeter, the listing of the most important stations provides valuable information about the nature and general location of the wall.

Debate has focused on whether such areas to the west and south as the Broad Wall, the Tower of the Ovens, and the Valley Gate were part of Nehemiah's Jerusalem. If the hill Gareb (Jer. 31:39) was located SW of Jerusalem, it was obviously outside the city in preexilic times, and would

Hasmonean tower built on a portion of Nehemiah's wall, traces of which can be seen in the lower courses of the tower and in other parts of the wall (W. S. LaSor)

not have been included in the fifth-century-B.C. construction, since according to Kenyon (*Archaeology in the Holy Land* [1960], p. 316) Nehemiah's walls followed the outline of those destroyed in 587 B.C. Kenyon's excavations at Jerusalem made all previous work obsolete. It now appears that the walls of the preexilic city did not enclose both the east and west hills, thus making Nehemiah's city smaller than originally imagined (K. M. Kenyon, *Jerusalem: Excavating 3000 Years of History* [1967], pp. 108-110). In his day the enclosed city was about 1140 m. (3750 ft.) in length and probably not more than 275 m. (900 ft.) wide at its greatest extent (at the north end). Thereafter it tapered to a width of about 165 m. (540 ft.) at the southern extremity. Further, Kenyon regarded as futile any attempt to correlate the description of the north and west walls in Nehemiah with the topography, a position supported by M. Avi-Yonah (in Y. Yadin, ed., *Jerusalem Revealed* [1976], p. 22; cf. Avi-Yonah, *IEJ*, 4 [1954], 239-248). By contrast, the archeological discoveries harmonize more readily with Nehemiah's description of the east wall, which was of solid construction, about 2½ m. (8 ft.) thick, and was newly built along the east ridge of the east hill.

The mention of business and professional guilds (Neh. 3:8-32) as participating in the work of reconstruction indicates the extent to which the pattern of preexilic life had been revived. The businessmen, the goldsmiths, and the perfumers were doubtless the most wealthy elements of society, and in consequence may have been more leisured than others in Judea. Professional guilds had their origin in the presettlement period of Israelite life, and guarded their occupational secrets jealously (cf. R. de Vaux, *Ancient Israel* [Eng. tr. 1961], I, 76-79). They came into increasing prominence in the postexilic period, and flourished in Greek and Roman times. So specialized had certain guild activities become by the period of Christ that to have a door installed required two carpenters, one to deliver the door and the other to install it on its hinges.

*See also* EZRA, BOOK OF.

***Bibliography.***–Comms. by P. R. Ackroyd (*Torch*, 1973); L. W. Batten (*ICC*, 1913); L. H. Brockington (*NCBC*, repr. 1977); F. C. Fensham (*NICOT*, 1982); D. Kidner (*Tyndale*, 1979); J. M. Myers (*AB*, 1965); W. Rudolph (*HAT*, 1949).

N. Avigad, *Discovering Jerusalem* (1983), pp. 61-63; A. Cowley, *Aramaic Papyri of the Fifth Century B.C.* (1923); F. M. Cross, *JBL*, 94 (1975), 4-18; R. W. Klein, "Ezra and Nehemiah in Recent Studies," in F. M. Cross, *et al.*, eds., *Magnalia Dei: The Mighty Acts of God* (*Festschrift* for G. E. Wright; 1976), pp. 361-376; H. H. Rowley, "Chronological Order of Ezra and Nehemiah," in *Servant of the Lord and Other Essays on the OT* (1965), pp. 135-168; "Nehemiah's Mission and Its Background," in *Men of God* (1963), pp. 211-245 (repr. from *BJRL*, 37 [1954/55], 528-561); "Sanballat and the Samaritan Temple," in *Men of God* (1963), pp. 246-276 (repr. from *BJRL*, 38 [1955/56], 166-198); G. Widengren, "Persian Period," in J. H. Hayes and J. M. Miller, eds., *Israelite and Judaean History* (*OTL*, 1977), pp. 489-538; E. Yamauchi, *Bibliotheca Sacra*, 137 (1980), 291-309

C. E. ARMERDING R. K. H.

**NEHEMIAS** nē-hə-mī'əs, nē-ə-mī'əs (1 Esd. 5:8, 40, AV). *See* NEHEMIAH.

**NEHILOTH** nə-hil'oth. The AV transliteration of Heb. *nᵉḥîlôṯ*, a technical musical term in the superscription to Ps. 5 (MT v. 1). The RSV translation, "for the flutes," is probably correct, assuming that *nᵉḥîlôṯ* is derived from *ḥālal*, "pierce," and is a cognate of *ḥālîl*, "play the flute." According to Mowinckel, the flute seems to have been associated with psalms of lamentation. *See* MUSIC III.B.2.

***Bibliography.***–Comms. on Psalms; S. Mowinckel, *Psalms in Israel's Worship* (Eng. tr. repr. 1979), II, 210; A. Sendrey, *Music in Ancient Israel* (1969), pp. 318-320.

**NEHUM** nē'hum [Heb. *nᵉḥûm*]. One of the twelve men whose names head the list of those who returned from the Exile with Zerubbabel (Neh. 7:7). In the par. Ezr. 2:2 (cf. 1 Esd. 5:8) the name appears as REHUM **1**.

**NEHUSHTA** nə-hōōsh'tə [Heb. *nᵉḥuštā'*–prob. 'serpent' (cf. *nāḥāš*) or 'brass' (*nᵉḥōšeṯ*)]. Mother of King Jehoiachin of Judah and daughter of Elnathan of Jerusalem (2 K. 24:8); exiled with Jehoiachin and his court when he surrendered to King Nebuchadrezzar of Babylon (vv. 12, 15; Jer. 29:2).

**NEHUSHTAN** nə-hōōsh'tän [Heb. *nᵉḥuštān*] (2 K. 18:4). Scholars have suggested two possible derivations of this name: (1) from *nᵉḥōšeṯ*, "copper" or "bronze," with afformative *ān*; (2) from *nāḥāš*, "serpent." (Some scholars point to a play on words with the verb *nāḥaš*, "practice sorcery" or "divine.") On the first explanation the meaning would be "a copper object" and could be a derogatory evaluation of the serpent (cf. KD; *IB*, III, 289f.). If this is correct the name Nehushtan would have been given by King Hezekiah (cf. H. Bauer and P. Leander, *Historische Grammatik der hebräischen Sprache* [1922, repr. 1965], p. 18). On the second meaning Nehushtan would be a proper name by which the serpent was commonly known, with no derogation intended. See Joines, pp. 61f.

Whatever its derivation, the Nehushtan is associated in 2 K. 18:4 with the "bronze serpent" (Heb. *nᵉḥaš nᵉḥōšeṯ*) that Moses elevated in the middle of the camp (Nu. 21:4-9). Anyone who looked upon the bronze serpent would recover from the snakebites inflicted on the people as punishment. 2 K. 18:4 appears to suggest that the bronze serpent had been kept since the Exodus and had become an object of idolatrous worship. As such, although it might have been a precious national relic or heirloom, Hezekiah was forced to destroy it in his reform.

Modern scholars have shown that a serpent cult was widespread in ancient Palestine (and in the entire Fertile Crescent) since at least the time of the Exodus (see Joines, pp. 62-73, 97-100). There are many representations of serpents associated with explicit sexual themes as well as more generally with fertility rites and symbols. (A less likely background is the ancient Greek association of the serpent with healing.) Its apparent association with the goddess Astarte (cf. Joines, pp. 61-67) would fit very well the mention of "high places" and "pillars" in 2 K. 18:4.

The existence of a serpent cult in the Near East, however, has raised for many scholars the problem of the relationship between the events recorded in Nu. 21:4-9 and 2 K. 18:4. Scholars offer two possible explanations of this data: (1) the traditional one given above, i.e., that an innocent relic from the Exodus had become an object of worship in Hezekiah's time; (2) the prevailing modern view that the serpent cult of the period of the monarchy was legitimized by the insertion of the etiological account of Nu. 21:4-9 in the story of the Exodus.

There has been much unnecessary speculation about when the Canaanite serpent cult entered the Israelite cult. Given the Israelites' repeated lapses into pagan practice during the monarchy, the serpent cult could have flourished at any time; e.g., possibly this cult had Assyrian origins and was instituted by Ahaz (2 K. 16:10ff.). If Judah already had a bronze serpent as a relic of national origins, or even just a tradition of which that serpent was a part, it would have been easy as well as shrewd to institute the new serpent cult upon the old tradition, especially for people who tended toward idolatry. There need be no irreconcilable difficulties between Nu. 21:4-9 and 2 K. 18:4.

One refinement of this picture revolves around the improbability that, given the Israelites' propensity toward idolatry, Moses would have kept the serpent for posterity. Nor does the list of temple items mention the serpent (e.g., 1 K. 7:40ff.). In short, there is no record of the serpent in the years between the Exodus and Hezekiah's reform. Assuming that the original serpent had been lost or destroyed, the clause "that Moses had made" would not necessarily mean that the serpents were the same object but that they were identified as such in the popular mind.

In conclusion, at the time of Hezekiah's reform Nehushtan or the "bronze serpent" had been given pagan, obscene, and idolatrous associations while retaining Mosaic associations. This dual association made it especially important for Hezekiah to destroy the serpent. The good symbol that is perverted may be more dangerous than the purely pagan symbol.

***Bibliography.***–Comms.; K. R. Joines, *Serpent Symbolism in the OT* (1974); H. H. Rowley, *JBL*, 58 (1939), 113-141, esp. 132-141.

H. VAN BROEKHOVEN, JR.

**NEIEL** nē-ī'əl [Heb. *nᵉʿîʾēl*; Gk. B *Inaēl*, A *Aniēl*]. A town in Asher near the border of Zebulun (Josh. 19:27). The list (vv. 24-31) names Neiel after Beth-emek, N of the valley of Iphtahel. It has been identified with Khirbet Yaʿnîn (*LBHG*, p. 440; *GP*, II, 67) on the eastern side of the Plain of Acco.

W. S. L. S.

**NEIGH; NEIGHING** [Heb. *ṣāhal* (Jer. 5:8; 50:11), *miṣhālôṯ* (8:16; 13:27)]; AV also BELLOW (50:11). Used figuratively by Jeremiah to describe the din of a mighty enemy army approaching from the north (8:16), Babylon's exultant delight at the capture of Judah (50:11), and the Israelites' adulterous desires and practices (5:8; 13:27).

**NEIGHBOR** [Heb. *ʿāmîṯ*–'fellow' (Lev. 6:2 [MT 5:21]; 18:20; 19:15; etc.), *qārôḇ*–'near (one)' (Ex. 32:27; Ps. 15:3), *rē(a)ʿ*–'comrade, fellow' (Ex. 11:2; 18:16; 22:7-11 [MT 6-10]; Lev. 19:13; etc.), *šāḵēn*–'neighbor' (Ex. 3:22; Dt. 1:7; Ruth 4:17; 2 K. 4:3; etc.), etc.; Gk. *geítōn*–'neighbor' (Lk. 14:12; 15:6, 9; Jn. 9:8), *plēsíon*–'near one, neighbor' (Mt. 5:43; 19:19; Acts 7:27; Rom. 13:9; etc.), part. of *perioikéō*–'dwell around' (Lk. 1:65), *períoikos*–'dwelling around' (v. 58), *héteros*–'other' (Rom. 13:8; 1 Cor. 10:24; Gal. 6:4)]; AV also ANOTHER, etc.

*I. In the OT.*–Most of the terms rendered by "neighbor" in the OT designate a fellow member of the community in covenant with Yahweh, i.e., one who shared in the rights and duties implied by membership in the covenant. All relations between members of the covenant community were sanctioned by divine law (cf. Job 16:21). So closely were God's covenant people bound together that a neighbor was to be treated as a brother (cf. the frequent use of "brother" and "neighbor" as synonyms, e.g., Dt. 15:2f., 12; Isa. 41:6; Jer. 31:34). In fact, one was to treat one's neighbor as one treated oneself (Lev. 19:18). It is not surprising, then, that most of the occurrences of Heb. *ʿāmîṯ*, *qārôḇ*, and *rē(a)ʿ* occur in legal and ethical contexts where specific laws and principles are applied to a variety of relationships between covenant neighbors. Since ethical principles and law were synonymous in the Israelite theocracy, we may consider these contexts as one.

By far the most popular term, *rē(a)ʿ* (a derivative of *rāʿâ*, "have dealings with [someone]") occurs in a variety of contexts; *ʿāmîṯ*, by contrast, occurs only in legal contexts in Leviticus. Although *šāḵēn* can also refer to fellow members of the covenant (e.g., Ps. 31:11 [MT 12]; Jer. 6:21; 12:14), it frequently refers to persons of nearby countries, e.g., taunting nations before whom God humbled disobedient Israel (Ps. 44:13 [MT 14]; 79:4, 12; 80:6 [MT 7]; 89:41 [MT 42]).

Disputes between covenant members were to be settled on the basis of God's statutes (cf. Lev. 19:15); if settlement in private was not possible (cf. the counsel of wisdom in Prov. 25:8-10), such disputes were to be settled by God's judges (cf. Ex. 18:16). The Decalogue forbade bearing false witness against a neighbor (Ex. 20:16; Dt. 5:20; cf. Lev. 19:16; Prov. 24:28; 25:18). Other sins of the tongue, e.g., slander (Ps. 101:5; Prov. 11:9), lying (Ps. 12:2 [MT 3]), reproachful (15:3) or deceitful speech (28:3; Jer. 9:5, 8 [MT 4, 7]), belittlement (Prov. 11:12), joking deception (26:19), and false flattery (27:14; 29:5), were singled out as destructive of personal relationships and of the societal fabric of God's covenant people in general (e.g., Ps. 15:3; Prov. 11:9). Divine punishment awaited those who behaved in such a fashion (e.g., Ps. 12:2-4; 101:5). Despising (Prov. 14:21; cf. Lev. 19:17) or planning evil against one's neighbor (Prov. 3:29) were likewise condemned as sinful.

The Decalogue also forbade coveting anything that belonged to a neighbor (Ex. 20:17; Dt. 5:21; cf. Eccl. 4:4). Frequently this commandment was associated with the sin of adultery. A good neighbor did not commit adultery with his neighbor's wife (cf. Lev. 18:20; Dt. 22:24, 26; Job 31:9-12; Prov. 6:29; Jer. 5:8; 29:23; Ezk. 18:6, 11, 15; 22:11; 33:26), for adultery, like bearing false witness, was a form of covenantal unfaithfulness (cf. Ezk. 16:15-52). It was destructive of society and represented a failure to live up to the holiness demanded by Yahweh's character (cf. Lev. 20:7). Hence it was a capital offense (e.g., 20:10).

Business relations between neighbors were also controlled by covenant law (cf. Lev. 6:2-5 [MT 5:21-24]). The

Decalogue prohibited stealing (Ex. 20:15; Dt. 5:19). Transactions involving buying and selling (Lev. 25:14f.), stored or borrowed property (Ex. 22:7-15 [MT 6-14]), collateral for loans (v. 26 [MT 25]; Dt. 24:10; cf. Prov. 6:1, 3; 17:18), debts (Dt. 15:2), wages (cf. Jer. 22:13; Ezk. 22:12), and property rights in general (Dt. 23:24f. [MT 25f.]; cf. 19:14; 27:17), were all governed by law.

Covenant law also forbade taking a neighbor's life (Ex. 20:13; Dt. 5:17) and specified penalties for murder (Dt. 19:11-13; cf. 27:24). Cities of refuge were provided for those who accidentally caused someone's death (4:41-43; 19:1-10; Josh. 20). The law also prescribed penalties for disfiguring a neighbor (Lev. 24:19f.).

The OT teaching about neighborliness is summarized in Lev. 19:18: "You shall not take vengeance or bear any grudge against the sons of your own people, but you shall love your neighbor [*rē(a)*ʿ] as yourself: I am the Lord." True neighborliness is a reflection of the character of God. It is wise behavior, a manifestation of sanctified common sense, which seeks the neighbor's good just as one seeks one's own good (cf. van Selms). It recognizes that God is the final judge in disputes between neighbors (cf. 1 K. 8:31f. par. 2 Ch. 6:22f.).

The prophets predicted that the erosion of neighborliness would precipitate divine judgment. Isaiah prophesied, "The people will oppress one another . . . every man his neighbor" (Isa. 3:5). In the midst of such oppression, Jeremiah and Micah warned against trusting one's neighbor (Jer. 9:4-9; Mic. 7:5f.). Conversely, the prophets foresaw a new age when true neighborliness would flow from the renewed hearts of God's people. In that day everyone would help his neighbor (Isa. 41:6). Jeremiah envisioned that God would write His covenant law on the hearts of His people; then people would not have to teach their neighbors to "know the Lord," for "they shall all know me, from the least of them to the greatest, says the Lord" (Jer. 31:34). Zechariah pictured the messianic age as a time when people would entertain their neighbors in peace and security under their vine and fig tree (Zec. 3:10; cf. Mic. 4:3f.).

***II. In the NT.***–The most common NT term for "neighbor" is Gk. *plēsíon,* the usual LXX translation of Heb. *rē(a)*ʿ. Unlike *rē(a)*ʿ, however, *plēsíon* in Greek literature was not restricted to a compatriot but could be applied to any fellow human being who was close at hand.

In Jesus' day there was an ongoing debate within Judaism concerning the definition of "neighbor" (*rē[a]*ʿ) in the love command of Lev. 19:18. Most restricted the obligation to loving one's fellow Israelites and full proselytes. Some (e.g., the Pharisees, the Qumrân community) even restricted it to members of their own group within Judaism, while a popular saying excluded personal enemies (cf. Mt. 5:43; see Jeremias, pp. 202f.). Certain Jewish teachers, however, favored an extension of the commandment to all fellow human beings, and this tendency may be reflected in the LXX's use of *plēsíon* to render *rē(a)*ʿ (see *TDNT,* VI, 315).

The command to love one's neighbor as oneself is the hallmark of NT ethics. It is described as the "royal law" in Jas. 2:8 and as the fulfillment of the law in Rom. 13:8-10; Gal. 5:14 (cf. Mt. 19:19). In Mt. 22:37-40 par. Mk. 12:29-31; Lk. 10:27 this command is combined with the command to love God above all (Dt. 6:5) to form a summary of the entire law. Jesus emphatically rejected the interpretation that limited one's obligation to loving relatives and friends; He demanded love even for enemies, on the model of God's love for all mankind (Mt. 5:43-48).

Jesus' teaching about loving others is presented graphically in His parable of the Good Samaritan (Lk. 10:30-37). The ongoing debate concerning the definition of "neighbor" lies behind the lawyer's question, "And who is my neighbor?" (v. 29). Jesus' parable was shocking in that it presented a despised outsider as the one who showed compassion. Jesus' concluding question, "Which of these . . . proved neighbor to the man. . . ?" (v. 36), reshaped the lawyer's question, focusing on the subject rather than the object of the love command (see Jeremias, p. 205). As T. W. Manson stated, the lawyer's question "is unanswerable, and ought not to be asked. . . . The point of the parable is that if a man has love in his heart, it will tell him who his neighbor is; and this is the only possible answer to the lawyer's question" (*Sayings of Jesus* [repr. 1979], pp. 261f.). K. Barth, following the early Church, interpreted the parable as pointing to Jesus Himself as the compassionate neighbor (*CD,* I/2, 417-19).

In addition to the direct citations mentioned above, the love command is alluded to in several passages that deal primarily with relationships within the Christian community. Paul exhorted the Corinthians, "Let no one seek his own good, but the good of his neighbor" (1 Cor. 10:24; cf. Rom. 15:2). Love for the neighbor also implies speaking the truth to one another (Eph. 4:25) and not being judgmental (Jas. 4:12; cf. v. 11).

*See also* LOVE.

***Bibliography.***–*CD,* I/2, 416-420; *DNTT,* I, 258f.; J. Jeremias, *Parables of Jesus* (Eng. tr., 2nd rev. ed., 1972), pp. 202-205; *TDNT,* VI, *s.v.* πλησίον (J. Fichter, H. Greeven); A. van Selms, *JNES,* 9 (1950), 65-75.

J. J. HUGHES N. J. O.

**NEKEB.** *See* ADAMI-NEKEB.

**NEKODA** nə-kō'də [Heb. *n*ᵉ*qôḏā'*; Gk. *Nekōda*].

**1.** [Gk. Apoc. *Noeba*]; AV, NEB, NOEBA. The head of a family of temple servants who returned from the Exile with Zerubbabel (Ezr. 2:48 par. Neh. 7:50; 1 Esd. 5:31).

**2.** [Gk. Apoc. *Nekōdan*]; AV, NEB, NECODAN. The head of a family of temple servants who returned from the Exile but could not prove that they were of Israelite descent (Ezr. 2:60 par. Neh. 7:62; 1 Esd. 5:37).

**NEMUEL** nem'ū-əl [Heb. *n*ᵉ*mû'ēl*].

**1.** A Reubenite; son of Eliab and brother of Dathan and Abiram (Nu. 26:9).

**2.** A son of Simeon and head of the Nemuelites (Nu. 26:12; 1 Ch. 4:24). The name is given as JEMUEL in Gen. 46:10; Ex. 6:15.

**NEMUELITES** nem'ū-əl-īts [Heb. *n*ᵉ*mû'ēlî*]. The family of NEMUEL (**2**) the Simeonite (Nu. 26:12).

**NEPHEG** nef'eg [Heb. *nepeg*–'heavy, slow'(?)].

**1.** A Kohathite Levite; son of Izhar and brother of Korah and Zichri (Ex. 6:21).

**2.** A son of David born in Jerusalem (2 S. 5:15; 1 Ch. 3:7; 14:6).

**NEPHEW.** *See* RELATIONSHIPS, FAMILY.

**NEPHI** nef'ī (2 Macc. 1:36, AV). *See* NEPHTHAR.

**NEPHILIM** nef'ə-lim [Heb. *n*ᵉ*pîlîm* (Gen. 6:4; Nu. 13:33)], AV GIANTS. The etymology of *n*ᵉ*pîlîm* is uncertain. The following explanations have been advanced with mixed reception. First, it may derive from the niphal of the verb *pālā'*, meaning "be extraordinary," i.e., "extraordinary men." Second, it may derive from the verb *nāpal,* "fall," in one of the following senses: (1) the "fallen ones" — from heaven, i.e., supernatural beings; (2) morally "fallen men"; (3) "those who fall upon," in the sense of invaders or hostile, violent men; (4) "those who fell by" the sword (cf. Ezk. 32:20f.); (5) "unnaturally begotten men" or bastards (cf. *nēpel,* "abortion" or "miscarriage"). None of these satisfies all scholars, and some consider *nᵉpīlîm* an unexplainable relic from an ancient, now-forgotten language. Contextual information is unfortunately limited to two enigmatic passages.

The Nephilim were apparently people of imposing physical stature when compared with the smaller Hebrews (Nu. 13:33). This particular reference is glossed by a statement which implies that the offspring of Anak in Canaan were descended from the renowned Nephilim of Gen. 6:4. The latter had gained a reputation as notable heroes in the antediluvian period, and apparently persisted after the Flood (*wᵉgam 'aḥªrê-ḵēn*). This could have occurred through migration, on the basis of a local Mesopotamian deluge, and in that case would account for their descendants living in Canaan.

The Anakim were a tall people (Dt. 2:21; *see* ANAK) with whom the REPHAIM, another pre-Israelite group in Canaan, were compared. The large stature of the individuals composing these groups suggests a condition such as hypertrophy of the long bones of the skeleton, or some other disorder of a genetic variety. This becomes even more likely if the Rephaim were being indicated by the use of a term such as *rāpā'* in 1 Ch. 20:6, 8, where genetic mutations are being described (cf. *rāpâ* in 2 S. 21:16, 18, 20, 22).

Genesis 6:1-4, while meaningful to the original recipients, has become obscure with the passing of time. It is impossible to be certain whether the Nephilim were the same as the "mighty men" (*gibbôrîm*) at the end of v. 4, or a separate group that overlapped chronologically. If they were identical, questions are then raised about the "sons of God" which procreated the "mighty men" (*see* SONS OF GOD [OT]). Some modern scholars have followed ancient Jewish tradition in supposing that the "sons of God" were "fallen ones," perhaps angels, who mated with women after being cast out of heaven, thereby giving origin to the "mighty ones" (but see J. Morgenstern, *HUCA,* 14 [1935], 76-107). Such a view generally presupposes that vv. 1-4 are an etiological fragment or a "myth" that helps to explain the character of antediluvian wickedness and the consequent need for the Flood.

That the material may conceivably be ancient Semitic historiography that contains important, if obscure, anthropological, demographic, or sociological information is a proposition that seems to be taken seriously only by some conservative scholars. They consequently oppose the "mythical" conception and interpret "sons of God" as a reference to the Sethite line (Gen. 5) or to the nobility (cf. Kline), whose mixed marriages to the "daughters of men" ("men" in a restricted sense as wicked or common people) contributed to a moral decline. They argue that "myth" is inconsonant with the perspective of the Pentateuch, that "angels" are pure in Genesis and sexless in the Bible as a whole (Mt. 22:30), and that people should not be punished (Gen. 6:3) for a sin that is primarily that of angels (v. 2).

Against the claim that "sons of God" (*bᵉnê hā'ᵉlōhîm*) is always used of angels, it should be noted that the equivalent phrase in Greek described a man (Adam) in Lk. 3:38, as did the comparable expression *bᵉnê 'elyôn* ("sons of the Most High") in Ps. 82:6. The unions would thus appear to be between two human groups, the males being perhaps of the Sethite line and the females possibly constituting neanthropic remnants that were exterminated by the Flood. Whether or not the "mighty men" were actually Nephilim, no particular sin seems to have been attached to their parentage. What was condemned was the violence and corruption that characterized contemporary society (Gen. 6:11f.).

The "demigod" explanation of the Nephilim, so popular in some circles (see Cassuto), seems therefore less preferable than a nonmythological, sociological explanation which sees the people described as specifically human groups engaged in relationships of deteriorating social and spiritual quality.

*See also* GIANTS.

***Bibliography.***–U. Cassuto, *Comm. on the Book of Genesis,* I (Eng. tr. 1961), 291-301; W. H. Green, *Presbyterian and Reformed Review,* 5 (1894), 654-660; M. G. Kline, *WTJ,* 24 (1962), 187-204; E. A. Speiser, *Genesis* (*AB,* 1964), pp. 44-46.

H. VAN BROEKHOVEN, JR. R. K. H.

**NEPHIS** nē'fis (1 Esd. 5:21, AV). *See* MAGBISH.

**NEPHISH** nē'fish; **NEPHISIM** nə-fī'sim; **NEPHISHESIM** nə-fish'ə-sim. *See* NAPHISH.

**NEPHTHALI** nef'thə-lī (AV Apoc.); **NEPHTHALIM** nef'thə-lim (AV NT). *See* NAPHTALI.

**NEPHTHAR** nef'thär [Gk. *Nephthar*] (2 Macc. 1:36); AV NAPHTHAR. The name given by Nehemiah and his associates to an extremely flammable substance, as recorded in 2 Macc. 1:19-36. The substance was discovered when Nehemiah sent priests to a dry cistern in which their priestly ancestors had hidden sacred altar fire at the time of their deportation. In the cistern, however, the postexilic priests found not fire but a "thick liquid" which, after they had sprinkled it on the sacrifice, ignited at exposure to the sun's rays. After the sacrifice had been consumed, Nehemiah ordered that the remainder of the liquid be poured upon large stones, and from these also flames shot up. Upon hearing a report of these events, the king of Persia declared as sacred the place where the liquid had appeared.

"Nephthar" is said to mean "purification" (v. 36), but its etymology is unknown. It is also identified with NAPHTHA, a flammable liquid familiar to the Persians (cf. Song Three 23) and also to the Greeks (e.g., Pliny *Nat. hist.* ii.109; Strabo *Geog.* xvi.1.15). It came to be associated with the postexilic purification rites of the temple (1 Macc. 1:18; cf. Nu. 31:23).

N. J. O.

**NEPHTOAH** nef-tō'ə [Heb. *neptô[a]ḥ*; Gk. *Naphthō*]. A place mentioned only in Josh. 15:9 and 18:15 as marking the northern boundary between Judah and Benjamin. Nephtoah has been identified with modern Lifta, located 5 km. (3 mi.) NW of old Jerusalem (*LBHG,* rev. ed., pp. 122f.), but this requires the double difficulty of a phonetic shift of *n* > *l* and the dropping of the final *ḥ*. Papyri Anastasi III, V, and VI also mention the "wells of Merneptah," which could be a reference to the "waters of Nephtoah," the modern Israeli name for the site (*LBHG,* rev. ed., pp. 184, 440), but this also requires manipulation of the text. The evidence of the LXX supports the MT.

J. MCKENNA

**NEPHUSHESIM** nə-fōō'shə-sim; **NEPHUSIM** nə-fōō'sim. *See* NAPHISH.

**NER** nûr [Heb. *nēr*–'lamp'] A Benjaminite; son of Abiel (1 S. 14:51) and father of Abner (1 S. 14:50f.; 26:5, 14; 2 S. 2:8, 12; 3:23, etc.; 1 K. 2:5, 32; 1 Ch. 26:28). 1 Ch. 9:35f. appears to list Kish and Ner as brothers (cf. 8:29f., where Ner is omitted), and some have therefore read 1 S. 14:50 as saying that Ner was Saul's uncle. But 1 Ch. 9:39 and 8:33 clearly state that Ner was the father of Kish the father of Saul, which means that Abner and Kish were brothers, that Ner was Saul's grandfather, and that Abner was Saul's uncle (1 S. 14:50f.; cf. 10:14-16). It is possible that there were two men named Kish, one being Ner's brother and the other his son (*see* KISH **1-2**).

**NEREUS** nir'i-əs [Gk. *Nēreus*]. A Roman Christian greeted by Paul (Rom. 16:15). He, his sister, and Olympas (possibly the children of Philologus and Julia) were members of a household church.

The name comes originally from a minor Greek sea-god, the father of the Nereids; it was found often throughout the Roman empire among freedmen and slaves, some of whom were in the imperial service. Nereus is also the name of one of the earliest Roman martyrs, though the Nereus in Romans cannot with any degree of certainty be identified with him. J. J. HUGHES

**NERGAL** nûr'gəl [Heb. *nērgal*; Akk. $^{d}$*ne*$_3$-*iri*$_{11}$-*gal*; Gk. *Nērigel*]. The god worshiped by the men of Cuth who had been relocated in Samaria by the king of Assyria (2 K. 17:30). Nergal was a Mesopotamian deity originally associated with fire and the heat of the sun (according to one text, "Nergal and Shamash are one," *Enc.Brit.* [1970], XVI, 229, and he bears the epithet *šarrāpu,* "the burner") who developed into the god of war, pestilence, and death, the god whose consort Ereshkigal ruled Irkalla (the nether world; cf. *CAD,* VII, 177). (For the myth of Nergal and Erishkigal cf. Am.Tab. 357; *ANET,* p. 103.)

The name is found in various forms, such as Sum. (DINGIR) U.GUR (Am.Tab. 35:13, 37), ĪR.RA (Code of Hammurabi, Prologue, ii.69; *ANET,* p. 165; cf. A. Deimel, *Šumerisches Lexikon,* III/1 [1934], 138), and Bab. *ne*$_3$-UNU.GAL, in which UNU.GAL can be read *urugal*$_2$ (glossed *u*$_2$-*ru-gal*) or *iri*$_{11}$-*gal* (with UNU glossed *i-ri*) (Code of Hammurabi reverse xxviii.24; *ANET,* p. 180). The values of the Sumerian signs can be translated "the mighty one of the great city," which correlates to the name of his consort, Ereshkigal, Sum. (DINGIR) NIN KI.GAL, "lady of the great land," i.e., "the land of no-return" (*Descent of Ishtar*, lines 1ff.; *ANET*, p. 107). The vocalization of the Hebrew, attested by the LXX, supports the reading *ne-iri-gal,* for none of the other writings would yield "Nergal."

Nergal was widely worshiped. Naram-Sin, grandson of Sargon of Akkad, gave credit to Nergal for his victory over Ebla, among other places (*CAH*$^3$, I/2, 325; *ANET,* p. 268). Shulgi, of the Third Dynasty of Ur (*ca.* 2000), named the temple of Nergal at Kutu E.MESLAM, literally "the house of Hades." Hammurabi called Nergal "the giver of preeminence to Kûtû" (Code of Hammurabi ii.69; *ANET,* p. 268). Kûtû is Cutha, the Cuth of 2 K. 17:30, modern Tel Ibrahim, about 45 km. (28 mi.) NE of Babylon. In pronouncing curses against any who would not heed the words on his stele, Hammurabi said "May Nergal, mighty among the gods, warrior who has no equal . . . by his great power, like angry fire in a bed of reeds, his people let him consume, with his mighty weapon may he split him [i.e., his people] open, his limbs like an image of clay let him smash" (Code of Hammurabi reverse xxviii. 24-39 [tr. from W. S. LaSor, *Handbook of Old Babylonian*]; cf. *ANET,* p. 180).

By a strange but not uncommon development, this god of death and pestilence also became the god to whom men offered gifts for protection of their cattle and fields, and the patron god of the hunter. In Assyrian texts of the 1st millennium he is described as one who restores the dead. Several theophoric names are compounded with Nergal, e.g., NERGAL-SHAREZER and Nergal-ushezib.

*Bibliography.*–M. Jastrow, *Religion of Babylonia and Assyria* (1898), pp. 65ff.; E. Dhorme, *Les religions de Babylonie et d'Assyrie* (1949), pp. 38-44; A. Deimel, *Pantheon Babylonicum* (1914); *ANET, passim*; A. Heidel, *Gilgamesh Epic* (2nd ed. 1949), pp. 129-132; R. W. Rogers, *Cuneiform Parallels to the OT* (1912), pp. 121-135. W. S. LASOR

**NERGAL-SHAREZER** nûr'gəl-shär-ē'zər [Heb. *nērgal śar-'eṣer,* in some MSS *-śar'eṣer*; cf. Akk. *nergal šar uṣur*–'may Nergal preserve the king']; NEB NERGALSAREZER. One (or two) of the "princes" of Nebuchadrezzar who "sat in the middle gate" when Jerusalem was captured (Jer. 39:3). A problem arises in v. 3 because the name occurs twice, the second time with the apposition "the Rabmag." The latter is the form that occurs also in v. 13. The possibility that these are the names of two different persons seems to be supported by the LXX, for the first is called in Greek *Nargalasar,* whereas the second is *Nagargasnaser Rabmag*. The Greek text (ch. 39 = LXX ch. 46) does not inspire confidence, however, since in v. 3 the other two names are considerably different from the Hebrew and vv. 4-13, including the second occurrence of the name, are omitted. If two different persons are meant, the second would be a lesser official (D. J. Wiseman, in *NBD,* p. 877; but cf. *CCK,* p. 38), a "Rabmag," Akk. *rab mu-un-gu* or *rab mu-ú-gu,* often (but questionably) translated "chief of the soothsayers."

Further support for the two-persons theory may be found in a prism of Nebuchadrezzar in which officials are listed, including the name "Nergalsharusur, the *Sîn-magir*" (*ANET,* p. 308; cf. E. Unger, *Babylon, die heilige Stadt* [1931], pp. 282-294). The name following Nergal-sharezer in Jer. 39:3 is given as Samgar-nebo. Some have objected that this is not a Babylonian name formation and have suggested that the MT has been garbled, that Samgar here has resulted from a misreading of Bab. *sîn-magîr* (cf. *IB,* V, 1079). Once again, the LXX appears to lend some support, for in the Greek text the second name is rendered as Samagoth and the "-nebo" element has become part of the third name.

Whether we read one or two Nergal-sharezers, the possible identification of this name with that of Neriglissar, king of Babylon 560-556, must also be considered. Until the publication of *CCK* little was known about this king, and not a great deal more is now available. He was not of the royal line but a nobleman, son of Bêl-šum-iškun (cf. S. Langdon and R. Zehnpfund, *Neubabylonischen Königinschriften* [1912], pp. 208ff.; *CCK,* p. 38 n. 6), who owned land at Babylon and Opis and was appointed to oversee the business affairs at E.BABBAR.RA ("the temple of the sun-god"; cf. *CCK,* p. 38 n. 10). Neriglissar married Nebuchadrezzar's daughter and subsequently seized the throne — but whether he was implicated in the plot that resulted in the death of Awîl-Marduk (Evil-merodach) or acceded to the throne as the legitimate heir (brother-in-law of Awîl-Marduk) is not clear. Upon his death (late April or early May, 556, according to R. A. Parker and W. A. Dubberstein, *Babylonian Chronology* [2nd ed. 1956], p. 12) he was succeeded by his son Labāši-Marduk, a youth who was assassinated after a reign of nine months. His successor was Nabonidus, a native of Haran. For further details see *CCK,* pp. 38-42, 74-77, 86-88.

W. S. LASOR

**NERI** nir'ī [Gk. *Nēri* < Heb. *nērîyâ*–'Yahweh is light'] (Lk. 3:27). An ancestor of Jesus. According to Lk. 3:27f. Neri was the father of Shealtiel and the son of Melchi, but according to Mt. 1:12 (and 1 Ch. 3:17) Jeconiah was Shealtiel's father. Cf. I. H. Marshall, *Gospel of Luke* (*New International Greek Testament Comm.*, 1978), pp. 163f.; R. H. Gundry, *Matthew* (1981), pp. 17f.; J. Jeremias, *Jerusalem in the Time of Jesus* (Eng. tr., rev. ed. 1969), pp. 290-97. *See also* GENEALOGY OF JESUS.

**NERIAH** nə-rī'ə [Heb. *nērîyâ*–'Yahweh is light' (Jer. 32:12, 16; 36:4, 8; 43:3; 45:1; 51:59), *nērîyāhû* (Jer. 36:14, 32; 43:6)]; **NERAIAH** [Gk. *Nērias*] (Bar. 1:1); AV NERIAS; NEB NERIAH. (The two Hebrew forms reflect a common variation of the theophoric element *yh*[*w*]; cf. the two forms of Jeremiah, Heb. *yirmᵉyâ* and *yirmᵉyāhû*.) Father of two sons: Jeremiah's scribe Baruch (Jer. 32:12) and the quartermaster Seraiah, who served as a messenger for Jeremiah (51:59).

**NERIAS.** *See* NERIAH.

**NERO** nē'rō [Gk. *Nerōn*]. The fifth Roman emperor, who was born at Antium in A.D. 37, began to reign October, 54, and died June 9, 68.

I. Parentage and Early Training
II. Reign
  A. "Quinquennium Neronis"
  B. Poppaea Sabina and Tigellinus
  C. Great Fire
  D. Persecution of Christians
  E. Conspiracy of Piso
  F. Visit to Greece
  G. Death
III. "Nero Redivivus"
IV. Nero and Christianity
  A. Nero and the NT
  B. Neronian Policy and Christianity

***I. Parentage and Early Training.***–Nero's father was Cnaeus Domitius Ahenobarbus ("brazen beard"), a man from an illustrious family but of vicious life. His mother Agrippina, daughter of Germanicus and the older Agrippina, was a sister of the emperor Caligula. Through her mother she was the great-granddaughter of the emperor Augustus, and this gave her son a strong claim to the throne.

Agrippina schemed to make Nero's imperial claim a reality. He was betrothed and later married to Octavia, daughter of Claudius, who succeeded his nephew Caligula as emperor. After the murder of Claudius's wife, Agrippina (by then widowed) wed Claudius, the law having been changed to allow her marriage to her father's brother. She persuaded Claudius to adopt Nero as his son, and the young man, formerly Lucius Domitius Ahenobarbus, became Nero Claudius Caesar Germanicus. Claudius agreed to make a will in favor of Nero, but when he began to regret disinheriting his own son Britannicus, Agrippina poisoned Claudius. Immediately Nero was proclaimed emperor by the praetorian prefect Burrus; the praetorian guard had been richly bribed. The senate weakly acknowledged the new emperor.

***II. Reign.***–*A. "Quinquennium Neronis."* The first five years (*quinquennium*) of Nero's reign were characterized by good government at home and in the provinces and by the emperor's popularity with the senate and people. Agrippina's influence over her son was lessened through the efforts of Burrus and Seneca the philosopher, who was Nero's tutor. One of her efforts to retain her power — a threat to present Britannicus as the rightful heir to the throne — resulted in Nero's having Britannicus poisoned and eventually banishing Agrippina from the palace. Seneca and Burrus brought about financial, social, and

Bust of the young Nero (Corinth Excavations, American School of Classical Studies; I. Ioannido and L. Bartziotou, photographers)

legislative reforms but allowed Nero to indulge in low pleasures and excesses and to surround himself with dissolute companions — habits that the emperor never abandoned.

*B. Poppaea Sabina and Tigellinus.* The wife of Otho, one of Nero's notorious companions, was Poppaea Sabina, a woman as ambitious as she was unprincipled. She was endowed, according to Tacitus, with every gift of nature except an "honorable mind." Beginning in 58 she used her husband as a tool to become Nero's consort. Under her influence Nero shook off all restraints, turned a deaf ear to his best advisers, and plunged deeper into immorality and crime. She allowed, if not persuaded, Nero to give Otho a commission in a distant province (Lusitania). With Nero's connivance she plotted Agrippina's death. Agrippina was induced to board a boat that had been carefully constructed to sink, but she saved herself by swimming ashore. She was subsequently killed on a pretext, however, and Nero claimed that she had committed suicide (Suetonius xxxiv; Tacitus *Ann.* cxli-cxlviii).

Having openly become Nero's mistress, Poppaea continued to eliminate her rivals. When Burrus died in A.D. 62, she forced Seneca to withdraw from the court. She had Nero divorce Octavia because of her barrenness and then banish her to the island of Pandateria on a false charge of adultery. Octavia was executed in 62 and her head brought to Poppaea. In 65 Poppaea herself died during pregnancy when Nero in a fit of rage cruelly kicked her.

After his extravagance had exhausted the well-filled treasury left by Claudius, Nero began to confiscate the estates of rich nobles against whom the new praetorian prefect Tigellinus could contrive the slightest charge.

Even this tactic did not prevent a financial crisis — the beginning of the bankruptcy of the Roman empire. Worst of all, the gold and silver coinage was depreciated, and the senate was deprived of the right of copper coinage.

*C. Great Fire.* The situation was immeasurably worsened by the great fire that began July 18, 64, in the Circus Maximus and that, with the aid of a high wind, consumed street after street of poorly built wooden houses. When after six days it had almost died down, another conflagration started in a different part of the city. Of the fourteen city regions, evidently seven were destroyed totally and four partially. Nero hurried back to Rome from Antium and superintended in person the work of the fire brigades, often exposing himself to danger. He took many of the homeless into his own gardens. Despite his efforts, numerous rumors accused him of arson (cf. Suetonius xxviii; Tacitus *Ann.* xv.38ff.). No serious modern historian, however, charges him with the crime.

*D. Persecution of Christians.* Since such public calamities were generally attributed to the wrath of the gods, everything was done to appease the offended deity. Tacitus recounted Nero's scheme to avert suspicion from himself. "He put forward as guilty [*subdidit reos*], and afflicted with the most exquisite punishments, those who were hated for their abominations [*flagitia*] and called 'Christians' by the populace. Christus, from whom the name was derived, was punished by the procurator Pontius Pilate in the reign of Tiberius. The noxious form of religion [*exitiabilis superstitio*], checked for a time, broke out again not only in Judea its original home, but also throughout the city [Rome], where all the abominations meet and find devotees. Therefore first of all those who confessed [i.e., to being Christians] were arrested, and then as a result of their information a large number were implicated [reading *coniuncti,* not *convicti*], not so much on the charge of incendiarism as for hatred of the human race. They died by methods of mockery; some were covered with the skins of wild beasts and then torn by dogs, some were crucified, some were burned as torches to light at night. . . . Whence [after scenes of extreme cruelty] commiseration was stirred for them, although guilty of deserving the worse penalties, for men felt that their destruction was not on account of the public welfare but to gratify the cruelty of one [Nero]" (*Ann.* xv. 44).

Such is the earliest account of the first gentile persecution (as well as the first gentile record of the crucifixion of Jesus). Tacitus clearly implied that the Christians were innocent *(subdidit reos)* and that Nero used them simply as scapegoats. Some regard the conclusion of the paragraph as a contradiction of this — "though guilty and deserving the severest punishment" *(adversus sontes et novissima exempla meritos)*. But Tacitus meant by *sontes* that the Christians were "guilty" from the point of view of the populace and that from his own standpoint, too, they merited extreme punishment, but not for arson. *Fatebantur* does not mean that they confessed to incendiarism, but to being Christians; *qui fatebantur* means that some boldly confessed, but others tried to conceal or perhaps even denied their faith.

*E. Conspiracy of Piso.* The tyranny of Tigellinus and his confiscations to meet Nero's expenses caused the nobles deep discontent, which culminated in the famous conspiracy of 64 headed by C. Calpurnius Piso. The plot was betrayed and an inquisition followed in which perished Seneca the philosopher, Lucan the poet, Lucan's mother, and later Annaeus Mela the brother of Seneca and father of Lucan (Tacitus *Ann.* xvi.21f.).

*F. Visit to Greece.* Having taken care of every suspected person, Nero abandoned the government in Rome to a freedman, Helius, and made a long visit to Greece (A.D. 66-68). There he took part in muscial contests and games; he won prizes from the obsequious Greeks, in return for which he bestowed on them the "freedom" of their province.

*G. Death.* In 66 began the revolt in Judea that would end in the destruction of Jerusalem, and in 68 the revolt of Vindex, governor of Lugdunum (Lyons) in Gaul, was put down. Shortly afterward came the fatal rebellion of Galba, governor of Hither Spain, who declared himself *legatus* of the senate and Roman people. Helius persuaded Nero to return to Rome. The emperor confiscated Galba's property and could have crushed him, but the doubts, fears, and distractions that overwhelmed him greatly helped Galba's cause. Nero lost the support of the praetorian guard that made him emperor. He committed suicide, bringing to an end the line of Julius Caesar.

***III. "Nero Redivivus."***–A freedman, two old nurses, and his cast-off concubine Acte cared affectionately for Nero's remains, and for a long time flowers were strewn on his grave (Suetonius lvii). Soon the strange belief arose that Nero had not really died but was living somewhere in retirement, perhaps in Parthia, and would return shortly to bring great calamity upon his enemies or the world (Suetonius lviii).

Some Jews amalgamated this belief with their concept of the antichrist. Asc. Isa. 4 (1st cent. A.D.) clearly identifies the antichrist with Nero; the idea repeatedly occurs in both Jewish and Christian sections of the Sibylline Oracles (3:66ff.; 4:117f.; 5:100f., 136f., 216f.).

How far the Christians regarded Nero as the historical personage of the antichrist is disputed. It would be natural if they had been inflenced by contemporary thought about the revival of Nero. W. Bousset (*Die Offenbarung Johannis* [1906], *in loc.*) regarded the beast of Rev. 13 as Rome and the smitten head "whose mortal wound was healed" as Nero; some scholars think that Rev. 17:10f. refers to Nero. Such passages in Revelation may refer to the spirit of Nero but certainly not to Nero himself. Some scholars have applied the number 666 in 13:8 to Nero, but it suits many other wicked rulers as well (cf. Farrar, ch. 28, 5). (*See* NUMBER VI.)

***IV. Nero and Christianity.***–*A. Nero and the NT.* Although the name Nero does not occur in the NT, he must have been the Caesar to whom Paul appealed (Acts 25:11) and at whose tribunal Paul was tried after his first imprisonment. Nero probably heard Paul's case in person, for he showed much interest in provincial cases. It was during the earlier "golden quinquennium" of Nero's reign that Paul addressed his Epistle to the Christians at Rome. Some have argued that Paul was probably martyred near Rome in the last year of Nero's reign (A.D. 68), but it is much more probable that Paul died in the first Neronian persecution of 64.

The NT never states that Peter visited Rome. The belief in such a visit arose later from tradition (cf. Clement of Rome, Ignatius, Papias, and later Tertullian, Clement of Alexandria, and the *Liber Pontificalis* [catalog of popes]). Although there is no reliable evidence that Peter was bishop of Rome, and while it is certain that if he went to Rome it was for brief period, it is highly probable that he visited the city in old age and was martyred there under Nero.

*B. Neronian Policy and Christianity.* Before Nero, the Roman government had been on friendly terms with Christianity, for it was not prominent enough to disturb society greatly and was probably confused with Judaism, a licensed religion (Tertullian *Apol.* 21). Paul urged the Christians of the capital to "be subject to the governing authorities" as "instituted by God" (Rom. 13:1f.). His high estimation of the Roman government as a power operating for the good of society was probably enhanced by his own experiences before his final imprisonment. By that time the difference between Christianity and Judaism had become apparent to the Roman authorities, perhaps because of the growing hostility of the Jews, or perhaps because of the alarming progress of Christianity, and policy had begun to change for the worse.

According to one view, the Neronian persecution was a unique attempt to satisfy the revenge of the mob and was confined to Rome. Christians were put forward as arsonists to remove suspicion from Nero. They were persecuted on account of false charges of Thyestean feasts, Oedipal incest, and nightly orgies; their withdrawal from pagan society and their exclusive manners caused the charge of "hatred of the human race." The evidence of Tacitus seems to support this view.

The preferable view, however, represented by Ramsay (*CRE*, ch. 11) and E. G. Hardy (*Studies in Roman History*, ch. 4), is that Christianity was permanently proscribed as a result of Nero's persecutions. In this view, the accounts of Tacitus and Suetonius are reconcilable; Tacitus gave the initial step, and Suetonius's inclusion of the persecution of Christians in a list of seemingly permanent police regulations (*Nero* xvi) indicates the outcome — an established policy of persecution. Ramsay maintained that Christians had to be tried and their crimes proved before they were executed, but Hardy argued that henceforth the Name itself was proscribed.

There is no reason to suppose that the Neronian persecution of 64 extended throughout the empire. The authorities for a general Neronian persecution and formal Neronian laws against Christianity are late. But the emperor's example in Rome would have greatly influenced the provinces; the persecutions established a precedent of great importance in the imperial policy toward Christianity.

*See* ROMAN EMPIRE AND CHRISTIANITY.

***Bibliography.***–*CAH*, X, ch. 21; L. H. Canfield, *Early Persecutions of the Christians* (1913); *CRE;* Eusebius *HE* ii.25; F. W. Farrar, *Early Days of Christianity* (1882); E.R. Goodenough, *Church in the Roman Empire* (1931), ch. 12; H. M. Gwatkin, *Early Church History*, I (1909); E. G. Hardy, *Christianity and the Roman Government* (1925); B. W. Henderson, *Life and Principate of the Emperor Nero* (1903).

S. ANGUS
A. M. RENWICK

**NEST** [Heb. (noun) *qēn* (Nu. 24:21; Dt. 22:6; 32:11; Job 29:18; 39:27; Ps. 84:3 [MT 4]; Prov. 27:8; Isa. 10:14; Jer. 49:16; Ob. 4; Hab. 2:9), (vb.) *qānan* (piel, Ps. 104:17; Isa. 34:15; Jer. 48:28; Ezk. 31:6; pual, Jer. 22:23), *šāḵan* (Ezk. 17:23); Gk. *kataskēnōsis* (Mt. 8:20 par. Lk. 9:58), *kataskēnóō* ("make nests," Mt. 13:32 par. Mk. 4:32; Lk. 13:19)]; AV also LODGE; NEB ROOST, SETTLE, "my powers unimpaired" (Job 29:18).

About half the references are to nests in general, but the following nests may be distinguished. (1) The nests of eagles or the griffon-vulture (Dt. 32:11; Job 39:27; Jer. 49:16; Ob. 4; Hab. 2:9; perhaps Nu. 24:21) are large, deep bundles of sticks and debris of deceptive strength. They are constructed in very inaccessible spots, high on cliffs or trees in the wilderness, providing a secure home for the young, which mature slowly (*see also* EAGLE). (2) Jer. 48:28 accurately describes the nests of the rock dove, built on little ledges on the face of the gorge and quite inaccessible (cf. Cansdale, p. 170). (3) It is uncertain whether Ps. 84:3 refers to nests of the swift or the swallow. Both birds are exclusively fliers with feet too underdeveloped to stand upon. They therefore build nests in niches or holes in vertical walls to which they can cling. Because they feed on insects that multiply around human settlements and because buildings provide suitable vertical walls, both birds are very much at home around people — and in the temple of God. (4) The scops-owl, which is native to Palestine and frequently nests in the ruins of human dwellings, fits the context of Isa. 34:15, although the NEB has "sand partridge" and the JB "viper."

The one literal reference to a nest is Dt. 22:6, where the law protects the nesting mother and thus the procreation of birds. The other references are usually metaphors for the security (or false security) of a person, city, or nation; e.g., the inhabitants of Lebanon "nest" among the cedars (Jer. 22:23) and the Edomites "nest" in their cliffs at Petra (49:16; Ob. 4). On the problematic Job 29:18, see the comms., especially R. Gordis (1978) and E. Dhorme (Eng. tr. 1966).

***Bibliography.***–G. S. Cansdale, *Animals of Bible Lands* (1970); G. R. Driver, *PEQ*, 87 (1955), 5-20, 129-140; A. Parmelee, *All the Birds of the Bible* (1959).

H. VAN BROEKHOVEN, JR.

**NET, SEINE.** Nets were used in Israel for HUNTING, FISHING, and fowling (*see* FOWLER).

(1) The most common word for net in the OT is *rešeṯ*. Nets were made out of cords (Ps. 140:5 [MT 6]) and were primarily used to catch the prey by the feet. This led to a figure of speech in which the wicked lay nets to trap the righteous, while the latter pray to God for deliverance (Ps. 10:9; 25:15; 31:4 [MT 5]; 140:5 [MT 6]; Prov. 29:5; Ezk. 19:8; Hos. 5:1) or even for a reversal, so that the wicked are caught in their own trap (Ps. 9:15 [MT 16]; 35:7f.; 57:6 [MT 7]; cf. Job 18:8). Several passages, however, indicate that a *rešeṯ* may have been used on occasion to bring down flying birds (Prov. 1:17; Hos. 7:12). In some instances, the Lord spreads a net to punish His people (Lam. 1:13; Ezk. 12:13; 17:20). *Rešeṯ* refers to a hunting net except in Ezk. 32:3, where it is used to catch a sea monster, and in Ex. 27:4f., where it ("network") refers to the grating that was placed upon the sacrificial altar.

(2) The Heb. *śᵉḇāḵâ* is mainly used to refer to some ornamental decoration on the capital of each of the two columns that stood in front of Solomon's temple. The RSV translates as "net" and "network," the AV as "net" and "wreathe," while the NEB is consistent with "network" (1 K. 7:17f., 20, 41f.; 2 K. 25:17; 2 Ch. 4:12f.;

Servants of King Ashurbanipal carry nets and stakes in a hunting scene from a Nineveh relief (*ca.* 640 B.C.) (Trustees of the British Museum)

Jer. 52:22f.). In 2 K. 1:2 it is translated as "lattice," referring to some type of window covering through which Ahaziah fell.

(3) The Heb. *ḥērem* was a net used in fishing. In a prophecy against Tyre, Ezekiel said that it would be destroyed, scraped bare, and become a place where fishermen would spread their nets (for drying; 26:5, 14). When speaking of blessings to come, Ezekiel prophesied that the Dead Sea (!) would be full of fish with fishermen spreading their nets along its now barren shores (47:10). This word for net was also used as a figure of speech to describe how the wicked snare the innocent (Eccl. 7:26; Mic. 7:2). In a prophecy of judgment the prophet related how the Lord would capture Pharaoh in His dragnet (AV "net"; NEB "meshes"; Ezk. 32:3). As Habakkuk described the evils of the Babylonians, he told how the king of Babylon ensnared his enemies in his net, and then offered sacrifices to his net in appreciation for his victories (Hab. 1:15ff.). Compare the picture of a Mesopotamian ruler who had snared his enemies in his net in *ANEP,* nos. 298, 307.

(4) Large nets (Heb. *miḵmār*) were used to hunt big animals such as antelope (Isa. 51:20). Various words meaning net, derived from this root, are used in Scripture. Fishermen in Egypt spread their nets upon the water (Heb. *miḵmōreṯ,* Isa. 19:8); the psalmist prayed that the wicked would fall into their own nets (Heb. *maḵmôr,* Ps. 141:10); and the king of Babylon captured his enemies in his seine (Heb. *miḵmereṯ*; AV "drag"; NEB "trawls"; Hab. 1:15f.).

(5) The Heb. *m*$^{e}$*ṣôḏâ* is used to refer to a fishing net (Eccl. 9:12). A related word, *m*$^{e}$*ṣûḏâ,* is used in a figure of speech in which God is portrayed as bringing difficult times upon His people (Ps. 66:11) or using the king of Babylon to take the "prince" of Jerusalem captive ("snare," Ezk. 12:13; 17:20). Job complains that God has closed

Eannatum, king of Lagash, holding enemies in a net. Fragments of the "stele of the vultures," mid-3rd millennium B.C., from Tello (Louvre)

Mycenean gold Vaphio cup showing a bull trapped in a net (ca. 1500 B.C.) (National Archaeological Museum, Athens)

His net (*m*$^{e}$*ṣûḏ*) about him (19:6), while a wicked woman has a heart that is a snare (*m*$^{e}$*ṣûḏ*; NEB "trap"; Eccl. 7:26).

The NT mentions three types of nets. The most common type is the *díktyon,* a general term that can include all kinds of nets. Two Greek words are used to describe the nets that the Galilean fishermen were mending when Jesus called them to be His disciples (Mt. 4:18ff.; Mk. 1:16ff.; Lk. 5:2ff.). The more general term *díktyon* dominates in these accounts, but in two instances the Gk. *amphíblēstron* is used along with *díktyon* (Mt. 4:18; Mk. 1:16). The former term referred to a bell- or pear-shaped net that had an opening 3 to 6 m. (10 to 20 ft.) in diameter. Around the circumference of the opening small weights were placed, and when the net was cast into the lake it sank to the bottom, trapping the fish inside.

In contrast to this usage of *díktyon* with *amphíblēstron,* by itself *díktyon* refers to a larger net in John's Gospel (21:6ff.), for in it the disciples caught 153 fish. This was probably a large seine. Seines were normally fitted with floats along the top while weights were placed on the bottom. These vertical nets could be attached to the shore, while a boat dragged it out into the water in a semicircular arc and then back to the shore again. Thus the fish would be trapped between the net and the shore line. It was also possible for two boats to complete a similar maneuver.

A seine (Gk. *sagḗnē*) is specifically mentioned in the parable of the net (Mt. 13:47-50). In it the kingdom of heaven is compared to a net (seine) in which all kinds of fish are caught. The good are kept while the bad are tossed away. Thus it will be at the close of the age, the evil being separated from the righteous.

*See also* NETWORK; SNARE. C. G. RASMUSSEN

**NETAIM** nə-tā'əm [Heb. *n*$^{e}$*ṭā*$^{c}$*îm*–'plantings'; LXX A *Ataeim*; B *Azaeim*; Lucian *Etaeim*] (1 Ch. 4:23); AV "plants." A city in Judah, mentioned with GEDERAH, which was in the Shephelah (Josh. 15:36). (The AV translated Heb. *n*$^{e}$*ṭā*$^{c}$*îm,* "plants," and *g*$^{e}$*ḏērâ,* "hedges," but the modern versions are correct in reading the words as place names.) W. F. Albright (*JPOS,* 5 [1925], 17-54, esp. pp. 50f.) suggested an identification of Netaim with Khirbet en-Nuweiti$^{c}$ S of the Wâdī Elah. Netaim was the abode of royal potters, who were descendants of Shelah son of Judah. E. M. COOK

**NETHANEEL** nə-than'i-əl. *See* NETHANEL.

**NETHANEL** nə-than'əl [Heb. *n^etan'ēl*–'God has given'; Gk. Apoc. *Nathanaēl, Nathanaēlos*]; AV, NEB, NETHANEEL, Apoc. NATHANAEL.

**1.** Son of Zuar; the leader of the tribe of Issachar who commanded 54,400 men and represented his tribe at the dedication of the tabernacle (Nu. 1:8; 2:5; 7:18, 23; 10:15).

**2.** The fourth son of Jesse; a brother of David (1 Ch. 2:14).

**3.** A priest who blew the trumpet before the ark when it was brought up from the house of Obed-edom (1 Ch. 15:24).

**4.** A Levite; father of Shemaiah the scribe (1 Ch. 24:6).

**5.** The fifth son of Obed-edom (1 Ch. 26:4); a Levite in the division of gatekeepers.

**6.** A prince sent by King Jehoshaphat to teach the law in the cities of Judah (2 Ch. 17:7).

**7.** A "chief of the Levites" who contributed to the Passover offering in the reign of King Josiah (2 Ch. 35:9 par. 1 Esd. 1:9).

**8.** Son of Pashhur; a priest who had married a foreign wife (Ezr. 10:22; called Nathanael in 1 Esd. 9:22).

**9.** A priest, head of the house of Jedaiah in the time of Joiakim the high priest (Neh. 12:21).

**10.** A priest who played a musical instrument at the dedication of the rebuilt walls of Jerusalem (Neh. 12:36); possibly the same as **8.** N. J. O.

**NETHANIAH** neth-ə-nī'ə [Heb. *n^etanyâ, n^etanyāhû*–'Yahweh has given'].

**1.** An Asaphite musician assigned by David to "prophesy with lyres, with harps, and with cymbals" (1 Ch. 25:2, 12).

**2.** A Levite sent by King Jehoshaphat to teach the law in the cities of Judah (2 Ch. 17:8).

**3.** The father of Jehudi (Jer. 36:14).

**4.** The father of Ishmael the murderer of Gedaliah (2 K. 25:23, 25; Jer. 40:8, 14f.; 41:1, etc.).

**5.** [Gk. Apoc. *Nathanias*]; AV, NEB, NATHANIAS. A layman who had married a foreign wife and was required to divorce her (1 Esd. 9:34; called Nathan in Ezr. 10:39).

**NETHER WORLD** [Heb. *'ereṣ taḥtîyôṯ* (Ezk. 26:20; 32:18, 24), *'ereṣ taḥtîṯ* (31:14, 16, 18); Eng. 'nether'–'lower']; AV "low parts of the earth," "nether parts of the earth"; NEB UNDERWORLD, WORLD BELOW, ABYSS. "Nether world" always refers to the abode of the dead, the destination of the people under God's judgment. In the NT it is called the "nether gloom" (Gk. *zóphos,* 2 Pet. 2:4, 17; Jude 6, 13; *see* GLOOM).

As Tromp pointed out (p. 180), *taḥtîṯ* can mean either "lower" (of two things) or "lowest" (of more than two). He concluded that since *'ereṣ* by itself denotes only "earth" and "underworld" in the OT, the adj. *taḥtîṯ* was added to clarify the sense of *'ereṣ*; thus *'ereṣ taḥtîṯ* is most accurately translated "nether world," i.e., lower world (cf. Eng. "underworld"). But Tromp's distinction between *taḥtîṯ* and *taḥtîyôṯ* ("the furthest extreme" of the underworld, pp. 182f.) is questionable (see A. Anderson, *Psalms* [*NCBC,* repr. 1981], I, 459), although 1 En. 22:9-13 certainly describes the underworld as being separated into various compartments. *See also* HADES.

On the theory (held by, e.g., Stadelmann and Tromp) that the Hebrews conceived of a three-story universe — heavens, earth, and underworld (i.e., Sheol = nether world) — *see* WORLD.

*See also* DEATH; GEHENNA; HELL; PIT; SHEOL.

***Bibliography*.**–W. Eichrodt, *Ezekiel* (Eng. tr., *OTL,* 1970), pp. 373-77; L. Stadelmann, *Hebrew Conception of the World (Analecta Biblica,* 39, 1970), esp. pp. 165-176; *TDOT,* IV, *s.v.* "'erets" (Bergman, Ottosson), esp. pp. 399f.; N. Tromp, *Primitive Conceptions of Death and the Nether World in the OT* (*Biblica et Orientalia,* 21, 1969), esp. pp. 180-83. G. A. L.

**NETHINIM** neth'ə-nim [Heb. *n^etînîm*–'given ones'; Gk. *Natheineim*]; AV NETHINIMS; RSV "temple servants"; NEB "temple-servitors." A group of temple servants (1 Ch. 9:2; Ezr. 2:43, 58, 70; 7:7; 8:17, 20; Neh. 3:26, 31; 7:46, 60, 73; 10:28 [MT 29]; 11:3, 21). The word always has the article and does not occur in the singular. The LXX usually transliterates but in one passage renders it "the given ones" (Gk. *hoi dedoménoi,* 1 Ch. 9:2). The Syriac (Pesh.) also transliterates the word in Ezra-Nehemiah but in 1 Ch. 9:2 renders it by a word meaning "sojourners." The meaning "given" is suggestive of a state of servitude, and Josephus seems to confirm the suggestion by calling the Nethinim "temple slaves" (Gk. *hieródouloi, Ant.* xi.5.1 [128]). Another form of the word, however, is used to describe the Levites, "*given* unto [Aaron] on behalf of the children of Israel" (Nu. 3:9; cf. 8:16, 19).

The preexilic history of the Nethinim is little known. Talmudic tradition identified them with the descendants of the Gibeonites, whom Joshua made "hewers of wood and drawers of water for the house of my God" (Josh. 9:23, 27; T.B. *Yebamoth* 78b-79). Ezr. 8:20, however, seems to indicate that David and his officials appointed them for the service of the Levites. Some of the names of the Nethinim indicate a foreign origin. The MEUNIM (Ezr. 2:50; Neh. 7:52) and the Nephisim (Ezr. 2:50; cf. Neh. 7:52; Gen. 25:15; 1 Ch. 5:19; *see* NAPHISH) were probably aborigines in Palestine who harassed the Hebrews from time to time (Jgs. 10:12; 1 Ch. 4:41; 2 Ch. 26:7). In both Ezra and Nehemiah the list of Nethinim is immediately followed by that of the servants of Solomon, whose duties were similar to and perhaps even humbler than theirs. These servants of Solomon appear to be descendants of the Canaanites whom Solomon employed in building (1 K. 5:15; 9:15-21). One may thus assume that the Nethinim were originally foreign slaves, mostly prisoners of war, who were given to the temple and assigned the lower menial duties there (R. de Vaux, *Ancient Israel* [Eng. tr. 1961], I, 89f.). Such was the custom among many ancient peoples, the closest parallel being the *širkûtu* of Babylon (*IB,* III, 584).

At the time of the return from the Exile the Nethinim had become important. Their number was considerable: 392 accompanied Zerubbabel at the first return (538 B.C.; Ezr. 2:58; Neh. 7:60). When Ezra some eighty years later organized the second return, he secured a contingent of Nethinim numbering 220 (Ezr. 8:20). In Jerusalem they enjoyed the same privileges and immunities as the other religious orders, being included by Artaxerxes' letter to Ezra among those who should be exempt from toll, custom, and tribute (Ezr. 7:24). A part of the city in Ophel, opposite the water gate, was assigned them as an official residence (Neh. 3:26, 31); the location was certainly appropriate if their duties at all resembled those of the Gibeonites (cf. Ryle, in *CBSC,* p. 57). They were also organized into a kind of guild under their own leaders (Neh. 11:21; cf. B. Levine, *JBL,* 82 [1963], 207-212, who claims they were a cultic guild of devoted but free persons; he notes parallels with Ugar. *ytnm*).

The Nethinim are not again mentioned in Scripture. It is probable that they, with the singers and porters, gradually were incorporated into the general body of Levites. Their name passed into a tradition, and the Talmud forbade intermarriage with them as un-Jewish.

J. B. GRAYBILL

**NETOPHAE** nə-tō'fī (1 Esd. 5:18, NEB). *See* NETOPHAH.

**NETOPHAH** nə-tō'fə [Heb. *neṭōpâ*–'dropping, drippings'; Gk. Apoc. B *Netebas*, A *Netōphae* (1 Esd. 5:18)]; NEB Apoc. NETOPHAE; **NETOPHATHITE** nə-tō'fə-thīt [Heb. *neṭōpāṯî*]; AV also NETOPHATHI (Neh. 12:28). A village 5 km. (3 mi.) SE of Bethlehem on the way to Tekoa, near Anathoth and the Herodium (cf. Ezr. 2:21-23; Neh. 7:26f.). It is probably the modern Khirbet Bedd Fālûḥ, which has a nearby spring, ʿAin en-Natûf, preserving the ancient name.

The Netophathites were descendants of Caleb through Salma (1 Ch. 2:54). The town itself has no real significance except as the home of three minor biblical characters. Maharai (2 S. 23:28 par. 1 Ch. 11:30) and Heled son of Baanah (or Heleb; 2 S. 23:29 par. 1 Ch. 11:30) were two of David's thirty mighty men; they commanded the 10th and 12th army divisions, respectively (1 Ch. 27:13, 15). Seraiah son of Tanhumeth supported Gedaliah after Nebuchadrezzar installed the latter as governor (2 K. 25:23). (The same account is in Jer. 40:8, but there it reads "Seraiah the son of Tanhumeth, the sons of Ephai the Netophathite," thus listing another group, "the sons of Ephai," as coming from Netophah.)

Netophah is also mentioned in connection with the Jewish resettlement after the Babylonian captivity. 1 Ch. 9:16 identifies several Levites who returned. (Netophah was not originally a levitical city, although nearby Anathoth was; cf. Josh. 21:9-12, 18.) These Levites were also called to celebrate the dedication of the wall of Jerusalem (Neh. 12:28). Ezr. 2:22 says that fifty-six Netophathites returned (cf. 1 Esd. 5:18, fifty-five). Neh. 7:26 says that 188 men returned to Bethlehem and Netophah (cf. Ezr. 2:21f., 179 returnees).

***Bibliography.***–A. Alt, *Palästina Jahrbuch* (1932), pp. 12, 47-54; Y. Aharoni, *IEJ*, 6 (1956), 102-111, 137-155.

W. D. MOUNCE

**NETOPHATHI** nə-tō'fə-thē. *See* NETOPHAH.

**NETTLES.**

(1) [Heb. *ḥārûl*] (Job 30:7; Prov. 24:31; Zeph. 2:9); NEB SCRUB (Job), WEEDS. True nettles (genus *Urtica*), which in Palestine are more virulent than in Europe, would scarcely suit the conditions in the text. The LXX of Job 30:7 has Gk. *phrýgana ágria*, "wild brushwood," indicating some perennial shrub. The most probable is some species of *Acanthus*, perhaps *A. spinosus* L. or *A. syriacus* Boiss., which occur commonly as weeds in the east. The "nettles" of Prov. 24:31 may be charlock, *Sinapis arvensis* L.

(2) [Heb. *qimmôś*; Gk. *ákantha*] (Isa. 34:13; Hos. 9:6); NEB also WEEDS (Hos. 9:6). Probably a species of true nettles, the four found in Palestine being *Urtica dioica* L., *U. caudata* Vahl., *U. pilulifera* L., and *U. ureus* L. They flourish in waste places and can attain a height of 2 m. (6 ft.).

R. K. H.

**NETWORK** [Heb. *maʿaśēh rešeṯ*–'working of a net' (Ex. 27:4; 38:4), *śeḇāḵâ* (1 K. 7:18, 20, 41f.; etc.)]; AV also WREATHEN WORK (2 K. 25:17), WREATH (2 Ch. 4:12f.). A grill or screen which was part of the altar of burnt offering in the wilderness tabernacle and the decorations made of woven chains on the tops of the pillars in front of Solomon's temple.

The single word net (Heb. *rešeṯ*) in the combination *maʿaśēh rešeṯ* is a rather general word for the kind of snare used to catch birds, fish, or even an enemy. It occurs, however, in Ex. 27:4f.; 38:4 to describe the grate or lattice work around the altar of burnt offering. According to most models of the TABERNACLE, this bronze screen allowed air in underneath the fire for better circulation.

Hebrew *śeḇāḵâ* is used once in the sense of trap (Job 18:8); elsewhere it refers to some kind of interlacing of ornamental bronze chains decorating the tops of the pillars on the porch of Solomon's temple (1 K. 7:18, 20, 41f.; 2 Ch. 4:12f.). 1 K. 7:17 contains the Hebrew word once in the plural ("nets") and once in the singular ("checker"). To complicate this difficult verse even further the RSV and NEB translators have twice read Heb. *šiḇʿâ*, "seven," as net (cf. LXX). Naturally there is little agreement as to how these architectural details looked. 2 K. 25:17 par. Jer. 52:22f. indicates that Nebuchadrezzar king of Babylon took these networks along with other trophies of war from the TEMPLE in 586 B.C.

R. L. ALDEN

**NEW; NEWNESS.** The idea of "new" in Scripture is connected primarily with three words: Heb. *ḥāḏaš* ("new, fresh") and Gk. *kainós* ("new" in the qualitative sense) and *néos* ("new" in the temporal sense). While the Greek words are sometimes used synonymously (cf. Mt. 9:17 par., where the wine is *néos* and the wineskins are *kainós* ["fresh"]; what is temporally new may well be qualitatively new also), in most instances they have a difference in nuance that provides insight into the theological significance of certain verses.

In the OT *ḥāḏaš* is often used simply to indicate that something (or someone) was not formerly present, e.g., a new king over Egypt (Ex. 1:8), new grain (e.g., Lev. 23:16), a new house (e.g., Dt. 20:5), new ropes (e.g., Jgs. 15:13), a new cart (e.g., 1 Ch. 13:7), a new sword (2 S. 21:16); *see also* NEW MOON; NEW YEAR. The prophetic literature uses the concept of newness in relation to God's saving work in Israel's future. The prophets anticipate a "new covenant" that God will establish with His people (Jer. 31:31-34), a "new heart" that He will place within them (e.g., Ezk. 36:26; *see* HEART III), and "new heavens and a new earth" that He will create (e.g., Isa. 65:17). God announces "new things" before they come into being (42:9) and places a "new song" on the lips of His people (42:10). Israel looks forward to a deliverance that will usher in a new and glorious age.

In the NT *néos* occurs eight times in the Synoptic Gospels ("new wine," Mt. 9:17 par.), twice in Paul's Epistles ("new lump [of dough]," 1 Cor. 5:7; "new self," Col. 3:10), and once in Hebrews ("new covenant," 12:24).

Greek *kainós* is used to describe wineskins (RSV "fresh," Mt. 9:17 par.), treasure (Mt. 13:52), fruit of the vine (Mt. 26:29 par.), a tomb (Mt. 27:60; Jn. 19:41), cloth (Mk. 2:21; cf. Lk. 5:36), etc. More significantly, *kainós* carries over the basic eschatological orientation of the OT prophets who spoke of the age to come, the new age of messianic fulfillment. Jesus' first coming introduced radical changes in salvation-history, inaugurating the new age anticipated by the prophets. When Jesus established the sacrament of the Lord's Supper, He announced, "this cup . . . is the new covenant [*hē kainḗ diathḗkē*] in my blood" (Lk. 22:20; the preferred MSS of the Matthaean and Markan parallels omit *kainḗ*). By His death, therefore, Christ fulfilled Jeremiah's promise of a new covenant written on the hearts of God's people (cf. Jer. 31:31-34; *see also* COVENANT, THE NEW) and introduced all sorts of new things. Everyone who is in Christ is a "new creation" (2 Cor. 5:17). By His death He abolished all artificial barriers and created "one new person" (Eph. 2:15). He has given a "new commandment" (Jn. 13:34; 1 Jn. 2:7f.), the commandment to love one another as He has loved us (*see also* COMMANDMENT, THE NEW).

As an eschatological concept, *kainós* appears repeatedly in Revelation. Believers are promised a new NAME (2:17; 3:12) and a new SONG (5:9; 14:3). The consummation of history will occur when God, the source of all newness, will make all things new (21:5). The present order will be replaced by "a new heaven and a new earth" (21:1; *see* HEAVENS, NEW), and God will dwell with His people in the "new Jerusalem" (21:2; *see* JERUSALEM IV.C). Meanwhile, Christians live between the inauguration and consummation of the messianic age.

It is significant that the body of canonical Christian writings produced in the 1st cent. A.D. is called the "New Testament" (or Covenant). These writings declare the fulfillment of the prophetic expectations for the new age, explain the historic basis for the new relationship between God and man, and point to the consummation when what now is new will be perfectly complete.

*See also* ESCHATOLOGY; NEW NATURE; REGENERATION.

***Bibliography.***–*DNTT,* II, 669-676; R. A. Harrisville, *JBL,* 74 (1955), 69-79; *TDNT,* III, *s.v.* καινός (Behm); IV, *s.v.* νέος (Behm); *TDOT,* IV, *s.v.* "chādhāsh" (North).

R. H. MOUNCE
C. B. HOCH, JR.

**NEW BIRTH.** *See* ANEW; REGENERATION.

**NEW COMMANDMENT.** *See* COMMANDMENT, THE NEW.

**NEW COVENANT.** *See* COVENANT (OT) IV.D; COVENANT, THE NEW.

**NEW CREATION** [Gk. *kainḗ ktísis*] (2 Cor. 5:17; Gal. 6:15); AV NEW CREATURE; NEB also NEW WORLD. *See* NEW NATURE; REGENERATION II.C.

**NEW EARTH.** *See* ESCHATOLOGY II-III.A; HEAVENS, NEW; REVELATION, BOOK OF IV.D.

**NEW GATE.** A gate of the TEMPLE (Jer. 26:10; 36:10). Its location is not certain.

**NEW HEART** [Heb. *lēḇ ḥāḏāš*] (Ezk. 18:31; 36:26). *See* HEART III; REGENERATION II.

**NEW HEAVENS.** *See* ESCHATOLOGY II-III.A; HEAVENS, NEW; REVELATION, BOOK OF IV.D.

**NEW JERUSALEM.** *See* JERUSALEM IV; CITY, BIBLICAL THEOLOGY OF.

**NEW LIFE.** *See* LIFE; REGENERATION.

**NEW MAN** [Gk. *kainós ánthrōpos*]; NEB NEW HUMANITY. This English expression occurs once in the RSV, where Paul says that Christ has abolished the barriers that divided mankind into two types of persons, Jew and Gentile, "that he might create in himself one new man in place of the two" (Eph. 2:15). "New man" is also used by the AV in 4:24; Col. 3:10. *See* NEW NATURE.

**NEW MOON** [Heb. *ḥōḏeš*–'new moon,' 'month'; Gk. *neomēnía* (Col. 2:16)]; AV, NEB also MONTH. Hebrew *ḥōḏeš* is derived from the verb *ḥāḏaš,* "make new"; it is never used simply to denote "newness" but always to designate the "new moon" (perhaps because it was a "fresh beginning") or the "month" (i.e., the period of time that begins with each new moon).

The Israelite calendar was lunar (*see* CALENDAR II.A.2); thus it is not surprising that the first day of each lunar month, like the sabbath, was a day set apart to worship God. The festivals of new moon and sabbath are often mentioned together in the OT (e.g., Isa. 1:13; 66:23; Ezk. 45:17; 46:1, 3; see de Vaux, pp. 476f.). As might be expected, the new moon of the seventh month carried special prominence (Lev. 23:24f.; Nu. 29:1-6; cf. 2 Ch. 5:3; Ezr. 3:6; Neh. 8:2); some have suggested, in fact, that this was the day of Israel's New Year Festival (see *TDOT,* IV, 235; cf. de Vaux, pp. 502-504).

The new moon observance was similar to that of a sabbath, but with a greater note of festive joy (cf. Hos. 2:11 [MT 13]). There was to be no mourning or fasting on this day (cf. Jth. 8:6); like the sabbath it was a day of rest from ordinary work (Am. 8:5). The various offerings prescribed for the new moon (Nu. 28:11-15) were significantly greater in quantity and quality than those for the sabbath (28:9f.), suggesting that — at least during one period in Israel's history — the new moon was a higher day than the sabbath. This day was considered an opportune time for offering peace offerings to Yahweh as a memorial (Nu. 10:10). A particular new moon could be chosen as the day for an annual family sacrifice (cf. 1 S. 20:5f., 28f.). Apparently Saul held a feast for his court the first two days of every month (cf. vv. 5, 18f., 24-27, 34); this account suggests that the new moon festival may have been celebrated for two days at certain times in Israel's history, perhaps because of the difficulty in determining precisely the day of the new moon.

As on any other feast day, God was thought to be especially near on the new moon; thus it was a good time to seek God's special guidance by consulting a prophet (2 K. 4:23). Interestingly, Ezekiel four times mentions receiving a vision on the first day of the month (Ezk. 26:1; 29:17; 31:1; 32:1).

The prophets often express a negative attitude toward the new moon and other festivals (e.g., Isa. 1:13f.; Hos. 2:11 [MT 13]; 5:7); they strongly reject the prevalent idea that these cultic observances could please God while social justice is neglected. Nevertheless, Isaiah employed the symbols of the new moon and the sabbath festivals to describe the joy that will characterize the new age to come: at that time all peoples will come to Jerusalem every sabbath and new moon to worship Yahweh (Isa. 66:23). In Ezekiel's picture of the ideal kingdom, the prince leads the people in worship on the new moon and sabbath (Ezk. 45:17; 46:1-7).

It is quite possible, as some have suggested, that the new moon received greater emphasis after the Exile, since in postexilic times Israel became primarily a religious community rather than a nation. The observation of the feasts, including the new moon, was resumed before the temple was rebuilt, beginning on the first day of the seventh month after the return under Zerubbabel (Ezr. 3:1-6 par. 1 Esd. 5:47-53). It was also on the first day of the seventh month that Ezra, during his reform efforts, read the law before the public assembly (Neh. 7:73b–8:2 par. 1 Esd. 9:37-40). The importance of the new moon and other festivals in postexilic Israel is also clear from Neh. 10:33 (MT 34).

That the new moon festival continued to be prominent in the NT era is suggested by Paul's exhortation to believers in Christ at Colossae: "Therefore, let no one pass judgment on you in questions of food and drink or with regard to a festival or a new moon or a sabbath. They are only a shadow of what is to come; but the substance belongs to Christ" (Col. 2:16f.). His point is that observances of special religious days is no longer binding on Christians, since Christ has fulfilled all that the law foreshadowed.

How the day of a new moon was determined is not known. Probably in the various communities a special watch was set at the appropriate time of the month; when the new moon was sighted, the surrounding countryside was informed through a system of relayed signals. At the central shrine a blast of trumpets announced the new moon (Nu. 10:10; Ps. 81:3 [MT 4]). In later times the rabbinic council set the dates of the new moon.

*See also* ASTRONOMY II.B; MOON.

***Bibliography.***–*ILC,* III-IV, 425-28; *TDOT,* IV, *s.v.* "chādhāsh, chōdhesh" (R. North); *TWOT,* I, 266; R. de Vaux, *Ancient Israel* (Eng. tr. 1961, repr. 1965), II, 469f.

J. E. HARTLEY

**NEW NATURE** [Gk. *kainós ánthrōpos* (Eph. 4:24), *néos* (*ánthrōpos*) (Col. 3:10)]; AV NEW MAN.

***I. Biblical Meaning.***–In contrast with the "old nature," which means the person that the Christian was "in Adam," before conversion, the "new nature" signifies the renewed being of the person who by faith is "in Christ," recreated inwardly, and indwelt by the Holy Spirit. The "old" nature is corrupt and expresses itself in evil deeds; the "new" bears the image of God and is marked by knowledge, righteousness, and holiness (Eph. 4:22ff.; Col. 3:9f.). *Néos* means new in the sense of "young," e.g., a newborn child; *kainós* means new in the sense of "renovated," e.g., a rebuilt house. One who has put on the *néos ánthrōpos* (lit. "new man") is "a babe in Christ" (cf. 1 Cor. 3:1); one who has put on the *kainós ánthrōpos* has undergone a decisive moral and spiritual change. Only Paul used this phrase, although the thought of renovation through new birth by the Spirit pervades the NT and goes back to Jesus (Jn. 3:3ff.; *see* REGENERATION).

"New nature" in Paul has a christological reference and points to a transforming relationship with the "last Adam," i.e., Christ; "old nature" points to mankind's fatal heritage from "Adam the first." Cullmann wrote on Col. 3:9f.: "The expression 'put on the new man', which is completely parallel to 'put on Christ' (Gal. 3:27; Rom. 13:14), shows that Paul thinks also of the objective basis for this transformation — Adam for the old man, Jesus for the new man" (*Christology of the NT* [Eng. tr. 1959], p. 174). The description of the "new nature" as created in God's image (a clear echo of Gen. 1:26) similarly contrasts Adam, in and through whose unfaithfulness to God mankind became unfaithful, and Jesus Christ, in whom God's image was perfectly displayed and through whom it is beginning to be displayed in mankind. "The 'Man', who alone is and has remained the image of the Creator, can form us according to this image when we 'put on the new man'" (Cullmann, p. 174).

This christological reference explains how Paul could give *kainós ánthrōpos* a corporate application in Eph. 2:15, which describes as "one new man" (RSV, AV) the new Jewish-Gentile community that Christ's reconciling action created. Paul's thought was that in and through Christ those who make up the new community are organically linked together; they are a new humanity, "all one in Christ Jesus" (Gal. 3:28); they share a given corporate life as "members one of another" (Eph. 4:25) and anticipate a promised corporate destiny whereby they will attain to "mature manhood, to the measure of the stature of the fulness of Christ" (v. 13). Meanwhile they must recognize their unity and express it by patient mutual love and service (4:1ff.; Rom. 12:4ff.; 1 Cor. 12; etc.).

The NT uses five different verbs to express the divine act involved when individuals put off the old nature and put on the new. (1) In Eph. 2:10 (cf. 4:24) the Christian is said to be "created in Christ" (*ktízō*), and in 2 Cor. 5:17 (cf. Gal. 6:15) he is called a "new creation" in Christ (*kainḗ ktísis*). (2) In Jn. 3:3-6; 1 Pet. 1:3, 23 and elsewhere the Christian is said to be "born anew" (*gennáō ánōthen, anagennáō*) by the Spirit through the Word as a fruit of Christ's resurrection, so that he is now one of God's "newborn babes" (1 Pet. 2:2). (3) In Eph. 2:5 and elsewhere the Christian is said to be "made alive" (*zōopoiéō*) through coresurrection with Christ, so that he is now brought "from death to life" (Rom. 6:13; cf. Eph. 2:1). (4) In Eph. 4:23 he who puts on the *kainós ánthrōpos* is "renewed" (*ananeóō*) spiritually, while (5) in Col. 3:10 he who puts on the *néos ánthrōpos* is being "renewed" ethically (*anakainóō,* as in Rom. 12:2; 2 Cor. 4:16). The correspondence of the anthropological idea of renewal and the christological concept of coresurrection is evident.

One who has put off the "old nature" and put on the "new nature" (the image is of changing clothes) has become the "spiritual" (*pneumatikós*) person of 1 Cor. 2:15; 14:37; Gal. 6:1 whose life is mastered by the indwelling Spirit, as distinct from the person "of the flesh" (*sarkikós*) and the "unspiritual" or "natural" (*psychikós*) person controlled by sensual appetites and graceless thoughts (Rom. 8:5-9; 1 Cor. 2:14; 3:1, 3f.; Eph. 2:3). (Christians become "of the flesh" if they lapse into sensual and graceless ways; the "unspiritual" or "natural" person, who lacks the Spirit, is "of the flesh" all the time.) The Christian's renewed self — which is his "heart" in the biblical sense — is his "inner nature" (2 Cor. 4:16; cf. Rom. 7:22; Eph. 3:16; 1 Pet. 3:4), the person that he now really is, even though he may sometimes fail to act in character. It is "according to the inner nature" that he seeks God, delights in God's law, and enjoys God's life through Spirit-given fellowship with Christ. His hope is that one day his "outer nature" (physical being, "members," cf. Rom. 6:13, 19; Col. 3:5) will be changed to match the "inner nature" on the pattern of the transformation of the physical in Jesus' resurrection and ascension, so that sin and decay will no more touch him (Rom. 7:22-25; 8:11-23; Phil. 3:20f.).

***II. Theological Bearing.***–The NT discussion points to the sovereignty of grace in regeneration. Though "put on" by human decision, the "new nature" (or "new man") is God's "new creation," brought about through Christ's resurrection and the sending of the Spirit. The "new man," which subjectively is one's identity as God's adopted child in Christ, is objectively the restoring and fulfilling of one's humanity through union with "the man Christ Jesus" (1 Tim. 2:5). Hereby one's "mind" — disposition, discernment, desire, comprehension, and commitment — is made new. Not by transubstantiation (change of substance), nor by transmutation (change of species), nor by transplant (change of natural organs), but by the indwelling presence of Christ through the Spirit, human beings are brought to behave in a quite new way — differently motivated, differently integrated, differently directed.

*See also* OLD NATURE; REGENERATION.

R. A. WEBB
J. I. PACKER

**NEW SPIRIT.** *See* REGENERATION II; SPIRIT.

**NEW TESTAMENT.** *See* BIBLE; CANON OF THE NT; CRITICISM.

**NEW TESTAMENT CANON.** *See* CANON OF THE NT.

**NEW TESTAMENT LANGUAGE.** *See* GREEK LANGUAGE OF THE NT.

**NEW TESTAMENT TEXT.** *See* TEXT AND MSS OF THE NT.

**NEW YEAR.** The starting point of a CALENDAR represents the New Year. In many cultures the turn of the year is marked by special celebrations, commonly designated the New Year Festival. The time and nature of these festivities varied considerably in the ancient Near East.

I. In the Ancient Near East
   A. Egypt
   B. Babylon
   C. Assyria
   D. Canaan
II. In Ancient Israel and Judah
   A. Autumnal New Year
   B. Spring New Year
III. In the NT
IV. In Postbiblical Judaism

***I. In the Ancient Near East.–A.*** *Egypt.* The Egyptian calendar commenced with the first day of the first month of the Season of Inundation. The inscriptions from the temple of Edfu (2nd cent. B.C.) provide the fullest description of the rituals associated with the New Year. The highlight was the removal of the image of Horus from his temple that it might be exposed to the sun's rays and thus effect the reunion of the deity's soul and body. Cf. *DBSup.*, VI, 555f. *See also* EGYPT VI.A.

*B. Babylon.* Although the *akītu* festival is often associated with the New Year, it is clear that in ancient Mesopotamia the event was celebrated in different cities and at different times of the year. In Babylon it was identified with the New Year observed near the vernal equinox on Nisan 1-11. Although no complete record of the rituals associated with the event has survived (*ANET,* pp. 331-34, describes the ritual for days 2-4), several important features of the festival can be identified: the entire epic of creation (*Enuma Elish*) was recited before Marduk; the temples of Marduk and Nabû were cleansed; the king was ritually humiliated in the temple; the statue of Marduk was taken to the Shrine of Destinies where the events of the coming year were decreed. In the most popular phase of the celebration the king "took Bēl [Marduk] by the hand," leading the grand procession of all the deities down Procession Street, the people bowing in awe before the great god. The images were installed in the *akītu* house outside the city, and a lavish banquet ensued; the sacred marriage (*hieros gamos*) was then celebrated (the exact time, place, and participants are not clear). On the final day the procession returned to Babylon, all the gods assembling at the Shrine of Destinies in Nabû's temple to fix "the destinies of the land." The next day Nabû's image was returned to its home in Borsippa, and the rest of the gods were dispersed to their respective shrines throughout the land.

The Babylonian New Year Festival was an elaborate affair, apparently incorporating aspects of several originally separate rituals. The event seems to have had several objectives: (1) to celebrate the supremacy and enthronement of Marduk; (2) to ensure the success of the enterprises of the coming year; (3) to affirm the king's status as high priest of Marduk; (4) to celebrate the enthronement of Nabû; (5) to mark the New Year on the calendar. It is doubtful that the Babylonian festival had anything to do with the death and resurrection of Marduk. Cf. J. A. Black, *Religion,* 11 (1981), 52f.

*C. Assyria.* The Assyrian *akītu* festivals probably bore some resemblance to the Babylonian celebrations. Sennacherib constructed an *akītu* house outside Asshur to be used in the month of Nisan. The actual purpose and rituals of the Assyrian festival remain unclear. Since the event was held in various cities at different times of the year, it is unlikely that the *akītu* festival functioned generally as a New Year celebration.

*D. Canaan.* The discovery of the mythological texts at Râs Shamrah has enabled some scholars to reconstruct an elaborate Canaanite autumnal New Year Festival. The ritual celebrated (1) the death and resurrection of the fertility-god, Baal; (2) the building of Baal's palace, indicative of his triumph over death (Mot); (3) the sacred marriage (*hieros gamos*) of Baal and Anath (enacted by the king and queen); (4) the victory of Baal over the chaotic forces (Yam); (5) and his enthronement as king over gods and men. Since Baal was the god of vegetation, it is generally agreed that the festivities were designed to ensure, by means of "imitative magic," prosperity in the new year.

Though this reconstruction is attractive, it is highly speculative. No Ugaritic texts to date are identified internally with the New Year Festival. Both the occasion of the composition of the texts and the times of their recitation are unknown. Many of the texts are fragmentary, and scholars disagree on the order in which they should be arranged.

The Phoenician and Canaanite texts in linear script discovered to date are silent on the New Year and its rituals.

***II. In Ancient Israel and Judah.***–Scholars disagree on both the time and the nature of the New Year Festival in Israel. W. Oesterley (in Hooke, ed., *Myth and Ritual,* p. 123) reflects a common opinion in arguing for an autumnal New Year before the Exile and a spring New Year thereafter. Others recognize the simultaneous use of two calendars, the spring New Year inaugurating the cultic year, the autumn festival starting the civil New Year.

*A. Autumnal New Year. 1. Evidence.* Evidence for an autumnal New Year is gathered from various sources.

(a) The extrabiblical Gezer Calendar (*ANET,* p. 320), reflecting the Palestinian calendar during the early monarchy, commences with the months of olive harvest, a fall agricultural activity.

(b) The Festival of Ingathering (*'āsîp*) is dated to "the going out of the year" (*bᵉṣē't haššānâ*) in Ex. 23:16 (cf. RSV, NEB, JB, NASB, NIV, "the end of the year"). In Ex. 34:22 the same feast is fixed at "the turn of the year" (*tᵉqûpaṯ haššānâ*). These instructions are held to reflect the oldest liturgical calendars. At the opposite side of the annual cycle, the time of year when kings customarily embarked on military activity is identified in 2 S. 11:1 (par. 1 Ch. 20:1) and 1 K. 20:22, 26 as "the return of the year" (*tᵉšûḇaṯ haššānâ*). A synchronism of 2 Ch. 36:10 with the Babylonian Chronicle, which recounts the appointment of Zedekiah as king in Jerusalem in the month of Adar, confirms the interpretation of this expression as the springtime. See A. K. Grayson, *Assyrian and Babylonian Chronicles* (1975), p. 102; but cf. N. H. Snaith, *Jewish New Year Festival* (1947), pp. 32f., for a dissenting view.

(c) The Sabbatical and Jubilee years commenced in the autumn (Ex. 23:10f.; Lev. 25:9). The latter was announced with the blowing of the ram's horn (Shofar), which in later Judaism was characteristic of the New Year celebration (Mish. *Rosh ha-Shanah* iv.1-9).

(d) Some scholars assert that the instruction that the month of Abib (= Nisan) is to be the first month of the year in Ex. 12:2 is a postexilic (P) alteration borrowed from the Babylonians.

(e) The expression "the head of the year" (*rō'š haššānâ*) in Ezk. 40:1 is identified with Tishri 10, or at least an autumnal beginning to the new year.

(f) Solomon is described as having begun the construction of the temple in the second month (Ziv) of his fourth regnal year (1 K. 6:1, 37) and to have completed the project in the eighth month (Bul) of his eleventh year. The entire task is said to have taken seven years (1 K. 6:38). By the inclusive system of reckoning time, whereby fractions are treated as full units, from the second month of the fourth year to the eighth month of the eleventh can equal seven years only by the Tishri-Tishri system; according to the Nisan-Nisan computation this would total eight years. See Thiele, pp. 28f.

(g) According to 2 K. 22:3 Josiah's repairs to the temple commenced in his eighteenth year. However, 2 K. 23:23 indicates that the climax of the reformation, the celebration of the Passover, also occurred in his eighteenth year. Since it is impossible that the intervening events could have happened in the two weeks required by the Nisan-Nisan calendar, Tishri 1 must have marked the beginning of his regnal year. See Thiele, pp. 29f.

(h) The duration between the command to Jeremiah to record his prophecies in the fourth year of Jehoiakim (Jer. 36:1) and Baruch's reading of the scroll in the ninth month (Kislev) of Jehoiakim's fifth year (36:9) appears to have been limited. Furthermore, since the king is warming himself in his winter house at the time of Baruch's reading, it must have been winter. By the Nisan-Nisan reckoning this would have required a minimum of nine months; with an autumnal New Year no more than nine or ten weeks is needed for the intervening period. See J. Morgenstern, "The New Year for Kings," in B. Schindler, ed., *Occident and Orient* (Gaster Anniversary Volume; 1936), pp. 439-456.

(i) According to Neh. 1:1 Nehemiah was in Susa in the month Kislev of the twentieth year of the king. In 2:1, however, the month of his royal service is Nisan, but it is still the twentieth year. This is possible only if the narrator was assuming an autumnal New Year, an apparent reversion to preexilic practice.

*2. Nature of the Israelite New Year Festival.* The most important argument for an autumnal New Year for many is the nature of the festival itself. The event is generally interpreted as one aspect of the much greater complex of fall celebrations which included the Feast of Ingathering, the Day of Atonement, and the Feast of Booths, all of which were observed during the month of Tishri. The reconstructed New Year Festival bore many resemblances to those already observed in Babylon and Ugarit. The evidence for these celebrations is drawn largely from the Psalms, many of which are viewed to have had their *Sitz im Leben* in these rituals.

Prominent in the liturgy of the New Year was the celebration of the enthronement of Yahweh. Following the lead of Mowinckel, many see *yhwh mlk* ("Yahweh has become king!") as the watchword of the occasion. This and similar expressions are frequent in the so-called enthronement Psalms (47, 93, 96–100). By annually reenacting the drama in the cult ritual the kingship of Yahweh was made a present reality. The festival recalled several dimensions to his kingship: (1) His lordship over the world was renewed in the dramatic reenactment of his creative (33:6-9; 95:3-5; 104:5-9) and providential (104:10-30) acts. (2) Similar to Marduk's victory over Tiâmat in Babylon, Yahweh's conquest of the unruly watery chaos, the forces of evil, was symbolized in the ritual combat (74:12-14; 89:9-12 [MT 10-13]; 93:3f.). (3) The cultic presentation of His victory over the nations, Israel's enemies, portrayed His providential care for Zion (2, 46–48). (4) His kingship over Israel, as expressed in His electing and saving acts, also featured prominently. Like Baal's supremacy in the Canaanite ritual, so Yahweh's kingship guaranteed Israel's continued prosperity (65:9-13 [MT 10-14]), as well as the maintenance of justice and righteousness (98:1-3; 99:4f.). The festival reached its climax with the bringing up of the ark, representing Yahweh's throne, to the temple on Zion.

These rituals did not merely commemorate Yahweh's past action; they actualized them for each generation of Israelites. Through the enthronement festival ancient Israel witnessed Yahweh's arrival as king and celebrated Him as the creator of the world, king of the whole earth, and savior of the nation.

In these dramatic reenactments the king played a special role. In the Psalms he functions as a divine figure: Yahweh places the crown on his head (21:3 [MT 4]) and promises him eternal life (21:4 [MT 5]; 72:5; 89:29, 36 [MT 30, 37]); the king is called a "son of God" (2:7; 89:27f. [MT 28f.]); he is addressed as God (45:6 [MT 7]); he may claim lordship over the world (72:8; 89:25 [MT 26]); for other kings to rebel against him is to rebel against Yahweh (2:1-9); he rules according to the principles of divine justice (45:6f. [MT 7f.]; 72:4, 12f.); his reign is characterized by fertility and prosperity (72:6f., 16). The New Year served to renew the covenant between Yahweh and the Davidic royal house. Because of this identification of the king and the deity some of the rituals were designed as assurances for the king himself (Ps. 110). Some have claimed that the ritual humiliation of the Babylonian kings also had its counterpart in the Israelite festival (Gottlieb, pp. 87-91).

In addition to these features, traces of the sacred marriage, echoes of which are seen in the Feast of Booths (Oesterley, in Hooke, ed., *Myth and Ritual,* pp. 139f.; Hooke, *Myth and Ritual,* p. 12), as well as the celebration of the death and resurrection of the deity (G. Widengren, in Hooke, ed., *Myth, Ritual, and Kingship,* pp. 190f.) have been recognized in Israel's New Year Festival (but cf. Gottlieb, pp. 77f., who rejected these claims).

This view of the complex rituals involved in the autumnal festival understands them to have been the high point of Israel's religious year. In this way Israel bade farewell to the old year and triumphantly welcomed the new.

*B. Spring New Year. 1. Response to the Claims for an Autumnal New Year.* Although the evidence for an autumn New Year in Israel is considerable, it is not as impressive as it first appears.

(a) The Gezer Calendar makes no claim to being an official calendar. It is simply a schedule of activities familiar to any farmer in ancient Palestine. Such a schedule may begin anywhere in the cycle, but it is natural in rural societies to measure time informally in relation to the harvest. In this case the olive harvest serves as an appropriate starting point. A similarly designed agricultural calendar has been discovered among the Elba tablets (3rd millennium B.C.; *see* TELL MARDIKH), but this calendar seems to have been replaced by a more official one (cf. G. Pettinato, *Archives of Ebla: An Empire Inscribed in Clay* [1981], pp. 147-153). Neither calendar claims to begin at an official New Year. Cf. the common modern practice in urban centers of computing time with reference to the annual vacation period.

(b) Concerning the expression *ṣēʾṯ haššānâ,* the correlative *bôʾ haššānâ* in 2 K. 13:20 seems to mean "springtime" (so RSV, NASB, NIV; contra J. Gray, *I & II Kings* [*OTL,* 2nd ed. 1970], p. 600, "late summer"). If the coming in of the year occurred in the springtime, the same must have been true of the end of the old year. The second correlative, *tᵉšûḇaṯ haššānâ,* also refers to the springtime (de Vaux, p. 190). This raises the question of how, in the context of Ex. 23, *ṣēʾṯ haššānâ* could be applied to an autumnal observance when the expression itself denotes the springtime. The answer is to be found in the analogy of the Gezer text. Ex. 23 says nothing about a calendar year; it has reference to the schedule of agricultural activities consisting of plowing, sowing, harvesting, and gathering in. The Feast of Ingathering terminates this cycle, not any official calendar year.

(c) Being essentially agricultural observances, the Sabbatical and Jubilee years fall naturally after the harvest. But to be precise, according to Lev. 25:9 the Sabbatical Year commences on Tishri 10, not on the postulated New Year on Tishri 1. Furthermore, Neh. 10:31 (MT 32) confirms the independence of the agricultural schedule from the calendar year by referring to the Sabbatical Year at a time when the spring New Year was being observed (Clines, *JBL*, 93 [1974], 30).

(d) The argument for Babylonian influence on Ex. 12:2 can be sustained only if one assumes the text is postexilic and represents an intentional polemic against the use of the old calendar with its purported autumn New Year. Neither assumption is certain. The syntax of the sentence suggests a description of an existing fact, not a new precept. It is assumed that already in Egypt the Israelites had counted the months of the year from Nisan (cf. U. Cassuto, *Comm. on the Book of Exodus* [Eng. tr. 1967], p. 137). But even if the text itself is postexilic, it may still be argued that the instruction represents a much older tradition, attached to Moses himself. As the leader in the Exodus event as well as its theological interpreter, he could readily have recognized its significance and attached the commencement of the Israelite calendar to the birthdate of the nation.

(e) Caution is advised in applying later usage to the meaning of the expression *rōʾš haššānâ* in Ezk. 40:1. The adoption of the phrase by later Judaism to designate New Year's Day need not reflect its significance for Ezekiel. It should be understood as "the beginning of the year," but in keeping with the prophet's consistent usage of the Babylonian system of reckoning elsewhere, a Nisan New Year is required. Cf. J. Finegan, *Handbook of Biblical Chronology* (1964), pp. 210-12.

(f) The seven years required for the construction of the temple in 1 K. 6:38 do not demand a Tishri New Year. The number may represent a stylized approximation, quite appropriate for a sacred task such as this, rather than an independent, precise statement of the duration of the project. Furthermore, in view of the apparent use of the exclusive system of reckoning in 1 K. 9:10, the appeal to inclusive usage here is not convincing. Cf. Clines, *JBL*, 93 (1974), 30-32.

(g) The celebration of Josiah's Passover in 2 K. 23:23 on the fourteenth day of the first month (cf. 2 Ch. 35:1) of his eighteenth regnal year, within a fortnight of the discovery of the Book of the Law (2 K. 22:3-13), is problematic only if one assumes that the narrator recounted the events of the reform in their chronological order of occurrence. 2 Ch. 34:1-8 suggests that the repairing of the temple represented one episode in a series of reforms begun ten years earlier (v. 3), rather than the motivation for those reforms as suggested by the order of 2 K. 22–23. The record of Josiah's campaign against any form of idolatry reads like an independent account without any reference to the discovery of the Book. The Book does not resurface until v. 21, where Josiah quite naturally leads the people in a covenant renewal ceremony by celebrating the Passover. Given the urgency of the situation, the immediate issuing of orders to make preparations for the Passover is to be expected. Since the accounts stress that the event was celebrated *in Jerusalem, by those who were present,* that is, *the inhabitants of Jerusalem* (2 K. 23:23; 2 Ch. 35:17f.), there was no need for a long period of preparation. Consequently, appeal to an autumnal New Year is unnecessary.

(h) Apparently Jer. 36:9, 22 describes Jehoiakim's reign on the basis of the spring New Year. The ninth month falls in the winter only by this scheme. Furthermore, the difficulty of finding an explanation for the nine-month delay in the reading of Jeremiah's scroll in the temple is not resolved by adopting an autumnal New Year. If Baruch needed to wait three months, why not nine? No compelling historical occasion can be found that would make the Tishri reckoning preferable.

(i) Admittedly the relationship of Neh. 1:1 to 2:1 is difficult to understand. An appeal to an autumn New Year for the editor of Nehemiah's memoirs is questionable in the light of the consistent assumption of a spring New Year by Ezekiel, the postexilic prophets, the narrator of Kings, "P," and the Chronicler. Thiele (p. 30) attributes this to "an intense spirit of nationalism." But this is valid only if the Israelites and Judeans had begun their official calendar year on Tishri 1 in the past. The foregoing suggests that there is little firm evidence for this. Furthermore, the Persian calendar with its spring New Year is employed consistently elsewhere in the book (2:1; 6:15; 7:72; 8:2, 14). How then are 1:1 and 2:1 to be reconciled? Any proposal which attempts to identify a terminus a quo other than the accession date of Artaxerxes, named in 2:1, is speculative. It is possible that the text of 1:1 has suffered in transmission. The absence of the name of the king looks suspicious. Perhaps the number nineteen has been mistakenly changed to twenty under the influence of 2:1. Or v. 1 may be an editorial addition to Nehemiah's autobiography. In any case, the passage is too problematic to be used in defense of an autumnal New Year.

The OT passages which speak clearly about the time of the New Year in the Hebrew calendar are disappointingly scarce. Indeed, apart from Ex. 12:2 the New Year is never specifically dated. If one excludes the debatable texts discussed above, however, the enumeration of a month *always* assumes an Abib/Nisan beginning of the year. Although the Israelites probably often dated their activities informally in relation to the high points in the religious calendar or the agricultural cycle for practical reasons, just as today students will speak in terms of the academic year or business people of the fiscal year, this should not be interpreted as the recognition of another calendar alongside the official one. From the earliest times, it appears, the Israelites adhered officially to a calendar whose beginning was associated with the vernal equinox. The observance of two simultaneously recognized New Year's days within the same lunisolar year is unlikely (but cf. J. B. Segal, *Hebrew Passover* [1963], pp. 135ff., who postulates an autumn royal New Year Festival and a spring popular festival; Y. Kaufmann, *Religion of Israel* [Eng. tr. 1960],pp. 306f., argues for a priestly spring New Year Festival and an autumn popular celebration).

*2. Nature of the Israelite New Year Festival.* Even if the Israelites had celebrated the onset of the New Year in the autumn, the reconstruction of the festivities as outlined above has serious weaknesses.

(a) From the perspective of methodology, the type of "patternism" which would recognize uniform cultic practices over widely scattered areas is open to challenge. The interpretation transfers Babylonian ideas and rituals involved in their *akītu* festivals to the Canaanite celebrations, and then via Canaan to Israel. Even if all three may have in principle been celebrating the same event, the turn in the calendar year, allowance should be made for variant conceptions of the roles of deities and kings.

(b) If the New Year Festival was as important a *Sitz im Leben* for many of the Psalms as it is claimed, why are there no unequivocal points of contact? But the original liturgical use of these Psalms, to say nothing of the original situation which spawned them, remains largely unclear. The problem is exacerbated by the total silence of the rest of the OT on the festival. Therefore, any reconstruction is purely hypothetical.

(c) The interpretation proposed for the expression *yhwh mlk,* found in many of these Psalms, is doubtful. Many of the so-called enthronement Psalms are monotheistic hymns in which the phrase declares, "It is Yahweh [not Baal or any other god] who is king!" rather than "Yahweh has become king!" Cf. E. J. Young, *Book of Isaiah,* III (1972), 550-52.

(d) Practices such as the sacred marriage in which the king plays the part of the deity, the reenactment of the deity's death and resurrection, and the ritual combat will be recognizable only to those who expect to find them. But even then, they can be identified only through allusions, suggestions, hints. For a critical response to the pre-Creation *Chaoskampf* interpretation of Ps. 74:12-17 see H. W. F. Saggs, *Encounter with the Divine in Mesopotamia and Israel* (1978), pp. 54-63.

(e) Finally, in Israel the autumn festival was first and foremost a harvest festival, not a New Year's celebration. The texts in which it is described make no allusions to the creation of the world, the conflict with the mythical primordial monster, or the sacred marriage of the king. Cf. Fohrer, p. 204.

In conclusion, the witness of the entire OT points to the commencement of the Israelite calendar in the springtime. In the context of a highly developed liturgical calendar, the silence of the records on any celebrations commemorating the turn of the year is remarkable. To be sure, the Passover falls within a fortnight of the event, but its primary significance has nothing to do with the end of the old year and the commencement of the new. It is to be expected that the Israelites would have welcomed the coming of the New Year in some way, but whatever these practices may have been, they were so overshadowed by the other celebrations of the religious calendar that not a trace remains. Indeed, when the New Year finally emerged as a significant festival in later Judaism its position in the lunisolar calendar had shifted a full 180 degrees, appearing now as an autumnal celebration.

***III. In the NT.***–Although the official calendar in the NT times was the Roman calendar, events are most often dated with reference to the Jewish religious year: the Passover (Jn. 13:1), the Feast of Tabernacles (7:2), Pentecost (Acts 2:1), the Sabbath (Mk. 2:27). However, the NT is silent on any type of New Year observance.

***IV. In Postbiblical Judaism.***–The Mishnaic tractate *Rosh ha-Shanah* speaks of four New Year's days: Nisan 1 for kings and feasts; Elul 1 for the tithe of cattle: Tishri 1 for the years (of foreign kings), the years of Release and Jubilee, and the planting of trees and vegetables; Shebat 1 (so Shammai; cf. 15, Hillel) for the tithing of trees and vegetables. In practice, however, Tishri 1 was celebrated as the "head of the year" (*rōʾš haššānâ*). How this date came to replace Nisan 1 is not clear. In contrast to the other festivals in the religious calendar, only Rosh ha-Shanah and Yom Kippur (Day of Atonement) were characterized by special solemnity. Although the celebration traditionally marked the creation of the world, the blasts of the ram's horn (Shofar), which figured prominently in the ritual, called the celebrants to soul searching and repentance. This was also a Day of Judgment (*Yom ha-Din*). All of humankind was viewed as passing before the throne of God, each person giving strict account of his or her actions during the past year and receiving assurance of mercy for the year to come. This was possible by virtue of the deeds of the fathers that are remembered by God (hence the designation *Yom ha-Zikkaron,* "Day of Remembrance").

***Bibliography.***–*General:* I. Engnell, *Studies in Divine Kingship in the Ancient Near East* (Eng. tr., 2nd ed., 1967); H. Frankfort, *Kingship and the Gods* (repr. 1978); T. H. Gaster, *Thespis* (rev. ed. 1961); S. H. Hooke, ed., *Myth and Ritual* (1933); *Myth, Ritual, and Kingship* (1958); H. Ringgren, *Religions of the Ancient Near East* (Eng. tr. 1973).

*On the date:* D. J. A. Clines, *Australian Journal of Biblical Archaeology,* 2 (1972), 9-34; *JBL,* 93 (1974), 22-40; E. R. Thiele, *MNHK.*

*New Year in Egypt: DBSup.,* VI (1960), 555f. (E. Drioton).

*New Year in Mesopotamia: DBSup.,* VI (1960), 556-597 (R. Largement); A. Falkenstein, "akitu-Fest und akitu-Festhaus," in R. von Kienle, *et al.,* eds., *Festschrift Johannes Friedrich* (1959), pp. 147-182; W. G. Lambert, *Iraq,* 25 (1963), 189f.; S.A. Pallis, *Babylonian Akitu Festival* (1926).

*New Year in Canaan:* J. C. de Moor, *New Year with Canaanites and Israelites* (2 vols., 1972).

*New Year in Israel: DBSup.,* VI (1960), 620-645 (H. Cazelles); J. H. Eaton, "The Psalms and Israelite Worship," in G. W. Anderson, ed., *Tradition and Interpretation* (1979), pp. 238-273; I. Engnell, *Rigid Scrutiny* (Eng. tr. 1969), pp. 180-84; H. Gottlieb, "Myth in the Psalms," in B. Otzen, *et al., Myths in the OT* (1980), pp. 62-93; A. R. Johnson, *Sacral Kingship in Ancient Israel* (2nd ed. 1967); S. Mowinckel, *Psalmenstudien,* II (1922); *Psalms in Israel's Worship* (2 vols., Eng. tr. 1962); H. Ringgren, *Israelite Religion* (Eng. tr. 1966), pp. 185-200; G. Widengren, *Sakrales Königtum im AT und im Judentum* (1955), pp. 62-79.

For critiques of this interpretation: G. Fohrer, *History of Israelite Religion* (Eng. tr. 1972), pp. 142-45, 202-205; H.-J. Kraus, *Worship in Israel* (Eng. tr. 1966), pp. 61-66; R. de Vaux, *Ancient Israel* (Eng. tr. 1961), pp. 502-506; E. J. Young, *Book of Isaiah,* I (1965), 494-99.

*New Year in Judaism: DBSup.,* VI (1960), 597-620 (A. Michel).

D. I. BLOCK

**NEZIAH** nē-zī'ə [Heb. *n^eṣî(a)ḥ*–'faithful, true'; Gk. Apoc. B *Nasi,* A *Nasith*]; AV Apoc., NEB Apoc., NASITH. The head of a family of temple servants (Nethinim) who returned from the Exile with Zerubbabel (Ezr. 2:54; Neh. 7:56; 1 Esd. 5:32).

**NEZIB** nē'zib [Heb. *n^eṣîḇ*; LXX *Naseib*]. A city of the Judean Shephelah (Josh. 15:43). It is plausibly identified with Khirbet Beit Neṣîb, about 13 km. (8 mi.) N of Hebron and 3 km. (2 mi.) S of KEILAH, with which it is mentioned in the city list in Josh. 15. E. M. COOK

**NIBHAZ** nib'haz [Heb. *niḇḥaz*]. A word written with a large final *z* (*zayin rabbāṯî*) in many Masoretic MSS and attested only in 2 K. 17:31, where it is recorded that the Avvites, a people settled by the Assyrians in Samaria, "made Nibhaz and Tartak." The reference may be to the Elamite gods Ibnakhaza and Dirtaq (F. von Hommel, *Orientalistische Literaturzeitung,* 15 [1912], 118), but omission of the Hebrew particle *ʾeṯ,* expected before a proper name, may indicate an otherwise unknown common noun or a textual problem. The proposal that *niḇḥaz* is a tendentious alteration of *mizbē(a)ḥ,* "altar," seems unconvincing. P. W. GAEBELEIN, JR.

**NIBSHAN** nib'shan [Heb. *hanniḇšān*; LXX A *Nebsan*; LXX B *Naphlazon*; Syr. *nʿšn*]. A city in the wilderness area of eastern Judea (Josh. 15:62). Cross and Milik identified Nibshan with Khirbet el-Maqârī SW of Qumrân, where fortifications and other structures from the 9th to 6th cents. B.C. have been found. But the narrow chronological span renders this site too late for Joshua's time (unless, like Cross, one is willing to date Josh. 15 in the 9th cent.).

The divergent forms of the LXX B and Syriac are probably errors in textual transmission, not a reflection of any ancient tradition.

***Bibliography.***–F. M. Cross and J. T. Milik, *BASOR,* 142 (Apr. 1956), 5-17; F. M. Cross and G. E. Wright, *JBL,* 75 (1956), 202-226, esp. 224. E. M. COOK

**NICANOR** nī-kā'nər, ni-kä'nôr [Gk. *Nikanōr*–'conqueror'].

**1.** A friend and general of Antiochus IV Epiphanes; son of Patroclus (1 Macc. 3:38; 2 Macc. 8:9). Nicanor hated the Jews (1 Macc. 7:26f.).

In 166 B.C. Lysias, regent of the western part of the Seleucidian domain (i.e., Syria), sent Nicanor and two other generals (Gorgias and Ptolemy) to put down the rebellion of Judas Maccabeus. So confident were they of victory that merchants followed to purchase Jewish slaves (1 Macc. 3:32-41; Josephus *Ant.* xii.7.2f. [296-98]). But Judas defeated them decisively at Emmaus and caused the Syrian soldiers to flee into Philistia (1 Macc. 4:1-22; Josephus *Ant.* xii.7.3f. [299-312]). 2 Macc. 8:34-36 (an account questioned by many scholars) embellishes the story by stating that Nicanor fled to Antioch in disguise.

When Antiochus IV died several years later, his nephew Demetrius escaped from Rome, seized and put to death both Lysias and Antiochus V, and assumed the throne of Syria as Demetrius I Soter (1 Macc. 7:1-4; Josephus *Ant.* xii.10.1 [389f.]). Demetrius sent Nicanor with an army to capture Judas and to confirm Alcimus (pro-Hellenist priest of the Aaronic line) as high priest in Jerusalem. Nicanor was appointed governor of Judea before he left (2 Macc. 14:12). Arriving in Jerusalem, he asked Judas to have a peaceful conference; his secret intention was to seize him during a meeting. Judas learned of the plot and would not meet with him a second time (1 Macc. 7:27-30; Josephus *Ant.* xii.10.4 [402-404]). Two battles followed. In the first, at Capharsalama (site uncertain), Nicanor suffered some losses (1 Macc. 7:31f.; Josephus *Ant.* xii.10.4 [405]). In the second, near Beth-horon and Adasa (villages NW of Jerusalem), Nicanor received some reinforcements but was slain early in the battle. His army fled to Gazara (32 km. [20 mi.] W of Jerusalem) and was destroyed by the Jews. The Jews cut off Nicanor's head and right hand and displayed them in Jerusalem. The day of Nicanor's defeat, 13 Adar 161 B.C. (Mar. 9), was annually celebrated by the Jews as "Nicanor's Day" (1 Macc. 7:33-49; 2 Macc. 15:25-36; Josephus *Ant.* xii.10.5 [406-412]). The author of 2 Maccabees closes his story on this triumphant note.

**2.** One of the seven men selected by the early Church to serve tables in order to free the apostles for other responsibilities (Acts 6:5). *See* SEVEN, THE.

***Bibliography***.–Y. Aharoni and M. Avi-Yonah, *Macmillan Bible Atlas* (1968), pp. 188, 195; J. R. Bartlett, *First and Second Books of the Maccabees* (*CBC*, 1973); *HJP*², I, 159, 169f.; S. Tedesche and S. Zeitlin, *First Book of Maccabees* (Eng. tr. 1950); *Second Book of Maccabees* (Eng. tr. 1954). H. W. HOEHNER

**NICODEMUS** nik'ə-dē-məs [Gk. *Nikodēmos*–'conqueror of the people' or 'victor over the people']. A Pharisee and member of the Sanhedrin ("a ruler of the Jews," Jn. 3:1), mentioned only in the Fourth Gospel, in connection with the discourse on the new birth (3:1-10), the last day of the feast (7:37-52), and the burial of Jesus (19:38-42). Nothing is known about his family background, although unsuccessful attempts have been made to identify him with Nicodemus ben Gorion in the Talmud.

Nicodemus shared the Jewish expectation of a political messiah who would deliver his people from the Romans. He was perplexed at Jesus' teaching about the spiritual nature of His kingdom. Nicodemus's cautiousness kept him from revealing openly his interest in Jesus and His teachings, but his curiosity compelled him to seek to know more.

By meeting Jesus at night he showed his unwillingness to be seen in His presence and to risk the disfavor of his fellow Pharisees, among whom Jesus was decidedly unpopular. He acknowledged, however, that Jesus was "a teacher sent from God" whose power came from God (Jn. 3:2). Jesus used the occasion to present to him truths concerning the new birth and the necessity of being born "of water and the Spirit" (v. 5) before one could enter the kingdom of God. Although a Pharisee and "teacher of Israel" (v. 10), Nicodemus did not understand even the basic principles of the kingdom. The interview did not result in his acceptance of Jesus openly, but it must have made a deep impression on his mind.

Some months before the crucifixion some of the chief priests and Pharisees denounced Jesus as an impostor and sought to have Him arrested. Nicodemus came to His defense and asked whether it was permissible, according to Jewish law, to judge a man without first giving him a hearing (Jn. 7:50f.). As a result of his seeking just and fair treatment of Jesus he was accused of having joined His Galilean followers. Not until the day of the crucifixion did he reveal more openly his support of the cause of Jesus when he and another member of the Sanhedrin, Joseph of Arimathea, gave the body of Jesus a decent burial (19:39). His providing much expensive myrrh and aloes for the burial implies that he was rich.

John used the Nicodemus interview to illustrate the statement in 2:25 that Jesus "knew what was in man." Jesus saw in Nicodemus a sincere seeker after truth to whom He could reveal a clearer and more complete knowledge of His mission than He could to many others. The statement that Nicodemus came to Jesus "by night" (3:2) fits John's frequent use of words capable of two meanings. Nicodemus came to see Jesus, not only under the cloak of physical darkness but also in a position of spiritual darkness. This leader and spiritual teacher's lack of spiritual understanding illustrates the condition of the Jewish nation as a whole. But he also represents the Jews sincere in their desire to know more about Jesus and the meaning of His mission.

The NT does not say whether Nicodemus ever became a Christian, but he probably did. Later Christian legend embellishes the NT account with stories of his baptism, hardships encountered because of his Christian faith, and his ultimate banishment from Jerusalem. The *Acts of Pilate* (4th cent.) was called the *Gospel of Nicodemus* in the Latin tradition after the 14th century. H. E. FAGAL

**NICODEMUS, GOSPEL OF.** *See* APOCRYPHAL GOSPELS III.B.

**NICOLAITANS** nik-ō-lā'ə-təns [Gk. *Nikolaïtēs*]. Followers of a deviant form of Christianity in Asia Minor, who were sharply condemned by John in his letters to Ephesus (Rev. 2:6) and Pergamum (2:15). The church in Ephesus is commended for its rejection of the Nicolaitans, who may stand in some relationship to the "false apostles" of v. 2. The group had gained a foothold, however, in Pergamum where, like Balaam of old, it encouraged the people to practice idolatry and sexual immorality (cf. Nu. 25:1-3; 31:16). Since the same practices were rampant in Thyatira, because of the influence of a certain prophetess "Jezebel" (Rev. 2:20), it is probable that the Nicolaitans, though not mentioned explicitly, were active there as well.

***I. Name.***–Nothing can be said with certainty about the origin of the name. Later Christian tradition linked the Nicolaitans with Nicolaus of Antioch, one of "the Seven" of Acts 6:1-6 (Irenaeus *Adv. haer.* i.26.3), attributing the heretical character of the movement either to Nicolaus himself (Hippolytus *Ref.* vii.24) or to misinterpretations of his teaching on the part of his followers (Clement *Misc.* ii.20; iii.4). Since there are related references to contemporary groups of Nicolaitans (see III below), and since

NT personages tended to be glorified rather than vilified in Church tradition, such an interpretation is not implausible. But, in the absence of any solid information on Nicolaus and on the subsequent history of the first-century Nicolaitans, it is advisable to approach this later tradition with caution.

Another approach, originating with C. A. Heumann (1712), is to see the term Nicolaitans as symbolic, resulting from an etymological play on the Hebrew name Balaam (*bilʿām* < *bālaʿ ʿam,* "he has destroyed the people," or *baʿal ʿam,* "lord of the people") that was then rendered into a Greek equivalent (*nikā́ laón,* "he has conquered the people"). Such an explanation should not be dismissed out of hand, especially for a writing like Revelation. While the appearance of the same wordplay in rabbinic tradition (T.B. *Sanhedrin* 105a) is probably too late to have probative value, wordplays on "Balaam" were not unknown in the 1st cent. (cf. Philo *De cherubim* 32). Furthermore, the other terms that appear in John's description of this group — Jezebel (v. 20) and Balaam (v. 14; while the syntax in v. 15 is difficult, it is probable that Balaam and Nicolaitan refer to the same group) — are his own symbolic characterizations, rather than terms used by the group of itself. But if such an explanation is judged to be too fanciful, then all that can be said is that the Nicolaitans owed their name to a Nicolaus about whom nothing is certain apart from his name.

*II. Characteristics.*–Any assessment of the nature of the Nicolaitan deviance must begin with Rev. 2:14f., where the teaching of Balaam is described as advocating the eating of "food offered to idols" (*eidōlóthyta*) and sexual immorality. The former accusation refers either to the purchase of previously consecrated meat on the open market or to actual participation in pagan religious festivals. The latter could be interpreted as metaphorical reference to idolatry, but should more probably be taken literally. Both practices are among those forbidden in the "Apostolic Decree" of Acts 15:28f.; 21:25.

Ramsay, attempting to put the motives of the Nicolaitans in the best possible light, saw them not as libertines but as well-meaning Christians prepared to make minor concessions in order to participate in the civic and economic life of Hellenistic society. While participation in Hellenistic life was no doubt a factor, the Nicolaitans were more probably advocates of an antinomian life-style, flaunting their "freedom" in a manner not unlike that of certain elements in the church at Corinth (cf. also the antinomian "followers of Balaam" in 2 Pet. 2:15; Jude 11).

The passage has several hints that the antinomian practice of the Nicolaitans might have been the fruit of a deeper doctrinal deviancy. The emphasis on "teaching," together with their claim to "know the deep things of Satan" (v. 24), suggests that Irenaeus was correct in characterising the Nicolaitans as a proto-Gnostic group (*Adv. haer.* iii.11.1).

*III. Subsequent History.*–Patristic references appear to imply the existence in the late 2nd cent. of a libertine Gnostic group known as Nicolaitans (Irenaeus *Adv. haer.* i.26.3; Tertullian *Adv. Marc.* i.29, *De praescr. haer.* 33; Hippolytus *Ref.* vii.24; Clement *Misc.* ii.20; iii.4; Eusebius *HE* iii.29). While most of these references are vague and insubstantial, Clement at least appears to have had solid information on a contemporary group claiming Nicolaus of Antioch as its founder. Current scholarly opinion, however, is skeptical that any link can be established between this group and that known to John. The most that can be reasonably conjectured is that the latter — whether "Nicolaitan" was a real party name or just John's own cryptic designation — was absorbed into some second-century manifestation of Gnosticism.

*Bibliography.*–W. M. Ramsay, *LSC,* pp. 298-302, 335-353; R. H. Charles, comm. on Revelation (*ICC,* 1920), I, 52f., 63f.; A. von Harnack, *JR,* 3 (1923), 413-422; M. Goguel, *RHR,* 115 (1937), 5-36; N. Brox, *VC,* 19 (1965), 23-30; E. S. Fiorenza, *JBL,* 92 (1973), 565-581; W. M. Mackay, *EQ,* 45 (1973), 111-15.

T. L. DONALDSON

**NICOLAS** nik'ə-ləs (AV, NEB, Acts 6:5). *See* NICOLAUS.

**NICOLAUS** nik-ə-lā'əs [Gk. *Nikolaos*–'conqueror of the people'] (Acts 6:5); AV, NEB, NICOLAS. One of the seven men chosen by the congregation of Jerusalem to assist the apostles by taking over the ministry of relief to the poor (i.e., "to serve tables," Gk. *diakonein trapézais,* Acts 6:2). These men are traditionally known as the first deacons; but they are not given any formal title in the text, and the subsequent activities of Stephen and Philip are broader than the normal work of a deacon. (*See* SEVEN, THE.)

We know nothing about Nicolaus from the NT except what can be gleaned from Acts 6:1-7. He is called a proselyte (*prosḗlytos*), i.e., a convert to Judaism rather than a Jew by birth. Luke also mentions that Nicolaus was from ANTIOCH (SYRIAN), which reflects Luke's interest in that city. This information about Nicolaus helps to set the stage for the mission to the Gentiles centered in Antioch (cf. 11:19-26; 13:1-3; etc.) Nicolaus must have been a man "of good repute, full of the Spirit and wisdom" (6:3), for these were the qualifications that the apostles set for the Seven.

From at least the time of Irenaeus (*Adv. haer.* i.26.3; cf. iii.11.1) there have been attempts to link this Nicolaus with the heretical NICOLAITANS referred to in Rev. 2:6, 15. The historical value of these attempts is debatable, and the paucity of information about either Nicolaus or the Nicolaitans makes such a connection questionable — especially in the light of Luke's portrayal of Nicolaus's Christian character. The earliest extant Latin comm. on Revelation (Victorinus of Pettau, *ca.* A.D. 300) says that the heretical group used the name of this Nicolaus, but it implies that he himself was not responsible for the heresy (see F. F. Bruce, *Book of the Acts* [*NICNT,* 1954], p. 129).

V. R. GORDON

**NICOPOLIS** ni-kop'ō-lis [Gk. *Nikopolis*–'city of victory']. A number of ancient cities — in Pontus, in Cilicia, in Bithynia, on the Thracian border, in Egypt, and elsewhere — were named Nicopolis in honor of victories. Nicopolis in Palestine was halfway between Jaffa and Jerusalem (1 Macc. 3:40, 57; 9:50). But the city at which Paul instructed Titus to meet him (Tit. 3:12) was most likely Nicopolis in Epirus, sometimes rather generally referred to as Nicopolis in Achaia. It was situated on the northern promontory that shuts in the gulf of Ambracia (now known as Arta) to the west. Augustus (Octavian) camped at the site prior to his battle with Antony at Actium (31 B.C.), which was situated directly S across the gulf. Because of a sudden storm that lashed Antony's navy and assisted

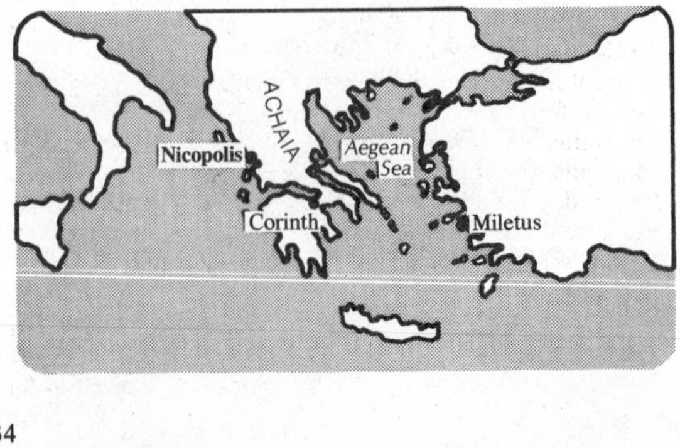

in bringing about his defeat, Augustus founded the city of Nicopolis, established it as a Roman colony, instituted a special festival to Apollo, and contributed to the building of a temple there with considerable support from Herod the Great (Josephus *Ant.* xvi.5.3 [147]).

Paul's intended visit to this city (after his release from prison) implies a plan to establish a Christian mission on the west coast of Greece — a task that had not been accomplished during the journeys recorded in Acts. Moreover, if Paul had passed through Miletus and Corinth (see 2 Tim. 4:20) on his way to Nicopolis, then probably he was arrested there and taken again to Rome. The postscript to Titus in Codex Alexandrinus stating that the Epistle was written from Nicopolis is late, however, and can hardly be accurate.

The city suffered early decline but was restored by Julian, and after a sacking by the Goths it was again restored by Justinian. In medieval times it decayed and was succeeded by Prebeza. The ruins are visible today.

See Pauly-Wissowa, XVII/1, 511-18.

G. L. BORCHERT

**NIGER** nī'jər [Gk. *Niger* < Lat. *niger*–'black']. Surname of SIMEON (5), who was one of the prophets and teachers at the church at Antioch (Acts 13:1). The surname may indicate that he was from North Africa, and some have conjectured that he was the Simon of Cyrene who carried Jesus' cross (Mt. 27:32 par.).

**NIGH.** *See* NEAR.

**NIGHT** [Heb. *laylâ, layil*] (e.g., Gen. 1:5); NEB also NIGHTFALL, OVERNIGHT, TONIGHT; [*lîn*–'pass the night'] (e.g., "spend the night," Gen. 19:2; 24:54; etc.); AV ABIDE, LODGE; [*'emeš*–'yesterday evening'] ("last night," Gen. 31:29, 42); AV YESTERNIGHT; NEB YESTERDAY; [*'ereḇ*–'evening'] (Job 7:4; Ps. 30:5); NEB EVENING, NIGHTFALL; [*'ašmûrâ*–'night-watch'] ("watch of the night," Ps. 63:6 [MT 7]); [Aram. *bûṯ*–'pass the night'] ("spend the night," Dnl. 6:18 [MT 19]); [Gk. *nýx*] (e.g., Mt. 2:14); NEB also NIGHTFALL, "as darkness fell," TONIGHT, etc.; [*phylakḗ*–'watch'] ("part of the night," Mt. 24:43); AV WATCH; [*dianyktereúō*–'spend the whole night'] ("continue all night," Lk. 6:12); [*agrypnía*–'sleeplessness, watching'] ("sleepless night," 2 Cor. 11:27); AV WATCHING, NEB "go without sleep"; [*nychthḗmeron*] ("a night and a day," 2 Cor. 11:25); NEB TWENTY-FOUR HOURS. That period of time without sunlight between dusk and dawn (approximately 6:00 P.M. to 6:00 A.M.).

The primary Hebrew word for night is *laylâ* (or the poetic form *layil*). The verb *lîn*/*lûn* is used most often in the literal sense of lodging for the night in some place (e.g., Gen. 28:11; 31:54; 32:13, 21 [MT 14, 22]; Josh. 3:1; Jgs. 19:6, 9, etc.); on the duty of providing overnight lodging for travelers *see* ENTERTAIN; INN). The primary NT term for night is Gk. *nýx*. In Greek literature *nýx* generally has a negative, ominous character. In mythology Nyx is the goddess of the night.

Night is first mentioned in the creation account of Gen. 1. On the first day God created light and separated it from the primeval darkness (1:3f.), and "God called the light Day, and the darkness he called Night" (v. 5). On the fourth day God created the sun to rule the day and the moon and the stars to rule the night (vv. 14-18; cf. Ps. 136:9); therefore both the day and the night belong to Him (Ps. 74:16).

During OT times the Hebrews divided the night into three night-watches (cf. Ps. 63:6 [MT 7]; Lam. 2:19; Jgs. 7:19; Ex. 14:24), but by NT times they had adopted the Roman custom of four night-watches (Lk. 12:38; Mt. 14:25 par.; cf. Mk. 13:35); *see* WATCH.

In the OT "night" often serves simply to indicate the time that an event occurred (e.g., Gen. 14:15; Nu. 11:9). Night was often the occasion of dreams (e.g., Gen. 20:3; 40:5), of visions (e.g., Dnl. 7:2; Zec. 1:8), and of other revelatory events (e.g., Gen. 26:24; Jgs. 6:40). The most memorable night in the OT was that of Passover, when Israel was delivered from bondage to Egypt (Ex. 11:4; 12:8, 12, 29-32, 42). During the desert wanderings God led His people by night with the pillar of fire (Ex. 13:21). Night was a favored time for clandestine activities (cf. Isa. 16:3). It was often chosen as a time for military deployment (e.g., Josh. 8:3; 10:9; Jgs. 9:34; cf. Isa. 15:1), for occult practices (1 S. 28:8), and for crimes such as thievery, sexual misdeeds, and murder (e.g., Job 24:14-17; Jer. 49:9; Gen. 19:1-5, 33-35; Jgs. 19:25; Prov. 7:8f.; Neh. 6:10). Night could therefore be a time of terror (Ps. 91:5f.). Yet those who trusted God did not need to fear the night (91:5f.); indeed, day and night are the same with God (139:11f.). During sleepless nights one was particularly vulnerable to feelings of dread (Job 4:13-21), worry (7:3f.), and grief (Ps. 6:6f. [MT 7f.]). But for the righteous the night could also be a productive time of personal meditation and spiritual refreshment (Ps. 63:6 [MT 7]; 77:6 [MT 7]; 92:2 [MT 3]; 119:55; cf. Josh. 1:8).

Figuratively, darkness and night symbolize the realm of evil, untruth, and judgment (Mic. 3:6; Wisd. 17:2-21). Zechariah prophesied that on the day of the Lord "there shall be continuous day . . . for at evening time there shall be light" (Zec. 14:7). In 2 Esdras several strange events at the end of the age occur at night (5:4, 7; cf. 7:38-42; the night is also the occasion of angelic visits [5:31; 6:12, 30, 36] and of dreams and visions [7:1; 11:1; 13:1]).

In the NT, as in the OT, "night" is used most often in the literal sense as an indication of time. Jesus walked on the water during the fourth watch of the night (Mt. 14:25). Sometimes He spent the whole night in prayer (Lk. 6:12; cf. Mt. 26:36-46 par.; see also Lk. 2:37; Acts 16:25). Nighttime was a frequent occasion for angelic visitations (Lk. 2:8f.; Acts 5:19; 12:7; 27:23) and for divine revelation through dreams (Mt. 2:12, 22) and visions (Acts 16:9; 18:9; 23:11).

The holy family fled to Egypt by night (Mt. 2:14). Likewise, it was under the cover of darkness that Paul and Silas escaped from Thessalonica (Acts 17:10) and that Roman soldiers escorted Paul from Jerusalem (23:23, 31). Nicodemus's decision to visit Jesus by night (Jn. 3:2) may have been prompted by "fear of the Jews" (cf. 19:38f.), but for John it also had a symbolic meaning: Nicodemus came out of the darkness of evil and untruth into the light of God's truth (cf. 3:19-21). Conversely, Judas left the light to go into the darkness on the night that he betrayed Jesus (13:30). It was at night, during the "power of darkness" (Lk. 22:53), that Jesus was arrested and brought to trial, abandoned by His disciples (Mt. 26:31), and denied by Peter (v. 34 par. Mk. 14:30).

In several NT passages "night" is employed in a purely figurative sense. Usually "night" corresponds to "darkness" (*see* DARK) as "day" corresponds to "light" (*see* LIGHT). In Jn. 9:4 Jesus, the "light of the world" (v. 5), cites a proverb to emphasize the urgency of completing His work on earth before the time arrives when such work is not possible, i.e., the time of His death on the closing of the age (cf. 11:9f.). Paul contrasts the "night" of the present age to the dawning "day" of the new age when God's rule will be consummated (Rom. 13:12). That day will come "like a thief in the night" (1 Thess. 5:2; cf. Mt. 24:42-44 par. Lk. 12:38-40; 2 Pet. 3:10; Rev. 3:3; 16:15; cf. also Lk. 17:34). But those who live in the light of divine revelation need not be taken unaware, because they are not in darkness (1 Thess. 5:4). Paul therefore exhorts the Thessalonian Christians to avoid the (moral and spiritual) sleep and drunkenness associated with the night and instead to remain alert and sober as befits the daytime (vv. 5-8).

The book of Revelation, like some of the OT prophets (cf. Isa. 13:10; Joel 3:15 [MT 4:15]), depicts a darkening of the sun, moon, and stars at the time of the final judgment (Rev. 8:12; cf. Mk. 13:24f.). In the new Jerusalem, however, there will be no more night, "for the Lord God will be their light" (Rev. 21:25; 22:5).

*See also* DAY AND NIGHT.

***Bibliography.***–*DNTT*, I, 420-25; J. Finegan, *Handbook of Biblical Chronology* (1964); *TDNT*, IV, *s.v.* νύξ (G. Delling); *TWOT*, I, 479f.

A. E. HILL

**NIGHT HAG** [Heb. *lîlîṯ*; Gk. *onokéntauroi*, normally a variety of ape, but in LXX Isa. 13:22; 34:11, 14 it apparently refers to a kind of demon found in deserted places; so LSJ, p. 1232] (Isa. 34:14); AV "screech owl"; NEB "nightjar." The Heb. *lîlîṯ* is ultimately derived from Sum. lil, "wind," "spirit" (cf. Akk. *lilu*, "demon," *lilītu*, "female demon"); it has no connection with Heb. *laylâ*, "night." Thus the RSV translation "night hag," though better than the AV and NEB translations referring to nocturnal birds, is inaccurate. Heb. *lîlîṯ* is also a cognate of Phoen. *llyn*, which occurs in an amulet from Arslan Tash (7th cent. B.C.) directing incantations against various demons (cf. F. M. Cross and R. J. Saley, *BASOR*, 197 [Feb. 1970], 46 and nn. 24f.; *ANET*, p. 658). Thus Heb. *lîlîṯ* refers to a malevolent supernatural being. In the OT Heb. *lîlîṯ* is found only in Isa. 34:14, where it is associated with other creatures who dwell in deserted places. This corresponds to the widespread belief that chaotic conditions and demonic beings inhabit the regions outside the perimeters of civilization.

The paucity of information makes it impossible to say anything definite about the night hag in the OT. In rabbinic literature, however, doubtless reflecting older folktales and folk beliefs, Lilith is regarded as a feminine demonic creature of the night, possessing wings and long flowing hair. According to legend Lilith was Adam's first wife, but remained with him for only a short time because she insisted on full equality with him (Ginzberg, I, 64-66). By pronouncing the divine name, Lilith flew away into the air and disappeared, and three angels sent by God could not persuade her to return to Adam, even though the penalty for not returning was the death of one hundred of her demonic children each day. Lilith now takes revenge on baby boys during the first night of their lives, and on baby girls for the first twenty days. In the talmudic period Lilith was thought able to take the form of a female *succubus* ("one who lies under") and impersonate a man's wife for the purpose of luring him into sexual relations. As a male *incubus* ("one who lies upon"), a Lili (the masc. sing. Aram. *lyly*) was thought able to impersonate a husband. Any children born of such irregular unions were thought to exhibit the effects of having a demonic parent.

The feminine and masculine forms of *lîlîṯ* occur frequently in the texts of the Aramaic incantation bowls. In one such text (No. 3, Isbell) the author seeks protection from "demons, demonesses, lilis, liliths, plagues, [evil sat]ans and all evil tormentors that appear." Such lists are meant to be as comprehensive as possible and reveal that the liliths were but one class of an elaborate taxonomy of malevolent spiritual beings. The sexually aggressive character of the lilis and liliths accounts for the fact that exorcistic texts are often expressed in formal divorce terminology, such as this text (No. 35, Isbell): "Again, bound and seized are you, evil spirit and powerful lilith. . . . But depart from their presence and take your divorce and your separation and your letter of dismissal. [I have written against] you as demons write divorces for their wives and furthermore, they do not return [to them]."

***Bibliography.***–T. H. Gaster, *Myth, Legend, and Custom in the OT* (1969), pp. 578-580; L. Ginzberg, *Legends of the Jews*, I (1909); C. D. Isbell, *Corpus of the Aramaic Incantation Bowls* (1975); J. Neusner and J. Z. Smith, "Archaeology and Babylonian Jewry," in J. A. Sanders, ed., *Near Eastern Archaeology in the Twentieth Century* (*Festschrift* N. Glueck, 1970), pp. 331-347.

D. E. AUNE

**NIGHT WATCH.** *See* DAY II; DAY AND NIGHT; WATCH.

**NIGHTHAWK** [Heb. *taḥmas*–probably 'violent one'] (Lev. 11:16; Dt. 14:15); NEB SHORT-EARED OWL. One of the abominable or unclean birds that the Israelites were forbidden to eat.

The identification of this bird is uncertain. "Night hawk" in British usage — reflected in the AV rendering — may refer to a small songbird called the nightjar, two species of which are to be found in Israel: the migrant European variety (*Caprimulgas europaeus*) and the resident Nubian species (*Caprimulgas nubicus*). If, however, the Hebrew term connotes a predator, the nightjar would be eliminated as a possibility. A species of owl would be more suitable (cf. LXX *glaúx*, "owl," in both passages).

*See also* ABOMINATION, BIRDS OF.

G. WYPER

**NIGHTJAR** (Isa. 34:14, NEB). *See* NIGHT HAG.

**NIGHT-MONSTER.** *See* NIGHT HAG.

**NILE** nīl [Heb. *yᵉʾôr*, prob. loanword < Egyp. *ỉtrw*, *ỉʾr(w)*, Copt. *eioor*, "watercourse"; cf. Akk. *iaʾuru*, "river Nile"; Gk. *potamós*, "river"]. The river of Egypt, to be distinguished from *nᵉhar miṣrayim*, "the river of Egypt," which refers to Wâdī el-ʿArîsh (Gen. 15:18, etc.). For the physical description of the Nile, *see* EGYPT III.A-D.

*I. Name.*–The early Egyptian name was *ḥʿpy*, later *ḥp*, which was also the name of the Nile-god, vocalized Ḥaʿpy in A. Gardiner, *Egyptian Grammar* (3rd ed. repr. 1978), p. 580. The word from which the Hebrew term is derived is *ỉtrw* (*ỉʾr*[*w*] from the 18th Dynasty on), "stream, river, watercourse," specifically referring to the Nile and its branches and channels (A. Erman and H. Grapow, *Wörterbuch der aegyptischen Sprache*, I [1926], 146; T. O. Lambdin, *JAOS*, 7 [1953], 151). The Greek *Neilos* and Latin *Nilus* have not been satisfactorily explained etymologically. The suggestion that Gk. *Neilos* was formed by adding the definite article *n-* to the word for river (cf. P. Montet, *Eternal Egypt* [Eng. tr. 1965], p. 6) cannot be accepted, since Coptic evidence proves that the *r* in *ỉʾrw* was phonemic and not an orthographic representation of *l*, as was sometimes the case in Egyptian. In the OT *naḥal miṣrayim*, literally "wadi of Egypt," does not refer to the Nile, for the Nile is never called a wadi, but refers rather to the Wâdī el-ʿArîsh (*see* BROOK OF EGYPT). But *nᵉhar miṣrayim*, "the river of Egypt" (Gen. 15:18), refers to the Nile, if the text is correct (cf. BDB, p. 625). The term Shihor is used also (Josh. 13:3; etc.), probably referring to the easternmost branch of the Nile in the Delta. The term *yᵉʾôr* is used exclusively of the Nile and its arms or canals with the exception of Isa. 33:21, "watercourses," and Dnl. 12:5-7, where it refers to the Tigris and is translated "stream" (cf. BDB, p. 384). The basic meaning of the Egyptian term that lay behind the Heb. *yᵉʾôr* is reflected in the LXX, which translates it consistently by *potamós*, "river," and never by *Neilos*.

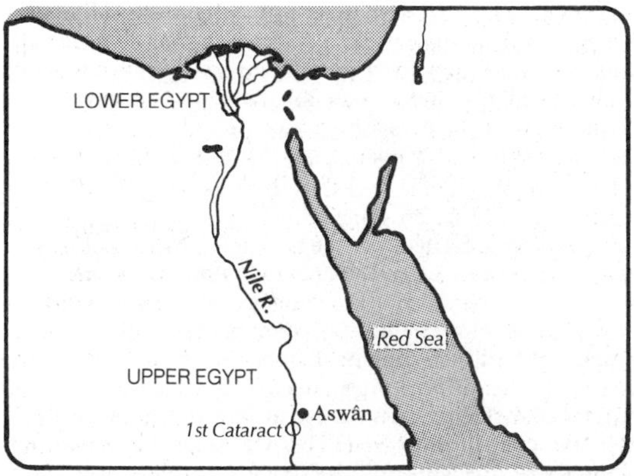


*II. Significance of the Nile.*–To the Egyptian the Nile began at the first cataract (Syene or Aswân). According to one bit of mythology, after emptying into the Mediterranean the river went into an underground Nile and returned to begin anew at Syene (cf. J. H. Breasted, *History of Egypt* [1919], pp. 55f.). This article, therefore, is limited to the portion of the Nile that was of importance to the ancient Egyptian. "Egypt is the gift of the Nile" — so, we are told, Herodotus expressed it (cf. ii.5). Water for irrigation of the fields, as well as for ordinary purposes, replenishing of the soil by the annual inundation, and the means of transportation were all supplied by the Nile. *See* Plate 45. It follows quite reasonably that the Nile was looked upon as a god.

Ḥapi (or Ḥapy) was the Nile-god. He-she is portrayed as a hermaphrodite, a figure with pendant breasts, the fertilizer male and nourisher female (cf. R. Patrick, ed., *All Color Book of Egyptian Mythology* [1972], Plate 1). It was fitting that offerings and prayers be made to the Nile for all the benefits he-she bestowed, and Ramses III recorded the offerings he made at Per-Ḥapi ("the house of Ḥapi," near modern Old Cairo) and other places. Ḥapi responded to such thanksgivings by manifesting him-herself in the annual flooding that renewed the fields and provided food for man and beast. The significance of the Nile to the ancient Egyptian can be seen in the "Hymn to the Nile" (cf. T. E. Peet, *Comparative Study of the Literatures of Egypt, Palestine, and Mesopotamia* [1931], pp. 77f.). It should be added that Osiris is often considered to be the god of the Nile and the causer of the Inundation (but cf. J. Černý, *Ancient Egyptian Religion* [1952], pp. 84f.), while at other times the crocodile-god Subek, or the dead king Unis appearing as Subek, is responsible for the annual flooding. Ḥapi is perhaps to be identified as one of the offspring of Osiris, but it must be admitted that Ḥapi has become all but lost in the Egyptian pantheon because of the prominence given to other deities.

*III. The Nile and the Bible.*–The story of the preservation of the infant Moses in a basket placed in the Nile (Ex. 2:3-10; Heb. *y*$^{e}$*'ôr* is translated "river" in RSV) needs no repetition. Less well known, perhaps, is the prominence of the Nile in the account of the plagues (7:17-19). According to one interpretation, several of the plagues resulted from an unusually high inundation of the Nile (cf. G. Hort, *ZAW*, 69 [1957], 84-103; 70 [1958], 48-59; W. S. LaSor, D. A. Hubbard, and F. W. Bush, *OT Survey* [1982], pp. 138-140; D. M. Beegle, *Moses, the Servant of Yahweh* [1972], pp. 96-118). But even if this "natural" interpretation is rejected, it must still be admitted that the striking of the Nile would be seen as a triumph of the God of the Hebrews over the Nile-god of the Egyptians, just as the tenth plague was seen as a judgment on all the gods of Egypt (12:12). The prophets Ezekiel (30:12) and Zechariah (10:11) foretold a future judgment on Egypt in which, among other things, the Nile would be dried up.

W. S. LaSor

**NIMRAH.** *See* Beth-nimrah.

**NIMRIM, WATERS OF** nim'rim [Heb. *nimrîm*]. A place in Moab associated with Zoar and Horonaim in the oracles against Moab in Isa. 15:1ff.; Jer. 48:1ff.

Eusebius (*Onom.* 138.21) identified the site with Bennamarim N of Zoar, and Jerome (comm. on Isa. 15) placed it on the Dead Sea with salt waters around it. Wâdī en-Numeirah, a stream flowing W into the Dead Sea about 13 km. (8 mi.) above its southern end, would fit the context. The suggestion of Wâdī Nimrîm, a stream flowing W into the Jordan about 13 km. (8 mi.) N of the Dead Sea, seems much less likely.

***Bibliography.***–*GP*, I, 178; II, 399; N. Glueck, *AASOR*, 15 (1935), 7f.; cf. 25 (1945), 36ff.

W. S. L. S.

**NIMROD** nim'rod [Heb. *nimrōḏ*]. A heroic figure listed as the son of Cush among the descendants of Ham in Gen. 10:8-12.

Nimrod is mentioned only three times in the OT: Gen. 10:8-12; 1 Ch. 1:10; Mic. 5:6 (MT 5). The Genesis tradition comprises an ancient fragment of Semitic historiography, which by its terseness is reminiscent of Sumerian history writing. In Gen. 2:13 Cush was described as a region surrounded by the "river" (better, "irrigation canal") known as Gihon. Although often identified with a region S of Egypt (the Ethiopia of ancient authors), it is actually unrelated to Cush (cf. E. A. Speiser, "River of Paradise," in *Festschrift Johannes Friedrich* [1959], pp. 473-485). Most probably the Cush of Gen. 2:13 was the district E of Mesopotamia from which the Kassites (the *Kuššû* of the Nuzi documents) emerged. The presence of Cush as the first name in the Hamite genealogy (Gen. 10:6; 1 Ch. 1:10) merely establishes the fact of his birth in Mesopotamia, and does not necessarily connect him with the land known in later times as Cush/Ethiopia. At the same time it does not preclude the possibility that his descendants may have migrated there.

Nimrod was "the first on earth to be a mighty man" (Gen. 10:8). His skill as a hunter inspired a proverb: "Like Nimrod a mighty hunter before the Lord" (v. 9). The phrase "before the Lord" is either the writer's indication that Nimrod's mighty deeds were in accordance with the will of Yahweh (Speiser) or is the equivalent of "on the earth" (G. von Rad, *Genesis* [Eng. tr., 2nd ed., *OTL*, 1972], p. 146).

Nimrod built a mighty kingdom in Mesopotamia (vv. 10-12). Its beginning was in the major cities of Babel, Erech, and Accad, all in the land of Shinar (the OT name for Sumer). Some translations have listed a fourth city, Calneh (so AV), but the Hebrew word could be read, with slight repointing, as *kullānâ*, "all of them" (so RSV, NEB; cf. KoB, p. 440). Nimrod's kingdom is also associated with Assyria (vv. 11f.). He founded four cities, two of which are identifiable and well known as Assyrian capitals (Nineveh and Calah). The AV reads these verses to indicate that a separate figure named Ashur founded the Assyrian cities, but this rendering is not defensible. The association of Nimrod with Assyria is supported by Mic. 5:6 (MT 5), which refers to Assyria as the "land of Nimrod."

Some commentators suggested that the Nimrod tradition in Gen. 10 is a fragment from the epic of some Babylonian deity (Ninurta is most frequently suggested), but the abundance of concrete detail in vv. 8-12 makes it far more likely that Nimrod was a historic personage. Speiser and other recent commentators regarded Tukulti-Ninurta I (*ca.* 1246-1206 B.C.) as the most likely choice, since he was the first Assyrian ruler to assert control over Babylonia as well. He was a widely celebrated figure, and his exploits could be the basis for the brief hero tradition of ch. 10. Nimrod could be related to the last half of the compound name, although this identification presents linguistic difficulties, as well as being much too late historically if the Genesis reference is in fact ancient Semitic historiography. Speiser also pointed out that classical sources seem to identify Tukulti-Ninurta I with the legendary figure Ninus, and postbiblical sources independently relate Ninus to Nimrod. No other historical identification seems to recommend itself strongly, although von Rad (p. 146), holding to the Hamitic connections of Cush, suggests Amenhotep III (1411-1375 B.C.), which seems to be at least a millennium too late.

*See also* CALNEH; CUSH; SHINAR.

See E. A. Speiser, *Eretz-Israel,* V (1958, Mazar Volume), 32-36.

B. C. BIRCH
R. K. H.

**NIMSHI** nim'shī [Heb. *nimšî*]. Grandfather of Jehu king of Israel (2 K. 9:2, 14). Jehu's usual designation, *ben-nimšî* ("son of Nimshi," 1 K. 19:16; 2 K. 9:20; 2 Ch. 22:7), apparently means "descendant of Nimshi."

**NINEVEH** nin'ə-və [Heb. *nînᵉwēh*; cuneiform *Ninua, Ninuwa*; Gk. (LXX, NT) *Nineuē,* (NT) *Nineui,* (Greek and Roman writers) *Ninos*]; AV also NINEVE (Lk. 11:32); [Gk. *Nineuitai*–'men of Nineveh'] (Mt. 12:41; Lk. 11:30, 32); AV, NEB, also NINEVITES. An ancient city of Mesopotamia and capital of Assyria.

I. Etymology
II. Biblical References
III. Location
IV. Excavations
V. History
VI. Library of Nineveh
  A. Royal Archives
  B. Literary Texts

***I. Etymology.***–The word appears in the cuneiform sources as *Ninua* and *Ninuwa*. The latter, which is the older form, is found in the Mari Letters (18th cent. B.C.) and seems to be the origin of the biblical form. Although *Ninuwa* may be of Hurrian origin, the cuneiform ideogram, composed of the sign for fish (*ḫa*) in an enclosure, shows that the name was early associated with the word for "fish" (Akk. *nūnu,* Heb. *nûn* [*nôn*]), an obvious allusion to the river-goddess Nina, whose emblem was the fish.

***II. Biblical References.***–Nineveh is first mentioned in the Bible in Gen. 10:11f., which states that Nimrod, a mighty hunter before the Lord, came from the land of Shinar (Babylonia) to Assyria and there built "Nineveh, Rehoboth-Ir [possibly a term describing Nineveh as a "city of wide streets"], and Calah, and Resen between Nineveh and Calah; that is the great city." Although the last phrase is used of Nineveh in Jonah 1:2; 3:3; 4:11, in this passage it probably refers to Calah, first, because of the word order of the Hebrew, and second, because Calah (modern Nimrûd) definitely outranked Nineveh in political importance at the time that Gen. 10 was probably written down. The statement in Genesis faithfully reflects the historical fact that Assyria was settled from Babylonia and that from the beginning it was closely attached, politically and culturally, to its southern neighbor.

2 K. 19:36 (par. Isa. 37:37) simply states that Sennacherib after his abortive attack on Jerusalem (19:35) returned to Nineveh, which he had made his capital.

Two contemporary prophets, Zephaniah (2:13-15) and Nahum, told of the fall of Nineveh (612 B.C.). Nahum's poem, which is called "an oracle concerning Nineveh" (Nah. 1:1), depicts in vivid and powerful language the impending doom of the city that had been the scourge of the earth. Its enemies are described as delirious with joy at the news of its crushing defeat (3:19).

In striking contrast with the account in Nahum of Israel's gloating vengeance over Nineveh's downfall is the story in Jonah of Nineveh's repentance and deliverance from the wrath of God. In this "missionary tract," divine mercy supersedes divine judgment upon Nineveh because the Ninevites heeded the preaching of God's messenger Jonah to forsake their violent and evil ways (3:8) and turn in humble contrition to God. The puzzling geographical notation that the great city of Nineveh was "three days' journey in breadth" (v. 3) may refer to the larger environs of the city known as the "Assyrian Triangle," which stretched from Khorsabad, about 23 km. (14 mi.) NE of Nineveh, to Nimrûd, about 37 km. (23 mi.) SE of Nineveh. In Mt. 12:41 (par. Lk. 11:30, 32) Jesus declared that the men of Nineveh to whom Jonah preached would arise at the last judgment and condemn the generation of Jesus' time.

***III. Location.***–The ancient ruins of Nineveh are located a short distance from the east bank of the Tigris River and opposite the modern city of Mosul, which is about 350 km. (220 mi.) NW of Baghdad. A small river, the Khoser, which traverses the plain from the mountains to the Tigris, flows between the two main tells, or mounds, of the site — Kuyunjik to the northwest and Nebi Yûnus to the southeast. The outline of the city walls, which are about 13 km. (8 mi.) in circumference and enclose an area of about 730 ha. (1800 acres), can still be traced.

Kuyunjik, the larger of the two tells, covers about 40 ha. (100 acres) at its base and rises abruptly from the level plain to a height of almost 30 m. (90 ft.). Already a ruin in the time of Xenophon, the mound was excavated on numerous occasions between 1842 and 1932.

Tell Nebi Yûnus, "the hill of the prophet Jonah," on the other hand, is only half as large as Kuyunjik. With the exception of a small sounding in 1954, it has escaped the archeologists' spade because it is occupied by a village, a burial ground, a mosque (formerly a Christian church), and the traditional tomb of Jonah.

***IV. Excavations.***–The mighty city with its huge palaces, magnificent temples, and colossal statuary, was so completely destroyed that the very site was in doubt until the 19th century. As the prophets had predicted (Zeph. 2:13-15; Nah. 3:7), Nineveh became "a desolation, a dry waste like a desert," and passed into oblivion for 2500 years.

The exploration of the site of Nineveh began in 1820 with C. J. Rich, Resident of the British East India Company at Baghdad. His excellent description of the Nineveh

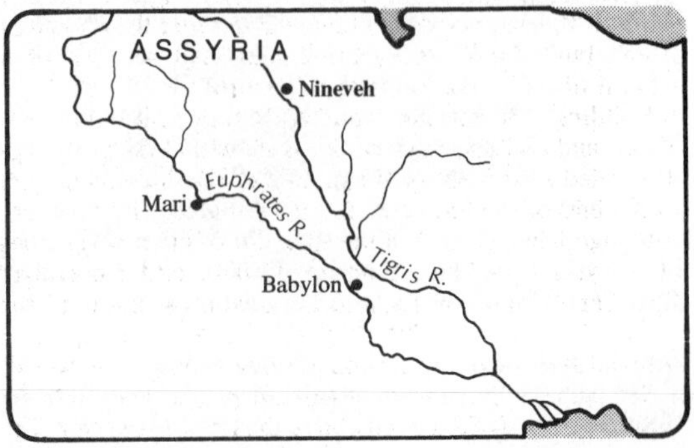

ruins included a map of the mounds. Rich was the first orientalist to arouse European interest in the lost civilizations of Mesopotamia.

A. H. Layard, the English archeologist and "father of Assyriology," discovered the great palace of Sennacherib king of Assyria (705-681 B.C.) in the southern corner of Kuyunjik in 1847. Excavations two years later revealed that this massive structure had at least seventy-one rooms, 3010 m. (9880 ft.) of walls covered with sculptured slabs, and twenty-seven gateways formed by colossal winged bulls and lion-sphinxes.

After Layard left Mesopotamia H. Rassam, a native Christian, carried on his work and in 1853 laid bare another great palace in the northern part of the tell that belonged to the Assyrian king Ashurbanipal (669-633 B.C.). The palace yielded vast treasures of sculpture and other works of art, and, most spectacular of all, the Royal Library with thousands of clay tablets (see VII below). The publication of these priceless texts was begun by G. Smith, an assistant in the British Museum.

Excavations continued sporadically at Kuyunjik after Layard and Rassam under the direction of E. A. W. Budge (1888-1891), L. W. King (1903), and R. C. Thompson (1927-1932), who with Hutchinson, Hamilton, and Mallowan explored the mound more scientifically and excavated the temple of Nabû.

*V. History.*–Although there is archeological evidence that the site of Nineveh was occupied as early as 5000 B.C., not until the 3rd millennium B.C. did signs of its importance as a religious, cultural, and political center begin to appear. Maništusu, a successor of Sargon I, erected a temple of Ishtar at Nineveh during the Semitic dynasty of Akkad (*ca.* 2360-2180). Its many restorations during the next two thousand years of Nineveh's history not only attest to the importance of this shrine of the city's main deity but also indicate that this may be the oldest building at Kuyunjik. A beautifully wrought lifesize bronze head, probably representing Sargon himself, was discovered in a sounding at Nineveh.

By 2000 Nineveh had merchants in an Assyrian colony at Kultepe in Cappadocia, where a text with the earliest known ideogram for Nineveh was discovered.

In the Early Assyrian period King Šamši-Adad I (1748-1716) rebuilt the temple of Ishtar at Nineveh and conquered the rival city of Mari, where he installed his son Yasmaḫ-Adad as governor. In the correspondence between the king and his son at Mari the name of Nineveh occurs several times (*ARM,* I, 35, 41, etc.). Shortly after the death of Šamši-Adad, however, Hammurabi king of Babylon subdued Assyria and made it a vassal state, as the prologue to his famous law code indicates (*ANET,* p. 165).

In the Middle Assyrian Kingdom (14th-12th cents. B.C.) Nineveh was the palace-city of several kings. Inscriptions discovered on the site show that Shalmaneser I (1265-1235), Tukulti-Ninurta I (1234-1197), and Tiglath-pileser I (1118-1078) had palaces at Nineveh, and that the temple of Ishtar, built a thousand years earlier, had been restored several times by the kings of this period.

Building inscriptions from both Kuyunjik and Nebi Yûnus and archeological evidence show that thirteen kings who ruled Assyria from the middle of the 2nd millennium to the end of the 7th cent. B.C. built palaces in Nineveh. Although Nineveh shared the splendor of other royal cities of Assyria — Asshur, Nimrûd (Calah), and Khorsabad (Dūr-Šarrukin) — throughout the centuries, not until the days of Sennacherib (705-681) did it become the capital of the land and one of the architectural wonders of the world.

Sennacherib pulled down the old palace and built his new one on a platform well above the level of the city. The site of the palace at the southern end of Kuyunjik has been dug extensively, but its full magnitude has not yet been determined. The remains of its scores of spacious rooms, large halls and courts, decorated walls with the sculptured history of Sennacherib's domestic accomplishments and military victories, and numerous entrances, guarded by colossal winged bulls weighing as much as 30 metric tons and by huge lion-sphinxes, give mute testimony to its majestic splendor. Clay tablets covered the floor of two palace rooms to a depth of a half-meter; the tablets were part of the Royal Library, whose main treasures were found in the palace of Ashurbanipal (669-633). Sennacherib was not exaggerating when he called his residence "the palace without a rival."

Bronze head, perhaps of Sargon. From Nineveh, last half of the 3rd millennium B.C. (Consulate General of the Republic of Iraq)

Sennacherib enlarged and beautified the city with temples, broad streets, and public gardens. Unique in the Near East were the dimensions and design of his aqueduct, which by its system of dams brought fresh water into the city from the mountains to the east. The king also built massive walls and fortifications around the city for protection against his enemies. Only Babylon in the ancient world surpassed Sennacherib's capital in magnificence and beauty.

After Sennacherib's death his son Esarhaddon ruled Assyria (681-669). Nineveh was his capital city also, but he built a new palace on the mound now known as Nebi Yûnus. Evidence of this structure was discovered in 1954 in a sounding made by the Director General of Antiquities in Iraq. Because the site is covered by a village further excavations are impossible.

Ashurbanipal, "the great and noble Osnappar" of Ezr. 4:10, succeeded his father Esarhaddon. Besides restoring the temples of Nabû and Ishtar, he built a new palace on the northern end of Tell Kuyunjik. H. Rassam excavated the site in 1853-54 and found the massive sculptures characteristic of Assyrian art and the famous "Lion Hunt" sequence carved in relief on the walls of the palace. The relief's realistic depiction of animals in action has never been excelled (*see* pictures in ASHURBANIPAL; ARCHEOLOGY OF MESOPOTAMIA). The greatest treasure from the site was of course the library of Ashurbanipal, which included thousands of clay tablets dealing with literary, religious, and historical subjects (see VI below).

In August, 612 B.C., the mighty city of Nineveh fell to the combined forces of the Babylonians under Nabopolassar and the Medes under Cyaxares. This date has been firmly established from Babylonian sources (the Babylonian Chronicle), which give a detailed description of the campaign against Nineveh: "they marched along the bank of the river Tigris and. . . . . .against Nineveh. . . .they encamped[?] From the month of Sivan to the month of Ab three *UŠ* [measures. . . . . .they advanced?] A strong attack they made against the city, and in the month of Ab, [the. . .th day the city was captured. . . . . .] a great defeat of the chief [people] was made. On that day Sin-šar-iškun, the Assyrian king. . . . . . . . The great spoil of the city and temple they carried off and [turned] the city into a ruin-mound and heaps of debris. . . . . ." (*CCK,* pp. 59, 61). The excavations at Kuyunjik have remarkably corroborated this description of Nineveh's complete destruction.

For the next three hundred years the site was not occupied, according to archeological evidence. Remains from the Seleucid, Roman, and Sassanian periods found on the tell point to sporadic settlements during these times. Benjamin of Tudela, a rabbi who visited Jewish communities in the East in the 12th cent. A.D., reported, "Nineveh now lies in utter ruins, but numerous villages and small towns occupy its former space" (T. Wright, ed., *Early Travels in Palestine* [1848], p. 94).

*VI. Library of Nineveh.*–One of the important buildings in Nineveh was the temple of Nabû on the northern part of the tell of Kuyunjik, at the southern corner of the palace of Ashurbanipal. R. C. Thompson discovered it in 1904-1905 and excavated it more extensively in 1927-28. Its origin is shrouded in mystery, but inscriptional material indicates that it was restored during the reigns of Adadnirari III (811-783 B.C.) and Ashurbanipal.

Nabû son of Marduk, the Nebo of Isa. 46:1, was the god of writing who knew all things. No shrine could have been more appropriate in a city whose ruins were to yield tens of thousands of clay tablets, numerous inscribed prisms, and long wall inscriptions. According to the colophons of several tablets this temple had a library in which the royal writings were deposited. Unfortunately, except for a few important fragments the elusive treasure of tablets has never been discovered on this site. It may lie hidden in some pocket near the temple, or it may have been dispersed among other sites, or it may even have been destroyed in the final sack of the city.

Large deposits of clay tablets did turn up in two places on Kuyunjik. Layard discovered one deposit in 1850 in two chambers of Sennacherib's palace, and H. Rassam found the other in 1853 in the palace of Ashurbanipal. According to R. C. Thompson 26,000 of these tablets have been cataloged, and most have been published.

Part of the Babylonian Chronicle telling of Nineveh's fall in 612 B.C. (Trustees of the British Museum)

Even if not the founder of the Nineveh library, Ashurbanipal was the real patron of science and learning. He collected the tablets for his library from places like Borsippa, Babylon, and Nippur, and he himself could read as well as copy these documents, as the colophon of almost every important tablet indicates: "Palace of Ashurbanipal, king of the world, king of Assyria. . . . The wisdom of Nabû. . . . I have inscribed upon tablets. . . . that I might see them and read them I have placed them within my palace. . . . Whosoever shall take (this tablet) away, or shall write his own name beside my name, may Ashur and Ninlil in wrath and fury cast him down, and may they blot out his name and seed from the land."

The tablets of the library were systematically numbered and cataloged in series whose headings were the first words of the first tablet of the series. The uniformity of the script and the accuracy of the texts suggests that the tablets were copied by a school of scribes, probably connected with the temple of Nabû.

The contents of the library may be divided into two main categories: the royal archives, and literary works in general.

*A. Royal Archives.* These archives contain letters written by the king, and others (which are in the majority) written to the king by sovereigns, princes, and state functionaries on all sorts of matters. Also found were contracts made with and by the royal house and economic texts dealing with every phase of palace life.

*B. Literary Texts.* The great majority of tablets are literary texts, which may be divided as follows.

*1. Philological.* Since the Assyro-Babylonian language was written in a script invented much earlier to record Sumerian, a non-Semitic language, and since many Sumerian literary works had been translated into the Assyro-Babylonian language, the scribes provided syllabaries, lexicons, and grammars of both languages for their students. Many of these texts, which are invaluable for the decipherment of the cuneiform script and the grammatical study of both these languages, have been found in the library at Nineveh.

*2. Juridical.* These legal texts deal with social practices and points of law concerning familial relationships, ownership of property, contractual agreements, etc.

*3. Historical.* The Assyrians were distinguished among the nations of the ancient world for their historical sense. Palace walls were lined with accounts and reliefs of military campaigns and victories, and prisms and statuary were inscribed with royal exploits. The annals of the kings were also written down on clay tablets, many of which were found in the library.

*4. Religious.* The religious texts from Nineveh are of primary importance for the study of the history of religion in the Near East and for biblical exegesis in particular. Here were first found the myths of creation, the Flood, etc., which many scholars think the Hebrews took over and adapted to their theology, particularly in Gen. 1–11. Also discovered were the literary patterns of hymns, prayers, lamentations, and wisdom motifs that were among the models for similar OT genres. Especially interesting is the way that the Babylonians and Assyrians adapted the ancient myths of Sumer to their own theological systems by changing the names of the gods. For instance, the Sumerian deity Enlil, the creator of the world and father of the gods, became Marduk in Babylonia and Ashur in Assyria.

Among the myths discovered in the library of Nineveh are the seven tablets of the Creation story; the twelve tablets of the Gilgamesh Epic, which deals with the age-old quest of mankind for eternal life and includes the Babylonian version of the biblical Flood story; the Legend of Etana, who flew to heaven on an eagle; the Story of Adapa, who squandered the opportunity for gaining immortality; the Myth of Zu the bird-god, who stole the Tablets of Destiny; the Descent of Ishtar to the Netherworld; and the legend of the birth of Sargon of Agade, who like Moses was saved as a young child by being put into a reed basket on the Euphrates River from which he was rescued by Akki. For the translation of these and other myth stories, see *ANET*, pp. 60-119, 501-518.

Also included among the religious tablets are the omen texts, which describe animal organs, especially the liver, and the movements of birds and heavenly bodies; incantation or magical texts used against demons and sicknesses of all kinds; ritual texts; and hymns, prayers, laments, and oracles for kings in times of trouble. A large corpus of wisdom literature includes proverbs, popular tales, and the story of the righteous sufferer, somewhat like Job in the OT.

*5. Scientific.* The five hundred tablets dealing with medicine indicate that it was an advanced science in Assyria. Diseases of all kinds are carefully described, and the prescriptions for their cure include some five hundred drugs. There are texts on botany, geology, chemistry, mathematics, and astronomy, as well as an invaluable treatise on the components of glass and the glazes for pottery.

The clay tablets from the library of Nineveh are not only the foundation of the science of Assyriology but also the clue to the intellectual and spiritual life of one of the greatest civilizations of the ancient Near East.

***Bibliography.***–E. A. W. Budge, *Babylonian Story of the Deluge and the Epic of Gilgamesh with an Account of the Royal Libraries of Nineveh* (1929); C. J. Gadd, *Fall of Nineveh* (1923); *Assyrian Sculptures* (1934); *Stones of Assyria* (1936); A. H. Layard, *Monuments of Nineveh* (1849); *Discoveries among the Ruins of Nineveh and Babylon* (1953); S. Lloyd, *Foundations in the Dust* (1949); A. Parrot, *Nineveh and the OT* (Eng. tr. 1955); *Nineveh and Babylon* (Eng. tr. 1961); H. W. F. Saggs, *Greatness that was Babylon* (1962); R. C. Thompson and R. W. Hutchinson, *Century of Exploration at Nineveh* (1929).

C. T. FRITSCH

**NINEVITES** nin'ə-vīts. The AV translation of Gk. *Nineuitai* (Lk. 11:30), designating the inhabitants of NINEVEH.

**NIPHIS** nī'fis (1 Esd. 5:21, RSV mg.). *See* MAGBISH.

**NIPPUR** ni-po͞or' [Sum. $^{d}$En-lil$^{ki}$; Akk. *Ni-ip pu-ru*]. An ancient holy city, called "the bond of heaven and earth" (Sum. dur-an-ki), and the principal religious center of southern Mesopotamia. Although Nippur is not mentioned in the Bible (despite the talmudic identification of Nippur with CALNEH), cuneiform tablets found there have been essential for knowledge of Sumerian literature and of the earliest cultural background of the OT.

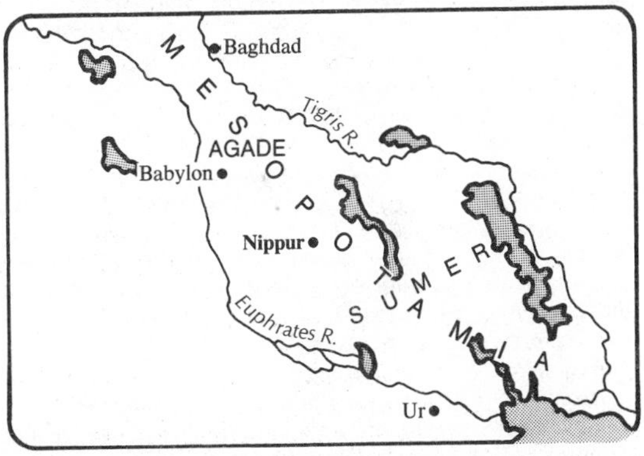


*I. Site.*–Covered with drifting sand dunes, bisected by a large wadi, and dominated by the crumbling ziggurat (temple tower) of Enlil ("Lord Storm"), a chief Sumerian god, is the desolate mound still called Nuffar. It is about 72 ha. (180 acres) in area, one of the most impressive mounds in the Near East. Lying midway between the Euphrates and Tigris rivers, Nippur is the center of a once-fertile irrigated region where the cities of southern Mesopotamia flourished for thousands of years. It is 150 km. (93 mi.) SE of Baghdad and 150 km. (93 mi.) NW of Ur, on an ancient waterway of the delta.

*II. Historical Significance.*–Like Delphi in Greece, Nippur was not a seat of political power. Many kings, however, including Naram-Sin of Agade (*ca.* 2150 B.C.), Ur-Nammu of Ur (*ca.* 2050), and Hammurabi of Babylon (*ca.* 1775), sought approval of the priests of Enlil at Nippur to legitimize their rule over Sumer and Akkad. They restored Enlil's shrine, the Ekur ("mountain house"), and

Three brick stamps from Nippur. The brick at right says "Naram-Sin, builder of the temple of Enlil"; the center brick reads "Šar-kali-šarri, king of Agade, builder of the temple of Enlil" (University Museum, University of Pennsylvania)

many other temples and brought inscribed statues and rich gifts. The Semitic conqueror Sargon (*ca.* 2250) conducted Lugalzagessi, the last Sumerian king of Uruk, to Nippur in a neckstock, and Sumerian literature regards the fall of Agade to the Gutians as retribution for Naram-Sin's desecration of the Ekur. The renown of Nippur is attested in "The Poor Man of Nippur," a broadly humorous tale inscribed on a late Neo-Assyrian tablet from Sultantepe near Urfa in Turkey and prominently featuring the "king of Nippur," a city that had no king (*Anatolian Studies,* VI, 145-162).

*III. Archeological Excavations.*–The English archeological pioneer A. H. Layard dug only briefly at the dreary site in 1851. After de Sarzec had discovered Sumerian civilization at Telloh in 1871, J. P. Peters of the University of Pennsylvania chose Nippur for excavation by the first American expedition to Mesopotamia. Between 1889 and 1900 four long campaigns under Peters, Haynes, and finally the distinguished Assyriologist Hilprecht endured severe hardships. Precise archeological data were not obtained, but occupation over a very long time was confirmed. Most importantly, about thirty thousand cuneiform tablets were recovered, the majority of which are now in the University of Pennsylvania Museum, with others in the Museum of the Ancient Orient in Istanbul and at the University of Jena in Germany.

After half a century of neglect, excavations were resumed in 1948, largely through the efforts of T. Jacobsen. The expedition, which was still active in 1982, at first involved the Oriental Institute of the University of Chicago, the University of Pennsylvania, and the American Schools of Oriental Research, and subsequently just the Institute. While much work remains to be done, the ziggurat, basically built by Ur-Nammu, and the temple of Enlil have been cleared, more tablets have been recovered, and an archeological sequence of more than five thousand years, from the Ubaid period (*ca.* 4500 B.C.) to 800 A.D., has been established. Excavation of a temple of the goddess Inanna has revealed twenty-two construction levels, probably the longest history for any known building.

Application in Mesopotamia of techniques more usual at American and European sites, such as geomorphology, paleobotany, and paleozoology, may disclose environmental factors that caused a marked decline in population at Nippur and other Mesopotamian cities during the "dark age" between the Old Babylonian and the Amarna periods (*ca.* 1600-1400 B.C.). The main contribution of Nippur, however, remains the epigraphic material.

*IV. The Tablets and Their Biblical Relevance.*–The content of the Sumerian texts is rich and varied. Most are economic and administrative: bills of sale, accounts, contracts, wills, and court decisions; there are also historical inscriptions and lexical lists of Sumerian words with Akkadian equivalents. But of primary importance are more than four thousand tablets and fragments containing literary compositions: myths, epic poems, hymns, laments, and proverbs. Although many of these texts were copied be-

Fragment of a hymn to Enlil, the god of Nippur (Isin period) (University Museum, University of Pennsylvania)

tween *ca.* 2000 and 1750 B.C., during the Isin-Larsa and Old Babylonian periods when Sumerian was no longer a spoken language, they accurately record compositions of unknown antiquity and comprise about 80 percent of known Sumerian literature.

The Nippur tablets have been indispensable for deciphering the difficult Sumerian language and for interpreting similar texts from other sites. Syntheses by S. N. Kramer and other scholars, notably T. Jacobsen in *Treasures of Darkness,* have demonstrated the great antiquity of Mesopotamian culture, firmly rooted in that of Sumer. Affinities with the Bible are readily apparent. Lamentations over the destruction of Ur and Agade may be compared with the biblical book Lamentations, wisdom texts with Proverbs, poems about a righteous sufferer with Proverbs and Job, and love lyrics of the goddess Inanna and her consort Dumuzi with Canticles. The very old custom of wailing for Tammuz (Dumuzi) is mentioned in Ezk. 8:14. Myths of creation and the flood show some striking similarities to the biblical accounts (*see* FLOOD VI). Far more impressive, however, is the distinctive quality of analogous OT texts. The Sumerian gods, fallible and capricious, formed man to labor for them and then sent plagues and famine to diminish the population. In contrast, the biblical material of each genre is infused and transformed by the ethical monotheism of Israel.

*See also* SUMER.

***Bibliography.***–D. E. McCown and R. C. Haines, *Nippur I: Temple of Enlil, Scribal Quarter and Soundings* (1967); D. E. McCown, *et al., Nippur II: The North Temple and Sounding E* (1978); *Archaeology,* 30 (1977), 26-37; S. N. Kramer, *Sumerian Mythology* (1961); *The Sumerians: Their History, Culture and Character* (1963); T. Jacobsen, *Treasures of Darkness, A History of Mesopotamian Religion* (1976); *ANET,* pp. 37-59, 455-463, 573-591, etc.; E. I. Gordon, *Sumerian Proverbs* (1959).

P. W. GAEBELEIN, JR.

**NISAN** nī'san, nē'sän [Heb. *nîsān*] (Neh. 2:1; Est. 3:7); [Gk. *Nisa(n)*] (Ad. Est. 11:2; 1 Esd. 5:6); AV also NISON (Ad. Est. 11:2). The first month of the year in the Hebrew CALENDAR, corresponding to March/April. The name is Babylonian in origin and appears in OT texts only after the Exile; in the Pentateuch it is called ABIB. *See also* NEW YEAR.

**NISROCH** nis'rok [Heb. *nisrōḵ*]. God of a temple in which Sennacherib was assassinated (2 K. 19:37; Isa. 37:38). The name, unattested in voluminous cuneiform sources, cannot easily be equated with Marduk or Nusku. Although any identification is problematical, sporadic omissions of *n* from transcriptions in the Greek MSS B, ℵ, and A, and analogies with Nimrod and Marduk, led the distinguished Assyriologist Landsberger to postulate the name of the national god Ass(h)ur with initial *n* and final *k* added.

***Bibliography.***–B. Landsberger and T. Bauer, *Zeitschrift für Assyriologie,* 37 (1927), 69f.; J. P. Lettinga, *VT,* 7 (1957), 105f.

P. W. GAEBELEIN, JR.

**NITRE** nī'tər (AV Prov. 25:20; Jer. 2:22). *See* LYE.

**NO** nō. The AV and NEB translation of Heb. *nō'* (Jer. 46:25; Ezk. 30:14-16; Nah. 3:8), rendered THEBES by the RSV.

**NOADIAH** nō-ə-dī'ə [Heb. *nôʿaḏyâ*–'Yahweh has met by appointment'; LXX *Nōadia*].

**1.** Son of Binnui; one of the Levites to whom Ezra entrusted the silver and gold and temple vessels that were brought to Jerusalem after the Exile (Ezr. 8:33; cf. 1 Esd. 8:63 [LXX 62], where he is called MOETH).

**2.** A prophetess associated with Tobiah and Sanballat in opposition to Nehemiah (Neh. 6:14).

**NOAH** nō'ə.

**1.** [Heb. *nō(a)ḥ*; Gk. *Noē*]; AV also NOE. The last of the antediluvian patriarchs and survivor of the Genesis Flood (Gen. 5:28–9:28).

***I. Name.***–The etymology of *nō(a)ḥ* is uncertain. Many commentators relate it to Heb. *nwḥ,* "to rest." In Gen. 5:29 the name is mentioned in assonance with the verb *nḥm* (piel), "comfort" (AV and RV) or "bring relief" (RSV), but *nwḥ* is closer to the name Noah.

***II. Genealogy and Longevity.***–Noah was the son of Lamech (Gen. 5:28f.; Lk. 3:36) and father of three sons, Shem, Ham, and Japheth (Gen. 5:32; 6:9; 9:18f.; 10:1), who were born before the Flood. The order preserved in these verses is not chronological. Ham was the youngest (9:24) and Japheth the second of Noah's sons.

Noah lived 950 years. Reinterpretations of the longevity of the ANTEDILUVIAN PATRIARCHS, such as appealing to the concept of family or dynasty identification rather than individual, are fraught with unresolved difficulties.

***III. Noah in a World Under Judgment.***–As a prelude to the story of the Flood, Gen. 6:1-7, 11f. paints a portrait of the wickedness of mankind (on the difficulty of identifying the "sons of God" *see* SONS OF GOD [OT]). The importance of this passage is its statement of the progression of evil. The Creator's response to a "corrupt" and "violent" civilization was one of grief and anger (6:5-7, 11-13). Judgment was imminent.

In the context of an already ruined civilization, Noah emerges as a man in step with God (6:9). He was righteous (*ṣaddîq*; cf. AV "just"); responding to events as yet unseen, he "became an heir of the righteousness which comes by faith" (He. 11:7). Noah was also blameless (*tāmîm*; cf. AV "perfect") "among the people of his time" (NIV, preferable to AV "in his generations"). *Tāmîm* signifies perfection in the sense of completeness or wholeheartedness (see BDB, p. 1071). Later writers would recall the days of Noah (Isa. 54:9; Mt. 24:37f.; Lk. 17:26f.) and would remember him as an exemplarily righteous man (Ezk. 14:14, 20; 2 Pet. 2:5).

***IV. The Flood.***–Noah was informed of the impending destruction 120 years beforehand (Gen. 6:3, 13; cf. 1 Pet. 3:20). The agency of judgment would be a flood (Heb. *mabbûl,* 6:17; 7:6, 7, 10, 17; see also Ps. 29:10). The LXX translates Heb. *mabbûl* by *kataklysmós,* which the NT also uses to refer to the Flood (Mt. 24:38f.; Lk. 17:27; 2 Pet. 2:5). Noah, the one who "found favor in the eyes of the Lord" (Gen. 6:8), this "herald of righteousness" (2 Pet. 2:5), and his family would be spared. The agency of their salvation would be an ark (*tēḇâ,* Gen. 6:14).

Every facet of the Flood narrative has been scrutinized with a view to logical explanation, including questions for which the text speaks not a word. The Genesis Flood is but one of many biblical events whose import has been diminished, if not lost, in the need for thorough explanation and empirical verification. These lines of inquiry may be legitimate, though extravagances abound, but it is more important to seek the intended emphasis and allow the text to speak in its own terms. *See also* FLOOD (GENESIS); ARK OF NOAH.

*A. Judgment.* The Flood bespeaks the certain judgment of a sovereign and righteous God on an ungodly world (see Kline, p. 89). This ordeal by water (2 Pet. 3:5f.) was a mere token of judgment when compared with the greater judgment that awaits not only the earth but all creation (cf. 2 Pet. 3:7, 10). The emphasis of Jesus' words in Mt. 24:36-41; Lk. 17:26-37, as He compared the days of Noah with those of the Son of man, was not on the sinfulness of Noah's contemporaries, but rather on the unexpectedness of impending doom (cf. Mt. 24:44).

*B. Salvation.* The Flood also bespeaks salvation to those

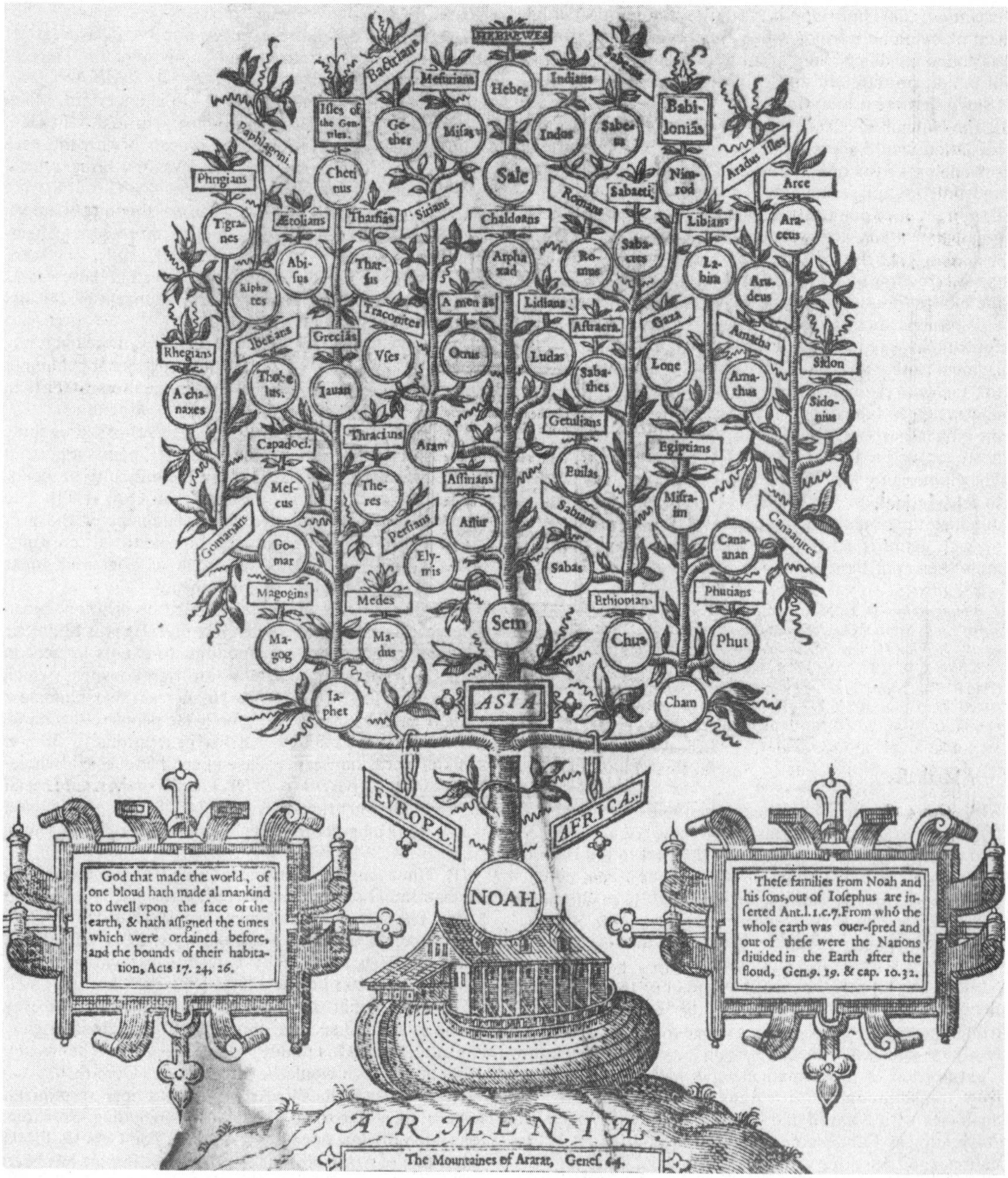


The ark, at rest on Mt. Ararat, and the genealogical tree of Noah (see Gen. 10). From the AV (London, 1611) (New York Public Library)

who put their faith in God (He. 11:7). Although the parallel between the deliverance of Noah and his family and salvation through Christ is not precise at every point, Peter compares the waters of the Flood with those of baptism in which the water symbolizes God's judgment on sin and deliverance into a new life (1 Pet. 3:20f.; *see also* BAPTISM VII.A). Peter emphasizes that the efficacy of baptism lies not in the outward symbolism of the "removal of dirt from the body" but in the inner response of faith to God.

*V. Noah's Counterparts in Cuneiform Sources.*–Although archeology has not provided empirical data for the Genesis Flood, excavations have unearthed many texts and fragments which preserve the story of a great flood, widely known among the civilizations of the ancient Near East. It is mentioned in the Sumerian King List (*ca.* 2000 B.C.; *ANET,* pp. 265f.; Kramer, pp. 328-331). A fragmentary Sumerian tablet from Nippur preserves the story of King Ziusudra, Noah's counterpart, who was warned that the gods had decided to destroy mankind with a flood. A great boat would provide Ziusudra's escape. The last extant lines of the text describe his deification (*ANET,* pp. 42-44).

The Epic of Atra-ḫasis (*ca.* 17th cent. B.C. in the earliest surviving copies) describes a deluge sent by the gods to destroy mankind after earlier attempts through drought had failed to control the increasing number of people and their noise (W. G. Lambert and A. R. Millard, *Atra-Ḫasīs:*

*The Babylonian Story of the Flood* [1969]). A small fragment of the Babylonian flood story referring to Atra-ḫasis was found at Râs Shamrah and dated to the 14th cent. B.C. (ibid., pp. 131-33).

Similar to the story of Atra-ḫasis is that preserved in the eleventh tablet of the Gilgamesh Epic (the best English translation with discussion of the biblical parallels is that of Heidel; see also *ANET,* pp. 72-99; S. N. Kramer, *JAOS,* 64 [1944], 7ff.). The story is, in part, that of Gilgamesh's quest for immortality which leads him to the island of Utnapishtim. This "Babylonian Noah" tells Gilgamesh the story of the flood which was prompted by Enlil's insomnia, as in the Atra-ḫasis Epic. Utnapishtim narrates how he alone was warned of the impending destruction and instructed to build a boat by which he and his family would be spared. The story leads to the granting of immortality to Utnapishtim, an event which will never recur.

The similarities between the biblical and Mesopotamian flood stories are striking, as are the differences (*see* FLOOD [GENESIS] VI; Heidel, pp. 224-269, esp. p. 269; T. Jacobsen, pp. 215-19). Opinions differ concerning the literary relationship between the biblical and Babylonian narratives. Many scholars consider the latter to comprise the raw materials from which the former was produced. Others contend that the two revert to an unknown common source. The similarities suggest a common recollection of an actual historical event. The differences bespeak the focus of divine inspiration. Genesis records the story of Noah in historical truth and imparts the theological significance of the Flood.

*VI. Noahic Covenant.*–Noah emerges from the ark and builds an altar of sacrifice. He offers burnt offerings, tokens of dedication and atonement, which produce a "sweet savour" to the Lord (Gen. 8:21, AV). Contrast the imagery of the Babylonian version at this point:

The gods smelled the savor
The gods smelled the sweet savor
The gods gathered like flies over the sacrifice.

What God had once commanded Adam (Gen. 1:28), He now reiterates to Noah and his sons (9:1; see Kline, p. 90). This COVENANT (Gen. 6:18; 9:8-17) is remarkable for its breadth (9:10; 12–13; 15; 17) and permanence. It is an everlasting covenant (Heb. *b^erîṯ ʿôlām,* 9:16), initiated by the beneficent Creator. He promised that never again would the world be destroyed by a flood (9:15). The rainbow (Heb. *qešeṯ,* usually denoting the weapon) was the covenant sign, a seal of the promise to mankind and a reminder to God of His commitments.

***Bibliography.***–A. Heidel, *Gilgamesh Epic and OT Parallels* (2nd ed. 1949); T. Jacobsen, *Treasures of Darkness* (1976), pp. 195-219; M. G. Kline, "Genesis," *NBC* (3rd ed. 1970); S. N. Kramer, *Sumerians* (1963); M. E. L. Mallowan, *Iraq,* 26 (1964), 62-82; A. R. Millard, *Tyndale Bulletin,* 18 (1967), 3-18; A. Parrot, *The Flood and Noah's Ark* (Eng. tr. 1955); G. J. Wenham, *VT,* 28 (1978), 336-348.

G. PRATICO

**2.** [Heb. *nōʿâ*]. One of the daughters of Zelophehad (Nu. 26:33; 27:1; 36:11; Josh. 17:3). *See* MAHLAH **1.** The names of the five women probably represented towns.

**NOAH, BOOK (APOCALYPSE) OF.** A lost pseudepigraphical document referred to and quoted in 1 Enoch and Jubilees. The Book of Noah, not a true apocalypse, contained a visionary description of purported events surrounding the birth of the biblical Noah, as well as an account of his death. A messianic notion of God's kingdom coming on earth forms the main theological theme. A special interest in fallen angels (such as those probably indicated in Gen. 6:1-4), who produced prodigious progeny with the daughters of men, structures the discussion of the problem of evil: demoralization of humanity, instigation of the Deluge and natural disasters, and setting the cosmos, angels, and people under awful judgment. The tension between the coming kingdom and the eschatological judgment seems to be the meaning of history.

The Book of Noah is mentioned in Jub. 10:13 and 21:10 and incorporated at length in Jub. 7:20-39; 10:1-15; 1 En. 6–11; 39:1-2a; 54:7–55:2; 60; 65–69; 106; and probably 107. 1 Enoch was written in Greek but preserved only in Ethiopic. Fragments in Aramaic, Hebrew, and Greek have been found in such sources as the Dead Sea Scrolls, as have fragments of the Book of Noah itself, in Hebrew. Since the Book of Noah is generally understood to be a source of 1 Enoch and Jubilees, it must predate *ca.* 150 B.C. The Hebrew Book of Noah is a different and later work based upon the selections of the Book of Noah preserved in the Hebrew, Greek, or Ethiopic version of Jubilees. That later work is treated in H. Rönsch, *Das Buch der Jubiläen* (1874), pp. 385-87, and R. H. Charles, *Ethiopic Version of the Hebrew Book of Jubilees* (1895), p. 179.

*See also* APOCALYPTIC LITERATURE.

See *APOT,* II, 163, 168, 170. J. H. ELLENS

**NO-AMON** nō-am'ən. *See* THEBES.

**NOB** nob [Heb. *nōḇ*; Gk. B *Nomba,* once *Nomma*; A *Noba,* once *Nobath*]. A village in Benjamin. The meaning of the name is unknown; perhaps it derives from *nûḇ,* "thrive"; cf. targumic *nôḇ,* "fruit."

After the Philistines destroyed Shiloh and its temple, some priests evidently migrated to Nob, which probably was part of the territory of Jerusalem. Under the Jebusite king they were protected from Philistine attacks.

According to 1 S. 21–22 a sanctuary was erected there. The ritual of the bread of the Presence was performed in the sanctuary (v. 6), and those who wished to undergo ritual purification stayed for some time in the temple precincts (v. 7). Votive offerings were stored in the building (21:9). It had an ephod by which the oracle could be consulted (21:9; 22:10); if the priest Ahimelech of these chapters is the same as Ahijah the great-grandson of Eli (14:3), which is very probable, priests from Nob carrying the instrument of oracle accompanied the people on military expeditions. Thus it seems that apart from the absence of the ark the whole cult-system of Shiloh was carried on in Nob.

The connections between David and the priests of Nob (cf. also Mt. 12:3f. par.) led to the massacre of all the inhabitants of the settlement, except for Abiathar, on the command of Saul. The eighty-five male adults killed by Doeg on Saul's command (1 S. 22:18) might justify an estimation of about 340 inhabitants of the settlement in those days. After the massacre Nob lost all importance as a "city of the priests." Fifty-two men among those who returned from the Exile with Zerubbabel traced their origin to the village, called (the other) Nebo in Ezr. 2:29; Neh. 7:33, and settled there again. After that event Nob disappeared from written sources. Josephus, who called it Naba, mentioned it only in connection with David's story. Isa. 10:32 does refer to a locality of the same name in the immediate neighborhood of Jerusalem, but whether it was inhabited in the prophet's days is not clear from this text. Probably Nebo in Ezr. 2:29; 10:43; Neh. 7:33 is the same place.

Jerome looked for Nob in the neighborhood of Aijalon, but Isa. 10:32 requires that Jerusalem was visible from Nob. Solomon's banishment of Abiathar, who originated from Nob, to his estate in Anathoth (1 K. 2:26) points in the same direction. Nob must have been on the road from Anathoth to Jerusalem, either the Râs el-Mesharif 3 km. (2 mi.) directly N of Jerusalem, Josephus's Scopus, or the Râs Umm et-Tala on the eastern slope of the same ridge.

There is no decisive archeological evidence at either place, however. The sanctuary proper may even have been on Mt. Scopus, but the houses were built somewhat to the east, where agricultural conditions are more favorable.

In 2 S. 21:16 "Ishbi-benob" perhaps is to be understood not as the name of a person but as a sentence, "they settled in Nob," but in this case one should read "Gob" (cf. vv. 18f.). The NEB reads, "Then Benob. . . ."

A. VAN SELMS

**NOBAH** nō'bə [Heb. *nōḇaḥ*].

**1.** A Manassite (Gk. *Nabau*) who conquered KENATH and renamed it Nobah (Gk. *Nobōth*) after himself (Nu. 32:42), therefrom a place with the same name.

**2.** A city in eastern Gilead W of the caravan route along which Gideon pursued the Midianites (Jgs. 8:11, LXX B *Nabeth*, A *Nabai*). This city was near JOGBEHAH, which Nu. 32:35 also mentions; hence there is no compelling reason not to identify it with **1** (v. 42).

W. S. L. S.

**NOBLE; NOBLEMAN; NOBILITY** [Heb. *'addîr, 'adderet̲, hāḏār, ḥōr, nāḏîḇ, nāgîḏ, partᵉmîm, gāḏōl*, niphal part. of *kāḇēḏ*; Aram. *yaqqîr*; Gk. *kalós, timḗ, eugenḗs (ánthrōpos)*]; AV also GOODLY, EXCELLENT, LIBERAL, HONOUR, PRINCE, etc.; NEB also CHIEFTAIN, LEADER, NOTABLE, RENOWNED, MAGNATE, FINE, CIVIL, HIGHLY BORN, etc.

As an adjective "noble" describes persons or things possessing outstanding qualities. It may denote great beauty or magnificent proportions, as of the temple (Gk. *kalós*, lit. "good, beautiful"; Lk. 21:5), the city of Jerusalem (Heb. *hāḏār*, lit. "splendor, grandeur"; Isa. 5:14), or the fruit-bearing vine (*'adderet̲*, lit. "majesty, glory") and cedar (*'addîr*, lit. "majestic, glorious") that represent Israel (Ezk. 17:8, 23). "Noble" can also denote superior moral qualities, as when it describes words of truth and wisdom (Heb. *nᵉgîḏîm*, Prov. 8:6), magnanimous deeds (*nᵉḏîḇôt̲*, Isa. 32:8; cf. v. 5), honorable conduct (Gk. *kalós*, Rom. 12:17; cf. *timḗ*, 2 Tim. 2:20f.), or a worthy task (*kalós*, 1 Tim. 3:1). Osnappar (Ashurbanipal?) is described as "noble" (so RSV; Aram. *yaqqîr*), but the NEB "renowned" probably better conveys the sense (Ezr. 4:10)

As a noun "noble" denotes a person of exalted rank. The abundance of Hebrew terms designating nobility in the later OT writings presents a sharp contrast to the egalitarian, tribal structure of Israelite society in premonarchial times. The institution of the monarchy contributed to the rise of a wealthy class who modeled themselves after foreign aristocrats. Although they did not form a nobility in the sense of a closed aristocracy of landowners into which one is born, these officials and heads of wealthy families did represent a distinct ruling class (see *BHI*, 3rd ed., p. 223; de Vaux, pp. 69f.).

The role of the Heb. *ḥōrîm* (lit. "freemen") is suggested by the term's frequent association with other terms for leaders in the monarchial and postexilic Israelite community, e.g., *zᵉqēnîm* ("elders," 1 K. 21:8, 11) and *sᵉgānîm* ("officials," Neh. 2:16; 4:14, 19 [MT 8, 13]; 5:7; 7:5; cf. also 6:17; 13:17). It occurs in parallel with *śārîm* ("princes") in Isa. 34:11f. (a prophecy fulfilled in Jer. 39:6; cf. 27:20 par. 2 K. 24:14).

*Nāḏîḇ* (lit. "willing, generous") originally designated one who gave himself voluntarily in the service of God or who — because of his exalted economic and social position — had a responsibility to do so. A true *nāḏîḇ* is generous and uses his resources wisely for the good of his community (cf. Nu. 21:18; Prov. 7:26; Isa. 32:5, 8). Often, however, *nāḏîḇ* is simply another term for a member of the ruling class, used in parallel with *śārîm* ("princes," Prov. 8:16; also Nu. 21:18) and *nᵉsîḵîm* ("princes," Ps. 83:11 [MT 12]); cf. its association with *meleḵ* ("king"), *śārîm* ("princes"), and *šô(a)ʿ* ("the rich") in Job 34:18f.

Other Hebrew terms for persons of high rank include *nāgîḏ* (used in preexilic texts to designate a leader chosen by God, but used in parallel with *śārîm* in Job 29:9f.), *'addîr* (lit. "majestic one," Jgs. 5:13; 2 Ch. 23:20; Neh. 3:5; 10:29; Ps. 16:3 [apparently referring to saints, but cf. A. A. Anderson, *Book of Psalms* (*NCBC*, repr. 1981), I, 142]; Nah. 3:18), *gᵉḏōlîm* (lit. "great ones," Jonah 3:7), *niḵbᵉḏîm* (niphal part. of *kāḇēḏ*, lit. "weighty or honored ones," Ps. 149:8), and *partᵉmîm* (a Persian loanword occurring only in Est. 1:3; 6:9; Dnl. 1:3).

Although Gk. *eugenḗs* (lit. "wellborn") originally denoted nobility of birth (Lk. 19:12; 1 Cor. 1:26), it also came to denote those qualities expected of nobility, i.e., generosity and broad-mindedness (Acts 17:11). On the AV of Jn. 4:46, 49 ("nobleman"), *see* OFFICER, OFFICIAL; on Acts 24:3; 26:25 (AV "most noble"), *see* EXCELLENT.

*See also* PRINCE.

***Bibliography.***–*BHI*, 3rd ed., pp. 220-24; R. de Vaux, *Ancient Israel* (Eng. tr. 1961, repr. 1965), I, 68-70, 72-74; *TWOT*, I, 327; II, 555.

N. J. O.

**NOD** nod [Heb. *nôḏ*; LXX *Naid*; Syr. *nwd*]. The land "east of Eden" into which Cain went after murdering Abel and being condemned by God (Gen. 4:16).

The word *nôḏ*, the infinitive absolute of the root *nwd*, means "wandering," and is probably intended to be symbolic; since Cain had been condemned to be a "wanderer" (*nāḏ*, vv. 12, 14), he would live in the "Land of Wandering" (*'ereṣ nôḏ*).

The odd LXX form *Naid* may imply that the Hebrew text used by the LXX translators was, or was read as, *nyd* or *n'd*, and vocalized as an Aramaic-type participle *nā'ēḏ*, "wanderer" (cf. Tg. Onk. *in loc.*). E. M. COOK

**NODAB** nō'dab [Heb. *nôḏāḇ*; Gk. *Nadabaioi*]. A Hagrite clan which, along with Jetur and Naphish, was completely defeated by the Transjordanian Israelite tribes (1 Ch. 5:19). In Gen. 25:15; 1 Ch. 1:31 the name Kedemah appears with Jetur and Naphish in a list of the sons of Ishmael (son of Hagar), suggesting that Nodab and Kedemah may be two names for the same clan or that one name may be a corruption of the other. The name Nodab is possibly preserved in Nudebe, a village in the Hauran.

**NOE** nō'ə (AV Mt. 24:37f.; Lk. 3:36; 17:26f.). *See* NOAH **1.**

**NOEBA** nō'ə-bə (AV, NEB, 1 Esd. 5:31). *See* NEKODA **1.**

**NOGAH** nō'gə [Heb. *nōgah*–'shining']. A son of David born at Jerusalem (1 Ch. 3:7; 14:6). In the parallel list in 2 S. 5:14f. the name is lacking. According to H. Williamson (*1 and 2 Chronicles* [*NCBC*, 1982], p. 56), Nogah is "a dittograph of the following name" (Heb. *nepeg*).

**NOHAH** nō'hə [Heb. *nôḥâ*]; AV also "with ease" (Jgs. 20:43), mg. MENUHAH; RSV mg. "resting-place"; NEB also "without respite." The fourth son of Benjamin (1 Ch. 8:2; but cf. Gen. 46:21, where the name is omitted) and, perhaps, the name of the place occupied by the clan of Nohah (Jgs. 20:43). In the latter passage the RSV follows LXX B (*apó Noua*) and emends the MT (*mᵉnûḥâ*, lit. "resting-place"; cf. RSV mg.) to read *minnôḥâ*, while the AV and NEB follow the MT (but cf. AV mg., NEB mg.). The syntax supports the RSV and NEB mg. reading, "from Nohah."

**NOISE, NOISY** [Heb. *qôl* (Ex. 32:17; 1 S. 4:6; 1 K. 1:40, 45; etc.), *rāwaʿ* ("make a joyful noise," Ps. 66:1; 95:1f.; 98:4, 6; 100:1), *šāʾôn* (Isa. 24:8; 25:5; Jer. 46:17; 51:55), *hāmôn* (Isa. 31:4; 33:3; Am. 5:23), part. of *hāmâ* (Prov. 9:13), hiphil of *hûm* (Mic. 2:12); Gk. *ēchéō* (1 Cor. 13:1), *rhoizēdón* (2 Pet. 3:10), *phōnḗ* (Rev. 9:9)]; AV also CLAMOROUS, SOUND, VOICE, etc.; NEB also SHOUT, SOUND, ACCLAIM, etc.

The Hebrew and Greek words for "noise" refer to any audible sound, pleasant or unpleasant. The RSV generally translates "noise" in contexts demonstrating either very loud sounds or sounds made by large numbers of animals or people. The RSV has used "noise" fifty fewer times than the AV, the chief difference being the rendering of the frequently used *qôl* as "sound" or "voice" rather than "noise." The RSV NT translates "noise(s)" on six occasions where the AV has either "sound(s)" or "voices" (1 Cor. 13:1; Rev. 8:5; 9:9 [2 times]; 11:19; 16:18).

The RSV OT uses "noise" to describe the sounds of warfare and God's judgment against the earth (Isa. 25:2; 29:6; 33:3; Jer. 4:29; 47:3; 50:22; Ezek. 26:10). There is also the "noise" of nature (Isa. 29:6; Jer. 51:55), as well as the "noise" of people: in worshiping the golden calf (Ex. 32:17), in preparation for battle (1 S. 4:6), in the coronation of a new king (1 K. 1:40, 45), and in heartless religion (Am. 5:23). Elsewhere, the psalmist admonishes God's people to "make a joyful noise" unto the Lord as they shout and sing in celebration and worship of God's perfect character and great deeds (Ps. 66:1; 95:1f.; 98:4, 6; 100:1).

Paul equates the "loveless" exercise of the gift of glossolalia with the "noisy gong" (*ēchéō*) characteristic of the unedifying din of pagan worship (1 Cor. 13:1; cf. 14:5-12, 19). Peter announces this present age will pass away with a "loud noise" (*rhoizēdón*, 2 Pet. 3:10). Like *ēchéō*, *rhoizēdón* is a unique NT word and connotes unexpected suddenness, plus a loud, rushing, crashing noise. Finally, "loud noises" (*phōnḗ*) are associated with the tribulation judgments (Rev. 9:9; cf. 8:5; 16:18) and the opening of God's temple in heaven (Rev. 11:19).

***Bibliography.***–*DNTT*, III, 111-14; *TDOT*, III, *s.v.* "hāmāh" (Baumann); "hāmam" (Müller). A. E. HILL

**NOISOME.** A term used by the AV in the archaic sense of "noxious" or "harmful," as a translation of Heb. *hawwâ* ("destruction") in Ps. 91:3 (RSV "deadly"; NEB "raging"), *raʿ* ("evil") in Ezk. 14:15, 21 (RSV "wild," "evil"; NEB "wild"), and Gk. *kakós* ("bad, evil") in Rev. 16:2 (RSV, NEB, "foul"). "Noisome" means "offensive" in the AV of 2 Macc. 9:9 (Gk. *barýnō*, "be burdensome"; RSV "felt revulsion"; NEB "was disgusted") and "malodorous" in the AV mg. of Job 31:40 (*see* COCKLE).

**NOMADISM.** Many different ways of life may properly be designated nomadism. This study is concerned with the nomadic cultures of the ancient Near East and, specifically, with the phenomenon of pastoral nomadism.

I. Pastoral Nomadism: Definition and Sources
II. Nomenclature
III. Ancient Near Eastern Pastoral Nomadism: The Mari Texts
IV. Archeological Evidence
V. Nomadism in the Bible
  A. Patriarchs
  B. Conquest and Settlement

***I. Pastoral Nomadism: Definition and Sources.***–Pastoral nomadism is a socioeconomic mode of life that is dependent primarily on the domestication and herding of animals and involves seasonal movement to new pasturelands. For further definition see Gottwald, "Nomads," p. 226.

The primary data for the study of pastoral nomadism in the ancient Near East come from Mesopotamia. Among the most significant are texts of the Third Dynasty of Ur (*ca.* 2060-1950 B.C.), the dynasties of Isin and Larsa (*ca.* 1960 B.C. and later), the Old Babylonian period (*ca.* 1830-1760 B.C.), and those from Upper Mesopotamia and Syria, principally in the Mari age (19th cent. B.C. and later).

***II. Nomenclature.***–Several terms are often used to designate the various types of migratory pastoral activity, such as full or camel nomadism, seminomadism, and transhumance (see Matthews, pp. 17-21). Full nomadism did not exist before the widespread domestication of the camel toward the end of the 2nd millennium B.C. Some scholars have suggested that only with the 1st millennium B.C. was the camel fully domesticated and that it was not until the 8th and 7th cents. B.C. that it became a common beast of burden (W. Dostal, *L'anticà società bedouina* [1959], p. 22; Matthews, p. 67 n. 7). But this does not mean that the mention of camels in Genesis (chs. 24 and 31) is anachronistic (*see* CAMEL; K. Kitchen, *Ancient Orient and OT* [1966], pp. 79f.).

Seminomadism is another designation applied to tribal people who engage in nomadic pastoralism. The movements of the seminomads, with their sheep, goats, and asses, were restricted by the availability of water sources. The grazing pastures were the steppes on the inner edge of the Fertile Crescent and the semidesert plains of Syria (J.-R. Kupper, *Journal*, p. 114; M. B. Rowton, *Oriens Antiquus*, 15 [1976], 20f.; P. E. L. Smith and T. C. Young, Jr., "The Evolution of Early Agriculture and Culture in Greater Mesopotamia: a Trial Model," in B. Spooner, ed., *Population Growth: Anthropological Implications* [1972], p. 22). Unlike the full or camel nomads, seminomads could not trek deep into the Arabian desert. Their migration was seasonal, following the retreating and advancing vegetation. As the name implies, seminomadism involved an intermixing of sedentary and nomadic living and also the introduction of nonpastoral activities in the tribal economy, such as hunting, gathering, and seasonal agriculture as supplementary forms of food extraction. Although somewhat of an oversimplification, the term seminomadism is used in modern anthropological literature to distinguish between sheep- and goat-breeding pastoralists and the camel nomads of the late 2nd and 1st millennia B.C. The terms seminomadism and pastoral nomadism are often used interchangeably (see Gottwald, *Tribes*, pp. 437-448).

Frequency and range of movement and type of habitation (traditions of more permanent architecture vs. temporary shelters) are generally valid criteria of distinction between the pastoral and camel nomad. Cf. the discussion of Gottwald (*Tribes*, pp. 440f.) on the tent as an accurate index of pastoral nomadism. He argues that the tent is not an unambiguous trait of pastoral nomadism as commonly understood.

The term transhumance, often used interchangeably with seminomadism, generally refers to all pastoral nomadism that involves seasonal movement of livestock to regions of different climate. Gottwald defines a narrower sense in which the term is used — a "form of intensive herd or flock breeding by communities which are primarily agricultural, have developed their crop cultivation intensively, and may even be advanced industrial societies. Pastoral role functions are restricted to a relatively small number of herdsmen-specialists who accompany the flocks and herds to seasonal pasturage, usually without their families" (*Tribes*, p. 445). The most common form of transhumant pastoralism in the Levant was winter steppe grazing with some late spring/summer upland grazing. Although the data are lean, Gottwald interprets Gen. 37:12-17; 2 Sam. 13:23;

and Gen. 38:12f. in the light of transhumant pastoralism.

Specialists do not agree on the criteria for differentiating among these three terms. A fundamental criterion, however, appears to be the degree and nature of the relationship between the nomadic groups and sedentary civilization (discussed under "socioeconomic morphemes" by Gottwald, *Tribes*, pp. 464-473; "dimorphic society" by M. B. Rowton, *JNES*, 32 [1973], 202f.).

The term "ass nomadism" (W. F. Albright, *BASOR*, 163 [Oct. 1961], 36-54), another designation for second-millennium pastoral nomadism, should be rejected (Van Seters, pp. 13f.; M. Weippert, *Bibl.*, 52 [1971], 407-432).

***III. Ancient Near Eastern Pastoral Nomadism: The Mari Texts.***–The ancient city of MARI was situated on the borders of the settled zone and the steppe; thus the Mari texts represent one of the most important sources for the study of pastoral nomadism and sedentarization in the ancient Near East. They reflect the social and political relations between the nomadic tribes and the urban centers.

J.-R. Kupper emphasized the importance of the Mari texts for the early history and diffusion of the West Semitic peoples (Amorites and Canaanites) and their languages. Kupper has been criticized for basing his study on old uncritical constructs of nomadism, with their faulty conceptions about the relation between pastoral nomads and settled peoples, and on nineteenth-century anthropological theory, which assumes that Semitic peoples passed from nomadic to sedentary stages of culture.

Utilizing anthropological models and ethnographic data from modern nomadic populations of the Middle East, M. B. Rowton has brought significant refinement to our understanding of pastoral nomadism, especially in terms of the relationship established between the social morphemes of "the town" and "the tribe." Rowton defined the symbiotic relationship between the sedentary and nomadic elements of the Mari kingdom as a "dimorphic society," i.e., one in which there was a double process of interaction between nomad and sedentary and between tribe and state. The basic dichotomy was thus not between the nomadic and sedentary peoples, as commonly emphasized, but between the "autonomous tribal chiefdom," composed of both pastoralists and villagers, and the great urban centers (*JNES*, 32 [1973], 202f.). This dimorphic sociopolitical system was, in large measure, the product of several environmental factors. The climate and geography of the region were such that the grazing areas utilized by the pastoral groups were "enclosed" within the area under the political control of the state of Mari (hence Rowton's designation "enclosed nomadism"). The state received a flow of reports from the provincial administrators concerning the movements and activities of the nomads. The pastoral nomads of Mari were thus in close contact with the sedentary community. Rowton commented that "dimorphic structure has its roots, not only in the physical environment, but also in the two apparently contradictory motives, mutual hostility and mutual need" (*Journal*, p. 30). Rowton referred to Mari tribalists, like the Yaminites or Haneans, as "integrated tribes," i.e., town-tribe confederations of which one segment was sedentary all year and another moved seasonally with the flocks in search of pasture (see Matthews, pp. 59-66).

In the light of recent studies on ancient Near Eastern pastoral nomadism/sedentarization, especially those dealing with the Mari texts and other second-millennium sources, the following points should be emphasized: (1) nomadic groups of the 2nd millennium were not true nomads but seminomadic pastoralists of the marginal steppe zones who came increasingly into commercial, social, and political contact with village and urban contexts; (2) sedentarization was not a process of unilinear evolution from desert to urban contexts but involved the "urbanization" of tribalists, "re-tribalization," and "withdrawal"; and (3) these circumstances produced a large, fluid population that constituted a social and political challenge to the urban centers. It must be emphasized that our understanding of ancient Near Eastern pastoral nomadism is far from complete. Our written sources are restricted, chronologically and geographically, and distorted in the sense that the perspective is invariably that of the urbanists. A complete picture will undoubtedly never come to light, though the TELL MARDIKH archives (ancient Ebla) offer the prospect of a better understanding (see G. Pettinato, *Archives of Ebla* [Eng. tr. 1981]).

Finally, a comment on the vexing problem of the AMORITES. The legitimacy of utilizing the images of Mari pastoral nomadism as a context for the study of nomadism in the Bible does not depend on a link between Amorite movements and the migration of Abraham nor even on the veracity of the "Amorite hypothesis." Although the picture of westward expansions by peoples speaking a West Semitic dialect offers an attractive historical context for the migration of Abraham from Ur to Palestine, such a connection is not demonstrable (J. J. Bimson, "Archaeological Data and the Dating of the Patriarchs," in A. R. Millard and D. J. Wiseman, eds., *Essays on the Patriarchal Narratives* [1980], pp. 59-62; W. G. Dever, "Palestine in the Second Millennium BCE: The Archaeological Picture," in J. H. Hayes and J. M. Miller, eds., *Israelite and Judaean History* [*OTL*, 1977], pp. 93-102). In fact, the very westward movements of the Amorites are disputed (Thompson, pp. 67-88). But as N. M. Sarna observed, "If Abraham's migration can no longer be explained as part of a larger Amorite migratory stream from east to west, it should be noted that what has fallen by the wayside is a scholarly hypothesis, not the Biblical text. Genesis itself presents the movement from Haran to Canaan as an individual, unique act undertaken in response to a divine call, an event . . . that inaugurates a new and decisive stage in God's plan of history. The factuality or otherwise of this Biblical evaluation lies beyond the scope of scholarly research" (*Biblical Archaeology Review*, 4/1 [1978], 52).

***IV. Archeological Evidence.***–It is important to note that the above portrait of the dimorphic society has been constructed by Rowton from written sources that are fragmentary at best. This picture has not been confirmed by archeology. Although archeology has produced a reasonably adequate picture of the urban aspect of the dimorphic society from lower Mesopotamia to Syria-Palestine, the village-pastoral aspect has not been documented for several reasons: (1) the marginal zones have not been investigated archeologically except for isolated surveys; (2) nomadic populations leave few traces for the archeologist's trowel; and (3) the translation of unwritten data into people and politics is methodologically an uncertain task (P. J. Parr, "Pottery, People and Politics," in R. Moorey and P. J. Parr, eds., *Archaeology in the Levant: Essays for Kathleen Kenyon* [1978], pp. 203-209). For what appear to be archeological reflections of the village-pastoral situation, see W. G. Dever, *op. cit.*, pp. 111f.; R. Cohen, *BASOR*, 236 (Fall 1979), 61-79. These data are meager and require caution in their interpretation.

***V. Nomadism in the Bible.***–The images of pastoral nomadism, as painted by second-millennium sources such as the Mari texts, provide the backdrop for the study of nomadism in the Bible. As noted above, this is particularly true for the period of the patriarchs, less so for the time of ancient Israel's wilderness, conquest, and settlement traditions. Although we shall concentrate on these periods, glimpses of the nomadic way of life (pastoral and full nomadism) are preserved in numerous biblical contexts (Gen. 4:20; 10; Ex. 2:15-22; 3:1; Dt. 26:5; Jgs. 5:24; 6:1-6; 1 S. 25:2ff.; Ps. 78:55; Jer. 25:24; 35:5ff.; 49:29). A period of nomadism figures in the history of several biblical peoples, such as the Edomites, Moabites, Ammonites, Midianites, Ishmaelites, Kenites, Arabs, and Arameans.

*A. Patriarchs.* The patriarchs of Genesis are clearly not depicted as full or camel nomads. Furthermore, though ethnological studies on the nomadic populations of the contemporary Middle East can be helpful, it would be methodologically inappropriate to impose the model of today's bedouin on the nomads of patriarchal times. The gap is too great between the patriarchs and the nomadic Arabs of today, whose lives have been radically changed by industrialization and twentieth-century economic and political structures. The most appropriate context for the study of patriarchal nomadism is provided by the Mari texts, although this model must also be used with caution. The nomadism of Genesis is not a mirror image of Mari pastoral nomadism; differences abound and the similarities must not be exaggerated. The political, economic, and social circumstances that prevailed during the period of the Mari kingdom were markedly different from those of Canaan during the time of Abraham, Isaac, and Jacob.

Any attempt to study the nomadism of the patriarchs in the context of the M.B. I-II period (Bimson, *op. cit.*, pp. 54-65; for a survey of the archeological nomenclature, see S. Richard, *BASOR*, 237 [Winter 1980], 5-34) must begin with recognition of the fragmentary nature of our sources, both written and unwritten. It must again be emphasized that our understanding of Mari pastoral nomadism is sketchy and written from the perspective of the urbanists. Furthermore, archeologists have only begun to piece together a cultural history of Syria-Palestine for this period. And perhaps most importantly, Genesis preserves little more than glimpses of the everyday lives of Abraham and his descendants. It is nevertheless clear that the patriarchs are depicted as nomadic herdsmen with recollections of the images of Mari pastoral nomadism.

Both societies are tribally organized. "Kinship is the principal glue in the social organization of nomadic peoples" (Matthews, p. 25). At Mari we read about the (Ben) Yaminites, Suteans, Haneans, and others. The tribal organization of the Genesis patriarchs is similarly clear.

The patriarchs camp in the vicinity of towns (Gen. 12:4-9; 13:1-18; 33:18-19; 37:12-17). They occasionally engage in agriculture (26:12-14). They raise sheep and goats (30:25-43) and dig wells (21:25-31; 26:15-22). There is close interaction, socially and economically, between the patriarchs and townspeople (21:25-34; 23:1-20; 26:17-33; 33:18-20). They move from one place of encampment and pasturage to another (12:8-9; 13:3). Under certain circumstances they dwell in towns as "resident aliens" (Heb. *gēr* and cognates; see 12:10; 15:13; 17:8; 19:9; 20:1; 21:23, 34; 23:4; 26:3; 28:4; 32:4; 35:27; 36:7; 37:1; 47:4, 9). Abraham was remembered as one who "by faith . . . sojourned in the land of promise, as in a foreign land, living in tents with Isaac and Jacob, heirs with him of the same promise" (He. 11:9).

Numerous texts in Genesis refer to the patriarchs living in tents (12:8; 13:3, 18; 18:1-10; 24:67; 31:25, 33f.). J. Van Seters (p. 14) considered these references an indication of the late origin of these narratives. For a rebuttal see D. J. Wiseman, "Abraham Reassessed," in Millard and Wiseman, eds., *Essays on the Patriarchal Narratives* (1980), p. 145.

Certain studies have proposed a first-millennium context for the patriarchal stories of Genesis and have minimized the applicability of second-millennium extrabiblical sources for the study of these narratives (Van Seters and Thompson; cf. the challenge of J. T. Luke, *JSOT*, 4 [1977], 35-47). Van Seters, for instance, addressed the widely espoused position that the patriarchal stories portray a nomadic way of life that can be documented from the textual remains of the second-millennium B.C. and concluded that "very little in the patriarchal stories . . . reflects the nomadic life of the second millennium" (pp. 16f.; see also p. 67 for a clear statement of his methodological premise for the comparative analysis of biblical and nonbiblical materials).

The adoption of Rowton's dimorphic model, which was constructed largely from the Mari texts, eliminates a number of Van Seters's objections to the application of second-millennium nomadic images to the patriarchal stories, such as (1) the use of Heb. *gēr,* "a term not entirely appropriate as a general designation for nomad" (Van Seters, p. 16); (2) the sedentary life of Abraham in Ur and Haran; (3) the theme of patrimony, which is "utterly foreign to the nomadic way of life but a fundamental principle of the settled economy"(p. 16); and (4) Isaac's practice of agriculture. Van Seters's objections to the mention of tents and camels have been addressed above. His dating of the patriarchal traditions to the Iron Age is based on the a priori assumption that they are late literary inventions.

*B. Conquest and Settlement.* The images of pastoral nomadism in ancient Israel's wilderness, conquest, and settlement traditions are not as apparent as those in the patriarchal traditions. The wilderness wanderings were not the product of regular seasonal movement in search of new pastureland but rather the sovereign hand of God miraculously directing the destiny of a people in fulfillment of promises made to their ancestors. Although we have little socioeconomic data on the Israelites of the Exodus, we may safely assume that survival in the wilderness would have involved ways of life reminiscent of nomadic peoples. This does not permit, however, the designation of this group as pastoral nomads. The narratives create the clear impression that this was a community unfamiliar with life in the wilderness and their survival was in large measure dependent on the Lord's provision (Ex. 13:17-22; 15:22-25; 16:1-21; 17:1-7). The events from Exodus to Conquest/Settlement cannot be explained from the perspective of natural cultural processes.

While rejecting N. K. Gottwald's view of the history of early Israel as an "indigenous revolutionary social movement," one may glean much from his provocative studies on "early Israelite pastoral nomadism" (*Tribes*, pp. 435-463; *Biblical Archaeology Review*, 4/2 [1978], 2-7). Utilizing the sociological models of G. Mendenhall, J. T. Luke, and M. B. Rowton, Gottwald concluded that most of the movements of the patriarchal families were migrations rather than seasonal treks. He acknowledged that "the socioeconomic data permit the interpretation that some or all of the patriarchal groups were transhumant pastoralists" (p. 452). Gottwald's view of Israel's early history as an indigenous social movement is constructed, in part, on the following conclusions relative to Israelite transhumant pastoralism: (1) it was a subsidiary subspecialization within the dominant socioeconomic mode of production, namely, intensive agriculture; (2) transhumant pastoralism of the patriarchal and Mosaic traditions was a sub-specialization indigenous to Syria-Palestine and not a culturally foreign intrusion from the outside; and (3) the transhumant pastoral element in early Israel "did not project a unified military attack against settled Syro-Palestinian peoples, nor a more covert infiltration, with the intent of annihilating or displacing the natives so as to take over their agricultural means of production, thereby advancing from a lower cultural level of pastoral nomadism to a higher cultural level of intensive agriculture" (pp. 460f.; cf. G. Mendenhall, *BA*, 25 [1962], 66-87 [repr. in *BA Reader*, III (1970), 100-120]).

Gottwald's fundamental diminishing of the cultural and historical significance of pastoral nomadism in the patriarchal period is unfortunate. Although refinements are necessary and assured conclusions are precluded for want of data, his basic rejection of the Exodus Israelites as pastoral nomads in the tradition of the Mari tribalists appears correct. His "parameters for the use of the earliest Israelite traditions in reconstructing the history and sociology of pre-monarchic Israel" must be rejected, however, together with the view of Israel's early history as an indigenous social movement.

***Bibliography.***–D. H. K. Amiran and Y. Ben-Arieh, *IEJ*, 13 (1963), 161-181; F. Barth, "A General Perspective on Nomad-Sedentary Relations in the Middle East," in C. Nelson, ed., *The Desert and the Sown* (1973), pp.11-21; J. Bottéro, *et al.*, *The Near East: The Early Civilizations* (1967), pp. 180-86; W. G. Dever, *HTR*, 64 (1971), 197-226; *BASOR*, 210 (Apr. 1973), 37-63; "The Beginning of the Middle Bronze Age in Syria-Palestine," in F. M. Cross, *et al.*, eds., *Magnalia Dei: The Mighty Acts of God* (*Festschrift* G. E. Wright; 1976), pp. 3-38; N. Gottwald, "Were the Early Israelites Pastoral Nomads?" in J. Jackson and M. Kessler, eds., *Rhetorical Criticism* (*Festschrift* J. Muilenburg; 1974), pp. 223-255; *Tribes of Yahweh* (1979); J.-R. Kupper, *Les Nomades en Mésopotamie au temps des rois de Mari* (1957); *Journal of the Economic and Social History of the Orient*, 2 (1959), 113-127; J. T. Luke, "Pastoralism and Politics in the Mari Period" (diss., University of Michigan, 1965); A. Malamat, *JAOS*, 82 (1962), 143-150; *BA*, 34 (1971), 2-22; V. H. Matthews, *Pastoral Nomadism in the Mari Kingdom* (1978); M. B. Rowton, *Studia Instituti Anthropos*, 28 (1976), 219-257; *JNES*, 36 (1977), 181-198; *Journal of the Economic and Social History of the Orient*, 17 (1974), 1-30; T. L. Thompson, *Historicity of the Patriarchal Narratives* (*BZAW*, 133, 1974); J. Van Seters, *Abraham in History and Tradition* (1975); M. Weippert, *Settlement of the Israelite Tribes in Palestine* (Eng. tr. *SBT*, 2/21, 1971).

G. PRATICO

**NON** non (1 Ch. 7:27, AV). *See* NUN (Person).

**NOOMA** nō'ə-mə (1 Esd. 9:35, NEB). *See* NEBO **2.**

**NOON; NOONDAY** [Heb. *ṣoh$^{o}$rayim*; Gk. *mesēmbría* (Acts 22:6)]; **NOONTIDE** [Heb. *d$^{e}$mî*] (Isa. 28:10); **MIDDAY** [Heb. *ṣoh$^{o}$rayim* (1 K. 18:29), *maḥ$^{a}$ṣîṯ hayyôm* (Neh. 8:3); Gk. *hēméras mésēs* (Acts 26:13)]; **SIXTH HOUR** [Gk. *héktos* (Mt. 20:5), *héktēs hṓras* (27:45), *hṓra héktē* (Mk. 15:33; Lk. 23:44; Jn. 4:6; 19:14; Acts 10:9)]; AV also "cutting off" (Isa. 38:10); NEB also BROAD DAYLIGHT (Dt. 28:29), "prime of life" (Isa. 38:10), "all afternoon" (1 K. 18:29), MIDDAY (Mt. 20:5; 27:45; Mk. 15:33; Lk. 23:44), NOON (Jn. 4:6; 19:14; Acts 10:9). These terms designate (1) the time that is midway between sunrise (about 6:00 a.m.; hence the sixth hour = noon) and sunset (about 6:00 p.m.) (Neh. 8:3; Acts 26:13), and thus (2) the time of day that is usually brightest, as *ṣoh$^{o}$rayim*, "brightness," indicates in 1 K. 18:29; Jer. 20:16; etc. Accordingly, usage may emphasize either: (1) temporal designation, i.e., "midday," "noon," "noontide," "sixth hour," as estimated from a sundial (e.g., Gen. 43:16, 25; 1 K. 18:26f.; *see also* HOUR); or (2) brightness in contrast to darkness (e.g., Dt. 28:29; Isa. 58:10; Am. 8:9).

A third meaning arises by extension of this emphasis on brightness, namely, that noon is a time when theophany is to be expected (Peter's vision, Acts 10:9; Paul's vision, Acts 22:6 and 26:13; the judgment made against Jesus, Jn. 19:14; cf. Ps. 37:6; Isa. 58:10). But noon may also be, contrary to all expectations, the time of worst confusion, darkness, and judgment (e.g., Job 5:14; Ps. 91:6; Isa. 59:10; Jer. 15:8; 20:16; Zeph. 2:4; Mt. 27:45 par.).

Of significance, particularly stressed in Jn. 19:14 (cf. Mt. 27:45; Lk. 23:44; contra Mk. 15:25, "the third hour"), is the time "about the sixth hour" on the eve of Passover when the trial of Jesus ended by His being handed over for crucifixion. The sun began to decline then from its apex toward evening, and priests could thus begin to slaughter paschal lambs for Passover, the feast that celebrates God's delivering His people in the Exodus (cf. R. E. Brown, *Gospel According to John XIII–XXI* [*AB*, 1970], pp. 882f., 895f.). This "sixth hour" on that day before Passover was revelatory in character, full of theological import about the irony of this people's rejection of their own divinely appointed deliverance (Jn. 17:1; cf. 2:4; 7:30; 8:20; 12:23, 27; 13:1; 16:21).

*See also* DAY; HOUR; TIME.

***Bibliography.***–C. K. Barrett, *Gospel According to St. John* (1955), pp. 39-41, 454; *TDNT*, II, *s.v.* ἡμέρα (von Rad, Delling); IX, *s.v.* ὥρα (Delling).

J. G. GIBBS

**NOPH** nof (AV, NEB, Isa. 19:13; Jer. 2:16; 44:1; 46:14, 19; Ezk. 30:13; AV 30:16). *See* MEMPHIS.

**NOPHAH** nō'fə [Heb. *nōpaḥ*] (Nu. 21:30, AV). A town in Moab, if the Hebrew text is to be followed. The LXX reads *kaí hai gynaíkes éti prosexékausan pýr epí Moab*, "and the women yet [again] poured fire upon Moab." The RSV and NEB, on the basis of the LXX and *npḥ' šr* in the Samaritan Pentateuch, emend to *npḥ 'š*, "fire was blown [= spread]." Grollenberg with reserve located the site N of Dibon (*GAB*, p. 158).

W. S. L. S.

**NORTH** [Heb. *ṣāpôn*]; NEB also ZAPHON (Ps. 89:12 [MT 13]; 48:2 [MT 3], NEB mg.); [*ś$^{e}$mō'l*–'left hand'] (e.g., Gen. 14:15; Josh. 19:27); AV LEFT HAND; [Gk. *borrás*] (Lk. 13:29; Rev. 21:13); **NORTH COUNTRY** [Heb. *'ereṣ ṣāpôn*] (e.g., Jer. 6:22; 10:22; Zec. 2:6 [MT 10]; 6:8). The RSV rendering "from the north" in Ezk. 23:24 is based on the LXX; the MT has an unknown word, Heb. *hōṣen* (<*haṣṣāpôn*?), which is translated "chariots" by the AV and is emended by the NEB to read "war-horses" (see comms.). In Job 37:9 the AV renders *m$^{e}$zārîm* (piel part. of *zārâ*, "scatter, fan") by "out of the north"; the RSV reads "scattering winds" and the NEB "rain winds."

Because the Israelites oriented themselves to the rising sun, the north was on the left; therefore it could be indicated by Heb. *ś$^{e}$mō'l* (*see* LEFT [HAND]; ORIENTATION). As a directional term "north" can be used to locate a specific object or identify a particular place; e.g., it may define a boundary line (Josh. 18:5) or specify a particular city gate (Ezk. 40:20, 23). "North" often is used with "south" as a merismus signifying the entire area between these two extremities (e.g., Ps. 107:3; Lk. 13:29). Sometimes it parallels "east" in references to Mesopotamia, which lay to the north and east of Israel (cf. Isa. 41:25).

Because Israel was protected by the desert on the east and the Mediterranean Sea on the west, and since the main highways ran N-S, Israel's enemies had to approach from either the north or the south. Because Egypt was weak during most of Israel's occupation of Palestine, Israel's enemies (Arameans, Assyrians, and Babylonians) generally came from the north. This fact, combined with the phenomenon that stormy weather from the west descends on Palestine from the north (cf. Prov. 25:23), gave "north" an ominous overtone for the Israelites: it represented a mysterious, unknown region, the location of hostile forces.

Jeremiah often prophesied that disaster from the north would befall Judah (Jer. 1:14f.; 4:6; 6:1). Although Assyria was still the dominant nation at the beginning of Jeremiah's prophecy (cf. Zeph. 2:13), by the height of his ministry the Babylonians had decimated the Assyrian empire. After

Nebuchadrezzar took Carchemish (605 B.C.) Jeremiah referred to Israel's enemy specifically as Babylon (e.g., 25:9-12; cf. references to Babylon as "the north" in Ezk. 26:7; Zec. 2:6f.). Jeremiah also prophesied that an enemy from the north would destroy Egypt (Jer. 46:20, 24), Philistia (47:2), and Babylon (Jer. 50:3, 9, 41 — a prophecy partially fulfilled by Persia's defeat of Babylon). Moreover, Jeremiah prophesied that Yahweh would one day bring Israel back to its homeland from the lands of the north (Jer. 3:18; 16:15; 23:8; 31:8; cf. Zec. 6:6, 8). These references indicate that for Jeremiah, "the north" symbolizes an evil, hostile force far more than a specific geographical location.

Building on Jeremiah's prophecies, Ezekiel depicts Israel's eschatological enemy as hordes from "the uttermost parts of the north" (Ezk. 38:6, 15; 39:2). Another apocalyptic oracle refers more specifically to the Seleucid king (ruler of one of the four nations resulting from the division of the Greek empire) as "the king of the north" (Dnl. 11:6-8).

In Ugaritic mythology Mt. Zaphon (Heb. *ṣāpôn*) is the sacred mountain of Baal, located in the far north. It is usually identified with Mt. Casius (Jebel el-'Aqraʿ), some 40 km. (25 mi.) N of the ancient city Ugarit (Râs Shamrah;) but the significance of Mt. Zaphon is more mythopoeic than geographical. A. S. Kapelrud postulated that the tower in Baal's temple was called Zaphon ("north"), for in mythical thought two locations endowed with the same sacred quality are identical regardless of their geographical distance. This mythopoeic meaning of *ṣāpôn* occurs several times in the OT. Ps. 48:2 (MT 3), which describes the temple mount as "Mount Zion, in the far north, the city of the great King" (RSV), would perhaps be better translated "like the utmost heights of Zaphon is Mount Zion" (NIV; cf. NEB mg.). A. Robinson takes Zaphon ("the north") to mean the heavenly place of Yahweh's rule, with Zion as its earthly counterpart. Thus Yahweh, the God who reigns over the entire world from Zaphon, His heavenly throne, is at the same time reigning from its earthly counterpart, His temple on Mt. Zion. In a taunt song picturing the downfall of the king of Babylon, Isaiah alludes to Zaphon as the mount of assembly of the gods: "I shall sit on the mount of assembly in the far north" (Isa. 14:13, RSV).

Some scholars have seen allusions to Mt. Zaphon in two accounts of theophanies accompanied by spectacular cloud displays coming out of "the north," in Job 37:22 (see M. Pope, *Job* [*AB*, 3rd ed. 1973], pp. 279, 286f.) and Ezk. 1:4 (see *IB*, VI, 70). In Job 26:7 "north" stands parallel to "earth," indicating that there it refers to the high heavens (cf. NEB "the canopy of the sky"); the verb *nāṭâ* ("stretch out," used of pitching a tent) supports this interpretation (see Roberts; for another view, cf. Pope, p. 183). Some scholars (e.g., M. Dahood, *Psalms*, II [*AB*, 2nd ed. 1973], 308, 314; cf. also NEB) have interpreted *ṣāpôn* in Ps. 89:12 (MT 13) to mean the cosmic mountain, particularly since Mt. Tabor and Mt. Hermon stand in the next stich; but the lack of any solid evidence that "south" has mythopoeic significance casts doubt on this view. The verse is saying that Yahweh created every part of the world, and no part of the universe is outside His rule.

*See also* ZAPHON, MOUNT.

***Bibliography.***–A. S. Kapelrud, *Baal in the Ras Shamra Texts* (Eng. tr. 1952); J. J. M. Roberts, *Bibl.*, 56 (1975), 554-57; A. Robinson, *VT*, 24 (1974), 118-123; J. de Savignac, *VT*, 3 (1953), 95f.; *THAT*, II *s.v.* צָפוֹן (W. H. Schmidt). J. E. HARTLEY

**NORTHEAST; SOUTHEAST.** The RSV translation of the Greek terms used in Acts 27:12 to describe the Cretan harbor called PHOENIX toward which Paul and his shipmates were bound for safe winter anchorage when they were driven west before a severe storm and shipwrecked on the shores of Malta. The harbor is described in Greek as: *bléponta katá líba kaí katá chṓron,* which is most naturally rendered "facing the southwest (wind) [*líps*] and the northwest (wind) [*chṓron*]." (Cf. the LXX use of *blépō* + *katá* + direction in Ezk. 11:1 and frequently throughout ch. 40.) The translation "southeast and northeast" most probably depends on the common identification of Phoenix with modern Loutro, a harbor on the south shore of Crete that corresponds most precisely to ancient references to Phoenix, except that it faces NE and SE. Suggested solutions to the problem include: (1) the assumption that Luke was mistaken about the actual orientation of the harbor; (2) attempts to identify ancient Phoenix with some harbor other than Loutro (e.g., Phenika, a small harbor on the west shore of the same peninsula that shelters Loutro); or (3) translation of the Greek idiom to represent the orientation of a ship entering the harbor rather than the harbor itself. This last seems quite unsupported by the evidence. G. H. WILSON

**NORTHEASTER** [Gk. *eurakýlōn* (*p*[74] א A B etc.), *euroklýdōn* (TR)]; AV EUROCLYDON. A sailor's term for the wind that blew Paul's ship off course on his voyage to Rome (Acts 27:14). It probably was a wind blowing off Mt. Ida across the open Bay of Messaria on the southern coast of Crete. Ramsay comments that it was typical of that area for a gentle southerly wind to "shift to a violent northerly wind" (*SPT*, p. 327).

The reading *eurakýlōn* is supported by the oldest MSS and is generally accepted as correct. It is a compound of Gk. *eúros* ("east wind") and Lat. *aquilo* ("northeast wind"; cf. *Oxford Latin Dictionary*, p. 158) and therefore designates the east-northeast wind (see MM, p. 264). The variant reading *euroklýdōn*, a compound of Gk. *eúros* ("[south]east wind") and *klýdōn* ("rough water, waves"), would designate a "southeast wind, that stirs up waves" (Bauer, rev., p. 325). Even apart from textual considerations this variant is not to be preferred, since the wind probably came from a northerly direction. Another variant, *euryklýdōn* (< Gk. *eurýs*, "broad," and *klýdōn*), means "the wind that stirs up broad waves" (Bauer, rev., p. 325).

*See also* PHOENIX; NORTHEAST; Vol. I, Map XXI.

***Bibliography.***–*HDB*, I, *s.v.* "Euraquilo" (W. P. Dickson); J. Smith, *Voyage and Shipwreck of St. Paul* (4th ed. 1880), pp. 119-125, 287-292; *SPT*. W. D. MOUNCE

**NORTHERNER** [Heb. *ṣᵉpônî*] (Joel 2:20); AV NORTHERN ARMY; NEB NORTHERN PERIL. One interpretation is that the "northerner" is an "army" of locusts that came from the north (cf. v. 25), as they did in A.D. 1915 (see Allen, pp. 88f.; Driver, pp. 60, 84-93). If so, most likely God used a wind to drive them away (cf. Ex. 10:19). *See also* LOCUST. But Childs and Wolff argued persuasively that "northerner" refers to an apocalyptic army that is described in terms of locusts; the "northerner" is the "enemy from the north" frequently mentioned in Jeremiah (1:13-15; 4:5-8; etc.) and Ezekiel (38:6, 15; 39:2).

***Bibliography.***–B. S. Childs, *JBL*, 78 (1959), 187-198; comms. on Joel by L. Allen (*NICOT*, 1976); S. R. Driver (*CBSC*, 1915); H. W. Wolff (Eng. tr., *Hermeneia*, 1977). G. A. L.

**NOSE, NOSTRILS** [Heb. *'ap*, also *nᵉḥîrayim* (Job 41:20 [MT 12])]; AV also FACE (Gen. 24:47); NEB also ANGER (Ex. 15:8), LIFE (Lam. 4:20); on Ezk. 8:17, NEB, see below.

Hebrew *'ap* is frequently translated "face," "anger," or "wrath" as well as "nose" or "nostril," perhaps because the nose is the most prominent feature of the FACE and readily reflects emotions such as Anger and Wrath. The cognate verb *'ānap* ("be angry") appears to have been connected originally with angry snorting (see *TDOT*, I, 351, 354). *N$^e$ḥîrayim* (dual form of *nāḥîr*) is related to the verb *nāḥar* ("blow"); cf. the cognate nouns *naḥar* (Job 39:20) and *naḥ$^a$râ* (Jer. 8:16), which denote the "snorting" of warhorses ready for battle. Yahweh's anger is depicted in poetic and figurative language as a blast of smoke or fire from His nostrils (Ex. 15:8; 2 S. 22:9, 16 par. Ps. 18:8, 15 [MT 9, 16]; Job 41:20 [MT 12]; cf. 4:9). Isa. 65:5 uses the image of "smoke in the nostrils" to describe God's anger at Israel's persistent disobedience (cf. Dt. 32:22; Jer. 17:4).

Like other ancient Near Eastern peoples, the Hebrews thought of the nose, rather than the lungs, as the organ of breathing (cf. Gen. 7:22; Lam. 4:20; Wisd. 15:15; 4 Macc. 15:19). Human beings have life only when the breath of God is in their nostrils (Gen. 2:7; Job 27:3). This dependence on breath, an aspect of human creatureliness and mortality, makes mankind of small account in comparison to the almighty, eternal God (Isa. 2:22; cf. Wisd. 2:2, which is part of the reasoning of ungodly persons [cf. 1:16–2:24]).

The nose is also referred to as the organ of smell — a sense not possessed by idols (Ps. 115:6). In Nu. 11:20 the clause "until it comes out at your nostrils" may indicate that the smell of the meat would become loathsome to the Israelites. Am. 4:10 refers to the stench of decomposing corpses. One form of torture that Antiochus used on Eleazar involved pouring a "broth of evil odour into his nostrils" (4 Macc. 6:25).

A Hook was sometimes put in the nose or jaw of a wild animal caught in a trap, so that it could be led away (cf. Job 40:24; 41:1 [MT 40:25]). Some ancient peoples (notably the Assyrians) had the cruel custom of humiliating their enemies in this way (cf. Ezk. 19:4, 9), and Isaiah used this figure to describe how Yahweh would lead Sennacherib back to Assyria (2 K. 19:28 par. Isa. 37:29; cf. Ezk. 38:4).

As a prominent facial feature, the nose is important to human beauty (cf. Cant. 7:4 [MT 5]). Nose Rings were worn as jewelry by Hebrew women (e.g., Gen. 24:47; Isa. 3:21; cf. the figurative use in Ezk. 16:12). The faces of prisoners of war were sometimes mutilated by cutting off their nose and ears (Ezk. 23:25).

The last clause of Ezk. 8:17 is very obscure. The AV and RSV translate the MT literally ("they put the branch to their noses"), while the NEB offers an unlikely interpretation ("they seek to appease me"). The text contains one of the "scribal corrections" (*tiqqûn sôp$^e$rîm*) made by the Masoretes in order to remove material considered disrespectful to God: the original *'appî* or *'appay* ("my nose") was changed to *'appām* ("their nose") (see BH). For the various interpretations that this text has received, see the comms. on Ezekiel, esp. KD and W. Eichrodt (Eng. tr., *OTL*, 1970); *see also* Gesture V.D.

See *TDOT*, I, *s.v.* "'ānaph" (J. Bergman, E. Johnson).

N. J. O.

**NOSE RINGS** [Heb. *nizmê hā'ap*–'rings of the nose'] (Isa. 3:21); AV NOSE-JEWELS. Heb. *nezem*, a general term for "ring," specifically designates a nose ring in Gen. 24:47 (cf. vv. 22, 30); Ezk. 16:12; and Prov. 11:22 (where a "beautiful woman without discretion" is compared to a *nezem zāhāḇ b$^e$'ap ḥ$^a$zîr* [RSV "gold ring in a swine's snout"]), as well as in Isa. 3:21. *See* Garments IX (esp. chart and picture); Ring.

**NOTABLE** [Heb. pass. part. of *nāqaḇ*–'distinguish, designate'] (Am. 6:1); AV NAMED; NEB OF MARK; [Gk.

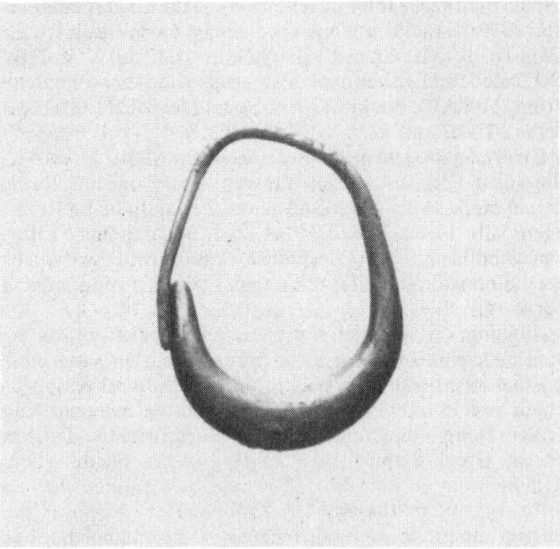

Gold nose- (or ear-) ring from Megiddo (Late Bronze Age). Actual size 18 mm. (0.7 in.) (Israel Department of Antiquities and Museums)

*gnōstós*] (Acts 4:16); **OF NOTE** [Gk. *epísēmos*] (Rom. 16:7); NEB EMINENT. Attracting notice, or worthy of attention.

The irony in Amos' reference to the ruling class of Israel as "the notable men of the first of the nations" (6:1) is made clear in v. 7: "Therefore they shall now be the first of those to go into exile. . . ." Paul described Andronicus and Junias (RSV; but perhaps "Junia"; cf. AV; BDF, § 125 [2]) as "*epísēmos* [prominent, outstanding] among the apostles" (Rom. 16:7); cf. Mt. 27:16, where *epísēmos* occurs in a negative sense to describe Barabbas (AV "notable"; RSV "notorious"). In 2 Macc. 3:26, AV, "notable" renders *ekprepḗs* ("outstanding"; cf. RSV "remarkably"; NEB "surpassing"), and in 6:28, AV, it renders *gennaíos* (cf. RSV "noble"; NEB "fine").

Sometimes "notable" is used in the sense of "conspicuous." The Sanhedrin found it impossible to refute the miracle performed by Peter and John because it was *gnōstós* ("known, clearly recognizable") and *phanerós* ("manifest") to all the inhabitants of Jerusalem (Acts 4:16). The AV uses "notable" to describe the horn(s) of the goat in Daniel's dream (Dnl. 8:5, 8; Heb. *ḥāzûṯ*; cf. RSV "conspicuous"; NEB "prominent") and the "day of the Lord" (Acts 2:20, Gk. *epiphanḗs*; cf. RSV "manifest"; NEB "resplendent"). Similarly, in 2 Macc. 26:33, AV, "notable" renders *epiphanḗs* (cf. RSV "splendid"; NEB "for all the world to see").

N. J. O.

**NOTE.** In Wisd. 19:18 (NEB "pitch") and 1 Cor. 14:7 (AV "sound"), Gk. *phthóngos* represents the "sound" or "tone" made by a musical instrument; cf. Rom. 10:18, where it denotes the sound of the human "voice" (AV "sound").

On Rom. 16:7 *see* Notable.

**NOTE; TAKE NOTE OF** [Heb. *yāḏa'*–'know' (1 S. 23:23; Jer. 5:1), hiphil of *nāḇaṭ*–'look at' (Ps. 10:14)]; AV TAKE KNOWLEDGE, BEHOLD, etc.; NEB FIND OUT, SEE, etc.; [Gk. *eídon* (Rom. 11:22), *skopéō* (16:17), *sēmeióō* (2 Thess. 3:14)]; AV also BEHOLD, MARK; NEB OBSERVE, "keep your eye on," MARK; **NOTICE; TAKE NOTICE OF** [Heb. hiphil of *nāḵar*] (Ruth 2:10, 19; 2 S.

3:36; Ps. 142:4 [MT 5]); AV also TAKE KNOWLEDGE, KNOW; NEB also "find (no) friend by my side"; [Gk. *katanoéō*] (Mt. 7:3 par. Lk. 6:41; Acts 27:39); AV CONSIDER, PERCEIVE, etc.; NEB also "with (never) a thought for"; **ESCAPE NOTICE** [Gk. *lanthánō*] (Acts 26:26); AV BE HIDDEN; NEB BE UNAWARE; **GIVE NOTICE** [Gk. *diangéllō* (Acts 21:26), *emphanízō* (23:15)]; AV SIGNIFY; NEB also APPLY TO.

"Note," "take note of," "notice," and "take notice of" generally mean to pay attention to something. Paul instructed his readers to be alert for those who opposed his teaching and to avoid such persons (Rom. 16:17; 2 Thess. 3:14). Gk. *katanoéō* is an intensified form of *noéō* ("perceive, understand"; cf. LXX Ps. 9:35 [Eng. 10:14]). Jesus warned against looking at the speck in another's eye while failing to inspect the log in one's own (Mt. 7:3 par.). The hiphil of Heb. *nāḵar* can signify treating someone with polite or friendly attention. Ruth was surprised when Boaz took an interest in her (2:10, 19); but the psalmist complained that no one showed the slightest concern for him (Ps. 142:4 [5]).

In Acts 21:26 "give notice" refers to a cultic announcement; in 23:15 it refers to an official communication with the Roman authority.

*See also* LOOK II; OBSERVE. N. J. O.

**NOTHING; NOUGHT.** Terms used synonymously to translate a variety of words in the OT and NT. The Hebrew terms include *'ayin* (e.g., Prov. 13:4; Eccl. 2:24; 3:12, 14), *'ep̄es* (e.g., Isa. 34:12; 41:29), *lō' me'ûmâ* (e.g., Gen. 40:15; Jgs. 14:6; 1 S. 25:21), *lō' ḏāḇār* (e.g., Gen. 19:8; 1 S. 20:2), *lō' ḵōl* (e.g., Gen. 11:6; Prov. 13:7), *tōhû* (e.g., Isa. 44:9; 49:4), *biltî* (e.g., Isa. 44:10; Am. 3:4), *heḇel* (e.g., Ps. 39:6 [MT 7]; "empty nothings," Job 21:34), *šāwe'* (e.g., Hos. 12:11 [MT 12]), etc. In the NT "nothing" most often represents Gk. *mēdeís* (e.g., Mt. 8:4; 27:19) or *oudeís* (e.g., Mk. 7:15; 11:13). "Nothing" and "nought" occur also in expressions such as "for nothing," "for nought" (Heb. *ḥinnām*, lit. "freely, without compensation"; e.g., Gen. 29:15; Ex. 21:2; Job 1:9; Isa. 52:3, 5), "nothing but" (*raq*, lit. "only"; e.g., Gen. 26:29), "bring to nothing" (hiphil of *māʿaṭ*, lit. "diminish," Jer. 10:24; Gk. *katargéō*, lit. "make ineffective," 1 Cor. 1:28), "come to nought" (Heb. *'āḇaḏ*, lit. "perish," Ps. 112:10; Prov. 10:28; 11:7; *'āp̄ēs*, lit. "be at an end," Isa. 29:20; hophal of *pārar*, lit. "be broken," Isa. 8:10), "have nothing to do with" (Gk. *paraitéomai*, lit. "decline, reject, avoid," 1 Tim. 4:7; 2 Tim. 2:23; Tit. 3:10), etc.

Job 26:7 describes God's omnipotence with the words, "He . . . hangs the earth upon nothing" (Heb. *beli-mâ*). "Nothing" and "nought" are often used to indicate the insignificance of a human life (e.g., Ps. 39:5 [MT 6]), of the nations and their rulers (e.g., Isa. 34:12; 40:17, 23; 41:11f.), and of false gods (e.g., 41:24, 29; 44:9f.) in contrast to the sovereign power of Yahweh, the Creator of the world and Ruler of history.

Qoheleth observes the monotonous cycles of the natural world and the futility of human toil and laments, "there is nothing new under the sun" (Eccl. 1:9), i.e., there is no evidence of change or progress (cf. Ps. 39:6 [MT 7]). In Ps. 73:25 the psalmist rejoices in the communion with God that makes all earthly delights and sorrows insignificant: "Whom have I in heaven but thee? And there is nothing upon earth that I desire besides thee."

An important theme in the Gospel of John is Jesus' total dependence upon His heavenly Father, and therefore the identification of Jesus' mission and authority with God's (Jn. 5:19, 30; 8:28, 54; 9:33). Likewise, Jesus' followers can do nothing apart from Him (15:5; cf. 16:23f.).

Reflecting a familiar OT theme, Paul points to the absurdity of human self-glorification in the light of God's sovereignty: "God chose what is low and despised in the world, even things that are not, to bring to nothing [Gk. *katargéō*] things that are, so that no human being might boast in the presence of God" (1 Cor. 1:28f.). In 13:2f. he reminds the Corinthians that all the other spiritual gifts have no value whatsoever if they are not controlled by the gift of love.

The Pastoral Epistles exhort their readers to exercise congregational discipline by "having nothing to do with" (i.e., avoiding or repudiating) "godless and silly myths" (1 Tim. 4:7), "stupid, senseless controversies" (2 Tim. 2:23), and "a man who is factious" (Tit. 3:10; cf. 2 Thess. 3:14, where "have nothing to do with" renders *mḗ synanameígnymi*, lit. "do not mingle").

P. L. BREMER N. J. O.

**NOTICE.** *See* NOTE, TAKE NOTE OF.

**NOURISH** [pilpel of Heb. *kûl*–'sustain, support,' piel of *gāḏal*–'grow'; Gk. *tréphō*–'feed, support,' *ektréphō*, *entréphō*–'bring up, train,' *epichorēgéō*–'give, support']; AV also FEED; NEB also CHERISH, MAKE GROW, NURSE, etc.

The biblical use of "nourish" generally has a spiritual or figurative sense. Thus in Ezk. 31:4 the image of a tree nourished by water or rain refers to Egypt (see comms., *BHS*; the AV and NEB follow the MT and read Assyria in v. 3; cf. Isa. 44:14). Zec. 11:16 refers to a worthless shepherd (vv. 15, 17) whom God raises up and who, instead of caring for his flock, devours them. Though he is an instrument of God's judgment, he will also be judged. In a more positive image the NT seer referred to God's care for the "woman" (the Church? Eve? Mary? see comms.) in Rev. 12:6, 14.

Spiritual nourishing is in view in Eph. 5:29, where Paul draws a parallel between care for one's own body (perhaps one's spouse; see comms.) and the way Christ cares for the Church. Cf. also Col. 2:19, where Paul uses the image of the body to describe the Church and its relation to Jesus Christ. In 1 Tim. 4:6 Paul uses the common image of the word of God as spiritual food (cf. Ezk. 2:8–3:3; Jn. 6:48-51), which Timothy has been fed since childhood (2 Tim. 3:15). G. A. L.

**NOVICE.** The AV rendering of Gk. *neóphytos* (lit. "newly planted"), which in 1 Tim. 3:6 means "recent convert" (so RSV; cf. NEB "convert newly baptized"). Because of the danger that rapid promotion may lead to pride and clouded judgment, recent converts are specifically listed among those who are disqualified from holding the office of bishop.

**NOW.** In the older English versions "now" occurs more than twelve hundred times. In the OT it most often translates Heb. *nā'* (a particle expressing urgency) or *ʿattâ*. The most important NT terms are Gk. *nýn* (and emphatic form *nyní*), *árti*, and *ḗdē* (which is also rendered "already"). What follows here are some of the major types of uses, with special emphasis upon those that appear in theologically significant statements.

English "now," like Gk. *nýn*, is primarily a temporal adverb; but it can also be used as a particle, noun, or adjective, and as an adverb it can be used to express logical or situational as well as temporal relationships. Hence a discussion of "now" in the Bible can best be divided into its nontemporal and temporal uses.

I. Nontemporal Usage
II. Temporal Usage
  A. Point in Time
  B. Period of Time
    1. Recent Past
    2. Imminent Future
    3. "Hour" of Jesus
    4. Time Between Christ's First and Second Comings
    5. "Then" and "Now" of Christian Experience

***I. Nontemporal Usage.***–"Now" has four common nontemporal uses. (1) It is frequently used as a connecting particle to express a logical connection or a point of transition in thought. Sometimes it is supplied by the RSV when the Hebrew or Greek has simply a coordinating conjunction (e.g., Gen. 16:1: "Now Sarai . . ."; Jn. 18:40: "Now Barabbas . . ."). But is also occurs as a translation of Heb. *nāʾ* or *ʿattâ* or of Gk. *nýn* (e.g., Lk. 11:39: "Now you Pharisees . . ."; Acts 10:33: "Now therefore . . .").

(2) It is also used as a particle of emphasis with interjections, requests, and commands. The AV often translates Heb. *nāʾ* literally while the RSV paraphrases or omits it (e.g., Gen. 12:11; 13:14); but cf. Isa. 1:18 (RSV "Come now . . ."). In the NT the RSV, as well as the AV, usually renders *nýn* as "now" in these expressions (e.g., Acts 4:29; 7:34; 13:11; Jas. 4:13).

(3) The expression "but now" (Gk. *nýn* [*nyní*] *de*) is used to denote a logical antithesis as when one posits the real or true state of affairs over against what is unreal or erroneous (e.g., Lk. 19:42; Jn. 8:40; 9:41; 15:22, 24; cf. Gen. 31:42). The RSV often translates the Greek phrase with "but in fact" (e.g., 1 Cor. 15:20), "but as it is" (1 Cor. 12:18, 20; He. 9:26), or some similar expression. In Rom. 3:21 the logical antithetical force of "but now" combines with the temporal eschatological meaning of "now"; but the temporal meaning is dominant, as v. 26 shows (Gk. *en tǭ nýn kairǭ*; RSV "at the present time").

(4) Frequently "now" expresses more of a situational than a temporal relationship, although an element of time may be involved. In such passages it means "in the present situation" or "as things now stand" (e.g., 1 S. 8:5: "you are old . . . now [Heb. *ʿattâ*] appoint for us a king"; cf. Gen. 29:32; Acts 15:10). At times it is difficult to determine whether the emphasis is on the temporal or the situational relationship. This ambivalence reflects the basic biblical perspective on time, in which the importance of a unit of time lies rarely in its chronological dimension but rather in what has happened, continues to happen, or will happen within it. E.g., when Paul affirms that "now is the day of salvation" (2 Cor. 6:2), he makes that affirmation in the light of God's recent reconciling work in Christ and the ongoing proclamation of the gospel of reconciliation.

***II. Temporal Usage.***–Strictly speaking, "now" designates a point in time between the past and the future. Thus it can designate the end of a period, the beginning of a period, or a specific point in time. It can also be extended to specify a duration of time; in the Bible it occurs frequently in this sense with a wide range of meanings.

*A. Point in Time.* The adverbial phrase "until now" is used frequently to designate the end of a period of time, when the eschatological enemies of Christ's kingdom are "already" at work (cf. 2 Thess. 2:6f.; 1 Jn. 2:18; 4:3). Gk. *héōs toú nýn* par.), or in a congregation's ministry (Phil. 1:5; *áchri toú nýn*).

"From now on" points to the beginning of a period of time. The RSV occasionally uses this phrase (e.g., Lk. 22:69; Acts 18:6; 2 Cor. 5:16), but usually it translates the Hebrew or Greek phrase (e.g., Heb. *mēʿattâ*; Gk. *apó toú nýn, apʾ árti*) by an equivalent expression such as "from this time forth" (Isa. 48:6), "henceforth" (e.g., Lk. 1:48; 5:10; Jn. 14:7; Rev. 14:13), or "hereafter" (e.g., Mt. 26:64). These beginning points may represent turning points in the history of redemption (Isa. 48:6; Mt. 26:64 par.), in the life of God's people (e.g., Lk. 5:10; Jn. 14:7; Rev. 14:13), and in the proclamation of the gospel to Gentiles (e.g., Acts 18:6).

Very frequently "now" simply denotes a specified point in time. This use appears in 1 Cor. 16:7: "I do not want to see you now (*árti*) just in passing" (cf. also *nýn* in v. 12; Gal. 3:3; He. 9:5; *nyní* in Philem. 9). Sometimes *árti* is also rendered as "just" (e.g., "My daughter has just died," Mt. 9:18) or "at once" (e.g., "and he will at once send me more than twelve legions of angels," 26:53).

*B. Period of Time.* In Jude 25 ("before all time and now [*nýn*] and forevermore") "now" probably refers to the whole time span of this present world order. "Now" is used in a variety of ways to refer to a long or short span of time. Where Gk. *nýn* is used as an adjective, the RSV usually translates it "present" (i.e., "the present time"; e.g., Rom. 3:26; 2 Cor. 8:14).

*1. Recent Past.* Used in this sense the term expresses vividly the close connection between past and present. Cf. Josh. 5:14 ("as the commander of the army of the Lord I have now come") and Acts 7:52 ("whom you have now betrayed and murdered").

*2. Imminent Future.* This usage appears frequently in the OT, e.g., Gen. 19:9 ("Now we will deal worse with you than with them"); 29:32 ("Surely now my husband will love me"); cf. Ex. 6:1; Isa. 49:19; etc. In the NT there may be a similar use in Phil. 1:20 ("now as always").

*3. "Hour" of Jesus.* In the Gospel of John "now" sometimes refers to Jesus' "hour," which 13:1 describes as follows: "when Jesus knew that his hour had come to depart out of this world to the Father, having loved his own who were in the world, he loved them to the end" (cf. also 2:4; 7:30; 8:20; 12:23, 27; 17:1). John later substitutes "now" (*nýn*) to refer to this "hour," which evidently includes Jesus' passion, death, resurrection, and ascension. Jesus says: "Now is the Son of man glorified . . ." (Jn. 13:31); "But now I am going to him who sent me" (16:5); "and now, Father, glorify thou me . . ." (17:5); "But now I am coming to thee" (v. 13; cf. 12:27); and "But now my kingdom is from another place" (18:36, NIV). Jesus' "hour" has its repercussions in the kingdom of darkness: "Now is the judgment of this world, now shall the ruler of this world be cast out" (12:31). This use of "now" may also be reflected in He. 9:24: "now to appear in the presence of God on our behalf" (cf. v. 26).

This "now" can also designate the time of Jesus' "hour" in the life of the disciples. Jesus says to them: "Where I am going you cannot follow me now; but you shall follow afterward" (Jn. 13:36; cf. *árti* in vv. 7, 37; 16:12; *nýn* in 14:29; 16:22). It can also indicate a time when the disciples had come to a new understanding through Jesus' proclamation (cf. 17:7; 16:31).

*4. Time Between Christ's First and Second Comings.* According to Rev. 12:10 the prophet John heard a loud voice in heaven saying: "Now [*árti*] the salvation and the power and the kingdom of God and the authority of his Christ have come, for the accuser of our brethren has been thrown down . . . ," and he "knows that his time is short" (v. 12). Paul affirms in 2 Cor. 6:2: "Behold, now [*nýn*] is the acceptable time; behold, now is the day of salvation." This is so because believers participate in the redeeming work of Christ; for "we are now [*nýn*] justified by his blood" and "reconciled to God by the death of his Son" (Rom. 5:9-11), and "in Christ" believers are "now" (*nýn*) free from condemnation (8:1). Nevertheless, "now" is also the time that believers continue to "live in the flesh" (Gal. 2:20) amid affliction and renewal (cf. 2 Cor. 4:16f.).

*a. The Christian and the Present World.* Although believers have citizenship already in heaven, they continue to live their lives of faith on earth (cf. Phil. 3:20; Col. 3:5). "Now" can describe three aspects of this present world.

(1) It is created by God and affected by sin. Jesus affirms: "My Father is working still [*héōs árti*, lit. "until now"], and I am working" (Jn. 5:17). This is God's world, but it has been subject to futility and the bondage of decay. Therefore "the whole creation has been groaning in travail together until now [*áchri toú nýn*]" and looks forward in hope to sharing in "the glorious liberty of the children of God" (Rom. 8:19-22). 2 Pet. 3:7 speaks of "the heavens and earth that now [*nýn*] exist" as having been stored up for fire.

(2) It is in bondage to the powers of darkness. Although Christ has come and has begun to rule, "we do not yet [*nýn dé oúpō*] see everything in subjection to him" (He. 2:8). Paul refers to "the prince of the powers of the air" as "the spirit that is now [*nýn*] at work in the sons of disobedience" (Eph. 2:2); this power continues to affect both Jew and Gentile outside of Christ (vv. 1-3). Paul can therefore speak of "the present [*nýn*] Jerusalem" that is in slavery with its children (Gal. 4:25). He also speaks of the Jews who "until today" have a veil over their hearts and do not understand the true meaning of the Torah (2 Cor. 3:14-16), and who are "now" (*nýn*) disobedient (Rom. 11:31; cf. Jn. 8:52; 15:22-24). 1 Jn. 2:9 says that anyone who claims to be in the light but hates his brother "is in the darkness until now [*héōs árti*]." In Lk. 6:25 woe is pronounced upon those who are "full now [*nýn*]" and "laugh now."

(3) It is where the Christian lives. The Christian "still" ("yet" or "now") lives in the old aeon. Paul refers to his life of faith as "the life I now [*nýn*] live in the flesh" (Gal. 2:20). This world is the arena in which salvation is enjoyed, but it is also a threatening situation for the Christian life. Because it is a time of "not seeing" Jesus Christ, "now" (*árti*) is a time of suffering (1 Pet. 1:6, 8). Paul sees this as especially true for the apostles "to the present hour" (*áchri tḗs árti hṓras*, 1 Cor. 4:11-13). It is a time of not yet (*ouk . . . ḗdē*, "not . . . already") having achieved perfection (Phil. 3:12). Furthermore, "now" is the time when the eschatological enemies of Christ's kingdom are "already" at work (cf. 2 Thess. 2:6f.; 1 Jn. 2:18; 4:3).

Yet the Christian in the present world has hope of ultimate victory and redemption, for "the sufferings of the present [*nýn*] time are not worthy to be compared to the glories that shall be revealed in us" (Rom. 8:18; cf. 2 Cor. 4:17–5:4; cf. 1 Pet. 1:6; Col. 1:24). And those who hunger and weep "now" (*nýn*) are blessed, for they shall be satisfied and shall laugh (Lk. 6:21).

*b. The Present Time of Salvation in Comparison with the Past.* (1) The present time of salvation stands in continuity with the former time. By way of allegory the children of promise of the new covenant correspond to the children of promise of the old (Gal. 4:29: "so it is now"). By way of type and antitype, baptism "now [*nýn*] saves you" in correspondence with God's action in the time of Noah and the Flood (1 Pet. 3:21; cf. He. 12:26: "then . . . now"). There is in this continuity also a "more than" in which the new excels the old (cf. He. 8:6: "But as it is [Gk. *nýn dé*], Christ has obtained a ministry which is as much more excellent than the old as the covenant he mediates is better . . ."; cf. the implied "more than" in 1 Pet. 3:20-22; He. 12:26-28).

(2) The present is a time of new revelation. In describing the gospel as a "mystery," Paul sometimes contrasts the "now" as a time of disclosure with the past as a time of concealment. The once hidden mystery of God (or of Christ) is now revealed (Rom. 16:25f.; Col. 1:26; cf. 2:2; 4:3; Eph. 3:5, 10). That mystery is rooted in Christ, is eschatological, and involved Christ's universal work. In other passages this new revelation is presented as the fulfillment of that to which the OT prophets pointed (1 Pet. 1:12; Lk. 2:29; cf. Eph. 3:5).

*c. The "Already" of Salvation as Anticipation of the Future.* Greek *ḗdē* is used primarily as an adverb of time meaning "now, already, by this time" (though occasionally it may denote logical proximity; cf. Mt. 5:28; 1 Cor. 6:7). Sometimes it designates the present time as the beginning of a process that has been anticipated for the future. It does not always refer to salvation. It can point to an eschatological error, as when some say that "the resurrection is past already" (2 Tim. 2:18) or think that they are "already filled" and "already rich" (1 Cor. 4:8). Paul expressly denies that he has already achieved the resurrection or been made perfect (Phil. 3:12). Sometimes the term is used of eschatological judgment already in process (Mt. 3:10; Lk. 3:9; esp. Jn. 3:18) and of the negative eschatological forces already at work, namely, the mystery of lawlessness (2 Thess. 2:7) and the spirit of the antichrist (1 Jn. 4:3; cf. 2:18).

But *ḗdē* can also be used in an important way to designate the "already" of eschatological salvation. The true light already shines (1 Jn. 2:8), the eschatological Elijah has already come (Mt. 17:12), those in Christ are already cleansed (Jn. 15:3), the sower already has a reward (4:36; or the alternative interpretation [v. 35]: "the fields are already white for harvest"), and, since salvation is near, it is already time for Christians to awaken from sleep and live as children of day (Rom. 13:11f.).

The present is described not only as a time of already possessing salvation but also as a time of expectation and hope, for in the NT the end time also has a future pole. Since we are now justified and reconciled in Christ, we can "much more" expect to be saved in the future (Rom. 5:9f.). Now we are the children of God, but when He appears "we shall be like him, for we shall see him as he is" (1 Jn. 3:2; cf. 1 Tim. 4:8).

The "now," although already a time of salvation, can therefore be contrasted with the future time when God's eschatological salvation will be enjoyed fully. "For now we see in a mirror dimly, but then face to face. Now I know in part; then I shall understand fully . . ." (1 Cor. 13:12). The fullness of the future that is promised makes pale by comparison the present experience of salvation, rich as it is.

*5. "Then" and "Now" of Christian Experience.* In a formalized way NT authors frequently contrast what "once" (Gk. *poté* or *tóte*) was true with what "now" (*nýn*) is true in their situation and experience as Christians. 1 Pet. 2:10 sets forth this stark contrast: "Once you were no people but now you are God's people; once you had not received mercy but now you have received mercy." This contrast is based on the work accomplished by Christ (cf., e.g., Col. 1:22; Eph. 2:13; Rom. 5:6-11), but the specific point of comparison lies in the experience of those who have become Christians. The emphasis is on what is now true for Christians and what therefore may appropriately be expected of them. In Eph. 2:11-13 Paul reminds the gentile Christians of the great gift of grace that is now theirs: "Therefore remember that at one time [*poté*] you Gentiles in the flesh . . . were . . . separated from Christ . . . having no hope and without God in the world. But now [*nyní dé*] in Christ Jesus you who were far off have been brought near in the blood of Christ." This gift of salvation involves an imperative: "for once [*poté*] you were darkness, but now [*nýn dé*] you are light in the Lord; walk as children of light . . ." (5:8). Other important passages that use the "then-now" formula are Rom. 6:19-23; 11:30-32; Gal. 1:23; 4:8-10; Col. 1:21f.; 3:7f.; Philem. 11. Passages that contain part of the formula include Rom. 5:8-11; 7:4-6; 1 Cor. 6:9-11; 2 Cor. 5:15f.; Gal. 2:13; 4:3-7, 29; Col. 2:13-15; 1 Tim. 1:13-16; Tit. 3:3-7.

We have seen, therefore, that a study of the temporal use of "now" sheds light on many aspects of the NT view of past, present, and future. The present time has its own importance in the history of redemption because it fulfils God's earlier redeeming activity. But it is also charged with greater significance and an existential quality because the past work of Christ is the beginning of the eschatological future. Rom. 13:11-14 expresses the eschatological character of the present time as follows: "Besides this you know what hour it is, how it is full time now for you to wake from sleep. For salvation is nearer to us now than when we first believed; the night is far gone, the day is at hand. Let us then cast off the works of darkness and put on the armor of light. . . ."

***Bibliography.***–J. Barr, *Biblical Words for Time* (rev. ed. *SBT*, 1/33, 1969); O. Cullmann, *Christ and Time* (Eng. tr., 3rd ed. 1962); S. J. De Vries, *Yesterday, Today and Tomorrow* (1975); *DNTT*, III, 833-39; P. Tachau, *"Einst" und "Jetzt" im NT* (1972); *TDNT*, IV, *s.v.* νῦν (ἄρτι) (G. Stählin); J. R. Wilch, *Time and Event* (1969).

A. J. BANDSTRA

## NUMBER.


I. Ancient Near Eastern Mathematics
II. Terminology and Signs
III. Basic Arithmetic
IV. Literary Use of Numbers
V. Symbolic Use of Numbers
  A. One
  B. Two
  C. Three
  D. Four
  E. Five
  F. Seven
  G. Six, Eight, Nine
  H. Ten
  I. Twelve
  J. One Thousand
VI. Gematria


In Hebrew the verbs *sāpar* (Gen. 15:5) and *mānâ* (Gen. 13:16) are commonly used for enumeration and counting. The derivative *mispār* (Ex. 16:16) is the most common noun for number, although *mik̲sâ* (Ex. 12:4) and the Aramaic *minyān* (Ezr. 6:17) also appear with this meaning. The passive participle of *pāqad̲* is used to designate the number of people counted in a census (Ex. 30:12f.). The LXX translates all these nouns by *arithmós,* which appears eighteen times in the NT (ten times in Revelation; cf. esp. 13:17f.; Jn. 6:10; Acts 4:4). Number as an indefinite count of people is indicated by *óchlos* ("multitude," Mk. 10:46; "company," Acts 1:15). The verb *psēphízō* appears with the meaning count in the sense of enumeration (so RSV "reckon") in Rev. 13:18.

***I. Ancient Near Eastern Mathematics.***–Biblical numbers and their use were no doubt influenced by the highly developed mathematical systems of Egypt and Mesopotamia. Although roughly equal to Mesopotamian mathematics in antiquity, Egyptian mathematics remained the more primitive and practically oriented, with little interest in mathematical theory. The Egyptians used a cumbersome decimal system that failed to discern that only ten symbols were needed to represent all possible numbers. They were, nevertheless, extremely effective in applying mathematics to practical needs, as witnessed in their building projects; e.g., they came very close to determining the exact value of pi.

In Mesopotamia both a decimal system, drawn from Semitic practice, and a sexagesimal system, introduced by the Sumerians, were known from very early times. The two blend together well, and the modern use of numbers still preserves elements of the sexagesimal system (divisions of time, degrees of a circle, a dozen). The Mesopotamians put mathematics to effective practical use, as evidenced by their building achievements and many extant business documents, but they were also interested in more theoretical mathematics. They could find square roots, knew the Pythagorean theorem, and developed basic principles of geometry and algebra. They influenced later Greek and thus modern mathematics and contributed much to the development of astronomy as a science.

***II. Terminology and Signs.***–The Hebrew OT and usually the Greek NT express numbers by words. The OT has words for each of the units, the tens, one hundred, two hundred, one thousand, two thousand, ten thousand, and twenty thousand. Both the Moabite Stone and the Siloam Inscription use words to express numbers, but the Samaria ostraca and the Lachish Letters provide some evidence for the existence of arithmetic figures. The Aramaic Elephantine papyri use figures (vertical lines for units and horizontal for tens), as do administrative documents from Ugarit and some Phoenician inscriptions. Thus Israel probably represented numerals with figures as well as words during the biblical period.

As early as Maccabean times (as indicated on coins) the Jews used the letters of the alphabet for numerical signs. Units were represented by the first nine letters, tens by the next nine letters, and one hundred to four hundred by the last four letters. The numbers fifteen and sixteen, however, were made by combining *ṭeth* (9) and *waw* (6) and *ṭeth* and *zayin* (7), respectively, since the letters *yod* (10) and *he* (5) or *yodh* and *waw* are shortened forms of the divine name Yahweh. The system of alphabetic notation still commonly denotes chapters and verses in the Hebrew Bible. The Greeks had a similar system of alphabetic notation, of which examples appear in the NT, e.g., the number for the beast in Rev. 13:18. (See the chart below for a view of these systems in Hebrew and Greek.)

Hebrew also has words for many of the ordinal numbers (first, second, etc.), and words for some simple fractions,

**TABLE OF ALPHABETIC NOTATION OF NUMERALS**

| | Hebrew | Greek | | Hebrew | Greek |
|---|---|---|---|---|---|
| 1 | א | A | 60 | ס | Ξ |
| 2 | ב | B | 70 | ע | O |
| 3 | ג | Γ | 80 | פ | Π |
| 4 | ד | Δ | 90 | צ | Ϙ |
| 5 | ה | E | 100 | ק | P |
| 6 | ו | F | 200 | ר | Σ |
| 7 | ז | Z | 300 | ש | T |
| 8 | ח | H | 400 | ת | Y |
| 9 | ט | Θ | 500 | תק | Φ |
| 10 | י | I | 600 | תר | X |
| 20 | כ | K | 700 | תש | Ψ |
| 30 | ל | Λ | 800 | תת | Ω |
| 40 | מ | M | 900 | תתק | Ͳ |
| 50 | נ | N | 1000 | א | /A |

e.g., one-third in Isa. 40:12. Certain words for parts of the body were used in biblical Hebrew to denote fractions or multiplication and sometimes both. *Yād,* "hand," indicates a fractional part in Gen. 47:24 ("four-fifths shall be your own"), but shows multiplication in 43:34 ("five times as much"). *Regel,* "foot," indicates multiplication in Nu. 22:28 ("three times"), and *peh,* "mouth" shows a fraction in Zec. 13:8 ("two-thirds shall be cut off"), but multiplication in Dt. 21:17 ("a double portion of all that he has"). The idiom *pî šᵉnayim,* "mouth of two," originally meant two-thirds but came to mean twice as much (2 K. 2:9). *Rō'š,* "head," sometimes means total or sum (Nu. 1:2).

*III. Basic Arithmetic.*–Simple enumeration accounts for most of the biblical references to numbers. Numbers range in size from one to 100,000,000 in the OT (Dnl. 7:10, "ten thousand times ten thousand stood before him") and 200,000,000 in the NT (Rev. 9:16, "twice ten thousand times ten thousand"). The highest number represented by one word is twenty thousand, *ribbōṯayim* (Ps. 68:17 [MT 18]). The Bible has no mathematical concept of infinity but does recognize numbers beyond the human capability for counting: Gen. 41:49, "he ceased to measure it, for it could not be measured"; Rev. 7:9, "a great multitude which no man could number."

Fractions were known and used in biblical times. There are separate Hebrew words for the fractions from a half to a fifth and for a tenth. One-tenth appears with special frequency in the Bible because of the importance of tithing in the biblical communities (Ex. 16:36; Nu. 18:26, 28; He. 7:1-10). It is also much used because of the decimal system of Hebrew mathematics, as were other decimal based fractions: two-tenths (Lev. 23:13), three-tenths (Lev. 14:10), and one-hundredth (Neh. 5:11). The fraction one-third appears fourteen times in Revelation where it always refers to one of three parts which was to be destroyed (Rev. 8). Other examples of biblical use of fractions include one-third (2 S. 18:2), one-half (Ex. 25:10, 17), one-fourth (1 S. 9:8), one-fifth (Gen. 47:24), and one-sixth (Ezk. 46:14).

Complementary fractions (the numerator is one less than the denominator) are frequently expressed in an indefinite manner reflecting Egyptian and Mesopotamian influence. Examples are: two-thirds expressed as a "double portion" (Dt. 21:17; 2 K. 2:9), four-fifths as "four parts" (Gen. 47:24), and nine-tenths as "nine parts" (Neh. 11:1).

The OT uses fractions only to designate portions of some larger whole, not in mathematical calculations. The Hebrews, like other ancient peoples, did not know how to convert mixed fractions to a common denominator. In the NT fractions are still used only in the simple manner known in the OT, although more sophisticated mathematical uses might have been available from Hellenistic culture.

The four basic arithmetical operations can be illustrated from the biblical material: addition (Gen. 5:3-31; Nu. 1:20-46), subtraction (Gen. 18:28-33; Lev. 27:18), multiplication (Lev. 25:8; Nu. 3:46-50), and division (Nu. 31:27-30). More complex mathematical operations are implied in Lev. 25:50; 27:18, 23.

Although Egyptian and Babylonian mathematics (and later Greek mathematics) were surely known widely in biblical times, the Bible shows little interest in complex mathematical operations and virtually no interest in mathematical theory. Its mathematics are of the simplest and most practical sort. The dimensions of the molten sea in Solomon's temple in (1 K. 7:23) indicate that the Hebrews still thought of the circumference of a circle as three times the diameter. This continued to be the reckoning in the time of the Mishnah (*Erubin* i.5).

*IV. Literary Use of Numbers.*–Numbers in the Bible do not always indicate exact totals or mathematical operations. They sometimes have literary (rhetorical) or symbolic uses. (For symbolic uses see V below.) Most of the literary and many of the symbolic uses discussed here have parallels elsewhere in the literature of the ancient Near East, particularly in Ugaritic literature (on the use of the numerical saying in Ugaritic and the OT see G. Sauer, *Die Sprüche Agurs* [1963]; Roth).

It is often difficult to tell whether the Bible intends a definite or an approximate number. In Hebrew the word for one (*'eḥāḏ,* fem. *'aḥaṯ*) is sometimes used to express the indefinite article (1 K. 13:11) or to mean "anyone, any one" (Lev. 4:2, 13, 22, 27; 2 S. 7:7). The number two is often used to mean "a few" (Nu. 9:22; 1 K. 17:12). Even more commonly the number three means simply a small number (Ex. 2:2; 10:22; Josh. 1:11; 1 K. 12:5; 2 K. 11:5; Isa. 16:14; Dnl. 1:5).

A sequence of two consecutive small numbers sometimes stresses the indefinite character of a number, e.g., "a day or two" (Ex. 21:21, "God speaks in one way, and in two" (Job 33:14). One and two also appear in sequence in 2 K. 6:10; Sir. 38:17; examples of two and three are Isa. 17:6; Hos. 6:2; Mt. 18:20. Both these pairs seem to indicate fewness. Of particular interest is the numerical saying, which often has the form "x . . . x + 1 . . ." (e.g., Prov. 6:16-19; cf. Dt. 32:30; Ps. 62:11 [MT 12]; Jer. 3:14; etc.). This device is common in Ugaritic literature as well (e.g., *UT,* 51:III:17-21; 1 Aqht 42-44; Krt 7-9, 16-20, 83f., 94f.). See Roth, p. 6, for a detailed analysis and explanation. Three and four appear together eight times in Am. 1:1–2:6, where they must indicate "several," since the number of sins listed for each nation is neither three nor four. A slightly different use of this pair is seen in Prov. 30:15-29, where the intent seems to be to emphasize the higher number, for a listing of four things follows the formula. Other pairs are four and five (Isa. 17:6), five and six (2 K. 13:19), six and seven (Job 5:19), seven and eight (Mic. 5:5), nine and ten (Sir. 25:7).

Two of the best known uses of approximate numbers appear in covenantal contexts: "visiting the iniquity of the fathers upon the children to the third and fourth generation of those who hate me, but showing steadfast love to thousands of those who love me . . . "(Ex. 20:5f.; cf. also Dt. 5:9f.; 7:9).

The Bible and other ancient literature commonly use round numbers to indicate approximate, traditional, or hyperbolic rather than exact sums. The number one thousand and its multiples are often rounded to signify a large amount and may often be hyperbolic (Lev. 26:8; 1 S. 18:7; Rev. 5:11). The failure to recognize this use has led to difficulties for those who take the numbers as exact sums. The census figures of Nu. 1 and 26 imply a population of two to three million, a figure that does not tally well with the notion that the Hebrews were "the fewest of all peoples" (Dt. 7:7), or that they were overwhelmed in numbers by the Canaanite cities they encountered on entry into the land. Large numbers for armies and the fallen in battle are also problematic. In 2 Ch. 17:12-19 Jehoshaphat's army consists of five divisions numbering 300,000, 280,000, 200,000, 200,000, 180,000, respectively. In 1 K. 20:29 a small army of Israelites is said to have killed 100,000 Syrians in one day.

The Heb. *'elep* ("thousand") may originally have meant "tribe," "clan," or "group," and did not necessarily indicate a group of exactly one thousand members (see N. Gottwald, *Tribes of Yahweh* [1979], pp. 269-284). Jgs. 6:15 clearly uses *'elep* in this way, and the use of the term for a military unit does not seem to mean the unit has a thousand members (Ex. 18:21; Dt. 33:17). W. F. Petrie (*Researches in Sinai* [1906]) first used this meaning to interpret the census lists in Nu. 1 and 26 as indications of families or tribal subgroups, thus allowing the more reasonable totals of 5550 and 5730 fighting men.

The plausible suggestion has also been made (see the articles by Clark and Wenham) that in many instances *'elep*, "thousand," is to be repointed *'allûp*, "officer" or "warrior." Such a revocalization would make sense of seemingly inflated numbers for armies or slain soldiers, and accords well with the practice of ancient times for mighty men to do much of the fighting (as with Goliath, 1 S. 17).

The most frequently used round number in the Bible is forty (Heb. *'arbā'îm*, Gk. *tessarákonta*), which has the sense of a relatively long period of time and more specifically is the traditional number of years in a generation. In the forty years that Israel spent in the wilderness the old generation died out and was replaced by the new (Ex. 16:35; Nu. 14:33f.; 32:13). A sense of completeness or maturity is attached to the number (perhaps because it is the product of four times ten). A man was considered to reach full adulthood at forty (Ex. 2:11; Josh. 14:7; 2 S. 2:10; Acts 7:23). In the Koran (*Sura* 46) a man is said to attain his strength at forty years, and according to tradition Muhammad came forward as a prophet at that age. Isaac and Esau married at forty (Gen. 25:20; 26:34). Moses' life was divided into three periods of forty years (Ex. 7:7; Dt. 34:7; Acts 7:23, 30, 36). Eli (1 S. 4:18), Saul (Acts 13:21), David (1 K. 2:11), Solomon (1 K. 11:42), and Jehoash (2 K. 12:1) all reigned for forty years. Periods of rest (Jgs. 3:11; 5:31; 8:28) and oppression (13:1) in the time of the judges commonly lasted forty years.

Forty days was a typical period of time for ritual observances: the fasting of Moses (Ex. 34:28), Elijah (1 K. 19:8), and Jesus (Mt. 4:2 par.); Moses' stay on Mt. Sinai (Ex. 24:18; cf. Dt. 9:9). The Flood lasted forty days (Gen. 7:4); the challenge of Goliath was forty days (1 S. 17:16). Jonah proclaimed, "Yet forty days, and Nineveh shall be overthrown" (Jonah 3:4), and there were forty days between the Resurrection and the Ascension (Acts 1:3). The abundant occurrences of the number forty indicate that it was used as a rounded rather than an exact figure.

*V. Symbolic Use of Numbers.*–Numbers in the Bible and other ancient literature often have symbolic or cultic meaning. Many of these have uses that are simultaneously literal and symbolic in meaning.

*A. One* (Heb. *'eḥāḏ*; Gk. *heís*). The number one naturally suggests unity. Thus it is basic to the concept of monotheism (Dt. 6:4, "The Lord our God, the Lord is One"; cf. also Wisd. 7:27; Mk. 12:32; 1 Cor. 8:6) and to the concept of human unity (Acts 17:26, "He made from one every nation"). Sin was brought into the world by one man, Adam (Rom. 5:12), but the gift of redeeming grace also by one man, Jesus Christ (v. 15). Jesus is one with the Father (Jn. 10:30).

The Church is one as the "body of Christ" (1 Cor. 12:12-14), thus one in unity with God, Christ, and each other (Jn. 17:21; Gal. 3:28). The unity expressed by the number one is central to the concept of the Church; "There is one body and one Spirit, just as you were called to the one hope that belongs to your call, one Lord, one faith, one baptism, one God and Father of us all..." (Eph. 4:4-6). In the Judeo-Christian tradition one also symbolizes the unity in marriage ("And the two shall become one flesh," Gen. 2:24; cf. Mt. 19:5; Eph. 5:31).

*B. Two* (Heb. *šᵉnayim;* Gk. *dýo*). This number is associated both with unity and with division or contrast. Examples of division are the alternatives implied in Elijah's taunt, "How long will you go limping with two different opinions?" (1 K. 18:21). There are the "two ways" of Mt. 7:13f. (cf. Mt.6:24; 21:28-32). In Rev. 1:16 a two-edged sword comes forth from the mouth of the risen Christ. The sword is often associated with the "word of God" (Eph. 6:17; He. 4:12; Rev. 19:13, 15), and in this instance seems to imply the double aspect of God's word proceeding from Christ, as both judging and redeeming word.

As a symbol of unity, two describes the unity of man and woman (Gen. 2:20, 24), the pairs of animals entering the ark (7:8f.), the two tablets of the law at Mt. Sinai (Ex. 32:15), and the pairs of disciples sent out by Christ (Mk. 6:7; Lk. 10:1). In Gen. 22:6, 8 Abraham and Isaac went "both of them together" in a poignant reference to their unity in spite of the coming sacrifice. A separate and common use of the number two arises out of the Hebrew legal tradition that there must be two witnesses to constitute adequate evidence in a court proceeding (Nu. 35:30; Dt. 17:6; 19:15). Thus two is the number associated with the theme of witness. In Jn. 8:17f. Jesus appeals to this rule of evidence and claims Himself and the Father as witnesses to His own authority. Several other NT references indicate this need for two witnesses (Mt. 18:16; 2 Cor. 13:1; 1 Tim. 5:19). The two unnamed witnesses in Rev. 11:3-12 seem to represent the Law and the Prophets and are probably intended to recall Moses and Elijah.

*C. Three* (Heb. *šālōš;* Gk. *treís*). Three was a common sacred number in the ancient Near East. As the number most distinctly marked with a beginning, middle, and end it seems to have been regarded as symbolic of a complete and ordered whole. Triads of gods are known from Egypt and Mesopotamia. The universe was in three parts: heaven, earth, and netherworld. Families consisted of three parts: father, mother, and child. It is not surprising that the number three in the Bible is second only to seven in the frequency of its symbolic use, although distinguishing exact from symbolic use is sometimes difficult.

Persons, things, or acts are often three in number: Noah's three sons (Gen. 6:10), Abraham's guests (18:2), Job's daughters (Job 1:2; 42:13) and friends (2:11), measures of meal (Gen. 18:6; Mt. 13:33), military companies (Jgs. 7:16, 20; 9:43; 1 S. 11:11; 13:17; Job 1:17), great cultic feasts (Ex. 23:14), night watches (Jgs. 7:19), daily prayers (Ps. 55:17 [MT 18]; Dnl. 6:10 [MT 11]), the threefold call of Samuel (1 S. 3:8), the three times Elijah stretched himself over the widow's child (1 K. 17:21), the keepers of the temple threshold (Jer. 52:24), the temptations of Jesus (Mt. 4:3ff. par.), His prayers in Gethsemane (Mt. 26:39, 42, 44 and par.), Peter's denials (Mt. 26:34, 75 par.), his threefold vision of the sheet (Acts 10:16), and Paul's triad of faith, hope, and love (1 Cor. 13:13).

Three is common in designating significant lengths of time, such as three days, three weeks, three months, or three years (Gen. 40:12f., 18; Ex. 2:2; 10:22; 2 S. 24:13; Isa. 20:3; Jonah 1:17; Mt. 15:32; Lk. 2:46; 13:7; Acts 9:9; 2 Cor. 12:8). Of greatest significance in Christian theology is reference to the Resurrection "on the third day" or "after three days' (Mt. 12:40; Jn. 2:19; 1 Cor. 15:4).

Other important uses of three are triple groupings in which the number itself is not mentioned: the threefold benediction of Israel (Nu. 6:24-26), the three cries of "holy" by the seraphim (Isa. 6:3; cf. Rev. 4:8), the trinitarian formula in Mt. 28:19; 2 Cor. 13:14. A threefold repetition of something not only has symbolic meaning but also is a method of expressing the superlative (e.g., Isa. 6:3).

*D. Four* (Heb. *'arba'*; Gk. *téssares*). Four is a sacred and symbolic number in most ancient cultures derived from the four points of the compass and from the square as the simplest plane figure. The number four is used most frequently as the symbol for comprehensive extent or completeness. In Babylonian mythology four figures of the Zodiac support the four corners of the firmament (Aquarius, Scorpio, Leo, Taurus). As early as the middle of the 3rd millennium B.C. Babylonian rulers assumed the title of "king of the four quarters," meaning the entire earth in all directions. This use of four to indicate the entire earth or universe is also common in the Bible. There is mention of the four winds (Jer. 49:36; Ezk. 37:9; Mt. 24:31), the four quarters or corners of the earth (Isa. 11:12; Ezk. 7:2; Rev. 20:8), the four rivers of Eden (Gen. 2:10-14), and the four corners in Peter's vision of the great sheet (Acts 10:11; 11:5).

There are four letters in the Hebrew spelling of the divine name Yahweh (*YHWH*), which is thus called the tetragrammaton. Four is common in reference to sacred precincts and their furnishing (Ex. 25–27; 1 K. 7:5, 19, 27, 30, 34, 38; Ezk. 41–43). There are the four horns, smiths, chariots, and horses in the visions of Zechariah (1:8 [LXX], 18ff.; 6:1ff.), four punishments (Jer. 15:3; Ezk. 14:21); four kingdoms in Nebuchadrezzar's dream (Dnl. 2:37ff.) and Daniel's vision (7:3, 17); four creatures transporting and guarding God's throne (Ezk. 1:1-26; 10:9-14, 21; Rev. 4:6f.; 5:6, 8, 14; 6:1; 15:7; 19:4). As shown by the location of the references above, four is an especially important number in apocalyptic literature.

Forty as a multiple of four is of great significance in the Bible (see IV above). Four hundred (Gen. 15:13) and four thousand (1 S. 4:2; Mt. 15:38; Acts 21:38) also appear as common round numbers. Forty thousand is a frequent round number for a great multitude (Josh. 4:13; 1 K. 4:26; 1 Macc. 12:41; 2 Macc. 5:14).

*E. Five* (Heb. *ḥāmēš;* Gk. *pénte*). The use of a decimal system makes five a common round number, and it need not have great symbolic significance. There are five books of the Law of Moses (Pentateuch); the book of Psalms is divided into five books; Canticles, Ruth, Lamentations, Ecclesiastes, and Esther are designated the Five Scrolls or Megilloth; and there are five sections of Jesus' teachings in the Gospel of Matthew. Five is common in legal penalties (Ex. 22:1 [MT 21:37]; Nu. 18:16), multiples of five are used for measurements (Ezk. 40:15) and administrative divisions (Ex. 18:21; Dt. 1:15). There are fifty days in the Feast of Weeks (Lev. 23:16) and fifty years in the Jubilee (Lev. 25:10f.), but these may be the square of the sacred number seven plus one. The woman at the well had five husbands (Jn. 4:18); Jesus fed the five thousand with five loaves (Mt. 14:17-21); there were five wise and five foolish virgins (Mt. 25:2).

*F. Seven* (Heb. *šeḇaʿ*; Gk. *heptá*). The number seven is the most significant symbolic number in the Bible, appearing in some manner in almost six hundred passages. It was a sacred number in virtually all the ancient Semitic cultures. Some attribute its importance to the worship of seven heavenly bodies: sun, moon, and five known planets. Others suggest, more probably, that it reflects the division of the lunar month into four seven-day weeks. In the OT the week has seven days with the seventh being the sabbath (Gen. 2:2f.). Seven is also important because it is the sum of two other numbers with sacred and symbolic importance, three and four.

Seven is very prominent in passages dealing with ritual observance and oath taking. Indeed, the Hebrew number seven (*šeḇaʿ*) and the verb "swear, take an oath" (*šāḇaʿ*) are etymologically related. Examples of the ritual importance of seven are: the number of lambs that confirmed an oath (Gen. 21:29f.), of Balaam's bulls, rams, and altars (Nu. 23:1, 14, 29), and of lambs for festal offering (28:11, 19, 27); the structure of sacred objects, such as the candlestick (Ex. 25:31-37; Zec. 4:2), temple furnishings (1 K. 7:17), the temple steps (Ezk. 40:22), and the width of the temple entrance (41:3). The consecration of priests (Ex. 29:30, 35, 37), the Feast of Unleavened Bread (34:18), seclusion for uncleanness (Lev. 12:2; etc.), the period before circumcision of a newborn (v. 3), and the Feast of Tabernacles (23:34) all lasted seven days. God promised sevenfold vengeance upon the slayer of Cain (Gen. 4:15); there was sevenfold sprinkling of blood in the ritual for the Day of Atonement (Lev. 16:14, 19), and sevenfold sprinkling or bathing for lepers (Lev. 14:7, 16, 27, 51; 2 K. 5:10, Naaman). The sabbath day and the sabbatical year were both the seventh.

Although in some instances the number seven may be meant literally, its symbolic significance is not far beneath the surface. Jacob served seven years for Rachel (Gen. 29:20) and bowed down seven times to Esau (33:3). There were seven years of plenty and seven of famine in Pharaoh's dream (Gen. 41:53f.). The Israelites marched seven days with seven priests blowing seven trumpets at Jericho (Josh. 6:8ff.). Samson had a seven-day marriage feast (Jgs. 14:12) and seven locks of hair (16:19) and was bound with seven bowstrings (v. 7). Jethro had seven daughters (Ex. 2:16) and Job seven sons and seven daughters (Job 1:2). Jesse (1 S. 16:10), Saul (2 S. 21:6), and Sceva (Acts 19:4) had seven sons. Elijah's servant ascended seven times to the top of Carmel (1 K. 18:43f.); Nebuchadrezzar had the furnace made seven times hotter (Dnl. 3:19) and was mad for seven times or years (Dnl. 4:16, 23, 25, 32). Anna enjoyed seven years of wedded life ( Lk. 2:36). There were seven loaves for the four thousand, and seven baskets of fragments (Mt. 15:34-37 par. ). There were seven demons cast out of Mary Magdalene (Lk. 8:2), and seven ministers of the church at Jerusalem (Acts 6:3ff.).

Seven is an especially prominent number in apocalyptic literature, e.g., in 1 and 2 Enoch and 2 Esdras, although it is curiously absent in the apocalyptic portions of Daniel. It is amazingly frequent in the book of Revelation: seven churches (1:4); seven golden candlesticks (v. 12); seven stars (v. 16); seven angels (v. 20); seven lamps of fire (4:5); seven spirits of God (1:4; 3:1; 4:5); a book with seven seals (5:1); a lamb with seven horns and seven eyes (v. 6); seven angels with seven trumpets (8:2); a dragon (12:3) and a beast (13:1) with seven heads; seven last plagues (15:1); and seven golden bowls (v. 7).

The Bible also has many examples, too numerous to mention, of sevenfold groupings in which the number seven is not explicitly employed.

Several multiples of seven are important. Seventy is the natural human life span (Ps. 90:10; Isa. 23:15). There were thought to be seventy nations on the earth (Gen. 10; 1 En. 89:59f.). This concept is involved in the translation of the Hebrew Bible into Greek for the seventy nations of the world, completed in legend in seventy days by seventy scholars and called the Septuagint (LXX) (cf. the Letter of Aristeas). The seventy disciples are probably to be seen as sent to the seventy nations (Lk. 10). We are to forgive seventy times seven (Mt. 18:22)). The genealogy of Jesus in Mt. 1 is organized into three groups of fourteen generations (v.17).

*G. Six* (Heb. *šēš*; Gk. *héx*), *Eight* (Heb. *šᵉmōneh*; Gk. *oktṓ*), *Nine* (Heb. *tēšaʿ*; Gk. *ennéa*). These numbers do not seem to play any great symbolic role in the Bible. Their importance seems to derive from their position before or after a significant sacred number (seven or ten).

The world is created in six days, with humanity created

on the sixth day (Gen. 1), the sabbath coming on the seventh (2:1-3). Hebrew slaves are to work for six years and be freed in the seventh (Ex. 21:2). There are six steps to the throne in Solomon's temple, but this is to provide for the symbolically more important twelve lions (1 K. 10:19f.).

Male children were circumcised on the eighth day (Gen. 17:12; Lev. 12:3; Lk. 1:59; 2:21; Phil. 3:5). The eighth day for the cleansing of a Nazirite (Nu. 6:10) and for the final assembly of the Feast of the Tabernacles (Lev. 23:36) is the day after a sacred period of seven days. 1 Pet. 3:20 notes that eight people were saved in the ark of Noah; Justin interpreted this allegorically (*Dial.* 138.1) to represent the eighth day of resurrection.

Nine lepers out of the ten healed failed to return for thanks (Lk. 17:17). The ninety-nine are significant as one less than a hundred (Mt. 18:12; Lk. 15:4).

*H. Ten* (Heb. *ʿeśer*; Gk. *déka*). Ten derives its main significance from being the basis of the decimal system, which no doubt derives from simple calculations on the fingers. Ten is thus a convenient rounded figure for an amount greater than a few. The most important uses of ten in the OT are the Ten Commandments or Decalogue (Ex. 20:2-17; Dt. 5:6-21) and the tithe (Gen. 14:20; Nu. 18:21, 26: Dt. 26:12).

Furnishings of the tabernacle or temple are often measured in ten or its multiples (Ex. 26; 1 K. 6–7; 2 Ch. 4; Ezk. 45). Ten righteous men would have saved Sodom (Gen. 18:32). There were also ten antediluvian patriarchs (Gen. 5), ten postdiluvian patriarchs (Gen. 11:10-30), ten plagues against Egypt (Ex. 7:8–11:10), ten testings of the Lord in the wilderness (Nu. 14:22), ten elders who accompanied Boaz (Ruth 4:2), ten temptations of Abraham (Jub. 19:8), ten virgins in the parable (Mt. 25:1), ten pieces of silver (Lk. 15:8).

The book of Revelation has a special interest in the number ten. Ten days of tribulation are predicted for the church at Smyrna (2:10), a red dragon and a beast with seven heads and ten horns (12:3; 13:1; 17:3, 7, 12, 16; cf. Dnl. 7:24), ten royal diadems (Rev. 13:1), and ten kings (17:12).

Ten played a prominent role in later Jewish life and practice. The tetragrammaton was uttered by the high priest ten times on the Day of Atonement. Ten persons constitute a congregation in the synagogue and must be present at a nuptial blessings. A row of comforters of the bereaved numbered ten.

*I. Twelve* (Heb. *šᵉnêm ʿāśār*; Gk. *dṓdeka*). In Mesopotamian cultures twelve was significant because of the twelve months in the lunar year, the twelve signs of the Zodiac, and the Sumerian sexagesimal numerical system. These factors may account for the importance of twelve in the Bible, since many scholars relate the number of Israel's tribes to the months of the lunar year and tribal responsibilities at the central sanctuary. Even if this was the original significance of the number twelve, its further significance in the Bible is based almost entirely on the fact that there were twelve tribes of Israel. The twelve tribes are surely reflected in the twelve pillars set up by Moses (Ex. 24:4), the jewels in the high priest's breastplate (28:11), twelve cakes of bread (Lev. 24:5), twelve spies (Nu. 13), twelve rods (17:2), twelve stones in the Jordan (Josh. 4:9), twelve officers of Solomon (1 K. 4:7), and the twelve stones in Elijah's altar (18:31).

Even in the NT the twelve apostles surely reflect the tribes of Israel (Mt. 10:1-5 par.). Paul, before Agrippa, asserts membership in the twelve tribes and claims the promises given them (Acts 26:7). The common use of twelve in the book of Revelation is also rooted, most probably, in the twelve tribes (Rev. 7:4-8; 12:1; 21:12, 14, 16, 21; 22:2). The number is associated with the completeness of divine election applied first to Israel and later to the Church as the New Israel. It derives some significance from being the product of the sacred numbers three and four. Philo called it a perfect number.

*J. One Thousand* (Heb. *ʾelep̄;* Gk. *chiliás* and *chílioi*). In the OT the number one thousand and its multiples are often used as a rounded or hyperbolic number for a large amount (already discussed in IV above). One thousand (or the plural thousands) is often used for numbers beyond counting. God shows steadfast love to thousands of those who love Him and keep his commandments (Ex. 20:6; Dt. 5:10; 7:9; Jer. 32:18). God's power is like "thousands upon thousands" of chariots (Ps. 68:17 [MT 18]). "A day in thy courts is better than a thousand elsewhere" (Ps. 84:10 [MT 11]). The difference between the divine and the human time scales is expressed in Ps. 90:4 (alluded to in 2 Pet. 3:8): "For a thousand years in thy sight are but as yesterday when it is past, or as a watch in the night."

The NT uses multiples of one thousand frequently. There were two thousand Gerasene swine (Mk. 5:13); five thousand were fed by Jesus on one occasion (Mt. 14:21 par.) and four thousand on another (Mt. 15:38 par.); three thousand were converted at Pentecost (Acts 2:41); five thousand believed the word (Acts 4:4). Paul mentions the seven thousand who did not bow the knee to Baal in the time of Elijah (Rom. 11:4; 1 K. 19:18), and the twenty-three thousand who died for their idolatry in the wilderness (1 Cor. 10:8; Nu. 25:1-18).

The book of Revelation makes frequent use of the number one thousand and its multiples. The heavenly hosts who praise God number "myriads of myriads and thousands of thousands "(5:11; cf. Dnl. 7:10). The number of the sealed is one hundred and forty-four thousand, twelve thousand out of each of the twelve tribes of Israel (Rev. 7:4-8; 14:1-3). A time of one thousand two hundred and sixty days ( = 3½ years?) is mentioned in 11:3 and 12:6. At the end of that time seven thousand will perish in an earthquake (11:13).

Six references to a period of a thousand years occur in Rev. 20:2-7. This is the period for which Satan is bound and after which will come the final conflict, the vanquishing of evil forces, and the establishment of God's kingdom. Already in the early Church this passage had given rise to the concept of a MILLENNIUM (Latin *mille,* "thousand" and *annus,* "year") as a thousand-year kingdom without evil prior to the end of history. It is attested in Barn. 15:3-9; Irenaeus *Adv. haer.* v.32-36; Justin *Dial.* 81; Tertullian *Adv. Marc.* 3.24; 4.31, but it is rejected by Origen *De prin.* 2.11.2 and Augustine *Civ. Dei* 20.7.

***VI. Gematria.***–This peculiar form of numerology was used for the interpretation of the Scriptures in later Judaism and adopted by some early Christians. The word itself is a Hebraized form of the Gk. *geōmetría,* used to mean "reckoning by numbers." The method employed the numerical values of the letters of the alphabet to find hidden meaning in scriptural passages (see the chart above). Only traces of the method can be found in the OT, but examples are more common in the Talmud and Midrashim, and the Cabalistic literature carries the unlimited possibilities of this method to incredible extremes. Rabbi Eliezer ben Yose the Galilean (*ca.* A.D. 130-160) listed gematria as the twenty-ninth of his thirty-two hermeneutical rules *(Sepher Kerithuth).*

Perhaps the best known of the possible examples of gematria in the OT is Gen. 14:14, in which 318, given as the number of Abraham's trained servants, equals the sum of the numerical equivalents for the Hebrew letter in the name Eliezer (אליעזר: 1 + 30 + 10 + 70 + 7 + 200). It is obvious that any desired meaning can be obtained simply by manipulating the letters of some scriptural passage. Unfortunately some still claim legitimacy for this interpretative method.

The only clear example of a biblical writer's use of gematria is the mysterious number of the beast, 666, or 616 in variant readings (Rev. 13:18). Most scholars are inclined to believe that these numbers represent a name whose letters add up to one of these numbers. The most likely name seems to be Nero Caesar, which because of two possible spellings can add up to either 616 or 666.

***Bibliography***.–O. Becker, *Das mathematische Denken der Antike* (1957); R. E. D. Clark, *Journal of the Transaction of the Victoria Institute*, 87(1955); 82-90; J. J.Davis, *Biblical Numerology* (1968); *DNTT*, II, (1976), 683-704; G. R. Driver, "Sacred Numbers and Round Figures," in F. F. Bruce, ed., *Promise and Fulfillment* (*Festschrift* S. H. Hooke; 1963), pp. 62-90; S. Gandz, "Complementary Fractions in Bible and Talmud," *Louis Ginsberg Memorial Volume* (1945), pp. 143-157; A. Heller, *Biblische Zahlensymbolik* (1936); K. Menninger, *Zahlwort und Ziffer*, (1957), 127ff.; O. Neugebauer, *Vorgriechische Mathematik* (1934); *Exact Sciences in Antiquity* (2nd ed. 1957); T. E. Peet, *BJRL*, 15 (1931), 409-441; W. Roth, *Numerical Sayings in the OT* (*SVT*, 13; 1965); *TDNT*, I, *s.v.* ἀριθμέω, ἀριθμός (O. Rühle); J. W. Wenham, *Tyndale Bulletin*, 18 (1967), 19-53.

B. C. BIRCH

**NUMBERING.** *See* CENSUS; ENROLLMENT; MUSTER.

**NUMBERS, BOOK OF.** The fourth book in the Pentateuch.

I. Introduction
   A. Title
   B. Outline
   C. Pentateuchal Context
   D. Sources, Composition, Author, Date
   E. Literary Structure
II. Theological Message
   A. Character of the People
   B. Character of God
   C. Importance of Cult and Ritual
   D. Recognition of the Authority of God's Chosen Leaders
   E. Gift of the Land
III. Special Problems
IV. Balaam Oracles
   A. Analysis
   B. Inscription from Tell Deir ʿallā
V. NT

***I. Introduction***.–*A. Title*. The English title is a translation of the Vulgate title, *Numeri*, which in turn is a translation (not transliteration) of the LXX title, *Arithmoi*. Several names were given to the book in Hebrew manuscripts. In modern Hebrew Bibles the title is the fourth major word in the first verse, *bᵉmiḏbār*, "in the wilderness." Another title used often is *wayᵉḏabbēr*, "and he [Yahweh] said," the first word in the MT. The LXX, Vulgate, and English titles were not well chosen, for they focus too heavily on the census lists of chs. 1 and 26 and the frequent occurrence of numbers elsewhere in the book. The Hebrew title *bᵉmiḏbār* is more suitable, for it indicates the geographical locale of most of the significant events that happened to Israel.

*B. Outline*. Numbers is a dynamic book permeated by a sense of movement. Its structure is discernible, though more difficult to demonstrate than the structure of some other OT books. The outline below attempts to show one viable way that the contents may be analyzed.

I. Preparations for Leaving (1:1–10:10)
   A. Israel and Tabernacle Arrangements (1:1–6:27)
      1. Census of Israel's Military Men (1:1–46)
      2. Arrangement of Israel Around the Tabernacle (1:47–2:34)
      3. Census, Placement, and Duties of Levites (3:1–4:49)
      4. Instructions to Keep the Camp Holy and Undefiled (5:1–6:21)
      5. Aaronic Benediction (6:22-27)
   B. Dedicatory Offerings and Consecration of Levites (7:1–8:26)
      1. Dedication of Altar (7:1-89)
      2. Consecration of Levites and Care of Lampstands (8:1-26)
   C. First Passover Kept (9:1-14)
   D. Preview and Anticipation of Leaving Sinai (9:15–10:10)
II. Israel's Wilderness Experiences (10:11–20:21)
   A. Events Before Kadesh (10:11–12:15)
      1. Tribes Set out from Sinai (10:11-36)
      2. People's Murmuring and Craving; God's Response (11:1-35)
      3. Moses' Uniqueness Challenged: Miriam and Aaron (12:1-15)
   B. Events Around Kadesh Highlighted (12:16–20:21)
      1. Unbelief and Evil Report of the Spies (12:16–13:33)
      2. Murmuring Against Moses and Aaron; God's Mercy and Judgment (14:1-38)
      3. God's Judgment; Israel's Arrogance and Chagrin Before Canaanites (14:39-45)
      4. Supplemental Legislation Pointing to Settlement in Canaan (15:1-41)
      5. Moses' Authority and Position Challenged: Korah, Dathan, Abiram (16:1-50 [MT 16:1–17:15])
      6. Aaron's Rod (17:1-13 [MT 16-28])
      7. Priestly and Levitical Duties Placed on Aaron and Sons (18:1-32)
      8. Purification of Person Defiled by a Corpse (19:1-22)
      9. Death of Miriam and Rebellion of Moses and Aaron (20:1-13)
      10. Edom Opposes Israel's Departure from Kadesh (20:14-21)
III. Israel's Experiences Approaching Canaan (20:22–36:13)
   A. Events Before Plains of Moab (20:22–21:35)
      1. Death of Aaron at Mt. Hor (20:22-29)
      2. Defeat of Canaanites at Hormah (21:1-3)
      3. People's Rebellion Against Moses and Aaron; Fiery Serpents (21:4-9)
      4. Journey to Bashan: Defeat of Sihon, Amorites, Og (21:10-35)
   B. Events in the Area of Moab (22:1–36:13)
      1. Balak and Balaam Episode: Israel Cannot Be Cursed (22:1–24:25)
      2. Apostasy at Baal of Peor (25:1-16)
      3. Second Census of Israel (26:1-65)
      4. Adaptation of Inheritance Laws and Moses' Successor Chosen (27:1-23)
      5. Recapitulation of Various Offerings; Sabbath Law Added (28:1–29:40 [MT 30:1])
      6. Instructions Concerning Women's Vows (30:1-16 [MT 2-17])
      7. Holy War Against Midian: Laws of Holy War Elaborated (31:1-54)
      8. The Transjordanian Lands Allotted (32:1-42)
      9. Review of Israel's Journeys from Egypt to Moab (33:1-56)
      10. Boundaries and Divisions of Canaan Delineated (34:1-29)
      11. Levitical Sites and Cities of Refuge (35:1-34)
      12. Further Adaptation of Inheritance Laws (36:1-13)

Because the major concern of the book is to trace

the theological significance of the journey of Israel as it moved toward the promised inheritance of Canaan, Israel is pictured on the go, or preparing to go, throughout the various sections of the book. Appropriate events and legal material punctuate the book whenever they relate to (1) danger of Israel's failure to receive the promises and hence forfeit its place as God's people, or (2) further development of Israel's preparedness to receive the promises. The content of the book is shaped to serve the above goals and purposes. From the start (1:1–10:10) Israel is goal (future)-oriented as it prepares to march toward the land of Canaan. Chs. 10:1–20:21 record the journey from Sinai and narrate the theologically important episodes that fill the way before Kadesh (10:11–12:16) and highlight the time at or near Kadesh (13:1–20:21). Events before the plains of Moab (20:22–21:35) and in Moab are described (chs. 22–36). The story is not consummated, however, finding its immediate denouement in the book of Deuteronomy and ultimately in Joshua-Judges. The content of Numbers is fully coherent and cogent only when its place in the broader theological, historical, and literary context of the Pentateuch (or Hexateuch) is recognized.

*C. Pentateuchal Context.* Numbers must be understood in the light of the whole Pentateuch, since it reflects several of the main concerns of the Pentateuch. For example, 1:1–10:10 completes at least three major themes introduced in Exodus: the necessary arrangement of Israel around the tabernacle and God's presence after its completion (Ex. 40; Nu. 2), the dedication of the altar (Ex. 27:1-8; 38:1-7; Nu. 7:1-89), the fulfillment of God's promise to multiply the people (Gen. 12:1-3; 15; cf. Ex. 1:1-7; Nu. 2). The journey toward Canaan fulfils many promises given in both Genesis and Exodus indicating that Israel would enter its own land (Ex. 3:17; 6:4, 8; 23:20-26; etc.). The legal material in Numbers is often a development or adaptation of laws found in Exodus or Leviticus or new legislation necessary as Israel developed and contemplated its inheritance. The Balaam oracles (Nu. 22–24; see IV below) reaffirm the immutable blessings of God upon His people (Gen. 12:1-3; 15; Ex. 1:7, 12) in faithfulness to His word, and also His cursing (Moab) of those who would curse Israel. The book points toward Deuteronomy in various ways, e.g., geographical location, theological preparedness, imminent death of Moses (cf. Nu. 27:12-14; Dt. 31:14-16; 34:1-12). Numbers does not appear to be a mere literary construct between Exodus-Leviticus and Deuteronomy, but rather a vital historical necessity (and a humbling one) that explains why Israel did not immediately enter the land of Canaan upon leaving Egypt. Many other connections between Numbers and other pentateuchal books will be evident in the discussion below.

*D. Sources, Composition, Author, Date.* Since these topics are interrelated, they will be treated together here.

Numbers is replete with nearly every type of biblical literature (see esp. M. Duvshani, *Beth Mikra,* 24 [1978], 27-32). Various literary types sometimes indicate various original sources; this seems to be the case in Numbers.

According to the book the original impetus for the recording of much of the material was from Moses. It indicates numerous times that Moses received instructions from God. It normally does not indicate whether Moses recorded these instructions in writing (Nu. 33:2 only demands that the writing took place at Moses' command). He may have written some or much of the material himself, or he may have had others record the material (cf. Ex. 18:13-23). It seems that he probably did both. In Nu. 31:21 Eleazar orally disseminates to others commands that Moses had evidently received. Aaron also received revelation from God (19:21), as did Eleazar (26:1, 63). In 5:31 a priest is to write down certain curses in a book (Heb. *sēp̄er*) upon instructions from Moses. It is clear that a priestly circle of influence helped shape the materials of Numbers before the present book was formed. Since priests and scribes (Heb. *sōp̄ᵉrîm*) were generally responsible for preserving the ancient traditions of their people, this situation in Israel is expected. Blocks of priestly material would have been available to a later composer, whether Moses himself, a contemporary, or a later compiler.

But both the content and style reflect more than a priestly ambience. The census lists in the book may have been produced by incipient bureaucratic levels of persons (cf. Ex. 18:13-23), but this is uncertain because the amount of such activity in Moses' time is not known in detail. This type of activity was paralleled in other ancient Near Eastern cultures (cf., e.g., E. A. Speiser, *BASOR,* 149 [Feb. 1958], 17-25; C. H. Gordon, *Ugaritic Literature,* [1949], pp. 124f.; Mendenhall). Boundary lists (Nu. 34; *LBHG,* rev., pp. 62, 69), spy reports (oral and written? — Nu. 13:25-33; cf. S. Wagner, *ZAW,* 76 [1964], 255-269), pagan narrative of unknown origin (Nu. 22–24; see W. F. Albright, *JBL,* 63 [1944], 207-233), ancient Israelite poetry (10:35f.; 21:14f., 17f., 27-30), some coming from an ancient Book of the Wars of Yahweh, war narratives (from the same book? — 21:1-3, 14f.; 31:1-54), and wilderness travel lists (33:1-49; Davies, *Tyndale Bulletin*) are part of the plethora of literary genres found in Numbers and in the ancient Near East before and after a probable composition date for the book. The multiplicity of sources and hands probably explains the tendency for those following the classical documentary approach to Numbers to affirm several ancient traditions and sources within and outside the accepted critical documents.

It is evident that many hands and oral traditions provided this diverse mix of literature. Ancient Near Eastern studies have shown that all of the above literary features of Numbers were in use by the 13th century. (See Y. Kaufmann, *Religion of Israel* [Eng. tr. repr. 1972], esp. pp. 153-211; he argues that much of "P" is quite old.) So one observes blocks of "priestly" material, narrative material (with legal and ritual material interwoven), technical official census lists, genealogical lists, "archival" materials and non-Israelite blocks of material (reworked to some extent by an Israelite compiler), and some of this is intertwined with snatches of ancient poetry of various kinds. In spite of this situation some basic literary structure is evident in the book. Moses could have assembled the material or he could have directed its utilization. (The use of the 3rd person does not negate Mosaic authorship.) The historical integrity and theological veracity of the material is still intact even if a person other than Moses put the material into its present form in order to dovetail into the larger context of the Pentateuch. Possibly a decision on the final date of the book's composition should await further discoveries.

In *Prolegomena to the History of Israel* (Eng. tr. 1878; repr. 1973) J. Wellhausen established the dominant critical position on the composition of the Pentateuch — the documentary hypothesis that divided the Pentateuch into four main sources, J, E, D, and P (*see also* CRITICISM II.D.5; PENTATEUCH IV.C). One of the most important commentaries based upon these results was by G. B. Gray. He divided the literature in Numbers among J, E, and P (pp. xxix-xxxix). He found different levels of P material in Numbers and attributed three-fourths of the book to this source. He used these symbols to show the different levels of P material in the book: $P^g$, the fundamental priestly work that focused on sacred institutions (*ca.* 5th cent. B.C.); $P^s$, material secondary to $P^g$ and later in origin; $P^x$, legal material not original to $P^g$ but not later than $P^g$.

The rest of the material was given to J and E sources (*ca.* 9th and 8th cents., respectively). The book reached its final form in the 3rd cent. B.C.

Several presuppositions of this position must be noted. One presupposition was that priestly (P) institutions and concepts of the kind found in most of the book of Numbers appeared very late in the ancient Near Eastern world. Israel's highly elaborate cult and ritual constructed around a central tabernacle was, therefore, an indication that the P content of Numbers must be a description of Israel's cult and ritual in the time of the compiler (*ca.* 4th cent.). Hence, the material was a retrojection of priestly traditions, after the Exile and return, back into an archetypal antiquity. The purpose of this retrojection was to "validate" the circumstance of the compiler's own day.

The critical view of Israel's early worship assumed that it was free, spontaneous, uninhibited, and simple, but gradually became encased in a tradition of cold, formal, rigid legalism. The P writer(s) represented the last stages of this religious development along with 1-2 Chronicles (postexilic books). This general presupposition was supported by appealing to the centralization of the cult assumed by P since centralization of the cult occurred under Josiah (2 K. 23 *ca.* 621 B.C.) some time earlier. (For a discussion of the supposed historical value of Numbers see Gray, pp. xlii-xlvii; Sturdy, pp. 4-6.)

M. Noth broke some new ground. His idea of the composition of Numbers is tied closely to his advocacy of a Tetrateuch (Genesis-Numbers) instead of a Pentateuch and to his understanding of the Deuteronomistic history (Deuteronomy-2 Kings). He noted that Numbers taken as a whole in isolation from the Pentateuch might seem to be "an unsystematic collection of innumerable pieces of tradition of very varied content, age and character ('Fragment Hypothesis')" (Noth, *Numbers,* p. 4). But Noth went on to describe a compositional makeup for Numbers that includes P as the dominant material, a Yahwistic source (J), E, which appears first in 21:21f., D (appearing basically late in the book and used to connect other materials to the "Deuteronomistic history"), and a good amount of late material (e.g., 5:1–9:14; chs. 25–31; 33–36 [includes some D material]) not susceptible to the usual source-analysis approach. He spoke of "old sources," meaning J and E, but these sources contain a bare minimum of ancient material, which would have had an oral history before being placed into the narratives of J and E.

The oldest material is the poetical material in chs. 22–24; 10:35f.; 21:27b-30. The spy story might be the remnant of an old tradition (chs. 13–14). Nevertheless, Noth maintained that Numbers contains an immense amount of late material, and "it certainly originated in the post-exilic cultic community in Jerusalem and is of interest and importance for our knowledge of the ordinances and concepts prevalent in that late period" (*Numbers,* p. 10).

J. Sturdy (pp. 1-9) supported a view of one original line of tradition that gave rise to the Pentateuch. He located this tradition in the monarchy under David and Solomon from whence it passed to the southern kingdom. This tradition gradually assimilated various traditions not already in the older tradition. The so-called evidence for E is in reality the inconsistencies caused by this assimilation of tradition by "J." This original line of tradition first crystallized *ca.* 1000-980 B.C. The P work absorbed this earlier tradition *ca.* 500-450 B.C. The historical worth of Numbers still is considered negligible according to Sturdy. The forty years of wanderings are merely J's theological reflection, and the tabernacle and its cult and ritual are the idealization of P. Both P and J seek to express the concerns of their day through drawing up theological stories in Numbers.

The above examples show that some details and some presuppositions of the original critical position have been modified and some scholars of this school allow for some reflection of preexilic practices even in the P material. The late origin of the various sources is still generally maintained, however, and a very low view of the historicity of the content of Numbers is asserted. Although some original historical veracity in tradition underlies the text, the story line of the present text is largely a theological construct.

Conservative scholars of the 20th cent. find no problems with the existence of sources used in the construction of Numbers. Above we concluded that several "sources" were used in the compilation of Numbers. One could call the priestly blocks of material "P," but the other material reflects many more kinds of self-contained sources dependent upon and interlocking with each other. This situation seems to argue for a final compiler and against separate original sources of the supposed nature of J E P. This also agrees with Sturdy's literary tendency to find a single line of tradition outside "P" with additions.

The material is put into a pattern to give a theological message, but this does not negate its historicity, which should be accepted until disproven. In Israel theology and history were inextricably linked to form an inseparable mosaic of meaning. The basic procedure of Israel's theology was to review history and draw great theological lessons from it.

The content of the history in Numbers no longer militates against its thirteenth-century historical provenance (cf. Gray, pp. xlii-xlvii). Much evidence from the ancient Near East coalesces to give the content an air of historical veracity (cf. Wenham, *Numbers,* pp. 23-25, for a good summary). These facts do not prove the historicity of Numbers, but as Wenham noted, "This evidence lends weight to the book's own testimony that the traditions on which it is based originated in the Mosaic period" (p. 24). R. Rendtorff (for Genesis; *Das überlieferungsgeschichtliche Problem des Pentateuch* [*BZAW,* 147, 1977]) and Wenham (for Numbers) also suppose that the biblical materials may profitably be looked at as original blocks of material that developed and were later combined by skilled compilers. This seems to be a viable explanation of the way Numbers may have come together. Connecting links would have been added and ancient poetry would have already been embedded in these blocks of ancient material. There is, however, no reason to suppose that the origination of the materials in Numbers could not have been in the Mosaic era. It is, of course, impossible to know when the material was molded into its present form, but dates from the early entry into Canaan (1250 B.C.) until the time of the breakup of the monarchy (*ca.* 931 B.C.) seem viable options at this time.

*E. Literary Structure.* The structure of Numbers is subordinated to the requirements of the theological-historical message, with the author's theological concern giving the book its structural continuity.

Some structural features of Numbers have been outlined above. The first major part of the book (1:1–10:10) records the preparation of Israel to move from Sinai toward Canaan. Material in 1:1–6:21 is placed before events in 7:1–9:16 even though the events in 1:1–6:21 actually took place after 7:1–9:16 (cf. 1:1; 7:1; 9:1, 15; 10:10; Ex. 40:1, 17). The sequence seems theologically, as well as literarily, acceptable, for the mustering of Israel around the tabernacle indicates the writer's concern for the central shrine of Israel. God's holiness permeates the camp and it must not be defiled (1:47-54). Before normal operations within the sphere of Yahweh's holiness can begin the congregation must be properly protected from Yahweh's holiness (1:53). Certain laws are added which are aimed at keeping the camp holy and undefiled lest Yahweh's holiness destroy the camp (5:1–6:21). The Aaronic benediction is fittingly placed at 6:22-27 because the holy congregation has been established. The dedication of the altar is subordinate to the establishment of Israel around the tabernacle (7:1-89). After the consecration of the Levites the people can keep the first Passover (9:1-14), and Israel's final preparation for moving out of the camp is described, including a specific description of how and when the people moved.

The writer has arranged the rest of his book to describe Israel's wilderness experiences (10:11–20:21) and its experiences in the approach to Canaan (20:22–36:13). To expect a perfectly "logical" arrangement of material in a book that purports to record the vicissitudes of Israel in the wilderness during a time of confusion and rebellion is perhaps unrealistic. However, the writer's material is arranged on principles within this broad dynamic structure: (1) rebellious and murmuring responses of the people cluster in various places to demonstrate theological lessons; (2) the movement of Israel from location to location is used to give the book action and continuity with events before Kadesh (10:11–12:15) and subsequently. God's judgment against Israel's unbelief is a major motif (14:39-45) that is fulfilled before Israel leaves the wilderness (26:64f.).

Various legal and ritual materials are added in 10:11–36:13. The principles that the writer(s) used for placing this material are not immediately clear. That it was vital to the existence of Israel is the reason for its inclusion and may reflect three considerations. (1) The material concerns Israel on the move and is reflective of Israel's developing community life. Legal and ritual material has an organic connection to life and hence develops as new understanding, needs, and demands arise. (2) The material is needed as the approach to and settlement of the land of Canaan are more fully contemplated. (3) The material also has exhortative value (esp. ch. 15); e.g., the strategic placement of the second census list gives emphasis to the fact that Israel's punishment for unbelief is over (26:64f.).

***II. Theological Message.***–The theological message of Numbers cannot be discussed in isolation from the rest of the Pentateuch. The chronological and geographical links among the books of the Pentateuch reinforce the fundamental theological themes of these books. Each book contributes in its own way to pentateuchal theology, but it is often a matter of emphasis rather than theological uniqueness that differentiates one book from the others. Numbers completes the establishment of God's ideal relationship to His people in 1:1–10:10. The travel narratives of the book show how these arrangements worked out on the road to Canaan.

*A. Character of the People.* The people were to reflect their God — He was holy, they were to be holy. The program set forth in Ex. 6:6; 19:5f.; Leviticus, *passim,* made God's goal the creation of a kingdom of priests and a holy nation. Although there were different levels of consecration to God (holiness) such as lay, Levitical, priestly, high priestly, and Nazirite, from the outset God's presence at the center of His people demanded that everyone be holy unto Him. In Numbers God's presence made the camp itself holy, and Israel was instructed in how to maintain this holiness (e.g., 1:50-54; ch. 5; etc.) through their obedience to God's instructions. However, what the people were, as opposed to what they should have been, is a theme clearly expressed in Numbers. The unbelief, murmuring, and rebellion of Israel as depicted by the author is in stark contrast to the characteristics that should have marked Israel (cf. chs. 11; 12; 13–14; 16; 20:1-13; 21:4-9; 25:1-4; 26:63-65). Even Moses did not escape censure from the Lord (20:12; 27:12-14). The failures of the people are part of the continuing saga of the stubbornness and rebelliousness of Israel already evident in Exodus (Ex. 5; 15:22–16:36; 17:1-7; 32; 33). The underlying sin of the people is their unbelief clearly revealed in the events of chs. 13–14. The Israelites, to be God's people, were to exercise the faith of their father Abraham. If they would not obey God, He would chastise them. The ultimate threat of the annihilation of the people in the wilderness is reached in 14:10b-12. The people were expendable before God and only the gracious character of God in response to Moses' magnificent intercession delivered them. Nevertheless, the destruction of that generation of people (twenty years old and over) in effect meant that because of unbelief the generation of Israel that could have inherited all the promises did not do so.

*B. Character of God.* Israel's God dwelt among them (Ex. 40:34-38; Lev. 26:11f.; Nu. 1:47-54; 9:15-23), both to sanctify them and to destroy the evil from among them (e.g., 11:1-3). This closeness between a people and their God was considered unique by Israel (Dt. 4:7f.). His guidance was always with them and He blessed them with visible signs of His presence and leadership (9:15-23). God's holiness had to be treated with meticulous respect; therefore the Levites camped around the tabernacle of the testimony to protect the rest of Israel from the holy wrath of God (1:47-54). God's holiness demanded Israel's holiness and faithfulness if His presence was to continue (cf. Ex. 33). His holiness made the camp and the land holy, and Israel was to be careful not to defile the land or make it unclean (e.g., 36:29-34). Uncleanness was to be cared for according to the instructions of Yahweh (e.g., ch. 19).

God was the provider and preserver of Israel. Although He judged the people according to His word, He loved and preserved them according to His nature. Israel was cared for during the forty years of wanderings in the face of serious threats (cf. ch. 26), surviving only by the grace of the One who was judging them.

God's gracious nature is revealed in His decision to hearken unto Moses rather than annihilating the rebellious people (ch. 13–14). The prayer of Moses and the description of the gracious character of God in 14:13-19 recapitulates Ex. 32:9-13. God's response to intercession by Moses (esp. Nu. 14:13-19) illustrates His concern for Israel's plight.

The sovereignty of God is apparent throughout the book, but especially in the Balaam oracles, which tie His sovereignty to His covenantal promises. Israel's first encounter with a famous Mesopotamian soothsayer (see V below) might have been intimidating at best and possibly disastrous. However, these oracles proclaim that no pagan religious system will be able to remove the blessing that God had placed upon Israel (Gen. 12:1-3; 15:1-20). The king of Moab falls under the curse of Yahweh's covenant with Israel: because he tried to curse Israel, Balak brought a curse upon his own people. God's sovereignty extends over all history according to His covenant with Israel (24:20-25), and only He can effect blessings and curses on nations and peoples.

*C. Importance of Cult and Ritual.* The book of Numbers continues to show the importance of cult and ritual in ancient Israel. Even after the extensive regulations of Leviticus the author of Numbers found it necessary to add to the religious practices of the people to ensure their prosperity before Yahweh. Approaching a holy God, avoiding uncleanness, purifying oneself if unclean, ministering before the Lord in the affairs of the tabernacle — all these matters seem foreign to us, but are clearly the heart of the matter for Israel as they worship before God with a good conscience from a stance of faith.

The support of the tabernacle and its workers was vitally

important (Nu. 18), and Israel's approach to God was to be one of respect and awe. Anthropological studies have helped us begin to understand the issues involved in this sacrosanct arena of ancient society (Gray, *Numbers*, pp. 47f.; Wenham, *Numbers*, pp. 25-39; Douglas). The holiness of God, contrasted with the unholiness and uncleanness of humanity, necessitated the cult and ritual, requiring God to delineate an acceptable way in which His people might approach Him without devastating consequences.

*D. Recognition of the Authority of God's Chosen Leaders.* Several episodes in Numbers establish the true line of religious authority within Israel. Moses, the priests, and the Levites are all confirmed in their positions. Chs. 12 and 16 illustrate the challenges that were placed before Moses. Each time confirmation was given to Moses' unique authority and position in God's economy of creating His own people (esp. 12:6-8; 16:25-50). Moses' position and plenary powers were not passed on to anyone in the way that he had embodied them. Moses exercised authority over Aaron the high priest, over the judges and military commanders, and over those empowered with the prophetic spirit. He exercised all the various powers of prophet, priest, and king (cf. esp. 15:32-36; 27; 31; 36). Ch. 17 confirms the Aaronic priests and the Levites as those who will "bear iniquity" for the people in regard to the sanctuary. Any others who take this ministry by force shall die (17:12f.; 18:7). The establishment of the structures of society and the lines of authority were highly important to the developing "kingdom of priests and a holy nation" of Israel.

*E. Gift of the Land.* The goal of the travel narratives of Numbers is Canaan. The land is as much a theological goal as it is a mere physical goal, however. The inheritance of the land consummates a vital part of the promise-fulfillment theme running through the Pentateuch.

Such inheritance is possible because God owns the land and gives it to whatever nation He wills. He therefore gives it freely to Israel (13:1f.; 14:8, 23, 39; 32:7-9; 33:53). But Israel because of unbelief failed to enter it the first time (14:11), and God refused to let Israel's rebellious invasion succeed (14:40-43). The land is a gift, the Lord owns the land, but Israel through exercise of faith must qualify to enter it (32:7-9, 15). Unbelief at Moab would have resulted in disaster again (32:14-15). Only if God went into the land with the people would they be successful in attaining possession (14:13-42; 32:20-22). Above all it is clear that possession of the land was ultimately dependent upon the moral and religious faithfulness of Israel to Yahweh and His Torah. The retention of the land was dependent upon Israel's faithfulness to the Mosaic instructions. The land would otherwise be defiled (e.g., 35:34) and Yahweh's continued presence that made the land holy would be in danger (33:56).

***III. Special Problems.***–A few of the most difficult problems encountered in a study of the book of Numbers have already been mentioned. Two issues deserve to be emphasized. A prominent concern has always been the exceedingly high numbers encountered in the book, especially in the census lists of chs. 1 and 26. The list in ch. 1 (v. 46) totals 603,550 men of twenty years of age or older. The total in ch. 26 is 601,730. This implies a total population of two to three million, a number that hardly seems appropriate.

It is hard to imagine the difficulties attendant upon sustaining two to three million people in the wilderness for forty years: food, sanitation, living space, morale. Some numbers appear internally inconsistent (e.g., the ratio of first-born males to all adult males was 1:27!). Each family would then appear to have had on the average twenty-seven sons and possibly as many daughters. Some verses indicate the smallness of Israel, such as Ex. 23:29f. where fear is expressed that Israel is too small to occupy the land if God drives out its inhabitants too fast. Dt. 6:6f. is somewhat ambiguous but seems to stress the small size of Israel compared to the inhabitants of Canaan. Nu. 13:27-29 indicates that Israel considered itself inadequate to overcome the inhabitants of the land. Finally, it is important to note that the whole population of the Promised Land was probably below three million people at this time (R. K. Harrison, *Intro. to the OT* [1969], p. 632). Several solutions have been offered to this knotty problem.

R. K. Harrison suggested (p. 633) that the numbers in the census lists rest upon some basis of understanding not now available to us. They represent "terms of relative power, triumph, importance" and are symbolic in some sense. They were meaningful to the ancients but we have lost the key. This suggestion is noteworthy. The fulfillment of Yahweh's promise to multiply Israel as the stars of heaven (Gen. 15:5) and the enormous deed of salvation at the Red Sea would call for some extraordinary expressions of God's deeds for Israel and His promise of fulfillment. A solution along these lines does not require a corrupt extant text and does not take the numbers in a strict literal sense.

Other scholars have been content to assert the literalness of the numbers. The physical multiplication of Israel to this extent was possible. The desert could have been much more supportive at an earlier date than it is now, although this is a moot issue since the miraculous intervention of God was precisely that which the text says preserved them several times in the face of sure destruction. This must remain a possibility but it hardly seems probable, based on archeological evidence of the demography of that time and geographical area (cf. Wenham, p. 67).

Several scholars have argued for the symbolic use of the numbers. M. Barnouin (*VT*, 27 [1977], 280-303) claimed that the numbers can be related to ancient Babylonian astronomical periods. But it seems highly doubtful that the biblical writer would have cared to relate the numbers to Babylonian astrology. It is also highly questionable that his original readers would have grasped or appreciated his point.

Several solutions to the problem have been offered based upon the assumption that the present text is corrupt. Some assume that *'elep̱* (usually signifying 1000) in the text was misunderstood by later copyists and the numbers have themselves become inaccurate because of this. In addition, the actual totals of the numbers may have been incorrectly passed on through the inadvertent dropping of noughts, etc. (For a full discussion see articles below by Clark, Mendenhall, J. Wenham.) One must conclude at present that objective material is needed before a solution will be possible

The historical or nonhistorical nature of the material in Numbers has occasioned warm controversy for some time. Numerous ancient Near Eastern archeological finds have tended to support the probablity of the historicity of numerous individual items and features of the book. The census lists no longer need to be considered fourth-century creations (see I.D above). Silver trumpets (Nu. 10) were used in Egypt at this time (K. A. Kitchen, *NBD*, p. 847) and ox-wagons were used by Egyptian pharaohs from 1470 B.C. Even the arrangement of Israel around the tabernacle with God in the center as king is reminiscent of the arrangement used by Rameses II in the 13th cent. when he went on campaigns (but cf. A. Kuschke, *ZAW*, 63 [1951], 74-105). The transmission of family records over long periods of time is found in Egyptian literature (Kitchen, *Tyndale Bulletin*, 5/6 [1960], 14-18). The design of the lampstand is found in the 15th-13th centuries. The use of spies in the land was an activity carried out also by the Hittites and Rameses II (cf. A. H. Gardiner, *Kadesh Inscriptions of Rameses II* [1960]). For the antiquity of the Balaam oracles see IV below. For the authenticity and coherence of the wilderness itinerary of Nu. 33 see Davies, *Way of the Wilderness*, pp. 58ff. The laws of Nu. 28–29 find a close resemblance in an Ugaritic ritual calendar from the 14th cent. B.C. (L. R. Fisher, *HTR*, 63 [1970], 485-501). This material could be multiplied, even though the goal has not been to prove the historicity of Numbers. This should be enough, however, to demonstrate the weakness of the position that would describe Numbers as neither authentic nor very ancient. The door is open to an assertion of the essential historicity of the book's content and perhaps especially of its P material.

Other problems abound in Numbers: the priesthood, the sometimes puzzling structure of the book, its legal material, etc., but here is not the place to discuss them in detail. E. E. CARPENTER

***IV. Balaam Oracles.**–A. Analysis*. The oracles are interesting from many standpoints. They represent an archaic form of Hebrew which witnesses to their antiquity. They sometimes describe God's past blessings on His people and at other points His unique future blessing of Israel.

The first poem (23:7-10) has a symmetrical pattern of synonymously parallel lines. The opening (v. 7a), middle (v. 9a), and closing (v. 10b) bicola consist of what Balaam has to say about himself: he was brought by the king of Moab, he is on the top of the rock to view the Israelites, and finally, he expresses the nostalgic thought that he would like to share in Israel's blessing in the end.

Flanking the middle bicolon are two quatrains about Israel. In the first (vv. 7a-8) Balaam expresses his frustration in not being able to curse them, and in the second (vv. 9a-10a) he observes the unique place that Israel has among the nations.

The second poem (Nu. 23:18-24) contains an introduction (v. 18) followed by two stanzas (vv. 19-21a, 21b-23) and a conclusion (v. 24). Here Balaam sees Yahweh as the one who forces him to bless Israel because Israel's deity is a God who must bring to pass His promised word. The figure of the stalking lion (v. 24) goes back to Jacob's prophetical oracle about Judah (Gen. 49:8-10). Indeed, Balaam will particularize the figure in the third oracle in 24:8f. At the beginning of stanza two (v. 21b), where the Hebrew text reads "the shout of the king," the LXX, the Tg. Onk., and the Sam. Pent. translate "royal majesty." Albright presented evidence to support the versions in this translation (p. 215 n. 43).

The third poem (24:3-9) has an introductory strophe (vv. 3f.) similar to that in the fourth poem (23:15f.). Then two stanzas flank the main oracle (v. 7b). A conclusion (v. 9b) answers back to v. 5, the opening line of the poem proper. These couplets are the only place where Israel is addressed in the poems (using the 2nd person sing.). The purpose of the poem is to predict Israel's coming monarchy. That is why the prophetic oracle is the apex of the poem (v. 7b).

The stanzas that flank the oracle present two contrasting views of Israel (these remind us of the peace and war standards from the Royal Tombs of Ur; see J. Finegan, *LAP*, Fig. 16; *ANEP*, nos. 303f.). Israel is described as a well-watered garden and flourishing cedars (vv. 5-7) and then as a warlike nation with the imagery of a wild ox and devouring lion (cf. Ezk. 19). The conclusion (v. 9) is a reminder of God's covenant promise to Abraham (Gen. 12:3), a promise that makes it impossible for God to turn His back on Israel at the whim of a Moabite king or a diviner from Mesopotamia.

The fourth poem has an introductory strophe almost identical to that of the third. In addition to his eyes being opened to see a vision, he hears the words of God (v. 16). The rest of this poem is oracular, i.e., the vision is descriptive of Israel's future king whose greatness has been alluded to in the apex of poem three (v. 7b). Now he is seen as the conqueror of the surrounding nations, especially Moab and Edom. The reference is, no doubt, to David and only in a secondary sense to the Messiah. The Dead Sea community made much of it as a prediction of the Messiah (1QM 11:6f.; see T. H. Gaster, *Dead Sea Scriptures* [rev. ed. 1964], pp. 296f.) but the NT does not. Note how Jeremiah in his curse on Moab integrates some of these words (v. 7b) with a quote from the poetic taunt of Moab in Nu. 21:27-30.

The rest of the Balaam poems (24:20-24) are short oracles concerning peoples whose history and destiny would overlap with Israel's. The Amalekites and Kenites are easily identified, but who are Asshur and Eber? And who are the sea-faring Kittim? At Qumrân the latter were identified as the Romans (F. M. Cross, *Ancient Library of Qumran* [rev. ed. repr. 1980], p. 124 n.). To others they are the Greeks or Philistines, but it seems wiser to leave these issues open. For example, Asshur need not be the Assyrians (cf. the Asshurites of Gen. 25:3 and 2 S. 2:9) and Eber here might conceivably be linked with Eber of Gen. 11:14-16. Cf. the 3rd-millennium king ʿEbrium of Ebla (Tell Mardikh), whose name is related to the root from which the term "Hebrew" (*ʿibrî*) comes. The latter originally had a wider meaning (social class?) than the term Israelite. *See* HABIRU.

*B. Inscription from Tell Deir ʿallā*. In 1967 at the Jordan Valley site of Tell Deir ʿallā archeologists found plaster fragments bearing a text in a language that exhibits both Canaanite and Old Aramaic features. The script is an Old Aramaic cursive type known also from certain Ammonite inscriptions. The fragments of plaster had originally been on a mud-brick wall or mud-brick stele within a sanctuary or other chamber where visitors could become acquainted with the message recorded. The writing was in two colors — red and black on white plaster — and archeologists have dated it to the end of the 8th and the beginning of the 7th cents. B.C. The *editio princeps* is by Hoftijzer and van der Kooij; see also the diss. by Carlton (Hackett).

The fascinating part of this text is the reference to Balaam the son of Beor as a religious leader who was obviously revered in Transjordan, just as we would expect from the biblical data. He is the leader of a cult that is not Yahwistic since the text clearly presents a polytheistic religion. The syntax and vocabulary are not unlike that of the OT; the text seems to be tied to Canaanite literary traditions (see McCarter).

Scholars have put the fragments together in two combinations (groups of fragments) and are still unsure of the relationship between them. The first tells of this man Balaam the son of Beor who was called a seer of the gods. He sees a vision at night when the gods speak to him and give him a message (all of which has not been preserved). The vision is so disturbing to Balaam that he wails and laments as he tells his people what the gods are going to do. A goddess, whose name begins with the letter *š* (the rest is lost), carries out the will of the gods, who are determined to cover the heavens with a cloud and bring darkness on the earth because of the shameful behavior of man.

In Nu. 24:4, 16 Balaam calls himself "the one who hears the words of *ʾEl* (God), the one who sees the vision of *Šadday* (the Almighty)." In the Deir ʿallā text these epithets are used in a *polytheistic* setting. According to Carlton (Hackett) *šdyn* is used as a divine name, similar to the

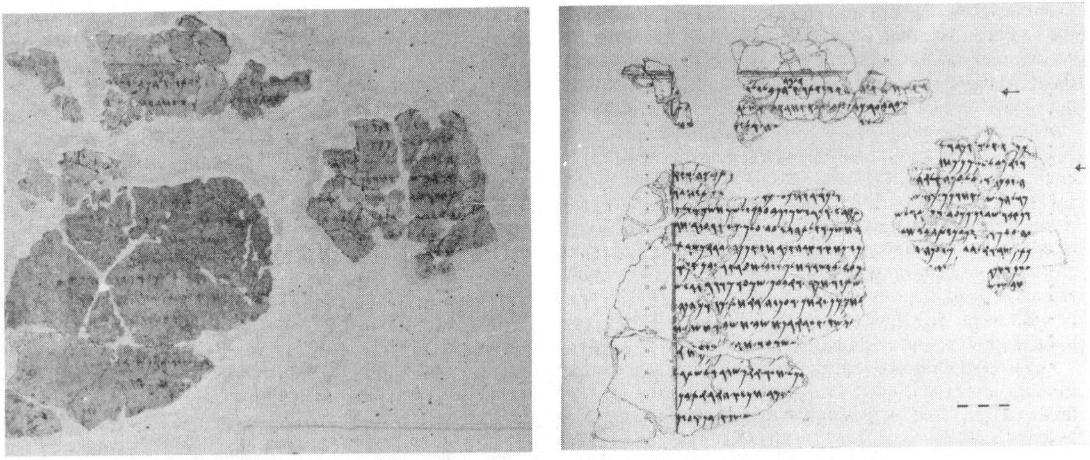

Actual fragments and line drawing (combination 1) of the Balaam text from Deir ʿallā (Department of Antiquities, Hashemite Kingdom of Jordan)

epithet *šadday* ("Almighty") used for God in the OT. The *šdyn* stand together as at an assembly of deities. In the period between the Exodus and the Conquest Israel "sacrificed to *šdym* and not to God, even gods they did not know" (Dt. 32:17). And in Ps. 106:37 the Israelites "sacrificed their sons and daughters to *šdym.*" In both cases the MT has vocalized the word *šēḏîm,* and it has traditionally been interpreted as "demons," a typical post-biblical (i.e., post-OT) way of handling earlier names of pagan deities (cf. Mt. 10:25; 12:24; Lk. 11:15).

The picture presented here shows Balaam among his own people while the biblical appraisal of Balaam is consistently negative. Even the story in Nu. 22–24 appears to be strongly ironic. Balaam, a man who might have gladly cursed Israel, finds himself unable to do so. As for the dating, the fragments evidently come from a wall or a stele. Such a monument must have preserved material that was already old to the people of the 8th or 7th cent. B.C. in whose context this document existed.

***Bibliography.***–W. F. Albright, *JBL,* 63 (1944), 207-233; A. Caquot and A. Lemaire, *Syria,* 54 (1977), 189-208; J. Carlton (Hackett), "Studies in the Plaster Text from Tell Deir ʿAlla" (diss., Harvard, 1980); J. Hoftijzer, *BA,* 39 (1976), 11-17; J. Hoftijzer and G. van der Kooij, *Aramaic Texts from Deir ʿAlla* (1976); P. K. McCarter, *BASOR,* 239 (Summer 1980), 49-60.

E. B. SMICK

*V. NT.*–Although the NT quotes from Numbers only three times (according to the United Bible Societies' Greek NT [3rd ed. 1975], 9:12 in Jn. 19:36; 16:5 in 2 Tim. 2:19; 30:2 in Mt. 5:33), the influence of Numbers is far greater in the NT than those few citations imply.

Jude 5-7 lists the rebellious generation that was destroyed in the wilderness along with the rebellious angels (v. 6) and the corrupt and apostate cities of Sodom and Gomorrah (v. 7) as a warning to the Christian saints to continue in their faith lest they too lose their first inheritance through unbelief. He. 3:1–4:13 continues along this same line to encourage Christians to continue to "hold fast our confidence and pride in our hope" (3:6). The major religious problem of the wilderness generation was their tendency to lose faith and hope in the face of adversity (3:12-19) and be confirmed and rejected in a state of unbelief. The Christians' challenge is to maintain their faith lest they too lose their inheritance and future hope (4:11-13). The future hope of Christians is parallel to the Promised Land of Canaan for Israel.

Paul's use of several episodes from Numbers in 1 Cor. 10:1-11 is indicative of his general assertion that "these things happened to them as a warning, but they were written down for our instruction . . ." (v. 11). Conditions at Corinth reminded Paul of certain events recorded in Numbers. God was not pleased with most of the people even after they had all experienced his mighty deeds of salvation (1 Cor. 10:1-5; Nu. 14:10-35). The whoredom of Israel at Baal of Peor (Nu. 25:1-18), the test of the Lord by the people (e.g., 21:5-6) and incessant murmuring (16:14, 49) are all listed as instructive to God's people at Corinth not to walk in the same rebellious way that Israel had walked. Paul affirms both the historical meaning and reality of the text ("happened *to them* as a warning") and its present significance at Corinth ("written down *for our* instruction").

The events of Numbers and the NT's use of them illustrate a typological significance that the OT had in some texts. Because of God's continued goals and purposes for mankind, because of His constant nature, because of mankind's constant failure and nature, a moral-religious cycle of relationship between God and mankind takes place in history. Inevitably, *unless* people remain faithful, the punishments of the covenant will come upon them. The marvelous provisions of God in the wilderness, however, remain as a challenge to trust His unparalleled care.

***Bibliography.***–*Comms.:* L. E. Binns (*Westminster,* 1927); H. Cazelles (*Bible de Jérusalem,* 3rd ed. 1971); G. B. Gray (*ICC,* 1903); KD; M. Noth (Eng. tr., *OTL,* 1968); N. H. Snaith (*NCBC,* 1967); J. Sturdy (*CBC,* 1976); G. J. Wenham (*Tyndale OT Comms.,* 1981).

*Other Studies:* U. Cassuto, "Sequence and Arrangement of the Biblical Sections," in *Biblical and Oriental Studies,* I (Eng. tr. 1973), 1-6; B. S. Childs, *Intro. to the OT as Scripture* (1979), pp. 190-201; R. E. D. Clark, *Journal of the Transactions of the Victoria Institute,* 87 (1955), 82-92; G. W. Coats, *Rebellion in the Wilderness* (1968); *CBQ,* 34 (1972), 135-152; G. I. Davies, *The Way of the Wilderness* (1979); *Tyndale Bulletin,* 25 (1974), 46-81; P. A. H. de Boer, *VT,* 32 (1982), 3-13; M. Douglas, *Purity and Danger* (1966); B. D. Eerdmans, "The Composition of Numbers," in *Oudtestamentische Stüdien,* 6 (1949), 101-216; M. Fishbane, *HUCA,* 45 (1974), 24-45; B. A. Levine, *In the Presence of the Lord* (1974); *JAOS,* 85 (1965), 307-318; G. E. Mendenhall, *JBL,* 77 (1958), 52-66; J. Milgrom, *Studies in Levitical Terminology,* I (1970); *JQR,* 69 (1978), 65-81; J. W. Wenham, *Tyndale Bulletin,* 18 (1967), 19-53.

E. E. CARPENTER

**NUMENIUS** nū-mēn'i-əs [Gk. *Noumēnios*]. Son of Antiochus and a Jewish ambassador. In 144 B.C. Jonathan (the Maccabee) sent Numenius and Antipater to Rome, Sparta, and other places where they successfully confirmed and renewed the friendship and alliances (1 Macc. 12:1-23) that had existed since the time of Judas (8:17ff.). After Jonathan's death, his brother Simon sent Numenius to Rome on a second embassy in 141 B.C., bearing as a gift a gold shield weighing nearly a thousand pounds (14:24). Josephus incorrectly dates this event in the time of Hyrcanus II (*Ant.* xiv.8.5 [143-48]), 47 B.C. Numenius returned in 139 B.C. with letters from the Roman consul Lucius declaring friendship with the Jews, forbidding neighboring states to harm the Jews, and requiring them to extradite any Jewish deserters (15:15-24). R. L. OMANSON

**NÛN** nōōn [נ, ן]. The fourteenth letter in the Hebrew alphabet, in *ISBE* transliterated as *n*. It was also used to represent the number fifty. *See* WRITING.

**NUN** nun [Heb. *nûn*–'fish'; Gk. Apoc. *Nauē*]; AV also NON (1 Ch. 7:27), Apoc. NAVE (Sir. 46:1). An Ephraimite, the father of Joshua (Ex. 33:11; Nu. 11:28; Dt. 1:38; Josh. 1:1; 1 K. 16:34; Neh. 8:17; etc.). Nun is also called the father of Hoshea (e.g., Nu. 13:8, 16; AV Oshea), of Jeshua (Neh. 8:17), of Jehoshua (e.g., Nu. 13:16, AV), and of Jesus (Sir. 46:1, AV); but all of these are other forms of the name Joshua.

**NURSE; NURSING** [Heb. qal part. of *yānaq* (Cant. 8:1; Joel 2:16), hiphil and hiphil fem. part. (*mêneqeṯ*) of *yānaq*, part. of *'āman*, part. of *sāḵan*; Gk. *tróphos* (1 Thess. 2:7)]; AV also SUCK, SUCKING, GIVE SUCK, CHERISH (1 K. 1:2, 4); NEB also SUCK, "at breast," WET-NURSE, SUCKLE, "take care of" (1 K. 1:2, 4), etc. To take or give nourishment at the breast; one who cares for children or the infirm.

Hebrew *yānaq* in the qal means "suck" and in the hiphil "give suck, suckle." Heb. *mêneqeṯ* generally refers to a wet nurse. Although Hebrew women usually nursed their own children (cf. 1 S. 1:23; 1 K. 3:21; Cant. 8:1), some families employed a wet nurse (e.g., the nurse of Joash [2 K. 11:2; 2 Ch. 22:11]; Jochebed, hired as a wet nurse for her own son by Pharaoh's daughter [Ex. 2:7-9]). Children were not weaned until they were two or three years old (cf. 1 S. 1:22-24). Often the wet nurse remained with the family as a trusted servant after her charge was weaned (e.g., Deborah, Rebekah's nurse [Gen. 24:59; 35:8]).

The part. of *'āman* (fem. *'ōmeneṯ*; masc. *'ōmēn*) has the more general sense of one who is entrusted with the care of children (e.g., Naomi [Ruth 4:16]; the nurse of Mephibosheth [2 S. 4:4]). Moses protested against being burdened with the responsibilities of a foster parent (*'ōmēn*) for the people of Israel (Nu. 11:12; cf. 1 Thess. 2:7, where Paul compares his care for the Thessalonian Christians to the tender affection that a nursing mother shows to her children). Deutero-Isaiah (49:23) prophesied a time when foreign kings and queens would attend to the needs of the Israelites like foster fathers (*'ōmᵉnîm*) and wet nurses (*mênîqôṯ*). (*See also* GUARDIAN.)

ABISHAG the Shunammite was chosen to be a *sōḵeneṯ* (part. of *sāḵan*, "be of service") for the aged King David (1 K. 1:2-4). Although the text explicitly states only that her task was to keep the king warm and that he did not have intercourse with her, some have seen in this story a parallel to the custom in certain tribal societies of deposing a king who is no longer virile. That Abishag was chosen for her beauty (vv. 3f.) gives some credibility to the theory that the passage describes a virility test that the king failed (v. 4), setting the stage for his successor to take the throne (cf. 1:5–2:46). (See J. Gray, *I & II Kings* [*OTL*, 2nd ed. 1970], p. 77.) N. J. O.

Bronze statuette of Isis nursing Horus (*ca.* 7th cent. B.C.) (University Museum, University of Pennsylvania)

**NURTURE.** The AV rendering of Lat. *erudio* (2 Esd. 8:12, RSV "instruct"), Gk. *paideúo* (Sir. 18:13, RSV "train"), and Gk. *paideía* (Wisd. 3:11, RSV "instruction"; Eph. 6:4, RSV "DISCIPLINE").

**NUT.**

**1. NUT ORCHARD** [Heb. *ginnaṯ 'ᵉgôz*; Gk. *kēpos karýas*] (Cant. 6:11); AV "garden of nuts"; NEB "garden of nut-trees." The reference is to the walnut tree (*Juglans regia* L.), indigenous to northern Persia and common in Palestine, particularly in the hills. The nuts are esteemed for food and for their oil content. Cf. M. Pope, *Song of Songs* (*AB*, 1977), pp. 574-79.

**2. PISTACHIO NUT** [Heb. *boṭnâ*; Gk. *terébinthos*] (Gen. 43:11); AV NUT. The *Pistacia vera* L., the *baṭam* of the Arabs. The LXX rendering is an error, since Gk. *terébinthos* invariably refers to Heb. *'ēlâ*, identified with *Pistacia*

*terebinthus* var. *palaestina* (Boiss.) Post, native to Gilead. *See* OAK. R. K. H.

**NUZI** nōō'zi. A city near modern Kirkûk, Iraq, which flourished in the middle of the 2nd millennium B.C. and whose inhabitants in that period were predominantly Hurrian. Parallels have frequently been drawn between the socio-juridical practices evidenced in the tablets found there and those of the patriarchal narratives of Genesis.

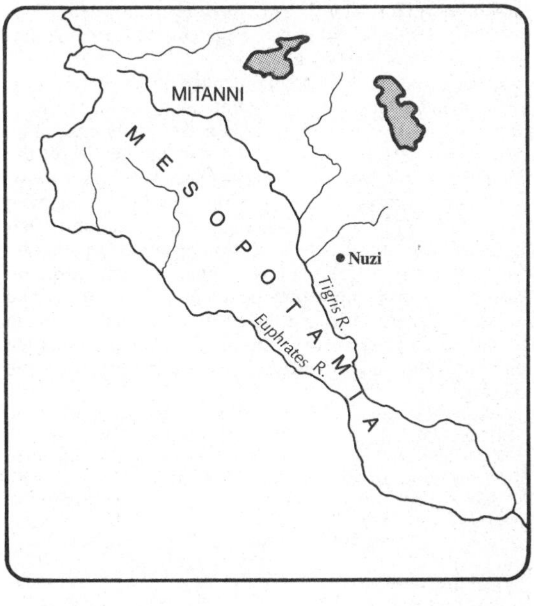


The mound of Yorghan (also Yoghlan) Tepe, containing the remains of ancient Nuzi, is located approximately 15 km. (9 mi.) SW of Kirkûk, ancient Arrapkha. It was excavated during 1925-31 by a team led by E. Chiera under the primary sponsorship of the American School of Oriental Research in Baghdad. Although remains were found dating from the early 4th millennium B.C. down to Roman times, the main periods of occupation were the late 3rd millennium, when the site had a primarily Akkadian population and was known as Gasur, and the mid-2nd millennium, specifically the 15th-14th cents. B.C. In the latter period the site was known as Nuzi and was part of a province of the kingdom of Mitanni. Its population was now overwhelmingly Hurrian, a development doubtlessly related in some way to the mass movement of Hurrian peoples that created the state of Mitanni during the second quarter of the 2nd millennium.

More than four thousand clay tablets were found in the excavations, some of them administrative records but most private family archives covering a period of some five generations. They were written in a dialect of Akkadian that was heavily influenced by the Hurrian language both in vocabulary and grammar. A wide variety of document types is represented in these archives. There are family-law documents comprising adoptions of various kinds, wills, and marriage contracts, as well as business records detailing the sale and transfer of land and the exchange of persons and goods. A number of lawsuits, both civil and criminal, have also been recovered.

From these texts scholars have gleaned much knowledge about the social customs and practices of these people, such as the ownership, exchange, and sale of land, the prices and sale of commodities of various kinds, the status and treatment of women and slaves, the nature and procedures of the legal system, and especially the nature and functioning of family law. Other genres of texts, giving information of a literary, political, or religious nature, are notably lacking, however, so that our knowledge in these areas is correspondingly slight. One implication of the nature of these texts needs to be stressed: since they are the records of actual transactions of a legal, business, and social nature between specific individuals, they record only the barest essentials pertinent to the situation, leaving much unsaid that was understood by all the parties involved. Therefore much in them is obscure and problematic, and they are only indirect evidence for the social and legal institutions, practices, and principles which governed the transactions involved. Thus they are capable of a wide latitude in interpretation and understanding.

Certain features of these socio-juridical customs provide parallels with biblical data, particularly the patriarchal narratives, but with varying degrees of exactness and probability. Only a partial list can be alluded to here. (1) In the area of inheritance rights, the granting of special privileges to an eldest son was widespread. At Nuzi and in Dt. 21:15-17 a double share is prescribed. (2) The regular term at Nuzi for the eldest son, *rabū*, "eldest," occurs in Gen. 25:23 (Heb. *raḇ*) instead of the usual Hebrew term (*b^e^ḵôr*, "first-born"). (3) In at least two texts from Nuzi a slave could be adopted in the absence of a son. This may provide an explanation of the status of Eliezer in Gen. 15. (4) In one marriage contract at Nuzi it is stipulated that the wife may provide a slave girl for her husband if she should prove to be barren, as was also done by Sarah, Rachel, and Leah (Gen. 16:1-4; 30:1-13). It is important to note that customs similar to all of these can also be found at sites other than Nuzi in this same era and some of them at much later times, including the 1st millennium. One very probable parallel occurs thus far only at Nuzi: the use of the idiom *kaspa akālu*, "to consume the money," with a meaning parallel to that of the cognate Hebrew phrase *'āḵal kesep* "to use up the money," in Gen. 31:15. Other suggested parallels also seem valid (see Selman).

A number of the parallels suggested in the past between Nuzi customs and those of the patriarchs must now be regarded as invalid. These include (1) a reputed wife-sister marriage as a background to the relationship between Abraham and Sarah (Gen. 12, 20), (2) the existence of a fratriarchy and a sistership adoption practice as a background for the relationship between Laban, Rebekah, and Abraham's servant in Gen. 24, and (3) the inheritance of household gods by the eldest son as the background to Rachel's theft of the teraphim in Gen. 29–31.

One line of argument for the historicity and date of the patriarchs that was based on these Nuzi parallels, particularly these last three, must now be significantly modified. In this approach many of these Nuzi customs were identified as specifically Hurrian on the basis of a presumed difference between them and the customs of the general Assyro-Babylonian culture of Mesopotamia, which otherwise formed the basic fabric of Nuzi society. This close parallel between patriarchal customs and these presumed Hurrian customs from Nuzi seemed particularly significant since the Hurrians' longest and deepest penetration into Mesopotamia occurred in the very area that the Bible presents as the homeland of the patriarchs, viz., northwest Mesopotamia in the general vicinity of Haran. This special connection between the patriarchal texts and specifically Hurrian Nuzi socio-juridical customs must be given up for clear and decisive reasons. First, a number of the customs that seemed most clearly idiosyncratic and so could be interpreted as Hurrian are now seen to stand in only a tenuous relation (if any) to Hurrian practice. Second, these particular customs were drawn from an interpretation of no more than twelve, most frequently only four or five, of the approximately three hundred Nuzi family-law texts known. Hence they can hardly be said to be representative even of the Nuzi texts themselves! Third, the Nuzi customs show much greater similarity to the socio-juridical practices of the Mesopotamian world at large than originally thought, and consequently the whole question of a specifically Hurrian pattern of family law is extremely suspect. The very criteria for determining when a particular custom is Hurrian in origin have yet to be worked out. Finally, it must be stressed that socio-juridical customs, even when valid parallels exist between the two groups of texts, are generally insufficiently precise chronologically to be used for dating purposes. A custom can only be chronologically significant if it can be shown to be confined to a reasonably limited period of time. In fact most socio-juridical customs in the ancient Near East were in use in various forms for long periods of time, frequently stretching through many centuries.

*See also* HURRIANS; PATRIARCHS.

***Bibliography.***–Archeology: R. C. S. Starr, *Nuzi. Report on the Excavations at Yorghan Tepe* (2 vols., 1939). Texts in transliteration and translation: R. H. Pfeiffer and E. A. Speiser, *One Hundred New Selected Nuzi Texts* (*AASOR*, 16, 1936). General: C. H. Gordon, *BA*, 3 (1940), 1-12; E. A. Speiser, "The Hurrian Participation in the Civilizations of Mesopotamia, Syria, and Palestine," in J. J. Finkelstein and M. Greenberg, eds., *Oriental and Biblical Studies* (1967), pp. 244-269; C. H. Mullo Weir, "Nuzi," in *AOTS*, pp. 73-86; M. Dietrich, *et al.*, *Nuzi-Bibliographie* (*Alte Orient und AT Studien*, II, 1972); T. L. Thompson, *Historicity of the Patriarchal Narratives* (*BZAW*, 133, 1974); M. J. Selman, *Tyndale Bulletin*, 27 (1976), 114-136; *Themelios*, 3 (1977), 9-16; R. de Vaux, *Early History of Israel* (Eng. tr. 1978), pp. 241-256; M. A. Morrison and D. I. Owen, eds., *Studies on the Civilization and Culture of Nuzi and the Hurrians* (*Festschrift* for E. R. Lacheman; 1981).

F. W. BUSH

**NYMPHA** nim'fə [Gk. *Nympha* or *Nymphas*; most likely an abbreviated form of Nymphius, Nymphodotus, or Nymphodorus]; AV NYMPHAS. An otherwise unknown but probably wealthy Laodicean Christian (Col. 4:15). This person was singled out because the church (or some part of it) met in his (or her) home.

Scholars disagree about the gender of *Nymphan*. This form, an accusative, can be accented either as fem. *Nýmphan* (nominative *Nympha*) or as masc. *NympҺán* (nominative *Nymphas*). The uncertainty of the gender of the noun resulted in a variation in the gender of the following possessive pronoun: "her" (RSV), "his" (AV), or even "their" (ASV) in some MSS. Lightfoot's contention that the feminine is improbable because of its Doric form (hardly to be expected at Colossae; cf. Moule) was answered by Moulton, who saw here an Attic feminine form. If a scribe altered "her" to "his" on the assumption that a woman would not be referred to in this way, "her" becomes the most difficult and therefore the preferred reading (see Lohse).

***Bibliography.***–Comms. on Colossians by J. B. Lightfoot (7th ed. 1884), pp. 242f.; E. Lohse (Eng. tr., *Hermeneia*, 1971), p. 174; C. F. D. Moule (*CGT*, 1957), p. 28 n. 1; see also J. H. Moulton, *Grammar of NT Greek*, I (3rd ed. 1908), 48; *Expos.T.*, 5 (1893-94), 66f.

J. J. HUGHES

# O

**OABDIUS** ō-ab'di-əs (1 Esd. 9:27, NEB). *See* ABDI **3.**

**OAK** [Heb. *'ēlâ, 'allâ, 'allôn, 'ēlôn, 'êlîm* (pl.); Gk. *terébinthos, drýs, bálanos*]; AV also "plain" (*'ēlôn*), TREES (*'êlîm,* Isa. 61:3), "hinds" (Ps. 29:9), "idols" (*'ēlîm,* Isa. 57:5), "ALLON" (*'allôn,* Josh. 19:33); NEB also TEREBINTH-TREE, TEREBINTH, Elon- (Josh. 19:33; Jgs. 4:11), "hinds" (Ps. 29:9), TREES (Isa. 61:3); **EVERGREEN OAK** [Gk. *prínos*] (Sus. 58); AV HOLM TREE; NEB "yew-tree" (for the sake of preserving pun in original; mg. "oak"); **TEREBINTH** [Heb. *'ēlâ*; Gk. *terébinthos*]; AV TEIL (Isa. 6:13), ELM (Hos. 4:13), TURPENTINE TREE (Sir. 24:16); NEB also OAK (Isa. 6:13). Several varieties of trees in the OT.

Hebrew *'ēlâ* (e.g., Jgs. 6:11, 19; 2 S. 18:9f., 14; Isa. 1:30; 6:13; Ezk. 6:13), Vulg. *terebinthus,* refers usually to the Palestinian terebinth *Pistacia terebinthus* var. *palaestina* (Boiss.) Post, though Gen. 35:4 probably refers to a true oak species. Cf. "valley of Elah" (1 S. 17:2, 19; 21:9) and "Elah" (Gen. 36:41; 1 K. 16:8). The *'allâ* (Vulg. *quercus,* Josh. 24:26) is an oak, perhaps *Quercus pseudococcifera* or *Q. palaestina.*

For Heb. *'ēlôn* the AV has "plain" (Gen. 12:6; 13:18; 14:13; 18:1; Dt. 11:30; Jgs. 4:11; 9:6, 37; 1 S. 10:3), but almost certainly the references are to species of the true oak, perhaps *Quercus coccifera* var. *pseudococcifera* (Desf.) Boiss., *Q. ilex* L., or *Q. aegilops.* In Josh. 19:33; Jgs. 4:11 the AV ("Allon") and NEB ("Elon-bezaanannim") take the same word as a proper name.

Hebrew *'êlîm,* perhaps the plural of *'ēlâ,* is probably *Q. coccifera* L., *Q. ilex,* or *Q. palaestina.* It occurs in Isa. 1:29; 57:5 (defective, AV "idols"); 61:3 (AV, NEB, "trees"). Heb. *'allôn* probably indicates the same varieties (Gen. 35:8; Isa. 2:13; 6:13; 44:14; Ezk. 27:6; Hos. 4:13; Am. 2:9; Zec. 11:2).

In Ps. 29:9 the RSV has "oaks," reading *'êlôṯ* for MT *'ayyālôṯ,* but probably the AV, RSV mg., and NEB are correct in translating "hinds."

Greek *prínos* (Sus. 58) is generally agreed to be the evergreen holm oak, *Quercus ilex* L., one of numerous kinds of oaks now growing in Palestine. *Q. ilex* is often stunted and bears glossy green leaves like the holly. The reference plays on the words *prínos* and *prísai,* "saw" (vv. 58f.). *See* SUSANNA.

There are two dozen kinds of oaks in Palestine, and in antiquity the Hebrews probably used a variety of terms for them. Confusion in identification may well arise from the similarity between the Hebrew words for "oak" and "terebinth." The Palestinian terebinth (Sir. 24:16, AV "turpentine tree") is a deciduous species attaining a maximum height of 7.6 m. (25 ft.) and is notable for the fragrant resinous juice in the leaves and branches. It is seldom found in clumps, thickets, or forests and grows in localities too warm or arid for the oak. The Cyprus turpentine of commerce is derived from this species. Since it was native to Gilead its resinous juice was probably part of the "spicery" carried by the Ishmaelite caravan to Egypt (Gen. 37:25). Some commentators have identified the "oak" of Jgs. 6:11; 2 S. 18:9; Am. 2:9 with the terebinth, but this is improbable.

Commonly found are the evergreen oaks, *Q. ilex, Q. palaestina,* and *Q. coccifera*; the deciduous oaks are principally *Q. aegilops, Q. cerris, Q. libani, Q. syriaca,* and *Q. lusitanica.* Of the evergreens, *Q. ilex* is shrublike, with prickly, dark-green leaves. *Q. coccifera* is somewhat larger and is distributed over the mountainous regions of Syria and Palestine. It is infested by a parasite, *Coccus ilicis* ("kermes"), which yields a scarlet dye (cf. Isa. 1:18).

The deciduous species *Q. cerris* is common in Palestine, attaining a maximum height of 18 m. (60 ft.). It bears large acorns and produces a hard, finely grained wood. *Q. aegilops,* the Valonea oak, has prominent oblong leaves and large acorns, whose cupules ("valonica") are used in

Terebinth (*pistaschia terebinthus*) in a corner of the Ḥaram esh-Sherîf (the temple mount in Jerusalem) (J. C. Trever)

tanning leather. *Q. lusitanica* seldom exceeds 9 m. (30 ft.) in height, and its branches are subject to infection with galls.

The oak was sometimes connected with a particular historical event, e.g., Abraham's oak at Hebron, and the "oak of weeping" (Gen. 35:8). The "groves" or trees surrounding Canaanite shrines have been interpreted animistically as the abodes of spirits that were venerated in worship, but Canaanite texts furnish little support for this view. The Hebrews certainly worshiped idols under oak trees (Isa. 1:29) in characteristic Canaanite fashion, and the oak may also have been a favorite place for outdoor divination (Gen. 12:16), not so much because of any inherent oracular features in the tree itself but because it afforded welcome shade from the sun. A famous Greek shrine was located at Dodona in Epirus, where the priests lay down among the oak groves to receive messages from the deities that supposedly spoke through the rustling leaves of the tree. R. K. H.

**OAK OF TABOR.** *See* TABOR, OAK OF.

**OAK OF THE PILLAR** [Heb. *ʾēlôn muṣṣāḇ*] AV PLAIN OF THE PILLAR; NEB OLD PROPPED-UP TEREBINTH. This tree was doubtless one of many solitary oaks of magnificent proportions that grew in ancient Palestine. It was a feature of the landscape at Shechem and witnessed numerous important civic ceremonies, including the coronation of Abimelech (Jgs. 9:6). The oak may have also been the very one under which Jacob buried the jewelry of his wives (Gen. 35:4), and perhaps the site of Joshua's monument to commemorate the covenant-renewal ceremony (Josh. 24:26). Whereas the RSV reads "oak" in the above references, the New King James Version has "terebinth" in Gen. 35:4 and Jgs. 9:6 (see NEB).

*See also* PILLAR. R. K. H.

**OAR.** *See* SHIPS.

**OATH.** The confirmation of a statement or promise by an oath occurs in all cultures of the world. It is usually associated with maledictions when it is broken (*see* CURSE), but with benedictions when it is kept (*see* BLESS). The oath is also associated with the promise, the contract between two parties, sometimes with legal enforcement and with the judgment of God. While generally spoken, it sometimes is accompanied by certain GESTURES to emphasize the seriousness of the occasion. An oath can be taken between two persons or parties, taken by a person to verify his promise to another, or taken in the name of God.

I. Oaths in the Ancient Near East
II. Terminology
III. Characteristics of the Oath
IV. The Oath Between Two Parties
V. The Oath Taken by the Lord
VI. The Oath in NT Times

***I. Oaths in the Ancient Near East.***–In Akkadian the oath is usually expressed by the technical term *nišum,* which is associated with *balāṭum,* "to live." This technical term is used in two ways: (1) *niš ilim,* "by the life of the god"; (2) *niš šarrim,* "by the life of the king." This can be interchanged by "may the god Šušinak live forever." In Am.Tab. 256 the following oath formula occurs: "As the king my lord lives, as the king my lord lives, Ayab is not in Pella" (*ANET,* p. 486). The repetition stresses the importance of the oath, which may be classified as religious because the Egyptian king was regarded as divine.

The oath was also used in Mesopotamia in the juridical sphere. The purification oath or ordeal oath played a very important role. The river ordeal is a well-known phenomenon where, e.g., a supposedly unfaithful wife was thrown into the river. If she succeeded in escaping the ordeal, she was purified and declared innocent. In Mesopotamian contracts the oath was not regarded as a necessity and in many instances it was not expected that witnesses would take an oath.

In Egypt the technical term for oath was *ʿnḫ,* "to live," or its substitute *w3ḥ,* as in Mesopotamia. Here also the oath could be taken in the name of the god or the king, e.g., "may the god live for me," or "may the king live for me." A person could even take an oath by himself, e.g., "may I live." In these cases it is understood to mean: "may the god live for me if I speak the truth."

In both these ancient cultures the danger of an oath was fully realized. There is evidence that in the Late Sumerian Period the oath was refused. In the Third Intermediate Period of Egypt the Wisdom of Amenemope (*ca.* 1000 B.C.) warned against the abuse of an oath. Still later the following pronouncement was made: "One who is quick to take an oath, will be quick to meet his death." Thus a negative reaction to an oath is older than many scholars have suspected.

The Hittites occasionally used the oath in their vassal treaties. If the oath was broken (*šarra-*), certain curses would come into effect, a general feature of most Ancient Near Eastern oaths. The Hittite military oaths exhibited the same characteristics (from *ca.* 1400 B.C.).

In the Canaanite-Phoenician world there is a strong resemblance between the oath and the vow (*ndr*). The vow occasionally occurs in Phoenician texts, suggesting that the vow must be regarded as an oath. In the Ugaritic Keret epic Keret makes a vow at the sanctuary of Asherah and Elat that if he acquires a wife, he will pay twice her price in silver and thrice her price in gold. When Keret does not meet his commitment, he becomes fatally ill. It is thus obvious that a curse accompanied the vow if it was broken, as with the oath.

***II. Terminology.***–In the OT the stem *šbʿ* in the niphal and hiphil expresses the idea "to take an oath," "to swear," or "to adjure," i.e., cause someone else to take an oath (2 S. 21:17; 1 K. 22:16 par. 2 Ch. 18:15; note also the use of the hiphil several times in Canticles for "adjure" as the heroine imposes an oath on the "daughters of Jerusalem"; on this oath *see also* GAZELLE). The noun is *š$^{e}$ḇûʿâ.* This stem occurs 216 times in the OT, demonstrating its importance. Not all its occurrences are associated with taking an oath. Sometimes it is closely linked with the curse. Another formula used to pronounce the oath is *kōh yaʿ$^{a}$śeh-l$^{e}$ḵâ ʾ$^{ĕ}$lōhîm w$^{e}$ḵōh yôsîp̱,* "may God do to me thus and add thus" (e.g., 1 S. 3:17). This oath is closely associated with the curse. Another term for the oath is *ḥālîlâ,* "may it be far from (me to do this or that)" (cf., e.g., Gen. 44:7, 17; Josh. 24:16; 1 S. 12:23). Still another formula for the oath is *ḥê-nap̱š$^{e}$ḵā,* "as your soul lives" (1 S. 17:55). Interesting is the double form of the oath in 2 S. 11:11, the words of Uriah to David: *ḥayyeḵā w$^{e}$ḥê nap̱š$^{e}$ḵā,* "as you live and as your soul lives" (cf. the example from Am.Tab. 256 cited above). This terminology has close affinities with that used in Mesopotamia and Egypt. In both these cases the oath is taken by the life of the king (cf. also Gen. 42:15). These formulas are sometimes followed by a negative or positive oath (the negative oath is usually introduced by *ʾim* and the positive oath by *ʾim lōʾ*; see GKC, § 149; *TWOT,* I, 48f.). Another term which can mean both oath and curse is *ʾālâ.* In Lev. 5:1 *ʾālâ,* "adjuration," refers to an oath or self-curse; one who makes such an oath sins (*ḥāṭāʾ*) if he does not testify as he said he would. The verb *nāḏar,* "take a vow," closely resembles the meaning "take an oath."

In the NT the most common term for oath is *hórkos* (Mt. 14:7, 9; 26:72; Mk. 6:26; Lk. 1:73; Acts 2:30; He. 6:16f.; Jas. 5:12). The related noun *horkōmosía* is also used (He. 7:20f., 28). Several related verbs are translated "adjure": *horkízō* (Mk. 5:7; Acts 19:13), *exorkízō* (Mt. 26:63), *enorkízō* (1 Thess. 5:27). The noun *anáthema* (lit. "curse") occurs once for "oath" (Acts 23:14), and its related verb *anathematízō* is translated "bind by an oath" in Acts 23:12, 14, 21. Finally, *opheílei* (<*opheílō*, "owe, be indebted") is also translated "bind by an oath" in Mt. 23:16, 18.

***III. Characteristics of the Oath.***–*A. Conditional.* The one who takes the oath can be exempted from it under certain circumstances. In Gen. 24 Abraham instructed his chief servant to fetch a wife for Isaac from Mesopotamia, rather than from the Canaanites. Because of possible difficulties in keeping the oath, Abraham exempted him from it if the woman was unwilling to return with him (Gen. 24:8). In Josh. 2:17 Rahab of Jericho requested the Israelite spies to swear that they should show kindness to her and her family when they conquered the city. The spies agreed on the condition that a scarlet cord should hang outside the window of her house where her whole family was assembled. If not, they would be exempted from their oath.

*B. Unconditional.* This is the most common oath in the OT. In Gen. 47:28-31 the aged Jacob requested Joseph not to bury him in Egypt, but with his fathers. Joseph took this unconditional oath to fulfil his father's wish and thus was bound by it. (50:5 notes that Joseph kept his oath.)

*C. Binding on later generations.* In Gen. 50:25 Joseph requested that the Israelites carry his bones from Egypt to Canaan for burial. Gen. 50:26 shows that the body of Joseph was embalmed and kept in Egypt until the Exodus, when his bones were taken for burial in Canaan. 2 S. 21:2 and 7 records the oath taken by the Israelites (Josh. 9) to spare the Gibeonites and conclude a vassal treaty with them. Saul, however, had broken this oath and annihilated them, causing a famine to rage during David's reign. David decided to make amends because of the binding force of the oath in the time of Joshua. The causality of the binding force of the oath is clearly important in this story. A. Malamat (*VT,* 5 [1955], 1-12) has shown that the same approach existed among the Hittites, where the calamities in the time of Mursilis II were interpreted as punishment for the breach of a treaty concluded by his father Šuppiluliuma with the Egyptians. An oath was clearly regarded as binding on later generations, and if broken required certain reparations. The breaking of an oath, or PERJURY, was regarded as a grave offense (cf. Jer. 7:9). Ps. 24 gives certain characteristics of a pious supplicant, including that he should not commit perjury (v. 4). People are warned not to take an oath lightly. If one makes a vow to God, one must not be slow to fulfil it, because it is better not to take a vow than to take it and not fulfil it (Eccl. 5:4ff.). This is a remarkable parallel to the story of Keret and to the Egyptian material cited above.

*D. Sacred and Profane Oaths.* It is sometimes difficult to determine whether an oath is profane or sacred, since certain descriptions of the taking of an oath do not mention God. Some scholars have thought that this must be understood, since there could hardly be an oath without indirect reference to the Lord. The one that takes an oath is always obliged to the Lord to keep it. Although this approach might be true for most examples of oath-taking, it is not uniformly so, as the instances where the oath is taken on the life of the king demonstrate (cf., e.g., 1 S. 17:55; 2 S. 11:11).

*E. Purification oath.* This was well known among the Israelites. It could be an oath taken at the sanctuary in the name of God to proclaim a person innocent (Ex. 22:8). To purify him from suspicion of the crime of theft, he had to go to the sanctuary to take an oath that he had not stretched out his hand to his neighbor's property (cf. also the Code of Hammurabi, §§ 125f., and esp. the Laws of Eshnunna, §§ 36f.). Another kind of purification oath is the ordeal. In Nu. 5:5ff. a woman suspected of adultery was forced to drink a concoction of water and dust and swear that she was innocent of adultery. If she swore falsely, the Lord would cause her thigh to waste away and her abdomen to swell. If she was innocent, this oath would purify her and nothing would happen to her (cf. the discussion above on the ordeal by river in Mesopotamia). It is clear that this oath, performed at the sanctuary in the presence of a priest with the Lord to execute the punishment in case of perjury, is placed in the religious sphere (cf. also 1 K. 8:31f.). It was not humanly possible to decide whether the wife was innocent. The same was true of the theft of movable property.

***IV. The Oath Between Two Parties.***–This kind of mutual oath could be executed between two persons, or between two countries in the international sphere. The former is best illustrated by the mutual oath of David and Jonathan to remain friends (1 S. 20:42; cf. David's lament on Saul and Jonathan in 2 S. 1, esp. v. 26).

In the sphere of international law parity and vassal treaties required both parties to take an oath. The vassal treaties show that the vassal was bound by an oath in the names of several gods to keep the stipulations of the treaty. If the treaty should be broken, the incorporated curses would take effect. This can be seen in the Hittite vassal treaties, the Assyrian vassal treaties of Esarhaddon, and the Aramaic vassal treaty of Sfire. That this custom was also known in Israel is clear from certain incomplete treaty contracts, e.g., Josh. 9 (notably vv. 14f.). The vassal treaty concluded between Israel and the Gibeonites was ratified by oath, which was later broken, bringing the curse of a famine in the time of David.

The oath that normally confirmed a covenant is absent from the oldest biblical form (Ex. 24). In Deuteronomy, however, the oath is mentioned, but then taken only by God (cf., e.g., Dt. 4:31). There may be traces of a possible mutual oath in Dt. 26:16-19. In such a case the stem *ʾmr* is used to express the taking of an oath. The Israelites have declared that the Lord is their God and that they will keep His commandments. The Lord has declared that Israel is His people, His treasured possession. The covenant formula is clearly present in both these expressions.

***V. The Oath Taken by the Lord.***–The oath is also used theologically, indicated by instances where the Lord is the subject of the verb *šāḇaʿ* (niphal), "swear." Nowhere is the Lord subject of the causative (hiphil) form of the verb, since people do not cause the Lord to swear. The formula used with the Lord as subject closely resembles the ordinary oath formula, viz., that one has to take an oath by someone or something. But the Lord takes an oath by Himself (cf. He. 6:13). This is expressed in various ways, e.g., by the preposition *bᵉ* (e.g., Gen. 22:16; Ex. 32:13; Jer. 22:5) or by *napšô* (Am. 4:2; Jer. 51:14). The Lord also swore by His holiness (Am. 4:2; Ps. 89:35 [MT 36]), by the pride of Jacob (Am. 8:7), and by His faithfulness (Ps. 89:49 [MT 50]).

In thirty-four instances God swears concerning the promise of the Holy Land, but elsewhere about the nation, the Davidides (e.g., Ps. 89:4 [MT 5]; 132:11), and the priestly king (Ps. 110:4). In all these cases the oath is taken to benefit people (Isa. 54:9ff.; Mic. 7:20; Josh. 21:44; Gen. 22:16ff.).

In a number of cases the oath of the Lord has a threatening character: against Israel (e.g., Nu. 32:10), the city of Jerusalem (Am. 6:8), or the Assyrians (Isa. 14:24ff.). It is also directed against individuals or families (1 S. 3:14), or groups such as the women of Israel, all of whom will be punished if they are disobedient.

*VI. The Oath in NT Times.*–The use of *šbʿ* in the Qumrân literature shows that the oath was still well known in the 1st cents. B.C. and A.D. A novice who was accepted as member of the community was obliged to take an oath to keep the laws of the community (1QS 5:8). The poets of the Qumrân *Hôḏāyôṯ* were obliged to promise not to sin (1QH 14:17), but a certain reticence to take an oath is observable.

The oath of confirmation plays an important role in the NT. Some scholars are of the opinion that the introductory formula *amēn* used by Jesus must be interpreted as a confirmation oath (see Talmon). Peter's self-curse in Mk. 14:71 must be interpreted as an oath. In his letters Paul occasionally uses the oath of confirmation, e.g., when he calls on God as witness that he remembers the Romans in his prayers (Rom. 1:9).

Covenant oaths are also mentioned in the NT. In Lk. 1:73 Zechariah refers to the oath God has sworn to Abraham; in Acts 2:30 Peter refers to God's promise of succession. Other examples (Rom. 14:11; He. 3:11, 18; 4:3; 6:13-17) reflect the OT conception of the divine oath.

In the passage dealing with swearing falsely and the prohibition of oath (Mt. 5:33-37; cf. also 23:16-22; Jas. 5:12), Jesus criticized all of the things used by the Jews for taking an oath. Instead He taught that it was better to avoid an oath by making a positive or negative decision on a person's attitude toward a certain problem. He stressed the seriousness of oaths because the oaths were made to the Lord (cf. Mt. 5:33).

*See also* COVENANT; SWEAR; VOW; WITNESS.

***Bibliography.****–Ancient Near East:* M. R. Lehman, *ZAW,* 81 (1969), 74-92; J. Pedersen, *Der Eid bei den Semiten* (1914); M. Weinfeld, "The Loyalty Oath in the Ancient Near East," *Ugarit-Forschungen,* 8 (1976), 379-414; J. A. Wilson, *JNES,* 7 (1948), 129-156.

*OT:* S. H. Blank, *HUCA,* 23 (1950-51), 73-95; H. J. Boecker, *Recht und Gesetz im AT und im Alten Orient* (1976); H. C. Brichto, *Problem of Curse in the Hebrew Bible* (1963); F. C. Fensham, *JBL,* 78 (1959), 160f.; *BA,* 27 (1964), 96-100; M. G. Kline, *By Oath Consigned* (1968); D. J. McCarthy, *Treaty and Covenant* (2nd ed. 1978); *TDOT,* I, *s.v.* "'ālāh" (Scharbert); "'rr" (Scharbert); H. C. White, *JBL,* 92 (1973), 165-179.

*NT:* S. Talmon, *Textus,* 7 (1969), 124-29; *TDNT,* V, *s.v.* ὀμνύω (J. Schneider); ὅρκος κτλ.: ὅρκος (J. Schneider).

F. C. FENSHAM

**OBADIAH** ō-bə-dī'ə [Heb. *ʿōḇaḏyâ*–'servant (or worshiper) of Yahweh'; Gk. *Abdiou*]. A common name in Israel comparable to "Christian" in English or "Abdullah" ("servant of Allah") in Arabic.

**1.** AV also ABDIAS (2 Esd. 1:39). The prophet (see the next article).

**2.** Ahab's chamberlain; he did his best to protect Yahweh's prophets from Jezebel, and carried the news of Elijah's reappearance to Ahab (1 K. 18:3-16).

**3.** A descendant of David (1 Ch. 3:31).

**4.** The son of Izrahiah and chief of the tribe of Issachar (1 Ch. 7:3).

**5.** The son of Azel, a Benjaminite, and a descendant of Saul (1 Ch. 8:38; 9:44).

**6.** A Levite descended from Jeduthun (1 Ch. 12:9); called Abda in Neh. 11:17 (*see* ABDA 2).

**7.** David's officer, a Gadite chief (1 Ch. 12:9 [MT 10]).

**8.** A chief of Zebulun, father of Ishmaiah (1 Ch. 27:19).

**9.** A prince of Judah sent by Jehoshaphat to teach the law in Judah (2 Ch. 17:7-9).

**10.** A Merarite who oversaw the repair of the temple under Josiah (2 Ch. 34:12).

**11.** AV, NEB, also ABADIAS (1 Esd. 8:35). The head of a family who went up with Ezra from Babylon (Ezr. 8:9).

**12.** One of the men who sealed the covenant with Nehemiah (Neh. 10:5 [MT 6]); perhaps the same as **10.**

**13.** A gatekeeper under Joiakim, the high priest in Nehemiah's time (Neh. 12:25). J. D. W. WATTS

**OBADIAH, BOOK OF.** The fourth of the Minor Prophets (fifth in the LXX). Obadiah is the shortest book in the OT: one chapter of twenty-one verses.

I. Name and Date
II. The Book
  A. Outline
  B. Composition
    1. Foreign Prophecy
    2. Prophetic Liturgy
    3. Relation to Jeremiah
  C. Meaning and Message
    1. The Dominion of Yahweh
    2. Edom
  D. Text

***I. Name and Date.***–The book is called "a vision" (Heb. *ḥāzôn*). This designates a prophetic book (cf. Isa. 1:1; Nah. 1:1) which interprets the work of God in history (cf. *TDOT,* IV, 283; here Jepsen defines *ḥāzôn* as "an event in which words are received"). OBADIAH is a fairly common name in Israel meaning "servant (or worshiper) of Yahweh." The short superscription adds nothing to identify which Obadiah is meant.

With no identifying marks for its author, the date of the book can be learned only from a study of the book itself. The focus of the book is obviously EDOM. The period of Edom's existence parallels that of Israel, and a number of conflicts erupted between them. Those who judge the order of books in the Minor Prophets to have been determined by chronology see events in the reigns of Jehoshaphat (872-852 B.C.) recorded in 2 Ch. 20 or those under Jehoram (852-845 B.C.) recorded in 2 K. 18–20 as possible backgrounds for an eighth-century date. Those who are not bound to an early date find more explicit correspondence in the destruction of Jerusalem in 586 B.C. when the city was plundered and refugees cut off in flight (2 K. 25:3-7). Bitter references in Lam. 4:21 and Ps. 137:7 seem to imply that Edomites participated in the plundering of the city that followed. If this is the reference in Ob. 10-14, the book must have come into existence after that.

The matter of dating becomes more complicated when the book is divided up into two or more separate oracles, as with J. A. Bewer (pp. 3ff.) and R. H. Pfeiffer (*PIOT,* pp. 585f.), or regarded as an anonymous assemblage of several fragmentary oracles (W. O. E. Oesterley and T. H. Robinson, *Intro. to the Books of the OT* [repr. 1958], pp. 370f.). Given such presuppositions, a date of *ca.* 400 B.C. or even later could be postulated for the finished work. The relationship between Obadiah and Jeremiah will also be an important factor in determining the date.

Obadiah 1-4 announces the imminent end of Edom. Its closing days came at the end of the 6th cent. and the beginning of the 5th when the Nabateans occupied the country. This marks the latest date for the book. Mal. 1:2-4 implies that Edom stands in ruins.

***II. The Book.****–A. Outline.* The book is composed of a series of prophetic words of different types, all about the coming fall of Edom and all leading up to the announcement of God's sovereign rule.

Superscription (v. 1a)
Audition: "Rise to battle!" (v. 1b-c)

First Announcement of Judgment (vv. 2-4)
Second Announcement of Judgment (vv. 5-10)
Indictment and Deprecation (vv. 11-14)
A Theological Explanation (vv. 15-16)
A Vision of Conditions to Follow (vv. 17-21)

*B. Composition.* The book is composed in a fashion that is familiar in the prophets.

*1. Foreign Prophecy.* A major feature of prophetic books in the OT is found in those prophecies relating to nations other than Israel and Judah. They witness to the universal rule of Yahweh. Major books have sections made up of these prophecies, while several complete books, including Obadiah, are prophecies about foreign nations.

Obadiah focuses on Edom, which appears in many other such prophecies. Edom is judged for misconduct against its "brother Jacob" and against Jerusalem. Pride has brought Edom down. So now on Yahweh's day for action against all the nations Edom is singled out for particular attention. This will show that the right of rule really does belong to Yahweh. The correct way to understand foreign prophecies is to see them as a part of Yahweh's royal exercise of authority as universal king.

*2. Prophetic Liturgy.* The composition of prophetic books is highly complex and is often difficult to understand. Many of them, like Obadiah, give evidence of being arranged in a way that fits liturgical presentation. When they are read in order, like a cantata, they display an artistic whole that is most effective. The audience is clearly Judeans and Israelites of the dispersion. The book brings a word from God.

Yahweh is understood to be the instigator of a call to battle against Edom (v. 1b-c). Twice Yahweh is quoted in direct announcement of judgment (vv. 2 and 4, and v. 8). The first two verses speak of judgment for Edom's arrogance and pride toward God. The last verse links the judgment to "violence done to their brother, Jacob."

The indictment is expanded in v. 11 while vv. 12-14 scold Edom for its actions "on the day of Israel's misfortune."

This historical judgment means much more to Israel than just vengeance on an enemy. It is set in the frame of Yahweh's great day in which justice is made real and the purpose of God's election of Zion and Israel will be fulfilled (vv. 15-18). For believing Israel, the sequence of events had implied an end to all God intended for it. Obadiah's message is that God will accomplish His purpose for His chosen through and beyond the tragic circumstances they endure. Justice that brings destruction to Edom is the same justice that gives Israel a future on Zion and in their own possession.

The final passage justifies the title of the book. It is a vision of things to come as elements of the dispersion move back to possess the promised land (vv. 19f.). Their leaders are called "saviors" who from Zion will rule over the land of Edom as in David's time (v. 21a). This will be a sign that the right of rule really does belong to Yahweh (v. 21b).

*3. Relation to Jeremiah.* Verses 1b-4 are remarkably similar to Jer. 49:14-16 and v. 5 to 49:9. In the nineteenth century, the literary relationship was analyzed by C. P. Caspari (pp. 7ff.), who concluded that Jeremiah had taken parts of an earlier oracle against Edom and reworked and expanded it in his own language. K. H. Graf (*Der Prophet Jeremia erklärt* [1862], pp. 559ff.) and S. R. Driver (*Intro. to the Literature of the OT* [repr. 1956], pp. 319f.) were among those who accepted this view, but Driver also followed H. Ewald (*Prophets of the OT* [Eng. tr. 1868], II, 277ff.) and Graf in thinking that, whereas Jeremiah had taken liberties textually with an earlier prophecy against Edom, Obadiah had cited it more faithfully. By contrast, Bewer concluded that Jeremiah had preserved the original oracle of Ob. 1-9 better than Obadiah himself did (p. 3), and T. H. Robinson concurred in this opinion. L. C. Allen (pp. 132f.) along with some other conservative authors, also considered Jer. 49 to be more primitive.

In addition to reflections of Jeremiah in Obadiah's prophecy, there appears to be a direct allusion in Joel 2:32 (MT 3:5) to Ob. 17. It is difficult to determine whether Joel was quoting the alleged earlier oracle which some scholars think both Jeremiah and Obadiah used, or whether he was actually citing one of these prophetic authors. If Joel was prophesying between 597 and 587 B.C. (cf. Joel 1:13f.; 2:15-17), he could have been reflecting the earlier prophecy rather than Jeremiah or Obadiah. But if Joel prophesied after the Exile, he may only have alluded in a general manner to one aspect of seventh-century B.C. prophetic eschatology rather than to the utterances of specific prophets of that period.

*C. Meaning and Message. 1. The Dominion of Yahweh.* The book has meaning when it is perceived as a prophetic and liturgical application of the OT understanding of God's rule over Israel and the nations (v. 21c). The OT teaches that Yahweh's dominion includes the nations, but that He has a special relation to Israel. This special relationship determines His relation to specific nations. The OT also teaches God's promise to unite Israel in Canaan.

God's acts toward the nations concern Israel because God uses the nations to accomplish His will for His people. If God fails to restrain the nations from pressure on Israel, it is seen as a judgment on Israel. When the nations are subdued, it is seen as God's acts on behalf of Israel. God holds the nations accountable for their acts toward Israel.

Within that setting, Obadiah sees the announced attack that will destroy the remnant of Edom as divine retribution for Edom's earlier attitude and action against Israel. Edom's destruction may also be seen as a sign of Yahweh's renewed dominion over the world, of His continued special relation to Israel, and of His loyalty to His promise to unite Israel again in Canaan.

*2. Edom.* Edom has theological significance in the OT. Edom is seen as the descendant of Esau (Dt. 23:7) and thus Israel's brother, both by blood and by treaty (Am. 1:11). But kinship and common interests also created conflict. David subdued Edom (2 S. 8:13f.) and Judah fought often with Edom (e.g., 2 K. 14:7). On other occasions they were allies against invaders (e.g., 2 K. 3).

In the Babylonian destruction of Jerusalem in 587 B.C. Edom was somehow involved in ways that Israel considered treacherous and unfair. Obadiah joins Ps. 137:7; Isa. 34:3-15; 63:1-6; Jer. 49:7-22; Lam. 4:21f.; Ezk. 35:3-15 (cf. Jth. 7:8, 18; 1 Esd. 4:45) in seeing God's judgment on Edom as a meaningful aspect of the Day of the Lord in which justice is finally done for an earlier wrong. This is evidence of God's faithfulness to do justice and to keep His promises concerning Israel's special relation to Him.

*D. Text.* The brevity of the prophecy has probably contributed to a reasonably good preservation of the text. Some scholars have postulated dislocations or transpositions in vv. 5, 15, and 21, along with certain early annotations to vv. 19f. In v. 6, the LXX, Syr., and Vulg. read the singular *niḥpaś* ("has been pillaged") for MT *neḥpᵉśû* (see AV). The LXX of v. 9 placed the final words "by slaughter" at the beginning of v. 10, making a couplet of "slaughter and violence," and this tradition was followed in the NEB (cf. AV, RSV). Verse 20 presents certain difficulties, with the MT reading "the captivity of this army" (see AV). This was rendered conjecturally by RSV as "the exiles in Halah" and by the NEB as "exiles of Israel." In v. 21, the LXX, Syr., and some versions had "those who have been saved" (interpreting MT *môšîʿîm* as a presumed hophal part., *mûšāʿîm*) for "saviors" (RSV, AV) and "those who find safety" (NEB).

*Bibliography.–Comms.:* L. C. Allen (*NICOT,* 1976); J. A. Bewer (*ICC,* 1911); C. P. Caspari (1842); J. H. Eaton (*Torch,* 1961); W. Rudolph (*KAT,* 1971); J. A. Thompson (*IB*); J. D. W. Watts (1969); Watts (*CBC,* 1975); H. W. Wolff (*BKAT,* 1977).

*Other Studies:* H. Bekel, *Theologische Studien und Kritiken,* 80 (1907), 315-343; G. Fohrer, "Die Sprüche Obadjias," in *Studia Biblica et Semitica* (*Festschrift* for T. C. Vriezen, 1966), pp. 81-93; J. W. Kornfeld, "Die judäische Diaspora in Ab. 20," in *Mélanges bibliques* (*Festschrift* for A. Robert, 1957), pp. 180-86; T. H. Robinson, *JTS,* 17 (1916), 402-408.

J. D. W. WATTS

**OBAL** ō'bəl [Heb. *ʿôḇāl*] (Gen. 10:28). Son of Joktan and ancestor of an Arabian tribe; called Ebal in 1 Ch. 1:22. The location of the tribe has not been identified (see M. F. Unger, *Archaeology and the OT* [1954], pp. 98f.).

**OBDIA** ob-dī'ə (AV, NEB, 1 Esd. 5:38). *See* HABAIAH.

**OBED** ō'bed [Heb. *ʿôḇēḏ, ʿōḇēḏ*–'worshiper'; Gk. *Iōbēd*].

**1.** Son of Ruth and Boaz; father of Jesse; grandfather of David; ancestor of Jesus (Ruth 4:17, 21f.; Mt. 1:5; Lk. 3:32).

**2.** Son of Ephlal, a descendant of Jerahmeel the Judahite (1 Ch. 2:37f.).

**3.** One of David's "mighty men" (1 Ch. 11:47).

**4.** A Korahite gatekeeper at the temple, son of Shemaiah; described as a man "of great ability" (1 Ch. 26:6f.).

**5.** Father of Azariah, one of the commanders who aided Jehoiada in deposing Queen Athaliah and crowning Joash (2 Ch. 23:1).

**6.** [Gk. Apoc. *Ōbēth*]; AV, NEB, OBETH. Son of Jonathan; one of the men who returned from Babylon with Ezra (1 Esd. 8:32); called Ebed in Ezr. 8:6.

**OBED-EDOM** ō'bəd ē'dəm [Heb. *ʿōḇēḏ ʾᵉḏôm*–'servant of Edom' (?)].

**1.** A Philistine living somewhere between Kiriath-jearim (where the ark of God had been for some twenty years, 1 S. 7:1f.) and Jerusalem (2 S. 6:10-12; 1 Ch. 13:13f.; 15:25). He was a Gittite (i.e., from Gath) who had taken up residence in Judah. After the sudden death of Uzzah — who had touched the ark while it was being transported to Jerusalem — David was afraid to move it further and left it at the house of Obed-edom. During the three months the ark remained with Obed-edom, he and his household were blessed by Yahweh. This was a clear sign to David that he should bring the ark to Jerusalem, which he did with much rejoicing.

**2.** A Levitical gatekeeper and musician; son of the musician Jeduthun (1 Ch. 16:38). His primary work was apparently that of gatekeeper (15:18, 24; 16:38), but he was also among those assigned to play the lyre before the ark of the covenant (15:21; cf. vv. 16-18; 16:5).

**3.** Head of a Korahite family of gatekeepers assigned to the south gate of the temple and the storehouse (1 Ch. 26:4, 8, 15). He was blessed of God in that he had sixty-two sons and descendants who served as gatekeepers, and they were men of great ability (26:4-8).

**4.** A temple servant in charge of its vessels and precious metals. Joash king of Israel took Obed-edom hostage when he defeated Amaziah of Judah in battle, sacked Jerusalem, and stole the sacred vessels and silver and gold of the temple (2 Ch. 25:24).

D. H. ENGELHARD

**OBEDIENCE.** *See* HEAR.

**OBEDIENCE OF CHRIST.**

*I. His Outward Obedience.*–At times the Gospels note Jesus' obedient response to the claims of human authority and custom, His subjection to His parents (Lk. 4:16), His observance of religious ordinances (Lk. 4:16), and His payment of tribute money (Mt. 17:24ff.). But the chief emphasis is that His whole earthly career was worked out step by step in perfect obedience to God's plan for Him as Savior (cf. Mt. 3:15). He lived under the constant constraint of fulfilling this career, which climaxed in His baptism in blood on the cross (Lk. 24:26). Knowing well from the start all that it involved (Mk. 2:20), He set His face unflinchingly in the direction of its fulfillment (Lk. 13:22). His whole career is described as "obedience" in Phil. 2:6ff.; He. 5:8. It is the fulfillment of the prophecy of Ps. 40:7 (MT 8) (cf. He. 10:7).

*II. His Inward Obedience.*–Christ's obedience was not automatic. He struggled greatly to overcome temptation from outside (cf. Mk. 1:13; Mt. 16:23) and to subdue what in Himself required stern and wholehearted discipline to bring it fully into line with God's purpose. He shrank from the agony involved in obedience (Mt. 26:38ff.). Although it was not possible for Him to sin, He nonetheless was tempted with a severity that He alone could resist triumphantly (cf. He. 4:15).

In making His obedient choice of God's will, He was completely without sin (Jn. 8:46; 2 Cor. 5:21; He. 4:15; 7:26). He claimed for Himself a perfect obedience in all the inward thoughts and tendencies of the heart: a continual openness of mind to learn what was God's will and a continual readiness to do it (Jn. 8:28), an inability to act without divine leading (5:19) or to judge anything apart from God (v. 30), a continual concern never to fail God in His work (9:4). He had such an identity of will with the Father that He could say: "The Father is in me and I am in the Father" (10:8; cf. 14:10). "I and the Father are one" (Jn. 10:30) is not simply a metaphysical statement. It is His affirmation that in Himself "there is no purpose of self; no element of self-will; no possibility, even for a moment, of the imagination of separateness" (Moberly, pp. 99f.).

*III. His Active and Passive Obedience.*–As well as having the active element of fulfilling a victorious career in the midst of the moral, spiritual, and other conflicts of life, His obedience had a passive aspect of acknowledging the judgment of God on sinners, with whom He more and more identified Himself, and of taking the responsibility for their sins. Such obedience ultimately meant submission to the shame and dereliction of the cross.

Thus in Christ's career and response to God an "active" and a "passive" obedience can be distinguished, as classical Protestant theology frequently does. But these two aspects of Christ's obedience cannot be separated. "They do not differ in time: both extend from the beginning of the incarnation to the death. Nor in subject; the same obedience is active and passive in a different respect" (Wollebius, in H. Heppe, p. 467).

*IV. The Place of Obedience in the Atonement.*–Due weight must be given to Rom. 5:19, "As by one man's disobedience many were made sinners, so by one man's obedience many will be made righteous," and to He. 9:14, "who through the eternal Spirit offered himself without blemish to God." It is obvious that the whole course of Christ's earthly obedience, as well as His death, contributes toward the full accomplishment of the atonement. Thus Calvin thought of the obedience of Christ as His merit and insisted that His reconciling and sanctifying work in human nature was carried out throughout His life on earth.

The Westminster Confession of Faith (cf. 8.5 and 11.3) distinguishes, almost sharply, between Christ's obedience and His death. Some have tended to attach His obedience to the work of sanctification and His death to the work of satisfaction. Moberly (pp. 98f.) suggested that the cancellation of the past should be attributed to the offering of atonement, and the sanctification of the present to the offering of obedience (cf. also Rom. 5:10).

No basis may exist, however, for such fine distinction. People require His obedience for their atonement, and fellowship with His death as well as with His life for their sanctification (cf. He. 10:10). As Denney said, "Obedience is the one term by which His work can always be described in relation to God" (*Death of Christ,* p. 232; cf. *Christian Doctrine of Reconciliation,* pp. 94-96). In the cross the obedience seems to be as important as the event; as P. T. Forsyth pointed out, what matters in it is not simply the "depth of agony" but also the "height of surrender" (p. 193).

Yet His saying (Lk. 12:50) "I have a baptism to be baptized with; and how am I constrained until it is accomplished" undoubtedly concentrates on His death as the focal point and fulfillment of His whole life's purpose. His death is significant as a deliberate act of "laying down" His life (Jn. 10:17). The blood by which people are saved from their sins is undoubtedly the *obedient life* poured out in death (Rev. 1:5; Rom. 3:25), but it is doubtful if the analogy of sacrificial blood would have been used unless a good deal of emphasis could be placed on the death in which the life is poured out.

***Bibliography.***–G. Aulén, *Eucharist and Sacrifice* (Eng. tr. 1958), pp. 147ff.; K. Barth, *CD,* IV/2, pp. 92ff.; E. Brunner, *The Mediator* (Eng. tr. 1947), pp. 496ff.; J. Denney, *Death of Christ* (repr. 1951), pp. 228ff.; *Christian Doctrine of Reconciliation* (1917), pp. 94-96; P. T. Forsyth, *Cruciality of the Cross* (repr. 1965), pp. 191ff.; H. Heppe, *Reformed Dogmatics* (Eng. tr. 1950); R. C. Moberly, *Atonement and Personality* (1910), pp. 99f.

R. S. WALLACE

**OBEISANCE** [Heb. *hištaḥ$^{a}$wâ*–'bow down deeply, prostrate oneself']; AV also BOW ONESELF, DO REVERENCE, WORSHIP, "humbly beseech" (2 S. 16:4); NEB also PROSTRATE ONESELF, BOW LOW, "I am your humble servant, sir" (2 S. 16:4); **PROSTRATE** [Heb. *hištaḥ$^{a}$wâ* (Isa. 49:7), *nāpal*–'fall down, throw oneself down' (Ps. 36:12 [MT 13]; hithpael, Dt. 9:18, 25), *šāḥaḥ*–'bow down' (Ps. 38:6 [MT 7])]; AV FALL DOWN, FALLEN, BOWED DOWN, WORSHIP; NEB also LIE, BOW DOWN. A gesture of respect or submission, which involved dropping to one's knees and touching one's nose and forehead to the ground. *See* picture in JEHU.

The Hebrew verb *hištaḥ$^{a}$wâ* was formerly understood as the hithpalel of *šāḥâ* (cf. BDB, p. 1005; KoB, p. 959). Modern scholarship, however, has discovered the Ugaritic verbal root *ḥwy,* which has a form *yšthwy,* "he prostrates himself"; and this has led to the conclusion that Hebrew once had a rare verbal root *ḥwh,* which has vanished except for the hishtaphel form *hištaḥ$^{a}$wâ* (*TDOT,* IV, 249). The form occurs 170 times in the OT (almost always translated *proskynéō* by the LXX). Its first meaning is the act of prostration, which can be performed before persons as a gesture of respect or submission or before Yahweh or other gods as an act of worship. Frequently it is used as a technical term for cultic worship (cf. the frequent prohibitions against "bowing down" [*hištaḥ$^{a}$wâ*] to other gods; e.g., Ex. 20:5; 23:24; Dt. 5:9; Josh. 23:7, 16; Ps. 81:9 [MT 10]). Thus the RSV most often renders it "worship" (e.g., Gen. 24:26, 48; Dt. 4:19; 8:19; 17:3; 26:10); the translation "bow (down)" is also common.

The RSV renders "do (or make) obeisance" in twenty-

Captive Elamites doing obeisance before Assyrian soldiers. Relief from Ashurbanipal's palace in Nineveh (*ca.* 645 B.C.) (Trustees of the British Museum)

one passages where the term denotes prostration before a person. Frequently it represents HOMAGE paid to a king or ruler, especially when one is making a request. Thus Joseph's brothers make obeisance before him in fulfillment of his dream (Gen. 43:28; cf. 37:7, 9f.; 42:6; 43:26). Likewise, David prostrates himself before Saul (1 S. 24:8 [MT 9]); and Mephibosheth (2 S. 9:6, 8), the wise woman of Tekoa (14:4), Joab (v. 22), Ziba (16:4), Araunah (24:20; cf. 1 Ch. 21:21), Bathsheba (1 K. 1:16, 31), Nathan (v. 23), and the assembly of Israel (1 Ch. 29:20) prostrate themselves before David; cf. 2 S. 1:2; 15:5; 18:28; 1 K. 1:53; 2 Ch. 29:20. Such a gesture of respect is also shown to visitors by Abraham (Gen. 18:2) and Lot (19:1), to Esau by Jacob and his family (33:3, 6f.), to Israel by Joseph (48:12), to Jethro by Moses (Ex. 18:7), to Boaz by Ruth (Ruth 2:10), to Jonathan by David (1 S. 20:41), to David by Abigail (25:23, 41), to Samuel by Saul (28:14), to his mother Bathsheba by Solomon (1 K. 2:19), etc. Mordecai incurred Haman's wrath by refusing to prostrate himself before him (Est. 3:2, 5).

*See also* ADORATION; POSTURES; WORSHIP.

***Bibliography.***–*TDNT,* VI, *s.v.* προσκυνέω (H. Greeven); *TDOT,* IV, *s.v.* "ḥwh" (H. D. Preuss); *TWOT,* I, 267-69.

N. J. O.

**OBELISK** ob'ə-lisk [Heb. *maṣṣēḇâ*–'pillar']; AV IMAGE; NEB SACRED PILLAR. Jeremiah 43:13 predicts Nebuchadrezzar's invasion of Egypt, prophesying that he will break the *maṣṣ$^{e}$ḇôṯ* of Beth-shemesh, which is in the land of Egypt. The Heb. *maṣṣ$^{e}$ḇôṯ* is appropriately rendered "obelisks" here (so RSV, JB, NAB) in view of the Egyptian context. Beth-shemesh, "house of the sun," is no doubt the Egyptian city of Yenew, "city of the column" (*see* ON), called by the Greeks Heliopolis, "city of the sun" (LXX "the pillars of Heliopolis, which are in On"). Located 9.6 km. (6 mi.) NE of Cairo, Heliopolis was the center of the sun-god Re (known also as Atum-Re). Seti I (*ca.* 1318-1304) boasted that he filled Heliopolis with obelisks.

According to the Heliopolitan theology the obelisk symbolized the primeval hill at the beginning of creation. It became the symbol of the sun-god, guaranteeing life and prosperity to the pharaohs. Pliny the Elder called the obelisks "symbolic representations of the sun's rays" (*Nat. hist.* xxxvi.14.64, *LCL*). As sacred objects, they had offerings made to them.

Egyptians called obelisks either *tekhen* or *benben*. The latter word is derived from the verb *wbn*, "shine," indicating its association with the sun. As a joke Greek visitors called these huge monuments *obelisks* (<*obelós*, "spit"), i.e., "little spits."

Obelisks can be traced back to the 5th Dynasty (*ca.* 2400 B.C.), and they continued in use (with some lapses) through the Ptolemaic period. The Romans removed many Egyptian obelisks for their own use, as well as erecting some new ones.

The best known example of the obelisk shape in America is, of course, the Washington Monument.

***Bibliography*.**–R. Engelbach, *Problem of the Obelisks* (1923); E. A. W. Budge, *Cleopatra's Needles and Other Egyptian Obelisks* (1926); S. Giedion, *Eternal Present II: The Beginnings of Architecture* (1964); A. Badawy, *History of Egyptian Architecture: The Empire* (1968); K. Martin, *Ein Garantsymbol des Lebens* (1977).

E. M. YAMAUCHI

**OBETH** ō'beth (AV, NEB, 1 Esd. 8:32). *See* OBED **6.**

**OBEY.** *See* HEAR.

**OBIL** ō'bil [Heb. *'ôḇîl*–'camel driver']. An Israelite who was in charge of King David's camels (1 Ch. 27:30).

**OBJECT.** The verb is used by the AV in the archaic sense of "accuse" in Acts 24:19 (RSV "make an accusation"); Wisd. 2:12 (AV "he . . . objecteth to our infamy the transgressions of our education"; RSV "he . . . accuses us of sins against our training").

**OBLATION.** The RSV translation of Heb. *minḥâ* (1 K. 18:29, 36), which often signifies the cereal offering, but may be used here in the general sense of an offering or sacrifice (cf. AV, NEB, "sacrifice"; also RSV of 2 K. 3:20). The time of the evening sacrifice was around 3 p.m.

The AV uses "oblation" more often. Sometimes it translates *minḥâ* (Isa. 1:13; 19:21; 66:3; Jer. 14:12; Dnl. 2:46; 9:21, 27). In Leviticus (also Nu. 18:9; 31:50) it is occasionally used for *qorbān*, a general term for all kinds of offerings. In 2 Ch. 31:14; Isa. 40:20; Ezk. 44–48 it renders *tᵉrûmâ* (AV usually "heave offering"; RSV "offering" or "wave offering").

*See* SACRIFICES AND OFFERINGS IN THE OT.

**OBOTH** ō'both [Heb. *'ōḇôṯ*–'waterskins']. A station of the Israelites in their journey from Mt. Hor to Moab (Nu. 21:10f.; 33:43f.). In Nu. 33 the sequence given is: Mt. Hor, Zalmonah, Punon, Oboth, Iye-abarim in the territory of Moab. In Nu. 21 the route is deliberately taken to avoid Edom, and Iye-abarim is described as in the wilderness "opposite Moab toward the sunrise" (21:11) and followed by the next location at the valley of Zered. The place therefore would seem to be E of Edom, between Feinân (Punon) and Wâdī el-Ḥesā (Zered). It has been suggested (*LBHG*, rev. ed., p. 55) that several stations on the King's Highway are named in the biblical account, and *Macmillan Bible Atlas* (Map 52) indeed does locate Oboth on this road, N of Bozrah. Abel marks it as the crossroads of the Gaza-Petra and the Tell el-Milḥ-Aqaba highways (*GP*, II, 401). The intention to circumvent Edom, however, suggests a location farther east, possibly on the Way of the Wilderness (the desert road or "Pilgrim Road"; cf. Baly, *GB*, rev. ed., p. 97). One suggested site, namely, ʿAin el-Weiba, based principally on a supposed similarity of the Arabic and Hebrew names and supported by the fact that it would be a suitable campsite (*GTTOT*, § 439), is actually located on the western side of the Arabah, opposite Feinân. It therefore is to be rejected on two counts: the Israelites would have reached that site before they came to Punon (cf. Nu. 33:43), and it is toward the west, not the east (cf. Nu. 21:11).

W. S. LASOR

**OBSCURITY.** A term used by the AV to denote total darkness. In Isa. 29:18 the AV renders "out of obscurity, and out of darkness" for Heb. *mē'ōpel ûmēḥōšeḵ* (RSV "out of their gloom and darkness"; NEB "out of impenetrable darkness"). Similarly, in 58:10; 59:9 "obscurity" renders *ḥōšeḵ* (RSV, NEB, "darkness") and "darkness" renders *'ōpel* (RSV "gloom"; NEB "dusk," "deep gloom"). In Prov. 20:20 "obscure darkness" renders *'îšôn ḥōšeḵ* (*K*) (lit. "eye of darkness"; cf. RSV "utter darkness"; the NEB "darkness comes" renders *'ᵉšûn ḥōšeḵ* [*Q*]).

The RSV uses "obscure" in the sense of "humble" or "unimportant" in Prov. 22:29 to render *ḥᵃšukkîm* (cognate of *ḥōšeḵ*; RSV "obscure men"; AV "mean men"; NEB "common men"), and in the sense of "impenetrable" or "unintelligible" in Isa. 33:19 for *ʿāmēq* (AV "deeper"; NEB "so hard to catch"; cf. Ezk. 3:5f., RSV "foreign").

N. J. O.

**OBSERVE.**

(1) [Heb. usually *šāmar*, also *ḥāgag* (Ex. 12:14), *ʿāśâ* (31:16), etc.; Gk. *tēréō* (Mt. 23:3; 28:20), *paratēréō* (Gal. 4:10), *phylássō* (Mt. 19:20 par.), *kratéō* (Mk. 7:3f.), *peripatéō* (Acts 21:21), *phronéō* (Rom. 14:6)]; AV also KEEP, REGARD, etc.; NEB also KEEP, DO, etc. In these passages "observe" means to practice, keep, or carry out. Heb. *šāmar* occurs frequently in the sense of "keep," especially with reference to obeying commands (e.g., Ex. 34:11; Lev. 19:37; 26:3; Josh. 22:5; Ps. 105:45) and celebrating feasts or holy days (e.g., Ex. 12:17; Dt. 5:12; 16:1). *Ḥāgag* ("celebrate a feast") and *ʿāśâ* ("do") are used in much the same way, as are also the NT terms.

(2) [Heb. *šāmar* (1 S. 1:12; 2 S. 20:10; Job 39:1; Eccl. 11:4; Isa. 42:20), *pāqaḏ* (Ex. 3:16), *yāḏaʿ* (Ruth 3:4), *bîn* (Ps. 33:15; Prov. 23:1), hiphil of *śāḵal* (Prov. 21:12), *nāṣar* (Prov. 23:26), *rā'â* (Eccl. 8:9; Jer. 33:24; Dnl. 1:13); Gk. *paratḗresis* (Lk. 17:20), *katanoéō* (Acts 11:6; Jas. 1:23f.), *anatheōréō* (Acts 17:23), *parakolouthéō* (2 Tim. 3:10)]; AV also MARK, CONSIDER, SEE, BEHOLD, etc.; NEB also "turn [my] eyes toward," "take note of," WATCH, KNOW, etc. Here "observe" means to see, notice, watch, or inspect. Heb. *šāmar* occurs in the sense of "watch." Some of the terms connote understanding as well as perception (e.g., *bîn*, *śāḵal*). Gk. *katanoéō* means "notice" or "inspect," while *parakolouthéō* means "follow," both with mind and in practice (2 Tim. 3:10). *See also* MARK II; SEE.

(3) Occasionally "observe" is used by the AV in an archaic sense; e.g., "his father observed [Heb. *šāmar*] the saying" (Gen. 37:11; RSV ". . . kept the saying in mind"); "observe [*šāmar*] lying vanities" (Jonah 2:8 [MT 9]; RSV "pay regard to"); "heard . . . and observed [*šûr*] him" (Hos. 14:8 [MT 9]; RSV ". . . and look after . . ."); "for Herod . . . observed [Gk. *syntēréō*] him" (Mk. 6:20; RSV ". . . and kept him safe").

N. J. O.

**OBSERVE TIMES.** *See* MAGIC II.A(5).

**OBSTINACY.** *See* STUBBORN.

**OCCASION.** The RSV translation of several terms with a wide range of meanings, e.g., Heb. *tᵉnû'â* ("grounds for opposition," Job 33:10), Gk. *chreía* ("need," Eph. 4:29), *aphormḗ* ("opportunity," 1 Tim. 5:14), and *tópos* (lit. "place," He. 8:7). In 1 S. 22:22 the AV and RSV render "I have occasioned" (i.e., "caused") for Heb. *sabbōṯî* (from *sāḇaḇ*, "turn, go around"), which many commentators (e.g., P. McCarter [*AB*, 1980], p. 363) emend to *ḥaḇtî* (from *ḥûḇ*, "be guilty"; cf. KoB, pp. 280, 647) on the basis of the LXX and Syriac.

**OCCUPATIONS** [Heb. *ma'ᵃśeh*] (Gen. 46:33; 47:3); [*mᵉlā'ḵâ*] (Jonah 1:8); NEB BUSINESS; [Gk. *hoi perí tá toiaúta ergátai*–'the workers who do such things' ("the workmen of like occupation," Acts 19:25); NEB ALLIED TRADES. Both *ma'ᵃśeh* and *mᵉlā'ḵâ* are general terms usually translated "work." Shepherd (Gen. 47:3) and silversmith (Acts 19:24) are only two out of about two hundred different occupations mentioned or implied in the Bible. *See* CRAFTS; WORK.

**OCCUPY.** A term used by the RSV in three different senses: (1) "engage someone's energy or attention" (Heb. piel of *hālaḵ* [Ps. 131:1; AV "exercise"; NEB "busy"], hiphil of *'ānâ* [Eccl. 5:20 (MT 19); AV "answer"; NEB "fill time"]; Gk. *synéchomai* [Acts 18:5; AV "pressed"; NEB "devoted"], *proséchō* [1 Tim. 1:4; AV "give heed to"; NEB "study"]); (2) "take possession of" (Heb. *yāraš* [Nu. 13:30; Dt. 2:31; 3:20; AV "possess," "inherit"]); (3) "reside in" (Heb. *bō'* [Neh. 2:8; AV "enter"]).

The AV uses "occupy" several times in the obsolete sense of "trade." In Ezk. 27:16, 19, 22 the AV renders Heb. *nāṯᵉnû bᵉ'izḇônāyiḵ* "they occupied thy fairs" (RSV "they exchanged for your wares"). In vv. 9, 27, AV, "occupy" and "occupiers" render forms of *'āraḇ* (RSV "barter," "dealers"), and in v. 21 a form of *sāḥar* (RSV "dealers"). In Lk. 19:13 "occupy" translates Gk. *pragmateúomai* (RSV "trade with").

Other unusual AV uses of "occupy" occur in Ex. 38:24 (Heb. *'āśâ*; cf. RSV "use") and in He. 13:9 (part. of Gk. *peripatéō*, lit. "walk," "behave"; RSV "adherents"). In 1 Cor. 14:16 "occupy" renders *anaplēróō* (lit. "fill up"); *see* OUTSIDER. N. J. O.

**OCCURRENT.** An obsolete form of "occurrence" used by the AV in 1 K. 5:4 (MT 18), rendering Heb. *pega'*, "chance" (RSV "misfortune"; NEB "attack").

**OCHIEL** ō-kī'əl [Gk. B *Ochiēlos*, A *Oziēlos*]; NEB OZIELUS. A Levite "captain over thousands" who furnished the Levites with cattle for the Passover in the time of King Josiah (1 Esd. 1:9); called JEIEL (7) in 1 Ch. 35:9.

**OCHRAN** ok'rən [Heb. *'oḵrān*–'trouble']; AV, NEB, OCRAN. The father of Pagiel, the leader of the tribe of Asher in the journey through the wilderness (Nu. 1:13; 2:27; 7:72, 77; 10:26).

**OCIDELUS** os-ə-dē'ləs (1 Esd. 9:22, AV). *See* GEDALIAH **3.**

**OCINA** ō-sī'nə [Gk. *Okina*] (Jth. 2:28); NEB OKINA. A town located somewhere along the Phoenician coast S of Tyre. The only clue to its exact location is its position in the list of cities: Sidon, Tyre, Sur, Ocina, Jamnia, Azotus, and Ascalon. Sandalium (Iskanderun) and various other places have been suggested but have little support. Both the name and location of Acco make it a likely possibility. Ocina is one of several cities named in Judith as representative of all the people along the eastern Mediterranean seacoast who were filled with terror when they heard of the approach of Holofernes, an Assyrian general sent by Nebuchadrezzar to devastate the lands that had revolted against him. D. H. MADVIG

**OCRAN** ok'rən (AV, NEB, Nu. 1:13; etc.). *See* OCHRAN.

**ODED** ō'ded [Heb. *'ôḏēḏ*–'restorer'].

**1.** The father of Azariah, who prophesied in the reign of Asa of Judah (2 Ch. 15:1). The conjecture that Oded was the same as Iddo (12:15; 19:29) has no tenable foundation. The difficulty of 15:8, which makes Oded himself the prophet, cannot be explained by dropping "Azariah the son of," for the phrase "the prophet" is still in the Hebrew absolute state. The only solution is to delete the words "Oded the prophet" from the text as a gloss (cf. KD, *in loc.*; GKC, § 127f).

**2.** A prophet of Samaria (2 Ch. 28:9) who lived in the reigns of Pekah of Israel and Ahaz of Judah. He protested the enslavement of Judahites captured during the Syro-Ephraimitic attack on the southern kingdom. Because chiefs of Ephraim supported him, the prisoners were treated kindly and escorted back to Jericho.

J. A. BALCHIN

**ODES OF SOLOMON.** *See* SOLOMON, ODES OF.

**ODOLLAM** ō-dol'əm (2 Macc. 12:38, AV). *See* ADULLAM **1.**

**ODOMERA** od-ə-mē'rə [Gk. B *Odomēra*, A *Odoarrēs*] (1 Macc. 9:66); AV ODONARKES. According to most LXX MSS, the victim of a surprise attack by Jonathan in the Judean wilderness near Bethbasi. He is usually understood to have been the chief of a bedouin clan or the leader of the pro-Greek party that incited Bacchides to attempt, unsuccessfully, to capture Jonathan and his forces (*ca.* 156 B.C.).

Two Greek MSS (V and 340), however, read *epétaxen* ("summoned," "commanded") in place of *epátaxen* (RSV "struck down"), and J. A. Goldstein (*I Maccabees* [*AB*, 1976], pp. 379, 395) has suggested that this is the correct reading. Odomera and his clansmen would then have been Nabateans who sympathized with Jonathan (cf. 5:25) and aided him in attacking Bacchides (cf. 9:67, RSV mg.: "Then they began to attack . . ."). This interpretation finds support in the parallel account of Josephus (*Ant.* xiii.1.5 [28]): "and [Jonathan] himself secretly went out into the country; then having gathered together a large force from among those who sympathized with him, he fell upon Bacchides' camp. . . ."

J. J. SCOTT, JR. N. J. O.

**ODOR** [Heb. *rê(a)ḥ*] (Gen. 8:21; Ex. 29:18, 25, 41; Lev. 1:9; etc.); AV SAVOUR; [hiphil of *bā'aš*] (Eccl. 10:1); AV SAVOUR; NEB RANCID; [Gk. *ózō*] (Jn. 11:39); AV STINKETH; NEB STENCH.

In forty-three of its forty-four occurrences in the RSV OT, "odor" translates *rê(a)ḥ* (lit. "breath," for scent is always air-borne) and always as it appears in the phrase "pleasing odor" (NEB "soothing odour"). This phrase was an old liturgical formula for the calming, pleasant smell of the ascending sacrifice before the Lord. This formula had very ancient roots but in time lost its literal sense and became simply a technical term for divine acceptance of (1 S. 26:19) or delight in (Am. 5:21) sacrificial offerings.

"Pleasing odor" appears often in Leviticus and Numbers in the context of priestly instructions for different categories of sacrifice. First, Lev. 1:1-17 mentions the "burnt offerings" of cattle (v. 9), the smaller animals (v. 13), and birds (v. 17). Each such offering is said to be "an offering by fire, a pleasing odor to the Lord" (cf. also Lev. 8:21, 28; Ex. 29:18). Second, Lev. 2:1-16 describes the "cereal offering" and again employs the formula "pleasing odor" (vv. 2, 9, 12), particularly with respect to the "memorial portion" (cf. Lev. 6:15, 21 [MT 8, 14]; Nu. 5:26), the small handful which was burned with oil and frankincense as a "pleasing odor" and which for the very poor could serve as a sin offering (Lev. 5:12). Third, Lev. 3:1-17 discusses the "peace offering," which is to be burned (v. 5) on top of the burnt offering as "a pleasing odor to the Lord." In Lev. 4:31 the same stock phrase is applied to a fourth category, the "sin offering," which atoned for unintentional sin. In Lev. 8:28 a similar phrase is applied to the "ordination offering" and in Nu. 15:7 to the "drink offering."

This long enduring anthropomorphic formula first appears in Gen. 8:21 (J). According to this passage, after the Flood Noah offered burnt offerings and "the Lord smelled the pleasing odor" and determined never again to send such a deluge. This language may bear a literary relationship to the sacrificial language and thought patterns of ancient Mesopotamia — the deity upon smelling the deliciously soothing odor of roasting food is delighted and relaxed and thereby assuaged of wrath (cf. the Gilgamesh Epic, tablet XI, lines 159-161; *ANET,* p. 95). Possibly, then, Hebrew sacrificial language ultimately derives from the ancient idea of sacrifice as feeding the deity, though this concept of sacrifice is certainly not Hebraic (cf. W. Eichrodt, *Theology of the OT,* I [Eng. tr., *OTL,* 1961], 141ff.). The OT also has a dimension of gratitude in sacrifice, clearly seen in the early example of Noah and no doubt also in that of his Mesopotamian counterpart Utnapishtim (cf. A. Heidel, *Gilgamesh Epic and OT Parallels* [1946], pp. 255-57).

The same liturgical formula ("pleasing odor") appears four times in Ezekiel. This is indicative of the prevalence of priestly terminology in that book. In three places (6:13; 16:19; 20:28) the prophet refers disparagingly to the sacrificial worship of idols as offering up a "pleasing odor" to them (reflecting surely the strong Deuteronomistic polemic against the high places and probably referring to the excesses of the notorious reign of Manasseh). In Ezk. 20:41 the old liturgical formula is again applied positively to Yahweh — "As a pleasing odor I will accept you, when I bring you out from the peoples."

Beyond this formula, "odor" appears only in Eccl. 10:1, for the hiphil of Heb. *bā'aš,* "stink." Here dead flies trapped in a bottle of precious ointment cause it to "give off an evil odor" (cf. NEB "turn rancid"), analogous to the way a small indiscretion may end up outweighing great honor and wisdom in a person.

The Greek verb *ózō,* "smell, emit an odor," occurs only once in the NT (Jn. 11:39) in the phrase *ḗdē ózei,* "by this time there will be an odor" (cf. NEB "stench"), spoken by the decorous Martha with reference to the body of her brother Lazarus, who had been dead for four days.

"Aroma" in 2 Cor. 2:15 (AV "savour"; NEB "incense") translates Gk. *euōdía,* which appears elsewhere in the NT only in the expression *osmḗ euōdías,* "odor of fragrance" (cf. Heb. *rê(a)ḥ nîḥô(a)ḥ*) in Eph. 5:2; Phil. 4:18 (*see* FRAGRANCE).

***Bibliography.***–*TDNT,* V, *s.v.* ὀσμή (Delling); R. Rendtorff, *Studien zur Geschichte des Opfers im alten Israel* (*WMANT,* 24, 1967); R. de Vaux, *Ancient Israel* (Eng. tr. 1961), II, 415-456; *Studies in OT Sacrifice* (Eng. tr. 1964).

D. G. BURKE

**OF.** In Anglo-Saxon "of" has the meaning "from," "away from" (as the strengthened form "off" has still), and is not used for genitive or possessive relations, which are expressed by special case forms. In the Norman period, however, "of" was used in place of French *de,* which among other things can indicate possession; this usage was well developed by the time of Chaucer. In the Elizabethan period both these senses were in common use. After *ca.* 1600 the later sense became predominant, and "of" in the earlier usage (which is now practically obsolete) was replaced by other prepositions. As a result, the AV often uses "of" in several ways that are no longer familiar.

(1) The AV commonly uses "of" in the sense of "from." In modern English "hear of" means "gain information about," as it does frequently in the AV (Mk. 7:25; Rom. 10:14; etc.). But more commonly in the AV the expression denotes the source of the information — e.g., "all things that I have heard of my Father" (Jn. 15:15); "to hear words of thee" (Acts 10:22); "We desire to hear of thee" (28:22; cf. 1 Thess. 2:13; 2 Tim. 1:13; 2:2; etc.; similarly "and learn of me," Mt. 11:29; cf. Jn. 6:45). In most of these cases the RSV substitutes "from."

Other AV passages where "of" means "from" include 2 Cor. 5:1 ("a building of God"; RSV "from"); Mk. 9:21 ("of a child"; RSV "from childhood"). A still more obscure passage is Mt. 23:25, "full of extortion and excess" (cf. RSV). Elsewhere in the AV and RSV "full of" refers to the contents (cf. vv. 27f.), but here the expression translates Gk. *ek,* "out of," and denotes the source (cf. NEB "which you have filled inside by . . ."). For other examples of this use of "of," cf. the AV of Jth. 2:21 ("they went forth of Nineveh"); 2 Macc. 4:34 ("forth of the sanctuary"); Mt. 21:25 ("The baptism of John, whence was it? from heaven, or of men?").

(2) In some places the AV uses "of" rather loosely to connect an act with its source or motive — e.g., Mt. 18:13 ("rejoiceth more of that sheep"; RSV "over"); 1 Cor. 7:4 ("hath not power of her own body"; RSV "over").

(3) "Of" is very commonly used by the AV to designate the agent — a use complicated by the AV's frequent use of "by" for the same purpose. Thus in Lk. 9:7 ("all that was done by him . . . it was said of some"; RSV ". . . said by some") the two words are used side by side for the same preposition (Gk. *hypó*; the AV follows a MS tradition that adds *hyp' autoú*). In some passages "of" may be wrongly interpreted as a possessive: e.g., "which were made eunuchs of men" (Mt. 19:12; RSV "by men"); "There are left some clusters of them that diligently seek through the vineyard" (2 Esd. 16:30; RSV "by those"). Other obsolete uses occur in 1 Cor. 14:24 ("He is convinced of all, he is judged of all"; RSV "by all" in both places); Phil. 3:12 ("I am apprehended of Christ Jesus"; cf. RSV "Christ Jesus has made me his own").

(4) In some cases the older English usage does not provide sufficient explanation for the AV. In Mt. 28:23 "take account of his servants" is better rendered by the RSV as "settle accounts with his servants." In Acts 27:5 the "sea of Cilicia" means the "sea which is off Cilicia" (cf. RSV). In 2 Cor. 2:12 "A door was opened unto me of the Lord" should be "in the Lord" (so RSV). In 2 S. 21:4 "We will have no silver nor gold of Saul, nor of his house," is very loose, and the RSV rewrites the verse entirely. In He. 11:18 Gk. *prós* is ambiguous and may mean either "to" (so RV) or "of" (so AV, RSV, NEB; cf. He. 1:7, where "of" is necessary).

B. S. EASTON

**OFFEND** [Heb. *ḥāṭā'*–'miss (a goal),' 'go wrong,' 'sin'] (Gen. 40:1); [*'āšam*–'offend,' 'be guilty'] (Ezk. 25:12); [*ḥāḇal*–'act ruinously, corruptly'] (Job 34:31); [*lā'â*–'be weary,' 'be impatient'] (Job 4:2); [Gk. *skandalízō*–'cause to sin,' 'give offense to'] (Mt. 11:6 par. Lk. 7:23; Mt. 13:57 par. Mk. 6:3; Mt. 15:12; 17:27; Jn. 6:61); [*hamartánō*–'do wrong, sin'] (Acts 25:8); AV also GRIEVE; NEB also INCUR GUILT, DO MISCHIEF, CAUSE OFFENCE, SHOCK, etc.; **OFFENDER** [Heb. hiphil part. of *ḥāṭā'*–'bring into guilt,' 'cause to sin'] ("who . . . make . . . out to be an offender," Isa. 29:21); [*ḥaṭṭā'*–'exposed to condemnation,' 'reckoned as offender'] ("counted offenders," 1 K. 1:21); [Gk. *opheilétēs*–'debtor'] ("worse offenders," Lk. 13:4); AV "make an offender," "counted offenders," SINNERS; NEB "charge with a sin," "treat as criminals," "more guilty"; **OFFENSE** [Heb. *peša'*–'rebellion,' 'transgression'] (Gen. 31:36; Prov. 10:12; 17:9; 19:11); [*ḥēṭ'*–'sin'] (Dt. 19:15; 22:26; Eccl. 10:4); [*mikšôl*– 'stumbling, means or occasion of stumbling'](Isa. 8:14); [*riš'â*– 'wickedness'] (Dt. 25:2); [Gk. *apróskopos*–'without offense, giving no offense'] (1 Cor. 10:32); AV also TRESPASS, SIN, TRANSGRESSION, STUMBLING, FAULT; NEB also MISTAKE, "which . . . shall run against"; **OFFENSIVE** [Heb. hiphil of *bā'aš*–'cause to stink'] ("make offensive," Ex. 5:21).

In the OT, Heb. *ḥāṭā'* and its derivatives represent the most common term for sin, but they have other nuances as well. Koch has questioned the classical basic meaning "miss (a mark)" (cf. Jgs. 20:16; Job 5:24; Prov. 8:35f.; 19:2) since this is found in late passages that reflect metaphorical uses (see *TDOT*, IV, 311). In Gen. 40:1 Heb. *ḥāṭā'* refers to rebellion against a king. This word often describes a wrong committed against another person (e.g., 1 S. 19:4; 24:11 [MT 12]; 26:21; 2 K. 18:14; Jer. 37:18). In Dt. 22:26 the cognate noun Heb. *ḥēṭ'* refers to a crime, and here to forcible rape, which was a capital offense (21:22). Dt. 19:15-21 is probably an elaboration of the ninth commandment (P. C. Craigie, *Book of Deuteronomy* [*NICOT*, 1976], p. 269), and v.15 stipulates the need of multiple witnesses to verify the commission of *ḥēṭ'*. The hiphil of Heb. *ḥāṭā'*, which means "cause to (or lead into) sin," occurs in Isa. 29:21. This same form is used in regard to Jeroboam, who "made Israel to sin" (1 K. 14:16; cf. 15:26, 30, 34). It is alleged in 1 K. 1:21 that if Adonijah were to become king he would perhaps use an accusation of treason to put away Bathsheba and Solomon. Though innocent, they would appear guilty and be "counted offenders."

The range of meaning for the qal of *'āšam* includes "act wrongly, become guilty, become culpable, atone for guilt" (*TDOT*, I, 435). In Ezk. 25:12 Heb. *'āšam* precedes an infinitive of the same root. This construction expresses either the intensity or the duration of the conflict between Judah and Edom.

In Job 34:31 "I will not offend any more" is syntactically parallel to "I will do it [iniquity] no more" in v. 32; therefore, "offend" (Heb. *ḥābal*) in v. 31 must also connote sin (cf. *TDOT*, IV, 186).

Several Hebrew nouns also deserve comment. In Gen. 31:36 Jacob asks Laban, "What is my offense? What is my sin . . . ?" Here "offense" translates Heb. *peša'* (< *pāša'*, "rebel," "transgress"). Prov. 10:12 states that "love covers all offenses," and indicates that "wrongs are endured and passed over for the sake of communal peace" (W. McKane, *Proverbs* [*OTL*, 1970; repr. 1977], p. 419). Similar to this is the thought of Prov. 17:9, which encourages a gracious silence about the shortcomings of others. And in Prov. 19:11 "to overlook an offense" favors the idea of a disciplined and magnanimous response toward provocation and personal insults. Heb. *mikšôl* (<*kāšal*, "stumble, stagger, totter") may have both a literal and a figurative sense. The literal sense is evident in Lev. 19:14; here it refers to a stumbling block over which the blind fall. But in Isa. 8:14 the sense is figurative; it refers to the Lord who once was Israel's security but now will be a cause of its fall (R. E. Clements, *Isaiah 1-39* [*NCBC*, repr. 1980], pp. 99f.; cf. Isa. 57:14).

"Offensive" in Ex. 5:21 translates the hiphil of Heb. *bā'aš*, which graphically describes something foul and repulsive. The qal of Heb. *bā'aš* is used in reference to the odious smells associated with various plagues, e.g., the "foul" smell produced by dead fish in the rivers (Ex. 7:18, 21) and the stench arising from dying frogs (8:14 [MT 10]).

In the NT, Gk. *skandalízō* has several nuances. For example, a person who becomes "offended" may be someone who is unwilling to believe (e.g., Mt. 13:57 par. Mk. 6:3; cf. also *apistía*, "unbelief," in Mt. 13:58; Mk. 6:6), someone who is losing confidence (e.g., Mt. 11:6 par. Lk. 7:23; cf. *TDNT*, VII, 350), or hindered in his belief (e.g., Jn. 6:61; cf. v. 64). The report in Mt. 15:12 that the Pharisees "were offended" by Jesus' saying means that they were actually angered by His parable because it challenged their traditions. On another occasion Jesus encouraged Peter to pay the temple tax rather than "give offense" (Mt. 17:24-17). Here Jesus' concern was to avoid providing an occasion for unbelievers to reject the message of the gospel (cf. R. H. Gundry, *Matthew* [1982], p. 357).

Paul enjoined his readers to "Give no offense to the Jews or to the Greeks or to the church of God" (1 Cor. 10:32). Apparently the dietary practices of some at Corinth caused problems. Paul's advice may have been twofold, viz., a plea for minimizing an excessive scrupulosity and a warning against a flagrant violation of Jewish dietary laws (cf. J. Héring, comm. on 1 Corinthians [Eng. tr. 1962], p. 99). For Paul the concern is not a matter of personal liberty (libertinism) or dietary restrictions (legalism), but the glory of God (v. 31).

The meaning of "offend" in Acts 25:8 is quite significant. The Jews made various charges against Paul (25:7) that must have been serious enough to warrant capital punishment (25:11); Paul, however, maintained his innocence, claiming that he had not "offended" or committed any crime against the laws of the Jews (cf. 21:21), the temple (cf. 21:28), or Caesar.

In Lk. 13:4 "worse offenders" translates Gk. *opheilétēs*, which is used figuratively for "one who is guilty, culpable, at fault" (Bauer, rev., p. 598). When used in relation to God it means "sinner" (cf. *hamartōloí*, Lk 13:2). According to Jewish thought, a causal relationship existed between personal tragedy and guilt (see G. F. Moore, *Judaism* [1927], II, 248f.; SB, II, 193-97). But Jesus' rhetorical questions (vv. 2, 4) with the subsequent answers (vv. 3, 5) flatly deny this concept of divine retribution.

*See also* STUMBLING BLOCK.

C. B. HOCH, JR.
G. L. KNAPP

**OFFER; OFFERING.** *See* SACRIFICES AND OFFERINGS IN THE OT.

**OFFICE.** In the OT "office" translates several Hebrew terms and expressions. Heb. *kēn* designates the original status or place of the restored chief butler (Gen. 40:13; 41:13). In Nu. 3:3 *lᵉkahēn*, "to act as priest," is translated "office." The phrase "who is in office" renders *'ᵃšer yihyeh*, which the AV translates literally ("that shall be," Dt. 17:9; 26:3). In 1 Ch. 9:22 the gatekeepers are established in their "office of trust" (*'ᵉmûnâ*); the duties of this position required that the gatekeepers be trustworthy (*see* GATEKEEPER). In Isa. 22:19 *maṣṣāb* ("station [so AV], garrison") refers to Shebna's office as steward or majordomo (cf. *'ᵃšer 'al habbayiṯ*, lit. "who is over the house," v. 15), which was a very important position in Israel (see Mettinger, pp. 70-110).

In the NT "tax office" (AV "receipt of custom"; NEB "custom house") renders Gk. *telṓnion* (Mt. 9:9 par. Mk. 2:14; Lk. 5:27). According to O. Michel (*TDNT*, VIII, 97 n. 93) this was a customs house, although in Mt. 9:9

it refers to a "simple exchange-table." Gk. *episkopē* is translated "office" both in Acts 1:20 (AV "bishoprick"; NEB "charge"), referring to the office of apostle, and in 1 Tim. 3:1 (NEB "leadership"), referring to the office of bishop. Col. 1:25 has "office" (AV "dispensation"; NEB "task") for *oikonomía,* perhaps referring to the bishop's office (see Bauer, rev., p. 559). In He. 7:5 "priestly office" translates *hierateía* (AV "office of the priesthood"), and in 7:23 "continuing in office" (AV "to continue") renders *paraménō* (see Bauer, rev., p. 620).

***Bibliography*.**–T. Mettinger, *Solomonic State Officials* (1971); *TDNT,* III, *s.v.* ἱερατεία (Schrenk); V, *s.v.* οἰκονομία (Michel).

G. L. KNAPP

**OFFICER** [Heb. *'addîr* (Nah. 2:5 [MT 6]), *'eḇeḏ* (Jer. 46:26), *neṣîḇ* (1 K. 4:19), *niṣṣāḇ, pāqîḏ, pāqûḏ* (Nu. 31:14, 48), *pequddâ* (2 Ch. 24:11), *rō'š* (1 Ch. 12:14, 18 [MT 15, 19]), *šālîš, śar, śar šālîšîm* (2 Ch. 8:9), *sārîs, šōṭēr*; Gk. *chilíarchos* (Mk. 6:21), *hypērétēs, práktōr* (Lk. 12:58 [twice]), *stratēgós* (Lk. 22:4, 52)]; AV also CAPTAIN(S), CHIEF (1 K. 14:27 par. 2 Ch. 12:10), EUNUCH (Jer. 52:25), GOVERNOR (1 Ch. 24:5 [twice]), etc.; NEB also CAPTAIN (Isa. 31:9), CHIEF (1 Ch. 12:14), CIVIL OFFICER (2 Ch. 32:3), etc.; **CHIEF OFFICER** [Heb. *nāgîḏ, pāqîḏ nāgîḏ* (Jer. 20:1), *raḇ* (Jer. 39:13; 41:1), *śar hanniṣṣāḇîm*]; AV CHIEF GOVERNOR (Jer. 20:1), PRINCE (Jer. 39:13; 41:1), RULER (*nāgîḏ*), etc.; NEB also CHIEF OVERSEER (2 Ch. 31:13), OFFICER (1 Ch. 9:11), OVERSEER (1 Ch. 26:24; 2 Ch. 31:12), PRINCIPAL OFFICER (1 Ch. 27:16); **OFFICIAL** [Heb. *'eḇeḏ,* piel part. of *šāraṯ* (Prov. 29:12), *'ōśeh hammelā'ḵâ* (Est. 9:3), *piqqē(a)h* (Ex. 23:8), *raḇ* (Est. 1:8), *sāgān, śar, sārîs* (2 K. 8:6; 24:15), part. of *šāṭar* (2 Ch. 34:13); Aram. *šilṭōn* (Dnl. 3:2f.), *ṭarpelāy* (Ezr. 4:9); Gk. *basilikós* (Jn. 4:46, 49)]; AV NOBLEMAN (Jn. 4:46, 49), OFFICER, PRINCE (*śar*), RULER, etc.; NEB also CHIEF MEN (Jgs. 8:6), CHIEF OFFICER (Ezr. 10:8; Zeph. 1:8), CLERK (2 Ch. 34:13), etc.; **CHIEF OFFICIAL** [Heb. *ri'šôn* (1 Ch. 18:17)]; AV CHIEF; NEB "eldest"; **HIGH OFFICIAL** [Heb. *gāḇō(a)h* (Eccl. 5:8 [MT 7]), *śar* (1 K. 4:2)]; AV PRINCE (1 K. 4:2), "he that is higher" (Eccl. 5:8); NEB OFFICER (1 K. 4:2), OFFICIAL (Eccl. 5:8); **PALACE OFFICIAL** [Heb. *sārîs* (2 K. 24:12; 1 Ch. 28:1)]; AV OFFICER; NEB EUNUCH.

Hebrew *śar* and *šōṭēr* designate a wide range of civil, military, and religious officials and sometimes function merely as generic terms for "officer." *Śar* is used collectively in 2 Ch. 32:21. Etymologically, *šōṭēr,* the part. of *šāṭar,* should mean "scribe" (cf. Akk. *šaṭāru,* "write"), and it does designate a scribal office in, e.g., 26:11.

Specific government officials are designated by Heb. *'eḇeḏ, niṣṣāḇ, ri'šôn,* and *sārîs*. The *'eḇeḏ* (lit. "servant") is a minister of the king in 1 K. 1:9; 9:22; 10:5 par. 2 Ch. 9:4; 2 K. 25:24; Jer. 46:26. The same word with like meaning is translated "servant" in 1 K. 1:47; 2 K. 5:6; 22:12 par. 2 Ch. 34:20. The *niṣṣāḇ* of 1 K. 4:5, 7, 27 is a royal governor of one of the twelve provinces into which Solomon divided Israel; cf. the *niṣṣāḇ* of Edom (RSV "deputy") under Jehoshaphat (1 K. 22:47). The *niṣṣāḇ* of 1 K. 5:16; 9:23; 2 Ch. 8:10 is a foreman of the drafted workers who constructed the temple. *Neṣîḇ* in 1 K. 4:19 is probably an error for *niṣṣāḇ,* since the usual meaning of *neṣîḇ* is "garrison," and the context seems to call for a royal governor of Judah equivalent to the twelve who ruled Israel (v. 7). Heb. *ri'šôn* in 1 Ch. 18:17 designates a high office of the royal service held by David's sons, though it can possibly be taken with "sons," as the NEB does, rendering it as the adjective "eldest." The *sārîs* is a EUNUCH (cf. Isa. 56:3-5); some, however, have rejected this meaning for Gen. 37:36; 39:1; 40:2, 7, since Potiphar

"Stele of the Necklaces" showing servants investing the high official Hor-Min with gold necklaces, a royal reward for great service. Pharaoh Seti I (1318-1301 B.C.) looks on (Louvre; picture M. Chuzeville)

was married — although married eunuchs are indeed attested. Eunuchs were employed especially as overseers of the king's harem (Est. 1:10; 2:3, 14f.; 4:4f.; cf. 2 K. 9:32) but could perform a number of functions in the king's court (1 K. 22:9 par. 2 Ch. 18:8; 2 K. 8:6; 25:19 par. Jer. 52:25; Dnl. 1:3).

The *nāgîḏ* of 1 Ch. 9:11, 20 (RSV "ruler"); 26:24; 27:16; 2 Ch. 31:12f.; 35:8; Neh. 11:11 (RSV "ruler"); Jer. 20:1 is the head of a department in the cultic administration. In 2 Ch. 28:7, however, *nāgîḏ* designates the "commander" of the palace, unless "palace" (Heb. *bayiṯ,* lit. "house") should here be rendered "temple."

Hebrew *'ōśeh hammelā'ḵâ* and *raḇ* as titles usually designate specific officials of the imperial governments of Mesopotamia and Persia, as do Aram. *šilṭōn* and *ṭarpelāy*. In Est. 3:9 the RSV translates the plural of *'ōśeh hammelā'ḵâ* literally: "those who have charge of the king's business." Similarly in 9:3 some sort of financial officer is meant. Heb. *raḇ* in 1:8; Jer. 39:13; 41:1 refers to the heads over the various classes of government officials. The word occurs four times in Jer. 39:13, although the translation obscures this. Nebuzaradan is head of the bodyguards; Nebushazban is the head eunuch; Nergalsharezer the head *māg*. These men acted in conjunction with the other head officers of the court. *Raḇ* similarly occurs in 2 K. 18:17; Jer. 39:3; Dnl. 1:3 (RSV "his chief eunuch"). The *raḇ* of Jonah 1:6 is head of the sailors, i.e., "the captain." Aram. *šilṭōn* in Dnl. 3:2f. designates the administrator of a province in Nebuchadrezzar's empire. Little is known of the *ṭarpelāy* of Ezr. 4:9. The suggestion that it is a Greek loanword meaning "the people of Tripolis" has not been generally accepted.

Greek *práktōr* in Lk. 12:58 designates the constable in charge of the debtors' prison. It is debated whether the term reflects Roman judicial procedure in contrast to the Jewish procedure implied by *hypērétēs* of the parallel passage, Mt. 5:25ff.

It is difficult to tell whether *sāgān,* which is used only in Ezra and Nehemiah, indicates a specific class of rulers or is merely a generic term for official. Although the rulers as a group were blamed for various undesirable conditions that prevailed, their specific functions are difficult to determine. *Sāgān* is translated "chief man" in Ezr. 9:2 and "official" in Neh. 2:16 (twice); 4:14, 19; 5:7, 17; 7:5; 12:40; 13:11.

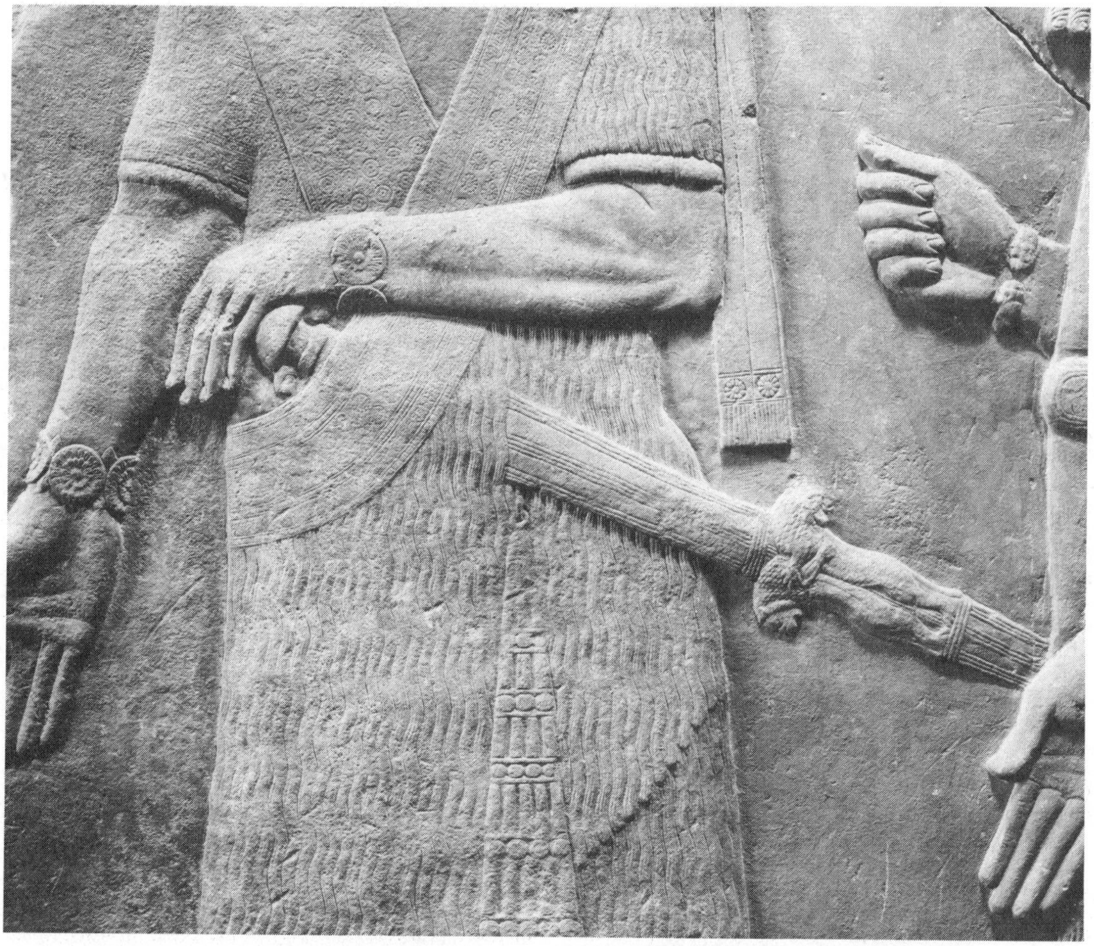

An officer of Sennacherib (704-681 B.C.) wears a sash and splendid sword decorated with two lions as a sign of his rank. Detail of an alabaster relief from Sennacherib's palace in Nineveh (Staatliche Museen, Berlin, DDR)

The piel part. of *šāraṯ*, *m*ᵉ*šārēṯ* (lit. "servant"), on the other hand seems to be a general term for subordinates or assistants. It is translated "chamberlain" in Est. 1:10. Heb. *pāqîḏ* is a general term for governmental commissioner, whether appointed by a higher official to carry out his wishes or chosen by a group of people as their leader and representative. It is translated "officer" in Jgs. 9:28; 2 Ch. 24:11; Est. 2:3 but "overseer" in Gen. 41:34; Neh. 11:9, 14, 22 and "leader" in Neh. 12:42. The words *pāqîḏ nāgîḏ* in Jer. 20:1 are probably not a compound title "chief deputy" but two separate titles. Pashhur was a deputy—specifically, the minister in charge of the temple of the Lord.

Greek *hypērétēs* in the NT is likewise a generic term for "deputy," "assistant." Jn. 7:32, 45f.; 18:3, 12, 18, 22; 19:6; Acts 5:22, 26 refer to the deputies of the chief priests and Pharisees, but Mt. 5:25 (RSV "guard") refers to the judge's deputy. In both cases, however, the deputies are officers of the law with police prerogatives. Similarly, the pl. of Gk. *stratēgós* (Lk. 22:4, 52) refers to the temple police (I. H. Marshall, *Gospel of Luke* [*New International Greek Testament Comm.*, 1978], p. 788) or overseers (J. Jeremias, *Jerusalem in the Time of Jesus* [Eng. tr. 1969], pp. 165f.; cf. MM, pp. 592f.).

A few specific terms occur for military officers. Of the *ʾaddîr* of Nah. 2:5 (AV "worthy") little is known. The word also designates a military officer in Jgs. 5:13; Nah. 3:18, translated "noble" both times by the RSV. A similar uncertainty prevails regarding the military use of *rōʾš* (lit. "head"; 1 Ch. 12:14, 18), and the *šālîš* of Ex. 14:7; 15:4; 2 K. 10:25 (twice); 2 Ch. 8:9; Ezk. 23:15, 23, etc. The LXX uses Gk. *chiliárchos* for the "commander of a thousand troops." In the NT it refers to the Roman *tribunus militum*, or commander of a cohort (= 600 men).

Hebrew *pāqûḏ* of Nu. 31:14, 18 seems to be a general term for any commissioned officer. It also occurs in this sense but is translated differently in 2 K. 11:15 par. 2 Ch. 23:14.

The RSV has taken as designations of officials a few words that have doubtful meanings or are best understood in another sense. Gk. *basilikós* (lit. "royal person") in Jn. 4:46, 49 may mean either "royal officer" or "member of the royal family." Heb. *p*ᵉ*quddâ* (2 Ch. 24:11) probably refers not to officials but to the royal treasury; cf. "what they have laid up" in Isa. 15:7. Heb. *gāḇō(a)h* in Eccl. 5:8 simply means "one who is in a high position" and is not really a title. Lastly, *piqqē(a)ḥ* (Ex. 23:8) should mean something like "the open-eyed" (cf. AV and NEB); i.e., a bribe blinds the one who really sees everything clearly, so that he pretends not to see.

*See also* ARMY; GOVERNMENT. E. D. WELCH

**OFFICES OF CHRIST.** *See* CHRIST, OFFICES OF.

**OFFSCOURING** [Heb. *s$^{e}$ḥî* (Lam. 3:45); Gk. *perípsēma* (1 Cor. 4:13)]; NEB also DREGS. "Offscouring" appears in the RSV OT only as a translation of the Hebrew hapax legomenon *s$^{e}$ḥî*. The noun, from the verb *sāḥâ*, "scrape" (which occurs only in Ezk. 26:4), means "sweepings" or "scrapings." In Lam. 3:45 the prophet recognizes that, due to God's judgment upon the sins of Israel, His chosen people are a picture of rejection and ridicule before the nations. Formerly in a position of favor, Israel is now represented as mere filth.

The Greek hapax legomenon *perípsēma* derives from the verb *peripsáō*, "wipe all around," "wipe clean." Thus the noun means "that which is wiped off." In literature outside the NT it may also refer to the means or instrument of wiping, or figuratively to the means of religious cleansing or expiation, sacrifice. In 1 Cor. 4:13 it is probably a term of contempt; Paul contrasts the apostles, who are regarded as filth among men, with the self-satisfied Corinthians.

*Bibliography.–DNTT*, I, 279; *TDNT*, VI, *s.v.* περίψημα (Stählin).

G. L. KNAPP

**OFFSET.** The term is used as a noun in two passages. In 1 K. 6:6 the Heb. *migrāʿ* (<*gāraʿ*, "diminish") denotes a shelf (AV "narrowed rests," NEB "rebates") in the wall of the side chambers of Solomon's temple, formed by decreasing the wall's width, so that the beams of the second and third stories would not penetrate the walls of the temple proper. The RSV also uses the term in Ezk. 41:6f., following the LXX, which understands a similar structural arrangement in the obscure details of Ezekiel's temple (so also the NEB, "intake"). The AV ("they entered") follows the corrupt MT version (*bāʾōṯ*) of the passage. See the comms., most of which follow the LXX, but cf. KD, *in loc*.

As a verb "offset" occurs in Hos. 12:8 (MT 9), but as the RSV mg. indicates, its reading is a conjecture based on the LXX (cf. NEB "pay"). The AV "find" is a literal translation of the Heb. *yimṣ$^{e}$ʾû*, which can also be translated "bring" (H. W. Wolff, *Hosea* [Eng. tr., *Hermeneia*, 1974], p. 207; cf. p. 214) or "catch up" (F. I. Andersen and D. N. Freedman, *Hosea* [*AB*, 1981], p. 594).

G. WYPER

**OFFSPRING** [Heb. *zeraʿ*–'seed,' also *ṣeʾ$^{e}$ṣāʾîm* (Job 5:25; 21:8; 27:14; Ps. 22:24 [MT 25]; etc.), *p$^{e}$rî*–'fruit' (Dt. 28:51, 53; Ps. 21:10 [MT 11]; Lam. 2:20), *nîn* (Gen. 21:23; Job 18:19; Isa. 14:22), part. of *yāṣāʾ yārēḵ*–'come out of the loins' (Gen. 46:26; Ex. 1:5; Jgs. 8:30), *bēn*–'child' (1 Ch. 7:13), *yeleḏ* (Job 39:3), *môleḏeṯ* (Gen. 48:6); Gk. *spérma*–'seed' (Gal. 3:16, 19, 29; Rev. 12:17), *génos*–'family, race' (Acts 17:28f.; Rev. 22:16)]; AV also SEED, FRUIT, "that came out of the loins," ISSUE, SON, etc.; NEB also CHILD, CHILDREN, FAMILY, ISSUE, DESCENDANTS, etc. The progeny of a person or animal. The biblical writers frequently use terms from plant life (Heb. *zeraʿ* and *p$^{e}$rî*; Gk. *spérma*) in a metaphorical sense to denote human children or descendants. While the RSV sometimes follows the AV in translating these terms "seed" or "fruit," it more often supplies the figurative sense of the term. In Acts 17:28f. Luke records a quotation by Paul from the Stoic poet Aratus (*Phaenomena* 5): "For we are indeed his offspring." Paul uses "offspring" not in the pantheistic sense intended by the Stoics but in the sense of being created by God in His image (see comms. on Acts, esp. F. F. Bruce [*NICNT*, repr. 1971], pp. 360f.).

*See* CHILD; FAMILY; FRUIT I.A.; SEED. N. J. O.

**OFTEN.** In the OT "often" is usually part of the phrase "as often as" in the RSV (AV "when," "after"; NEB also "when," "whenever"). It translates the Hebrew *middê*, "as often as" (e.g., 1 S. 1:7; 18:30; 1 K. 14:28; 2 Ch. 12:11; Isa. 28:19; Jer. 31:20). The RSV uses "how often" twice to translate *kammâ* (Job 21:17; Ps. 78:40). An additional use of "often" is found in Prov. 29:1, where "he who is often reproved" (RSV) renders Heb. *ʾîš tôḵāḥôṯ*, literally "a man of reproofs." Similarly, "had often been at war" (2 S. 8:10; 1 Ch. 18:10) translates *ʾîš milḥ$^{a}$môṯ*, "a man of wars."

In the NT "often" generally renders the Greek adverb *pollákis*, "many times, frequently, often" (Mt. 17:15; Mk. 5:4; 9:22; Jn. 18:2; Acts 26:11; Rom. 1:13; 2 Cor. 8:22; 11:23, 27; Phil. 3:18; 2 Tim. 1:16; He. 6:7). The RSV uses "how often" three times to translate *posákis*, "how many times, how often," in the questions posed in Mt. 18:21; 23:37; Lk. 13:34. The phrase "as often as" translates *hosákis*, "as many times as," in 1 Cor. 11:25f.; Rev. 11:6. Also, "often" translates *pyknós* (Lk. 5:33), *pyknóteron* (neut., comparative of *pyknós*, Acts 24:26), and "so often" (AV "much"; NEB "all the time") renders *tá pollá* (Rom. 15:22; var. *pollákis*).

The use of *hosákis* is significant in 1 Cor. 11:25f. Some apply vv. 25f. to any common meal (Orr and Walther, p. 273) or to any occasion when wine was available (see Barrett, pp. 269f.), but the immediate context limits the reference to the Lord's Supper (Robertson and Plummer, p. 247). The verbs "eat" and "drink" in vv. 25f. have an anticipatory mood and continuative verbal aspect. Therefore, this memorial ought to be repeated; however, the presence of *hosákis* makes the frequency of future observances indefinite.

*Bibliography.*–Comms. on 1 Corinthians by C. K. Barrett (*HNTC*, 1968); W. F. Orr and J. A. Walther (*AB*, 1976); A. Robertson and A. Plummer (*ICC*, 2nd ed. 1914).

G. L. KNAPP

**OG** og [Heb. *ʿôg*, *ʿōg*]. Amorite king of the territory of BASHAN; last of the giant REPHAIM race. Og's empire E of the Jordan was conquered by Moses and the Israelites in preparation for the invasion W of the Jordan (Nu. 21:33-35; Dt. 3:1-12). Bashan was assigned mainly to the half-tribe of Manasseh, though partly to Reuben and Gad (Nu. 32:33; Dt. 3:12f.).

After they conquered the kingdom of Sihon (Nu. 21:21-32), the Israelites headed north to the fertile region of Bashan (a territory extending from Mt. Hermon to the river Jabbok). At Edrei, Og and his army met the Israelites (Nu. 21:33). Bashan was powerful, noted for its sixty fortified cities, with "high walls, gates, and bars" (Dt. 3:4f.). But God encouraged Israel, and in the ensuing battle Og and his sons were killed (Nu. 21:35), thus ending the line of the Rephaim.

Og's great stature is evidenced by reference to his *ʿereś barzel*, translated variously "bedstead of iron" (RSV, AV) or "sarcophagus of basalt" (NEB), which measured about 2 m. by 4 m. (6 ft. by 13½ ft.). It came into the possession of the Ammonites and was on display at their capital, Rabbah, at the time of the writing of Dt. 3:11. Since many basalt sarcophagi have been found in the general region of Bashan, and since black basalt is an ironlike rock, the conjecture that Og's "bedstead" was really a sarcophagus has gained popularity. Against this interpretation is the fact that *ʿereś* never means sarcophagus elsewhere. At any rate, the outsized bedstead or sarcophagus would indicate only that Og's stature was larger than normal, and affords no precision as to his actual height.

The conquest of Og and his kingdom is remembered in

the OT as one of Israel's greatest victories (Dt. 1:4; 4:47; 29:7 [MT 29:6]; 31:4; Josh. 2:10; 9:10; 12:4; 13:12, 30f.; 1 K. 4:19; Neh. 9:22; Ps. 135:11; 136:20). D. STUART

**OHAD** ō'had [Heb. *'ōhaḏ*]. Third son of Simeon (Gen. 46:10; Ex. 6:15). The name is lacking in the parallel lists in Nu. 26:12-14; 1 Ch. 4:24f.

**OHEL** ō'hel [Heb. *'ōhel*–'tent']. A son of Zerubbabel, descendant of David (1 Ch. 3:20).

**OHOLAH** ō'hə-lä [Heb. *'oh$^o$lâ*]; AV AHOLAH. A symbolic name for Samaria. Ezk. 23 presents an allegory in which Samaria ("Oholah") and Jerusalem ("Oholibah"), i.e., the northern and southern kingdoms, respectively, are sisters married to the Lord, but faithless to Him from the beginning of their relationship. Although both Oholah and OHOLIBAH are clearly connected with Heb. *'ōhel,* "tent," the precise meanings are obscure (see comms., esp. W. Eichrodt, *Ezekiel* [Eng. tr., *OTL,* 1970], pp. 321f.).

Both sisters entangled themselves in profligate harlotries — in political mésalliances with Assyria (vv. 5, 12) and in religious debaucheries in Molech worship (v. 37). Thus both Oholah and her lewd sister were marked for judgment (v. 49). Oholah was delivered to her lover Assyria (vv. 9f.), where she was shamefully treated. Her sister Oholibah failed to learn the lesson of the results of being faithless to Yahweh. She became even more corrupt in her inordinate lust for foreign entanglements than was her sister (vv. 11-21).

Ezekiel 16 presents a similar allegory on Israel's spiritual nymphomania, her unbridled lust for other lovers (gods).

R. B. ALLEN

**OHOLIAB** ō-hō'li-ab [Heb. *'oh$^o$lî'āḇ*–'father's tent']; AV, NEB, AHOLIAB. A Danite, son of Ahisamach, appointed by Moses to assist Bezalel in supervising the construction of the tabernacle and its furniture. He and Bezalel are described as divinely inspired master craftsmen (Ex. 31:6; 35:34; 36:1f.; 38:23).

**OHOLIBAH** ō-hō'li-bə [Heb. *'oh$^o$lîḇâ*–'my tent is in her'(?)] (Ezk. 23:4, 11, 22, 36, 44); AV AHOLIBAH. An opprobrious and symbolic name given by Ezekiel to Jerusalem (23:4) in an allegory depicting Judah's unfaithfulness to Yahweh and the judgment that awaited her. Like her sister OHOLAH (Samaria), Oholibah played the HARLOT with heathen nations — i.e., she formed political alliances with them and adopted their idolatrous practices, including religious prostitution. Like her sister, she was promised the judgment of destruction at the hands of her "lovers" (cf. vv. 22-35). For another allegory using harlotry as a symbol of Jerusalem, see ch. 16; cf. also Jer. 3:6-11.

N. J. O.

**OHOLIBAMAH** ō-hō-li-bä'mə [Heb. *'oh$^o$lîḇāmâ*–'tent of the high place']; AV AHOLIBAMAH.

**1.** Daughter of Anah and granddaughter of Zibeon the Horite ("Hivite," Gen. 36:2); one of Esau's wives (vv. 2, 5, 14, 18, 25). Curiously, her name is missing from the lists of Esau's wives in 26:34 and 28:9. No satisfactory explanation has been given for these apparently conflicting traditions.

**2.** An Edomite clan chief (Gen. 36:41; 1 Ch. 1:52).

**OIL** [mainly Heb. *šemen*; Gk. *élaion*; but see below].

***I. Terms.***–By far the most common term is Heb. *šemen* <*šāman,* "to grow fat." It appears often with *zayiṯ,* "olive" (Ex. 27:20; 30:24). Heb. *šemen* refers to olive oil except in Est. 2:12, which specifically mentions oil of myrrh. Heb. *yiṣhār* <*yāṣhar,* "shine" (cf. Job 24:11), occurs less frequently (e.g., 2 K. 18:32). The etymological reference is to either the light-giving qualities of the oil or the brightness of newly pressed oil. Aram. *m$^e$šaḥ* occurs twice (Ezr. 6:9; 7:22) and has the same root as "Messiah," "the Anointed One." Gk. *élaion* is the NT term, a neuter noun <*elaía,* "olive," related to Eng. "oil" (cf. Lat. *olea,* "olive").

***II. Production.***–Almost all the oil used by the Israelites came from the beautiful and plentiful olive tree. The olive harvest, which terminated the season, ripened about October-November, although for the fine-quality "beaten oil" (Heb. *šemen kāṯîṯ,* Ex. 27:20; Nu. 28:5; 1 K. 5:11) some of the berries were picked before they were fully ripe. They were then gently pounded in a stone mortar and carefully decanted to remove every possible impurity. This oil had special uses; see III.E,F below. Such a process would have been uneconomical for general use, so a different method was adopted for most of the berries. The ripe olives (black or almost so) were either shaken or beaten from the trees with long poles (Dt. 24:20), although sometimes they were picked by hand, and then carried in baskets on the head — or if necessary by asses — to the place of processing. The olives that remained on the trees were left for the poor (Dt. 24:20).

There were various methods for crushing or bruising the berries, which was necessary before the oil could be extracted. These included treading the fruit with the bare feet (Mic. 6:15) as for grapes, pounding in a mortar, and crushing with a stone roller. For larger quantities a mill was used.

The mill consisted of a circular stone basin about 2.5 m. (8 ft.) in diameter, fitted with a vertical millstone revolving around a central pivot. A long pole extended from the center of the vertical stone, which was attached to the pivot about a foot from the end. Two people pushing the other end of the beam could then revolve the stone around the lower basin. Some of the oil was squeezed out and collected in vats or jars; the remaining pulp was carried on reed or goat-hair mats or in baskets to the presses.

There were various kinds of presses. The most common probably consisted of a pole whose lower end was wedged into a hole in the rock and upper end weighted with stones. The crushed olives in their containers were placed on a "table" of stone, and the pole was placed on top. When pressure was exerted the oil would drip from the pulp into an excavated stone basin near the table. The oil was carefully refined by allowing it to settle for some time, and it was then stored. Another method was sprinkling the pulp with hot water so that the oil came to the surface and could easily be collected.

Domestic oil was stored in small jars or cruses (1 K. 17:12; 2 K. 4:2); oil for religious purposes such as anointing was often kept in horns (1 S. 16:13; 1 K. 1:39). Larger amounts were stored in 380- to 760-liter (100- to 200-gallon) jars or in cisterns (1 Ch. 27:28; 2 Ch. 11:11; Neh. 13:5-8). The royal treasury boasted large amounts (2 K. 20:13). A supply of pure oil was always kept in the temple (Josephus *BJ* v.13.6 [565]).

Traces of oil-processing equipment dating from earliest times to the beginning of the Christian era have been found in Palestine. The Mishnah (*Menahoth* viii.4) claimed that the oil of Tekoa was best.

***III. Uses.***–*A. Commodity of Exchange.* Since olive oil could retain its sweetness for years when properly stored, it served as good merchandise both for home trade (2 K. 4:7; Lk. 16:6) and export (Solomon annually gave 20,000 cors of "beaten oil" to Hiram of Tyre for his help in building the temple [1 K. 5:11; cf. 2 Ch. 2:10]). See also Ezr. 3:7; Isa. 57:9; Ezk. 27:17; Hos. 12:1; Rev. 18:13.

*B. Toiletry.* Oil was and still is used abundantly as a cosmetic. In the desert regions of the East it kept the skin and scalp soft. Generally it was used after the bath (Ruth 3:3; 2 S. 12:20) and was often scented. It was also a useful protection against sunburn, flies, and vermin. On arrival at a feast the guests' feet were washed and their heads anointed with oil. Pliny claimed that it was a useful protective against the cold. See also Est. 2:12 ("oil of myrrh"); Ps. 104:15; Ezk. 16:9; Mic. 6:15; Lk. 7:46. To abstain from using oil was a sign of mourning (2 S. 14:2).

*C. Food.* Oil took the place of butter and animal fat to a very large extent in the diet of the people of Mediterranean countries. It was used with meal for making cakes (1 K. 17:12, 14, 16), although sometimes oil was poured over the cooked dough (*see* BREAD IV). It is often mentioned with other items of food such as wine (Rev. 6:6), fine flour (Lev. 2:1, 4f., etc.), and honey (Ezk. 16:13). See also Nu. 11:8; Prov. 21:17; Hag. 2:12.

*D. Medicine.* Olive oil has certain curative qualities and is still used in modern medicine. Celsus mentioned its use for fevers, and Josephus (*Ant.* xvii.6.5 [172]) said that Herod was given an oil bath in an attempt to cure him of his deadly disease. Isaiah wrote of it as softening wounds (1:6). The Good Samaritan mixed it with wine and poured the resultant antiseptic fluid into the wounds of the stricken traveler. Mk. 6:13 and Jas. 5:14 are concerned with its symbolic significance more than its curative qualities, though the latter are not to be excluded. The application of a substance in certain cases, such as the clay used by Jesus (Jn. 9:6), served to reinforce the evidence of the ear (the prayer for the sick man), and such may be the purpose of the use of oil in Jas. 5:14. On the other hand, anointing with oil may be a symbol of the life-giving Holy Spirit (1 Jn. 2:27) and thus comparable to laying on of hands.

*E. Light.* Only oil was used for lighting in biblical times. Most of the houses faced north because of the heat and glare of the sun, and the apertures in the walls were certainly not for lighting. Hence an oil lamp was kept burning continuously. Hundreds of specimens of lamps have been excavated, the most common being the saucer with a lip (*see* LAMP). A special supply of "beaten oil" was kept for the lamps in the tabernacle and the temple (Ex. 25:6; 27:20). See also Mt. 25:3f., 8.

*F. Ritual.* Apart from the lamps in the holy place mentioned above, pure oil was used in a number of religious rites, particularly offerings and consecration. "Beaten oil" was used in the continual burnt offering or offering by fire (Ex. 29:38-42; cf. Nu. 28:3-6. Oil had to be mixed with or poured over almost all food offerings (Ex. 29:40; Lev. 2:1ff.; Nu. 28:5; Ezk. 45:24). The exceptions were the sin offering (Lev. 5:11) and the jealousy offering (Nu. 5:15). Oil was also used in the offering for the purification of leprosy (Lev. 14:10ff.), the offering of firstfruits (Dt. 18:4; 2 Ch. 31:5; Neh. 10:37, 39 [MT 38, 40]; 13:5, 12), and tithes (Ezk. 5:14; 45:25).

The oil used for religious anointing is described in Ex. 30:22-25. It had a variety of constituents, including olive oil, and was used to consecrate the tabernacle and its furniture (Ex. 40:9ff.), priests (Ex. 29:7ff.; Lev. 8:12), Kings (1 S. 10:1; 1 K. 1:39; 2 K. 9:1, 3, 6; Ps. 89:20 [MT 21]), prophets (1 K. 19:16), and weapons of war (2 S. 1:21). Jacob's stone (Gen. 28:18) and pillar (35:14) were also anointed, although not with this special preparation.

*G. Burial.* The Egyptians, Greeks, and Romans used oil to embalm the dead, and the Jews also may have known the custom, although the OT does not mention it. Jesus referred to it in connection with His own burial; that oil, however, was only the basis of a more costly unguent (Mt. 26:12; Mk. 14:3-8; Lk. 23:56; Jn. 12:3-8; 19:40).

*IV. Figurative Uses.*–Abundant oil indicated general prosperity (Dt. 32:13; 33:24; 2 K. 18:32; Job 29:6; Joel 2:24), while lack of it signified economic distress (Joel 1:10; Hag. 1:11). It symbolized joy and gladness (Ps. 45:7 [MT 8]; He. 1:9), especially in connection with the gospel (Isa. 61:3). It is spoken of in connection with friendship and fellowship (Ps. 133:1f.) and restoration of strength (92:10 [MT 11]). Words of deceit are softer than oil (55:21 [MT 22]; Prov. 5:3). The wicked curse as readily as oil soaks into bones (Ps. 109:18, perhaps a reference to the medicinal use of oil; see the comms.). The careful use of oil indicates wisdom (Prov. 21:17, 20). It may also be a symbol of the Holy Spirit as life-giving agent, although this is not stated specifically (cf. 1 S. 16:13; Isa. 61:4).

J. A. BALCHIN

**OIL, ANOINTING** [Heb. *šemen hammišḥâ*] (Ex. 25:6; 29:7, 21; etc.). Also referred to as "holy anointing oil" or simply "holy oil" (Nu. 35:25; Ps. 89:20 [MT 21]).

In Ex. 30:22-33 Moses is instructed to use myrrh, cinnamon, aromatic cane, cassia, and olive oil to make a special anointing oil, holy to Yahweh "throughout your generations." It was to be used for anointing the tent of meeting with all its furnishings, the ark, and the altar, and for consecrating Aaron and his sons as priests. Any use of it with "ordinary men" was a grave offense (vv. 32f.). The instructions for its use are repeated in Ex. 40:9-15 and carried out in Lev. 8:10-13. Ex. 37:29 indicates that the craftsman Bezalel made the first anointing oil; the responsibility later passed to Eleazar son of Aaron (Nu. 4:16). In many passages the anointing oil is connected with the fragrant incense prepared for use in the tabernacle (Ex. 30:34-38). It is not stated whether the same oil was used for anointing kings in Israel, although Ps. 89:20 seems to claim this for David.

*See also* ANOINT; OIL. B. C. BIRCH

**OIL, BEATEN.** *See* OIL II.

**OIL, HOLY.** *See* ANOINT; OIL III.F; OIL, ANOINTING.

**OIL, MAKING.** *See* OIL II; OLIVE TREE.

**OIL, OLIVE.** *See* OIL; OLIVE TREE.

**OIL PRESS.** *See* OIL II; OLIVE TREE; WINE PRESS.

**OIL TREE.** *See* OLEASTER.

**OINTMENT** [Heb. *šemen* (Eccl. 7:1; 10:1), *merqāḥâ* ("pot of ointment," Job 41:31 [MT 23]), *tamrûq* (Est. 2:3, 9, 12); Gk. *mýron* (Jth. 10:3; Mk. 14:3-5 par.; Lk. 23:56) *myrismós* (Jth. 16:8 [LXX 7]) *smḗgma* (Sus. 13:17)]; AV also "things for purifying/purification," "washing balls"; NEB also COSMETICS, PERFUME, OIL, SOAP. Ointments were made from a basic olive OIL to which were added various ingredients, sometimes spice (Ex. 25:6; Lk. 23:56) such as cassia (Ex. 30:24), or PERFUME (Ex. 30:25; Jn. 12:3) such as from the pistachio nut (Mk. 14:3; Cranfield takes *pistikḗs* [ RSV "pure"] as a transliteration of the Aram. *pístāqā'*, "pistachio nut"). The ingredients were crushed and mixed together, then boiled in the oil (hence the image in Job 41:31), which would absorb the odors of the ingredients.

An alabaster or glass flask or jar was used as a container (Mk. 14:3; Lk. 7:37), especially when the ointment was expensive (Mk. 13:3-5 par.), alabaster being considered the best material for this use (Pliny *Nat. hist.* xiii.19; see A. McNeile, comm. on Matthew [1915], *in loc.*, for more references), as large disoveries of such jars show. Since the container was sealed, it was necessary to break the jar in order to pour out the contents (Mk. 14:3): doing so meant the whole contents were used at once (cf. *TDNT*, IV, 801), hence the criticism of the woman as extravagant.

Ointments had various uses and symbolic values: (1) as a body lotion to protect the skin in a dry climate (Sus. 13:17) and to add sexual attraction (Est. 2:3, 9, 12; Jth. 10:3f.; 16:8; cf. Cant. 1:3); (2) as an act of hospitality, especially when a guest's head and feet were parched from traveling in the sun on hot, dusty roads (Lk. 7:36-39: the failure of Jesus' host to provide ointment was a lack of hospitality); (3) as a part of the burial rite (Lk. 23:56).

Probably the most important passages describing the use of ointment are those in which a woman anoints Jesus (Mt. 26:6-13; Mk. 14:3-9; Lk. 7:36-50; Jn. 12:1-8). These passages have many similarities but also important differences, in both the setting and the significance of the anointing. In all the Gospels but Luke the theological significance of the anointing is Jesus' death, specifically His burial. The woman's act of devotion suggests (unwittingly for her) embalmment, thus prophesying Jesus' death. This is especially true in John's account (which is preceded by the Sanhedrin's condemnation of Jesus to death), where the *feet* are anointed: Brown suggests this is more likely for a dead person than for a living one, who would be anointed on the head, as in Mark's account. (The feet are anointed in Luke's account as well, first with tears, then perfume. Marshall explains this anointing of the feet as accidental, though kissing the feet was a sign of deep reverence, e.g., for teachers.)

Luke's account attaches a different significance to the anointing: it speaks of the woman's love and devotion as a consequence of having been forgiven. It is a sacrificial gift, costing almost a year's wages (though Luke does not mention the high cost, which in the other accounts leads to criticism of the woman), testifying to the strength of the woman's awareness of how much she has been forgiven. Lk. 7:47 speaks of her love as evidence of prior forgiveness, not as the grounds on which she is about to be forgiven (Marshall). Her deep devotion, showing keen awareness of much forgiven, stands in stark contrast to the host's perfunctory reception of Jesus, showing his lack of awareness of being forgiven or even of needing

Egyptian unguent dish of (fossilized) ivory with turquoise glaze (18th Dynasty). On its sides are scenes from the afterlife. Actual size: 2.5 cm. (1 in.) high, 7 cm. (2¾ in.) long, 4.4 cm. (1¾ in.) broad (Louvre)

forgiveness. This contrast is illustrated by the parable of Lk. 7:41-43 (see Marshall).

*See also* pictures in COSMETICS; FLASK.

***Bibliography.***–R. E. Brown, *Gospel According to John*, I (*AB*, 1966); C. E. B. Cranfield, *Gospel According to St. Mark* (*CGT*, 1966); A. Legault, *CBQ*, 16 (1954), 131-145; I. H. Marshall, *Gospel of Luke* (*NIGTC*, 1978); *TDNT*, IV, *s.v.* μύρον, μυρίζω (Michaelis).

W. J. MOULDER

**OKINA** ō-kī'nə (Jth. 2:28, NEB). *See* OCINA.

**OLAMUS** ō'lə-məs (AV, NEB, 1 Esd. 9:30). *See* MESHULLAM **12.**

**OLD AGE.** The nearest biblical equivalents of the modern definition of old age are Heb. *ḥeleḏ*, "life," "lifetime," and Gk. *hēlikía*, "full age" or "manhood." The Hebrews sometimes used *yôm*, "day," to express age, as with Jacob (Gen. 47:28), but in Job 5:26 *kelaḥ* means "ripe old age" (NEB "sturdy old age"). The adjective *zāqēn* also described an aged person (2 S. 19:32; Job 32:9; Jer. 6:11; etc.) as well as an "elder" of Israel.

The NT also used *presbýtēs* for "aged" (Tit. 2:2; Philem. 9); *presbýtis* for "aged woman" (Tit. 2:3); *gēras* for "old age" (Lk. 1:36), and *probebēkōs en hēmérais* for "advanced in days" (Lk. 2:36).

The orientals honored the aged (cf. Lev. 19:32) and greatly desired the blessings of old age, regarding them as a mark of divine approval (Gen. 15:15; Ex. 20:12; Job 5:26; etc.). Thus old age was anticipated in faith and hope (Ps. 71:9, 18). Superior wisdom was credited to the aged (Job 12:20; 15:10; 32:7); hence positions of authority were given to the "elders." R. K. H.

**OLD GATE** [Heb. *šaʿar hayšānâ*] (Neh. 3:6; 12:39); NEB JESHANAH GATE, mg. "gate of the Old City." *See* JERUSALEM III.F.2.a.

**OLD MAN.** *See* OLD NATURE.

**OLD NATURE; OLD SELF** [Gk. *palaiós ánthrōpos*–'old man']; AV OLD MAN; NEB also OLD HUMAN NATURE; "man we once were." Paul used the Greek phrase three times to signify the unrenewed, sin-dominated self, i.e., the person that the Christian was in Adam before conversion. Paul said that one's "old nature" has been both "crucified with Christ" (Rom. 6:6) and "put off" by a deliberate decision in response to the gospel summons (Eph. 4:22; Col. 3:9). This "putting off" is the negative side of "putting on the new nature," i.e., accepting the new identity offered in Christ through coresurrection with Him (cf. Col. 3:10 with 2:12f.; 3:1-4; Eph. 4:24 with 2:5f.). The two phrases together reveal the christological content and significance of repentance and faith, whereby people pass from "the present evil age" (Gal. 1:4), in which they bear Adam's image, are ruled by sin, and stand under judgment, into the new age, in which they bear Christ's image, share His life, and by His Spirit enter into knowledge of God and holiness of conduct (Col. 3:10; Eph. 4:24).

*See also* SPIRITUAL MAN; NEW NATURE.

J. I. PACKER

**OLD PROPHET.** A prophet from Bethel during the reign of Jeroboam I (931-910 B.C.) and a central character in one of the most perplexing, and important, prophetic narratives in the OT (1 K. 13:11-32). The background for this narrative is 12:25–13:11, which relates Jeroboam's establishment of cult centers at Bethel and Dan, the denunciation of the Bethel altar by a "man of God" from Judah,

Jeroboam's initially violent reaction, divine intervention, Jeroboam's attempt at reconciliation through hospitality, and the Judahite's rejection of that hospitality. The Judahite begins his journey home, but the old prophet from Bethel, having heard of the incident at the altar, catches up with the Judahite and offers him hospitality (just as Jeroboam had). At first the Judahite refuses, but he relents when the old prophet claims (falsely) to have "a word of the Lord" countermanding the Judahite's previous "word of the Lord." After their meal the old prophet receives a genuine word from God, a judgment on the Judahite for disobeying God's original instructions. The Judahite departs, but a lion kills him on the way; when the old prophet hears of it he retrieves the body, buries it in his own grave, and instructs his sons to bury his body beside the Judahite's. The postscript to this story comes in 2 K. 23:15-18, during Josiah's reformation. At that time the prediction made by the man of God from Judah (1 K. 13:2f.), and confirmed by the old prophet from Bethel (vv. 31f.), was fulfilled.

This summary does not do justice to the many twists and turns of the story, nor to the story's details that have interesting parallels elsewhere in Scripture (see esp. Barth, Simon). The puzzling character of the story has exercised scholars for many years. It has been called a parable (Rofé, pp. 158-163), a midrash (Montgomery and Gehman, pp. 259-265), a prophetic legend (Gray, p. 324; Long, pp. 150f.), or a *vaticinium ex eventu* (prophecy after the event; see A. Guillaume, *Prophecy and Divination* [1938], pp. 421-23). Since the work of Noth, renewed scholarly interest in the so-called Deuteronomistic History has prompted much discussion of this narrative's place in that work (see Dozeman, Lemke, Long). The purpose of the narrative has also been debated: to denounce Jeroboam's cult (Jepsen), to distinguish between true and false prophets (Dozeman, Crenshaw), to demonstrate the supremacy of God's word (Simon, p. 86; cf. *CD*, II/2, 409).

Each of these proposals has some merit, but none explains the various features of the story as well as Barth's analysis, which shows how the story may be interpreted in the larger context of Scripture, how it fits into the central theme of Scripture. Barth treated this passage as an "illustration of the differentiating election of God," which he viewed as the "sum of the Gospel" (*CD*, II/2, 3) and therefore implicit in all Scripture (p. 341). The man of God from Judah — first elected to bear the divine word of judgment against the Bethel cult and then rejected for disobedience — and the old prophet from Bethel — first part of the rejected Bethel cult and then the bearer of the divine word of judgment against the Judahite — may be regarded as together prefiguring Jesus Christ, who was elected for rejection (pp. 351, 353f.). Thus 1 K. 13 is prophecy, fulfilled in Jesus Christ (p. 409).

Some have identified the man of God from Judah as the Iddo (or Yadon) mentioned in 2 Ch. 13:22 (see Josephus's embellished account in *Ant.* viii.8.5–ix [230-245]), while others have identified him with Amos (see Crenshaw, pp. 41f.; cf. Lemke, pp. 315f.). But such identifications must remain speculative.

***Bibliography***.–K. Barth, *CD*, II/2, 393-409; J. L. Crenshaw, *Prophetic Conflict* (*BZAW*, 124; 1971), pp. 39-49; T. Dozeman, *CBQ*, 49 (1982), 379-393; J. Gray, *I & II Kings* (*OTL*, 2nd ed. 1970); A. Jepsen, "Gottesmann und Prophet," in H. W. Wolff, ed., *Probleme Biblischer Theologie* (*Festschrift* G. von Rad; 1971), pp. 171-182; W. Lemke, "The Way of Obedience: 1 Kings 13 and the Structure of the Deuteronomistic History," in F. M. Cross, *et al.*, eds., *Magnalia Dei* (*Festschrift* G. E. Wright; 1976), pp. 301-326; B. Long, *1 Kings* (*Forms of OT Literature*, IX; 1984); J. Montgomery and H. Gehman, comm. on Kings (*ICC*, 1951); A. Rofé, "Classes in the Prophetical Stories," in *Studies on Prophecy* (*SVT*, 26; 1974), pp. 143-164; U. Simon, *HUCA*, 47 (1976), 81-117.

G. A. LEE

**OLD SELF.** *See* OLD NATURE.

**OLD TESTAMENT.** *See* BIBLE; TEXT AND MSS OF THE OT.

**OLD TESTAMENT CANON.** *See* CANON OF THE OT.

**OLD TESTAMENT LANGUAGES.** *See* ARAMAIC; HEBREW LANGUAGE.

**OLEASTER** ō-lē-as'tər. Hebrew *'ēṣ šemen,* which appears in 1 K. 6:23, 31-33; Neh. 8:15; Isa. 41:19 (and possibly 1 Ch. 27:28), is rendered in various ways by the versions (AV "olive tree," "pine," "oil tree"; RSV "olivewood," "wild olive," "olive"; NEB always "wild olive"); but in each case it probably refers to the narrow-leaved oleaster, *Elaeagnus angustifolia* L., a graceful shrub with fragrant flowers and grey-green leaves. The wood is hard and finely grained and was used in antiquity for images and idols. Although sometimes designated "wild olive," it bears no relation to the true olive. The oleaster yields an inferior oil, probably mentioned in Mic. 6:7. R. K. H.

**OLIVE.** *See* OLIVE TREE.

**OLIVE BERRIES.** *See* OLIVE TREE.

**OLIVE, CULTIVATED** [Gk. *kalliélaios*] (Rom. 11:24); AV GOOD OLIVE. *See* GRAFT; OLIVE TREE.

**OLIVE, GRAFTED.** *See* GRAFT; OLIVE TREE.

**OLIVE TREE** [Heb. *zayiṯ*; Ugar. *zt*; Gk. *elaía*]. One of the most valuable trees in ancient Palestine, the olive (*Olea europaea* L.) was often the only tree of any size in the locality. It was the first-named "king" of the trees (Jgs. 9:8), which attests to its economic importance in antiquity. *See also* ORCHARD; Plate 57.

The olive was apparently native to western Asia. It symbolized beauty, strength, peace (cf. Gen. 8:11), friendship, prosperity, and divine blessing. Jer. 11:16; Hos. 14:6 refer to its beauty, and Ps. 128:3 to its fruitfulness. The oil was used in the sacrificial offerings and as an emblem of sovereignty was prominent at coronations.

The olive is a slow-growing tree requiring years of patient work before attaining maturity. The branches of the wild olive are stiff and spiny, but the cultivated tree is a multi-branched evergreen with a gnarled trunk covered with a smooth ash-colored bark. The leaves are leathery and oblong. The fleshy portion of the large, oval-shaped fruit is usually eaten raw and yields the valuable commercial olive oil. At maturity the tree can exceed 6 m. (20 ft.) in height and is difficult to kill merely by cutting, since new sprouts arise from the stump and roots to form as many as six new trunks. Old trees send up shoots in this manner; and if the parent trunk is undecayed, the shoots should be pruned away, since they are of the wild olive variety and need grafting before they can be of use.

The olive tree flowers about May, and when the blooms fall (Job 15:33) the fruit begins to form, maturing between September and December, depending on the locality. The trees are beaten with long sticks (Dt. 24:20), and the immature fruit is left behind (cf. Isa. 17:6) for the poor to glean (Dt. 24:20). The yield is unpredictable, and in antiquity a poor season often brought great hardship.

Olive oil was widely used in cooking and as a cosmetic, fuel, unguent, and article of commerce. It was extracted in biblical times by crushing olive berries in the hollow of a stone (cf. Ex. 27:20) or treading them underfoot (Mic. 6:15). As larger stone presses were devised, they were set up by the olive yards. Donkeys carried baskets of berries to the presses, and the oil was extracted by a circular millstone revolving upright around a central pivot. *See* OIL.

An abundant oil harvest signified divine blessing (Joel 2:24; 3:13 [MT 4:13]). People displayed faith when they could rejoice in the Lord despite losses among their olive trees (Hab. 3:17). The palmerworm or locust (Am. 4:9) devastated the olive tree along with other green vegetation. Although the trees are still plentiful in Palestine, they were much more abundant in antiquity.

In its wild state the olive fruit is small and worthless and is made plentiful only by grafting in branches from good stock. Paul stressed the obligations of the Gentiles to the true Israel (Rom. 11:17) by showing that, contrary to nature (11:24), God had grafted wild olive shoots onto good stock. *See also* GRAFT.

On 1 K. 6:23, 31-33; Neh. 8:15; Isa. 41:19; *see* OLEASTER.

R. K. H

**OLIVE, WILD** [Heb. *ʿēṣ šemen*–'tree of oil'; Gk. *agriélaios*]; AV also PINE (Neh. 8:15). The Heb. *ʿēṣ šemen*, which is rendered "wild olive" always by the NEB but only once by the RSV (Neh. 8:15), probably refers to the OLEASTER, which is not related to the true olive. The Gk. *agriélaios* (Rom. 11:17, 24), on the other hand, refers to the uncultivated OLIVE TREE. *See also* GRAFT.

**OLIVES, MOUNT OF** [Heb. *har hazzêṯîm*–'the mountain of olive trees' (Zec. 14:4), *maʿᵃlēh hazzêṯîm*–'the ascent of olive trees' (2 S. 15:30); Gk. *tó óros tṓn elaiṓn*–'the mountain of the olive trees' (Mt. 21:1, etc.)]; **OLIVET** [Gk. *tó óros tó kaloúmenon elaiṓn*–'the mountain called "of olive trees,"' (Lk. 19:29; 21:37), *toú elaiṓnos*–'of the olive grove' (= Olivet) (Acts 1:12; but cf. Bauer, rev., p. 248)]. The name of the ridge, or portion of the ridge, E of Jerusalem.

I. Names
II. Location and Description
III. OT
IV. NT
V. Subsequent History and Tradition
VI. Eschatology

*I. Names.*–The common name for the ridge, or a portion of it, is related to words for "olive, olive trees, olive grove," as indicated above. There is discussion concerning the reading in some texts, since Gk. *elaiṓn* can be the pl. gen. of *elaía*, "olive tree," or the sg. masc. of *elaiṓn*, "olive grove, orchard," but the meaning is scarcely affected. The plural "olive trees" certainly conveys the same idea as the singular "olive grove." The term "Olivet" comes from the Lat. *olivetum*, "olive grove." Josephus uses both "Olivet" (*toú Elaiṓnos óros, Ant.* vii.9.2 [202]; *BJ* v.12.2 [504] and "the mount called 'Olivet'" (*tó Elaiōn kaloúmenon óros, BJ* v.2.3 [70]; *óros tó prosagoreuómenon Elaiōn, Ant.* xx.8.6 [169]. In T.P. *Taanith* 69a the same term is used, Aram. *ṭûr zêṯāʾ*, "mountain of the olive grove." The expression used in 2 S. 15:30 (RSV "the ascent of the Mount of Olives") doubtless refers to a road or path that received its name because it traversed the ridge in that area.

2 Kings 23:13 refers to high places which Solomon built "to the south of the mount of corruption" (*har hammašḥîṯ* <*šḥt*, "to destroy"). This name appears to be a play on words, based on a proposed original *har hammišḥâ*, "mount of anointing oil" (<*mšḥ*, "to anoint"). More recently the ridge has been called Jebel eṭ-Ṭûr ("the mountain of the tower [or mountain]"), Jebel Ṭur ez-Zait ("the mountain of the mount of olives"), and Jebel ez-Zaitun ("the mountain of the olive trees"). In Jewish usage it was also called "the mountain of lights," since it was the location of the signal fire that announced, by means of similar fires on other hills, the appearance of the new moon (T.B. *Rosh Ha-Shanah* 22b). In Christian usage it is sometimes called "mount of the Ascension," since it is designated in the NT as the location of Christ's ascension (Acts 1:9, 12).

*II. Location and Description.*–The ridge is a spur of the Central Mountain Range (*see* PALESTINE) about 3 km. (2 mi.) in length, which is divided from the principal range by Wâdī ej-Jôz, the Kidron Valley, and Wâdī en-Nâr (*see* JERUSALEM II.B). In turn the spur is divided into three summits by lesser valleys or depressions. From north to south these summits are: (1) Mt. Scopus, although this name is somewhat incorrect. Josephus referred to *Skopos* as a place (not a mountain; cf. *BJ* ii.19.4 [528], 7 [542]; v.2.3 [67]; 3.2 [106, 108]) that lay N of the city, calling it also "Lookout" (Gk. *Saphein* [*Ant.* xi.8.5 (329)], probably < Aram. *ṣāpîn*; cf. Heb. *ṣōpîm*, "watchmen" [1 S. 14:16], whence the modern *har haṣṣōpîm*, where Hebrew University is located). G. A. Barrois pointed out that this name properly refers to the entire ridge (*IDB*, III, 597). Mt. Scopus today is identified with Ras el-Mesharif, 820 m. (2690 ft.), one of the highest points in the Jerusalem area. The summit to be included in the Mt. of Olives, then, would more correctly be Ras Abū Kharnub, location of the German hospice and possibly the site of Nob. South of this summit the ancient Roman road

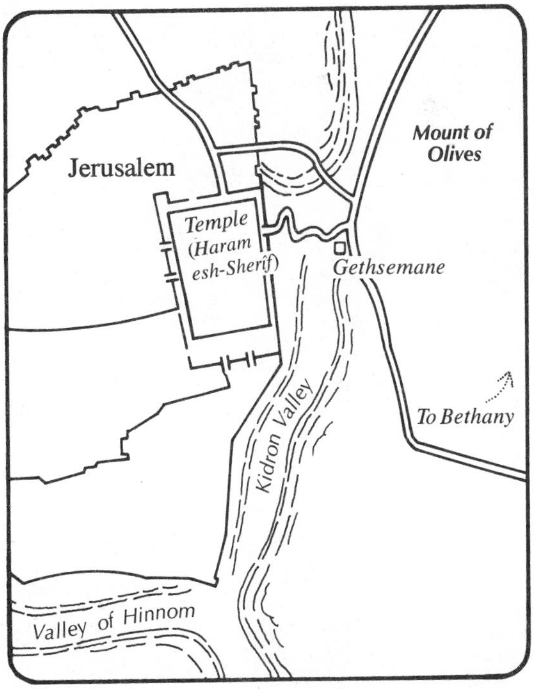

to Jericho passed through a saddle, and the modern road from the northeast corner of the old city turns at this place to go to the Mt. of Olives.

(2) Jebel eṭ-Ṭûr, 818 m. (2684 ft.) is the Mt. of Olives proper, located E of the temple area (Ḥaram esh-Sherîf, the Dome of the Rock). To the south of this summit there is a more noticeable saddle through which the modern highway to Jericho passes.

(3) Jebel Bāṭn el-Hawā ("the mountain of the womb of the wind"), possibly the Mt. of Corruption (2 K. 23:13; *see* CORRUPTION, MOUNT OF). It is generally identified as *Mons Scandali,* the mountain of offense. On the western flank of this hill the village of Silwān is located, while the southern end falls off to Wâdī en-Nâr, which is formed by the confluence of the Kidron and Hinnom valleys.

The main ridge is capped with nari (Arab. *kaʿkuli*), beneath which is soft chalk and chalky limestone containing flint. The flint was used by settlements of paleolithic man; the limestone decomposed to form soil that is good for orchards, particularly olives. The western flanks receive moisture from the rains and dews, but the eastern flanks, facing the Wilderness of Judea and the Jordan Ghor, become suddenly arid. In the early morning, before heat haze forms, the view from the Mt. of Olives to the Jordan Valley, the Dead Sea, and the mountains of Moab is spectacular.

***III. OT.***–The account of David's flight from Absalom (2 S. 15–16) contains several geographical details. After "the king crossed the brook Kidron" (15:23), he "went up the ascent of the Mt. of Olives" (v. 30) and "came to the summit, where God was worshiped" (v. 32). Beyond the summit he "came to Bahurim" (16:5), and finally he "arrived weary at the Jordan" (v. 14). All the details cannot be precisely established, but there is no doubt that the route traversed the Mt. of Olives. The location of BAHURIM is not certain, but it would seem to be to the N or NE of the Mt. of Olives, and the route would probably be close to the Roman road to Jericho built a millennium later. The place of worship likewise cannot be established with precision. If Nob is to be located on Mt. Scopus (i.e., Ras Abū Kharnub), it is tempting to identify this with the place of worship (cf. 1 S. 21:1; 22:9-11).

Solomon built high places for Chemosh and Molech "on the mountain east of Jerusalem" (1 K. 11:7). These high places are further described as "east of Jerusalem, to the south of the mount of corruption" (2 K. 23:13). The suggestion that this name was deliberate irony, based on "mount of anointing oil" (cf. T.B. *Shabbath* 56b and comms. of Rashi and Radak), has been mentioned, and the location certainly agrees with that of the Mt. of Olives. The ascription of the name *Mons Offensionis,* "mount of offense," however, cannot be traced back before Quaresmius in the 17th century.

Ezekiel saw the glory of God depart from the temple to stand "upon the mountain which is on the east side of the city" (Ezk. 11:23). In his vision of the new Jerusalem, he saw this glory return and enter the temple (43:2-5). It is commonly understood that the mountain referred to is Olivet.

In Zechariah's description of the Day of Yahweh (Zec. 14), he states: "On that day his [i.e., the Lord's] feet shall stand on the Mount of Olives which lies before Jerusalem on the east; and the Mount of Olives shall be split in two from east to west by a very wide valley; so that one half of the Mount shall withdraw northward, and the other half southward" (14:4). He goes on to say, "On that day living waters shall flow out from Jerusalem, half of them to the eastern sea and half of them to the western sea; it shall continue in summer [the dry season] as in winter" (v. 8).

***IV. NT.***–Most of the NT references to the Mt. of Olives are connected with the final week of Jesus' earthly ministry ("Passion Week"). The only exceptions are Jn. 8:1 (the passage on the woman taken in adultery, the inclusion of which at this point in the Fourth Gospel is seriously questioned) and Acts 1:12 (cf. Lk. 24:50-53, the reference to the Ascension). It is reasonable to assume that the incident with Mary and Martha (Lk. 10:38-42) also occurred in Bethany on the eastern side of the Mt. of Olives, but the place is not named. The raising of Lazarus (Jn. 11) likewise took place at Bethany, which is described as "near Jerusalem, about fifteen stadia [2.8 km. or 1.8 mi.] distant" (11:18), but again, the Mt. of Olives is not named. Likewise, the feast "six days before the Passover" was held at Bethany (12:1; cf. Mt. 26:6-12; Mk. 14:3-9).

The feast at Bethany was followed the next day (Jn. 12:12) by the palm-strewn procession to Jerusalem (vv. 13-15). This is specifically located with reference to Bethphage and the Mt. of Olives (Mt. 21:1-11; Mk. 11:1-10; Lk. 19:28-39). As Jesus approached the city, He wept over it (Lk. 19:41-44) at a place traditionally marked by the Dominus Flevit chapel.

According to Lk. 21:37 Jesus did not lodge in Jerusalem during that week, but "at night he went out and lodged on the mount called Olivet." This is supported by other accounts. For example, the "cursing of the barren fig tree" took place the day after the Triumphal Entry as Jesus was returning to the city from Bethany (cf. Mt. 21:17-19; Mk. 11:11-14, 19f.). The Olivet Discourse on the signs of the end of the age (Mt. 24; Mk. 13) was given "on the Mount of Olives opposite the temple" (Mk. 13:3; cf. Mt. 24:3), as Jesus was returning from Jerusalem (Mk. 13:1; Mt. 24:1). He sent Peter and John "into the city" (Mt. 26:18; Lk. 22:8) to prepare the Passover, and when it was evening He and the other disciples observed the Feast (Mt. 26:20; Mk. 14:17; Lk. 22:14). After the meal they sang a hymn and "went out to the Mount of Olives" (Mt. 26:30; Mk. 14:26; Lk. 22:39; cf. Jn. 18:1). They came to a place called Gethsemane (Mt. 26:36) where Jesus underwent His agony, and later was seized by the soldiers and taken to trial (Jn. 18:12, cf. Mt. 26:47-57; Mk. 14:43-50; Lk. 22:47-54).

***V. Subsequent History and Tradition.***–The Mt. of Olives and the portion of the Kidron Valley which is immediately adjacent, often identified as the Valley of Jehoshaphat (cf. Joel 3:2 [MT 4:2]), are of primary significance to Jews, Christians, and Moslems (cf. W. S. LaSor). In the Haggadah this mount was the location where the dove that had been released by Noah plucked the olive leaf (Midr. *Gen. Rabbah* xxxiii.9; *Lev. Rabbah* xxxi.8; *Lam. Rabbah* ii.5). The ritual of the burning of the red heifer (cf. Nu. 19:2) was performed on the Mt. of Olives (Mish. *Parah* iii.6). Storehouses for the temple were located on the Mount (T.P. *Taanith* iv.5). The signal fire to indicate the new moon has already been mentioned; a similar signal was used for the time of the burning of leaven on the eve of Passover (T.B. *Pesahim* 14a). And because of the importance of the Valley of Jehoshaphat on judgment day, where the resurrection is to take place, in order for those who have been buried elsewhere to get to the site, "The Holy One, Blessed be He, makes subterranean passages for them, and they burrow and roll in them until they come under the Mount of Olives" (from M. Hacohen; cf. T.P. *Ketubim* 35b, quoted in C. G. Montefiore and H. Loewe, *Rabbinic Anthology* [repr. 1974], p. 600, no. 1651; cf. also G. F. Moore, *Judaism* [1927], II, 379f.). On the slopes of the mount overlooking the Kidron is a vast Jewish burial ground, reputed to be the largest Jewish cemetery in the world.

Christian tradition concerning the Mt. of Olives is largely

related to the NT events, which have been discussed above. In addition, the identification of "the exact spot" has often been added. (For sources of many of these traditions, cf. D. Baldi, pp. 383-426, 752-780, and notes in LaSor.) The identification of the Valley of Jehoshaphat with the Kidron is mentioned by the Pilgrim of Bordeaux (A.D. 333). The Breviary of Jerusalem (A.D. 530) is the first to identify the "Galilee" of Mt. 28:16 with a place on the Mt. of Olives known as *Viri Galilaei* (the words taken from Acts 1:11), now marked by a church. According to one tradition, mentioned by Rauwolf (A.D. 1573), this was where pilgrims to Jerusalem from Galilee encamped. A basilica erected by Constantine as a memorial to his mother Helena marked the spot of the Ascension; St. Paulinus Nolanus (A.D. 403) mentions the basilica and also the footprints left by Jesus, which are at present shown to the visitor to the Chapel of the Ascension. Aetheria (A.D. 395) mentions a church called the Martyrium under which was a grotto where the Lord taught the disciples. The foundations of the basilica are located at the Eleōna, where the Carmelite Cloister of the Pater Noster was later erected. On the walls of this cloister the Lord's Prayer is recorded in sixty languages (E. Hoade, p. 323). The chapel of the Ascension, at the summit of the mountain, was built in 1834 near the earlier Church of the Ascension which had been turned into a mosque in 1187. A stone with the footprints of Jesus is located in the octagonal chapel.

The site of Gethsemane is marked by a Franciscan complex, which includes the garden with its gnarled olive trees and the Church of All Nations with the Stone of the Agony in front of the altar. Because of the importance of the Valley of Jehoshaphat with reference to the resurrection, there is an extensive history of Christian burials, as well as Jewish and Moslem, on the Mt. of Olives. The anonymous Placentius (A.D. 570) mentions that James, Zebedee, and many of the saints lie in this mountain, and the tomb of Mary is mentioned in an Armenian description of the holy places dating from the 7th century. Grethenios (A.D. 1400) believed that the tombs of Joachim and Anna, parents of Mary, were in the same place that marked the tomb of Mary, and Greffin Affagrat (A.D. 1533) held that in addition there was another tomb "which some say to be that of St. Joseph, spouse of the virgin Mary." The Armenian Gethsemane, opposite that of the Fransciscans, is the present location of the tomb of Mary.

In Moslem tradition the Grand Assize of all mankind will take place in the Kidron Valley between the Dome of the Rock and the Mt. of Olives. Ibn el-Gaqih describes it: "The Mount of Olives faces the Mosque [el-Aqsa], and between them is found the Valley of Ben Hinnom, and from it ʿIsa [Jesus] ascended to Heaven. And on the Day of Judgment all souls will be gathered to it and they will cross the bridge over the Valley of Jehoshaphat, some to Paradise and some to Gehennam." Burhān ed-Dîn el-Farkah of Damascus (d. 1329) wrote that the sanctity of the place "rests on a deed of Saffiya, the wife of the prophet who went up on the mount and prayed there." There are many Moslem tombs on the western slopes of Wâdī Sitti Maryam (the Arab name of that portion of the Kidron Valley E of Ḥaram esh-Sherîf).

*VI. Eschatology.*–The eschatological significance of the Mt. of Olives is based on the prophecies in Ezekiel and Zechariah, to which have been added Jewish, Christian, and Moslem interpretations and traditions. Ezekiel saw the glory of the Lord (in later Jewish terminology, the Shekinah) depart from the temple and stand above the Mt. of Olives (Ezk. 11:23). This, however, was not the end of the covenantal relationship, for in his vision of the new Jerusalem Ezekiel saw the glory of Yahweh coming "from the east" (where the Mt. of Olives was located, 11:23) and entering the temple, to make it His throne (43:2-7). When this prophecy is added to the vision of the Day of the Lord which Zechariah records (Zec. 14:1-9), the gathering of the nations before Jerusalem to destroy it and the coming of the Lord to the Mt. of Olives to destroy them become part of the eschatological scheme. If, then, the prophecy of the gathering of the nations in the Valley of Jehoshaphat (Joel 3:2) is added, the basis for Jewish, Christian, and Moslem beliefs about the importance of the Mt. of Olives in the end times is established.

***Bibliography.***–W. S. LaSor, *Christian News from Israel*, 13,3/4 (1962), 16-23; M. Hacohen, *Har Hazeitim* (1962); E. Hoade, *Guide to the Holy Land* (7th ed. 1973), pp. 305-331; D. Baldi, *Enchiridion Locorum Sanctorum* (1955), pp. 383-426, 752-780; H. Vincent and F.-M. Abel, *Jérusalem Nouvelle* (1914-1926), II, chs. 13-14, pp. 328-419; Hd. Sauvaire, *Histoire de Jérusalem et d'Hébron* (1876), p. 19; A. Katsh, *Judaism in Islam* (1954), *passim*.

W. S. LASOR

**OLIVET** ol'i-vet. *See* OLIVES, MOUNT OF.

**OLIVEWOOD.** *See* OLEASTER.

**OLIVEYARD** [Heb. *zayiṯ*]. *See* OLIVE TREE; ORCHARD.

**OLYMPAS** ō-lim'pəs [Gk. *Olympas*; perhaps an abbreviated form of *Olympiodōrus*] (Rom. 16:15). An unknown slave or freedman; one of five members of a Roman household church. Philologus and Julia may have been his parents, and Nereus and his sister were perhaps Olympas's siblings. J. J. HUGHES

**OLYMPIAN ZEUS** ō-lim'pē-ən zo͞os [Gk. *Dios Olympios*]; AV JUPITER OLYMPIUS. An epithet of the Greek god ZEUS, and the name given to the temple in Jerusalem by Antiochus Epiphanes in 168 B.C. as part of his attempt to hellenize the Jews (2 Macc. 6:2). The epithet came from Mt. Olympus in Thessaly, where Zeus was thought to preside over the court of the gods.

**OLYMPIUS** ō-lim'pē-əs (2 Macc. 6:2, AV). *See* OLYMPIAN ZEUS.

**OMAERUS** om-ə-ē'rəs (1 Esd. 9:34, AV). *See* AMRAM **2.**

**OMAR** ō'mär [Heb. *'ômār* < *'āmar*–'speak'(?)]. Son of Eliphaz and grandson of Esau; an Edomite clan chief (Gen. 36:11, 15; 1 Ch. 1:36).

**OMEGA.** *See* ALPHA AND OMEGA.

**OMEN** [Heb. *naḥaš*–'divination,' 'enchantment,' 'omen'] (Nu. 24:1); AV ENCHANTMENT; NEB DIVINATION; [*nāḥaš*–'practice divination'] ("watch for an omen," 1 K. 20:33); AV "observe whether anything would come"; [*'ôṯ*–'sign'] (Isa. 44:25); AV TOKEN; NEB SIGN; [*môpēṯ*–'sign, wonder'] ("good omen," Zec. 3:8); AV "wondered at"; [Gk. *éndeixis*–'sign, omen, proof'] ("clear omen," Phil. 1:28); AV EVIDENT TOKEN; NEB SURE SIGN. Any phenomenon that is believed to portend a future event. Isa. 44:25f. affirms that Yahweh, the Creator and sovereign Lord of history, makes nonsense out of the predictions of the diviners (possibly the Babylonian *bārû* priests) based on "signs" or "omens," but brings to pass the words spoken by His messengers, the true prophets. On Nu. 24:1 and 1 K. 20:23, *see* MAGIC II.A (6). *See also* DIVINATION; PROPHECY I.C; II.C.

In two other passages "omen" has no divinatory connotations but simply denotes a sign of something that will happen in the future. Zec. 3:8 prophesies that Joshua (who has just been absolved of his guilt and made fit for the high priesthood) and his fellow priests are "good omens" (Heb. *môpēṯ,* usually translated "wonder"; see *TDOT,* I, 168), i.e., they are signs of a happy future, when God's grace will be more fully revealed in the messianic age. In Phil. 1:28 Paul states that the Philippian Christians' steadfastness in the face of persecution is a clear sign to their adversaries of their adversaries' ultimate destruction and the Christians' ultimate salvation, since it is proof that the Christians have God on their side (cf. Acts 26:14).

*See also* SIGN.

*Bibliography.*–*IB,* V, 517f.; VI, 1067-1070; J. Lindblom, *Prophecy in Ancient Israel* (1962), pp. 85-88, 138; *TDOT,* I, *s.v.* "'ôth" (F. J. Helfmeyer). N. J. O.

**OMER** ō'mər [Heb. *'ōmer*] (Ex. 16:16-36). A dry measure equivalent to a tenth of an ephah. *See* WEIGHTS AND MEASURES.

**OMNIPOTENCE** om-nip'ō-təns. The condition of being all-powerful; an attribute of God.

BIBLICAL BASIS OF THE DOCTRINE

***I. Terms and Usage.***–The noun "omnipotence" is not found in the English versions, nor is any noun exactly corresponding to it in the original Hebrew or Greek. The adjective "omnipotent" occurs in Rev. 19:6, AV, for Gk. *pantokrátōr,* "all-powerful." This word (RSV always "almighty") appears also in 1:8; 4:8; 11:17; 15:3; 16:7, 14; 19:15; 21:22; and 2 Cor. 6:18. It is found frequently in the LXX, especially in the rendering of the divine names Yahweh Sabaoth and El Shaddai.

***II. The Concept in OT Names of God.***–The formal conception of omnipotence as worked out in theology does not occur in the OT. The substance of the idea is conveyed in various indirect ways. The notion of strength is inherent in the OT conception of God from the beginning, being already represented in one of the two divine names inherited by Israel from ancient Semitic religion, 'El. According to one etymology strength is also inherent in the other name, 'Elohim, which by its plural form brings out the fulness of power in God and marks an approach to the idea of omnipotence (cf. *TDOT,* I, 273).

The concept of might occupies a prominent place in the patriarchal religion, as is indicated by the name characteristic of this period, 'El Shaddai (cf. Gen. 17:1; 28:3; 35:11; 43:14; 48:3; 49:24f.; Ex. 6:3). This name, however, designates the divine power as standing in the service of His covenantal relation to the patriarchs, as transcending nature and overpowering it in the interests of redemption.

Another divine name that signals this attribute is Yahweh Sabaoth (RSV "Lord of hosts"). This name, characteristic of the prophetic period, describes God as the king surrounded and followed by the angelic hosts (Heb. *ṣᵉḇā'ôṯ*). Since the might of an oriental king is measured by the splendor of his retinue, God is of great, incomparable power, the King Omnipotent (Ps. 24:10; Isa. 2:12; 6:3-5; 8:13; Jer. 46:18; Mal. 1:14).

Other names expressive of the same idea are 'Abir, "Strong One," compounded with Jacob or Israel ("Mighty One," Gen. 49:24; Ps. 132:2-5; Isa. 1:24; 49:26; 60:16), and 'El Gibbor, "God Hero" ("Mighty God," Isa. 9:6 [of the Messiah]; cf. Jer. 20:11). God is figuratively designated as *ṣûr,* "rock," in Dt. 32:4, 15, 18; Ps. 18:2, 31, 46 (MT 3, 32, 47); 19:14 (MT 15); 89:26 (MT 27); Isa. 17:10; 26:4; 30:29; Hab. 1:12. The specific energy with which the divine nature operates finds expression also in the name of 'El Ḥay, "Living God," which God bears over against the impotent idols (1 S. 17:26-36; 2 K. 19:4-16; Ps. 18:46; Jer. 23:36; Dnl. 6:20-27 [MT 21-28]). References to God's "hand," "arm," and "finger" anthropomorphically describe His power; e.g., in Dt. 5:15; 7:19; etc., God delivers Israel from Egypt by His "mighty hand" and "outstretched arm." *See* GOD, NAMES OF.

***III. Other Modes of Expression.***–Some of the attributes of God have an intimate connection with His omnipotence. Under this head, God's nature as Spirit and His holiness especially may be considered. The representation of God as Spirit in the OT does not primarily refer to the incorporeality of the divine nature but to its inherent energy. The physical element underlying the conception of Spirit is that of air in motion, and in this at first not the invisibility but the force forms the point of comparison. The opposite of "spirit" in this sense is "flesh," which expresses the weakness and impotence of the creature over against God (Isa. 2:22; 31:3).

The holiness of God in its earliest and widest sense (not restricted to the ethical sphere) describes that majestic, specifically divine character of His being, that which evokes in mankind religious awe. Holiness is not a single attribute coordinated with others, but a peculiar aspect under which all the attributes can be viewed, that which renders them distinct from anything analogous in the creature (1 S. 2:22; Hos. 11:9). In this way holiness becomes closely associated with the power of God, indeed sometimes becomes synonymous with divine omnipotence (Ex. 15:11; Nu. 20:12). In Ezekiel, especially, God's "holy name" is often equivalent to His renown for power, hence interchangeable with His "great name" (Ezk. 36:20-24). The Spirit as a distinct essence and as the agent and a person of the Godhead also represents the divine power (Isa. 32:15; Mt. 12:28; Lk. 1:35; 4:14; Acts 10:38; Rom. 15:19; 1 Cor. 2:4).

***IV. Unlimited Extent of the Divine Power.***–All these expressions predicate a great and unique power of God. Statements that explicitly affirm the absolutely unlimited extent of this power are rare. The reason, however, lies not in any actual restriction placed on this power, but in the concrete, practical form of biblical thinking, which prevents abstract formulation of the principle. The point to be noticed is that not one statement exempts anything from the reach of divine power. Nearest to a general formula come such statements as "Nothing is too hard for [God]" (Jer. 32:17; cf. Gen. 18:14) and "whatever the Lord pleases he does, in heaven and on earth" (Ps. 135:6; cf. 115:3). The thought is also phrased negatively: no one "can hinder" God from carrying out His purpose (Isa. 43:13); God's hand is not "shortened" (Nu. 11:23). NT expressions are "with God all things are possible" (Mt. 19:26 par. Mk. 10:27; Lk. 18:27) and "with God nothing will be impossible" (Lk. 1:37; RV "no word from God shall be void of power"). God's omnipotence is indirectly implied in the effect ascribed to faith (Mk. 9:23 par. Mt. 17:20, "all things are possible to him who believes"), because faith puts the divine power at the disposal of the believer. On its subjective side, the principle of inexhaustible power finds expression in Isa. 40:28: God is not subject to weariness. Because He is conscious of the unlimited extent of His resources, nothing is marvelous in His eyes (Zec. 8:6).

***V. Forms of Its Manifestation.***–The distinctive quality of the divine power that renders it omnipotent becomes apparent chiefly through its forms of manifestation. The divine power operates not merely in single concrete acts but is comprehensively related to the world. In nature and in history, in creation and in redemption, this power produces, controls, and directs everything that comes to pass. Nothing in the realm of actual or conceivable things can withstand it (Am. 9:2f.; Dnl. 4:35); it extends and masters all details of reality, even to the minutest and most recondite sequences of cause and effect (Mt. 10:30; Lk. 12:7). Nothing happens by chance (1 S. 6:9; cf. v. 12; Prov. 16:33). Divine power need not operate through second causes; it itself underlies all second causes and makes them what they are.

Divine power is creative, producing its effect through a mere word (Gen. 1:3ff.; Dt. 8:3; Ps. 33:9; Rom. 4:17; He. 1:3; 11:30). Among the prophets, Isaiah emphasized this manner of the working of God's power in its immediateness and suddenness (Isa. 9:8; 17:13; 18:4-6; 29:5). All the processes of nature are ascribed to the causation of God (Job 5:9ff.; 9:5ff.; 38–39; Isa. 40:12ff.; Am. 4:13; 5:8f.; 9:5f.), especially God's control of the sea (Ps. 65:7 [MT 8]; 104:9; Isa. 50:2; Jer. 5:22; 31:35).

God also has power over the processes of history. He sovereignly uses not merely Israel but all nations, even the most powerful, e.g., the Assyrians, as His instruments for the accomplishment of his purpose (Am. 1:1–2:3; 9:7; Isa. 10:5-15; 28:2; 45:1; Jer. 25:9; 27:6; 43:10). The prophets do not ascribe to God merely relatively greater power than the gods of the nations; rather, the prophets show that His power extends into the sphere of the nations, and they ignore the heathen gods in estimating His might (Isa. 31:3).

Even more than the sphere of nature and history, that of redemption reveals the divine omnipotence, from the point of view of the supernatural and miraculous. Thus Ex. 15 celebrates the power of God in the wonders of the Exodus. It is God's exclusive prerogative to do wonders (Job 5:9; 9:10; Ps. 72:18); He alone can make "a new thing" (Nu. 16:30; Isa. 43:19; Jer. 31:22). In the NT the great embodiment of this redemptive omnipotence is the resurrection of believers (Mt. 22:29; Mk. 12:24) and specifically the resurrection of Christ (Rom. 4:17, 21, 24; Eph. 1:19ff.). God's power is evidenced in the whole process of redemption (Mt. 19:26; Mk. 10:27; Rom. 8:31; Eph. 3:7, 20; 1 Pet. 1:5; Rev. 11:17).

***VI. Its Significance for Biblical Religion.***–The significance of the idea of divine omnipotence may be traced along two distinct lines. First, it appears as a support of faith. Second, it is productive of that specifically religious state of consciousness which Scripture calls "the fear of the Lord." Omnipotence in God is that to which human faith addresses itself. In it lies the assurance that He is able to save, as in His love lies the assurance that He is willing to save (Ps. 65:5f. [MT 6f.]; 72:18; 118:14-16; Eph. 3:20).

As to the other aspect of its significance, the divine omnipotence in itself, and not merely for soteriological reasons, evokes a specific religious response. This is true, not only of the OT, where the element of the fear of God stands comparatively in the foreground, but remains true also of the NT. Even in Our Lord's teaching, the prominence given to the fatherhood and love of God does not obscure the transcendent majesty of the divine nature, including omnipotence, which is made a potent factor in the cultivation of the religious mind (Mt. 6:9). The beauty of Jesus' teaching on the nature of God consists in His keeping the exaltation of God above every creature and God's loving condescension toward the creature in perfect equilibrium, and His making this exaltation and condescension fructified by each other. Religion is more than the inclusion of God in the general altruistic movement of the human mind; it is a devotion at every point colored by the consciousness of that divine uniqueness in which God's omnipotence occupies a foremost place.

***Bibliography.***–A. B. Davidson, *Theology of the OT* (1904), pp. 163f.; E. König, *Geschichte der alttestamentlichen Religion* (1912), pp. 135-37, 391, 475; G. F. Oehler, *Theology of the OT* (Eng. tr. 1883), pp. 88, 911, 126.

G. VOS

### History of the Doctrine

I. Church Fathers
II. Schoolmen and Reformers
III. Modern Theologians

***I. Church Fathers.***–The doctrine of God's omnipotence as expressed by the fathers derived naturally from the doctrine of God's creation of the world and sovereignty over it. One of the earliest Christian writings, the Didache (10:3), adopted the concept of God as almighty, which found its way into the Apostles' Creed. 1 Clement has a passing reference to God's mastery over all things (8:2). Justin Martyr introduced attributes from contemporary philosophy — "the everlasting, ineffable, impassible, and ingenerate nature of God" (*Apol.* 1.9) — which strongly reinforced the idea of God's omnipotence, while Theophilus (*Ad Autolycum* ii.4) found a clear manifestation of the divine power in God's making of all things precisely as He desired and willed. Against the Gnostic theory of a limited demiurge as the maker of this world, Irenaeus stressed the equation of the Creator with the true God, for "otherwise the title 'Almighty' will be reduced to nought" (*Adv. haer.* ii.1.5). He, too, located the supremacy of the divine power in the ability of God not merely to fashion existing materials but also to furnish the very stuff of the world itself, thus making all things out of nothing (ii.10.4).

In the 3rd cent. Origen raised a central question about the omnipotence of God when discussing the rationality of prayer (*On Prayer* 5): if God in His almightiness ordains all that happens, what place can there be for prayer? According to the appointed order of the universe, the sun, for example, will rise in any case, and therefore praying that it do so seems pointless. Human responsibility, however, implies freedom of action, which in turn apparently imposes a limit on the omnipotence of God. To avoid this implication, Origen suggested that God's omnipotence must extend to the freedom of human choice and providentially comprehends it. Prayer and other acts that presuppose and express human freedom constitute elements in the overruling of divine omnipotence.

In the more developed fourth-century theology represented, e.g., by Cyril of Jerusalem in his *Catecheses,* the divine omnipotence comprises seven main elements. First is the noncontingency of the divine will; God in His willing is not subject to any extraneous events, fate, or chance (4.5). Second is God's absolute supremacy; He has "none mightier than Himself, no successor to drive Him out of His kingdom" (6.7). Third is the universal extent of the power of God; it covers all things and all people and cannot be restricted, e.g., to heaven alone or simply to the soul (8.1-3). Fourth is the divine forbearance of evil; God's omnipotence is not limited by opposition but teleologically tolerates it in order to achieve the greater victory (8.4). Fifth is the divine overruling of all things to serve both God and His people; in this regard Cyril warned his congregation against saying that money or property is the devil's and taught them to regard them as something that may and should be used for God (8.5-7). Sixth is the analogous expression of the divine omnipotence in the powerful works of the natural world that God has made (9.2). Seventh is full manifestation of God's omnipotence in the Son and the Spirit no less than in the Father, since the Son and the Spirit stand outside the things that merely serve God (8.5). The plenitude of power is seen in the Son as the Creator and as the risen, ascended, and returning Lord (11.10, 22f.), and is seen in the Spirit as the all-powerful Giver whose ministry includes baptism, tongues, healing, preaching, sanctification, and forgiveness (16.22; 17.14-38).

At the end of the patristic age John of Damascus added the following points to the discussion. First, he equated the divine omnipotence more completely with the operation of the Holy Spirit, whom he described as living, endowed with will, self-moving, active, exercising His power in the prosecution of every design in accordance with His will (*De fide orthodoxa* i.7). Second, he related God's power very strictly to His will, by which alone it is measured; omnipotence is the ability of God to do what He wills to do (i.7). Third, he linked omnipotence to the Greek term for God, *théos,* derived from the word for "run," *théō,* thus denoting God's power to run through all things, and care for them (i.9). John, too, found the power of God preeminently displayed in the divine victory over death in the death of Christ (4.4,11), though he did not bring out as clearly as Gregory of Nyssa had done in his *Oratio catechetica* (24) that the divine omnipotence is so great that at the cross it could take the paradoxical form of impotence and thus express itself with all the greater force.

*II. Schoolmen and Reformers.*–Medieval theology saw some significant but not uniformly helpful developments in the relation to the divine omnipotence. Anselm in his *Proslogion* tackled the apparent contradiction that Scripture says the omnipotent God cannot do certain things, e.g., tell a lie or change His nature. He pointed out that this implies consistency rather than contradiction, for things such as lying are negative and passive expressing impotence rather than omnipotence. God's inability to do things of this kind is thus the greater evidence of His almightiness (7).

Thomas Aquinas raised the issue of limitation in a different way. Asking whether God can do things that He has not done as well as those that He has, Aquinas concluded that He can; thus he came to distinguish between God's absolute power, which covers such acts, and His ordained power, which extends to that which He has in fact done. While intrinsically correct, this answer should not be reinterpreted as positing a distinction between God's extraordinary power, manifested, e.g., in miracles, and His ordinary power, expressed in the natural order. Nor should it be used to set up for God a new group of impossibilities relating, not to Himself, but to His creation, e.g., to a reversal of the law of noncontradiction or of the established mathematical structure of the universe (cf. *Summa Theol.* i.25.3). In such matters the real issue is not whether there can be such a reversal, but why there cannot be. God's omnipotence is not limited by an external impossibility imposed upon Him; the restriction is rather that of an impossibility that He Himself imposes. Later nominalists like William of Occam developed this principle to the point of suspending everything — the structure of morality as well as reality — on the omnipotent but apparently arbitrary will of God, whose free decision it is that right should be right and wrong wrong, but who hypothetically might have reversed things.

Among the leading Reformers, Calvin, in his comparatively few references to the divine omnipotence, retained the emphasis upon God's will but did so with a much more theological than philosophical concern. He evinced no interest in the inner omnipotence of God and focused on its outer manifestation, which he discovered extensively in creation and providence (*Inst.* i.5.1, 9). He believed firmly that Satan and sinners in no way limit this divine power by their opposition, for it is "dependent upon God's sufferance," so that even Satan can "do only those things which have been divinely permitted to him," "his malice being directed to the fulfilment of divinely appointed goals" (i.18.1). Like the fathers, Calvin saw the power of God at work specifically in the ministry of Christ in creation and redemption (i.13.12f.) and also in the work of the Holy Spirit in regeneration, sanctification, and the bestowal of power, grace, and gifts (i.13.14). For Calvin omnipotence meant God's continuous action whereby all that occurs does so by His knowledge and deliberation (i.16.3). He made this point succinctly in the *Genevan Catechism* when answering the question of the meaning of almightiness: "Not only has God might He does not exercise but He also has all things under His power and hand" (*LCC,* XXII, 93f.). In his *Brief Reply* (*ibid.,* p. 339) he stressed that even reprobation manifests God's omnipotence, for "as regards themselves the wicked did what God did not will, but as regards God's omnipotence they were by no means to prevail against His will, so that through them, even as they did what was against the will of God, His will was done." God would never let evil be done — a thought of Augustine is echoed here — "unless as omnipotent he were able to make good out of the evil."

*III. Modern Theologians.*–During the 17th cent. theologians devoted much time and energy to discussions of the divine omnipotence. Heidegger defined it as the attribute by which God adequately carries out whatever He wills in accordance with His nature (cf. H. Heppe, *Reformed Dogmatics* [Eng. tr. 1950; repr. 1978], p. 95). Mastricht equated it with the very essence of God and therefore described it as eternal, infinite, and independent (in Heppe, pp. 99f.). What is possible or impossible for it is determined by the divine glory; all that will glorify God is possible, while what will not is impossible. What lies outside the divine omnipotence is thus nonexistent. Heidegger advanced the important thesis that speaking of impossiblities in no way implies a limitation of divine omnipotence but rather suggests the perfection of God's power, which God Himself will never contradict. Being "omnipotent is doing what he wills, not suffering what He does not will" (*ibid.,* pp. 101f.). Braun argued similarly that God cannot perform contradictions because "they are nothing" and would overturn His perfection. Thus God cannot produce an infinitely perfect creature, for infinite perfection includes the necessity of existence, which by nature a creature cannot have (*ibid.,* pp. 102). Heidegger agreed with Aquinas in distinguishing between absolute and ordered (or actual) power. He also saw a difference between power (*potentia*) and the right by which God uses it (*potestas*), which itself subdivides into absolute right, God's absolute power of free will, and ordered right, i.e., God's right to act in accordance with what He has ordained. In all these discussions omnipotence is handled exclusively in relation to the world and not to God in Himself, so that although Wollebius (*Compend* I, 3) found omnipotence in the inner work of God, this tended to be isolated from creaturely action and narrowly equated with the divine omnicausality.

The problem of God's general omnipotence was compounded by the vigorous controversy that arose in the later 16th and 17th cents. over the relation between divine and human action in grace and salvation. Arminianism and Molinism seemed to many to threaten a strict doctrine of divine omnipotence. Although Molinism had a more direct bearing on the related question of divine omniscience (or prescience), it carried the implication of a restriction of the divine power. Both Arminians and Molinists tried in different ways to protect human freedom against divine almightiness, but in so doing they seemed to weaken the almightiness. Thus they produced a reaction that tended to equate the divine omnipotence with an abstract predetermination of all things but that compensated by allowing for a system of conditions within the fixed and irrevocable order (F. Gomarus, *Works* [1644], III, 34), the "secondary causes" to which the Westminister Confession refers in 3.1.

Emphasis on human freedom caused divine omnipotence to be questioned in the 17th cent. and the problem of evil intensified the challenge in the eighteenth. The problem, which was not new, took the simple form that evil ought not be to be present in the creation of an all-loving and all-powerful God. For a time the philosophical optimism of Leibniz's *Theodicy* — that all is ultimately for the best in the best of all possible worlds — offered an apparently satisfactory solution to the difficulty, although with a hint at some limitation of the Creator's power. But the Lisbon earthquake in the middle of the century and Voltaire's merciless ridiculing in his *Candide* of a facile and fatuous optimism revived the uneasiness of the period and opened the door, not to the concept of a limited or hostile God, but to doubt about the very existence of God.

An enhanced concern for the humanity of Jesus produced a new line of thought in the 19th century. The so-called kenotic Christology associated with I. A. Dorner, G. Thomasius, F. H. R. Franck, and C. Gore divided the divine attributes into two groups: attributes of majesty (e.g., omnipotence), and more moral or personal attributes (e.g., love). Christ in His incarnation supposedly abandoned the attributes of the first group, which were incompatible with real humanity, but retained those of the second group, which were compatible. In the person of Christ, who did the work of revelation and reconciliation, God thus surrended Himself to external forces in a supreme and victorious expression of His never-failing love.

Early in the 20th cent. the philosopher A. N. Whitehead, attempting to provide Christianity with a metaphysical basis, advocated a concept of God in which He shares in the universal process of being and thus suffers from necessary restriction even while exercising a certain measure of control. Whitehead's views received little support at first, but the representatives of process theology revived them virtually unchanged in the second half of the century. In the meantime the horrors of National Socialism forced Dietrich Bonhoeffer to a radically new vision of the omnipotence of God in the light of Christ's crucifixion. Human autonomy, he thought, renders God "weak and powerless in the world, and that is precisely the way, the only way, in which he is with us and helps us" (*Letters and Papers from Prison* [Eng. tr. 1971], pp. 360ff.). Yet Bonhoeffer was not surrendering the divine omnipotence. In a manner similar to that of Gregory of Nyssa, and to early concepts and illustrations of Christ's redeeming work, he was redefining it as an omnipotence that paradoxically triumphs in and through its very impotence.

Karl Barth expressed the same thought in his massive treatment of reconciliation in *CD,* IV (esp. IV/1). He, too, stressed that in order to exercise His lordship in our behalf, God in Christ became a servant (§59), and that in order to carry through His decisive action, He submitted voluntarily to the Passion. Nowhere, in fact, did God demonstrate His omnipotence more fully than by showing that even in the impotence of suffering and death He could still be almighty and accomplish His own purposes, not just in spite of, but precisely by means of the apparently victorious might of His opponents. Taking up the same point in *Christian Faith* (Eng. tr. 1979), H. Berkhof selected what he took to be a more accurate title, "The Defenseless Superior Power," for the section (21) that an older dogmatician would have put under the heading "Omnipotence."

Barth, however, realized that this insight could not altogether supersede the older theologians' view of omnipotence. He took care to avoid onesidedness by balancing the newer view of divine power with a treatment of divine constancy in a long subsection (§ 31.2) of *CD* II/1. He fully considered the biblical data and earlier theological discussions and made a number of significant points. (1) God as omnipotent differs from the changeable, which cannot do all that it wills and can do what it does not will. (2) God as omnipotent differs from the unchangeable, which suffers from a restriction of possibility and thus from final incapacity. (3) God as omnipotent is Lord of all creation, whether in life or in death. (4) God defines His own omnipotence rather than being defined by it. (5) Omnipotence covers both physical possibility *(potentia)* and moral or legal possibility *(potestas).* (6) It extends to more than God's past, present, and future works and hence should not be too directly equated with His omnicausality. (7) Omnipotence is God's power to be Himself and to live in and by Himself as Father, Son, and Holy Spirit; it is thus delimited by His essence and nature. (8) It is power over everything; and thus it limits and determines all other powers, is not itself limited or determined by them, and is always absolute power (God's ongoing choice) even though it may take the form of ordered power (a particular choice). (9) It is the omnipotence of the divine knowing, willing, and loving as these are known by revelation. (10) Its revelation-defined character dispels all erroneous notions that it impairs or threatens the independence of the creature. (11) Omnipotence is known as active, historical, and personal power; the particularity of its exercise protects it against abstract generality but in no way excludes its universality as power over all things. (12) Its exercise has a specific center or location from which God lovingly knows and wills and which in Barth's view is ultimately to be identified as Jesus Christ, the personal Logos or incarnate Word. "This centre is the omnipotent Word by which He created and governs and upholds the world, withstands its rebellion, and restores it to Himself . . . . omnipotently [even in the impotence of the cross and Passion as well as in the naked power of the Resurrection] bringing it back to peace with Himself."

The full import of Barth's presentation does not seem to have been grasped by theologians who are preoccupied with the complementary ideas of human power, divine weakness, and cosmic process. Barth reminds us that while some redefinition or refocusing may be necessary, the themes with which earlier scholars wrestled have a genuine biblical basis and still deserve a place in theological study. There is no need, of course, to follow Barth slavishly either in his assessment of others or in his own reconstruction. There is a need, however, to keep all aspects of the divine omnipotence in view, to hold God's omnipotence in balance with its specific expression in the work of the incarnate Son, to work out the concept in authentically biblical terms, and to protect it against the constant pressure of dissolution in philosophical abstractions.

G. W. BROMILEY

**OMNIPRESENCE** om-ni-prez′ əns. The condition of being present everywhere at once; an attribute of God.

Biblical Basis of the Doctrine

*I. Terms and Usage.*– Neither the noun "omnipresence" nor the adjective "omnipresent" occurs in Scripture, but the idea that God is everywhere present is throughout presupposed and sometimes explicitly formulated. God's omnipresence is closely related to His omnipotence and omniscience: that He is everywhere enables Him to act everywhere and to know all things, and conversely, through omnipotent action and omniscient knowledge, He has access to all places and all secrets (cf. Ps. 139). Thus conceived, the attribute is only the correlate of the monotheistic conception of God as the Infinite Creator, Preserver and Governor of the universe, immanent in His works as well as transcendent above them.

*II. Philosophical and Popular Ideas.*–The philosophical idea of divine omnipresence is that of exemption from the limitations of space, subjectively as well as objectively. God is subjectively omnipresent in that His consciousness and knowledge do not depend on sense perception of the spatial world. He is objectively omnipresent in that space relations in the created world do not limit His presence and operation. This metaphysical conception of transcendence above all space is, of course, foreign to the Bible, which in regard to this, as in regard to the other transcendent attributes, clothes the truth of revelation in popular language and speaks of exemption from the limitations of space in terms and figures derived from space itself. Thus the very term "omnipresence" in its two parts "everywhere" and "present" contains a double inadequacy of expression, for both parts express spatial concepts.

The mode of divine omnipresence is another point at which the popular nature of the biblical teaching must be kept in mind. In treating the concept philosophically, it is important to distinguish among its applications to the essence, to the activity, and to the knowledge of God. The Bible does not draw these distinctions in the abstract. Although sometimes it refers to the pervasive immanence of God's being, it frequently contents itself with affirming the univeral extent of God's power and knowledge (Dt. 4:39; 10:14; Ps. 139:6-16; Prov. 15:3; Jer. 23:23f.; Am. 9:2).

*III. Divine Omnipresence of Being.*–The last observation has given rise to the theories of a mere omnipresence of power or omnipresence by an act of will, as distinct from an omnipresence of being. But plainly such a distinction is foreign to the intent of the biblical statements. The writers of these passages contented themselves with describing the practical effects of omnipresence without reflecting upon the difference between these and the attribute's ontological aspect; the latter is neither affirmed nor denied. Jer. 23:23f. shows that no denial of the omnipresence of being is intended. The first statement in v. 24, that no one can hide from God, expresses the omnipresence of v. 23 in terms of omniscience; in the second statement in v. 24, that God fills heaven and earth, omniscience finds ontological expression. The presence of God's being in all space is similarly affirmed in Ps. 139 (cf. v. 2 and vv. 13-16 with vv. 7-12) and in 1 K. 8:27; 2 Ch. 2:6; Isa. 66:1; Acts 17:28.

*IV. Omnipresence in Earlier Parts of the OT.*–Since omnipresence is the correlate of monotheism, it is said to be lacking in the earlier parts of the OT by those who date the development of monotheism to the prophetic period (8th cent. B.C.). It is undoubtedly true that the earliest narratives speak very anthropomorphically of God's relation to space, of His coming and going. But it does not follow from this that the writers conceived of God as being circumscribed by space. Their anthropomorphic statements refer to God's visible presence in theophany, not to His presence in general. If one inferred from the local elements in these descriptions that God is limited by space, then one might with equal warrant, on the basis of the physical elements in the descriptions, impute to the writers the view that God is corporeal.

*V. Special Redemptive and Revelatory Presence of God.*–The theophanic form of appearance does not disclose what God is ontologically in Himself but merely how He condescends to appear and work for the redemption of His people. It establishes a redemptive and revelatory presence in definite localities without detracting from the divine omnipresence. Hence theophany is not confined to one place; the altars built by the patriarchs to commemorate theophanies coexisted in several places, each and all offering access to the special divine presence.

It is significant that as early as the patriarchal period these theophanies and the altars connected with them were confined to the Holy Land. This shows that the idea embodied in them had nothing to do with a crude conception of the deity as locally circumscribed but marked the beginning of that gradual restoration of the gracious presence of God to fallen humanity, the completion of which forms the goal of redemption. Thus God is said to dwell in the ark, in the tabernacle, on Mt. Zion (Nu. 10:35; 2 S. 6:2; 2 K. 19:15; Ps. 3:4 [MT 5]; 99:1); in the temple (1 K. 8; Ps. 20:2 [MT 3]; 26:8; 46:5 [MT 6]; 48:2 [MT 3]; Isa. 8:18; Joel 3:16, 21 [MT 4:16, 21]; Am. 1:2); in the Holy Land (1 S. 26:19; Hos. 9:3); in Christ (Col. 2:9); in the Church (Jn. 14:23; Rom. 8:9, 11; 1 Cor. 3:16; 6:19; Eph. 2:21f.; 2 Pet. 2:5); in the eschatological assembly of His people (Rev. 21:3).

The presence of God in heaven must similarly be understood not as an ontological presence but as a specific theocratic manifestation (1 K. 8:27; Ps. 2:4; 11:4; 33:13-15; 104:3; Isa. 6:1-3; 63:15; 66:1; Hab. 2:20; Mt. 5:34; 6:9; Acts 7:48f.; Eph. 1:20; He. 1:3). How little the idea of heavenly presence is meant to exclude God's presence elsewhere may be seen in references to God's self-manifestation both in heaven and in the earthly sanctuary (1 K. 8:26-53; Ps. 20:2-6 [MT 3-7]; Am. 9:6). It has been alleged that the idea of God's dwelling in heaven marks a comparatively late attainment in the religion of Israel, of which no trace in the preprophetic period can yet be discovered (so B. Stade, *Biblische Theologie des AT* [1905], I, 103f.). But a number of passages in the Pentateuch bear witness to the early existence of this belief (Gen. 11:1-9; 19:24; 21:17; 22:11; 28:12). God comes, according to the belief of the earliest period, with the cloud (Ex. 14:19f.; 19:9, 18; 24:15; Nu. 11:25; 12:5). That even in the opinion of the people God's local presence is an earthly sanctuary need not have excluded Him from heaven follows also from the unhesitating belief in His simultaneous presence in a plurality of sanctuaries. Since in the biblical view God's presence is not confined to a certain sanctuary, it follows that He can be simultaneously in heaven and on earth (cf. H. Gunkel, comm. on Genesis [*Hand Kommentar zum AT,* 4th ed. 1917], p. 157).

*VI. Religious Significance.*–Both from a generally religious and from a specifically soteriological point of view the omnipresence of God is of great practical importance for the religious life. In the former respect it guarantees that the actual nearness of God and a real communion with Him may be enjoyed everywhere, even apart from the places hallowed for such purposes by a specific gracious self-manifestation (Ps. 139:7-12). In the other respect divine omnipresence assures the believer that God is at hand to save in every place where from any danger or foe His people need salvation (Isa. 43:2). *See also* PRESENCE; PRESENCE OF GOD.

*Bibliography.*–A. B. Davidson, *Theology of the OT* (1904), p. 181; E. König, *Geschichte der alttestamentlichen Religion* (1912), pp. 197-200; G. F. Oehler, *Theology of the OT* (Eng. tr. 1883), p. 111.

G. VOS

HISTORY OF THE DOCTRINE

I. Patristic Period
II. Scholastic Period
III. Reformation Period
IV. Modern Period

*I. Patristic Period.*–The earliest Christian theologians accepted without difficulty the doctrine of God's omnipresence. The doctrine of creation enabled them to resist any temptation toward a localization of God (even in heaven), while their belief in the Incarnation plainly ruled out any absence of God from His world. Hence the fathers' strong insistence on divine transcendence, which for the Apologists had a philosophical as well as biblical support, found its most comfortable expression in the thought of the God whom nothing contains but who Himself contains all things and is thus present in and to all things.

The attribute of noncircumscription (or incomprehensibility) played an important role in the patristic understanding of omnipresence. It formed a powerful argument against the idolatry of the age and the related concept of localized deity. Clement of Alexandria, e.g., pointed out that God has no bodily shape and cannot therefore be circumscribed (*Misc.* vii.5). Origen contended for the same truth in his discussion of the statement "who art in heaven" in the Lord's Prayer (*On Prayer* xxiii.1f.). This phrase cannot mean that heaven contains God, for "all things are contained and held together by Him." He said that the ascension of Jesus similarly must be understood in a mystical, not a spatial, sense. Localization implies divisibility, materiality, and corporeality and thus contradicts God's nature as disclosed by the Bible. So firmly did the fathers resist God's localization, except in the Incarnation, that they hazarded the dubious paradox that God is both everywhere and nowhere, which would seem to imply omniabsence as well as omnipresence.

A later theologian like Cyril of Jerusalem (4th cent.) formulated the divine omnipresence more cautiously. He established God's transcending of space and time by stating that God is not circumscribed in any place. The heavens as well as the earth are His work. Transcendence, however, does not mean absence. On the contrary, being transcendent, God is "in all things and about all" (*Catecheses* iv.5). Cyril repeated the point in a list of the divine perfections, arguing that as the creator of space God knows no limitation by it, existing in all things but circumscribed by none (vi.8). Because God cannot be contained, Hilary of Poitiers could say at the same period that apart from revelation He "is far beyond the power of comprehension" (*De trinitate* i.7). Augustine echoed Hilary's thought (*Trinity* xv.13 [22]). John of Damascus forcefully asserted the underlying divine transcendence (*De fide orthodoxa* 1.4), explaining that where God is said to be in a place, the meaning is that "His operation is plainly visible, God Himself being wholly in all things and over the universe." Like his predeceessors, John related omnipresence to incorporeality. He recognized, of course, that God could take a body and thus restrict His omnipresence, as in the incarnation of the Son. But this does not imply essential coporeality or impair God's eternal omnipresence by nature.

*II. Scholastic Period.*–Among the early schoolmen, Anselm of Canterbury expressed his belief that all spiritual beings are uncircumscribed and eternal but that God is uniquely so, for He alone is everywhere and always (*Proslogion* 13). While accepting God's omnipresence, Peter Lombard introduced a threefold differentiation of His presence: (1) a general presence in all things, (2) a more excellent presence by grace in holy spirits, and (3) a most excellent presence of all in the man of Jesus, not by the grace of adoption but by the grace of union. Although this distinction raised problems of its own, it offered a safeguard against pantheism and protected the uniqueness of the presence of God in the incarnate Son.

*III. Reformation Period.*–In keeping with the general tenor of reformation theology, Calvin offered no abstract discussion of the omnipresence of God. He related the divine presence to the work of salvation, first through the covenant people, then through Christ and the Holy Spirit. He stated, e.g., that in the benefits conferred by Christ "the pious mind perceives the very presence of God" (*Inst.* i.13.13). Similarly, he claimed, that the Holy Spirit, "everywhere diffused, sustains all things. . . . Because he is circumscribed by no limits, he is excepted from the category of creatures; but in transfusing into all things his energy . . . he is indeed plainly divine" (i.13.14). The thought of the constant presence of God gave Calvin confidence in the trials of life (iii.2.21). He saw prayer to God as an invoking of the presence "of his providence. . . , and of his power . . . and of his goodness . . . and, in short, it is by prayer that we call him to reveal himself as wholly present to us" (iii.20.2).

A special problem that greatly exercised the Reformers was that of the nature of the presence of Christ's humanity at the Lord's Supper. They agreed that in virtue of His omnipresence Christ was present according to His divine nature. They also agreed that the medieval idea of a real presence of the human nature by transubstantiation, i.e., the replacement of the substances of bread and wine by those of Christ's physical body and blood, should be rejected. Luther, however, continued to confess a real presence of the body and blood alongside the bread and wine. He defended this conviction on the ground that because Christ's human and divine natures interact as one essence, His divine nature enables His human nature also to be omnipresent. Beginning with Zwingli, the Reformers resisted this form of ubiquitarianism, as they called it. They denied neither the presence of the divine Christ nor, indeed, the presence of the human Christ through the Holy Spirit to faith, but they rejected both the literal presence of the body and blood and the christological understanding on which it rested.

*IV. Modern Period.*–The Protestant theologians of the 17th cent. discussed omnipresence with great thoroughness. Heidegger related it to infinity, of which eternity was the temporal aspect and omnipresence the spatial aspect (in H. Heppe, *Reformed Dogmatics* [Eng. tr. 1950; repr. 1978], pp. 64f.). Polanus equated omnipresence with immensity, which signifies that the divine essence is not "limited, circumscribed, or bounded by any place" but penetrates and fills all places everywhere and is present to all things (in Heppe, pp. 64f.). Riissenius, however, distinguished between the two, describing immensity as an eternal attribute but relating omnipresence to creation as "a dwelling locally which exists in time" (in Heppe, pp. 64ff.).

Alsted said that omnipresence is a containing of all places rather than a dwelling in them. S. van Til described omnipresence as "the very actuality of existing related to corporeal creatures." Polanus insisted that it excludes spiritual and supernatural as well as physical circumscription, God being neither in a circumscriptive place, like corporeal beings, nor in a definitive place, like such intelligent forms as souls or angels. Riisseninus observed that, although God is also outside the world, He is not in some other space; rather, He is outside it "So far as all the spaces in the world do not exhaust the immensity of God." Polanus added the further delimitation that omnipresence differs from infinite extension, since God is both within all things and outside all things. Marck preferred the term immensity to omnipresence because the latter suggests that the divine immeasurability is tied to creation instead of being essential to God. Mastricht tried to make the same point by stating that the divine omnipresence is not just operative but is an essential all-presence in the world (in Heppe, pp. 66-69).

The Lutheran and Reformed theologians of this age continued a sharp debate on ubiquity in relation to the eucharist. Gerhard argued for the eucharistic presence of Christ's body and blood in virtue of the hypostatic union, although he conceded that the human Christ has no omnipresence by essence or nature. Polanus, however, accepted the ubiquity of the whole Christ, both human and divine, but laid great stess on the humanity of Christ by taking its limitation more seriously, by locating it at the right hand of the Father between the Ascension and the Second Coming, and by finding at the Supper only a presence by the Holy Spirit, along the lines suggested by Calvin and his generation.

During the 18th cent. an upsurge of pantheism or panentheism, due in no small measure to the influence of Spinoza, brought with it a tendency to play down God's transcendence in favor of His immanence. Schleiermacher represented this development in *Reden über die Religion* (Eng. tr., *On Religion,* 1958) in the first edition of which (1799) he replaced the term God by the tendentious term *universum.* Even when God's omnipresence was not so strictly related to the world, an abstract and negative concept of infinity tended to crowd out the thought of the personal God who is over all things and yet also present with and to them. Thus Schleiermacher in his more mature work, *Der christliche Glaube* (1821-22; Eng. tr., *Christian Faith,* 1928), defined eternity and omnipresence as a timeless causality that conditions time and space and everything in them (§§52f.). Similarly, Biedermann in *Dogmatik* (1869, p. 627), saw in these divine qualities the internal essence of the ground of the world. Wickelhaus in *Lehre der heiligen Schrift* (1892, p. 339) advocated much the same understanding when he spoke of the retreat of time and space and the manifestation of an essence that is utterly other. Almost imperceptibly, then, a type of impersonal transcendence replaced the equally impersonal immanence of the pantheistic equation. Omnipresence was incidently included among the attributes of majesty that Christ supposedly renounced in His self-emptying *(kenosis),* but in contrast to omniscience and omnipotence it played little role in the development of kenotic Christology.

The 20th cent. brought with it an interesting but not very successful attempt to banish spatial terminology from the doctrine of God. This attempt naturally accepted the divine omnipresence but disputed the idea of a transcendent God who is "up or out there." In contrast, it had a tendency, as in Paul Tillich, to depersonalize or subjectivize the divine omnipotence by finding God especially "in here" as the ground of individual being. By focusing on the divine immanence in this form, the movement had a definite contribution to make, but it suffered from two disadvantages. Superficially, it could not avoid a measure of self-contradiction, for spatial terminology is not avoided by the replacing of God out there by a God within. More seriously, this concept of the immanence of God could hardly do justice to the full range or the implied sovereignty of God's omnipresence, although J. A. T. Robinson (*Honest to God* [1963], p. 46) conceded that God is in principle more and other than "the infinite and inexhaustible depth of the ground of all being."

A more conservative and comprehensive treatment of omnipresence may be found in Barth's stimulating discussion in "The Perfections of the Divine Freedom" in *CD,* II/1, § 31.1. Barth paired God's omnipresence with His unity and grounded the former in the divine uniqueness and simplicity (p. 461). But he also regarded omnipresence as the presupposition of God's sovereignty, there being in creation "no presence without His presence: a presence with all the wealth and unity of His perfections; His presence as Himself in the sequence and simplicity in which He is Himself." Barth pointed out that the concept of divine omnipresence adds to that of divine unity the idea of a universe to which God is present (p. 462). Divine omnipresence also helps to show how God is love, an idea that cannot be explained simply by His unity. Yet the relation between omnipresence and love is reciprocal, for God does not have to be present to others but is so in the freedom of His love. Thus there would be no other at all were it not for the love of God, but there would also be no love were not God freely present to the other (p. 463).

Diverging from the dogmaticians of the 17th cent. Barth opposed the subsuming of omnipresence and eternity under the more general category of infinity, which does not properly define the nature of God (p. 464). Attempting his own definition, Barth advanced the thesis that omnipresence is the perfection in which God is present and in which, distinct from all else and preeminent over it, "He possesses His own place" (p. 468). He discarded the idea of God's nonspatiality, arguing that God is spatial "always and everywhere in such a way that His spatiality means the manifestation and confirmation of His deity" (pp. 468f.). Along these lines he found he could not agree with the conclusion that God is nowhere as well as everywhere. "There is nowhere where God is not, but He is not nowhere.... He is always somewhere... from there seeking man and there to be sought by man, there in His remoteness and from there drawing near, present here as the One who is there" (p. 471). Yet Barth accepted the thought of a differentiated presence, i.e., God's freedom to be present in a specific way (pp. 472f.).

As characteristics of God's omnipresence Barth listed (1) His possession of a space that is exclusively His own and in which He is present exclusively to Himself (p. 474); (2) His presence in creation, which is both general, invoking distinction and relationship, and special, occurring in the context of the divine work of revelation and reconciliation (pp. 471f.); and (3) The Incarnation, as the "basis and constituent centre" of the special presence (pp. 483f.). The final form of God's omnipresence led Barth to the positive conclusion that the God who is present to Himself as the Triune God, being present in Jesus Christ, not only gives humanity created space from His own uncreated and creative space but also gives it His own space. He thus "reveals Himself to be omnipresent in Himself, and as such outside Himself, in His special work (whose centre is His action in... the man Jesus Christ) and in His general work which is subservient to this special work, finding its goal and completion and therefore its meaning and origin in it" (p. 487).

By way of appendix Barth considered the ubiquitarian issue in eucharistic theology. He tried to preserve the qualities and avoid the defects of both sides by (1) agreeing to a human presence, the presence of the undivided Mediator, (2) differentiating the spiritual mode of this presence from that of the proper and original presence at God's right hand, and (3) insisting that in this mode He is no less here than there, but "really present both there and here, in both places the whole Christ after His divine and also after His human nature" (p. 490).

G. W. BROMILEY

**OMNISCIENCE** om-nish'əns. The condition of knowing everything; an attribute of God.

BIBLICAL BASIS OF THE DOCTRINE

***I. Terms and Usage.***–The term itself does not occur in Scripture, either in its nominal or its adjectival form. The OT expresses omniscience in connection with such words as Heb. *da'aṯ,* "knowledge," *bînâ* and *teḇûnâ,* "understanding," and *ḥoḵmâ,* "wisdom." "Seeing" and "the eye," "hearing" and "the ear" occur as figures for God's knowledge, just as "arm," "hand," and "finger" are used in metaphors of His power. The NT terms that express omniscience are Gk. *ginōskein* and *eidénai,* "know," *gnōsis,* "knowledge," and *sophía,* "wisdom."

*II. Tacit Assumption and Explicit Affirmation.*–Scripture everywhere teaches the absolute universality of the divine knowledge. The historical books, although lacking any abstract formula and occasionally referring anthropomorphically to God's knowledge of things (Gen. 11:5; 18:21), nonetheless presuppose divine omniscience in relating how God knows what people are doing, hears prayer, and discloses the future (1 S. 16:7; 23:9-12; 1 K. 8:39; 2 Ch. 16:9). Explicit affirmation of omniscience is made in the Psalter, the Prophets, the wisdom literature, and the NT. This is due to the increased internalizing of religion, by which its hidden side, to which the divine omniscience corresponds, receives greater emphasis (Job 26:6; 28:24; 34:21f.; Ps. 139:12; 147:5; Prov. 15:3, 11; Isa. 40:26; Acts 1:24; He. 4:13; Rev. 2:23).

*III. Extension to All Spheres.*–The absolute universality of divine knowledge is affirmed with reference to the categories that comprise all that is possible or actual. God knows His own being, possessing perfect consciousness of it; the unconscious finds no place in Him (1 Jn. 1:5). God also knows what exists outside Himself, the created world in its totality. This knowledge extends to small as well as to great affairs (Mt. 6:8, 32; 10:30); to the hidden heart and mind of mankind as well as to that which is open and manifest (Job 11:11; 34:21, 23; Ps. 14:2; 17:2f.; 33:13-18; 102:19f. [MT 20f.]; 139:1-4; Prov. 5:21; 15:3; Isa. 29:15; Jer. 17:10; Am. 4:13; Lk. 16:15; Acts 1:24; 1 Thess. 2:4; He. 4:13; Rev. 2:23). It extends to all the divisions of time, the past, present, and future alike (Ps. 56:8 [MT 9]; Isa. 41:22; 44:6-8; Jer. 1:55; Mal. 3:16). It embraces that which is contingent from the human viewpoint as well as that which is certain (1 S. 23:9-12; Mt. 11:22f.).

*IV. Mode of Divine Knowledge.*–Scripture connects God's knowledge with His omnipresence. Ps. 139 is the clearest expression of this. Omniscience is the omnipresence of cognition (Jer. 23:23ff.). It is also closely related to God's eternity, which makes Him in His knowledge independent of the limitations of time (Isa. 43:8-12). God's creative relation to all that exists is represented as underlying His omniscience (Ps. 33:15; 97:9; 139:13; Isa. 29:15). His all-comprehensive purpose forms the basis of His knowledge of all events and developments (Isa. 41:22-27; Am. 3:7).

God's knowledge of things, however, is not identical with His creation of them, as Augustine and others have suggested. The act of creation, while necessarily connected with the knowledge of that which is to be actual, is not identical with such knowledge or with the purpose on which such knowledge rests, for in God, as well as in man, the intellect and the will are distinct faculties. In the last analysis, God's knowledge of the world has its source in His self-knowledge. Since the world is a revelation of God, all that is actual or possible in it is a reflection in created form of what exists uncreated in God. Thus the knowledge of the creation becomes a reproduction of the knowledge of the mind of God (Acts 17:27; Rom. 1:20). The divine knowledge of the world also is like the divine self-knowledge in that it is never dormant.

The Bible nowhere represents God as attaining to knowledge by reasoning but everywhere as simply knowing. For embracing the multitude and complexity of the existing world He does not depend on such mental processes as abstraction and generalization. From what has been said about the immanent sources of the divine knowledge, it follows that such knowledge is not a posteriori derived from its objects, as all human knowledge based on experience is, but is exercised without receptivity or dependence. In knowing, as well as in all other activities of His nature, God is sovereign and self-sufficient. In cognizing the reality of all things He needs not to wait upon the things but draws His knowledge directly from the basis of reality as it lies in Himself. Although God's knowledge of Himself and knowledge of the world are thus closely connected, it is nevertheless important to distinguish between them and also between His knowledge of the actual and His knowledge of the possible. These distinctions mark off the theistic conception of omniscience from the pantheistic conception. God's life is not bound up with the world in such a way that He has no scope of activity beyond the world.

*V. God's Omniscience and Human Free Will.*–Since Scripture includes in the objects of divine knowledge the issue of human exercise of free will, the problem arises how the contingent character of such decisions and the certainty of divine knowledge can coexist. It is true that the knowledge of God and the purposing will of God are distinct, and that only the latter determines the certainty of the outcome of an event. Consequently the divine omniscience adds or detracts nothing in regard to the certainty; it does not produce but presupposes this certainty. But precisely because omniscience presupposes certainty, it appears to exclude every conception of contingency in the free acts of human beings and thus to render them in every essence determined. The knowledge of the issue of an act must have a fixed point of certainty to terminate upon, if it is to be knowledge at all. Those who make the essence of freedom absolute indeterminateness must, therefore, exempt this class of events from the scope of divine omniscience. But this is contrary to all the testimony of Scripture, which distinctly makes God's absolute knowledge extend to such acts (Acts 2:23).

Some have attempted to construe a peculiar form of divine knowledge, the *scientia media,* which would relate to this class of acts specifically. It would be distinguished from the *scientia necessaria,* which has for its object God Himself, and the *scientia libera,* which terminates upon the certainties of the world outside God, as determined by His free will. This *scientia media* would then be based on God's foresight of the outcome of the free choice of man. It would involve a knowledge of receptivity, a contribution to the sum total of what God knows that would derive from His observation of the world process. That is to say, *scientia media* would be knowledge a posteriori in essence, although not in point of time. It is, however, difficult to see how such a knowledge can be possible in God, when the outcome is psychologically undetermined and undeterminable. The knowledge could originate no sooner than the determination originates through the free decision of a person. It would, therefore, necessarily become a posteriori knowledge in time as well as in essence. The appeal to God's eternity as bringing Him equally near to the future as to the present and enabling Him to see the future decisions of human free will as though they were present cannot remove this difficulty, for when once the observation and knowledge of God are made dependent on any temporal issue, divine eternity itself is thereby virtually denied. Nothing remains but to recognize that God's eternal knowledge of the outcome of the free will choices of human beings implies that there enters into these choices, notwithstanding their free character, an element of predetermination, to which the knowledge of God can attach itself.

*VI. Religious Importance.*–Divine omniscience is most important for the religious life. The very essence of religion as communion with God depends on His all-comprehensive cognizance of the life of every person at every moment. Hence the irreligious characteristically deny the omniscience of God (Ps. 10:11f.; 94:7-11; Isa. 29:15; Jer. 23:23; Ezk. 8:12; 9:9). Especially along three lines this fundamental religious importance reveals itself: (1) it lends support and comfort when the pious suffer from misunderstanding and misrepresentation; (2) it acts as a deterrent to those tempted by sin, particularly secret sin, and becomes a judging principle to all hypocrisy and false security; (3) it furnishes the source from which mankind's desire for self-knowledge can obtain satisfaction (Ps. 19:12 [MT 13]; 51:6 [MT 8]; 139:23f.).

*See also* KNOW; FOREKNOW; PREDESTINATION.

***Bibliography.***–A. B. Davidson, *Theology of the OT* (1904), p. 180; G. F. Oehler, *Theology of the OT* (Eng. tr. 1883).

G. VOS

HISTORY OF THE DOCTRINE

I. The Early Church
II. The Medieval Church and The Reformation
III. The Modern Era

***I. The Early Church.***–The omniscience of God, like His omnipotence and omnipresence, stands in close relationship to His creative sovereignty. In making and controlling the world, God in His wisdom knew and knows all things in it. He can thus take into account all factors and possibilities and will not be surprised, checked, or defeated by any eventuality. Omniscience is both a prerequisite and a consequence of the divine omnipotence.

The early fathers accepted the omniscience of God without question, but it was left to later theologians to state and formulate the doctrine more specifically. Cyril of Jerusalem (4th cent.), e.g., stressed two aspects in his *Catecheses*. First, God in His omniscience knows the intents of the human heart. Thus the heart's response must be sincere, for a mere assent of the lips cannot deceive God. Discerning "who is genuine and who is only acting a part," God "is able both to keep the sincere safe and to make a believer of the hypocrite" (*Procatechesis* 17). Second, the divine omniscience extends to all things and implies the noncontingency of the divine will. God "knows all things . . . not being subject to any sequence of events or nativity or chance or fate" (*Catecheses* iv.5). Cyril kept the divine omniscience in balance by noting that all God's attributes are perfect, so that omniscience is the complete knowing not only of His wisdom but also of His goodness and greatness. God possesses "wisdom and loving-kindness in like measure," "not abounding on one side and deficient on another."

John of Damascus developed another aspect of the omniscience of God by relating it to His beneficent providence. Knowing all things, God provided ("foresaw") for all of us according to our needs. This applied to revelation too, which God adapted to what we can bear, making known to us "what it was expedient for us to know" (*De fide orthodoxa* i.8). The preexistent element in the divine knowledge also claimed John's attention. Discussing the possible derivation of the word *theós* (God) from *theásthai* (to see), he explained that nothing escapes God: "He saw all things before they came to pass" and "conceived of them independently of time" (i.9). For John the divine knowledge included the divine self-knowledge. Whereas God is incomprehensible and undefinable for us, He has "a clear vision of Himself" (i.13). As regards creation, God sees all things at once "with His divine, all-seeing, and immaterial eye"; hence He does not experience the temporal (or spatial) limitation of knowledge familiar to His creatures.

The strong element of foreknowledge in God's omniscience raised problems with regard to human freedom. Origen dealt with the obvious question whether there is any point in bringing petitions to God if He already knows our needs and the way to meet them (*On Prayer* 5). He said that rational creatures have been given the gift of self-movement, which implies self-will, and that this freedom, far from conflicting with God's knowledge, is included within it: "With all else it has been known to God" (6). John of Damascus, tackling the same general issue, accepted the premise that "every rational being is free" (*De fide orthodoxa* ii.3). He then explained the divine predestination in terms of the divine omniscience. In moral choices "God in accord with His foreknowledge justly cooperates with those who in right conscience choose the good," but He "abandons those who choose and do what is bad." Hence John distinguished sharply between foreknowledge and predestination. God foreknows all things but does not predestine them all, predestination being "the result of the divine command made with foreknowledge" (i.30). Some matters, of course, do not ultimately depend on human decision, e.g., the attainment of salvation, and here predestination and foreknowledge coincide, for "through His foreknowledge God has already decided all things beforehand in accordance with His goodness and justice." It will be seen that John, like Cyril, avoided any isolation of God's omniscience from His other perfections.

***II. The Medieval Church and the Reformation.***–Although the theologians discussed omniscience in great detail, they did not greatly develop the doctrine. Thomas Aquinas, for example, related it to providence in much the same way as Origen and John of Damascus. That God knows all things may imply necessity in some areas but not in all, since contingent causes are provided for some effects just as necessary causes are for others (*Summa Theol.* i.22.3). In matters of salvation, Thomas recognized the divine freedom of election. Foreknown merits are not the cause of predestination but at most only the effects. The number of the elect is materially foreordained as well as foreknown by God (i.23.5).

The Reformers decisively changed the later scholastic emphasis on philosophical rather than theological considerations in discussions of the divine omniscience. Although the Reformed confessions gave brief lists of the attributes of God, they tended to subsume God's omniscience under His wisdom. Thus the *French Confession* (1559) described God as "all-wise, all-good, all-just, and all-merciful" (art. I), the *Belgic Confession* (1561) called Him "perfectly wise" (art. I), the *Scots Confession* (1560) spoke of His "eternal wisdom" (art. I), and the *Anglican Articles* (1571) stated that God is "of infinite power, wisdom, and goodness" (art. I). Only the later and more expansive *Westminster Confession* (1647) developed the theme of omniscience, but even this document did not employ the term in the statement "His knowledge is infinite, infallible, and independent upon the creature, so as nothing is to Him contingent or uncertain" (art. II, 2).

Among the leading Reformers, Calvin evinced little interest in the theoretical issues of omniscience. He tied the knowledge of God very strictly to His will, which is the cause of all things. Rejecting the idea of a purely passive or permissive will of God in the case of wicked human acts (*Inst.* i.18.1), Calvin made several important deductions from the divine omnivolence (all-willingness). First, the righteousness of what God does must be accepted. Whatever He wills, by the very fact that He wills it, must be considered righteous even when human beings do not understand it (i.17.2). Second, the will of God may appear to be manifold, but in reality it is a unity (i.18.3). Third, God uses the wicked for His own purpose, which He Himself knows, although this does not mean that the wicked are "excusable, as if they had obeyed his precept" (i.18.4). Hidden though the ways of God may often be, one can have confidence that His wisdom or all-encompassing knowledge informs all that He wills and does.

When he turned to the more direct matters of salvation, Calvin made two points of great significance. First, election rests on God's will alone, so that He does not have to give reasons for it that mankind can understand (iii.23.11). Second, foreknowledge and foreordination are both to be placed in God, but they must neither be confused nor one subordinated to the other. Calvin plainly equated foreknowledge with omniscience: "We mean [by it] that all things always were, and perpetually remain, under his eyes, so that to his knowledge there is nothing future or past, but all things are present . . . in such a way that he not only conceives them through ideas, . . . but he truly looks upon them and discerns them as things placed before him." This knowledge extends "throughout the universe to every creature." Predestination, in contrast, is God's eternal decree for each person, eternal life being foreordained for some and eternal damnation for others (iii.21.5). Calvin discussed the order of foreknowledge and foreordination in his commentary on Acts (2:23). Foreknowledge comes first, since God contemplates what He will ordain before He ordains it. But Luke put God's decree first "to teach us that God neither wills nor decrees anything without having long before directed it to its proper end." In this way Scripture refutes the error that "even while God foresees everything, he lays no constraint upon his creatures." "It belongs to God, not only to know the future, but also to ordain by his will whatever he wants to be done." With special reference to salvation Calvin ruled out any idea of God's electing being simply an acceptance "of those whom he foresaw as worthy of his grace." The truth according to Rom. 8:28-30 is that "God's knowing the elect rests upon his own good pleasure, because he foreknew nothing outside himself which led him to will the adoption of sons." By means of the divine will Calvin thus linked the all-knowing God to His self-knowing.

***III. The Modern Era.***–The dogmatic theologians of the 17th cent. regarded knowledge and will as the essence of the life of God. They defined knowledge as cognition and intelligence, seeing in it the perfection of God's intellect whereby He uniquely understands and knows all things outside Himself — past, present, future, and possible (Heidegger, in H. Heppe, *Reformed Dogmatics* [Eng. tr. 1950; repr. 1978], p. 69). This knowing is absolute and comprises knowledge of God Himself as well as of things outside Himself. As in the case of all the divine attributes, God is Himself knowledge; He does not merely have the capacity for it, as human creatures do. Knowledge, then, is for God neither a potentiality nor a faculty but an act in which He does not simply have knowledge but knows. In consequence His knowledge is eternal and intuitive (Heppe, p. 70). He does not take up things from outside into His knowledge, which would be to change, expand, or modify Himself. As a single act, God's knowledge is not successive but simultaneous, not acquired through a survey of things but itself conditioning them and arising out of the divine self-knowledge (Keckerman, in Heppe, p. 70). In a comprehensive definition God's omniscience may thus be described as "one, absolutely simple, unconditioned, infinite, simultaneous, eternal, unchangeable, and absolutely perfect and certain intuition" (Heppe, p. 71).

While the divine knowledge is unitary, it has different aspects which call for notice. First is God's natural and necessary knowledge, a direct awareness of His own being and of all possibilities of being insofar as He is their conditioning cause. Second is His free knowledge, an awareness comprising all realities and resting on the absolute decree of His will. Third is the knowledge of vision, the seeing of all things as present, the knowledge of them in their secondary causes, and the knowledge of their essence (Voetius, in Heppe, pp. 72f.). Fourth is the knowledge of simple intelligence, by which "God knows the things which might eventuate, but which never eventuate, which will never exist," so that He does not know them "in willing them, because He does not will them to eventuate, or in their secondary causes (they do not have any), or in themselves, because they will never exist" (Polanus, in Heppe, p. 74).

The foreknowledge (or prescience) of God demands special treatment because in a sense it does not exist in itself but only in human perception of the matter. In virtue of His absoluteness God knows the future. Only what is possible and what God allows are future. It is as God determines things that He knows the future. In this knowledge, however, He sees it as present. His prescience is thus infallible and in its determinative character immutable. In this determinative character it is a special aspect of God's knowledge, extending only to things that are still to be, and in this sense subordinate to His will (Bucanus, in Heppe, pp. 74f.). Prescience, then, rests on the divine decree, so that a twofold necessity arises for the future, "the one that of necessity, since it is a decree, the other that of infallibility as regards prescience" (Hottinger, in Heppe, p. 76).

Along these lines Reformed theology distinguished prescience from permission, which Arminian and Jesuit teaching postulated as a kind of "middle knowledge," i.e., "a conditional knowledge of future contingencies by which from eternity, not absolutely but contingently, God knows what men and angels would be doing with their freedom in given circumstances" (Voetius, in Heppe, p. 77). The Arminian concept of election, that God predetermines the salvation of believers in Christ but only foreknows and does not foreordain the act of belief itself, conforms to the idea of "middle knowledge," which Reformed orthodoxy rejected.

The theology of the 16th-17th cents. devoted a separate section to the intimate relation between the all-willing and the all-knowing of God. It equated God's will with His being and thus ascribed to it, as to God's knowledge, absolute singleness, eternity, infinity, immutability, and activity (Mastricht, in Heppe, pp. 81ff.). While differentiating God's will from His knowledge, it saw the two as coincident, the former being the obverse of the latter. Like the divine knowledge, the divine will is both a willing of God Himself and a willing of things outside Him; God wills Himself necessarily and creatures freely, in such a way that "no element in creaturely life can be a determining reason for the divine will." Various distinctions could be made relative to God's will for His creatures, especially between His perceptive will and His discerning will, which itself could be subdivided into His effective will and permissive (but still active) will by which God lets evil happen to reveal His glory. Heidegger also distinguished between the revealed will of God (in Scripture and experience) and His hidden or secret will that has still to be disclosed (in Heppe, pp. 88ff.). In every form God's will stands in the closest possible relation to His knowledge, as it does also to His holiness, righteousness, and goodness.

The Arminian controversy greatly influenced the discussion of God's omniscience. Against the wedge that Arminius was driving between God's foreknowledge and His foreordination, the projected *Lambeth Articles* (1595) claimed that the foreknowledge of faith is not the moving or effective cause of predestination to life. The Synod of Dort (1619) similarly argued that election does not mean that God, foreseeing all possible qualities of human actions, elected certain of these as a condition of salvation (I, 9). Later, the *Westminster Confession* stated that effectual calling is "of God's free and special grace alone, not from anything at all foreseen in man" (X, 2). The point of these assertions was not to deny God's foreknowledge but to prevent its isolation from His foreordination, as though God were simply predestinating to salvation those whom in His omniscience He knew in advance would believe.

Echoes of this controversy could still be heard in the 18th cent., as in the debate between Wesley and the Calvinists, but attention gradually shifted to other problems of omniscience, especially those of theodicy and incarnation. As regards theodicy, philosophical optimism promoted the view that God in His omniscience, foreseeing all possibilities, created the best of all possible worlds in which even the unavoidable element of evil contributes to the general good. A growing realization of the extent of evil, both natural and historical, shattered what seemed to many to be the intolerable complacency of this optimism but in so doing cast doubt on the divine goodness, the divine power, or the divine knowledge, or possibly all three. Some circles sought relief in the deistic concept of a God who is indeed omniscient but who has left the world of His creation to its own devices. Others abandoned the idea of a transcendent God in favor of pantheism, whereby God is equated with the universe itself.

In the 19th and 20th cents. some thinkers took the more drastic course of postulating a transcendent being of limited powers. Process theology, heavily influenced by evolutionism, developed the concept of a God who is Himself implicated in the world process, so that even with His superior resources He has to face new and unforeseen contingencies and problems. More orthodox theology, of course, was not prepared to accept such forfeitures of the divine omniscience.

As regards the Incarnation, the kenotic theologians of the 19th cent. (e.g., I. A. Dorner, G. Thomasius, and C. Gore) perceived an incompatibility between the true humanity of Jesus and His divine omniscience. Drawing a distinction between God's moral or essential attributes and His attributes of majesty, they argued that in the self-emptying *(kenosis)* of the Incarnation Jesus retained the former (e.g., love, righteousness, and mercy) but relinquished the latter (e.g., omnipotence, omnipresence, and omniscience). In His life, then, as the incarnate Son, Jesus shared in the limitation of knowledge that all humans experience, enjoying a gift of discernment but in the great intellectual disciplines having no advantage over contemporaries in His own sphere of life. Whether this restriction of knowledge included misinformation or error became a matter of heated discussion when the authority of Jesus was invoked, e.g., for the Mosaic authorship of the Pentateuch. In some circles this appeal was ruled out on the ground that Jesus knew no more about such matters than anyone else, that He shared traditional beliefs about them without being committed to their correctness, and that He had not in any case come into the world to give superior information on literary and historical issues. Others were prepared to accept that the incarnate Son voluntarily restricted His use of knowledge, but not that His knowledge itself was limited, so that He would have held or imparted erroneous information.

Preoccupation with individual issues of this kind tended to inhibit more comprehensive dogmatic discussion of omniscience, but the 20th cent. saw a reversal of this trend with the extensive treatment of the divine perfections by Karl Barth in *CD*, II/1, § 31.2. Barth divided the perfections into two groups, those of love and those of freedom, but kept the groups in close relationship; he dealt with the divine omniscience within the context of the divine omnipotence, which as a perfection of love he paired off with the constancy of God, which is a perfection of freedom. (He had a separate discussion of the wisdom of God, a perfection of freedom, in connection with the perfection of patience, in II/1, pp. 422ff.) An interesting point here is that in contrast to the kenotic theologians Barth did not group God's omnipresence, omnipotence, and omniscience apart from His love but saw precisely in these three (along with omnivolence) attributes of love rather than of freedom.

Omniscience forms part of God's omnipotence because the latter was for Barth the specific omnipotence of His knowing (omniscience) and His willing (omnivolence) (p. 545). In relation to this omniscience of omnipotence Barth made the following points: (1) Omniscience displays God's revelation, for in revelation God speaks about Himself, about us, and about all things, thus showing Himself to be One who knows, and letting us know ourselves as those who are known by Him (p. 546). (2) Knowledge of God's omniscience arises in the fellowship with Him that He has granted us despite our sin, for this is also a fellowship of knowledge (p. 546). (3) Being so closely tied to God's redeeming purpose, God's omniscience presents itself to us as "a complete act of will" which is "the supreme contingency in the essence of God," unlimited by any extraneous necessity (p. 547). (4) In view of this link between God's knowledge and His will, sharing God's knowledge cannot be a purely intellectual affair but involves conformity to His will (p. 548). (5) God's knowledge, like His other perfections, is God's being, God Himself, as His being is also His knowledge (p. 549). (6) Knowledge and will may be cautiously equated in God, since both are God, but not so as to deprive God of the particular characteristic of either, nor so as to ascribe a primacy to either (p. 551). (7) God's omniscience and omnivolence are both free in the sense of being superior to everything distinct from God (p. 552). (8) God's omniscience is complete in its range but should not be called infinite, since it is defined by itself and by God's will, establishing its own limit beyond which everything is null and void (p. 552). (9) Human beings cannot escape God's omniscience, for all things are open to God and every possible path of escape lies within the realm of His knowledge (p. 554). (10) Like God's knowledge, His will is exhaustive (though not infinite), extending to all that opposes it and allowing no escape by hostility or attempted neutrality (pp. 555f.). (11) The prescience in omniscience affirms God's eternal supremacy: "The 'fore' denotes the absolute priority and superiority of God Himself to every possible existence distinct from His own, His dignity as the Creator of being and as the Lord and master even of non-being" (p. 556). It also expresses the eternity of God's knowledge: "All things in all ages are foreknown by God from all eternity . . . no less and no different in their future than in their past and present" (p. 559). (12) In the divine omnivolence what corresponds to the divine foreknowledge is freedom, God's will taking precedence of all else apart from God Himself, but in such a way that creatures may have a relative freedom as well as relative necessity (pp. 560ff.). (13) The character of the divine willing and knowing manifests the truth of the divine personhood in which God is Lord of His own power, putting His will and knowledge to work in a differentiated use of it (pp. 566f.). (14) All valid distinctions in God's knowledge are grounded in God Himself and not in outside objects: "As the One who is over all things He knows all things, and as the One who knows He has power over Himself and all things" (p. 567). (15) The divine will is similarly manifested in its exercise in a free and living act of the divine person, especially in our reconciliation in which God acts for us "without any deserts on our part," not being compelled to do what He does, but doing it "because He wills it" (pp. 588f.).

An important feature of Barth's discussion is that his strict relating of omniscience to revelation and his accompanying emphasis on differentiation offer a solution to the incarnational problem of the apparent incompatibility of omniscience and humanity. In this view God's omniscience, like His omnipotence and omnipresence, is not abstractly infinite but is defined by God Himself. With no extraneous limits, God has all the capacity that He wills and needs both to be Himself and to accomplish all aims outside Himself. When, therefore, the eternal Son assumed humanity in order to fulfil the divine purpose of revelation and reconciliation, His omniscience took the particular form appropriate to this purpose and action. Jesus Christ did not relinquish omniscience and even restrict it. His incarnation involved no alteration or diminution of His deity. As God, He continued to enjoy and exercise the knowledge that He shares eternally with the Father and the Holy Spirit. As man, however, He enjoyed and exercised it in the specific way that involves no incompatibility with His true humanity (which was, of course, real humanity in contrast to our fallen humanity). This view poses no difficulty unless it is erroneously assumed either that omniscience is always abstractly infinite or that because human knowledge cannot take a divine form, divine knowledge cannot take a human form. The former assumption makes the mistake of defining God by omniscience instead of omniscience by God, while the latter errs by imposing a human definition on both.

G. W. BROMILEY

**OMRI** om'rī, om'rē [Heb. *ʿomrî*; Gk. *Ambri*; similar names in Arabic, indicate that it derives from a triliteral root *ʿmr*– 'thrive,' 'live long'].

**1.** One of the great kings of the northern kingdom of Israel, who founded a dynasty that lasted some fifty years. The sources for the reign are 1 K. 16:16-30; 20:34; Josephus *Ant.* viii.12.5 [309-313]; the Moabite Stone set up by King Mesha and the Assyrian inscriptions (*ANET*, pp. 320f., 280, 284f.).

Scholars have assigned rather different lengths to Omri's reign, depending upon the point from which the sources reckoned his kingship. 1 K. 16:15-17 recorded that Omri, the Israelite commander, besieged Tirzah, where Zimri had assassinated Elah of Israel (*ca.* 885 B.C.). Though Zimri, a commander of chariotry who had aspirations to the throne, reigned only a week before committing suicide, he precipitated a period of civil instability during which yet another claimant, Tibni, arose but was ultimately defeated (vv. 21f.). Following this, Omri became king in the thirty-first year of Asa of Judah, and reigned for twelve years (v. 23). Yet that same source also recorded that he reigned at Tirzah for six years, implying that Omri was not king over the entire nation at that time. Omri doubtless occupied Tirzah when Zimri died, but needed some four years to consolidate his position against Tibni before becoming king "over Israel" with his undisputed capital at Samaria. The correlation with Asa of Judah indicates a reign of eight years (vv. 23, 29), but when the four years of conflict with Tibni are added, the period of twelve years mentioned in v. 23 is still correct. Overall dates for Omri would thus be *ca.* 885-873 B.C.

Part of the wall of Omri's palace at Samaria (J. C. Trever)

Omri had demonstrated his military abilities both against the Philistines prior to the assassination of Elah, and also against the ambitious Tibni, who had claimed a surprising measure of popular support. But once established as king of Israel, Omri founded a new dynasty, the *Bit-Ḫumri* (house of Omri) of Assyrian records. He was the father of Ahab, another vigorous military leader who also promoted the commercial growth of the northern kingdom. His might, as the Bible phrases it, appears in his friendly alliances with Judah and Phoenicia and in his construction of the new capital, Samaria, on a very strategic site, an isolated hill. It was so strong that the Assyrians captured it only after a three-year siege.

Omri's military prowess was also seen clearly in his subjugation of Moab, which was forced to pay heavy tribute to Israel (2 K. 3:4) during the reigns of Omri and Ahab. The Moabite view of the situation was inscribed on the MOABITE STONE, the oppression by Omri being attributed to the displeasure of the national deity Chemosh with his land. The inspired historian of Kings, writing some years later, was not impressed by any of these things; the alliance with Phoenicia and the marriage of the crown prince Ahab to the daughter of Ethbaal priest-king of Sidonia only opened the door for Baal-worship.

While Omri had evidently lost some territory in the north to Ben-hadad (1 K. 20:34), supplementing that already acquired by the Syrians in the time of Baasha of Israel (1 K. 15:20), his successful attack on the Moabites may have deterred Ben-hadad from further thoughts of territorial expansion in Israel. His position in relation to the Aramean dynasty was strengthened further when he entered into a highly profitable trading alliance with Phoenicia, thereby making access to the Mediterranean by the Syrians considerably more difficult.

Omri was succeeded *ca.* 873 B.C. by Ahab his son, who followed the political, social, and religious patterns established by his father. Three decades later the name of Omri was still being commemorated in the Black Obelisk of Shalmaneser III (*ca.* 842 B.C.) in a reference to Jehu, a man who had overthrown the *Bit-Ḫumri*. In Mic. 6:16 the allusion to the "statutes of Omri" saw the prophet blaming him for the replacement of Sinaitic covenant religion in Israel by the gross idolatry of Canaanite worship.

***Bibliography.***–J. W. Crowfoot, K. Kenyon, and E. L. Sukenik, *Buildings at Samaria* (1943); *Objects from Samaria* (1957); *ANET*, pp. 320f.

Panel from the Black Obelisk of Shalmaneser III (859-824 B.C.) showing Jehu of Israel's Omride dynasty bowing before the king (Trustees of the British Museum)

**2.** A Benjaminite, son of Becher (1 Ch. 7:8).

**3.** A Judahite, descendant of Perez and father of Ammihud (1 Ch. 9:4).

**4.** The tribal chief of Issachar in David's time (1 Ch. 27:18). R. K. HARRISON

**ON** on [Heb. *'ôn*]. Son of Peleth; a Reubenite who joined with Korah, Dathan, and Abiram in their revolt against Moses and Aaron (Nu. 16:1). If PELETH (**1**) is the same as Pallu (cf. 26:5, 8-10), then On would have been the uncle of Dathan and Abiram; but some commentators have suggested that "On" is a textual corruption and should be deleted (see, e.g., G. B. Gray, comm. on Numbers [*ICC*, 1903], pp. 194f.).

**ON** on [Heb. *'ôn*; Gk. *ōn*; Egyp. *iwnw*]. An Egyptian city, also called HELIOPOLIS, center of the ancient cult of Atum-Re, the sun god. Its ruins have been excavated 16 km. (10 mi.) N of modern Cairo.

After his rise to power in Egypt, Joseph married Asenath, daughter of "Potiphera priest of On" (Gen. 41:45, 50; 46:20), undoubtedly a priest of Re, as his name implies. The prophets refer to On in different ways. In his prophecy against Egypt Jeremiah pronounces judgment on the "pillars of *bēṯ šemeš*," the "house of the sun" (Jer. 43:13; RSV "obelisks of Heliopolis"), i.e., On. In an oracle against the cities of Egypt Ezekiel refers to the "young men of *'āwen*," "wickedness," a pejorative vocalization of On (Ezk. 30:17; cf. AV Aven).

For the question of whether Isa. 19:18 refers to On, *see* CITY OF THE SUN.

*See also* EGYPT. E. M. COOK

**ONAM** ō'nam [Heb. *'ônām*–'vigorous'].

**1.** Fifth son of Shobal and ancestor of a Horite clan group in Edom (Gen. 36:23; 1 Ch. 1:40).

**2.** A Judahite, son of Jerahmeel by Atarah (1 Ch. 2:26, 28); possibly related to ONAN son of Judah.

**ONAN** ō'nan [Heb. *'ônān*–'vigorous']. Second of the three sons of Judah and the Canaanite Bath-shua (Gen. 38:4, 8f.; 46:12; Nu. 26:16; 1 Ch. 2:3). When the Lord slew his elder brother Er, because of his wickedness, Er's wife Tamar was given to Onan (*see* MARRIAGE IV.A.2; TAMAR). Onan's continuing refusal to impregnate her was displeasing and thus he too was slain by the Lord. C. G. RASMUSSEN

**ONE.** *See* NUMBER.

**ONESIMUS** ō-nes'ə-məs [Gk. *Onēsimos*]. A name occurring twice in the NT (Philem. 10; Col. 4:9) in reference to one person. The name means "useful" and as such was a common Greek name for slaves (see Bauer, rev., p. 570). Paul plays on the meaning of the name when he says (Philem. 11; cf. v. 20) that Onesimus was formerly "useless" to his master but is now "useful" both to his master and to Paul (presumably as a companion and helper to the imprisoned apostle). Paul is nevertheless unwilling to retain Onesimus in his service without first asking Onesimus's owner, usually assumed to be Philemon (though it could be Archippus, or even Apphia, to whom the Epistle of Philemon is also addressed), the favor of permitting Onesimus to serve Paul on Philemon's behalf (vv. 12-14).

Paul shows great care in dealing with this matter: he gently (or perhaps not so gently; cf. Church, p. 27) urges Philemon to receive the slave who "was parted" from him — a delicate reference to Onesimus's running away. Paul's care in presenting his case certainly indicates the sensitivity of the situation for Philemon personally (Church, p. 21, calls it a "difficult," "discreditable," or "scandalous" case) — though the letter is a "public" one. There may also have been a growing sensitivity to the practice of slave ownership by Christians (see below). At any rate, Paul sends Onesimus back to his master with the letter to Philemon. (On the same journey Onesimus and Tychicus [Col. 4:9] took the Epistle to the Colossians; that Philemon lived in Colossae is known from the names of five persons greeted in both Philem. 23f. and Col. 4:10-14.) Paul requests that Onesimus be sent back to him (perhaps implying that Onesimus be given his freedom; cf. Stuhlmacher, *in loc.*), reminding Philemon of his indebtedness to Paul (Philem. 19b). Onesimus's debt to his master — a debt that Paul promises to repay — may have involved not only the inconvenience and loss of service incurred by the slave's flight, but perhaps also robbery to finance it.

Paul notes three positive results of Onesimus's running away and subsequently being converted by Paul (Philem. 10): (1) the formerly "useless" slave (because he ran away?) is now "useful" both to his master and to Paul (vv. 11, 20); (2) the master, parted from Onesimus "for a while," will now have him "forever" (v. 15); and (3) before Onesimus was a "slave," but now he is a "beloved brother" (v. 16). The implications of the last statement for the institution of slavery (the contradiction of holding a brother as a slave) may be more obvious to the modern reader than they were to the early Christian community (*DNTT*, III, 595f.). Manumission of a fellow Christian was certainly not automatic (Col. 3:22–4:1; Eph. 6:5-9; 1 Pet. 2:13-25). Nevertheless, some elements in the early Church (e.g., the Corinthian "enthusiasts"; see Gayer) may have urged the abolition of slavery. Paul's approach, however, is not to attempt to abolish slavery as an institution but to call Christians to live out the implications of their common status as members of the redeemed community. Thus he sowed the seeds for a "spiritual" — rather than bloody — revolution. (*See also* SLAVE.)

The great affection in which Paul holds Onesimus is seen in Philem. 10, where he calls Onesimus his child (a reference to Onesimus's Christian conversion under Paul's influence), and in v. 16, where he calls Onesimus a "beloved brother, especially to me." In Col. 4:9 Paul praises Onesimus's character, calling him a faithful and beloved brother. If Onesimus is the ONESIPHORUS of 2 Tim. 1:16-18, the reasons for Paul's appreciation are clear: "He has often refreshed me and he was not ashamed of my chains but eagerly sought me out in Rome."

Some readers connect Onesimus with the bishop praised by Ignatius of Antioch in his letter to the church at Ephesus in the early 2nd century. As in Philemon, there is a pun on the name of the commended bishop. If he was the same Onesimus, he must have been advanced in years — even had he been a youth when he ran away and met Paul in Rome.

*See also* PHILEMON; PHILEMON, EPISTLE TO; SLAVE.

***Bibliography.***–F. F. Church, *HTR*, 71 (1978), 17-33; R. Gayer, *Die Stellung des Sklaven in den paulinischen Gemeinden und bei Paulus* (1976); P. Stuhlmacher, *Der Brief an Philemon* (*Evangelisch-katholischer Komm. zum NT*, 1975). W. MOULDER

**ONESIPHORUS** ō-nes'ə-fōr'əs, on'ə-sif'ə-rəs [Gk. *Onēsiphoros*–'profit-bringer' (2 Tim. 1:16; 4:19)]. Onesiphorus, well known to both Paul and Timothy, made a significant contribution to the Ephesian church and also to Paul during his final imprisonment (2 Tim. 1:15-18). Paul laments that "all" the Asians were ashamed of him in his imprisonment and had deserted him. But in contrast to these, Onesiphorus came to Rome, searched diligently for Paul, and ministered to him. This involved much effort and personal danger, for during the Neronian persecution in the mid-60's it was not only difficult to track down a prisoner, but also dangerous to approach one imprisoned because of the persecution. Paul praised Onesiphorus for this frequent ministry of refreshment (*anapsýchō*) as well as his service in Ephesus (cf. 2:1).

A puzzling fact is that Paul does not speak of Onesiphorus in the present tense but only in the phrase "the house [*oíkos*] of Onesiphorus" (1:16; 4:19). There are no personal greetings for Onesiphorus even in the context of such greetings (4:19-21). This, along with the tone of the prayer in 1:18, has led many scholars to conclude that Onesiphorus was now dead (e.g., see J. N. D. Kelly, *Pastoral Epistles* [*HNTC*, 1963], pp. 169f.). Others suggest that he was absent from home or was to be included in the phrase "house of Onesiphorus" (see, e.g., E. K. Simpson, *Pastoral Epistles* [1954], p. 129). The evidence is inconclusive, but it is possible that Onesiphorus had died.

If Onesiphorus was dead, Paul's prayer in 1:18 is the earliest prayer for the dead in Christian literature, as well as the only one in the NT (cf. 1 Cor. 15:29). There was a Jewish precedent in 2 Macc. 12:43-45, and prayers on behalf of the dead did become a common practice in the early Church. If Paul is to be understood this way, it is a general prayer simply asking God for mercy for the deceased. No doctrine of prayer for the dead can be erected on this isolated passage, nor does it offer solid scriptural support for the practice.

More detailed information about Onesiphorus is not forthcoming. Attempts to identify him with ONESIMUS are not convincing. There is mention of Onesiphorus in later pseudepigraphical literature (e.g., Acts of Peter and Andrew, Acts of Paul and Thekla), but this material is of little value historically. Finally, personal references like this are difficult to explain if not authentically Pauline, whether by his own hand, the hand of an amanuensis, or the work of a later disciple using genuine material.

V. R. GORDON

**ONIARES.** *See* ONIAS.

**ONIAS** ō-nī'əs [Gk. *Onias*].

**1.** (AV also ONIARES, 1 Macc. 12:19). Onias I, son of the high priest Jaddua and father of the high priest Simon I according to Josephus (*Ant.* xi.8.7 [347]; xii.2.5 [43f.]). He was high priest from 320 to 290 B.C., when Arius was king of the Spartans (309-265 B.C.). According to 1 Macc. 12:7-24 Arius wrote a letter to Onias declaring an alliance and friendship with the Jews. Josephus incorrectly states that this letter was sent to the high priest Onias III (*Ant.* xii.4.10 [225]). If this letter was written late in the reign of Arius, the recipient would have been the high priest Onias II (J. A. Goldstein, *I Maccabees* [AB, 1976], pp. 455f.).

**2.** Onias II, son of Simon I. Too young to succeed his father directly as high priest, Onias II became high priest only after his uncle Eleazar (*Ant.* xii.2.5 [40-50]) and his great uncle Manasseh (*Ant.* xii.4.1 [156-58]). Josephus portrays him as "small-minded and passionately fond of money" (*Ant.* xii.4.2 [161f.]) and states that he refused to pay Ptolemy of Egypt the twenty talents of silver that his predecessors had paid. (This was Ptolemy III Euergetes. For discussion of the chronological problems, cf. Tcherikover, *Hellenistic Civilization*, pp. 128-130.) Apparently Onias's refusal to pay the tax was related to his pro-Seleucid stance during the Third Syrian War. When Ptolemy threatened to invade Judea and parcel out the land to his soldiers, Joseph the son of Tobiah and nephew of Onias intervened with the king. From this time on, the Tobiads were a strong rival of the high priest's family, the Oniads.

***Bibliography.***–V. Tcherikover, "The Political Situation From 332 to 175 B.C.E.," in A. Schalit, ed., *World History of the Jewish People*, VI (1972), 76f.; *Hellenistic Civilization and the Jews* (Eng. tr. 1959), pp. 127-134.

**3.** Onias III, son of Simon II and grandson of Onias II, high priest during the reign of Seleucus IV Philopator (187-175 B.C.). Onias III was a pious man (2 Macc. 3:1) who gained the respect even of Seleucus IV. But a disagreement between the high priest, who was pro-Ptolemaic, and Simon, the captain of the temple, led Simon to turn to Apollonius, governor of Coelesyria and Phoenicia, with the claim that large amounts of money that did not belong to the account of the sacrifices were in the temple treasury and could be taken by King Seleucus. When the king learned of this, he sent one of his high officials, Heliodorus, to Jerusalem to confiscate the money. Onias met Heliodorus, explained that Simon had misrepresented the facts, that the amount of money was much smaller and belonged to widows and orphans, and to Hyrcanus son of Tobias. Despite Onias's objections, Heliodorus entered the temple, whereupon "the Sovereign of spirits and of all authority caused so great a manifestation" that he would have died had not Onias prayed for his recovery (2 Macc. 3:1-40).

After this incident, Simon continued to plot against Onias. Finally, the high priest made a trip to Antioch to plead his case before the king; but before he arrived Seleucus IV was assassinated and his brother Antiochus Epiphanes became king in 175 B.C. (2 Macc. 4:1-6). The historical sources do not relate what happened between Onias and Antiochus, but it is clear that Onias was not successful. His own brother Jason bought the office of high priest from the king and "at once shifted his countrymen over to the Greek way of life" (2 Macc. 4:7-20). Three years later Menelaus, the brother of the abovementioned Simon, bought the office of high priest for himself. Menelaus then stole some of the temple's golden vessels in order to use them as payment to secure his own position. When Onias publicly reproached Menelaus, Menelaus plotted Onias's death (2 Macc. 4:23-34).

The fate of Onias is disputed by scholars. According to 2 Macc. 4:34, Andronicus, the king's deputy, was prompted by Menelaus to trick Onias out of his sanctuary at Daphne and murder him (cf. Dnl. 9:26). Josephus, however, states that Onias fled to Egypt, where King Ptolemy warmly received him and gave him land at Heliopolis on which to build a temple (*BJ* i.1.1 [33]; vii.10.2-3 [421-432]).

***Bibliography.***–S. Tedesche and S. Zeitlin, *Second Book of Maccabees* (1954), pp. 9-15, 140f.; V. Tcherikover, *Hellenistic Civilization and the Jews* (Eng. tr. 1959), pp. 156-172, 469.

4. Onias IV, son of Onias III and builder of the Jewish temple in Leontopolis according to some accounts (Josephus *Ant.* xii.9.7 [388]; xiii.3.1-3 [62-73]). When Antiochus V killed Menelaus and made Alcimus high priest (*Ant.* xii.9.7 [385f.]), Onias IV fled to Egypt and built a temple with the permission of the Egyptian monarch. He justified the building of this temple by the prophecy of Isa. 19:19: "In that day there will be an altar to the Lord in the midst of the land of Egypt. . . ." Josephus's accounts are contradictory. In *BJ* he credits Onias III with building the temple in Egypt; in *Ant.* xii, xiii he credits Onias IV.

See V. Tcherikover, *Hellenistic Civilization and the Jews* (Eng. tr. 1959), pp. 276-281.

5. Onias, a high priest. Also known as Menelaus, he usurped the office of high priest from Jason by buying it from Antiochus IV (2 Macc. 4:23-26). In 2 Macc. 4:23 Jason and Onias III are identified as brothers; and Menelaus and Simon, the temple captain, are called brothers in 4:7. Josephus, however, refers to Onias-Menelaus as a brother of Jason and Onias III (*Ant.* xii.5.1 [237-39]; xv.3.1 [41]). Probably Onias-Menelaus was a cousin (Gk. *exádelphos*) of Onias III. *See also* MENELAUS.

***Bibliography.***–F.-M. Abel, *Les Livres des Maccabées* (1949), pp. 337f.; S. Tedesche and S. Zeitlin, *Second Book of Maccabees* (1954), pp. 78-80.

R. L. OMANSON

**ONIONS** [Heb. *beṣālîm*; Gk. *krómmyor*]. An Egyptian delicacy for which the Israelites longed (Nu. 11:5). The onion (*Allium cepa* L.), a staple item of diet, was widely cultivated in ancient Syria, Egypt, and Palestine.

R. K. H.

**ONLY BEGOTTEN.** The AV translation of Gk. *monogenḗs* in six NT passages (Jn. 1:14, 18; 3:16, 18; He. 11:17; 1 Jn. 4:9), usually in the phrase "only begotten Son" (all the references except that in He. 11:17 are to Jesus' relationship to God). The RSV and NEB render *monogenḗs* by "only" — a translation supported by the use of *monogenḗs* in the LXX. In each of its four occurrences in the LXX OT, *monogenḗs* translates Heb. *yāḥîḏ* (lit. "only one," "solitary," "beloved"): Jgs. 11:34 (AV, RSV, "only child"); Ps. 22:20 (MT 21; LXX 21:20; AV "darling," mg. "dear life"; RSV "life," mg. "only one"); 25:16 (LXX 24:16; AV "desolate"; RSV "lonely"); 35:17 (LXX 34:17; AV "darling," mg. "dear life"; RSV "life"); cf. also the use of *monogenḗs* in Tob. 3:15; 6:11; 8:17. Elsewhere the LXX renders Heb. *yāḥîḏ* by Gk. *agapētós* (lit. "[only] beloved"; see Gen. 22:2, 12, 16; Jer. 6:26; Am. 8:10; Zec. 12:10).

Scholars are divided over the legitimacy of the AV rendering "only begotten" in the six passages mentioned above. The position against the AV translation was stated clearly by D. Moody, who insisted that *monogenḗs* means "one," "only," or "unique" rather than "only begotten." Moody's major arguments include the following. (1) The standard lexicons support this meaning (e.g., see MM, pp. 416f.; Bauer, rev., p. 527). (2) The Old Latin MSS rendered *monogenḗs* by Lat. *unicus* ("only") rather than *unigenitus* ("only begotten"). In the Vulgate Jerome changed *unicus* to *unigenitus* ("only begotten") for theological reasons, i.e., to ensure the doctrine that Jesus was "begotten, not made." (In passages that lack this theological interest [Lk. 7:12; 8:42; 9:38] he kept *unicus* as the translation of Gk. *monogenḗs*.) The Vulgate exercised a formidable influence on the AV and subsequent English translations. (3) The LXX use of *monogenḗs* for Heb. *yāḥîḏ* and NT usage of the term in Lk. 7:12; 8:42; 9:38; He. 11:17 clearly support the meaning "only." (4) The reference in 1 Clem. 25:2 to the phoenix bird (which was neither born nor begotten) as *monogenḗs* demands the meaning "only one of its kind." (5) John's emphasis on Jesus' uniqueness as *monogenḗs* is underscored by his reservation of the term *huiós* to Jesus alone; believers he calls *tékna,* "children."

Other scholars who have taken this position include J. H. Bernard, R. E. Brown, C. H. Dodd, L. Morris, B. F. Westcott, and D. G. Vanderlip. Brown, e.g., stated: "Literally the Greek means 'of a single [*monos*] kind [*genos*].' Although *genos* is distantly related to *gennan,* 'to beget,' there is little Greek justification for the translation of *monogenēs* as 'only begotten.'" The word describes Jesus' uniqueness, "not what is called in Trinitarian theology his 'procession'" (p. 13).

A contrary position has been argued by C. K. Barrett, J. B. Bauer, F. Büchsel, R. H. Lightfoot, B. Lindars, and R. Schnackenburg. While admitting the linguistic strength of the preceding view, these scholars have argued that in the Johannine passages *monogenḗs* denotes Jesus' origin in addition to His uniqueness. Jesus is not only the "only" Son of the Father: He is the "begotten" Son because He derives His being from the Father. Barrett, e.g., insisted that the Son proceeds from the Father in personal though never independent existence (p. 166). J. B. Bauer held that in John *huiós* designates Jesus' origin and contains the idea of His eternal begetting by God (p. 868).

The interpretation of *monogenḗs* is further complicated by the textual problem in Jn. 1:18. Whereas some witnesses (including later Greek MSS, versions, and some church fathers) read *monogenḗs huiós,* the earliest Greek MSS $p^{66}$ א B C) have *monogenḗs theós*. Textual critics and exegetes are divided over the proper reading of the text. Exegetes preferring *monogenḗs huiós* include C. K. Barrett, F. Büchsel, R. Bultmann, M. Dods, and R. Schnackenburg; those preferring *monogenḗs theós* include J. H. Bernard, R. E. Brown, and L. Morris. While those who translate *monogenḗs* by "only begotten" can make sense of *monogenḗs huiós* ("only begotten Son"; cf. Jn. 3:16, 18; 1 Jn. 4:9), they run into enormous theological difficulties with *monogenḗs theós* ("only begotten God").

In conclusion, an assessment of the linguistic evidence seems to indicate that "only" or "unique" may be an adequate translation for all occurrences of *monogenḗs* in the Johannine literature (see Bauer, rev., p. 527). Discussions about the origin or derivation of the Son in relationship to the Father should be conducted along theological rather than linguistic lines.

***Bibliography.***–C. K. Barrett, comm. on John (2nd ed. 1978); J. B. Bauer, *Encyclopedia of Biblical Theology* (1981); Bauer, rev., p. 527; J. H. Bernard, comm. on John, I (*ICC,* 1928); R. E. Brown, *Gospel According to John,* I (*AB,* 1966); R. Bultmann, *Gospel of John* (Eng. tr. 1971); *DNTT,* II, 725; C. H. Dodd, *Interpretation of the Fourth Gospel* (repr. 1968); M. Dods, *Expos.G.T.,* I (1961); F. C. Grant, *ATR,* 36 (1954), 284-87; R. H. Lightfoot, *St. John's Gospel* (1956); B. Lindars, *Gospel of John* (*NCBC,* repr. 1981); D. Moody, *JBL,* 72 (1953), 213-19; L. Morris, *Gospel According to John* (*NICNT,* 1971); R. Schnackenburg, comm. on John, I (Eng. tr. 1968); *TDNT,* IV, *s.v.* μονογενής (F. Büchsel); B. F. Westcott, *Epistles of St. John* (repr. 1966); comm. on John (1908); M. F. Wiles, *The Spiritual Gospel* (1960); D. G. Vanderlip, *Christianity According to John* (1975).

C. B. HOCH, JR.

**ONO** ō'nō [Heb. *'ônô*; Gk. B *Ōnan,* A *Ōnō*]; AV and NEB Apoc. ONUS (1 Esd. 5:22). A biblical Palestinian town identified as modern Kefr ʿAnā NW of Lydda. Neh. 11:35 associates Ono with "the valley of the craftsmen." It is named along with Lod as being built by descendants of Benjamin (1 Ch. 8:12). "The sons of Lod, Hadid, and

Ono" were among the Jews who returned from the Babylonian Captivity (Ezr. 2:33; Neh. 7:37). During the rebuilding of the wall of Jerusalem, Sanballat and Geshem proposed that Nehemiah confer with them in "one of the villages in the plain of Ono," but Nehemiah recognized the invitation as an attempt against him (Neh. 6:2). Benjaminites reoccupied Ono in the resettlement of the country (11:35). C. E. DE VRIES

**ONUS** ō'nəs. *See* ONO.

**ONYCHA** on'i-kə [Heb. *šᵉḥēleṯ*; LXX *ónyx*]; NEB AROMATIC SHELL. One of five substances making up the composition of the INCENSE which was burned on the gold altar in the tabernacle (Ex. 30:34f.). The Gk. *ónyx* means "nail" or "nail shaped" and has been taken to refer to the shell of a cockle or mollusk. Mollusks are found in the shallow waters of the Mediterranean and Red seas. Such shells give off a pungent odor when burned. C. G. RASMUSSEN

**ONYX** on'iks. *See* STONES, PRECIOUS.

**OPEN.** In the OT usually the translation of Heb. *pāṯaḥ*. Other OT terms include *pāṣâ* (of opening the mouth, e.g., Gen. 4:11; Jgs. 11:35f.; Ezk. 2:8), *pāqaḥ* (of opening the eyes, e.g., Gen. 21:19; 2 K. 4:35), *gālâ* (lit. "uncover," e.g., Job 33:16; Ps. 119:18 [piel]), *rᵉḥōḇ* ("open square," e.g., Jgs. 19:15, 17; AV "street"; *see* SQUARE), *pᵉnê* (lit. "face of," esp. of an open field, e.g., Lev. 14:7, 53), *śāḏeh* ("open country," e.g., Dt. 21:1; AV "field"; *see also* FIELD). In the NT "open" usually translates Gk. *anoígō*, which is used of opening the heavens (e.g., Mt. 3:16), the mouth (e.g., Lk. 1:64), the eyes (e.g., Jn. 9:10), a door (e.g., Acts 16:26), a scroll (e.g., Rev. 5:3), etc. Other NT terms include *dianoígō* (e.g., Mk. 7:34f.), *schízō* (lit. "rend," Mk. 1:10), *anaptýssō* (lit. "unroll," Lk. 4:17), *trachēlízō* (lit. "twist the neck," He. 4:13), etc.

**OPEN PLACE.** The AV translation "in an open place" in Gen. 38:14 is based on a misunderstanding of Heb. *bᵉpeṯaḥ ʿênayim,* which was taken to mean "in an opening openly" (cf. AV "openly," v. 21, for *ʿênayim*) instead of "in an opening of Enaim." The RSV reading, "at the entrance to Enaim," is supported by Tg. Onk., Syr., and Vulg., which understand the phrase to mean the road junction for ENAIM (see comms., esp. E. A. Speiser, *Genesis* [*AB,* 2nd ed. 1964], p. 298). Cf. the NEB rendering, "where the road forks in two directions."

**OPENLY.** *See* PLAIN, PLAINLY.

**OPERATION.** *See* WORK.

**OPHEL** ō'fəl [Heb. *hāʿōpel*] (2 Ch. 27:3; 33:14; Neh. 3:26f.; 11:21; without the definite article the Heb. *ʿōpel* is translated "hill" in Isa. 32:14; Mic. 4:8). In all the references with the article the RSV has simply "Ophel," except in 2 K. 5:24 (see below), but the AV mg. adds "the tower." When the Hebrew has no article, the RSV renders it "hill" and the AV and NEB have various suggestions in text and margin: "hill," "tower," "stronghold," "secret place," "citadel." The root of the word indicates a "bulge" or "swelling"; the same noun is rendered "tumor" in 1 S. 5:9; etc. Evidently it could be applied to a mound and in some cases became a proper name (JB always treats it as a proper name).

A site clearly described as on the east hill of Jerusalem S of the temple was named Ophel (2 Ch. 27:3; 33:14; Neh. 3:26f.). Josephus stated (*BJ* v.4.2 [142-45]) that the eastern wall of the city ran from Siloam "and reaches as far as a certain place which they call Ophlas when it was joined to the eastern cloister of the temple." In *BJ* v.6.1 (254) he stated, "John held the temple with much of the environs, Ophla and the valley called Kedron." This place is not identical with the "Acra" and "Lower City," which were held by Simon. The name Ophel cannot be applied, as has been so commonly done, to the whole southeastern hill.

It is disputed whether the Ophlas of Josephus was identical with the OT Ophel. The OT references make clear that Ophel was a quarter of Jerusalem to whose defenses such kings as Jotham and Manasseh paid great attention. Excavations have revealed remains of fortifications erected at widely differing dates.

See J. Simons, *Jerusalem in the OT* (1952), pp. 60-67; *see also* JERUSALEM III.D.5.r; F.2.t.

Another "Ophel," translated "hill" by the RSV, was situated apparently in Samaria (2 K. 5:24), where Gehazi took his ill-gotten presents from the hands of the servants of Naaman the Syrian. According to J. Gray (*I & II Kings* [2nd ed., *OTL,* 1970], p. 510), the definite article with Heb. *ʿōpel* here suggests a more specific feature than simply a hill, perhaps the citadel of Samaria. For a similar use Gray appeals to the reference in the MOABITE STONE, an inscription of Mesha king of Moab, contemporary with Omri. Mesha said (lines 21f.): "I built QRḤH . . . and the wall of the citadel [or Ophel]." Most scholars (e.g., W. F. Albright in *ANET,* p. 320) translate *hʿpl* here rather than transliterate it as a proper name (contra *IDB,* III, *s.v.* [G. A. Barrois]). E. W. G. MASTERMAN D. F. PAYNE

**OPHIR** ō'fər [Heb. *'ôpîr*]. A son of Joktan, descendant of Shem (Gen. 10:29; cf. 1 Ch. 1:23) and presumably eponymous settler of the region of Ophir.

**OPHIR** ō'fər [Heb. *'ôpîr*; Gk. *Ōpheir, Oupheir, Sōpheir, Sōpheira, Sōphēra, Soupheir, Souphir*]. A region, the gold of which was proverbial, located in or near the southern Arabian peninsula, named for a son of Joktan, descendant of Shem (Gen. 10:29).

In the Bible, "gold of Ophir" is considered among the most precious of substances (Isa. 13:12; Ps. 45:9 [MT 10]; Job 28:16; Sir. 7:18). Indeed, in one verse (Job 22:24) "Ophir" is used as a metonymy for "gold." It is possible that the "gold of Uphaz" of Jer. 10:9 and Dnl. 10:5 is a textual error for "gold of Ophir" (so NEB).

Ophir is mentioned most prominently in the account of the joint expedition of the men of Solomon and Hiram of Phoenicia (1 K. 9:26-28). Solomon outfitted a fleet at Ezion-geber on the Gulf of Aqaba and Hiram supplied expert sailors for it. The fleet returned from Ophir bearing 420 talents of gold. The parallel account in 2 Ch. 8:17f. implies that Hiram supplied the fleet itself as well as the men and reports the amount of gold as 450 talents. The cargo of the fleet is further specified in 1 K. 10:11f. (par. 2 Ch. 9:10f.) as "almug wood [sandalwood] and precious stones." Jehoshaphat's attempt to mount a similar expedition to Ophir met with failure (1 K. 22:48; but cf. 2 Ch. 20:35-37, which gives a different account).

The notice in 1 K. 10:22 (par. 2 Ch. 9:21) that every three years the Israelite-Phoenician "ships of Tarshish" would bring a cargo of "gold, silver, ivory, apes, and baboons" (RSV mg.) is commonly associated with the Ophir expedition, but there is no real reason to connect the two — Ophir is not mentioned in the verse — and thus no evidence in these exotic goods for the location of Ophir. (Indeed, the parallel passage in 2 Chronicles says the ships went *to* Tarshish.) If the tradition recorded in 1 Ch. 29:4 is to be taken at face value David in his day was able to obtain gold from Ophir. It seems likely that Hiram was the middleman here as in so many of Israel's commercial ventures.

Ophir is also mentioned in an inscribed potsherd from Tell el-Qasîleh, N of Tel Aviv on the plain of Sharon, perhaps biblical APHEK: "Gold of Ophir for Beth Horon, 30 shekels." It is unclear whether this is really gold from Ophir, or simply fine gold; but Aphek's position athwart the main north-south caravan route in Palestine would make it an ideal distribution point for goods coming from Ezion-geber to all points north, including Phoenicia.

The location of Ophir is much disputed. The biblical writers themselves associate Ophir with the Arabian peninsula. In the Table of Nations of Gen. 10, Ophir as one of the sons of Joktan is placed among names of Arabian tribes. And it is perhaps no mistake that the account of the Ophir expedition in 1 Kings is interrupted by a lengthy description of the visit by the Queen of Sheba, an Arabian kingdom (1 K. 10:1-10). The attribution of gold, sandalwood, and precious stones to Ophir is consistent with a location in south Arabia. But there was a tradition, albeit postbiblical, in ancient times that Ophir was to be sought in India. The otherwise inexplicable transliterations of the LXX (see above) may point to ancient Supara, a locality N of Bombay. This Indian theory is attested also in Josephus (*Ant.* viii.6.4 [163f.]) and Jerome (in translating Job 28:16). But this seems to be nothing more than an example of the widespread (then and now) desire to actualize the text by identifying an otherwise unknown location with one known to the reader.

Inscribed potsherd from Tell el-Qasîleh mentioning "gold of Ophir" (Israel Department of Antiquities and Museums)

Other proposed locations in Africa and the Near East (see G. Ryckmans) are based on the evidence of 1 K. 10:22, which, as noted above, is debatable.

***Bibliography.***–BDB, *s.v.* "*'ôpîr*"; *DBSup.*, vol. VI (1959), 744-751 (Ryckmans); B. Maisler, *JNES*, 10 (1951), 265-67.

E. M. COOK

**OPHNI** of'nī, of'nē [Heb. *ʿopnî*; Gk. (Lucian) *Aphnē*, lacking in LXX] (Josh. 18:24). A town in the territory allotted to Benjamin. In Joshua's list of Benjaminite cities (18:21-28) it is named between Chephar-ammoni (site unidentified) and Geba, modern Jebaʿ, 9 km. (5½ mi.) N of Jerusalem. Ophni is thus often identified with Jifna, about 5 km. (3 mi.) NW of Bethel on the route descending from Bethel to Aphek near its intersection with the Jerusalem-Shechem highway (*LBHG,* rev., p. 60; *GTTOT,* § 327, p. 174). Jifna is the Gophna of Josephus (*BJ* iii.3.5 [55]), which was then head of one of the eleven toparchies in Judea. If this identification is correct, it implies a northward bulge in the territory of Benjamin, which is not in agreement with Josh. 18:12 (cf. *GTTOT,* § 326, p. 171).

D. E. WARING

**OPHRAH** of'rə [Heb. *ʿoprâ*–'young hind']. A man of the tribe of Judah, son of Meonothai (1 Ch. 4:14).

**OPHRAH** of'rə [Heb. *ʿoprâ*–'young hind'; Gk. B *Iephratha,* A *Aphra*].

**1.** A city in the territory allotted to Benjamin (Josh. 18:23). The other cities listed suggest a location NE of Jerusalem. Ophrah is also mentioned in 1 S. 13:17f., as the destination of one of the three raiding parties sent out by the Philistines. From Michmash one party went toward Beth-horon on the west, one toward the wilderness on the east, and the third toward Ophrah and SHUAL, presumably to the north, since Saul was camped at Geba to the south.

Ophrah is generally identified with the Ephron of 2 Ch. 13:19, the Ephraim of 2 S. 13:23; Jn. 11:54, and the Aphairema of 1 Macc. 11:34 (*GAB,* p. 158). The proximity of Ephron to Bethel and of Ephraim to Baal-hazor helps to determine a more precise location.

Jerome, identifying Ophrah with Ephraim, placed it 5 Roman miles (7.4 km., 4.6 mi.) E of Bethel. This location supports an identification with modern eṭ-Ṭaiyibeh, a site about 6.5 km. (4 mi.) NE of modern Beitîn (Bethel) and 8 km. (5 mi.) N of ancient Michmash. Since Hebrew names from the roots *ʿpr* (e.g., Ophrah) and *ḥpr* resemble Arab. *ʿifrit,* "demon," they are commonly changed to the euphemistic name *eṭ-Ṭaiyibeh,* "the favor" (cf. *LBHG,* rev., p. 121).

**2.** A city in the territory W of the Jordan allotted to Manasseh; it belonged to the clan of Abiezer (Jgs. 6:11,

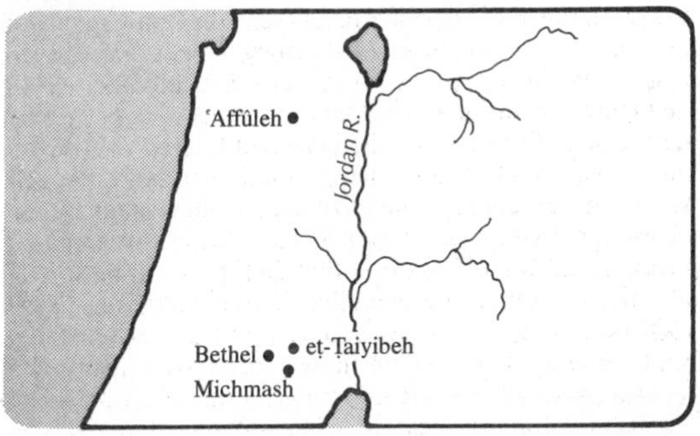


15, 24, 34; 8:32; 9:5; cf. Josh. 17:2; 1 Ch. 7:18). Ophrah was the home of Gideon and the place where he received a divine commission to deliver Israel from the oppressing Midianites, built an altar to Yahweh, and destroyed the local high place (Jgs. 6:11-32). Under Gideon it became a tribal cultic center, but the golden ephod that he set up there proved a snare to his house and to all Israel (8:22-28). At Ophrah Gideon's son Abimelech slew seventy of his brothers whom he saw as possible rivals to his claim of kingship; only Jotham escaped alive (9:1-6).

The location of Ophrah is uncertain. Many suggestions have been made, including Ferʿata, W of Shechem; Tell el-Fârʿah, NE of Shechem; Silet ed-Dahr, N of Shechem; the eṭ-Ṭaiyibeh S of Tul Karm; and the eṭ-Ṭaiyibeh NW of Beth-shean. Ophrah has usually been identified with the latter eṭ-Ṭaiyibeh, which is NE of the hill of Moreh and near the well of Harod, the Jezreel Valley, and Tabor — places that figure in the events of Jgs. 6–8. It has also been argued that eṭ-Ṭaiyibeh is more likely the site of the Hapharaim belonging to Issachar (Josh. 19:19) and that Ophrah should possibly be identified with ʿAffûleh, which is SW of the hill of Moreh and in the center of the Jezreel Valley. This site seems to agree with the *ʿ-p-r* in the list of Thutmose III (no. 53) and also fits the testimony of Eusebius (*Onom.* 28.25), who placed *Aphraia* about 9 km. (6 mi.) N of Legio. In addition, a tell with both Bronze and Iron Age remains is at ʿAffûleh. Although the Abiezer clan is known to have been located in Mt. Ephraim, possibly some of them had migrated to the Jezreel Valley in the north. In support of this position, Josh. 17:11 may hint at a territorial expansion of Manasseh at the expense of Issachar (*LBHG*, rev., pp. 263f.). D. E. WARING

**OPINION** [Heb. *seʿippâ*–'division,' 'branch'] (1 K. 18:21); NEB "sit on the fence"; [*dē(a)ʿ*–'knowledge'] (Job 32:6, 10, 17); NEB also KNOWLEDGE; [*lēḇ*–'heart'] (Prov. 18:2); AV HEART; NEB WIT; [Gk. *dialogismós*–'thought, reasoning, argument'] (Rom. 14:1); AV, NEB, DOUBTFUL; [*gnṓmē*–'mind,' 'opinion,' 'judgment'] (1 Cor. 7:25); AV, NEB, JUDGMENT. A personal judgment, appraisal, or belief that may or may not be generally shared.

In 1 K. 18:21 Elijah taunts the prophets of Baal as he addresses the people, "How long will you go limping [*pāsaḥ*] with two different opinions?" (the NEB modernizes, "sit on the fence"). Heb. *seʿippîm* serves as a fine paronomasia: the people's indecision between allegiance to Baal or to Yahweh is matched by the torturous dance of the prophets of Baal (cf. piel of *pāsaḥ*, "limp [in the dance]," v. 26). While the general sense of the expression is clear, the precise meaning of *seʿippîm* is uncertain. The cognate noun *sāʿîp* can denote a "cleft" (e.g., Jgs. 15:8, 11) or a "branch" (e.g., Isa. 17:6); the piel of *sāʿap* means to "cut down (branches)." If the basic meaning is "cleft," then the expression might be translated "hobble between two forks (of a road)," i.e., between two opinions or allegiances. J. Gray (p. 396) prefers the translation "hobble on two crutches (made from branches)," but this rendering detracts from the word-play.

Three times in the speeches of Elihu the AV and RSV translate *dē(a)ʿ* "opinion" (Job 33:6, 10, 17). Several commentators, however, prefer the literal translation "knowledge" (e.g., F. I. Andersen, S. R. Driver and G. B. Gray, H. H. Rowley). Elihu shows deference to his elders in waiting his turn to speak, but he is fully confident that what he has to say is "knowledge" imparted by God (v. 8), and that it is superior to the wisdom of his elders (vv. 9-15).

The meaning of Prov. 18:2 is clear: the fool has no interest in understanding but only in spewing out his own ideas, feelings, and opinions (*lēḇ*); therefore he speaks impulsively without bothering first to listen to others (v. 13) or to acquire knowledge (cf. v. 15), and his rash words often lead to ruin (vv. 6f.).

In Rom. 14:1 the RSV translates Gk. *eis diakríseis dialogismṓn* "for disputes over opinions" (AV "to doubtful disputations"; NEB "attempting to settle doubtful points"). Paul's point seems to be that the Roman Christians are to receive into their fellowship those whose faith is weaker (i.e., those who have scruples about eating and drinking, observance of special days, etc.) without provoking disputes about these scruples (see J. Murray, pp. 174f.).

Because he has no ruling from the Lord concerning virgins, Paul simply gives his own "opinion" or "judgment" (AV, NEB) about the matter; but he wants his advice to be taken seriously because of his own trustworthiness (1 Cor. 7:25).

***Bibliography.***–F. I. Andersen, *Job* (*Tyndale OT Comms.*, 1976), pp. 246f.; S. R. Driver and G. B. Gray, Comm. on Job (*ICC*, repr. 1977), pp. 279f., 282; J. Gray, *I & II Kings* (*OTL*, 2nd ed. 1970), p. 396; W. McKane, *Proverbs* (*OTL*, 1970), pp. 515f.; J. Murray, *Epistle to the Romans*, II (*NICNT*, 1965), 174f.; H. H. Rowley, *Job* (*NCBC*, rev. ed. 1976, repr. 1980), p. 208.

R. B. ALLEN N. J. O.

**OPOBALSAMUM** o-pō-bal'sə-məm. *See* BALM OF GILEAD; STACTE.

**OPPRESS; OPPRESSION; OPPRESSOR** [Heb. *ʿāšaq*] (e.g., Lev. 19:13); AV also DEFRAUD, DO WRONG TO, DECEIVE, DECEITFULLY; NEB also "keep back the wages of," ILL-TREAT, CHEAT, ROB, etc.; [Heb. *ʿōšeq*] (e.g., Eccl. 7:7); NEB also CALUMNIES, SLANDER, SLANDEROUS WORDS, DEVIOUS, TYRANNY; [Heb. *ʿošqâ*] (Isa. 38:14); NEB "pay heed"; [Heb. *ʿāšôq*] (Jer. 22:3); [Heb. *ʿašûqîm*] (Job 35:9; Eccl. 4:1; Am. 3:9); [Heb. *maʿašaqqâ*] (Prov. 28:16; Isa. 33:15); NEB GRASPING, EXTORTION; [Heb. *yānâ*] (e.g., Dt. 23:16 [MT 17]); AV also VEXED; NEB also FORCE, ILL-TREAT, TYRANT, CRUEL; [Heb. *lāḥaṣ*] (e.g., Ex. 3:9); AV also AFFLICT; NEB also BE HARD UPON, HARASS, HARRY, MAKE SUFFER; [Heb. *laḥaṣ*] (e.g., Ex. 3:9); NEB also BRUTALITY, DISTRESS, SUFFERINGS; [Heb. *nāgaś*] (e.g., Isa. 3:5); AV also EXACT; NEB DEAL HARSHLY WITH, MAKE WORK HARDER, TASK-MASTER, DRIVER, MONEY-LENDER; [Heb. *rāṣaṣ*] (e.g., Jgs. 10:8); NEB also CRUSHED; [Heb. *ʿānâ*] (Gen. 15:13; Ex. 1:12; Zeph. 3:19); AV AFFLICT; NEB also HARSHLY TREATED; [Heb. *ʿānāw*] (Ps. 69:32 [MT 33]; 76:9 [MT 10]); AV HUMBLE, MEEK; NEB HUMBLE FOLK, HUMBLE MEN; [Aram. *ʿanēh*] (Dnl. 4:27 [MT 24]); AV POOR; NEB WRETCHED; [Heb. *tōḵ*] (e.g., Ps. 10:7; 55:11 [MT 12]); AV DECEIT, DECEITFUL

MEN; NEB also VIOLENCE, WRONG; [Heb. *dāḥaq*] (Jgs. 2:18); AV VEX; NEB ILL-TREATMENT; [Heb. *dak*] (Ps. 9:9 [MT 10]; 10:18); NEB also DOWNTRODDEN; [Heb. *ḥāmôṣ*] (Isa. 1:17; 16:4 [see *BHS*]); AV also "extortioner"; NEB also "extortion"; [Heb. *ʿāqâ*] (Ps. 55:3 [MT 4]); NEB "shrill clamor"; [Heb. *ʿāmāl*] (Isa. 10:1); AV GRIEVOUSNESS; NEB BURDENSOME DECREES; [Heb. *ʿōṣer*] (Ps. 107:39; Isa. 53:8); AV also PRISON; NEB also "without protection"; [Heb. pl. of *ʿārîṣ*] (Job 6:23; 27:13); AV also MIGHTY; NEB RUTHLESS MEN; [Heb. hiphil part. of *ṣûq*] (Isa. 51:13); [Heb. part. of *ṣārar*] (Nu. 10:9); NEB HARD-PRESSED; [Heb. *šōḏ*] (Ezk. 45:9); AV SPOIL; NEB ROBBERY; [Gk. *katadynasteúō*] (Acts 10:38; Jas. 2:6); NEB also "insulted"; [Gk. *kataponéomai*] (Acts 7:24); NEB omits; [Gk. *thraúō*] (Lk. 4:18); AV BRUISED; NEB BROKEN VICTIMS.

The OT is everywhere concerned about oppression. The Law, the Prophets, and the Writings join their voices in their condemnation of the oppressor, their exhortation not to oppress, and their comforting assurance to the oppressed that God is on their side.

*I. Vocabulary of Oppression.*–A wide variety of Hebrew words are translated "oppress," "oppression," and "oppressor." The most common word is *ʿāšaq*, which usually signifies the oppressor's enriching himself by violating a neighbor's property rights. Thus in the law it is in a series with "fraud," "robbery," and "deception" about found articles (Lev. 6:2ff.). It parallels "false balances" in Hos. 12:7 and stands in apposition to "coveting" and "seizing one's fields and house" in Mic. 2:2. One delivers the robbed from his "oppressors" (Jer. 21:12; 22:3); in 22:17 *ʿāšaq* stands to "dishonest gain" as "violence" stands to "shedding innocent blood." The word sometimes refers explicitly to withholding the wages of the worker (Lev. 19:13; Dt. 24:14f.; Mal. 3:5), but by extension it can cover any form of oppression. Indeed, the derivative Heb. *ʿošqâ* is used in Hezekiah's prayer (Isa. 38:14) as an emotive cry of distress even though no rights have been violated.

Hebrew *yānâ* has general reference to ill treatment. Other Hebrew words indicate various oppressive uses of power: *nāgaś*, exacting and driving tyranny; *ʿārîṣ* and *ḥāmôṣ*, formidable ruthlessness; *šōḏ*, ruinous violence; and, more mildly, *ṣûq*, constraint, and *ʿōṣer*, restraint.

Hebrew *ʿānâ* and its derivatives suggest the humiliation effected. *Tōḵ* refers to the injury inflicted, *ʿāmāl* to the trouble caused, and *ṣārar* to the hostility shown.

Hebrew *lāḥaṣ*, "squeeze" or "press," *rāṣaṣ*, "crush," *dak*, "crushed," *dāḥaq*, "crowded," and *ʿāqâ*, "pressure," are used figuratively.

*II. Oppression of the Nation.*–Oppression may characterize relations between or within nations. The victims are typically Israel or Judah (except Sidon, Isa. 23:12; Egypt, Jer. 46:16; and Babylon, Jer. 50:16 — all oppressed in judgment and reversal) and the poor and powerless.

The oppression of the Jews by other peoples is important in salvation history. The patriarchs, the Exodus, the judges, the kingdom, the Exile — in the whole story of oppression and deliverance God's covenantal faithfulness is seen, celebrated, and trusted. The song of Asaph celebrates God's covenantal faithfulness in His protection of the wandering patriarchs (1 Ch. 16:21 par. Ps. 105:14, Heb. *ʿāšaq*). The Exodus is remembered and celebrated as God's deliverance from the oppressor Egypt (e.g., Gen. 15:13, in the promise to Abraham, Heb. *ʿānâ*; Ex. 3:9, in the call of Moses, *laḥaṣ* [E; cf. *ʿonî*, "affliction," 3:7; *ʿaḇōḏâ*, "bondage," 6:6]; Dt. 26:7, in the ancient confession of faith at the offering of first fruits, *laḥaṣ*). The Deuteronomic historians recall the cycle of oppression, repentance, and deliverance in order to lead a threatened people to repentance and recovery. Typically the Lord was moved by pity for His groaning people to raise up judges to deliver them from oppression, but after deliverance the people returned to their unfaithful ways and fell into the hands of oppressors again (Jgs. 2:18f.; cf. 4:3; 6:9; 10:12; 1 S. 12:8ff.; 2 K. 13:4, 22). The song of the covenant, Ps. 106, especially vv. 42-45 (Heb. *lāḥaṣ*, v. 42), sums up the history. Psalmists also celebrated God's deliverance of the nation from oppression (76:9; 107:38f.), expressed their confidence in God as "a stronghold for the oppressed" (9:9), and lamented their present oppression and called to God for deliverance (44:24). The prophets threatened to invoke oppression of the nation as judgment for the people's faithlessness to the covenant (Am. 6:14; Hos. 5:11; cf. the covenant curse of Dt. 28:29, 33), but they were confident that God remained the faithful deliverer of the oppressed (Isa. 9:4; 52:3; Jer. 50:33f.). They thus promised an eventual end of oppression. Sometimes that end is depicted in terms of God's deliverance (Zeph. 3:19; Jer. 30:20), sometimes in terms of the deliverance brought by God's agent (Zec. 9:8). Sometimes the deliverance brought a great reversal, with the oppressed exalted over their oppressors (Isa. 14:2, 4; 60:14; the oppressor Moab pleading for protection from Zion is a gentle form of the same theme, 16:4). Sometimes the promised destruction of the oppressors is gruesomely described (49:26), but sometimes their fate is quite left out of view (54:14). On the other hand, 19:19-25 beautifully tells of an end to oppression; Egypt, Assyria, and Israel, the oppressors and the oppressed, would together worship God.

Even when God delayed deliverance from the oppressor He blessed the people (Ex. 1:12). The whole story serves the prophetic appeals that the people repent and trust God rather than fear the fury of the oppressor (Isa. 51:13).

*III. Oppression Within the Nation.*–Within the nation the oppressors were the rich and powerful, and their victims were the poor and powerless, the orphan and widow, the slave, the sojourner, and the helpless. The law stands against such oppression (apodictic commands: Ex. 22:21; 23:9; Lev. 19:13; Dt. 23:16; 24:14; casuistic law: Lev. 6:2-5). The context in law sometimes specifies the act, sometimes the victim. An explicitly proscribed act is usually an offense against property (Lev. 6:2-5; 19:13, Heb. *ʿāšaq*). The particular groups mentioned in laws against oppression are poor or powerless (the stranger, Ex. 22:21; 23:9; the slave, Dt. 23:16).

The prophets stood with the law in condemning such oppression (e.g., Isa. 58:3 [Heb. *nāgaś*], where the victims are the workers; Jer. 6:6 [*ʿōšeq*]; 9:6 [*tōḵ*]; Ezk. 22:29 [*yānâ*], where the victims are the poor and needy; Hos. 12:7 [*ʿāšaq*]; Mic. 2:2 [*ʿāšaq*]; Zec. 7:10 [*ʿāšaq*], where the victims are the widow, the fatherless, the sojourner, and the poor; Mal. 3:5 [*ʿāšaq*], where the victims are the hireling, the widow, and the orphan). Perhaps the most memorable condemnation is Amos's line about the cows of Bashan "who oppress the poor, who crush the needy, who say to their husbands, 'Bring, that we may drink'" (Am. 4:1). The prophets pronounced God's sentence against such oppression. In Isaiah the sentence is that God leaves the people in their oppression; in 3:5, 12 oppression and the resulting chaos evince the wrathful judgment of God. Oppression makes worship a mockery and blasphemy (1:12-17 [*ḥāmôṣ*]; 58:5-8 [*rāṣaṣ*]; Jer. 7:4-7 [*ʿāšaq*]). Such oppression is included explicitly by Isaiah (59:13 [*ʿōšeq*]) and implicitly by all the classical prophets among the heinous national sins.

The rulers had a special obligation to stop oppression. Jeremiah exhorted the king to "deliver from the hand of the oppressor he who has been robbed" (Jer. 21:12; 22:3), and he judged Jehoiakim sternly (22:17). Ezekiel condemned the oppression by the princes of Israel and promised a time when princes would "no more oppress my people" (Ezk. 45:8f.). Even Nebuchadrezzar was exhorted to show mercy to the oppressed (Dnl. 4:27). Ps. 72, a royal Psalm, petitions God, "Give the king thy justice" (v. 1), "may he defend the cause of the poor of the people, give deliverance to the needy, and crush the oppressor" (v. 4; cf. v. 14).

For all the importance of the rulers, it is finally God who is and can be trusted to deliver the oppressed. The king was only to reflect God's siding with the oppressed, as Ps. 72 makes clear. Even while he lamented the arrogance of the oppressor, the psalmist was certain that God would "do justice to the fatherless and the oppressed, so that man who is of the earth may strike terror no more" (10:18). The hymns praise and invite others to praise God, for He "works vindication and justice for all who are oppressed" (103:6; cf. 146:7). Jesus revealed Himself as God's agent when in His inaugural address He announced that His mission included the liberation of the oppressed (Lk. 4:18, quoting Isa. 61:1f.).

Wisdom literature is not based on the law or covenant traditions and does not have grand visions of an eschatological future. But it, too, denounces oppression. The theological emphasis in wisdom literature falls on God the Creator and Sustainer rather than on God the deliverer and lawgiver. Wisdom literature generally sees mankind not as distressed but as sharing responsibility for the well-being of God's creatures. Wisdom's stance toward oppression is caught nicely in Prov. 14:31, "He who oppresses a poor man insults his Maker" (cf. 29:13).

Sometimes the stress on God as Creator and Sustainer and the consequent order in the world led Wisdom to make naive appeals to the prudence of righteousness over against oppression (Prov. 22:16; the Hebrew is very difficult, however). The author of Ecclesiastes, of course, was anything but naive, and one of his complaints against the world was the abuse of power and the resultant unrelieved suffering: "Behold, the tears of the oppressed, and they had no one to comfort them! On the side of their oppressors there was power, and there was no one to comfort them" (Eccl. 4:1). An appeal to the prudence of wicked and vain oppressors is naive because for them self-interest rather than the justice of God, which is written in the covenant and announced by the prophets, determines what is prudent. A more firmly based appeal to prudence shows that oppression is contrary to the order intended by God the Creator.

Characteristically, Luke said more about the oppressed than did any other NT writer. Among the Synoptists only Luke included the account of Jesus' synagogue reading of Isa. 61:1f., in which liberating the oppressed is stressed (Lk. 4:18f.; cf. Acts 10:38; also I. H. Marshall, *Gospel of Luke* [*NIGTC*, 1978], p. 182, who pointed out a similar use of Isa. 61:1f. at Qumrân with reference to the teacher of righteousness). In Acts 7:34 Stephen noted Moses' role as the liberator from oppression. Finally, James pointed out to his readers that the rich were oppressing them and thus deserved no special privileges (Jas. 2:1-7).

*See also* EXTORTION.

***Bibliography***.–T. Hanks, *God So Loved the Third World* (1983); Y. Kim, "The Vocabulary of Oppression in the OT" (Ph.D. Diss., Drew, 1981); J. Pons, *L'Oppression dans l'AT* (1981); E. Tamez, *Bible of the Oppressed* (Eng. tr. 1982). A. D. VERHEY

**OR.** Used in an archaic sense by the AV and RSV once for Heb. *'ô*, "either" (NEB, NIV), "whether" (JB, NAB), in 1 S. 26:10 (but cf. KD). In Ps. 90:2 the AV and RSV translate Heb. *w*[e] as "or ever" (cf. AV in Eccl. 12:6; Cant. 6:12; Dnl. 6:24; Sir. 18:19).

**ORACLE.** *See* PROPHECY IV.B.

**ORACLES, SIBYLLINE** sib'ə-lēn. *See* PSEUDEPIGRAPHA V.F.

**ORATION** [Gk. *dēmēgoréō*] ("make an oration," Acts 12:21); NEB HARANGUED; **ORATOR** [Heb. *laḥaš*] (Isa. 3:3, AV); RSV "(expert in) charms"; NEB "enchanter"; [Gk. *rhḗtōr*] (Acts 24:1, AV); RSV SPOKESMAN; NEB ADVOCATE.

The verb *dēmēgoréō* is a hapax legomenon in the NT meaning "deliver a public address." In Acts 12:21 it was Herod who "made an oration" to the crowd (cf. 4 Macc. 5:15; Josephus *Vita* 17 [92]).

In Isa. 3:3 the phrase *n*[e]*ḇôn laḥaš* (lit. "one who perceives a whisper") is translated "eloquent orator" in the AV. However, *laḥaš* derives from the verb *lāḥaš*, "whisper" or "charm," which probably denotes snake charming in Ps. 58:5 (MT 6). Thus in Isa. 3:3 the noun probably refers to one skillful in muttering charms or magical incantations (cf. Eccl. 10:11; Jer. 8:17), not to speech in general.

Used generally to mean "public speaker" (Philo *De Vita Contemplativa* 31; Josephus *Ant*. xix.2.5 [208]), *rhḗtōr* also meant "advocate, lawyer." The latter sense is attested in an early papyrus MS (Oxy. P. 37, i, 4, N.D.). Tertullus is called *rhḗtōr* in Acts 24:1, AV. The Sanhedrin enlisted him since he was familiar with Roman and Jewish law (E. Haenchen, *Acts of the Apostles* [Eng. tr. 1971], pp. 652, 657). Here he registers a formal complaint before Felix against Paul. G. L. KNAPP

**ORCHARD** [Heb. *pardēs* < Pers. *pairi-daēza* (cf. Gk. *parádeisos*)–'paradise,' 'park, forest'] (Cant. 4:13); [*ginnâ*–'garden'] (Cant. 6:11); AV, NEB, GARDEN; **OLIVE ORCHARDS** [*zayiṯ*–'olive tree, olive plantation']; AV OLIVE-

Terraced orchard of fig trees outside Bethlehem (TWA)

YARD, OLIVES; NEB OLIVE-GROVE, OLIVE YARD, OLIVE-TREES.

Palestine was known in the ancient Near East as a land rich in fruit trees. When the Israelites took possession of the land, they inherited the orchards of the Canaanites (cf. Dt. 6:11; 8:8; Neh. 9:25). These were so important to the economy that the Israelites were forbidden to destroy them even in time of war (Dt. 20:19f.). Most important of the cultivated trees was the OLIVE TREE. Olive orchards and vineyards are frequently mentioned as vital to the economy of Israel (e.g., Ex. 23:11; Dt. 28:39f.; 2 K. 5:26; 18:32; 1 Ch. 27:27f.). Next in importance was the FIG tree (see Jotham's parable, Jgs. 9:7-15; cf. Am. 4:9; Hab. 3:17). The POMEGRANATE was another favorite fruit (cf. Nu. 13:33; Dt. 8:8; Cant. 4:13; Joel 1:12; Hag. 2:19). Other cultivated trees included the ALMOND and other NUT trees (cf. Cant. 6:11), the PALM TREE, and the SYCAMORE fig. *See also* FRUIT II; Vol. II, Plates 10, 13, 14.

All the kings of the ancient Near East owned vast estates that included orchards. Samuel warned the Israelites that a king would take their orchards and give them to his servants to work (1 S. 8:15). This happened as early as the reigns of Saul, David, and Solomon (cf. 1 S. 22:7; 1 Ch. 27:26-28; cf. also Eccl. 2:4-6, where *pardēsîm* [v. 5] is rendered "parks" by the RSV). Although in the ideal picture of peace and prosperity every Israelite family lived off the fruit of its own plot of land (cf. 1 K. 4:25; 2 K. 18:31; Isa. 36:16; Mic. 4:4; Zec. 3:10), the confiscation of lands and orchards by unscrupulous creditors was a problem throughout Israel's history (cf. Neh. 5:11).

*See also* GARDEN. N. J. O.

**ORDAIN** [Heb. *millē' yāḏ*–'fill the hand'] (Ex. 28:41; 29:9, 29, 33, 35; 32:29; Lev. 8:33; Nu. 3:3); AV CONSECRATE; NEB INSTALL, INSTALLATION, CONSECRATE; [*ṣāwâ*–'order, command'] (2 S. 17:14; Ps. 44:4 [MT 5]; Lam. 2:17; 3:37); AV COMMAND, APPOINT; NEB also PURPOSE, BIDDING, "forbid"; [*'āśâ*–'make, appoint, institute'] (Nu. 28:6; 1 K. 12:33); NEB "regular," INSTITUTE; [*nāṯan*–'give, set'] (2 K. 23:5); NEB APPOINT; [*śûm*–'set, place'] (Hab. 1:12); NEB APPOINT; [*šāpaṭ*–'set'] (Isa. 26:12); NEB BESTOW; [piel of *qûm*–'impose, institute'] (Est. 9:27); NEB RESOLVE; [*mišpāṭ*–'legal decision,' 'justice'] (1 Ch. 15:13); AV "due order"; NEB "as we should have done"; supplied contextually by the RSV in 2 Ch. 2:4 (MT 3); 22:7; [Gk. *horízō*–'determine,' 'appoint'] (Acts 10:42; cf. 3 Macc. 6:36); NEB DESIGNATE; [*diatássō*–'order, direct, command'] (Gal. 3:19); NEB PROMULGATE; [*tássō*–'assign'] (Acts 13:48); NEB MARK OUT; [*protássō*–'fix, determine'] (2 Macc. 8:36); AV, NEB, GIVE; [*dídōmi*–'give, grant'] (1 Esd. 1:32); AV ORDINANCE; NEB PROCLAIM; [*plēróō tás cheíras*–'fill the hands'] (Sir. 45:15); AV CONSECRATE; [*gráphō*–'write'] (Tob. 1:6); NEB PRESCRIBE; [*kosméō*–'adorn,' 'set in order'] (Sir. 42:21); AV GARNISH; NEB SET IN ORDER.

Of the Hebrew terms cited, only the expression *millē' yāḏ* refers to consecration of individuals for functions within the community. None of these Hebrew or Greek terms bear the specialized meaning that "ordain" has come to have in postcanonical ecclesiastical circles, namely, appointment to, or installation in, an office that is both limited to recipients of a specific rite and dependent for its validity upon authorization from recognized channels within an ecclesiastical structure.

In the English versions "ordain" is used with at least three different shades of meaning. (1) "Set in order," "arrange." This sense (cf. Lat. *ordināre*), now obsolete, occurs several times in the AV (e.g., Ps. 132:17; Isa. 30:33; Heb. *'āraḵ*; RSV "prepare"). In the RSV it occurs only at Sir. 42:21. (2) "Establish," "bring about," "issue a decree." This is the most common meaning of "ordain" in the RSV OT and Apocrypha. Most often it refers to divine purposes, judgments, or decrees (e.g., 2 S. 17:14; Ps. 44:4 [MT 5]; Is. 26:12; Lam. 2:17; 3:37; Hab. 1:12), although it occasionally refers to a human action (e.g., 1 K. 12:33; Est. 9:27). In Gal. 3:19 it denotes angelic instrumentality. (3) "Set apart (for a special function)," "appoint." "Ordain" in this sense occurs frequently in the AV (e.g., 1 Ch. 9:22; 2 Ch. 11:15; Jer. 1:5; Dnl. 2:24; Jn. 15:16; Acts 14:23; 17:31), and the RSV has usually changed it to "appoint." The RSV uses "ordain" in this third sense only to translate Heb. *millē' yāḏ* (cf. Sir. 45:15; see *TWOT*, I, 363), an expression used primarily of the consecration of priests; in the NT "ordain" occurs in this third sense only twice, both times with God as the subject (Acts 10:42; 13:48).

In technical ecclesiastical usage "ordain" and "ordination" ordinarily refer to special status accorded ministers or priests through officially sanctioned rites, with associated emphasis on authority to proclaim the Word or to administer sacraments, or to do both. Underlying such terminology is usually a distinction between clergy and laity — a distinction that fails to do justice to the broad spectrum of function and service enjoyed by the people of God (see, e.g., Rom. 12:4-8; 1 Cor. 12:4-31; Eph. 4:7-16), including also ministry by women (e.g., Jn. 20:18; Acts 18:26; Rom. 16:1; 1 Cor. 11:5; Phil. 4:3).

The principal biblical passages that have been cited to support a specialized ordination include Mk. 3:14; Jn. 15:16; 20:21-23; Acts 6:1-6; 13:1-3; 14:23; 1 Tim. 4:14; 2 Tim. 1:6. Of these, neither Mk. 3:14 nor Jn. 15:16 refers to a rite, and the RSV appropriately renders Gk. *poiéō* and *títhēmi* by "appoint" instead of "ordain" (AV). The point of Jn. 20:21-23 is not to specify channels of consecration for declaring forgiveness but to teach the Christian community's independence from Jewish cultic tradition in dealing with sin. According to Acts 6:1-6 the apostles chose the "Seven," on the basis of the gifts they already possessed, to administer distributions to widows; and to ratify this decision the apostles laid their hands on them. This laying on of hands is not a hierarchical prerogative; for subsequently (13:1-3) Barnabas and Saul (Paul) were "set apart" (*aphorízō*; AV "separate") by prophets and teachers, not for an office but for fresh tasks. Despite their rejection by traditionalist Jews (14:19), Barnabas and Paul continued their evangelizing efforts and "appointed" (*cheirotonéō*; AV "ordained") elders (v. 23). No specific rite is indicated. The use of *kathístēmi* to denote official action is amply attested in the Hellenistic world; but in Tit. 1:5 (AV "ordain"; RSV "appoint") there is no hint of any special rite. In keeping with the perspective of Rom. 12:6, the author of 1 Tim. 4:14 affirmed that Timothy received a special gift (*chárisma*) for functioning in the manner outlined in vv. 11-13, when elders assembled and laid hands on him. Similarly, in 2 Tim. 1:6 Timothy received assurance that Paul's own spirit of courageous action, affection, and prudence had been conveyed to him through Paul's hands. Neither passage endorses ecclesiastical prerogative. The referent for the laying on of hands in He. 6:2 cannot be determined (see comms.).

Evidence for the ways in which early Christian communities publicly recognized those who were already functioning or were about to function in various capacities is admittedly slender. Nor can any consistent pattern be established; but fasting, prayer, and laying on of hands appear to be primary features.

In view of the fluidity of practice in the early Christian communities and the technical meanings that "ordain" has acquired, it is probably best to avoid the use of this term in rendering biblical terms that deal with appointments to various types of service. Awareness of this hazard of anachronism should not, on the other hand, prejudice the privilege of each Christian community to adopt such practices and rites as may assist the Church in expressing and discharging its principal responsibility, the proclamation of the gospel. *See also* BISHOP; HANDS, LAYING ON OF.

***Bibliography.***–M. Dibelius and H. Conzelmann, *Pastoral Epistles* (Eng. tr., *Hermeneia,* 1972), pp. 55-57, 70f.; E. Lohse, *Ordination im Spätjudentum und im NT* (1951); *RGG,* IV, *s.v.* "Ordination"; E. Schweizer, *Church Order in the NT* (Eng. tr., *SBT* 1/32, 1961); K. Stendahl, *The Bible and the Role of Women* (1966); C. Stuhlmueller, *Women and Priesthood* (1978); M. Warkentin, *Ordination* (1982).

F. W. DANKER

**ORDER.** A term used as both a noun and a verb, with a variety of meanings: (1) the arrangement of persons, objects, or events in their proper places in relation to one another; (2) a proper condition, in which things are harmoniously arranged or regulated according to a set pattern or rule; (3) a classification; (4) an authoritative directive or command.

(1) The arrangement of persons, objects, or events in their proper places in relation to one another. The Hebrew verb *ʿāraḵ* often means setting in layers or rows: e.g., arranging wood or offerings on an altar (Gen. 22:9; Lev. 1:7f., 12; 6:12 [MT 5]; 1 K. 18:33; cf. *maʿarāḵâ,* Jgs. 6:26), the bread of the Presence on the table (Ex. 40:4, 23; Lev. 24:8), lamps in the tabernacle (Lev. 24:3f.), stalks of flax on a roof (Josh. 2:6).

In Job 33:5 *ʿāraḵ* has the sense of setting forth arguments in a legal case (cf. 13:18; 23:4; 32:14; 37:19). It has a similar forensic meaning in 2 S. 23:5, where David praises God for having made a covenant that is "ordered in all things" (*ʿarûḵâ ḇakkōl*); i.e., its terms are fully set forth. The same verb is used of lining up troops in battle ARRAY (cf. 1 Ch. 12:38 [MT 39], *maʿarāḵâ;* AV "rank"). In Nu. 10:28 the RSV and NEB render "order of march" for the plural of *massaʿ* (cognate of *nāsaʿ,* "set out," v. 28b; cf. AV "journeyings"). A chronological sequence of generations is indicated by *tôlēḏôṯ* (Gen. 25:13; Ex. 28:10). Gk. *kathexḗs* indicates that events are narrated in chronological or logical sequence ("orderly," Lk. 1:3; "in order," Acts 11:4). The frequently occurring phrases "in order to" and "in order that" express a causal sequence, and therefore purpose.

In some instances the verb "order" has the sense of "arrange or regulate to bring about order." Wisd. 8:1 praises Wisdom because "she orders [Gk. *dioikéō,* lit. "keep house, manage"] all things well." The AV frequently uses the verb in this sense: e.g., Aaron "shall order [Heb. *ʿāraḵ*] the lamps upon the pure candlestick before the Lord continually" (Lev. 24:4; cf. v. 3; Ex. 27:21; Jer. 46:3; cf. also Ps. 119:133 and Isa. 9:7, where "order" renders the hiphil of *kûn,* "establish" [RSV "keep steady," "establish"]). Sometimes "to order" means to regulate one's own life or behavior. "So Jotham became mighty, because he ordered [hiphil of *kûn*] his ways before the Lord his God" (2 Ch. 27:6). In Ps. 50:23 Yahweh promises, "To him who orders [*śîm,* "sets, fixes"] his way aright I will show the salvation of God." In Gen. 41:40 Pharaoh promises Joseph that all the Egyptians "shall order themselves as you command." The MT *ʿal-pîḵā yiššaq* literally means "shall kiss you on the mouth"; most versions follow the LXX (*hypakoúsetai*), emending the Hebrew verb to *yāšōq* or *yaqšēḇ.*

(2) A proper condition, in which things are harmoniously arranged or regulated according to a set pattern or rule. In the OT it was considered important that worship be conducted in an orderly fashion. The Levites in charge of the service of song performed their duties "in due order" (Heb. *kemišpāṭ,* lit. "according to custom [or judgment]," 1 Ch. 6:32 [MT 17]). Paul also taught that worship should be conducted "decently and in order" (Gk. *euschēmónōs kaí katá táxin,* 1 Cor. 14:40). In Col. 2:5 *táxis* describes disciplined Christian behavior, while in 1 Cor. 7:35 *euschḗmōn* denotes moral conduct that will not offend unbelievers (see *TDNT,* II, *s.v.* εὐσχήμων [H. Greeven]). A house that is "put in order" (*kosméō,* Mt. 12:44 par. Lk. 11:25) is one that is tidied (cf. NEB), but the Greek verb may also mean "decorate" (hence AV "garnished'; cf. Lk. 21:5, RSV "adorned").

The phrase "set your house in order" (Heb. *ṣaw leḇêṯeḵâ*), used of Hezekiah (2 K. 20:1; Isa. 38:1) and Ahithophel (2 S. 17:23), means to give final instructions to one's household or to make one's will. Cf. Gen. 49:29 (Jacob) and 1 K. 2:1 (David), where the same verb (RSV "charged") denotes the final injunctions of a dying man. Although usually read as the piel of *ṣāwâ* ("command"), the verb may be a cognate of Arab. *waṣiya,* "make a last testament" (see J. Gray, *I & II Kings* [*OTL,* 2nd ed. 1970], p. 697).

(3) A classification. "Second order" (Heb. *mišneh,* "second") designates a secondary division of priests (2 K. 23:4) or musicians (1 Ch. 15:18). Gk. *tágma* (1 Cor. 15:23) is a military term designating rank. Paul taught the Corinthians that there would be two resurrections: first that of Christ, and then, at His coming, that of the second rank, composed of those who belong to Him.

Psalm 110, traditionally interpreted as a messianic Psalm, speaks of a priest "after the order of Melchizedek" (Heb. *ʿal-diḇrāṯî malkî-ṣeḏeḵ,* v. 4). The author of Hebrews quotes the LXX of this text (*katá tḗn táxin Melchisedek*) five times and applies it to Christ (He. 5:6, 10; 6:20; 7:11, 17). Here "order" refers to the higher rank and "the entirely different nature of Melchizedek's priesthood compared with that of Aaron" (Bauer, rev., p. 804; see comms.; *see also* MELCHIZEDEK).

(4) An authoritative directive or command. In the RSV OT the verb "order, give orders" frequently translates the Heb. piel of *ṣāwâ* (Gen. 12:20; 42:25; 2 S. 14:8; 18:5; Est. 4:5, 17; Jer. 36:5, 8; 37:21; AV usually "command" or "give a commandment"). When used of a ruler or person in authority, *ʾāmar* ("say") sometimes has the sense of "order, command" (e.g., 2 K. 1:11; 10:20; Neh. 13:9, 19; Est. 6:1; 9:25; cf. Aram. *ʾamar,* Dnl. 3:19f.). Other verbs are the piel of *yāsaḏ* (Est. 1:8; AV "appoint"; NEB "lay it down"), the piel of *dāḇar* (lit. "speak," Nu. 32:27), and Aram. *šelaḥ* (lit. "send an order," Ezr. 6:13; cf. AV, NEB). Nouns rendered "order" include Heb. *yāḏ* (lit. "hand," 1 Ch. 25:6; 2 Ch. 23:18), *ʿēṣâ* (lit. "advice," Ezr. 10:8), *dāḇār* (lit. "word," Est. 1:19; 2:8; 3:15), and Aram. *millâ* (lit. "word," Dnl. 3:22). In Jer. 31:35f. *ḥuqqîm* is rendered "fixed order," i.e., Yahweh's "decrees" (AV "ordinances") that govern the operation of the universe (*see also* HEAVEN, ORDINANCES OF).

In the NT "order" or "give orders" most often renders Gk. *keleúō* (Mt. 8:18; 14:19; 18:25; 27:58, 64; Acts 5:34; 12:9; etc.; AV usually "command"). Other verbs (usually rendered "command" by the AV) are *epitimáō* (lit. "warn," Mt. 12:16; Mk. 3:12), *epitássō* (Mk. 6:27), *diatássō* (Acts 24:23), *parangéllō* (Acts 23:30; NEB "instructed"), and *diastéllō* (He. 12:20). In Jn. 11:57 "orders" (AV "commandment") renders the noun *entolḗ.*

N. J. OPPERWALL

**ORDINANCE** [Heb. *mišpāṭ*]; AV also JUDGMENT, MANNER, CEREMONY (Nu. 9:3), etc.; NEB also MANNER, CUSTOM, LAW, etc.; [Heb. *ḥōq, ḥuqqâ*]; NEB also RULE, LAW, JUDGMENT, etc.; [Aram. *qeyām*] (Dnl. 6:7, 15 [MT 8, 16]); AV STATUTE; NEB DECREE;

[Gk. *dikaíōma* (Lk. 1:6), *dógma* (Eph. 2:15)]; NEB also REGULATION. An established religious rite, a statute enacted by a legitimate governing authority, a prescribed order of things, or an authoritative command. The word "ordinance" has an unmistakable legal connotation, apparent in its frequent use in lists alongside such words as "statutes," "testimonies," "commandments," "charges," and "laws" (cf. Dt. 4–30; 1 K. 2:3; 8:58).

The words *ḥōq* and *ḥuqqâ* are derived from a Semitic root meaning to inscribe or engrave. These words are often also translated "statute" or "decree," suggesting that this type of law is specifically prescribed in writing. The word *mišpāṭ* has a much broader meaning, ranging from "justice" (i.e., the desired ideal) to "judgment" to "custom" (i.e., the practiced norm). Behind these nuances perhaps lies the notion that the ideal is the norm in the community ruled by God; customs are not valued for tradition's sake alone but because they provide a channel for the realization of justice. In summary, the word "ordinance" may suggest a specific written code in some instances, while at other times it seems to refer to general, commonly held norms.

(1) In cultic contexts the word "ordinance" designates *an established religious rite*. More specifically, it appears to refer to the customary guidelines and procedures for performing certain rituals and ceremonies, such as the Passover (Ex. 12; Nu. 9; 2 Ch. 35:13), the Feast of Booths (Neh. 8:18), and regular Sabbath observances (Ezk. 20). It also covers the prescribed liturgical practices of temple worship (Ezk. 43:11, 18; 44:5), including the proper manner for performing sacrifices (Nu. 15:16, 24; Nu. 29) and burnt offerings (Lev. 5:10; 9:16; Ezr. 3:4; Ezk. 46:14). While the Israelites believed all these rites and ceremonies to be ordained and established by God, the temple priests undoubtedly were the authoritative interpreters and enforcers of these ordinances. It is quite possible that texts in the Jerusalem temple described in detail the proper liturgical practice of these ordinances (cf. Lev. 1–16).

(2) The word "ordinance" can designate *a statute enacted by legitimate governing authority* (i.e., a specific and binding policy of law). A king had the legal authority to establish an ordinance (see Dnl. 6:7, 15, where a signed document is involved), but he also had the more informal authority of prestige to set a precedent by his own example (cf. 1 S. 30:25; 2 Ch. 8:14).

(3) "Ordinance" is also used in the restricted sense of *a prescribed or "given" order of things*. Behavior that is consistent and predictable is sometimes attributed to underlying laws that govern and control it. The regularity of some natural phenomena suggests underlying laws which govern nature; the Bible declares these to be ordinances established or prescribed by God (Job 38:33; Jer. 33:25). Similarly, human traditions, customs, and norms (which constitute a fairly predictable part of the given social order) belonging both to the faithful (2 Ch. 35:25) and to pagans (Ezk. 5:7; 11:12) are also called "ordinances."

(4) The most comprehensive definition of the word "ordinance" is *an authoritative command*, the authoritative command of God, especially as it relates to the appropriate social behavior of His people. Ancient Israel did not sharply distinguish between the secular and the sacred; everyday conduct was to be shaped according to the ordinances of God (cf. the "Holiness Code," Lev. 18–26).

In some instances God's authoritative command for human conduct seems to have been understood in the narrow legal context of written codes (Josh. 24:25; 2 K. 17:37). In other instances, however, God's authoritative commands appear to have been understood more broadly. God's ordinances were identified more generally with God's ways (Dt. 5:31-33; Ps. 18:21f. [MT 22f.] Isa. 58:2), God's word (Ps. 119:13; 147:19), and the fear of the Lord (Ps. 19:9 [MT 10]). As such, God's ordinances are based upon His gracious activity (Dt. 6:20ff.) and are an integral part of the bond of love uniting God and His people (Dt. 11:1; Ezk. 11:20). They are viewed as the source of life and salvation (Lev. 18:5; 2 Ch. 7:17ff.; Ezk. 20:11, 13). God's ordinances can be viewed less as a formal legal code of commands and prohibitions and more as a fully integrated, deliberate, and disciplined reorientation of life away from self-centered desires (Dt. 8:11ff.). Obedience to God's ordinances therefore is not simply a matter of human effort to conform to a code; rather it reflects the indwelling presence of God's Spirit (Ezk. 36:26ff.).

The tension between God's ordinance as a written, legal code and as a spiritual, righteous will is reflected in Ezk. 20:25, where God seems to admit candidly that legal codes at best have a limited effect in producing true righteousness, and that often they mirror more of the degenerate human condition than they do the transcendent will of God (cf. Mk. 10:2-9). The tension is partially resolved in the NT (cf. Rom. 2:25-29), where righteousness is declared to have appeared in Christ, independent of the law (Rom. 3:21). Reconciliation with God is therefore achieved not through ordinances but through Christ, who abolished the law of commandments and ordinances (Eph. 2:15).

G. A. HERION

**ORDINANCES OF HEAVEN.** *See* HEAVEN, ORDINANCES OF.

**ORDINATION.** *See* ORDAIN.

**ORDINATION, RAM OF** [Heb. *'êl hammillu'îm*] (Ex. 29:22 [without the definite article], 26f., 31; Lev. 8:22, 29); AV RAM OF CONSECRATION; RAM OF INSTALLATION. The "ram of ordination" was the second of two rams sacrificed in the installation ceremony of Aaron and his sons. Because Aaron and his sons had not yet assumed office, the right thigh — normally the priest's portion — was burned on the altar and the breast was eaten by Moses, who was officiating as priest.

*See also* ORDAIN; PRIESTHOOD; SACRIFICES AND OFFERINGS IN THE OT V.

**ORE** [Heb. *'eḇen*–'stone'] (Job 28:2f.); AV STONE. Ore was plentiful in the Arabah (cf. Dt. 8:9); thus Job 28 reflects the Edomite setting of the book. The human capacity to dig deep mine shafts and smelt precious metals from the ore (vv. 1-11) is contrasted here with people's inability to find wisdom (vv. 12-28).

**OREB** ôr'əb [Heb. *'ōrēḇ* or *'ôrēḇ*–'raven']. A Midianite leader captured and killed by Gideon and the men of Ephraim. It is also the name of a rock where Oreb was killed.

Judges 7:25 concludes the chapter which describes Gideon's miraculous rout of the Midianite army from the valley near the hill of Moreh by the use of only three hundred soldiers armed with trumpets and torches. Along with Zeeb, another leader, the Ephraimites captured and killed Oreb at a rock named after him (no longer identifiable). The Ephraimites, at first angry with Gideon because he did not include them in the original battle, were pacified by Gideon's praise of their capture and execution of these Midianite leaders (8:3). Ps. 83:11 (MT 12) and Isa. 10:26 recall that victory in petition and praise to God.

R. L. ALDEN

**OREB** ôr'əb (2 Esd. 2:33, AV). *See* SINAI.

**OREN** ôr'ən [Heb. *'ōren*–'laurel']. A son of Jerahmeel and descendant of Judah (1 Ch. 2:25).

**ORGAN** [Gk. *mélos*–'part,' 'limb'] (1 Cor. 12:18f.); AV MEMBER. *Mélos* is elsewhere rendered "member" (e.g., vv. 12, 14, 25-27) or "part" (vv. 20, 22) by the RSV. *See* MEMBER.

The AV uses "organ" to translate Heb. *'ûgāḇ* (or *'ugāḇ*) in Gen. 4:21; Job 21:12; 30:31; Ps. 150:4 (RSV "pipe"). *See* MUSIC II.C.2.

**ORGIES** [Heb. *hāmôn*–'tumult,' 'crowd'] (Jer. 3:23); AV MULTITUDE; NEB CLAMOUR. The AV and NEB are much more literal here than the RSV, which interprets this verse in the light of vv. 6-10 (see KD, *in loc.*). Thus according to the RSV, Jeremiah regarded with shame the Canaanite fertility rites practiced by Judah during his time. *See also* HIGH PLACE; RELIGIONS OF THE BIBLICAL WORLD: CANAANITE.

**ORIENTATION.** The means of fixing directions.

*I. OT.*–In the OT world several methods of fixing directions were used and fluidly combined. (1) Directions are often designated relative to the perspective of the person giving the directions. In this case *qeḏem* signifies what is "in front of" or "before" one, while *'āḥôr* refers to that "behind" or "to the rear." (The concept of four primary directions extending out from the individual or object is clearly expressed in Ezk. 1:17, Heb. *'arba'aṯ riḇ'êhen,* "their four sides," translated in the RSV as "their four directions.") *Śemô'l,* "left (hand)," and *yāmîn,* "right (hand)," complete the four primary directions. The limitations of such a system are obvious. The directions expressed are not absolute, but relative to the position of the individual and therefore cannot provide fixed reference points.

(2) Directions based on solar movements are also known in the OT and provide a first step toward fixed or absolute reckoning. Here *mizrāḥ,* "place of coming forth" (cf. Nu. 21:11; Ps. 113:3), and *môṣā',* "going out" (Ps. 75:6 [MT 7]), designate the "place of (the sun's) rising," while the corresponding "place of setting" is indicated by "place of entering of sun" (Dt. 11:30), *meḇô' šemeš* or by *ma'arāḇ* (1 Ch. 7:28; Ps. 75:6).

(3) The combination of these systems provides a more complete method of determining direction based on solar orientation. This is accomplished by fixing the direction one "faces" toward the sunrise. Thus *qeḏem* becomes synonymous with *mizrāḥ* and regularly signifies "east." In consequence, the other relative terms are fixed as well: *'āḥôr* = *ma'arāḇ* = west; *śemô'l* = north; *yāmîn* = south. Points of the compass between these major coordinates are not usually expressed.

(4) Geographical and topographical features were also employed to produce a system that was absolutely fixed, at least for the locality served. Under this system certain topographical features served to mark the compass points while directions were fixed in relation to them. For Israel in Canaan, west came to be associated with *yām,* "sea," in reference to the Mediterranean, its most prominent topographical feature and the country's western boundary. Similarly north was called *ṣāpôn* from the mountain of the same name that was visible in that area. (Mt. Saphon is identified as Mons Cassius, located in Syria.) Following this pattern, south was designated *negeḇ* for the dry, desert region that marked the southern border of Israel. East does not seem to have a consistent designation, though the term *hā'arāḇâ* or perhaps *'ēḇer hayyārdēn* may have served this purpose (Gen. 50:10). Most often the terms *mizrāḥ* and *qeḏem* continue to be used (see Josh. 12:1, where *mizrāḥ* serves to qualify both *'ēḇer hayyārdēn* and *hā'arāḇâ*).

(5) In a more limited sense, direction (or motion) toward or from a particular point can be expressed in a variety of ways. First, simple prepositions, either separable or inseparable, may be used. Thus motion to or toward a point is regularly indicated by the use of the prepositions *'el, 'aḏ,* and the inseparable preposition *le-*. Motion away from a point is expressed most frequently by the various forms of the preposition *min*. On other occasions the inseparable preposition *be-* (which normally indicates motion within a sphere of action) can, in combination with the prepositions *'aḏ, le-*, and with *hê locale,* indicate motion "away from" a given point (Dt. 1:44, *beśē'îr 'aḏ ḥormâ,* "from Se'ir to Hormah").

*II. NT.*–In the NT world two systems of orientation were commonly used: solar-stellar and a nautical system relying on wind direction.

*A. Solar-stellar Orientation.* Here, as in the OT, orientation is fixed according to solar movements. East is *anatolḗ* or "rising" and sometimes occurs with *hḗlios* ("sun") explicitly expressed. West by correspondence becomes *dysmḗ,* "setting [of the sun]" (Mt. 8:11). In addition to these two obvious solar directions, the Greek employs *mesēmbría,* "midday," to indicate south, the position of the sun at noon (Acts 8:26). Since there is no appropriate solar position to mark the final compass point, Greek employs the stellar terminology *árk(t)os,* "the bear" (i.e., Ursus Major, connected with the Polar Star) to designate north.

*B. Nautical Orientation.* The Greeks were master sailors and thus well acquainted with the winds on which their navigation depended. It is not surprising, therefore, that the most frequently employed means of orientation was based on wind direction. Names were given to the winds that emanated from certain points of the compass: north = *aklýdōn*/*akýlōn* (Lat. *aquilo*; sometimes known as *borrás,* Lk. 13:29; Rev. 21:13); south = *nótos* (Lat. *notus*); east = *eúros* (Lat. *eurus*); west = *zéphyros* (Lat. *zephyrus*). It was also possible to designate intermediate winds between these points: northwest = *chṓros* (Lat. *corus*; Acts 27:12); southwest = *líps* (Lat. *africus*; Acts 27:12); northeast = *eurakýlōn* (between *eúros* and *akýlōn*; Lat. *euro-aquilo*; Acts 27:14); southeast = *eúro-nótos* (between *eúros* and *nótos*; Lat. *phoenix*/*vulturnus*).

See O. Eissfeldt, *Baal Zaphon, Zeus Kasios, und der Durchzug der Israeliten durchs Meer* (1932).

G. H. WILSON

**ORION** ō-rī'ən [Heb. *kesîl*] (Job 9:9; 38:31; Am. 5:8). A brilliant constellation (the translation of *kesîl* in Isa. 13:10) of stars dominating the winter night sky in northern latitudes, named after the mythical Greek hunter. The three OT references mention it as demonstrating the transcendent creative power of the Lord. See G. R. Driver, *JTS,* 7 (1956), 1-11.

Most commentators (see the comms. on Job by KD, Driver and Gray [*ICC*], Rowley [*NCBC*], Pope [*AB*]; comms. on Amos by Driver [*CBSC*], Wolff [Eng. tr. *Hermeneia*]) have explained that *kesîl,* "Orion," is directly related to *kesîl,* "fool," i.e., the ancients viewed Orion as a foolish giant (cf. Syr. *gabbārā',* "giant," in Job 9:9; 38:31) who offended the gods and was punished with death. Cf. T. Gaster, *Thespis* (2nd ed. 1961), pp. 260, 320-29.

*See also* ASTRONOMY. N. GREEN G. A. L.

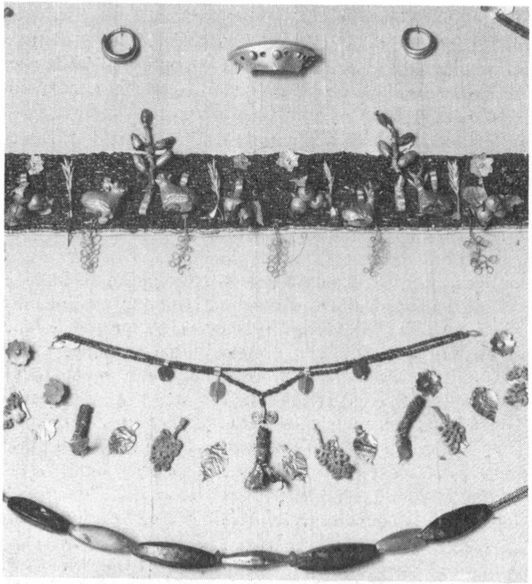

Various ornaments from the tomb of Queen Shubad (Ur, *ca.* 25th cent. B.C.) (University Museum, University of Pennsylvania)

**ORNAMENT** [Heb. *ʿaḏî* (Ex. 33:4-6; 2 S. 1:24; etc.); NEB also JEWEL, JEWELLERY, FINERY; [*ḥalî*] (Prov. 25:12); NEB NECKLACE; [*meged*–'precious gift'] ("costly ornament," Gen. 24:53); AV PRECIOUS THING; NEB COSTLY GIFT; [*tôr*–'string (of jewels)'] (Cant. 1:10f.); AV ROW (OF JEWELS), BORDER; NEB PLAITED TRESS, BRAIDED PLAIT. A decorative article used for personal adornment. In the RSV "ornament" usually represents Heb. *ʿaḏî*, a general term derived from *ʿāḏâ*, "adorn" (e.g., Jer. 2:32; 4:30). Archeological excavations have uncovered many fine examples of jewelry in Palestine and other countries of the ancient Near East. In biblical times both men and women wore ornaments fashioned from gold, silver, and semiprecious stones (*see* GARMENTS IX; JEWEL; STONES, PRECIOUS; pictures in GARMENTS and GOLD; *see also* individual articles ARMLET; BRACELET; EARRING; NECKLACE; PENDANT; RING).

The precise meaning of *tôrîm* in Cant. 1:10f. is uncertain. If it is derived from the stem *twr*, "go around, turn," it may refer to a round object, a series or string of objects (see *CHAL*, p. 388; cf. AV), or something plaited (see KoB, p. 1023; cf. NEB; RV "plait"). Most commentators agree that *tôrîm* represents some sort of ornamentation worn on the cheeks of a horse or a woman (see M. Pope, *Song of Songs* [*AB*, 1977], pp. 343f.). N. J. O.

**ORNAN** ôr'nən. *See* ARAUNAH.

**ORPAH** ōr'pə [Heb. *ʿorpâ*–perhaps 'neck'; LXX *Orpha*.] Ruth's sister-in-law.

The family of Elimelech had left Bethlehem during a famine in the period of the judges (Ruth 1:1). After Elimelech died (v. 3), his two sons, Mahlon and Chilion, married Moabite women, Ruth and Orpah, respectively (cf. 4:10). Ten years later both sons died (1:5). When Naomi heard that the famine in Judah was over, she decided to return to her homeland. Her daughters-in-law were determined to go with her, but Naomi urged them to return to their homes, where they might have the opportunity to remarry (vv. 8-13). In an intensely emotional scene Orpah relented and returned to her people and to her gods (vv. 14f.), but Ruth would not be dissuaded from following Naomi (vv. 16f.).

Though the biblical text does not condemn her — indeed, only praises her (v. 8) — her behavior contrasts sharply with the devotion of Ruth. Thus in Jewish tradition the name Orpah acquired a negative meaning because of her action of turning her back on the Lord (Midr. *Ruth Rabbah* ii.9).

*See also* RUTH. R. B. ALLEN

**ORPHAN** [Heb. *yāṯôm*; Gk. *orphanós*]; AV, NEB, also FATHERLESS (CHILD).

The Heb. *yāṯôm* occurs three times (Ex. 22:22 [MT 21]; Hos. 14:3 [MT 4]; Mal. 3:5) in the singular and once (Lam. 5:3) in the plural. The remedying of social abuses involving orphans and widows had formed an important part of social reform movements in Sumer during the 3rd millennium B.C., led by such rulers as Urukagina of Lagash (*ca.* 2350 B.C.) and Ur-Nammu, the founder of the Third Dynasty of Ur (*ca.* 2100 B.C.; cf. *ANET*, p. 524). Hammurabi claimed to promote justice for the orphan (*ANET*, p. 178). The Ugaritic myths also stress the virtue of caring for orphans (*ANET*, pp. 148, 151, 153).

The law of Moses showed special concern for the fatherless (Ex. 22:22; Dt. 10:18; 24:17-22; etc.), pleading for justice on their behalf (P. C. Craigie, *Deuteronomy* [*NICOT*, 1976], pp. 206, 310f.). This concern was rooted in God's redemption of Israel from Egypt.

Orphans were included with widows, resident aliens, and Levites as beneficiaries when the special tithe was apportioned at the end of a three-year period (Dt. 14:29; 26:12). At harvest time the workers were encouraged to leave some fallen fruit, small sheaves, or incompleted mowings for the widows, orphans, and aliens. These "gleanings" helped such underprivileged classes to feel an integral part of the covenant community of Israel (Craigie, p. 311), and assured them that justice in society existed for them also. Strong humanitarian concerns were an important characteristic of the Torah, expressing the nature of a God who was the "father of the fatherless" (Ps. 68:5 [MT 6]; cf. 10:14).

Orphaned daughters were especially vulnerable in the ancient Near East, and even though they might have inherited ancestral property in the absence of brothers, they could still fall prey to the greedy and unscrupulous. Consequently legislation was enacted in the Torah (Nu. 27:7-11) that safeguarded the rights of such women in Israel with all the authority of "statute and ordinance."

The tradition of providing for orphans and widows was a continuing feature of Israelite life. The preexilic prophets, following the doctrines of the Mosaic law, were insistent in their demands for justice for the "fatherless" (Isa. 1:17; cf. R. E. Clements, *Isaiah*, I [*NCBC*, 1980], 34; Jer. 22:3; Zec. 7:10). Hosea affirmed that the orphan found mercy at God's hands (14:3). In Sirach a man was instructed to be like a father to orphans, and in this way would become like a son of the Most High (4:10; cf. 2 Esd. 2:20). In the Maccabean period, when the Jewish forces defeated the soldiers of Nicanor in battle, they included the widows and orphans of the district among the recipients of plunder (2 Macc. 8:28, 30). The Talmud regarded as most worthy of commendation any act of charity to orphans.

The biblical orphan is usually the child of the widow. There is no clear case where the term implies the loss of both parents. Hence the translation "orphan" instead of "fatherless" is arbitrary (except in Lam. 5:3, where it is chosen for stylistic reasons); the connotations of "orphan" are the same as those of "fatherless."

The widow and orphan typify the helpless and defenseless among God's people. In exile Israel called itself an orphan to express its helplessness (Lam. 5:3). Like the orphan, Israel confessed that God alone could help it (Hos. 14:3). Thus "orphan" becomes associated with the redemption promised by God. The prophet promised that the Day of the Lord would bring vindication for the widow and orphan and judgment for their oppressors (Mal. 3:5).

Greek *orphanós* occurs twice in the NT (Jn. 14:18; Jas. 1:27). In Jn. 14:18 the term is often not translated "orphan" (AV "comfortless"; RSV "desolate"; NEB "bereft"; but cf. JB, NIV, NAB, NASB). Some scholars suggest that a similar usage is found in Greek and rabbinic literature, which apply "orphan" to disciples whose teacher or rabbi has died (e.g., cf. B. Lindars, *Gospel of John* [*NCBC*, repr. 1981], p. 480). The gospel, however, presents Jesus as more than a teacher and implies that he used *orphanós* to assure His disciples that His departure would not cancel the vindication promised by the OT prophet.

James's definition of true religion continues the OT requirement to protect the widow and orphan (Jas. 1:27; cf. Dt. 24:17f.). The redemption received by God's people obligates them to assist and to seek justice for those who are oppressed and cannot help themselves.

*See also* FATHERLESS; WIDOW.

D. E. HOLWERDA R. K. H.

**ORTHOSIA** or-thō-sē'-ə [Gk. *Orthōsias*]; AV ORTHOSIAS. The city to which Trypho fled from Dora, where he was besieged by Antiochus Sedetes (1 Macc. 15:37). According to Pliny (*Nat. Hist.* v.17) Orthosia lay S of the river Eleutherus and N of the city of Tripolis. The Peutinger Tables place it 12 Roman mi. (18 km., 11 mi.) N of Tripolis and 30 Roman mi. (43 km., 28 mi.) S of Antaradus on the Phoenician coast. Its approximate location is indicated by Ard Artuzi, or a place near it, at the mouth of Nahr el-Barid.

B. HOVEY

**OSAIAS** ō-sā'yəs (1 Esd. 8:48, AV). *See* JESHAIAH **5**.

**OSEA** ō-zē'ə. The AV translation of Lat. *Oseae* in 2 Esd. 13:40 (RSV, NEB, "Hoshea"). *See* HOSHEA **5**.

**OSEAS** ō-zē'əs. The AV translation of Lat. *Osee* in 2 Esd. 1:39 (RSV, NEB, "Hosea"). *See* HOSEA.

**OSEE** ō'zē (Rom. 9:25, AV). *See* HOSEA.

**OSHEA** ō-shē'ə (Nu. 13:8, 16, AV). *See* HOSHEA **1**; JOSHUA **5**.

**OSIRIS** ō-sī'rəs. *See* RELIGIONS OF THE BIBLICAL WORLD: EGYPT.

**OSNAPPAR** os-nap'ər [Heb. *'osnappar*]; AV ASNAPPER; NEB ASNAPPAR. An Assyrian king who deported and resettled foreign peoples in Samaria (Ezr. 4:10). He is usually identified with ASHURBANIPAL.

**OSPREY** os'pri [Heb. *'oznîyâ*] (Lev. 11:13; Dt. 14:12); AV OSPRAY; NEB BEARDED VULTURE. One of the birds of abomination.

Because the osprey (*Pandion haliaetus*) is a fish-eating bird, and since fish are to be found only in a few places in Palestine, the short-toed eagle (*Circaetus gallicus*), which closely resembles the osprey, has sometimes been a preferred identification.

The NEB rendering "bearded vulture" (*Gypaetus barbatus*) may be appropriate enough in that that bird is a resident Palestinian species, but it is doubtful that the ancients could have approached that creature closely enough to have observed the so-called beard (G. Cansdale, *Animals of the Bible* [1970], p. 145). Some type of vulture, though, would seem suitable in the context of birds prohibited as food. The vulture's habit of feeding on carrion would have been sufficient to include it on the list of proscribed foodstuffs.

*See also* ABOMINATION, BIRDS OF.

G. WYPER

**OSSIFRAGE** os'ə-frāj [Heb. *peres*–'breaker'] (AV Lev. 11:13; Dt. 14:12). *See* VULTURE.

**OSSUARIES** osh'ə-wār-ēz [Gk. *ostophágoi*; Lat. *ossuarium*–'for bones']. Small clay or limestone chests, usually 50-75 cm. (20-30 in.) long, 30-50 cm. (12-20 in.) wide, and 25-40 cm. (10-16 in.) deep, used for burial of human bones. The corpse was buried in a cave or tomb in the rocks until it decomposed enough for the bones to be gathered into a small receptacle for reburial; this procedure was followed to make room for new burials. Hundreds of these bone-boxes have been found near Jerusalem and Nablus and in Galilee, most of which date before A.D. 70. In 1945 E. L. Sukenik found several in a family tomb in a Jerusalem

Side of a limestone ossuary (Israel Department of Antiquities and Museums)

Aramaic inscription, "Simeon, builder of the sanctuary," on an ossuary from Giv'at ha-Mivtar (Israel Department of Antiquities and Museums)

suburb, Talpioth, on the road to Bethlehem; one contained a coin of Herod Agrippa dating to A.D. 42-43. Others which reflect the Chalcolithic period (4300-3150 B.C.) have been found in Haderah, Bene-berak, and Azor. The ossuary was used as late as the Gaonic period (6th-11th cents. A.D.).

Some ossuaries are plain; others have paneled framework and decorations of plants, buildings, gates, cross-hatchings, or rosettes. The lids are flat, rounded, or gabled. Some of the chests are shaped like a four-legged receptacle with a vaulted roof, a door with a bolt in the facade, and windows in the rear. Some facades even have the appearance of human faces.

Many of the ossuaries have brief inscriptions in Greek or Aramaic, or both, that give the names and sometimes the professions of the departed. One ossuary found at Givʿat ha-Mivtar in 1968 is inscribed with the name "Simon" followed by Aramaic words, which are problematic but seem to be translatable as "one of the builders of the sanctuary." Thus Simon was probably one of the master masons or engineers who worked on Herod's temple. Another ossuary is inscribed, "The bones of the sons of Nicanor, who made the door." Possibly these were the workers on the doors of the Nicanor Gate in the second temple.

Another interesting inscription is one presented by S. Klein (1929), which reads, "Herein were placed the bones of Ussia, the King of Judah. And [the ossuary] is not to be opened." *See* picture in UZZIAH. Many other names on ossuaries are also known from the Bible, e.g., "Jesus son of Joseph" in an Aramaic inscription, which dates to the 1st cent. A.D. but has no bearing on the belief in the resurrection of Jesus, since both names were common at that period.

The ossuary found at Givʿat ha-Mivtar, mentioned above, was only one of fifteen found in three burial caves. These contain the remains of thirty-five individuals. Five ossuaries contain evidence of death by violence: by crucifixion, conflagration, a blow from a mace, starvation, and once death in childbirth. The case of crucifixion is of particular interest, since the bones include two pierced by a large iron nail; this evidence has a bearing on the position of the body and the techniques used in crucifixion. *See* CROSS VI.B.

These ossuaries are important because they indicate the physical characteristics of the people who lived in Jerusalem just prior to the destruction of the second temple and because the skeletal remains in them bear certain marks of violence, which lend emphasis to the chaotic events of that time.

***Bibliography.***–M. Burrows, *What Mean These Stones?* (1941), pp. 240, 243; K. Galling, *Biblisches Reallexikon* (1937), cols. 404-407; N. Haas, *IEJ*, 20 (1970), 38-59; S. Klein, *Jüdisch-palästinisches Corpus Inscriptionum* (1920); C. H. Kraeling, *BA*, 9 (1946), 16-20; J. Naveh, *IEJ*, 20 (1970), 33-37; L. Y. Rahmani, *IEJ*, 18 (1968), 220-25; *IEJ*, 22 (1972), 113-16. B. R. AND P. C. PATTEN

**OSTRACA** osʹtrə-kä. Potsherds, specifically those used as writing materials. Gk. *óstraka* is the plural of *óstrakon*, a term used in the LXX (Job 2:8; Ps. 21:16 [Eng. 22:15]; Isa. 30:14) and elsewhere to refer to a POTSHERD (piece of broken pottery). Unglazed pottery was common in antiquity, and potsherds, which could be picked up in any rubbish heap, were often used (and sometimes reused after washing) for ephemeral records such as school exercises, letters, receipts, memoranda, bills, and short-term contracts. Ostraca could be used even by the poorest classes, who could not afford anything else to write on.

Ostraca were commonly used in Egypt from the Old Kingdom (*ca.* 2650-2150 B.C.) on, though the majority are of New Kingdom date (*ca.* 1550-1050 B.C.). Although the writing on most ostraca is in ink, some are incised. Their use in Mesopotamia was more limited because potsherds were more suitable for scripts easily written with pen and ink (such as Aramaic) rather than for those usually inscribed with a stylus (such as cuneiform).

Front (left) and rear (right) view of a house-shaped ossuary from Azor (Chalcolithic Period) (Israel Department of Antiquities and Museums)

Since ostraca tend to be preserved under conditions that would readily destroy parchment, leather, or papyrus, they have been found even in Palestine. Excavators in Israel and Jordan are taking greater care now, and increasing numbers of ostraca are being discovered. Such finds are valuable for linguistic and paleographic study as well as for revealing the life of the common person in both the ancient and classical worlds.

In ancient Greek cities ostraca were used for casting votes. Thousands of these potsherds inscribed with the names of candidates for banishment have been discovered in Athens; thus "ostracize" (Gk. *ostrakízein*) came to mean voting for the banishment of an accused person (cf. Aristotle *Constitution of Athens* xxii.6).

***I. Hebrew and Aramaic Ostraca.***–In 1908-1910 the excavation of a palace storeroom in SAMARIA uncovered more than sixty Hebrew ostraca containing memoranda related to the delivery of wine and oil from districts in western Manasseh to the Israelite royal court. The exact dating of these texts is in dispute. Suggestions range from the first half of the 9th cent. B.C. to the second half of the 8th cent. B.C. If as late as the latter, these texts, inscribed with ink in a Paleo-Hebrew script, may reflect the tribute exacted by King Menahem in 738 B.C. in order to appease Tiglath-pileser III, king of Assyria (2 K. 15:19f.).

In 1935 and 1938 excavations in the gatehouse at Tell ed-Duweir (LACHISH) revealed twenty-one ostraca from the early 6th cent. B.C. in Paleo-Hebrew script. One is dated in the ninth year of King Zedekiah (589/588), when Nebuchadrezzar besieged and destroyed Jerusalem (2 K. 25:1). These ostraca, containing a series of reports to the military commander of Lachish, reflect the situation of Jer. 34:6f., when Lachish and Azekah were the only Judean cities that remained standing against the Assyrian armies. Two of the documents refer to the "the prophet." Though there are other candidates, many scholars believe him to have been Jeremiah. In any case, the tetragrammaton appears and the Yahwistic religious context of these ostraca is clear. (*See also* LACHISH LETTERS.)

Excavations at ARAD (begun in 1962) uncovered over a hundred ostraca, some incised but most written in ink. Roughly half were written in Hebrew from various periods of the Iron Age; most of these are letters and dockets. Some letters refer to rations for the KITTIM, known from both the OT and the Dead Sea Scrolls, and one letter mentions the *byt yhwh,* "house of Yahweh," thus providing the first direct reference to the Jerusalem temple in

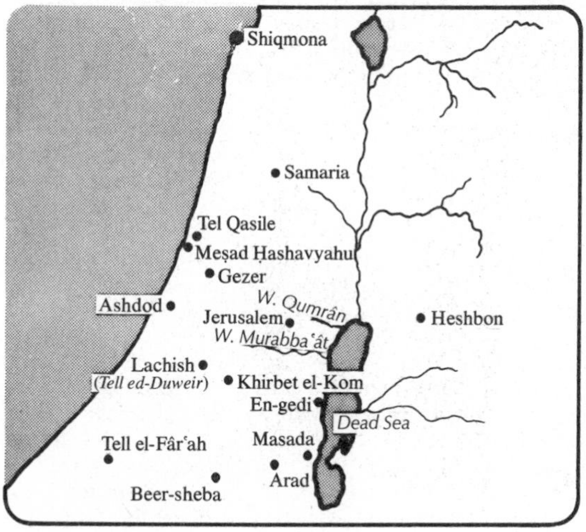


Hebrew epigraphy. Other ostraca had only a name inscribed, but two of these names are known from the Bible; the priestly families of Meremoth and Pashhur. The Aramaic ostraca, from *ca.* 400 B.C., are mostly dockets of the Persian garrison.

Excavations at Masada have yielded eleven ostraca bearing personal names, including Ben Yaʾir, probably referring to Eleazar ben Jairus, the commander of the Zealot stronghold destroyed in A.D. 74 by Silva and his Roman legionnaires. These ostraca present grim evidence of the casting of lots by Eleazar and his ten leaders for the executioner's role in the final stage of the besieged defenders' mass suicide (Josephus *BJ* vii.9.1 [389-401]; *see also* MASADA IV). Other important Dead Sea ostraca of the Roman period come from Wādî Qumrân and Wādî Murabbaʿât.

In addition to the major groups of Palestinian ostraca mentioned above, the following smaller finds are noteworthy: examples as early as the 16th cent. B.C. come from Gezer and Lachish; from the 8th cent. B.C. the "Ophir ostracon" from Tel Qasile (Tell el-Qasîleh) and the "Simeon ostracon" from Beer-sheba; from the 7th cent. B.C., an ostracon illustrating Ex. 22:26f. found at Meṣad Ḥashavyahu as well as the "Ophel ostracon" from Jerusalem; from the 6th cent. B.C., a whole series of Ammonite ostraca from HESHBON (Tell Ḥesbân); from the 5th cent. B.C. agricultural ostraca from Ashdod and Tell el-Fârʿah (S); from the 5th/4th cent. B.C., "barley" ostraca from Arad and an abecedary from Shiqmona; and from the 4th cent. B.C., Aramaic ostraca from Tell el-Kheleifeh, En-gedi, and Beer-sheba. Though they were found in Egypt, the Aramaic ostraca from Elephantine (5th cent. B.C.) are extremely important for Palestine.

***II. Greek and Coptic Ostraca.***–The earliest Greek inscription found in Palestine was the third-century B.C. bilingual (with Aramaic) ostracon from Khirbet el-Kôm. But the great bulk of Greek ostraca, many preserving documents of various kinds (chiefly tax receipts), have been found in Egypt. The texts of more than four thousand have been published, including major collections held by the United Kingdom, Belgium, Germany, Canada, and the United States. These texts illustrate in unexpected ways the everyday Greek speech of the common people of Egypt through the Ptolemaic, Roman, and Byzantine periods. Like the papyri, they help to illumine the syntax and lexicography of the NT as well as daily life in the ancient world. No remains of classical literature have been found on ostraca except for excerpts that were apparently used for school exercises, and possibly a quotation of some Sappho verses (cf. G. Vitelli, *et al.*, eds., *Papiri greci e latini* [1912-], no. 1300).

In some instances Christian literary texts are preserved on Egyptian ostraca. Most remarkable is a series of twenty ostraca of various sizes, probably from the 7th cent. A.D., inscribed with the Greek texts of parts of Matthew, Mark, Luke, and John. The longest continuous text is Lk. 22:40-71, written on ten numbered pieces. The texts, written in three different hands, attest the poor's interest in the NT text at the time of the Arab conquest. They also display an early form of the NT text that was widespread in Egypt — a form supported by the distinguished codices Vaticanus and Sinaiticus. Although these ostraca were cataloged among NT MSS by C. R. Gregory (0153), they are not MSS in the technical sense and have not been treated as such in subsequent inventories by K. Aland and others.

Coptic ostraca are numerous, especially from the Byzantine period, and of even more interest for Christian history than Greek ostraca. A Sahidic ostracon preserves the pericope on the woman taken in adultery (Jn. 7:53–8:11), which is otherwise unattested in the Sahidic MSS of the NT. A Christian hymn to Mary, akin to the canticles in Luke, and many Christian letters have been found. Coptic ostraca provide unusually valuable information on the religious and economic history of Egypt from the time of the Arab conquest onward.

*Bibliography.*–Y. Aharoni, *Arad Inscriptions* (Eng. tr. 1981); W. F. Albright, *BASOR,* 92 (Dec. 1943), 16-26; J. Černý, *Chronique d' Egypte,* 6 (1931), 212-224; F. M. Cross, *Andrews University Seminary Studies,* 13 (1975), 1-20; Deiss. *LAE,* pp. 50-60; L. T. Geraty, *BASOR,* 220 (Dec. 1975), 55-61; W. C. Hayes, *Scepter of Egypt,* II (1959); R. Hestrin, *et al.,* eds., *Inscriptions Reveal* (rev. ed. 1973); A. Lemaire, *Inscriptions Hébraïques, I: Les Ostraca* (1977); S. Moscati, *L'Epigrafia Ebraica Antica 1935-1950,* (1951); J. F. Oates, *et al., Bulletin of the American Society of Papyrologists,* 11 (1974), 1-35; A. F. Rainey, *PEQ* (1967), 32-41; A. A. Schiller, *Bulletin of the American Society of Papyrologists,* 13 (1976), 99-123; W. Shea, IEJ, 27 (1977), 16-27; H. Torczyner, *et al., Lachish I: The Lachish Letters* (1938); H. E. Winlock, *Monastery of Epiphanius at Thebes* (repr. 1973).

E. J. GOODSPEED L. T. GERATY

**OSTRICH** [Heb. *baṯ hayyaʿ^a^nâ*–'daughter of greed' or 'daughter of the desert'] (Isa. 13:21; 34:13; 43:20; Jer. 50:39; Mic. 1:8); AV OWL; NEB DESERT-OWL, OWL; [*Q yāʿēn*–'greedy one' or 'desert one'] (Lam. 4:3); [*r^e^nānîm*–'ringing cries'] (Job 39:13); AV PEACOCK. The largest bird now living (*Struthio camelus*); once an inhabitant of all the semi-desert regions of the Near East from Egypt to Mesopotamia, but now confined (in the wild) to Africa. Standing 2-2½ m. (6-8 ft.) tall and weighing up to 140 kg. (300 lbs.), the ostrich does not fly but runs very swiftly, using its wings as sails. It has been known to reach speeds of 80 km. per hour (50 mph) in open country.

The ostrich was hunted in the ancient Near East both for its feathers and for food. In the OT, however, it is listed among the "unclean" birds that the Israelites were forbidden to eat (Lev. 11:16; Dt. 14:15). In most of the other OT references the ostrich is associated with other wild creatures (esp. the jackal) that frequent uninhabited areas such as deserts and ruins. Two passages refer to its plaintive night cry (Job. 30:29; Mic. 1:8).

Although the identification of the *baṯ hayyaʿ^a^nâ* with the ostrich goes back to the Targums and the LXX (cf.

Assyrian cylinder seal showing a man, bow and arrow on his back and sword in hand, throttling an ostrich (9th-8th cent. B.C.) (The Trustees of the Pierpont Morgan Library)

*strouthós* in Lev. 11:16; Dt. 14:15; Job 30:29), G. R. Driver rejected this translation (though he accepted it for *yāʿēn* and *r^e^nānîm*) and argued that the expression denotes a type of owl (*HBD, s.v.* "Ostrich," "Owl"; *PEQ,* 87 [1955], 12f.; *see also* ABOMINATION, BIRDS OF). Many scholars have followed his suggestion (e.g., cf. NEB, NIV; see also *CHAL,* p. 138; Cansdale, pp. 190f.), although others continue to support the traditional identification with the ostrich. Some relate the terms *yaʿ^a^nâ* and *yāʿēn* to an Arabic term meaning "barren ground, desert" (the ostrich's habitat); others relate these terms to a Syriac term meaning "greedy" (perhaps from the ostrich's habit of swallowing any object it can find, even if it is inedible).

The hapax legomenon *r^e^nānîm* may be a poetic name for the ostrich derived from its disturbing cry (see BDB, p. 943). Although the Hebrew text of Job 39:13 is unintelligible and so has spawned numerous emendations and translations (see comms.), most scholars agree that *r^e^nānîm* refers to the ostrich. Verses 14f. probably refer to the female habit of covering her eggs with sand and leaving them to be warmed by the sun in the heat of the day. The eggs have a thick shell (about 6 mm. or ¼ in.), and thus only a few animals can destroy them. It is usually the male, with his darker plumage, who incubates the eggs at night. Extra eggs are placed near the incubated ones to serve as food for the young. When danger approaches, both the cock and the hen run off in an attempt to divert attention from the nest; the chicks' feathers provide good camouflage when they lie still. It was perhaps misunderstanding of these habits that led to the female ostrich's reputation for cruelty to her young (v. 16; cf. Lam. 4:3). The charge of stupidity (Job 39:17) may have derived from the ostrich's tendency to swallow hard objects or from its well-known habit, when cornered, of lowering its head rather than attempting to escape. In open country, however, an ostrich can easily outstrip a horse and its rider (v. 18; see Bodenheimer).

*Bibliography.*–F. S. Bodenheimer, *Animal and Man in Bible Lands* (Eng. tr. 1960), pp. 59f.; G. Cansdale, *Animals of Bible Lands* (1970), pp. 190-93; A. Parmelee, *All the Birds of the Bible* (1959), pp. 204-208, 225.

G. WYPER N. J. O.

**OTHNI** oth'nī [Heb. *ʿoṯnî*]. Son of Shemaiah; a Levitical gatekeeper (1 Ch. 26:7).

**OTHNIEL** oth'ni-əl [Heb. *ʿoṯnîʾēl*]. Reputations for good or ill are sometimes gained in a single important event in one's life. Othniel is remembered for his military victory over Debir (Josh. 15:17; Jgs. 1:13). Debir, previously known as Kiriath-sepher, had initially been conquered by Joshua (Josh. 10:38f.), but apparently needed to be recaptured after the tribal inheritances had been allotted. Caleb had been granted a portion in Judah (Josh. 15:13) and needed help capturing Debir. He promised his daughter Achsah as a wife to whoever would smite Debir. Othniel, Caleb's younger relative (either brother or nephew), rose to the challenge and captured Debir. At the urging of Achsah and through her request, Caleb gave her and Othniel the "upper and lower springs" as land for their use (Josh. 15:19; Jgs. 1:15).

In addition to this military exploit, Othniel is remembered as the first judge and deliverer of Israel following the death of Joshua. Without a theocratic mediator, Israel followed the desires of its heart and was quickly enticed to worship Baal, the native deity of the land (Jgs. 3:7). A certain Cushan-rishathaim, king of Mesopotamia, was the instrument of God's wrath into whose hand Yahweh sold Israel (Jgs. 3:8). For eight years Israel was "slave" of Cushan-rishathaim, but Israel's cries for help were answered by Yahweh in raising up a deliverer for His people — Othniel.

He was the first of many such deliverers, and the pericope (Jgs. 3:7-11) detailing Othniel's role is paradigmatic of successive deliverers. That the deliverer and judge is raised up by Yahweh indicates that the Lord's leadership is paramount and not that of the deliverer. Whatever personal and military qualities Othniel may have had, his role in this event is determined not by the people's choice but by Yahweh's selection. Yahweh's kingship is served by a leader of His choosing.

Furthermore, the "Spirit of the Lord" (Jgs. 3:10) came upon Othniel to enable him for his task as it did his successors Gideon (6:34), Jephthah (11:29), and Samson (14:6). The Spirit of the Lord frequently was granted those who were Yahweh's co-workers in the working out of His plan of salvation in history. Othniel was endowed with this Spirit so that he could judge Israel, set it on the pathway of obedience, and wage warfare against the enemies of the Lord and His people. The benefits of the Spirit such as wisdom, understanding, counsel, might, and fear of the Lord were apparently granted Othniel as he judged (i.e., set on the right course) Israel and overcame its oppressor.

Othniel's work resulted in a period of "rest" for forty years (Jgs. 3:11), a characteristic refrain in Judges. The unrest of Israel was a consequence of disloyality to its covenant suzerain (2:20). Apostasy from Yahweh, forgetting Yahweh's saving acts which gave it birth (2:10), mingling with the people of the land, and adopting their ways (2:6–3:6) all contributed to making the land of promised rest a land of unrest. The deliverers thus had to do more than win battles against external foes — they had to redirect the loyalties of the people as well. Othniel's judging was more than condemnation; it was also a work of leading to reconciliation. Othniel delivered Israel from external oppression (Cushan-rishathaim) and saved it from its own evil ways. Only then could the land return to the true rest.

D. H. ENGELHARD

**OTHONIAH** oth-ə-nī'ə [Gk. *Othonias*]; AV, NEB, OTHONIAS oth-ə-nī'əs. A layman who had married a foreign woman and was required to divorce her (1 Esd. 9:28); called MATTANIAH (**11**) in Ezr. 10:27.

**OUCHES.** An archaic term designating a setting for a precious stone, used by the AV to translate Heb. *mišbᵉṣôṯ* in Ex. 28:11, 13f., 25; 39:6, 13, 16, 18 (RSV "settings"; NEB "rosettes"). The Hebrew term is probably derived from the verb *šāḇaṣ*, "weave in a pattern"; thus the settings were not of solid gold but were formed of gold wire woven around the stones (cf. RSV "settings of gold filigree" when *mišbᵉṣôṯ* is combined with *zāhāḇ*, "gold"; *see* FILIGREE). Ex. 39:3 describes how this wire was produced.

**OUTCAST** [ Heb. niphal of *nāḏaḥ* and *dāḥah*–'be cast out, scattered']; AV also EXPELLED, DRIVEN OUT; NEB also BANISH, BANISHMENT, SCATTERED SONS, DRIVEN OUT, HOMELESS (PEOPLE), DISPERSED. As used by the RSV, "outcast" generally refers to a people who have been expelled from their homeland. The Israelites were warned that their apostasy would be punished by banishment from their land (cf. Dt. 28:63f.) — a threat that was fulfilled when they were taken into exile by Assyria and Babylon (*see* CAPTIVITY). When they repented, however, they were promised a restoration to their homeland (cf. Dt. 30:3-5; Isa. 11:11f.; 56:8; Jer. 30:17f.; Zeph. 3:19; cf. also Ps. 147:2). Many of Israel's neighbors and enemies also suffered banishment (e.g., Moab, Isa. 16:3f.; cf. Jer. 30:16).

Absalom chose banishment to the Aramean kingdom of Geshur, the home of his maternal grandfather (2 S. 13:37f.), to escape punishment for murdering his half-brother Amnon (vv. 28f.; *see* PUNISHMENTS); but through the intervention of Joab and a woman of Tekoa, David was later persuaded to restore Absalom to his own home (14:13f., 21-24).

*See also* FUGITIVE; DISPERSION. N. J. O.

**OUTER COURT.** *See* TEMPLE; *see also* floor plan in EZEKIEL.

**OUTER DARKNESS** [Gk. *skótos exṓteron*]; NEB THE DARK. An expression occurring only in Matthew (8:12; 22:13; 25:30), describing the future state of those who because of their unfaithfulness have been denied entrance into the brightly lit banquet hall that symbolizes the joy of the Kingdom. In Jewish literature "darkness" was associated with the place of eternal punishment (cf. 1 En. 103:5-8: "Woe to you, ye sinners, when ye have died, . . . and into darkness and chains and a burning flame where there is grievous judgement shall your spirits enter; and the great judgement shall be for all the generations of the world . . ." [*APOT,* II, 275]; for rabbinical references, see SB, IV, 1075-83), and Jesus was apparently using it in the same sense.

*See also* DARK; GNASH; HELL. N. J. O.

**OUTER NATURE** [Gk. *éxō ánthrōpos*] (2 Cor. 4:16); AV OUTWARD MAN; NEB OUTWARD HUMANITY. *See* INNER MAN; NEW MAN.

**OUTER TENT.** The RSV translation of Gk. *hē prṓtē skēnḗ* (lit. "the first tent/tabernacle"; cf. AV, NEB) in He. 9:2, 6, 8. The outer tent (HOLY PLACE) was the first part of the TABERNACLE that was entered by the high priest on the Day of Atonement; it was separated from the "second" (*deutéra,* v. 7; i.e., the Holy of Holies) by a curtain (cf. vv. 2f.). Many commentators, with the RSV, interpret the phrase in v. 8 in the same way as in vv. 2 and 6 (e.g., J. Moffatt [*ICC,* 1924]; cf. also *TDNT,* VII, *s.v.* σκηνή [W. Michaelis]); according to this view, the Holy Place was a *parabolḗ* (v. 10, RSV "symbolic"), because it blocked the people's access to the presence of God. Others, however, with the NEB ("the earlier tent"), have interpreted the phrase to mean that the entire tabernacle with its Levitical ritual (cf. v. 1) was a sign that free access to God was not yet possible (e.g., F. F. Bruce [*NICNT,* 1964]; P. E. Hughes [1977]). N. J. O.

**OUTGOINGS** [pl. of Heb. *môṣā'*] (Ps. 65:8 [MT 9]). The Heb. *môṣā'* (<*yāṣā'*, "go forth") here probably refers to the place from which the morning and evening go forth, i.e., the east and the west, and hence is an expression (merismus) for the whole earth (so A. A. Anderson, *Psalms,* I [*NCBC,* repr. 1981], p. 470; BDB, p. 425). Others, however, think it refers to "the limits of the day, and so the goings out of morning and evening worship in the temple" (C. A. Briggs and E. G. Briggs, comm. on Psalms, II [*ICC,* 1907], 82; on p. 85 Briggs notes that *môṣā'* in Ps. 19:6 [ MT 7] refers to dawn). G. A. L.

**OUTLANDISH.** Used by the AV with its original meaning "out of the land," i.e., "foreign" (RSV, NEB), translating Heb. *noḵrî* (Neh. 13:26). Nehemiah used the argument from the history of Solomon and his foreign wives (cf. 1 K. 11:1-10) to convince the Jewish leaders of the extreme danger brought in by intermarriage with foreigners.

**OUTRAGE; OUTRAGEOUS.** The adjective in Prov. 27:4, AV, translates Heb. *šeṭep,* "flood." "Anger is overwhelming" (RSV) and "anger is a deluge" (NEB) are better translations. The RSV uses the verb in He. 10:29

to translate Gk. *enybrízō*, "insult, offend, outrage" (AV "hath done despite unto"; NEB "affronted").

**OUTROADS.** An obsolete term (cf. its opposite, "inroads," still used in modern English) used by the AV to translate Gk. *exodeúō*, "go forth, march out," in 1 Macc. 15:41 ("that . . . they might make outroads upon the ways of Judea"; cf. RSV "make raids"; NEB "patrol").

**OUTSIDER** [Heb. *zar*] (Ex. 29:33; 30:33; Lev. 22:10, 12f.); AV STRANGER; NEB UNQUALIFIED PERSON; [Gk. *idiṓtēs*] (1 Cor. 14:16, 23f.); AV UNLEARNED; NEB PLAIN MAN, UNINSTRUCTED PERSON; RSV mg. "him that is without gifts" (v. 16); [*ho éxō* (1 Cor. 5:12; Col. 4:5; 1 Thess. 4:12), *ho éxōthen* (1 Tim. 3:7)]; AV "them that are without"; NEB also "those outside your own number," "the non-Christian public."

*Hoi éxō* and *hoi éxōthen* clearly refer to those outside the Christian fellowship (cf. "those outside," Mk. 4:11). The meaning of *idiṓtēs*, however, is disputed. Bauer (rev., pp. 59f., 370) interprets literally the expression *ho anaplērṓn tón tópon toú idiṓtou*: "he who takes the place of the inquirer" (i.e., a group of proselytes or catechumens — distinct from both the *pistoí* ["believers"] and the *ápistoi* ["unbelievers"; cf. vv. 22-24] — who had a part of the room reserved for them). Most scholars, however, interpret the expression as referring figuratively to those in the position of the non-ecstatic who could not understand tongue-speaking (*see* Tongues, Gift of). Some identify the *idiṓtai* with the *ápistoi* ("unbelievers") with whom they are mentioned in vv. 23f. (e.g., see *TDNT*, III, *s.v.* ἰδιώτης [H. Schlier]; cf. H. Conzelmann, *1 Corinthians* [Eng. tr., *Hermeneia*, 1975], pp. 238f.).

*See also* Stranger (OT). N. J. O.

**OUTWARD MAN; OUTWARD HUMANITY.** *See* Outer Nature.

**OVEN** [Heb. *tannûr*; Gk. *klíbanos*]; NEB also FURNACE, STOVE. The Heb. *tannûr* refers to the small domestic oven (Ex. 8:3 [MT 7:28]; Lev. 11:35) used for baking breads of various types (Lev. 2:4; 7:9; 26:26). It is seen blazing with fire as a sign of Yahweh's wrath (Ps. 21:9 [MT 10]; Mal. 4:1 [MT 3:19]; cf. "furnace" in Isa. 31:9). The results of Yahweh's wrath are seen in Lam. 5:10, where the people's skin is as hot as an oven, due to a scorching famine. A portable, smoking *tannûr* (RSV "fire pot") is a symbol of Yahweh's presence before Abraham in Gen. 15:17. In Hos. 7:4, 6f. wicked ones in Israel burn hot like an oven with evil deeds and intrigue. The LXX translates *tannûr* by *klíbanos* except in Isa. 31:9. The NT also uses *klíbanos* (Mt. 6:30 par. Lk. 12:28). (On Neh. 3:11 and 12:38, *see* Ovens, Tower of the.)

Many different cooking devices are known from all over the Near East, from earliest times to the present. The *tannûr* was the most common baking oven, with two basic types, both made of clay. One was cylindrical or slightly conical, about 70-100 cm. (27-39 in.) high and 50-60 cm. (20-24 in.) wide, with an open top. It was usually placed in the ground, either indoors or with a small cubical hut above it to keep out the rain. The other was about the same size, but more egg-shaped, even pointed, with small openings in the top and the base. It was usually above ground, topped with a flat stone or clay cover. Large, inverted water jugs were sometimes used as substitutes.

A fire was first built on a layer of small stones on the oven floor. Then the coals were raked or scooped out so that the bread dough could be placed against the hot inner walls (though occasionally outside as well), or on the

Small oven at Qumrân (W. S. LaSor)

hot stones, and peeled off when done. In some cases, the walls were covered with mud or potsherds the better to preserve heat. The common fuels were wood, charcoal, dried grasses and weeds (cf. Mt. 6:30 par. Lk. 12:28), straw, and animal dung (cf. Ezk. 4:12, 15).

See also Bread IV; Furnace.

***Bibliography.***–G. Dalman, *Arbeit und Sitte in Palästina*, IV (1935), 1-152 and plates 17-25a; R. J. Forbes, *Studies in Ancient Technology*, VI (1966), 58-67; C. Singer, *et al.*, eds., *History of Technology*, I (1954), 272f.; II (1956), 118-121.

D. M. HOWARD, JR.

**OVENS, TOWER OF THE** [Heb. *migdal hattannûrîm*]; AV TOWER OF THE FURNACES. A tower in the wall of Jerusalem, rebuilt under Nehemiah (Neh. 3:11; 12:38). It was in the northwestern corner of the city, near the Broad Wall (cf. 3:8; 12:38). Very likely it was the tower built as a fortification of the Corner Gate by King Uzziah (2 Ch. 26:9). The name suggests that baker's ovens were located in this vincinity (*see* Bakers' Street). *See also* Jerusalem III.F.2.d.

**OVERCHARGE.** A term used twice by the AV in the archaic sense "to weigh down with an excessive load." It translates Gk. *barýnomai* (lit. "be weighed down" [so RSV]) in Lk. 21:34 and *epibaréō* (lit. "weigh down"; RSV "put it too severely") in 2 Cor. 2:5.

**OVERCOME** [Heb. niphal of *hāyâ*–'happen, occur' (Dnl. 8:27), *hālam*–'strike' (Isa. 28:1), *ḥāzaq*–'be strong' (1 K. 16:22), *yākōl*–'be able to, can' (Nu. 13:30; Jer. 20:10f.), hiphil of *nāḵâ*–'strike, hit,' 'conquer' (1 S. 30:1), *'āḇar*–'cross, go over' (Jer. 23:9), *qûṣ*–'feel disgust, dread' (Nu. 22:3), *rûḏ*–'roam' (Ps. 55:2 [MT 3])]; AV also "faint," "smite," (BE) DISTRESSED, "mourn"; NEB also "prove stronger," CONQUER, "catch," ATTACK, etc.; [Gk. *nikáō* (1 Jn. 2:13f.; 4:4; 5:4f.; etc.), *katalambánō*–'seize', *kataphérō*, *hēttáomai*–'be defeated (by), succumb (to)']; AV also "astonished," "comprehended," "sunk down"; NEB also OVERPOWER, MASTER, CONQUER, DEFEAT, BE VICTOR OVER, "be beside oneself."

The RSV OT uses "overcome" in several different contexts. In military contexts "overcome" refers to the conquest of one people or faction by another. Thus the Amalekites conquer Ziklag (1 S. 30:1), and Omri's followers prove too strong for Tibni's supporters (1 K. 16:22). The great numbers of the Hebrews apparently caused the Moabites to be overcome with fear (Nu. 22:3; cf. Ex. 1:12, where the same verb is used to describe the Egyptians' dread of the rapidly multiplying Hebrews). In Nu. 13:30 Caleb confidently predicts that the Hebrews can conquer Canaan. Here *yāḵôl nûḵal* (lit. "to be able we are able"), the infinitive absolute followed by a finite verb form, expresses emphasis, which the RSV, AV, and NEB amplify a bit more than the Hebrew form warrants (cf. more accurate translations in the NIV, JB, NAB).

The Heb. *yāḵōl* also occurs in the context of a more personal or individual use of "overcome": Jeremiah's enemies hoped to silence his opposition to them, but he was confident that, since the Lord was on his side, he would not be overcome (Jer. 20:10f.; cf. v. 7, where the same verb is translated "prevail"). Similarly, the psalmist prayed for help because he was overwhelmed by his troubles (Ps. 55:2), which apparently refers to oppression by enemies (v. 3). Although the form and precise meaning of MT *'ārîḏ* are problematic (see comms.), the context seems to require a meaning like the RSV. Another problematic text is Dnl. 8:27, where the RSV translates the niphal of *hāyâ* as "overcome" (AV "fainted" and NEB "strength failed" are similar). Usually this form of the verb means "was fulfilled, brought about," but that meaning hardly fits the context here. Although scholars have suggested various explanations and emendations (see comms.), none is satisfactory.

Two texts speak of being overcome by wine. In both instances the verbs used are unusual. In Isa. 28:1 the prophet pronounces a woe against the drunkards of Ephraim (i.e., the northern kingdom), who are "overcome by wine" (Heb. *h^alûmê yāyin,* lit. "those struck [down] by wine"; usually *hālam* means simply "hit"). In Jer. 23:9 Jeremiah likens his prophetic experience to drunkenness; cf. the similar use of *'āḇar* with water (i.e., a flood that overwhelms a person) in Jonah 2:4 (cf. also Ps. 38:4 [MT 5]).

The most common NT term is Gk. *nikáō,* the usual Greek word for gaining victory in individual physical conflict (as in Lk. 11:22) or war. It is related to the nouns for "victory," *níkē* (1 Jn. 5:4) and *níkos* (Mt. 12:20; 1 Cor. 15:54f., 57). In the NT it is usually applied to winning in spiritual or eschatological conflict, either by Christ (e.g., Jn. 16:33) or the believers (e.g., Rom. 12:21; cf. the translation "prevail" in 3:4). Bauernfeind correctly says that in the NT it is "a word of promise, an eschatological word" (*TDNT,* IV, 945). In addition to the six times it appears in 1 John, *nikáō* is used often in Revelation (2:7, 11, 17, 26; 3:5, 12, 21; 5:5; 6:2; 11:7; 12:11; 13:7; 15:2; 17:14; 21:7; RSV always "conquer"). At the close of each of the seven letters of Rev. 2–3 the believer who "conquers" is promised an eschatological reward. *See also* CONQUER.

In Jn. 1:5 the term is *katalambánō,* which can mean "win, make one's own," "suppress," or perhaps even "grasp" in an intellectual sense, i.e., "comprehend." This term is only one part of a difficult verse that has received varying interpretations. For more complete discussion see the comms.; also Bauer, rev., p. 413.

In Acts 20:9, the story of Eutychus, both "sank into (a deep sleep)" and "being overcome (by sleep)" use passive forms of Gk. *katapherō.* The first use is in the present tense, probably indicating the process of falling asleep, while the second use is a past tense (aorist) that would indicate being sound asleep (cf. F. F. Bruce, *Acts of the Apostles* [2nd ed. 1952], p. 373).

"What overcomes a man" in 2 Pet. 2:19 represents Gk. *hǭ . . . tis hḗttētai,* lit. "by which (thing) . . . someone is defeated." The same verb is translated "(be) overpowered" in the next verse.

In Mk. 5:42 RSV "overcome" is used to avoid an awkward rendering of the Gk. *exéstēsan ekstásei megálȩ̄* (lit. "amazed with great amazement"), probably an example of Semitic influence on the style of NT Greek (cf. BDF, §198[6]).

R. H. MOUNCE
G. A. L.

**OVERLAY** [Heb. *ṣāpâ*] (Ex. 25–27; 30:3, 5; 36–37; 38:2, 6, 28; 1 K. 6:20ff.; 10:18; 2 K. 18:16; 2 Ch. 3:4; 4:9; 9:17); NEB also PLATE; [*ṣippûy*] (Ex. 38:17, 19); [*ṭû(a)ḥ*] (1 Ch. 29:4); [*ḥāpâ*] (2 Ch. 3:8f.); [*rāqa'*] (Isa. 40:19); AV SPREAD OVER; NEB "covers with plate"; [*tāpaś*] (Hab. 2:19); AV LAID OVER; NEB ENCASED. Both the tabernacle and the temple extensively used overlay of gold, silver, and bronze. In 2 K. 18:16 Hezekiah stripped the overlay from the doors of the temple to provide the thirty talents of gold demanded by Sennacherib. Isa. 40:19 and Hab. 2:19 refer to the custom of overlaying wooden idols with gold.

**OVERPASS.** An obsolete verb used three times by the AV as a translation of Heb. *'āḇar* ("pass over"). In Ps. 57:1 (MT 2) and Isa. 26:20 it has the meaning "pass" or "pass by" (cf. RSV, NEB). In Jer. 5:28 it means "pass over the boundaries" (cf. RSV "know no bounds").

**OVERPLUS.** The AV translation of Heb. *hā'ōḏēp̄* (part. of *'āḏap,* "remain over"), i.e., "that which remains over, surplus," in Lev. 25:27 (RSV "overpayment"; NEB balance").

**OVERSEER; OVERSIGHT.** In the RSV OT, usually the translation of a form of Heb. *pāqaḏ* ("appoint"; e.g., hiphil in Gen. 39:4f.; hophal in 2 K. 12:11 [MT 12]) or one of its cognates: *pāqîḏ* ("officer," e.g., Gen. 41:34) and *p^equddâ* ("commission," e.g., Nu. 3:32). Other OT terms are *mišmereṯ* ("custody, service," Nu. 3:32) and the piel of *nāṣaḥ* ("supervise," 2 Ch. 2:18 [MT 17]; Ezr. 3:8f.). These terms designate various types of supervisors or officers; e.g., a steward in charge of an Egyptian officer's house (Joseph, Gen. 39:4f.); foremen assigned to supervise slave levies (2 Ch. 2:2, 18); overseers of various tasks in the tabernacle and temple (e.g., Nu. 3:32; 2 Ch. 31:13; cf. Ezk. 44:11).

In the NT Gk. *epískopos* is rendered "overseer" by the AV and some editions of the RSV in Acts 20:28; cf. also the RSV mg. of Phil. 1:1 (AV, RSV, NEB, "bishop"). The AV (cf. RSV mg.), following certain ancient MSS, renders "take oversight" for *episkopéō* in 1 Pet. 5:2. *See* BISHOP: GENERAL II; GUARDIAN.

N. J. O.

**OWL** [Heb. *kôs*] (Lev. 11:17; Ps. 102:6; Zeph. 2:14 [emended reading of the Hebrew text, which has *qôl,* "voice"]; "little owl," Dt. 14:16); AV also "voice" (Zeph. 2:14); NEB also TAWNY OWL; [*yamšûp, yamšôp*] (Isa. 34:11; "great owl," Dt. 14:16); NEB SCREECH-OWL; [*qippôz*] (Isa. 34:15); NEB SAND-PARTRIDGE. The name of the nocturnal birds of prey forming the order *Strigiformes.* All owls are characterized by a large head and eyes, a short hooked bill, and powerful talons.

Identifying Hebrew terms for owls has always caused problems for translators, as the widely varying translations show. Most scholars agree that Heb. *kôs* and *yamšûp* designate owls, although there is disagreement about the species they refer to. There is less agreement about *qippôz* (Isa. 34:15), which has often been translated "arrowsnake" (cf. ASV "dart-snake"; JB "viper"), based on a derivation from Aram. *q^epaz* ("leap, spring"); others, however, prefer the translation "owl," since the arrow snake does not incubate eggs (cf. BDB; KoB; KD). The NEB's translation "sand-partridge" follows the suggestion of G. R. Driver. Many scholars also believe that Heb. *baṯ ya'^anâ* (RSV "ostrich") designates a species of owl (so AV, NEB; *see*

Silver hemiobol showing an owl. The inscription reads "Yehezekiah the satrap" (Jerusalem, *ca.* 350 B.C.) (Israel Museum, Jerusalem)

OSTRICH). On the AV's rendering "screech owl" for Heb. *lîlîṯ* in Isa. 34:14, *see* NIGHT HAG

Owls are listed among the "birds of abomination" that the Israelites were forbidden to eat (Lev. 11:17 [here the RSV renders *kôs* "owl" but, inexplicably, renders *yamsûp* IBIS]; Dt. 14:16). Probably they were considered unclean because they eat flesh with blood in it. G. R. Driver (*PEQ*, 87 [1955], 5-20) attempted a scientific analysis of the birds on these lists (Lev. 11:13-19; Dt. 14: 11-20) and concluded that no less than eight of the terms refer to various kinds of owls, beginning with the largest species and ending with the smallest (*see* ABOMINATION, BIRDS OF; see also *HDB*). The NEB has largely followed his suggestions. These identifications must remain tentative at best, however. Because owls are basically nocturnal birds, it is unlikely that ancient peoples could have observed them closely enough to identify so many species; moreover, several of the birds on Driver's list appear in Palestine only rarely or in migration. Furthermore, as Driver himself conceded, "some of the words may be alternative or local names for the same bird" (*HDB*).

While all identifications of Hebrew terms with particular species of owls remain tentative, it is quite possible that the OT writers were familiar with some of the species that are now present in Palestine. The most common is the little owl (*Athene noctua*), which is only about 27 cm. (10½ in.) long and can be found nearly everywhere, especially in lonely places such as thickets, tombs, and ruins. "Little owl" is the AV and RSV translation of *kôs* in Dt. 14:16 (Driver used this translation for *tinšemeṯ;* see NEB Lev. 11:18; Dt. 14:16; cf. RSV "water hen"). The eagle owl *(Bubo bubo),* the largest and fiercest of the owls in Palestine (about 45 cm., 18 in. long), is common in semi-desert areas covered with scrub; it is Driver's translation of *baṯ yaʿanâ* (Lev. 11:16; Dt. 14:15; RSV "ostrich"). The tiny scops owl *(Otus scops),* only about 20 cm. (8 in.) in length, is a summer visitor to Palestine. Although it is seldom seen, its call is often heard. Driver suggested this as the bird designated by *qāʾāṯ* (RSV "pelican," Lev. 11:18; Dt. 14:17). The tawny owl (Driver's translation of *qāʾaṯ* (see NEB Lev. 11:17; Dt. 14:16), about 40 cm. (16 in.) in length, is a fairly common resident in Palestine; but like the scops owl it is heard much more often than it is seen. The screech owl (Driver's translation of *yanšûp*; cf. RSV "great owl," Dt. 14:16), about 33 cm. (13 in.) in length, is also abundant in Palestine. Although seldom seen by day, it is easily recognized by its peculiar hissing or snoring noises and its raucous screech in flight. The short-eared owl (Driver's translation of *taḥmās,* Lev. 11:16; Dt. 14:15; RSV "night hawk") migrates through Palestine, and the long-eared owl (Driver's translation of *šāḥap*, Lev. 11:16; Dt. 14:15; RSV "sea gull"), rarely seen, visits the forests of Palestine during the winter. The fisher owl (Driver's translation of *šālaḵ*, Lev. 11:17; RSV "cormorant") is not known to reside in Palestine.

Apart from the references in Lev. 11 and Dt. 14, owls appear in the OT only figuratively. Along with other wild creatures that haunt wastelands and ruins, the owl symbolizes the loneliness of a tormented psalmist (Ps. 102:6 [MT 7]) and the desolation of nations upon which the judgment of the Lord has descended (Edom, Isa. 34:11, 15; Assyria, Zeph. 2:14).

***Bibliography.***–G. Cansdale, *Animals of Bible Lands* (1970), pp. 147-49, 175f.; *HDB*; A. Parmelee, *All the Birds of the Bible* (1959), pp. 106, 110f.; G. R. Driver, *PEQ*, 87 (1955), 5-20. N. J. O.

**OWL, SCREECH.** *See* NIGHT HAG; OWL.

**OX** ōx [Gk. *Ōx*]. Grandfather of Judith; father of Merari; descendant of Israel (Jth. 8:1).

**OX; OXEN** [Heb. *šôr*] (Gen. 32:5 [MT 6]; 49:6; Ex. 20:17; etc.); AV also BULLOCK, "wall" (reading *šûr*, Gen. 49:6); NEB also BULL, CATTLE, HERD; [*bāqār*] (Gen. 12:16; 20:14; 21:27; etc.); [*ben-habbāqār*–'son of the herd,' 'calf,' 'ox'] (Isa. 65:25); AV BULLOCK; NEB CATTLE; [*par*–'young bull'] (Ex. 24:5); NEB BULL; [pl. of *'elep*–'cattle'] (Ps. 8:7 [MT 8]; Isa. 30:24); [Aram. *tôr*] (Dnl. 4:25, 32f. [MT 22, 29f.]; 5:21); [Gk. *boús*–'bull,' 'cow'] (Lk. 13:15; 14:5, 19; Jn. 2:14f.; 1 Cor. 9:9; 1 Tim. 5:18); NEB also CATTLE; [*taúros*–'bull'] (Mt. 22:4; Acts 14:13); NEB also BULLOCK; [*móschos*–'calf,' 'young bull,' 'ox'] (Rev. 4:7); AV CALF. A domesticated, horned, bovine mammal descended from *Bos primigenius* (called the aurochs in Europe; *see* WILD OX); more specifically, a full-grown male ox. Heb. *bāqār* (also rendered "herd," "cattle," etc.) is a collective term for bovine cattle, which can include bulls, cows, calves, and heifers. Heb. *šôr* and the Aramaic cognate *tôr,* on the other hand, usually denote the adult male of the species, i.e., a bull or steer. *See* CATTLE.

On Dt. 22:10, *see* YOKE; on Dt. 25:4 (LXX quoted in 1 Cor. 9:9; 1 Tim. 5:18), *see* MUZZLE. N. J. O.

**OX-GOAD.** *See* GOAD.

**OXYRHYNCHUS SAYINGS OF JESUS.** *See* LOGIA II.

**OZEM** ō'zəm [Heb. *'ōṣem*].

**1.** The sixth son of Jesse and older brother of David (1 Ch. 2:15). The LXX (*Asom*) and Vulgate readings suggest that his name should be pointed *'āṣōm*.

**2.** The fourth son of Jerahmeel, a descendant of Judah (1 Ch. 2:25).

**OZIAS** ō-zī'əs.

**1.** (AV, NEB, Jth. 6:15f.; 7:23; 8:9; etc.). *See* UZZIAH **2.**

**2.** (2 Esd. 1:2, AV). *See* UZZI **7.**

**3.** (Mt. 1:8f., AV). *See* UZZIAH **1.**

**OZIEL** ō'zi-əl [Gk. *Oziēl*]. An ancestor of Judith (Jth. 8:1).

**OZIUS** ō-zī'əs (1 Esd. 5:31, NEB). *See* Uzzah **5.**

**OZNI** oz'nī [Heb. *'oznî*–'my ear'(?)]. A descendant of Gad and head of the family of the Oznites (Nu. 26:16). He is called Ezbon in Gen. 46:16.

**OZNITES** oz'nīts [Heb. *hā'oznî*]. The clan descended from Ozni (Nu. 26:16).

**OZORA** ō-zôr'ə (1 Esd. 9:34, AV). *See* Ezora.

# P

**P.** The Priestly source in the Pentateuch, according to the Graf-Wellhausen development hypothesis. P is generally dated after the Babylonian Exile. *See* CRITICISM II.D.5.

**PAARAI** pā'ə-rī [Heb. *paʿᵃray*]. An ARBITE; one of David's valiant men known as the "thirty" (2 S. 23:35). He is called "Naarai the son of Ezbai" in 1 Ch. 11:37.

**PACATIANA** pā-kə-ti-ā'nə, pak-ə-tī'ə-nə. The AV follows certain late Greek MSS in adding a subscription to 1 Timothy: "The first to Timothy was written from Laodicea, which is the chiefest city of Phrygia Pacatiana [Gk. *Pakatianē*]." The name did not appear until *ca.* A.D. 300, when Diocletian divided the province of Asia into seven parts; two of the new provinces were named Phrygia Prima (Pacatiana) and Phrygia Secunda (Salutaris). See *HDB,* III, 865.

**PACE** [Heb. *regel*–'foot'] (Gen. 33:14); AV GO, "be able to endure"; [infinitive of *rāḵaḇ*–'ride'] (2 K. 4:24); AV RIDING; [*ṣaʿaḏ*] (2 S. 6:13); NEB STEP. A rate of movement (walking [Gen. 33:14]; riding an ass [2 K. 4:24]); or a distance based on one human step (2 S. 6:13).

**PACHON** pā'kōn [Gk. *Pachōn*]. The name of the ninth month (April 26-May 25) in the Egyptian calendar (3 Macc. 6:38).

**PADAN; PADDAN** pad'ən. *See* PADDAN-ARAM.

**PADDAN-ARAM** pad'ən-ā'ram or -âr'əm [Heb. *paddan ᵓᵃrām*; Gk. *Mesopotamia, Mesopotamia Syrias*]; AV PADAN-ARAM. The region of Harran in upper Mesopotamia. "Paddan-aram" and "Haran" may be dialectical variants for the same locality, since *padānu* and *ḫarrānu* are synonyms for "road" or "caravan route" in Akkadian. It should not be identified with Tell Feddan, which R. O'Callaghan called "a factitious localization of Paddan Aram in later Syrian tradition" (*Aram Naharaim* [1948], p. 96).

In the Bible the name designates the home of Bethuel, father of Isaac's wife Rebekah (Gen. 25:20). Jacob was sent there by his father to find a wife and to escape his brother Esau's wrath (ch. 28). Jacob lived in Paddan-aram about twenty years, tending the flocks of his father-in-law Laban as the bride price for his wives Leah and Rachel. In this way he also earned a sizable flock for himself before returning to the land of Canaan. This area is referred to simply as "Paddan" in 48:7, but this may be a textual error (cf. the NEB); the LXX, which includes *tḗs Syrias,* may indicate a text that read "Paddan-aram" (the Sam. and Syr. also support this reading). The people who lived in the area were called "Arameans" (31:24) and the language was "Aramaic" (v. 47). D. H. MADVIG

**PADDLE.** *See* STICK.

**PADON** pā'don [Heb. *pāḏôn*; Gk. Apoc. *Phadōn, Phalaios*]; AV Apoc., NEB Apoc., PHALEAS. The head of a family of temple servants (NETHINIM) who returned from exile with Zerubbabel (Ezr. 2:44 par. Neh. 7:41; 1 Esd. 5:29).

**PAEDIAS** pə-dī'əs (1 Esd. 9:34, NEB). *See* BEDEIAH.

**PAGANS.** A term increasingly used in modern versions as an occasional rendering for Gk. *éthnē,* which the AV translates "Gentiles." Moffatt used "pagans" rather frequently in the OT and four places in the NT (Mt. 5:47, where the original is *ethnikoí*; 1 Cor. 10:20; 12:2; Eph. 4:17). Goodspeed used "heathen" in such passages. "Pagans" appears in Mt. 5:47 (JB, NIV); 1 Cor. 5:1 (RSV, NEB, JB, NIV); 10:20 (RSV, NIV); 12:2 (NASB, NEB, JB, NIV); Eph. 2:11 (JB); 4:17 (NEB, JB); 1 Thess. 4:5 (NEB, JB, NIV); 1 Pet. 2:12 and 4:3 (NEB, JB, NIV). The guiding principle in most instances is that when *éthnē* is used in communications addressed to churches that are mainly gentile in such a way as to distinguish the *éthnē* from the readers, then the rendering "pagans" is appropriate.

*See also* NATIONS. E. F. H.

**PAGIEL** pā'gi-əl [Heb. *pagʿîᵓēl*–'fortune of God' (?)]. Son of Ochran and leader of the tribe of Asher (Nu. 1:13; 2:27; 7:72, 77; 10:26). He was one of twelve tribal leaders who assisted Moses in taking the census and who made offerings at the dedication of the tabernacle.

**PAHATH-MOAB** pā'hath mō'ab [Heb. *paḥaṯ môᵓāḇ*–'governor of Moab'; Gk. *Phaathmōab*]; AV Apoc. also PHAATH MOAB (1 Esd. 5:11); NEB Apoc. PHAATH-MOAB. Possibly the tribal name of the 2,812 descendants, divided among the clans of Jeshua and Joab, who returned from the Babylonian captivity under the leadership of Zerubbabel (*ca.* 538 B.C.; Ezr. 2:6; Neh. 7:11 has 2,818). An additional two hundred males from the tribe of Pahath-moab, led by Eliehoenai, traveled with Ezra from Babylon to Judah (*ca.* 458 B.C.; Ezr. 8:4). After Ezra denounced mixed marriages, some of the members of the tribe put away their foreign wives (Ezr. 10:30). During the governorship of Nehemiah (*ca.* 445 B.C.), Hasshub (a son of Pahath-moab), and presumably his associates, repaired a portion of the wall of Jerusalem as well as the "Tower of the Ovens" (Neh. 3:11). Eventually an individual named Pahath-moab, perhaps the clan chief, was among those who affixed their names to the covenant document drawn up during the days of Nehemiah (Neh. 10:14 [MT 15]).

It has been suggested that the tribal name was derived from someone who had in fact been the governor of Moab. B. Mazar (*IEJ*, 7 [1957], 232) has plausibly suggested that some of the Reubenites who had settled in the area of Moab (1 Ch. 5:3-8) and who had been captured and deported by Tiglath-pileser III (*ca.* 733 B.C.) were the core of this tribe. The returnees noted above would thus be descendants of these early exiled Israelites.

C. G. RASMUSSEN

**PAI** pā'ī, pī [Heb. *pā'î*; Gk. *Phogōr*]. The royal city of Hadad or Hadar, king of Edom (1 Ch. 1:50). The name should probably be read "Pau" (Heb. *pā'û*, "groaning," "bleating"; so Lucian, Syr., Vulg., Tg.), as in Gen. 36:39. Neither verse indicates its location; it has not been identified.

**PAIN; PAINFUL** [Heb. *kā'aḇ*] (Job 14:22; Ps. 69:29 [MT 30]); AV also SORROWFUL; NEB "becomes black," DISTRESS; [Heb. *ke'ēḇ*] (Job 16:6; Isa. 17:11; 65:14; Jer. 15:18); AV, NEB, also SORROW; [Heb. *maḵ'ōḇ*] (Job 33:19; Ps. 38:17 [MT 18]; Eccl. 2:23; Jer. 30:15; 45:3; 51:8); AV also SORROW, GRIEF; NEB also SUFFERING, SORE, TRIALS, WOUND; [Heb. *ḥîl*] (Jer. 6:24; 22:23; 50:43); AV also PANG; NEB ANGUISH, PANGS; [Heb. *ḥûl*] (Job 15:20; Jer. 4:19; 51:29) AV also TRAVAIL, SORROW; NEB ANXIETY, WRITHING; [Heb. *ḥîlâ*] (Job 6:10); AV SORROW; NEB ANGUISH; [Heb. *ḥēḇel*] (Job 21:17; Isa. 66:7); AV also SORROW; NEB also SUFFERING; [Heb. *'eṣeḇ*] (Gen. 3:16; probably Ps. 13:2 [MT 3] with the support of the Syr.; MT *'ēṣâ*–'counsel'); AV SORROW, "counsel"; NEB "labour," ANGUISH; [Heb. *'iṣṣāḇôn*] (Gen. 3:16); AV SORROW; NEB "labour"; [Heb. *'ōṣeḇ*] (1 Ch. 4:9; Isa. 14:3); AV SORROW; [Heb. *ṣîr*] (1 S. 4:19; Dnl. 10:16); AV also SORROW; NEB "labour," "pierced"; [Heb. *mar*] (Nu. 5:24, 27); AV "bitter"; NEB omits; [Heb. *rā'â*] (Eccl. 11:10); NEB TROUBLES; [Heb. *'ānî*] (1 Ch. 22:14); AV, NEB, TROUBLE; [Heb. *'āraq*] (Job 30:17); AV "sinews"; NEB "throbbing in my veins"; [Gk. *lypéō*] ("cause pain," 2 Cor. 2:2, 4f.); AV MAKE SORRY, BE GRIEVED, CAUSE GRIEF; NEB also OFFENDED, INJURY; [Gk. *lýpē*] (2 Cor. 2:1, 3; He. 12:11; 1 Pet. 2:19); AV "heaviness," GRIEVOUS, GRIEF; [Gk. *pónos*] (Rev. 16:11; 21:4); [Gk. *askéō*] (Acts 24:16); AV "exercise"; NEB "train"; [Gk. *básanos*] (Mt. 4:24); AV TORMENTS.

None of these words allow any clear division between somatic and psychic pain or between social and individual suffering. Since humans are a unity and always part of a community, the same words refer to the pain of the body and the pain of the spirit, to the pain of individuals and the pain of communities.

Thus Heb. *kā'aḇ*, e.g., can designate the pain of circumcision ("sore," Gen. 34:25) and the pain of being unjustly insulted and reproached (Ps. 69:29). Heb. *maḵ'ôḇ* can mean either Israel's pain in exile (Jer. 30:15) or the individual anguish of Baruch (45:3). Heb. *ḥûl* and *ḥîl* and the associated words refer to the bodily movements of twisting and writhing caused by severe pain, often that of childbirth (cf. Isa. 26:17; Jer. 6:24; 22:23; 50:43). Far from being restricted to individual bodily pain, however, these words often describe, either directly or metaphorically, the mental anguish of individuals (Job 6:10; 15:20; 21:17, although the text of this last reference is questionable) as well as the severe pain and anguish of kings (Jer. 50:43), nations (6:24; 22:23), and even the earth (51:29, at the judgment of Babylon). Even Heb. *'ōṣeḇ* and words related to it, which rarely mean physical pain, can in one instance refer to an individual's physical pain (1 Ch. 4:9, travail; cf. Gen. 3:16) and in another to national servitude (Isa. 14:3, with reference to the Exile). Gk. *lýpē* refers to the pain associated with childbirth ("sorrow," Jn. 16:21) as well as to the pains of the strained relationship between Paul and the Corinthian church (2 Cor. 2:1ff.; "grieve," 7:8ff.).

Pain, like the unity of humanity, is multidimensional in Scripture. People and human pain have physical, biological, psychological, mental, communal, and historical dimensions in Scripture. It is possible, important, and legitimate to focus on one or another of these dimensions at any particular time, but it is essential to remember that they are always related. The curse brought pain for both male and female (Gen. 3:16, "I will greatly multiply your pain [Heb. *'iṣṣāḇôn*] in childbearing; in pain [Heb. *'eṣeḇ*] you shall bring forth children"; v. 17, "in toil [Heb. *'iṣṣāḇôn*] you shall eat of it [the ground] all the days of your life"). This pain is not merely physical but multidimensional, pointing to people's estrangement from one another, from God, and from nature.

The prophets assumed the intimate relationship between sin and pain suggested by the curse when they explained or predicted the judgment of pain upon Israel's sins (e.g., Jer. 30:15). But this relationship can be distorted to presume a strict correlation between particular offenses and specific pains (*see* EVIL). This is the presumption of Job's friends (Job 15:20; 33:19), but Job refuses to accept it (16:5f.; 21:17). This is also the presumption of trial by ordeal (Nu. 5:24, 27); although the multidimensional unity of mankind may give such an ordeal effectiveness because of psychological suggestion, judging a person guilty if he feels pain is certainly a presumption and a distortion.

Pain is never presented as something to be sought. Eccl. 11:10 sagely advises the young person to "remove vexation from your mind, and put away pain from your body," for youth is fleeting. Paul sought assiduously to avoid another painful visit to the Corinthians (2 Cor. 2:1-5). But pain is accepted. The author of Ecclesiastes knew that it is characteristic of this world (2:23). Paul reached the higher vision that pain may be risked and borne by those who pursue the cause of God and accept the passion of Christ in this world (2 Cor. 2:4, "For I wrote you out of much affliction and anguish of heart and with many tears, not to cause you pain but to let you know the abundant love that I have for you"). Christians are to be willing to bear pain for the sake of love but to strive not to cause it. Thus Paul admonished the reconciled Corinthians to forgive and to comfort the one that they had been punishing (2 Cor. 2:7f.). 1 Pet. 2:19 instructs slaves, "One is approved if, mindful of God, he endures pain while suffering unjustly," for "to this you have been called, because Christ also suffered for you, leaving you an example" (v. 21). The Christian standing toward pain is thus somewhat paradoxical; it is a consequence of sin, evil, and humanity's estrangement, but it is accepted as part of the Christian calling. Other doctrines of pain, including the lofty examples of Buddhism and Stoicism, seek to avoid pain and strive to become insensitive to it and dispassionate (Berdyaev, pp. 117-19; on the Stoics, see *TDNT*, IV, 315f.). Paul never ceased to be passionate toward the Corinthians, and although he did not seek pain, he endured it voluntarily because he loved them. This attitude is quite far from the Buddhist refuge in nonbeing or the Stoic retreat to *apátheia*.

Just as people and human pain are multidimensional unities in Scripture, so the balm for pain is a multidimensional unity. The hope for balm is a hope for a multidimensional unity of salvation and health (Rev. 21:4). This hope is the backdrop against which the healings of Jesus are performed and recorded (Mt. 4:24; cf. 9:1-9). They point beyond themselves to the one Healer, the one Savior.

***Bibliography***.–N. Berdyaev, *Destiny of Man* (Eng. tr., repr. 1960); C. S. Lewis, *Problem of Pain* (1962); *TDNT*, IV, *s.v.* λύπη (Bultmann).

A. D. VERHEY

**PAINT; PAINTED; PAINTING** [Heb. *pûḵ, kāḥal, māšaḥ*]; NEB also ANTIMONY (Jer. 4:30). In two instances *pûḵ* means "black eye paint": Jezebel painted her eyes with it when she heard that Jehu was coming after her to kill her (2 K. 9:30), and Jerusalem is seen as a harlot "enlarging" her eyes with it (Jer. 4:30). It also occurs in the name of one of Job's daughters, Keren-happuch (lit. "the horn of eye paint," Job 42:14). Ezk. 23:40 describes Oholibah as a harlot representing Jerusalem, who paints (*kāḥal*) her eyes as she awaits her lovers. In Jer. 22:14 *māšaḥ*, usually translated "anoint," refers to painting cedar walls with a bright red paint.

Cosmetic eye paints were common in the ancient Near East, with the most detailed information coming from Egypt. Their earliest use was for magico-religious purposes — for protection by the gods. Later they were used as beauty aids (cf. Jer. 4:30). The most common Egyptian eye paint was made of galena (not stibium or antimony; see Lucas and Harris, pp. 80ff., 195ff.; Cohen), a dark gray lead sulfide (Egyp. *msdmt*; cf. Akk. *guḫlu*; Heb. *kāḥal*, probably also *pûḵ*; Arab. *koḥl*). Prior to the 2nd millennium B.C. it was applied to the upper eyelid with a finger, and later with a "kohl stick," a small rod of wood, bone, ivory, metal, or glass that was moistened and dipped into the cosmetic powder. Malachite, a green copper ore, was commonly applied to the lower eyelid. Akkadian texts occasionally refer to yellow eye paints and even the use of red ochre.

These cosmetics were stored in crude form in small linen or leather bags. Prepared forms (powders, or pastes made with water-soluble gums [fats, oils, or resins were not used]) were stored in shells, sections of hollow reeds, or small vases, or wrapped in plant leaves.

It is interesting that the Bible so rarely mentions artistic painting per se. Bright, red-lead paint (*šāšar*; not vermilion; see Forbes, p. 221) is mentioned in Jer. 22:14 (see above) and Ezk. 23:14, where the Chaldeans are painted in red on murals. In the intertestamental period the Wisdom of Solomon mentions painting idols with red paint (13:14) or various colors (15:4). 2 Macc. 2:29 refers to painting and decorating a house, and 4 Macc. 17:7 shows knowledge of painting of pictures.

The art of painting is well attested in the biblical world, however. Egyptian painting survives from most periods; most notable are the elaborate and colorful tomb paintings. Less is left from Mesopotamia, but colorful frescoes and even traces of paint on stone reliefs do remain. In Palestine the principal surviving painting is on pottery, although painting on walls of rich homes is known from the vicinity of NT Jericho and Samaria. Extant Greek painting is also primarily from pottery, but Greek art (along with Etruscan) influenced the later Roman tomb painting, as well as the spectacular Roman murals of the 1st cents. B.C. and A.D. found on the walls of private homes and public buildings, most notably at Pompeii. Jewish synagogues had colorful floor mosaics and wall paintings; the earliest evidence for these comes from the 3rd cent. A.D.

Ancient painters had well-developed crafts. For example, some fifteen colors were standard in Egypt. Painting was done on pottery, plaster, stone, wood, canvas, papyrus, ivory, metal, and even semiprecious stones. Various palettes and mortars and pestles for mixing of paints survive, as do different brush types, usually of reeds, grasses, or fibrous wood, with ends frayed by soaking in water. Many media were used in different periods, including gums, gelatine, milk curds, egg whites, and beeswax; varnishes or wax often covered the paintings.

*See also* ART; INK; WRITING.

***Bibliography***.–R. Amiran, *Ancient Pottery of the Holy Land* (2nd ed. 1982); R. D. Barnett, *Assyrian Palace Reliefs* (1959, 1970); J. M. Baumgarten, "Art in the Synagogue: Some Talmudic Views," in J. Gutmann, ed., *Synagogue* (1975), pp. 79-89; H. R. Cohen, *Biblical Hapax Legomena in the Light of Akkadian and Ugaritic* (1978), pp. 117f.; R. J. Forbes, *Studies in Ancient Technology*, III (1965), 17-20, 210-264; G. Gassiot-Talabot, *Roman and Palaeo-Christian Painting* (1965); J. L. Kelso, *Excavations at NT Jericho* (*AASOR*, XXIX-XXX, 1955), pp. 45-49; L. Koehler, *Theologische Zeitschrift*, 3 (1947), 314-18; A. Lucas and J. R. Harris, *Ancient Egyptian Materials and Industries* (4th ed. 1962), pp. 80-85, 133f., 195-99, 338-366; A. Maiuri, *Roman Painting* (1953); A. Mekhitarian, *Egyptian Painting* (1954); M. Robertson, *Greek Painting* (1959); C. Singer, *et al.*, eds., *History of Technology*, I (1954), 238-245, 470f.; II (1956), 359-364; Y. Tomabechi, *JNES*, 42 (1983), 123-131.

D. M. HOWARD, JR.

**PALACE** [Heb. *'armôn* (Isa. 23:13; 25:2; 32:14; etc.), *bayiṯ*–'house' (1 K. 4:6; 2 K. 10:5; 11:6; etc.), *bîrâ* < Akk. *birtu*–'citadel' (1 Ch. 29:1, 19), *bîṯān* < Akk. *bitānu* (Est. 1:5; 7:7f.), *hêḵal* < Akk. *ekallum* < Sum. É.GAL–'big house' (1 K. 21:1; 2 K. 20:18; 2 Ch. 36:7; etc.); Aram. *hêḵal* (Ezr. 4:14; Dnl. 4:4, 29 [MT 1, 26]; 5:5; 6:18 [MT 19]; Gk. *aulḗ* (Mt. 26:3; Mk. 15:16; Lk. 11:21)]; AV also HOUSE, HOUSEHOLD, TEMPLE, HALL; NEB also HOUSE, CASTLE, MANSION, etc. A building or complex of buildings that serves as the residence of a king, a prince, a governor, or other dignitary. It is usually of exceptional size with lavish furnishings and decorations.

We have several sources of information on ancient palaces. Homer describes the splendid Mycenaean palaces, the OT describes Solomon's palace, and Josephus describes Herod's many residences. Royal inscriptions of Assyria and Persia, in particular, give details about the workers and materials used in the construction of palaces. From standing ruins and excavations we have foundations, walls, and occasionally fragments of columns and roofs. In a few cases magnificent frescoes and stone reliefs have been recovered, e.g., from Minoan and Assyrian palaces.

***I. In the Ancient Near East***.–Although a number of palaces have been excavated, only a few will be mentioned here. *See also* ASSYRIA VIII; BABYLON IV.E; CRETE; MARI II; PERSEPOLIS; TELL MARDIKH.

About twenty Neo-Assyrian palaces have been found, including those from the provincial capitals and from the major capitals of Nimrûd (CALAH), Khorsabad (Dūr-Šarrukin), and Nineveh. Of these only about a third have been excavated extensively. Most of these palaces were arranged around two courts. The *bābānu* (< Akk. *bābu*, "gate") or forecourt had administrative offices, service quarters, and storerooms. The *bitānu* (< Akk. *bītu*, "house") or inner court had the reception and residential rooms. The throne room was located between these courts.

The most thoroughly investigated Assyrian palace is that of Sargon II at Khorsabad, 25 km. (15 mi.) NE of Nineveh. This palace, covering 10 ha. (24 acres), was erected on a huge brick platform. It contained over two

Aerial view showing excavations of Herod's palace at Jericho (site excavated by Dr. Ehud Netzer on behalf of the Hebrew University in Jerusalem) (E. Netzer)

hundred rooms. The ceremonial court covered a quarter of an acre; the throne room measured 49 by 11 m. (161 by 36 ft.). The palace was equipped with granaries, kitchens, bakeries, and wine cellars. The entrances were guarded by stone statues of the Lamassu, winged bulls 4 m. (13 ft.) high. Floors were paved with brick tiles and the walls were decorated by some 500 sq. m. (6000 sq. ft.) of stone reliefs (*see* pictures in BIT; HUNTING).

NINEVEH was the great Assyrian capital on the Tigris River to which Jonah was sent. Over a dozen Assyrian kings built at the site, but the two principal palaces at Kuyunjik (the larger of the two mounds on the site) are those of Sennacherib (704-681) in the southwest and of Ashurbanipal (662-628) in the north. Sennacherib's "palace without a rival" covered 2 ha. (5 acres) and contained seventy halls. The halls were adorned with more than 3000 m. (10,000 ft.) of sculptured stone slabs (*see* pictures in COMMERCE; GESTURE). Of particular interest are the reliefs of room 36, now in the British Museum, which depict the king's conquest of the Judean city of Lachish (2 K. 18:13-17). The most significant discovery was the famous library of Ashurbanipal, who collected all the literature of previous generations, including the Babylonian flood story contained in the Gilgamesh Epic. His palace was also adorned with frescoes; *see* pictures in ARABIA; ARCHEOLOGY OF MESOPOTAMIA; ASHURBANIPAL; CART; EAT; HORSE.

SUSA was the site of the story of Esther in the days of Ahasuerus, i.e., Xerxes (485-465). The author of Esther refers to the gate of the king (2:19), the outer court (6:4), the inner court (4:11), the house of the women (2:9), and a second area for concubines (2:14). The use of the word *bîṯān* is striking; in context (1:5; 7:8) it may mean garden kiosk. Darius made Susa the administrative capital of the Persian empire in 522. From a detailed inscription we know that from 518 to 512 Darius built a palace on the Apadana mound by employing materials and workmen from every part of his realm. The remains of the Apadana palace as we see them today belong to the reconstruction of Artaxerxes II (404-359). The building included a square central hall, 59 m. (194 ft.), with six rows of six columns and porticoes on three sides. The columns were 20 m. (65 ft.) high, capped by double bull protomes.

*II. In Palestine.*–Saul, the first king of Israel, rebuilt a fortress-palace at the site of GIBEAH (Tell el-Fûl), 5 km. (3 mi.) N of Jerusalem (1 S. 15:34ff.). The site was excavated by W. F. Albright in 1922-23 and 1933 and by P. Lapp in 1964. As reconstructed from the preserved corner the fortress would have been 52 by 35 m. (171 by 115 ft.).

All that we know about David's palace is that it was constructed with the aid of cedar beams, carpenters, and stone masons sent to him by Hiram king of Tyre (2 S. 5:11; 1 Ch. 14:1). Hiram later sent similar supplies and workmen to aid Solomon in his construction of the temple (1 K. 5:1-11), and presumably also for the building of his palace.

A detailed description is given of the construction of Solomon's palace in 1 K. 7:1-12. We learn that whereas Solomon spent seven years in building the temple (6:38), he spent thirteen years in building his palace (7:1). Several distinctive structures are described:

(1) The House of the Forest of Lebanon (vv. 2-5) was a great hall, 100 cubits long, 50 broad, and 30 high (46 by 23 by 13.5 m.; 150 by 75 by 45 ft.), which received its name from forty-five cedar columns. There is some uncertainty as to whether these were arranged in four rows (MT) or in three (LXX, Vulg.). This building evidently served as an armory for the storage of weapons (1 K. 10:17, 21; Isa. 22:8) and as a treasury for precious objects (2 Ch. 9:20).

(2) A colonnade, 50 cubits by 30 (23 by 13.5 m.; 75 by 45 ft.) with a porch may have served as a waiting room or reception hall (1 K. 7:6).

(3) The throne room served as the Hall of Judgment (v. 7). It was paneled from the floor to the ceiling with cedar. The interspersing of timber courses among the courses of stone (vv. 9-11) was designed as protection against earthquakes. Solomon's throne was inlaid with ivory and gold (2 K. 10:18-20).

Jerusalem Model of Herod's palace (W. S. LaSor)

(4) Of the residences themselves we are simply told that he built a similar palace for himself and a separate one for the pharaoh's daughter (1 K. 7:8; 10:24), who was the most important of his foreign wives.

In his expanded description of Solomon's palaces Josephus (*Ant.* viii.5.2 [137f.]) speaks of "a very splendid hall for feasts and banquets, filled with gold."

Unfortunately archeologists have been unable to recover any of Solomon's buildings at Jerusalem, with the possible exception of a fragmentary wall uncovered by K. Kenyon. But two palaces attributed to Solomon have been identified by Y. Yadin at Megiddo. The south building 1723, measuring 23 by 21 m. (75 by 69 ft.), was surrounded by a large court with a plastered floor. The outer walls were made of finely drafted ashlars in alternating headers and stretchers. Two proto-Aeolic capitals were recovered. The northern palace, building 6000, resembled the *hilāni* palaces of Neo-Hittite Syria, i.e., a rectangular room that was a pillared forehall with its entrance on one of its long sides.

Ahab's palace at Samaria was excavated by J. Crowfoot and K. Kenyon. They uncovered finely drafted header-and-stretcher ashlars that were probably the work of Phoenician masons employed by Jezebel from her homeland. About two hundred ivory plaques, comparable to those found at Nimrûd and Arslan Tash, illustrate the ostentatious luxury denounced by Amos (Am. 6:4; 1 K. 22:39; Ps. 45:8 [MT 9]).

Jeremiah (22:13-19) upbraided Jehoiakim for exploiting his people by building a great palace with spacious upper rooms. Y. Aharoni believed that he uncovered this palace at Beth-haccherem (Ramat Raḥel) just S of Jerusalem. The inner citadel or palace covered an area 90 by 50 m. (295 by 164 ft.). Aharoni recovered four proto-Aeolic capitals, some imported Assyrian palace ware, the painting of a bearded king on a sherd, and decorations from windows that correspond to those described in Jeremiah's diatribe (v. 14).

Herod the Great (40-4 B.C.) was one of the most prodigious builders of antiquity. Josephus describes numerous palaces built by Herod (e.g., at Caesarea, *BJ* i.21.5 [408]), some of which have been uncovered by archeologists. *See also* MASADA III.

At the artificially heightened hill of Herodian near Bethlehem, Herod was finally laid to rest. According to Josephus *BJ* i.21.10 [420]: "The enclosure was filled with gorgeous palaces, the magnificent appearance of which was not confined to the interior of the apartments, but outer walls, battlements, and roofs, all had wealth lavished upon them in profusion." Excavations by V. Corbo uncovered remains of a triclinium or dining hall, 15 by 11 m. (49 by 36 m.), baths, and mosaic pavements. Excavations by E. Netzer since 1972 at the base of the steep hill have revealed a complex of subsidiary palaces, including a huge audience hall, 130 by 55 m. (427 by 180 ft.) overlooking a hippodrome.

Near the present site of the Jaffa Gate in Jerusalem Herod erected three magnificent towers called Hippicus, Phasael, and Mariamme (Josephus *BJ* v.4.3 [161-69]). The base of Phasael is still preserved in the so-called David's Tower. It was just S of these towers that Herod erected his palace, which according to Josephus (*BJ* v.4.4 [176-181]) defied description. It contained "immense banqueting-halls and bed-chambers for a hundred guests." There were also groves of trees, canals, and ponds. Excavations in the area of the Armenian Gardens by M. Broshi and D. Bahat have revealed that the palace was erected on a podium about 350 by 60 m. (1080 by 190 ft.). Only a few rooms in the northwest were preserved; Corinthian and Ionic capitals were recovered.

The wealthy Sadducean high priests had their palatial homes in the Upper City of Jerusalem. Jesus was brought at night before the residences of Annas and Caiaphas (Mt. 26:3, 58, 69; Mk. 14:54; Lk. 22:55; Jn. 18:15). Gk. *aulḗ,* which the AV translates "palace" in these passages, means "court" or "courtyard."

The Hasmoneans built a palace W of the temple in Jerusalem. Herod Agrippa II, who made additions to the palace in the reign of Nero (A.D. 54-68), enjoyed viewing the proceedings in the temple from this palace. This provoked the priests who built a wall to block his view

(Josephus *Ant.* xx.8.11 [189-193]). During the siege of Jerusalem by the Romans the Jewish insurgents burned down the palace because they resented Agrippa II's collaboration with the Romans (Josephus *BJ* ii.17.6 [426]).

*See also* PRAETORIUM.

***Bibliography.***–P. Amiet, *Syria,* 51 (1974), 65-73; R. Amiran and A. Eitan, *IEJ,* 22 (1972), 50f.; *AOTS*; R. D. Barnett, *Assyrian Palace Reliefs* (1970); *DBSup.,* VI, 976-1021 (J. M. Fenasse); *EAEHL*; P. Garelli, ed., *Le palais et la royauté* (1974); K. Kenyon, *Royal Cities of the OT* (1971); S. Lloyd, *Archaeology of Mesopotamia* (1978); A. Parrot, *Nineveh and the OT* (1955); D. Ussishkin, *BA,* 36 (1973), 78-105; Y. Yadin, ed., *Jerusalem Revealed* (1975).

E. M. YAMAUCHI

**PALAL** pā'lal [Heb. *pālāl*–'judge']. Son of Uzai, and one who helped Nehemiah to rebuild the wall of Jerusalem (Neh. 3:25).

**PALANQUIN** pal-ən-kēn', pə-lan'kwin [Heb. *'appiryôn*; LXX *phoreíon*]; AV CHARIOT. A canopied portable couch or throne, carried on men's shoulders by means of poles (Cant. 3:9). Heb. *'appiryôn* is a hapax legomenon, and there have been many theories about its origin and some debate about its meaning. According to G. Gerleman (comm. on Canticles [*BKAT,* 17, 1965], pp. 139-142) the description suggests a building rather than a throne or litter; he proposed an etymology from Egyp. *pr,* "house." Others have sought a similar sense by emending the text to read *'appeḏen,* a Persian loanword meaning "palace" (cf. M. Pope, *Song of Songs* [*AB,* 1977], pp. 441-43). Still other scholars derive it from Gk. *phoreíon,* "litter," but this would require a date for the Song after *ca.* 300 B.C., since that is the earliest known usage of *phoreíon.*

G. A. L.

**PALATIAL TENTS** [Heb. *'ohᵒley* (sic; see *BHS*) *'appaḏnô*] (Dnl. 11:45); AV TABERNACLE OF HIS PALACE; NEB ROYAL PAVILION. The "palatial tents" pitched by the hostile king of the north were meant to serve as his headquarters. Heb. *'appeḏen* derives from Akk. *appadān,* which is a loanword from Old Pers. *apadāna,* "palace." Cf. Aram. *'appaḏnā',* used in the Tg. of Jer. 43:10 to translate Heb. *šaprîr,* "royal canopy"; cf. also Syr. *'āpadnā',* "palace, citadel." For a picture of the Apadana at Persepolis, *see* Vol. I, Plate 1.

G. A. L.

**PALESTINA** pal-ə-stī'nə [Heb. *pᵉlešeṯ*] (AV Ex. 15:14; Isa. 14:29, 31); **PALESTINE** pal'ə-stīn (Joel 3:4, AV). *See* PHILISTIA.

**PALESTINE** pal'ə-stīn [Heb. *pᵉlešeṯ*–'Philistia'; Gk. *Palaistínē* (sometimes with *Syríe*–'Palestine Syria']. A term used for the Philistine coastal region, for the Cisjordan region occupied by the Israelites ("the land of the Canaanites"), and for a larger area including a portion of Transjordan; hence not a clearly definitive term.

I. Names
  A. Palestine
  B. Syria
  C. Canaan
  D. The Land
  E. Judah/Judea
  F. Beyond the River
II. General Description
  A. Location
  B. Size
  C. Importance
III. Geology
  A. Formative Periods
  B. Pluvial Ages
IV. Geography
  A. North-South Divisions
    1. Coastal Plain
    2. Shephelah
    3. Western (Central) Mountain Range
    4. Plain of Esdraelon (Valley of Jezreel)
    5. Negeb
    6. Jordan Rift
    7. Eastern (Transjordanian) Plateau
  B. Mountains and Valleys
  C. Seas and Rivers
  D. Roads
  E. Cities
  F. Tribal Portions
V. Climate
  A. Seasons
  B. Former and Latter Rains
  C. East Wind
  D. Other Features
  E. Effects of Latitude and Topography
  F. Has The Climate Changed?
VI. Biota
  A. Flora
  B. Fauna
VII. Cultural Ages
  A. Lower Paleolithic
  B. Middle Paleolithic
  C. Upper Paleolithic
  D. Mesolithic
  E. Neolithic
  F. Chalcolithic
  G. Bronze
  H. Iron
VIII. History
  A. Prehistoric
  B. Pre-Israelite
  C. Biblical Period
  D. Postbiblical Period
  E. Population
IX. Languages and Writing
  A. Cuneiform
  B. Alphabetic Writing
  C. Proper Names
X. Religion
XI. Cultural Contributions
XII. The Land in Prophecy

***I. Names.**–A. Palestine.* The use of the name Palestine for the region W of the Jordan Rift (Cisjordan) became popular in the time of the British Mandate (1918-1948; after World War I Iraq, Transjordan, and Palestine were mandated to the British, while Syria and Lebanon were placed under French control). It is not so used in the Hebrew OT. In Ex. 15:14; Isa. 14:29, 31, Heb. *pᵉlešeṯ* (AV "Palestina") should be translated "Philistia" (cf. RSV, NEB). In Joel 3:4 (MT 4:4) the term is clearly used for the coastal region of Philistia. Gk. *Palaistínē* does not occur in the NT.

The earliest known use of the name Palestine occurs in Herodotus, who used the expressions "in Palestine Syria" (i.105; ii.106), "the Syrians which are in Palestine" (ii.104; vii.89), and "the Palestine Syrians" (iii.5). It is not clear, however, what territory Herodotus intended to include. In one passage the term seems limited to the coastal region: "These Phoenicians . . . now inhabit the seacoast of Syria; that part of Syria and as much of it as reaches to Egypt, is all called Palestine" (vii.89). Josephus, who also used the expression "Palestine Syria" (*Ant.* viii.10.3 [260]), distinguished Palestine from Coelesyria (i.6.4 [145]) but did not specify what he included in the term. In *CAp* i.22 (171) he spoke of the Jews as "inhabitants of Palestine"; but since this occurs in a discussion of Herodotus, it is not clear how Josephus was using the term. Jerome spoke of "the land of Judea, which is now called Palestine" (*In Ezechiel* 37:17, quoted by F.-M. Abel [*GP,* I, 313], who said that this usage became official in the Roman and Byzantine Chancellery, and even included the southern portion of Transjordan).

The Heb. *pᵉlešeṯ* and the gentilic *pᵉlištî(m)* ("Philistine[s]") can be traced to one of the sea-peoples who invaded the coastal regions early in the 12th cent B.C. They are referred to in Egyptian records as *prst* (Egyptian lacked a symbol for *l*; cf. inscriptions of Ramses III and references to sources in *ANET,* p. 262) and in Assyrian as *palaštu* (inscriptions of Adad-nirari III; cf. *ARAB,* I, §§ 734, 739). Their name took prominence among those of the sea-peoples and ultimately was applied to the hinterland as well as to the coastal region.

*B. Syria.* In the LXX *Syria* was used to translate Heb. *ʾᵃrām* ("Aram"), and the term is considered a corruption of "Assyria," referring to lands placed under Assyrian control. (Thus certain Christians in the Near East who use the Syriac Scriptures refer to themselves as "Assyrians.") Herodotus confirmed this tradition when he said of the Assyrian army, "These are called by Greeks Syrians, but by the barbarians they were called Assyrians" (vii.63). But he distinguished Syria as a geographical entity that bordered on Egypt and was inhabited by the Phoenicians (ii.116). Xenophon listed Syria, Assyria, Phoenicia, and Arabia as separate regions (*Anabasis* vii.8.25).

Syria was divided into two parts. Upper Syria (Gk. *hē ánō Syria*) stretched from Babylonia to Cilicia; it was known in the OT as Heb. *ʾᵃram nahᵃrayim,* "Syria between the Rivers" ("Mesopotamia," Gen. 24:10). (For the various meanings that *ʾᵃrām,* i.e., Upper Syria, could have in the OT, see BDB, p. 74.) Under the Seleucids Syria became a political unit that extended from eastern Asia Minor to Persia and for a time included Palestine. In 64 B.C. Syria became a Roman province with its capital at Antioch (cf. Acts 15:23, 41; Gal. 1:21). The name COELESYRIA ("hollow Syria") was used of the region S of the lower Orontes basin and the great bend of the Euphrates, extending to Ashkelon and Jerusalem. It was so named because of the numerous valleys throughout much of Coelesyria (cf. *GP,* I, 8-11, 310-12).

*C. Canaan.* Abram (Abraham) migrated to "the land of Canaan" (Gen. 12:5), and God promised to give him "this land" (v. 7). Later it was defined as "the land of the Kenites, the Kenizzites, the Kadmonites, the Hittites, the Perizzites, the Rephaim, the Amorites, the Canaanites, the Girgashites, and the Jebusites" (15:19-21), or simply "all the land of Canaan" (17:8).

The etymology of the words Canaan and Canaanite (Heb. *kᵉnaʿan, kᵉnaʿanî*) is disputed (*see* CANAAN I). The most plausible explanation may be a derivation from *kinaḫḫu,* a word meaning "blue or purple colored cloth" in the Nuzi letters (cf. M. Noth, *OT World,* pp. 51f.; *GTTOT,* § 45). This theory has been challenged by B. Landsberger (*JCS,* 21 [1967], 166f.); but Landsberger's suggestion that this word is related to Akk. *uqnû* and Gk. *kyános* is not convincing. The *ʿayin* in Heb. *kᵉnaʿan* was probably an original *ghayin* (since it is reflected in Akkadian as *ḫ,* whereas *ʿayin* is reflected as *ʾaleph*), and the *ghayin* is found in the Hurrian word that lies behind *kinaḫḫu* at Nuzi. Moreover, the word occurs in Akkadian also as *kinaḫnu* (apparently meaning "merchant"), which would seem to be the original form from which *kinaḫḫu* developed by assimilation. If this etymology is sustained, the "Canaanite" was originally a merchant who traded in cloth dyed in blue-purple (cf. Gk. *phoiníke,* "Phoenicia" < *phoinikoús,* "purple-red").

The use of the word to refer to the land rather than the trade (cf. B. Maisler [Mazar], *BASOR,* 102 [Apr. 1946], 7-12) may go back at least to the time of the Ebla tablets. Dagan is called "the god of Canaan" (G. Pettinato, *Testi amministrativi della biblioteca L.2769* [*Materiali Epigrafici di Ebla,* 2; 1980], text 3, verso III.4; text 48, verso V.4), Canaan being spelled in syllabograms as *ka₂-na-na-um* and *ka₂-na-na-im,* respectively. But the absence of an *ʿayin/ghayin* makes this identification suspect. The word *knʿny* ("Canaanite") does occur in the 14th cent. B.C. in Ugaritic (*UT,* 311:7). In the Amarna Tablets from the same period the name is apparently used of the land; in the expressions ᵐᵃᵗ*ki-na-aḫ-ḫi,* ᵐᵃᵗ*ki-na-aḫ-ni* (and other spellings), the determinative *mat* could alternatively be read as a noun in construct, "the land of the Canaanites" (Am.Tab. 8:15, 17); but in 30:1 ("to the kings of ᵐᵃᵗ*ki-na-a-aḫ[-ḫi]*"), where the land is divided among petty kingdoms, and in 36:15 (*[p]i-ḫa-ti ša ki-na-ḫi,* "the district of Canaan"), it clearly seems to be a place name. (*See also* CANAAN II.)

Because the Phoenicians are often considered the descendants of the Canaanites (cf. S. Moscati, *World,* pp. 3-7), and because Ugaritic is often referred to as a Canaanite language (cf. W. F. Albright, *Yahweh and the Gods of Canaan* [repr. 1969], p. 115), the question may be raised whether "Canaan" was used only of the coastal region. Isaiah so uses the term in an oracle against Tyre (23:11), and Zephaniah speaks of Canaan as "land of the Philistines" (2:5). But in the OT "Canaan" was also applied to Galilee, the plain of Jezreel, Ephraim, Judah, the Shephelah, and the Negeb (cf. Gen. 12:6; 24:3; 38:2; Nu. 21:1; Jgs. 1:3, 9f., 27, 29, etc.). Nicolas of Damascus is quoted by Josephus as referring to the land where Abraham settled as "then called Canaan but now Judaea" (*Ant.* i.7.2 [160]), and Josephus repeatedly used "Canaan" to describe the land of the patriarchs (*Ant.* i. *passim*). The NT uses "Canaan" for the land of the fathers (Acts 7:11) as well as for the Phoenician area (Mt. 15:22; cf. par. Mk. 7:26). (Cf. Noth, *OT World,* pp. 49-53; E. A. Speiser, *AASOR,* 16 [1936], 121f.; A. Goetze, *JCS,* 10 [1956], 10.)

*D. The Land.* A very common expression in the OT is "the land" (Heb. *hāʾāreṣ,* e.g., Ruth 1:1), often qualified as "the land of Canaan (or the Canaanites)" (e.g., Gen. 12:5; Ex. 3:17), "the land of the Hebrews" (Gen. 40:15; cf. *Ant.* vii.12.2 [303]), "the land of Yahweh" (Hos. 9:3), "the land which he promised them" (Dt. 9:28), "the land of Israel" (mostly postexilic, e.g., Ezk. 7:2), and "the holy land" (only in Zeph. 2:5). The NT uses several expressions that include Gk. *gḗ*: "the land of Canaan" (Acts 13:19), "the land of Israel" (Mt. 2:20), "the land of Judea" (Mk. 1:5; as in Mt. 2:6, however, this may refer only to the southern portion of Palestine), "the land" (Lk. 21:23), and "the land of promise" (He. 11:9). Other expressions use *chṓra,* which is sometimes translated "land" but more properly means "region, district" (cf. Mk. 1:5; Acts 26:20; see Bauer, rev., p. 889); Josephus seems to prefer *chṓra* (*Ant.* vii.12.2 [303]; viii.13.7 [353]). The modern state of Israel is called *ʾereṣ yiśrāʾēl* ("the land of Israel"), commonly abbreviated to *hāʾāreṣ* ("the land").

*E. Judah/Judea.* In the LXX *Ioudaia* ("Judea") is used to translate Heb. *yᵉhûḏâ* ("Judah," i.e., the southern kingdom; e.g., 1 S. 23:3), and after the return from exile this was somewhat expanded to include a portion of what had been Israel (the northern kingdom; cf. Neh. 3; Jth. 4:1, 3; 1 Macc. 3:34). Gradually "Judea" was extended to include the land inhabited by the Jews (cf. Josephus *CAp.* i.22 [179], where it is traced to Aristotle through Clearchus in an unlikely story; also *Ant.* i.6.2 [133]; xiv.1.3

[9]). This usage is reflected in 1 Thess. 2:14 and Acts 26:20; in Mt. 19:1 the term includes a portion of Transjordan. Coins minted by Vespasian bore the inscription *Judea capta*. In a narrower sense Judea denoted a southern part of Palestine, distinct from Idumea, Samaria, Galilee, Perea, and other regions (cf. Mk. 3:7; Acts 1:8; 9:31). Josephus speaks of "Judaea and the three toparchies adjoining it, Samaria, Galilee, and Peraea" (*Ant.* xiii.2.3 [50]). (*See also* JUDAH, TERRITORY OF; JUDEA.)

*F. Beyond the River.* In the Persian period the satrapy of Aram. *ʿᵃḇar-nahᵃrâ* (Gk. *péran Euphratou/potamoú*), "Trans-Euphrates" or "Beyond the River," included Syria, Phoenicia, Palestine, and Cyprus (*CAH*, IV [1930], 195-97). It is mentioned in Ezr. 4:17, etc.; Neh. 2:7, 9.

*II. General Description.–A. Location.* Palestine lies within the region between the Mediterranean Sea and the Arabian Desert (34°–36° east longitude) and between Sinai and the mountains of Lebanon (29° 30′ – 33° 30′ north latitude), within the southern portion of the Temperate Zone. Situated at the eastern end of the Mediterranean Sea, it is part of the Levant (the Levantine states are usually considered Syria, Lebanon, and Palestine or Israel). Palestine is located at the southwestern end of "the Fertile Crescent," the fertile lands extending along the Tigris-Euphrates valley and the Levant.

An almost continuous chain of mountain ranges extends from the Pyrenees (between France and Spain) to the Himalayas (between India and Tibet), affording protection to the lands along the southern flanks of the mountains from the colder and wetter climate of the Eurasian land mass. Similarly, the deserts of northern Africa and Arabia form a southern separation of the Mediterranean region. Thus the shores and islands of the Mediterranean form a somewhat homogeneous area in terms of climate, peoples, and biota. Palestine is an integral part of this Mediterranean world. At the same time, passes such as the Danube and the Nile valleys afforded relatively easy communication between the Mediterranean world and Europe to the north and Africa to the south.

The Arabian desert is generally considered the home of the Semites (an oversimplification that needs qualification). The attraction of the more fertile regions lying to the north and west of Arabia is believed to have been an important element in the periodic migrations of Arabian (Semitic) peoples into Mesopotamia, Syria, and Canaan. This is sometimes presented as the tension between "the Desert and the Sown." Abram's migration to the land of Canaan is often related to population movements that resulted from this tension; however, the Bible nowhere indicates that Abram was part of such a migration but rather presents his journey as that of a single family led by what Abram believed to be a divine impulse (Gen. 11:31–12:7).

The TABLE OF NATIONS (Gen. 10) portrays the population of the "earth" after the Flood as comprising three divisions descended from the three sons of Noah and their descendants. The Japhetic peoples, so far as they can be identified, occupied the regions to the north of the Semites, and the Hamitic peoples the regions to the south. It is important to distinguish, however, between the ethnic relationships (given in Gen. 10) and the linguistic relationships; e.g., some of Ham's descendants are considered "Semitic" because they came to speak Semitic languages (e.g., Canaan, Sheba, Babel, etc.), and at least one of the Semites (Elam) is classified linguistically as non-Semitic.

*B. Size.* Because of the imprecision of what is included as "Palestine" it is necessary to describe the size in various ways. The distance "from Dan to Beer-sheba" (1 S. 3:20; etc.) is 240 km. (150 mi.), from Beer-sheba to Ezion-geber 200 km. (125 mi.), and from Dan to Hamath (Nu. 13:21; but *see* HAMATH) 225 km. (150 mi.). From the River of Egypt to the Euphrates (Gen. 15:18) is nearly 700 km. (435 mi.; all distances are air-line). From the Mediterranean Sea to Dan is 40 km. (25 mi.), while from Joppa to the Jordan River is 80 km. (50 mi.), and at the latitude of Beer-sheba the land is 130 km. (80 mi.) in width. Cisjordanian Palestine is 15,500 sq. km. (6000 sq. mi.) and if Transjordan is added it is 26,000 sq. km. (10,000 sq. mi.). The Negeb adds about 9000 sq. km. (3500 sq. mi.; the figures differ in different works, depending on what is included). Cf. P. Lemaire and D. Baldi, *Atlante storico della Bibbia* (1955), pp. 22f.; Israel 1:100,000 maps published by the State of Israel, Survey of Israel (1977).

*C. Importance.* Palestine occupies a strategic part of the only land-bridge connecting Europe and Asia with Africa, and before the creation of the Suez Canal it was the only means of connecting maritime trade between East and West. Thus ancient Palestine lay at the crossroads of the world of its day. Trade routes, which go back a millennium or more before written records, connected Egyptian with European and Asiatic trade centers. These merchants must of necessity have passed through Palestine. Armies also marched through Palestine: Egyptian and Ptolemaic armies moving against northern foes, and Babylonian, Persian, and Roman armies against enemies to the south; thus Palestine was often occupied by armies of other nations. With the development of maritime trade, largely by the Phoenicians (of which Tyre is symbolic; cf. Ezk. 28), the sea routes connecting merchant centers brought Palestine into closer contact with both the positive and negative elements of the highly developed civilizations. At the same time, because of Palestine's generally mountainous topography, the main highways were located to the east along the edge of the desert (sometimes called the Way of the Kings or the King's Highway) and to the west along the coast (often called the Way of the Sea; see IV.D below). As a result, Palestine is sometimes depicted as situated in "splendid isolation" (*WHAB*, p. 6). Both internationalism and isolationism can be found in the history of Palestine; the latter applies more to the southern portion (Judah), while the former applies more to Samaria and especially to lower Galilee.

*III. Geology.*–In this article only those geological elements that are particularly relevant to understanding the Bible will be considered (for a fuller discussion, see the thorough chapters in *CAH*, I/1 [3rd ed. 1971], esp. p. 2 and chs. 2, 3, and 5; cf. also *GB* [rev. ed. 1974]). *See* Plate 46.

*A. Formative Periods.* Geologists commonly divide the earth's geological history into four principal eras, to which one or two others are prefixed:

- Archeozoic Era, 4.5 billion years B.P.
  (B.P. = Before the Present)
- Proterozoic (Pre-Cambrian) Era, 1.5 billion years B.P.
- Primary (Paleozoic) Era, 600 million B.P.
  - Cambrian Period, 600-500 million B.P.
  - Ordovician, 500-440 million B.P.
  - Silurian, 440-400 million B.P.
  - Devonian, 400-350 million B.P.
  - Carboniferous, 350-270 million B.P.
  - Permian, 270-220 million B.P.
- Secondary (Mesozoic) Era, 220 million B.P.
  - Triassic Period, 220-180 million B.P.
  - Jurassic Period, 180-135 million B.P.
  - Cretaceous Period, 135-70 million B.P.
    - Cenomanian Epoch
    - Turonian Epoch
    - Senonian Epoch
- Tertiary (Cenozoic) Era, 70 million B.P.

Paleocene Period, 70-60 million B.P.
Eocene Period, 60-40 million B.P.
Oligocene Period, 40-25 million B.P.
Miocene Period, 25-12 million B.P.
Pliocene Period, 12-1 million B.P.
Quaternary Era, 1 million B.P.
Pleistocene Period, 1 million to 10,000 B.P.
Holocene (Recent) Period, 10,000 B.P. to present

There is some variation in the dates and names assigned to the various divisions. Some geologists consider the Quaternary as part of the Cenozoic, or identify it with the Pleistocene Period. The eras are subdivided into either "periods" or "systems," and these are further subdivided into "epochs" (for which some scholars use "systems").

It is generally believed that the hard, crystalline rock that forms the Arabian platform was laid down in the Archeozoic (Pre-Cambrian) era. Life forms consisting of fish, insects, and reptiles (cf. Gen. 1:20f.) appeared in the Paleozoic and continued into the Mesozoic. According to some geologists, Africa, Arabia, and the Deccan of India formed a land mass that has been named Gondwanaland (others believe that this was several land masses in juxtaposition); this was separated from the Russian platform on the west by a great sea called Tethys Sea (of which the Mediterranean Sea is a remnant). The advances and regressions of the sea during the Triassic, Jurassic, and Cretaceous periods left sedimentary deposits. In the Sinai basin these were mostly of limestone, 1500 m. (5,000 ft.) thick; the wilderness of Judea received thick deposits of Nubian sandstone. During the Cenomanian, Turonian, and Senonian epochs of the Upper (Later) Cretaceous period deposits of limestone and chalk formed the basic structure of Palestine. (*See* Plate 48.) In this period there were also outpourings of lava through rifts in the basaltic and granitic layers of the earth's surface, and perhaps the same tectonic forces separated the African-Arabian part of Gondwanaland from the Indian part (*CAH,* I/1 [1971],119).

During the Cenozoic era land vegetation approached its modern aspect. An uplifting of the land caused the Tethys Sea to recede. Modern birds and mammals appeared in the Paleocene and the Eocene periods (cf. Gen. 1:22-24). The Eurasian and Afro-Arabian land masses seem to have been joined in the Oligocene period. The Miocene period saw the folding of the earth's surface, the elevation of the mountains, doming and the beginning of rifting, along with the opening of the eastern Mediterranean. Most of the present-day genera were present in the Pliocene period, during which time the kurkar of the Palestinian coast, the Mousterian red sandstone of Sharon, and the wind-blown deposits of loess around Gaza were laid down.

In the Quaternary era the Palestine rift was formed. Most present-day species were present, and man appeared (cf. Gen. 1:26; the present writer distinguishes between "man" as defined anthropologically and "the Adam" as presented in the Bible). The glacial periods in the more northerly regions were approximately paralleled by pluvial periods in the Mediterranean and Near Eastern regions.

*B. Pluvial Ages.* Students of European and North American geology report four successive periods of glaciation (named respectively Gunz, Mindel, Riss, and Würm), when ice covered the northern latitudes of these continents. In Palestine (and regions of equal latitude) these periods were times of excessive rainfall and hence are called Pluvial ages. But there is evidence of only three such ages in Palestine: Pluvial A (Grand Pluvial, 600,000–300,000 B.P.), corresponding to the first two glacial ages; Pluvial B (200,000–120,000 B.P.), corresponding to Riss; and Pluvial C (70,000–14,000 B.P., broken by an interstadial period 48,000–32,000 B.P.), corresponding to Würm. Interpluvial periods corresponded to the interglacial periods.

Apart from the Bible scholars who identify the biblical Adam with the anthropoid creatures that existed prior to the glacial/pluvial ages, and who identify the Noachian Flood with one of these ages, biblical scholarship generally places all the biblical events from the creation of Adam after the last glacial/pluvial period. Our discussion of Palestine will therefore be confined largely to the latter part of the Quaternary, commonly called the Holocene or Recent period, which is dated from the end of the glacial/pluvial period.

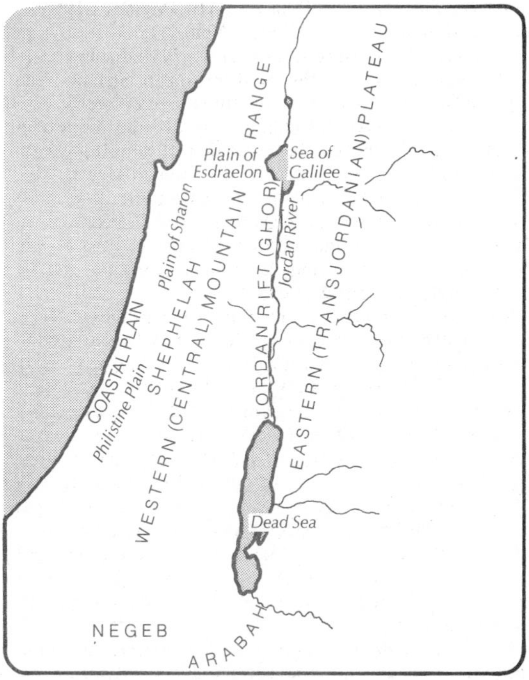


The highest mountain in the Palestine area, Jebel Rām (about 45 km. [28 mi.] E of Elath), a mass of red Nubian sandstone on a pre-Cambrian granite platform (A. D. Baly)

| | Geological | Climatic | | Archeological and Cultural Anthropological |
|---|---|---|---|---|
| 600,000 B.P. | Early Pleistocene | Grand Pluvial | | Lower Paleolithic |
| 300,000 B.P. | Middle Pleistocene | First Interpluvial | | |
| 200,000 B.P. | | Pluvial B | | |
| 120,000 B.P. | | Last Interpluvial | | |
| 70,000 B.P. | Late Pleistocene | Pluvial C | Early Pluvial C | Middle Paleolithic |
| 48,000 B.P. | | | Gottweig Interstadial | |
| 32,000 B.P. | | | Late Pluvial C | Upper Paleolithic |
| 14,000 B.P. | Food-producing activities begin | | | |
| | Holocene (Recent) | Postpluvial | | Mesolithic - - - Neolithic |
| 8000 B.C. | Food-producing activities become dominant | | | |
| 5000 B.C. | | | | Chalcolithic |
| 3200 B.C. | | | | |

Geological, Climatic, and Archeological/Cultural Anthropological Ages (after a chart from E. Anati, *Palestine Before the Hebrews*)

*IV. Geography.–A. North-South Divisions.* Four features running approximately N-S are common to the entire Levant: (1) the littoral or coastal plain; (2) a western (sometimes called central) mountain range; (3) the rift-valley; (4) an eastern mountain range or high plateau. These features, with some local variations, are characteristic of Palestine. Three portions of these regions — the Shephelah, the Valley of Esdraelon, and the Negeb — must be considered separately. (*See* Vol. I, Map II; cf. *HGHL,* pp. 52-62; *WHAB,* pp. 17-20.)

Kurkar ridge of cliffs along the coast of Ashkelon (A. D. Baly)

*1. Coastal Plain.* This littoral plain extends practically the entire length of Palestine. At the northern end, at Ras en-Naqûrā (Rōsh ha-Niqrāh), the coastal plain is broken by a mountain spur that reaches the sea (the "Ladder of Tyre," 1 Macc. 11:59; cf. *Ant.* xiii.5.4 [146]; *BJ* ii.10.2 [188]). The plain is also broken at the foot of Mt. Carmel. The littoral of Palestine accordingly is divided historically and geographically into three parts. (1) The plain of Asher extends S from the Ladder of Tyre to Mt. Carmel, where the plain widens to about 10 km. (6 mi.); it is known today as the plain of Zebulon. (2) The plain of SHARON (Isa. 33:9; 65:10) extends S of Mt. Carmel from the Crocodile River (Nahr ez-Zerqā) to the Yarkon (Naḥal Yarqôn), a distance of about 50 km. (31 mi.) N-S and from 10 km. (6 mi.) to 15 km. (9 mi.) E-W. It is characterized largely by sand dunes (kurkar ridges) from the Pliocene period. In the central part of the plain an outcropping of Mousterian red sand, once covered with oak, rises to about 55 m. (180 ft.). Watered by perennial rivers and seasonal wadis, Sharon was capable of fertility (cf. 1 Ch. 5:16; Isa. 65:10) and indeed has become fertile in modern times. (3) The rest of the coast of Palestine is loosely identified as the Philistine plain (Jgs. 1:19, 34), which extends to Gaza (70 km., 42 mi.). The plain broadens to about 30 km. (18 mi.) in the southern

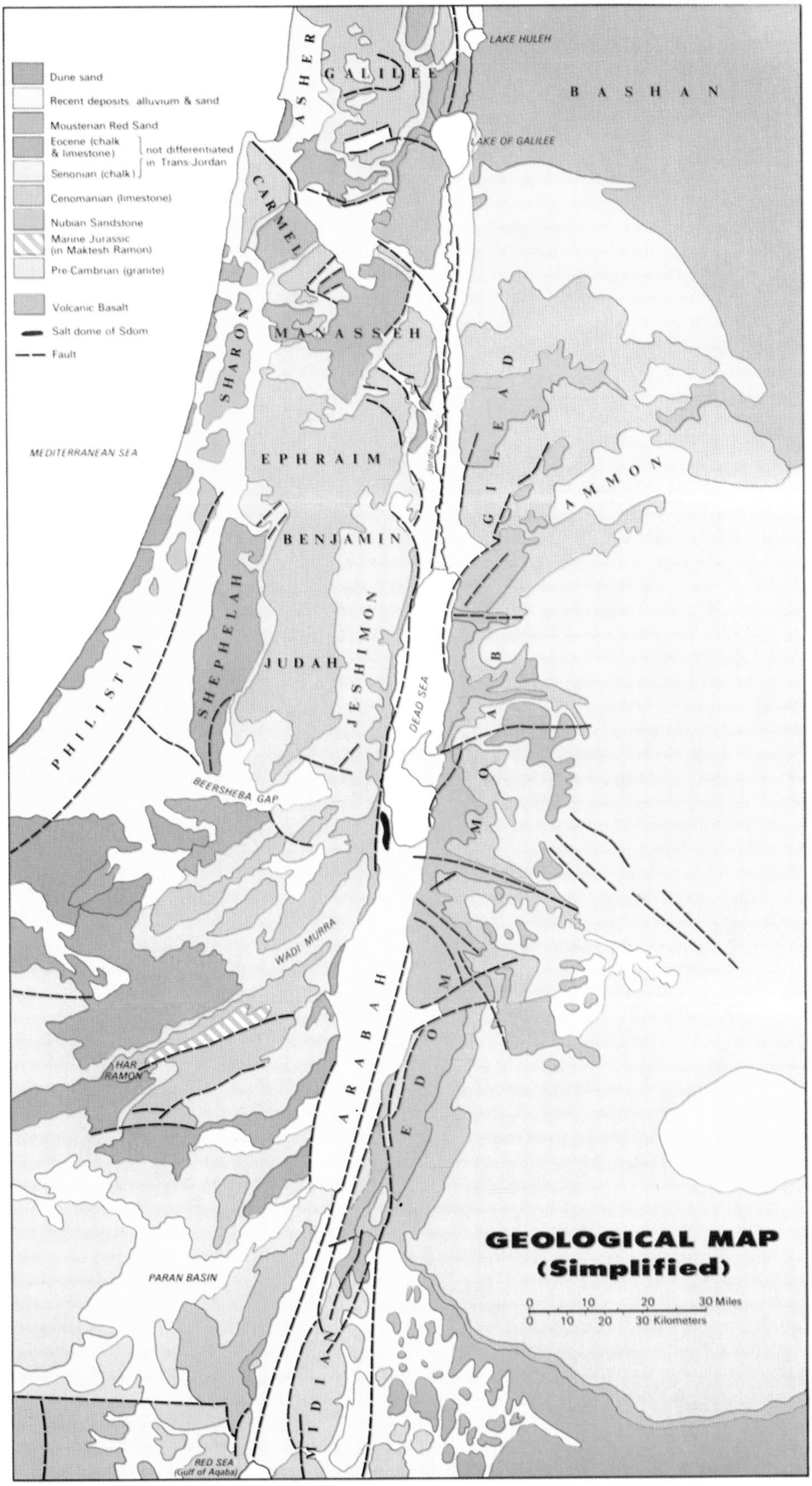


*Plate 46.* From A. Denis Baly, *Geography of the Bible*, 2nd edition, Harper and Row. Copyright 1974 by A. Denis Baly

*Plate 47.* The forested mountains of Gilead (A. D. Baly)

*Plate 48.* Wâdī Beidan, a Senonian chalk valley that leads from Shechem to Tirzah (A. D. Baly)

*Plate 49.* The old road from Jerusalem to Jericho (W. S. LaSor)

*Plate 50.* The wooded slopes of Mt. Hermon (Jamie Simson, Das Photo)

*Plate 51.* The plain of Gennesaret at the northwest end of the Sea of Galilee (W. S. LaSor)

*Plate 52.* The source of the Jordan River near Dan (W. S. LaSor)

*Plate 53.* The Mediterranean Sea west of Silifke (about 120 km., 75 mi., SW of Tarsus) (D. H. Condit)

*Plate 54.* The rugged Judean countryside near Bethlehem. Note the natural terracing of the Cenomanian limestone developed into agricultural terraces (A. D. Baly)

*Plate 55.* The mound of Heshbon in early spring (B. VanElderen)

*Plate 56.* The mound of Heshbon in early summer (B. VanElderen)

part. Sand dunes, some 45 m. (150 ft.) in height, were once thought to be formed of sand from the Nile, but now they are explained as soft chalk and limestone brought down from the Shephelah by the numerous wadis (cf. *GB*, p. 136). The five principal cities of the Philistines (Ashdod, Ashkelon, Gath, Gaza, and Ekron; cf. 1 S. 6:17) were in this plain. (See *GB*, pp. 121-143; *HGHL*, pp. 101-143.) 101-143.)

Because of the nature of the coastal plain, the only good natural harbor was at Acco. The Philistines (or earlier peoples) made use of the Yarkon at Tell el-Qasîleh (*LBHG* [rev. ed. 1979], pp. 273, 275); this may also have been used by the Phoenicians bringing materials for Solomon's temple. At the Phoenician fortification known as Strato's tower Herod constructed a city and harbor, which he renamed CAESAREA (*Ant.* xv.7.3 [217], 9.6 [331-341]; cf. Acts 18:22).

2. *Shephelah* (pronounced shə-fē'lə). Between the coastal plain and the central mountain range are sections of piedmont or foothill: E of the plain of Zebulun (the Shephelah of Galilee; cf. *GB*, p. 162), E of the Sharon plain (the Shephelah of Israel; cf. Josh. 11:16; *GB*, p. 141), and most notably E of the Philistine plain (the Shephelah of Judah, commonly called simply the Shephelah). The name Shephelah (Heb. *š$^e$pēlâ*) was obviously given to the area by people who lived on the mountain range, for it means "lowland" (cf. Josh. 11:16). The Shephelah (of Judah) is about 45 km. (27 mi.) long and 15-20 km. (9-12 mi.) in width, and is very fertile; hence it was the region of frequent battles between the Philistines and the Hebrews.

The Shephelah is cut by several valleys that formed routes between the coastal region and the cities on the mountain range. Among these are the valley of Aijalon (Josh. 10:12), the valley of Sorek (Wâdī eṣ-Ṣarâr) (Jgs. 16:4), and the valley of Elah (Wâdī es-Sanṭ) (1 S. 17:2).

(See *GB*, pp. 121-130; *HGHL*, pp. 112-143; *see also* SHEPHELAH.)

3. *Western (Central) Mountain Range*. This range extends the length of Palestine except for the plain of Jezreel (Esdraelon). D. Baly has pointed out that the range is actually composed of a number of uplifts or domes in regions that run approximately NE-SW, cut by faults and depressions (*GB*, pp. 7f., 28-30). To the visitor untrained in geology, however, it appears to be an almost continuous range, with high points at Har Meron in Upper Galilee (1208 m., 3962 ft.), at Mt. Ebal in Samaria (940 m., 3084 ft.), and in the south toward Hebron (1012 m., 3320 ft.). The range continues SW into the "high Negeb," where several peaks rise above 1000 m. (3300 ft.), the highest being Har Ramôn (1033 m., 3389 ft.). North of Galilee the western range is named the LEBANON and the eastern the Hermon (*see* HERMON, MOUNT), but because the Hermon lies in a northeast-southwest plane, it sometimes gives the appearance of belonging to Cisjordan more than to Transjordan; indeed, as Baly has shown (*GB*, p. 7 map 3), the mountains of Upper Galilee and the Anti-lebanon to which the Hermon belongs are part of the same geological pattern. *See* Plate

The northern portion of the western range has been known historically as GALILEE, including Upper and Lower Galilee (*see* Vol. II, Plates 15, 19) and the plain of Esdraelon. The continuation of the western range from the southern edge of the plain of Esdraelon to about the latitude of Jerusalem was known as Samaria (Ob. 19; Ezr. 4:7; *see* SAMARIA, COUNTRY OF) after the capital founded by Omri (1 K. 16:24); prior to that it was the region of Manasseh and Ephraim (cf. 12:25). The southern portion of the range came to be called JUDAH after the principal tribe (cf. 12:17). South of Beer-sheba the region was called the Negeb (or Negev; Gen. 20:1).

The Israelites lived principally in the mountains of Galilee, Samaria, and Judah. A major north-south road, sometimes called the Way of the Water-parting (*GB*, p. 98) — although unnamed in the Bible — wound between mountain heights and climbed over lesser hills. There were no rivers — only seasonal watercourses (wadis). But there were a number of springs of "living waters" (Heb. *ʿayin*, "spring, source"), which together with dug wells (Heb. *b$^e$'ēr*, "well") provided water. Place names with ʿAin (ʿEn), however, do not always indicate the presence of a spring (*HGHL*, p. 72 n. 1).

The western slopes of the central range are gentle and well watered, often forming the "lowlands" or Shephelah. The eastern slopes, on the other hand, are steep, arid, and forbidding. Apart from some lesser-known and difficult ways, the only roads connecting the central range with the Ghor (the rift-valley between the Sea of Galilee and the Dead Sea) were at the valley of Jezreel, the valley formed by Wâdī Fârʿah, and the valley from Bethel to Jericho. *See* Plate 49.

(See *GB*, pp. 152-190; *HGHL*, pp. 171-240.)

4. *Plain of Esdraelon (Valley of Jezreel)*. The valley that extends from the Mediterranean to the Jordan, separating the hills of Lower Galilee from the complex formed by Mt. Carmel, the mountains of Samaria, and Mt. Gilboa, is in the Bible called Heb. *ʿēmeq yizr$^e$ʿē'l* ("Valley of Jezreel," Josh. 17:16) or *biqʿaṯ m$^e$giddôn* ("plain of Megiddo(n)," Zec. 12:11, if indeed this refers to the same place; but cf. W. S. LaSor, *The Truth about Armageddon* [1982], pp. 141, 144f.). In Jth. 1:8 this appears as Gk. *pedíon Esdrēlōn* ("plain of Esdraelon"). Further complicating the nomenclature, some modern scholars have applied the name "plain of Esdraelon" or "plain of Megiddo" to the western portion of the valley and "Valley of Jezreel" to the eastern — a convenient distinction but without any biblical support. The modern name, ʿEmeq Yizreʿel, is applied to the entire valley. *See* JEZREEL, VALLEY OF.

The valley is divided by the watershed, with the Kishon River (Nahr el-Muqaṭṭaʿ) flowing W to the Mediterranean, and the Harod River (Nahr Jālûd) flowing E to the Jordan near Beth-shan. Until modern times the valley was poorly drained and therefore a swamp in the wet season (cf. 1 K. 18:44; Jgs. 4:13-16; 5:19-21). The western part, from the narrow gap between Mt. Carmel and the hills of Galilee at Harosheth eastward to Zerʿîn (Jezreel), is roughly triangular in shape, about 40 km. (25 mi.) on the northern and southern sides. It is bordered on the north by the

Wadi between Jericho and Jerusalem (B. VanElderen)

scarp of the hills of Lower Galilee, Nazareth being a prominent city. At the southwest corner, Mt. Carmel rises steeply from the plain and runs SE, joining with the mountains of Samaria. The watershed is approximately at Jezreel, which is often considered the eastern end of the plain of Megiddo (Esdraelon). At this point the plain suddenly narrows from about 20 km. (12 mi.) to enter what is today called the valley of Jezreel (in distinction from the plain of Megiddo, as mentioned above) — a valley of never more than 3 km. (2 mi.) in width. With the hill of Moreh forming the northern border and Mt. Gilboa the southern (*see* Vol. II, Plate 16), the valley descends rather sharply to the Jordan Ghor near Beth-shan, reaching sea level at the spring of Harod (ʿAin Jālûd; cf. Jgs. 7:1) and dropping to 225 m. (740 ft.) below sea level at the Jordan, a distance of only about 25 km. (15 mi.). The western portion of the plain of Esdraelon belonged to Zebulon, the eastern portion to Issachar. The coastal region at the western end was part of the plain of Asher (known today as the "plain of Zebulon").

The plain of Esdraelon was thus mostly landlocked, and the means of ingress and egress were few but nevertheless very important. A main route to the west passed through the gap into the plain of Asher (Zebulon) and the gulf of Acco; the route to the east passed through the narrow valley to Beth-shan. The road to the north went past Mt. Tabor, forming part of the major highway from Damascus to Egypt that was often called the Way of the Sea (see IV.D below). To the south there were several exits; the best known was guarded by Megiddo and went via Wâdī ʿAra (Naḥal ʿIrôn) to the plain of Sharon; NW of Megiddo a fortified exit at Jokneam (Josh. 12:22) guarded the route leading to Dor; SE of Megiddo a route guarded by Taanach (Jgs. 5:19) also led to the plain of Sharon; and still further SE a road went up by the ascent of Gur (2 K. 6:13) to Ibleam, Dothan, and Samaria.

(See *HGHL,* pp. 246-266; *GB,* pp. 144-151.)

*5. Negeb.* The region S of Beer-sheba is referred to as the NEGEB (pronounced and sometimes spelled "Negev"). It has been suggested that the word came from a root meaning "parched," but it is usually defined as "south." Heb. *negeḇ* can be used either as a proper noun for the region S of Palestine (e.g., Jgs. 1:16) or as a common noun meaning "south" (e.g., Gen. 13:14). Because the term is often associated with Heb. *miḏbār,* "desert," the Negeb is sometimes thought of as an empty, perhaps sandy, wilderness. But *miḏbār* refers to a region of marginal rainfall, with soil composed more often of shingle than of sand — a region capable of supporting settlements if some method of collecting dew (e.g., rock mulching) or of irrigaton is employed. The Wilderness of Zin (*miḏbar ṣin,* not to be confused with the Wilderness of Sin, Ex. 16:1) is in the Negeb (Nu. 13:21).

The Negeb is shaped like an elongated triangle with its apex to the south. Its northern limit follows approximately the line formed by Gaza-Beer-sheba-Sodom, about 110 km. (70 mi.); its eastern border is the Arabah from the Dead Sea to the Gulf of Aqabah, about 170 km. (105 mi.); and its southwestern border runs from a location about 30 km. (20 mi.) S of Gaza to Eilat on the Gulf of Aqabah, about 210 km. (130 mi.). It has the physical features of the rest of Palestine: a coastal plain (in modern times known as the Gaza Strip), the Shephelah, the central mountain range (skewed toward the southwest in the Negeb and often called the "high Negeb"), and the rift-valley, here known as the Arabah. Its highest points include Har Ramôn (1033 m., 3389 ft.) near the present Sinai border; Har Saggî (1006 m., 3300 ft.), 18 km. (13 mi.) S of Har Ramôn; and numerous peaks above 900 m. (2950 ft.). In general the central (or western) range descends from just S of Hebron and then begins to rise again around Dimonah (opposite the south end of the Dead Sea); the highest points are at the Sinai border, at which point the range descends quite sharply to the Wilderness of Paran (*miḏbar pārān*).

(See *HGHL,* pp. 189-195; *GB,* pp. 99-111, 247-251; N. Glueck, *Rivers in the Desert* [1959].)

*6. Jordan Rift.* The Jordan Rift is part of a huge geological rift that extends from the KaraSu valley in Turkey to the Zambesi River in Africa. Within Palestine it extends from the foot of Mt. Hermon to the Gulf of Aqabah, about 420 km. (260 mi.). In biblical times the streams flowing from Mt. Hermon formed a lake in the Huleh basin (Lake Semechonitis/Semachonitis in *Ant.* v.5.1 [199]). Lake Huleh was approximately 70 m. (230 ft.) *above* sea level (at some point in the past a mapmaker erroneously indicated that it was below sea level, and this error has been reprinted in countless Bibles and atlases), the same as present-day low spots in the Huleh basin. (In modern times the lake has been drained and the waters contained in a channel.) From there the Upper Jordan River cuts its way through a basalt plug (in comparatively recent times named Jisr Banât Yaʿaqub, "Bridge of the Daughters of Jacob"), descends about 250 m. (800 ft.), and empties into the Sea of Galilee (210 m., 688 ft. below sea level), a lake 12 km. (7 mi.) wide and 21 km. (13 mi.) long. *See also* GALILEE III.E; Plate 51.

The Jordan River proper originates with the waters from the Sea of Galilee, to which are added the Yarmûk and Jabbok (Wâdī Zerqā) and numerous lesser wadis that drain the Transjordan plateau, as well as the Wâdī Fârʿah and other (almost insignificant) wadis that descend from the western range. The river, except in flood, is contained in a narrow, meandering valley. This is located in a wider valley that the Arabs call the Zôr but which is called the "pride" or "jungle" of the Jordan in Jer. 12:5; 49:19; Zec. 11:3 (perhaps better translated "the swelling of the Jordan," since it is the portion of the Ghor that has been cut by the swollen flood waters). *See* JORDAN; *see also* Plate 52.

The KaraSu Valley in Turkey where the Great Rift begins (W. S. LaSor)

The Jordan empties into the Dead Sea (Salt Sea, Gen. 14:3; sea of the Arabah, Dt. 3:17; eastern sea, Ezk. 47:18; Lake Asphaltitis, *BJ* i.33.5 [657]) at about 393 m. (1292 ft.) below sea level (this measurement varies from year to year). The Dead Sea is 83 km. (52 mi.) long and 16 km. (10 mi.) wide, and its bottom — the lowest point of the rift — is about 800 m. (2600 ft.) below sea level. Its northern end is at the latitude of Jerusalem; its southern end is about 16 km. (10 mi.) S of the latitude of Beer-sheba.

The valley S of the Dead Sea is called the ARABAH

(a name given also to other portions of the rift; cf. BDB, p. 787). From the Dead Sea to the Gulf of Aqabah the Arabah is about 170 km. (105 mi.) long. It rises gradually from the level of the shore of the Dead Sea to a point about 90 m. (300 ft.) above sea level (at about the latitude of Petra) and then descends gradually to sea level at the head of the Gulf of Aqabah (Ezion-geber; cf. Nu. 33:35; 1 K. 9:26-28).

The rift (Ghor) becomes increasingly arid from the region where the Jabbok enters, and the Jordan draws salts from the valley. All water entering the Dead Sea leaves by evaporation, with the result that the salt content of the Dead Sea is exceedingly high (estimated at 25-30 percent). (See N. Glueck, *River Jordan* [1946]; *GB*, pp. 191-209; *HGHL*, pp. 284-331.)

7. *Eastern (Transjordanian) Plateau.* A high plateau stretches from the Jordan Rift eastward to the Arabian Desert. It lies at an average elevation of 600 m. (2000 ft.) and is cut by a complex drainage system of numerous wadis that form several deep gorges as they descend to the Jordan River or the Dead Sea. These gorges divide Transjordan into distinct regions. From north to south the gorges are: the Yarmuk, separating Bashan and the Golan from the dome of Gilead; the Jabbok (Wâdī Zerqā), separating Gilead from Ammon (Dt. 3:16); the Arnon (Wâdī el-Môjib; *see* Plate 43), at times the natural boundary between Ammon and Moab (Nu. 21:13, although Moab often extended further north; cf. v. 26); and the Zered (Wâdī el-Ḥesā), a natural boundary between Moab and Edom (cf. Dt. 2:13). The Arnon empties into the Dead Sea 35 km. (22 mi.) S of its northern end, and the Zered empties into it near its southern tip. Numerous other wadis cut the western scarp of the Transjordan plateau, the most important of which are the Kufrinjeh and the Râjeb in Gilead, the Nimrîn (Shuʿeib), Kefrein, and Ḥesbân in the plains of Moab, and the Zerqā Māʿîn 18 km. (11 mi.) N of the Arnon, with which it is sometimes confused (cf. Abel, *GP,* I, 171-78).

BASHAN, the region N of the Yarmuk, as a result of volcanic activity, was covered by very rich soil. The

Cracked surface of mud flats in the Arabah (A. D. Baly)

The Yarmûk River in upper Transjordan (B. VanElderen)

The Jabbok River (W. S. LaSor)

Volcanoes in the area of Jebel ed-Druze. In the foreground is a hard volcanic plug and in the background are softer cinder cones (A. D. Baly)

Jebel edh-Dhakar, a mass of volcanic basalt that forced its way through the Kurnub sandstone of the Zered region (A. D. Baly)

volcanic activity also resulted in great heights, with the range known as Jebel ed-Druze or Jebel Ḥaurân reaching an altitude of 1765 m. (5789 ft.), the highest point in either Cisjordan or Transjordan (*see* HAURAN). Between the Yarmuk and the Jabbok is the region of GILEAD (although at some periods the name included territory S of the Jabbok). The terrain is rugged and in biblical times was well forested (cf. Jer. 22:6; *see* Plate 47). The territory between the Jabbok and the Arnon is often simply called AMMON, and the region between the Arnon and the Zered, MOAB. But although the physical geography is established by the river gorges, the historical picture is considerably more complex. South of the Zered (Wâdī el-Ḥesā) was EDOM, which at some periods extended across the Arabah into the Negeb. Although historically it is not beyond question, the southern limit of Edom is generally taken to be just south of the head of the Gulf of Aqabah (which in modern times is the boundary between the Hashemite Kingdom of Jordan and Saudi Arabia).

*B. Mountains and Valleys.* Some of the highest peaks in Palestine have already been mentioned. The Bible, however, names many others, usually in connection with significant events. These include the following: Abarim in Moab (e.g., Nu. 33:44); Carmel N of Sharon (Jer. 46:18); Ebal in Samaria (Dt. 27:13); Jearim on the northern border of Judah (Josh. 15:10); Jerusalem (or Zion; often); Moriah (Gen. 22:2; generally identified with the temple mount); Nebo in Moab (Dt. 32:49); Olivet E of Jerusalem (Lk. 21:37); Pisgah in Nebo (Nu. 21:20); Seir in Edom (Gen. 32:3 [MT 4]); Shepher in the wilderness (Nu. 33:23); Sinai (Ex. 19:11); Sirion (Senir, Hermon, Dt. 3:9); Tabor in Galilee (Ps. 89:12 [MT 13]); Zalmon near Shechem (Jgs. 9:48); and Zemaraim in Ephraim (2 Ch. 13:4). It is important to note that the term "mountain" (Heb. *har*; Gk. *óros*) can be used not only of high mountains (e.g., the Hermon) but also of what may commonly be called hills. Thus, for example, "Mount" Tabor rises to an elevation of only 562 m. (1843 ft.). *See also* HILL; Plate 50.

The importance of valleys in a mountainous land such as Palestine cannot be overestimated. Valleys and plains of Cenomanian and Turonian rock that has broken down and weathered into terra rossa provide fertile areas for agriculture (*see* Plate 54), while valleys of Senonian chalk, not suitable for agriculture, are usually smooth and dry and afford good roads. Many valleys are named (over thirty by one count); but the subject is complicated by the variety of Hebrew and Greek words translated "valley." It would seem that Heb. *ʿēmeq,* from a root meaning "to be deep," should denote a depth, a low place, and that *biqʿâ,* from a root meaning "to cleave," should denote a cleft or a narrow valley. But both words seem to be used without regard to the root meanings. The plain of Megiddo is called *biqʿaṯ meḡiddô* (2 Ch. 35:22), but the valley of Jezreel where it spreads out by the hill of Moreh is called *ʿēmeq* (Jgs. 7:1; cf. 6:33). Isa. 40:4 (". . . and the rough places [shall become a] plain") uses *biqʿâ* for "plain." Heb. *naḥal* ("torrent, torrent-valley, wady," BDB, p. 636) is properly a seasonal riverbed; yet it can be used of the Arnon, which is a deep gorge with water in all seasons (Dt. 2:36), as well as for the Valley of Eshcol, a gentle valley with a seasonal river (Nu. 13:24). Heb. *gayʾ* is used both of the valley of Hinnom (Josh. 15:8) and of the "valley of the craftsmen" in the southern part of the plain of Sharon (Neh. 11:35; cf. 1 Ch. 4:14 mg.); it is unlikely that a valley similar to the Hinnom would be found in the Sharon.

The LXX is not consistent in translating these terms. It uses Gk. *pháranx* ("chasm, ravine") for *gayʾ* (Hinnom, Josh. 15:8), for *naḥal* (Zered, Nu. 21:12), and for *ʿēmeq* (Aijalon, Josh. 10:12); Gk. *cheímarros* ("winter-flowing," hence a wadi) for *naḥal* (Arnon, Dt. 2:36) and for *biqʿâ* (Dt. 8:7); Gk. *koilás* ("hollow") for *ʿēmeq* (e.g., Jezreel, Josh. 17:16); and Gk. *pedíon* ("plain") for *biqʿâ* (Megiddo, 2 Ch. 35:22). The neat differentiation in usage suggested by S. R. Driver (*HDB*, III, *s.v.* "Plain"; IV, *s.v.* "Vale, Valley") does not appear to be supported by the evidence.

*C. Seas and Rivers.* Hebrew *yām* may denote a sea, a lake, or even a river. In Palestine there are no large seas. The land borders on the MEDITERRANEAN SEA, which is called "the sea" (Nu. 13:29), "the Great Sea" (Nu. 34:6), "the western sea" (lit. "the sea behind"; east was always "before"; Dt. 11:24), and "the sea of the Philistines" (Ex. 23:31). The DEAD SEA is called "the Salt Sea" (e.g., Gen. 14:3), "the sea of the Arabah" (Dt. 3:17), and "the eastern sea" (lit. "the sea in front," Ezk. 47:18). The Sea of Galilee (*see* GALILEE, SEA OF) is most commonly called by that name, although it is also known as "the sea of Chinnereth" (Nu. 34:11; Josh. 12:3), "the Sea of Tiberias" (Jn. 6:1), and "the lake of Gennesaret" (Lk. 5:1). The Dead Sea and the Sea of Galilee, like the Mediterranean, can be called simply "the sea" (Isa. 16:8; Mt. 4:13). Lake Huleh (Semechonitis in *BJ* iii.10.7 [515]; iv.1.1 [2f.]; in Arabic known as Baḥret el-Ḥûleh) is not named in the Bible. It is often identified with the "waters of Merom" (Josh. 11:5), but this is questionable, since the location was not suitable for the military campaign described in Josh. 11:1-9 (*see* MEROM, WATERS OF). The RED SEA is a translation of Heb. *yām sûp* (lit. "sea of reeds," Ex. 13:18); it is probably also "the sea of Egypt" (Isa. 11:15). Heb. *hayyām* ("the sea") can also denote the Nile (RSV "the Nile"; lit. "the sea," Isa. 19:5) and the Euphrates (Isa. 21:1; Jer. 51:36; but the reference in Isa. 21:1 may be to the Persian Gulf; cf. BDB, p. 411).

Some of the rivers in Palestine have already been discussed. Heb. *nāhār* ("ever-flowing stream, river") is not used of rivers within Palestine. The single great river in Palestine is, of course, the Jordan, which is called simply "the Jordan" (Heb. *hayyardēn*; Gk. *ho Iordanēs*). Cisjordan has no rivers of great size; but numerous brooks or rivers — some of which have water only in the rainy season — are named, e.g., the Kishon (Jgs. 4:7), the Kidron (2 S. 15:23), and the Cherith (1 K. 17:5). The BROOK OF EGYPT (Nu. 34:5) probably refers to the Wâdī el-ʿArîsh in Sinai. (On the watercourses that flow into the Jordan from Cisjordan, see *GP,* I, 169f.; on the great rivers that flow into the Jordan and Dead Sea from Transjordan, see IV.A.7 above; cf. *GP,* I, 171-78.)

*See* Vol. I, Map II.

*D. Roads.* The principal roads in Palestine generally ran N-S. Because of the mountainous character of Cisjordan and the deep gorges in Transjordan, the trunk roads of necessity were either in the Mediterranean littoral or toward the east in the Transjordanian plateau. A major highway from very ancient times joined Damascus (and points to the east) with Egypt; it proceeded along the southeastern flanks of Hermon, crossed the Upper Jordan just before it enters the gorge at "the Bridge of the Daughters of Jacob" (see IV.A.6 above), and thence ran across Galilee to the plain of Esdraelon via one of the passes that cut the Carmel range (probably Wâdī ʿAra, alongside Megiddo), into the Sharon plain, and S to Gaza and Egypt. This, or some part of it, was called the Way of the Sea (Via Maris; cf. Isa. 9:1); since "sea" was a common term for "west," the name may have meant simply "the western road." At its southern end it was known as the "way of the land of the Philistines" (Ex. 13:17). Toward the east of the Transjordanian plateau the KING'S HIGHWAY (Nu. 20:17) led from Damascus to the head of the Gulf of Aqabah. Rebuilt by Trajan (*ca.* A.D. 106), it was known also as Trajan's Road, and by Arabs as Tariq es-Sulṭan (the Sultan's Highway). The modern highway was relocated further to the east; it follows more or less the "Pilgrim's Road," which avoids some of the deep river valleys crossed by the King's Highway (see *GB,* p. 95 map 40).

There were other north-south roads. In Cisjordan one ran along the Jordan Valley and another along the waterparting of the central mountain range. Numerous east-west roads had great local importance but were little used by international merchants or military forces. These followed

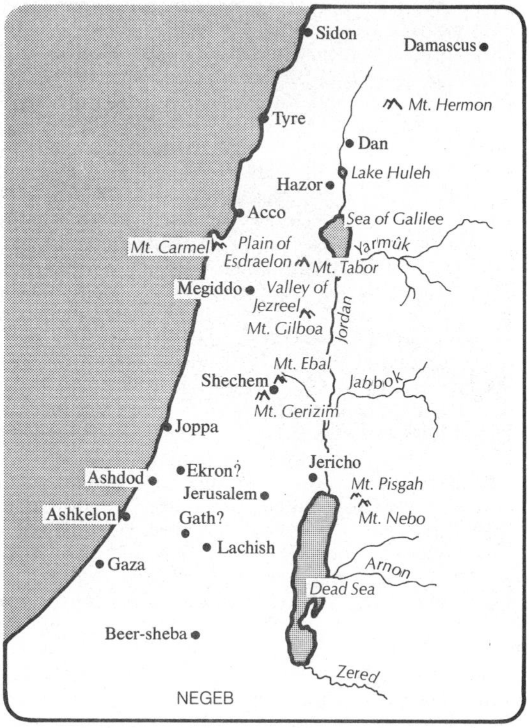


the valleys that led from the central range either to the Jordan Ghor or to the coastal plain. Principal cities were located on these routes. (See IV.A.4 above; *see also* Vol. I, Map V.)

*E. Cities.* There were nc great cities in Palestine; nevertheless, the Bible refers to scores of cities, towns, and villages, and many significant persons and events in the Judeo-Christian tradition are connected with these places. The principal city was the capital, JERUSALEM. The cities of the Philistine Pentapolis (Ashdod, Ashkelon, Gath, Gaza, and Ekron) are named several times, as are the capital cities of Ammon (Rabbah, Josh. 13:25; Dt. 3:11) and Moab (Kir-haresheth, 2 K. 3:25) and some of the cities of the DECAPOLIS. Cities that guarded passes or roads leading into the central highlands are referred to more for their strategic locations than for their size or cutural contributions (e.g., Jericho [Josh. 7:2], Lachish [10:31], Hazor [11:10], and many others; see also IV.A.4 above). Some of the communities mentioned in the Bible were so insignificant that their locations can no longer be determined; and some places of political significance were deemed hardly worthy of notice in the Bible (e.g., Omri's capital at Samaria). These facts underscore the observation that the Bible is concerned with the revelatory and redemptive acts of God and the responses of His people, rather than with a history of Palestine.

See G. A. Barrois, *Manuel d'archéologie biblique,* I [1939], 127-212; *GB,* pp. 182-190; *see also* CITY.

*F. Tribal Portions.* The tribes of Asher, Zebulun, Naphtali, and Issachar were allotted portions in Galilee. Later Dan was relocated in the extreme north of that region. The tribes of Ephraim and Manasseh were located in Samaria; Manasseh was also given a portion in northern Transjordan (Gilead). Also apportioned land in Transjordan were Reuben (Moab and Ammon) and Gad (Ammon). Judah, Simeon, and Dan were located in the southern part of Palestine (later called Judah, since Judah appears to have absorbed Simeon, and Dan was relocated in the north). The tribe of Benjamin occupied a region on the somewhat poorly defined border between Judah and Samaria. (*See* Vol. I, Map VI; see also *WHAB*, pp. 42-44; *GAB*, pp. 58-61, Map 11; *LBHG*, pp. 191-285.)

*V. Climate.*–We are concerned here with climatic conditions (i.e., characteristic weather patterns) in Palestine from approximately the end of the last pluvial age to postbiblical times. Local weather conditions at any specific point in time are governed by a number of factors: the season of the year, location in relation to large land or sea masses, latitude, topography, air movements, etc. The combination of all these factors over a period of time produces the climate of the region.

*A. Seasons.* Because it lies within the temperate zone, Palestine might be expected to have four seasons; but in fact it has only two, due to several factors: (1) it is bordered on the west by the Mediterranean Sea; (2) it is located relatively close to two large continental masses (Europe and Africa) that have considerable differences in temperature and moisture; (3) it is on the edge of the region affected by the monsoons of southern Asia and the Indian ocean, which produce a two-season year. Palestine's two seasons are dry ("summer," e.g., Gen. 8:22; Am. 3:15) and wet ("winter," e.g., Gen. 8:22; Jer. 36:22). Due in part to the rotation and the inclination of the earth, winds in Palestine are prevailingly from the west: from the northwest in WINTER and from the southwest in SUMMER. These are known as "Etesian [periodic] winds." In summer they are affected by the warm, dry climate of northern Africa and in winter by the cold, moist climate of Europe. The presence of the Mediterranean, however, moderates these conditions so that extremes of temperature and rainfall are within relatively narrow limits. The seasonal climate is comparable to that of the western part of southern California. *See* Plates 55, 56.

*B. Former and Latter Rains.* Because of the frequency of these terms in the Bible, it is sometimes thought that Palestine had two rainy seasons — an error apparently resulting from unfamiliarity with the land and misunderstanding of the biblical terms. The rainy season is separated from the dry by transitional periods during which some rain may fall. Between summer (June-September) and winter (December-March) such rains are the "former rains," and between winter and summer they are the "latter rains." RAIN regularly falls in winter, usually in two- or three-day periods at intervals of about one week, and this was accepted as normal by the people of the Bible. The early (former or autumn) rains (e.g., Dt. 11:14; Jer. 5:24; Joel 2:23) afforded the farmer a period for preparing the fields and planting, and the latter (or spring) rains (e.g., Jer. 5:24; Hos. 6:3) extended the growing season. These were looked upon, if abundant, as a blessing from the Lord (Dt. 11:14); lack of them was viewed as punishment. Times of drought or "no rain" were probably years in which early and latter rains were lacking and winter rainfall was subnormal rather than completely absent, based on the fact that no year of complete absence of rain has been recorded in modern Palestine.

*C. East Wind.* During the transitional seasons (April-early June, September-early November) there are seasons of excessive dry heat, described as the "east wind" (e.g., Jonah 4:8), "hot wind" (e.g., Jer. 4:11), and "south wind" (e.g., Lk. 12:55). In modern times this is called the *sirocco* or *khamsin* (Arab. *ḫamsin* means "fifty"; at one time it was thought there were fifty such days a year); in modern Hebrew it is the *šaraḇ*. The wind blows from the southeast (or east or south), the temperature rises by 10° C (18° F) or more, the air becomes filled with very fine sand and takes on the color of lead, the humidity falls, vegetation wilts, and human beings and animals become irritable. It usually lasts two or three days but may last a week or more. To the people of the Bible this was a warning or figure of God's judgment (cf. Hos. 12:1 [MT 2]; Isa. 27:8; Ezk. 17:10). (*See also* WIND.)

*D. Other Features.* DEW was a very important feature of the climate, often furnishing moisture when there was no rain, particularly on the windward slopes. An abundance of dew was a blessing from the Lord (Dt. 33:28), whereas its absence was a curse (Hag. 1:10). It could be heavy enough at night to soak a garment (cf. Jgs. 6:38) and hang like a cloud (Isa. 18:4), but it disappeared quickly after the sun came up (Hos. 13:3). SNOW falls only rarely in Palestine, and then only on the higher portions of the Cisjordanian and Transjordanian ranges. HAIL, which results from the rapid currents in heavy formations of cumulus clouds, was likewise considered a punishment from the Lord (Ezk. 13:11, 13), although on occasion it was seen as His intervention on behalf of His people (Josh. 10:11). Since such cloud formations are unusual in Palestine, hail is not common. The WHIRLWIND was a phenomenon of indefinite characteristics, ranging from dust devils to tornado-like winds; the latter were usually along the coastal plain.

*E. Effects of Latitude and Topography.* In general, rainfall decreases from N to S and from higher to lower altitudes in Palestine; but this statement must be modified by other factors. Since the wind is prevailingly from the west, and since it gathers moisture only when it moves over bodies of water, more rain falls on the western slopes of the central mountain range and on the Transjordanian plateau than on the eastern slopes (known as the "rain shadow"). Likewise, since the Jordan Ghor is below sea level, the northern part of it is drier than surrounding regions and the southern part is without rain during almost the entire year, largely because it lies within the rain shadow. The almost total absence of weather fronts means that whatever rainfall there is must come from condensation of moisture in the clouds as they move over higher elevations. As a result the low-lying coastal region (which is nearest the source of the moisture) gets less rainfall than the Shephelah, the windward side of the central range, or even the western portion of the Transjordanian plateau.

*F. Has the Climate Changed?* Because the Bible contains statements stressing the fecundity of the land (e.g., "flowing with milk and honey," Nu. 13:27), some have theorized that the climate of Palestine has changed since biblical times. This is strongly denied by certain other writers who state that the climate has not changed in the last eight or nine thousand years — certainly well before any description of Palestine in the Bible. D. Baly (*GB*, pp. 64-76) makes the most acceptable statement: "The answer to this very vexed question is both yes and no" (p. 64). The biblical period had a fairly uniform climate, bracketed by an earlier wetter period (prior to 4000 B.C.) and a later wetter period (*ca.* 400 B.C. to the first part of the common era). There have been climatic fluctuations or cycles, although none has been anything like the change that occurred at the end of the pluvial ages.

But certain factors have altered the land's floral and faunal characteristics and to some extent its fertility. The principal factor has been human occupation. With the shift from nomadism to settled communities, certain animals withdrew. Trees were cut down to provide space for planting and grazing (Josh. 17:14-18), as well as for building materials and firewood (this was greatly accelerated under the Ottoman empire, which imposed a tax on trees). Goats were widely raised, and they destroyed young trees and other vegetation. The diminishing of the forests led to a decrease in the retention of moisture as well as to some increase in wind and rain erosion. These and similar factors resulted in conditions that have sometimes appeared to be the result of climate changes. In the last few decades these effects have been noticeably reversed through cultivation of the land, irrigation, and reforestation. (*See also* FLORA II.)

(See C. E. P. Brooks, *Climate Through the Ages* (1949); H. H. Lamb, *The Changing Climate* (1968); A. D. Crown, *JNES*, 31 [1972], 312-330; *GP*, I, ch. V; *GB*, chs. 4–6; *HGHL*, pp. 62-88.)

*VI. Biota.–A. Flora.* Within the short space of 200 km. (125 mi.) almost every kind of vegetation from arctic (on Mt. Hermon) to subtropical (Sea of Galilee, Jordan Ghor, and Dead Sea basin) is present in Palestine. Writing of the plain of Gennesaret, Josephus stated with understandable exaggeration: "There is not a plant which its fertile soil refuses to produce, and its cultivators in fact grow every species. . . . One might say that nature had taken pride in thus assembling, by a *tour de force*, the most discordant species in a single spot, and that, by a happy rivalry, each of the seasons wishes to claim this region for her own" (*BJ* iii.10.8 [516-18]). One does find typical Mediterranean flora along the littoral and into the Shephelah, vegetation of the temperate zone on the central and eastern heights, and tropical vegetation in the rift-valley from the Sea of Galilee to the lower end of the Dead Sea, wherever water is plentiful (e.g., Jericho and En-gedi). Desert varieties are found in the Negeb and in arid regions of the Jordan Ghor and Transjordan.

Certain regions are noted in the Bible for their particular vegetation. Olives, vines, and grain were common in the Shephelah as well as in other regions (cf. Hos. 2:8 [MT 10]; Jgs. 15:5). The oaks of Bashan were proverbial (Isa. 2:13; Ezk. 27:6; Zec. 11:2). Because of the close connection between vegetation and weather, the prophets often spoke of the abundance or the destruction of trees and vegetation as a manifestation of Yahweh's blessings and punishments (cf. Joel 1; Hos. 2:9 [MT 11]).

A word of caution is in order. The names for plants and trees given in the standard Bible translations are not always reliable. As a comparison of English versions will show, much uncertainty exists over the meanings of some biblical terms, especially the Hebrew, and the LXX and Vulg. equivalents are sometimes misleading.

(*See* FLORA; see also *MPB*; G. E. Post, *Flora of Syria, Palestine, and Sinai* [2nd ed., 2 vols., 1932-1933].)

*B. Fauna.* Because of its geographical location, Palestine has been as open to animal migrations as to human, especially those from southern Europe, southwestern Asia, and northern Africa. Accordingly, the remains of a great many species have been found, and the biblical record refers to many "kinds" of FISH, BIRDS, CATTLE, creeping things, and beasts of the earth (cf. Gen. 1:21-25).

Again, caution is necessary, for the precise meanings of some of the Hebrew words is not known, and some of the identifications made in Modern Hebrew are inaccurate; thus the various translations of these terms are confused and misleading. Caution and humility are also required by a recognition that changes have occurred in the fauna of Palestine. The climatic changes that occurred in the Quaternary, particularly during the Pluvial periods, caused faunal relocations. The domestication of animals that characterized the Neolithic caused further disturbances in the faunal situation, for the husbandmen attempted to drive off predators, while other species withdrew from the vicinity of human communities.

Domesticated animals mentioned in the Bible include the horse (Gen. 47:17), ass (12:16), mule (2 S. 13:29), pig (an abominable thing; cf. Isa. 65:4), camel (Gen. 32:15 [MT 16]), and small and large cattle (e.g., sheep, ox; cf. Gen. 13:2, 5-7). It is often claimed that both the horse and the camel are mentioned anachronistically in the Bible. Current knowledge supports the presence of these animals in Palestine well before the patriarchal period, but the date of domestication is still in question. Wild animals include the wolf (Gen. 49:27), jackal (possibly the term includes the fox; cf. Ps. 63:10 [MT 11]), bear (2 S. 17:8), lion (Isa. 30:6), and possibly the leopard or cheetah (cf. Hab. 1:8). The bear and the lion are now extinct in Palestine.

(*See* ZOOLOGY; see also F. S. Bodenheimer, *Animal and Man in Bible Lands* [Eng. tr. 1960]; *GP*, I, 219-233.)

***VII. Cultural Ages.***–Physical anthropologists have given names to certain periods based on the material used for tools. The Stone Age is divided into the Old Stone Age (Paleolithic), the Middle Stone Age (Mesolithic), and the New Stone Age (Neolithic). In Palestine the Paleolithic Age extended throughout the Pleistocene (2,000,000-14,000 B.P.). (*See* Chart on p. 636.)

*A. Lower Paleolithic.* During the Lower Paleolithic Age (600,000-70,000 B.P.) three principal traditions of stone industries have been identified: the Chopper (Pebble) tradition, the Bifacial tradition, and the Tayacian tradition (called Tabunian in the Near East, after Tabun in Mt. Carmel). Remains of the Pebble tradition have been found in sites from the Grand Pluvial periods in the Jordan Valley, and also on the shores of what was probably an early Quaternary lake in the same valley (cf. E. Anati, pp. 59f.). Remains of the Bifacial tradition are quite extensive in Palestine. These people were hunters of large animals (elephants, rhinoceroses, hippopotamuses), and they learned to master fire. Evidence from Pluvial B (*ca.* 200,000 B.P.) is found in the upper Jordan Valley and in the Judean desert. Other finds were made on the northern coast of Israel, in the Negeb, and on the Transjordanian plateau (see Anati, pp. 62-70). The Tabunian tradition is also found at Umm Qatafa in the Judean desert and at Yabrud on the eastern slopes of the Anti-lebanon. Some scholars believe that the makers of these tools were food-collectors rather than hunters. In the late Tabunian (Pluvial C) new types of tools are found, some of which appear to be transitional to the Mousterian culture (Anati, p. 76).

*B. Middle Paleolithic.* Several hundred sites of this age, often called Mousterian, have been found in Palestine. It originated about the beginning of Pluvial C (the Würm glaciation in Europe, *ca.* 70,000 B.P.) and continued for about 40,000 years. Radiocarbon datings from Tabun date Level C at *ca.* 41,000 B.P. and Level B at 39,500 B.P. Many new species of animals are attested, including bears, foxes, hares, squirrels, and wolves; very likely they migrated

Skeleton of Skhul man (W. S. LaSor)

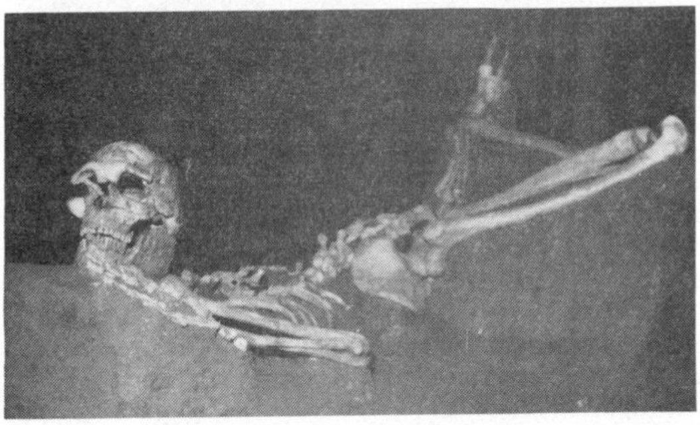

from Europe to escape the cold. This faunal break occurred between Levels B and C at Tabun, hence sometime after the Gottweig Interstadial period (between Early and Late Pluvial C) had begun. Human skeletal remains from Tabun and from Skhul (Sukhul) — two sites separated by less than 125 m. (400 ft.) — also show notable differences, suggesting to some scholars that a different species of hominid entered the land during the same period. The Skhul man, moreover, was different from both the Neanderthal of the Middle Paleolithic and the Homo Sapiens of the Upper Paleolithic (a problem that is further complicated by the fact that scholars are not yet in agreement in dating or defining Homo Sapiens). (See *AP* [rev. 1960], pp. 49-64.)

*C. Upper Paleolithic.* This age began with the late stages of the Würm glaciation (*ca.* 28,000 B.P.). The introduction of a new culture S of the chain of mountain ranges separating northern Europe from the Mediterranean region suggests that people were seeking a milder climate. They were of a new physical type, apparently of a higher intelligence, and left traces of the earliest man-built structures, living in either tents or huts. They had an aesthetic or artistic sense, clothed themselves, and fashioned a figurine that seems to represent a goddess of fertility. This culture spread over much of the northern hemisphere and lasted 20,000-25,000 years. It ended suddenly and was followed by what some have pictured as a dark age.

*D. Mesolithic.* The Middle Stone Age is a transitional period and is not even considered a separate age by many anthropologists. The greatest concentration of Mesolithic sites in southwestern Asia is found in western Palestine, where the dominant culture is called Natufian. Primitive boats enabled people to reach offshore islands; the invention of the rope led to the discovery that mechanical power could be generated by tightening and releasing the rope; and the invention of the bow and trap made hunting less dangerous. Mankind was on its way to becoming a food-producer, the characteristic of the "Neolithic revolution" (Anati, pp. 139-214).

*E. Neolithic.* The New Stone Age began approximately with the end of the Glacial and Pluvial ages and is generally considered the dividing point between the Pleistocene and the Holocene (Recent) periods. According to available data the earliest evidence of food production is dated *ca.* 11,000 B.P. ( = 9000 B.C.), at which time it was limited to the region SW of the Zagros and SE of the Taurus mountains. In the Jordan Valley the Neolithic Age began *ca.* 7500 B.C. The earliest stage of Neolithic is called Aceramic (or Pre-pottery), so named because human beings had not yet discovered how to make pottery. Pre-pottery Neolithic is found at Jericho and at Beidha, which lies 8 km. (5 mi.) S of Petra in Transjordan. The lowest carbon-14 date for Pre-pottery Neolithic at Jericho is *ca.* 5850 B.C. The cultures at Jericho, Yarmuk, and the coastal region (in the vicinity of Byblos) all developed pottery traditions. Carbon-14 dates of *ca.* 4600 B.C. have been obtained for the coastal culture. Megalithic monuments (e.g., DOLMENS) were erected during this period in Palestine — the only place in the world where they are found so early (Anati, p. 279). (See *FSAC,* pp. 135-37.)

*F. Chalcolithic.* This age is so named because bronze (actually, copper) tools and instruments began to appear alongside the stone tools. Agriculture and cattle-raising were fairly well developed. In the coastal tradition burials have been found in pottery vases that were stored in caves dug in Kurkur. In the late 34th and 33rd cents. northern cultural influences reached northern Palestine (Anati, p. 295), preparing the way for the new Urban Age. Other groups of people entered the south in the western Negeb, the region around Beer-sheba, the Judean desert, and Moab (including the site of Teleilât el-Ghassûl, where fully sedentary village life is attested [Anati, p. 306]). (See *FSAC,* pp. 137-146; *AP,* pp. 65-79.)

*G. Bronze.* With the Urban Age (which was — and often is still — called Early Bronze) we enter the "historical" period. Urban settlements have been found in Palestine at an earlier date than in the European Bronze Age. New tribes and peoples entered Palestine. The dominant race was (Proto-)Mediterranean, probably descended from the Mesolithic Natufian people; but other peoples — Alpine, Armenoid, and Eurafrican — can be distinguished, so that E. Anati has observed, "The picture we obtain is that of a great racial and cultural symbiosis equaled in no other historic or prehistoric period" (p. 323; cf. *GAB,* p. 15). In the light of this evidence there appears to be no sound basis for the theory that Gen. 10 is based on a late tradition representing conditions of the 1st millennium B.C. (See *CAH,* II/1 [1973], 77-116; *AP,* pp. 80-109.)

*H. Iron.* With the introduction of iron as a common material for making tools, the Iron Age opened (*ca.* 1200 B.C.). Since this falls well within the historical period, physical anthropology is of diminishing relevance for the present article.

(See P. Lemaire and D. Baldi, *Atlante storico della Bibbia* [1955], table on p. 15; C. C. McCown, *Ladder of Progress in Palestine* [1943], pp. 18-84; V. G. Childe, *New Light on the Most Ancient East* [1935], pp. 21-84; J. Mellaart, *Earliest Civilizations of the Near East* [1965], pp. 11-63; *BHI,* pp. 24-44.)

***VIII. History.***–The history of Palestine is reconstructed from archeological and literary evidence, the latter including both biblical and extrabiblical. For our purposes Palestine's history can be divided into (1) prehistoric, (2) pre-Israelite, (3) biblical (including the OT, intertestamental, and NT periods), and (4) postbiblical.

*A. Prehistoric.* To speak of "prehistoric" history may seem to be a contradiction of terms, but an outline of events, in greater or lesser detail, can be constructed from geological, anthropological, and archeological evidence (see VII above; *see also* ARCHEOLOGY OF PALESTINE AND SYRIA). It is clear that Palestine was inhabited from the Lower Paleolithic, and that hominids of higher intelligence appeared in the Upper Paleolithic and spread widely in the Mesolithic. Communities that can be called cities are found in the Neolithic, and evidence of walls and a large tower have been uncovered at Jericho. The "Urban" period, however, begins with Early Bronze, *ca.* 3200 B.C. At that time the population of Palestine was quite diverse, probably with Natufian descendants and also Alpine, Armenoid, and Eurafrican peoples. (See *AP,* pp. 49-79; *FSAC,* pp. 128-168.)

*B. Pre-Israelite.* When the Israelites entered Palestine it was inhabited by a number of peoples, such as those named in Gen. 15:19-21. Among these, the Canaanites, Amorites, and Jebusites appear to have been the most important, and the designation of Palestine as "the land of Canaan" suggests that the Canaanites were the most significant.

According to Gen. 10:15-20 Canaan was descended from Ham; linguistically, however, the Canaanites are identified as Semitic. Three considerations help to explain this problem. (1) Peoples from northern Africa were undoubtedly among the mixture of tribes and peoples in prehistoric Palestine (see VII.G above). This can be demonstrated not only by anthropological and archeological evidence but also by the comparative study of ancient Egyptian and Semitic languages, which show marked similarities in morphology, syntax, and vocabulary (see W. S. LaSor, "Semitic Phonemes" [Diss., Dropsie College, 1949]; cf.

*CAH,* I/1 [1971], 132-36). If the Canaanites were originally Hamitic as the biblical tradition indicates, the language does not present a serious problem, for it would not be the only time that an immigrant people — whether by peaceful means or by conquest — adopted the language of their new homeland. (2) If, as suggested above (I.C), "Canaanite" is related to the word for "purple," the term underwent semantic development; originally it probably indicated either (a) the people of the land where the purple dye was produced, or (b) a merchant or trader (cf. Hos. 12:7; Isa. 23:8; *ANET,* p. 246 n. 29). (3) "Canaanite" was quite likely not this people's original name, for the names of peoples are usually given to them by others (a well-established example is the name "Hittite"). The homogeneity of the Canaanites (cf. *AP,* p. 109) has to be viewed as resulting from an ethnic if not racial mixture, as is indicated in Gen. 10:15-19. (See S. Moscati, *Ancient Semitic Civilizations* [Eng. tr. 1958], pp. 99-123; *Face of the Ancient Orient,* pp. 203-229; E. Anati, pp. 411-437.) *See also* CANAAN.

Second in importance were the AMORITES, who are generally identified with the Amurru ("westerners") of cuneiform records (Sum. mar-tu; Akk. *amurru*). These people apparently moved westward from Mesopotamia and occupied parts of Syria and Palestine, perhaps in the middle of the 3rd millennium. The earliest cuneiform references (latter part of the 3rd milennium) indicate that the Amurru were a culturally inferior group of nomads or seminomads located in Syria; they are later portrayed as petty states with powerful kings (*CAH,* I/2 [1972], 562-66). They were responsible to some degree for the end of Ur III; later they established the Amorite dynasty in Babylon, of which Hammurabi is the best-known ruler. In the middle of the 2nd millennium Amurru was the northernmost administrative district of Egypt, bordering on the north of Canaan (*CAH,* II/1 [1973], 472), and after this it came under Hittite control (cf. *ANET,* pp. 203-205). The Amarna letters (e.g., 60, 70, 158) refer to a number of Amorite city-states. With the invasions of the sea-peoples and the Hittite wars the Amurru vanish from history.

Biblical evidence, on the other hand, suggests that the Amorites were a Canaanite tribe (Gen. 10:15f.; Ex. 3:8), that they dwelt in the mountains (Dt. 1:19) whereas the Canaanites dwelt in the valleys and plains, and that they had "kingdoms" in Transjordan at Heshbon and Bashan (Josh. 9:10). It is within the realm of possiblity that two or more different names have become mixed, since Heb. *'aleph, hê, ḥêṯ* (= Arab. *ḥa* but not *ḫa*), and *'ayin* (but not *ghayin*) are all reflected in Akkadian by *'aleph* (or simply an initial vowel). That the traditions of the Amurru and the biblical Amorites are interrelated cannot be denied, but to assume that the terms are everywhere identical is unwarranted (cf. Noth, *OT World,* pp. 77, 237f.).

The Jebusites occupied JEBUS, the city that later became the Israelite capital under David (*see* JERUSALEM III.A, B). According to the biblical account the Jebusites were descendants of Canaan (Gen. 10:16). In Josh. 10:5 Adonizedek, the (Jebusite) king of Jerusalem, is named as one of five Amorite kings.

The HORITES, described as the original inhabitants of Seir (Gen. 14:6), are usually identified with the HURRIANS, a non-Semitic people who were present in Alalakh in the 18th cent. and in Palestine in the 16th cent. (see I. J. Gelb, *Hurrians and Subarians* [1944]). This identification is not, however, without problems. That non-Semitic peoples were in Palestine before the patriarchal period is undeniable; but the theory that "Horites" in Gen. 14:6 is a proleptic reference to the later Hurrian invasion is not convincing. Similarly, the HITTITES (Gen. 15:20; "sons of Heth," 23:3 [RSV "Hittites"]) present a problem that has not been satisfactorily solved. The history of the Hittites is so complicated by the use of various names ("Hittite," "Hattic," "Proto-Hittite") and by the various peoples that enter into the early history (cf. O. R. Gurney, *Hittites* [1952], pp. 15-21) that it is necessary to ask, "What is meant by 'Hittite'?" The Hittites of Genesis should not necessarily be equated with the Hittites of the 16th cent. B.C., nor is it certain that the "Heth" of Gen. 10:15 is the physical ancestor of the "sons of Heth" in 23:3, since "father of" and "son of" in the Semitic languages can have expanded meanings.

Palestine during the 3rd millennium was thus inhabited by peoples of different descent, some of them living in city-states and maintaining separate ethnic or tribal names. In the 2nd millennium Palestine came under Egyptian influence, as witnessed by the AMARNA TABLETS.

(See K. M. Kenyon, *Amorites and Canaanites* [1966]; J. Gray, *Canaanites* [1964]; Moscati, *Face of the Ancient Orient,* pp. 161-233; *World,* pp. 1-110; Anati, pp. 317-437; Noth, *OT World,* pp. 49-104; A. T. Clay, *Amurru* [1909; needs much updating]; *CAH,* I/2 [1971], 208-237, 538-594; II/1 [1973], 77-116, 526-556; G. Buccellati, *Amorites of the Ur III Period* [1966]; A. Haldar, *Who Were the Amorites?* [1971].)

*C. Biblical Period.* Abraham entered the land of Canaan near the end of the 3rd or beginning of the 2nd millennium (some scholars would date this event as late as the middle of the 2nd millennium, if indeed they recognize it as having happened at all). The patriarchal period gives evidence of numerous tribes and several petty kingdoms (cf. Gen. 14:1f., 8f., 18) as well as of Egyptian influence (12:10-20), especially toward the end of the patriarchal period (chs. 42–50). The Israelite "conquest" of Canaan occurred after the middle of the 2nd millennium (*see* EXODUS, DATE OF THE), when there were still numerous city-states, and Canaanite enclaves continued to exist long after the Israelites were established in the land (cf. Jgs. 1; 3:1-5). At the beginning of the 12th cent. the sea-peoples occupied a number of locations in the littoral, and conflict between the Philistines and the Israelites was frequent (cf. Jgs. 14:4; 1 S. 17) until the reign of David (cf. 2 S. 19:9). (See *BHI,* pp. 67-182; *LBHG,* pp. 133-285; Noth, *OT World,* pp. 234-245; *NHI,* pp. 53-163; LaSor, *et al., OT Survey,* pp. 68-226.)

The consolidation of the land into a kingdom was the result of David's military efforts (*ca.* 1000 B.C.) and Solomon's administrative genius. At that time Israel's borders were extended beyond the limits of what is defined in this article as Palestine. After Solomon the kingdom was divided into the northern kingdom (Israel) and the southern kingdom (Judah). Israel was captured by the Assyrians (Samaria fell in 722/21), and Judah was captured by the Babylonians (Jerusalem fell in 597 and was destroyed in 586; *see* JERUSALEM III.E). Egyptian influence was seriously threatened and finally terminated by the Babylonians; and, following the conquest of Babylon by the Persians, Palestine became part of the Persian satrapy of "Beyond the River" (see I.F above). The Judahites who returned from Babylonian captivity (by that time known as Judeans or Jews) occupied portions of Palestine, while other parts were occupied by Samaritans, Idumeans (Edomites), and other peoples. (See *LBHG,* pp. 286-423; *BHI,* pp. 184-464; *NHI,* pp. 164-356; LaSor, *et al., OT Survey,* pp. 227-297; *CAH,* II/1 [1973], 54-64, 417-525; II/2 [1975], 49-116, 152-273, 307-330, 359-378, 443-481, 507-536, 537-605.)

With the break-up of Alexander's kingdom, Egypt became the portion of Lagos and his descendants the Lagides

(Ptolemies), and Syria became the portion of Seleucus and the Seleucids. The Ptolemies controlled Palestine until 198 B.C., at which time the Seleucid Antiochus III took over Coelesyria, including Palestine. The Hasmonean (Macabbean) revolt occurred in the time of Antiochus IV and his successor, and there was a nominal Jewish kingdom until the Roman Pompey took Jerusalem in 63 B.C. The Idumean Herod became king of the Jews under the aegis of Rome in 37 B.C., and the Herodian family continued to rule all or parts of Palestine under increasing control by Roman governors and legions until the destruction of Jerusalem in A.D. 70. The land was divided politically into ethnarchies and tetrarchies in the NT period (*Ant.* xvii.9.5–11.4 [218-320]; *BJ* ii.2.1–6.3 [14-100], etc.; Lk. 3:1). Geographically, the main areas in Cisjordan were Galilee, Samaria, and Judea; in Transjordan (or Perea) they were the cities of the Decapolis. (See *BHI,* pp. 343-464; *NHI,* pp. 300-428.)

*D. Postbiblical Period.* Roman rule of Palestine continued until the division of the empire into East (Byzantium) and West (Rome); in A.D. 324 Palestine became part of the Byzantine empire. Moslem rule commenced in 638 and continued (with the Crusader interruption, 1099-1187) until 1250. This was followed by the Mameluke period (1250-1517) and then the Ottoman Turkish rule (1517-1917). Palestine came under the British Mandate in 1917. When Great Britain terminated this and the United Nations established a Jewish State in November, 1947, the stage was set for increased Arab-Jewish hostilities and several wars. The State of Israel was established in May, 1948.

Throughout this entire postbiblical period there were Jewish settlements in Palestine at Modein, in Galilee, and elsewhere. The large Jewish center at Tiberias in Galilee produced the Palestinian Talmud during the early centuries of the Common Era. The "western Masorah" was also the product of Tiberian Masoretes.

*E. Population.* The figures for the population of Palestine in biblical times vary considerably in scholarly works. Three methods are commonly used, but each has weaknesses. One method is based on population density, i.e., the average number of inhabitants per unit of area. Although often presented as "scientific," this method is demonstrably unreliable, as evidence from Ebla has shown (*see* JERUSALEM III.D.5.b). A second method is based on the figures in the Bible. Nu. 1:1-46 states that at the first census after the Exodus there were 603,550 able-bodied men; adding the women, children, and those unfit for military duty would give a total population estimated at two to three million (cf. 26:1-63, which gives the census at a later date as 601,730). David's census (2 S. 24:9) lists the men fit for war as 800,000 in Israel and 500,000 in Judah, for a total of 1,300,000. Using the average of one man of military capability for every five persons, this would give a total population of 6,500,000. To challenge these figures is not, however, to deny the authority of the Bible, for biblical statements make it clear that the Israelites were not the most numerous or most powerful people in the region (Dt. 7:7; cf. Ex. 23:29); rather, the peoples in Canaan were described as "seven nations greater and mightier than yourselves" (Dt. 7:1). When the Israelites entered the land of promise they were unable to drive out the nations that dwelt there (cf. Jgs. 1), and this does not fit well with the figure of 600,000 fighting men. A third method of estimating the population is to compare it with modern Israel, which is over three million. But this method also is open to question, due in part to the large number of Jewish immigrants in the 20th century.

Biblical statements lead us to conclude that the number of Israelites who entered the land under Joshua was not greater than that of the people already dwelling there and that this figure did not increase dramatically in the following centuries — for Saul was unable to suppress the Philistines, and the forces of Ahab were not significantly greater than those of Hadadezer of Damascus or Irḫuleni of Hamath (according to Shalmaneser's figures; see *ARAB,* I, § 611; *ANET,* pp. 278f.; cf. LaSor, *et al., OT Survey,* p. 168 n. 11). To attempt to give a figure to this population is futile, as is demonstrated by the wide disparity in estimates of the population of Jerusalem in the time of Jesus (ranging from 20,000 to 12,000,000; *see* JERUSALEM III.H.30).

***IX. Languages and Writing.***–Long gone are the days when scholars could say that Palestine was a backward region with little culture and that writing could not have developed earlier than Homer. Writing was known in the Levantine area from the middle of the 3rd millennium, and several forms of writing in several languages were in existence in the first half of the 2nd millennium. Where evidence is lacking for the language itself, some conclusions can be drawn from the study of personal and divine names.

*A. Cuneiform.* The use of CUNEIFORM (wedge-shaped) writing dates back before 3000 B.C. in Mesopotamia. The large number of tablets discovered at Tell Mardikh (Ebla) gives evidence of the use of this medium of writing (using syllabograms and logograms) in Syria from *ca.* 2300 B.C. But the fact that Ebla was a center of commerce and that its mercantile activities stretched over a large area in the Near East, including a number of places in Palestine named in the documents, implies that there were scribes in Palestinian cities who were capable of reading Eblean (or Eblaite) cuneiform. Cuneiform Akkadian was the medium of communication in the Near East throughout the 2nd millennium, but our most important evidence of its use in Palestine comes from the AMARNA TABLETS. These documents, written on clay tablets and dating from the middle of the 14th cent. B.C., were found in Egypt; but they include about three hundred letters written by scribes in the Levant, of which approximately half were written either to or from Palestine. Cuneiform documents have been found also in Palestine (at Hazor, Megiddo, Taanach, Shechem, Jericho, and Gezer), dating from *ca.* 1450-1350 B.C., and one Amarna-type letter has been found at Tell el-Ḥesī (cf. G. A. Barrois, *Manuel d'archéologie biblique,* 2 [1953], 149-153; *see* EGLON III). Two other systems might be mentioned here: the inscriptions from the early 2nd millennium in Syria and Palestine (e.g., at Tell ed-Duweir), named "pseudo-hieroglyphic" by M. Dunand (cf. *AP,* p. 185), which may be an early development of hieroglyphic writing into syllabograms; and the alphabetic cuneiform of Ugarit from the middle of the 2nd millennium (see IX.B below).

*B. Alphabetic Writing.* The invention of the alphabet is usually attributed to the Phoenicians, though this has been challenged on the grounds that the alphabet is not phonemically (and phonetically) suited to Phoenician. Whatever the origin of the Phoenician alphabet, there can be no doubt that it became the basis of a great many other alphabets (Noth, indeed, says "all of the alphabetic scripts in the entire world" [*OT World,* p. 211]), including Aramaic (the "square letters"), Syriac, Arabic, Greek, Cyrillic, Latin, and others, doubtless through the widespread mercantile colonies and shipping routes of the Phoenicians and Greeks. Although the Phoenician centers were located to the north of Palestine (Acco, Tyre, Sidon, Byblos, Arwad), their effects were quickly and deeply felt in Palestine. It can be stated unequivocally that several systems of writing were known in Palestine in the 2nd millennium, some of which were certainly in use at many locations by the early 1st millennium B.C. (cf. *FSAC*, p. 43).

The earliest efforts to develop an alphabetic system of WRITING are often traced to the INSCRIPTIONS at the turquoise mines at Serābîṭ el-Khâdim in Sinai. These inscriptions, dated between 1900 and 1500 B.C., have not yet been satisfactorily deciphered, and the question whether such a revolutionary idea as an alphabet could have been invented by "an ignorant mine boss" (C. C. McCown, *Ladder of Progress in Palestine* [1943], p. 112; cf. A. Gardiner, *PEQ* [1929], 48-55) has not been convincingly answered. One theory traces the development of the alphabet to acrophonic use of Egyptian hieroglyphs (i.e., using the symbol to represent its first sound). Certainly an alphabet, written in cuneiform characters, was in use at Ugarit (Râs Shamrah in Syria) by the 14th century. It consisted of thirty consonantal characters, three of which were various vocalizations of *aleph* (*aleph, ileph, uliph*; *see* table in CUNEIFORM). It is true that both Serābîṭ el-Khâdim and Ugarit are at some distance from Phoenicia (or Palestine) and that these systems may not have penetrated to this region (although texts in a shorter form of the Ugaritic alphabet have been found near Mt. Tabor and at Taanach and Beth-shemesh; see P. C. Craigie, *Ugarit and the OT* [1983], p. 50). Their influences, however, may have contributed to the development of the Phoenician alphabet.

Early Hebrew inscriptions include the GEZER CALENDAR (10th cent. B.C.) and a quantity of Hebrew and Phoenician inscriptions found at Kuntillet ʿAjrūd in Sinai, which are dated to the 9th and 8th centuries. Early Phoenician inscriptions on arrowheads are dated to the 12th cent. (Moscati, *World*, pp. 89f.), while the Ahiram inscription dates from *ca.* 1000 B.C. and the Mesha Inscription in Moabite (*see* MOABITE STONE) makes use of the same alphabet (mid-9th cent.).

With the hellenization of the Near East, and especially with the Seleucid rule over Palestine, Greek came into use. It would be equally erroneous to assume either that all Jews spoke Greek or that none spoke it. Contrary to a popular view, Greek rather than Latin, was used widely by the Romans (cf. the works of Josephus, addressed to his Roman patron but written in Greek; Paul's Epistle to the Romans was likewise written in Greek). It is commonly assumed that by NT times Aramaic was the common language of Palestinian Jews, and where the word "Hebrew" occurs in the NT it is usually interpreted to mean "Aramaic." But the extensive use of Hebrew by the Qumrân community, even for its Manual of Discipline and its commentaries, and the almost complete absence of Aramaic, have led some scholars to conclude that Hebrew was the more common language, at least through the 1st cent. A.D. In the Byzantine period Greek was presumably still used by the governmental representatives and probably also by certain other persons. With the Moslem conquest Arabic came to be used; ultimately it became one of the three official languages of modern Palestine under the British mandate, along with Hebrew and English.

*C. Proper Names.* The study of names (whether of persons or deities), while not providing sufficient evidence to reconstruct otherwise unknown languages, has shed considerable light on the movements of peoples and their languages. Hittite, Hurrian, and Amorite names have been identified at various sites in Palestine, lending a measure of support to the biblical accounts that Hittites, Horites (possibly orthographically corrupted to "Hivites" in some passages), and Amorites were among the many peoples of Palestine. The Philistines were probably related to or identical with the Pelasgians, an Aegean people. Thus we may conclude that Palestine at various times was inhabited by or had extensive relations with peoples of Indo-European, Indo-Aryan, and various Semitic origins, and that these languages and cultures left their marks on the peoples of Palestine. (See *CAH*, II/1 [1973], 1-41; II/2 [1975], 252-273, 507-536; see also W. L. Moran, "Hebrew Language in Its Northwest Semitic Background," in *BANE*, pp. 54-72; *AP*, pp. 177-203; M. Sprengling, *The Alphabet: Its Rise and Development from the Sinai Inscriptions* [1931]; *CAH*, I/1, [1970] 136-138; W. F. Albright, *Proto-Sinaitic Inscriptions and Their Decipherment* [1966]; H. B. Huffmon, *Amorite Personal Names in the Mari Texts* [1965].)

*X. **Religion.***–A small country populated by so many peoples of diverse backgrounds must as a matter of course have included not only many religions but also eclectic or syncretic mixtures of these systems. It is a gross oversimplification, entirely without biblical support, to suppose that the Israelites had a common and pure religion of Yahwism. Their ancestors were worshipers of pagan gods (Josh. 24:2). The Hebrews who left Egypt brought elements of Egyptian religion with them (Ex. 32:7f.), and Moses warned them against turning to the gods in the land they were about to enter (Dt. 8:19). Joshua admonished them to put away their foreign gods (Josh. 24:23), and the days of the Judges saw repeated apostasies (Jgs. 3:5f.; etc.). Solomon not only tolerated and encouraged the cultic practices of his foreign wives (1 K. 11:1-8) but even turned from Yahweh to these pagan deities himself (vv. 9, 23). The prophets continually preached against the religious beliefs and practices of the Israelites who had mixed false doctrine with their Yahwism or had turned to serve Baals (cf. Isa. 2:6-8; Jer. 5:4-11; etc.). The people were punished for their apostasy by exile in Assyria and Babylon (Isa. 10:5f.; Jer. 21:10). After their return from the Babylonian Exile the Jews appear to have forsaken idolatry, for this sin is not mentioned again in biblical texts (although there is evidence of religious eclecticism in the Aramaic papyri from Egypt and other sources). As a result of Ezra's reforms zealous legalism or cold indifference replaced idolatry, and the inroads of hellenization during the rule of the Seleucids resulted in the reaction of the Hasidim and their successors, the Pharisees. The NT witnesses to the same tendency of human beings to construct their own forms of religion; even many of Jesus' followers left Him when it became apparent that His teachings differed from their hopes (Jn. 6:66). Apostasy takes many forms (cf. Mal. 3:5-7), as is demonstrated by anti-Semitism, militarism, and the introduction of many elements of pagan religions into Christianity.

The once-popular History of Religions School attempted simplistically to trace the development of religion from animism to monotheism, altering the biblical account to fit the theory (cf. W. O. E. Oesterley and T. H. Robinson, *Hebrew Religion* [2nd ed. 1937]). More careful study has produced a much more complex picture, with a mixture of Aryan, Indo-European, Semitic, and other deities, as theophoric names attest. Accordingly some cultic practices in Israel were quite likely taken over (and "sanctified") from a pagan source (e.g., circumcision, and the Feast of Unleavened Bread). Some vestiges of animism may indeed have remained (cf. the terebinth at Mamre [Gen. 13:18]; the water at Bethesda [Jn. 5:7]; the pillars at the entrance to the temple [2 Chr. 3:17]). A remnant of polytheism may be seen in the Hebrew word *ʾēlîm* (lit. "gods") in passages such as Ps. 29:1 (lit. "sons of gods") or Ex. 15:11. Some terms are so veiled in obscurity that there is no consensus concerning their origin or meaning (cf. "Azazel,"

Lev. 16:7-28; "Lilith" [RSV "night hag"], Isa. 34:14). The Israelites were repeatedly reproved for resorting to the "high places" (*bāmôṯ*), "groves" (*'ᵃšērôṯ*), and Baals. Deities such as Ashtoreth, Chemosh, and Milcom (1 K. 11:5,7; 2 K. 23:13) are also named. The discovery of the Ugaritic religious literature has shed much light (and some nonsense) on the study of Israelite religion, particularly the Canaanite influences on it. (*See also* IDOL; IDOLATRY; RELIGIONS OF THE BIBLICAL WORLD: CANAANITE.)

To mention such data is not to deny the unique character of Yahwism. The God of Israel is portrayed by the Bible as One who takes His people in whatever circumstances they may be, speaks their language and uses their figures and images, and ultimately leads them from ignorance to knowledge, from falsehood to truth. Unless the Israelites were in bondage to false gods, the OT prophets were little more than haranguers. That the people had for the most part continued to ignore and persecute the prophets was the charge made by John the Baptist and by Jesus.

To attribute the survival of Israel's religion to "the Semitic genius for religion" is either a truism or an absurdity. There were other Semitic religions, and some of them existed within the same geographical and temporal framework as Israel; but the verdict of history is clear: they have not survived. The religion of Israel survived and ultimately spread beyond Palestine because of two factors, the first of which is an item of faith: the God of Israel is a living God who works in historical situations to make Himself and His redemptive purpose known; second, the people who worship this God believe that He is such a God.

(See H. H. Rowley, *Worship in Ancient Israel* [1967]; H. Ringgren, *Israelite Religion* [Eng. tr. 1966]; T. C. Vriezen, *Religion of Ancient Israel* [Eng. tr. 1967]; W. F. Albright, *Yahweh and the Gods of Canaan* [1968]; P. C. Craigie, *Ugarit and the OT* [1983], pp. 67-90; R. de Vaux, *Ancient Israel* [Eng. tr. 1961], II.)

***XI. Cultural Contributions.***–Palestine in antiquity was largely an agricultural nation. It did have a few mercantile centers, outposts of commercial nations such as Ebla. But until comparatively modern times Palestine did not make great contributions in arts and crafts, trade and commerce, or industry and science. Because the coast offered no suitable harbors (except at Acco) there was little maritime trade. At certain periods of Israelite history the Gulf of Aqabah, with its port at Elath, became the terminus of a trade route, but the sailors were not Israelite (cf. 1 K. 10:22). Likewise, the skilled craftsmen who built Solomon's capital were Tyrians (5:1-6 [MT 15-21]; 7:13-45; this "Hiram" [or "Huram(abi)," 2 Ch. 2:13; 4:11], is to be distinguished from King Hiram). Galilee had a major highway (the Way of the Sea) that connected Egypt and the port at Acco with Damascus, and a trade route ran from Gaza to Edom at the southern end of Palestine; but the trunk roads lay near the coast on the west of Cisjordan and toward the desert on the east of Transjordan, leaving Palestine largely free from stimuli that might have developed arts and crafts.

The Egyptians and Greeks made great contributions in architecture and sculpture, the Ebleans and Assyrians and later the Phoenicians and Greeks in trade and commerce, the Hittites and Anatolian peoples in metallurgy, the Persians and Romans in government — but what was the distinctive contribution of Palestine? The answer must lie in historiography and Yahwistic monotheism, with the sense of history largely if not totally dominated by belief in the redemptive activities of Israel's God.

This unique contribution brought about other cultural developments in the course of history. The Psalms gave rise to psalmody; the imagery of the Scriptures encouraged representations in ikons and sculptures; and the concern for the poor, the widow, and the orphan led to charitable organizations. The tradition of worship in the temple gave rise to the synagogue and the church, and in turn to architectural and cultic forms to satisfy the need for corporate worship. Nascent Judaism originated in Palestine; the rabbis' grapplings with the implications of the Scriptures produced rabbinic literature and the Palestinian Talmud; and the scribes at Tiberias helped to preserve the correct reading of the Hebrew Bible through the Masorah. Even the alphabet is indebted to the Judeo-Christian Scriptures for its widespread use (e.g., Syriac, Cyrillic, and many modern adaptations used to publish the Scriptures in modern tongues).

*See also* ART VI.

***XII. The Land in Prophecy.***–The concept of the LAND first appears in the call of Abram (Gen. 12:1, 7). The promise was repeated to Abram/Abraham (13:14-17; 15:18-21; 17:8), to Isaac (26:34), to Jacob at Luz (48:4), and was known to Joseph (50:24). Statements that Yahweh "swore" or performed an oath to "give" the "land" occur repeatedly in the first seven books of the OT. In the Decalogue the only commandment with promise speaks of the possession of the land (Ex. 20:12); the implicit threat of exile from the land is made explicit in other passages, notably Dt. 28 (cf. vv. 36, 64-67). Israel, which had been "planted" in the land, would be "plucked up" (Dt. 28:63; Jer. 12:14), "rooted up" (1 K. 14:15), "cut off from" (9:7), "exiled from" (2 K. 17:23; 25:21; Jer. 52:27), and would "perish from" this land (Josh. 23:13, 16).

But Yahweh's word could not be voided. Several prophets refer to the replanting, rebuilding, or return to the land. Ezk. 37 (part of the longer eschatological passage that includes chs. 34–39) promises the resurrection of both Israel and Judah (37:19-22) and an "everlasting covenant" (vv. 26-28); this is followed by the Gog-Magog conflict (chs. 38f.) — a figure that is taken up in Revelation's description of the end time (Rev. 20:7-10). Likewise the book of Zechariah depicts the restoration of Judah and Joseph/Ephraim (= Israel) and the return from exile (10:6-11) in connection with the end time events (cf. 9:9; 14:4-9). Other passages in the prophets refer to blessings involving the land "in the latter days." The promise of a "Wonderful Counselor" (Isa. 9:6) is immediately associated with the throne of David (v. 7) and the "remnant" that will return (10:21). The messianic promise in 11:1-5 is followed by a picture of an idyllic kingdom (vv. 6-9) and the return of the remnant of Israel and Judah (vv. 11-16). Joel's prophecy of the outpouring of the Spirit specifically mentions Mt. Zion, Jerusalem, the valley of Jehoshaphat, Tyre, Sidon, and other place names (Joel 2:28–3:21 [MT 3:1–4:21]). Jeremiah's prophecy of the new covenant (Jer. 31:31-34) is in a context that speaks of the rebuilding of Jerusalem with specific geographical details (vv. 38-40). Many additional passages could be cited.

Jewish interpreters and some Christian interpreters (early Chiliasts and recent Premillennialists) have held that the promises of the restoration of the Jews to the land, the reign of the messianic king in Jerusalem (Zion; cf. Ps. 2:6; 110:2), the desire of the Gentiles ("nations") to learn the way of the Lord from Israel (Isa. 2:2-4; Mic. 4:1-3), peace on earth and the concomitant blessings of the messianic age, are to be fulfilled, with a literalness that is temporal and spatial (allowing for some poetic language). Other Christian interpreters would claim that the Jews lost these promises when they rejected their Messiah and that the Church is now the "Israel of God" (cf. Gal. 6:16; *see also* ESCHATOLOGY IX). This hermeneutical problem cannot be solved here (cf. W. S. LaSor, *The Truth about Arma-*

*geddon* [1982], pp. 75-89, 150-174), but the question must be faced: does not the common Christian interpretation fail to grapple exegetically with the passages that include the land promise? The land of Palestine is an integral part of the covenant with Abraham, just as the throne of David is an integral part of the covenant with David (cf. Jer. 33:20-22). According to the NT the covenant with Abraham is still in force (Gal. 3:15-18; Rom. 4:13-24), as is the covenant with David (Lk. 1:32f.; cf. Acts 2:25-36). The new covenant, which includes the possession of the land (Jer. 31:27-34), is now in force (He. 8:8–9:15). The hermeneutical problem requires careful attention, and a serious effort should be made to reach an exegetically satisfactory solution. Meanwhile it must be recognized that, however the relevant passages are to be understood, the redemption of sinful humanity and the blessings of righteousness and peace have their basis in time and space in the land of Palestine. (*See also* GEOGRAPHY, BIBLICAL.)

***Bibliography.***–Y. Aharoni and M. Avi-Yonah, *Macmillan Bible Atlas* (1968); E. Anati, *Palestine Before the Hebrews* (Eng. tr. 1963); *AP* (rev. ed. 1960); *CAH*; D. Baly and A. D. Tushingham, *Atlas of the Bible World* (1971); *BHI* (3rd ed. 1981); G. Eichholz, *Landscapes of the Bible* (Eng. tr. 1963); *Enc. Brit.* (1970), XVII, *s.v.* "Syria and Palestine, History of" (K. Kenyon, P. Parr); H. T. Frank, *Discovering the Bible World* (1975); *FSAC* (rev. ed. 1957); *GAB*; *GB* (rev. ed. 1974); *GP*; *GTTOT*; *HGHL* (rev. ed., repr. 1966); W. S. LaSor, *et al.*, *OT Survey* (1982); *LBHG* (rev. ed. 1979); S. Moscati, *Face of the Ancient Orient* (Eng. tr. 1962); *World of the Phoenicians* (Eng. tr. 1968); *NHI* (Eng. tr. 2nd ed. 1960); M. Noth, *OT World* (Eng. tr. 1966); *WHAB*.

W. S. LASOR

**PALLET.** *See* BED.

**PALLU** pal'o͞o; **PALLUITES** pal'o͞o-īts [Heb. *pallû'* < *pālā'*–'be conspicuous, extraordinary']; AV also PHALLU. The second son of Reuben (Gen. 46:9; Ex. 6:14; Nu. 26:5; 1 Ch. 5:3), and the father of Eliab (Nu. 26:8). The patronymic (Palluites) occurs in Nu. 26:5.

**PALM (OF THE HAND)** [Heb. *kap*]. The Hebrew term properly denotes the "hollow of the hand" (cf. the metaphorical use of *kap* for a concave DISH). It is usually translated "hand" by the English versions (e.g., cf. the gesture of stretching out the *kappîm* in prayer; *see* GESTURE I), but the translation "palm" occurs four times in the RSV (e.g., 2 K. 9:35). In Lev. 14:15, 26 it refers to the cupped left hand of the priest, into which sacrificial oil is poured. In Isa. 49:16 Yahweh assures Zion of His constant love for her by the use of a beautiful metaphor: He has carved her name on His hand so that He will never forget her (for other examples of this type of practice, *see* MARK I).

*See also* HAND. N. J. O.

**PALM TREE** [Heb. *tāmār*; Gk. *phoínix*]. The many references to palm trees are unquestionably to the date palm (*Phoenix dactylifera* L.), one of the most characteristic trees of the Orient. The date palm ranges extensively from India to North Africa and is the principal desert foodplant. In oriental architecture palm figures were used as ornamentation (cf. 1 K. 6:29, 32; Ezk. 40:31); the palm was a symbol of grace, elegance, and dignity (*see* TAMAR). The large leaves were used in making roofs or repairing fences, smaller ones became containers, and the integument in the crown furnished material for rope.

The dates, hanging down in immense clusters, were the chief food of many ancient peoples, as they are for some modern peoples. The Babylonians made intoxicating liquor by extracting the syrupy content of the spathe surrounding the flowers. This liquor was probably the "strong drink" of Lev. 10:9; Nu. 6:3; Jgs. 13:4; Isa. 5:11; Mic. 2:11; etc. It was also known euphemistically as "honey" (Heb. *d^e^baš*) and as such is doubtless intended in Gen. 43:11; 1 S. 14:25; Isa. 7:15; Cant. 4:11; Rev. 10:9; etc. Strabo, Pliny, and Herodotus recorded that the Orientals made wine and honey from the date palm.

Griffin-demons scraping and collecting sap from a palm tree; the sap was used to anoint the king to enhance his fertility. From the palace of Ashurnasirpal II at Nimrûd, 9th cent. B.C. (Trustees of the British Museum)

From early times the staminate (male) flowers were used in artificial fertilization of the pistillate (female) flowers. Assyrian sculptures and Egyptian bas-reliefs depict winged figures shaking a bunch of male flowers over female blooms. Names like Baal-tamar, Hazazon-tamar, and Bethany ("house of dates") indicate the date palm's abundance in ancient Palestine. Jericho was called the "city of palm trees" (Dt. 34:3; Jgs. 1:16; 3:13; 2 Ch. 28:15).

The righteous flourish like the palm tree (Ps. 92:12-15 [MT 13-16]). Its branches indicated the highest of the people (Isa. 9:14 [MT 13]; 19:15) as contrasted with the rush, or lowest people. Palm branches were used at the Feast of Tabernacles (Lev. 23:40; cf. Neh. 8:15; 2 Macc. 10:7) and by the multitudes who escorted Christ to Jerusalem (Jn. 12:13). In Rev. 7:9 the uncounted multitude stood before the Lamb holding palm branches.

In Ps. 65:11 (MT 12) the NEB reading "palm trees" for MT *ma'gāleykā* (RSV "tracks of your chariot") is not supported by either the MT or LXX and must be regarded as strictly conjectural.

*See* Plate 59. R. K. H.

**PALMER WORM.** The AV translation of Heb. *gāzām* (lit. "cut") in Joel 1:4 (RSV "cutting locust"); 2:25 (RSV "cutter"); Am. 4:9 (RSV "locust"). The palmer worm is a caterpillar that appears in great numbers and devours vegetation; but the reference here is apparently to a type of LOCUST (cf. NEB), or the locust at a particular stage of development.

**PALMYRA.** *See* TADMOR.

**PALSY.** The AV translation of Gk. *paralytikós* and *paralelyménos* (pf. pass. part. of *paralýō*). Eng. "palsy" is a sixteenth-century form derived from French *paralysie* (< Lat. *paralysis*); today it is usually replaced by Eng. "paralysis" or "paralyzed" (cf. RSV, NEB; *see* PARALYTIC). Palsy designates various conditions characterized by a loss of ability to move or to control movements of the body. It generally results from damage to the brain or spinal cord or from a disease of the central nervous system. *See* DISEASE IV.B.

**PALTI** pal'tī [Heb. *palṭî*–'Yahweh delivers' or 'my deliverance']; AV also PHALTI (1 S. 25:44).

**1.** Son of Raphu; as a leader of the tribe of Benjamin, he was one of the twelve spies sent by Moses to explore the land of Canaan (Nu. 13:9).

**2.** Son of Laish, from Gallim in Benjamin; the man to whom Saul gave his daughter Michal, David's wife, when David was outlawed (1 S. 25:44). Later, however, through the intervention of Abner, Michal was taken from her grief-stricken husband (here called Paltiel) and restored to David (2 S. 3:15f.).

**PALTIEL** pal'ti-əl [Heb. *palṭî'ēl*–'God delivers' or 'God is my deliverance']; AV also PHALTIEL (2 S. 3:15).

**1.** Son of Azzan; a leader of the tribe of Issachar appointed to assist Eleazar and Joshua in dividing the land W of the Jordan among the tribes of Israel (Nu. 34:26).

**2.** An alternate form of PALTI **2.**

**PALTITE** pal'tīt [Heb. *palṭî*–'Yahweh delivers' or 'my deliverance'; Gk. A *Phellōnei,* B *Kelōthei*]; NEB "from Beth-pelet." A descriptive adjective applied to Helez, one of David's valiant men called the "thirty" (2 S. 23:26). Paltite may be a patronymic of Palti; but more probably it means an inhabitant of BETH-PELET in the Negeb of Judah. In 1 Ch. 11:27; 27:10 Helez is called "the Pelonite"; most scholars agree that the text is corrupted in these places and should be emended to "the Paltite" (cf. *BHS*; but *see* HELEZ **1**; PELONITE).

**PAMPHYLIA** pam-fil'ē-ə [Gk. *Pamphylia*]. A highly fertile alluvial plain in Asia Minor bordered on the south by the Mediterranean and on the north by Pisidia, and enclosed by the two massive outcrops of the Taurus Mountains that constitute Lycia to the west and Cilicia Tracheia to the east. Its physical features greatly resemble those of its eastward counterpart, Cilicia Pedias, but it is much smaller and had virtually no strategic significance in the history of Asia Minor. Two great rivers, the Cestrus and the Eurymedon as they were called in antiquity, drain the Pisidian hinterland and with the lesser Catarrhactes and Melas at the western and eastern extremities, respectively, have built up the plain. The land was rich in fruit and crops and was a center of pharmaceutical products.

A chain of five major Greek cities, set in a slight arc in relation to the seacoast, spanned about 64 km. (40 mi.) of the Pamphylian plain. The greatest and most recent (as its name, honoring the second-century-B.C. dynasty of Pergamum, makes clear) was Attaleia, modern Antalya, at the western end of the gulf. (The older Olbia, still farther W, was apparently dispossessed to make way for the new foundation. To the east lay an obscure Magydus, also eclipsed, although revived in the NT period.) Perga was a little inland to the east; next, across the Cestrus, came Sillyum, then Aspendus (on the Eurymedon), and finally Side, on the eastern end of the gulf. These last

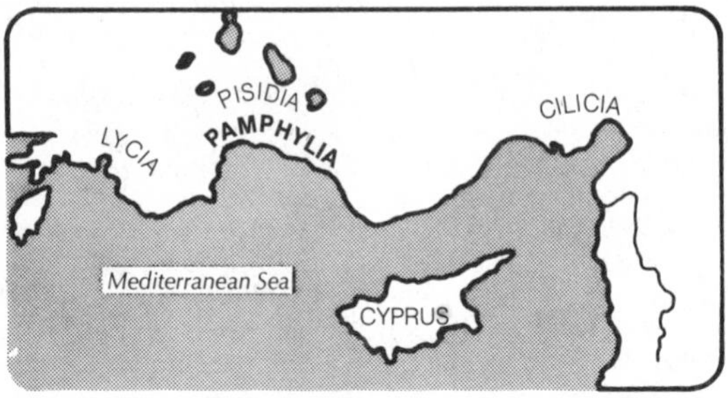


four cities (with the two overshadowed by Attaleia) were ancient foundations whose tradition went back to the migrations after the Trojan War. The miscellany of peoples in the region allegedly accounted for the name Pamphylia, the place "of all peoples." The peculiar dialectical features of their coinage lend some support to the claim of such antiquity and also indicate the mixing of Greek and non-Greek in what was then a remote frontier of Greek settlement.

Pamphylia came under Roman sovereignty at the end of the 2nd cent. B.C., when the Cilician pirate menace compelled Roman intervention. It was later attached to the province of Asia and then to Galatia; in A.D. 43 Claudius made it and its western neighbor Lycia into a new province.

What took Paul to Pamphylia after he left Paphos in Cyprus (Acts 13:13) is not specified. But since Pamphylian Jews were at Pentecost (2:10), one would naturally assume that he expected to preach in their synagogues. There must have been some value attached to working in Pamphylia if one is to explain the defection of Mark when Paul decided to go to Pisidian Antioch and Lycaonia in the interior. The breach with Mark is the only recorded happening in Pamphylia (13:13; 15:38); this fact and the way that 14:25 mentions the preaching on the return journey imply that no church had been formed in Perga. The visit to Attaleia (v. 25) was apparently for convenience of travel; again, no details are given. Certainly Pamphylia does not attract any subsequent concern of Paul's, as one would expect had a successful mission been conducted there.

***Bibliography.***–Strabo xiv.4.1-3; Pauly-Wissowa; *RRAM*, I, 260-63; *CERP*, pp. 124-147; *SPT*, pp. 89-97.

E. A. JUDGE

**PAN** [Heb. *kîyôr*] (1 S. 2:14); NEB CAULDRON; [*maśrēṯ*] (2 S. 13:9); [*marḥešeṯ*] (Lev. 2:7; 7:9); AV FRYINGPAN; [*ṣēlāḥâ*] (2 Ch. 35:13). A cooking utensil used for preparing various items of food.

The term *kîyôr* is used twenty-three times in the OT, but is translated "pan" only once. It most often refers to the LAVER in the temple, so the term most likely indicates some large container for holding liquids. In 1 S. 2:14 it is used for cooking the sacrifices at the Shiloh sanctuary where the boiling of meat is mentioned in v. 13. The *kîyôr,* when used for cooking, was probably a large boiling pot.

The term *maśrēṯ,* used only in 2 S. 13:9, seems to have been a utensil for baking cakes (probably very much like pancakes). It may have been a flat sheet, a frying pan, or even a convex sheet intended to stretch over a small fire of brush much like that which the modern Arab village housewife uses for the local flatbread.

Use of the *marḥešeṯ* seems to have been similar to that of the *maśrēṯ,* except that it occurs only in ritual contexts for preparing cereal offerings. The verbal root means "moving" or "stirring," indicating that the contents were meant to be stirred.

The *ṣēlāḥâ,* mentioned only in 2 Ch. 35:13 (but cf. *ṣalaḥaṯ,* "dish," e.g., 2 K. 21:13), was used for boiling offerings at Josiah's Passover. The vessel was thus probably a type of closed cooking pot.

*See also* GRIDDLE; PLATE; POT.

L. G. HERR

**PANEL** [Heb. *misgereṯ*] (1 K. 7:28ff.); AV BORDER; [*sap*] (Ezk. 41:16a); AV DOOR POST; [*śᵉḥîp*] (Ezk. 41:16b); AV CIELED; [*sāpan*] (Jer. 22:14; Hag. 1:4); AV CIELED; NEB also WELL-ROOFED. Hiram of Tyre made for Solomon's temple ten large bronze stands having panels figured with lions, oxen, and cherubim (1 K. 7:28ff.). Jer. 22:14 and Hag. 1:4 use different forms of the verb *sāpan,* "cover"; in the context the RSV "paneling" appears preferable to the AV "cieled." The RSV "paneled" of

Ezk. 41:16a is a conjecture based on the LXX *pephatnōména,* which presupposes *s^epûnîm* (cf. *BHS*) for MT *hassippîm* ("doorsill, threshold"). G. WYPER

**PANNAG** pan'ag. In Ezk. 27:17 the AV transliterates Heb. *pannag* as a place name, but from the context it is obviously some kind of food. The RSV "early figs" is based on the reading *pagag* and does fit the context well. But the Tg. *qôlyā',* "parched grain," as well as the Akkadian cognate *pannigu,* "meal, flour," suggests some kind of grain product (cf. NIV "confections"; NASB "cakes"). H. Cohen (*Biblical Hapax Legomena in the Light of Akkadian and Ugaritic* [1978], p. 118) noted that in one text Akk. *pannigu* occurs with *dišpu,* "honey," a cognate of Heb. *dāḇaš*, which follows *pannag* in Ezk. 27:17. G. A. L.

**PAP.** An obsolete term used by the AV to translate Heb. *šaḏ* in Ezk. 2:21 (RSV, NEB, "breast") and Gk. *mastós* in Lk. 11:27; 23:29; Rev. 1:13 (RSV, NEB, "breast"). Heb. *šaḏ* means "female breast"; Gk. *mastós* has a wider meaning, inlcuding the male chest. *See* BREAST.

**PAPER** [Gk. *chártēs*] (2 Jn. 12); NEB paraphrases "black and white." *See* PAPYRUS; WRITING.

**PAPER REEDS.** The AV translation of Heb. *'ārôṯ* in Isa. 19:7. According to KoB (p. 734), the noun *'ārâ* means "(bul)rush." But other scholars read it as a derivative of the verb *'ārâ,* "be naked or bare" (see BDB, p. 788; cf. KD); thus the RSV rendering "bare places." For the NEB's use of "lotus," see T. W. Thacker, *JTS,* 34 (1933), 163-65.

**PAPHOS** pā'fos [Gk. *Paphos*]. A town on the southwest coast of Cyprus. Old Paphos (now known as Kouklia) seems to have been settled by Greek colonists during the Mycenaean period, although some attribute the original settlement to the Phoenicians. New Paphos, 16 km. (10 mi.) NW of Old Paphos, developed as the port of the old city and became the more important of the two during the Ptolemaic period. The Paphos of Acts is the New Paphos.

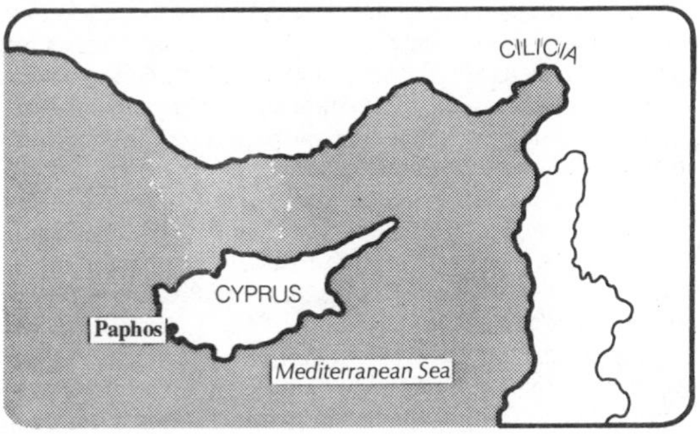


The ancient fame of Paphos was tied to the worship of the Greek goddess of love, Aphrodite. It became a popular place of pilgrimage when the legend of her birth was localized there. When Cyprus came under Roman control in the mid-1st cent. B.C., it was treated administratively as a part of the province of Cilicia. Some twenty-five years later it was made a separate imperial province with its own military governor. Shortly thereafter its status was again changed to a senatorial province under a proconsul. Paphos was the government seat and hence the residence of Sergius Paulus (Acts 13:7). During the Byzantine period the capital was changed from Paphos to Constantia (Salamis).

The story of the visit of Paul and Barnabas to Paphos (Acts 13:4-12) and the resulting conversion of Sergius Paulus marks the first time that a ruler became a Christian. Cyprus thus was the first territory to be governed by a Christian ruler.

*Bibliography.*–Pauly-Wissowa, XIII; *Oxford Classical Dictionary* (1949), *s.v.*; R. Gunnis, *Historic Cyprus* (1936); H. Luke, *Cyprus* (1965); P. Newman, *Short History of Cyprus* (1940).

R. A. GWINN

**PAPIAS.** *See* APOSTOLIC FATHERS VIII.

**PAPYRUS** pə-pī'rəs [Lat. *cyperus papyrus*–'the Egyptian papyrus'; Heb. *gōme'*] (Job 8:11); AV RUSH; [Gk. *býblos, bíblos*–'papyrus plant or roll made of papyrus'], whence "book" (Mk. 12:26). A plant and the writing material that was made from it.

The papyrus was a marsh or water plant, abundant in Egypt in ancient times, that served many purposes in antiquity. The papyrus tuft was the emblem of the northern kingdom in Egypt and, like the lotus, was a favorite design on the capitals of columns. Ropes, sandals, and mats were made from its fibers (cf. Homer *Od.* xxi.391; Herodotus ii.37, 69), and bundles of the long stalks were bound together into light boats (Isa. 18:2).

Illustration of the construction of a boat from papyrus reeds. From a tomb at the pyramids.

I. Papyrus Paper
II. Egyptian Papyri
III. Greek Papyri
  A. Discovery
  B. Literary
  C. Documentary
  D. Septuagint
  E. NT
  F. Theological
IV. Aramaic and Hebrew Papyri
V. Other Papyri
VI. Contribution to Biblical Study

***I. Papyrus Paper.***– From the papyrus plant early Egyptians made the tough and inexpensive paper that became the common writing material of the ancient world. The white cellular pitch of the long, triangular papyrus stalk was stripped of its bark or rind and sliced into thin strips. Two layers of these strips were laid at right angles to each other on a hard surface, forced together by pounding, dried, and smoothed with pumice. The sheets thus formed were pasted together to form a roll of any length desired. Pliny the Elder described the process and the product (*Nat. hist.* xiii.11-13).

***II. Egyptian Papyri.***–Extant Egyptian papyrus rolls date from the 27th cent. B.C. and no doubt papyrus had been manufactured for centuries before. The Egyptian rolls were sometimes very long and were often beautifully decorated with colored vignettes *(The Book of the Dead).*

Four columns of hieratic script from the Harris Papyrus: the last two columns of "The Taking of Joppa" (right; see *ANET*, pp. 22f.) and the first two columns of "The Tale of the Doomed Prince" (left; see W. K. Simpson, ed., *Literature of Ancient Egypt* [1973], pp. 85-91) (Trustees of the British Museum)

Egyptian documents of great historical value have been preserved on these fragile rolls. The Ebers Papyrus of the 16th cent. B.C. sums up Egyptian medical lore from the time of Amenhotep I. The Harris Papyrus, 41 m. (133 ft.) long in 117 columns, dates from the mid-12th cent. B.C. and records the benefactions and achievements of Ramses III. Papyri of the 19th, 20th, and 21st Dynasties are relatively numerous, and their contribution is important for Egyptian history, life, and religion. By 1000 B.C. papyrus was used for writing far beyond the limits of Egypt. The Wen-Amon Papyrus (11th cent. B.C.) relates that five hundred rolls of papyrus were among the goods sent from the Delta to the prince of Byblos, but except in rare instances papyri have escaped destruction only in Upper Egypt, where the dry climate favored their preservation.

***III. Greek Papyri.***–With Alexander's conquest of Egypt (332 B.C.) and the subsequent Ptolemaic dynasty, Greeks came more than ever before into Egypt, and from Greek centers like Alexandria and Arsinoë in the Faiyûm the Greek language began to spread. Greek papyri are abundant from the Ptolemaic (323-30 B.C.), Roman (30 B.C.-A.D. 292/3), and Byzantine (A.D. 292/3-642) periods, i.e., from the death of Alexander to the Arab conquest. The three hundred Aphrodito Greek and Coptic papyri, published by Bell and Crum, date from A.D. 698-722 and show how Greek persisted in the Arab period.

*A. Discovery.* The first important discovery of Greek papyri in modern times was made in 1752 among the ruins of Herculaneum, near Naples. There in a house that had been destroyed and buried by volcanic ash from Vesuvius (A.D. 79) was found a whole library of papyrus rolls, charred by the heat. With the utmost pains many of these carbonized rolls were unrolled and deciphered, and the first part of them was published in 1793. They consist almost wholly of works of Epicurean philosophy.

The first Greek papyri discovered in Egypt were forty or fifty papyrus rolls that local residents claimed to have unearthed in a box of sycamore wood in Giza. One roll, purchased by a dealer, was presented to Cardinal Stefano Borgia in 1778; the others were destroyed as worthless. N. I. Schow published the Borgia Papyrus ten years later;his edition included the first documentary text on papyrus, a list of certain peasants forced to work on the Nile embankment at Tebtunis in A.D. 192.

In 1820 natives found papyri, mainly from the 2nd cent. B.C., in an earthen pot at the site of the Serapeum in Memphis. The papyri fell into various hands and are now in the museums of London, Paris, Leiden, and Rome. With them papyri began to flow steadily into the British and Continental museums. The present period of papyrus recovery dates from 1877, when an immense mass of Greek and other papyri, most documentary rather than literary, was found at the mound (*kom*) el-Faris in the Faiyûm, on the site of the ancient Arsinoë. The bulk of this collection passed into the hands of Archduke Rainer at Vienna; the museums of Paris, London, Oxford, and Berlin secured minor portions. These texts belong mainly to the Byzantine period.

Most of these discoveries were made by natives digging for fertile earth (*sebakh*) at ancient sites and occasionally finding antiquities to sell to tourists or dealers. By this time, however, the Egypt Exploration Fund (later Society) had begun its operations in Egypt, and Flinders Petrie was at work there. Digging among Ptolemaic tombs at Gurob in 1889-1890, Petrie found many mummies, with mummy-casings made of "cartonnage," papyri pasted together. Scholars hailed the Petrie papyri as the most important found to that time, for they were mainly from the 3rd cent. B.C. and included a copy of Plato's *Phaedo*. The British Museum secured papyri of the lost work of Aristotle, *Constitution of Athens,* the lost *Mimes* of Herodas, a fragment of an oration of Hyperides, and extensive literary papyri of works already extant. The Louvre acquired the larger part of the *Oration Against Athenogenes,* the masterpiece of Hyperides. In 1894 B. P. Grenfell of Oxford began working with Petrie in the Egyptian excavations and secured papyri, with D. G. Hogarth, for England.

With A. S. Hunt of Oxford, Grenfell excavated in 1896-1897 at Behnesa, the Roman Oxyrhynchus, and unearthed the greatest mass of Greek papyri of the Roman period thus far found. Their discovery in 1900 of a great mass of Ptolemaic papyri at Tebtunis in the Faiyûm was comparable in importance to their Oxyrhynchus find. One of the most productive sources of papyri at Tebtunis was the crocodile cemetery, where many mummies of the sacred crocodiles were wrapped in papyrus cartonnage. Grenfell and Hunt also excavated important Ptolemaic

Plato *Phaedo* 67E-69A. From cartonnage at Gurob (Trustees of the British Museum)

texts imbedded in mummy cartonnage in 1902 at Hibeh, and P. Jouguet made similar finds in 1901 at Ghoran and in 1902 at Medinet en-Nahas. Excavations by Grenfell and Hunt at Oxyrhynchus in 1903-1907 produced results almost as astonishing and quite as valuable as those of the first excavations there. The work of L. Borchardt and a German team at Abusir in 1902 has exceptional interest, for it uncovered the then-earliest Greek papyrus text, a fourth-century papyrus roll of the verses of Timotheus of Miletus. The Timotheus roll held this precedence until 1962, when a fourth-century papyrus roll containing an allegorical commentry on the Orphic hymns was discovered in the funeral pyre of a tomb at Derveni near Thessalonica in Greece. The acquisition of papyri by purchase and excavation continues to the present, chiefly in Egypt but also occasionally elsewhere, e.g., at Dura-Europos on the Euphrates and at numerous sites in the Judean desert.

*B. Literary.* More than 1500 Greek literary papyri, great and small, of works other than biblical and theological have been published. That about one-half are Homeric attests the great popularity of the *Iliad* and *Odyssey* in Greco-Roman times. These are now so abundant and extensive that they make an important contribution to Homeric textual studies. Rather less than one-third preserve works of other ancient writers that were already known through medieval or modern copies. Among these are works of Plato, Demosthenes, Isocrates, Thucydides, Euripides, Sophocles, Aeschines, and Herodotus. Another extensive group preserves works or fragments of works that were usually regarded as lost or were unknown. They include portions of Alcman, Sappho, and the lost *Antiope* and *Hypsipyle* of Euripides, fragments of the comedies of Menander and the Iambi of Callimachus, *Mimes* of Herodas, poems of Bacchylides, Aristotle's *Constitution of Athens,* the *Persae* of Timotheus, and six orations, one of them complete, of Hyperides.

*C. Documentary.* The overwhelming majority of published Greek papyri — more than 15,000 — have been documentary. This category embraces every kind of public and private text, including letters, accounts, wills, receipts, contracts, leases, deeds, complaints, petitions, notices, and invitations. The value of these contemporary and original documents for the illumination of ancient life can hardly be overestimated. The life of Upper Egypt in Ptolemaic and Roman times is now probably better known than that of any other period of history down to recent times. Among the most important of the Ptolemaic documentary papyri are the revenue laws of Ptolemy Philadelphus (259 B.C.) and the forty-seven decrees of Ptolemy Euergetes II (118 B.C., 140-139 B.C.). In 1910 a papyrus now in Hamburg supplied the *Constitutio Antoniniana,* by which Roman citizenship was conferred upon the *peregrini* (non-Italians) of the empire. The private documents are even more important illustrations of the life of common people in antiquity.

*D. Septuagint.* More than 150 papyri of the LXX have been discovered. Perhaps the most important is the Berlin Genesis (3rd or 4th cent. A.D.) in a cursive hand, purchased at Akhmîm in 1906. Other papyri preserving parts of Genesis among the Amherst, British Museum, and Oxyrhynchus papyri date from the 3rd or 4th century. British Museum 230 (3rd cent.) preserves Ps. 12:7–15:4. A Berlin papyrus contains Ps. 40:26–41:4. An Amherst papyrus (7th cent.) shows parts of Pss. 108, 118, 135,138–140. Of the Prophets the chief papyrus is the Heidelberg Codex (7th cent.), which contains Zec. 4:6 to Mal. 4:5. The John Rylands Library of Manchester has papyrus fragments of Dt. 23–28 from mummy cartonnage dating from the 2nd cent. B.C.; with a Fuad papyrus of Dt. 31:36–32:7 they comprise the earliest witnesses to the LXX. The important Chester Beatty collection in Dublin contains portions of several LXX codices, including two of Genesis (3rd cent. and 4th cent.), Numbers and Deuteronomy (2nd cent.), Isaiah (3rd cent.), and Ezekiel and Esther (3rd cent.). Papyrus fragments of the LXX discovered in caves near Khirbet Qumrân date from the 1st cent. B.C. (*see* DEAD SEA SCROLLS). The great antiquity of some of these documents gives special interest to their readings.

*E. NT.* Eighty-three papyri containing parts of the Greek NT have been discovered in Egypt. They vary in age from the 2nd to the 7th cents. and in extent from scraps of a few verses to almost complete codices of a Gospel, Acts, or the Pauline letters. The fragment of Jn. 18:31-34, 37f. in the John Rylands Library, dated *ca.* 125, is the oldest witness to the NT text. Another remarkable MS is Bodmer Papyrus XIV and XV, a third-century codex containing most of Luke and John. It preserves an early and important text-type found in the famed Codex Vaticanus. The Bodmer collection of Geneva includes another important papyrus codex of John from *ca.* 200. The last leaves of this codex belong to the Chester Beatty collection, which also has a valuable codex of the Gospels and Acts from the 3rd cent. and a codex from *ca.* 200 originally containing Romans, Hebrews, 1 and 2 Corinthians, Ephesians, Galatians, Philippians, Colossians, and 1 and 2 Thessalonians, in that order.

Eighty of the known NT papyri are parts of codices. The three remaining papyri are parts of rolls that originally carried classical and OT texts and were inscribed later on their backs (verso) with NT passages.

*F. Theological.* Of the numerous Greek theological papyri that have come to light, thirty-one fragments of NT

LXX text of Ezk. 16:57-63 (left) and Est. 3:13 (including the long LXX additions) (Chester Beatty Library; picture P. Davison International Ltd.)

apocryphal writings have been published. The Oxyrhynchus sayings of Jesus, dating from 2nd and 3rd cents., are probably the best known (*see* LOGIA). Other Oxyrhynchus papyri preserve parts of the Apocalypse of Baruch (chs. 12–14; 4th or 5th cent.); the Acts of John (4th cent.); and Irenaeus *Adv. Haer.* iii.9 (3rd cent.). The Shepherd of Hermas is now attested by numerous papyrus fragments from the 2nd to 6th centuries. Among the valuable theological papyri discovered in 1941 at Tura were the lost commentaries on the Psalms, Job, and Zechariah by Didymus the Blind (6th or 7th cent.) and several works of Origen, including commentaries on Exodus and Romans, a homily on 1 Kings, *Contra Celsum,* and the lost *Dialogue with Heracleides*, all from the 6th and 7th centuries. Several Greek papyri from the 3rd to 5th cents. contain the *Homily on the Passion* by Melito of Sardis. The papyri continue to furnish important texts of patristic literature as well as early Christian homilies, hymns, prayers, letters, and amulets.

The oldest extant NT manuscript: fragments of Jn. 18:31-34, 37f. (John Rylands Library, Manchester)

*IV. Aramaic and Hebrew Papyri.*–From 1893 to 1908 numerous Aramaic papyri, dating from the 5th cent. B.C., were found on Elephantine (Egyp. *Yeb*), an island near Aswân (Egyp. *Sewen;* cf. SYENE [Heb. *s*ᵉ*wēnēh*] of Ezk. 29:10, denoting the southern border of Egypt). The literary papyri contain portions of the Book of Ahiqar and an Aramaic version of Darius's Behistun inscription. The documentary texts reflect the affairs of a colony of heterodox Jews doing business and serving as a military outpost under Persian control and worshiping their god Yahu in a temple, in which they made meal, incense, and burnt offerings. When Egyptian priests destroyed the temple of Yahu in 410 B.C., the Jews appealed for redress to the Persian governor, under whose patronage the temple was rebuilt by 399 B.C.

In 1942 an Aramaic papyrus letter that has been dated *ca.* 603/602 B.C. was discovered at Saqqârah (Memphis). In it the Palestinian king Adon (of Ashkelon?) sought military aid from Pharaoh Neco II against the invading armies of the Babylonian Nebuchadrezzar. Other important Aramaic papyri were discovered in 1962 and 1963 in two caves of the Wâdī Dâliyeh N of Old Jericho. These texts, dating from 375 to 335 B.C., contain about forty fragments of contracts, loan agreements, and other business documents written in Samaria.

Beginning in 1947 and continuing for more than a decade, Aramaic and Hebrew manuscripts were found near Qumrân and other ancient sites in the wilderness of Judea

W of the Dead Sea (*see* DEAD SEA SCROLLS). Although most of these materials are leather, some are papyrus. The Aramaic papyri consist chiefly of documentary texts dating from the First and Second Jewish Revolts. The Hebrew papyri derive largely from the same periods and contain several remarkable letters of Simon bar Cochba, the legendary leader of the Second Jewish Revolt against Rome. These finds near the Dead Sea include the oldest papyrus found outside Egypt, a Hebrew letter dated *ca.* 750 B.C. found in a cave of Wâdī Murabbaʿât (P. Mur. 17). This letter, reused in antiquity to record a list of contributors, belongs to the period of King Uzziah's economic activity in the Judean desert and the Negeb (2 Ch. 26:2, 7, 10).

***V. Other Papyri.***–*A. Coptic.* Coptic papyri have made special contributions to early Christian literature. C. Schmidt published a considerable Coptic fragment of the Acts of Paul and a Coptic (Akhmîmic) codex of 1 Clement, almost complete. Texts of Psalms, Proverbs, and homilies were discovered at the White Convent near Panopolis (Akhmîm); indeed, biblical papyri in Coptic are fairly numerous and are being rapidly enriched by such discoveries as the Bodmer Papyri III (John and Genesis), XVI (Exodus), XVIII (Deuteronomy), and XIX (Matthew and Romans). The library of Coptic papyrus codices found near Nag Hammadi in 1945 is a remarkable collection of Jewish and Christian gnostic writings (*see* NAG HAMMADI).

*B. Arabic.* Arabic papyri, from the period after the Arab conquest, A.D. 640, first began to appear from Egypt in 1825 when three pieces were brought to Paris and published by S. de Sacy. Not until the great papyrus finds of 1877-1878, however, did any considerable number of Arabic papyri find their way into Europe. The chief collections are at Vienna (Rainer Collection), Berlin, and Cairo. Large archives of Arabic papyri were discovered at the turn of the century in Aswân (Syene). A few fragments of documentary and magical Arabic papyri from the 10th cent. were found among the manuscripts in Wâdî Murabbaʿât.

*C. Latin.* Latin papyri are comparatively rare. Of the one hundred literary papyri that have been published, Vergil's *Aeneid* is most frequent, with the works of Cicero next best attested. Latin papyri, chiefly after Diocletian, were discovered in Egypt, although some texts came to light at Herculaneum, Dura-Europos in Mesopotamia, and Palestine. The literary texts are accompanied by Latin-Greek glossaries, lexica, and grammars reflecting the schools of Roman Egypt. Nonliterary Latin papyri have become especially valuable in elucidating Roman military and legal traditions.

***VI. Contribution to Biblical Study.***–The papyri have made a valuable contribution to textual criticism of both the OT and the NT. For early Christian literature their testimony has been of unusual interest (the Oxyrhynchus Logia and Gospel fragments). Both literary and documentary papyri have illuminated the religious and cultural environment of the Bible: parallel structures and expressions in the papyri have made biblical literary forms clearer.

A series of uncial MSS from the six centuries preceding the Codex Vaticanus bridges the gap between what were the earliest uncials and the hand of the inscriptions and allows more accurate dating of uncial MSS. Minuscule or cursive hands, too, so common in the NT MSS of the 10th and later cents., appeared in a new light when such writing was seen not as a late invention arising out of the uncial but as the ordinary hand, as distinguished from the literary or book hand, that had existed side by side with the uncial from at least the 4th cent. B.C. *See* WRITING.

The philological contribution of the documentary papyri has been considerable. Like the NT writings, they reflect the common as distinguished from the literary language of the times, and words that had appeared exceptional or unknown in Greek literature have been shown to have been in common use. The problems of NT syntax are similarly illuminated.

Specific historical notices sometimes light up dark points in the Bible. For example, a British Museum decree of Gaius Vibius Maximus, prefect of Egypt (A.D. 104), ordered all who were out of their districts to return to their homes in view of the approaching census (cf. Lk. 2:1-5). Most important of all is the contribution of the papyri to a sympathetic knowledge of ancient life. They present a veritable gallery of biblical characters. A strong light is sometimes thrown upon the social evils of the time, of which Paul and Juvenal wrote so sternly. The child, the prodigal, the thief, the host with his invitations, the steward with his accounts, the thrifty householder, the soldier on service receiving his *viaticum* or retired as a veteran upon his farm, the husbandman, and the publican, are met at first hand in the papyri, which often they themselves had written. The worth of this material for the historical interpretation of the Bible is very great.

***Bibliography.***–*Collections:* P. Benoit, *et al.*, *DJD* (1960-1965); B. P. Grenfell, *et al.*, *Oxyrhynchus Papyri* (1898-1927); F. G. Kenyon, *Chester Beatty Papyri* (1933-1941); F. G. Kenyon and H. I. Bell, *Greek Papyri in the British Museum* (1893-1917); V. Martin, *et al.*, *Bibliotheca Bodmeriana* (1954-1964); K. Preisendanz, *Papyri Magicae Graecae* (1941); W. Schubart, *et al.*, *Aegyptische Urkunden aus den Staatlichen Museen zu Berlin, Griechische Urkunden* (1919-1937); W. Schubart, *et al.*, *Berliner Klassikertexte* (1904-1923); V. A. Tcherikover and A. Fuchs, *Corpus Papyrorum Judaicarum* (1957-1964).

*Periodicals* (the first two important for bibliographies): *Aegyptus; Chronique d' Égypte; Archiv für Papyrusforschung.*

*Reference Works:* L. Mitteis and U. Wilcken, *Grundzüge und Chrestomathie der Papyrusforschung* (1912); F. Preisigke, *et al.*, *Berichtigungsliste der griechischen Papyrusurkunden aus Aegypten* (1922-); *Sammelbuch griechischen Urkunden aus Aegypten* (1919).

*Specific Sections of This Article: I:* N. Lewis, *Papyrus in Classical Antiquity* (1974).

*III:* K. Aland, ed., *Repertorium der griechischen christlichen Papyri*, I: *Biblische Papyri* (1976); A. S. Hunt and C. C. Edgar, *Select Papyri* (1932-1934); F. G. Kenyon, "Fifty Years of Papyrology," in *Actes Ve Congrés de Papyrologie* (1938), pp. 1-11; R. A. Pack, *Greek and Latin Literary Texts from Greco-Roman Egypt* (2nd ed. 1965), pp. 1-144, 152-55; K. Preisendanz, *Papyrusfunde und Papyrusforschung* (1933); E. G. Turner, *Greek Papyri: An Introduction* (1968); J. G. Winter, *Life and Letters in the Papyri* (1933).

*IV:* P. Benoit, *et al.*, *Les Grottes de Murabbaʿât* (*DJD*, 2, 1961); A. Cowley, *Aramaic Papyri of the Fifth Century B.C.* (1923); F. M. Cross, *BA*, 26 (1963), 110-121; A. Dupont-Sommer, *Semitica*, 1 (1948), 43-68; E. G. Kraeling, *Brooklyn Museum Aramaic Papyri*, (1953); A. Vincent, *La Religion des Judéo-Araméens d'Eléphantine* (1937); Y. Yadin, *BA*, 24 (1961), 34-50, 86-95.

*V:* A. Calderini, *Papiri Latini* (1945); R. Cavenaile, *Corpus papyrorum latinarum* (1958); A. Grohmann, *Einführung und Chrestomathie zur arabischen Papyruskunde* (1955); *From the World of Arabic Papyri* (1952); W. Kammerer, *Coptic Bibliography* (1950); A. A. Schiller, *Bulletin of the American Society of Papyrologists*, 13 (1976), 99-123.

*VI:* BDF; H. I. Bell, *Cults and Creeds in Graeco-Roman Egypt* (1953); Deiss.*LAE;* B. M. Metzger, *Text of the NT* (2nd ed. 1968); MM; B. Olsson, *Papyrusbriefe aus der frühesten Römerzeit* (1925); W. Schubart, *Griechische Paläographie* (1925); E. Würthwein, *Text of the OT* (Eng. tr., rev. ed. 1979).

E. J. GOODSPEED
I. A. SPARKS

**PARABLE** [Heb. *māšāl*–'saying'; cf. niphal of *māšal*–'be like'] (Ps. 78:2); NEB "story with a meaning"; [piel of *dāmâ*] (Hos. 12:10 [MT 11]); AV SIMILITUDE; [Gk. *parabolḗ*–'comparison'] (Mt. 13 par.; 22:1; Mk. 3:23; 7:17 par.; 12:1, 12 par.; Lk. 5:36; 6:39; 12:16; 13:6; etc.). A metaphor or simile often extended to a short narrative; in biblical contexts almost always formulated to reveal and illustrate the kingdom of God.

I. OT
II. Intertestamental Period
III. Jesus' Ministry
 A. Synoptic Gospels
  1. History of Interpretation
   a. Epochs in Research
   b. Current Syntheses
  2. Classification
 B. Gospel of John
 C. Gospel of Thomas
IV. The Rest of the NT
V. Rabbinic Literature

*I. OT.*–Although "parable" occurs only twice in the RSV OT, Heb. *māšāl* occurs thirty-nine times with a broad semantic range. It can mean "byword" or "taunt" in an expression of irony or contempt (1 K. 9:7; Job 17:6; Ezk. 14:8); "proverb," either as a short popular saying (1 S. 10:12; Ezk. 18:2) or as a concise word of wisdom (1 S. 24:13; Prov. 1:1; 10:1; 25:1); "allegory" (Ezk. 17:2; 24:3); or prophetic or didactic "discourse" (Nu. 23:7; Job 27:1). In many instances the *māšāl* draws much of its force and relevance from its historical context, confronting its hearers with a comparison or figurative saying that sheds new light on a contemporary situation, often a crisis. In Ps. 78:2a "parable" parallels "dark sayings" in v. 2b; the psalmist declares that he will reveal the hidden significance of Israel's history. In Hos. 12:10 (MT 11) "I . . . gave parables" translates the piel of *dāmâ*, "make comparisons," which in this verse parallels the "visions" that the Lord "multiplied."

Several OT narratives, not specifically labeled as *mᵉšālîm*, form close parallels to Jesus' parables. Some are actually fables, involving talking plants and animals (usually as symbols for kings and their nations — Jgs. 9:8-15; 2 K. 14:9f.); others more closely approximate the nature parables of Jesus (Isa. 5:1-7, which probably forms the background for Mk. 12:1-9 par.; and Ezk. 17:22-24; cf. Mk. 4:32). By far the closest parallel in form is Nathan's parable of the ewe lamb, which convicted David of his sins against Uriah and Bathsheba (2 S. 12:1-7); the point is grasped only when the main point of comparison is recognized at the end of the parable.

***II. Intertestamental Period.***–In Judaism *māšāl* and its Aramaic equivalent *maṯlā'* took on an even wider variety of meanings: "parable, similitude, allegory, fable, proverb, apocalyptic revelation, riddle, symbol, pseudonym, fictitious person, example, theme, argument, apology, refutation, jest" (Jeremias, p. 20). In the Apocrypha *mᵉšālîm* were predominantly proverbs, especially in the Wisdom of Solomon and Sirach. In the RSV "parable" occurs in Sir. 3:29 as the object of a wise man's rumination; in 39:2f. as a parallel to discourses and proverbs, with "subtleties" and "obscurities" to interpret; and in 47:15, 17, along with riddles, songs, proverbs, and interpretations, as characteristic of Solomon's wisdom. 2 Esd. 8:2f. presents a similitude remarkably parallel to synoptic teaching in both form and content, comparing the small amount of gold dust out of all the earth's clay to the few who will be saved out of all God's creation. 2 Esd. 4:47, on the other hand, uses "parable" to refer to a symbolic vision that the Lord reveals to His seer. Such visions recur regularly in the Pseudepigrapha, especially in the apocalyptic literature. The most famous collection of these is 1 En. 37–71, known as the Parables or Similitudes of Enoch. The highly symbolic and allegorical revelations are quite different from the parables of Jesus; but they do provide important background for the symbolism of NT eschatology and (if their pre-Christian origin can be maintained) for Jesus' use of the title "Son of man." Gk. *parabolḗ* in the LXX always reflects an underlying Heb. *māšāl*, so "parable" by NT times had clearly inherited a broad semantic range. In classical Greek literature, that range was much narrower; Aristotelian definition limited "parable" to a comparison of a known to an unknown object that made exactly one main point (*Rhet.* 2.20).

***III. Jesus' Ministry.***–All the RSV NT uses of "parable" occur in the Gospels. Jesus' mastery of the art of telling parables is demonstrated by the complete lack of any attempt by any other NT character or writer to imitate Him. Even in post-NT Christian literature, only a few narratives receive the label "parable," and these (e.g., Shep. Herm. Sim. 1–9) resemble the similitudes of intertestamental apocalyptic more than the teaching of Jesus. The criterion of "dissimilarity" has thus often been invoked to establish the authenticity of the parables as the core of Jesus' teaching, even by those who doubt the genuineness of many of the Gospel sayings attributed to Him.

*A. Synoptic Gospels. 1. History of Interpretation.* Several different trends of interpretation have dominated successive periods of church history; current scholarship is trying to consolidate and synthesize the contributions of each of these trends.

*a. Epochs in Research.* Although distinctions can be drawn between the periods of the early church fathers, the Middle Ages, and the Reformation and its legacy (Stein, pp. 42-52), the dominant form of parable interpretation during the eighteen centuries from *ca.* 100 to 1900 was "allegorizing" (*see* ALLEGORY). Symbolic significance was discovered for as many details as possible in each parable. The most famous example of this method is Augustine's interpretation of the parable of the Good Samaritan (Lk. 10:25-37); the man going down from Jerusalem was Adam leaving the city of heavenly peace; the robbers beating him were the devil and his angels, persuading the man to sin; the priest and the Levite stood for the Law and the Prophets; the Samaritan was Christ; the oil and wine, comfort and exhortation; the beast, the body of Christ; the inn, the Church; and the innkeeper, the apostle Paul (*Quaestiones Evangeliorem* ii.19). To be sure, commentators debated the significance of such details, but all agreed that hidden meanings were present.

Around the turn of this century A. Jülicher's magisterial *Die Gleichnisreden Jesu* broke with these centuries of tradition, arguing that, as in classical Greek usage, each parable may have only one *tertium comparationis* (point of comparison). He also introduced a threefold distinction between the similitude (Ger. *Gleichnis*), a short present-tense comparison; the parable (*Parabel*), a complete story, usually in past tense; and the example-story (*Beispielerzählung*), a parable in which the "moral" is more secular than religious (Jülicher, I, 112-17). Again, commentators disagreed concerning the main point of a given parable — usually on the basis of their differing understandings of Jesus' eschatology (*see* ESCHATOLOGY; the history of interpretation described there closely parallels that of the parables) — or concerning which parables fell into which of the three categories, but the majority of twentieth-century scholars have preferred Jülicher's principles to those of his predecessors. The parable of the Good Samaritan, e.g., is now often viewed as an example-story of which the main point is to imitate the Samaritan's neighborliness.

The most famous pioneer of form criticism (*see* CRITICISM III), R. Bultmann, initiated a complementary approach that examined tendencies in the oral transmission of teachings like those attributed to Jesus in the Synoptics.

The typical form of a parable includes conciseness of narrative and numbers of characters, the use of direct speech and soliloquy, climactic repetition, and the law of end-stress (*HST,* pp. 188-192). J. Jeremias, whose work remains the most important study of the parables still in print, built on both Jülicher's and Bultmann's insights to formulate ten "laws" governing the "transformation" of Jesus' original words in early Church tradition and by the Evangelists' redaction: (1) translation into Greek; (2) changing imagery to communicate better with a Hellenistic audience; (3) embellishment of details; (4) introduction of themes from the OT and folk literature; (5) addressing to the Church parables originally intended for Jesus' opponents; (6) a shift from eschatology to exhortation; (7) application to missionary contexts; (8) allegorical interpretation; (9) collecting and conflating parables, and (10) inventing settings and generalizing conclusions where none was provided in the tradition (Jeremias, pp. 113f.). Returning to the example of the Good Samaritan, most form and redaction critics consider Lk. 10:25-29 and 37b an artificial context that did not originally belong to the parable itself.

Recent parable research has emphasized literary more than historical analysis. The "new hermeneutic" (*see* INTERPRETATION, HISTORY OF IV.H.3) highlights the power of Jesus' parables and enjoins expositors to give their attention not to intrepreting them so much as to re-creating the "language event" (*Sprachereignis*) that Jesus' original audiences experienced (Linnemann). Structuralism applies the categories of modern linguistics to analyze "surface" and "deep" structures of the texts, based on, e.g., the type of plot (see Via's excellent work on "comedy" and "tragedy"), the functions of the various "actants" (roughly equivalent to "characters"), and the types of opposition and resolution in the various "sequences" of the narratives (Patte). K. E. Bailey's recent works call attention to often unnoticed parallelism (esp. chiastic or inverted parallelism) within the various parables. The result of all these literary analyses for the example of the Good Samaritan is that a good case can be made for the historical unity and authenticity of all of Lk. 10:25-37, for the narrative as a pure parable and not an example-story, and for the main point being that even one's enemy is one's neighbor (see Bailey, *Poet,* pp. 72-74; Funk, pp. 29-34; P. Jones, p. 228).

*b. Current Syntheses.* Many Gospel passages closely match the form of the principal narrative parables, even though they are not specifically introduced as parables (see below). Conversely, Luke can apply the term *parabolḗ* even to a saying as short as "Physician, heal yourself" (4:23). In Lk. 4:23 the RSV translates *parabolḗ* as "proverb," while the saying labeled a "parable" in 6:39 ("Can a blind man lead a blind man? Will they not both fall into a pit?") is not much more than a proverb. Clearly, the word "parable" as used by almost all interpreters includes both more and less than what the Synoptics specifically call parables (for an appeal to abandon this approach, see Sider). C. H. Dodd's classic definition remains unsurpassed: "a metaphor or simile drawn from nature or common life, arresting the hearer by its vividness or strangeness, and leaving the mind in sufficient doubt about its precise application to tease it into active thought" (Dodd, p. 16). This definition can be overly pressed; the parables contain key "atypical features" (Huffman) as well, which need not be jettisoned as inauthentic. Twentieth-century interpreters often forget the shock value of a Samaritan hero, a justified tax-collector (Lk. 18:14), or a father running to welcome his prodigal son (15:20).

Perhaps no issue has dominated parable research as much as the relationship between parable and allegory. Jülicher's reaction against centuries of abuse was an overreaction; the Hebrew as well as the Greek background for *parabolḗ* must be retained. More scholars have come to recognize that Jesus' parables often have important details with hidden symbolism, and that the mistake of past interpreters was more one of anachronistic allegorizing than of allegorical interpretation as such (see esp. Klauck). Especially where component metaphors allude to well-known OT passages and stock Jewish symbols, the interpreter must be open to a partially allegorical approach, such as Jesus Himself employed for the parables of the Sower (Mk. 4:3-9, 14-20 par.) and of the wheat and tares (Mt. 13:24-31, 37-43). (On the authenticity of this type of interpretation, which has often been challenged, see Payne.) In fact, according to purely literary criticism, any "extended metaphor in narratory form" is an allegory (Boucher, p. 20); the only narrative parables of Jesus that are not allegories are His example stories, which are extended synecdoches.

Another key issue in interpreting parables is their purpose. Clearly Jesus used the parabolic form of speech to illustrate and clarify the nature of the kingdom of God. Yet in Mk. 4:11f., He tells His disciples that "for those outside everything is in parables; so that they may indeed see but not perceive, and may indeed hear but not understand; lest they should turn again, and be forgiven." Apparently Jesus intended to conceal as well as to reveal. This passage has regularly been labeled a creation of Mark, or of church tradition before him, or at least as out of context. Of those who accept its authenticity in this context, some have tried to avoid the problem of its apparent meaning by explaining the *hína*-clause ("so that . . .") as result rather than purpose, or as part of the OT quotation on which it is based (Isa. 6:9f.); but neither of these suggestions evades the force of the *mḗpote*-clause ("lest . . ."). It is best to allow the full weight of these words to be felt. Jesus' teaching confronted people with radical demands, and not all were willing to comply. Some followed Him in discipleship, but others were actually driven further from the Kingdom (cf. Mt. 12:34f. par.). The key is not in the meaning of "so that" but in the phrases "see but not perceive, . . . hear but not understand." It is not intellectual but volitional blindness and deafness that is in view (cf. Lk. 20:19). Klauck puts it best: "they understand the provocative claim of the parables very well, but they are not prepared to accept it. For Mark, Jesus' speaking in parables is not a riddle as such. What is perplexing is the behavior that it calls forth — that man can see salvation personified and nevertheless not come to conversion and belief" (p. 251).

Finally, many of Jeremias's "laws of transformation" have been questioned. The interpreter need not feel misled by the audience or interpretation assigned to the parable by the Synoptist (Blomberg, *Trinity Journal,* N.S. 3 [1982], 11-14). Although Jesus' exact words (*ipsissima verba*) have been altered, as a comparison of Gospel parallels demonstrates, the essential meaning or authentic voice (*ipsissima vox*) behind them has not been changed. (For the best, most comprehensive discussion of each Synoptic parable and its parallels with defense of this viewpoint, see Kistemaker.) The Evangelists' differing redactional styles and interests become clearly visible in their renditions of the double- and triple-tradition parables (see Carlston), but their revisions are mostly paraphrastic, explanatory, and abbreviating in nature. The most drastic differences and apparent distortions often come between pairs of parables that may not be variants of one original after all, but two separate narratives from different occasions in Jesus' life (e.g., Mt. 22:1-14 and Lk. 14:16-24; Mt. 25:14-30 and Lk. 19:12-27; Mt. 18:12-14 and Lk. 15:4-7; see Blomberg, *WTJ* [1984]).

2. *Classification*. Of the Synoptic passages specifically called parables, some are really simple metaphors or comparisons rather than genuine "parables" as the word is generally used: Mt. 15:13f. par. (the blind leading the blind); Mk. 3:23-27 (plundering the strong man's house); 7:14-16 (on defilement); Lk. 5:36-39 (wineskins and garments); and 21:19-31 (the budding fig tree). Here the influence of Heb. *māšāl* broadens the application of the more technical Gk. *parabolḗ*. Many other teachings of Jesus fall into this broader category, e.g., the lamp and bushel (Mk. 4:21 par.), savorless salt (Mk. 9:50), weather signs (Lk. 12:54-56 par.), the city on a hill (Mt. 5:14), and the lamp of the body (Mt. 6:22 par.). (For longer lists, see Hunter, *Parables*, pp. 121f.; Perkins [who calls these "parables derived from proverbs"], pp. 10-12; *DNTT*, II, 749-751.)

The remaining occurrences of "parable" appear with full narratives of the type usually associated with this term. These have often been classified according to content, e.g., the "coming," "grace," "men," and "crisis" of the Kingdom (Hunter, *Parables*); or the "Kingdom as present," "Kingdom as demand," "God of the parables," and "final judgment" (Stein). More natural groupings arise out of recent literary and structural analyses, as in Crossan's threefold classification of parables of "advent," "reversal," and "action," or Via's twofold comic/tragic division. Special studies have also analyzed such subgroups as "servant" or "parousia" parables (Weiser, Schneider). M. D. Goulder has even grouped the parables by Gospel, arguing that the narratives in Matthew and Luke are so shaped by those Evangelists' own distinctive styles and interests that only the narratives in Mark are authentic. A better case can be made for seeing earlier (pre-Markan) collections of similar parables as sources for the Evangelists' redactions (cf. Mk. 4; Mt. 13; parts of Lk. 9:51–18:34; see Blomberg, "Midrash"). The following classification combines the insights of several of these methods.

"Nature parables" include the Sower (Mk. 4:1-9 par.), the seed growing secretly (4:26-29), the mustard seed (4:30-32 par.), and the leaven (Mt. 13:33 par.). These all illustrate the remarkable growth of the Kingdom from small beginnings. The most elaborate of these is the first. Theologians have wrestled with the significance of the four soils, especially for the doctrine of the "perseverance of the saints," but it is unlikely that the imagery can resolve the debate. The parable of the fig tree (Lk. 13:6-9 also employs agricultural imagery, but deals with potential death rather than growth. As a stock symbol for Israel and its leaders, the fig tree graphically depicted the impending judgment on the Jews who did not repent.

"Discovery parables" include the hidden treasure (Mt. 13:44), the pearl of great price (vv. 45f.), and the dragnet (vv. 47-50). These tie in closely with Matthew's collection of nature parables, but they make a slightly different point: the value of God's kingdom is so great that its discovery leads wise people to abandon all for its sake.

"Contrast parables," of which there is a large number, compare one or two examples of negative attitudes or actions related to God's kingdom with a positive example — or vice versa. Those with "comic" (happy) endings include the lost sheep, coin, and son (Lk. 15:4-32 — although the last of these has an open-ended conclusion as the father awaits the reaction of the prodigal's older brother), the Good Samaritan (10:25-37), and the Pharisee and publican (18:9-14). All illustrate God's surprising mercy for the lost, outcast, and dispossessed. Those with "tragic" (usually judgmental) endings include the two builders (Mt. 7:24-27 par.), the faithful and unfaithful servants (24:45-51), the talents/pounds (25:14-30; Lk. 19:11-27), the unforgiving servant (Mt. 18:23-35), and the rich man and Lazarus (Lk. 16:19-31; this parable has spawned numerous unjustified descriptions of the afterlife, and the interpreter must avoid confusing the worlds depicted here with reality; Jesus' imagery is probably borrowed from Egyptian and Jewish folklore; see *TDNT*, I, 146-49). In several instances, contrast parables balance positive and negative examples so evenly that it is difficult to assign emphasis to either (the two sons, Mt. 21:28-32; the two debtors, Lk. 7:40-43; the wheat and tares, Mt. 13:24-30; the ten virgins, 25:1-13). Although it is usually possible to identify one overarching point in a contrast parable, this point is often elaborated best under two or three subheadings corresponding to the main characters or groups of characters portrayed. Thus the parable of the prodigal teaches not only the joy of repentance but also God's welcome for sinners, and it further warns against the hard-heartedness that resents God's mercy for others.

Contrast parables can be divided not only into comic and tragic, but also into "expected" and "unexpected" types. The reward and punishment of the faithful and unfaithful servants surprised no one, but the justification of the publican and condemnation of the Pharisee upended all social convention. Several other parables that focus on a single character or group also present surprising switches. These "reversal parables" include the great dinner and wedding feast (Lk. 14:16-21 and Mt. 22:1-14), in which the invited guests' refusal excludes them from the banquet; the wicked husbandmen (Mk. 12:1-12 par.), in which the (presumably Jewish) tenants' rejection of their landlord's servants and son leads to the vineyard being leased to others (Gentiles?); the laborers in the vineyard (Mt. 20:1-16), where last-minute workers receive a full day's wage; the rich fool (Lk. 12:16-21); and the places at table (Lk. 14:7-11).

"A fortiori parables" refer to those that employ the logic of "how much more . . . ?" or "from lesser to greater" (Heb. *qal wāḥômer*), which if missed can result in grave misinterpretation. God is *not* reluctant to give like the sleeping man in the parable of the friend at midnight (Lk. 11:5-8); Jesus' appended comments make this clear: "how much more will the heavenly Father give . . . ?" (v. 13). The same logic is implicit in the parables of the unjust judge (Lk. 18:1-8), the unjust steward (Lk. 16:1-13; it is only the shrewdness that the master praises), the unprofitable servants (17:7-10), the tower-builder and warring king (14:28-33), the asking son (11:11-13), and the animals in the well (14:5). Several of these shorter parables share the additional feature of interrogative form, introduced by *tís ex hymṓn* ("which one of you [would do such and such]?"), which expects an emphatically negative response. The a fortiori logic is thus made clear: if even human beings would not act in a certain evil or foolish way (or conversely, if they would act positively), how much more can God be depended on to behave righteously!

*B. Gospel of John*. The word "parable" does not occur in John, but "figure" in 10:6; 16:25, 29 translates *paroimía* ("riddle" or "wise saying") — a term used by the LXX in several instances for *māšāl*. These Johannine uses apply the term to Jesus' metaphors of the Good Shepherd (10:1-5) and the woman in travail (vv. 20-24), which closely parallel the shorter Synoptic similitudes. A. M. Hunter (*John*, pp. 78f.) has in fact identified thirteen "parables" in John (3:8, 29; 4:35-38; 5:19-20a; 8:35; 10:1-5; 11:9f.; 12:24, 35f.; 13:1-15; 14:2f.; 15:1f.; 16:21). None of these approximates in form the longer narrative parables in the Synoptics, but

Jesus' characteristic style of teaching is still discernible. The Johannine "parables" provide an important link with Synoptic tradition for establishing the historical continuity between the Fourth Gospel and its predecessors.

*C. Gospel of Thomas.* The main extracanonical source for parables attributed to Jesus is the Gospel of Thomas (*see* APOCRYPHAL GOSPELS V.J.1). Of its 114 sayings, over half have parallels in the NT Gospels, including eleven of its thirteen parables: 8 (dragnet), 9 (sower), 20 (mustard seed), 57 (wheat and tares), 63 (rich fool), 64 (great dinner), 65 (wicked husbandmen), 76 (pearl of great price), 96 (leaven), 107 (lost sheep), and 109 (hidden treasure). Two previously unknown parables compare the Kingdom to a woman with a broken jar of meal that loses its contents without her knowledge as she walks home (97; a warning against taking "salvation" for granted?) and to a would-be assassin who practices sword thrusts into the wall of his house before leaving to slay his monarch (98). This latter parable closely parallels Lk. 14:28-33 on counting the cost, and many scholars consider both new parables authentic. The eleven parables with NT parallels have incited more controversy. Two basic approaches compete for acceptance. One views Thomas as having preserved versions more original than those found in the Synoptics, because its versions are consistently shorter and simpler. Others find in Thomas clear signs of dependence on the canonical Gospels and of Gnostic redaction, and they attribute Thomas' accounts to at least a second-century date. Arguments for the latter view generally appear stronger (see Lindemann; Blomberg, "Thomas").

***IV. The Rest of the NT.***–The term "parable" does not occur elsewhere in the RSV NT, but Gk. *parabolḗ* does reappear twice. In He. 9:9 (lit. "a parable") and 11:19 (lit. "in a parable") the RSV translates the Greek as "symbolic" and "figuratively speaking," respectively. The metaphor in 9:9 compares the tabernacle and the sacrifices to the "present age," which is passing away; 11:19 compares Isaac's reprieve from slaughter to the resurrection of the dead.

***V. Rabbinic Literature.***–Literally hundreds of passages in the Midrashim, Tosefta, and Talmuds begin with the label *māšāl*, and they often use introductory formulas identical to those found in the Synoptics ("it is like . . . ," "to what shall it be compared . . . ?" etc.). Similar imagery also affords sometimes striking parallels with Jesus' parables. (Cf., e.g., T.B. *Shabbath* 153a [about a king who announced an impending banquet and the division between servants who clothed themselves for the festivity and those who did not] with Mt. 22:1-14 and 25:1-10. Those who argue against the authenticity or unity of composition of these Synoptic parables might need to reconsider.) The rabbinic *mᵉšālîm* make plentiful use of stock symbols such as father, king, judge, and shepherd for God; vineyard, vine, and sheep for God's people; the enemy for the devil; harvest and grape gathering for the final judgment; and weddings, feasts, and festal clothing for the eschatological consummation. They also regularly conclude with explanatory comments. These factors alone should caution interpreters against refusing to see similar "allegorical" elements and "generalizing conclusions" in Jesus' parables as authentic. It is simply false to claim that a master storyteller need never interpret his parables; the psychological states of his audience regularly require it (see Magass).

On the other hand, the parables of the early Rabbis (Tannaim) reveal significant differences from those of Jesus. The most important difference is that parables in the rabbinic literature almost always illustrate or expound a biblical (OT) text that is mentioned in the introduction or conclusion of the narrative. The NT parables, however, almost never function in this way; Jesus came not to exegete Scripture, but to reveal the new age of God's kingdom.

*See also* FIGURE.

***Bibliography.***–K. E. Bailey, *Poet and Peasant: A Literary-Cultural Approach to the Parables in Luke* (1976); *Through Peasant Eyes: More Lucan Parables* (1980); C. L. Blomberg, *Trinity Journal*, N.S. 3 (1982), 3-17; "Midrash, Chiasmus, and the Outline of Luke's Central Section," in R. T. France and D. Wenham, eds., *Gospel Perspectives*, III (1983), 217-261; "Tradition and Redaction in the Parables of the Gospel according to Thomas," in *Gospel Perspectives*, V (1984); *WTJ*, 46 (1984), 78-103; M. Boucher, *The Mysterious Parable* (1977), C. E. Carlston, *Parables of the Triple Tradition* (1975); J. D. Crossan, *In Parables: The Challenge of the Historical Jesus* (1973); *DNTT*, II, 743-760; C. H. Dodd, *Parables of the Kingdom* (1935); P. Fiebig, *Die Gleichnisreden Jesu im Lichte der rabbinischen Gleichnisse des neutestamentlichen Zeitalters* (1912); D. Flusser, *Die rabbinischen Gleichnissen und der Gleichniserzähler Jesus*, I (1981); E. Fuchs, *Studies of the Historical Jesus* (Eng. tr. 1964); R. W. Funk, *Parables and Presence* (1982); M. D. Goulder, *JTS*, 19 (1968), 51-69; *HST*; N. A. Huffman, *JBL*, 97 (1978), 207-220; A. M. Hunter, *Interpreting the Parables* (1960); *According to John* (1968); J. Jeremias, *Parables of Jesus* (Eng. tr., rev. ed. 1972); G. V. Jones, *Art and Truth of the Parables* (1964); P. R. Jones, *Teaching of the Parables* (1982); A. Jülicher, *Die Gleichnisreden Jesu* (2 vols., 1899; 2nd ed. 1910, repr. 1969); W. S. Kissinger, *Parables of Jesus: A History of Interpretation and Bibliography* (1979); S. Kistemaker, *Parables of Jesus* (1981); H.-J. Klauck, *Allegorie und Allegorese in synoptischen Gleichnistexten* (1978); A. Lindemann, *ZNW*, 71 (1980), 214-243; E. Linnemann, *Parables of Jesus* (Eng. tr. 1966); W. Magass, *Linguistica Biblica*, 36 (1975), 1-20; I. H. Marshall, *Eschatology and the Parables* (1963); W. O. E. Oesterley, *Gospel Parables in the Light of Their Jewish Background* (1936); D. Patte, *What is Structural Exegesis?* (1976); P. B. Payne, "The Authenticity of the Parable of the Sower and Its Interpretation," in R. T. France and D. Wenham, eds., *Gospel Perspectives*, I (1980), 163-207; P. Perkins, *Hearing the Parables* (1981); N. Perrin, *Jesus and the Language of the Kingdom* (1976); G. Schneider, *Parusiegleichnisse im Lukasevangelium* (1975); J. W. Sider, *Bibl.*, 62 (1981), 453-470; R. H. Stein, *Intro. to the Parables of Jesus* (1981); D. W. Suter, *Tradition and Composition in the Parables of Enoch* (1979); A. C. Thiselton, *SJT*, 23 (1970), 437-468; *TWOT*, I, 191f., 533f.; D. O. Via, *The Parables: Their Literary and Existential Dimension* (1967); H. Weder, *Die Gleichnisse Jesu als Metaphern* (1978); A. Weiser, *Die Knechtsgleichnisse der synoptischen Evangelien* (1971).

C. L. BLOMBERG

**PARACLETE.** The transliteration of Gk. *paráklētos*, a noun that occurs four times in John's Gospel (14:16, 26; 15:26; 16:7, all rendered "Paraclete" in the NAB). The word has been translated as "Comforter" (AV), "Counselor" (RSV, NIV), "Advocate" (JB), "your Advocate" (NEB), and "Helper" (Today's English Version). Its only other NT occurrence is in 1 Jn. 2:1, where it is rendered "advocate" (AV, RSV), "intercessor" (NAB), or "one to plead our cause" (NEB). In John's Gospel Jesus uses *paráklētos* as a designation of the "Holy Spirit" (14:26) or "Spirit of truth" (14:16; 15:26; 16:7), while 1 Jn. 2:1 applies the term to Jesus Himself, now in the presence of God the Father.

The first NT occurrence of *paráklētos* refers to the Spirit as "another Paraclete" (Jn. 14:16, NAB), apparently in relation to Jesus Himself. The meaning is either that Jesus in His earthly ministry was actually the first "Paraclete" or that He is promising "another Person . . . as your Paraclete" without implying that the title belonged to Him first (cf. His cryptic references to "another" in Jn. 5:32, 42). Although 1 Jn. 2:1 refers to Jesus as *paráklētos* specifically in His exalted state, it can be assumed that *paráklētos*, like the accompanying term *díkaios* ("righteous one"), applies to the whole scope of Jesus' ministry both before and after His resurrection. Whether or not Jesus explicitly applied the term to Himself, He clearly used it to designate the Spirit as His successor and continuing representative on earth after His departure.

The noun *paráklētos* is derived from the verb *parakaléō*, "call for," "make an appeal," "comfort," or "counsel." Such noun formations are normally understood in a passive sense, i.e., "one who is called for or summoned" (cf. Lat. *advocatus* in the Vulg. of 1 Jn. 2:1). In John's Gospel the Paraclete is introduced precisely as one summoned, a messenger sent from the Father in answer to Jesus' prayer (Jn. 14:16; cf. also v. 26; 15:26; 16:7). These considerations tend to justify such translations as "Advocate," "Helper," or "Mediator." But because *parakaléō* is an important verb in the NT, some scholars have argued that the verbal noun has an active sense: "one who appeals, counsels, or consoles"; hence the popular translations "Comforter" or "Counselor."

Undoubtedly the Paraclete in John's Gospel does carry out some functions that are aptly expressed by the verb *parakaléō*. Yet the Paraclete's role is best understood not by sketching the range of meaning of *parakaléō* (which does not occur in the Johannine writings) but by noting the verbs actually used by John to describe what the Paraclete will do:

(1) In relation to Jesus' disciples, the Paraclete will *be with* them forever (14:16f.) to *teach* and *remind* them of what Jesus has already taught (v. 26). "He" (the masculine article and pronoun indicate personality, not gender) will *testify* to them, and through them to the world, about Jesus (15:26f.). He will *guide* them into all the truth and will *glorify* Jesus by *speaking* what He hears from the Father. He will even *predict* things to come (16:13-15).

(2) In relation to the world, the Paraclete will act as God's advocate, to *convict* the world of sin and *prove it wrong* in its standards of justice and judgment (16:8-11).

Because a survey of the predicates describing the Paraclete's activity provides a better understanding of His nature than an analysis of the term *paráklētos* itself, the term's "background" in Jewish and Hellenistic thought is not of great significance for its NT usage. There is in fact no real conceptual background for Jesus' distinctive use of *paráklētos* — neither in the figure known as the *Yawar*, or "Helper," in the late Gnostic Mandean literature (as Rudolf Bultmann and others have proposed), nor in Hellenism, nor in the OT, nor in Jewish apocalyptic or rabbinic literature, nor in the writings of the Qumrân community. None of these could provide the conceptual background for the use of *paráklētos* in John's Gospel, for the Paraclete is the successor of Jesus. The Paraclete's nature and function presuppose the historical career of Jesus and depend on that career for their meaning.

One does find in Jewish literature, however, the conceptual background for at least two specific elements of Jesus' teaching about the Paraclete. (1) The Scriptures provide several examples of two successive figures with the second either completing or fulfilling the work of the first, e.g., Moses and Joshua, Elijah and Elisha, Moses and the "prophet like Moses" (Dt. 18:15-18), John the Baptist and "the Coming One" (as John expected Him), John the Baptist and Jesus (as He actually appeared in history). Sometimes the first is the "greater," while at other times the second is greater; sometimes there are simply parallels between the two, while other examples present contrasts as well. In some cases (though in different ways) the Spirit of God provides the link between the two figures (Dt. 34:9; 2 K. 2:9, 15; cf. Mk. 1:8). (2) Late Jewish angelology provides parallels for the function of angels or "spirits" as revealers (in Jewish apocalyptic literature) and as defenders of God's people (in the Qumrân documents, sometimes with the designation "Spirit of truth").

Nowhere except in the Gospel of John do these two elements come together. As in the case of John the Baptist and "the Coming One," a flesh-and-blood historical person (Jesus) is to be succeeded by a supernatural figure (the Paraclete). But what makes the latter succession unique is that Jesus never says, as John does, "He who comes after me ranks before me" (Jn. 1:15) or "is mightier than I" (Mk. 1:7). Jesus does not testify about the Paraclete but promises that the Paraclete will testify about Him. Although Jesus does not specifically address the issue of relative greatness, His own role is the primary one while the Paraclete's role is derivative ("He will glorify me, for he will take what is mine and declare it to you," Jn. 16:14).

The link between the Spirit and the historical Jesus is stronger in these passages than in similar passages in which the term *paráklētos* does not occur: e.g., Jesus' promise of the Spirit to His disciples in times of persecution (Mk. 13:11; Mt. 10:19f.; Lk. 12:11f.), the references in 1 Jn. 2:20, 27, to an anointing (*chrísma*) from God given to teach the disciples and guard them against lies and false doctrine, and the reference in 2 Jn. 2 to "the truth which is in us and will be with us forever" (cf. 1 Jn. 5:6, "the Spirit is the truth"). "Paraclete" as a title for the Holy Spirit is limited to passages in which the Spirit functions specifically as Jesus' successor and testifies specifically about Jesus. The term seems to have been applied first to Jesus — either by Himself or by His disciples — but only as an informal designation of His role (*paráklētos* without the definite article, Jn. 14:16; 1 Jn. 2:1), not as a title or technical term (*ho paráklētos*, "the Paraclete," in all other NT uses). The formal title was reserved for the Spirit; once Jesus had introduced the "Spirit of truth" as *állos paráklētos*, the titular form prevailed in the Johannine farewell discourses. The effect was to emphasize both the Spirit's personality and the Spirit's continuity with Jesus.

Other NT writers did not use *paráklētos*, but they occasionally made a similar point by using phrases such as "the Spirit of Jesus" (Acts 16:7), "the Spirit of Jesus Christ" (Phil. 1:19), or "the Spirit of Christ" (Rom. 8:9; 1 Pet. 1:11; cf. 2 Cor. 3:17). In the figure of the Paraclete more than anywhere else, the Spirit of God wears a human face, and it is the face of Jesus.

***Bibliography***.–O. Betz, *Der Paraklet* (1963); R. E. Brown, *NTS*, 13 (1967), 113-132; *Gospel According to John*, II (*AB*, 1970); 1135-1144; G. Johnston, *Spirit-Paraclete in the Gospel of John* (1970); *TDNT*, V, *s.v.* παράκλητος (J. Behm); H. Windisch, *Spirit-Paraclete in the Fourth Gospel* (Eng. tr. 1968). J. R. MICHAELS

**PARADISE** par'ə-dīs [Gk. *parádeisos* (Lk. 23:43; 2 Cor. 12:4; Rev. 2:7; 2 Esd. 4:7; 6:2; 7:36, 123; 8:52)]; NEB also GARDEN (Rev. 2:7). Paradise is a Persian loanword (*pairi-daēza*) which was taken over by Hebrew (*pardēs*), Greek, and Aramaic (*pardēsā'*). The Persian word originally meant "an enclosure" and came to mean "a park surrounded by a wall." The loanword thus came to mean "park, garden," often with the idea of being surrounded by a wall. The three OT occurrences (Neh. 2:8; Eccl. 2:5; Cant. 4:13) follow this secular meaning. Xenophon first used the Greek word to refer to the parks of Persian kings and their nobility. By the 3rd cent. B.C. *parádeisos* was a general term for "park."

The LXX used *parádeisos* forty-seven times, translating four Hebrew words (*pardēs, gan, ganâ, 'ēpen*). While the LXX sometimes used *kēpos* to translate *gan*, in Gen. 2 and 3 it used *parádeisos* all thirteen times. Thus, the garden of Eden became increasingly identified in the Jewish mind with *parádeisos*. In addition to these thirteen uses, the LXX also used *parádeisos* another seven times (3 in Isaiah; 4 in Ezekiel) to refer to a garden of God. These twenty uses of *parádeisos* show a significant shift from secular to religious meaning.

*Parádeisos* developed into a specific eschatological concept in the Jewish intertestamental writings, especially in the apocalyptic literature. The starting point for all Jewish thinking about paradise, under the influence of the LXX, was the garden of Eden. A recurring theme in the apocalyptic literature is the return of the beginning in the last days (as God says in Barn. 6:13, "Behold, I make the last things as the first"). Thus a natural development of the concept of paradise occurred.

The identification of the future paradise with Eden became widespread in the apocalyptic literature. The first instance is T. Levi 18:10 (probably 2nd cent. B.C.; cf. Isa. 51:3 and Ezk. 36:35 for the closest OT parallels). *Parádeisos* shortly became a technical term. This idea that the future paradise is identical with the original paradise led to the further notion that paradise must exist now. Thus paradise was seen not only as a future home for the righteous, but as existing in the present, between creation and the final age, although now in hidden form (first found in 1 En. 60:7f., 23; 61:12; 70:4).

There are three stages of the one paradise: the ancient garden, the present paradise which is hidden, and the future paradise. *Parádeisos* in the apocalyptic literature usually refers explicitly to one of these three stages. The word is often used of the present intermediate state of the righteous dead, best defined as the home or abode of the departed righteous (Apocalypse of Moses 37:5; Testament of Abraham 20A). But this intermediate resting place is also their future home in the final age, i.e., the future paradise of the final consummation of blessedness (T. Levi 18:10f.; T. Dan 5:12; 1 En. 25:4f.; 2 Esd. 7:36, 123; 8:52).

Another development also took place. Now the departed righteous no longer dwell in Sheol (*šᵉʾôl*) but in paradise. Only the ungodly are in Sheol or Hades (*hádēs*). Actually, both the old view (all the dead are in Hades) and the new view (only the ungodly dead are in Hades) can be found in first-century Jewish literature (cf. Josephus *Ant.* xviii.1.3 [14]; *BJ* ii.8.14 [163]; iii.8.5 [375]; Lk. 16:19-31).

The NT concept of paradise is dependent on the Jewish intertestamental use. The word occurs three times, always of an eschatological paradise and never of a garden or park as in secular Greek.

*Parádeisos* is found once in the Gospels. Jesus says to the thief on the cross, "Truly, I say to you, today you will be with me in Paradise" (Lk. 23:43). The thief asks Jesus to remember him at the parousia, i.e., "when you come in your kingly power" (23:42). Jesus responds with the gracious and surprising "*amen*" saying. The forgiveness of the new age that God now provides through Christ is unlimited. Clearly, this use of *parádeisos* reflects the Jewish apocalyptic idea of a present, hidden paradise. The "today" reinforces the idea that Jesus is speaking of an intermediate abode of the righteous. Although *parádeisos* is not used, this same understanding of existence after death can be seen in Lk. 16:19-31 where the intermediate abode of the righteous (Abraham's bosom, v. 22) and the ungodly (Hades, v. 23) are found together (cf. 2 Esd. 7:36).

All Jesus tells the thief about existence in paradise is that it will entail fellowship with Him. This may seem to be difficult in the light of other NT passages that suggest that Jesus descended into Hades before His resurrection (Mt. 12:40; Acts 2:27, 31; Rom. 10:7; Eph. 4:8-10[?]; 1 Pet. 3:19). However, this difficulty comes from pressing the language of apocalyptic imagery too far and "is more imaginary than real" (I. H. Marshall, *Gospel of Luke* [*NIGTC*, 1978], p. 873). The saying should probably be seen in the light of T. Levi 18:10f., which says that the Messiah "will open the gates of Paradise . . . and give the saints to eat of the tree of life." Jesus, acting as the Messiah, opens paradise for His followers through His death and resurrection. The gates are now open and Jesus assures the thief of immediate entry.

In 2 Cor. 12:4 Paul also uses *parádeisos* of the present, hidden home of the departed righteous. In the context of reluctant boasting to defend his apostleship, Paul speaks of his "visions and revelations of the Lord" (12:1). He focuses on a particularly impressive instance of fourteen years ago when he was caught up into the third heaven and paradise, either in or out of the body (12:2f.). Commentators are largely agreed that no differentiation is to be made between "the third heaven" and paradise. (2 En. 8:1 [B] and Apocalypse of Moses 37:5 locate paradise in the third heaven. There is not enough evidence here to make judgments about Paul's enumeration of the heavens.) Although Paul cannot relate the content of this revelation (12:4), he seems to be saying that he heard and possibly saw Christ in paradise (12:1f., 4). "Paul is granted in this life an experience of this aspect of heaven which thus anticipates both 'the intermediate state' and the glory of the final consummation" (Lincoln, p. 80).

The only NT use of *parádeisos* for the future and final home of the righteous is in Rev. 2:7. Jesus promises to grant to him who conquers "to eat of the tree of life" in "the paradise of God." As often in the apocalyptic literature (T. Levi 18:10f.; 1 En. 25:4f.; 2 Esd. 8:52), the tree of life is located in paradise (cf. Gen. 2, 3; Rev. 22:1-5, 14). In this eschatological paradise humanity will enjoy fellowship with God as it was in the beginning.

Thus the NT concept of paradise participates in the development of *parádeisos* which begins in the LXX and flowers in Jewish apocalyptic. The key characteristic of the intermediate paradise is, as always in the NT, fellowship with Christ (Acts 7:59; 2 Cor. 5:8; Phil. 1:23). John looks forward to the final consummation when all the people of God will dwell together with God in the eternal paradise (Rev. 22:1-5). Jesus and the NT writers give new understanding to the present hidden paradise and the future paradise by characterizing it primarily as fellowship with Christ. This content, and not the concept of paradise itself, was what was important to the NT writers. The concept of paradise was open to the abuse of grandiose speculation (which began to happen in the second-century Church), and this may explain its rarity in the NT. "What really matters is not the felicity of Paradise, but the restoration of the communion with God which was broken by Adam's fall" (Jeremias, p. 773).

***Bibliography.***–C. K. Barrett, *Second Epistle to the Corinthians* (*HNTC*, 1973), pp. 305-312; *TDNT*, V, *s.v.* παράδεισος (J. Jeremias); A. T. Lincoln, *Paradise Now and Not Yet* (1981), esp. pp. 71-86.

V. R. GORDON

**PARAH** pä'rə [Heb. *pārâ*–'heifer'(?); Gk. B *Phara,* A *Aphar*]. A town in the territory allotted to Benjamin (Josh. 18:23). Parah is usually identified with the modern Khirbet el-Fârah, located about 9 km. (5½ mi.) NE of Jerusalem and near the spring ʿAin Fârah, which is the source of Wâdī Fârah and provides water for the Old City of Jerusalem. It is also possible that Parah is the location of the biblical brook of Perath (Jer. 13:4-7, NEB; Heb. *pᵉrāṯâ*; AV, RSV, "Euphrates") as well as the valley of Pheretae of Josephus (*BJ* iv.9.4 [512]); but cf. *GTTOT,* §81, p. 33 n. 13.

D. E. WARING

**PARALEIPOMENA, PARALIPOMEA.** *See* CHRONICLES, BOOKS OF.

**PARALYTIC** [Gk. *paralytikós*] (Mt. 4:24; 9:2, 6; Mk. 2:3-5, 9f.); AV "sick of the palsy"; NEB PARALYZED (MAN); **PARALYZED** [*paralelyménos* (pf. pass. part. of *paralýō*) (Lk. 5:18, 24; Acts 8:7; 9:33), *paralytikós* (Mt. 8:6)]; AV "taken with palsy," "sick of the palsy"; NEB also PARALYSIS; [*xērós*] (Jn. 5:3); AV WITHERED. *See* DISEASE III.C; IV.B.

**PARAMOUR** [Heb. *pilleḡeš*]; NEB MALE PROSTITUTE. The Hebrew term usually designates a female concubine (e.g., Gen. 22:24), but in Ezk. 23:20 it is applied to a male lover. KoB (p. 761) and others have suggested that the MT be emended to *pᵉlištîm* (Philistines); but the passage is concerned with Judah's pro-Egypt policy (cf. v. 27), and a reference to the Philistines would be out of place.

**PARAN** pä-ran' [Heb. *pā'rān*]. A biblical term used geographically with reference to ill-defined areas of desert to the S and SW of Palestine. Although Paran usually designates an area of wilderness or desert, the term apparently forms a part of a place name EL-PARAN in Gen. 14:6, and Dt. 33:2 and Hab. 3:3 refer to Mt. Paran. Although the latter passages are poetic, Mt. Paran may reasonably be interpreted as another appellation for Mt. Sinai (*see* SINAI, MOUNT).

In the earliest reference to Paran, El-paran marks the southern limit of Chedorlaomers's campaign (Gen. 14:6). El-paran, possibly Elath at the head of the Gulf of Aqabah, is said to be "by [Heb. *'al*] the wilderness." Ishmael lived in the Wilderness of Paran after his expulsion by Abraham (Gen. 21:21). Later, the Israelites journeyed to the Wilderness of Paran from the Wilderness of Sinai after the giving of the Law (Nu. 10:12; 12:16). Three sites — Taberah, Kibroth-hattaavah, and Hazeroth — are mentioned in connection with the journey (e.g., 11:3, 34f.) and probably should be located in the Wilderness of Paran. Unfortunately, none can be identified with certainty, although Hazeroth has been equated by some with 'Ain Khaḍrā, a site NW of Jebel Mûsā in southern Sinai.

Moses sent the twelve spies into Canaan from the Wilderness of Paran, and they returned to Kadesh, which by implication is located in the Wilderness of Paran (Nu. 13:3, 26). Yet in other passages Kadesh is stated to be in the Wilderness of Zin (Nu. 20:1). Interestingly, the wilderness itinerary of Nu. 33 does not include a reference to Paran in the text, although the LXX includes the Wilderness of Paran and identifies it with Kadesh (LXX Nu. 33:36). *See* KADESH **1**.

Later references include 1 S. 25:1, which relates that David went to the Wilderness of Paran. One version of the LXX, however, reads the "wilderness of Maon," a more likely reading since the village of Maon in Judah is mentioned in 25:2. Finally, Hadad the Edomite fled from Midian through Paran to Egypt (1 K. 11:18).

These passages furnish some general information helpful in delimiting the Wilderness of Paran. Paran must be W of Midian and E of the Wilderness of Shur on the border of Egypt. Paran may have extended to the southern borders of Judah if the MT of 1 S. 25:1 is correct. Most references, however, associate the Wilderness of Paran with the area between Mt. Sinai and the region of Kadesh-barnea and Elath. Depending on where one locates Mt. Sinai, this area would include portions of central and northeastern Sinai. Many scholars identify the Wilderness of Paran with portions of the desert et-Tīh, a rugged high plateau drained by the Wâdī el-'Arîsh. This would be on the route of Hadad as he fled to Egypt (1 K. 11:15) and fits the biblical description of "that great and terrible wilderness" Israel traversed on the way from Mt. Sinai to Kadesh (Dt. 1:19).

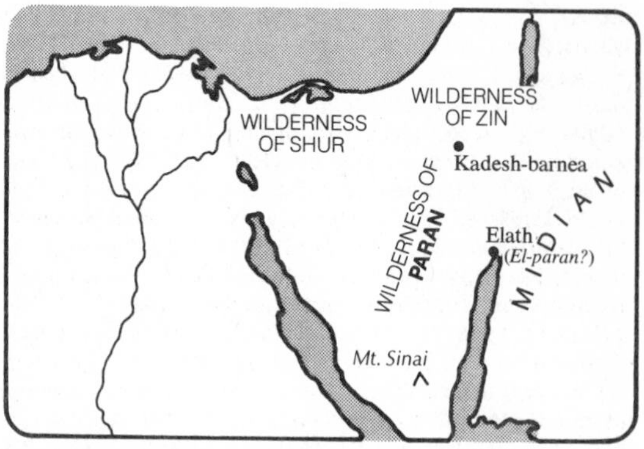


Aharoni suggested that Paran is a more general term that originally referred to most or all of the Sinai Peninsula. He argued that this would explain the absence of Paran in the list of Nu. 33, since this list includes only specific locales. Further, if Paran refers to a much larger region, this would explain how Kadesh could be alternately said to be in the Wilderness of Paran and Zin, for Paran could include Zin.

***Bibliography.***–Y. Aharoni, *LBHG* (rev. ed. 1979), p. 199; B. Rothenberg, *God's Wilderness: Discoveries in Sinai* (1961), pp. 165-69.

T. V. BRISCO

**PARAPET** [Heb. *ma'ᵃqeh*] (Dt. 22:8); AV BATTLEMENT. The term seems to be related to Arab. *'q'*, "hinder," and denotes a low wall or protective railing built around the edge of a flat roof to prevent people from falling.

**PARBAR** pär'bär [Heb. *parbār*; pl. *parwārîm*; LXX *pharoureím*]. Four gatekeepers were assigned for the "parbar" (AV, RV, RSV) at the road in the area to the west of the temple and two in the "parbar" itself (1 Ch. 26:18). This may have been an open pavilion or court (NEB "colonnade"; NIV "court"; cf. Ezk. 41:12).

In 2 K. 23:11 the plural form (AV "suburbs"; RSV, NAB, "precincts"; NEB "colonnade"; NIV "court") designates the location of the chamber of Nathan-melech, in the area where Manasseh had kept the horses and chariots dedicated to the sun.

Though it is difficult to accept such an etymology for the 2 Kings passage, scholars have derived the word from the Pers. *parwār,* meaning etymologically "having light" and designating an open summerhouse or kiosk. In 1916 E. Littmann published an Aramaic-Lydian inscription from Sardis which uses the word *prbr* for the open anteroom of a tomb (*Sardis,* VI/1, 25). In the Mishnah and the Targumim the word signified "suburbs."

J. M. Allegro interpreted item 31 in the Copper Scroll from Qumrân as an "open pavilion" or "summer house" (*Treasure of the Copper Scroll* [1964], p. 137).

*See also* PRECINCT. E. M. YAMAUCHI

**PARCEL.** Used by the AV in the sense of a "piece of land" to translate Heb. *ḥelqâ* (Gen. 33:19; Josh. 24:32; Ruth 4:3; 1 Ch. 11:13f.) and Gk. *chōríon* (Jn. 4:5). The RSV changes it to "piece," "portion," "plot," or "field," but keeps "parcel" in Ruth 4:3.

**PARCHED** [Heb. *qālâ* (Lev. 2:14; "parched grain," Josh. 5:11), *qālî* ("parched grain," Lev. 23:14; Ruth 2:14; 1 S. 17:17; 25:18; 2 S. 17:28), *ṣᵉḥîḥâ* (Ps. 68:6 [MT 7]), *ṣiheh* (Isa. 5:13), *ṣîyâ* (Ps. 107:35; Hos. 2:3 [MT 5]; Joel 2:20), *'āyēp̄* (Ps. 143:6), *ḥārab̲* (Isa. 19:5; Hos. 13:15), niphal of *ḥārar* (Ps. 69:3 [MT 4]), *ḥᵃrērîm* ("parched places," Jer. 17:6), *nāšaṯ* (Isa. 41:17), *ṣāmā'* ("parched ground," Jer.

48:18)]; AV also DRY, THIRSTY, BARREN, etc.; NEB also ROASTED, SCORCHING, SORE, THIRSTY, etc.

The seven RSV instances where "parched" translates *qālâ* and *qālî* all refer to roasted GRAIN. Two methods of parching were used: a small bundle of stalks of grain could be held over an open fire (Lev. 2:14) until the heads of grain were thoroughly roasted, after which the hulls could be rubbed off and the grain eaten; or the heads could be put in a pan over a fire until they were roasted enough to eat. Previously prepared parched grain was a popular ready-to-eat food for persons away from home (Ruth 2:14; 1 S. 17:17; 25:18; 2 S. 17:28; cf. also Lev. 23:14; Josh. 5:11).

The other instances where the RSV employs "parched" refer to excessive dryness, and these occur in contexts of judgment and mercy. Those who rebel against God (Ps. 68:6; Jer. 17:6) or refuse to repent (Isa. 5:13; Hos. 2:3; 13:15) shall dwell in a parched land (cf. also Isa. 19:5; Jer. 48:18; Joel 2:20). But God will quench the thirst of the oppressed and deliver them from parched lands (Ps. 107:35; 69:3; Isa. 41:17; cf. Ps. 143:6). Like all peoples who live near deserts, the Hebrews knew the destructive force of the dry climate and the vital importance of relief from that dryness. E. WALHOUT G. A. L.

**PARCHMENT** [Gk. *membrána* (2 Tim. 4:13); Lat. *membrana*]. The word "parchment" is derived from Lat. *pergamena* (Gk. *pergamēnós*), pertaining to PERGAMUM, an ancient city in Mysia of Asia Minor. There, according to Marcus Varro (*ca.* 116-27 B.C.) as cited by Pliny (*Nat. hist.* xiii.21f.), King Eumenes developed parchment for WRITING material in the 2nd cent. B.C. Since parchment documents from other sites can be dated to earlier times Varro's legend probably reflects the widespread fame of Pergamum as a parchment trade center rather than the actual invention of parchment in that city.

Parchment is made chiefly from the skins of sheep and goats. The hair and fleshy portions of the skin are removed as in tanning by first soaking the skin in limewater and then dehairing, scraping, and washing it. In contrast with the process of tanning a LEATHER skin (Gk. *diphthéra*), the skin for parchment is then stretched on a frame, treated with an absorptive agent such as chalk or alum to remove the fatty substances, and dried. It is finally given a smooth surface by rubbing it with pumice and dressing it with chalk. A finer grade of parchment, vellum, is made from the skins of calf and kid.

Parchment was used extensively in the Greco-Roman world for rolls, codices, legal documents, etc., vying with the less expensive papyrus for that purpose. Due to its greater beauty, erasability, and durability, parchment supplanted papyrus as the basic book material in the 4th cent., after which almost all Christian codices were of parchment. Two of the most widely renowned biblical MSS in Greek are Codex Sinaiticus and Codex Vaticanus, parchment codices of the 4th cent. that display an early and important type of NT text, one also preserved in some NT papyri from Egypt; these codices have served as the basis for most modern critical editions of the Greek NT.

Parchment continued in use as the chief material for book production through the late Middle Ages, at which time paper began to displace it. With the introduction of printing, parchment was relegated to use in book binding and ceremonial documents.

The only biblical reference to parchment (2 Tim. 4:13) is so elusive that it precludes positive identification. The "parchments" requested have been taken to mean a collection of blank writing sheets, a collection of the author's notes, a set of official documents attesting his citizenship, or a special class of books. The last seems most plausible, for the author omits "and" before "above all" (contra RSV; cf. NEB, NIV, JB). If the reference is to books, however, their content must remain a subject of conjecture.

*Bibliography*.–T. Birt, *Das antike Buchwesen* (1882, repr. 1959), pp. 46-126; R. De Vreese, *Introduction à l'étude des manuscrits grecs* (1954), pp. 11-16; K. J. Lüthi, *Das Pergament, seine Geschichte, seine Anwendung* (1938); H. J. Plenderleith, *The Conservation of Antiquities and Works of Art* (1956), pp. 44-50; W. Schubart, *Das Buch bei den griechen und Römern* (3rd ed. 1961), pp. 23-28.

I. A. SPARKS

**PARDON** [Heb. *sālaḥ*–'pass over' (Ex. 34:9; Nu. 14:19f.; Dt. 29:20 [MT 19]; etc.), *nāśā'*–'lift up' (Ex. 23:21; 1 S. 15:25; Job 7:21; Mic. 7:18), piel of *kāpar*–'cover' (2 Ch. 30:18), *kāsaḥ*–'cover' (Ps. 85:2 [MT 3]), niphal of *rāṣâ*–'be paid off' (Isa. 40:2); Gk. *chárin déomai*–'ask favor' ("beg pardon," Wisd. 18:2), *paraitéomai*–'ask to be excused' ("beg pardon," 3 Macc. 6:27), *syngnōstós estin*–'is pardonable' (Wisd. 6:6), *lýō*–'set free' (Sir. 28:2), *aphíēmi*–'cancel, forgive, pardon' (1 Macc. 13:39); Lat. *ignoscō*–'pardon, forgive, excuse' (2 Esd. 7:139)]; AV also SPARE, COVER, FORGIVE; NEB also FORGIVE, TAKE AWAY (Mic. 7:18), BE PAID (Isa. 40:2), "beg as a favour" (Wisd. 18:2), FORGIVENESS.

As used by the RSV OT ("pardon" does not occur in the RSV NT), there is little difference in meaning between "pardon" and "forgive(ness)." In some contexts "pardon" may have a somewhat narrower focus than "forgiveness": "pardon" may signify simply the releasing of an offender from the penalty for the offense, whereas "forgiveness" tends to emphasize the relinquishment of resentment toward the offender, opening the way to a restoration of fellowship. All the Hebrew terms rendered "pardon" are elsewhere rendered "forgive" or "forgiveness" by the RSV, with the exception of the niphal of *rāṣâ* (Isa. 40:2; the NEB translation is more accurate: "be paid").

*See* FORGIVENESS. N. J. O.

**PARENT.** *See* CHILD II; CRIME: Parents, Crimes Against; EDUCATION II; FATHER II; MOTHER; RELATIONSHIPS, FAMILY.

**PARK** [Heb. *pardēs*; cf. Akk. *pardīsu*; Avestan *pairidaēza*; Gk. *parádeisos*] (Eccl. 2:5); AV ORCHARD. A wooded enclosure. Most scholars assume that Heb. *pardēs* is a loanword from Avestan *pairidaēza*, "circular enclosure" (cf. M. Ellenbogen, *Foreign Words in the OT* [1962], p. 136).

**PARLOUR.** The AV translation of Heb. *ḥeḏer* (1 Ch. 28:11; RSV "chamber"; NEB "court"), *liškâ* (1 S. 9:22; RSV "hall"; NEB "dininghall"), and *ʿalîyâ* (Jgs. 3:20-25; RSV, NEB, "roof chamber"). *See* CHAMBER; HALL; HOUSE V.

**PARMASHTA** pär-mash'tə [Heb. *parmaštā'*]. One of the ten sons of Haman (Est. 9:9).

**PARMENAS** pär'mə-nəs [Gk. *Parmenas*, possibly a shortened form of *Parmenidēs*–'steadfast']. One of the Seven chosen by the Jerusalem church to assist the apostles in the daily distribution of charitable relief (Acts 6:5). According to tradition he was martyred at Philippi during the reign of Trajan.

**PARNACH** pär'nak [Heb. *parnāḵ*]. Father of the Zebulunite leader Elizaphan, who was appointed by Moses to assist Eleazar and Joshua in the division of the land W of the Jordan among the Israelite tribes (Nu. 34:25).

**PAROSH** pâr'osh [Heb. *parʿōš*–'flea' (cf. 1 S. 24:14)]; AV also PHAROSH (Ezr. 8:3).

**1.** [Gk. Apoc. *Phoros,* B *Phares* (1 Esd. 8:30)]; AV PHOROS, PHAREZ; NEB PHOROS. Head of a family that returned from the Exile in part with Zerubbabel (Ezr. 2:3 par. Neh. 7:8; 1 Esd. 5:9) and in part with Ezra (Ezr. 8:3 par. 1 Esd. 8:30). Some members of the family had married foreign women and were required to divorce them (Ezr. 10:25 par. 1 Esd. 9:26).

**2.** A chief who sealed the covenant with Nehemiah in the time of Ezra (Neh. 10:14).

**3.** Father or ancestor of Pedaiah, who helped to rebuild the wall of Jerusalem in the time of Nehemiah (Neh. 3:25); possibly the same as **1** or **2.**

**PAROUSIA** pär-o͞o-sē'ə, pär-o͞o'zhi-ə. A Greek word used by theologians as a technical term for Christ's return at the end of the age. The basic meaning of *parousía* is "presence," from which "coming to be present" derives. In the NT it sometimes simply means "presence" (e.g., 2 Cor. 10:10), but the more usual meaning is "arrival," "coming." In six instances it is used of common human arrivals: of Paul (Phil. 1:26), of Titus (2 Cor. 7:6f.), of Stephanus and his friends (1 Cor. 16:17). It refers once to the coming of "the lawless one" (2 Thess. 2:9) and once to that of "the day of God" (2 Pet. 3:12). On all other occasions the term is used of Christ: once of His coming at the Incarnation (2 Pet. 1:16) and fifteen times of His coming again at the end of the age (e.g., Mt. 24:3). In modern times it has become customary to refer to His "Second Coming" or "Second Advent," but these terms are not found in the NT (though He. 9:28 says that Christ "will appear a second time"); the expression "Second Coming" seems to have originated with Justin Martyr in the 2nd century. In the NT Christ's coming at the end of the age is simply "the coming." *Parousía* was in use as a technical term for the arrival of the emperor or other dignitary when he visited his subjects (Deiss.*LAE*, pp. 368ff.). This was a great event, sometimes marked by the striking of special coins or the erection of monuments. The word thus has overtones of greatness that should be kept in mind when it is used of Christ's return.

I. Terms Used of Christ's Coming
II. The Manner of the Coming
III. Modern Views
  A. Realized Eschatology
  B. A Present and a Future Kingdom
  C. The Delay of the Parousia
    1. The Teaching of Jesus
    2. Lukan Eschatology
    3. Pauline Eschatology
    4. Other Considerations
  D. Imminence
IV. The Millennium
  A. Premillennialism
  B. Postmillennialism
  C. Amillennialism
V. Conclusion

***I. Terms Used of Christ's Coming.***–Among the other terms — in addition to *parousía* — used of Christ's coming is the verb *érchomai.* Jesus is described as "he who comes" or "the coming one" with reference both to His first coming (Mt. 21:9; Lk. 7:19f.) and to His second (2 Thess. 1:10; Rev. 1:7; 22:7). He is distinctively "the coming one." On the first occasion He came (in fulfillment of prophecy) to accomplish the divine work of salvation; on the second He will come in fulfillment of further prophecy) to bring God's saving purpose to its consummation.

The term *apokálypsis,* "revelation" (1 Cor. 1:7; 2 Thess. 1:7), points to the decisive "making known" of Christ. At present He is in the realm of the unseen; it is possible for people to deny that He saves or even that He exists. When He returns, however, His reality will be clear to all (Mt. 24:30; Rev. 1:7). The term *epipháneia,* "manifestation" or "appearance" (2 Thess. 2:8; 1 Tim. 6:14), is used in a number of religions to denote "a visible manifestation of a hidden divinity" (Bauer, rev., p. 304). It often includes the notion of manifestation in splendor. As things are, people do not see Christ, but at the Parousia He will become manifest to all and be manifest as a supreme, glorious being.

The same event may be referred to with some combination using the word "day," e.g., "the day of God" (2 Pet. 3:12); "the day of the Lord" (1 Thess. 5:2); "the day of the Lord Jesus" (2 Cor. 1:14); "the day of our Lord Jesus Christ" (1 Cor. 1:8); "the day of Jesus Christ" (Phil. 1:6); "the day of Christ" (Phil. 2:16); "[the Son of man's] day" (Lk. 17:24); "the day of redemption" (Eph. 4:30); "the day of wrath" (Rom. 2:5; better, "day of wrath and revelation . . ."); "the day of judgment" (2 Pet. 2:9); "the last day" (Jn. 6:39); "the great day" (Jude 6); "that day" (2 Thess. 1:10); or simply "the day" (Rom. 13:12). In the OT "the day of the Lord" is often looked for as the day of God's decisive and final intervention in history to destroy all evil. On that day all people will be judged and God's will will be done perfectly. The NT clearly applies this expectation to the activity of Christ at the end of this age. All terminology that stresses the "day" points to the critical time, the consummation of God's purpose throughout the history of the world.

There are still other ways of describing the same event. It is the time when Christ will "be manifested," "be revealed" (pass. of *phaneróō,* Col. 3:4; 1 Pet. 5:4). Once Jesus spoke of the Twelve as sitting on twelve thrones and judging Israel in "the new world" (Mt. 19:28; *palingenesía,* "rebirth," which may be used of the world or of people). Sometimes the coming is referred to with nontechnical words (e.g., Phil. 3:20; 4:5; 1 Thess. 1:9f.; 4:14). Thus "our blessed hope" (Tit. 2:13) uses no technical language but surely points to the coming of Christ that is the hope of all believers. In this spirit the NT Christians prayed for the coming (1 Cor. 16:22; Rev. 22:20).

From all this it is clear that the Parousia was a concept of great importance for the early Christians. They spoke about it in a variety of ways and referred to it often, probably more often than to any other single doctrine in the NT. They looked with eager longing for the day when Jesus would return.

***II. The Manner of the Coming.***–It is important to recognize the limitations of our knowledge when attempting to describe in detail what will happen at Our Lord's return. That He will return, the NT leaves no doubt. But concerning what will precede or follow the Parousia, much is not clear. There is room, therefore, for a decent humility and a readiness to consider the insights of others.

At the time of the Ascension angels told the disciples, "This Jesus, who was taken up from you into heaven, will come in the same way as you saw him go into heaven" (Acts 1:11). This apparently means that the Parousia will be a personal and visible return, one visible on the widest scale (Mt. 24:27). It will be seen by unbelievers as well as believers, for "all the tribes of the earth will mourn" when they see the Son of man coming, after which He will send His angels to gather His elect (Mt. 24:30f.). Sometimes it is said that He will come "on the clouds" (Mt. 24:30; 26:64; cf. Lk. 21:27; Rev. 1:7). This will be no localized event, for that day "will come upon all who dwell upon the face of the whole earth" (Lk. 21:35; cf. 17: 24). Jesus will come in glory and will be attended by angels (9:26). His coming will be "with a cry of command, with the archangel's call, and with the sound of the trumpet of God" (1 Thess. 4:16). Clearly the NT envisages a public, open, and splendid event — something very different from His lowly first coming.

The coming will be quite unexpected (Mk. 13:35-37). Preoccupied with worldly affairs, unbelievers will be surprised like those on whom the Flood came or those who were destroyed in Sodom (Lk. 17:26-30, 34). The Parousia will be as sudden and unexpected as the coming of a thief (1 Thess. 5:2, 4; 2 Pet. 3:10). Neither the incarnate Son nor the angels know the time of it (Mk. 13:32), thus it is obviously quite impossible for human beings to determine it. But though we cannot know exactly when Jesus' coming will occur, we are informed of certain signs that will precede it. "The gospel must first be preached to all nations" (Mk. 13:10; cf. Acts 1:7f.). There will be widespread apostasy (Mt. 24:10; 2 Tim. 3:1-9; 2 Pet. 3:3f.), an increase in wickedness and a growing cold of love (Mt. 24:12). A being will appear called "the man of lawlessness" (2 Thess. 2:3f.), probably to be identified with the "antichrist" (1 Jn. 2:18; 4:3). John's use of the plural indicates that more than one being can manifest the essential qualities of antichrist, and some have suggested that Nero, e.g., may be regarded as a type or foreshadowing of antichrist. Jesus Himself spoke of "false Christs and false prophets" arising and showing "signs and wonders" in those days (Mk. 13:22; cf. v. 6). It seems clear to most scholars, however, that in addition to these false messiahs the Bible points to one especially evil and powerful being who will arise in the last days.

The troubles of that time will be so great that Jesus said, "in those days there will be such tribulation as has not been from the beginning of the creation which God created" (Mk. 13:19). Widespread calamities will strike, e.g., wars, rumors of wars, earthquakes, famines (vv. 7f.), and signs in the heavens (vv. 24f.). We read also of persecutions of believers (v. 9) and a mysterious reference to "the desolating sacrilege set up where it ought not to be" (v. 14). But despite the fulfillment of such predictions people will still scoff at the idea of Christ's coming (2 Pet. 3:3f.; cf. Lk. 18:8). The signs are evidently not meant to enable accurate predictions of the time of the coming. Indeed, the function of prophecy in general is not so much to enable us to predict future events as to assure us of the hand of God in the events foretold. Who could have informed us, OT in hand, of even the main outline of the life and work of the incarnate Christ? Yet again and again the Gospels tell us that things happened "that what was spoken by the prophets might be fulfilled."

At Christ's coming the dead will be resurrected. Some passages speak as though all will be raised, believers and unbelievers alike (e.g., Jn. 5:28f.), but others mention only believers (e.g., Jn. 6:40; 1 Cor. 15:23; 1 Thess. 4:16). Those still alive at that time will undergo change (1 Cor. 15:51-57). All will be judged, both the living and the dead (2 Tim. 4:1; 1 Pet. 4:5); some passages even speak of angels as undergoing judgment (2 Pet. 2:4; Jude 6). The judgment will be God's (Rom. 2:2; He. 10:30; 12:23), although some passages refer to Christ as the judge (Jn. 5:22; Acts 10:42). Perhaps it is best to understand that the Father will judge through the agency of the Son (Acts 17:31; Rom. 2:16). Paul makes it clear in 1 Cor. 15 that the new order that will follow the resurrection will be quite different from any that exists at present. Several passages speak of the present universe ceasing to exist (Mt. 24:35; 2 Pet. 3:7, 10), and Rev. 21–22 describes in some detail the new heaven and the new earth (cf. Isa. 65:17; 66:22).

Christians are instructed to maintain an attitude of watchfulness (Mk. 13:35-37; Lk. 21:28; 1 Cor. 1:7) and of eager expectation, "waiting for and hastening the coming of the day of God" (2 Pet. 3:12). Christians are those who "have loved his appearing" (2 Tim. 4:8) and are "awaiting our blessed hope, the appearing of the glory of our great God and Savior Jesus Christ" (Tit. 2:13).

***III. Modern Views.***–The NT contains much teaching about the coming. But in modern times there is considerable dispute about how this material should be understood. Liberalism gave little attention to this strand of NT teaching. Many scholars held that Jesus did not originate the teaching ascribed to Him on this subject, but that it had been produced by the early Church and read back onto the lips of Jesus. Those scholars who did ascribe this teaching to Jesus Himself saw it as a piece of nonessential trimming attached to the fringes of His real message. But A. Schweitzer compelled the theological world to take Jesus' eschatology seriously (*QHJ*). He taught that Jesus saw the kingdom of God in apocalyptic terms and thought that He would establish it Himself, but He died in the attempt to make it a reality. Not many scholars have agreed with Schweitzer's basic position, but all who have written since his monumental work have had to reckon with the eschatological element in Jesus' sayings.

*A. Realized Eschatology.* One way of dealing with the problem of Jesus' eschatology has been to ascribe teaching on the Parousia to the early Church and to see Jesus as teaching "realized eschatology." According to this view Jesus held that the action of God was to be seen in His ministry: "The *eschaton* has moved from the future to the present, from the sphere of expectation into that of realized experience" (C. H. Dodd, *Parables of the Kingdom* [rev. ed. 1961], pp. 40f.). Scholars such as Dodd have held that Jesus may well have predicted that He would survive death and that the cause of God would triumph, but the Church understood Him not in the way that He meant this but in the light of its own experience. "Where He had referred to one single event, they made a distinction between two events, one past, His resurrection from the dead, and one future, His coming on the clouds" (Dodd, *Parables*, pp. 76f.). The Parousia is thus seen as the invention of the Church, not the authentic teaching of Jesus. Jesus is supposed to have been concerned solely with what God was doing in His ministry during His life on earth.

It is probably true that in the past Christians have paid too little attention to the present aspect of the kingdom of God. Thus Dodd and others have rendered a service in highlighting this aspect of Jesus' teaching. But it is unbalanced to claim that this is all that Jesus taught.

A similar objection may be made to other views, e.g., that of J. A. T. Robinson. He contended that Jesus emphasized two major themes: vindication and visitation. In the Resurrection and Ascension we see Him vindicated before God, and at the end of the age God will visit His people in judgment (see *Jesus and His Coming* [1957]). This view, too, understands the Parousia as a creation of the Church. Such a view allows for more than realized eschatology but rejects the idea that Jesus taught that He would come again. To eliminate the idea of the Parousia from Jesus' teaching, however, requires much critical surgery. If the Gospels give anything like a reliable account of what He said, then He did teach that He would return at the end of the age.

*B. A Present and a Future Kingdom.* Recent scholarship has widely recognized that the kingdom of God has a future aspect as well as a present aspect and that Jesus did teach that He would come back to inaugurate the future aspect. The two aspects are inextricably linked. The Parousia and the events associated with it are the culmination of the work of salvation seen in the life, death, resurrection, and ascension of Christ. The expression "inaugurated eschatology" points to the truth that the kingdom was begun during Jesus' earthly ministry but its consummation awaits His return. Exactly what "return" means, however, is not clear in much writing. For most critical scholars the NT concept of the Parousia is illusory, whether it was taught by Jesus or not. Many hold that the early Church expected the Parousia within a few years of Jesus' death, certainly within the lifetime of many of His contemporaries; but it did not happen. For such scholars, therefore, the whole concept was mistaken. Jesus never intended to return or, if He did, He was wrong. They maintain that a piece of first-century Jewish apocalyptic like this should have no place in a genuinely Christian theology.

Such opinions, however, proceed from the climate of modern secular thinking rather than from a study of the NT. Any doctrine alluded to in the NT as frequently as this one must be accepted as an integral part of the Christian way — unless one proposes to rewrite Christianity to make it conform to twentieth-century thought. The Parousia cannot be discarded on any fair representation of NT teaching, although it may need to be interpreted carefully. It enshrines the very important truth that in the end good will triumph over evil and God's will will be perfectly done. To accept as the final state of affairs the evil we see working so powerfully in the modern world is to despair. However one understands the Parousia, it stands for the final, decisive intervention of God and the total overthrow of evil. If one surrenders this, what is left is not authentic Christianity.

*C. The Delay of the Parousia.* Many scholars contend that the first Christians expected Jesus to return speedily and that the delay of the Parousia was an embarrassment for the early Church. This problem is thought to have influenced or even shaped the theology of the later NT writers. But it is not easy to demonstrate that the first Christians expected an imminent parousia and later abandoned the idea. The evidence often allows more than one interpretation. R. J. Bauckham has also pointed out that the problem is not peculiar to Christianity. For a long period Jewish apocalyptic taught the imminence of God's eschatological salvation, and its failure to arrive did not discredit apocalyptic (*Tyndale Bulletin,* 31 [1980], 3-36). Christians such as the writers of 2 Peter and Revelation were accustomed to the tension between imminence and delay. Thus one should not exaggerate the problem that this tension presented.

*1. The Teaching of Jesus.* Did Jesus teach that He would return within the lifetime of His hearers? Attempts to find this in the words of Our Lord usually center on passages such as Mk. 9:1 and Mt. 10:23. In the former Jesus says, "Truly, I say to you, there are some standing here who will not taste death before they see that the kingdom of God has come with power." The coming of the kingdom with power is taken to mean the Parousia with its attendant events. But the passage is far from being an unambiguous reference to the Parousia. Many see a reference to the Transfiguration and hold that the way the Evangelists arrange their material shows that this was their view. Those who espouse "realized eschatology" read it as expressing the truth that the kingdom has come already (e.g., Dodd, *Parables,* pp. 37f.). Others think of an event such as the destruction of Jerusalem or the Day of Pentecost. These and other interpretations that have been suggested show that His saying does not offer clear proof that Jesus expected to return during the lifetime of His hearers.

In Mt. 10:23 Jesus says, "you will not have gone through all the towns of Israel, before the Son of man comes." This is a puzzling passage, and again many interpretations have been proposed. Some, e.g., see a reference to the exaltation of Jesus in the Resurrection, others to the events associated with the fall of Jerusalem. Perhaps the best interpretation has been offered by S. S. Smalley: "In this case we are presented with a further example of the double perspective already encountered in the teaching of Jesus, in which the fall of Jerusalem becomes proleptic of the end" (*JBL,* 83 [1964], 47).

Neither of these passages, then, proves that Jesus expected an early parousia (though, of course, both would be consistent with such an idea if it could be demonstrated elsewhere). An examination of other passages would yield the same conclusion. Running throughout the teaching of Jesus is a tension between the present and the future, and there is no point in trying to minimize it. N. Perrin finds it in such a familiar and well-loved source as the Lord's Prayer (*Kingdom of God in the Teaching of Jesus* [1963], pp. 191ff.). Neither side of this tension may safely be neglected, nor may the tension be dismissed by asserting that for Jesus "the future" meant "the immediate future." The simplistic line of ascribing to Jesus the expectation that all would be over within a year or two resolves the problem no more than interpreting His teaching as pure apocalyptic or pure realized eschatology.

*2. Lukan Eschatology.* A further problem arises with Luke's eschatology. A common view among scholars posits that Luke inherited a tradition containing teaching about the imminence of the Parousia, but that by the time he wrote Luke-Acts the nonfulfillment of this expectation had become an agonizing problem. Luke's solution was to minimize the teaching on the imminence of the Parousia and to replace it with something else. H. Conzelmann asked, "If Luke has definitely abandoned belief in the early expectation, what does he offer on the positive side as an adequate solution of the problem?" And he answered, "An outline of the successive stages in redemptive history according to God's plan" (*Theology of St. Luke* [Eng. tr. 1961], p. 135). According to H. Flender, Luke replaced a belief in an imminent parousia with an emphasis on two things: the heavenly reality and earthly history. A problem exists, in that "redemption has become an event in the past. . . . His solution is to give simultaneous expression to the supernatural mystery and the earthly visibility of Christ and his history" (*St. Luke: Theologian of Redemptive History* [1967], p. 167). E. Käsemann held that Luke replaced the vivid expectation of the Parousia with an emphasis on the Church as an institution, resulting in what is called "early catholicism" (*Frühcatholizismus*).

The difference between Luke and the other Synoptists should not be exaggerated, however. Matthew and Mark also know of a delay before Jesus comes, and imminence is not their total eschatology. Further, it is simply not true that Luke's interest is in the institution rather than eschatology. To start at the beginning, Luke retains words of John the Baptist that speak of the coming judgment (3:9, 17). Luke sees the approach of the kingdom of God in the ministry of Jesus and reports (as the other Synoptists do not) that Jesus instructed the Seventy to say, "The kingdom of God has come near to you" (Lk. 10:9; cf. similar words to the Twelve in Mt. 10:7). The words, "nevertheless know this, that the kingdom of God has come near," are reported by Luke (10:11) but are lacking in Matthew's similar passage (Mt. 10:14). Luke alone has the passage about the servants being ready for the Master's return (Lk. 12:35-38; cf. vv. 39f. par. Mt. 24:43). Luke records a note of urgency in connection with judgment and the coming of the Son of man (Lk. 13:6-9; 18:8). In the great eschatological discourse he distinguishes more clearly than the other Synoptists between those sayings that refer to the Parousia and those that refer to the fall of Jerusalem. After the words, "And then they will see the Son of man coming in a cloud with power and great glory," only Luke adds, "Now when these things begin to take place, look up and raise your heads, because your redemption is drawing near" (21:27f.). Further, he retains some words that look for the Parousia as definitely as any in the NT: "Truly, I say to you, this generation will not pass away till all has taken place" (21:32). Similarly, in Acts 1:11 he records the angels' prediction that Christ would come back in the same way as He went. Luke reports Peter's words about looking for God to send Christ at the appointed time (Acts 3:20f.) and about Christ being judge of the living and the dead (10:42); he also has Paul's words about God judging the world by Christ (17:31). Acts ends with Paul "preaching the kingdom of God" (28:31).

In the face of this evidence it is difficult to maintain that Luke had no interest in the Parousia. He omits some teaching about it that is found in the other Synoptic Gospels, but he also has some references to it that the others lack. Luke has his own way of dealing with the Parousia and associated events. Although he gives the Parousia a different emphasis from some of the other NT writers as he brings out its significance in his own way, he certainly does not abandon it.

*3. Pauline Eschatology.* Those who hold that the first Christians thought of the Parousia as taking place within their lifetimes usually appeal to Paul's words: "then we who are alive, who are left, shall be caught up together with them in the clouds to meet the Lord in the air" (1 Thess. 4:17). It is argued that these words show that Paul expected to be alive at Christ's return. But exactly the same line of reasoning, if applied to other passages (e.g., 1 Cor. 6:14: "God raised the Lord and will also raise us up by his power"; so also 2 Cor. 4:14; Phil. 3:11; cf. Acts 20:29; 2 Tim. 4:6f.), would show that Paul expected to be dead at that time. As early as 1 Thess. 5:10 Paul saw his own death as a possibility: Christ "died for us so that whether we wake or sleep. . . ." This simply demonstrates that Paul had the habit of classifying himself with those to whom he wrote. Such expressions prove nothing about his expectation of being alive at the Parousia. Furthermore, Paul's exhortations to upright living in his early writings (e.g., 1 Thess. 4:1-12; 2 Thess. 3:6-12) imply an interval before the Parousia during which his correspondents could practice these ethical virtues. And Paul nowhere indicates the length of the interval. That his expectation of the Parousia did not fade is clear from its presence in Philippians, which all agree is among the later letters (e.g., Phil. 1:6; 2:16; 3:20f.; 4:5).

*4. Other Considerations.* Dating the NT documents is not easy, and the experts are far from being in agreement. But whichever document is dated late, one is apt to find in it the expectation of the Parousia. In addition to the passages noted so far, we may observe this expectation in Mt. 24; Lk. 21; Jn. 5:28f.; 6:44; Acts 1:11; Eph. 4:30; Col. 3:4; He. 10:25; Jas. 5:8; 1 Pet. 1:5; 2 Pet. 3; 1 Jn. 3:2; Rev. 1:7; etc. In fact, it is found in every NT book except Galatians and the short Philemon, 2 John, and 3 John. Any balanced reading of the NT reveals that the future Parousia is part of the teaching of Jesus and that it was retained in the early Church. Perhaps there were some in the early Church who thought that the Parousia would take place very soon. This has been a common phenomenon throughout the history of the Church, and there is no reason to doubt that it occurred also in the first days of the Church. But nothing recorded in the NT compels belief that the Parousia was to take place in the immediate future, as A. L. Moore has shown quite plainly (*Parousia in the NT* [1966]). The expectation of the Parousia may have receded to some extent during the NT period, but we can scarcely say more than that.

By contrast with the scholars we have been considering, theologians such as J. Moltmann (*Theology of Hope* [Eng. tr. 1967]; *The Experiment Hope* [Eng. tr. 1976]) and W. Pannenberg (*Jesus — God and Man* [Eng. tr. 1968]; *Basic Questions in Theology* [3 vols., Eng. tr. 1970-73]) have put considerable emphasis on the future. For them the thought of the future consummation is all-important. Although they do not stress the Parousia as such, their emphasis on the future hope is a great improvement over theologies that see nothing beyond the here and now.

*D. Imminence.* We must reckon with the fact that the NT does use the language of imminence. "Surely I am coming soon" said the risen Lord to the seer (Rev. 22:20), and similar words can be found elsewhere. Such words, of course, could mean that the Parousia is near on our ordinary time scale. But it is also possible that the language of imminence is used of the Parousia because it refers to an action of God rather than of man, and the imminence is on God's time scale, not man's. However delayed it may be by our measurements, it has always the characteristic of being imminent. R. L. Saucy speaks of "the always-impending intervention of God with its strong ethical exhortation for life" (*Expositor's Bible Comm.*, I [1979], 104). To live in the conviction that the Parousia is imminent does not mean to be in a continuous ecstasy of enthusiasm. It means to have a deep-seated hope and to occupy oneself in doing what pleases the Master so that when He comes His servant will be found ready.

***IV. The Millennium.***– Among Evangelicals there has been much discussion about the way the Parousia relates to the MILLENNIUM (< Lat. *mille,* "thousand," and *annus,* "year"), the thousand-year reign spoken of in Rev. 20. The millennium itself is understood in several ways.

*A. Premillennialism.* Significant differences exist among premillennialists, but common to them all is the view that the Parousia will inaugurate a thousand-year reign of Christ with His saints (Rev. 20:4), and that this reign will take place here on earth. The Parousia precedes the reign; hence the name "premillennial." Premillennialism rejects the postmillennialist view that the millennium will be a long reign of goodness before Christ comes. Premillennialists point to the parable of the Wheat and the Tares as envisaging the presence of evil on the earth to the end of the age (Mt. 13:24-30, 36-43). Evil will be strong in the last days, and this will be the state of affairs right up to the time that Christ comes (cf., e.g., 2 Tim. 3:1-5; 2 Pet. 3:3-13). The millennium will be a time of worldwide peace, righteousness, and prosperity, with Christ as King of the whole earth. During the thousand years Satan will be "bound" (Rev. 20:1-3). Opinions differ about how this binding should be understood, but premillennialists are certain that it signifies a severe curtailment of the activities of the evil one, with the result that goodness will have a wide scope such as we can only dream of in present conditions.

Although they are in general agreement on the millennium itself, premillennialists are not united on other questions, notably the relationship of the Rapture to the Great Tribulation. The Rapture (< Lat. *rapiō,* "snatch up") is the catching up into the air of believers who are alive at the Parousia, so that they will be with Christ forever. The primary basis for this doctrine is 1 Thess. 4:17: "then we who are alive, who are left, shall be caught up together with them in the clouds to meet the Lord in the air; and so we shall always be with the Lord." The Bible also speaks of sufferings and difficulties in the last times (e.g., Isa. 60:2; Jer. 30:7; Dnl. 12:1; Mt. 24:6-12, 21; Mk. 13:19; 1 Tim. 4:1-3; 2 Tim. 3:1-5; 2 Pet. 3:3f.; Jude 17-19; Rev. 7:14). These texts point clearly to a Great Tribulation, though its duration is not specifically mentioned. It is usually identified with the seventieth week of Daniel's prophecy (Dnl. 9:24-27). If a "week" in this prophecy denotes a week of years, this gives seven years as the length of the Great Tribulation.

What Scripture does not make clear is whether this time of trouble precedes or follows the rapture of the saints. Pretribulationists hold that the Rapture takes place before the Great Tribulation so that the Church does not go through it, while posttribulationists maintain that the Rapture follows the troubles and that the Church endures the Tribulation along with the rest of the world.

Classic premillennialism takes the latter path. It emphasizes that the NT nowhere says that the Rapture will take place at the beginning of or before the Great Tribulation, and that the natural reading of the relevant passages is that the Rapture will follow the Great Tribulation. They agree, however, that the Church will not suffer the wrath of God, which is at the conclusion of the Tribulation (Rev. 15:1); they hold either that the Church will be protected by God during this time or that the Rapture will take place immediately before the outpouring of the divine wrath. C. R. Erdman, setting out the premillennial position, could write: "There is no support in Scripture for the theory that this Rapture of the Church is to be 'secret,' that it is imminent, that it may be 'at any moment,' that it will precede the Apostasy, and Great Tribulation, and indeed will occur 'three and a half years' or 'seven years' before the actual Reappearing of Christ" (*ISBE,* IV, 2251E). He further maintained that, according to Rev. 20:4-6, those martyred during the Great Tribulation would be included among those who undergo the first resurrection. This, of course, means that the Rapture must follow the Great Tribulation. In this form of premillennialism the Parousia is followed immediately by the judgment of all, good and evil alike (Mt. 25:31-46; Rev. 20:11-15). Finally comes the rule of Christ. Those who hold such views maintain firmly that signs will precede the Parousia, and thus it cannot occur "at any moment." Paul recognized toward the end of his life that he would die (2 Tim. 4:6-8) and made no mention of any possibility that Christ might return to deliver him. But such premillennialists do not therefore conclude that Christians may ignore the NT calls for watchfulness and postpone the Parousia into some remote future. The signs are such that they might well occur in any generation. Therefore believers must always be on the watch, for the signs may be beginning before their very eyes.

Pretribulationists are premillennialists who hold that the Church will not go through the Great Tribulation, for before it begins they will be caught up in the Rapture. The Rapture is "secret" in that the world will know nothing of it; Christians will be caught up to meet the Lord, and unbelievers will know only that the believers are no longer on earth. This view divides the Parousia into two phases: Christ's coming for His saints at the Rapture and His coming for judgment at the end of the Great Tribulation. Those who hold this view point out that the passages that deal with the Tribulation contain no references to the Church and nothing to indicate that the Church will be involved in these terrible experiences. Neither the descriptions of what will happen nor the warnings to the Church in the Epistles instruct church members about how they should conduct themselves during those trying days or admonish them to beware of these days and be ready for their coming. Often pretribulationists point to Rev. 3:10: "Because you have kept my word of patient endurance, I will keep you from the hour of trial which is coming on the whole world, to try those who dwell upon the earth." They hold that the most likely meaning is that the Church will be kept out of the Great Tribulation. Furthermore, they maintain that the Rapture does not fit easily with the events at what might be called the Second Coming proper. The inference is that there are two events which, while connected, are not identical. Pretribulationists sometimes also use an argument based on the NT teachings about the imminence of the coming. If a whole series of events must precede the Parousia, then it is difficult to see how it is imminent. But if the Rapture is the next great event to take place, then we may well speak of Christ's coming as though it might happen at any moment.

Most of the discussion seems to take place between pre- and posttribulationists. But some premillennialists take up neither position. The duration of the Great Tribulation is usually understood to be seven years, i.e., the "seventieth week" of Daniel's prophecy. But Daniel speaks not only of "one week" but also of "half of the week" (Dnl. 9:27; cf. 7:25; 12:7), which is paralleled in Revelation by a number of expressions denoting a period of three and a half years (Rev. 11:2f.; 12:6, 14; 13:5). Some premillennialists think that the Parousia will take place in the middle of this week of Tribulation; as a result they are called midtribulationists. The first part of the seven years will be a time of comparative peace and security; it is at the midpoint that the real trouble will begin. At this point Christ will come and snatch up His Church (cf. 1 Thess. 5:3). The position resembles that of the posttribulationists in deferring the Rapture to a point well past the beginning of the seven years. But its upholders are one with the pretribulationists in maintaining that the Church will not pass through the Great Tribulation.

All premillennialists emphasize the importance of taking literally the teaching of Rev. 20 about the millennium. They reject interpretations that see this part of Scripture as metaphorical, claiming that the words of the Bible must always be understood in their literal sense unless there is some compelling reason to understand them otherwise. They find no such reason here. Thus we must see a reign of Christ on earth with His saints for a literal thousand-year period following the Parousia. The reference to the "first resurrection" (Rev. 20:5f.) shows that more than one group will be raised. The only natural understanding, they maintain, is that the faithful are raised first and unbelievers are raised at a later time. Satan is to be restrained during this period of blessedness (vv. 1-3), but at its conclusion he will be released for a short period (vv. 3, 7). As a result of his activities the forces of evil designated "Gog and Magog" (v. 8) will be gathered for one final rebellion against God and God's people. But these forces will be destroyed by fire from heaven, and the devil and his helpers will be cast into the lake of fire (vv. 9f.). Then follows the judgment at the great white throne (vv. 11-15), after which comes the setting up of the new heavens and the new earth (chs. 21–22).

Some premillennialists greatly emphasize the place of the Jews in God's plan. They point out that many OT prophecies envisage Israel having its own land and prospering therein (e.g., Gen. 15:18-21; Nu. 23:9) and see the nations of the world learning of God's ways from His dealings with Israel (e.g., Ps. 102:14-16 [MT 15-17]; Ezk. 39:21-29). Some have objected that these prophecies refer only to the OT period, for the NT states that "he is not a real Jew who is one outwardly" but "He is a Jew who is one inwardly" (Rom. 2:28f.). They suggest that as a result of the work of Christ the people of God is now the Church and that there is therefore no significant place for Israel as a nation: Jews are now on the same footing as everyone else. But these premillennialists counter that in the NT the Jews do have a special place. Jesus spoke of a time when He would return and the Twelve would "sit on twelve thrones, judging the twelve tribes of Israel" (Mt. 19:28). Some of the songs in the first part of Luke's Gospel speak of the greatness of Christ in terms of Israel, which seems to indicate a continuing role for that nation (Lk. 1:32f., 54f., 68-79). At the Ascension the disciples ask Jesus, "Lord will you at this time restore the kingdom to Israel?" and Jesus seems to respond only to the question of when this will take place (Acts 1:6f.). Again, Paul makes it clear that God has not rejected the Jews (Rom. 11:1f.). The apostle looks for a time when "all Israel will be saved; as it is written, 'The Deliverer will come from Zion, he will banish ungodliness from Jacob . . .'" (v. 26).

Jerusalem will be "trodden down by the Gentiles," but this is only "until the times of the Gentiles are fulfilled" (Lk. 21:24; cf. Rev. 11:2). Then the Lord will return (Mt. 24:30), and the deliverance spoken of in Rom. 11:23-31 will be brought to pass. The Great Tribulation is "the time of Jacob's trouble" (Jer. 30:7, AV). Putting all this together, some premillennialists conclude that Israel will come to recognize Jesus as the true Messiah when He comes back in glory. The "veil" will be taken from their minds and they will turn in faith to Christ (2 Cor. 3:15f.). This does not mean that Israel will escape the Great Tribulation. Indeed, it is precisely then that the Jews will have a most important function. Since the Church has been removed at the Rapture, converted Israel is the only part of mankind left on earth that is faithful to God. So the purposes of God, specifically His missionary purposes, are worked out through Israel. That nation will occupy a key position during the events of the end time.

*B. Postmillennialism.* Postmillennialists put strong emphasis on biblical passages that speak of the advance of the gospel. Jesus Christ commissioned the Church to evangelize the world and the Holy Spirit gave it the power to carry this out. The parable of the leaven suggests that the Kingdom will steadily transform the world (Mt. 13:33). The gospel will be preached and more and more people will be converted until the entire world is christianized. The millennium will be a long period of peace and righteousness at the end of which Christ will return. Postmillennialists do not agree on whether the millennium will last for precisely a thousand years or will be much longer. And they do not suggest that the world will ever be perfected: there will be some whose Christianity will be purely nominal and others who do not respond to the gospel at all (although these will not be typical). They are certain, however, that the conversion of millions will bring enormous changes and that in the end the whole world will be christianized.

Postmillennialists emphasize that they are not speaking of a humanist ideal of progress by purely human effort. They do not look for a natural evolution of institutions and culture into a kind of secular heaven on earth. Rather, they envisage spiritual progress in the power of God. They point out that in the Great Commission Jesus commanded His followers not only to preach but also to "make disciples of all nations" (Mt. 28:19). This, they say, means more than that the gospel be preached as a form of witness to the nations (though that is included; cf. Mt. 24:14): it means that the preaching will be effective, that people will be converted and transformed. Since "all authority" has been given to Christ for the accomplishment of this commission, postmillennialists hold that it would be presumptuous to doubt that the commission can be fulfilled. Christians are not called to carry out a kind of experiment in preaching, the outcome of which is problematical, but to evangelize in the name of Christ and in the power of the Holy Spirit: thus they are certain of the gospel triumph. Postmillennialists often chide the Church and particularly themselves for slowness in carrying out the command of Christ.

In addition to the scriptural basis of their position, postmillennialists often point out that the world today, despite its many shortcomings, is better than it used to be. They contrast the cruelties, superstitions, and needless sufferings of earlier days with conditions at the present time. Opponents of this view point out that the present time, with its world wars, depressions, starvation, etc., is far from ideal. Postmillennialists reply that progress is never uniform, and there have always been times when people have regressed. Thus a long perspective is needed. Despite the presence of much evil, there is abundant evidence that God is at work in our world and that progress is being made.

Postmillennialism holds that when the millennium of peace, progress, and spiritual power has been accomplished, Christ will return. His coming will inaugurate not a millennial reign on earth but rather a general resurrection of saved and unsaved alike, the judgment of all mankind, and entrance into heaven or hell. Postmillennialists sometimes stress that the biblical picture of the judgment cannot easily be reconciled with the premillennial view of a rapture of the saints followed by the judgment of the wicked. The Bible usually pictures the judgment of all persons as one event; if there is a separation of judgments, the parable of the Tares puts the judgment of the wicked before the gathering of the saints (Mt. 13:30). Also, if the wicked are destroyed and the saints gathered in, no subjects will remain for the millennial reign.

Postmillennialists further point out that while the return of Christ is connected directly with judgment in official declarations of the Church, e.g., the Apostles Creed, the Nicene Creed, the Athanasian Creed, the Augsburg Confession, the Westminster Confession, and the Thirty-nine Articles, no part of the Church has an official statement of belief that includes a millennial reign on earth by Christ with the saints. Premillennialism in all its forms remains a private speculation and in its pretribulation form a very late speculation (not found before the 19th cent.).

Postmillennialism is not as popular as it once was, but its strength should not be underestimated. Those who hold this view take seriously certain important scriptural passages of which all must take due account.

*C. Amillennialism.* In Greek the letter *alpha* (*a*) is a negative prefix like "un-" in English; "amillennial" accordingly means "not millennial." The amillennial view is that there will be no literal millennium either before or after the Parousia, that the language about the millennium is metaphorical and must be understood as such. Amillennialists point out that the millennium is mentioned in only one passage of the Bible, Rev. 20. They find this a flimsy foundation on which to build a worthwhile edifice. They point out that no book of the Bible has more symbolic and metaphorical language than Revelation, and that "a thousand" has every appearance of being symbolic: it is the cube of ten, the number of completeness, and symbolizes something like the complete time that God has determined. Moreover, not even the most ardent millennarians, despite their claims, interpret all of Rev. 20 literally; e.g., Satan cannot be bound by a literal chain and thrown into a literal pit (vv. 1-3). Amillennialists see it as relevant also that those who reign with Christ are "souls" (not resurrected bodies as the millennial system requires) and that "the second death" cannot mean literal death. Furthermore, they point out that Rev. 20 says nothing about the coming of Christ, and the words to which appeal is made in the preceding chapter say nothing about His coming and may well be interpreted otherwise. They claim that nothing in Rev. 20 shows that the thousand-year reign is to take place on earth; the description of the participants as "souls," as well as John's use of "throne," accords better with the reign taking place in heaven. They conclude, purely on the basis of exegesis, that Rev. 20 refers to the heavenly triumph of the faithful martyrs rather than to a millennial reign on earth by all the saints. With this basis for millennial theory thus removed, amillennialists find nothing to substantiate the theory. Although certain other scripture passages may not contradict the idea of the millennium, none of them proves it.

Amillennialists find a considerable objection to any millennial view in that, while the NT mentions the second coming repeatedly (probably more than any other doctrine), it mentions the millennium explicitly only in Rev. 20. If this doctrine is so important, they ask, why is it so widely ignored? Furthermore, the great apostasy (see II above) presents a great problem if one looks for a literal millennial reign of Christ on earth. If, as some premillennialists say, Christ will have reigned on earth for a thousand years and all mankind will have known the blessings of His rule during this time, how is it that so many will turn away from Him at the first opportunity? And if evangelism is to make the whole world Christian, as postmillennialists say, where will Satan find his recruits (especially if one believes in the perseverance of the saints, as do many postmillennialists)?

A further problem found in premillennial views is that the way the Bible refers to the resurrection of mankind seems to envisage all rising simultaneously, not in two groups separated by a thousand years (e.g., Dnl. 12:2; Jn. 5:28f.; but cf. LaSor, *Truth about Armageddon,* pp. 150-179). Likewise, the repeated references to the judgment of the righteous and the unrighteous give no indication that these will be separated by a thousand years (e.g., Mt. 13:30, 41-43; 16:27; 25:31-46; Rom. 2:5-10, 16; 1 Cor. 3:12-15; 2 Cor. 5:10; 2 Thess. 1:6-10; Rev. 20:11-15). Amillennialists find no place for a millennial reign on earth in passages that speak of the destruction of this earth and the coming of a new heaven and earth (e.g., 2 Pet. 3:10), because the renewal of the world seems to be connected with judgment rather than a millennial kingdom (Mt. 19:28). Moreover, to amillennialists the whole concept of a millennial reign is Jewish rather than Christian. The concept occurs unambiguously in passages such as 2 Esd. 7:27-29, but the NT emphasizes not a material kingdom but a kingdom of "righteousness and peace and joy in the Holy Spirit" (Rom. 14:17; cf. Col. 1:13f.). In accordance with this, some passages appear to indicate that Christ's kingdom is a present reality rather than a reign at the end of the world (e.g., Acts 2:30f.). To amillennialists, the premillennial insistence on a literal fulfillment of many scriptural prophecies appears to be a repetition of the Jews' error at Jesus' first coming. Those Jews looked for a literal, physical kingdom of David with Jerusalem as its capital, and they never did understand that Jesus' kingdom is "not of this world" (Jn. 18:36).

Some of these points are objections to one of the millennial views and some apply to both. Taken together, they convince amillennialists that the Bible has no solid evidence for a thousand-year reign of Christ and the saints on earth, either before or after the Parousia. They see the struggle between good and evil as continuing in the world up to the time of Christ's coming. Meanwhile, the Church must be active in evangelism, but not with the idea that it is bringing in the millennium (as postmillennialists hold). In the end, at His appointed time, Christ will return. This will be followed not by a millennial reign on earth (as premillennialists teach) but by the resurrection of all mankind, the final judgment, and the entrance into heaven or hell.

*V. Conclusion.*–From all of this it is plain that the Parousia is of the first importance in NT teaching. It will be the consummation of the whole process of salvation that Jesus Christ inaugurated when He came to earth. The death of Jesus, the means whereby sins are put away, shows the depths of God's love (Jn. 3:16; Rom. 5:8) and His determination to bring salvation to sinful people. The Parousia provides assurance that the work that was begun at such cost will not be allowed to fail. In His own good time God will bring this world with all its evil to an end and will bring in that perfect kingdom where His will is completely done. The purpose of the Parousia is not to cause Christians to occupy themselves with working out the precise way in which these prophecies will be fulfilled. Rather, it is God's assurance that He will allow nothing to stand in the way of the final fulfillment of His purpose. Christ will return. All evil will be put away as "the kingdom of the world" becomes "the kingdom of our Lord and of his Christ, and he shall reign for ever and ever" (Rev. 11:15).

***Bibliography.***–For an extensive bibliography of critical works, see *DNTT,* II, 932-35; see also O. T. Allis, *Prophecy and the Church* (1945); G. R. Beasley-Murray, *Jesus and the Future* (1954); L. Boettner, *The Millennium* (1957); H. Conzelmann, *Theology of St. Luke* (Eng. tr. 1960); J. E. Fison, *The Christian Hope* (1954); H. Flender, *St. Luke: Theologian of Redemptive History* (Eng. tr. 1967); T. F. Glasson, *Second Advent* (2nd ed. 1947); W. Hendriksen, *More than Conquerors* (1939); J. M. Kik, *Revelation Twenty* (1955); G. E. Ladd, *Blessed Hope* (1956); *Crucial Questions about the Kingdom of God* (1952); W. S. LaSor, *Truth about Armageddon* (1982); A. L. Moore, *Parousia in the NT* (1966); *TDNT,* V, *s.v.* παρουσία (A. Oepke); J. A. T. Robinson, *Jesus and His Coming* (1957); R. L. Saucy, "Eschatology of the Bible," in *Expositor's Bible Comm.,* I (1979), 103-126; A. C. Thiselton, *Tyndale Bulletin,* 27 (1976), 27-53; J. F. Walvoord, *Millennial Kingdom* (1959); *The Rapture Question* (1957).

L. MORRIS

**PARSHANDATHA** pär-shan-dā'thə [Heb. *paršandāṯā'*– 'made for battle'(?)]. The first of the ten sons of Haman (Est. 9:7). The name is Persian and has been explained in various ways. H. S. Gehman (*JBL,* 43 [1924], 327) translated it "the inquisitive one," from Avestan *frašna,* "question," plus *dāta,* "given to"; cf. other explanations in L. B. Paton, comm. on Esther (*ICC,* 1908), p. 70.

**PARSIN.** *See* MENE, MENE, TEKEL, AND PARSIN.

**PART.** The noun is a general term designating one of a number of units or subdivisions that together constitute a whole. It is frequently supplied by the RSV in rendering a Hebrew or Greek genitive construction (e.g., cf. Ex. 29:12, 20f.; AV, lit., "take of the blood"; cf. also 1 Cor. 12:15f.; AV, lit., "not of the body"). Elsewhere it represents a variety of terms, including Heb. *dāḇār* (lit. "thing"; 1 K. 6:38), *ḥelqâ* (lit. "plot of land"; Ruth 2:3), *beṯer* (lit. "piece [of sacrificial meat]"; Jer. 34:18f.), *ḥeder* ("inner [most] parts," Prov. 18:8; 20:27, 30; etc.), *qāṣeh* ("outlying parts," Nu. 11:1; "uttermost parts," Dt. 30:4), *yᵉrēḵâ* ("farthest parts," Jer. 6:22; 25:32; etc.; "innermost parts," 1 S. 24:3 [MT 4]; Am. 6:10; "uttermost parts," Ezk. 32:23; etc.), *'aḥᵃrîṯ* ("uttermost parts," Ps. 139:9). In the NT it most often renders Gk. *méros* (lit. "part, portion, region"; e.g., Lk. 11:36; Jn. 13:8; 19:23); but cf. *merís* in

Acts 8:21 and *mélos* in 1 Cor. 12:20, 22 (*see* MEMBER). The RSV uses "take part" to translate *koinōnós* (Mt. 23:30; AV "partaker"), *koinōnía* (2 Cor. 8:4; AV "fellowship"), and *synkoinōnéō* (Eph. 5:11; Rev. 18:4; AV "have fellowship with," "be partaker of"), and "take [my] part" to render *paragínomai* (2 Tim. 4:16; AV, lit., "stand by"). On the expression "do the part of the next of kin" (Ruth 3:13), *see* KIN I. The AV uses "part" interchangeably with "portion" as a translation of Heb. *ḥēleq,* while the RSV more consistently uses the latter term (*see* PORTION).

The verb "part" generally means to divide into parts (e.g., Lev. 11:4-7, etc. [Heb. hiphil of *pāras*]; 2 K. 2:8, 14 [niphal of *ḥāṣâ*]; Jn. 19:24 [Gk. *diamerízō*]) or to separate from or take leave of someone (e.g., Josh. 22:9 [Heb. *yālak̲*]; Lk. 9:33 [Gk. pass. of *diachōrízō*]; 24:51 [*diístēmi*]; Acts 21:1 [*apospáō*]; Philem. 15 [*chōrízō*]). The AV uses the verb in several ways that are no longer familiar: e.g., for Heb. *ḥālaq* in 1 S. 30:24 (cf. RSV "share") and for the piel of *pārad̲* in Prov. 18:18 (cf. RSV "decide between").

N. J. O.

**PARTHIANS** pär'thi-ənz [Gk. *Parthoi* < Old Pers. *Parthava*] (Acts 2:9). The people inhabiting the area southeast of the Caspian Sea (its exact ancient boundaries are uncertain). They apparently came from the same peoples as the Turanians and entered Iran from Central Asia. They fell under the rule of various ancient nations: Assyrians, Medes, Persians, Greeks (Alexander), Seleucids, Romans, and finally the Persian Sassanids *ca.* A.D. 226. Nevertheless, they were responsible to a great extent for the failure of Alexander's successors to maintain and enlarge their eastern territories.

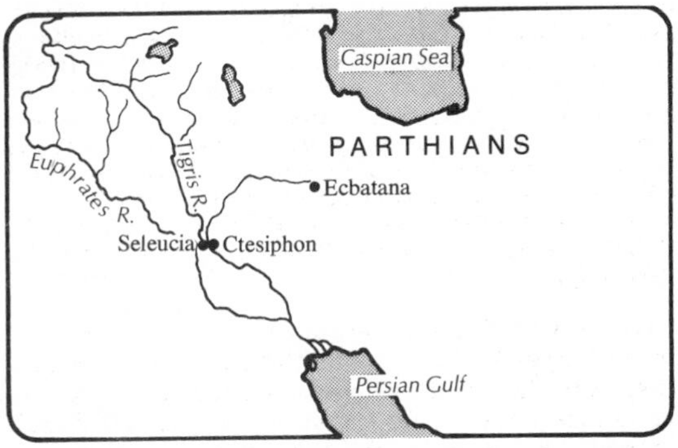


The Behistun inscription of Darius I (*ca.* 520 B.C.) first mentions the name *Parthava*. Parthia's history as a Persian satrapy is not well known. It was still a province of the Persian empire when Alexander the Great conquered Persia (332 B.C.). After the breakup of Alexander's empire the Parthians were under the Seleucids until 250 B.C., when Arsaces freed them from the Seleucids and launched the kingdom of the Parthians. Arsaces became king and his brother Tiridates followed him and took his name. Henceforth the name "Arsaces" became the generic name of succeeding Parthian kings. The classical sources aid us greatly in identifying these kings by using their individual names. The Parthian kings traced their ancestry back to the Persian king Artaxerxes II. The Parthian kingdom was made up of small vassal kingdoms that referred to the Parthian king as "king of kings." By the time the Romans appeared in the East the Parthian empire reached the Euphrates. The first great Parthian king was Mithradates I (*ca.* 171-138 B.C.). He extended the kingdom's rule to Babylon, and at its height the kingdom stretched across modern Iran to the Indus River.

Inevitably the Romans and Parthians became the two dominant competing powers in the Orient. Several wars were fought, but in 53 B.C. Crassus and his Roman army were totally defeated and their Roman standards were lost at Carrhae (Ḥarrân). Crassus had despoiled the Jewish temple and the Jews began to look upon the Parthians as possible liberators from the Roman yoke and Greek cultural tyranny. Later Mark Antony also suffered defeat at the hands of the Parthians. The Parthian military became famous for its cavalry and the accuracy of its bowmen — "a Parthian shot" being coined as a proverb because of certain strategies of the Parthian cavalry. The Roman legions (on foot) were often effectively harassed by the Persian cavalry in desert areas. Indeed, the most original contributions of the Parthians were in their military prowess and strategy. The Parthians were also famous for their horses.

The Roman emperor Trajan carried on war successfully against the Parthians (A.D. 114-117). The Romans retreated under Hadrian and Roman power did not extend farther east again. Several cities served as capitals during the Parthian era: Dara (under Arsaces probably the first capital), Ecbatana, Seleucia (on the Tigris River), and Ctesiphon. The fate of the nation fluctuated from A.D. 117 to 217 until the Persian Artaxerxes defeated the Parthians and thereby created the Persian Sassanian Empire (A.D. 226).

The Parthians did not establish a significant civilization. They took most of their culture, such as they had, from the Greeks, Persians, and Babylonians. Their religion was Persian — they served Ahura-Mazda — and they spoke Pahlavi (north Persian dialect). They themselves seemed to be quite tolerant in religious matters and the Jews were not persecuted in Parthia for religious reasons. For a brief time the Jews looked upon the Parthians as deliverers from the power of Rome, especially in 40-37 B.C. when they helped establish Antigonus as the last Hasmonean king of the Jews. But other events seem to indicate that any realistic hope of ultimate deliverance from Rome by Parthia was unlikely.

Josephus noted that many Jews settled in Parthian territory (*Ant.* xv.2.1f. [11-17]). They spoke an Aramaic dialect and sent tribute to the Jerusalem temple (*Ant.* xviii.9.1 [310-13]). He relates two stories that show the unfortunate hostility that arose from time to time between the Jews in Parthia and their neighbors. One concerns the foolish behavior of two Jewish brothers and the other the terrible massacre of fifty thousand Jews by indignant Syrians and Greeks in Seleucia on the Tigris (*Ant.* xviii.9.1-9 [310-379]). The stories show that help from the Parthians in the Jews' struggles against Rome was largely illusory.

The Parthians are mentioned in 1 En. 56:5 as the object of divine judgment. The NT book of Acts states that Parthians were in Jerusalem on Pentecost (Acts 2:9-11). These may have been Jews or proselytes. The book of Revelation (13:3; 17:8, 17, etc.) is said by some to refer to a legend that had grown up about Nero (cf. comms. by R. Mounce [*NICNT*, 1977], pp. 252f.; G. R. Beasley-Murray [*NCBC*, rev. ed. repr. 1981], pp. 210f.). Nero was expected to return from the East at the head of the Parthian army as antichrist. Rev. 6:1-8 may have the famous Parthian horsemen and bowmen as its model.

***Bibliography.***–F. F. Bruce, *Acts of the Apostles* (1951); N. C. Debevoise, *Parthia* (1938); F. J. F. Jackson, *Josephus and the Jews* (repr. 1976); B. Reicke, *NT Era* (Eng. tr. 1968).

E. E. CARPENTER

**PARTIALITY; SHOW PARTIALITY; BE PARTIAL** [Heb. hiphil of *nāk̲ar* + *pānîm* (Dt. 1:17; 16:19; Prov. 24:23; 28:21; Isa. 3:9), *nāśā' p̄ānîm* (Lev. 19:15; Dt. 10:17; Job 13:8, 10;

32:21; etc.), *maśśō' pānîm* (2 Ch. 19:7), *hāḏar* (Ex. 23:3); Gk. *prósōpon lambánō* (Lk. 20:21; Gal. 2:6), *prosōpolēmpsía* (Rom. 2:11; Eph. 6:9; Col. 3:25; Jas. 2:1), *prosōpolēmptéō* (Jas. 2:9), *prosōpolḗmptēs* (Acts 10:34), *prósklisis*–'inclination' (1 Tim. 5:21)]; AV also RESPECT OF PERSONS, ACCEPT ONE'S PERSON, COUNTENANCE, etc.; NEB also (SHOW) FAVOUR, TAKE ONE'S PART, etc.

The Hebrew phrase *nāśā' pānîm* (lit. "lift up the face") originally referred to the graciously accepting act of raising up the face of one who had prostrated himself (cf. Gen. 40:13, 20; "accept," 32:20; *see also* FAVOR). As a judicial expression, however, the phrase came to be used pejoratively to denote unjust preferential treatment (*THAT,* II, 442). A similar development occurred with the phrases *hikkîr* (hiphil of *nāḵar,* lit. "pay attention to") *pānîm* and *hāḏar* (lit. "show respect, honor") *pānîm* (cf. *hāḏar pānîm* [RSV "defer"] used in parallel with *nāśā' pānîm* ["be partial"] in Lev. 19:15; *hāḏar* occurs alone in Ex. 23:3; see *TDOT,* III, 341). Through the LXX the Hebraism *prósōpon lambánō* (lit. "take or accept the face") entered NT Greek. This phrase and the compound forms derived from it (Gk. *prosōpolēmpsía,* etc.) have not been found in pre-Christian secular Greek.

In biblical times judges were continually tempted to pervert justice by showing favoritism. Most often the temptation was to favor the rich and powerful (cf. the association of partiality with taking bribes in Dt. 10:17; 16:19; 2 Ch. 19:7; Sir. 35:12); but covenant law also forbade discrimination in favor of the poor (Ex. 23:3; Lev. 19:15; cf. Dt. 1:17). The evil of judicial partiality was denounced by wisdom teachers (e.g., Prov. 18:5; 24:23-25; 28:21; cf. 17:15; Job 13:8, 10; etc.) and by the prophets (e.g., Isa. 3:9; cf. Ps. 82:2; Mal. 2:9 condemns priestly partiality). The early Christian community continued to struggle with the problem of discrimination based on worldly social distinctions (Jas. 2:1-9; cf. 1 Tim. 5:21).

The standard for human justice is the righteousness of God, who "shows no partiality" in His dealings with rich and poor (Job 34:19; cf. Dt. 10:17f.; 2 Ch. 19:7; Sir. 35:12f.), Jew and Gentile (Acts 10:34; Rom. 2:11), masters and slaves (Eph. 6:9; Col. 3:25), and those of small or great reputation (Gal. 2:6), but "judges each one impartially [Gk. *aprosōpolḗmptōs*] according to his deeds" (1 Pet. 1:17). In Lk. 20:21 the scribes and chief priests (with simulated sincerity) address Jesus as a *didáskalos* who teaches "the way of God" without partiality.

*See also* JUDGE; JURISPRUDENCE, ABUSE OF.

***Bibliography.***–P. Davids, *Epistle of James* (*NIGTC,* 1982), pp. 105-116; *DNTT,* I, 585, 587; *TDNT,* VI, *s.v.* πρόσωπον κτλ.: προσωποληµψία κτλ. (E. Lohse); *TDOT,* III, *s.v.* "hādhār" (G. Warmuth); *THAT,* II, *s.v.* פָּנִים (A. S. van der Woude).

N. J. O.

**PARTICULAR; PARTICULARLY.** The adverbial phrase "in particular" occurs twice in the AV, both times with the obsolete meaning of "individually": 1 Cor. 12:27 (Gk. *ek mérous*; RSV "one by one") and Eph. 5:33 (*hoi kath' héna hékastos*; AV "every one of you in particular"; RSV "each one of you"). The adverb "particularly" occurs in the same sense in the AV of Acts 21:19 (*kath' hén hékaston*; RSV "one by one"). In He. 9:5, AV, it renders *katá méros* (lit. "part by part"; RSV "in detail"); cf. the AV's use of the plural noun to render the same Greek phrase in 2 Macc. 2:30 (RSV "with details"). The adjective occurs in the sense of "special" (Vulg. *peculiares*) in the first Prologue to Sirach, AV (the whole section is omitted by the RSV).

D. M. EDWARDS

**PARTRIDGE** [Heb. *qōrē'*] (1 S. 26:20; Jer. 17:11).

Three species of partridge are to be found in Palestine: the rock or Greek partridge or chukar (*Alectoris graeca*), the desert or sand partridge (*Ammoperdix heyi*), and the black partridge or francolin (*Francolinus francolinus*), found in marshes or dense vegetation.

One ancient method of hunting these stout-bodied game birds appears in the psalmist's reference to the snare of the fowler (Ps. 91:3; cf. 1 S. 26:20). Another method involved the use of tame partridges as decoys (Sir. 11:30). But whether inhabiting the rocky highlands, the deserts, or marshy areas, these birds were adept at hiding both themselves and their eggs from those that preyed upon them.

Explanations of the allusion to the actions of partridges in Jer. 17:11 are numerous. Perhaps the meaning is that more than one hen laid eggs in the same nest (V. C. Holmgren, *Bird Walk through the Bible* [1972], p. 134). The hen that completed the incubation process would thus hatch a mixed brood, some of which did not belong to her.

G. WYPER

**PARTY** [Gk. *haíresis*] (Acts 5:17; 15:5; 26:5; Gal. 5:20, "party spirit"); AV SECT, HERESIES (Gal. 5:20); NEB also GROUP; [*méros*] (Acts 23:9); AV PART; **CIRCUMCISION PARTY** [*hoí ek (tḗs) peritomḗs*–'those from the circumcision'] (Acts 11:2; Gal. 2:12; Tit. 1:10); AV THEY THAT WERE OF THE CIRCUMCISION; NEB THOSE WHO WERE OF JEWISH BIRTH, ADVOCATES OF CIRCUMCISION, JEWISH CONVERTS. A group of persons committed to certain religious or philosophical teachings and practices. Sometimes the word occurs in a pejorative sense.

In classical usage *haíresis* and its cognate verb *hairéō* may refer to the capture of a town (Herodotus iv.1), the act of taking or choosing, or the choice made (i.11). A plan, purpose, thought, or course of action can also be denoted (Plato *Phaedrus* 256c). In the middle voice (*hairéomai*) the word may denote joining a party (Herodotus i.108) or adopting an opinion (iv.137). Hence *haíresis* came to mean those who "chose" to associate with a political party, a philosophical school, or a religious community espousing a particular view. Thus Josephus mentioned Herod's murdering forty-five men of Antigonus's "party" (*Ant.* xv.1.2 [6]); he also described the three major religious groups (*treís hairéseis*) in Judaism prior to Christianity: the Pharisees, the Sadducees, and the Essenes (*BJ* ii.8.2-14 [119-166]).

The NT likewise mentions the "parties" of the Pharisees and Sadducees (Acts 5:17, *haíresis tṓn Saddoukaiōn*; 15:5, *tḗs hairéseōs tṓn Pharisaiōn*), with the Pharisees referred to as "the strictest party" (26:5, *katá tḗn akribestátēn haíresin*). These two parties held conflicting opinions on certain theological matters, e.g., resurrection and the reality of angels (23:6-10). *Méros* (lit. "part") in Acts 23:9 denotes the part of the crowd that were Pharisees in opposition to the Sadducees.

The term "circumcision party" (Acts 11:2; Gal. 2:12; Tit. 1:10) calls for comment. B. H. Throckmorton, Jr. (*IDB,* III, *s.v.*) and J. N. D. Kelly (*Pastoral Epistles* [*HNTC,* 1963], p. 234) interpreted this phrase to denote Jewish Christians. This is unsatisfactory, however, since some other Jewish Christians (e.g., Paul) would probably not have pressed for stringent obedience to the law, especially as regards circumcision, even before the Apostolic Council ruled that it was not necessary. F. F. Bruce (*Comm. on the Book of the Acts* [*NICNT,* 1954], p. 234) stated that Acts 11:2 denotes Jewish Christians zealous for the law, whereas Acts 10:45 denotes nothing more than "Jews."

H. Conzelmann (*Die Apostelgeschichte* [*HNT*, 1963], p. 66) claimed that "circumcision party" denotes the entire (Jewish) Christian community in Jerusalem. But one wonders whether every Jewish Christian in Jerusalem would be so militant.

"Circumcision party," especially as it occurs in Acts 11:2, may best be interpreted in the light of Acts 15:5, where the instigation for circumcision came from "some believers who belonged to the party of the Pharisees." Like 11:1f., Acts 15:1-5 mentions both the circumcision issue and Judea, the residence of those who would be most concerned about circumcision: the believers among the Pharisees. Gal. 2:12 may also be interpreted in the light of Acts 15:1-5. Though the controversy took place in Antioch, Paul's opponents had come from James in Jerusalem. These opponents were Pharisees who had professed belief in Jesus as Messiah, but desired all adherents to the faith to keep the laws of Moses, especially circumcision (so M. Hengel, *Acts and the History of Earliest Christianity* [Eng. tr. 1979], p. 116).

*Haíresis* when used pejoratively denotes a group whose belief or practice differs from what is considered orthodox. This use is found in both Hellenistic Judaism and apostolic Christianity. The Hebrew antecedent here is *mîn,* which in biblical Hebrew means biological kind or species (Gen. 1:11f.; cf. CD 12:14). Later, however, the term came to denote varieties of iniquity (CD 4:16, *lšlwšt myny hṣdq,* "three kinds of whoredom") and the practitioner of the unorthodox (including Jewish Christians): "Who is a *min*? (A Jew) who worships idols" (T.B. *Horayoth* 11a).

Thus the rabbis used *mînîm* as a common noun to describe religious movements that they opposed, such as Jewish Christianity (T.B. *Berakhoth* 28b), Gnosticism, and heretical Judaism (*Jew. Enc.,* VIII, 594f.; Jastrow, p. 775). This kind of thinking is identical to that of Paul's accusers in Acts 24:5, who charged him with being a "ringleader of the sect of the Nazarenes." In v. 14 Paul defended the teaching of the primitive Church, "the Way, which they call a sect [*hairesin*]." This new "Way" claimed a definite continuity with OT revelation, shared some of the important doctrines of rabbinic Judaism (e.g., the resurrection of the body, the age to come, the inspiration of the Scriptures), and exhibited many characteristics of the scriptural exegesis of the early rabbis. It did not, however, consistently or rigorously observe certain pharisaic practices such as circumcision, strict sabbath observance, and ritual cleansing.

The NT authors also used *haíresis* to denote groups at variance with the teachings and practices of the apostolic Church. In Gal. 5:20 "party spirit" is grouped with "selfishness" (*eritheíai*) and "dissension" (*dichostasíai*) as "works of the flesh." The *haíresis* ("faction") in 1 Cor. 11:19 is the group that is not "approved" (AV; cf. NIV; Gk. *dókimos*) and that separates itself from the body of Christ. 2 Pet. 2:1 similarly depicts "false teachers" (*pseudodidáskaloi*) and "false prophets" (*pseudoprophḗtai*), who will introduce "destructive heresies" (*haíreseis apōleías*). In the postapostolic age *haíresis* became a technical term for heresy (e.g., Ign. Eph. 6:2).

***Bibliography.***–*Jew. Enc.,* VIII, *s.v.* "Min" (I. Broyde); *TDNT,* I, *s.v.* αἱρέομαι κτλ.: αἵρεσις (Schlier).

R. J. WYATT

**PARUAH** pə-ro͞o'ə [Heb. *pārû(a)ḥ*]. Father of the Jehoshaphat who was one of the twelve officers assigned to provide food for Solomon's household; Issachar was his district (1 K. 4:17).

**PARVAIM** pär-vā'əm [Heb. *parwāyim*]. A region famous for its gold, which was used as one of the decorative elements in the temple (2 Ch. 3:6). Suggested identifications of this source of gold include *Farwa* in south Arabia or *el-Farwein* in north Arabia. On the basis of rabbinic statements it has also been suggested that it had a reddish hue (Midr. *Cant.* 3:10), or that the reference is to some miraculous golden trees which bore golden fruit (T.B. *Yoma* 21b, 39b). Parvaim also appears in a scroll from Qumrân (1QapGen 2:23) as the "home" of Enoch.

***Bibliography.***–P. Grelot, *VT,* 11 (1961), 130-38; 14 (1964), 155-163; H. E. del Medico, *VT,* 13 (1963), 158-186.

C. G. RASMUSSEN

**PASACH** pā'sak [Heb. *pāsaḵ*]. Son of Japhlet, descendant of Asher (1 Ch. 7:33).

**PASCHAL LAMB.** *See* PASSOVER.

**PAS-DAMMIM** pas-dam'əm [Heb. *pas dammîm*]. The site of one of David's victories over the Philistines (1 Ch. 11:13). *See* EPHES-DAMMIM.

**PASEAH** pə-sē'ə [Heb. *pāsē(a)ḥ*–'limping']; AV also PHASEAH (Neh. 7:51).

**1.** Son of Eshton, descendant of Judah (1 Ch. 4:12).

**2.** [Gk. Apoc. *Phinoe*]; AV PHINEES; NEB PHINOE. The head of a family of temple servants (*see* NETHINIM) who returned from the Exile with Zerubbabel (Ezr. 2:49 par. Neh. 7:51; 1 Esd. 5:31).

**3.** Father of Joiada who helped to repair the Old Gate of Jerusalem (Neh. 3:6).

**PASHHUR** pash'ər [Heb. *pašḥûr* < *paššāḥ*–'destruction' + *s^eḥôr*–'all around' (see J. A. Thompson, *Book of Jeremiah* [*NICOT,* 1980], p. 455), or possibly Egyp. *Pš Ḥōr* (KoB, p. 784)]; AV PASHUR.

**1.** Son of Immer; a priest and chief officer in the temple in the time of Jeremiah (Jer. 20:1). His function was apparently to maintain order in the temple precincts. He punished Jeremiah for his gloomy prophecy by beating him and putting him in stocks (v. 2). Following his release, Jeremiah pronounced on Pashhur the judgment of seeing his family and nation carried into exile by Babylon because he had prophesied falsely (vv. 3-6). Jeremiah also gave him a new name, MAGOR-MISSABIB (RSV "Terror on every side"), which is a wordplay on "Pashhur" (v. 3). He was probably one of the officials deported in 598 B.C., because soon after that his position was occupied by Zephaniah son of Maaseiah (29:25f.). This Pashhur may be the same as **2** below.

**2.** Father of Gedaliah, one of the princes who attempted to have Jeremiah executed (Jer. 38:1-6); possibly the same as **1** above.

**3.** Son of Malchiah; a prince of Judah. When Jerusalem was under siege by Babylon, he was sent by King Zedekiah to request an oracle from Jeremiah (Jer. 21:1f.); but Jeremiah's response was a prophecy of doom (21:3ff.). Later he was among those who heard Jeremiah's advice to capitulate to Babylon and sought King Zedekiah's permission to have Jeremiah executed for treason (38:1-6). One of his descendants (Adaiah) was among the priests who lived in Jerusalem after the Exile (1 Ch. 9:12 par. Neh. 11:12).

**4.** [Gk. Apoc. *Phassour, Phaisour*]; AV PHASSARON, PHAISUR; NEB PHASSURUS, PHAESUS. Head of a priestly family that returned from the Exile with Zerubbabel (Ezr. 2:38 par. Neh. 7:41; 1 Esd. 5:25). Some members of this family had married foreign women (Ezr. 10:22 par. 1 Esd. 9:22).

**5.** A postexilic priest who sealed the covenant with Nehemiah (Neh. 10:3). N. J. O.

**PASS** [Heb. nouns: *maʿᵃḇār* (1 S. 13:23), *maʿbārâ* (e.g., 1 S. 14:4)]; AV also PASSAGE; [Heb. verbs: usually *ʿāḇar*–'pass by, through, or over,' also *pāsaḥ*–'skip over,' *hālaḵ*–'go,' *ḥālap*–'pass by or away' (e.g., Job 9:11), *ʿāḏâ*–'walk over' (28:8), qal and hiphil of *bāraḥ*–'pass through' (e.g., Ex. 26:28), *yāṣâ*–'go forth' (e.g., Nu. 34:4), qal and hiphil of *bôʾ* (e.g., "come to pass," Dt. 13:2; "bring to pass," 2 K. 19:25), *hāyâ*–'be' (e.g., 1 K. 1:21), piel of *kālâ*–'finish' (Prov. 16:30), etc.]; AV also GO ON, ABIDE, etc.; NEB also CONTINUE, GO, CROSS, AVOID, VANISH, etc.; [Gk. *érchomai*–'go' (Mt. 15:29), *parérchomai*–'pass by or away' (e.g., Mt. 5:18), *antiparérchomai*–'pass by on the other side' (Lk. 10:31f.), *diérchomai*–'pass through' (e.g., Mt. 12:43), *apérchomai*–'go away' (e.g., Rev. 9:12), *proérchomai*–'go forward' (Acts 12:10), *paraporeúomai*–'pass by' (e.g., Mt. 27:39), *diaporeúomai*–'go through' (Rom. 15:24), *ekporeúomai*–'go out' (Mk. 7:19), *parágō*–'pass by' (e.g., Mt. 9:9, 27), *diágō*–'draw through,' 'live' (Tit. 3:3), pass. of *katargéō*–'nullify, abolish' (e.g., 1 Cor. 2:6), *diabaínō*–'go through' (Lk. 16:26), *metabaínō*–'pass over' (e.g., Jn. 5:24), *diodeúō*–'travel through' (Acts 17:1), *ekbállō*–'throw out' (Mt. 15:17), *chōréō*–'go out' (15:17), *páresis*–'passing over,' 'remission' (Rom. 3:25), *hypérechō*– 'be above' (Phil. 4:7), *gínomai*–'happen' (e.g., Mk. 11:23), *diagínomai*–'go through' (e.g., Mk. 16:1), pass. of *plēróō*– 'fill up' (Acts 7:30; 9:23)]; AV also BE PERFORMED, COME, JUDGE, CEASE, etc.; NEB also DISAPPEAR, VANISH, VISIT, etc.; **PASSAGE** [Heb. inf. of *ʿāḇar*] (Nu. 20:21); NEB CROSS; [*liškâ*–'hall'] (Ezk. 42:4, 11f.); AV CHAMBER; [Gk. *periochḗ*–'portion (of Scripture)'] (Acts 8:32); AV PLACE; [*epí*–'at, on'] (Mk. 12:26; Lk. 20:37); AV "in"; NEB "in the story of"; **PASSER-BY** [Heb. part. of *ʿāḇar* (Ezk. 16:15, 25); Gk. part. of *parágō* (Mk. 15:21)]; AV, NEB also, PASS BY.

As a noun, "pass" denotes a narrow route through mountainous terrain (e.g., 1 S. 14:4; Isa. 10:29; *see also* MICHMAS; cf. the use of *maʿᵃḇār* and *maʿbārâ* to denote a place where one crosses a body of water; *see* FORD). "Passage" occurs in three different senses: (1) permission to pass through someone's territory (Nu. 20:21), (2) a long, narrow hall in the temple (Ezk. 42:4, 11f.), and (3) a specific portion of Scripture (Mk. 12:26; Lk. 20:37; Acts 8:32).

As a verb, "pass" (in the OT, usually Heb. *ʿāḇar*) most often denotes movement from one place to another. Persons or nations "pass through" a land (e.g., Gen. 12:6; Dt. 2:4, 18; Jgs. 11:17, 19) or "pass over" a river (e.g., Dt. 27:12; Josh. 3:14). For Israel the crossing of the Jordan (cf. Josh. 3–4), the last barrier before the Promised Land, signified the fulfillment of God's promises (cf. Dt. 9:1; 11:31; 27:2; etc.). This "passing over" the Jordan is reminiscent of Israel's "passing over" the Red Sea (Josh. 4:23). Heb. *ʿāḇar* signifies judgment, however, when on the night of Israel's liberation the Lord "passes through" (*ʿāḇar*) the land, slaying the firstborn of the Egyptians, but "passes over" (*pāsaḥ*) the Israelite houses that had blood on the doorposts (Ex. 12:12f., 23, 27; *see also* PASSOVER). Picking up this image, Amos later prophesies that a time will come when the Lord will no longer "pass by" (*ʿāḇar*) Israel (Am. 7:8; 8:2) but will "pass through" (*ʿāḇar*) the land in judgment (5:17; see Mays, pp. 99, 133). Ezekiel likewise prophesies judgment on Judah for foolishly playing the harlot with passers-by (Ezk. 16:15, 25; cf. Prov. 9:15). Laid waste so that none can "pass through" (*ʿāḇar,* Jer. 9:12), Judah becomes an object of horror and hissing for all who "pass by" (*ʿāḇar,* 18:16; this fate also awaits Edom [49:17] and Nineveh [Zeph. 2:15]). Yet this is not God's last word for His chosen people, for He promises that "when you pass through the waters I will be with you" (Isa. 43:2).

The expression "it came to pass" occurs thousands of times in the AV as a translation of Heb. *wayᵉhî* (Gk. *kaí egéneto* in the NT), an introductory formula used to connect sections of narrative. The RSV most often omits the formula, but it occasionally uses "come to pass" or "bring to pass" to emphasize God's action in causing historical events and fulfilling prophecies (e.g., 2 K. 15:12; 19:25; Isa. 37:26; 46:11; Lam. 3:37; cf. Mk. 11:23; Lk. 1:20; 1 Cor. 15:54).

In the NT Gk. *parérchomai* sometimes has the literal sense of "pass by" or "go by," e.g., used of Jesus walking past the disciples on the lake (Mk. 6:48) or walking through a city (Lk. 18:37). But it occurs more often in the figurative sense of "pass away" or "disappear," especially in passages with a strong eschatological note (e.g., 2 Pet. 3:10). Paul speaks of the old condition that has "passed away" (i.e., lost force, become invalid) when a person becomes a "new creation" in Christ (2 Cor. 5:17). Jesus promised that while heaven and earth will "pass away," His words will remain (Mt. 24:35; Mk. 13:31; Lk. 21:33; cf. *apérchomai,* Rev. 21:1, 4).

Greek *páresis* occurs in the NT only at Rom. 3:25 (RSV "pass over"; AV "remission"; NEB "overlook"). In classical Greek it sometimes meant simply "passing over," but it also occurred with the legal meaning "letting go unpunished" (Bauer, rev., p. 626; *see* FORGIVENESS I; also W. G. Kümmel, *Journal for Theology and the Church,* 3 [1967], 1-13; J. Murray, pp. 119f.; *TDNT,* I, 511).

The author of the Epistle to the Hebrews draws a comparison between Jesus and the Aaronic high priests. Whereas the latter were given the privilege of passing through the veil into the holy of holies once each year, Jesus, the "great high priest," has "passed through [*diérchomai*] the heavens" to the very throne of God (4:14; see Bruce, p. 85).

***Bibliography.***–F. F. Bruce, *Epistle to the Hebrews* (*NICNT,* repr. 1981); J. Gray, *Joshua, Judges and Ruth* (*NCBC,* rev. ed. 1977); J. L. Mays, *Amos* (*OTL,* repr. 1976); J. Murray, *Epistle to the Romans,* I (*NICNT,* 1960); *TDNT,* I, *s.v.* ἀφίημι κτλ. (R. Bultmann); II, *s.v.* ἔρχομαι κτλ.: διέρχομαι, παρέρχομαι (J. Schneider).

D. K. MCKIM
N. J. O.

**PASSING OF MARY.** *See* APOCRYPHAL GOSPELS II.F.

**PASSION; PASSIONS** [Heb. *qinʾâ*–'jealousy, ardor'] (Prov. 14:30); AV ENVY; [Gk. *epithymía*] (Rom. 6:12; Eph. 2:3; 2 Tim. 2:22; Tit. 2:12; 3:3; 1 Pet. 1:14; etc.); AV LUSTS; NEB DESIRES, SENSUALITY, IMPULSES, etc.; [*hēdonḗ*] (Jas. 4:1, 3); AV LUSTS; NEB BODILY DESIRES, PLEASURES; [*órexis*] (Rom. 1:27); AV, NEB, LUST; [*páthos*] (Rom. 1:26; Col. 3:5; 1 Thess. 4:5); AV AFFECTIONS, INORDINATE AFFECTION, LUST; NEB also "giving way"; [*páthēma*] (Rom. 7:5; Gal. 5:24); AV MOTIONS, AFFECTIONS; [*thymós*] (Rev. 14:8; 18:3); AV WRATH; NEB FIERCE, mg. WRATH; [*páschō*] (Acts 1:3); NEB DEATH; [*pyroúmai*–'be burned'] ("be aflame with passion," 1 Cor. 7:9); AV BURN; NEB "burn with vain desire"; [*hypérakmos*] ("passions are strong," 1 Cor. 7:36); AV "pass the flower of her age"; NEB "instincts are too strong," mg. "ripe for marriage."

These terms are used in the RSV with three basic meanings.

***I. Suffering.***–This is the original meaning of "passion," which is derived from Lat. *passio* ("suffering"), from the verb *patior,* a cognate of Gk. *páschō* ("suffer," "undergo, experience"). This use of "passion" is now obsolete except in reference to Jesus' SUFFERING. In Acts 1:3 "after his passion" (RSV, AV, and most earlier English versions) is influenced by the Vulg. *post passionem suam,* which translates Gk. *metá tó patheín,* literally "after he had suffered." In this context *patheín* (aorist infinitive of *páschō*) refers specifically to Jesus' death (cf. NEB; cf. also *páschō* in the sense of "die" in Lk. 24:26, 46; Acts 3:18; 17:3; 26:23), which is contrasted with His resurrection (see *TDNT,* V, 913).

The Passion narratives are those sections of the Gospels that deal with Jesus' suffering during the last few days of His earthly life, including the Last Supper, His agony in Gethsemane, His arrest and trial, and His crucifixion. *See* LORD'S SUPPER; JESUS CHRIST IV.D; JESUS CHRIST, ARREST AND TRIAL OF; CROSS VI.

***II. Intense Sensual Desire.***–The RSV uses "passion" or "passions" once in the OT (Prov. 14:30) and twenty-five times in the Epistles to indicate lust for bodily pleasures, e.g., sex, drunkenness, and material possessions. The most common term, Gk. *epithymía,* can represent "desire" in a morally neutral or positive sense (cf. Jn. 8:44; Phil. 1:23; 1 Thess. 2:17; 1 Tim. 3:1); but in the NT it usually indicates an evil desire — or, more precisely, the inability to renounce or control, for the sake of obedience to God, desires that may in themselves be natural. *Hēdonḗ* (cf. *hēdýs,* "sweet") can simply mean "pleasure" (cf., e.g., Lk. 8:14; 2 Pet. 2:13; *see* PLEASE), but in the NT it usually denotes "desire for sensual pleasure." Thus *epithymía* and *hēdonḗ* are closely related and can be used as synonymous parallels (Tit. 3:3).

*Páthēma* (from *páschō*) usually means "suffering" and is so rendered by the RSV elsewhere (e.g., Rom. 8:18; 2 Cor. 1:5-7; Phil. 3:10; Col. 1:24). But in Gal. 5:24 (cf. also Rom. 7:5) the *pathḗmai* ("passions") and *epithymíai* ("desires") of the *sárx* ("flesh") clearly represent the impulse to engage in the vices listed in 5:19-21. The cognate *páthos* can also mean "suffering," "experience," or "emotion" in a general sense (cf. *homoiopathḗs,* lit. "of similar experiences or feelings," Acts 14:15; Jas. 5:17; AV "[of] like passions"; RSV "of like nature"). Paul, however, used it only in the sense of "passion" — specifically "erotic passion" (e.g., Rom. 1:26). In Col. 3:5 *páthos* ("passion") appears with *epithymía kakḗ* ("evil desire") in a list of vices, and in 1 Thess. 4:5 *en páthei epithymías* is rendered "in the passion of lust" (AV "in the lust of concupiscence"; NEB "giving way to lust").

*Órexis,* which occurs only once in the NT, is related to the verb *orégomai,* which is used in a positive sense in 1 Tim. 3:1 ("aspire") and He. 11:16 ("desire") but in a negative sense in 1 Tim. 6:10 ("craving"); in Rom. 1:27 the noun denotes "sexual desire." In 1 Cor. 7:36 Paul's use of *hypérakmos* (from *hypér,* "beyond," and *akmḗ,* "highest point" or "prime") is ambiguous: it could refer either to the man's sexual desire (cf. RSV, NEB) or to the woman's maturity (cf. AV, NEB mg.), but the context makes the former more likely.

The authors of the NT Epistles viewed sensualism as a serious threat to the Christian community, and they strongly opposed those who taught that bodily actions were a matter of moral indifference (*see* GNOSTICISM VI.C). Uninhibited indulgence of sensual desires is characteristic of the old nature — of living according to the flesh rather than the Spirit (e.g., Rom. 7:5; Gal. 5:16-21; Eph. 2:3; 1 Pet. 2:11). Those who make their "own passions" (*ídiai epithymíai,* 2 Pet. 3:3; "own likings," 2 Tim. 4:3; "own desire," Jas. 1:14) the goal of their lives are "ungodly" (Jude 14-19), because they have chosen to follow their own will instead of God's (cf. 1 Pet. 4:2). They are "lovers of self . . . lovers of pleasure [*philḗdonoi*] rather than lovers of God" (2 Tim. 3:2-4). Their LICENTIOUS life-style promises freedom, but it makes them slaves to sin and death (Rom. 6:16; 2 Pet. 2:18f.). When *hēdonḗ* (lust for sensual pleasures) rules one's life, it creates conflict within oneself (Rom. 7:18-23), with other persons (Tit. 3:3; Jas. 4:1f.), and with God (4:3f.; cf. 1 Jn. 2:15-17). Freedom from its enslavement can be found only by dying to the old sinful self and rising through Christ to a new life ruled by the Spirit (Rom. 6:6-11; 8:1-11; Gal. 5:22-24; Eph. 4:22-24; cf. Col. 3:5-10; *see* NEW MAN; OLD SELF).

*See also* DESIRE; FLESH III.B; LUST; SLAVE.

***III. Wrath.***–In Rev. 14:8; 18:3 the RSV renders Gk. *toú oínou toú thymoú tḗs porneías* "the wine of her impure passion." The AV's literal translation, "the wine of the wrath of her fornication," is more accurate. In the NT *thymós* always means WRATH, and in Revelation it almost always means divine wrath (e.g., Rev. 14:19; 15:1, 7; 16:1; cf. the synonym *orgḗ* in 6:16f.; 11:18; 16:19; 19:15). In 14:8; 18:3 two images are combined: "the wine of God's wrath," which must be drunk by all who have worshiped the beast (14:9f.), and "the wine of fornication" of the great HARLOT (Rome, symbolized by Babylon), drunk by the kings of the earth (17:2). "The wine of wrath" represents God's judgment upon those who have been seduced by Rome's corrupt practices (cf. Jer. 25:15-29, which pictures divine punishment as a "cup of the wine of wrath" which the nations are forced to drink).

***Bibliography.***–Bauer, rev.; *DNTT*, I, 105-113, 456-461; *TDNT*, II, *s.v.* ἡδονή, φιλήδονος (G. Stählin); III, *s.v.* θυμός κτλ. (F. Büchsel); V, *s.v.* πάσχω κτλ. (W. Michaelis).

N. J. OPPERWALL

**PASSION, THE.** A term that refers to Jesus' suffering during the last two days of His earthly life, especially His crucifixion. *See* PASSION I. As an adjective "Passion" is used of the last week (or last two weeks) of Lent and of musical settings and plays that deal with Jesus' suffering and death.

**PASSOVER** [Heb. *pesaḥ*; Gk. *páscha*; cf. Aram. *pisḥā'*; note also Eng. "paschal"]. A major festival held in the spring to commemorate Israel's deliverance from Egypt. The term is often used of the entire festival celebration (e.g., Ex. 12:48; 2 K. 23:21). It may also designate the Passover sacrifice to be eaten (Ex. 12:11; 2 Ch. 30:18) and the animal victim, i.e., the "Passover lamb" (Ex. 12:21; 2 Ch. 30:15).

I. Origin
II. In OT Times
III. In NT Times
IV. Passover Today

***I. Origin.***–*A. Etymology.* The noun *pesaḥ* is derived from the verb *pāsaḥ*. Its etymology, however, is much disputed, and various theories have been proposed.

Many scholars have argued that *pāsaḥ* may come from two separate roots (so BDB, p. 820). The first root means "pass" or "leap over" (Ex. 12:13, 23, 27). At the time of the Exodus, each Israelite household that had blood smeared on its doorposts was "passed over" (i.e., omitted, left out) by God when He struck down the Egyptians. A second Hebrew verb (using the same radicals but coming from a different root) means "be lame, limp." It is often distinguished from the former meaning in several passages unrelated to the context of the Passover (see 2 S. 4:4; 1 K. 18:21, 26). Some scholars, however, have sought to derive all the meanings of *pāsaḥ* from this second root (cf. *CHAL,* p. 294). Thus, in comparison to the limping dance of the prophets of Baal (1 K. 18:21, 26), God is seen "to skip by, spare" the houses of the Israelites on the eve of the Exodus (Ex. 12).

Glasson argued that the three occurrences of *pāsaḥ* in

Ex. 12 should not be rendered "passover," but "defend, protect" (thus the alternate reading to Ex. 12:13, NEB, "to stand guard over"). This interpretation is based largely on the use of *pāsaḥ* in Isa. 31:5, where it parallels words meaning "defend, protect." The context pictures a bird protectively hovering over its nest guarding its young. Isaiah thus depicts the Lord as Israel's protector, defending each home by forbidding the destroyer to enter (Ex. 12:23; cf. He. 11:28). The LXX and Tgs. give additional support to this sense.

Attempts have also been made to link *pesaḥ* to a variety of non-Hebraic roots. For example, *pesaḥ* has been tied to Akk. *pašāḫu*, "to appease, placate" (a god). Others have tried to relate it to Egyp. *peš*, "to spread wings over" (in order to protect), or to Egyp. *p3 sḥ*, "blow, stroke," supposedly an allusion to the tenth plague that struck dead the firstborn of the Egyptians. Such non-Hebraic etymological hypotheses are extremely tenuous, and while the etymology is evasive, earlier explanations are more plausible.

*B. Background.* Passover is the oldest of Jewish festivals, originating over three thousand years ago. Passover appears originally to have conflated two separate spring festivals. One rite involved unleavened bread, the other a sacrificial lamb. The OT (Ex. 34:18, 25) distinguishes the festivals by using the terms "Feast of Unleavened Bread" (*ḥag hammaṣṣôṯ*) and "Passover Feast" (*ḥag happāsaḥ*). The NT (Mt. 26:17; Mk. 14:1; Lk. 22:1) refers to both of these as "the Passover" (*tó páscha*) and the "Feast of Unleavened Bread" (*tá ázyma* or *hē heortḗ tṓn azýmōn*). These festivals were held in immediate sequence. Passover was celebrated at twilight of the 14th day of the month (Ex. 12:6) and the Feast of Unleavened Bread for the seven days following, namely, the 15th to the 21st (Ex. 12:15; Lev. 23:5f.; Nu. 28:16f.; 2 Ch. 35:1, 17). Toward the end of the NT era, however, the one term, "Passover" was generally used to designate the integrated celebration of what had begun as two festivals. Though, by that time, the title "Feast of Unleavened Bread" had not disappeared, Josephus (*Ant.* xiv.2.1 [21]; xvii.9.3 [213f.]) indicates that "Passover" was commonly used to refer to both festivals. The mishnaic tractate *Pesahim* reveals a similar popular combining of the feasts.

Some scholars have postulated a prehistory to the Passover from references in Exodus, e.g., "Let my people go, so that they may hold a festival to me in the desert" (5:1; cf. 10:9). This may have reference to a shepherd's festival kept by Semitic nomads in the spring as they would head for new pastures before the start of the dry season. The Feast of Unleavened Bread may have had its origin in an agricultural festival related to the spring barley harvest. After entering Canaan, the Israelites may have adopted aspects of this feast from the Canaanites (cf. de Vaux, 490-93).

The critical view has held that these separate festivals were not combined or historicized (connected to the actual Exodus) until about the time of the Exile or later. This line of reasoning, of course, is conjecture. Whatever the exact prehistory of the Passover, the festival cannot be separated from that historic moment in Israel's past that brought miraculous deliverance from Egypt.

***II. In OT Times.***–The Exodus was the redemptive event par excellence in the life of God's covenant people. The Passover reenacted annually the greatest miracle Yahweh performed out of grace for His chosen; it was to become the focal point of Jewish history. The Passover celebration retold the story of freedom after more than four hundred years of Egyptian bondage. The frequent OT allusions to that deliverance indicate that it was a source of hope for the nation's future redemption.

Instructions regarding the observance of Passover are found mainly in the Pentateuch. The account in Ex. 12:1–13:16 outlines the historical setting and ordinances governing the last meal in Egypt: (1) Celebration was to be at the full moon (Ex. 12:6) on "the first month" (Ex. 12:2) of spring (i.e., Abib; cf. Ex. 13:3f.; Dt. 16:1; later called Nisan). It marked the start of the barley harvest. (2) On the 10th day of the month a year-old male lamb or kid, without defect, was to be selected according to the size of the household (Ex. 12:3-5). (3) On the 14th of the month at twilight (lit. "between the two evenings") the lamb was to be killed (12:6). (4) Blood from a basin must be applied by hyssop (a leafy plant) to the doorframes and lintels of the houses where the people gathered to eat the lambs (vv. 7, 22). (5) The lamb must be roasted over the fire — head, legs, and inner parts, no bones broken (vv. 9, 46). (6) Bitter herbs (*m^e^rōrîm*) and bread made without yeast (*maṣṣôṯ*) must also be eaten (v. 8). (7) Any remains of the meal not consumed were to be burned (v. 10). (8) The meal was to be eaten in haste with cloak tucked into belt, sandals on feet, and staff in hand (v. 11). (9) All future generations of Israelites were to celebrate Passover as a lasting ordinance (vv. 14, 24, 42, 47). (10) Slaves and resident aliens were permitted to join the meal, provided they had been circumcised (vv. 44, 48).

On the next day, the 15th of Abib (Nissan), the Feast of Unleavened Bread began. This observance, distinct from Passover, was to last seven days. During this time all bread made with yeast was to be destroyed and only unleavened bread eaten (12:15, 17-20; 13:6f.). The first and seventh days were for holding sacred assemblies; no work was to be done, except to prepare food (12:16).

The Passover was to be an opportunity for the father to teach his children. He (not a substitute) was obliged to explain the meaning of the ceremony when his children asked (12:26f.; 13:8, 14). From this practice of ritual questioning the term *Haggadah* (lit. "explaining, telling") took on increased importance in the life of the community. (Today the term is used for the book that explains the meaning of the celebration at the Passover meal.) The importance played by recital of the magnalia (the great redemptive events of biblical faith) throughout Israelite history (e.g., Dt. 26:5-9; Josh. 24; 1 S. 12; cf. Acts 7) was vital in preserving memory of the Exodus "for generations to come" (Ex. 12:42).

Other major pentateuchal references to the Passover (Lev. 23:5-8; Nu. 28:16-25; Dt. 16:1-8) indicate that the Feast of Unleavened Bread was closely integrated to it. Various offerings were specified throughout the week (Nu. 28:19-24). *Maṣṣôṯ* is now referred to as the "bread of affliction" (Dt. 16:3). Though Passover began as a family festival of the home (Ex. 12:21-23, 46), Deuteronomy anticipates the time when wilderness wanderings would lead to permanent residence in Canaan, with worship at a central sanctuary (Dt. 16:2, 6f.). The changed circumstances were to transmute the Passover into a pilgrimage festival at which all adult males were to appear (cf. Ex. 23:14-17; 34:23). The law of Moses also makes provision for a second Passover, or "minor Passover" as it was called in the rabbinic period. This was celebrated a month later (14th day of the second month) for any who were ceremonially unclean or away on a journey at the regular time (Nu. 9:1-14; cf. 2 Ch. 30:2).

Various Passover celebrations are recorded in the OT, beginning from the moment Israel entered Canaan. On the plains of Jericho, prior to the Conquest, Passover was conducted under the leadership of Joshua (Josh. 5:10-12). Solomon celebrated the three pilgrimage festivals that now centered in Jerusalem (2 Ch. 8:13). From this point on, Passover focused upon a permanent central sanctuary, the blood of the paschal lamb now sprinkled by priests on the altar of burnt offering. Being more of a public ceremony, Passover was sometimes given strong support by religiously sensitive national leaders.

The Chronicler records two great Passover celebrations at the temple in Jerusalem (2 Ch. 30:1-27; 35:1-19; cf. 2 K. 23:21-23). These followed revivals during the reigns of King Hezekiah (716-687 B.C.) and King Josiah (640-609 B.C.). The magnitude of these observances was unparalleled in Israel for centuries (2 Ch. 30:26; 35:18). The last historical text to mention the Passover festival is Ezra. After rebuilding the temple upon return from exile, the people celebrated Passover with considerable joy (Ezr. 6:19-22). The OT prophets have no specific references to Passover feasts apart from one projected by Ezekiel in his description of the new temple (Ezk. 45:21-24).

During the intertestamental period, despite Seleucid and Roman control of Jerusalem, it appears that Passover was still celebrated with some regularity. Two noncanonical writings from the 2nd cent. B.C. give emphasis to the Passover theme. 1 Esdras opens with an account of Josiah's Passover (1:1-22; cf. 2 Ch. 35:1-19), and Jubilees gives detailed procedures about the Passover festival (49:1-23).

***III. In NT Times.***–Our understanding of the Passover during the NT era comes largely from the writings of Josephus, the mishnaic tractate *Pesahim,* and the NT itself. Pilgrimages were made annually to Jerusalem for the Passover sacrifice until the temple was destroyed in A.D. 70. Following this time, many Jews found themselves in *gālûṯ* (exile), scattered in communities among the nations of the world. Passover ceased being a pilgrimage festival at a central sanctuary. Once again, as in pharaonic Egypt, the Passover feast began to center upon the family in the home, a place where it has remained for more than nineteen centuries.

Passover in NT temple days was a spectacle of excitement and devotion. Pilgrims near and far ascended to the holy city in large numbers (cf. Jn. 11:55). Considering the area of Jerusalem at this time, scholars look on Josephus's figure of about three million Jews present for Passover (*BJ* ii.14.3 [280]; vi.9.3 [420-25]) as extremely exaggerated. Many historians have suggested a more realistic figure would be under 200,000. Accommodations for both sleeping and feasting were sought out in every available space (cf. Mk. 14:15). In lieu of rent hosts entertaining pilgrims in their homes were given the hides of the animals slaughtered and consumed by their guests (T.B. *Yoma* 12a). Perhaps to help defuse the smoldering Jewish resentment of their presence, local Roman authorities released a prisoner at Passover time (Mk. 15:6-15; cf. Mish. *Pesahim* ix.6a).

Days before Passover began, Jerusalem was a hubbub of commercial activity. Many pilgrims who were also merchants arrived early to sell or barter their wares (cf. Mt. 21:12f.; Jn. 2:13-16). Beggars stationed themselves strategically by the bustling gates of the city. Jerusalem became not only an emporium for such domestic goods as clothing, jewelry, and exotic ointments, but also for spices, herbs, condiments, wheat, fish, and wine used throughout the week-long festivities. Of utmost importance to pilgrims, however, was the purchasing of sheep and goats for sacrifice at the temple. The animal (preferably a lamb) was selected on the 10th of Nisan (*Pesahim* ix.5). The size of the lamb varied since a single individual was forbidden to eat an entire animal. Family groups, or companies of at least ten people (e.g., the disciples with their Master), were required to eat the entire lamb at one sitting (T.B. *Pesahim* 64b). No part of the animal was to remain until the next day.

Before the family meal on Passover eve, the day was filled with preparation for the event. A full contingent of priests — twenty-four divisions instead of the usual one — came early to the temple. Their first task was the burning of the leaven (*ḥāmēṣ*). This had been searched for by candlelight in each home the night before and then removed for burning the next morning (*Pesahim* i-iii). By midday all work stopped.

The afternoon was set aside for the ritual slaughtering of the lamb. The offering of the Passover sacrifice at the temple began about 3:00 P.M. (*Pesahim* v.1), and was conducted in three massive shifts. When the temple court was filled with the first group of offerers, the gates of the court were closed. The ram's horn was sounded and the sacrifice began (*Pesahim* v.5). Each Jew slaughtered his own lamb. The priests stood in two rows, one holding gold basins, and the other silver. After the blood was drained into a basin, it was tossed against the base of the altar (*Pesahim* v.6). While the offerings were going on, the Levites sang the Hallel (Pss. 113–118). Each lamb was then skinned and its fat with kidneys removed for burning on the altar (*Pesahim* v.9f.; cf. Lev. 3:3-5). Before leaving the temple, each offerer slung his lamb — wrapped in its own hide — over his shoulder (T.B. *Pesahim* 65b). He then departed with his company to prepare the Passover meal. Immediately, the next division of offerers filed into the temple court and the ritual was repeated.

The Passover evening meal was held at home or in a room within the city reserved for the occasion (cf. Mt. 26:17-19 par.). In the courtyard of the home the carcass of the lamb, with legs unbroken, was roasted. It was placed in a clay oven on a skewer of pomegranate wood (*Pesahim* vii.1). Inside, the company gathered, festively dressed in white. The room was prepared with floor cushions for reclining and small tables for serving. At the head of the room sat the one leading the ritual meal.

By NT times the Passover observance had features added to those already specified in the OT. A *seder*, meaning a set "order of service," was now followed (cf. *Pesahim* x.1-9). It was a festival that celebrated freedom, hence celebrants ate reclining (cf. Ex. 12:11). Each had to "regard himself as if he came forth himself out of Egypt" (*Pesahim* x.5). The meal included various symbolic elements, each consumed at specified points throughout the evening. These included roasted lamb, bitter herbs, unleavened bread, *ḥ$^a$rōseṯ* (pasty mixture of nuts, fruit, and wine), and a raw vegetable dipped into a tart liquid. At various intervals four cups of wine, a symbol of joy, were consumed. The wine was probably mixed with water and heated (cf. *Pesahim* vii.13). Ritual hand-washings, prayers, and portions of the Hallel (Pss. 113–118) also punctuated the observance. A key point of instruction in Israelite tradition came when the son asked his father the ceremonial question, "Why is this night different from other nights?" (*Pesahim* x.4). The father responded by giving a historical synopsis of God's redemptive dealings with Israel that led to deliverance from Egypt. The ceremony concluded late, but many feasters then returned to the streets of Jerusalem to continue their celebration. Others returned to the temple mount to await the reopening of the temple gates at midnight so that they might spend the rest of the night in worship and prayer (cf. Josephus *Ant.* xviii.2.2 [29]).

Scholars have debated whether the Last Supper was a Passover meal (see standard NT comms.). The Synoptic Gospels state that it was (Mt. 26:17 par.), but Jn. 19:14 has cast some doubt on this. The Johannine passage need not be in conflict with the Synoptic tradition, however, if the expression "day of Preparation of the Passover" (RSV) be understood as "day of Preparation of Passover Week" (NIV). In this context, "day of preparation" would refer to Friday, since every Friday was the day of preparation for the weekly Sabbath. The term "Passover" would be used here to include reference to the week-long Feast of Unleavened Bread, which by this time had merged by popular usage with Passover into one long feast (see G. Archer, *Encyclopedia of Bible Difficulties* [1982], pp. 375f.; cf. I. H. Marshall, *Last Supper and Lord's Supper* [1981], pp. 57-75).

From the NT record it seems clear that Jesus instituted the Lord's Supper by associating it with the third cup of wine, which came after the Passover meal was eaten (cf. 1 Cor. 11:25). It was known as the "cup of redemption," linked in rabbinic tradition to the third of the fourfold promise of redemption in Ex. 6:6f., "I will redeem you." Jesus associated this cup of red wine with His atoning death in saying, "This cup which is poured out for you is the new covenant in my blood" (Lk. 22:20; cf. 1 Cor. 11:25). According to some scholars (e.g., W. Lane, comm. on Mark [*NICNT,* 1974], pp. 508f.; *see also* LORD'S SUPPER III, IV.A) He refused, however, to drink the fourth cup (Mk. 14:25 par.; cf. *Pesahim* x.7), referred to as the "cup of consummation" (cf. Ex. 6:7) based on the promise that God will take His own people to be with Him (cf. V. Taylor, comm. on Mark [repr. 1959], p. 547; cf. also J. Jeremias, *Eucharistic Words of Jesus* [Eng. tr., rev. ed. 1977], pp. 84-88, 207-218). The unfinished meal of Jesus was a pledge that redemption would be consummated at that future messianic banquet when he "drinks it anew in the kingdom of God" (Mk. 14:25; cf. Mt. 26:29; Rev. 3:20; 19:6-9). The Lord's Supper concluded with the singing of a hymn (Mt. 26:30; Mk. 14:26), doubtless the second half of the Hallel (Pss. 115–118).

In referring to His death as a sacrifice, Jesus was comparing Himself to the Passover lamb (cf. Rev. 5:12, "Lamb who was slain"). John the Baptizer calls him "the Lamb of God" (Jn. 1:29, 36). Paul reflects this same rich symbolism: "For Christ, our Passover lamb, has been sacrificed" (1 Cor. 5:7). Peter describes God's children as redeemed "with the precious blood of Christ, a lamb without blemish or defect" (1 Pet. 1:18f.). This blood-redeemed community is called a new lump of "unleavened dough" (1 Cor. 5:7). The prophetic significance of Christ's death, "Not one of his bones will be broken" (Jn. 19:36), is a fulfillment of Scripture that states the bones of the Passover lamb were not to be broken (Ex. 12:46; Nu. 9:12; cf. Ps. 34:20 [MT 21]).

*IV. Passover Today.*–Only the Samaritans, a small community of several hundred located near Shechem (modern Nablûs), still observe annually the blood sacrifice of the Passover lamb. Unchangingly committed to the Law of Moses since Bible times, the entire Samaritan community gathers on the slopes of the "chosen place" (cf. Dt. 16:2, 6f.), Mt. Gerizim, where they live for the full festival. For the Jewish community, however, since the destruction by Rome of Mt. Zion and the temple, sacrifices have ceased and Passover has once again returned to the home. In the contemporary Passover meal (called a seder [< Heb. *sēḏer*, "order"]), in order to bring to mind the days of the temple, a shankbone and roasted egg are placed on the seder plate. These symbolize the roasted paschal sacrifice and the festival offering brought when the temple was still standing.

The modern Passover seder makes use of a written explanatory text called a *Haggadah.* It is traditional on the first night of Passover to hold a family seder at home, and on the next night to hold a community seder at the synagogue. On the seder table is placed the "cup of Elijah," a goblet of wine poured, but not drunk. According to scriptural tradition, Elijah, who ascended to heaven in a fiery chariot (2 K. 2:11f.), would return as the herald and messenger of the coming Messiah (Mal. 4:5 [MT 3:23]).

An engraved pewter seder plate with symbols associated with Passover, representations of the required foods, and some details from the *Haggadah* (Israel Museum, Jerusalem)

Page from the *Birds' Head Haggadah* (Germany, *ca.* A.D. 1300). The birds' heads were used to avoid depicting human features (Israel Museum, Jerusalem)

Thus, in Jewish belief, messianic hope is kindled more strongly during Passover than at any other season for it is the "season of redemption" (cf. Midr. *Ex. Rabbah* 15:12).

Synagogue liturgy at Passover includes several special emphases. On the first day of Passover a prayer for dew is recited, a reminder that in Israel the rainy season has now ended and the dry season is fast approaching. The second night of Passover begins the "Counting of the *Omer*" (lit. "sheaf" [of barley]). This period of seven weeks culminates in the festival of *Shavuot* (Weeks), often called Pentecost, which means fiftieth day. Also during the Passover festival the book of the Canticles is read. Alluding to the beauty of springtime (Cant. 2:11-13), the very season of Passover, the rabbis interpreted this book as a picture of God's love for His people Israel. Toward the end of Passover week, the Torah reading in the Synagogue is the Song of Moses (Ex. 15:1-18), an ancient, poetical paean of praise rehearsing the triumphant deliverance of Israel through the waters of the Red Sea.

*Bibliography.*–R. de Vaux, *Ancient Israel* (Eng. tr. 1961), II, 484-493; H. Donin, *To Be A Jew* (1972); *Encyclopedia Judaica,*

Bitumen stone "cup of Elijah" (Israel Museum, Jerusalem)

XIII, *s.v.* (A. Kanof); T. H. Gaster, *Passover* (1949); T. Glasson, *JTS*, 10 (1959), 79-84; *ILC*, III-IV, 383-415; M. Klein, ed., *Passover* (1973); H. Schauss, *Guide to Jewish Holy Days* (1938); J. Segal, *Hebrew Passover* (1963); *TDNT*, V, *s.v.* πάσχα (J. Jeremias).

M. R. WILSON

**PASTOR** [Gk. *poimḗn*–'shepherd']. One of five gifts given to the Church for leadership by the ascended Lord (Eph. 4:8, 11). Whereas apostles, prophets, and evangelists minister in the Church at large, pastors and teachers serve in the local congregation. By these gifts Christ guides the Church to realize the riches of its election (1:17ff.), by being equipped, built up (4:12), growing into the fulness of His stature (v. 13), all of which results in holy living (vv. 22-24).

As used by the NT, "pastor" designates both an endowment for ministry and the one who fills that ministry, but it implies no fixed office. The pastoral ministry may be performed by a *presbýteros* (1 Pet. 5:1f.), an *epískopos* (1 Tim. 3:2), or even both (cf. Acts 20:17, 28). Rather than an office, it suggests a moral or spiritual relationship. A pastor must be faithful to Christ the Chief Shepherd (1 Pet. 2:25; cf. He. 13:20), self-sacrificing (cf. Jn. 10:11), seeking the lost (cf. Mt. 18:12-14). Secular usage also connotes governance. So Paul instructs the Ephesian elders "to care for" (Gk. *poimaínein*) the church of God and to protect it from heretical "wolves" (Acts 20:28f.).

Use of "pastor" as a title for the congregation's leader derives substantially from the Geneva Bible. Following Calvin's sharp, formal distinction between *poimḗn* (Lat. *pastor*) and *didáskalos* ("teacher," Lat. *doctor*) in his commentary (comm. on Ephesians [Eng. tr. 1965], pp. 179f.; cf. also *Inst.* iv.3.1-8), the Geneva translation adopted the Latin term instead of "shepherd," which both Wyclif and Tyndale had used.

*See* SHEPHERD; MINISTRY.

***Bibliography.***–Comms. on Ephesians by T. K. Abbott (*ICC*, 1899), p. 118; M. Barth (*AB*, 1974), pp. 429-441, 477-484; B. F. Westcott (repr. 1979), pp. 169-171; also H. von Campenhausen, *Ecclesiastical Authority and Spiritual Power in the Church of the First Three Centuries* (Eng. tr. 1969), pp. 55-75; R. Y. K. Fung, *EQ*, 52 (1980), 195-214; D. Moody, *Interp.*, 19 (1965), 168-181; *TDNT*, VI, *s.v.* ποιμήν (J. Jeremias).

W. R. HARRIS

**PASTORAL EPISTLES.**

I. Title
II. Characteristics
III. Authenticity
  A. External Attestation
  B. Internal Claims
    1. Historical Background
    2. Ecclesiastical Situation
    3. Mention of Heresies
    4. Doctrinal Considerations
    5. Linguistic Considerations
  C. Alternative Theories
    1. Fragment Theory
    2. Fiction Theory
  D. Conclusion
IV. Date
V. Purpose
VI. Important Topics
  A. Christology
  B. Man and His Need
VII. Contents

***I. Title.***–The two Epistles to Timothy and the Epistle to Titus have been known collectively as the Pastoral Epistles since the 18th century. They bear this title as letters written by Paul, the chief pastor, to alert the recipients to their pastoral duties. Their many similarities necessitate treating them as a whole, since most of the problems that arise for one arise also for the others, although each has its own special characteristics. In considering the variety of issues relating to them, one can therefore deal with them sometimes separately and sometimes together.

***II. Characteristics.***–All three Epistles are addressed to individuals, and this at once marks them out from the Pauline letters written to churches. They are evidently intended, however, to have wider implications than has merely private correspondence. They were to strengthen the hands of the apostle's lieutenants and are therefore especially valuable for the insight that they give into Paul's advice to his helpers. It would be correct to call them semipersonal and perhaps semiecclesiastical.

Each Epistle contains some teaching on ecclesiastical problems and information on conditions within the early Church. 1 Timothy and Titus have directions regarding choice of church officers, and all three give guidelines for Christian behavior and activity within the Church. Yet intermixed with this semiofficial material are more personal exhortations intended for the individuals addressed. Timothy is more than once encouraged to deal courageously with all the problems confronting him. All three Epistles contain exhortations regarding false teachers and various other admonitions.

While each Epistle has revelations of the author's character and personality, these are most pronounced in 2 Timothy. In ch. 4 the many personal details throw much light on the conditions of the apostle's closing days and lend themselves to imaginative reconstruction. Paul had left behind a cloak at Troas and asked for his parchments to be collected. Such details add pathos to an Epistle that has been not inappropriately called "Paul's swan song." Because these Epistles are the apostle's latest literary productions they make a significant contribution to knowledge of his outlook, particularly as he contemplated the finish of his earthly race.

***III. Authenticity.***–There have been stronger attacks upon the authenticity of these Epistles than upon any other letters bearing the name of Paul in the NT. In fact, these Epistles are still widely regarded as non-Pauline; thus all the factors affecting authenticity must be carefully assessed.

*A. External Attestation.* Many traces of these Epistles are in the early Apostolic Fathers, although the loose citation of NT books during this period makes it difficult to prove that authors like Clement of Rome and Ignatius knew the Epistles. It is at least probable that they did. The many similar phrases in the Pastorals and Clement are more adequately explained by Clement's use of the former than vice versa, in spite of the claims of, e.g., B. H. Streeter (*Primitive Church* [1929], p. 153). Most scholars, however, have been cautious about postulating Clement's or Ignatius's use of the Pastorals.

It is difficult to deny that Polycarp showed acquaintance with these Epistles, at least with 1 and 2 Timothy (cf., e.g., Polyc. Phil. 4:1 and 1 Tim. 6:7, 10; Polyc. Phil. 5:2 and 1 Tim. 3:8; 2 Tim. 2:12). Some scholars, like A. E. Barnett (*Paul Becomes a Literary Influence* [1941], pp. 182-84), have claimed that both Polycarp and the author of the Pastorals drew from a common source, but this is an unsatisfactory method of dealing with external evidence because it allows the early attestation of any NT book to be summarily dismissed.

After Polycarp the evidence becomes more impressive both in clarity and quantity. It is reasonably certain that Justin Martyr (*Dial.* cxviii), Athenagorus (*Supplicatio* xvi), and Theophilus (*Ad Autolycum* ii.16) all knew and esteemed these letters. In fact, Theophilus took for granted that they came from the divine Word. Irenaeus's testimony is indisputable. By his time the authority of these Epistles was unchallenged; further proof is the MURATORIAN FRAGMENT, which shows that the church of Rome highly esteemed them.

This testimony reveals no early doubts about the authenticity of the Epistles. None of the witnesses mentioned raised any dissenting voice. In fact, there is evidence of only one second-century writer on the NT who rejected them — Marcion (according to Tertullian *Adv. Marc.* v.1, 21), who hardly represents any general ignorance of or rejection of these Epistles in that century. Certain parts of the Pastorals would have been against Marcion's presuppositions (e.g., 1 Tim. 1:8 on the goodness of the law). Moreover, Marcion customarily cut out the biblical books that did not appeal to him, e.g., all the Gospels except Luke, and even those that he accepted he extensively amended.

Scholars have stressed the absence of the Pastorals from the Chester Beatty codex $p^{46}$ as evidence that they were questioned during the 3rd century. The evidence of

A facsimile of Codex Sinaiticus (4th cent. A.D.) showing 1 Tim. 6:9–2 Tim. 1:15 (Trustees of the British Museum)

these papyri, however, is inconclusive. The codex of the Pauline Epistles is incomplete. It has been calculated that the rest of the codex would not have had room for the Pastorals; but the scribe could have reduced the size of his writing toward the end or could have added MS pages — a procedure known in the ancient world — and thus could have included the Pastorals.

It is against such a firm background of acceptance of authenticity and of Pauline authorship that the problem of authorship will be discussed. The next consideration will be the internal claims of the letters.

*B. Internal Claims.* All three of these Epistles purport to come from the apostle Paul, in a manner completely in harmony with the claims of the other Pauline letters. But those who on other grounds have disputed the Pauline authorship have regarded Paul's name as pseudonymous. It should at once be observed that this is the only alternative to taking the claims of the Epistles at their face value. Many pseudonymous works were indeed produced by Jewish and Christian (Gnostic) writers, but epistolary imitations are very difficult and were generally avoided in favor of gospels, acts, and apocalypses. Those who postulate a pseudonymous origin for the Pastorals cannot ignore this factor. Moreover, the self-claims of any literary work should be given some weight unless they can be shown to be historically unlikely or false on other grounds.

In addition to the name of Paul in the opening greetings, each Epistle has many other indications that the author is Paul. The first-person singular is used quite naturally and reflects a personal acquaintance of the author with the person addressed (e.g., 1 Tim. 1:3, 18; 3:14; 5:21; 6:14; 2 Tim. 1:3ff.; 2:9; 3:10ff.; 4:1, 6ff.; Tit. 1:5; 3:8, 12ff.). The presence of other pronounced personal allusions (1 Tim. 1:12ff.; 2:7; 2 Tim. 1:2; 2:10; 4:7) in a manner typical of Paul adds considerable support to the self-claims of the salutation. Even many who have not maintained Pauline authorship have recognized that these reminiscences are strongest in 2 Timothy and have postulated that the Epistle incorporates genuine fragments of Pauline material (see III.C below).

In spite of these internal claims many scholars have challenged Pauline authorship on a number of grounds, which must be weighed carefully. They may conveniently be grouped under five headings.

*1. Historical Background.* The Pastorals contain a group of historical allusions that must be placed in their historical context. The attempt to do so has caused such difficulties that some scholars have declined to regard the allusions as historical at all or have fitted each allusion separately into some known Pauline situation, although recognizing the impossibility of fitting them in as a whole.

The historical data may be summarized as follows. Paul had left Timothy at Ephesus and Titus at Crete to have them carry out certain church arrangements (1 Tim. 1:3; Tit. 1:5). In 1 Timothy Paul indicated that he had moved on to Macedonia; in Tit. 3:12 he spoke of spending the winter at Nicopolis (evidently in Epirus). In 2 Timothy, however, he mentioned that Onesiphorus had sought him out while he was at Rome (1:17) and referred to having left his cloak behind at Troas, apparently rather recently (4:13), and to having left the ill Trophimus at Miletus. Moreover, by the time he wrote 2 Timothy the apostle had become a prisoner, although there is no evidence of this in 1 Timothy and Titus. In fact, in 1 Timothy Paul was looking forward to visiting Timothy at Ephesus soon (3:14).

All these details suggest considerable movement by Paul and his companions. The question naturally arises of how these movements fit the framework of Acts. In spite of a variety of ingenious attempts, it must be recognized that the existing accounts of Paul's journeys do not allow all the data mentioned above to be fitted in with any credible sequence. The main problem is that 2 Timothy must be assigned to a Roman imprisonment but 1 Timothy and Titus to a period when Paul was still engaged in his Asiatic ministry, which according to Acts must have been several years earlier. But if 2 Timothy dates from the close of Paul's Roman imprisonment, it is odd that Paul requested his cloak to be brought from Troas or mentioned leaving Trophimus at Miletus, cities that he would have last visited several years before. Furthermore, Acts never refers to Paul's visiting Crete or Nicopolis, and it is difficult to suggest any occasion within the framework of Acts when these visits could have been made.

What then are the alternatives? If these Epistles are genuinely Pauline there is only one solution possible — that all three were written after Paul's Roman imprisonment recorded in Acts. This solution, however, involves a theory that Paul was released from this imprisonment, enjoyed a further period of freedom, and was then arrested a second time and taken back to Rome, where he suffered execution.

Such a solution, which does not conflict with the known facts, has been challenged on various accounts. The silence of Acts is considered a major objection. The same might be said, however, of the theory that Paul was executed immediately after the house arrest mentioned in that book. Moreover, if Paul's imprisonment had not terminated when Acts was written, its silence on further activity is self-explained. A further criticism of this traditional solution is the character of patristic references to Paul's further activity. Eusebius (*HE* ii.22.1f.) reported it in a way that might suggest disbelief, although he appeared to be commenting on what he had received from others. Much earlier is Clement of Rome's obscure allusion to the apostle Paul's preaching as far as the boundary of the West (1 Clem. 5:7). Whether Clement meant that Paul went to Spain or whether he simply regarded Rome as the boundary, the fact remains that his words do not exclude a period of Paul's further activity in the East, even if they do not testify to it. The release hypothesis, in short, does not depend upon the veracity of the Spanish visit.

Furthermore, it must be investigated whether the apostle's release would have been probable. The evidence from Acts on the charges against Paul suggests that under the normal course of Roman justice the apostle would have been released. But many have assumed that an appeal to so infamous an emperor as NERO may not have resulted in a favorable verdict. Indeed, Nero's persecution of the Christians in Rome beginning in 64 suggests that he would have been poorly disposed toward Paul. Lack of data leaves the whole matter inconclusive, but the release theory is not impossible or improbable.

*2. Ecclesiastical Situation.* Since all these Epistles refer to church officials and to ecclesiastical procedure and discipline, the question arises whether the situation suggested by this evidence could have sufficiently developed during Paul's lifetime. Some scholars have believed that the Epistles reflect a later period, so that Pauline authorship is impossible. To assess the position rightly the character of the internal evidence must first be noted. Three offices are mentioned, bishops, elders, and deacons, but Tit. 1:5-7 shows clearly that the bishops were not altogether distinct from the elders. In fact, the most obvious interpretation of this evidence is that bishops exercised a special function within the elder system and that there were actually two groups of officials, elders and deacons. But such an arrangement does not reveal a particularly developed state of affairs. In the church at Philippi bishops and deacons held office, as the salutation of Paul's letter to that church makes clear. Moreover, the Acts accounts of Paul's appointment of elders, as at Galatia (14:23), and of his direct dealings with elders, as at Ephesus (20:17ff.), suggest that the appointment of elders was part of the procedure within the primitive Church. B. S. Easton (p. 226) has maintained that the ecclesiastical situation is 2nd cent. and has regarded the Acts references as anachronistic, but this is a most unsatisfactory method of disposing of unfavorable data.

But the question arises whether Paul was at all interested in church organization. If he was not, Pauline authorship of the Pastorals would be difficult to maintain. Those, like Easton, who find the ecclesiastical references in these Epistles too highly organized for Paul proceed from certain presuppositions that are themselves open to challenge. It is assumed that Paul's own data must be examined independently of Acts, with the result that the Acts testimony is discounted, as mentioned above, and the testimony of the Pauline Epistles becomes the sole source of information. On such a basis Paul's lack of interest in church order can of course be maintained. But the evidence of Acts cannot be so summarily dismissed, and although the Pauline Epistles certainly do not support uniformity of government in all Pauline churches, they do not necessarily demand the theory of Paul's disinterestedness in church order. The apostle evidently did not believe in rigidity in ecclesiastical matters, but this does not mean that he was not interested in ecclesiastical organization. Evidently both Ephesus and Crete already had an elder system, and Paul was most anxious to ensure that suitable candidates would continue to be appointed. Moreover, he wanted the Christian traditions to be adequately handed down and conceived that a well-chosen elder system was the best means of achieving this. It can hardly be imagined that Paul was so shortsighted that he never envisaged the necessity of such officials.

Another imagined difficulty is the reference to novices being excluded from the candidates eligible for the bishop's office at Ephesus (1 Tim. 3:6). This seems to be an indication of a long-established church and thus seems to require a date well after the apostolic age (cf. E. F. Scott, p. 32). But such an approach fails to account for the circumstances of primitive communities. A large community would have been much more able than a small one to decline the appointment of a novice, and it is significant that this injunction is omitted from the instructions to Titus at Crete (1:7-9), where the church was in all probability more recently founded than the church at Ephesus.

The suggestion that Timothy and Titus are a pseudonymous disguise for bishops of a monarchial type is quite improbable (contra *IB*, XI, 344f.). Such monarchial episcopacy did not develop until the time of Ignatius and was evidently not widespread even then. Moreover, the general indications of the ecclesiastical situation in the Pastorals, e.g., the elementary requirements for candidates for office, suggest a much more primitive period than that reflected in Ignatius's epistles. In any case, there is no explanation why Timothy and Titus should have been chosen as typical representatives of monarchial bishops. It is much more reasonable to regard the letters as actually addressed to the persons named.

*3. Mention of Heresies.* There are many scattered indications in these letters that false teachers were then causing trouble at Ephesus and Crete. Paul had little time for their teaching and urged both Timothy and Titus to deal with them summarily. But does this fact reveal a non-Pauline approach, in view of the apostle's method of refuting heresy actively by presenting the Christian answer? If Paul's treatment of the Colossian heresy was a norm and if his approach to any heresy could not deviate from this norm, then there would be some justification for concluding that the Pastorals do not reflect Pauline practice. But these two assumptions may certainly be challenged. An examination of the heresy referred to in the Pastorals is sufficient to show that Paul is not likely to have combatted a heresy with so little positive content.

The heresy's major feature seems to have been its pointless teaching, which is variously described as myths, endless genealogies (1 Tim. 1:3-7), wordy wrangles, evil surmisings, perverse disputations (6:3-5), and godless chatter (v. 20). These characteristics would not have impressed Paul as being worthy of refutation.

The Pastorals give very little hint of any doctrinal error in the heresy. In fact, the only definite reference is to the denial of the resurrection, and even this seems to have been restricted to two people, Hymenaeus and Philetus (2 Tim. 2:17ff.). Paul further alluded to Hymenaeus and Alexander making shipwreck of their faith (1 Tim. 1:19f.), but he offered no information about the nature of their error. No doubt this was unnecessary, since Timothy would have been well acquainted with these people.

According to Tit. 1:14 the myths were Jewish, which suggests that the false teachers were probably Judaizers. The false teachers desired to teach the law although they lacked understanding of it (1 Tim. 1:7). Paul's exhortation that Titus himself avoid arguments about the law (3:9) may indicate the practice of the false teachers. The practical outworking of this heresy was mainly ascetic, according to 1 Tim. 4:1-5, which predicts abstinence from both marriage and food. Although the future tense is used, traces of this tendency could already have been in evidence.

Nothing in the evidence so far adduced requires a post-Pauline date, although some scholars (e.g., E. J. Goodspeed, *Intro. to the NT* [1937], p. 338) have supposed that second-century Gnosticism was in mind. They have appealed to the reference in 1 Tim. 6:20 to "antitheses," which is known to have been the title of a book by Marcion. But if the supposedly second-century author had Marcionism in mind, he dealt with it most ineffectively. It is more probable that "antitheses" was a current technical term and that Marcion's use of it is no proof of any close connection. It may be concluded that the heresy alluded to in the Pastorals gives no evidence of being postapostolic.

A comparison of this heresy with that at Colossae makes Paul's different approach in the Pastorals unsurprising (*see* COLOSSIANS, EPISTLE TO THE II). Moreover, it is natural that when he addressed his own close companions he did not enter into a detailed refutation. The different character of the heresy and the different recipients of the Pastoral Epistles sufficiently account for Paul's changing the method that he used in Colossians. There is nothing improbable in the apostle's handling of the situation.

*4. Doctrinal Considerations.* Even the most enthusiastic opponents (e.g., P. N. Harrison, pp. 87ff.) of Pauline authorship generally have admitted that the theology of the Pastorals has a Pauline flavor, though these scholars maintain that mixed with the Pauline emphases is much that is non-Pauline. The Pastorals' omission of theological elements important in the other Pauline Epistles illustrate this point. The Pastorals' conception of God is said to differ from the other Epistles. There are some finely expressed descriptions of God, notably 1 Tim. 1:17; 6:15f., which call Him King of the ages, King of kings, and the only Sovereign and characterize Him as invisible and immortal. These descriptions mix Jewish and Hellenistic ideas and are not Paul's usual conception. The well-loved title Father occurs only in the opening salutation of 1 Timothy. Scholars have doubted that Paul could so radically modify his conception of God by the time that he wrote the Pastorals.

On the other hand, any modifications are of emphasis rather than of content; no ascriptions to God definitely contradict Pauline theology. But this is a kind of negative argument that cannot assist one in estimating the Pastorals' theology. From the positive side it can be said that there is much in these letters that portrays the fatherly acts of God even if the title itself is lacking (cf. 1 Tim. 1:1; 2:3; 4:10; Tit. 1:3; 2:10; 3:4, which mention God's redemptive acts). These allusions alone sufficiently show that the God of the Pastorals is certainly not as remote as has been alleged.

Similarly it has been maintained by J. Moffatt (*Intro. to the Literature of the NT* [1915], p. 412) that the Pauline concept of mystic union with Christ is lacking, for although the phrase "in Christ" occurs it describes qualities rather than persons. This objection is not a serious ground for disputing the Pauline authorship of these Epistles, since qualities "in Christ" are unintelligible apart from some mystic union "in Christ" (cf. 2 Tim. 1:1; 3:12; Rom. 6:11, 23; 8:2).

These illustrations suffice to show that basing any argument on characteristic omissions is precarious. It may be surprising that the great doctrine of justification is omitted (although Tit. 3:7 hints at the idea), but Paul must not be expected to have reflected all the facets of his Christian beliefs in letters written to personal friends who would presumably have been thoroughly acquainted with his doctrinal expositions.

Another line of attack is that doctrine in the Pastorals is stereotyped. It had been formulated into creeds that could be passed on by suitably qualified and authorized people. This formulation is described as "the faith," "the deposit," and "sound teaching." It had fixed limits and allowed no creative thinking within its concepts. With such arguments an objector to Pauline authorship like Easton (p. 203) supports his contention that the terms mentioned above conflict with the dynamic approach of Paul.

This challenge appears to be a real difficulty at first sight but is offset by two important considerations. Sometimes in other Epistles Paul referred to a body of doctrine, notably in Rom. 6:17, which mentions a form of doctrine that had been delivered to the readers. Phil. 1:27 refers to "the faith of the gospel," Col. 2:7 to "the faith" in which believers are rooted, and Eph. 4:5 to "one faith," clearly used objectively. The other important consideration is the presumption that Paul would have recognized the necessity for accurately transmitting the body of Christian doctrine. It is surely not strange to suppose that Paul would have had a relatively fixed idea of what he meant by "the deposit" or "the faith," and Timothy and Titus would no doubt have been acquainted with that idea.

But why should Paul suddenly have used the adjective "sound," since he did not use it elsewhere? It would certainly be most appropriate when contrasting the truth with error, which may well be conceived of as a disease (cf. 2 Tim. 2:17, which calls the teaching of Hymenaeus and Philetus "gangrenous").

Some scholars have found a difficulty in the introduction of five passages as "FAITHFUL SAYINGS" (1 Tim. 1:15; 3:1; 4:9; 2 Tim. 2:11; Tit. 3:8) because this phrase may reflect a time when doctrine had been reduced to acceptable sayings (M. Dibelius and H. Conzelmann, p. 9). But it is uncertain when the Christian Church first saw the need for such approved statements, and it is possible that doctrines were formulated in Paul's lifetime. Similarly, the Christian hymn of 1 Tim. 3:16 can be an early formulation, since citations from hymns may occur in the other Pauline Epistles (e.g., Phil. 2:5ff.; Col. 1:15ff.; Eph. 5:14). If the first two of these references are not accepted by all, the third can hardly be disputed as a hymnic fragment in view of its introductory formula and rhythmic form. It is reasonable to suppose that Paul recognized the value of Christian doctrine in set form that could be repeated or sung at gatherings for Christian worship. (*See also* HYMNS IN THE NT.)

*5. Linguistic Considerations.* Opponents of Pauline authorship have always paid considerable attention to linguistic criteria in analyzing literature and especially in comparing two or more works to ascertain common authorship. The major weakness of much of this criticism is that as yet it has no agreed canons of linguistic criticism, which would be a valuable restraint on inaccurate inferences.

The linguistic problem of the Pastorals involves two main branches of study: that of words occurring only in these Epistles among Pauline writings, and that of common prepositions, pronouns, and particles, which are thought to indicate an author's style. A subsidiary consideration is the Pastorals' lack of many characteristic Pauline expressions.

The Pastorals contain 175 words occurring only once in the NT (hapax legomena). Whereas some hapax legomena occur in each Pauline Epistle, the number is much higher in proportion to the letter's length in the Pastorals than in any other Epistle. P. N. Harrison examined this difficulty in detail. He concluded that the Pastorals were quite distinct from the other Epistles attributed to Paul and thus had a different author. The Pastorals contain in addition to hapax legomena 130 words used elsewhere in the NT but not by Paul. This fact is also supposed to support non-Pauline authorship.

Harrison (pp. 36f.) placed even more emphasis on the prepositions, pronouns, and particles (numbering 112) which he considered characteristic of Paul's letters but which are absent from the Pastorals. He pointed out that many of these occur with some frequency and that their absence from the Pastorals should therefore be regarded as significant. Harrison also maintained that since the language of the Pastorals shows kinship with the vocabulary of the Apostolic Fathers and the Apologists, the author belongs to this period and could not have been Paul.

Many have thought that the cumulative evidence denies Pauline authorship of these Epistles. But there are considerations that must be set over against this evidence. Statistical computations of the number of hapax legomena used in the Pastorals and in the other Pauline Epistles undoubtedly demonstrate a difference of vocabulary, but statistics cannot conclusively explain the differences. When the subject matter, purpose, or persons addressed change, new words may be expected. The limited amount of Pauline literature precludes certainty about what kind of language might be expected from Paul in various circumstances. Moreover, Paul's own vocabulary might have enlarged as a result of changing circumstances. Much more Pauline literature would be needed for a satisfactory basis for statistical comparisons. The vocabulary of a person of Paul's intellectual stature must have considerably exceeded the approximately 2400 words used in the existing Epistles.

The problem of the 112 omitted prepositions, pronouns, and particles is lessened when it is realized that other recognized Pauline letters contain very few of them (e.g., Colossians and 2 Thessalonians). Thus the apostle could have written Epistles using very few of what are deemed to be his characteristic words. When the prepositions, pronouns, and particles that do occur in the Pastorals are included in the list, the comparison with the other Epistles is much more favorable (see D. Guthrie, *The Pastoral Epistles and the Mind of Paul*; *Pastoral Epistles*, pp. 212ff., for a fuller discussion of Harrison's linguistic theories).

The attempt to show that the language of the Pastorals is similar to that of the Apostolic Fathers and Apologists is no more successful. Many of the Pastoral hapax legomena that Harrison claimed to find also in these second-century works occur there only once and cannot therefore be cited as representative second-century vocabulary. Moreover, many of them also occur in the LXX, to which Harrison paid little attention. To support his arguments he brought in many second-century secular writers, but it can be shown that most of the words under review also occur in the secular vocabulary of the 1st century. In fact, very few cannot be paralleled in any writings prior to the mid-1st century. Thus the evidence does not demonstrate that the Pastorals' language is 2nd century. There is as much evidence, in fact, for a first-century date.

*C. Alternative Theories.* Those who dispute that Paul wrote the Pastorals have proposed two main theories of authorship. The first theory supposes that some genuine material was incorporated, while the second regards all the material as fiction. For convenience these will be called, respectively, the fragment and fiction theories. The following comments will show that many considerations render these alternative theories far less probable than Pauline authorship.

In addition to these major alternatives, there are modifications of Pauline authorship that maintain authenticity of the original Epistles but not of the extant form. In other words, the Pastorals were edited by one of Paul's associates. F. F. Bruce has suggested that Timothy and Titus themselves edited Pauline material in their possession (*see* PAUL THE APOSTLE II.D). It would be better to suppose that another of Paul's companions had done the editing or perhaps that Paul used an amanuensis. An amanuensis would account for linguistic differences, although it is impossible to know what degree of license the apostle would have allowed his secretary. It is easier to suppose an amanuensis theory for official church epistles than for semipersonal letters. Nevertheless, knowledge of Paul's literary habits is not sufficient to exclude the possibility that many of the peculiarities of these Epistles are due to his secretary.

*1. Fragment Theory.* The fragment theory was evolved to avoid a dilemma. Some parts of the Pastorals sound too genuinely Pauline to be dismissed as unauthentic; consequently their authenticity has been admitted by many who do not regard the Epistles as a whole as Pauline. There have been many different identifications of the so-called genuine fragments. The most widely followed is that of P. N. Harrison (*Expos.T.,* 67 [1955], 80), who isolated Tit. 3:12-15; 2 Tim. 4:9-15, 20, 21a, 22b; and 2 Tim. 1:16-18; 3:10f.; 4:1, 2a, 5b-8, 16-19, 21b-22a on the ground that they lack the linguistic peculiarities of the rest of the Epistles. A careful scrutiny of these "genuine notes" will show, however, that they consist largely of salutations and offer far less opportunity for any observable deviation from the style of the other Epistles than do the didactic portions. Another motive for Harrison's theory is the desire to fit the personal allusions into the context of Acts, which can be done only if they are treated piecemeal.

There are some serious objections to this kind of theory. Extraction of these "genuine notes" tends to be so subjective that a wide variety of theories results. Moreover, a theory like Harrison's creates real difficulties when the methods of compilation are considered. It cannot adequately explain, e.g., the editor's rearrangement of the genuine notes in 2 Tim. 4, or his omission of all genuine fragments from 1 Timothy. The uneven distribution of fragments also lacks satisfactory explanation.

Another problem, clearly more acute for the fragment theory than for any other, is the order in which the three Epistles were written. It is important to analyze the motives for using different quantities of genuine material. Did the writer produce 1 Timothy before 2 Timothy and then decide that some genuine notes would add verisimilitude to his next pseudonymous productions? Or was 2 Timothy with its quantity of genuine notes first published and then the other Epistles issued with decreasing concern for verisimilitude? Either way presents difficulties if not impossibilities.

Since not all personal allusions in these Epistles are included in the "genuine notes," the writer must have invented some. Once admit this, however, and the basis of the fragment theory is much less secure, for suspicion is at once aroused as to why the author could not have invented them all. Such doubts lead to the fiction theory (see C.2 below). Yet another problem for Harrison's theory is accounting for the preservation of the fragments, which appear to have been rather scrappy and not easy to preserve in the form in which they were used. The problem is most acute if the writer gained possession of them in loose pieces, although, if one presupposes that the writer received them in a body, it is also hard to explain how they became so jumbled up in composition.

The fragment theory contains many psychological problems that make it far less credible than is often supposed. For example, the writer must have been a curious mixture of devotedness to Paul and inability to appreciate his theology. He is supposed to have incorporated many echoes of Paul's Epistles and yet to have omitted his most characteristic doctrines. It is surely more credible that Paul himself wrote these letters, in which case the echoes of former Epistles are not surprising.

Another unavoidable problem for the theory of genuine fragments is its need of an adequate motive for their incorporation into letters purporting to be entirely from Paul. It is not enough to appeal to the widespread practice of producing pseudepigrapha and then to assume that such a procedure would have been regarded as almost axiomatic within the Christian Church. No pseudepigraphic parallel is close enough to establish even the probability that the Christian Church would have regarded the publication of letters under the assumed authorship of the apostle Paul as a legitimate procedure. There are only two examples of known epistolary pseudepigrapha in Christian history with any obvious parallels to NT Epistles: the so-called 3 Corinthians incorporated in the Acts of Paul, and the much later Epistle to the Laodiceans. In both cases external evidence is quite sufficient to establish their spurious character, and it is clear that the authors' aims, however well intentioned, were not acceptable to the Church at large. There are certainly no parallels at all to the practice of incorporating genuine notes in pseudepigrapha. If the theory is correct it marks a new religious literary practice, which requires justification. Works with the stamp of orthodoxy would not have needed such a questionable device to establish them. Why then did the author resort to such a practice? Is it credible to suggest that he attributed his letters to Paul out of modesty, because he had drawn his inspiration from Paul's genuine letters and had incorporated genuine Pauline fragments? This modesty explanation of pseudepigraphy has been enthusiastically embraced in recent times (e.g., by B. S. Easton and P. N. Harrison). It has even been suggested that the writer's use of pseudonymity was virtuous, since he would have been dishonest to publish the letters in his own name. But the Christian attitude toward pseudepigraphy assumed in this type of theory is only a hypothesis demanded by the presuppositions of the theories themselves.

*2. Fiction Theory.* The fiction theory, as advocated, e.g., by J. Holtzmann (*Die Pastoralbriefe* [1880]), presents much the same problems, although it may be slightly easier to conceive of a wholehearted literary invention unaided by genuine material. If an author invented whole Epistles, he should have been capable of inventing the so-called genuine fragments. Yet the difficulty that many have found with a fiction theory is that the result in some parts (e.g., 2 Tim. 4) is so realistic as to be improbable. Such a conviction about certain passages implies authenticity of the whole Epistle. Indeed, the strength of support for the fragment theory is a sufficient indication of the difficulties of a fiction theory.

*D. Conclusion*. In spite of the peculiarities of the Pastorals, the maintenance of Pauline authorship presents far fewer difficulties than any of the alternative theories. It must be conceded that the early Church's unquestioned acceptance of these letters as genuinely Pauline is a more certain indication of authorship than modern speculation about what Paul could or could not have written.

*See also* PAUL THE APOSTLE II.D.

***IV. Date.***–If the genuineness of these Epistles is assumed, they need to be dated in the last year or two of the apostle's life, i.e., after his release from his first Roman imprisonment. 1 Timothy and Titus probably belong close together and must be placed within the period of Paul's further activity in the East, while 2 Timothy clearly dates from Paul's final imprisonment, when death appears to have been imminent.

On the other hand, any denial of Pauline authorship leaves few indications for precise dating. Alternative theories date these Epistles from the latter part of the 1st cent. to the middle of the 2nd. The main basis for a second-century date is the claim that the heresies reflected in the Epistles are Gnostic, but if this theory is rejected there is no reason to deny a first-century date. The strength of the arguments for Pauline authorship mentioned above makes A.D. 63-64 the most probable date.

***V. Purpose.***–In 1 Timothy the apostle's exhortations to his faithful helper cover aspects of church order and practice and contain much personal advice, not only about Timothy's own life and behavior but also about the handling of the different groups within the church. In 3:14f. Paul stated clearly why he had written. The letter was to be regarded as a prelude to his proposed visit to Ephesus; in case that visit was delayed the letter would guide Timothy's behavior in the church. Probably Paul had already given much of the material in this letter to Timothy orally, but its written form would have strengthened his position. Paul's urging Timothy to bold action more than once suggests that the latter was either timid by nature or intimidated by reason of his youth.

In writing to Titus Paul had as one of his aims urging Titus to join him at Nicopolis, where he had decided to spend the winter. He gave Titus instructions very similar to Timothy's, although modified to suit the different situation in Crete. An indication that Titus's assignment was tougher than Timothy's is the description of the Cretans in Tit. 1:10-16.

2 Timothy is in effect Paul's farewell letter. It is obvious that he expected his end very soon. He thought of his course as already finished and longed to see Timothy again, although he was apparently uncertain that he could. Even in this final letter he found it necessary to exhort Timothy to exercise courage in the work to which he had been called. The apostle added several personal reminiscences and testimonies that he clearly intended as a spur to the younger man. The many personal allusions in this letter reveal much of the apostle's character; ch. 4 particularly shows his frame of mind as he faced martyrdom.

***VI. Important Topics.***–Because the Pastorals are generally practical in character, many have overlooked their theological content. It may not be as evident as in Paul's other Epistles, but it is nevertheless present.

*A. Christology*. The Pastorals mention both the humanity (1 Tim. 2:5) and the lordship of Christ, although the latter is more dominant. Our Lord's descent from David (2 Tim. 2:8) and His trial before Pilate (1 Tim. 6:13) are referred to, but the interest does not center in the earthly life of Jesus. More than one passage has an exalted conception of lordship, particularly the doxology of 1 Tim. 6:15f. This passage probably applies to the Father, but others clearly ascribe lordship to Christ.

All these Epistles stress Christ's mission as Savior, although it is worth noting that saving is also frequently attributed to God. The divine action in sending Christ to be Savior is most clearly brought out in Tit. 2:11, where salvation is the result of the grace of God and where Paul's reference to its appearing must mean the Incarnation. In 2 Tim. 1:9 salvation and thus Christ's coming are the result of God's mercy initiated according to His own purpose.

The more precise teaching about Christ's saving activity is somewhat more limited. 1 Tim. 2:5 mentions His office as mediator and conceives of His sacrifice as a ransom. This passage is closely linked with the idea of the redemptive activity of Christ that comes into focus in Tit. 2:14. His incarnation brought about the abolition of death (2 Tim. 1:10) through His resurrection (2 Tim. 2:8, 11). Salvation is seen as all-embracing.

Another aspect of Christ in these Epistles is His position as judge. Distinguishing the judgment activity of God from that of Christ is not always easy. This difficulty is seen particularly in 2 Tim. 4:1, which attributes the act of judging to both. Christ alone judges in v. 8, at a time described as "that day."

Allusions in the Pastorals imply the preexistence of Christ. He intentionally came into the world to save sinners (1 Tim. 1:15). He was manifest in the flesh (3:16). Even more clearly does the thought occur in 2 Tim. 1:9, which says that grace was given in Christ before the world began.

The glorification of Christ clearly appears in the christological hymn in 1 Tim. 3:16. His present kingly activity is brought out in the faithful saying in 2 Tim. 2:12 ("if we endure, we shall also reign with him"). Believers will share this glory of Christ, as is evident from Paul's statement in 4:8 that the crown of righteousness is reserved for those who love His appearing. The heavenly kingdom is the apostle's ultimate goal (v. 18).

*B. Man and His Need*. 1 Timothy 4:4 makes evident that man was placed in a good world made by a good Creator, but a number of passages show that man is nevertheless sinful. Paul called himself the chief of sinners (1:15). Christ's having the mission to save (2:4) implies man's need of salvation. 2:14 hints that the origin of this condition is Eve's sin, but the doctrine of original sin is not developed. The three Epistles' numerous references to moral decadence sufficiently prove what kind of creature man becomes in his natural state. Most of the sins specifically mentioned are clearly recognizable as moral perversions.

The powers behind the world of sin are demonic, and Paul saw by the Spirit an increase in such activity (1 Tim. 4:1). In fact, the "last days" are described as perilous times of moral laxity and materialism (2 Tim. 3:1ff.).

***VII. Contents.***

1 Timothy

A. Greeting (1:1f.)
B. Reminiscences (1:3-20)
   1. Timothy is reminded of his task at Ephesus, with special reference to false teachers (1:3-11).
   2. He is reminded of Paul's experience of the gospel in order to reassure him (1:12-17).

3. He is reminded of past prophecies about his vocation and exhorted to carry on spiritual warfare (1:18-20).

C. Regulations for Church Life (2:1–6:2)
   1. Public prayer is to be universal in scope because of God's desire for the salvation of all (2:1-8).
   2. Women must be modest and silent in worship. This instruction appeals to the story of Adam and Eve (2:9-15).
   3. Timothy is instructed how to select qualified bishops and deacons; care is necessary because the Church is God's special concern (3:1-13). Paul introduces a hymn to Christ (3:14-16).
   4. Timothy is told how to combat false teaching and other threats to the Church. Paul offers his personal example (4:1-16).
   5. Timothy is told how to discipline and deal with different groups within the Ephesus church, especially widows (5:1-16). Elders are to be honored according to their work and protected from indiscriminate charges (5:17-20). Timothy must discipline himself as well as others (5:21-25). He is told how to treat slaves of Christian and of non-Christian masters (6:1f.).

D. Concluding Instructions (6:3-21)
   1. Timothy is again told to avoid false teachers (6:3-5).
   2. He is warned about the perils of wealth, since the false teachers are covetous (6:6-10).
   3. He is exhorted to develop spiritual qualities that befit his high calling as a man of God (6:11-16).
   4. He is to charge the rich not to trust in their possessions (6:17-19).
   5. He is again told to guard the deposit of truth and to avoid error and teachers of it (6:20f.).

2 Timothy

A. Greeting (1:1f.)

B. Paul's Thanksgiving for Timothy's Faith and Desire to See Him (1:3-5).

C. Exhortations Based on Experience (1:6-14)
   1. Timothy must kindle his gift into a flame and remember the nature of the Spirit that he received (1:6f.).
   2. Accordingly he must be unashamed in witnessing (1:8).
   3. He has access to God's power and grace (1:8f.).
   4. To encourage him, Timothy is reminded of the shame that Paul has suffered for the sake of his own calling and of Paul's confidence in God (1:10-12).
   5. Timothy should hold fast to the truth by the Spirit's power (1:13f.).

D. Example of Others (1:15–2:1)
   1. The Asiatics, who had deserted Paul, are a warning to Timothy against disloyalty (1:15).
   2. Onesiphorus, an example of Christian affection and help, is a reminder to Timothy to be strong in grace (1:16–2:1).

E. Timothy's Task (2:2-13)
   1. Timothy is to commit the true teaching to those with proven ability to pass it on (2:2).
   2. He is to resolve to endure trials as do the soldier, athlete, and farmer (2:3-6).
   3. He is to draw encouragement from the Gospel and from Paul's own sufferings for it (2:7-10). A faithful saying tells of the recompense for suffering for Christ's sake (2:11-13).

F. Exhortations about False Teachers (2:14–3:9)
   1. Timothy must warn Christians about false teaching and must become an efficient expositor of the truth (2:14f.).
   2. Paul advises the shunning of irrelevant discussions that lead only to disaster, as the case of Hymenaeus and Philetus shows (2:16-19). Timothy should pursue Christian virtues, avoid foolish questions, and deal courteously with opponents to win them for Christ (2:20-26).
   3. Paul warns about the perils to come. He vividly describes those who will arise in the last days and claim to be devout but lack the power of a godly life. Timothy is told to avoid such people if they arise in his lifetime (3:1-9).

G. Further Exhortations Based on Experience (3:10–4:5)
   1. Timothy is reminded of Paul's teaching, his life, and particularly his sufferings (3:10f.).
   2. He is reminded that suffering is the lot of all Christians and that seducers and deceivers will increase rather than decrease (3:12f.).
   3. He is reminded of the value of Scripture in his early training and its continued profitability for his work for God (3:14-16).
   4. He is therefore to fulfil his calling as a preacher of the Word. This will require diligent application at all times, since people will not welcome sound doctrine (4:1-5).

H. Paul's Farewell (4:6-22)
   1. In sacrificial language Paul expresses his readiness to depart (4:6).
   2. He makes a personal confession that his race is run and that the crown of righteousness is already reserved for him and for all who love Christ's appearing (4:7f.).
   3. Paul gives some personal messages (4:9-22).

Titus

A. Lengthy Greeting and Statement of Paul and Titus's Common Faith (1:1-4)

B. Appointment of Officials (1:5-16)
   1. Titus has already been commissioned to appoint elders in Crete (1:5).
   2. He is reminded of the moral and spiritual qualifications required (1:6-9).
   3. He is warned about the opponents whom the elders must refute and about the Cretans' reputation for lying and material gluttony (1:10-16).

C. Christian Behavior (2:1-10)
   1. Titus is to encourage aged people to be soberminded and sound in faith (2:1-3).
   2. Younger people are to be taught self-control, and wives are to concentrate on domestic happiness (2:4-6).
   3. Titus himself is to provide an example in speech and doctrine (2:7f.).
   4. Slaves are to be obedient to masters and dependable in order to further Christian doctrine (2:9f.).

D. Doctrine as a Basis for Behavior (2:11-15)
   1. God's grace is the teacher for Christian living (2:11f.).
   2. Hope for the second advent should give a further impetus (2:13).
   3. The mainspring of purity is the redemptive activity of God (2:14).
   4. These are the things that Titus is called to speak (2:15).

E. Social Responsibilities (3:1-7)
   1. Loyal citizenship, sober behavior, and humility are to be enjoined on all Christians (3:1f.).
   2. There is nevertheless a contrast between Chris-

tianity and its environment. Paul points to what Christians were (3:3) and then to what they have become—heirs of an eternal inheritance—through God's mercy and the renewing of the Holy Spirit (3:4-7).

F. Final Exhortations to Titus (3:8-15)
   1. The value of good works is pressed on him (3:8).
   2. He is to avoid empty arguments with those devoted to vain speculations after at least two attempts to reclaim them have failed (3:9-11).
   3. He is exhorted to join Paul for the winter at Nicopolis when Artemas or Tychicus has arrived to relieve him (3:12).
   4. He is to assist Zenas and Apollos on their journeys (3:13).
   5. He is to see that the Cretans maintain good works (3:14).
   6. Greetings are exchanged and the benediction is pronounced (3:15).

***Bibliography.***–Comms. by C. K. Barrett (1963); J. H. Bernard (*CGT,* 1899); M. Dibelius (*HNT,* 3rd ed. 1937); M. Dibelius and H. Conzelmann (*HNT,* 4th ed. 1966; Eng. tr., *Hermeneia,* 1972); B. S. Easton (1948); R. Falconer (1937); F. Gealy (*IB,* XI, 343-551); D. Guthrie (*Tyndale NT Comms.,* 1957); A. T. Hanson (*NCBC,* 1982); W. Hendriksen (1957); J. Jeremias (*NTD,* 6th ed. 1953); J. N. D. Kelly (*HNTC,* 1964); A. R. C. Leaney (1960); W. Lock (*ICC,* 1924); A. Plummer (*Expos.B.,* 1888); E. F. Scott (*MNT,* 1936); E. K. Simpson (1954); C. Spicq (*EtB,* 1948); R. A. Ward (1974); B. and J. Weiss (7th ed. 1907); N. J. O. White (*Expos.G.T.,* 1910); G. Wohlenberg (3rd ed. 1923).

E. Bertrand, *Essai critique sur l'authenticité des Epîtres Pastorales* (1887); K. Grayston and G. Herdan, *NTS,* 6 (1959), 1-15; D. Guthrie, *The Pastoral Epistles and the Mind of Paul* (1956); A. T. Hanson, *Studies in the Pastoral Epistles* (1968); P. N. Harrison, *Problem of the Pastorals* (1921); F. R. M. Hitchcock, *Expos.T.,* 41 (1930), 20-23; J. D. James, *Genuineness and Authorship of the Pastoral Epistles* (1906); G. W. Knight, *The Faithful Sayings in the Pastoral Epistles* (1968); S. de Lestapis, *L'Énigme des Pastorales de Saint Paul* (1976); B. M. Metzger, *Expos.T.,* 70 (1958), 91-94; W. Michaelis, *Pastoralbriefe und Gefangenschaftsbriefe* (1930); C. F. D. Moule, *BJRL,* 47 (1965), 430-453; F. Torm, *ZNW,* 17 (1918), 225-243; P. Trummer, *Die Paulustradition der Pastoralbriefe* (1978); S. G. Wilson, *Luke and the Pastoral Epistles* (1979).

D. GUTHRIE

**PASTURE; PASTURING** [Heb. *rāʿâ, mirʿeh, marʿîṯ, migrāš, nāwâ, nāweh, dōḇer* (Mic. 2:12), *kar* (Ps. 37:20; 65:12; Isa. 30:23), *nahᵃlōl* (Isa. 7:19); Gk. *nomḗ* (Jn. 10:9)]; AV also FOLD, HABITATION, HOUSE, etc.; NEB also FLOCK, GRAZING GROUND, HERBAGE, etc.

The RSV calls the portions of common land surrounding the Palestinian villages and towns (Heb. *migraš*) "pasture lands" in the records of their allocation to the Israelite tribes (Nu. 35:2ff.; Josh. 14:4; 21:2ff.; etc.) and elsewhere "common land," "open land (space, country)." Such areas were used freely as common grazing ground by the shepherds and herdsmen of the community.

The Heb. *nahᵃlōl* occurs only in Isa. 7:19; it probably means "watering hole" (cf. Arab. *manhal,* "watering place" < *nahila,* "drink"). It would doubtless be marked by the presence of a few bushes (see AV) or low brambles, upon which the invading insects would settle in large numbers.

In Ezekiel's instructions for the allocation of land in connection with his ideal temple, a specific portion of pastureland was to be set aside for the sanctuary (Ezk. 45:4). The devastation of the pastures (cf. Lam. 1:6; Ezk. 25:5) was symbolic of the utter desolation of the land. By contrast, the spiritual prosperity of the saved is indicated in Jn. 10:9 under the figure of rich pasturage.

R. K. H.

**PATARA** pat'ə-rə [Gk. *Patara*] (Acts 21:1). One of the main cities of Lycia, which is the mountainous outcrop of southern Asia Minor between Rhodes and Cyprus, SW of Pamphylia. Strabo described Lycia as "exceedingly well supplied with harbors and inhabited by decent people." The latter point is his way of distinguishing it from its eastern counterpart, Cilicia Tracheia, notorious for piracy. The Lycians always stood in high regard in antiquity because Homer listed them as Trojan allies (*Iliad* ii.876f.). Yet they were not Greek, and the Lycian language long resisted the hellenization that took place during a century of Ptolemaic control. After brief periods of Seleucid and Rhodian administration the cities of Lycia were recognized as independent by Rome and became one of the best known and most unusual examples of republican federalism. As many as twenty-three cities had seats in a representative assembly, one, two, or three, according to their size. Since there were thirty-six cities in Pliny's day and many more are known from their inscriptions, it is assumed that the smaller cities were grouped together for purposes of representation. The system was preserved when Lycia in A.D. 43 was joined with Pamphylia to make a new Roman province.

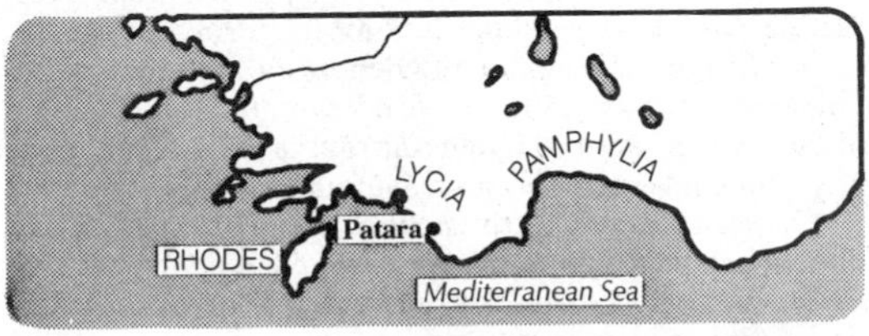


Patara, on the southwest coast facing Rhodes, possessed one of Lycia's best harbors, E of the Xanthus River mouth and protected by a headland with a lighthouse. Paul's party changed ships here, after leaving Rhodes, for the voyage to Tyre. Patara was one of the six members of the confederacy big enough to have three representatives in the assembly, but there is no record of a church in the NT period.

***Bibliography.***–Strabo *Geog.* xiv.3.1-10; *CERP,* pp. 96-110; *RRAM,* pp. 516-539.

E. A. JUDGE

**PATE** [Heb. *qoḏqōḏ*] (Ps. 7:16 [MT 17]); NEB HEAD. The top of the head. "Pate" has been used here by the RSV, AV, and most of the early English versions since Coverdale probably for poetic effect, since it parallels "head" (*rōʾš*). *See* CROWN OF THE HEAD.

**PATH** [Heb. *ʾōraḥ, nᵉṯîḇâ, nāṯîḇ, maʿgāl, mišʿôl* ("narrow path," Nu. 22:24), *šᵉḇîl* (Ps. 77:19 [MT 20]), *mᵉsillâ* (Joel 2:8), *ḥᵃlaqlaq* ("slippery path," Jer. 23:12), *dereḵ* (Jer. 31:9), *tāmaḵ* ("follow the path," Prov. 5:5); Gk. *hódos, tríbos, trochía*]; AV also WAY, LAND (following MT *ʾereṣ* in Ps. 143:10), GOINGS, RANKS (Joel 2:7); NEB also COURSE, WAYSIDE, ROAD, LINE, FOOTPATH, etc. A route of travel; frequently a metaphor for the direction, pattern, or experiences of a person's life.

"Path" occurs in only one OT narrative passage to describe a literal beaten track (Nu. 22:24). Elsewhere it is used only in poetic passages (apart from Gen. 49:17, only in WISDOM literature [Job, Psalms, and Proverbs] and in the Prophets) with various figurative meanings. The most common term, Heb. *ʾōraḥ,* is rendered "path" about thirty times. It can refer figuratively to a land route upon which people can walk (cf. Isa. 41:3; Hos. 2:6 [MT 8]), to the route that fish follow through the sea (Ps. 8:8 [MT 9]), or to the sun's "course" (RSV) through the sky (Ps.

19:5 [MT 6]). Most often, however, it is a metaphor for the course of a person's life. In this sense it often occurs in synonymous parallelism with *derek*, which is usually rendered "way" (e.g., Gen. 49:17; Ps. 27:11; Isa. 30:11; *see* WAY). The two terms are not, however, totally synonymous. That *derek* usually occurs in the singular while *'ōraḥ* appears more often in the plural (cf. Prov. 2:8, 20) suggests that a *derek* may be made up of several *'ᵒrāḥôṯ* (cf. Isa. 3:12, where the RSV renders *derek 'ōrᵉḥōṯeykā* "the course of your paths"; see *TDOT*, III, 281).

In seventeen passages "path" represents the feminine noun *nᵉṯîḇâ* and in four the masculine *nāṯîḇ*. These terms can refer figuratively to a track on the ground (e.g., Job 18:10; 28:7; cf. "bypath," Jer. 18:15) or even to a "wake" produced on the surface of the water (Job 41:32 [MT 24]; Isa. 43:16; cf. *šᵉḇîl*, Ps. 77:19 [MT 20]); but most often, like *'ōraḥ*, they are metaphors for the course that one chooses for one's life, occurring frequently in synonymous parallelism with *derek* (e.g., Job 24:13; Prov. 1:15; 3:17; Isa. 42:16). In ten instances "path" translates *ma'gāl* (possibly < *'ᵃgālâ*, "chariot, cart"; cf. RSV "tracks of thy chariot," Ps. 65:11 [MT 12]). This term also occurs frequently in parallel with *derek* (e.g., Prov. 4:11; cf. v. 26; 5:21; Isa. 59:8) and usually refers to a pattern of behavior that determines a person's destiny (cf. Prov. 2:9, 15, 18; etc.). *Mᵉsillâ*, which generally denotes a built-up road or "highway" (cf. Isa. 40:3), is used figuratively in Joel 2:8 of the course followed by an "army" of locusts (cf. *'ōraḥ* in v. 7).

A person's "path" can variously represent (1) one's direction in life, (2) one's behavior or manner of life, or (3) all that one experiences in the course of one's life. In the first sense, wisdom literature saw only two paths between which every person must choose: the path of obedience to God and the path of disobedience. The wise/righteous seek to conform their lives to the pattern revealed by God in His commandments. Thus the psalmist prays, "Make me to know thy ways, O Lord; teach me thy paths [*'ōrᵉḥōṯ*]" (Ps. 25:4; cf. 17:5; 119:35; Isa. 2:3 par. Mic. 4:2; Isa. 26:8). The paths of such persons are level (Ps. 27:11; 143:10; Prov. 15:19; Isa. 26:7; 42:16) and straight (Prov. 3:6; Jer. 31:9; cf. Wisd. 10:10) and light (Ps. 119:105; Prov. 4:18; Isa. 42:16; cf. Sir. 50:29), whereas the paths of the foolish/wicked — those who forget God (Job 8:13) and turn aside from His revealed will (Isa. 30:11; cf. 3:12; Wisd. 5:7f.; 12:24; Bar. 4:13) — are crooked (Prov. 2:15; Isa. 59:8) and slippery and dark (Jer. 23:12; Prov. 2:13), so that "they do not know over what they stumble" (Prov. 4:19; cf. Job 18:10). Moreover, obedience to God's commandments leads to righteousness (Ps. 23:3; Prov. 2:9; 4:11), justice (Prov. 2:8f.; 8:20), and peace (3:17; Isa. 59:8). Ps. 25:10 confesses, "All the paths of the Lord are steadfast love and faithfulness. . . ." The direction or pattern of life that one chooses will determine one's destiny. The path of wisdom/righteousness leads to life, while the path of error/wickedness leads to death (cf. Ps. 16:11; Prov. 2:18f.; 5:5f.; 7:25; 10:17; 12:28; 15:24). Thus the wisdom teachers warned, "Take heed to the path of your feet, then all your ways will be sure" (4:26).

The OT writers confessed that a person's "paths," in the sense of one's deeds or manner of life, are all known by God (e.g., Ps. 139:3; Prov. 5:21; cf. Job 13:27; 33:11). In some passages "path" seems to refer simply to what one experiences in the course of one's individual life; thus calamity can be depicted as one's path being made impassable (Job 30:13; cf. Hos. 2:6) or being enveloped in darkness (Job 19:8). The psalmist complained of his enemies: "In the path where I walk they have hidden a trap for me" (Ps. 142:3 [MT 4]).

In the RSV NT "path" occurs only in the parable of the sower and in several quotations from the LXX. In Jesus' parable (Mt. 13:4, 19 par. Mk. 4:4, 15; Lk. 8:5, 12) Gk. *hodós* (the usual LXX translation of Heb. *derek*) refers to a footpath along the edge or through the middle of a field. In Palestine sowing preceded plowing; thus the farmer sowed seed on the path that he intended to plow up later (see J. Jeremias, *Parables of Jesus* [Eng. tr., 2nd rev. ed. 1972], pp. 11f.).

"Path" (*hodós*) has a figurative sense in Acts 13:10, which combines the words of the LXX of Prov. 10:9 and Hos. 14:9, and in Rom. 3:16, which quotes from the LXX of Isa. 59:7. He. 12:13 applies the exhortation of Prov. 4:26 to the entire Christian community, urging that "paths" (*trochiaí*) be made straight so that all may finish the race (cf. v. 1). All the Synoptics quote from the LXX of Isa. 40:3 (with a slight change in wording): "Prepare the way [*hodós*] of the Lord, make his paths [*tríboi*] straight" (Mt. 3:3 par. Mk. 1:3; Lk. 3:4). Whereas Isa. 40:3 had poetically depicted the construction of a "highway" (Heb. *mᵉsillâ*) across the desert in preparation for the exiles' exodus from Babylon, the Gospel writers applied this imagery figuratively to John's ministry of preparation for the coming of the Messiah — the true fulfillment of the promised deliverance.

*See also* WALK.

***Bibliography.***–J. L. Crenshaw, *OT Wisdom* (1981), pp. 79f.; J. Muilenburg, *The Way of Israel* (1961), pp. 33-36; *TDNT*, V, *s.v.* ὁδός (W. Michaelis); *TDOT*, III, *s.v.* "derekh" (J. Bergman, A. Haldar, H. Ringgren, K. Koch).

N. J. OPPERWALL

**PATHEUS** pə-thē'əs (1 Esd. 9:23, AV). *See* PETHAHIAH **2.**

**PATHROS** path'ros [Heb. *paṯrôs* < Egyp. *p3-t3-rs[y]*–'the southland'; Gk. *gḗ Pathourēs*]; **PATHRUSIM** path'ro͞o-sēm [Heb. *paṯrusîm*]. A designation of Upper (i.e., southern) Egypt, the Nile Valley area between Memphis (cf. Jer. 44:1), near modern Cairo, and Syene (modern Aswân). It is invariably mentioned together with Egypt in the OT (Jer. 44:15; Ezk. 29:14; 30:14); its plural gentilic, Pathrusim, occurs in the Table of Nations in Gen. 10:14 (= 1 Ch. 1:12). Especially significant is Isa. 11:11, which refers to *miṣrayim* (Lower or northern Egypt), *paṯrôs*, and *kûš* (Nubia) in the same N-S geographical order as the *muṣru-pāturîsu-kûsu* of the somewhat later Assyrian inscriptions of Esarhaddon.

R. F. YOUNGBLOOD

**PATHRUSIM.** *See* PATHROS.

**PATIENCE; PATIENT; PATIENTLY.** In the RSV "patience" is almost always a human disposition. It is tempting to consider patience simply as a virtue to be cultivated, but it is first of all a divine disposition. Indeed, the patience of God frequently serves as the source and pattern for human patience.

*I.* **Makrothymía** ***of God.***–The patience of God is included in the catalog of His attributes that runs through the OT like a refrain, "a God merciful and gracious, slow to anger [Heb. *'erek 'appayim*], and abounding in steadfast love and faithfulness" (Ex. 34:6; cf. Nu. 14:18; Neh. 9:17; Ps. 86:15; 103:8; 145:8; Jer. 15:15; Joel 2:13; Jonah 4:2; Nah. 1:3). The LXX translates Heb. *'erek 'appayim* quite literally as Gk. *makrothymía*, *makrothyméō*, and *makrothýmōs*. Thus a word with little significance in nonbiblical Greek was given a good deal of importance and a new depth in biblical Greek.

God's patience, or slowness to anger, does not dismiss His wrath or give up the claims that are legitimately His (see Nu. 14:18; Nah. 1:3). But His patience delays His wrath, so people ought not to misuse it. His patience allows and calls for repentance (cf. Joel 2:13). The traditional OT confession of God's patience is radically interpreted by Jonah (4:2) to include the whole world, the Ninevites as well as the Israelites.

The NT materials are quite consistent with that pattern of patience. 2 Pet. 3:9 explains the delay of the Day of the Lord as due to God's patience: He "is patient [Gk. *makrothyméō*; RSV "forbearing"] toward you, not wishing that any should perish." Neither God nor the author dismisses the day of wrath and glory; it is delayed so that all might repent.

The parable of the unforgiving servant in Mt. 18:23-35 presupposes this pattern of patience. The lord forbears with his servant (18:26f.) but his entitlement to a "reckoning" (v. 24) is not given up (vv. 32-34). The reference to "anger" (v. 34) shows the influence of the Hebrew expression translated "slow to anger." In this parable the servant misuses his master's patience by refusing to live in the kind of repentance that would cause his relations with others to reflect the Lord's patience (v. 29).

Paul presupposed the same pattern of patience and the same relation between the patience of God and the patience of people in Rom. 2:4, which contrasts the behavior of the judgmental Christians in Rome with the patience of God. Their refusal to be slow to judge and slow to anger presumed upon God's patience. God's wrath against the gentile unrighteousness is not dismissed (1:18-32). But the "judges" neither reflected God's patience nor used it to be led to repentance themselves. Rather, they abused it by judging the gentile Christians harshly and by boasting about their own righteousness. Therefore they presumed "upon the riches of his kindness and forbearance and patience" (2:4) and by their "impenitent heart" stored up wrath for themselves (v. 5).

The pattern of Rom. 9:22 may look different initially. (J. Horst, *TDNT,* IV, 382, denied that God's patience here allows for and intends repentance and conversion.) But the elements of the pattern — the delay (but not the dismissal) of wrath, the possibility of misusing the patience by pretending to have some special claims on God's favor, the possibility of repentance, and the intention of the final conversion of all (11:32) — all are present in the extended argument of chs. 9–11. The implication that Jewish and gentile Christians in Rome should imitate God's patience is always just below the surface.

The Pastoral Epistles contain a quite remarkable sequence of patience. Christ as the agent of God displayed His "perfect patience" (1 Tim. 1:16) in Paul by delaying wrath against the blasphemer and persecutor for the sake of calling him to repentance and missionary service. This patience is an "example," presumably for the communities' dealings with other persecutors who act ignorantly in unbelief. Paul in turn as an agent of Christ became an example of patience (2 Tim. 3:10; cf. 2 Cor. 6:6), and, finally, Timothy was instructed to be "unfailing in patience and in teaching" (2 Tim. 4:2). The chain extended from Christ as God's agent to Paul as Christ's agent and to the young pastor Timothy. Nowhere along the chain are the claims either of God's righteousness or of the unrighteous abandoned. Nowhere is patience reduced to a kind of apathetic tolerance; everywhere anger, wrath, and any final judgment are delayed for the sake of repentance. God's patience, which is also in those whom He engages in His disposition, refuses to dismiss either His righteousness or the unrighteous. It is God's determination to bless a people in and with His righteousness.

*II.* **Makrothymía** *of Mankind.*–God's patience stands behind human patience as its pattern and the first link in a chain. Human patience is not first of all a virtue achieved but a gift received. It is listed among the fruits of the Spirit (Gal. 5:22). It comes when one is strengthened with the power of God (Col. 1:11). But that gift, that empowerment, is also an obligation (Gal. 5:25); thus patience is also listed among those virtues that the Christian is to "put on" (Col. 3:12) and among those that describe "a life worthy of the calling to which you have been called" (Eph. 4:1f.). Christians are exhorted to be patient (1 Thess. 5:14; Jas. 5:7).

In each of these contexts Gk. *makrothymía* is patterned after God's patience, but different aspects of that pattern are emphasized. 1 Cor. 13:4 associates patience with love; it is love that is patient (Gk. *makrothyméō*). (It is worth observing that the predicate adjectives of the English translations of vv. 4f. translate Greek verbs; the works of love rather than the attributes of love are enumerated.) Indeed, "love is patient" is the first thing said about love and one of the most important things that one can say about patience. Patience is also associated with love in Gal. 5:22, the list of the fruit of the Spirit, and in 2 Tim. 3:10, the description of Paul's ministry. In 1 Cor. 13:4; 2 Cor. 6:6 (RSV "forbearance"); Gal. 5:22, Gk. *makrothymía* appears alongside "kindness" (Gk. *chrēstótēs, chrēsteúomai* [1 Cor. 13:4]). It is associated with "lowliness," "meekness," "forbearing one another" (Gk. *tapeinophrosýnē, praýtēs, anechómenoi allḗlōn* [Eph. 4:2; Col. 3:12]). In 1 Thess. 5:14 it stands alongside "admonish the idle, encourage the fainthearted, help the weak." A person whose patience reflects God's patience refuses to dismiss either the righteousness of God or the unrighteous, the idle, the fainthearted, and the weak. Patience delays judgment and anger; it does not repay "evil for evil" (1 Thess. 5:15).

Sometimes because of its associations Gk. *makrothymía* comes very close to the meaning of Gk. *hypomonḗ*. It is linked with "faith" in He. 6:12-15, where Abraham exemplifies one who waits in the confident expectation of the fulfillment of God's promises. In Jas. 5:7-11, a section devoted to the exhortation "be patient," it is associated with Gk. *kakopatheía* and *hypomonḗ,* perseverance and endurance (RSV "suffering" and "steadfastness"). In these places the emphasis falls, as with *hypomonḗ,* on courageous endurance rather than on restraint of anger and retaliation. In James, however, the pattern of divine patience is still operative, for the exhortations about patience include, "Do not grumble, brethren, against one another, that you may not be judged" (Jas. 5:9). The patience of God must not be misused but should rather be an occasion for repentance, which involves being patient with each other.

*III.* **Hypomonḗ.**–Greek *hypomonḗ* is also translated "patience." J. B. Lightfoot (comm. on Colossians and Philemon [rev. ed. 1904], p. 138) suggested that in general the distinction between *hypomonḗ* and *makrothymía* can best be seen in their opposites — respectively, cowardice or despondency, and wrath or revenge. Exceptions are the use of *makrothymía* in Hebrews and James. Unlike *makrothymía, hypomonḗ* was already a firmly established word in nonbiblical Greek. Plato contrasted *hypomeínai,* having courage (to hear out an argument), to *phygeín,* running away (*Theaetetus* 177b). NT use is consistent with such a classical emphasis on courage and is influenced by the sense of *makrothymía* as well as by the model of the afflicted OT saints who put their trust in God. Ps. 37:7, e.g., calls for the saints to "wait patiently" (following Aq. *apokarodokéō,* which suggests Heb. *yāḥal* rather than *ḥûl*) for the action of God against the evil and for the humble poor. (The OT already aligned this disposition with patience in the sense of Gk. *makrothymía,* for Ps. 37:8 instructs, "Refrain from anger and forsake wrath.") In Ps. 40:1 (MT 2) the emphatic Hebrew construction of infinitive absolute and finite verb, Heb. *qawwōh qiwwîṯî*, is translated by the Vulg. *expectans expectavi*; an approximate translation is "I waited waitingly [for someone to help] or the NEB "I waited, waited. . . ." The RSV translation, "I waited patiently," seems best if one remembers that such patience is courageous endurance in expectation of God's action, not apathy or despondency.

Patient endurance of unjust suffering has God's favor (1 Pet. 2:20). In v. 21 *hypomonḗ* comes close to *makrothymía*, for the example of such patient endurance is Christ, who "did not revile in return" and "did not threaten" (v. 23). The book of Revelation reminds communities in the midst of persecution of the gift and responsibility of courageous endurance with expectation (Rev. 1:9; 2:2f., 19; 3:10).

As *makrothymía* is especially related to love, so *hypomonḗ* is especially related to hope. In the context of the cosmic hope of Rom. 8:18-25, Paul declared, "The sufferings of this present time are not worth comparing with the glory that is to be revealed to us" (v. 18). For that glory the creation and the Christian community wait with "eager longing" and "patience" that is courageous endurance with expectation, not apathy or fatalism (vv. 19, 25). *Hypomonḗ* is also associated with hope in 12:12, "Rejoice in your hope, be patient in tribulation." (Cf. 1 Thess. 1:3, the patience [*hypomonḗ*; RSV "steadfastness"] of hope.)

Such patience is, finally, no merely passive waiting. Its expectation bears fruit. It is a courageous persistence in well-doing (Rom. 2:7; Lk. 8:15; and in the apostolic activity of Paul himself, 2 Cor. 12:12).

***IV. Patience in the Wisdom Literature.***–"Patience" has a quite secular sense in the wisdom literature, being advocated because it is prudent, not because one ought to be patient like God. Prov. 25:15 teaches that being patient (*'ōreḵ 'appayim*, lit. "long of nose" or "long to anger") helps one be persuasive. Eccl. 7:8b contrasts the patient (*'ereḵ rû[a]ḥ*, lit. "long of spirit/breath") and the proud. The preceding context (v. 8a) demands that this contrast be relevant to the long and sometimes tedious wait between the beginning of a thing and its end. The end is better than the beginning, and patiently waiting for that end is better than haughtily seizing it prematurely, perhaps by violent means. The prudent person is patient, exercises self-control, and is "not quick to anger" (v. 9).

In Prov. 14:17 the RSV prefers the LXX to the MT. The MT reading, Heb. *yiśśānē'*, contrasts the quick-tempered person who is not hated for his shortness of temper with the devious person who plans and executes revenge coldly and dispassionately and who is hated. The RSV and LXX, like v. 29, compare the short-tempered and the patient person. (The LXX seems to presuppose a text reading *yiśśā'*, a change of one consonant; cf. W. McKane, *Proverbs* [*OTL*, 1970], p. 468.)

In Job 6:11 a quite literal translation would have Job ask, "Why should I prolong [hiphil of *'āraḵ*] my life [*nepeš*]?" (so AV). The RSV quite legitimately takes *nepeš* as the seat of the emotions or passions (cf. H. W. Wolff, *Anthropology of the OT* [Eng. tr. 1974], pp. 15-18) and so translates "Why should I be patient?" The sense of the question in either case is, "What's the point of enduring, of calmly waiting for the end?" The patience called for is courageous endurance with expectation, but Job has lost his spirit and wants only to die (v. 13).

"Patiently" [Gk. *makrothýmōs*] has a quite secular sense of dispassionately holding one's emotive reactions in check in Acts 26:3, where Paul appears before Agrippa.

*See also* FORBEAR.

***Bibliography.***–*TDNT*, IV, *s.v.* μακροθυμία κτλ. (Horst); W. Meikle, *Expos.*, 8th ser., 19 (1920), 219-225; 304-313.

A. D. VERHEY

**PATMOS** pat'məs [Gk. *Patmos*]. A small Greek island of the group Dodecanese, about 45 km. (28 mi.) SSW of Samos in the Aegean Sea, mentioned once in the Bible: "I, John . . . was on the island called Patmos on account of the word of God and the testimony of Jesus" (Rev. 1:9). Revelation is the only NT book whose author stated its place of writing.

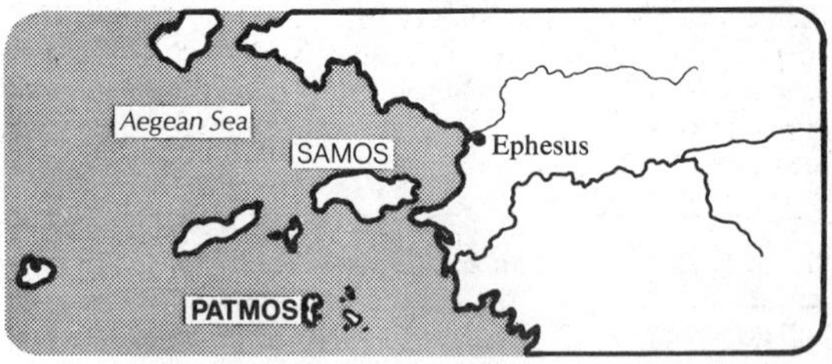


The island is 16 km. (10 mi.) long from north to south and about 10 km. (6 mi.) broad along the northern coast. It is volcanic, rocky, and mostly treeless. The highest point is Mt. Elias, which rises over 250 m. (800 ft.). *See* Plate 61.

In antiquity Thucydides (iii.33) and Strabo (*Geog.* x.5) mention Patmos. It was one of the many places to which Rome banished exiles. According to a tradition preserved by Irenaeus (*Adv. haer.* v.30), Eusebius (*HE* iii.18-20), Jerome (*De vir. ill.* 9), and others, John was exiled there in the 14th year of the reign of Domitian (A.D. 95) and returned to Ephesus on the accession of Nerva (A.D. 96). Traditions concerning John's exploits on Patmos have survived in *Acts of John by Prochorus*, a work attributed to John's scribe but actually composed in the 5th century. The grotto that legend identifies as the site of John's visions is the most venerated of the island's score of shrines and chapels.

The famous monastery of St. John the Theologian was founded by St. Christodoulos in 1088. Nearby is the Patmian Theological School, founded in 1713 and still attended by students from all parts of Greece. Although only part of the once-valuable library in the monastery is left, it contains about three hundred parchment and six hundred paper MSS, chiefly biblical and patristic, and is one of the major collections of Byzantine MSS in Greece.

*See also* JOHN THE APOSTLE; REVELATION, BOOK OF.

***Bibliography.***–V. Guérin, *Description de l'île de Patmos et de l'île de Samos* (1856), pp. 1-120; J. Sakkelion, *Patmiake Bibliotheke* (1890); H. F. Tozer, *Islands of the Aegean* (1890), pp. 178-195; C. Diehl, *Byzantische Zeitschrift*, 1 (1892), 488-525.

I. A. SPARKS

**PATRIARCHS.** The forefathers of the people of Israel. The term can be used in a broad sense, referring, e.g., to David (Acts 2:29), to the list of eleven revered ancestors from Abraham to Daniel (1 Macc. 2:51-60), or even to the ANTEDILUVIAN PATRIARCHS. However, the patriarchs par excellence are Abraham, Isaac, Jacob, and Joseph and his brothers. This article concerns these patriarchs, whose story is presented in Genesis.

I. Structure of the Patriarchal Narratives
II. Theme and Theology of the Patriarchal Narratives
  A. Promise
    1. Blessing
    2. Posterity and Land

B. Covenant
C. Faith and Righteousness
III. Background and Historical Nature of the Patriarchal Narratives
A. Religion
1. God of the Father
2. God as 'El and Yahweh
3. Religious Practices
B. Life-style
C. Date and Historicity

*I. Structure of the Patriarchal Narratives.*–The story of the patriarchs of Israel is set forth in Gen. 12–50. This corpus is structured by the second series of five occurrences of the formula, "These are the generations [descendants or stories] of . . ." (the first five occurrences structure Gen. 1–11), as follows:

| Division | Introducing Narrative | Introducing Genealogy |
|---|---|---|
| The Terah Cycle (Abraham) 11:27 → 25:18 | 11:27 Terah and his story (Abraham) | 25:12 Ishmael and his descendants |
| The Isaac Cycle (Jacob and Esau) 25:19 → 37:1 | 25:19 Isaac and his story (Esau and Jacob) | 36:1, 9 Esau and his descendants |
| The Jacob Story (Joseph) 37:2 → 50:26 | 37:2 Jacob and his story (Joseph) | |

Note how the major divisions that can be discerned on the basis of content are set off by this recurring formula: each of the cycles of patriarchal narratives is introduced as the story of the father of the principal character of that section, viz., the Abraham cycle is introduced as the story of Terah (11:27), the Jacob cycle as the story of Isaac (25:19), and the long narrative about Joseph as the story of Jacob (37:2). This is probably to be explained (at least in the last two cases) by the highly patriarchal nature of Israelite society. Even though the major content of the narrative concerns the sons, it is properly the story of the patriarch becuse he is still alive and functioning as the head of the family; it is *his* story because it is *his* family. It should also be noted how each of the two cycles of stories, the Abraham cycle and the Jacob cycle, closes with a genealogical section (introduced by this formula) that brings to a conclusion the role of the secondary character of that section: Ishmael at the end of the Abraham cycle (25:12-18) and Esau at the end of the Jacob cycle (36:1-43). Finally, this structure reveals the secondary importance of the role of Isaac in the patriarchal traditions, for no separate cycle of stories deals with him. (The division entitled "The Isaac Cycle" deals with Jacob and Esau.)

***II. Theme and Theology of the Patriarchal Narratives.**–A. Promise.* After a transitional passage consisting of an expanded or annotated genealogy, which gives a very few (but nonetheless important) familial facts (11:27-32), the major theme of the patriarchal narratives is given at the very beginning in the call and election of Abraham. Gen. 12:1-3 sets forth the basic elements of the promise to the patriarchs and is of programmatic significance for the nature and purpose of the stories of the patriarchs that follow. Their theme throughout is the progress, the vicissitudes, and the partial fulfillment of those promises that here stand like a rubric at their beginning.

Although numerous elements have been isolated from the various formulations of the promise (see, e.g., Westermann, pp. 132-160), three are prominent in 12:1-3: the promise of blessing (vv. 2f.), the promise of posterity ("a great nation," v. 2), and the promise of land (v. 1).

*1. Blessing.* The theme of God's blessing reverberates through the following narratives. It is sometimes stated independently (e.g., 35:9; 48:3), but most often it is connected with the promises of posterity (17:16, 20f.; 22:17; 26:24; 28:3) and of land (26:3; 28:4). An important corollary of this blessing of God is that through the patriarchal line blessing will come upon humankind in general (12:3; 26:4; 28:14). It is at this point that the patriarchal theme is most closely tied to the universal prehistory of Gen. 1–11, for in the creation ordinances (1:28) and in their restatement after the Flood (9:1) God blesses humankind and commands them to be fruitful and fill the earth.

*2. Posterity and Land.* When the significance of these two great promises in the call of Abraham has been perceived, the point of the narrative flow becomes transparent. Abraham is to become a great nation (12:2), but Sarah is barren (11:30); the land of Canaan belongs to his descendants (12:1, 7), but the Canaanites occupy it (12:6b). Right at the beginning the narrator consciously juxtaposes God's promise and Abraham's circumstances. The whole great promise of innumerable descendants is reduced to the single but staggering question: will Sarah bear Abraham a son? This question is the overarching, all-consuming interest of chs. 12–21. The promise is stated in the most extravagant way: Abraham's descendants are to be as the dust of the earth (13:16), as numerous as the stars in heaven (15:5). Abraham and Sarah, childless, attempt stratagems to fulfill the promise: he adopts a slave born in his own house (15:2f.); Sarah, to protect her position as his wife, provides her maid Hagar as a secondary wife, through which union Ishmael is born (ch. 16). But each of these attempts meets with God's promise of a son through Sarah (15:4; 17:18f.). Finally, when old age makes the promise seem impossible in human terms, "the Lord visited Sarah as he had said" (21:1) and Isaac is born. Even the haunting narrative of the sacrifice of Isaac (ch. 22) relates to the same theme: Abraham is called to an obedience that jeopardizes the promise should he fail, but that, by demanding Isaac's life, also jeopardizes the promise should he carry out his awful instructions.

The Isaac cycle (relating mainly the story of Jacob and Esau), 25:19–37:1, resonates with the same theme. It begins with the account of the birth of Jacob and Esau (25:21-26). Their destiny and story are foreshadowed in two ways; first, by the oracle to Rebekah (v. 23), which reveals that it is two *nations* that struggle in her womb and that the younger shall supplant the elder; second, by the following brief but pregnant account of Esau's sale of his birthright to Jacob (vv. 27-34). Immediately thereafter the specific promises given to Abraham in 12:1-3 are repeated to Isaac in 26:2-5. The long story that follows — the endangering of the ancestress (26:6-11), Jacob's theft of Esau's blessing (ch. 27), the resulting fraternal rivalry that endangers the life of the heir of the promise (27:41-45), the barrenness of Rachel and the rivalry between her and Leah to produce sons for Jacob (29:31–30:24), and especially the specific reaffirmation of the Abrahamic promises to Jacob at Bethel on his way out of the land of promise (28:13-15) and again at the same place on his return (35:9-12) — all these events reveal that the central theme here also is the fulfillment or nonfulfillment of the promises of land and of posterity.

The Jacob story, whose main content is the extended

and carefully constructed narrative of Joseph, is different in form from the Abraham and Jacob cycles of stories but relates to the same theme. It begins immediately with Joseph's dreams (37:5-11), which once again foreshadow the ascendancy of the younger over his elder brothers. The long story that follows relates how these dreams do indeed come true, as Jacob seems to have suspected they would (37:11b). Whatever other lessons it teaches, however, its present meaning expressly relates to the preservation of the expanding people of the promise: it is Joseph himself who knows that God sent him ahead to preserve for his family "a remnant on earth" and "many survivors" (45:5-8), and that, though his brothers intended evil, God meant it for good, to preserve alive many people (50:20).

Thus the patriarchal period is supremely the time of the promise. But it is a promise that is strangely, almost perversely, postponed. The vision may be that of descendants like the dust of the ground (13:16), the stars of the heaven (15:5), or the sand of the sea (22:17), but the reality is Abraham's long vigil for one son, Jacob's long exile for fear of his life, and at the end but seventy people (46:27). The land is to belong to them and their descendants, but they wander like resident aliens (Heb. *gērîm*) through the "land of their sojourning" (Heb. *māgûr*; 17:8; 28:4; 37:1; 47:9), which is owned by the Canaanites (12:6b; 13:7b). The only land they ever possessed was one field for a burial plot (23:17-20) and another for an altar (33:19f.). As Clines observed (p. 46), the experience of Abraham presages the whole patriarchal story, for he arrives in the land (12:5) only to walk straight through it, out the other side, and down into Egypt (12:10). And so, at the end of the patriarchal period, through the beautifully told story of Joseph, the patriarchal family are no longer even sojourners in the land. They have removed to Egypt. Indeed, it is in this way that these narratives are closely tied to what follows, for the promise has not been realized and the goal has not been reached. The fulfillment of the promises of land and of posterity will be realized only by the dramatic events of the Exodus and Conquest that follow, as the text itself frequently sets forth (e.g., Ex. 6:4-8).

*B. Covenant.* The chief means by which God set up and normalized a relationship betwen Himself and the patriarchs was His COVENANT. A covenant is the establishment of a particular relationship or the commitment to a particular course of action, not naturally existing, which is given sanction by an oath normally sworn in a solemn ceremony of ratification.

God's covenant with the patriarchs is established with Abraham in two passages, Gen. 15:7-21 and 17:1-21. In Gen. 15 the covenant is sealed and ratified by God in a solemn and mysterious ceremony in which God places Himself under oath by passing between the halves of sacrificed animals in the awe-inspiring form of a flaming torch and a smoking furnace, ominous symbols also used in magical ritual (see E. Speiser, *Genesis* [*AB*, 1964], pp. 113f.). Here God condescends to place Himself symbolically under a curse (for the demonstration of which see Jer. 34:19-22) in order to affirm to Abraham the certainty of the promises He has made. Although using somewhat different vocabulary and ideas, ch. 17 also sets forth the covenant with Abraham, but it stresses primarily the promise of posterity (17:4-6, while ch. 15 centered on the promise of land), and it adds the requirement of circumcision, the sign of the covenant. It is important to stress that in this covenant it is God who takes the oath. Nothing is required of Abraham (circumcision is the *sign* of the covenant, 17:11). It is in this way that the Abrahamic covenant differs from that with Moses in Ex. 20. In the covenant with Abraham it is *God* who lays Himself under obligation; whereas in the Mosaic covenant it is *Israel,* the recipient of the covenant, which takes the oath and is thereby placed under stringent stipulations.

*C. Faith and Righteousness.* In the stories of Abraham, as we have noted, the promise of innumerable descendants is reduced to the single, absorbing question of one son, the fulfillment of which is singularly postponed while the promise is stated in ever more extravagant terms. Clearly a major point of these stories is Abraham's faith and obedience. This can be seen in the account of his call. The summons to Abraham is radical: he is to abandon all his roots — land, kindred, and immediate family (12:1) — and that for a most uncertain destination, "a land that I will show you" (v. 1). Modern westerners, who live in a mobile society where the bonds of family and family residence are so easily broken, need to recall here that it was very difficult for ancient people, rooted in patriarchal and patrilocal culture, to relocate. So when, after the call, the narrator presents Abrahams's response in terse and utter simplicity ("So Abram went as the Lord told him," v. 4), it is clear that Abraham is presented to us as a model, a paradigm of faith and obedience.

That the text intends to teach about the relationship between faith and righteousness can most clearly be seen in 15:6: "And he [Abraham] put his faith in the Lord and he reckoned it to him as righteousness." The importance of this verse is signalled by the fact that it is not part of the narrative of what happened between God and Abraham (vv. 1-5), but is the narrator's summarizing word that Abraham's righteousness consisted in the fact of his faith in God's promise. If righteousness is conceived, as in modern western society, as conformity to an abstract moral code, this equation is indeed hard to understand. In the Bible, however, righteousness is not a norm prescribing ethics, but faithfulness to a relationship. The righteous person is faithful to the claims of all his or her relationships. Therefore, according to this passage, God judges that a person's righteousness in relation to Him is fullfilled when that relationship is characterized by faith (see Rom. 1:16f.; 4:1-25; Gal. 3:6-9).

***III. Background and Historical Nature of the Patriarchal Narratives.***–*A. Religion.* The narratives of Gen. 12–50 do not provide a complete picture of the religious beliefs and practices of the patriarchs; the purposes of the narratives are theological, dwelling on the divine call and promises and their fulfillment (and nonfulfillment). We can gather enough, however, to give a general description and to set the religion of the patriarchs in its cultural context which archeological discoveries have illuminated. The Bible clearly indicates that Abraham received a polytheistic heritage from his immediate ancestors (Josh. 24:2f.; cf. 24:14; Gen. 31:19-35; 35:2). We cannot in any way trace Abraham's religious experience, for the Bible tells almost nothing about what he once was. But it stresses in a remarkable way the new intervention in human affairs that God's call of Abraham in Gen. 12:1-3 represents. Although he still moved in the religious milieu of his day, as we shall observe, his departure for Canaan at the bidding of God was also a departure from the polytheism of his past into a single-minded devotion to the one God who revealed Himself to him.

*1. God of the Father.* The most important feature of patriarchal religion is revealed by the characteristic identification of the Patriarchal God as the "God of my/your/his father(s)" (31:5, 29; 43:23; 46:23; 50:17; and esp. Ex. 3:6, 13, 15). With this must be connected the frequent formulas that use a proper name, e.g., "the God of Abraham" (Gen. 31:53; cf. 26:24; 28:13; 32:9 [MT 10]), "the God of Isaac" (28:13; cf. 32:9; 46:1), "the God of Nahor" (31:53), and the later and more developed "the God of Abraham, the God of Isaac, and the God of Jacob" (Ex. 3:6, 15). These titles show that the patriarchal God was conceived as the clan's patron deity, to which each patriarch referred by a special name, indicating a close personal tie between the patriarch and his God. This can clearly be seen in Gen. 31:36-54, where Jacob swears by the "Fear of his father, Isaac" (*see* FEAR II.C), and Laban by the "God of Nahor" (31:53f.). Besides the "Fear of Isaac," God is also known as the "the Mighty One of Jacob" (49:24). This "God of the father" terminology has close parallels in the Cappadocian, Mari, and Amarna texts (all 2nd millennium B.C.) as well as less exact parallels in texts from Arabic and Aramean peoples from the later intertestamental and early Christian periods. The early parallels demonstrate that such terminology is appropriate to patriarchal times. A further illustration of the personal and clan relationship between the patriarch and the deity is the appearance of a group of personal names using as divine epithets the terms *'aḇ,* "father," *'aḥ,* "brother," and *'am,* "family, kinsman (on father's side)," e.g., *Abiram/Aḥiram* means "my (divine) father/brother is exalted." These names are abundant also among Israel's Northwest Semitic neighbors, and they become rare both there and in the Bible after the 10th cent. B.C. As J. Bright observed (p. 99), these names illustrate splendidly the patriarchs' keen sense of kinship between clan and deity.

*2. God as 'El and Yahweh.* Another important feature of the patriarchal knowledge of God is revealed by the fact that they worshiped God under a variety of 'El names, i.e., 'El Shaddai (17:1; 27:3; 35:11; 43:14; etc.), 'El 'Elyon (14:18-22), 'El 'Olam (21:33), 'El Ro'i (16:13), and 'El Beth-el (31:13; 35:7). *See* GOD, NAMES OF II.B. The great majority of the patriarchal narratives use either the generic term *'Elohim,* "God," or the personal name *Yahweh* (usually translated "Lord"). But the usual translation of Ex. 6:3 ("I appeared to Abraham, to Isaac, and to Jacob, as God Almighty ['El Shaddai], but by my name the Lord [Yahweh] I did not make myself known to them") seems to teach that the patriarchs knew God as 'El Shaddai, not Yahweh, a name that was revealed only to Moses (Ex. 3:13-15). The frequent use of "Yahweh" in the Genesis narratives has been explained by understanding "name" in the sense of "character" or translating Ex. 6:3 in such a way that it asserts that the patriarchs knew the name of Yahweh.

G. J. Wenham ("The Religion of the Patriarchs," in Millard and Wiseman, pp. 161-195) studied the use of Yahweh in Genesis and observed that in the Joseph story the name Yahweh is restricted to narrative framework, while the dialogues use 'Elohim or 'El Shaddai. Thus the editor held that the patriarchs did not know the name Yahweh though he believed that Yahweh was their God. The Abraham and Jacob cycles, while presenting more ambiguous evidence, can also be interpreted in this manner. In these texts the name Yahweh does occur in the dialogues (although more frequently in the narrative framework), but Wenham showed that it is unnecessary to conclude that the patriarchs knew God as Yahweh, especially given the strong evidence cited above that the patriarchs did not know the name Yahweh. Rather, Wenham posited that the editor of Genesis was so convinced of the identity of Yahweh and the God who revealed Himself to the patriarchs that he not only used "Yahweh" in the narrative but also more sparingly in reporting human and angelic speech, and used great reserve in modifying divine utterances. Sometimes the evidence is quite clear. Thus Hagar is told to name her son "'Ishma*el;* because the Lord [*Yahweh*] has given heed to your affliction. . . .' So she called the name of the Lord [*Yahweh*] who spoke to her, 'Thou art a God of seeing ['*El* Ro'i] . . . '" (16:11, 13). Very suggestive evidence in the same direction are several names of the patriarchs and of tribal leaders from the patriarchal period (Nu. 1–2) compounded with 'El and Shaddai, e.g., Ishmael, Israel, Elizur, Zurishaddai, but none with Yahweh.

Thus the evidence seems very strong that the patriarchs worshiped and knew God as *'El,* which is the generic word for "god" in all the Semitic languages except Ethiopic. Among the Semitic peoples of Syria and Canaan in the patriarchal period, 'El was the preeminent god, head of the pantheon, who presided as king over the divine assembly in the farthest north. He was called "creator of the earth" and "creator of creatures" in Canaanite literature of the period, being represented as wise and kind, the ideal king. It seems very likely that this Canaanite tradition represents the cultural background against which the patriarchs identified as *'El* the God who called them and gave them His promises and His covenant. If so (as R. de Vaux noted, *Early History,* p. 282), it must be stressed that, as the patriarchal narratives and the rest of Israel's religious history reveal, none of 'El's mythological aspects or other characteristics was adopted apart from his identity as the supreme power of the universe. It is also important to note that the name Baal is not mentioned in the patriarchal narratives — not even one name is compounded with that title as the epithet. In the extrabiblical texts Baal rose to prominence late in the patriarchal period and became, as the Bible presents as well, the major figure in the debased fertility religion of Canaan from the period of the Judges onward (see de Vaux, *Early History,* pp. 9f.). It would appear that Baal was so incompatible with the God who revealed Himself to the patriarchs that they totally eschewed the name.

*3. Religious Practices.* The texts give little information about the religious practices of the patriarchs. They built altars (Gen. 12:7f.; 13:18; 26:25; etc.) and offered sacrifice (31:54; 46:1; cf. ch. 22), often at places that already functioned as sacred places among the Canaanites (e.g., 12:7) and that later functioned as important sanctuaries for Israel, such as Shechem, Bethel, Mamre (Hebron), and Beer-sheba. Associated with these sites were sacred stones (*maṣṣēḇôṯ*) (28:18, 22; 31:45; 35:20) and sacred trees (12:6; 13:18; 21:33), cultic objects that later became so identified with the Canaanite fertility religion that they were proscribed (Ex. 34:13; Dt. 7:5; 12:2; Hos. 4:13, etc.). We know very little about the method and cultic nature of patriarchal sacrifice, but it is important to note that, contrary to later Israelite practice, patriarchal sacrifice required no priesthood and was limited to no special place. An important aspect of their religious practice was circumcision, a rite that marked their covenant identity (Gen. 17). They also offered libations (28:18) and engaged in prayer (25:21), often prostrating themselves in the common ancient Near Eastern manner (17:3, 17; 24:52).

Thus, for the patriarchs, God associated Himself with persons, not with places as in Canaanite religious conceptions. The patriarchs clearly conceived God as *one*. Isaac worshiped the God of his father (26:23ff.), as did Jacob (31:5, 42, 53). Thus the same conception was transmitted from generation to generation. This God is unique, without colleagues or consort, and the family of Jacob must put away the strange gods they brought with them from Aram-Naharaim (35:2). Whether we can call this belief monotheism is a debate that is foreign to the OT conception. The patriarchal belief is much more explicit about what it affirms than what it denies, and we should perhaps with H. H. Rowley (*Worship in Ancient Israel* [1967], p. 21) call this a *practical* monotheism.

*B. Life-style.* Another area that has led to considerable discussion and diverse interpretations has been the patriarchal way of life. Since, as has been stressed above, the narratives were written for other than sociological purposes, the information given is limited and incomplete. Briefly summarized the basic data are as follows. The patriarchs were primarily herdsmen, possessing sheep and goats (13:5-7; 30:32ff.; etc.), and cattle as well (15:9; 18:7; 46:32), although cattle figure only in stories from Canaan itself. Whenever animals are mentioned in connection with journeys to or presence in Mesopotamia, only sheep and goats are spoken of (chs. 29–31). The patriarchs moved freely from Canaan to Mesopotamia and back and from encampment to encampment within Canaan (13:3-6; 33:18; 35:6, 16-27). The sons of Jacob traveled with their flocks to Shechem (37:12) and on to the plain of Dothan (v. 17), while their father dwelled at Hebron (35:27). They lived in tents (12:8; 18:1ff.; 31:24-34), and to provide water they dug wells (21:30; 26:15-22). Yet they also cultivated the soil (26:12; 37:6f.), and they regularly settled near towns (20:1ff.; 23:1-20; 33:18). They were very wealthy, possessing flocks and herds, silver and gold, male and female slaves (12:16; 26:13f.), and Abraham could muster 318 trained men to rescue Lot (14:14).

Given these factors, and others more incidental, scholars have interpreted the patriarchal way of life very diversely. Some have proposed that the patriarchs were merchants or caravanners (see, e.g., W. F. Albright, *BASOR,* 163 [Oct. 1961], 36-54). But the most prevalent interpretation has been that the patriarchs were nomads or seminomads. Formerly, the nomadic life-style was generally understood by adopting as a model the sociological patterns of the camel-mounted Arab bedouin of the modern era. Since the 1970's, however, new theories of NOMADISM have been developed by social and cultural anthropologists that seem to provide a hopeful new line of research for patriarchal backgrounds (see Luke; Matthews). Points of contact between the biblical tradition and Mari appear to be numerous and significant (see Dever, pp. 114-17, and esp. de Vaux, pp. 229-233), including: (1) the "dimorphic" society of the villager-pastoralist type (*see* NOMADISM V.A); (2) tribal organization, consisting of interrelated extended families and a patriarchal social structure; (3) cognate technical vocabulary (e.g., Mari *ummatum* = Heb. *'ummâ,* "tribe"; Mari *nawûm* = Heb. *nāwēh,* "pasture"); (4) social and religious customs (e.g., covenant).

Although detailed studies of both the Mari texts and the patriarchal narratives against the background of this new understanding of nomadism in the ancient world wait to be done, these preliminary comparisons strongly suggest that both texts reflect very similar life-styles and that the Mari texts may supply a historical context into which the patriarchal narratives fit very well. Certainly past attempts to dismiss the patriarchal picture as unhistorical on the basis of comparisons with the traditional understanding of nomadism will have to be radically revised.

*C. Date and Historicity.* With the triumph of the Wellhausenian views of literary criticism at the close of the 19th cent., the evaluation of the historical worth of the patriarchal narratives was negative in the extreme; their religious content was viewed as reflecting the beliefs of the period in which they were written, either the early monarchy in the 9th-8th cent. B.C. (J, E) or the postexilic period in the 6th-5th cent. B.C. (P). The patriarchs themselves were regarded as figures of astral mythology, Canaanite deities, heroes drawn from pre-Israelite folklore, or personifications of tribes whose history is reflected in their movements and relationships. Thus they were often accorded no real historical existence. When these views were developed, the history and culture of the 3rd and 2nd millennia B.C. were virtually unknown. Since that time an extraordinary amount of material has thrown light on the period. Dozens of sites have been excavated in Palestine, Syria, and Mesopotamia, while literally thousands of texts from the period have been unearthed (see J. J. Bimson, "Archaeological Data and the Dating of the Patriarchs," in Millard and Wiseman, pp. 53-89). This wealth of material has given us a great deal of knowledge of the history of 2nd millennium B.C., far more than our predecessors could have dreamed possible. The main periods can now be delineated with considerable clarity, particularly in the areas of Mesopotamia and Egypt, where the nature of the writing methods and the climate have enabled numerous texts to survive. Thus we are moving in the area of history (written records), not prehistory. Nonetheless, even in these areas, gaps and uncertainties are numerous.

When we turn to the area of Palestine, we are on much less certain ground. Part of the reason for this is the "accidents" of discovery, of course, but much of it is due to the inherent nature of the physical culture of Palestine itself (see Dever, pp. 74f.). Canaan was always culturally far behind the great centers of civilization, and its position as the land bridge between them meant that it regularly suffered from the depredations of invasion, war, and pillage, which left only sparse and very poorly preserved materials. Also the damp climate has normally prevented the preservation of the usual writing materials of papyrus, parchment, and broken pottery. Thus for the whole period prior to 1000 B.C. we are really dealing with prehistory rather than history. Since almost all of the events of the patriarchal narratives take place within Palestine proper, the above facts make it antecedently very difficult to locate the patriarchs in the stream of contemporary history. Nevertheless, the discoveries mentioned above produced a much more positive assessment of the historical value of the patriarchal narratives (see esp. the treatments by Albright, Bright, Rowley, and de Vaux).

In Germany, however, Albrecht Alt and Martin Noth, among others, espoused a much less positive assessment of the historical worth of Gen. 12–50. While not ignoring the results of archeology, Alt and Noth were primarily interested in the study of the preliterary history of the narratives, and of the oral traditions from which they supposedly emerged; thus they made extensive use of form and redaction criticism. Accordingly, the patriarchs appear as shadowy historical figures who had received divine promises of land and posterity and established cults at sacred altars *outside* Palestine commemorating these events; Noth could find no evidence "for making any definite historical assertions about the time and place, presuppositions and circumstances of the lives of the patriarchs as human beings" (*NHI,* p. 123).

These emphatically different approaches came into open conflict in a series of articles (for a summary see de Vaux, "Hebrew Patriarchs"), resulting in some modification of the two positions. Hence Noth later wrote that "the origins of Israel are rooted in historical conditions that are proved by archeological discoveries to be located in the middle of the 2nd millennium" (*SVT,* 7 [1960], 269). Thus scholars reached a considerable consensus regarding this issue, even though they differed in details about the extent of the historical assertions that could be made and the date of the patriarchs in the general period of the first half of the 2nd millennium B.C.

In the mid-1970's this consensus came under sharp attack. The works of T. L. Thompson and J. Van Seters attempted to show on a number of grounds, both from the literary nature of the material (Van Seters) and from the extrabiblical evidence (Thompson), that the text of Genesis is in no way a historical document (see also Dever, pp. 94f.). Now there is no question that a number of the lines of evidence used by a generation of scholars in support of the consensus noted above have been overstated and on occasion are invalid, and the works just mentioned have performed a valuable service in demonstrating this fact (particularly that of Thompson). But it is a gross overreaction to deny to these narratives any historical value (see J. Goldingay, "The Patriarchs in Scripture and History," in Millard and Wiseman, pp. 1-34). The Bible and extrabiblical texts offer more than sufficient evidence that the narratives' historicity is a warrantable conclusion.

First, both a surface reading and a literary study of the patriarchal narratives reveal their historiographical nature and intent, which are determined by literary and theological motives rooted in the past experience of the community, in historically based traditions. Further, a comparison with other ancient Near Eastern narrative works shows that the patriarchal narratives stand closest in literary type to historically based narratives.

Second, and significant in the light of its correlation with the biblically derived chronology that places the patriachs about 400 years before the Exodus (Gen. 15:13; Ex. 12:40), some evidence suggests that the patriarchal narratives reflect authentically the conditions pertaining in the ancient Near East in the first half of the 2nd millennium. This evidence includes the similarities between patriarchal names and Amorite names, patriarchal life-style and the life-style reflected in the Mari texts (see III.B above), and patriarchal religion and second-millennium Semitic religion (see III.A above). For a more detailed discussion of these points, see LaSor, *et al.*, pp. 98-109; M. J. Selman, "Comparative Customs and the Patriarchal Age," in Millard and Wiseman, pp. 91-139.

Therefore we may conclude that the patriarchs were indeed historical figures. This does not imply that a single person or event in the patriarchal stories has been found in extrabiblical sources — nor is it likely that one of them will be, simply because the patriarchal narratives are family history. The patriarchs themselves were chiefs of pastoral-nomadic clans, whose lives affected the political events of their era not at all.

But if their political impact in their own day was negligible, their religious impact on the world has been momentous. First, Gen. 12–50 says much about the style of life that must characterize the people of God: it is to be a life of trust and faith in and obedience to Him who calls. Second, these chapters present the basic facts of the beginning of redemptive history: God has freely chosen one man and his descendants through whom "all the families of the earth shall be blessed" (12:3), and He solemnly promises them land and posterity. The significance of this redemptive history is set forth in part by its explicit presentation as the answer to the universal problem of human alienation from God and one another through sin set forth in Gen. 1–11. But the fulfillment of these promises and the salvation-history here begun waits for its partial realization in the dramatic events of the deliverance from slavery in the Exodus story and for its final consummation in the Son of Abraham (Mt. 1:1) who draws all men to Him (Jn. 12:32), thus providing the blessing for all the families of the earth promised at the beginning of the patriarchal story.

***Bibliography.***–W. F. Albright, *Biblical Period from Abraham to Ezra* (1963), pp. 1-10; *FSAC*, pp. 236-249; A. Alt, "The God of the Fathers," in *Essays on OT History and Religion* (Eng. tr. 1966), pp. 3-77; J. Bright, *BHI* (3rd ed. 1981), pp. 67-103; D. J. A. Clines, *Theme of the Pentateuch* (*Journal for the Study of the OT, Supp.*, 10, 1978); F. M. Cross, *Canaanite Myth and Hebrew Epic* (1973); W. Dever, "Palestine in the Second Millennium *BCE:* The Archaeological Picture," in J. H. Hayes and J. M. Miller, eds., *Israelite and Judaean History* (1977), pp. 70-120; K. M. Kenyon, *CAH*, 2/1 (3rd ed. 1971), 77-116; W. S. LaSor, D. A. Hubbard, and F. W. Bush, *OT Survey* (1982), pp. 88-116; J. T. Luke, *Journal for the Study of the OT*, 4 (1977), 35-47; V. H. Matthews, *Pastoral Nomadism in the Mari Kingdom ca. 1830-1760 B.C.* (1978); A. R. Millard and D. J. Wiseman, eds., *Essays on the Patriarchal Narratives* (1980); M. Noth, *NHI*, pp. 121-27; H. H. Rowley, *BJRL*, 32 (1949/50), 44-79 (repr. in *Servant of the Lord* [1965], pp. 281-318); M. J. Selman, *Tyndale Bulletin*, 27 (1976), 114-136; T. L. Thompson, *Historicity of the Patriarchal Narratives* (*BZAW*, 133, 1974); J. Van Seters, *Abraham in History and Tradition* (1975); R. de Vaux, *Early History of Israel* (Eng. tr. 1978), pp. 161-287; "The Hebrew Patriarchs and History," in *The Bible and the Ancient Near East* (Eng. tr. 1971), pp. 11-121; C. Westermann, *Promises to the Fathers* (Eng. tr. 1980).

F. W. BUSH

**PATRIARCHS, TESTAMENTS OF THE TWELVE.** *See* APOCALYPTIC LITERATURE III.C.

**PATROBAS** pat'rə-bəs [Gk. *Patrobas*; an abbreviated form of *Patrobios*]. An otherwise unknown member of a household church that included Asyncritus, Phlegon, Hermes, and Hermas (Rom. 16:14). It is also the name of a well-known, influential, and unpopular freedman of Nero who was put to death by Galba (Tacitus *Hist.* i.49; ii.95; Dio Cassius *Hist. Epit.* xliv.3f.; Suetonius *Galba* 20). The Patrobas of Romans may have been a dependent of this person (see F. F. Bruce, *Paul: Apostle of the Heart Set Free* [1977], p. 387).

J. J. HUGHES

**PATROCLUS** pə-trō'kləs [Gk. *Patroklos*]. Father of Nicanor, one of the Syrian generals sent to fight against Judas Maccabeus (2 Macc. 8:9).

**PATROL** [Heb. hithpael of *hālaḵ*] (Zec. 1:10f.; 6:7); AV WALK, "walk to and fro through"; NEB "range through," "range over." The figure is that of a military patrol traversing the earth and reporting to an angel; cf. the similar use of the hithpael of *hālaḵ* in Josh. 18:4, 8 (of Joshua's surveyors); Job 1:7 and 2:2 (of Satan's patrolling the earth [cf. NAB]); Gen. 3:8 and Job 22:14 (of God's "walking").

**PATTERN** [Heb. *taḇnîṯ, mar'eh*; Gk. *týpos, hypotýpōsis, hypódeigma*]; AV also EXAMPLE (He. 8:5), FASHION (Acts 7:44), FORM (2 Tim. 1:13); NEB also COPY (He. 9:23), DESIGN (Ex. 25:9, 40), DETAILED PLAN (2 K. 16:10, OUTLINE (2 Tim. 1:13).

Exodus 25:9, 40 use Heb. *taḇnîṯ*, referring to shape or form, for the pattern that God gave Moses at Sinai for building the tabernacle in the wilderness (cf. the similar use of *taḇnîṯ* for a pattern of a pagan altar in 2 K. 16:10). Nu. 8:4 uses *mar'eh* (a sight, or the appearance of something) for this pattern, which Aaron followed in building the golden lampstand. The NT uses *týpos* ("type," "pattern," "model") in He. 8:5 (quoting Ex. 25:40, LXX); Moses saw a representation of the true tabernacle in heaven (He. 8:2) after which the one on earth was to be modeled. It was made clear that although people would make the tabernacle, God determined its shape and form. Since God would be approached through the tabernacle and its services, the pattern had to be followed in every detail. Any deviation would result in the people's loss of the spiritual truths that a right approach to God would provide. He. 9:23 uses *hypodeígmata* for the "copies" (AV "patterns") of heavenly things in the wilderness tabernacle that as representations of heavenly realities foreshadowed the work of Jesus as the great high priest.

Titus was admonished not only to teach sound doctrine

but also to show himself in every way a "model" (*týpos*; AV "pattern") of good works (Tit. 2:7). The Christians of Crete had the right to expect that their pastor would set them and their pagan neighbors an example by his self-restraint and disciplined Christian living. The probability that Titus himself came from a pagan background enabled him to provide a "flesh-and-blood" example for Christians and pagans alike.

1 Timothy 1:16 sets forth Paul as "foremost of sinners" not only because he had persecuted God and His church but also because he was an "example" (*hypotýpōsis*; AV "pattern") of what God can do with any convert regardless of his past. If God had enough patience and love to forgive a blasphemer and persecutor such as Paul, He can do the same for all those who place no confidence in themselves but submit their will to His desires from day to day. Paul's experience is not the only example of God's perfect patience; rather, in every converted person God displays afresh the pattern that He follows when He reveals His love and patience to sinners. H. E. FAGAL

**PAU** pä. *See* PAI.

**PAUL, APOCALYPSE OF.** *See* APOCRYPHAL APOCALYPSES II.D.

**PAUL THE APOSTLE** [Gk. *Paulos*]; in Acts before his conversion and for some time afterward, SAUL [Gk. *Saulos, Saoul*].

- I. Sources
  - A. Acts of the Apostles
  - B. Pauline Epistles
    - 1. Paul As a Letter Writer
    - 2. Dating the Epistles
  - C. Acts and the Epistles Compared
    - 1. In Reference to Paul Himself
    - 2. In Reference to Paul's Career
- II. Problems in Paul's Epistles
  - A. Group One
    - 1. Galatians
    - 2. Thessalonians
  - B. Group Two
    - 1. Corinthians
    - 2. Philippians
    - 3. Romans
  - C. Group Three
    - 1. Philemon
    - 2. Colossians and Ephesians
  - D. Group Four: Pastoral Epistles
- III. Pauline Corpus
- IV. Paul and Early Christian Preaching and Teaching
- V. Paul and Jesus
- VI. Chronology of Paul's Career
- VII. Life and Ministry of Paul
  - A. Paul the Roman Citizen
  - B. Paul the Pharisee
  - C. Paul Begins to Be a Christian
  - D. Paul and Barnabas
  - E. Paul in Macedonia and Greece
  - F. Paul Completes His Aegean Ministry
  - G. Paul Comes to Rome

***I. Sources.***–The sources of information on the life and teaching of Paul are the Acts of the Apostles and the Pauline Epistles. These provide contemporary views of the apostle from the outside and from the inside, respectively.

*A. Acts of the Apostles.* For the date, authorship, and historical character of this book *see* ACTS OF THE APOSTLES. If the author of Acts was Luke the physician of Syrian Antioch, the portrait of Paul in Acts was drawn by one of his close friends and companions. Paul's complicity in the condemnation and execution of Stephen is mentioned in Acts 7:58 and 8:1a, and his persecution of the Jerusalem church in 8:3. 9:1-30 records his conversion and its immediate aftermath. Then, after an indefinite period of time, 11:25-30 tells of his association with Barnabas as a teacher in the new gentile church of Antioch and of the famine-relief mission to Jerusalem with which the Antiochene church entrusted him and Barnabas. 12:25 relates their return after the accomplishment of that mission. From there to the end of Acts Luke gives little more than a record of Paul's apostolic ministry in Cyprus, Galatia, and the provinces bordering on the Aegean Sea until at last, after two years' imprisonment in Judea, the apostle reached Rome. He spent two more years under house arrest there, still "preaching the kingdom of God and teaching about the Lord Jesus Christ" to all who visited him, without pause or hindrance (28:30f.).

One of Luke's motives in describing Paul's apostolic career up to his arrival in Rome was apologetic; he was concerned to defend Paul (and the Christianity that Paul proclaimed) against charges of disaffection. Thus Acts shows that in Paul's travels throughout the Roman world he usually established good relations with the gentile authorities. At Ephesus he was on friendly terms with the Asiarchs, and the town clerk declared his innocence. In Philippi the magistrates had to eat humble pie for beating and imprisoning him. His Jewish opponents tried to prejudice the minds of the authorities against him but were usually unsuccessful. At Corinth Gallio refused to listen to them. In Palestine Felix and Festus found no basis for their accusations, and Herod Agrippa II was convinced of Paul's innocence. The closing verses of ch. 26 show complete agreement on that point among Festus, Agrippa, Bernice, and their assessors. So marked is this apologetic tendency that some have inferred that Acts (or even Luke-Acts as a whole) was written to supply the information required for Paul's defense before the imperial tribunal in Rome (cf., e.g., M. Aberle, *Theologische Quartalschrift*, 37 [1855], pp. 173ff.; 45[1863], pp. 84ff.); D. Plooij, *Expos.*, 8th series, 8 [1914], 511ff.; 13 [1917], 108ff.; J. I. Still, *St. Paul on Trial* [1923], pp. 84ff.; Duncan, p. 97). A defense, however, can hardly have been the main purpose of the book; the theological motifs, e.g., would then have been irrelevant. The apologetic purpose of Acts was probably wider. There was an intelligent reading public, or rather listening public, at Rome; Luke may have availed himself of the opportunity to rebut in the imperial city itself the popular charges brought against Christianity by insisting on its complete and acknowledged innocence before the law of the empire.

It is plain that throughout Acts Paul is Luke's hero; indeed, the main object of some passages is apparently to show how Paul stands head and shoulders above other men. For example, in the voyage and shipwreck story of ch. 27, Paul stands out as master of the situation at the most critical juncture. But Acts not only reveals the greatness of Paul's character; it also establishes the validity of his apostleship. This tendency of Acts is the more important when one considers how Paul's apostleship was compared disadvantageously with that of the Twelve in several quarters, as the Galatian and Corinthian correspondence testifies. Luke seems therefore to have selected incidents that show how Paul's apostleship was confirmed by the same signs as was Peter's. Peter healed a lame man (3:2ff.), but so did Paul (14:8ff.). Peter's shadow had healing power (5:15), but so had Paul's kerchiefs (19:12). Peter exorcized (5:16), but so did Paul (16:18). Peter had a victorious encounter with a sorcerer (8:18ff.), but so had

Paul (13:6ff.). Peter raised the dead (9:36ff.), but so did Paul (20:9ff.). An objection to Paul's apostolic claim was that it was founded on visions, whereas the Twelve had been personal companions of Jesus "in the days of His flesh." This objection is explicit later in the *Clementine Homilies* (xvii.13), but it is reflected in some passages in the Epistles where Paul vindicated his apostleship (cf. 1 Cor. 9:1; 2 Cor. 12:1). Luke, however, showed that although Paul was commissioned in a vision to go as an apostle to the Gentiles (Acts 22:17-21), it was also in a vision that Peter received his commission to preach to the Gentile Cornelius and his household (10:9ff.).

But Luke's confirmation of Paul's apostleship does not rest on this parallelism between the "Acts of Paul" and the "Acts of Peter." It depends rather on his straightforward account of Paul's apostolic labors and journeys. No one could accept Luke's testimony and doubt the reality of Paul's apostleship.

The measure of Luke's success in his vindication of Paul's apostolic claims was early recognized. Tertullian, e.g., pointed out to the heretics who rejected Acts while accepting the Pauline Epistles that the former is the only independent evidence for the apostolic authority of the latter: "Here let me say to those who reject the *Acts of the Apostles*: 'It is first necessary that you show us who this Paul was, both what he was before he was an apostle, and how he became an apostle' — so very great is the use which they make of him in respect of other questions also" (*De praescr. haer.* 23).

*B. Pauline Epistles. 1. Paul As a Letter Writer.* Of the twenty-seven documents that make up the NT, thirteen are Epistles or letters that name Paul as their author. The majority of these Epistles were written probably before any other NT document; the earliest of them may go back to A.D. 48.

The circumstances of letter writing in the 1st cent. A.D. may illuminate certain aspects of Pauline study — particularly the style and language of his Epistles and their textual history. Even if a form of shorthand was used (such as the *notae Tironianae* of Cicero's secretary), writing was a slow business compared with writing in modern times — although not so slow as O. Roller argued in *Das Formular der paulinischen Briefe* (1933). (On this point see E. Percy's critique of Roller in *Probleme der Kolosser- und Epheserbriefe* [1946], p. 10 n.) J. Jeremias, e.g., surely exaggerated when he said (following Roller), "The composition of a letter of the length of 2 Timothy demanded of the ancient art of writing not hours but days of laborious work" (*Die Pastoralbriefe* [*NTD*, 1953], p. 5).

According to Roller the roughness of the writing material (especially papyrus) and the inadequacy of the reed pens and of the ink all contributed to the difficulty of the procedure. When a letter or even a longer document was dictated, the scribe often took down the gist of it on wax tablets and then composed the fair copy at leisure in his own handwriting and style. The sender sometimes checked it to make sure that it conveyed the sense of what he wished to say and added a few words of greeting in his own hand to certify the authenticity of the document (cf. 1 Cor. 16:21; Gal. 6:11; Col. 4:18; 2 Thess. 3:17).

Paul, it is clear, regularly used amanuenses in his letter writing. Yet for the most part he did not give them the general sense of his communication and leave them free to write it up in the conventional epistolary style. The individual style of most of his Epistles tells its own tale. Paul dictated, and the scribe copied his words verbatim as best he could. The work of copying would not have been so difficult when Paul developed a careful argument in a relatively calm mood; at other times the impetuous torrent of his thought carried him swiftly on, and one can only imagine how the amanuensis fared. Paul's mind ran ahead of his utterance, and the words sometimes seem to have overleaped a gap in order to catch up with his thought.

Usually, one may suppose, one of Paul's friends rather than a professional letter writer acted as his amanuensis. The only amanuensis whose name is given is Tertius, who sent his greetings in the first person in Rom. 16:22. Tertius may have been a professional amanuensis, since Romans is rather more formal than most of Paul's letters; even so, he was evidently a Christian, since he sent his greetings "in the Lord." From the frequency with which Timothy's name is joined with Paul's in the superscription of letters (2 Corinthians; Philippians; Colossians; 1 and 2 Thessalonians; Philemon) it has been conjectured that he commonly acted as the apostle's amanuensis. Indeed, it is a matter of considerable interest that most of the letters in which Timothy's name is thus conjoined with Paul's (Philippians; Colossians; 1 and 2 Thessalonians) are marked off from the other Pauline letters as a distinct group exhibiting one particular sentence-length pattern (W. C. Wake, *HibJ*, 47 [1948-49], 50ff.). It is in features like sentence-length and the use of connective particles that the individuality of the amanuensis is especially likely to appear.

An author writing letters with a view to publication is naturally more careful about their finished style than one whose letters are simply intended to inform, instruct, or greet the recipients. Paul's letters were primarily composed for the people to whom they were addressed, although there is evidence that he intended some to be read by others as well. In either case, Paul's Epistles do not come into the literary category of the epistles of Cicero or Pliny; and yet in Paul's letters the author's personality comes through as clearly as in the classical epistles. Here was a man with something to say, and what he had to say was so much part of himself that there could be nothing artificial or merely conventional about the way that it was expressed.

If a certain letter bearing Paul's name differs stylistically from other letters, the possibility that the amanuensis occasionally exercised a greater measure of stylistic freedom should dictate caution in using this criterion alone to determine the genuineness of such a letter.

*2. Dating the Epistles.* Paul's letters have not come down to modern readers in chronological order. Their present order — beginning with Romans and ending with Philemon — is based on a twofold principle. First, Paul's letters to churches precede those to individuals; second, within these two groups, the letters are arranged in descending order of length, from Romans to 2 Thessalonians in the first group and from 1 Timothy to Philemon in the second. (The main exception to this rule is that Galatians precedes Ephesians, although Ephesians is slightly longer; this exception may be due to an incident in the early history of the Pauline corpus.)

Two kinds of criteria guide scholars in arranging the letters chronologically. One kind is the personal references in some letters that indicate quite clearly to which point in Paul's career they belong. Thus he evidently wrote 1 Thessalonians soon after leaving Thessalonica, either during his stay in Athens or (more probably) shortly after he had settled in Corinth (cf. 1 Thess. 3:1-6 with Acts 17:1–18:5). He clearly wrote 1 Corinthians during his Ephesian ministry (1 Cor. 16:8) and 2 Corinthians shortly after the close of that ministry (2 Cor. 1:8ff.; 2:12f.). Romans was written when Paul was about to set out for his last visit to Jerusalem (Rom. 15:25).

But such definite time indications are not always available. Sometimes, as in Gal. 1:18–2:14, Paul's autobiographical references relate to the past, and it is not clear whether this is the immediate past or the more remote past. At other times his personal notes relate to the present but are not explicit enough to be set unambiguously in the available outline of his life. Thus Paul when writing Philippians, Colossians, Philemon, and Ephesians (the Captivity Epistles) was evidently a prisoner, but it is not immediately obvious to which of his frequent imprisonments (2 Cor. 11:23) these letters may belong.

Where the time indication is an insufficient criterion, scholars must fall back on the more uncertain one of the development of Paul's thought. Here one must be careful not to argue in a circle, determining the development of Paul's thought from the order of his Epistles and determining the order of his Epistles from the development of his thought. But if a definite progression of thought can be established from the Epistles datable by more objective criteria, it can sometimes be used to suggest the probable dates of the other Epistles. Even so, one must beware of assuming anything so simple as "linear progression" when one tries to trace the advancing thought of such a man as Paul.

With this and every other proper proviso, the history of Paul's thought may be considered in relation to two quite different subjects: his eschatological expectation and his conception of the Church as the body of Christ.

*a. Eschatological Expectation.* Along with the other elements in the primitive kerygma, Paul had "received" the belief that Jesus, whose messianic office had been confirmed by His resurrection, would return in due course as divinely appointed judge of the living and the dead (cf. Acts 10:42; 17:31). A favorable verdict in that judgment, Paul held, was assured for those who were justified in the present world by faith in Jesus. At Thessalonica Paul taught his converts to wait for Jesus' return from heaven but used terms that some misunderstood to mean that this event would take place while they were all still alive. Perhaps because of his hasty departure before he had completed the instruction he hoped to give them (Acts 17:10), they did not realize that the resurrection of the just (which would coincide with the Parousia) would include not only the faithful of OT times but also believers in Jesus like themselves if they died before He returned. When Paul wrote to reassure them about those of their number who had died already, he appeared to associate himself with those who would survive until the Parousia: "We who are alive, who are left until the coming of the Lord, shall not precede those who have fallen asleep" (1 Thess. 4:15).

His language in this connection is markedly apocalyptic: the Lord is to be attended at His appearing by all His holy ones (1 Thess. 3:13); He "will descend from heaven with a cry of command, with the archangel's call, and with the sound of the trumpet of God" (4:16); "the dead in Christ will rise first," and living believers will then "be caught up together with them in the clouds to meet the Lord in the air" (v. 17). The apocalyptic note is even more pronounced in the second Epistle: in addition to the apocalyptic pericope in 2 Thess. 2:3ff., which foretells the Lord Jesus' destroying the man of lawlessness "by his appearing and his coming," there is the statement in 1:7ff. that He will be "revealed from heaven with his mighty angels in flaming fire" to execute vengeance on the ungodly and "to be glorified in his saints."

But in all the eschatological content of these two Epistles the dominant note is ethical. Even if the Parousia is near at hand, it must not be used as an excuse for slacking and failing to earn an honest living; still less must it be used for failing to maintain the highest standard of Christian morality. Paul presented the Parousia preeminently as a grand incentive to holiness and sobriety of life.

1 Corinthians, written about four years later than the Thessalonian correspondence, has substantially the same eschatological teaching as 1 Thessalonians, but apocalyptic terminology is not so prominent. It pays more attention to the resurrection of the dead as the harvest of which Christ's resurrection was the firstfruits; Paul's treatment of this topic arose out of the tendency of some members of the Corinthian church to drop the doctrine of resurrection from their creed. On the day of resurrection, he said, a "spiritual body" will be raised, and simultaneously "we shall be changed" — i.e., "we" who have not passed through death shall receive immortal bodies "in a moment, in the twinkling of an eye, at the last trumpet" (1 Cor. 15:52). Here the conception of a "spiritual body" marks a notable advance on current Jewish ideas. Although in this passage Paul still seems to have associated himself with those who will be alive on earth at the Parousia, elsewhere in the same Epistle he associated himself with those who will be raised from the dead then (6:14). Yet, he said, the time would not be long delayed, and this had implications for present family and secular relationships (7:29ff.). When the time comes, Christ will exercise His judicial authority and apportion praise and blame (4:4f.; 5:5), and His people will share His judicial and royal dignity (6:2f.).

Similarly, in Philippians Paul could say "The Lord is at hand" (4:5, which, however, may intend His personal and continual nearness rather than the imminence of His parousia), or, in greater detail, that from heaven "we await a Savior, the Lord Jesus Christ, who will change our lowly body to be like his glorious body, by the power which enables him even to subject all things to himself" (3:20f.). Here certainly too much emphasis should not be placed on his use of "we," for it is plain from other parts of this Epistle that he viewed with equanimity either continued life or early death. While he thought that his prolonged life would be better for his friends and converts, his personal preference was "to depart and be with Christ, for that is far better" (1:23). He did not think of the interval between death and resurrection as a hiatus in his fellowship with Christ.

2 Corinthians 1–9 reveals a further advance. As in 1 Cor. 6:14, Paul associated himself with those who will be raised from the dead (2 Cor. 4:14). But the resurrection principle is already at work in the servants of God; the spiritual body is even now being formed, as the inner man undergoes daily renewal (v. 16), and death will mean (one gathers) the immediate receiving of "our heavenly dwelling, so that by putting it on we may not be found naked" (5:2f.). Possibly the deadly peril in which Paul found himself shortly before the writing of these words (1:8ff.) had led him to consider more urgently than before what the believer's prospects at death would be. To be "away from the body" would mean being "at home with the Lord" (5:8). But it remains true that "we must all appear before the judgment seat of Christ, so that each one may receive good or evil, according to what he has done in the body" (v. 10).

In Romans Paul stressed the inward participation in Christ's risen life that His people experience in the present world, having been baptized into His death and raised with Him to "walk in newness of life" (Rom. 6:3f.). This experience is communicated through the Spirit, whose indwelling presence is the pledge and "first instalment" of full and final resurrection — "the redemption of our bodies" (8:11, 23). Paul still saw the Parousia as the day of judgment and review (2:16; 14:10ff.), of salvation and glory (8:17; 13:11). But he also saw it as the day for which all creation eagerly waits — the day when the universe will be liberated from its bondage to frustration and futility to share "the glorious liberty of the children of God" (8:19ff.).

This cosmic vision prepares one for the teaching of Colossians and Ephesians that Christ is the one in whom God proposes to reconcile the universe to Himself (Col. 1:20) and to consummate its unity (Eph. 1:9f.). Yet at the end of Paul's great period of letter writing, as at its beginning, his main purpose in presenting the Parousia was to let it have its sanctifying effect on the earthly lives of Christians: since they will be manifested in glory with Christ, their true life, when He appears (Col. 3:4), they must in the present world reject what is unworthy of that prospect and pursue what befits it (cf. Eph. 4:1).

Along with this progression in Paul's thought about the last things, some scholars have recognized in Colossians and Ephesians a growing appreciation of the positive worth of family relationships. This is specially obvious in Paul's treatment of marriage. Having made all due allowances for varying conditions of context and life-setting, one finds an unmistakable difference in tone between 1 Cor. 7:1-8, 26-38 and Col. 3:18f.; moreover, Eph. 5:22ff. treats the married state as a divinely designed analogy of the relation between Christ and the Church.

Paul's eschatological thinking, then, gives some reason for dating Philippians — or at least Phil. 3:2–4:9 — along with the Corinthian correspondence, but Colossians and Ephesians appreciably later.

*b. The Body of Christ.* An even stronger argument for dating Colossians and Ephesians some time after the Corinthian and Roman Epistles is the apparent progression in Paul's conception of the Church as the body of Christ.

The common life of Christians is first likened to the interdependent functioning of the various parts of a body in 1 Cor. 12:12ff., where the head is one member among others, and an individual member of the Church is compared to the head or to a part of the head — an ear or an eye. Rom. 12:4f. similarly compares the mutual and cooperative responsibilities of church members to the diverse functions performed by the different parts of the body as they work together for the health and efficiency of the whole. But in Col. 1:18; 2:19; Eph. 1:23; 4:12ff.; etc. Paul thought rather of the relationship that the Church as the body of Christ bears to Him as the head. Here comparing an ordinary member of the Church to the head or to part of the head is impossible; here, too, the body ceases to be a mere simile and becomes the most effective term that the apostle can find to express the vital bond uniting the life of the people of Christ with His own risen life. It is uncertain whether this was a spontaneous and inevitable advance in Paul's thinking about the relation between Christ and His people, or the datum of a further revelation, or the result of some special stimulus. The form of his teaching on the subject in Colossians likely reflects his vigorous reaction to the Colossian heresy. But it is very difficult to think of Paul writing in these terms to Colossae about the same time that he wrote his successive letters to the Corinthians and before he wrote to the Romans.

It has, indeed, been suggested that Romans in substance is earlier than the date implied by its personal references, and that its composition may have been spread out over a considerable time (cf. G. S. Duncan, *Expos.T.*, 67 [1955-56], 164). No doubt the main argument of Romans is the product of long experience and reflection, but its actual form belongs to the beginning of A.D. 57, and it appears to have had special relevance to the situation in the Roman Church at that time.

The cosmic significance of Christ and the Church is not absent from other Epistles (e.g., 1 Cor. 8:6; Rom. 8:19ff.), but Colossians and Ephesians present a more developed exposition of it. Paul's thinking in this realm may again have been stimulated by the necessity of giving the Christian answer to the cosmic speculations of the Colossian heresy. In any case, it is difficult to suppose that Paul's fuller statement in these two Epistles of the cosmic implications of the gospel belongs to the same period as the more inchoate adumbrations in 1 Corinthians and Romans. While these two aspects of Paul's thought have limited value for dating his Epistles, since they leave a number of chronological questions unanswered, they do suggest that the following grouping of the Epistles be adopted as a working arrangement.

| | |
|---|---|
| **Group One** | |
| Galatians | Written from Syrian Antioch, A.D. 48 (?) |
| 1 Thessalonians | Written from Corinth, A.D. 50 |
| 2 Thessalonians | Written from Corinth, A.D. 50 |
| **Group Two** | |
| 1 Corinthians | Written from Ephesus, A.D. 55 |
| Philippians 3:2–4:9 | Written from Ephesus, A.D. 55 (?) |
| 2 Corinthians | Written from Macedonia, A.D. 56 |
| Romans | Written from Corinth, A.D. 57 |
| **Group Three** | |
| Philippians 1:1–3:1; 4:10-23 | Written from Rome, A.D. 60/61 |
| Colossians | Written from Rome, A.D. 60/61 (?) |
| Philemon | Written from Rome, A.D. 60/61 (?) |
| Ephesians | Written from Rome, A.D. 60/61 (?) |
| **Group Four** | |
| Titus | Written from Ephesus, after A.D. 62 (?) |
| 1 Timothy | Written from Macedonia, after A.D. 62 (?) |
| 2 Timothy | Written from Rome, A.D. 65 (?) |

*C. Acts and the Epistles Compared. 1. In Reference to Paul Himself.* The nineteenth-century Tübingen School of NT historical criticism (represented by F. C. Baur, A. Schwegler, and E. Zeller) found the presentation of Paul in Acts to be radically inconsistent with that in the four Pauline letters whose authenticity they acknowledged (Romans, Galatians, 1 and 2 Corinthians). Reading these four letters in the light of the Hegelian dialectic interpretation of history, with its pattern of thesis, antithesis, and synthesis, these scholars recognized in Acts the synthesis, the latest stage, that belonged to the latter half of the 2nd century. The thesis and antithesis were represented by Peter and Paul, who violently opposed one another, Paul advocating complete liberty from the Jewish law, Peter insisting on its continued observance by gentile believers as well as by Jews. Obviously, if this interpretation of history is true, then Acts must be unhistorical; but the picture of events in these four Pauline Epistles must then be equally unhistorical. While in Galatians Paul insisted that he had received the gospel and his commission to preach it directly from God, through no human mediation, in 1 Cor. 15:11 he equally insisted that the gospel he preached was essentially the same as that preached by the original apostles. This is implied even in Galatians, the Epistle that seemed to lend most color to the Tübingen thesis. When Peter, John, and James gave Paul and Barnabas the right hand of fellowship (Gal. 2:9), there was no hint of any difference in the substance of the preaching; the only difference related to the constituencies each group was to serve. Paul pronounced a solemn and repeated anathema on any who preached a different gospel from that which he preached (Gal. 1:8f.), but he never implied that the Jerusalem apostles were liable to his anathema.

The picture of Peter in Galatians accords well with that in Acts, and both differ from the fictitious Peter of Tübingen imagination. According to Gal. 2:11ff. Peter's personal conviction, like Paul's, was that no distinction should be made, even socially, between Jewish and gentile believers. In Antioch, "before certain people came from James, he ate with the Gentiles; but when they came, he withdrew and separated himself" — not because he had changed his convictions, but "fearing those of the circumcision." What had previously convinced Peter the orthodox Jew that there was nothing wrong in eating with Gentiles? The explanation is in Acts 10, which relates how he had learned not to call common what God had cleansed. Peter's action at Antioch was a lapse from his better judgment and practice.

Besides maintaining that the writer of Acts had made Peter too Pauline, the Tübingen critics also insisted that he had made Paul too Petrine in his attempt to reconcile the irreconcilable. They found in Acts the Paul who accepted the decisions of the Apostolic Council, circumcised Timothy, and undertook to perform a rite in the temple to calm those who were alarmed at rumors of his rejection of all ritual obligations. This Paul was, to them, far removed from the uncompromising controversialist of Galatians. Is the Paul of Acts really the Paul of the Epistles? In Galatians one must remember that Paul was dealing in white-hot urgency with a situation threatening the very foundations of the gospel. For the Paul of the Epistles outward acts in themselves are neither good nor bad; only the intention makes them so. The truly emancipated person is not in bondage to his liberty. If he wishes for certain proper purposes to perform a ritual act not sinful in itself he will do so, not as under an obligation, but freely. If meat offered to idols is set before him, and there is no risk of causing offense to others by eating it, he will eat it and give God thanks; to him an idol is nothing. If expediency demanded that a half-Jew be circumcised for his greater usefulness in the gospel, Paul would circumcise him; in such a case circumcision was simply a minor surgical operation performed for a practical purpose. But narrower minds will never grasp the difference between doing such things freely and doing them as religious obligations with a view to securing divine favor. To them Paul's behavior appears as rank inconsistency. So it appeared to his Judaizing and other opponents in his own day; so it has appeared to many biblical critics in more recent times, and they have therefore dubbed Acts unhistorical. An apostle must not be inconsistent! But the consistency that some expect from Paul is the "foolish consistency" that Emerson in his *Essay on Self-Reliance* called "the hobgoblin of little minds, adored by little statesmen and philosophers and divines." "This charge of lack of consistency is a delight to men of limited intelligence, who desire someone whom they can understand, and will always say exactly what they expect of him. As they cannot find such a man in Paul, his utterances often appear to them to be illogical. But this is not because he is really inconsistent, for no one held to great principles more consistently, but because of his exceptional breadth of view, and his power of seeing that there is more than one side to every question" (Foakes Jackson, p. 15).

On the foundation principles of Christianity Paul was uncompromising; where these were not affected he was the most adaptable of persons. He circumcised Timothy but solemnly warned the Galatian Christians against the practice because they were being taught to regard it as necessary to complete their salvation. Such an attitude would bind them to the rites and ceremonies from which Christ had made them free. But even in Galatians Paul insisted that circumcision in itself is unimportant (5:6); only when performed as a religious act does it carry with it the obligation to do the whole law. Cf. 1 Cor. 7:18f., where he evidently meant that converted Jews like himself need not cease to observe ancestral customs (cf. Acts 21:21, 24).

Similarly, one who ate meat offered to idols and was aware of the idol might violate his conscience in so doing; Paul said that he should therefore refrain. But one to whom the meat was just a piece of meat like any other and to whom the idol meant nothing at all might eat freely, although the grace of Christ would lead him to refrain if another's conscience might be injured by his action (1 Cor. 8). Paul himself endeavored to be in Jerusalem for various festivals and associated himself with purificatory rites; yet he challenged the Galatians: "You observe days and months and seasons and years" (Gal. 4:10). The difference lay in the intention; their action would lose them the very liberty of which Paul availed himself. Paul's attitude to such matters is given in Rom. 14:5f.: "One man regards one day above another; another judges every day alike. Let every man be fully persuaded in his own mind. He who regards the day, regards it unto the Lord; and he who eats, eats unto the Lord, for he thanks God; and he who does not eat, unto the Lord he does not eat, and thanks God."

In his attitude to the Jews the Paul of Acts is also the Paul of the Epistles. The Paul who repeated in Rom. 1:16; 2:9f., "To the Jew first, and also the Greek," is the Paul who in Acts visited the synagogues first, in city after city, and who in Pisidian Antioch declared to the hostile Jews: "It was necessary that the word of God should be spoken to you first." The Paul who suffered so much from Jewish hostility in Acts is the Paul who spoke so severely of the Jews in 1 Thess. 2:15ff. But at the same time the Paul who in Acts persisted to the end of the narrative in pressing the claims of Christ upon his brethren according to the flesh despite their opposition is the Paul who in Rom. 9:2f. told of his great sorrow and unceasing anguish of heart at their refusal to receive the gospel and was willing himself to be accursed, if only his heart's desire and prayer to God for their salvation might be accomplished.

It may be surprising at first that the apostle to the Gentiles preached to Jews at all, in view of the demarcation agreement of Gal. 2:9. But in his evangelization of the gentile lands Paul could have scarcely made a point of excluding Jews from his gospel preaching. Since in so many cities the gentile "God-fearers" who attended the Jewish synagogue provided Paul with his point of contact with the gentile population and formed the nucleus of the local church that he formed, he inevitably preached to Jews as well as to Gentiles. The demarcation of Gal. 2:9 may have been intended geographically and not in a strict racial sense; the Jerusalem apostles were not forbidden to evangelize Gentiles residing in Judea.

The Paul who in Acts 9:15 was the Lord's "chosen vessel" to bear His name before the Gentiles in the Epistles claimed to have been divinely set apart, even from birth, for this very purpose (Rom. 1:1ff.; Gal. 1:15f.). The Paul who in Acts labored with his hands in Corinth and Ephesus and bade the Ephesian elders learn a lesson from him in this respect (Acts 18:3; 20:34) in the Epistles showed

House on a wall in Damascus. From such a place Paul was lowered in a basket (Acts 9:25) (W. S. LaSor)

the same example and taught the same lesson to the Thessalonians and Corinthians (1 Thess. 2:9; 2 Thess. 3:8; 1 Cor. 9:18; 2 Cor. 11:7). The Paul who in Acts adapted so readily to Jew and Gentile, learned and unlearned, Areopagus and Sanhedrin, synagogue audience and city mob, Roman governor and King Agrippa, is the Paul who said in 1 Cor. 9:19ff., "Though I am free from all, I have made myself the slave of all, that I might win the more. To the Jews I was as a Jew, that I might win the Jews; to those under the law, as under the law (not being myself under the law), that I might win those under law; to those without law, as without law (not being without law toward God, but under the law of Christ), that I might win those without law; to the weak I was weak, that I might win the weak; I have become all things to all men, that by all means I might save some."

Luke in narrating Paul's apostolic ministry summarized several of the apostle's speeches. Of these the most important are his synagogue address in Pisidian Antioch (Acts 13:16-41), his speech before the Athenian Areopagus (17:22-31), his farewell exhortation to the elders of the Ephesian church (20:18-35), his defense before the unruly crowd in the outer court of the Jerusalem temple (22:1-21), and his later defense before the younger Agrippa at Caesarea (26:2-29). These speeches provide a little more material for comparing the Paul of Acts with the Paul of the Epistles. The first two are sample addresses to Jewish and gentile audiences, respectively (on the latter see VII.E below); the last two are apologetic, addressed also to non-Christian audiences. The only Pauline speech in Acts addressed to Christians — the farewell speech to the Ephesian elders — might be expected to have closer affinities to his Epistles than the other speeches have, and this is what one finds. So abundant, indeed, are the parallels between this speech and the whole range of Pauline Epistles, that the speech might be explained as a cento compiled from the Epistles, were it not that the author of Acts elsewhere shows no sign of dependence on the Epistles and almost certainly did not know them.

*2. In Reference to Paul's Career.* Since the Pauline Epistles do not appear to have served as source material for the narrative of Acts, they provide independent information on a number of crucial issues that arise in Luke's account of Paul's career. Conversely, some Epistles can be read with greater understanding against the background that Luke supplies; e.g., his narratives of Paul's evangelization of Thessalonica (Acts 17:1-9) and Corinth (18:1-18) supply helpful introductions to the Thessalonian and Corinthian Epistles.

Here and there in his Epistles Paul made an autobiographical digression that illuminates something left obscure in Acts. Thus the Epistles tell even more clearly than Acts that the central element in his conversion experience was the risen Christ's actual *appearance* to him (1 Cor. 15:8; 9:1). The account of his persecuting zeal in Gal. 1:13ff. tallies well with Acts. In the Epistles and Acts alike his conversion and earliest Christian activity are associated with Damascus, although Galatians includes reference to a stay in Arabia (1:17). In 2 Cor. 11:32f. his escape from Damascus in a basket is told as in Acts 9:24f., but while Acts says that the Damascene Jews watched the city gates to catch him, Paul said that the ethnarch of the Nabatean King Aretas did so (cf. VII.C below). Whereas Acts says that his first postconversion visit to Jerusalem took place "when many days had passed" (9:23), Paul said more precisely that it was "after three years" (Gal.

1:18). Whereas Acts says that Barnabas "brought him to the apostles" (9:27), Paul said (Gal. 1:18f.) that the only apostles whom he met on that occasion were Peter and James the brother of Jesus; he added that his visit lasted fifteen days, which he spent with Peter. His statement "I was still not known by sight to the churches of Christ in Judea" (Gal. 1:21) is less easy to square with Acts 9:28f. Paul's statement that he went from Jerusalem "into the regions of Syria and Cilicia" (Gal. 1:21) agrees with the evidence of Acts 9:30 that he was shipped home to Tarsus (the information that he was a native of Tarsus comes from Acts). The autobiographical narrative of Galatians suggests further that Paul was engaged in missionary activity among Gentiles even before he joined Barnabas at Antioch. The latter episode is recorded only in Acts (11:25ff.) but is supported by the appearance in the Epistles of Paul and Barnabas as colleagues (cf. Gal. 2:1; 1 Cor. 9:6).

The next incident to which Paul made autobiographical reference is his Jerusalem visit of Gal. 2:1ff. However this visit should be dated (see VII.D below), Galatians gives valuable information about a conference not recorded in Acts, at which the Jerusalem "pillars" agreed that Paul and Barnabas should continue their gentile ministry while they would concentrate on apostolic witness to the Jews.

The account of the controversy during Peter's visit to Antioch (Gal. 2:11ff.) has no parallel in Acts, although it may be linked with the arrival of Judaizers from Judea (Acts 15:1). Acts, moreover, never relates that Paul had to face a situation like that with which he dealt in Galatians. The silence of Acts on such matters is no doubt bound up with Luke's purpose and plan; but despite all his information on the rise and progress of early Christianity, scholars' knowledge of the field covered by Acts would have serious gaps were it not for the firsthand information in Paul's Epistles.

Similarly, Acts does not detail the tensions to which the Corinthian correspondence bears witness. One might well wish that this correspondence had been preserved entirely — not only all Paul's letters to the Corinthians but also their letter to him (cf. 1 Cor. 7:1). As it is, the surviving correspondence gives a vivid impression of the war that Paul had to conduct against legalists and libertines simultaneously (see VII.E below).

Paul's references to Apollos in 1 Corinthians are illuminated by the short account of him in Acts 18:24-28.

Paul's Ephesian ministry of nearly three years is sketched briefly in Acts 19; only a few outstanding incidents are detailed (principally the riot in the theater). The Epistles written in that period throw further light on Paul's words to the elders of Ephesus in Acts 20:19, where he reminded them of his tears and the trials that befell him "through the plots of the Jews"; these letters also ease one's sense of surprise at his forecast in 20:29f. that after his departure his converts would be exposed to invasion by "fierce wolves" and to seduction by false teachers within. On the problem of Paul's special perils during his Ephesian ministry (cf. 1 Cor. 15:30-32; 2 Cor. 1:8-11; 11:23-29) see VII.F below. Paul's summary of hazards in 2 Cor. 11:23ff. shows how incomplete is extant information about his apostolic ministry.

The Epistles also make evident that Paul was greatly concerned at this time about the collection that he was organizing in his gentile churches as a gift and token of fellowship for the Jerusalem church. 1 Cor. 16:1ff. first mentions it, in terms suggesting that the Corinthians had already been informed about it. Paul had also instructed the churches of Galatia about it (1 Cor. 16:1), probably when he had returned that way from his flying visit to Palestine in A.D. 52 (Acts 18:23). He reverted to the subject in 2 Cor. 8:1ff., where (writing in Macedonia) he stimulated his Corinthian readers by telling them of his boast to his Macedonian friends that "Achaia has been ready since last year" (9:2) and by describing how zealously the Macedonian Christians despite their poverty had begged for the favor of sharing in this good work. By the time that he wrote Romans the collection of the money was almost complete, and he revealed something of its importance for him (Rom. 15:25ff.). He was not sure if it would achieve its purpose and be "acceptable to the saints" in Jerusalem; he asked the Roman Christians to pray that this might be so and that he might be "delivered from the unbelievers in Judea" (15:31). The necessity of this last prayer is clear from Acts 21–26.

But Acts says hardly anything about the collection, although the references to it in the Epistles explain a few points in Luke's narrative. (1) Why did Paul resolve, after passing through Macedonia and Achaia, to visit Jerusalem before Rome (Acts 19:21)? He wished to see the collection safely delivered. (2) Why did so many gentile Christians accompany Paul on his last journey to Jerusalem (Acts 20:4)? They were delegates from the contributing churches (cf. 1 Cor. 16:3f.). (3) What were the "alms and offerings" that Paul told Felix he had brought to his nation (Acts 24:17)? They were the contributions of the gentile churches. Luke's reticence about the collection may have an apologetic motive; perhaps the collection itself was an item in the indictment of Paul, being represented by his prosecutors as a diversion of money that ought to have been paid into the temple fund at Jerusalem.

Many interesting points about "undesigned coincidences" between Acts and the Pauline Epistles were made by W. Paley in *Horae Paulinae* (1st ed. 1790).

***II. Problems in Paul's Epistles.***–The tentative chronological grouping of Paul's Epistles suggested above (I.B.2) raises a number of problems that call for brief ventilation; they are dealt with more fully in the articles on the individual Epistles.

*A. Group One. 1. Galatians.* Placing Galatians in Group One as the earliest of Paul's extant letters has the obvious disadvantage of detaching it from the Pauline letter to which it has the closest affinity — Romans. Yet the main outline of Paul's understanding of the gospel as expressed in both these Epistles may well have taken definite shape within a short time from his conversion. Galatians even on the earlier dating did not precede Romans by more than nine years.

The early dating of Galatians, to a time shortly after Paul's return to Syrian Antioch (Acts 14:27), is bound up with the following theses. (1) Gal. 1:2 addresses the churches of Pisidian Antioch, Iconium, Lystra, and Derbe, which Paul and Barnabas planted on their first missionary journey in Asia Minor; (2) Paul's statement in Gal. 4:13 that he had preached the gospel to them "at first" (i.e., the first time or the former time) alluded to his journey from Pisidian Antioch to Derbe via Iconium and Lystra (Acts 13:14–14:21a). The implied second visit had immediately followed the first, for Paul and Barnabas, having reached the frontier between Roman Galatia and the kingdom of Antiochus, retraced their steps and revisited the churches that they had so lately founded (Acts 14:21b-23). (3) The Council of Jerusalem (Acts 15) had not yet met; otherwise Paul could scarcely have failed to mention its decision in confirmation of his argument in Galatians. (4) Paul's Jerusalem visits of Gal. 1:18; 2:1 correspond respectively to those of Acts 9:26; 11:30.

All these theses can be contested, but the arguments against them are no more conclusive than the arguments in their support. A more serious argument against the early dating of Galatians is that of C. H. Buck, Jr. (*JBL*, 70 [1951], 113ff.). Buck maintained that Galatians, which uses both the "flesh/spirit" antithesis and the "works/faith" antithesis, must be later than 2 Cor. 1–9, which uses only the former antithesis. If Paul had formulated the "works/faith" antithesis before he wrote 2 Cor. 1–9, Buck continued, he could scarcely have avoided using it at least once in these chapters, since they have a "vehement anti-legal position." The situation of 2 Cor. 1–9, however, is not on the same footing as that of Galatians and does not call for the "works/faith" antithesis. Another anti-legal antithesis found in 2 Cor. 1–9 is letter/Spirit (3:6f.), which reappears in Romans (2:9; 7:6), but is absent from Galatians despite that letter's "vehement anti-legal position."

*2. Thessalonians.* On the Thessalonian correspondence, see the discussion above. Despite all the difficulty of relating the second Epistle satisfactorily to the first, alternative suggestions to the Pauline authorship of 2 Thessalonians raise more problems than they solve. The same is probably true of the hypothesis that 1 Thessalonians was written after 2 Thessalonians (cf. T. W. Manson, *Studies in the Gospels and Epistles* [1962], pp. 259ff.).

*B. Group Two. 1. Corinthians.* The problems presented by Paul's Corinthian correspondence illustrate the difficulties under which the collection of his letters was first undertaken.

The first Epistle appears to be intact. But it was not the first letter that Paul sent to the Corinthian church; another, mentioned in 1 Cor. 5:9, apparently preceded it. It is unlikely that Paul was using the "epistolary aorist" in this verse; he was probably referring to an earlier letter dealing particularly with sexual morality. This earlier letter may be designated A; it must be regarded as lost. The view that a fragment of it is embedded in 2 Cor. 6:14–7:1 is not only bibliographically improbable but open to the objection that these verses do not deal with the specific subject of A.

The extant 1 Corinthians may be designated B. It was sent to Corinth from Ephesus (1 Cor. 16:8), possibly by the hand of Timothy (4:17; cf. 16:10f.).

2 Corinthians again refers to a previous letter — a severe one from Paul to the Corinthian Christians that cost him much pain as he wrote it and that, once it had left his hands, he regretted having sent, lest his readers suffer too much pain when they received it. In it he presented them with something in the nature of an ultimatum, testing their obedience by demanding disciplinary action against a certain member of their church. The letter's effect, however, was so unexpectedly good that it brought about a complete reconciliation between Paul and the whole Corinthian church, in which a strong opposition to his leadership had been growing (cf. 2 Cor. 2:3-11; 7:8ff.).

1 Corinthians lacks the features ascribed to the severe letter and can hardly be identified with it. The person against whom the severe letter demanded disciplinary action is probably not the incestuous man whose excommunication is enjoined in 1 Cor. 5:13. The severe letter was more probably a distinct document, written between 1 Corinthians and 2 Corinthians, and may be designated C, in which case 2 Corinthians may be designated D.

But, according to some scholars, C may not be totally lost. There is a marked break in argument and temperament between 2 Cor. 9 and 10; the note of gladness and reconciliation apparent up to the end of ch. 9 suddenly gives way to sharp remonstrance and almost violent defense of Paul's apostleship. Several features of 2 Cor. 10–13 correspond to what can be gathered about the severe letter from references to it in chs. 1–9. It is not surprising that many commentators have concluded that chs. 10–13 represent the end of C, while chs. 1–9 (with the possible exception of 6:14–7:1, sometimes, though improbably, identified with A) contain the bulk of D (whose ending has somehow been lost). (Cf. the exposition of this view in J. H. Kennedy, *Second and Third Epistles to the Corinthians* [1900]; for the unity of 2 Corinthians cf. comms. by J. Denney [*Expos.B.*, 1894]; A. Menzies [1912]; P. E. Hughes [*NICNT*, 1962].)

Even if 2 Cor. 10–13 represents C, it can represent only part of it, for these chapters say nothing about the strong disciplinary action that the severe letter demanded (2:5ff.; 7:12). It can be argued more convincingly that chs. 10–13, far from being part of a letter antedating chs. 1–9, is part of an even later letter; this is an unavoidable conclusion if (as is probable) 12:18 refers back to the mission of Titus announced in 8:6ff. This later letter would have to be designated E, and C regarded as completely lost.

However that may be, why should 2 Corinthians have come down to us in this disorganized state? One suggestion is that the church of Corinth, *ca.* A.D. 96, had its interest revived in the letters that Paul had written to it forty years before by receiving a letter from Clement of Rome. Seeing how a leader in the church of Rome valued one of Paul's letters to Corinth (Clement invoked the authority of 1 Corinthians in his expostulation with the Corinthians), the leaders of the Corinthian church may have set themselves to retrieve all they could of the remains of Paul's correspondence with their predecessors. These remains were mutilated by that time, but they pieced the fragments together to the best of their ability, putting what was obviously the opening salutation of a letter at the beginning and what was obviously the concluding greeting at the end. Thus they produced 2 Corinthians, which is actually a combination of D and at least one other letter. But all this is highly speculative.

*2. Philippians.* Philippians (or part of it) is placed in Group Two along with 1 and 2 Corinthians on the ground that it most probably dates from Paul's Ephesian ministry. Some scholars (e.g., G. S. Duncan) have assigned all the Captivity Epistles to the Ephesian period, and others (e.g., C. H. Dodd) to Paul's Roman captivity — not to mention those (e.g., E. Lohmeyer) who have assigned them to his two years' custody in Caesarea. Still others have separated Philippians in date and place from Ephesians, Colossians, and Philemon. Of this last group, some (e.g., P. N. Harrison) have preferred a Roman dating for Philippians while admitting an Ephesian setting for the others; some (e.g., C. J. Cadoux) have dated Philippians in the Ephesian period but Ephesians, Colossians, and Philemon in the Roman period.

That Philippians is a Captivity Epistle is clear: "It has become known," said Paul, "throughout the whole praetorium that my imprisonment is for Christ" (Phil. 1:13). It seems certain that he was imprisoned at the place from which he wrote. If (with RV and RSV) one takes "praetorium" to mean the "praetorian guard," one must think of Rome (cf. AV "in all the palace"); but elsewhere in the NT the word denotes the headquarters of a Roman governor appointed by the emperor, with military forces under his command. No instance can be adduced of the use of "praetorium" for the headquarters of a senatorial province like Asia, as opposed to an imperial province. (Advocates of a Caesarean provenience can, of course, point to Acts 23:35, which expressly says that Paul was kept under guard "in Herod's praetorium" at Caesarea, the seat of government of the imperial province of Judea.) The Christians "of Caesar's household" (Phil. 4:22) were not necessarily attached to the imperial palace in Rome; the civil service of the empire was staffed by freedmen of the emperor, and such *Caesariani* were to be found in many provinces. Timothy's planned visit to Philippi (Phil.

PAUL THE APOSTLE

2:19) could have been associated with Paul's sending him and Erastus from Ephesus to Macedonia (Acts 19:22). The "true yokefellow" of Phil. 4:3 could have been Luke, who appears to have been in Philippi during Paul's Corinthian and Ephesian ministries — if this is a sound inference from the closing of the first "we" section of Acts in Philippi (Acts 16:17) and the opening of the second one there (20:5f.).

On the other hand, the description of Paul's environment in Phil. 1:12-18 (quite apart from the mention of the "praetorium") suits Rome better than any rival location. In favor of a Roman provenience, moreover, certain similarities in language between Philippians and 2 Timothy are adduced, as though the possibility of Paul's life being poured out as a libation (Phil. 2:17) had become a certainty by 2 Tim. 4:6a, and his desire to be released (Phil. 1:23) was on the point of being fulfilled by 2 Tim. 4:6b. Those who have denied that this section of 2 Timothy might itself be of Ephesian provenience have urged that in Ephesus Paul must have had a chance of appealing to Caesar, whereas 2 Timothy suggests no such loophole of hope. But if Paul was somehow involved in the troubles accompanying the assassination of M. Junius Silanus proconsul of Asia in A.D. 54 (cf. VII.F below), an appeal to Caesar would have increased his danger.

Although there is no explicit evidence for Paul's imprisonment in Ephesus, his claim at the end of his Ephesian ministry to have endured "far more imprisonments" than his traducers (2 Cor. 11:23) shows that he must have been imprisoned on many more occasions than the one recorded in Acts 16:23ff.

The terms in which he acknowledged the gift from the Philippians (Phil. 4:10ff.) suggest that the interval since their last gift to him was long. But Paul makes it plain that no negligence is attributed to them: "you had no opportunity," he says (4:10). Perhaps it was Paul himself who deprived them of any opportunity. More than once, immediately after his first leaving Philippi, the church there sent him gifts (4:15). But Paul soon learned that, if he accepted material aid for himself from his converts, this was taken by others as evidence of a mercenary spirit. Hence he requested his converts not to send money for his personal use, and this request was reinforced when he began to organize the relief fund for Jerusalem. He was anxious that all available gifts from his churches should be channeled into that fund. But by the time of his Roman imprisonment the fund had been closed and the money taken to Jerusalem. Paul's changed circumstances may have moved the Philippians to judge that "now at length" it would be opportune to send him a gift. Even so, its delivery was delayed because of the illness of their messenger, Epaphroditus (cf. C. O. Buchanan, *EQ*, 36 [1964], 157ff.).

The eschatological criterion, which has been considered in I.B.2.a above, indicates that the perspective of Phil. 3:2–4:9 is rather close to that of 1 Corinthians.

Most of Philippians is devoted to friendly encouragement. Little in the Philippian church required correction, apart from some personal friction among its members. Hence ch. 2 contains a general exhortation to likemindedness that is reinforced by the example of Christ's self-denial (vv. 6-11 may be an early Christian hymn on the humiliation and exaltation of the Servant of the Lord), and 4:2 specifically exhorts Euodia and Syntyche to "agree in the Lord." But 3:2-21 introduces a note so unlike the rest of the Epistle that these verses have sometimes been regarded as part of a separate letter. Indeed, if the bibliographical improbability involved in such a hypothesis can be surmounted, there is much to be said for regarding 3:2–4:9 as part of a separate letter dating from Paul's Ephesian period, and for setting the rest of Philippians in the context of the Roman imprisonment.

The people against whom he put the church on guard in Phil. 3:2ff. were not necessarily at Philippi then, but a warning was in order because their visits to other churches of his had resulted in trouble and controversy. They evidently included Judaizers of the class dealt with in Galatians but also, at the opposite extreme, exponents of "Christian" libertinism (v. 19). The vigor of Paul's language in v. 2 (cf. Gal. 5:12) might suggest that if one accepts C. H. Dodd's theory of a psychological watershed in Paul's Christian life (dated in the latter part of his Ephesian ministry), Philippians comes before rather than after it. Certainly his tone is milder toward those who "preach Christ from envy and rivalry" in 1:15ff.; it is not necessary to identify these rival preachers with the "dogs," "evil-workers," and "mutilators of the flesh" of 3:2. The group of 1:15ff. may be compared to those who fostered party spirit at Corinth (1 Cor. 1:12), but Paul would probably not have admitted that the people of Phil. 3:2 were preaching the gospel at all. That "those who mutilate the flesh" (3:2) were not his straightforward Jewish opponents but rather Judaizing Christians trying to undermine his apostolic authority seems plain (1) from the consideration that the Philippian Christians would have required little warning against Jewish opponents of Christianity, and (2) from his following caution about "confidence in the flesh." The parallel with his self-vindication in 2 Cor. 11:16ff. is obvious, and the language of Phil. 3:2ff. may very well reflect the apostle's state of mind at that time.

*3. Romans.* Romans can be dated rather easily; it was sent to Rome in anticipation of Paul's projected visit there (cf. Acts 19:21), on the eve of his setting out for Judea with the gentile churches' contributions for the Jerusalem church. It is thus an "occasional" letter in that it was written to prepare the Christians of Rome for his visit; on the other hand, it is less of an occasional letter than most of his other Epistles, for its main argument — an exposition of the gospel as Paul understood and proclaimed it — is not directed to a particular situation in the church addressed. Because of its general character, the letter was apparently judged suitable for circulation among other churches, with the omission of the personal greetings of ch. 16 (which the closing doxology's position at the end of ch. 15 in $p^{46}$ suggests; an even shorter recension of the Epistle, which omits chs. 15–16, is probably Marcionite in origin).

*C. Group Three.* This group comprises the later Captivity Epistles — Philemon, Colossians, and Ephesians. It has been suggested already (see I.B.2.b above) that the development in Colossians and Ephesians of the conception that the Church is the body of Christ accords better with a later (Roman) dating than with an earlier dating.

*1. Philemon.* Philemon manifestly has the same date as Colossians (cf. Col. 4:9). The argument that Onesimus, running away from his master in the Lycus Valley, would have more likely hidden in the nearest big city, Ephesus, than in distant Rome can be countered by the equally probable argument that he may well have thought distant Rome a safer hiding place than Ephesus. Paul's request to Philemon to prepare a guest room for him (Philem. 22) because he hoped to be released and to pay him a visit is also intelligible on either hypothesis.

It is unclear how Onesimus communicated with Paul. But Paul's delicately insinuated hope in writing to Onesimus's master Philemon was that Onesimus would be sent back to continue the personal service that Paul valued so highly. The very survival of the letter is strong evidence that Paul had his way. Moreover, its inclusion in the Pauline corpus has been taken, especially by J. Knox (*Philemon among the Letters of Paul* [1935]), as evidence that Onesimus himself had a hand in the compilation of the corpus.

*2. Colossians and Ephesians.* Paul wrote Colossians after learning from Epaphras that the church of Colossae was in danger of accepting a Jewish-Hellenistic syncretistic teaching that was willing to accommodate some Christian elements. In his reaction to this "specious make-believe" (as he called it) Paul developed beyond its previous point his presentation of the cosmic role of Christ and the gospel. The "principalities and powers," which played a decisive part in the "Colossian heresy," were inferior to Christ (1) because they owed their existence to Him, the agent in creation, and (2) because they were vanquished by Him when they tried to overwhelm Him on the cross.

The doctrine of the cosmic Christ was not new to Paul. He and his fellow Christians believed in "one Lord Jesus Christ, through whom are all things and through whom we exist" (1 Cor. 8:6); this Christ was "the power of God and the wisdom of God" (1:24). God through the Spirit had imparted to His people that hidden wisdom, "decreed before the ages for our glorification," through ignorance of which the superhuman world rulers had "crucified the Lord of glory" and thus compassed their own doom (2:6-10). The liberation that Christ procured by His death was not restricted to mankind but would ultimately be displayed in its cosmic outreaching (Rom. 8:19-22). But what these and other Epistles hint at is expounded more fully and systematically in Colossians and Ephesians.

Justification by faith, although fundamental to Paul's thinking, does not exhaust his message. The Reformation inevitably paid special attention to the principle by which the individual soul is accepted as righteous in God's sight. But it is regrettable that a tendency developed among Protestant theologians to equate Paulinism so absolutely with the emphasis of Galatians and Romans that the corporate and cosmic insights of Colossians and Ephesians were considered non-Pauline. There is room in true Paulinism — and in true Christianity — for both these emphases.

The difference in vocabulary that has been detected between these two Epistles and their predecessors may be due in part to Paul's employing the technical terms of a controverted system of thought to confute it. An apologist to the Gentiles, Paul was a pioneer in meeting opponents on their own ground and adapting their language to Christian use in order to show that the problems to which an answer was vainly sought elsewhere found their satisfying solution in the gospel.

It has been suggested above (I.B.2.b) that in replying to the Colossian heresy Paul developed his earlier metaphor of a Christian fellowship as interdependent parts of a body to the view in Colossians and Ephesians of the Church as the body whose head is Christ. With this view he brought out not only the living communion among the members but also the dependence of all the members on Christ for their common life and power. He vindicated the supremacy of Christ against a theosophy that set Him on a lower plane than other celestial powers. In consequence these two Epistles use "body" in correlation with "head" rather than (as in the earlier Epistles) in correlation with "spirit"; this is no argument, however, against their Pauline authorship.

While Colossians and Ephesians stand together over against the earlier Epistles, they significantly differ from each other. Yet these differences should not be overstressed. That the technical terms of Colossians have new senses in Ephesians does not prove diversity of authorship; one need only think of the variety of senses in which Paul used Gk. *nómos,* "law," in Romans. It is a well-attested feature of less formal literature that "a single word or phrase persists in the writer's mind by its own force, independently of any sense-recurrence" (E. Laughton, *Classical Philology,* 45 [1950], 75).

From the theme of the cosmic Christ Paul went on to consider the cosmic role of the Church as the body of Christ. After showing Christ as the reconciler of mankind to God, he thought about Christ's role as the reconciler of human beings to one another and especially of Jews to Gentiles. In Colossians he unfolded the "mystery" that Christ dwells in gentile (as well as Jewish) Christians as their hope of glory; in Ephesians he further unfolded the "mystery" of the union in one body of those who are thus indwelt by Christ — Jews and Gentiles alike. To Paul with his Jewish parentage, this could never cease to be the crowning wonder of God's grace.

If the author of Ephesians was not Paul, he was the greatest Paulinist of all time. That such a genius left no further trace in early Christian history is scarcely credible, for Ephesians is a distinctive work with its own unity of theme. An atomistic study may make it look like a compilation from Paul's other letters, but when viewed as a whole it has a unity no such compilation could attain. It may justifiably be described as an exposition of "the quintessence of Paulinism," but it is more than that: it brings the teaching of Paul's earlier Epistles to a further state of revelation and application, saying what Paul would have said had he advanced from his portrayal of the cosmic Christ in Colossians to treat the cosmic role of the Church. Some of its stylistic features would be explained by an amanuensis with a more classical style than the transcriber of Colossians (who was probably Timothy).

The significant differences between Colossians and Ephesians are not inconsistent with the view that Paul, having completed his reply to the Colossian heresy, allowed his thoughts to run on in a less controversial vein until he was gripped by the vision that finds expression in Ephesians and began to dictate its contents in an exalted mood of inspired meditation, thanksgiving, and prayer. The resultant document was then carried as a general letter — one might even say as Paul's testament — to the churches of Asia by the messengers entrusted with the Epistle to Colossae.

*D. Group Four: Pastoral Epistles.* The problem of the authorship of the Pastoral Epistles (1 and 2 Timothy, Titus) remains unsolved. Although most scholars have not considered the extant Epistles Pauline, others have ably restated the case for their authenticity.

The main points urged against their Pauline authorship are (1) their polemic against heresies that have a second-century gnostic (and even Marcionite) hue; (2) their more stereotyped theological outlook, presuming a fixed body of orthodox doctrine called "the faith"; (3) the developed state of church organization that they reflect; (4) the difficulty of finding a suitable setting for them in Paul's lifetime; (5) the fact that early external evidence is not so strong for them as for the other Epistles attributed to Paul; (6) indications of borrowing from the other Epistles; (7) their divergence in style and vocabulary from the other Epistles and affinity to second-century Christian writings.

The heresies envisaged in these Epistles, however, do not have the fully developed character found in the 2nd century. The reference, e.g., in 1 Tim. 6:20 to the "contradictions [Gk. *antítheses*] of what is falsely called knowledge [*gnō̂sis*]" appears unrelated to Marcion's *Antitheses.* The emergence of a recognized body of belief by A.D. 60-70 is not surprising; generally undisputed Epistles of Paul have traces of credal and catechetic summaries. The ecclesiastical organization in the Pastoral Epistles had not reached the stage of development represented in the Ignatian epis-

PAUL THE APOSTLE

tles (*ca.* A.D. 115). The threefold ministry had not yet been established; the government of the churches by bishops (or elders) and deacons found in the Pastorals is attested as early as Phil. 1:1. A second-century date for these Epistles (whether in general terms or specific, such as their recent ascription to Polycarp of Smyrna) is too late.

It is admittedly difficult to find a setting for the Pastorals in Paul's lifetime as known from Acts and the Pauline Epistles. But since they are in any case later than the other Epistles attributed to Paul, they must (if Pauline) belong to the closing years of his life, about which scholars are poorly informed. To place them in Paul's closing years may involve a "flight into *terra incognita*" (M. Dibelius), but that does not constitute an adequate argument against this dating.

The strongest argument against a Pauline date and authorship is that from style and vocabulary, presented in its most cogent form by P. N. Harrison in *Problem of the Pastoral Epistles* (1921). Harrison's thesis has contributed more than anything else toward widespread disbelief in their authenticity. Yet the statistical presentation of the linguistic evidence from such a restricted field as the Pauline corpus is of limited validity; other conclusions than Harrison's may account not only for the Pastorals' linguistic peculiarities but also for other distinctive features (*see* PASTORAL EPISTLES III.B.5).

If it is difficult to accept all three in their present form as letters written or dictated directly by Paul, they may be held to represent the posthumous recension of a number of *disiecta membra* (scattered parts) of Paul's correspondence (esp. with Timothy and Titus), and other fragments, possibly together with some notes of his oral instruction on church order. (Such a situation will best be appreciated by those who have actually collected, edited, and published someone else's literary remains.) Timothy or Luke may have been especially active in this regard. Timothy was associated with Paul in the writing of other Epistles, and Luke was Paul's only companion and evidently his amanuensis when 2 Tim. 4:11 was written. (See C. F. D. Moule, *Birth of the NT* [3rd ed. 1981], pp. 281f.)

***III. Pauline Corpus.***–The earliest collection of Paul's Epistles for which explicit information is available is that drawn up by Marcion at Rome *ca.* A.D. 144 as the second part of his canon. Part I was "The Gospel" (a specially edited form of Luke). Part II, "The Apostle," consisted of ten Pauline Epistles (all except the three Pastorals) edited in accordance with Marcion's hypothesis that Paul was the only true apostle of Jesus, since the Jerusalem apostles had adulterated His teaching with OT and Jewish elements, from which it was originally entirely free. It is implied in Tertullian's critique of Marcion (and generally confirmed by the express testimony of Epiphanius) that in Marcion's canon the Epistles appeared in this order: Galatians, 1 and 2 Corinthians, Romans, 1 and 2 Thessalonians, Ephesians (called by Marcion "the Epistle to the Laodiceans"), Colossians, Philippians, Philemon. If the Corinthian correspondence is reckoned as one composite letter, and the Thessalonian correspondence similarly, then (apart from Galatians) the Epistles are arranged in descending order of length. (It is interesting to observe how largely this principle has continued to control the traditional order of the Pauline Epistles.) A. Harnack supposed that Galatians was placed first because its argument was so particularly congenial to Marcion's interpretation of the gospel. J. Knox suggested that Marcion found the Pauline corpus of ten letters already arranged with Ephesians at the head and Galatians immediately before Colossians and that he transposed Galatians and Ephesians (*Marcion and the NT* [1942]). This suggestion has to be appreciated in the light of the view of E. J. Goodspeed and his school that Ephesians was composed as a statement of Paulinism to stand as an introduction to the Pauline corpus when it was first collected and published (cf. E. J. Goodspeed, *Key to Ephesians* [1956]).

The catholic leaders reacted to Marcion's teaching by defining their own canon, in which the NT did not supersede but stood alongside the OT. This canon also had not just Luke but a fourfold Gospel, not only the Gospel narrative but its sequel in Acts, not only Pauline Epistles but Epistles of apostles, and not merely ten but thirteen Epistles of Paul. Since the end of the 2nd cent. the thirteen Epistles bearing Paul's name have invariably formed part of the NT canon.

But efforts to envisage the formation and history of the Pauline corpus before Marcion's time have little success. The corpus of ten Epistles was probably something that he inherited; $p^{46}$ (late 2nd cent.) has apparently the same ten Epistles and Hebrews but lacks the three Pastorals.

It seems clear that the collection of Paul's Epistles had begun by A.D. 96, when the Epistle of Clement of Rome to the Corinthians was written, for Clement quoted 1 Corinthians as readily as Romans and appeared to know Ephesians and Philippians as well. There is some reason to think that he did not have access to 2 Corinthians, since it contains passages so in harmony with his argument that he would almost certainly have quoted them had he known them. The suggestion that his evident knowledge and appreciation of 1 Corinthians stimulated the Christians of Corinth to gather the surviving fragments of Paul's correspondence in their church archives has been mentioned above (see II.B.1). But it certainly looks as though some of Paul's letters were interchanged and circulated before the ten-letter corpus was published. Whatever the date of 2 Peter may be, it presupposes a considerable collection of Paul's Epistles (3:15f.). On the other hand, scholars must reckon with the practical certainty that Paul's Epistles were not used as a source by the author of Acts. Perhaps, as Goodspeed suggested, the publication of Acts *ca.* A.D. 90 led to a revival of interest in Paul, in consequence of which his literary relics were collected. Whether, in addition, they were collected at Ephesus (so Goodspeed, *Intro. to the NT* [1937], pp. 217ff.; C. L. Mitton, *Formation of the Pauline Corpus of Letters* [1955], pp. 44ff.) or at Alexandria (so G. Zuntz, *Text of the Epistles* [1954], p. 278), and whether the publication of the first Pauline corpus led to the formation of other Christian epistolary corpora (so A. E. Barnett, *Paul Becomes a Literary Influence* [1944]) are hypotheses that cannot be verified with the available evidence.

Possibly the second and enlarged edition of the Pauline corpus (thirteen letters) circulated for a considerable time alongside the shorter ten-letter corpus; it may even have been published before the time of Marcion. Ignatius, for instance, appears to have been acquainted with the Pastoral Epistles. Tertullian's statement (*De praescr. haer.* 38) that the Gnostic Valentinus "appears to have used the entire canon" (unlike his contemporary Marcion) possibly implies a certain recognition of the second-century catholic canon of the NT, including the thirteen Pauline Epistles, even before the publication of Marcion's canon.

At any rate, the letters of Paul were in circulation throughout the Christian world early in the 2nd cent. and the publication of the Pauline corpus, together with the fourfold Gospel and Acts as the "pivot" book, formed an initial and essential stage in the shaping of the completed NT canon.

Even before the last decade of the 1st cent., churches had probably begun to exchange Paul's letters to them.

Indeed, Paul himself had encouraged such an interchange. However the "letter from Laodicea" of Col. 4:16 is identified, it is evident that the Colossian and Laodicean churches were called upon to exchange their letters from Paul. It is probable, too, that Ephesians from the start and Romans in one of its recensions had the character of general epistles, not confined to one community only. Galatians was addressed to "the churches of Galatia," not to one church. The reference in Gal. 6:11 to Paul's distinctive handwriting makes it probable that one copy was sent to be passed on from one church to another.

The various witnesses for the text of the Pauline Epistles must be reexamined to discover whether they all represent a textual tradition stemming from the publication of the first Pauline corpus or whether some textual evidence of at least some Epistles that antedated their publication in the corpus may not have survived. The conclusion cannot be certain. F. G. Kenyon's measurements of agreement and disagreement between $p^{46}$ and other principal MSS, however, reveal significant variations from one Epistle to another; Romans, in particular, stands apart (*Chester Beatty Biblical Papyri*, Fasciculus III Supplement [1936], pp. xv ff.). This state of affairs can best be explained if the textual tradition of Romans at least goes back to a time when the individual Epistles circulated separately. There is some evidence, too, that the "Macedonian" Epistles (1 and 2 Thessalonians and Philippians) formed a small collection on their own before the publication of the larger corpus.

*IV. Paul and Early Christian Preaching and Teaching.*– The Epistles of Paul are the earliest written source of information on the apostolic preaching in the first days of Christianity. Since they were written for people who had already heard and believed this preaching, they refer to it only occasionally, when Paul wished to remind his readers of something. Even so, the main outline of the preaching could be reconstructed if necessary from these Epistles alone.

In his early preaching Paul emphasized Christ's crucifixion (1 Cor. 2:2; Gal. 3:1), His resurrection, and His role at the Parousia (1 Thess. 1:9f.). The most notable kerygmatic passage in his Epistles is 1 Cor. 15:3ff., where (to introduce an argument for the truth of resurrection) he reminded his readers of three essential elements in the message that they had received from him (as he himself had received it earlier) — Christ's death for their sins, His burial, and His resurrection on the third day. His death and resurrection are said to have taken place "in accordance with the scriptures"; several eyewitnesses of His resurrection are listed, among whom Peter and James are mentioned by name. Paul's added reference to his own belated vision of the risen Christ is probably his personal contribution to the message that all the apostles proclaimed. He insisted that on the basic facts his preaching did not differ from that of the other apostles (1 Cor. 15:11).

Further references in this and other Epistles help to fill out the summary of the preaching. 1 Cor. 11:23ff. is Paul's account of the institution of the Eucharist — again, something that he had "received" himself before he "delivered" it to his converts. (This is the earliest extant account of the institution, antedating Mk. 14:22-25 by several years.) The rest of Paul's message may be summarized thus: "God in the fulness of time and in accordance with prophetic Scripture has sent His Son Jesus as the Christ, who was born of the seed of David, lived under the law, taught the truth of God, was betrayed and crucified, dying the death that incurred the divine curse in order to redeem others from the curse incurred by sin. He was buried, was raised again the third day, appeared to many witnesses, and was exalted to God's right hand, where He intercedes for His people. He will reappear in glory to judge the world, to raise the faithful departed, to consummate for His people the salvation that He won for them, and to bring enduring bliss to all creation."

The outline of the early preaching that can be reconstructed from Paul's Epistles is generally the same as the one traceable in other NT Epistles, in the apostolic speeches reported in the first half of Acts, and in the Gospels — notably in the framework of Mark (see C. H. Dodd, *NT Studies* [1953], pp. 1ff.; *Apostolic Preaching and Its Developments* [1936]).

If Paul's Epistles show that he was at one with the other apostles on the basic facts of the gospel, even if he interpreted and applied them in a way distinctively his own, they also show that his Christology was essentially the same as theirs. Such a significant feature as the application to Jesus of OT passages that speak of Yahweh (e.g., Isa. 45:23 in Phil. 2:10f.) is not peculiar to Paul; cf. the application of Isa. 8:12f. in 1 Pet. 3:14b-15a, and of Ps. 102:25-27 in He. 1:10-12. The "wisdom" Christology of Col. 1:15ff. is paralleled in the prologue of John and in He. 1:2f. Paul introduced it in a confessional context (Col. 1:13ff.; cf. Eph. 1:7f.) that appears to represent a wider Christian usage than his own — e.g., it mentions the "remission (Gk. *áphesis*) of sins," whereas Paul's own preference was for more positive terms that speak of God's justifying grace. The "wisdom" Christology may reasonably be taken as another thing that Paul "received" before handing it on to others.

The portrayal of Christ's humiliation and exaltation in Phil. 2:5-11 reflects a "Servant of the Lord" Christology (cf. II.B.2 above). E. Lohmeyer detected in this christological passage a pre-Pauline hymn and emphasized its appropriateness to the context. What is important is that in his Christology (as in his soteriology) Paul was not the complete innovator that some have imagined; he shared with other Christians fundamental beliefs that he and they ultimately "received from the Lord."

Paul's Epistles are also the earliest written source (though some would except James) for Christian ethical teaching. That this teaching goes back to the teaching of Jesus seems clear.

One cannot fail to observe the close logical connection brought out by Paul between the ethical teaching and the facts of the preaching. Because his converts had accepted the truth of the gospel story, it was incumbent on them to live in conformity with the mind of Christ. The Pauline "therefore" implies this in, e.g., Rom. 12:1; Eph. 4:1; Phil. 2:12; Col. 3:5.

But these Epistles bear witness, too, that at an early date Christian ethical teaching received a catechetical form for the more effective instruction of converts — the "form of teaching" of Rom. 6:17 (RV). The catechetical teaching of Col. 3:5–4:6, e.g., falls into four paragraphs that may be collected under the captions "put off" (3:5-11), "put on" (3:12-17), "be subject" (3:18–4:1), and "watch and pray" (4:2-6). That is to say, converts to Christianity must "put off" old vices and "put on" new virtues, they must display a spirit of yieldingness and mutual consideration in their relations with one another (not least within the domestic circle), and their general behavior must be characterized by vigilance and prayerfulness. The recurrence of such "forms," under these or similar catchwords, in non-Pauline as well as in Pauline Epistles is best explained by a common body of catechetical instruction rather than by literary dependence of certain Epistles on others. Even so, Paul revealed his distinctive lines of thought in his treatment of such common Christian property — e.g., in his use of the terms "put to death" or "reckon as dead" as alternatives to "put off" (cf. Rom. 6:11; 8:13; Col. 3:5).

*V. Paul and Jesus.*–Paul's letters were written neither to record the facts of Jesus' life and ministry nor to give a detailed account of his kerygma. They were addressed to people who already knew the gospel story; their acquaintance with the details of the kerygma is presupposed. Paul's lack of interest in the life and teaching of Jesus before His passion has often been exaggerated, especially when this exaggeration is linked with a false interpretation of 2 Cor. 5:16. When Paul said there, "Even though we once regarded Christ from a human point of view, we regard him thus no longer," he was contrasting his present knowledge of the exalted Lord with his estimate of Him before his conversion. He was not comparing his present knowledge of the exalted Lord with the knowledge of Him possessed by the Jerusalem apostles and others who had been His companions during His ministry, or implying that this companionship conferred no advantage on them. Paul, the other apostles, and all their fellow believers, whether or not they had known Jesus "in the days of his flesh," knew Him now as the exalted Lord, who communicated His presence and power to His followers by the Spirit. They looked at all the events before the Crucifixion from the standpoint of Easter and Pentecost. This perspective did not mean that they represented the works and words of Jesus less accurately, but that they understood them more adequately. Paul was no doubt indebted to Peter and others for much of his information about the earthly life of Jesus, and the vivid depiction of the crucifixion story implied in Gal. 3:1 was probably based on the testimony of eyewitnesses.

Although Paul insisted on the divine preexistence of Jesus (Phil. 2:6; Col. 1:15ff.), he viewed Him nonetheless as a real man born of woman (Gal. 4:4), and as a descendant of Abraham (Rom. 9:5) and David (1:3). He was a poor man (2 Cor. 8:9); He lived under the Jewish law (Gal. 4:4). The time came when He was betrayed, and on that night He instituted a meal of bread and wine to be taken as a memorial (1 Cor. 11:23ff.). He endured the Roman penalty of death by crucifixion (1 Cor. 1:23; Gal. 3:1; etc.) — 1 Tim. 6:13 gives His judge's name as Pontius Pilate, before whom He is said to have "made the good confession" — yet Jewish representatives had some responsibility for His death (1 Thess. 2:15). He was buried, rose the third day, and was thereafter seen alive by many eyewitnesses on various occasions, including one occasion on which He was so seen by over five hundred, most of whom were alive nearly twenty-five years later (1 Cor. 15:4ff.). In this summary of the evidence for the reality of Christ's resurrection Paul showed a sound instinct for the necessity of marshaling personal testimony to support what might well appear an incredible assertion.

Paul knew the Lord's original apostles (Gal. 1:17ff.; etc.), of whom Peter and John are mentioned by name as "pillars" of the Jerusalem community (2:9), and His brothers, of whom James is similarly mentioned. He knew that the Lord's brothers and apostles, including Peter, were married (1 Cor. 9:5) — an incidental agreement with the Gospel story of the healing of Peter's mother-in-law (Mk. 1:30). He quoted sayings of Jesus on occasion, e.g., His teachings on marriage and divorce (1 Cor. 7:10f.) and on the right of gospel preachers to have their material needs supplied (1 Cor. 9:14; 1 Tim. 5:18; cf. Lk. 10:7), and Christ's words at the institution of the Lord's Supper (1 Cor. 11:24f.).

Paul moreover carefully distinguished situations in which he could quote a direct and authoritative ruling of Jesus, which put an end to all disputing, from those in which, in default of such a ruling, he expressed his own judgment, which he recommended but would not impose. Contrast "not I but the Lord" in the prohibition of divorce (1 Cor. 7:10f.) with "I . . . , not the Lord" and "I have no command of the Lord" in statements on related problems (vv. 12, 25). This careful distinction suggests that the early Church was not so ready to devise sayings of Jesus bearing upon situations that arose as some form critics have suggested.

Although Paul did not always quote the actual sayings of Jesus, he showed throughout his works how well acquainted he was with them. A comparison of the ethical section of Romans (12:1–15:7), where Paul summarized the practical implications of the gospel for the lives of believers, with the Sermon on the Mount particularly shows how thoroughly imbued the apostle was with the teaching of his Master. Besides, Paul's chief argument in his ethical instruction there and elsewhere is the example of Christ Himself, and Paul's understanding of Christ is in perfect agreement with His character as portrayed in the Gospels. Paul's mention of "the meekness and gentleness of Christ" (2 Cor. 10:1) echoes Our Lord's own words, "I am meek and lowly in heart" (Mt. 11:29). The self-denying Christ of the Gospels is the one of whom Paul said, "Even Christ pleased not himself" (Rom. 15:3). Just as the Christ of the Gospels called on His followers to deny themselves (Mk. 8:34), so the apostle insisted that, after the example of Christ Himself, "We who are strong ought to bear with the infirmities of the weak, and not to please ourselves" (Rom. 15:1). He who said, "I am among you as the servant" (Lk. 22:27), and performed the menial task of washing His disciples' feet (Jn. 13:4ff.) is He who according to Paul "took the form of a slave" (Phil. 2:7). When Paul wished to commend to his readers all those graces that adorn the Christ of the Gospels he did so in language like this: "Put on the Lord Jesus Christ" (Rom. 13:14).

*VI. Chronology of Paul's Career.*–Chronological notes are rare in Paul's letters — outstanding are the "three years" of Gal. 1:18, the "fourteen years" of 2:1, and the other "fourteen years" of 2 Cor. 12:2. Other incidental notes are "I will stay in Ephesus until Pentecost" (1 Cor. 16:8) and "Achaia has been ready since last year" (2 Cor. 9:2; cf. 8:10).

In Acts chronological references are less rare but are more plentiful for the later part of Paul's ministry than for the earlier part. After Barnabas brought Paul to Antioch, they met with the church there "for a whole year" before they were sent on their famine-relief mission to Jerusalem (Acts 11:25). Luke as an Antiochene would remember this, but for most of the narrative that he could not control by personal knowledge his sources gave him little chronological help, and he marked an interval of time by transitional formulas like "after some days" (15:36). His chronological details are most precise when he described his voyages with Paul; then his diary reads like a logbook (cf. 16:11; 20:6-16; 21:1-8; 27:1-39; 28:11-17). For the rest, he said that Paul spent eighteen months in Corinth (18:11), between two and three years in Ephesus (19:8-10; 20:31), and three months in Greece immediately before his last journey to Palestine (20:2f.). Later he mentioned the two years that elapsed between Paul's arrest and Felix's recall from the procuratorship of Judea (24:27; this, and not the duration of Felix's procuratorship, is certainly what is meant), the three months' wintering in Malta (28:11), and Paul's two-year house arrest in Rome (v. 30). Between these specified periods, however, are periods of unspecified duration.

The whole of Paul's Christian career as related in Acts clearly must fall between A.D. 33 (or whatever alternative

St. Paul's Bay at Lindos on Rhodes (Acts 21:1) (W. S. LaSor)

year may be regarded as the year of his conversion) and 64, when the Neronian persecution began. The Judean famine of Acts 11:28 is dated in the reign of Claudius (41-54) — more particularly, as the position of ch. 12 suggests, near the death of Herod Agrippa I in 44. To the reign of Claudius also must be dated Paul's Corinthian ministry. When he arrived in Corinth Paul met Aquila and Priscilla, who had recently left Italy because of Claudius's edict expelling Jews from Rome (18:2) — an edict for which Orosius's date of 49, based on other grounds, is probable. More precise information is provided by the statement that Gallio's proconsulship of Achaia coincided with or at least overlapped Paul's stay in Corinth (v. 12). Gallio's proconsulship probably lasted no longer than a year, being terminated by an attack of malaria (Seneca *Ep. mor.* 104.1); it is dated rather closely by a reference to him as proconsul of Achaia (either currently or very recently) in a rescript of Claudius to the citizens of Delphi dated to Claudius's twenty-sixth acclamation as *imperator* (W. Dittenberger, *Sylloge Inscriptionum Graecarum,* II [4th ed. 1960], no. 801). Other inscriptional evidence (*CIL,* III, 476; VI, 1256) points to the first seven months of 52 as the period of this acclamation. Since proconsuls normally entered their office on July 1, Gallio probably became proconsul of Achaia on July 1, 51. Paul's Corinthian ministry may thus have run from the autumn of 50 to the spring of 52, and his Ephesian ministry (which was separated from his Corinthian ministry by a hasty visit to Palestine) from the autumn of 52 to the summer of 55.

Festus's supersession of Felix as procurator of Judea may be dated to 59 by a change in provincial coinage in Nero's fifth year (cf. F. W. Madden, *History of Jewish Coinage* [1864], p. 153). Since Paul was sent by sea to Rome shortly after Festus's arrival in Judea, another, more tenuous argument in support of that year is that in A.D. 59 the Day of Atonement appears to have fallen rather late (Oct. 5), as Acts 27:9 suggests: "even the fast [the Day of Atonement] had already gone by."

With these few aids to fixed dating, the following tentative chronological outline of Paul's career may be drawn up.

| | |
|---|---|
| Conversion | A.D. 33 |
| First Postconversion Visit to Jerusalem | 35 |
| Joins Barnabas at Antioch | 45 |
| Famine-Relief Visit to Jerusalem | 46 |
| Accompanies Barnabas to Cyprus and Asia Minor | 47-48 |
| At the Council of Jerusalem | 49 |
| Journey with Silas and Others to Philippi, Thessalonica, and Corinth | 49-50 |
| In Corinth | 50-52 |
| In Ephesus | 52-55 |
| At Troas (2 Cor. 2:12) | autumn 55 |
| In Macedonia and Illyricum | 55-56 |
| In Corinth | winter 56-57 |
| Arrival and Arrest in Jerusalem | May 57 |
| Detention in Caesarea | 57-59 |
| Voyage to Rome | 59-60 |
| Under House Arrest in Rome | 60-62 |
| Outbreak of Neronian Persecution | 64 |
| Last Imprisonment, Trial, and Execution | 65 (?) |

***VII. Life and Ministry of Paul.***–*A. Paul the Roman Citizen.* "Saul, who is also called Paul" (Acts 13:9), was born about the beginning of the Christian era in Tarsus, the principal city of Cilicia in southeast Asia Minor (9:11; 22:3). His description of himself as a "Hebrew" (2 Cor. 11:22), "a Hebrew born of Hebrews" (Phil. 3:5), shows that his parents though living in the Diaspora among the Greeks were far from being assimilationist Jews, but remained faithful to the language and customs of Palestinian Jewry. An incidental confirmation of this is Paul's statement in Acts 26:14 that the voice on the Damascus road addressed him "in the Hebrew [probably Aramaic] language" — probably because Hebrew was *Paul's* mother tongue rather than because it was *Jesus'* habitual speech. According to Jerome (*De vir. ill.* 5) Paul's ancestors belonged to Gischala in Galilee and migrated to Tarsus at the time of the Roman conquest of Palestine (63 B.C.); the accuracy of this tradition is uncertain. Although born into an orthodox Jewish family Paul was born a Roman citizen (22:28); thus his father must have been a Roman citizen before him.

How the citizenship came into Paul's family is not known. Paul's native Cilicia fell within the *provincia* of more than one Roman general in the 1st cent. B.C. — e.g., Pompey and Antony — and the grant of citizenship to approved individuals was included in the *imperium* conferred on these generals by law. But whether one of these generals or someone else granted Roman citizenship to Paul's family and why it was so granted are unknown. In a letter dated February 18, 1953, Sir William Calder said of Paul: "Had not his father (or possibly grandfather) been made a citizen by Antony or Pompey? Were they not a firm of *skēnopoioi* [tentmakers], able to be very useful to a fighting proconsul?" This suggestion is as reasonable as any that could be made on this point, but the evidence is uncertain.

As a Roman citizen Paul had three names — *praenomen* (first name), *nomen gentile* (family name), and *cognomen* (additional name) — but only his *cognomen,* Paullus, is known. His *nomen gentile* if known might give some clue to the circumstances of his family's acquisition of the citizenship (for new citizens commonly assumed their patron's *nomen gentile*). His *cognomen* may have been chosen because of its assonance with his Jewish name Saul — Heb. *Šā'ûl,* in the NT sometimes spelled *Saoul* and more often *Saulos,* the latter form rhyming with Gk. *Paulos.* Since he belonged to the tribe of Benjamin (Phil. 3:5) his parents may have named him Saul after the most illustrious member of that tribe in their nation's history, Israel's first king.

On more than one occasion Paul appealed to his rights as a Roman citizen — at Philippi (Acts 16:37), to protest his having been beaten with rods by the lictors attendant on the chief magistrates of the colony before he had received a proper trial; some years later, at Jerusalem (22:25), to avoid being scourged (much more murderous than a beating with rods) by authorities who wanted to know how he had enraged the Jews in the temple court. He later availed himself of his citizen rights when he appealed to Caesar (25:11); see VII.G below. The rights of Roman citizens were laid down in a long succession of laws (most recently the *lex Julia de vi publica*), going back traditionally to the *lex Valeria* of 509 B.C. They included exemption from certain ignominious forms of punishment, protection against summary execution, and the right of appeal to the sovereign authority.

When a man claimed his citizen rights — when he said *civis Romanus sum* ("I am a Roman citizen") or its equivalent in Greek — how did he prove his claim? Certainly it was a capital offense to claim falsely to be a Roman citizen, but how did an official know whether the claim was true? A new citizen might have a duly witnessed copy of his certificate of citizenship; auxiliary soldiers received such a document when they were enfranchised, and civilians may have been given something similar. But Paul was not a new citizen. He might, however, have produced a diptych containing a certified copy of his birth registration. Each legitimate child of a Roman citizen had to be registered within (it appears) thirty days of birth (cf. F. Schulz, *Journal of Roman Studies,* 32 [1942], 78ff.; 33 [1943], 55ff.). If he lived in the provinces, his father or some duly appointed agent made a declaration in the appropriate record office that the child was a Roman citizen (*civem Romanum esse professus est*); the declaration was recorded in the official register, and the father or agent received a copy in diptych form, properly certified by witnesses.

It is doubtful that an itinerant Roman citizen customarily carried this diptych around with him. F. Schulz was sure that Paul did so and produced it for corroboration when he claimed civic privileges (*Journal of Roman Studies,* 33 [1943], 63f.). A. N. Sherwin-White, however, thought it more likely that such certificates were normally kept in the family archives (*Roman Society and Roman Law in the NT* [1963], p. 149; cf. *Roman Citizenship* [1939]).

A further point to consider is that registration of Roman citizens at birth was apparently enacted by the *lex Aelia Sentia* of A.D. 4 and the *lex Papia Poppaea* of 9; if Paul was born even a year or two before the earlier enactment, he might not have been registered in this way.

*B. Paul the Pharisee.* Although Tarsus was an outstanding center of Greek culture, ranking next to Athens and Alexandria, and "no mean city" in other respects (Acts 21:39), it was not to its schools of philosophy or rhetoric that Paul was sent for his education. Instead, he went to Jerusalem and became a pupil of the elder Gamaliel, leader of the school of sacred learning founded in the previous generation by Hillel. Since Paul's parents were themselves adherents of the party of the Pharisees (23:6), their son was naturally entrusted to the tuition of the most illustrious Pharisee of his day.

At what age Paul came to Jerusalem from Tarsus is difficult to decide. The most relevant reference, Acts 22:3, may be variously interpreted according to the alternative punctuations. Earlier interpreters tended to assume that he lived at Tarsus long enough to be deeply influenced by its Hellenistic way of life and modes of thought and moreover by Mithraism as practiced in Cilicia. W. C. van Unnik later argued that the words "born indeed at Tarsus in Cilicia, but brought up in this city [Jerusalem]" mean that Jerusalem was the city of Paul's boyhood. He could certainly have acquired an elementary knowledge of Greek culture from Gamaliel, who probably gave his disciples prophylactic courses in this subject (cf. W. L. Knox, *Some Hellenistic Elements in Primitive Christianity*, p. 33).

The question of Paul's indebtedness to Hellenistic or Jewish influences has been unnecessarily complicated by a failure to recognize that Hellenism and Judaism were not sealed off from each other in watertight compartments. Hellenism was influenced by Judaism, and for centuries Judaism had been deeply influenced by Hellenism not only in the Diaspora but also in Judea and Jerusalem. Practically from its earliest days the church of Jerusalem included Hellenists as well as Hebrews (Acts 6:1), and Paul, "Hebrew" as he declared himself to be, must have imbibed many of the Hellenistic elements in the cultural atmosphere of his day. The main features of Stoic belief were commonplace among thinking people; some technical terms of the mystery cults had become part of everyday language. Quotations from the great Greek poets came as naturally to the lips of Greek speakers as snatches of Shakespeare come to English speakers', often without the realization that they are Shakespearean. Some current ideas, as Paul's letters to Corinth and Colossae show, contained inchoate forms of what later became full-blown Gnosticism. To Paul this kind of *gnōsis* was of no account in comparison with *agápē* — "'knowledge' puffs up," he said, "but love builds up" (1 Cor. 8:1) — but he was perfectly willing to use its vocabulary in a "disinfected" sense if he could thereby establish the truth of the gospel more effectively (cf. H. Chadwick, *NTS,* 1 [1954/55], 261ff., esp. 272).

The day has gone by, however, when Paul could be regarded as the man who hellenized the gospel of Jesus and in so doing transformed it almost beyond recognition. Far and away the most powerful influence on his thinking up to the moment of his conversion was Judaism, and rabbinic Judaism at that. The truth of this can scarcely be contested since the publication in 1948 of W. D. Davies's *Paul and Rabbinic Judaism*; the evidence there is ample and conclusive. Other streams of Judaism no doubt exercised some influence on him; Colossians and Ephesians in particular show affinities of language with Jewish "nonconformity," whose significance must be a subject for further study (cf. K. G. Kuhn, *NTS,* 7 [1960/61], 334ff.). But what was destined to become the "main stream" was determinant for his outlook, as might be expected in Gamaliel's pupil.

Paul's main concern in the school of Gamaliel was to become as proficient as possible in the ancestral traditions of his people. He claimed indeed to have outstripped his contemporaries in the knowledge and practice of the Jewish religion (Gal. 1:14). The way of acceptance with God was obedience to the law — not only the written law with its 613 precepts but the oral tradition, transmitted by generations of rabbis and preserved by the School of Hillel, which interpreted those precepts and applied them in detail to every department of contemporary life. "As to righteousness under the law," according to his later, Christian assessment of this earlier stage of his life, he was "blameless" (Phil. 3:6), living "before God in all good conscience" (Acts 23:1). But for his conversion he might well have made his name as the greatest Pharisee of all time.

Almost certainly Paul was in Jerusalem during the last phase of Jesus' Palestinian ministry. Whether he ever set eyes on Jesus is impossible to know, but his attitude toward Him appears plainly enough in his violent opposition to the infant church of Jerusalem. He mentioned his persecution of the Church as the high-water mark of his zeal for the law (Phil. 3:6; cf. Gal. 1:13). To his mind this new movement threatened everything that he held dear. In particular, he found blasphemous the disciples' claim that the crucified Jesus — who, in the light of Dt. 21:23, had died under the curse of God — was Israel's Messiah.

Acts makes Paul's persecuting activity begin with the trial and execution of Stephen. When the men who had testified against Stephen laid aside their outer garments to take the initiative in stoning him, as the law required (Dt. 17:7), Paul guarded their clothes and thus gave practical proof of his approval of their action (Acts 7:58; 8:1).

(Luke's narrative does not necessarily imply that Paul was a member of the Sanhedrin.) Since Stephen had been active in the Jerusalem synagogue, which Jews from Cilicia, among others, attended (6:9), it was probably Stephen's arguments that brought home to Paul the necessity of destroying this new movement, if his ancestral traditions were to survive. The temporizing course favored by his master Gamaliel (5:34ff.) was not what the situation demanded.

The Hellenists in the Jerusalem church were evidently the principal target of the persecution. They were forced to flee from Jerusalem or Judea across the provincial frontiers, and even there Paul endeavored to round them up. While he was on his way to the synagogues of Damascus with letters of extradition signed by the high priest, bent on arresting the disciples who had sought refuge in that city and bringing them back to Jerusalem for trial and punishment, he encountered the risen Jesus and was turned into the zealous champion of the faith that he had been trying to obliterate.

Nowhere is it suggested that while Paul was in full career as a persecutor he entertained any misgivings about the rightness of his course. The goads against which his kicking was useless (so the risen Christ warned him) were the stimuli that henceforth drove him in a direction exactly contrary to his previous one. Up to that moment he knew, or believed he knew, what the law required, and he fulfilled its requirements to the best of his understanding and ability. Once he became a believer in Christ, indeed, his former persecuting zeal appeared to him as the sin of sins in his life. "I am the least of the apostles, unfit to be called an apostle, because I persecuted the church of God. But by the grace of God I am what I am . . ." (1 Cor. 15:9f.). What he says of his fellow Jews in Rom. 10:2f. had been equally true of himself: "I bear them witness that they have a zeal for God, but it is not enlightened. For, being ignorant of the righteousness that comes from God, and seeking to establish their own, they did not submit to God's righteousness." But as long as he sought to establish his righteousness before God on the basis of the law, his conscience was clear, even — or rather, especially — amid his persecuting activity (see K. Stendahl, *HTR*, 56 [1963], 199ff.).

What is the relevance in this connection of the debated passage in Rom. 7:7-25? The autobiographical interpretation of the passage has become unfashionable, largely in consequence of W. G. Kümmel's study *Römer 7 und die Bekehrung des Paulus* (1929), to a point where it is described as "now relegated to the museum of exegetical absurdities" (P. Démann, cited in F. J. Leenhardt, comm. on Romans [Eng. tr. 1961], p. 181; cf. Munck, pp. 11f.).

The passage falls into two parts: vv. 7-13, which are in the past tense, and vv. 14-25, which are in the present. In the former part, which is more relevant here, Paul retold the story of the fall; but in doing so he told his own story: "here Paul's autobiography is the biography of Everyman" (T. W. Manson, in *Peake's Comm. on the Bible* [rev. ed. 1962], p. 945). He would not have used the first-person singular had he not recognized the fall as an authentic description of his own history as well as of the history of mankind. In this sense at least he knew himself to be "the Adam of his own soul" (2 Bar. 54:19), beguiled into covetousness by sin, which used as its weapon of assault the very commandment that forbids covetousness. But one must remember that this is Paul's *Christian* diagnosis of an early crisis in his life, which did not appear to him in the same light at the time that he experienced it. Whatever that time may have been — possibly his bar mitzvah initiation — the youthful Paul had learned to come to terms with the law and kept it without blame and with a conscience void of offense. "The true meaning of sin was not discovered at the feet of Gamaliel but at the foot of the cross" (E. K. Lee, *A Study in Romans* [1962], p. 27).

*C. Paul Begins to Be a Christian.* Paul's conversion was followed almost immediately by his call to be Christ's apostle to the Gentiles. Although this call may have been communicated to him in part by Ananias of Damascus, a private believer like Ananias could have been no more than the mouthpiece of the risen Lord. Paul knew and maintained thenceforth that his apostolic commission came from the risen Lord whom he had seen on the Damascus road, without the mediation of the Jerusalem apostles.

Paul's own account of the matter suggests that he lost no time in beginning to discharge his commission. Some time, however, must be allowed for him to have come to terms with his new situation. When the law was suddenly dislodged from its central position in his thought and life, all the elements in his thinking that had taken their appropriate place in relation to the law were shaken apart, but they quickly came together in a new pattern around the new center of Paul's thought and life, Christ. The arguments that Paul had formerly regarded as conclusive against the truth of the disciples' claims had to be related to the fact, no longer to be doubted, that these claims were true. Jesus' dying the death on which the divine curse rested no longer meant that He could not be the Messiah but instead had to be related to His *being* the Messiah. The solution stated in Gal. 3:13, "Christ redeemed us from the curse of the law, having become a curse for us," must have commended itself to Paul early in his inward readjustment to the revelation that he had received.

What precise form of eschatological expectation Paul had been brought up to hold must be a matter for inference; most probably he had been taught that the present age would be separated from the age to come (the resurrection age) by the "days of the Messiah." If so, this expectation required to be modified in one most material particular, for the Messiah, as he realized, had already come. The death and resurrection of Jesus had inaugurated the "days of the Messiah," for He was now enthroned in glory, exercising His messianic reign until all His enemies were subdued. He would annihilate the last enemy of all, death, at the final resurrection (1 Cor. 15:26). The people of the Messiah would then be introduced into the heritage of glory that lay in store for them. This glory would be a sharing in His glory, and as His glory was the sequel to His sufferings, so for them — and not least for Paul himself (Col. 1:24) — sharing in His sufferings on earth was the indispensable prelude to sharing His glory hereafter (Rom. 8:17).

For the present, on earth, Christians live in hope, but this hope is a living hope because the presence of Christ is made real to them by His indwelling Spirit. The Spirit keeps the hope of glory alive within them; He is the pledge of resurrection; He aids their prayer life; He cooperates in all things for good with those who love God; He imparts to them the power to live as befits the people of Christ, liberating them from the law of sin and death that dominates the children of the present age (Rom. 8:1-28). Moreover, He unites them to Christ; in this one Spirit they have all been baptized into one body, so that Christ's eternal life lives in them and they live in Him (Rom. 6:4; 1 Cor. 12:13; Gal. 3:27).

Over and above all that, those who are "in Christ Jesus" face the prospect of the judgment day with confidence, because they have already been justified by faith in Him. "If the days of the Messiah have commenced, those of the Torah came to their close. On the other hand, if the

Law, the Torah, still retained its validity, it was proclaimed thereby that the Messiah still had not appeared" (L. Baeck, *JJS*, 3 [1952], 93ff., esp. 106). Therefore "Christ is the end of the law, that every one who has faith may be justified" (Rom. 10:4), and a return to the principle of justification by the works of the law, such as provoked the Epistle to the Galatians, is tantamount to a denial that Jesus is the Messiah (hence the "anathema" of Gal. 1:8f.).

Paul probably had to continue readjusting his thinking to the implications of the Messiah's having come in Jesus during his sojourn in "Arabia," to which he departed soon after his conversion (Gal. 1:17). But his own implication is that he went to Arabia to proclaim Christ. The Arabia to which one would go from Damascus was the Nabatean kingdom, stretching along the eastern frontier of the Roman sphere of influence from Damascus S to the Gulf of Aqabah. A suggestion that Paul's visit to that territory was not devoted entirely to quiet contemplation is the hostile interest that the Nabatean king Aretas IV (9 B.C.–A.D. 40), or at least his representative in Damascus, took in him when he returned to that city (2 Cor. 11:32f.).

Not until the third year after his conversion did Paul revisit Jerusalem. He went there, he said, "to visit Cephas [Peter]," and spent a fortnight with him. The only other "apostle" whom he met then was James the Just, the Lord's brother (Gal. 1:18f.). The verb that Paul used of his visiting Peter is interesting: "I went up," he said, "*historēsai Kēphan*" — "to get to know Cephas" (NEB), and not only to get to know the man himself, but to get to know things that Peter was specially competent to impart. For all Paul's insistence on his independence of the Jerusalem apostles, he recognized Peter as a prime informant on matters about which it was important that he become well informed — the facts about Jesus, the *parádosis* or deposit of teaching that derived its authority from Him, the "tradition" about which Paul could later say to his converts: "I received from the Lord what I also delivered to you" (1 Cor. 11:23). Peter could obviously impart to Paul much information — more than James could, since James had not been a disciple of Jesus during His ministry — but one thing, Paul insisted, Peter did not and could not impart to him, and that was apostolic authority.

Paul must have distinguished in his mind between the sense in which the gospel came to him "through a revelation of Jesus Christ" — the sense in which, he said, "I did not receive it from man, nor was I taught it" (Gal. 1:12) — and the sense in which it was something that he had "received" (1 Cor. 15:3). His gospel was indeed both "revealed" and "received" (cf. O. Cullmann, *Early Church* [Eng. tr. 1956], pp. 59ff.), but sometimes the apologetic or polemic requirements of the moment made him emphasize one aspect to the practical exclusion of the other.

Paul himself, if asked to elucidate the distinction between the two aspects, would probably have said that the core of the gospel, "Jesus Christ the risen Lord," was imparted to him directly on the Damascus road, when God, as he said, "was pleased to reveal his Son in me" (Gal. 1:16). Although he knew others who were in Christ before him (Rom. 16:7), including some who were apostles before him (Gal. 1:17), he did not learn the gospel from them. But the historical details of the teaching of Jesus, the incidents of Holy Week, the resurrection appearances, and the like were related to him by those with experience of them.

The summary of resurrection appearances in 1 Cor. 15:5ff. (excluding that to Paul himself) falls into two series: (1) to Peter, to the Twelve, and to over five hundred at one time; (2) to James, to all the apostles. Each series goes back in all probability to the testimony of the man whose name introduces it; i.e., Paul received this information from Peter and James, almost certainly during his fortnight in Jerusalem in the third year after his conversion, when he met them both.

But if he preached the gospel before he received this information from Peter and James, what did he preach? On the basis of his knowledge of the OT interpreted in the light of his Damascus-road experience, he was able to proclaim Jesus Christ the risen Lord without any delay. This explanation agrees with Luke's account that Paul "for several days" after his conversion "was with the disciples at Damascus; and in the synagogues immediately he proclaimed Jesus, saying, 'He is the Son of God'" (Acts 9:19f.). After his interview with Peter and James, however, he was able to fill in further details, delivering to others what he himself had received.

*D. Paul and Barnabas.* After visiting Jerusalem Paul returned to his native Cilicia, and there he disappeared from NT records for some years. They were not idle years, for the news kept reaching the ears of the disciples in Judea that their former persecutor was propagating the faith that he had once attempted to destroy (Gal. 1:23). To this period (*ca.* A.D. 42) belong the ecstatic experience described in 2 Cor. 12:2ff., which left its mark on Paul forever afterward, and at least some of the five beatings inflicted on him by synagogue authorities (11:24).

The most acute phase of the inward struggle so vividly portrayed in the present tense in Rom. 7:14-25 likely occurred in this period, too. The autobiographical reference of this passage, as of the seven verses that precede it, has been questioned; however, the poignant description of someone who loves the law of God and longs to do it but is forced by a stronger power than his own to do things that he detests is surely no "abstract argument but the echo of the personal experience of an anguished soul" (M. Goguel, *Birth of Christianity* [Eng. tr. 1953], pp. 213f.). This description is a more vivid version of Gal. 5:17, "The desires of the flesh are against the Spirit, and the desires of the Spirit are against the flesh; for these are opposed to each other, to prevent you from doing what you would." The man who disciplined his body lest he be disqualified himself after acting as herald to others (1 Cor. 9:27) had no undue confidence in himself. One can well believe that a man of Paul's imperious zeal found it no easy matter to "crucify the flesh" and to win the victory over a hasty tongue, a premature judgment, a feeling of resentment at any encroachment by others on the sphere of his own apostolic service. In later years he could entreat his friends "by the meekness and gentleness of Christ" (2 Cor. 10:1), but this meekness and gentleness did not come to him naturally. The man who pressed on to the goal of God's upward calling in Christ Jesus (Phil. 3:14) knew that the run for the immortal garland was "not without dust and heat." Paul was too fond of portraying the way of holiness as a race to be run, a battle to be fought, for one to suppose that victory came to him suddenly. The tension could never be completely resolved while he lived simultaneously in the present age and in the age to come (as every Christian must do in this overlapping interval "between the times"), but he learned that victory was his when he ceased to fight the battle in his own strength and relied upon the liberating "law of the Spirit of life in Christ Jesus" (Rom. 8:2).

This obscure phase of Paul's Christian career ended *ca.* A.D. 45 when Barnabas fetched him from Tarsus to join him in the care of the young church of Syrian Antioch, where a group of Hellenistic believers had some time previously embarked on an extensive program of gentile evangelization (Acts 11:19-26). Such an evangelistic and teaching ministry among Gentiles was the very kind of work to which Paul knew himself called, and he took his place with Barnabas and other colleagues in this congenial task.

About 46 the Antiochene Christians charged him and Barnabas to convey a gift to their Jerusalem brethren at a time when Judea was hard hit by famine (Acts 11:27-30). Probably on this occasion the two of them had the meeting with the leaders of the Jerusalem church recorded in Gal. 2:1-10. (This meeting has often been identified with the Council of Jerusalem described in Acts 15, but the two narratives have very little in common, apart from the identity of the protagonists on both occasions. *See* APOSTOLIC COUNCIL.) Paul dated this meeting "after fourteen years" (Gal. 2:1), which might mean the fourteenth year after his Jerusalem visit of 1:18 but more probably the fourteenth year after his conversion. The interview with the Jerusalem leaders — James, Peter, and John (and it is noteworthy that now James heads the list) — was held in private, and, said Paul, "I laid before them . . . the gospel which I preach among the Gentiles, lest somehow I should be running or had run in vain" (2:2).

This is an extraordinary admission, on the face of it; Paul seemed to agree that without the recognition or at least the fellowship of the Jerusalem leaders his apostolic service would be fruitless. Evidently, while his commission was not derived from Jerusalem, it could not be discharged effectively except in fellowship with Jerusalem.

One reason for this attitude was surely Paul's horror of schism. If a complete cleavage took place between the Jerusalem church and the gentile mission Christ would be divided, and His cause, divided against itself, would come to grief. All the energy that Paul had devoted, and hoped to devote, to gentile evangelization would be in vain if the apostolate to the circumcision and that to the uncircumcision did not recognize each other.

All went well at this interview, however. The Jerusalem "pillars" acknowledged that Barnabas and Paul had been called by God to evangelize Gentiles as truly as they themselves had been called to the Jewish apostolate, and the two sides shook hands in joint recognition of their respective spheres of labor.

Nothing was said about circumcision on this occasion, Paul declared, although the opportunity to raise that question was present: Barnabas and he were accompanied by Titus, a young gentile Christian from Antioch. Circumcision became a live issue only later, at the Council of Jerusalem.

All that the Jerusalem leaders asked Barnabas and Paul to do was to continue to remember "the poor" of the mother church. Paul, who had already been active in this regard, treated this as a serious moral obligation throughout his ministry.

Shortly after their return to Antioch Barnabas and Paul were sent by its church, in response to a prophetic utterance, to evangelize the areas to the west and northwest — more particularly, the island of Cyprus and the southern part of the Roman province of Galatia in central Asia Minor. There they preached the gospel and planted churches, among which those of Pisidian Antioch, Iconium, Lystra, and Derbe are mentioned by name (Acts 13:14–14:23). This work was an extension of their mission in Syrian Antioch, which remained their home base at this stage, and they reported to the church of Syrian Antioch the progress of their mission when they returned.

It was probably this unforeseen extension of the gentile mission that caused some of the more conservative believers in Judea to insist that gentile converts be circumcised and accept the attendant obligation to keep the Jewish law. The prospect of a decisive gentile majority in the church filled them with serious and not unnatural misgivings. Accordingly some of them visited Syrian Antioch and her newly founded daughter churches to press their views.

When a deputation of these people first visited Antioch, Peter was temporarily living there. Paul described what happened in Gal. 2:11-14. One of them, an envoy from James, appears to have told Peter that his practice of eating at the same table as gentile Christians in Antioch was an embarrassment to his colleagues in Jerusalem; Peter, probably from motives of conciliation, desisted from this practice, at least for a time. Paul reacted sharply because he saw that Peter's action would be interpreted to mean that uncircumcised gentile believers were at best second-class Christians, even if it did not compromise the gospel principle of salvation by grace. This principle was certainly in danger of being compromised in the churches of south Galatia, where Paul's converts were disposed to listen to those who insisted on circumcision (in addition to faith in Christ) as necessary for membership in the saved community. In Paul's eyes any such addition to the gospel message deprived it of its gospel character.

The dispute had to be settled "at the highest level," and Barnabas and Paul led a deputation from the church of Antioch to discuss the matter with the apostles and elders at Jerusalem. James, who summed up the debate, gave his judgment that no conditions were to be imposed on Gentiles as necessary for salvation beyond the condition of faith in Christ, with which God had clearly shown Himself to be satisfied. But when this question of principle had been settled, there remained the practical problem of making the day-to-day fellowship between Jewish and gentile converts in mixed communities as unencumbered as possible. At James's insistence, the letter sent from the Council to the church of Antioch and her daughter churches included a ruling that gentile Christians should abstain from certain kinds of food that their Jewish brethren would find offensive, and conform to the Jewish marriage laws.

These requirements contained nothing per se to which Paul would have objected, for where basic principles were not compromised he was the most conciliatory of persons, and he repeatedly inculcated the Christian duty of respecting the scruples of others in such matters (cf. Rom. 14:1ff.; 1 Cor. 8:1ff.). Admittedly he never appealed to the Jerusalem decrees when dealing with such subjects in his letters. For one reason, the letter from Jerusalem was addressed "to brethren who are of the Gentiles in Antioch and Syria and Cilicia" (Acts 15:23), and even if these terms could be stretched to include the south Galatian daughter churches of Antioch, Paul's letter to those churches may have been written before the Council of Jerusalem. For another reason, Paul was not disposed to support his injunctions to his gentile churches by appealing to the authority of a document issued by Jerusalem, especially since Christians from Jerusalem and Judea constantly and, indeed, increasingly invaded his gentile mission field and attempted to undermine his apostolic authority in the eyes of his converts. This put it out of the question for Paul even to appear to be subject to the authority of Jerusalem.

*E. Paul in Macedonia and Greece.* Shortly after the Council of Jerusalem Paul parted company with Barnabas and no longer made Syrian Antioch his missionary base. According to Luke, the parting between him and Barnabas was due to their failure to agree whether to take Mark, Barnabas's cousin, with them on a further visit to the recently founded churches of Asia Minor. Mark had set out with them on their previous journey to Cyprus and Asia Minor but had left them in the course of the journey and had returned to Jerusalem. It could also be suggested that Barnabas's following of Peter's example when the latter withdrew from table fellowship with gentile Christians at Antioch (Gal. 2:13) was partly responsible for this decision to part company; but Paul's subsequent references to Barnabas (cf. 1 Cor. 9:6) do not suggest any permanent breach of friendship, although there was no further collaboration between the two.

With Silas (Silvanus), a like-minded member of the Jerusalem church who appears to have been a Roman citizen like Paul himself, Paul revisited the churches of south Galatia. The westward way to Ephesus, which apparently they had hoped to take, was barred to them, so, turning north and northwest, they reached the Aegean coast at Troas and crossed the sea to Neapolis in Macedonia. By this time they had two further companions — Timothy, a young convert of Lystra, who was henceforth Paul's faithful lieutenant, and Luke, the gentile physician of Antioch, who modestly indicates his presence with Paul and the others at this stage by using the pronoun "we" instead of "they" in his narrative (Acts 16:10-17).

After landing in Macedonia they made short stays in Philippi and in Thessalonica, the capital of the province. Churches were quickly planted in both cities, and these continued to thrive, although the missionaries, and particularly Paul, were compelled to leave sooner than they wished. In Philippi he and Silas were accused before the Roman magistrates (Philippi being a Roman colony) of interference with citizens' property rights; this was one of the occasions on which Paul (as well as Silas) appealed to his Roman citizenship. In Thessalonica the charge against him and his companions was more serious. The Thessalonian citizens who had given hospitality to Paul were brought before the politarchs and charged with harboring the men who had "turned the world upside down," flouted Caesar's decrees, and proclaimed a rival emperor, one Jesus (Acts 17:6f.). The wording of the accusation, as Luke recorded it, suggests that subversive characters had been active elsewhere among the Jewish communities of the empire, and Paul and his companions were represented as being of their number. Paul's friends took him out of Thessalonica quickly for his own safety — and theirs. The accusation was a most serious one, and the politarchs could not afford to treat it lightly. Apart from its special mention of Jesus, the language of the accusation fits very well into the general picture of movements within the Judaism of the day, more or less "messianic" in character, that constituted a threat to public order in places with Jewish communities, and that were deplored and denounced by those responsible Jews who knew the importance of maintaining acceptable relations with Rome. Paul the Roman citizen was certainly as appreciative of the *pax Romana* as any of those Jews, but it could not be denied that his apostolic progress from city to city was usually attended by public disturbances, which could easily be turned to his detriment.

Paul's two letters to the Thessalonian church, which were written only a few weeks or at most months after his departure from their city, bear witness to an intense eschatological excitement among the Christians there, and perhaps among the Jews also. In both Epistles Paul found it necessary to insist on a more sober outlook on the last things and pointed out that certain events precede the day of the Lord: "That day will not come, unless the rebellion comes first, and the man of lawlessness is revealed, the son of perdition, who opposes and exalts himself against every so-called god or object of worship, so that he takes his seat in the temple of God, proclaiming himself to be God. Do you not remember that when I was still with you I told you this? And you know what is restraining him now so that he may be revealed in his time. For the mystery of lawlessness is already at work; only he who now restrains it will do so until he is out of the way" (2 Thess. 2:3-7).

The life-setting and meaning of these words can be quite reasonably stated thus. The personal "abomination of desolation, standing where he ought not," foretold by Jesus in Mk. 13:14, must have appeared to many to be on the point of emerging ten years before Paul wrote, when the emperor Gaius in A.D. 40 ordered the erection of his image in the Jerusalem temple. This order was canceled just in time, but the terror and anxiety of those days left an abiding impression on Jews and Christians alike and colored their views of what would happen when the antichrist did in fact arise. When Paul visited Thessalonica *ca.* 50 he told his converts there about the coming day when lawlessness would manifest itself in all its evil, incarnated in "the man of lawlessness" who would go so far as to enthrone himself in the temple of God and claim divine honors beyond those paid to anyone or anything else. The quoted passage repeats this teaching and adds that the day of the Lord will not come until the antichrist appears to lead the great eschatological rebellion against God. At present the forces of lawlessness and anarchy are already active beneath the surface, but a restraining power prevents them from breaking forth. One day, however, this restraining power will be removed, and those evil forces will riot unchecked.

Paul told his readers that they knew what this restraining power actually is; perhaps he had already told them by word of mouth. The context suggests that at that time imperial law and order were a check on the turbulent forces always threatening to break loose. This identification is further suggested by the fact that the restraining power is referred to both by the neuter article and participle *tó katéchon,* "what is restraining [him]" (2 Thess. 2:6), and by the masculine article and participle *ho katéchōn,* "he who [now] restrains [it]" (v. 7). The imperial power was embodied in the emperor and could thus be described in personal as well as in impersonal terms. This too could explain the very guarded hints at the restrainer's identity. To speak openly in a letter about the coming removal of the imperial power or of the emperor himself would have been impolitic; in view of the charges of seditious activity recently pressed against Paul and his friends in Thessalonica, the consequences for the Thessalonian Christians would have been serious if a letter that seemed to support these charges fell into the wrong hands. But if another interpretation is adopted — e.g., O. Cullmann's and J. Munck's suggestion that Paul was referring to himself and his own apostolic ministry as the restraining agency — there is no obvious reason why Paul should not have stated his meaning plainly.

From Thessalonica Paul went to Beroea in Thessaly, and when similar trouble threatened to break out there, he was sent by sea to Athens. There he waited for his companions Silas and Timothy to rejoin him. (Luke apparently remained in Philippi.) The apologia before the Athenian Areopagus that Luke ascribed to him (Acts 17:22-31) has frequently been adjudged to be un-Pauline because it teaches a "God-mysticism" instead of the Pauline "Christ-mysticism" (A. Schweitzer, *Mysticism of Paul the Apostle,* pp. 6ff.; cf. M. Dibelius, *Studies in the Acts of the Apostles,* pp. 26ff.). But the address was delivered to pagans, not to Christians, and Paul knew well enough that in building a bridge between his hearers and himself he must start building at their end, not at his own. The *Areopagitica*'s appeal to the revelation of God in creation and providence and its criticism of idolatry are essentially the same as those in the early part of Romans, when the different audiences are borne in mind; in both echoes of the book of Wisdom may be detected. As expounded in the speech, the creative power of God, His care for His creatures, and His independence of them but their entire dependence on Him are firmly rooted in the OT. Paul's mind was too comprehensive and versatile for one to suppose that he must continually harp on one string; he is greater than all the Paulinisms.

But Athens was only a temporary halting-place; after a few days Paul moved on to Corinth, a busy seaport and chief city of the province of Achaia. There for the first time since leaving Antioch he found a base where he could stay for a considerable time and both plant and consolidate a center of Christian witness. Some months after his arrival in Corinth an attempt was made to restrain him; the leaders of the Jewish community of Corinth accused him before Gallio proconsul of Achaia of "persuading men to worship God contrary to the law" (Acts 18:13). The charge, as reported by Luke, is ambiguous; which law — Jewish or Roman — was Paul accused of breaking? It is more likely that he was accused of breaking Roman law. Gallio on dismissing the case told the prosecutors that he did not want to be a judge in questions of Jewish law, but they would have known that already. Their hope lay in convincing him that Paul's activity constituted a contravention of Roman law, which it was Gallio's business to maintain. They charged Paul with propagating an illegal religion — the implication being that what he was preaching was certainly not Judaism, which enjoyed the recognition and protection of imperial law except when its practice or propagation endangered public order.

Gallio, however, summed up the situation quickly; to him Paul was a Jew like his accusers and spoke the same sort of language as they did. Any differences between Paul and them concerned interpretations of Jewish law and religion, and it was no part of Gallio's responsibility to pronounce judgment on such questions. If public order had been endangered, if crime or misdemeanor had been involved, he would certainly have taken the matter up, he said. He had the prosecutors ejected from the court and turned a blind eye when bystanders mobbed the ruler of the synagogue.

Gallio's ruling, which in effect extended to Christianity the freedom that Judaism enjoyed under Roman law, probably created a precedent for other magistrates and allowed Paul to prosecute his apostolic mission with the assurance of the benevolent neutrality of the imperial authorities for several years to come. Certainly if Gallio had ruled against Paul, this verdict would have been invoked by Paul's opponents for the rest of his life; a precedent established by so exalted and influential a magistrate would have carried great weight. Gallio's ruling may also have confirmed Paul's good opinion of Roman justice and influenced Paul's very positive attitude in Rom. 13:1-7 toward "the powers that be" as "ministers of God" — not to speak of its influencing his later decision to appeal to Caesar.

Gallio's ruling encouraged Paul to continue in Corinth; in all he spent eighteen months there, until the spring of A.D. 52. By that time there was a large and gifted, if volatile, church in Corinth, consisting mostly of converts from paganism whose earlier life had accorded with the moral laxity for which their city was notorious in that day. Paul was faced with the practical problem of deciding on the best means of teaching such people the Christian way of life.

Many of his fellow Christians and critics in Jerusalem would have assured him that his only wise course was to impose the Jewish law on these converts as a fundamental condition of their acknowledgment as Christians. But Paul had learned in his own experience that all the law-keeping in the world could never bring assurance of salvation and peace with God — and he knew more about law-keeping than most of his critics did. But the moment that he surrendered his life to Christ, he knew that he had found the true way of salvation and peace. And he contended that when persons yielded themselves to the living Christ and the power of His Spirit, their inward beings were so changed that from that time forth they would spontaneously fulfil "the just requirement of the law" (Rom. 8:4) and produce "the fruit of the Spirit" (Gal. 5:22f.).

Many Christians thought that Paul was being impossibly optimistic. This conception, they said, might work all right with people who already had a stable moral foundation, but how could it work with a crowd of immoral pagans such as had been swept into church fellowship in Corinth and similar places? Paul maintained that it could work, even among people whose background and environment were so unpromising; in the long run Paul's way was vindicated. But at the time many of his friends (not to speak of his opponents) seriously thought that his course of action was weakening the ethical standards of the gospel. In justification of their criticism they could point to moral lapses among Paul's converts.

Paul deplored these lapses more than anyone else, for he knew that his apostolic reputation was bound up with his converts' behavior — his apostolic reputation not so much in the eyes of men as in the sight of God. Repeatedly he told his converts that he could look forward with confidence to the day when he must give an account of his stewardship before the tribunal of Christ only if they stood firm in their faith and proved the genuineness of their Christianity by the quality of their lives. But he treated them as mature children of God; instead of imposing a code of rules on them he set before them the perfect standard of Christ — Christ being not merely an external example but being reproduced within them by the power of the Spirit. This standard, which Paul called "the law of Christ" (1 Cor. 9:21; Gal. 6:2), is a law written in human hearts and not on stone or parchment. It is a law that forbids Christians to live irregular lives, to quarrel with one another, to interfere in other people's business, to live at other people's expense when they are perfectly able to earn their own living. But it is not in essence a negative law; it is the positive law of Christian love. Jesus had not only summed up the OT law in the two great commandments of love to God and love to one's neighbor; His whole life had embodied this law of love and had provided His followers with a standard for their own emulation. If then the power of the indwelling Spirit of God reproduces the character of Christ in the lives of His people, they will spontaneously follow the law of love. This was Paul's ambition for his converts.

It was no easy way that he chose, but it was the noblest way, and he never doubted that it was the only right way for men and women who had come of age spiritually through faith in Christ. It was a way that brought him repeated disappointment, as his converts failed to respond to "the upward call of God in Christ Jesus" (Phil. 3:14), but it never brought him disillusionment. His many disappointments were more than matched by the readiness with which the majority of his converts — even those newly liberated from idolatry — embraced his teaching and exhibited the law of Christ in their lives, which shone like bright lights in the surrounding darkness.

Paul's task was rendered the more difficult because he had to wage war on two fronts: against those who thought that the gospel emancipated them from all ethical conventions, and against those who (partly, no doubt, by way of reaction to the former) went to the opposite extreme and tried in the name of Christianity to set up taboos against marriage, against animal food, and so forth. Thus while Paul was doing all he could to restrain those who misinterpreted Christian liberty to mean license to do anything they chose, he was obliged to deal firmly with those who wanted to introduce a new set of prohibitions that would have banished Christian liberty altogether. This double struggle must be borne in mind if one is to understand the arguments he employed now on this side and now on that. He went as far as he could with both sides, until the point came where he had to stand fast and vindicate the principles of the gospel. He agreed with much that the libertarians said about Christian freedom but reminded them of its attendant responsibilities. He agreed with much that the ascetic party said about self-denial — he himself practiced self-denial far beyond what they did — but he insisted that self-denial must be a voluntary discipline, not to be imposed on others against their will, and not to be imposed on oneself in a spirit of legalism or with the idea of acquiring special merit in God's sight. To the one group he said, "Liberty, not license"; to the other he said, "Liberty, not bondage." Christians living in a non-Christian environment were to remember that the public reputation of Christianity, and indeed of Christ Himself, depended on their behavior. But there was an even higher incentive; they were to remember above all that they were called to please Christ. To win Christ's approval mattered supremely for Paul in his own life, and he was eager that it should matter supremely in theirs. To this end, then, he gave them every encouragement.

For the rest, Paul's policy was to preach the gospel and plant churches in important centers like Corinth and along the main lines of imperial communication in the provinces that he evangelized. He had no time to do more if he was to accomplish his task, which was at this stage in his ministry the evangelization of the Aegean lands and after that the evangelization of the rest of the Mediterranean world, insofar as others had not already preached the gospel there. He knew that "the gospel must first be preached to all nations" (Mk. 13:10) before the Parousia could be expected. This was sufficient reason for magnifying his office as apostle to the Gentiles, but his gentile apostleship had this further importance in his eyes, that it would pave the way for the turning of his fellow Israelites to Christ — a consummation (perhaps, as he thought, coincident with the Parousia) for which he longed and prayed unceasingly (Rom. 9:1ff.; 10:1; 11:13ff.).

*F. Paul Completes His Aegean Ministry.* Leaving Corinth in the spring of A.D. 52, Paul paid a brief visit to Palestine and then traveled overland to Ephesus, chief city of the province of Asia, which he made his base for the next phase of his activity, lasting nearly three years (Acts 20:31). There with a number of helpers he preached and taught so assiduously that "all the residents of Asia heard the word of the Lord, both Jews and Greeks" (19:10). The church in the province of Asia, in fact, endured without a break from those years until the disruptive exchange of populations between Turkey and Greece in A.D. 1923.

Some disciples of Jesus had indeed settled in Ephesus before Paul's arrival there — representatives of another stream of Christian advance than those whose progress is recorded in Acts. But it was with Paul's arrival that the Christianization of the province began in earnest.

For all the success of his work, he had many obstacles to overcome. The riot in the Ephesian theater (Acts 19:23ff.; *see* Plate 60) illustrates how commercial interests were liable to be affected by new religious movements; there was opposition from the local Jewish community (20:19). In short, as Paul himself put it, the city presented "a wide door for effective work" together with "many adversaries" (1 Cor. 16:9). Some of those adversaries offered more serious threats to Paul's liberty, and even to his life, than might be gathered from a cursory reading of Acts and the Epistles. Of the many imprisonments to which he alluded in 2 Cor. 11:23 (written toward the end of his Ephesian ministry) one at least was probably endured in Ephesus. The cryptic reference in 1 Cor. 15:32 to his having "fought with wild beasts at Ephesus" suggests some deadly peril; he mentioned another deadly peril in 2 Cor. 1:8ff.

What these deadly perils were cannot be known with certainty. One attractive suggestion is that Paul may have somehow been jeopardized by the events attendant on the assassination of Marcus Junius Silanus proconsul of Asia. Nero's mother Agrippina had plotted this death shortly after Nero's accession to the imperial throne in October, 54 (cf. Duncan, *St. Paul's Ephesian Ministry,* pp. 102ff.). Certainly the language of 2 Cor. 1:8ff. implies more than a nearly fatal illness. Quite possibly, as C. H. Dodd argued (*NT Studies,* pp. 80ff.), this experience marked a spiritual watershed in Paul's Christian experience, but it cannot safely be made a criterion for dating his Epistles on one or the other side of the watershed.

In addition to such external troubles, Paul bore as a daily weight his "anxiety for all the churches" (2 Cor. 11:28). His Corinthian correspondence, which belongs to this period, provides sufficient commentary on these words. After Paul had left Corinth there was a deliberate campaign there to subvert his authority by belittling his apostolic status. Paul, it was well known, had not been one of Jesus' companions during His Palestinian ministry but claimed to have been commissioned later, in a vision. Some belittlers of Paul's apostleship compared his status unfavorably with other apostles', particularly Peter's. Whether Peter himself ever visited Corinth or even knew that some church members there had formed a party claiming his leadership cannot be inferred with certainty from Paul's references to those Corinthian Christians who said, "I belong to Peter" (1 Cor. 1:12). But if Peter did know or approve of their party in any measure, Paul could regard it as a breach of the agreement that he and Barnabas had reached with Peter and the other "pillars" at Jerusalem. Those who claimed to act in Peter's name at Corinth represented themselves as building on the foundation that Paul had laid (3:10ff.). There was a way of doing this that Paul did not resent; he seems to have been quite happy about Apollos's activity at Corinth after his own departure, although he deprecated the tendency to make Apollos a party leader, just as he refused to be regarded as a party leader himself. But the Petrine party, in claiming to build on Paul's foundation, did so in a manner that disparaged Paul's work. Although they did not follow the cruder methods used by the Judaizers earlier in the churches of Galatia, immediately pressing on gentile Christians the necessity of circumcision and the other requirements of the Jewish law, Paul perhaps regarded their activity as accordingly all the more dangerous. How careful Paul himself was not to "build on another man's foundation" (Rom. 15:20) may be seen from the delicacy of his approach in Romans, where he wrote to a Christian community he had no part in forming.

After his departure from Ephesus in the summer of 55 Paul spent some time revisiting the churches of Macedonia and Achaia. This stage of his activity is not narrated in detail; an indication that it was more extensive than Acts 20:1-3 might lead one to suppose is his statement in Rom. 15:19 that he had preached the gospel as far west as Illyricum — the Roman province bordering the eastern shore of the Adriatic Sea, NW of Macedonia. The interval following his Ephesian ministry is the only one into which a visit to Illyricum can be fitted. Besides, the context in which Paul mentioned the visit implies that it was the latest episode in his missionary activity at the time of writing — *ca.* early 57.

One reason that Paul wrote to the Roman Christians then was to prepare them for a visit that he hoped shortly to pay them. But he told them that before he could set out for Rome he had to discharge a commission in Jerusalem — the delivery to the Christians there of a monetary contribution that he had been organizing in the churches of his gentile mission field for three or four years (Rom. 15:25ff.; cf. 1 Cor. 16:1ff.; 2 Cor. 8:1ff.).

This "ministry" to Jerusalem was part of Paul's overall apostolic program; in addition, some ten years earlier the Jerusalem leaders had requested Barnabas and Paul, as they ministered to the Gentiles, not to forget "the poor" (Gal. 2:10) — a term that became practically synonymous with the believing community in Jerusalem (cf. the later Jewish-Christian community of Ebionites, from the Heb. *'eḇyôn,* "poor").

This contribution was a means of bringing home to the gentile Christians their indebtedness to Jerusalem. Since the gospel had come to them from there, it was a small return on their part to contribute to the material needs of the mother church of Christendom. Moreover, Paul regarded the gift as a means of strengthening the fellowship that ought to be maintained between Jerusalem and the gentile churches. He knew that many members of the Jerusalem church looked with suspicion on his gentile mission, while some went so far as to try to win his converts over to a conception of Christian faith and life more in keeping with that held by the rank and file of the Jerusalem disciples. What Paul thought and felt about the activities of such people is evident from his onslaught against them in 2 Cor. 11:13 as workers of deceit who masqueraded as apostles of Christ. But he could not tolerate the idea of a permanent cleavage between Jerusalem and the gentile churches. Anything of this kind would be a disaster for the cause of Christ in the world, and he set himself to overcome it by a generous gesture of brotherly love.

One may wonder, indeed, if Paul and the Jerusalem leaders understood the contribution in the same light. For Paul it was a spontaneous gesture of brotherly love, a token of grateful response by his converts to the divine grace which had brought them salvation. But in the eyes of the elders of the Jerusalem church it might have been a form of tribute, a duty owed by the daughter churches to their mother, comparable to the half-shekel that Jews throughout the world paid annually to maintain the Jerusalem temple.

In Paul's eyes, however, it was something more even than a grateful gesture by the gentile churches or a means of strengthening the fellowship between them and Jerusalem. It was the climax of his own ministry in the eastern Mediterranean and an act of worship and dedication to God before he set out for the western Mediterranean. It was the outward and visible sign of the "offering up of the Gentiles" that crowned his priestly service as Christ's apostle among them (Rom. 15:16). For this reason he attached great importance to his accompanying the delegates who were to carry their churches' gifts to Jerusalem and there to present this offering to God, perhaps by an act of worship at the very place in the temple where once Christ had appeared to him and sent him "far away to the Gentiles" (Acts 22:21). Then, and not till then, would he be ready to set out for Rome.

*G. Paul Comes to Rome.* According to Luke, Paul's plan to visit Rome was formulated toward the end of his Ephesian ministry: "Paul resolved in the Spirit to pass through Macedonia and Achaia, saying, 'After I have been there, I must also see Rome'" (Acts 19:21). The reason for Paul's plan appears clearly enough from his letter to the Romans, where he told the Roman Christians that he had completed his apostolic task in the Aegean lands and hoped to repeat in Spain what he had done in Macedonia and Achaia, Galatia and Asia. His settled policy of preaching Christ where the gospel had not previously been heard, his unwillingness to "build on another man's foundation," ruled out most of the other Mediterranean lands as areas for his further apostolic activity. But evidently no one had carried the Christian message to Spain. To Spain, then, Paul would go. And on his way to Spain he would have an opportunity to realize a long-cherished desire to see Rome, and not only to see it, but, by the goodwill of the Christians there, to make it his base for his Spanish mission (Rom. 1:11-15; 15:14-32).

Luke had nothing to say of Paul's plan to evangelize Spain. Rome is the terminus of Luke's history; he reached his goal when he brought Paul there, and there he left him still preaching the gospel. The purpose of Luke-Acts as a whole is bound up with the note on which the narrative comes to an end. For Luke, Paul's words "I must also see Rome" anticipate the goal of Luke's own narrative, whereas for the apostle Rome was but a temporary halting-place on his way farther west.

The circumstances in which Paul reached Rome were different from any that he could have foreseen. When he wrote to the Roman Christians he evidently had some misgivings about the reception he would have in Jerusalem: pray, he said, "that I may be delivered from the unbelievers in Judea, and that my service for Jerusalem may be acceptable to the saints" (Rom. 15:31). While he and the delegates from the gentile churches received a friendly welcome from James and his fellow elders, he was set upon in the temple by some Jews from the province of Asia and charged with violating its sanctity. He was taken into custody by members of the Roman garrison in the adjoining Antonia fortress, and when their commander discovered that Paul was a Roman citizen he sent him under armed escort to Felix procurator of Judea at Caesarea. The Jewish authorities sent a deputation to Caesarea to press two charges against Paul — the particular charge of sacrilege, which could not be substantiated because the witnesses failed to appear, and the more general charge of being a subverter of public order throughout the whole Diaspora. To both charges Paul returned a firm plea of Not Guilty, but Felix deferred sentence until his recall from office in 59. His successor Festus reopened the case with every intention of acting in accordance with the highest standards of Roman justice. When, however, he spoke of holding the trial at Jerusalem and not at Caesarea, Paul was afraid that through the new governor's inexperience he might be put into the power of his enemies. Accordingly he availed himself of a Roman citizen's privilege and appealed to Caesar (Acts 25:11).

The right of appeal (*provocatio*) to the emperor appears to have grown out of the earlier right of appeal to the sovereign people. According to Dio Cassius (*Hist.* li.19), Augustus in 30 B.C. was granted the right to judge on appeal. In this period, too, was enacted the *lex Julia de vi publica* (see VII.A above), which forbade any magistrate vested with *imperium* or *potestas* to kill, scourge, chain, or torture a Roman citizen, or to sentence him if he had appealed to the emperor, or to prevent him from going to Rome to lodge his appeal within a fixed time. It appears that, from the date of this enactment, a Roman citizen anywhere in the empire was protected against arbitrary magisterial coercion, although the provincial magistrate might deal with cases involving a plain breach of established statute law, which Paul's case manifestly did not (cf. A. H. M. Jones, *Studies in Roman Government and Law* [1960], p. 96). (The picture given in Acts of Paul's appeal is true to the dramatic date of the book, accords with what is known of conditions in the late 50's of the 1st cent. A.D., and is worthy indeed to be treated as a substantial addition to the available evidence.)

The provincial judge had to send an explanatory statement (*litterae dimissoriae,* "letter of dismissal") along with the accused man, and the inexperienced Festus was certainly glad to have the aid in drafting this document of the younger Agrippa, king of the areas NE of the Roman province of Judea that had formerly constituted the tetrarchies of Philip and Lysanias. Agrippa had come to Caesarea to pay his respects to the new procurator on the morrow of Paul's appeal to Caesar (Acts 25:13ff.). (From 48 to 66 the Jewish high-priesthood was in Agrippa's gift, and he was reputed to be well versed in Jewish religious practice.) This king had an opportunity of hearing Paul for himself and agreed that he could not reasonably be convicted on any of the serious charges brought against him; indeed, he might have been discharged there and then had he not appealed to Caesar, but for Festus to prejudge the issue now by discharging him would have been impolitic, if not *ultra vires* (beyond his authority) (Acts 26:32). To Rome, then, Paul was sent, under the custody of the centurion Julius (27:1ff.).

Why did Paul appeal to Caesar? He did not do so while Felix was in office, presumably because Felix had virtually decided on his innocence and was simply postponing his formal acquittal and release. One day (Paul might have hoped), Felix's procrastination would come to an end, and he would be discharged and be able to carry out his long-cherished plan of traveling to Rome and the West. But with the recall of Felix and his supersession by Festus a new and dangerous situation was developing for Paul; hence he made his momentous decision.

One may be sure that the uppermost consideration in Paul's appeal to Caesar was not his own safety, but the interests of the gospel. Seven or eight years previously he had experienced the benevolent neutrality of Roman law in the decision of Gallio proconsul of Achaia that there was nothing illegal in his preaching since (so far as Roman law was concerned) it was a variety of Judaism. He might reasonably have expected a similarly favorable verdict from the supreme court in Rome. But even a man of smaller intelligence than Paul must have realized that the consideration that moved Gallio would not be valid much longer. Thanks in a large measure to Paul's own activity, it would soon be impossible to regard Christianity as a variety of Judaism, since it was now manifestly more gentile than Jewish. A favorable hearing from the emperor in Rome might win recognition for Christianity, if not as the true fulfillment of Israel's ancestral religion (which Paul believed it to be), at least as a *religio licita* (a lawful religion) in its own right. Besides, if Nero in person heard Paul's defense, what might the outcome not be? The younger Agrippa had politely declined to admit the logic of Paul's argument, but Gentiles had regularly shown themselves more amenable to the gospel than Jews, and a Roman emperor might be more easily won than a Jewish client-king. It would be precarious to set limits to Paul's high hopes, however impracticable they may appear to us in retrospect.

Although Paul had appealed to Nero, the emperor would not inevitably have heard the case in person. According to Tacitus (*Ann.* xiii.4.2) Nero announced at the beginning of his principate that he would not judge cases *in propria persona* (personally), as his predecessor Claudius had done; indeed, during his first eight years he generally delegated them to others (cf. *Ann.* xiv.50.2). Thus Paul's case, especially if it came up before 62, was probably heard by someone other than Nero, perhaps the prefect of the praetorian guard, "representing the Emperor in his capacity as the fountain of justice, together with the assessors and high officers of the court" (Ramsay, *SPT,* p. 357). If the hearer was the prefect, it would have made a great difference whether he was the honest Afranius Burrus or his infamous successor Tigellinus. But one cannot be sure to whom Paul's case was delegated, if it was delegated at all.

Luke recorded in considerable detail Paul's voyage to Rome, shipwreck on the way, and a three-month winter stay in Malta (Acts 27:1–28:10); his narrative is interesting for many reasons (not least as an important documentary source for knowledge of ancient seamanship), among them especially its portrayal of Paul in trying circumstances of a kind that displays a person for what he really is. Paul kept his head and faith high amid the mounting despair and imparted some of his own indomitable courage to his fellow passengers.

When at last he and the other prisoners on board reached Rome, they were handed over by the centurion who had charge of them to the "stratopedarch," according to the Western text of Acts 28:16. This official may have been the camp commandant of the praetorian guard. All forms of the text agree that Paul "was permitted to stay by himself with the soldier who guarded him."

Paul lived in Rome for two full years at his own expense (or on his own earnings). Whether or not the AV "in his own hired house" can be accepted as a translation of *en idíō misthṓmati* (Acts 28:30), he probably did remain under house arrest, i.e., he was not kept in custody in the headquarters of the praetorian guard but "outside the camp," as many Western authorities add. He was thus free to receive visitors, although he could not move about freely himself. Luke mentioned among Paul's earliest visitors a deputation of Roman Jews, whose debate with the apostle forms the last scene of Luke's history — plainly with programmatic intent. The pattern of Jewish refusal of the gospel and gentile acceptance of it, which recurred earlier in Luke's history, is recorded definitively in Rome, with Paul's conclusive last word (after his quotation of Isa. 6:10): "Take knowledge, then, that this salvation of God has been sent to the Gentiles; *they* will listen to it" (Acts 28:28).

But what of the "two full years" of Paul's detention? What happened at the end of this period? Some have assumed quite confidently that it ended with Paul's trial, conviction, and execution (cf. J. V. Bartlet, *Expos.,* 8th ser.,

St. Paul's Bay, Crete, where Paul was shipwrecked en route to Rome (W. S. LaSor)

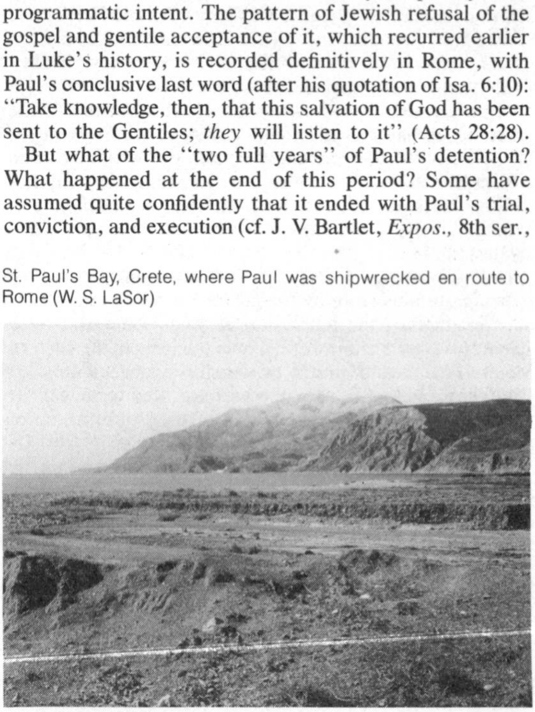

5 [1913], 464ff.). Others have thought that it ended with his release, either because he was tried and acquitted or because the case went against his accusers by default (cf. K. Lake, *Interpreter,* 5 [1908/09], 147ff.; W. M. Ramsay, *Teaching of Paul in Terms of the Present Day,* pp. 346ff.; H. J. Cadbury, *BC,* V, 297ff., esp. 326ff.).

On the one hand, if Paul's two-year detention was followed immediately by his condemnation and death, Luke's failure to say anything about these events is inexplicable. On the other hand, there does not appear to be first-century evidence for any procedure permitting a case to lapse automatically by default. The available evidence suggests that everything was done to compel the appearance of prosecutors and defendants and to prevent the abandonment of charges. A prosecutor who did not appear in court within a reasonable time would probably be penalized, but that would not imply the automatic discharge of the defendant.

The prolongation of Paul's stay in Rome over two full years could have been due to congestion of court business as much as anything else; if indeed he was discharged without being tried, this act could have resulted from Caesar's exercising his *imperium.* "Perhaps Paul benefited from the clemency of Nero, and secured a merely casual release. But there is no necessity to construe Acts to mean that he was released at all" (A. N. Sherwin-White, *Roman Society and Roman Law in the NT* [1963], p. 119). Paul's Epistles must be examined to discover if they throw any more light on the question than Acts does.

If Paul *was* released after his two years of captivity in Rome, where did he go next? His letter to Philemon (if it belongs to his Roman captivity) indicates that he expected soon to be discharged and to revisit his friends in the province of Asia. "Prepare a guest room for me," he said, "for I am hoping through your prayers to be granted to you" (Philem. 22). The Pastoral Epistles provide unmistakable references to some activity by Paul in the eastern Mediterranean, which cannot well be dated anywhere before his arrest in Jerusalem and voyage to Rome. In addition to the province of Asia, he appears to have visited Macedonia (1 Tim. 1:3), Crete (Tit. 1:5), and Epirus (Tit. 3:12). It is true that according to Luke he told the elders of the Ephesian church when he took his leave of them at Miletus that they would never see him again (Acts 20:25, 38), but at that time he was planning to set out for Spain as soon as he had completed his business in Jerusalem and did not foresee the disruption in his plans that his arrest in Jerusalem would cause.

Was he ever able to fulfil his hope of preaching the gospel in Spain? To this question no certain answer can be returned. Two Roman documents suggest that he did go there. Clement of Rome in his epistle to the Corinthians (*ca.* 96) reminded them how Paul "went to the limit of the West" and bore his testimony before rulers before he departed from the world (1 Clem. 5:7). Whether Clement meant "the limit of the West" or was speaking simply of Paul's reaching "his goal in the West," as a Roman writer he likely was referring to a place farther west than Rome. The Muratorian Canon (*ca.* 190) also seems to say that Luke omitted both Peter's martyrdom and Paul's departure from the capital for Spain (lines 37-39). This apparent assumption that Paul did set out for Spain could, however, be nothing more than an inference from Rom. 15:24, 28; indeed, the same might be said, though with less probability, of Clement's mention of his going to "the limit of the West." The question must remain open.

On the final scene of Paul's life there is more certainty. The Roman Christian writer and presbyter Gaius (late 2nd cent.) said that he could point out on the Vatican hill and by the road to Ostia the "trophies" (funeral monuments) of

Statue of Paul in St. Peter's Square, Rome (W. S. LaSor)

the apostles (i.e., Peter and Paul, respectively). Eusebius, who quoted Gaius to this effect (*HE* ii.25.7), also mentioned how Dionysius bishop of Corinth (*ca.* 170) in a letter to the Roman church recalled the martyrdom of Peter and Paul in Italy around the same time — presumably, as tradition asserts, in the persecution under Nero that broke out in 64. 2 Tim. 4:6-18 may well refer to a second imprisonment and trial of Paul at Rome which issued in his condemnation and execution. As a Roman citizen, Paul would have been beheaded with the sword. But that would have been a small matter in the eyes of one who had long recognized that "to die is gain" (Phil. 1:21); what filled him with joy was that his appearance in court gave him one more opportunity to bear witness to the gospel: "the Lord stood by me and gave me strength to proclaim the word fully, that all the Gentiles might hear it" (2 Tim. 4:17).

*See also* ROMAN LAW; Vol. I, Maps XVIII-XXI.

***Bibliography.***–(See also B. M. Metzger, *Index to Periodical Literature on the Apostle Paul* [1960].) A. B. D. Alexander, *Ethics of St. Paul* (1910); B. W. Bacon, *Jesus and Paul* (1921); *Story of St. Paul* (1905); W. Barclay, *Mind of St. Paul* (1958); C. K. Barrett, *From First Adam to Last* (1962); H. N. Bate, *Guide to the Epistles of St. Paul* (1926); F. C. Baur, *Paul, His Life and Works* (2 vols., Eng. tr. 1876); F. W. Beare, *St. Paul and His Letters* (1962); G. Bornkamm, *Paul* (Eng. tr. 1971); F. F. Bruce, *Paul* (1977); R. Bultmann, *Theology of the NT,* I (Eng. tr. 1952); L. Cerfaux, *Christ in the Theology of St. Paul* (Eng. tr. 1959); *Church in the Theology of St. Paul* (Eng. tr. 1959); W. D. Davies, *Christian Origins and Judaism* (1962); *Paul and Rabbinic Judaism* (2nd ed. 1955); A. Deissmann, *Paul, A Study in Social and Religious History* (Eng. tr., 2nd ed. 1926); M. Dibelius, *Die Geisterwelt im Glauben des Paulus* (1909); *Studies in the Acts of the Apostles* (Eng. tr. 1956); M. Dibelius and W. G. Kümmel, *Paul* (Eng. tr. 1953); C. H. Dodd, *Meaning of Paul for Today* (1920); *NT Studies* (1953), pp. 67-128; J. W. Drane, *Paul: Libertine or Legalist?* (1975); G. S. Duncan, *St. Paul's Ephesian Ministry* (1929); E. E. Ellis, *Paul and His Recent Interpreters* (1961); *Paul's Use of the OT* (1957); F. J. Foakes Jackson, *Life of St. Paul* (1927); A.

Fridrichsen, *Apostle and His Message* (1947); T. R. Glover, *Paul of Tarsus* (1925); M. Grant, *Saint Paul* (1976); D. Guthrie, *NT Intro.* (1961), pp. 386-684; N. Q. Hamilton, *Holy Spirit and Eschatology in Paul* (1957); A. M. Hunter, *Interpreting Paul's Gospel* (1954); *Paul and His Predecessors* (2nd ed. 1961); R. Jewett, *A Chronology of Paul's Life* (1979); *Paul's Anthropological Terms* (1971); E. Jüngel, *Paulus und Jesus* (1962); E. Käsemann, *Perspectives on Paul* (Eng. tr. 1971); H. A. A. Kennedy, *St. Paul and the Mystery Religions* (1913); *St. Paul's Conception of the Last Things* (1904); *Theology of the Epistles* (1919); S. Kim, *Origin of Paul's Gospel* (1981); J. Klausner, *From Jesus to Paul* (Eng. tr. 1944); J. Knox, *Chapters in a Life of Paul* (1950); *Marcion and the NT* (1942); *Philemon among the Letters of Paul* (1935); W. L. Knox, *St. Paul and the Church of Jerusalem* (1925); *St. Paul and the Church of the Gentiles* (1939); *Some Hellenistic Elements in Primitive Christianity* (1944); K. Lake, *Earlier Epistles of St. Paul* (2nd ed. 1914); *Paul, His Heritage and Legacy* (1934); J. G. Machen, *Origin of Paul's Religion* (1947); T. W. Manson, *On Paul and John* (1963); *Studies in the Gospels and Epistles* (1962); C. L. Mitton, *Formation of the Pauline Corpus of Letters* (1955); J. Munck, *Paul and the Salvation of Mankind* (Eng. tr. 1959); A. D. Nock, *Early Gentile Christianity* (2nd ed. 1964); *St. Paul* (1938); F. Prat, *Theology of St. Paul* (Eng. tr. 1959); W. M. Ramsay, *Cities of St. Paul* (1907); *Pauline and Other Studies* (1906); *SPT*; *Teaching of Paul in Terms of the Present Day* (1913); H. N. Ridderbos, *Paul and Jesus* (Eng. tr. 1957); *Paul* (Eng. tr. 1975); J. A. T. Robinson, *The Body: A Study in Pauline Theology* (*SBT*, 1/5, 1952); E. P. Sanders, *Paul and Palestinian Judaism* (1977); W. Schmithals, *Paul and James* (Eng. tr. 1965); R. Schnackenburg, *Baptism in the Thought of St. Paul* (Eng. tr. 1964); H. J. Schoeps, *Paul: The Theology of the Apostle in the Light of Jewish History* (Eng. tr. 1961); G. Schrenk, *Studien zu Paulus* (1954); A. Schweitzer, *Mysticism of Paul the Apostle* (Eng. tr. 1931); *Paul and His Interpreters* (Eng. tr. 1912); C. A. A. Scott, *Christianity According to St. Paul* (1927); *Footnotes to St. Paul* (1935); *St. Paul, the Man and the Teacher* (1936); J. Smith, *Voyage and Shipwreck of St. Paul* (Eng. tr. 1880); W. D. Stacey, *Pauline View of Man* (1956); K. Stendahl, *Paul Among Jews and Gentiles* (1976); J. S. Stewart, *A Man in Christ* (1935); P. Stuhlmacher, *Das paulinische Evangelium* (1968-); H. St. J. Thackeray, *Relation of St. Paul to Contemporary Jewish Thought* (1900); W. C. van Unnik, *Tarsus or Jerusalem?* (Eng. tr. 1962); G. Vos, *Pauline Eschatology* (2nd ed. 1952); D. E. H. Whiteley, *Theology of St. Paul* (1964); A. Wikenhauser, *Pauline Mysticism* (Eng. tr. 1960).

F. F. BRUCE

## PAULINE THEOLOGY.

- I. Natural Theology
  - A. The Case Against Pauline Natural Theology
  - B. The Case for Pauline Natural Theology
- II. Special Revelation
  - A. Its Nature
  - B. Its Extent
  - C. Its Necessity
  - D. Evidence
- III. The Trinity
- IV. Jesus Christ
  - A. His Deity
  - B. His Humanity
- V. Man and Sin
  - A. Man as Creature
  - B. Man as *Sarx*
  - C. Man as Sinner
- VI. Redemption
  - A. Righteousness of God
  - B. Justification by Faith
  - C. Law and Grace
- VII. The Church
  - A. Its Nature
  - B. Visible and Invisible
- VIII. Eschatology
  - A. Parousia
  - B. Resurrection
  - C. Judgment
- IX. Summary

Paul is the most influential theologian of all time. Although his theology does not adulterate the content or even the expression of the theology presented in the Gospels, it is clearly more systematic. He may not have established his missions on any other person's foundations, but his theology rests squarely on the teaching of the OT and of his Lord Jesus Christ. Nevertheless he went beyond both; Christ's promise of the Spirit—"He will guide you into all truth" (Jn. 16:13) — was fulfilled uniquely in Paul. So here we shall follow somewhat systematically this guidance, considering consecutively Paul's doctrines of natural theology, special revelation, the trinity, Jesus Christ, man and sin, redemption, the Church, and the future.

*I. Natural Theology.–A. The Case Against Pauline Natural Theology.* Many scholars have denied that Paul had a natural theology, i.e., a doctrine of God constructed from nature, including human nature, independent of special revelation. Among them are B. Gärtner, G. Bornkamm, N. B. Stonehouse, O. Cullmann, K. Barth (e.g., *CD*, I/2, 167), D. Bonhoeffer, G. Berkouwer, R. Reitzenstein, and J. de Zwaan.

First, in making their case some, including Bornkamm (*NTS*, 4 [1957/58], p. 94), have denied the authenticity of the Areopagus (Mars' Hill) address. But their denial is due mainly to its "natural theology," which is the question under discussion. Furthermore, the unquestionably authentic Rom. 1–2 even more clearly appears to teach natural theology.

Second, it has also been observed (cf., e.g., M. E. Andrews, "Paul, Philo, and the Intellectuals," in J. S. Kepler, ed., *Contemporary Thinking about Paul* [1950], pp. 400f.) that Paul was not really among the *literati*, did not display the "philosophic calm" of the typical natural theologians, the Stoics, and was more mystically oriented, though in a different way, than Philo. These interesting points may be quite true without militating against Paul as a natural theologian. All Stoics may be philosophers but not all philosophers are Stoics.

Third, R. Reitzenstein (*Poimandres* [1904], p. 118) argued that Gk. *gnṓsis theoú* in Paul is not knowledge (*Wissen*) but insight or feeling (*Schauen, Fühlen*). While this is an interesting and significant observation, it scarcely proves Paul to be anti-intellectual. Feeling and intuition imply knowledge. An emphasis on feeling does not preclude intellection and apparently assumes it. Furthermore, as Bornkamm observed, "Our investigations have shown that Paul is much more concerned with man's rationality... than is usually recognized" (p. 100).

Fourth, some have pointed out that Paul's teachings concerning the means of salvation, spiritual community, the resurrection body, and final judgment are not found in the Stoic enchiridion. This does not prove, however, that all Pauline doctrines (e.g., natural theology) are absent from the Stoic enchiridion.

Fifth, de Zwaan observed (543f.) that Pauline revelation is not concerned with the *stoicheía* but with righteousness, election, and the like themes; if the word "merely" is inserted before "concerned" no objection can be taken, but then neither can any argument against natural theology be made. In any case, the meaning of *stoicheía* is too uncertain to allow the word's use in argument. (*See* ELEMENT.)

Sixth, more serious is the constant contention that the God of the Greek philosophers and Stoics is impersonal. The assumption is that if Paul were an amateur natural philosopher, his God too would be impersonal: since his God was not, he did not philosophize or attempt to prove God. But this contention falsely assumes that all Greek philosophizing led only to an impersonal deity and that all philosophizing could lead only to a Greek conclusion.

Seventh, it is contended that when Paul argued from the visible things (Gk. *toís poiḗmasin*) to the invisible God (*tá aórata*) in Rom. 1:20 he was a Christian believing in the personal God and Father of Our Lord Jesus Christ. Certainly Paul was a Christian believer when he wrote this text. But, (1) it does not follow that he was here assuming the God he sought to prove; (2) there is no evidence in the context that he was assuming God; (3) just the opposite, there is every evidence that he did not assume Him; for (4) he appealed only to natural revelation, not to special revelation, as manifesting the invisible God; so that (5) people in general "know God."

Eighth, the exegesis that Gk. *phanerón* ("manifest," Rom. 1:19; RSV "plain") points not to human speculation but to divine revelation is both true and false. It is true that revelation is what makes manifest, but it is false that revelation is not made manifest to human speculation or insight. Revelation's "transparent" character is shown in people's "knowing" God and being "inexcusable" for not worshiping Him.

Ninth, if Paul had a natural theology he would have had to teach that salvation was identical with right thinking (Gärtner, p. 143). It is clear that people's wrong thinking was traceable to their sinful condition. They were given up to a "reprobate mind" because they "would not" have God in their thinking; they would not worship Him. The implication is clear that if their hearts were right their minds could easily see the revelation. Indeed, they did see it in spite of themselves and immediately proceeded to suppress it. Obviously, if this wilful blindness were taken away, they would think rightly; salvation of the mind *is* part of total salvation.

Tenth and finally, many have noted that Paul as a student of and believer in the OT, which assumes rather than argues the existence of God from Gen. 1:1 on and disdains Greek rationalizing of God, could not turn apologist in his own writings. We will not press the point that the anti-intellectualism of the OT may be overdone but will note, first, that the Jews developed an apologetic, as seen, e.g., in the wisdom literature of Job, Psalms, Proverbs, and Ecclesiastes; second, that the man who became all things to all people that he might win some would not likely have used an irrelevant Jewish approach to Gentiles; and third, that he would not have charged them with being "inexcusable" for not knowing a God whom they could not have known.

*See* STOICS.

*B. The Case for Pauline Natural Theology*. In favor of a Pauline natural theology have been a host of scholars, including M. Dibelius, G. Lüdemann, E. J. Price, A. Fridrichsen, H. Lietzmann, T. Wilson, H. Daniel-Rops, and K. F. W. Prior. The positions of R. Bultmann and M. Pohlenz are somewhat ambiguous or ambivalent. Whitely (p. 56) simply notes that mankind had sufficient natural knowledge to be blameworthy.

Among the arguments favoring this position are first, that Paul's *Sitz im Leben* (life-setting) predisposes one to admit the possibility, if not to anticipate the actuality, of a Pauline natural theology. Both his Jewish and his pagan backgrounds are relevant. A natural theology, as shown above, was to be expected of a Diaspora Jew whose kinsmen had lived in Tarsus for a century and a half (T. Wilson, p. 41). If the Hebrew OT could be translated into Greek, if the wisdom literature could argue as Plato's *Timaeus* did, if the Alexandrian contemporary Philo could synthesize Moses and Plato, then an evangelist of Paul's intensity would have left no intellectual stones unturned to capture the gentile mind for Christ.

Second, not only Paul's good, Hellenistic Greek but his actual arguments were congenial to, if not produced by, paganism. The Gentiles in Platonism, Orphism, and Stoicism has already arrived at a rational monotheism. The confluence of Paul in this stream has led E. J. Price, B. Weiss, M. Dibelius, and others to express judgments similar to Wilson's: Paul had "the same doctrine of natural revelation" (p. 54). The apostle was able to subdue the Lystrian idolaters by an appeal to natural theology (Acts 14:12ff.); he did not break up the gospel meeting before the Areopagus with his natural theology, in which he used proof texts from Aratus and Epimenides, but only with his speaking of a resurrection and judgment, items of revealed theology.

Those who have supposed that his later resolution to know only Christ and Him crucified (1 Cor. 2:2) implies an abandoning of natural theology fail to explain why Paul would reject an approach that had served him well. Moreover, as Bornkamm has commented (p. 94), in 1 Cor. 1:18f. Paul disparages human wisdom in the context of proofs (p. 94), and 1 Cor. 1–3 is against worldly wisdom and not against true wisdom or reason. When Paul argues that the "foolishness" of God is wiser than men, can one suppose that Paul is charging the all-wise God with real folly? The "wisdom of men" is folly (cf. "claiming to be wise, they became fools," Rom. 1:22) in its refusal to submit to the special revelation of God. Plato, who longed for the revelation that the apostle received, would presumably have put the same estimate on his own speculation when in the presence of revealed wisdom. In other words, those listening to Paul before the Areopagus erred not in having a natural theology but in a non sequitur of which no natural theologian should ever be guilty: because natural revelation disclosed no bodily resurrection or specific final judgment, it was therefore opposed to these doctrines. That is, there is nothing in natural *theology* against *the possibility* of a bodily resurrection. On the contrary, if there is a God, which natural theology proves, the possibility of a miracle is proved along with Him. Thus not Paul, the advocate of special revelation, but his auditors, who gloried in general revelation, broke with natural theology at the end of the Mars' Hill sermon. The "wisdom of men" is foolishness and the "foolishness of God" wisdom.

Third, in general the independent theistic arguments of Paul resemble closely those of the Stoic Sextes (Gärtner, p. 110). Sextes reasoned from common consent, which does not differ from the general character of Rom. 1; Acts 14 and 17. Mankind knows God (Gk. *gnóntes tón theón,* Rom. 1:21) by nature and by nature knows the decree (Gk. *dikaíōma*) of God (Rom. 1:32). The Stoic used the order of nature as a cue to its designer, which Paul closely approximates in Acts 17:24f. Sextes stressed the consequences of denying God as an argument for His existence. Paul likewise closely related ungodliness (Gk. *asébeia*) and wickedness (*adikía,* Rom. 1:18). Paul showed the Athenians the fatuity of supposing that the Maker of all things could be made with hands and seemed to think that proving that unbelievers worship the creature rather than the Creator proves that their worship is patently absurd. He did not generally take the "rational" grounds of unbelief very seriously but on the contrary insisted that people's minds become reprobate because they are not willing (Rom. 1:21) to have God in their thinking.

Fourth, perhaps the most fundamental argument that Paul assumed natural theology is that no one can intelligibly deny that he did. All students of Rom. 1–2 find Paul teaching natural revelation. On that there is no divergence, nor could there be. Natural theology, however, in distinction from natural revelation, is affirmed by some, denied by others. But can it be denied? For if all grant that Paul's man *stifles* this natural revelation of God so that it never becomes natural theology, must not all also grant that man stifles this *knowledge* of natural revelation? Nor can this knowledge be eradicated, for as even Gärtner noticed (p. 79) God is continuously revealing it.

Thus, according to Paul, mankind has a will to blot out while God has a will to reveal. The result must be a reluctant natural theology—a grudging admission and a continuous effort to obliterate this admitted knowledge. So against those who think that mankind is led to God by natural revelation Paul points out the stubborn, wicked, inexcusable refusal of mankind; against those who think that mankind is not even dragged to natural theology Paul points out the inescapable, persistent, kind, and forbearing manifestation of God within and among people.

***II. Special Revelation.***–If it is reasonably clear that Paul taught a natural revelation constraining hostile mankind to a natural theology distorted almost, but not quite, beyond recognition, it is virtually undisputed that he taught and stressed a special, written supernatural revelation. The nature, extent, necessity, and evidence of this revelation will be noted.

*A. Its Nature.* B. B. Warfield (*DCG,* II, 585) showed that the characteristic expression for this revelation is *graphḗ,* which occurs fifty times in the NT and throughout indicates "something which the Holy Ghost has spoken through the mouth of its human authors [Acts 1:16]." Paul employed the expression in Rom. 1:2; 4:3; 9:17; 10:11; 11:2; 15:4; 16:26; 1 Cor. 15:3; Gal. 3:8; 3:22; 4:30; 1 Tim. 5:18; 2 Tim. 3:16. Ellis (p. 21) noted that *theópneustos,* "God-breathed," in 2 Tim. 3:16 also accords with the usage of contemporary Judaism and the early Church. Thus the invisible God, who is manifested by the things He made, now "opens his own sacred mouth" (Calvin).

*B. Its Extent.* The *graphḗ* extended to the Bible, the whole Bible, and nothing but the Bible. G. Schrenck (*TDNT,* I, *s.v.* γράφω κτλ.), after noting that a number of NT references apply to particular verses, concluded that such instances may mean "the Scripture (taken as a whole) says at this particular place," as indeed Warfield demonstrated (*DCG,* II, 585f.). For extracanonical references cf. Ellis (pp. 74f., 83), who refuted A. Schweitzer's statement that Paul appealed similarly to Jewish Haggadah (*Paul and His Interpreters* [Eng. tr. 1948], p. 46).

The Pauline Scripture is not restricted to the OT; 1 Tim. 5:18b cites Mt. 10:10; Lk. 10:7. That Paul was as conscious as 2 Pet. 3:15f. that Paul was delivering "Scripture" may be seen from 2 Thess. 3:14f., where he regarded obedience to his writing as a prerequisite of continued church fellowship, and from 1 Cor. 4:16, where his preached and "delivered" word is connected with the Corinthians' salvation (cf. N. B. Stonehouse, pp. 83f.). Although the inspiration applies extensively to the entire Bible, the question remains how intensively it applies. The *pása graphḗ* ("all scripture," 2 Tim. 3:16) admits of no exception, and even if it did no Pauline canon for distinguishing is offered. Thus by explication and implication *theopneustía* (divine inspiration) is attributed to every word of Scripture with the same precision taught by Paul's Lord (Mt. 5:18; Jn. 10:35). Paul's relatively "free" citing of the LXX (for tabular listing see F. Prat, I, 411-14, and Ellis, pp. 150-188) may appear to militate against such an interpretation; but, first, it is virtually impossible to distinguish between an allusion and a quotation; second, most changes in the OT text are to suit the new context; third, punctuation, quotation marks, and such modern devices for reproducing exact wording did not exist in antiquity (cf. R. Nicole, "NT use of the OT," in Henry, ed., *Revelation and the Bible,* pp. 144f.); and, finally, Paul himself claimed (as noted above) the authority of an inspired messenger of the God whose Sovereign right to cite and modify His Word as he chose was as indisputable as that Word's infallibility, in whatever precise form it took. In addition to the numerous citations and allusions to the Scripture in the apostle's writings, there is "not a paragraph," as A. D. Nock observed, "which does not include subconscious recollections of the Greek OT just as every paragraph of *Pilgrim's Progress* echoes the King James Bible" (*Saint Paul* [1938], p. 183). Again, Paul's distinguishing between the *epitagḗ* of the Lord and his own *gnṓmē* (1 Cor. 7:25), in the light of his claim to being an agent of Christ and revealer of His Word, must be a distinction of source and not of authority, i.e., a distinction between the word of Christ that issued from Christ's own lips and the word of Christ that was transmitted through the apostle's mind and pen.

*C. Its Necessity.* Even though God has revealed Himself since the foundation of the world by the things He has made, further revelation is still needed because natural revelation does not have the "power of God for salvation" that is associated with the gospel (Rom. 1:16). The world learned from created things the "power and divinity" of God (v. 20); this knowledge, although not salvific, made mankind "without excuse" (v. 21). Thus the world could gain wisdom (v. 22; 1 Cor. 1:21). But by wisdom the world "did not know God" (1 Cor. 1:21; cf. Acts 17:23); on the contrary, "they [the people of the world] have turned into fools" (Rom. 1:22, Goodspeed, *Student's NT*). They knew God (v. 21), yet they knew not God; they knew about God but did not know the "thoughts of God" (1 Cor. 2:11). They could discover from nature what God by His power had done but could not know what by His evangel He would do. How could they, for who knows even "a man's thoughts except the spirit of the man which is in him? So also no one comprehends the thoughts of God except the Spirit of God" (v. 11).

*D. Evidence.* What evidence is there that God has revealed "the things of God"? Apparently Paul and his readers assumed the inspiration of the *graphḗ.* He rested his argument on inspiration rather than resting inspiration on argument. There seems to be nothing comparable in his treatment of *graphḗ* with his close reasoning in Acts 14:15f.; 17:24f.; Rom. 1:18f. for the reality of the natural revelation of God. One may not infer, however, that he proceeded the same way in winning gentile converts and establishing Christian congregations as he did when addressing the "household of faith." The *theopneustía* of Scripture, apparently unchallenged by Jewish and pagan converts, required no defense. But may one not infer that Paul as well as Peter stood ready to defend, "to any one who calls you to account for the hope that is in you" (1 Pet. 3:15), the *theopneustía* no less than the bodily resurrection (1 Cor. 15:1ff.), justification by faith alone (Rom. 4:5ff.), and, more to the present point, his own apostleship (2 Cor. 12:1ff.)?

Paul's apostleship began with Jesus Christ's appearance to him on the way to Damascus (Acts 9:1ff.; 22:5ff.; 26:12ff.). As Rengstorf observed (*TDNT,* I, 438), for Paul this was "an act of God, an objective event, not a visionary experience" (Gal. 1:15; Rom. 1:1); it made him conscious of a calling such as the OT prophets, particularly Jeremiah, received. Paul, however, did not rest his authority entirely on the supernatural Damascus appearance that began his apostolate. When necessary he also appealed to the continuing evidence of Christ powerfully at work through him. He reminded the Corinthians of his "signs and wonders and mighty works" (2 Cor. 12:12) on his earlier visits and promised on his return a similar display of the power of Christ if they demanded proof that Christ was speaking in him (13:3f.). While we agree again with Rengstorf that Paul used 2 Cor. 12:12 "only to demonstrate the justice of his cause and not the significance of his person" (p. 440), we do insist that Paul is not above providing external proof of his divine commission. His argument is that the proved supernatural accreditation of his person evinces the supernaturalness of his message. "Am I not an apostle? Have I not seen our Lord Jesus Christ?" Although he admitted that others also displayed supernatural powers (1 Cor. 12:27-30), these miracle workers claimed no Damascus road experience nor appointment to the apostolate.

In sum, Paul fully endorsed the OT as infallible Scripture and indicated the same of some representative NT materials. He meanwhile certified his own sanctioning and supplying of Scripture by his supernatural endowment with the apostolate.

***III. The Trinity.***–There is one God exhibiting many attributes and existing in three persons. True to the OT doctrine in Dt. 6:4, Paul insisted on the unity of the Godhead (1 Cor. 8:4, 6; 1 Tim. 1:17), usually calling God "Father." "There is not one single letter that he ever wrote in which Paul does not call God *Father* (1 Thess. 1:1; 2 Thess. 1:2; Gal. 1:3; 1 Cor. 1:3; 2 Cor. 1:2; Rom. 5:7; Eph. 1:2; Col. 1:2; Philem. 3)," wrote W. Barclay (*Mind of St. Paul* [1958], pp. 32f.; cf. F. Amoit, *L'Enseignement de St. Paul* [1946], I, 59). God is all in all (1 Cor. 15:24-28), the living source of all (1 Cor. 8:6; 1 Thess. 1:9; Rom. 11:36. Rengstorf (*TDNT,* I, 439f.) observed that Paul was the first apostle to recognize the call of Christ as from God, omnipotent and sovereign (Eph. 1:11; Rom. 9:18), omniscient (Rom. 11:33-36; 1 Cor. 1:21; Eph. 3:10), righteous (Rom. 3:5, 25; Acts 17:31), eternal (Rom. 1:20; 1 Tim. 1:17), invisible but manifest in Christ, the Christlike God (2 Cor. 5:19; Col. 1:15; 3:6; 1 Tim. 1:17), wrathful (Rom. 1:18; Eph. 2:3; 5:6; 1 Thess. 1:10; 5:9), merciful and peaceful (Rom. 2:9; 2 Cor. 5:19f.; 13:11; 2 Thess. 3:16).

Paul's monotheism is explicit, his trinitarianism implicit. No less emphatic than his insistence on the unity of God (Amoit, I, 59) is his ascription of personality to three divine persons—the Father, the Son, and the Holy Spirit. (See preceding paragraph for discussion of the Father's personality; see IV below for discussion of the Son's.)

The NT contains 379 references to the Spirit and His distinct divine personhood; 146 references are Paul's (R. B. Hoyle, *Holy Spirit in St. Paul* [1928], p. 25). His personality and divinity are assumed rather than proved. Ascribed to Him are knowledge (1 Cor. 2:10f.), will (1 Cor. 12:11), purpose or thoughts (Gk. *phrónēma,* Rom. 8:27), feeling (Rom. 15:30; Eph. 4:30). He leads, teaches, intercedes, cries out; with reference to what mere energy or influence could such language fitly be used? Equally evident is Paul's belief in the divinity of the Spirit. In Acts 28:25-27 he ascribes to the Spirit language that Isa. 6:8-10 ascribes to "the King, the Lord of hosts." Many of the passages imply the Spirit's possession of divine attributes such as omnipresence (Rom. 8:11; 1 Cor. 12:13; Tit. 3:5).

This exposition seems sufficient answer to W. Beyschlag (*NT Theologie* [1896], II, 204) and others who have seen in such passages merely another instance of Paul's personalizing of the impersonal, and to A. Sabatier (p. 338), who recognized the tripersonal but reduced its significance to an expression of the sequence of redemption: the love of the Father manifested in the grace of the Son and wrought in the soul by the Spirit. Paul's identification of the Spirit and Christ (2 Cor. 3:17) must refer to essence or substance, not to person as assumed by modalism, an error that E. F. Scott thoroughly refuted (*The Spirit in the NT* [1923], pp. 180-83; unfortunately N. Q. Hamilton, *Holy Spirit and Eschatology in Paul* [1957], p. 83, appears to have seen only a "dynamic" unity). The Westminster Larger Catechism (Answer 9) may be resting too much on 2 Cor. 13:14 but not on Pauline theology as a whole when it says: "There be three persons in the Godhead, the Father, the Son, and the Holy Ghost; and these three are one true, eternal God, the same in substance, equal in power and glory; although distinguished by their personal properties."

***IV. Jesus Christ.***–Jesus Christ was Paul's very life. It was not the apostle but Christ who lived in him (Gal. 2:20). For Paul to live was Christ (Phil. 1:21). To gain at any cost "the surpassing worth of knowing Christ Jesus my Lord" was his one goal (3:7f.), and to know Christ and Him crucified was his total method (1 Cor. 2:2). His favorite self-designation was "slave" (Gk. *doúlos*) of Christ. It was Jesus who had appeared to him while he was planning to exterminate Christians. This episode received more attention from Paul than any other in his life (Acts 9:1-19; 22:4-16; 26:9-18) and actually occupies more space in the NT than any other narrative except the passion of Jesus Christ itself. Describing this Christ utterly overwhelmed the apostle, and about thirteen times he gave up, using the expression "the unsearchable riches of Christ."

*A. His Deity.* Although unsearchable and inexhaustible, Christ is not unknowable, and Paul says much about Him. Most important, Jesus Christ is divine. We note briefly five lines of evidence together with challenges and attempted refutations. First, the most characteristic designation of Jesus, namely, *kýrios,* "Lord," not to mention combinations, was employed 144-146 times (B. B. Warfield, *Lord of Glory,* p. 223). Since *kýrios* is the LXX word for *YHWH,* Jesus for Paul was the covenant God of Israel (J. G. Machen, p. 307). This mere fact is answer enough to Sabatier's erroneous deduction from 1 Cor. 15:28 that Christ is Lord only during the period of redemption, (p. 334) and to W. Foerster's suggestion that in Phil. 2 the confession of Jesus as *kýrios* is limited by its being "to the glory of God" (*TDNT,* III, 1089). "Son of God" is used less often but tellingly enough to justify W. Morgan (*Religion and Theology of Paul* [1917], p. 56), Warfield, and others in insisting that the title is metaphysical. The contention of H. Weinel (*St. Paul, The Man and His Work* [Eng. tr. 1906], p. 324) and others that it is messianic is a further explication, not a contradiction; i.e., the Son of God's essential divinity does not prevent His graciously assuming a messianic role.

Closely related to *kýrios* is the designation "first-born," Gk. *prōtótokos,* not *protókistos* (Col. 1:15). "First born" is manifestly a correlative of the term "Father" (which is virtually always applied to the first person of the Godhead) inasmuch as the two terms are mutually dependent, as Athanasius observed against the Arians of the early Church and B. M. Metzger urged against the Arians of today, the Jehovah's Witnesses (*Theology Today,* 10 [1953], 76f.). "First-born" indicates not a beginning in time but priority in rank.

That Christians are called "sons of God" is an infinitely different matter. Even Sabatier is constrained to confess: "Christ, in short, is God's own Son, essentially His. We are, and shall always be so by adoption only" (pp. 334f.). Christ is the image (*eikṓn*), the form (*morphḗ*) and glory (*dóxa*) of God (1 Cor. 2:7; 2 Cor. 4:6; Phil. 2:6; Col. 1:15). These terms of themselves could mean no more than the image of God in mankind, but in Paul's context they indicate the unique and identical character of God. For example, in Phil. 2:6 the "form of God" in which Christ eternally exists is utterly different from the "form of a servant" which He took or the "likeness of a man" which He became.

At first glance it appears striking and disappointing that the apostle did not designate Christ principally by the term God (Gk. *theós*), since His deity is infinitely the more important aspect of His being. However, first, God by any other name is still God, as shown above. Second, since there are three persons in the trinity the distinctiveness of each is not deity. Third, the name *theós* is characteristically the designation, virtually a proper name, for the first person, who at the same time is distinguished as "Father." Fourth, "Lord" is the characteristic name, "trinitarian name," which affirms deity in common with the other persons of the Godhead and is also the Son's personal distinction. Fifth, Paul does apply the designation *theós* to Christ sufficiently to leave no doubt of his doctrine if one judged from that term alone. Rom. 9:5, whatever its syntactical ambiguity, by its context indicates the reference of *theós* to *Christós* so clearly that modern scholarship is returning to the orthodox view of the early fathers (Sanday-Headlam [comm. on Romans (*ICC*, 5th ed. 1902)], Prat, E. Stauffer, *et al.* [*TDNT*, III, *s.v.* θεός κτλ.]). The ambiguous text of Tit. 2:13, which the AV translates "... the glorious appearing of the great God, and our Saviour Jesus Christ..." has been translated, since 1798 when Granville Sharp detected and formulated a certain rule of Greek syntax, "...the appearing of the glory of our great God and Savior Jesus Christ" (RSV; cf. B. M. Metzger, p. 79). Thus the same person, Jesus Christ, is called God and Savior. Again, if God was in Christ reconciling the world (2 Cor. 5:19) Christ must be identical with God, for who else could reconcile the world? Thus E. Andrews (p. 125) and A. C. McGiffert, whom he cited, were saying more than they seemed to realize when they used this text to explain the sense in which Christ is divine. Moreover, Gk. *morphḗ toú theoú* in Phil. 2:6 is tantamount to "very God of very God" and as such virtually an appropriation of *theós* as a name of Christ. Likewise, "the church of God which he got at the cost of his own life" (Acts 20:28, Goodspeed), referring as it indisputably does to Jesus Christ, inferentially calls Him *theós*.

In addition to such direct references to the deity of Christ are the oblique assumptions of the same, clues (in their own way even more impressive, because more casual) to the thinking of Paul. To Christ Paul prayed (2 Thess. 3:5; 2 Cor. 12:8f.), to Christ he ascribed the glorious manifestation of God (2 Cor. 5:19), to Christ he assigned the role of Creator (Col. 1:16f.), and to Christ belongs the "day of the Lord," which according to OT usage is the day of Yahweh, God (1 Thess. 5:2; 2 Thess. 1:10; 2:2; 1 Cor. 1:8b).

Worthy of separate notice is the oft-observed agreement of the apostolic Church with Pauline Christology (R. J. Knowling, *Testimony of St. Paul to Christ* [1905; 3rd ed., 1911] p. 44; Machen, pp. 25ff.; H. N. Ridderbos, *Paul and Jesus* [Eng. tr. 1958], p. 53). Modern form criticism has remarkably confirmed the high doctrine of Christ found in the Church from the beginning (Wrede, "Mark is as bad as John"; cf. F. F. Bruce, *The NT Documents: Are They Reliable?* [1943], pp. 32f.; J. Jeremias [*Der Schlüssel zur Theologie des Apostels Paulus* (1971)], O. Michel [*Paulus und seine Bibel* (1929)], O. Cullmann [*Christology of the NT* (Eng. tr., rev. ed. 1959)], and many others find many already crystallized creeds reiterated by Paul). The presence of such a view and the absence of controversy with Paul argue that his christology was the same as the Church's.

Two objections are frequently offered to the interpretation of Paul as a high Christologist. It is irrelevant that the apostle did not deal in "speculation" and "abstractions" (E. Andrews, p. 14; D. Somerville, *St. Paul's Conception of Christ* [1897], p. 183), since a person can communicate precise truth without resorting to a technical scholastic methodology, and Paul did not shun to make deductions (cf. Romans and Galatians *passim*). The first objection is that although allegations of adoptionist Christology are generally to be given up, one still can find subordinationism in Paul (E. Andrews, pp. 131f.). Warfield has definitively refuted this objection (*Lord of Glory*, pp. 213-18, which Andrews cites without answering it).

The second objection is that the Kenosis of Phil. 2:7 shows that Paul's Christ emptied Himself in some way or degree of His deity. The text, however, says nothing of the sort. Christ's *morphḗ toú theoú* ("form of God") is permanent (*hypárchōn*), and the "emptying" is taking the *morphḗ doúlou* ("form of a servant"). The emptying, in other words, is not Christ's divesting of deity but His investing Himself with the infinitely inferior humanity. Christ's humanity is even further humiliated (to the death of the cross) and again later exalted (vv. 9f.), while the *morphḗ toú theoú* continues unchanged through all the human vicissitudes (cf. J. J. Müller, comm. on Philippians and Philemon [NICNT, 1955], pp. 80-85; A. Oepke, *TDNT, III, s.v.* κενός; J. H. Gerstner, *BDTh, s.v.* "kenosis"). In any case, the LXX usage suggests that "emptied himself" simply means "poured out himself," i.e., in death.

*B. His Humanity.* Arguments that Paul's Christ was not truly human have been broached by a number of scholars, including H. von Soden, *Theologische Abhandlungen* (1892), p. 115; M. Kähler, *Der sogenannte historische Jesus* (2nd ed. 1956); R. Bultmann, *Theology of the NT*, I (Eng. tr. 1955), 238f. Some of the arguments are ostensibly drawn from Paul himself, and some from his background, Rom. 8:3, "sending his own Son in the likeness of sinful flesh," is sometimes cited as a hint of Pauline docetism. The rare use of the name "Jesus" without the modifiers "Christ" or "our Lord" (e.g., Rom. 3:26; 2 Cor. 4:10f.; Eph. 4:21; 1 Thess. 4:14) is considered suspicious; but 2 Cor. 5:16 ("though we once regarded Christ from a human point of view [*katá sárka*] we regard him thus no longer") is the *locus classicus* used against Paul's acceptance of the true humanity of Christ. Paul is thought to have had the Philonic *lógos* (Word) or the Hellenistic primal man in view when he spoke of the man Christ Jesus, the Last Adam, or the Heavenly Man.

The statements of Paul that seem to reveal an indifference to the human Christ will be considered first. Goodspeed translated Rom. 8:3 *homoiṓmati sarkós* as our "physical form." A. Schlatter (comm. on Romans [2nd ed. 1952], *in loc.*) remarked that *sárx* indicates "concrete" form and that "docetic concepts should not be intruded." The rare use of the name "Jesus," if it could not be explained, would not count against the human Christ. Paul probably was assuming the Gospel narrative with which all were familiar and was giving an interpretative development that presented "Jesus" as the "Lord," which was the all-important point of view. "Christ" in Paul had become a proper name, and to call Christ "Lord" was the work of the Spirit (1 Cor. 12:3). That Paul called Christ "Lord," of course, implied not that the Lord Christ was not the man Jesus but rather that the Lord Christ was more than merely the man Jesus. The latter implication seems to be the key to 2 Cor. 5:16. Even Bultmann granted that *katá sárka* modifies *egnṓkamen* rather than *Christón* ("we know according to the [our] flesh Christ" rather than "we know Christ according to the [His] flesh"). However, he finds *katá sárka* knowledge about Christ not essentially different from knowledge about Christ *katá sárka*. P. Althaus (*Fact and Faith in the Kerygma of*

*Today* [1959], p. 35) rightly insisted on a difference between knowledge of Christ *in carne* and *secundum carnem*. Goodspeed made this point very plain, although his translation as a whole may be questioned: "So from that time on, I have estimated nobody at what he seemed to be outwardly; even though I once estimated Christ in that way, I no longer do so." The parallelism here between once knowing and no longer knowing people *katá sárka* and once knowing and no longer knowing Christ clearly indicates that a historical Christ is in view just as historical people are. This is no "other-than" but a "more-than" human view, and in the case of Christ it is strongly reminiscent of Mt. 16:17.

As for the primal man derivation of a Pauline nonhistorical or existential Christ, the objections are insurmountable to all but the hardiest Bultmannians. First, no one has established the existence of such a concept prior to Paul. Mr. Black said, "There is no unequivocal evidence pointing to the existence of such a conception in Pre-Christian sources, particularly within Judaism" (*SJT*, 7 [1954], 177). Second, if such evidence was discovered, its influence on Paul would still need to be shown. Third, proof would be required that more than Paul's terminology was influenced. Fourth, if even that substantial influence was shown, a mere coincidence between an idea of such a being and the historically existing being of Paul's writings would need to be disproved. Such considerations have led most modern scholars to abandon the chase.

Having suggested the futility of pinning docetism on the apostle, we briefly will indicate the impressive amount of help Paul affords the quest for the historical Jesus. E. Renan said that one could construct a small Life of Jesus from Pauline sources. First, it is possible that Paul met Jesus and that the "we once knew" of 2 Cor. 5:16 intends this meeting, especially since it is compared with the knowledge he had of other people. Second, the narratives of the Damascus road conversion indicate that Paul actually saw and heard Jesus (Acts 9:1-19; 22:4-16; 26:9-18). Third, there may be a hint of the Virgin Birth in Rom. 1:3 compared with the Luke account, as G. A. Danell suggested (*Studia Biblica*, IV [1951-52], 94ff.); at any rate, Christ took flesh (Rom. 8:3). Fourth, He was born of a woman. Fifth, He was made under the law (Gal. 4:4). Sixth, He was a teacher (1 Tim. 5:18). Seventh, He preached the kingdom (Rom. 14:7). Eighth, He was the embodiment of love, for as Jonathan Edwards has said (*Charity and its Fruits*), 1 Cor. 13 is a brief biography of Jesus. Ninth, He died (Acts 20:28). Tenth, He was raised bodily from the dead (1 Cor. 15). Eleventh, He was exalted above all (Phil. 2:11).

In fact, Paul was interested in the humanity of Christ because he was especially interested in His divinity. The mind of Christ Jesus was His willingness, although divine, to condescend to become man. The emphasis in such a passage as Phil. 2:5ff. is that Christ's condescension was so very great precisely because, as God, He is so very great, and as man, obedient to death, He became so very low. Had He been merely like God the stoop would not have been so enormous; had He been merely like man there would have been no condescension at all.

*V. Man and Sin.–A. Man as Creature.* "God created man in his own image" (Gen. 1:27). Paul teaches this, e.g., in 1 Cor. 11:7: "[Man] is the image and glory of God; but woman is the glory of man." S. V. McCasland (*JBL*, 69 [1950], 85f.) inferred that the apostle denied the account in Gen. 1:26f. that woman, too, was created in the divine likeness in favor of the Gen. 2:4–3:24 account. The two Genesis accounts, however, do not contradict but rather explicate one another. Moreover, in 1 Cor. 11:7 woman is the glory (*dóxa*) of the man, who is the glory of God. The resemblance of man and woman to God is the same here as in Gen. 2:4–3:24, which shows that Eve, no less than Adam, was created by God, of the very substance of her husband (which, if we wish to quibble, is a much higher stuff than the dust of the earth from which he was made, Gen. 2:7). Furthermore, one could infer from Eph. 4:24 that *ánthrōpos* (man in general, not man as male) was created in the image of God.

Did mankind lose the image of God by the fall? While Rom. 5:12-21 does not explicitly declare that through Adam's disobedience the divine image was lost, still, if condemnation, death, and judgment do not involve this image, what do they involve? As will be shown below, mankind's present state of *sárx* cannot be the state of a person created in the image of Paul's God. In Eph. 4:24 the work of grace consists of the creation of the new man *katá theón* ("put on the new nature, created after the likeness of God in true righteousness and holiness"; cf. Col. 3:10). As shown above, Paul received the OT as the *graphḗ* of God. Since it teaches that God created mankind in His own image, the statement in Ephesians appears to be merely a definition of the contents of that image.

What is the nature of man? Paul's man has (or is) a vast set of characteristics, qualities, faculties, such as: *thélēma* (will, 1 Cor. 7:34; Eph. 2:3); *kardía* (heart, 1 Thess. 2:4; Rom. 8:27; 1 Cor. 14:25); *noús* (mind, Rom. 1:28; 1 Cor. 14:15; Phil. 4:7); *pneúma* (spirit, Rom. 8:4; Gal. 5:16; 1 Thess. 5:23); *sárx* (flesh, Rom. 7:18; 1 Cor. 1:26; Gal. 2:16; Eph. 2:3; Col. 1:24); *syneídēsis* (conscience, Rom. 2:15; 2 Cor. 4:2; 5:11); *sṓma* (body, Rom. 12:1; 1 Cor. 6:13; Gal. 6:17); *psychḗ* (soul, Rom. 2:9; 1 Cor. 15:45; 1 Thess. 2:8).

*B. Man as Sarx.* Probably the most important and certainly a unique Pauline description of mankind is *sárx*. *TDNT* (VII, *s.v.* σάρξ κτλ. [Schweizer, Baumgärtel, Meyer]) devotes no less than fifty-four pages to this word, of which fourteen deal expressly with Paul's doctrine (including Colossians, Ephesians, and the Pastorals). E. Schweizer found seven (a couple more, but not so important, in the Epistles particularly mentioned) Pauline uses of this one word: first, body; second, earthly sphere; third, "flesh and blood" or humanity; fourth, object of human confidence; fifth, *katá sárka* with the verb; sixth, subject of sin; seventh, the overcome or subdued flesh. W. D. Stacey (*Pauline View of Man* [1956], pp. 183ff.) listed characteristics corresponding to the first, third, and sixth above. W. P. Dickson tended in the same direction with an emphasis on what the word does not mean (*St. Paul's Use of the Terms Flesh and Spirit* [1883], pp. 310ff.). A. Ritschl stressed the whole man in opposition to the divine *pneúma*, (pp. 69ff.; cf. Dodd, p. 57). E. Schweizer and others have seen that emphasis as especially Colossian ("the essence of God-alienated man"). J. A. T. Robinson neatly distinguished between *sárx* as "in the world" and as "for the world" (which is the creature's sinful "distance from God," p. 25). Despite the many texts and the equally numerous minute scholarly studies of them, it is still difficult to improve upon Calvin's comment on Rom. 7:18: "Under the term *flesh* Paul always includes all the endowments of human nature, and everything that is in man, except the sanctification of the Spirit.... Both terms, therefore, *flesh* and *spirit*, are applicable to the soul. The one relates to that part which has been regenerated and the other to that which still retains its natural affection." Man as *sárx* is man-as-man, or man-as-sinner, but never in the vast array of texts referring to a mere human does *sárx* mean man-as-saint.

Here a postponed point in Paul's doctrine of Christ's

humanity must be faced. Christ took *sárx* (Rom. 8:3), was manifested in the *sárx* (1 Tim. 3:16), and in *sárx* was crucified (Col. 1:22). Because *sárx,* whenever it is viewed morally by Paul, comes under condemnation, the question arises whether even Christ, as *sárx,* is a sinner. It cannot be doubted that Paul's own reply to such an insinuation from his teachings would be a vehement "God forbid!" But we must be more academic. First, Paul nowhere said that Christ is a sinner. Second, on the contrary, Christ "knew no sin" (2 Cor. 5:21). Third, He is specifically contrasted with Adam—who did sin, was disobedient, and brought death into the world—as the one who did not sin, was obedient, and brought justification (Rom. 5:12-14). Fourth, Rom. 3:25f.—Christ Jesus, "whom God put forward as an expiation by his blood, to be received by faith. This was to show God's righteousness, because in his divine forbearance he had passed over former sins; it was to prove at this present time that he himself is righteous and that he justifies him who has faith in Jesus"—defies interpretation if Jesus Himself were unrighteous. Fifth, it has been shown that *sárx* is sometimes used of man-as-man without the necessary connotation of man-as-sinner. Sixth, the assumption, therefore, that man-as-man (*sárx*) must be man-as-sinner (*sárx*) is gratuitous.

Other important terms in Pauline psychology are *sōma, psychḗ,* and *pneúma. Sṓma,* while sharing much of the same territory with *sárx,* is never intrinsically evil, just as *psychḗ* is never intrinsically good (cf. Rom. 12:1 and 2:9); their mixed characters show that Paul's theology is biblical, in contrast to Greek psychology-morality (E. J. Price tended to select only those Pauline passages that superficially served his purpose of establishing a parallel between Paul and Plato). J. A. T. Robinson's statement, "One could say without exaggeration that the concept of the body forms the keystone of Paul's theology" (p. 9), is based on the confusion of a figure of speech with a figure (cf., e.g., Rom. 12:1, where *sṓma* is patently a synecdoche for the total personality). The trichotomy suggested by 1 Thess. 5:23 ("spirit [*pneúma*] and soul [*psychḗ*] and body [*sṓma*]") is precluded by the interchangeability of *pneúma* and *psychḗ* in other texts (cf. 1 Cor. 14:14, "my spirit [*pneúma*] prays"; Eph. 6:6, "doing the will of God from the heart [*psychḗ*]"; Phil. 1:27, "stand firm in one spirit [*pneúma*]"; Col. 3:23, "work heartily [*psychḗ*], as serving the Lord"). The denial of dichotomy by many moderns who would read an existentialist-*gestalt* pattern into Paul is precluded by 2 Cor. 5:1ff.

*C. Man as Sinner.* The discussion of *sárx* above serves incidentally as an introduction to the Pauline doctrine of sin. That the same word could be used for man-as-man and for man-as-sinner is a sure cue. The linguistic use of *sárx* suggests that man could become something other than he was created (man-as-*sinner*) but yet not altogether other (*man*-as-sinner). But the persistent use of *sárx* for man-as-sinner suggests that, at least for the present, this is his normal state. The apostle by no means leaves readers to inference and conjecture. The man-as-sinner meaning of *sárx* is abundantly exhibited (Rom. 7:18, 25; 8:13; 13:14; Gal. 5:16, 19f.; cf. *TDNT,* VII, 131-34 [Schweizer]).

If sin is man's present state, how did he fall into it? Through Adam, is Paul's plain answer (Rom. 5:12ff.; 1 Cor. 15:22). As C. Hodge neatly summarized: "One thing is clear—Adam was the cause of sin in a sense analogous to that in which Christ is the cause of righteousness" (comm. on Romans [rev. ed. 1886; repr. 1976], p. 146).

Paul's most exhaustive post mortem on fallen mankind is Eph. 2:1-10. Man is dead in the sphere of outward transgressions and inner principles; accordingly he goes on and on in the course of an evil world (v. 1) under the dominion of Satan (v. 2). Not only were the gentiles thus depraved; the people of God, the Jews, also served the flesh, even in the area of the mind, with the result that all people were, not by circumstances but by nature, not in relation to mankind but in relation to God, "children of wrath" (v. 3). Verses 4-7 show that nothing less than the resurrecting power of Christ was used to make such spiritual corpses live. Many modern scholars question Paul's authorship of Ephesians. M. Barth, however, said of the differences of Ephesians from the rest of the Pauline corpus, which cause many to doubt its authenticity: "Only the master himself was free...not to follow what may look like a party's platform. An imitator would have wished to give the impression of being a true Paulinist" (*Interp.*, 17 [1963], 3; cf. *Ephesians* [*AB,* 1974], 36-50). Thus it is necessary to indicate that Paul renders the same negative verdict against fallen man elsewhere, especially in Rom. 3:10-20.

***VI. Redemption.***–*A. Righteousness of God.* The righteousness of God (Gk. *dikaiosýnē theoú*) is the key concept for Paul's doctrine of redemption. Since in the gospel the righteousness of God is revealed (Rom. 1:17), defining the *dikaiosýnē theoú* is of crucial importance. Some scholars construe this expression as meaning the righteousness that God bestows on the believer, whom He approves accordingly. Against this view, to which no grammatical objection may be urged, is its logical incoherency. If this righteousness is something wrought in the believer it must possess an objective character that is inherent in the term. Thus the righteousness in the believer is the righteousness that is in God initially. Righteousness is communicable to the believer, but it is *God's* righteousness that is communicated.

More particularly, the *dikaiosýnē theoú* is communicated to persons through the work of Christ. For God to bestow righteousness on unworthy persons is, on the face of it, the unrighteousness of God. The Judge of all the earth would appear to do wrong. What was a stumbling block to the Jews in Paul's time (1 Cor. 1:23) had constituted something of an obscurity from the time that sinful persons were first saved. To this the apostle speaks directly in Rom. 3:24f.: "Christ Jesus, whom God put forward as an expiation [Gk. *hilastḗrion*] by his blood, to be received by faith. This was to show God's righteousness, because in his divine forbearance he had passed over former sins." Here Paul's reasoning seems clear. God is just, not unjust, in passing over (or forgiving, Gk. *páresis*) sins done in ancient times, because Christ is now set forth as the propitiation, i.e., Christ is the divine basis (retroactive, in this instance) for the forgiveness of sins. If this action "was to show God's righteousness," then the righteousness of God must have been transmitted from the *hilastḗrion* to the sinner. If the sinner did not thus become righteous (by definition, he could not have made himself such), he would have been unrighteous still, and for God to regard him otherwise would have made Him unrighteous.

Thus the context, showing forth God's righteousness, appears to have much more bearing on the meaning of *hilastḗrion* than some commentators have noticed. Christ's blood is seen as a sacrifice that satisfies divine justice; it propitiates God, who thereby may accept the sinner without compromising His righteousness, and in fact it forms a display of His righteousness. If the *hilastḗrion* is not construed in such a manner, its relevance to its context is difficult to see.

Paul speaks less fully but even more pointedly to this matter in 2 Cor. 5:21, "For our sake he made him to be sin who knew no sin, so that in him we might become the righteousness of God." This statement is unclear unless one assumes, as one may, that Paul has in mind here what he spells out in Rom. 3:25. Denying Paul the analogy-of-faith principle may lead to an absurd interpretation well illustrated by Sabatier: "...God sees in Christ that which is in us,—namely, sin; and in us that which is in Christ—namely, righteousness. No doubt this is a logical contradiction" (p. 330). Again, what reason is there for referring to the "blood of God" in Acts 20:28 except to make clear the righteousness of God in the "purchase" of the Church?

Other Pauline terms also indicate or are congenial to the idea that Christ is the "satisfaction" that makes God righteous in "reckoning" sinful believers in Christ as righteous. On the use of Gk. *katallásein* see D. Whiteley (*JTS*, 8 [1957], 241), who admitted at least the possibility of the substitutionary meaning. On Gk. *lýtron* and cognate forms see Morris, *APC*, pp. 26ff.; on *hypér* see A. T. Robertson, *Grammar of the Greek NT* (5th ed. 1931), pp. 573f.; and E. Mayser, *Grammatik der Griechischen Papyri aus der Ptolemäerzeit*, II, 2 (1934), 460, cited by Morris, p. 62.

*B. Justification by Faith*. God's righteousness received in Christ is man's justification (Gk. *dikaíōsis*). Just as this doctrine was the *articulus stantis aut cadentis ecclesiae* (doctrine by which the Church stands or falls) of Luther, so for Paul it constituted the gospel, "for in it the righteousness of God is revealed through faith for faith" (Rom. 1:17). Actually, however, the term *dikaiosýnē theoú* is used only eight times and exclusively in Romans, Galatians, and Philippians (ch. 3). Many have noticed that these passages are concerned with Judaizers (A. B. Bruce, *St. Paul's Conception of Christianity* [1894], pp. 46f.; J. Jeremias, *Expos.T.*, 66 [Oct. 1954–Sept. 1955], 368). We conclude that Paul stresses this doctrine among Judaizers because of their legalistic tendencies and leaves the theme less developed elsewhere not because the doctrine is unimportant but because its further exposition is unnecessary. At any rate, for Paul the *en christṓ* relationship to justification is so close as to be almost identical. To be in Christ is to be in righteousness; Christ is our righteousness (1 Cor. 1:30; cf. Rom. 8:31f.). Paul's steps to salvation seem to be: first, man as *sárx* is against the *dikaiosýnē theoú* and therefore under *orgḗ theoú*; second, Christ, who is God and of course the righteousness of God, took humanity and became a "propitiation" ("became sin") for sinners; third, sinners coming to Christ (*en christṓ*) come into Christ's (God's) imputed righteousness and out of their own expiated sinfulness.

Paul calls this coming to Christ *pístis* (faith). The frequent occurrence of this term in Pauline letters emphasizes the "trust" (fiducial) aspect of faith. So clear is this stress that A. Deissmann saw the term as equivalent to union with Christ: "of Jesus Christ" is the "mystical genitive" (*Paul* [Eng. tr., 2nd ed. 1926], p. 163). Five different metaphors are used to express this central truth (pp. 167f.). Calvin used the analogy of marriage, which unites one person with another (*Inst.* iii.13). Jonathan Edwards used the same simile of marriage (*Works* [Dwight], V, 261). F. Neugebauer, rightly rejecting Bultmann's all-too-externalistic notion that faith is obedience (*In Christus* [1958], p. 158), insisted that it is faith alone and perceptively noted that Paul almost never speaks of faith in Christ, probably because it is so obviously understood as to be a tautology (p. 173; "for *en christṓ* defines what *pístis* means!" [p. 174]).

*C. Law and Grace*. The relation of the law to justification, both before and after, is a prime concern of Paul's. The keeping of the *nómos* (law) is at once a preparation for the *dikaiosýnē theoú* and a consequence of it. The law was a preparation for the gospel, the custodian of believers until the heir came (Gal. 3:24) because, Paul says, "I through the law died to the law, that I might live to God" (2:19). Thus the propaedeutic use of the law is to convict of sin, to kill to the law, to demonstrate that salvation cannot come from the law. "By the works of the law shall no one be justified" (2:16). "All who rely on works of the law are under a curse....No man is justified before God by the law (3:10f.). "If a law had been given which could make alive, then righteousness would indeed be by the law. But the scripture consigned all things to sin, that what was promised to faith in Jesus Christ might be given to those who believe" (vv. 21f.; cf. Rom. 3:19f.). Paul's own poignant experience with the law seems to be set forth in similar terms in Rom. 7:9-11: "I was once alive apart from the law, but when the commandment came, sin revived and I died; the very commandment which promised life proved to be death to me. For sin, finding opportunity in the commandment, deceived me and by it killed me."

The keeping of the law is the consequence of, no less than the preparation for, the righteousness of God. Now endowed with the righteousness of God, adopted into the family of God (Gal. 4:6f.), having the Spirit of God (Rom. 5:5), the Christian begins to fulfil the law. The antinomian accusation, "Do we then overthrow the law by this faith?" is answered by Paul with an expostulation, "By no means! On the contrary, we uphold the law" (Rom. 3:31). A fuller explanation is given in Rom. 6:1-4 ("How can we who died to sin still live in it?").

Although justified Christians are for the first time fulfilling the law (Rom. 8:3f.), they are not doing so perfectly. Even Paul himself, in whom the grace of God abounded most abundantly and who could command the Philippians to "join in imitating me" (3:17), regarded himself not as having attained but merely as pressing on (Phil. 3:12, 14). When he examines this imperfection more minutely and autobiographically, he reveals it as an intensely agonizing struggle. One can wish that a host of scholars such as A. Ritschl (pp. 69ff.), W. G. Kümmel (*Man in the NT* [Eng. tr. 1963], pp. 49ff.), and P. Althaus (*Paulus und Luther über den Menschen* [1938], p. 41), who viewed Rom. 7:14f. as an experience of the burdened sinner rather than of the redeemed saint, as Augustine once did, would see, as Augustine later did, that this passage cannot describe anyone but a true believer (cf. A. F. N. Lekkerkerker, *Römer 7 und Römer 9 bei Augustin* [1942]).

We submit several reasons for the apparent necessity of this interpretation. First, the description of Rom. 7:13f. is not basically different from the indisputably Christian experience of Phil. 3:12, 14, where Paul does not consider himself as having attained but agonizes on, or from 1 Cor. 9:27, where he must continue savagely to beat his body lest while he preach to others he himself be a castaway. Second, as noted previously, fallen man is hostile to God, dead in the realm of trespasses and sins, seared in conscience. Such a person does not strive after holiness as is depicted in Rom. 7:13f. Third, Paul specifically states in 3:11 that no natural, unconverted person seeks after God. Fourth, 7:25 shows that the agonizing person of v. 24 is delivered through Jesus Christ his Lord. If v. 25 was to refer to some other state of the person, it would be difficult to explain why it immediately follows the agonized query: "Who will deliver me from the body of this death?"

Rom. 8:1 simply continues the consolation of 7:25, assuring Paul and all saints who are in Christ Jesus that there is "now no condemnation." In other words, 7:13f. poignantly states in terms of Paul's own experience the imperfection of sanctification in this present world and at

PAULINE THEOLOGY

the same time reveals this imperfection to be consistent with the assurance of future (perfect) deliverance and present justification. The passage may be seen as an expanded autobiographical commentary on Phil. 2:12f., "Work out your own salvation with fear and trembling, for God is at work in you."

While thoroughly repudiating legalism, and intransigently inculcating evangelical doctrines of justification and sanctification, Paul not only insists that the law as a standard will be kept by those who are dead to the law as a way of salvation (cf. Rom. 3:21 and 6:14), but also spells out the details. That is, a Christian informed with the Spirit of Christ has moral, legal righteousness exceeding that of the scribes and Pharisees (cf. Mt. 5:20). At this point Paul's moral codes in Gal. 5:19-24; 1 Cor. 6:9f.; Phil. 4:8f.; Eph. 6:10-20; etc. should be consulted.

Thus Paul sets forth Christianity as a religion of pure grace with an unbending perfectionist moral ideal. While the most strenuous efforts must constantly be made, serenity fills the believer's soul with the knowledge that there is now no condemnation. One is utterly free of the bondage of the law as a system while one strives after full conformity to its most rigorous demands. While the law as a master is killed, it is established in its rightful place as the servant of the grace of God. Sailing successfully between the Scylla of legalism and the Charybdis of antinomianism, Paul's Christianity is on the high seas of lawful (the element of truth in legalism), free (the element of truth in antinomianism) evangelicalism (the gospel lacking in both legalism and antinomianism).

***VII. The Church.***–We have noted above that justification comes about *ek písteōs,* which is another way of saying *en christō̂.* These terms describe the justification of the individual. If one considers that many individuals have this experience, one has Paul's doctrine of the Church, i.e., the "body" of Christ, the body of believers.

*A. Its Nature.* The nature of this body or Church consists of Christ and believers vitally and inseparably but not indistinguishably united together. P. Benoit (*RB,* 63 [1956], 30) showed that this doctrine is taught in Paul's earlier Epistles but reaches full development only in Colossians and Ephesians. L. Cerfaux's statement that this Church "is neither Jewish or non-Jewish, but a *tertia gens*" (*Christ in the Theology of St. Paul,* [Eng. tr. 1959]; cf. N. Flanagan, *CBQ,* 19 [1957], 479; M. Barth, "Das Volk Gottes," in M. Barth, *et al., Paulus — Apostat oder Apostel?* [1977], pp. 45-134) requires modification. While Paul's Church is not exclusively Jewish or non-Jewish, it is continuous with the OT Jewish church (Rom. 11:17ff.), which was not itself strictly "Jewish." The notion of a *tertia gens* would give an erroneous idea indeed, for the apostle knew of only one people of God in all ages, not even two, much less three. O. Cullmann (*Christ and Time,* pp. 186f.) and O. Perels (*TLZ,* 76 [1951], 396) rightly observed, further, that the Church of Ephesians and Colossians is no different from Paul's Church elsewhere, but it is viewed from the standpoint of union with Christ rather than that of its struggle with the world.

One comes to be in the body of Christ internally, by believing, and externally, by baptism and the Lord's Supper. The discussion above showed that faith or trust was tantamount to union with Christ. The apostle, however, speaks somewhat similarly of baptism and the eucharist. In Gal. 3:27 he writes: "For as many of you as were baptized into Christ have put on Christ" (cf. also Rom. 6:3; 4:11; Col. 2:12; 3:4; 1 Cor. 10:7). These and other such strong sacramental teachings understandably led Flanagan (p. 483) to write: "It is union with Christ's physical body that makes us Christ's mystical body." This idea of union, however, is manifestly not Paul's intention, for then there would be an identification of all Israel as true Israelites, which he positively repudiates by saying: "For not all who are descended from Israel belong to Israel, and not all are children of Israel because they are his descendants....This means that it is not the children of the flesh who are the children of God, but the children of the promise are reckoned as descendants..." (Rom. 9:6-8). If Flanagan were correct, the apostle's clear differentiation between circumcision of the flesh and of the heart would be impossible (Rom. 2:28f.). Likewise, if communing in the body and blood of the Lord were identical with receiving the eucharist, Paul could not warn the Corinthians against eating and drinking damnation to themselves (1 Cor. 11:29).

*B. Visible and Invisible.* Does Paul allow that a person may have the internal experience without the external sacrament or the sacrament without the experience? That is, does Paul conceive of an "invisible" as well as a "visible" Church? In Ephesians, the principal Epistle for his doctrine of the Church, Paul apparently distinguishes those who are truly Christians, i.e., who are in the mystical body of Christ, from those who merely profess Christianity and are in the visible Church only. Paul addresses the Epistle to "saints" (1:1) but writes in 4:21: "assuming that you have heard about him [Christ] and were taught in him, as the truth is in Jesus." The RV has essentially the same translation, and Goodspeed reads: "if you have really become acquainted with him and have been instructed in him." It is clear that Ephesians is referring to hearing not in the ordinary sense but in a mystical sense, which Goodspeed renders as "become acquainted with." Thus not all in the Church have necessarily "heard" Christ, have become His sheep (cf. Jn. 10:4), are necessarily Christians, or are in the mystical body of Christ. Paul conveys the same idea in Eph. 6:24: "Grace be with all who love our Lord Jesus Christ with love undying"; not all in the Church necessarily love the Lord Jesus Christ in sincerity, i.e., as true Christians; see also Rom. 9:7; 2 Tim. 2:20.

Christ, whom Paul recognized as the authoritative Son of God, also taught this mixed character of the visible church. Not all the fish in the gospel net are good (Mt. 13:47f.); not all on the gospel threshing floor is true wheat (Mt. 3:12). Not all in the field are wheat, some are tares (Mt. 13:24ff.); Not all who profess to be waiting for the Son of man are wise virgins, some are foolish and will be rejected (Mt. 25:1ff.); "Not every one who says to me, 'Lord, Lord,' shall enter the kingdom of heaven" (Mt. 7:21). Thus it seems clear that not all who are in the visible church are of it, not all who have heard of Christ have "heard" Christ, not all who are outwardly baptized are buried with Christ, and not all who partake of the eucharist discern the Lord's body (1 Cor. 11:29).

Paul's prison Epistles, especially Ephesians, reveal other characteristics of the Church as well as develop the above ideas of it. Note, for example, how full is the discussion of the Church in Eph. 2:11–4:16: the Church's unity of Jews and Gentiles, of Christ and believers is expounded in 2:11-22, its mystery in 3:1-13, and its unified, diversified, edified membership in 4:1-16.

***VIII. Eschatology.***–*A. Parousia.* Parousia, although it is concerned primarily with the end time, was Paul's emphasis in his earliest ministry. Thus the Thessalonian letters contain the fullest treatment of this doctrine; this doctrine, unlike others, did not change or even undergo basic development during the apostle's ministry (J. A. Beet, *Expos.,* 4th ser., 10 [1894], 110). Gk. *parousía* appears to derive from *páresti,* "be present." Although Christ's presence or appearing is the central conception (1 Thess. 1:10; 2:19; 3:13; 4:15; 5:23; 2 Thess. 2:1, 8f.; 1 Cor. 15:23), it is visible and audible and associated with the judgment of the "Son of Destruction" as well as with the resurrection and salvation of believers.

*B. Resurrection.* Paul teaches in 1 Cor. 15:44 that the resurrection of Christ was corporeal and implies that man's resurrection will also be. Gk. *sōma* here may mean more than mere body but never less than that. The resurrection produces a "spiritual body." J. P. Lange (comm., *in loc.*) correctly explained Paul's thinking in this passage: "The phrase natural body indicates the body with its vital principle or *psuche* that relates it to the present material or terrestrial order. On the other hand, the spiritual body is the body with its vital principle (*pneuma*) that relates it to the new or celestial order." Paul's statement in v. 50, "Flesh and blood cannot inherit the kingdom of God," underlines his doctrine that the *sōma* will not be as now but will change into a spiritual body in which it will inherit the kingdom of God. R. Bultmann (H. W. Bartsch, ed., *Kerygma und Mythos,* I [3rd ed. 1954], 144) and K. Barth agreed on Paul's teaching about the resurrection of Christ; Barth wrote, "To be exegetically accurate we must understand corporeally risen; and thus, if we are not to make so bold as to substitute for the apostolic witness another one altogether, there cannot be any talk of striking out the empty grave." Again, "The tomb is doubtless empty, under every conceivable circumstance empty!" (*Resurrection of the Dead* [Eng. tr. 1933], p. 138). Even a radical thinker like S. J. Case (*Origins of Christian Supernaturalism* [1946], pp. 192f.) concurred on this interpretation of Paul.

Paul's Damascus road experience cited above also implies a bodily resurrection of Christ. First, the appearance was visible, being brighter than the noonday sun and blinding Paul. Second, Jesus' voice was heard by all, though understood only by Paul. Third, Paul was qualified to become an apostle, a prerequisite for which was that a person had "seen the Lord." Finally, in an important passage (Rom. 8:23) Paul teaches the "redemption of our bodies."

*C. Judgment.* Paul provides no general descriptive picture of the final judgment (H. B. Carré, *Paul's Doctrine of Redemption* [1914], p. 156) like Our Lord's teaching, especially in Mt. 25:31ff., probably just because Christ did provide one. But Paul often refers to that climactic event (1 Thess. 5:3; Rom. 2:9; 6:23; 1 Cor. 3:17; 5:5; 6:9; 15:50; Phil. 1:28; 3:19) at which Christ Himself will be the judge (Rom. 2:16; 1 Cor. 4:5; 2 Cor. 5:10; Acts 17:31).

How is the judgment related to the wrath of God (Gk. *orgḗ toú theoú*)? E. Stählin (*TDNT,* V, 423) stated, "Wrath is an essential and inalienable trait in the biblical and NT view of God"; he added that in most instances *orgḗ* refers to judgment, at which point it is concentrated. God's actual wrath can no more be denied than his *agápē* (love) and *éleos* (mercy). In support of this view Stählin cited Rom. 1:18; 9:22 and then proceeded, without warrant, to suggest that wrath and love are not mutually exclusive. On the contrary, these must be mutually exclusive not merely in the basic meaning of terms but in the Pauline and biblical doctrine of the diverse destinies of people determined by the judgment. These diverse destinies have been shown above. Now we must draw the inference that wrath and love are not opposite sides of the same coin, for then they would lead to the same rather than diverse destinies. If wrath were a function of love, it would produce the same ultimate felicity which Paul, so far from envisaging, categorically denies.

Thus we have seen that the Resurrection will follow the Parousia and that at the final judgment the wrath of God will be revealed (Rom. 1:18) and will begin to burn to the uttermost against all who are not in Christ. For those in Christ—e.g., Paul himself—death will be gain (Phil. 1:21) and the future judgment will be the great acquittal and introduction to the perfect state.

*IX. Summary.*–Paul's theology logically begins with a natural knowledge of God, who infallibly reveals Himself in sacred Scripture as a divine trinity. Human sin and judgment are such that redemption is possible only through the incarnation of the second person of the trinity, the Lord Jesus Christ, who identified Himself with the guilt of His people, who, in turn, are justified only by faith in Him. But when by faith they are united with Christ they not only begin to produce the ethical fruits of this union but constitute the true body of Christ, the Church. As such they live in the Church and in the world until the great separation and judgment, occurring after the Parousia of the Son of God, the Savior and Judge of the end times.

*See also* PAUL THE APOSTLE.

***Bibliography.***–E. Andrews, *The Meaning of Christ for Paul* (1949); O. Cullmann, *Christ and Time* (Eng. tr., rev. ed. 1964); H. Daniel-Rops, *Saint Paul, Apostle of Nations* (Eng. tr. 1953); J. de Zwaan, *Zeitschrift für systematische Theologie,* 8 (1930/31), 539ff.; M. Dibelius, *Paul* (Eng. tr. 1953); C. H. Dodd, *Meaning of Paul for Today* (repr. 1970); E. E. Ellis, *Paul's Use of the OT* (1957); J. Fitzmyer, *Pauline Theology* (1967); A. J. Fridrichsen, *The Apostle and His Message* (Eng. tr. 1947); V. P. Furnish, *Theology and Ethics in Paul* (1968); B. Gärtner, *The Aeropagus Speech and Natural Revelation* (Eng. tr. 1955); L. Goppelt, *Theology of the NT,* II (Eng. tr. 1982); D. A. Hagner and M. J. Harris, eds., *Pauline Studies: Essays Presented to F. F. Bruce* (1980); G. F. Hasel, *NT Theology: Basic Issues in the Current Debate* (1958), pp. 62-67, 90-95, 144-49; M. D. Hooker and S. G. Wilson, eds., *Paul and Paulinism* (1982); L. E. Keck, *Paul and His Letters* (1979); S. Kim, *Origin of Paul's Gospel* (1982); H. Lietzmann, *Paulus* (1934); R. N. Longenecker, *Paul, Apostle of Liberty* (1964); G. Lüdemann, *Paulus, der Heidenapostel,* I (1980); J. G. Machen, *Origin of Paul's Religion* (1925); F. Prat, *Theology of St. Paul* (2 vols., Eng. tr. 1959); E. J. Price, *HibJ,* 16 (1918), 263ff.; K. F. W. Prior, *Gospel in a Pagan Society* (1975); E. Renan, *Saint Paul* (Eng. tr. 1869); H. Ridderbos, *Paul: An Outline of His Theology* (Eng. tr. 1975); A. Ritschl, *Entstehung der altkatholischen Kirche* (1857); J. A. T. Robinson, *The Body — A Study in Pauline Theology* (*SBT,* 1/5, 1952); A. Sabatier, *Apostle Paul* (Eng. tr. 1891); N. B. Stonehouse, "Special Revelation as Scriptural," in C. F. H. Henry, ed., *Revelation and the Bible* (1958); B. B. Warfield, *Lord of Glory* (1907); D. E. H. Whitely, *Theology of St. Paul* (1974); T. Wilson, *St. Paul and Paganism* (1927); W. Wrede, *Paul* (Eng. tr. 1962).

*See also* the bibliography for PAUL THE APOSTLE.

J. H. WEBSTER J. H. GERSTNER

**PAULUS** pol'əs, **SERGIUS** sûr'ji-əs [Gk. *Sergios Paulos*] (Acts 13:7). Proconsul of Cyprus (A.D. 47/48). Paul, Barnabas, and Mark met him in Paphos where he summoned them to tell him "the word of God." He was the first Roman official mentioned in Acts to hear the gospel. Elymas, known also as BAR-JESUS, sought to turn the proconsul from the faith. After seeing Elymas blinded in accordance with Paul's curse (Acts 13:9-11), Sergius Paulus "believed . . . , for he was astonished at the teaching of the Lord" (v. 12). The nature of his belief (i.e., whether he became a Christian) is disputed (cf. "believed" in Acts 8:13 — Simon Magus).

The *nomen* Sergius and the *cognomen* Paulus (more correctly Paullus) were not uncommon. Luke failed to give his *praenomen.* This has led to much speculation regarding his identity. Three different inscriptions must be considered. (1) *Inscriptiones Graecae ad res Romanas pertinentes,* III, 930, found at Soli on the north coast of

Cyprus, gives a dateline "in the proconsulship of Paulus." The earliest this Greek inscription can be dated is A.D. 50, making this consulship too late to fit into Pauline chronology. (2) A Latin inscription (*CIL,* VI, 31545) refers to a Lucius Sergius Paullus, one of the curators of the Banks of the Tiber during the reign of Claudius. Many scholars surmise he later became proconsul of Cyprus and is to be identified with the Sergius Paulus of Acts 13:7. Ramsay argued for this identification and maintained that L. Sergius Paullus became a well-known Christian. But this is speculation; no evidence has been found to prove (or disprove) that this Lucius Sergius Paullus ever went to or was proconsul of Cyprus. If he was his term would have begun in A.D. 48, a date that seems incompatible with Pauline chronology. (3) In its restored form a fragmentary Greek inscription from Kythraia in north Cyprus mentions a Quintus Sergius Paulus as proconsul, probably during the reign of Claudius (*Inscriptiones Graecae ad res Romanas pertinentes,* III, 935). It is possible that the Sergius Paulus of Acts 13:7 is this man (see Van Elderen).

***Bibliography.***–W. M. Ramsay, *Bearing of Recent Discovery on the Trustworthiness of the NT* (1915), pp. 150-172; B. Van Elderen, "Some Archaeological Observations on Paul's First Missionary Journey," in W. W. Gasque and R. P. Martin, eds., *Apostolic History and the Gospel* (*Festschrift* for F. F. Bruce, 1970), pp. 151-56.

J. J. HUGHES

**PAVEMENT** [Heb. *riṣ<sup></sup>pâ, ma<sup></sup>ăśeh, malbēn*]. A surface made firm and level to facilitate movement, or the materials used for this purpose. The most common of the Hebrew words is *riṣᵉpâ* (2 Ch. 7:3; Ezk. 40:17f.; 42:3), which originally referred to the fitting together of stones and could include the "mosaic pavement" of Est. 1:6.

In Ex. 24:10 the Hebrew term is *maʿᵃśeh,* lit. "work," so that the whole expression *maʿᵃśēh liḇnaṯ hassappîr* means literally "a work of flagstone of sapphire."

In Jer. 43:9 RSV "pavement" appears in a passage so difficult that the LXX left it untranslated. Both the word translated "mortar" (Heb. *meleṭ*) and the word translated "pavement" (Heb. *malbēn*) are problems. The first is a hapax legomenon of uncertain meaning. It could refer to the clay used in making bricks as well as to the same material used between bricks (*see* MORTAR). Heb. *malbēn,* which otherwise means "brick kiln," "brick mold," or "brick making," here seems to mean "terrace of bricks" (KoB, p. 527). Some commentators think that the two words may be variants, so that J. Bright translates "in the clay flooring [?], in the pavement [?]" (comm. on Jeremiah [*AB,* 1965], pp. 259, 263; cf. also J. A. Thompson, comm. on Jeremiah [*NICOT,* 1980], p. 670).

For Jn. 19:13 *see* PAVEMENT, THE. E. W. S.

**PAVEMENT, THE** [Gk. *lithóstrōton*[ (Jn. 19:13). The part of the praetorium in which Pilate judged Jesus, also called GABBATHA (Gk. *Gabbatha* perhaps for Aram. *gabbaṯāʾ*).

The Greek word is an adjective meaning "paved with stoneblock," "made of tesserae," hence, of a mosaic or tessellated pavement. As a noun designating an area of the praetorium the term obviously refers to a pavement, either of large stones or tesserae. Albright interpreted Aram. *gabbaṯāʾ*, apparently reflecting some feature of the floor or area, as "ridge," "elevated terrain" (*AP,* p. 245). R. E. Brown (*Gospel According to John,* II [*AB,* 1970], 882), noting that John did not intend the Greek and Aramaic words to be equivalents (cf. Jn. 5:2), favored this meaning for the Aramaic and cited a parallel from Josephus (*BJ* v.2.1 [51]).

The public trial of Jesus could not be conducted in the palace proper lest the Jews defile themselves before the feast. Hence Pilate located his JUDGMENT SEAT outside in the courtyard where this pavement was (Jn. 19:13).

In the excavations of the Fortress Antonia located NW of the temple area an impressive pavement of large stone blocks was uncovered (Aline de Sion, *La Forteresse Antonia* [1956], pp. 107-118). This discovery is one of the factors favoring the identification of the PRAETORIUM with the Fortress Antonia. This large central courtyard measures about 32 m. (104 ft.) E-W and 48 m. (156 ft.) N-S. The limestone blocks of the floor range in thickness from 25 to 51 cm. (10 to 20 in.); some are about 1 m. (3 ft.) square, and others are rectangles about 1 by 2 m. (3 by 6 ft.). The stones along the south side of the courtyard are grooved — apparently a roadway striated to prevent animals from slipping. Other stone blocks have inscribed outlines, possibly of games played by the soldiers stationed there (*ibid.,* pp. 119-142). Underneath the courtyard is a large double cistern about 14 by 51 m. (45 by 170 ft.) and about 9 m. (30 ft.) deep; channels in the pavement drained water from it into the cistern. The vaulted ceiling of the cistern supported the pavement above.

This well-constructed and large pavement found in what appears to be the Fortress Antonia seems to locate with some certainty the pavement of Jn. 19:13 and likewise the praetorium. *See also* JERUSALEM III.H.10.

B. VANELDEREN

**PAVILION.** Used several times by the AV and RSV to render Heb. *sukkâ* ("covert," "booth," or "tent"). In Job 36:29, RSV, it refers to the thick thunderclouds that screen God from human view (AV "tabernacle"; cf. AV 2 S. 22:12 par. Ps. 18:11 [MT 12]; *see* CANOPY). In Isa. 4:5, RSV (MT, AV, 4:6), it is a protective covering that will shield the restored city of Jerusalem from the sun and rain (AV "tabernacle"; NEB "shelter"). In the AV of Ps. 27:5 (RSV "shelter"; NEB "roof"); 31:20 (MT 21) (RSV "covert"; NEB "cover") "pavilion" is used figuratively of the security found in Yahweh's presence; some commentators see it as a specific reference to the tabernacle or temple as a place of refuge (see comms.). N. J. O.

**PAW** [Heb. *kap*] (Lev. 11:27); NEB FLAT PAW; [*yāḏ*] (1 S. 17:37); NEB omits; [*ḥāpar*] (Job 39:21). In Lev. 11:27 animals with soft paws (*kappîm,* lit. "palms") are distinguished from those with hooves. *Yāḏ,* the usual term for HAND, appears three times in 1 S. 17:37 in a common figurative expression ("from the hand of") denoting deliverance. The verb *ḥāpar,* used of the horse in Job 39:21, usually means to "dig" (e.g., Gen. 21:30: Dt. 23:13 [MT 14]) or "search out" (e.g., Josh. 2:2f.).

**PAY; PAYMENT** [Heb. *šālam*] (Ex. 21:36; 22:1, 4, 7, 9 [MT 22:37; 23:3, 6, 8]; Dt. 23:21 [MT 22]; 2 S. 15:7; 2 K. 4:7; Job 22:27; Ps. 22:25 [MT 26]; etc.); AV also RESTORE (Ex. 22:1, 4), PERFORM (Ps. 61:8 [MT 9]); NEB also "make good," REPAY, RESTORE, FULFILMENT, etc.; [*nāṯan*] (Ex. 21:19, 22; Nu. 20:19; 1 K. 5:6 [MT 20]; 2 K. 12:15 [MT 16]); AV also GIVE, BESTOW; [*šûḇ*] ("pay back," Gen. 50:15; Lev. 25:27; Prov. 24:29); AV REQUITE, RESTORE, RENDER, etc.; NEB also REQUITE; [*šāqal*] (Ex. 22:17 [MT 16]; 1 K. 20:39; Est. 3:9; 4:7); [*nāśāʾ ʿōneš*] ("pay the penalty," Prov. 19:19); AV "suffer punishment"; NEB "brings punishment"; [*ʿāśar*] (Dt. 26:12); AV TITHE; NEB "take (a tithe)"; [*gāmal*] ("pay back," Joel 3:4 [MT 4:4]); AV RECOMPENSE; [*kesep*] (Ex. 21:11; Job 31:39; Lam. 5:4); AV MONEY; NEB BUY; [*ʾeškār*] (Ezk. 27:15); AV PRESENT; [*qorbān*] (Lev. 22:18); AV OBLATION; NEB FULFILMENT; [Aram. *nᵉtan*] (Ezr. 4:13); [Gk. *dídōmi*] (Mt. 22:17; Mk. 12:14f.); AV GIVE; [*apodídōmi*] (Mt. 18:25ff.; 20:8; Lk. 7:42; Rom. 13:7); AV also GIVE, RENDER; [*dapanáō*] ("pay [their] expenses," Acts 21:24); AV "be at (their) charges"; [*teléō*]

Part of a relief from Kuyunjik (Nineveh) showing a royal tent (pavilion); the inscription above it reads "Tent of Sennacherib, king of Assyria." To the left Sennacherib sits on a throne receiving the leaders of Lachish, whom he had just captured (Trustees of the British Museum)

(Mt. 17:24; Rom. 13:6); [*dōreán*] ("without pay," Mt. 10:8; 2 Th. 3:8); AV FREELY, FOR NOUGHT; NEB also WITHOUT COST, WITHOUT CHARGE; [*apéchō pánta*] ("I have received full payment," Phil. 4:8); AV "I have all"; NEB "I give you my receipt for everything."

*Šālam,* often used in the expression "pay (my) vows" (e.g., Dt. 23:21; 2 S. 15:7; Job 22:27; Ps. 22:25; 50:14; 61:8; 66:13), occurs in the piel with the meanings "make good (a vow)," "restore" (e.g., Ex. 22:1ff.), "reward." The RSV of Isa. 65:6 renders it "repay"; this idea is also implicit in the Hebrew of v. 7.

*Šûḇ* conveys the idea of returning or restoring something. The AV literally translates Lev. 27:8, "If he be poorer than thy estimation," but the RSV correctly interprets this as "If a man is too poor to pay your valuation"; i.e., if a man could not raise the amount set by Moses to redeem himself, he could have the priest set a value on him. This regulation made it possible for a poor man to make a special vow.

Greek *apéchō* is a technical term used in commercial transactions that means to receive a payment and to give a receipt for it. Only the church at Philippi had entered into such a "partnership" with Paul (cf. v. 15).

N. J. O.

**PÊ** pā [פ]. The seventeenth letter of the Hebrew alphabet, transliterated in *ISBE* as *p* with daghesh and as *p̱* without daghesh. It also came to be used for the number eighty. *See* WRITING.

**PEACE** [Heb. *šālôm*]; AV also FAVOUR, PROSPEROUS; NEB also SAFETY, FAREWELL, WELFARE, WELCOME, PROSPER(ITY), UNHARMED, GREETINGS, GOOD NEWS, SOUND, HARMONY, etc.; [*berāḵâ*] (2 K. 18:31; Isa. 36:16); AV "agreement . . . by a present"; [*menûḥâ*] (1 Ch. 22:9); AV REST; [*regaʿ*] (Job 21:13); AV MOMENT; [*mêšārîm*] (Dnl. 11:6); AV AGREEMENT; NEB MARRIAGE; [Aram. *šelām*] (Ezr. 5:7; Dnl. 4:1 [MT 3:31]; 6:25 [MT 26]); NEB GREETINGS, PROSPERITY; [Gk. *eirḗnē*]; AV also REST, QUIETNESS; NEB also SAFE, TERMS, GOOD WISHES, BLESSINGS, HAPPILY, GOOD LUCK; [*siōpáō*] (Mk. 4:39); NEB HUSH; **HOLD ONE'S PEACE** [Heb. qal and hiphil of *ḥāraš*]; AV also HOLD ONE'S TONGUE (Est. 7:4); NEB also SAY NOTHING, MONTH (1 S. 10:27; emending to *ḥōḏeš,* following LXX), KEEP TO ONESELF, KEEP SILENCE, BE SILENT; [*dāmam*] (Lev. 10:3); NEB BE DUMBFOUNDED; [hiphil of *ḥāšâ*]; NEB also SAY NO MORE; **MAKE PEACE; BE AT PEACE; LIVE IN PEACE** [Heb. qal, hiphil, and hophal of *šālēm*]; NEB also COME TO TERMS, PROSPER; [*šālâ*] (Job 12:6); AV PROSPER; NEB BE LEFT UNDISTURBED; [Gk. *eirēneúō*] (Mk. 9:50; 2 Cor. 13:11; 1 Thess. 5:13); [*eirēnopoiéō*] (Col. 1:20); **GIVE PEACE** [Heb. hiphil of *nû(a)ḥ*] (1 Ch. 22:9, 18; 23:25;

2 Ch. 14:6f. [MT 5f.]); AV GIVE REST; NEB also SECURITY; **PEACEABLE; PEACEFUL** [Heb. *šālēm*] (2 S. 20:19); [*šālôm*]; AV also COUNSEL OF PEACE; NEB also TRANQUIL, CONCORD; [*šālēw*] (1 Ch. 4:40); [Gk. *eirēnikós*] (He. 12:11; Jas. 3:17); NEB also PEACE-LOVING; [*hēsýchios*] (1 Tim. 2:2); NEB QUIET; **PEACEABLY** [Heb. *šālôm*]; AV also IN PEACE; NEB KIND WORD, IN PEACE, WELL, AS A FRIEND, AMICABLY; **LIVE PEACEABLY** [Gk. *eirēneúō*] (Rom. 12:18).

***I. In the OT.***–The concept of peace in the OT is most often represented by the Hebrew root *šlm* and its derivatives. The noun *šālôm*, one of the most significant theological terms in Scripture, has a wide semantic range stressing various nuances of its basic meaning: totality or completeness. These nuances include fulfillment, completion, maturity, soundness, wholeness (both individual and communal), community, harmony, tranquillity, security, well-being, welfare, friendship, agreement, success, and prosperity.

Peace is often understood as the opposite of war (Eccl. 3:8; Ps. 120:7) or linked with the absence of war (Jgs. 11:13; 21:13; 2 S. 20:19; 1 K. 2:5; 4:24 [MT 5:4]; 2 Ch. 15:5; Ps. 35:20; Prov. 16:7; Jer. 12:12; 14:13; 28:9). In this sense, peace is desirable for nations (Jgs. 4:17; 1 K. 4:24 [MT 5:4]; 5:12 [MT 26]; 22:44 [MT 45]; Ezr. 9:12; Isa. 33:7), tribes or clans (Josh. 9:15; Jgs. 21:13; 1 S. 7:14; 29:7; see also 1 Ch. 12:18, in which the willingness to negotiate is implicit), or cities (Dt. 20:10-12; Jgs. 8:9; 1 K. 20:18).

Such peace can result from military victory, as in Jgs. 8:9; 1 Ch. 22:18; Isa. 9:6f. (MT 5f.); Jer. 43:12; Mic. 5:5 (MT 4); Zec. 9:10. In 1 K. 22:27f. the king's coming "in peace" means his coming "in victory," "with his purpose accomplished." Surrender is often concomitant with the end of military hostilities and is therefore an element in the resulting peace (2 S. 10:19; 1 K. 20:18; 1 Ch. 19:19; Isa. 27:5; Dnl. 11:17, LXX). But peace can also result from diplomacy (e.g., Est. 9:30; 10:3; cf. Jer. 6:14; 8:11), and this demonstrates its intimate connection with the biblical concern for the total well-being of the individual as well as of the community (1 S. 25:6; in Dt. 23:6 [MT 7] *šᵉlōmām wᵉṭōḇāṭām*, "their peace [and] their prosperity," corresponds to Akk. *sulummû u ṭūbtu* in similar contexts). The ratification of treaties was intended to produce peace (Gen. 26:28-31; Josh. 9:15; 1 S. 16:4f.). Formal and informal agreements of nonbelligerence and/or nonviolence were frequently made in ancient times (Dt. 2:26-29; 20:10-12; Josh. 10:1-4; 11:19; Jgs. 4:17; 1 S. 7:14; 1 K. 5:12 [MT 26]; 2 K. 9:17-22, 31; 18:31 par. Isa. 36:16; Dnl. 11:6), and the phrase "covenant of peace" was employed in a variety of situations (Nu. 25:12; Isa. 54:10; Ezk. 34:25; 37:26; Mal. 2:5; cf. Sir. 45:24). Such covenants of *šālôm* ("completeness" or "fulfillment") served to unite the wills of the opposing parties, creating a common will that was expected to be maintained by scrupulous adherence to the covenant stipulations.

Psalm 119:165 stresses the sense of serenity and contentment possessed by all who love (i.e., obey; cf. vv. 166-168) the divine law. Prominent in the OT is the teaching that God is the giver of peace in all its fullness (Lev. 26:6; 1 Ch. 12:18; 22:9 [note the pun on the name Solomon, "peaceful one"]; 23:25; 2 Ch. 14:6f. [MT 5f.]; Job 22:21; 25:2; Ps. 4:8 [MT 9]; 29:11; 37:37; 122:6-8; 147:14; Prov. 3:17). The prophets declare emphatically that God Himself is the source of true peace (Isa. 26:12; 52:7 [cf. Nah. 1:15 (MT 2:1)]; Ezk. 34:25; 37:26; Zec. 6:13; 8:12; Mal. 2:5f.). Without a righteous life, made possible by God's help, no one is able to find peace (Isa. 48:22; 57:1f., 21; 59:8); therefore peace and righteousness are frequently linked together (Ps. 72:7; 85:8, 10 [MT 9, 11]; Isa. 9:7 [MT 6]; 32:17f.; 48:18; 60:17); cf. also the association of peace with justice in Isa. 59:8; Zec. 8:16.

The sense of well-being and fulfillment that comes from God is dependent on His gracious presence (Gen. 28:20f.; Jgs. 6:23f.; 18:6; 1 K. 2:33). It is in this light that "peace" is sometimes invoked as a spiritual blessing upon another (e.g., Ex. 4:18; 1 S. 1:17; 20:42; 2 S. 15:9, 27; Zec. 8:19; cf. 1 K. 2:6). The key passage associating peace with the divine presence is the conclusion of the Aaronic benediction: "The Lord lift up his countenance upon you, and give you peace" (Nu. 6:26; cf. 1 Ch. 23:25; Ps. 122:6-8); this has formed the basis of such prayers as the well-known synagogue benediction: "May the Lord God bless his children and all mankind with peace."

Harmony between God and His creatures (Isa. 27:5) and among His creatures themselves (1 S. 16:4f.; Job 5:23; Zec. 6:13) is at the heart of the OT emphasis on peace as community. Such community results when people treat one another with goodwill and love, but no peace is possible where there is malice (cf. Gen. 37:4; 2 S. 3:21-23; 17:3; 1 K. 2:13; 2 K. 9:17-22, 31; Ps. 120:6f.; Cant. 8:10; Jer. 9:8 [MT 7]). When a community is at peace its members can experience safety and prosperity (Isa. 26:3 [RSV translates *šālôm šālôm* as "perfect peace"; *see* PERFECT I]), although a superficial peace can lead to a false sense of security and contentment (2 K. 20:19 par. Isa. 39:8; 1 Ch. 4:40; Job 12:6; 21:13). Whereas peace is found by doing good (Ps. 34:14 [MT 15]), its absence can be equated with judgment (Jer. 12:12; 14:19; 16:5; 25:37; Lam. 3:17; Ezk. 7:25). In contrast to the false prophets who announced peace when there was none, the true prophets proclaimed a peace that brought healing (Isa. 57:19; Jer. 6:14; 8:11, 15; 14:13; 28:9; Ezk. 13:10, 16; Mic. 3:5).

The use of "peace" as a word of greeting implies a desire for the addressee's well-being in the widest sense. Such usage was common in ancient Semitic culture. Cognates of Heb. *šālôm* (Jgs. 19:20; 1 S. 25:6; 1 Ch. 12:18; Dnl. 10:19) include Aram. *šᵉlām* (Ezr. 5:7; Dnl. 4:1 [MT 3:31]; 6:25 [MT 26]), Ugar. *šlm*, Akk. *šulmu*, and Arab. *salâm* (which is still used today; also derived from the same root are the part. *muslim* and the infinitive *islâm*, both denoting "submission [to God]"). Heb. *šālôm* could also be used as an expression of farewell or as a description of someone's departure, often including the idea of contentedness or serenity (Gen. 26:29, 31; Ex. 18:23; 1 S. 25:35; 29:7; 2 S. 15:9; 1 K. 22:17 par. 2 Ch. 18:16; 2 K. 5:19; Isa. 55:12). To die "in peace" connotes that one has completed a full and satisfying life (Gen. 15:15; 2 K. 22:20 par. 2 Ch. 34:28; Jer. 34:5). To achieve this completeness, having fulfilled the divine purpose for one's life, is virtually equivalent to salvation; thus *šālôm* was often written on Jewish gravestones, and Gk. *en eirḗnē* was similarly used in early Christian cemetery inscriptions.

***II. In the NT.***–Corresponding to Heb. *šālôm* in the OT, Gk. *eirḗnē* and its derivatives form the dominant NT word-group expressing the ideas of peace, well-being, rest, reconciliation with God, and salvation in the fullest sense. In classical Greek *eirḗnē* primarily signified the absence of conflict (especially in a political or military sense), the antithesis to war; it could also connote the conditions resulting from the cessation of war, or the condition of law and order that results in the blessings of prosperity for land and people (exemplified by the *pax Romana* during the reign of Caesar Augustus). In NT references to the political and military spheres, *eirḗnē* is used in the classical sense to denote the opposite of war (Mt. 10:34 par. Lk. 12:51; 14:32; Acts 12:20; 24:2; Rev. 6:4). In Lk. 19:42 Jesus may be reflecting on the perennial yearning for peace in Jerusalem expressed in passages such as Ps. 122:6-8. In general, however, the NT's use of *eirēnē* is influenced much more by that of the LXX, where the term is used almost invariably to translate Heb. *šālôm*. Thus *eirēnē* in the NT has taken on the broader connotations of well-being, completeness, inner satisfaction, the contentment and serenity that derive from having lived a full life, etc. The peace that Jesus gives is qualitatively different from that which the world can give (Jn. 14:27).

As the source of all peace, God is frequently referred to in the Epistles as the "God of peace" (Rom. 15:33; 16:20; Phil. 4:9; 1 Thess. 5:23; He. 13:20; cf. also 1 Cor. 14:33; 2 Cor. 13:11; 2 Thess. 3:16). Peace is included among the gifts of the Holy Spirit to believers (Rom. 8:6; 14:17; 15:13; Gal. 5:22). The NT expects peace to be the normal state of affairs among Christians (Mk. 9:50; Rom. 14:17, 19; 1 Cor. 14:33; 16:11; 2 Cor. 13:11; 1 Thess. 5:13; 2 Tim. 2:22; 1 Pet. 3:11; 2 Pet. 3:14), and especially between husband and wife (1 Cor. 7:15). Peace with God (Rom. 5:1) is essential to unity within the Church (Eph. 2:14-17; 4:3; 6:23) and among all persons (Rom. 12:18; Col. 1:20; He. 12:14; Jas. 3:17f.).

Peace is associated with various other gifts, virtues, and states of being: with receptiveness to God's salvation (Mt. 10:13 par. Lk. 10:5f.), with freedom from distress and fear (Jn. 14:27; 16:33; cf. also 1 Tim. 2:2), with healing, both spiritual and physical (Mk. 5:34; Lk. 7:50; 8:48; cf. 11:21), with love (2 Cor. 13:11), with heavenly wisdom (Jas. 3:17), and with security (1 Thess. 5:3). Inner peace is a vital aspect of Christian experience (Phil. 4:7; Col. 3:15); it is closely related to and issues from a life of righteousness (He. 12:11; also 7:2; cf. Rom. 3:10, 17).

Jesus Christ is the mediator of peace (Col. 1:20). Peace with God is the result of being justified through faith in Christ (Rom. 5:1). The good news of salvation, which is called "the gospel of peace" (Eph. 6:15) because it reconciles believers to God and to one another (cf. 2:12-18), forms part of the "whole armor of God" (6:11, 13) that enables the Christian to withstand the attacks of the spiritual forces of evil. This "good news of peace by Jesus Christ" (Acts 10:36) is an important element in the evangelistic motivation and message of the Church (cf. 9:31); it is intimately related to Christ's commission of His disciples as ambassadors to a lost world (Jn. 20:19-21, 26). The song of Zechariah (Lk. 1:68-79), the Gloria in Excelsis Deo (2:14), and the Nunc Dimittis (2:29-32) all demonstrate that peace in its full dimensions is the fulfillment of the messianic expectations of God's people (e.g., 1:79; 2:14, 29; cf. 19:38; Isa. 9:6f. [MT 5f.]). Peace is likewise an essential part of the eschatological hope of Christians (Rom. 2:9f.; cf. 14:17; 16:20; 1 Thess. 5:23).

Like Heb. *šālôm* in the OT, *eirēnē* is used both in greetings (Lk. 10:5f. par. Mt. 10:13; Jn. 20:19, 21, 26) and in valedictory formulas (Mk. 5:34; Lk. 7:50; 8:48; Acts 16:36; cf. Lk. 2:29; Acts 15:33; 1 Cor. 16:11; Jas. 2:16). The hendiadys "grace and peace" (sometimes also including "mercy") forms a part of the opening greeting in all the Pauline Epistles (Rom. 1:7; 1 Cor. 1:3; 2 Cor. 1:2; Gal. 1:3; Eph. 1:2; Phil. 1:2; Col. 1:2; 1 Thess. 1:1; 2 Thess. 1:2; 1 Tim. 1:2; 2 Tim. 1:2; Tit. 1:4; Philem. 3) and also in 1 Peter (1:2), 2 Peter (1:2), 2 John (v. 3), Jude (v. 2), and Revelation (1:4). "Peace" also appears in closing greetings and benedictions (Rom. 15:33; 2 Cor. 13:11; Eph. 6:23; 2 Thess. 3:16; 1 Pet. 5:14; 3 Jn. 15; cf. Gal. 6:16; 1 Thess. 5:23; He. 13:20). Such usage is clearly in line with Judeo-Christian tradition and practice down through the ages, as exemplified in the Eighteen Benedictions, which forms the daily prayer pattern of observant Jews: "Blessed art Thou, O Lord, the One who blesses His people Israel with peace."

*See also* PEACEMAKER; PROSPER.

***Bibliography.***–*DNTT,* II, 776-783; J. I. Durham, "שָׁלוֹם and the Presence of God," in J. I. Durham and J. R. Porter, eds., *Proclamation and Presence: OT Essays in Honor of Gwynne Henton Davies* (1970), pp. 272-293; W. Eisenbeis, *Die Wurzel* ŠLM *im AT* (*BZAW,* 113, 1969); P. L. Hammer, *Shalom in the NT* (1973); D. J. Harris, *Shalom! The Biblical Concept of Peace* (1970); *ILC,* I-II, 263-335; C. G. Montefiore and H. Loewe, eds., *Rabbinic Anthology* (repr. 1974), pp. 530-38; *TDNT,* II, *s.v.* εἰρήνη κτλ. (W. Foerster, G. von Rad); *THAT,* II, *s.v.* שלם (G. Gerleman); H. C. White, *Shalom in the OT* (1973); D. J. Wiseman, *VT,* 32 (1982), 311-326.

R. F. YOUNGBLOOD

**PEACE OFFERING.** *See* SACRIFICES AND OFFERINGS IN THE OT.

**PEACEMAKER** [Gk. *eirēnopoiós*] (Mt. 5:9). One who seeks to end strife and establish harmony, particularly between oneself and one's neighbors. The noun is rare in classical Greek, but it is sometimes used of rulers who have established peace in the empire (e.g., Xenophon *Hellenica* vi.3.4; Plutarch *Moralia* 279b; cf. its application to God in Philo *De specialibus legibus* ii.192; cf. also the application of the verb *eirēnopoiéō* to Christ's work of cosmic reconciliation in Col. 1:20).

The background for *eirēnopoiós* in Mt. 5:9 (its only NT occurrence), however, is to be found in Hebrew rather than classical Greek tradition (*see* PEACE). Although *eirēnopoiós* does not appear in the LXX, the verb *eirēnopoiéō* does, in Prov. 10:10, LXX (cf. also Isa. 27:5, Aq., Symm., Th.; the LXX has *poiéō eirḗnēn*). Rabbinic literature refers frequently to the virtue of "making peace" (Heb. *ʿāśâ šālôm*) in the sense of ending strife. There is a famous saying of Hillel: "Be of the sons of Aaron, loving peace and pursuing peace, loving mankind and bringing them nigh to the Law" (*Aboth* 1.12; see SB, I, 217; *TDNT,* II, 409). Closely related to the teaching of Mt. 5:9 is that of Jas. 3:18, which uses Gk. *hoi poioúsin eirḗnēn* for those who promote unity and reconciliation within the Christian community. The Beatitude makes clear that those who strive for an end to discord and the establishment of harmony (Heb. *šālôm*) within the human community are doing the will of God and are therefore worthy to be called God's children.

***Bibliography.***–*DNTT,* II, 782; SB, I, 215-18; *TDNT,* II, *s.v.* εἰρήνη κτλ.: εἰρηνοποιός (W. Foerster).

R. F. YOUNGBLOOD N. J. O.

**PEACOCK** [Heb. *tukkîyîm*] (1 K. 10:22 par. 2 Ch. 9:21); NEB MONKEYS.

Two species of peafowl are to be found in southeastern Asia, *Pavo muticus* and the more beautiful *Pavo cristatus*. The latter occurs in the jungles of India and Ceylon. The Hebrew term is sometimes believed to have originated in that area, being derived from the Tamil *tokei*. 1 K. 10:22 par. 2 Ch. 9:21 lists peacocks as part of the cargo brought to Solomon by his merchant vessels. The birds were also brought to Egypt, Assyria, and Greece in ancient times. Their inclusion among the imports to Israel is therefore not impossible.

But W. F. Albright (*ARI,* pp. 212f. n. 16) derived the Hebrew rather from the Egyp. *ky*. In the Story of the Shipwrecked Sailor from the Middle Kingdom (translation in W. K. Simpson, ed., *Literature of Ancient Egypt* [1973], pp. 50-56), the king of Punt gives the sailor a variety of presents. At the end of the list of these luxuries occur *qf* and *ky,* apes and baboons, the Egyptian equivalents of the last two items in Solomon's cargo, *qōpîm* and *tukkîyîm*. In the early 15th cent. two species of monkeys were recorded as being imported to Egypt from Punt.

G. WYPER

**PEARL** [Heb. *p^e^nînîm* (pl.)] (Job 28:18b); AV RUBY; NEB RED CORAL; [Gk. *margarítēs*]. (For AV "pearl" in Job 28:18a *see* STONES, PRECIOUS.) A hard, shiny concretion of shell material formed as an abnormal growth in some mollusks.

Pearls have long been highly valued because of their beauty and rarity. Thus they appear with jewels and other luxurious materials in several biblical lists (1 Tim. 2:9; Rev. 17:4; 18:12, 16; 21:21). Their great value gives meaning to the comparison with wisdom in Job 28:18 and to the parable in Mt. 13:45f.

**PEASANTRY** [Heb. *p^e^rāzôn*] (Jgs. 5:7, 11); AV VILLAGES; NEB CHAMPIONS. The meaning of Heb. *p^e^rāzôn* is uncertain. KoB (p. 777) understands *p^e^rāzôn* as "dwellers of open country." The AV, following a few MSS, emends *p^e^rāzôn* to *p^e^rāzôṯ*, "open, rural country" (cf. the use of *p^e^rāzôṯ* in Est. 9:19; Ezk. 38:11; Zec. 2:4 [MT 8]), but this sense is hardly satisfactory. G. Garbini (*JSS*, 23 [1978], 23f.) attempted to relate Heb. *przn* to Epigraphic (Old) South Arabian *frzn*, "iron" (thus v. 7, "iron ceased in Israel" [cf. v. 8; 1 S. 13:19-22]; and figuratively, v. 11, God's acts of justice made Israel as strong as iron, "the triumphs of his [God's] iron"), but this seems forced. More plausibly, J. Gray (*Joshua, Judges and Ruth* [*NCBC*, 1977], p. 217) suggested two other possibilities. He noted that the LXX *dynatoí* suggests an original Heb. *rôz^e^nîm*, "rulers" (cf. the LXX's use of *dynástou* for *rāzôn* in Prov. 14:28), a reading that makes much better sense in the context. He also noted a possible cognate to *przn* in Arab. *barrāz*, "champion in single combat" (cf. NEB). If valid, the latter possibility would also explain the LXX's use of *dynatoí* in Hab. 3:14, where MT *pāraz* has been problematic.

G. A. L.

**PECULIAR.** A term used by the AV only in its original sense of "belonging exclusively to one person or group" (from Lat. *pecūlium*, "private property"). Thus Qoheleth says that acquiring the "peculiar treasures" (Heb. *s^e^gullâ*, lit. "personal property"; RSV, NEB, "treasure") of kings and provinces is vanity (Eccl. 2:8; cf. v. 11). The AV also renders *s^e^gullâ* by "peculiar" or "peculiar treasure" in four passages referring to Israel as God's chosen people: Ex. 19:5; Dt. 14:2; 26:18; Ps. 135:4 (RSV "own possession"; NEB "special possession," "special treasure"). Tit. 2:14 quotes from the LXX of these passages (Gk. *perioúsios*, lit. "rich," "special," "chosen"; AV "peculiar"; RSV "of his own"; NEB "marked out for his own"). But in 1 Pet. 2:9, AV, "peculiar" (cf. RSV "own," mg. "own possession"; NEB "claimed . . . for his own") represents Gk. *peripoíēsis* (lit. "possessing, possession"), the LXX rendering of *s^e^gullâ* in Mal. 3:17 (AV mg. "peculiar treasure"; cf. AV "jewels"; RSV "special possession"; NEB "own possession"), which speaks of the righteous as God's special people. The AV also uses the term in Wisd. 19:6, where it renders Gk. *taís saís epitagaís* by "the peculiar commandments that were given unto them" (cf. RSV, NEB, "thy commands").

*See also* POSSESS.

N. J. O.

**PEDAHEL** ped'ə-hel [Heb. *p^e^ḏah'ēl*–'God has redeemed']. Son of Ammihud; a leader of Naphtali chosen to assist Joshua and Eleazer in dividing up the land W of the Jordan (Nu. 34:28).

**PEDAHZUR** pə-dä'zər [Heb. *p^e^ḏâṣûr*–'(the) rock has redeemed']. Father of Gamaliel, who was the leader of Manasseh in the wilderness of Sinai (Nu. 1:10; 2:20; 7:54, 59; 10:23).

**PEDAIAH** pə-dā'yə, pə-dī'ə [*p^e^ḏayāhû, p^e^ḏāyâ*–'Yahweh has redeemed'].

**1.** Father of Joel, who was the officer in charge of the half of Manasseh W of the Jordan during King David's reign (1 Ch. 27:20).

**2.** A native of Rumah; father of Zebudah mother of Jehoiakim (2 K. 23:36).

**3.** Descendant of David and son of Jeconiah (1 Ch. 3:18). According to v. 19 he was the father of Zerubbabel (cf. LXX, which substitutes Shealtiel here); but Pedaiah's brother Shealtiel is called the father of Zerubbabel in Ezr. 3:2, 8; 5:2; Neh. 12:1; Hag. 1:1, 12, 14; 2:2, 23. A common explanation of this discrepancy is that Shealtiel died childless, and in levirate marriage Pedaiah fathered Zerubbabel by Shealtiel's widow (see KD).

**4.** Son of Parosh; one who helped to rebuild the wall of Jerusalem after the Exile (Neh. 3:25).

**5.** [Gk. Apoc. A *Phaldaios*, Lucian *Phadaias*]; AV PHALDAIUS; NEB PHALDAEUS. One of those who stood at Ezra's left hand when the law was read to the people (Neh. 8:4; 1 Esd. 9:44).

**6.** A Levite appointed by Nehemiah as a treasurer over the storehouses of food to be distributed to the Levites (Neh. 13:13).

**7.** A Benjaminite; son of Kolaiah, father of Joed, and ancestor of Sallu, who was among those who lived in Jerusalem after the Exile (Neh. 11:7).

**PEDDLER** [Gk. part. of *kapēleúō*–'trade in, peddle'] (2 Cor. 2:17); AV "corrupt"; NEB HAWKING. This pejorative term describes two abuses, with either or both of which Paul's opponents at Corinth may have charged him: (1) selling the word of God for profit, as some itinerant Greek philosophers disreputably sold their ideas for monetary gain (*TDNT*, III, 603f.; Barrett, p. 103; Hughes, p. 83 n. 22; Plummer, pp. 73f.); and (2) adulterating the word of God, as wine traders watered down their product (see Isa. 1:22, LXX), or as some Jewish missionaries compromised their religion by spreading their doctrines while selling merchandise (cf. W. D. Davies, *Paul and Rabbinic Judaism* [4th ed. 1980], p. 133 n. 1). Both abuses appear together in Lucian's description of philosophers who sell their teaching (*Hermotimus* 59).

Paul had not received financial support from the Corinthians for his ministry there (1 Cor. 9:12b, 15; cf. Mt. 10:8f.), though he believed he had a right to it (1 Cor. 9:3-14; cf. Mt. 10:10; 1 Tim. 5:18; *see also* TENTMAKER). So, unlike peddlers, Paul preached the gospel "free of charge" (1 Cor. 9:18). But the point he makes may be the broader one that he, with Silvanus and Timothy (2 Cor. 1:19), had preached the gospel not with dishonest practices or mixed motives but "as men of sincerity, commissioned by God" (2:17b).

***Bibliography.***–Comms. on 2 Corinthians C. K. Barrett (*HNTC*, 1973); P. E. Hughes (*NICNT*, 1962); A. Plummer (*ICC*, repr. 1966); also *TDNT*, III, *s.v.* καπηλεύω (H. Windisch).

W. J. MOULDER

**PEDESTAL** [Heb. *kēn*]; AV BASE; NEB LEVEL EDGE. Heb. *kēn* is usually rendered "base" by the RSV (cf. Ex. 30:18, 28; 31:9; etc.). It represents the BASE (4) of each LAVER (II) in the temple of Solomon (1 K. 7:31).

**PEDIGREE.** The AV translates the hithpael of Heb. *yālaḏ* (lit. "show one's birth") "declared their pedigrees" in

Nu. 1:18 (RSV "registered themselves"; NEB "registered their descent"). The keeping of pedigrees (i.e., genealogical records) was very important in Hebrew tradition. *See* GENEALOGY III.

**PEDIMENT** [Heb. *marṣepeṯ*] (2 K. 16:17); AV PAVEMENT; NEB BASE. The term refers to the stone base supporting the temple "sea" that Ahaz substituted for the bronze oxen, which he used to pay his tribute to the king of Assyria.

**PEEL; PILL.** Two verbs that originally had different meanings: (1) "peel" (cf. Lat. *pellis,* "skin") meant to strip off the skin, while (2) "pill" (cf. Lat. *pilus,* "hair") meant to remove the hair. But in Elizabethan English the two were confused. Thus the AV uses "pill" in Gen. 30:37f. (Heb. piel of *pāṣal,* lit. "peel [bark]"; so RSV, NEB) and Tob. 11:13 (Gk. *lepízō,* lit. "strip off [skin, flakes, etc.]"; RSV "scale off"; NEB "peel off"), where "peel" is clearly meant. The second meaning may be implied, however, in Isa. 18:2, 7, where the Ethiopians are described by the AV as "peeled" (cf. NEB "smooth-skinned"; RSV "smooth"; Heb. pual part. of *māraṭ;* cf. also *māraṭ* in Ezr. 9:3; Neh. 13:25; Isa. 50:6, where it means "pull out hair"). In Ezk. 29:18 the qal pass. part. of *māraṭ* is used to describe the shoulders of the Babylonian soldiers (AV "peeled"; RSV "rubbed bare"; NEB "chafed").

B. S. EASTON N. J. O.

**PEEP.** The AV translation of Heb. *ṣāpap* in Isa. 8:19; 10:14 (RSV "chirp"; NEB "squeak," "chirp"). On 8:19, *see* DIVINATION III.G.

**PEKAH** pē'kə [Heb. *peqaḥ*–'opening,' i.e., release from bondage and subjection; Gk. *Phakee*] (2 K. 15:25-31). The son of Remaliah, an ex-court official, and eighteenth king of Israel (*ca.* 737-732). He seized the throne after murdering his predecessor Pekahiah (*ca.* 742-740 B.C.) in Samaria while acting as Pekahiah's "captain," a title denoting high military rank. Pekah was then credited with a twenty-year reign over Israel (2 K. 15:27), which if reckoned from his succession to Pekahiah in *ca.* 740 B.C. would have taken him well beyond the fall of Samaria to Assyria in 722 B.C., as well as excluding the reign of Hoshea of Israel (*ca.* 732-722 B.C.) completely.

Some understanding of this apparent discrepancy may be gained by endeavoring to trace Pekah's prominence back to the short-lived reigns of Zachariah and Shallum (*ca.* 753/752 B.C.). At that time he was probably already a military officer in control of some Israelite forces in Gilead (cf. 2 K. 15:25), and may well have formed an unofficial alliance with Rezin of Syria, since both faced the threat of a resurgent Assyria under Tiglath-pileser III (*ca.* 745-727 B.C.).

Certainly when Pekah succeeded Pekahiah he lost no time in implementing a formal military relationship with Rezin, the Philistine states, and some of the Transjordanian kingdoms in an attempt to contain the Assyrian advance and restore prosperity to Israel. Pekah could therefore have spent over a decade building up the military resources of Israel in Gileadite territory, and still have been serving in an important military capacity in the time of Pekahiah.

It is possible that part of the reason for Menahem's quick submission to Tiglath-pileser III (2 K. 15:9) was to forestall Pekah's rise to the position of commander of Israel's entire forces and thereby to prevent him from making any attempt to usurp the throne with Syrian help. In the end Pekah did achieve this goal, but with very little force and in the absence of external assistance, the deed being done in the short reign of Pekahiah, Menahem's son and successor.

If, therefore, by speaking of the length of Pekah's "reign" as twenty years the source in Kings is actually describing his period of military power in Israel, the apparent historical difficulty is removed. From the time of Zachariah and Shallum (*ca.* 753 B.C.) to the accession of Hoshea in *ca.* 732 B.C. (cf. 2 K. 15:30) is a period of just over twenty years, while Pekah's actual rule as king of Israel would extend from the time of Pekahiah's assassination (*ca.* 740 B.C.) to Hoshea's accession, an interval of about eight years (*ca.* 740-732 B.C.). This would imply that the author of 2 Kings understood Pekah to have been a military commander in the Transjordan area for some twelve years. A wine-jar handle (8th cent. B.C.) recovered from the mound at Hazor bore Pekah's name, and thus attested to his rule in Israel.

Pekah was a fiery anti-Assyrian; his predecessors' policy of truckling to Assyria was to him and his Gileadite patriots a betrayal of Israel's national interests, a threat to its independence, and thus a policy to be reversed at all costs. This he attempted to do by creating an anti-Assyrian confederacy, of which he and Rezin king of Damascus were the principal leaders. The armies of this confederacy attacked Ahaz king of Judah, who refused to join them and appealed to Tiglath-pileser.

The Israelites struck Judah from the north, inflicting a heavy blow and carrying off many prisoners, who, however, were later sent back home after prophetic intervention (2 Ch. 28:8-15). Reaching Jerusalem, the confederates began a siege (2 K. 16:5; Isa. 7). Their plan was to take Judah, annex parts of it, and make their lackey ben Tabeel king of Judah. In addition to the attacks from the north Judah was subjected to two other onslaughts; the Philistines swarmed over the Shephelah and Negeb and seized a number of cities, and the Edomites captured Elath (2 Ch. 28:17f.).

Tiglath-pileser, who had conquered Hamath some years before, set out to crush the members of the confederacy one by one. It appears that he struck at Israel twice — a preliminary assault and then an all-out attack. Isa. 9:1 refers to the battles, which are summarized in 2 K. 15:29, as two campaigns. Tiglath-pileser first came down, as one of the inscriptions states, by the coast of the "upper sea" and, driving inland, fell upon Zebulun and Naphtali. In the south he subjugated the Philistine state of Gaza and imposed tribute. If this campaign was to isolate Israel from Egypt and the southern states, then the second was to isolate Damascus. Tiglath-pileser came down the seacoast this time and, advancing inland, occupied Gilead and Galilee, leaving Israel a mere skeleton of a kingdom, consisting of Mt. Ephraim and the royal capital. The cities taken were Ijon, Abel-beth-maacah, Janoah, Kedesh, and Hazor. These territories were incorporated into newly created Assyrian provinces; their Israelite inhabitants were carried off into exile and slavery in Babylon.

Pekah was not allowed to survive the national disaster for which he was responsible. He was assassinated by Hoshea son of Elah, a pro-Assyrian conspirator and the last occupant of the throne of Israel.

***Bibliography.***–*ANET,* pp. 283f.; J. Gray, *I & II Kings* (*OTL,* rev. ed. 1970), pp. 64-68, 626; *MNHK,* pp. 79-81; H. Tadmor, *JCS,* 12 (1975), 22-40, 77-100.

M. S. SEALE R. K. H.

**PEKAHIAH** pē-kə-hī'ə [Heb. *p^eqaḥyâ*–'Yahweh has opened,' i.e., God has brought relief or release; Gk. *Phakeias*] (2 K. 15:22-26). The son of Menahem and king of Israel for two years (*ca.* 740 B.C.), whose short rule was correlated in 2 K. 15:23 with the fiftieth year of

Azariah (Uzziah) of Judah. This man had evidently begun his rule *ca.* 791 B.C. as co-regent with Amaziah (*ca.* 796-767 B.C.), and accordingly his fiftieth year would be *ca.* 741 B.C., which establishes an approximate date for Pekahiah.

Political instability marked his brief tenure of office. Pekahiah continued his father's pro-Assyrian policy, which was to maintain the throne at the price of tribute-paying vassalage. This policy ran counter to patriotic sentiment, however, and a ruler who exhibited any sign of weakness, on the field of battle or otherwise, was liable to be murdered by Israelite patriots. Pekahiah was the sixth king to be thus dispatched. He was attacked in his palace at Samaria by Pekah son of Remaliah, a court officer, who was assisted by fifty fellow conspirators from Gilead (Dt. 3:13f.). Pekahiah, like the other kings of Israel, is censured for clinging to the perversions introduced by Jeroboam. He was one of the Israelite kings who was not mentioned in Chronicles, and this might indicate an adverse opinion by the Chronicler regarding his religious outlook.

The presence of Argob and Arieh (Jair), which are place-names, in the MT of 2 K. 15:25, should not be regarded as a dislocation from v. 29 (so RSV mg.), even though the MT reads a little awkwardly. If the two names are placed after the MT "sons of" (RSV "men of"), the difficulty is removed and the verse then reads, "and Pekah the son of Remaliah, his captain, conspired against him, and smote him in Samaria in the citadel of the king's house, and with him were fifty men of Argob and Jair, Gileadites." The prophetic strictures of Hosea (6:8) against Gilead as a "city . . . tracked with blood" were thus entirely appropriate. M. S. SEALE R. K. H.

**PEKOD** pē'kod [Heb. *p^eqôḏ*; Akk. *puqūdu*]. One of the larger Aramean tribes that had settled in southeastern Babylonia between the lower Tigris and Elam by the 8th cent. B.C. The economy of the Puqudu was based on agriculture and animal husbandry. The Assyrian royal inscriptions record that Tiglath-pileser III (745-727 B.C.), Sargon II (721-705 B.C.), and Sennacherib (704-681 B.C.) subdued the Puqudu (Akk. *^lúpuqūdu*). Nebuchadrezzar (605-562 B.C.) claimed to control the land of Puqudu (Akk. *māt puqūdu*). Tiglath-pileser III may have deported them to Kar-Ashur, a newly built city, which was probably situated E of the Tigris and N of the Diyâlā rivers.

In an oracle against Babylon, Jeremiah refers to an attack on "the inhabitants of Pekod" (Jer. 50:21), in which Pekod is a geographic territory in Babylonia (cf. Nebuchadrezzar's reference to *māt puqūdu*). Ezekiel prophesies that Pekod will be one of the peoples (cf. Tiglath-pileser's, Sargon's, and Sennacherib's references to *^lúpuqūdu*) of Mesopotamia who will turn against Jerusalem (Ezk. 23:23).

The Puqudu gave their name to both a city and a canal, which are referred to in Neo-Assyrian documents and in T.B. *Betzah* 29a, *Ketuboth* 27b, *Hullin* 127a.

*Bibliography.*–J. A. Brinkman, *Orientalia*, 46 (1977), 305-308; *Political History of Post-Kassite Babylonia 1158-722 B.C.* (1968), pp. 229, 240, 274-76, *et passim*; G. A. Cooke, comm. on Ezekiel (*ICC*, 1936); M. Dietrich, *Die Aramäer Südbabyloniens* (1970), pp. 5f. *et passim*; F. Delitzsch, *Wo lag das Paradies?* (1881), pp. 181, 195, 238-240; S. Langdon, *Die neubabylonischen Königsinschriften* (1912), 146f.; A. Neubauer, *La Géographie du Talmud* (1868), pp. 363-65; S. Parpola, *Neo-Assyrian Toponyms* (1970), pp. 280f.; S. Schiffer, *Die Aramäer* (1911), pp. 126-130; E. Schrader, *Cuneiform Inscriptions and the OT* (Eng. tr. 1888), pp. 117, 120; *Keilinschriftliche Bibliothek*, II (1890), 12f., 40f., 70f., 106f.

M. J. HORSNELL

**PELAIAH** pə-lā'yə, pə-lī'ə [Heb. *p^elā'yâ*–'Yahweh is marvelous'].

**1.** Son of Elioenai, a descendant of David (1 Ch. 3:24).

**2.** [Gk. Apoc. A *Phiathas*]; AV BIATAS; NEB PHIATHAS. A Levite who was present at Ezra's public reading of the law and assisted him by expounding the law to the people (Neh. 8:7; 1 Esd. 9:48). He also took part in sealing the covenant with Nehemiah (Neh. 10:10 [MT 11]).

**PELALIAH** pel-ə-lī'ə [Heb. *p^elalyâ*–'Yahweh has judged']. A priest whose grandson Adaiah lived in Jerusalem after the Exile (Neh. 11:12).

**PELATIAH** pel-ə-tī'ə [Heb. *p^elaṭyâ, p^elaṭyāhû*–'Yahweh delivers'].

**1.** A "chief of the people" who witnessed the sealing of the covenant (Neh. 10:22 [MT 23]).

**2.** Grandson of Zerubbabel and descendant of David (1 Ch. 3:21).

**3.** One of the sons of Ishi who led a band of Simeonites into the hill country of Seir, drove out the Amalekites, and settled there themselves (1 Ch. 4:42f.).

**4.** Son of Benaiah; one of two Judean princes among twenty-five men against whom Ezekiel prophesied (Ezk. 11:1-13). These men, who apparently formed some sort of council, were condemned for giving "wicked counsel" (v. 2; possibly counsel to revolt against Babylon) and shedding innocent blood (v. 6). When he heard Ezekiel's prophecy of judgment (vv. 7-12), Pelatiah fell dead (v. 13).

**PELEG** pel'eg [Heb. *peleg*–'watercourse,' 'division'(?); Gk. *Phalek*]; AV also PHALEC (Lk. 3:35). The son of Eber and the father of Reu (Gen. 10:25; 11:16-19; 1 Ch. 1:19, 25), thus an ancestor of Abraham and Jesus (Lk. 3:35). The meaning of the statement "in his days the earth was divided [Heb. *nipl^egâ*]" (Gen. 10:25) is disputed. It could refer to the division of humanity into linguistic and/or geographical groupings after the tower of Babel incident (Gen. 11:9; so KD), to the use of irrigation techniques by Peleg and his descendants (cf. Akk. *palgu*, "irrigation canal"), or to the division of the countryside into districts (cf. Akk. *puluggu, pulungu*, "district") during his days. Several attempts have been made to relate the personal name to the following geographical names: Phalga, located in Mesopotamia at the junction of the Euphrates and Habor rivers (see W. F. Albright, *JBL*, 43 [1924], 387f.); el-Falj, a district in northeast Arabia; el-Aflāj, S of Jebel Tuwaiq in central Arabia (see J. Skinner, *ICC* on Genesis [1910], p. 220). C. G. RASMUSSEN

**PELET** pe'let [Heb. *pelet*–'escape, deliverance'].

**1.** A Calebite, son of Jahdai (1 Ch. 2:47).

**2.** Son of Azmaveth (cf. NEB "men of Beth-azmoth"); one of the warriors who joined David at Ziklag when he was in hiding from King Saul (1 Ch. 12:3).

**PELETH** pe'leth [Heb. *peleṯ*–'swiftness'].

**1.** A Reubenite; father of On, who joined Korah, Dathan, and Abiram in revolting against Moses and Aaron (Nu. 16:1); probably the same as PALLU son of Reuben, who was the grandfather of Dathan and Abiram (cf. 26:5, 8-10). Some commentators have suggested that "On" is a textual corruption and should be deleted, since the name does not reappear (see comms.).

**2.** Son of Jonathan, a Jerahmeelite (1 Ch. 2:33).

**PELETHITES** pel'ə-thīts [Heb. *p^elēṯî*]. Certain armed men who along with the Cherethites served as David's bodyguard (2 S. 8:18; 20:23; 1 Ch. 18:17). This name may be a variant form of *p^elištî*, "Philistine," with the *š* assimilating to the *t* (so J. Montgomery, comm. on Kings [*ICC*, 1951], pp. 85f.; he thought that the LXX *Pheleththei* reflected the original pronunciation). Thus the origin of these people seems to be from the same background as the Philistines or sea-peoples.

The Pelethites were faithful to David during his later years when Absalom and Sheba rebelled. They played a decisive role in the war against Absalom's forces in which Absalom lost his life (2 S. 15:16-22). They also participated along with David's regular troops under Joab's command in successfully suppressing the insurrection of Sheba (2 S. 20:6f.). When their leader Benaiah, along with Zadok the priest and Nathan the prophet, supported Solomon's claim to the throne, the Pelethites followed him and no doubt ensured the victory of Solomon over Adonijah (1 K. 1:38, 44).

G. KROEZE

**PELIAS** pə-lī'əs. The AV's misspelling of Gk. *Pedias* (1 Esd. 9:34), rendered BEDEIAH by the RSV because of the parallel in Ezr. 10:35.

**PELICAN** [Heb. *qā'āṯ*; Gk. *pelekán*] (Lev. 11:18; Dt. 14:17); NEB HORNED OWL. Any member of the genus *Pelecanus* — large, web-footed birds possessing a membranous pouch hung from the lower beak and used for scooping fish from swamps, lakes, and rivers.

The pelican (mainly *Pelecanus onocrotalus*) was certainly known from early times as an inhabitant of ancient Near Eastern waterways, but its identification in the OT is uncertain. Heb. *qā'āṯ,* usually taken to mean "the vomiter," could well designate the pelican since the mother feeds her young on fish regurgitated from her crop. In the lists of birds of abomination (Lev. 11:18; Dt. 14:17) most translations have read the word as "pelican," as does the LXX. All birds that feed on carrion or fish are included in these lists as unclean.

Three other references are less clear. In Ps. 102:6 (MT 7) the AV reads "pelican of the wilderness" and the RSV "vulture of the wilderness." The AV reads the same term as "cormorant" in Isa. 34:11 and Zeph. 2:14; the RSV reads "hawk" and "vulture," respectively. All these passages picture a bird perched alone in the wilderness or among the ruins of Edom or Nineveh as a symbol of desolation. Many have thought that this wilderness setting rules out the pelican, which lives near water. Pelicans, however, are often found perched in isolation, seemingly far from water, when in actuality, being large and powerful birds, they are within easy flight of a lake or stream. Another intriguing possibility (Holmgren) is that the "pelican of the wilderness" is the marabou (Arab. *murabit,* "hermit") a wilderness bird whose throat pouch may have caused the pelican's name (*qā'āṯ*) to be applied to it. It might then also be this wilderness bird that is referred to in Isa. 34:11 and Zeph. 2:14.

G. R. Driver in an article on the "birds of abomination" identified *qā'āṯ* with the Scops Owl. Although there is but slender evidence for this reading, it seems to have influenced the NEB, which reads "horned owl" for *qā'āṯ* in all passages. *See* ABOMINATION, BIRDS OF.

In the earliest Christian centuries the pelican became widely used as a symbol of Christ's sacrifice for His Church. This symbolism has its origin in an ancient belief that the bird punctured her breast to feed the young on her own blood. Some species of pelican have a red-tipped upper beak that is pressed against the crop in regurgitating food for the young; this practice gave rise to the tradition. The pelican appears regularly in Christian art and heraldry. The artist who designed the title page for the AV in 1611 included a depiction of a pelican feeding its young.

***Bibliography***.–F. S. Bodenhemer, *Animal and Man in Bible Lands* (1960), p. 64; G. R. Driver, *PEQ* (April, 1955), p. 16; V. C. Holmgren, *Bird Walk Through the Bible* (1972).

B. C. BIRCH

**PELLA** pel'ə. The impressive site of Pella, locally known as Tabaqat Faḥl, is situated in the foothills of the northern Jordan Valley, about 3 km. (2 mi.) E of the Jordan River. Its central feature is an oval tell (mound) 30 m. (100 ft.) high, at the southern base of which a powerful spring flows into a small valley known today as the Wâdī Jurm. Immediately to the south a large dome-shaped natural hill called Tell el-Ḥuṣn rises more than 60 m. (200 ft.) above the Wâdī Jurm.

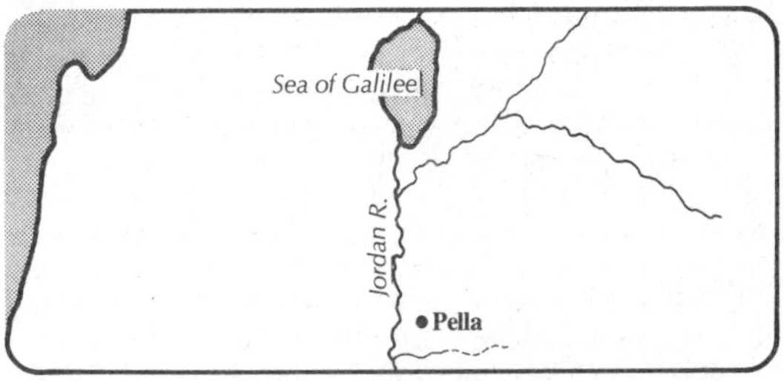


It is not yet known when the first settlement was made beside the spring, but sherds and stone implements indicate that the site was occupied in the Neolithic, Chalcolithic, and Early Bronze Ages. The city of Pahila, or Pihil(um), is mentioned in Egyptian texts as early as the 19th cent. B.C. Tombs found in the hills that surround the city have shown that during most of the 2nd millennium B.C. Pella's culture was essentially Canaanite.

There is archeological evidence of occupation during the Iron Age (1200-600 B.C.), a period during which the Israelites controlled Palestine. Although little is yet known of Pella's government, religion, and culture during that

Tomb of the Canaanite period (17th cent. B.C.) at Pella (courtesy of The College of Wooster; picture D. Kuylenstierna)

time, it would seem that the Israelites never exercised strong control over the city. From 600 to 200 B.C. Pella may have been only a village, for few remains of those centuries have been found.

In the 2nd cent. B.C., perhaps after a refounding under the Seleucid monarchy of Syria, the city underwent explosive growth. Earlier cultural affinities largely gave way, at least superficially, to Hellenistic culture. The old Semitic name of the city was replaced in Greek by Pella, the name of the city in which Alexander the Great was born. The invasion and looting of the city in 83/82 B.C. by soldiers of Alexander Janneus, the Hasmonean ruler of Palestine, left the city in ruins. It was not until the 1st cent. A.D. that Pella began a new spurt of growth, this time under the cultural influence of Rome.

Although not mentioned in the Bible, the city was a refuge for Jewish Christians fleeing Jerusalem *ca.* A.D. 67 during the First Jewish Revolt. These Christians later returned to Jerusalem, but Christianity remained established at Pella. Toward the end of the 1st cent. the city began to issue its own coinage, and constructed a small theater (probably an odeon) near the spring. A number of tombs of the 3rd and 4th cents. have been found, many of them rich in glass vessels.

Pella reached its greatest expansion during the Byzantine period (A.D. 325-635), when residential areas crept into the valleys and up the slopes that surrounded the city. Christianity rapidly became virtually the only religion that was tolerated. Several churches were built, including not only the large West Church and Civic Complex Church but a small church high on the eastern hill overlooking the city. The theater was closed and its stone slab seats were reused for a monumental stepped approach to the Civic Complex Church from the west.

The ecclesiastical institutions of the city underwent rapid decline after the Islamic Conquest of A.D. 635, which followed the "Battle of Fiḥl" (Pella) between Byzantine and Arab armies. A massive earthquake devastated the city on January 18, 746/47, burying many persons and animals in the collapsing buildings. The survivors, lacking the resources to rebuild their city, wandered away forever.

Courtyard of the Civic Complex Church at Pella, constructed about the 5th cent. A.D. (courtesy of The College of Wooster; picture D. Kuylenstierna)

Much of what is known about ancient Pella has come through excavations conducted since 1967, initially by The College of Wooster in Ohio and subsequently in cooperation with Sydney University, with the assistance of the Department of Antiquities of Jordan.

*Bibliography.*–*EAEHL*, III, *s.v.* (L. I. Levine); R. H. Smith, *Pella of the Decapolis, Vol. I: The 1967 Season of The Wooster Expedition to Pella* (1973); "Pella of the Decapolis," *Archaeology*, 34 (1981), 46-53; A. McNicoll, R. H. Smith, and B. Hennessy, *Pella in Jordan, I: An Interim Report on The Joint University of Sydney and The College of Wooster Excavations at Pella, 1979-1981* (1982).

R. H. SMITH

**PELONITE** pel'ō-nīt [Heb. *pᵉlônî, pᵉlōnî*] (1 Ch. 11:27, 36; 27:10). A title applied to Helez and Ahijah, two of David's heroes who fought with him against the Philistines. In the parallel list (2 S. 23:26) Helez is called a Paltite, i.e., a native of Beth-pelet, which is in the Negeb. In 1 Ch. 27:10, however, Helez is said to be an Ephraimite. A comparison of the two lists suggests that Ahijah is identical with Eliam, who is called a Gilonite in 2 S. 23:34. Many scholars have attempted to solve this confusion by concluding that the Chronicles text is in error. See KD on 2 S. 23:26.

G. KROEZE

**PELUSIUM** pə-lo͞os'i-əm [Heb. *sîn*–'clay'?; Egyp. *sìn*; Gk. *Pēlousios*]; AV SIN; NEB SIN, SYENE. Roman name for the Egyptian stronghold which in ancient times guarded the northeast frontier of Egypt. Pelusium lay on the strategic coastal route known later as the "Way to the Land of the Philistines." It was situated approximately 1.5 km. (1 mi.) inland from the sea and about 32 km. (20 mi.) E of modern Port Said. Ramses II (*ca.* 1287-1220 B.C.) is said to have constructed a wall from Pelusium to Heliopolis to defend against Asiatic invasions.

The Heb. *sîn* (Ezk. 30:15f.) is thought to be an exact rendering of the original Egyp. *sìn*. Pelusium, however, is derived from the Gk. *Pēlousios* (<*pēlós*, "clay"), which may be based on a mistaken translation of the Hebrew (cf. Aram. *sᵉyān*, "clay"). Others relate the Greek to an Egyptian religious term (*peremūn*, "house of Amun") connected with the site, which might also explain the origin of the modern designation, Tell Faramâ.

Actual identification of the city mentioned in Ezekiel (30:15f.) is complicated by the LXX's use of two separate names: *Sain* (30:15 = *sîn* = Pelusium; see AV) and *Syēnē* (30:16 = Syene, Aswân; see NEB). The city is mentioned in Egyptian texts of the Old Kingdom and noted as well in such foreign sources as Herodotus (ii.15, 141).

*Bibliography.*–W. Spiegelberg, *Zeitschrift für Ägyptische Sprache und Altertumskunde*, 49 (1911), 81-84; A. H. Gardiner, *JEA*, 5 (1918), 253f.; *GTTOT*, § 1434.

G. H. WILSON

**PEN** [Heb. *ʿēṭ*] (Job 19:24; Ps. 45:1 [MT 2]; Jer. 8:8; 17:1); NEB also "tool"; [Gk. *kálamos*] (3 Jn. 13); **PENKNIFE** [Heb. *taʿar hassōpēr*–'razor of the scribe'] (Jer. 36:23).

Hebrew *ʿēṭ* is applied to any writing instrument, whether an iron chisel for cutting letters in stone (Job 19:24), a stylus with a point of hard stone or metal for engraving deeply (Jer. 17:1), or a brush which could be used on ostraca, leather, or papyrus (cf. Jer. 36:18; cf. also the ostraca from Arad, Lachish, and Samaria). Any hard point would be used for scratching names on pots or other objects. Most documents, however, were written with pen and ink on leather, papyrus, or potsherds.

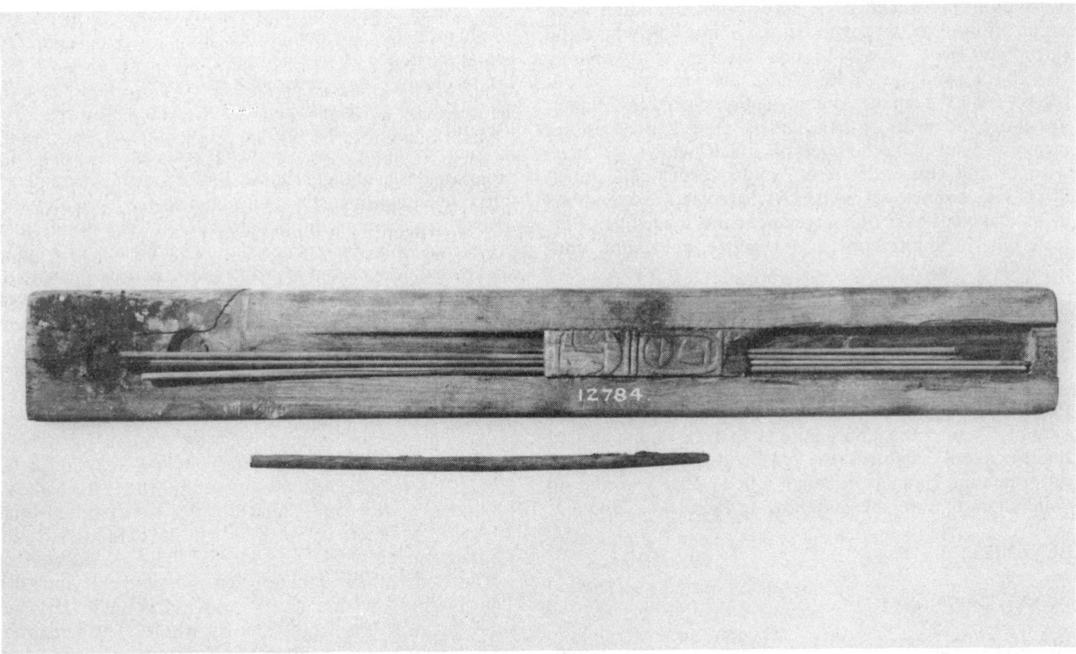



Scribe's palette with sharpened reeds (pens). The circular hollow (left) held ink or paint. The inscription reads "Ahmose I" (18th Dynasty, 1550-1350 B.C.) (Trustees of the British Museum)

The pen was made from a selected reed, cut and dried. One end was cut diagonally and the point was carefully shaved thin and then split, as in the modern fountain pen. Finally the very point was clipped off squarely with a sharp penknife (cf. Jehoiakim's rather different use of the penknife, Jer. 36:23).

The AV has "pen" for Heb. *ḥereṭ* in Isa. 8:1 (Heb. *ḥereṭ ʾᵉnôš,* AV lit. "with a man's pen"), but the RSV prefers to translate "in common characters" and the NEB "in common writing" (mg. "with an ordinary stylus"). In Jgs. 5:14 the AV mistakenly translates Heb. *šēḇeṭ* as "pen" (no doubt due to *sōpēr,* "scribe," which follows); the NEB "musterer's staff" is perhaps preferable to the RSV's "marshal's staff" (*sōpēr,* usually translated "scribe," sometimes refers to a military official in charge of mustering; cf. 2 K. 25:19).

The common Greek word for a pen was simply *kálamos,* "reed" (3 Jn. 13).

*See also* INK; SCRIBE; WRITING.

See G. R. Driver, *Semitic Writing* (3rd ed. 1976), pp. 17-33, 85f.

A. R. MILLARD

**PENANCE.** *See* REPENT.

**PENCE.** The plural of "penny." *See* MONEY.

**PENCIL** [Heb. *śereḏ* (Isa. 44:13)]; AV "line"; NEB SCRIBER. Hebrew *śereḏ* is a hapax legomenon and occurs in a difficult context, so its meaning is uncertain. Most scholars agree that it is some kind of marker (NASB, *CHAL,* p. 354, "red chalk"; NAB, BDB, p. 975, "stylus"; cf. modern Heb. *śereḏ,* "marking tool, stylus").

**PENDANT** [Heb. *nᵉṭîpâ*] (Jgs. 8:26; Isa. 3:19); AV COLLAR, CHAIN; [*ʿᵃnāq*] (Prov. 1:9); AV CHAIN; NEB CHAIN OF HONOUR. An ornament suspended from the ears or the neck. Heb. *nᵉṭîpâ* is derived from *nāṭap̱* ("drip") and probably denotes a drop-shaped EARRING (*see also* GARMENTS IX). Prov. 1:9 compares parental

Canaanite-style, gold pendant earrings from an anthropoid sarcophagus at Deir el-Balach (13th cent. B.C.) (Israel Museum, Jerusalem)

instruction to *ʿanāqîm,* some sort of ornamentation worn about the neck of a young man (cf. Cant. 4:9, where the sing. *ʿanāq* [RSV "jewel"] refers to a part of a woman's NECKLACE, and Jgs. 8:26, where the fem. pl. *ʿanāqôṯ* [RSV "collars"] denotes ornamentation placed by Midianites about the necks of their camels [cf. v. 21]). A similar metaphor is used by the book of Sirach, which describes wisdom and education as a "golden ornament" (6:30; 21:21; Gk. *kósmos chryseós*). Archeological excavations in biblical lands have uncovered pendants made of various materials, including bone, iron, bronze, gold, and semiprecious stones.

*See also* AMULET; CRESCENTS; STONES, PRECIOUS.

N. J. O.

**PENIEL** pə-nī'əl. *See* PENUEL, PENIEL.

**PENINNAH** pə-nin'ə [Heb. *peninnâ*–'coral'(?)]. Second wife of Elkanah the Ephraimite (1 S. 1:2). Peninnah had both sons and daughters (vv. 2, 4), and she took pleasure in tormenting Hannah, Elkanah's first wife, who had no children (v. 6) until she gave birth to Samuel (v. 20).

**PENKNIFE.** *See* PEN.

**PENNY.** *See* MONEY.

**PENSION.** The AV translation of Gk. *klḗros* in 1 Esd. 4:56. The Greek term means a "portion assigned by lot" and here denotes a piece of land (cf. RSV, NEB, "land").

**PENTATEUCH** pen'tə-to͞ok [<Gk. *pénta*–'five' + *teúchos* 'book']. The first five books of the Bible.

- I. Introduction
- II. Contents
  - A. Theological Message
  - B. Historical Dimension
  - C. Literary Character
- III. Significance
- IV. Origin, Composition, Authorship, and Nature
  - A. Precritical Positions
    1. OT
    2. NT
    3. Church Fathers (A.D. 100-*ca.* 600)
    4. Pre-Reformation Era
    5. Reformation
  - B. Early Critical Observations: Enlightenment (17th-18th Cents.)
  - C. Development of Critical Theories
    1. Antecedents of Graf-Wellhausen
    2. Graf, Kuenen, Wellhausen
  - D. Responses to Graf-Wellhausen (19th Cent.)
    1. Critical School
    2. Conservative School
  - E. Development of Pentateuchal Studies (20th Cent.)
    1. Ancient Near Eastern Studies
    2. Form Criticism
    3. Tradition Criticism
    4. Canonical Criticism
    5. Graf-Wellhausen Hypothesis
  - F. Conservative Scholarship
    1. Ancient Near Eastern Studies
    2. Affirmation of Unity
    3. Historicity
    4. Basic Mosaicity
    5. Representative Positions

***I. Introduction.***–The term Pentateuch comes to us from the ancient Greek translation of the Scriptures called the Septuagint (LXX) through the Latin Vulgate (*ca.* A.D. 400). The Jewish custom of referring to the five-fifths of the Torah probably lies behind the choice of this term. The actual existence of five distinct literary works (Genesis–Deuteronomy) may have been necessary because of the need to limit the length of a scroll. The Jews called this literature the Torah (*hattôrâ* < the verb *yārâ,* "teach, instruct," "shoot"), which means instruction, a most appropriate designation since the Torah contains the authoritative teaching or instruction given to the Israelites that constitutes them as the people of God. The Torah comprises not only ancient legislation given through God's spokesman Moses, but also an equally impressive amount of historical narrative that forms the context for the legal material. Thus the Torah is the most important section of the Jewish canon.

The English names of the individual books also come to us from the LXX via the Latin Vulgate. The Hebrew method of designating these books follows ancient Near Eastern usage and simply calls each book by its first significant word(s). Hence Genesis is *berēʾšîṯ,* "in the beginning"; Exodus is *weʾēlleh šemôṯ,* "these are the names"; Leviticus is *wayyiqrāʾ,* "and he [the Lord] called (unto Moses)"; Numbers is *bemiḏbar,* "in the wilderness"; and Deuteronomy is *ʾēlleh haddeḇārîm,* "these are the words."

This body of literature appears to be of great antiquity. The fivefold division of its contents is secondary and subordinate to the larger literary whole. The Samaritan Pentateuch, however, attests to both the antiquity of the fivefold division and the ancient nature of the whole work (*see* PENTATEUCH, SAMARITAN). On various grounds modern scholars (beginning *ca.* A.D. 1800) have sometimes tried to substitute a Hexateuch (Genesis–Joshua) or Tetrateuch (Genesis–Numbers) for the Pentateuch. These approaches tend to challenge the integrity of the Pentateuch as the constitutive basis for the rest of the OT, as well as for the existence and purpose of the nation of Israel and mankind. Some discussion of these issues is presented below.

***II. Contents.***–*A. Theological Message.* The Pentateuch relates God's teleology for the world and humankind as He works with them in the flow of history, at first on a universal scale and then on a more particular level with Israel, through whom He aims to redeem all peoples (Gen. 12:1-3).

The biblical writer reports God's creation in two magnificent chapters that logically precede the later revelation of God as Redeemer to Israel. In highly charged theological-historical language reflecting the ancient world of the author, these unparalleled chapters profoundly delineate God's goals and purposes in creation. God brings all things into existence, even primal matter from which He fashions all things. The primary purpose of creation is to create human beings in God's image, in a right relationship to Him, so that He might be with them and be their God. Of great importance is the perfect environment in which Adam and Eve are placed. Their subsequent fall and frustration from this state of innocent perfection, with all the attendant ramifications, are traced through Gen. 3–11. God's judgment of mankind's corrupt and rebellious ways is highlighted twice, in the Noachian Flood (Gen. 6–8) and in the story of mankind's attempted self-exaltation and autonomous religious achievement (Gen. 11). Mankind's corrupt moral and religious condition is clearly painted (6:5; 8:21-24), but the continued potential for relationship with God is affirmed (5:1-3; 9:6).

The dismal swamp of hopelessness in which mankind finds itself in Gen. 3–11 is lighted with hope because of God's gracious preservation of humanity (chs. 6–9) and His ultimate gracious condescension to act to save mankind through a designated program (12:1-3; cf. 11:1-9). With the call of Abram (12:1-3) God begins His special salvific program for the reclamation of the human race through Abram and his desendants. Gen. 12–50 relates how God provides for and preserves His chosen people and the specific covenants which He made with them (e.g., chs. 15, 17) so that He could do through Abram all that He had promised (12:1-3).

Thus one soon realizes that various themes run through the Pentateuch and form its basic groundwork (*Grundstrucktur*): creation, judgment, deliverance, promise, election, covenant, law, land, people. All these motifs are realities grounded in history. They testify to the close-knit unity of this multifaceted work and are united in the broader scheme of God's main purpose of making a people as His word effects the promise-fulfillment scheme reflected in His own faithfulness to His goals and purposes.

As noted, the providential care of the chosen people is related in Gen. 12–50, and in Egypt God continues to fulfil His promises in the midst of adversity as He multiplies the few souls who went down to Egypt into a mighty throng of people (Ex. 1:1-7). The book of Exodus recounts the historical and theological birth of the people of Israel from a "people that was no people" — the salvation event par excellence in the OT. The Exodus group is constituted at Sinai (Ex. 19–23) as the people with whom God will dwell; they will be His people (6:6f.; 19:5f.). Here at last God renews a people who will reflect His image and show His character. The logical, if not chronological, priority of Israel's doctrine of creation to the salvific event of the Exodus is evident in that at Sinai this people is lifted toward the very possibility of being the image of their Creator, a religious-moral people in relationship to Him once again. This people is to be God's unique possession among the nations of the earth and be to Him a "kingdom of priests and a holy nation" on the basis of all of the Mosaic covenant.

The remainder of Exodus and Leviticus describes how God makes Ex. 6:7-9; 19:5f. a historical religious-moral reality. Ex. 20–31 record various laws for Israel's instruction and the information needed to build the tabernacle where God will dwell, as well as the ordination of Aaron and his sons as a holy priesthood to span the gap between God and mankind. Ex. 35–40 record the construction of the tabernacle and God's gracious appearance among His people to dwell with them (40:16-38). Leviticus takes up the continuing theme of God's creation of Israel as His unique priestly people among mankind. The priesthood makes communication with God possible and sets up Israel as the unique religious-moral nation on earth, through whom all other nations can find blessing from Israel's God; all this in fulfillment of God's promise to Abraham, Isaac, and Jacob. A major purpose of all of the law, the call of Israel, etc., is to cause the Israelites to love their God supremely and their neighbor and the alien among them as they love themselves (Dt. 6:4-6; Lev. 19:18-34); thus will they be His people.

Further legislation in the vicinity of Sinai is related in the book of Numbers. But Numbers also relates two other important points. One has to do with Israel's disobedience and rebellion in the wilderness, especially in failing to enter the land because of unbelief. The second is concerned with Israel's preparation to enter and take the Promised Land after forty years of judgment and discipline because of disobedience.

Deuteronomy follows as a logical consequence and is an integrated literary unit with the first four books, for it shows that Israel is in essence God's religious-moral people even without the land. On the other hand, Deuteronomy emphasizes obedience to the Mosaic covenant as the only way that Israel can inherit the land of Canaan (a clear parallel to Eden). By the end of Deuteronomy Israel has experienced the amazing faithfulness of God, who fulfilled every promise and covenantal obligation. The giving of the land, based upon Israel's obedience to the Torah, is the story of Joshua–Judges. Hence the Pentateuch gives Israel its *raison d'être*: Israel exists for God's glory, to reflect His image before mankind — ultimately to achieve the salvation of the world.

*B. Historical Dimension.* It is clear from the doctrine of creation that history is basically the interaction that takes place between God's working to create a people by His word and that people's reaction to His gracious advances within a created framework of reality. This interaction of God, mankind, and the world is the essence of biblical historical reality. Mankind, in its *imago dei* capabilities as religious-moral being, determines to a significant extent the flow of the linear development of history, for the path of history depends upon religious and moral issues. Reality for mankind, the issues of life and death, lies in the arena of God's creation where mankind meets God — in history. Though human beings bear the *imago dei,* they bear it in earthen vessels of creation; they meet their Creator, even as *imago dei,* as created entities in history and subject to finitude and the vicissitudes of historical reality.

The nine basic pentateuchal themes mentioned above are tied to movement and involvement in God's created world, to history. They are not timeless abstract ideas but deal with particular theological or historical realities that exist when God relates to His image-bearing creatures. So the religious-moral message of the Pentateuch cannot be divorced from the fact that God has given His message through events in history to mankind, which is encased in history and meets God in history. Mankind is part of creation; the speaking of God to mankind through the created orders in an ongoing way is historical revelation. Thus if the historical bedrock of God's dealings with mankind is dissolved, then the message of God evaporates into thin air (or at best into abstract religious concepts). It is, in short, not possible to hold to the religious-moral message of the Pentateuch without holding to its basic historicity, which constitutes a necessary but not a sufficient condition for its truth. Hence, in the Pentateuch we understand that, because of the nature of God, mankind, and the world, we are not dealing with myth, fable, mere astrological tales, or literary creations, but with the truth communicated by God to mankind through history in concrete word and concrete event. But as the preceding section has shown, the biblical writers and compilers wrote history from a theological or religious-moral point of view to bring out, as part of God's communication to mankind, the meaning of His mighty acts in the events of history.

*C. Literary Character.* The Pentateuch is a literary document similar to many other literary documents, except, of course, that God has spoken through the form(s) that it has taken during its compositional history. It is complex, containing scores of literary genres. It is made up of law and narrative, poetry and prose, drama and story; it is in form ancient, not modern; it is complex linguistically, and full of sources of various kinds, yet a unified work. It is literarily sophisticated at times and literarily simple at other times. It is the word of God in human words that numerous hands have worked on to record, preserve, and pass on. Some signs of compilation and growth are evident, as are clear signs of literary arrangement. Its order is at times clear, at times confusing; no cogent reasons can be given for all its literary structures. Some of its language is still not understood, and the method by which it was compiled is far from sure. It speaks in the language of its day, but the generic humaneness of its message and God's constant purposes and goals for mankind make it relevant to any and all ages and cultures. The profound religious-moral message of the document, its ancient historical nature, and its complexity, both as to its final literary form and the compositional process by which it reached its final form, have combined to make this part of Holy Scripture one of the most discussed portions of the OT.

*III. Significance.*–The significance of the Pentateuch for understanding the Bible can hardly be stressed too much. It sustains a vital relationship to the rest of the OT and to the NT. Its canonical function is of major importance.

Within the Pentateuch itself, God constitutes Israel as His people by giving them the law without the land. As Deuteronomy emphasizes, acquisition of the land of Canaan is dependent upon Israel's faithfulness to the covenant of Sinai. This conditional relationship of Israel to the land is clearly reminiscent of the relationship between mankind in the beginning and his inheritance of and dominion over the created order. That is, if human beings had been the religious-moral beings God desired, the creation would have been theirs to inherit as a gift of the Creator. This key insight into the nature of the relationship between God and mankind — on the religious-moral level — is determinative for the rest of the OT and the NT as well. The historical books of the OT delineate a history of Israel written from a theological perspective, which is furnished by the Mosaic covenant (God's religious-moral principles for His people). The words of God as recorded in the Torah provide the plumb line by which the historical writer evaluates the vicissitudes of Israel's history before God (esp. 2 K. 17–23). The key to Israel's success lay in the people's obedience to the stipulations of the Sinai covenant. The wisdom and poetical books share much with the surrounding cultures of the ancient Near East, but the basis of success before God and mankind is ultimately found to be the law of Moses, the Torah, which is able to make one successful in daily living, as well as wise and pleasing to God (Prov. 1:7; Ps. 119; etc.). The inspired prophets themselves call the people back to the law of God as revealed in the Torah. And, although they despair of real success in their venture and paint pictures of a new covenant (Jer. 31:31-34), a new creation and new people (Isa. 40–66), and a new heart (Ezk. 34), they still conceive of the new future in terms reminiscent of the old covenant at Sinai; for this picture, in effect, is a final realization of the goals and purposes of God in creation and in the covenant of Moses with Israel. In short, the rest of the OT is simply incomprehensible without the presupposition of the great events of God's revelation and the relationship of God to mankind and Israel as depicted in the Pentateuch. The universal problems of mankind in Gen. 1–11 find a universal solution, not outlined in detail in the prophets, but certainly clearly adumbrated in God's eschatological dealings with the whole earth.

The relationship of the Pentateuch to the NT is just as vital as its relationship to the rest of the OT. As Bush has noted (LaSor, Hubbard, Bush, pp. 3f.), the absolute importance of the Pentateuch is seen in that the NT often refers to events in it (e.g., creation, the call of Abraham) as some of the most significant events that provide the type for the antitypical new creation of the Word of God in the NT. No other OT analogy to what God has done and is doing in Christ is sufficient except the creation itself. The nature of God's creation is indeed the necessary and sufficient logical presupposition for God's new creation in Christ. God's redemptive activity in and through Abraham finds its fulfillment in the NT.

*IV. Origin, Composition, Authorship, and Nature.–A. Precritical Positions.* Views about the Pentateuch have been many and varied. A relatively brief historical survey of the views past and present is offered below. (For a fuller treatment of this part of pentateuchal studies see the standard intros. to the OT.)

*1. OT.* A canonical view of the Pentateuch took shape within the OT itself, but it is difficult to determine whether expressions like "the law of Moses," "God's law," etc. refer to a part or the whole of the present Pentateuch. In the historical books (Joshua–2 Kings) the references to the Pentateuch may be to an early form of the legal sections of the Pentateuch, to an early form of the Pentateuch, or mainly to Deuteronomy. It is possible, however, that these references are to the Pentateuch in essentially its present form. The texts are offered here for examination: "the book of the law," Josh. 1:8; 8:34; 2 K. 22:8; "the book of the law of God," Josh. 24:26; "the law of Moses," 1 K. 2:3; "the law that Moses commanded them," 2 K. 21:8; "the commandments which the Lord commanded Moses," 2 K. 18:6; "the law of Moses," 2 K. 23:25. A point to consider in studying these references is that it seems highly unlikely that we should think of the "laws of Moses" without also thinking of at least some basic surrounding narrative accompanying those laws, especially since Israel's understanding of God's revelation always entailed placing it in a historical-cultural setting which could not be divorced from the giving of the revelation. Moses' name is so closely connected with these laws that he is in some way considered as the one through whom they were given to Israel.

The many references to the Pentateuch in the Chronicler's history (Ezra–2 Chronicles) are more clearly to what seems to be a law of Moses reflecting essentially the present form and content of our Pentateuch. Again, essential Mosaic authorship is clearly implied, whatever that may have meant in the ancient Near Eastern world. These references are: "the law," Ezr. 10:3; Neh. 8:2, 7, 14; 10:34 (MT 35); 12:44; 13:3; 2 Ch. 14:4; 31:21; 33:8; "the book of the law," Neh. 8:3; "the book of the law of Moses," Neh. 8:1; "the book of Moses," Neh. 13:1; 2 Ch. 25:4; 35:12; "the law of the Lord," Ezr. 7:10; 1 Ch. 16:40; 2 Ch. 31:3; 35:26; "the law of God," Neh. 10:28f. (MT 29f.); "the book of the law of God," Neh. 8:18; "the book of the law of the Lord," 2 Ch. 17:9; 34:14; "the book of the Lord their God," Neh. 9:3; cf. also "the law of Moses the servant of God," Dnl. 9:11, 13; "the law of Moses," Mal. 4:4 (MT 3:22). Whether these references support a clear developmental view of the Pentateuch in which first only some laws, then Deuteronomy, and finally the whole Pentateuch were attributed to Moses is possible, but far from certain. And again it is difficult to imagine the laws without a basic narrative context surrounding them. The canonical claim of the OT is clear in its assertion that Moses is the essential author of the Pentateuch. This biblical fact cannot be set aside *a priori*.

*2. NT.* NT references to the Pentateuch continue along the lines already established in the OT but include specific references to Moses' writing activity (e.g., Jn. 1:45; 5:46): Mt. 12:5; Mk. 12:26; Lk. 2:22-24; 10:26; 16:16; Jn. 7:19, 23; Gal. 3:10; etc. These references constitute an internal canonical tradition that points to the divine and human authorship of the Pentateuch, but also just as strongly affirm that the human dimension of its origin and composition cannot be thought of apart from Moses. The internal evidence of the Pentateuch itself as it bears upon its origin and composition will be discussed below.

*3. Church Fathers* (A.D. 100-*ca.* 600). The first few centuries of the Christian Era were precritical, as far as biblical studies are concerned. The church fathers accepted the divine origin of the Pentateuch and believed that it was written ultimately by Moses. Some church fathers after the third century, however, seemed to accept the legend of Ezra's miraculous reproduction of the law and other ancient Jewish books recorded in 2 Esd. 14:19-48. It is interesting that in this legend Ezra *dictates* the books as the Holy Spirit moves him and as God enlightens his mind. The inscripturation is effected by five chosen scribes trained to write rapidly. Nevertheless, in this process Ezra is considered the one who authors the books originally recorded by Moses (this seems to be the implication of the text for the church fathers). An interesting concept of authorship, authority, and compositional method is evident here that reflects ancient Near Eastern and biblical thinking. However, the unreliability of 2 Esdras as a historical document and the failure of the church fathers to be critical or accurate in numerous historical and scientific matters are well known, as is their tendency to fanciful interpretation of Scripture and unquestioning acceptance of legendary traditions.

Most early negative concepts of the Pentateuch came from religious or philosophical groups that were considered apostate by both Jews and Christians. E. J. Young, who made a careful study of these early centuries, noted the Nazirites and Ebionites who questioned the Mosaic authority of the Pentateuch in whole or in part. Certain writers, however, indicate that questions were arising about the Pentateuch, especially by the end of the 7th century. Some pentateuchal "problems" were appearing. Already the great church father Jerome (*ca.* 400) had asserted the ultimate Mosaic authorship of the Pentateuch, but did allow for its final form to come from Ezra's time (i.e., 4th cent. B.C.); he did so on the basis of internal criticism of the text of the Pentateuch (e.g., Gen. 35:4; Dt. 34:5-12). He felt that Deuteronomy was the book found in the temple during Josiah's reform (see de Wette below), but did not date the book to Josiah's time.

*4. Pre-Reformation Era.* During the pre-Reformation era no serious critical approaches were taken toward the Pentateuch, although a few scholars continued to suggest that some material in the Pentateuch came later than the time of Moses. And the unlikely fact that Moses wrote of his own death (Dt. 34) continued to be pointed out (e.g., Ibn Ezra, 1092-1167, and Ibn Ḥazm of Cordova, 994-1064). The scholars of those centuries were still unequipped to deal with the rigorous demands of scientific criticism. However, the beginning of the Renaissance and the resulting study of ancient documents in several languages (Greek, Hebrew, Latin, Arabic) set the stage for the more emphatic concerns of the Enlightenment, a more critical examination of the biblical texts.

*5. Reformation.* Even the Reformation era did not see the flowering of a serious critical stance toward the biblical materials, although some interesting and strange observations were made by A. Bodenstein, a Catholic (Carlstadt, 1480-1541). He was sure that since Moses could not have written of his death in Dt. 34:1-12, and since the rest of the Pentateuch reflected the literary style of these Deuteronomic verses, then the rest of the Pentateuch was not from the hand of Moses. B. Pereira (1589) suggested that scribal additions had been made in Genesis, and that the Pentateuch had undergone revision and interpretation. Some again suggested that the Pentateuch as a whole was the work of Ezra, who probably used scribal notes. That certain portions of the Pentateuch (at least interpolations) were written by a later hand was generally accepted.

*B. Early Critical Observations: Enlightenment (17th-18th Cents.).* The deepest roots of much of nineteenth-century criticism lie in the 17th-18th cents., when the "sciences of man" were beginning to be developed. Modern philosophy began with Descartes in France and the rise of Empiricism in Britain (Hobbes, Locke, *et al.*). The Enlightenment was the human attempt to understand this world from several nontheistic points of view. This aspect of the Enlightenment placed the human being at the center of all things and tried to understand him from a humanistic point of view; but a parallel attempt to understand the world, indeed the cosmos, also developed and was a precursor to nineteenth-century positivism. The supernatural and revealed religion were challenged, while a religion of reason was supported (cf. Deism), textual criticism had its beginnings, a concern for history and history writing was engendered, and a general feeling of the gradual growth, development, and progress of mankind was held by many. The people of the Enlightenment tended to see the past barbarous eras of mankind superseded by the present era, in which mankind was finally coming of age. All other past histories and peoples were considered inferior to the present age.

This attitude became inimical in various degrees and various ways to a revelatory and, hence, supernatural book like the OT. Johann Semler (*Abhandlung von freier Untersuchung des Canon* [1771-75]) advocated an approach to the Bible that treated it as any other book, but not as a book of revealed religion. The ancient writings of the Hebrews were even considered inferior and devalued. Not all people during the Enlightenment accepted this devaluation of all past history, however, nor did everyone raise reason above all else (e.g., Rousseau, Jacobi). J. G. Herder (1744-1803) was an intellectual giant who wrote a philosophy of history (*Ideen zur Philosophie der Geschichte der Menschheit* [1784-1791]) to prove the falsity of such a position (cf. also J. G. Hamann, F. H. Jacobi).

Several names are of interest here because of their pronouncements concerning the Pentateuch. In keeping with the tendency of the *Zeitgeist* Thomas Hobbes in *Leviathan* (1651) attempted to study the Pentateuch objectively and from his philosophical point of view. He did not disavow Mosaic authorship to those parts of the Pentateuch attributed to Moses, but he did believe that others were reporting about Moses. Baruch Spinoza (1632-1677), who drew out Descartes' idealism to its logical end, denied the Mosaic authorship of the Pentateuch in *Tractatus Theologicopoliticus*. He developed a systematic approach to the investigation of the Pentateuch and concluded that Ezra compiled the Pentateuch using older material, some of which came from Moses. Deuteronomy was the legal code promulgated by Ezra. Like Hobbes he ascribed to Moses only those portions which the Pentateuch ascribes to him. He also noted the presence of doublets in the Pentateuch. R. Simon, an Oratorian, noted stylistic variations, and both logical and chronological discontinuity in the Pentateuch (*Critical History of the OT* [Eng. tr. 1682]). His solution to the complexity of these puzzling issues was to date the Pentateuch relatively late, although the writer used various sources. A Protestant theologian, Le Clerc, placed the composition of the Pentateuch before the Samaritan schism (4th cent. B.C.). By this time, the *Zeitgeist* of the 17th-18th cents. and the continuing puzzlement of many of the investigators of the Pentateuch clearly indicated that someone would soon attempt a more complete and satisfying solution to the origin, authorship, and composition of the Pentateuch.

*C. Development of Critical Theories. 1. Antecedents of Graf-Wellhausen.* In 1753 Jean Astruc attempted to solve the enigma of these pentateuchal issues by an inductive approach (*Conjectures sur les mémoires originaux dont il paroit que Moyse s'est servi pour composer le livre de la Genèse*). Astruc picked up on an earlier suggestion by C. Vitringa (1689) that Moses had probably used sources in compiling the Pentateuch. The sources were likely very ancient; some may have come originally from Abraham, who brought them from Mesopotamia.

Thus, according to Astruc, Moses wrote Genesis using ancient memoirs or sources. The basic criterion that Astruc used to separate out these sources was the divine names 'Elohim and Yahweh, 'Elohim appearing in what Astruc called his A source and Yahweh in a B source. Astruc developed further criteria in order to divide the rest of the Pentateuch into sources. Moreover, he found it necessary to postulate several other sources (e.g., Gen. 14) and an interpolator in order to divide Genesis fully into sources. He speculated that Moses had arranged his material in orderly columns, but that these columns had been confused and the present difficult text had resulted. In all this he did not question the authority of the Pentateuch or its Mosaic authorship. His main fault lay in his presuppositions. His investigations were carried on without an understanding of the nature of ancient Near Eastern literature, and he wrongly assumed that he had the tools to discern the various sources of an ancient document. Finally, his treatment of the Pentateuch as an eighteenth-century piece of Western European literature doomed his investigations to failure from the start. Nevertheless, his analysis of Genesis into sources marks a major development from the confused surmising of the preceding centuries and pointed the way that critical pentateuchal studies would proceed in the future.

Johann G. Eichhorn pursued Astruc's speculations and wrote a three-volume introduction (1781-83) in which he used documentary approaches through Leviticus similar to Astruc's, including the admission that in addition to the J and E sources other sources were also evident that did not conform to a J-E documentary approach. He eventually rejected Mosaic editorship or a Mosaic literary production. Eichhorn's position is often termed the *early documentary* hypothesis.

Another German scholar, K. D. Ilgen, continued this approach to pentateuchal studies by claiming to have delineated up to seventeen different sources in Genesis alone (*Die Urkunden des Jerusalemischen Tempelarchivs*, I [1798]). He divided these "documents" among three different authors: $E^1$, $E^2$, and J, and was the first to find two sources within the E document. He did argue with Astruc's division of the various sources between J or E, even assigning Astruc's J in Gen. 1–11 to his $E^2$. He continued to expand the criteria used in describing the various source documents, for he felt that the use of the divine names was not a sufficient criterion.

Several scholars near the end of the 18th cent. and the first half of the 19th cent. developed similar approaches to the origin, authorship, and composition of the Pentateuch. Some advocated a "fragmentary" approach, which described the Pentateuch as the combination of a number of fragments rather than documents. Alexander Geddes, W. M. L. de Wette, and J. S. Vater developed the fragment hypotheses, and several scholars defended it (e.g., A. Th. Hartmann, *Historisch-kritische Forschungen über die Bildung, das Zeitalter und den Plan der fünf Bücher Mosis* [1831], who questioned whether writing was developed in the time of Moses; Peter von Bohlen, *Intro. to the Book of Genesis* [Eng. tr., 2 vols., 1855]). Astruc had noted the "fragmentary" nature of his sources and had postulated that this phenomenon was the result of an unfortunate mixing of originally distinct sources. Geddes (*Holy Bible* [*ca.* 1792]; *Critical Remarks* [1800]) discerned in the memoirs what he felt were the original fragments, which a redactor had put together to form the Pentateuch. These fragments reflected two different series which could be separated by various criteria, of which the use of Yahweh or 'Elohim was the main one. Moses had nothing to do with authorship of the Pentateuch. These fragments came from various times, some before Moses' time, some after. The final product was placed in the time of Solomon. Geddes also advocated a Hexateuch (Genesis–Joshua) rather than a Pentateuch, since Joshua is of necessity an appendix to Genesis–Deuteronomy. Geddes was strongly influenced by the rationalism which tended to dominate biblical studies for the next fifty years.

J. S. Vater found thirty-eight or more fragments in the Pentateuch and dated it in the Exile (*Comm. über den Pentateuch* [4 vols., 1802-1805]). Deuteronomy was earlier, from the time of David or Solomon.

De Wette was highly influenced by Kantian thought and Kant had little use for the OT. Like Geddes, a philosophical (Kantian) approach characterized his work. He stressed the historical nature of the Bible, and he saw language largely as symbols through which true religious ideas could be expressed. At first de Wette supported the fragmentary approach (*Beiträge zur Einl. in das AT* [2 vols., 1806-1807]), but by 1840 he had switched his support to the supplementary hypothesis (*Lehrbuch der historisch-kritischen Einl. in die Kanonischen und apokryphischen Bücher des AT* [6th ed. 1845]). Of particular importance was de Wette's theory that Deuteronomy was the book found in the temple when Josiah's reform was in progress (cf. Geddes, Jerome).

Heinrich Ewald, both a great biblical theologian and a great critic of the 19th cent., criticized de Wette's early position (*Die Komposition der Genesis kritisch untersucht* [1823]). Ewald saw the Achilles' heel of a fragmentary approach to the Pentateuch to be the amazing unity of a book like Genesis, and this principle extends to the allusions of one part of the Pentateuch to another part. For a time Ewald advocated a supplementary hypothesis, which posited an E or Elohist document as the basic source into which parts of a parallel J source had been inserted. This combined source constituted the later basic E document. Ewald changed his mind (as shown in *Geschichte de Volkes Israel* [1843]) when he moved to a crystallization hypothesis, which was highly complex but whose basic principle was that various parts of the first six books of the OT served as centers around which other parts clustered for the final Hexateuch (*ca.* 600-500 B.C.). Many narrators and editors took part in this process. Ewald's change of view was prompted by his isolation of various materials which did not belong to the Yahwist, Elohist, or even the Deuteronomist. Ewald's work effectively stopped the early appearance of a fragmentary approach to the Pentateuch. He did not advocate Mosaic authorship of Genesis, but thought a unity of authorship alone explained its character and ancient features. Thus, although he held to the supplementary position, his stress on the unity of the Pentateuch separated him from scholars like Geddes, de Wette, and Vatke.

Although de Wette had already used Kantian philosophy as a framework for his biblical theology and for doing some of his critical work, with Wilhelm Vatke the Hegelian system of philosophy became dominant, and the OT materials were made to fit into the Hegelian scheme of developmental historiography. Wellhausen later would say that he learned "the most and the best" from Vatke. Vatke forced the religious history of the biblical materials into Hegel's famous scheme of the development of religion. Three stages are thereby discernible in the history of Israel's religion: (1) a religion of nature in which God is nature in some way or, at least, less than spirit, (2) a religion in which God is a personal spirit, (3) and a religion in which God is an infinite spirit (Christianity) who is both immanent and transcendent. Vatke's rearrangement of the biblical materials to fit this scheme was as follows: (1) judges and early monarchy = primitive and naturalistic stages (thesis), (2) prophets and later monarchy = personal spiritual stage (antithesis), and (3) the postexilic period = the institutionalization and legalization of the legislation and religion of Israel (synthesis). With the faulty views of religious development in Vatke's day, along with the absence of sufficient ancient Near Eastern archeological evidence to curtail speculative theories and a *Zeitgeist* largely determined by Hegelianism (less so by Fichte, Schelling, Schleiermacher, Mach) and early evolutionary thought, Vatke's move to interpret Scripture the way he did is understandable, but unfortunate.

Vatke dated the biblical documents late with abandon since Mosaic monotheism and priestly religion were, according to him, necessarily late whatever the documents implied. The Mosaic theocracy was not actual history. The law was produced by a political-religious state already in existence. Much of the basic literary material of the Pentateuch according to his scheme should be dated much later than it was usually dated (cf. de Wette). Vatke was more radical than many, and his basic work (*Die biblische Theologie wissenschaftlich dargestellt* [1835]) was neglected for nearly a generation, but he set the pace that would be picked up later.

Two main documents had supposedly been isolated by this time, E and J, J being delineated in various ways. Two men projected this documentary approach further to reach the immediate forerunner of the modern view of the documentary theory. Herman W. Hupfeld (*Die Quellen der Genesis und die Art ihrer Zusammensetzung von neuem untersucht* [1853]), found three documents which he called $E^1$, $E^2$, and J. Basic to the discovery was his conviction that J was a continuous source intertwined with a source that he called $E^2$. $E^1$ was the original *Grundschrift* and provided the basic framework for the Pentateuch. So the sources became $E^1$, $E^2$, and J in that order. E. Riehm isolated Deuteronomy (*Die Gesetzgebung Mosis im Lande Moab* [1854]) as an independent source. This preliminary documentary theory was $E^1$, $E^2$, J, D. Eventually it would become J E D P ($E^2$ = E, $E^1$ = P), indicating a new nomenclature and sequence of sources. Hupfeld's $E^1$, $E^2$, J, P were compiled by a final redactor, and thus some literary problems remained in the text. He also agreed with de Wette that Deuteronomy came from the time of Josiah. Many scholars supported Hupfeld's solution, but several adjustments were made to this basic documentary hypothesis before it was finally accepted by a great mass of biblical scholars.

*2. Graf, Kuenen, Wellhausen.* Three men, K. H. Graf, A. Kuenen, and J. Wellhausen, refined the documentary hypothesis into its modern form. Graf originally maintained that $E^1$ ($E^1$ $E^2$ J D) was the *Grundschrift* of the Pentateuch that J had supplemented. When he proceeded to use D (621 B.C.) as a fulcrum around which to date other legislative and priestly materials (e.g., he dated the Book of the Covenant before Deuteronomy since the latter presupposed the former's laws), he assigned detailed Levitical laws in $E^1$ to the time of Ezra, although he ascribed the so-called Holiness Code (H) to Ezekiel. $E^1$, mostly narrative now, still came first, but through criticism from Riehm and Nöldeke and correspondence with Kuenen he became convinced that all of $E^1$ should be dated late since the narrative could hardly be separated from the laws imbedded in it. Hence he came to favor a sequence of sources reflecting $E^2$ J D $E^1$ and asserted that J was a document in its own right and that $E^2$ J or J $E^2$ were the oldest documents of the Pentateuch. $E^2$ and J were combined by a redactor with D. The Priestly Code (including Lev. 17–26) was compiled by Ezra in exile and later combined with $E^2$ J D to form $E^2$ J D $E^1$. Aside from the unlikely literary expertise and acumen which these men professed to share and by which they divided up the Pentateuch, it is most important to observe the extrabiblical Hegelian philosophy and evolutionary presuppositions used to remold, rewrite, and conform the ancient Scriptures to nineteenth-century thought. The bounds of sound literary criticism were exceeded and historical theory and criticism came into play. A. Kuenen (*De Godsdienst van Israël* [1869-70]; Eng. tr. *Religion of Israel*) settled the dispute as to whether $E^2$ J or J $E^2$ was the correct chronological sequence by supporting and effectively establishing the J $E^2$ D $E^1$ sequence.

Julius Wellhausen presented with great cogency (for those who accepted his presuppositions) the J E D P documentary developmental hypothesis and brought it to dominance and clarity. He was able to present the culmination of the work of decades by many scholars in an effective *magnum opus* (*Komposition des Hexateuchs*). Wellhausen maintained that J and E documents made up the earliest part of the Pentateuch, J being mainly a well-written narrative. He dated J *ca.* 850 B.C. and held that it originated in the southern kingdom. E was dated to 750 B.C. and came from the northern kingdom. A redactor $R^{JE}$ put these two documents together near 650 B.C. after the fall of the northern kingdom. D(euteronomy) came from Judah during the reform of Josiah (621 B.C.). The $R^D$ redactor put D together with J E *ca.* 550 B.C., and finally the priestly document ($E^1$ = P) was composed well after the Exile and combined with J E D by another redactor to form J E D P. Minor modifications and editorial material were incorporated so that it was not until 200 B.C. that our final Pentateuch was completed. As has been noted, a definite scheme of Israel's historical development lay at the bottom of this reconstruction, and the documentary hypothesis and the developmental hypothesis were wedded by Wellhausen, Hegelian and evolutionary teachings being reciprocal reinforcing influences.

The reader is directed to the basic OT intros. for an adequate presentation of the detailed criteria used to separate J E D P, etc., and a more detailed description of the presuppositions underlying the Graf-Wellhausen hypothesis (e.g., S. R. Driver, *PIOT,* R. K. Harrison, G. Ch. Aalders, A. Robert and A. Feuillet). An attempt to present these criteria here in so short a space would oversimplify the issue. *See also* CRITICISM.

According to Wellhausen the Pentateuch had no actual historicity and nearly all the priestly legislation was merely a retrojection of the cultus that existed in the postexilic community during and after the time of Ezra. Mosaic authorship was out of the question — the man Moses was practically turned into a handy cipher that the real biblical writers had created and used. The claims of Mosaicity in some parts of the Pentateuch were neglected and the canonical and extracanonical tradition of Mosaic authorship was considered totally inaccurate. The progressive revelatory development of Israel's religion and history presented by the biblical literature was rejected almost in toto. The enigma of the origin, authorship, and composition of the Pentateuch *as it stands in Scripture* was not solved. An ancient Near Eastern book was merely made to conform to nineteenth-century literary, philosophical, religious, historical, speculative hypotheses that rejected Scripture's witness to itself and that were uninformed, or refused to be informed, by knowledge from the ancient Near Eastern world that was accumulating. A clear naturalism dominated Wellhausen's hypothesis; supernaturalism was disallowed as an explanation for any parts of the Pentateuch. The principle that institutions described in a document were basically no older than the time of the composition of the document was accepted, or if "ancient" events were described therein, no historical worth was likely to be preserved in the record because of the great distance of time separating the event and its inscripturation. Scholars had undue faith in their ability to analyze and separate out sources and certainly undue faith in the critics' claim to understand how the writer(s) "should have written" their book.

The Wellhausen hypothesis triumphed in nearly all scholarly circles by the end of the 19th century (e.g., see the intros. by C. Cornhill [7th ed. 1913] and C. Steuernagel [1912] in Germany; the works of W. R. Smith and S. R. Driver in England and America). It seemed that the main problem of the Pentateuch had been solved and only details and a few uncertain matters remained. The younger generation of Bible scholars everywhere was overwhelmed by this new solution.

Several scholars attempted to challenge some conclusions of the Graf-Wellhausen explanation, however. The various divergences of opinion among scholars before Vater, Vatke, de Wette, Graf, Kuenen, and Wellhausen were almost insignificant compared to the chasm that was created between older views of the Pentateuch and those of the Graf-Wellhausen persuasion. The work of Graf and Wellhausen resulted in a revolution in OT theology and history. It is interesting to note, however, that the results of Assyriology and Egyptology were already challenging the new hypothesis in its infancy. The ancient nature of the material in P was being supported by E. Schrader (*Cuneiform Inscriptions and the OT* [2 vols., 1885-88]) and, hence, the late dating of P was questioned. Although some would say that the new Graf-Wellhausen position wiped out the Mosaic period, F. Hommel (*Ancient Hebrew Tradition as Illustrated by the Monuments* [Eng. tr. 1897]), an adherent to the school of Wellhausen and scholar of ancient cultures, could say that Abraham and the stories surrounding him were "historic facts."

*D. Responses to Graf-Wellhausen (19th Cent.). 1. Critical School.* From 1880 to 1925 scholars who shared many positions with the Graf-Wellhausen school questioned various aspects of the solution. Some argued for an earlier date for P (Riehm, Dillmann, Kittel, Delitzsch, Nöldeke, Klostermann), others argued for an earlier date for Deuteronomy (J. B. Griffiths, *Problems of Deuteronomy* [1911]; Klostermann, *et al.*), and Dillmann and Baudissin argued for an earlier date for H, the so-called Holiness Code (Lev. 17–26). Delitzsch placed the formation of much of the legal material in the time of Joshua–Judges, Klostermann argued for an earlier rescension of JE, and Klostermann, Eerdmans, and Möller attacked the general scheme and presuppositions of the developmental theory of Wellhausen.

Several followers of Wellhausen suggested adjustments of the literary analysis. R. Smend supported an earlier suggestion by K. Budde (*Urgeschichte* [1883]) that $J^1$ and $J^2$ are parallel authors discernible in Gen. 1–11. Smend also argued for greater unity of E. His suggestions are referred to sometimes as the *new documentary hypothesis*.

*2. Conservative School.* Conservative scholars had begun to respond at the beginning of the 19th century. E. W. Hengstenberg, an avowed supernaturalist, wrote a comprehensive rebuttal to the antisupernatural approaches of Vatke, de Wette, and Vater that is still valuable today. Hengstenberg effectively showed how the present arrangement of the biblical material implies and presupposes the authenticity of the Bible's own presentation of God's dealing with mankind and the world (e.g., monotheism is early, the law is implied and alluded to in Joshua-Judges, the law is already in existence as shown by an examination of the prophets, revelation is a vital part of the warp and woof of OT history, etc.). M. Drechsler developed the unity and genuineness of the book of Genesis (*Die Einheit und Echtheit der Genesis* [1838]) and thus argued strongly for an author who created this literary architecture. C. F. Keil (*Manual of Historico-Critical Intro. to the Canonical Scriptures of the OT* [Eng. tr. 1869]) also met the critical school head-on. He did use some historical and archeological facts to buttress his case, but he was writing before Wellhausen's work. H. Ewald also helped stem the total victory of the movement of Wellhausen and his predecessors. He was not in the same school as the others that we have mentioned, but his more respectful approach to the Scriptures and his supplementary and subsequent crystallization theory of the composition of the Pentateuch, along with his nonantagonistic approach to supernaturalism, show how his presuppositions enabled him still to date Genesis materials very early. He refused to surrender totally the internal and traditional integrity of the text.

The reactions of conservatives continued, although their voices were largely unheeded by the majority of OT scholars. The basic foundations of the Graf-Wellhausen hypothesis were attacked by E. Bissell (*Pentateuch. Its Origin and Structure* [1885]), and Geerhardus Vos (*Mosaic Origin of the Pentateuchal Codes* [1886]) claimed essential Mosaicity for the Pentateuch and rejected the literary analysis. Möller picked up on the unity of the Pentateuch and stressed it further.

The general impact of archeology among conservative scholars was to confirm the basic historicity of the biblical accounts, and people like A. H. Sayce, a former adherent to "higher criticism," wrote as impartial archeologists. The facts of the monuments seemed to him to confirm biblical historicity (*Higher Critics and the Verdict of the Monuments* [1894]; *Monuments, Facts, and Higher Critical Fancies* [5th ed. 1927]).

The criteria used to analyze the documents were seriously questioned by J. Dahse, *Archiv fur Religionswissenschaft*, VI [1908] 305-319). He also used the growing archeological evidence to challenge the late dating of the priestly material and to point out the advanced nature of other ancient Near Eastern cultures. In several works H. Wiener (*Essays in Pentateuchal Criticism* [1910]; *Origin of the Pentateuch* [1910]), pointed out differences between the MT and the LXX in the use of the divine names. J. Skinner answered many of these charges by Wiener and Dahse in *Divine Names in Genesis* (1914).

James Orr, a noted conservative polymath, dealt with the critical scheme severely. He used keen reasoning and some archeology and put forth his own hypothesis about the authorship, origin, and composition of the Pentateuch. While admitting the complexity of the Pentateuch, he affirmed full confidence in its unity and historical credibility. He saw evidence of different writers, different styles and stages of compilation, but no need to separate J and E, most of which he said went back to Moses or immediate post-Mosaic times. Deuteronomy is ancient, historical, and the discourses genuine. It was probably an independent work originally, but clearly reflects knowledge of the Mosaic Book of the Covenant (Ex. 21–23), the J E material, and presupposes part of the Levitical legislation. P contains laws from the Mosaic age and is basically Mosaic in origin. The early laws of P date the history early. P was not likely a continuous document, but was rather a framework for

J E that also included independent comment at places. Genesis is probably all pre-Mosaic. When the Israelites came from Egypt they were not a backward, primitive people but were relatively advanced. The patriarchs even knew of books and writing, and "at an early period, in Egypt under Joseph, if not before, attempts were made to set down things in writing." In the beginning, *at an early date* of the formation of the Pentateuch, Orr saw collaboration and cooperation of the original composers, *not much later* in the process (p. 369). Ezra (or some other figure) gave the Pentateuch its final revision.

Orr's work was meticulous and well done. He grasped the essence of historical criticism, and his attempted solution to the problem of the Pentateuch is still echoed in some conservative works. The repeated charge that *no* conservative scholar has tried to present an alternate working hypothesis is plainly false. Orr's attempt is admirable, but no critical scholar ever replied to his suggestions. Most fundamentalists rejected his solution as liberalism, even though he retained the basic historicity and Mosaicity of the Pentateuch and its picture of Israel's history and religion.

A more conservative and well-reasoned defense of the traditional idea of the Pentateuch was presented by W. H. Green, but conservative scholars, as well as critical speculators, were simply not able to put forth a compositional hypothesis of the Pentateuch because the knowledge of how books were made in the ancient Near East was not yet clear. The work of Schrader, Orr, Sayce, Kyle (others could be listed), shows that ancient Near Eastern archeology and philology were beginning to have an impact on biblical studies.

*E. Development of Pentateuchal Studies (20th Cent.).* Several new types of biblical criticism have developed during the 20th cent., and although the Graf-Wellhausen hypothesis still dominates pentateuchal studies, it does so in many cases — both as to documents and presuppositions — in a modified form. A great number of its adherents reject the original developmental aspect of the critical position and also its nineteenth-century Hegelian garb. Many adherents emphasize the trustworthiness of the historical framework of the Pentateuch (see, e.g., the essays in *BANE*). Although documents are still dated late, the traditions in the documents are considered ancient and quite trustworthy. Some scholars prefer to use certain aspects of the Graf-Wellhausen hypothesis (e.g., J) and feel that even the evidence of ancient Near Eastern studies supports it rather than a greatly modified view (cf. T. L. Thompson). Others, however, criticize and reject the documentary hypothesis and suggest a supplementary hypothesis in its place (Van Seters, Rendtorff). Moreover, among critical scholars a renewed stress on the thematic unity is evident. Conservative scholars are gradually developing the expertise to suggest viable alternatives to the modified Graf-Wellhausen hypothesis rather than merely criticizing it.

*1. Ancient Near Eastern Studies.* The development of archeology had seriously challenged the assumption of the Graf-Wellhausen hypothesis that the biblical writers of the Pentateuch were often simply calling forth a world that did not exist. By 1930 it was clear that the Pentateuch was not a mere literary construct, but that it called to remembrance a world that had actually existed and had provided the framework within which the ancestors of Israel's faith truly lived and moved and died. At last an external check was being developed by which the gratuitous speculation of many higher critics could be judged. The ancient Near Eastern world was opened up by archeological developments (begun in the 18th cent.) in Egypt, Babylon, Assyria, Syria, Palestine, and Asia Minor. *See* articles on the archeology of various areas for full reviews of this fascinating development.

A few observations about this topic will give the reader some idea of the importance of this field for pentateuchal studies. Although a sound scientific approach to archeology was developed only around the turn of the 20th cent., it is clear that archeological materials were available to nineteenth-century scholars and should have created at least a greater respect for the authenticity of ancient sources and traditions. Schrader's work along with Sayce's work was mentioned earlier (cf. also H. Hilprecht, *Recent Research in Bible Lands* [1897]). George Smith had published Babylonian texts in 1876 (*Chaldean Account of Genesis*), such as the Babylonian Genesis, and part of a Sumerian flood and creation story was found at Nippur (1893-1896). More material from the Sumerians, Assyrians, and others that deals with creation and a great flood has been unearthed from the 19th cent. till the present. The ancient cuneiform script had been deciphered by 1857. Numerous archeological finds confirming the factuality of the historical books of the Bible were known in the 19th cent., but the mass of ancient Near Eastern discoveries began in the 20th century.

In 1901 V. Sheil found a stele at Susa, a former capital of Elam, that had the ancient law code of Hammurabi inscribed on it. The code dates *ca.* 1750 B.C., thus antedating the laws of Moses by several centuries but reflecting the even more ancient laws of Eshnunna (2000 B.C.) and Lipit-Ishtar (*ca.* 1850 B.C.), a Sumerian.

The ancient city of Ur had been excavated as early as 1854, but it was C. L. Woolley who brought the splendor of this ancient wonder to light (1922-1939). He found that education was highly developed and that the Ur III period (2070-1960 B.C.) was possibly the time during which Abraham resided in this great civilization. Writing was already over a thousand years old by the time of Ur III. Ur-Nammu, the founder, was responsible for a law code from this era. It appeared that not only Moses but Abraham also would possibly have been able to write. At the site of Nuzi, SE of Nineveh, the American Schools of Oriental Research found many clay tablets from private homes that paralleled some of the social customs and traditions reflected in the patriarchal narratives of the Bible (sale of birthright, oral blessing, treatment of concubines, adoption, etc.). The date of these tablets was *ca.* 1500 B.C. Old Babylonian texts (*ca.* 2000-1600 B.C.) also furnish good parallels to patriarchal customs. Equally significant finds were unearthed at Tell el-Ḥarîrî (Mari) on the Euphrates (1933-1939). Names were found in these texts that reflect those found in Gen. 11:16, 23f., e.g., Peleg, Serug, Nahor. Other finds at Mari are relevant to pentateuchal studies: texts reflecting the ancient character of priestly practices, the building materials in some structures (reflecting Gen. 11:3), the mention of Ḫabiru and Benjaminites (both may reflect some relation with the Hebrews of the OT) as well as the Arramu (= OT Arameans, e.g., Gen. 24:29; 29:5; Dt. 26:5).

This early tendency to find parallels between the Bible and the ancient Near East in order to confirm the historicity and authenticity of the Scriptures is seen now as somewhat simplistic by some scholars. More will be said on this issue below. Of course, most of the archeological finds do not bear directly or even indirectly upon biblical writings, but they do provide some general context for the Bible.

Finds from Syrio-Palestinian archeological endeavors did not begin until *ca.* 1910. The Alalakh Tablets from northern Syria (15th cent. B.C.), though they do not bear directly on the OT, do contribute to our understanding of what culture, religion, language, etc. were like at that time. For example, covenant making and covenant contracts, narrative style, Ḫabiru, kingship, marriage contracts, scribal activity, and various other matters are elucidated.

Perhaps the most helpful find so far has been the materials unearthed at the ancient site of Ugarit (Râs Shamrah) in 1929ff. and 1948ff. The polytheistic world of the ancient Near East is clearly delineated, especially in a number of mythological texts. But just as significant is the bearing that the Ugaritic language, which is an alphabetical cuneiform, is having on the understanding of the Hebrew language and the biblical text. Much of this Ugaritic literature coming from the 15th cent. B.C. parallels the writing style and form of the Hebrew Bible (cf. P. C. Craigie, *Ugarit and the OT* [1983]).

The finds at ancient Ebla (Tell Mardikh) in Syria (beginning esp. in the mid-1970's) may continue to increase our understanding of the ancient Hebrew language and script and will certainly increase our understanding of the ancient Near East. Despite the early claims made about the verification of certain OT facts, the full and exact bearing that these materials from Ebla may have on biblical studies is far from certain at the time of writing (*see* TELL MARDIKH).

Egyptian archeological finds began at a very early date. Egyptian hieroglyphic writing, a mixture of phonetic, ideographic, and alphabetic symbols, was deciphered over a period of fourteen years (1808-1822) of intensive study by J. F. Champollion. Egyptian studies have provided indirect confirmation of the authentic Egyptian flavor of the Joseph stories in Genesis and to many features of the material in the book of Exodus. The Amarna Tablets, first discovered in 1887, reflect social and political conditions in Palestine and Egypt possibly during the time of the late patriarchal period and the sojourn in Egypt (some would date the conquest of Canaan during the Amarna period). Excavations at Tanis and Qanṭîr suggest that the biblical record reflects a date for the Exodus during the 19th Dynasty under Rameses II (1304-1290 B.C.). The "Israel Stele" of Merneptah (*ca.* 1220) mentions a people in Canaan bearing the name Israel.

Hittite materials have opened up a new world of the ancient Near East that offers some excellent possibilities for OT studies. When Hilprecht edited his book in 1896 Hittite had not been deciphered, although a fair amount was known about the presence of Hittites in various areas of the ancient Near East. B. Hrozný deciphered the language in 1915, and now the Hittite civilization is recognized as one of the great ancient powers of its time. Hittite treaties from the 2nd millennium may offer a key to the "treaty" nature of Ex. 20, Josh. 24, or even the whole book of Deuteronomy (see Craigie, Clines). Hittite prayers, their idea of sin, and a "deuteronomic" view of national disasters are especially important for OT studies (cf. *AOTS*, pp. 105-114).

Several generations of ancient Near Eastern and OT scholars have worked indefatigably to show the way ancient Near Eastern studies illuminate, illustrate, and confirm (most always indirectly) the biblical materials (Bright, Wright, Albright, Speiser, Livingston, Wiseman, Millard, *et al.*). The result of twentieth-century archeological activity is that many scholars (both liberal and conservative) feel that the data agree with and largely support the OT view of its own history rather than speculative systems that challenge the Bible's own understanding of the history and message that it bears.

However, not everyone has accepted the general consensus that the patriarchal history should be placed in the 1st half of the 2nd millennium. Since the late 1960's some scholars have seriously challenged this almost universal conclusion. Moreover, archeological finds sometimes have raised problems rather than solved them, and it must be remembered that we are talking about indirect confirmation of biblical materials most of the time. Hence, there is room for some divergence of opinion about the implications of the archeological evidence. Evidence can be interpreted in various ways. It is actually surprising, since only a very small fraction of possible archeological work has been done, that the material relevant to OT studies is as abundant as it is. See further below.

2. *Form Criticism.* Form Criticism (*Formgeschichte*) arose after a sufficient amount of knowledge and interest had accumulated dealing with the ancient Near East and other ancient cultures. H. Gunkel is considered the pioneer of this study in the biblical areas, along with H. Gressmann. Some refinement of the method has occurred since Gunkel wrote *Schöpfung und Chaos in Urzeit und Endzeit* (1895), in which he applied his form-critical method. Although Gunkel accepted the J E D P documents proposed by Wellhausen, he made a revolutionary move in his evaluation of the content contained in the documents. He maintained, e.g., that although P in Gen. 1 as a document is late, many of the traditions (oral and written) used by the composer of the document are very ancient. The possible implications of this approach for the historical value of biblical traditions is evident, and of course, this was simply a little different way of saying what the ancient Near Eastern archeological finds seemed to be saying. Themes such as creation were traced by Gunkel from their first appearance through their final presentation, the changes in message and structure being carefully noted. The method attempted to allow the text "to live again" to some extent. The use of form criticism, however, did not always necessarily buttress the historicity of biblical texts. In fact, as employed by many scholars, it challenges any essential historicity of the events reported in the biblical text (cf. Van Seters, T. L. Thompson).

The OT itself was considered to be largely compositions made up of smaller literary units. The form-critical method tried to show how the smaller units originated and how the larger books (documents) were built up from the smaller literary units. The delineation of the oral traditions behind the literary forms was vital to this approach. The agenda of discerning the various literary types and forms was good, but the attempt to discern the original *Sitz im Leben* (life-setting) behind the beginnings of certain literary forms was questionable, given the speculative principles necessarily used. The *Sitz im Leben* of the biblical text was often ignored. The unity of the final canonical biblical composition tended to be disregarded and the text atomized into disjunctive units. The composer was thought to reveal not his own isolated mind, but much more the social, religious, cultural, and historical dimensions of his time.

Some unfortunate methodological problems arose, however, because of the failure to utilize ancient Near Eastern literary models sufficiently. The actual parallels used were too often taken from much later literature. Some scholars made uncritical assertions of the biblical writers' "borrowings" from other surrounding cultures, but Gunkel himself tried to show the unique religious thought of Israel as well. The tendency of form criticism to see biblical units as products of fertile human minds and cultures, rather than reflections of historical events and people, was inherent to the usual form-critical approach. Controls needed to be found. The revelational and inspirational element of the biblical writings could hardly be discerned at times in the mass of legends, sagas, forms, etc. that were encountered by this method. This is not necessarily the fault of the method, but may reflect operational presuppositions and a lack of control over the method. Undue attention is often given to the text or situation behind the text, and the evident meaning of the final text is missed or relegated to unimportance or changed by the esoteric factors gained by the investigation behind the text. The "historical kernel" of the various developed themes and genres uncovered often played no necessary or sufficient part in the theological content or form of the final text. The evolutionary scheme of the literary units, from small primitive units to larger complex units, is open to question and not evident at all in much ancient Near Eastern literature. And it is clear that a final form can be used in more than one religious, social, or general cultural setting (hence *Sitz im Leben* is to be used cautiously) and could even originate in various settings.

Many scholars have contributed to the development and use of this method of doing OT studies (see H. F. Hahn, pp. 119-156; K. Koch, *Growth of the Biblical Tradition* [Eng. tr. 1969]; J. Hayes, ed., *OT Form Criticism* [1974]). M. Noth and A. Alt used this approach to study OT law and the tribal beginnings and history of Israel. Although their speculative reconstructions of the patriarchal period have been challenged, they affirmed the ancient nature of some of the material itself. J. Hempel (*Die althebräische Literatur* [1930]), A. Lods (*Histoire de la littérature hébräique et juive* [1950]), and G. von Rad have developed form-critical studies. Von Rad identified the "ancient credos" hinted at in Dt. 6:20-24; 26:5f. with the primitive stage of the development of the Pentateuch. Working with J E D P he said that the Yahwist (J) put more fully developed traditions together and hence was the one who gave the Pentateuch its essential form.

Numerous challenges have been leveled against the studies of Alt, Noth, and von Rad. According to Van Seters any extensive preliterary stage of the pentateuchal material is unfounded. The form-critical method tends to challenge the unity and historicity of the materials if not used along with archeological controls and an awareness of the unitary themes of the Pentateuch. Some form-critical scholars have given the theological nature of biblical writing a more proper emphasis. Alt, von Rad, and Noth affirmed a basic historicity of the pentateuchal material, but both Van Seters and T. L. Thompson, who also used form criticism, denied the basic historicity of the ancient patriarchal traditions. Nevertheless, when used along with the necessary controls of ancient Near Eastern literary and historical materials, a respect for biblical traditions, and an appreciation for larger literary forms and themes, the form-critical method tends to show the historicity, authenticity, unity, and uniqueness of the biblical materials at substantive levels, and to delineate the clear ancient Near Eastern character and ambience of the OT.

*3. Tradition Criticism.* Gunkel himself had emphasized the oral stages of the traditions that were eventually written down. The study of these preliterary traditions came as a natural step within form criticism. This discipline is termed the history of tradition (*Traditionsgeschichte*). The oral formation and transmission of the various traditions of the OT are studied, but oral tradition is given priority and writing is seen as a late phenomenon in the ancient Near East. Hence, the pentateuchal traditions would have existed for centuries in gradually evolving oral form until they were written down quite late (*ca.* 400 B.C.), according to tradition criticism. M. Noth postulated an early period of oral tradition for the pentateuchal materials before they were recorded in writing, but this has been denied strongly by Van Seters, who has little sympathy for any stress on oral tradition.

Several Scandinavian scholars (H. S. Nyberg, H. Birkeland, S. Mowinckel, I. Engnell) have been largely responsible for the growth and development of this approach to OT studies. However, G. Widengren (*Literary and Psychological Aspects of the Hebrew Prophets* [1948]), himself a Scandinavian, has argued for the parallel use of written and oral tradition, even giving written tradition pride of place. The best introduction is still Eduard Nielsen, *Oral Tradition* (see also J. Lindblom, *Prophecy in Ancient Israel* [Eng. tr. 1962], pp. 220-291). Other writers dealing with traditions outside the OT (e.g., in NT studies, H. Riesenfeld, *Jésus transfiguré* [1947]; B. Gerhardsson, *Memory and Manuscript* [Eng. tr. 1961]) have tended to support a view opposed to the tradition-history school; namely, that it is most likely that important events, traditions, etc. were written down at the beginning (cf. Albright), not the end, of the ancient transmission process. This conclusion seems confirmed by various ancient Near Eastern materials.

Several criticisms have rightly been leveled at this whole enterprise. It sometimes sounds as if those who use the method are absolutely sure of their results; this cannot be the case. The method itself is highly subjective; it is an art and not a science at this stage. A greater use of ancient Near Eastern materials as a control over theory is needed. And more often than not, examples do not come from the ancient Near East. The term tradition history is ambiguous and, as many have noted, the dissemination (2 Ch. 17:9f.) of a work must be differentiated from the oral transmission of a work. This approach sometimes subordinates historicity to faith. The scholar begins to write the record of Israel's faith as it was passed down, not Israel's "event-word" background. But this methodological approach is not able to postulate historicity or nonhistoricity by itself. Some check upon the probable historical truth of pentateuchal traditions *and* the presuppositions of the reader of those traditions must still be furnished by ancient Near Eastern archeological material. Finally, the extant cuneiform documents in the hundreds of thousands surely attest to the great importance of writing at an extremely early period in the ancient Near East. This method, if followed in its critical application, would seem to date the *recording in writing* of the biblical materials much too late. Nevertheless, it has provided valuable insights into the probable oral preservation of some biblical materials before being written down and has emphasized the need to understand how the ancients composed books. This approach helps us gain a great appreciation and understanding of some of the pentateuchal traditions.

*4. Canonical Criticism.* Brevard Childs's works have put forth a concern to regain the OT Scriptures for the Church while maintaining a proper stance of critical biblical scholarship toward the Bible itself. Canonical criticism presupposes and makes use of all of the types of biblical criticism enumerated above, but tries to avoid the excesses found in each one, e.g., minute analyses of texts, detailed identification of J, E, D, etc., undue concern about the text behind the text. It works seriously with inner-biblical categories in defining authorship, historicity of texts, etc. Authorship and authority, e.g., are to be understood in relation to tradition received, developed, and molded by a community of faith. The received *form* of the canonical corpus is of great importance and hence the problem of Pentateuch, Tetrateuch, or Hexateuch becomes crucial. A positive feature of this method of doing biblical criticism is that it does not pontificate upon historicity or nonhistoricity of the biblical texts, but tries to discern what is of concern and significance to the biblical writer — the theological message of the text is of paramount importance. Childs himself sides neither with those who demand absolute historical accuracy of the biblical events nor with those who require no historical event to lie behind the biblical materials. Rather, his concern is to let the canonical text determine the degree to which we are concerned with this issue when doing exegesis for the Christian community. Canonical criticism draws attention to the fact that it is the final form of the text that has canonical authority for the religious community. A further advantage of this approach is that the overall literary work being studied, be it a chapter, book, or group of books, must be seen in a reciprocal way. For the Pentateuch the method allows great fluidity in interpreting the various literary genres found in this body of literature. Cf. Childs, *Intro.*; *Myth.*

5. *Graf-Wellhausen Hypothesis.* It is clear that much has happened in the field of biblical studies since 1900 to change and challenge the Graf-Wellhausen hypothesis, but much has happened also to challenge any fundamentalist approach to the highly complex pentateuchal puzzlements. Except for a few cases, a general consensus prevails that archeological evidence implies and helps establish the basic historicity of pentateuchal traditions. Form criticism and its offshoots also argue for much ancient material in the Pentateuch. Linguistic evidence argues for the ancient nature of various parts of the Pentateuch: Nu. 23–24, the Balaam Oracles; Dt. 33, Moses' Blessing; Ex. 15, the Song of Miriam; Gen. 49, the Blessing of Jacob; Jgs. 5, the Song of Deborah and Barak. Various legal and covenantal forms are seen to reflect ancient documents (Book of the Covenant, Decalogue, Deuteronomic laws, etc.). It must be remembered, however, that this has taken seventy years to establish. Many still accept some modified form of the Graf-Wellhausen hypothesis. The various forms of OT criticism have sometimes influenced and even dictated the changes in this method. The *reductio ad absurdum* of the documentary analysis was reached when B. Baentsch (*Exodus-Leviticus-Numeri* [*Handkommentar zum AT,* 1903]) found about seventeen documents or authors in Leviticus (seven different P sigla were used by him!). More moderate adjustments were to come, however, and each document was analyzed and often redated accordingly. The history of each document alone became as complicated and involved as the composition of the whole Pentateuch had been thought to be earlier.

G. Hölscher and R. H. Kennett (*Deuteronomy and the Decalogue* [1920]) dated D later than Josiah. T. Östreicher (*Das Deuteronomische Grundgesetz* [1923]) and A. Welch (*Code of Deuteronomy* [1924]) dated D earlier than Josiah and noted the ancient nature of the traditions contained in the book. Östreicher understood Deuteronomy (*locus classicus,* Dt. 12) to be pursuing cultic purity, not cultic unity as the Wellhausen theory argued. E. Robertson (*OT Problem* [1950]) dated Deuteronomy to the time of Samuel. Some had noted basic differences in J so that $J^1$ and $J^2$ were suggested. O. Eissfeldt (*ZAW,* 48 [1930], 66-73; *Hexateuch-Synopse*) separated out L (a Lay source), and felt that it reflected nomadic ideals and dated it to the time of Elijah. J. Morgenstern (*HUCA,* 4 [1927], 1-138) discerned what he called a K document and dated it *ca.* 900 B.C. R. Pfeiffer (*ZAW,* 48 [1930], 66-73) found an S (Seir or South) source with additions (S2). Von Rad (*Priesterschrift*) separated P into $P^a$ $P^b$, and M. Noth, while using J E D P, felt that a G (*Grundschrift*) source lay at the base of the Pentateuch. Yehezkel Kaufmann (*Religion*) argued vehemently for the recognition of P as more ancient than D and even E or J. Moreover, the existence of some of the traditional sources (J E D P) was challenged, and the supplementary theory was nearly resurrected again. P. Volz and W. Rudolph (*Der Elohist als Erzähler: Ein Irrweg der Pentateuchkritik?* [*BZAW,* 63, 1933]) argued against the existence of E as a narrative source. Volz also denied that P was a narrative source, and thus asserted J as the basic source, while Rudolph accepted P (see also Rudolph, *Der 'Elohist' von Exodus bis Josua* [*BZAW,* 68, 1938]).

In varying degrees these scholars used form criticism, tradition criticism, and archeological materials from the ancient Near East. And some not only tried to modify the documentary hypothesis but even rejected it; especially important were J. Pedersen (*ZAW,* 49 [1931], 161-181) and the Uppsala scholars who were noted above. Pedersen affirmed that the various strands in the Pentateuch were parallel and contained exilic, but also preexilic, material, some of it very ancient. He saw the central core of the Pentateuch as Ex. 1–15, a cult legend that is not an "exposition of ordinary events." It is embellished material, and the original events and *Sitz im Leben* behind it are not accessible to documentary and form criticism. The Uppsala scholars challenged the Graf-Wellhausen construction and called it a modern creation that did not take into account the true nature of the material with which it was dealing. I. Engnell, the leading spokesman for this group, concluded that the Pentateuch is made up of a "P-work" and Deuteronomy, the first part of "the Deuteronomic history work"; both works in their written from may date from the time of Ezra-Nehemiah.

Both von Rad and Noth were highly influenced by form criticism and tradition criticism while still using the standard sigla in their work. Von Rad worked with a Hexateuch, while Noth favored a Tetrateuch (Genesis–Numbers). Both men allowed for a period of oral tradition behind the written materials of each document (J E D P, plus G (?) for Noth). Noth's *Überlieferungsgeschichte des Pentateuchs* is largely concerned with the oral tradition that lies behind the current documents of the Pentateuch, especially the G source (behind J and E), which may have been oral, not written (cf. J. Bright, "Modern Study of OT Literature," in *BANE,* pp. 13-31; C. R. North, "Pentateuchal Criticism," in *OTMS,* pp. 48-83).

However, three scholars have challenged many basics of this whole enterprise as it has moved gradually to assert a "basic historicity" of the biblical traditions. And even more serious criticisms of the various aspects of the original Graf-Wellhausen hypothesis have been forthcoming. J. Van Seters used literary and form-critical analysis to date the traditions of Abraham (Gen. 12–25). He gave priority to this evidence over archeological evidence but used first-millennium B.C. archeological evidence to firm up his form-critical and structural studies of the patriarchal stories. He viewed archeological evidence as analogical and not capable of proving the date of anything. The oral forms associated with Abraham could have first been attached to him when written down. He accepted J and dated it to the exilic period; P is a post-exilic literary supplement to J; J gives frequent clues to his own time. He saw tradition criticism as helpful but needing control by form criticism. He concluded that the usual criteria of source criticism are not adequate to separate out sources, and the existence of the traditional E source in the Pentateuch is highly questionable. Van Seters in effect asserted a supplementary hypothesis centering on J.

T. L. Thompson suggested that the nature of the stories as literature should be the focus of discussion, not the historicity of the events. According to him the patriarchal traditions were taken up into J at the end of the 10th or during the 9th cent. B.C. The traditions do not reflect any "basic historicity." They are based on a late scheme of theology that projects a very unhistorical world view. The question is "whether we are prepared to see literary forms which are foreign to us . . . as media of truth" (*Historicity,* p. 328). For Thompson archeology has not proven a single patriarchal event to be historical.

R. Rendtorff has suggested a different way of doing source analysis as well as different terminology. He preferred to work with primeval history (Gen. 2–11), Exodus history (Ex. 1–15), Sinai material (Ex. 19–24), and cycles of material centering on Abraham, Isaac, Jacob, and Joseph. These strands of material are parallel in the Pentateuch and joined end to end. Much of the formative work was done during the time of Solomon. The various blocks of traditional material have a level of genuine historicity lying behind them (he respected and approved the use of archeological control data), but have been retold again and again and so altered as to stress the important features fundamental to Israel's faith (*God's History* [Eng. tr. 1962]). These combined sources probably underwent a P and a final D redaction. This approach helps explain the unity of the pentateuchal materials and also militates against the older source analysis of J E D P that often split unified and coherent wholes in an irrational way. Rendtorff's helpful approach, along with Van Seters's and Thompson's new attempts to deal with pentateuchal issues, shows the correctness of his observation that "We possess hardly any reliable criteria for dating pentateuchal literature. Every dating of the pentateuchal sources rests on purely hypothetical assumptions, which only have standing through the consensus of scholars" (*Problem,* p. 169).

Various scholars who accept J E D P in a twentieth-century modified form and who have great respect for the historicity of the ancient traditions contained in the late documents have criticized Thompson and Van Seters severely (e.g., *BHI* [3rd ed. 1981], pp. 67-103; N. Sarna, *Biblical Archeology Review,* 3/4 [1977], 5-9). And leading archeologists (e.g., Y. Yadin) have continued to affirm a very positive relationship between the Bible and archeological data.

*F. Conservative Scholarship.* Conservative scholars have traditionally been quick to argue against excessive biblical criticism, but slow to develop viable alternative hypotheses. Happily this situation has begun to be remedied, especially since the 1960's. A strong conservative position is developing that neither merely affirms a precritical position on pentateuchal issues nor merely criticizes the other side. Emphasis here will be given to some positive work toward a conservative synthesis of pentateuchal issues. These conservative positions allow for diversity of views, but they share some important basic points: they affirm the basic Mosaicity, historicity, and authenticity of the Pentateuch, and strive to define pentateuchal authority, authorship, and composition according to true inner-biblical categories and ancient Near Eastern models coming from the milieu, ambience, and time of the Scriptures. Important aspects of this position are shared by scholars across the lines of the traditional conservative-liberal dichotomies; the position is arising by force of the evidence. Scholars are seeking to control their syntheses by basing them on solid evidence from the enormous amount of ancient Near Eastern studies that has accumulated during the 20th century. Competent solutions are being offered without recourse to hypotheses which undermine the historical truth of Scripture (the necessary condition for the truth of the scriptural message) or the theological truth and dimension of Scripture (the sufficient condition for the authenticity and truth of Scripture). The supernatural is given its proper place. No full-scale pentateuchal conservative synthesis has yet occurred, but, for all that, neither has a new twentieth-century full-scale synthesis of the pentateuchal issues from any posture been achieved. Especially helpful from the conservative side are the new commentary series published and in process at this time (e.g., *Tyndale OT Comms.*; *NICOT*; *Word Biblical Comms.).* Some sampling of various conservative approaches are noted below. These works have steered away by and large from the extremes on pentateuchal issues and are breaking new ground, and giving younger conservative scholars some solid hypotheses to build on, develop, change, and improve.

It is now recognized that the relationship that existed between biblical compositions and their author(s) is a highly complex issue, and its solution (if possible at all) involves literary form, literary sources, growth and development, oral tradition, ancient Near Eastern concepts, etc. Authorship is to be defined carefully by inner-biblical categories (Childs) and by ancient Near Eastern categories that help illumine the biblical categories. The final evaluation of these issues must be such that the Pentateuch retains its canonical significance for the rest of the OT documents, for the faith of ancient Israel, and for the Church. The Pentateuch must be seen as constitutive of Israel's faith and life (historical books, wisdom books, prophets).

*1. Ancient Near Eastern Studies.* All scholars are agreed that ancient Near Eastern studies are required for one to answer the questions regarding pentateuchal authorship, origin, composition, and genre. It should be made clear, however, that these studies are not sufficient for us to understand or believe the religious-moral (theological) message of the Pentateuch. Ancient Near Eastern studies are used to control theories about some pentateuchal issues and to help us think in categories appropriate to this ancient piece of literature (Kitchen, Livingston, Segal, Harrison, Millard, Wiseman, Craigie, Wenham, Goldingay, Kidner). Any approach using modern critical methods must respect the theological and historical integrity of the text (unless there is adequate reason for doing otherwise) and be controlled as much as possible by information coming from ancient Near Eastern studies. These studies themselves are not to be used to destroy the uniqueness of the biblical materials. Some form-critical studies have given results that cut across traditional documentary theories and stress the unity of the literature of the Pentateuch (Livingston, Wenham, Craigie).

*2. Affirmation of Unity.* In general the unity of the Pentatuech is being affirmed with new vigor (e.g., B. W. Anderson, *JBL,* 100 [1981], 5-21; D. W. Baker, "Diversity and Unity in the Literary Structure of Genesis," in Millard and Wiseman; Clines). Various types of sources are indeed recognized (Wenham, Kidner, Harrison), and that many inspired hands have worked to bring us the Pentateuch is admitted. Even within one book (e.g., Genesis) numerous literary genres are present (Gen. 1:1–3:4; 4–11; 12–50, etc.). Of paramount importance, however, is not the individual books of the Pentateuch, but the final product — the Pentateuch as a whole (see II.C above).

*3. Historicity.* This issue has already been covered sufficiently but again it should be noted that the historicity of the Pentateuch is a necessary condition for the acceptance of the truth content of the Pentateuch, but not a sufficient cause. Conservative scholars recognize clearly that the Pentateuch is a theological-historical document (Goldingay, Kidner), so while the historicity of the biblical story is a necessary condition for its authority, an inspired theological dimension is the only sufficient basis for its authority in all matters of faith and practice.

*4. Basic Mosaicity.* Very few, if any, modern conservative scholars see the Pentateuch as a composition whose every word, oral and written, came from Moses. Such a position is hardly viable based upon the inner-biblical witnesses (e.g., Genesis, post-Mosaica) or upon ancient Near Eastern concepts of authorship (Bush, Harrison, etc.). The pentateuchal issues to a great extent do center upon Moses, but his "authorship" or activity must be correctly defined. Both growth and development (e.g., Josh. 24:26; Nu. 26:28-36; 27:1-11; 36:1-9) are probable, and the use of sources by Moses is certain. But the unique religious and moral profundity of the pentateuchal materials was given by revelation and inspiration through Moses in conjunction with tradition(s) available in that day and is not to be leveled to ancient Near Eastern concepts, nor seen as an outgrowth of ancient Near Eastern culture. The constitutive nature of the message of God through Moses to Israel means that the Pentateuch in its essential content (perhaps not final form) is early as a whole, not late. According to what we know about ancient Near Eastern literary composition, Moses could have written much of the material himself, but just as likely he could have dictated much of it to scribes or he could have supervised the compositional process as numerous hands utilized various materials (see below).

The inner-biblical tradition asserts that Moses wrote (e.g., Ex. 17:14; 20:21-23; 24:4-8; Nu. 33:1f.; Dt. 1:6–4:40; 5–26), that he spoke extensively, and that sometimes he orally disseminated what he wrote (Dt. 31:9-11, 19, 30, 32). It is clear that he composed various types of material: law, poetry, and prose narrative. According to ancient biblical tradition he was a highly gifted and well-trained man (Ex. 1–12; cf. *NBD, s.v.* "Moses"). Significant literary activity is predicated of Moses; however, the Pentateuch as a whole is anonymous. Any theories about the origin and subsequent composition and development of the Pentateuch must remain theories open to future adjustment and change. Indeed, only since the early 1960's has real progress been made in understanding authorship in the ancient Near East and how books were put together.

While these materials have been listed it must be noted that Moses' exact relationship to the material in its *final form* is difficult to determine, and conservative scholars differ, and rightly so, on such a hard issue. It is indeed necessary that Moses be the one in whom and through whom God worked as Scripture attests, but it is sufficient to affirm that an inspired writer and *possibly* not Moses was privileged to write down the Mosaic traditions along with many other ancient traditions. The unit of revelation in the OT is indeed the divinely inspired interpreted event (H. W. Robinson, *Inspiration and Revelation in the OT* [1946]). Inner-biblical tradition sufficiently attributes to Moses writing and other activity such that without him there would be no Pentateuch. Several possible relations between the total Pentateuch have been affirmed by conservative scholars, and some are noted below. Demonstrably the integrity and authority of the Pentateuch are maintained and unimpaired.

*5. Representative Positions.* Several conservative positions on the date of the individual books of the Pentateuch and the Pentateuch as a whole have been offered recently, and each synthesis should receive a hearing. Although the possibilities for the final date of the Pentateuch range rather widely, nearly all agree that the final date of the whole work is not nearly so important as the date, origin, and historicity of its contents. Its authoritative theological canonical function is not contested.

Certain general positions about the final form of the Pentateuch are discernible: (1) Those who give the Pentateuch a date in the Mosaic era, but allow for varying degrees of post-Mosaica. Extensive reference is made to the use of ancient Near Eastern control material and the presence of material already ancient to Moses is allowed in varying degrees. R. K. Harrison, K. A. Kitchen, and others represent this position. Harrison's approach views the Pentateuch holistically as an intimately integrated body of material subject to growth and development during the Mosaic era. He avoids extremes (e.g., Moses did not exist; Moses wrote every syllable of the Pentateuch). He notes that men capable of producing a literary work such as the Pentateuch were present in Egypt. He credits Moses with the bulk of the materials specifically attributed to him, noting that Moses may have dictated some of this material. It is an open question as to how many laws of the Pentateuch are original with Moses and how many are a product of Israel's pre-Settlement history. Priests helped preserve parts of the text and these materials were put together later. The laws must be seen as dynamic, not static (cf. Nu. 26:28-36; 27:1-11; 36:1-9). Josh. 24:26 shows that later additions were made to the text. Final unity was achieved by Moses or a compiler. Alteration and addition could occur later, a common ancient Near Eastern literary procedure. Editorial activities resulted in explanatory glosses, linguistic changes, etc. in accordance again with recognized ancient Near Eastern practices. The whole in virtually its final form was complete by Samuel's day. K. A. Kitchen suggested that the consonantal text of the Pentateuch existed almost in its present form soon after the death of Moses (notes on "Lectures on Pentateuchal Studies" [n.d.], p. 49). Minor revisions were made later (Gen. 36:31b; Dt. 34:10-12). Orthographical changes took place also. Hence from *ca.* 1200 B.C. the books constituting the Pentateuch existed. Many conservative scholars follow this approach to pentateuchal issues.

(2) Those who hold that most of the material in the Pentateuch is Mosaic and goes back to Moses as "author" defined in ancient Near Eastern terms, but believe that the final form of the Pentateuch is later than Moses and includes substantial amounts of post-Mosaica. *Terminus ad quem* dates range from the time of Joshua to generally the time of Solomon. Ancient pre-Mosaica, post-Mosaica, and later editorial activity are allowed.

M. H. Segal, a Jewish scholar, holds that it is clear that a critical examination of the Pentateuch will conclude that Mosaic authorship is not a viable position for the whole Pentateuch. Considerable parts explain, supplement, and even develop older material. He believes, however, that "the traditional claim of the Mosaic authorship should become the basis of a new study of the problem" (p. 25). These materials are not mere literary inventions, but coming from the Oral Torah they are Mosaic traditions recorded by inspired authors.

G. C. Aalders allows for the material specifically attributed to Moses, but also notes that probably most of the legal material of Exodus, Leviticus, Numbers, and Deuteronomy goes back to Moses as author (p. 151). The present form of these books indicate both post-Mosaica and a-Mosaica. The third-person portions probably were organized by a later hand (cf. Harrison and Kitchen). He allows a "greater freedom in the part of the compiler in dealing with the Mosaic material" (p. 152). Ex. 15 may or may not be Mosaic. The pre-Mosaic material in Genesis does not claim Mosaic authorship, and various sources were used to compose Genesis (cf. Wright, Wiseman, Naville, Kidner). Gen. 14 appears to be a non-Israelite source. The entire antediluvian history (Gen. 1–6) was probably written during the sojourn in Egypt or earlier. Several post-Mosaic documents are noted by Aalders (Book of the Wars of the Lord, Nu. 21:14f., 17f., 27-30; Balaam oracles, Nu. 23–24). The final revision of the Pentateuch was in the early years of David's reign. The final statement to be made about the Pentateuch is that God is its ultimate and true author.

(3) Those who date the final form fairly late (9th-7th cents.), but recognize genuine ancient traditions in the composition of the Pentateuch. Pre-Mosaica, post-Mosaica, editorial comment, and additions are suggested, but the original constitutive dimension of the Pentateuch for Israel's faith at an early stage is not lost. J. A. Thompson (*Deuteronomy*), while holding that a substantial part of Deuteronomy stems from long before the 7th cent., brought out the important point that it was probably necessary for a "representation" of the words of Moses at important key moments in Israel's history. The final form, therefore, of Deuteronomy and of the Pentateuch could stem from as late as the 7th cent. B.C., although its essential form came from a time during the united monarchy (pp. 67f.).

F. Bush finds several formative periods for the Pentateuch (LaSor, Hubbard, Bush, pp. 54-67). He mentions the period of slavery in Egypt as a likely time when the patriarchal stories were preserved orally. They were later written down during the Mosaic period. The events of the Exodus and the wilderness wanderings were recorded in writing during the early monarchy. The final form of the Pentateuch stems from the time of Ezra in the 5th cent. B.C. Ultimately, however, it is not the date of the Pentateuch as we have it that is of most significance, but the final product, which, early or late, embodies God's inspired word and ancient traditions from pre-Mosaic to post-Mosaic times.

More scholars representative of these three basic stances could be discussed (Wiseman, Kidner, Wright, Goldingay, Wenham, Cole, Livingston, Hamilton, *et al.*), but enough has been said to indicate some of the vital agreements among conservative scholars about pentateuchal issues and also to note some important disagreements. Although no new synthesis or a conservative consensus on all pentateuchal issues has arisen, it appears that conservative beginnings in this area are promising. The alternative positions being proffered — critical attempts to achieve a cogent replacement for the outdated and inaccurate twentieth-century modification of the Graf-Wellhausen hypothesis — are weak. Some rapprochement between conservative and liberal scholars is discernible. Generally speaking, conservative work has been even more fruitful in the study of the individual books of the Pentateuch (see bibliography below; *see also* GENESIS; EXODUS, BOOK OF; LEVITICUS; NUMBERS, BOOK OF; DEUTERONOMY; MOSES; TEXT AND MSS OF THE OT; CRITICISM). When these various excellent positions concerning the individual books of the Pentateuch can be synthesized, a more worthy conservative working hypothesis for pentateuchal studies will be achieved.

***Bibliography.***–*Introductions:* G. C. Aalders, *Short Intro. to the Pentateuch* (Eng. tr. 1949); W. W. Baudissin (1901); B. S. Childs (1979); S. R. Driver (repr. 1972); O. Eissfeldt (Eng. tr. 1965); R. K. Harrison (1969); A. Kuenen (1890); W. S. LaSor, D. Hubbard, and F. Bush (1982); R. Pfeiffer, *PIOT*; A. Robert and A. Feuillet (Eng. tr. 1968); E. Sellin and G. Fohrer (Eng. tr. 1968); E. J. Young (rev. ed. 1964).

*Commentaries:* U. Cassuto, *Comm. on the Book of Genesis* (Eng. tr. 1961); *Comm. on the Book of Exodus* (Eng. tr. 1967); B. S. Childs, *Book of Exodus* (*OTL,* 1974); R. Cole, *Exodus* (*Tyndale OT Comms.,* 1973); P. C. Craigie, *Book of Deuteronomy* (*NICOT,* 1976); F. Delitzsch, comm. on Genesis (Eng. tr. 1888); A. Dillmann, *Die Bücher Numeri, Deuteronomium, und Josua* (*Kurzgefasstes exegetisches Handbuch zum AT,* 1886); H. Gunkel, *Genesis* (5th ed. 1922); R. K. Harrison, *Leviticus* (*Tyndale OT Comms.,* 1980); D. Kidner, *Genesis* (*Tyndale OT Comms.,* 1967); Moses ben Nahman, *Comm. on the Torah* (Eng. tr. 1971-76); M. Noth, *Exodus* (Eng. tr., *OTL,* 1962); *Leviticus* (Eng. tr., *OTL,* 1977); *Numbers* (Eng. tr., *OTL,* 1968); G. von Rad, *Genesis* (Eng. tr., *OTL,* rev. ed. 1973); *Deuteronomy* (Eng. tr., *OTL,* 1966); J. A. Thompson, *Deuteronomy* (*Tyndale OT Comms.,* 1974); G. Wenham, *Book of Leviticus* (*NICOT,* 1979); *Numbers* (*Tyndale OT Comms.,* 1981).

*Other Studies:* W. F. Albright, *ARI*; *FSAC*; A. Alt, *Essays on OT History and Religion* (Eng. tr. 1966); G. W. Anderson, ed., *Tradition and Interpretation* (1979); A. G. Auld, *Expos. T.,* 91 (1980), 297-302; J. J. Bimson, *Redating the Exodus and Conquest* (1978); J. Bright, *BHI* (3rd ed. 1981); W. Brueggemann and H. W. Wolff, *Vitality of OT Traditions* (1975); U. Cassuto, *Documentary Hypothesis and the Composition of the Pentateuch* (Eng. tr. 1961); B. S. Childs, *Myth and Reality in the OT* (*SBT,* 1/27, 1960); R. E. Clements, *God's Chosen People: A Theological Interpretation of the Book of Deuteronomy* (1968); "Pentateuchal Problems," in Anderson, ed., *Tradition and Interpretation,* pp. 96-124; D. Clines, *Theme of the Pentateuch* (1978); F. M. Cross, *Canaanite Myth and Hebrew Epic* (1973); B. D. Eerdmans, *Alttestamentliche Studien* (4 vols. 1908-1912); O. Eissfeldt, *Hexateuch-Synopse* (1922); I. Engnell, *Gamla Testamentet* (1945); J. Goldingay, "Patriarchs in History and Scripture," in Millard and Wiseman, eds., *Essays on the Patriarchal Narratives,* pp. 11-42; C. Gordon, *Ancient Near East* (3rd ed. 1965); K. H. Graf, *Die geschichtlichen Bücher des AT* (1865); "Die sogenannte Grundschrift des Pentateuchs," in A. Merx, ed., *Archiv für wissenschaftliche Erforschung des AT,* I (1869), 466-477; W. H. Green, *Higher Criticism of the Pentateuch* (1895, repr. 1978); *Unity of Genesis* (1895, repr. 1979); H. F. Hahn, *OT and Modern Research* (1966); V. P. Hamilton, *Handbook on the Pentateuch* (1982); E. W. Hengstenberg, *Dissertations on the Genuineness of the Pentateuch* (Eng. tr., 2 vols., 1847); G. Hölscher, *ZAW,* 40 (1922), 161-255; A. Hurvitz, *RB,* 81 (1974); 24-65; Y. Kaufmann, *Biblical Account of the Conquest of Palestine* (Eng. tr. 1953); *Religion of Israel* (Eng. tr. 1961); K. Kenyon, *Archaeology in the Holy Land* (4th ed. 1979); K. A. Kitchen, *Ancient Orient and OT* (1967); *Bible in Its World* (1977); G. Kittel, *History of the Hebrews* (Eng. tr., 2 vols., 1895-96); A. Klostermann, *Der Pentateuch* (1893); A. Kuenen, *Religion of Israel* (Eng. tr., 3 vols., 1874-75); M. G. Kyle, *Problem of the Pentateuch* (1920); G. H. Livingston, *The Pentateuch in Its Cultural Environment* (1974); W. J. Martin, *Stylistic Criteria and the Analysis of the Pentateuch* (1955); D. J. McCarthy, *Treaty and Covenant* (rev. ed. 1978); A. R. Millard and D. J. Wiseman, eds., *Essays on the Patriarchal Narratives* (1980); W. Möller, *Wider den Bann der Quellenscheidung* (1912); E. Naville, *Higher Criticism in Relation to the Pentateuch* (1923); E. Nielsen, *Oral Tradition* (*SBT,* 1/11, 1954); T. Nöldeke, *Untersuchungen zur Kritik des AT* (1869); C. R. North, "Pentateuchal Criticism," in *OTMS,* pp. 48-83; M. Noth, *Deuteronomistic History* (Eng. tr. 1981); *History of Pentateuchal Traditions* (Eng. tr., repr. 1981); *Laws in the Pentateuch and Other Studies* (Eng. tr. 1966); *Überlieferungsgeschichte des Pentateuchs* (1948); J. Orr, *Problem of the OT* (1906); J. Pedersen, *ZAW,* 49 (1931), 161-181; *ILC*; G. von Rad, *Die Priesterschrift im Hexateuch* (1934); *Problem of the Hexateuch and Other Essays* (Eng. tr. 1966); *Studies in Deuteronomy* (Eng. tr., *SBT,* 1/9, 1951); R. Rendtorff, *Das überlieferungsgeschichtliche Problem des Pentateuchs* (*BZAW,* 142, 1977); H. H. Rowley, *From Moses to Qumran* (1963); *OTMS*; M. H. Segal, *Pentateuch* (Eng. tr. 1967); M. J. Selman, *Themelios,* 3 (1977), 9-16; R. Smend, *Die Erzählung des Hexateuchs auf ihre Quellen untersucht* (1912); W. R. Smith, *OT in the Jewish Church* (1881); *Religion of the Semites* (repr. 1972); E. Speiser, *Oriental and Biblical Studies* (1967); R. J. Thompson, *Moses and the Law in a Century of Criticism since Graf* (*SVT,* 19, 1970); T. L. Thompson, *Historicity of the Patriarchal Narratives* (*BZAW,* 133, 1974); J. H. Tigay, *JBL,* 94 (1975), 329-342; J. Van Seters, *Abraham in History and Tradition* (1975); R. de Vaux, *Ancient Israel* (Eng. tr. 1961); *Bible and the Ancient Near East* (Eng. tr. 1972); *Early History of Israel* (Eng. tr. 1978); J. Wellhausen, *Prolegomena to the History of Ancient Israel* (Eng. tr., repr. 1957); *Die Komposition des Hexateuchs* (1879); J. W. Wenham, "Moses and the Pentateuch," in *NBC* (rev. ed. 1970), pp. 41-43; G. E. Wright, *WBA*; *BANE*.

E. E. CARPENTER

**PENTATEUCH, SAMARITAN.** The Scripture of the Samaritan sect.

I. Outline of Samaritan History
II. Origins of the Samaritan Pentateuch
III. Knowledge of the Samaritan Pentateuch
IV. The Nâblus Scroll

V. Character of the Samaritan Pentateuch
VI. Qumrân and the Samaritan Pentateuch
VII. Conclusion

*I. Outline of Samaritan History.*–The Samaritan community that has existed in Nâblus for many centuries seems to have originated after the conquest of Samaria by Sargon II in 722 B.C. That Assyrian monarch made the area around Samaria into the province of Samerena and repopulated it by replacing the Israelites taken captive to Babylonia with people from Cuthah, Avva, Babylon, Hamath, and Sepharvaim who were loyal to the Assyrian regime (2 K. 17:24). These and later deportees (Ezr. 4:2,10) intermarried with the surviving Israelites and adopted their faith syncretistically (2 K. 17:32f.), being instructed by a Hebrew priest sent back to Bethel by Esarhaddon for that purpose.

These descendants of the Mesopotamian expatriates became known as Samaritans, after the territory that they occupied. These people claimed kinship with the Jews, but the Jews repudiated the relationship as coincidental, regarding the Samaritans as little better than Gentiles. Yet the Jews could not dismiss conclusively the principal thing that they shared: the Torah with the cultic enactments based upon its prescriptions. And when the successors of ancient Judah ultimately succumbed to the Romans in A.D. 70, the Samaritans, whose own existence had been turbulent, survived as a community and to this day celebrate the Passover in Nâblus according to the rites laid down in the Pentateuch. Their most precious cultic possession is a Torah scroll, written in Paleo-Hebrew characters, for which they claim great antiquity.

*II. Origins of the Samaritan Pentateuch.*–On purely historical grounds, the Samaritans and their copy of the Torah (presumably brought from Babylonia at the time of Esarhaddon) could not have existed as a cultic unit before *ca.* 720 B.C. Samaritan traditions deny this late date, however, claiming instead that they originated from those Israelites who had remained loyal to the location prescribed by Moses, Mt. Ebal (cf. Dt. 27:4), when the rest of the nation had adopted the rival site at Shiloh where the ark had been deposited (Jgs. 18:1). The Samaritans gained some archeological support in 1983 when A. Zartel unearthed a large stone altar in a compound on Mt. Ebal that was filled with ashes and sheep bones dated to the 12th cent. B.C. Whether this is the altar of Josh. 8:30 cannot be determined with certainty, but Zartel assigned it to the period of Joshua with great probability, since no other sites dating to the biblical period have been found on Mt. Ebal. Without question the location was a ritual site of great importance and unique in character.

In this connection it is noteworthy that the shrine on Mt. Ebal was the only one built according to Moses' instructions and that the great Hebrew lawgiver clearly did intend that the nation's worship be centered on the Ebal/Gerizim area (cf. Dt. 27:4; Josh. 8:30-35) and not on Jerusalem, which was a Jebusite stronghold until David's time (cf. C. H. Gordon, *Intro. to OT Times* [1953], pp. 132f. [=*World of the OT* (1958), p. 146]; J. Macdonald, *Theology of the Samaritans* [1964], p. 17).

The Samaritans claim similar antiquity for their Pentateuch, regarding it as having originated with Abishua, the great-grandson of Aaron (1 Ch. 6:3f.). While this claim is obviously exaggerated, the canon of the Samaritan Pentateuch was indeed in existence long before the schism promoted by Nehemiah (444 B.C.), since it constituted the sole scriptural material of the community both before and after that time (Roberts, p. 188). The highly conservative nature of the Samaritans guaranteed the transmission of their scriptural text in a form only slightly different from the original and governed by procedures that will be mentioned below. Thus the Samaritan Pentateuch is an important witness to one of the very ancient text-forms of the Hebrew Pentateuch that was current at least as early as the 5th cent. B.C. and that could even reach back to the period of the Hebrew monarchy.

*III. Knowledge of the Samaritan Pentateuch.*–Of the Greek fathers, Origen knew of it and noted two insertions that do not appear in the MT, Nu. 13:1 and 21:12, drawn from Dt. 1:2 and 2:18. Eusebius of Caesarea in his *Chronicon* (J. Karst, ed., *Die griechischen Christlichen Schriftsteller, Eusebius Werke,* V [1911], 40) compared the ages of the patriarchs before Abraham given in the LXX with those given in the Samaritan Pentateuch and the MT. Epiphanius was aware that the Samaritans acknowledged the Pentateuch alone as canonical. Cyril of Jerusalem noted agreement of the LXX and the Samaritan Pentateuch in Gen. 4:8. These are the principal evidences of knowledge of the Samaritan Pentateuch among the Greek fathers. Jerome noted some omissions in the MT and supplied them from the Samaritan Pentateuch. The Talmud shows that the Jews retained a knowledge of the Samaritan Pentateuch longer than Christians, and speaks contemptuously of the points in which it differs from the MT. Since the differences observed by the fathers and the Talmudists are to be seen in the present form of the Samaritan Pentateuch, they afford evidence of authenticity of that form.

After nearly a millennium of oblivion the Samaritan Pentateuch was restored to the knowledge of Christendom by Pietro de la Valle, who in 1616 purchased a copy from the Samaritan community that then existed in Damascus. This copy was presented in 1623 to the Paris Oratory and shortly after published in the *Paris Polyglot* under the editorship of Morinus, a priest of the Oratory who had been a Protestant. He emphasized the difference between the MT and the Samaritan Pentateuch in order to prove the need for the Church to decide which texts are Scripture. A fierce controversy resulted, in which various Protestant and Catholic clergymen took part.

Now many copies of the Samaritan Pentateuch can be found in Europe and America. All of them may be regarded as copies ultimately of some Nâblus prototype, though not necessarily of the Abisha scroll. These copies are in the form not of rolls but of codices or bound volumes. They are usually written in two columns to the page, one column being the Targum or interpretation, which is sometimes in Aramaic and sometimes in Arabic. Some codices show three columns with both Targums. Probably nearly 100 of these codices are in various libraries of Europe and America. They are all written in the Samaritan script and differ only by scribal blunders.

*IV. The Nâblus Scroll.*–This ornate (Abisha) scroll has been described as being made "of parchment, written in columns, 13 in. deep, and 7½ in. wide. The writing is in a fair hand, rather small; each column contains from 70 to 72 lines, and the whole roll contains 110 columns. The name of the scribe is written in a kind of acrostic, running through these columns, and is found in the Book of Dt. The roll has the appearance of very great antiquity, but is wonderfully well preserved, considering its venerable age. It is worn out and torn in many places and patched with re-written parchment; in many other places, where not torn, the writing is unreadable. The skins of which the roll is composed are of equal length and measure each 25 in. long by 15 in. wide " (J. Mills, *Three Months' Residence at Nablus, and an Account of the Modern Samaritans*

[1864], p. 382). The parchment has been written only on the hair side, and the roll is preserved in an elaborately decorated silk case. The genuineness of the Abisha scroll was questioned from the time of G. Genenius's study (*De Pentateuchi Samaritani origine, indole et auctoritate* [1815]), which demonstrated the superiority of the MT in a rather sweeping manner that has necessitated a subsequent modifying of some of the original conclusions. P. Kahle regarded the manuscript as mixed in character, combining ancient elements with fourteenth-century ones. A Samaritan Pentateuch manuscript from the 7th cent. formed part of the *Paris Polyglot* (1632) and Walton's *London Polyglot* (1675), whereas A. F. Von Gall's five-volume edition *(Der hebräische Pentateuch der Samaritaner* [1914-1918]) drew largely on medieval manuscripts. Studies of photographs of the Abisha scroll have supported the great antiquity of the text (R. E. Moody, *Boston University Graduate Journal,* 10 [1957], 158-160).

***V. Character of the Samaritan Pentateuch.***–The script is different from the square "Aramaic" characters of a modern Hebrew Bible, being instead a primitive type of rounded script formerly described as Phoenician. This divergence from the early *ʿiḇri* letters enabled hostile Jews of a later period to recognize the uncultured origins of the Samaritans for what they really were (T. B. *Sanhedrin* 21b). Political and religious considerations apart, however, the style of the Samaritan Pentateuch's lettering is a form of Paleo-Hebrew, and the various extant manuscripts make it clear that this ancient version had its own developed vocalization and an unusual type of paragraph division (cf. E. Robertson, *Catalogue of the Samaritan Manuscripts in the John Rylands Library at Manchester* [1938], cols. xxi-xxii: *Notes and Extracts from the Semitic Manuscripts in the John Rylands Library, III, Samaritan Pentateuch Manuscripts* [1937]).

Extracts from Dt. 6:4; 23:15; 28:6 in Samaritan script. From a limestone block that perhaps stood in a doorway (like a mezuzah). From Nâblus, 13th cent. A.D. (Trustees of the British Museum)

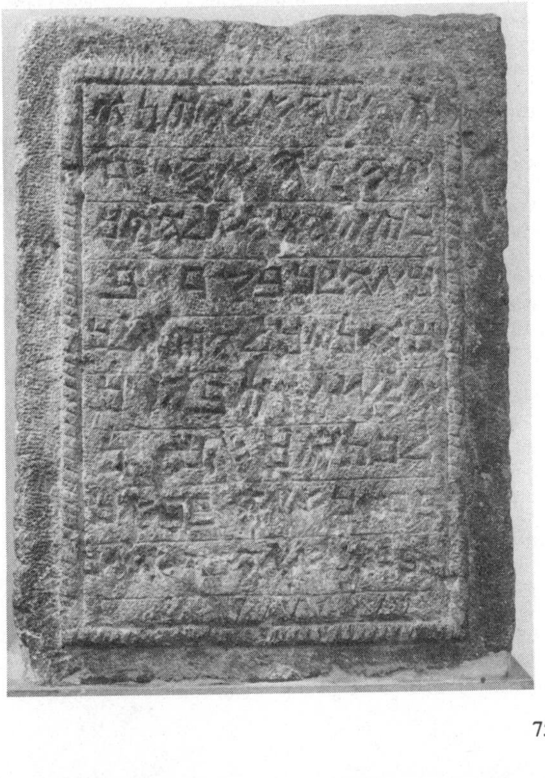

The way in which the Samaritan Pentateuch differs textually from the MT suggests that the Samaritans did not have a body of professional scribes such as the *sōp̄erîm* of the Hebrews. The Samaritan Pentateuch has an estimated 6000 textual variants from the MT, and in 1900 instances it agrees with the LXX (P. Kahle, *Theologische Studien und Kritiken,* 88 [1915], 399-439; cf. A. Sperber, *HUCA,* 14 [1939], 161-249.) While some Samaritan Pentateuch readings appear to be genuine variants, perhaps representing an early divergent tradition of the MT, others reflect Samaritan doctrinaire tendencies, e.g., the stress on the sanctity of Mt. Gerizim. Thus a slightly modified form of Dt. 27:4, in which that mountain was substituted for Mt. Ebal, is inserted in the text of Gen. 20. In Nu. 25:4f. the Samaritan Pentateuch harmonizes the command of the Lord with the actions of Moses, so as to remove any possible conflict. Probably in the interests of propriety, the Samaritan Pentateuch changed the text of Gen. 50:23 from *ʿal-birkê yôsēp* ("born upon Joseph's knees" [RSV]) to *bîmê yōsêp* ("born in the days of Joseph"). Again, in Dt. 25:11, the Samaritan Pentateuch read a euphemism (*bᵉśārô,* "his flesh") instead of the more explicit MT *mᵉḇušāyw* ("his genitals"). Many changes are orthographic, with the style of the Samaritan Pentateuch exhibiting a fuller spelling than the MT, as is characteristic of the Chronicler as well as of the later Hasmonean period. Early Hebrew used the letter *he* for a final long *ô* of the third masculine singular pronominal suffix as in Gen. 9:21, where the MT has *ʾhlh* but the Samaritan Pentateuch reads *ʾhlw*. The use of *scriptio plene* ("full spelling") writing occurred more consistently in the Samaritan Pentateuch than in the MT. In morphology, the short form of the imperfect verb with *waw*-consecutive was replaced in the Samaritan Pentateuch with the long form of the imperfect. Occasionally the *waw*-consecutive-and-the-perfect of the MT was replaced in the Samaritan Pentateuch by the *waw*-conjunctive and the normal verb form. Another morphological procedure was to replace the infinitive absolute of the verb with an imperative or a finite verb form, thus reversing a grammatical trend familiar in the Amarna Age. At various points in the tradition the scribes glossed the text to obtain greater clarity by such devices as inserting subjects, appositives, prepositions, and particles, and at the same time removed discrepancies in syntax. In common with the scribes of other ancient Near Eastern nations, the Samaritans modernized their Scriptures by replacing archaic Hebrew forms with constructions and terminology of a later period. Accordingly, it must be remembered that a "Hasmonean" form in the Samaritan Pentateuch need not be regarded as original, and thus an argument for a late date of the version, but merely as an item of scribal revision, and therefore only an indication of the date of the particular recension in which it occurs. As in other ancient manuscripts, there are some variants that appear to be the result of a scribe confusing letters that look alike in the Samaritan and Hebrew scripts used in more recent times. But in Ex. 1:11, where the Samaritan Pentateuch reads *piṯōn* for MT *piṯōm,* the confusion may well have arisen if the scribe of the Samaritan Pentateuch was copying from a Torah scroll written in the ancient angular script of the Siloam inscription (*ca.* 701 B.C.), in which *m* and *n* are very similar in form.

Some scholars have adopted a date as late as the 1st cent. B.C. (W. F. Albright, *FSAC,* pp. 345f.; F. M. Cross, *Ancient Library of Qumran and Modern Biblical Studies* [2nd ed. 1961], p. 172) for the origin of the Samaritan recension and its archaizing script, but M. Greenberg (*JAOS,* 76 [1956], pp. 161-63) and others have opted for a date in the 4th cent. B.C. The late date for the Samaritan Pentateuch as a sectarian recension is based partly on paleographic evidence that suggests that in the Hasmonean period there began a separation of the paleo-Hebrew script into branches, one of which was the archetype of the Samaritan script (F. M. Cross, "Development of the Jewish Scripts," in *BANE,* pp. 133-202, esp. 189 n. 4). Additional support is thought to be found in the argument that the Samaritan Pentateuch, like the Hasmonean-era Dead Sea Scrolls, exhibited such orthographic features as the full use of the *matres lectionis,* but as has been observed above, this was also a feature of the Chronicler's orthography. Such Samaritan Pentateuchal peculiarities as the use of *aleph* as an additional *mater lectionis* for *ā,* the abbreviated spelling of certain suffixes and pronouns, the general omission of the *he locale,* and the use of the so-called "pseudo-cohortative" form are more consistent with a scribal modernizing of the text in Hasmonean times than the creation of a new sectarian document at that late date.

In fact, there is a sense in which the Samaritan Pentateuch was sectarian in nature from its inception. Scholars should consider its origins rather than late recensions. Thus, to compare the oldest extant examples of Samaritan lapidary inscriptions with what appears on the surface of coins of the Hasmonean period, as Albright did in an attempt to establish the "lateness" of the Samaritan sectarian recension (*FSAC,* pp. 345f., n. 12), is surely misguided. Inscriptions engraved on durable material, whether stone or the surface of a die, demand by the very nature of that material a different approach to the reproduction of the inscribed symbols than would be the case for a record of events made on a papyrus or leather surface, where a much more flexible scribal technique is possible. A better approach would be to abandon evidence that is patently late and concentrate instead upon comparing the Samaritan script with that of the 5th cent. B.C. Aramaic papyri from Elephantine, the Siloam Inscription, or even the Lachish Letters (*ca.* 590 B.C.), rather than with the more stylized Hasmonean lapidary materials. In view of the suggestion that the Samaritan recension was written in an archaized script, a practice also employed at Qumrân, it should be remembered that the Samaritan scribes did not need to "archaize" the script used because their tradition knew of no other form, unlike the MT, which moved from Paleo-Hebrew to the square "Aramaic" characters.

The simplest explanation of the provenance of the Samaritan Pentateuch is that the Samaritans took over a text that was already in existence and put their own distinctive imprint upon it, as indicated by the sectarian and other readings. That text seems to have been Palestinian in origin rather than Egyptian (as was the case with the LXX), but it was closely related to both the MT and the LXX. It is quite possible that it was dependent upon or influenced by one of the textual types that underlay the LXX. In any event, the circumstances that marked the history of the Samaritan sect point to an early rather than a late period for the characteristic alterations in the Samaritan Pentateuch.

Contrary to the view of some scholars, there is no evidence that the Samaritans first acquired a copy of the Torah as a consequence of the altercation between Nehemiah and one of the sons of Joiada (Neh. 13:28). By 300 B.C. Ben Sira was making sarcastic comments about the Shechemites (Sir. 50:26), and in the Hasmonean period relations between Samaritans and Jews had become so embittered, especially after John Hyrcanus destroyed the Samaritan temple on Mt. Gerizim (Josephus *Ant.* xiii.9.1 [256]; *BJ* 1.2.6 [63]) in 128 B.C., that contact between the two peoples at a religious level for the purpose of making a "Samaritan sectarian recension" would have been unthinkable. It is equally difficult to imagine the Samaritans preserving the entire Torah in oral form until a late period of their history, and the attempt to date their recension toward the beginning of the 1st cent. B.C. appears to be an accommodation to the more extreme form of the Graf-Wellhausen hypothesis, which would have the Pentateuch appearing in its final redaction about 200 B.C. But if the Torah was in substantially its present state by the early monarchy, as conservative scholars frequently maintain, there is no reason why a copy of the Law could not have been circulating among the expatriates at Samaria in the days of Esarhaddon, particularly if a priest from the captivity instructed the Samaritans in the ancient Hebrew law from such a scroll. Orthographic considerations also suggest an earlier rather than a later time of origin for the Samaritan recension, if only because some scribal variations seem best explained by the copying into Samaritan script of a Hebrew Torah already extant in a script similar to that of the Siloam Inscription. Indeed, the Samaritan alphabet seems to be only a slightly more developed form of the Hebrew script current in the days of Hezekiah (716-686 B.C.), which would be sufficiently archaic for all normal scribal purposes. Thus the view that the Samaritan sectarian recension was made in an archaized script resurgent about 110 B.C., as J. D. Purvis (*Samaritan Pentateuch and the Origin of the Samaritan Sect* [1968], pp. 16-87) and others have suggested, is beset by great difficulties.

***VI. Qumrân and the Samaritan Pentateuch.***–From the fourth cave came many fragments of an early recension of Exodus, designated 4QEx[a]. P. W. Skehan (*JBL,* 74, [1955], 182-87) stated that they bore a clear relationship to the Samaritan Pentateuch, being written in a form of script antecedent to that found in the Abisha Scroll and other copies of the Samaritan Pentateuch. In addition, the Qumrân fragments of Exodus exhibited the same peculiarities as the corresponding Samaritan Pentateuchal text. Skehan indicated that 4QEx[a] attested to the antiquity of the Samaritan textual tradition and its constancy of transmission, but did not assert the priority of the Samaritan Pentateuchal text over its Hebrew counterpart. It has therefore been conjectured that the fragments probably formed part of a first-century B.C. private collection that was incorporated into the Qumrân library. Were this the case, it would indicate that the Samaritan Pentateuch enjoyed with the MT a correspondingly long period of textual transmission, and that if copies of the Samaritan Pentateuch were extant in the 1st cent. B.C. the autograph must of necessity have originated very much earlier, as is also the case with the book of Isaiah (*see* ISAIAH VIII.F). Again the fragments raise the question about why any scribe would desire to "archaize" deliberately a recension of the Samaritan Pentateuch when there was already at least one in circulation in 110 B.C., which was extant in an even older type of script.

***VII. Conclusion.***–The Samaritan Pentateuch embodies an ancient text that has been updated periodically in accordance with the generally accepted canons of scribal practice in the ancient Near East. When the Samaritan Pentateuch agrees with the LXX against the MT, both testify to the existence of a pentateuchal recension going back at the very least to the 5th cent. B.C. Even this source had undergone scribal revisions in process of transmission, making for a very venerable archetype. While the Samaritan Pentateuch, when used in conjunction with the LXX, can furnish useful information in an attempt to restore an "original text," the readings of the Samaritan Pentateuch must be evaluated with great care if improvements upon the MT are being sought, since it tends in any case to demonstrate the purity of the MT. Most of all, the value of the Samaritan Pentateuch to the scholar is the manner in which it attests to the antiquity and textual integrity of the Torah.

*See also* SAMARITANS.

***Bibliography.***–B. J. Roberts, *OT Text and Versions* (1951); F. G. Kenyon, *Our Bible and the Ancient Manuscripts* (rev. ed. 1958), esp. pp. 89-94; P. Kahle, *Cairo Geniza* (2nd ed. 1959); R. K. Harrison, *Intro. to the OT* (1969), pp. 220-26; B. K. Waltke, "Samaritan Pentatuch and the Text of the OT," in J. B. Payne, ed., *New Perspectives on the OT* (1970), pp. 212-239; in R. K. Harrison, *et al., Biblical Criticism: Historical, Literary and Textual* (1978), pp. 47-82.

J. E. H. THOMSON R. K. HARRISON

**PENTECOST** pent'ə-kost. Greek *pentekoste* means "fiftieth" and came to designate the fiftieth day after Passover. The OT does not use the term, but instead refers to the festival as the "feast of weeks" (Ex. 34:22). On this day the Church was born.

I. OT Roots
II. NT Witness
  A. Actual Event?
  B. Divine Visitation?
  C. Components
III. NT Exposition
  A. Peter's Exposition
  B. Salvation
  C. New Community
  D. Mission
  E. Spiritual Gifts
IV. Contemporary Judaism

***I. OT Roots.***–According to the Jewish calendar all males were obligated to appear before the Lord three times each year (Dt. 16:16). Pentecost was the second of these national festivals and took place fifty days or seven full weeks after Passover (vv. 9f.). It was designated the "feast of weeks" since it concluded the interval that began with the presentation of the first harvest sheaves, thereby marking the end of the grain harvest. It was celebrated with much joy, the cessation of hard work, and the ritual presentation of a "cereal offering of new grain" in the form of two loaves of leavened, salted bread (Lev. 23:16f.; Nu. 28:26) along with freewill offerings. It was also inevitably an occasion for covenant renewal. Year by year as the Israelites participated in this agrarian festival they gave thanks to Yahweh for showing His faithfulness by providing another harvest to sustain them through the coming year, and they thereby reaffirmed their covenant bond to Him. *See also* FEASTS.

***II. NT Witness.***–*A. Actual Event?* Was the outpouring of the Holy Spirit at Pentecost a historical event or merely a theological construction by Luke? Some have argued (e.g., Haenchen, pp. 172f.) that inasmuch as no uniform tradition existed about the coming of the Spirit (see Jn. 20:22), Luke contrived an implied correspondence between God's breathing life into man at Creation and His Spirit's creating the new man in Christ at Jerusalem. But the evidence is overwhelming that the Church began in Jerusalem shortly after Jesus' resurrection, and that the "pillar apostles" (Peter, James, and John), although Galileans (Acts 1:11; 2:7), assumed leadership of the Church in Jerusalem, not Galilee. The apostle Paul did not challenge this situation. Luke drew from a uniform tradition: something tremendous happened in Jerusalem that transformed the apostles into men of conviction and courage and provided them with a spiritual impetus that enabled the Christian movement to expand rapidly, so that in a few decades vital congregations were in all the major cities of the Roman Empire (Dunn, *Jesus*, pp. 138f.). The reality of Pentecost could not have been contrived: "This was not done in a corner" (Acts 26:26).

*B. Divine Visitation?* Critical scholars make much of the more striking features of Luke's account — wind, fire, and speaking in tongues — and regard them as theological constructions more than realities. Emotional tension and prolonged expectation have often precipitated communal visions. But there is no evidence that Luke was influenced by the burning bush or the Sinai traditions (Ex. 3:2; 19:18). What the disciples were looking for was "the Son of man coming in clouds of glory." Fire, wind, and speaking in tongues were totally unexpected; the event cannot be explained in psychological terms. As for the last phenomenon, the number of people who claim to have spoken in foreign languages and the testimony of those who have recognized their words must be considered. Although the contemporary phenomenon of glossolalia should not be equated with the unique miracle of Pentecost, there is sufficient overlap to establish the possibility, if not actuality, of the pentecostal event (Dunn, *Jesus*, p. 151).

*C. Components.* This pilgrimage feast of Israel gained new significance for Christians because it coincided with the birthday of the Church. On that day the Holy Spirit baptized 120 disciples of Jesus as they awaited His coming, doubtless in an upper room in the temple (Lk. 24:53). This event marked the climax of Jesus' ministry, for the sending forth of the Holy Spirit followed His ascension and thus fulfilled John the Baptist's ultimate prediction that the Messiah would baptize "with the Holy Spirit and with fire" (Mt. 3:11 par. Lk. 3:16) after He had become "the Lamb of God, who takes away the sin of the world" (Jn. 1:29). Although only 120 saw the vision and received this initial empowering, before that day ended 3000 were added to their number.

This gift of the Spirit to the people of God is not unlike divine visitations in the OT, with their signs of wind and fire (1 K. 18:38; 19:11-13; Ezk. 37:9-14). But it is distinctive in that its recipients both worshiped God and bore witness to Him in tongues (Acts 2:3f.), and there is the added miracle that many pilgrims in Jerusalem heard their witness "each . . . in his own language" (v. 6).

***III. NT Exposition.***–The day of Pentecost (Acts 2) marks the shifting of God's redemptive purpose from a particular people (the descendants of Abraham via Isaac and Jacob) to all peoples. On that day the Church was formed and empowered for its worldwide mission; the event thus marks the resumption of universal history, with which the Bible begins (Gen. 1–11). Accordingly, Pentecost has primary importance to all who are concerned with the nature and purpose of the Church, particularly its mandate to preach the gospel of the kingdom throughout the world as a witness to all nations; "and then the end will come" (Mt. 24:14).

*A. Peter's Exposition.* Fortunately, Peter's sermon on that day (Acts 2:14-36) has preserved the apostolic understanding of the event. Most significant is his stress not on the Holy Spirit but on Jesus Christ, not so much on His earthly ministry and crucifixion as on His resurrection and exaltation as Lord and Christ. Peter began with a refutation of the charge that the Spirit-filled apostolic community was acting in a disorderly fashion (vv. 15f.). He then quoted Joel 2:28-32 (MT 3:1-5) to indicate that Pentecost marks the beginning of the messianic age, the Day of the Lord, that is sure to come to glorious consummation in God's time (vv. 16-21). Peter's main concern was to focus attention on Jesus Christ: His humanity (v. 22), His death (v. 23), and His attestation as deity by "mighty works and wonders and signs" (v. 22), particularly His resurrection (vv. 24-36). Peter unabashedly used Ps. 16 (cf. Lk. 24:44) to establish David's prediction of the Resurrection. When his hearers came under conviction because of his charge that they had consciously participated in Jesus' condemnation, Peter called for repentance and, using the "keys of the kingdom" (Mt. 16:19), extended the promise of forgiveness and the gift of the Holy Spirit (Acts 2:37-40).

*B. Salvation.* Pentecost marks the completion of Christ's redemptive work. Following His resurrection He ascended into heaven and presented Himself as the first fruits of a coming harvest. On that occasion He took "into the Holy Place . . . his own blood, thus securing an eternal redemption" for His people (He. 9:12). In this sense Pentecost both consummates Easter and represents its fulness. When the Father accepted this sacrifice "for the sins of the whole world" (1 Jn. 2:2) and exalted Him on high, the Father and the Son together sent forth the Spirit — the gift of the new covenant. Pentecost thereby marks "a watershed in salvation history," the beginning of a new age under a new covenant. An analogy can be drawn between Jesus' baptism and anointing at the Jordan River and what the disciples experienced on that memorable day (Dunn, *Baptism,* p. 40).

*C. New Community.* At Pentecost the people of the new covenant were consolidated into a new body, which is the body of Christ, a messianic eschatological community, the Church. But a new religious institution was not extracted from the larger social order to become a self-sustaining, separated-unto-God community of faith. Rather, Pentecost marks the initial fulfilling of the prophetic vision of the uplifted temple in Zion, and the Torah's going forth from its innermost sanctuary as the message of God's mighty, redemptive act in reconciling the world to Himself (cf. Isa. 2:2f.; Mic. 4:1f. with Jn. 2:19f.; 12:32; 2 Cor. 5:19). In response the nations began to turn to Yahweh in repentance and faith. A new people of God was formed: the Church, consisting of Jews, proselytes, and "all that are far off, every one whom the Lord our God calls to him" (Acts 2:39).

The very essence and vitality of this new community were "integral and essential to its witness" (Kraus, p. 27). Their loving acceptance of one another and their selfless sharing (*koinōnía*) were nothing less than the universalization of Jesus' ministry by the Spirit in and through each member. All sensed His call to participate in the new social reality that He was sending forth into the world. All expressed their spiritual oneness by "devot[ing] themselves to the apostles' teaching and fellowship, to the breaking of bread [the eucharist] and the prayers" (Acts 2:42). Their love for one another enabled them to affirm their communal relationship "in Christ" by loving service "to all, as any had need" (v. 45).

*D. Mission.* After the Resurrection and before the coming of the Holy Spirit the apostles had been instructed about the kingdom of God (Acts 1:3). This instruction involved missionary obligation (v. 8) and included the promise that, being energized by the Spirit, they would become witnesses to the resurrected Christ. They would begin this witness in Jerusalem but would not stop until they reached "the end of the earth." Samaria was specifically identified as a reminder that all the fragmented human race must be reached, even those easily overlooked because of reputed cultural or religious inferiority (v. 8). The proclamation of Peter, "standing with the eleven," was the first expression of Christian obedience to this missionary task (2:14). "The first cry of life from the newborn Church was the proclamation that Jesus is the Lord of heaven and earth, as well as the Messiah of the Jews" (v. 36; Kraus, p. 26).

When Peter inaugurated the giving of a new Torah and a new day of salvation, in which men and women, young and old, could become new creatures in Christ (cf. Jer. 31:33; Ezk. 36:27; 2 Cor. 5:17), his intention was that they too might participate in the worldwide mission of the Church. Indeed, the manifestation of tongues in the presence of "devout men from every nation under heaven" (Acts 2:5) was an expression of God's universal redemptive purpose; Peter's appeal (vv. 38-40) marks the beginning of the Spirit's new work: "to gather into one the children of God who are scattered abroad" (Jn. 11:52). Inasmuch as the majority of those in Jerusalem could probably understand Aramaic or Greek, scholars have wondered about the need for this phenomenon. Can it be that God was thereby giving His Church a linguistic mandate: that each separate people should hear the gospel in its primary language — the one closest to the individual heart?

This phenomenon of tongues that were intelligible to people of diverse languages also underscores the Church's essential obligation to bear witness "by word and deed" (deeds need words of explanation, and words need deeds of confirmation; see, e.g., Jn. 5:36; Rom. 15:19). The subsequent coming of the Spirit upon the Roman centurion Cornelius and his household (Acts 10:44f.) and upon some remnants of John the Baptist's revival movement (19:1f.) is additional evidence of glossolalia.

It should be noted that the Spirit was not given just to enable the people of God to pursue personal holiness and enjoy corporate worship and fellowship. Indeed, those concerned with such dimensions of sanctification will not automatically serve their own generation according to the will of God unless they recognize that the Spirit was also given to energize corporate waiting on God for missionary outreach. Acts is replete with references to the Spirit's centrality in the evangelistic activity of the Church (4:8; 13:2; 15:28; 16:6; etc.). Thus the initial pentecostal event is to be distinguished from the subsequent infillings of the Holy Spirit when He came upon those who were missionary minded and empowered them to extend the knowledge of Jesus Christ beyond the frontiers of faith (e.g., 13:52–14:1).

All this adumbrates the worldwide missionary movement, which in turn reminds the Church of its eschatological hope in the coming of the kingdom and the final triumph of God in human history. Missionary outreach provides the divine reversal of the scattering and hostility of the nations that followed the judgment at Babel (Gen. 11:1-9). Once men and women of diverse backgrounds are "in Christ," they become "of one heart and soul" (Acts 4:32) — one family — the household of faith.

There has been considerable debate among scholars over the source of the apostles' missionary motivation: was it Jesus' resurrection appearances, the Great Commission, or their pentecostal experience? Actually, all three contributed. The impulse to witness arises from one's understanding of the nature of the Church and from the constraint of the risen Christ's love upon one's heart and life (2 Cor. 5:14f.). As Boer stated: "The descent of the Spirit at Pentecost made the disciples apostles, i.e., missionaries. One might say it branded them as apostles. The world-embracing missionary vision is expressed in prophetic reality in the speaking with tongues. At Pentecost the whole of God's redemptive purpose for the world was for a moment set off in bold relief" (p. 62).

*E. Spiritual Gifts.* Pentecost marks the beginning of the bestowal of spiritual gifts on all the redeemed so that each may participate in the life of Christ in the midst of the

Church and in the Church's witness to the nations. In this sense it represents God's answer to Moses' prayer: "Would that all the Lord's people were prophets, that the Lord would put His spirit upon them!" (Nu. 11:29). From Pentecost onward all Christians are to regard themselves as called to the full-time task of making Jesus Christ known, loved, and served throughout the world. All have been given spiritual gifts to make this service possible (1 Cor. 12:4f.). Each local congregation should covet the "higher gifts" that will enable it to become what God intends — a community of the Spirit in the midst of the nations, "a new social embodiment of the Spirit of Christ where everyday patterns of life together enhance the new order of the Spirit" (vv. 27f.; Kraus, p. 62). This mission will continue until the gospel has been preached to all nations. It uniquely represents "the sign of [Christ's] coming and of the close of the age" (Mt. 24:3).

*IV. Contemporary Judaism.*–In the years that followed the birth of the Church, particularly after the destruction of the second temple in A.D. 70, the Jewish community gradually transformed its understanding of the simple harvest festival of Pentecost into a commemoration of the giving of the law at Sinai, which is said to have occurred fifty days after the Passover that marked the Exodus from Egypt (Ex. 19:1). This change in emphasis was possibly a reaction to the Christian celebration of Pentecost, although there is some evidence that the association with the Sinaitic covenant is pre-Christian (Harrison, p. 53). In the English-speaking churches Pentecost is often called Whitsunday because it was a chief day for baptisms and the baptized were clothed in white.

***Bibliography.***–H. R. Boer, *Pentecost and Missions* (1961); F. F. Bruce, *Book of Acts* (*NICNT,* 1954); J. Dunn, *Baptism in the Holy Spirit* (*SBT,* 2/15, 1970); *Jesus and the Spirit* (1975); L. Goppelt, *Apostolic and Post-Apostolic Times* (Eng. tr. 1970); E. Haenchen, *Acts of the Apostles* (Eng. tr. 1971); E. F. Harrison, *Acts, the Expanding Church* (1975); C. N. Kraus, *Community of the Spirit* (1974); A. Schlatter, *Church in the NT Period* (Eng. tr. 1955); J. Weiss, *Earliest Christianity,* I (Eng. tr. 1959).

A. F. GLASSER

**PENUEL** pen-yo͞o'əl [Heb. *pᵉnû'ēl, pᵉnî'ēl* (*K,* 1 Ch. 8:25)].

**1.** The cognomen of a clan chief of Judah (1 Ch. 4:4) who was the father of Gedor.

**2.** The name of a Benjaminite who was one of the eleven sons of Shashak (1 Ch. 8:25). On the *K-Q* problem, see GKC, § 90K.

**PENUEL** pen-yo͞o'əl, **PENIEL** pə-nī'əl [Heb. *pᵉnû'ēl, pᵉnî'ēl*–'face of God' (Gen. 32:30); Gk. *eídos (toú) theoú*–'appearance of God' (Gen. 32:30f.), elsewhere *Phanouēl*]. The name that Jacob gave to a place in Transjordan where he wrestled with "a man" (Gen. 32:24-31), located on the Jabbok (Nahr ez-Zerqā) E of Succoth, near Mahanaim. When Gideon was pursuing the Midianites, he asked the men of Penuel for food, and they "answered him as the men of Succoth had answered." On his return, he destroyed the city (Jgs. 8:8f., 17). Possibly it lay in ruins until Jeroboam I "built" it (1 K. 12:25). The expression, however, may mean that Jeroboam strengthened its fortifications to make it an outer line of defense for his capital Shechem.

The name has been identified as #53 in Shishak's list (Aharoni, *LBHG,* p. 285), and may also be the Panili of Late Assyrian texts. Scholars have placed the site E of the twin mounds Tulûl edh-Dhahab, 6.8 km. (4.25 mi.) above Tell Deir ʿAllā (= Succoth?). Cf. *AASOR,* 18 (1939), 232-35.

W. S. L. S.

**PENURY.** *See* POVERTY.

**PEOPLE** [Heb. *ʿam, lᵉ'ōm* (e.g., Prov. 11:26; 14:28); Gk. *laós, óchlos*–'crowd,' *ánthrōpos*–'man,' *dēmos, génos*–'race,' 'descendants,' *plēthos*–'multitude' (Lk. 8:37; Acts 5:16; 14:4; 25:24)].

*I. OT.*–The term *ʿam* was common Semitic, being related to a root meaning "paternal uncle." In its broadest sense *ʿam* referred to the human population of the earth (Isa. 24:4f.), then the inhabitants of a given area (e.g., "the people who are [live] in the city," Josh. 8:16; Jer. 29:16; 36:9). The plural form, *ʿammîm,* "peoples," usually refers to foreign national and ethnic groups, being frequently interchanged with *gôyîm. See* NATIONS.

Of special interest is the expression "people of the land" (*ʿam hāʾāreṣ*). Some have interpreted this as a technical expression for a special class of people, the owners of property and those with political influence, as opposed to the masses (e.g., E. Würthwein, *Der ʿamm haʾarez im AT* [1936]; M. H. Pope, *IDB,* I, 106f.). In most contexts, however, the general sense, "the population of the land," is preferable (Gen. 23:12f., Hittites; 42:6, Egyptians; Ex. 5:5, Israelites in Goshen; Lev. 20:2, 4, Israel; Nu. 14:9, Canaanites; 2 K. 11:14, *et passim* in 2 Kings, Judah). In Jeremiah "people of the land" is often juxtaposed with references to kings, princes, and priests (1:18; 34:19; 37:2; 44:21; 52:6, 25; cf. also Ezk. 7:27; etc.). Ezr. 4:4 applies it to the non-Jewish population of Jerusalem and its environs, in contrast to the returned exiles. The plural form, "peoples of the land," occurring in several late texts (Est. 8:17; Ezr. 3:3; 10:2, 11; Neh. 9:24; 10:31f.; 1 Ch. 5:25; cf. "nations of the land," Ezr. 6:21), usually refers to the same groups. The "people*s* of the land*s*" are specifically named in Ezr. 9:1f., 11. For defenses of this broader interpretation see E. W. Nicholson, *JSS,* 10 (1965), 59-66; G. Buccellati, *Cities and Nations of Ancient Syria* (1967), pp. 168ff.

The term *ʿam* was also applied to smaller groups: the emissaries sent by Israel to Eglon (Jgs. 3:18), Philistine banqueters (Jgs. 16:30), Saul's acquaintances (1 S. 10:11), Solomon's alien labor force (1 K. 5:16 [MT 30]), the returnees from exile with Ezra (Ezr. 8:15), party factions gravitating around specific leaders (e.g., 2 S. 13:34; 15:12; 1 K. 1:39; etc.). In fact, it appears that any time two or more individuals were united in any way, they could legitimately be identified as an *ʿam,* "people."

Occasionally *ʿam,* "people," serves as a military term, having reference to any army or group of warriors (e.g., Jgs. 8:5; cf. *ṣāḇāʾ,* "army," in v. 6). The most explicit expression is "people of war" (*ʿam hammilḥāmâ*) in Josh. 10:7; 11:7; etc. In 2 K. 13:7 the *ʿam* ("army") is broken down into units of cavalry, chariotry, and infantry. Foreign armies are usually described as belonging to a person, or accompanying him (e.g., Pharaoh's people, Ex. 14:6; Sihon's people, Nu. 21:23; etc.). Armies attached to city-states are identified as "the people of the king of a geographic locality," rather than "the people of the geographic locality" (Josh. 8:14; "army," 1 Ch. 19:7).

Several other special uses of *ʿam* should be noted. In Gen. 19:4 and Josh. 5:4f. the term refers exclusively to men. Isa. 24:2; Hos. 4:9; and Ezr. 9:1 use *ʿam* for laymen in contrast to the priests. The expression *bᵉnê hāʿām,* lit. "sons of the people," refers to the "common people" or "lay people" (2 Ch. 35:5, 7). Jer. 17:19 identifies the gate used by the common folk as "the gate of the sons of the people" (so JB; cf. AV, NIV, NASB; RSV, NEB, "Benjamin Gate," requires a slight emendation).

The original kinship significance of the root is also remembered in some contexts. Members of a household, including family and servants, were sometimes designated just as "people" (Gen. 14:16; 1 K. 19:21) or as the "people who were with [the head of the house]" (Gen. 32:7 [MT 8]; 33:15). When a suffix is added *ʿam* may bear the sense "relative" (2 K. 4:13; Ps. 45:10 [MT 11]). One's countrymen are called "sons of my/your people" (Gen. 23:11; Lev. 19:17f.; cf. Jgs. 14:16). This kinship sense is reflected also in two stereotyped idioms found in the Pentateuch. "To be gathered to one's people," which occurs ten times (e.g., Gen. 25:8), should be interpreted this way because: (1) the translation "peoples" for *ʿammîm* is inappropriate; (2) biforms of the expression replace *ʿammîm* with *ʾābôṯ*, "fathers" (e.g., Jgs. 2:10); (3) death was commonly viewed as a reunion with one's predeceased ancestors. (*See also* GATHER.) "To be cut off from one's people(s)" appears twenty-two times. The phrase signifies not only excommunication from the cultic community (Ex. 12:15, 19; Nu. 19:13, 20), but also execution (Ex. 31:14; Lev. 20:3). In distinguishing between the direct descendants of Abraham and other members of the household, the context of Gen. 17:14 confirms the kinship overtones of the expression.

*II. NT.*–The RSV translates five Greek terms with "people." *Ánthrōpos* is treated generically in Jn. 4:28; 6:10, 14; Rev. 11:13. *Dḗmos,* which generally translates *mišpāḥâ,* "race, family," in the LXX, occurs only four times in the NT. In each instance the reference is to the population of a city: Jerusalem (Acts 12:22), Thessalonica (Acts 17:5), Ephesus (Acts 19:30, 33). This use of *dḗmos* reflects Heb. *ʿam* more than *mišpāḥâ,* a development that surfaces as early as Dnl. 8:24; 9:16 (LXX), and the intertestamental writings. In 2 Cor. 11:26 and Gal. 1:14 *génos* is rendered "my people," i.e., countrymen (cf. also Phil. 3:5).

The most important term for "people" in the NT is *laós*. Apart from the kinship overtones of the latter, the semantic range of *laós* parallels roughly that of *ʿam* in the OT. The national significance, common in the LXX, is reflected in the eight plural occurrences (Lk. 2:31; Acts 4:25, 27[?]; Rev. 7:9; 10:11; 11:9; 17:15). Elsewhere, however, the popular sense, "crowd, population, people," predominates. In Mt. 27:25 *laós* is used interchangeably with *óchlos,* "mob."

In the LXX *óchlos* and *plḗthos* translate a variety of Hebrew terms (*hāmôn, ḥayil, ʿam, qāhāl, rabbîm*) and most often refer to "a crowd, host, mob of people," or "an army." In the NT *óchlos* is restricted to the Gospels, Acts, and Rev. 7:9; 19:1, 6, while *plḗthos* is used especially in Luke-Acts. In general, *óchlos* signifies the throngs, the masses, sometimes in contrast to the authorities (e.g., Mt. 14:5; Mk. 15:11; etc.). In John the term acquires a special sense, recalling *ʿam hāʾāreṣ,* "people of the land," in many OT contexts. See esp. Jn. 7:31-49. The plural form *óchloi* in Rev. 17:15 bears a more national meaning, "peoples," opposite *laoí, éthnē* "nations," and *glṓssai,* "tongues."

D. I. BLOCK

**PEOPLE OF EDEN** [Heb. *bᵉnê ʿeḏen*–'sons of Eden' (so NASB)]; AV CHILDREN OF EDEN. The expression occurs only on the lips of the Assyrian emissary, Rabshakeh, in 2 K. 19:12 par. Isa. 37:12. In his own language the expression would have been rendered *mārū Adini.* In Akkadian texts this phrase is reserved for the members of the Bīt-Adini branch of the Aramean Bīt-Dakkūri tribe in Babylonia (J. A. Brinkman, *Political History of Post-Kassite Babylonia* [1968], pp. 244, 264ff.). This appears to support an identification of the "people of Eden" with these southern Arameans (so M. C. Astour, *IDBSupp.,* p. 251). It seems preferable, however, to identify this Eden with another Bīt-Adini, a northern Aramean state on the upper Euphrates, W of the Balîkh tributary, for several reasons. (1) In 2 K. 19:12 it is associated with Gozan, Haran, and Rezeph. (2) Telassar (Akk. *Til Aššuri*) need not be tied too closely to Eden; it merely identifies the place to which the "people of Eden" were exiled. (3) The expression *bᵉnê ʿeḏen* may refer to the members of the dynasty of Adini, after whom the state was named, rather than to the citizens of the nation. (The practice of naming Aramean states after the founder of a dynasty is paralleled in Bīt-Agusi [Arpad]; so J. A. Fitzmyer, *Aramaic Inscriptions of Sefire* [1967], pp. 40f. Here the members of the ruling family are called the *bny*-Gush, "sons of Gush." Cf. *KAI,* no. 222, A:15ff.; B:1ff. Note also Hadadezer, who is identified as "the son of Rehob, king of Zobah" [2 S. 8:3, 12]. In 2 S. 10:6 Zobah is identified with Beth-rehob.) This interpretation concurs with the reference to the disappearance of a series of kings from the same general area in 2 K. 19:13. One known king of Bīt-Adini, Aḫuni, is identified as a "son of Adini" (*ᴵa-ḫu-ni mār ᴵa-di-ni, Welt des Orients,* 4 [1967], 36). Significantly, the dynastic name, BETH-EDEN, is preserved in Am. 1:5. (For a defense of the identification of this Beth-eden with Bīt-Adini, cf. Malamat, contra Astour.) The shortened form of the name, Eden, occurs in Ezk. 27:23, where this state is depicted as a trading partner with Tyre, alongside Haran, from the same general region.

Much of the history of Bīt-Adini is unknown. Ashurnasirpal II (885-859 B.C.) identifies Aḫi-yababa, of Bīt-Adini, as the new king, installed by rebels, over Bīt-Halupi (A. K. Grayson, *Assyrian Royal Inscriptions,* II, no. 547). Bīt-Adini itself appears to have arisen about a century prior to the attack by Ashurnasirpal on Kaprabu, the fortified city of Aḫuni the king (*Assyrian Royal Inscriptions,* II, nos. 582ff.). In 856 B.C. the royal city, Til-Barsip, fell to Shalmaneser III, and the state was incorporated into the empire. Til-Barsip was renamed Kar-Shalmaneser and was destined to play an important role in the administration of the western part of the Assyrian empire. Malamat suggests that Shamshi-ilu was the governor over this region at the time of Amos's prophecy.

***Bibliography.***–E. Honigmann, *Reallexikon der Assyriologie,* II (1938), 33f.; Y. Ikeda, *Iraq,* 41 (1979), 77-79; A. Malamat, *BASOR,* 129 (Feb. 1953), 25f.; *The Aramaeans in Aram Naharaim and the Rise of their States* (1952), pp. 39-47; D. Ussishkin, *Orientalia,* 40 (1971), 431-37.

D. I. BLOCK

**PEOPLE OF GOD** [Heb. *ʿam (hā)ʾᵉlōhîm* (Jgs. 20:2; 2 S. 14:13; etc.); Gk. *laós toú theoú* (He. 4:9; 11:25; cf. 1 Pet. 2:9f.)]. Although the phrase "people of God" does not occur often in the Bible (cf. also *ʿam YHWH,* Jgs. 5:11; 2 S. 1:12; etc.), the concept is presupposed in the phrases "my people," "his people," or "thy people" (depending on the speaker), which are found roughly two hundred times each in Scripture. In the OT Israel is called out from the nations to be God's people, holy as He is holy, separated to the Lord, and ultimately commissioned to communicate His offer of salvation to the world. In the NT this role passes on to the Christian Church. Throughout the development of the concept in Scripture, the people of God is seen as a corporate, holy, interacting, sharing, worshiping community in the world, God's continuous method of communicating His mind to mankind through mankind.

In Exodus God chooses Israel as His people over against those of Pharaoh (3:7–11:10, esp. chs. 8–9) The theme is "Let my people go!" and the declaration is that the Egyptians "shall know that I am the Lord." Subsequently, in the wilderness after Israel's failure, Moses pleads for the people in terms of God's relationship with them, which gives them their national distinctiveness (Ex. 33:16).

In Deuteronomy the concept develops ethical dimensions.

The "people of God" are to be "holy unto the Lord," a covenant people with a special mission, and committed to observe His commandments (Dt. 7:6-11; 14:2; 27:9f.; 28:9; 29:12f.).

The concept is found throughout the historical books in passages that tell of Israel's conquest of the land (e.g., Jgs. 5:11), salvation from oppressors (e.g., 1 S. 9:16f.; 2 S. 3:18; 5:2; 7:7-11; 1 K. 6:13; 8:16; 14:7; 16:2; 1 Ch. 17:6-10; 2 Ch. 6:5-7; 7:13f.), or the establishment of the house of David (2 S. 7:23f.; 1 Ch. 17:21f.).

The notion of a specific people of God is clear in the eighth-century prophetic oracles and allegories. Israel is continually reminded that it is a covenant people and the cardinal sin is unfaithfulness, by which "My people" becomes "Not my people" (Hos. 1:9f. [MT 1:9–2:1]; 2:23 [MT 25]). The strongest prophetic analogy is the broken marriage relationship (cf. Am. 7:8, 15; 8:2; 9:10, 14; Mic. 1:9; 2:4-9; 3:5; 6:3, 5; Hos. 4:6-12; 6:11; 11:7; Isa. 3:12, 15; 5:13; 32:13, 18).

In the 6th cent. Jeremiah and Ezekiel strongly articulated the figure about fifty times in passages that deal with Israel's turning to foreign idols and forgetting the covenant relationship as the people of God. But even in judgment the prophets retained the phrase. Two other elements are found in this corpus of material about God's people: the moral requirement of holiness (Ezk. 11:20; 38:16; 39:7; 44:23) and the promise of the continuing character of the people of God in spite of captivity — "a remnant shall be saved" (Jer. 24:7; 30:3; 31:31-34; Ezk. 37:11-14). The concept of the people of God occurs in the Psalms, also, as God personally admonishes His people (e.g., Ps. 78:1; 81:8f. [MT 9f.]).

The prophetic use of the concept develops in the second part of Isaiah, which uses the term with endearment and encouragement, e.g., "Comfort my people." The motivation for God's election of Israel is revealed in the series of "His actions" — creating Israel, redeeming Israel, calling Israel, and commissioning Israel as His witness to the nations (43:1-13; cf. 40:1; 43:20; 47:6; 51:4, 16; 52:4-6; 53:8; 57:14; 58:1; 65:10).

Christ reinterpreted the concept in the light of His own ministry and mission to the world, and the CHURCH became heir to the promises of Israel. Directly and indirectly the NT claims the transfer of the role of "people of God," with its responsibilities and promises, to the Church.

The transfer is implied in several NT passages. One is the angelic annunciation to Zachariah (Lk. 1:17) that John the Baptist is "to make ready for the Lord a people prepared." Lk. 24 implies that Jesus understood the words of the prophets to apply to His own work and mission. At the Jerusalem Council Peter testified that God had visited the Gentiles "to take out of them a people for his name" (Acts 15:14).

The transfer is also implied by Paul's apparent use of "Israel of God" for Christians in Galatia (Gal. 6:16). That Christians are newly taken into the people of God is indicated by use of both the imagery of God's temple and the theology of adoption in the same passage (2 Cor. 6:16-18). In Rom. 11, when Paul asks rhetorically if God has rejected His people (v. 1), he answers by speaking of the remnant, chosen by grace (v. 5) from the Gentiles (v. 12). Paul also speaks of the glory of Christ's salvation, His self-giving for redemptive purposes "to purify unto Himself a people of his own" (Tit. 2:14).

The whole typology of the Letter to the Hebrews shows how the institution of the old Israel and their spiritual functions are to pass on in a better form through Christ to the Christian community and how the God-and-people relationship continues (8:10). The gift of the Holy Spirit is another new element that makes Christian believers a corporate, sharing, worshiping community, which Peter describes as "a chosen race, a royal priesthood, a holy nation, God's own people," specifying their roles of praise and witness as "God's people" (1 Pet. 2:9f.).

The Church is thus the "people of God," called as the community of the risen Lord to live the holy life, to minister to the needy world, and to offer salvation to mankind in the name of Christ.

On the level of practical theology, the phrase "people of God" serves as a useful corrective against excessive western individualism. The Church is a community, not of isolated individuals but of participating, interacting partners (Gk. *koinōnoí*), sharing each others' burdens and building up each others' faith. The Church's witness — in the ministries of service, human liberation, and mission — must be a corporate witness.

The phrase may be used of the Church at large in the world or of any operating *koinōnía* when a group sees itself as part of the "body of Christ," performing His ministry and witness in a particular place.

It is quite wrong to use the term "people of God" in a superior, exclusivistic, or isolationist sense ("holier than thou"), as has happened. This is to misuse the "of God" part of the phrase, which makes the goal an outreaching, corporate ministry in the execution of God's purpose in the world — something that calls for humble obedience, not superior isolation. Moral holiness is demanded because God Himself is holy. The people of God must strive for this holiness, although their hope lies not in their own works but in the merits of Christ, through whom alone they may claim the status of people of God (Tit. 2:11-14; 2 Cor. 6:16-18).

Finally, the concept of the people of God extends beyond time and place, for the promise of the fellowship of this company is eternal. All who know Him on earth may participate in this fellowship as a pledge and foretaste of more to come (Rev. 21:1-3; cf. He. 4:9-11a; Eph. 1:13f.).

***Bibliography.*–*TDNT*, IV, *s.v.* λαός (Strathmann, Meyer); *THAT*, II, *s.v.* גּוֹי/עַם (A. R. Hulst).

A. R. TIPPETT

**PEOR** pē'ōr or pē'ər [Heb. $p^{e}$ʿ*ôr*; Gk. *Phogōr*].

**1.** A mountain in Moab, the third and last place to which Balaam was taken by Balak in order to curse Israel (Nu. 23:28). Eusebius (*Onom.*) located it on the way from Livius to Heshbon, 7 Roman mi. (10 km., 6.4 mi.) from the latter. Since the camp of Israel in the plains of Moab was visible (Nu. 24:2), it must have been located near Mt. Nebo. Peor was also the site of the Israelites' idolatrous worship of the local Baal (Nu. 25:3, 5, 18; Dt. 4:3; Josh. 22:17; Ps. 106:28). *See* BAAL IV.

**2.** A town in Judah added to the MT's list of towns in Josh. 15:58 by the LXX (included by NEB). It has been identified with Khirbet Faghur SSW of Bethlehem.

**3.** The LXX reading for MT *paw* in Gen. 36:39; *see* PAU.

W. S. L. S.

**PERAZIM** pə-rā'zim [Heb. $p^{e}$*rāṣîm*–'bursting forth' (BDB, p. 829)]. A mountain mentioned only in Isaiah's prophecy of judgment upon the rulers of Jerusalem (28:21). It may be identified with BAAL-PERAZIM (1 Ch. 14:11), where after defeating the Philistines David said, "the Lord has broken through [*pāraṣ*] my enemies before me, like a bursting [*pereṣ*] flood" (2 S. 5:20). Isaiah may thus be referring to the meaning of the mountain's name when he says that just as God's judgment burst upon the Philistines, so now He will "rise up as on Mount Perazim" and His judgment will burst forth on the rulers of Jerusalem.

See E. J. Young, *Book of Isaiah*, II (1969), 292.

W. D. MOUNCE

**PERDITION** [Heb. *b$^e$lîya‘al*] (2 S. 22:5 par. Ps. 18:4 [MT 5]); AV UNGODLY MEN; NEB DESTRUCTION; [Gk. *apṓleia*] (Jn. 17:12; 2 Thess. 2:3; Rev. 17:8, 11); NEB also "who must be lost" (Jn. 17:12). A term generally used to denote a state or place of utter and eternal destruction.

Various etymological explanations for *b$^e$lîya‘al* have been proposed (see *TDOT,* II, 132f.), but none has proved totally satisfactory. In 2 S. 22:5 par. Ps. 18:4 the phrase "torrents of *b$^e$lîya‘al*" occurs in parallelism with "cords of Sheol [*š$^e$’ôl*]" and "snares of death [*māweṯ*]," both of which are personified figures associated with the realm of the dead (*see* DEATH III; SHEOL). Since the underworld is often depicted as a watery, chaotic abyss (*see* DEEP), "torrents of *b$^e$lîya‘al*" appears to be a poetic figure personifying the powers of CHAOS, i.e., all the evil forces that undermine the divine order for human life (see *TDOT,* II, 134f.; *ILC,* I-II [repr. 1964], 431f., 463f.). This would also help to explain why lawless persons can be called *b$^e$nê-b$^e$lîya‘al* (lit. "sons of Belial" [cf. AV]; e.g., Dt. 13:13 [MT 14]; Jgs. 19:22; 20:13; 1 K. 21:10, 13; RSV "base fellows"; NEB usually "scoundrels"; *see* BELIAL). (Heb. *ben-* is often used to describe a person's character or fate; *see* BEN-.)

Occurring eighteen times in the NT, Gk. *apṓleia* is most frequently translated "destruction" by the RSV (e.g., Rom. 9:22; *see* DESTRUCTION II, III). In the LXX it is sometimes used in a personified sense to translate Heb. *’$^a$ḇaddôn* (e.g., Job 26:6; 28:22; Ps. 88:11 [MT 12; LXX 87:12]; *see* ABADDON). Of the four times the RSV renders it "perdition," two are in the expression "son of perdition." In 2 Thess. 2:3 it refers to the "man of lawlessness," God's apocalyptic enemy (*see* ESCHATOLOGY V; LAWLESS). In Jn. 17:12 Jesus tells His Father that He has lost no one except the "son of perdition," i.e., Judas Iscariot, who as the tool of Satan is about to betray Jesus. The phrase here denotes both a person's character and his fate: it refers to "one who belongs to the realm of damnation and is destined to final destruction" (Brown, p. 760). In Rev. 17:8, 11, like 2 Thess. 2:3, "perdition" is used with reference to a creature fulfilling an apocalyptic role of opposition to God. The "beast" is said to "go to perdition" (Gk. *hypágō eis apṓleian*; cf. *eimí eis apṓleian,* Acts 8:20 [RSV, AV, "perish"; NEB "go . . . to damnation"]; cf. also Phil. 3:19; Mt. 7:13 [NEB "perdition"]; AV "perdition" in Phil. 1:28; 1 Tim. 6:9; He. 10:39; 2 Pet. 3:7). This seems to be synonymous with his being cast alive into the LAKE OF FIRE (Rev. 9:20) along with the devil, the false prophet, and all whose names are not found in the book of life; there he will "be tormented day and night for ever and ever" (20:10, 14f.). Thus, those who oppose God and reject His salvation face the terrible destiny of eternal punishment.

*See also* ANTICHRIST; ETERNAL; PERISH.

***Bibliography.***–R. E. Brown, *Gospel According to John,* II (*AB,* 1970); *DNTT,* I, 462-65; *TDNT,* I *s.v.* ἀπόλλυμι, ἀπώλεια (A. Oepke); *TDOT,* II, *s.v.* "b$^e$liyya‘al" (B. Otzen).

C. PINCHES N. J. O.

**PEREA** pə-rē′-ə [Gk. *Peraia,* unused in the NT except var. Lk. 6:17 ℵ* W]. A portion of Transjordan included in the kingdom of Herod the Great, and included with Galilee in the tetrarchy of Herod Antipas.

*I. Name.*–The Gk. *Peraia* appears to have been derived from the more common name *péran toú ’Iordanou,* "across the Jordan" (Dt. 1:5; Mt. 4:25), a translation of Heb. *‘ēḇer hayyardēn* and Aram. *‘aḇrēh d$^e$yardēnā’*, both meaning "beyond the Jordan" or "Transjordan." The Greek expression came to be treated as an indeclinable substantive, as in the phrase *en tǭ péran toú ’Iordanou* ("in [the] Transjordan," Dt. 3:20, LXX) and *eis tḗn péran toú ’Iordanou* ("to [the] Transjordan," Josephus *Ant.* xii.4.9 [222]). Josephus frequently used *Peraia* (e.g., *BJ* ii.4.2 [57]); more specifically *hē hypér ’Iordanēn Peraia,* "the beyond-Jordan Perea" (*BJ* ii.3.1 [43]).

*II. Location.*–Josephus defines the region thus: "Perea extends in length from Machaerus to Pella, in breadth from Philadelphia to the Jordan" (*BJ* iii.3.3 [46]), and states that it is bounded on the east by Arabia, Heshbonitis, Philadelphia, and Gerasa (§47). Since Pella belonged to the Decapolis, Josephus's statement, "the northern frontier is Pella" (§47), must mean that Perea extended northward to, but did not include, Pella; the Wâdī el-Yâbis (on which Jabesh-Gilead is located) formed a northern boundary, and the Arnon a southern boundary (*see* Vol. I, Maps XVII, XXII). In his explorations in Transjordan N. Glueck concluded that the eastern boundary was W of Medeba and he would correct Josephus's statement about the breadth of the region to read "from Jordan to about one half the way to Philadelphia" (*Explorations in Eastern Palestine,* III [*AASOR,* 18-19, 1939], 140, 143). Josephus describes Perea as "for the most part desert and rugged and too wild to bring tender fruits to maturity," but he added that there were tracts of finer soil and the country was watered by torrents descending from the mountains and by springs which never dry up (*BJ* iii.3.3 [45]).

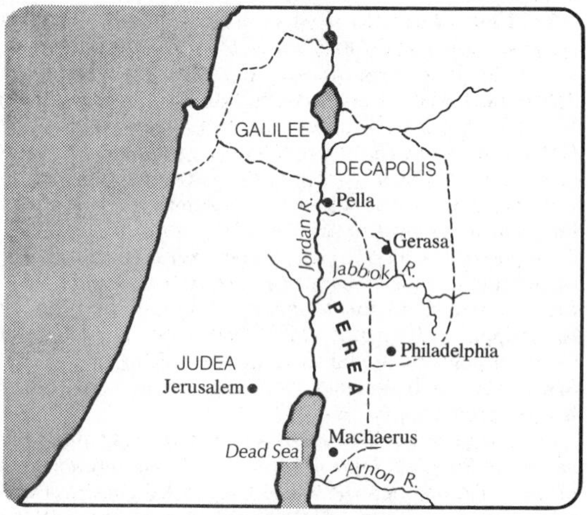


The capital of Perea, according to Josephus, was Gadara (*BJ* iv.7.3 [413]). Some have identified this with Umm Qeis (Muqeis), which was in the Decapolis and too far north to be Perea (*see* GADARA). A more probable location is Gadora (Tell ‘Ain Jedûr) near eṣ-Ṣalṭ (*LBHG,* rev., p. 370 n. 129; cf. H. Thackeray, *Josephus,* III [*LCL*], 120f. note b). Other places in Perea that are mentioned are: Amatha (one of the most important fortresses in Transjordan; *BJ* i.4.2 [186]), Zia (15 Roman mi. W of Philadelphia; *Ant.* xx.1.1 [2]), Bethennabris (opposite Jericho [could this be "Bethany beyond Jordan," called "Bethabara" in a variant reading of Jn. 1:28?]; *BJ* iv.7.4 [420]), Abila (Abel-shittim, 8 km. [5 mi.] S of Bethennabris; *BJ* iv.7.6 [438]), Betharamtha (or Bethramphtha, Betharam [Josh. 13:27], which later became Livia and then Julia; *BJ* ii.4.2 [59]; *Ant.* xviii.2.1 [27]), Esbus (Essebos, Essebonitis, Heshbon; *Ant.* xii.4.11 [233]), Medeba (Medaba; *BJ* i.2.6 [63]), Calirrhoe (*BJ* i.33.5 [657]), and Machaerus (*BJ* i.16.6 [317-320]). Medeba and Heshbon were at times outside the districts of Perea.

*III. History.*–Transjordan is prominent in the OT, and it is subdivided into regions (Gilead, Ammon, Moab, etc.), but there is no indication of a region corresponding to Perea. Judas Maccabeus and his brother Jonathan crossed the Jordan to aid the Jews whom the Gentiles were attempting to destroy (1 Macc. 5:9-13, 24, 40-44; cf. Aharoni and M. Avi-Yonah, *Macmillan Bible Atlas* [rev. ed. 1977], Map 189). By *ca.* 152 B.C., as a result of Jonathan's conquests, Judea controlled a region in Transjordan that has come to be known as Perea (1 Macc. 11:33, 57-74; *Macmillan Bible Atlas,* Map 199). Demetrius II granted independence to Judea in 142 B.C. In 129 Antiochus VII was killed in battle, and John Hyrcanus seized the opportunity to take over as much territory as possible. His first conquests were in Perea, where the Jews had maintained a foothold since the time of Jonathan, and he extended this region by taking a portion of the Nabatean holdings (*Ant.* xiii.9.1 [254f.]; *Macmillan Bible Atlas,* Map 208).

Pompey liberated gentile cities that had been occupied by Jews since the time of John Hyrcanus, and Gabinius, proconsul of Syria 57-55 B.C., attempted to split the Jewish state into five districts: Galilee, Jericho, Jerusalem, Adora (Eastern Idumea), and Perea. Perea's capital was at Ammathus (*Ant.* xiv.4.4 [75f.]; xiv.5.4 [91]; identified with Tell ʿAmmatā, a few miles NE of the junction of the Jabbok and the Jordan, in R. Marcus, *Josephus,* VII [*LCL*], 405 note d). The Roman effort failed in its purpose of dividing the Jewish people, and the concept of five districts soon disappeared.

In 31 B.C. Herod the Great was confirmed by Octavian (Augustus) in his kingdom and added many other regions, so that by 20 B.C. his domain was at its greatest extent. At Herod's death Augustus divided the kingdom among Herod's three surviving sons, and Herod Antipas received Galilee and Perea (*BJ* ii.6.3 [93-95]). Agrippa I, grandson of Herod the Great, received the tetrarchy of Philip in A.D. 37, that of Antipas in 39, and the rest of Herod's kingdom in 41 (*Ant.* xviii.6.10 [237]; xviii.7.2 [252]; *BJ* ii.9.6 [181-83]; ii.11.5 [214f.]). When Agrippa died in A.D. 44 the rule of Judea was turned over to the Roman procurators, but in 53 the tetrarchy of Philip was granted to Agrippa II (*BJ* ii.12.8 [247]), and under Nero he also received portions of Galilee and Perea (*BJ* ii.13.2 [252]). When Agrippa II died (*ca.* 95) Perea became part of the Roman province of Syria.

***IV. Jewish and NT Perea.***–This section is so titled because the Perea of the NT (*péran toú 'Iordanou*) was part of the kingdom of Herod and, as described above, of certain of his successors. According to the Mishnah (*Baba Bathra* iii.2) Perea was one of three Jewish provinces, the others being Galilee and Judea (cf. Mt. 4:25). It was therefore possible — and indeed customary — for Jews to travel from Galilee to Judea by the way of Perea, without passing through Samaria (Josephus *Ant.* xx.6.1 [118]). Jn. 4:4 is a remarkable exception, the significance of which should not be lost when commenting on the passage.

In Mt. 19:1 we read: "Jesus . . . went away from Galilee and he entered the region of Judea beyond the Jordan [*péran toú 'Iordanou*]." Some have suggested that this be emended to conform with some MSS of Mk. 10:1 that insert another "and" (Gk. *kaí*) to read "the region of Judea *and* Across-Jordan." While this reading has the support of the great uncial MSS, ℵ and B, the route would make no sense, for Jesus would hardly have gone from Galilee to Judea and then to Perea. It is the *kaí* in Mk. 10:1 that is suspect (note that the *United Bible Societies' Greek NT* has put it in brackets and given the reading a value of "C", meaning "a considerable degree of doubt"). "Judea beyond and Jordan" or "Transjordan" is an NT name for Perea and probably was the common term among the Jews of the time.

John was baptizing in "Bethany beyond Jordan" (Jn. 1:28), which might be translated "Perean Bethany" or "Bethany of Perea." According to Josephus, John was put into the dungeon at the fortress of Machaerus, and later put to death there (*Ant.* xviii.5.2 [116-19]). Details of the imprisonment and death of John given in the NT, however, have raised questions about Josephus's accuracy on this point.

The long Lukan insertion (Lk. 9:51–18:34) has sometimes been called "the Perean Ministry." More recent scholars doubt that this records a continuous sequence of teachings that occurred during the last journey from Galilee to Jerusalem. Some of the events, however, did take place in Perea. The refusal of the Samaritans to receive Jesus and His disciples (9:53) does not suggest that He continued on through Samaria to Judea, but rather that the route was then shifted to avoid Samaria, hence through Perea. Lk. 17:11, "he was passing along between Samaria and Galilee," suggests a route through the Cisjordan Decapolis (Scythopolis, Beth-shean), in order to enter Perea by the ford of the Jordan near Scythopolis. Lk. 18:31 suggests that Jesus and His disciples had arrived in the Jordan Valley opposite Jericho (cf. 18:35; 19:1).

Jesus and His disciples were in Perea when Lazarus was taken ill (Jn. 10:40; 11:7), and they made the trip from there to Bethany. The Ephraim to which Jesus retired after raising Lazarus (Jn. 11:54) was "near the wilderness," possibly indicating a location in Perea (cf. Mk. 1:4 [lit. "John was baptizing in the wilderness"]). The common identification of Ephraim with Aphairema on the southern edge of Samaria raises the question of whether under the circumstances Jesus and His disciples could be secure in a location in Judea. The suggestion that the teachings of Mt. 19; Mk. 10:1-31; Lk. 18:15-30 belong to this interlude faces two objections: the interval, according to John, appears to have been quite brief; and Jesus and His disciples seem to have been alone (Jn. 11:54) and not engaged openly in teaching.

W. S. LASOR

**PERES** per'ēz [Aram. *p^e^rēs*] (Dnl. 5:28, AV). *See* MENE, MENE, TEKEL, AND PARSIN.

**PERESH** per'esh [Heb. *pereš*]. Son of Machir and his wife Maacah; grandson of Manasseh (1 Ch. 7:16).

**PEREZ** per'ez [Heb. *pereṣ*–'a bursting forth, breach'; Gk. *Phares*]; AV OT also PHAREZ, AV NT PHARES; **PHARES** [Gk. *Phares*] (1 Esd. 5:5); **PEREZITES** per'ə-zīts [Heb. *parṣî*] (Nu. 26:20); AV PHARZITES. Twin son (with Zerah) born of the incestuous relationship between Tamar and her father-in-law Judah (Gen. 38). Perez was the father of Hezron and Hamul (Gen. 46:12; Nu. 26:21; 1 Ch. 2:4f.) and the ancestor of the Perezites (Nu. 26:20).

Perez received his name because of the unusually violent nature of his birth. As Tamar was about to give birth to her twins, one son presented his hand. The midwives placed a scarlet thread on this hand to mark the firstborn. The hand was then withdrawn, and the brother "burst forth"; hence the name Perez (Gen. 38:28-30). Critical scholars such as G. von Rad (*Genesis* [Eng. tr., rev. ed., *OTL,* 1972], p. 356) regard the birth narrative of Perez as an etiology, an explanation developed in later times for the prominence of the line of Perez over that of Zerah. Prominent families in Jerusalem traced their ancestry from Perez in postexilic times (1 Ch. 9:4; 27:3; Neh. 11:4, 6).

The village women of Bethlehem invoked the name Perez in their blessing of Ruth when she married Boaz (Ruth 4:12), a blessing doubly appropriate because of the levirate marriage and the non-Israelite origins of both Ruth and Tamar.

The line of David (Ruth 4:18-22; cf. 1 Esd. 5:5: Phares = Perez) and of Jesus is traced through Perez (Mt. 1:3 par. Lk. 3:33).

R. B. ALLEN

**PEREZ-UZZA** per'ez ōōz'ə [Heb. *pereṣ ʿuzzā'*–'breach of Uzzah'] (1 Ch. 13:11); **PEREZ-UZZAH** [Heb. *pereṣ ʿuzzâ*] (2 S. 6:8). An unknown site located somewhere W of Jerusalem on the road to Kiriath-jearim. It received its name to commemorate the occasion when Uzzah steadied the ark of the covenant as David was endeavoring to move it to Jerusalem. For this breach of priestly propriety Uzzah was struck dead. Even though his action was most probably inadvertent, the shock of contact with Israel's most sacred cultic object could have been sufficient to provoke a terminal circulatory accident.

R. K. H.

**PERFECT; MAKE PERFECT; PERFECTION** [Heb. *tāmîm* (Lev. 22:21; Dt. 32:4; 2 S. 22:31; Job 36:4; etc.), also *tām* (Cant. 5:2; 6:9), *šālôm* (Isa. 26:3), *kālîl* (Lam. 2:15; Ezk. 16:14; 27:3; 28:12), *kālal* (Ezk. 27:4, 11), *miḵlāl* (Ps. 50:2), *tiḵlâ* (Ps. 119:96), *taḵlîṯ* (Ps. 139:22); Gk. often *téleios, teleióō*, also *teleiótēs* (Phil. 3:12), *teleíōsis* (He. 7:11), *katartízō*–'prepare, make complete' (Mt. 21:16), *holoklēría* ("perfect health," Acts 3:16), *epiteléō*–'finish, complete' (2 Cor. 7:1), *pás*–'all, whole' (2 Cor. 7:16; Tit. 3:2), *teléō*–'finish' (2 Cor. 12:9), *hápas*–'all' (1 Tim. 1:16), perfect pass. part. of *plēróō*–'fill full, complete' (Rev. 3:2)]; AV also CONSECRATED (He. 7:28), UNDEFILED (Cant. 5:2; 6:9), ALL (e.g., 2 Cor. 7:16); NEB also COMPLETE, SOUND, CONSUMMATE, UNDYING, PEACE, WHOLENESS, FULL STRENGTH, GOODNESS, ALL, CONSISTENTLY, "go the whole way" (Mt. 19:21), "complete the whole" (Col. 3:14), "a balanced character" (Jas. 1:4).

The RSV uses "perfect" far less often than the AV, especially in passages referring to human beings. This is probably because in Modern English the term is often used in an ideal, absolute sense (i.e., total sinlessness) that is usually not present in the Hebrew or Greek terms it represents.

***I. In the OT.***–The Hebrew term most often rendered by "perfect" is *tāmîm* (lit. "complete," "without defect"), derived from the root *tmm* ("be complete, finished"). In over half of its occurrences *tāmîm* refers to animals that are physically sound or "without blemish" (the usual RSV translation; *see* BLEMISH) and therefore acceptable for sacrifices (cf. Lev. 22:21).

The RSV OT uses "perfect" to desribe a human being only in Job 36:4, where Elihu claims that he is "perfect [*tāmîm*] in knowledge" because he is divinely inspired (cf. 32:8; 33:3f.; 37:16). The OT (esp. Psalms and Proverbs) frequently employs *tāmîm* to describe human conduct that is completely obedient to God's will. Although the AV sometimes translates it "perfect" in such passages, the RSV always employs a term such as "blameless" (e.g., Gen. 17:1; Dt. 18:13; Ps. 101:2, 6; Prov. 2:21 [RSV "men of integrity"]; 11:5; Ezk. 28:15).

Apart from Lev. 22:21 and Job 36:4, the RSV translates *tāmîm* by "perfect" only in references to God: to His work (Dt. 32:4), His way (2 S. 22:31 par. Ps. 18:30 [MT 31]), His knowledge (Job 37:16), and His law (Ps. 19:7 [MT 8]).

Another derivative of *tmm, tām* (lit. "complete," "sound," "pure"), is similar in meaning to *tāmîm*. It is rendered "perfect" by the RSV only in Cant. 5:2; 6:9; here it probably refers to the flawless beauty of the Shulammite, although other interpretations have been suggested (cf. AV "undefiled"; KD "wholly devoted"). The AV translates *tām* "perfect" in nine passages referring to human character or conduct (Job 1:1, 8; 2:3; 8:20; 9:20-22; Ps. 37:37; 64:4). The fact that *tām* is used to describe Job, and *tāmîm* to describe Noah (Gen. 6:9), neither of whom was totally without sin (cf. Gen. 9:21; Job 42:1-6), shows clearly that these terms do not denote perfection in in the absolute sense. Rather, they point to a person's integrity of character; they describe a person who is singlemindedly obedient to God's will as expressed in His commandments.

Another term sometimes rendered "perfect" by the AV, Heb. *šālēm* (lit. "complete, whole, full"), expresses a similar idea. Frequently it is used with *lēḇ* ("heart") to describe a person whose heart is "wholly true" to Yahweh, i.e., one whose loyalty to Yahweh is undivided (cf. RSV 1 K. 8:61; 11:4; 15:3, 14; 2 K. 20:3; 1 Ch. 28:9; 29:9, 19; Isa. 38:3, etc.). The cognate noun *šālôm* describes the wholeness, fulfillment, and peace experienced by one who enjoys this kind of unimpaired relationship with God. According to Isa. 26:3, the Lord keeps "in perfect peace" (AV, RSV; Heb. *šālôm šālôm*) the nation that has fixed its trust in Him.

Eight times the RSV uses "perfect" or "perfection" to render terms derived from the root *kll* ("be complete, perfect, whole"). In each case the reference is to unblemished beauty: that of Jerusalem (Ezk. 16:14; Lam. 2:15), of Tyre (Ezk. 27:3f., 11; 28:12), of Zion (Ps. 50:2). "Perfect" and "perfection" are each used once by the RSV to render a derivative of *klh* ("accomplish, finish, end"); both *taḵlîṯ* and *tiḵlâ* express the idea of totality or completeness. Ps. 139:22 speaks of "perfect" (i.e., "total") hatred, while 119:96 contrasts the limitless breadth of God's law with the limited nature of all other things, however complete.

***II. In Intertestamental Judaism.***–Hebrew *tāmîm* is a prominent term in the writings of the Qumrân community. In the Manual of Discipline (1QS) alone, *tāmîm* occurs eighteen times, especially in the expression "(walking) in perfection of way," which denotes a "full observance" of God's will as revealed in the statutes of the community (see, e.g., 1QS 8:10, 18, 21; cf. 2:2; 3:9f.; 9:19; etc.). Sometimes *tāmîm* denotes members of the community (e.g., 1QS 3:3; 4:22; 1QM 14:7; 1QH 1:36). The expression *lēḇ šālēm* ("undivided heart") occurs in 1QH 16:7, 17 (cf. T. Jud. 23:5).

In the RSV Apocrypha "perfect," "perfectly," and "perfection" usually represent Gk. *téleios* or one of its cognates (e.g., Wisd. 4:13, 16; 6:15; 9:6; Sir. 24:28; 31:10; 34:8; 44:17; etc.; for the meaning of *téleios*, see III below). Exceptions are *akmḗ kállous* (lit. "acme of beauty") in Ad. Est. 15:5 (LXX 5:1b) and *hygíeia iáseos* (lit. "health of healing") in Sir. 1:18.

***III. In the NT.***–The most common terms for "(make) perfect" and "perfection" in the RSV NT are Gk. *teleióō* ("finish," "complete," "make perfect") and its cognates *téleios* ("complete," "mature," "perfect"), *teleiótēs* ("completeness," "perfection," "maturity"), and *teleíōsis* ("fulfillment," "perfection"). In the NT as in the OT, the AV uses "perfection" and "perfect" more often than the RSV; e.g., cf. the AV and RSV translations of *akribṓs* (lit. "accurately," "carefully") in Lk. 1:3; Acts 18:26; 23:15, 20; 24:22; 1 Thess. 5:2; of *katartízō* ("restore," "make complete," "create," "prepare") in Lk. 6:40; 1 Cor. 1:10; 2 Cor. 13:11; 1 Thess. 3:10; He. 13:21; 1 Pet. 5:10; of *katartismós* ("equipping," "training") in Eph. 4:12; of *katártisis* ("completion, being made complete") in 2 Cor. 13:9; and of *ártios* ("complete," "proficient") in 2 Tim. 3:17. Whereas the AV consistently translates *téleios* by "perfect," the RSV often uses "mature" (see below).

*Téleios* (a cognate of *télos,* "end," "goal," and *teléō,* "bring to an end, complete") is one of the terms used by the LXX to render Heb. *tāmîm* and *šālēm;* thus it is not surprising that the NT sometimes uses *téleios* in the LXX sense of "undivided commitment to God" and "complete obedience to His will." *Téleios* is used in this sense in Matthew. In 19:21 Jesus challenges a rich young man, "If you would be perfect, go, sell what you possess and give to the poor . . . ." The young man was obviously not undivided in his commitment to God: his riches were a stumbling block to singleminded discipleship. In 5:48 Jesus instructs His disciples, "You, therefore, must be perfect, as your heavenly Father is perfect" (cf. Dt. 18:13, where the RSV renders Heb. *tāmîm* "blameless"). The context in Mt. 5 indicates that by "perfect" Jesus means completeness of love: His disciples are to display the kind of undifferentiated love toward both friends and foes that God shows toward all mankind (cf. Lk. 6:36, which has *oiktírmōm,* "merciful," instead of *téleios*). (See comms., e.g., D. Hill, *Gospel of Matthew* [*NCBC,* repr. 1981], p. 131).

In the Epistle of James *téleios* also means "whole" or "complete,"sometimes in the specific sense of "mature." In 1:4 it appears twice: "And let steadfastness have its full effect [*érgon téleion*], that you may be perfect [*téleios*] and complete [*holóklēros*], lacking in nothing [*en mēdení leipómenoi*]." In other words, believers have not reached "completeness" or "maturity" until their faith, through testing, has produced steadfastness, and steadfastness has shown itself in a "complete work" (*érgon téleion*), i. e., "total obedience." Such obedience involves not only hearing but also doing the "perfect [*téleios*] law, the law of liberty" (v. 25). The "perfect" law may mean the "whole" law as summarized in the love commandment (cf. 2:8; see *TDNT,* VIII, 74f.), or it may mean the OT law as "completed" by Christ's reinterpretation (see Davids, pp. 99f.). Another sign of "wholeness" is self-control, especially in speech (3:2). Jas. 1:17 states that "every perfect gift is from above," i.e., God's gifts (perhaps referring especially to the gift of wisdom; cf. vv. 2-8, 12-14) are "wholly" good and intended to enable believers to persevere in trials; hence God cannot be accused of sending the evil that tempts people to fall (cf. v. 13).

1 John uses *teleióō* (perfect pass.) four times with reference to a Christian's love being "perfected" (2:5; 4:12, 17f.). John's idea seems to be that God's love (2:5 [not RSV "love for God"]; 4:12), which He demonstrated by sending His Son to be an expiation for sins (4:9f.), is "brought to completion" in Christians who obey Jesus' command to love one another (cf. 2:3-11; 3:10-18; 4:7-12, etc.; see also *teleióō* [RSV "perfectly"], Jn. 17:23). Such "perfected" love results in confidence on the day of judgment (4:17; *téleios,* v. 18).

The Pauline epistles use *téleios* several times in the specific sense of "mature" (cf. RSV 1 Cor. 2:6; 14:20; Eph. 4:13; Phil. 3:15; Col. 1:28; 4:12). In other passages it basically means "whole" or "complete." In Rom. 12:2 Paul exhorts his readers to be transformed by the renewal of their minds so that they may know the "perfect" (i.e., "whole") will of God. In 1 Cor. 13:9-12 Paul contrasts the "partial" (*ek mérous,* vv. 9f., 12; RSV "imperfect," "in part") knowledge that Christians have in the present with the "full" or "complete" (*téleios,* v.10, RSV "perfect") revelation that awaits them at the Parousia. In Phil. 3:12, the only passage in which Paul uses *teleióō,* he appears to be using the language of opponents who claimed that they had already reached the goal of perfect bliss. Col. 3:14 describes *agápē* as *sýndesmos tēs teleiótētos* (RSV "[which] binds everything together in perfect harmony"; AV "the bond of perfectness"), apparently meaning that love is what binds the community together into the unity of the body of Christ, producing the complete wholeness and maturity that is the goal of Christ's body (cf. Eph. 4:13-16).

The *teleióō* word group appears most frequently in the Epistle to the Hebrews. The author often uses *teleióō* in a way not found in the other NT writings: in the specialized LXX sense of "qualify (a priest) for cultic service" or, more generally, "qualify (anyone) to stand before God" (see *TDNT,* VIII, 82f.). "Perfection" thus denotes "unimpeded access to God and unbroken communion with Him" (Bruce, p. 44). The author shows how Jesus, through His suffering (2:10; 5:8f.; cf. 2:17f.) and His offering of Himself as an unblemished sacrifice for sin (7:26-28; cf. 9:14), has been qualified to be the eternal High Priest for His people. By entering the "more perfect" tabernacle (the heavenly sanctuary, i.e., the very presence of God; 9:11) and by offering Himself as a once-for-all sacrifice (cf. vv. 25f.), Jesus has accomplished the "perfection" that was unattainable through the law (7:19; 10:1) or the Levitical priesthood (7:11; 9:9) and was therefore unavailable to the OT saints except through Christ (11:40; 12:23): He has cleansed His people from sin and qualified them to come into God's presence with confidence (10:14, 19-22). In the cultic terminology of Hebrews, then, "perfection" applies both to Jesus' qualification as the eternal High Priest and to Christians who can now stand before God cleansed of sin. (*See also* PERFECTER.)

It is apparent, therefore, that among the NT authors the concept of "perfection" (as reflected in the use of the *teleióō* word group) has a variety of nuances. For none of these writers do these terms mean "total sinlessness." Nonetheless, it is clear that these writers view "perfection" (whether conceived of as undivided loyalty to God, an unimpeded relationship with God, wholehearted obedience to God's will, fully developed love, or an advanced level of maturity in Christ) as a goal toward which the Christian strives with the utmost seriousness.

On the idea of perfection in Christian theology, see J. Wesley, *Plain Account of Christian Perfection* (1766); B. B. Warfield, *Studies in Perfectionism* (1931); R. N. Flew, *Idea of Perfection in Christian Theology* (1934).

***Bibliography.***–J. Bogart, *Orthodox and Heretical Perfectionism in the Johannine Community as Evident in the First Epistle of John* (1977); F. F. Bruce, *Epistle to the Hebrews* (*NICNT,* 1964, repr. 1981); P. Davids, *Epistle of James* (*NIGTC,* 1982); *DNTT,* II, 59-66; P. J. du Plessis, ΤΕΛΕΙΟΣ: *The Idea of Perfection in the NT* (1959); H. N. Ridderbos, *Paul: An Outline of His Theology* (Eng. tr. 1975), pp. 265-272; B. Rigaux, *NTS,* 4 (1957/58), 237-262; *TDNT,* VIII, *s.v.* τέλος κτλ. (G. Delling). N. J. OPPERWALL

**PERFECTER.** A term used by the RSV in He. 12:2 to translate Gk. *teleiōtḗs* (AV "finisher"; NEB "finish"), which is derived from the verb *teleióō,* "bring to completion, make perfect" (*see also* PERFECT). The author exhorts readers to run the race of faith with their full attention on Jesus, "the pioneer and perfecter of our faith" (since "our" does not occur in the Greek, NASB "perfecter of faith" is probably a better translation). In Jesus the faith illustrated by the OT saints mentioned in ch. 11 has been "perfected" or "brought to completion," for throughout His earthly life He exhibited complete trust in God and devotion to God's will (cf. 2:13; 10:7-10). He is therefore the supreme example of persevering faith and a source of strength to those who are presently "running the race."

***Bibliography.***–Comms. on Hebrews by F. F. Bruce (*NICNT,* repr. 1981), P. E. Hughes (1977), and J. Moffatt (*ICC*, repr. 1948); *TDNT*, VIII, *s.v.* τέλος κτλ.: τελειωτής (G. Delling). N. J. O.

**PERFORM** [Heb. *'āśâ* (Ex. 18:18; etc.), piel, pual, and hiphil of *šālam* (Isa. 19:21; etc.), hiphil of *qûm* (1 S. 15:11, 13; etc.), *pā'al* (Ps. 44:1 [MT 2]; Isa. 41:4), *šāmar* (Lev. 8:35; Nu. 3:7; Neh. 12:45), *ṣāḇā'* (Nu. 8:24), *'āḇaḏ* (Josh. 22:27; Ezk. 29:18), etc.; Gk. *poiéō* (Lk. 1:72; etc.), *gínomai* (Acts 4:16, 22, 30; 8:13), *teléō* (Lk. 2:39), *apoteléō* (Lk. 13:32), *epiteléō* (He. 9:6), *prássō* (Acts 26:20), *ergázomai* (Jn. 6:30), *katergázomai* (2 Cor. 12:12), *apodídōmi* (Mt. 5:33)]; AV also DO, KEEP, SHOW, PAY, PRACTICE, WORK, etc.; NEB also DO, CARRY OUT, OBSERVE, OBEY, PAY, DISCHARGE, WORK, etc.

English "perform" is derived from Old French *perfournir* (*per*–"thoroughly" + *fournir*–"to complete"), and thus its original meaning is "bring to completion, finish entirely." Sometimes the AV uses "perform" in this sense, e.g., for Heb. *gāmar* (Ps. 57:2 [MT 3]; RSV, NEB, "fulfil"), for the piel of *bāṣa'* (Isa. 10:12; RSV, NEB, "finish"), and for Gk. *epiteléō* (Rom. 15:28; 2 Cor. 8:11; RSV "complete"; NEB "finish"); cf. the AV "performance" for Gk. *teleíōsis* (Lk. 1:45; RSV, NEB, "fulfil[ment]").

In some instances the RSV continues this use of "perform." The various forms of Heb. *šālam*, which carry the idea "bring to completion," are several times rendered "perform" in connection with vows (piel in Ps. 76:11 [MT 12]; Isa. 19:21; pual in Ps. 65:1 [MT 2]) and counsel (hiphil in Isa. 44:26). The idea seems to be that a vow (or advice) is not complete until it has been entirely carried out or acted upon. Cf. also (see heading above) RSV "perform" for Gk. *teléō* ("complete"), *apoteléō* ("complete, finish") and *epiteléō* ("complete," "accomplish").

In modern English, however, "perform" has lost this narrower focus on completing an act and can simply indicate doing an act. Thus the English versions (including AV) frequently use "perform" for Heb. *'āśâ* (lit. "do," "make"; cf. RSV Lev. 25:18; Dt. 4:13; etc.) and its Greek equivalent *poiéō* (e.g., RSV Jn. 11:47; Acts 7:36; Rev. 16:14); for Heb. *pā'al* ("make" [see heading above]); for the hiphil of *qûm* ("carry out"; cf. RSV 2 K. 23:3; Neh. 5:13; Jer. 11:5; etc.), and for Gk. *gínomai* ("be made, be done, take place"), *prássō* ("do, accomplish"), *ergázomai* ("do, work, accomplish, carry out"), and *katergázomai* ("accomplish, do, produce").

In Dt. 25:5, 7 (cf. also Gen. 38:8) "perform the duty of a husband's brother" translates the piel of Heb. *yāḇam* and refers to the levirate law, which expected a man to marry his deceased brother's widow. *See* HUSBAND'S BROTHER; RELATIONSHIPS, FAMILY. N. J. O.

**PERFUME; PERFUMER** [Heb. *rôqē(a)ḥ* (Ex. 30:25, 35; 37:29; Eccl. 10:1), *raqqāḥ* (1 S. 8:13; Neh. 3:8), *mirqaḥaṯ* (2 Ch. 16:14), *riqqû(a)ḥ* (Isa. 57:9), *rî(a)ḥ* (Ex. 30:38), *nûp* (Prov. 7:17), *q^eṭōreṯ* (Prov. 27:9), *m^equṭṭereṯ* (Cant. 3:6), *bātê hannep̄eš* ("perfume boxes," Isa. 3:20), *bōśem* (Isa. 3:24)]; AV also APOTHECARY, CONFECTIONARY, SMELL, SWEET SMELL, TABLETS; NEB also "for pleasure," "sprinkled," "from burning," "lockets."

The value and universal appeal of perfume can be seen in almost all the ancient literatures. Prov. 27:9 declares that "oil and perfume make the heart glad." The Talmud states that "happy is he whose craft is that of a perfumer" (T.B. *Kiddushim* 82b). Perfumes are commonly used in figures of speech to make favorable comparisons (e.g., Cant. 1:13; 4:10-14; 2 Cor. 2:14-16; Eph. 5:2; Phil. 4:18; cf. Sir. 24:15; 49:1). Perfumes were used in three general areas: medicine, cosmetics, and religion.

The dry, scorching heat of Egypt and Palestine made the use of aromatic oils and ointments a virtual necessity of life. Egyptian texts show widespread use in all levels of society, and claim that "oil is the remedy for the body" (Forbes, p. 2). Both men and women anointed the hair and body with oils after bathing to protect the scalp and skin (Ruth 3:3; 2 S. 12:20; Ezk. 16:9; cf. Jth. 10:3). The pharmacist-perfumer (*myrepsós*; cf. Sir. 49:1) is mentioned alongside the physician in Sir. 38:8.

The line between hygienic and cosmetic uses of perfumes is sometimes rather indistinct; the latter assumed greater importance over time as the fragrances became more desirable in and of themselves. They were important in love-making (Est. 2:12; Cant. 1:3, 13; 5:5; 7:12f.) and were often applied to clothes and bedroom furniture (Ps. 45:8 [MT 9]; Prov. 7:17; Cant. 3:6; 4:11). Even scented breath was valued (Cant. 7:8), perhaps produced by spiced wine (Cant. 8:2; cf. Mk. 15:23), among other things.

Perfume containers mentioned in the Bible include a bag of myrrh "that lies between my breasts" (Cant. 1:13), "perfume boxes" (Isa. 3:20), and alabaster flasks (Mt. 26:7; Mk. 14:7; Lk. 7:37). Many glass, alabaster, stone, and lead jars are mentioned in Egyptian, Mesopotamian, and classical texts, and many survive today, especially from Egypt, a few sealed ones with traces of perfume still present.

In the religious sphere, fragrant oils and spices were used in burying the dead, e.g., Jacob and Joseph (Gen. 50:2f., 26), Asa (2 Ch. 16:14), and Jesus (Jn. 19:39f.; cf. Mk. 26:1; Lk. 23:56; 24:1). Cf. also Herod's elaborate funeral (Josephus *Ant.* xvii.8.3 [199]). Jesus states that even the anointing of His head and feet by the women (but cf. Lk. 7:36-50) anticipates His burial (Mt. 26:6-13

Two eastern Greek terra-cotta statuettes representing Aphrodite. The one with the spoutlike opening (left) is a perfume bottle (*ca.* 550 B.C.) (Trustees of the British Museum)

par. Mk. 14:3-9; Jn. 12:1-8). Mourners, on the other hand, would refrain from using perfumes (2 S. 12:20; Dnl. 10:3; cf. Ad. Est. 14:2; Jth. 10:3).

Aromatic oils were also important in religious ritual in all biblical cultures. The Egyptians, for example, called their perfumes the "fragrance of the gods" (Forbes, p. 8). The sacred anointing oil and holy incense in Israel were made of the finest spices, "blended as by the perfumer" (Ex. 30:23-25, 34f.). Neither was to be made or used for other than the prescribed purposes (30:32f., 37f.).

The art of perfumery was practiced by a professional class of craftsmen: the perfumer is known from the texts of Ebla, Mesopotamia, Egypt, and Ugarit, as well as Greece and Rome, and even from Egyptian reliefs. Biblical references to the process include the recipes in Ex. 30:22-38; 37:29 (where Bezalel is the first-mentioned perfumer); Neh. 3:8; 1 Ch. 9:30; and 1 S. 8:13 (where Israel's daughters would be put to work as perfumers, among other things).

The manufacturing process, detailed in numerous Egyptian and classical recipe texts, used various oils and fats as bases to carry the fragrances. These oils and fats were extracted from flowers, seeds, gum-resins, fragrant woods, etc., by one of several means: (1) balls or cones of animal fat were covered with layers of flower petals until saturated with the scent (enfleurage); (2) the herbs were heated in oil and the mixture strained while hot, or else boiled in water and oil poured over them (maceration); and (3) oil presses were used to extract liquid fragrances (expressing). Note also the dried forms of Cant. 1:3 and 3:6.

Most perfumes come from tropical countries. Of the biblical ones, balsam (BALM), CAMEL'S THORN, HENNA, labdanum (RSV "myrrh," Gen. 37:25; 43:11), STACTE, and GUM (tragacanth) were native to Palestine. Others originated elsewhere: ALOES in East Africa and India; BDELLIUM in India or North Africa; CALAMUS in India; CASSIA in Ceylon and the East Indies; CINNAMON in Ceylon; FRANKINCENSE in Arabia and East Africa; GALBANUM in India; MYRRH in Arabia and East Africa; spikenard (NARD) in Nepal and the Himalayas; SAFFRON in India and the East Indies. ONYCHA, the only animal fragrance mentioned in the Bible, came from mollusks in the Red Sea. The Bible also shows knowledge of the ubiquitous "spice-routes" over which these passed (Gen. 37:25; Ezk. 27:19, 22; cf. 1 K. 10:2, 10, 25).

*See also* ANOINT; FLORA III, IV; FRAGRANCE; INCENSE; OIL; OINTMENT; SPICE.

***Bibliography.***–M. S. Balsam, "Fragrance," in M. S. Balsam and E. Sagarin, eds., *Cosmetics: Science and Technology,* II (2nd ed. 1972), 599-634; A. Brenner, *JSOT,* 25 (1983), 75-81; G. Dalman, *Arbeit und Sitte in Palästina,* IV (1935), 251-55, 259-268; V (1937), 266f., 274, 339; R. J. Forbes, *Studies in Ancient Technology,* III (1965), 1-17, 26-50; R. K. Harrison, *Healing Herbs of the Bible* (1966), pp. 41-54; I. Löw, *Die Flora der Juden* (4 vols., 1924-1934); A. Lucas and J. R. Harris, *Ancient Egyptian Materials and Industries* (4th ed. 1962), pp. 85-97; *MPB*; W. A. Poucher, *Perfumes, Cosmetics, and Soaps,* I (6th ed. 1959); E. Sagarin, *Science and Art of Perfumery* (2nd ed. 1955); C. Singer, *et al.*, eds., *History of Technology,* I (1954), 285-298; G. W. Van Beek, "Frankincense and Myrrh," in E. F. Campbell, Jr. and D. N. Freedman, eds., *BA Reader,* II (1964), pp. 99-126; M. Zohary, *Plants of the Bible* (1982).

D. M. HOWARD, JR.

**PERGA** pûr'gə [Gk. *Pergē*]. A major Greek city of Pamphylia in southern Asia Minor, located a few kilometers upstream from the mouth of the Cestrus and about 8 km. (5 mi.) W of the river itself, an advantageous location in an era of piracy (2nd and 1st cents. B.C.). That shipping had direct access to Perga, in spite of the changed circumstances of the river today, is confirmed by Paul and Barnabas's traveling there by sea from Cyprus (Acts 13:13);

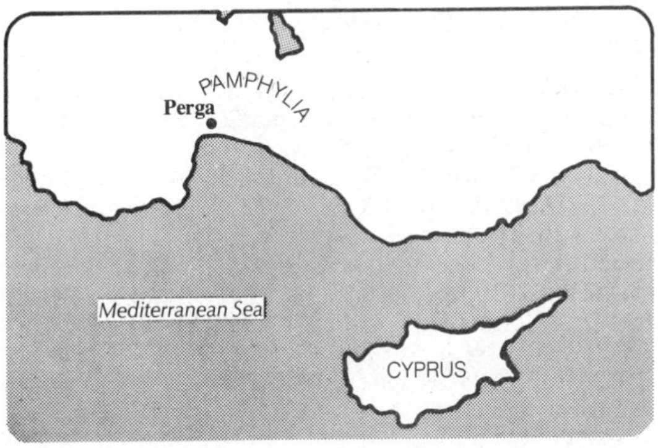


however, their departure from Attalia (14:25f.), the more recent coastal foundation to the southwest, perhaps already represented the normal route (*see* picture in ASIA MINOR). Perga occupied a central position in the chain of Pamphylian cities; from there ran the most direct route north up the Cestrus Valley into Pisidia and the great plateau of Anatolia. According to Ramsay, the modern name of ancient Adada, Kara Bavlo, may preserve a tradition that Paul and Barnabas took this route to Pisidian Antioch (13:14). It was a perilous hinterland and the likely scene of some of Paul's journeying ordeals (2 Cor. 11:26f.).

The city itself was, however, both long established and prosperous. The substantial ruins at Murtana justify its reputation for splendor. At least three aqueducts served the city, and its theater, seating at least twelve thousand people, was one of the largest known from the ancient world. According to tradition Greeks from the Argolid and Lacedaemon settled the city, but its coins show the persistence of an ancient dialect into the 2nd cent. B.C. Subsequently came extensive Italian settlement; one-third of the names on inscriptions from Perga are Roman. The

Ruins of the theater at Perga (B. K. Condit)

Inscription in Latin and Greek mentioning Diana (Artemis) and Plancia Magna, the Roman benefactress of Perga (2nd cent. A.D.) (B. K. Condit)

main national cult was that of the Queen of Perga, no doubt a pre-Hellenic nature-goddess, who was identified with Artemis as at Ephesus and honored as the patroness of the city, her temple having asylum rights.

What happened on the two visits of Paul and Barnabas to Perga is obscure. Acts 13:13 mentions only the breach with Mark, who returned to Jerusalem. Ramsay suggested that Paul contracted malaria (his "thorn in the flesh"?) in the sultry climate and for this reason abandoned a plan to work there in favor of the healthier Galatian cities of Lycaonia (Gal. 4:13). Perga presumably had a synagogue (Pamphylia was a well-attested home of Jews), which initially would have attracted the apostles to Perga and in which they would have preached on their second visit (Acts 14:25). The silence of Acts and later tradition imply, however, that no church was formed.

***Bibliography.***–Strabo *Geog.* xiv.42; Pauly-Wissowa, XIX/1, 694-704; *RRAM*, pp. 1134f.; W. Ramsay, *SPT*, pp. 89-97; *CRE*, pp. 16-24.

E. A. JUDGE

**PERGAMUM** pûr′gə-məm [Gk. *tó Pergamon* or sometimes *hē Pergamos*; also *ho Pergamos* in Polybius xxi.8.10; xxii.3.10]. One of the seven cities of Asia Minor whose "angel" is addressed as the opening device of Revelation (1:11; 2:12). The city is praised for the spirit symbolized in its martyr Antipas but blamed for a few members who approve food sacrificed to idols and other so-called NICOLAITAN deviations (2:13-17). The designation of Pergamum as the place where "Satan's throne" is (v. 13) probably refers to Pergamum's being the official Asian center for the imperial cult (see comms. on Revelation, esp. R. H. Charles, I [*ICC*, 1920], 61; R. Mounce [*NICNT*, 1977], pp. 96f.; H. B. Swete [3rd ed. repr. 1968], pp. 34f.; cf. G. Beasley-Murray [*NCBC*, rev. ed. repr. 1981], p. 84).

Pergamum (modern Bergama) was 24 km. (15 mi.) inland from the northeast Aegean shore and 110 km. (70 mi.) N of Smyrna. On a 300-m. (1000-ft.) height, it commanded a magnificent view of the bay of Lesbos. It lay between the Selinus (to the west) and Cetius tributaries of the navigable Caicus/Bakir 3 km. (2 mi.) south, which formed the border between seacoast Mysia and inland Lydia. Archeological finds in the neighborhood date from the epoch of nearby Troy, 1200 B.C.; from Vergil *Aen.* ii.555f. exegete C. à Lapide thought Troy and Pergamum were the same.

Founded by Greek colonists, the town had a local coinage

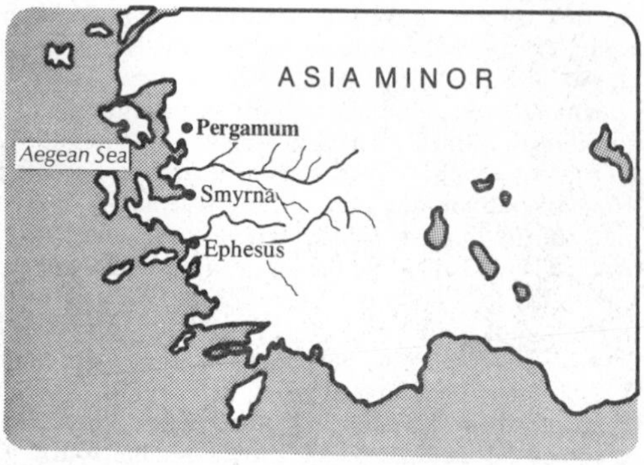


before 420 B.C. and is mentioned in Xenophon (*Anabasis* vii.8.8). During Alexander's conquest Antigonus seized Pergamum, and at the latter's death in 301 Lysimachus of Thrace gained control of Asia Minor. In 283 Lysimachus entrusted this strategic *pérgamon* or "fortress" to Phileterus, who bequeathed it as an independent Seleucid vassal state to his nephew Eumenes I in 263.

Eumenes paid taxes to the warlike Galatians, but after 241 his nephew Attalus I overthrew their domination. This event is commemorated by monuments both here and in Athens, including the famous "Dying Gaul" statue of which a Roman copy is in the Ludovisi collection of Rome's Thermae Museum. Attalus strengthened his position and that of his city-state by supporting Rome against Macedon. He enriched his capital with splendid buildings and extended his rule toward Ankara and Antalya-Perga, 480 km. (300 mi.) ESE (cf. E. Hansen, *Attalids of Pergamon* [1947]; R. Wenning, *Galateranatheme* [1976]).

Eumenes II (197-159 B.C.) attained such great power that he could dictate the succession to the Seleucid throne in 175. He brought his dynasty to its peak, and his capital became a center of artistic and literary culture. His LIBRARY of 200,000 scrolls rivaled Alexandria's and in place of Egyptian papyrus it popularized as writing material the goatskin sheets that thus came to be known as *pergamēnḗ*, corrupted into English as "parchment." The frequent and even ancient assertions that parchment was invented here (Pliny *Nat. hist.* xiii.21 [70]) do not constitute proof, since earlier Assyrians sometimes used skins instead of clay.

A very large theater was erected at the top of the Acropolis, near the library and beside temples of Dionysus, Athena, and Demeter. The most splendid monument of Pergamum was the "altar of Zeus," 12 m. (40 ft.) high, that once crowned its acropolis and was later reconstructed in East Berlin as a result of the archeological enterprises

Reconstruction of the temple of Zeus at Pergamum (Staatliche Museen zu Berlin, DDR)

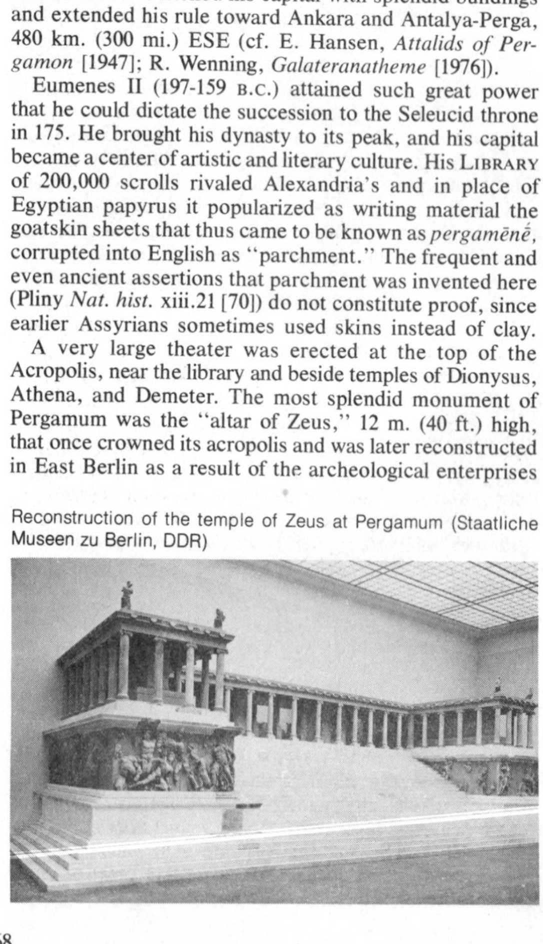

Theater at Pergamum (B. K. Condit)

of K. Humann in 1873, continued by W. Dörpfeld (*Altertümer von Pergamon* [1895-1923]; M. Pfanner, *Archäologischer Anzeiger* [1979], pp. 46-57). This lofty pagan shrine could have been the "Satan's throne" of Rev. 2:13, either because it was of imposing height (see Beasley-Murray) or because it symbolized Rome's power administered at Pergamum from 190 until transferred to Ephesus by Hadrian A.D. 129 (R. North, *Verbum Domini,* 28 [1950], 65). Although Attalus I had adorned the Zeus-altar pedestal with statuary, it is debated whether Eumenes II or his successor had the pedestals constructed. *See* Plate 65.

Attalus II (159-138) founded under his own name the momentous south Turkey seaport of Attalia (now Antalya; *see* picture in ASIA MINOR) but saw his power decline. Prusias II of Bithynia took his city, and he died poisoned. The last monarch, Attalus III (138-133), completed liquidation of the long-proud state. Weak and cruel, and seeing Rome's will about to emerge in the agrarian reform of Tiberius Gracchus, he perhaps cynically "bequeathed" his domain to Rome at his death (R. Boulanger, *Guide Bleu: Turquie* [1958], p. 283). Under Rome Pergamum became the capital of an administrative unit called in a somewhat special sense just Asia, the "fat and fertile" of Cicero's Pompey oration (cf. *RRAM*).

From the Roman period on, the city's building activity moved down the hillside to the plain where modern Bergama sprawls. At the south end of this plain grew up the Asclepium or healing center, famous throughout the world since 350 B.C. Its attendants, though fostering superstitious beliefs, also showed genuine sympathy for the sufferers and sometimes could help them with a surprisingly adequate stock of medical lore acquired through years of observation. Galen, a native of Pergamum who received his early training there (*ca.* 160 B.C.), along with his rival Hippocrates founded scientific medicine.

The German excavations, continued in 1900-1913 and 1927-1939 under T. Wiegand (O. Deubner, *Das Asklepieion* [1938]), were resumed in 1958 at the healing sanctuary (E. Boehringer, *Neue deutsche Ausgrabungen* [1959], pp. 121-171; O. Ziegenauer, *Das Asklepieion 2* [1975]). A theater was a small adjunct of the Asclepius sanctuary. Another adjunct was the library built by Flavia Melitena *ca.* 190 B.C.

Pergamum, drained of its treasury by the Roman takeover, supported Mithridates against Rome in 88 B.C. and saw its library handed over to its hated rival Alexandria by Cleopatra's friend Antony. Josephus (*Ant.* xiv.10.22 [247-255]) told of a Roman letter in 139 and a Pergamum senate decree in 130 defending the Jewish community already installed in Pergamum as in many neighboring cities of Asia Minor (see, e.g., *LSC,* pp. 142-157). The several years of Paul's ministry in Ephesus *ca.* A.D. 53 may have enabled him to bring Christianity to the Jews in Pergamum, 160 km. (100 mi.) north. The Pergamum monuments bring to mind events in the ministries of Paul or John: the theaters, for which the admission ticket was sometimes "a white stone" (Rev. 2:17); the extensive triple gymnasium, where youths trained not only in sport (1 Cor. 9:24) but also in philosophy, while walking ("peripatetic") among the colonnades (*stoá*).

Recorded martyrs besides Antipas are Carpus, Papylus, and Agathonike under Decius (*LTK,* VIII, 273). A ruin called Red Basilica in the plain beneath the lower agora of the Pergamum Acropolis, excavated in 1934-38, may have been a temple built to Egyptian Serapis before 200 B.C. but transformed into a Byzantine church of St. Paul (Boulanger, p. 289). Hadrian visited Pergamum in A.D. 123 (Pauly-Wissowa, I/1, 505). Three temples to Roman emperors explain Pergamum's title of "thrice temple-warden" (Pauly-Wissowa, XIX/1, 1235-63).

Zenobia's rise to power at Palmyra in A.D. 269 weakened Asia Minor's resistance. Archeologists have retrieved four churches built at Pergamum before 717. Leo the Isaurian and his son *ca.* 740 rebuilt the city after Moslem invasions; the Crusaders occupied it in 1212 and Timur in 1402. The Ottomans installed since 1330 enriched the town with fifteen mosques, one allegedly an earlier Sancta Sophia church. Today Bergama has also a small museum amid its unequaled magnificence of standing ruins.

*Bibliography.*–J. Finegan, *Archeology of the NT* (1981), pp. 172-74; *LSC*, pp. 281-315. R. NORTH

**PERICOPE** pə-ri'kō-pē [Gk. *perikopḗ*–'cutting around']. A term used by Greek church fathers and later scholastics for an excerpted Scripture passage or a shorter classical text. Based on synagogue and early Church use of shorter readings in worship services, later Christian lectionary collections became known as pericopae.

In modern biblical studies, chiefly through the development of form criticism, "pericope" became a technical term for a Scripture unit said to have originally circulated independently. Such units were supposed to have been gathered by the Synoptic writers and implanted in a historical-biographical framework of the Evangelists' own invention. In current exegesis the term is used for any passage of one to three paragraphs studied as a unit (e.g., Mk. 1:40-44).

R. KROEGER

**PERIDA** pə-rī'də [Heb. *p^e^rîḏā'*] (Neh. 7:57); **PERUDA** pə-ro͞o'də [Heb. *p^e^rûḏā'*; Gk. *Pherida, Phadoura,* Apoc. *Pharida*] (Ezr. 2:55; 1 Esd. 5:33); AV Apoc. PHARIRA; NEB Apoc. PHARIDA. Head of a family of Solomon's servants that returned from the Exile with Zerubbabel (Ezr. 2:55 par. Neh. 7:57; 1 Esd. 5:33).

**PERISH** [Heb. *'āḇaḏ* (e.g., Lev. 26:38), niphal of *kāraṯ*–'cut' (Gen. 41:36), *nāp̄al*–'fall' (Ex. 19:21), *tāmam* + inf. of *gāwaʿ* (Nu. 17:13 [MT 28]), niphal of *šāmaḏ* (e.g., Dt. 28:51), niphal of *sāp̄â* (e.g., 1 S. 26:10), *ʿāḇar*–'pass (over)' (Job 36:12), *kālâ* (Isa. 31:3; Ezk. 13:14; etc.), niphal of *dāmâ* (Ps. 49:12, 20 [MT 13, 21]; Hos. 10:7), qal and hiphil of *dāmam* (Jer. 8:14), niphal of *šāmam* (Lam. 4:5); Gk. *apóllymi* (Mt. 18:14; etc.), *eínai eis apṓleian* (Acts 8:20), pass. of *aphanízō* (Acts 13:14); *apothnḗskō* (Mt. 8:32), *phthorá* (Col. 2:22); *phthartós* (1 Cor. 9:25)]; AV also "be consumed with dying" (Nu. 17:13), DESTROY, FAIL, BE SILENT, BE CONSUMED, BE DESOLATE, BE CUT OFF; NEB also MEET ONE'S END, VANISH, WIPE OUT, BE ANNIHILATED, PAY WITH ONE'S LIFE, BE DOOMED, BECOME EXTINCT, BE LOST (Mt. 18:14), GO TO DAMNATION (Acts 8:20), etc.

***I. In the OT.***–The main Hebrew verb translated by "perish," *'āḇaḏ,* in the qal has two dominant meanings: "wander off, be lost," and "perish, be destroyed." Sometimes the first meaning is used literally in reference to animals that have wandered away from the herd and are likely to be killed (e.g., 1 S. 9:3, 20; RSV "be lost"). Occasionally this use occurs in a figurative sense: Israel is like sheep whose shepherds have left them and who wander about aimlessly (RSV "lost," Jer. 50:6; Ezk. 34:4, 16; *see* LOSE). This use of *'āḇaḏ* corresponds closely to one English meaning of "perish": "go destructively" (< Lat. *per-ire*).

More frequently *'āḇaḏ* means "perish, be destroyed," or, in the piel or hiphil, "cause to perish, destroy" (e.g., Dt. 7:24; Ezk. 25:7). The transitive forms of the verb (usually rendered "destroy" by the RSV) occur most often in a military context, very frequently with God Himself as the author of destruction. Behind many of the intransitive (qal) uses of the verb also lies the idea that divine judgment brings about the destruction of nations (e.g., Lev. 26:38; Dt. 4:26f.; 11:17; 30:18; Josh. 23:13, 16; Job 4:9; Ps. 2:12; 10:16; 73:27; Isa. 41:11). Used in this sense, as in the sense of "wander off, be lost," *'āḇaḏ* always implies an element of personal responsibility for one's own destruction (see *TDNT,* I, 394f.). The reason for the divinely willed ruin is neglect of or opposition to God's law (cf. Dt. 8:19f.; 28:20). *See also* DESTRUCTION III.

In certain prophetic texts *'āḇaḏ* describes the disappearance during evil times of the good qualities of life, e.g., truth (Jer. 7:28), wisdom (Isa. 29:14; Jer. 49:7), and godliness (Mic. 7:2).

A striking derivative of *'āḇaḏ* is the noun *'^a^ḇaddôn* (ABADDON), the place of destruction in the afterlife (Job 26:6; etc.). In this connection the question arises whether *'āḇaḏ* and its derivatives ever refer to eternal destruction or always simply to the ruinous end of this life. Esther's statement, ". . . I will go to the king, though it is against the law; and if I perish, I perish" (4:16), plainly has in view only her self-sacrificing death. But certain passages, especially in the Psalms, suggest horizons beyond the grave (cf. Ps. 73:27 in the light of v. 24; 83:17; etc.; see M. Dahood, *Psalms,* III [*AB,* 1970], xli-lii; G. C. Berkouwer, *Return of Christ* [Eng. tr. 1972], pp. 171-79). In any case it is God — not the grave — who finally decides a person's destiny (cf. Ps. 49:14f.).

***II. In the NT.***–The key NT term rendered by "perish" is Gk. *apóllymi* (the usual LXX translation of Heb. *'āḇaḏ*). Like Heb. *'āḇaḏ, apóllymi* can be used intransitively with the sense either of "lose" or "be destroyed." When read in the light of its LXX usage, *apóllymi* evokes the image of a sheep that separates itself from the flock, gets entangled in the shrubbery, and starves to death or is eaten by wild animals. It implies an element of initial wilfulness and later helplessness. Thus the loss of one's life can be attributed at least in part to one's own will (cf. "lose," Mt. 10:39 par.). But whereas *'āḇaḏ* usually connotes only physical death, *apóllymi* frequently refers to a definitive and unending destruction that is contrasted with everlasting life (see *TDNT,* I, 394-96). This contrast is clearly observable in Jn. 3:16: in a world that God loves and in which the gospel is preached, the alternatives are either to perish or to have eternal life (cf. 10:28; see R. E. Brown, *Gospel According to John,* I [*AB,* 1966], 134).

Greek *phthorá* ("corruption, destruction") and *phthartós* ("corruptible") refer to subjection to death as an ongoing process. Corruption characterizes existence controlled by flesh (cf. Isa. 40:6: "All flesh is grass"; *see* FLESH I.G). By contrast God is immortal (*áphthartos,* 1 Tim. 1:17), and the Christian inheritance is imperishable (*áphthartos,* 1 Pet. 1:4).

The extended passage on resurrection in 1 Cor. 15:42-55 is governed by the contrast between the perishable and the imperishable. What is sown (human life from conception onward) is "perishable" (v. 42), i.e., subject to corruption in its process and end-result; what is raised (the human body which bears "the image of the man of heaven" [v. 49]) is "imperishable" (*aphtharsía*), i.e., outside the sphere of death and corruption (cf. vv. 53f.).

In 1 Peter the same contrast is at work, but in widely differing contexts. Here the seed of regeneration is the imperishable Word (1:23); the saving blood of Christ is contrasted with perishable silver and gold (1:18f.); a gentle and quiet spirit is called an "imperishable jewel" (3:4); and the promised salvation is an imperishable inheritance (1:4).

*See also* DEATH; LIFE; PERDITION.

*Bibliography.*–*TDNT*, I, *s.v.* ἀπόλλυμι κτλ. (A. Oepke); IX, *s.v.* φθείρω κτλ. (G. Harder); *TDOT,* I, *s.v.* "'ābhadh" (B. Otzen); *TWOT,* I, 3f. J. VRIEND

**PERIZZITE** per'ə-zīt [Heb. *p^e^rizzî*; Gk. *Pherezaios* (except in Ezr. 9:1, LXX A *Pherezi*, B *Pheresthei*)]; AV Apoc. PHERESITE, PHEREZITE. One of the peoples occupying Canaan from patriarchal times (Gen. 13:7; 15:20; 34:30). Because of the sin of these various peoples (15:16) God commissioned Israel in the period of the Conquest to execute His temporal judgment against them (e.g., Dt. 7:1ff.). Israel's fidelity to this charge was erratic (cf. Josh. 9; 13:13; Jgs. 1; 3:5); thus many Perizzites and other non-Israelites survived till Solomon's time, when he conscripted them for his slave labor force (1 K. 9:20f. par. 2 Ch. 8:7f.).

The vagueness of the biblical references has led to scholarly disagreement about the precise geographical distribution and identity of the Perizzites. The Perizzites are merely listed with other Canaanite groups, typically the Canaanites, Hittites, Amorites, Hivites, and Jebusites (see Ishida for discussion of the various lists). The lack of convincing extrabiblical references to this population adds to the problem (cf. Wiseman, pp. xv-xvi).

Joshua 11:3 groups the Perizzites with the Amorites, Hittites, and Jebusites, and locates them in the hill country of northern Canaan (cf. also Gen. 13:7; 34:30). Other passages suggest the Perizzites also inhabited the highlands further south (Josh. 16:10, LXX; Jgs. 1:4f.). Finally, some infer from Josh. 17:15 that the Perizzites inhabited the forested region of Carmel (so A. H. Sayce, *ISBE,* IV, *s.v.*) or of the Transjordan (so Soggin, p. 183). But other studies defend a location in Israel's central highlands (so Woudstra, p. 268; Miller, p. 244).

A plausible etymology relates "Perizzite" to the Heb. *p^e^rāzôṯ, p^e^rāzî,* "rural country" (the LXX renders two of the three occurrences of this term as "Perizzites"). Thus many scholars consider "Perizzite" simply as an appellative — hence, "villagers." The pairing of "Canaanites and Perizzites" (Gen. 13:7; 34:30; Josh. 16:10, LXX; Jgs. 1:4f.) may support this view (cf. Boling, *Judges,* p. 54). While not necessarily excluding an appellative use or derivation (cf. M. Liverani in Wiseman, pp. 101ff.), the general biblical use of Perizzite seems to be ethnic.

Of the two common scholarly proposals, the first identifies the Perizzites as a Hurrian subgroup. Favoring this approach is the possible identification of a few names of Hurrian background: *pire/izzi,* an envoy of the Hurri-Mitanni King Tušratta to Pharaoh Amenhotep IV (Am.Tab. 27-29). Since Am.Tab. 27 includes a hieratic Egyptian note *pirasi* for this name, the related names of various slaves (e.g., *pirisim, pirisija*) may also be relevant. Finally the Hurrian personal name *pirzu* is found at Nuzi (cf. *Encyclopedia Judaica, s.v.*).

The second proposal identifies the Perizzites as a subgroup of Amorites (in some contexts, a term which is broad enough to include Hurrians and other non-Semitic groups). Favoring the Amorite proposal is the recognition that the invading population of Canaan at the dawn of the M.B. Age was generally Amorite (see esp. Dever, *HTR, contra* Lapp, p. 115, that the Perizzites were originally Central Asians). Dever and others argue that this earlier Amorite wave was made up of seminomadic groups from the fringes of Syria (hence "Perizzite" = "rustic") as opposed to the later Amorite wave which brought the distinctive urban culture of M.B.II.A. Some such distinction, or perhaps a distinction of geographical distribution, would explain the separate listing of Perizzites and Amorites in Scripture.

*See also* CANAAN, esp. III.

***Bibliography.***–R. Boling, *Judges* (*AB,* 1975); R. Boling and G. E. Wright, *Joshua* (*AB,* 1982), p. 166; W. G. Dever, *HTR,* 64 (1971), 197-226; "The Beginning of the M.B. Age in Syria-Palestine," in F. M. Cross, *et al.*, eds., *Magnalia Dei* (*Festschrift* for G. E. Wright, 1976), pp. 3-38; H. L. Ginsberg and B. Maisler (Mazar), *JPOS,* 14 (1934), 234-267; T. Ishida, *Bibl.*, 60 (1979), 461-490; P. W. Lapp, *Dhahr Mirzbaneh Tombs* (1966); J. M. Miller, "Israelite Occupation of Canaan," in J. H. Hayes and J. M. Miller, eds., *Israelite and Judaean History* (*OTL,* 1977), pp. 213-284; J. A. Soggin, *Joshua* (Eng. tr., *OTL*, 1972); D. J. Wiseman, ed., *Peoples of OT Times* (1973); M. H. Woudstra, *Joshua* (*NICOT,* 1981).

G. P. HUGENBERGER

**PERJURER** [Gk. *epíorkos*] (1 Tim. 1:10). One who swears falsely. In 1 Tim. 1:10 the term is found in a list of vices, as is "perjury" (*epiorkía*) in Wisd. 14:25. It is related to the verb *epiorkéō,* "swear falsely," in Mt. 5:33. *See also* OATH; SWEAR.

**PERPETUAL** [Heb. *ʿôlām*] (Ex. 28:43; Lev. 3:17; Nu. 10:8; etc.); AV often FOR EVER, also EVERLASTING (Ex. 40:15; Nu. 25:13); NEB usually FOR ALL TIME, also FOR EVER, IN PERPETUITY, UNENDING (Jer. 51:39, 57), IMMEMORIAL (Ezk. 35:5), etc.; [*tāmîḏ*] (Ex. 30:8); NEB REGULAR; [*neṣaḥ*] (Ps. 74:3); NEB "beyond repair"; [niphal part. of *nāṣaḥ*] (Jer. 8:5); NEB "incurable"; **PERPETUALLY** [*ʿaḏ*] (Am. 1:11); NEB UNCEASING; **PERPETUATE** [hiphil of *qûm*–'establish'] (Dt. 25:7; Ruth 4:10); AV RAISE UP; [niphal of *qārā'*–'be called, named'] (Gen. 48:16); AV "name"; NEB "called by (my name)"; [niphal of *zāraʿ*–'be sown, impregnated'] (Nah. 1:14); AV SOW; NEB "scatter"; **PERPETUITY** [*ṣ^e^mîṯuṯ, ṣ^e^miṯuṯ*–'forfeiture of right to repurchase'] (Lev. 25:23, 30); AV FOR EVER; NEB also "outright."

"Perpetual" usually translates *ʿôlām,* a term that is more frequently translated "for ever" or "everlasting." In the OT *ʿôlām* does not, however, represent an abstract, philosophical concept of eternity. Rather, its primary meaning seems to be "the whole duration of a life span." When referring to God or anything grounded in God's nature, it denotes an unending duration (*see* AGE **1**; ETERNAL I; ETERNITY II). But elsewhere it can denote the entire life span of a person (e.g., a slave [Ex. 21:6]; Samuel [1 S. 1:22]; David [27:12]), a nation (cf. Ex. 31:16; Josh. 4:7), a relationship (cf. Ezk. 35:5), an institution (e.g., the Aaronic priesthood), etc. The translation "perpetual" highlights the temporality of institutions such as the priesthood (e.g., Ex. 28:43; 29:9, 28; 40:15; etc.), the sacrificial system (e.g., Lev. 3:17), and the sabbath (e.g., Ex. 31:16). Heb. *ʿaḏ* and *neṣaḥ* are basically synonyms of *ʿôlām,* while *tāmîḏ* is an adjective or adverb that is usually translated "continual" or "continually."

N. J. O.

**PERSECUTE; PERSECUTION** [Heb. *rāḏap*–'pursue,' *śāṭam*–'bear a grudge against' (Job 30:21); Gk. *diṓkō*–'pursue,' *diōgmós*–'pursuit,' *diṓktēs*–'pursuer' (1 Tim. 1:13), *thlípsis*–'affliction' (Acts 11:19)]; AV also OPPOSE, FOLLOW; NEB also PURSUE, HUNT, HOUND. In Ps. 49:5 (MT 6) the RSV ("persecutors") and NEB ("treacherous foes") read *ʿōq^e^ḇay* for MT *ʿ^a^qēḇay* (lit. "my heels," so AV; see comms.). Persecution is the suffering or pressure, mental, moral, or physical, which authorities, individuals, or crowds inflict on others, especially for opinions or beliefs, with a view to their subjection by recantation, silencing, or, as a last resort, execution. The importance of this subject is indicated by the frequent use of the terms in both the OT and the NT.

I. OT
II. Intertestamental Period
III. NT
  A. Christ
  B. The Church
IV. Gentile Persecutions
V. Results of Persecution

*I. OT.*–Persecution was common in OT times, although in view of the close ties between people and religion it is often hard, especially before the Exile, to distinguish between ethnic and religious oppression. During and after the Exile plain examples occur in Daniel, which reports the attempts of alien rulers to force the three young men, and then Daniel himself, to betray their religious beliefs or abandon their religious practices (Dnl. 3). Apart from external pressures, the righteous in Israel suffered persecution by their own people, as testified by Jesus (Mt. 23:35) and Stephen (Acts 7:52). The prophets in particular suffered persecution of this kind, e.g., Elijah and other prophets of God under Ahab (1 K. 18) and Uriah and Jeremiah under Zedekiah (Jer. 26:20-24). The Psalms, too, are full of pleas to God made by those who suffer persecution because of their faithfulness to God and His commandments (e.g., Ps. 119:84-87, 150, 157, 161).

*II. Intertestamental Period.*–In the period between the Testaments the Jews often suffered severely because of their refusal to accept idolatry and their loyalty to God and the law. The attempt of Antiochus Epiphanes of Syria to replace Israel's religion by pagan worship led to wholesale martyrdom (1 Macc. 1:44ff.) until the successful revolt of the Maccabees remedied the situation. Jews of the Dispersion, too, were always open to attacks because of what seemed to be their strange beliefs and customs and their refusal to comply with the prevailing religious syncretism. The afflictions of those who maintained fidelity in spite of vicious pressures are aptly summed up in He. 11:33-38.

*III. NT.–A. Christ.* Christ Himself suffered persecution as many efforts were made to silence Him by force (Lk. 4:29) or cunning (Mt. 22:15ff.). From one standpoint His arrest, trial, and crucifixion might be regarded as a supreme instance of persecution. Christ also warned His disciples that they would suffer persecution as He did (Mt. 5:11; 10:16ff.; Jn. 15:20). Persecution would serve as a test. Thus in Mk. 4:17, in the parable of the Sower, those who have no root in themselves fall away when persecution comes because of the Word. At the same time, persecution carries the possibility of blessing for those who endure. One of the Beatitudes refers to those that are persecuted for righteousness' sake. Their special blessing is that the Kingdom is theirs (Mt. 5:10).

The forms that persecution may take in the NT are varied, whether in relation to Christ Himself or to His disciples. Prominent are false accusation (Mt. 5:11), disparagement (Jn. 8:48), excommunication (Lk. 6:22), contemptuous treatment (Mk. 15:16ff.), and, of course, arrest and flogging (Mt. 10:17) and, in the last resort, execution (Jn. 21:18f.).

*B. The Church.* The first persecutions of the Church were at the hands of Jewish authorities. They began shortly after Pentecost, partly because of some general hostility to the message and mission of the apostles, but chiefly because of Sadducean opposition to the proclamation of the resurrection of Jesus (Acts 4:2; 5:17). The Pharisees at first adopted a more tolerant attitude (5:34-39), and the addition of many priests to the Church shows that the people as such did not instigate early attempts to suppress the gospel (6:7). Indeed, the NT itself specifically states that the people held the apostles in high honor (5:13), and it leaves the impression of a popular movement that only the religious leaders were trying to quell (5:14; 6:7). The first arrests proved unsuccessful, and serious persecution began only with the stoning of Stephen, whose exposition of OT history incensed synagogue opponents, was misinterpreted to the people, and infuriated the members of the high council (6:9ff.; 7:54ff.). The ensuing attack on the Jerusalem church scattered its members, and Paul came into prominence for the persecuting zeal that he then regarded as service of God but would later see as his great sin (cf. Acts 8:1ff.; 9:1ff.; 22:4; 1 Cor. 15:9). The execution of James, the first apostolic martyr, came shortly afterward under Herod Agrippa (Acts 12:1f.), and Peter, imprisoned when James was killed, escaped a similar fate only through the intervention of the angel (12:3-11).

After these first years the NT has little evidence of continued persecution in Palestine, but Paul on his missionary journeys frequently met with opposition from Jews who rejected the Christian message. Active hostility drove him out of Thessalonica (Acts 17:5ff.), and at Corinth charges were preferred against him before the proconsul Gallio (Acts 18:12ff.), although without success. On some unspecified occasions the Jews flogged Paul (2 Cor. 11:24), and finally in Jerusalem he was subjected to rough treatment (Acts 21:30ff.), a plot was made to assassinate him (23:12ff.), and the accusations of the council led to his imprisonment, his appeal to the emperor, his transfer to Rome, and perhaps to his ultimate execution at gentile hands.

Shortly afterward James the Lord's brother met his death in Jerusalem (probably by stoning), and during the Jewish War Christians in the capital escaped more serious repression only by their flight to Pella. After A.D. 70, however, the Jews lost any active power of persecution except briefly during the turbulent years of the Bar Cochba revolt (A.D. 132-135).

*IV. Gentile Persecutions.*–During the first years of missionary expansion the Church enjoyed comparative peace from the Roman authorities, partly due to the general imperial policy of religious toleration, and partly due to the supposed privileged position of Christianity as a sect of Judaism. Sporadic hostility arose when vested interests were thought to be threatened, as at Philippi and Ephesus (Acts 16–19), but Paul's Roman citizenship proved a potent deterrent in the one case, and fear of government action served as a useful brake in the other. Paul was certainly kept under arrest by Felix, who wished to maintain good relations with the Jewish leaders, but when the hearing took place before Festus and Agrippa, the two judges could not see that Paul had done any wrong. Rome at first seems to have repeated the verdict, for according to the witness of the Pastorals Paul was able to resume his missionary work for a limited period.

A drastic change came in July of A.D. 64, when Nero, accused of setting a disastrous fire in Rome and unable to clear himself by gifts or sacrifices, decided to make the Christians his scapegoats, and started a persecution which for its cruelty would evoke censure even from those who regarded Christianity as a debased superstition (Tacitus *Ann.* xv.44). References to this persecution may perhaps be found in 1 Peter, and also in 2 Timothy, in which Paul mentions his trial and impending death. 1 Clem. 1:1 also refers to the martyrdom of Peter and Paul at this time, and Eusebius (*HE* ii.25.5ff.) adds that Peter suffered death by crucifixion and Paul by beheading. If Revelation belongs to the age of Nero, the persecution extended to Asia Minor, for the opening letters mention pressures and martyrdoms (2:2, 10, 13, 19; 3:8), and the author himself suffered exile for the word of God and the witness of Christ (1:9). It is possible, of course, that this persecution took place some years later under Domitian, but in Revelation Rome had certainly assumed the persecutor's role (16:6; 17:6; 18:24; 19:21; 20:4). The state that should be the minister of divine justice (Rom. 13:1ff.) had become the beast from the abyss (Rev. 13), the new Babylon whose fall would be an occasion for rejoicing (ch. 18).

Under Trajan at the beginning of the 2nd cent. the question of Christianity arose in a letter sent to the emperor by Pliny the Younger, proconsul of Bithynia. Faced with a great increase of the Church that had caused the temples to be deserted and the trade in offerings to fall off, Pliny had followed up anonymous accusations, called upon accused persons to renounce their faith and worship the imperial statue, and either managed to enforce compliance or imposed severe punishment. He wished to know whether he had taken the right course. Trajan in his reply recognized that punishing known believers was the correct thing to do, but he insisted that any who recanted should be released, and he provided some protection for Christians by stating that they should not be tracked down and that anonymous accusations should be disregarded (Pliny [the Younger] *Ep.* x.96f.). In general, persecution seems not to have been either common or severe in Trajan's time, although Ignatius of Antioch, who wrote his famous letters on the way to execution at Rome, was a notable victim.

The more relaxed attitude of Trajan persisted under his great successors Hadrian and Antoninus Pius. Hadrian in a rescript to the proconsul of Asia (*ca.* A.D. 125) added the further protection that any who falsely accused others of being Christians should suffer even more stringent punishment than those they accused (Eusebius *HE* iv.9). The more favorable climate of the period encouraged the Apologists to offer their arguments for Christianity and its recognition, although it is doubtful how far those in power paid attention to the various pleas. Undoubtedly the Church enjoyed peace in many areas at this time. Isolated martyrdoms still occurred, of course, e.g., that of Polycarp in Smyrna (A.D. 156) and that of Justin in Rome (A.D. 165). In the records, the issue was not the illegality of Christianity as such but the refusal of Christians to give proof of loyalty, as all others would do apart from the Jews who were specifically exempt, by making some offering to a statue of the divine emperor. Popular rumors, e.g., that the Christians were atheists, cannibals, and incestuous persons, helped to inflame ordinary citizens against the Church, especially in times of emergency through earthquake, famine, fire, or flood, and the steadfast rejection of idolatrous offerings gave some substance to at least the first of these charges.

Toward the end of the Antonine period, Marcus Aurelius, although a great emperor in other respects, took a more hostile attitude to the faith. The terrible outbreak of mob violence in South Gaul in A.D. 177 (Eusebius *HE* v.1, 3ff.), which produced some of the heroic martyrs of the early Church, marred the reputation of an otherwise sagacious and conscientious ruler.

The 3rd cent. brought an intensification of persecution broken by long periods of virtual toleration. As Tertullian claimed in his *Apologeticum*, the Church enjoyed rapid expansion as the 2nd cent. progressed. More systematic policies were developed, first to check its growth, and then, if possible, to secure its eradication. The edict against conversion under Septimius Severus in A.D. 202 caused temporary disruption, e.g., in Alexandria, from which Clement fled, and where Origen suffered the loss of his father. More seriously, Decian in A.D. 250 decreed that all persons should make offerings on penalty of torture or death, the aim being to execute the more forceful leaders and to force the rest into apostasy. Those who obeyed the edict received certificates of compliance as a check. The policy proved surprisingly successful, for while many Christians stood out against the imperial demand, large numbers of nominal believers either obeyed it or secured certificates by bribery, and divisions arose within the Church over what to do with apostates who desired to renew their membership on the death of Decius in 251. In 257 Valerian renewed the persecution with particular attacks on the clergy and believers of higher social rank, and also with the confiscation of church property. Several leading Christians, including Cyprian of Carthage, suffered martyrdom as a result. Valerian, however, reigned only briefly, and in 261 Gallienus, who had been co-emperor but now reigned alone, not only granted toleration but gave the Church official recognition by restoring its property.

The final struggle came with Diocletian in A.D. 303 when the policies of Decian were reactivated, churches were destroyed, and Christians were also ordered to hand over their sacred books and vessels for destruction. This last great Roman persecution, which continued intermittently for many years, took a serious toll, especially in the more heavily populated eastern part of the empire where Galerius pressed it more severely. It also led to renewed controversies over the status of clergy who handed over the sacred books (the so-called *traditores*) or who were ordained by those who did so. Yet this persecution proved in the event to be the darkest hour before the dawn, for eventually even Galerius, the most savage of the persecutors, was forced of his "most mild clemency" (as he put it) "to offer his speediest indulgence, that Christians may exist again, and may establish their meeting houses" (A.D. 311). More secure peace came in A.D. 313 when Constantine and Licinius, the emperors in West and East, issued the famous Edict of Milan, which granted liberty of opinion and practice to all religious persuasions. Licinius, it is true, commenced a new persecution in 319, but he was overthrown in 324 by Constantine, who as sole emperor proceeded to reaffirm his policy of toleration for all beliefs, although now with some measure of scorn for those who preferred their "temples of falsehood" to "the glorious edifice" of God's truth.

*V. **Results of Persecution.***–For all the misery it caused, persecution served some valuable purposes. It discouraged people from joining the Church except out of sincere conviction. It raised up witnesses whose faith commended itself because of their obvious sincerity of commitment. It purged the Church when in more peaceful periods nominal adherents increased and Christianity became more fashionable. It proved the power of the gospel against the worst that a great imperial power like Rome could do. It provided leaders who could withstand heresies like Arianism as they had withstood oppression. It proved to those who suffered under it the truth of Christ's promise to be present with His people and of His assurance that they could be of good courage in affliction in virtue of His own overcoming of the world.

Naturally there were problems and failures. Persecution not only brought havoc to individual lives but devastated churches, led to apostasy, and brought divisions that were potentially more disruptive than persecution itself. Even more seriously and sadly, perhaps, Christians failed to learn from persecution that they themselves had no right to become persecutors when they came into a position to be so, as happened when they secured the favor of Constantine, and the attempted suppression of the schismatic Donatists formed the first of a shameful series of similar acts both within the Church and outside it. Nevertheless, the survival of the Church under persecution, which seemed almost a miracle of resurrection to those who went through the Diocletian era, showed that God could indeed overrule human wrath to His own glory and the well-being of His Church and its ministry. As Christians have still had to suffer persecution in later centuries and across different continents, they can thus take heart from the experiences of their predecessors in the NT communities and the early Church.

*Bibliography*.–H. Bettenson, *Documents of the Christian Church* (1963); L. H. Canfield, *The Early Persecution of the Christians* (1913); B. J. Kidd, *Documents Illustrative of the History of the Church,* I (1920); J. Stevenson, *A New Eusebius* (1960); H. B. Workman, *Persecution in the Early Church* (n.d.).

G. W. BROMILEY

**PERSEPOLIS** pûr-sep'ə-lis [Gk. *Persepolis, Persaipolis, Persopolis*–'city of Parsa']. A city in ancient Persia.

Persepolis, Susa, Ecbatana, and Babylon were the four capitals of the Achaemenian empire (550-330 B.C.). Situated in the province of Fars, the place of origin of the dynasty, about 50 km. (31 mi.) N of Shiraz, Persepolis stretched out over the vast plain of Marvdasht crossed by the Polvar River.

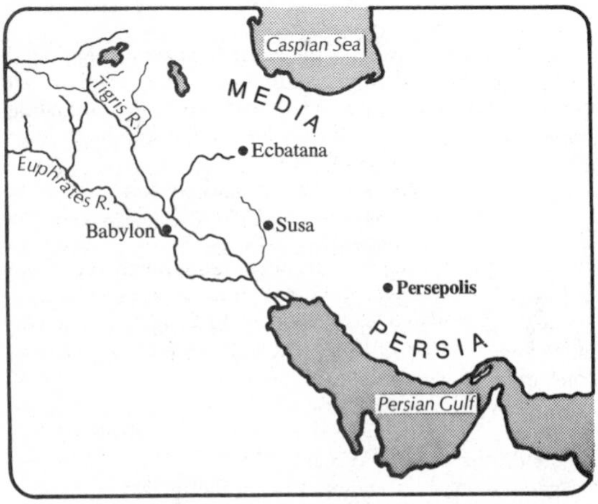


The royal part of the capital, conceived and in part realized by Darius (522-486 B.C.), was an artificial terrace resting against Kouh-è Rahman, the "mountain of pardon." This gigantic platform, 452 by 352 m. (1485 by 1155 ft.), rising 12 m. (40 ft.) above the plain, was formed by joining the spurs of the mountain by a mass of polygonal blocks dovetailed with iron and lead pins.

The principal access to the terrace was made from the west side by a majestic double stairway with very low steps, which permitted a horseman to ascend. The terrace supported great official buildings in the north part and residential buildings in the south part. The buildings had walls of coarse, sunbaked bricks, but the doors, windows, recesses, and columns were carved in stone brought from nearby quarries.

In the north part of the terrace the approaches of two great halls, the Apadana and the "hundred columns," were controlled by the propylaeum of Xerxes. The Apadana, where the king received nobles of the two master peoples, the Persians and Medes, was a great square hall surrounded by three porticos. Seventy-two columns, each 8 m. (27 ft.) high, supported its roof, made of cedar beams from Lebanon. Two stairways on the northern and eastern sides leading to this hall were decorated in relief: on one side a deployment of the royal court, with guards, army, horses, and chariots (*see* second picture in ARCHEOLOGY OF IRAN; *see also* Vol. I, Plate 1), and on the opposite side a procession of twenty-three delegations of nations that constituted the first world empire, from the Ethiopians

Relief from the Apadana at Persepolis showing some of the delegations from twenty-three nations bringing tribute to Xerxes (L. A. Willis)

Relief from the Apadana at Persepolis showing Median (with high rounded hats) and Persian (with high fluted hats) dignitaries alternating in procession to Darius (L. A. Willis)

to the Scythians of Central Asia and from the inhabitants of Asia Minor to those of India. All were bringing to the Great King the products of their lands, the most precious of which were laid at the foot of the throne of the vast hall of "the hundred columns."

This decoration, like a grandiose poster, announced the spectacle that was to take place below in the plain at the foot of the terrace, under the eyes of the Great King. The king was seated on the edge of the Apadana, where stood the (equestrian?) statue of Xerxes that was later overturned and broken by the soldiers of Alexander the Great in their capture of Persepolis.

The north part of the terrace was joined to the south part by a building with three doors (the Tripylon), which also served as a propylaeum. Darius had built the Tripylon when the edifices of the north part were still far from completed. At the south were the palaces of Darius, of Xerxes, and of Artaxerxes III(?), the harem of Xerxes, and in the eastern angle the Treasury. *See* third picture in ARCHEOLOGY OF IRAN.

The name of Persepolis in Old Persian, mentioned in Xerxes' inscription on his propylaeum, was Parsa; "Persepolis" comes from the Greeks, whose writings, however, do not mention the city before Alexander the Great.

Aeschylus (*The Persians*) ignored this capital and spoke only of Susa (16, "the Old Kissian Ramparts," or 120, "the Citadel of the Kissians") and Ecbatana. Ctesias, the personal physician of Artaxerxes II, who resided at the court several years, also did not mention Persepolis. The foreign ambassadors were received especially at Susa and also at Ecbatana but apparently never at Persepolis. The character of this capital, which differed from that of modern capitals, explains these facts.

The court of the Great King left Susa and came to Persepolis for the festival of New Year's Day (March 21). At that time delegations from all countries of the Persian empire brought as offerings their most famous products. By this gesture these nations assured the Great King of their loyalty to the crown. Parsa was therefore a sacred dynastic place where the union of the peoples who formed the empire was sealed with its rulers.

Darius conceived and in part carried out the general plan of Persepolis. His palace, the Tripylon, the foundations of the Apadana, and at least two-thirds of the Treasury date from his reign. Xerxes (486-465 B.C.) completed the Apadana, as well as his propylaeum and palace. The hall of the hundred columns dates from the reign of Artaxerxes I (465-424 B.C.), and an unfinished palace is attributed to Artaxerxes III (359-338 B.C.). To the extent projected, Persepolis was never finished.

Several thousand tablets found in the surrounding wall and in the Treasury were written in Elamite (except some rare tablets in Aramaic and in Greek) and traced the long period of building activity on the terrace under the three kings — Darius, Xerxes, and Artaxerxes I. The specialists of the various crafts at any one time numbered over thirteen hundred, and included many nationalities. The tablets revealed an unexpected aspect of the economic life of the country and an important reform of Darius; he introduced into Persia the use of money, which gradually replaced payment of the workers in kind.

The royal terrace, which was neither the acropolis nor the citadel, was no more Parsa than the Louvre is Paris. This city, one of the greatest in ancient Persia, stretched far toward the west and certainly also toward the north, probably as far as Naqsh-i-Rustam. There, carved in the high rock, are the tombs of Darius and his three successors. The tomb of Darius III is unfinished. *See* second picture in DARIUS.

In February, 330 B.C., Persepolis fell into the hands of Alexander the Great. He had its treasure transported to Ecbatana by "10,000 pairs of mules, and 5,000 camels" (Plutarch *Alexander* 68). The Macedonian lived there for four months while leading several operations against mountain tribes. At the end of their sojourn the Macedonians set fire to the tapestries during a drinking bout. The fire completely destroyed the palaces, which were thereafter totally abandoned.

The first attempt to excavate the terrace was made in 1878 by F. Mirza, Governor General of Fars, in the hall of the hundred columns. Modern scientific research began in 1931 with the mission of the Oriental Institute of Chicago under the direction of E. Herzfeld, who was followed by E. Schmidt. The Iranian mission has pursued this work since 1939.

Near Eastern studies are indebted to the work of the Achaemenian kings at Persepolis. Each royal builder left several inscriptions carved on the stone of the monuments in cuneiform signs and in three languages, Old Persian, Elamite, and Babylonian (*see* Vol. I, Plate 5). These inscriptions, which western travelers noticed in the 17th cent. and copied in the 18th cent., enabled scholars of several countries, who worked independently of one another, to decipher cuneiform writing in the first half of the 19th century. This remarkable achievement has made it possible to lift the veil that had hidden thousands of years of history of many Middle East civilizations.

According to 2 Macc. 9:1f. Antiochus Epiphanes entered Persepolis and tried to rob the temples there and control the city, but he was repulsed by the inhabitants. Since Persepolis was destroyed and abandoned in 330, this account is probably in error (2 Maccabees is not always reliable). Perhaps the event in 2 Macc. 9:1f. is the same as that described in 1 Macc. 6:1-4 and Polybius xxxi.11; i.e., the reference then should be to ELYMAIS, not Persepolis.

*See also* PERSIA.

***Bibliography.***–J. P. Morier, *Journey through Persia, Armenia and Asia Minor* (1812); C. F. M. Texier, *Description de l'Arménie, la Perse et la Mésopotamie* (3 vols., 1842-1853); E. N. Flandin and P. Coste, *Voyage en Perse* (1 vol. text and 4 vols. plates, 1843-1854); F. Stolze, *Persépolis* (2 vols., 1882); F. Sarre and E. Herzfeld, *Iranische Felsreliefs* (1910); A. Moortgat, *Hellas und die Kunst der Achaemeniden* (1926); J. Breasted, *National Geographic Magazine,* 64 (Oct. 1933), 381-420; E. Herzfeld, *Archaeological History of Iran* (1934); *Iran in the Ancient East* (1941); A. Olmstead, *History of the Persian Empire* (1948); G. G. Cameron, *Persepolis Treasury Tablets* (1948); E. Schmidt, *Persepolis*, I-II (1953-57); R. North, *Guide to Biblical Iran* (1956), pp. 79-92; R. Ghirshman, *Art of Ancient Iran* (1964); W. Culican, *The Medes and the Persians* (1965), pp. 83-111; G. Walser, *Die Volkerschaften auf den Reliefs von Persepolis* (1966).

R. GHIRSHMAN
tr. W. S. L. S.

**PERSEUS** pûr'sē-əs [Gk. *Perseus*].

Perseus, the last king of the Macedonians, is mentioned along with his father Philip (V) at 1 Macc. 8:5 as an example of the foreign powers vanquished by the expanding Roman armies prior to the middle of the 2nd cent. B.C. (cf. Josephus *Ant.* xii.10.6 [414]).

Our primary sources on Perseus are Polybius xxvii-xxix, Livy xlii-xliv, and Plutarch *Aemilius Paullus*. Perseus was born *ca.* 212 B.C. to Philip and Polycrateia of Argos. As the heir to the throne Perseus became apprehensive of the designs of his younger half-brother Demetrius, who as a hostage at Rome had made some influential Roman friends. When Perseus accused his brother of attempting to assassinate him, Philip reluctantly had Demetrius executed.

Upon Philip's death in 179, Perseus acceded to the throne. In the following year he married Laodice, daughter of Seleucus IV. His foes, e.g., Eumenes of Pergamum, called Rome's attention to what they perceived as Perseus's aggressive expansionism. Alarmed by these accusations, in 171 Rome declared the Third Macedonian War against Perseus.

After three years of indecisive fighting, the war came to a swift close at the famous battle of Pydna in Thessaly on June 22, 168. The actual site of the battle was probably SW of the modern town of Katerini some 16 km. (10 mi.) S of Pydna, the city to which the king fled. As in the battle of Cynoscephelae fought nearby in 197 by Philip, the Roman legions under Aemilius Paullus once again proved more flexible than the Macedonian phalanxes. With only a few losses on their side, the Romans killed twenty thousand men and captured nearly ten thousand.

The consequences of the battle at Pydna were far-reaching. Perseus was displayed in Paullus's triumph at Rome in 167, and died in captivity five years later. The monarchy in Macedonia was replaced by four separate republics. On his way home Paullus ravaged Epirus (Albania), which had sided with Perseus, and brought home 150,000 Epirote prisoners to be sold as slaves. The Macedonian booty was so bountiful that Rome was able to cancel its land taxes. "After the battle of Pydna, there can have been few who seriously doubted that Rome had risen to world power" (Errington, p. 226).

Immediately after the Roman victory at Pydna the consul Popilius Laenus was emboldened to order Antiochus IV peremptorily out of Egypt. When the Seleucid king hesitated, the Roman legate drew a circle about him and ordered him to make up his mind before he left the circle.

Knowledge of the Roman victories over Philip and

Perseus influenced Judas Maccabeus to send envoys to seek a treaty of friendship with Rome. Though the exact contents of the letter recorded in 1 Macc. 8:23-32 have been disputed, most scholars no longer doubt the fact of such a treaty negotiated in 161 between the Jews and the Romans.

***Bibliography.***–P. Meloni, *Perseo e la fine della monarchia Macedone* (1953); M. Cary, *History of the Greek World 323-146 B.C.* (1963), pp. 199-203; J. Briscoe, *Historia*, 18 (1969), 49-70; R. M. Errington, *Dawn of Empire: Rome's Rise to World Power* (1972), chs. 15-16; *HJP*², I, 151-172; E. Gruen, *Greek, Roman and Byzantine Studies*, 15 (1974), 221-246; *Chiron*, 6 (1976), 73-95; J. A. Goldstein, *I Maccabees* (*AB*, 1976); F. W. Walbank, *Historical Comm. on Polybius*, I-III (1957-79).

E. M. YAMAUCHI

**PERSEVERANCE** [Gk. *proskartérēsis*] (Eph. 6:18); [*hypomonḗ*] (He. 12:1); AV PATIENCE; NEB RESOLUTION; **PERSEVERE** [Gk. *paraménō*] (Jas. 1:25); AV CONTINUE; NEB "lives in its [the perfect law's] company." Persistence in the face of discouragement or opposition.

Rare in Hellenistic Greek, *proskartérēsis* occurs in the NT only at Eph. 6:18, where it refers to persistent, persevering prayer as part of the Christian's spiritual armor. The related verb, *proskarteréō*, underscores the element of steadfastness in the Christian life (cf. "devote oneself," Acts 2:42; 6:4), and especially in prayer (cf. Acts 1:14; "be constant," Rom. 12:12; "continue steadfastly," Col. 4:2). Throughout the NT Christians are exhorted to persist in prayer (e.g., Lk. 18:1-8; Phil. 4:6; 1 Thess. 5:17).

The author of Hebrews uses the image of a race (cf. 1 Cor. 9:24; Phil. 3:12) to summon Christians facing persecution to "perseverance" (*hypomonḗ*, "patience, endurance, steadfastness") in their faith so that they, like Christ, might attain the prize (He. 12:1f.). (*See also* ENDURE; STEADFASTNESS.)

In Jas. 1:25 *paraménō* has the sense of "continuing" (cf. Phil. 1:25; He. 7:23) to allow the "perfect law, the law of liberty," to rule one's life, i.e., to do it as well as to hear it.

In theology "perseverance" appears in the phrase "perseverance of the saints," which is sometimes equated with "the security of believers" or "eternal security." Citing passages such as Jn. 6:37; 10:28; 17:6-11; Rom. 8:31-39, some interpreters hold that once one has been saved, one cannot subsequently forfeit salvation. Others maintain that only those who persevere to the end are saints. They cite passages such as Lk. 8:9-15; Gal. 5:4; He. 2:1-4; 3:7–4:13; 6:4-6 as evidence that one can renounce faith in Christ Jesus and hence forfeit one's salvation.

Whereas the Calvinists, with their theory of predestination, find it inconceivable that a saint (i.e., one of the "elect") would not persevere, the Arminians, with their doctrine of the freedom of the human will, maintain the possibility that salvation might be lost. According to I. H. Marshall (p. 207), the NT "knows neither the rigid logic of Calvinism nor the 'casualness' of Arminianism." Rather, the NT writings must not be pressed to give a logically rigid answer. "The NT is content to hold together the facts of perseverance and apostasy in paradox, and to rest the confidence of the believer not on a logical argument but on the faithfulness of God in whom he must continually trust" (*ibid.*).

***Bibliography.***–*TDNT*, III, *s.v.* καρτερέω κτλ. (W. Grundmann); IV, *s.v.* μένω κτλ.: παραμένω, ὑπομένω, ὑπομονή (F. Hauck); I. H. Marshall, *Kept By the Power of God* (1969).

R. L. OMANSON

**PERSIA** pûr′zhə [Heb. *pāras*; Gk. *Persis*; Old Pers. *Pārsa*; Akk. *Parsu, Parsua*; Late Egyp. *Pars(a)*; Pers. *Pārs, Fārs*]; **PERSIAN** pûr′zhin [Heb. *parsī*; Aram. *parsay*; Gk. *Persai*; Old Pers. *Pārsa*].

- I. Biblical References
- II. The Land
  - A. Central Plateau
  - B. Climate
- III. History
  - A. Prehistory
  - B. Kingdom of Elam
  - C. Rise of Medes and Persians
  - D. Median Kingdom
  - E. Achaemenians
    1. Cyrus
    2. Cambyses II
    3. Darius
    4. Xerxes
    5. Decline of the Empire
  - F. Greeks
  - G. Parthians
  - H. Sassanians
- IV. Language
  - A. Old Persian
  - B. Medic

***I. Biblical References.***–The term Persia is used in the Bible mainly in the phrase "king of Persia" (Ezr. 1:1f., 8; 3:7; 4:3, 5, 7, 24; 6:14; 7:1; 9:9; Dnl. 10:1, 13). Frequently it appears in combination with "Media" or "Medes" (Est. 1:14, 18f.; 10:2; Dnl. 5:28; 6:8, 12, 15 [MT 9, 13, 16]; 8:20). It is used as an adjective only in Neh. 12:22 and Dnl. 6:28 (MT 29). It denotes properly the modern province of Fārs, not the whole Persian empire. This is supported also by Ezk. 27:10 and 38:5, where Persia is listed along with Put, Lydia, and Cush. Daniel possibly used "Persia" to denote the whole empire in 10:13, 20; 11:2. The empire itself was called Airyana, the present Iran, from a term in the *Avesta* based on the Sanskrit word *arya*, "noble." The province of Parsa (Persis to the Greeks, now known to Arabs as Fārs), lay E of Elam (modern Khuzistan).

***II. The Land.***–Persia and Iran have been used interchangeably to designate the same geographical area. Modern Iran covers 1,647,000 sq. km. (636,000 sq. mi.) of varied climatic and geographical extremes, stretching across deserts and mountains from Iraq to Afghanistan and from the Caspian Sea to the Persian Gulf.

*A. Central Plateau.* The greater part (about 777,000 sq. km., 300,000 sq. mi.) is a vast plateau consisting of a series of high valleys and arid basins which lie at an altitude of 900-2500 m. (3000-8000 ft.) above sea level. The plateau is hemmed in on the west by a great spine of the Zagros Mountains which stretches more than 1600 km. (1000 mi.) southeastward from Azerbaijan and separates the inner basin from the Tigris-Euphrates lowlands. The Elburz range rims the southern shores of the Caspian Sea and walls in the plateau on the north. These mountains

The Zagros Mountains (L. A. Willis)

rise precipitously from below sea level (Caspian Sea is 28 m. [92 ft.] below sea level) to a maximum height of 5771 m. (18,934 ft.) at Mt. Damavand. To the northeast of Tehran are the "Caspian Gates," which link the plateau with the Caspian Sea. On the east the Elburz range merges into the Kopet Dagh range, which continues southward and separates Iran from Afghanistan. On the south the circuit is completed by the Makran, Sistan, and Baluchistan ranges. The central plateau, though fertile in spots, is extremely dry. The two large salt-caked deserts, the Dasht-i-Kavir to the north and Dasht-i-Lut to the south, are considered to be the most arid regions in the world. These deserts have always acted as a barrier to east-west communication. To the southwest of the Zagros is the plain of Khuzistan (ancient Susiana) through which the Karūn River flows to the Persian Gulf. This area, an extension of Mesopotamia, is the largest stretch of lowland in modern Iran.

*B. Climate.* The landscape and climate offer general resemblances to those of the American Southwest. The extremes of geography also make for extremes of climate. Except for the northern coast, rainfall is meager, averaging annually 20 cm. (8 in.) or less on the eastern plateau and 38 cm. (15 in.) on the western. Rainfall does not exceed 5 cm. (2 in.) in the Lut. Temperature varies from −18° C. (0° F.), on occasion, to an average of 20-32° C. (70-90° F.) in summer on the plateau, and to a blistering 50° C. (120° F.) or more along the Persian Gulf. On the north, along the Caspian, the climate is subtropical, and, with heavy rainfall, luxuriant forests grow. These forests are called *jangal* in Persian, a word from which English "jungle" is derived.

***III. History.***–The history of Persia before 1000 B.C., when the MEDES and Persians arrived, is limited almost exclusively to the history of ELAM, the southwest portion of Iran. Only from this area have come documents worthy of mention from the pre-Persian period. Few other documents are found before Zoroaster appeared in the 7th century. Enmebaragesi of the First Dynasty of Kish records a successful campaign against the land of Elam (before 2600 B.C.).

*A. Prehistory.* Archeological evidence takes us back much further. The Zagros region was ideally suited for the so-called Neolithic Revolution (*ca.* 9000 B.C.), for here were prototypes of the earliest domesticated plants and animals. Sites such as Ganj Dareh and Tepe Guran (in Iranian Khuzistan and Luristan) give evidence of the increasing cultivation of barley and wheat and the raising of sheep and goats. This led to an increase in human population and the development of village communities which began to use irrigation. Evidence has also been found of similar development in Fārs, southern Turkestan, northeast Iran, and at Sialk, S of Tehran.

Tepe Sialk has yielded some of the earliest traces of human presence on the Iranian plateau. This community grew up around a spring, and two adjacent mounds (tells, tepes) were formed. The earliest houses (on the northern hill) were made of reeds or branches covered with mud. A few teeth of cattle and sheep, together with sickles formed of bone and flint, suggest some kind of agriculture and stock breeding. Painted pottery can be linked with the Hassuna IB ware in Mesopotamia. Metal came in towards the end of the period. Sialk II shows marked progress as crude bricks replaced puddled clay for building, trade with areas hundreds of kilometers away is attested, and pottery shows greater refinement. Sialk III is represented on the southern hill where a new village grew up after the northern hill was abandoned. It is a continuation of Sialk II, and is almost identical with the lower levels of Tepe Hissar I.A. Pottery was still made by hand, but the kiln made its appearance in the later periods. The pottery was decorated in a greater variety of ways than before, and metal occurred more frequently. By Sialk III.4, copper began to be forged (until then it was hammered), and the potter's wheel appeared — a technological breakthrough because it allowed greater regularity of form and greater production. Stone seals, used for indicating ownership, also appeared in Sialk III.4. The question remains as to whether these were invented in the Iranian mountains.

It is evident that the material progress of early agricultural settlements in Iran can be compared favorably with those of Mesopotamia, but the geographic restrictions of the country were not conducive to the emergence of larger political units. The most likely area for this type of development was the low-lying region between the Zagros foothills and the Euphrates (modern Khuzistan).

*See also* ARCHEOLOGY OF IRAN; *see* Plate 67.

*B. Kingdom of Elam.* In this plain the kingdom of Elam was formed, a country rich in raw materials. It supplied early Sumer with metals (silver, copper, tin, and lead), stone (obsidian, alabaster, diorite, and steatite), precious gems, horses, and timber.

Very few documents are available from the pre-Persian era. Partly in Akkadian and partly in Elamite, most have come from Susa, the capital of Elam. The Elamites recorded the name of their country in cuneiform as *Ḫaltamti* or *Ḫatamti,* which may mean "God's land." The Sumerians and Akkadians referred to Elam as "highland" because the country included not only the low plain of Susiana but the mountains and plateaus to the north and east. This linkage of plains and mountains is a chief characteristic of Elamite history that endured for thousands of years until the Medes and Persians conquered all the mountain territory *ca.* 600 B.C.

*C. Rise of Medes and Persians.* Early waves of Indo-European tribal groups brought the Achaians to Greece, formed the Hittite kingdom in Asia Minor and the Mitannian kingdom in northern Mesopotamia, and contributed to the Hyksos chiefs in Syria and Egypt. Toward the end of the 2nd millennium B.C. tribes from Transoxiana — the steppes of southern Russia E and S of the Caspian Sea — migrated in large numbers and began to settle in Iran and S of the Black Sea. These are known by the term Aryan ("noble"). This new wave, associated with the Cimmerians and Scythians, included the Medes and Persians, who by the 9th cent. had established themselves in northwest Iran between Lake Urmia and the plain of Ecbatana (Hamadân). Further immediate expansion was stifled by the existing powers of Urartu to the northeast, Assyria to the west, Babylonia to the south, and Elam at the head of the Persian Gulf.

The first references to the Medes and Persians occur in an inscription of Shalmaneser III. He referred to them all as Medes and deported thousands of them in 837 B.C. The Medes and Persians also paid tribute to Tiglath-pileser III and Sargon II.

*D. Median Kingdom.* The Medes gradually consolidated their position, changing from tribal to village administration. Repeated attacks by Assyrians, Urartians, and Mannians forced them to unite in the 7th cent. B.C. The Median capital was ECBATANA (Hamadân), founded by Deioces or Dayakku according to Herodotus (i.98). Deioces had been taken to Assyria in 715 by Sargon II, and was subsequently exiled to Hamath in Syria. Phraortes or Khshathrita (675-653 B.C.), his successor, extended his control over the Persians to the southwest, but either in an attack on Nineveh against Ashurbanipal or in conflict with the Scythians, he lost his life. The SCYTHIANS dominated Media for twenty-eight years until they were defeated by the successor of Phraortes, Cyaxares or Uvakhshtra (653-585), who was a master of military strategy. In alliance with Nabopolassar of Babylon, and with the aid of Scythian mercenaries, he sacked Nineveh after a siege of several months. Babylon and Media shared equally in the spoils. A treaty was concluded, and Amytis, the granddaughter of Cyaxares, was married to Nebuchadrezzar II, son of Nabopolassar. It was for her that the "Hanging Gardens" of Babylon were built.

*E. Achaemenians.* The Persians moved from the area W and SW of Lake Urmia to Luristan, E of Elam, and finally to Parsa, where they settled. Their dynasty was founded by Achaemenes or Hakhamanish *ca.* 700 B.C. His successor, Teipses, was able to add Anshan to his kingdom. On his death his two sons were each given a share: Ariaramnes or Ariyaramna (*ca.* 640-590) received Parsa, and Cyrus or Kurash I (*ca.* 640-600) the western part, including Anshan. The first inscription of the Achaemenian family is attributed to Ariaramnes. On a gold tablet written in Old Persian cuneiform he calls himself king of Parsa, and describes Parsa as "a land of fine horses and good men." The son and heir of Cyrus I, Cambyses or Kanbujiya I (*ca.* 600-559), though still subordinate to the Medes, proclaimed himself "king of Anshan." Mandane, daughter of Astyages, was married to Cambyses, and to this union was born Cyrus II.

*1. Cyrus.* CYRUS became the vassal king of Anshan and ruled from Pasargadae. With the support of the Persian tribes and Nabonidus, Cyrus revolted against Astyages, his grandfather and Median overlord (549 B.C.). The Median army under Harpagus defected to Cyrus, and the army commanded by Astyages mutinied and handed him over to Cyrus. Media ceased to be an independent kingdom. Cyrus now was heir to Assyria, Syria, Armenia, and Cappadocia. He showed rare ability in blending diplomacy with military skill, tolerance, and wisdom. The Persians called him "father"; the Greeks respected him; the Jews saw him as "shepherd" and God's "anointed" (Isa. 44:28; 45:1). By all measurements he is one of the outstanding figures of the Achaemenian dynasty.

The demise of Media meant that Persia was in direct conflict with Babylonia. Nabonidus, however, concentrated on westward expansion. He built a palace at Tema in the Arabian peninsula and left Babylon under the control of his son Belshazzar. Cyrus turned his attention first to the north and west. Assyria and Cilicia yielded, Asshur and Haran were captured, and an indecisive battle was fought with Croesus of Lydia. Although winter was near, Cyrus pushed on to Sardis, which he took after a fourteen-day siege (547 B.C.). The subjugation of the Ionian Greek cities was accomplished by Harpagus in a three-year campaign.

The Persian empire now covered most of Asia Minor. The eastern frontiers were extended to include the Aryan tribes, Parthia, and the Bactrian tribes as far as Samarkand. Cyrus now was strong enough to deal with Babylonia. To protect his capital, Nabonidus had brought the images of most of the gods of Babylonia to Babylon. This alienated the priests, who were already at odds with him. Gobryas or Ugbaru, governor of Gutium and formerly an outstanding general of Nebuchadrezzar, defected to Cyrus. It was he who entered Babylon without battle on October 13, 539 B.C. The gods were returned to their proper temples and the various peoples were sent back to their respective homes, including the Jews to Judea. Cyrus, who ruled the greatest empire the world had known, died nine years later in a battle on the eastern frontier against the Massagetae.

*2. Cambyses II.* CAMBYSES II (529-522 B.C.), "king of Babylon" and eldest son of Cyrus, had been recognized already as regent. At the news of his father's death, he assumed the full titulary, "king of Babylon, king of lands." Almost immediately he prepared to invade Egypt. With the fall of Pelusium and Memphis, Egyptian resistance was broken, and Cambyses was acknowledged as king and legitimate pharaoh. Attempts to penetrate Nubia to the south and beyond Cyrenaica to the west were unsuccessful. The throne of Persia, in his absence, was seized by Gaumata, who pretended to be Smerdis or Bardiya, the younger brother whom Cambyses had secretly assassinated. Cambyses died under questionable circumstances on his way home (522 B.C.).

*3. Darius.* DARIUS (Daryavaush) son of Hystaspes (Vishtaspa), the satrap of Parthia, acted swiftly, and within two months Gaumata was taken prisoner and executed. Two years or more were required to deal with revolts throughout the empire. In commemoration of his victory, a huge bas-relief was cut in a high cliff above the old caravan route between Ecbatana and Babylon at the small village of Bisitun (BEHISTUN) on the plain of Kermanshah. Under the protection of Ahura-Mazda, who is depicted arising out of a winged sun-disk, Darius tramples underfoot the false pretender to the throne, while nine rebel leaders, fastened together with a rope around their necks, stand before him. The Behistun inscription, written in Old Persian, Akkadian, and Elamite, identifies Darius as "the great king, king of kings, king of Persia, king of countries, son of Hystaspes, grandson of Arsames, an Achaemenian," who gained his position with help from "Ahura-Mazda and the other gods."

Darius was an excellent administrator, and he spent much of his energy on reorganization of the empire. Twenty satrapies under Persian officials were established. A military commander and a tax official, answerable directly to the king, were placed in each satrapy. Inspectors, called "the ears of the king," made periodic and unannounced visits. A network of roads was created to facilitate travel and communication. A new palace was built at SUSA (521 B.C.), and an entirely new capital was founded at PERSEPOLIS (518 B.C.). The extent of his campaigns in the east is unknown, but he claims to have extended his rule over the Scythians on the other side of the sea. By diplomacy and military action he reestablished control over the Greek cities of Ionia, but in his attempt to conquer the Greek mainland he was defeated at Marathon in 490 B.C.

Darius died in 486 B.C. Under him the Persian empire attained the height of its power and glory. He ruled from the Indus and Jaxartes rivers in the east to Egypt and the Aegean in the west, from the Persian Gulf in the south to the Caspian and Black seas on the north. Throughout the next century and a half (486-538) his successors were concerned with the preservation of the empire he had consolidated and organized.

*4. Xerxes.* Xerxes (the AHASUERUS of Ezra and Esther),

The Behistun bas-relief (W. S. LaSor)

who had gained experience as viceroy of Babylon, lacked the tolerance of his predecessor and treated harshly both Egypt and Babylon. He would have preferred to direct his energies toward building palaces and monuments, but the Greek problem would not go away. In 480 B.C. a Persian army accompanied by ships manned by Phoenician, Ionian, Egyptian, and Cypriot allies moved against Greece. A canal was dug through the isthmus of Sane to avoid the dangerous promontory of Athos. After a delay at Thermopylae, Thebes and Athens were taken by the Persians, but the Greeks inflicted a disastrous defeat on the Persian fleet at Salamis, then near Miletus, and again at Plataea and Mycale. Xerxes was forced to relinquish everything beyond Asia Minor. He was assassinated in his palace in 465 B.C.

*5. Decline of the Empire.* The three succeeding kings, ARTAXERXES I Longimanus, Darius II Ōchos, and Artaxerxes II Mnēmōn, managed to hold the empire together, more by the outlay of gold than by those positive qualities expected of kings. Artaxerxes III Ōchos was ambitious, ruthless, and brutal. He put down revolts and restored Egypt to the empire. After reigning for about twenty years (359-338), he was poisoned by Bogoas, who in turn was poisoned by Darius III Codomanus, the last of the Achaemenian kings and a distant cousin of Artaxerxes III. Darius might have restored the empire if he had not overestimated his own strength and underestimated the strength of Alexander, who defeated him in battle at Gaugamela or Arbela (331 B.C.). The Persian empire passed over to the Greeks.

*F. Greeks.* Alexander the Great quickly occupied the Achaemenian capitals of Ecbatana, Susa, and Babylon. Persepolis was looted and burned, perhaps in retaliation for Persian action against Greek cities. Some would call Alexander the last of the Achaemenians because he married Roxane, daughter of the Satrap of Bactria, a Sogdian chief, and coerced thousands of his troops into marrying Persian women at Susa. After the death of Alexander in 323 B.C., his empire was divided through conflict among his generals. Seleucus I Nicator fell heir to most of the territory of Persia, but the Seleucids held it for only a short time. The attempt to bring unity to the area failed,

Impression of an Achaemenian cylinder seal showing the royal hero (Darius?) standing on sphinxes and holding lions in a triumphant gesture (Cylinder Seal no. 824; The Trustees of the Pierpont Morgan Library)

The plain of Issus in Asia Minor. Here Alexander won a major battle over Darius and set the stage for the final battle at Gaugamela (W. S. LaSor)

and constant wars with other states and internal rivalry led to the weakening of the central authority and to the loss of the eastern satrapies, beginning with Bactria.

*G. Parthians.* The PARTHIANS probably belonged to the Parni tribe, one of a number of Scythian tribes which roamed the steppe country between the Caspian Sea and the Aral Sea. *Ca.* 250 B.C. they invaded Parthia, slew the local satrap, and set up their own dynasty under Tiridates, a member of the house of Arsacid. His successor, Artabanus I, suffered a defeat at the hands of Antiochus III, but Phripatius (195 B.C.) capitalized on the Roman defeat of Antiochus and reconquered the provinces south of the Caspian Sea. Mithradates I, the true founder of the Parthian empire, greatly expanded his territorial control between 160 and 140 B.C., until, at the time of his death (*ca.* 137 B.C.), he ruled an empire stretching from the Euphrates to Herat. The Parthians felt themselves to be the restorers of the Achaemenian empire and adopted the title "Great King."

*H. Sassanians.* A movement even more closely identified with the Achaemenians originated in Parsa. These kings claimed to be descendants of the Achaemenians and rightful heirs to the empire. Their revolt against the Parthians in A.D. 224 led to a new dynasty, the Sassanian, named after Sassan, the grandfather of Ardashir, the first king. Ardashir defeated the Parthians and killed Artabanus V. Zoroastrianism became the state religion, and the Sassanians claimed from Ahura-Mazda the divine right to rule. The empire was strong enough to withstand and defeat the Romans and the Byzantines. They in turn fell to the Arab invasion in A.D. 642.

***IV. Language.***–Persian, both ancient and modern, is Aryan, a branch of Indo-European. It is closely akin to Vedic Sanskrit and Armenian. There were two main dialects in the ancient language: (1) that of the Persians (known from inscriptions of Achaemenian kings) and (2) that of the Medes (known from the *Avesta* and a few isolated words in Greek writers).

*A. Old Persian.* This dialect was used between 550 and 330 B.C., and consists of about 5800 words in one thousand lines of texts. With the exception of the inscriptions of Darius on his tomb and at Behistun, these are mainly repetitious statements about kingship and lists of peoples and places, so that fewer than five hundred different words are actually available. Evidence seems to point to the fact that Elamite was written in Elam (several thousand tablets from the archives at Persepolis) and Babylonian in Babylon, but in Persia Persian was written in Aramaic. A probable procedure at Persepolis is described by Ghirshman: "The order came in Persian from a high court official; the scribe translated it into Aramaic and wrote it on papyrus; the text was then passed to a second scribe, who translated it into Elamite and inscribed it upon a tablet" (R. Ghirshman, p. 164). Inscriptions in Persian are carved in a cuneiform script which consists of forty-four characters, of which seven are ideographs or contractions. The remaining signs are syllabic, consisting of a consonant and a vowel, except for the separate vowels. The text was written from left to right as are other cuneiform syllabaries. Cyrus the Great has left one sentence in Persian: *Adam Karush Khshayathiya Hakhamanishiya,* "I am Cyrus the King, the Achaemenian." There are several long inscriptions of Darius I (including one at Suez), a few of Xerxes at Persepolis, and some short ones of Artaxerxes I, Artaxerxes Mnēmōn, and Artaxerxes Ōchus. Modern Persian has developed from Achaemenian or Old Persian through Pahlavi and Dari.

*B. Medic.* This dialect is represented by the Avesta, the sacred books of the Zoroastrians. None of the original manuscripts has survived, and what is extant comes from a much later period. The Avesta is composed of three parts: (1) *Yasna,* which contains the hymns (*Gathas*) attributed to Zoroaster himself; (2) *Yashts,* which are hymns to various deities; and (3) *Videvdat* (law against demons), which contains moral precepts.

*See* RELIGIONS OF THE BIBLICAL WORLD: PERSIA.

***Bibliography.***–G. G. Cameron, *Persepolis Treasury Tablets* (1948); A. T. Olmstead, *History of the Persian Empire* (1948); R. G. Kent, *Old Persian* (1950); R. Ghirshman, *Iran* (1954); *CAH,* IV (1953), 1-346; *CAH* (3rd ed.), II/1 (1973), 256-288, 686-715; II/2 (1975), 379-416, 482-506; W. Culican, *Medes and Persians* (1965); J.-L. Huot, *Persia I: From the Origins to the Achaemenids* (1965); D. N. Wilber, *Persepolis: The Archaeology of Parsa, Seat of the Persian Kings* (1969); R. Collins, *Medes and Persians: Conquerors and Diplomats* (1974); B. Dicks, *Ancient Persians: How They Lived and Worked* (1979).

R. E. HAYDEN

**PERSIAN RELIGION.** *See* RELIGIONS OF THE BIBLICAL WORLD: PERSIA.

**PERSIANS** (Ezr. 4:9, RSV). *See* APHARSITES.

**PERSIS** pûr'sis [Gk. *Persis*–'Persian woman']. A name used of freedwomen and especially of female slaves throughout the Roman empire but mentioned only once in the Bible (Rom. 16:12). She is greeted with two other female "workers in the Lord," Tryphaena and Tryphosa (perhaps twin sisters), but is accorded an eminence greater than theirs as "the beloved." The past tense (aorist indicative) *ekopíasen,* "who has worked hard," suggests an older lady who had done a considerable amount of Christian work.

J. J. HUGHES

**PERSON.** In the RSV OT "person" most often represents Heb. *nepeš,* which occurs 755 times and has a broad range of meanings (including "throat," "breath," "soul," "living being," "[an individual's] life," etc.; see KoB, pp. 626-28; *see also* SOUL). The RSV renders it "person" about sixty-five times, most frequently in contexts of casuistic law (e.g., Ex. 12:15, 19; Lev. 7:20f., 27; 17:10, 12, 15; 18:29; Nu. 5:6; 9:13) and in enumerations of people (e.g., Gen. 46:18, 22, 25-27; Ex. 1:5; 12:4; 16:16; Nu. 31:40). (See Johnson, pp. 1-22; *TDNT,* IX, 620; *TWOT,* II, 589f.; H. W. Wolff, pp. 21f.)

In several instances "person" represents Heb. *'āḏām* ("mankind," "human being"), e.g., in passages where human beings are distinguished from animals of various sorts (Nu. 31: 28, 30, 47; Jonah 4:11; etc.). The expression *nepeš 'āḏām* is rendered "persons" in Nu. 31:35, 40, 46 and "persons of men" (referring to slaves) in Ezk. 27:13. Unlike *'āḏām,* Heb. *'îš* specifically denotes a man as opposed to a woman or child (Nu. 19:18; 1 S. 9:22; 22:18; 2 K. 10:6f., 14; Job 32:21). Because the face identifies a person and reflects that individual's disposition, Heb. *pānîm* (lit. "face") is often used to represent a person. The expression *nāśā' panîm* (lit. "lift up the face") means to show someone respect or favor (Dt. 28:50), and *pāneyḵā hōlᵉḵîm baqᵉrāḇ* (lit. "your face going into battle") means to go to battle "in person" (2 S. 17:11).

In some OT passages the RSV supplies "person" for a smooth translation where a corresponding Hebrew term is lacking (e.g., Lev. 27:4-8). In other cases it supplies "person" in rendering various Hebrew nouns (e.g., *negaʿ,* "disease," Lev. 13:4, 12, 17; *neṯeq,* "skin disease," 13:33; *negaʿ hanneṯeq,* v. 31) and adjectives (e.g., *ṭāhōr,* "clean," Nu. 19:19; *ṭāmē',* "unclean," v. 22).

In several NT passages the RSV uses "person" to translate Gk. *ánthrōpos* (Rom. 7:1; 1 Cor. 2:11; 7:26; Jas. 1:7; 1 Pet. 3:4). The term denotes "mankind" or "human being" as a species distinct from the animals and from God; frequently it emphasizes the transitoriness of human life and the limited nature of human knowledge (*TDNT,* I, 364). In three passages "person" represents Gk. *psychḗ* (the usual LXX translation of Heb. *nepeš*; frequently rendered "life" or "soul" by the RSV): Acts 27:37 and 1 Pet. 3:20 use it in enumerations of people, and in Rom. 13:1 it simply refers to an individual person.

Most uses of "person" in the RSV NT, however, are supplied by the translators for smooth renderings of Greek pronouns (e.g., *tis,* "some," "a certain"; *toioútos,* "such"; *hékastos,* "each") and adjectives (e.g., *polloí,* "many"; *sebómenoi,* "devout"; *asebeís,* "ungoldly"). Two other terms are each translated "person" once: Gk. *ónoma* (usually "name") in Acts 1:15 (see Bauer, rev., p. 573) and Gk. *prósōpon* (lit. "face"; cf. Heb. *pānîm*) in 1 Thess. 2:17, where Paul contrasts his absence from his Thessalonian friends "in person" (*prosṓpǭ*; cf. "face to face," v. 17b) to his presence with them "in heart" (i.e., in thought and concern). For the biblical concepts of personality, *see* ANTHROPOLOGY; PSYCHOLOGY.

***Bibliography.***–*DNTT,* II, 564-69; A. R. Johnson, *Vitality of the Individual in the Thought of Ancient Israel* (2nd ed. 1964); D. Lys, *Nephesh* (1959); *TDNT,* I, *s.v.* ἄνθρωπος (J. Jeremias); IX, *s.v.* ψυχή κτλ. (G. Bertram, *et al.*); *TDOT,* I, *s.v.* "'ādhām" (F. Maass), "'îsh" (N. P. Bratsiotis); *THAT,* II, *s.v.* נֶפֶשׁ (C. Westermann); *TWOT,* II, 587-591; H. W. Wolff, *Anthropology of the OT* (Eng. tr. 1974).

N. J. O.

## PERSON OF CHRIST.

I. History of Interpretation
  A. Creeds and Orthodoxy
  B. Quest of the Historical Jesus
  C. Contemporary Debate
II. Method in Interpretation
III. Synoptic Gospels
  A. Mark
  B. Matthew
  C. Luke
IV. Apostolic Preaching and Teaching
  A. Peter and the Jerusalem Church
  B. 1 and 2 Peter, James, and Jude
  C. Paul
V. Hebrews
VI. Johannine Writings
  A. Gospel of John
  B. Johannine Letters
  C. Revelation
VII. Conclusion

For a survey of christological controversies from the patristic age to the present, *see* CHRISTOLOGY; CREEDS AND CONFESSIONS. For fuller discussion of the life and ministry of Jesus, *see* JESUS CHRIST. The aim of the present article is to discuss the identity of Jesus Christ on the basis of the NT writings and in the light of the controversies that this question has provoked.

***I. History of Interpretation.***–*A. Creeds and Orthodoxy.* Orthodox Christian beliefs concerning the person of Christ were defined by the creedal statements of the ecumenical councils of the 4th and 5th centuries. Leading up to these definitions were a series of involved controversies that variously interpreted Jesus in the light of the religious syncretism known as Gnosticism, ideas drawn from Jewish monotheism, and Greek philosophy. The formulations of the creeds must therefore be understood in terms of the questions that they were addressing and the language used in the debates of the times.

The Gnostics thought of Christ as the emissary of the supreme spiritual being, sent to bring redemption from the material, evil world. The Gnostic redeemer brought knowledge of the world of light. Gnosticism took numerous forms. (For the Gnostic texts and the views of the church fathers, see W. Foerster, *Gnosis* [Eng. tr., 2 vols., 1972-1974].) Jesus was sometimes seen as a righteous man who received power from above in order to elude the wicked creator of the material world and enable others to do the same. Others claimed that the Christ descended upon Jesus at His baptism, enabling Him to preach "the unknown Father." In Gnostic thought the Christ either temporarily inhabited a human body but left it before the crucifixion or merely assumed human appearance. Christian anti-Gnostic writers, like Irenaeus, Tertullian, and Hippolytus, replied by stressing the identity of the supreme God with the Creator, the goodness of creation, and the reality of the earthly life of Jesus, especially His crucifixion and resurrection.

One expression of the effort to safeguard monotheism is seen in the EBIONITES, a sect of Jewish Christians who believed that Jesus was the male offspring of Joseph and Mary on whom the Holy Spirit descended at His baptism. Also since the time of Novatian (*ca.* 250) the term Monarchianism has been used to describe two separate ways of stressing the unity of God ("monarchy") while maintaining the divinity of Christ (*On the Trinity,* 30). Dynamic Monarchianism or Adoptionism taught that Jesus was a man on whom descended the power (Gk. *dýnamis*) of God at His baptism. This power enabled Jesus to perform miracles. The resurrection and ascension of Jesus completed His elevation to divine status. Modalism or Sabellianism (so called after Sabellius) viewed God as a single reality who manifested Himself under different modes. Just as the light and heat of the sun were ultimately identical, so the Son and the Spirit were but different manifestations of the Father.

Philosophical ideas affected the teaching of the fathers in different ways. The Logos doctrine of the Apologists combined an appeal to the teaching of Jn. 1:1-18 concerning the Word *(lógos)* with the Stoic idea of the dissemination of Reason *(lógos)* in all things, particularly in human beings. Christ was thus the particular incarnation of "the true light that enlightens every man" (Jn. 1:9). The Logos that enabled Socrates to condemn demons "took form and became man and was called Jesus Christ" (Justin Martyr *Apol.* i.5). The Apologists saw a further analogy between the utterance of words and the Incarnation (cf. Justin *Dial.* 61; Tertullian *Adv. Prax.* 5). The spoken word was the expression of the speaker's mind. In a sense it was distinct from the speaker; yet at the same time it was the expression of the speaker himself. In making this point the fathers stressed that the uttered word was not a creature. They thought of it as the offspring of the one who spoke.

The Trinitarianism of Origen (*ca.* 185-254) was a reinterpretation of the Church's traditional faith in terms of the Middle Platonism that flourished in Alexandria (see esp. *De prin.* i and ii). The Father was God in a unique sense, but the generation of the Son was eternal and comparable with the brilliancy of the sun (*De prin.* i.2.4). But there were also hints of a subordination of the Son to the Father and the Spirit to the Son. Origen used the Platonic idea of the preexistence of the soul in order to explain the Incarnation. Whereas other souls fell in a premundane fall, the one soul adhered to the divine Logos with a perfect love, and as a reward became the soul of Christ (*De prin.* ii.6.3f.).

Subordinationism was carried to its logical conclusion by Arius, a presbyter of Alexandria, who accused his bishop, Alexander, of Sabellianism. Arius argued that since the Son was begotten by the Father, He must have been a distinct being and that there must have been (a time) when the Son was not. In other words, He was a creature. The council of Nicea (325) was convened to settle the controversy, which threatened to split the Church and destroy the peace of the Roman empire. The council ultimately condemned Arius. Its creed stressed that Jesus Christ, the Son of God, was "begotten, not made, of one substance [Gk. *homooúsios*] with the Father." It also asserted the humanity of Christ, drawing attention to His birth, suffering, resurrection, and ascension.

The next half century saw numerous attempts to change and modify the Nicene Creed and with it the teaching of the Church. The Nicene position was stoutly defended by Athanasius and the Cappadocian Fathers from the standpoint of soteriology. Jesus had to be God in order to save and restore humankind. But He also had to be truly human, for what had not been assumed by Him could not be saved. Hence, He had to be fully God and fully man. Nicene orthodoxy finally triumphed at the Council of Constantinople (381). The creed known today as the Nicene Creed is actually the modified and strengthened form of the Creed believed to have been ratified by the Council of Constantinople.

In the 4th cent. the question of the divinity of Christ began to be overshadowed by that of the precise relationship of His divinity to His humanity. Two major schools of thought emerged. The School of Antioch stressed what has been called a Word-man Christology, which emphasized the reality of the two natures but left aside questions about the reality of their union. The Alexandrian School taught a Word-flesh Christology, which stressed the reality of their union but appeared to compromise the integrity of Christ's humanity. The Nestorians, who belonged to the Antiochene School, were accused by their Alexandrian opponents of teaching that there were two separate beings in the person of Christ. Nestorius's rejection of the term *theotókos,* "God bearing" or "Mother of God,"which was applied to the Virgin Mary, was seen by the Alexandrians as an attempt to revive Adoptionism.

The Alexandrian School, on the other hand, gave rise to the heresies of Apollinarianism and Eutychianism. Apollinaris sought to explain the Incarnation by suggesting that, in the case of Jesus, the rational soul was replaced by the divine Logos. This helped to explain the single nature of Christ, His Virgin Birth, sinlessness, and supernatural powers. The orthodox pointed out, however, that such a Christ was not fully human since He lacked a human, rational soul. He could not therefore be the agent of salvation. "What has not been assumed cannot be restored; it is what is united with God that is saved" (Gregory of Nazianzus *Epistula* 101.7). Apollinaris was condemned at Constantinople (381). Eutyches taught an extreme version of the Alexandrian doctrine that Christ had one incarnate nature *(phýsis).* This echoed the teaching of Cyril of Alexandria, whose one-nature doctrine appeared to suggest a synthesis of the divine and human natures, but was intended to mean that Christ had one single, concrete existence. In the hands of Eutyches, it verged on a docetic Christology in which the human nature of Jesus was absorbed into the divine.

The *Tome* of Pope Leo (449) endorsed the condemnation of Eutyches and gave classical expression to the Christology of the Western Church. The *Tome* was accepted by the Council of Chalcedon (451) together with Cyril's letters to Nestorius and to the Easterns. The council reaffirmed the creeds of Nicea and Constantinople and also issued its own definition, which precluded the heresies of the rival schools and asserted that Jesus Christ was "of one substance with the Father as touching the Godhead, the same of one substance with us as touching the manhood, like us in all things apart from sin." While rejecting the confusion of the two natures, the council insisted that their distinction was in no way abolished because of the union, "but rather the characteristic property of each nature being preserved, and concurring into one Person and one subsistence [*hypóstasis*], not as if Christ were parted or divided into two persons, but one and the same Son and only-begotten God, Word, Lord, Jesus Christ." The council did not resolve the problem of Christology, but gave it more precise definition and stated the parameters of orthodox thought in terms of the questions that were being asked.

Throughout this period and afterward, orthodox theologians were concerned to stress the immutability and impassibility of God. This is reflected in the careful phraseology of Chalcedon that rejected the thought of change in the divine nature. Underlying this concern was the conviction that change implied imperfection, and therefore God could not be thought of as changing. Somewhat earlier the impassibility of God found vigorous defense in Tertullian's *Adversus Praxeam,* which accused Praxeas of teaching Patripassianism. The logical implication of Praxeas's Modalism is seen in the thought that the Father suffered on the cross. But Tertullian repudiated this. He allowed that Christ suffered only as a man; in His divine nature He did not suffer *(Adv. Prax.* 29).

The teaching of Chalcedon found general acceptance in the Western Church but its equation of "nature" with "substance" failed to satisfy not only the followers of Eutyches but also many followers of Cyril. Monophysitism, the doctrine that Christ had one nature, continued to flourish in the East, where many theologians equated "nature" with hypostasis rather than "substance." In the 6th cent. the anti-Monophysite theologian Leontius of Byzantium sought to interpret Chalcedon in the tradition of Cyril's Christology. His doctrine of Enhypostasia taught that the humanity of Christ did not have an independent *hypóstasis* or person. The one hypostasis is that of the divine Logos. The idea was further developed by John of Damascus (*ca.* 675-759).

Much of the terminology of the Western Church derives from Tertullian, whose use of Lat. *persona* helped to establish "person" as a term for a member of the "trinity" (a term that he also helped to establish). In early usage "person" did not carry with it the thought of personality and the overtones of self-awareness, rationality, will, and freedom. Rather it denoted an individual, i.e., that which individuates or gives concrete reality to a substance. Thus God has one substance which exists concretely in three persons. When applied to Christ, "person" concretizes the divine and human substances. In Greek theology the term that ultimately gained acceptance was *hypóstasis.* It denoted a mode of being *(trópos hyparxéōs),* not in the Modalistic sense of a temporary appearance but in the sense of a mode in which God was God.

Although Boethius (*ca.* 480-*ca.* 524) defined "person" as "the individual substance of a rational nature" (*Liber contra Eutychen et Nestorium* 3), the great theologians of the Western Church did not read into the term modern notions of personhood. It was a manner of speech that was not to be pressed. To Augustine, the formula of three divine persons had been coined not to give an explanation but to avoid remaining altogether silent (*De trin.* v.9). It served to show that the Father was not the Son, and the Spirit was neither the Father nor the Son (*De trin.* vii.4). To Anselm, God was "an ineffable plurality" and "an ineffable unity" (*Monologion* 38; 79). The three "persons" must on no account be thought of as three separate beings. To Aquinas, "divine person" signified "relation as something subsisting" (*Summa Theol.* i.29.4). Similarly,

Calvin defined "person" as "a 'subsistence' in God's essence, which, while related to the others, is distinguished by an incommunicable quality" (*Inst.* i.13.6). In other words, the great theologians of the Western Church repudiated tritheism. When they spoke of the trinity and the person of Christ, they did not have in mind a picture of three divine beings. When they spoke of the Incarnation, they did not picture one of the divine beings temporarily changing into a man or perhaps appearing in the guise of a man. Rather, there was an external threefoldness in God, and it was in His eternal and inseparable threefoldness that God was in Christ reconciling the world to Himself.

To the great theologians of the Western Church the discussion of these questions was not a matter of abstract speculation. It was bound up with a concern to worship God in truth and to understand the meaning of Scripture and the faith of the Church. It was further linked with a concern to approach the person of Christ from the standpoint of redemption and salvation. Anselm's *Cur deus homo* presented a classic account of the Incarnation on the grounds that God had actually to become a human being in order to save humanity. The Reformation preserved this emphasis. On the one hand, the ecumenical creeds of the Church were endorsed on the grounds that they could be proved by warrant of Scripture. On the other hand, the necessity of the Incarnation was defended in terms of mankind's need of God to become human in order to redeem humanity. The thought was further developed in terms of the three offices of Christ as prophet, priest, and king (*see* CHRIST, OFFICES OF).

*B. Quest of the Historical Jesus.* Already in the 16th cent. some cast doubt on Christian orthodoxy. In his writings on the trinity, M. Servetus (1511-1553) urged that biblical language concerning God, His Word, and His Spirit had been misuderstood. The Socinians denied the eternity of Christ and insisted that "God is but one person" (*Racovian Catechism* 3.1). Although OT prophecy applied to Christ, "it would not hence follow that he possessed a divine nature" (4.1). Such criticisms sought to undermine the orthodox understanding of the person of Christ, but it was not until the 18th cent. that the quest of the historical Jesus began in earnest.

It is customary to date the beginning of the quest from the publication by G. E. Lessing of some posthumous *Fragments of an Unknown Author*. The final Fragment was entitled "On the Intentions of Jesus and his Disciples" (1778). The piece was actually an extract from an unpublished manuscript by H. S. Reimarus (1694-1768), entitled *Apology or Defence of the Rational Worshipers of God*. In it Reimarus launched a full-scale attack on the Bible. He viewed Jesus as a Jewish reformer who had no desire to found a new religion. His preaching of the Kingdom of God embroiled Him in politics and led Him to an untimely death. Afterward the disciples invented the story that He had risen from the dead and that He would return in judgment. Thus the entire fabric of Christian beliefs is based on the fraudulent scheme of the disciples to perpetuate their situation. The work provoked great outcry, but it was not as original as has been often supposed. Reimarus himself was deeply indebted to English Deism, which he had come to know first hand in England a half century earlier. In the 1720's, Anthony Collins had attacked Christian claims that Jesus fulfilled OT prophecy, insisting that justification for those claims could be found only if prophecy were interpreted allegorically. Shortly afterwards Thomas Woolston ridiculed the Gospel miracles, especially the resurrection of Jesus, which he accounted for by the claim that the disciples stole the body of Jesus. D. Hume's celebrated essay, "Of Miracles" (*Enquiry Concerning Human Understanding* [1748], § 10), was an oblique attack on Christian truth-claims based on miracles. Since miracles were by definition violations of the laws of nature, they were self-refuting and no amount of historical testimony would suffice to establish them. By the time that Lessing published the *Fragments,* these ideas were well known in Britain and in Germany.

The Age of Enlightenment in the 18th cent. and the emergence of philosophical Idealism in the 19th cent. produced a climate of opinion that favored radical reappraisal of the person of Christ. The views of the Deists and Reimarus were themselves expressions of Enlightenment thought. The Age of Enlightenment found its culmination in the teaching of I. Kant (1724-1804), who maintained that metaphysical and theological questions must remain outside the scope of human reason. Kant effectively placed an embargo on theology except as a way of teaching practical morality. Kant's *Religion within the Limits of Reason Alone* (1793) presented Jesus (though without mentioning His name) as "the personified idea of the good principle" and a "wise teacher" of rational religion. Idealism, on the other hand, rejected the Christian theistic view of God's existence over and above the world. Hegel's *Phenomenology of Spirit* (1807) represented the world as the process of the self-determination of the Spirit. In Hegel's reinterpretation of Christianity, the death of Christ meant the death of the abstraction of the divine Being. The Incarnation was the embodiment of the Idea of the union of the absolute Spirit of humankind.

The theology of F. Schleiermacher (1768-1834) was in part an attempt to circumvent the embargo that Kant had placed on metaphysical knowledge. It was also a restatement of orthodoxy that avoided having to treat the Bible as propositional revelation. For Schleiermacher the essence of religion lay in the human awareness of being dependent. God was posited as the correlate of the sense of utter dependence, and sin was presented as man's attempt to be independent when he should be dependent. In place of the God-man of the Creeds, Schleiermacher depicted Jesus as a man who was like all others in His human nature "but distinguished from them all by the constant potency of His God-consciousness, which was a veritable existence of God in Him" (*Christian Faith* [2nd ed. 1830-1831; Eng. tr. 1928], no. 94, p. 385). As such Jesus was the sinless mediator of the consciousness of God. At the close of his work Schleiermacher called for a reappraisal of the traditional doctrines of the trinity and the person of Christ, which would avoid the problems that he felt were presented by terms like "person" and "nature" (no. 96, pp. 391-98). Schleiermaher was the first German theologian to lecture on "The Life of Jesus." His lectures were published posthumously in 1864 (Eng. tr. 1975). In the meantime, a steady stream of lives of Jesus had been published, ranging from the devotional and pious to the fictional accounts of K. F. Bahrdt and K. H. Venturini, which involved elaborate Essene plots to take over Jewish society. In 1828 H. E. G. Paulus had published his *Life of Jesus,* which was perhaps the most important rationalistic treatment. Paulus accepted the main outlines of the Gospel narratives but sought rationalist explanations for the miracles of Jesus. He explained the resurrection by suggesting that Jesus was not really dead and had revived in the tomb.

Such explanations were ridiculed by D. F. Strauss (1808-1874) in his *Life of Jesus Critically Examined* (1835-1836; Eng. tr. repr. 1972), which attributed the supernatural miracle working to the myth-making tendency in religion. In some ways Strauss anticipated the History of Religions school and the approach of form criticism. He argued that the figure of Christ presented in the NT was the product of myth-making tendencies that viewed Jesus in terms of concepts taken from the OT and represented Him as the fulfillment of OT expectations. Although Strauss allowed for psychosomatic factors in the healings attributed to Jesus, he rejected the supernatural. Drawing on Hegelianism, he saw the beliefs of the early Church as the symbolic representation of the idea of the Absolute Spirit in history. But in his *New Life of Jesus* (1864), which was written on a more popular level, the Hegelianism was dropped and Jesus was presented as one of the great improvers of humankind.

Strauss's earlier work provoked considerable controversy, and ended his academic career. Even his former teacher at Tübingen, F. C. Baur (1792-1860), dissociated himself from Strauss, complaining that Strauss wanted to be critical without engaging in the critical inquiry that the NT writings demand. Baur's own approach was deeply influenced by his *Tendenz* Criticism, which appraised writings in the light of the tendencies that they displayed. He saw a fundamental conflict between Hellenistic Christianity led by Paul and Judaic Christianity led by Peter. Writings showing evidence of this conflict were dated earlier and those that did not were given a late date. Baur dated all four Gospels late. His understanding of the person of Jesus bore marked resemblance to that of Schleiermacher.

The mid-19th cent. saw numerous attempts to desupernaturalize Jesus and present Him as a strong religious personality or moral teacher. In France, E. Renan's *Life of Jesus* (1863) created the same kind of sensation that Strauss's work had done a generation earlier. Perhaps the nearest British counterpart was J. R. Seeley's *Ecce Homo* (1865). The theology of A. Ritschl (1822-1889) stressed the moral character of the Kingdom of God and the role of Christ in establishing it. In a similar vein, the great liberal church historian A. von Harnack maintained that Jesus' message was not concerned with Himself but with the kingdom of God and its coming, God the Father and the infinite value of the human soul, and the higher righteousness and commandment of love (*What is Christianity?* [Eng. tr. 1901], p. 51). In *Messianic Secret in the Gospels* (1901; Eng. tr. 1971), W. Wrede argued that the Gospels, especially Mark, present Jesus as deliberately concealing His messiahship and power until the close of His ministry. Wrede maintained that this was the work of the Evangelist and not of Jesus Himself, who did not claim to be the Messiah at all. The Gospels were thus a reading back into the life of Jesus of later beliefs about His person (cf. C. M. Tuckett, ed., *Messianic Secret* [1983]).

The History of Religions school, which flourished between 1880 and 1920, sought to interpret the Bible against the background of contemporary religions, which, they maintained, deeply influenced the ideas found in Scripture. In *Kyrios Christos* (1913, Eng. tr. 1970) W. Bousset (1865-1920) argued that the eschatological ideas underlying terms like "Messiah" and "Kingdom of God" came largely from other religions. He traced the title "Lord" to Hellenistic religion and saw the ascription of divinity to Jesus as the result of alien influences. Somewhat earlier, A. Schweitzer (1875-1965) wrote *The Quest of the Historical Jesus* (1906, Eng. tr. 1912), tracing the story from Reimarus to Wrede. He concluded that most of the scholars engaged in the quest to recover Jesus were guilty of turning Him into someone who corresponded to their own religious and moral ideas. The reason for this was that they had neglected eschatology. Schweitzer pictured Jesus as someone who preached the imminent coming of the Kingdom of God on earth and who saw Himself as God's messianic agent in bringing it about. Jesus' teaching was not to be spiritualized. It was, however, conditioned by an obsolete world view and mistaken in its expectations. Schweitzer ended his work on a mystical, existential note. Although we can find no designation that expresses what Jesus is to us today, those who obey His call will learn "as an ineffable mystery" who He is (p. 403).

In Britain H. P. Liddon's *Divinity of Christ* (1867) represented a major defense of orthodoxy. In contrast with the growing trend to stress Jesus' character as an individual man, the Catholic theologian John Henry Newman (1801-1890) urged in the manner of the early Alexandrian School that Christ should be thought of as man, rather than as *a* man. Christ's human nature had no personality belonging to it; His humanity was not substantive or independent. Rather, it was something possessed by the second person of the trinity, like an attribute or organ (cf. R. Strange, *Newman and the Gospel of Christ* [1981], pp. 43-67).

In response to the new ideas in philosophy and criticism, several attempts were made to modify and restate orthodoxy. The school of Mediating Theology followed Schleiermacher. Many of its members stressed the sinlessness of Jesus, but the movement also gave rise to a more speculative approach in the teaching of Richard Rothe (1799-1867) and I. A. Dorner (1809-1884). Dorner concluded his massive *History of the Development of the Doctrine of the Person of Christ* (1845-1846; Eng. tr., 5 vols., 1861-1863) with a statement of his own approach, which drew on philosophical ideas. He combined a dynamic view of God with the idea of Christ as the head and representative of mankind. The Incarnation was necessitated not by sin but by the loving self-communication of the trinity. Dorner, like other members of the school, was concerned with the true humanity of Christ and its growth and development. But it was his speculative system that gave his view a theological necessity.

The doctrine of KENOSIS proved to be one of the major battlegrounds of nineteenth-century theology. The term means "emptying" and alludes to the self-emptying of Christ referred to in Phil. 2:7 ("[He] emptied himself [*heautón ekénōsen*], taking the form of a servant, being born in the likeness of men"). The idea figured in post-Reformation and early evangelical piety in connection with Christ's state of humiliation during the period of His earthly life, as contrasted with the state of exaltation that began with His resurrection and ascension. Kenotic Christology gained increasing popularity in the 19th century. In *Christ's Person and Work* (3 vols., 1853-1861), G. Thomasius used kenosis to defend orthodoxy against the charges of critics like D. F. Strauss, who claimed that it was inconceivable that an omnipotent, omnipresent, and omniscient God could become incarnate in an individual human being. Thomasius's answer was that Christ emptied himself of these divine attributes during the period of the Incarnation, though He was divine in other respects. German kenotic Christology was popularized in the English-speaking world by A. B. Bruce in *Humiliation of Christ* (1876). Charles Gore used it to help explain why Jesus' views on the OT were different from those of modern scholars ("Holy Spirit and Inspiration," in C. Gore, ed., *Lux Mundi* [1889], pp. 230-266). In becoming man the second person of the trinity accepted the limitations of a genuinely human life. This meant that Jesus had to learn in the same way that others do, and that the scope of His knowledge was affected by the prevailing general state of knowledge. Thus Jesus could not be expected to have the same critical understanding of the OT that modern scholars have. In later writings Gore saw kenosis as a key to understanding God's ways with human beings in general. God deals with them not in His omnipotence but with the same self-restraint that is exemplified in the Incarnation. The doctrine was further developed by P. T. Forsyth in *Person and Place of Jesus Christ* (1909) and H. R. Mackintosh in *Doctrine of the Person of Jesus Christ* (1912), both of which stressed a complementary growth and self-fulfillment alongside the self-limitation of Christ.

The advocates of kenosis saw themselves as moderate defenders of orthodoxy. Their aim was to defend the reality of the Incarnation against the criticism of those who saw Jesus as no more than a religious personality. But to more conservative theologians kenosis posed a threat to the very foundations of faith. If Jesus' knowledge was limited, could He not have been mistaken in other aspects of His teaching? If He was wrong about the authorship of certain books and believed in the historicity of people and events that modern critics deem unhistorical, could He not have been wrong in His teaching about the Kingdom, judgment, salvation, and the Father? If Jesus was limited in His intellectual knowledge, could He not also have been limited in other respects? Could the same argument be applied to the question of whether He was sinless?

Advocates of kenosis drew attention to the obvious facts concerning Jesus' humanity as depicted in the Gospels. He ate, drank, slept, wept. He "increased in wisdom and in stature, and in favor with God and man" (Lk. 2:52). He was repeatedly tempted but did not succumb. He confessed that not even the Son knew the hour of Parousia (Mk. 13:32). He was clearly not omnipresent. Nor did he avail Himself of divine omnipotence either in the temptations recorded in Mt. 4 and Lk. 4 or in meeting His opponents.

Nevertheless, kenosis is open to serious objections. It has been criticized for treating the divine attributes of omnipotence, omnipresence, and omniscience as if they were optional extras that God could readily dispense with. But since these attributes constitute the being of God, without them God would not be God. As E. L. Mascall has pointed out, kenoticism is a kind of inverted Monophysitism (*Christ, the Christian and the Church* [1946], p. 12): in ancient Monophysitism the divine nature of Christ absorbed the human; in kenoticism, the human nature of Christ absorbs the divine. Moreover, kenoticism raises the question of what became of the cosmic functions of the second person of the trinity during the period of the Incarnation. Scripture identifies Him not only as the Creator but as the sustainer of the universe (Jn. 1:1-5; He. 1:1-3). If He emptied Himself of the divine attributes, how was the world sustained during the Incarnation? In reply to this question, the advocates of kenosis questioned the feasibility of the idea that Christ retained these cosmic functions during His earthly life, especially during His infancy and childhood.

The conflicting alternatives seem to present an insoluble dilemma. But the dilemma rests on certain misconceptions. As William Temple observed, "All these difficulties are avoided if we suppose that God the Son did indeed most truly live the life recorded in the Gospel, but added this to the other work of God" (*Christus Veritas* [1924], p. 143). Kenosis mistakenly assumes that the humanity of Jesus functioned like a receptacle in which the second person of the trinity had to be contained, so that what could not be thus contained must somehow be abandoned. Temple's reply is consistent with the teaching of Athanasius, Augustine, and classical theologians down the ages. In Reformed theology this position came to be known as the *Extra Calvinisticum,* which insisted upon the activity of the Word outside the Incarnation as well as within it. As Calvin pointed out, "Even if the Word in his immeasurable essence united with the nature of man into one person, we do not imagine that he was confined therein" (*Inst.* ii.13.4, *LCC*).

It may well be that the debate about kenotic Christology presupposed an essentially tritheistic view of God that treated the three divine persons as separate individual beings. It thus gave rise to the problem of how God could function as God if one of the three divine beings virtually ceased to function as such for a period of time. The problem suggests the need for a more adequate model for understanding the trinity. Related to this is the question of how far Jesus was conscious of His divine person and powers. W. Sanday suggested an approach using the psychological concept of the unconscious mind (*Christologies Ancient and Modern* [1910]; *Christology and Personality* [1911]). He suggested that the seat or locus of all divine indwelling and divine action upon the human soul is the subliminal consciousness. Thus, Jesus as a man was consciously aware only of what the Father chose to bring into His conscious mind.

The question of kenosis and the interpretation of Phil. 2:5-11 continues to be keenly discussed (see R. P. Martin, *Carmen Christi* [2nd ed. 1983]). The passage is widely thought to be a hymn cited by Paul, and perhaps composed by him, to which he appeals as a model for Christian behavior. It may be, however, that v. 7 is not a description of the Incarnation but an allusion to the death of Christ using the language of Isa. 53:12, where the Servant is said to have "poured out his soul to death." The passage may also reflect the temptations of Jesus (Mt. 4:1-10; Lk. 4:1-12), which turn on His being addressed as the Son of God. Jesus renounced the misuse of divine power and chose the role of the obedient servant that led to the cross. If this is so, the passage would have nothing to do with the metaphysical speculation of kenotic Christology.

One of the most important nineteenth-century contributions to Christology came from the Danish philosopher Søren Kierkegaard (1813-1855), whose thought became more widely known only through twentieth-century translations of his writings. Kierkegaard is frequently represented as a pioneer existentialist who had a minimal belief in the historicity of Jesus and who was more concerned with existential response than with historical truth. But close study of works like *Philosophical Fragments* (1844), *Concluding Unscientific Postscript* (1846), and *Training in Christianity* (1850) show that this is a misconception. Kierkegaard did not question the historicity of the NT, but his main concern lay in grasping the implications of the transcendence of God for philosophy, theology, and daily life. God's transcendence means that God is wholly other: He is not an object in time and space or a being alongside other beings. But this means that, even in revelation, God remains transcendent and therefore hidden, for divinity cannot be transformed into an object that can be perceived by the senses. When people saw and heard Jesus, they saw a man. In the Incarnation God appears *incognito*. There is an absolute paradox, because the very act of divine self-revelation involves an act of self-veiling. In order to unveil Himself to mankind, God has to veil Himself in human form. Since our human language is the language of time and space, the relationship between our language and God can be only an indirect one. Basically Kierkegaard was maintaining an orthodox view of Christ without using the vocabulary of orthodoxy. He was wrestling, on a level much deeper than that of his contemporaries and successors, with the implications of divine transcendence for the Incarnation and Christian living.

*C. Contemporary Debate.* The 20th cent. has witnessed widely divergent interpretations of the person of Christ.

Karl Barth (1886-1968), notably in his multi-volume *Church Dogmatics,* attempted a monumental reinterpretation of theology in terms of Christology. In response to theological liberalism, Barth presented Christ as the sole mediator of revelation (cf. Mt. 11:27; Jn. 1:1-18; 14:1-11; He. 1:1-5). As the Word incarnate, Christ is God's word to man. In order to be God's Word, He had to be divine. This led Barth to a doctrine of the trinity, grounded in revelation, in which the Word was the objective reality and the Spirit the subjective reality of the Father's self-revelation. In the later volumes of the *Church Dogmatics* Barth came to view the Incarnation as the key to God's own person, the creation, and reconciliation. On the basis of the union of God and man in the person of Jesus Christ, Barth posited a covenant between God and all mankind. For the sake of this union the creation had come into being. This idea led Barth to a doctrine of double predestination in which Christ was the elect for all and the reprobate for all. Although Barth did not acknowledge that universalism was the logical outcome of his position, many of his readers saw no other alternative.

Barth's contemporary, Rudolph Bultmann (1884-1975), adopted a radically different view. Using the tools of form criticism and the History of Religions school, Bultmann came to the conclusion that it was impossible to know what Jesus was like. One could know only that He had existed. In his programmatic essay, "NT and Mythology" (1941; Eng. tr. in H. W. Bartsch, ed., *Kerygma and Myth* [1953], pp. 1-44), Bultmann argued that the entire thought world of the NT was mythological, the sources of the myths being Jewish apocalyptic and Gnosticism. This thought world was obsolete and unacceptable to modern minds, and thus to make way for the true offense of the gospel the NT needed to be demythologized. The preaching of the cross and resurrection of Christ (which could not be demythologized) presented men and women with the possibility of understanding themselves and entering into an authentic existence in which they were liberated from the quest for tangible security.

Paul Tillich (1886-1965) drew on the critical work of Schweitzer and Bultmann, but made his own restatement of nineteenth-century Idealism. He rejected a theistic view of God in favor of an immanent Ground of Being. Tillich's *Systematic Theology* (3 vols., 1951-1963) viewed humanity as alienated from the Ground of its Being. The Christ was the symbolic figure who had overcome this alienation and was thus, as the Bearer of the New Being, able to mediate reconciliation to others.

At present there is considerable dissatisfaction with the conclusions of Barth, Bultmann, and Tillich. Barth's dogmatic thought made much of the Incarnation but showed less interest in the purely historical Jesus. Tillich's views were bound up with his existential ontology, which now appears equally remote from the concerns of contemporary philosophy and of the Christian Church at large. Subsequent scholarship has reversed Bultmann's view that the NT idea of Christ as a heavenly redeemer was drawn from Gnosticism. Bultmann's sources were all considerably later than the NT, and it is now apparent that the Gnostic idea was derived from Christianity. Several of Bultmann's students came to think that their teacher was much too skeptical with regard to the historical Jesus. Their own work has given rise to what has been called a new quest of the historical Jesus (see James M. Robinson, *A New Quest for the Historical Jesus and Other Essays* [1983]). The philosophical questions raised concerning myth and the interpretation of language have given fresh impetus to the discipline of hermeneutics (see A. C. Thiselton, *Two Horizons* [1980]).

Ever since the English Deists, repeated attempts have been made to compare Jesus with the so-called "divine men" of the ancient world in order to show that Jesus was really a figure like Apollonius of Tyana or other holy men (cf. L. Bieler, ΘΕΙΟΣ ΑΝΗΡ [2 vols., 1935-1936; 1 vol. repr. 1967]). Some have detected different Christologies in the NT and have represented the Gospel of Mark, with its emphasis on the suffering Son of man, as an attempt to combat the wonder-working "divine man" Christology attributed to the disciples (cf. T. J. Weeden, *Mark—Traditions in Conflict* [1971]). In the 1979 reprint of his work, however, Weeden himself acknowledged the inadequacy of the "divine man" concept. Recent research has shown that the term "divine man" (*theíos anḗr*) did not necessarily imply the divinization of a holy man and was not associated with miracle-working (D. L. Tiede, *Charismatic Figure as Miracle Worker* [1972]; C. R. Holladay, Theios Aner *in Hellenistic-Judaism* [1977]). The figure of Apollonius continues to be the subject of research. He is thought to have lived in the 1st. cent. A.D. Philostratus's *Life of Apollonius* iv.45 tells of an event that invites comparison with Lk. 7:11-17. Although many have suggested that the *Life of Apollonius* affords evidence for widespread belief in the wonder-working powers of holy men in the ancient world, the work itself is evidently a piece of anti-Christian polemic, commissioned by the Empress Julia Domna in order to foster the cult of Apollonius as a rival to Christianity (cf. J. Ferguson, *Religions of the Roman Empire* [1960], pp. 181-183). Thus the historical value of the work is open to serious doubt.

In *Jesus the Magician* (1978) Morton Smith revived the ancient accusation that Jesus was really a magician, maintaining that the "official portrait" of Jesus in the Gospels was really propaganda designed to cover up the truth. Smith's case bears a marked resemblance to that of the Jewish leaders who accused Jesus of casting out demons by Beelzebul (Mk. 3:22; Mt. 12:24; Lk. 11:15). Contemporary Jewish scholarship, however, is inclined to take a more positive view of Jesus. G. Vermes depicted Jesus as a Galilean charismatic who clashed with the more formal religion of the Pharisees (*Jesus the Jew* [1973]). Other Jewish writers have sought to give recognition to Jesus while denying the Christian ascription of divinity to Him (cf. Hagner, *Jewish Reclamation of Jesus).*

Various writers have attempted to interpret Jesus as a political revolutionary. In *Jesus and the Zealots* (1967) S. G. F. Brandon saw connections between Jesus and the Zealot movement in its struggle for liberation from Roman rule. Liberation theology has called for a thorough reappraisal of Christology with the aim of stressing Christ's role as a social and political reformer who called into question the oppressive structures of society (cf. Sobrino, *Christology at the Crossroads;* L. Boff, *Jesus Christ Liberator* [1978]; J. Andrew Kirk, *Liberation Theology* [1979]). In *The Crucified God* (1974) J. Moltmann stressed God's identification with suffering in and through Christ and the importance of this for the Church's understanding of God and of its role in the world. The attempts to turn Jesus into a political revolutionary have been refuted by A. Richardson (*Political Christ* [1973]) and M. Hengel (*Was Jesus a Revolutionist?* [Eng. tr. 1971]; *Victory over Violence* [Eng. tr. 1973]; *Christ and Power* [Eng. tr. 1977]; *Charismatic Leader and His Followers* [Eng. tr. 1981]). Nevertheless, the social and ecclesial implications of Christology remain a vital concern.

An attempt to reinterpret the person of Christ in terms of Process Theology has been made by D. R. Griffin in *A Process Christology* (1973). From the Roman Catholic standpoint, E. Schillebeeckx has attempted contemporary restatements in *Jesus: An Experiment in Christology* (1979) and *Christ: The Christian Experiment in the Modern World* (1980). In *Jesus the Christ* W. Kasper provided a Catholic statement along more traditional lines. The most radical British Protestant account of the person of Christ appeared in *Myth of God Incarnate,* ed. J. Hick (for replies, cf. E. M. B. Green, ed., *Truth of God Incarnate* [1977]; Goulder, ed., *Incarnation and Myth: The Debate Continued*). Hick and his colleagues questioned whether the whole idea of Incarnation was not obsolete and irrelevant. They asked whether belief in Christ's divinity was not the product of the mythical thinking of later Christians, and they suggested parallels with the deification of the Buddha. When stripped of the alleged myths, Jesus emerged as a great humanitarian.

A significant alternative to such skepticism was provided a generation earlier by D. M. Baillie in *God Was in Christ* (1948). Baillie emphasized the need to think of Jesus as a man in the fullest sense of the word. He was also deeply impressed with the emphasis that Barth, Brunner, and Bultmann placed on revelation. But he refused to divorce revelation from God's actions in the earthly life of Jesus, which he believed to be the revelation of God to mankind. The works of Jesus were the works of the Father (cf. Jn. 5:19, 30; 14:10; cf. 2 Cor. 5:19). As a model for understanding the Incarnation, Baillie put forward the Christian's experience of the paradox of grace, in which the believer is aware of being both human and responsible and, at the same time, the recipient of God's free grace. Jesus remained fully human but was also aware of the Father's presence in His life. Baillie drew attention to NT passages that stressed the kinship of Jesus with believers (Jn. 17:20-26; 20:17; Rom. 8:29; Col. 1:18; He. 2:11), but he repudiated any suggestion that anyone could be a Christ if he or she were so minded. The Incarnation depended solely on divine initiative. At the same time, Baillie's account of the Incarnation leaves the impression of a veiled unitarianism. Although he alludes to the trinity, he appears to see this simply as the Church's way of speaking of its experiences of God. In the end it is the Father Himself who is Incarnate in Christ. Baillie's Christology was ultimately a restatement of Schleiermacher's basic position.

A most significant statement of Christology appeared in Pannenberg's *Jesus — God and Man.* Pannenberg described the traditional approach as Christology "from above" because of its attempt to view Christ from God's perspective. Christology "from above" tends to be docetic and lacking in interest in the human person of Jesus and His historical background. But since we are earthly, historical beings, we need to discover reasons in history for our christological confession. Pannenberg proposed a Christology "from below" that would avoid presuppositions of divinity and begin with the historical activity of Jesus. He saw Jesus as standing in the apocalyptic tradition and as one for whom the kingdom of God was the single pulsating reality.

Pannenberg accepted the views of German NT scholars who denied that Jesus applied to Himself such christological titles as Son of man, Son of God, Christ, and Lord. Only in retrospect were these titles seen to apply truly to Him. Jesus was concerned with actualizing the kingdom of God, which became a present reality in Him. He was put to death for blasphemy, but the real blasphemy was that of His opponents. In a real sense, Jesus died in their place. The resurrection is God's vindication of Jesus. As such it establishes God's essential unity with Jesus from the beginning. In retrospect it can thus be seen that Jesus was God and Man. Pannenberg disliked the traditional language of the two natures of Christ and preferred to say that He was truly God and truly man. Pannenberg's approach, like that of D. M. Baillie, raises questions about the reality of the trinity, and it may be asked whether, after all, his approach is not essentially a restatement of Schleiermacher's basic approach to Christology.

Moreover, it may be doubted whether a Christology "from below" is truly viable. Pannenberg's Christology was not consistently "from below." With the resurrection of Jesus he invoked divine validation of Jesus "from above." Although he discounted the transcendent implications of concepts such as Son of God and Christ, he gave a central place to the kingdom of God — another concept "from above." The "blasphemy" for which Jesus was condemned clearly has a divine reference and thus expresses a value judgment "from above." In short, Pannenberg did not expunge all transcendent concepts from his account of Jesus' life before the Resurrection. He appears to have been arbitrary in those that he accepted and those that he rejected. Moreover, it must be conceded that even after the Resurrection the Church remains as much "below" as before. The problem of the transcendent in history cannot be solved in the simplistic way that Pannenberg suggested. Jesus' earthly ministry, no less than the Resurrection itself, raises transcendent, theological questions, and it is arbitrary to impose on this period a historical frame of reference that precludes from recognition the very features that indicate the action and presence of God in Christ.

Whereas Baillie and Pannenberg pose the question of whether it is ultimately the Father who became incarnated, "Spirit Christology" raises the question of whether it is the Spirit who became incarnate in Jesus. In Lampe's *God as Spirit,* "Spirit" appears to be a synonym for God, thus giving his Christology a unitarian stamp. The question is more open in the work of Dunn, *Jesus and the Spirit* and *Christology in the Making.* In His earthly ministry, Jesus is the recipient of the Spirit; thereafter He is the bestower of the Spirit. Dunn stressed the role of the Spirit in Jesus' baptism and subsequent ministry. After the Resurrection and Ascension the Spirit is the Spirit of Christ and, as such, the medium of God's presence in the Church.

***II. Method in Interpretation.***–It is apparent from the above survey that one's views about the person of Christ are vitally affected by one's presuppositions and method of approach. Much depends upon whether the Gospels are treated as history or are regarded as relatively late, culturally conditioned expressions of the faith of the early Church. Many NT scholars whose views of the historical value of the Gospels are not so pessimistic as Bultmann's are nevertheless influenced by his criteria in their redaction criticism. Thus, R. H. Fuller observes, "As regards the sayings of Jesus, traditio-historical criticism eliminates from the authentic sayings of Jesus those which are paralleled in the Jewish tradition on the one hand (apocalyptic and Rabbinic) and those which reflect the faith, practice and situations of the post-Easter church as we know them from outside the gospels" (*Foundations of NT Christology,* p. 18; cf. N. Perrin, *Rediscovering the Teaching of Jesus* [1967], pp. 42f.; R. Bultmann, *History of the Synoptic Tradition* [Eng. tr. 1963], p. 205). To these two criteria a third is frequently added. Authentic sayings of Jesus should be "conceivable as developments within Palestinian Judaism" and "use its categories, and if possible reflect the language and style of Aramaic" (Fuller, p. 18). But to many scholars, such criteria now seem to be virtually valueless (cf. R. T. France, "Authenticity of the Sayings of Jesus," in C. Brown, ed., *History, Criticism,*

PERSON OF CHRIST

*and Faith,* pp. 101-142). The first criterion presupposes that Jesus could have had nothing in common with Jewish tradition; the second presupposes that His teaching and practice could have had nothing in common with that of the post-Easter Church; the third not only appears to contradict the first but also rules out sayings and words that have been translated into idiomatic Greek.The use of such criteria in the historical investigation of the person of Christ inevitably calls into question the results of the research.

Many scholars who have used such methods have professed to discover an evolution of Christology within the NT. Thus, the later writings are said to contain a deified Christ who is worshiped as divine, whereas the historical Jesus is presumed to have been a prophetic figure with an apocalyptic message of the Kingdom. Jesus' titles — e.g., Son of Man, Son of God, Christ, and Lord — are thought by some scholars to have been applied to Him retroactively by the post-Easter Church (cf. H. E. Tödt, *Son of Man in the Synoptic Tradition* [Eng. tr. 1965]; F. Hahn, *Titles of Jesus in Christology*). On the other hand, scholars like O. Cullmann (*Christology of the NT*) and C. F. D. Moule (*Origin of Christology*) have seen a development (implying an essential continuity) rather than an evolution (implying a change from one species into another) within the NT. Despite his espousal of the above-mentioned criteria, R. H. Fuller also recognizes a direct line of continuity between Jesus' self-understanding and the Church's christological interpretation of Him. A similar approach may be noted in M. Hengel, *Son of God.*

Many questions pertinent to understanding the person of Christ lie outside the scope of this article. Among them are the date and composition of the NT writings. One's view of these matters clearly affects how one interprets what these writings say about Christ. The account that follows must eschew such questions, however, and confine itself to an analytic description of the person of Christ as found in various NT writings. The synoptic Gospels are treated first, not because they were necessarily written before the other NT writings, but because they give an account of Jesus' life and ministry.

A detailed examination of the titles of Jesus likewise falls outside the scope of this article. But because one's interpretation of the titles significantly affects one's view of the person of Christ, some account of them must be given here. In the past it has frequently been assumed that "Son of Man" refers to Jesus' humanity and that "Son of God" implies His divinity. Thus, to prove Christ's divinity it was necessary to show that the title Son of God fitted Him and that Jesus Himself used the title as a claim to divinity. But this procedure is an anachronistic oversimplification. Even within the NT, SON OF GOD is not necessarily a divine title. Adam is called "the son of God" in Luke's genealogy of Jesus (Lk. 3:38). Hos. 11:1 (cited in Mt. 2:15) alludes to the nation of Israel as God's son. Nathan's prophecy to David contains God's promise to David's successor: "I will be his father, and he shall be my son" (2 S. 7:14). The passage occurs in a collection of testimonies at Qumrân (4QFlor 10f.). In Ps. 2:7 the king is addressed: "You are my son, today I have begotten you" (cited in Acts 13:33; He. 1:5; 5:5; cf. 2 Pet. 1:17). This passage is the source of the identification of Jesus with God's Son by the Bath Kol (voice from heaven) after Jesus' baptism (Mk. 1:11; Mt. 3:17; Lk. 3:22; cf. Jn. 1:34). The Bath Kol also identifies Jesus with the chosen servant in whom God delights (Isa. 42:1; cf. also Mt. 12:18-21). In the light of these contexts the title Son of God is not first of all an expression of personal divinity but a designation of messianic kingship.

The title SON OF MAN has provoked considerable discussion in recent years (in addition to the works of Tödt, Hahn, Cullmann, and Moule already noted, see F. H. Borsch, *Son of Man in Myth and History* [1967]; *Christian and Gnostic Son of Man* [*SBT*, 2/14, 1970]; R. N. Longenecker, *Christology of Early Jewish Christianity* [*SBT*, 2/17, 1970]; F. J. Moloney, *Johannine Son of Man* [1976]; A. J. B. Higgins, *Jesus and the Son of Man* [1964]; *Son of Man in the Teaching of Jesus* [1980]; M. Casey, *Son of Man: The Interpretation and Influence of Daniel 7* [1979]; M. D. Hooker, *Son of Man in Mark* [1967]; F. F. Bruce, "Background to the Son of Man Sayings," in Rowdon, ed., *Christ the Lord,* pp. 50-70; Moule, *Essays in NT Interpretation,* pp. 75-90; Kim, *"The 'Son of Man'" as the Son of God*; Lindars, *Jesus Son of Man*). Interpretations range from claiming that Son of Man is nothing more than a circumlocution for "I," or that it is deliberately vague, to suggesting that it denotes a supernatural, apocalyptic figure (thought to be found, e.g., in 1 En. 37–71). Many, including the present writer, find in Dnl. 7 an essential clue to the meaning of the term in the Gospels. In Dnl. 7 the figure of the Son of Man represents either the saints of the Most High (e.g., the people of Israel) or the angelic guardian of the saints. The figure is vindicated and given an everlasting dominion after withstanding the attacks of the enemies of the Ancient of Days. The figure of the Son of Man in 1 Enoch is clearly an elaboration of the picture in Daniel.

A characteristic feature of the Son of Man sayings in the Gospels is the word "the." Jesus speaks of Himself as "the" Son of Man. C. F. D. Moule makes the fruitful suggestion that for Jesus the title describes His vocation. Jesus saw Himself as the one called to be the Son of Man as described by Daniel. If this is so, He may have been assuming the role of the saints who were summoned to remain faithful to Yahweh and who would ultimately be vindicated; alternatively, He may have been saying that it was He Himself, not an angelic being, who was the guardian of Israel. This latter point might explain why the writer to the Hebrews was at pains to distinguish between Jesus and the angels, pointing out the superiority of the Son (He. 1–2).

The title may well have further overtones. In Ezekiel the prophet is frequently addressed as "son of man." He too was summoned to be Yahweh's loyal representative in a time of trial and upheaval (Ezk. 2:3; 3:4-11). He was called to consume the Word of God and then declare it (3:1-11). He was filled and led by the Spirit of God in his vocation (2:2; 3:12, 14, 24, etc.). Moreover, the punishment of the house of Israel is laid upon him (4:4). Both Ezekiel and Daniel are set in the exilic period from which they both ultimately derive.

Finally, the title Son of Man points back to Adam. In biblical Hebrew *'āḏām* denotes Adam and is the ordinary word for "man." Originally Adam, or mankind as the image of God, was given dominion over the earth (Gen. 1:26-30; cf. Ps. 8). The Israelites traced their descent to Adam, who figured a great deal in intertestamental literature (on this and Adam in the NT, see Dunn, *Christology in the Making,* pp. 98-128). There may well be in the title Son of Man a hint that the Son of Man is the true descendant of Adam (cf. Lk. 3:38), to whom therefore dominion is given. If this is so, there is a convergence of meaning in the titles Son of God and Son of Man. Both indicate Yahweh's appointed righteous servant to whom is given authority to reign over the earth. Two further titles applied to Jesus may point in the same direction. The title "image of God" is best interpreted as meaning God's representative to whom is given stewardship and authority over the earth (cf. D. J. A. Clines, *Tyndale Bulletin*, 19 [1968], 53-103). The title "Christ" (Gk. *christos*) or "Messiah" (Heb. *māši[a]ḥ*) means "the anointed one." Prophets (Ps. 105:15; 1 K. 19:16; 1QM 11:7f.; CD 2:12; 6:1; etc.) and priests (Ex. 40:13; Lev. 4:3, 5, 16; 6:22; Zec. 4:14; possibly Dnl. 9:25f.; 1QS 9:11; etc.) were anointed. But anointing was also associated with kingship, the anointed son of David, and in turn kingship figured in political messianism (1 S. 10:1; 15:1; 16:13; Isa. 9:6f.; 11:1-10; 45:1; Jer. 23:5f.; Ezk. 34:23f.; Ps. Sol. 17–18; Eighteen Benedictions; cf. G. Vermes, *Jesus the Jew* [1981], pp. 129-159). In the Testaments of the Twelve Patriarchs, the Messiah was seen as prophet, priest, and king (T. Reub. 6:7-12; T. Levi 8:14; T. Jud. 24:1-3; T. Dan 5:10f.; T. Jos. 19:8-12). If the messianic concept was fairly open in Jewish thought generally, kingly motifs predominated in the expectation of Palestinian Judaism. The title Son of David may well have been only a more specific synonym for the messianic Son of God.

In and of itself the title MESSIAH or Christ does not necessarily imply divinity. It means "the anointed one." But this raises the question: By what and by whom is the Christ anointed? As we shall see below, the NT writers leave no doubt that they believe it was God Himself who anointed Jesus in such a way that God was personally identified with Jesus. The title LORD is also ambiguous. It could be used as a polite form of address without any divine connotations (e.g., Mt. 21:30 [RSV "sir"]; Mk. 7:28). But it was also a title for God. The LXX uses *kýrios* ("Lord"), following the Hebrew avoidance of speaking the divine name (Heb. *yhwh*). The use of Aram. *maráná thá* ("Our Lord, come") in 1 Cor. 16:22 (cf. Rev. 22:20) suggests that this was a prayer used from the early times in the Aramaic-speaking churches. The title was not generally applied to Jesus during His earthly ministry, though Mt. 7:21f.; 22:34-46; Mk. 12:35-37 (cf. Ps. 110:1) allude to His Lordship. The Lordship of Jesus was asserted by the early Church in view of His resurrection (Acts 2:36; Rom. 1:4; 14:9; Phil. 2:10f.), which demonstrated His cosmic Lordship (1 Cor. 8:6; Col. 1:15-20). Probably the earliest Christian confession was the formula "Jesus is Lord" (Rom. 10:9; 1 Cor. 12:3; Phil. 2:11).

*III. Synoptic Gospels.–A. Mark.* The theme of Jesus' messianic sonship is central to Mark's Gospel. It figures in the opening title (Mk. 1:1). Peter's confession of Jesus as the Christ (8:29) forms a climax to Jesus' public ministry. It is followed by the transfiguration and God's acknowledgment of Jesus as "my beloved Son" (9:7). At Jesus' trial the high priest asks Him, "Are you the Christ, the Son of the Blessed?" (14:61). The question clearly links the concept of the Christ with that of the Son of God ("the Blessed" is evidently a circumlocution for the divine name). Jesus not only answers affirmatively but also identifies the Christ and Son of the Blessed with the Son of Man, using the imagery of Dnl. 7:13: "I am; and you will see the Son of man sitting at the right hand of Power, and coming with the clouds of heaven" (Mk. 14:62). After Jesus' death the centurion confesses, "Truly this man was a son of God" (15:39).

The theme of messianic sonship is linked with other themes. Peter's confession is followed by Jesus' prediction of His suffering, death, and resurrection (8:31-33). The Transfiguration is followed by similar sayings (9:9-13). Jesus responds to James's and John's desire to sit at His right and left hands in glory by speaking about His baptism and reminding them that "the Son of man also came not to be served but to serve, and to give his life as a ransom for many" (10:45). This saying identifies Jesus with the suffering servant of Isa. 53:12, as does the Last Supper (14:22-25; cf. O.Cullmann, *Christology of the NT*, pp. 64f.). Moreover, the voice from heaven had already identified Jesus with God's Son after the Spirit descended upon Jesus following His baptism (Mk. 1:11; cf. Ps. 2:7; Isa. 42:1).

A neglected but important feature of Mark's Christology is the prophecy of John the Baptist: "I have baptized you with water; but he will baptize you with the Holy Spirit" (Mk. 1:8). A widely held view assumes that John is talking about Pentecost and the bestowal of the Spirit upon the Church, and that this prophecy is the same as that in Acts 1:5; 11:16. But in Acts Jesus gives the promise to His disciples, while in Mark it is John who speaks of what Jesus will do to His hearers. The focus in Mark is not Pentecost (which is not mentioned in the Gospels) but the ministry of Jesus. In fact, a major theme of Mark's Gospel is to show how Jesus, as the messianic Son of God, fulfilled this prophecy. The prophecy is followed by an account of Jesus' baptism, the descent of the Spirit, Jesus' identification by the voice from heaven, and Jesus' being led by the Spirit into the wilderness to be tempted (Mk. 1:9-13). Baptism signifies cleansing, death, and renewal. The subsequent events recorded by Mark show how Jesus baptizes His hearers with the Spirit through His exorcisms, healings, cleansings from sin, and teaching (on this theme in all four Gospels, see C. Brown, *Miracles and the Critical Mind,* pp. 300-325). Jesus' first act of public ministry involves exorcizing a man with an unclean spirit (1:21-28). The account contains an implicit contrast between the Holy Spirit and the unclean spirit who recognizes Jesus as "the Holy One of God" but is rebuked and driven out of the man. Further healings and cleansings are reported in the remainder of Mk. 1. In 2:2-12 Jesus claims authority as Son of Man to forgive sins, an act that the scribes see as blasphemous. Conflicts with the Pharisees center on the issue of Jesus' relationship with sinners (2:15-17), fasting (2:18-22), and the sabbath (2:23-28). After Jesus heals a man with a withered hand on the sabbath, the Pharisees plan with the Herodians to destroy Him (3:1-6).

The Pharisees' motive for planning Jesus' death is not simply petty jealousy. The Law laid down strict precepts for dealing with prophets who performed signs and wonders in order to lead people astray. Such a prophet was to be put to death "because he has taught rebellion against the Lord your God" (Dt. 13:5; cf. Mish. San. 7, 10). (On the importance of this and other passages from Deuteronomy in the trial and condemnation of Jesus, see A. Strobel, *Die Stunde der Wahrheit* [1980].) Because of His different interpretation of the Law, Jesus was perceived as a self-styled messianic prophet who was leading the people astray. This prompted the charge that Jesus was "possessed by Beelzebul, and by the prince of demons he casts out the demons" (Mk. 3:22). Jesus responded to this accusation by pointing to its patent falsity and self-contradictory character and also by warning against the unforgivable sin of blaspheming against the Holy Spirit. Mark adds the comment, "for they had said, 'he has an unclean Spirit'" (3:30). This comment indicates that blasphemy against the Holy Spirit is attributing to Satan what is patently the work of the Holy Spirit; the comment also identifies the works of Jesus with the works of the Holy Spirit.

By presenting Christ in these terms Mark has been developing a Spirit Christology. But at the same time he has developed a Word Christology. Jesus preached "the gospel of God" (Mk. 1:14). He taught and commanded with divine authority (1:17, 25, 27, 41; 2:5, 10; 3:14f.). Following the discussion of the charge that Jesus is possessed by Satan, Mark relates Jesus' parable of the sower as a summary of His ministry thus far (4:2-9). Lest there be any doubt about what Jesus is doing, the explanation is given: "The sower sows the word" (4:14). It is the enemies of Jesus, who snatch away the word that He has sown, that are the agents of Satan (v.15).

R. P. Meye has made a strong case for understanding the miracle stories in the middle section of Mark in terms of Ps. 107 ("Psalm 107 as 'Horizon' for Interpreting the Miracle Stories of Mark 4:35–8:26," in R. A. Guelich, ed., *Unity and Diversity in NT Theology* [*Festschrift* G. Ladd; 1978], pp. 1-13). The Psalm depicts Yahweh as deliverer in various life-threatening situations. Through the miracle stories Mark shows how Jesus fulfills the role of Yahweh in His own person.

The stories lead up to Peter's confession of Jesus as the Christ (Mk. 8:29). The disciples report that Jesus has been identified with John the Baptist (perhaps suggesting the practice of necromancy), Elijah (reflecting the expectation of Elijah's return before the Day of the Lord; cf. Mal. 4:5f. [MT 3:23f.]; Mk. 9:12f.), or one of the prophets. All three possibilities indicate that Jesus is thought of as a prophet. But Peter rejects these suggestions and confesses Jesus as the Christ. This raises the question noted earlier: By what or by whom is Jesus anointed as the Christ? The answer has already been given: Jesus was anointed by the Spirit at His baptism and identified as the messianic Son of God. In other words, the title Christ carries with it an implicit reference to the Holy Spirit. Thus each use of the title Christ contains an allusion to the Spirit's unique manifestation in the life of Jesus. The confession of Jesus as the Christ stands in direct contradiction to the religious leaders' claim that Jesus is possessed by Satan.

The so-called messianic secret, Jesus' command to His disciples to tell no one about Him (Mk. 8:30; 9:9), was doubtless bound up with several considerations. Jesus did not want people to misunderstand the nature of His messiahship by identifying it with political aspirations. He wished to avoid a premature confrontation with His adversaries. He refused the testimony of demonic spirits (1:25, 34), for such spirits were not competent witnesses, and to ally Himself with their testimony would have given credence to the charge that He was possessed by, and working in league with, Satan. Jesus wished to let His deeds speak for themselves. His injunction to silence is of a piece with His teaching in parables: the message was plain to all who had ears to hear. Jesus' reticence to claim messiahship publicly may also have been related to the ancient Jewish belief that no man could claim to be the Messiah until he had accomplished the task of the anointed one. Nevertheless Jesus implicitly asserted His messianic kingship by His entry into Jerusalem and the temple (11:1-11). He raised the question of the identity of the Christ but answered it only indirectly (Mk. 12:35-37; cf. Ps. 110:1). He also warned about false Christs and prophets in terms that recall Dt. 13 (Mk. 13:22), and He encouraged the disciples by promising that the Son of Man would come to gather up the elect (Mk. 13:26f.; cf. Dnl. 7:13). But Jesus did not publicly acknowledge His messiahship until the high priest confronted Him at His trial with the direct question, "Are you the Christ, the son of the Blessed?" (for literature and discussion, see *DNTT*, III, 506-511; C. M. Tuckett, ed., *Messianic Secret* [1983]).

The question of defilement and the true nature of cleansing comes to the fore in Mk. 7:1-23. Here again Jesus and the Pharisees stand diametrically opposed. The latter are concerned with the ritual purification and washings (*baptismoí*, 7:4); Jesus is concerned with the heart (vv.19-23). The theme of baptism becomes explicit once more in Jesus' cleansing of the temple (11:15-33), which comes at the climax of His public ministry. Like many of Jesus' actions (e.g., His entry into Jerusalem), it is an enacted sign. When the chief priests, scribes, and elders demand to know His authority for doing this, Jesus replies by asking whether John's baptism was from heaven (i.e., from God) or from men. The question is not simply a device to confuse His questioners. The authorities are reluctant to deny that John's baptism was from God, for they know that the people believe John to have been a real prophet. But acknowledging that John's baptism was from God would implicitly give them the answer to their own question, and they know that Jesus will ask, "Why then did you not believe him?" For John had said, "I have baptized you with water; but he will baptize you with the Holy Spirit" (1:8). Therefore, acknowledging that John's baptism was from God would mean recognizing that Jesus' actions are the fulfillment of John's prophecy, and thus that He is indeed baptizing or cleansing as the Spirit-anointed Christ. Hence Jesus' cleansing of the temple is a baptism of the temple in the power and authority of the Spirit; moreover, it carries with it His claim to be the Spirit-anointed Christ.

The religious leaders condemn Jesus for what they deem to be blasphemy, i.e., His claim to be the messianic Son of God and the Danielic Son of Man to whom ultimate authority has been given (Mk. 14:61f.; cf. Dnl. 7:13). They evidently associated these claims with prophecy (Mk. 14:65) and kingship (Mk. 15:2-20, 26-32). Their attitude toward Jesus is clearly derisive, yet there is irony in their calling Him "King of Israel," a title also applied to Yahweh (e.g., Isa. 44:6; cf. Ps. 47:6 [MT 7]). Although Mark does not explicitly state this, the circumstances and mode of Jesus' death can only mean that in the Jewish context He is a false pretender who is accursed by God and rightly put to death to avoid defiling the land (cf. Dt. 21:23). The verdict might seem to be supported by Jesus' cry of desolation (Mk. 15:34), though the entire context of Ps. 22 shows that this cry is ultimately a confession of faith in God. The negative verdict on Jesus is reversed by the rending of the curtain of the temple (Mk. 15:38), the centurion's confession ("Truly this man was a son of God," v.39), and Jesus' resurrection (16:1-8; appearances of the risen Christ are described only in the variant endings of Mark).

Mark's account of the person of Christ is paradoxical. Jesus is clearly a human figure. He knows human emotions (Mk. 3:5; 6:6, 34; 8:2f., 12; 9:19; 10:14). He requests information (6:38; 8:27; 9:21) and professes His ignorance about the time of the Son of Man's coming (13:32). But Jesus' human emotions may also be seen as embodying God's own compassion and wrath, and His actions and words as embodying God's actions and words. Mark presents Jesus as the messianic Son of God. As the Son of Man He is also the servant who came "not to be served but to serve, and to give his life as a ransom for many" (10:45). Jesus' messiahship involves rejection, suffering, death, and resurrection (8:31; 9:12, 31; 10:33f.; 12:7f.). Implicitly, Mark presents the way of Jesus as the way of Yahweh, so that rejecting Jesus means rejecting Yahweh. Mark does not attempt a theoretical explanation of the Incarnation; rather, he treats Jesus' origin enigmatically by recording the question, "Is not this the carpenter, the son of Mary . . . ?" (6:3). He allows Jesus' actions, words, and fate to speak for themselves and to define the nature of His sonship.

*B. Matthew.* Matthew's account of the person of Christ is widely regarded as having made use of Mark. Jesus' humanity clearly stands out, but Matthew is particularly concerned to draw out the divine, supernatural aspects of Jesus' story. Occasionally this means passing over some of the human traits noted by Mark; e.g., both Matthew and Luke omit the anger and surprise mentioned in Mk. 3:5 and 6:6. Matthew stresses Jesus' healings and miracles (Mt. 8:16f.; 9:35; 12:15; 14:21; 15:38; 21:19). He gives special attention to Jesus' fulfillment of OT prophecy and typology (Mt. 1:22f. [cf. Isa. 7:14]; 2:15 [cf. Hos. 11:1]; 2:17f. [cf. Jer. 31:15]; 2:23 [cf. Isa. 11:1]; 4:14f. [cf. Isa. 9:1f.]; 8:17 [cf. Isa. 53:4]; 12:17-21 [cf. Isa. 42:1-4]; 13:35 [cf. Ps. 78:2]; 21:4f. [cf. Isa. 62:11; Zec. 9:9]; 26:54, 56; 27:9f. [cf. Zec. 11:12f.; Jer. 32:6-15; 18:2f.]). In addition to explicit references to fulfillment, Matthew gives numerous allusions to the OT. Thus, Jesus' response to John the Baptist's disciples, who ask whether Jesus is the one who is to come, draws attention to His own works (Mt. 11:5f.), which indeed are the works prophesied of the Lord's anointed (Isa. 35:5f.; 61:1; cf. Lk. 4:18f.). Matthew identifies John the Baptist himself as the messenger who prepares the way of the Lord (Mt. 11:10; cf. Mal. 3:1; Mk. 1:2) and as the "Elijah who is to come" (Mt. 11:14; cf. Mal. 4:5; Mt. 17:10-13; Jn. 1:21; Lk. 1:17).

Matthew's Christology is directed toward Jewish or former Jewish readers who are thoroughly conversant with the OT. It aims to show how Jesus fulfills Jewish expectation. Matthew traces Jesus' genealogy back to Abraham (Mt. 1:2) and concludes it by naming "Joseph the husband of Mary, of whom Jesus was born, who is called Christ" (1:16). Here "Christ" appears to be in transition to becoming not only a title but a personal name. Matthew's use of titles of Jesus suggests that he understands them to have a significance that transcends Jewish national interests. He explains the name "Jesus" by adding "for he will save his people from their sins" (1:21). Matthew clearly stresses Jesus' messiahship. The title "Son of David" occurs more frequently in Matthew than in the other Gospels (1:20; 9:27; 12:23; 15:22; 20:30; 21:9, 15)."Son of God" may be simply a synonym for "Christ." Peter's confession, "You are the Christ, the Son of the living God" (16:16), is best understood as a Jewish parallelism in which both clauses make the same point but in different words.

Matthew's use of "Son of God" in the temptations (Mt. 4:3, 6) is also best understood as messianic. This narrative follows the account of Jesus' baptism, the descent of the Spirit, and the declaration "This is my beloved Son, with whom I am well pleased" (Mt. 3:13-17; cf. Ps. 2:7; Isa. 42:1). Jesus' temptations reduplicate Israel's temptations as God's son in the wilderness wanderings (cf. B. Gerhardsson, *Testing of God's Son* [1966]; *DNTT*, III, 798-808). As such, they are not temptations to misuse His personal divinity but are rather tests of His messianic sonship. Whereas Israel as God's son had failed, Jesus, as the messianic Son, lives by every word that proceeds out of the mouth of God, refuses to tempt the Lord His God, and worships and serves God alone.

"Son of God" does not express pure divinity but rather focuses on a true humanity that is rightly related to God. In this sense Jesus alone is the true Son of God. As noted above (II), this title converges with "Son of Man" in both the Adamic and Danielic senses. Therefore, the Son of God has dominion (cf. His dominion over the waters, Mt. 14:33). It is to this dominion that Satan's temptations are directed. But Jesus shows Himself to be the true Son of God by refusing to misuse His dominion for selfish ends. In His passion, Jesus is again challenged to save Himself by virtue of being Son of God (27:40, 42). But again He refuses to use His divine authority to save himself. Matthew's account of the trial and passion juxtaposes the titles Christ, Son of God, Son of Man, and King (26:63–27:54). Jesus is condemned for what appear to His adversaries to be blasphemous pretensions to messianic kingship. But (as was noted in III.A above) there is implicit irony in the mocking application to Jesus of the title "King of Israel" (27:42), which properly belongs to Yahweh: in rejecting Jesus, His enemies are rejecting Yahweh Himself.

Matthew's account of Jesus gives even greater prominence to the Spirit than does Mark's. Like Mark, Matthew records the descent of the Spirit, the prophecy of John the Baptist, the voice from heaven, and the Spirit leading Jesus into the wilderness to be tempted (Mt. 3:11–4:1). Likewise, the cleansing of the temple figures at the climax of Jesus' ministry (21:12-27), with the implication that Jesus is acting in the power and authority of the Spirit. But Matthew repudiates any suggestion of adoptionism in his account of Jesus' conception by the Holy Spirit (1:20). Furthermore, he gives a fuller account of the Beelzebul controversy (12:15-32; cf. also 9:33f.) and of Jesus' pronouncement on blasphemy against the Holy Spirit. He presents Jesus' healings and exorcisms as the fulfillment of Yahweh's promise to put His Spirit upon His servant, who will bring justice to the Gentiles (Isa. 42:1-4; Mt. 12:18-21; cf. 3:17). In Matthew's account Jesus Himself attributes His casting out of demons to the Spirit of God and states that this work proves that "the kingdom of God has come upon you" (12:28; cf. 4:17). Thus, Jesus' work is presented not only as a sign that the eschaton has dawned, but also as a transition to the gentile mission that begins when the risen messianic Son of Man, declaring that all authority in heaven and on earth have been given to Him, commands His disciples to go and "make disciples of all nations . . . " (28:19f.).

This commission, which links the Son with the Father and the Spirit (Mt. 28:19), takes up the theme of Jesus' unique relation with the Father and consequent unique mediatorship of the knowledge of the Father (cf. 11:25-30). Another prominent theme in Matthew is that of wisdom (cf. F. Christ, *Jesus Sophia* [1970]; M. Jack Suggs, *Wisdom, Christology and Law in Matthew's Gospel* [1970]; R. G. Hamerton-Kelly, *Pre-Existence, Wisdom and Son of Man* [1973]; J. M. Robinson, "Jesus as Sophos and Sophia: Wisdom Tradition and the Gospels," in R. L. Wilken, ed., *Aspects of Wisdom in Judaism and Early Christianity* [1975], pp. 1-16). This emphasis is shared by Luke, and thus some scholars attribute it to the Q source, which, like wisdom literature generally, may have been a collection of sayings containing the wisdom of the teacher. Jesus is depicted as not only a teacher of wisdom but the personal manifestation of God's wisdom in action (Mt. 11:18f. par. Lk. 7:33-35; Mt. 11:25f. par. Lk. 10:21; Mt. 11:27 par. Lk. 10:22; Mt. 12:41f. par. Lk. 11:31f.; Mt. 23:34-37 par. Lk. 11:49-51; 13:34f.). Because Jesus is the wisdom of God incarnate, He can issue the invitation to come to Him and take His yoke (Mt. 11:28-30; cf. the striking parallel in Sir. 51:23-27). In wisdom literature wisdom plays a role comparable to that of the word of God elsewhere in Scripture. Wisdom functions both in creation and in the enlightenment of humankind (cf. Prov. 8). It is associated with the human spirit and God's Spirit (Job 32:8; Prov. 1:23; 20:27; Wisd. 1:1-15; 7:22–8:1; cf. G. T. Montague, *Holy Spirit* [1976], pp. 91-110). It is also associated with salvation history (Wisd. 10:1–11:1). In the light of this Jewish background, the NT references to wisdom have profound significance for understanding the person of Christ. Jesus is not simply a wise man; He is the incarnate wisdom of God.

*C. Luke.* Luke's Christology also gives prominence to the Holy Spirit and to wisdom. Like Matthew, though drawing on entirely different stories, Luke draws attention to the Holy Spirit's role in the conception of Jesus (Lk. 1:35). He mentions the Spirit in connection with the ministry prophesied for John the Baptist (1:15, 17) and also with the prophetic utterances of Elizabeth (1:41), Zechariah (1:67), and Simeon (2:25-27). Luke is concerned to correct any impression that the Spirit first comes upon Jesus after His baptism. His account thus precludes adoptionism or the possibility that Jesus might simply be a prophet or a charismatically gifted figure. Luke's emphasis on wisdom has already been noted (for references, see III.B above). Just as Luke stresses that the Spirit is present prior to Jesus' baptism, so also he stresses that Jesus is filled with wisdom from childhood (2:40, 52). Like the other evangelists, Luke records John the Baptist's prophecy concerning Jesus' baptism with the Holy Spirit (3:16), the descent of the Spirit, and Jesus' identification by the voice from heaven (3:21f.). Not only is Jesus "full of the Holy Spirit" and led by the Spirit into the wilderness to be tempted by the devil (4:1f.), but subsequently He returns "in the power of the Spirit into Galilee," where He begins His ministry (4:14). Between the account of the Spirit's descent and Jesus' subsequent identification as the Son of God, and the account of the temptation, Luke inserts his genealogy, which traces Jesus back to Adam, "the son of God" (3:38). This sequence portrays Jesus as the eschatological Son of God who, in contrast to Adam, triumphs over temptation and exercises true dominion.

In his account of Jesus' visit to Nazareth (Lk. 4:16-30), Luke further identifies Jesus with the servant of the Lord who is anointed by the Spirit (4:18f.; Isa. 61:1f.). The passage indicates that Jesus' messiahship is to be thought of in terms of His anointing by the Spirit after His baptism, and that this is constitutive for His ministry.

Luke's Gospel is characterized by his consistent attempt to balance Jesus' teaching and miracles (cf. P. J. Achtemeier, "Lukan Perspective on the Miracles of Jesus: A Preliminary Sketch," in C. H. Talbert, ed., *Perspectives on Luke-Acts* [1978], pp. 153-167). He frequently eliminates detail in order to focus on Jesus. In Jesus' response to John the Baptist's question whether Jesus is "he who is to come," Luke emphasizes Jesus' current miracles (Lk. 7:18-23 par. Mt. 11:2-6; cf. Lk. 7:1-17). Jesus' mighty works, whether performed by Him or by the disciples under His authority, show that the kingdom of God is present and demand a positive response (Lk. 10:9, 11, 13-20; 11:14-23; 17:20f.). The works performed by the seventy are indicative of Satan's downfall (10:17-20) and are an occasion for Jesus' rejoicing in the Holy Spirit (10:21). Luke detaches the saying on blasphemy against the Spirit from the Beelzebul controversy (12:10), but he nevertheless gives the controversy a central place (11:14-26). He stresses that it is by the Spirit that Jesus works and by the Spirit that Jesus' disciples are to live and work (11:13, 20; 12:12; 24:49). (The expressions "finger of God" [11:20] and "promise of my father" [24:49] are ways of speaking about the Spirit.) His disciples will also be given God's wisdom (21:15).

Alongside this emphasis on Jesus being the Spirit-anointed Messiah, Luke draws attention to Jesus' humanity. Jesus knows the pain of rejection and grief (Lk. 22:15, 39-46). He is tempted (4:13; 22:28) and divinely strengthened (22:43). He communes with God in prayer (6:12; 11:1; 22:32, 41, 44) and commends His spirit into the Father's hands (23:46). He is compassionate to outcasts (7:36-50; 19:1-10), Samaritans (9:51-56; 10:29-37; 17:11-19), and sinners (5:29f.; 18:9-14). At the same time. He makes the most stringent demands on His followers — demands that transcend family ties (9:23-26, 57-62; 14:25-35).

Luke's selection of stories and use of the titles of Jesus indicate that he sees in them a universal significance. At the Annunciation the angel tells Mary, "The Holy Spirit will come upon you, and the power of the Most High will overshadow you; therefore the child to be born will be called holy, the Son of God" (Lk. 1:35). To the shepherds the angel declares, "Be not afraid; for behold, I bring you good news of a great joy which will come to all the people; for to you is born this day in the city of David a Savior, who is Christ the Lord" (2:10f.). In general, Luke uses the title Christ more frequently than Mark, though he rarely introduces it into the sayings of Jesus. In 24:26, 46 "Christ" is connected with suffering and death. "Son of Man" also occurs more frequently than in Mark, partly due to the sayings used by Luke but not by Mark. On occasion Luke interprets sayings for his gentile readers (e.g., cf. Lk. 22:69 par. Mk. 14:62; Lk. 23:47 par. Mt. 27:54; Mk. 15:39). Nevertheless he uses "Lord" more frequently than the other Evangelists. He not only records the enigmatic reply, "The Lord has need of it" (Lk. 19:31; cf. Mt. 21:3; Mk. 11:3), but finds it natural to refer to Jesus as "the Lord" (Lk. 7:19; 10:1; 11:39; 12:42; 17:5f.). Luke's usage suggests that he sees a deeper retrospective significance in the incidents that he relates in the light of the Resurrection and the Church's reception of the Spirit from the Father at Jesus' behest (24:49). Thus the stories that he recounts, whose truth he has researched (1:1-4), take on a new meaning and receive a higher ratification in the light of Jesus' exalted status.

*IV. Apostolic Preaching and Teaching.–A. Peter and the Jerusalem Church.* The preaching in Acts has been the subject of considerable discussion (for review, see *DNTT,* III, 57-58). A number of scholars have argued that the sermons in Acts represent Christian teaching that is considerably earlier than any of the NT writings themselves. Based on his analysis of passages in Acts (e.g., 2:14-39; 3:13-26) and the Pauline Epistles (e.g., Gal. 1:3f.; 3:1; 4:6), C. H. Dodd sought to establish a basic pattern of apostolic preaching (*Apostolic Preaching and Its Developments* [1936]; *see* PREACH II.B.1.b.). He noted certain differences between Paul's preaching and the preaching associated with Peter and the Jerusalem Church (the "Jerusalem kerygma"). The Jerusalem apostles do not appear to have used the title Son of God. In Acts (9:20) Paul is the first to use the title, though it seems likely that the Pauline phrase "Son of God in power" (Rom. 1:4) means substantially the same as "Lord and Christ" in the Jerusalem kerygma. The Jerusalem preaching relates the forgiveness of sins to Christ's death and resurrection but does not say explicitly that Christ died "for our sins." Nor does it develop the thought of the continued intercession of the exalted Christ. But many elements are common to the peaching of Peter in Acts and the teaching of Paul in his Epistles, including the Davidic descent of Jesus, establishing His human qualification for messiahship; His death and resurrection according to the Scriptures; His consequent exaltation to the right hand of God as Lord and Christ; His deliverance from sin and judgment into new life; the call to repentance; and warning of judgment (see Dodd, pp. 25f.).

Although critics have challenged Dodd's contention that Peter's speeches in Acts represent the earliest apostolic preaching, many of their objections are not substantial. Nevertheless, the record of Stephen's preaching (Acts 7), Philip's testimony (8:26-40), Paul's preaching at Athens (ch. 17), his address to the elders of Ephesus (20:17-35), and his defenses before Felix (ch. 24) and Agrippa (ch. 26) indicate that other forms of preaching existed alongside the Jerusalem kerygma. What Dodd identified as the apostolic kerygma is not an all-purpose presentation of the Christian message but is preaching directed specifically to the Jewish situation. Its aim therefore is to establish Jesus' messiahship. Despite Jesus' rejection by the Jewish leaders, His resurrection shows that He is indeed the Christ and Lord of all (10:36; cf. 2:34-36). In His lifetime Jesus was anointed by the Spirit and empowered to perform wonders (2:22; 10:38), and it is Jesus who, in exalted state, bestows the Spirit upon His disciples (2:33, 38; cf. 10:44-48).

The theme of the Spirit's role in Jesus' earthly ministry and exaltation also figures in Stephen's preaching (7:51-56). Both Peter and Stephen identify Jesus with the prophet foretold by Moses (3:22; 7:37; cf. Dt. 18:18). This identification repudiates the implicit charge that Jesus was a false prophet and blasphemous messianic pretender who was rightfully put to death. The whole book of Acts displays a strong interest in proving that Jesus is the Christ in the sense of the Spirit-anointed Messiah. Jesus is God's Christ (Acts 2:31; 3:18; 5:42; etc.) who "must suffer" (17:3; 26:23). He is "the Righteous One" (3:14; 7:52; 22:14), the stone rejected by the builders which has been made the head of the corner (4:11; cf. Ps. 118:22; Rom. 9:32f.; 1 Pet. 2:5-8). In view of the Resurrection and the outpouring of the Spirit there is no more question of a messianic secret. Peter boldly declares, "Let all the house of Israel therefore know assuredly that God has made him both Lord and Christ, this Jesus whom you crucified" (Acts 2:36).

Acts proclaims that, instead of being the evildoer whom the authorities put to death for His blasphemies, Jesus is the holy, anointed, suffering servant of prophetic expectation (3:13, 26; 4:27, 30; 8:30-35; 17:3; 26:23; cf. Isa. 53). Above all, Jesus is Lord. Acts speaks of Him as "the Lord Jesus," "the Lord Jesus Christ," "our Lord Jesus Christ," and simply "the Lord." The Resurrection and outpouring of the Spirit have vindicated His lordship (2:36). Stephen addresses Him as Lord over life and death when he prays, "Lord Jesus, receive my spirit (7:59). Christians are characterized as those who call upon His name (9:14; cf. 2:21; 22:16). Believers are baptized in the name of Jesus Christ and through Him receive the Spirit (2:38; 8:12, 17; 10:44-48; 19:5f.; etc.). Healing (3:6; 4:7, 10) and exorcism (16:18; 19:13) are performed in His name. He is the Author of life (3:15), the Leader and Savior whom God has exalted to His right hand "to give repentance to Israel and forgiveness of sins" (5:31). "There is salvation in no one else, for there is no other name under heaven given among men by which we must be saved" (4:12).

*B. 1 and 2 Peter, James, and Jude.* E. G. Selwyn drew attention to many parallels in thought and phrase between 1 Peter and Peter's preaching in Acts (*First Epistle of St. Peter* [2nd ed. 1947], pp. 33-36). He saw the connection not as literary but as historical, going back to the teaching of Peter himself. A common feature is the emphasis on Jesus' resurrection, which is related to His vindication and baptism (1 Pet. 1:3, 21; 3:18-22). In contradistinction to the view of the Jewish hierarchy, Jesus' death is seen as the redemptive death of the righteous for the unrighteous (1:18f.; 2:21, 24; 3:18). Jesus is the cornerstone, the stone that causes unbelievers to stumble and that was rejected by the builders (2:4-8; cf. Ps. 118:22; Isa. 8:14; 28:16; Mt. 21:42 par.; Acts 4:11; Rom. 9:33). But this stone is in fact the foundation of the new temple into which believers are built, so that they become a holy priesthood offering spiritual sacrifices to God through Jesus Christ (1 Pet. 2:5).

Although 1 Peter does not use the term "servant" of Jesus, 2:22-25 clearly draws on the portrait of the suffering servant in Isa. 53:5f., 9, 12 (cf. Acts 3:13, 26; 4:27, 30). Jesus suffers as the righteous one who provides the example for His followers (1 Pet. 1:11; 2:21; 4:1, 13; 5:1).

In 1 Peter "Jesus Christ" and "Christ" have become personal designations. "The Son," "His Son," and "Son of God" do not occur, but "Lord" is applied to Jesus four times (1:3; 2:3, 13; 3:15). The dominion of Christ, which figures elsewhere in connection with His sonship and lordship, is expressed in 1:8 (where He is the object of unqualified worship); 3:22; 4:11; 5:11. God calls human beings "to his eternal glory in Christ" (1 Pet. 5:10).

The Christologies of 2 Peter, James, and Jude focus attention on Jesus as Lord and Savior. In 2 Pet. 2:9, 11; 3:8f. "the Lord" means God, but in 3:2, 10, 15 it denotes Christ (cf. "our Lord" in 1:2, 8, 11, etc.). In these Epistles "Son" appears only in 2 Pet. 1:17 in a reference to the Transfiguration. In the light of the previous discussion concerning sonship as a designation of kingship (see II above) and the teachings of 2 Peter in general, it seems likely that this passage is meant to attest to what has already been said about "the eternal kingdom of our Lord and Savior Jesus Christ" (1:11).

In James every reference to Christ includes the title "Lord." Jesus is called "the Lord Jesus Christ" in 1:1 and "our Lord Jesus Christ" in 2:1; otherwise He is not mentioned by name. James sometimes uses "Lord" as a synonym for God (1:7; 3:9; 4:10, 15; 5:4, 10f.), but he uses it to denote Christ in 1:1; 2:1; 5:7f., 14f.

The usage in Jude is similar. "Lord" denotes God in vv. 9 and 14; it refers to Christ in vv. 4, 17, 21, and 25. The letter concludes with the doxology: "to the only God, our Savior through Jesus Christ our Lord, be glory, majesty, dominion, and authority, before all time and now and for ever. Amen" (v. 25).

The use of "Savior" to describe Jesus is comparatively rare in the NT. The majority of instances occur in 2 Peter (1:1, 11; 2:20; 3:2, 18) and the Pastoral Epistles (2 Tim. 1:10; Tit. 1:4; 2:13; 3:6). Otherwise it occurs in Lk. 2:11; Jn. 4:42; Acts 5:31; 13:23; Eph. 5:23; Phil. 3:20; 1 Jn. 4:14. V. Taylor ascribes its restricted and delayed currency to its use in Greek religion and Caesar-worship (*Names of Jesus,* p. 109). The same could not be said, however, of the title "Lord." Its currency and controversiality may depend not on its meaning in Hellenistic circles but its meaning in Judaism. It may also be noted that the idea of "Savior" is present in the name Jesus itself, which is a form of the name of Joshua ("Yahweh is salvation," "Yahweh saves," or "Yahweh will save").

*C. Paul.* It is an open question whether Paul ever saw or met Jesus during His earthly life (see F. F. Bruce, *Paul: Apostle of the Heart Set Free* [1977], pp. 95-112). If Paul was educated in Jerusalem, he may well have encountered Jesus, though at that time he sided with Jesus' opponents and became an active persecutor of the Church (Acts 7:58; 8:1; 9:1-5, 13f.; 22:3-5; 26:9-11). But Paul's attitude was completely transformed by his encounter with the risen Christ on the Damascus road, an encounter that led to his apostleship (cf. S. Kim, *Origin of Paul's Gospel* [1981]). Paul was clearly not an apostle in the same sense that the Twelve were; for eleven of them had been disciples chosen by Jesus, while Matthias had been a follower from the beginning of Jesus's ministry (Acts 1:21f.). Paul also lacked the qualification of having witnessed to Jesus' resurrection before His ascension. But he insisted that Christ had appeared to him "as one untimely born" (1 Cor. 15:8) and had given him a special apostleship to the Gentiles (1 Cor. 15:9; Gal. 1:12; 2:8; cf. Acts 9:15; 22:14f.; cf. also the opening greetings of Paul's letters).

Moreover, Paul insisted that his teaching was not his own invention but was based on what he had "received" (1 Cor. 15:3). Some passages in the Epistles read like

PERSON OF CHRIST

fragments of creeds or catechisms, suggesting a pre-Pauline body of teaching concerning Christ that Paul helped to shape (cf. O. Cullmann, *Earliest Christian Confessions* [Eng. tr. 1949]; J. N. D. Kelly, *Early Christian Creeds* [3rd ed. 1972], pp. 6-29; V. F. Neufeld, *Earliest Christian Confessions* [1963]). The Pauline Epistles stress the Resurrection, which vindicates Jesus and completes His saving work (1 Cor. 15:3-8; Rom. 1:3f.; 8:34; Phil. 2:6-11; 1 Tim. 3:16; 2 Tim. 2:8; cf. 1 Pet. 3:18-22). Other formulations are bipartite, linking God and Jesus Christ, sometimes alluding to Christ's reconciling work (Rom. 4:24; 1 Cor. 8:6; 1 Tim. 2:5f.; cf. 1 Pet. 1:21) and sometimes alluding to Christ as the judge of all (1 Tim. 6:13f.; 2 Tim. 4:1). The greetings of the Epistles frequently link God the Father and the Lord Jesus Christ as the source of grace (Rom. 1:7; 1 Cor. 1:3; 2 Cor. 1:2; Gal. 1:3; Eph. 1:2; etc.). The phrase "the God and Father of our Lord Jesus Christ" has the character of a formula of Christian confession (Rom. 15:6; 2 Cor. 1:3; 11:31; Eph. 1:3; cf. 1 Thess. 3:11; 2 Thess. 2:16; etc.). Occasionally the Spirit is also mentioned alongside God the Father and the Lord Jesus Christ (1 Cor. 12:3-5; 2 Cor. 1:21f.; 13:14; Eph. 2:18; 4:4-6; etc.).

Some scholars have argued that Paul had no interest at all in the historical Jesus (cf. R. Bultmann, *Faith and Understanding* [Eng. tr. 1969], pp. 220-246). According to Bultmann, Christ is to be found only in the kerygma of the cross and Resurrection. Paul appears to take only slight interest in Jesus' life and teaching, although he does refer to Jesus' Davidic descent (Rom. 1:3), His birth (Gal. 4:4), His gentleness (2 Cor. 10:1), His humiliation and self-denial (Rom. 8:3; 15:3; 2 Cor. 8:9; Phil. 2:6-11), His teaching (Rom. 12:19-21 [cf. Mt. 5:43-48]; Rom. 13:9f. [cf. Mt. 19:16-21; 22:39f.]; 1 Cor. 7:10f. [cf. Mt. 19:3-9 par. Mk. 10:2-12]), the Last Supper (1 Cor. 11:23-25), His concern for the support of His followers (1 Cor. 9:14; cf. Lk. 10:7), and an otherwise unknown saying (Acts 20:35).

Some have appealed to 2 Cor. 5:16 in support of the claim that Paul was not interested in the historical Jesus: "... even though we once regarded Christ from a human point of view, we regard him thus no longer." But this passage must be seen in the light of Paul's former attitude to Jesus and of his train of thought elsewhere. "Christ crucified" is "a stumbling-block to the Jews and folly to the Gentiles" (1 Cor. 1:23). The slogan "Jesus be cursed!" (12:3) represents the official attitude of the Jerusalem hierarchy — an attitude that had clearly spread in the diaspora. The form of Jesus' death was a self-evident sign to the Torah-respecting Jew that Jesus was cursed (Gal. 3:13; cf. Dt. 21:23). But Paul had come to see that this was a human judgment. Instead of being the definitive proof that Jesus was under the divine curse, the cross became the means of redemption, reconciliation, and salvation (2 Cor. 5:21; cf. Rom. 3:24-26). To curse Jesus is *ipso facto* proof that one does not possess the Spirit; conversely, one can acknowledge Him only in the power of the Spirit (1 Cor. 12:3). The gift of this knowledge is comparable to the creation of light (2 Cor. 4:6). It brings about the kind of radical transformation that Paul himself had experienced (cf. 5:17).

This new experience of Christ in the Spirit shows that Jesus is indeed the Spirit-anointed Christ and that the interpretation of Jesus' enemies (including, formerly, Paul) is wrong. Thus 2 Cor. 5:16 indicates not a lack of interest in the earthly Jesus but rather the reverse. It is a condemnation of judgments about Jesus that are not prompted by the Spirit (cf. 1 Cor. 2:1-16; 2 Cor. 3:12–4:15). Likewise, Paul's decision to "know nothing among you except Jesus Christ and him crucified" (1 Cor. 2:2) reflects a determination to know the Jesus who was crucified for His claims to be the Spirit-anointed Messiah. Paul's apostolic ministry focused on the proclamation of Jesus' significance in the light of His death, resurrection, and bestowal of the Spirit. But he took with him on his missionary journeys persons such as Mark (e.g., Acts 12:12, 25) and Luke (e.g., 2 Tim. 4:11; Philem. 24), who either knew at first hand of the events surrounding Jesus or were involved in compiling accounts of them.

To Paul, therefore, Jesus is the vindicated Messiah. He was qualified for this by His human Jewish descent (Rom. 1:3; 9:5); but His messiahship depends ultimately on God's personal presence in Him (2 Cor. 5:19). His identity as the messianic Son of God is established beyond doubt by the Spirit: Jesus is "designated Son of God in power according to the Spirit of holiness by his resurrection from the dead, Jesus Christ our Lord" (Rom. 1:4; cf. 8:11).

Paul refers to Christ as the "Son of God" only four times (Rom. 1:4; 2 Cor. 1:19; Gal. 2:20; Eph. 4:13). He also calls Him "the Son" once (1 Cor. 15:28) and "his Son" twelve times (Rom. 1:3, 9; 5:10; 8:3, 29, 32; 1 Cor. 1:9; Gal. 1:16; 4:4, 6; Col. 1:13; 1 Thess. 1:10). In addition, he makes implicit references to sonship in passages that speak of the Father of Jesus Christ (e.g., 2 Cor. 1:3). Even so, references to Christ's sonship are few compared with references to Him as "Lord" (a title applied to Jesus approximately 222 times in the Pauline corpus). The reason for this great discrepancy may be that "Son of God" said less than "Lord" did. To Jewish ears "Son of God" had messianic overtones, but at the same time it set the Messiah over against God. To Paul, Jesus was indeed the Messiah; hence Paul could freely use the term "Christ." But God was in Christ in a way that justified Christ being called "Lord," a title that properly belonged to Yahweh. This title was already applied to Jesus by Peter and the Jerusalem church (see IV.A above). "Jesus is Lord" was evidently the basic Christian confession (Rom. 10:9; 1 Cor. 12:3; Phil. 2:11) and was the essence of Paul's preaching (2 Cor. 4:5; cf. 1 Cor. 8:6; Rom. 11:36; Col. 1:16). Christ's status, therefore, is the status of God Himself. The judgment that belongs to God alone is committed to Christ (Rom. 14:9f.; 2 Cor. 5:10; cf. Acts 17:31; 1 Cor. 15:24-28). All human beings will bow and confess Jesus Christ as Lord, thereby giving glory to the Father (Phil. 2:11). Christ is in fact "the Lord of glory" (1 Cor. 2:8); "for in him all the fullness of God was pleased to dwell" (Col. 1:19).

It is a matter of debate whether Paul ever explicitly calls Christ "God." The RSV translates Rom. 9:5 "to them belong the patriarchs, and of their race, according to the flesh, is the Christ. God who is over all be blessed for ever. Amen." But the RSV mg. renders the last part "Christ, who is God over all, blessed for ever. . . ." The passage might be a doxology (as in the RSV text), but the description of Christ as God would be in harmony with Paul's teaching elsewhere (cf. B. M. Metzger, "Punctuation of Rom. 9:5," in Lindars and Smalley, eds., *Christ and Spirit in the NT*, pp. 95-112). For Paul applies to Christ various metaphors and phrases that properly apply to God. In Acts 17:28 Paul identifies God in terms of a quotation thought to be drawn from Epimenides: "In him we live and move and have our being." The same could be said of Christ. Elsewhere, however, Paul says, "For me to live is Christ" (Phil. 1:21), and "I have been crucified with Christ; it is no longer I who live, but Christ who lives in me" (Gal. 2:20). This is true of all believers: "For you have died, and your life is hid with Christ in God . . ." (Col. 3:3; cf. references to Christ "in you," e.g., Rom. 8:10; 2 Cor. 13:3, 5; Gal. 4:19; Col. 1:27). This language presents a striking parallel to the promise of God that constitutes the essence of OT religion: "I will live in them and move among them, and I will be their God and they shall be my people" (2 Cor. 6:16; cf. Ex. 29:45; Lev. 26:12; Jer. 31:1, 33; Ezk. 37:27).

This thought, that the divine indwelling is now realized through Christ and the Spirit of Christ, underlies Paul's use of the metaphor of the temple. Believers have taken the place of the Jerusalem temple as the dwelling place of God (2 Cor. 6:16; cf. 1 Cor. 3:16f.; see R. J. McKelvey, *The New Temple* [1969]). In Eph. 2:11-22 Paul takes the thought of the temple even further. The Gentiles are brought into the temple through Christ's death, which reconciles Jew and Gentile to God and to each other. The "household of God" is "built upon the foundation of the apostles and prophets, Christ Jesus himself being the chief cornerstone, in whom the whole structure is joined together and grows into a holy temple in the Lord" (2:19-21).

Another OT metaphor depicts Israel as the bride of Yahweh (Jer. 2:2; cf. Isa. 49:18; 62:5). To Paul the Church is the bride of Christ (2 Cor. 11:2; Eph. 5:22-32). These allusions may well be traced back to Jesus' references to the bridegroom and the wedding feasts (Mk. 2:19f. par.; Mt. 22:1-10 par. ; 25:1-13; cf. Jn. 3:29).

Even more prominent than the idea of Christ indwelling the believer is that of the believer being "in Christ" (e.g., Rom. 8:1; 1 Cor. 15:22; 2 Cor. 5:17; Gal. 3:26, 28; Eph. 1:4, 7; Phil. 2:5; 4:13; Col. 2:6, 10). The meaning of Gk. *en* ("in") is very broad (cf. Moule, *Origin of Christology,* pp. 54-69; *DNTT*, III, 1192f.), embracing suggestions of incorporation, reference, cause, agency, mode, location, and authority. Common to these varied meanings is the idea that the Christian's identity and relation to God is defined in terms of being "in Christ."

Related to this idea is the metaphor of the body (for literature and discussion, see R. H. Gundry, Sōma *in Biblical Theology with Emphasis on Pauline Anthropology* [1976]). Paul refers to the Church as the body of Christ (e.g., Rom. 12:4f.; 1 Cor. 10:17; 12:12-27; Eph. 3:6; 4:13-16; 5:30; Col. 1:18, 24; 2:19; 3:15). The metaphor includes the ideas of mutual interdependence, growth, and Christ's headship. There are grounds for thinking that Paul did not invent this metaphor. Paul's contemporary, Seneca, addressed the Roman emperor Nero as "the soul of the republic and it is your body" (*De Clementia* i.5.1; cf. ii.2.1; *Epistulae* 92.30). Philo said that the high priest settled disputes and offered sacrifice so that all parts of the nation might be united in one fellowship "as a single body" (*De specialibus legibus* iii.23 [131]; for further examples, see Moule, *Origin of Christology,* pp. 83-85).

It is possible that Paul developed this body metaphor in opposition to ideas of corporate identity that he found in paganism and Judaism. The concept of the "flesh" may have played a part in this development. For the Judaizers the ritual removal of the flesh in circumcision defined membership in the covenant people of God. To Paul this was no more than a mutilation of the flesh (Phil 3:2). God's action in Christ is a "circumcision" that replaces the circumcision of the flesh (3:3; Col. 2:11f.). In place of the Judaizers' concern with the flesh, Paul is concerned to hold fast "to the Head, from whom the whole body, nourished and knit together through its joints and ligaments, grows with a growth that is from God" (Col. 2:19).

Paul's Epistles also contain a wisdom Christology (cf. the discussion of wisdom in Matthew, III.B. above). Although Christ crucified is a stumbling-block to the Jews and folly to the Greeks, He is "the power and the wisdom of God" (1 Cor. 1:24). God "is the source of your life in Christ Jesus, whom God made our wisdom..." (v.30). 1 Cor. 8:6; 10:4; Rom. 10:6-8 may also contain references to wisdom (see Dunn, *Christology in the Making,* pp. 162-196). Paul assigns to Christ the role in the creation and sustenance of the world that pre-Christian Jewish thought assigns to wisdom (1 Cor. 8:6; cf. Prov. 3:19; Wisd. 8:4-6; Philo, *Quod deterius potiori insidiari solet* 16). Perhaps the most striking passage is Col. 1:15-20, which is widely regarded as a pre-Pauline hymn. Whereas wisdom literature describes wisdom as "an image of God's goodness" (Wisd. 7:26; cf. Philo *Legum allegoriae* i.14) and as the first or firstborn in God's creation (Prov. 8:22-31; cf. Sir. 24:9; Philo *Quaestiones et solutiones in Genesin* iv.97; *De ebrietate* 8; cf. also Ps. 104:24), Col. 1:16f. assigns the creative role to Christ. Just as God's "fullness" (*plērōma*) is manifested in His wisdom in creation and providence, so all the fullness of God dwells in Christ "bodily" (Col. 2:9; cf. 1:19). In the sense that the *plērōma* of God was eternal, Christ pre-existed eternally.

The Pauline Epistles do not use the title Son of Man, but the contrasting parallel between Christ and Adam figures prominently at certain crucial points (see Barrett, *From First Adam to Last*; Dunn, *Christology in the Making*, pp. 98-128). In addition to explicit references to Adam in Rom. 5 and 1 Cor. 15, implicit allusions occur in Rom. 1:18-25 and Phil. 2:6-11. The Christ-hymn in Phil. 2, which is not a piece of theological speculation about Jesus' self-divestiture of divine attributes (see the discussion of kenosis in I.B above), appears to be a meditation that draws an implicit contrast between Jesus as the Christ and Adam, who looked to his own interests and sought equality with God. The reference to Jesus' being "in the form of God" (v.6) probably corresponds to the first man's being made in the "image" and "likeness" of God (Gen. 1:26). In Hebrew thought the visible form of God is His glory. Unlike Adam, Jesus did not count equality with God a thing to be grasped (Phil. 2:6; cf. Gen. 3:5); rather, "taking the form of a servant," He "emptied himself" (Phil. 2:7; cf. the prophecy of the Suffering Servant who "poured out his soul to death," Isa. 53:12). Whereas the first man's disobedience brought death into the world and deprived humankind of God's glory, Christ's obedience brings reconciliation, life, and the restoration of glory (Rom. 5:12-21; cf. 1:23; 3:23; 8:17f., 30; 1 Cor. 15:21f., 43, 50-57; Phil. 3:21).

Thus the first man, Adam, is relativized by the person and work of Christ. Human beings were created as God's image, i.e., to be God's representatives with stewardship and dominion over the earth (Gen. 1:26-30; 5:1f.; 9:6; cf. D. J. A. Clines, *Tyndale Bulletin,* 19 [1968], 53-103). But for Paul it is not Adam who is the image and glory of God, but Christ (1 Cor. 15:49; 2 Cor. 4:4, 6; cf. 3:18; 1 Cor. 11:7; Col. 1:15). God's purpose in predestination is that human beings might be "conformed to the image of his Son, in order that he might be the firstborn among many brethren" (Rom. 8:29).

The contrast between Christ and Adam is also seen in the close association of Christ with the Spirit of God. The first man Adam became merely a "living being," but the "last Adam" became a "life-giving Spirit" (1 Cor. 15:45; cf. 2 Cor. 3:17f.). Elsewhere Paul contends that no one can say that Jesus is Lord except by the Holy Spirit (1 Cor. 12:3), that the Spirit's gifts are given for the growth and edification of the body of Christ (12:4–14:40; cf. Rom. 12:4-11; Eph. 4:4-16), and that it is the Spirit who enables people to know the wisdom of God in Christ (1 Cor. 2). In His earthly ministry Jesus was the Christ anointed by the Spirit of God; as Lord it is Jesus who bestows the Spirit.

The identification of Christ with the Spirit appears also

in Paul's description of the Christian life. Christ gives life (1 Cor. 15:45); so does the Spirit (2 Cor. 3:6). Jesus enjoyed a unique sonship in which He familiarly addressed God as "Abba" (Mk. 14:36; cf. Luke's version of the Lord's Prayer [Lk. 11:2], which probably reflects this use). Through the Spirit believers receive adoption as God's children and so are able to address God in the same way (Rom. 8:15f.; Gal. 4:6). Thus the Christian life may be characterized either in terms of one's relationship with Christ (e.g., Rom. 5:11; 6:4; 8:1, 29; 1 Cor. 2:2; 3:11; 4:1; Gal. 2:20) or in terms of being led by and indwelt by the Spirit (Rom. 8:9-17; 14:17; 1 Cor. 3:16; Gal. 3:2). The Church drinks of both Christ and the Spirit (1 Cor. 10:4; 12:13). The Spirit is the agent of the resurrection of Christ and of believers (Rom. 1:4; 8:11). The "spiritual body" (1 Cor. 15:44, 46), i.e., resurrection body, is a body vivified by the Spirit. Believers are justified "in the name of the Lord Jesus and in the Spirit of our God" (1 Cor. 6:11). The Spirit is associated not with the law but with Christ, who sets people free from the law of sin and death (Rom. 8:2; cf. 2 Cor. 3:6, 17f.).

In Paul's writings, therefore, the Spirit of God is irrevocably identified with the Lord Jesus Christ (cf. 2 Cor. 13:14). It is through Christ in the one Spirit that both Jew and Gentile have access to the Father (Eph. 2:18).

Although the Apostle Paul does not formulate the doctrine of the trinity (i.e., he does not use terms such as "trinity," "person," and "substance," and does not say explicitly that the Father, Son, and Spirit are of equal essence), the role that he ascribes to Christ and the Spirit in relation to the Father provides the basis for subsequent Christian trinitarian and incarnational thought.

*V. Hebrews.*–Whether Hebrews is actually a letter is a matter of debate. It is evidently a public document, designed to set out the significance of Jesus against a background of Jewish beliefs about angels, sacrifice (especially the Day of Atonement ritual), and the covenant. The author's typology, contrasting the historical institutions of Israel with the final reality of Christ, has prompted the suggestion that the writer was a converted Christian Platonist, working in the traditions of Philo's exegesis. The book's dire warnings against lapsing from the faith, especially in the light of possible persecution, indicate the threat of hostility to the Church.

The author begins by showing the superiority of Jesus over the prophets and the angels (He. 1:1-4). This suggests that some were ready to grant that Jesus was a prophet. It also indicates a veneration of angels in the Jewish community. The author's stress on Jesus' humanity as the Son of God would have added significance if the work was written against the background of belief that the apocalyptic "one like a son of man" was an angelic being.

The author's high Christology is announced in the opening thesis, which asserts Christ's divinity in terms that echo wisdom and *lógos* theology (see VI.A below). As the Son, Christ is "the heir of all things" (v. 2). God not only created the world through Him; Christ continues to uphold the universe "by the word of his power" (v.3). F. F. Bruce has stated: "Just as the image and superscription on a coin exactly correspond to the device on the die, so the Son of God 'bears the very stamp of his nature' (RSV). The Greek word *charaktēr,* occurring here only in the New Testament, expresses this truth even more emphatically than *eikōn,* which is used elsewhere to denote Christ as the 'image' of God (II Cor. 4:4; Col. 1:15). Just as the glory is really in the effulgence, so the substance (Gk. *hypostasis*) of God is really in Christ, who is its impress, its exact representation and embodiment. What God essentially is, is made manifest in Christ. To see Christ is to see what the Father is like" (*Epistle to the Hebrews* [*NICNT*, 1964], p. 6).

Elsewhere in the NT sonship has strong overtones of kingship and "Christ" connotes the Messiah. But in some places "Christ" has become virtually a name as well as a title. This may be the case in Hebrews, where it is a designation of Jesus (3:6, 14; 5:5; 6:1; 9:11, 14, 24; etc.). The use of Ps. 45:6f. [MT 7f.] in He. 1:8f., however, suggests that the sense of "Christ" as "the Anointed One" is fundamental to the author's argument (cf. L. C. Allen, "Psalm 45:7-8 (6-7) in Old and New Testament Setting," in Rowdon, ed., *Christ the Lord,* [1981], pp. 220-242). The title Lord is also rare (He. 2:3; 7:14; 12:14; 13:20). Perhaps this relative lack of emphasis on the messianic kingship and lordship of Jesus results from the writer's concern to emphasize Jesus' high priesthood. More precisely, the author sees Jesus as a high priest after the order of Melchizedek, "king of Salem, priest of the Most High God" (He. 7:1; cf. 5:6, 10; 7:11, 15-17). This priesthood includes within it the notion of kingship. Moreover, in Jewish thought high priesthood is superior to kingship, in that the high priest has an access to God that is denied to kings and a power that transcends the political sphere.

Hebrews links Christ's sonship with His high priesthood, and it is on account of His high priesthood that He reigns. The author quotes Ps. 2:7 twice in connection with Jesus' sonship: in He. 1:5 to demonstrate the Son's superiority over the angels (here 2 S. 7:14 is also cited), and in He. 5:5 with regard to His high priesthood. The author also demonstrates the Son's superiority over the angels by applying to Him the psalmist's address to the king, "Thy throne, O God, is for ever and ever . . . " (He. 1:8f.; cf. Ps. 45:6f. [MT 7f.]). But as the argument develops, Christ's sonship is associated with His high priesthood (He. 4:14; cf. 6:6; 7:3; 10:12). Jesus has become a priest after the order of Melchizedek, "not according to a legal requirement concerning bodily descent but by the power of an indestructible life" (7:16). Christ has made atonement once and for all by His own self-offering, thus making obsolete the rituals of the old covenant (8:13–9:28; 10:19-22; cf. Lev. 16). His death and resurrection as the kingly high priest establish the new and eternal covenant (7:22; 8:8-13; 9:15; 10:16-18; 13:20; cf. Jer. 31:31-34). As the kingly high priest He is "seated at the right hand of the throne of the Majesty in heaven" (8:1; cf. Ps. 110:1; He. 1:3, 13; 10:12f.; 12:2).

Hebrews emphasizes not only Christ's divine being, but also His true humanity. In this sense, also, Christ is distinguished from the angels. For the world to come was subjected not to the angels but to humankind (He. 2:5-8; cf. Ps. 8:4-6 [MT 5-7]). Though for a while Jesus was made "lower than the angels," He was later enthroned "because of the suffering of death, so that by the grace of God he might taste death for every one" (He. 2:9). Jesus partook of human nature "that through death he might destroy him who has the power of death, that is, the devil" (2:14). Christ's full humanity is thus as necessary for salvation as His divinity. His humanity also enables Him to sympathize with human weaknesses, for He is a high priest "who in every respect has been tempted as we are, yet without sinning" (4:15). He also knows human agony and fear (5:7). "Although he was a Son, he learned obedience through what he suffered; and being made perfect he became the source of eternal salvation to all who obey him" (5:8f.). Having endured the cross and the hostility of sinners, He has become "the pioneer and perfecter of our faith" (12:2f.). He suffered "outside the gate in order to sanctify the people through his own blood" (13:12).

*VI. Johannine Writings.*–The questions of the relationship among the various writings associated with John lie outside the scope of this article (*see* JOHANNINE THEOLOGY; JOHN, EPISTLES OF; JOHN, GOSPEL ACCORDING TO; JOHN THE APOSTLE; REVELATION, BOOK OF). The following discussion does not prejudge such questions but merely seeks to note the treatment of the person of Christ in these writings.

*A. Gospel of John.* The discussion of the Synoptic Gospels (see III above) noted that Matthew, Mark, and Luke begin with what might be called an explicit Spirit Christology. They all stress the role of the Spirit in connection with Jesus' messiahship. But they also develop an implicit Word Christology. Jesus speaks the Word of God, not simply as a prophet but with the authority of God Himself. The Fourth Gospel reverses the emphasis. It begins with an explicit Word Christology and develops an implicit Spirit Christology.

John begins with the declaration, "In the beginning was the Word [*lógos*], and the Word was with God, and the Word was God. He was in the beginning with God; all things were made through him, and without him was not made anything that was made" (Jn. 1:1-3). John goes on to explain Jesus's sonship in terms of the Word become flesh (1:14). The opening words of the Fourth Gospel thus clearly recall the opening words of Genesis, which attribute the creation of all things to the Word of God that brings them into being. As the Gospel develops, it presents Jesus as the Son who does the work of the Father who sent Him (Jn. 5:17-27; 7:28f.; 9:3f.; 17:3f.; cf. 15:24; 20:30f.). Jesus' works show that He is in the Father and that the Father is in Him (10:37f.; 14:10f.; 17:21). His words are not spoken on human authority but are the words that the Father has taught Him (8:28; 12:49f.; 14:10; cf. 7:17; 8:38).

The meaning of "word" (*lógos*) in John has been much debated (cf., e.g., C. H. Dodd, *Interpretation of the Fourth Gospel* [1955], pp. 263-289; J. D. G. Dunn, *Christology in the Making*, pp. 213-250). John's identification of the *lógos* with the creative and revealing Word of God in the OT is unmistakable. But there may well be further overtones. In wisdom literature Wisdom is the medium of creation and revelation; it does what the Word does in other OT writings. Wisdom literature presents numerous striking parallels to what is said of the Word in Jn. 1:1-14 (e.g., cf. Prov. 3:19; 8:22, 30, 35; Wisd. 7:22, 25-30; 8:1; Sir. 24:6; see Dodd, pp. 274f.).

Whether John was also aware of Philo's teaching concerning the *lógos* is debatable. *Lógos* occurs over 1400 times in Philo's works. Drawing on Greek philosophy to interpret the OT, Philo understood the *lógos* as the thought of God coming to expression. As such it plays a prominent part in his teaching on creation (*De opificio mundi* 16-44). John, however, does not speculate about the *lógos* in the same way that Philo did. The most that can be said is that *lógos,* representing Word or Wisdom, was a term that had deep meaning in the Jewish world of the 1st century.

To presuppose a Gnostic background for John's thought (as did R. Bultmann, *Gospel of John* [Eng. tr. 1971]) is unnecessary and anachronistic. The sources on which Bultmann built his case are considerably later than the NT (cf. E. M. Yamauchi, *Pre-Christian Gnosticism: A Survey of the Proposed Evidences* [1973]). It now appears that developed Gnosticism itself drew on Christian teaching and was not in the first instance a contributory factor to the composition of the NT.

Another suggested background for John's *lógos* teaching is Stoicism. In Stoic thought the *lógos* was the principle of rationality and order in the world. It was the immanent divine reason in a philosophical scheme that was basically pantheistic. If John was aware of Stoic thinking, his own presentation of Jesus as the preexistent *lógos*-become-flesh is as much a corrective to Stoicism as it is an endorsement.

John's declaration "and the Word was God" (*kaí theós ḗn ho lógos,* Jn. 1:1) has provoked much debate. In common Greek usage nouns are regularly given the definite article, and it has sometimes been suggested that the absence of the definite article before *theós* implies that the Word was in some sense divine without actually being God. Others see this as John's attempt to avoid modalism. The passage conforms, however, to a recognized grammatical pattern in the NT, in which definite nouns that precede the verb regularly lack the definite article (E. C. Colwell, *JBL,* 52 [1933], 12-21; C. F. D. Moule, *Idiom Book of NT Greek* [2nd ed. 1959, repr. 1968], pp. 115f.; for other literature, see *DNTT,* II, 81). Thus the grammatical construction does not in itself imply that the Word was anything less than God, and the argument of the Gospel as a whole shows that the author presents Jesus as God incarnate.

Jesus' identification as God incarnate is evident when Thomas greets the risen Jesus, "My Lord and my God!" (Jn. 20:28). Somewhat earlier Jesus says to Philip, "He who has seen me has seen the Father" (14:9). The divine title "Lord" (*kýrios*; cf. Jn. 1:23; 12:13, 38) is also given to Jesus, not only in the post-Resurrection narratives (20:2, 13, 18, 20, 28; 21:7; etc.), but also in narratives of Jesus' ministry (where it is sometimes rendered "master"; cf. 4:1; 6:23, 68; 9:38; 11:2; 13:13-16; 15:15, 20; cf. 12:21 [RSV "Sir"; here it may be simply a polite form of address]). In some of the latter passages John's use of "Lord" reflects his post-Resurrection understanding; nonetheless, Jesus' lordship is clearly present in His actions and teaching.

The Greek formula *egṓ eimi* (lit. "I am"; RSV "It is I" or "I am he") echoes a divine self-affirmation found in Deutero-Isaiah (Jn. 4:26; 6:20; 8:24, 28, 58; 13:19; cf. Mk. 6:50; 13:6; 14:62; Isa. 43:10; 48:12). It also echoes the revelation of the divine name to Moses (Ex. 3:14). The great "I am" discourses in the Fourth Gospel identify Jesus with God's salvation. Jesus is the bread of life (Jn. 6:35, 41, 48, 51); the light of the world (8:12); the door (10:7, 9); the good shepherd (10:11, 14); the resurrection and the life (11:25); the way, the truth, and the life (14:6); and the true vine (15:1, 5). These images take up OT themes and transcend them. It is not manna but Jesus who is the true bread from heaven (6:32f., 49-51; cf. Ex. 16:4; Ps. 78:24; 105:40). The vine is a symbol of Israel (Ps. 80:8-16 [MT 9-17]; Isa. 5:1-7; Jer. 2:21; Ezk. 15; 19:10-14; Hos. 10:1); thus, in identifying Himself as the true vine Jesus is claiming to be the true Israel. In calling Himself the good shepherd, Jesus is assuming a role that properly belongs to Yahweh (cf. Ps. 23:1-4; Isa. 40:10f.). Those to whom Yahweh had previously delegated this role had proved to be unfaithful (Isa. 56:9-12; Ezk. 34), but Yahweh promised to set up over His people "one shepherd, my servant David," who would provide for His people's needs (34:23).

The signs that Jesus performs likewise reveal Him as Creator and Savior, the Son of God, and in so doing they bring life (Jn. 20:30f.; cf. 2:1-11; 4:46-54; 5:1-18; 6:1-14, 16-21; 9:1-14; 11:1-44). His works manifest the preexistent divine glory and thereby bring glory to God (1:14; 2:11; 5:41, 44; 7:18; 8:50, 54; 11:4, 40; 17:4f., 22, 24). Jesus supersedes the tabernacle as the dwelling place of God's glory (1:14; cf. vv. 17f.; Ex. 33:7, 9-11, 18-23; 40:34f.; *see also* SHEKINAH). He also transcends the Torah (Jn. 1:17;

5:39-47; 7:19-23) and the temple (2:18-22). In John, as in the Synoptic Gospels, Jesus' works are an enactment of His teaching on the sabbath (Jn. 5:9-18; 7:22f.; 9:14-16). They force the question of whether Jesus is the Christ, as He revealed Himself to the Samaritan woman (4:25f.; cf. 7:31), or whether He is performing signs and wonders in order to lead the people astray, as Caiaphas argues (11:47-53). Whereas in the Synoptics Jesus is accused of casting out demons by Beelzebul, in John He is accused of being a Samaritan and having a demon (8:48; cf. 7:20; 10:20). Like the Synoptics, John shows that the suggestion that Jesus' works are demonic is self-refuting (10:21; cf. 3:2; 7:31). But whereas in Matthew and Luke Jesus refers His works to the Spirit of God, in John He relates them to the Word of God (7:16f.; 8:51-58; 14:10). In the Synoptics the attribution of Jesus' works to Satan is seen as blasphemy against the Holy Spirit; in John false accusation of Jesus is attributed to the devil (8:44).

It was noted above that John, in contrast to the Synoptic Gospels, begins with an explicit Word Christology. Nevertheless, he develops alongside it an implicit Spirit Christology. As in the Synoptics, Jesus' ministry is understood as a ministry of the baptism with the Holy Spirit (Jn. 1:32f.). For thematic reasons John describes the cleansing of the temple at the outset of Jesus' ministry (2:13-22). John's comment about the Spirit's not having been given because Jesus had not yet been glorified (7:39) does not imply that the Spirit was inactive in Jesus' ministry. It refers rather to the inner experience of the Spirit by believers (cf. v. 38). As the Gospel proceeds, a theology of the Spirit in relation to Jesus unfolds. To see the Kingdom one must be born of the Spirit (3:5-8). True believers (whether Jews or Samaritans) worship God in Spirit and in truth (4:24). The picture of drinking the Spirit through Jesus (7:37f.) is already implicit in 4:10-14 (cf. 1 Cor. 10:4; 12:13).

At the end of the Gospel, Jesus performs an act of prophetic symbolism when He breathes on the disciples and says, "Receive the Holy Spirit" (Jn. 20:22). Underlying the symbolism is the fact that Spirit in Greek (*pneúma*) and Hebrew (*rû[a]ḥ*) means "wind" or "breath." In breathing on the disciples, Jesus bestows on them the divine breath, that is, His own life and energy. As human words are articulated by human breath, God's Word is articulated by the divine breath, which as such communicates life (6:63; cf. Ps. 104:29f.).

The Paraclete sayings of Jn. 14:16f., 25f. and 16:7-15 constitute a bridge between Jesus' unique possession of the Spirit and His bestowal of the Spirit on the Church. The meaning of PARACLETE (*paráklētos*) has been much discussed. Common to its various occurrences is the sense of "helper." That the Spirit is "another Paraclete" implies that Jesus Himself is the first Paraclete. The Spirit's activity is an extension of Jesus' own activity. The Spirit will abide with the disciples after Jesus' departure to teach them, to remind them of Jesus' words, and to guide them into truth. The Spirit will bear witness to Jesus through the disciples and will convict the world of sin, righteousness, and judgment. The translation of *paráklētos* by "Advocate" is justified by John's forensic structure (cf. G. B. Caird, *Language and Imagery of the Bible* [1980], p. 159). The author takes up the OT theme of God's lawsuit. The first witness to be called is John the Baptist (Jn. 1:6-8). He is followed by Jesus (3:31f.). But since no one can expect to be believed on his own testimony alone, Jesus' testimony is corroborated by the works that the Father has given Him (5:31-36) and by the evidence of the Scriptures (5:39-45). Applying the law of evidence, Jesus invokes the testimony of the Father (8:17f.). The climax of the case comes with Jesus' death. Satan, representing the world of which he is prince, loses his case because he has no hold over Jesus and those for whom He died (12:31f.; 14:30). It is not Jesus who is in Satan's grip but Satan's agents. Although Satan has lost, his agents still try to vindicate their cause and defend their actions. But the disciples will not be on their own in their witness to Jesus. They will have as their Advocate the Spirit of Truth whom the world (i.e., Jesus' opponents) cannot receive (14:17). The Spirit will be in the disciples, bearing witness with them to Jesus (15:26f.) and convicting the world of sin because it does not believe in Jesus (16:9), of righteousness "because I go to the Father" (v.10), and of judgment "because the ruler of this world is judged" (v.11).

The question of Jesus' sonship in John has been much debated (for a survey, *see* JOHANNINE THEOLOGY, IV.A-C; more fully, C. H. Dodd, *Interpretation of the Fourth Gospel,* pp. 228-262; F. J. Moloney, *Johannine Son of Man* [1976]). It is frequently suggested that the titles Son of Man and Son of God have acquired a somewhat different sense in the Fourth Gospel. Nevertheless, it should be noted that John gives prominence to Jesus' messiahship, which is a thoroughly Jewish concept. At crucial points Christhood and Sonship are juxtaposed in a way that suggests that they mutually define each other (Jn. 1:17f.; 20:31). John also stresses Christ's messianic kingship over Israel (1:49; 12:13; 18:33-38; 19:3, 14-22). He is king, not in the sense of having an earthly kingdom (18:36; cf. 6:15; 19:12, 21), but in the sense of being the agent of God's dominion over the world. As such He is also the Son. Jesus' sonship is the result of the Word having become flesh (1:14). Although judged and condemned by men, He is in the bosom of the Father (v.18).

John stresses Jesus' messiahship. Prior to his account of Jesus' ministry, John records a dialogue between John the Baptist and representatives of the Pharisees in which John the Baptist emphasizes that he is not the Christ (Jn. 1:20, 25-27; cf. 3:28). Jesus does not trust Himself to people at large (2:24f.), but He does to inquiring individuals like Nicodemus (3:1-21) and the Samaritan woman (4:7-26). The Samaritan woman is expecting the Messiah (which John translates "Christ" for his non-Jewish readers, 4:25; cf. 1:41). She knows that the Messiah is not simply a political ruler for she defines Him as the one who "will show us all things." The Samaritans who hear her testimony and go on to believe Jesus' word confess, ". . . we have heard for ourselves, and we know that this is indeed the Savior of the world" (4:42). This confession points to the apolitical, universal character of Jesus' messiahship. The big question for the Jews is whether Jesus is in fact the Messiah (7:26f., 31, 41f.; 9:22; 10:24; 12:34; cf. 4:29). The purpose of the Fourth Gospel is to show that "Jesus is the Christ, the Son of God, and that believing you may have life in his name" (20:31). This is the confession of the godly throughout Jesus' ministry, from the very first disciples (1:41) to Martha at the death of Lazarus (11:27), whose raising forms the climax of Jesus' ministry, revealing Him as the Lord and Savior of life.

The themes of Jesus as the Christ, Son of Man, and Son of God are closely interwoven. As Son of Man, Jesus is the primal, archetypal man, but John does not indulge in metaphysical speculation on this point. His allusions echo OT themes that find their fulfillment in Jesus. The reference to "the angels of God ascending and descending upon the Son of man" recalls Jacob's ladder (Jn. 1:51; cf. Gen. 28:12). The special intimate relationship with God that was promised to Israel finds its focus in Jesus as the Son of Man. The titles Son of Man and Son of God occur in the dialogue with Nicodemus in Jn. 3. Nicodemus evidently does not share the skepticism of his fellow Pharisees, but his confession (3:2) falls short of attributing messiahship to Jesus. Although the title Christ is not mentioned, the themes of the Spirit and the Kingdom figure prominently in Jesus' reply (vv.5-8). The reference to the Son of Man descending from heaven (v.13) does not necessarily imply His preexistence. It is rather an assertion that He has come from God (cf. v.2; 6:62). This leads to the theme that the Son of Man must be "lifted up" for the salvation of those who believe in Him, as Moses lifted up the serpent in the wilderness (3:14f.; cf. Nu. 21:9). As this theme is developed, the Son of Man is identified with the unique Son of God (Jn. 3:16-18).

Underlying these references to the Son of Man is the thought of Dnl. 7 (see II above). As the Son of Man Jesus is also the judge (Jn. 5:27; cf. 3:16-21) and the giver of life (6:27, 54, 63). As in the Synoptics, the Son of Man will be vindicated (8:28). Jesus' use of the title in connection with His healing of the man born blind (9:35-39) shows that Jesus is more than a prophet and brings into focus the issue between Him and the Jews. The cross is not simply the means by which Jesus is executed; it is the means by which the Son of Man is glorified (12:23, 28; 13:31f.; cf. 17:1-5; 19:5). It is the act upon which salvation depends; thus it manifests God's glory and vindicates both the Father and Jesus.

Son of God is a title expressing messianic kingship (see II above), and the juxtaposition in John of "Christ" with "Son of God" indicates that this identification remains. The context of these designations is not to be defined in the abstract, however, but by what the Gospel says about Jesus and His relationship with the Father. Whereas other human beings may be called "children" (*tékna*) of God through Jesus (Jn. 1:12; 11:52; cf. 8:37-44), Jesus alone is the "Son" (*huiós*). In fact, He is the "only" Son (1:14, 18; 3:16, 18; cf. 1 Jn. 4:9; on *monogenḗs* as "only" and not "only begotten," cf. ONLY BEGOTTEN; D. Moody, *JBL*, 72 [1953], 213-19; *DNTT*, II, 725). The Son comes from the Father (Jn. 3:17; 11:27). As the Son, Jesus does only the works of the Father, and to honor the Son is to honor the Father (5:19-23). Their relationship is one of mutual love (3:35; 5:20). Contrary to what the Jews think, Jesus' works are acts of loving obedience (5:19; cf. 4:34; 5:30; 6:38; 7:16-18; 8:28; 10:36f.). The Father dwells in the Son and the Son in the Father (10:38; 14:10f.; 17:23). To see Jesus the Son is to see the Father (12:45; 14:9).

Jesus' unique relationship with the Father is expressed in His consciousness as the Son. But this does not imply a docetic Christology. The prayers of Jesus express both an intimacy with the Father and also a separateness (Jn. 11:41; 12:27f.; 17:1). Although John omits much of the historical realism in Mark (e.g., the accounts of the baptism, temptation, agony, exorcisms, and the limitations implied in Mk. 6:5 and 13:32), he draws attention to Jesus' weariness and thirst (Jn. 4:6f.). He mentions that Jesus bore His own cross (19:17) and that blood and water came from His side (19:34). It would therefore be incorrect to say that John has no interest in Jesus' humanity. On the other hand, his interest in Jesus' person from first to last is theological and soteriological (1:14; 20:30f.).

*B. Johannine Letters.* Many scholars have maintained that the letters of John were written against a background of Gnosticism or incipient Gnosticism. This view is based on an interpretation of 1 John in the light of later Gnostic teaching. Support is drawn from Irenaeus's statement that John was an opponent of Cerinthus, whose teaching displayed Gnostic adoptionist tendencies (*Adv. haer.* i.26.1; iii.3.4, 11.1). Comparison of Cerinthus's teaching with the ideas refuted in 1 John indicates wide divergencies between the two. Moreover, the letters themselves do not mention Cerinthus. It has therefore been suggested that the false teachers described in 1 John are some kind of proto-Gnostics who stress the spirit and perfection, and that John counters them by stressing the reality of the Incarnation and the Atonement, together with the need to love and to avoid sin.

A more attractive interpretation, however, sees as the background to 1 John the fundamental conflict between the Church and Judaism. On this view, John's opponents are charging the Church with lawlessness: having abandoned the Torah, Christians are *ipso facto* sinners who walk in darkness, living reckless lives. These opponents deny that Jesus is the Christ and regard His death as proof that He was a heinous lawbreaker who deserved His fate. They furthermore claim that it is they who possess the Spirit.

In response to these charges 1 John emphasizes Jesus' messianic sonship and the principles of conduct that characterize Christian faith. One cannot have fellowship with the Father apart from fellowship with "his Son Jesus Christ" (1 Jn. 1:3). By implication, this fellowship supersedes the law and the covenant community of Israel. Christians do not pretend to be sinless; rather they walk in fellowship with God and with one another, confessing their sins and receiving forgiveness and cleansing from Jesus His Son (1:6-9). Moreover, they have "an advocate" (*paráklētos*) with the Father, "Jesus Christ the righteous" (2:1), whose death is the propitiation (*hilasmós*) for the sins of the whole world (2:2; cf. 4:10). Those who deny Jesus' messiahship (described as antichrists, 2:18, 22) deny both the Son and the Father (2:22f.). Believers, on the other hand, have an anointing (*chrísma*) from "the Holy One" (2:20; cf. the application of this title to Yahweh Himself in Isa. 1:4; etc.). This assertion alludes to Christ's anointing by the Spirit and His gift of the Spirit to believers (cf. 1 Jn. 2:27; 3:24; 4:13).

1 John asserts that believers are not lawbreakers because they are Christians. Everyone who commits sin is guilty of lawlessness (1 Jn. 3:4), but Jesus "appeared to take away sins, and in him there is no sin" (v.5). Moreover, "no one who abides in him sins" (v.6). Mindful of the charges that Jesus was in league with the devil (cf. Jn. 7:20; 8:48, 52; 10:20; Mt. 9:34; 10:25; 12:24; Mk. 3:22; Lk. 11:15), John points out that the very opposite is true. The Son of God came to destroy the works of the devil (1 Jn. 3:8). "No one born of God commits sins; for God's nature abides in him, and he cannot sin because he is born of God" (3:9; cf. 5:18). The statement is not an assurance of the believer's sinless perfection, though it is true of Jesus as the Son of God. The statement contains an assurance that what matters is to be born of God, regardless of whether one is in the community of Israel or not. But this is not a license to sin. Actions attest whether one is a child of God or of the evil one (3:9f.). Obedience to God's commandments is the sign that one knows God (2:3-17) and abides in Him (3:11-24). God's love in sending His Son requires the response of love for God and one's neighbors (4:7-21; cf. 3:16-18).

1 John stresses the importance of recognizing and believing the Spirit's testimony that Jesus is the messianic Son of God. The test of whether a spirit is of God is the confession, "Jesus Christ has come in the flesh" (1 Jn. 4:2). The Spirit of God abides in all who confess that Jesus is the messianic Son of God (4:15). Such believers are God's children (5:1) and share in Christ's victory over the world (5:4). God Himself has given three witnesses that Jesus is the Christ, the Son of God: the water, the blood,

and the Spirit (5:6-8; the meaning of these "witnesses" has been much debated; see the comms.). Indeed, to reject this testimony is to make God a liar (v.10). But those who do believe in Jesus as the Son of God know the true God and have eternal life (vv.11-13, 20).

2 John, like 1 John, warns against false teachers who reject Jesus' messianic sonship (cf. 2 Jn. 3). One who "will not acknowledge the coming of Jesus Christ in the flesh" is called an "antichrist" (v.7). "Any one who . . . does not abide in the doctrine of Christ does not have God; he who abides in the doctrine of Christ has both the Father and the Son" (v.9).

*C. Revelation.* The book of Revelation is unique in genre in the NT. It describes itself as an "apocalypse" (*apokálypsis*) or "revelation" of Jesus Christ (Rev. 1:1), but it also calls itself "prophecy" (1:3; cf. 10:11; 19:10; 22:6-19). It shares with Jewish apocalyptic literature the features of visions, symbolism, and interpretation of the course of history from a divine perspective. But there are also important differences. The medium of the revelation is not a remote figure like Enoch, but John, who is known to his readers as a fellow Christian and sufferer for Jesus (1:1, 4, 9). The work embodies a letter form (1:3; 2:1–3:22; 22:6-21). It is a message of visionary consolation, interpreting Jesus Christ in the light of OT symbolism and history in the light of Jesus Christ. Its theology appears to be related in some way to that of the Fourth Gospel and the Johannine letters, but the precise relationship is the subject of much discussion.

The book of Revelation interprets history in the light of the exalted Christ. It identifies Him as "one like a son of man" (Rev. 1:13; 14:14; cf. Dnl. 7:13; 10:5; 1 En. 46:1-4). He is thus the righteous one to whom dominion is given. Whether or not the figure in Daniel was originally an angelic being, Revelation makes it clear that the figure finds fulfillment in Jesus, to whom the angels are themselves subject (Rev. 1:1, 20; 2:1, 8, 12, 18; 3:1, 7, 14; 7:1–10:7; etc.). Jesus Christ fulfills the vision of Dnl. 7 in that he is "the faithful witness, the firstborn of the dead, and the ruler of kings on earth" (Rev. 1:5). He is "alive for evermore," having "the keys of Death and Hades"(1:18). He is the Son-King who rules the nations (2:27; 12:5; 19:15; cf. Ps. 2:8f.). Whereas other NT writings quote Ps. 2:7 to identify Jesus as the messianic Son of God (Mt. 3:17; Acts 13:33; He. 1:5; 5:5; 2 Pet. 1:17), Revelation uses the psalm in its prophetic vision of Jesus Christ as the judge and ruler of the world (cf. Rev. 1:7; 14:14, 18-20; 19:11-16; 22:12).

The title Son of God occurs only once (Rev. 2:18), in a context that suggests judgment and kingship and culminates in an echo of Ps. 2. It suggests that Christ's sonship is to be understood in terms of Jesus' exalted messianic kingship. Likewise, other passages that focus on Christ's dominion refer to God as Jesus' Father (Rev. 1:6; 2:27; 3:5, 21; 14:1). At the same time the one who rules is called the Lamb of God. In the Fourth Gospel John the Baptist calls Jesus "the Lamb [*amnós*] of God, who takes away the sin of the world" (Jn. 1:29; cf. v.36). Similarly, Revelation describes Jesus' death as the slaying of the Lamb (*arníon*) of God. Indeed, the title becomes a major category for understanding Jesus' messiahship (Rev. 5:6-13; 6:1, 16; 7:9f., 14, 17; 12:11; 13:8; 14:1, 4, 10; 15:3; 17:14; 19:7, 9; 21:9, 14, 22f., 27; 22:1, 3). As the Lamb, Jesus is both the sacrificial victim and the shepherd-king (5:6-14; 7:17; 14:1, 4).

The book of Revelation closely associates the Spirit with Christ. John receives his visions of Christ "in the Spirit" (1:10; 4:2; 21:10; cf. 14:13; 19:10; 22:6, 17). The words of the exalted Christ are also identified as the words of the Spirit (2:7, 11, 17, 29; 3:6, 13, 22).

At first sight, Revelation's use of the title "Word [*lógos*] of God" (19:13) to describe the warrior Messiah seems somewhat remote from the Fourth Gospel's use of *lógos* (cf. Jn. 1:1). The usage here is more closely related to that in Wisd. 18:15f. (cf. Philo *De somniis* i.157-59). Nevertheless, in the development of the Gospel of John the Word incarnate is also He who is King, Judge, and Lord.

Revelation preserves both Christ's identity with and His separateness from God. Christ is described as "the Amen, the faithful and true witness, the beginning of God's creation" (Rev. 3:14; cf. Col. 1:15, 18). But it is God who is worshiped as Creator (Rev. 4:11; 14:7). Nevertheless, it is granted to Christ to sit with the Father on His throne (3:21; 7:15-17; 22:1, 3). He receives worship like that addressed to God (cf. 4:11; 5:12f.). The book opens with a distinction between Jesus and God (1:1). But this does not mean that the author is implicitly denying the divinity of Christ. Rather, the author appears to use "God" where other NT writers use "Father." The reason for this seems to lie in the author's stress on the sovereign majesty of God, who is the ruler and judge of all beings. As we have noted, "Father" occurs in passages that focus on the kingdom and dominion of the Son — passages that have as their background the filial relationship of the king as the Son of God. Thus the distinction between Christ and God reflects the fact that the Father is not identical with the Son; it also recognizes that Christ in His humiliation and His exaltation is human as well as divine.

In other passages Christ is described in terms that properly apply to God. The description of the "one like a son of man" (Rev. 1:13-15) corresponds to that of the "ancient of days" in Dnl. 7:9. His voice is like the voice of God (Rev. 1:15; cf. Ezk. 1:24). God Himself is the Alpha and Omega, the first and the last (Isa. 44:6; 48:12; Rev. 1:8; 21:6; cf. Ex. 3:14), but so is Jesus Christ (Rev. 1:17; 22:13). The final visions depicting the new Jerusalem as the bride of the Lamb (Rev. 21–22) make clear that God's covenant promise to dwell with His people is realized only in and through the Lamb (e.g., 21:22f.; 22:12f.). Grace and peace come from God and from the Lord Jesus Christ (1:4f.; 22:21). Appropriately, the book opens and closes with this theme.

***VII. Conclusion.***–Radical scholars see in the NT an evolution of Christology. Such theology presupposes that Jesus was originally no more than a devoutly religious figure who was transformed by Christian faith into a divine being. The present writer, however, sees not an evolution (which suggests a change of one species into another) but a development or series of developments (for this view, see C. F. D. Moule, *Origin of Christology*, pp. 1-10), e.g., a progressive understanding of a reality that was present to begin with. The reality to which the NT testifies is that God Himself was personally present in Jesus of Nazareth. He who made and sustains the universe was present in this human life in a unique way, inviting all human beings to share the fullness of life in Him through the gracious reconciliation brought about by His life, death, resurrection, and ascension. This presence of God in Christ has to be understood through Jesus' words and actions and in terms of the NT thought-forms, which need to be interpreted in the context of their meaning in the NT text. In other words, one's understanding of the person of Christ should be read out of the NT rather than read into it.

This review of NT Christology has at various points drawn attention to Spirit Christology and Word Christology. Spirit Christology draws attention to the Holy Spirit's anointing of Jesus as the Christ and the Spirit's activity in and through Christ. Word Christology focuses on Jesus as the one who not only speaks the Word of God but *is* the Word of God incarnate. Similarly, Wisdom Christology presents Jesus as the incarnation of the Wisdom of God. These approaches to Christology are ultimately complementary. In the OT Yahweh did not deal with His people directly, for no one could see God's face and live. He spoke to them in His Word or wisdom and was present in His life-giving Spirit (Heb. *rû[a]ḥ* or Gk. *pneúma*, both meaning "wind" or "breath"). The Word of God is uttered by the breath of God. Thus Word and Spirit are not identical but they are inseparable. They represent the mind of God and the life of God. In Jesus Christ, the Son of God, the Word of God was made incarnate by the Spirit of God.

Later Christian thinkers spoke of the trinity and the Incarnation. These terms are not found in the NT itself. Rightly understood, however, they express the witness of the NT. The NT witness refuses to separate the trinity from the Incarnation and the Incarnation from the trinity. It invites us, rather, to find the Father through the Son in the power of the Spirit.

***Bibliography.***–P. Althaus, *The So-Called Kerygma and the Historical Jesus* or *Fact and Faith in the Kerygma of Today* (Eng. tr. 1959); C. C. Anderson, *Critical Quests of Jesus* (1969); *Historical Jesus* (1972); H. Anderson, *Jesus and Christian Origins* (1964); G. Aulén, *Jesus in Contemporary Historical Research* (Eng. tr. 1976); D. M. Baillie, *God Was in Christ* (1948); E. Bammel and C. F. D. Moule, *Jesus and the Politics of His Day* (1984); C. K. Barrett, *From First Adam to Last* (1962); *Jesus and the Gospel Tradition* (1967); H.-W. Bartsch, ed., *Kerygma and Myth, Volumes I and II Combined* (1972); G. K. A. Bell and A. Deissmann, eds., *Mysterium Christi* (1930); G. C. Berkouwer, *Person of Christ* (Eng. tr. 1954); J. Bowker, *Jesus and the Pharisees* (1973); C. E. Braaten and R. A. Harrisville, eds., *Historical Jesus and the Kerygmatic Christ* (1964); C. Brown, *Jesus in European Protestant Thought, 1778-1860* (1985); *Miracles and the Critical Mind* (1984); ed., *History, Criticism and Faith* (1976); R. E. Brown, *Jesus God and Man* (1967); F. F. Bruce, *Jesus and Christian Origins outside the NT* (1974); G. W. Buchanan, *Jesus, the King and His Kingdom* (1984); R. Bultmann, *Jesus and the Word* (Eng. tr. 1934); *Jesus Christ and Mythology* (Eng. tr. 1958); H. J. Cadbury, *The Peril of Modernizing Jesus* (1937); E. C. Colwell, *Jesus and the Gospel* (1963); H. Conzelmann, *Jesus* (Eng. tr. 1973); O. Cullmann, *Christology of the NT* (Eng. tr. 1959; rev. ed. 1963); C. H. Dodd, *Founder of Christianity* (1970); F. G. Downing, *The Church and Jesus* (*SBT*, 2/10, 1968); J. D. G. Dunn, *Jesus and the Spirit* (1975); *Christology in the Making* (1980); J. W. Fraser, *Jesus and Paul* (1974); H. W. Frei, *Identity of Jesus Christ* (1975); R. H. Fuller, *Foundations of NT Christology* (1965); R. H. Fuller and P. Perkins, *Who is this Christ?* (1983); R. W. Funk, *Jesus as Precursor* (1976); L. Goppelt, *Jesus, Paul, and Judaism* (Eng. tr. 1964); M. D. Goulder, ed., *Incarnation and Myth: The Debate Continued* (1979); R. C. Gregg and D. E. Groh, *Early Arianism* (1981); A. Grillmeier, *Christ in Christian Tradition*, I (Eng. tr., 2nd ed. 1975); D. Guthrie, *Jesus the Messiah* (1972); D. A. Hagner, *Jewish Reclamation of Jesus* (1984); F. Hahn, *Titles of Jesus in Christology* (Eng. tr. 1969); A. E. Harvey, *Jesus and the Constraints of History* (1982); M. Hengel, *Son of God* (Eng. tr. 1976); *Between Jesus and Paul* (Eng. tr. 1983); C. F. H. Henry, ed., *Jesus of Nazareth* (1966); J. Hick, ed., *Myth of God Incarnate* (1977); J. Jocz, *Jewish People and Jesus Christ* (2nd ed. 1952); M. Kähler, *The So-called Historical Jesus and the Historic, Biblical Christ* (Eng. tr. 1964); W. Kasper, *Jesus the Christ* (Eng. tr. 1976); L. E. Keck, *A Future for the Historical Jesus* (1971); S. Kim, *"The 'Son of Man'" as the Son of God* (1983); J. D. Kingsbury, *Matthew: Structure, Christology, Kingdom* (1975); *Christology of Mark's Gospel* (1983); W. Kramer, *Christ, Lord, Son of God* (Eng. tr. 1966); G. W. H. Lampe, *God as Spirit* (1977); X. Léon-Dufour, *The Gospels and the Jesus of History* (Eng. tr. 1968); B. Lindars, *Jesus Son of Man* (1983); B. Lindars and S. S. Smalley, eds., *Christ and the Spirit in the NT* (1973); H. K. McArthur, ed., *In Search of the Historical Jesus* (1970); C. C. McCown, *Search for the Real Jesus* (1940); I. H. Marshall, *Origins of NT Christology* (1976); *I Believe in the Historical Jesus* (1977); E. L. Mascall, *Theology and the Gospel of Christ* (1977); C. F. D. Moule, *Origin of Christology* (1977); *Essays in NT Interpretation* (1982); D. L. Pals, *Victorian "Lives" of Jesus* (1982); W. Pannenberg, *Jesus — God and Man* (Eng. tr. 1968); G. Parrinder, *Jesus in the Qur'ān* (1965); A. E. J. Rawlinson, *NT Doctrine of the Christ* (1926); J. Reumann, *Jesus in the Church's Gospels* (1968); H. N. Ridderbos, *Paul and Jesus* (Eng. tr. 1958); J. M. Robinson, *A New Quest of the Historical Jesus and Other Essays* (1983); H. H. Rowdon, ed., *Christ the Lord* (1982); E. P. Sanders, *Jesus and Judaism* (1985); E. Schillebeeckx, *Jesus* (Eng. tr. 1979); *Christ* (Eng. tr. 1980); A. Schweitzer, *The Quest of the Historical Jesus* with new introduction by J. M. Robinson (1968); R. V. Sellers, *Two Ancient Christologies* (1940); *Council of Chalcedon* (1953); E. M. Sidebottom, *Christ of the Fourth Gospel* (1961); M. Smith, *Jesus the Magician* (1978); J. Sobrino, *Christology at the Crossroads* (Eng. tr. 1976); G. N. Stanton, *Jesus of Nazareth in NT Preaching* (1974); S. W. Sykes and J. P. Clayton, eds., *Christ, Faith and History* (1972); G. H. Tavard, *Images of the Christ* (1982); V. Taylor, *Names of Jesus* (1953); *Person of Christ in NT Teaching* (1958); H. E. W. Turner, *Jesus, Master and Lord* (1953); *Jesus the Christ* (1976); H. G. Wood, *Jesus in the 20th century* (1960); F. M. Young, *From Nicaea to Chalcedon* (1983).

C. BROWN

**PERSUADE** [Heb. piel of *šāsaʿ*] (1 S. 24:7 [MT 8]); AV STAY; NEB REPROVE SEVERELY; [hiphil of *bārâ*–'give food for comfort'] ("persuade to eat," 2 S. 3:35); AV "cause to eat"; [hiphil of *nāṭâ*–'turn aside'] (Prov. 7:21); AV "cause to yield"; NEB "lead [one] on"; [Gk. *peíthō*] (Mt. 27:20; Acts 12:20; 14:19; 18:4; 19:26; 2 Cor. 5:11); AV also "make [one's] friend"; NEB also WIN OVER, TRY TO CONVINCE, "with propaganda," "address [one's] appeal"; [*anapeíthō*] (Acts 18:13); NEB INDUCE; **BE PERSUADED** [Heb. pual of *pāṯâ*–'be corruptible'] (Prov. 25:15); [Gk. mid. or pass. of *peíthō*] (Acts 17:4; 21:14; 26:26; Rom. 14:14); AV also BELIEVE; NEB also BE CONVINCED, BELIEVE; **PERSUASION** [Gk. *peismonḗ*] (Gal. 5:8); **PERSUASIVENESS** [Heb. *leqaḥ*–'teaching,' 'gift of persuasion'] (Prov. 16:21, 23); AV LEARNING; NEB KNOWLEDGE, LEARNING.

"Persuade" can be used in either the positive sense of "convince" or the negative sense of "mislead" or "seduce." The AV OT uses "persuade" in the negative sense for the Heb. piel of *pāṯâ* in 1 K. 22:20-22 (RSV, NEB, "entice") and the hiphil of *sûṯ* in 2 K. 18:32; 2 Ch. 18:2; 32:11, 15; Isa. 36:18 (RSV "mislead," "induce"; NEB "mislead," "incite").

The MT of 1 S. 24:7 (MT 8) is difficult, because most commentators have agreed that *yešassaʿ* (lit. "tore to pieces") is too strong for the context, even if it is taken figuratively (but cf. NEB; KoB [p. 999] suggests "disperse"). Various emendations have been suggested (see comms.); the RSV follows the LXX (*peíthō*).

Greek *peíthō* occurs with a variety of nuances in the NT. It can have the negative sense of "mislead" or "seduce" (e.g., Mt. 27:20; Acts 12:20; 14:19; 19:26; cf. *anapeíthō* in 18:13; *peismonḗ* in Gal. 5:8). Positively it can mean "convince" or "be led to a firm conviction" (cf. Acts 17:4; 18:4; Rom. 14:14; 2 Cor. 5:11). The AV also renders *peíthō* "persuade" in Mt. 28:14 (RSV "satisfy"; NEB "put matters right"); Acts 13:43 (RSV, NEB, "urge"); 19:8 (RSV "plead"); 28:23 (RSV "try to convince"; NEB "seek to convince"); Gal. 1:10 (RSV "seek the favor of"; NEB "canvas for support"). The AV often has "be persuaded" for the middle or passive of *peíthō* (e.g., Lk. 16:31; 20:6; Rom. 8:38; 15:14; He. 6:9; etc.).

Agrippa's answer to Paul in Acts 26:28 has received many translations and interpretations. The text with the strongest MS support has Gk. *en olígǭ me peítheis Christianón poiḗsai*. The AV, reading *genésthai* ("to be") in place of *poiḗsai* ("to make"), renders, "Almost thou persuadest me to be a Christian." The RSV, reading *peíthę̄* ("you think") in place of *peítheis* ("you persuade" or "you try to persuade"), offers, "In a short time you think to make me a Christian!" Perhaps the best translation is Haenchen's: "Soon you will convince me to play the

Christian" (*Acts of the Apostles* [Eng. tr. 1971], p. 689; see also other comms.). N. J. O.

**PERUDA** pə-ro͞o'də. *See* PERIDA.

**PERVERSE; PERVERSELY; PERVERSENESS** [Heb. *yāraṭ* (Nu. 22:32), hiphil and niphal of *ʿāqaš*–'be, make, or prove crooked' (Job 9:20; Prov. 28:18), *ʿiqqēš*–'crooked' (Dt. 32:5; 2 S. 22:27; etc.), niphal part. of *hāpak̠*–'turn' (Prov. 17:20), *tahpuk̠ôṯ*–'perverse things' (Dt. 32:20; Prov. 2:14; etc.), niphal part. of *ʿāwâ*–'do wrong, distort, disturb' (1 S. 20:30; Prov. 12:8), hiphil of *ʿāwâ* (1 K. 8:47; 2 Ch. 6:37), niphal part. of *lûz*–'go the wrong way' (Prov. 3:32; Isa. 3:12), *sûg*–'deviate' (Prov. 14:14), piel of *ʿāwal*–'act wrongfully' (Isa. 26:10), *selep*–'deceit' (Prov. 15:4); Gk. perfect pass. part. of *diastréphō*–'twist about' (Mt. 17:17 par. Lk. 9:41; Acts 20:30; Phil. 2:15)]; AV also FROWARD-(NESS), BACKSLIDER, DO AMISS, etc.; NEB also MUTINOUS, CROOKED, WARPED, CORRUPT, etc. Turned away from what is morally right or good.

The predominant context of "perverse" in the RSV OT is wisdom literature, especially Proverbs. It is particularly related to the concept of the WAY or PATH, which is a metaphor for the course or direction of one's life. Most broadly, two alternatives are open to humanity: the way of the Lord (Ps. 18:21; etc.), which is good and right (1 S. 12:23); or the way of evil (Prov. 2:12; 8:13; etc.), which is the way of sinners and the unrighteous (Ps. 1:1). *See also* WISDOM.

The various Hebrew terms rendered "perverse" describe the evil way and those who follow it. The way of the perverse is full of thorns and snares (Prov. 22:5) and will lead them into the pit (28:18). On the other hand, those who walk in integrity will be delivered (28:18) and are "better," though poor, than the rich who are perverse (v. 6). An interplay between outward, physical direction and inward, spiritual condition may be intended in the story of Balaam, where the "angel of the Lord said to him . . . 'Behold, I have come forth to withstand you, because your way is perverse before me'" (Nu. 22:32). Here Heb. *yāraṭ* means literally "precipitate" or "steep." Thus the meaning may be either that Balaam was proceeding recklessly without heed to divine warnings, or that the sides of the road were steep and the walls prevented a turning aside — or it could mean both of these (see N. H. Snaith, *Leviticus and Numbers* [*NCBC*, repr. 1977], p. 290).

The perverse person "spreads strife" (Prov. 16:28) and is "filled with the fruit of his ways" (14:14). Such a person is plainly "an abomination to the Lord" (3:32). Job in his extremity complained bitterly of God's apparent injustice: "Though I am innocent, my own mouth would condemn me; though I am blameless, he would prove me perverse" (Job 9:20); but David confessed, "with the pure thou dost show thyself pure; and with the crooked thou dost show thyself perverse" (2 S. 22:27; Ps. 18:26 [MT 27]). Perverseness is associated with the heart (Ps. 101:4), the eyes (Prov. 16:30), the mind (11:20; 12:8; 23:33), and speech (19:1; cf. Acts 20:30) — particularly the mouth (Prov. 10:32) and tongue (v. 31; 15:4; 17:20). A perverse heart results in perverse actions (cf. 1 K. 8:47 par. 2 Ch. 6:37; Prov. 2:14; Isa. 26:10; 30:12). Saul in a fit of anger hurled the epithet at Jonathan: "You son of a perverse [niphal part. of *ʿāwâ*, lit. "bewildered, distressed, agitated"], rebellious woman" (1 S. 20:30).

The term CROOKED is sometimes used in conjuction with "perverse" (e.g., Prov. 17:20), most notably in the phrase "crooked and perverse generation," which indicates conduct that is twisted or corrupted from the way of God's righteousness and favor. The phrase is used by Moses to describe apostate Israel (Dt. 32:5; cf. v. 20) and by Paul (alluding to Dt. 32:5) to describe the pagan world in which the Philippian Christians lived (Phil. 2:15). Jesus may also have been alluding to Moses' words when He exclaimed, "O faithless and perverse generation, how long am I to be with you?" (Mt. 17:17 par. Lk. 9:4). Scholars disagree as to whether Jesus was primarily addressing the father of the epileptic boy, the disciples, the crowd, or all those who were present (see comms., esp. J. A. Fitzmyer, *Gospel According to Luke*, I [*AB*, 2nd ed. 1983], 809). While this judgment is specifically applied to those present, Matthew and Luke are "perhaps seeking to extend it to the unbelieving, non-Christian world" in general (*TDNT*, VII, *s.v.* στρέφω: διαστρέφω [G. Bertram]).

D. K. MCKIM

**PESHITTA.** *See* VERSIONS.

**PESTILENCE** [Heb. *deb̠er*; Gk. *loimós*; also Heb. *māweṯ* (Job 27:15; Jer. 43:11); Gk. *thánatos* (Rev. 6:8; 18:8)]; AV also DEATH (Job 27:15; Jer. 43:11; Rev. 6:8; 18:8). A sudden fatal epidemic, generally regarded as a divine visitation. The reference to pestilence in Ps. 91:6, "walking in darkness," alludes to its obscure etiology. In the wilderness wanderings the rebellious Israelites were frequently threatened with pestilence (cf. Nu. 14:12; Dt. 28:21), which appears to have materialized on certain occasions (Nu. 11:33; 16:46; 25:8). Solomon's prayer of dedication (1 K. 8:7) sought the removal of pestilence when national repentance was apparent. Am. 4:10 compares pestilence with the Egyptian plagues; in Hab. 3:5 it heralds divine judgment (cf. Ex. 5:3; 9:15; Lev. 26:25; etc.). The apocalyptic discourse of Lk. 21:11 (Mt. 24:7, AV) couples pestilence (Gk. *loimoí*) with famine.

The Latin term *pestilentia* is connected with *pestis* ("plague"), but the ancients appear to have distinguished plague from pestilence. Of the infectious diseases such as typhoid, cholera, dysentery, bubonic plague, and smallpox that scourged the ancient Near East, the one most frequently described as "plague" was bubonic infection. "Pestilence," sometimes described as "noisome," was often associated with besieged cities, suggesting such diseases as enteric fever (typhoid) or cholera resulting from contaminated water supplies.

*See also* PLAGUE. R. K. H.

**PESTLE** [Heb. *ʿelî*] (Prov. 27:22). Usually a cylinder or rounded cone to be held in the hand for pounding in a MORTAR.

The term pestle is used only once in the Bible, and there the normal function of the pestle is clear. Pestles are frequent finds on archeological excavations. They are usually made of magmatic stone or of hard limestone, though metal pestles were probably used with metal mortars.

L. G. HERR

**PETER** [Gk. *Petros*, for *Kēphas* < Aram. *kêpā'*]. A disciple of Jesus and apostle of the early Church.

The NT literature gives prominent place to Peter, whose life and ministry fall conveniently into the three categories indicated by O. Cullmann's comprehensive study, *Peter: Disciple-Apostle-Martyr.*

- I. Disciple
  - A. Early Days
  - B. Call to Discipleship
  - C. Role in Jesus' Ministry
- II. Apostle
- III. Martyr

***I. Disciple.***–*A. Early Days.* Occasional references to

Peter' original name Symeon (Gk. *Symeōn*; see Acts 15:14; 2 Pet. 1:1 in one MS tradition) show that he belonged to the Jewish community. His home was in Galilee, at Bethsaida (Jn. 1:44). While this locality was Jewish, it was also cosmopolitan (so O. Cullmann, *The NT* [Eng. tr. 1968], p. 107). Both Andrew, Peter's brother, and Philip, who also came from Bethsaida, bear Greek names; and the bilingual setting arising from Greek culture explains why Simon became his adopted name, grecized from Symeon.

His father's name was Jonah = John (Mt. 16:17; Jn. 1:42). (The notion that Bar-Jona means "anarchist, zealot" is an unfortunate eccentricity.) At some unspecified point in his life he had married (Mk. 1:30) a wife who in later days accompanied him on his missionary tours, evidently to Corinth, where she was known (1 Cor. 9:5).

His trade, both at Bethsaida on the east bank of the Jordan River and at Capernaum, a port on Lake Gennesaret, was fishing (Mk. 1:16-21). Lk. 5:1-11 indicates something of this trade, which he resumed for a while in the later part of the gospel story (Jn. 21:1-3).

Concerning his cultural attainments, Acts 4:13 should not be pressed unduly. Probably, if C. H. Dodd is correct (*Interpretation of the Fourth Gospel* [1953], p. 82), the description of Peter and John as "uneducated, common men" means no more than that they were ignorant of the finer points of the rabbinical interpretation of the Jewish Torah. Exposure to Hellenistic culture in Bethsaida is a counterbalancing argument in favor of Peter's general education. He spoke his native language with a special, recognizable accent (Mk. 14:70; Mt. 26:73).

Both Peter and his brother Andrew were followers of John the Baptist (Jn. 1:40-42), as indeed were a considerable number of the original disciples (Acts 1:22) before their call to service by Jesus.

*B. Call to Discipleship.* The Fourth Gospel preserves an authentic tradition of Jesus' Judean ministry, part of which included the summons of Jn. 1:40-42. This context has the first replacement of the name "Simon" by "Peter." The middle term is Aram. *kêpā'* (Gk. *Kēphas*), meaning "stone" or "rock." This was to be his new name, symbolizing a change of character. Hereafter he would be a new man, consolidated by his relationship to Christ his Lord. The name is probably proleptic, anticipating the time when Peter would take his place as a pillar apostle (Gal. 2:9) and a foundation stone, which he and the other apostles were to be as original witnesses to the gospel (Eph. 2:20; Rev. 21:14). "Kephas" (Cephas) is Paul's normal appellation of him, except in Gal. 2:7f.

The reference to Cephas in 1 Cor. 15:5 is important in this context. There is general agreement that Paul here

Traditional site of Peter's house in Capernaum (W. S. LaSor)

quotes from a Jewish-Christian (or less likely a Hellenistic-Christian) creed that he received from his predecessors, probably Jewish-Christian believers. If so, the use of the Semitic name Cephas in the post-Resurrection appearance to Peter bears witness to the time when the name-changing took place, suggesting that it was as the risen Lord showed Himself to "Simon" (cf. Lk. 24:34: "The Lord has risen indeed, and has appeared to Simon") that Simon became Cephas (or Peter, as the name became rendered into Greek). This suggestion is taken up in Mt. 16 and explains the importance of Peter's confession.

The first introduction to Jesus in Judea makes more intelligible the subsequent response Peter made when Jesus called him to abandon his trade and become His full-time disciple (Mk. 1:16f.; 10:28; an expanded version of this call is in Lk. 5:1-11). A further invitation to belong to the inner group of the Twelve is given in Mk. 3:13ff., and the new name is mentioned at that time. Mark calls him Simon up to 3:16; thereafter Mark refers to him as Peter.

*C. Role in Jesus' Ministry.* Still another honor was his as Jesus permitted a group of three disciples to accompany Him on special occasions. Peter is included in the trio along with James and John (see Mk. 5:37; 9:2; 13:3; 14:33). In the lists of the Twelve, Peter stands at the head (Mk. 3:16, etc.; cf. Acts 1:13).

Mark's Gospel has a distinctive role for Peter. Although he is ranked as the first of the disciples and is regarded as the chief spokesperson of the Twelve, Mark singles him out for blame at critical points in the narrative. At Mk. 1:35-37 Peter leads the way to find Jesus and tries to press on Him the role of a popular teacher. At Caesarea Philippi (8:27-33) Jesus receives Peter's confession of messiahship with a certain reserve, and announces that Peter's subsequent remonstrance is the work of Satan. The following incident of the Transfiguration (Mk. 9:2-10) contains at least one puzzling verse (6): in response to Peter's suggestion to erect three booths, the parenthetic note says, "For he did not know what he should answer." Strictly taken, this statement suggests that there was an implied rebuke, and Peter is dumbfounded and unable to respond. A reason for a rebuke, that Peter's suggestion of the booths — associated with nationalistic triumph — has offered Jesus a painless way to His messianic glory, is given by some interpreters of Mark (see R. P. Martin, *Mark: Evangelist and Theologian* [1972], p. 130), endorsing B. W. Bacon's startling observation that Mark "never introduces the Apostle to the circumcision for any individual part without making him the target for severe reproof and condemnation" (*Is Mark a Roman Gospel?* [1919; repr. 1969], p. 76).

Other examples of Peter's role being less than flattering are his being singled out for reproach in Gethsemane (Mk. 14:37) and his denials (Mk. 14:66-72), which are recounted in such a way as to include the suspicion that he may have "cursed" his Lord (v. 71) — a cardinal offense in the early Church (1 Cor. 12:3; M. Polyc. 9:3). There is a brighter side in the promise of Mk. 16:7 — unique to this Gospel — when the risen Lord sends a message to Peter.

At face value, Mark was being painfully honest in portraying Peter's humanity and weakness, and eventual recovery. But perhaps this passage shows an early stage of the story of Peter, one in which his subsequent glory as martyr and apostolic hero has not yet thrown its light on this first phase of his relationship with his master.

Matthew's Gospel offers a picture of Peter modified by ecclesiastical developments. We can see this trend in the way Peter is made more prominent as inspired leader and the disciple credited with a role of intermediary between

Jesus and the other members of the Twelve (see Mt. 15:15; 17:24-27; 18:21f.). In two special incidents Peter plays a unique role, both in action (14:23-33) and in word (16:17-19).

The first, the "walking on the water" incident, which in Matthew's account includes Peter's request to accompany Jesus and his subsequent lapse of faith, is part of this Evangelist's intention to show both the dignity and the frailty of Peter. Because his weakness is only too apparent, it cannot be that Matthew wishes to exalt him as the uniquely preeminent apostle (so P. Benoit, *L'évangile selon St. Matthieu* [*Sainte Bible*; 3rd ed. 1961], and other Roman Catholic commentators), even if Matthew does give Peter a distinctive status. More likely is Cullmann's view that Peter here is a typical disciple who achieves greatness only in dependence on the Lord. His role is exactly that of "spokesman for the Twelve," not more nor less (*Peter,* pp. 23-27). Yet it cannot be denied that the enlarged pericope is introduced for hortatory purposes, with Peter playing the role of the model disciple who looks to his Lord in time of danger.

H. J. Held sees a deeper meaning in the part given to Peter here. He maintains that not only is Christ portrayed as deliverer from need and danger, he also "gives his disciple a share in his power to walk on the water," and so Matthew enhances Peter's role as leader of the Twelve (G. Bornkamm, G. Barth, and H. J. Held, *Tradition and Interpretation in Matthew* [Eng. tr. 1963], p. 272).

The confession at Caesarea Philippi (16:17-19) is more problematical. The authenticity of the pericope has been challenged on textual grounds. A. von Harnack ("Der Spruch über Petrus als der Felsen der Kirche," *Sitzungsbericht der Berliner Akademie der Wissenschaft* [1918], pp. 637ff.) tried to show that the passage is an interpolation into the original text, made at Rome in the time of Hadrian (A.D. 117-138). But this is a vain plea, without any external support. Moreover, the Semitic coloring of the passage testifies to its primitive character.

A second argument objects that linguistically the term for "church" (Gk. *ekklēsía*) is an anachronism. Linguistic researches show, however, that the true equivalent of *ekklēsía* is the Heb. *ʿēḏâ* ("assembly") or Aram. *kᵉnîštāʾ* ("gathering"). Thus it is more appropriate to translate the Greek word by "people of God" than "church" (so J. Jeremias, *NT Theology* [Eng. tr. 1971], p. 168), in this way meeting the argument that Jesus could not have envisioned an institutional body when using the words recorded in Mt. 16:18 and 18:17. No such concept is required, since He more reasonably had in view the eschatological people of God that He had come to gather in His ministry and beyond.

A third objection raises the issue of the subsequent history of the Church. It is said that Peter did not occupy the authoritative position that this logion of Jesus in v. 19 would inevitably have secured for him. The argument hinges on the meaning of the "power of the keys" (*see* KEYS, POWER OF THE). For the Jewish background, the comms. on Lk. 11:52 par. Mt. 23:13 should be consulted. Evidently what is meant here is "the spiritual insight which will enable Peter to lead others in through the door of revelation through which he has passed himself" (R. N. Flew, *Jesus and His Church* [2nd ed. 1943], p. 95); and this "key" was not the exclusive possession of Peter — even if Mt. 16:19 contains a promise directed particularly to him — though on the day of Pentecost by common consent he was the first to use it. And in Acts 10 he opened the door of faith to Cornelius as the firstfruits of the Gentile mission (see Acts 11:18). On the Jewish setting of the terms "binding" and "loosing," see *TDNT,* II, *s.v.* δέω (Büchsel).

Peter's confession was the turning point in Jesus' ministry. To him was accorded by divine revelation the insight into the mystery of Jesus' person, whom he acknowledged as Israel's Messiah and the divine Son. The subsequent rebuke (Mt. 16:21-23) is directly related to Peter's misunderstanding of what messiahship involved and his attempt to dissuade Jesus from the path to the cross. Mark preserves the vivid narration (Mk. 8:32f.) that exposes Peter's frail humanity, which was open to Satanic influence and resulted in his becoming the mouthpiece of Jesus' enemy, once defeated in the wilderness temptation (Mt. 4:1-11).

On the other hand, Matthew's account of the incident at Caesarea Philippi, by its inclusion of Peter's faith in Jesus as Son of God and the encomium he received as the rock, does give the apostle a special place in the divine economy. This description has suggested to some scholars that the locus of the revelation (Mt. 16:17) and the conferring of the honor as "rock"-man is better placed in the time of the Resurrection appearances. Such a dislocation of the Gospel narrative cannot be supported from the text itself, which, however, may hold some hints that Peter's attestation of faith looks forward to the situation as it developed in the later Church, especially Matthew's church, where Peter was evidently a revered teacher. There is a fairly strong consensus that Matthew's community regarded itself as a "school" (K. Stendahl, *School of St. Matthew* [1954]) or a "study-group" (C. F. D. Moule, *Birth of the NT* [1962], p. 88), patterned on the Jewish idea of the synagogue as *bêṯ hammiḏrāš,* "house of learning." Matthew may well have been regarded as an honored teacher in that situation (cf. 13:52), so it is not surprising that he would wish to exalt Peter's role and so claim apostolic sanction for those elements in his Gospel that set out answers to pressing issues in his day, namely, the opposition of Pharisaic Judaism in the post-Jamnia period (W. D. Davies, *Setting of the Sermon on the Mount* [1963], p. 315) and the inroads of antinomian — and maybe charismatic — leaders (G. Barth, in G. Bornkamm, G. Barth, and H. J. Held, *Tradition and Interpretation in Matthew* [Eng. tr. 1963], pp. 159-164) who were challenging Matthew's authority as a church teacher. The appeal to Peter's office (at Antioch?) would therefore be important in the shaping of the Gospel tradition in the church of Matthew's constituency. M. Hengel (*Acts and the History of Earliest Christianity* [Eng. tr. 1979], p. 98) has argued that the church at Antioch came increasingly under Petrine influence after Paul had declared his position regarding gentile freedom from the Jewish kosher laws and suffered a sense of isolation from his Syrian base. Hengel thus accounts for the special role played by Peter in Matthew (14:28f.; 16:16-19; 17:24; 18:21) and suggests that Antioch was the home of both that Gospel and its teaching on Peter's status.

An integral part of the confession at Caesarea Philippi is the subsequent experience of the Transfiguration (note the date-connection, so rare in the Gospels, Mk. 9:2 par.). Peter is again spokesperson for the three, and again misguided and fallible (Mk. 9:5). Later reflection showed the reality of this vision, and Peter benefited from hindsight (1 Pet. 5:1; 2 Pet. 1:16-18). His proud claims to loyalty are shown up as hollow mockery by the events in Gethsemane, and his threefold denial (Mk. 14:66-72) is painfully told. The end is not without hope, for the promise of *au revoir* (Mk. 14:28) is confirmed by a personal message to Peter (Mk. 16:7) and is followed by a personal appearance of the living Christ (Lk. 24:34; 1 Cor. 15:5).

*II. Apostle.*–After Pentecost Peter became the leading figure in the apostolic Church. Here we are in touch with the role of Peter in Lukan Christianity. The Gospel of

Luke portrays Peter in a more favorable light than Mark's account. There is no rebuke of Peter for his false messianic presuppositions (Lk. 9:20-22), and Luke has Peter's confession in a limpid, verbless form as though to make it a proto-creed of the Church (see R. P. Martin, "Salvation and Discipleship in Luke's Gospel," in J. L. Mays, ed., *Interpreting the Gospels* [1981], pp. 214-230).

Peter's eventual restoration is given more shape in the garden scene (Lk. 22:31f.), and Peter's role as leader is clearly to the fore, as part of Luke's interest in what has been termed the first exercise in "pastoral theology" (J. C. O'Neill; details in Martin, "Salvation and Discipleship in Luke's Gospel," pp. 227-230). The Lukan depiction of Peter emphasizes the parenetic elements in his character (esp. in 5:1-11) as a prelude to Luke's fuller description of him in Acts as church leader and Jewish-Christian missionary.

Acts 1–12 shows that Peter was clearly the dominant influence, both in decision making and public preaching (see 1:15-22; 2:14-40; 3:12-26; on his Pentecostal address see R. F. Zehnle, *Peter's Pentecost Discourse* [1971]).

Before the Jewish authorities (Acts 4:5ff.) Peter is spokesperson; and his many-sided role included that of forceful leader (5:1-11) and miracle worker (5:15). The evidence, however, should not be exaggerated, and H. Conzelmann's attempt (comm. on Acts [*HNT,* 1963], p. 39) to find in 5:3 traces of a characterization of Peter as a "divine man" who knows all human secrets is to be refused. The Holy Spirit's endowment of the apostle is a better explanation, and it is this factor that accounts for the dramatic change between Peter's character in Gethsemane and in the courtyard and his new boldness (4:13) as a Christian witness.

Peter is presented as a church leader in his handling of the situation at Samaria and his encounter with Simon (Acts 8:14-24; on the exegetical problems involved see J. D. G. Dunn, *Baptism in the Holy Spirit* [*SBT,* 2/15, 1970], ch. 5). The historian evidently decided to give prominence to the conversion of Cornelius by the way the narrative is set down, with great fulness of detail and repetition for emphasis (Acts 10–11). Peter's Jewish susceptibilities were overcome and his convictions redirected as he came to learn that "God shows no partiality" (10:34) and that Gentiles such as Cornelius were suitable recipients of the gospel message, offered and received on the basis of trust in Christ, without any ceremonial requirement. Peter's sermon, dramatically cut short (cf. 11:15) by the gracious interposition of God (10:44-47), announced the good news, which was accepted gratefully and movingly. Peter's association with the embryonic gentile mission is clear. Luke evidently wanted to depict him as a link between Jewish Christianity (which in Luke's day was part of past history, yet still important as demonstrating the Jewish origins of the Church in the salvation-historical process) and the now dominant gentile Christianity. Peter serves, for Luke, as the model of a "bridge-man" (J. D. G. Dunn, *Unity and Diversity in the NT* [1977], p. 385; cf. Bruce, pp. 42f.; this description is already noted in Brown, *et al.,* p. 162).

But Peter's sympathies lay more with a mission to his Jewish compatriots, if we place the concordat with Paul (Gal. 2:7-10) in the period before the Jerusalem Council. His native weakness peeps through in the vacillations he practiced at Antioch, and he needed the stern reproof of Paul (Gal. 2:14-21). If Galatians is a pre-Council letter, written A.D. 48-49, subsequent events at Jerusalem show that Peter profited from this rebuke, as is demonstrated by his gentile interest in 1 Peter (see F. F. Bruce, *Epistle to the Galatians* [*NIGTC,* 1982], pp. 55f.).

Peter's arrest in Jerusalem at an earlier date (Acts 12:1-17) led to imprisonment and marvelous release. The apparent hopelessness of his plight as a prisoner of Herod is described to highlight the need for him to leave Jerusalem. This he did, and "departed and went to another place" (v. 17).

The role of Peter at the Jerusalem Council is a matter of continuing debate. One likely view is that we should separate the discussion in Acts 15:1-19 from what is reported in the later verses that describe the formulation and propagating of the so-called decree. The mutual agreements in the first part of the narrative that united Peter and Paul, who had already sealed an agreement in the meeting of Gal. 2:4, 7, were ratified by James on the basis of his appeal to Am. 9:11f. (LXX). This proposal by James was a *modus vivendi* in the interests of gentile freedom and access to the gospel without Jewish restrictions. The details of the decree spelled out in the subsequent verses, however, relate to the single item of table fellowship. Paul and Peter may not have been present when the decree was announced, since Paul never alludes to it in his letters and James's reference to it in Acts 21:18-25 carries the impression that it is announced as something new to Paul.

This reconstruction, which has some problems, notably the presence of the apostles' names in Acts 15:22, 25f. (though it should be observed that the decree is committed to Judas and Silas to transmit), explains one feature regarding Peter's behavior at Antioch. It was the Jewish Christians who, armed with the decree, attacked Peter's lax table fellowship and occasioned Peter's vacillation (Gal. 2:13f.). The issue was whether Jewish laws were binding on gentile believers. Under pressure, Peter and Barnabas gave in when faced with the explicit terms of the decree and they in turn tried to enforce it on the Antioch congregation. Paul regarded this action as a betrayal of the gospel and a move away from the concordat of Gal. 2:1-10 made earlier. Paul's position hardened at this juncture; it set him in opposition to the "pillar" apostles, whose emissaries we may see in 2 Cor. 10–13, and isolated him from Antioch, where Peter's influence continued and became canonized in the publication of Matthew's Gospel some decades later. (For an illuminating discussion of these issues see D. R. Catchpole, *NTS,* 23 [1976/77], 428-444.)

Aside from a brief reappearance at the Jerusalem Council (Acts 15:7-11), Peter now vanishes from the NT story of the Church. Attempts have been made to argue that he left Jerusalem for Rome, there to become the first bishop. But these are countered by the fact that, when Paul wrote his letter to the Romans, he had no knowledge of Peter's presence in the imperial city; and Roman Catholic writers have become more flexible in leaving this identification of "another place" with Rome as an open question (see O'Connor, pp. 10f.; Brown, *et al.,* ch. 4). No certain answer is possible; the text may mean no more than that Peter temporarily left the Christian meeting place. The rise of James in his absence, however, requires that Peter soon moved away from the Holy City and engaged in missionary work elsewhere (Gal. 2:9), possibly Corinth (1 Cor. 1:12) and the regions of Pontus-Bithynia (1 Pet. 1:1). If the historical reconstruction made earlier has some cogency to it, Peter made his home in Antioch and acted as an intermediary between two factions, the Jewish Christianity led by James and the gentile congregation established by the apostle Paul. Peter's subsequent arrival in Rome is clearly attested, and the bond between Rome and communities of Asia Minor (seen in 1 Peter) is equally well established by the essay of J. H. Elliott, "Peter, Silvanus and Mark in 1 Peter and Acts," in W. Haubeck and M. Bachmann, eds., *Wort in der Zeit: Festschrift für K. H. Rengstorf* (1980), pp. 250-267.

Statue of Peter in St. Peter's Square, Rome (W. S. LaSor)

*III. Martyr.*–The apostolic authorship of 1 Peter requires that Peter wrote his Epistle from Rome, if (as is very likely) "Babylon" in 1 Pet. 5:13, conceals the name of the imperial city (*see* PETER, FIRST EPISTLE OF II). The link between Peter and Rome is firmly made in 1 Peter, even if we see that document as a deposit or testament of Petrine teaching collected by a member of his school, either in his later life (Silvanus is usually the name associated with the activity of an amanuensis) or after his lifetime. Contemporary study of 2 Peter views it as a later record of that Petrine school in the final decades of the 1st cent. (see the arguments for this in R. J. Bauckham, *Jude, 2 Peter* [*Word,* 1983], pp. 151-163, who goes further and suggests as author either Linus, mentioned in 2 Tim. 4:21 and regarded in the early Roman bishop succession lists [deriving from Hegesippus] as bishop of Rome after Peter, or Anencletus [Cletus], Linus's successor and Clement's predecessor). Dating 2 Peter is problematical, and suggesting both a *Sitz im Leben* and an author is risky, but it does seem clear that all the data — literary, tradition-historical, and theological — point to Rome as the setting and place of publication of "Peter's testament," which is enshrined, if considerably modified, in that letter.

Christian tradition speaks with a divided voice about Peter's stay in Rome. Irenaeus (*Adv. haer.* iii.1.1) makes the two apostles Peter and Paul the founders of the church there, but this cannot be so, in view of Paul's letter in A.D. 55 or 58 to the Roman church, which he had not then visited (Rom. 1:13). More reliably, Eusebius (*HE* ii.25.8, citing Dionysius) witnesses to the cooperative work of the two men in Italy when Paul was a prisoner there, presumably the period described at the close of Acts.

The Neronian persecution in A.D. 65 marks the turning point, though our sources of information about the apostles are not clear. 1 Clem. 5–6 speaks of Christian martyrs at Rome in such a way as to fit the description of Tacitus (*Ann.* xv.44) that it was during Nero's pogrom that Paul and Peter perished. This would preclude any release of Paul and further ministry after Acts 28, unless the date of the two-year confinement in "free custody" is brought forward to make possible a release and further missionary work in the West (so Eusebius *HE* ii.22.2). Many scholars accept the direct evidence of 1 Clem. 5–6 and insist that the two apostles were martyred in Nero's outburst: so Harnack, (*Geschichte der altchristlichen Literatur bis Eusebius* [1897-1904], II/1, 242), Lietzmann (*Petrus und Paulus in Rom* [2nd ed. 1927], p. 238), Cullmann (*Peter*, pp. 91-110), and G. Ogg (*Odyssey of Paul* [1968], pp. 194-200). But there is a way to steer a middle course through these conflicting church traditions. J. J. Gunther (*Paul: Messenger and Exile* [1972], ch. 6) argues that Paul was tried and sentenced to *relegatio,* or exile, at the close of his detention in Rome (Acts 28). When he heard of the fire at Rome in A.D. 64 he returned to the city and was rearrested and executed in the following year along with Peter. For more detail see R. P. Martin, *NT Foundations,* II [1978], 298-300.

The tradition that Peter was crucified head downward (found in the apocryphal Acts of Peter) appears to be an embroidered version of Jn. 21:18f.

Evidently the burial sites of the apostles were well known, according to Eusebius *HE* ii.25.7, who quotes Gaius, at the time of Bishop Zephyrinus, A.D. 198-217: "You will find the trophies [Gk. *trópaia*] of those who founded this church." See the discussion by J. Lowe, *St. Peter* (1956), pp. 33-45, for the archeological evidence, to be supplemented by O'Connor. The maximum conclusion to be drawn from these Vatican excavations is that Peter's memorial was cherished near the spot where he

Relief depicting Peter's crucifixion head downward (Rome) (W. S. LaSor)

died. His body was never recovered — therefore all talk of Peter's bones is chimerical (in spite of the announcement by Pope Paul VI on June 26, 1968, that such a discovery and identification had been made; see G. F. Snyder, *BA*, 32 [1969], 2-24) — but with the later concern for relics Christians piously believed, for apologetical reasons, that his exact grave could be located (O'Connor, p. 209).

***Bibliography.***–R. E. Brown, K. P. Donfried, and J. Reumann, eds., *Peter in the NT* (1973); F. F. Bruce, *Peter, Stephen, James, and John* (1979); O. Cullmann, *Peter: Disciple — Apostle — Martyr* (Eng. tr., 2nd ed. 1962); A. A. de Marco, *The Tomb of St. Peter* (1964); D. W. O'Connor, *Peter in Rome* (1969).

R. P. MARTIN

**PETER, APOCALYPSE OF.** *See* APOCRYPHAL APOCALYPSES II.B, C.

**PETER, FIRST EPISTLE OF.**

I. Title and Attestation
II. Author, Date, and Provenance
III. Theological Themes
IV. Ethical Admonitions
Special Appendix: The Composition of 1 Peter

***I. Title and Attestation.***–Since the 18th cent. the letters of James, Jude, 1 and 2 Peter, and 1, 2, and 3 John have been designated "Catholic Epistles." The term "catholic" (Gk. *katholikḗ*), a term used by Eusebius for at least some of these Epistles (*HE* ii.23.25; v.18.5; vii.25.7), means "universal" and carries the sense that these letters were directed in the first place to the Christian Church as a whole and not to specific congregations or to certain individuals. In the case of 1 Peter, however, "catholic" is less appropriate, since 1:1 gives a definite geographical area for the original addressees. These first readers, who lived at the northeast end of the Roman world of NT times, are later known to us from the correspondence between the emperor Trajan and the governor Pliny (A.D. 111/12). They are referred to throughout the letter as a group of Christian congregations who face a set of specific circumstances and are marked off from the rest of "Christendom" scattered throughout the ancient world (5:9).

Some valuable attestation of the letter comes in 1 Clement and Polycarp, especially the latter, who quotes from the Epistle several times in his letter to the Philippians. Eusebius (*HE* iii.25.1-3) placed the letter among the accepted parts of the NT canon of his day (*ca.* A.D. 300), and there is no suggestion that its authenticity was ever challenged in the early Church.

The first witness to its authorship comes in 2 Pet. 3:1. This identification is open to doubt because the addressees of the two Epistles are not the same (T. Zahn, *Intro. to the NT* [Eng. tr. 1909], II, 202). R. J. Bauckham, however, agreed with the majority of commentators that 2 Pet. 3:1 refers to 1 Peter, suggesting that the author of 2 Peter had two reasons for the reference: (1) he was a member of the same Petrine circle in Rome that produced 1 Peter; (2) after a long section (2:10b-22) in which he condemned the false teachers in his day, he needed to reestablish the link with the apostle Peter and claim his authority for so writing (*Jude, 2 Peter* [*Word,* 1983], pp. 285f.). But no explicit ascription of the document to the apostle Peter is made until Irenaeus, *ca.* A.D. 185 (*Adv. haer.* iv.9.2; 16.5; v.7.2).

***II. Author, Date, and Provenance.***–The letter itself offers evidence of apostolic authorship (1:1), with a claim duly registered to eyewitness testimony of the Lord's passion and possibly His resurrection and/or transfiguration, seen as a forestate of the glory of His parousia (5:1).

According to Selwyn, "This impression of eyewitness runs through the Epistle, and gives it a distinctive character" (comm., p. 28). Of the items of common interest that unite the Peter of the Gospels and the author of this letter, the following are the most noteworthy. (1) The allusion to the "testing of faith" (1 Pet. 1:7) naturally suggests a reference to the apostle's own experience (Lk. 22:31). (2) Peter's own recovery and recommissioning (implied in the fourfold Gospel tradition, e.g., Mk. 16:7) may well be read in his poignant words of 1 Pet. 5:10. (3) The shepherd-sheep imagery (2:25; 5:2f.) recalls a similar feature in both the Synoptics (e.g., Mk. 14:27f.) and John (Jn. 21:15-17), with special application to Peter. (4) The common praise of humility as necessary in Christian living is inculcated in both explicit teaching (1 Pet. 5:5) and dramatic action-parable (Jn. 13:1-10). In the latter episode Peter is the interlocutor with the Lord, and it cannot be coincidental that the Greek verb *enkomboústhai,* "clothe," in 1 Pet. 5:5 calls to mind the picture of a person attiring himself in a garment tied onto his body, as in Jn. 13:4, where Jesus wrapped a towel used by slaves around Himself as a prelude to His washing the disciples' feet. An incidental detail like this suggests that Peter is consciously reminiscing in his later writing.

F. W. Beare, however, argued against the inferences drawn by Selwyn on the ground that the author of 1 Peter had read the Fourth Gospel, including Jn. 21, and stood consciously under its influence (2nd and 3rd eds. of his comm., p. 191). Thus the relationship behind the common expressions and motifs is literary and not personal. For example, on 1 Pet. 2:21-25 Beare denied any evidence of a personal reminiscence and saw rather the case of a writer "whose knowledge of the Passion is literary and theological . . . since it is framed wholly in phrases of the Second Isaiah and the Apostle Paul; there is not a shred of personal reminiscence" (*loc. cit.*). This explanation drawing on the OT prophecy is rather weak, since we may ask what impulse prompted the author to cite the servant passage (which is only rarely attested in the NT) if it was not a conscious recall of Jesus' bearing as a harmless lamb led to the slaughter. Also, Paul's meager use of the Servant of God prophecy in Isa. 53 suggests that the author of 1 Peter is not indebted to Paul at this point.

There is also close correspondence between the language of Peter as reported in Acts and the language of this Epistle. (1) The character of God as the impartial judge is designated in 1 Pet. 1:17 by the word "not-respecting-persons" (Gk. *aprosōpolḗmptos*), which is found in Acts 10: 34 in slightly different form *(ouk éstin prosōpolḗmptēs).* (2) What has been called "the stoneship of Christ" — an allusion to Cyprian's collection of biblical references in his *Testimonies* (Treatise 12) ii.16 — is attested by such verses as Acts 4:10f. and 1 Pet. 2:7f., both of which draw upon Ps. 118:22. To be sure, the Pauline literature (Rom. 9:32f.; Eph. 2:20) also appeals to this Scripture proof text on Christ as the rejected and exalted stone but not so explicitly to Ps. 118 as do these two passages in Acts and 1 Peter. (3) The way in which the Lord's "name" is made central in both documents cannot be accidental. It occurs in Acts 3:6, 16; 4:10, 12; 5:41; 10:43 — all of which have Peter playing a distinct role — and in 1 Pet. 4:14, 16. (4) Peter's speech in Acts 3:18, 24 places great emphasis on the way God has fulfilled the OT prophetic Scripture in sending the Messiah; an identical position in regard to messianic prophecy is taken in 1 Pet. 1:10-12.

Why, then, has Petrine authorship been denied? (1) There are similarities of language between this Epistle and literature ascribed to Paul, especially Ephesians. C. L. Mitton's investigation (*Epistle to the Ephesians* [1951]) sought to date Ephesians later than 1 Peter because of alleged dependence of the former on the latter. This was countered by more recent study (seen in J. H. Elliott, *JBL*, 95 [1976], 243-254, esp. 247f.), which noted that the common matter relates mainly to liturgical interest (e.g., 1 Pet. 1:3ff.; Eph. 1:3ff.) and suggested that it is best to account for the parallels by crediting both writers with access to a common fund of liturgical and catechetical material, perhaps located at Rome (so E. Best, comm., pp. 32-36). This would also account for the links between 1 Peter and 1 Clement, also a document emanating from the church in Rome. (See Special Appendix below for the liturgical origin of 1 Peter.)

(2) The literary style of 1 Peter raises doubt, for some of the vocabulary is undeniably classical (see A. H. McNeile and C. S. C. Williams, *Intro. to the Study of the NT* [2nd ed. 1953], p. 220 n. 1 for a list of words in this tradition), and the OT is cited in the LXX version. The issue is whether a Galilean fisherman, known to be an "uneducated, common man" (Acts 4:13), could have written in the style and manner of these chapters.

Two replies may be made to this doubt. First, Acts 4:13 probably means only that Peter and John were not versed in rabbinic lore. According to C. H. Dodd (*Interpretation of the Fourth Gospel* [1953], p. 82 n. 1) the Greek terms in Acts 4:13 represent the rabbinic *bôr wᵉheḏᵉyôṭ* and mean that the apostles were ignorant of the Torah in the eyes of official Judaism. These terms say nothing, however, about the apostles' cultural background or linguistic expertise. Second, O. Cullmann (*The NT* [1968], p. 99) argued that Peter's village of Bethsaida (Jn. 1:44) was cosmopolitan, open to cultural influences that may well have equipped him for the task of composing letters.

As an alternative to the second reply, and not necessarily to its exclusion, some have proposed that the polished literary format and style of 1 Peter is the work of an amanuensis (secretary). This seems to be implied in 5:12: "By Silvanus, a faithful brother as I regard him, I have written briefly to you." Selwyn (pp. 9-17, 369-384) extracted the maximum from this text in defense of the idea that Silvanus (the Silas referred to in Acts) was the real author of the letter, writing out Peter's teaching in his own style and language. This alternative would relieve the need to attribute to Peter a literary competence beyond that of a Galilean fisherman. The argument that appeals to Silvanus is not clear-cut, however, since its proponents find a connection between 1 Peter and 1 Thessalonians, which is also attributed to Silvanus, at least in part (1 Thess. 1:1). This last factor really embarrasses more than aids the case for an amanuensis, as W. L. Knox was quick to point out in response to Selwyn (*Theology*, 49 [Nov. 1946], 342-44). Also, B. Rigaux, in his commentary on 1 Thessalonians (*EtB* [1956], p. 107), noted that "the appeal to Silvanus is in vain . . . since words, grammar, phrases, and ideas are Paul's." Beare, too, agreed (pp. 189f.), and his criticism moved on to one further point: "The fatal objection to this hypothesis . . . lies in the character of the teaching, most conspicuously in the meagreness of the references to the doctrine of the Spirit" (p. 28). But this last objection is by no means realistic, for one of the leading theological ideas in 1 Peter is precisely the teaching on the Holy Spirit!

(3) Scanty references to Jesus' earthly life do not comport with the reminiscences that some expect of the chief of the apostles. But this objection overlooks such allusions as are there (see above) and assumes that Peter intended to give his memoirs in letter form, which is not the case. His purpose in writing is expressed in 5:12: "exhorting and declaring that this is the true grace of God; stand fast in it."

(4) Some claim that the nature of the persecutions reflects a time after the apostolic age. F. W. Beare built much of his positive contribution on this claim, arguing that 4:12-16 can mean only that Christians were being accused of a political charge and were suffering *propter nomen* ("on account of the name" of Christ) as sedition-mongers and enemies of the state. (B. Reicke's similar view of 1 Peter as directed against a Christian "zealot" movement involved in overthrowing the Roman government (comm., pp. 95-100) was effectively challenged by C. F. Sleeper, *Nov.Test.*, 10 [1968], 270-286.) This implies a situation when Christians were openly branded as a political group, subversive of the Roman state. Emperors who did show hostility to the Church were Nero (A.D. 64), Vespasian (d. 79), Domitian (81-96), and Trajan (111/12). Beare maintained that, of this list, the only possible persecutor whose enmity matches the evidence in 1 Peter is Trajan. Pliny's correspondence in A.D. 111/12 shows that Christians in Pontus-Bithynia were being accused simply of being Christians, a situation that appears to match precisely the charge implied in 1 Pet. 4:16. This is a neat link, and Beare exploited it fully.

But Beare's hypothesis has some serious weaknesses. (a) Nothing in 1 Peter indicates an official state persecution as a settled policy. After reviewing the evidence of the letter itself, Kelly concluded that because "there is no evidence for any very extensive persecution initiated by the government in the 1st or early 2nd cents.," there is no reason to quarrel with "the impression which the letter as a whole conveys [which] is not of juridical prosecutions by the government (these seem ruled out by the references themselves, by the statement that the ill-treatment is world-wide [see (c) below], and by the respect shown to the emperor), but of an atmosphere of suspicion, hostility and brutality on the part of the local population which may easily land Christians in trouble with the police" (comm., pp. 10, 29).

(b) 1 Peter has no explicit reference to official inquisition or torture, such as was practiced in Pontus-Bithynia in Pliny's time (*Ep.* x.96f.). The descriptions of the trials the readers were suffering (1:6) and the ill treatment meted out to them (3:13-17), along with the "fiery ordeal" (4:12-19), suggest that the hardships were private and confined to the area, "originating in the hostility of the surrounding population. The technical terms for official persecution (*diōgmos*,etc.) are noticeably absent, nor is there any unambiguous mention of formal accusation *(katēgoria)*, much less of imprisonment or execution" (Kelly, p. 10).

(c) The sufferings of Christians are part of the general attitude taken to them in other places, if we take seriously the remark in 5:9. This is rightly regarded as of "crucial significance," thus endorsing the notion that "the troubles referred to in iv. 12ff. are in no way exceptional but have their counterpart in a great many places" (Kelly, p. 10). Local outbursts of mob violence may well explain the cause and nature of these pinpricks (suggested by 4:1-4). See further C. F. D. Moule's discussion in *Essays*, pp. 142f.

As we attempt to reach a conclusion about the Epistle's authorship and provenance it is important to take note of the letter's composition (see Special Appendix below), which embodies much liturgical matter drawn from the common literary materials of the early Church (e.g., 2:4-8 is related literarily to Rom. 9:33; cf. Selwyn, comm., pp. 268-277). Also there is specific evidence in 5:12 of the use of a scribe and (possibly) an editor.

With regard to date, the unspecific nature of the persecutions is in keeping with a setting in the decade of the 60's, before the outbreak of the Neronian persecution at Rome in which Peter and Paul perished (A.D. 64). If 1 Peter was published with Peter's personal authorization and as representing his own apostolic teaching, as seems very probable, a date in the 60's is required.

The place of publication is almost certainly to be identified as Rome, especially in view of the most plausible explanation of the cryptogram in 5:13, where "Babylon" means the imperial city, as in Rev. 14:8; 17; 2 Esd. 3:1f., 28, 31 (see Cullmann, pp. 83-86).

Alternative locations have been proposed, however. (1) A literal Babylon was championed by R. G. Heard (*Intro. to the NT* [1950], p. 171), who called attention to Josephus's remarks on the large number of Jewish communities there (*Ant.* xv.2.2 [14]). But Josephus's evidence is doubtful, and there is no positive confirmation that Babylon did not fall into disrepair and ruin (see D. J. Wiseman, *NBD*, p. 118).

(2) A symbolic value was attached to the name "Babylon" by Moule (*Essays*, p. 142), who argued that the place name was selected to draw a simple parallel with ancient Babylon as the place to which God's people had been exiled.

(3) The most ambitious attempt to find a definite locale for 1 Peter was made by M.-E. Boismard (*RB*, 64 [1957], 181), who opted for Antioch in Syria on the grounds that the teaching of the "descent into Hades" was established early in the churches of Syria; that the title "Christian" is found in the NT only in those places that speak of the Church in Syria (Acts 11:26; 26:28) and in 1 Pet. 4:16; and that the *Apostolic Tradition* of Hippolytus both has a Syrian background and reflects the language of 1 Peter.

The last point is countered by the finding that the *Apostolic Tradition* clearly emanated from Rome (G. J. Cuming, *Hippolytus: A Text for Students* [1976]). Moreover, 1 Peter has closer literary affinities with 1 Clement (see Kelly, p. 12), which is indubitably associated with Rome. Finally, the absence of the Epistle's influence on Ignatius of Antioch is a telling counterobjection.

More recent study of 1 Peter has opened up new lines of investigation regarding the provenance and authorship of 1 Peter. The traditional view sees 1 Peter as a genuine hortatory letter, possibly using baptismal language (Moule, *Essays*, p. 137) and even parts of a baptismal catechism (Selwyn), intended to address and encourage persecuted believers in Asia Minor. Selwyn championed the apostolic authorship, though allowing the role of Silvanus as scribe; he thought the Epistle emanated from Rome in A.D. 63. In dependence on P. Carrington's study on *The Primitive Christian Catechism* (1940), Selwyn believed that Peter drew on a deposit of ethical teachings common to Colossians, Ephesians, and James, in turn based on the Levitical code (Lev. 17–19, the so-called Holiness Code). F. W. Beare, as noted above, took exception both to this setting of the letter and the case for an apostolic authorship.

E. Lohse (*ZNW*, 45 [1954], 86-89; cf. also *Formation of the NT* [Eng. tr. 1981], pp. 212f.) led the opposition to the view of 1 Peter as a baptismal liturgy developed by H. Windisch and H. Preisker (see Special Appendix below). In its place Lohse, for whom neither baptism nor catechism was the leading theme, put the general subject of persecution. The letter, he maintained, was intended to offer encouragement to a beleaguered church in the throes of persecution. The author adapted traditional teaching to meet his readers' need. The letter was written from Rome. This understanding is shared by D. Hill (*Nov.Test.*, 18 [1976], pp. 181-89), for whom the ruling motif of the letter is exhortation to stand firm in the face of actual physical and emotional suffering caused by loss of civil rights and threat of punishment, including death. The genre of the letter is strictly parenetic; its catechetical overtone is incidental.

Goppelt's 1978 commentary began a new approach. Goppelt remarked that 1 Peter is the only NT writing that addresses systematically and thematically the matter of Christian alien residence within the structure of contemporary society (comm., p. 41). Writing at Rome anywhere between A.D. 65 and 80, the author offered exhortation in the light of growing persecution, the origin of which is not the police (Kelly) or the state (Beare) but popular slander (1 Pet. 2:12; 3:16; 4:4, 14) caused by Christians not conforming to the world's standards because of their loyalty to Christ. The letter's response to this situation is (a) to show the difference between the Church and the pagan society around it (1:1–2:10); then (b) to develop the paradox that, although Christians are "strangers" and "aliens" in their society, they will share in its social responsibility and not become either revolutionaries or ascetics (2:11–4:11); yet (c) to acknowledge realistically that the Christians are bound to collide with the prevailing ethos, and receive the reward of suffering, thus participating in Christ's sufferings (4:12–5:14).

Goppelt's contribution was his identification of the social dimension of the reader's needs as a major item, not as a side-issue subordinate to the theological or ethical concerns of their community. In this he was followed by J. H. Elliott, *A Home for the Homeless* (subtitled *A Sociological Exegesis of 1 Peter, Its Situation and Strategy*, and containing a bibliography of pertinent studies), and D. L. Balch. These writers agreed in basic position, though they differed over details. The thesis is that "the *oikos* or household constituted for the Christian movement as well as for its environment a chief basis, paradigm and reference point for religious and moral as well as social, political, and economic organization, interaction, and ideology" (Elliott, *Home*, p. 213). Applied to the understanding of 1 Peter, this approach suggests that the aim of the document is apologetic. It was written when Roman Christians of the Petrine circle were expressing concern for their brethren in Asia (Elliott) or when Christian slaves and wives became converted to Christianity and were provoking the state authorities on the charge of being "seditious" (Balch, p. 95). The author(s) of 1 Peter, whom Elliott linked with Mark and Silvanus, former colleagues of the now martyred Peter (see his essay, "Peter, Silvanus and Mark in 1 Peter and Acts," in W. Haubeck and M. Bachmann, eds., *Wort in der Zeit: Festschrift für K. H. Rengstorf* [1980], pp. 250-267), dealt with the problems by appealing to the Church as God's house or family to accommodate the needs of a socially deprived and ostracized social group in Asia (Elliott), or more particularly the needs of Christian women living in partially Christian households whose ethos was prescribed by Roman insistence on submission, order, and harmony (Balch).

One result has emerged from this latest phase of Petrine studies: 1 Peter owes little to Pauline Christianity, and represents a separate and distinct entity within the pluriform and socially diverse examples of what we tend to run together as social groups forming the Church in NT times.

***III. Theological Themes.***–Probably no document in the NT is so theological as 1 Peter, if "theological" is taken in the strict sense of teaching about God. The author's mind "begins from and returns constantly to the thought of God as Creator, Father and Judge, as the One whose will determines all that comes to pass, who shapes the destiny and determines the actions of those whom He has chosen for His own, who sustains them through the sufferings which He sends to test them, and who at the last will vindicate them and reward them eternally" (Beare, p. 33). This is a noble statement and is amply justified.

While 1 Peter has more than a little to say about the other cardinal Christian doctrines, its emphasis does fall on the character and action of God, who is the Holy One (1:15), the Father (1:17), the Creator (4:19), and Judge

(4:5). Faith is directed to Him (1:21; 3:18) through the mediation of Christ His Son.

Jesus Christ is pictured on an OT background as the true paschal lamb (1:19) and servant of Yahweh (2:22-24). The twin poles of His existence are His sufferings and death (2:23f.) and His exaltation (1:3, 21). Peter accentuates the sufferings of the Lord as a prelude to His death on the cross, partly to show that His death was real and partly to make the exemplary point that He is thereby kin to the Epistle's readers, who were in the throes of suffering on account of their faith in Christ (see F. V. Filson, *Interp.*, 9 [1955], 400-412). In 3:18-22 he provides a succint statement of the theme of Christ's exaltation (see the thorough treatment by W. J. Dalton, *Christ's Proclamation to the Spirits* [1965]).

The value of His death is stated in terms of access to God. Also, by that sacrifice on our behalf Christians are supplied a power to follow in his steps and be dedicated to God. His ascension is reported after a reference to that mysterious period of three days of death, in which the events of 3:19 and 4:6 are set. Most likely this refers to Christ's role as the new Enoch (so Kelly), in which He visited the underworld and announced the fate of wicked superbeings, thereby assuring the Church that their regime was ended and their dominion broken. The chief point in favor of this interpretation is that it gives an immediate moral application to the persecuted Christian community to whom Peter is writing. (*See also* PRISON, SPIRITS IN.)

At present Christ is Lord (3:15), whose parousia is awaited (1:7, 13; 4:13; 5:1). An imminent end time motivates the author (4:7) and gives his ethical teachings a distinctive color. This seems clearly to reflect a life-situation in the apostolic age.

More debatable is the issue whether 1 Peter is removed from the apostolic era on account of a singular absence of the doctrine of the Holy Spirit. For F. W. Beare (p. 36) this is a decisive factor. He comments, "The Spirit has fallen into eclipse . . . in First Peter." But the case is not so cogent, since there are four references to the Spirit, 1:2, 11, 12; 4:14, all of which seem to betray an early date and refer to a primitive statement of the Spirit's power.

On another test case, the use made in 1 Pet. 2:22-24 (and 1:19?) of the *'ebed YHWH* figure in Isa. 53 anchors this teaching in a sector of primitive Christianity (see Cullmann, *Peter*, pp. 66-68), for there is evidence that this title for Jesus was short-lived in the early Church.

We may conclude that much of the above teaching belongs to a time of consolidation and suggests a statement of the Christian faith for new believers of gentile origin. This is confirmed by their geographical address (1:1). The readers are unknown to Peter, who at 1:12 marks himself off from the preachers in the area. The readers have only recently been evangelized (2:2) and baptized (3:21) — unless these texts fit into a baptismal service on which 1 Peter is the running commentary (F. L. Cross's view, which is open to criticism [see Special Appendix below]). That they were Gentiles seems clear from 1:14; 2:10-12; 4:3. It is doubtful, however, that Peter's readers had been adherents of a Hellenistic mystery cult who were familiar with the taurobolium (bath in a bull's blood) or the cult of Cybele or Isis, as Perdelwitz infers from 1:3f. (This entire reconstruction of initiation rites in the mystery religions has been critically scrutinized by G. Wagner, *Pauline Baptism and the Pagan Mysteries* [Eng. tr. 1967].)

***IV. Ethical Admonitions.***–To get to the root of Peter's moral instruction given to his readers, we need to come to some firm conclusions concerning the setting of the letter and its format.

(1) Modern study has veered in the direction of regarding the references to "persecutions" in the letter (seen to be a truly epistolary composition, even if it incorporates catechesis, hymns, and creeds of the primitive Church and finds its natural setting in baptism as a baptismal homily; see Special Appendix below) as relating to some local outburst of opposition more than to an official state policy. (For a useful summary of the possibilities see E. G. Selwyn, *Studiorum Novi Testamenti Societas Bulletin*, nos. 1-3 [repr. 1963], 35-50.) Therefore we shall more properly regard Peter's call to steadfastness and a good conscience under provocation as part of his general counsel for the Christian life, spoken of as a "tribulation" (as in Acts 14:22), rather than as part of an "interim ethic" addressed to a Church caught in the grip of a tyrannous government. See Kelly, pp. 25f., who noted how the author's purpose is seen as one of "sustaining and encouraging the Asian Christians" whose "troubles are the ever-felt background of every paragraph [he writes]." Kelly proceeded to identify two aspects of his moral theology as significant: first the strongly eschatological perspective in which he places the experiences of his readers; then the emphasis on exemplary behavior that characterizes the Epistle.

(2) The literary question turns on the possibility that there is a break at 4:11. Moule (*Essays*, pp. 134-145) uses this possibility to support the view that in 2:11–4:11 the sufferings are in prospect but in 4:12–5:11 they are actual. In this way he accounts for the change in tense of the verbs, and the change in tone from a more placid to a more fearful mood between the earlier and later sections, which represent two originally distinct versions of the letter (pp. 140-45). Kelly criticized this line of reasoning on linguistic and contextual grounds and argued that the entire letter is shot through with the persecution motif, to be understood as the type of hostile treatment to be expected by minority groups living in a pagan environment. It is this element pervading the letter that gives it the character of a persecution tract, offering encouragement and guidance to Christians in the slave group who were undergoing the threat of serious reprisals on account of their faith (pp. 5-11). We may add to this the evidence that they seem to be newly won converts, and on that account persecution and deprivation would come all the harder to understand and to bear.

Peter's advice may be treated under five headings. (1) The Christian life is centered in hope (1:3) and sustained by faith in a God whose purposes are known in Christ (1:2). This is Peter's starting point and cardinal principle of theology, both doctrinal and practical.

(2) The call to self-control (1:13) is meant to issue in a display of the qualities of Christian living that will make it attractive to others in the pagan society around the believers (2:11, 16). Even when they are unjustly provoked and harassed, let Christians be courteous and patient (3:8-17); slaves who are maltreated without cause will be especially open to the temptation to fight back (2:18-25).

(3) The Christian attitude to the ruling authorities is set down in 2:13-17, with a warning in 4:15-19 directed against those who would commit antisocial acts.

(4) Humility is a Christian grace (3:8; 5:5f.) that is to characterize God's people both in the outside world and in the Church. In the Church this summons to lowliness especially fits those who aspire to ecclesiastical office (see J. H. Elliott, *CBQ*, 32 [1970], 367-391), reminding leaders that their office is one of service, not dictatorship.

(5) The summons to endurance (4:7, 19; 5:8-11) fastens on a typical NT grace applicable specifically in a time of testing (cf. Mk. 13 par.). If the terminology is somewhat different, clearly the admonitions to patience, persistence,

and prayerful vigilance are common to this stratum of NT ethical teaching. By strange irony, it was just this "determination" (Gk. *hypomonḗ*) and refusal to give in to trial and unfaithfulness that later was misunderstood by the Roman magistrates when Christians were arraigned on charges of sedition. It was regarded as inflexible obstinancy (Lat. *pertinacia*). What was to be the Christian's right attitude in these circumstances in the mid-first century is classically expressed in 3:15.

Special Appendix: the Composition of 1 Peter

Modern study of 1 Peter has concentrated on the literary structure of the document as part of the more general interest in form criticism of the Epistles. The intention in this discipline is to investigate the literary deposits (e.g., blessings, hymns, admonitions) assumed to be embedded in the NT letters in order to discover the religious and theological situations out of which these preepistolary traditions emerged. (This corresponds to identifying the *Sitz im Leben* in the canonical Gospels.) Such situations are mainly cultic, sacramental, and parenetic (i.e., relating to the Church's instruction of Christians and giving warnings and encouragements in the believers' personal and social lives). The composition of 1 Peter has been viewed in three chief ways. The following is a summary of a fuller discussion (with bibliography) in R. P. Martin, *VE,* 1 (1962), 29-42.

*A. Epistle that Embodies Hymnic Material.* The traditional view of the literary form of 1 Peter, that it is a genuine Epistle, written by a single person, and addressed to various Christian communities in Asia, does not preclude the possibility that fragments of hymns, creeds, and confessions, or even pieces of sermonic material could have been inserted into such an Epistle. Should 1 Peter prove to contain such material it would not be unique, for it seems fairly clear that Paul incorporated previously existing fragments into his letters.

An illustration of this sort of thing in 1 Peter is 2:4-8, which Selwyn examined in detail in one of the celebrated Notes appended to his commentary (pp. 268-277). The conclusion of this study is that underlying these verses is an early Christian hymn or rhythmical prayer, common to both Peter and Paul (in Rom. 9:33). Selwyn's analysis produced a hymn of seven lines, covering vv. 6-8. This analysis differed from Windisch's arrangement, which produced from vv. 1-10 "a hymn on the holy destiny of Christendom, in four strophes, 1-3, 4f., 6-8, 9f." Selwyn justly criticized this view on the ground that it used the term "hymn" too widely, "for there is nothing hymnodic in structure in verses 4, 5" (p. 276 n. 2).

A strong reason for believing that a Christian adaptation of certain OT passages produced a cultic psalm is the presence in v. 6 of the phrase *periéchei en graphȩ̄́*, which Selwyn took to mean "it stands in writing," comparing Sir. 44:5 (comm., pp. 163, 273). This could very well mean "as it is contained in the hymn." Then the introductory formula would be equivalent to that in Eph. 5:14, and possibly that in Phil. 2:5, if E. Lohmeyer's interpretation of "which was also in Christ Jesus" as "a sort of formula of citation" has any plausibility (see R. P. Martin, *Carmen Christi, Phil. 2:5-11* [rev. 1983], pp. 63-84).

Windisch proposed several other hymns in 1 Peter. He described 1:3-12 as an *Eingangshymnus* (entrance-hymn) made up of five seven- or five-line strophes joined together by relative pronouns. The likelihood that the letter opens with a long prayer introduced by the solemn blessing—after the manner of the Jewish *bᵉrāḵôṯ* — of v. 3 is becoming increasingly acceptable in view of researches that show that the letters of the apostles were intended to be read in public worship.

Windisch also wrote or implied that three parts of the letter may be isolated as *Christuslieder* ("Christ-hymns"): 1:18-21; 2:21-25; and 3:18-22. He designated 2:21-25 "the second Christ-hymn," making a parenthetical reference to 1:18-21 that implies that it is the first hymn addressed to Christ. There is little to support this suggestion if we interpret strictly the term "hymn." The language admittedly is cultic and exalted, and the setting of 1:20 as a "two-member Christ-text" is just possible, but it would be precarious to say that it owed its origin to a separate hymn, of which it is a postulated fragment.

Windisch regarded 3:18-22 as a baptismal hymn to Christ in four strophes (the exhortation in 3:13-17, interrupted by 3:18-22, is continued in 4:1); although perhaps not all of 3:18 belongs to the hymn. He gave no formal analysis and it is not certain whether he meant that Peter in 3:18-22 was quoting from a hymn familiar to the Church or that Peter was led by certain associations to break spontaneously into verse form himself.

In his 1947 essay, "Confessional and hymnic fragments in 1 Peter," Bultmann built on the foundation laid by Windisch. Bultmann held that, in the passages under consideration, the author had before him an actual quotation, but that not all of 3:18-22 is a quotation. The author added comments on an existing text, whether a hymn or a creed. The contribution of Bultmann's essay is that he not only identified certain parts of the letter as hymnic or confessional, he also held that the author of the document known as 1 Peter had before him a series of credal or hymn-like forms on which he commented by means of certain glosses. The role of the author, in certain passages of this letter, is that of glossator.

The reconstructed whole of the original version of 1:20; 2:21-24; 3:18-22, before the glossator "spoiled" the simple symmetry, would have looked like this:

(? I believe in the Lord Jesus Christ,)
Foreknown before the world's foundation,
But manifested at the end of the times;

Who suffered once for sins,
To bring us to God;

Put to death in the flesh,
But made alive in the spirit,
in which He also preached to the imprisoned spirits;
(But) having gone into heaven He sat at the right hand
of God,
Angels and authorities and powers under His control.

In comment on Bultmann's reconstruction, R. Leivestad (*Christ the Conqueror* [1954], p. 177) regarded it as "quite plausible," and E. Schweizer (*Erniedrigung und Erhöhung* [1955], p. 105) also accepted it. The main writers who spoke against Bultmann were J. Jeremias (*ZNW*, 42 [1949], 194-201, esp. 195f.) and Lohse, both accusing him of the same thing. The price he paid for his attempt to secure a completely balanced arrangement of the text was too high. His alterations were too unrestrained and unwarranted, especially when he tore asunder vv. 19 and 20ff. Even this recasting of the material failed to produce the desired result of a completely symmetrical arrangement, as may be seen by noting the inordinate length of v. 22. His use of the gnostic redemption myth to explain vv. 20ff. was unrequired. The summary judgment is "not convincing" (Lohse), and his joining together of 1:20 and 3:18-22 was pronounced by Jeremias "most improbable"; Cranfield said exactly the same (*Expos.T.*, 69 [1958], 369).

Later writers dealt more critically with Bultmann's proposal to find in 1 Peter a unified hymn in three parts. In spite of the efforts of M.-E. Boismard (*Quatre hymnes*) to trace in these verses (1:20; 3:18, 22; 4:6) a connected seven-line Christ-hymn, parallel in structure to 1 Tim. 3:16, the main verdict on Bultmann's enterprise has been negative. The most that R. Deichgräber conceded (*Gotteshymnus und Christushymnus in der frühen Christenheit* [1967], pp. 140-43) was that in 2:21-24 there are four short sections, joined by the relative pronoun ("who") but lacking reference both to Christ's preexistence (1:20) and to His exaltation (a theme picked up in 3:18-22). These hymnic fragments (identified mainly because v. 25 looks beyond its immediate context) are unique in describing the earthly life of Jesus and drawing upon Isa. 53. Deichgräber placed the section in a Hellenistic setting, since the LXX is quoted. He also cautiously suggested a eucharistic background for the use of the passage in the church's worship, rejecting Boismard's idea of a baptismal setting on the ground that v. 24b, "dying to sin, living to righteousness," is secondary and not part of the hymnlike structure.

K. Wengst (*Christologische Formeln und Lieder des Urchristentums* [1972], pp. 83-86) was less impressed by Bultmann's proposal to regard 2:21-25 as a hymn-form and thought that since the death of Christ leads to an ethical admonition (esp. in vv. 21, 24), we should regard the pericope as a "catechetical instruction" based on Christ as a model (Gk. *hypogrammós*; cf. Polyc. Phil. 8:1f., which cites 1 Pet. 2:24 and then applies it: "Let us then be imitators [*mimētaí*] of His endurance [*hypomonḗ*] . . . for this is the example [*hypogrammós*] He gave us in Himself, and this is what we have believed"). The link between Christ's suffering and endurance and the parenetic call to follow Him in the same attitude is clear from 1 Pet. 2:20, and formed a theme in later ethical exhortation (Barn. 5:1, 5; 2 Clem. 1:2). The application to Peter's readers would be apparent, and Wengst made a good case for the use of Isa. 53 in a hortatory — rather than hymnic or liturgical — context.

The response to Bultmann is more emphatic with regard to 1 Pet. 3:18-22. Deichgräber (pp. 169-173) doubted that we should label these verses a confession of faith or a hymn. He was especially critical of Boismard's proposal (*Quatre hymnes*, pp. 103-109) to extend the hymn to include 4:6 and regard 3:18–4:6 as a baptismal creed. The chief objection arises from Deichgräber's recognition that there are "mixed" styles of writing — both prose and poetry — in 3:18-22, and there is little warrant for Bultmann's method of recasting the text to form a symmetrical whole. Deichgräber allowed that there are hymnic fragments in vv. 18b and 22, both verses rich in participial verb forms, but the two examples do not necessarily belong to the same earlier composition (as Wengst, *Christologische Formeln*, pp. 163f., was to argue). His strong point, taken up by J. T. Sanders (*NT Christological Hymns* [1971], pp. 17f.), was to observe the parallel of v. 18b with 1 Tim. 3:16. Sanders helped to endorse the literary contacts by paralleling v. 22 with 1 Tim. 3:16, whose last line runs, "[He] was taken up into glory." Thus 1 Pet. 3:18f., 22 turns out to be a preformed early version of a hymnic formula of which 1 Tim. 3:16 is a more complete or refined version. Certainly there are more rhetorical traits in 1 Tim. 3:16 than in the Petrine text, even if both texts share the same feature of *parallelismus membrorum* (or couplet) at their center, that is, "incarnate/put to death in the flesh," "vindicated/made alive in the spirit."

Wengst (p. 163) attempted to trace a "way of Christ" in six steps from preexistence through epiphany and death to resurrection, exaltation, and lordship over the cosmic powers as in other NT hymnic specimens (e.g., Phil. 2:6-11). While data for this proposal may be here (messianic canticles would have grown to full-blown Christ-hymns as a response to a gnostic threat; cf. R. P. Martin, *Expos. T.*, 94 [1983], 132-36), it is difficult to find persuasive Bultmann's and Wengst's argument that these credal-hymnic elements are scattered throughout 1 Peter.

Somewhat more convincing is the proposal of S. E. Johnson (*JBL*, 69 [1960], 48-51) to regard 3:18-22 as organically connected with the opening verses of ch. 4. The text is a good example of chiasmus on a large scale, for the argument proceeds from the example of Christ's passion and resurrection in 3:18f. to a statement of what happened in the early days of human history as a type of present salvation. Then the author returns at 3:20b to proceed point by point through the antitype of Christian baptism, and concludes with a statement in 4:6 of what Christ has accomplished by His death and resurrection. In the pattern that Johnson sets out, all this appears very neat and tidy — perhaps too much so — but at least it has a merit that Bultmann's schema lacked, that it leaves the text unmanipulated in the interests of the theory. The interrelation of kerygma and ethical appeal (in 3:18-22 and 4:1f.) is certainly an interesting point, and the parallel with Phil. 2:5-11 and 2:14-16 should be noticed.

*B. Baptismal Document.* A second theory of the composition of 1 Peter sees it as a baptismal document. A clear statement of this view is given by Windisch: "The main part of the letter 1:3–4:11 represents a baptismal address" (comm. [1930], p. 82). The connection of the letter with the rite of baptism is universally accepted, especially in light of the section 3:18-22, which has just been examined. Kelly spoke for many NT and liturgical scholars when he said that this text "reads like a part-paraphrase and part-quotation of an instruction preparatory to baptism. The insertion in verses 20ff. of a short account of the meaning of the sacrament bears this out" (*Early Christian Creeds* [1950], p. 18).

For some writers, such as Selwyn, Lohse, Moule, Goppelt, and D. Hill (*Nov. Test.*, 18 [1976], 181-89), however, the references to baptism are incidental, as in many other places in the NT, especially in the Pauline corpus. The document is then essentially a message of encouragement, written to harassed or persecuted believers, as 4:12 makes plain. The allusions to baptism are more or less extraneous to the main concern of the document, which is correctly designated an Epistle.

Both the references to baptism and the messages of encouragement are included in a novel hypothesis first proposed by Perdelwitz in 1911. His argument needs close inspection, especially since it was accepted with enthusiasm by B. H. Streeter (*The Primitive Church* [1929], p. 122), who added some speculation of his own.

The linchpin of this theory is the supposition that the letter has a clear break at 4:11. Perdelwitz gave four arguments for this idea. (1) The sufferings of Christians are described in 4:12 as present, whereas in the earlier part of the letter (1:6; 3:13f., 17) they are hypothetical. Verses 3:17 and 4:19 show the contrast. (2) In 1:6, 8 the joy is offered as a present reality, but in 4:12f. it lies in the future. (3) The "Amen" in 4:11 is not unexpected when we note that the connection between 4:11 and 4:12 is weak; and there is a complete change of situation between what is future and what is present. (4) The assumption that 1 Peter contains two separate parts can explain the "briefly" in 5:12, which could hardly be used of the whole document, some 1675 words.

Perdelwitz concluded that 1 Peter was originally in two parts. In support of this hypothesis, later scholars have noted that 1:3–4:11 has no genuinely epistolary characteristics. It lacks reference to places and people. The style is polished and balanced, with long measured sentences; the impressive opening in 1:3-9 is matched by an equally

*Plate 57.* Valley of olive trees between Bethlehem and Beit Jālā (J. C. Trever)

*Plate 58.* A fruitful branch of a pomegranate tree (G. Wenham)

*Plate 59.* Palm trees at ʿAin Mûsā, an oasis in the Sinai peninsula that some identify with Marah (Ex. 15:23) (W. S. Lasor)

*Plate 60.* The famous theater at Ephesus (cf. Acts 19:29, 31) (W. S. LaSor)

*Plate 61.* The island of Patmos (A. D. Baly)

*Plate 62.* The Egnatian Road from Kavalla (Neapolis) to Philippi (W. S. LaSor)

*Plate 63.* The mouth of the Dog River (Nahr el-Kalb) on the Phoenician (Lebanese) coast between Beirût and Byblos (W. S. LaSor)

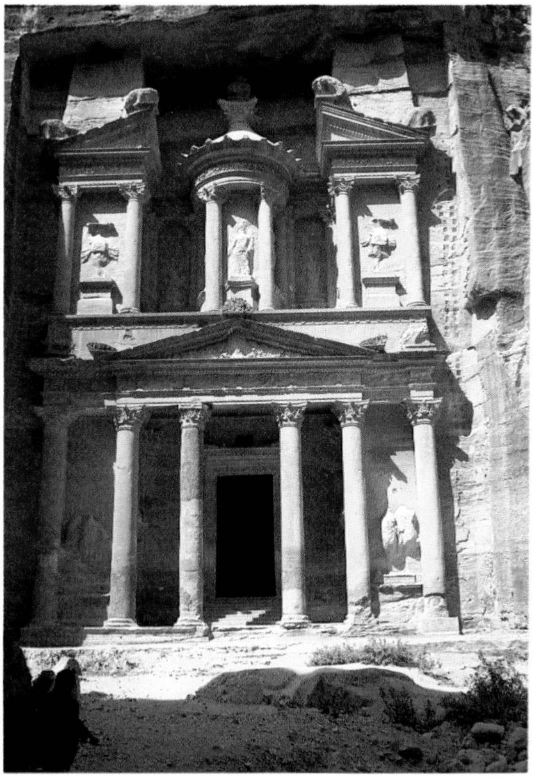

*Plate 64.* The Khazneh Far'un, the most magnificent monument at Petra (W. S. LaSor)

*Plate 65.* The altar of Zeus on the acropolis at Pergamum (W. S. LaSor)

*Plate 66.* Some of the rock-carved tombs at Petra (W. S. LaSor)

*Plate 67.* Persian gold disk (less than 12 cm., 3 in., in diameter) with repousse design. From Amlash, early 1st millennium B.C. (Rosenthal Art Slides)

*Plate 68.* Bichrome amphora with vertical handles. From Cyprus, *ca.* 700-475 B.C. (R. H. Johnston)

*Plate 69.* Early Bronze Age juglets with red slip from Bâb edh-Dhrâʿ. Left juglet has fishnet design (R. H. Johnston)

*Plate 70.* Bronze Age pottery from Bâb edh-Dhrâʿ (*ca.* 3000-2000 B.C.). Decorations include red slip, ledge handles, lug handles, punctate design, and beaded bands (R. H. Johnston)

impressive conclusion, with doxology and Amen. On the other hand, the section 4:12 to the end "breathes an entirely different atmosphere. The style is direct and simple. There are no carefully constructed periods or nicely balanced rhythms and antitheses... it has the quick language of a letter written in haste and under tension" (Beare, p. 7).

The most plausible *Sitz im Leben* of the earlier homiletical document would have been a baptism. Many signs, as Perdelwitz observed, point to the address as having been given to a group of recently baptized neophytes. The converts in mind are living in the first flush of their Christian experience. Thus their joy is still undaunted and exuberant (1:8); 2:1ff. is a clear description of the first stages of their faith and incorporation into Christ and His people. "As a scarlet thread the particle 'now' runs through all the statements of the author," says Perdelwitz (p. 18). And this is an important factor in interpreting 3:21: "Baptism... *now* saves you." One of the most impressive arguments for the origin of 1 Peter as a baptismal sermon is the evidence of the use of catechetical forms in the earlier part of the Epistle.

It seems that this is as far as we can go in placing the document in the worshiping life of the early communities of believers. But two closely allied views try to take the description of the *Sitz im Leben* considerably farther.

*C. Baptismal Liturgy*. The views of Preisker and Cross are treated together because of the way in which the second has sprung out of the first, although they might be mutually exclusive.

In his revision of the commentary by Windisch, Preisker understood 1 Peter as not simply the report of a baptismal service or the incorporating of baptismal material into a genuinely epistolary form but as the transcript of an actual baptismal service, in progress at the time of writing. It is an eyewitness account of the rite in its several stages and embodies the various contributions made by those who take part. Thus Preisker called 1 Peter "the oldest document of a primitive Christian divine service." The first question that comes to mind in reading this startling description is, "How did such a service report come to get mixed up, without explanation, with a document that purports to be a letter sent to churches in Asia and written in the name of a single individual?" This question is still unanswered when we have read all that Preisker and his supporters have told us in defense of their theory. This surely is the gaping hole in the side of this hypothesis, as Moule observed (*Essays*, p. 137). Best asked pertinently what interest Christians in Asia Minor would have in the baptismal liturgy of the church at Rome. "It is impossible to envisage the situation in Asia Minor which would have called out the need for the liturgy, nor the circumstances in Rome which would have led to its communication" (comm., p. 22).

Preisker's analysis has been summarized in the writings of Beare, Best, Cross, Cranfield, Moule, and Walls. This discussion will treat only those points on which criticism has fastened. One of the main supporting beams for this thesis is the distinction in verb tenses. In 1:3-21 the sanctification is future, but at 1:22f. it is taken as something fully achieved. Therefore, Preisker boldly concluded that the baptism took place between 1:21 and 1:22 but is not reported openly because it belongs to the secret training (*disciplina arcani*) of the Church. This looks suspiciously like an excuse to avoid an obvious criticism of the theory! The text hardly supports the theory anyway. The present participles must be taken as anticipating the future privileges of those being baptized, but, as Beare says, "it seems quite arbitrary to neglect the aorist *anagennēsas* (1:3) and to treat the present participle (in 1:5) as a future." The rigid division of ch. 1 into the two tenses of future (looking forward to baptismal act) and past (in recognition of what it has accomplished) will not hold. The tense in 1:3 is past, and there are ethical exhortations in 1:22.

Another supporting beam in Preisker's reconstruction is the presence of "stylistic peculiarities." He writes that the document contains "separate, self-contained sections, laid side by side, without transitions, each with its own stylistic peculiarities" (p. 157). In this way he is able to report, as though he himself had been present at the baptism, who spoke each part of the service. Characters flit across the stage in a bewildering array. When the neophytes have been baptized they take a brief vow (1:22-25), but the three-strophe hymn of 2:1-10 is sung by a Spirit-possessed individual. A "new preacher stands up in the community" at 2:11 and delivers a piece of exhortation that culminates in a hymn to Christ (2:21-24). Here Preisker accepts without demur Bultmann's conclusion that the author of this hymn took over a previously existing hymn. But this raises a difficulty: Are we to think of the hymn as coming spontaneously to the lips of the congregation (as is presumably the case in the record of 1 Cor. 14) or as their reciting, with adaptation, of something traditionally known in the Church? At 3:13 the style changes and another figure, an apocalyptist, comes forward to give an eschatological word as his contribution. This extends to 4:7a. The remaining verses to 4:11 are the final prayer of the baptism service. To account for the rest of the document Preisker held that the whole congregation is brought in at that point for a concluding service, which includes an eschatological address (4:12-19), an exhortation to the elders and young people, and finally a piece of "didactic instruction" from the presbyter, rounded off by a concluding blessing from another presbyter, who, said Beare rather drily, has evidently been sitting in the corner all the time.

The argument from linguistic style is notoriously uncertain (cf. C. F. D. Moule, *Epistles to the Colossians and Philemon* [1957], pp. 61f.); and the one place in his discussion where Preisker brought forward some objective criteria (in his attempt, on stylistic grounds, to posit a "common authorship" of 2:11–3:12 and the *paráklēsis* of vv. 1-9) is far from persuasive.

That there are differences of style in the entire letter is one thing, and this we may freely grant; but it is quite another thing to assign the various strands of the document to putative speakers (with Preisker) or to allocate them to different provenances (as Lohse proposes). With Beare it is better to say that the author of 1 Peter is a writer who evinces "the variations of a good prose stylist," at the same time giving due weight to the possibility that he has incorporated into his treatise fragments of hymns and confessions that may have been part of the common property of the early churches. But anything resembling the patchwork that Preisker or Lohse suggests seems to be imposing a theory on the evidence. Beare's conclusion best explains the literary phenomena of 1 Peter: "Rather than the direct use of fragments of a liturgy, the evidence seems to me to indicate a sermon developed along lines suggested by the structure of the liturgy, perhaps with an occasional outright quotation of familiar credal formulas, but as a rule freely expressed in the writer's own words and style" (p. 226).

Citation of this conclusion tends to prejudge the issue of Cross's modification of Preisker's arrangement. Cross built upon the hypothesis of his predecessor and sought ostensibly to improve it in one important respect. Accepting 1:3–4:11 as a baptismal liturgy reporting an actual baptism in progress, Cross believed that we can more precisely identify the document as the celebrant's part in the Easter baptismal service.

Cross found his chief support in the notion that the key to much of the imagery of the document is the Easter celebration of the primitive Church. He traced many Easter (or paschal) motifs in the language of the letter. The typology of the Exodus pervades much of the text: e.g., in 1:18f. (as indeed in many of the allusions in 1:3-21) the background is clearly that of the Passover. Similarly, in 2:9f. the language is borrowed directly from Ex. 19:5f., which describes the giving of the Torah by which the Exodus deliverance was completed. The "Paschal theology," as Cross called it, is summarized in the exordium of vv. 3-12, which embodies the whole meaning of the Easter message. This assumption is obviously fundamental to Cross's hypothesis. This basic supposition of the paschal background of the letter has been assailed by T. C. G. Thornton in *JTS*, 12 (1961), 14-26; but see A. R. C. Leaney, *NTS*, 10 (1963/64), 238-251, for a contrary view.

By a skillful blending of the conclusions that he either reached or adopted, Cross went on to state his final verdict on 1 Peter. It is a liturgical document, as far as 1:3–4:11 is concerned. He confessed to an embarrassment when faced with the remainder of the letter. He felt that Preisker's suggestion that it contains an address to the whole company then assembled is lacking in conviction, but he had nothing to offer to take its place. But any literary theory that is left with 4:12–5:14 on its hands as a kind of inconvenient surd is under a cloud of suspicion.

As far as the structure of the formula is concerned, Cross's revision and new setting require alterations in Preisker's analysis. In the main, these modifications are in the form of attributing an author to the principal sections of the document, and it is the role of the celebrant that dominates the scene in Cross's reconstruction. Thus Cross has virtually fathered a new hypothesis altogether. He placed all the addresses in one mouth and ignored many of the hymns that earlier scholars had confidently classified. The result is that the "baptismal liturgy" theory is gone — if by that is meant the record of a service in progress. Instead we have, as J. W. C. Wand put it, "not so much the liturgy itself as the Bishop's running commentary on the liturgy" (*Interp.*, 9 [1955], 388). It is a serious weakness in the baptismal liturgy theory that its advocates are thus divided in the way in which the text is apportioned to the different participants in the rite. This divergence diminishes confidence in the theory as a whole; and both Preisker's and Cross's arrangement must meet Moule's objection that it is difficult to imagine "how a liturgy-homily, shorn of its 'rubrics'... but with its changing tenses and broken sequences all retained, could have been hastily dressed up as a letter and sent off (without a word of explanation) to Christians who had not witnessed its original setting" (*Essays*, p. 137). This point is made in the course of Moule's thorough examination of the Preisker-Cross hypothesis. The result of this examination is that alternative explanations can be provided for all the evidence that they bring forward in support. This lends extra weight to the observation made above. The final judgment, therefore, on this stimulating proposal must be "not proved."

This verdict is shared by Best (comm., pp. 22f.), who argued that 1:3–4:11 is more like a baptismal sermon than a liturgical sequence. He noted the cluster of baptismal ideas in 1:3, 23; 2:2, with 2:1 a possible allusion to a person's putting off clothing before the baptism (p. 24). Credal forms may be embodied in the baptismal hymns of 1:3-5: 3:18-22. In this assessment Best was joined by a number of scholars, e.g., Kelly (pp. 17-20) and Blevins. Blevins accepted Moule's earlier theory that 1:3–4:11 represents a baptismal sermon preached to new converts, whereas 4:12–5:11 may well be a sermon to the larger congregation already involved in a later persecution. But Best was soundly critical of so dividing the letter, and Goppelt offered an analysis of the letter that requires no such partitioning (comm., p. 42).

*D. Some Conclusions.* (1) The epistolary form of 1 Peter must be our fixed starting point, and only the strongest reasons will compel us to regard it as other than what it purports to be: an apostolic letter.

(2) There is ample precedent in the Pauline corpus for the belief that a genuine letter may embody sections of catechetical and cultic material. The researches of Seeberg, Carrington, and Selwyn in regard to the catechetical material, and Hunter, Cullmann, and Lohmeyer in respect of the cultic material, have amply demonstrated that the NT writers took over and incorporated into their literature pieces of parenesis, psalms and hymns of Christian worship, and rudimentary confession of faith and catechetical material. The rite of initiation in baptism was exactly the occasion when much of this material was used and transmitted to the convert. The presence of liturgical terms, the exalted, hieratic language, and the lyrical turns of expression in 1 Peter may be accounted for in this way.

The data of catechetical material in 1 Peter drawn from a wide variety of sources have been shown in some notable studies. Lohse investigated the pre-Christian elements in the parenetic tradition. The main interest, however, has centered on the relation of the teaching in 1 Peter to the Gospel tradition, both Synoptic and Johannine. E. Best has an important discussion, concluding that some evidence, though not much, points to an intimate connection between 1 Peter and the apostle Peter's teaching reported in Acts and in Mark's Gospel (*NTS*, 16 [1969/70], 95-113; summarized in his comm., pp. 52-54). R. H. Gundry, however, in two essays examined echoes of the words of Christ in 1 Peter and concluded that the letter was dictated by Peter in Rome (*NTS*, 13 [1966/67], 336-350; *Biblica*, 55 [1974], 211-232). Best's denial of 1 Peter's close dependence on the Synoptic tradition and Goppelt's remark (comm., p. 53, endorsed by Blevins, p. 408) that the Fourth Gospel has no visible contact with 1 Peter are both challenged by G. Maier, "Jesustradition in 1. Petrusbrief," to be published in R. T. France and D. Wenham, eds., *Gospel Perspectives*. The debate evidently continues.

The use of catechetical material paralleled in the Pauline corpus and other NT hortatory literature has also been scrutinized. The closest agreements are between 1 Peter and Romans (data in Best, comm., pp. 32-34; Best traces the affinity to a tradition common in the church at Rome, though conceding that Peter got to know Paul's theology before he came to Rome, where he was martyred; 1 Peter, however, seems unaffected by the most distinctive influences traceable to the Pauline theology) and between 1 Peter and Ephesians (see C. L. Mitton, *Epistle to the Ephesians* [1951]; *Ephesians* [*NCBC*, 1976], pp. 17f., arguing that the author of 1 Peter used Ephesians; also J. Coutts, *NTS*, 3 [1956/57], 115-127, who sees behind 1 Pet. 1:3-12 and Eph. 1:3-14 a common liturgical tradition comprising a baptismal prayer; similarly M. -E. Boismard, *Quatre Hymnes*, pp. 15-56). Best (comm., pp. 35f.), moreover, supported this dependence and argued that the author of 1 Peter knew both Romans and Ephesians; or, as the present consensus dictates, the Petrine circle, which cherished Peter's memory and sought to apply his teaching to their situation, drew upon shared catechetical instruction found in the church at Rome.

One discordant note to make this chorus (joined by J. H. Elliott, *Home*) less than universal is the observation that there are parallels between 1 Peter and the Epistle of James in their respective parenetic emphases, so 1 Peter "gives testimony to sources available to the early church emerging from the Palestinian background and breaking into the Greek world" (Blevins, p. 408).

While the origin of catechetical traditions may be in dispute, there is a strong body of opinion that sees 1 Peter as containing identifiable baptismal teaching, whether liturgical or sermonic. This position has been challenged by those who find their chief clue to 1 Peter's composition in its function as an apologetic tract addressed to a community undergoing social ostracism, not as a liturgical document (see II above). Nevertheless, we aver that the connection with the baptismal rite is evident and we explain much of the liturgical data as the borrowing of material from such a service, although the borrowing may be unconscious and indirect and may have passed through the author's mind, making it thereby his very own.

(3) On this basis it may be possible to avoid giving too prominent a place to those verses that seem to require the letter's partitioning. If liturgical forms are incorporated, some of the cogency of the view that there is a break at 4:11 is destroyed, especially if W. Nauck has proved his point that there is no need to think of a change in the type of distress that had come upon the Church in the two parts of the Epistle. The case for the letter's unity is still arguable (see W. Nauck, *ZNW,* 46 [1955], 80; and W. J. Dalton, *Christ's Proclamation to the Spirits* [1956], who also vindicates the Epistle's unity).

(4) In conclusion, the issue of the literary origins of 1 Peter is stated in G. W. H. Lampe's words: "That 1 Peter makes use of baptismal material and is concerned with baptism is generally agreed. It remains an open question whether it is a genuine epistle, or whether it is indeed a liturgy embodied in a kind of letter" (*Expos.T.*, 71/12 [1960], 361). The evidence offered is such that the second alternative is not imperatively required; and the peculiarities of the letter may be attributed to the use of a special source. 1 Peter stands as a genuine letter but as including two baptismal homilies, one delivered before the other after the rite (see O. S. Brooks, *Nov.Test.*, 16 [1974], 290-305).

***Bibliography.***–Comms. by F. W. Beare (3rd ed. 1969); E. Best (*NCBC*, repr. 1982); C. Bigg (*ICC*, 2nd ed. 1910); C. E. B. Cranfield (*Torch,* 1950); L. Goppelt (*KEK,* 1978); U. Holzmeister (1937); J. N. D. Kelly (*HNTC,* 1969); R. Knopf (*KEK,* 1912); A. R. C. Leany (*CBC,* 1967); H. Preisker — see Windisch; B. Reicke (*AB,* 1964); H. Rendtorff (7th ed. 1951); K. H. Schelkle (*HTK,* 1961); J. Schneider (*NTD,* 9th ed. 1961); E. Schweizer (2nd ed. 1949); E. G. Selwyn (2nd ed. 1947, repr. 1981); A. M. Stibbs and A. F. Walls (*Tyndale NT Comms.*, 1959); H. Windisch (*HNT,* 1930; 3rd ed. [rev. H. Preisker] 1951); G. Wohlenberg (*KZNT,* 3rd ed. 1923).

D. L. Balch, *Let Wives Be Submissive: The Domestic Code in 1 Peter* (1981) (review by R. P. Martin, *Journal for the Study of the NT,* 117 [1983], 103-105); W. Bieder, *Grund und Kraft der Mission nach dem 1. Petrusbrief* (1950); J. L. Blevins, *Review and Expositor,* 79 (1982), 401-413; M. -E. Boismard, *Quatre hymnes baptismales dans la première épître de Pierre* (1961); R. Bultmann, *ConNT,* 11 (1947), 1-14; F. L. Cross, *1 Peter: A Paschal Liturgy* (1954); O. Cullmann, *Peter: Disciple — Apostle — Martyr* (Eng. tr., 2nd ed. 1962); J. H. Elliott, *The Elect and the Holy* (1966) — 1 Pet. 2:4-10; *Home for the Homeless* (1981); E. Lohse, *ZNW,* 45 (1954), 68-89 (repr. in *Die Einheit des NT* [1973], pp. 307-328); C. F. D. Moule, "The Nature and Purpose of 1 Peter," in *Essays in NT Interpretation* (1982), pp. 133-145 (repr. from *NTS*, 3 [1956/57], 1-11); R. Perdelwitz, *Die Mysterienreligionen und das Problem des 1. Petrusbriefes* (1911); B. Reicke, *Disobedient Spirits and Christian Baptism* (1946) — 1 Pet. 3:19; A. Schlatter, *Petrus und Paulus nach dem ersten Petrusbrief* (1937).

R. P. MARTIN

**PETER, GOSPEL OF.** *See* APOCRYPHAL GOSPELS III.A.

## PETER, SECOND EPISTLE OF.

I. Contents
II. Attestation
III. Form
IV. Theological Themes
V. Historical Setting

***I. Contents.***–*A. Words of Greeting (1:1f.).* The author writes as an apostle to those who have come to share the faith of the apostles. The use of the word "knowledge" (*epignṓsis,* 1:2) serves as the transition to the body of the letter.

*B. The Things Necessary for Life and Godliness (1:3-11).* The things of which Peter speaks are the eight virtues listed in 1:5-7. These virtues begin with "divine power" (1:3) and end with participation in the "divine nature" (1:4) and entrance into God's eternal kingdom (1:12). God's "precious and very great promises" (1:4) are fulfilled in Christians' ability to escape the world's corruption and blindness (1:4, 9) and by the virtues to be confirmed in the knowledge of God (1:3, 8).

*C. Guarantees of the Promises (1:12-21).* Both the exhortations and the promises are solemn reminders of what the readers already know. They come with the unique authority of one about to die (1:12-15). Beyond this, they come from an eyewitness of the transfigured Christ (1:16-18). Finally, they are prophetic words like the inspired utterances of the OT prophets (1:19-21).

*D. Warnings Against False Teachers (2:1-22).* The mention of prophecy leads Peter to speak of false prophets and teachers, soon to infect the Church (2:1-3). He insists first on the certainty that they will be punished (2:3), citing as examples the evil angels, the generation that perished in the flood, and the cities of Sodom and Gomorrah (2:4-8), and concluding with a general principle (2:9). Then he describes the false teachers: they are mindless defiers of authority (2:10-12), bent on pleasure and greed (2:13-16), promising freedom but bringing only slavery and corruption (2:17-22).

*E. Vindication of God's Promise (3:1-18).* The readers are to hold fast to the tradition they have received (3:1f.) in the face of a specific threat: the heretics will scoff at the hope of Christ's coming (3:3f.), forgetting the lesson of the flood (3:5-7) and the difference between God's timetable and mankind's (3:3-10). Christians, knowing how the world will end, must faithfully await the sure fulfillment of God's promise (3:11-18).

***II. Attestation.***–In spite of the famous name it bears, 2 Peter has occupied a modest and at times tenuous place in the canon. In the ancient Church it was the least known of all the NT books and among the last to be accepted into the canon.

The first mention of 2 Peter by name is found in Origen, who already knew of problems surrounding it: "Peter . . . left behind one acknowledged Epistle, and, it may be, a second one; for it is doubted" (*Comm. on John* v.3). Other references by Origen (e.g., *Hom. on Joshua* vii.1) indicate that he himself accepted it as genuine, but these occur only in the later and not always reliable Latin translation by Rufinus. In the 4th cent. Eusebius (*HE* iii.25.3) listed 2 Peter among the "disputed books" (*antilegómena*). He also furnished the information that before Origen, Clement of Alexandria may have known 2 Peter. In his

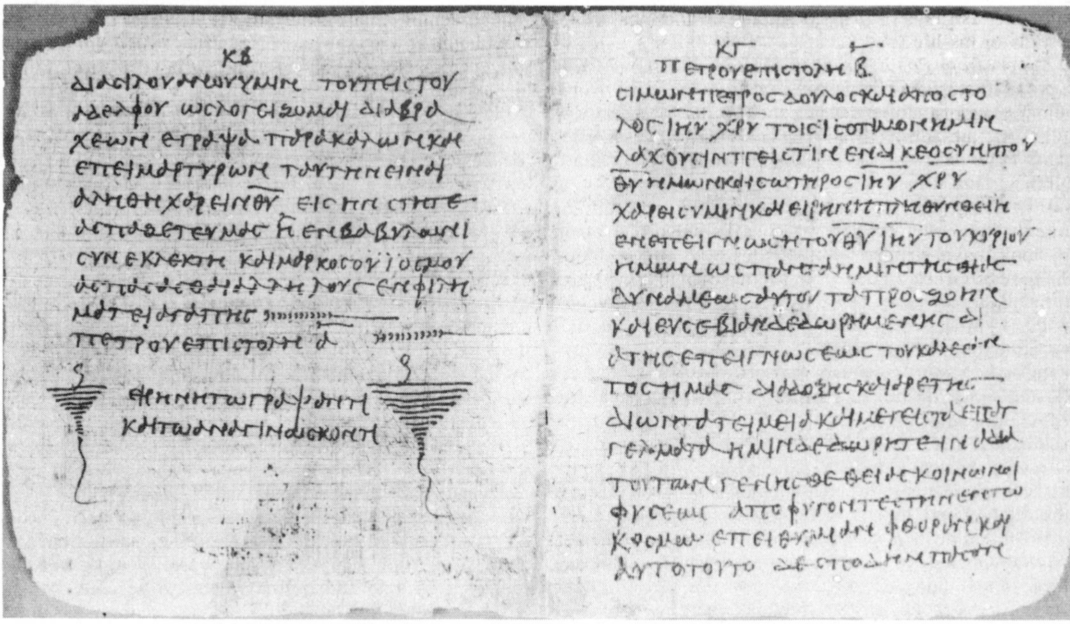

Bodmer Papyrus VII (*ca.* A.D. 300) showing 1 Pet. 5:12-14; 2 Pet. 1:1-5 (Foto Biblioteca Vaticana)

brief commentaries (*Hypotypōseis*) Clement did not pass over "even the disputed writings [*antilegómena*], I mean the Epistle of Jude and the remaining Catholic Epistles, and the Epistle of Barnabas and the Apocalypse known as Peter's" (*HE* vi.14.1). But caution must be used in drawing conclusions from Eusebius's witness, for only fragments of Clement's *Hypotypōseis* have been preserved, and none of these deals with any part of 2 Peter. Moreover, Eusebius's inclusion of Barnabas and the Apocalypse of Peter among the "disputed" books suggests that he was not here referring to the categories with any exactness, for in *HE* iii.25.3 he listed these works as "rejected" (*nóthoi*).

The evidence for the early use of 2 Peter is somewhat increased by the publication in 1959 of the Bodmer papyri VII-IX ($p^{72}$). This third- or fourth-century codex from Egypt contains 1 and 2 Peter and Jude (all copied by the same scribal hand) along with Pss. 33 and 34 and a seemingly miscellaneous collection of noncanonical works. Such a grouping makes it difficult to use $p^{72}$ as evidence of 2 Peter's canonicity, but does suggest its association in the Egyptian Church with 1 Peter and with the Epistle of Jude. This helps to explain (a) how the Alexandrian theologians Clement and Origen could have known 2 Peter, and (b) why Jude and both the Petrine Epistles were included when the NT was translated into Coptic (the language of Egypt) in the 3rd century.

Efforts have been made to find allusions to passages from 2 Peter in the literature of the 2nd cent., but none of the suggested parallels has met with general agreement. Perhaps the closest similarities are those found in the Apocalypse of Peter, dating from the mid-2nd cent. (e.g., in the Akhmim Fragment of that work: v. 1, "Many of them shall be false prophets and shall teach ways and diverse doctrines of perdition" [cf. 2 Pet. 2:1]; v. 21, "another place . . . very gloomy" [cf. 2 Pet. 1:19]; vv. 22, 28, "blaspheming the way of righteousness" [cf. 2 Pet. 2:2, 21]). Knowledge of 2 Peter would of course be expected in those circles where the apostle Peter was honored and where legends grew up around him. What is remarkable is not that a few parallels exist, but that they are not closer or more numerous than they are. Essentially the Church up to A.D. 200 is silent about 2 Peter. The Epistle was not attacked; it was simply ignored and seems to have remained virtually unknown until the time of Origen.

*III. Form.*–Second Peter presents itself unmistakably as the work of the apostle Peter (1:1). The author claims to have been an eyewitness of Jesus' glory on the mount of transfiguration (1:16-18), and he can speak of the apostle Paul as "our beloved brother" (3:15). But more specifically, 2 Peter presents itself as Peter's *testament*. A testament is a well-known and easily identifiable literary form. It is a farewell discourse of one who is about to die. Biblical examples include the farewell of Jacob (Gen. 49), of Moses (Dt. 31–33), of Jesus (Mt. 24–25; Jn. 14–16), and of Paul (Acts 20:17-38; 2 Timothy). Apocryphal testaments were assigned in Jewish and/or Christian tradition to Adam, Abraham, Job, Isaac, Solomon, and the twelve sons of Jacob.

The most common elements in this literary form are: (1) a prediction of one's death; (2) reminiscences of the past; (3) predictions of what is to come, often with special emphasis on "hard times" (e.g., tribulation and apostasy); (4) exhortations to the hearers (i.e., the readers) to be faithful through all these things; (5) some kind of positive disclosure of final victory or vindication. These elements are present in 2 Peter. The Apostle cites as his reason for writing the fact that he is soon to die, just as Jesus had told him (1:12-14; cf. Jn. 21:18f.). He warns against false teachers who will come to destroy the Church with their heresies (ch. 2; 3:3-7). He exhorts his readers to guard themselves against this threat and to build lives of faithfulness and virtue (e.g., 1:1-12; 3:11-18), knowing that in the end God will triumph (1:4, 11; 3:8-13). Although 2 Peter bears all the marks of a real letter (address, salutation, closing doxology), it could also have been appropriately named the Testament of Peter.

The classification of 2 Peter as a testament says nothing regarding its authenticity. A testament can be a mere literary device by which an author clothes his message in words falsely attributed to some great man of the past. This is what has happened in the apocryphal testaments of late Judaism. Or a testament can be the genuine product of a man's last days or years summing up the most vital concerns of his life (cf. perhaps D. Bonhoeffer's *Letters and Papers from Prison* [Eng. tr., 3rd ed. 1967]).

Several factors have combined to convince the overwhelming majority of modern scholars that the apostle Peter is *not* the author of 2 Peter in a literary sense:

(1) 2 Peter lacks any wide attestation in the ancient Church.

(2) The language and style of 2 Peter not only differ markedly from 1 Peter, so that it is unlikely that the same man could have written both Epistles, but also include a number of Greek religious and philosophic terms that seem unlikely to have come from a Galilean fisherman like Peter. Moreover, the Epistle exhibits in places an exaggerated rhetorical style more characteristic of Hellenistic Asia Minor than of primitive Christianity.

(3) The situation that is presupposed is indicated by a number of details in 2 Peter that point to a date later than the apostle Peter's death (believed to have been in the 60's): e.g., at least some of Paul's letters have been collected and seem to be regarded as Scripture (3:15f.); the author looks back on the apostles as if they belong to an earlier generation (3:2); he knows of the existence of 1 Peter ("this *second* epistle," 3:1) and, it is urged, capitalizes upon it to gain acceptance for his own writing; most important, perhaps, the first generation of Christians has passed away and the second coming of Christ has been long delayed (3:3ff.).

(4) 2 Peter shows dependence on Jude. A close comparison of these two Epistles suggests (a) a literary relation between them and (b) the priority of Jude. If Jude dates from the 70's or 80's, 2 Peter cannot be much earlier than A.D. 100 and is perhaps considerably later.

On the basis of such arguments, 2 Peter is frequently regarded as the latest of all the NT writings (according to some critics as late as 140 or 150). Denial of traditional views of authorship of particular biblical books is not necessarily accompanied by denial of their authority or religious value. But in the case of 2 Peter, linguistic and historical arguments are sometimes joined with certain negative theological judgments, so that to some extent it is appropriate to speak of a critical "attack." Many scholars of an earlier generation who denied Petrine authorship were careful and sober in their criticism, and very thorough in building their case (e.g., F. H. Chase and J. B. Mayor), but this has not always been true of their successors. The Epistle is often said to move on a distinctly lower ethical plane than most of the rest of the NT (esp. with regard to charity toward one's opponents), and to neglect the central features of the Christian message (the cross and the resurrection of Jesus Christ).

Before such criticisms are accepted, several moderating factors must be kept in mind.

(1) As a testament, 2 Peter speaks clearly of the apostle's approaching death. Early tradition states almost unanimously that Peter died as a martyr in the persecution of the Church by the Emperor Nero *ca.* A.D. 64. Yet the Epistle contains no development of the theme of martyrdom. This is surprising if it is indeed a second-century document, for Christian literature of this period tended more and more to glorify the martyrs. Their heroism and faithfulness to Christ in the face of threats and torture served as an example to Christians everywhere. Before A.D. 100 Clement of Rome could write specifically of Peter's martyrdom: "Let us set before our eyes the good apostles: Peter, who because of unrighteous jealousy suffered not one or two but many trials, and having thus borne witness as a martyr went to the glorious place which was his due . . ." (1 Clem. 5:3f.). It is remarkable that a second-century tract pretending to be Peter's testament would omit any reference to his glorious martyrdom. Such reticence is more what we would expect if Peter were himself the author.

(2) It can be argued that the theme of martyrdom is not developed because 2 Peter is not written (as was 1 Peter) to strengthen the readers against persecution. Rather, it is a polemical tract against certain heresies that confront the Church. But when we think of Peter combating heresy, we cannot but think of the traditional archheretic Simon Magus. Simon comes into contact with the apostle only briefly in the NT (Acts 8:9-24), but a wealth of legend surrounds him in later tradition. In the second- and third-century narrative cycles found in the Acts of Peter and the Pseudo-Clementine Recognitions and Homilies he becomes Peter's constant foe in philosophical debate and in contests of miraculous power. It seems strange that an antiheretical tract in Peter's name from the 2nd cent. would have missed an opportunity to make reference to Simon Magus. But there are none of these legendary features in 2 Peter.

(3) In general 2 Peter is free of the legendary and apocalyptic details that characterize the apocryphal Petrine literature (i.e., the Gospel, the Apocalypse, and the Acts of Peter). In this respect at least, 2 Peter is more like 1 Peter than like any other writing that bears the Apostle's name.

(4) It is doubtful that the mention in 2 Pet. 3:1 of itself as a "second" Epistle implies a reference back to 1 Peter. The author clearly indicates that *both* Epistles in view are reminders of apostolic tradition (perhaps with emphasis on warning about heresy, cf. Jude 17). But this description does not fit 1 Peter, which never refers back to the apostles.

(5) Though the author of 2 Peter claims to be an apostle, he does not model his claim upon that of 1 Peter. His use of the Jewish designation "Symeon (instead of Simon) Peter" is hard to explain as a later fiction. It is a rare form of the name, occurring elsewhere in the NT only on the lips of James (Acts 15:14). By itself, however, it is no proof that 2 Peter is early. The Pseudo-Clementine writings are evidence that primitive Jewish-Christian terms and thought forms survived even in the 2nd and 3rd centuries.

(6) It is by no means certain that 2 Peter is dependent on Jude. It is clear that a literary relation of some sort exists, but the matter of priority is difficult to settle. Is priority to be assigned to the more elaborate and wordy 2 Peter or to the more coherent and compactly written Epistle of Jude? Would a reviser be more likely to expand his source or to abridge it? Examples of both can be cited (e.g., Matthew has expanded Mark's Gospel with material of his own, yet in many individual pericopes he has abridged the earlier Gospel for the sake of conciseness and emphasis on one main point). Sometimes obscure verses in 2 Peter are clarified by their parallels in Jude (e.g., 2:11; cf. Jude 9), while in other cases the reverse is true (e.g., Jude 11; cf. 2 Pet. 2:15f.). It has been argued that 2 Peter is later because it has suppressed Jude's two references to noncanonical literature: 1 Enoch in Jude 14, and (according to Clement and Origen) the Assumption of Moses in Jude 9. But the reasoning is precarious, (a) because in avoiding apocryphal material, 2 Peter stands squarely with most of the rest of the NT, and (b) because later works of the 2nd and 3rd cents. do on occasion make extensive use of noncanonical Jewish literature, often reediting and circulating it for the edification of Christians. Thus the matter of priority remains unresolved. The references to apostolic tradition in Jude 17f. and 2 Pet. 3:2 suggest the possibility that the two Epistles may have used as their common source some antiheresy tract (or tracts) attributed to the apostles. But if there was such a source the parallels are

unfortunately not close enough to permit its reconstruction.

All these considerations indicate that the question of 2 Peter's authenticity is by no means as simple as is sometimes thought. Both the traditional view of Petrine authorship and the modern critical conclusion that this is a second-century tract falsely claiming apostolic origin face serious difficulties. Beyond these two alternatives, only conjectures can be offered. It is possible that 2 Peter may represent a compendium or anthology of traditional Petrine material put together in the form of a testament by one or more of the apostle's followers after his death. Posthumous publication in Peter's name does not necessarily imply any intent to deceive. If the tradition behind 2 Peter was genuinely Petrine (or even if it was thought to be), then the only kind of compiler of the material who might be guilty of fraud would be one who presumptuously signed *his own* name to the apostle's teaching.

There are clues in the Epistle itself that this compendium theory may have some merits. For example, the very passage that stamps this work as a testament hints at a double time perspective. Speaking as Peter, the author makes two distinct statements:

(a) "I think it right, *as long as I am in this body,* to arouse you by way of reminder . . ." (1:13).

(b) "And I will see to it that *after my departure* you may be able *at any time* to recall these things" (1:15). The contrast between Peter's lifetime and the period after his death is striking. The second statement could refer to some other document, unknown to us, which Peter intended to write but never did. If so, it is most plausibly understood as coming from Peter himself. (Who would bolster a false apostolic claim by a vague reference to a nonexistent document?) But it is also possible that 2 Peter embodies within itself *both* stages of the work of bringing to remembrance — "as long as I am in this body," and "after my departure . . . at any time." This might explain why the heretics are predicted as yet to come (2:1) but described as if already present (2:12-19). Moreover, in 3:1ff. it is remarkable that the writer would present himself as Peter by referring to "this second epistle" while in the very same sentence looking back at "your apostles" as figures of the past. Perhaps the term "second" or "secondary epistle" is used in relation not to 1 Peter, but to the traditional Petrine teachings out of which 2 Peter has been built. If so, then the writer has not slipped here by inadvertently speaking of the apostles as past; instead he is consciously and openly speaking from within the framework of his own time. In accordance with Peter's wishes as expressed in the tradition recorded in 2 Pet. 1:15, he attempts to bring Peter's teaching and personality to bear on increasingly complex problems that arose after the apostle's death. The relation of 2 Peter to the historical Peter would then be somewhat analogous to the relation of the Gospel writers to Jesus as they preserved His teaching while adapting it to their own needs. Though the compendium theory explains a number of things, including the stylistic problems of 2 Peter, the slowness with which it became known and accepted, and especially the double time perspective which shows through at times, it falls short of proof and must remain a hypothesis.

***IV. Theological Themes.***–Despite its brevity, 2 Peter has a number of features that give its theology a distinctive stamp. An element in ch. 2 that distinguishes 2 Peter from Jude is that he appeals to the OT for illustrations of God's deliverance of the righteous as well as of His judgment of the wicked (2:9). In accord with a principle grounded in the words of Jesus, the last days will parallel the days of Noah and of Lot (2:5-9; cf. Mt. 24:37ff.; Lk. 17:26-28). Like these ancient figures, Christians live in a world ripe for judgment. Negatively they are those who have escaped the world's corruption (1:4; 2:18, 20), while positively they await a "new heaven and a new earth" (3:13).

History, for 2 Peter, falls into three ages: "the ancient world" (2:5; 3:6), "the present heavens and earth" (3:7), and the world to come (3:10, 13). The dividing points are Noah's flood, and the expected "coming of the day of God" (3:12). As Noah was a "herald of righteousness" in his day, so Christians are heralds of a new world "in which righteousness dwells" (3:13). They look for a day parallel in its import to the flood, but parallel in kind to the judgment on Lot's city of Sodom, a day when "the heavens will pass away with a loud noise and the elements will be dissolved with fire" (3:10). History is thus divided by means of outward physical events that change the course of nature rather than by invisible realities such as redemption or the Spirit. When the author speaks of Jesus, he fastens upon the Transfiguration, with its visible display of Jesus' glory, as a sign of divine power and of Christ's future coming (1:16-18). He claims to have seen Jesus enthroned as king on the "holy mountain" (cf. Ps. 2:6) before his very eyes. This, together with the swift certainty of God's judgment in the past, assures him that the divine promise will be fulfilled. Yet he never revels in the spectacular for its own sake; he appeals to it in the face of a specific threat, but his positive counsel is to grow in the knowledge of God by erecting upon faith a whole ladder of virtues culminating in love (1:5-7). This, as much as the grim warnings that follow, belongs to the substance of his testament.

***V. Historical Setting.***–To say that in some respects the historical setting of 2 Peter looks beyond the lifetime of the apostle does not solve the problem of determining what that setting was. The earliest attestation of the Epistle suggests that it may have come from Egypt, and it is natural to connect the warnings about false teachers with the Gnosticism that flourished in Egypt in the 2nd century. But the author attacks the heretics more for immorality than for false doctrine: they are bent on lust and pleasure (2:2, 13f.), and are greedy for gain (2:14f.); they make extravagant claims for themselves (2:18) while blaspheming angelic beings (2:10ff.); for all this they are doomed to destruction (2:3, 9). These features agree remarkably with certain traditions surrounding the earliest attested form of Gnosticism. This was Simonian Gnosticism, which claimed Simon Magus as its founder. Simon too was charged with immorality and blasphemy of angels (Irenaeus *Adv. haer.* i.23.3f.) and was remembered for his extravagant claims, his greed for money, and his certain destruction (Acts 8:9-24). But since many of these same features became standard elements in the ancient Church's description of heretics, no precise identification of the opponents is possible.

At any rate, no connection can be established between Simon and the scoffers who denied Christ's coming (Irenaeus, par. 3, in fact attributes to Simon a view, shared by 2 Peter, that the world was to be dissolved). Their objections were based mainly on disappointment of eschatological hopes. This problem may have had its origin in Jewish attacks on primitive Christianity. Christians claimed that in Christ the messianic age had dawned, yet it was clear that the world had not been visibly transformed. This made the Church vulnerable to Jewish charges that nothing had really changed since the days of "the fathers" and that therefore the Christian claim was false. Elsewhere, in the NT, "the fathers" uniformly refers to OT figures. It is possible that by the time 2 Peter was written the charge had been taken up even by some within the Church, for whom "the fathers" might have included the first generation of Christians, but this passage should not be pressed too far as evidence for a late date. Its basic idea is ancient enough to be expressed in an anonymous source (Jewish or Christian) cited as "the scripture" by Clement of Rome before A.D. 100, and therefore traceable back almost to the time of Peter (1 Clem. 23:3f.; cf. also 2 Clem. 11:2f.).

Unfortunately 2 Peter is too brief to allow a fuller reconstruction of its historical setting. Unanswered questions remain, particularly regarding the precise relation between chs. 2 and 3. Clearly the same group is in view in both places, but whether the denial of the eschatological hope is the root of all the false teaching, or simply one deviation among many, is not easily determined.

***Bibliography.***–Comms. by A. E. Barnett (*IB*); R. Bauckham (*Word*, 1983); C. Bigg (*ICC*, 2nd ed. 1910); J. Chaine (*EtB*, 1939); C. E. B. Cranfield (*Torch*, 1960); M. Green (*Tyndale NT Comms.*, 1968); J. N. D. Kelly (*HNTC*, 1969); R. Knopf (*KEK*, 7th ed. 1912); A. R. C. Leaney (*CBC*, 1967); J. B. Mayor (1907; repr. 1965); J. Michl (Regensburger NT, 2nd ed. 1968); J. Moffatt (*MNT*, 1928); B. Reicke (*AB*, 1964); K. H. Schelkle (*HTK*, 1961); J. Schneider (*NTD*, 9th ed. 1961); J. Skilton (*NICNT*, 1972); F. Spitta (1885); W. Vrede (4th ed. 1932); J. W. C. Wand (1934); H. Windisch (*HNT*, 3rd ed. 1951); G. Wohlenberg (*KZNT*, 3rd ed. 1923).

E. M. B. Green, *2 Peter Reconsidered* (1961); E. Käsemann, "Apologia for Primitive Christian Eschatology," in *Essays on NT Themes* (Eng. tr., *SBT*, 41, 1964), pp. 169-195; J. H. Neyrey, *JBL*, 99 (1980), 407-431; E. I. Robson, *Studies in the Second Epistle of St. Peter* (1915).

J. R. MICHAELS

**PETHAHIAH** peth-ə-hī'ə [Heb. *p$^e$taḥyâ*–'Yahweh opens'].

**1.** The head of a priestly family, assigned in David's time to the nineteenth division of temple service (1 Ch. 24:16).

**2.** [Gk. Apoc. *Pathaios*, A *Phathaios*]; AV PATHEUS; NEB PHATHAEUS. A Levite who had married a foreign woman and was required to divorce her (Ezr. 10:23 par. 1 Esd. 9:23); probably the same Levite who assisted Ezra in leading a public service of confession after the Israelites had "separated themselves from all foreigners" (Neh. 9:5; cf. vv. 1-3).

**3.** Son of Meshezabel, descendant of Judah; adviser to Zerubbabel in postexilic Jerusalem (Neh. 11:24).

**PETHOR** pē'thôr [Heb. *p$^e$ṯôr*; Gk. *Phathoura*]. Home of Balaam son of Beor, near the Euphrates (Nu. 22:5). In Dt. 23:4 it is further described as being in Aram-naharaim (Mesopotamia), and Nu. 23:7 speaks of Aram and the eastern mountains. Pethor is identified with the Pedru found in geographical lists of Thuthmose III (15th cent. B.C.) and with Pitru, the Hittite name for the Assyrian Ana-Aššurutîr-aṣbat (meaning "I founded [it] anew for Aššur"), a city which Shalmaneser III captured in his third year (857 B.C.) and where he received tribute from the kings of Carchemish, Commegene, Melitene, and other districts. Shalmaneser places Pitru "on the other side of the Euphrates, on the river Sagur" (*ANET*, p. 278). The modern Sājūr flows into the Euphrates from the northwest about 90 km. (60 mi.) NE of Aleppo. Pethor would thus be on the west bank of the Euphrates, probably at the site of Tell el-Aḥmar, 19 km. (12 mi.) S of Carchemish.

R. E. HAYDEN

**PETHUEL** pe-thōō'əl [Heb. *p$^e$ṯû'ēl*]. Father of Joel the prophet (Joel 1:1).

**PETITION** [Heb. *š$^e$'ēlâ, šēlâ*]; NEB PRAYER, PRAY, REQUEST, ASK; [*miš'ālâ*] (Ps. 20:5 [MT 6]); NEB ASK; [*nāśā' pānîm*–'lift (someone's) face'] (1 S. 25:35); AV "accept thy person"; NEB "grant your request"; [Aram. *b$^e$ʿâ, b$^e$ʿā'*–'request, ask, pray' (Dnl. 6:7, 11-13 [MT 8, 12-14]), *bāʿû*–'petition, prayer' (6:7, 13 [MT 8, 14])]; AV also PRAY; NEB also PRAYER; [Gk. *entyncháno*] (Acts 25:24); AV DEAL; NEB APPEAL. A request or appeal made to a powerful ruler or to God.

"Petition" is the language of the court. Queen Esther approaches King Ahasuerus on behalf of her people using a Persian ceremonial formula of making a petition (*š$^e$'ēlâ*; cf. *šā'al*, "ask") and a request (*baqqāšâ*; Est. 5:6-8; 7:2f.; 9:12). In 1 S. 25:23-31 Abigail prostrates herself before David and intercedes with him for the life of her husband Nabal. David responds with kingly FAVOR, "I have hearkened to your voice, and I have granted your petition [lit. "raised your face"]" (v. 35; *see also* PARTIALITY). The concept of appealing to a ruler is present also in Acts 25:24, where Festus tells King Agrippa that "the whole Jewish people petitioned me" concerning the apostle Paul (see *TDNT*, VIII, *s.v.* τυγχάνω κτλ.: ἐντυγχάνω [O. Bauernfeind]).

Elsewhere "petition" occurs in the sense of PRAYER. King Darius issued a decree prohibiting anyone from making "petition to any god or man for thirty days," except to Darius himself (Dnl. 6:7). Thus, for one month the king alone was to be the god to whom all religious petitions were directed (see comms., e.g., *IB*, VI, 440f.). Because Daniel rejected this idolatry and was found "making petition and supplication before his God" (v. 11 [MT 12]) three times daily (vv. 12f. [MT 13f.]), he was thrown into the den of lions as the interdict prescribed (v. 16 [MT 17]). In 1 S. 1:10f. Hannah, old and barren, prayed that God would give her a child. Eli the priest blessed her, "Go in peace, and the God of Israel grant your petition [Heb. *šēlâ*] which you have made to him" (v. 17). When Hannah brought the young Samuel to Eli, she proclaimed God's faithfulness, "For this child I prayed; and the Lord has granted me my petition [*š$^e$'ālâ*]" (v. 27). In the same spirit the community intercedes on behalf of the king, "May the Lord fulfil all your petitions!" (Ps. 20:5 [MT 6]). Interestingly, the only other passage that uses *miš'ālâ* (Ps. 37:4; RSV "desire") also speaks of the Lord fulfilling the prayerful desires of one who trusts in Him during times of trouble (see *TWOT*, II, 892).

D. K. MCKIM
W. R. HARRIS

**PETRA** pe'trə. Capital city of the Nabateans, commonly identified with biblical SELA. Petra ("the rock") is located in a semi-landlocked valley some 80 km. (50 mi.) S of the Dead Sea. The valley owes its modern name, Wâdī Mûsā ("the valley of Moses"), to local folklore identifications with the Mosaic tradition. The nearest modern village, and the starting point for tourist visits today, is el-Ji (the Gaia of Eusebius *Onom.*). Access to the site is generally through the eastern ridge (el-Kubtha) via the Sîq ("cleft"), a narrow, winding geologic fissure.

If we assume its identity with Sela, the city is first mentioned in historical times in connection with Amaziah's defeat of "the men of Seir" (2 K. 14:7; 2 Ch. 25:11f.). At

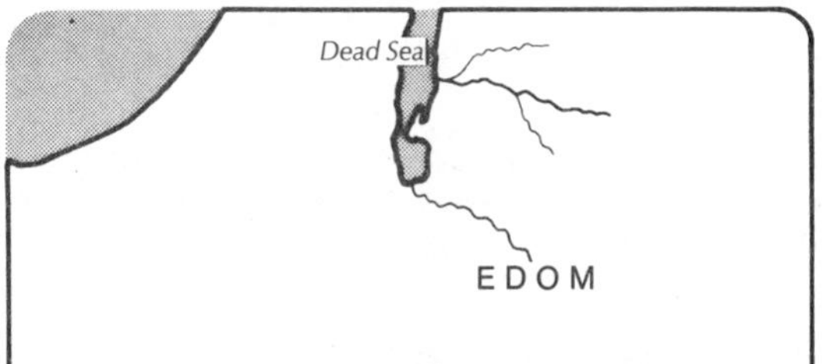

that time it was an Edomite stronghold near the King's Highway, the major communication route in Transjordan. How much earlier the Edomites had taken over the site has not yet been determined, but it appears to have coincided with the early Iron Age in Syro-Palestine. The presence of Upper Paleolithic and Neolithic remains in the vicinity of the site, and especially at nearby Beidha, indicates a considerable early occupation.

Nothing more is known of the site, however, until 312 B.C., when the Greeks raided the area, according to Diodorus Siculus (*see* NABATEANS). By that point Petra had already become a Nabatean center; it would rise in the next few centuries to become the capital of one of the greatest commercial kingdoms known in the ancient Near East. The next report of the city and its people comes from the early 2nd cent. B.C. (2 Macc. 5:8). By then the Nabatean kingdom had begun to press on Jewish-held territory to the north, and the Nabateans had begun to be involved in the intrigues of the Hasmonean court. Here the influence of Antipater, whose wife was a Nabatean, figures greatly.

After Petra fell to the forces of Trajan in A.D. 106, it was honored by the title of *colonia* and beautified with a few public buildings but was actually in its final stages of decline. The capital of Provincia Arabia eventually shifted elsewhere, and in strategic commercial importance Petra was superseded by other cities.

During the Byzantine period some slight Christian occupation of Petra took place, as inscriptions and architectural remains suggest. Yet this was negligible, and no real resurgence of urban power developed. The episcopal see that bore the name of Petra did not even refer to Petra at all but to nearby Kerak. Enough Christian influence remained, in the form of monasticism, however, for the "monks of St. Aaron" to be found in the area as late as the Crusades.

During the early period of the Crusades Petra regained strategic value and was refortified. The ancient name of the site had been lost, however; the fortress, at el-Wuʿeira just outside the Sîq, was known as the fortress of the "valley of Moses." Petra's resurgence was based upon the same factor that had made it a major commercial center under the Nabateans — the convergence of the land caravan routes from the south that led west to Gaza and the sea and north to Damascus. The Latin kingdom was in dire need of financial sustenance. Hence minor installations were established inside the ancient city area to police the caravan routes, and the caravans were taxed as a source of revenue from time of Baldwin I (A.D. 1100-1118) onward. The disastrous defeat of the Crusader forces at the Horns of Hattin in A.D. 1187 was felt at Petra as well; once more its position was no longer strategic, as Islamic control returned over the whole area.

Rediscovered in 1812 by J. L. Burckhardt, Petra — "the rose-red city half as old as time" — was visited by a number of learned travelers and scholars until it became a major tourist attraction in modern times. It is primarily known today for its fantastic natural beauty and the hundreds of rock-carved facades left by the Nabateans. Among the best known of these are the Khazneh Farʿun (the "treasury of the pharaoh"), ed-Deir ("the monastery"), and the "royal tombs." Dozens of others exist, mostly off the usual tourist trails, as well as scores of rock-hewn stairways, cultic places, and religious carvings. Among the cultic places, the "great high place," discovered by Robinson early in the present century, is one of the finest examples of open-air cultic centers in the Near East. *See* picture in HIGH PLACE.

The enormous Roman temple, ed-Deir, about 50 m. (175 ft.) high, was carved by the Roman conquerors of this Nabatean stronghold in the 3rd cent. A.D. (Jordan Information Bureau)

Roman-style amphitheater at Petra carved out of red sandstone (B. VanElderen)

In addition to these structures, a monumental theater near the Sîq entrance to the city has been excavated by an American expedition in cooperation with the Department of Antiquities of Jordan. The theater's seating area was rock-carved, with stage and scenery of built masonry, and it could hold seven thousand spectators. Only since the excavations under the direction of P. C. Hammond has the

Nabatean origin of this Roman-style structure been proved. Later Roman restyling had obscured its original builders' identity.

The Roman remains of Petra have become more apparent only in the last few years, as the Jordan Department of Antiquities uncovered, restored, and preserved some of them. The paved Roman street, with colonnade and shop fronts, the massive triple-arched gate, and the temple called Qasr Bint Farʿun have been given attention. Likewise, various clearings of rubble, tourist trails, and other features have been undertaken, including the restoration of the ancient barrage at the mouth of the Sîq. The latter work was both a restoration and a safety measure, since the barrage diverts flood waters from the Sîq through an original tunnel and around the city.

The hydraulic engineering skill of the Nabateans at Petra and elsewhere has also come under scientific study. At Petra the remains of vast cisterns, old runnels, catchment basins, and a vast system of pressure pipes may still be seen.

Excavations at Petra have been undertaken by G. Horsfield, W. F. Albright, M. Murray, P. Parr, D. Kirkbride, P. C. Hammond, and others. Much completely new material on the life, culture, language, numismatics, and historical connections of the Nabateans and their capital city has been brought to light. As a consequence, the extraordinary commercial and cultural role of Petra among the great caravan cities of the ancient Near East has become more recognized and appreciated.

*See also* Plates **64**, **66**.

***Bibliography.***–*EAEHL*, *s.v.* "Petra"; P. C. Hammond, *BA*, 23 (1960), 29-32; *The Nabataeans–Their History, Culture and Archaeology* (1973); A. Kammerer, *Pétra et la Nabatène* (2 vols., 1929-30); A. Kennedy, *Petra, Its History and Monuments* (1925); *see also* NABATEANS, Bibliography. P. C. HAMMOND

**PEULLETHAI** pē-ul'ə-thī [Heb. *peʿullᵉṯay*–'reward of Yahweh'(?)]; AV, NEB, PEULTHAI pē-ul'thī. A Levite, eighth son of Obed-edom; a gatekeeper of the temple storehouse (1 Ch. 26:5; cf. v. 15).

**PHAATH-MOAB** fā'ath mō'ab (AV, NEB, 1 Esd. 5:11; NEB 8:31). *See* PAHATH-MOAB.

**PHACARETH** fak'ə-reth (1 Esd. 5:34, AV, NEB). *See* POCHERETH-HAZZEBAIM.

**PHAESUS** fē'səs (1 Esd. 9:22, NEB); **PHAISUR** fā'zər (AV). *See* PASHHUR **4.**

**PHALDAEUS** fal-dē'əs (1 Esd. 9:44, NEB); **PHALDAIUS** fal-dā'əs (AV). *See* PEDAIAH **5.**

**PHALEAS** fə-lē'əs (1 Esd. 5:29, AV, NEB). *See* PADON.

**PHALEC** fā'lek (Lk. 3:35, AV). *See* PELEG.

**PHALLU** fal'o͞o (Gen. 46:9, AV). *See* PALLU.

**PHALTI** fal'tī (1 S. 25:44, AV). *See* PALTI **2.**

**PHALTIEL** fal'ti-əl.

**1.** [Lat. *Phalthihel, Salathiel*]; AV SALATHIEL. A "chief of the people" who came to Ezra between his first and second visions (2 Esd. 5:16).

**2.** (2 S. 3:15, AV). *See* PALTIEL **2.**

**PHANTOMS** [Heb. *ṣelem*–'image'] (Ps. 73:20); AV IMAGE; NEB IMAGES IN SLEEP. This difficult verse reads literally, "As a dream when one awakes, O Lord, in the city their image you shall despise." Heb. *ṣelem* often refers to an idol ("image," 1 S. 6:5, 11; 2 K. 11:18), although it is also used in a less concrete sense ("shadow," Ps. 39:6 [MT 7]). Thus D. J. A. Clines (*Tyndale Bulletin*, 19 [1968], 74f.) states that *ṣelem* here means "an insubstantial non-physical object, a dream-object; yet it is recognizably the shape or configuration of something." See the comms. for other interpretations of this verse. G. A. L.

**PHANUEL** fan'yo͞o-əl, fə-no͞o'əl [Gk. *Phanouēl* (= Heb. *pᵉnû'ēl*)–'face of God'; *see* PENUEL]. Parent (probably father) of Anna the prophetess (Lk. 2:36).

**PHARAKIM** fâr'ə-kim [Gk. B *Pharakem*, A *Pharakeim*]; AV PHARACIM. Head of a family of temple servants who returned from the Exile with Zerubbabel (1 Esd. 5:31). The name is omitted in par. Ezr. 2:51; Neh. 7:53.

**PHARAOH** fā'rō, fā'rā-ō [Heb. *parʿōh*; Gk. *Pharaṓ*; Egyp. *pr-ʿ3*–'great house']. The common OT title for the kings of ancient Egypt. It derives from a phrase used for the royal palace and court until the New Kingdom when, in the mid-18th Dynasty, it came to be used of the king himself. It first so occurs under Thutmose III and IV (15th cent. B.C.), then with Ikhnaton (*ca.* 1360), and thereafter frequently. (See W. C. Hayes, *JEA*, 46 [1960], 41f.; A. H. Gardiner, *Egyptian Grammar* [3rd ed. 1957], p. 75 and n. 10; J. Vergote, *Joseph en Égypte* [1959], pp. 45-48.)

The biblical and Egyptian uses of "pharaoh" correspond closely. Thus in the Pentateuch "Pharaoh" is used without a proper name precisely as in Egypt in the later 14th to 10th cents. B.C. (thus including Moses' time). From the 10th cent. B.C. onward "Pharaoh" plus a proper name became common usage; cf. Pharaoh Hophra and Pharaoh Neco. The phrase "Pharaoh king of Egypt" is a purely Hebrew phrase (parallelistic) and so not datable by reference to Egyptian sources.

Since pharaohs before the time of Solomon are not mentioned by their own names in the OT, their identities can only be approximated on general chronological grounds. Thus Abraham's pharaoh (Gen. 12) probably belonged to the 12th Dynasty, and Joseph's to the Hyksos (15th Dynasty) or their immediate predecessors. The pharaoh(s) of the oppression preceded and terminated in the pharaoh of the Exodus; these rulers were most likely Ramses II and his predecessors (esp. Seti I and perhaps Harmhab; *see* EXODUS, DATE OF THE). The date of Bithiah and her father (1 Ch. 4:18) is unknown. The pharaoh that took Gezer and gave it with his daughter's hand to Solomon (1 K. 3:1; 9:16) belonged to the 21st Dynasty and was perhaps Siamun; *see* EGYPT II; PHARAOH'S DAUGHTER. To that line would also belong the Edomite Hadad's host (1 K. 11). For kings SHISHAK, SO, TIRHAKAH, NECO, and HOPHRA, *see* separate articles; Zerah was not a king but a general.

Isaiah 19:11 well reflects Egyptian pride in the continuity of pharaonic tradition, for every pharaoh was the successor to the whole line of earlier kings and joined their august company at death (cf. H. W. Fairman, "Kingship Rituals of Egypt," in S. H. Hooke, ed., *Myth, Ritual, and Kingship* [1958], pp. 99f., 103f.).

Pharaoh was a god by office yet himself human (cf. G. Posener, *De la divinité du Pharaon* [1960]; J. G. Griffiths, *JEA*, 49 [1963], 189-192); he was considered responsible for the welfare of Egypt, even including the Nile (cf. Ezk. 29:3; sources quoted by S. Morenz, *Die Heraufkunft des Transzendenten Gottes in Aegypten* [1964], p. 48 and n. 2). K. A. KITCHEN

**PHARAOH HOPHRA.** *See* HOPHRA.

**PHARAOH NECO.** *See* NECO.

**PHARAOH'S DAUGHTER** [Heb. *baṯ-parʿōh*].

**1.** The woman who rescued and adopted Moses (Ex. 2). She was probably one of many members of a harem at a delta pleasure palace. She would be a daughter (not necessarily the sole one) of a predecessor of Ramses II, the most probable pharaoh of the Exodus.

**2.** A wife of Solomon (1 K. 3:1; 7:8; 9:16, 24; 11:1). Since Shishak ruled Egypt twenty years before raiding Palestine in Rehoboam's fifth year, he acceded about year 25 of Solomon's reign. Shishak's predecessor Psusennes II ruled about fourteen years (acceding about year 11 of Solomon). Hence in his first few years Solomon probably married a daughter of the preceding king, Siamun. Her name is unknown because no contemporary records of Siamun's family have been recovered. Marriage with a pharaoh's daughter was a special honor.

*Bibliography.*–A. Malamat, *JNES*, 22 (1963), 9-17; *BA*, 21 (1958), 96-102 (repr. in *Biblical Archaeologist Reader*, II [1964], 89-94).

**3.** Bithiah, who married Mered (1 Ch. 4:18). Her date and identity are unknown. K. A. KITCHEN

**PHARATHON** fär'ə-thon [LXX Gk. *Pharathon*]; AV PHARATHONI. The LXX reads *kaí tḗn Thamnatha Pharathōni* (see NEB) but Josephus (*Ant.* xiii.1.3 [14-16], which spells the name *Pharanthō*) and the Syriac insert an "and" between the two names, thus listing two separate cities. (The LXX may have omitted the *kaí tḗn* before *Pharathōni*; so Rahlfs, *Septuaginta*.)

Pharathon is a city in Judea which was fortified by Bacchides (1 Macc. 9:50), and housed a garrison which harassed Jonathan (v. 51). Some would identify it with PIRATHON, a city in the hill country of Ephraim (Jgs. 12:15), the home of a minor judge named Abdon (Jgs. 12:13) and of Benaiah, one of David's thirty men (2 S. 23:30; 1 Ch. 11:31; 27:14; not Benaiah of Kabzeel described in 2 S. 23:20-23). The problem with identifying these two names with the same city is that Pharathon was in Judea (1 Macc. 9:50) but Pirathon was in Ephraim (Jgs. 12:15; 1 Ch. 27:14). W. D. MOUNCE

**PHARES** fâr'ēz [Gk. *Phares*]. The Greek form of PEREZ son of Judah. "Phares" is used by the AV, RSV, and NEB in 1 Esd. 5:5, but by only the AV in Mt. 1:3; Lk. 3:33 (RSV, NEB, "Perez").

**PHAREZ** fâr'ēz.

**1.** An AV OT form of PEREZ.

**2.** (1 Esd. 8:30, AV). *See* PAROSH **1.**

**PHARIDA** fə-rī'də (1 Esd. 5:33, NEB); **PHARIRA** fə-rī'rə (AV). *See* PERIDA.

**PHARISEES** fâr'ə-sēz [Gk. *pharisaíoi*]. A prominent religious party in Judaism during the late Second Temple period (*ca.* 100 B.C. - A.D. 70), the party most frequently mentioned in the NT.

- I. Name
- II. Description
  - A. "Traditional" View
  - B. Pharisees in Josephus
  - C. Pharisees in the NT
  - D. Pharisees in Rabbinic Literature
  - E. A Comparison of the Sources
- III. Historical Development
  - A. Antecedents
  - B. Sadducean-Pharisaic Rivalry
  - C. Roman Period
- IV. Anti-Pharisaic Criticism
- V. Pharisees in the NT
  - A. Jesus and the Pharisees in the Gospel Tradition
  - B. Pharisees in Acts and Paul

***I. Name.***–"Pharisees" is an anglicized transliteration of Gk. *pharisaíoi*, which in turn derives from Heb. *pᵉrûšîm* or *pᵉrûšîn* or Aram. *pᵉrišayyaʾ*. Two suggestions for the meaning of this name have not received much support. One, by T. W. Manson (*BJRL*, 22 [1938], 153-59), is that the word *pᵉrûšîm* may be construed to mean "Persianizers," a taunt or epithet devised by their opponents to stigmatize them for believing in demonic spirits, angels, and the resurrection of the body, all of which are paralleled in Persian religion. Another remote possibility is that, since *prš* can also mean "expound" (Jastrow, pp. 1241-44), there would be a connection between "Pharisees" and biblical exegesis. This view could be supported by Josephus's statement that the Pharisees were "the most accurate exegetes of the law" (*BJ* ii.8.14 [162]; cf. W. O. E. Oesterley, *The Jews and Judaism during the Greek Period* [1941], p. 246).

Usually, however, the root *prš* means "separate," "detach." Thus the Pharisees were probably the "separated ones," but "separated from what or whom is an unresolved question" (Martin, I, 85). Two answers to the question have been suggested, one in terms of a religio-political schism that occurred earlier in the Second Temple period, another in terms of more purely religious concerns — the withdrawal from, or customary avoidance of, the unclean. Support for the first answer is found in the reign of John Hyrcanus (134-104 B.C.), when the Pharisees withdrew support from him and thus from the Hasmonean dynasty. Thus the name would have denoted "separatists."

But the most common view is that *pᵉrûšîm* refers in some way to religious practices of the group that involved separation from ritual uncleanness. This outlook may be illustrated by the statement of *Siphra* to Lev. 11:44 (39a), "'Be holy ones (*qedošim*) for I am holy' (*qadoš*), that is: 'As I am holy (*qadoš*) so should you be holy ones (*qedošim*); as I am a separated one (*paruš*) so should you be separated ones (*perušim*).'" The *Mekilta* on Ex. 19:6 is similar: "'You should be to me a kingdom of priests, a holy nation:' 'Holy' — holy, hallowed, separated from the peoples of the world and their detestable things." Although this exegesis is not attributed specifically to the Pharisees, "it is easy to see how those who made it their end to fulfill this ideal might take its name *Pĕrūshīm* as a less presuming title than *Ḳĕdōshīm*" (Moore, *Judaism*, I, 61).

***II. Description.***–*A. "Traditional" View.* The "traditional" view of the Pharisees has been that they were a Jewish sect or party whose members voluntarily took upon themselves a strict regimen of laws pertaining to purity, sabbath observance, prayer, and tithing. They joined together in *ḥᵃḇûrôṯ*, Pharisaic communities, to which initiates were admitted after a probationary period (Tosefta *Demai* ii.12, 48). Those who belonged to the *ḥᵃḇûrôṯ* were *ḥᵃḇerîm*, "Pharisaic brothers." The Pharisees or *ḥᵃḇerîm* restricted their dealings with the *ʿam hāʾāreṣ*, "people of the land," whom the Pharisees considered lax in observance of the law. A large number of Pharisees may have been members of the school of Hillel or later followers of the traditions associated with him (cf. Neusner, *Politics to Piety*, pp. 13-44). Many of the Pharisees were scribes also, though most were not (Jeremias, pp. 246-251). This accounts for the NT reference to two groups, scribes and Pharisees, along with occasional mention of "scribes of the Pharisees" (Mk. 2:16; Acts 23:9). A Pharisee was usually a layman without scribal education, whereas a scribe was trained in rabbinic law and had official status. The Pharisees and scribes observed and perpetuated an oral tradition of laws handed down from the former teachers and wise men of Israel (cf. Mish. *Aboth* i-ii). This oral law, or Halakah, was highly venerated by the Pharisees and scribes. They taught that it had been handed down from Moses and was to be given the same respect as the written laws of the Pentateuch. By gathering into *ḥᵃḇûrôṯ*, by strict observance of scribal Halakah pertaining to purity, fasting, tithing, prayer, and by separating from the unclean, the Pharisees sought to fulfill the injunction of Lev. 11:44 and Ex. 19:6: to be a holy nation and a kingdom of priests. Their goal was to replicate the laws of temple purity in the home (Neusner, *Politics to Piety*, p. 89).

This picture of the Pharisees, ably and comprehensively documented by Jeremias, has been challenged. Neusner has shown that the study of the Pharisees has often suffered from academic deficiencies, scholarly biases, and a party spirit (*Rabbinic Traditions*, III, 320-366). Also, more recent studies of the Pharisees, especially those of Bowker, Rivkin, and Neusner, have shown that the presentations of the Pharisees in the three major sources — Josephus, the NT, and the rabbinic literature — are not entirely consistent. Josephus presents the Pharisees in a generally positive manner but says little about their beliefs and practices. The NT gives more information about them but often, though not always, presents them negatively, often characterizing them as "hypocrites." The rabbinic literature must be used with caution, for it stands farthest in time from the events it reports about the Pharisees; most of its material was written much later than the NT. These studies have demonstrated that an accurate description of the Pharisees can be attained only by a comparison of the three major sources.

*B. Pharisees in Josephus.* The first-century Hellenistic-Jewish historian JOSEPHUS mentioned the Pharisees forty-two times in three of his writings. In *Vita* 2 (10-12) he claimed to have subjected himself to the religious training of the Essenes, the Sadducees, the Pharisees, and a certain Bannus (apparently a desert ascetic of some sort) between the ages of sixteen and nineteen. After spending most of this period with Bannus, he returned to the Pharisees. (The chronology here is not quite clear and the events seem somewhat compressed [Neusner, pp. 46f.].)

Josephus characterized the Pharisees in several passages that deal with the "philosophical schools" of the Jews. They were the "leading sect" (*BJ* ii.8.14 [162]), whose views were so influential that all forms of prayer and religious service were performed in conformity with them (*Ant.* xviii.1.3 [15]). Even the Sadducees conformed in certain respects to pharisaic practice, for "otherwise the masses would not tolerate them" (xviii.1.4 [17]). The Pharisees were considered "the most accurate interpreters of the law" (*BJ* ii.8.14 [162]) and "experts in their country's laws" (*Vita* 38 [191]). They excelled the rest of the nation in observing religious customs (*BJ* i.5.2 [110]).

The Pharisees believed that God controls events, though men also choose their course of action (*BJ* ii.8.14 [163]; cf. *Ant.* xiii.5.9 [171-73]), and that human souls live on after death, good ones in another body and bad ones in eternal punishment (*BJ* ii.8.14 [163]). Pharisees lived simply and did not pursue luxury (*Ant.* xviii.1.3 [12]). They were agreeable and hospitable to each other (*BJ* ii.8.14 [166]). In certain situations they sent out deputations to deal with various problems (*Vita* 39 [196]).

It could be inferred from *Vita* that there were ranks among the Pharisees, for there is mention of those who were leaders (*hoi prṓtoi tṓn pharisaíōn* [5 (21)]). In addition, some of them were priests (39 [198]).

Of particular interest are passages that mention political activities of the Pharisees. In *Ant.* xiii.10.5f. (288-298) Josephus reported the schism between John Hyrcanus, Jewish ruler and high priest, and the Pharisees. Hyrcanus quit the Pharisees and joined the Sadducees after a certain Pharisee named Eleazar told Hyrcanus that he should give up the high priesthood and be content as king. The basis for Eleazar's statement was that "we have heard from our elders" that Hyrcanus's mother had been a prisoner (and presumably raped) during the reign of Antiochus Epiphanes. (Hyrcanus would therefore be ineligible for the high priesthood; cf. Lev. 21:14.) Hyrcanus, outraged at the allegation and influenced by a Sadducean friend, quit the Pharisees and joined the Sadducees. He also abolished the pharisaic practices that had been enacted as laws and began to punish those who observed them (*Ant.* xiii.10.6 [296]). The passage also states that "even when they [the Pharisees] speak against the king or high priest, they immediately gain credence" (xiii.10.5 [288]). In addition, Josephus stated here that the Pharisees had passed on (Gk. *parédosan*) regulations to the people "handed down by the fathers" (Gk. *ek patérōn diadochḗs*) that are not written in the laws of Moses. The Sadducees rejected this pharisaic oral law and accepted only that which was written. For this reason the Pharisees and Sadducees had serious differences (xiii.10.6 [297f.]).

The accounts of the death of Alexander Janneus (*Ant.* xiii.15.5-16.2 [398-415]; *BJ* i.5.2 [110]) are similar in some respects to that of the death of Hyrcanus. The great influence of the Pharisees over the people is emphasized (*Ant.* xiii.15.5 [401-404]) as are the pharisaic regulations "introduced . . . in accordance with the tradition of their fathers" (Gk. *katá tḗn patrǭ́an parádosin*, xiii.16.2 [408]). After the transition of power from Alexander Janneus to his wife, Alexandra Salome (76 B.C.), the Pharisees came to hold sway over her and "became at length the real administrators of the state, at liberty to banish and to recall, to loose and to bind, whom they would" (*BJ* i.5.2 [111]). In a position to avenge earlier persecution and criticism from the pro-Sadducean faction, "they proceeded to kill whomsoever they would" (i.5.3 [113]). In *BJ* they appear as a group already in existence that came to exercise political power, but their doctrines and practices are not described.

During the reign of Herod the Great the Pharisees refused to take an oath of loyalty to Herod and the Roman government. Josephus described the Pharisees as "a group of Jews priding itself on its adherence to ancestral custom and claiming to observe the laws of which the Deity approves" (*Ant.* xvii.2.4 [41]). Herod unsuccessfully attempted to fine them for their refusal to take the oath and then had several of them executed for bribing members of his court (44).

The beginning of *Antiquities* xviii has important information about events leading up to the rebellion against Rome (A.D. 66-70). It reports that the revolt of Judas the Galilean was aided by a certain Pharisee named Saddok (xviii.1.1 [3]). Judas established what Josephus called a "fourth philosophy" that "agrees in all other respects with the opinions of the Pharisees, except that they have a passion for liberty that is almost unconquerable, since they are convinced that God alone is their leader and master" (xviii.1.6 [23]). Though Josephus passed on this information, which clearly relates a faction of pharisaism to the beginnings of the revolutionary Zealot party, he felt that this was not a true pharisaism. This revolutionary development of pharisaism was "a lesson that an innovation and reform in ancestral traditions [lit. "the things of the fathers," Gk. *hoi pátrioi*] weighs heavily in the scale in leading to the destruction of the congregation of the people" (xviii.1.1 [9]).

*C. Pharisees in the NT.* The word "Pharisee" occurs about a hundred times in the NT (depending on how one understands the variant readings). The vast majority of these occurrences are found in the Gospels, especially the Synoptics.

Scholars sometimes (e.g., Weiss, *TDNT,* IX, 36; Rivkin, pp. 79-83) begin their discussion of the Pharisees in the NT by noting the polemical tone with which they are condemned in certain passages, especially by Jesus. Thus Rivkin grades Mark, Matthew, and Luke, respectively, as "least hostile," "most hostile," and "midway" according to how much data each relates about the Pharisees. A more accurate approach, however, would take into account not only the polemical passages but also those that describe pharisaic interest in Jesus and those in which many Pharisees are depicted as having joined the movement started by Jesus (cf. Jn. 3:1; Acts 15:5). One must also point out that harsh criticism of the Pharisees is not at all unique to the NT (see IV below). The Pharisees were also criticized both by their own successors, the rabbis of the post-70 era, and by the group at Qumrân. In many instances the disagreements between Jesus and the Pharisees are comparable to those between various rabbis and their schools and have some of the characteristics of rabbinic debate. Therefore a kind of intra-Jewish criticism may account for the strident tone of certain passages in the NT, rather than a Christian bias or anti-semitism.

Several stories dealing with the Pharisees are grouped together near the beginning of Mark (2:15–3:6), probably with the intention of showing the original readers the differences between Jesus' teaching and pharisaic regulation. In 2:15-17 the issue is table fellowship; in vv. 18-22 it is fasting; in 2:23–3:6 it is the legality of certain activities done on the sabbath. All of these would have been regulated by pharisaic and scribal Halakah. Mk. 2:16 is noteworthy because the best MSS read "scribes of the Pharisees," indicating that the terms "scribes" and "Pharisees," though mentioned together often, are not completely synonymous, as Rivkin would have it (pp. 104-111).

Mark 7:1-13 (par. Mt. 15:1-9) is very important in describing the Pharisees. Here the Pharisees and "some of the scribes who had come from Jerusalem" (again, two different groups) objected that Jesus and the disciples ate with unwashed hands. They "did not walk according to the tradition of the elders" (Gk. *ou peripatoúsin . . . katá tḗn parádosin tṓn presbytérōn*). The word "tradition" (Gk. *parádosis*) occurs five times in this passage. It was a tradition of "the elders," i.e., it had been handed down from previous teachers and was considered binding by the scribes and Pharisees. Another important word here is "walk." The Semitic term here would be *hālaḵ,* "(to) walk," from which is derived Halakah, the oral law, the "walk" of pharisaic practice. Thus the question is why Jesus and His disciples do not observe the Halakah, the handed-down tradition that in this case pertains to the washing of hands before meals.

In Matthew "hypocrite" is virtually synonymous with "Pharisee" (*TDNT,* VIII, 566-68). The passage that contributes most to the NT description of the Pharisees is ch. 23, a series of criticisms in which "hyprocrite" is ascribed to both scribes and Pharisees. In spite of the polemical tone, the passage gives some valid information about pharisaic and scribal practice. In vv. 2f. Jesus acknowledges that the scribes and Pharisees sit in Moses' seat. This must surely indicate that Jesus is ascribing to them a great deal of influence, if not the primary place of religious authority, in His day. This chapter also indicates that the scribes, most of whom were Pharisees (Jeremias, p. 243), attended banquets (v. 6), made proselytes (v. 15), gave legal rulings about oath-taking (v. 16), tithed herbs (v. 23), and (as Mk. 7:1-13 has already shown) were concerned about the cleansing of eating utensils (vv. 25f.).

Since Mt. 23 consistently condemns the scribes and Pharisees together, Rivkin concluded that they are synonymous. Jeremias, however, had already shown that Mt. 23, interpreted in the light of Lk. 11:37-53, "falls into two parts: the first (vv. 1-22, 29-36) is levelled at the scribes, and the second (vv. 23-28) at the Pharisees." Matthew seems to blend the two groups slightly but does make a clear distinction in 23:25-26 with the words "'Woe unto you, scribes and Pharisees,' then continuing (v. 26) with the single phrase: 'thou blind Pharisee'" (p. 254).

In the parallel passage in Luke (11:37-53), Jeremias noted that the condemnations heaped on the scribes and Pharisees are also of two different kinds. In vv. 46-52 the scribes are condemned for imposing upon the people strict laws that they themselves do not follow, for building the tombs of the prophets while being ready to condemn to death contemporary men sent by God, for taking away "the key of knowledge" and not making use of it themselves, and for a prideful religiosity (taking the best seats at the synagogues, etc.). The condemnations of the Pharisees in Lk. 11:39-42, 44 are not identical. They are accused of hypocrisy in practicing the laws of purity, since they are impure inwardly, and of hypocrisy in the laws of tithing. They tithed herbs, not required by the written law, and neglected the moral obligations that were in the written law. As Jeremias put it, "We can see that these reproaches have absolutely nothing to do with a theological education; they are levelled at men who lead their lives according to the demands of the religious laws of Pharisaic scribes" (pp. 253f.).

Luke has other material dealing with the Pharisees that is not in the other Gospels. In 7:36-50, the story of Simon the Pharisee who invited Jesus to dinner, the pharisaic concern about contact with the *ʿam hāʾāreṣ* is illustrated in 7:39 (cf. Mk. 2:16; Mish. *Demai* ii.2f.). The parable of the Pharisee and the publican (18:9-14) shows that fasting and tithing were important to the Pharisee. The going up to the temple to pray may indicate observance of certain times of prayer, an important pharisaic regulation (cf. Jeremias, p. 249).

Luke's second volume has further references to the Pharisees. Acts 5:34 describes Gamaliel, a Pharisee, as "a teacher of the law, held in honor by all the people." Such a description indicates that he was a pharisaic scribe, a leader among the Pharisees. Acts 15:5 mentions Pharisees as members of the early Church who accepted Jesus as the Messiah but who felt it necessary to circumcise gentile converts and have them keep the law of Moses. In 23:6-10 Paul, a Christian Pharisee, raises the issue of the resurrection of the body in a mixed group of Pharisees and Sadducees. Luke adds, "for the Sadducees say that there is no resurrection, nor angel, nor spirit, but the Pharisees acknowledge them all" (v. 8). It is also important to note that v. 9 clearly demarcates "the scribes of the Pharisees' party," indicating that some Pharisees, but not all, were scribes.

The Gospel of John adds little to this picture, but several points may be made. The Pharisees appear first in Jn. 1:19-28 as senders of a deputation from Jerusalem to evaluate John the Baptist. The sending of a deputation is paralleled in Josephus *Vita* 39 (196). The Pharisees of the Fourth Gospel are often associated with the "chief priests" (7:32; 18:3). This is not surprising, for many of the Pharisees in Jerusalem would either have been priests themselves or would have recourse to those who were responsible for the legal aspects of temple worship. Thus the Pharisees of John would have been leading pharisaic scribes, like Nicodemus (Jn. 3:1; cf. Josephus *BJ* ii.17.3 [411]), and in addition may also have been priests (*Vita* 39 [197f.]).

Finally, Paul's self-designation in Phil. 3:5, "As to the law, a Pharisee," is related to his former observance of the Halakah mentioned in Gal. 1:14.

*D. Pharisees in Rabbinic Literature.* Multiple problems are involved in searching through this body of literature for a description of the Pharisees. As Bowker stated, "even a brief acquaintance with the rabbinic sources makes it clear that the sense in which the Pharisees were the predecessors of the rabbis is by no means simple or direct" (p. 1). No clear historical picture shows either where pharisaism ends and rabbinic Judaism begins or what changes and alterations of tradition this transition brought. Unlike Josephus and the NT, the rabbinic literature is much later than the events it narrates about the Pharisees. Its problems of historical development and literary interdependence are still largely unresolved. A more specific problem is that the rabbinic literature does not simply use Gk. *pharisaíoi,* as do Josephus and the NT, but *p^erûšîm,* "separated ones," *sôp̱^erîm,* "scribes," and *ḥ^akāmîm,* "sages," or "wise men." And it is uncertain what these three terms mean and whether they denote one, two, or three groups. In fact, *p^erûšîm* itself may denote more than one group.

As Bowker (pp. 12-15) and Rivkin (pp. 131-143) have demonstrated, a reliable point of departure is that group of texts in which *ṣ^eḏûqîm* or Sadducees are opposed to *p^erûšîm* or Pharisees. As noted, both Josephus (*Ant.* xiii.10.6 [297f.]) and the NT (Acts 23:6f.) show the Sadducees and the Pharisees in a number of serious disagreements. Some passages in the rabbinic literature do the same. For this reason Rivkin referred to them as the "unambiguous texts" (p. 133). The dialogue often begins with the stereotyped formula, "we complain against you *p^erûšîm* because," followed by, "we complain against you *ṣ^eḏûqîm* because." In Mish. *Yadaim* iv.6, for example, the debate is whether the handling of holy Scripture causes the hands to become ceremonially unclean (so Pharisees). Continuing in *Yadaim* iv.7, the Sadducees complain against the pharisaic ruling that makes an unbroken stream of liquid clean. The Pharisees then complain against the Sadducees for ruling that a stream emanating from a cemetery is clean. Another debate follows, with the two parties arguing whether the owners of slaves are free from responsibility for damage done by their slaves (Pharisees) or whether the owners are accountable (Sadducees). Two similar texts without the stereotyped formula are T.B. *Yoma* 19b and Tosefta *Hagigah* iii.35. Both passages mention differences between the *p^erûšîm* and the *ṣ^eḏûqîm* about the performance of certain temple rituals. T.B. *Yoma* 19b tells of a Sadducean high priest who prepared incense outside the Holy of Holies and then entered, contrary to pharisaic interpretation. After a few days he was struck dead (by God) for this deviation. His father had warned him, saying, "Although we are Sadducees, we fear the *p^erûšîm,*" but he defied pharisaic practice anyway and suffered for it.

These texts, in which the *p^erûšîm* are contrasted with the *ṣ^eḏûqîm,* are indeed "unambiguous," and, as Rivkin claimed, "the term *Perushim* must be translated 'Pharisees' since the meaning of *Perushim* is guaranteed by the proper noun *Zedukim,* 'Sadducees'" (p. 131). Problems arise, however, when Rivkin goes on to claim that *p^erûšîm* is completely synonymous with *ḥ^akāmîm* and *sôp̱^erîm* in other passages. For example, T.B. *Niddah* 33b, a passage dealing with purity regulations for women, reads, "[She] assured him that although they were wives of Sadducees they paid homage to the Pharisees [*p^erûšîm*] and showed their blood to the Sages [*ḥ^akāmîm*]... There was only one exception, a woman who lived in our neighbourhood... but she died" (tr. Slotki, Soncino ed.). Rivkin apparently believed it self-evident that *ḥ^akāmîm* as used here denotes the same group as the *p^erûšîm,* but this is not at all obvious. In fact, the text can be easily read, retaining coherency, if one defines the *ḥ^akāmîm* as "the majority of scholars as opposed to another group or a single authority" (so L. Ginzberg, "Hakam," *Jew.Enc.*, VI [1904], 160f.). I. W. Slotki, editor of the Soncino edition of *Niddah,* likewise assumed that the text referred to two different groups (p. 234 n. 1).

Rivkin's position is weakened by another passage that clearly distinguishes *ḥ^akāmîm* from *sôp^erîm*: "Whosoever according to the words of the Scribes [*sôp^erîm*] requires immersion, conveys uncleanness to Hallowed Things and renders Heave-offerings invalid . . . .So R. Meir. But the Sages [*ḥ^akāmîm*] say . . ." (Mish. *Parah* xi.5f., ed. Danby). Here it is clear that Rabbi Meir accepts a ruling of the *sôp^erîm* (scribes) in opposition to that of the *ḥ^akāmîm* (sages).

Rivkin claimed that the synonymity of *p^erûšîm* and *ḥ^akāmîm* is demonstrated by a comparison of Mish. *Yadaim* iii.2, in which Rabbi Joshua differs with the *ḥ^akāmîm* about the Scriptures causing uncleanness of hands, and iv.6, where the same Halakah is found in a dialogue concerning Pharisees vs. Sadducees. It is true, as Rivkin claimed, that the same Halakah is the basis of discussion. This fact, however, falls far short of proving that the *ḥ^akāmîm* in iii.2 are synonymous with the *p^erûšîm* of iv.6. The two passages, aside from use of the same Halakah, are very different. In iv.6 Rabbi Johanan ben Zakkai is depicted debating with the Sadducees by taking the side of the Pharisees. His question, "Have we nothing against the Pharisees except this?" certainly implies both that he probably did not consider himself a Pharisee and that others did in fact "have something against the Pharisees." In contrast, iii.2 closes with the *ḥ^akāmîm* admonishing Rabbi Joshua: "Ye may infer nothing about the words of the Law from the words of the Scribes [*sôp^erîm*] . . . and nothing about the words of the Scribes from [other] words of the Scribes" (Danby). This statement appears to put Rabbi Joshua and the *sōp̱^erîm* in opposition to the *ḥ^akāmîm,* further supporting a distinction between the two groups.

In addition, Rivkin claimed that the Boethusians and the Sadducees were also synonymous. A quick comparison of T.B. *Yoma* 19b and Tosefta *Yoma* i.8 supports this contention. The Boethusians and Sadducees, however, were probably completely different groups with some common features, the Boethusians synonymous not with the Sadducees but with the Herodians of Mk. 3:6; 12:13. The Herodians and Boethusians were both temple-oriented, had a hereditary high priesthood, and were non-pharisaic, among other things.

The many parallel passages constitute a fundamental problem in establishing a description of the Pharisees from the rabbinic texts. Some of these passages are identical and others are not. Rivkin attempted to solve this problem by identifying the different terms: the *p^erûšîm* are synonymous with the *ḥ^akāmîm* and the *sôp^erîm*; the Boethusians and Sadducees are identical also. Much of the evidence, however, does not support this solution. The passages examined above often show a distinction between the *pᵉrûšîm, ḥᵃkāmîm,* and *sôpᵉrîm.* Such a multiplicity of terms resists being reduced to two groups, Pharisees-Scribes-Sages vs. Boethusians-Sadducees. Rather, the various terms point to a more complicated history of development and rivalry of various parties that originated during the Second Temple period. After the fall of Jerusalem and during the codification of the rabbinic literature, the distinctions between the groups became blurred.

*E. A Comparison of the Sources.* What can be learned of the Pharisees from a comparison of the three major sources? First, the Pharisees were the rivals of the Sadducees. At the time of the ministry of Jesus, the Pharisees were the leading party and held so much influence over the common people that the Sadducees were often forced to conform to pharisaic practice (Mt. 23:2; Josephus *Ant.* xviii.1.4 [17]; T.B. *Yoma* 19b). Second, the Pharisees in the NT are definitely a group distinct from the scribes, though some Pharisees were scribes. This lack of complete synonymity is also reflected in the rabbinic literature, where the *pᵉrûšîm, sôpᵉrîm,* and *ḥᵃkāmîm* are often found as separate groups (T.B. *Niddah* 33b; Mish. *Parah* xi.5f.). Third, the Pharisees followed and perpetuated an oral law, the "tradition of the elders," which, they believed, had also come from Moses (Mish. *Aboth* i.1-12; ii.8). For example, they believed in the resurrection of the body, a concept, among others, that the Sadducees rejected (Acts 23:6-9). In addition, the Pharisees followed a strict system of religious practices (Josephus *BJ* i.5.2 [110]). They fasted (Mt. 6:16; Lk. 18:12), made proselytes (Mt. 23:15; Josephus *Vita* 2 [11f.]; Mish. *Demai* ii.12), prayed (Mt. 6:5; Lk. 18:12; Baraitha to T.B. *Berakoth* 47b), and tithed their goods (Lk. 11:42; 18:12; Mish. *Demai* ii.12). There were ranks among their members, including those who were initiates and others who were leaders (*Vita* 5 [21]; Jn. 3:1-10), scribes (Mk. 2:16; Acts 23:9), and priests (*Vita* 39 [198]). They sent out deputations to examine individuals who did not conform to their policies or doctrines (*Vita* 39 [196]; Jn. 1:19-24). They were very zealous for their vision of Judaism (Gal. 1:14) and, on occasion, ruthlessly opposed their enemies, real or imagined, by means of bribery, incarcerations, and executions (cf. Josephus *BJ* i.5.3 [113f.]; Jn. 18:3; Acts 8:1; 9:1f.).

This summary coheres largely with the view of the Pharisees presented by Jeremias. The pharisaic communities (*ḥᵃḇûrôṯ*), however, of which Jeremias made so much (pp. 247-250), find no mention in the NT or Josephus.

*III. Historical Development.–A. Antecedents.* Although solid historical data can lead to differing conclusions, the origins of pharisaism can probably be traced to the early postexilic period. The reforms of Ezra and Nehemiah set in motion a Judaism concerned, in intent at least, with a strict observance and study of the Scriptures (cf. Mal. 3:16). Evidence within the OT itself indicates a growing trend toward biblical exposition by qualified teachers and an emphasis on correct interpretation and application of the law (Ezr. 7:11; 8:16; Neh. 8:7-9; 1 Ch. 25:8; 27:32). Prominent teachers and their disciples began to meet together regularly for Scripture study and to argue various points of interpretation. Sir. 51:23 gives evidence of such a "teaching house," which was probably the equivalent of the "midrash house" (Heb. *bêṯ hammiḏrāš*) of later rabbinic times. The pharisaic schools of Hillel, Shammai, and others were a later part of this trend.

The reforms of Ezra and Nehemiah provided what Thoma (pp. 255f.) called the "primary spiritual-religious impulse" of the HASIDEANS, who were probably the direct antecedents of the Pharisees. Such a link is not entirely certain but is supported by 1 Macc. 2:42, which states that the Hasideans joined in the Maccabean revolt "willingly for the law." They definitely wanted to maintain religious devotion and obedience to the Torah, which was being threatened by an encroaching Hellenism.

The alliance of the Hasideans and the Maccabees was short-lived. Although the temple was purified in 164 B.C. (cf. 1 Macc. 4:36-58), Judas Maccabeus was not content with the greater religious freedoms he had obtained but continued to press for political autonomy. The Hasideans, however, were content with what the revolt had obtained — restoration of Jewish religious practices, including temple worship. When the Syrians installed a certain Alcimus as high priest the Hasideans were willing to accept him, being persuaded that he was of the Aaronic line. Alcimus, however, turned against the Hasideans and killed sixty of them (1 Macc. 7:12-18). The Hasideans again threw their support behind Judas Maccabeus. 2 Macc. 14:6 indicates that the Hasideans continued in the Maccabean revolt and even mentions Judas Maccabeus as their leader, but this may be a garbled Syrian account of the situation.

*B. Sadducean-Pharisaic Rivalry.* Although evidence is scant, it is probable that, as part of the aftermath of the Maccabean revolt, the party of the Sadducees developed around the hereditary high priesthood established by Judas Maccabeus. When the Pharisees first appear in Josephus's narrative, in the account of the charge against John Hyrcanus by Eleazar (see II.B above), they are the opponents of the Sadducees. Although the account mentions personal reasons for this schism between the Pharisees and the Hasmonean dynasty, the earlier uneasiness of the Hasideans over Hasmonean political power and the pharisaic opposition to a hereditary high priesthood may be part of the historical background of this incident (M. Black, *IDB*, III, 779).

At the time of Hyrcanus's death (104 B.C.) pharisaic fortunes were at a low point and did not improve during the reign of his successor Alexander Janneus (103-76 B.C.). Janneus, too, was opposed in his administration of high-priestly duties, as Josephus made clear (*Ant.* xiii.13.5 [372f.]). Janneus retaliated in anger and killed several thousand of his enemies. An insurrection developed later, and Janneus nearly lost control of his kingdom (xiii.14.2 [379]). He managed to salvage the situation, however, and again took revenge on those Jews who had opposed him, crucifying eight hundred of them and slaying their wives and children while they looked on (xiii.13.2 [380f.]). Although Josephus did not specifically identify them, Janneus's enemies must have included Pharisees, as may be inferred from his death-bed advice to his wife Alexandra, that she give power to the Pharisees again, since no one could rule peaceably without their support (xiii.15.5 [400-402]). In addition, T.B. *Kiddushin* 66a states that it was the result of Eleazar's scandalous remarks (made against Janneus according to this passage) that "all the hakamim were massacred," and these *ḥᵃkāmîm* would certainly have included some who were Pharisees.

Alexandra took her husband's advice, giving the Pharisees greater power and influence than ever before. The "tradition of their fathers" (Gk. *hē patrōá parádosis*), abolished by her father-in-law Hyrcanus, was reintroduced, and the people were commanded to follow it (Josephus *Ant.* xiii.16.2 [408]). Alexandra's reign, 76-67 B.C., was a kind of "golden age" of pharisaism. Firmly in control, the Pharisees proceeded to destroy their Sadducean enemies, executing so many that a pro-Sadducean faction, led by Janneus's son Aristobulus, appealed to Alexandra for help.

*C. Roman Period.* When Alexandra died (67 B.C.) civil war broke out between her sons Aristobulus II and Hyrcanus II. Rome, in an expansionist phase, settled the dispute by annexing Palestine and the adjoining areas. The Roman general Pompey entered Jerusalem in 63 B.C. and set up Roman rule. The Pharisees and Sadducees never again enjoyed the political power they had previously attained. Jewish subservience to Rome probably had the effect of making their differences "less and less political and more distinctively religious" (M. Black, *IDB,* III, 780).

Josephus mentions the Pharisees several times during the reign of Herod the Great (37-4 B.C.). They refused to take an oath of loyalty to Herod and the Romans, but on account of their influence over the people he merely attempted to fine them rather than resort to more drastic punishments (*Ant.* xvii.2.4 [42]). Yet he did execute some leading Pharisees suspected of bribing key officials (*Ant.* xvii.2.4 [43-45]). After Herod's death (4 B.C.) his son Archelaus ruled for ten years (4 B.C.-A.D. 6). Abuse of power led his subjects, Jews and Samaritans alike, to complain to Augustus. In A.D. 6 Judea became a province of Rome administered by a prefect. This had the effect of making Roman rule more direct. Although major issues were decided by the Roman authorities, the SANHEDRIN retained control over some internal affairs. The Sadducees were probably in control of the Sanhedrin, but Josephus wrote that they had to submit "to the formulas of the Pharisees since otherwise the masses would not tolerate them" (*Ant.* xviii.1.4 [17]).

The Pharisees maintained considerable influence during this period. Jesus described them as "sitting in Moses' seat" (Mt. 23:2), that is, occupying the place of supreme religious authority. Though most of the Pharisees were probably opposed to Jesus and His teaching, some were at least willing to have table fellowship with Him and discuss His teaching (Lk. 7:36; 14:1). After some of the leading Pharisees, in collusion with other authorities, succeeded in having Jesus executed (cf. Jn. 18:3), a number of them were won over to the movement started by Jesus (Acts 15:5). Even Saul of Tarsus, a Pharisee particularly zealous for the preservation of the oral law (Gal. 1:14) and a student of Rabbi Gamaliel (Acts 22:3), joined the movement and became one of its ablest spokesmen.

According to Josephus, the outbreak of the Jewish war (A.D. 66-70) originated in a revolutionary "fourth philosophy" (see II.B above), which was opposed by Pharisees of a more moderate outlook who attempted to dissuade the others from rebellion (*BJ* ii.17.3 [410]). The revolutionary faction gained support, however, and war with Rome ensued, ending in disaster for the Jewish nation.

Although pharisaism is often seen as continuing after the revolts of A.D. 66-70 and 135, such a conclusion is questionable. T. B. *Baba Bathra* 60b does indeed mention some *p^erûšîm* who fasted after the temple was destroyed (A.D. 70). In Mish. *Yadaim* iv.6-8, however, Rabbi Johanan ben Zakkai, the leader of the rabbinical school at Yavne (Jamnia) and an important figure in maintaining the legacy of pre-70 Judaism, seems to distinguish himself from the Pharisees, though he defends one of their views against Sadducean criticism. If one of the most prominent leaders of post-70 Judaism did not consider himself a Pharisee, it is questionable that the pharisaism of the Second Temple period survived the revolt. The Pharisees as a definite group probably came to an end, along with the Sadducees and Essenes. What some assume to be a post-70 pharisaism may be an altered form of it, a newer rabbinical scribal movement that inherited the best that the *p^erûšîm* had to offer and attempted to preserve it (cf. Neusner, *Politics to Piety,* pp. 97-100), but which avoided any direct association with Pharisees because of pharisaic involvement in the disastrous revolt and other excesses that had stigmatized them as hypocrites (Mt. 23:23f.; T.B. *Sotah* 22b).

*IV. Anti-Pharisaic Criticism.*–Even while the Pharisees had dominant status, they came under increasing criticism. Anti-pharisaic sentiment is associated with various passages in the Gospels, especially Mt. 23. Thus Rivkin claims that Matthew has an all-consuming hatred for the Pharisees (p. 83). Severe criticism, however, is also found in some of the documents from Qumrân and in the rabbinic literature.

The Qumrân community rejected pharisaism because it frequently nullified the law while trying to protect it from transgression. If the Damascus Document (CD) is an Essene product (so Meyer, *TDNT,* IX, 29f.; Jeremias, 3rd ed.), then those described in CD 1:18–2:1 who "presented false expositions" may well be the Pharisees and pharisaic scribes of Jerusalem. Similarly, 1QH 4:10 speaks of those who seek to exchange the teaching of God for "smooth words." Meyer suggested with some plausibility that the "babbler," the "windbag," and the "false prophet" of CD 4:19 (7:1); 8:12ff. (9:21ff.); 29:15ff. might imply a pharisaic leader such as Shimeon ben Shatach or Hillel. Hillel established a legal formula (*prozbul*) that, in effect, annulled the law of remission in Dt. 15:2. Such an exegesis, aimed more at circumventing the text than expounding it, "represents precisely what the anti-Pharisaic criticism of the Zadokites calls a 'deceitful exposition of the Torah'" (Meyer, p. 31).

The NT criticism of the Pharisees is in some ways similar to that from Qumrân. Jesus accused the Pharisees of being "blind guides" (Mt. 23:16). He also rebuked them for nullifying the word of God by means of their tradition, closing His remarks with, "and many such things you do" (Mk. 7:6-13). Apparently He could have given examples other than the Corban issue, in which pharisaic Halakah contradicted the intended meaning of Scripture. Another similarity is in the criticism on the subject of divorce. CD 4:20f. rebukes those who take two wives in their lifetimes and Jesus (Mk. 10:2-9) condemns divorce "for any cause." Both passages cite Gen. 1:27 to prove that God's original intent was that marriage should be with one partner only. In addition, Jesus frequently referred to the Pharisees as "hypocrites," implying not that Jesus saw their teaching as always wrong but that they failed to follow it themselves.

The criticism of the Pharisees in the rabbinic literature is neither as sharply focused nor as plentiful as that found in the Dead Sea Scrolls or in the NT. Since, however, the rabbis who rebuilt Judaism after the fall of Jerusalem seem to have avoided associating themselves with the name "Pharisee," embarrassment on the part of these direct heirs of the spiritual legacy of pharisaism calls for an explanation.

A rather obscure reference is Mish. *Sotah* iii.4, which states, "a foolish saint, a wicked man with cunning, a woman who is *perushah,* and the wounds of the Pharisees [Heb. *makkôṯ p^erûšîm*], these wear out the world." While it is not clear what the *makkôṯ p^erûšîm* are, they are certainly uncommendable in the eyes of Rabbi Joshua. Another example is T.B. *Sotah* 22b, in which Alexander Janneus exhorts his wife, "Fear not the Pharisees and the non-Pharisees but the hypocrites who ape the Pharisees; because their deeds are the deeds of Zimri but they expect a reward like Phineas" (tr. A. Cohen, Soncino ed.). Seven kinds of Pharisee, most of them insincere, appear in T.P. *Berakoth* ix.5. Two who are sincere are the *pārûš* who loves like Job and the *pārûš* who loves like Abraham. The others are interested in fulfilling their obligation to the law only if they have the time or if in doing so their sin and guilt may be counterbalanced. The *makkôṯ pᵉrûšîm* are more clearly described in T.P. *Sotah* iii.4, where they designate the practices of those who use casuistry to take advantage of someone. Two examples are given. In one, a group of children uses pharisaic legal advice in attempting to wrest financial control of the estate from their widowed mother. This parallels Jesus' accusation in Mk. 12:40 that the Pharisees "devour widows' houses."

It is certainly possible, judging from these examples, that the later rabbis felt that some of the earlier Pharisees had engaged in hypocrisy and casuistry. Another possible reason for the avoidance of direct association with pharisaism may have been the proximity of zealotism to pharisaism (see II.B above). Thus, after the fall of Jerusalem, "Pharisee" may have connoted either a hypocrite or a hothead committed to a hopeless revolutionary idealism that had ruined the nation by the ill-fated revolt against Rome. Pharisaism had often presented a contrived biblical exegesis that avoided, or even worse contradicted, the intended meaning of the law and the prophets. Righteousness became equated with a mechanistic repetition of certain religious functions such as fasting, the keeping of set times of prayer, and tithing. Such a state of affairs did not totally permeate pharisaism, but it was prevalent enough to give rise to the kind of criticism found in CD, the NT, and the rabbinic literature.

*V. Pharisees in the NT.–A. Jesus and the Pharisees in the Gospel Tradition.* The presentation of the Pharisees in the Gospels is generally negative. Jesus is seen to be disputing with them continually, which suggests that His teaching was the antithesis of pharisaism. Closer investigation, however, does not support this suggestion. The NT evidence shows Jesus in agreement with beliefs and practices vitally important to the Pharisees. He taught and defended the concept of the resurrection of the body, thus differing from the Sadducees (Mk. 12:18-27). He accepted the temple cult in Jerusalem as the proper place of worship for national Judaism. In this He differed from the Samaritans (Jn. 4:23). He and His disciples attended the synagogue and participated in the Jewish feasts regularly (Mk. 1:21; Lk. 4:16-30; Jn. 5:1; 7:10; Lk. 22:8-23; etc.). Unlike those who belonged to the community at Qumrân, He worked within the existing institutions of Judaism (cf. Wilcox, p. 174). Furthermore, He did not support revolutionary zealotism with its fierce anti-Roman sentiment. On the contrary, He once pronounced a Roman centurion full of faith and worthy of the kingdom of God (Mt. 8:5-13; cf. Lk. 22:51; Mt. 26:52).

While these similarities to pharisaic distinctions from other groups do not make Jesus a Pharisee, some evidence points in that direction, though it is not conclusive. First, He was addressed as Rabbi and had a group of disciples who were His "school," similar to the rabbinic schools of Hillel and Shammai. There is disagreement about how similar Jesus' "school" was to those of the other rabbis, but, as Wilcox pointed out, "individual differences at any time and between any two Rabbis and their students would vary widely," so some differences do not necessarily rule out any comparison (p. 175). Second, the overriding of the Sabbath, allowed by Jesus in certain circumstances (cf. Mk. 3:1-6; Lk. 13:10-17; Jn. 5:1-18; 7:19-24), is paralleled in the Talmud (T.B. *Yoma* 85b) and Tosefta (*Shabbath* xv.16; see Wilcox, pp. 176f. n. 247). Third, the Golden Rule, a summary statement of the essence of the OT law, is found both in the teaching of Jesus and in that of Hillel, where it is similar but stated in a negative form (T.B. *Shabbath* 31a). Fourth, Neusner pointed out a similarity between the teaching of Jesus in Mt. 9:13; 12:7 and that of Rabbi Johanan ben Zakkai in *Aboth de Rabbi Nathan* 4. In both of the Gospel passages Jesus cites Hos. 6:6 in disputes with the Pharisees, the first over table fellowship with "sinners" and the second over the abrogation of the sabbath. Jesus said, in effect, that God is more interested in a merciful heart than in an outward religiosity. The use of Hos. 6:6 by Rabbi Johanan is similar. Fifth, Jesus' teaching on divorce in Mt. 19:3-9 is similar to that attributed to the school of Shammai. Wilcox noted how the Gospel account presupposes the debate on this matter within Judaism (p. 177 n. 251).

In spite of NT evidence that Jesus and the Pharisees shared many of the traditions of Judaism of their day, there were two major differences between Jesus and the majority of the Pharisees. First, Jesus held to a more conservative approach to OT interpretation. His teaching, judging from the examples given in the Gospels, was often more directly derived from the intended meaning of the OT than that of His opponents. His teaching on divorce (Mt. 19:3-9) restricts divorce to the one cause of immorality rather than allowing a multiplicity of grounds, some of them rather flimsy, such as the school of Hillel allowed (cf. T.B. *Gittin* 90a; Mish. *Gittin* ix.10). In Mk. 7:1-13 Jesus attacks the misuse of Corban whereby some Pharisees evaded the responsibility of caring for aged parents by claiming to have given their money to serve God, a tradition that led to a violation of Ex. 20:12. Mk. 7:1-13 puts into sharp focus Jesus' opposition to transgression of Scripture by means of an oral tradition supposedly derived from Scripture. Furthermore, Jesus taught that His practice of healing on the sabbath, though it violated pharisaic prohibitions, was not in conflict with the OT Scripture. On the contrary, it was compatible with the intent of the sabbath: to give a day in which to rest from fatigue and to be revived (Mk. 2:27). Second, Jesus had, as Wilcox put it, "a heightened sense of personal piety" (p. 181). He emphasized that defilement is an inner condition of the heart (Mk. 7:14-23). The attempt to attain righteousness by means of an elaborate oral tradition that specified explicitly how to wash, tithe, pray, and maintain "cleanness," as taught by the Pharisees, was therefore useless, since it did not address the real problem.

Of these two basic departures from the pharisaic outlook, the first, Jesus' reliance on a more direct appeal to the OT text, proved to be the more serious. If it had been merely a question of Jesus having a few differences of opinion with the Pharisees over various points of Halakah, He still would have been part of the variegated stream of pharisaic tradition, in which the various teachers often disagreed on particular points of practice and exegesis. Opposition to Jesus arose, however, when He began to make statements about Himself that had definite messianic implications (Mk. 12:36), even to the point of claiming to have a special relationship with the Father (cf. Mt. 11:27; Jn. 10:14-23). Jesus supported His claims by a direct appeal to various OT texts. An important example is Jn. 10:34-36, in which Jesus claimed to be the Son of God by appealing to Ps. 82:6. In a manner similar to that of Mt. 5:17, Jesus claimed that "scripture cannot be broken" (10:35). He used a literalist (*pᵉšaṭ*) form of interpretation common to the rabbis by not allowing the passage in question to be diluted by substituting "angels" or "judges" for "sons of God," a practice attested by the ancient versions (Targums, Syriac) and by the rabbinic literature (*Midrash on Psalms* 82:1; *Numbers Rabba* 16:24; etc.). By avoiding the customary, evasive exegesis associated with this passage, Jesus followed the most conservative use of the text, and the obvious implication of His argument — that He is entitled to be the son of God in a special, messianic sense (cf. 10:24) — angered the authorities. These direct appeals to Scripture (cf. Mk. 12:35-37), combined with His ability to work numerous miracles, brought Jesus into an irreconcilable conflict with the authorities (Jn. 10:33, 39; 11:47). A plan was devised to eliminate Jesus, and some of the Pharisees, probably those who were connected with priestly functions in Jerusalem, were clearly involved in it (Jn. 11:47-53; 18:3).

*B. Pharisees in Acts and Paul.* Although the majority of the Pharisees had probably been opposed to Jesus and His teaching, many of them did become part of the Church at an early date. Acts 15:5 tells of believing Pharisees who, not surprisingly, advocated circumcision of Gentiles and the keeping of the law of Moses. Christian Pharisees may also have been included in the group mentioned in 21:20: "... the Jews of those who have believed; they are zealous for the law." Gamaliel, a leading Pharisee of the council who was probably also an ordained scribe (Jeremias, pp. 253-56), is mentioned twice in Acts. He first appears in 5:34-39, urging restraint in dealing with the apostles. Gamaliel appears again in 22:3-21, Paul's account of his conversion, as Paul tells of his education in Jerusalem "at the feet of Gamaliel, educated according to the strictest manner of the law of our fathers" (v. 3).

Though Paul was probably a leading Pharisee, judging by his own accounts of his credentials (Phil. 3:5f.) and by his persecution of the Church (Gal. 1:13f.), it is difficult to determine with certainty the extent to which his background influenced the formulation and expression of his faith in Jesus of Nazareth as the Messiah. Jeremias made a case for the influence of Hillel on Paul by observing that Paul often used seven hermeneutical rules attributed to Hillel ("Paulus als Hillelit," in E. E. Ellis and M. Wilcox, eds., *Neotestamentica et Semitica* [*Festschrift* for M. Black; 1969], pp. 88-94, esp. 92-94; cf. Longenecker, pp. 33-35; 117f.). For example, Hillel's first rule, "light to heavy," is illustrated in Rom. 5:12-21: if death reigned through Adam, how much more shall God's grace result in life through Christ. Hillel's second rule is illustrated in Rom. 4:1-12, where Paul joins Gen. 15:6 and Ps. 32:1f. on the basis of the common word "reckoned."

Although Paul articulated his new faith under the influence of a pharisaic background, he did not consistently apply pharisaic practices in his ministry. For example, he rebuked Peter for withdrawing from table fellowship with gentile Christians (Gal. 2:11-14). He did not insist on circumcision of Gentiles, but advocated only a faith in Jesus Christ that brought about righteousness. Furthermore, he advocated tolerance on the keeping of certain days of worship, eating of various foods (Rom. 14:2-6), and he did not advocate a definite system of tithing (2 Cor. 9:6-10). Thus, in his ministry to the gentile churches, Paul dispensed with the outward distinctives of pharisaism: tithing, sabbath regulations, and various forms of ritual purity. He did, however, maintain some of these practices while in Jerusalem (Acts 21:26; 1 Cor. 10:20).

***Bibliography.***–J. Bowker, *Jesus and the Pharisees* (1973); L. Finkelstein, *The Pharisees* (2 vols., 3rd ed. 1962); R. T. Herford, *The Pharisees* (1924); *HJP,* II/2, 10-28; M. Jastrow, *Dictionary of the Targumim, Talmud Babli, Yerushalmi, and Midrashic Literature* (1971); J. Jeremias, *Jerusalem in the Time of Jesus* (Eng. tr. 1969); R. Longenecker, *Biblical Exegesis in the Apostolic Period* (1975); R. Marcus, *JR,* 23 (1952), 153-164; R. P. Martin, *NT Foundations* (2 vols., 1975-1978); G. F. Moore, *Judaism in the First Centuries of the Christian Era* (repr., 2 vols., 1946); J. Neusner, *Rabbinic Traditions about the Pharisees before 70* (3 vols., 1971); *From Politics to Piety: The Emergence of Pharisaic Judaism* (1973); H. Odeberg, *Pharisaism and Christianity* (1964); E. Rivkin, *A Hidden Revolution* (1978); *TDNT,* IX, *s.v.* φαρισαῖος (R. Meyer, K. Weiss); C. Thoma, "Der Pharisaïsmus," in J. Maier and J. Schreiner, eds., *Literatur und Religion des Frühjudentums* (1973), pp. 254-272; M. Wilcox, "Jesus in the Light of His Jewish Environment," in W. Hasse, ed., *Aufstieg und Niedergang der Römischen Welt,* 2.25.1 (1982), 131-195.

R. J. WYATT

**PHAROSH** fâr'osh (Ezr. 8:3, AV). *See* PAROSH **1.**

**PHARPAR** fär'pär [Heb. *parpar*]. One of the two rivers of Damascus mentioned by Naaman (2 K. 5:12). It is difficult to determine the exact location of this river. Two possibilities have been suggested. Some believe ABANA and Pharpar are two tributaries of the Nahr Baradā, which flows through Damascus. It is more common, however, to identify these two rivers as those which flow through the Damascus plain approximately 16 km. (10 mi.) S of Damascus. In this case "Damascus" would refer to the whole plain. The Nahr Baradā is usually identified with the Abana and the Nahr el-Aʿwaj is identified with the Pharpar. The Nahr el-Aʿwaj originates in the foothills of Mt. Hermon and flows eastward in a very crooked path through the plain of Damascus until it finally enters the salt lake, Baḥret el-Hijāneh. The fresh waters of this river coming from the melting snow off the mountains would be understandably more attractive to Naaman than the frequently muddy waters of the lower Jordan.

G. KROEZE

**PHARZITES** fär'zīts (Nu. 26:20, AV). *See* PEREZ.

**PHASEAH** fə-sē'ə (Neh. 7:51, AV). *See* PASEAH **2.**

**PHASELIS** fa-sē'lis [Gk. *Phasēlis*] (1 Macc. 15:23). A city of Lycia on the south coast of Asia Minor. It was located on the extreme end of a promontory with high mountains isolating it politically, ethnically, and geographically from the rest of Lycia. In 1 Macc. 15:23, a letter of a Roman consul refers to Phaselis in a list of cities in the Lycian League in 130 B.C., although it was independent of this league.

Because of its three small harbors, Greek colonists from Rhodes established Phaselis as a trading city in the 7th cent. B.C. Shortly thereafter it was inhabited by settlers from Naucratus in Egypt; it shared in Greco-Egyptian trade from 570 to 526 B.C. Under the Persian standard it struck its own coins, which had the prow and stern of a war galley as an emblem, until 466 B.C., when it joined the Athenian League. From 276 to 190 B.C. it fell under partial rule of the Ptolemies and Seleucids. It finally lost all independence and commercial importance in history when the Roman proconsul Servilius subjected it for harboring Cilician pirates. It was occupied into Byzantine times and was the seat of a bishop before it died completely. In its prime Phaselis was famous for its attar of roses and temple of Athene which was said to have contained the sword of Achilles.

The modern hamlet of Tekrova adjoins the site, which is marked by the ruins of a few Greek tombs, a flattened acropolis, a temple built by Trajan, a crumbling Roman aqueduct, and a hidden Greek temple.

***Bibliography.***–*CAH,* IV, VII; *HDB,* III, *s.v.* (W. M. Ramsay); F. Stark, *Lycian Shore* (1960).

R. T. HARRISON

**PHASIRON** fas'ə-ron [Gk. *Phasirōn,* var. *Pharisōn*] (1 Macc. 9:66); NEB PHASIRITES. According to most LXX MSS, the ancestor or chief of a bedouin clan that was attacked near Bethbasi in the Judean wilderness. But according to two Greek MSS (V and 340) the "sons of Phasiron" were "summoned" (*epétaxen*) rather than "struck down" (*epátaxen*) by Jonathan. *See* ODOMERA.

**PHASSARON** fas'ə-ron (1 Esd. 5:25, AV); **PHASSURUS** fas'ə-rəs (NEB). *See* PASHHUR **4.**

**PHATHAEUS** fə-thē'əs (1 Esd. 9:23, NEB). *See* PETHAHIAH **2.**

**PHEBE** fē'bē (Rom. 16:1, AV). *See* PHOEBE.

**PHENICE** fə-nī'sə.

**1.** (AV Acts 11:19; 15:3). *See* PHOENICIA.

**2.** (Acts 27:12, AV). *See* PHOENIX.

**PHENICIA** fə-nish'ə (Acts 21:2, AV). *See* PHOENICIA.

**PHERESITES** fer'ə-sīts (1 Esd. 8:69, AV); **PHEREZITES** fer'ə-zīts (AV Jth. 5:16; 2 Esd. 1:21). *See* PERIZZITE.

**PHIATHAS** fī'ə-thəs (1 Esd. 9:48, NEB). *See* PELAIAH **2.**

**PHICOL** fī'kōl [Heb. *pîḵōl*–'mouth of all'(?); Gk. *Phikol*]; AV PHICHOL. Commander of the Philistine army in the time of Abraham (Gen. 21:22, 32) and Isaac (26:26). The mention of both the Philistine king, Abimelech, and the Philistine commander, Phicol, in similar events involving Abraham and Isaac is one factor that has led some to view the two accounts as "a single incident which was differently reported in two independent sources [i.e., E and J]" (E. A. Speiser, *Genesis* [*AB*, 1964], pp. 203f.). Other explanations are possible, however. One, although improbable, is that the same Philistines were involved with both patriarchs, for long lives were not uncommon in patriarchal times, according to biblical records (e.g., Abraham lived to 175 [Gen. 25:7] and Isaac to 180 [35:28]). Another is that Abimelech and Phicol were Philistine titles rather than personal names (*see* ABIMELECH). G. A. L.

**PHILADELPHIA** [Gk. *Philadelph(e)ia*]. The Hellenistic name of two localities.

**1.** The NT Decapolis city previously called Rabbah or Rabbah of the Ammonites (*see* RABBAH **1**); the modern Amman, capital of Jordan. Its name meant not "brotherly love" but "in honor of Philadelphus," i.e., PTOLEMY II, who married his sister (Arsinoe II, "lover [*phílos*] of her brother [*adelphós*]") according to Egyptian royal custom.

**2.** (Rev. 1:11; 3:17). A city in Anatolia; the modern Alaşehir, "red city" or perhaps "city of Allah." It was named for the founders' sponsor, King Attalus of Pergamum (159-138 B.C.), whose surname Philadelphus meant "loyal to his brother [Eumenes]." It is 32 km. (20 mi.) E of Sardis and 97 km. (60 mi.) E of Smyrna, on a 210-m. (700-ft.) plateau extending from the north slopes of the Tmolus/Boz Mountains toward the Hermus River, today called Gediz but along this stretch Cogamıs. A settlement named Callatebus seems to have existed here from *ca.* 900 B.C. and was invaded by Cyrus on his march to Sardis in 546.

Though Sardis was so near, Attalus thought that a new center of population was needed in this fertile heartland of Lydia. He imported Macedonian veterans to settle there, as the shields on its coinage before 100 B.C. imply. Like Sardis Philadelphia was helped by Tiberius after the earthquake of A.D. 17 (Strabo *Geog.* xiii.4.10) and showed its gratitude by adding Neocaesarea to its name. The city became Philadelphia Flavia under Vespasian Flavius and in 214 added the title *Neokoros,* "(emperor-cult-)temple-keeper" (Pauly-Wissowa, XIX/2, 2091).

Philadelphia's temples merited it a prosperous stream of pilgrims, so that by A.D. 400 it was known as "little Athens." Like Smyrna it had a synagogue regarded by the Christians as notably uncooperative (Rev. 3:9). Yet the warm invitation held out to Philadelphia involves unusually Hebraic imagery: the key of David (v. 7); the name of Jerusalem (v. 12).

Ignatius of Antioch wrote to Philadelphia from Smyrna. Philadelphia's own first bishop may have been Demetrios of 3 Jn. 12 (Apos.Const. vii.46.9; *LTK,* VIII, 441). On the "prophetess Ammia," see Eusebius *HE* v.17.2; on "Philadelphia and Montanism," W. Calder, *BJRL,* 7 (1922), 309-354.

About 8 km. (5 mi.) E of Alaşehir in Badınca, Roman remains were found and partly removed to the museum in Manisa (*CBQ,* 18 [1956], 35). The Byzantine rampart inside Alaşehir is still visible; from 1109 to 1379 the Byzantine rulers resisted efforts of the Seljuk Moslems to incorporate the town into their surrounding domains. The town, with a population of 20,000-25,000 remains partly Greek. R. NORTH

**PHILARCHES** fil-är'kēz. The AV transliteration of Gk. *phylárchēs* (lit. "ruler of a *phylḗ* ['tribe' or 'tribal military contingent']") in 2 Macc. 8:32. The AV takes it as a proper name. The RSV ("commander [of forces]") and the NEB ("officer commanding [the forces]") more correctly interpret it as the title of a military officer. Cf. 1 Esd. 7:8, where it designates a "tribal leader" (RSV; AV "chief of the tribes"; NEB "patriarch").

**PHILEMON** fī-lē'mən [Gk. *Philēmōn*]. A "fellow worker" of Paul, to whom he addressed an Epistle (Philem. 1). Our only knowledge of the man is by inference from this letter, taken in conjunction with the closely related Epistle to the Colossians.

We infer that Philemon was a resident in the small city of Colossae in the upper Lycus Valley, some 16 km. (10 mi.) upstream from Laodicea, and that the Colossian church or some part of it met in his house. He was a man of standing whose hospitality is warmly commended in the Epistle (Philem. 7). He had evidently been converted through Paul (v. 19), but the circumstances of their previous acquaintance are unknown. He was ostensibly the owner of the runaway slave Onesimus, who occasioned the letter. The persons mentioned in v. 2 were presumably members of his family. Apphia was perhaps his wife. Her name is uncommon, although cognate forms were characteristic of this part of Phrygia; yet it is actually attested among the few known inscriptions of Colossae (R. Cagnat, *et al., Inscriptiones Graecae ad res Romanas pertinentes,* IV, 868). Archippus, mentioned also in Col. 4:17, may have been his son. The juxtaposition of this name with the injunctions concerning the Laodicean church in Col. 4:16 lends force to the suggestion that Archippus held some special responsibility at Laodicea (J. B. Lightfoot, *Colossians and Philemon* [1879], p. 307). Unless, however, we follow J. Knox in identifying the letter of Col. 4:16 with Philemon, it is natural to conclude from Col. 4:9 that Onesimus, and therefore the household of Philemon, belonged to Colossae, not Laodicea.

The relation between the apostle and Philemon was so close that Paul may press him to forgive Onesimus the wrongs he had done to the extent of receiving his repentant slave in a new relationship of brotherhood in Christ that transcended the relationship of master and slave.

The traditional reconstruction of the family and circumstances of Philemon has been challenged at several points by E. J. Goodspeed and especially by J. Knox (*see* PHILEMON, EPISTLE TO).

The traditions about Philemon and his family contained in the Apostolic Constitutions (vii.46) and in the Martyrologies are without merit (see Lightfoot, comm., p. 304; *Ignatius* [2nd ed. 1889], II, 535). C. J. HEMER

**PHILEMON, EPISTLE TO.**

I. Contents
II. Authenticity
III. Occasion and Date
IV. Views of Knox
V. Value and Significance

*I. Contents.*–(a) Paul and Timothy salute Philemon and his family, and the church that meets in his house (vv. 1-3). (b) Paul offers thanksgiving and prayer for Philemon, whose love and fellowship have been a blessing to others (vv. 4-7). (c) He tactfully requests that Philemon receive Onesimus, who formerly, despite a name meaning "profitable," was an unprofitable servant, but now, converted through an apostle in bonds, is true to his name (vv. 8-13). Paul will not, however, retain Onesimus as a helper without his master's consent. It may be that his temporary departure will result in Philemon's having him back forever in a new relationship (vv. 14-16). (d) If Onesimus has wronged his master, let the latter reckon the account against Paul, though on the score of debt Philemon owes his own spiritual life to Paul (vv. 17-19). (e) Paul has confidence in Philemon's compliance, and requests a lodging for himself (vv. 20-22). (f) Greetings from Paul's companions, and conclusion (vv. 23-25).

*II. Authenticity.*–The standing of this Epistle is inseparable from that of Colossians. These two letters, with Philippians and Ephesians, make up the four "imprisonment Epistles." Philippians was written apparently on a different occasion, but the other three ostensibly reflect the same circumstances. Colossians and Philemon were evidently sent together by the same messengers to the same destination. The genuineness of this beautiful personal appeal has rarely been doubted: it stands rather as Paul's signature to the authenticity of Colossians. Its place in the canon has only twice been seriously questioned: in the 4th and 5th cents. some thought it too slight to be Pauline, or if Pauline too lacking in edification to be considered worthy of canonicity; in the 19th cent. it was rejected by F. C. Baur and the Tübingen School, for whom its inauthenticity was a corollary of their rejection of Colossians.

External attestation is fairly strong. The earliest reference may be in Ign. Eph. 2, where a similar wordplay is made on the name Onesimus, and where Knox found other significant echoes (pp. 51ff.; see below). Tertullian knew Philemon and testified that Marcion accepted it without tampering with its text (*Adv. Marc.* v.21). The epistle is listed in the Muratorian Fragment, and Origen quoted v. 14 as Pauline (*Hom. in Jer.* 20).

The earlier attack on the letter was decisively answered by Jerome and by Chrysostom. Baur's rejection of it rested on the very different ground that it was a Christian fictional romance, the vehicle for a moral homily of reconciliation. Some of his followers found other objections. Pfleiderer and Weizsäcker treated it as allegorical; Holtzmann and others adopted interpolation theories. Steck claimed that an unknown writer used the younger Pliny's correspondence with Sabinianus, where he pleaded his friend's forgiveness for an erring freedman (Pliny *Ep.* ix.21, 24, written *ca.* A.D. 108). This idea was developed by van Manen (*EB*). He rejected all the Pauline Epistles, arguing here that the form showed an unnatural confusion between a personal letter and one addressed to a household church.

These excesses of skepticism have not found acceptance. The transparent genuineness of Philemon is seen rather as corroboration at least of Colossians. There are unsolved problems in the short note, but these are rooted in our imperfect inferential knowledge of the real-life situation that called forth this vivid appeal.

*III. Occasion and Date.*–Three different views have been held about the time and place of the Pauline imprisonment from which Colossians and Philemon were written: (a) a hypothetical imprisonment in Ephesus, *ca.* A.D. 54-55; (b) Caesarea, *ca.* A.D. 57-59 (Acts 24:26f.); (c) Rome, *ca.* A.D. 60-62 (Acts 28:16, 30).

Traditionally all the imprisonment Epistles (or Captivity Epistles) have been assigned to Rome, but the difficulties of this assumption, especially in the case of Philemon, have led many to look elsewhere. The Caesarean view has been supported for over a century, e.g., by Lohmeyer, and more recently by B. Reicke ("Caesarea, Rome and the Captivity Epistles," in W. W. Gasque and R. P. Martin, eds., *Apostolic History and the Gospel* [1970], pp. 277-286). It has difficulties of its own: it is understandable that a runaway should seek anonymity in Ephesus, the nearest great city, or in Rome, the distant capital, but why should he have gone to Caesarea? Reicke argued that he went to seek Paul's protection; but it seems more likely that he would rather have taken pains to avoid his master's associates, and that his conversion was, as traditionally supposed, a change of heart consequent upon an unintended meeting with Paul.

The claims of Ephesus have had a greater recent vogue, and were ably pressed a generation ago by G. S. Duncan (e.g., *St. Paul's Ephesian Ministry* [1929]). They hinge upon the actuality of the supposed Ephesian imprisonment. Such passages as 1 Cor. 15:32 and 2 Cor. 1:8 point to Paul's having undergone some special extremity of danger in Ephesus. There is no evidence that this involved imprisonment, and if it did such imprisonment is likely to have been a brief but rigorous condition pending trial or execution of sentence. The circumstances of prolonged custody or house arrest as at Caesarea or Rome were unusual and cannot be too easily assumed here.

The traditional Roman view has been championed by C. H. Dodd, and still remains the most satisfactory. We know that Luke and Aristarchus (Acts 27:2) sailed with Paul for Rome, and both sent greetings in these Epistles. Luke, however, was apparently absent from the Ephesian ministry, to judge from the incidence of the "we passages." Some have urged against Rome its great distance and the improbability of Paul's arranging lodging from there, but such arguments are not decisive. For the runaway Onesimus the distance may have seemed an advantage. Both C. F. D. Moule and F. F. Bruce inclined to a Roman origin. Bruce, acknowledging the difficulty of arguing from Philemon in isolation, favored Rome on the basis of the development in Paul's concept of the Church as reflected in Colossians.

The date is essentially determined by the view taken of the place of writing. In the case of Rome a further detail merits attention. A great earthquake devastated the Lycus Valley during Nero's reign. Tacitus (*Ann.* xiv.27), our earliest authority, dated it A.D. 60. Eusebius (*Chron.*) and Orosius (vii.7, 12) placed a similar disaster after the fire of Rome in 64 but were probably influenced by a later Christian tradition that made it a judgment on the pagan world for the Neronian persecution. Colossians and Philemon betray no knowledge of the disaster. Arguments from silence are always suspect, but we can scarcely doubt that Paul's loving concern would have been expressed here if bad news had recently arrived. There are many uncertainties in the case, but his silence may perhaps point to a setting early in the Roman imprisonment. Subsequent news of the earthquake, coupled with the unanticipated prolongation of his own case, may have radically altered the situation. We cannot tell if he ever fulfilled his plan to visit Colossae.

*IV. Views of Knox.*–Interest in Philemon has been stimulated by J. Knox, *Philemon among the Letters of Paul,* in which he developed ingeniously some of the ideas of E. J. Goodspeed. Knox (a) reconstructed differently the background of the letter, and (b) argued for a wholly new conception of its importance in the NT canon.

(a) The owner of the slave was not Philemon at all, but Archippus, who is made the main addressee of the letter, Philemon being the overseer of all the Lycus churches and probably resident in Laodicea. The "letter from Laodicea" of Col. 4:16 is asserted to be Philemon, which had first been delivered there to Philemon, the first though not the primary addressee, whose prior intercession with Archippus was being enlisted. The "ministry" Archippus is admonished to fulfil (Col. 4:17) was that of acceding to Paul's request, which was to restore Onesimus to him as a helper. (b) Arguing from the possible reminiscences of Philemon in Ignatius, where the Ephesian bishop is named Onesimus, Knox maintained that this was the same slave in later life (*ca.* A.D. 110), that he was responsible for collecting the corpus of the Pauline letters at Ephesus, and that he selected for inclusion the brief note Philemon which so closely concerned himself.

This series of plausible conjectures is hard to reconcile with a straightforward reading of the texts, from which we must suppose that Philemon is the main recipient and the slave owner. Archippus's ministry is surely to be understood of some active responsibility in the church. And Col. 4:16 evidently contemplates an exchange of letters addressed respectively to the churches of Colossae and Laodicea. The identity of the "letter from Laodicea" is an open question: possibly it was our Ephesians, treated as an encyclical; it could hardly have been Philemon (see further Moule, pp. 14-18).

The application of this reconstruction to support Goodspeed's theory of the Pauline corpus is yet more speculative. It is an interesting observation that Ignatius's address to his Ephesian Onesimus is so reminiscent of Philemon, but Onesimus was a common slave name, and it is precarious, if attractive, to argue that the two men were the same. For criticism of Goodspeed's views of the canon, which postulate that Onesimus himself wrote Ephesians as an introductory exposition of Paulinism, see D. Guthrie, *NT Intro.* (1970), pp. 647-653.

*V. Value and Significance.*–The views so far discussed seem influenced by the desire to justify the existence of Philemon by finding some hidden significance in it. But this letter about a slave is a precious document of Christian freedom in its own right.

Masters had an absolute power over their slaves, even if in practice Roman law and custom were becoming more humane. The generous provision for the fugitive enjoined in Dt. 23:15f. found no echo in pagan society: action could be taken even against any who harbored him (Oxy. P. 1422, 1643). These are closer parallels than the letter of Pliny, which concerns an emancipated dependent over whom his patron had renounced such absolute claims.

Paul did not question the institution of slavery. Elsewhere he laid down principles for the conduct of Christian masters and slaves (1 Cor. 7:20-24; Eph. 6:5-9; Col. 3:22-25) and made the themes of servitude and manumission the vehicle of rich spiritual teaching (cf. also Rom. 8:15-17; Gal. 4:5-7). But here, in a case where he could himself have been liable for harboring a fugitive, he pleaded for an abolition of human categories and penalties between a master and slave who had been brought into a new basis of relationship in Christ, for "there is neither slave nor free, . . . for you are all one in Christ Jesus" (Gal. 3:28). This view was not disruptive of existing society, but it introduced a spirit in which the institution of slavery could only wither.

A careful reading of Paul's request suggests that he was making a twofold plea, first for a reconciliation of master and slave, then perhaps that Philemon might be willing to release Onesimus to assist Paul in the overriding priority of the work of the gospel. He did not press the latter point, nor would he force Philemon's hand. Knox argued (p. 5) that in Philem. 10 the expression *parakalṓ perí* means "ask for" rather than "ask on behalf of" in late Greek idiom, but his parallels are not conclusive. Paul's second request is not so explicit.

The preservation of the letter testifies to the recognition of its value in the early Church, and probably also to Philemon's compliance.

***Bibliography.***–Comms. by H. M. Carson (*Tyndale NT Comms.*, 1960); M. Dibelius (*HNT,* 3rd ed. 1953); E. Eisentraut (1928); P. Ewald (*KZNT,* 2nd ed. 1910); G. Friedrich (*NTD,* 9th ed. 1962); J. Gnilka (1980); J. Knox (*IB*); A. R. C. Leaney (*Torch,* 1960); J. B. Lightfoot (6th ed. 1882); E. Lohmeyer (*KEK,* 1957); E. Lohse (*KEK,* 1968; Eng. tr., *Hermeneia,* 1971); C. F. D. Moule (*CGT,* 1957); J. J. Müller (*NICNT,* 1955); E. F. Scott (*MNT,* 1930); K. Staab (Regensburger NT, 3rd ed. 1959); A. Suhl (1981); M. R. Vincent (*ICC,* 1897).

F. F. Bruce, *BJRL,* 48 (1965), 81-97; C. H. Dodd, *NT Studies* (1953), pp. 83-128; G. S. Duncan, *Expos.T.*, 46 (1934/35), 293-98; E. J. Goodspeed, *Intro. to the NT* (1937), pp. 109-124; J. Knox, *Philemon among the Letters of Paul* (1935). C. J. HEMER

**PHILETUS** fī-lē'təs [Gk. *Philētos*] (2 Tim. 2:17). An early heretic, probably from the province of Asia. Along with HYMENAEUS (cf. 1 Tim. 1:20) he was accused of deviating from the truth and upsetting the faith of some by maintaining an over-realized eschatology, saying (as some of the Corinthians had before; cf. 1 Cor. 4:8; 15:12) that the resurrection had already occurred (2 Tim. 2:18). In spiritualizing the resurrection, Philetus and Hymenaeus may have taught that it occurred at baptism (based on a misunderstanding of Rom. 6:1-11; Col. 3:1; cf. Jn. 17:3) or during the instruction given at baptism.

J. J. HUGHES

**PHILIP** fil'ip [Gk. *Philippos*].

**1.** Philip II, king of Macedonia (359-336 B.C.) and father of ALEXANDER THE GREAT (1 Macc. 1:1; 6:2). Shortly after he became king, Philip transformed Macedonia into a powerful kingdom, and all of Greece fell under his control after his victory at Chaeronea in 338 B.C. He expanded his kingdom eastward by gaining control of the Straits of the Hellespont and the Bosphorus, thereby gaining control of the maritime route from the Aegean Sea to the Black Sea. Such expansion at the western border of Persia's empire signaled an imminent war with Persia. Philip was assassinated by one of his own officers while preparing for this war. He was succeeded on the throne by his twenty-year-old son, Alexander.

**2.** Philip V, king of Macedonia (220-179 B.C.). After the Syrian defeat of the Ptolemaic kingdom in 198 B.C., Philip received control over part of the former Ptolemaic kingdom in Thrace and Asia Minor. Rome, concerned about the rise of powerful Hellenistic states such as Macedonia and the Seleucid kingdom, defeated Philip in 197 at Cynoscephalae. After his death in 179, his son Perseus became king and was in turn defeated by the Romans in 168 (1 Macc. 8:5).

**3.** Philip, a Phrygian appointed governor of Jerusalem by Antiochus Epiphanes (*ca.* 170 B.C.), after the latter ravaged Jerusalem and the temple and returned to Antioch (cf. 1 Macc. 1:20-42; Dnl. 11:28; 2 Macc. 5:1-23). Philip was charged with implementing the king's policy concerning the Jews. According to 2 Macc. 5:22, he was "in character more barbarous" than Antiochus Epiphanes. He had pious Jews burned who had hidden in caves in order "to observe the seventh day secretly" (6:11). When Philip perceived the growing military success of Judas Maccabeus, he enlisted the aid of Ptolemy, governor of Coelesyria and Phoenicia (8:8).

**4.** Philip, trusted courtier of Antiochus Epiphanes and perhaps his foster brother. The word *sýntrophos* used in 2 Macc. 9:29 may mean "foster brother," but may also mean "intimate friend" (cf. Abel, p. 406; Bauer, rev., p. 793). Prior to his death, Antiochus Epiphanes appointed Philip, who was with the king in Persia, as regent and guardian of the king's young son, Antiochus V (1 Macc. 6:14-17), apparently deposing Lysias from all the offices earlier conferred on him (cf. 1 Macc. 3:32-36). When Lysias learned that Philip had returned from Persia and Media with the intention of seizing control of the government, he abandoned his siege of Jerusalem, restored religious rights to the Jews, and quickly returned to Antioch to protect his own position (6:55-63; 2 Macc. 13:23).

Goldstein (p. 324) thinks that the Philip of 1 Macc. 6:14-17 is not the same Philip who was opposed by Lysias. According to Josephus (*Ant.* xii.9.7 [386]), Philip was killed in Antioch by Lysias and Antiochus V Eupator, but according to 2 Macc. 9:29 he fled to Egypt, the enemy of Syria, for protection.

**5.** Philip the tetrarch (Lk. 3:1), son of Herod the Great and Cleopatra of Jerusalem. *See* HEROD VI.

**6.** Herod Philip, the brother of Herod Antipas, and the first husband of Herodias (Mt. 14:3 par. Mk. 6:17). *See* HEROD V.B.2.

**7.** One of the Twelve. *See* PHILIP THE APOSTLE.

**8.** One of the Seven. *See* PHILIP THE EVANGELIST.

*Bibliography.*–F.-M. Abel, *Les Livres des Maccabées* (1949); J. A. Goldstein, *I Maccabees* (AB, 1976).

R. L. OMANSON

**PHILIP, GOSPEL OF.** *See* APOCRYPHAL GOSPELS V.J.2.

**PHILIP THE APOSTLE** [Gk. *Philippos*]. One of the original twelve apostles. He appears fifth in every listing of the apostles (Mt. 10:3; Mk. 3:18; Lk. 6:14; Acts 1:13).

Philip appears as a distinct personality only in the Gospel of John. He was the first disciple directly called by Jesus (Jn. 1:43). It cannot be determined whether Jesus found Philip before leaving for Galilee or after He had arrived there. If Jesus found him before going to Galilee, Philip may have been one of the disciples of John the Baptist (Jn. 1:35). Philip's home was Bethsaida ("Fishertown"), a small fishing village on the north shore of the Sea of Galilee. John's note that this was also the hometown of Andrew and Peter may explain why Philip is usually mentioned in close conjunction with Andrew (Jn. 6:8; 12:22).

After Jesus had found him and he had responded to the call, Philip quickly found Nathaniel (Jn. 1:45). Philip was apparently well versed in the Scriptures and saw the fulfillment of the OT promises concerning the Messiah in Jesus of Nazareth. When Nathaniel hesitated, questioning if anything good could come from Nazareth, Philip invited him to come and see (v. 46). In Jn. 6:4-7 Philip demonstrated that he himself did not fully see. Jesus tested the extent of his faith by asking him how they were to buy bread for the multitude that had been following Him. Philip, still immersed in the workaday world, responded in terms of expenses. He could accurately appraise the value of the bread required for each person to receive something to eat, but he badly underestimated the miraculous power of Jesus.

In Jn. 12:21 some unnamed Greeks approached Philip to serve as an intermediary in their request for an audience with Jesus. Philip then consulted with Andrew and they both informed Jesus (v. 22). Philip may have been singled out by the Greeks because he spoke Greek. He and Andrew were the only disciples who had Greek names; they were also the only disciples reported to have brought another to see Jesus. Whether their entreaty was granted is not recorded.

At the Last Supper Jesus shared His reflections on the Father and the meaning of His ministry with His disciples. Through Him they had known the Father (14:7). Philip at this point expressed his own wish to see the Father (v. 8). Philip's misunderstanding reflected an earthly-mindedness that desired a sign from heaven, a tangible vision of the true God akin to an OT theophany (cf. Ex. 24:9-11; 33:12-23). His request was similar to Moses' petition, "Show me thy glory" (Ex. 33:18). Philip's spiritual dullness provoked Jesus to respond with some exasperation (vv. 9-11). Philip had been privy to far more than a shadowy theophany; he had witnessed the very incarnation of God. The one who had seen Jesus had seen the Father. Although Philip had been with Jesus from the start, this truth had quite escaped his notice.

Later tradition tended to confuse Philip the evangelist with Philip the apostle. For example, Tertullian referred to the Philip who witnessed to the Ethiopian eunuch in Acts 8 as an apostle (*De bapt.* 18). In his epistle to Victor of Rome, Polycrates the bishop of Ephesus referred to Philip as one of the luminaries of Asia who lived there with his two daughters and was buried in Hierapolis. Another daughter was said to have been buried in Ephesus (Eusebius *HE* iii.31.3). (It is possible that the interest in Philip reflected in the Fourth Gospel is due to its Ephesian provenance.) Eusebius reported that the daughters of Philip had related to Papias an account of the miracles of a resurrection of a dead body and of a man who drank a deadly poison with no ill effects (*HE* iii.39.9). Philip was also identified as the disciple whom Jesus commanded to follow Him instead of burying his father (Clement of Alexandria *Misc.* iii.4, 25).

Philip plays a prominent role in the Pistis Sophia, a late third-century Gnostic work (*see* APOCRYPHAL GOSPELS V.G). Reportedly, he wrote down all "the discourses which Jesus spoke" and "all that he did." This may be an allusion to the Gospel of Philip, which was forged in his name (*see* APOCRYPHAL GOSPELS V.J.2). According to Epiphanius *Haer.* 26.13.2f. this Gospel was used by Egyptian Gnostics. In the Acts of Philip (a fourth- or fifth-century romance), Philip is completely confused with Philip the evangelist and even described as a son of thunder, quick tempered and vindictive. He is also reported in this work to have been martyred by crucifixion head downward in Hierapolis.

D. E. GARLAND

**PHILIP THE EVANGELIST** [Gk. *Philippos*]. One of the seven men chosen to minister to the neglected Greek-speaking widows in the church at Jerusalem (Acts 6:1-6). Though the name "Philip" is Greek and he was selected to act in the interest of the widows of the Hellenists, it is difficult to ascertain whether he himself was a Hellenist. His selection to a function of service does not necessarily constitute what later became known as the "diaconate" despite the fact that "deacon" and "serve" (Acts 6:2) derive from the same root.

The next mention of Philip is in Acts 8:4. The persecution directed against the church in Jerusalem led to its dispersion and the spread of the gospel. Philip himself went to the territory of Samaria. Due to textual difficulties it is uncertain whether his endeavor led him to Sebaste (formerly the ancient city of Samaria), or to another city of Samaria, perhaps Gitta, the birthplace of Simon Magus according to Justin Martyr (*Apol.* i.26; cf. F. F. Bruce, *Book of the Acts* [*NICNT*, 1954], p. 177; B. Metzger, *Textual Comm. on the Greek NT* [1971], pp. 355f.).

In response to the preaching of Philip in Samaria many were healed and freed from unclean spirits (Acts 8:7). The significance of Philip's ministry in Samaria is that it highlighted the universal application of the gospel (cf. 1:8) even to the extent of healing the ancient schism between the Jews and Samaritans (cf. Jn. 4:9). Further, the signs and miracles performed by Jesus, the apostles (e.g., Acts 3:1-7; 5:12f.), and Philip announced the coming of the kingdom of God (8:6, 12).

While in Samaria Philip also encountered Simon, a pretentious practitioner of magic who had gained a large group of adherents; however, Philip's preaching of the gospel resulted in the conversion and baptism of numerous men and women, and even Simon himself, though his repentance may be questioned (8:9-13, 18-24; on legends regarding Simon see *BC*, V, 151-163). In response to Philip's ministry among the Samaritans, the apostles in Jerusalem sent Peter and John so that the new believers might receive the Spirit and be assured that they were truly incorporated into the new community (8:14-17).

A heavenly messenger then directed Philip southward to the Gaza-Jerusalem road where he met the Ethiopian eunuch, a court official to the queen of Ethiopia, also called by the hereditary title Candace. As a eunuch he could not achieve the status of a full proselyte (cf. Dt. 23:1; but also Isa. 56:3-5), but he may have been a "God-fearer" (cf. Acts 2:10; 10:2; *see* ETHIOPIAN EUNUCH). The eunuch's query on Isa. 53 provided Philip with an opportunity to identify the Suffering Servant and to speak "the good news of Jesus." The eunuch was converted and baptized (8:26-39). Then the Spirit "caught up" Philip (cf. the similar experience of Elijah, 1 K. 18:12, and Ezekiel, e.g., Ezk. 3:12), and he "was found" at Azotus (ancient Philistine Ashdod) heading north to Caesarea while preaching the gospel in the towns.

Some twenty years later Philip is mentioned again, now as a resident of Caesarea and father of four unmarried daughters who are prophetesses (Acts 21:8f.). Here Philip provided lodging for Paul and his companions who were on their way to Jerusalem. In this "we" section of Acts Luke relates the events at Caesarea, and it is likely that he received information for earlier portions of Acts from the accounts supplied by Philip and his daughters (cf. *SPT*, p. 379).

Later traditions often confused Philip the evangelist with PHILIP THE APOSTLE, but in Acts 21:8 Luke makes a special attempt to distinguish this Philip as "the evangelist, who was one of the seven" (cf. esp. J. B. Lightfoot, comm. on Colossians and Philemon [repr. 1979], p. 45). One tradition states he died at Hierapolis (Eusebius *HE* iii.31), while another asserts he became bishop of Tralles where he eventually died (*PL*, CXVII, 103).

G. L. KNAPP

**PHILIPPI** fil'ə-pī, fi-lip'ī [Gk. *Philippoi*]. A city of Macedonia, today in ruins.

I. Geographical Setting
II. History
III. Archeology
IV. Philippi and the NT
V. Later History

*I. Geographical Setting.*–Philippi was situated near the eastern end of the Egnatian Road (Via Egnatia), the major overland route traversing the Balkan peninsula. To the south, 15 km. (9 mi.) away but separated by a coastal mountain range (Symbolon), lay Philippi's port city of NEAPOLIS (known today as Kavalla and in medieval times as Christopolis). To the north are the foothills of the Balkan highlands, to the east rises Mt. Orbelos, and to the west Mt. Pangaeum (Pangaion).

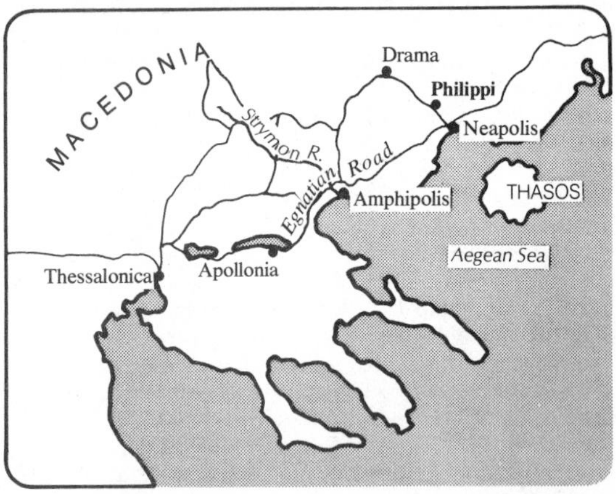


The broad flat plain in which Philippi is located extends generally to the northwest. In antiquity this plain was rather marshy, but today much of the area has been reclaimed, and former swamps yield both fruit and grain. Surrounded by mountains on almost every side, close to the sea, and near the borders of Thrace, Philippi naturally became a strategic city in the Greek empire. This inland valley is sheltered from the brisk sea winds, yet the climate of the plain is typical of the North Aegean area, being moderately hot in summer but raw and cold in winter.

*II. History.*–Gold was discovered at Mt. Pangaeum, and settlers from the island of Thasos (S of Neapolis) seized the area, which had previously been under Greek or Thracian control, and founded their city near the site of Philippi. They called it Krenides (from Gk. *krēnēde,* "spring"), undoubtedly because of the spring-fed river and marshlands (cf. Strabo *Geog.* vii, fragments 34, 41f.; Diodorus xvi.3.7f.). Diodorus said that the exiled Athenian statesman Callistratus was the leader of the original Thasian settlers. Although Appian (*Bell. civ.* iv.105) linked Krenides with Daton, it is more likely that Daton included the larger surrounding area, since Philippi is about 15 km. (9 mi.) inland and according to Strabo Daton encompassed an "admirably fertile territory, a lake, rivers, dockyards and productive gold mines."

Following his ascension to the throne Philip II of Macedon, the father of Alexander the Great, realized the strategic importance of Krenides and captured and rebuilt the city, renaming it Philippi. The Thasian settlers were driven out or assimilated into the large influx of Macedonian inhabitants. The city was walled even to the Acropolis (the ruins are still visible) and strongly fortified. A Greek theater was constructed that probably was used during Paul's time. (The ruins visible today are from the Aurelian reconstruction and probably seated about 50,000 people.) The gold mines were worked with vigor and produced over a thousand talents a year (Diodorus xvi.8), supplying the means by which Philip outfitted his army.

After the battle of Pydna (168 B.C.), Macedonia passed into Roman hands. L. Aemilius Paullus, the Roman consul, divided Macedonia into four major regions or districts (Livy xlv.29). Philippi was situated in the first district, whose capital became Amphipolis. Much discussion has centered upon the problematic description in Acts 16:12 (cf. א, A, C, etc., followed roughly by most English versions) of Philippi as "the first (or leading) city of the district of Macedonia," since Amphipolis continued to be the capital of this district. Blass and others have suggested that the Gk. *prṓtē* ("first") be emended to the genitive *prṓtēs* and thus read "a city of the first district of Macedonia," which would accord more with the Roman structure. Such a solution has its own problems. The suggestion of W. M. Ramsay (*SPT,* pp. 206f.), however, probably best represents Luke's thinking: whether or not the capital of the first district was established at Amphipolis, the citizens of Philippi had good reason to claim that their large *colonial* city was in reality the leading city of the district.

After the Roman conquest, the gold being exhausted, Philippi declined "to a small settlement" (Strabo vii.331 fr. 41) by the time of Caesar, but in a strange twist of history Philippi again became important because on its plains the future of the Roman republic was decided. In 42 B.C. Brutus and Cassius, assassinators of Caesar, met Octavian (later Augustus) and Antony. Antony defeated Cassius, while Brutus won the first battle with Octavian but was later defeated at Philippi. In honor of this victory Philippi was made a Roman colony (Colonia Victrix Philippensium), and many veterans settled there. After Octavian defeated Antony at the battle of Actium (31 B.C.), Philippi received an influx of Antony's followers, who had been dispossessed of their Italian property (Dio Cassius li.4). The colony was then renamed Colonia Iulia Philippensis to honor the cause of Julius Caesar, and later (27 B.C.), when Octavian was designated Augustus, the colony's name was changed again to Colonia Augusta Iulia (Victrix) Philippensium, equating the cause of Augustus with that of Caesar. Philippi was at that time given the right to the Law of Italy (*ius Italicum*) together with many privileges and immunities — especially the immunity from taxation. As might be expected, the residents of Philippi became very conscious of their Roman heritage (cf. Acts 16:20f.).

*III. Archeology.*– The major archeological work at Philippi was done between 1914 and 1918 by the French (École Française d'Athènes). The work has since been continued by the Greeks, who have established at Kavalla (Neapolis) a fine museum of artifacts recovered from Philippi and the surrounding area.

In the general plan of Philippi the Egnatian Road running E-W bisected the city, which was built on a spur of Mt. Orbelos. In the north sector, the highest part of the city, is located the theater and the Acropolis, on the west side of which are several pagan shrines. In the south sector, paralleling the Egnatian Road, is the forum, which has been excavated. It is about 100 m. (300 ft.) long and 50 m. (150 ft.) wide. Although it dates from the period of Marcus Aurelius, 2nd cent. A.D., it was undoubtedly built on the site of a previous forum known to Paul and his com-

Part of the Egnatian Road at Philippi (E. LaSor)

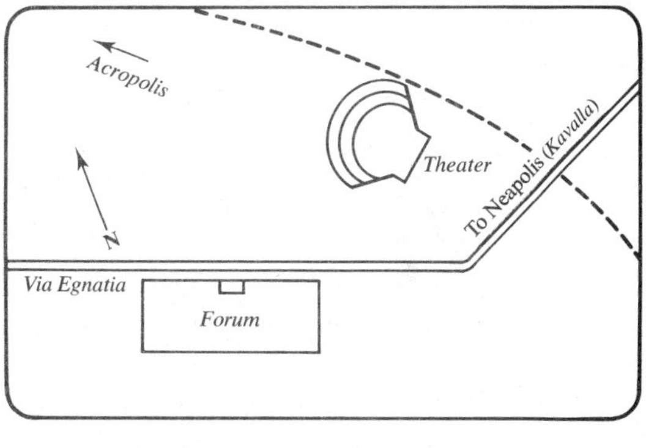


panions. In the middle of the north side of the forum are preserved four steps, which must have led to the speaker's platform or judgment seat (Gk. *bēma*). If Paul and Silas were sentenced from a tribunal platform, these steps may have been part of it (Davies, p. 96), since the forum complex does not seem to have been radically altered in rebuilding (McDonald, p. 21). At the northwest and northeast corners of the forum are the ruins of the temples of Antonia and Faustina. Other civic buildings such as grain shops and a library, together with fountains and a Roman stoa, surrounded the forum. Probably the city prison where Paul and Silas spent an eventful night (Acts 16:23ff.) was in this area.

About a kilometer NW of the city on the Egnatian Road the ruins of a colonial arch were discovered. Such arches were often erected to indicate the privileged status of Roman colonies.

*IV. Philippi and the NT.*–Following his vision and the Macedonian call (Acts 16:9ff.) Paul, together with Silas (also called Silvanus), Timothy, and Luke, set sail from Troas in Asia Minor and arrived the following day at Neapolis. Paul's strategy seemingly was to concentrate on the large cities of the Egnatian Road. Setting out almost immediately, he crossed the Symbolon ridge, which rises sharply to a pass of 500 m. (1600 ft.) and then descends to the plain. The graphic account of Paul's first visit to Philippi is recorded in Acts 16:12-40.

On the sabbath, according to his custom, Paul sought out the worshiping Jews and god-fearers. The Egnatian Road crossed the Gangites (Gangas) River not far beyond the arch. Thus the riverside where the Jews and god-fearers gathered for prayer and where the gospel was first preached in Europe (Acts 16:13) can be identified with fair certainty, although a branch of the Krenides is a possible alternative. The Jews' place of worship may have been determined by the Roman practice of tolerating, but sometimes excluding from colonial limits, religious practices that were inconsistent with their state. The colonial limits of Philippi, including the space outside the walls enclosed by the pomerium (the outer line of the colony), apparently extended to the arch. Thus the worshipers would have been practically by the Gangites before they were outside the city. The river may also have been important for Jewish lustration rites, and in this vicinity Paul probably baptized his first converts in Europe (v. 15).

The absence of any reference to men among the worshipers seems to indicate that the Jewish community was weak numerically. Although Luke legitimately could use the term "prayer" (Acts 16:13) as a figurative description for a synagogue (Cadbury, p. 87), the absence of men from the sabbath service of prayer greatly weakens this idea since at least ten men were necessary for a synagogue to function. The RSV is probably correct in rendering the uncertain Greek as "where we supposed there was a place of prayer" (*see also* PRAYER, PLACE OF), for at this time there was probably no synagogue in Philippi. Apparently the women who were meeting for prayer were led by one Lydia (whose name means "the Lydian woman"; cf. F. F. Bruce, *in loc.*). This woman marketed purple dyed products for which her native city in Lydia, THYATIRA, was famous. Probably a woman of means, perhaps a widow, she and her household were the first to accept the apostolic message, and she prevailed upon the missionaries to stay with her while they were at Philippi. How long Paul remained is not clear, but his stay was suddenly shortened.

On the way to prayer the Christians encountered a woman possessed of a strange spirit. F. F. Bruce (*in loc.*) suggests that Gk. *pýthōna,* translated "divination," may indicate that the Philippians considered her inspired by Apollo, the Python god. Her cries that the Christians were "servants of the most high God" were countered by Paul with a command in the name of Jesus for the spirit to leave her (cf. exorcisms by Jesus, Lk. 8:28ff.). The men who profited from this woman's possessed state seized Paul and Silas and dragged them to the forum (Gk. *agorá,* "marketplace") and accused them before the magistrates of advocating illegal practices in the Roman colony (Acts 16:21). Although the two magistrates of a Roman colony normally were designated as *duumvir,* Cicero indicated (*De lege agraria* ii.93) that they were often dignified with the title *praetor,* which Luke employed. Paul and Silas were mobbed, stripped, beaten with rods (fasces, carried by the lictors or sergeants), cast into prison, and placed in stocks. That night an earthquake jarred loose both stocks and prison doors. Paul saved the jailer from suicide, and the members of his household received the apostolic message and were baptized.

The next day the magistrates ordered the prisoners released, but Paul refused to accept such a dismissal since as a Roman citizen he was exempt from scourging and was entitled to a proper trial. Roman citizenship was undoubtedly pleaded during the disorderly trial but went unheeded. It is difficult to know with certainty whether Paul carried a portable certificate or diptych in order to prove his citizenship (cf. Cadbury. pp. 71f.; F. Schulz, *Journal of Roman Studies*, 33 [1943], 58-64; but *see* PAUL THE APOSTLE VII.A). The lictors reported the fact of citizenship to the magistrates, who made appropriate apologies but begged Paul to leave their city.

The missionaries set out for Thessalonica, but they seem to have left Luke behind, because the "we" section of Acts ends in ch. 16 and is not resumed until 20:5, when Paul again leaves Philippi for Jerusalem. The presence of Luke during the five-year interval may explain the growth and strength (in affliction) of the church at Philippi (2 Cor. 8:1f.; Phil. 1:29f.). Although not specifically stated, Paul probably visited Philippi on his way to Greece during his third journey, waiting for the coming of Titus (2 Cor. 7:5f.) and probably writing 2 Corinthians there (8:1ff.; 9:2-4). On his return from Greece to Syria he was forced to go by way of Philippi because of a plot on his life. At that time Luke rejoined him. From Phil. 2:24 and 1 Tim. 1:3 one may surmise that he intended to visit Philippi again, and he possibly did so in connection with a visit to Troas (2 Tim. 4:13). The communication between Paul and Philippi was not limited to visits, however; the Philippians sent gifts of money at least on two occasions (Phil. 4:16; 2 Cor. 11:9; Phil. 2:25). Paul's limiting his correspondence with this church to one letter therefore is unlikely (cf. Polyc. Phil. 3:2 and J. B. Lightfoot's note on Phil. 3:1).

*V. Later History.*–After Paul's death little is heard of Philippi, except that Polycarp bishop of Smyrna addressed an encouraging letter to the church after Ignatius stopped there on his way to martyrdom in Rome. The ruins of five ancient churches have been identified in the vicinity of Philippi, including one from the 4th cent. near the river site traditionally associated with the "place of prayer." The prosperity of later Christianity in this area is attested by the two large basilicas that were erected in the 5th-6th centuries. The first was evidently destroyed by earthquake, and the second collapsed because of faulty construction (Davies, pp. 97-100). The small crypt of the first church has been erroneously linked to the prison where Paul and Silas spent their eventful night. Of the destruction of Philippi no account is available, and the site is now uninhabited.

***Bibliography.***–F. F. Bruce, *Acts of the Apostles* (2nd ed. 1952), pp. 312-323; H. J. Cadbury, *Book of Acts in History* (1955); *CIL*, III, 1, 633-707; Suppl. 7337-7358; P. E. Davies, *BA*, 26 (1963), 91-106; Ecole Française d'Athenes, reports appearing in vols. 44-49, 52, 54-55, 57-62 of *Bulletin de correspondence hellénique*; E. Haenchen, *Acts of the Apostles* (Eng. tr. 1971), pp. 492-504; R. F. Hoddinott, *Early Byzantine Churches in Macedonia and Southern Serbia* (1963), pp. 99-106; *The Thracians* (1981), pp. 87, 106, 170f.; R. Longenecker, *Expositor's Bible Commentary*, IX (1981), 458-467; W. A. McDonald, *BA*, 3 (1940), 18-44; Pauly-Wissowa, XIX, 2206-2244; *SPT*.

G. L. BORCHERT

**PHILIPPIANS, EPISTLE TO THE.**

I. Paul and the Church of Philippi
II. Origin of the Epistle
III. Structure
IV. Impact

***I. Paul and the Church of Philippi.***–According to Acts, Paul founded the church of Philippi during his second journey, shortly after his first arrival in Europe *ca.* A.D. 50.

He came with Timothy and Silas to Troas, and had a vision of a Macedonian man who asked him to preach the gospel in Macedonia (Acts 16:8-10). Paul and his friends immediately sailed to Samothrace and to Neapolis, the seaport of eastern Macedonia; then, following the Roman Egnatian Road (which connected Epirus with Byzantium), they went some 16 km. (10 mi.) northwest and reached Philippi, where they decided to stay (vv. 11f.).

PHILIPPI had the form of a rectangle. Its northeastern quarters were on the slope of the acropolis, under which the Egnatian Road ran diagonally between the eastern and the western city gates; its southwestern quarters were on the plain where Antony had defeated the murderers of Caesar in 42 B.C. The inhabitants were proud of their

Traditional site of Paul's prison in Philippi (W. S. LaSor)

Roman citizenship, which they had received after the battle of Actium in 31 B.C. when Augustus made Philippi a colony of Roman veterans (Acts 16:12, 21). Paul alluded to this by contrasting political and religious citizenship (Phil. 1:27; 3:20).

There were also Jews and God-fearing women in Philippi but, evidently because of the strong Roman consciousness of the citizens, the Jews were not allowed to have a synagogue within the city walls, so they had only a place of prayer outside the west gate at a river (Acts 16:13). This river was either the Gangites, 2.4 km. (1.5 mi.) W of the city (Collart), or a streamlet of the Krenides just outside the gate (Lemerle).

Paul spoke to some of the God-fearing women assembled here, and the first to become a Christian was a female wholesaler by the name of Lydia who imported purple textiles of Thyatira. She was baptized, and became the hostess of Paul and the other Christians (Acts 16:13-15). Lydia and her friends are the first evidence of a Christian church in Europe, besides some Jewish Christians of Rome, who may have included Aquila and Priscilla before this couple had to leave for Corinth in A.D. 50 (Acts 18:2; cf. Suetonius *Claudius* 25.5).

Paul's great success in Philippi caused the Romans there to react against the influence of what they supposed to be Judaism, and the duumviri of the city arrested Paul and Silas (Acts 16:16-24). Seeing that Claudius had driven out the Jews of Rome in A.D. 50 (as mentioned above), the Greeks of Alexandria were inspired in A.D. 52 to accuse the Jews of stirring up society. It was in this connection that Paul and Silas were accused in Philippi of introducing Jewish customs unworthy of Romans (16:20f.). They were flagellated and imprisoned, but the jailer was converted, and the magistrates had to apologize and then asked Paul to leave their city (16:25-40). Paul followed the Egnatian Road to Thessalonica (17:1; 1 Thess. 2:2), where he received material support more than once from Philippi, perhaps especially from Lydia (Phil. 4:15f.). The Philippians also supported him in Corinth (2 Cor. 11:9).

During his third journey Paul was attacked in a similar way by the Gentiles in Ephesus (Acts 19:23-40). He visited Macedonia again in A.D. 57 (Acts 20:1; 1 Tim. 1:3). If he wrote 2 Corinthians at Philippi, it was mainly in that city that he was occupied with his great collection for Jerusalem (2 Cor. 8:1; 9:2; Rom. 15:26). A third visit to Philippi occurred at Easter, A.D. 58, on Paul's return from his collection activity in Greece (Acts 20:3, 6). Those scholars who assign the custody mentioned in Philippians (Phil. 1:7, 12-17) to Ephesus make the new journey to Philippi, which the apostle mentioned as a possibility (Phil. 1:27; 2:24), coincide with the first of these collection visits. The combination is dubious, however (see II below). There is no indication of any captivity in Ephesus, but merely of a tumult (Acts 19:23-40; cf. 1 Cor. 15:32, Gk. *ethēriomáchēsa*). On that occasion Timothy was already in Macedonia (Acts 19:22), not with Paul (Phil. 1:1). Paul must therefore have been looking forward to visiting the Philippians on a later occasion. It is uncertain, though, whether he did go to Philippi a fourth time, as he desired. No text mentions such a visit (1 Tim. 1:3 refers to that earlier occasion mentioned above). If the apostle was able to visit Spain after A.D. 62 (the plan to do so is mentioned in Rom. 15:24, 28, and the journey is probably referred to in 1 Clem. 5:6f.), there was not much time left for a new visit to Philippi before his martyrdom in 64 or 65 (1 Clem. 5:6f.).

***II. Origin of the Epistle.***–As is true of all Pauline Epistles, Philippians has given rise to a great variety of theories regarding the circumstances under which it was composed. Yet it seems possible to answer some fundamental questions with a considerable degree of probability.

(1) Modern scholars no longer attempt to deny the Pauline authorship of the Epistle. The greeting names Paul and Timothy as its senders; and there is no reasonable ground to discredit the notice about the writer and his assistant since the diction and ideas are very much in harmony with other Pauline Epistles, in particular with 1 Corinthians and Romans, but also with Ephesians and Colossians (C. L. Mitton, comm. on Ephesians [1951], pp. 107-110, 322-332). Paul had received fresh information about the situation of the Philippians from Epaphroditus, their fellow Christian, and sent him back with the Epistle (2:25-30; 4:18). In spite of the linguistic identity of their names, Epaphroditus and Epaphras (Col. 1:7; 4:12; Philem. 23) were two different persons, as is evident from their special connections with different congregations.

(2) In accordance with German and French traditions of literary criticism, several attempts have been made to attack the literary integrity of the Epistle (references in W. G. Kümmel, *Intro. to the NT* [Eng. tr., 2nd ed. 1975], pp. 322f.). They are intended to remove what theologians with a high regard for Paul as a theologian consider contradictions and unevennesses. These attempts give rise to many new difficulties and enigmas, partly because quite different and subjective explanations have been suggested, and partly because the literary procedure becomes less understandable by involving a series of secondary factors.

In some cases Paul is supposed to have made a revision himself. The question here is why Paul would have made rearrangements or additions in his MS when he knew that his time was short. Paul always wrote to a local church and in this case was eager to send Epaphroditus with the letter, so that it must be supposed to have been rather soon in the hands of its readers. Had he wanted to improve his message, he would have done so under the impression of fresh prophetic inspiration, and then he would have sent another letter but never would have dreamed of calling back his MS for revision, as if he were a modern scholar.

Should instead some disciple be accused of having changed the wording of the original? Those who think so have spoken not of textual variants, which may have been caused by later scribes, but of a deliberate revision. In this connection many different suggestions to restore an original sequence have been made (e.g., 4:10-23; 1:1–3:1; 4:4-7; 3:2-4, 8f.; or 4:10-20; 1:1-26; 2:17f.; 1:27–2:16; 4:1-3; 2:19-30; 3:1a; 4:4-7; 4:21-23; 3:2-21; 4:8f.). The great variety of theories makes the picture confusing, and because of the circumstances any solution of this kind seems improbable. What interest would have directed this inventive redactor? It cannot have been to make the letter more complicated than it was. Once the letter was read and circulated by its recipients, that activity of the supposed redactor would have been rejected as falsification. Some think, however, that various local letters of Paul were combined by somebody who desired to make them of interest to the whole Church. One must ask why this man left out original prescripts and inserted secondary transitions but was so careless that he did not give the result of his work a really catholic, ecumenical character, letting all those local and personal details remain.

The many attempts to destroy the integrity of Philippians are too divergent and subjective to be convincing. A personal letter written in a short time and under special conditions should not be expected to be consistent like a theological treatise. The literary manipulations now in vogue again raise difficulties greater than those their originators were trying to solve.

(3) Paul wrote his letter to Philippi in custody ("fetters," Phil. 1:7, 13f., 17). Modern scholars consider Philippians, together with the Captivity Epistles written to Christians in Asia Minor (Ephesians, Colossians, and Philemon), to have been written from either Ephesus, Caesarea, or Rome. This problem has to be discussed without any prejudicial opinion that Philippians and the other Captivity Epistles must relate to the same prison.

(a) Ephesus is often said to be the place of captivity behind Philippians, Ephesians, Colossians, and Philemon. This is arbitrary, for the NT indicates several arrests (2 Cor. 6:5; 11:23; Rom. 16:7) and yet does not contain the slightest allusion to any imprisonment in Ephesus. On the contrary, Luke said that the city tumult raised there by the artisans (Acts 19:23f.) *ca.* A.D. 56 was stopped by the magistrates (19:35-40; 20:1), and Paul looked back on this desperate struggle but not on any imprisonment (1 Cor. 15:32). There is also the difficulty that Timothy is said to have left for Macedonia before this disturbance happened (Acts 19:22), but is mentioned in Phil. 1:1 as being with the apostle.

(b) Paul's imprisonment in Caesarea *ca.* A.D. 58-60 (Acts 23:33; 24–26) may very well be regarded as the background of the three Captivity Epistles sent to Asia Minor with Epaphras, Tychicus, and Onesimus: Ephesians, Colossians, and Philemon. The chronological reason for this view is that Paul represented his imprisonment as involving a new factor in his life ("now also a prisoner," Philem. 9), and his only long-lasting imprisonment began in Jerusalem and Caesarea *ca.* A.D. 58. This view is also supported by the geographical circumstances. The situation is most easily conceivable if the slave Onesimus escaped from Colossae to Caesarea and was urged by Paul to return there with Tychicus (Philem. 11, 15, 17; Col. 4:7-9). In this way they would simply have passed from Colossae to Caesarea and back again in a short time and on foot, which would not have been possible if Paul had been in Rome. Furthermore, in Caesarea the apostle may very well have been hoping to be freed rather soon and to pass Colossae (Philem. 22) on his way to Rome and Spain (Rom. 15:23f., 28). The projected visit to Colossae would contradict his Spanish plans if the apostle had written the three Epistles from Rome.

(c) In all these respects Philippians is evidently based on a different situation. Hence its background seems to be Rome and the years 60-62 (Acts 28:16, 30).

With regard to chronology, the apostle's trial is not a new factor but a long story now approaching its end (Phil. 1:7, 12, 26; 2:24; 4:10). Paul did not call himself a prisoner who had to suffer in chains (Eph. 3:1; 4:1; 6:20; Col. 1:24; 4:18; Philem. 1, 9) together with some fellow prisoners (Col. 4:10; Philem. 1, 9), but only spoke of "bonds," implying that he was arrested or in custody (Phil. 1:7, 13f., 17). No other prisoner is mentioned; Paul on the contrary indicated that he could receive and send out collaborators at his discretion (2:19, 25, 28; 4:18). This was his situation in Rome A.D. 60-62 when he lived in a private house guarded by a soldier (Acts 28:16, 23, 28).

Geographical details also point toward Rome. The distance between Rome and Philippi is not greater than that between Caesarea and Philippi. The good roads would have allowed the Philippians to send Epaphroditus with money to Rome and to be informed about his illness within six or eight months (Phil. 2:25-30; 4:18), and Paul spent two years in the Roman custody. Also indicative of a Roman provenance is Paul's statement that his case had "become known among the whole praetorium and all the others" (Phil. 1:13). The expression "praetorium" cannot refer to a building (as in the Gospels), but must indicate some people, comparable with "the others." Several

Greek inscriptions use the word praetorium in a personal sense to designate the praetorian guard of the emperor in Rome (L. Heuzey and H. Daumet, *Mission archéologique* [1876], nos. 130f.; *Inscriptiones Graecae,* XIV [1890], no. 911; W. Dittenberger, *Orientis graeci inscriptiones,* II [1905], no. 707). This corresponds to a normal Latin literary usage (Pliny *Nat. hist.* xxv.6 [17]; Suetonius *Nero* 9; Tacitus *Hist.* i.20; etc.). During the first Christian centuries the praetorian guard was always garrisoned in Rome, although part of it would have provisionally accompanied the emperor abroad. Inscriptions found at other places (as also those quoted above) have to do only with individuals who had earlier been members of the Roman bodyguard. *See also* PRAETORIUM; PRAETORIAN GUARD.

Representatives of the Ephesus theory believe that inscriptions found on a road near this city prove that a praetorian detachment was garrisoned in Ephesus. This is wrong, for the documents in question (*CIL* 6085 = 7135 and 7136) were made for a veteran who had been a member of the guard and now served at this road as a rural policeman (*stationarius*). The praetorian guard itself had to be where the emperor was, and for the days of Paul this implies nothing but Rome.

It is also most natural that Paul should use the Latin loanword *praetorium* while in Rome and while addressing Christians of a Roman veteran colony familiar with military conditions in Rome. Because of some details given by Josephus in his report on the arrest of Agrippa in Rome (Josephus *Ant.* xviii.6.6f. [179-204]), the soldier who guarded Paul in Rome (Acts 28:16) must be supposed to have served in the praetorian regiment and to have fulfilled his function of a policeman by order of the prefect (commander in chief) of the praetorians, who was personally responsible for the arrest of state prisoners. During the Roman custody of Paul and until A.D. 62 the prudent equestran politician Burrus held this office. Tacitus referred to occasions when Burrus used praetorian soldiers as policemen in Rome, sometimes in opposition to the cruel tendencies of Nero (*Ann.* xiii.48; xiv.7-10; etc.). According to a popular biography, the prefect Aelianus is said to have felt sympathy for the imprisoned oriental philosopher Apollonius, who had been accused of spreading foreign doctrines (Philostratus *Apoll.* vii.16-28). The personal conversation of this prefect with the prisoner sheds light on the circumstances under which Paul may have become convinced that "the whole praetorium" was aware of his being under trial for the sake of Christ.

Another indication of Rome and Nero's court is the greeting at the end of the Epistle from "those of the house of Caesar" (Phil. 4:22). While clients and servants of the emperor and his family did live in other places, such people were mainly found in Rome, which also had a Jewish synagogue of Augustenses (J. Frey, *Corpus inscriptionum Judaicarum,* I [1936], pp. LXXIIIf.). The point is lost if one does not see that Paul is happy to confer a greeting from such a group directly connected with the imperial court to readers in a Roman colony where the leading elements were proud of their connections with the capital.

As stated above, the apostle may very well have expected in A.D. 59 that his captivity in Caesarea would soon be over so that he would be able to visit Colossae (Philem. 22), then sail from Ephesus to Rome and later to Spain (Rom. 15:23f., 28). This natural project would have been more complicated if Philippians had been written from Caesarea, for a visit to Philippi (Phil. 1:27; 2:24) would be a detour. If the Epistle was written from Rome, the situation is simplified. Without assuming that Paul gave up his Spanish plans while being on trial, one may observe that Rome would have been the most natural place for his contemplating both projects: first a journey to Spain, then a new visit to the East.

*III. **Structure**.*–Philippians is both a genuine personal letter containing intimate information, and an Epistle offering theological instruction and ethical admonition.

Except for the letter to Philemon, it may be called the most personal writing in the NT, for it both emphasizes the friendly connections of Paul and the Philippians and brings several reports of what the apostle, his disciples, and the readers had recently done or were going to do. This does not prevent Philippians from being a theological writing, a rich source of Christian doctrine and an excellent instrument of apostolic teaching, especially with regard to Christ and the Church. These two aspects of Philippians — personal letter and theological Epistle — are represented in turn in the document. Accordingly, the contents of Philippians may be divided into the following sections, alternating between information and admonition.

1:1-26: *Information.* Paul is grateful because the Philippians have given him material support (1:1-11). He is also hopeful because the praetorium and other people know that he has been arrested for the sake of Christ and the gospel, and because he is convinced that his trial is making progress (1:12-26).

1:27–2:16: *Admonition.* There must be spiritual unity and mutual service among the members of the church (1:27–2:4). Christ is the model in this regard because of His voluntary humiliation or "kenosis," which found expression when He laid aside His divine glory, took on a human shape, and obediently appeared in the function of a servant, even permitting Himself to be crucified (2:5-11, often regarded as a hymn based upon some formula of confession; cf. V. Neufeld, *Earliest Christian Confessions* [1963]). Thus every Christian must show obedience in this world until the day of Christ (2:12-16).

2:17-30: *Information.* Paul is full of joy though he knows that he might be sacrificed because of his ministry (2:17f.). Timothy will soon be sent to Philippi to look after the readers, but Epaphroditus will come first (2:19-24). He brought some gifts (perhaps money and clothes) from the readers to Paul, and then fell ill, as the readers know, but now he is returning with the present Epistle.

3:1–4:9: *Admonition.* The readers should rejoice in the Lord, with regard to His coming glory (3:1). They are warned against inclinations to legalistic Judaism (3:2-6), which implies looking backward instead of forward (3:7-17). Another aspect of this false propaganda is that its representatives cultivate materialistic and even political ambitions instead of looking upward to Christ in His glory (3:18–4:1). In opposition to all sorts of self-assertion and provocation Paul implores two women and the whole congregation to let themselves be dominated by peace and other virtues (4:2-9).

4:10-23: *Information.* Paul thanks his readers for the support they have given him recently through Epaphroditus (4:10-20). He is happy to confer greetings especially from some clients or servants of Nero and his family (4:21-23).

*IV. **Impact**.*–Both the personal and the theological interests of Philippians are valuable for devotion.

(1) Philippians is a personal document illustrating the relations between the apostle of the Gentiles at the summit of his life and the congregation that he regarded as nearly ideal. The Epistle is characterized by repeated expressions of joy and exhortations to rejoicing (Phil. 1:4, 18, 25; 2:2, 17f., 29; 3:1; 4:1, 4). These are partly due to Paul's satisfaction with the readers and gratitude for their help. But there is more than a personal interest behind this emotion of happiness. Paul is dealing with the joy of faith that has an eschatological accent: he is conscious that Christ has come and will come again to bring consummation. This is

the cause and the object of Christian joy so much emphasized in this Epistle.

(2) Philippians is also a theological document offering essential contributions to the study of NT Christology, ecclesiology, and eschatology.

Christ is first of all mentioned as the subject of apostolic preaching (1:13-17). Paul was arrested for the sake of the gospel; but this has encouraged many to preach the kerygma of Christ in an often hostile environment, and what is important is only that Christ is made known everywhere. Suffering brings the believer closer and closer to his Redeemer (1:20-23). Against the background of his exhortations to a behavior worthy of the gospel (1:27–2:4) the apostle quotes the "kenosis" hymn (2:5-11), which is the most essential christological passage found in all the Pauline Epistles. Here the humiliation and exaltation of Christ are not meant to be a topic of dogmatics and are referred to not for any doctrinal reasons, but with a pronounced ethical interest. Paul has just spoken of mutual Christian *diakonía* (2:1-4). Christ's incarnation is then represented as the model of such unselfish service. Though He existed in the state of God, He did not regard being equal with God as something "to be grasped" (2:5f.). Since the Greek word used here (*harpagmós,* "robbery") is normally active, whereas passive meanings (something [being] stolen) are found only in later contexts and secondary expositions, the meaning is that Christ did not use His majestic position to commit robbery in the sense of enforcing His authority upon other beings. An old Greek catena has indicated the correct translation of the phrase by quoting the expression "the ministry is not an opportunity for robbery" (Gk. *ouk harpagmós hē timḗ*; P. Poussines, *Catenae graecorum patrum* [1673], p. 233).

Christ renounced the divine fulness and omnipotence that belonged to Him as the Son of God and instead dispossessed Himself (2:7a). This is called His kenosis ("emptying"), i.e., Christ's laying off of His divine fulness, dignity, and power so that He "emptied" Himself at His incarnation. It is meaningless to ask whether this is a pre-Pauline or a Pauline topic. The apostle may possibly have adopted some formula or hymn familiar to the readers, but in this case he quotes the words in a free way and gives every detail a meaning in the present exposition. Attempts to reduce the kenosis passage to pre-Pauline and non-Pauline traditions are popular, but the result is another kenosis, insofar as the words of Paul are deprived of their meaning.

With a special reference to Christian *diakonía* Paul then reminded the readers that Christ took on the form of a servant (2:7b). The point is that a completely unselfish service is most glorious in the eyes of God, as shown in Isaiah's Servant prophecies that Jesus fulfilled. The readers were certainly familiar with these classical prophecies, so that Paul did not have to insert any literary quotation. It is dubious whether he used the LXX text, but even if this was the case, the slight difference of the words for "servant" does not imply any real difficulty. Paul deliberately used the Gk. *doúlos* (like the LXX in Isa. 49:3f. and corresponding with *douleúōn* in 53:11). He could not possibly have said *país* (like Isa. 42:1; 49:6; 50:10; 52:13), for in the phrase "the form of a servant" this expression would have been understood as "child," whereas Paul wanted to clarify that Christ is the model of Christian service. This is also why he pointed out the humiliation and sacrifice of the incarnate Son of God (2:7c-8): in complete obedience Christ took on human nature, humbled Himself, and permitted Himself to be killed in a miserable way on a cross. Here is the basis of His subsequent exaltation to universal sovereignty (2:9-11). Thus Christians have to be His successors in obedience and blamelessness (2:12-16). Paul himself endeavors to be united with Christ in His suffering in order to participate in His resurrection (3:10-12) and in this context wants to be a pioneer for the believers (3:17; 4:9).

The church of Philippi was administered by functionaries called bishops and deacons (1:1, Gk. *epískopoi, diákonoi*). In earlier Pauline Epistles these categories are not mentioned together; there are only indications of specialists in *diakonía* (Rom. 12:7; 16:1). A few years before writing Philippians, the apostle is reported to have called the presbyters of Ephesus "bishops" (Acts 20:28). Since he addressed the bishops of Philippi similarly in the plural, it seems they were not monarchic officers but rather honorary authorities like presbyters who collaborated in the administration of community life. The deacons of Philippi were probably functionaries responsible for social work, like the deacons mentioned in other contexts. Paul appears to have addressed them, along with the bishops, especially with regard to their help when he arranged the collection in Macedonia. The combination of bishops and deacons represented by Philippians is also found in 1 Tim. 3:2, 8 and not long afterward it became a normal system (1 Clem. 42:2; Did. 15:1).

Paul is extraordinarily satisfied with the Christians of Philippi because of their *diakonía,* and the Epistle is characterized by expressions of his gratitude and happiness (1:3-7; 2:2, 12; 4:10, 15-18). The Philippians do not have the same perfection and harmony on the level of doctrine, but a certain inclination to individualism and even heresy. For this reason Paul emphasizes his desire that the Christian love so well represented by the readers may help them more and more to acquire Christian knowledge and righteousness (1:9-11). His heartfelt concern is their behavior in society (Gk. *politeúesthe,* 1:27), which should be worthy of the gospel and without any disharmony in spite of all external difficulties (1:27-30).

As usual Paul sees the remedy in his ecumenical program: the purity of Christian love and the unity of the Holy Spirit (2:1-4). The necessary predisposition is not any special confession, philosophy, or hermeneutics, but the perfection of Christian *diakonía* that will bring about the spontaneous improvement of Christian doctrine. Christ is the prototype of *diakonía* (2:5-11), and if the believers follow Him they will have spiritual unity and doctrinal harmony, each respecting the attitude of the other (2:3).

But no tolerance of heretics who destroy Christian peace is permitted. Paul had been irritated by Christian troublemakers in Rome (cf. Rom. 16:17f.) who used the gospel for intrigues and provocation (Phil. 1:15-17). Clement further illustrates this by saying that jealousy and envy in the environment caused the martyrdom of Peter and Paul (1 Clem. 5:1-7), as later also the fall of Jerusalem (6:4). He evidently thinks of zealotic propagandists and intriguers within Christianity who had relations with Judaism. It is very probable that Jewish zealotism, which was quite powerful *ca.* A.D. 60, had influenced Christians who preached against the Gentiles and the authorities. At any rate, Paul had similar fanatics in mind when he complained that envy and intrigues characterize the preaching of provocative elements who cause him difficulties in his trial (Phil. 1:15a 17). He also warned the Philippians against rapacious propagandists, whom he called "dogs" and "evil workers" (3:2a). Since the apostle had just had difficulties in Rome with such Christian troublemakers, whom Clement describes as zealots, there is reason to assume that Paul thought of similar troublemakers in Philippi, i.e., provocative fanatics or zealots. There is also reason to understand them as Christian Judaizers, because Paul says they represent fleshly mutilation in opposition to spiritual circumcision (3:2b-3). They may also be compared with those Christian zealots for the Jewish law whom Paul had found in Galatia and in Jerusalem (Gal. 1:7; Acts 21:20).

Against such nomists Paul remarks that his Jewish background is an asset that he counts as "refuse," and that a Christian must forget what is behind him and pursue only what lies before him (3:13). It is not difficult to recognize that Paul speaks of the same Judaizers when, a few verses later, he summarizes his criticism by warning the readers against many who are the enemies of Christ's cross and have only material interests (3:18f.). For natural reasons, Christians dominated by Jewish ideals endeavored to suppress the actual passion of Christ, to emphasize dietary observances ("whose god is their belly," as in Rom. 16:15), and to achieve the earthly triumph of the Church. Paul expressly criticizes such a materialization of eschatology (they are "concerned with earthly things") by pointing out that the object of Christian hope is no political community on earth, but the eschatological kingdom of Christ (3:20f.).

Hope is thus a topic of special importance for Paul in Philippians. It is connected with his repeated expressions of joy (1:4, etc.). The starting-point is what God has already done for the believers: this is a warrant for their approaching perfection when Christ comes (1:6, 10f., 20). Paul is happy to live for Christ but even more is yearning to die in Him (1:21-23). The progress of the readers (1:25) also means approaching eternal salvation sent by God (1:28). Working for this salvation is necessary because it is God who does the work (2:12b-13). Paul hopes the readers will be an honor for him on the day of Christ (2:16). By rejoicing in Christ (3:1), i.e., with His coming in mind, they will avoid the dangers of Judaistic heresy (3:2). Of sole importance is the progression and perfection of the unity with Christ (3:8-17). The readers must look forward to their glorification, which comes from heaven and from the future (3:2-21). As the Lord is quite near (4:5), they will have the peace of God in the present (4:7) and be able to give all honor to Him (4:20).

***Bibliography.***–Comms. by K. Barth (Eng. tr. 1962); F. W. Beare (*HNTC*, 1959); J.-F. Collange (Eng. tr. 1979); P. Collart (1937); R. E. Davies (1958); M. Dibelius (*HZNT*, 1925); G. Friedrich (*NTD*, 8th ed. 1963); K. Grayston (*Epworth Preacher's Comms.*, 1957); W. Hendriksen (1962); P. Lemerle (1945); J. B. Lightfoot (1896); E. Lohmeyer (*KEK*, 1961); R. P. Martin (*New Century Bible Comm.*, 1976; repr. 1980); J. H. Michael (*MNTC*, 1929); E. Peterson (1962); E. Thurneysen (1943).

E. Lohmeyer, *Kyrios Jesus* (on 2:5-11) (1928); G. Delling, *RGG*, V (1961), cols. 333-36; J. Schmid, *LTK*, VIII, cols. 457f.; A. Ehrhardt, *Framework of the NT Stories* (1964), pp. 37-43; D. Georgi, "Der vorpaulinische Hymnus Phil 2,6-11," in E. Dinkler, ed., *Zeit und Geschichte: Dankesgabe an R. Bultmann* (1964), pp. 263-293; O. Hofius, *Der Christushymnus* (1973).

G. Bornkamm, "Der Philipperbrief als paulinische Briefsammlung," in *Neotestamentica et Patristica* (*Festschrift* O. Cullmann; *Nov.Test. Supp.*, 6, 1962), 192-202; C. O. Buchanan, *EQ* (1964), pp. 157-166; F. F. Bruce, *BJRL*, 46 (1964), 326-345; 48 (1965), 81-97; D. G. Dawe, *SJT*, 15 (1962), 337-349; V. Furnish, *NTS*, 10 (1963), 80-88; H. Koester, *NTS*, 8 (1961), 317-332; L. Krinetzki, *TQ*, 139 (1959), 157-193, 291-336; B. S. Mackay, *NTS*, 7 (1960), 161-170; R. P. Martin, "The Form-analysis of Philippians 2, 5-11," *SE*, II (1964), 611-620; B. Reicke, "Unité chrétienne et diaconie, Phil ii I-II," in *Neotestamentica et Patristica* (*Festschrift* O. Cullmann; *Nov.Test. Supp.*, 6, 1962), 203-212; W. Schmithals, *ZTK*, 54 (1957), 297-341; G. Strecker, *ZNW*, 55 (1964), 63-78.

B. REICKE

**PHILISTIA** fə-lis'tē-yə [Heb. *p^eléšeṯ*] (Ex. 15:14; Ps. 60:8 [MT 10]; 83:7 [MT 8]; 87:4; 108:9 [MT 10]; Isa. 14:29, 31; Joel 3:4 [MT 4:4]); [*p^elištîm*] (Zec. 9:6); AV also PALESTINA, PHILISTINES, PALESTINE; NEB also PHILISTINE(S). The region later known as Palestine, whose people were the PHILISTINES. During the reign of Ramses III, a group of Aegeo-Cretan tribes attempted an invasion of Egypt and were repulsed. Some of them landed on the coastal region of Palestine, among them the *prst*. Egyptian orthography had no separate character to indicate the phoneme /l/, using either the character for *n* or that for *r*. Later evidence from Coptic indicates that the *l*-sound was present in Egyptian; hence the Heb. *p^eléšeṯ* suggests that the Egyptian word was pronounced something like **pilist* or **peleset*. The Peoples of the Sea, as these invaders have come to be known, were part of a migration of Indo-European peoples that occurred in the late 13th and early 12th cents. that greatly affected the history of the Near East. The tradition that CRETE (Caphtor) was one of their places of origin is preserved in the Bible in Am. 9:7 and Jer. 47:4 (cf. also Dt. 2:23). Cf. W. S. LaSor, D. A. Hubbard, and F. W. Bush, *OT Survey* (1982), pp. 119-122; *CAH* II/2 (3rd ed. 1975), 359-378, esp. 371-78.

W. S. L. S.

**PHILISTIM** fil-is'tim, fil'ə-stim (Gen. 10:14, AV). *See* PHILISTINES.

**PHILISTINES** fə-lis'tinz, fil'ə-stēnz [Heb. *p^elištî*, pl. *p^elištîm*]; **PHILISTIA** fə-lis'tē-ə [Heb. *p^eléšeṯ*]. The people of the coastal plain of southern Palestine, generally from Joppa to Gaza, and portions of the adjacent foothills, from whom the name "Palestine" is derived.

I. In the Bible
   A. Names
   B. Territory Defined
   C. In the Patriarchal Period
   D. At the Time of Occupying the Land
   E. During the Monarchy
   F. After the Division of the Monarchy
II. In Extrabiblical Sources
   A. Documentary Evidence
   B. Other Archeological Evidence
III. Synthesis
   A. Overall View
   B. Patriarchal "Philistines"
   C. Conquest of Canaan and the Philistines

***I. In the Bible.***–*A. Names.* The Hebrew name *p^eléšeṯ*, "Philistia, Palestine," occurs only eight times in the OT. In the AV the word is sometimes translated "Palestine" (Joel 3:4 [MT 4:4]) or "Palestina" (Ex. 15:14; Isa. 14:29, 31), although the term "Palestine" did not come into common use until Herodotus (i.105; mid-fifth cent. B.C.). *See* PALESTINE. A preferable translation is "Philistia," which the AV uses in Ps. 60:8; 87:4; 108:9, and which is regularly used in the RSV. The gentilic, sing. *p^elištî*, "Philistine" (used only of Goliath [1 S. 17:8, etc.] and of the one slain by Abishai [2 S. 21:17]), pl. *p^elištîm*, "Philistines," occurs frequently (255 times, according to KoB, p. 764), referring to the people of that region. As a general rule the plural does not take the definite article, which may account for the translation into Greek as *allóphyloi*, "foreigners." The LXX sometimes translates with various forms, such as *Phylistieim*, "Philistia" (Ex. 15:14), and *Philistiaios*, "Philistines" (1 K. 17:23 A), or uses other names, such as *Gerara* (Gen. 26:8) or *Goliad* (1 K. 17:42 B). (Other versions [Aq., Symm., Th.] seem to prefer spellings with *upsilon* rather than *iota* [but not exclusively].) But in the great majority of cases, the LXX translates with forms of *allóphylos*, "foreign, foreigner, Gentile." The English use of the word "Philistine" to mean "one who lacks culture or esthetic refinement" and other pejorative ideas is supported neither by biblical nor extrabiblical data and should be abandoned.

In passages constructed with parallelism the Cherethites are mentioned with the Philistines (cf. Ezk. 25:16; Zeph. 2:5). In the prophetic messages the Philistines are connected with Caphtor (cf. Jer. 47:4; Am. 9:7). Both Hebrew words, *kᵉrēṯî* and *kaptôrîm,* are identified with Crete by modern scholars (see II.A below). David had a guard that included Cherethites and Pelethites (and also 600 Gittites, or men from Gath, 2 S. 15:18); since "Cherethites" seems to mean "Philistines," and Gath was the site of one of the Philistine rulers, it seems reasonable to assume the Pelethites were also in some way related to the Philistines. It would follow that David had come to know these men and had drawn them to him during the time that he was associated with Achish king of Gath (1 S. 27:3).

*B. Territory Defined.* In Josh. 13:3 the Lord tells Joshua of the land remaining to be conquered: "all the regions of the Philistines, and those of the Geshurites (from the Shihor, which is east of Egypt, northward to the boundary of Ekron, it is reckoned as Canaanite; there are five rulers of the Philistines, those of Gaza, Ashdod, Ashkelon, Gath, and Ekron), and those of the Avvim, in the south, all the land of the Canaanites." This passage has some difficulties, but the general meaning is clear. The Shihor has been identified with Pelusiac (i.e., the easternmost branch of the Nile. According to Dt. 2:23 the Avvim were the occupants of the southern part of the region (including Gaza), whose villages had been destroyed by "the Caphtorim, who came from Caphtor," who then settled in the same area. The Geshurites were probably a tribe in the south, which had been there "from of old" in the region "as far as Shur, to the land of Egypt"; at any rate, David conducted raids on them, as well as on the Girzites and the Amalekites, when he was located in the country of the Philistines (1 S. 27:8). The five cities mentioned are often called "the Philistine pentapolis"; Gaza was the southernmost, and Ekron (if the identification with Khirbet el-Muqennaʿ is accepted) the northermost. Ashkelon alone was on the Mediterranean coast; Gaza and Ashdod were on the Via Maris, which, because of the sand dunes, was located from 4 to 6 km. (2.4 to 3.6 mi.) inland from the sea. The locations of Gath and Ekron have long been disputed; current scholarship tends to identify them with Tell eṣ-Ṣâfī and Tell el-Muqennaʿ, respectively, at the eastern edge of the coastal plain where it joins the foothills (the Shephelah).

There were many other Philistine locations, some of which will be discussed below (II.B), and the OT mentions a number of "wars" or military campaigns in various places, suggesting that the Philistines at various times extended their control as far north as Beth-shean and Mt. Gilboa (1 S. 31:1) and into the Shephelah to Michmash and

Aijalon (14:31), and indeed even to the vicinity of Jebus (Jerusalem) (2 S. 5:17). The portion of Palestine that is commonly called "the Philistine plain" (*see* PALESTINE IV.A.1) is a satisfactory identification of the region occupied by the Philistines.

*C. In the Patriarchal Period.* Genesis 21 gives an account of a dispute over water rights between Abraham and Abimelech. The location was on the edge of the Negeb at a place thereafter known as Beer-sheba (v. 31). When the dispute was settled, Abimelech and Phicol the commander of his army "returned to the land of the Philistines" (v. 32). It is also recorded that "Abraham sojourned many days in the land of the Philistines" (v. 34). Clearly, Abimelech was a man of authority, probably the king of a city-state, and "the land of the Philistines" included the region around Beer-sheba. The problems of reconciling the date of this dispute with the earliest known presence of Philistines in the area will be discussed below (III.B).

According to Gen. 26:1 "Isaac went to Gerar, to Abimelech king of the Philistines," because there was famine in the land. This famine is distinguished from that which occurred in the days of Abraham (26:1), and in the sequence of events as presented in chs. 21–25 it is unlikely that it is the same Abimelech (however, the commander of his army was also called "Phicol"). We note that Abimelech is called "king" (Heb. *meleḵ*), which is not the title used of the "rulers" *(sᵉrānîm)* of the Philistine cities. Gerar is on the eastern edge of the coastal plain between Gaza and Beer-sheba. Isaac dwelt at Gerar and prospered, although the wells which Abraham had dug had been stopped up by the Philistines (26:15). Finally, Abimelech said to Isaac, "Go away from us; for you are much mightier than we" (26:16). In the ensuing events Abimelech followed Isaac even to Beer-sheba, which thus may have been part of the Philistine region.

These are the only two texts that mention the Philistines in the patriarchal period. In both accounts the "Hittities" also are mentioned (23:3-20; 26:34), further complicating the chronological problem.

*D. At the Time of Occupying the Land.* Exodus 23:31 makes a passing reference to "the sea of the Philistines," but the next time the Philistines come into the biblical story is in connection with the occupation of the land of Canaan. "The regions of the Philistines" were named as part of the land that remained to be possessed (Josh. 13:2). A similar statement is found in Jgs. 3:1-3, where the Philistines, among others, are for "a testing of Israel, to know whether they would obey the commandments of the Lord" (Jgs. 3:4; cf. 10:6-11). Again we note that the Hittites are also mentioned (3:5).

The five Philistine cities are named and the five "rulers" are mentioned in such a way as to suggest that they were the only Philistine rulers. The Hebrew word is *sᵉrānîm* (used only in the plural), translated "rulers" in Josh. 13:3, but "lords" in Jgs. 3:3, RSV; it is used only of Philistine rulers (cf. Jgs. 16:5; 1 S. 6:16-18; a total of 21 times in the MT). It is generally thought to be a loanword, related somehow to Gk. *týrannos,* but the chain of relationship is not clear.

*E. During the Monarchy.* Intermittent warfare with the Philistines continued from the time of the occupation of Canaan until David was able to subdue this enemy, although the only references prior to the time of King Saul are, as we have seen, in Josh. 13 and Jgs. 3 and 10. The tribal allotment of Dan was originally in the Shephelah and the plain, including the cities occupied by the Philistines (Josh. 19:40-46), but the Danities were forced out by the Amorites (Jgs. 1:34), who were probably pushed from their former territory by the Philistines, and Dan subsequently located in the extreme north (Josh. 19:47f.).

The Philistines are introduced again in 1 S. 4: "Now Israel went out to battle against the Philistines; they encamped at Ebenezer, and the Philistines encamped at Aphek" (v. 1). The Israelites were defeated, and someone suggested that they take the ark of the covenant into battle (v. 3). But the Philistines were again victorious and even captured the ark (v. 11), which was taken to Ashdod and placed in the temple of their god Dagon (5:2). On the following day the figure of Dagon was found face downward on the floor (v. 3). After a series of terrifying events the people of Ashdod sent the ark to Gath (v. 8). Again, the results caused the people to send the ark to Ekron (v. 10), then to Beth-shemesh (6:12, 14), where there were Israelites. From there it was transferred to Kiriath-jearim where it remained for some twenty years (7:1f.). The Philistines were subdued, and the Israelites recaptured cities which had been taken "from Ekron to Gath" (v. 14). If we accept the suggestion of B. Mazar, this Gath was in the northern Shephelah, possibly the Gittaim of 2 S. 4:3 (Ras Abū Ḥumeid, near Gezer) or the Gath-padalla in the Sharon plain inland from Caesarea (cf. Ch. 7:21; *see* GATH III; but see also Aharoni, *LBHG*, rev., p. 382 n. 68, who suggested the possibility that it was Philistine Gath), hence the recovered cities lay in the region north of the Philistine pentapolis (*GTTOT*, § 659, p. 309).

Samuel called for a national repentance, that the Lord might "save us from the hand of the Philistines" (1 S. 7:8). But the people wanted a king (8:66). Samuel received a revelation from the Lord that "a man from the land of Benjamin" would save Israel from the hand of the Philistines (9:15f.). Saul became king, but he was unable to subdue the enemy; rather, his reign was marked by many small wars with the Philistines: at Geba (13:3); with three raiding parties from Michmash (13:17); "beyond" Beth-aven and "from Michmash to Aijalon" (14:31); between Soco and Azekah (17:1), a battle which was climaxed by the single-combat encounter of David and Goliath (17:8f.) and the Israelites' pursuit of the Philistines "as far as Gath" and Ekron (17:52); at Keilah (23:8); and finally at Shunem and Gilboa (28:4), where Saul and his three sons lost their lives (31:8). Although the biblical account records repeated victories over the Philistines, it is clear that these were local skirmishes, for the Philistine menace continued throughout Saul's reign.

David's first encounter with the Philistines took place during Saul's reign, in the valley of Elah, where he killed Goliath (17:50). Following this stirring victory, he led Israelite forces against the Philistines with such success that Saul became jealous (18:7-9). As a result David became a political refugee who finally took asylum in Gath along with "the six hundred men who were with him" (27:2f.). It is reasonable to assume that his time with the Philistines, together with his raids on Israel's enemies to the south (27:8f.), prepared him to deal effectively with the Philistines when he became king of Israel.

David was at first king of "Judah," probably meaning the enlarged tribe that had absorbed Simeon, and located his capital at Hebron (2 S. 2:1-4). Since that region was controlled by the Philistines (or so the records seem to imply), it is possible that this step was taken with the consent of the Philistine rulers. But, when the Philistines received the news that David had been made king of Israel and had located his capital in Jerusalem, they moved against him (5:17). David's first victory (v. 20) was apparently inconclusive, and the Philistines again came to the valley of Rephaim (v. 22). This time David's forces routed them, and smote them "from Geba to Gezer" (v. 25). During the following months (and years?) a number of Philistines gathered around David: the Cherethites and Pelethites, as well as the six hundred men from Gath (15:18). We note again that the "Hittites" come into the story (1 S. 26:6; 2 S. 11:6; 24:6). If the Philistines had been subdued, they were not yet completely beaten, for there were wars with them at an unnamed location (2 S. 21:15), at Gezer (1 Ch. 20:4; 2 S. 21:18 reads "Gob"), at Gob (2 S. 21:19, where Elhanan the Bethlehemite slew Goliath the Gittite), and at Gath (21:20), where there was a hexadactylic giant who was slain by Jonathan the son of Shimei (21:21). The account in 2 S. 21 presents a number of difficulties, as a study of the commentaries on this passage will show. There are also accounts of skirmishes with the Philistines at Lehi (2 S. 23:11) and at Bethlehem (24:14).

*F. After the Division of the Monarchy.* Since there is no record of conflict between the Philistines and the Israelites under Solomon, it is often asserted that David brought an end to the Philistine power. Some would date this to the victory recorded in 2 S. 5. If they were not a serious threat, however, the Philistines were still a hostile force.

Gath was apparently a vassal state. The term *seren,* "tyrant, ruler," is no longer used, but instead Achish is called *meleḵ,* "king" (1 K. 2:39). Gezer had been taken by an Egyptian pharaoh and given as dowry to his daughter, Solomon's wife (9:16f.). Among the cities which Rehoboam (931-913 B.C.) fortified, Gath is named (2 Ch. 11:8; but *see* GATH II. B. 2, where A. F. Rainey holds that this should be read as Moresheth-gath), but these were later (*ca.* 928) captured by Shishak of Egypt (2 Ch. 12:2-4). Baasha assassinated Nadab of Israel (*ca.* 909) at Gibbethon, "which belonged to the Philistines"; Nadab had been besieging the city (1 K. 15:27), hence it must have been an enemy enclave. Israelite troops were encamped at Gibbethon at the time of Omri's coup (*ca.* 880; 1 K. 16:15), and again it is recorded that Gibbethon "belonged to the Philistines," possibly implying that the Israelite troops were there to keep peace. Some Philistines paid tribute to Jehoshaphat king of Judah (*ca.* 873–848; 2 Ch. 17:11), and in the days of Jehoram (*ca.* 853-841) a coalition of Philistines and Arabs invaded Judah and carried off the king's possessions, sons, and wives (2 Ch. 21:16f.). This coalition continued to be powerful until the days of Uzziah (*ca.* 767-740), who made war on the Philistines, broke down the walls of Gath, Jabneh, and Ashdod, built cities in Philistine territory, and subdued the Philistines and the Arabs (2 Ch. 26:6f.).

The Philistines are included in prophetic messages. Amos (*ca.* 753) proclaimed a word of the Lord against the cities of the Philistines: Gaza, Ashdod, Ashkelon, and Ekron, "because they carried into exile a whole people to deliver them up to Edom" (Am. 1:6-8). In the fourth year of Jehoiakim (*ca.* 605) Jeremiah uttered a prophecy that included "all the kings of the lands of the Philistines," naming Ashkelon, Gaza, Ekron, "and the remnant of Ashdod" (Jer. 25:20). Zephaniah (7th cent.) prophesied against the Philistine cities of Gaza, Ashkelon, Ashdod, and Ekron (Zeph. 2:4), and declared woes against the "inhabitants of the seacoast," the "nation of the Cherethites," "Canaan, land of the Philistines," and mentioned again Ashkelon (Zeph. 2:5-7). Zechariah (6th cent.) delivered an oracle that included "the pride of Philistia," naming Ashkelon (twice), Gaza (twice), Ekron (twice), and Ashdod (Zec. 9:5-7). It is noteworthy that Gath is not mentioned in these prophecies, from which it may be inferred that Gath ceased to be of any major significance after the time of Uzziah (cf. Am. 6:2, where Gath is included among places that have been ruined). In Assyrian records, likewise, Ashdod, Ashkelon, Ekron, and Gaza are named, but Gath does not appear; thus Sennacherib (705-681): "Ashdod, Ashkelon, Ekron, and Gaza"

(ARAB, II, § 312); Esarhaddon (681-669): Gaza, Ashkelon, Ekron, and Ashdod (*ARAB*, II, § 690); and Ashurbanipal (669-627): Gaza, Ashkelon, Ekron, and Ashdod (*ARAB*, II, § 876). Within the next few centuries the location of Gath had become unknown.

***II. In Extrabiblical Sources.***–Because the biblical accounts of the Philistines do not everywhere agree with data from extrabiblical sources, it seemed wise to separate the two in this article and thus avoid a constant interplay of the two sources or interruptive attempts at harmonization.

*A. Documentary Evidence.* In the Table of Nations (Gen. 10) Mizraim (Egypt) is named as the father of (among others) Casluhim (whence came the Philistines) and Caphtorim (v. 14). Some scholars perceive a textual dislocation here, and assert that the parenthetical statement about the Philistines should follow "Caphtorim" (cf. *BHS*). This would bring the statement into agreement with Am. 9:7, "Did I not bring . . . the Philistines from Caphtor. . . ?" The Caphtorim are mentioned as those who displaced the Avvim in Dt. 2:23, and the Philistines are called "the remnant from the coastland of Caphtor" in Jer. 47:4. The location of Caphtor, however, for many years was not certainly known.

Some have tried to identify the Philistines with the Pelasgians who were originally from the region of the Hellespont and then invaded Greece (Herodotus i.57; ii.51). This suggestion gave way to others: the Philistines originally came from Crete, or Cyprus, or a coastal region of Asia Minor (in articles published from 1913 to 1956 G. A. Wainwright maintained that Crete/Keftiu was in Anatolia; cf. *CAH*³, II/2, 969, IV.19-23.) The question seems to have been settled by a topographical list of Amenhotep III *ca.* 1400 (cf. J. Vercoutter, *L'Égypte et le Monde Égéen Préhellénique* [1956], pp. 40ff., 407, 417), and many scholars now accept the identification with Crete. Egyptian "Keftiu ships" carried on commerce with Cyprus, Cilicia, Crete, Ionia, Aegean islands, and perhaps mainland Greece as early as the days of Thutmose III (1482-1450) (*CAH*³, II/1, 387).

In an Ugaritic text concerning the abode of Kotharwa-Ḫasis, the god of artisans, the word *kptr* occurs: *kptr ksu ṯbth ḥkpt arṣ nḥlth,* "Caphtor is the throne of his sitting, *Ḥkpt* the land of his inheritance" (*UT,* ʿnt VI:14-16). The passage seems to preserve a memory of a connection with Crete as the home of their crafts; *Ḥkpt* may be another name for Crete or one of its regions. Economic texts from Mari speak of *Kaptara,* and an Akkadian text from Ugarit refers to ships arriving from *Kapturi*. C. H. Gordon had raised the question whether the words *kpt-r* and *ḥ-kpt* may include some morphological elements, a preformative *ḥ-* and a sufformative *-r,* leaving *kpt* as the basic word (*Ugaritic Literature* [1949], p. 23 n. 1), and relating this to Egyptian *kft-yw*. But the persistence of *r* in Hebrew, Akkadian, and Ugaritic forms, plus the fact that final *-r* could become *-yw* by phonetic decay (*see* CAPHTOR II), rather support *kptr/kftr* as the original word. This would be further supported by the parallelism of Cherethites (Heb. *kᵉrēṯî,* "Cretan") and Philistines in Zeph. 2:5, and by the inclusion of Cherethites along with the men of Gath among David's guard (2 S. 15:18).

Merneptah (*ca.* 1224-1214) recorded an attempt of Libyans and the sea-peoples to invade Egypt from Libya in his fifth regnal year. He mentioned the Sherden, Sheklesh, Tursha, and Akawasha, but does not name either the Philistines or the Tjekker.

In the Great Harris Papyrus, Ramses III (*ca.* 1182-1151) boasts of extending the frontiers of Egypt and overthrowing them that had attacked: "I slew the Denyen in their islands, while the Tjeker and the Philistines were made ashes. The Sherden and the Weshesh of the Sea were made nonexistent" (*ANET,* p. 262; J. Breasted, *Ancient Records of Egypt, IV* [1907], §§ 403f.). History gives the lie to the gross exaggerations of this claim. A relief on the mortuary temple of Ramses II at Medinet Habu has an account of the attempt of the sea-peoples to invade Egypt (cf. A. Gardiner, *Egypt of the Pharaohs* [1961], pp. 282-87, fig. 11). They were repulsed, and some of them landed on the shore of Djahi (which included Phoenicia and Palestine). Among these sea-peoples were the *prst* (Philistines), *ṯkr* (Tjekker), *škrš* (Shekelesh), *dnyn* (Denyen), and *wšš* (Weshesh). It is well-known that Egyptian, lacking an orthographic representation of *l,* used either *n* or *r* to represent the sound (*see* EGYPT V.E), hence *prst* would be used for **plst*. The different peoples are distinguishable by their headdresses: a Philistine warrior is represented wearing a "feathered" headdress, consisting of a leather cap and a headband with curving strips standing upright, variously identified as feathers, reeds, leather strips, or "some bizarre hairdo" (see *ANEP,* no. 7; cf. Dothan, *Biblical Archaeology Review,* p. 26).

The Onomasticon of Amenemope, dated to the end of the reign of Ramses IX (1134-1117), names Ashkelon, Ashdod, and Gaza, and then mentions three sea-peoples, Shardana, Tjekker, and Philistines (cf. *CAH*³, II/2, 378 n. 1; A. Gardiner, *Ancient Egyptian Onomastica* [1947], p. 1). The Tale of Wen-Amon (*ca.* 1050) locates the Tjekker at Dor, on the coast S of Mt. Carmel, where excavations have been conducted. The Sherden may have been located at Akko (Dothan, *Biblical Archaeology Review,* p. 44).

In an inscription Adadnirari III (810-783) claims he imposed tribute upon many peoples, including Israel (the land of Omri), Edom, and "Palestine *(Pa-la-as-tu),* as far as the shore of the Great Sea of the Setting Sun" (*ANET,* p. 281). In addition to references in the records of Sennacherib, Esarhaddon, and Ashurbanipal mentioned above (I. F), Philistine cities are named in the inscriptions of Tiglath-pileser III (747-727; cf. *ANET,* pp. 283f.), Sargon II (721-705; *ANET,* p. 286; Gath is mentioned, if *Gi-im-tu* is properly interpreted), and Nebuchadrezzar (605-562; *ANET,* p. 308). In an Aramaic papyrus found at Saqqârah a Philistine ruler pleads for help against Nebuchadrezzar (*CCK,* p. 28 and n. 5).

*B. Other Archeological Evidence.* Earlier scholars' statements that Philistine remains were rare now have to be corrected. Philistine remains from very many sites have been recovered. (See map of principal sites in Dothan, *Biblical Archaeology Review,* p. 27, marking some 44 locations.) But the most important of all archeological discoveries, namely, texts with which to interpret the finds, have not yet been found. A stamp seal with characters similar to Cypro-Minoan script was recovered at Ashdod, and a number of clay tablets were found at Tell Deir ʿallā (Succoth?) in the Jordan Ghor, about 36 km. (22 mi.) SSW of Beth-shean, written in a similar script. Some scholars have tentatively called this "Philistine." On the reliefs on the mortuary temple of Ramses III at Medinet Habu the Philistines can be distinguished not only by their headdress but also by their dress, consisting of a corselet of leather or metal over a shirt and a short panelled kilt with hem and tassels (cf. *CAH*³, II/2, 373). Military chariots were manned by a driver and two warriors, had six-spoked wheels, and were drawn by two horses. The infantry fought in phalanxes of four men each, three of them armed with a long, straight sword and a pair of spears, and the fourth with only a sword. All carried round shields. The Philistine camp included not only the chariotry and infantry, but also civilians, men, women, and children, who traveled in two-wheeled carts drawn by four oxen. Philistine ships are also portrayed, single-masted and with only steering-oars. Both the chariots and the ships are similar to those of the Egyptians (cf. A. Gardiner, *Egypt of the Pharaohs* [1961], pp. 282-87; Dothan, *Biblical Archaeology Review*, pp. 24-26).

Of the Philistine pentapolis only Ashdod has been thoroughly excavated, although Gaza and Ashkelon are definitely identified, and Ashkelon has undergone considerable excavation. At Ashdod the Egyptian-Canaanite fortress of level XIV was destroyed and replaced by a Philistine community (level XIII) which included a potter's workshop and locally made Mycenaean III C1 pottery. This type of pottery is found at a number of Philistine sites, as well as at sites in the Aegean and the Mediterranean, and is clearly indicative of a marked cultural change between Mycenaean II (LH [Late Helladic] II) and Mycenaean or LH III. It also marks the end of the Bronze Age. Levels XII and XI present a Philistine city with two building complexes divided by a street. A gold disk of Aegean style and seals in a type of orthography resembling Cypro-Minoan were found, and a figurine which is the earliest known Philistine cult goddess, now called "Ashdoda," with similarities to figurines of the "Great Mother" of Mycenaean sites. The latest level at Ashdod (level X) is dated *ca.* 1050 B.C. (shortly before the beginning of Saul's reign over the Israelites) and is the largest and most prosperous, with a lower city outside the acropolis, and pottery that shows assimilation into the local types.

At Tell el-Qasîleh on the Yarkon (Nahr el-ʿAujā), just N of Tel Aviv, a Philistine city was founded in the early part of the 12th century. Three temples were superimposed in levels XII-X, the first clearly Philistine temples to be discovered. These temples are unlike any discovered in Canaan and show similarities to temples found at Kition (Cyprus) and at Mycenaean sites on mainland Greece and on the island of Melos. A buried cache of cult vessels was found in a pit in the level XI temple.

Philistine painted jug with a strainer spout. From a tomb at Tell el-Fârʿah (Sharuhen) (12th cent. B.C.) (Israel Museum, Jerusalem)

Philistine pottery: painted jug and stirrup cup with geometric designs (University Museum University of Pennsylvania)

It has been commonly believed that the Philistines brought iron metallurgy to Canaan and maintained a strict monopoly (cf. *CAH*³, II/2, 516). This was based largely (if not entirely) on 1 S. 13:19-21, although iron is not mentioned in that passage. There are, however, statements concerning iron tools at earlier periods, and in Josh. 17:16 the "Canaanites of the plain" appear to be Philistines with iron chariots (cf. Jgs. 1:19). Archeological discoveries include tools and weapons made of iron dating back to mid-third millennium (*see* IRON). Excavations of Philistine sites in Palestine have uncovered no evidence of iron metallurgy, nor even any substantial amount of iron (*LBHG,* rev., p. 274). The metallurgy of iron was an Anatolian (Hittite or pre-Hittite) craft, and the Philistines were probably more closely related to the Aegean than to Anatolia.

Anthropoid coffins that had been identified as "Philistine" are now known to have been introduced by an Egyptian for the burial of an Egyptian officer. The method was taken over by Philistines and adaptations were made.

Philistine pottery, like other cultural items, shows a gradual assimilation to local customs. The earliest was Mycenaean IIIC, although tests on the clay from which it was made indicate that it was of local origin. But later pottery has elements of Egyptian and Canaanite pottery.

Similarly, the Philistine cult gives evidence of a goddess like the mother-goddess of the Aegean region, but there are also evidences of the worship of several male and female deities of the Canaanite region, including Dagon, Ashtaroth, and Beelzebub.

***III. Synthesis.–A. Overall View.*** It is premature to attempt to write a history of the lands of the eastern Mediterranean in the latter half of the 2nd millennium. What is clear, however, is that there was widespread migration, whether willing or forced, whether caused by military or socioeconomic events, or perhaps a combination of several factors. There are even attempts to link the collapse of the Late Bronze Age in Greece and Anatolia with a major climatic change or the volcanic eruption of Santorini (Thera) and a resulting tidal wave (cf. R. Carpenter, *Discontinuity in Greek Civilization* [1966]; L. Pomerance, *Final Collapse of Santorini [Thera]* [1970]).

The Hyksos had invaded the eastern delta of Egypt, and after a century or more their dominance had come to an end and the 18th Dynasty was established. At approximately the same time, there was a transition from Middle Bronze, Middle Minoan, and Middle Helladic to Late Bronze/Minoan/Helladic, pottery and other remains indicating a notable cultural difference in the relative regions. LH I was contemporary with the coming of the Achaeans (i.e., the Greeks or Mycenaeans) to the Greek Peloponnesus from Asia Minor; LM I was marked by the destruction of Phaestos and Hagia Triada on Crete. Shortly thereafter Knossos was destroyed, and the use of Linear A writing came to an end. The Hittites were on friendly terms with the Aḫḫiyawa, considered by many to be the Achaeans (a name the Greeks often used for themselves; cf. ACHAIA). But the Mycenaeans (or Greeks or Achaeans) were in a process of conquest or relocation. Troy (level VIIA) was destroyed (the Trojan War of Homer's *Iliad*), Crete and Cyprus were invaded, there was a Mycenaean settlement at Ugarit, and similar settlements elsewhere are known. Just how much the Dorian invasion of Greece (probably from the north) was responsible for the sudden movements of population cannot yet be measured. Mycenae was destroyed, and the Mycenaeans fled. Hattusas (Boghazköy) was destroyed and the Hittite empire came to an end. Hittites fled eastward and subsequently reestablished the Syro-Hittite kingdom. Other places that fell included Miletus, Mersin, Tarsus, Carchemish, Ugarit, Açana, Sidon, and places on Cyprus. In several of these sites the discovery of Mycenaean IIIC pottery indicates a connection with the sea-peoples. It is clear that Mycenaeans, Hittites, Cretans, Cypriots, and peoples of other regions in Anatolia and the islands of the Mediterranean were all on the move. The cultural level is marked as LM[inoan] IIIC in Crete and LH[elladic] IIIC (or Mycenaean IIIC) in Mycenaean areas.

Merneptah records a victory in Libya in his fifth year (*ca.* 1223), in which there were sea forces from many places. Among those named are Lukka (Lycians) and Achawasha (Achaeans?), as well as others that may be identified with peoples in Anatolia or the islands (*CAH*[3], II/2, 366-371). As noted above, Ramses II lists a number of peoples who tried to invade the eastern Delta. Evidence from places that had been conquered indicates that the invasion by sea was part of a larger movement that included an invasion by land — rather a migration, for the invaders were bringing with them their families and household belongings. When this population shift was complete, the Bronze Age would come to end and the Iron Age would be ushered in.

*B. Patriarchal "Philistines."* How do we fit the biblical references to the Philistines into this larger story? It is clear that the "Philistines" of the days of Abraham and Issac were not part of the great migration of the 13th and 12th centuries. But this appears to be the climax of population movements that had begun at least several centuries earlier, including the Amorites, the kingdom of the Mitanni, and the Asiatics who are known best as Hyksos. Two explanations are readily available (to dismiss the biblical accounts as anachronistic is to sidestep the problem).

(1) The Philistines of the patriarchal age may have been a people with a similar name — at least in translation. After all, the earliest reference to the Philistines of the 12th cent. is the Egyp. *prst*. It is an assumption that this was pronounced "pelest." Now, it is not impossible that an earlier people called "Palishti" lived in southern Canaan, and that the name was later transferred to the *prst*. Moreover, there seems to be an identification of the patriarchal Philistines with the Canaanites (note the interchange of "Philistines" and "Canaanites" in Josh. 13:2-4 and Jgs. 3:3; note also the expression "the Canaanites who dwell in the plain" [Josh. 17:16], almost certainly a reference to the Philistines, since they had chariots of iron). A similar statement could be made for the Hittites of the same period with even greater plausibility, for the name Ḫatti/Hittite properly belonged to the people who were displaced by the Indo-European "Hittites" (cf. HITTITES I.).

(2) The name may have been proleptic, i.e., a later author or editor simply used that name for the people who lived in the region later occupied by the Philistines.

*C. Conquest of Canaan and the Philistines.* It is also evident that the occupation of Canaan by the Israelites — whether we date it in the 15th or the 13th cent. — occurred at a time when the lands of the eastern Mediterranean were in turmoil. It would be misleading, however, to attempt to identify the Israelite migration with any one of the others (as, e.g., has frequently been done with Abraham's migration and that of the Amorites). The biblical accounts nowhere indicate that the Israelites moved from Egypt to Canaan as part of a larger population shift. On the other hand, it is likely that the general unrest provided a favorable time for the occupation of Canaan, since Egypt was not in a position to exercise any considerable authority over that region.

If we assume a fifteenth-century date for the "conquest of Canaan" (*see* EXODUS, DATE OF THE), this would allow the Israelites about two centuries in Canaan before the Philistine occupation. On the other hand, if we assume a thirteenth-century date, the Israelites would hardly have gotten settled in the land and have completed their tribal apportionments when the Philistines appeared on the scene. This seems to fit better with the descriptions in Josh. 13:1-7; 19:40-48; Jgs. 2:6–3:6.

But regardless of the date for the Exodus, the biblical account of the continuing conflicts between the Israelites and the Philistines fits well with what we know of the Philistines. The locations of Gaza, Ashkelon, and Ashdod are beyond dispute. Gath disappeared early from the scene, possibly in the days of Uzziah, and has not been positively identified at the time of writing this article. Ekron had revolted against Assyria in the days of Hezekiah and Sennacherib invaded the region (*ARAB*, II, § 240), obtained the release of Padi king of Ekron (who had been deposed by the people), restored him to his throne, and enlarged the territory. The identification of Khirbet el-Muqenna' with Ekron appears to satisfy both the location as described in the Bible (Josh. 15:10f.) and the size of the city as described by Sennacherib (*ARAB*, II, § 312), although some scholars still would identify Ekron with 'Aqir (cf. *CAH*[3], II/2, 509 n. 3).

***Bibliography.***–G. Bonfante, *American Journal of Archeology*, 50 (1940), 251-262; *CAH*[3], II/2 (1975), 127-536, esp. 371-78, 507-516; M. Dothan, *Archaeology*, 20 (1967), 178-186; "Ashdod of the Phoenicians," in D. N. Freedman and J. C. Greenfield, eds., *New Directions in Biblical Archaeology* (1969), pp. 15-24; T. Dothan, *Biblical Archaeology Review*, 8/4 (1982), 20-44; *The Philistines and Their Material Culture* (Eng. tr. 1982); C. H. Gordon, *Antiquity*, 30 (1956), 22-26; K. A. Kitchen, "Philistines," in D. J. Wiseman, ed., *Peoples of OT Times* (1973), pp. 53-78; R. A. S. Macalister, *The Philistines: Their History and Civilization* (1913, repr. with notes by A. Silverstein 1965); B. Mazar, "The Philistines and Their Wars with Israel," in B. Mazar, ed., *The World History of the Jewish People*, III: Judges (Eng. tr. 1971), pp. 164-179; N. K. Sandars, *The Sea Peoples, Warriors of the Ancient Mediterranean* (1978).

W. S. LASOR

**PHILISTINES, LORDS OF THE.** *See* LORDS.

**PHILISTINES, SEA OF THE.** *See* MEDITERRANEAN SEA.

**PHILO JUDAEUS** fī'lō jōō-dā'əs. A Hellenistic Jewish philosopher in Alexandria.

I. Introduction
II. Life and Work
III. Some Leading Themes
IV. Significance

*I. Introduction.*–Philo of Alexandria, a contemporary of Jesus and the apostles, is the one Jewish author belonging to the Dispersion whose works have been preserved in any considerable quantity. Quite apart from the influence exercised by his writings on later Christian thought and exegesis, his works are a primary source of information for the Judaism of the Dispersion, for the ideas current in NT times, for the ways in which Jews of the period could react to the thought and culture of a predominantly gentile environment, and for the extent to which it was possible to harmonize the OT with Greek philosophy. At the same time, our lack of material for comparison makes it hard to say how far he is truly representative, how widely these ideas were shared. Even in Alexandria not every Jew would have had Philo's particular background and interests, and what was typical of Alexandria was not necessarily typical of the Dispersion as a whole. There is always a danger of making him more representative than he really was. On the other hand, it would be a mistake to regard him as an isolated figure. His references to his predecessors show that he stood in a tradition, while the appearance of some of his ideas in other writers, who probably would not have been influenced by his works, indicates that these ideas at least were widespread.

*II. Life and Work.*–The one fixed point for the chronology of Philo's life is the embassy sent by the Alexandrian Jews to Caligula in the winter of A.D. 39-40. Josephus wrote (*Ant.* xviii.8.1 [259f.]) that Philo was the leader of the delegation. Philo himself, in his account of the mission, implied that he was then fairly well advanced in years. Since he wrote at least two treatises after his return, however, he cannot have been a very aged man at this time. Accordingly, his birth is generally dated *ca.* 20-25 B.C., and his death *ca.* A.D. 45-50.

Philo belonged to a prominent and wealthy family in the Jewish community of Alexandria, of which his brother Alexander was a leading figure. Philo's nephew Tiberius Alexander was to carve out for himself a career in the Roman imperial service, including terms of office as procurator in Palestine and as prefect of Egypt. Little is known of Philo's own career, apart from the inferences that may be drawn from occasional hints in his writings.

It may be presumed that he received the normal training of a Jewish boy, but there is no indication that his knowledge of Hebrew, if he had any, was at all profound. He discussed the meanings of Hebrew proper names, but he both wrote and thought in Greek, using as his text the Greek version of the Jewish Scriptures. He could even speak of Greek as "our language." Certainly he had enjoyed a Greek education, in itself an indication of the standing of his family, since admission to the *gymnasium* appears to have been a privilege jealously guarded (see Tcherikover-Fuks, *Corpus papyrorum Judaicarum,* I [1957], 37ff., 60ff.). He was versed in Greek history and literature and familiar with the philosophers, although here it is open to question whether his knowledge was really profound or based on the epitomes of the doxographers. For the rest, he appears as a man of scholarly tastes and reflective turn of mind, drawn almost against his will into the world of practical affairs; yet he was no recluse. Although he expressed his distaste for political activity, his writings reveal his keen and observant interest in and appreciation of the varied aspects of the busy life of the city.

Alexandria at this period was the intellectual capital of the ancient world and also the home of one of the largest Jewish communities in the Dispersion. The relations between the Alexandrian Jews and their gentile neighbors were not, however, the best, as may be seen from Philo's own writings (cf. *In Flaccum,* ed. Box [1939]; *De legatione ad Gaium,* ed. Smallwood [1961]), and Alexandria was also one of the centers of anti-Jewish propaganda. This has an important bearing on the character of his work. Living as they did in a predominantly gentile environment, exposed daily to the attractions of Hellenistic culture, the Jews of Alexandria were constantly tempted to abandon their ancestral faith and conform to the customs of their neighbors. The case of Tiberius Alexander is significant, since he could not have held the offices he did without relaxing his observance of the Jewish faith. There were presumably others who, whether for the material advantages to be gained or because of the attractions of an apparently superior culture and philosophy, turned away from Judaism and became completely assimilated to their gentile neighbors.

From this point of view, Philo's writings can be seen as a defense of Judaism, designed to assure such Jews of the superiority of their own tradition and restrain them from apostasy. Whether the attraction was that of a mystery cult or that of Greek philosophy, Philo set himself to meet and overcome it by presenting Judaism as the true mystery, the true philosophy. The allegorical method of interpretation, itself taken over from the Stoics, enabled him to read his philosophy into the Scriptures. Passages that on the surface appear absurd or meaningless are shown to be the vehicles of a deeper truth. The philosophy of Plato, the numerical speculations of the Pythagoreans, and the ethics of the Stoics all are to be found in the inspired teachings of Moses; indeed, the Greeks borrowed all they knew from Moses. At the same time, this defense could also appeal to the Gentile, answering the slanders of anti-Semitism and seeking to convince him of the validity of the Jewish faith. Unfortunately it is not possible to say how effective Philo's work was from a missionary point of view. The preservation of his writings was due to the interest of Christian, not of Jewish, successors. There is no indication that his works exercised any lasting influence on Jewish thought, although this may be due to the deficiency of our sources; the material assembled by Goodenough (*Jewish Symbols*) seems to show that Philo's type of Judaism might have been more widespread and survived much longer than once was thought.

Philo was not, however, merely a propagandist. His works are on a different level from the fragments of Jewish literary propaganda preserved by Eusebius. He was also a deeply religious thinker with a strong vein of mystical piety running through his work. From this point of view the fundamental element in his writings is his firm and steadfast loyalty to Judaism, and this not only in theory but in observance. Although his allegorical method allowed him to present the characters and events of the Pentateuch as symbols of philosophical truths, he could also roundly condemn those who spiritualized the law at the expense of the observance of the letter (*De migratione Abrahami* 89f.). Pagan religion with its polytheism and idolatry he rejected, although he was well aware of the contemporary trends toward monotheism in pagan thought.

The mystery religions and their rites Philo mentioned only rarely, and always with contempt. It is therefore the more remarkable that some modern scholars have suggested that he transformed Judaism into a mystery religion; but here attention must be paid to definition of the terms. That Philo should have transformed Judaism into one of the cults he so despised, even to present it as the true mystery, seems quite incredible; yet he used mystery terminology, spoke of initiation, regarded Moses as the hierophant who led men to the hidden meaning of the sacred utterances. The truth is that the term "mystery" and related words had long been used by philosophers, more or less figuratively, to describe their own teachings, the "mysteries" of philosophy. It is in this sense that Philo used the term, as he could also speak of Judaism as the ancestral philosophy of his people.

This means, however, that he was reading his Jewish Scriptures through Greek eyes. It is indeed not the least interesting and significant aspect of his writings that he was so completely hellenized and yet remained fundamentally loyal to Judaism. Athens and Jerusalem are often thought to be irreconcilable. It is suggested that all Jews were either hellenizing apostates or fanatical Zealots who would have no dealings with the gentile world, but Philo shows this rigid alternative to be wrong. As Goodenough put it, the two traditions were so blended in Philo's mind that debate as to whether he was more Jew or Greek has little meaning; "Philo's group was 'neither Jew nor Greek,' but a new creature in being both" (*Intro.*, pp. 10, 122). What marks him off from other "hellenizing" Jews is that for all his Hellenism he remained loyal to the faith of his fathers. Unfortunately we have no means of determining how many thought as he did, in Alexandria or in the Dispersion at large. So far as Judaism is concerned, the tradition he represents went into eclipse after the fall of Jerusalem in A.D. 70.

In philosophy Philo was not an original thinker, and Wolfson's description of him as "no mere dabbler in philosophy, but a philosopher in the grand manner" errs on the side of enthusiasm. Philo's thought is eclectic, drawing now upon one school, now upon another. The dominant philosophy of the time was the Platonizing Stoicism, or Stoicizing Platonism, commonly associated with the name of Posidonius of Apamea; and this philosophy Philo read between the lines of the OT. As Colson has said, if the ingenuity of his deductions is undeniable, so also is their fancifulness and even perversity, by the standards of sound exegesis. Within certain limits, however, there is justice in Wolfson's estimate: Philo's real contribution to the history of thought is his combination of Greek philosophy with biblical revelation, which prepared the way for the Christian Platonists of Alexandria, and through them for a whole tradition reaching down to the Middle Ages.

Philosopher, apologist, religious thinker, mystic, versed in Greek learning yet loyal to the Jewish tradition, Philo was clearly a man of many aspects. To single out any one of them as the norm would do him less than justice. When we recall the period in which he lived, a period that saw the dawn of the Roman empire and the birth of the Christian mission; when we consider the trends and currents of thought of the time, the meeting of East and West, the interplay of Greek philosophy and oriental religion, the maelstrom of contemporary syncretism, then we begin to appreciate his significance. Philo's writings provide important insights into these different aspects of the world into which the gospel came.

*III. Some Leading Themes.*–Philo was not a systematic writer. Nowhere did he present a detailed and comprehensive statement of his theories; nowhere did he develop a system of philosophy or of theology. Exegete rather than philosopher, expositor rather than systematic theologian, he was concerned to explain the Scriptures, and his ideas on any given subject have to be pieced together from isolated references scattered throughout his works. As might be expected, there are inconsistencies, even contradictions, in his statements, and it is sometimes difficult to say what he really believed. Thus summary accounts of his opinions are often subject to qualification. Some modern systematizations have owed almost more to their authors than to Philo himself.

On a number of points, however, the material is sufficiently abundant, and sufficiently consistent, to allow the formation of a fairly clear conception of his views. One notable feature is the almost complete neglect of the messianic hope, possibly in part the result of prudence in one who lived in a gentile city where anti-Jewish feeling was strong, but also the result of a spiritualizing of the expectation; the Messiah has become the philosopher-king, and the materialistic aspects of the hope have been transformed into symbols of moral progress. Israel's destiny lies not in conquest but in priesthood: the Jews are to the world at large what priests are to the state. It should be noted that Philo's primary concern was with the Pentateuch, not with the prophets or with apocalyptic. It is Moses, law giver, philosopher, priest, and king, who is the central human figure.

Philo's theology may be conveniently summarized under the traditional heads of God, the world, and man. Contemporary pagan thought, as already noted, was moving toward monotheism, and here we can see a certain convergence of gentile and Jewish belief. The Greeks, however, tended to think of God as immanent and impersonal, an abstract philosophic deity; and this introduced a certain duality into Philo's thought: he could speak not only of "Him who is" but also of "that which is"; or, like the Stoics, he could speak of "nature" when we should expect a reference to God. Greek influence thus introduced a tendency toward an impersonal conception of God, but here we must beware of forcing Philo into the categories of later thought. As Goodenough observed (*Intro.*, p. 87), the question of "personality" in God had not yet been raised, and Philo apparently saw no incompatibility between the abstract Supreme Being of philosophy and the personal God of Judaism. Both have their place in his thinking.

Another tension is that of immanence and transcendence. The Stoics thought of God as immanent in the world, and Philo had no doubt of God's care and concern for the world; yet as abstract Being God must be beyond and above the world. This tension Philo tried to resolve by his doctrine of the Logos and the powers: God's nature forbade contact with matter, so He made use of His powers instead. Though transcendent, God has filled the universe with Himself, by causing His powers to extend themselves throughout.

Alone, unique, and all-sufficient, God has no needs and is wholly exempt from passion of any kind; He alone enjoys perfect happiness and bliss. Plato in the famous passage *Timaeus* 28c had spoken of the difficulty of attaining to a knowledge of God, and in this Philo followed him. God is not apprehensible to the mind, save in that He exists; yet this is no reason for abandoning the search. Although God Himself needs no name, He has nonetheless vouchsafed it to the human race, and made it possible for the race to ascend toward Him. The search for God is itself felicity; to see that God is incapable of being seen is itself a boon. Here Philo's thought of course has OT links as well, but even this brief summary may serve to show the interaction of Greek and Jewish thought in his mind.

The world we know owes its creation to the goodness of God, and Philo roundly denounced the impious falsehood of those who admired the cosmos rather than its Creator. In point of fact, a gulf is fixed between the world, which is material, and the transcendent God; only the immaterial is truly real. Again, God is the author of good only, and is not directly the cause of evil. To account for the origin of evil Philo had recourse to the theory of subordinate powers. The plural "Let us make" in Gen. 1:26 allowed him to infer that man was not made by God alone, but in part by lesser beings. The effect is to reserve to God the credit for what is good and perfect, but at the same time to remove from Him the responsibility for imperfection. Of these powers the chief is the Logos, the mediator between creature and Creator, at once the reason of God and the image of God and also the archetype of the human mind and the source and spring of noble conduct.

The first stage in the creation of the world is the formation of an intelligible universe. To describe this formation Philo used the analogy of an architect forming the plan of a city in his mind, before he ever sets it down on paper, much less begins to build. This intelligible universe is no other than the Logos of God when God was already in the act of creating; through the agency of the Logos the visible world came into being. The two stories of the creation of mankind in Genesis enabled Philo to go further: the man of Gen. 1, the image of God, is the Logos; the man of Gen. 2, who was molded from the dust, is a stage further removed, created "after the likeness," and an inferior copy. Philo's doctrine of man, however, is by no means uniform; Goodenough could speak of "what even in Philo is a surprising jumble of contradictions." Mortal with respect to his body, man is immortal with respect to his mind. He has in his mind the closest copy on earth of the eternal archetype. Yet even the perfect man, insofar as he is a created being, never escapes from sinning; and mind, the highest part of man, may be misled by pleasure into unhallowed union with sense. One clue here lies in earlier Greek philosophy: as Philo put it, there are two kinds of soul, one that is the intelligent and reasonable, and another that operates through the senses. When he spoke of "mind," he sometimes had one of these in view, sometimes the other. Elsewhere he used the Platonic figure of the charioteer and his horses. In short, he could use various Greek philosophical systems, as best suited his purpose.

The body is the tomb of the soul, and it is not possible for one whose abode is in the body to attain to being with God. The business of wisdom is to become estranged from the body and its cravings, for the body is wicked and a plotter against the soul, a composition of clay, a molded statue, carried as a corpse from birth to death. This disparagement of the body has obvious links with later Gnostic thought, but it would probably be wrong to reckon Philo a Gnostic, although he marks a stage in that direction.

Space does not permit discussion of other interesting aspects of Philo's works: his portrayal of the patriarchs as incarnations of the laws, his use of the symbolism of the high priest's robes, his mystical aspirations, the conception (apparently his own invention) of that "sober intoxication" which is divine inspiration. Nevertheless, the summary above may convey some idea both of his thought and of the influences that lie behind it. The rest is best learned from direct study of his writings. His works fill twelve volumes in the Loeb edition and are too numerous to mention individually. (For a survey cf. Goodenough, *Intro.*, pp. 30-51.) Most are devoted to exposition of an allegorical commentary on the Pentateuch, but there are also the two "political" works mentioned above and a treatise "On the Contemplative Life," which is interesting for its assessment of an ascetic group, the Therapeutae, who were in some ways akin to the Essenes.

*IV. Significance.*–When such early fathers as Clement of Alexandria and Origen sought to reconcile their Christian faith and Greek philosophy, they found in Philo one who had already prepared the way. Through the works of these and later fathers the Philonic tradition was to be continued for centuries. This in itself is enough to make Philo a significant figure in the history of thought. In addition he gives us glimpses into the mental climate of the NT period, shows us the ideas that were current, at least in certain circles, and the influences that were at work in the world to which the gospel came. He is thus important for the general background of NT times, although the very bulk of his writings, and the comparative absence of other material, exposes us to the danger of making him too much the mirror of his times. In particular he provides evidence, now confirmed by the Dead Sea Scrolls, that Judaism in the NT period was by no means so rigidly uniform as once was thought. Reconstructions based solely upon rabbinic sources may present a distorted picture, even though these sources may contain material very much older than the time of their own writing. Philo helps toward a balanced judgment.

Philo's influence on the Alexandrian Christian tradition is unquestioned; it can be documented by direct quotations in Clement and in Origen. The question of his influence on earlier Christian writers is, however, much more delicate. How early did the conditions become operative that prompted the Alexandrian synthesis of Christianity and philosophy? Justin, for example, had a Logos doctrine, but did he derive it from Philo? On at least one occasion he maintained a view that Philo had explicitly rejected, which suggests not a relationship of dependence but a common background of tradition.

In the NT itself the obvious links are with the Fourth Gospel, but here again the same holds good. There are numerous parallels, not merely in relation to the Logos (cf., e.g., C. H. Dodd, *Interpretation of the Fourth Gospel* [1953], pp. 54ff.); but do they reflect the influence of Philo's writings? At any rate, Philo could never have written "The Logos became flesh." Parallels are also to be found in Paul, but again a common background appears to be a more natural explanation than literary dependence. With Hebrews, however, the question is more open: not only are there parallels, but the style, the patterns of thought, the methods of exegesis all recall the Philonic. This would be the more interesting if Apollos, "born at Alexandria, an eloquent man and mighty in the scriptures," was in fact the author.

Philo's thought has points of contact with the second-century Gnostics, but it would probably be a mistake either to consider him a Gnostic or to ascribe Gnosticism purely to Philonic influence. Once again it is rather a matter of common background. Philo shows the mental climate in which Gnosticism could arise but was himself rather pre-Gnostic than Gnostic in the strict sense. In general, his works provide valuable insights into a range of aspects of ancient thought about which we should otherwise know nothing.

***Bibliography.**–Texts:* Standard ed. of Greek text: L. Cohn and P. Wendland, index by H. Leisegang (7 vols., 1886-1930); Greek (or Armenian) text with Eng. tr.: F. H. Colson, G. H. Whittaker, and R. Marcus (12 vols., *LCL*, 1929-1962).

*Bibliographies:* H. L. Goodhart and E. R. Goodenough, in Goodenough, *Politics of Philo Judaeus* (1938), pp. 125-321; L. Feldman, *Studies in Judaica: Scholarship on Philo and Josephus (1937-1962)* (1963); E. Hilgert, *Studia Philonica*, 1 (1972), 57-71; 2 (1972), 51-54.

*General:* H. A. A. Kennedy, *Philo's Contribution to Religion* (1919); Pauly-Wissowa, XX/1, 1-50 (H. Leisegang); H. A. Wolfson, *Philo* (1948); E. R. Goodenough, *Intro. to Philo Judaeus* (2nd ed. 1962); S. Sandmel, *Philo of Alexandria* (1979).

*Specific Topics:* R. M. Wilson, *The Gnostic Problem* (1958); R. P. C. Hanson, *Allegory and Event* (1959); R. Williamson, *Philo and the Epistle to the Hebrews* (1970). R. M. WILSON

**PHILOLOGUS** fi-lol'ə-gəs [Gk. *Philologos*–'lover of learning']. A Roman Christian greeted by Paul (Rom. 16:15). He was possibly the husband of Julia and the father of Nereus, his sister, and Olympas. If so, this family may have formed the nucleus of a house church (cf. vv. 15b-16). Philologus was a common slave name, found frequently in Greek and Latin inscriptions, including those of the imperial household.

**PHILOMETOR** fil-ə-mē'tôr [Gk. *Philomḗtōr*] (2 Macc. 4:21). *See* PTOLEMY VI.

**PHILOSOPHY; PHILOSOPHER** [Gk. *philosophía, philósophos*].

- I. Background
  - A. Greek
  - B. Judaic
- II. In the Bible
  - A. OT
  - B. NT
- III. In Church History
  - A. Early Church
  - B. Middle Ages
  - C. Reformation
  - D. Modern Era
- IV. Conclusion

***I. Background.***–*A. Greek.* Composed of the two words *phílos*, "love," and *sophía*, "wisdom," the noun *philosophía* and its cognates (*philósophos*, "lover of wisdom," and the verb *philosophéō*, "love wisdom") seem to have come into use in the 5th cent. B.C. Although the meaning "love of wisdom" remained the same, the understanding of what it entailed varied with the different schools of Greek thought. For the Sophists it meant the study of things with a view to practical insight. Plato saw in it a profound desire for truth, yet not without relation to educational and political action. Aristotle equated it with a methodical attempt to explain sensory reality. The Epicureans perceived true philosophy in culture fulfilled in detachment. The Stoics regarded it as a mastery of reality culminating in progress in right conduct. For Middle Platonism it was a developing likeness to God, sometimes achieved by the practicing of death. In the wisdom speculation of Hellenism, philosophy could also incorporate mythological elements. Thus salvation could be closely linked to knowledge, mediated in some cases by revelation, so that the goal of investigation was not scientific information but the grateful adoration of deity.

*B. Judaic.* Along lines similar to those of Hellenism in general, Hellenistic Judaism (e.g., in 4 Maccabees) could claim that Jewish faith and worship represented true philosophy. Philo developed this insight with his philosophical interpretation of the OT, though he stressed the superiority of biblical teaching to that of the philosophical schools. He certainly saw an integral relation between *philosophía* and *sophía*, but he also saw a distinction, for the former was simply the royal way to the latter, which could not be attained in any case without divine revelation. Josephus adopted a similar standpoint, but with a greater emphasis on the institutional aspect. Rabbinic Judaism found the rabbis engaged in many dialogues with Hellenistic philosophers. By and large, however, they made it their main concern to state the superiority of Jewish teaching, though they did not hesitate to incorporate appropriate insights from philosophy into their writings.

***II. In The Bible.***–*A. OT.* Four brief points may be made in relation to the OT. First, a great deal is said about wisdom, and it is obviously an object of earnest and affectionate search. Second, wisdom in the OT is plainly to be differentiated from the wisdom of Greek philosophy, for, while it has a similar if even more emphatic practical orientation, it has a theological root in the fear of God. Third, in the Greek translation of the OT (the LXX) the *philosophía* word-group plays no significant role. Fourth, in the LXX, terms and concepts from Greek thought are almost necessarily chosen to render certain Hebrew words in areas where the themes of Greek philosophy and OT teaching converge, but in general these terms and concepts derive their significance from the Hebrew originals rather than from Hellenic usage.

*B. NT. 1. General.* Written in Greek, and using the LXX as Scripture, the NT also unavoidably uses words and concepts with a Greek or Hellenistic background, although how far the authors were conscious of this is debatable. Forms of thought from the world of physics may thus be found in statements about God, Christ, and creation, as in Jn. 1:1-18; Col. 1:15-20; He. 1:3. Similarly, anthropological and ethical expressions occur in missionary preaching, as in Rom. 1:20; 2:15, in exhortation, as in 1 Cor. 9:24; 2 Pet. 1:5-7. Adoption of these terms, however, does not imply commitment to their philosophical content. The terms are vehicles for the presentation, elucidation, and application of a message which is independent of philosophy, in some sense antithetical to philosophy's principles, methods, and ideas, and incompatible with many of its systems, e.g., materialism or dualism (whether of soul and body or of opposing cosmic forces).

*2. Specific.* A detached, if not critical, attitude toward philosophy dominates the only NT use of the noun *philosophía*, in Col. 2:8: "See to it that no one makes a prey of you by philosophy or empty deceit, according to the elemental spirits of the universe, and not according to Christ" (cf. 1 Tim. 6:20; "what is falsely called knowledge"). Here, of course, the author was plainly not condemning all philosophy. He was specifically warning against the Colossian heresy with its apparent appeal to special insights and its imposition of special rules. Apparently the group under attack was trying to advance its cause either by claiming to be philosophy or by using philosophical concepts or methods. For this reason an element of "empty deceit" marked the enterprise, with which philosophy could be linked in this context. Resisting these techniques, however, the apostle implicitly differentiated the gospel from philosophy even if he did not repudiate philosophy as such. Christianity was certainly a form of *sophía* but it made no claim whatever to be *philosophía*. As the gospel of Christ, whom "God made our wisdom" (1 Cor. 1:30) and in whom "are hid all the treasures of wisdom and knowledge" (Col. 2:3), Christianity could often use similar words, but it built a totally different structure on a totally different foundation.

The use of *philósophos* in Acts 17:18 follows similar lines. The reference in "some of the Epicurean and Stoic philosophers" was obviously neutral as such. A distinction might also be discerned, perhaps, in the reaction to Paul's initial comments, for while one group (possibly the Epicureans) dismissed him as a "babbler," another (possibly the Stoics) saw in him "a preacher of foreign divinities." In the ensuing Areopagus address Paul made no attack on philosophy as such. Indeed, he proclaimed the general nearness of God and quoted a pagan author to the effect that all of us live and move and have our being in Him (17:28). Nevertheless, there was obviously an implied criticism of the philosophers when it came to the knowledge and service of God. With all their intellectual searching they had neither found the true God nor prevented the idolatrous worship that characterized even such a cultural center as Athens. At the climax of his speech, therefore, Paul issued a call for repentance oriented to the risen and returning Christ, about whom the philosophers had nothing to tell, and for whom some of them at least could find no place (17:32).

***III. In Church History.**–A. Early Church.* As educated people, especially those trained in philosophy, became Christians, they naturally tried to fuse their faith and philosophy, incompatible though these might have been in Scripture. Interestingly enough, the *philosophía* word-group played little part in Gnostic writings, except when Acts of Thomas 139 called philosophia, defined as love of God's wisdom, a cardinal Christian virtue. Tertullian was close to the mark, however, when he attributed the Gnostic perversion of the gospel, e.g., its dualism to a philosophical source (*De praescr. haer.* 7). More soberly, and with a claim to be true philosophers, the second-century Apologists adopted the method of philosophical discussion and made some equation of Christian and philosophical concepts, e.g., the Logos (Justin *Apol.* i.46; ii.13). Even Tertullian, although he rhetorically opposed Jerusalem to Athens, was prepared to use philosophical terms to belabor opponents with philosophical arguments and apparently to espouse a philosophical notion like the materiality of the soul.

Meanwhile Clement of Alexandria, himself a philosopher whose search had finally led him to Christ, took the bolder course of intentionally putting the gospel in philosophical rather than biblical terms and concepts in order to facilitate the work of evangelism and Christian education in cultured circles (*Misc.* vii.1.1). For philosophy, he believed, had been raised up by God as a schoolmaster to bring us to Christ (i.5.28.1-3). Clement recognized, of course, that Scripture is the first principle of Christian truth, that simple people may use a short cut to this truth, and that philosophy itself cannot lead to truth and salvation apart from the ministry of the Word and Spirit (vii.16.95ff.).

In the centuries that followed, as Christians trained in Greek and Hellenistic thought assumed theological leadership, philosophy continued to have an ambivalent status and to play an ambivalent role. On the one hand, it undoubtedly underlay the Trinitarian and christological heresies and infused some dubious elements even into the thinking of such orthodox masters as Augustine. On the other hand, it provided the terms and concepts, e.g., substance, person, and nature, which went into the formulation of biblically based orthodoxy, not only in theological treatises, but also in such credal affirmations as the Nicene Creed and the Chalcedonian Definition. The accuracy and appropriateness of such language, of course, are still subjects of theological debate.

*B. Middle Ages.* The outburst of theological activity usually designated Scholasticism brought perhaps the most ambitious of all Christian attempts to apply philosophy to the gospel. Anselm, adopting the principle of faith seeking understanding and inheriting some of the Platonism of Augustine, set out to demonstrate the rationality of such basic beliefs as the existence and nature of God (*Proslogion*) and the atonement (*Cur deus homo*). The rediscovery of Aristotle then produced a brilliant restatement of Christianity by Thomas Aquinas, who found a place for philosophical argument (the Five Ways) in his preambles, and then proceeded to discuss and present the historical dogmas with the aid of philosophical methods, terms, and concepts. Thomas, of course, recognized the limits of philosophy. Its proof of God is by no means indispensable, for it can lead only a few, with considerable difficulty, to the belief in God's existence that simple people may know by revelation alone. Furthermore, it cannot lead past this belief to a knowledge of God's nature and work. In all the great doctrines, it can supply the tools of interpretation or support, but the content must be taken from the authoritative tradition found primarily in Scripture and secondarily in the fathers and councils. Thus for Thomas, as for all the Schoolmen, exposition of Scripture formed the crown of theological endeavor. The later Nominalists (e.g., William of Occam) were, if anything, even more skeptical about the contribution of philosophy than Anselm and Aquinas. They used and sharpened its tools in the form of logical analysis, argument, and presentation, but they had little confidence in its ability to supply reliable content.

*C. Reformation.* Influenced by the revival of biblical studies which came with the Renaissance (cf. Erasmus and Reuchlin), the Reformers had an acute sense of the discrepancy between the language and methods, as well as the content, of Scripture on the one side, and those of philosophy and philosophical theology on the other. This led to a wariness toward philosophy which could even become pronounced hostility in Martin Luther, who spoke scathingly about Aristotle, had little but contempt for scholastic theologians, advised a quick study of philosophy (as a worthless skill) simply to achieve the ability to destroy it, and contrasted the philosophical view of creation and its mechanics with Paul's theology of a groaning but expectant creation in Romans 8 (*Luther's Works*[1972], XXV, 360ff.). Cranmer, too, consistently made it his aim in England to establish a biblically based doctrine and church life as distinct from the "sophistries" in which he had been "nozzled" and the resultant corruptions. His ally Ridley, while not unskilled in the use of logical forms, complained bitterly of the empty wranglings which passed for theology at the Sorbonne, devoting himself instead to an assiduous study of the NT in Greek. Calvin, with his humanist background, perceived some elements of truth in the writings of the great philosophers, but he could see no possibility of any knowledge even of God the Creator unless our weak or blinded eyes are assisted by the spectacles of Holy Scripture. When it came to a full knowledge of God and the self, he stated no less categorically than Luther that without God's Word and Spirit the greatest geniuses are as blind as moles. (*Inst.*1.1ff.; 2.2.12ff.). Zwingli, for all his high estimation of philosophers and his use of philosophical preambles, shared the same fundamental conviction, as may be seen from his harsh condemnation of medieval philosophizing in *The Clarity and Certainty of the Word of God* and his appeal to Scripture alone in *The Sixty-Seven Articles*. In general, the Reformers made two decisive changes in the relation between theology and philosophy. They established the primacy of Scripture with a new rigor and consistency and they evolved a new theological style which drew more directly on the content of Scripture.

*D. Modern Era.* Even in the later Reformation period, however, a revival of philosophical interest may be discerned, e.g., in the curriculum of the Geneva Academy under Beza, or the influence exerted by Petrus Ramus, who substituted his own logical system for that of Aristotle. During the 17th cent. Protestant theologians, both Lutheran and Reformed, developed a scholasticism of their own, in which they preserved the essential content of Reformation teaching but readopted philosophical styles of presentation and made a modest use of Aristotle and Descartes by way of preamble or basis. Once started, this trend proved difficult to check. It led on the one side to the increasing rationalization of theology, as in the comprehensive system that Christian Wolff in Germany erected on a Leibnizian foundation, or in the attempted balancing of reason and revelation that Butler in England sought in his *Analogy*. It led on the other side either to an absorbing of revelation into natural religion, as in the English Deists or the German Neologists, or to an open break with revealed religion, as in the French Encylopedists. In the 19th and 20th cents., then, theology made it a primary concern to adapt Christianity to such varying philosophical movements as Romanticism (Schleiermacher), Idealism (Biedermann, the Cairds), Existentialism (Bultmann), and Evolutionism (Drummond, Teilhard de Chardin, and Whitehead). The two problems with all such reinterpretations, as perceived, e.g., by Karl Barth, are (1) that the biblical content does not fit naturally into these alien schemes, and (2) that by its very nature the biblical revelation resists the claim of philosophy to offer a comprehensive system of truth. Barth himself, of course, was willing to make use of philosophical terms and concepts from various sources, as the fathers and the biblical authors had done. He was also prepared to grant full recognition to philosophy as one of the humanities. But he would not commit himself as a theologian to any single philosophical system. Nor would he allow the equation or confusion of philosophy with divinity. Divinity, he believed, is possible only as God makes Himself known in His saving work and enlightens and restores darkened and fallen reason so that it will perceive and accept this revelation.

***IV. Conclusion.***–As the biblical data suggest, and the historical experience of the Church confirms, philosophy is to be approached and handled with a certain ambivalence. On the one hand, Scripture does not categorically invalidate philosophy, reject the philosophical quest as a way to faith, exclude philosophical terms and thought-forms, or rule out the possibility of putting the content of revelation in the vocabulary of other times and cultures as the task of proclamation demands. On the other hand, Scripture teaches plainly that full and true knowledge of God, self, and the world comes only by way of God's self-revelation, that the higher rationality of this self-revelation can be perceived only as reason is illumined by the Holy Spirit, that the restatement of this self-relevation must be firmly and finally controlled by the terms and concepts divinely selected for it in the written Word, and that the content of it must not be attenuated or altered by adjustment to human systems of thought with their various monistic or dualistic principles.

In the last analysis, of course, the biblical message involves a reinterpretation of its own. Judaism grasped this already with its insight into the true nature of wisdom. The NT took a further step with its equation of the divine wisdom and Christ. Christians may still find a place for classical or modern philosophy as an academic discipline. Even as they do so, however, they realize that for them philosophy itself has an added or new dimension. Love of Christ is the true philosophy which is indeed coterminous with Christianity itself. G. W. BROMILEY

**PHINEAS** fin'i-əs. *See* PHINEHAS.

**PHINEES** fin'i-əs.

**1.** (AV 1 Esd. 5:5; 8:2, 29; 2 Esd. 1:2b; 1 Macc. 2:26; Sir. 45:23). *See* PHINEHAS **1.**

**2.** (2 Esd. 1:2a, AV). *See* PHINEHAS **2.**

**3.** (1 Esd. 8:63, AV). *See* PHINEHAS **3.**

**4.** (1 Esd. 5:31, AV). *See* PASEAH **2.**

**PHINEHAS** fin'ē-əs [Heb. *pînᵉḥās,* prob. < Egyp. *p'nḥsy,* "the Nubian" or "the Negro" (see Cody, p. 70)]; **PHINEAS** [Gk. *Phinees* (1 Esd. 8:29; 4 Macc. 18:12), *Pheinees* (1 Esd. 8:2)]; AV Apoc. PHINEES; NEB Apoc. also PHINEAS.

**1.** The distinguished priest who was the son of Eleazar, the son of Aaron, the brother of Moses (Ex. 6:25; 1 Ch. 6:4, 50 [MT 5:30; 6:35]). Phinehas rose to prominence because of his righteous response to the apostasy of Israel at Shittim (Nu. 25). There at the last encampment before crossing the Jordan, Israel was seduced by Moabite and Midianite women to engage in cultic prostitution and to offer idolatrous sacrifices to the Baal of Peor. In His well-deserved wrath, the Lord sent a plague among His people in which 24,000 ultimately died. To avert His wrath, the Lord directed Moses to execute any of Israel's leaders who had been responsible for this sin and expose their corpses. But apparently before this purge could be implemented, atonement was made and the plague brought to a sudden end: Phinehas followed Zimri, the son of a tribal leader of Simeon, and Cozbi, the daughter of a prominent Midianite leader, into the tabernacle (Heb. *qubbâ,* RSV "inner room"; see F. M. Cross, "Priestly Tabernacle," in G. E. Wright and D. N. Freedman, eds., *Biblical Archaeologist Reader,* I [1961], 218f.) and put them to death. This he accomplished with a single spear thrust through Zimri and into Cozbi's belly with the obvious implication that they were caught in the very act of their ritual prostitution.

God rewarded Phinehas for his "cleansing" of the tabernacle by extending to him a "covenant of peace" that promised a lasting priesthood to his progeny (cf. the similar occasion of the promotion of the Levites in Ex. 32:25-29; later interpreted in terms of a covenant in Jer. 33:21; Mal. 2:4ff.). That the text does not explicitly record any conditions need not imply that this promise to Phinehas and his descendants was entirely unconditional (e.g., cf. the various accounts of the covenant with David in 2 S. 7; 1 Ch. 22:12; 28:7; also cf. the general principle of Jer. 18:7-10 and Ezk. 33:13-16). Furthermore, it is not clear from its wording that the original promise intended to restrict the legitimate succession of high priests solely to the house of Phinehas.

Nevertheless, from the biblical record, supplemented with the available extrabiblical evidence, it appears that Phinehas's progeny did enjoy a lasting priestly ministry and that, in particular, they also provided the succession of high priests from his own day down to the time of Eli (of the family of Ithamar according to 1 Ch. 24:3). This succession of high priests resumed with Zadok in the days of David (so 1 Ch. 6:1ff., 50ff.; see Olyan's discussion of Zadok's debated ancestry). And it continued down through Ezra (Ezr. 7:5) at least until 171 B.C. when Antiochus IV transferred the priesthood to Menelaus (2 Macc. 4:23; cf. Bruce, pp. 58f.).

Cross has offered a stimulating but still problematic challenge to the older documentary hypothesis, which assigned Nu. 25:1-5 to JE and vv. 6-18 to P (or some other late priestly source). He reinterprets Nu. 25 as a reflex of a later polemic defending the legitimacy of an Aaronic priestly family (though not exclusively descendants of Phinehas) against the presumed counterclaims of a Mushite priestly family (Cross, *Myth,* pp. 195-215). *See* PRIESTS AND LEVITES for further discussion.

In Nu. 31:6 Phinehas brings the articles of the tabernacle and signaling trumpets to aid in the battle against the Midianites that God declared to avenge the Baal-peor incident. Still later Phinehas led a diplomatic mission to the eastern tribes of Reuben, Gad, and the half-tribe of Manasseh (Josh. 22). Finally, in Jgs. 20:28 Phinehas ministered before the ark at Bethel.

The Abrahamic ascription (Gen. 15:6) in Ps. 106:30f. commemorates the zeal of Phinehas that brought an end to the plague: "This was credited to him as righteousness for endless generations to come" (NIV; cf. also 1 Macc. 2:26, 54; 4 Macc. 18:12). Likewise, Phinehas is honored, at least indirectly, in Josh. 24:33, which states that his father Eleazar was buried on a hill (or town; so RSV) named after the son, "Gibeah of Phinehas in the hill country of Ephraim."

The striking commendation in the canonical tradition becomes extravagant praise in the intertestamental literature. Sir. 45:23-25 includes Phinehas in the list of famous men, extolling him as "third in glory" after Moses and Aaron. And the praise in the intertestamental literature becomes pure legend in the rabbinical period, where, for example, the Pseudo-Jonathan Targum asserts that twelve miracles accompanied Phinehas's act of zeal.

**2.** The younger son of Eli and brother of Hophni (1 S. 1:3). Phinehas and Hophni outraged the public conscience in their contempt for the sacrificial laws, which prescribe the priest's portion and insist that fat first be burned as the Lord's own portion (1 S. 2:12-17), and also for their seeming practice of cultic prostitution (1 S. 2:22). Scripture records Eli's feeble attempt to rebuke his sons, who totally ignored him (1 S. 2:22-25). The point is often missed, however, that Eli stands condemned not because he failed to use, say, the stronger measure of "the rod." (His sons were themselves fully grown and married!) Rather, Eli failed (perverting justice much as David would later do out of favoritism toward children) to exercise his proper judicial office as priest and execute his sons for their capitally punishable offenses. An unnamed prophet brought God's message of judgment, later confirmed by Samuel.

Sometime later, Hophni and Phinehas in their presumption took the ark into a doomed battle against the Philistines at Aphek and subsequently lost the ark and their lives to the enemy (1 S. 4:11). When this news was brought back to Eli, he too died, and the wife of Phinehas immediately went into labor and died after naming their son Ichabod, meaning "where is the glory?" (1 S. 4:21).

*See also* HOPHNI AND PHINEHAS.

**3.** The father of a priest named Eleazar (Ezr. 8:33; 1 Esd. 8:63). He, Meremoth, and others evaluated the silver and gold and other sacred articles that were returned to the temple under Ezra's leadership in their attempt to be sure that these all arrived safely. Some have taken this as a reference not to Eleazar's immediate father but to his remote ancestor, the great Phinehas mentioned in **1.**

***Bibliography.***–F. F. Bruce, *NT History* (1969); A. Cody, *History of OT Priesthood* (1969); F. M. Cross, *Canaanite Myth and Hebrew Epic* (1973); *JBL,* 94 (1975), 4-18; M. Noth, *Numbers* (Eng. tr., *OTL,* 1969); S. Olyan, *JBL,* 101 (1982), 177-193.

G. P. HUGENBERGER

**PHINIS** fin'is (1 Esd. 5:21, NEB). *See* MAGBISH.

**PHINOE** fi-nō'ə (RSV mg., NEB, 1 Esd. 5:31). *See* PASEAH **2.**

**PHLEGON** fleg'on [Gk. *Phlegōn*–'burning']. A Roman Christian to whom Paul sent greetings (Rom. 16:14). His was a common name among slaves and freedmen.

**PHOEBE** fē'bē [Gk. *Phoibe*–'pure, bright, radiant'] (Rom. 16:1); AV PHEBE. A Christian woman who had a ministry at the church in Cenchraea (a port city 11 km. [7 mi.] E of Corinth on the Saronic Gulf), known only from Rom. 16:1f. Paul calls her an *adelphḗ* ("sister," indicating that she is a Christian) and a *diákonos* (RSV "deaconess"; AV "servant"; NEB "who holds office"). *Diákonos* may be a technical term referring to a fixed office (cf. RSV "deacon," Phil. 1:1; 1 Tim. 3:8, 12), or it may simply refer to services on behalf of the church community (cf. RSV "minister," Eph. 3:7; Col. 1:7; etc.; "servant," 1 Cor. 3:5; 1 Thess. 3:2; etc.). That an order of deaconesses existed by the early 2nd cent. is clear, but the NT nowhere else refers to such an order, except possibly in 1 Tim. 3:11. Nevertheless, one should not rule out the possibility that an ecclesiastical office is intended here.

Paul requested that the Christians in Rome (although some interpreters regard Rom. 16 as a separate letter sent to Ephesus, not to Rome) "help [*parastḗte*] her in whatever she may require from you," perhaps implying that she had a specific task to perform. Part of the motive for helping her is that she has been a *prostátis* (RSV "helper"; AV "succourer"; NEB "good friend") for Paul and many other Christians. The masc. *prostátēs* is often a technical term for a legal representative of a foreigner, which would suggest a person of wealth and status. But no evidence indicates that women could perform this legal function, and it is probably best to understand *prostátis* as "helper," corresponding to the "help" the congregation is enjoined to give her.

Phoebe probably carried the letter to Rome (if we assume that ch. 16 was originally part of this letter). She was likely a Gentile, as her name carries strong associations with the mythology of Apollos (Phoebus) and Artemis. The specific ways in which she helped Paul and many others remain a matter for speculation.

*See also* DEACON, DEACONESS; MINISTER.

***Bibliography.***–C. E. B. Cranfield, *Epistle to the Romans,* II (*ICC,* 1979), 780-83; H. Gamble, *Textual History of the Letter to the Romans* (*Studies and Documents,* 42, 1977), pp. 84-95; E. Käsemann, *Comm. on Romans* (Eng. tr. 1980), pp. 409-411.

R. L. OMANSON

**PHOENICIA; PHOENICIANS** fə-nish'ə, -enz [Gk. *Phoinikē, Phoinikēs*–'purple-red']. A country at the eastern end of the Mediterranean, approximately where modern Lebanon is located, and the people of that country.

I. Name
II. Region
III. Language and People
IV. Demography and Economy
V. Commerce and Colonization
VI. Political History
VII. Religion

***I. Name.***–In modern historical use, Phoenicia designates the Syrian coast, and Phoenicians the Northwest Semitic inhabitants of that region in the period from 1200 B.C. to about the end of the Roman era. The words "Phoenicia" and "Phoenician" are Greek, attested certainly as early as Homer (J. Muhly, *Berytus,* 19 [1970], 19-66), therefore from the 8th cent., and still used in Acts 11:19; 15:3; 21:2. The terms are presumed to be connected with the word *phoínix,* which means "red-purple" (also "date palm") and is attested already in Mycenean documents of the 13th cent. (*po-ni-ki-ya* as determinative of a "purple" cart). The Greek word seems to be etymologically grounded in the Indo-European sphere (cf. *phónos,* "murder," and similar terms tied to the concept of "blood" or "red"). The terms "Phoenicia" and "Phoenicians" have not been traced to the languages of the ancient Near East, for the assonance of the Egyptian toponym *fnḫw,* which refers to an indefinable region in Syro-Palestine and is attested only in the Old Kingdom, is probably not phonetically correct.

The inhabitants of the region called themselves and were called by their immediate neighbors either "Sidonians" (cf. Josh. 13:6; Jgs. 3:3), the designation that properly belonged to the inhabitants of the principal city of the area, or "Canaanites" (Akk. *kinaḫnu* or *kinaḫḫu* for the region; Egyp. *p3 knʿn* for the region; Ugar. *knʿny* for the people; Phoen. *knʿn* for the region; Heb. *kᵉnaʿan* for the region and *kᵉnaʿᵃnî* for the people). "Canaanite" does not exactly correspond to "Phoenician"; the former applies to the larger entity, whether from a chronological viewpoint, since it is attested from the 15th cent., or from a geographical viewpoint, since it is applicable to a zone of the interior, especially in Palestine (on the latter cf. R. de Vaux, *JAOS*, 88 [1968], 23-30). It is nevertheless interesting that in the Akkadian of Nuzi (15th cent.) the term *kinaḫḫu* designates "red-purple" (possibly by Hurrianization of the Akkadian term for "purple," *uqnu* > **ukniaḫḫu* > *kinaḫḫu*); there would then be a connection between the name of the color and the name of the region (and its inhabitants), exactly as in the case of the name the Greeks gave to Phoenicia (cf. E. Speiser, *Language*, 12 [1936], 121-26).

The usage of either the more generic term (Canaanite) or the more specific term (Sidonians), and the absence of a local name to indicate this people, corresponds to the actual historical situation. For the Phoenicians were always subdivided politically into city-states (hence the political entities "Tyre" and "Sidon," but no political entity "Phoenicia"), and not clearly distinguishable on the cultural or ethno-linguistic level from the population of the hinterland, but rather characterized clearly by their thrust toward the sea and the West. The Greeks, however, saw this people as unitary and characterizable Phoenician.

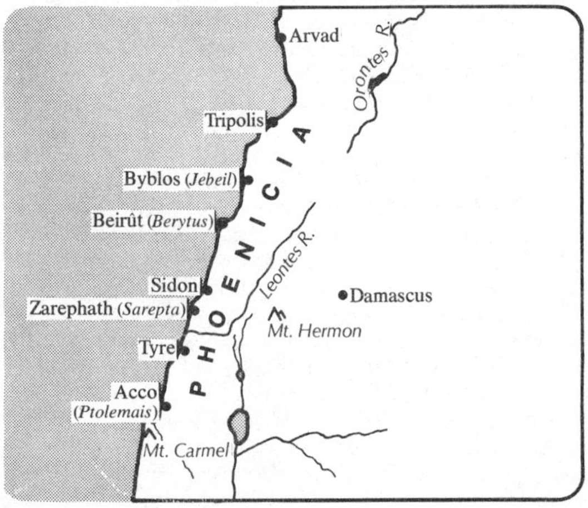


***II. Region.***–Phoenicia is a strip of land between the Mediterranean and the mountains (the Lebanon, altitude 3088 m. [10,130 ft.]; Jebel Anṣarīya, altitude 1583 m. [5,193 ft.]) that extends from Mt. Cassius (Jebel el-ʿAqraʿ) on the north to Mt. Carmel on the south, for a length of about 300 km. (185 mi.). The width is variable, depending on the distance of the mountains from the coast, but always rather narrow, becoming nonexistent where a mountain spur meets the sea in the form of a promontory (on physical geography, cf. E. de Vaumas, *Le Liban*, I-II [1954], with bibliography). Actually, an alternation of coastal plains and mountain spurs produces a territorial fragmentation of the region that makes land communication difficult; the fragmentation is especially marked when each coastal plain is used as the agricultural hinterland of a port city that is neither an economic nor a political center. From north to south we can distinguish the following zones:

(1) South of Mt. Cassius, woody and adjacent to the sea, is a broader zone, with coastal plains, and hilly regions with valleys (notably that of Nahr el-Kebîr, which debouches near the present Latakia). In the 2nd millennium this region saw the flourishing of the kingdom of Ugarit, but in the Phoenician period (properly speaking) this area had no historic importance.

(2) The aforementioned zone is closed at the southern end by a mountain spur that comes to the sea (near Qalʿat er-Russ); soon after, a broad coastal plain opens up with its modern centers at Jebeil and Bâniyâs and its chief centers in the Phoenician age at Siannu (Tell Siano) and Usnu, the successors of the kingdom of Siyannu-Usnatu of the 2nd millennium. The best-known archeological site is Tell Suqas (on this region cf. P. I. Riis, *Tell Sūkās*, I-VI [1970-1979]). The plain is closed toward the southern end by a branch of Jebel Anṣarīya that descends and interrupts the coastal plain near Qalʿat Marqab.

(3) From Marqab to the promontory of Mantar there is no plain; a confusion of hills results in rather meagre agricultural resources for the region. The modern center is Tartūs, but the ancient center was Arvad (Erwâd), located on a small island 2.5 km. (1.5 mi.) from the coast (H. Frost, *Annales Archéologiques de Syrie* [hereafter *AAS*] 14 [1964], 67-74; 16 [1966], 13-28), mentioned in Gen. 10:18 and Ezk. 27:8, 11. A series of centers on the mainland, such as Antarados (Tartūs) and Marathus (Amrît; cf. M. Dunand, *Bulletin de Musée de Beyrouth* [hereafter *BMB*], 7 [1944-45], 99-107; 8 [1945-48], 81-107; *AAS*, 4-5 [1954-55], 189-204; 6 [1956], 3-8), are attested only later. The difficulty of communication with the hinterland and the sparseness of agricultural resources determined a maritime vocation for Arvad.

(4) South of Mantar a vast coastal plain opens up, the plain of ʿAkkar, well irrigated by several watercourses. The principal centers were Ṣimirra (Tell Kazel; cf. *AAS*, 7 [1957], 3-16; 14 [1964], 3-14) and Arqa/Irqata (Tell ʿArqah; cf. *Syria*, 54 [1977], 25-30; 55 [1978], 136-139; *BMB*, 30 [1978], 61-75), both of which had already flourished in the 2nd millennium and again in the Phoenician era, and are named in Gen. 10:17-18 (Arkites and Zemarites). Other centers flouishing before 1200 (particularly Ullaza = Tell Kastina) had no role in the Phoenician age. The region, basically agricultural and with good communications with the interior (the depression between Jebel Anṣarīya and the Lebanon that leads to the Orontes valley), is not projected toward the sea: Ṣimirra and Arqa are not on the coast, but more toward the interior.

(5) Next, a stretch of rather jagged coast, corresponding to the adjoining slopes of the Lebanon, is a region between the two promontories that are the locations of the modern cities of Tripolis and Beirût. Tripolis is of relatively recent founding (5th cent. B.C.), and is suspected of covering the Phoenician Maḫallata (H. Salamé-Sarkis, *Mélanges de l'université Saint-Joseph* [hereafter *MUSJ*], 49 [1975/76], 549-563). Beirût is already attested in the 2nd millennium, but was of secondary importance until the Hellenistic age (N. Jidejian, *Beirut Through the Ages* [1973]). In the Phoenician period the center of this zone was rather Byblos (modern Jebeil; Gebal in Ezk. 27:9; Josh. 13:5; cf. R. Dussaud, *Syria*, 4 [1923], 300-315), the best-known Phoenician city archeologically, although the remains belong primarily to the Bronze Age and the Roman period (P. Montet, *Byblos et l'Égypte* [1928]; M. Dunand, *Fouilles de Byblos* [1939-1954]; *BMB*, 17 [1964], 21-36; 19 [1966], 95-101; 20 [1967], 21-26). A series of lesser centers gravitated toward Byblos, attested chiefly in the Amarna Letters: Batrūna (Batrūn), Šigata (Šaqqa), ʿAmmiya (ʿEnfe), etc. *See also* Plate 63.

(6) South of Râs Beirût the coastal plain opens once more and then a hilly region ending at Ṣarafand (OT Zarephath, NT Sarepta). The chief center is Sidon (modern Ṣaidā; cf. N. Jidejian, *Sidon Through the Ages* [1972]; M. Dunand, *BMB*, 26 [1973], 7-25), "firstborn" of Canaan

Amarna Letter from Rib-addi, prince of Byblos, to Pharaoh (Louvre; picture M. Chuzeville)

(Gen. 10:15). The entire region from Beirût to Sidon is sprinkled with minor centers, cited in Assyrian texts and known archeologically: Khalde (R. Saida, *BMB,* 19 [1966], 51-90; 20 [1967], 165-69; *Berytus,* 20 [1971], 130-34), Kherayeb (M. Chehab, *BMB,* 10 [1951-52]; 11 [1953-54]; B. Kaukabani, *BMB,* 26 [1973], 41-58), etc. Noteworthy in the south is Sarepta (modern Ṣarafand; cf. J. B. Pritchard, *Sarepta* [1975]; *Recovering Sarepta, A Phoenician City* [1978]), attested in the 2nd millennium (Papyrus Anastasi I) and ending in the classical age (called Zarephath in 1 K. 17:9).

(7) In the mountainous region beginning at Ṣarafand and ending at the promontories of Râs el-ʿAbyadh and Râs en-Nakûrah ("Ladders of Tyre"), where coastal communications are practically broken, lies a beautiful coastal plain into which the Litani (classical Leontes) empties and in which are the centers of Maḥalēb (Mahalab, Josh. 19:29; cf. Ahlab, Jgs. 1:31), Ushu (classical Palaetyrus, modern Tell Rašîdîya; cf. K. Galling, *ZDPV,* 69 [1953], 91-93, perhaps biblical Hosah of Josh. 19:29). The chief center is Tyre (Ṣûr), on a small island facing the coast and joined to the mainland in the Hellenistic age (H. J. Katzenstein, *History of Tyre* [1973]). Toward Râs en-Nakûrah is the Hellenistic center of Umm el-ʿAwāmîd, of archeological note (M. Dunand and R. Duru, *Oumm el-ʿAmed* [1962]).

(8) A final broad coastal plain stretches between Râs en-Nakûrah and the Carmel, well watered with various watercourses (among them the Kishon). The center of the region is ʿAkkā (OT Accho; modern Tell el-Fukhkhâr) a port already attested in the 2nd millennium and flourishing in Phoenician (cf. Jgs. 1:31), Roman (NT Ptolemais), and medieval times (St. John of Acre). Other centers are: Achzib (modern ez-Zîb; on excavations cf. M. Prausnitz, *IEJ,* 15 [1965], 256-58) and Tell Abū Hawâm (cf. R. Hamilton, *Quarterly of the Department of Antiquities in Palestine,* 3 [1934], 74-80; 4 [1935], 1-69; B. Maisler [Mazar], *BASOR,* 124 [Dec. 1950], 21-25), near modern Haifa. This region, because of easy communications with the interior and the overhanging Galilee hills, was the most exposed to penetration by the Israelite tribes (cf. the "blessings of Jacob," Gen. 49, relevant to Zebulun, Issachar, and Asher; cf. also Josh. 19:29; Jgs. 1:31f.).

***III. Language and People.***–The language spoken in the region is included in the Northwest Semitic group, and is closely related to Hebrew (less so to Aramaic). It can be traced essentially from a local dialectical development of Amorite (also called the Northwest Semitic of the first half of the 2nd millennium), characterized in part by elements that developed indigenously and in part by elements common to Hebrew. Some principal phonetic elements are: reduction of the parent consonants with the shift of *ḫ* > *ḥ*, *ǵ* > *ʿ*, *ṯ* > *š*, *ḏ* > *z* (as in Hebrew); alterations in the syllabic structure (but less than in Hebrew, maintaining the patterns *qatl, qitl, qutl* without segholization), especially as a consequence of the loss of the final vowel; vocalic changes with the shift of accented long *ā* > long *ō* (more active than in Hebrew: **yatōn* and **malōk* instead of **nātān* and **mālāk*) and with the reduction of diphthongs (**bayt* > *bêt,* Heb. *bayiṯ;* **mawt* > *môt,* Heb. *māweṯ*). On the morphological level: the end of noun declension and the introduction of the article *h-*, used, however, less regularly than in Hebrew; the end of the system of verbal moods and alteration of the system of "tenses"; the causative *yiqtil* (contrasted with Hebrew *hiqtil*). On the lexical plane: peculiarities in the demonstrative (*ʾz*), relative (*ʾš*), and pronominal elements (*-y* 3rd sing., *-m* and *-nm* 3rd pl., vis-à-vis Heb. *-h* and *-hm*); preference for words that differ from those usually used in Hebrew ("to be," *kn* instead of *hyh;* "to make," *pʿl* instead of *ʿśh;* "gold," *ḥrṣ* instead of *zhb;* "no," *bl* instead of *lʾ*; etc. — in a number of instances, the word used in Phoenician is the same as, or similar to, the word used in Hebrew poetry or parallelism).

One may explain the racial and linguistic elements by assuming that the Phoenicians were the descendants of the population formerly in the region (if not always, at least for the historically documented period). The continuity of the indigenous peoples (Byblos, Tyre, Sidon, and in general all the Phoenician cities existed already in the pre-Phoenician age) and the complete cultural homogeneity of the Phoenician period with respect to the preceding, such as in the rather pure language and in other parts of the culture (religion, political and social structure, figurative traditions, etc.), suggest a substantial continuity with obvious innovations the result of internal development and not of outside introductions.

In the period between 1200 and the Roman age Phoenicia was inhabited by a population that by physical traits (which naturally have nothing to do with its ethnic and cultural characteristics) is included in the "Mediterranean" type common to a large part of the Near East (cf. W. Shanklin and M. Ghantus, *BMB,* 19 [1966], 91-94). Naturally the ancient authors (from Herodotus i.1 and vii.89 on) fantasized on the provenience of the Phoenicians (from the Persian Gulf), because the historiographic theories of antiquity were based on the simplistic concept of "origins" and "provenience" and took into account only population shifts that had already developed their own characteristics. Today, since the complexity of the constitutive process of ethnic entity is differently presented, and the cultural data are distinguished from the political and racial, the perpetuation of such theories (unfortunately related in some authorative works) is unacceptable (cf. S. Moscati, *Rendiconti dell'Accademia Nazionale de Lincei,* 18 [1963], 483-506; *Problematica della civiltà fenicia* [1974]). On the contrary it is necessary to demonstrate through the historical process that the people of Phoenicia were constituted in (relative) ethnic autonomy toward 1200, emerging from a more undifferentiated relationship to the wandering "Canaanite" that in the Late Bronze embraced all Syria-Palestine. It was a process of identification that began from the comparison of and in opposition to the identification of other neighboring ethnic entities: that formed by Israelites, Arameans, Moabites, etc., with their own political formation and with their own linguistic and cultural characteristics, helped also to single out the Phoenician ethnos. Among these, the Phoenicians are the most direct heirs of the preceding "Canaanite" world, since the other peoples were affected by the phenomenon of nomadic sedentarization that carried even more substantial mutants in the social and political body.

In this process of differentiation, obviously long and progressive, a decisive turning point was the invasion of the peoples of the sea (*ca.* 1190; cf. R. deVaux, *MUSJ,* 45 [1969], 481-498), for such invasions with all the political and economic consequences (destruction of cities, interruption of trade, fall of the Egyptian and Hittite empires, etc.) not only signaled a profound fracture in Syrian history but was also the occasion for a more decisive concretization of the innovative factors formerly latent (e.g., diffusion of the alphabet, metallurgy of iron, etc.). It is therefore reasonable to put the beginning of Phoenician history *ca.* 1200; and it is obviously easy to see the end in the Roman era, when the use of the local language gave way to Greek and Aramaic, and every element of cultural autonomy ceased, the culture having been progressively eroded during the centuries of dependence first on the oriental empires and afterward on the Hellenistic.

Between these two chronological limits one may single out a Phoenician people with its own history and its own culture that, though in the process of coming into being, nevertheless manifested characteristic traits. If the lack of political unity rendered difficult the emergence of a firm national conscience, nevertheless those with whom the Phoenicians came into contact recognized them as a unity (whether "Phoenicians," "Sidonians," or "Canaanites") and distinguished them from their neighbors (by language, by economic activity, by cultural elements, by religious faith), the Neo-Hittites and Arameans, the Israelites and Philistines. Especially in the west the Phoenicians were presented as active navigators, merchants, artisans, assuming a sort of national image, recurring from Homer to Poenulus of Plautus and to the stories of the Punic wars with an evaluation that passed from admiration to ill will and to scorn. Similarly, the attitude of Israel toward the Phoenicians passed from admiration of their technical ability and the desirability of economic collaboration at the time of Solomon, later to hatred and scorn, expressed particularly by Ezekiel (Ezk. 26–28; cf. also Joel 3:4-8 [MT 4:4-8]; Am. 1:9f.). This change may be attributed on the one hand to economic pressures exercised by the Phoenician merchants on the poorer interior of Palestine, and on the other to the opinions of the ambient Yahwists, to whom the Phoenician cult was impious and immoral (cf. 1 K. 16:31-33; 2 K. 23:13; cf. already 1 K. 11:5-8; 11:13).

*IV. Demography and Economy.*–With drastic simplification one can imagine that in the 1st millennium the mountains of Lebanon and Jebel Anṣarīya were for the most part still covered with woods and trees of great height (the celebrated cedars) or at least with Mediterranean maquis, while the coastal plains were completely free for agricultural use (M. B. Rowton, "The Topological Factor in the *Ḥapiru* Problem," in H. G. Güterbock and T. Jacobsen, eds., *Studies in Honor of Benno Landsberger* [1965], pp. 375-387). From this to the basic cereal culture were added in notable measure the typical Mediterranean arboreal cultures of the vine and the olive, which provided wine and oil. Likewise the wooded areas were exploited to provide timber for construction (of ships, of roofs, and for reinforcing brick walls, etc.) and for smaller objects (furniture, handles) as well as for resins (H. Klengel, *Das Altertum,* 13 [1967], 67-76; J. Brown, *Lebanon and Phoenicia, I: The Physical Setting and the Forest* [1969]). Oil, wine, and especially timber were exported at the time of the great kings of Egypt and Mesopotamia, which for obvious climatic and historical reasons were lacking in forest resources. Since very ancient times (3rd millennium) the interest of the great empires in wood and other products of the region is attested, and such interest was continually present in the Phoenician era proper, with obvious economic advantages but also with grave danger to political independence.

The distribution of the population was clearly distinguished between the small coastal plains, which were densely populated, and the mountainous zones at some distance from the coast, almost uninhabited. The forms of settlement tell nothing about the villages that housed the basic farmer population. The cities on the other hand reveal some proper urban characteristics, partly reconstructible from the topographical and archeological data (cf. B. Isserlin, *Rivista di studi fenici,* 1 [1973], 135-152). With few exceptions (Ṣimirra, Irqata, Sianu) the cities were on the coast, and by preference made use of the rocky promontories (Tell Suqas, Byblos, Sidon, Acco, etc), sometimes islands (Tyre, Arvad), always with the aim of providing anchorage secure against winds and currents, sheltered by the aforementioned promontories or by the lines of cliffs that in places fronted the coast. The Phoenicians sought to reproduce this type of settlement also in the zones of their commerical expansion, choosing promontories and small islands facing the coast, anchorages sheltered by the capes or between lagoons. The Phoenician cities were obviously surrounded by walls (imposing remains from the Persian era at Byblos and Arvad); unfortunately all of the internal makeup of the cities is not known — the location of the temples among the more noteworthy edifices, together with the public buildings, markets, etc., and the royal palace. Extraurban sanctuaries were characteristic (as that of Amrît and like the temple of Eshmun at Sidon), connected with springs or with woods, or situated on the hills (the numerous Roman sanctuaries of Lebanon go back certainly to the Phoenician era). Likewise the necropoleis were outside the cities, mostly dug in areas of rock outcroppings.

The population, as in general in the preclassical Near East, was subdivided in two segments: (1) a peasant segment, united by the community life of the village, dedicated to the activity of the direct production of food (agriculture and arboriculture, and in Phoenicia probably also fishing but not pastoralism); and (2) an urban segment, centralized within the royal palace and dedicated to specialized economic activities, especially in the sectors of transformation and distribution (artisans, merchants) and in the service of the organizations of the state (admin-

Phoenician ivory formerly decorated with lapis lazuli, gold, and carnelian. From Nimrûd, 721-705 B.C. (Trustees of the British Museum)

Phoenician ivory plaques from Nimrûd (British Museum; picture W. S. LaSor)

istration, cultus, etc.). From the community of the village the produce flows to the city, as the center of political power, the surplus of the products being necessary for the maintenance of the persons not involved in the direct production of food. In the particular case of Phoenicia, however, it seems that the activity of transformation and exchange of the products was of particular importance, not being sustained only by the surplus of the immediate interior, and not destined only for the sphere of the local royal palace; but being sustained also by the influx of raw materials from great distances, and being sent also to distant royal palaces and to foreign "markets"; i.e., Phoenicia produced also for export. Typical in this sense was the working of ivory: the raw material came from afar (the Syrian elephant was already extinct in the 1st millennium), was worked in Phoenicia by the specializing workshops, and reexported as objects of value either to the east (Samaria, Arslan Tash, Nimrûd; cf. esp. R. D. Barnett, *Catalogue of the Nimrud Ivories* [1957]; I. Winter, *Iraq,* 38 [1976], 1-22) or to the west (Cyprus: V. Karageorghis, *Salamis in Cyprus* [1969]; Greece; and as far as Spain: J. Bonsor, *Early Engraved Ivories* [1928]). The same applied to artistic working of bronze (cf., e.g., O. Negbi, *Tel Aviv,* 1 [1975], 159-172): items of armament, daggers, cauldrons, and especially plates, discovered on the one hand in Assyria, and on the other at Cyprus (cf. esp. E. Gjerstad, *Swedish Cyprus Expedition,* IV/2 [1948]) and as far as Greece and Italy; cf. also 1 K. 7:13-47. The same can be said for the working of glass, a product of value that had in Phoenicia, if not its origin (which dates from the Syrian Late Bronze), certainly a center of development and diffusion. The same applies above all to wool stuff dyed purple, which in antiquity was considered the typical product of Phoenicia and, in spite of the almost total lack (due to the obvious deterioration of the material) of direct archeological attestation, has been confirmed by texts. The wool certainly came from the surrounding Syro-Palestinian interior; the purple dye (in various shades from red to violet as indicated by different terminology; see B. Landsberger, *JCS,* 21 [1967], 155-173) was extracted from a mollusk (*murex brandaris* and *trunculus*; cf. L. B. Jensen, *JNES,* 22 [1963], 104-118); indeed, little hills of conch shells of the murex, residue of the work, still attest to the intensity of such activity.

This inclusion of Phoenician artisanship in a complex commercial system is generally considered to be the reason for a presumed lack of artistic "originality." In fact, the symbolic representations used are of diverse and often external origin (esp. Egyptian), but in general their entrance into the Syro-Palestinian artistic repertory goes back to the 2nd millennium and therefore was an element of local tradition for the Phoenicians. More than a commercial fact, Phoenician iconographic eclecticism was a well-rooted cultural fact. The prestige of Phoenician artisanship is proved not only by the export of objects but also by the presence of craftsmen in the building of the temple at Jerusalem (9th cent.) and the palace of Ashurnasirpal (8th cent.); and in the west since Homeric times the Phoenicians were famous not only as merchants and pirates but also as most clever artisans.

***V. Commerce and Colonization.***–Already in the period between 1500 and 1200 the coastal cities of Syria-Palestine had developed a notable commercial activity by maritime routes (J. M. Sasson, *JAOS,* 86 [1966], 126-138) besides ass-caravans to the Syrian, Anatolian, and Mesopotamian hinterlands. But their trade was rather circumscribed, developing on one side toward the great Egyptian market to the south, on the other toward Cyprus, the Cilician coast, and then to the Aegean on the west. They were therefore

Gold pectoral from Byblos showing Egyptian influence (19th cent. B.C.) (Louvre; picture M. Chuzeville)

technically constricted by a navigation exclusively coastal and one-directional, and were economically characterized in the same way by an exchange of products of luxury between centers endowed with an analogous palatine structure, besides the transportation of some raw materials (Cypriote copper, Lebanese timber) always within the same system. The routes to more distant lands, a preurban structure, and the access to other more costly and exotic raw materials were in the hands of other commercial organizations: on one side Egypt had monopolized (if not made of it a notable economic force) access through the Red Sea to southern Arabia and to east Africa (Punt), and therefore the influx of gold and of products such as ebony, incense, etc. On the other hand Mycenean commerce, accustomed by geographical necessity to more complex routes in the open sea, had controlled the nascent Mediterranean traffic, the volume of which and interest in which increased with the addition of side products (amber, obsidian, etc.) of metal research (tin, silver, etc.) in the Sardinian and Spanish west.

The turbulence produced by the invasion of the peoples of the sea, and in particular the collapse of the Mycenean commercial organization and the retreat of Egypt from the international scene, contrary to what one might expect, left substantially intact the commercial potential of Phoenicia, which knew how to take advantage of the occasion, succeeding on the one hand the Egyptians in the Red Sea routes to the lands of gold and incense, and on the other hand the Myceneans in routes toward countries of silver, tin, and iron ore. The methods of this phase of Phoenician commerce are shown especially in biblical passages about the joint enterprises of Hiram of Tyre and Solomon (*ca.* 950; cf. G. Bunnens, *Journal of Economic and Social History of the Orient,* 19 [1976], 1-31): the ships came and went on a triennial cycle, without the need of establishing along the way any point of fixed support (1 K. 9:26-28; 10:22; cf. 2 Ch. 8:17f.). It was therefore a commerce without colonization, and the reports of classical authors on the early foundations of Utica and Cadiz *ca.* 1100, if they have any value (all the reports that Greek chronological tradition has linked to the Trojan War are suspect), must be related to frequent visits to intermediate landing places (Utica) or to points of contact with the natives (Cadiz) to effect the exchange (cf. K. Galling, *ZDPV,* 88 [1972], 1-18, 140-181).

This traffic with countries so distant and poorly known from semilegends, in the extreme south (Ophir) and the extreme west (Tarshish), resulted in the flow of raw materials or essentials for the technology of the era (metal) or valuables on the plane of personal prestige (exotic products) or of the cultus (incense). The Phoenicians were therefore economically attuned to the difference of value that the countries of origin and those of the destination attributed to such products: the "native" Somalis or Iberians were satisfied with necklaces of glass paste or at most with some clothing (of which only the pins remain), while the imports into the Near East brought to the Phoenicians notable profits. The case of Phoenician commerce in highly cultural regions (Egypt, Assyria, Greece, Cyprus) was different; these regions absorbed products of luxury (ivory, bronze, purple stuff, etc.). Not least in importance among the effects of commercial contacts with Greece was the introduction of the Phoenician alphabet (9th-8th cents.), an introduction connected with contributions in the fields of myth and art.

The situation changed in the 8th cent. through the concomitance of diverse factors. The economic and cultural stimulus of the commerce of metals helped create in the metalliferous countries of the Mediterranean (Cyprus, Sardinia, Etruria, south Spain) the major concentrations of wealth and therefore the major outlet of the market, with local aristocracies already exiting from the Bronze Age (Tartessic Spain, Noragic Sardinia, Etruria), in which, however, other areas remained (all northern Africa and W of Egypt). Contemporaneously Greece alongside Phoenicia was making use of maritime routes, in the search for and distribution of metals, with access to the great markets of Egypt and the Orient. Finally, in Phoenicia motives perhaps analogous to those of a socioeconomic nature known by Greece as well as political motives (Assyrian imperialistic pressures) stimulated emigration (G. Kestemont, *Oriens antiguus,* 11 [1972], 137-144; S. Frankenstein, in M. T. Larsen, *Power and Propaganda* [1979], 263-294). The combination of these various factors changed the Mediterranean commercial system (the route of Ophir was temporarily abandoned, its place taken by the continuous going and coming of caravans between south Arabia and Transjordan); it passed from a navigation that was based on a point of support perhaps habitual but certainly urbanistically inconsistent to the foundation of true colonies; from searches for raw materials that took on the aspect of raids *(razzia)* harmful of the natives to a commerce of markets, with export to a local public more economically qualified and with organizations of the culture according to the needs of the motherland; from a free though adventuous navigation to a concurrence and contraposition of Phoenician and Greek routes, especially of the markets reserved for the Phoenicians and of the markets reserved for the Greeks.

The chronology of Phoenician colonization has long been a problem. The critical tendency formerly refuted the dates of the classical authors and on archeological grounds assigned the colonization to the 8th cent. (from the classic studies of J. Beloch, *Rheinisches Museum,* 49 [1894], 111-132, to R. Carpenter, *American Journal of Archeology,* 62 [1958], 35-53; *et al.*). But W. F. Albright's arguments for the earlier date (*BASOR,* 83 [Oct. 1941], 14-22; cf. also "Role," pp. 341-49) have prevailed (summarized by: W. Culican, *Abr Nahrain,* 1 [1960], 16-55; G. Garbini, *Cultura e Scuola,* 7 [1963], 92-97). Yet clearly the situation in the 11th cent. was profoundly diffferent from that of the 8th cent., and the adoption of a chronology cannot disregard the historic situation. In the historico-economic picture presently delineated the true and proper Phoenician colonization cannot be conceived if it was not substantially coeval with that of the Greeks, and crowded into areas that were diverse and competitive. The Phoenician colonies (prevalently of Tyre, according to the reports of the classical authors) were localized on the southeast coast of Cyprus (Kition), in northern Africa and W of Sirta (Utica, Carthage, Hadrumetum, Hippo, and many others extending to Lixus on the Atlantic), at Malta, in western Sicily (Motya, Palermo, Solunto), in southeast Sardinia (Nora, Sulcis, Tharros, Cagliari, etc.), in the Balearic Islands (Ibiza), in southern Spain (Cadiz and others). What little is known of the political structure of the colonies seems to concern only magistracies of the collegial type (the "judges," *špṭm,* Lat. *sufetes;* the popular assembly, *ʿm;* cf. M. Sznycer, *Semitica,* 25 [1975], 47-68), which are characteristic of local, nonautonomous communities, while there is nowhere a trace of a true "king" (unless at Carthage by secondary phenomenon). It is therefore probable that the colonies were initially constituted as politically dependent directly on the motherland, even if it is obvious that quite soon they were detached in self-government, conferring political authority on their communal magistrature.

The vigorous emergence of Carthage (in the 6th cent.),

which constituted a political unity and a western Phoenician cultural world ("Punic"), including its relationship with the natives in both the commercial and the cultural sector, its means of demographic and military penetration toward the interior, and its rapport with the Greeks and then with the Romans, constitute such important problems that the history can no longer be considered as properly Phoenician. From the diverse expressions of these factors in the various regions and various periods a Punic world resulted that was well diversified, both internally and especially with respect to the eastern motherland, but from which are perpetuated language and writing, political and religious elements, economic and artistic elements, leading to an era somewhat advanced, when it came to be progressively absorbed in the provincial Roman world.

Hence after the detachment of the colonial world Phoenicia remained a commercial center of primary importance. An oracle of Ezekiel on Tyre (Ezk. 27; cf. H. van Dijk, *Ezekiel's Prophecy on Tyre* [1968]) gave a picture of the commercial network of the Phoenician city *ca.* 580-570 that included the Mediterranean (from Spain to Ionia and Cyprus), Egypt and the Libyan coast, the Syro-Palestinian interior, Assyria, central and eastern Anatolia and Armenia, Arabia stretching to Yemen. The ties with Egypt were based on the constant pharaonic support of the struggles of the Phoenicians to maintain their independence in the face of Assyro-Babylonian pressures. Assyro-Babylonian documents prove the commercial presence of Phoenicia in Mesopotamia (cf. A. L. Oppenheim, *City Invincible* [1960], p. 174; *JCS,* 21 [1967], 236-254) that was certainly the basis of the Achemenian interest in commercial development of Phoenicia, in opposition to the Greeks. Neither was the more properly explorative aspect of Phoenician navigation stopped: a natural continuation of the ancient route to Ophir was the circumnavigation of Africa accomplished in three years (*ca.* 600); on behalf of Pharaoh Neco Phoenician ships departed from the Red Sea and returned by the Mediterranean (Herodotus iv.42). And in the reverse direction the Carthaginian Himilco (*ca.* 450) continued the ancient route from Tarshish with expeditions that went through the Pillars of Hercules, turned north and finally reached the English coast (Avieno *Ora maritima*); and Hanno (*ca.* 425) sailed along the coast of western Africa as far as the Gulf of Guinea (C. Muller, *Geographi Graeci Minores* [1855], I, 1-14; J. Ramin, *Le périple d'Hannou* [1976]; J. Blomquist, *Date and Origin of the Greek Version of Hanno's Periplus* [1979]).

***VI. Political History.***–After the invasion of the peoples of the sea and the rapid constitution of a Phoenician ethnic entity (in the sense indicated above), the historic documentation began in a heterogeneous manner. An Egyptian source in the 11th cent. (the account of Wen-Amon, who was taken to Phoenicia to procure timber; W. F. Albright, "The Eastern Mediterranean about 1060 B.C.," in G. E. Molynas, ed., *Studies Presented to D. M. Robinson* [1951], pp. 223-231; G. Bunnens, *Rivista di studi fenici,* 6 [1978], 1-16; H. Goedicke, *The Report of Wenamun* [1975]), and local inscriptions in the 10th cent. (of kings Ahiram, Abibaal, Elibaal, Yehawmilk, Šiptibaʿal; cf. W. F. Albright, *JAOS,* 67 [1947], 153-160) refer to Byblos. The Assyrian king Tiglath-pileser I (*ca.* 1100) made an expedition to Arvad to procure timber (E. Weidner, *AfO,* 18 [1957-58], 341-360; cf. *ARAB,* I, § 360). Of Sidon we have only a glimpse of an ancient predominance that passed to Tyre *ca.* 1000. The chief notices about Tyre come from the OT, with reference to the participation of Hiram king of Tyre in the construction of the temple at Jerusalem and to the commercial expeditions to Ophir (2 S. 5:11; 1 K. 5:15–7:51; 9:10-14, 26-28; 10:11, 22; cf. 2 Ch. 2:2-15; 9:10, 21). This was the period of greatest prestige for Tyre, which dealt favorably with the cities of the interior of Syro-Palestine and with the Egyptian and Assyrian empires, which could threaten Tyre militarily. It was also the period of the first commercial enterprises in distant lands.

Succeeding phases (9th-7th cents.) have more precise reports about Tyre, among which the extracts of the "Annals" of small city-states that Josephus cited from Menander of Ephesus (F. Jacoby, *Die Fragmente der griechischen Historiker,* III, C [1958], no. 783; cf. Josephus *CAp* i.18 [116-120]) could be considered reliable (though the coincidence with the accounts of the OT known to Josephus, but not with the Assyrian texts unknown to him, is reason to be suspicious). Meander gives the list of the kings with the years of reign and some notices; the OT provides some detail, obviously on the connections with Israel (1 K. 16:29-32; 2 K. 23:13).

But the most significant reports are from the Assyrian texts. The purely commercial relationships in the time of Tiglath-pileser I passed to a weightier and unbalanced presence with Ashurnasirpal II and Shalmaneser III (9th cent.): the Assyrian kings sought to procure needed raw materials by means of military pressure and the payment of tribute. The Phoenician cities, with rare exceptions, preferred to pay tribute rather than undertaking an armed resistance of dubious outcome and perhaps greater expense.

The final aggravation of the situation came in the 8th cent., with Assyria's progressive establishment of a provincial system that put an end to all local autonomy and placed the region under the direct control of Assyrian functionaries and garrisons. In 743 Tiglath-pileser III made northern Phoenicia (as far as, but excluding, Byblos) into a province with its center as Ṣimirra; only Arvad remained autonomous because of its island nature (cf. B. Oded, *ZDPV,* 90 [1976], 38-49). In 700 Sennacherib took Sidon from King Luli of Tyre (cf. *ARAB,* II, §239) and enthroned an Assyrian vassal at Sidon; when Sidon rebelled in 677, Esarhaddon destroyed it and made the area an Assyrian province, while imposing on Tyre a treaty of vassalage (cf. *ARAB,* II, §§511, 527; G. Pettinato, *Rivista di studi fenici,* 3 [1975], 145-160). In 671 Tyre rebelled, and Assyrian intervention resulted in the formation of a third province in southern Phoenicia, with its center at Ushu. The final encounter of Assyria with Arvad and Tyre was indecisive. At the end of the Assyrian empire the situation was as follows: three Assyrian provinces (Ṣimirra, Sidon, Ushu) comprising almost the whole territory, only the two small islands of Arvad and Tyre and the small city-state of Byblos remaining autonomous.

The Neo-Babylonian kingdom inherited these situations and succeeded then to have final autonomy with Nebuchadrezzar's conquest of Tyre in 573. In the 6th cent. the culmination of the process of political subjugation, of economic exploitation, and of the demographic climax that characterized the entire Syro-Palestinian area under the Mesopotamian empires seemed to take place. With the rise of the Persian empire (538), however, the Phoenician cities revived (cf. J. Elayi, *Baghdader Mitteilungen,* 9 [1978], 25-38), through the Achemenian kings' political awareness of the military and commercial opposition of the Phoenician fleet to that of the Greeks (e.g., the battle of Salamis, 480). The Achemenian policy seemed to have reevaluated especially Arvad, Sidon, Tyre, and Kition. Arvad had control of all northern Phoenicia from the mouth of the Orontes to the plain of ʿAkkar, through its dependencies (Marathus, Antaradus, Ṣimirra,

Shalmaneser III exacted tribute from the fortified (island) city of Tyre (upper left). Bronze overlay from gates at Tell Balawat (just N of Nimrûd), 9th cent. B.C. (Trustees of the British Museum)

etc.); the colossal wall of Arvad and the monumental tombs of Amrît document the prosperity of the area in the 5th-4th cents. B.C. Sidon controlled the coast from Byblos (autonomous with kings Šipti-baʿal III, Yehawmilk, and Bat-noʿam, all of whom have left inscriptions) to Sarepta, had dependencies in Palestine (Dor, Jaffa), and was the seat of a provincial Persian palace. The remains of the great temple of Eshmun and some inscriptions of the local kings (Eshmunʿazar, Tabnit, Bod-ʿAstarte) belong to this time (cf. M. Dunand, *MUSJ*, 69 [1975/76], 489-499). Southern Phoenicia, from Sarpeta to Carmel, was in the hands of Tyre, which also controlled Ashkelon in Palestine (H. J. Katzenstein, *BA*, 42 [1979], 23-74). The predominance of Arvad, Sidon, and Tyre is also confirmed by the fact that these three cities joined in the founding of Tripolis (N of Byblos). A fourth large Phoenician center under Persian dominion was Kition on the island of Cyprus: an ancient Tyrian colony, Kition in the 5th-4th cents. extended its control to the mineral areas of the interior, annexing Idalion and Tamassos, as the titulary usage of kings Baʿal-milk, ʿOz-baʿal, Milkyaton, Pummayyaton shows in their inscriptions.

In the middle of the 4th cent. the continuous struggles sustained by Egypt and Cyprus with the help of the Athenians against the Achemenians involved also the Phoenicians: the Persians harshly repressed two revolts of the kings of Sidon, Straton "Philhellene" (362) and Tennes (346). The Greek commercial penetration (witnessed by the importing of Attic ceramic), the presence of Greek mercenaries, and the opposition to the Persian empire found their culmination and their outlet with the expedition of Alexander, who met with favor from all the Phoenician cities save Tyre, which was besieged and conquered (333). With the introduction of the Hellenistic kingdoms (Ptolemaic for Phoenicia S of Tripolis, Seleucid for the more northern region, with some fluctuations) Phoenicia was exposed to the Greek demographic penetration (which was concentrated in the more vacant northern region: the founding of Laodicea and Antiochia), and even more by the commercial and cultural penetration, with the introduction into a world more vast that spoke Greek and used Greek money. The political history ceased to have an autonomous character: the replacement of the monarchies with collegial governments (the "people," *ʿam*), the beginning of the local "eras" (Arvad 259, Beirût 197, Tyre 126, Sidon 110) in connection with the recovery of certain autonomies and the affirmation of the Roman dominion are all events that the Phoenician cities endured together with the neighboring Hellenistic world.

*VII. Religion.*–Phoenician religion was the direct continuation of "Canaanite" religion of the Late Bronze Age (known esp. from the Ugaritic texts) having been left in the safety of the contributions of the seminomadic populations, which took the upper hand in the rest of the interior of the country in 1200, introducing at the official level elements of the pastoral religiosity. The Phoenician religion therefore remained typical of the surrounding agricultural environment, centered on the problem of the punctual and correct repetition of the seasonal vegetation cycle and of the reproductive cycle of the animate creatures. The essential nucleus of the pantheon was constituted by a pair of dieties: one feminine, in the figure of a mother-goddess, represented the element of the earth; and the other a male, in the figure of a young god, represented the element of vegetation. The relationship between these two

Phoenician inscription of King Bod-ʿAstarte in the temple of Eshmun at Sidon (Beirut Museum; picture W. S. LaSor)

deities secured the correct repetition of the vegetative cycle. The alternation of a dry season with a rainy, with the consequent death and reflorescence of the vegetation, was symbolized by the death and resurrection of the young god. The figure of a father-god of cosmological character (the creator of the world) was less "active" in the cult and in the myth. The stabilization of these three elements in a fixed "triad" was a late and artificial achievement, but the three elements were much older, even pre-Phoenician.

In various cities these divine figures were called by different names, which in general were rather epithets, and therefore susceptible of variation and of application to the same entity. Thus the young god at Tyre had the name of Melqart (*ml[k] qrt,* "king of the city"), at Sidon he was Eshmun (*'šmn*), at Byblos Adonis ("lord" in Grecized form); the mother-goddess was Astarte (*ʿštrt*) at Tyre, Baalat (*bʿlt,* "lady") at Byblos; the father-god was El *('l)* at Byblos, Baal Shamaym (*bʿl šmym,* "lord of heaven") at Sidon, etc. The fluidity of the epithets entailed some diachronic variation: thus Melqart and Eshmun are not attested early in the Phoenician era, Adonis only in the Hellenistic and Roman periods. Other deities attested in Phoenicia (and also in the rest of the Syro-Palestinian world, already in the 2nd millennium), such as Resheph (*ršp*), Dagon (*dgn*), and Elyon (*ʿlyn*), were within certain limits amenable to the fundamental elements of the triad. It is particularly noteworthy that the epithet of the young god Baal (*bʿl,* "lord") was often qualified more specifically, assuming local forms such as *Baal Qarnaym* ("lord of the two horns"), *Baal Marqōd* ("lord of the dance"), *Baal Ṣûr* ("lord of Tyre"), etc.

The scant notices preserved by inscriptions (and related almost exclusively to the pantheon) can be integrated with the references in the OT (on the penetration of the cult of Baal and Ashtoreth at Jerusalem and Samaria: Jgs. 10:6; 1 K. 11:4-8, 33; 16:31f.; 2 K. 23:13), and especially with the references in the classical authors, which although late (and subject to some misunderstandings) have their interest. In particular the theogony that Philo of Byblos records (*ca.* A.D. 100; text in F. Jocoby, *Die Fragmente der griechischen Historiker,* III, C. [1958], no. 790), attributing it to a certain Sanchuniathon, priest of Beirût at the time of the Trojan War, has been reevaluated as to its reliability in the light of some agreement with the Ugaritic texts (O. Eissfeldt, *Ras Schamra und Sanchujaton* [1939]; *Sanchujaton von Berut und Ilumiku von Ugarit* [1952]; cf. R. Oden, *PEQ,* [1976], 115-126; J. Barr, *BJRL,* 57 [1976], 17-68; L. Troiani, *L'opere storiografice di Filone da Byblos* [1976]; A. I. Baumgarten, *Phoenician History of Philo of Byblos* [1983]). Also, available classical texts (from Theocritus to Lucian) refer to the festivals for the death and resurrection of Adonis that must have formed the fulcrum of the religious life of Phoenicia. On the cultus we have archeological data (such as the remains of the great sanctuaries at Sidon and Amrît) to be integrated with the literary notices: the divine presence was generally localized in springs, woods, tops of mountains, and the sanctuaries are often "open" apertures, inserted in natural passages.

In the colonies there are later innovations, especially through the influence of the local populations, and then through the stronger exposure to Hellenistic and Roman culture: at Cyprus Resheph was preeminent, through assimilation with a local god (Apollo in Greek clothing); at Malta the temple of Astarte succeeded one of the prehistoric mother-goddess and then was replaced by one of Hera-Juno; in Sicily Astarte Erycine was the Punic transposition of a divine figure of the Elymi; in Sardinia the Phoenician god Sid assumed an unusual role by assimilation to the local Sardus Pater; at Carthage in the 5th and 4th cents. Astarte was succeeded by Tanit (of Libyan etymology and origin; cf. F. Hridberg-Hansen, *La Déesse TNT* [1979]). Tanit and her companion Baal Hammon (perhaps "lord of the burning-incense"; identified with Kronos-Saturn and as such still venerated in the late Roman period) are especially known through the worship paid to them in the proper sanctuary called Tophet where live sacrifices of children were brought. Such sacrifices were typical at Carthage (and amply described by Diodorus xx.14.6), but were already attested in the East (the name appears in 2 K. 23:10). Archeological remains of such sanctuaries have been excavated in Sicily (Motya), Sardinia (Sulcis, Tharros, etc.), and Africa (Carthage, Hadrumetum, etc.). True human sacrifice *(mlk 'dm)* progressively gave way to the sacrifice of a substitute (*mlk 'mr,* "sacrifice of a lamb"); the term *mlk,* "sacrifice" (*yiqtil* participle of *hlk*), has nothing to do either with "king" or with a presumed god Moloch, which in reality never existed (O. Eissfeldt, *Molk als Opferbegriff im Punischen und Hebräischen und das Ende des Gottes Moloch* [1964]; R. de Vaux, *Studies in OT Sacrifice* [Eng. tr. 1964], pp. 73-90).

*See also* RELIGIONS OF THE BIBLICAL WORLD: CANAANITE.

***Bibliography.***–See the general syntheses of G. Contenau, *La civilisation phénicienne* (1949); D. Harden, *Phoenicians* (3rd ed. 1980); S. Moscati, *World of the Phoenicians* (Eng. tr. 1968). Cf. also W. F. Albright, "Role of the Canaanites in the History of Civilization," in *BANE,* pp. 328-362; *CAH,* II/2, 516-526; D. R. Ap-Thomas, "Phoenicians," in D. J. Wiseman, ed., *Peoples of OT Times* (1973), pp. 259-286; P. K. Hitti, *History of Syria* (1951); B. Peckham, "Israel and Phoenicia," in F. M. Cross, *et al.,* eds., *Magnalia Dei: The Mighty Acts of God* (*Festschrift* G. E. Wright; 1976), pp. 224-248; W. Ward, ed., *Role of the Phoenicians in the Interaction of Mediterranean Civilizations* (1968); *Atti del I Congresso Internazionale di Studi Fenici e Punici,* I-III (1983); *Studia Phoenicia* (2 vols., 1983); G. Garbini, *I Fenici: storia e religione* (1980). On Language: J. Friedrich and W. Röllig, *Phönizische-punische Grammatik* (rev. ed. 1970); S. Segert, *Grammar of Phoenician and Punic* (1976); older, briefer, but still useful, Z. Harris, *Grammar of the Phoenician Language* (1936; repr. 1971); see also R. Tomback, *Comparative Semitic Lexicon of the Phoenician and Punic Languages* (1978); M. J. Fuentes Estañol, *Vocabulario fenicio* (1980). Onomastics: F. L. Benz, *Personal Names in the Phoenician and Punic Inscriptions* (1972). Writings: J. B. Peckham, *Development of the Late Phoenician Scripts* (1968); P. K. McCarter, *Antiquity of the Greek Alphabet and the Early Phoenician Scripts* (1975). On commerce: W. Culican, *The First Merchant Venturers* (1966). On the colonies: S. Gsell, *Histoire ancienne de l'Afrique du Nord,* I-IV (1921-24) is still basic; more recently, in general: G. Bunnens, *L'expansion phénicienne en Mediterranée* (1979). Carthage: G. Picar, *Le monde de Carthage* (1956); B. Warmington, *Carthage* (1960); S. Moscati, *Fenici e*

*Cartagine* (1972). Cyprus: V. Karageorghis, *Kition* (1976); O. Masson and M. Sznycer, *Recherches sur les Phéniciens à Chypre* (1972); E. Gjersted, *Report of the Director/Department of Antiquities, Cyprus*,(1979), pp. 230-254. Sardinia: S. Moscati, *Fenici e Cartaginesi in Sardegha* (1968). Spain: J. M. Blázquez, *Tartessos y los origines de la colonización fenicia en Occidente* (1975).

M. LIVERANI
tr. W. S. L. S.

**PHOENIX** fē'niks [Gk. *Phoinix*]; AV PHENICE. The harbor of Crete where, it was hoped, Paul's ship could winter on the trip to Rome (Acts 27:12).

Acts 27 tells how the ship set sail from Caesarea and went along the southern coast of Asia Minor and down the southern coast of Crete to a harbor called Fair Havens, near the town Lasea. Since this port was not adequately sheltered from the winds, the ship set sail for a harbor called Phoenix in order to winter there. But Paul never reached Phoenix because the northeastern winds blew the ship off course, and it eventually ran aground on Malta.

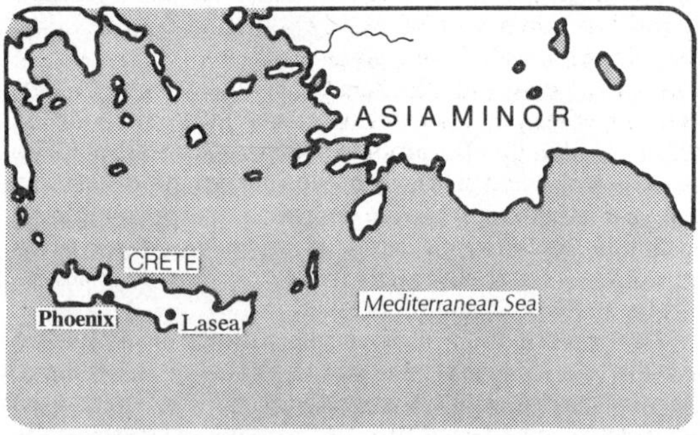


The general location of Phoenix is quite certain. It is on the southern coast of Crete, further west than Lasea. But possibly the northeastern wind that blew them off course came down off Mt. Ida (near ancient Troy) and across the open Bay of Messaria; thus Phoenix would have been further west than the bay. In his discussion of ancient writers J. Smith (pp. 93f.) said that Hierocles located Phoenix near the island Clauda in the vicinity of the towns Aradena and Anopolis; Strabo (*Geog.* x.4.3) placed it "on the south side of the narrow part of Crete, . . . on the north side of which is Amphimalla"; and Ptolemy (*Geog.* iii.17.3) placed it 55 km. (34 mi.) E of Cape St. John, which is on the west end of Crete, and 170 km. (106 mi.) W of Cape Salmone (i.e., 55 km., 34 mi., W of Cape Matala; see Smith; cf. *HDB*, III, *s.v.* [Ramsay]; Ogilvie, pp. 308-310). Beyond this, the exact location of Phoenix is debatable, the two most likely candidates being the modern towns of Lutros (also Loutro[s]) and Phineka.

Cape Mouros is a narrow peninsula, 53 km. (33 mi.) from the west end of Crete, which extends about 1.5 km. (1 mi.) south into the sea and widens at its southern end. The east side of the peninsula forms the bay of Lutros, and the town is on the northeast side of the peninsula. On the strength of Smith's arguments, Lutros has been the preferred location for ancient Phoenix. It is within the general location described above, being due N of Clauda and near the towns of Aradena and Anopolis (p. 94; cf. E. Haenchen, *Acts of the Apostles* [Eng. tr. 1971], p. 700 n. 7). On the basis of statements by Spratt ("It is the only bay to the westward of Fair Havens in which a vessel of any size could find shelter during the winter months") and Brown ("It is the only secure harbour in all winds on the south coast of Crete"), which he confirmed by personal observation, Smith argued that Lutros is the only possible harbor in the area (p. 92n.). The high mainland N of the harbor and the island in the harbor's mouth prevent the easterly winds from disturbing its waters. Spratt added that an inscription in Lutros (cited in Ogilvie, p. 311) confirms that Egyptian grain ships used to winter there.

The major problem with identifying Phoenix with Lutros is Luke's description that the harbor faces "both southwest and northwest" (NIV; *katá líba kaí katá chōron*). Greek *líps* is the wind coming up from the southwest, and *chōros* is the wind coming down from the northwest (cf. Goodspeed). Lutros faces east, and therefore its entrances to the sea open up toward the northeast and southeast. Smith argued that the Greek means that the harbor is open "to the point *towards* which it [i.e., the wind] blows — that is, it is not open to the south-west but to the north-east" (p. 88). This is, however, a very unnatural reading of the Greek; *katá* means "down," so that the harbor faces down the direction from which the wind is coming, i.e., "down the south-west wind and down the north-west wind" (Bruce, p. 457; cf. Bauer, rev., pp. 475, 891).

On the west side of the peninsula that forms Cape Mouros is the harbor called Phineka, which most scholars now identify with Phoenix. This harbor not only satisfies all the general requirements, since it is close to Lutros, but also accords with Luke's description, since it faces west. Its name preserves the ancient form of Phoenix. Ptolemy also said that the harbor Phoenix is W of the town, whereas the harbor Lutros is E of the town Lutros.

The problem with the identification of Phoenix with Phineka is that today the west harbor is too shallow for large ships. Bruce said that possibly the two rivers entering the harbor have silted it up (p. 457), although Ogilvie claimed that there is no evidence of silting (p. 312). Ramsay left open the possibility that the shoreline has altered since Paul's time (*HDB*, III, *s.v.*). Spratt argued that the seismic disturbances in the 6th cent. A.D. tilted the island of Crete and raised the area of Lutros 4.11 m. (13.5 ft.). Ogilvie, followed by Haenchen (p. 700 n. 7), continued this reasoning and argued, on the basis of shell and rock formations, for a raise of 4.2 m. (14 ft.). Paul's ship probably drew about 2 to 3 m. (7 to 9 ft.) and a depth 4.2 m. (14 ft.) lower would therefore have been sufficient for the ship to enter the harbor (pp. 312f.).

Ogilvie also pointed out that the west harbor originally had two inlets, which faced northwest (not visible today) and southwest, and it would have been sufficiently deep. Also, the jetty protecting the bay originally extended 45 to 90 m. (150 to 300 ft.) further west and would have more completely protected the bay.

*See also* NORTHEASTER; Vol. I, Map XXI.

***Bibliography.***–F. F. Bruce, *Acts of the Apostles* (2nd ed. 1952); J. Finegan, *Archeology of the NT* (1981), pp. 196f.; E. J. Goodspeed, *Expos.*, 6th ser., 8 (1903), 130-141; C. Lattey, *Scripture*, 4 (1949-51), 144ff.; R. M. Ogilvie, *JTS*, N.S. 9 (1958), 308-314; J. Smith, *Voyage and Shipwreck of St. Paul* (1880; repr. 1978); T. A. B. Spratt, *Travels and Researches in Crete* (1865), II.

W. D. MOUNCE

**PHOROS** fôr'əs (AV, NEB 1 Esd. 5:9; 9:26; NEB 8:30). *See* PAROSH 1.

**PHRYGIA** frij'i-ə [Gk. *Phrygia*]. A large ancient country of central Asia Minor. It is mountainous and has tablelands reaching 1200 m. (4000 ft.) in height. Its name is derived from the Phryges, a Thracian tribe that in early times invaded the country and drove out or absorbed the earlier Asiatic inhabitants. The Phrygians established a powerful kingdom traditionally associated with the royal names Gordius and Midas. It was overthrown *ca.* 700 B.C. by Cimmerian raids and the ascendancy of Lydia. Phrygia

passed successively under the empires of Persia, Alexander, and the Seleucids. After 190 B.C. it formed part of the Attalid kingdom of Pergamum, and most of it was included in the Roman province of Asia in 116 B.C.

Josephus (*Ant.* i.6.1 [126]) related Togarmah (Gen. 10:3; etc.) to the Phrygians, but this name is now more usually referred to Armenia or to Tilgarimmu, modern Gürün, in eastern Cappadocia. The boundaries of Phrygia varied greatly at different periods. The name Hellespontine Phrygia was long applied to a region adjoining the Dardanelles. In NT times, however, Phrygia proper comprised the western part of the Anatolian plateau and the mountains and valleys to its immediate west, but it was administratively divided between the provinces of Asia and Galatia. The Lycus Valley cities of Laodicea, Hierapolis, and Colossae were at the southwest extremity of Asian Phrygia, which extended N to the borders of Bithynia beyond Dorylaeum (Eskişehir). Galatian Phrygia, a smaller area S of the Sultan Dağ range, included Pisidian Antioch and Iconium and adjoined Pisidia and Lycaonia.

The presence of influential Jewish communities in a pagan environment in Phrygia helps to explain its early evangelization and rapid Christian development. Josephus (*Ant.* xii.3.4 [147-153]) said that Antiochus III (223-187 B.C.) settled two thousand loyal Jewish families in Phrygia and Lydia, and Cicero (*Pro Flacco* 28) alluded to the vast sums confiscated from the Jews in Apamea and Laodicea in 62 B.C.

The NT mentions Phrygia without qualification only in Acts 2:10. Jews from Phrygia were in Jerusalem at Pentecost. In Acts 16:6 and perhaps 18:23 the Gk. *Phrygian* is to be understood adjectivally. The phrase *tḗn Phrygian kaí Galatikēn chṓran* in 16:6 has long been a focus of controversy. J. B. Lightfoot (comm. on Galatians [10th ed. 1890], p. 22) and W. M. Ramsay (*Expos.*, 4th ser., 9 [1894], 48ff.) agreed in taking *Phrygian* adjectivally. Two adjectives were then bracketed under a common article to refer to a single compound entity, "the Phrygian and Galatian country," not "Phrygia and the Galatian country." Lightfoot, who wrote before the definitive statement of Ramsay's "South Galatian" view, was unable to attach convincing geographical value to this understanding of the phrase. Ramsay argued that it denotes "Galatian Phrygia." This term, describing the district of Pisidian Antioch and Iconium where Phrygia overlapped the Roman province of Galatia, is not recorded in that form, but is precisely paralleled by "Asian Phrygia" and "Galatian Pontus," both well attested. This interpretation is a cardinal point in the geography of the South Galatian view.

J. Moffatt (*Intro. to the Literature of the NT* [3rd ed. 1918], p. 93) and K. Lake (*BC,* V, 231), followed by E. Haenchen (*Acts of the Apostles* [Eng. tr. 1971], p. 483) and others, have denied that *Phrygian* could be an adjective here, Lake on the ground, that the adjective was two-terminational in later Greek, so that this separate feminine form did not exist. This denial is erroneous, however; there are numerous attestations of the feminine adjective, and the natural construing of the phrase with the common article favors the rendering on which Lightfoot and Ramsay agreed (cf. C. J. Hemer, *JTS,* N.S. 27 [1976], 122-26; *JTS,* N.S. 28 [1977], 99-101).

The interpretation of Acts 18:23 is more difficult, and less crucial. *Phrygian* there could be adjective or noun, and the phrase may denote the same or a different complex of territories. But even if rendered there "the Galatian country and Phrygia," both elements are likely to refer to parts in the south. Acts 16:6, in particular, is important as referring to the area first visited as reported in ch. 13. Paul's first coming to Pisidian Antioch in Galatian Phrygia (13:14) corresponds with his first preaching in Galatia (Gal. 4:13). This fits a synthesis with a dating of Galatians before the events of Acts 15 and the direct identifications of the Jerusalem visit of Acts 9 with Gal. 1 and that of Acts 11 with Gal. 2. Acceptance of this reconstruction counters a persistent attack on the historical value of Acts that sometimes builds extensively on Lake's error noted above. Although the problems of the Jerusalem visits are complex, and a total solution is not to be offered simplistically or glibly, the linguistic and geographical assumptions on which North Galatian views are often joined with historical skepticism to exclude alternatives can be shown to be misconceived.

Paul's coming to Pisidian Antioch with Barnabas marked his first entry both into Phrygia and into the province of Galatia (cf. Gal. 4:13). His first address there is reported at some length (Acts 13:16-41), perhaps as marking the beginning of his systematic mission to the Gentiles. He revisited Galatian Phrygia with Silas and Timothy on his second journey (16:6); he was forbidden to preach in Asia but must have crossed Asian Phrygia toward Bithynia before being prevented from entering that land (v. 7). His route may have been NW from Pisidian Antioch to Dorylaeum and thence W across the province of Asia to Troas. After working again in Galatian Phrygia on his third journey he traveled to Ephesus "through the upper country" (19:1), perhaps by the direct upland road. This route may account for his being unknown by sight to the Colossians and Laodiceans of the great trade route (Col. 2:1). Asian Phrygia, especially the Lycus Valley, was probably evangelized by associates of Paul during his residence at Ephesus.

Christianity spread rapidly in the larger cities but sometimes assumed strange forms influenced by the heterogeneous and enthusiastic nature of the population. Remarkable early epigraphic evidence attests its presence. Phrygia was the center of the Montanists, to whom the uniquely defiant public Christian profession of the third-century epitaphs from the Tembris Valley in northwest Phrygia has been ascribed. Many other inscriptions exist whose Christianity is carefully veiled. Eusebius recorded the massacre of a whole Christian city, probably Eumenea, in the persecution by Diocletian (*HE* viii.11.1).

***Bibliography.***–*CERP*: *Monumenta Asiae Minoris Antiqua* (1928); Ramsay, *CBP.*

C. J. HEMER

**PHUD** fud (Jth. 2:23, AV). *See* PUT.

**PHURAH** fū'rə (Jgs. 7:10f., AV). *See* PURAH.

**PHURIM** fū'rim (Ad. Est. 11:1, AV). *See* PURIM.

**PHUT** fut (AV Gen. 10:6; Ezk. 27:10). *See* PUT.

**PHUVAH** fū'və (Gen. 46:13, AV). *See* PUVAH.

**PHYGELUS** fī'jə-ləs [Gk. *Phygelos*–'fugitive'] (2 Tim. 1:15); AV PHYGELLUS. Phygelus was a Christian in the province of Asia who, along with HERMOGENES and others, turned away from Paul (2 Tim. 1:15). Whether the desertion was due to theological differences, fear of having to share his lot, or failure to support Paul during his trial is unknown.

B. R. and P. C. PATTEN

**PHYLACTERY** fə-lak'tə-rē [Gk. *phylactērion*]. A small box containing Scripture verses. One was bound on the forehead and another on the arm during prayer.

The word "phylacteries" occurs in the Bible only in Mt. 23:5. The Greek word means "safeguard," "means of protection," "amulet," and as used in Mt. 23:5 is generally identified as the *tefillin* (lit. "prayers"), small boxes containing Scripture verses and worn during prayer, although a less common view identifies the phylacteries of Mt. 23:5 as magical charms or amulets (e.g., Bowman, pp. 523-538; cf. Goodspeed's translation, "They wear wide Scripture texts as charms . . .").

*Tefillin* were worn by every adult male at the daily morning prayers in either the home or synagogue except on the Sabbath and high festivals, though originally they were probably worn all day. Women, slaves, and minors, as well as those persons whose dead lay unburied, were exempt from wearing *tefillin* (for other exceptions, see *Jew.Enc.*, X, 25). In the 1st cent. A.D. they were probably worn by a minority of the people.

The hand-*tefillah* was put on first. This cube-shaped leather case contained one piece of parchment on which were written these four texts: Ex. 13:1-10, 11-16; Dt. 6:4-9; 11:13-21. This *tefillah* was fastened on the inside of the bare left arm just above the elbow so as to be near the heart. The long leather straps that passed through flaps on the box were twisted three times to form the letter *shin* (שׁ), and the following prayer was said: "Blessed art thou, O Lord our God, King of the universe, who hast sanctified us with the commandments and enjoined us to put on *tefillin*." Then the straps were twisted seven times around the arm, forming two *shins,* one with three prongs and one with four.

Modern Jew with prayer shawl and phylactery (W. Braun)

Next the head-*tefillah* was put on in the center of the forehead and this prayer was recited: "Blessed are thou, O Lord our God, King of the Universe, who hast sanctified us with thy commandments and enjoined upon us the command about *tefillin.*" The head-*tefillah* was divided equally into four compartments with one of the four passages (Ex. 13:1-10, 11-16; Dt. 6:4-9; 11:13-21) placed in each compartment. The box was sewn to the strap with twelve stitches, one for each tribe of Israel. On the right side was the letter *shin,* an abbreviation of *Shaddai* (the Almighty). On the left side was a four-pronged *shin,* a reminder of the four Scripture texts. The head strap was knotted in back in the form of the letter *daleth*; and the arm strap was in the shape of the letter *yodh.* Together with the *shin,* these three letters formed the consonants of the name *Shaddai.*

Discoveries of *tefillin* capsules and fragments at Qumrân and Murabbaʿât suggest that prior to A.D. 135 the common content of the *tefillin* was five sections of Scripture: Dt. 5:1–6:3 (the Decalogue); 6:4-9; 10:12–11:21; Ex. 13:1-10, 11-16 (cf. also Mish. *Sanhedrin* xi.3). Mishnaic reform sometime prior to A.D. 135 led to exclusion of the Decalogue. According to both the Palestinian and Babylonian Talmuds (T.P. *Berakoth* 3c and T.B. *Berakoth* 12a), the Decalogue was omitted from the daily morning prayer before the end of the 2nd cent. in order to counter the attacks of the heretics (*Minim*) against the divine origin of the whole Torah, "So that they may not say, 'only these words [the Ten Commandments] were given by God to Moses on Sinai.'" The Midrash *Sifre* on Deuteronomy required the Decalogue to be omitted both from the morning prayer preceding the Shema and from the phylacteries.

These *tefillin* from Qumrân and Murabbaʿât also shed light on the phrase "they make their phylacteries broad" (Mt. 23:5). Previously this phrase had generally been understood to mean that the straps were made broad, and such in fact is the translation of this verse in two Syriac MSS from the 4th and 5th centuries. But these *tefillin* from the 1st cent. A.D. show that the head *tefillin* were not cubical, but rectangular, with the breadth across the forehead varying much more than the length.

The custom of wearing *tefillin* has its origin in the injunctions of Dt. 6:8; 11:18; Ex. 13:9, 16. The "frontlets" (Heb. *ṭôṭāpōṯ*) are usually considered as the forerunners of the *tefillin* (note that the Tg. translates *ṭôṭāpōṯ* by *tᵉpillîn*), though the precise meaning of *ṭôṭāpōṯ* is debated. Some connect it to Akk. *ṭaṭāpu,* "surround, encircle," and Arab. *ṭafa,* "go about," "circle" (so BDB, p. 377; cf. E. A. Speiser, *JQR,* 48 [157/58], 208-217), hence something wrapped around the head or arm. It served as a symbol (cf. *'ôṯ,* "sign") or reminder (cf. *zikkārôn,* "memorial") of God's deliverance.

Opinions vary as to whether these verses were intended to be obeyed in a literal sense. If "these words" (Dt. 11:18) refer to all of Dt. 5–11, then a literal fulfillment is not intended. It is also unclear whether "these words" in Ex. 6:8 refer only to vv. 4f. or to the whole subsequent sermon. On the other hand, the injunctions in Ex. 13 are primarily matters of ritual practice and are meant to be obeyed literally.

It is not known when the custom began. It was unknown among the Samaritans; hence one view concludes that the custom must have developed after the Samaritan-Jewish schism (3rd cent. B.C.?). Yet the Letter of Aristeas (*ca.* 130 B.C.) refers to the practice as already old (v. 159). Rabbinic literature indicates that the *tefillin* were equivalent to amulets or charms for some wearers, yet for many others they were a memorial of God's commandments and a witness to pagans that the Jews "are called by the name of the Lord" (T.B. *Menahoth* 35b). Jesus did not criticize the practice, only the excesses which led to larger phylacteries for pious show.

***Bibliography.***–*Jew.Enc.*, X, *s.v.* (J. H. Greenstone, L. Blau, and E. G. Hirsch), is still valuable for its references to relevant passages in the rabbinic literature. See esp. T. B. *Menahoth* 34a-44a. See also J. Bowman, "Phylacteries," *SE* (1959 = *TU*, 73), pp. 523-538; J. H. Tigay, *HTR*, 72 (1979), 45-53; G. Vermes, *VT*, 9 (1959), 65-72.

R. L. OMANSON

**PHYSICAL** [Gk. *psychikós* (1 Cor. 15:44, 46), *sárx*–'flesh' (Rom. 2:28)]; **PHYSICALLY** [Gk. *phýsis*–'nature'] (Rom. 2:27); AV NATURAL (1 Cor. 15:44, 46), FLESH (Rom. 2:28), BY NATURE (Rom. 2:27); NEB ANIMAL (1 Cor. 15:44, 46), FLESH (Rom. 2:28), NATURAL STATE (Rom. 2:27). Each of the texts contrasts the physical or earthly with the spiritual. In Rom. 2:27-29 Paul points out that the circumcision of the flesh (*sárx*, v. 27) is only physical (*phýseōs*, v. 28), and what is needed, "true circumcision," is a spiritual matter (v. 29). In 1 Cor. 15:42-50 Paul discusses the resurrection of the dead and clearly differentiates the earthly, physical (*psychikós*) body from the spiritual (*pneumatikós*) body (cf. H. Clavier, "Brèves remarques sur la notion de σῶμα πνευματικόν," in W. D. Davies and D. Daube, eds., *Background of the NT and Its Eschatology* [*Festschrift* for C. H. Dodd, 1964], pp. 342-362).

G. A. L.

**PHYSICIAN** [Heb. part. of *rāpā'*–'heal'; Gk. *iatrós*]; NEB also "stitching" (Job 13:4), DOCTOR. The earliest practitioners of the healing arts appear to have been priest-physicians. The Sumerian priest-physicians employed largely empirical methods and frequently utilized psychological suggestion in their treatment of diseases. An extant Sumerian pharmacopoeia (*ca.* 2000 B.C.) contains some recognizable substances of a carminative, astringent, and emollient nature. This range of medicinal substances was extended later by the Babylonian priest-physicians, who also set fractures, reduced dislocations, and removed cataracts from eyes in the so-called prescientific period of medicine. Some sections of the Code of Hammurabi (§§ 215-221) deal with contemporary therapeutics (*see* HAMMURABI V.C). Egyptian priest-physicians also used herbs, splinted fractures, extracted teeth, and attended to wounds. In the ancient Near East sickness was uniformly ascribed to the activity of evil spirits working in the body; this made necessary the use of magical incantations, potions, and spells in the treatment of disease. (*See* DISEASE I; HEAL I.)

The Hebrews were forbidden to use magic; instead they were instructed to regard God as the giver of health and disease alike (Dt. 32:39; cf. Job 5:18). They were unique in that they had no tradition of physicians until many centuries after Moses. (The Egyptian "physicians" who attended Jacob and Joseph [Gen. 50:2, 26] were in fact embalmers.) Based on the belief that Yahweh alone is the Healer (Ex. 15:26), Mosaic legislation assigned to the priest the task of inspecting diseases (e.g., Lev. 13f.). Folk remedies were doubtless used by the Hebrews. Isaiah (38:21), e.g., employed a type of poultice that was also used at Ugarit (C. H. Gordon, *Ugaritic Literature* [1949], p. 129; cf. also 2 K. 20:7). The BALM OF GILEAD (cf. Jer. 8:22) was celebrated in antiquity for its healing properties and was undoubtedly prescribed by herbalists. The healing that Joram of Israel sought in Jezreel (2 K. 8:29) evidently involved normal recovery from battle wounds without the services of a physician; it is possible, however, that his wounds were dressed with astringent and emollient substances to promote healing. Asa king of Judah is reported to have sought help from physicians (2 Ch. 16:12); but the Chronicler clearly disapproves of Asa's trust in physicians rather than in God. The general Hebrew estimate of physicians appears to be reflected by the remark of Job 13:4.

In the intertestamental period magic and superstition increased significantly among the Jews. This coincided with the greater prominence of physicians, who, however, seem to have been little more than herbalists. Even Ben Sira (2nd cent. B.C.), who acknowledges the physician's abilities and usefulness, recognizes that both the medicines and the skill to prescribe them were created in the first place by God (Sir. 38:1-8). Thus God is the true source of healing, and the appropriate response to sickness is prayer by both the sick person and the physician, whose skills are at best very limited (vv. 9-15; cf. 10:10). (See also G. von Rad, *OT Theology*, I [Eng. tr.1962], pp. 274f.)

The talmudic tradition records the presence on the temple staff of a physician who cared for the priests (Mish. *Shekalim* v. 1). Physicians were also present in the cities (T.B. *Gittin* 12*b*) and were licensed by the local authorities (T.B. *Baba Bathra* 21*a*). Despite such measures, physicians were not always helpful (Tob. 2:10; Mk. 5:26 par. Lk. 8:43), and Christ may well have quoted a criticism of local physicians in His Galilee ministry (Mt. 9:12 par. Mk. 2:17; Lk. 5:31; cf. 4:23: "Physician, heal yourself"). In Col. 4:14 LUKE is identified as the "beloved physician," but very little is known about his background.

*See also* DISEASE; HEAL.

R. K. HARRISON

**PIBESETH** pī-bē'seth [Heb. *pî-ḇeseṯ*; Gk. *Boubastos*; Egyp. *Pr-B3st*–'house of Bastet,' the cat-goddess]; AV, NEB, PI-BESETH. An ancient city in northeast Egypt, identified with Tell Basṭa, about 1.5 km. (1 mi.) SE of Zagazig. The Bubastic branch of the Nile was named for this city on its banks.

In his oracle against Egypt, Ezekiel predicted that the "young men" (soldiers) of Pi-beseth would die in battle (30:17). Egyptian records indicate that the military commander who dealt with lands to the northeast lived in this city, which occupied a strategic position at the beginning of Wâdī Ṭumilât, a valley leading from the Nile Valley through the desert to the eastern border of Egypt. Pi-beseth was a capital of Egypt during the Bubastite dynasties, the 22nd and 23rd (*ca.* 950-750 B.C.). After Bubastis fell before the army of Artaxerxes III of Persia the other cities of Egypt surrendered (Diodorus xvi.49-51).

Another reason that Ezekiel marked Pi-beseth for judgment may be that it, like On, which is mentioned in the same verse, was a pagan religious center. Herodotus referred to the festival celebrated annually with great revelry in the city (ii.59f.), to the mummification and burial of cats there (ii.67), and to its beautiful temple of Bubastis (Bastet) and a smaller temple (ii.137f.). Excavations have disclosed the bones of many cats buried in pits and the ruins of the temples described by Herodotus.

***Bibliography.***–E. Naville, *Bubastis* (1891); *Festival Hall of Osorkon II* (1892); L. Habachi, *Tell Basta* (1957, *Supplément aux annales du service des antiquités de l'Égypte*, 22); H. Kees, *Orientalische Literaturzeitung*, 53 (1958), cols. 309-312.

JOHN ALEXANDER THOMPSON

**PICKS** [Heb. *ḥªriṣîm*; *ḥªrîṣîm*] (2 S. 12:31; 1 Ch. 20:3); AV HARROWS; NEB SHARP IRON TOOLS. Sharp instruments of iron, mentioned only here. The related adjective (*ḥārûṣ*, "sharp") is used in Isa. 28:27; 41:15; Am. 1:3 of the sharpness of threshing sledges. These picks are listed with saws and iron axes as tools with which David made his defeated Ammonite enemies work at making bricks. (Note the Akkadian parallel in *CAD*, IX, 9.) Older versions (e.g., AV) and commentators have David torturing them with these implements, in line with their own savagery (1 S. 11:2; 2 S. 10; Am. 1:3) and sacrificial practices (2 K. 23:10; Jer. 32:35). The text is difficult at several points, however. Very few versions (older or modern) note that *malbēn* (*Q*), usually read as "brickkilns," is sing. and more properly refers to a brick-mold (so *CHAL*, p. 197; cf. Akk. *nalbanu, nalbattu*); this would support the recent readings. See S. R. Driver, *Notes on the . . . Books of Samuel* (2nd ed. 1913), pp. 294-97.

***Bibliography.***–R. J. Forbes, *Studies in Ancient Technology*, VII (1966); C. Singer, *et al.*, *History of Technology* I (1954), 618-622; J. F. A. Sawyer, *Transactions of the Glasgow University Oriental Society*, 26 (1978), 96-107. D. M. HOWARD, JR.

**PICTURE.** The term occurs twice in the RSV. Ezk. 23:14f. describes the kind of wall paintings and engravings probably viewed by ambassadors of Judah on visits to Assyria and Babylon: depictions of (RSV "a picture of"; Heb. *d*^e^*mûṯ*, lit. "image, likeness" [cf. Isa. 40:18]; AV "after the manner of"; NEB "looked like") war scenes and triumphal processions of Babylonian rulers and soldiers. Such displays of imperial splendor so impressed Judah that she sought an alliance with Babylon (Ezk. 23:16; see comms., esp. KD). On 8:12, *see* PICTURES, ROOM OF.

"Pictures" occurs three times in the AV. In Nu. 33:52 (*see* FIGURED STONE) and Prov. 25:11 (RSV "setting [of silver]"; NEB "[silver] filigree") it represents Heb. *maśkîṯ*, which denotes some kind of carved work. In Isa. 2:16, AV, "pictures" represents *ś*^e^*ḵîyôṯ*, a hapax legomenon interpreted by the AV and some commentators (e.g., KD) as a cognate of *maśkîṯ*. Others, following the LXX, obtain a closer parallel with v. 16a by reading it as a type of ship (cf. RSV "craft"; NEB "dhow"), either by deriving the term from Egyp. *śk.tj* ("ship"; KoB, p. 921) or by emending the MT (see comms.). N. J. O.

**PICTURES, ROOM OF** [Heb. *ḥaḏrê maśkîṯ*–'rooms of an image'; Gk. *koitṓn kryptós*] (Ezk. 8:12); AV CHAMBERS OF IMAGERY; NEB SHRINE OF (ONE'S OWN) CARVED IMAGE. The meaning of this phrase is uncertain in the absence of biblical or other contemporary parallels. It may mean secret rooms (MT; "room" in LXX, Syr., Vulg., Tg.) containing collections of images of gods or perhaps pictures on the walls (cf. Ezk. 8:10; 23:14). Heb. *maśkîṯ* (< *śāḵâ*, "look") points to an image or figure, probably related to pagan religion (cf. Lev. 26:1; Nu. 33:52); but conceivably it could be used for wall carvings, in which case the "creeping things, and loathsome beasts, and all the idols of the house of Israel" (Ezk. 8:10) are perhaps the objects portrayed.

The seventy elders of the house of Israel are envisioned in one large room in the previous verses, so if v. 12 refers directly to that scene, the versions with singular "room" must be followed (so *BH*). Heb. *'îš* and the singular suffix, however, seem to indicate separate rooms for each man, and the previous context is then no longer a certain guide as to the contents of the rooms (cf. AV, NEB; see comms.). J. W. D. H.

**PIECE.** In the OT, the translation of a large number of Hebrew terms, many of which have approximately the same significance, e.g., *gezer* (Gen. 15:17), *nēṯaḥ* (Ex. 29:17; Lev. 1:6; etc.), *paṯ* (Lev. 2:6; 1 S. 2:36; etc.), *pelaḥ* (1 S. 30:12; etc.). It is used frequently in paraphrastic renderings, especially with verbs such as BREAK and DASH. The RSV and NEB sometimes use "of one piece with" to render *min-* ("out of, from"; e.g., Ex. 25:19, 31, 35f.). In the NT "broken pieces" translates the plural of Gk. *klásma*, "fragment (of bread)"; *see* FRAGMENTS.

**PIECE OF MONEY.** *See* MONEY.

**PIECE OF SILVER.** *See* MONEY.

**PIERCE** [Heb. *nāqaḇ* (2 K. 18:21; Job 40:24; 41:2 [MT 40:26]; Isa. 36:6; Hab. 3:14), *dāqar* (Nu. 25:8; Zec. 12:10; 13:3), polel of *ḥālal* (Job 26:13; Isa. 51:9), *ḥālap*–'pass through' (Jgs. 5:26), pual of *ṭā'an* (Isa. 14:19), *yāṣā'*–'go,' 'come out' (2 K. 9:24), *māḥaṣ*–'smite through, wound severely' (Nu. 24:8), piel of *pālaḥ*–'cleave' (Prov. 7:23)]; AV also BORE, STRIKE THROUGH, THRUST, FORM, WOUND, etc.; NEB also PUT A HOOK, TRANSFIX, BREAK, RUN THROUGH, etc.; [Gk. *ekkentéō* (Jn. 19:37; Rev. 1:7), *diérchomai*–'go through' (Lk. 2:35), *diiknéomai*–'pierce, penetrate' (He. 4:12), *nýssō*–'prick, stab, pierce' (Jn. 19:34; Mt. 27:49 var.), *peripeírō*–'pierce through,' 'impale' (1 Tim. 6:10)]; AV also PIERCE THROUGH; NEB also STABBED, SPIKED; Heb. *kā'*^ă^*rî* in Ps. 22:16 [MT 17] is problematic and variously emended (cf. P. C. Craigie, *Psalms*, I [*World Biblical Comm.*, 1983], 196 n. 17.b).

The majority of OT passages refer to the killing of human beings with weapons that include the spear (Nu. 25:8), sword (Isa. 14:19; cf. Jgs. 9:54; 1 S. 31:4 par. 1 Ch. 10:4), arrow (Nu. 24:8; 2 K. 9:24; cf. Job 20:24), and, possibly, tent stake (Jgs. 5:26; cf. 4:21). Hab. 3:14 presents a graphic description of the destruction of enemies by arrow-like weapons ("shafts" for Heb. *maṭṭeh*; cf. Hab. 3:9). The original meaning of the "pierced one" in Zec. 12:10 is lost and remains a matter of scholarly speculation. In the NT (Jn. 19:37; Rev. 1:7) it is understood as a messianic reference (cf. F. F. Bruce, *NT Development of OT Themes* [1969], pp. 110-13). "Pierce" in Zec. 13:3 refers to the purging of prophets from Jerusalem by execution (cf. Dt. 13:1-5).

Other OT passages refer to animals that are "pierced," i.e., either taken captive or killed. The futile attempts of men to capture either the Behemoth (Job 40:24; cf. v. 15) or Leviathan (41:2) illustrate the contrast between human finite abilities and God's limitless power. Elsewhere, Job describes God's omnipotence over creation and His defeat of the "fleeing serpent" (26:13; cf. Isa. 27:1). Similarly, Isaiah recounts God's defeat of "Rahab" and the "dragon," which are either symbolic representations of Egypt or mythological creatures (Isa. 51:9; on the Ugaritic parallels *see* DRAGON; LEVIATHAN; cf. *ANET*, pp. 67, 130f.).

"Pierce" also occurs in several figurative expressions. In Isa. 36:6 Assyria warns Israel that reliance on Egypt, which is called a broken reed, will only "pierce" the hand of those who "lean on" Egypt (cf. 2 K. 18:21). Also, Prov. 7:23 compares a man who is seduced by an adulteress to an animal whose internal organs are penetrated by an arrow.

In the NT the literal and figurative uses of "pierce" are similar to those in the OT. In Jn. 19:37 the author quotes Zec. 12:10 (see above) as being fulfilled in the thrusting of the spear into Jesus' side (Jn. 19:34; cf. Josephus *BJ* iii.7.35 [335]; Sib. Or. 8:296; Irenaeus *Adv. haer.* iii.22.2). Perhaps John intended to highlight the efficacy of Jesus' atoning work by including this detail (cf. C. K. Barrett, *Gospel According to John* [2nd ed. 1978], pp. 556f.). While in Jn. 19:37 "pierce" emphasizes the lance thrust, in Rev. 1:7 it underlines the entire act of crucifixion. The assimilation of Jn. 19:34 best accounts for the textual variant in Mt. 27:49.

Figurative uses of "pierce" occur in Lk. 2:35; 1 Tim. 6:10; and He. 4:12. Lk. 2:35 expresses the effect of Jesus' rejection and passion on His mother Mary, namely, pain and anguish in her soul (but cf. J. A. Fitzmyer, *Luke,* I [*AB,* 1981], 429f.). According to 1 Tim. 6:10, while in the pursuit of money some believers defected from their faith; consequently they "pierced their hearts," i.e., they inflicted a pained conscience on themselves. The NT hapax legomenon Gk. *diiknéomai* in He. 4:12 describes the efficacious action of "the penetration of God's word to the innermost depths of man's personality" (P. E. Hughes, *Hebrews* [1977], p. 165). H. WOLF G. L. K.

**PIETY** [Gk. *dikaiosýnē, eusébeia*]; AV ALMS, HOLINESS; NEB RELIGION, GODLINESS; **IMPIOUS** [Heb. *nāḇāl*; Gk. *asebḗs*]; AV FOOLISH, UNGODLY; NEB also SAVAGE, BRUTAL; **IMPIOUSLY** [Heb. *ḥānēp*]; AV HYPOCRITICAL; NEB BRUTES.

"Piety" generally denotes "devoutness" or "reverence for God" (cf. *eusébeia,* Acts 3:12); but it can also signify "conspicuous religiosity," as in Mt. 6:1 (Gk. *dikaiosýnē,* lit. "righteousness"; cf. RSV 5:20; 6:33; etc.), where Jesus warns against ostentatiousness in the three main areas of Jewish piety: almsgiving (vv. 2-4), prayer (vv. 5-15), and fasting (vv. 16-18).

For the Greeks "piety" (*eusébeia* and cognates) consisted of reverence for the gods (also for one's country, ancestors, etc.) and careful observance of cultic duties. But in the OT (and subsequently the NT) true piety is the "fear of the Lord" (Heb. *yir'aṯ yhwh*; rendered by Gk. *eusébeia* in the LXX of Prov. 1:7; 13:11; Isa. 11:2; 33:6), which always involves active obedience to a personal God. Thus the "impious" are those who are contemptuous of God and His commandments. Ps. 35:16 cries out against those who "impiously" (Heb. *ḥānēp*; *see* GODLESS [MEN]) persecute the righteous. Ps. 74:18, 22 describes those who scoff at God as *nāḇāl* (lit. "foolish" in a moral and spiritual sense; *see* FOOL I). 1 Pet. 4:18 quotes the LXX of Prov. 11:31, applying it eschatologically to the suffering that awaits the "impious" (Gk. *asebḗs,* LXX for Heb. *rāšā'*, "wicked") at the final judgment.

*See also* FEAR II.B, IV; GODLINESS; RELIGION; UNGODLY.

***Bibliography.***–*DNTT,* II, 91-95; *TDNT,* VII, *s.v.* σέβομαι κτλ: εὐσεβής, εὐσέβεια, ἀσεβής (W. Foerster). N. J. O.

**PIGEON** [Heb. *gôzāl*] ("young pigeon," Gen. 15:9); NEB FLEDGLING; [*yônâ*] (Lev. 1:14; 5:7, 11; 12:6, 8; 14:22, 30; 15:14, 29; Nu. 6:10); [Gk. *peristerá*] (Mt. 21:12; Mk. 11:15; Lk. 2:24; Jn. 2:14, 16); AV also DOVE.

The distinction between pigeons and doves is not easy to make. Usually species with blond or brownish coloring are designated "doves" while those of darker hues are called "pigeons." The difficulty in distinguishing these birds is also to be seen in Scripture in that, of the several varieties found in Palestine, only the turtledove (*Streptopelia turtur*) is given a separate name (Heb. *tôr*).

In Israelite sacrifices turtledoves and pigeons could be offered instead of animals from the herd or flock. This was a provision for the poorer members of the nation (Lev. 5:7). In certain cases of sacrifices for purification, i.e., at childbirth (12:6, 8), from a skin disease (14:22, 30), from a bodily discharge (15:14, 29), and after a necessary violation of the Nazirite vow (Nu. 6:10), turtledoves and pigeons were the required victims, not optional ones. The exclusive use of these birds by Mary and Joseph at the presentation of Jesus in the temple (Lk. 2:22-24), however, highlights their relative poverty.

The use of pigeons and doves in sacrifices meant that they were domesticated in Israel (Isa. 60:8). The sacrificial victim had to be owned by the offerer. He could not offer a wild animal or bird. The need arose, therefore, for the sale of doves and pigeons to prospective offerers. It is to vendors of such that Jesus said, "You shall not make my Father's house a house of trade" (Jn. 2:16).

*See also* DOVE. G. WYPER

**PI-HAHIROTH** pī-ha-hī'roth [Heb. *pî-haḥîrōṯ*] (Ex. 14:2, 9; Nu. 33:7); **HAHIROTH** [Heb. *haḥîrōṯ*] (Nu. 33:8, RSV, but some Heb. MSS, ancient versions, the AV, and the NEB read Pi-hahiroth in this verse also). A town in the east delta of Egypt. The LXX in Ex. 14:2, 9 translates this name by Gk. *apénante tḗs epaúleōs,* "opposite the encampment," in Nu. 33:7 by *stóma Eirōth,* "mouth of Eiroth," and in Nu. 33:8 by *Eirōth.* Some of the many suggestions for the Egyptian source of this name are: *ḥnt-ta-ḥrt* (Daressy), *pr-Ḥtḥrt,* "house of the goddess Hathor" (Clédat), *pa- ḥwyr* (Cazelles), and two hypothetical names, *pr-ḫrty,* "house of the god Ḫrty" (Spiegelberg), and *pr-Ḥrt,* "house of the goddess Ḥrt" (Albright).

During the Exodus the Israelites after leaving Etham encamped near Pi-hahiroth (Ex. 14:2), where the pursuing Egyptians overtook them (v. 9). From this place the Israelites set out to pass through the sea (Nu. 33:9).

The biblical texts locate Pi-hahiroth "between Migdol and the sea" (Ex. 14:2) and "in front" (vv. 2, 9) or "east" (Nu. 33:7) of Baal-zaphon. Most scholars place Pi-hahiroth on the Isthmus of Suez, but proposals for the exact site vary: a marsh between Maghfar and Lake Timsâḥ (Daressy); Jebel Abu Haṣa, which has ruins of a temple of Hathor (Clédat); the area of al-Qantarah (Albright); and lakes in the eastern part of Wâdī Ṭumilât (Cazelles).

***Bibliography.***–W. F. Albright, *BASOR,* 109 (Feb. 1948), 15f.; H. Cazelles, *RB,* 62 (1955), 350-57; J. Clédat, *Bulletin de l'Institut Français d'Archéologie Orientale,* 21 (1919), 206-219; G. Daressy, *Bulletin de l'Institut d'Égypte,* 5 (1911), 6; P. Montet, *Egypt and the Bible* (Eng. tr. 1968), pp. 60-64; W. Spiegelberg, *Ägyptologische Randglossen zum AT* (1904), pp. 25-27; C. de Wit, *Date and Route of the Exodus* (1960), pp. 13-20.

JOHN ALEXANDER THOMPSON

**PILATE, ACTS OF.** *See* APOCRYPHAL GOSPELS III.B.

**PILATE, PONTIUS** pī'lət, pon'shəs. Roman governor of Judea A.D. 26/27-36, who presided at the trial of Jesus.

***I. Information.***–The history of Pontius Pilate is known chiefly from the account of his governorship of Judea in Josephus (*Ant.* xviii.2.2 [35]; 3.1f. [55-62]; 4.1f. [85-89]; *BJ* ii.9.2-4 [169-177]), from an incident related by Philo (*De legatione ad Gaium* 299-305), and from the record of the trial of Jesus in the four Gospels. These documents are supplemented by an inscription from Caesarea that gives the correct form of his title, *praefectus Iudaeae* (*Année epigraphique* [1964], n. 39; *see* picture in CAESAREA; *see also* PROCURATOR). The inscription, which is incomplete, records his two known names but does not give his first name (*praenomen*). The family name of Pontius was fairly common throughout central and northern Italy at all social levels and was the name of one consul of A.D. 17 and of another of A.D. 37. But the cognomen Pilatus (meaning either "armed with a javelin," or "bald," or by another derivation, "shaggy") is extremely rare; hence the family connections of Pilate remain uncertain. Pilate's role in the trial of Jesus is mentioned also by the independent Latin historian Tacitus in his brief reference to the "execution of Christus, author of that sect, by the procurator Pontius Pilate in the reign of Tiberius" (*Ann.* xv.44.4).

***II. Governorship of Judea.***–Philo implied that Pilate had a political connection with the *éminence grise* Sejanus (*De* *legatione ad Gaium* 159), commander of the praetorian guard. Pilate might have been a protégé of the consul of A.D. 17. As an equestrian official, he must previously have served as a military tribune or staff officer in a Roman legion and possibly in other units before proceeding directly from the army to the governorship of Judea in A.D. 26/27. As governor he had five infantry cohorts and a cavalry regiment under his command (perhaps some five thousand men in all) for the maintenance of order, an unusually large force for a province that had no serious external commitments and was bordered by dependent kingdoms, the Herodian tetrarchies and the Nabatean kingdom. He was subordinate to the general authority of the legate of Syria, the supreme military commander in the East. But he had absolute authority in managing his own province, of which Caesarea, not Jerusalem, was the administrative center. *See* PROVINCES, ROMAN.

Josephus narrated three incidents of Pilate's governorship that illustrate the difficulties faced by the Roman rulers in Judea. When Pilate sent a military unit to garrison duty in Jerusalem, the population took offense because within the Holy City the army used standards that displayed images of the emperor, contrary to previous Roman practice in Judea as well as to Jewish law. According to Josephus this was a deliberate offense. At first Pilate refused to withdraw these symbols of the imperial majesty — which late sources exaggerated to include an imperial statue placed in the temple (see comms. on Matthew by Origen [17:25] and Jerome [24:15]. After a display of force, however, he yielded to the pressure of a popular demonstration (*Ant.* xviii.3.1 [55-59]; *BJ* ii.9.2f. [169-174]).

Pilate later tried to placate Jewish hostility by organizing a water supply for Jerusalem. His attempt to finance his project from temple funds caused a violent demonstration, which Pilate suppressed by police action, instructing his soldiers to use their batons instead of swords. Disregard of his orders caused several deaths. This affair may be the mysterious massacre of Galileans, "whose blood Pilate had mingled with their sacrifices" (Lk. 13:1).

In his tenth year of office Pilate found it necessary to suppress an armed concourse of fanatics who gathered in the territory of Samaria to excavate the holy vessels of Moses that were supposedly buried on Mt. Gerizim. The mob was ambushed, many died, and many of the survivors were executed. The city council of Samaria protested the action to the governor of Syria, who sent Pilate back to face an investigation by the emperor at Rome (*Ant.* xviii.4.1f. [85-89]).

Philo, who regarded Pilate as the agent of the anti-Jewish policy of Sejanus, recorded an earlier and less serious incident (*De legatione ad Gaium* 299-305). Pilate set shields bearing an innocuous dedication to the emperor on the walls of his residence at Jerusalem. The infuriated Jewish leaders sent a mission of protest to Tiberius in Italy, and Tiberius ordered the removal of the shields to the temple of Augustus in pagan Caesarea.

It was Tiberius's policy, seldom followed by other emperors, to retain successful officials in the same post for many years, instead of the usual three or four. He must have been satisfied with Pilate's management of a difficult province because he kept Pilate, like his predecessor as prefect, in charge for ten years. Josephus's attitude toward Pilate was unfavorable, but unlike Philo, who accused Pilate of every vice, Josephus was not violently hostile. He found only a single disastrous action to impute to Pilate in ten years. Modern scholars (e.g., Schürer and Smallwood) have tended to echo the attitudes of either of the Jewish sources. But it was Pilate's duty to maintain order over a surly subject people, who were even more unruly because their land had been annexed rather than conquered — Pompey in 63 B.C. had besieged and captured only the temple precinct at Jerusalem; there had been no general resistance later, but only local and dynastic rebellions.

*III. Trial of Christ.*–Christ's trial before Pilate had nearly all the features of a normal provincial trial by the *cognitio* (investigation) of the governor. The prosecution was initiated and conducted by independent prosecutors (*delatores*) — the high priest and his colleagues (Mt. 27:26; Mk. 15:3; Lk. 23:1, 4). The governor sat on his judgment seat (Mt. 27:19; Jn. 19:12) and gave direct sentence of punishment (Mt. 27:26; Mk. 15:15; Jn. 19:16). The charge was formulated not as the infringement of a particular law but as an indictment of actions that the governor was required to evaluate (Mt. 27:11; Mk. 15:2-5; Lk. 23:2). Only a mention of the governor's assessors (*consilium*) is lacking. Pilate's repeated questioning of Jesus about His alleged kingship was in a form regularly employed to determine the guilt of a prisoner who refused to plead; Christian martyrs were questioned in this way in the earliest recorded trials (Pliny *Ep.* x.96.2f.; Eusebius *HE* v.1.202).

Josephus portrayed Pilate as a governor who was determined to maintain Roman supremacy and to secure its recognition. Although given to unwise initiatives and quick to act against manifest dissidence, Pilate was ready to investigate and to yield to the unfamiliar prejudices of his subjects. Josephus's portrait accords with the view of Pilate in the Gospel accounts of the trial of Christ. Both in the Synoptic Gospels and in John, Pilate carefully questioned the prisoner about His political role. But he eventually yielded to the strong pressure of the Jewish clergy to convict Jesus. The Jews' explicit threat against Pilate, "If you release this man, you are not Caesar's friend" (Jn. 19:12), hints at an investigation on a charge of *maiestas minuta* — neglect of the security of the state. Such investigations were frequent in Rome in this period; Pilate escaped one for the trial of Christ, but a later action caused him to be sent to Rome for imperial interrogation.

Christ and Barabbas before Pilate. From Codex Rossanensis (6th cent.) (B. M. Metzger)

The Gospel narratives stress the responsibility of the Jewish clergy for Christ's death and diminish that of Pilate. Many have argued that their tone gives a false picture of the clergy's role and that the whole responsibility was Pilate's. The governor in some modern interpretations merely sentenced one agitator who had been involved in local riots, i.e., the cleansing of the temple, and pardoned another, Barabbas (Mk. 15:7-15; Lk. 23:18-25). But the outline of Roman procedure in the Gospels is correct. The governor would have taken the initiative only in circumstances of open riot, as in the Samaritan affair, when direct action replaced criminal procedure. The judicial prosecution of a malefactor for past actions required the formal initiative of a third party (*delatio*), as in the various trials of Paul (e.g., Acts 24:1-9; 25:1-27). Hence extreme interpretations of the trial that underplay the role of the clergy are not well founded. For the difficult question whether the high priest possessed the power of capital jurisdiction, which would have removed the necessity to work through the governor's court, *see* PROCURATOR.

*See also* JESUS CHRIST, ARREST AND TRIAL OF.

***IV. Death of Pilate.***–Pilate, sent to Rome by the governor of Syria to explain his slaughter of the Samaritans, reached the city after the death of Tiberius. The Christian tradition of Eusebius (*HE* ii.7) credibly records that "calamities forced him to an unavoidable suicide" in the reign of Gaius (37-41). As was common in this period, Pilate probably killed himself after his trial and condemnation, perhaps when in exile at Vienna-on-Rhone, with which later tradition connects his death.

***V. Later Reputation.***–Apart from the accounts of Christ's trial the NT mentions Pilate only to place certain events chronologically. Acts 3:13 briefly summarizes the Gospel version of Pilate's unwillingness to convict Christ, although in 4:27 the author conjoins Pilate, Herod, and the clergy in complicity. Luke alone reports the massacre of the Galileans (Lk. 13:1) but regards it as a natural calamity, a manifestation of God's wrath for which Pilate should not be blamed. Luke also mentions the disagreement and reconciliation of Pilate and Herod, which is not recorded in Josephus. An incidental reference to Pilate occurs in 1 Tim. 6:13.

The NT writers' lack of hostility toward Pilate is reflected in the later Apologists. Tertullian called him "a Christian by conscience" (*Apol.* 21.24) and attributed to him a letter commending the faith. Origen described Pilate's wife as a convert, and the Coptic church ultimately canonized Pilate himself. Eusebius, who cited in part Josephus's account of Pilate, attributed the governor's suicide to divine justice but did not comment directly on his responsibility for the crucifixion. Later tradition produced the fictitious Acts of Pilate (*see* APOCRYPHAL GOSPELS III.B) and colorful accounts of his death.

***Bibliography.***–*Année epigraphique* (1964), n. 104; Pauly-Wissowa, XX/2, 1322f.; E. Schürer, *HJP*², I, 383-87; A. N. Sherwin-White, *Roman Society and Roman Law in the NT* (repr. 1980); E. M. Smallwood, *Jews under Roman Rule* (1976), pp. 106ff.

A. N. SHERWIN-WHITE

**PILDASH** pil'dash [Heb. *pildāš*] (Gen. 22:22). A son of Abraham's brother Nahor and Milcah. The etymology of the name is uncertain. Some scholars (e.g., R. de Vaux, *Early History of Israel* [Eng. tr. 1978], pp. 212, 240) have regarded Nahor's sons as the ancestors of the Aramean tribes.

**PILE** [Heb. (verbs) niphal of *ʿāram* (Ex. 15:8), piel of *yāsaḏ*–'found' (2 Ch. 31:7), hiphil of *kûn*–'prepare' (Job 27:16f.), *sālal*–'heap up' (Jer. 50:26), *dûr* (Ezk. 24:5), (noun) *meḏûrâ* (Ezk. 24:9)]; AV also "be gathered together" (Ex. 15:8), "lay the foundation" (2 Ch. 31:7), "prepare" (Job 27:16f.), CAST (Jer. 50:26), "burn" (Ezk. 24:5); NEB also "stand . . . like a bank" (Ex. 15:8), "deposit" (2 Ch. 31:7), GET PILES (Job 27:16), "get" (Job 27:17), "pack" (Ezk. 24:5), "fire-pit" (Ezk. 24:9).

The root *ʿrm* (I) occurs only in Ex. 15:8, but its meaning is clear from both the context and the rabbinical Hebrew and Syriac cognates ("heap up, dam up"). The uses of *yāsaḏ, kûn,* and *sālal* are fairly common, but *dûr* and *meḏûrâ* are rare words. Both come from the root *dwr,* "circle," and are related to *dôr,* "generation" (life cycle). In Ezk. 24:5 W. Zimmerli's translation, "pack round," illustrates well the sense of *dûr* (*Ezekiel 1* [Eng. tr., *Hermeneia,* 1979], p. 493). The AV follows the LXX *hypokaíō,* "burn," perhaps because the context clearly indicates a fire. A similar instance of contextual inference is apparent in the NEB's translation of *meḏûrâ* in v. 9; the only other occurrence of *meḏûrâ* is Isa. 30:33 (RSV "pyre"), and in both contexts it clearly refers to a pile of wood.

G. A. L.

**PILEHA** pil'ə-hä (Neh. 10:24, AV). *See* PILHA.

**PILFER** [Gk. *nosphízō*] (Tit. 2:10); AV PURLOIN. Paul here advises Titus to instruct Christians who are slaves not to steal from their masters. As is clear from its use in the LXX and other Greek literature (see Bauer, rev., pp. 543f.), *nosphízō* means to misappropriate something for oneself that should or does belong to someone else. Cf. Acts 5:2f., where Ananias and Sapphira "kept back" (Gk. *nosphízō*) some of the money from a sale of property but claimed that they were giving it all. Cf. also Josh. 7:1, 19-21; in v. 1 the LXX uses *nosphízō* to describe Achan's retention of some of the spoils that were all to be devoted to the Lord.

G. A. L.

**PILGRIMAGE** [Heb. *māgôr* < *gûr*–'sojourn'] (Ps. 119:54). According to most commentators *māgôr* is used as a metaphor for one's earthly, transient existence (cf. v. 19, where "sojourner" translates the related Heb. *gēr*; cf. esp. Gen. 47:9, where "sojourning" renders *māgôr*; cf. E. A. Speiser, *Genesis* [*AB,* 1964], p. 351, who said that such an explanation is "unduly sophisticated"). The NEB "wherever I make my home" and the NIV "wherever I lodge" reflect some of the uncertainty inherent in the root *gwr* (see G. von Rad, *Genesis* [Eng. tr., *OTL,* 1972], pp. 407f.). These interpretations are more plausible than the JB and NAB "exile," which reflects the supposed exilic background of the Psalm but are inappropriate to the sense of *māgôr.*

G. A. L.

**PILHA** pil'hä [Heb. *pilḥāʾ*–'millstone'] (Neh. 10:24 [MT 25]); AV PILEHA. A man who signed Nehemiah's covenant.

**PILL.** A verb used in English dialect, meaning to strip off or PEEL. The term occurs in the AV of Gen. 30:37f.

**PILLAR** [Heb. *maṣṣēḇâ*] (Gen. 28:18, 22; 31:13, 45, 51f.; 35:14, 20; Ex. 23:24; 24:4; 34:13; Dt. 7:5; 12:3; 16:22; etc); AV also IMAGE, GARRISON (Ezk. 26:11); NEB also SACRED PILLAR; [*ʿammûḏ*] (Ex. 13:21f.; 14:19, 24; 26:32, 37; 27:10ff.; 33:9f.; 35:11, 17; 36:36, 38; 38:10ff.; Nu. 3:36f.; etc.); NEB also POST, BEAM; [*neṣîḇ*] (Gen. 19:26); [hophal of *nāṣaḇ*–'be set up'] (Jgs. 9:6); NEB "propped-up"; [*māṣûq*] (1 S. 2:8); NEB FOUNDATION; [*šāṯ*] (Isa. 19:10); AV "purpose"; NEB "spinner"; [Gk. *stýlos*] (Gal. 2:9; 1 Tim. 3:15; Rev. 3:12; 10:1).

Pillars had a number of uses among the ancient Hebrews. The tradition of setting up memorial or sacred pillars (commonly designated by Heb. *maṣṣēḇâ*) dates from the patriarchal period. The unworked memorial that was raised over Rachel's burial place (Gen. 35:20) was so well known that its location was still remembered as late as the time of Saul (1 S. 10:2), being described as on the border of Benjamin at Zelzah. The pillar set up by the childless Absalom to perpetuate his name (2 S. 18:18) was less memorable, however, and has been incorrectly identified with the "Tomb of Absalom" (1st cent. B.C.) in the Kidron Valley of Jerusalem. To commemorate visibly the covenants between Jacob and Laban and also between God and Israel (Gen. 31:45-54; Ex. 24:4; Josh. 24:26f.) suitable monuments were erected.

Pillars frequently constituted sacred objects. In Gen. 35:14, e.g., Jacob set up a stone structure that commemorated God's presence and was designated "House of God" (Bethel). Moses erected twelve pillars and an altar at the foot of Mt. Sinai to symbolize the spiritual unity of the twelve Hebrew tribes when the covenant was ratified (Ex. 24:4). Joshua erected twelve stones at Gilgal, on the east side of Jericho, to mark the safe crossing of the Jordan and to serve as a witness to God's mighty power (Josh. 4:20-24). The origin of the pillar at Shechem (Jgs. 9:6) is uncertain, but may go back to the patriarchal period (*see* OAK OF THE PILLAR). A messianic prophecy in Isa. 19:19 states that a *maṣṣēḇâ* will be erected to the Lord on the Egyptian border to demonstrate God's control of foreign peoples. In the following century Jeremiah predicted the destruction of the sacred pillars (RSV "obelisks," Jer. 43:13) of Re at Heliopolis.

Canaanite shrines invariably contained one or more pillars, which were so closely identified with the idea of deity, especially male gods, that they themselves were often venerated as objects of worship. The pillars were normally associated with other pagan cultic objects, one of which was the *ʾᵃšērâ*. This was apparently a wooden pole or stele thought to symbolize the goddess of fertility, and thus mentioned in conjunction with the *maṣṣēḇâ* (Ex. 23:24; Lev. 26:1; Dt. 7:5; 12:2; Hos. 3:4; etc.). Many upright stones, described archeologically by the term menhir, have been found in the Levant, notable Palestinian examples occurring at Gezer, Byblos, and Râs Shamrah (Ugarit). The menhir was normally left in a rough form, although occasionally it appeared to have been partly shaped. At Hazor a damaged upright pillar was recovered from the entrance to an important building in the fortified Canaanite city, while excavations at a lower level (13th cent. B.C.) revealed a number of miniature stone slabs in a shrine. The invading Israelites may well have been responsible for the damage inflicted at this particular level.

The Heb. *ʿammûḏ* is often rendered "pillar" in the sense of a structural member supporting a roof, i.e., a column. Excavations at Gezer and elsewhere suggest that the pillars

Pillars near an altar (of Baal? Molech?) at Byblos (*ca.* 2500 B.C.) (D. H. Condit)

Collection of stelae from the Canaanite orthostat temple at Hazor (1500-1200 B.C.) (Israel Museum, Jerusalem)

that Samson pulled down at the time of his death (Jgs. 16:29f.) were made of wood and set on bases of stone. Several buildings with rows of pillars incorporated into their structure have been recovered from the period of the Israelite monarchy. The Solomonic palace-temple complex included a building described as the "house of the forest of Lebanon" (1 K. 7:2), perhaps an armory, that was supported on cedar pillars. This building was then linked by a pillared hall to the throne-room. Quite clearly the wooden pillars were being used as structural components, and therefore cannot be likened to the row of standing basalt stones recovered from the Canaanite shrine at Hazor (13th cent. B.C.). These artifacts had rounded tops, and one of them bore a rough engraving suggesting worship.

Solomon's temple had two large freestanding bronze pillars at the entrance (1 K. 7:15-22), but their significance is uncertain. Perhaps they were analogous to a freestanding column about 2.5 m. (8 ft.) high that was also recovered from Hazor. They may have been cressets or fire-altars, and evidently played some part in preexilic cultic worship in Israel (cf. 2 K. 11:14; 23:3). *See* JACHIN AND BOAZ. The remains of ten pillars at Gezer, apparently erected when the city was refortified under Solomon, have been dissociated from the high place and are regarded instead as a row of markers attesting to the unity of the refounding clans (see Graesser). From the early Israelite period at Tell Arad came a rectangular shrine with a high place and a *maṣṣēḇâ* (see *EAEHL*, I, 85f.), indicating that the pillar exercised some function in the worship at the shrine before it was removed in the 7th cent. B.C.

At Megiddo stone pillars were used in a building formerly described as "Solomon's stables," which is now dated to the time of Omri (885-874 B.C.) and Ahab (874-852 B.C.). The structure itself may not even have been a stable, but was perhaps an armory or a storehouse (cf. Y. Yadin, *BA*, 23 [1960], 62-68). The rectangular pillars in the royal palace at Samaria had carved proto-Aeolic or Ionic capitals, perhaps reflecting Phoenician concepts of design. There is no doubt that the Greeks assigned great importance to the use of pillars in the construction of temples, public buildings, and private residences of the wealthy, a feature that was also prominent in the palaces of the Persian rulers at Susa (cf. Est. 1:6) and Persepolis. The ruined temples at Baalbek and Gerasa testify to the abundant use of pillars in shrines and other buildings of Hellenistic origin.

A figurative use of *ʿammûḏ* occurs in Prov. 9:1, where the house of wisdom was said to have seven pillars. Perhaps the author employed this imagery to enhance the glory and beauty of the wisdom that he was commending, and to show its perfection by using the number seven, which for the Hebrews signified what was consummate and complete. Another figurative use occurs in Job 26:11, which mentions the "pillars of heaven," i.e., the mountains (cf. the comms., many of which assume that this passage reflects a primitive world-view). Cf. also Ps. 75:3 (MT 4). *See* WORLD I.A.

In the NT "pillar" occurs only occasionally and in a figurative sense. James, Cephas, and John were reputedly "pillars" of the Jerusalem church (Gal. 2:9), i.e., foundational figures, while 1 Tim. 3:15 describes the Christian Church as "the pillar and bulwark of the truth." The imagery of basic structural components describes accurately people of spiritual substance, reliability, and dependability. The one who is victorious in the Christian life is to become a pillar in God's temple (Rev. 3:12). A powerful angel is described in Rev. 10:1 as having legs "like pillars of fire."

*See also* PILLAR OF CLOUD AND PILLAR OF FIRE.

***Bibliography*.**–G. A. Barrois, *Manuel d'Archéologie Biblique*, II (1953), 346-48, 358-363; C. F. Graesser, *BA*, 35 (1972), 34-63; Y. Yadin, *BA*, 19 (1956), 2-12; 21 (1958), 45. R. K. HARRISON

**PILLAR, OAK OF THE.** *See* OAK OF THE PILLAR.

**PILLAR OF CLOUD AND PILLAR OF FIRE.** The visible manifestation of the divine presence during the Exodus. The Lord went before the Israelites "by day in a pillar of cloud [Heb. *ʿammûḏ ʿānān*] to lead them along the way, and by night in a pillar of fire [*ʿammûḏ ʾēš*] to give them light . . . the pillar of cloud by day and the pillar of fire by night did not depart from before the people" (Ex. 13:21f.; cf. 14:19, 24; Nu. 14:14). When the congregation was at rest, the cloud stayed over the tabernacle (Ex. 40:36; Nu. 9:17; 14:14). When the Lord wished to communicate His will to Moses, the pillar descended to the door of the tent of meeting (Ex. 33:9-11; Nu. 12:5; Dt. 31:15).

Scholars have offered various rationalistic explanations of these pillars. M. Noth (*Exodus* [Eng. tr., *OTL*, 1962], p. 109) supposed that the pillar of cloud and the pillar of fire reflected the volcanic activity of the Sinai area. U. Cassuto (*Comm. on the Book of Exodus* [Eng. tr. 1967], p. 158) saw a parallel with the ancient practice of carrying smoke and fire signals at the head of caravans as a guide.

Two other theories draw parallels from the ancient Near East. T. Mann (*JBL*, 90 [1971], 15-30; see also *Divine Presence and Guidance in Israelite Traditions* [1977], pp. 132f., 256f.) pointed out the weaknesses of the above theories and offered an alternative explanation on the basis of Ugar. *ʿnn*, which is usually translated "messenger" or "servant." Mann suggested that *ʿnn* is better translated "cloud" or perhaps "cloud-messenger"; in Ugaritic mythology the storm-god Baal has messengers (usually in pairs) who take the form of clouds. According to Mann this mythology provides the background for the Israelite traditions. G. Mendenhall (*Tenth Generation* [1973], pp. 32-66, 209-213) also appealed to Ugar. *ʿnn* but identified it more closely with the deity. He suggested that the term is the semantic equivalent of Akk. *melammu*, the "aureole . . . surrounding that which is divine" (p. 52). Thus he called Heb. *ʿānān* the mask of Yahweh, i.e., a manifestation of His presence. The *ʿānān* was later identified with the divine messenger or angel (Heb. *malʾāḵ*, Ex. 14:18; cf. 33:9-11). R. Good ("Cloud Messengers?" *Ugarit-Forschungen*, 10 [1978], 436f.), however, has criticized such interpretations of Ugar. *ʿnn*. He pointed out that Ugaritic has two different words *ʿnn*, one meaning "servant" (< *ʿnw/y*, "submit") and the other meaning "cloud"; in the texts that Mann and Mendenhall cited, Ugar. *ʿnn* clearly means "servant." Thus neither of these explanations is satisfactory.

G. A. L.

**PILLAR OF SALT.** *See* LOT II.B.

**PILLAR, PLAIN OF THE.** *See* OAK OF THE PILLAR.

**PILLARS OF THE EARTH; PILLARS OF HEAVEN.** *See* WORLD I.A.

**PILLOW** [Heb. *kāḇîr*] (1 S. 19:13, 16); NEB RUG. A support for the head of a reclining person. Heb. *kāḇîr* occurs only in this passage and, as noted in the RSV mg., its meaning is uncertain. The context and cognates (e.g., *kᵉḇārâ*, "sieve," Am. 9:9) suggest something "woven" from goats' hair. It was placed "at its [the image's] head" (*mᵉraʾᵃšōṯāyw*), apparently to serve as a wig (cf. Cant. 4:1, where a woman's hair is compared to a flock of goats). See P. K. McCarter, *I Samuel* (*AB*, 1980), p. 326.

The AV uses "pillow" in five additional places. In Gen. 28:11, 18 it renders *mᵉraʾᵃšōṯāyw* (see above) "for his pillows" (cf. RSV "under his head"; NEB "a pillow for his head," "on which he had laid his head"; cf. the same term in 1 S. 26:7, 11f., 16). In Ezk. 13:18, 20, AV, "pillows" represents Heb. *kᵉsāṯôṯ* (RSV, NEB, "magic bands"; *see* MAGIC II.A [7]). On Mk. 4:38, *see* CUSHION. N. J. O.

**PILOT** [Heb. *ḥōḇēl* (Ezk. 27:8, 27-29); Gk. part. of *euthýnō* (Jas. 3:4)]; AV also GOVERNOR (Jas. 3:4); NEB HELMSMAN. A person who steers a boat.

The Heb. *ḥōḇēl*, which occurs only in Ezk. 27 and Jonah 1:6, no doubt refers to the one who manipulates the sail lines (cf. *ḥeḇel*, "rope"; see *TDOT*, IV, 178; *see also* SHIPS). The use of *raḇ haḥōḇēl* in Jonah 1:6 suggests that the RSV, AV, and NEB translations of *ḥōḇēl* in Ezk. 27 may be too exalted (see also LXX *kybernḗtēs*); i.e., it is perhaps better to follow JB, BDB (p. 287), and *CHAL* (p. 94) and translate "sailor" (see W. Zimmerli, *Ezekiel*, II [Eng. tr., *Hermeneia*, 1983], 59; cf. E. M. Good, *Semitics*, 1 [1970], 84 n. 15).

James uses two images to illustrate that just as relatively small objects can influence much larger ones, so the tongue can influence the whole person. His examples, a horse's bit and a ship's rudder, were often used for illustrations. See M. Dibelius and H. Greeven, *James* (Eng. tr., *Hermeneia*, 1976), pp. 185-190, for a full discussion of this imagery. G. A. L.

**PILTAI** pil'tī [Heb. *pilṭāy*–'(Yahweh is) my deliverer'] (Neh. 12:17). One of the priests in the days of the high priest Joiakim. Piltai was the head of the father's house of Moadiah (i.e., Moadiah's family; see N. Gottwald, *Tribes of Yahweh* [1979], pp. 285-292, for a definition of a "father's house"). Similar names occur in Punic (*plṭbʿl*, "Baal is my deliverer"), Ugaritic, and Akkadian (see F. Benz, *Personal Names in the Phoenician and Punic Inscriptions* [1972], pp. 390f.). G. A. L.

**PIM** pim. *See* WEIGHTS AND MEASURES.

**PIN** [Heb. (noun) *yāṯēḏ* (Jgs. 16:13f.), (verb) hiphil of *nāḵâ*–'strike' (1 S. 18:11; 19:10; 26:8)]; AV also SMITE (1 S. 18:11; 19:10; 26:8); NEB also BEATER (Jgs. 16:13f.). The pin in Jgs. 16:13f. is a cylindrical piece of wood or metal used in WEAVING to beat up (hence the NEB) the woof, i.e., tighten the weave, in the loom. The MT in vv. 13b and 14a is apparently corrupt (see the comms., esp. G. F. Moore [*ICC*, 1895], pp. 353-55; cf. KD, *in loc.*); the RSV is based on the LXX, but the AV follows the MT.

The three occurrences of the verb in 1 Samuel all concern David and Saul. In his jealous rage Saul tried to impale David with his spear, but David escaped harm (18:11; 19:10). In 26:8 Abishai, one of David's faithful men, wanted to strike down the sleeping Saul, but David stayed his hand. See P. K. McCarter, *I Samuel* (*AB*, 1980), pp. 305f., 325, 405, 407f., for literary and text criticism and socio-political background. G. A. L.

**PINE AWAY** [Heb. *dûḇ* (Lev. 26:16), *zûḇ* (Lam. 4:9), *māqaq* (Lev. 26:39; Ezk. 24:23), *rāzî* (Isa. 24:16)]; AV also "sorrow" (of heart) (Lev. 26:16), "leanness" (Isa. 24:16); NEB also "fail" (appetite, Lev. 26:16), "villainy" (Isa. 24:16), "waste away" (Lam. 4:9); the AV and NEB have "pine away" in Ezk. 33:10 (Heb. *māqaq*; RSV "waste away"), and the AV uses the phrase to render Gk. *xēraínō* in Mk. 9:18 (RSV "become rigid"; NEB "go rigid").

In these passages Heb. *māqaq* means "decay, rot away" because of sin. Heb. *dûḇ* in Lev. 26:16, with its object *nepeš*, is "sorrow of heart" in the AV, "pining away of life" in the RSV, and "failure of appetite" in the NEB. Cf. Dt. 28:65, where the RV has "pining of soul."

In Isa. 24:16 the MT has Heb. *rāzî-lî*, which the AV translates "my leanness" and the RSV "I pine away." *BH* suggests *reẓî*, and some versions render "my secret" (cf. LXX mg.; Aram. *rāz*, "secret," Dnl. 2:18ff.; 4:9). Most commentators derive *rāzî* from Heb. *rāzâ*, "be lean" (cf. E. J. Young, *Book of Isaiah*, II [*NICOT*, 1969], 170-74); but the form is difficult to explain (thus KoB, p. 883, simply says "unexplained").

For the starving persons of Lam. 4:9 Heb. *zûḇ* is used, meaning "dry up," "wear away," or "be exhausted by morbid discharges."

The "pining sickness" (Heb. *dallâ*) of Isa. 38:12, AV, is a wrong translation. The AV and RV margins correctly read "from the thrum," and the RSV rendering is "from the loom." God removes Hezekiah's life from the earth just as readily as the weaver takes fabric from the loom.

On Mk. 9:18 *see* EPILEPSY; MEDICINE. R. K. H.

**PINE (TREE)** [Heb. *teʾaššûr*] (Isa. 41:19; 60:13; Ezk. 27:6); AV BOX TREE, "Ashurites" (Ezk. 27:6); NEB BOX, BOXWOOD; [Heb. *berôṯ*] (Cant. 1:17); AV, NEB, FIR. Hebrew *teʾššûr* (Ugar. *tšrm*) should normally be regarded as the designation of the slender cypress *Cupressus sempervirens* L. If it can be demonstrated that boxwood is actually meant, the only species that grew in Palestine was the *Buxus longifolia* Boiss., an attractively grained wood that the Romans used for cabinetwork and ivory inlays. In Ezk. 27:6 the MT has *baṯ-ʾaššurîm* (lit. "daughter of Ashurites"; see AV), but the RSV follows the generally accepted repointing *biṯʾasssurîm* (lit. "with pines").

Hebrew *berôṯ* in Cant. 1:17 most probably refers to a species of juniper, evidently the Phoenician juniper, and not to the Aleppo pine (*Pinus halepensis* Mill.), as some botanists have thought, even though the latter is native to the Mediterranean area.

*See also* CYPRESS; FIR TREE; OLEASTER; PLANE TREE. R. K. H.

**PINING SICKNESS** (Isa. 38:12, AV). *See* PINE AWAY.

**PINION** pin'yən [Heb. *ʾēḇer*, *ʾeḇrâ*] (Dt. 32:11; Job 39:13; Ps. 68:13 [MT 14]; 91:4; Ezk. 17:3); AV WING, FEATHERS; NEB also WING.

Pinions form the terminal sections of a bird's wings. Poetically the term may refer to the wings themselves (thus the RSV translates *ʾēḇer* "wing" in Ps. 55:6 [MT 7]; Isa. 40:13; cf. also the parallelism with "wing" in Dt. 32:11; Ps. 91:4), especially when the birds are in flight. Pinions, therefore, become the symbol of both strength and protection (Dt. 32:11; Isa. 40:31). G. WYPER

**PINNACLE.** The highest point; in architecture, a small turret or spire. The term rendered "pinnacles" in Isa. 54:12 (AV "windows"; NEB "battlements") is the plural of Heb. *šemeš* ("sun"), which suggests those parts of the buildings in restored Jerusalem that will reflect the sun. In Mt. 4:5 par. Lk. 4:9, Gk. *pterýgion* (lit. "little wing," but elsewhere "tower," "rampart," "pinnacle"; cf. Vulg. *pinnaculum*, "little wing") designates a part of the TEMPLE. It has traditionally been identified with the southeast corner of the outer court, which overlooked the Kidron valley and was so high that "if anyone looked down from the rooftop, combining the two elevations, he would become dizzy . . ." (Josephus *Ant.* xv.11.5 [412]). Another suggestion is the lintel of a gate of the temple, which may have been in the form of a balcony. (See comms.)

N. J. O.

**PINON** pī'nən [Heb. *pînōn*] (Gen. 36:41; 1 Ch. 1:52). One of the chiefs of Edom. Some (e.g., KD) connect Pinon with the place PUNON, one of Israel's camps in the wilderness (Nu. 33:42f.).

**PIONEER** [Gk. *archēgós*] (He. 2:10; 12:2); AV CAPTAIN, AUTHOR; NEB LEADER, "on whom (faith) depends from start (to finish)." In these passages and in its other two NT occurrences (Acts 3:15; 5:31) Gk. *archēgós* refers to Christ. It has two main senses that often merge: (1) "leader," "chief"; (2) "founder," thus "initiator," or in a bad sense "instigator." Both senses are well attested in pagan literature and in the papyri. Christ is *archēgós* of "salvation" (He. 2:10) and of "faith" (12:2); in each case the nuance "founder" seems apposite (cf. Vulg. *auctor*, "originator"). For the thought in Hebrews cf. 5:9, where Christ is called "source [*aítios*] of eternal salvation"; 6:20, where He is a "forerunner [*pródromos*] on our behalf." He is the "pathfinder" who has blazed the trail as His people's representative and forerunner; He has run the race to its triumphant finish (12:1f.).

***Bibliography.***–F. F. Bruce, *Epistle to the Hebrews* (*NICNT*, 1964), pp. 40-44, 351f.; E. K. Simpson, *EQ*, 18 (1946), 35f.; *TDNT*, I, *s.v.* ἄρχω κτλ.: ἀρχηγός (Delling). C. J. HEMER

**PIPE** [Heb. *ṣanteʾrôṯ*] (Zec. 4:12). In Zechariah's vision of a lampstand he saw, next to the lampstand, two olive trees with branches beside which were two golden pipes. These pipes apparently supplied oil to the lamp from the olive trees.

This text has several problems. (1) Since Heb. *ṣanteʾrôṯ* is a hapax legomenon, its meaning is not clear. Most scholars relate it to *ṣinnôr*, "channel, shaft" hence "spout" (see, e.g., KD; BDB, p. 857; cf. Targumic Aram. *ṣanterîn*, "spouts, tubes"). North suggested "funnel" (p. 187). (2) The MT states that these pipes poured out "gold"; most scholars take this to be a reference to golden oil (so Baldwin, pp. 123f.; Kimchi, p. 45). (3) The meaning of the vision is somewhat debated, but the two olive trees apparently represent Zerubbabel and Joshua, the civil and religious leaders; the lampstand represents Israel; and the oil the Spirit of God. See the comms. for further discussion.

For musical pipes, *see* MUSIC II.C.

***Bibliography.***–J. Baldwin, *Haggai, Zechariah, Malachi* (*Tyndale OT Comms.*, 1972); A. M'Caul, *Rabbi David Kimchi's Commentary on the Prophecy of Zechariah* (1937); R. North, *Bibl.*, 41 (1970), 183-206; R. Smith, *Micah-Malachi* (*Word Biblical Comm.*, 1984). G. A. L.

**PIRAM** pī'rəm [Heb. *pirʾām*–'wild ass' or 'zebra'(?)] (Josh. 10:3). King of Jarmuth, who along with Adoni-zedek of Jerusalem and three other Amorite kings (v. 5) attacked Gibeon because the Gibeonites had made peace with Israel (v. 1). Gibeon turned to Joshua for help (v. 6), and he responded with an all-night march from Gilgal. His army then routed the Amorite forces (on the miracle here, *see*

Beth-horon, Battle of). The kings escaped to a cave near Makkedah (v. 16) but there were trapped and killed (vv. 18-27). G. A. L.

**PIRATHON** pir'ə-thon; **PIRATHONITE** pir'ə-thon-īt [Heb. *pirʿāṯon, pirʿāṯônî*; Gk. B *Pharathōm,* A *Phraathōm, Pharathyneitēs*]. The home of Abdon son of Hillel, a judge (Jgs. 12:13, 15), as well as the home of Benaiah, one of David's chief captains (2 S. 23:30; 1 Ch. 11:31; 27:14). It was "in the land of Ephraim, in the hill country of the Amalekites" (Jgs. 12:15). It is probably to be identified with Farʿâtā, about 9.5 km. (6 mi.) SW of Shechem. Some have located the site in Benjamin on the basis of the geographical references to Abdon as a Benjaminite in 1 Ch. 8:23, 30; 9:36, but these references are to different persons named Abdon. It is doubtful that Pirathon is the Pharathon fortified by Bacchides (1 Macc. 9:50; Josephus *Ant.* xiii.1.3 [14-16]), since this town is in Judea; there is also a textual problem: some MSS read Timnath-Pharathon (so NEB), a compound name, rather than two separate names (see J. A. Goldstein, *I Maccabees* [*AB,* 1976], p. 386). R. P. DUGAN, JR.

**PISGAH** piz'gə [Heb. *happisgâ,* always with the definite article and always in combination (see discussion below); Gk. *Phasga,* although the LXX does not always render the term as a proper noun but sometimes uses *hē laxeutḗ* or *tó lelaxeuménon*]. A mountain (range or peak) in Moab opposite Jericho, identical with or closely joined to Mt. Nebo (Dt. 34:1).

Four times the word occurs in the expression *rō'š happisgâ,* "the top (head) of the Pisgah": Nu. 21:20; 23:14; Dt. 3:27; 34:1. In the last two passages the term refers to the place where Moses went to view the Promised Land. Four times the word is found in the expression *'ašdōṯ happisgâ,* "the slopes of Pisgah" (RSV; AV reads Ashdoth-pisgah, except in Dt. 4:49 where it reads "the springs of Pisgah"): Dt. 3:17; 4:49; Josh. 12:3; 13:20. Each of these passages uses the compound form as a term of geographical significance. The LXX rendering of *pisgâ* by forms of *laxeúō,* "hew, dress stone" (Nu. 21:20; 23:14; Dt. 3:27; 4:49), may be significant. This rendering is not limited to either of the compound terms, for three times it is used where the Hebrew has *rō'š happisgâ,* and once where the Hebrew reads *'ašdōṯ happisgâ.* Jerome (*Onom. s.v. Asedoth*) translates *Fasge* by Lat. *abscisum,* "steep," "broken off," thus deriving Pisgah from the verb *pāsag,* "split, cut off." This translation suggests that *happisgâ* was read "the cutting off, the cleft" (cf. Gk. *tó lelaxeuménon*).

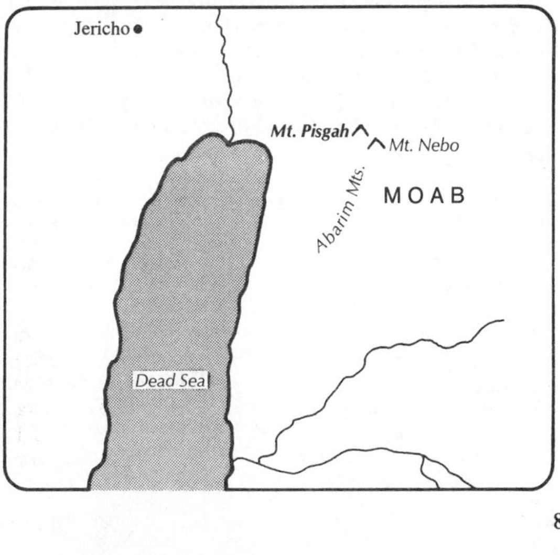


Viewed from the east, the edge of the Transjordan plateau overlooking the Dead Sea certainly gives this appearance.

It is impossible to determine whether "the Pisgah" was the name of the entire range (now the Abarim Mountains) or of a single peak. If a peak, the identification with Râs es-Siâghah (or Jebel Siâghah) commends itself, for this peak, slightly lower than Mt. Nebo and to the northwest, is joined to Nebo by a saddle.

*See also* Nebo, Mount. W. S. L. S.

**PISHON** pī'shon [Heb. *pîšôn*; Gk. *Ph(e)isōn*; AV PISON]. One of the four rivers of Eden, mentioned only in Gen. 2:11. It is said to have flowed around the whole land of Havilah. Conjectures about the identification of Pishon are numerous and no conclusion is generally accepted (see the comms.). The mention of Havilah is of little help, since its location is unclear. It appears to be associated with northeastern Arabia in Gen. 25:18 but with southwestern Arabia in Gen. 10:28. D. E. WARING

**PISIDIA** pə-sid'i-ə (Gk. *Pisidia*). A highland area of south central Asia Minor (Acts 13:14; 14:24). In Acts 13:14 ℵ A B C $p^{45}$ read Gk. *Antiocheian tḗn Pisidian,* "the Pisidian Antioch"; most other MSS read *Antiocheian tḗs Pisidias,* "Antioch of Pisidia." The former, followed by the NEB, is most likely original and correctly describes geographical facts of the time when Paul traveled in the country (see below).

Pisidia as a strict geographical term was the name given to a huge block of mountain country (190 km. [120 mi.] E-W and 80 km. [50 mi.] N-S) stretching northward from the Taurus and bordered by Pamphylia on the south, Lycia on the southwest, Phrygia on the north and west, and Isauria on the east, though the frontier on that side was never strictly drawn. The name is so used by Xenophon, who recorded that the Pisidians were independent of the Persian king at the end of the 5th cent. B.C. (*Anabasis* i.1.11).

Alexander the Great had difficulty in reducing Pisidia, and throughout ancient history the area is described as the home of a turbulent and warlike people given to robbery. The task of subjugating them was entrusted by the Romans to the Galatian King Amyntas, and at his death in 25 B.C. Pisidia was included in the Roman province of Galatia organized from his former territories.

Augustus undertook seriously the pacification of the Pisidian and Isaurian mountains. He established a chain of military colonies at Cremna, Comana, Olbasa, Parlais, and Lystra and connected them by military roads with the main garrison city of Antioch. This had been founded by the Seleucids and lay in Galatian Phrygia, near the northern border of Pisidia. Augustus established the Roman *colonia* there in *ca.* 25 B.C. (accepting Ramsay's dating) and the city was thenceforth passionately loyal to him. As the military organization of Pisidia centered upon this city on its border, Antioch derived the title "the Pisidian," which served to distinguish it from other cities named Antioch.

An inscription shows that P. Sulpicius Quirinus, who is mentioned in Lk. 2:2 as governor of Syria in the year of Christ's birth, was an honorary magistrate of the colony of Antioch; his connection with Antioch dated from his campaign *ca.* 8 B.C. against the Homonades, who had resisted and killed Amyntas.

Pisidia remained part of the province of Galatia until A.D. 74, when the greater (southern) part of it was assigned to the new double province of Lycia-Pamphylia and the cities in this portion of Pisidia then ranked as Pamphylian. The northern part continued to belong to Galatia until the close of the 3rd cent., when Diocletian formed a new province of Pisidia, with Antioch as capital, that included the southern part of the old province of Galatia and the districts of Lycaonia and Asia. Antioch was for the first time correctly described as "of Pisidia," although there is reason to believe that the term "Pisidia" had already been extended northward in popular usage to include at least part of the Phrygian region of Galatia. This usage perhaps explains the reading "Antioch of Pisidia" in Codex Bezae, whose readings usually reflect conditions of the 2nd cent. A.D. in Asia Minor. The use of the term in this way was political and administrative; ethnically Antioch remained Phrygian and retained its Phrygian identity into the 3rd cent. A.D. (see W. M. Calder, *Journal of Roman Studies,* 2 [1912], 84). During NT times Antioch was very much a Roman outpost. It was governed by *duumviri* and a municipal council whose membership was restricted to the Roman colonists. The quarters into which the city was divided bore Latin names; the city was dominated by the temple in honor of Augustus. Latin was the official language and many inscriptions of this period are in Latin. The *incolae,* Greek or Phrygian inhabitants, were regarded as separate and inferior to the "coloni."

Paul crossed Pisidia on the journey from Perga to Antioch mentioned in Acts 13:14 and again on his return (14:24). Of those journeys no details are recorded in Acts, but Conybeare and Howson suggested that the "perils of rivers" and "perils of robbers" mentioned in 2 Cor. 11:26 refer to his journeys across Pisidia. Ramsay pointed out in confirmation of this view that many Pisidian inscriptions refer to the armed policemen and soldiers who kept peace in the region, while others refer to conflict with robbers and to an escape from drowning in a river (*CRE,* pp. 23f.; cf. *Journal of Roman Studies,* 2 [1912], 82f.). The Turks call the site of Adada, a city on Paul's probable route from Perga to Antioch, Kara Bavlo; "Bavlo" is the Turkish pronunciation of "Paulos," and the name is probably reminiscent of an early tradition connecting the city with Paul.

Rural Pisidia remained unaffected by Hellenic civilization and apart from Antioch itself Jewish communities appear to have been few. The Roman occupation of the time was purely military. It is therefore unlikely that Paul preached extensively during his progress through the country. Pisidia differs from Phrygia in that none of its Christian inscriptions, except at the extreme northwest, dates from before the legal recognition of Christianity under Constantine. In the brief but savage repression of Christianity under Maximin Daia (311-312) the inscription on the sarcophagus of Bishop Eugenius of Laodicea Combusta (Ladik) shows that Valerius Diogenes, *Praeses* of Pisidia, carried out persecuting measures against Christian officials under him (W. M.Calder, ed., *Monumenta Asiae minoris antiqua,* I [1928], no. 170; and H. Dessau, ed., *Inscriptiones Latinae selectae* [3 vols., 1892-1916], no. 9480).

***Bibliography.***–*CRE,* pp. 18ff.; W. M. Calder and J. M. R. Cormack, eds., *Monumenta Asiae Minoris Antiqua,* VIII (1962); K. Lanckoronski-Brzezie, *Städte Pamphyliens und Pisidiens* (1890); *RRAM*; W. M. Ramsay, *Historical Geography of Asia Minor* (1890); *Journal of Hellenic Studies,* 50 (1930), 283-87; B. Levick, *Anatolian Studies,* 8 (1958), 219-222; A. Kryzanowska, "Monnaies coloniales d'Antioche de Pisidie," *Textes et Travaux,* 7 (1970); A. S. Hall, *Anatolian Studies,* 18 (1968), 57-92; S. Mitchell, *Journal of Roman Studies,* 66 (1976), 106-131.

W. H. C. FREND

**PISON** pī'son (Gen. 2:11, AV). *See* PISHON.

**PISPA** pis'pə [Heb. *pispâ*–'cut off, separate'(?)] (1 Ch. 7:38); AV, NEB, PISPAH. A son of Jether from the tribe of Asher.

**PIT** [Heb. *bôr, bᵉʾēr, gûmmāṣ* (Eccl. 10:8), *paḥaṯ, šaḥaṯ, šûḥâ, šîḥâ* (Ps. 57:6 [MT 7]), *šᵉḥûṯ, šᵉḥîṯ* (Lam. 4:20), *mahᵃmōrôṯ* (Ps. 140:10 [MT 11]), *mikreh* (Zeph. 2:9); Gk. *bóthynos, phréar, ábyssos, hypolḗnion* (RSV "pit for winepress," AV "place for winevat," NEB "winepress")]; AV also DUNGEON (Lam. 3:53, 55), CORRUPTION, DESTRUCTION, DITCH, GRAVE; NEB also DUNGEON (Isa. 24:22; Zec. 9:11), MUD (Job 9:31), GRAVE, "pit of death" (Ps. 103:4), ABYSS (e.g., Ps. 69:15), etc. In Prov. 28:18 the RSV follows Syr. and emends MT *ʾeḥāṯ* to *šaḥaṯ* (see *BHS*); AV and NEB follow MT. Hos. 5:2 is textually corrupt: the RSV emends to "pit of Shittim" (see *BHS* and comms.); the AV follows MT *šāḥaṭ,* "make slaughter," and the NEB paraphrases. In 2 Pet. 2:4, the RSV and NEB follow ℵ A B C etc., *seiroís,* "pits"; AV "chains" follows K L P p72 etc., *seiraís*; see R. J. Bauckam, *Jude, 2 Peter* (*Word Biblical Comm.,* 1983), pp. 244, 249.

In the OT "pit" translates two major families of words. One (*bôr*/*bᵉʾēr*) denotes the literal sense in narrative and legal sections, while used as part of the vocabulary for discussing death in prophetic and poetic material. The second (*šaḥaṯ,* and cognates of *šû[a]ḥ*; cf. BDB, p. 1001) connects "pit" exclusively with the realm of death, being found only in the prophets, Psalms, Job, and Proverbs. The NT follows the same distinction between narrative and prophetic usages.

A pit may be any cavity in the ground, though *bᵉʾēr* especially refers to a cistern, hewn to collect winter rains. Large enough to hide a person (e.g., Joseph, Gen. 37:22ff.; David, 2 S. 17:9), they were a potential danger for livestock (Ex. 21:33ff.; Mt. 12:11) as well as for people. Such a cistern could trap a lion (2 S. 23:20), or be a convenient and dishonorable grave (for Absalom, 2 S. 18:17; for the princes of Ahaziah, 2 K. 10:14; for the king of Babylon, Isa. 14:19). *See also* CISTERN.

The danger of an open, unguarded pit is a traditional metaphor for wicked or foolish schemers (Prov. 26:27; 28:10, 18; Eccl. 10:8), the unwary before the harlot (Prov. 22:14; 23:27), and the spiritually blind (Mt. 15:14; Lk. 6:39). The pit becomes their own trap (Ps. 7:15 [MT 16]; cf. Rom. 3:20), resulting in destruction (e.g., Jer. 18:22; Ezk. 19:8; Ps. 35:7; 57:6 [MT 7]).

Most importantly, "pit" forms part of the Hebrew vocabulary of death and seems to be a synonym for SHEOL (hence the RSV often capitalizes it). The common participial phrase, *yôrᵉḏê bôr,* "those who go down to the pit" (e.g., Ps. 28:1; Prov. 1:12; Isa. 38:18; Ezk. 26:20) is part of a larger literary formula: one goes down to Sheol (Ps. 55:15 [MT 16]), to the dust (Job 17:16), *šaḥaṯ* — the realm of death (Ps. 30:9 [MT 10]) and the nether world (Ezk. 32:24ff.). The formula follows Ugar. *yrdm ʾrṣ,* "going down to the (nether) world" (see Tromp). The pit is dark and deep (Ps. 88:6 [MT 7]), desolate (Ps. 40:2 [MT 3]), where one cannot praise (Ps. 30:9 [MT 10]), filled with filth (Job 9:31), a dreadful end (Ezk. 26:21), beneath even the deep (Jonah 2:6 [MT 7]; Ps. 69:15 [MT 16]). *See also* DEATH.

The pit (*šaḥaṯ*) is the realm of death (Ps. 49:9 [MT 10]) metaphorically as well as physically. To Yahweh belongs redemption from its despair or from an untimely end (Job 33:22ff.; Ps. 16:10 [MT 11]; 103:4; Isa. 51:14ff.). To Yahweh also belongs judgment. The pit is prepared for the wicked (Ps. 94:13) and for Israel's enemies (Ezk. 32:18ff.).

In the NT the pit is the home for the fallen angels (2 Pet. 2:4), the eschatological abode of the beast (Rev. 11:7) and of Satan (Rev. 9:11). God nonetheless holds the key to this bottomless pit (Rev. 9:1; 20:1, 3). *See also* ABYSS.

***Bibliography.***–M. Pope, *JBL*, 83 (1964), 269-278; N. J. Tromp, *Primitive Conceptions of Death and the Nether World in the OT* (1969), pp. 66-71; *TDOT*, I, *s.v.* "be'ēr" (Heintz).

W. R. HARRIS

**PITCH** [Heb. *kōper*] (Gen. 6:14); [*zepeṯ*] (Ex. 2:3; Isa. 34:9); NEB also TAR (Ex. 2:3). A viscous, sticky, flammable, hydrocarbon substance distilled from petroleum or coal tar and used for water-proofing, pavements, roofing and, in ancient Mesopotamia, mortar.

In Gen. 6:14 the term *kōper* clearly refers to the caulking material for Noah's ark. It is a loanword from Akk. *kupru*, which was used by Utnapishtim, the Babylonian Noah, in caulking his "ark." It probably should not be equated with the common Hebrew root, *kpr*, meaning "to cover," although its consonantal structure is identical. That the word indicates "pitch" comes primarily from the LXX which translates it with *ásphaltos*.

The second term, *zepeṯ*, is also used as a caulking material in Ex. 2:3 along with BITUMEN (Heb. *ḥēmār*). The distinction between "bitumen" and "pitch" in this context is unclear. In Isa. 34:9 it flows and burns like brimstone. Because the context places this action in Edom, it may refer to the bitumen fields S of the Dead Sea still visible today.

*See also* MORTAR. L. G. HERR

Proto-Hittite gold pitcher from Alašia (Cyprus), 23rd cent. B.C. (Hittite Museum, Ankara; picture W. S. LaSor)

**PITCHER** [Heb. *kaḏ*] (Eccl. 12:6); [*gāḇî(a)*ʿ] (Jer. 35:5); AV POT; NEB BOWL.

The Heb. *kaḏ* is translated "pitcher" by the AV in most of its thirteen occurrences. Nine of those occurrences are in Gen. 24, the story of Rebekah at the well, and clearly refer to water jars, not pitchers as we know them today. Even in Eccl. 12:6 the context is that of fountain activity, making "water jar" a better translation. In daily use it would probably have been considered a woman's vessel, because it was the woman who normally drew water. Many such water jars are found at the bottom of excavated cisterns. The term was used in the Gideon story (Jgs. 7) to indicate the vessel covering the torches.

The Heb. *gāḇî(a)*ʿ usually refers to a cup (e.g., Gen. 44:2, 12, etc.), but the context in Jer. 35:5 seems to call for a larger vessel. According to J. Kelso (*Ceramic Vocabulary of the OT* [*BASOR Supp. Studies*, 5/6, 1948], p. 17), both cup and pitcher may have had a calyx shape (cf. Ex. 25:31-34). L. G. HERR

**PITFALL** [Heb. *śeḇāḵâ*] (Job 18:8); AV SNARE; NEB PIT; [*šîḥâ*] (Ps. 119:85); AV PITS; NEB "(spread) tales"; [*paḥaṯ*] (Lam. 3:47); AV SNARE; NEB PIT; [Gk. *skándalon*] (Rom. 11:9); AV, NEB, STUMBLING BLOCK. "Pitfall" is a figurative rendering of terms that the AV translates literally. In Job 18:8 *śeḇāḵâ* is parallel to *rešeṯ*, "net," and probably refers to a grid or network laid over a pit. *Śeḇāḵâ* elsewhere is used only of a lattice work or grating ("net," 1 K. 7:17; "network," 7:20, 41f.; 2 Ch. 4:12f.; Jer. 52:22f.) in the temple; as J. Gray (*I & II Kings* [*OTL*, 2nd ed. 1970], p. 185) noted, a similar semantic variance occurs in the Arabic cognates *šabaka*, "net," and *šubbak*, "window" (both < *šabaka*, "interjoin, interweave"). *Šîḥâ* refers to a PIT dug in the ground for catching wild animals. The Gk. *skándalon* literally means a trap but is used figuratively of anything that might lead one to fall into error, sin, or destruction. Note that Rom. 11:9 is a quote from the LXX (Ps. 68:23 = 69:22 [MT 23]), which often uses *skándalon* to translate Heb. *môqēš*, "trap."

*See also* STUMBLING BLOCK. G. A. L.

**PITHOM** pi'thəm [Heb. *piṯōm*]. One of the two store-cities built by the Hebrews during their bondage in Egypt. Pithom occurs only in Ex. 1:11, but RAMESES, the other store-city, is mentioned four times (Ex. 1:11; 12:37; Nu. 33:3, 5).

Pithom is the Hebrew rendering of the Egyp. *pr ỉtm* or

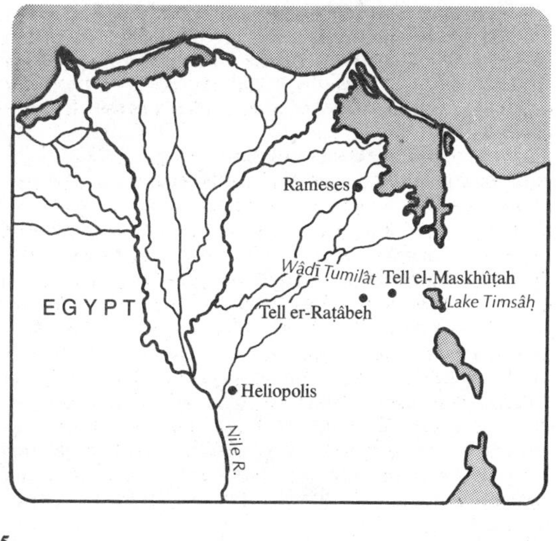

*Pr-Tm* (*Per Tum*). *Per*, meaning "house," was used to denote nonfunerary temples dedicated to a god. Uphill has argued that the term had a much wider administrative context and was used to designate a town containing a temple dedicated to a major god. Thus Thebes, sacred to Amun, could be termed "Per-Ammun." *ìtm* certainly refers to the great god Atum, a god who personified the sun, whose chief cult center was Heliopolis (biblical On, also Beth-shemesh, Jer. 43:13; Egyp. Iunu). Today the site is in the northeast suburbs of modern Cairo. Circumstantial evidence links Pithom with a city bearing the Greek name *Hērōōnpolis*. In Gen. 46:28 the LXX reads "*Hērōōn polis* in the land of Ramses" for the MT "Goshen." Interestingly, the Bohairic Coptic version reads "Pithom in the land of Ramses," thus substituting Pithom for the LXX *Hērōōn polis*. Both Naville and Gardiner argued that the god Ero (Latin Hero) was linked with Atum and consequently Pithom and Heroonpolis should be equated. Such an equation is accepted by many scholars.

The location of Pithom continues to be a matter of debate. Most of the discussion has centered on two sites, Tell er-Reṭâbeh and Tell el-Maskhûṭah, both of which are located in the eastern end of the Wâdī Ṭumilât. The latter is a fertile finger of land extending to Lake Timsâḥ from the Nile Valley. Historically the Wâdī Ṭumilât served as an important conduit into Egypt from the east; Asiatics frequently used this route coming from Palestine and Edom. Most discussions of the location of Pithom are predicated on the assumptions that Ramses, the point from which the Exodus began (Ex. 12:37), is located in the Wâdī Ṭumilât and that Pithom must be located nearby. A third assumption in much of the discussion is that the Exodus occurred in the 13th cent. B.C. Therefore, building remains from the time of the late fourteenth- or early thirteenth-century pharaohs, e.g., Ramses I, Seti I, or Ramses II, should be adduced. Three major options have been proposed.

In 1883 Naville excavated Tell el-Maskhûṭah, located 15 km. (9 mi.) W of Ismailia, and subsequently identified the site with Pithom on the basis of several lines of evidence. Inscriptional material from the site mentions Per-Atum along with the more frequent *Ṭkw(t)*. The former term occurs only in late inscriptions. Monuments from the times of Ramses II (1290-1224 B.C.) found at the site established that Atum was worshiped there. Two Roman inscriptions linked the site to Ero or Heroonpolis and thus Pithom. Naville also found architectural features which he interpreted as "store chambers." He noted that the facilities were built, in part, of bricks produced without straw. These factors led Naville to identify Tell el-Maskhûṭah with Pithom, an identification still accepted by some scholars today. Others have identified the site with biblical Succoth.

Sir Alan Gardiner was one of the first to raise serious objections to Naville's thesis. He noted that the term *Ṭkw(t)* was the more frequent designation of the site. Uphill has pointed out that although *Ṭkw(t)* is certainly the capital of the eighth nome of Egypt, it does not follow necessarily that *Ṭkw(t)* was known as Pithom. It must be admitted, however, that *Ṭkw(t)* appears in some cases to have a regional connotation; thus Pithom could be in *Ṭkw(t)*. Peet noted that Naville's "store-chambers" were more likely the typical foundations of Egyptian fortresses. Further, bricks produced without straw are not unique to Tell el-Maskhûṭah.

Gardiner located Pithom at Tell er-Reṭâbeh, a site excavated in 1906 and located 14 km. (9 mi.) W of Tell el-Maskhûṭah. He postulated this identification largely on the basis of his reading of a Roman milestone found at Tell el-Maskhûṭah by Naville that mentioned Ero. The inscription, Gardiner noted, did not indicate that Tell el-Maskhûṭah was Ero, rather that Tell el-Maskhûṭah was located about 14 km. (9 mi.) on the road from Ero to Clysma (Suez). Ero, and therefore Pithom, must be located W of Tell el-Maskhûṭah. Gardiner believed that Tell er-Reṭâbeh was ideally situated.

Petrie's excavation at Tell er-Reṭâbeh demonstrated that the site was built prior to the New Kingdom. Ramses II and Ramses III were responsible respectively for a temple, probably dedicated to Atum, and an enclosure wall. One scene from the temple shows Ramses II smiting an Asiatic by the strength of Atum. Little else is known of the site, but W. F. Albright and several of his pupils have accepted Gardiner's proposal that the site be identified with Pithom.

Uphill has proposed a third possibility and would equate Pithom with Heliopolis, the Egyptian Iunu, near Cairo. He maintained that Per-Atum would be understood by an Egyptian as a reference to the chief cult center of Atum and the surrounding district sacred to that god. Petrie excavated the site and found a large temenos, possibly built by Ramses II. It must be noted, however, that the great temple of Heliopolis was sacred to Rē -Harakhti, another solar deity, and that a "house" (Per) of Atum at the site is only conjectured.

Thus the location of Pithom remains uncertain. Of the three proposals, that of Uphill has not won wide acceptance. Current scholarship remains divided over Tell er-Reṭâbeh and Tell el-Maskhûṭah, with perhaps an edge given to the former. Further excavation seems the only hope of clarification.

***Bibliography.***–A. Alt, "Die Deltaresidenz der Ramessiden," in *KS*, III, 176-185; B. Couroyer, *RB*, 53 (1946), 75-98; A. H. Gardiner, *JEA*, 5 (1915), 242-271; *JEA*, 10 (1924), 95f.; W. Helck, *VT*, 15 (1965), 35-48; P. Montet, *Les Enigmes de Tanis* (1952); E. Naville, *The Store-City of Pithom and the Route of the Exodus* (3rd ed. 1903); *JEA*, 10 (1924), 32-36; T. E. Peet, *Egypt and the OT* (1924); W. M. F. Petrie, *Hyksos and Israelite Cities* (1906); *Heliopolis, Kafr, and Shurafa* (1915); D. B. Redford, *VT*, 13 (1963), 401-418; E. P. Uphill, *JNES*, 27 (1968), 291-316; *JNES*, 28 (1969), 15-39.

T. V. BRISCO

**PITHON** pī'thon [Heb. *pîṯôn*] (1 Ch. 8:35; 9:41). A great-grandson of Saul through Merib-baal (Mephibosheth) and Micah. The meaning of the name is uncertain; Noth (*IP*, p. 254) suggested that it is related to the postbiblical Heb./Aram. *piṯnā'*, "adder," but this seems tenuous.

**PITIFUL.** A term used by the AV three times in the archaic sense of "full of pity," "compassionate": Lam. 4:10 (RSV "compassionate"); Jas. 5:11 (RSV "compassionate"); 1 Pet. 3:8 (RSV "tender heart"). *See* COMPASSION; HEART VI.

**PITY** [Heb. *ḥāmal* (Ex. 2:6; 2 S. 12:6; Job 27:22; Zec. 11:5f.; etc.), *ḥûs* (Dt. 7:16; 19:13; Ps. 72:13; etc.), *nûḏ* (Ps. 69:20 [MT 21]), piel or pual of *rāḥam* (Ps. 102:13 [MT 14]; 103:13; Isa. 49:10; Hos. 1:6-8; 2:1, 4, 23 [MT 3, 6, 25]; etc.), *raḥ*ª*mîm* (Ps. 106:46; Am. 1:11), niphal of *nāḥam* (Jgs. 2:18; Ps. 90:13; Jer. 20:16; etc.), *ḥānan* (Job 19:21; Ps. 86:16; 102:14 [MT 15]; 109:12), *ḥemlâ* (Isa. 63:9); Gk. *splanchnízomai* (Mt. 18:27; 20:34; Mk. 1:41; 9:22), *eleeinós* ("most to be pitied," 1 Cor. 15:19)]; AV also COMPASSION, REPENT, LO-RUHAMAH (Hos. 1:6, etc.), MERCY, FAVOR, etc.; NEB also LO-RUHAMAH (Hos. 1:6, etc.), SHOW FAVOR, RELENT, WARM INDIGNATION, etc.; **PITIABLE** [Gk. *eleeinós*] (Rev. 3:17); AV MISERABLE; NEB PITIFUL.

*I. Biblical Terms.*–The Hebrews did not distinguish between emotions and the actions stimulated by those emotions; thus the Hebrew terms represented by "pity" mean not merely to feel sympathy for one who is suffering or helpless but also to come to the aid of that person. Heb. *ḥûs* ("have pity, compassion") and *ḥāmal* ("spare," "be sorry for") occur frequently in juridical contexts where they denote pity resulting in the mitigation or suspension of punishment. The niphal of *nāḥam* (AV usually "repent") occurs frequently of Yahweh's relenting from judgment and showing mercy to His people. *Ḥānan* (lit. "be gracious"; cf. *ḥēn,* "grace, favor") frequently means to show kindness to the poor and needy. The verb *rāḥam* is related to the noun *reḥem,* "womb." The Hebrews regarded the abdominal region as the seat of tender emotions (see *ILC,* I-II, 309, 525). The verb *rāḥam* and the cognate noun *raḥ$^a$mîm* generally denote the natural feelings of love and tenderness that are aroused in the strong (e.g., parents) by the helplessness and dependence of the weak, especially within the family. The Greek verb *splanchnízomai* is derived from the noun *splánchna* ("inward parts, entrails," then "seat of the emotions"; cf. Eng. "heart"). Although *splánchna* occurs rarely in the LXX, in later intertestamental Jewish writings it came to be used as a translation of Heb. *raḥ$^a$mîm* (*TDNT,* VII, 550-53). *Eleeinós,* "pitiable" (cognate of *éleos,* "mercy," and *eleéō,* "show mercy"), is used to describe the miserable condition of two groups of "Christians" whose attention is fixed too much on this life rather than on the resurrection hope (1 Cor. 15:19; Rev. 3:17).

***II. In the OT.***–The showing of pity is, above all, a characteristic of God. God's pity is an expression of His Steadfast Love (Heb. *ḥeseḏ,* e.g., Ex. 20:6; 34:6f.) toward His covenant people. On the basis of the covenant, the Israelites could appeal to God's compassion (Ps. 86:15f.; 90:13; cf. 106:44-46). They knew Him as a God who pities the weak and needy (Ps. 72:12-14; cf. 103:13f.). When His people were afflicted or oppressed, God promised salvation (Jgs. 2:18; Isa. 63:7-9; cf. Ps. 102:13f. [MT 14f.]). To a repentant people in a devastated land He promised forgiveness as well as grain, oil, and wine (Joel 2:18f.). To His people in exile He promised a return to Palestine and the provision of food and water on the journey through the desert (Isa. 49:9f.). While God was especially compassionate toward His covenant people, He showed pity also toward those outside the covenant — especially children — and even to animals! (Jonah 4:11).

God could also be motivated to withhold His pity from His covenant people because of their unfaithfulness (e.g., Lam. 2:17; 3:43; Zec. 11:6). By naming his child "Not pitied" (Hos. 1:6, 8; cf. 2:4; *see also* Lo-ruhamah), Hosea signified that God was withdrawing His fatherly protection from Israel. Yet he also prophesied that on a day of eschatological renewal the Lord would again show compassion toward His people (2:1, 23 [MT 3, 25]). The formula (or a variant), "my eye will not spare [*ḥûs*], nor will I have pity [*ḥāmal*]," occurs frequently in Ezekiel (5:11; 7:4, 9; 8:18; 9:5, 10; cf. 20:17, where *ḥûs* ["spare"] is used in a positive sense; cf. also Jer. 13:14; 21:7), always with reference to God's judgment against His unfaithful covenant people. The formula, which indicates that a punishment is to be carried out without mitigation, may have originated in the procedures of sentencing and execution. Deuteronomy uses a similar expression in prescribing the death penalty for various crimes: "Your eye shall not pity [*ḥûs*] . . ." (Dt. 7:16; 13:8 [MT 9]; 19:13, 21; 25:12).

Humans, as well as God, can show pity. It was expected that one would be compassionate toward members of one's own family; thus Edom's (Esau's) "casting off all pity" toward its brother Israel (Jacob) was an action deserving of judgment (Am. 1:11). Anyone in a helpless or dependent condition merited pity, e.g., children (cf. Isa. 13:18; Ezk. 16:4f.), especially orphans (Ps. 109:12), also captives (Ps. 106:46), the poor (2 S. 12:6). Pharaoh's daughter took pity on the infant Moses and acted to deliver and provide for him (Ex. 2:6-10). Struck down by tragedy and intense physical suffering, Job pleaded for compassion from his "friends," but he found none (Job 19:21; cf. Ps. 69:20 [MT 21]; 17:10).

***III. In the NT.***–In the NT it is primarily Jesus who demonstrates pity through His parables (e.g., Mt. 18:27; cf. "have compassion" [*splanchnízomai*], Lk. 10:33; 15:20) and through His miracles of healing and exorcism. Moved with pity, Jesus healed the blind men by the road to Jericho (Mt. 20:34), a leper (Mk. 1:41), and a child possessed by a demon (9:22-27). By His parables and healing acts Jesus displayed the compassion of God, thus revealing His messianic character as the one in whom the divine mercy was present (see *TDNT,* VII, 553-55).

*See also* Compassion; Mercy.

***Bibliography.***–*DNTT,* II, 599f.; J. L. Mays, *Amos* (*OTL,* 1969), pp. 35f.; *Hosea* (*OTL,* repr. 1976), pp. 28f., 34, 53; *TDNT,* VII, *s.v.* σπλάγχνον κτλ. (H. Köster); *TDOT,* IV, *s.v.* "chûs" (S. Wagner), "chāmal" (M. Tsevat). J. J. HUGHES N. J. O.

**PLACE.** The translation of a great many Hebrew and Greek terms, but most often of Heb. *māqôm* in the OT and Gk. *tópos* (the usual LXX translation of *māqôm*) in the NT. According to H. Köster the terms have slightly different emphases (*TDNT,* VIII, 193f.). Heb. *māqôm* always represents the "site" of a thing or event; i.e., it is defined in relation to something that is there or belongs there or takes place there. Frequently it denotes the dwelling place of a person or people (cf. Gen. 18:33; Ex. 16:29; Nu. 24:11, 25; 1 S. 14:46; 26:25); as such it can refer to a country (e.g., Ex. 3:8; 2 S. 7:10) or to a town (e.g., Gen. 18:24; 19:12-14). It can also designate a person's bed (e.g., 1 S. 3:2, 9), seat (e.g., 20:25, 27), or standing-place (cf. 5:3). In a broader sense it can denote any site (e.g., Gen. 28:11 [three times], 16f.; Ex. 3:5; Nu. 22:26; cf. 1 S. 21:2 [MT 3]).

Although its use in the Apocrypha and NT is heavily influenced by its LXX usage, Gk. *tópos* originally lacks the strong sense of possession generally present with Heb. *māqôm.* Instead it primarily denotes a geographical space. It can designate any area: "a lonely place" (Mt. 14:13, 15; etc.), "waterless places" (Mt. 12:43 par. Lk. 11:24), "various places" (e.g., Mt. 24:7 par.), etc. (cf. simply "the place," Lk. 10:32; 19:5; 22:40; 23:33). Sometimes it refers to a town or district (e.g., Act 16:3; cf. Lk. 10:1).

The use of *tópos* in Revelation reflects OT influence. Created things such as the earth and sky (20:11), mountains and islands (6:14), have their divinely assigned places (cf. Job 6:17; 8:18; 9:6; 14:18; etc.); but they are only transitory: at the end of the age they will dissolve to be replaced by the new heaven and new earth (cf. Rev. 21:1). The threatened removal of the lampstand from a disobedient church denotes the end of its existence as a part of the Church of Christ (2:5). God's promise to sustain the Church is depicted by His provision of a place of refuge for the woman during persecution (12:6, 14). Satan and his angels, however, must forfeit forever their allotted place in heaven (v. 8); cf. Acts 1:25: Judas forfeited his place among the apostles to go to "his own place" (a euphemism for hell; see comms.).

*See also* Broad Place; Clean and Unclean II.E; Dwell; High Place; Holy Place; Lonely.

See *TDNT,* VIII, *s.v.* τόπος (H. Köster). N. J. O.

**PLACE, BROAD.** *See* Broad Place.

**PLACE, HIGH.** *See* High Place.

**PLAGUE** [Heb. (vb.) *nāgap,* (nouns) *nega',* *negep,* *makkâ,* *maggēpâ,* *deber*; Gk. *mastíx,* *plēgḗ*]; AV also PESTILENCE, MURRAIN, SORE; NEB BLOW, CALAMITY, DISEASE, PESTILENCE, SICKNESS. The word "plague" occurs more than fifty times in the RSV and over a hundred times in the AV.

While the term can be used of any disease resulting in high mortality, it is most commonly associated today with bubonic infection, an affliction that was widespread in the ancient world. Its incidence was generally sudden and devastating, the infecting organism, *Pasteurella pestis,* being conveyed to people by the rat-flea. Plague is characterized by high fever, glandular swellings, extreme prostration, and a high mortality rate, often exceeding eighty percent. The enlarged inguinal lymph buboes have given the disease its characteristic designation. Bubonic plague spreads quickly along lines of communication and is fostered by filth and unsanitary conditions.

The tenth Egyptian plague (Ex. 11:4ff.) has been regarded as a bubonic outbreak, but this seems improbable because of the selective nature of the pathogenic agency. *See also* PLAGUES OF EGYPT. Though the same term (Heb. *nega'*) was used by the Philistines for the Egyptian plagues (1 S. 4:8), it obviously here refers to affliction in general. The affliction of Kibroth-hattaavah (Nu. 11:33) was most probably food poisoning rather than bubonic plague, even though animals other than rats can disseminate plague. The diseases that overtook the spies (Nu. 14:37) and destroyed Korah's sympathizers (16:47) are too obscure to identify. The plague of 25:8ff. (cf. 26:1; 31:16; Job 22:17; Ps. 106:29f.) was probably bubonic rather than venereal in nature, despite the licentious character of Moabite religious devotion. The affliction that decimated the Philistines (1 S. 5:6) and that suddenly destroyed Sennacherib's army (2 K. 19:35; Isa. 37:36) was probably bubonic. It is noteworthy that Herodotus (ii.141) spoke of rodent activity in connection with the destruction of Sennacherib's army. Plague, however, was not endemic in ancient Palestine, despite its prevalence in the southeast.

The term plague is used in various instances of an affliction other than bubonic or pneumonic plague. The prophets and psalmists spoke of various punitive incidents in that manner, while Hosea (13:14) described death as a human plague, a sentiment enlarged upon and modified by Paul (1 Cor. 15:55). In Rev. 16:21; 18:4; 21:9; 22:18, *plēgḗ* was used metaphorically in the sense of calamity.

*See also* AFFLICTION; DISEASE III.H; PESTILENCE.

R. K. H.

**PLAGUES OF EGYPT.**

I. Introduction
II. The Ten Plagues
III. Interpretation

***I. Introduction.***–A series of ten signs or wondrous judgments from God performed upon Pharaoh and Egypt through the agency of Moses and Aaron (Ex. 7–12). The central task laid on Moses through God's call (Ex. 3:1–4:17) was to go to Pharaoh and bring the people of Israel out of Egypt (3:10). In the course of this call God warned Moses that Pharaoh would not let Israel go "unless compelled by a mighty hand. So," He said, "I will stretch out my hand and smite Egypt with all the wonders which I will do in it" (Ex. 3:19f.). After Pharaoh refused Moses' initial demand (Ex. 5:1f.) and subsequently retaliated with an increase in the Israelites' work load (5:5-18), God again charged Moses to demand that Pharaoh let Israel go (7:1f.). He then added, "but I will harden Pharaoh's heart, and though I multiply my signs and wonders in the land of Egypt, Pharaoh will not listen to you; then I will lay my hand upon Egypt . . ." (7:3f.). What followed was a dramatic and classic confrontation between the power and authority of God and the stubborn will and hard heart of Pharaoh. After the initial sign of the rod that became a serpent and swallowed up the rods of the Egyptian sorcerers, to which Pharaoh paid no heed (7:8-13), God's power and authority were made known through a series of ten catastrophes, termed "plagues" in Ex. 9:14, whence the traditional name. Through these plagues both Israel (6:7) and Pharaoh (7:5) were to learn who the Lord is. After each of the first nine catastrophes God "hardened Pharaoh's heart" (7:3) and he refused to let Israel go. With the tenth, the death of all the Egyptian first-born throughout all the land, however, Pharaoh finally relented (12:29-32) and allowed Israel to depart (12:33-37).

***II. The Ten Plagues.***–The ten plagues are as follows:

(1) The water in Egypt was turned to blood (7:14-25). This happened when Aaron struck the water of the Nile with his rod in the sight of Pharaoh and his servants. It extended to the tributaries of the Nile, the canals, ponds, pools, and even the water standing in pots (vv. 19f.). All the fish died and the water became foul and undrinkable (v. 21). The magicians of Egypt then did the same (v. 22). Some of the complexity of the text is indicated by the fact that v. 17 implies that it was Moses who used the rod rather than Aaron.

The Heb. *dām* is the ordinary word for human and animal blood, but it is possible that it is used metaphorically. It is interesting and perhaps significant to note that no reversal of this condition is related. The text simply states that seven days passed after this event (v. 25).

(2) Frogs covered the land (8:1-15 [MT 7:26–8:11]), entering houses, climbing into beds and kitchen utensils and even into ovens (v. 3). This plague also occurred when Aaron stretched out his hand with the rod over the waters of Egypt (vv. 5f.), and the Egyptian magicians repeated the feat (v. 7). Pharaoh then requested that the plague be removed and stated that he would let the people go (v. 8). Moses interceded and the frogs died; then they were gathered in heaps and polluted the land (vv. 12-14), whereupon Pharaoh changed his mind (v. 15). Although the Hebrew word for "frogs," *ṣ^e^pardē(a)'*, occurs only in the plague passages and in Ps. 78:45 and 105:30, there is no question about its meaning.

(3) Gnats or mosquitoes plagued man and beast (8:16-19 [MT 12-15]). Like the first two, this plague came without warning and occurred when Aaron struck the dust of the ground with his rod (vv. 16f.). The text specifically states that all the dust of the earth became gnats. The Egyptian magicians attempted to reproduce this feat also, but could not and so confessed to Pharaoh that it was the work of God (vv. 18f.). The exact meaning of the Hebrew word translated "gnats" (*kinnîm*) is difficult to determine, but some form of stinging insect is indicated. Some scholars prefer the translation "lice."

(4) Swarms of flies covered the land (8:20-32 [MT 16-26]). As in the first plague, Moses met Pharaoh at the river and warned him. A new element then appeared: the Israelites in the land of Goshen were spared the plague of flies (vv. 22f.). Moses and Pharaoh entered into negotiations. Pharaoh offered a concession: Israel may go to sacrifice but must stay within the land (v. 25). To this Moses objected that the Egyptians would find the Israelite sacrifices so offensive as to create trouble between them (vv. 26f.). Pharaoh then assented to the original demand, ending lamely, "you shall not go very far away" (v. 28). When the flies were removed, he again reneged (v. 32). The precise meaning of the Hebrew term for "flies" (*'ārōb*) here is also uncertain. The etymology, however, suggests insects that come in swarms.

(5) A severe plague fell upon all the Egyptian animals

(9:1-7). This plague began like the second, with God's command to Moses to go in to Pharaoh and warn him (vv. 1-3). Similar to the last plague, the animals of the Israelites were spared (v. 4). The exact nature of the disease is quite unspecified since the word used (*deḇer*) is the general Hebrew term for any plague or pestilence.

(6) Boils (or inflammations) breaking out in sores came upon people and animals (9:8-12). Like the third plague this came without warning. It was caused by the action of Moses, who was commanded to throw the soot or ashes of a furnace (or kiln) into the air, so that the resulting dust created the skin lesions. Again the exact nature of the disease is uncertain, for the word translated "boils" (*šᵉḥîn*) means something like "inflammations" and is connected with a number of different diseases (Isa. 38:21; Lev. 13:18f.; Job 2:7), while the second word "sores" (*ʾᵃḇaʿbuʿōṯ*) occurs only here.

(7) Very heavy hail struck down people and animals and destroyed the vegetation (9:13-35). The pattern of the first and fourth plagues is here repeated: Moses was commanded to appear before Pharaoh and warn him of the impending catastrophe. Here the purpose of the plagues is clearly enunciated: to show God's power and to declare His name throughout all the earth (v. 16). In addition a means of escaping the catastrophe was offered to those Egyptians who had come to fear the word of the Lord: they were commanded to find shelter for their animals (vv. 19-21). Once again this plague did not fall on the Israelites in Goshen (v. 26). A development also occurred with Pharaoh. He admitted his sin and affirmed that the Lord was in the right and he and his people in the wrong (v. 27). But when the hail stopped he once again hardened his heart.

(8) Locusts devoured the land (10:1-20). Parallel to the second and fifth plagues Moses was commanded to go in to Pharaoh and warn him (10:1). In this plague Pharaoh's servants interceded with him (v. 7) and prevailed upon him to relent partially: he now negotiated over who would go and offered to let the men alone depart (vv. 9-11). Once again the plague was brought on by Moses stretching forth his rod over Egypt (v. 13). Pharaoh again admitted his sin, but now prayed that "only this once" the plague would be removed (vv. 16f.). Clearly the conclusion was drawing near, but once again the Lord hardened Pharaoh's heart.

(9) A deep darkness that "could be felt" spread over the land (10:21-29). Similar to the third and sixth plagues, the darkness came without warning (vv. 21-23). It was brought on by Moses stretching out his hand toward heaven (v. 22). This plague also did not affect the Israelites (v. 23). Pharaoh now offered to let adults and children leave, but demanded that the cattle stay (v. 24). Moses refused (vv. 25f.) and the negotiations broke off completely, with Pharaoh warning Moses that, if he ever saw him again, he (Moses) would die (v. 28). Moses agreed they would not meet again, obviously implying that he would be gone (v. 29). The narrative abruptly breaks off, not even recounting the removal of the darkness. All was thus ready for the final and decisive climax — the last plague.

(10) The death of the first-born (11:1–12:50). The form of the announcement of the last plague (11:1-10) does not fit any of the three patterns, each thrice repeated, of the previous nine plagues. Some of the complexities of the text are again evident here. After God informs Moses that He will bring one more plague and gives instructions for the despoiling of the Egyptians (vv. 1f.), there follows a speech in which Moses is clearly addressing Pharaoh (cf. the second-person address in vv. 8f.). Yet no new indications of time or place have been given. It must be understood that the arrangement here is topical rather than chronological and that this speech follows 10:29 at the end of the confrontation over the ninth plague. The first nine plagues are viewed as signs and wonders that God brought on Egypt to reveal His power and authority (7:3 and esp. 9:15f.), but the tenth, the death of the first-born, is regarded as God's judgment on Pharaoh and Egypt (7:3f.; 12:12). It is described in a passage that also narrates and gives regulations for the Passover (12:1-50).

***III. Interpretation.***–The complexities in the text, two of which were briefly referred to above, have led to the hypothesis that at least two, and probably three or more, different sources lie behind the present text. Proponents of this view are in general agreement about the separation of a Yahwist (or J) source, containing seven plagues, and a Priestly (or P) source, containing five (see, e.g., Childs). Considerable difference of opinion exists, however, as to whether the remaining material constitutes a separate source, usually identified as that of the Elohist (or E), or individual additions from another source or sources. (For a representative presentation, see Childs, pp. 130-151.) In opposition to this approach, however, some recent treatments have stressed elements that show a structure and balance that cut across the supposed sources. These synthetic elements suggest a greater unity than the theory of sources allows or can explain. Thus the first nine plagues are structured by a literary device that groups them into three sets of three plagues each (cf. the observations in the description of the plagues above). In the first plague in each set Moses is commanded to appear before Pharaoh at the river; in the second he is to "come before Pharaoh" (possibly meaning an audience at the palace); and in the third he is simply to make a gesture that brings the plague without any warning to Pharaoh. This can be diagrammed as shown below.

Another study has taken a completely different approach. G. Hort has posited that these plagues fit the natural phenomena of Egypt rather exactly, forming a sequence of unusually severe natural events that exhibit a cause-and-effect relationship between them (except for the hail) in precisely the order in which they are related in the biblical text. The sequence of phenomena in brief is as follows: The plagues begin with an abnormally high inun-

| | **Plague No.** | **Plague** | **Plague No.** | **Plague** | **Plague No.** | **Plague** | **Structure** |
|---|---|---|---|---|---|---|---|
| First Set | 1 | blood | 4 | flies | 7 | hail | Moses appears before Pharaoh in the morning at the river |
| Second Set | 2 | frogs | 5 | animal pestilence | 8 | locusts | Moses "comes before" Pharaoh |
| Third Set | 3 | gnats | 6 | boils | 9 | darkness | Moses does not appear but uses only a symbolic gesture |

dation of the Nile due to excessive rains on the Abyssinian plateau, which forms the headwater region of the Blue Nile, the principal source of the water of the Nile at flood stage. These extremely high waters would have washed down large quantities of the characteristic bright red earth of the Abyssinian and Ethiopian plateau plus reddish-colored microorganisms called flagellates. The combined effect would be to turn the Nile bloodred and create conditions that would kill the fish (the first plague). The decomposing fish would cause the frogs to desert the river banks (the second plague), after having infected them with the disease organism *Bacillus anthracis,* which would thrive in the swampy soil and the decaying fish and cause the sudden death of the frogs. The third and fourth plagues would be mosquitoes and a fly, *Stomoxys calcitrans,* both of which would breed freely in the ideal conditions created by the stagnant waters of the retreating Nile flood. The cattle disease of the fifth plague would be anthrax, caused by the dead frogs infested with *Bacillus anthracis* spores; and the "boils that break out into sores" on people and cattle (the sixth plague) would be skin anthrax, a disease principally transmitted by the bite of the *Stomoxys* fly of the fourth plague. Hail and thunderstorms (the seventh plague) coming in the time of the year that the above sequence of events requires would destroy flax and barley but leave the wheat and spelt (9:31) for the locusts (the eighth plague), whose immense numbers ("as neither your fathers nor your grandfathers have seen," 10:6) would be favored by the same Abyssinian rains that had caused the initial, abnormally high flood. Finally, the "darkness so thick that it can be felt" (10:21, the ninth plague) is an apt description of an unusually strong Khamsin, or desert sandstorm, which strikes Egypt from the south in late February or early March, usually lasting two to three days. In this case the effect would have been especially severe due to the thick layer of fine red Abyssinian dust left over the whole land by the retreating waters of the exceptionally high Nile flood.

In this interpretation it must be recognized that the miraculous consists in the fact that the events are unusually severe and that Moses has foreknowledge of each and can time his demands upon Pharaoh to fit. The events themselves are fully explainable given the climatological, geographical, and microbiological facts of the Egyptian area. Apart from the hail, they would have continued in an inexorable chain once set in motion by the abnormally severe rainfall in the Abyssinian plateau and the consequent unusually high Nile flood.

It is very hard, however, to make such an inexorable, naturally-conditioned chain of events fit the facts of the biblical account. The biblical narrative clearly and unequivocally depicts most of these scourges as happening at the express command of Moses and Aaron and in a number of cases brought on virtually instantaneously by a gesture: thus water turns to blood "in the sight of Pharaoh," 7:20; frogs cover the land, 8:6; the dust on the ground turns to gnats, 8:17; the ashes thrown in the air "before Pharaoh" become boils on man and beast, 9:10; etc. It is also very difficult to accommodate this naturalistic explanation with the fact that the Egyptian magicians duplicate the feat of the first two plagues of blood and frogs. On the other hand, both historical evidence for the occurrence of similar plagues down through Egyptian history and this empirically based hypothesis for a sequence of severe natural events show that the plagues do indeed fit precisely the natural phenomena of Egypt. It would appear that one must, on the one hand, posit that this naturalistic explanation is an unwarranted rationalization and the plagues were a series of miraculous events performed by God through Moses and Aaron, which, however, were deliberately made to fit the known physical conditions and biological realities of Egypt. Or one must, on the other hand, posit that some such sequence of natural events forms the basis for the plague narratives, and that these events were interpreted as signs of God's power in such a way that Pharaoh was constrained to allow Israel to depart; but these accounts, transmitted over many generations, were embellished by the folk traditions of the community in order to heighten the direct and miraculous action of God as a testimony to the great victory He obtained over Egypt in delivering His people from Pharaoh's bondage and power.

The first alternative seems preferable given that the last plague, the death of the first-born, is one that has no "natural" explanation. It is God's judgment on Pharaoh and Egypt and Egypt's gods (12:12) and finally convinces Pharaoh to let Israel go (12:30-32).

***Bibliography.***–U. Cassuto, *Comm. on the Book of Exodus* (Eng. tr. 1967), pp. 92ff.; B. S. Childs, *Book of Exodus* (*OTL,* 1974), pp. 121-177; K. A. Kitchen, *Ancient Orient and OT* (1966), pp. 157f.; G. Hort, *ZAW,* 69 (1957), 84-103; 70 (1958), 48-59; F. V. Winnett, *Mosaic Tradition* (1949), pp. 3ff.

F. W. BUSH

**PLAIN; PLAINLY** [Heb. pual of *pāraš*–'explain' ("make plain," Nu. 15:34), piel of *bāʾar*–'make clear' (Dt. 27:8; Hab. 2:2); Aram. pass. part. of *p*$^{e}$*raš* (Ezr. 4:18); Gk. *phaneróō*–'reveal, make known' ("make plain," 2 Cor. 11:6; pass., "be plain," 1 Jn. 2:19), *phanerós*–'visible' (Rom. 1:19; Gal. 5:19), *dḗlos*–'evident' (1 Cor. 15:27), *ékdēlos*–'quite evident' (2 Tim. 3:9), *orthṓs*–'rightly' (Mk. 7:35), *parrhēsía*–'openness,' 'outspokenness' (Mk. 8:32; Jn. 10:24; 11:14; 16:25, 29)]; AV also MANIFEST, OPENLY, etc.; NEB also CLEAR, CLEARLY, MAKE KNOWN, etc.; the RSV also employs "plainly" to render the infinitive absolute (used for emphasis) of several Hebrew verbs: *rāʾâ,* "see" (Gen. 26:28), *ʾāmar,* "say" (Ex. 21:5), and the hiphil of *nāgaḏ,* "tell" (1 S. 10:16). An adjective and adverb used to indicate clarity of speech, writing, knowledge, or actions.

In Dt. 27:8 and Hab. 2:2 the piel of *bāʾar* indicates that the words of Yahweh are to be engraved on tablets in such a way that they are easily legible. Whitewash was used on the tablets to make the writing clearly visible (Dt. 27:2, 4).

Most often, however, these words are used of clear, understandable speech. Clarity was especially important in legal contexts, e.g., Yahweh's instructions concerning the manner of capital punishment for sabbath-breaking (Nu. 15:34) and a slave's decision to remain a slave for life (Ex. 21:5). In Ezr. 4:18 Aram. *m*$^{e}$*pāraš* is the pass. part. of *p*$^{e}$*raš*, "separate, distinguish" (KoB, p. 1114); it could mean either that the letter was read "distinctly," with a pause after each word, or that it was read with a Persian translation after each section (cf. Heb. *m*$^{e}$*pōrāš*, Neh. 8:8; RSV "clearly," mg. "with interpretation"). Mk. 7:35 employs Gk. *orthṓs* to indicate that a man had been healed of a speech impediment and could now speak normally.

Greek *parrhēsía* occurs in the dative nine times in the Gospel of John. In five instances it describes speech or actions done in public (RSV "openly," e.g., 7:4, 13; 11:54). Jesus taught not secretly but "openly" in the temple and synagogues (7:26; 18:20; cf. Acts 28:31). But the term can also describe speech that is unambiguous and nonfigurative. Most of Jesus' public teaching was in parables or figurative speech that could be understood only by faith (Jn. 10:24; cf. Mk. 4:2, 10-13, 33f. par.), but He sometimes spoke to His disciples "plainly" (Jn. 11:14;

Mk. 8:32). Even they, however, could not understand His teaching fully until they had received the "Spirit of truth" (Jn. 16:25, 29-32; cf. vv. 12-15; also 14:25f.; see R. E. Brown, *Gospel According to John,* II [*AB,* 1970], 734-36; *TDNT,* V, 880f.). *See also* BOLD; CONFIDENCE.

Elsewhere in the NT "plain" and "plainly" mean "clearly known" or "manifest." On the meaning of *phaneróō* and *phanerós, see also* MANIFEST.

***Bibliography.***–*DNTT,* II, 734-37; *TDNT,* V, *s.v.* παρρησία (H. Schlier). N. J. O.

**PLAIN** (noun) [Heb. *ʿarāḇâ*–'desert' (Nu. 22:1; 26:3, 63; etc.)]; NEB LOWLAND, ARABAH (Zec. 14:10); [Heb. *biqʿâ*–'valley' (Gen. 11:2; 2 Ch. 35:22; Neh. 6:2; etc.)]; AV also VALLEY; NEB also VALE; [Heb. *kikkar*–'circle,' 'region' (Dt. 34:3; 2 S. 18:23; 1 K. 7:46; etc.)]; NEB also NEIGHBORHOOD (Neh. 3:22); [Heb. *mîšôr*–'level place' (1 K. 20:23, 25; 2 Ch. 26:10; etc.)]; NEB also TABLE-LAND (Jer. 48:8); [Heb. *ʿēmeq*–'valley' (Jgs. 1:19, 34)]; AV VALLEY; NEB VALE; [Heb. *'ereṣ hāʿēmeq*–'land of the valley' (Josh. 17:16)]; AV LAND OF THE VALLEY; NEB VALE; [Aram. *biqʿâ* (Dnl. 3:1)].

Most of the plains mentioned in the OT are identifiable. First there is the broad expanse of Mesopotamia where the first human beings lived (Gen. 11:2). Later Ezekiel had visions on a plain where the river Chebar flowed (Ezk. 3:22f.; 8:4). Dnl. 3:1 mentions the plain of Dura, which was probably near Babylon.

The flat areas on both sides of the Jordan Valley are called plains. 1 K. 7:46 (par. 2 Ch. 4:17) probably refers to the west bank while 2 S. 18:23 refers to the east. The plain of Jericho clearly is that lower and broader part of the valley in which Jericho is situated (Dt. 34:3; Josh. 4:13; 5:10; 2 K. 25:5; Jer. 39:5; 52:8). The plains of Moab are on the opposite or east side (Dt. 34:1, 8; Josh. 13:32; etc.).

Between Mt. Carmel and Beth-shean a valley runs from northwest to southeast. It is called the plain of Megiddo in 2 Ch. 35:22 and Zec. 12:11 and the Valley of Jezreel in Josh. 17:16. The war between Israel and Syria (1 K. 20:23-25) probably took place here.

The coastal plain, especially that part S of Joppa, is yet another major geographical feature of Palestine. Clearly Jgs. 1:19, 34 refer to this area. Neh. 6:2 mentions the plain of Ono, a localized part of the coastal plain a few miles SE of Joppa. The reference in 2 Ch. 26:10 is general but may indicate the coast as well.

In Neh. 3:22 the "plain" was apparently a region in Jerusalem (see NEB; *see also* JERUSALEM III.D.5.d-e). Likewise, the "plain" in Jer. 21:13 was probably a specific area of Jerusalem; in the context it appears to be the location of the king (note "house of David," v. 12; "rock," v. 13), possibly the high, level area adjacent to the temple mount.

Two texts use the image of topographical changes to illustrate the overcoming of obstacles. Isa. 40:3f. declares that the rough places shall become a plain preparatory to the coming of the Lord (cf. Lk. 3:4f.), i.e., all obstacles to His coming will be removed. In Zec. 4:7 the angel of Yahweh promises that the "mountain" of obstacles confronting Zerubbabel in his efforts to rebuild the temple will be removed.

*See also* PALESTINE IV.A.1, 4; B. R. L. ALDEN W. S. L. S.

**PLAIN, CITIES OF THE.** *See* CITIES OF THE VALLEY.

**PLAIN OF THE PILLAR** (Jgs. 9:6, AV). *See* OAK OF THE PILLAR.

**PLAIN OF THE VINEYARDS** (Jgs. 11:33, AV). *See* ABEL-KERAMIM.

**PLAINS OF MOAB** [Heb. *ʿarḇôṯ môʾāḇ*]. The waste region immediately N of the Dead Sea and E of the Jordan River that served as the staging area for the Israelite invasion of Canaan (Nu. 22:1; 36:13). It was here that Moses delivered to Israel his final series of sermons, which are recorded in Deuteronomy (1:1; 34:1, 8). *See* Vol. I, Map II; *see also* ARABAH; MOAB. G. H. WILSON

**PLAISTER.** *See* PLASTER.

**PLAITING** [Gk. *plékō*]; AV PLATTED. Interweaving or braiding of strands. The term is used to describe how the CROWN OF THORNS was made by the Roman soldiers who mocked Jesus (Mt. 27:29 par. Mk. 15:17; Jn. 19:2). The AV uses "plaiting" in a reference to the elaborate hair-styles worn by women in Greco-Roman society (1 Pet. 3:3; RSV, NEB, "braiding"; Gk. *emplokḗ*).

**PLAN** (verb) [Heb. *ḥāšaḇ*–'think, account' (2 S. 14:13; Ps. 140:2, 4 [MT 3, 5]; Prov. 16:30; Jer. 48:2; piel, Prov. 16:9; 24:8), *yāʿaṣ*–'advise, counsel' (Ps. 62:4 [MT 5]; Prov. 12:20; Isa. 14:24; niphal, 2 Ch. 32:3), *yāṣar*–'shape' (Isa. 22:11; 37:26 par. 2 K. 19:25), piel of *dāmâ*–'imagine, think, devise' (2 S. 21:15), *zāmam*–'think, plan' (Jer. 51:12), *ḥāraš*–'cut in, engrave,' 'plough' (Prov. 3:29), *nāṭâ*–'stretch out, extend' (Ps. 21:11 [MT 12]), *śûm*–'set, station' (Jer. 9:8 [MT 7]); Aram. peal of *ʿašiṯ*–'think, plan' (Dnl. 6:3 [MT 4]); Gk. *bouleúō*–'resolve, decide' (Jn. 12:10; Acts 27:39; 2 Cor. 1:17, "make plans"), *poiéō*–'do, make' (Acts 25:3)]; AV DEVISE, THINK, PURPOSE, CONSULT, FORM, etc.; NEB also PLOT, CONSULT, AIM, DESIGN, etc.; (noun) [Heb. *maḥašāḇâ/maḥašeḇeṯ*–'thought, device' (Ps. 33:10; Prov. 20:18; Jer. 18:11f.; 29:11; Dnl. 11:24; etc.), *yēṣer*–'form' (1 Ch. 28:9), *ʿēṣâ*–'advice, counsel' (Neh. 4:15 [MT 9]; Ps. 14:6; 20:4 [MT 5]; Isa. 19:3; 25:1; Jer. 19:7; 49:20, 30; 50:45; Mic. 4:12), *taḇnîṯ*–'construction,' 'pattern,' 'figure' (1 Ch. 28:11f., 18f.), *dāḇār*–'speech, word' (2 Ch. 30:4), *zimmâ*–'intention' (Job 17:11)), *maʿarāḵ*–'arrangement' (Prov. 16:1), *mišpāṭ*–'judgment' (Ex. 26:30), *sôḏ*–'counsel' (Ps. 83:3 [MT 4]), *ʿeštōneṯ*–'thought, plan' (Ps. 146:4); Gk. *boulḗ*–'resolution decision' (Acts 2:23; 4:28; 5:38, 27:42), *oikonomía*–'management,' 'arrangement' (Eph. 1:10; 3:9)]. An infinitive that shows purpose (cf. GKC, §§114f.) accounts for the rendering "planning to kill" (from Heb. *hārag,* "kill") in Gen. 27:42. In 2 Ch. 7:11 the RSV and NEB use "plan" to render Heb. *bā' ʿal-lēḇ* (lit. "came into the heart"; so AV). In Ps. 55:9 (MT 10) "their plans" (*ʿaṣātām*) is absent in the MT but supplied by the Targum. Also, the RSV "plan" in Ezk. 43:10 derives from the LXX rather than the MT (cf. W. Zimmerli, *Ezekiel,* II [Eng. tr. 1983], 410 n. 10c). Various Hebrew and Greek terms rendered "plan" refer to divine purposes, human purposes (both good and evil), architectural designs, and preparations for warfare.

In Ps. 20:4 the writer acknowledges God as the fulfiller of human plans. He is also able to overrule human intentions (Ps. 33:10), and ultimately His purposes will prevail (Prov. 19:21).

The Lord is also sovereign in regard to the nations. For example, it was His purpose for Assyria to be an instrument of judgment upon Israel (Isa. 37:26 par. 2 K. 19:25; cf. Isa. 10:5). Not only did the Lord intend for Babylon to be an instrument for judgment upon Israel (Mic. 4:15), but He also purposed to judge Babylon for its cruelties and injustices toward Israel (Jer. 50:45).

Using the Medes God planned to overthrow Babylon (Jer. 51:12). God's purposes for unrepentant Israel included not only their judgment (Jer. 18:11) but also their restoration (Jer. 29:11).

According to Prov. 15:22 human plans need careful consideration and the guidance of others (cf. 20:18). Also, it is better to be careful in planning than to be hasty (21:55). But human plans also include another aspect, for they are effectual only when they coincide with the Lord's plans (12:20). Nevertheless, a person's plans sometimes seem shattered when the end of life appears imminent (Job 17:11). And the psalmist affirms that people's intentions die with them (Ps. 146:4).

That people often intend evil towards others is a fact repeatedly confirmed in the Scriptures (Prov. 3:39; cf. Prov. 6:14, 18; 12:20; 14:22). The enemies of God devise evil plots (Ps. 83:3 [MT 4]). The psalmist recognizes that evil often is the object of human planning (Ps. 21:11 [MT 12]). In response to this the psalmist asks for divine protection from those who both plot against him and seek his downfall (140:2, 4 [MT 3, 5]). Prov. 6:18 clearly states that the Lord hates those who devise evil plots (*see* PLOT).

Several OT passages use "plan" in the sense of a mechanical drawing or blueprint. For example, David gave Solomon the "plans" for the temple that he received from the Lord (1 Ch. 28:11f., 18f.). An unusual use of Heb. *mišpāṭ* occurs in Ex. 26:30, where it refers to a pattern for the tabernacle structure (cf. 1 K. 6:38; Jer. 30:18).

Another use of "plan" occurs in passages that pertain to military maneuvers. For example, Saul intended to wage a battle against the Gibeonites (2 S. 21:5). Jer. 48:2 describes the orchestration of an attack against Heshbon. Dnl. 11:24 mentions military plans for war, while "plans" in Prov. 20:18 seems to have the same military sense.

In the NT Gk. *boulḗ* refers to both human and divine plans. In reference to the ministry of the apostles Gamaliel advises the Sanhedrin that human plans may eventually lapse, whereas divine plans cannot be overthrown (Acts 5:38). In Acts 2:23 Peter proclaimed that Jesus' death happened according to the "definite plan" of God, for it was in His plan that Messiah should suffer (cf. Lk. 24:25, 46; Acts 17:3; 26:22f.).

The translation of Gk. *oikonomía* in Eph. 1:10 and 3:9 by "plan" is debatable. Some scholars understand this term as a reference to God's plan of salvation, i.e., His arrangements for redeeming humankind (e.g., Bauer, rev., p. 559; cf. Ign. Eph. 18:2; 20:1). Others suggest that the term refers to "the manner in which God's purpose is worked out in human history" (F. F. Bruce, comm. on Ephesians [*NICNT*, 1984], p. 262; cf. M. Barth, *Ephesians* [*AB*, 1974], I, 86-88). G. L. K.

**PLANE TREE** [Heb. *ʿarmôn*; Gk. *plátonos, elátē*] (Gen. 30:37; Ezk. 31:8); AV CHESTNUT; [Heb. *tiḏhār*] (Isa. 41:19; 60:13); AV PINE; NEB FIR. Heb. *ʿarmôn* is probably the massive oriental plane tree (*Platanus orientalis* L.), which stands over 18 m. (60 ft.) and has a trunk girth of about 4 m. (14 ft.). The Hebrew root *ʿrm,* "be bare," may refer to the annual peeling of the tree's bark.

Hebrew *tiḏhār* is from a root meaning "revolve," which may allude to the somewhat whorled nature of pine and fir branches. The word is rare in Hebrew, and its identification is therefore rather difficult. Perhaps one of the juniper species is indicated. *See also* FIR TREE.

The common chestnut, *Castenea sativa* Mill., is not indigenous to Palestine, though it is found elsewhere in the Near East; the AV translation probably reflects a simple misunderstanding of the Hebrew term.

In Gen. 30:37 Jacob used the incompletely peeled rods from several kinds of trees, including the plane tree, to produce selective breeding among goats. Distinctively marked animals were thought to be harbingers of good fortune, and were esteemed accordingly. Jacob appeared to be influenced by the widespread folk-belief in maternal impressions, i.e., that some startling experience occurring at or shortly after conception would influence the appearance of the fetus. This belief has now been disproved by modern studies, in the realization that fetal abnormalities very frequently have a genetic basis. The sheep did not need to see the partly peeled rods, but only the dark goats, to breed the required color of animal. Crossbreeding of sheep and goats was attempted frequently in ancient Mesopotamia, and the offspring that resulted were valued highly. R. K. H.

**PLANES** [Heb. *maqṣuʿôṯ*] (Isa. 44:13). Carpenter's tools for scraping, planing, or removing wood, mentioned only here, in connection with the fashioning of an idol. (The NEB renders this noun verbally, "he planes the wood.") The verbal root (*qṣʿ,* "scrape") is used at least once, in Lev. 14:41, where any contaminated plaster on the inside of a leper's house was scraped off in a cleansing ceremony. Many such tools of stone and various metals are known from the ancient Near East, but these planes have not been specifically identified.

*Bibliography.*–C. Singer, *et al.*, eds., *History of Technology,* I (1954), 618-621, 687-690; II (1956), 228-231.

D. M. HOWARD, JR.

**PLANETS.** The AV and NEB translation of Heb. *mazzālôṯ* in 2 K. 23:5. The term probably denotes "constellations" (so RSV). *See* ASTRONOMY II.B, C; ASTROLOGY.

**PLANK** [Heb. *śᵉḏērâ* (1 K. 6:9), *lû(a)ḥ* (Ezk. 27:5); Gk. *sanís* (Acts 27:44)]; AV BOARD; NEB also COFFERING (1 K. 6:9), TIMBER (Ezk. 27:5); **BOARD** [Heb. *lû(a)ḥ* (Ex. 27:8; 38:7), *ṣelaʿ* (1 K. 6:15f.)]; AV also PLANK (1 K. 6:15b); NEB also PLANK (Cant. 8:9), "shell" (Ex. 27:8; 38:7). The meanings of the various Hebrew words are all determined by their contexts; in other contexts they mean quite different things. Thus *lû(a)ḥ* usually means "tablet," of stone, wood, or metal. *Ṣelaʿ* usually means "side." *Śᵉḏērâ* can mean the orderly arrangement of rank (of soldiers; cf. *sēḏer,* "order, arrangement"). In Ezk. 27:5 the MT has the dual *luḥōṯayim,* which makes no sense and is usually emended to *luḥōṯayiḵ,* "your planks," on the basis of the Targum (see *BHS*). The Gk. *sanís* is a hapax legomenon in the NT, but its meaning is clear from its use in other Greek literature (see Bauer, rev., p. 742). G. A. L.

**PLANT** (vb.) [Heb. *nāṭaʿ*]; [*šāṯal*–'transplant'] (Ps. 1:3; 92:13 [MT 14]; Jer. 17:8); [*śûm*–'set, place'] (Ezk. 4:2); AV SET; NEB BRING; [*nāṯan*–'put, set'] (Ezk. 17:5); [Gk. *phyteúō*]; (noun) [Heb. *ʿēśeḇ*–'herb']; AV HERB; NEB also WILD PLANT (Gen. 3:18), GROWING THING (Ex. 9:22, 25), VEGETATION (10:12, 15), GREEN THING (Ps. 104:14); [*ḥāṣîr*–'green grass, herbage'] (Job 28:12); AV HERB; NEB GREEN PLANT; [*neṭaʿ*–'planting, plantation']; NEB also GARDEN (Isa. 17:10), "towers" (Ps. 144:12); [*maṭṭāʿ*–'planting'] (Ezk. 17:7; 34:29); AV, NEB, also PLANTATION; [*qîqāyôn*]; AV, NEB, GOURD; [*yônēq*–'sapling'] ("young plant," Isa. 53:2); AV TENDER PLANT; [*ṣeʾᵉlîm*] (Job 40:21); AV SHADY TREE; NEB THORNY LOTUS; [*śî(a)ḥ*] (Gen. 2:5); NEB SHRUB; [*ṣemaḥ*] (Ezk. 16:7); AV BUD; NEB "something growing"; [Gk. *phyteía*] (Mt. 15:13); [*chórtos*] (Mt. 13:26); AV BLADE; NEB CORN; **PLANTER** [Heb. part. of *nāṭaʿ*] (Jer. 31:5).

The frequent use of agricultural imagery reflects the nature of Palestinian society. The agrarian orientation dates from as early as 7500 B.C., as the excavations at Jericho indicate (*see* AGRICULTURE I).

The nearly seventy occurrences of the root *nāṭaʿ* may be divided between literal and figurative uses. When employed in the literal sense "plant" includes references to people planting trees (Gen. 21:33; Lev. 19:23; Eccl. 2:5), gardens (Jer. 29:5, 28), and vineyards (Gen. 9:20; Dt. 20:6; Prov. 31:16; Eccl. 2:4).

In anthropomorphic language the Lord is depicted as planting a garden (Gen. 2:8). In this instance the emphasis is not the creation of vegetation but God's provision for His created beings (cf. C. Westermann, *Genesis 1–11* [Eng. tr., 1984], p. 208).

Figurative usage accounts for about thirty occurrences of Heb. *nāṭaʿ*. In Jer. 12:1-6 the prophet Jeremiah, like Job, wrestles with the perplexing question, "Why do the wicked prosper?" That the wicked who now flourish were "planted" by the Lord (v. 2) further aggravates the problem for Jeremiah. Though righteous, he himself suffers, while the wicked "grow and bring forth fruit" (v. 2). Jeremiah's lament and plea provide classic expression to the problem of evil.

The common metaphor of Israel as a plant often demonstrates Yahweh's sovereign action for His people. For example, the psalmist depicts Israel as a vine brought by the Lord from Egypt and planted in the land of conquest (Ps. 80:8 [MT 9]; cf. Isa. 5:1-7). Similarly, the Lord promised David that He would provide a permanent place for His people (2 S. 7:10 par. 1 Ch. 17:9). Jeremiah also affirms that the Lord of hosts "planted" Israel (Jer. 11:17). The Lord's planting is a sovereign act, which He will undo if a nation is disobedient (18:9f.). In 24:6 the images of planting and building parallel each other. Here the Lord promises not to "tear down" or "uproot" the exiles of Judah, but rather to "build them up" and "plant them." And in Am. 9:14f. the Lord promises ultimate restoration of His people: "I will plant them upon their land, and they shall never again be plucked up out of the land which I have given them."

Also Heb. *šāṯal* depicts Israel (Ezk. 17:22f.) and the righteous (Ps. 1:3; 92:13 [MT 14]; Jer. 17:8) as planted trees. Ps. 92:12f. portrays the righteous as a flourishing palm and a strong cedar that are planted in the house of the Lord (i.e., the temple). Even in old age they experience fruitfulness and strength (A. Weiser, *Psalms* [Eng. tr., *OTL*, 1962], p. 616; cf. Ps. 1:3; Jer. 17:8; 1QH 8:4-11). Clearly, the "planting" done by the Lord was a common OT metaphor. The various OT authors pressed it into service to illustrate the care and control of Yahweh over His creation.

Nearly half of the thirty-three occurrences of Heb. *ʿēśeḇ* are in the Pentateuch, where it figures in the Creation account (Gen. 1:11f., 29f.; 3:18) and in the account of the plagues upon Egypt (Ex. 9:22, 25; 10:12, 15). This word designates food for people (Gen. 9:3) as well as food for the cattle (Dt. 11:15; Ps. 106:20). Heb. *ḥāṣîr* in Job 8:12 is a type of grass that flourishes after the seasonal rains but quickly wilts in the dryness of summer, thereby exemplifying the transitory state of human life (cf. Ps. 37:2; 129:6; Isa. 40:6-8). (*See also* GRASS.)

Suggestions for the identity of *qîqāyôn* in Jonah 4:6f., 9f. include ivy (Jerome), squash, and pumpkin; however, it most likely represents the foliant castor-oil plant, *Ricinus communis* (see NEB mg.; cf. *MPB*, pp. 203f.; *see also* GOURD 1). Heb. *ṣeʾĕlîm*, which the RSV renders "lotus plant" in Job 40:21 but "lotus tree" in 40:22, is somewhat obscure, but it probably represents *Zizyphus Lotus*, a thorny tree common in Syria and Africa (cf. H. H. Rowley *Job* [*NCBC*, rev. ed. repr. 1980], p. 257).

Greek *phyteúō*, the common NT verb rendered "plant," often refers to cultivated vineyards (Mt. 21:33 par.; Lk. 13:6; 1 Cor. 9:7). In 1 Cor. 3:5-9 Paul employs agricultural metaphors to present several essential facets of establishing churches. Paul plants, Apollos waters, but God alone effects growth (v. 6). G. L. KNAPP

**PLANTATION** [Heb. *maṭṭāʿ*] (Ezk. 34:29); AV PLANT. A place of planting is indicated (*maṭṭāʿ* < *nāṭaʿ*, "to plant"), but not in the technical U. S. or West Indian sense of a large estate farmed by resident laborers. Cf. the translations "place of planting" for *maṭṭāʿ* in Mic. 1:6, and "planting" in Isa. 61:3.

**PLASTER** (noun) [Heb. *ʿāpār*] (Lev. 14:41f., 45); AV DUST, MORTER; NEB DAUB; [*śîḏ*] (Dt. 27:2, 4); AV PLAISTER; [Aram. *gîr*] (Dnl. 5:5); AV PLAISTER; (verb) [Heb. *ṭû(a)ḥ*] (Lev. 14:42f., 48); AV PLAISTER; NEB REPLASTER; REDAUB; [*śîḏ*] (Dt. 27:2, 4); AV PLAISTER; NEB also COVER OVER. The noun is a white substance usually made from a lime and water mixture which hardens as the water evaporates; used for coating wall and floor surfaces. The verb refers to the process of applying plaster.

The Heb. *śîḏ* normally means "to boil." Its use to indicate plaster refers to the slaking of lime in boiling water. It appears as both a verb and a noun in Dt. 27:2, 4. Here it is used to cover a stone for purposes of writing, a practice which was common in ancient Palestine (note the Chalcolithic paintings done in plaster at Ghassul and the Iron Age inscriptions from Kuntillet ʿAjrūd).

The basic meaning of the verb *ṭû(a)ḥ* is "overlay" or "coat." It is translated "plaster" in Lev. 14:42 because the context indicates coating with a mud plaster; the niphal is used in vv. 43, 48.

The noun *ʿāpār* normally means "dust" in Hebrew, and in the context probably indicates some form of mud plaster frequently used by the lower classes.

The Aram. *gîr* is used in the context of Belshazzar's feast where writing activity takes place on the plaster. Excavations in Babylon have shown that Nebuchadrezzar's (and thus probably Belshazzar's) throne room was covered with a fine, white plaster.

Plaster has been in use from Neolithic times (the plastered heads of Jericho and the plaster floors and statues found at ʿAin Ghazal in Jordan) to the present. Its use, however, proliferated from the beginning of the Iron Age (*ca.* 1200 B.C.) in cisterns, which enabled the settling Israelites to construct towns in the mountains of Palestine where there were no springs. Only the richest houses were coated with fine-grade plaster. Most floors were unplastered.

In Isa. 38:21 the AV translates Heb. *māraḥ* as "lay it for a plaister" (RSV, NEB, "apply"). Although *māraḥ* appears only here in the OT, the context and the use of *māraḥ* in rabbinical Hebrew indicate that it means "rub."

*See also* LIME.

***Bibliography.***–*EAEHL*, II, *s.v.* "Jericho" (K. Kenyon, *et al.*); IV, *s.v.* "Tuleilat el-Ghassul" (J. R. Lee); Z. Meshel and C. Meyers, *BA*, 39 (1976), 6-10. L. G. HERR

**PLATE** [Heb. *qeʿārâ*] (Ex. 25:29; 37:16; Nu. 4:7; 7:13, etc.); AV DISH, CHARGER; NEB DISH; [*ṣîṣ*] (Ex. 28:36; 39:30; Lev. 8:9); NEB ROSETTE; [*maḥaḇaṯ*] (Ezk. 4:3); AV PAN; NEB GRIDDLE; [*paḥ*] (Nu. 16:38 [MT 17:3]); [Gk. *paropsís*] (Mt. 23:25f.); AV PLATTER; NEB DISH. A flat household utensil used for holding food; a flat, hammered piece of metal used for decorative purposes.

None of the above Hebrew terms is equivalent to our modern household plate. Ceramic plates are rare in the archeological record; people seemed to have eaten out of shallow bowls, because their food consisted mostly of sauces or stews into which they dipped bread. The silver *qeʿārâ* listed fourteen times in Nu. 7 weighed 130 shekels, or 1.48 kg. (3.25 lbs.). We should probably visualize a large, bowllike vessel, perhaps a krater.

The *maḥaḇaṯ* of Ezk. 4:3 was an iron baking pan. In Lev. 7:9 (RSV GRIDDLE) it is used for baking cereal offerings.

The *paropsís* was a shallow bowl or plate used for eating in the Roman period. Many examples of such a utensil made of finely burnished red ware have been found in Roman Palestine.

The normal RSV translation for *ṣîṣ* is "flower," indicating that the "plate" involved in Ex. 28:36 and Lev. 8:9 was a rosette made out of plate metal. It was used to decorate the turban of the high priest.

The *paḥ* of Nu. 16:38 should be understood as gold leaf. See Ex. 39:3 where the RSV has translated LEAF.

L. G. HERR

**PLATFORM** [Heb. *kîyôr*] (2 Ch. 6:13); AV SCAFFOLD; [*gōḇah* < *gāḇah*–'be high'] ("raised platform," Ezk. 41:8); AV HEIGHT; NEB RAISED PAVEMENT; [hophal part. of *nû(a)ḥ*] ("part of the platform which was left free," Ezk. 41:9, 11); AV "that (which) was left"; NEB "unoccupied area"; [*bêṯ ṣelāʿôṯ*] ("between the platform," Ezk. 41:9); AV "place of the side chambers"; NEB "beside the terrace." A structure from which Solomon prayed before the assembly of Israel during the dedication of the temple. Albright related *kîyôr* to Sum. ki-ùr, literally "foundation of the earth," which signifies a foundation platform or the entrance to the underworld (*ARI*, pp. 152-54). That derivation has been disputed by R. Clifford (*Cosmic Mountain in Canaan and the OT* [1972], p. 180 n. 109), who preferred to see the cognate as Akk. *kiuru*, "metal basin." Elsewhere in the OT Heb. *kîyôr* refers to the bronze lavers used in the tabernacle and temple.

The MT of Ezk. 41:8-11 is corrupt. Ezekiel's ideal temple was built on a platform (*gōḇah*). *Munnaḥ*, the hophal participle of *nû(a)ḥ*, "let alone," denotes open space. The RSV apparently emends v. 9b to read *bên haggōḇah*, "between the platform."

G. WYPER

**PLATTER** [Gk. *pínax*] (Mt. 14:8, 11 par. Mk. 6:25, 28); AV CHARGER; NEB DISH. A large, shallow dish normally used for serving food.

All four instances of this word occur in the context of John the Baptist's beheading when his head is served up to Salome on a platter; no doubt this horrible irony was suggested by the banquet setting. There is no hint as to whether the vessel was metal or earthenware. Apparently it was large enough to hold a severed head. The finely slipped and burnished red ware of the Roman period called *terra sigilata* was at times made into large plates that could fit this description. Fragments of such platters are found at most early Roman sites where well-to-do individuals lived. Because it was used primarily by the rich and would have been in the palace of Herod, it may have been such a vessel that was used by John the Baptist's executioners.

In Luke 11:39 the RSV translates the same Greek term as DISH, because the context seems to indicate the ordinary eating utensil of the day.

L. G. HERR

**PLAY.** *See* GAMES; HARLOT; MUSIC.

**PLEA; PLEAD** [Heb. *rîḇ* (e.g., 1 S. 24:15; Ps. 74:22; Prov. 22:23; 23:11; Isa. 51:22; Jer. 18:19; 50:34; 51:36; Mic. 7:9), niphal of *šāpaṭ*–'go to court' (1 S. 12:7; Jer. 12:1), *teḥinnâ*–'supplication' (Jer. 37:20; 38:26), *taḥanûnîm*–'supplication' (Jer. 3:21), *tōhû*–'nothingness' ("empty plea," Isa. 29:21; 59:4), piel inf. of *dāḇar*–'speak' (Isa. 32:7), hiphil of *pāgaʿ*–'make entreaty' (Jer. 15:11), *qôl*–'voice' (Lam. 3:56); Gk. *peíthō* (Acts 19:8), *entynchánō*–'appeal, petition' (Rom. 11:2)]; AV also CONTEND, SUPPLICATION, VOICE, ENTREAT, PERSUADING, MAKE INTERCESSION, etc.; NEB also PETITION, CRY, MAINTAIN ONE'S CAUSE, PERSUASION, etc.

Although "plea" and "plead" can simply denote an earnest entreaty (e.g., Jer. 3:21), in the RSV OT they are almost always used, either literally or metaphorically, in a context of legal proceedings. The most important term, the verb *rîḇ*, is occasionally used of a legal dispute between human beings. Thus Isa. 1:17 urges pleading on behalf of widows as an example of "doing good," and Prov. 25:8f. advises, "do not hastily bring into court [*rîḇ*]. . . . Argue your case [*rîḇeḵā rîḇ*] with your neighbor himself . . ." (cf. 1 S. 12:7, where Samuel contends [niphal of *šāpaṭ*] with the Israelites after they had sinned by asking for a king).

Most often, however, the legal dispute occurs between God and His covenant people. Much has been written on the use of *rîḇ* in the prophetic literature to denote a LAWSUIT brought by Yahweh against His people for their violation of the covenant (e.g., B. Gemser, "The *rib*- or controversy pattern in Hebrew mentality," in M. Noth and D. Winton Thomas, eds., *Wisdom in Israel and in the Ancient Near East* [*SVT*, 3; 1955], pp. 120-137). In Mic. 6:1f. Yahweh summons Israel to answer charges and calls upon the mountains to act as witnesses: "Arise, plead your case [*rîḇ*] before the mountains. . . . Hear, you mountains, the controversy [*rîḇ* as noun] of the Lord . . . for the Lord has a controversy [*rîḇ*] with his people . . ." (cf. Hos. 4:1). Hos. 2:2 (MT 4) allegorically portrays Yahweh in the role of plaintiff — a husband who takes legal proceedings against his adulterous wife (Israel) and summons her children (individual Israelites) to bring complaints against her also: "Plead with [*rîḇ be*, better translated "accuse, complain against"] your mother, plead — for she is not my wife" (i.e., she has broken the marriage/covenant; see J. L. Mays, *Hosea* [*OTL*, 1969], pp. 35-38). On the other hand, Jeremiah files a legal complaint (*rîḇ*, RSV "complain") against Yahweh for allowing injustice to flourish (Jer. 12:1; see W. L. Holladay, *Jeremiah: Spokesman Out of Time* [1974], pp. 92f.). Similarly, Job uses the language of the law court in his complaints against God's apparent injustice (Job 13:6; cf. v. 3; ch. 9) and sarcastically accuses his friends of patronizing God by pleading God's case dishonestly: "Will you show partiality toward him, will you plead the case [*rîḇ*] for God?" (13:8).

Often the OT portrays God as an advocate or judge who defends His people against their persecutors (e.g., Isa. 51:22; Jer. 50:34; 51:36). Those who are oppressed and helpless — e.g., the poor and the fatherless (Prov. 22:23; 23:10f.) and victims of dishonest lawsuits (cf. Isa. 29:21; 59:4) — look to God to plead their cause (e.g., 1 S. 24:15; Ps. 119:154; Jer. 18:19). Speaking on behalf of Israel, Micah acknowledges God's just judgment upon the nation's sin but also anticipates that God's judgment will reach its ultimate purpose in salvation: "I will bear with the indignation of the Lord because I have sinned against him, until he pleads my cause and executes judgment for me" (Mic. 7:9). Thus legal language is employed "to interpret the history of judgment as a process in which the judge marvellously becomes advocate and defender" (J. L. Mays, *Micah* [*OTL*, 1976], p. 159).

In Acts 19:8 Gk. *peíthō* (RSV "plead"; cf. AV "persuade") describes Paul's attempts to "convince" (see

Bauer, rev., p. 639) the Ephesians "about the kingdom of God." In Rom. 11:2, however, "plead" is used in the juridical sense as in the OT, referring to Elijah's accusation against Israel in 1 K. 19:10, 14.

D. K. MCKIM N. J. O.

**PLEASANT PLANTS** [Heb. *niṭʿê naʿ$^{a}$mānîm*–'plants of the pleasant ones'] (Isa. 17:10); NEB "gardens in honour of Adonis." Most scholars have concurred with the NEB rendering (see also JB), which interprets *naʿ$^{a}$mānîm* as a descriptive title of the god ADONIS (the Greek form of Heb. *'āḏôn*). Adonis's numerous manifestations in the fertility cult may account for the plural form *naʿ$^{a}$mānîm*.

Although such an interpretation fits the context well, it has some problems. First, little is known about the "gardens of Adonis," which are treated briefly in only a few Greek texts (see Pauly-Wissowa, I/1, 385f., 387f.; VII/1, 807f.). Second, the LXX translates the Hebrew text *phýteuma ápistis,* not *Adōnidos kēpoi,* the regular Greek expression for the gardens of Adonis. Finally, the appeal to Ugar. *nʿm* (see L. A. Snijders, *Oudtestamentische Stüdien,* 10 [1954], 45-47) as an epithet for a deity akin to Adonis has little value, since *nʿm* is not applied to Baal, the Ugaritic counterpart of Adonis. Thus it seems best to follow the RSV rendering and interpret the reference as to some vegetation cult, perhaps a forerunner of the Adonis cult (J. Pedersen, *ILC,* III-IV, 473, suggested the Tammuz cult).

G. A. L.

**PLEASE; BE PLEASED** [Heb. *ṭôḇ* 'good' (*b$^{e}$ʿênê*–'in the eyes of,' *ʿal*–'with respect to,' or *lipnê*–'before'), *yāṭaḇ (b$^{e}$ʿênê)*–'go well (in the eyes of),' *yāšar b$^{e}$ʿênê*–'be right in the eyes of,' *rāʿâ b$^{e}$ʿênê*–'evil in the eyes of' ("not please," Gen. 28:8; Ex. 21:8), *māṣāʾ ḥēn b$^{e}$ʿênê*–'find favor in the eyes of' (Gen. 47:25), *rāṣâ*–'be pleased with, favorable to,' *rāṣôn*–'favor, liking' (Est. 9:5; Dnl. 8:4), hiphil of *yāʾal*–'agree to,' *ḥāpēṣ*–'desire,' 'delight in,' *ʿāraḇ* (Hos. 9:4), hithpael of *pāʾar*–'prove oneself glorious' ("be pleased to command," Ex. 8:9 [MT 5]), *nāʾ* (particle of urgency; Jgs. 16:6, 10), *maḥmāḏ*–'something desirable' (1 K. 20:6); Aram. *š$^{e}$par*–'seem good,' 'please' (Dnl. 6:1 [MT 2]); Gk. *aréskō, arestós*–'pleasing' (Acts 12:3; 1 Jn. 3:22), *euarestéō* (He. 11:5f.), *euárestos* (2 Cor. 5:9; Col. 3:20), *kalṓs*–'well' (Jas. 2:3), *thélō*–'wish' (Mt. 17:12; Mk. 9:13), *eudokéō*–'be well pleased,' *eudokía*–'good will' (Lk. 2:14)]; AV also "be good in (one's) eyes," SEEM GOOD, BE CONTENT (hiphil of *yāʾal*), FAVOUR, APPROVE, DELIGHT, GOOD WILL, etc.; NEB also WILL, LIKE, FAVOUR, WISH, BE SATISFIED, RESOLVE, SUIT, BE CONTENT, etc.; **PLEASING** [Heb. *nîḥô(a)ḥ*–'soothing,' *ṭôḇ* (1 K. 14:13; Est. 8:5), *ʿāraḇ, nōʿam*–'kindness' (Prov. 15:26), *ḥēpeṣ*–'joy, pleasure' (Eccl. 12:10); Gk. *euárestos, euarestéō* (He. 13:16), *arestós* (Jn. 8:29), *areskeía*–'satisfaction' (Col. 1:10)]; AV also SWEET (*nîḥô[a]ḥ*), GOOD, PLEASANT, ACCEPTABLE, etc.; NEB also SOOTHING (*nîḥô[a]ḥ*), GOOD, FAVOUR, DELIGHT, ACCEPTABLE, etc.; **PLEASANT; PLEASANTNESS** [Heb. niphal part. of *ḥāmaḏ*–'desirable' (Gen. 2:9), *ḥemdâ*–'something desirable,' *ḥemeḏ*–'charm, beauty,' *maḥmāḏ* ("pleasant place," Isa. 64:11 [MT 10]), *nāʿam*–'be pleasant, agreeable,' *nāʿîm*–'agreeable, pleasant,' *nōʿam* (Prov. 3:17; 16:24), *naʿ$^{a}$mānîm* (Isa. 17:10), *ṭôḇ, māṯēq*–'sweetness' (Prov. 16:21), *šaʿ$^{a}$šûʿîm*–'delight' (Isa. 5:7), *ʿāraḇ* (Jer. 31:26), *ʿōneg*–'enjoyment' (Isa. 13:22), *taʿ$^{a}$nûg*–'enjoyment' (Mic. 2:9); Gk. *chará*–'joy' (He. 12:11)]; AV also GOOD, SWEET(NESS), "red wine" (reading *ḥemer* in place of *ḥemeḏ* at Isa. 27:2), JOYFUL; NEB also DELIGHT(FUL), GOOD, COMFORT, KIND, WINNING, "in honor of Adonis" (*naʿ$^{a}$mānîm,* Isa. 17:10), GORGEOUS, etc.; **PLEASURE** [Heb. *ḥāpēṣ, ḥēpeṣ, rāṣâ, rāṣôn, ṭôḇ, śāmē(a)ḥ*–'rejoice' (Eccl. 2:10), *śimḥâ*–'joy' (Prov. 21:17; Eccl. 2:1f., 10), *ʿeḏnâ*–'(sexual) pleasure' (Gen. 18:12), *nepeš*–'desire,' 'will' (Ps. 105:22), *ʿāraḇ* (Ezk. 16:37), *nāʿîm* (Ps. 16:11), *ʿāḏîn*–'voluptuousness' (Isa. 47:8); Aram. *r$^{e}$ʿû*–'will, decision' (Ezr. 5:17); Gk. *hēdonḗ*–'pleasure,' 'enjoyment,' *philḗdonos* ("lover of pleasure," 2 Tim. 3:4), *eudokéō, dokéō*–'think' (He. 12:10), *eudokía* ("good pleasure," Phil. 2:13), *spataláō* ("live in pleasure," Jas. 5:5), *apólausis*–'pleasure' (He. 11:25), *chará* (2 Cor. 1:15)]; AV also DELIGHT, LIKE, MIRTH, GOOD, BENEFIT, etc.; NEB also WANT, FAVOUR, WISH, ASSET, WILL, BENEFIT, etc.

The terms "please," "pleasant," and "pleasure" are all related etymologically (<French *plaisir* <Lat. *placēre*) and are used to translate many of the same biblical terms (see above). The verb "please" means to "give pleasure (i.e., delight, enjoyment, gratification)," the adjective "pleasing" (usually occurring in the phrase "pleasing odor"; *see* ODOR) describes something that gives pleasure, and the adjective "pleasant" indicates qualities that tend to give pleasure. For a discussion of some of the more important biblical terms, see *DNTT,* II, 814-820; *TDNT,* I, *s.v.* ἀρέσκω (W. Foerster); II, *s.v.* εὐδοκέω (G. Schrenk), ἡδονή (G. Stählin); *TDOT,* V, *s.v.* "ḥapeṣ" (G. Botterweck), "ṭôḇ" (I. Höver-Johag).

Hebrew idiom often indicates that something is pleasing by referring to the gratification that it gives to the eyes (cf. the expression *ṭôḇ b$^{e}$ʿênê, yāṭaḇ b$^{e}$ʿênê,* etc.). That which is right in one's sight (*yāšar b$^{e}$ʿênê*) is pleasing because it is seen to be fitting, acceptable, and edifying.

One who pleases another finds favor with that person (e.g., 2 S. 3:36; cf. Prov. 16:7). A man who finds a young woman pleasing desires to marry her (Jgs. 14:3, 7; Est. 2:4, 9). Similarly, one acts favorably on advice or counsel that one finds pleasing (2 S. 17:4; Est. 1:21; 2:4; etc.; Jth. 7:16; 11:20; 1 Macc 1:12; 8:21; Acts 12:3). In positive relationships one person seeks to please another, e.g., one's parents (Gen. 28:8f.; Col. 3:20), one's master (cf. Ex. 21:8; Jth. 12:14), the king (Neh. 2:5, 7; Est. 1:19; 3:9), and God (Prov. 16:7). Those who please God find His favor and intimate fellowship with Him (He. 11:5; Sir. 35:16). They also escape the snares of evil (cf. Eccl. 7:26). "When a man's ways please the Lord, he makes even his enemies to be at peace with him" (Prov. 16:7).

Whatever is beautiful, enjoyable, productive, or edifying can be described as "pleasant," e.g., houses (Ezk. 26:12), vineyards (Isa. 5:7; Am. 5:11), sleep (Jer. 31:26; 3 Macc. 5:12), speech (Prov. 16:21, 24; 23:8), knowledge (Prov. 2:10; 22:18), aromas (Sir. 24:15), voices and melodies (Sir. 6:5; 40:21), a maiden (Cant. 7:6 [MT 7]), a life of obedience (Job 36:11), and brothers living in harmony (Ps. 133:1). A city located in a beautiful, secure setting is said to have a pleasant situation (2 K. 2:19). Palestine as the promised land was frequently called a pleasant land (Ps. 106:24) because it was a beautiful, fertile land that could support God's people well. But the prophets proclaimed that, because the people had disobeyed God, He would turn the pleasant land into a desolation (Jer. 12:10; 23:10; cf. Zec. 7:14). On the translation of Heb. *naʿ$^{a}$mānîm* in Isa. 17:10, *see* PLEASANT PLANTS.

Several OT passages discuss the pursuit of sensuous pleasure. The writer of Ecclesiastes decided to experiment with pleasure in order to test its value (Eccl. 2:1). He stated: "I kept my heart from no pleasure" (v. 10). Although he found a degree of satisfaction in his work (2:10, 3:13), in the end he concluded that the pursuit of pleasure is futile (2:11). His conclusion, "What use is it?" (2:2), implies the answer, "of no use." Prov. 21:17 warns, "He who loves pleasure will be a poor man." Sexual pleasure is referred to in Ezk. 16:37 and probably also in Gen. 18:12 (cf. Wisd. 7:22).

The NT repeatedly warns against pursuing the sensuous pleasures of this world (cf. also Sir. 18:31). In Jesus' parable of the Sower, the pursuit of the "cares and riches and pleasures of life" chokes out the word of God (Lk. 8:14). Those who "have lived on the earth in luxury and in pleasure" have "fattened [their] hearts in a day of slaughter" (Jas. 5:5). Pleasure in unrighteousness enslaves a person (Tit. 3:3) and leads to condemnation (2 Thess. 2:12). The author of Hebrews recalls that Moses became a great example of faith by choosing to endure hardship with God's people rather "than to enjoy the fleeting pleasure of sin" (He. 11:25). *See also* PASSION.

In many passages "pleasure" bears the connotations of "will" (e.g., 2 S. 19:18 [MT 19]; Neh. 9:37). This is particularly true when the reference is to God. God's pleasure and His will are one; there is no gap between His pleasure and His deeds (cf. Sir. 41:4). God "does whatever he pleases" anywhere in the universe (Ps. 115:3; cf. 135:6). God states, "I will accomplish all my purpose" (AV "pleasure," Isa. 46:10b). This positive, dynamic concept underscores the principle that God's will is to seek continually what is good and pleasurable for all of His creation. Because the Servant of God suffered a cruel, unjust death according to God's pleasure (AV Isa. 53:10; RSV "will"), many are justified by the merits of His vicarious death. Truly God's foremost pleasure is to bless His people (Nu. 24:1), especially those who live uprightly (1 Ch. 29:17). He is pleased to give them victory over all who oppress them (Ps.149:4; cf. 40:13 [MT 14]).

God's pleasure is often an expression of His sovereign grace. Yahweh's choice of David as king of Israel, e.g., is based solely on the fact that He takes pleasure in David (1 Ch. 28:4). Thus, people experience God's pleasure not because of any talent they possess but because they have faith in God and hope in His loyal love (Ps. 147:10f.). Nevertheless, God directs His concern to all. In Ezk. 33:11 God says, "I have no pleasure in the death of the wicked" (cf. 18:32). In the NT Jesus assures His disciples that it is God's "good pleasure" to give the Kingdom to everyone who follows Him (Lk. 12:32).

At Jesus' baptism (Mt. 3:17 par.) and at His transfiguration (Mt. 17:5 par.) God the Father acknowledged that His Son was well-pleasing to Him, i.e., God accepted His Son's obedience and set His approval on Jesus' work. Col. 1:19 gives profound theological expression to Jesus' incarnation with the words, "in Him all the fullness of God was pleased to dwell." During Jesus' earthly ministry and especially during His passion, He did not seek to please Himself (Rom. 15:3). Rather, His purpose was always to do what was pleasing to God (Jn. 8:29).

The NT exhorts each believer, like Christ, to do what is pleasing to God by bearing the fruit of good works and growing in the knowledge of God (Col. 1:10; cf. Eph. 5:8-10). The sacrifices that are "a pleasing aroma" to God under the new covenant are good works and the sharing of what one has (He. 13:16; cf. Rom. 15:26f.; Phil. 4:18). Frequently Christians must set aside the search for self-pleasure in order to edify their neighbors (Rom. 15:1-3). It is in this spirit that Paul writes, "I try to please all men in everything I do, not seeking my own advantage, but that of many, that they may be saved" (1 Cor. 10:33). Nevertheless, believers must sometimes choose between satisfying the desires of human beings and those of God. In such cases they must always seek to please God, no matter what the cost (1 Thess. 2:4; cf. Gal. 1:10).

Whatever is done to please God must be done in faith, "for without faith it is impossible to please him" (He. 11:6). Moreover, Christians can live the life of faith solely because God is at work in them, willing and working His good pleasure (Phil. 2:13). One who does what is pleasing to God and keeps His commandments has great power in prayer (1 Jn. 3:22).

*See also* DESIRE; ENJOY; FAVOR; PURPOSE.

J. E. HARTLEY

**PLEDGE** [Heb. *ʾāsar ʾissār*–'bind a binding' ("bind by a pledge," Nu. 30:2-5, 7, 10f. [MT 3-6, 8, 11f.]), *ʾissār* (Nu. 30:12 [MT 13]), *ʾ$^{ĕ}$sār* (Nu. 30:14 [MT 15]), *ḥāḇal* ("take in [for a] pledge," Dt. 24:6, 17; Job 24:3, 9; "taken in pledge," qal pass. part., Am. 2:8; "exact a pledge," Job 22:6; "hold in pledge," Prov. 20:16b; 27:13b), *ḥāḇal ḥ$^{a}$ḇōl* ("take in pledge," Ex. 22:26 [MT 25]), *ḥ$^{a}$ḇōl* (Ezk. 18:12, 16; 33:15), *ḥ$^{a}$ḇōlâ* (Ezk. 18:7), *ʿ$^{a}$ḇaṭ ʿ$^{a}$ḇôṭ* ("fetch a pledge," Dt. 24:10), *ʿ$^{a}$ḇôṭ* (Dt. 24:11-13), *ʿaḇṭîṭ* (Hab. 2:6), *ʿērāḇôn* (Gen. 38:17f., 20; perhaps Job 17:3a), *nāṯan yāḏ*–'give a hand' (Ezr. 10:19; "pledge allegiance," 1 Ch. 29:24), *tāqaʿ kap*–'strike a palm (of a hand)' ("give a pledge," Prov. 6:1b; 17:18a; 22:26a); Gk. *pístis*–'faith' (1 Tim. 5:12)]; AV also BOND, SUBMIT, "strike the hand," etc.; NEB also (GIVE A) GUARANTEE, (BINDING) OBLIGATION, etc.; **SECURITY** [Heb. *t$^{e}$śûmeṯ yāḏ* (Lev. 6:2 [MT 5:21]); Gk. *hikanós* (Acts 17:9)]; AV also "fellowship" (Lev. 6:2); NEB CONTRACT, BOUND; **SURETY** [Heb. *ʿāraḇ* ("be/become/give surety," Gen. 43:9; 44:32; Ps. 119:122; Prov. 6:1a; 11:15; 17:18b; 20:16a; 22:26b; 27:13a); Gk. *éngyos* (He. 7:22)]; AV also "strike the hand," (TAKE A) PLEDGE; NEB also PLEDGE, GUARANTOR; **SURETYSHIP** [Heb. *tôq$^{e}$ʿîm*] (Prov. 11:15); AV SURETISHIP; NEB STAND SURETY. *See also* SECURITY and SURETY for other senses of these words.

Taking or giving a pledge has two main foci in the OT: (1) security, and (2) personal obligation. Security was presented to guarantee the fulfillment of a transaction; e.g., Judah gave Tamar his signet, cord, and staff for security until he could pay her a kid from the flock in return for her sexual favors (Gen. 38:12-20). The OT has strict legislation to protect the poor in matters of security. A poor man's outer garment, which was often his only covering for the night, was never to be kept after sundown (Ex. 22:26f.; Dt. 24:12f.; cf. Mt. 5:40; Lk. 6:29). A widow's garment could not be taken even for a few hours (Dt. 24:17). The creditor could not secure anything that related to the earning of a debtor's livelihood, e.g., a millstone (Dt. 24:6). Neither could a lender enter a house to find a pledge; the pledge remained under the control of the debtor until he brought it out (Dt. 24:10f.). The wisdom literature discourages the astute youth from giving or becoming a pledge for another, especially a stranger (Prov. 6:1-5; 22:26f.). But the one having business with a person who has become security for a foreigner needs to keep that person's garment as a pledge (Prov. 20:16; 27:13). See W. McKane, *Proverbs* (*OTL*, 1970), pp. 542f.

Humankind has a strong tendency to find a loophole in the law. Some used the laws regulating security to enhance their own wealth by outdoing the poor and the simple (Hab. 2:6; cf. Job 22:6). Others blatantly violated the law against keeping pledged garments (Am. 2:8). Particularly perverse were those who took a poor man's child in pledge (Job 24:9). Thus it becomes evident why restoring a pledge was a sign that a person truly repented of his evil ways and was seeking God (Ezk. 33:14-16; 18:5-17).

Pledging also involved personal obligation; a person bound himself, often by a ceremonial gesture, to follow a certain course of action. Heb. *nāṯan yāḏ* (lit. "give a hand"; e.g., 1 Ch. 29:24; Ezr. 10:19) and *tāqaʿ kap* (lit. "strike a hand"; e.g., Prov. 22:26) denote the sealing of an obligation; hence each phrase is translated "pledge," or "be a surety." The leaders and the sons of David obligated themselves publicly to support King Solomon (1 Ch. 29:24). Under the inspiration of the teaching of Ezra the priests who had entered into mixed marriages pledged to put aside their foreign wives (Ezr. 10:19).

An adult male was free to obligate himself to a course of action by making a vow to God. But only a widowed or divorced woman had the same freedom. An unmarried woman's pledge was negated if her father expressed disapproval on the same day that he heard of it, and a husband could veto his wife's pledges in the same way (Nu. 30).

The concept of pledge also appears in regard to one's faith in God. In a strong affirmation of faith Job pled with God to give surety so that he could be released from his suffering while he waited for his vindication (Job 17:3).

When Jason and his friends were brought before the local authorities of Thessalonica for harboring Paul, a suspected troublemaker, they had to give security before they were released (Acts 17:1-9). This security was either an oath or some other kind of guarantee, perhaps a deposit of money. Most likely they promised to send Paul away from the city and not to entertain him again in one of their homes.

In 1 Tim. 5:11f. Paul instructed Timothy not to enroll younger widows, those under sixty, on an official list of widows. Those who were entered on this list received support from the church and bound themselves by an oath or pledge to serve Christ through good works and not to remarry. Paul discouraged a younger widow from being admitted to this order, lest after a time she, yielding to desire, remarry and come under condemnation for breaking her earlier pledge (Gk. *pístis*). In this case *pístis* means an agreement; no doubt it was sealed by vows taken before the local assembly of believers.

*See also* DEBT; GUARANTEE. J. E. HARTLEY

**PLEIADES** plē′ə-dēz [Heb. *kîmâ*] (Job 9:9; 38:31; Am. 5:8); AV also "seven stars" (Am. 5:8). An open cluster of stars, part of the zodiacal constellation of Taurus the Bull. In Greek mythology the Pleiades were the seven daughters of Atlas who were pursued by Orion and changed into stars just as Orion was about to catch them. The three OT passages mention the constellation to contrast mankind's weakness and the Lord's creative might.

Although the meaning and etymology of Heb. *kîmâ* are obscure, the versions generally support the translation "Pleiades." See the comms., esp. E. Dhorme on Job (Eng. tr. 1967), p. 132; H. W. Wolff on Amos (Eng. tr., *Hermeneia*, 1977), p. 241; see also G. Schiaparelli, *Astronomy in the OT* (1905), p. 62.

*See also* ASTRONOMY. N. GREEN

**PLENTY; PLENTEOUS; PLENTIFUL; PLENTIFULLY** [Heb. *śāḇāʿ*–'satiety'] (Gen. 41:29-31, 34, 47, 53; Prov. 3:10); NEB also "corn," "good years"; [qal of *śāḇē(a)ʿ*–'be sated, satisfied'] (Prov. 12:11; 20:13; 28:19; Jer. 44:17); AV also "be satisfied with"; NEB also ENOUGH, "lead to," "your fill"; [*rōḇ*–'greatness, abundance'] (Gen. 27:28; 1 K. 10:27; 2 Ch. 1:15; 9:27; 31:10; Job 26:3); NEB also "to spare," "foolish"; [hiphil of *rāḇâ*–'multiply'] (Ps. 130:7); NEB "great"; [*šāmēn*–'fat'] (Isa. 30:23); [*karmel*–'orchard'] (Jer. 2:7); NEB FRUITFUL; [qal of *ʾāḵal*–'eat'] (Joel 2:26); NEB "your fill"; [*day*–'enough'] (Est. 1:18); AV "too much"; NEB ENDLESS; [Gk. *polýs*–'many, much'] (Mt. 9:37 par. Lk. 10:2); AV also "great"; NEB "heavy"; [*euphoréō*–'be fruitful'] (Lk. 12:16); NEB "heavy"; [*perisseúō*–'abound, be rich in'] (Phil. 4:12).

The Heb. *śāḇāʿ* occurs six times in Gen. 41, where the RSV translates it "plenty" and "plenteous" with reference to the famous seven years of plenty in the Joseph narrative. Prov. 3:10 teaches that a consequence of honoring the Lord with one's substance and first fruits will be barns filled with "plenty" and vats "bursting with wine" (cf. Heb. *śāḇāʿ wᵉṯîrôš*, lit. "plenty and new wine"); i.e., the full life will come to those whose lives are properly disposed toward stewardship and respect of God. Here the NEB translates *śāḇāʿ* as "corn" in the light of the LXX *plēsmonḗs sítǭ*, "filled with grain"; cf. the Phoenician inscription of Azitawadda, line A.III.9, where the same pairing, *śbʿ wtrš*, occurs with the meaning "grain and new wine" (*KAI*, I, 6; II, 38; *ANET*, p. 654; cf. M. Dahood, *Proverbs and Northwest Semitic Philology* [1963], p. 9).

In five instances the RSV renders the cognate Hebrew verb *śāḇē(a)ʿ* as "have plenty." Prov. 12:11 contrasts the industrious farmer who, though finding life a struggle, at least has "plenty" to eat, with the thoughtless dreamer who "spends his time chasing rainbows" (R. B. Y. Scott, *Proverbs* [*AB*, 1965], p. 89). (See also Prov. 28:19; cf. Prov. 20:13 and "The Instruction of Amen-em-opet," ch. 6, in *ANET*, p. 422).

The common Hebrew substantive *rōḇ* is twice translated by the RSV as "plenty" — in Gen. 28:27, referring to an abundance of grain, and in 2 Ch. 31:10, concerning food left over. It is also rendered "plentiful" in 1 K. 10:27 (par. 2 Ch. 1:15; 9:27) in reference to the cedars made abundant by Solomon. In Job 26:3 *wᵉṯûšîyâ lārōḇ hôḏāʿtā* is translated by the RSV "and plentifully declared sound knowledge" (cf. NEB, "what sound advice to the foolish?"; see comms.).

The words of Yahweh in Jer. 2:7 picture the entry into Canaan thus: "And I brought you into a plentiful land" (Heb. *ʾereṣ hakkarmel*; only here is Heb. *karmel* translated "plentiful" in the RSV). In the phrase *waʾᵃḵaltem ʾāḵôl wᵉśāḇôa(a)ʿ*, "You shall eat in plenty and be satisfied" (Joel 2:26), the infinitive absolute immediately follows the cognate finite verb, a common Hebrew syntactical device for adding a durative nuance to the verbal action. Thus here it literally means "you shall continually eat," or the like, hence the RSV "eat in plenty."

In the NT "plenty" occurs only in Phil. 4:12, where it renders Gk. *perisseúō*, "abound, be rich in, be more than enough." Here *perisseúō* is paired antithetically with *tapeinóō*, "lower, humble, lack" (itself more commonly paired with *hypsóō*, "lift up, exalt"): "I know how to be abased, and I know how to abound."

The Gk. *polýs* is translated "plentiful" in Mt. 9:37 par. Lk. 10:2 with regard to the full readiness of the eschatological harvest. Jesus' charge, "The harvest is plentiful, but the laborers are few," addressed to the Seventy in Luke, in Matthew is given to the disciples just prior to the mission of the Twelve.

The Gk. *euphoréō*, a hapax legomenon in the NT, appears in the parable of the barn-building fool (Lk. 12:16) in reference to the yield of abundant crops from his lands (cf. NEB "heavy"). D. G. BURKE

**PLEROMA** plā′rō-mə [Gk. *plḗrōma*]. A Greek word, used seventeen times in the NT, that has at least three possible meanings: "that which is filled"; "that which fills or fills up," i.e., "completes"; and "that which is brought to fulness or completion."

The first meaning does not seem to occur in the Scriptures, but the other two meanings play an important role in certain key biblical texts. Examples of the second meaning include the citation of Ps. 24:1 (LXX) in 1 Cor. 10:26; Mt. 9:16 where *plērōma* refers to a "patch" that fills up the hole in a torn garment; Mk. 6:43; 8:20.

Under the third meaning should be placed Rom. 11:25, the "full number, totality" (of the Gentiles), and 15:29, the "full measure" (of Christ's blessing). Rom. 13:10 describes love as the *plērōma* of the law. This has been construed as "the sum total of the law's prescriptions and demands"; but it is possible that the correct meaning here is "fulfillment," i.e., that love, like the Lord Jesus, is the "end" of the law (Rom. 10:4; cf. Gal. 5:14; 6:2) in that love brings the law to its full realization and perfect completion (cf. Mt. 5:17; 26:56; Mk. 1:15). This nuance leads to those verses in Colossians and Ephesians in which the precise meaning of *plērōma* is disputed.

Colossians 1:19 and 2:9 are best taken together. The meaning of *plērōma* in 2:9 is clear from its modification by *tḗs theótētos*; it undoubtedly means "the fulness of deity," i.e., the totality of the Godhead that dwells in Christ; and this meaning may be decisive in correctly interpreting *pán tó plḗroma* in 1:19. One way to interpret 1:19 is to take *plērōma* as a quasi-technical term of early gnostic speculation, which used it to denote the region inhabited by the "full number" of intermediary beings that were thought to exist between the Creator God and the created world. (Cf. Ernst, pp. 41-50, for the background of *plērōma* in gnostic thought. The more important texts, drawn from the Valentinians, are cited and discussed by Lohse, pp. 57f.) The alternative is to take *plērōma* as meaning "God in His fulness," "the entirety of God's attributes, His full divinity," which was pleased to dwell in Christ (so RSV, supplying "of God").

According to the first view, Paul is combating speculative teachers at Colossae who reduced Christ to a member of the celestial hierarchy. The apostle responds to this teaching by asserting that Christ is the fulness of these intermediary beings. They are subsumed in Him, for He is the *plērōma* of them all. (See R. P. Martin, *Colossians and Philemon* [*NCBC*, repr. 1981], pp. 59f., 79f. for further comment.) This view, which assumes that Paul and the Colossian heretics used a common term, has been supported by many scholars, e.g., Lightfoot, Scott, R. Bultmann (*Theology of the NT,* II [Eng. tr., 1955], 149ff.), and (with modification) Lohse.

Opposition to this view has taken several forms. The older arguments focused on the lack of convincing evidence for an early gnostic creed in the 1st century. While this position is still viable, the data of the Nag Hammadi finds give some indication that incipient "gnosticism" (or, better, gnostic religion) arose apart from second-century Christianity and developed alongside the Pauline gospel in Hellenistic society contemporaneous with the apostolic communities. More convincingly, P. D. Overfield (*NTS,* 25 [1978/79], 384-96) has insisted that Paul in Colossians is not indebted to gnostic ideas for his understanding of *plērōma.* He argued that God Himself is called *plērōma* in the text; *plērōma* does not refer to the vast space separating God from the world. Moreover, there is no descent of the Redeemer from the *plērōma* in Pauline incarnational Christology (see E. Schweizer, "Paul's Christology and Gnosticism," in M. D. Hooker and S. G. Wilson, eds., *Paul and Paulinism: Essays in Honour of C. K. Barrett* [1982], pp. 115-123).

Another group of interpreters (e.g., Kehl, p. 119; O'Brien, p. 52) have perceptively observed that the tautologous expression "all the *plērōma*" appears to have been chosen for polemical purposes. This full expression was evidently meant to deny what some were asserting at Colossae, namely, that Christ was only one emanation of deity and not the fulness of divine life and power. Thus Paul may well be reacting to a Colossian term and redefining it. Recognizing that the use of *plērōma* in Stoic thought and the Hermetic writings is not a real parallel, a considerable body of recent scholarship (e.g., Masson; Moule, pp. 164-69; Kehl, pp. 116-125; J. G. Gibbs, *Creation and Redemption* [1971], pp. 107f.; O'Brien, p. 52) has argued that one need not look beyond the OT for the source of Paul's use of *plērōma*. This group interprets *plērōma* as the Greek equivalent of Heb. *m$^e$lō'* (for the LXX usage see Ernst, pp. 22-30; the most important texts are Ps. 24:1; Jer. 8:16; 47:2; Ezk. 12:19; 19:7; 30:12). God Himself, moreover, fills the universe (Jer. 23:24; Ps. 72:19) with His glory (Isa. 6:3; Ezk. 43:5; 44:4, where the cognate *plḗrēs,* "full," occurs). This view sees Paul's use of *plērōma* as parallel with the logos Christology of Jn. 1:1-18, conveying the christological thought of God's essence now embodied in Christ: in Christ the total of divine attributes dwells and is revealed and communicated to humankind.

In Ephesians *plērōma* is understood by some commentators as applying to the Church as well as to Christ. This would confirm the view that Paul does not use *plērōma* in any technical "gnostic" sense. In Eph. 1:10 (cf. "fulfil," Mt. 5:17 and Mk. 1:15; "fully," Gal. 4:4) the thought is that God's foreordained plan, at the climax of salvation history ("the fulness of time"), has been consummated in that the entire universe is placed under the cosmic Christ.

Ephesians 1:22f. may be interpreted in a number of ways, which have been listed with admirable clarity by R. Yates (*Expos.T.,* 83 [1972], 146-151). The real question is whether *plērōma* ("fulness," v. 23) refers to the Church (so AV, RV, RSV), which is then to be taken actively as that which completes Christ who is filling all things (corresponding to Eph. 4:10; so J. Dupont, *Gnosis: la connaissance religieuse dans les épîtres de Saint Paul* [1949], p. 424 n. 1) or passively as that which is filled by Christ; or whether *plērōma* should be treated as in apposition to "him" in v. 22 and so taken to apply to the Lord Himself as the one who has been designated by God the Father as the fulness of the Godhead who fills all in all (as in 1 Cor. 15:28). This latter interpretation has the advantage of harmonizing with the rest of the Epistle (4:10) and with the teaching of *plērōma* in Colossians noted above. See Moule for a defense of this view; Synge also takes *plērōma* as a reference to Christ.

Ephesians 3:19 confirms the understanding of *plērōma* as a christological title. This verse is another expression of the hope that "Christ may dwell in your hearts by faith" (3:17); 4:12f. envisions the whole body of believers coming into such an experience.

Another interpretation pays close attention to the voice of the verb (passive or middle) in Eph. 1:23. Christ is being fulfilled or is filling Himself; but by or with whom? One answer is that He is fulfilled by the Christians who, as members of His body, "complement" the head and together form the "whole Christ" (so J. A. Robinson [*Ephesians* (1903), pp. 42-45, 152, 255-59]; F. W. Beare, *IB,* X, 636). On the other hand, W. L. Knox (*St. Paul and the Church of the Gentiles* [1939], pp. 186f.), L. S. Thornton (*Common Life in the Body of Christ* [1941], ch. 10), and J. A. T. Robinson propose the translation "that which is filled by him who is always being filled (by God)," i.e., the Church is constantly receiving from Christ its head the complete fulness that Christ receives from the Father (see J. A. T. Robinson, p. 65 n. 3).

***Bibliography.***–M. Barth, *Ephesians,* I-II (*AB,* 1974); J. Ernst, *Pleroma und Pleroma Christi* (1970); F. Fowler, *Expos.T.,* 76 (1965), 294; N. Kehl, *Der Christushymnus im Kolosserbrief* (1967); J. B. Lightfoot, *St. Paul's Epistles to the Colossians and to*

*Philemon* (3rd ed. 1897), pp. 255, 271; E. Lohse, *Colossians and Philemon* (Eng. tr., *Hermeneia*, 1971); C. Masson, *L'épître de Saint Paul aux Colossiens* (*Comm. du NT*, 1950); C. F. D. Moule, *Epistles of Paul the Apostle to the Colossians and to Philemon* (*CGT*, 1957), Appendix IV; *SJT*, 4 (1951), 79-86; P. T. O'Brien, *Colossians-Philemon* (*Word Biblical Comm.*, 1982); P. D. Overfield, *NTS*, 25 (1978/79), 384-396; E. Percy, *Die Probleme der Kolosser- und Epheserbriefe* (1946); J. A. T. Robinson, *The Body* (*SBT*, 1/5, 1952), pp. 65-72; E. F. Scott, *Epistles to the Colossians, to Philemon and to the Ephesians* (*MNTC*, 1930); F. C. Synge, *Epistle to the Ephesians* (1941). R. P. MARTIN

**PLOT** (vb.) [Heb. *ḥāšaḇ*–'think, account'] (Est. 9:24; Ps. 36:4 [MT 5]; 52:2 [MT 4]; Jer. 18:18; Nah. 1:9 [piel], 11); AV IMAGINE, DEVISE; NEB MAKE PLOTS, DECIDE, etc.; [*zāmam*–'think, plan'] (Ps. 31:13 [MT 14]; 37:12), AV also DEVISE; [*hāgâ*–'devise, plan'] (Ps. 2:1); AV IMAGINE; [*kārâ*–'dig'] (Prov. 16:27); AV DIGGETH UP; NEB REPEATS; [*ʿāśâ*] (Isa. 32:6); AV WORK; NEB HATCH; [*qāšar*–'bind, league together'] (Neh. 4:8 [MT 2]); AV CONSPIRE; NEB BAND; [hiphil part. of *ḥāraš*–'cut in, engrave,' 'plough,' 'devise'] (1 S. 23:9); AV SECRETLY PRACTISE; NEB PLAN; [niphal of *dāḇar*–'speak'] (Ps. 119:23); AV SPEAK; NEB SCHEMING TOGETHER; [Gk. *symbouleúō*–'consult, plot'] (Acts 9:23); (noun) [ Heb. *maḥᵃšāḇâ*–'thought, device']; AV DEVICE; NEB also "what to do" (Jer. 18:18); [*ḥēpeś*–'(shrewd) device, plot'] (Ps. 64:6 [MT 7]); AV SEARCH; NEB etc.; [*zāmām*–'plan, device'] ("evil plot," Ps. 140:8 [MT 9]); AV WICKED DEVICE; NEB "designs against me"; [*rōḵes*–'league, band'] (Ps. 31:20 [MT 21]); AV PRIDE; NEB "in league together"; [*sôḏ*–'council,' 'counsel'] (Ps. 64:2 [MT 3]); AV COUNSEL; NEB FACTIONS; [*ʿēṣâ*–'counsel, advice'] (Jer. 18:23); AV COUNSEL; [Gk. *epiboulḗ*–'plot, conspiracy']; AV "lying in wait"; NEB also PLANS (Acts 9:24), MACHINATIONS (20:19); [*systrophḗ*–'plot, conspiracy'] (Acts 23:12); AV, NEB, "(a) banding together." The Hebrew and Greek terms primarily refer to the activity of planning and the plan itself, usually with the negative connotation of scheming.

The verb most frequently translated "plot" by the RSV is Heb. *ḥāšaḇ*. Basically the root means "plan, devise," and refers to the cognitive activity of people as well as God. It also reflects such nuances as "meditate" (e.g., Mal. 3:16), "invent" (e.g., Ex. 31:4), "impute" (e.g., Gen. 15:6), and "esteem" (e.g., Isa. 53:4). But when the context indicates that the planning has evil intent it is translated "plot."

Similarly, though Heb. *zāmam* may have a good sense (e.g., the virtuous woman who "considers" a field in Prov. 31:16), it often refers to the evil intentions of wicked persons (e.g., Gen. 11:6; Dt. 19:19; Prov. 30:32). Often Heb. *kārâ* figuratively expresses plotting against others (e.g., Ps. 7:15 [MT 16]; 57:6 [MT 7]; 119:85; Prov. 26:27; Jer. 18:20, 22). Similarly, the qal of Heb. *ḥāraš* occasionally means "devise" in a bad sense (e.g., Job 4:8; Prov. 3:29; 6:14, 18; 12:20). In Ps. 119:23 "plotting against" translates the niphal of Heb. *dāḇar* with the preposition *bᵉ*. This construction approximates *bᵉ* with the piel of Heb. *dāḇar*, which the RSV translates "speak against" (e.g., Nu. 12:1, 8; 21:5, 7; Ps. 50:20; 78:19).

The Hebrew noun *maḥᵃšāḇâ* (<*ḥāšaḇ*, "think, account") has several meanings. When translated "plot" in the RSV it connotes "schemings" (Est. 8:3; 9:25; Jer. 18:18; Dnl. 11:25). But it also may simply mean "thoughts," e.g., the Lord's thoughts (Jer. 29:11), the thoughts of the wicked (Gen. 6:5), or the thoughts of the righteous (Prov. 12:5). Also, Ex. 31:4 and 35:32, the "artistic designs" (Heb. *maḥᵃšāḇōt*) of the tabernacle created by the divinely enabled craftsmen (cf. Ex. 35:33, 35).

Usually the word "plot" in the RSV reflects the idea of scheming. Plotting is associated with the wicked. The godless premeditate their evil actions before effecting them (Ps. 36:4 [MT 5]). Their plans are secretive (64:2) and intended for destruction (52:2 [MT 4]) and evil (Prov. 16:27). According to Isa. 32:6 the fool is the one who machinates evil.

Several individuals and groups in the OT figure as victims of evil plans. David was the object of Saul's schemings (1 S. 23:9). During the Exile, Jeremiah suffered from conspiracies against him (e.g., Jer. 18:18, 20, 22f.). Likewise the Jews endured schemes during the postexilic period (e.g., Est. 8:3; 9:24, 25). While rebuilding the wall around Jerusalem, Nehemiah and his workers faced plannned opposition from the Samaritans (Neh. 4:7-23 [MT 1-17]). The psalmist lamented that some plotted to take his life (Ps. 31:13 [MT 14]).

But the psalmist reminds the righteous to expect the wiles of the wicked and not to react with alarm (37:12). He commits himself to God's statutes (119:23f.), and invokes God to shelter him from the secret plans of the wicked (64:2 [MT 3]; cf. 83:3 [MT 4]) and to frustrate their schemes (140:8 [MT 9]). Elsewhere (31:20 [MT 21]) he thanks God for His benevolence toward the righteous and for His protection of the righteous from schemers (see the comms. for the proposed revocalizations of *zāmām* in 140:8 and the disputed meaning of *rōḵes* in 31:20).

The psalmist realizes that the plans of the wicked are futile and useless (Ps. 2:1). Though plotting against others (Prov. 16:27), the wicked may eventually fall into the pits dug by their own hands (Ps. 7:15f. [MT 16f.]; 57:6 [MT 7]; cf. Prov. 26:27). Nevertheless, God in His goodness is able to protect the righteous from conspirators (Ps. 31:20 [MT 21]). Ultimately the wicked will receive just recompense for their craftiness (37:2, 9f., 13-15, 20, 38).

In the NT Paul was the object of various plots. After Paul's conversion the Jews planned to kill him (Acts 9:23), but Paul learned of their plan (Gk. *epiboulḗ*) and escaped. Acts 20:3 records a similar incident while Paul was in Greece. Later at Miletus Paul recalls his previous experiences of persecution by the Jews (20:19). He senses that a dubious future awaits him as he prepares for a return to Jerusalem (20:22f.). Because of a conspiracy by the Jews against his life, Paul was escorted by Roman soldiers to Caesarea (Acts 23:12-35), where he appeared before Felix (ch. 24).

Interestingly, the actions of the Jewish religious leaders who persecuted Paul resemble the maneuvers of the chief priests and elders who sought to arrest and kill Jesus (cf. Gk. *symbouleúō* in Mt. 26:4 and Acts 9:23).

*See* CONSPIRACY; PLAN. G. L. KNAPP

**PLOT** [Heb. *ḥelqâ*–'portion of ground'] (2 S. 23:11f.; 2 K. 9:25f.; 1 Ch. 11:13f.); AV PIECE, GROUND, PORTION, PLAT, PARCEL; NEB also FIELD; in Ezk. 45:2 the RSV and NEB supply "plot." A piece of land.

The Heb. *ḥelqâ*, related to *ḥālaq*, "divide, apportion," is often used with *śāḏeh*, "field," and translated "plot of ground." *See also* PORTION.

In Ezk. 45:2 the RSV and NEB supply "plot" for a smooth translation; the MT *mᵉrubbāʿ sāḇîḇ* (lit. "square all around"; cf. AV) appears redundant, since a square area is by definition the same all around; but Ezekiel had a penchant for using *sāḇîḇ*, often for emphasis.

**PLOW** [Heb. (vb.) *ḥāraš* (Dt. 22:10; 1 S. 8:12; Job 4:8; etc.), *ʿāḇaḏ* (Dt. 21:4); Gk. (noun) *árotron* (Lk. 9:62), (vb.) *arotriáō* (Lk. 17:7; 1 Cor. 9:10)]; AV also EAR (Gen. 45:6; Ex. 34:21; 1 S. 8:12); NEB also TILL (Dt. 21:4), "drive" (Ps. 129:3); **PLOWER** [Heb. *ḥāraš* (part.)] (Ps. 129:3); NEB PLOUGHMAN; **PLOWMAN** [Heb. *'ikkar* (Isa. 61:5), *yāgab̲* (2 K. 25:12; Jer. 52:16), *ḥāraš* (part.) (Am. 9:13)]; AV also HUSBANDMAN (2 K. 25:12; Jer. 52:16); NEB also LABOURER (2 K. 25:12; Jer. 52:16), "till the land" (Isa. 61:5); [Gk. *arotriáō* (part.) (1 Cor. 9:10)]; **PLOWSHARE** [Heb. *'ēt̲* (Isa. 2:4; Joel 3:10 [MT 4:10]; Mic. 4:3), *maḥareše̲t* (1 S. 13:20f.)]; AV also SHARE (1 S. 13:20), MATTOCK (1 S. 13:21); NEB also MATTOCK (Isa. 2:4; Joel 3:10; Mic. 4:3). The plow must have been invented soon after draft animals were domesticated (before 3000 B.C.), but the hoe or digging stick continued in use for many years. The plow was developed from the hoe by lengthening the hoe shaft so that the beasts could be harnessed and by adding a handle for guidance. The blade or share was of hard wood or metal and was easily worn or damaged in stony country (cf. 1 S. 13:20). Iron plowshares began to be widely used in Palestine early in the 1st millennium B.C. (*see* picture in IRON). An example was found at Gibeah (Tell el-Fûl) in ruins identified with Saul's fortress (see *AASOR*, 34-35 [1960], pl. 19A).

The simple plow was made from a young tree of oak or from another hardwood tree with a diameter of 7.5-10 cm. (3-4 in.). The tree was severed just below a good-sized branch and again 40-50 cm. (15-20 in.) above. The upper end of the severed trunk was pointed to form the share or the attachment for a metal share. Between this end and the side branch was fitted a brace. The branch, trimmed

Fertility-god sits on a throne and holds a plow. Cylinder seal impression from *ca.* 2360-2180 B.C. (Staatliche Museen zu Berlin, DDR)

Drawing of men plowing (with a seed plow) and sowing. From a Babylonian seal impression, 14th cent. B.C. (University Museum, University of Pennsylvania)

3-3.5 m. (10-12 ft.) from the trunk, became the pole. A lighter stick, about 1 m. (3 ft.) long, projected upward from the share to form the handle. In a slightly different type of plow the handle and share are one continuous piece, cut so that there is a slight bend at the middle; the pole is of two pieces joined end to end and the thicker end is notched to attach it firmly to the share. The whole is so light that it can easily be carried on a man's shoulder. These plows literally scratched the soil, as implied by Heb. *ḥāraš*. The plowman guided his plow with one hand, and with the other he could goad the oxen or with the chisel end of his goad break away the lumps of earth that impeded the plow.

In Mesopotamia the seed plow was in common use. A funnel behind the share directed the seed from a container into the furrow as soon as it was opened (see *ANEP*, nos. 86-88). To produce a straight and even furrow the plowman had to fix his gaze forward and not for one instant glance aside. This necessity gave rise to the simile for the Christian (Lk. 9:62; cf. Phil. 3:13).

One special law is mentioned in connection with plowing, namely, that an ox and an ass should not be yoked together (Dt. 22:10). Oxen were principally used for plowing (Job 1:14); often several yokes of oxen followed each other, making parallel furrows across the field (cf. 1 K. 19:19). The land cannot be plowed before the rains (cf. Jer. 14:4). Since plowing was a hard and routine task, it was often given to slaves (cf. Prov. 20:4); the Hebrew verb *'ābad̲*, "work," could also mean "plow" (Dt. 21:4; cf. Lk. 17:7; Hos. 10:11; Isa. 61:5).

Many metaphors and similes are taken from this common action. The famous sign of God's peace, making plowshares (Heb. *'ēt̲*) from swords (Isa. 2:4; Mic. 4:3), and the warlike converse (Joel 3:10), find their explanation in 1 S. 13:19-21, where the oppressed Israelites were forbidden the smiths who might manufacture either implement or effect the simple transformation. The expression "the plowers plowed upon my back" indicates deep affliction (Ps. 129:3; cf. 141:7, NIV, NAB, NASB). The agricultural image of plowing iniquity and reaping trouble or injustice (Job 4:8; Hos. 10:13 [cf. the comms.]; 1 Cor. 9:10) is still popular today. When the opponents of Samson used his wife to discover the answer to his riddle he said, "If you had not plowed with my heifer . . ." (Jgs. 14:18). The destruction foretold for Zion was to be so complete that the site could be plowed as a field (Jer. 26:18). In a time of prosperity the soil would be so fertile that the plowman would overtake the reaper (Am. 9:13). In a parable Isaiah uses the variety in agriculture to point up the various ways God deals with His people (Isa. 28:23-29). Among the improbabilities of Am. 6:12 should probably be read, "Will one plow the sea with oxen?" following a very slight alteration of the MT (see the comms., esp. H. W. Wolff [Eng. tr., *Hermeneia*, 1977], pp. 284f.).

A. R. MILLARD

**PLUCKING OUT HAIR.** *See* HAIR VII; PUNISHMENTS IV.L.

**PLUMB LINE; PLUMMET.** *See* MEASURING LINE.

**PLUNDER** [Heb. *bāzaz*] (Gen. 34:27; 2 K. 7:16; Ps. 109:11; Isa. 11:14; Jer. 20:5; 50:37; Ezk. 39:10; Am. 3:11; Zeph. 2:9); AV SPOIL, ROB; NEB also SPOIL, SEIZE, THROWN DOWN; [*baz*] (Ezk. 29:19; 36:5; 38:12f.); AV PREY; NEB also SEIZED; [*bizzâ*] (2 Ch. 14:14; Ezr. 9:7; Neh. 4:4; Est. 9:10, 15f.; Dnl. 11:24, 33); AV SPOIL, PREY; NEB also SPOIL, REPROACH; [*šāsas*] (Jgs. 2:14; 1 S. 17:53; Isa. 13:16; Zec. 14:2); AV SPOIL, RIFLED; NEB also

RIFLED; [*šāsâ*] (Jgs. 2:16; 1 S. 14:48; Isa. 10:13; 17:14; Jer. 50:11); AV SPOIL, ROBBED, DESTROYERS; NEB also MARAUDING BANDS, HOSTILE RAIDS, RAVAGED; [*m^ešissâ*] (Isa. 42:22; Zeph. 1:13); AV SPOIL, BOOTY; NEB also SPOIL; [*šālāl*] (Est. 3:13; 8:11; Isa. 10:6; Jer. 50:10; Hab. 2:8; Zec. 2:8f. [MT 12f.]); AV SPOIL; [*ḥālaṣ*] (Ps. 7:4 [MT 5]); AV DELIVERED; NEB SET FREE; [*šāḏaḏ*] (Isa. 21:2; Ob. 5); AV, NEB, SPOIL, ROBBERS; [*bāqaq*] (Nah. 2:2, 9 [MT 3, 10]); AV EMPTIERS, SPOIL; NEB PLUNDERING HORDES, SPOIL; [*ṭerep*] (Nah. 3:1); AV, NEB, PREY; [Gk. *harpázō*] (Mt. 12:29); AV SPOIL; [*diarpázō*] (Mt. 12:29; Mk. 3:27); AV SPOIL; NEB also "making off with," RANSACKING; [*harpagḗ*] (He. 10:34); AV SPOIL; NEB SEIZURE; **PILLAGE** [niphal of Heb. *ḥāpaś*] (Ob. 6); AV "searched out"; NEB RANSACKED.

Plunder is used as a verb for robbing or looting as an act of war and also as a noun denoting gains from such actions. Heb. *ḥālaṣ* can mean "set free" or "deliver," but the piel form in this context seems to require the meaning of "strip by violence" or "plunder."

Soldiers of the victorious armies in the ancient Near East gained their "wages" through plundering the dead on the battlefield, the remains of abandoned enemy camps, and the towns conquered in their attack. All valuables, including flocks and herds, women and children, were theirs for the taking (Gen. 34:27-29; Jgs. 5:30); *see* picture in CART. Under the direction of God, such taking of spoil could be an indication of His judgment brought upon His own people (Isa. 10:5f.) or upon foreign powers (Jer. 50:10).

Not only organized armies but also bands of raiders exacted their toll on the settlements vulnerable to attack. The Sabeans and Chaldeans plundered Job's possessions (Job. 1:14-17). The Amalekites stormed and plundered David's city of Ziklag, but David pursued and defeated them and divided the spoil (1 S. 30:1-3, 18-31).

By analogy with armies and marauders, the leaders and the wealthy class in Israel are said to loot widows and orphans through their oppression and injustice (Isa. 10:1f.).

Christ's parable concerning Satan's dominion in Mt. 12:22-32 par. Mk. 3:22-30 refers to still another type of looting, namely, burglary. When a thief enters the house of the strong man, only after binding the owner can he carry out his criminal intent. G. WYPER

**POCHERETH-HAZZEBAIM** pō-ker'əth-haz-ə-bā'əm [Heb. *pōḵereṯ haṣṣ^eḇāyîm*–'binder (fem.) of the gazelles'] (Ezr. 2:57; Neh. 7:59; 1 Esd. 5:34); AV POCHERETH OF ZEBAIM, PHACARETH . . . SABI (1 Esd. 5:34); NEB also PHACERETH . . . SABIE (1 Esd. 5:34). One of the sons of Solomon's servants who was head of a postexilic family. The fem. part. *pōḵereṯ* may denote an office (cf. *qōheleṯ*, "preacher"; see GKC, § 122r).

**PODS** [Gk. *kerátia*–'little horns'] (Lk. 15:16); AV HUSKS. The pods of the carob tree or locust tree (*Ceratonia siliqua* L.), a leguminous evergreen tree common in Palestine, Syria, and Egypt that attains a height of 9 m. (30 ft.). Abundant in April and May, the pods are flat and horn-shaped, containing numerous beanlike seeds in a mucilaginous pulp. When ripe the sweet pods were eaten by the poor and were also used as cattle and pig fodder. K. Bailey (*Poet and Peasant* [1976], pp. 171-73) distinguishes between the wild (thorny) carob, used mainly for firewood, and the sweet (Syrian) variety that can be eaten.

The tradition that the "locusts" of Mt. 3:4; Mk. 1:6 were carob pods has been preserved in the popular name for carob bread, "St. John's bread," but is uncertain.

R. K. H.

**POET.** The translation of Gk. *poiētḗs* in Acts 17:28, where Paul cites Greek poets in an apologetical speech to Epicurean and Stoic philosophers at the Areopagus in Athens. From the Greek text it is not clear whether "as even some of our poets have said" refers to the preceding line ("In him we live and move and have our being," v. 28a), to the following line ("For we are indeed his offspring," v. 28b), or to both. The first line may be a quotation from Epimenides the Cretan (cf. RSV mg.), the same poet who is quoted in Tit. 1:12 (see Bruce, *Acts*; but cf. also other comms.). The second line is a quotation from the Stoic poet ARATUS (*Phaenomena* 5, part of an introductory dedication to ZEUS, the Supreme Being of Greek philosophy). A similar expression occurs in Cleanthes *Hymn to Zeus* 4. Paul rejects the pantheistic sense intended by the Stoic poets but quotes them to corroborate his teaching about the proper worship owed to the Creator God by all His creatures. *See also* STOICS.

*Bibliography.*–F. F. Bruce, *Acts of the Apostles* (2nd ed. 1952; repr. 1970), pp. 338f.; *Paul, Apostle of the Heart Set Free* (1977), pp. 238-243; W. Neil, *Acts of the Apostles* (*NCBC*, 1973), pp. 191f.

N. J. O.

**POETRY, HEBREW.**

I. Introduction
II. Meter
III. Parallelism
IV. Repetition
V. Other Devices
VI. Construction from Formal, Material, and Liturgical Units
VII. General Characterization
VIII. More Recent Studies

***I. Introduction.***–More than one-third of the OT was written in poetic form, including some of the best-loved passages in all of Scripture. The Hebrew text itself was not placed in poetic lines, but the Masoretes did employ a special poetic accentuation in the books of Job, Proverbs, and Psalms, whose first letters (in Hebrew) were combined to form the acronym *'emeṯ*, "truth." None of the ancient versions translated the Bible into poetic form, but the first-century Jewish historian Josephus did acknowledge that Moses and David made use of poetic verse (*Ant.* ii.16.4 [346]; iv.7.44 [303]; vii.12.3 [305]). In 1952 the RSV became the first English translation to utilize indented lines in order to identify clearly the poetic material. Since then, many other modern versions have followed this practice.

Other poetical books are Ecclesiastes, Canticles, and Lamentations, along with large parts of the prophetical books. Isaiah contains some of the most powerful poetic passages found anywhere and is almost entirely written in poetic form. Jeremiah is equally divided between prose and poetry. It seems that the Spirit of God often used poetry as He lifted the prophets to the highest of spiritual experiences. In the historical books we find occasional sections of poetry; see, e.g., Gen. 4:23f.; ch. 49; Ex. 15; Nu. 21:14f., 27-30; chs. 23–24 (oracles of Balaam); Dt. 32–33; Josh. 10:12-14; Jgs. 5; 9:8-15; 1 S. 2:1-10; 2 S. 1:19-27; 3:33f.; ch. 22; 23:1-7.

What is the difference between Hebrew prose and Hebrew poetry? Certainly what holds for literature in other languages holds also for Hebrew literature: it is not easy to specify the features distinguishing prose from poetry (see Kugel).

We must look further at the questions that arise here. In so doing we shall limit ourselves generally to formal considerations, though it is true, of course, that in these formal differences between prose and poetry we meet with differences of other sorts. Thus, e.g., it is often true that what fills the heart reveals itself more directly and more intensely in poetry than in prose.

The characteristics of Hebrew poetry are nowhere more clearly set forth than in the Psalms. The Psalms, therefore, along with Isaiah, the most poetic of the prophets, will receive particular attention in this article.

In the study of Hebrew poetry the book by Bishop Robert Lowth, *De sacra poësi Hebraeorum* (1753; Eng. tr. *Lectures on the Sacred Poetry of the Hebrews,* 1815), is particularly important. More or less disjointed reflections on the characteristics of Hebrew poetry were made already in earlier centuries, but Lowth laid the foundations for more systematic studies. He was convinced that Hebrew poetry had a real meter, but that our ignorance of the manner in which Classical Hebrew was spoken has made it impossible for us to reconstruct the meter. Hence Lowth concentrated on another feature: the *parallelismus membrorum,* "parallelism of members." Here he distinguished three types of parallelism: synonymous, antithetic, and synthetic — a division that is still used in its main lines (but cf. Kugel).

***II. Meter.***–At the end of the 19th cent. several German scholars made studies of the meter in Hebrew poetry. Since that time a tremendous amount of work has been done to determine this meter, but no universally accepted conclusions have been reached.

In two respects there is virtual unanimity: (1) Hebrew poetry has an accentual meter, not a quantitative meter like that of Greek and Latin poetry (i.e., the question of whether a syllable is long or short is of far less importance in Hebrew poetry than in Greek or Latin). (2) A serious obstacle for ascertaining the meter is our continuing ignorance of the original Hebrew pronunciation. In this respect, it is significant that recent investigations (e.g., the study of the Qumrân Scrolls) have increased our knowledge of pre-Masoretic pronunciation of the Hebrew language.

In scanning Hebrew poetry three main systems have been employed. It is not possible to give here an adequate description of these, and the following comments are designed only to offer an impression. Some authors, following J. Ley and E. Sievers, are of the opinion that the anapest foot (⏑ ⏑ -) is basic to Hebrew meter. Room must be made, however, for many irregularities. Thus the number of syllables receiving no accent is in principle two; in fact, however, this may fluctuate between none and four. Building on the work of G. W. H. Bickell and G. Hölscher, S. Mowinckel suggested that the Hebrew meter is in principle iambic (⏑ -). According to Mowinckel there is an alternation system — an interchange of stressed and unstressed syllables. Between two stressed syllables comes only one unstressed, but in many cases this unstressed syllable may be missed (syncope). In contrast, the system of Sievers can be called the accentuation system; the metrical accent coincides with the natural word-stress. Against this view, Mowinckel argued that the rhythmical accent can fall on the naturally unstressed syllables as well. As a result of this difference, the accents characterizing Hebrew poetic lines are heavier in the system of Sievers than in that of Mowinckel.

A third approach to meter is the syllable-counting system developed by F. M. Cross and D. N. Freedman and followed by M. Dahood, D. Stuart, and S. Geller. According to Cross and Freedman parallel lines tend to have the same number of syllables even when the number of accented syllables is not the same. Hence, there is no regular pattern of unstressed syllables corresponding to stressed syllables, but the total number of syllables in parallel lines does tend to be equal. Lines which have eight to thirteen syllables are considered "long" and those with three to five syllables are "short." Stuart noted that a scansion based on a syllable count is very accurate and makes it easier to identify regular and irregular meter and balanced and unbalanced couplets. A verse such as Nu. 23:24 turns out to be nicely balanced when one looks at the syllables in each line rather than the semantic equivalents.

A word of caution should be given to alert the reader about a serious problem in terminology with reference to poetic lines and verses. A verse is composed of two or three parts or limbs called lines, stichs, or cola. A two-line verse is referred to as a couplet, a distich, or a bicolon, and a three-line verse is a triplet, tristich, or tricolon. In the printed editions of the Hebrew Bible a whole verse is usually printed on one line, with a gap called a "caesura" between the parallel parts. For this reason some scholars refer to the whole verse as a poetic line (or "period" or "stich"), and the parts are called hemistichs or cola.

The discovery of the Râs Shamrah (ancient Ugarit) tablets in 1929 was welcome, for a number of these texts were poetical. Like Hebrew, Ugaritic poetry is largely composed of lines that have two or three stresses. But G. D. Young and W. S. LaSor have supported C. H. Gordon's contention that there do not seem to be any regular patterns of rhythm or meter in the Ugaritic or Hebrew materials. Stuart has pointed out that Hebrew lines tend to be a syllable or two shorter than Ugaritic lines.

Since the time of K. Budde (1882) attention has been given especially to the meter of the dirge, the *qînâ* meter; see, e.g., Am. 5:2 and Lam. 3:25-27. According to Sievers the formula of this is 3 + 2 (counting "accents" or "stresses"); according to Mowinckel it is 4 + 3. Stuart agrees that *qînâ* meter is certainly an unbalanced one, but on occasion the shorter line can precede the longer one. According to Cross, the *qînâ* meter does not appear in the earliest Israelite poetry.

Most Hebrew verses reflect a 3 + 3 or 2 + 2 pattern but many other variations occur. According to Sievers, Hebrew verse has many combinations: 2 + 2, 3 + 3, 4 + 4, 4 + 3, 3 + 4, 3 + 2, 2 + 3, 2 + 2 + 2. Mowinckel referred to the *mashal*-meter as a 4 + 4 pattern, which he said was used in all wisdom literature.

***III. Parallelism.***–A feature that appears continually in Hebrew poetry, and has been regarded as its most prominent characteristic, is *parallelismus membrorum,* or parallelism. A poetic line consists usually of two members or parts that in one way or another run parallel to each other and correspond with each other. In those instances where one or more terms in a line are obscure, the repetition inherent in parallelism often allows the interpreter an opportunity to understand the words correctly.

Continued repetition brings with it the peril of a certain monotony, but the Hebrew poets knew how to escape this danger by using parallelism with great freedom and variation. Such variation is sometimes achieved by giving the poetic lines varying lengths (see, e.g., Ps. 3:7a, b, and 8 [MT 8a, b, 9]). It is possible to distinguish various kinds of parallelism by using either material or formal criteria. That is, one can ask how both members of a poetic verse relate themselves to each other when examined in terms of their content or in terms of their form. If material criteria are used, however, every distinction may be defective because there are so many variables; one must, therefore, proceed with caution. In making use of *material* criteria one can distinguish the following types.

In *synonymous parallelism* the expression of the first member is repeated by the second in different words.

POETRY, HEBREW

Cf. Ps. 2:3:

"Let us-burst their bonds asunder *a b c*
and-cast their-cords from-us." *a' b' c'*

Sometimes one or more terms from the first line have no corresponding term in the second line, and this is referred to as incomplete synonymous parallelism. Usually if one term is omitted, another will be lengthened to "compensate" and help balance the line (hence the term "ballast variant"). In Ps. 103:7 the term "people of Israel" (represented by C') compensates for the omission of the verb in the second line:

"He-made-known his-ways to-Moses *a b c*
his-acts to-the-people-of-Israel." *b' C'*

The same form is found in Ps. 105:10, which ends with the ballast variant "everlasting covenant":

"which-he-confirmed to-Jacob as-a-statute, *a b c*
to-Israel as-an-everlasting-covenant." *b' C'*

*Emblematic parallelism* is a specific kind of synonymous parallelism in which one line contains a simile or metaphor. Cf. Ps. 103:13:

"As a father pities his children,
so the Lord pities those who fear him."

Most verses which are parallel on a material (semantic) level are also parallel on a grammatical (formal) level; i.e., the person, gender, and number of the verb tend to be the same and the nouns may have the same suffix. Geller and Collins have pointed out, however, that sometimes we find grammatical parallelism without semantic parallelism. In Ex. 15:7, e.g., the statement "thou overthrowest thy adversaries" is parallel to "thou sendest forth thy fury." The verbs are both second person singular and the objects each have the same suffix, but the corresponding terms do not have the same meaning.

In *climactic parallelism* (also known as "repetitive," "staircase," or "step" parallelism) one or more elements from the first line are repeated in the second line, and the main emphasis or "climax" comes at the end of the verse. Often the first line contains a term in the vocative case (e.g., Ps. 29:1):

"Ascribe to-the-Lord, O-heavenly-beings, *a b c*
ascribe to-the-Lord glory-and-strength." *a b d*

Psalm 94 has three examples of climactic parallelism in vv. 1, 3, and 23. V. 23 is different from the others in that the final line is clipped with its repetition of "will wipe them out." This abrupt ending is appropriate for the final verse of the psalm.

Climactic parallelism is also characteristic of Ugaritic poetry, as the following example (*UT* 68:8f.) shows:

"Lo, thy-enemies, Baal, *a b c*
lo, thy-enemies thou-shalt-slay." *a b d*

In the famous song of Deborah in Jgs. 5:27 we find perhaps the most dramatic instance of this form in the description of the death of Sisera at the hands of Jael:

"He sank, he fell,
he lay still at her feet;
at her feet he sank, he fell;
where he sank, there he fell dead."

The threefold repetition of "sank" and "fell" in this quatrain allows the full emphasis to fall on the final word, "dead."

Ugaritic poetry also illustrates the use of parallel words that tend to occur in the same order. H. L. Ginsberg and U. Cassuto identified a number of word-pairs found in both Ugaritic and Hebrew, terms such as "head" (*rō'š*) and "crown" (*qoḏqōḏ*) (Ps. 68:21 [MT 22]), "enemy" (*'ōyēḇ*) and "foe" (*ṣār*) (Ps. 81:14 [MT 15]), and "thousand" (*'elep*) and "ten thousand" (*r$^e$ḇāḇâ*) (Ps. 91:7). Other scholars have demonstrated that many such word-pairs exist in Hebrew poetry (see Gevirtz and esp. Dahood).

When the lines of a verse express a contrast, the relationship is called *antithetic parallelism,* and the second line is usually introduced with "but." Often the second member emphasizes the reverse side of the thought set forth in the first. In some parts of Proverbs this sort of parallelism is particularly common. Cf. Prov. 10–15; 28–29; e.g., 10:1:

"A wise son makes a glad father,
but a foolish son is a sorrow to his mother."

Most of the verses in Prov. 10–15 illustrate antithetical parallelism, and there are a number of examples in the Psalms. Ps. 1:1 and 2 have an antithetical relationship, and v. 6 is likewise cast in this form.

A modification of synonymous parallelism is the so-called *synthetic parallelism,* in which the second line develops or completes the thought in a way that could not be determined from the first line. The parallelism is looser and the corresponding terms do not line up as neatly. For example, the second line of Ps. 1:2 ("and on his law he meditates day and night") advances the thought of the first line ("but his delight is in the law of the Lord"). In Ps. 51:13 (MT 15) the line "and sinners will return to thee" is the result of "Then I will teach transgressors thy ways." Ps. 1:1 shows a progression from "walks" to "stands" to "sits." Some scholars, such as Geller, use the word "list" to describe this relationship, citing Ps. 148:9:

"Mountains and all hills,
fruit trees and all cedars!"

"List" could also apply to Pss. 24:4 and 15:2f. LaSor refers to the progressive destruction due to locusts in Joel 1:4 as a kind of synthetic parallelism called "the chain figure."

G. B. Gray preferred the term *formal* to *synthetic* because of the lack of genuine parallelism in some instances. Actually, *formal parallelism* could be a separate category altogether since the two lines are really one run-on line (enjambment):

"For the stars of the heavens and their constellations
will not give their light" (Isa. 13:10).

The same is true of Ps. 2:6:

"I have set my king
on Zion, my holy hill."

Such "nonparallelism" can sometimes pinpoint verses which the poet wishes to emphasize. Ps. 110, a short but difficult poem and the Psalm most quoted in the NT, has several verses with only formal parallelism (cf. vv. 1, 3, 4, 7).

In all that has been said about parallelism we have had in mind the sort of parallelism that can be ascertained in successive lines. This is *internal parallelism.* But often two successive couplets (distichs) are parallel to each other. This is *external parallelism.* Cf. Ps. 27:1:

"The Lord is my light and my salvation; *a*
whom shall I fear? *b*
The Lord is the stronghold of my life; *c*
of whom shall I be afraid?" *d*

We can say that between lines a and b, and between c and d, there is a (synthetic) parallelism; but actually it makes more sense to point out that there is a (synonymous) parallelism between a and c, and between b and d. (To enliven the style the parallelism between a and c is imperfect, with a ballast variant.) Cf. Ps. 127:1; Isa. 1:10.

All sorts of variations are possible with external parallelism. Thus we find in Prov. 23:15f., e.g., external parallelism in a chiastic arrangement:

"My son, if your heart is wise,
my heart too will be glad.
My soul will rejoice,
when your lips speak what is right."

In Lam. 1:1 the poet does the same thing in more elaborate fashion. Lines 1, 3, and 6 are parallel, as are lines 2, 4, and 5. The inversion of lines 5 and 6 produces a climactic ending.

In making use of parallelism the Hebrew poets not only availed themselves of considerable variation; they also allowed themselves a large amount of freedom. There are, in other words, a good many irregularities. Sometimes there are not two but three parallel members in a poetic verse, producing a tristich (tricolon). Cf. Ps. 1:1:

"... who walks not in the counsel of the wicked,
nor stands in the way of sinners,
nor sits in the seat of scoffers."

Moreover, it happens with some frequency that in an unexpected manner the parallel member is lacking. Many regard this as a corruption of the text, but this is an unwarranted conclusion. Ps. 6 consists entirely of statements that are parallel two by two; but this pattern is broken in v. 6a (MT 7a), where the parallel member is omitted. In this way the poet attains a certain "effect": he is too fatigued, we might say, to repeat the same thing over again. See also, e.g., Ps. 29:7; 37:20. Especially at the beginning and end of a Psalm — or of a part of a Psalm — this phenomenon can be observed repeatedly. See, e.g., the end of Ps. 2, the "initial strokes" in Ps. 31:1, 7, 9, 11, 15a, 21 (MT 2, 8, 10, 12, 16a, 22), and the "concluding stroke" in Ps. 20:5c (MT 6c). Cf. also Ps. 22:11a, 15c, 16c, 26c, 29c (MT 12a, 16c, 17c, 27c, 30c). A line, word, or phrase that stands apart from the parallelism is said to be in *anacrusis*. Examples of anacrusis cited by Collins are the introductory "What do you mean" in Isa. 3:15 and "saying" in 46:10.

A further point is to be noted. In Ps. 1:3 the phrases "that yields its fruit in its season" and "its leaf does not wither" are clearly parallel. But in regard to "He is like a tree planted by streams of water," the question arises: Must a caesura or pause be made after "tree" or "planted"? If not, there is no parallelism here. If a caesura is made then it becomes a case of synthetic or formal parallelism; it is clear that this is parallelism only in a very much weakened sense ("purely formal parallelism"). In any event, "In all that he does, he prospers" has no parallelism.

Such cases are numerous. This freedom, this irregularity in the use of parallelism in no way detracts from the beauty of the poem. It would be better to say that in this way the poets display greater beauty by combating monotony.

***IV. Repetition.***–This, too, has a very important function in Hebrew poetry. One might say that the use of parallelism also implies repetition, but it will become evident that the latter term refers to another phenomenon. This does not mean, of course, that these two devices are not related.

In general one avoids as much as possible using a word or an expression more than once in the same immediate context. But in certain circumstances such repetition of a word, or words, or even of an entire sentence, can have an aesthetically pleasing effect.

Notice first two forms of this phenomenon that are found in Hebrew poetry and that appear often elsewhere; the *refrain* and the *inclusio,* or correspondence of beginning and end. For the refrain see Ps. 8:1, 9 (MT 2, 10); 24:7-10; 39:5, 11 (MT 6, 12); 42:5,11 (MT 6, 12); 43:5; 46:7, 11 (MT 8, 12); 62:1f., 5f. (MT 2f., 6f.); 67:3, 5 (MT 4, 6); 80:3, 7, 19 (MT 4, 8, 20); 99:5, 9; 107:8, 15, 21, 31; cf. also, e.g., Isa. 9:11, 16, 20 (MT 12, 17, 21); 10:4; Am. 1:3, 6, 9, 13; 2:1, 4, 6; 4:6, 8-11.

According to Liebreich, the beginnings of seventy-four Psalms correspond with their ends, forming a kind of inclusio. (This figure may be too high but the number of cases is certainly great.) Besides simple instances found in, e.g., Pss. 20, 21, 30, 103, and 139, see, e.g., Ps. 17:1f., 15; 25:1-3, 19-21. It should be remembered that there can be correspondence between the beginning and end not only of a Psalm as a whole but also of a section of a Psalm; cf., e.g., the opening words of Ps. 22:1 (MT 2) with the concluding words of v.10 (MT 11).

We must also take into account other forms of this device. Consideration must be given, first, to the phenomenon of "stairlike" parallelism: an expression is used in one line or part of a line, and used again in a later line or part of a line. In ancient times this pattern had a very important function in a part of Semitic poetry, as is evident from Ugaritic poetry and also from the Song of Deborah (Jgs. 5, which many regard as one of the oldest examples of Israelite poetry; see, e.g., vv. 19-21, 23f.; cf. G. Gerleman, *VT,* 1 [1951], 168-180). In regard to the Psalms, this pattern is particularly characteristic of the pilgrimage Psalms, Pss. 120–134. See further Jgs. 9:8-15; Ex. 14:12-23; Pss. 29; 93.

M. Buber and F. Rosenzweig pointed out that generally in the OT, and particularly in the Psalms, the phenomenon of "key words" has an important function. A vigorous statement on this is found in Buber's *Good and Evil* (Eng. tr. 1953), p. 52: "The recurrence of the key-words is a basic law of composition in the Psalms. This law has a poetic significance, rhythmical correspondence of sound values, as well as a hermeneutical one: the Psalm provides its own interpretation, by repetition of what is essential to its understanding. This is why it often refuses to vary the expression of a certain subject." Thus one may note as key words, e.g., "righteous" in Ps. 11, "be far" in Ps. 22 (used at the beginning of the three sections into which vv. 1-21 [MT 2-22] may be divided, viz., vv. 1, 11, and 19), and "ways," "paths," "teach" in Ps. 25.

We have thus given four forms in which the device of repetition appears. The distinctions among these are often not clear and the forms sometimes overlap. More important is that many examples of this device cannot be subsumed under any one of these four forms. How are we to explain these?

In most poems certain words are used more than once. This is inevitable, and in very many cases no special significance should be attached to such a practice. But since the device of repetition has, most assuredly, an important function in the Psalms, it must also be assumed that in many cases repeated usage of words is intentional. The Hebrew poet liked to play with a word, to set it in more than one context, in order to expose its various shades of meaning.

We may take a few random examples. Ps. 33:10-12 shows a peculiar structure in that each of the words "counsel," "devices," "nation," and "people," is used twice. Concerning Ps. 25 — and various other Psalms — we can say that the "stairlike" parallelism, though it is not characteristic, has nevertheless left its mark: note the "be ashamed" in vv. 2f. and the "remember" of vv. 6f. It would seem, at the same time, that the wordplay in these verses is more deliberately thought out than, e.g., in Jgs. 5. In Ps. 11 not only is the word "righteous" a key word (see above), but also there is a definite intent, e.g., in the double usage of the word "behold." The eyes of the Lord "behold" the children of men to try or to test (v. 4); and whoever in this divine testing is found righteous receives the privilege that he might "behold" (v. 7) the face of the Lord (here the ASV and RSV are more accurate than the AV). Because "test" is found both in vv. 4 and 5 we have a case of "stairlike" parallelism. Similarly, in Ps. 133 the word *yōrēḏ* occurs three times in succession, twice with reference to the oil "running down" upon Aaron's beard and robes (v. 2) and once with reference to the dew of Mt. Hermon "falling" on Zion (v. 3). Cf. the repetition of "beard" in v. 2.

Repetition plays an important role also in many of the ACROSTIC psalms. Often the lines subsumed under the first letter state the poem's basic theme, which is subsequently looked at from many different angles. In Ps. 119 the emphasis upon obeying the law of the Lord found in the first stanza (*aleph,* vv. 1-8) is carried on throughout the entire poem — nearly every verse contains some reference to the word of God. Ps. 34 repeatedly speaks of the Lord as One who hears prayer (vv. 4, 6, 15, 17 [MT 5, 7, 16, 18]) and who delivers His people (vv. 4, 7, 11, 19 [MT 5, 8, 12, 20]). In Ps. 37 the poet warns the righteous not to fret over the prosperity of the wicked (vv. 1, 7, 8), for evil men will soon fade away and vanish from the scene (vv. 2, 10, 20, 36). The godly are urged to trust in the Lord (vv. 3, 5), because the wicked will be "cut off" (vv. 22, 28, 38). No less than five times the righteous are assured that they will "possess the land" (vv. 9, 11, 22, 29, 34). Ps. 145 emphasizes the attributes of God as the psalmist reflects upon God's power and mighty deeds (vv. 4, 6, 11f.; cf. Ps. 111:2, 6f.). Since a number of the alphabetic psalms deal with "wisdom" themes, it is fitting that the book of Proverbs ends with an acrostic poem eulogizing the ideal wife (31:10-31).

*V. Other Devices.*–Several other stylistic devices appear more commonly in Hebrew poetry than in Hebrew prose. Among the more important are chiasm and climax.

*Chiasm* refers to an inverted arrangement so that the parallel terms are in reverse order: e.g., "the father is wise" followed by "strong is the son" (not "the son is strong"). Chiasm is particularly common in Hebrew poetry and is another of the means the poets used to escape the peril of monotony in parallelism. Note the following instances as found in the first book of Psalms alone. (In this connection one must remember that most translations take very little — indeed, too little — account of this device.) See 1:1b, c, 6; 2:1f., 5, 8; 3:4, 7 (MT 5, 8); 5:1, 6, 9 (MT 2, 7, 10); 6:6, 9 (MT 7, 10); 7:5, 13, 15f. (MT 6, 14, 16f.); 8:5f. (MT 6f.); 9:5, 15, 18 (MT 6, 16, 19); 13:5 (MT 6); 15:3f.; 17:1, 8; 18:4-8, 13, 33f. 39f., 42, 47-49 (MT 5-9, 14, 34f., 40f., 43, 48-50); 19:1 (MT 2); esp. 20:2-5 (MT 3-6); 21:8 (MT 9); 22:12, 15f., 18, 22, 24 (MT 13, 16f.,19, 23, 25); 25:3, 6f.; 26:3-5, 12; 28:4; 29:5f., 8, 10f.; 31:2-4 (MT 3-5); 32:5, 10; 33:1f., 4f., 8, 10f.,16f.; 34:18 (MT 19); 35:17-19; 36:5, 8, 11 (MT 6, 9, 12); 37:6, 14, 17, 19, 21; 38:2, 7, 9f., 12, 18f., 21 (MT 3, 8, 10f., 13, 19f., 22); 40:11, 17 (MT 12, 18); 41:6 (MT 7).

The book of Isaiah also contains several examples of chiasm. In 6:10 the words "heart," "ears," and "eyes" occur in three successive lines followed by three more lines that refer to the "eyes," "ears," and "heart." This pattern can be represented as a b c c' b' a'. A similar arrangement is found in Isa. 40:12:

> "Who has measured in the hollow of his hand
> the waters,
> and the heavens with a span has marked off."

Each line has a verb, a prepositional phrase, and an object, but the order is reversed in the second line. When Isaac blessed Jacob and Esau in Gen. 27:29 and 39 he used chiasm, though the chiastic elements are separated by ten verses. Both verses have the phrases "the dew of heaven" and "the fatness of the earth," but in reverse order.

Chiastic construction is also found repeatedly in larger units. Thus, e.g., in Ps. 17, vv. 1-8 refer to the poet, vv. 9-12 to his enemies, vv. 13f. to his enemies, and v. 15 to the poet; in Ps. 36, v. 10 (MT 11) refers back to vv. 5-9 (MT 6-10), v. 11 (MT 12) to vv. 1-4 (MT 2-5); in Ps. 37, vv. 5f. are an elaboration of vv. 3f., while v. 7 develops vv. 1f. See further, e.g., H. H. Walker and N. W. Lund, *JBL,* 53 (1934), 355-370.

The use of parallelism led easily to the rise of the *climax* as a poetic device. The climax is sometimes formed by one poetic verse (see, e.g., Ps. 1:1; 7:5 [MT 6]; 9:3, 5 [MT 4, 6]; 31:2 [MT 3]. It can also be formed by a larger unit (see, e.g., Ps. 5:4-6 [MT 5-7]; 8:7f. [MT 8f.]; 11:4-6; 31:7f. [MT 8f.]; 35:1-10, 13f.; 40:1-3, 14f. [MT 2-4, 15f.]).

Related to the climax is "the style of successive *ramification*" (Alonso-Schökel). As an example we take Ps. 16. In vv. 1f. we have, so to speak, the "bud"; in what follows we see the "petals" unfolding themselves. In detail, v. 5a unfolds in 5b, 6; vv. 5f. as a whole unfold in vv. 7-11, etc.

Rhyme has no essential function in Hebrew poetry, although now and then one gets the impression that the poet purposely used it: see Ps. 146:6-9, where we find first a triple *-ām,* then seven times *-îm,* finally twice *-ēḏ* (*-ēṯ*). One can also point to the theefold use of *-î* in Gen. 49:3, to "Heshbon" and "Sihon" in Nu. 21:27, and to the five uses of the *-ênû* ending in Jgs. 16:24.

Of greater importance is the use of *assonance,* which occurs repeatedly in poetic contexts. Isa. 24:17 contains *paḥaḏ, paḥaṯ,* and *paḥ* for the "terror, and the pit, and the snare" that await earth's inhabitants. Another threefold combination that also employs *alliteration* is the *mehûmâ, mebûsâ,* and *mebûkâ* of Isa. 22:5, the "tumult and trampling and confusion" associated with the day of the Lord. Other examples of assonance or alliteration are found in Isa. 21:2; 33:1; Joel 1:10; Nah. 2:11 (MT 12); Ps. 1:1; 6:10 (MT 11); 18:7, 12 (MT 8, 13); 32:7; 33:7; 34:2 (MT 3); 37:20.

An illustration of *onomatapoeia* is contained in the galloping of the horses, the *dahᵃrôṯ dahᵃrôṯ* of Jgs. 5:22. In Isa. 17:12 the prophet uses a number of "m" and "n" sounds and especially the words *hᵃmôn* and *šeʾôn* to compare the uproar of the nations to the raging of the sea.

The prophets were also fond of wordplay or *paronomasia*. Amos was shown a basket of summer fruit (*qayiṣ*) as a sign that the end (*qēṣ*) had come upon Israel (8:1f.), and Jeremiah saw an almond branch (*šāqēḏ*) that indicated that God was watching (*šōqēḏ*) to see that His word of judgment was fulfilled (1:11f.). When Isaiah sang his song of the vineyard (Isa. 5), he ended with a strong denunciation of Israel (v. 7): God "looked for justice [*mišpāṭ*], but behold, bloodshed (*miśpāḥ*); for righteousness [*ṣeḏāqâ*], but behold, a cry [*ṣeʿāqâ*]!" The words sounded so similar but their meaning was so different! Also compare the reference to "destruction from the Almighty" (*šōḏ miššadday*) in Isa. 13:6.

*Hyperbole* is a poetic device using exaggeration for effect, so one must guard against an overly literal interpretation. When David was oppressed by Saul he described his plight as being encompassed with the cords of death, entangled with the cords of Sheol (Ps. 18:4f. [MT 5f.]). One could easily infer that David had died and gone to the grave, but most likely he was overstating his plight in graphic terms. When Jonah found himself drowning in the Mediterranean Sea, the same terminology was closer to reality (Jonah 2:5f.). For the Hebrew, anyone whose life was threatened, discomfited, or constricted by sickness, distress, or enemies was in the sphere and power of death.

In Isaiah the king of Assyria uses hyperbole when he boasts that "I dried up with the sole of my foot all the streams of Egypt" (37:25). He means that he was able to

POETRY, HEBREW

cross those streams and continue his invasion of Egypt. Similarly, highly figurative language may be involved in the description of the new Jerusalem in Isa. 54:11f. with its foundations of sapphires, gates of jewels, and walls made of precious stones.

Since the Israelites made less distinction between animate and inanimate nature than we are accustomed to do, it is not surprising that the Scriptures sometimes employ *personification*. Isaiah was particularly fond of this device. He spoke of the mountains and trees breaking out in song when the Lord redeems Jacob (44:23; 49:13), "and all the trees of the field shall clap their hands" (55:12). The sun and moon will be ashamed when the Lord reigns on Mt. Zion (24:23). Cities and countries are referred to as "daughters" (even "virgin daughters"; cf. 23:12; 37:22; 47:1) or "widows" (47:8; 54:4), depending on whether they have been destroyed. Even the abstract qualities of "justice" and "truth" are personified in Isa. 59:14f., and "wisdom" and "folly" are two women seeking to influence the naive in Prov. 8 and 9. In Ps. 23:6 "goodness and mercy shall follow me all the days of my life." The gates of Jerusalem lament and mourn over the collapse of Jerusalem (Isa. 3:26), but the cedars of Lebanon rejoice when Babylon falls (Isa. 14:8).

A special effect called *apostrophe* is attained when that which is personified is furthermore made an imaginary object of address; see Ps. 24:7ff.; 68:16 (MT 17); 114:5f.; etc. For other examples of apostrophe, see Josh. 10:12; 2 S. 1:24, 26; Nah. 2:9 (MT 10); Ps. 52:1ff. (MT 3ff.); 94:8ff.; etc. (cf. also König, pp. 230, 243).

***VI. Construction from Formal, Material, and Liturgical Units.***–Is there in Hebrew poetry a composition of poems from strophes? If one does not take this word "strophe" in too strict a sense, one can only answer affirmatively.

In Ps. 119 the first eight verses begin with the first letter of the Hebrew alphabet, the next eight with the second letter, etc. Clearly, then, Ps. 119 is composed of strophes, each of eight verses. For the same or similar reasons it may be said Pss. 9 and 37 and Lam. 4 consist of strophes each of two verses; and that Lam. 1, 2, and 3 are composed of strophes each of which has three poetic verses. Since these acrostic poems all follow the Hebrew alphabet they should each have twenty-two strophes. In the case of Ps. 37 this is not reflected very well in the English versification, because vv. 7, 20, and 34 each contain two Hebrew verses (distichs) and another strophe begins in the middle of v. 28. As a result there are only forty verses instead of the expected forty-four. Lam. 2–4 reverses the normal order of the *ayin* and the *pe* (an extrabiblical example of this variant order has been found on an abecedary from ʿIzbet Ṣarṭah; see E. Würthwein, *Text of the OT* [Eng. tr., 4th ed. 1979], pp. 218f.).

Sometimes a refrain will divide a lyrical unit into strophes. Pss. 42 and 43, which may once have constituted one psalm, have a lengthy refrain starting with "Why are you cast down, O my soul." The whole five lines are repeated in 42:5, 11, and 43:5. Cf. also Pss. 46, 80, 107; Isa. 9:7–10:4. Unfortunately the word SELAH, which is probably some kind of musical notation, cannot be used safely to divide psalms into strophes. Several other psalms can be divided into strophes owing to their symmetrical structure. Ps. 2 is apparently made up of four sections, each with three verses, with a shift of speakers in each section. In Ps. 139 the four units, each six verses long, explore the attributes of God. Ps. 132 is divided into two equal units celebrating the choice of Jerusalem and the Davidic dynasty. Cf. esp. vv. 1 and 10, 2 and 11, 9 and 16.

There is need for caution, however, when one speaks of strophes in connection with Hebrew poetry. One can only regard a pericope as a real strophe if it forms a unit not only from a material point of view but also in some sense from a formal point of view. But Hebrew poems can rarely be divided into formal units.

They often consist of material units. Close examination of Hebrew poems, esp. the Psalms, shows time and again that the separate sentences do not stand arbitrarily next to each other, such as might sometimes seem to be the case at a first glance. They arrange themselves in units. There is a progression in thought. The best general analogy to the Psalms is not the common one of a string of pearls in which one is strung next to the other, but that of a building in which each part rests on another.

A few examples will illustrate this progression (*see also* PSALMS V.C). A simple but remarkable case is Ps. 3. This begins with a bitter complaint, vv. 1f. Verses 3-6 can be called "expressions of confidence." Only then comes the real prayer (v. 7a, b), very brief, consisting of two short cries for help. In v. 7c, d the poet sees deliverance already before him. Verse 8 was possibly spoken by a ministrant of the sanctuary.

Especially remarkable is the place of the prayer, which is introduced by complaint and expressions of confidence. Such a preparation for the real entreaty is encountered quite frequently. It is common for the poet to begin a Psalm of urgent need with a song of thanksgiving or praise. See, e.g., Ps. 40 and esp. Ps. 89; the poet, so to speak, does not plunge immediately into the matter but first lays a foundation on which he then stands to offer his petition.

In this connection it might be well to look at Ps. 44. Already for reasons of content this Psalm must be divided into vv. 1-8 (hymn), 9-16 (complaint), 17-22 (evidence of righteousness), and 23-26 (the real prayer). But from a formal vantage point we are confronted by the striking fact that the subsections consist, consecutively, of ten, eight, six, and four verses. This can hardly have occurred by chance. The Psalm rises up like a ziggurat, a Mesopotamian temple tower, built in stages; and only when the poet has come to the topmost flight does he raise up his prayer to God.

Psalm 17 is built up in a different way. The first part (a prayer for justice, vv. 1-5) clears the way for the second (a prayer for preservation from enemies, vv. 6-12); the first and second parts together support the prayer in the third part (vv. 13-15).

The construction of Ps. 22 is particularly ingenious. Of the many comments that could be made on this Psalm, we will limit ourselves to the lament of vv. 1-21. The introduction (in vv. 1-10) comprises a complaint (vv. 1f.) and a song of praise (vv. 3-5), then again a complaint (vv. 6-8) and a song of praise (vv. 9f.). The songs of praise function as motifs; the first one takes its point of reference in the first complaint, the second in the second complaint; moreover, the two complaints complement each other, as do the two songs of praise. The second part of the Psalm (vv. 11-18) contains the first direct petition, which is very short (v. 11a), and a long complaint made up of a short introduction (v. 11b) and two separate sections (vv. 12-15 and 16-18). The masterful whole formed by vv. 1-18 serves as foundation for the real prayer that comes only in vv. 19-21. Notice in passing the use of "to be far" in vv. 1, 11, and 19.

Psalm 33 has three sections: vv. 1-3, 4-19, 20-22. Purely material considerations suggest a division of vv. 4-19 into 4f., 6-12, 13-19. It then appears that vv. 6-12 and 13-19 each consists of seven poetic verses — which, it would seem, may be regarded as an *a posteriori* vindication for the rightness of the division suggested.

Various Psalms are composed of liturgical units. Thus it may be assumed that vv. 1-5 of Ps. 20 were uttered by a ministrant of the sanctuary who spoke on behalf of the congregation, v. 6 by another who related a divine revelation, vv. 7f. by the first ministrant, and v. 9 by the entire congregation. See further Pss. 2, 12, 28, etc.

*VII. General Characterization.*–Many of the foregoing remarks can be true only if Israel had *trained poets*. But why should this not have been the case? True, we know little or nothing of the schooling these poets received, but we do know that special training was given among surrounding peoples. It was given already in ancient Sumer (cf. S. N. Kramer, *From the Tablets of Sumer* [1956], p. 4).It has been observed that Sumerian poetry is characterized by a precisely worked out rhetoric. It is, therefore, improbable that the Israelite poets, whose verse shows similarity to that of surrounding nations, produced their poetry without some prior schooling.

Israelite poets also apparently acquired a sort of "rhetoric." This manner of writing verse became part of their very life. It is natural, therefore, that without any particular exertion on their part they more or less intentionally incorporated into their poetry a variety of poetic phenomena and skills that we rediscover today only at the cost, perhaps, of considerable effort.

No one will deny that Hebrew poetry gives expression to deeply rooted emotions. But Israel's poets gave vent to these emotions not in an unruly, uncontrolled way. They let themselves be guided by a definite manner of writing verse, by a particular style. It may perhaps be said that this mode of making poetry bore to some extent an *intellectual character*. To verify this claim one need only reflect on the ingenious construction of these poems, on the stylistic devices of repetition and chiasm, on the acrostic poems, etc. The formulation of these poems — here, too, one thinks especially of the Psalms — was under the control of a formulating intellect. See here further the generalized statement of M. Buber and F. Rosenzweig, *Die Schrift und ihre Verdeutschung* (1936), p. 238: "All genuinely poetic art is in this sense rational — in that by a formative law of reason [*Gestaltgesetz der Vernunft*] it constructs and forms what is rudimentary."

The adage is sometimes heard: art is the most individual expression of the most individual emotion. If such be the ideal, the Israelite poets never strove after it. They never intended to expound highly individual emotions, and they never sought for highly individual expressions. Rather, they let themselves be *led by tradition*. Certainly one can speak of the originality of Israel's poets not only in content but also in form; but to determine this one must use different criteria from those usually applied today. The peculiarity of a poet, to the Hebrew mind, consisted in his giving new variations to traditional forms, in his setting a traditional image or figure in a new context, etc.

A single example will suffice. Ps. 23 has unmistakably its own peculiar ring. But one can hardly say that the image of the shepherd is original. In the ancient Near East it was common for a king to be called "shepherd" (see, e.g., 2 S. 5:2). The most important reason for this traditional character of Israel's poetry is certainly that in Israel's spiritual life the individual occupied a far less prominent place than in Western culture. N. H. RIDDERBOS

H. M. WOLF

*VIII. More Recent Studies.*–Several studies have appeared since 1980 that depart radically from, or add new dimensions to, the traditional approaches to Hebrew poetry.

The massive, complex tome of M. O'Connor (*Hebrew Verse Structure* [1980]) applies modern linguistics and comparative poetics to Hebrew poetry in an attempt to move the study of Hebrew poetry away from its focus on parallelism and meter to a focus on syntax. He points out the weaknesses in the traditional approaches (e.g., the well-known problem of meter, including the problems with syllable counting) and offers a whole new type of analysis in an effort to be more "scientific." Naturally, accompanying his new approach is new terminology. For example, since he rejects the presence of meter in Hebrew poetry he talks about "syntactic constraints" that shape Hebrew poetry (e.g., p. 65). Instead of the vague category "parallelism," he talks about "tropes," "a group of phenomena which occur regularly and serve as part of the verse structure" (e.g., p. 87). His basic poetical unit is the "line," but his concept of a line is difficult to define. More importantly, one wonders whether O'Connor has lost sight of the poetry in his attempt to analyze it scientifically; by ignoring or downplaying the semantic aspect of poetry he seems to have missed something essential.

J. Kugel also offers a major study of Hebrew poetry that reexamines the traditional approach, specifically parallelism (*The Idea of Biblical Poetry: Parallelism and Its History* [1981]). Like O'Connor he denies that Hebrew poetry has meter and he rejects syllable counting. But more importantly he challenges the notion of synonymous, antithetic, and synthetic parallelism. Although the category of synthetic parallelism has long been problematic (see S. Geller, *Parallelism in Early Biblical Poetry* [1979], pp. 375-385), while synonymous and antithetic parallelism have been widely accepted, Kugel turns the whole discussion on its head by rejecting the synonymous and antithetic classifications, instead asserting that all Hebrew poetry is actually synthetic (pp. 57f.): "it consists of A, a pause, and A's continuation B"; that is, the character of Hebrew poetry is "seconding." It involves a pausal sequence and is characterized by binary sentences, terseness, and a high degree of semantic parallelism. Kugel also provides a history of the study of parallelism, beginning with the church fathers and rabbis and concluding with the modern discussion (with an appendix on O'Connor's book).

Two studies by W. LaSor look at other dimensions of Hebrew poetry: the Masoretic accentual system ("An Approach to Hebrew Poetry through the Masoretic Accents," in A. Katsch and L. Nemoy, eds., *Essays on the Occasion of the Seventieth Anniversary of the Dropsie University (1909-1979)* [1980], pp. 327-353) and an analysis of other early Semitic poetry ("Samples of Early Semitic Poetry," in G. Rendsburg, *et al.*, eds., *The Bible World: Essays in Honor of Cyrus H. Gordon* [1980], pp. 99-121).

In the former article LaSor examined the divisions of the Masoretes in OT passages that were generally recognized as poetry. Though these were considerably later than the original compositions, two facts must be admitted: (1) The Masoretes attempted to preserve the division of the passages as they were traditionally recited, and liturgical compositions retain their original forms even generations after words have undergone semantic alteration or accent shift. (2) The MT that we have is at least somewhat more objective than the textual emendation or reconstruction to a text that we do not have. The evidence is clear that "parallelism" exists in the MT, as marked by the accents. However, there are not only distichs (bicola, a statement divided into two parts), but even tristichs and tetrastichs (statements in three or four parts), which Kugel mentions only briefly (pp. 26f.). Furthermore, there is no evidence of metrical regularity in any extended passage. One noteworthy observation resulted from the study of a portion of Lamentations, namely, that the *qînâ* meter, which is widely accepted as consisting of 3 + 2 stressed syllables, rarely occurs in the book after which it is named (*qînâ*, "lamentation"). In fact, the opposite 2 + 3 is more common, but certainly not regular (p. 332).

In the latter article LaSor analyzed the structure of poetic portions of materials from Akkadian (Babylonian and Assyrian), Ugaritic, Aramaic, Qumrân Hebrew, Sumerian, and Arabic. It is apparent that some kind of parallelism occurs regularly, in patterns remarkably similar to those that are generally identified in Hebrew poetry. Acrostic structures are found early in the Babylonian period (using the same cuneiform symbol for the beginning of each stich or line). Tristichs and tetrastichs are present in the poetic structure. Again, there is no evidence of regular meter or line length.

One may conclude that parallelism of thought — by whatever term it is called — is found in Hebrew poetry. Meter, whether defined in classical forms or by some method of syllable counting, is not found. The concept of "poetry" is due to recognition of an elevated style which does not conform to classical or western ideas of poetry, and it is therefore possible for an author to move from the more mundane ("prose") to the loftier style ("poetry"), or even somewhere in between, in the same composition.

W. S. L. S.

***Bibliography***.–Discussions of Hebrew poetry can be found in the introductions to the OT (e.g., O. Eissfeldt, *The OT: An Introduction* [Eng. tr. 1965]) and in the comms. on the OT poetical books. See esp. M. Dahood, *Psalms*, I-III (*AB*, 1966-70), and C. H. Bullock, *Intro. to the OT Poetic Books* (1979).

Various aspects of Hebrew poetry are illuminated in E. König, *Stilistik, Rhetorik, Poetik in Bezug auf die biblische Literatur* (1900); T. H. Robinson, *Poetry of the OT* (1947); "Hebrew Poetic Form," *SVT*, 1 (1953), 128-149 (including references to a wide field of literature, also covering the meter); F. Horst, *TR*, 21 (1953), 97-121; L. Alonso-Schökel, "Die stilistische Analyse bei den Propheten," in *SVT*, 7 (1960), 154-164; *Estudios de poética hebrea* (1963); S. Gevirtz, *Patterns in the Early Poetry of Israel* (1964); F. M. Cross and D. N. Freedman, *Studies in Ancient Yahwistic Poetry* (1975); W. S. LaSor, D. A. Hubbard, and F. W. Bush, *OT Survey* (1982), pp. 307-318; W. Watson, *Classical Hebrew Poetry: A Guide to Its Techniques* (1984); A. Berlin, *Dynamics of Biblical Parallelism* (1985). In addition, the annual *Ugarit Forschungen* offers many studies discussing various aspects of Hebrew and Ugaritic poetry.

*Meter:* E. Sievers, *Metrische Studien*, I-III (1901-1907); S. Mowinckel, *Psalms in Israel's Worship* (Eng. tr. 1962), II, 159-175; *Real and Apparent Tricola in Hebrew Psalm Poetry* (1957); also G. D. Young, *JNES*, 9 (1950), 124-133; S. Segert, "Problems in Hebrew Prosody," in *SVT*, 7 (1960), 283-291; R. C. Culley, "Metrical Analysis of Classical Hebrew Poetry," in J. Wevers and D. Redford, eds., *Essays on the Ancient Semitic World* (1970), pp. 12-28; D. K. Stuart, *Studies in Early Hebrew Meter* (1976).

*Parallelism:* G. B. Gray, *Forms of Hebrew Poetry* (repr. 1972, with Prolegomena by D. N. Freedman); M. Dahood, "Ugaritic-Hebrew Parallel Pairs," in L. Fisher, ed., *Ras Shamra Parallels*, I (1972), 71-382; II (1975), 3-39; T. Collins, *Line-forms in Hebrew Poetry* (1978); S. A. Geller, *Parallelism in Early Biblical Poetry* (1979); J. L. Kugel, *The Idea of Biblical Poetry: Parallelism and Its History* (1981); M. O'Connor, *Hebrew Verse Structure* (1980).

*Style of repetition: chiasm:* M. Buber and F. Rosenzweig, *Die Schrift und ihre Verdeutschung* (1936); J. Muilenburg, "A Study in Hebrew Rhetoric," in *SVT*, 1 (1953), 97-111; L. J. Liebreich, *HUCA*, 27 (1956), 181-192; H. W. Lund, *AJSL*, 49 (1933), 281-312.

*Strophic structure:* C. F. Kraft, *Strophic Structure of Hebrew Poetry as Illustrated in the First Book of the Psalter* (1938); E. J. Kissane, *Book of Psalms*, I (1953), pp. XXXIX-XLII; P. van der Lugt, *Strofische Structuren in de Bijbels-Hebreeuwse Poëzie* (1981).

*General characterization:* S. Mowinckel, *HUCA*, 23/1 (1950-51), 205-231.

N. H. RIDDERBOS
H. M. WOLF

## POETRY IN THE NT.

*I. Poetry Drawn from OT Models.*–Since Hebrew poetry is based not on quantitative meter but on the stress required by the grammatical forms in the lines, it is not to be expected that these phenomena (e.g., assonance, paranomasia, acrostic) should carry over into the Greek of the NT. We should rather look for stylistic features in the Hebrew Bible that exert their force when a NT writer seeks consciously to compose in the style of the OT or includes a piece of "translation Greek" in dependence on an OT text or paradigm.

A good example of this type of writing is seen where the NT takes over some of the most common stylistic forms of the OT, e.g., parallelism (the complementary or antithetical juxtaposition of poetical lines). Ps. 104 uses parallelism, mainly synonymous, to produce a powerful effect. The influence of this style is traceable in Luke's opening chapters (Lk. 1–2), which preserve some early canticles doubtless treasured in the Jewish-Christian community. In the opening stichos of the Magnificat Mary says:

My soul magnifies the Lord,
and my spirit rejoices in God my Savior. (1:46f.)

Later in the same song is an example of antithetical parallelism:

He has put down the mighty from their thrones,
and exalted those of low degree. (v. 52)

Lk. 2:14 shows not only antithetical parallelism but also a rudimentary form of a Greek rhetorical device, chiasmus:

Glory to God in the highest
and on earth peace among men with whom he is pleased!

The antitheses "in the highest" and "on earth" fall at opposite ends of their respective lines and thus form an X (Greek letter *chi*; hence chiasmus).

*II. Greek Rhetorical Forms in the NT.*–The NT uses antithesis to good effect, especially in the short, creedlike statements that express the two stages of Christ's existence. These are denoted by the terms flesh and spirit. See Rom. 1:3f. for an example drawn presumably from pre-Pauline Christianity. 2 Cor. 5:16 shows its influence on Paul's thinking. More sophisticated uses of this formula are 1 Tim. 3:16; 1 Pet. 1:20; 3:18.

1 Timothy 3:16 contains a number of other rhetorical forms, which were first studied by E. Norden, *Agnostos Theos* (2nd ed. 1923). The authority for these terms is the Roman rhetorician Quintilian in his *Institutio Oratoria*. The repetition of the verb at the beginning of each line and in the same grammatical form produces a species of rhythm known as *parison* and *homoeoptoton* (ix.3.76, 78). In the first couplet the verbs have the same syllabic length (5 beats), and this leads to *isocolon* (ix.3.80). Moreover, the phrases that close the lines of the couplet, *en sarkí* (in the flesh)/*en pneúmati* (in the spirit), have similar-sounding endings; this device is known as *homoeoteleuton* (ix.3.77). These poetic forms make the short verse one of the most precious instances of a literary piece in the entire NT. Commentators have not been slow to recognize this, since it is often referred to as possessing "un rythme hiératique" (J. Schmitt, *Jésus ressuscité dans la prédication apostolique* [1949], p. 100) and a lyrical quality that defies translation into English. As B. S. Easton commented (*The Pastoral Epistles* [1948], p. 136), "The Greek assonances cannot be reproduced and the crisp allusiveness is lost on modern ears."

Philippians 2:6-11 yields to the same literary analysis. Since Lohmeyer's innovative study in 1928 (*Kyrios Jesus*) this passage has long been recognized as hymnic in form and capable of division into strophes (Lohmeyer postulated six such stanzas). Later attempts to improve on this produced a three-strophe hymn in which the device of *parallelismus membrorum* (i.e., arrangement into couplets, sometimes triplets, or even quatrains) was utilized, and a tacit acceptance was made of Aristotle's judgment that a perfect literary composition requires "a beginning, a middle and an end" (*Poet.* 1450 b 26; see L. Cooper, *Aristotle on the Art of Poetry* [1913], p. 28). This is held to correspond to the three states of Christ: preexistence, incarnation, enthronement (so J. Jeremias, "Zur Gedankenführung in den paulinischen Briefen," in J. N. Sevenster and W. C. van Unnik, eds., *Studia Paulina* [1953], pp. 152-54). The permanent contribution of Jeremias is his discovery that the entire hymn is built up in couplets, though his analysis suffers from some weaknesses (noted and discussed by R. P. Martin, *Carmen Christi* [1967], pp. 32-35). Yet another proposal is to discard the entire notion of a hymn set in stanzas and see the passage as structured in the form of a set of couplets (so Martin, pp. 36ff.). When this is done, the several literary devices observed in 1 Tim. 3:16 are also seen here (details in *Carmen Christi,* pp. 36-38 and later discussion of the literary form of Phil. 2:6-11 in R. P. Martin, *Philippians* [*NCBC,* repr. 1980], pp. 109-112).

One further section of the Pauline corpus that has been inspected with a view to discovering literary traces of a poetic character is Col. 1:15-20. The most elaborate analysis is that offered by C. Masson (*Comm. du NT,* 10 [1950]), who pressed into service the element of metrical quantity and syllabic length. He found a pattern of meter caused by the regular sequence of syllabic length, and in his hands this christological hymn offered to the cosmic Christ becomes the nearest specimen in the NT to a Greek poem, with both rhythm and rhyme.

Ephesians 5:14 is another good example of Greek poetic structure. The text divides into three lines (a feature ignored by the RSV), and there is a swinging trochaic rhythm that cannot be reproduced exactly in English. The nearest we get to it is offered in the paraphrase,

Awake, O Sleeper,
From the grave arise.
The light of Christ upon you shines.

But even that rendering fails to capture the assonance of the final syllables of lines 1 and 2, *katheúdōn*/*tṓn nekrṓn,* which employs the device of *homoeoteleuton.* It is interesting that it was precisely this triplet form that was used in the initiation chants of the Hellenistic mystery cults (see the data of the Attis formula in H. Schlier, comm., *in loc.*). F. F. Bruce noted, "It has been suggested that Christians took over the rhythm for use in the act of Christian initiation, and that we have here a primitive baptismal hymn" (*Epistle to the Ephesians* [1961], p. 108).

Other sections of the NT that contain poetical forms are 1 Cor. 13:1-13; 15:54-57 (with many instances of antithetical parallelism; see J. Weiss, *History of Primitive Christianity* [Eng. tr. 1937], for a full study of Paul's literary usages, esp. in this passage) and Phil. 3:3-10. (Cf. the more recent study of 1 Cor. 13 by O. Wischmeyer, *Der höchste Weg: das 13. Kapital des 1 Korintherbriefes* [1981], esp. pp. 175-223.)

***III. Poetry in the Language of Jesus.***–Falling into a special category is the *ipsissima vox* of Jesus. By this term is meant the traits of language and idiom that may be recovered by recasting into their presumed original Aramaic form the Greek portions of the Gospels that contain the words of Jesus. In a series of fruitful studies from G. Dalman (*The Words of Jesus* [Eng. tr. 1902]) to M. Black (*An Aramaic Approach to the Gospels and Acts* [3rd ed. 1967]), this line of inquiry has been pursued with measurable success. The gains are harvested by J. Jeremias (*NT Theology* [Eng. tr. 1971], I), who stressed that Jesus' spoken mother tongue shows many signs of poetic quality, both in structure (assonance, alliteration, and rhythm) and content (use of the riddle [*māšal*] or gnomic saying, parallelism, and poetic anticlimax, as in Mt. 7:24-27). Many of these studies, including the well-known book by C. F. Burney, *The Poetry of Our Lord* (1925), are technical works that can be evaluated only by those acquainted with Aramaic; however, the popular treatments of W. A. Curtis, *Jesus Christ the Teacher* (1943), and R. H. Stein, *The Method and Message of Jesus' Teachings* (1978), may be generally recommended for an insight into Jesus' poetic manner of speech.

***IV. Poetic Quotations in the NT.***–From the world of contemporary literature the NT writers occasionally draw allusions. In Acts 17:28 Paul's statement "For we are also his offspring" derives from his fellow Cilician Aratus (*Phainomena* 5), and the earlier part of that Pauline statement, "For in him we live and move and have our being," is apparently indebted to a poem of Epimenides the Cretan. The same Cretan poet wrote the hexameter castigating the character of the Cretans that appears in Tit. 1:12. Cleanthes' famed *Hymn to Zeus* also contains a reminiscence of the Aratus quotation as part of the Stoic philosophy. The moral tag "Bad friends ruin the noblest people" (JB) in 1 Cor. 15:33 comes from *Thais* by the Athenian comic playwright Menander (4th cent. B.C.).

R. P. MARTIN

**POINTS, IN ALL.** An expression occurring twice in the AV. In Eccl. 5:16 (MT 15) ("In all points as he came, so shall he go") it renders Heb. *kol-ʿummâ* (RSV "just as"; NEB "exactly as"). Human beings leave the world in all regards as helpless as they entered it, no matter what they may have gained or accomplished during their lives.

In He. 4:15, AV, it renders Gk. *katá pánta* (RSV "in every respect"; NEB "every way") in the phrase, "[Jesus] was in all points tempted like as we are, yet without sin." Jesus successfully resisted temptation at all points of his nature, in body, soul, and spirit (cf. 2:14, 17f.). *See* TEMPTATION OF CHRIST.

M. O. EVANS

**POISON; VENOM** [Heb. *ḥēmâ, rō'š*; Gk. *thymós, iós*]; AV also GALL, HEMLOCK; NEB also GALL. Although poisons were commonly encountered in ancient Palestine in various forms, they were seldom employed for destructive purposes. The suicide of Ptolemy Macron (2 Macc. 10:13) was a notable exception. Some authorities have conjectured that the "water of bitterness" (Nu. 5:16-28) was a poisonous drink, but if it consisted merely of dust from the tabernacle floor mixed with water it was not likely poisonous. More probably the priest was relying upon a developed ritual of psychological suggestion to achieve the desired effect. The administration of poisons in trial by ordeal seems to be indicated in Mk. 16:18, although most modern commentators favor a less dramatic interpretation. It should be remembered that the Hebrews regarded any bitter-tasting substance as poisonous.

Very few of the poisonous Palestinian plants such as henbane, belladonna, and the opium poppy are mentioned in Scripture. Exceptions are the "poisonous weeds" (AV, RV, "hemlock") of Hos. 10:4 (*Artemisia judaica* L., or a related species), used in a simile for the judgment that falls on Israel, and the poisonous gourd of 2 K. 4:39 (*Citrullus colocynthis* L.). The former is a rather woody plant with a strong aromatic odor and bitter taste, related to the common mugwort. The latter is a trailing vine whose pulpy fruit is intensely bitter and has drastic cathartic qualities. The "vine of Sodom" with its "grapes of poison" (Dt. 32:32) appears to be the same plant, used metaphorically.

OT poisons were normally of animal, reptile, or insect origin (Dt. 32:24, 33; Job 20:16; Ps. 140:3) and were irritants, producing a fever and usually resulting in death. Some thirty varieties of serpents have been reported from Palestine, many of them poisonous; the eight different Hebrew terms employed to describe the *Ophidae* reflect the range of species. The reference in Ps. 140:3 preserves the popular belief that the forked tongue of the snake carried the poison (cf. Jas. 3:7f.), whereas it is actually contained in the fang, a fact known to Pliny the Elder (*Nat. hist.* xi.62).

*See also* GALL; WORMWOOD. R. K. H.

**POLE** [Heb. *b^eri(a)ḥ*–'bar' (Ex. 40:18), *môṭ* (Nu. 13:23), *môṭâ* (1 Ch. 15:15), *nēs*–'standard' (Nu. 21:8f.), pl. of *baḏ*]; AV also STAFF (Nu. 13:23; usually pl. STAVES), BAR (Ex. 40:18); NEB also CROSSBAR (Ex. 40:18), STANDARD (Nu. 21:8f.). The plural of Heb. *baḏ* usually refers to poles used to carry sacred objects, including the ark, which because of its holiness was not to be touched (2 S. 6:7); only the Levitical sons of Kohath were to carry it (Nu. 4:1-13; 1 Ch. 15:15). These poles were made of acacia wood, which was very durable, and were overlaid with gold (Ex. 25:13; 37:4f.). Similar poles were made to carry the table used in the tabernacle for the bread of the Presence (5:28; 37:14f.), the altar of incense (30:4f.; 37:28), and the altar of burnt offering, although those for the latter altar were overlaid with bronze, not gold, to match the bronze altar (27:6f.; 38:5-7). The lengths of the various poles are not known, but those for the ark are said to have been so long that in Solomon's time their ends could be seen "from the holy place before the inner sanctuary" (1 K. 8:8 par. 2 Ch. 5:9). These poles were never to be removed from the ark (Ex. 25:15; 1 K. 8:8), but the use of *môṭâ* rather than *baḏ* in 1 Ch. 15:15 may indicate that the original poles had worn out and had been replaced by new ones (see below on *môṭ*).

Hebrew *nēs* is a banner or standard and is thus appropriately used for the pole with the bronze serpent that Moses held up for the people during the fiery-serpent episode (Nu. 21:8f.). The *b^eri(a)ḥ* of the tabernacle (Ex. 40:18) probably refers to part of the framework for the tabernacle; the same word is used in the description of that framework ("bar," Ex. 26:26-29; 36:31-34). Thus the AV and NEB are more consistent in their translations than the RSV. Heb. *môṭ* (<*mûṭ*, "waver, shake") may imply that the pole laden with grapes was wobbly (Nu. 13:23), although G. B. Gray's suggestion (comm. on Numbers [*ICC*, 1903], p. 37) that it means a board with a large, flat surface upon which objects could be set has some merit (cf. "carrying frame" in Nu. 4:10). G. A. L.

**POLICE** [pl. of Gk. *rhabdoúchos*–'one who carries a rod' (Acts 16:35, 38)]; AV SERJEANTS; NEB OFFICERS. The Gk. *rhabdoúchoi* refers to Roman lictors (cf. Bauer, rev., p. 733; Diodorus v.40.1), who carried the *fasces*, a bundle of twelve birch rods bound with a red thong, as a sign of their authority.

Paul met these officers in the forum at Philippi (Acts 16:19ff.). Before the *stratēgoí* (*see* MAGISTRATE) and their attendant lictors, he was accused of disturbing the peace; then he was stripped, beaten (with the rods of the lictors; cf. 2 Cor. 11:25), and imprisoned. The next day the magistrates sent their lictors to release Paul. Only then were Paul's protests of Roman citizenship finally heard.

This account accords well with our knowledge of Philippi and the role of lictors generally. As a Roman colony under *ius italicum*, the city enjoyed the full range of civic and religious offices. So the city's twin magistrates, the *duumviri* (or *duoviri*), as holders of imperial authority, were each attended by two lictors (a consul had twelve lictors, and after Domitian, the emperor had twenty-four).

Although an office common to the ancient world (e.g., Polybius v.26.10), lictors proper held a distinctive office within the imperial apparatus. Their role was to speak for the magistrate, to clear his way, and to effect his right of arrest, summons, and punishment.

Modern life lacks a clear parallel to this office. The AV "serjeant" is accurate, if taken in the obsolete sense of one who carries out the orders of a court or of another authority. The RSV "police" suggests the appropriate function, but implies a greater autonomy than lictors enjoyed, as well as missing their ceremonial aspects. Our closest parallel may be that of a marshal or an officer of the court.

*Bibliography.*–*BC*, IV, 200; A. N. Sherwin-White, *Roman Society and Roman Law in the NT* (1963), pp. 71-82; *Dictionnaire d'Archéologie Chrétienne* (1939), XIV/1, *s.v.* "Philippes" (P. Collart).

W. R. HARRIS

**POLICY** [Heb. *śeḵel* (Dnl. 8:25); Gk. *panoúrgos* (Jth. 11:8), *boulḗ* (1 Macc. 8:4), *stratḗgēma* (2 Macc. 14:29), *stratēgéō* (2 Macc. 14:31)]. The AV uses this term in an obsolete way for "cunning" (Dnl. 8:25), "strategy" (Jth. 11:8), "planning" (1 Macc. 8:4), "stratagem" (2 Macc. 14:29), and "outwit" (2 Macc. 14:31).

**POLL.** Both the noun and verb have obsolete usages in the AV. The noun translates Heb. *gulgōleṯ* (lit. "skull"), which the RSV renders "census" (Nu. 1:2), "head by head" (vv. 18, 20, 22), "apiece" (3:47), and "individual" (1 Ch. 23:24). The verb "poll" means to cut or trim hair (2 S. 14:26; Ezk. 44:20; Mic. 1:16).

**POLLUTION** [Heb. *ṭum'â* (Ezr. 6:21), *niddâ*–'something detestable' (9:11)]; AV FILTHINESS; NEB also UNCLEANNESS; [Gk. *alísgēma*] (Acts 15:20); NEB "polluted by contact with"; **POLLUTE; POLLUTED** [Heb. qal and hiphil of *ḥānēp* (Nu. 35:33; Ps. 106:38; Isa. 24:5; Jer. 3:1f., 9), piel of *ḥālal*–'profane' (1 Ch. 5:1; Jer. 16:18), qal, niphal, and piel of *ṭāmē'* (2 Ch. 36:14; Ezk. 20:43; 23:17, 30), hophal of *šāḥaṯ* (Prov. 25:26), piel and pual of *gā'al* (Mal. 1:7, 12), *'iddâ*–'menstruation' (Isa. 64:6 [MT 5])]; AV also DEFILE(D), CORRUPT, FILTHY (Isa. 64:6 [MT 5]); NEB also DEFILE(D), "commit incest" (1 Ch. 5:1), DESECRATED, TAINTED, FILTHY; [Gk. *bdelýssomai*] (Rev. 21:8); AV ABOMINABLE; NEB VILE. To make something ritually or morally impure. Most of the terms are discussed under CLEAN AND UNCLEAN; DEFILE; and PROFANE. Heb. *ḥānēp* generally occurs in connection with the defilement of the land (*see* CLEAN AND UNCLEAN II.E).

The "pollutions of the peoples of the land" from which the participants in the Passover had to separate themselves (Ezr. 6:21) were the idolatrous practices of foreign peoples who had entered Judah during the Exile. The quotation in 9:11f. is a composite drawn from passages such as Ex. 34:12-16; Lev. 18:24-30; Dt. 7:1-4. (*See also* FILTH.) In Mal. 1:7, 12 "polluted" simply means "blemished," i.e., food of inferior quality. The "pollutions of idols" from which the gentile Christians were asked to abstain (Acts 15:20) refers to meat that has previously been sacrificed to idols. The "polluted" who are condemned in Rev. 21:8, however, are those who have participated in the abominable practice of emperor worship.

*See also* HOLINESS; PURE. N. J. O.

**POLLUX** pol'əks. *See* TWIN BROTHERS.

**POLYCARP.** *See* APOSTOLIC FATHERS.

**POLYGAMY** pə-lig'ə-mē [< Gk. *polloí*—'many' plus *gaméō*–'marry']. While the term literally implies multiple marriage by one member of either sex, in general usage it describes a man who has numerous wives concurrently in the same family group. This situation is more correctly described as *polygyny*, which signifies a man who has numerous wives. The converse of this is *polyandry*, denoting a woman with several concurrent husbands.

Polygyny became subsumed under polygamy early in Hebrew history, despite the marital ideal laid down in Gen. 2:24. Contrary to conventional liberal scholarship, this admonition seems to be very early rather than late, since it reflects prepatriarchal social configurations such as the matriarchate, whereby men, not women, left home at marriage. In any event, the Genesis dictum established monogamy as a working principle for mankind, and originally it was meant to signify the union of a male and a female who were counterparts to each other. The wife was in no way regarded as inferior to her husband, being considered in the first instance as specifically the "essence of his essence" (Gen. 2:23). Whether such a relationship was to be regarded as prescriptive or descriptive depends upon the retention or omission of the "shall" or "will" in v. 24. The former emphasis was espoused by the KJV, the NIV, and the New King James Version, while the RSV and the NEB retained a present, descriptive tense.

Once the fall occurred, however, a difference in the marital relationship took place, with the male becoming the dominant partner in the union (3:16). The wife was placed in a subordinate position, and immediately was vulnerable to exploitation, one form of which was polygyny. This type of marital relationship occurred under a variety of circumstances. Women captured in battles between city-states or larger countries (cf. Dt. 21:10-14) became part of the victors' spoils. While some women were taken as wives, others were reduced to brutal concubinage, ministering to the captors' lusts while their legal wives bore the legitimate family offspring. In the ancient Near East, women who found themselves serving as slaves for other reasons frequently became the object of sexual exploitation in households by men who regarded them as inferior "wives." In the OT, the earliest example of polygyny/polygamy was the marriage of Lamech to Adah and Zillah (Gen. 4:19). Lamech's boastful "sword-song" seems to have perpetuated the spirit of his ancestor Cain, and this apparently extended to polygamy also. In ancient Mesopotamia, marriage contracts frequently specified that a wife who proved infertile should give her handmaid to her husband in order to produce children for the household. This situation underlies the procedure whereby Sarah's handmaid Hagar was given by her to Abraham as a wife (Gen. 16:3) for purposes of procreation. In accepting this polygamous relationship Abraham was acceding to local custom rather than obeying the divine decree or trusting God's promise to him concerning descendants.

From a very early period of human history there seems to have been a preponderance of females in society, and this was apparently presenting certain problems by the patriarchal period. Esau in mid-life married two Hittite women (who may either have been of indigenous Hatti stock, or a migrant group from some area of the subsequent Hittite empire), and spitefully augmented the family disturbance that they caused (Gen. 26:25) by marrying into the family of Ishmael (28:9). Jacob, by contrast, became polygamous by default initially, falling victim to Laban's marital scheme for his unattractive daughter Leah (29:16-30). He became openly polygamous subsequently when he took Bilhah, Rachel's maid, as a concubine (30:3), an event that was followed by Leah's giving her maid, Zilpah, to Jacob as a wife to produce children for the family (30:9-13) in addition to the seven that she herself had produced.

By the Mosaic period polygamy was being legislated for as though it was a current social institution. Dt. 21:15-18 prescribed that a man had to treat the offspring of a disfavored wife equally with the son of a loved wife, indicating some of the tensions arising within a polygamous marriage (cf. Gen. 29:20-31). King David was unashamedly polygamous (2 S. 5:13-16), even stooping to murder to satisfy his lust (2 S. 11:15, 27), while Solomon's huge harem (1 K. 11:3) included foreign wives that were the result of political alliances. Marriage of this kind had been prohibited in the Torah (cf. Ex. 34:16) because of the dangers of idolatry being introduced into Israel from such sources. These sexual extravagances ultimately brought grave economic problems to Israel, and at Solomon's death the kingdom divided, never to unite again in this age (1 K. 11:12).

One form of polygamy, however, was provided for in the Law. This was the marriage institution known as the levirate (from *levir,* "a husband's brother") and was apparently sanctioned in the interests of endogamous marriage and the continuation of the family line. Levirate MARRIAGE (Dt. 25:5-10) provided that a deceased man's brother should take the widow as his wife and raise a family to perpetuate his brother's name and keep inherited land in the family. Social ostracism was the penalty incurred if a surviving brother was unwilling to enter into such a marriage for whatever reason.

One form of the levirate involved Judah and Tamar (Gen. 38), while a more celebrated one was that between Boaz and Ruth (Ruth 4), even though the procedure differed somewhat from the Deuteronomic formulation. Levirate marriage appears to contravene the legislation prohibiting marriage with one's brother's wife (Lev. 18:16; 20:21), but in other respects was actually a humane way of dealing with what was frequently the desperate plight of widows by keeping them within the family and tribe, without which they would almost certainly have starved or been callously exploited.

There are thus numerous reasons for the rise of polygamy/polygyny, which apart from sensuous considerations included the need to maintain endogamous marriages, the desire to increase the Israelite population, the necessity for providing for destitute widows in order to avoid slavery, prostitution and the like, and the maintaining of the nation's working force. These factors notwithstanding, the ideal Hebrew marriage continued to be monogamous, despite the examples set to the contrary by royalty. The admonitions of Proverbs, thought by some to be teaching given to the sons of the wealthy, furnish no hint of polygamy (cf. 12:4; 19:13), while at the same time condemning prostitution openly (7:6-23). By the 5th cent. B.C. the ideal of fidelity to the original spouse was still being promoted as a paradigm of the relationship that ought to exist between Israel and her God (Mal. 2:13-16).

The NT teachings on marriage presupposed monogamy, and while Christ conceded that Moses had allowed divorce "because of the hardness of your hearts" (Mt. 19:8), He emphasized that such was not the original intent of marriage. In point of fact, divorce would have been rare in Christ's time because the cost to the husband of returning his wife's dowry and arranging for financial support for her and any children of the marriage would have been prohibitive under normal conditions (*see* DIVORCE). While polygamy was tolerated among the rich and powerful, it was recognized as a violation of that covenantal fidelity that God demanded of Israel His bride at the highest level (cf. Hos. 2:2), and that Christ also demanded of the Church (cf. 2 Cor. 11:2). This latter consideration is of fundamental importance, since God has spoken His final word in His Son, and now demands repentance, obedience, and unswerving fidelity from His people.

*Bibliography.*–M. Burrows, *Basis of Israelite Marriage* (1936); L. M. Epstein, *Marriage Laws in the Bible and the Talmud* (1942); D. R. Mace, *Hebrew Marriage* (1953); R. de Vaux, *Ancient Israel,* I (Eng. tr. 1961). R. K. HARRISON

**POMEGRANATE** [Heb. *rimmôn*; Akk. *armannu*; Gk. *rhóa, kṓdōn*]. The many references are to one of the most characteristic Near Eastern trees, the *Punica granatum* L.

Core-formed vase in the shape of a pomegranate. Actual height: 7.6 cm. (3 in.). From Cyprus, 1440-1350 B.C. (Corning Museum of Glass)

Tripod with pomegranate decorations. From Ugarit, 15th-14th cent. B.C. (Louvre)

Native to Persia and India, it was grown in Palestine at an early period. *See* Plate 58.

Moses told the Israelites that pomegranates, along with wheat, barley, vines, and figs, were to be found in the Promised Land (Dt. 8:8; cf. Hag. 2:19), and Israelite spies indeed brought some from Eshcol (Nu. 13:23). When in the Sinai the Israelites longed for the grain, vines, figs, and pomegranates of Egypt (Nu. 20:5). In Joel 1:11f. the withering pomegranate is an object of lamentation.

The tree is shrublike but may occasionally attain 9 m. (30 ft.) in height. It bears bright-green oblong leaves and brilliant scarlet blossoms (cf. the metaphorical use in Cant. 4:13; 7:12 [MT 11]). The ripe globular fruit contains an acid pulp in which red seeds are embedded. In antiquity the expressed juice was made into a sweet wine (8:2). Pomegranate rind is rich in tannic acid, and in ancient Egypt it was burned in temples and houses as a fumigant.

Pomegranate flowers formed a popular decorative motif, appearing on Aaron's garments (Ex. 28:33f.; 39:24f.; cf. Sir. 45:9) and in the brass work of the Solomonic temple (1 K. 7:18-20, 42; 2 K. 25:17; 2 Ch. 3:16; 4:13). The pomegranate tree of Migron (1 S. 14:2) may have been a place, Rimmon. Other localities that were doubtless named after pomegranate trees included Gath-rimmon (Josh. 19:45), Rimmon-perez (Nu. 33:19f.), En-rimmon, and Rimmon (Josh. 19:7, 13).

In Greek mythology, a single pomegranate seed eaten by the hungry Persephone (Korê) while she was a prisoner of Hades (Pluto) in the underworld proved to be her undoing. Although she was released, she was condemned to return there each winter for three months until the spring flowers emerged. The rituals of Demeter (Earth-Mother) and the Maiden (Persephone) were the oldest of the Eleusinian Mysteries, and were being enacted annually in Greece long before the Hebrew exile. They attracted a large following, mainly of women, but there is no reference to the rituals in the NT. R. K. H.

**POMMEL** [Gk. *hypōpiázō*–'strike under the eye,' 'give a black eye'] (1 Cor. 9:27). A term that continues the boxing metaphor of v. 26, here used figuratively of self-control.

For the noun "pommel" in 2 Ch. 4:12f., AV, *see* BOWL.

**POMP** [Heb. *y^eqār*] (Est. 1:4; Ps. 49:12, 20 [MT 13, 21]); AV HONOUR; NEB also "like oxen" (Ps. 49:12, 20); [*gā'ôn*] (Isa. 14:11); NEB PRIDE; [Gk. *phantasía*] (Acts 25:23); NEB "full state." Heb. *y^eqār* literally means "preciousness" and thus probably indicates ostentatious luxury. Cf. M. Dahood, *Psalms I* (*AB,* 1965), p. 299, who suggests that *y^eqār* in Ps. 49:12, 20 is a term for the nether world; though such a meaning fits the context well, it is based on very tenuous evidence and should not be accepted. Similarly, the NEB's emendation of MT *bîqār* ("in pomp") to *kabbāqār* ("like oxen") has little to commend it. The idea expressed here and in Isa. 14:11 is that pomp and wealth without the knowledge of God are empty; death removes them.

The Gk. *phantasía,* used only in Acts 25:23 in the NT, may refer to the whole procession rather than just the ostentation of Agrippa and Bernice (see the comms.).

G. A. L.

**POND.** *See* POOL.

**PONDER** [Heb. hiphil of *śāḵal*–'understand'] (Ps. 64:9 [MT 10]); AV WISELY CONSIDER; NEB LEARN (THEIR) LESSON; [hithpolel of *bîn*–'understand'] (Isa. 14:16); AV CONSIDER; [*hāgâ*–'consider,' 'mutter'] (Prov. 15:28); AV STUDY; NEB THINK; [Gk. *symbállō*] (Lk. 2:19); [*dienthyméomai*] (Acts 10:19); AV, NEB, THINK. To consider carefully or weigh in one's mind. The AV uses "ponder" also to render the piel of Heb. *pālas* in Prov. 4:26; 5:6, 21 (RSV "take heed to," "watch"; NEB "look out for," "watch for") and *tāḵan* in 21:2; 24:12 (RSV "weigh"; NEB "fix a standard").

**PONTIUS PILATE.** *See* PILATE, PONTIUS.

**PONTUS** pon'təs [Gk. *Pontos*]. An important territory in northeast Asia Minor, lying along the south shore of the Black Sea. The name was not ethnical but geographical, designating the part of Cappadocia that bordered on the Pontus (Euxine), as the Black Sea was then termed. Pontus proper extended from the Halys River (Kızıl Irmak) on the west to the borders of Colchis on the east, its inland boundaries meeting those of Galatia, Cappadocia, and Armenia. The chief rivers besides the Halys were the Iris, Lycus, and Thermodon. The fertile land of their valleys and of the narrow coastal margin was separated from the interior by mountains, once heavily forested, which have always impeded communication with the plateau. Important products included fruit, corn, olives, and timber.

The earliest history of Pontus is obscure. There are traces of Assyrian culture from the 3rd millennium B.C.; Hittite occupation may be seen in the surviving tumuli and rock tombs. The home of the legendary Amazons, originally Hittite warrior-priestesses, was located by the river Thermodon. About the 7th cent. B.C. Greeks from Miletus colonized the strategic site of Sinope (Sinop), strictly in Paphlagonia, and from there Amisus (Samsun) and Trapezus (Trabzon, Trebizond), where Xenophon's Ten Thousand reached the sea. The interior was meanwhile occupied by diverse native tribes, of whom the Chalybes were traditionally the first workers in iron; the Moschi and Tibareni, mentioned by Herodotus, have sometimes been identified with Meshech and Tubal (Gen. 10:2). The principal settlements were then around temples, notably that of Mâ at Comana Pontica, near modern Tokat.

When the Persians established supremacy in Asia Minor with the overthrow of Lydia in 546 B.C., Pontus was loosely joined to the great empire and was ruled by Persian satraps. In the 4th cent. B.C. Ariobarzanes and Mithridates laid the foundation of an independent kingdom, whose capital was first at Amasia (Amasya) in the Iris Valley, later famous as the birthplace of the geographer Strabo in the 1st cent. B.C. Greek culture, however, was slow to penetrate the interior.

Pontus reached its zenith under its most famous king, Mithridates VI Eupator (120-63 B.C.). In 88 he overthrew Roman authority in Asia Minor and ordered the massacre of eighty thousand Romans. Sulla restored Roman fortunes in the first war (88-84); in a third war (74-65) Mithridates was successively opposed by Lucullus and Pompey. After his defeat by Pompey his dominions were incorporated in the territories of the Roman republic. The aged king died in exile in the Crimea. The Mithridatic dynasty was finally destroyed after Caesar's lightning victory over Pharnaces at Zela (Zile) in 47 B.C.

Most of Pontus was then administratively united with the Roman province of BITHYNIA (forming Bithynia-Pontus); the eastern part, however, became a separate kingdom (termed Pontus Polemoniacus) under Polemo of Laodicea and his house (36 B.C.–A.D. 63), and the southwest was incorporated into the province of Galatia (Pontus Galaticus). Bithynia-Pontus was constituted a senatorial province under a proconsul in 27 B.C.

Allusions to Pontus in the NT probably refer to this provincial area. Philo attested to the widespread settlement of Jews there (*De Legatione ad Gaium* 36). Some of them were present in Jerusalem at Pentecost (Acts 2:9) and may have been the earliest evangelists in the province. Paul was prevented from entering Bithynia (16:7); possibly others were already working there. Paul's associate Aquila was a Jew of Pontus (18:2). It is not clear whether he and his wife Priscilla were already Christians at their meeting with Paul at Corinth.

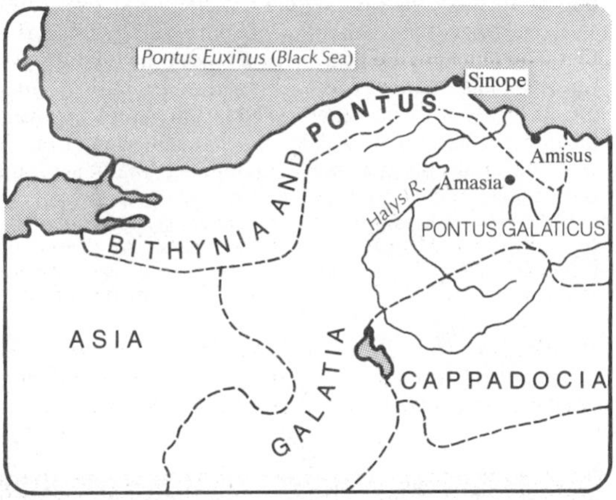


The inclusion of the sojourners of the Dispersion in Pontus, with those of four other provinces in Asia Minor, in the address of 1 Pet. 1:1 again points to a rapid early expansion of Christianity there. The faith must have been established quickly in the Greek coastal cities, arriving either by the sea route or overland by the trade artery from Caesarea Mazaca in Cappadocia. F. J. A. Hort argued that the sequence of names in 1 Peter represents Silvanus's route around the churches, beginning from Sinope in Pontus (*First Epistle of St. Peter I.1–II.17* [1898], pp. 157-184). The hinterland of Sinope is, however, mountainous and difficult, and it seems more likely that the starting point was further east at Amisus. Amisus commanded the best route to the interior through Amasia, chief city of Pontus Galaticus, where it crossed the principal longitudinal road of inland Pontus. From there, after traversing the eastern end of provincial Galatia, Silvanus would have reached Caesarea in Cappadocia (Hemer, pp. 239-243). The recent sociological approach to 1 Peter by J. H. Elliott (*A Home for the Homeless* [1982]) posits a readership of non-citizen aliens in a largely rural setting at a somewhat later date. This seems contrary to the probabilities of early Christian expansion, which was along the coasts and principal roads, whereas the country people seem to have resisted the new religion. The names of provinces also suit the period before Vespasian reorganized the eastern frontiers, combining an enlarged Galatia with Cappadocia in A.D. 72. The difficulties of using this kind of evidence, in either direction, must be recognized, of course. While he was special imperial commissioner in Bithynia-Pontus (A.D. 111-113) Pliny found Christians under his authority in such numbers that pagan temples had become deserted. Ramsay argued that Pliny's famous letter to the emperor Trajan seeking guidance in the matter (x.96), while broadly relevant to the whole double province, was primarily occasioned by conditions in Amisus (*CRE,* pp. 224f.; *see also* PERSECUTE IV).

Some light is thrown on the second-century religious situation in Pontus by Lucian's account of the charlatan Alexander of Abonuteichus, who considered Christians among his principal opponents. The heretic Marcion was a native of Sinope. Aquila, a Jewish proselyte of Pontus, made a slavishly literal Greek rendering of the Hebrew OT to counteract the Christian use of the LXX.

The reference to Queen Tryphaena in the apocryphal Acts of Paul and Thecla may be of historical value. Ramsay identified her with the Pontic queen of the Polemo dynasty (*CRE,* pp. 382-391).

Pontus was partitioned in the provincial reorganization of Diocletian. The area remained part of the Byzantine empire until the foundation of the empire of Trebizond in 1204. It fell under Ottoman rule in 1461.

***Bibliography.***–W. J. Hamilton, *Researches in Asia Minor, Pontus and Armenia* (2 vols., 1842); *CRE*, ch. 10; J. A. R. Munro, *Journal of Hellenic Studies*, 21 (1901), 52-66; W. Leaf, *Journal of Hellenic Studies*, 36 (1916), 1-15; *CAH*, IX (1932), chs. 5, 8; XI (1936), 575-580; *CERP*, ch. 6; C. J. Hemer, *Expos.T.,* 89 (1977/78), 239-243.

C. J. HEMER

**POOL; POND** [Heb. *b$^{e}$rēḵâ, b$^{e}$rāḵâ*; Arab. *birkat*] (2 S. 2:13; 1 K. 22:38; Isa. 7:3; 36:2; Nah. 2:8 [MT 7]; etc.); [Heb. *'$^{a}$gam*–'marsh'] (Isa. 14:23; etc.); [Heb. *mayim*] (Jer. 41:12); AV WATERS; [Heb. *mayim '$^{a}$gam*] (Ps. 107:35; 114:8); AV STANDING WATER; [Heb. *miqweh*–'gathering'] (Ex. 7:19; cf. Gen. 1:10); [Heb. *gēḇ*] (2 K. 3:16); AV DITCH; [Gk. *kolymbḗthra*–'place of diving'] (LXX; Jn. 5:2, 4, 7; 9:7).

Lakes or ponds are very rare in Palestine. The word for a natural pond or marsh (Heb. *'$^{a}$gam*) refers to pools of the Nile (Ex. 7:19; 8:5) or to the transformation of the desert into a place of springs, rivers, and pools (Ps. 107:35; 114:8; Isa. 35:7; 41:18; 42:15) rather than to actual pools within Palestine. Pools in Palestine (Heb. *b$^{e}$rēḵâ*) were typically man-made (cf. 2 K. 20:20; Neh. 3:16; Eccl. 2:6), built to collect the scant or irregular rain or spring water for both irrigation and drinking. Pools, in contrast to cisterns, were usually open, large, public or government installations, and, from Roman times at least, rectangular and wider than they were deep.

In Jerusalem, channels brought water from Gihon, the biblical name for the main spring east of the city (Isa. 7:3; 36:2). It was to avoid this exposed route outside the city wall that Hezekiah cut the Siloam tunnel through solid rock to a new pool at the southern edge of Ophel (2 K. 20:20; 2 Ch. 32:30; cf. the NT reference to the Roman-period pool of Siloam in Jn. 9:7). The "upper pool" (2 K. 18:17; Isa. 7:3; 36:2), the "lower pool" (Isa. 22:9), the "old pool" (22:11), the "King's Pool" (Neh. 2:14), and the "Pool of Shelah [AV Siloah] of the king's garden" (Neh. 3:15) all seem to be connected with water from Gihon and its channels. (*See* JERUSALEM II.C; III.D.2.e-g, 5.j, t; III.F.2.e-h.)

Part of the Jerusalem Model showing the pool of Siloam at the lower end of David's City (W. S. LaSor)

One of the Pools of Solomon near Bethlehem (W. S. LaSor)

The pool of Beth-zatha (Bethesda) has been identified at the north of the city in what are now the grounds of the Church of St. Anne (cf. Jn. 5:2). The three great "Pools of Solomon" near Bethlehem, the largest almost 180 m. (600 ft.) long and 15 m. (50 ft.) deep, also supplied water to Jerusalem by aqueduct, at least from the Roman period (Josephus *Ant.* xviii.3.2 [60-62]). The OT also refers to pools at Gibeon (2 S. 2:13), Hebron (4:12), and Samaria (1 K. 22:38).

Pools and water-holding systems were also made by damming watercourses in which water flowed after rain showers. Examples of these are found at Dhībân and Medeba in Moab, in the Judeah Buqê'ah west of Qumrân, and frequently in the Negeb (cf. *BASOR,* 142 [1956]; 155 [1959]).

Some pools had purposes other than drinking, washing, and irrigation. At Qumrân there were several types of water containers. From a main reservoir distribution channels (some with sedimentation basins) led to pools, some of which were for baptizing. "Waters of washing" are mentioned (1QS 5:13f.) and "waters of impurity" (3:9), but their precise significance is not clear. Early commentators on the Dead Seas Scrolls tended to use the word "baptism," leading those not familiar with Judaism to think of the rite as initiatory (i.e., required for admission to the sect). The texts, however, rather limit the use of the waters to those who were already members, possibly in connection with an annual examination (cf. W. S. LaSor, *Dead Sea Scrolls and the NT* [1972], pp. 72f.).

When Masada was excavated, first one and then another MIQVAH was uncovered. Y. Yadin, the archeologist, told of the concern of the rabbis that these miqvot complied with rabbinic measurements (*Masada* [1966], pp. 166f.). Excavations at the south wall of the Temple Mount in Jerusalem have uncovered a number of miqvot. According to one interpreter, persons who wished to go into the temple enclosure were required to purify themselves at these miqvot. Another has suggested that these miqvot were where the three thousand were baptized on the day of Pentecost. Both suggestions need further confirmation.

A sect called Therapeutae ("healers") used pools as a

Pool at Herod's later palace at Jericho (site excavated by E. Netzer for the Hebrew University of Jerusalem; picture Z. Radovan)

means of healing, and hot springs at Tiberius were (and still are) considered to have healing value.

There were also swimming pools (Herod had one in his palace at Masada and another at Jericho) and fishing pools in ancient Palestine.

In figurative use, the eyes of the beloved are likened to pools of Heshbon (Cant. 7:4 [MT 3]), and the doomed city of Nineveh resembles a pool going dry (Nah. 2:8).

*See also* CISTERN; LAKE; WATER.

***Bibliography.***–J. J. Simons, *Jerusalem in the OT* (1952); J. B. Pritchard, *BA*, 19 (1956).

D. W. HARVEY W. S. L. S.

**POOLS OF SOLOMON.** *See* POOL.

**POOR.** A term referring primarily to persons of low social and economic status, but sometimes designating God's righteous people, the humble and meek who call upon God for deliverance.

- I. In the OT
  - A. Terms
  - B. Teaching
    1. Rights of the Poor
    2. Righteousness and the Poor
    3. The Poor as the Oppressed
    4. Hope of the Poor
    5. The Poor as the People of God
- II. In the NT
  - A. Terms
  - B. Teaching
    1. Hope Realized: Gospel for the Poor
    2. Righteousness and the Poor
    3. The Poor as the Oppressed
    4. The Poor as the People of God

***I. In the OT.***–*A. Terms.* God's concern for the poor looms large on the pages of Scripture because poverty results primarily from unrighteous conduct by either the poor individuals or the larger community. While a variety of Hebrew terms is used to designate the poor, little emphasis falls on the distinctive nuances of each term. Often they are used synonymously (cf. Ps. 82:3f.). The major Hebrew terms are:

(1) *ʿĀnî, ʿānāw,* "oppressed," "poor," "humble" (e.g., Lev. 19:10; Dt. 15:11; Job 29:12; Ps. 10:9; 74:19; Isa. 3:14f.). These terms are used to designate one who suffers not from a deserved, self-inflicted poverty but from a poverty caused by wrongful impoverishment or dispossession. God is the helper and deliverer of such poor (the *ʿᵃnāwîm*). *See* HUMBLE I. B.

(2) *ʾEḇyôn,* "in want, needy, poor" (e.g., Dt. 15:4-11; Job 31:19; Ps. 132:15; Prov. 14:21; Jer. 2:34). This term originally referred to a beggar seeking alms but was later used more generally for the very poor and homeless. In some of the Psalms it is linked with *ʿānî* ("poor [*ʿānî*] and needy [*ʾeḇyôn*]") to designate all the righteous who petition God as their deliverer from need of any kind (Ps. 37:14; 40:17 [MT 18]; 70:5 [MT 6]; 74:21; etc).

(3) *Dal,* "weak," "thin," "low," "poor" (e.g., Ex. 23:3; 1 S. 2:8; Job 5:16; Ps. 113:7; Prov. 19:17; Am. 8:6). This term can refer to physical weakness (e.g., Gen. 41:19), but more often it refers to those who are powerless due to low social status, e.g., the poorest class of peasants left behind during the Babylonian captivity (*dallâ,* 2 K. 25:12; Jer. 40:7; 52:15f.).

(4) *Rāš,* "poor, needy." This term (part. of *rûš,* "be poor") is used in a purely social or economic sense, especially in wisdom literature (2 S. 12:1, 3f.; Prov. 13:8; 14:20; 18:23; 22:7; etc.).

(5) *Miskēn,* "dependent, socially inferior." This term (cf. Akk. *muškênu,* "beggar") is related to the self-designation still used by Arab beggars. It occurs only in Ecclesiastes; interestingly, in each occurrence the *miskēn* is wise (Eccl. 4:13; 9:15f.).

*B. Teaching.* The OT teaches that God is scandalized by poverty and wills its abolition: "There will be no poor among you . . . " (Dt. 15:4). But although God's will is unequivocal, its fulfillment depends upon God's blessing, which is conditional upon the obedience of His people: ". . . if only you will obey the voice of the Lord your God . . . " (v. 5). Sadly, because Israel does not obey, "the poor will never cease out of the land" (v. 11). Therefore, Israel was commanded to respond to the poor at all times with open hand and heart and was warned that to do anything less than this was sin (vv. 7-11). The year of release was the institutionalized expression of God's will that poverty be abolished, for in this year all debts were to be cancelled (vv. 1f.; *see* SABBATICAL YEAR). God's expressed will for the poor was never fully actualized in history, but it became the basis for the prayers of the poor and for the hope that it would become a reality in the future (cf. Ps. 9:18 [MT 19]; 132:15). Consequently, God's will that there be no poor in the land continues to be mandated for the "new Israel" as the obedience required by the Kingdom that has been and will be given (Lk. 12:32f.).

*1. Rights of the Poor.* The Mosaic legal code established that the poor had certain rights (cf. Isa. 10:2). While anyone in Israel could eat from a neighbor's vineyard or field to satisfy hunger (Dt. 23:24f.), the poor were given additional rights. Each year the gleanings of field, orchard, and vineyard belonged to the poor, including the border of the field, the sheaf forgotten in the field, and whatever grew spontaneously in the Sabbatical Year (Lev. 19:10; 23:22; Dt. 24:19; Ex. 23:11). No interest was to be exacted on loans to the poor (Ex. 22:25; Lev. 25:36), nor was the cloak given in pledge to be kept overnight (Dt. 24:12), nor was food to be sold for a profit to the poor who could not maintain themselves (Lev. 35:37). If because of poverty an Israelite sold himself, he was not to be treated harshly as a slave, but was to be treated as a hired servant who would gain his freedom in the year of release (Dt. 15:12-18) or in the Year of Jubilee (Lev. 25:39-43). Poor hired servants were to be paid their wages on the day they earned them (Dt. 24:14f.). The poor who sold their property or themselves retained the right of redemption either by another, by themselves, or by release in the Year of Jubilee (Lev. 25:25-28, 47-55). These stipulations sought to provide the poor with an economic base necessary to guarantee a livelihood and personal liberty. While the court was not to be partial to the poor (Ex. 23:3), it was to see that the justice due the poor was not perverted (Ex. 23:6; Lev. 19:15). Finally, because the poor had equal rights with the rich to appear before God (the price of atonement was the same, Ex. 30:15), they were allowed to present less costly sacrifices (Lev. 14:21f.; 27:8).

These rights were an integral part of God's covenant with Israel rooted in the Exodus. The refrain, "they are my servants whom I brought forth out of the land of Egypt," or "you shall remember that you were a slave in the land of Egypt," grounds both the rights of the poor and Israel's obligation to maintain those rights in God's redemptive act (Lev. 25:38, 42, 55; Dt. 25:18, 22). As the servants of the Lord redeemed from slavery in Egypt, the poor were entitled to share in Israel's inheritance, which included the land, its produce, and freedom. The law of release intended to guarantee that each possessed what was essential for the maintenance of human life and liberty, that no one for reasons of wealth oppressed another, and that each stood in a relationship of liberty and brotherhood to his or her neighbor (cf. Jer. 34:13-17).

The covenant code was rooted also in the creational order (even Sodom was condemned by the prophet because it "did not aid the poor and needy," Ezk. 16:49). The rights of the poor were grounded not only in the Exodus event but also in the goodness and justice that could be discerned in the order of creation. This perspective is evident especially in the wisdom literature. Both rich and poor are equal before God because "the Lord is the maker of them all" (Prov. 22:2; cf. 14:31; 17:5; Job 34:19). The righteous person is one who discerns this creational order and acts in accordance with it; such a person "knows the rights of the poor" and always seeks to vindicate those rights (Prov. 29:7; cf. 31:9). Thus the rights of the poor are established by both the creational and the redemptive acts of God.

2. *Righteousness and the Poor.* The obligation to defend the rights of the poor is an essential part of the biblical way of righteousness for individuals and governments. The righteous individual and the righteous king are expected to know these rights and defend them (Prov. 29:7; 31:9). The king who judges the poor with equity is promised that his throne will be established forever (29:14); likewise, the righteousness of the individual who has distributed freely and given to the poor will endure forever (Ps. 112:9; cf. Dt. 24:13). The king (Messiah) who embodies the righteousness of God will be found on the side of the poor, defending them, judging their cause with justice, crushing their oppressor, and delivering "the needy . . . , the poor and him who has no helper" (Ps. 72:2, 4, 12; cf. 83:3f. [MT 4f.]). Thus "a just and well-regulated government will be distinguished for maintaining the rights of the poor and afflicted" (J. Calvin, comm. on Ps. 82:3). The mere performance of religious ritual and cult does not fulfil the way of righteousness, for the fast that God approves is the removal of oppression: "to share your bread with the hungry, and bring the homeless poor into your house" (Isa. 58:6f.). Knowing the Lord is equated with caring for the poor: "He [Josiah] judged the cause of the poor and needy; then it was well. Is not this to know me? says the Lord" (Jer. 22:16). Blessing is promised to those who walk this way of righteousness, for "he who is kind to the poor lends to the Lord, and he will repay him for his deed" (Prov. 19:17; cf. 14:21; 22:9; 28:27; 31:20). Nevertheless, wisdom literature presents also the case of Job, who acted righteously toward the poor and yet experienced affliction (Job 29:12, 16; 30:25; 31:16, 19).

3. *The Poor as the Oppressed.* Although wisdom literature warns that poverty may be self-inflicted (Prov. 6:6-11; 21:17: 23:21), in the OT it is primarily the wicked who deprive the poor of their rights. The poor hide themselves because the wicked thrust them off the road, take their infants in pledge, and even seek to kill them (Job 24:4, 9, 14). Although sometimes the poor oppress the poor (Prov. 28:3), usually it is the rich who oppress them (22:7, 16, 22; 28:15). "The fallow ground of the poor yields much food, but it is swept away through injustice" (13:23).

The prophets condemned Israel because "the spoil of the poor is in your houses" (Isa. 3:14f.) and "on your skirts is found the lifeblood of guiltless poor" (Jer. 2:34). In a time of rising prosperity and increasing class distinctions, Amos denounced Israel for buying "the poor for silver and the needy for a pair of sandals" (Am. 8:6; cf. 2:7; 4:1; 5:11; 8:4). After the Exile Zechariah prophesied that the Lord "scattered them with a whirlwind among all the nations which they had not known" (Zec. 7:14) because they had been neither kind nor just but had oppressed the poor (vv. 8-13). Thus the prophets announced the judgment of exile not only because fertility cults had corrupted Israel's worship but also because Israel had not maintained the rights of the poor.

4. *Hope of the Poor.* Because the hopes of the poor were not realized and injustice continued to reign, the poor placed their hope in the promises of God: "'Because the poor are despoiled, because the needy groan, I will now arise,' says the Lord. 'I will place him in the safety for which he longs'"(Ps. 12:5 [MT 6]; cf. 9:18 [MT 19]). The Lord is called the "refuge" or "stronghold" of the poor (Ps. 14:6; Isa. 25:4), their "helper" and "deliverer" (Ps. 40:17 [MT 18]; 70:5 [MT 6]), the one who saves them out of all their trouble (34:6 [MT 7]); for the Lord "raises the poor from the dust and lifts the needy from the ash heap" (113:7; 1 S. 2:8). Nonetheless, the complete realization of the hope of the poor is promised only for the messianic age, when the Servant-King "shall judge the poor with righteousness and decide with equity for the meek of the earth" (Isa. 11:4; cf. 29:19; 41:17; Ps. 132:15).

5. *The Poor as the People of God.* The helpless poor, who depended on God as judge to defend their rights and to vindicate them when they were oppressed, came to be viewed as synonymous with the righteous people of God (cf. Ps. 14:5f.; Isa. 3:15; 14:32). Similarly, the oppressed people of God identified themselves as the "poor" who depended upon God for their vindication (cf. Ps. 37:14; 74:19; Hab. 3:13f.). In fact, the phrase "poor and needy" became a designation of the people of God who trusted in Him to deliver them out of all their troubles (Ps. 40:17 [MT 18]; 70:5 [MT 6]; 74:21; 86:1).

***II. In the NT.**–A. Terms.* In classical Greek two terms designate the poor: *pénēs* denotes the working poor who own little or no property, and *ptōchós* signifies the beggar, one who is totally dependent on others for help. Although the LXX uses both terms to translate the various Hebrew terms, the NT uses *ptōchós* almost exclusively, the two exceptions being *pénēs* in a quotation of Ps. 112:9 (2 Cor. 9:9) and *penichrós* in a description of the poor widow (Lk. 21:2). The NT use of *ptōchós* is not restricted to its classical Greek meaning but is shaped by OT use.

*B. Teaching.* Because the NT declares that the kingdom of God is already present, it proclaims God's concern for the poor with even greater vigor than the OT (cf. Lk.

12:32f.). Although the Christian Church has always recognized the biblical concern for the poor, it has tended to spiritualize the concept "poor" in certain key passsages (e.g., Lk. 4:18; 6:20; 7:22), so that it becomes a synonym for "sinner." More recently, certain Liberation theologies have materialized or politicized the concept of "poor" so that it becomes synonymous with the abject poor, the paupers who are dispossessed because of political or economic oppression. While both "sinner" and "pauper" are aspects of "poor" in the biblical concept, to make either the *exclusive* meaning is to obscure the biblical teaching.

*1. Hope Realized: Gospel For The Poor.* The NT proclaims that the hope of the poor is realized in Jesus' inauguration of the eschatological Year of Jubilee. Luke's Gospel especially, based on Isaiah's prophecy (Isa. 61:1f.) of the anointed servant who will proclaim Jubilee's promise of release and forgiveness ("the acceptable year of the Lord"), recounts Jesus' ministry according to the themes of Jubilee. Jesus is anointed by the Spirit "to preach good news to the poor" (Lk. 4:18), who are also the "captives," the "blind," and the "oppressed" (cf. 7:22; Mt. 11:5). While originally a description of Israel's condition awaiting release from exile, this prophecy became an eschatological symbol of God's oppressed people awaiting release in the final Year of Jubilee in the end-time (cf. 11QMelch in the Qumrân Scrolls). The good news proclaimed to the poor is the gospel of the kingdom of God (Lk. 4:43), the announcement of that realm in which the great reversal of all injustice and oppression would become a reality. Because the prophecy of Isa. 61:1f. (cf. 58:6) is shaped by the language of the Jubilee (Lev. 25; Dt. 15), Luke's emphasis falls on release from actual social, economic, and political oppression. The biblical promise of release is always, however, connected with forgiveness of sins. The OT Year of Jubilee was proclaimed on the Day of Atonement; therefore its release was predicated upon God's release (forgiveness) of Israel from its sins. Similarly, Isaiah's promise and Luke's announcement of the eschatological Jubilee is predicated upon the forgiveness of sins (cf. Lk. 24:47). God's word of forgiveness creates the basis for reversal of injustice and the deliverance of the poor.

The same Jubilee perspective shapes the Lukan beatitudes: "Blessed are you poor, for yours is the kingdom of God" (Lk. 6:20). Here also the poor are defined further by the subsequent beatitudes addressed to those who hunger, weep, and are oppressed (vv. 21f.). Whereas Luke emphasizes the reversal of the social and economic condition of the poor, Matthew's emphasis falls more upon the spiritual and ethical condition of the poor; the "poor in spirit" are the meek, those who hunger for righteousness, the merciful, the pure in heart, the persecuted (Mt. 5:3-11). Both Matthew and Luke, however, have the same persons in view, for the poor are the disciples of Jesus who, like the *ʿanāwîm* of the OT, know real poverty and oppression, but who as the humble and meek look to the Lord for their salvation. Thus interpretations of the "poor" that understand Matthew in exclusively spiritual categories or Luke in exclusively material categories overlook the *ʿanāwîm* piety and status that is the background for both.

Although God's forgiveness of sins in Jesus' name has been granted (Lk. 24:27) and Jesus has inaugurated the eschatological Year of Jubilee (4:21; 6:20), the kingdom of God has not yet fully arrived. The complete reversal of the condition of the poor awaits the future, but already under the symbol of a joyful banquet the promise is given that the "poor and maimed and blind and lame" will have a place in the Kingdom (14:21). Since this is so, those who give banquets on earth should invite "the poor, the maimed, the lame, the blind" (v.13), because those who hope to attend the eschatological banquet must reveal that the Jubilee reversal promised in the future Kingdom has already begun.

*2. Righteousness and the Poor.* The forgiveness of sins that inaugurates the Kingdom entails the obligation to begin the Jubilee reversal of poverty. Jesus instructed His disciples in response to the gift of the Kingdom to sell their possessions and give alms (Lk. 12:33), and the church in Jerusalem did precisely that in order to care for the poor and needy (Acts 2:44f.; 4:34f.; cf. Dt. 15:4). In response to the salvation brought by Jesus, Zacchaeus declared as a sign of repentance that he would give (present tense as a future expressing resolve) half of his goods to the poor (Lk. 19:8) — far more than the 20 percent encouraged by the rabbis. Jesus once accepted an extravagant act of devotion seemingly in disregard of the poor (Mt. 26:6-13 par. Mk. 14:3-9; Jn. 12:1-8), but this did not compromise His concern for the poor. He called the anointing a beautiful act because it was done in preparation for His burial. Such extravagance was appropriate as an exceptional act, whereas giving to the poor should occur continuously. In fact, the exception proves the rule that devotion to Jesus is expressed through caring for the poor.

Throughout His ministry Jesus maintained the OT teaching that the way of righteousness includes caring for the poor, and the disciples assumed that this was so (cf. Mk. 14:15; Jn. 13:29). In the parable of the rich man and Lazarus (Lk. 16:19-31), Jesus taught that someone who ignored the OT teaching about sharing with the poor was so morally blind that he would not be convinced of its necessity even by one raised from the dead. On another occasion Jesus instructed a rich young man to sell his possessions and "give to the poor"; for although he claimed to have kept the commandments, his wealth interfered with true love for the neighbor and thus prevented his becoming a disciple of Jesus (Mt. 19:16-22 par. Mk. 10:17-22; Lk. 18:18-23). In the sequel Jesus promised that those who followed Him, leaving behind family and property (which in context may imply giving one's wealth to the poor), would share in the great reversal that has already begun and will be completed in the age to come (Mt. 19:23-30 par. Mk. 10:23-31; Lk. 18:24-30). Thus the NT way of righteousness as caring for the poor fulfils that of the OT, for in the presence of the Kingdom Jesus' disciples are called to manifest in their relationship to the poor the grand reversal that God has promised.

*See also* ETHICS: THE ETHIC OF JESUS III.C; ETHICS: NT ETHICS II.C.1.

*3. The Poor as the Oppressed.* Although Jesus' parable about the rich man and Lazarus depicts the miserable condition of the helpless poor (Lk 16:20f.), it is especially James who condemns the rich for having gained their wealth at the expense of the poor (Jas. 5:1-6). James warns the rich within the Church (1:9-11; cf. 2:1-4); but he also identifies the poor as those chosen by God to inherit the Kingdom and the rich as unbelievers who oppress the believers and blaspheme the name of Jesus (2:5-7). The poor are oppressed both because of their economic poverty and because they, like the OT *ʿanāwîm*, are the ones rich in faith; cf. the Beatitudes (Mt. 5:3-12; Lk. 6:20-23), which also identify the oppressed poor with the persecuted disciples of Christ.

*4. The Poor as the People of God.* While "poor" can be used simply to denote an economic condition (cf. the merismus "rich and poor," which is used to describe the totality of humankind; e.g., Rev. 13:16; Ps. 49:2 [MT 3]; cf. Ruth 3:10), "poor" is often used as a synonym for "people of God." The poor widow who gave two copper coins is a notable example of the piety that depends totally on God (Lk. 21:1-4). Strikingly, the name Lazarus, the poor man in Jesus' parable (Lk. 16:19-31), means "he whom God helps." The "poor" to whom Jesus promises the Kingdom are disciples (Lk. 6:20; Mt. 5:3; cf. Jas. 2:5). Thus the people of God can be identified as the "poor" for various reasons: social and economic deprivation, voluntary poverty (cf. Mt. 19:23-30 par.), persecution, and total dependence upon God for deliverance from every need (including deliverance from spiritual poverty; cf. Rev. 3:17). Jesus is Himself the ground and model for the people of God both in their identification as the poor and in their caring for the poor. For He had "nowhere to lay his head" but depended on God and others for support (Lk. 9:58); He became poor so that others might become rich (2 Cor. 8:9); and He is present in the poor brethren who are the hungry, the thirsty, and the naked (Mt. 25:35-40). Jesus was Himself one of the *ʿanāwîm* (cf. "humble," Heb. *ʿānî,* Zec. 9:9). In imitation of Christ, the apostles were "poor, yet making many rich" (2 Cor. 6:10).

Some scholars (e.g., see Fitzmyer, p. 10) have proposed that "the Poor" (Rom. 15:16; Gal. 2:10) was a self-designation of the Jerusalem congregation. This thesis, however, cannot be substantiated; the circumstantial evidence is inadequate. While it is true that a Jewish Christian sect of the 2nd cent. called itself "the Poor" (EBIONITES) and claimed to trace its origin to the Jerusalem church, Irenaeus (*Adv. haer.* i.26.2), the first writer to mention them by name, classified them as heretics. Likewise, while the Qumrân community viewed itself as the poor people of God and in one instance called itself "the Congregation of the Poor" (4QpPs37), it did so, not because of its insistence on community of goods, but primarily becuase in its oppressed condition it readily identified with the "poor and needy" in the Psalms (esp. Ps. 37). Consequently, the existence of community of goods in the Jerusalem church does not in itself imply that its members called themselves "the Poor." In addition, neither of the two texts used to substantiate this thesis is conclusive. Paul was asked by the Jerusalem church "to remember the poor" (Gal. 2:10), and later he journeyed to deliver the "contribution for the poor among the saints at Jerusalem" (Rom. 15:26). Since in Rom. 15:25 Paul speaks of "going to Jerusalem with aid for the saints," some have argued that v. 26 should be read as "the poor, who are the saints." The more likely reading, however, is that there were many poor among the saints in Jerusalem. Because God Himself was righteous in giving to the poor (cf. 2 Cor. 9:9), Paul was also eager to do this (Gal. 2:10), and he encouraged others to give cheerfully (2 Cor. 9:6-15). Thus Paul's collection, gathered from the gentile churches for the poor in Jerusalem, was an act of charity rendered in obedience to the command and example of Christ — an act that expressed also the hope of reconciling the Jewish and gentile branches of the Church.

*See also* POVERTY; ALMS.

***Bibliography***.–A. Causse, *Les "pauvres" d'Israël* (1922); J. Fitzmyer, "The Qumran Scrolls, the Ebionites, and Their Literature," in K. Stendahl, ed., *The Scrolls and the NT* (1957), pp. 208-231; *TDNT,* VI, *s.v.* πτωχός (F. Hauck, E. Bammel); A. Gelin, *Poor of Yahweh* (Eng. tr. 1964); L. Keck, *ZNW,* 56 (1965), 100-129; 57 (1966), 54-78; K. F. Nickle, *The Collection: A Study in Paul's Strategy* (*SBT,* 1/48, 1966); J. Jeremias, *Jerusalem in the Time of Jesus* (Eng. tr. 1969), pp. 87-119; *NT Theology* (Eng. tr. 1971), pp. 108-121; G. Gutierrez, *Theology of Liberation* (Eng. tr. 1971), pp. 287-306; G. von Rad, *Wisdom in Israel* (Eng. tr. 1972), pp. 74-96; *TDOT,* I, *s.v.* "'ebhyôn" (G. J. Botterweck); M. Hengel, *Property and Riches in the Early Church* (Eng. tr. 1974); M. Dibelius and H. Greeven, *James* (Eng. tr., *Hermeneia,* 1976), pp. 39-45; *DNTT,* II, 820-29; *THAT,* II, *s.v.* ענה II (R. Martin-Achard); R. Sloan, *Favorable Year of the Lord* (1977); J. D. Gort, "Gospel for the Poor," in T. Baarda *et al.*, eds., *Zending op weg naar de Toekomst* (*Festschrift* J. Verkuyl, 1978), pp. 80-109; E. Dussel, *International Review of Missions,* 68 (1979), 115-130; D. H. Engelhard, *Calvin Theological Journal,* 15 (1980), 5-26; E. Lohse, *ZNW,* 72 (1981), 51-64.

D. E. HOLWERDA

**POPLAR** pop'lər [Heb. *libneh*–'whiteness'; LXX *styrákinos,* i.e., "storax" (Gen. 30:37), *leúkē*–'white' (Hos. 4:13)]. A Palestinian tree that was highly prized for its shade. It flourished under the same topographical conditions as oaks and terebinths (Hos. 4:13), and was one of the trees planted in the groves where pagan Canaanite worship occurred.

The tree may possibly have been the Storax (*Styrax officinalis* L.), a common shrub in ancient Palestine that occasionally grew as high as 6 m. (20 ft.). The undersurfaces of its oval green leaves were covered with whitish hairs, which might have accounted for the Hebrew name. This light color was also characteristic of the pure white flowers, similar to orange blossoms, which covered the tree in spring.

While some botanists prefer to identify the poplar with the Storax, many biblical scholars think of it in terms of the white poplar (*Populus alba* L.), which also bears shiny green leaves that have a white coloration on the underside. This tree flourished throughout Palestine in antiquity, often towering to a height of 18 m. (60 ft.) and producing a heavily shaded area. The buds and flowers exhibit a delightful fragrance each spring, which would add to the attractiveness of the poplar as a shade tree. Jacob used the peeled, creamy white poplar branches along with branches from other trees to produce supposed prenatal impressions upon ewes in a program of selective breeding (Gen. 30:37).

In Hos. 14:5 (MT 6) the RSV and NEB emend MT *lᵉbānôn,* "Lebanon" (so AV) to *libneh,* "poplar," apparently to provide a better parallel to "lily" and a more sensible complement to "strike root." But the reference to Lebanon could simply be an instance of synecdoche, since the forests of Lebanon were so well known (cf., e.g., 1 K. 5:6 [MT 20]; 7:2; Isa. 10:34). Cf. also Hos. 14:6 (MT 7), which refers to Lebanon in a similar fashion.

See *MBP,* pp. 181-83.

R. K. H.

**PORATHA** pō-ra'thə [Heb. *pôrāṯā'*] (Est. 9:8). One of Haman's ten sons killed by the Jews on orders from Mordecai, who had been authorized by King Ahasuerus to issue such orders as a means of protecting the Jews (cf. 8:11; 9:2-10, 16). The name Poratha is apparently Persian; according to H. S. Gehman (*JBL,* 43 [1924], 327) it is from Old Pers. *pauru,* "much," + *dā,* "giving," i.e., "liberal one"; cf. L. B. Paton, comm. on Esther (*ICC,* 1908), p. 70, for other possible Persian derivations.

G. A. L.

**PORCH.** A term used by the RSV only in 1 K. 7:6; Ezk. 8:16 to render Heb. *'ûlām* (but used frequently by the AV for this term; RSV usually "vestibule") and in Mt. 26:71 for Gk. *pylōn.* "Porch" is also an AV translation of Heb. *misdᵉrôn* in Jgs. 3:23 (RSV "vestibule"), Gk. *proaúlion* in Mk. 14:68 (RSV "gateway"), and *stoá* in Jn. 5:2; etc. (RSV "portico"). *See* GATEWAY; TEMPLE; VESTIBULE. On "Solomon's porch" (RSV "Solomon's Portico"), *see* JERUSALEM III.H.22.

**PORCIUS FESTUS.** *See* FESTUS, PORCIUS.

**PORCUPINE** [Heb. *qippōḏ*] (Isa. 34:11); AV BITTERN; NEB BUSTARD. If the Hebrew is related to the Arab. *qunfuḏ*, "hedgehog" (the RSV rendering of *qippōḏ* in Isa. 14:23; Zeph. 2:14), the reference would be to the insect-eating mammal *Erinaceus europeus*. A small mammal about 25 cm. (10 in.) long, it is covered with short spines and rolls itself into a ball when disturbed or attacked. The porcupine (*Hystrix cristata*), also known by the Arabic term *qunfuḏ* in some areas, is an herbivorous rodent that is more than twice the length of the hedgehog, and has long spines. In Isa. 34:11 "porcupine" is probably a correct rendering of the *qippōḏ* that was to scavenge in desolated Edom.

*See also* HEDGEHOG. R. K. H.

**PORPHYRY** pôr'fi-rē [Heb. *bahaṭ*] (Est. 1:6); AV RED (MARBLE); NEB MALACHITE. The term porphyry is from Ionic Gk. *porphýra/ē*, meaning purple. The term refers historically to a specific kind of maroon- or purple-colored rock. In modern petrographic use porphyry is an igneous rock in which a texture of conspicuously large crystals exists in a fine-grained matrix, regardless of color (cf. LXX *smaragdítēs*, a green lithic or gemstone). The Esther passage implies an architectural flooring analogous to the later Roman *opus sectile*, a geometric cut-rock surface pattern. R. G. BULLARD

**PORPOISE** [Heb. *taḥaš*]; RSV GOAT(-SKINS); AV BADGER. The term is usually found with Heb. *'ôr*, "skin (of)," and refers to a fine-quality leather used in the coverings of the tabernacle (Ex. 25:5; 26:14; 35:7, 23; 36:19; 39:34) and its sacred furniture (Nu. 4:6-25) as well as for the fabric of Jerusalem's symbolic shoes (Ezk. 16:10).

The precise meaning of *taḥaš* is not certain. It may have been a sea animal (cf. Arab. *tuḥas*, "dolphin" or "dugong"; also "sea-cow" as in NEB or "manatee") or a land animal (most likely a goat). The LXX, Josephus, and talmudic tradition do not agree on a definition.

*See also* LEATHER. D. STUART

**PORT.** A term used once by the AV in the obsolete sense of "gate" (Neh. 2:13; on the Dung Gate, *see* JERUSALEM III.F.2.c). The RSV uses "ports" once in the sense of "harbors" as a translation of the plural of Gk. *tópos* (lit. "[inhabited] place"; Acts 27:2; AV "coasts").

**PORTENT** [Heb. *môp̄ēṯ*] (Ps. 71:7; Joel 2:30 [MT 3:2]); AV WONDERS; NEB also SOLEMN WARNING; [*'ôṯ*] (Isa. 8:18; 20:3); AV SIGN; [Gk. *sēmeíon*] (Rev. 12:1, 3; 15:1); AV WONDER, SIGN. In these passages "portent" denotes a person (Ps. 71:7; Isa. 8:18) or event (e.g., in the heavens) whose distinguishing features indicate that God is acting or is about to act. Isaiah served as a portent through his name ("Yahweh is salvation"), through the names of his children (cf. 7:3 mg.; 8:1 mg., 3f.), and through his actions (20:1-5). *See also* SIGN; WONDER.

**PORTER.** A term used by the AV in the older sense of GATEKEEPER.

**PORTICO, SOLOMON'S.** *See* JERUSALEM III.H.22; TEMPLE IV.C.2.

**PORTION** [Heb. *ḥēleq* (e.g., Gen. 31:14; Lev. 6:17 [MT 10]; Neh. 2:20; Isa. 61:7), *ḥelqâ* (Dt. 33:21; Josh. 24:32; Job 24:18; Jer. 12:10), piel of *ḥālaq* ("portion out," Isa. 34:17; "divide a portion," 53:12), hiphil of *ḥālaq* ("receive a portion," Jer. 37:12), *maḥ^alōqeṯ* (Ezk. 48:29), *ḥeḇel*–'rope, line' (Josh. 17:5, 14; 19:9; 1 Ch. 16:18; Ps. 105:11; Ezk. 47:13), *mānâ* (e.g., 1 S. 1:4f.; 9:23; 2 Ch. 31:19; Neh. 8:10, 12; Est. 2:9; 9:19, 22; Ps. 16:5; Jer. 13:25), *m^enāṯ* (e.g., Ps. 11:6), *'azkārâ* ("memorial portion," Lev. 2:2, 9, 16; 5:12; 6:15; 24:7; Nu. 5:26), *maś'ēṯ*–'lifting up,' 'offering' (Gen. 43:34), *dāḇār*–'word,' 'thing,' 'affair' (Ex. 16:4; 2 K. 25:30; Dnl. 1:5), *t^erûmâ*–'contribution, offering' ("priests' portion," Ex. 29:27f.; "[holy] portion," Ezk. 45:1, 6; etc.), *t^erûmîyâ*–'contribution' ("special portion," 48:12), *peh*–'mouth' (Ps. 49:13 [MT 14]; "double portion," Dt. 21:17), *'eḥāḏ*–'one' ("one portion," Ezk. 48), *ḥōq* ("allotted portion," 16:27; "fixed portion," 45:14), *qōḏeš*–'holy' (e.g., "holy portion," Ezk. 45:4), *rē'šîṯ*–'first' ("choice portion," 48:14), *'ešpār* ("portion of meat," 2 S. 6:19 par. 1 Ch. 16:3), piel of *māḏaḏ* ("portion out," Ps. 60:6 [MT 8]; 108:7 [MT 8]); Gk. *merís* (Lk. 10:42), *sitométrion* ("portion of food," 12:42)]; AV also PART, LOT, RATE, HEAVE OFFERING, OBLATION, MESS, etc.; NEB also PART, SUPPLY, PERQUISITE, SHARE, HOLDING, RESERVE, etc.; in a few instances "portion" is supplied by the RSV for ease of translation (Gen. 4:4; Lev. 7:35; 2 Ch. 31:15). An individual's or group's SHARE in something; used most often in reference to the distribution of land (see below) or food (e.g., Gen. 43:34; 1 S. 1:4f., 9:23f.; Lk. 12:42).

The Hebrew root *ḥlq* means primarily "(give or receive) the share that is allotted to one." The verb *ḥālaq* is used of "dividing" or "distributing" various kinds of goods, such as land (e.g., Nu. 26:53), food (2 S. 6:19), and spoils of battle (Isa. 53:12). Likewise, the noun *ḥēleq* can denote various types of "portions," including battle spoils (Nu. 31:36), food (e.g., Dt. 18:8), and even one's destiny, apportioned by God (e.g., Job 20:29; 27:13; 31:2; Ps. 17:14; Eccl. 9:9; Isa. 17:14).

In its most specialized sense, however, *ḥēleq* denotes a share of land allotted to a tribe or family (e.g., Josh. 15:13). (*Ḥelqâ*, a fem. form of *ḥēleq*, always has this sense.) In this sense the "portion" has fundamental importance in a clan-based, agricultural society, because for each individual or small group it represents both the basic means of livelihood and also a sign of belonging to the people as a whole (see *TDOT*, IV, 448f.). Cf. the complaint: "We have no portion [*ḥēleq*] in David" (2 S. 20:1; cf. 1 K. 12:16) — i.e., no share in the common life and power of the royal house.

When Israel entered Palestine, each tribe except Levi was allotted a portion of land (Josh. 18:10; cf. chs. 13–19) as an inheritance from Yahweh, the original and true owner of all the LAND (Lev. 25:23; cf. Dt. 32:9; Jer. 12:10, where Israel is described as Yahweh's "portion"; cf. also the expression "have a portion in Yahweh [i.e., Yahweh's land]," Josh. 22:25, 27). G. von Rad (pp. 85f.) suggested that this belief in Yahweh's ownership of the land formed the background for the practice of apportioning it by casting LOTS — a "cultic" means of determining the divine will. The procedure, which also made use of the *ḥeḇel* (*see* MEASURING LINE), is described in Josh. 18:4-6; Isa. 34:17; Mic. 2:4f. (cf. Ps. 16:5f., which uses the metaphor of a person who rejoices to see that he has received a good portion, because "the lines have fallen for me in pleasant places"). By extension the terms *ḥeḇel* ("line") and *gôrāl* ("lot") came to be used synonymously with *ḥelqâ* and *ḥēleq* (often in parallelism with *naḥ^alâ* ["inheritance, heritage"]; *see* INHERIT) to denote a piece of land that has been measured and allotted (*see also* ALLOTMENT).

The priestly tribe of Levi received no "portion" (*ḥēleq*) in Canaan, i.e., it was not entitled to own land (Nu. 18:20; Dt. 10:9; 12:12; 14:27, 29; 18:1; Josh. 14:4; 18:7). Instead, Yahweh was Levi's "portion" (Nu. 18:20; cf. Dt. 10:9). In a practical, economic sense this meant that the Levites obtained their living through "portions" of sacrifices and offerings that were reserved for them (e.g., Lev. 6:17 [MT 10]; Nu. 18; *see also* FIRST FRUITS; TITHE; cf. also the terms *mānâ* [a portion (usually of food) assigned to someone; e.g., Ex. 29:26; Lev. 7:33; 8:29], *m^e^nāṯ* [e.g., 2 Ch. 31:4; Neh. 12:44, 47; 13:10], *t^e^rûmâ* [general term for an offering or contribution; e.g., Ex. 29:27f.; Nu. 18:8], and *qōḏeš* [lit. "holy"; cf. "holy portion," Lev. 24:9; "sacred portion," Dt. 26:13]). But the statement "I [Yahweh] am your portion" pointed to much more than the source of the Levite's material sustenance: it was the promise of a special, unbreakable relationship with Yahweh, the source and sustainer of all life.

The theme that Yahweh is the "portion" of the devout Israelite finds expression also in some of the Psalms (16:5; 73:26; 119:57; 142:5 [MT 6]) and in Lam. 3:24 (cf. also Jer. 51:19). Ps. 73:23-28 contains an especially beautiful elaboration of this confession. (See von Rad, pp. 260-66, for the idea that these Psalms originated in a community of spiritually alert Levites.) Jesus' statement that "Mary has chosen the good portion [Gk. *merís*]" (Lk. 10:42) should also be understood against this background. *Merís* is a common LXX translation of Heb. *ḥēleq, ḥelqâ, mānâ,* and *m^e^nāṯ* (*DNTT,* II, 303f.).

Ezekiel's vision of the restoration of Israel in the messianic age (chs. 40–48) includes a description of an idealized reallotment of the land of Palestine, "one portion" (Heb. *ʾeḥāḏ,* lit. "one") of equal size going to each tribe (48:1-7, 23-27; cf. *ḥēleq* [RSV "tribal portion"] in 45:7; 48:8, 21). Much detail is given regarding a sacred district that is to be set apart for Yahweh (*t^e^rûmâ*; AV, lit., "oblation"; RSV usually "holy portion"; NEB "[sacred] reserve"; cf. 45:1, 6; 48:8-12, 18-22), which will include the temple area and living quarters for the Levites and Zadokite priests (cf. 45:4f.).

The meaning of Heb. *ʾešpār* in 2 S. 6:19 par. 1 Ch. 16:3 is uncertain. Most scholars (e.g., *CHAL,* p. 30) translate it "cake of dates" (so NIV) rather than "portion (or piece) of meat" (so RSV, NEB, AV); see the comms. (though he concludes that its meaning is uncertain, S. R. Driver, comm. on Samuel [2nd ed. 1913], pp. 270f., offers the most thorough discussion).

***Bibliography.***–G. von Rad, "The Promised Land and Yahweh's Land in the Hexateuch," in *Problem of the Hexateuch and Other Essays* (Eng. tr. 1966), pp. 79-93; see also pp. 260-66; *TDOT,* IV, *s.v.* "ḥbl I" (H.-J. Fabry); "chālaq II" (M. Tsevat).

N. J. OPPERWALL

**PORTRAY** [Heb. *ḥāqaq*] (Ezk. 4:1; 8:10; 23:14); NEB DRAW, CARVED; [*ṣûrâ*] (Ezk. 43:11); AV "shew . . . the form of"; NEB DESCRIBE; [Gk. *prográphō*] ("publicly portray," Gal. 3:1); AV "evidently set forth"; NEB OPENLY DISPLAY. Heb. *ḥāqaq* as used by Ezekiel means "engrave." In Ezk. 43:11 the AV, RSV, and NEB follow the LXX, which has Gk. *diagráphō*; Heb. *ṣûrâ* literally means "ground plan."

Scholars disagree about the precise meaning of *prográphō* in Gal. 3:1. Some commentators, e.g., Calvin, have held that it means "portray publicly," i.e., present a verbal picture (cf. NEB, NIV, NAB, NASB), while others, e.g., E. Burton (*ICC,* 1920), have denied that possibility and take it to mean "proclaim publicly" (cf. JB, Moff.; also G. Schrenk, *TDNT,* I, 771). See further H. D. Betz, *Galatians* [*Hermeneia,* 1979], p. 131; F. F. Bruce, *Epistle to the Galatians* [*NIGTC,* 1982], pp. 147f.

**POSIDONIUS** pos-i-dō'ni-əs [Gk. *Posidōnios*].

**1.** One of the three envoys sent by the Seleucid general Nicanor to arrange a truce with Judas Maccabeus and to give and receive pledges of friendship with the Jews (2 Macc. 14:19).

**2.** A distinguished Stoic philosopher and historian from Apamea (*ca.* 135-51 B.C.), named by Josephus (*CAp* ii.7 [79]) as an anti-Semitic writer. J. J. SCOTT, JR.

**POSSESS; POSSESSION** [Heb. *yāraš* (Gen. 15:7f.; 22:17; etc.; "strip of possessions," Zec. 9:4), *y^e^ruššâ* (Dt. 2:5, 9, 19; etc.), *môrāš* (Isa. 14:23; Ob. 17), *môrāšâ* (Ex. 6:8; Dt. 33:4; Ezk. 11:15; etc.), niphal of *ʾāḥaz* (Josh. 22:9; "gain possession," Gen. 47:27; "have possession," Nu. 32:30; "take possession," Josh. 22:19), *ʾ^a^ḥuzzâ* (Gen. 23:9, 20; 47:11; 49:30; etc.), *miqnâ* (Gen. 23:18), *miqneh* (Gen. 26:14), *qinyān* (Gen. 31:18; Ps. 105:21; in Zec. 13:5 the RSV emends MT *hiqnanî,* the hiphil of *qānâ,* to *qinyānî*; see RSV mg.), *nāḥal*–'inherit' (hithpael, Isa. 14:2; hiphil, "cause to possess," Zec. 8:12), *naḥ^a^lâ*–'inheritance' (Dt. 4:20), *r^e^ḵûš* (Gen. 12:5; 13:6; 15:14; 36:7; 2 Ch. 21:14, 17; 31:3; 32:29; 35:7), *n^e^ḵāsîm*–'riches, wealth' (Eccl. 5:19 [MT 18]; 6:2), *meḡeḏ* ("valuable possessions," 2 Ch. 21:3), *y^e^ḇûl* (Job 20:28), *mimšāq* ("a land possessed," Zeph. 2:9), *b^e^yāḏ* ("in possession," Ex. 21:16; 22:4 [MT 3]), *l^e^* (alone or with *hāyâ* or *nāṯan*) (e.g., Job 22:8), hiphil of *ḥāzaq* ("get possession," Dnl. 11:6), *lāḇaš*–'clothe' ("take possession," 2 Ch. 24:20), *s^e^gullâ* (Ex. 19:5; Dt. 7:6; 14:2; 26:18; Ps. 135:4; "my special possession," Mal. 3:17); Aram. *ḥ^a^san* (Dnl. 7:18), *ḥ^a^lāq*–'share' (Ezr. 4:16)]; AV also INHERIT, (GIVE) INHERITANCE, etc.; NEB also PATRIMONY, PROPERTY, TERRITORY, etc.; [Gk. *ktáomai, ktēma* (Mt. 19:22; Mk. 10:22; Acts 2:45), *hypárchō, hýparxis* (He. 10:34), *échō, katéchō* (2 Cor. 6:10), *peripoíēsis* (Eph. 1:14), *pneumatikós* (1 Cor. 2:13); contextual in 1 Cor. 8:7]; AV also HAVE, GOODS (Mt. 24:47), SUBSTANCE (He. 10:34), etc.; NEB also OWN, HAVE, WEALTH, PROPERTY, etc.; **POSSESSOR** [Heb. *baʿal* (Prov. 1:19); Gk. *ktḗtōr* (Acts 4:34)]; AV also OWNER; NEB THOSE WHO GET, HAVE; **DISPOSSESS** [Heb. *hāyâ y^e^rēšâ* (Nu. 24:18), *yāraš* (Nu. 21:32; Dt. 2:12, 21f.; 9:1; 11:23; 12:2, 29; 18:14; 19:1; 31:3; Jer. 49:1f.); hiphil of *yāraš* (Nu. 32:39; Dt. 7:17; Jgs. 11:23; 24b); *pûṣ* (Ezk. 46:18); Gk. *katáschesis* (Acts 7:45)]; AV also BE A POSSESSION, DRIVE OUT, SUCCEED, etc.; NEB also DRIVE OUT, OCCUPY, POSSESS, etc.

Possessions in biblical times consisted primarily of flocks and herds as well as parcels of land (Gen. 47:11). Abraham bought a "possession" for a burial place from the Hittites (Gen. 23:9, 20). The law is called a possession of the assembly of Jacob (Dt. 33:4).

Much of the language of possession in the OT is related to the covenant. An essential part of a covenant is an inheritance. The promises given to Abraham were that his descendants would become a great nation and that they would inherit the land. Before Israel could possess Canaan, however, they had to defeat and remove its occupants; thus *yāraš* is translated both "possess" and "dispossess." When Israel took possession of the land, other nations were defeated and lost their possession of the land. The procedure used is evident according to the verbs of Josh. 19:47: the Danites fought, captured, put to the sword, took possession, and settled the land. Once the land was divided among the tribes, it remained to each family in perpetuity (Lev. 25:34; Dt. 4:40; Josh. 14:9). Should anyone lose his land because of debt, carefully laid-out laws caused the land to revert to its original owners at the Jubilee Year. The tribe of Levi, however, did not inherit a unit of land, but certain cities; God Himself was considered their inheritance (Dt. 10:9). In regard to the king, a Psalm anticipated the time when the farthest parts of the earth were to be in his possession (Ps. 2:8).

Among the OT books, Deuteronomy in particular stipulates how the Israelites were to take possession of the land that God had promised them and then conduct themselves there. Although they had to be active on the battlefield, God would defeat the enemy (Dt. 7:1f.). There was a balance between God's gift and the people's response. God's gift was foundational, but the people had to put their lives on the line to receive it. To insure God's dynamic presence for success the people were exhorted to observe carefully the statutes and ordinances taught by Moses (4:1; 11:8); their continued occupation of the land was contingent upon their observance of the law (4:5). The people's faithfulness would move God to bless the land so that it would produce abundant crops to satisfy their desires (28:11-14). The right to inhabit the land thus depended on the people's moral and religious strength rather than on their military prowess.

Psalm 37 describes those who will possess the land as "those who wait for the Lord" (v. 9), "the meek" (v. 11), and "the righteous" (v. 29; cf. Isa. 60:21). The OT taught that when the people sinned, the land no longer supported them; they were subject to being dispossessed by another nation (cf. Lev. 18:24-30). But the people could realize their sin and seek God, and He would restore them to their inheritance (Dt. 30:1-11). Consequently the prophets comforted the people taken into captivity by declaring that they would return and again possess the land (Jer. 30:3; cf. Isa. 57:13). These principles no doubt provided the background for the Beatitude, "Blessed are the meek, for they shall inherit the earth" (Mt. 5:5). As stated in Dnl. 7:18, "the saints of the Most High shall receive the kingdom, and possess the kingdom for ever, for ever and ever."

Throughout the OT Israel is referred to as God's private possession (*s^egullâ*). They became unique by entering into covenant with him at Sinai (Ex. 19:5). They were chosen solely because of God's love (Dt. 7:6-8). As a special people they were to be holy unto Yahweh and to keep His commandments, with the result that He would bring them praise, fame, and honor (Dt. 26:18f.). 1 Pet. 2:9f. transfers this concept to the believers, who now are God's own possession. (*See also* PECULIAR.)

The NT emphasizes that true possessions are stored up in heaven (Mt. 6:19-21). Jesus said, "A man's life does not consist in the abundance of his possessions" (Lk. 12:15). Covetousness thereby is avoided. Consequently many members of the early Church sold their possessions to help each other and to spread the gospel (Acts 2:45; 4:34).

*See also* DEMONOLOGY; HEIR. J. E. HARTLEY

**POSSESSION, DEMONICAL.** *See* DEMONOLOGY; EXORCISM.

**POST.**

(1) [Heb. *m^ezûzâ*] (Jgs. 16:3; Ezk. 45:19; 46:2). The side post of a door or gate. *See* HOUSE III.C; GATE; FORTIFICATION II.

(2) [Heb. *ʿammûḏ*] (Cant. 3:10); AV PILLAR; NEB POLE. The legs or canopy-supports (or both) of Solomon's palanquin.

(3) [Heb. *mišmereṯ*] (2 Ch. 7:6; Isa. 21:8); AV OFFICE, WARD; NEB also STATION; [*māqôm*–'place'] (1 K. 20:24); AV PLACE; NEB COMMAND; [*ʿōmeḏ*] (2 Ch. 30:16); AV, NEB, PLACE. The station or duty to which a guard or officer is assigned (*see* GATEKEEPER; WATCHMAN). 1 K. 20:24 apparently refers to Ben-hadad's consolidation of the Syrian army under military commanders in place of tribal chiefs ("kings").

(4) A term used by the AV in the obsolete sense of "courier," translating Heb. *rāṣ* (lit. "runner"; part. of *rûṣ*). *See* COURIER; GUARD. N. J. O.

**POSTURES; ATTITUDES.** The postures or attitudes by which the Hebrews showed respect or worshiped reflected the cultures of the Fertile Crescent during biblical times. Although the Israelites' religion, which was a revealed religion, had many distinctive features, the postures they assumed in showing respect to persons in authority and in worshiping resembled those of their neighbors in many ways.

Various Hebrew and Greek terms describe the postures assumed by Israelites as well as by Gentiles to show respect or to worship. The context necessarily indicates whether worship is involved. Four physical postures that appear in the Bible include standing, bowing, kneeling, and "falling on the face" or prostrating oneself.

*I. Standing.*–Archeological evidence from Assyria, Babylonia, and Egypt indicates that standing erect, often with head bowed, was a common position assumed in the presence of a revered person. The Hammurabi stele shows this great king standing to receive the law code from the sun-god (*see* picture in HAMMURABI). Babylonian and Assyrian seals picture priests standing before the throne of Sin or Šamaš. Persons in the OT who stood before rulers include Joseph in Egypt (Gen. 41:46), the advisers in Israel (2 Ch. 10:6, 8), Esther in the Persian court (Est. 5:22; 8:4f.), and Daniel and others in the Babylonian court (Dnl. 1:19; 2:2).

Several passages in the OT mention various persons who were praying while they stood before the Lord. In 1 S. 1:26 Hannah told Eli that she was the one who was "standing" (Heb. niphal of *nāšaḇ*, "be stationed, stand") in his presence when she prayed to the Lord to give her a child (cf. 1 S. 1:1-20). During the dedication of the temple Solomon "stood" (<Heb. *ʿāmaḏ*, "stand") before the altar with his hands uplifted while he prayed to the Lord (1 K. 8:22; cf. vv. 23-53). The RSV "stood" also translates Heb. *ʿāmaḏ* in Neh. 9:2, where the assembly of Israelites "stood and confessed their sins. . . . "

In the NT "standing" as a posture of prayer appears several times. In Mt. 6:5 Jesus exhorts, "And when you pray you must not be like the hypocrites; for they love to stand and pray in the synagogues and at the street corners. . . . " Jesus' exhortation was not a restriction on one's posture during prayer, since Jews customarily stood during prayers (cf. SB, I, 401f.). For example, Jews stood during the recitation of the Eighteen Benedictions, i.e., the Shemoneh Esreh (Mish. *Berakoth* iii.5; v.1; *Taanith* ii.2). Also, the school of Shammai said that in the morning one should stand to recite the Shema, but in the evening one should recline (Mish. *Berakoth* i.3; for the prayer texts cf. *HJP*², II, 454-463). What Jesus did condemn was the ostentatious attitude of the hypocrites, since they prayed in order "that they might be seen by men" (Mt. 6:5). Also, the verbal tense of "stood" in Mt. 6:5 indicates an extended period of time during which the hypocrite hoped to be observed by others (R. A. Guelich, *Sermon on the Mount* [1982], p. 281). The parable of the publican and the Pharisee (Lk. 18:9-14) contrasts the prayer of a proud, pious Pharisee, who pompously "stood and prayed thus with himself" (v. 11), with that of a humble, despised tax collector, who, "standing far off" (v. 13), perhaps in the outer court of the temple (SB, II, 246), pleaded with God for mercy.

*II. Bowing.*–Bowing is often noted in the biblical records, though the exact posture is not always clearly indicated. When persons bowed they might touch their forehead or their breast with their hand, fold their arms, or place their hands on their knees. Reverence and submission are repeatedly associated with bowing. The RSV OT often translates three basic Hebrew terms by "bow" or "bow down." Heb. *qāḏaḏ*, "bow down, kneel down," occurs often where people "bow down" and worship the Lord (e.g., Gen. 24:26, 48; Ex. 4:31; 12:27; 34:8; 1 Ch. 29:20; Neh. 8:6). In 1 K. 1:16, 31 Bathsheba "bowed" and did obeisance to King David. Heb. *kāraʿ* also refers to "bowing down" before God (e.g., 2 Ch. 7:3; 29:24; Ps. 95:6), before human kings (Est. 3:2, 5), and before false gods (1 K. 19:18). The hishtaphel of Heb. *ḥāwâ* (see *TDOT,* IV, 249 on the origin of this form; it was formerly thought to be the hithpalel of *šāḥâ;* see KoB, p. 959; BDB, p. 1005) refers to "bowing" before other persons (Gen. 18:2; 23:7; 33:6f.; 1 S. 25:23, 41; 37:10; etc.), before angels (Gen. 19:1), before human kings (2 S. 24:20; 1 K. 1:23; cf. v. 53), and before idols (Ex. 20:5; 23:24; Lev. 26:1; Nu. 25:2; Dt. 5:9).

The RSV NT most frequently translates Gk. *kámptō* by "bow." In Rom. 11:4 (quoting 1 K. 19:18); 14:11 (quoting LXX, Isa. 45:23); Eph. 3:14; and Phil. 2:10, Gk. *kámptó* combines with Gk. *góny,* "knee," to give "bow the knee." The phrase expresses "the adoration and veneration which is due to God alone and not to any idol (Rom. 11:4); the recognition of God as the supreme judge (Rom. 14:11) or the acknowledgment that Jesus, in his universal majesty and cosmic significance, is Lord of all (Phil. 2:10)" (*DNTT,* II, 859). Also, 1 Clem. 57:1 suggests that repentance is accompanied by "bending the knees [*kámpsantes tá gónata*] of your hearts."

Various Jewish prayers, e.g., the Amidah (<*ʿāmad,* "stand") include a "slight symbolic bow" (Heinemann, p. 274 n. 44); however, the Amidah itself is said while one assumes a standing position (W. W. Simpson, *Jewish Prayer and Worship* [1965], p. 30). *See* GESTURE IV.

***III. Kneeling.***–This is often the posture of people engaged in prayer. In the OT Heb. *bārak̲,* "kneel down," and Heb. *kāraʿ,* "bow down," are the words often used to portray this posture. For example, in 2 Ch. 6:13 Solomon "knelt upon his knees" (Heb. *wayyib̲rak̲ ʿal-birkāyw*) until he finished his prayer of dedication (1 K. 8:54; Heb. *mik-ᵉrō[a]ʿ ʿal-birkāyw,* lit. "from kneeling on his knees"). In Ezr. 9:5 Ezra "fell upon [his] knees" (Heb. *wāʾek̲rᵉʿâ ʿal-birkay*) prior to prayer and confession (cf. 10:1). Daniel also "got down upon his knees" (lit. "kneeled upon his knees") three times a day and "prayed and gave thanks before his God" (Dnl. 6:10 [MT 11]).

In the NT Jesus assumes a kneeling position while praying in the garden of Gethsemane (Lk. 22:41). Matthew says that Jesus "fell on his face" (Mt. 26:39), while Mark states that he "fell on the ground" (Mk. 14:35). Possibly Jesus first fell to His knees and then bowed forward so that His face touched the ground. In Lk. 22:41 Gk. *theís tá gónata* (lit. "after he placed the knees"; cf. Acts 7:60; 9:40; 20:36; 21:5) "is Lucan, and the unusual attitude for prayer . . . stresses the urgency and humility of Jesus" (I. H. Marshall, *Gospel of Luke* [*NIGTC,* 1978], p. 830; cf. SB, II, 259-262).

***IV. Prostrating Oneself.***–Another intensive manner of showing deep reverence or of appealing to a superior was by prostrating oneself, i.e., lying flat on the ground, or kneeling with one's face and hands on the ground. (*See* picture in JEHU.) Abject subjection was frequently involved and could be based either on genuine respect or on a fear of judgment. It is uncertain whether each of the following instances was attended with prayer, but each example does occur in contexts of worshiping God or of submitting to human authorities. Heb. *nāpal,* "fall," is often used to show this action. For example, Abraham fell on his face before God, expressing submission and adoration (Gen. 17:3, 17). Moses and Aaron assumed this position during times of intercession (e.g., Nu. 16:45; 20:6). Joshua also assumed this position when he interceded before the Lord on behalf of the people (Josh. 7:6). Other persons who "fell on their faces" in submission and respect before people include David before Jonathan (1 S. 20:41), Abigail before David (25:23), and Esther before a Persian king (Est. 8:3). Also, Job worshiped God in a position of prostration (Job. 1:20). The prophets Ezekiel (Ezk. 1:28; 3:23; etc.) and Daniel (Dnl. 8:17) fell upon their faces after seeing certain visions.

In the NT Gk. *píptō* is often used for falling down or prostrating oneself before another in adoration. For example, the wise men "fell down" before Mary's child and worshiped Him (Mt. 2:11), Cornelius "fell down" at the feet of Peter (Acts 10:25), and various individuals in the book of Revelation "fall down" and worship (Rev. 4:10; 5:8, 14; 19:4).

For several Jewish prayers prostration was the usual posture. Worshipers in the temple assumed this posture during the rite of the daily whole-offering (Mish. *Tamid* vii.3; cf. Heinemann, pp. 125, 134, 145). Worshipers recited the Alenu prayer from a prostrate position (cf. Heinemann, pp. 271, 273, 274 n. 44). Also, the prayers offered in the temple "in thanksgiving for the deliverance of the Temple from the hands of gentiles" were called the thirteen prostrations (H. Danby, *Mishnah* [1933], p. 592 n. 2; cf. Mish. *Shekalim* vi.3; *Middoth* ii.3, 6). *See* ADORATION II.A; OBEISANCE.

*See also* PRAYER; WORSHIP.

***Bibliography.***–J. Heinemann, *Prayer in the Talmud* (1977); *TDNT,* III, *s.v.* κάμπτω (Schlier); *TDOT,* II, *s.v.* "brk" (Scharbert); IV, *s.v.* "hwh" (Preuss); *TWOT,* I, 267-69, 456; II, 784f., 914f.

S. J. SCHULTZ G. L. KNAPP

**POT** [Heb. *sîr*] (Ex. 27:3; 2 K. 4:38-41; etc.); AV also PAN, CALDRON; NEB also CAULDRON; [*pārûr*] (Nu. 11:8; Jgs. 6:19; 1 S. 2:14); AV also PAN; [*dûd̲*] (Job 41:20 [MT 12]); NEB CAULDRON; [*merqāḥâ*] (Job 41:31b [MT 23b]); NEB MIXING-BOWL; [*nēb̲el*] (Lam. 4:2); AV, NEB, PITCHER; [*kîyôr*] (Zec. 12:6); AV HEARTH; NEB BRAZIER; [Gk. *xéstēs*] (Mk. 7:4); NEB JUG; [*keramikós*] (Rev. 2:27); AV VESSEL; NEB EARTHENWARE; **FIRE POT** [Heb. *tannûr*] (Gen. 15:17); AV FURNACE; NEB BRAZIER. A vessel usually used in cooking, but the term can also be used to indicate a variety of ceramic vessels.

The *sîr* was a typical cooking pot made of either metal (Ex. 27:3) or, in common domestic use, earthenware. Many references indicate its use for the boiling of meat, especially in ritual contexts. The *pārûr* was apparently similar in form and function and cannot be distinguished from the *sîr*. The term *dûd̲,* usually translated "basket" by the RSV, connotes a vessel for boiling in Job 41:20. The other occurrences of the word seem to indicate storage; the vessel may thus have been a very large cooking pot or krater. The *merqāḥâ* is a pot used for holding ointment. *Nēb̲el* seems to be a term for a vessel in general with no specific form, function, or ware intended; elsewhere the RSV translates the word as "skin," "waterskin," "jar," "flagon," "vessel." The *kîyôr* usually refers to the temple LAVER but Zec. 12:6 seems to indicate any hot cooking vessel. The Heb. *tannûr* is a loanword from Akk. *tanūru,* "oven"; usually it refers to the portable oven used generally for cooking (e.g., Lev. 2:4). In the covenant ceremony in Gen. 15:17 apparently Abraham saw an object resembling this oven which looked like "a large inverted bowl without any bottom" (J. Kelso, *Ceramic Vocabulary of the OT* [*BASOR Supp. Studies,* 5/6, 1948], p. 31).

The *xéstēs* seems to have been a common cooking vessel kept clean by pious Jews. The term *keramikós* simply means "ceramic ware" and cannot be defined more specifically. Rev. 2:27 emphasizes its fragility. L. G. HERR

**POTASH** (Isa. 1:25, NEB). *See* LYE.

**POTENTATE.** One who wields great power. The term is used by the AV to render Gk. *dynástēs* (RSV, lit., "sovereign"; cf. NEB "holds sway") in 1 Tim. 6:15, referring to God: "the blessed and only Potentate, the King of kings and Lord of lords." *Dynástēs* is used of God also in the Apocrypha (e.g., Sir. 46:5 [RSV "Mighty One"]; 2 Macc. 15:3, 23 [RSV "Sovereign"]), of Zeus in Sophocles *Antigone* 608, and of men in Lk. 1:52 (pl.; AV, RSV, "the mighty"; NEB "monarchs") and Acts 8:27 (AV "of great authority"; RSV "minister"; NEB "high official"). *See also* SOVEREIGN.

**POTIPHAR** pot'ə-fər [Heb. *pôṭîpar*]. The Egyptian officer to whom the Midianites sold Joseph (Gen. 37:36; cf. 37:25, 27f.; 39:1; Jgs. 8:24) and in whose household Joseph rose to a position of authority (Gen. 39:1-6). The form of the name of Potiphar is Egyp. *p3-dî-p3-Rʿ*, "he whom Re [the sun-god] has given," and is probably an abbreviated form of POTIPHERA with loss of the final *ayin* (Gen. 41:45, 50; 46:20).

Potiphar is described in Gen. 37:36 and 39:1 as a *sārîs*, "officer" (NEB "eunuch") and a *śar haṭṭabbāḥîm*, "captain of the guard" (NEB mg. "executioner") These titles deserve comment. The "butler" and the "baker" of Gen. 40:2, 7 are also designated by Heb. *sārîs*, a term which elsewhere in the OT often means "eunuch" (2 K. 9:32; 20:18; Isa. 39:7; Jer. 29:2; 34:19). This meaning is problematic in this context, for Potiphar was married (Gen. 39:1), and eunuchs were not prominent in ancient Egypt (Vergote, pp. 40-42). Heb. *sārîs* has its origin in the Akkadian title *ša rēši* or *ša rēš šarri*, literally "the one of the (king's) head" or "(court) official." By the 1st millennium B.C. the term had come to mean "eunuch." It has been observed that the earlier meaning of "official" or "courtier" accords well with the Joseph contexts whereas the later, narrower meaning of *sārîs* is more appropriate in biblical contexts belonging to the 1st millennium B.C. *See* EUNUCH II. B.

The precise meaning of the title *śar haṭṭabbāḥîm* is uncertain, for Egyptian sources provide no exact equivalent. The RSV "captain of the guard" is perhaps correct and would accord with Potiphar's implied command of the prison (Gen. 39:20; 40:3ff.). A nearly identical title is applied to the Babylonian Nebuzaradan (*raḇ ṭabbāḥîm*, "captain of the guard") in 2 K. 25:8 and Jer. 52:14. This translation appears likely in this context (the NEB mg. "executioner" is unwarranted; see Vergote, pp. 31-35).

Joseph's success in Potiphar's house is credited throughout the narrative to the presence and blessing of the Lord. Even Potiphar observed "that the Lord was with him, and that the Lord caused all that he did to prosper in his hands" (Gen. 39:3). Joseph was later imprisoned by Potiphar as a result of the attempted seduction by Potiphar's unnamed wife (39:6-23). Similarities have long been observed between this story and the seduction scene preserved in the Egyptian myth of Bata and Anubis, the so-called Tale of Two Brothers (*ANET*, pp. 23-25; W. K. Simpson, ed., *Literature of Ancient Egypt* [1973], pp. 92-107). But this incident is the only point of contact between the two narratives. Even in the circumstances of Joseph's wrongful imprisonment, "the Lord was with Joseph and showed him steadfast love, and gave him favor in the sight of the keeper of the prison" (Gen. 39:21).

See J. Vergote, *Joseph en Égypt* (1959). G. PRATICO

**POTIPHERA** po-tif'ə-rə [Heb. *pôṭî peraʿ*]; AV POTIPHERAH. Joseph's father-in-law (Gen. 41:45, 50; 46:20). His daughter Asenath (perhaps "she belongs to Neit") Joseph received in marriage from Pharaoh. Manasseh and Ephraim were born of this union (41:50-52).

Potiphera is Egyp. *p3-dî-p3-Rʿ*, "he whom Re has given." Re was the sun-god who was worshiped at On, a city later named Heliopolis by the Greeks. Potiphera's title, *kōhēn ʾōn* (priest of On), may indicate that he was high priest of this center of Egyptian sun-worship.

Although this form of name does not appear in Egypt until the 10th cent. B.C., one cannot rule out earlier use, since many inscriptions from the time of the Hyksos (approximately Joseph's time) were destroyed.

*See also* POTIPHAR. G. PRATICO

**POTSHERD** [Heb. *ḥereś* (Job 2:8; 41:30 [MT 22]; Ps. 22:15 [MT 16])]; AV also STONE (Job 41:30); NEB also PIECE OF A BROKEN POT (Job 2:8), SHERD (Job 41:30); **SHERD** [Heb. *ḥereś*] (Isa. 30:14); NEB SHARD. A piece of broken pottery. Its sharp edges could be used to scrape boils or pus (cf. the LXX) from the skin (Job 2:8), and the underbelly of Leviathan was so rough that it was like "sharp potsherds" (41:30). Somewhat larger pieces could be used for carrying hot coals or water (Isa. 40:13). The dry climate of the Near East made the potsherds dry as well (Ps. 22:15). Potsherds were also a common WRITING surface (*see also* OSTRACA); their greatest importance is in dating, for frequent changes in pottery style and the presence of sherds all over the ancient Near East allow archeologists to establish a relative chronology. *See* ARCHEOLOGY VI. G. A. L.

**POTSHERD GATE** [Heb. *šaʿar haḥarsîṯ*–'gate of the earthenware pots'; Gk. *pýlēs tḗs charsith* (B *tharseis*)] (Jer. 19:2); AV EAST GATE; NEB GATE OF THE POTSHERDS. A gate of Jerusalem leading to Topheth and the Potter's Field at the east end of the Valley of Hinnom, possibly the same as the Dung Gate. *See* JERUSALEM III.D.5.

**POTTAGE** [Heb. *nāzîḏ*–'boiled food'](Gen. 25:29, 34; 2 K. 4:38-40; Hag. 2:12); NEB BROTH, POT; in Gen. 25:30 the RSV renders "that red pottage" for Heb. *hāʾāḏōm hāʾāḏōm hazzeh* (cf. *AB* "that red stuff"). Eng. "pottage" denotes a soup made of vegetables. *See* FOOD II, IV.

**POTTER; POTTERY.**

I. Introduction
II. Materials
III. Techniques
IV. Characteristics of Palestinian Pottery
V. Potters, Pottery, and the Bible
VI. Archeological Significance
VII. Analytical Methods
VIII. Conclusion

***I. Introduction.***–The "Neolithic revolution," when the culture changed from a food-gathering society to a food-producing society, introduced a need for storage vessels of all sizes. Groups of potters provided the pots and pans of antiquity and containers for a vast array of needs. The working of clay and the making of pottery is among the oldest of the crafts and is the only technology that has changed very little from early times.

Potters built the first silos for silage to feed animals, and large ceramic vessels were made to contain various grains used in households for food. Potters formed the cups, plates, bowls, jugs, bottles, and cook pots used by all. Water bottles were made that actually kept the water cool. This was especially important in desert lands where the

Model of a potter's shop from a tomb at Saqqârah (The Metropolitan Museum of Art)

heat was intense and oases were far apart. Clay was used to cover roofs and to build kilns. Clay was even used to make the wheel heads on which the ancient potter turned his clay. Clay containers contained the cosmetics that women used and, at times, stored out-of-season clothing. Ritual vessels were manufactured for religious purposes, and of course ceramic vessels played an important part in death rituals. The potter provided his skill to meet the daily human needs from birth to death. He was a prominent figure with importance to his community.

*II. Materials.*–The basic material used by potters is CLAY. Clays are basically alumino-silicates with many other minor but important components; among these, oxides. Chemically speaking, clay is a hydrated silicate of aluminum ($Al_2O_3{*}2SiO_2{*}2H_2O$) mixed with various impurities which may run as high as 50 percent. In a popular sense, clay is a fine-grained rock which becomes sticky when wet. A concise definition is offered by the American Ceramic society as follows: "Clay is a fine-grained rock which, when suitably crushed and pulverized, becomes plastic when wet, leather-hard when dried, and on firing is converted to a permanent rock-like mass."

The word "ceramics" is derived from Gk. *keramikós*, which simply means earth or earthen. The potter makes articles from naturally occurring earths. Clays come from weathered rocks that are broken down by the influences of air, water vapor, and other ingredients contained in the air; by the action of water as in rain, rivers, hail, lakes, or the sea; by the action of snow and ice; or by the action of plants and animals in their growth and decay.

Clays are moved from their point of origin by sedimentation along the course of a river; by large masses of ice, e.g., a glacier; or by air. (Anyone who has traveled in the Middle East or the Far East has encountered wind-blown deposits of clay called loess.) Clay could be deposited at the mouth of a river, in a freshwater lake, or in a sea or an ocean.

Clay is abundant all over the earth, and throughout the Middle East there are clays that can be used by the potter, the brickmaker, the roofmaker, or the image-maker. Many of the Middle Eastern clays have a high iron content along with concentrations of calcium, lime, and salts. The presence of irons in the clay produces a range of color from brown-black to salmon buff to dusty white depending on the firing variables of time, temperature, and atmosphere. In some areas potters mix and blend different clays together to form a clay body suitable for their needs. At times materials such as dung or straw were added to the clay to make it more porous or more workable (see III below). Most clays in the biblical region are thixotropic clays, i.e., clays that become more plastic and softer the more the potter works them but harden up quickly when allowed to stand. These properties are vital for potters who are building vessels by hand or on the wheel, especially if they are manufacturing large storage vessels.

Potters sought out deposits of clays that contained contrasting oxides, and after water-levigating the clays from one settling basin to another, finally produced a micrograined clay that could coat the exterior of a vessel or be applied with a crude brush into designs. This material is called "slip" in potters' terminology. Some Early Bronze Age and Iron Age pottery was decorated with slips (see below).

*III. Techniques.*–During the long period of Neolithic cultures in the Syro-Palestinian area (the Pre-pottery Neolithic B Period) the use of clay was well established in nonpottery functions. This was a developmental period that occurred prior to the 6th millennium B.C. During this Pre-Pottery Neolithic B Period fired clay was used as a fine-grained plaster on walls and floors of large rectangular rooms (e.g., at the "Jericho" settlement). These walls were often cream or pinkish in color and highly burnished.

Burnishing is a technique much used by early potters. Clay that has slightly hardened but not totally dried is in a state called "leather-hard." The clay is hard but feels cold. If clay in this state is rubbed briskly with a smooth stone or bone or a polished piece of wood it develops a sheen. This is caused by a fine microlayer of clay being brought to the surface and being polished. Burnishing can produce a high gloss on clay. At times it has been misread as a layer of clay slip or a glaze. In addition to using clay as a plaster, human skulls were built up and decorated by plastering clay over the skull itself and at times inserting stones as a form of mosaic. Clay figurines were also formed of unfired clay; in fact, clay anthropomorphic and zoomorphic images go far back into human development — as far back as 30,000 B.C. People have always formed images of their own likenesses, images of the world in which they lived, and images of their gods. They created

Zoomorphic clay figure from Cyprus (700-475 B.C.) (R. H. Johnston)

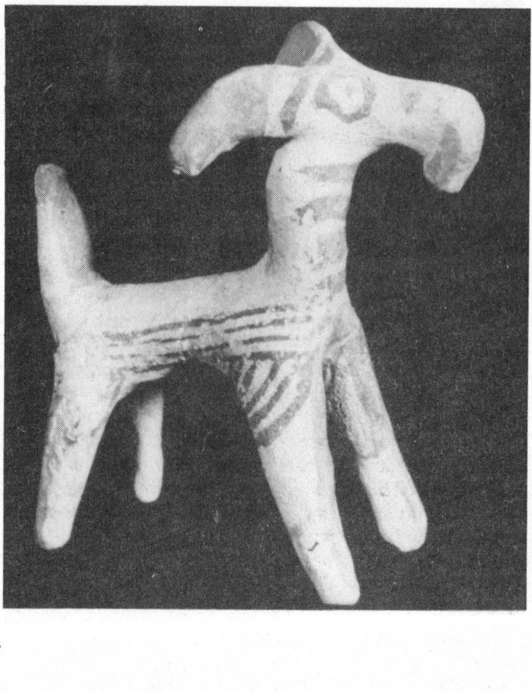

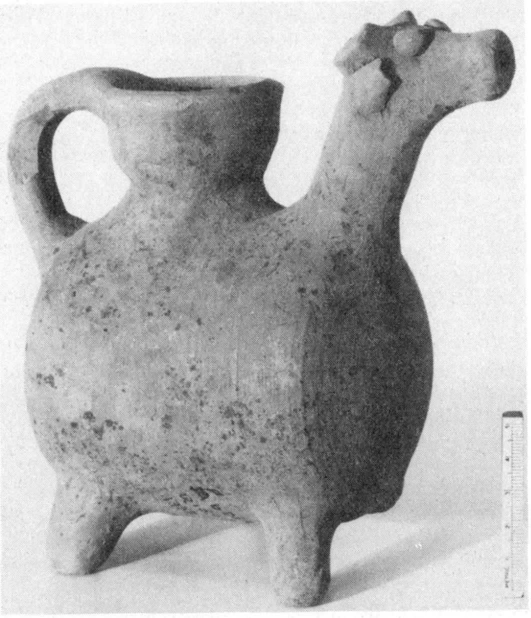

Zoomorphic vessel from Megiddo (Oriental Institute, University of Chicago)

these images for fertility rituals, magic rituals to explain and control their environment, and to develop a god/magic relationship — the beginnings of shamanism.

The making of clay vessels and the discovery that clay can be made hard by fire developed in some unknown manner. There are many theories. The closest ceramic tradition to the Syro-Palestinian tradition of clay would be from southwestern Anatolia. Particularly the sites of Hacılar and Çatal Hüyük have great parallels. The ceramic tradition at these sites goes back to 9000-7000 B.C. This is among the earliest uses of clay vessels and the steps toward fired clay. Early potters added tempering material (aplastic material) to their wares as well as straw. The use of threshing-floor straw is well documented in the OT when the Jews were in bondage in Egypt and employed as brickmakers (Ex. 1:14; 5:7-14). The addition of aplastics to a clay body can reduce the thermal shock to ceramic ware used as cooking pots. It also can reduce the expansion and contraction and breakage during firing in pit firings or in simple updraft kilns. Straw added to clay produces a more porous body — very important to assist in firing survival and in the making of water bottles. A porous body will allow the contained water to leach through the walls of the vessel. As it does, the water coming to the exterior of the vessel evaporates and thus by a natural process of refrigeration cools the water contained inside the vessel. The addition of dung and straw to the clay body also acts as a binder in the manufacturing process and helps hold a poor quality clay together as it is being formed. Some believe that bacteria added to clay in dung also help to make a clay body more plastic.

The preparation of clay for making of pottery is simple. The clay is dug and brought to the potter's work area. It is crushed by beating it with logs or rolling over it with a heavy roller. The large stones are removed. A pit is dug and lined with stones or plastered. The clay is dumped in and water added to produce a slurry. The heavy stones settle to the bottom and the clay can be skimmed off to get rid of excess water. The clay is allowed to stand in its plastic state for several days to age. It is then ready for use. The potter will have his assistant work the clay into small pugs that are the appropriate size for the vessel that is to be made. The potter or his helper de-airs, or wedges, the clay by slapping pieces of it together or by kneading the clay like bread dough. Failure to remove the air results in increased breakage in the firing process — the air becomes steam and expands during the temperature increase, eventually exploding the piece.

The earliest pottery from Pottery Neolithic and the Early Bronze I and II periods was handmade. The potter shaped the ware with his hands only; no wheel was used and the tournette had not yet been invented. The potter pinched and paddled the clay to form the shape he wanted. He could make large vessels by adding coils on top of coils of clay, smoothing each coil into the vessel form. Vessels 2 m. (6 ft.) and larger in height were made by this technique. The forms were smoothed with sticks and bones to a refined shape and then polished or burnished when the ware reached the leather-hard state. Decoration was incised or scratched into the vessels and, at times, punctate dots were pushed into the vessel with a round stick. Herringbone, zigzag lines, and bands of parallel incisions were also used.

Early in the making of pottery vessels the use of slip painting was discovered. Slip is a very fine-grained colored clay. A light colored slip could be painted over a rough dark clay or vice versa. Designs could be incised through the slip-covered vessel to expose the contrasting color underneath, or designs could be painted on with colored slip. The slip itself could be burnished. The only tools used were the potter's hands, some sharp sticks, polished stones or bones, and crude brushes sometimes made by chewing the ends of plant material and exposing the bristlelike fiber. Handles were added by using coils of clay, thus enabling better and safe handling of the vessel as well as allowing the vessel to be hung from a peg or a house beam. The bases of early vessels were rounded since they were placed in concave depressions in early households or placed in clay or woven tripods or ring holders. Since few surfaces were flat, flat-bottomed vessels were of little use.

Another decorative technique used by the earliest potters was combing. Both horizontal and vertical bands of combing were used as well as wavy combing. Combing was done by dragging a stick with teeth cut into it over the surface of a vessel. The combing could be used to help refine the shape of the pot. Perhaps the most common technique of early potters is the paddle-and-anvil technique. Anvils made of clay, wood, or stone could be used inside the pottery while a wooden or clay paddle could be used on the exterior to shape and thin the pottery sides. If designs have been carved into the paddle, the pottery can be decorated with an overall pattern as it is being shaped and formed. By using the paddle and anvil the potter could make pieces that were quite thin-walled and cylindrical.

Early firing was probably done by pit firing. A pit was dug and at times lined. Then pottery and fuel were stacked in the pit and fuel over the pit. Using brush, straw, or dung cakes for fuel, earthenware temperatures were easily reached. Later, simple updraft kilns were constructed with a firing chamber under a chamber for holding pieces to be fired. The floor of the pottery chamber was pierced with carefully placed holes to insure a more even temperature. Again, earthenware temperatures could easily be reached, but since the heat could be better controlled, there was less distortion in the fired pieces and less breakage.

The next step in the manufacturing process was the introduction of a tournette. The tournette allowed the pot-

Village potter in Cyprus working on a tournette (R. H. Johnston)

ter to rotate the piece as he worked, and with the help of an assistant the potter could make more pieces in a given workday. Tournettes were made of clay, wood, or stone. Several examples of tournettes have been found.

Sometime during the E.B. II period (2900-2650 B.C.) the true potter's wheel was invented. Pottery from this time shows that it was made on a centrifugal wheel (cf. Jer. 18:3f.). Wheels like this could be spun by an assistant or turned by the potter's feet. The potter could place a pug of clay on the wheel, center it while it was spinning, and open, draw up, form, and finish a vessel in a short period of time. No one is certain exactly when or where the potter's wheel was invented, but it appears in the Middle East at many places *ca.* 2750 B.C. Wheel-made pottery shows distinctive signs of the method of manufacture. The marks of the potter's hands are evident in the inside drawing rings left there when the potter formed the piece.

The technique of the ancient Palestinian potters when using a kick wheel can be described by the following steps or procedures: (1) The potter or his assistant wedges (de-airs) the clay and forms it into a pug. The pug size varies depending on the size of the pot to be made. (2) The pug of clay is fastened to a "bat" made of wood or fired clay that is in turn fastened to the wheel head. (3) As the wheel is turned, the pug is centered. (4) The pug is opened by forcing the hand down into the pug while the wheel is spinning. (5) The opened form is raised up by exerting pressure inside against the outside with the potter's hands. The centrifugal force of the turning wheel thins the clay between the potter's hands and stretches the clay upward. (6) The potter opens or closes the form, making the desired shape. (7) Handles are added with coils or bands of clay. (8) Decorative elements are applied using combs, sticks, colored slip, or roulette. (9) The form can be refined by the paddle-and-anvil technique. (10) The finished piece is removed from the wheel and put aside to dry; later it will be trimmed to its final shape. (11) The piece is dried and prepared for the firing. The making of an averaged-size pitcher form can take 5 to 10 minutes. The wheel enables the potter to make many pieces very quickly.

The press mold was a technique often used to make figurines such as the Astarte of the Canaanites during the time of Joshua (*see* pictures in GODS; IDOLATRY). Parts of press-molded figures could be added to hand-formed parts. An example might be adding a press-molded head to a hand-formed figurine. Press molds were made of wood, clay, or stone. Wet clay is pressed into the mold to receive the negative cut-mold impressions. If a head is to be made, it is press molded in two halves that are joined together while the clay is plastic. Press molds were also used to make seal-like forms that could be added to a clay vessel as decorative elements. This technique is called sprigging. For example, animal or plant forms can be press molded and attached to a newly formed clay vessel. A mold or stamp can also be used to make seals. These seals were trademarks or signs of royal ownership.

***IV. Characteristics of Palestinian Pottery.*–*A.*** *Neolithic* (*ca.* 9000-4300 B.C.). The use of fired clay or pottery is found during this era. The vessels were handmade with relatively simple forms, often basket-like, bowl-shaped, and in small and large jar shapes. Much of the clay fabric is coarse with indications of straw temper. Incised decorations included chevron and herringbone with triangular elements; punctate decorations also appear. Handles are formed of crude coils of clay or of knob, ledge, or lug shapes. Some vessels have zoomorphic forms as handles. During Neolithic times there are also examples of finer ware made of a finer clay, with smoothed surfaces, at times coated with burnished slip. There are also examples of burnished designs. Bases were often flat.

*B. Chalcolithic* (*ca.* 4th millennium). The pottery from this period is represented by the Ghassulian and Beer-sheba cultures. The lines between the Neolithic and the Chalcolithic cultures are elusive at best. Wares are thinner and show evidence of a better knowledge of pyrotechnology, better kilns, and less added aplastic material. Forms are more refined and complex. There are u-shaped bowls, bowl-chalices, cornets, goblets, jars (medium necked and holemouth jars), incense burners, and large pithoi. Rope decorations appear and punctate decorations continue. Handles are ledge, knob, and coils of clay; some handles had a small hole through which rope could be passed. The use of redslip is widespread, as is burnishing. Incised designs persist. Churns appear as a more complex ceramic form.

*C. Early Bronze* (*ca.* 3100-2200 B.C.). This is a complex period in ceramic history and an era of change, development, and refinement. Forms appear to be handmade. Later in the Early Bronze era the tournette begins to be used, and later still the potter's wheel. The ledge handle starts as a plain handle, becomes thumb indented, then is pushed up, and later folded over (scalloped). Flat-bottomed jars with spouts appear, as do juglets of all sizes, bowls (some with an "omphalos" in the center), pedestaled bowls, teapots, platter amphoriskoi, twin bowls (some connected by a hidden channel), and incense burners (some bases are round). Decorative elements include typical E.B. I red-burnished slip, net painting, brown-burnished slip, painted slip decorations (bands, diagonal lines, crosshatch, vertical and horizontal bands), punctate decorations, and rope decorations. *See* Plates 68, 70. Current work being done at Bâb edh-Dhrâʿ, Numeira, Ṣâfī (Zoor), Feifa, and Khanazir will add new dimensions to the study of Bronze Age pottery.

*D. Middle Bronze* (2000-1500 B.C.). Middle Bronze pottery is best studied from reports from Tell Beit Mirsim, Lachish, Megiddo, Jericho, and Tell el-Fârʿah (Sharuhen). Vessels are spherical and barrel-shaped with less defined shoulders. Pottery has flat bases or no distinct base at all. There are less handles with the exception of some loop handles. Firing techniques and clay preparation appear to be more sophisticated. Evidence of the tournette is reflected in vessels with handmade bodies and with wheel-turned necks. Vessel joins are easily detected, showing the making of separate parts of the vessel. Typical forms are the caliciform jar and bowl lamps with four pinched spouts, carinated bowls, some with a trumpet foot, button-based juglets, double-handled jugs, elongated dipper juglets, teapots, and lamps. The centrifugal wheel is apparent in M.B. II with a much greater refinement of form. These include open rounded bowls, goblets, high-footed goblet-chalices, kraters, storage jars, bottles, and juglets of all sizes and shapes. The forms are not only richer but more elaborate and graceful. *See* picture in ARCHEOLOGY OF PALESTINE AND SYRIA.

*E. Late Bronze* (1550-1200 B.C.). During the later stages of M.B. II and into the L.B. period there was an influx of pottery from Cyprus ("bilbils," "milk bowls") and from Mycenae (stirrup jars, pyxides, and piriform jugs). This is the period of bichrome ware and ware in the shape of and decorated with animal forms and geometric designs. The potter's centrifugal wheel is evident in the shape of vessels and in the band decorations of the vessels. Bowls (*see* picture in BOWL), goblets, chalices, kraters, storage jars, cooking vessels, pithoi, amphoriskos shapes (*see* Plate 70), mugs, amphora, and Astarte plaques are common. Decorative elements include banding, birds, fish, geometric forms, bulls, tree of life, goats, *et al.* The pilgrim flask appears to originate during this period and has become one of the most characteristic forms of this period.

Painted jug with band decorations. From Râs el-ʿAin (just E of Tel Aviv), M.B. II-L.B. (Israel Department of Antiquities and Museums)

Two jugs from Tell el-ʿAjjûl. This bichrome ware was a high point in pottery art (M. B. II.C-L.B. I) (Israel Department of Antiquities and Museums)

Handleless pottery vessel in the form of a fish. The decorative technique is typical of pottery from Tell el-Yehudiyeh, a Hyksos stronghold in the Delta (Israel Museum, Jerusalem)

Goblet decorated in chocolate-on-white style. Note the geometric designs and ibex (Israel Department of Antiquities and Museums)

A pilgrim flask (R. H. Johnston)

Duck-shaped vase from Cyprus (850-600 B.C.) (R. H. Johnston)

Hellenistic "teapot" from Mareshah (Israel Department of Antiquities and Museums)

*F. Iron I* (1200-1000 B.C.). Pottery types reflect the Bronze Age. This is the period of Philistine pottery. Typical are bichrome bowls with alternating red and black bands, trefoil-mouth jugs and juglets, black burnished vessels, chalices, geometric slip decoration, including burnished and slip-painted forms as well as natural forms and birds. Some imported wares or cultural influences are from Phoenicia, Cyprus, and the Aramean kingdom. In addition to red and black slip, we also find yellow and brown slip sometimes covering most of the vessel and at times highly burnished.

*G. Iron II* (1000-587 B.C.). The skills of the potters using the centrifugal potter's wheel are evident by mass production of vessel types. Wheel burnishing is apparent. Bowls are made with alternating red and black rings similar to the preceding period (*see* Plate XX). Some deep bowls have stump legs, some have coiled legs, and some have band handles. Some vessels are perforated like sieves. Burnishing continues as does slip painting, both by hand and on the wheel. One-handled cups appear. The bases of vessels clearly show the cutoff marks caused by cutting them loose from a turning wheel with a string. There are oil jugs, chalices, cups, pitchers, cook pots, wares, goblets, kraters, pithoi, decanters, spouted jugs, and figurines.

*H. Exilic-Persian* (*ca.* 587-332 B.C.). Black-polished ware appears, slip-coated, reduction-fired, and polished to a high sheen glossy black. Bottles, jars, bird-beaked vessels, tripod vessels with three legs, cluster pottery, zoomorphic vessels, lamps, figurines, basket handles, lug handles, and zoomorphic handles are characteristic. Decorative elements include geometric painted designs, animals and bird representations, plant forms, colored bands, wavy lines, and impressed elements done with stamps.

*I. Hellenistic* (*ca.* 332-63 B.C.). Imported black ware as well as imitated local copies are common. There were Rhodian type jars, inscribed (stamped) handles, wheel-thrown lamps, molded (piece molded) lamps with molded decorations, unguentania and bowls, plates, and bottles of all sizes.

*J. Roman* (63 B.C.-A.D. 324). This period saw an influx of terra sigillata, wheel-made and wheel-trimmed precise forms, polished, fine-grain, red-slipped clay. Clay was probably water-levigated to sort out fine clay particles. Forms have well-defined shoulders and base detail. Rims are carefully finished. There is much use of rouletting as decoration as well as use of stamped and sprigged decoration. Nabatean ware in Jordan is extremely thin and aesthetic with painted floral decorations. There were Herodian spouted lamps, ribbed ware, jugs, bottles, flasks, juglets, and figurines. Some decorative elements were either imported or copied from Italy. Perhaps Roman potters came to Palestine to work. Roman ware is a high point in pottery in the Syro-Palestine area in terms of technique and in the use of decorative elements.

*K. Byzantine* (A.D. 324-630). Incised lines and ribbing are common decorative elements. There are long-necked vessels with twisted handles — at times, perhaps, copies of metal vessels. Combed patterns are common, perhaps a reflection of Bronze Age techniques. There are pedestal lamps and button-based vessels. Pottery takes on a more Eastern flavor. Cooking vessels and jars use the ribbing technique mentioned earlier. Some bowls are pedestal bowls. Christian symbols are used on lamps, *et al.*

*See also* the chart in ARCHEOLOGY.

***V. Potters, Pottery, and the Bible.***–The OT differentiates between native clays (dry or wet) and clays specially sought out and prepared for the making of pottery. According to Kelso (whose *Ceramic Vocabulary* is the best discussion of the OT material) Job 10:9 is the best illustration of the different words for clays: "Remember that thou has made me of clay [*ḥōmer*] and wilt thou turn me to dust [*ʿāp̱ār*] again?" *Ḥōmer* is the Hebrew word for a worked clay or a potter's clay, or in some phrases, a wet refuse clay (cf. "mire" in Job 30:9; Isa. 10:6). It is also used for brick clay ("mortar," Ex. 1:4; Isa. 41:25; Nah. 3:14), and in Job 38:14 it may refer to the clay used for stoppers of wine jars or storage jars. (cf. E. Dhorme, *Comm. on the Book of Job* [Eng. tr. 1967; repr. 1984], pp. 581f., who identifies it with terra sigillata). A seal was often stamped in the wet clay to denote ownership. (Archeologists carefully study these seals and often are thereby able to establish a relative chronology.) In addition to its common meaning "dust," Heb. *ʿāp̱ār* can also refer to potter's clay, the only kind of "dust" that can be used to fashion a figure or image (Kelso, p. 5); thus several texts use it in the imagery of God as potter (Isa. 29:16; 45:9; 64:8 [MT 7]; Jer. 18:1-4; cf. Gen. 2:7, 19).

The Hebrew word for wet clay is *ṭîṭ,* which seems to refer to a native wet clay with no preparation being done to make it into a workable potter's clay (see III above). Thus it is cast up by the sea ("dirt," Isa. 57:20) and may be found on river banks ("mire," Job 41:30 [MT 22]). It is also found in the bottom of a cistern ("mire," Jer. 38:6), and several texts refer to the "mire of the streets" (2 S. 22:43 par. Ps. 18:42 [MT 43]; cf. "mud," Zec. 9:3; 10:5), which Kelso (p. 5) called wet refuse clay, formed from crumbled bricks that had gotten wet. It is also used of a bog (Ps. 40:2 [MT 3]; 69:14 [MT 15]). Aram. *ṭîn* (cognate of Heb. *ṭîṭ*) is also used of clay in Daniel's interpretation of Nebuchadnezzar's vision of a great image, whose feet and toes were partly of potter's clay *(ḥᵃsap̱ dí-pᵉḥār)* or miry clay *(ḥᵃsap̱ ṭînā')* (Dnl. 2:41, 43).

Two other words for clay are *'ereṣ* and *'ᵃḏāmâ.* Both words usually refer to the land or the earth or the ground in general, but a few texts may have more specific, concrete substances in view. Thus in Ps. 12:66 (MT 7) *'ereṣ* may refer to a fired clay (see M. Dahood, *Psalms,* I [*AB,* 1966], 74f.); cf. also Lam. 2:21 ("dust"). In Jgs. 6:37-40 *'ereṣ* ("ground") may refer to the marly clay used on a threshing floor (see Kelso, pp. 5, 42). Heb. *'ᵃḏāmâ* may also have the meaning of a dry native clay; cf. Isa. 45:9, *ḥarśê 'ᵃḏāmâ,* "earthen vessel," and Gen. 2:19, where God forms all the creatures from the "ground" (Heb. *ᵃḏāmâ;* cf. v.7).

Other words used to describe pottery are: Heb. *ḥereś,* which describes fired clay, pottery ("earthen vessel," Prov. 26:23; "vessel," Isa. 45:9), or a potsherd (Job 2:8; 41:30 [MT 22]; Ps. 22:15 [MT 16]; "sherd," Isa. 30:14); *kᵉlî ḥereś,* pottery or a fired ware that has gone through the kiln to make it more durable ("earthen vessel," Lev. 6:28); *kᵉlî yôṣēr* ("earthen vessel," 2 S. 17:28; "potter's vessel," Ps. 2:9); *niḇlê ḥereś* ("earthen pots," Lam. 4:2); *nēḇel yôṣēr* ("potter's vessel," Isa. 30:14); Aram. *ḥᵃsap̱,* which corresponds to Heb. *ḥereś* and thus denotes a fired clay or terra cotta. According to Kelso (p. 7) "clay" in Dnl. 2:33-35, 42, 45 refers to terra-cotta inlays that were built into the iron feet of the image (cf. *ḥᵃsap̱ dí-pᵉḥār,* "potter's clay," and *ḥᵃsap̱ ṭînā',* "miry clay," in Dnl. 2:41, 43).

The potter is called a *yôṣēr* (< *yāṣar,* "to form, shape") in Hebrew (Isa. 29:16; 41:25; Jer. 18:2-4, 6; etc.) and *pᵉḥār* in Aramaic (Dnl. 2:41). *Yôṣēr* is one of several Hebrew terms for craftsmen who make objects of clay, wood, metal, or other materials. According to Kelso (p. 7) it is the potter to whom this term is most often applied. 1 Ch. 4:23 seems to refer to royal potters (see I. Mendelsohn, *BASOR,* 80 [Dec. 1940], 17-21), but their connection with the *lmlk* inscriptions is problematic (contra Kelso: cf. H. G. M. Williamson, *1 and 2 Chronicles* [*NCBC,* 1982], p. 61).

Other technical terms include *rāmas,* "to tread (clay)" (Isa. 41:25; Nah. 3:14; note that in both instances the term for clay is *ṭîṭ*); *qāraṣ,* "to pinch (off)," used only in Job 33:6 in this technical sense of pinching off a pug of clay from the large prepared batches of clay (cf. KoB, p. 857, which notes the cognate Akkadian expression, *qarāṣa ṭîṭa,* "shape clay"; see also the comms., many of which note that this Akkadian expression occurs in the Gilgamesh Epic when Aruru creates Enkidu from clay [*ANET,* p. 74]). The *bêṯ hayyôṣēr,* "potter's house," served both as dwelling and workshop (Jer. 18:2; Kelso, pp. 8f.).

The only specific reference to a potter's wheel is Jer. 18:3. Here the term is *'oḇnāyim,* a dual form that no doubt refers to the traditional kick wheel used at that time. The potter turns the wheel with his feet and works the clay on an attached smaller wheel located on the top of the wheel shaft. Pottery was also made by hand, e.g., by the paddle-and-anvil technique and by the tournette. Jer. 18:4 offers more about the craft of manufacturing pottery: "And the vessel he was making of clay was spoiled in the potter's hand, and he reworked it into another vessel, as it seemed good to the potter to do." When working on the potter's wheel the clay can become too wet and collapse or the object being made can get off center and fly off the wheel head. Air bubbles can ruin a piece, as can many other factors. The potter, like many other craftsmen, is careful not to waste his raw material, so he will reform the piece into a clay ball and make another object from the clay.

Terms for "kiln" include *tannûr,* which really means oven (Lev. 2:4; 26:26) but which could also be applied to the firing of pottery (cf. Kelso, p. 9, on Neh. 3:11; 12:38); *kiḇšān* (Ex. 9:8, 10; 19:18; "furnace," Gen. 19:18), which according to Kelso (pp. 40f.) is a smelting furnace; and Aram. *'attûn* (Dnl. 3), which Kelso (p. 38) said was probably a brick kiln. The early kilns were simple updraft kilns with a riddle floor separating the firing chamber for the pottery from the fire pit, where the kiln was stoked using straw, dung cakes, or wood as fuel. Kilns such as these can be found all over the Middle East today, still being used to fire pottery. *See also* FURNACE; OVEN.

The glazing of pottery did not occur in Syro-Palestine

Potter's kick wheel made of clay and wood. From Afghanistan (R. H. Johnston)

during biblical times. Pottery was decorated using colored clays, colored slips, or at times was entirely covered with colored slip and burnished to a relatively high gloss. This gloss is retained after the firing. The use of the term "glaze" in Prov. 26:23 ("Like the glaze covering an earthen vessel") is a conjecture; the MT reads *kesep sîgîm,* "silver dross." The conjecture is based on supposed Hittite *(zapaga[y]a)* and Ugaritic *(spsg)* evidence. Despite the appropriateness of the image for the context, further research has suggested that the Hittite and Ugaritic terms mean "bowl," not "glaze" (see H. Cohen, *Biblical Hapax Legomena in the Light of Akkadian and Ugaritic* [1978], pp. 122f. n. 40). There has been no evidence of the use of a lead or tin glaze in OT times. We do know that the bricks of the Lion Wall in Babylonia were glazed. These date to the time of King Nebuchadrezzar II (605-562 B.C.). Mention must also be made of Egyptian faience ware such as the famous turquoise hippopotamus that dates back to 2000-1700 B.C.

Some glazed tiles have been found from the Egyptian Predynastic period, prior to 3200 B.C. These glazes used an alkaline flux and were fired very low. Glazed ware was, however, not widely made in ancient Egypt. The Egyptian faience body was high in silica- and borax-type fluxes. As ware dried, the soluble fluxes were drawn to the surface, forming the glaze-like coating in the firing. Copper greens and turquoise were used in the early period, and by 2000 B.C. cobalt blue and manganese black were used. By 1500 B.C. other colors emerged, such as manganese purples, chrome yellows and orange, iron reds and opaque white from tin oxide. Again, the writer does not know of any of this techonology during OT times in Syro-Palestine ware. With the rise of Islam after A.D. 622, one begins to see the spread of a variety of Islamic glazes.

***VI. Archeological Significance.***–Of all the material excavated, the largest amount is ceramic. On a large excavation literally thousands of ceramic pieces are found. Clay is durable, resistant to change, and the key to the dating of any modern site. In 1890 Sir Flinders Petrie excavated the site of Tell el-Ḥesī. In his publication of a corpus of pottery he recognized the chronological value of ceramic material in a stratified excavation. He established a scale of dated sherds. Since that time the process of establishing chronologies through the stratified ceramic yield has been intensified and expanded. A trained ceramic archeologist can sift through sherds or fragments of ceramic objects and "date" a site. In many cases this dating will be more definite than carbon-14, potassium-argon, or thermoluminescent dating.

Pottery being excavated in a temple doorway at Tell Kittan (Israel Department of Antiquities and Museums)

As ancient civilizations grew, as needs changed, and as foreign influences moved in, the style of pottery changed. When an ancient city was conquered one of the prizes was the craftsmen of that city; this provided interchange between the conquerors and the conquered. Technology changed too and is an important aspect in studying ceramics. Trade among towns and cities, among countries, and among continents resulted in changes in identifiable ceramic forms. The ceramic yield can provide clues to diet, produce, animal husbandry, and, at times, clues to weapons, games, and cultural mores.

Much Syro-Palestinian pottery was earthenware pottery, which is quite porous. Some of the Hebrew dietary laws may have resulted from the type of vessels used. For example, milk stored in an earthenware bottle will soak into the pores of the clay, turning sour and allowing bacteria to build up. This would cause the vessel to be "unclean." Earthenware plates and cups would suffer from the same problems. We are dealing with ceramic material that not only provided the pots and pans but light, heat, shelter, *et al.* No wonder this is the most studied material on any excavation. Ceramic specialists are a part of every major excavation now in progress. They apply their knowledge and skill to the knowledge and skills of all the specialists that make up an excavation team. The ceramic study can go on for years after a site has been dug. New techniques have helped to glean even more information from clay objects.

***VII. Analytical Methods.***–In addition to the ecological approach combined with the study of the archeological present, an extensive array of scientific and mathematical techniques is being applied to the in-depth study of material being excavated. The computer allows one to do statistical studies and to develop three-dimensional models. The process of neutron activation can isolate and identify rare trace elements in clay bodies, assisting in the study of domestic vs. imported ware by relating or not relating trace elements to a specific geographic area or relating groups of clay vessels to each other. X-ray and xeroradiographic studies and analysis allow the scholar to look at the inner structure of vessels with a nondestructive technique. The petrographic microscope with polarized light allows one to examine microthin sections to determine specific and general mineral content, which helps in establishing the locale of the manufactured ancient pottery. In addition, thermoluminescence, atomic absorption study, gas chromatograph analysis, carbon-14 and tree-ring dating techniques, the application of the X-ray analyzer, soil sample studies, clay sample studies (including pyrotechnical studies of fired clay samples where the impact of time, temperature, and atmosphere variables are tested, noted, and compared to ancient fired material), ethnographic study, and the establishment of site typology through comparative study all aid the study of pottery. This listing of scientific and mathematical techniques is not at all complete but gives the reader some idea of the complexity and intensity of archeological ceramic research.

***VIII. Conclusion.***–An effort has been made to inform the reader of the spread of ceramic material found and studied on a Syro-Palestinian site. New material is constantly being found and new studies made. The study of Syro-Palestinian ceramic material and pottery is an ongoing study. Much of the knowledge that we have about biblical times and places is due to the study of excavated material, much of which is ceramic. New excavators emerge from academia each year armed with new techniques and fresh approaches. Added to the accumulated skills and knowledge of the past, these will add new dimensions to our study of the Bible. The excavator of the future will have to have even more awareness and knowledge of science, mathematics, and technology than ever before. The excavator will have to be familiar with the uses and applications of computers. The advent of the mini- and microcomputers operating on battery power and being quite portable brings the computer right onto the excavation as a recording and note-taking device. Information recorded in the field can be sent electronically to a mainframe computer for more sophisticated use. The amount of information will increase and require the excavation director to sort out the specific data needed to answer specific questions. With the advent of new computers specifically designed for graphics, much of the laborious hand drawing will come to an end. The new technologies will ease the toil and labor required of all excavators and speed up the time needed to publish new mterial. The new technology will not replace the need for classic learning but add to it and offer new dimensions in biblical study.

*Bibliography.*–W. F. Albright, *Recent Discoveries in Bible Lands* (1955); R. Amiran, *Ancient Pottery of the Holy Land* (1970); P. Delougaz, *Plano-convex Bricks and the Methods of their Employment* (1953); *EAEHL;* G. M. Foster, *Traditional Cultures and the Impact of Technological Change* (1962); H. J. Franken, *In Search of the Jericho Potters* (1974); H. J. Franken, ed., *Potters of a Medieval Village in the Jordan Valley* (1975); R. W. Grimshaw, *The Chemistry and Physics of Clays* (1980); R. Hampe and A. Winter, *Bei Topfern und Topferinnen in Kreta Messenien und Zypern* (1962); *Bei Topfern und Zieglern in Suditalien Sizilien und Griechenland* (1965); H. Hodges, *Artifacts* (1964); R. H. Johnston, *BA,* 37 (Dec. 1974), 86-106; "The Development of the Potter's Wheel: An Analytical and Synthesizing Study in Material Culture, Styles, Organization, and Dynamics of Technology," in H. Lechman and R. Merrill, eds., *1975 Proceeding of the American Ethnological Society,* pp. 169-210; R. H. Johnston and R. E. Alexander, *Xeroradiography of Ancient Objects* (1972); J. L. Kelso, *Ceramic Vocabulary of the OT* (*BASOR Supp. Studies* 5-6, 1948); J. L. Kelso and J. Palin Thorley, "The Potter's Technique at Tell Beit Mirsim Particularly in Stratum A," in W. F Albright, ed., *Excavation of Tell Beit Mirsim,* III (*AASOR,* 21-22; 1941-43); K. M. Kenyon, *Archaeology of the Holy Land* (4th ed. 1979); F. Matson, ed., *Ceramics and Man* (1965); R. T. Schaub, "The Early Bronze 1A-1B of the Bab edh Dhra Cemetery, Jordan" (Ph. D. diss., University of Pittsburgh); A. O. Shepard, *Ceramics for the Archaeologist* (1971); G. E. Wright, *The Pottery of Palestine from the Earliest Times to the End of the Early Bronze Age* (1937); *WBA* (2nd ed. 1970).

R. H. JOHNSTON

**POTTER'S FIELD** [Gk. *agrós toú keraméōs* (Mt. 27:7, 10)]. A burial ground outside Jerusalem for foreigners. Before hanging himself, the repentant Judas threw down in the temple the thirty pieces of silver he had received for betraying Jesus. Since the silver was "blood money" (i.e. money paid for a man's life), it could not be put into the temple treasury; hence the purchase of the field. Matthew's reference to it as the "potter's field" probably means it was bought from a potter, though scholars have suggested that this was where the potters got their clay or dumped their refuse. Easy confusion of the Hebrew term for treasury *('ôṣār)* with the term for potter *(yôṣēr)* may account for the alternative uses of the money that the priests considered.

Matthew's reference to this event as the fulfillment of "the prophecy of Jeremiah" has provoked much discussion. Several OT allusions seem to be mixed here: Jeremiah's visit to the potter's house (Jer. 18:1-5; cf. 19:1-13), his purchase of a field from his cousin for seventeen silver pieces (32:9), and Zechariah's contribution to the treasury of his wages — thirty shekels — according to God's command (Zec. 11:12f.). See the discussions in Gundry, pp. 555-58; Moo, pp. 189-210.

According to Acts 1:18f. (which refers to this field as AKELDAMA) Judas had bought the field with the money received for turning Jesus over to the chief priest. The association with blood (Akeldama is the Greek transliteration of Aram. *ḥᵃqēl dᵉmā',* "field of blood") differs from that in Mt. 27:7: Judas fell into this field and "all his bowels gushed out" (Acts 1:18); hence the gruesome name. Scholars have advanced various theories to explain the differences in these accounts. Some have called them contradictory (see the comms. by F. Beare [1981], pp. 525f.; A. McNeile [repr. 1980], pp. 407-409; A. Plummer [repr. 1953], pp. 385f.), and others attempt to harmonize them (cf. D. Carson, pp. 561f.). Cf. Barth's attempt to maintain the tension between the two accounts (*CD,* II/2, 463-471).

The traditional site of this field since the 4th cent. has been the south slope at the east end of the Hinnom Valley. The pilgrim Antoninus Martyr (6th cent.) knew this as a burial place for foreigners, and pilgrims were buried here at least until the 17th century.

*Bibliography.*–D. Carson, "Matthew," in F. Gaebelein, ed., *Expositor's Bible Comm.,* 8 (1984); R. Gundry *Matthew* (1982); D. Moo, *OT in the Gospel Passion Narratives* (1984).

W. J. MOULDER

**POUND.** *See* WEIGHTS AND MEASURES.

**POVERTY** [Heb. *rêš* (Prov. 10:15; 13:18, 24:34), *rē'š* (6:11; 30:8), *rîš* (28:19; 31:7), *rûš* (10:4), *yāraš* ("come to poverty," 20:13; 23:21)]; AV, NEB, also POOR; [Gk. *hystérēsis* (Mk. 12:44), *hystérēma* (Lk. 21:4), *ptōcheía* (2 Cor. 8:2, 9; Rev. 2:9)]; AV also WANT, PENURY; NEB also POOR, "less than enough."

- I. Biblical Terms
- II. Sociology of Poverty in Scripture
  - A. In the Seminomadic Economy
  - B. In the Agricultural Economy
  - C. During the Monarchy
  - D. From the Exile to Roman Colonialism
  - E. Responses to Poverty in First-century Palestine
  - F. Jesus and Poverty
    - 1. Jesus' Social Standing
    - 2. Jesus and the Poor
  - G. The Early Church and Poverty
    - 1. Social Standing of the Early Christians
    - 2. Paul and Poverty
    - 3. Poverty and Persecution
  - H. Conclusion
- III. Liberation Theology

***I. Biblical Terms.***–Hebrew *rêš* and its cognates and Gk. *hystérēsis* and *hystérēma* describe a condition of economic lack or insufficiency, a condition of having "less than enough." In dealing with poverty, however, Scripture more commonly uses concrete, picturesque, and evocative language. It is not "poverty" that commands attention in the Bible as much as "the poor" (*see* POOR). The terminology for the poor pictures real people reduced to begging (Heb. *'eḇyôn;* Gk. *ptōchós*; the noun *ptōcheía* means lit. "beggarliness"), humiliated and oppressed (Heb. *'ānî*), weak, frail, and drained of strength (Heb. *dal*). Such language does not merely describe; it evokes sympathy and summons protest. The prophets and evangelists were not indifferent to poverty. When they spoke of it, their terminology reflected their compassion for the poor and their condemnation of oppression and injustice. The less colorful and more neutral terminology — words that call attention to a condition rather than to people made wretched by the condition — is used almost exclusively in proverbs that regard poverty as a result of laziness (Prov. 6:11; 10:4; 20:13; 24:34), unrestrained desire for rich food and strong drink (23:21), frivolous pleasure-seeking (28:19), or generally refusing the prudent instructions of the wise (13:18).

*II. Sociology of Poverty in Scripture.–A. In the Seminomadic Economy.* According to the biblical narratives the patriarchs first lived a seminomadic existence, wandering with flocks and herds and pitching their tents where water and pasture invited. Among seminomads the fundamental social unit was the family, three or four generations descended from a surviving male parent. The bonds of blood reached still further back: clans were groups of families who claimed common descent from a more remote ancestor, and tribes were related through a still more remote ancestor. Individuals owned no land. The flocks and herds belonged to the extended family for whom the patriarch held the animals in trust. Personal property was limited to items like weapons and ornaments. There were, in effect, no rich and no poor in the family or clan. Status in the clan was determined not by one's possessions but by one's position in the family. Even slaves were economically members of the clan — but without the status of blood kinship.

While there were no rich or poor within the clan, the clan itself could be rich or poor. The size of the family and of its flocks and herds were measures of its wealth. But even wealthy families lived a difficult and precarious existence, constantly contending against the threats of nature and marauders. Poor clans might be reduced to the status of ʿApiru, that class of landless people who survived by hiring themselves out in military service or by selling themselves as slaves; their life had neither place nor dignity. While the tribes of Israel cannot be simply identified with ʿApiru (*see* HABIRU), some of them surely had the status of ʿApiru in Egypt, doing slave labor at Pithom and Raamses (Ex. 1:11).

The Israelites never forgot their seminomadic origins. The Exodus account recalls that God saw the Israelites' poverty in Egypt — their "affliction" (Ex. 3:7), their "oppression" (v. 9), their "bondage" (6:6) — and He rescued them and kept His promise to give them a land for their own possession. God's redemption of the Israelites from poverty (from the status of ʿApiru) remained a paradigm for their own treatment of the poor (cf., e.g., Dt. 15:12-15). The memory of a society within which there were no rich or poor provided a standard for later economies and an image of renewal, a nomadic ideal. Indeed, the nomadic way of life persisted into the late monarchy in the life of countercultural clans like the Rechabites, who pledged not to own vineyards, till the soil, or build houses (Jer. 35).

*B. In the Agricultural Economy.* The settlement in Canaan caused profound changes in the Israelite economy. Settled agricultural life required the cultivation of field crops, orchards, and vineyards. The arts of cultivation, at least as the Canaanites practiced them, required proper reverence for the *beʿālîm*, the fertility-gods whose favor assured the crops. Heb. *baʿal* meant "owner," and associated with reverence for the *beʿālîm* was a system of ownership and an attitude toward possessions that differed radically from the nomadic economy. In the new economy the land was privately owned. Its produce yielded prosperity for some, while the less fortunate began to merge with the conquered and dispossessed classes, creating distinctions between rich and poor within Israelite society. Moreover, an emphasis on localities gradually supplemented or challenged the ties of kinship, and the villages became a new focus for loyalty in addition to the clan.

The religious struggle between Yahweh and the *beʿālîm* involved an understanding of agriculture and the economy and also a response to the emergence of poverty within society. Israel understood the land as God's gift and saw the economic growth and security it provided as God's blessing. Nevertheless, faithfulness to God and to His covenant required not only rejecting the *beʿālîm* but also protecting the poor in the land from oppression and exploitation. The Covenant Code (Ex. 20:22–23:33) already contains a number of provisions to prevent or at least alleviate poverty. The fundamental conviction that the land was God's (e.g., Lev. 25:23) was based on the fundamental principle that it was inalienable from the families to whom God had apportioned it. Among the procedures that reflected and protected that principle (and the importance of kinship) were JUBILEE and the option of redemption by a kinsman (*see* REDEEMER). In these ways Israel established an agricultural way of life that presumed a fundamental equality to be God's design and that regulated and limited the economic process in the interest of protecting the poor.

*C. During the Monarchy.* Another social and economic revolution occurred with the transition to monarchy. David's reign marked the beginning of an urban and commercial way of life that opened a huge gap between the rich and the poor. With the conquest and assimilation of the remaining Canaanite cities and the establishment of a capital city in Jerusalem, the culture and the economy became increasingly urban. The royal court and the standing army were innovations that needed to be supported by taxation and conscription (see 1 S. 8:11-17). International commerce and industrial developments brought about a remarkable prosperity, a "golden age," but it was not shared equally. The king, his court favorites, the urban merchants, and businessmen all profited, but the small peasant farmer did not. The poor became poorer. They suffered under a heavy burden of taxation, conscription, inflation, and powerlessness. So, while some lived in great luxury, many more fell into poverty, first mortgaging their lands and then losing them and becoming landless tenants or slaves.

In principle the king was subject to the laws of the covenant that he publicly vowed to uphold. In practice, however, royal despotism often displaced the covenant as the basis of social obligation. Ideally, then, the king was the defender of the poor (e.g., Ps. 72), but in reality he was often among their oppressors. The story of Naboth and his vineyard (1 K. 21) is paradigmatic of the conflict between royal despotism and covenant law. Elijah's condemnation of Ahab for rejecting the covenant law's protections for the poor is a paradigm of the prophetic social criticism. With vivid realism the prophets described the violation of the covenant, the oppression and injustice of the social order. They condemned the kings and other authorities who failed to protect the poor (Jer. 22:13-17; Hos. 5:1f., 10); they protested against the professional prophets, priests, and sages who said what their clients wanted to hear instead of what the justice of God required (Jer. 8:8-10; Hos. 4:4-6; Am. 7:10-17; Mic. 3:5-7); they ridiculed the vain women who lived in luxury careless of the cries of the poor (Isa. 3:16-26; Am. 4:1-3); they sentenced dishonest and avaricious merchants (Am. 8:4-6), selfish and heartless creditors (5:11), covetous landowners (Isa. 5:8; Mic. 2:1-4), and venal judges (Isa. 1:23; 3:13-15; Am. 5:7, 10, 12) to the judgment of God. They announced that God was on the side of the poor, that He was their ally, that they were His people (Isa. 3:15), and that His covenant law stood as an alternative to and judgment upon a social order that simultaneously generated brutalizing poverty and unrestrained luxury. The prophetic social criticism climaxed in the identification of the poor with the righteous remnant that will survive God's judgment (see Zeph. 3:12), in making "the humble" and "the poor" equivalent (*see* HUMBLE).

The social criticism of the prophets was not joined to a practical political program, but it was not without political effect. The reforms of Hezekiah and Josiah were, in part at least, responses to the prophets' message. The prophetic social criticism also left its mark on Israelite cultic life; in the Psalms the righteous frequently refer to themselves as the "poor" (e.g., Ps. 40:17 [MT 18]; 70:5 [MT 6]; 86:1; 109:22) whom God has sworn to protect. Even the wisdom tradition was affected. It is true that the sages appealed to experience rather than the covenant law and frequently traced poverty to the indolence and folly of the poor rather than to injustice and the oppression of the rich (e.g., Prov. 6:11; 10:4; 13:18; 20:13; etc.); nevertheless, their advice often reflected the concerns of covenant law (e.g., Prov. 22:28; 23:10 [cf. Dt. 19:14]; Prov. 11:1 [cf. Dt. 25:13-16]). They recognized God's advocacy of the cause of the poor (Prov. 22:22f.) and saw benevolence to the poor as a critical test of the piety of the rich (Job. 29:12, 16; Ps. 112:9). The sage desired "neither poverty nor riches" but what is necessary and sufficient (Prov. 30:8).

*D. From the Exile to Roman Colonialism.* When Jerusalem fell to the Babylonians, its political, economic, and intellectual leaders were exiled to Babylon. There they had, of course, the social status of conquered aliens, but they seem not to have suffered severe economic hardship. In Judah the remaining population lived in desolating poverty (Lam. 5:1-18). The era of resettlement under Persian dominion evidently saw renewed tensions between the wealthy landowners and the peasant farmers and landless tenants. A succession of poor harvests made the situation still more desperate for the poor, who mortgaged their fields to pay the taxes due Persia or even to buy grain for themselves. Many lost their land; others fell into slavery for their indebtedness. Nehemiah instituted a social reform according to the familiar pattern of the covenant, prohibiting interest on loans to the poor, liberating the slaves, and returning their land to them (Neh. 5:1-13).

The conquests of Alexander looted the treasures of the Persian empire and established colonial policies throughout the captive territories. Greek was enforced as the language of commerce, and Hellenistic merchants and businessmen capitalized on their advantage. The constant warfare that followed Alexander's death ruined the prosperity of Greek and Asian cities and taxed the resources of the countryside. Slave trade increased, and competition with slave labor drove down the wages of the free.

The brief period of Jewish independence began with great promise. The rule of Simon was celebrated for its compassion for the poor and needy, a veritable fulfillment of God's promise (1 Macc. 14:8-15; cf. Mic. 4:4). Under subsequent Hasmonean rulers, however, Israel saw a return of the old conflicts between covenant law and royal despotism with its concentration of wealth in a Jerusalem aristocracy.

Roman rule only deepened the divide between the rich and the poor. Jerusalem was a city of both great extravagance and great poverty. Herod's court, the priestly aristocracy, and wealthy merchants and landowners lavishly displayed their wealth, e.g., by giving alms to the many mendicants who lived in Jerusalem. In the countryside absentee landlords held great estates that were managed by administrators. The peasant farmers were once again reduced to the status of slaves and day laborers. Pliny (*Nat. hist.* xviii.35) said that the great estates were the ruin of Italy (*latifundia perdidere Italiam*); they did their damage in the provinces of the empire as well.

*E. Responses to Poverty in First-century Palestine.* The rabbis responded to poverty by repeating and interpreting the teachings of the Torah. They encouraged private generosity and kindness toward the poor, almsgiving and the "works of love." They denounced noncompliance with the rights of the poor during harvest (Mish. *Aboth* v. 9) and even broadened the regulations that protected the poor (*Baraitha Baba Kamma* 80b-81a). Hillel's *prozbul* (Mish. *Shebiith* x.4) provided a legal mechanism for evading the remission of debts in the Sabbatical Year, but some of the other rabbis denounced this along with other evasions. The rabbis began a system of public assistance for the poor. The tithe for the poor (Dt. 14:28f.; 26:12) provided the basis in Halakah for a welfare system administered by special officers of the synagogue. A "poor basket," to which weekly gifts were made, supported a community chest from which the needs of the poor were met (Mish. *Peah* vii.2-9; viii.7). The rabbinic response did much, it seems, to alleviate the hardships of poverty. Since the rabbis were not paid for their instruction, they themselves depended on the tithe and on the generosity of their students and others; sometimes they supported themselves by engagement in a trade or as day laborers. Some of the rabbis became prosperous — especially after the defeats of rebellions in A.D. 73 and 135, when religious and social leadership and status fell to them.

The rebellions themselves were, in part at least, responses to the social tensions in Palestine. In the 1st cent. the Zealot movement reflected and capitalized on the resentment of the poor toward Rome and the priestly and lay nobility. When they took Jerusalem in A.D. 66, the Zealots destroyed the city archives with their records of land transactions and indebtedness. In 68 the rebels declared the emancipation of Jewish slaves. The Zealot position grew out of the ancient convenantal claim that the land belonged to God and was inalienable from the families to whom God has entrusted it. The movement found support among the Galilean and Judean peasants; it was opposed by the priestly aristocracy and the wealthy. The poverty of the times also gave rise to a less political (and less religious) violence: robbers presented a serious problem in the 1st cent.

The community at Qumrân had its own response to the social tensions of the times. Their zeal for the law did not lead them into rebellion but into withdrawal. On the shores of the Dead Sea they established a congregation of God's elect, a "congregation of the poor" (4QpPs37 1:5, 10), whose common life stood as judgment on the priestly aristocracy in Jerusalem for amassing wealth at the expense of the poor (1QpHab 12:3, 6, 10); it also stood as a promise of God's eschatological renewal of social life by overcoming the division between rich and poor through community of goods (1QS 1:11; 6:19, 22, 25; 4QpPs37 1:10).

The social tensions of the Hellenistic and Roman periods nurtured an apocalyptic expectation of the abolition of poverty and an expectation of judgment against the rich oppressors (e.g., T. Jud. 25:4; Jub. 23:18-23). These expectations sustained sometimes a countercultural common life (e.g., the community at Qumrân), sometimes an uncalculating revolutionary zeal (e.g., the Zealots), but most often deeds of love and almsgiving until the end (e.g., some of the rabbis). (Later rabbis, less commonly poor and more restrained in their eschatology, did not share such expectations; cf. T. B. *Berakoth* 34b.)

*F. Jesus and Poverty. 1. Jesus' Social Standing.* Jesus was not from the poorest of the poor in Galilee. His father was a craftsman, not a day laborer or a slave. But the family was poor. The sacrifice made for purification was "a pair of turtledoves or two young pigeons," the offering prescribed for those too poor to offer a lamb (Lk. 2:24; cf. Lev. 12:2–8). Jesus probably apprenticed in carpentry; but when He entered upon His public ministry, like the rabbis He depended upon the generosity of others (Mt. 8:20 par. Lk. 9:58). The accounts of Jesus' dependency upon the hospitality of the "righteous" (e.g., Lk. 7:36; 11:37) and upon the gifts of notable women (8:1-3) represent a reliable memory of His career. The same dependency was true of the disciples (Mk. 6:7-13 par.). There was nothing ascetic about Jesus' poverty as the contrast with John the Baptist (Mt. 11:18-19 par.) makes clear. Jesus did not glorify poverty; rather, He lifted up the poor.

*2. Jesus and the Poor.* Jesus announced the kingdom of God in the midst of considerable social tension. The announcement of the coming reign of God brought news of a great reversal: the humble would be exalted and the poor would be blessed. The great reversal was "good news to the poor" (Lk. 4:18; cf. 7:22 par. Mt. 11:5). Already that coming reign of God made its power felt in Jesus, and to receive Him, to welcome God's kingdom, meant to share what one had with the poor. Jesus' vision of a great reversal surely contributed to His initial popularity among the common people and to His eventual rejection by the wealthy priestly aristocracy.

Jesus' word, "You always have the poor with you" (Mk. 14:7 par. Mt. 26:11; Jn. 12:8), does not compromise His announcement of good news for the poor. His saying quotes Dt. 15:11, where it is clear that "the poor will never cease out of the land" only because of the community's refusal to keep the covenantal stipulations for alleviating poverty (Dt. 15:1-11; cf. Lk. 16:29-31). Jesus rebukes the woman's accusers, to be sure, but not for being concerned about the poor. He rebukes them for presumptuously singling out this one woman, for self-righteously judging her when the very presence of the poor judges the whole community. The woman's carefree disposition toward her possessions was her way of welcoming the coming reign of God; in Jesus' absence the same freedom from the tyranny of possessions will be turned toward generosity to the poor.

*See also* ETHICS: THE ETHIC OF JESUS III. C; POOR IV.

*G. The Early Church and Poverty. 1. Social Standing of the Early Christians.* Early in this century the socialist historian K. Kautsky (*Foundations of Christianity* [Eng. tr. 1953]) claimed that early Christianity was essentially a proletarian movement. The first converts, drawn from the ranks of the poor, were moved by economic and social distress. A. Deissmann's response (Deiss. *LAE*) acknowledged that the early Christians were poor but provided a romantic, rather than proletarian, portrait of their poverty. Only recently has a "new consensus" (see Malherbe) emerged that the early Christians came from a broad spectrum of social levels and that the early Church was more nearly a cross section of society than either Kautsky or Deissmann had thought. Within the context of Roman society — which was marked by what R. MacMullen (p. 99) called "verticality," an oppressive and pervasive sense of "high" and "low" social standing based primarily on wealth — the social integration found in the early Church was remarkable; sometimes it was a cause of conflict within congregations (see Theissen).

The fellowship (Gk. *koinōnía*) of the early Church joined rich and poor together in table fellowship and in the sharing of possessions. Paul rebukes the Corinthians for allowing social distinctions to disrupt and distort their table fellowship, i.e., their participation (Gk. *koinōnía*) in the body and blood of Christ (1 Cor. 10:16; 11:17-34). In the Jerusalem church possessions were sold to meet the needs of the poor (Acts 2:44f.; 4:34-37). In contrast to the community of goods practiced at Qumrân, the Jerusalem church's sharing was not defined by statutes and protected by sanctions fixed by community regulations; rather, it was voluntary and spontaneous. The *koinōnía* was the decisive thing, not organization.

It was a fellowship that transcended and broke down the hierarchical, "vertical" patterns of Roman society and constituted a new Israel, a new covenanted community in which "there was not a needy person among them" (Acts 4:34; cf. Dt. 15:4, 11). The voluntary and spontaneous sharing moved toward institutionalized forms of concern for the poor as the Church grew and needs persisted. E.g., when the needs of the widows among the Hellenists were not being met, the Church appointed seven men to the duty of caring for them (Acts 6:1-6; 1 Tim. 5:3-16 makes an effort to limit the number of widows supported by the Church).

*2. Paul and Poverty.* Paul worked with his hands, as he more than once reminded his churches (in self-defense [1 Cor. 9] and in an object lesson [2 Thess. 3:7-12]). He had known "want" (Gk. *hystérēsis,* Phil. 4:11) and he gratefully accepted the generous gifts of congregations (4:15-18). His general attitude to both plenty and poverty was "contentment" (vv. 11f., Gk. *autárkeia;* cf. 1 Tim. 6:6-9).

Paul warns his congregations against "covetousness" (Gk. *pleonexía,* e.g., Eph. 5:3; Col. 3:5) but not against wealth itself. His epistles contain no mention of an apocalyptic reversal of social status. His teachings seem much closer to the middle-class respectability of Stoic morality than to the teachings of Jesus. Paul's principle seems to be the Gk. *autárkeia* (self-sufficiency, autonomy, contentment) so highly valued by Cynics and Stoics. He exhorts the Thessalonians to work diligently in order to provide for themselves and to "be dependent on nobody" (1 Thess. 4:11f.). All individuals, in order to maintain their independence, must have enough to care for their own needs and to be "content" with what they have. Paul's contentment stands, however, in a different moral context from the contentment of the Stoics. In Stoic philosophy one achieved contentment by willing whatever happened; in that way one participated in the great reason (Gk. *lógos*) at work in the world. Paul's contentment, however, was rooted in God's eschatological act in Jesus Christ. The Christian participates in the cross and Resurrection — not in cosmic reason — and thereby in the eschatological cause of God. So Paul discerns the relative insignificance of plenty and of poverty (cf. Phil. 4:5f., where "have no anxiety about anything" follows directly upon "the Lord is at hand"), but he rejects the enthusiastic disowning of financial responsibilities practiced by idlers at Thessalonica (1 Thess. 4:11f.; 5:14; 2 Thess. 3:6-12).

God's cause includes the fellowship of rich and poor. Paul never says that "in Christ there is neither rich nor poor," nor does he call for a community of goods. But he does evidently expect the wealthy Christians in freedom and in fellowship to contribute to the needs of the poor within the congregations, to practice hospitality (Rom. 12:13; cf. 16:23), to use their gifts as members of one body in Christ (Rom. 12:4-8). As mentioned above, Paul rebukes the wealthy in the Corinthian community for forming groups along social class lines at the common meal; by this practice they "despise the church of God and humiliate those who have nothing" (1 Cor. 11:22).

Paul's commitment to a fellowship that transcended and broke down the verticality of Roman society as well as the division between Jew and Gentile can perhaps be seen most clearly in his appeals for the collection. This offering for "the poor" in Jerusalem was a part of Paul's mission among the Gentiles from the time of the Jerusalem Council (Gal. 2:10). In exhorting the Corinthians to give generously to the collection, Paul reminds them of the "the grace of our Lord Jesus Christ, that though he was rich, yet for your sake he became poor, so that by his poverty you might become rich" (2 Cor. 8:9). Paul does not infer from this pattern that the Corinthians are to give everything away so that "others should be eased and you burdened" (v. 13); rather, he moves toward "equality" (Gk. *isótēs*), to a community of voluntary fellowship where the needs of those in poverty (Gk. *hystérēsis*) are met out of the abundance of others (v. 14). He corroborates his argument by appealing to God's provision of manna for the Israelites (2 Cor. 8:15; cf. Ex. 16:18), i.e., to an economic order in which hoarding was futile, daily needs were met, and God had to be trusted to provide. As manna was a familiar eschatological symbol, such a "manna economy" would be a mark of the churches' participation in a new age that would transcend the verticality of Roman society and the division between Jews and Gentiles.

*3. Poverty and Persecution.* Under Domitian (A.D. 81-96) the imperial cult was rigorously enforced, and the Christian movement endured the hardships of petty persecution — including evidently, economic harassment (cf. Rev. 13:17). The experience of alienation and oppression gave rise — as it had before — to apocalyptic literature, specifically to the book of Revelation. In Revelation's protest against oppressors and consolation for the oppressed, judgment falls on "the kings of the earth and the great men and the generals and the rich and the strong" (6:15).

Not every church in Asia Minor was driven into poverty in this period; Revelation recognizes Smyrna's poverty (2:9) but warns Laodicea against the security provided by wealth (3:17f.) — wealth that may have been gained at the cost of compromising with the imperial cult. The "patient endurance" (Gk. *hypomonḗ*; 1:9; 2:2f. 19: 3:10; 13:10; 14:12) to which the churches are called is not a freedom to accommodate the claims of Domitian and so to live comfortably (as the false teachers probably held); it is rather a freedom from conventional standards of prosperity and power, a freedom to accept poverty and powerlessness in faithful loyalty to Jesus Christ and in expectation of His final triumph and blessing.

Revelation describes several visions that depict Roman oppression and the judgment on Rome: the vision of the third horseman with the images of an inflation that robs the poor of sustenance (6:5f.); the vision of the beast's use of economic power to exploit and oppress (13:16f.), and, at the climactic vision of Babylon's (i.e., Rome's) fall (17:1–18:24). Babylon's splendor, at which even the seer "marveled" (17:6), provided no protection. The fall of Babylon is lamented by those who are powerful and wealthy according to her standards and with her aid ("the kings of the earth" [18:9f.], "the merchants" [vv. 11-17a, esp. the slave-traders] and "the shipmasters" [18:17b-19]); but God's people celebrate it as the apocalyptic announcement of God's reign and of the great reversal that reign brings.

*H. Conclusion.* The Scriptures never merely describe poverty. The terminology, the images, and the messages evoke sympathy for the poor and summon protest against oppression. The treatment of poverty is not romantic or ascetic, neither is it impartial or "objective." The biblical writers did not simply expound atemporal ideas and doctrines; rather, they responded to historical and communal developments in protest, in advocacy, in hope for God's unchallenged rule and promised blessing.

***III. Liberation Theology.***–If Scripture is not impartial and "objective" about poverty, then can it be genuinely heard and obeyed if the contemporary churches and their theologians adopt — for the sake of either "spiritual transcendence" or "scholarly objectivity" — an attitude of neutrality on the issues of oppression and poverty? That is the question being raised anew by theologies of liberation.

Liberation theologies claim that the churches and their theologians have always been working either for or against the oppressed, wittingly or unwittingly. If that is so, then any attempts to achieve spiritual neutrality and scholarly objectivity concerning exploitative sociological structures are self-deceptive. Liberation theologies candidly adopt as their methodological starting point a "partial" perspective, a bias: they begin with the stance of advocating the cause of the poor and oppressed, a posture of protest against the arbitrary power of dominant groups. They accept alliances with admittedly partial ideologies (e.g., the socioeconomic theories of Karl Marx) as a historical and social necessity for serving the cause of the poor.

Liberation theologies come in a great variety. Among the causes championed are those of the poor, of Blacks in South Africa and North America, and of women. These theologies have all reminded the churches of their past failures, namely, their collusion with oppressive power and structures (even if unwittingly in the name of spiritual transcendence or scholarly objectivity); they have all called upon the churches to disown the gnostic, "spiritualized" version of the real freedom intended by the God who liberated the Israelites from bondage in Egypt and raised Jesus from death; and they have all challenged the churches to read and use Scripture in the light of Scripture's own advocacy of the poor and oppressed. These contributions of liberation theology have been important.

Theologies of liberation have also had their critics, however. The fundamental criticism concerns the issue of theological control. Some reviewers charge that liberation theologies too uncritically give up control over the theological enterprise and the praxis of the Church to the ideological perspective with which the theology is allied. These critics have observed that it is one thing to call attention to the ideological presuppositions of any interpretation of Scripture; it is quite another to yield control unreservedly to any set of ideological presuppositions. To give up biblical and theological control over the use of any social perspective is to give up the possibility of critical reconstruction and transformation of the culture. And yielding biblical and theological control over the praxis of the churches means that ideological considerations, rather than integrity with the identity of the people of God, will govern the means that the churches use to achieve their scripturally sanctioned goals.

The question of control is important, but if it is raised with respect to liberation theologies, then it must also be raised with respect to the theologies of the rich and powerful. To criticize liberation theologies for their lack of self-criticism regarding ideological alignments is somewhat like pointing out the sliver in their eye while ignoring the beam in the eye of conventional first-world theologies. The fundamental question put by liberation theology to the churches remains to be answered: if Scripture itself is not impartial about poverty and does not simply trade in atemporal doctrines but in protest, in advocacy, and in hope for God's unchallenged rule and blessing, then can the people who learn their identity and calling from Scripture be faithful in any way other than in advocacy, protest, and hope for the poor?

***Bibliography.***–R. Batey, *Jesus and the Poor* (1972); J. H. Cone, *Liberation: A Black Theology of Liberation* (1970); N. A. Dahl, "Paul and Possessions," *Studies in Paul* (1977), pp. 22-36; N. K. Gottwald, *Tribes of Yahweh* (1979); F. C. Grant, "Economic Background of the NT," in W. D. Davies and D. Daube, eds.,

*Background of the NT and Its Eschatology* (*Festschrift* C. H. Dodd, repr. 1964), pp. 96-114; G. Gutiérrez, *Theology of Liberation* (Eng. tr. 1973), pp. 287-306; M. Hengel, *Property and Riches in the Early Church* (Eng. tr. 1974); J. Jeremias, *Jerusalem in the Time of Jesus* (Eng. tr. 1969); J. A. Kirk, *Liberation Theology* (1980); R. MacMullen, *Roman Social Relations* (1974); A. Malherbe, *Social Aspects of Early Christianity* (2nd ed. 1983); W. Meeks, *First Urban Christians* (1983); R. R. Reuther, *New Woman/New Earth: Sexist Ideologies and Human Liberation* (1975); E. Schüssler Fiorenza, *Invitation to the Book of Revelation* (1981); R. B. Y. Scott, *Relevance of the Prophets* (rev. ed. 1968); J. L. Segundo, *Liberation of Theology* (1976); *TDNT,* VI, *s.v.* πτωχός κτλ. (F. Hauck, E. Bammel); VIII, *s.v.* ὕστερος κτλ. (U. Wilckens); G. Theissen, *Studien zur Soziologie des Urchristentums* (1979).

A. D. VERHEY

**POWDERS** [Heb. *'aḇqaṯ*–'fragrant powder(s)' (of the merchant)]; NEB POWDERED SPICES. The word, a fem. sing. noun used collectively, occurs only at Cant. 3:6, where Solomon's litter is pictured coming out of the desert carrying his intended bride (see the parallel to v. 6a at 8:5 and Pope, pp. 423-431). She is perfumed with myrrh, frankincense, and the rest of the merchant's complement of aromatic powders, and is ceremoniously escorted by a band of sixty warriors.

The masc. form of the noun (*'āḇāq*) occurs six times and is best translated as "fine dust." It has the texture of soot (Ex. 9:9; cf. Ezk. 26:10), is finer than the common dust of the ground (*'āp̄ār*) (Dt. 28:24; cf. Nah. 1:3), and scatters like chaff in the wind (Isa. 29:5; cf. 5:24). In each case, it is flying or swirling dust, and the use of *'aḇqaṯ* is similar: the bride is enveloped in the fragrance of these powders.

***Bibliography***.–R. J. Forbes, *Studies in Ancient Technology* III (1965), 1-26; M. Pope, *Song of Songs* (*AB*, 1977).

D. M. HOWARD, JR.

**POWER; MIGHT.** These words are used by the RSV virtually interchangeably to translate a broad range of Hebrew and Greek terms. This article also discusses the adjectives "powerful" (used by the RSV only ten times) and "mighty," which is used more than four hundred times to describe deeds, persons, or other entities that demonstrate great strength.

- I. In the OT
  - A. Hebrew Terms
  - B. Bearers of Power
    1. Nonpersonal Entities
    2. Human Beings
    3. God
    4. Other Spiritual Beings
  - C. Attitude Toward Power
    1. Divine Power
    2. Human Power
- II. In the NT
  - A. Greek Terms
  - B. Bearers of Power
    1. God
    2. Other Spiritual Beings and Forces
    3. Jesus Christ
    4. Human Beings
  - C. Power and Weakness

***I. In the OT.***–*A. Hebrew Terms.* Many Hebrew terms are rendered "power," "might," and their adjectives. The most common are *kō(a)ḥ* (e.g., Ex. 9:16), *'ōz* (e.g., Lev. 26:19), *ḥayil* (e.g., Ps. 59:11 [MT 12]; see *TDOT,* IV, 349-355), *ḥāzāq* (e.g., Ex. 3:19; see *TDOT,* IV, 305), *geḇûrâ* (e.g., 1 Ch. 29:11), and cognates of these terms. *Geḇûrâ* in plural form refers in ten of eleven instances to the "mighty deeds" ("mighty acts," etc.) of God (e.g., Dt. 3:24; see *TDOT,* II, 372f.). *Gibbôr* ("hero") is often rendered "mighty one" or "mighty man" (e.g., Gen. 6:4). The substantive *'āḇîr,* "Mighty One" of Jacob/Israel, occurs six times and is applied only to God (e.g., Gen. 49:24). Both *yāḏ,* "hand" (e.g., Dt. 32:36), and *zerô(a)',* "arm" (e.g., Ps. 79:11; see *TDOT,* IV, 133-140), may represent the power of human beings or of God.

*B. Bearers of Power. 1. Nonpersonal Entities.* For the most part the OT has a very concrete conception of power. Occasionally power is accorded to abstract entities such as transgression (Job 8:4; Heb. *yāḏ*) and Sheol (e.g., Ps. 49:15 [MT 16]; Hos. 13:14), but usually it is accorded to concrete beings or objects that have the capacity to perform specific deeds. This may include instruments of power (e.g., "the power [*yāḏ*] of the sword," Job 5:20; Jer. 18:21) and even by analogy the sun who "rises in his might" (*geḇûrâ,* Jgs. 5:31). Might or power is ascribed to animals such as the horse (*ḥayil,* Ps. 33:17) and the lion (*yāḏ,* Dnl. 6:27 [MT 28]) and to natural forces such as the waters of the sea (e.g., *'addîr,* Ex. 15:10; Ps. 93:4 [twice]).

*2. Human Beings.* Human beings are said to possess might or power in a variety of senses. First, "might" can simply mean human vitality concentrated on a particular task. Thus Israel was commanded to love the Lord their God with all their heart, soul, and might (*me'ōḏ,* Dt. 6:5), and David "danced before the Lord with all his might" (*'ōz,* 2 S. 6:14). Second, "power" can represent the ability to carry out an action toward someone else, whether for good (*'ēl,* Prov. 3:27) or ill (*'ēl,* Gen. 31:29). Third, both terms are often used in a military sense to designate collective forces (*kō[a]ḥ,* Josh. 17:17) and individual warriors. Prominent fighters or heroes (*gibbôrîm*) are often called "mighty men" (e.g., 2 S. 10:7), "the mighty" (e.g., 2 S. 1:19-27), etc., in the RSV and AV. The term was especially applied to "the mighty men of David" (*see* MIGHTY MEN). Fourth, since political and military power are closely associated, "power" sometimes includes the idea of political force and authority. Thus it is the king who exercises "royal power" (*mamlāḵâ,* 2 K. 14:5; AV, lit., "kingdom"). The books of Kings employ a formula that summarizes a king's reign in terms of his "acts," his "might" (*geḇûrâ*), and "all that he did" (or some of his deeds; e.g., 2 K. 10:34; 13:8, 12). Feats of warfare are sometimes highlighted (e.g., 1 K. 22:45), but so is the building of cities (15:23).

*3. God.* In the OT power and might are ascribed above all to God (e.g., *'ōz,* Ps. 62:11 [MT 12]). God's power is shown both in the fact that He created the world (e.g., *kō[a]ḥ,* Jer. 10:12) and remains more powerful than all the forces within it (e.g., *'addîr,* Ps. 93:4) and also in His mighty acts of salvation (e.g., *geḇûrōṯ,* Ps. 150:2). Some of the names of God point to His power (*see* GOD, NAMES OF). Above all, it is by showing His power that God reveals Himself as Yahweh (*geḇûrâ,* Jer. 16:21). In the Exodus Yahweh shows His "power" (*kō[a]ḥ*) not only over Pharaoh (Ex. 9:16) and the forces of nature, but over all the gods of Egypt (cf. 12:12). Because of such acts of redemption, God can be called "the Mighty One [*'āḇîr*] of Jacob (or Israel)" (e.g., Gen. 49:24; Ps. 132:2, 5; Isa. 1:24; 49:26).

Through His power as Creator, Redeemer, and Judge, God is seen to exercise His rule, not only over Israel, but over all nations (*'ōz,* Ps. 77:14 [MT 15]) and over heaven as well (*kō[a]ḥ, geḇûrâ,* 2 Ch. 20:6). it is He who fights for Israel as a warrior (Ps. 24:8; Isa. 42:13), performs marvelous acts of salvation (Ps. 74:13; 78:4), and in judgment causes Israel to be defeated by its enemies (2 Ch. 36:15f.); who imparts riches, honor, and strength (1 Ch. 29:12); who empowers judges (Jgs. 2:16), kings (1 S. 2:10; Ps. 20:6 [MT 7]; Dnl. 2:37), and prophets (Mic. 3:8), at times giving them the power to do miracles (Ex. 4:21;

cf. Dt. 34:10-12). One of the titles given to the messianic king prophesied by Isaiah is "Mighty God" (*'ēl gibbôr,* Isa. 9:6 [MT 5]). *See also* OMNIPOTENCE.

*4. Other Spiritual Beings.* Some OT passages seem to imply the existence of other gods, but Yahweh is clearly seen as above them all (e.g., Ps. 95:3). Other passages, however, especially in the Prophets, show that idols are nothing precisely because they are powerless while Yahweh is all-powerful (cf. Dt. 32:15-18, 36-39; Isa. 40:18-20, 25f.; 41:21-24; etc.; *see* IDOLATRY II.D). The OT refers also to other spiritual beings such as angels (called Heb. *gibbōrê ḵō[a]ḥ* [lit. "warriors of strength"; RSV "mighty ones"] in Ps. 103:20) and demons. While they sometimes engage in very significant actions, such beings are not worshiped or greatly feared, because they have no independent power but rather act only under the authority of God. This applies even to SATAN, who is seldom mentioned in the OT (cf. *yāḏ,* Job 1:12; 2:6).

*C. Attitude Toward Power. 1. Divine Power.* While the power of God is cause for humans to FEAR Him, ultimately only the wicked need fear in the negative sense. God's might is not simply raw power but is "saving power" (*yᵉšûʿâ,* Ps. 67:2 [MT 3]) directed by His love. Therefore God's power is the basis for both the celebration (Ps. 147:5) and the petition (80:2 [MT 3]) of His people. Times of anguish because of God's harsh judgments (e.g., Lamentations), seeming indifference (Ps. 74), or even apparent cruelty (Job 30:21), give way to the hope that God will employ His power for the redemption of His people. This faith inspires the great doxologies such as that of David: "Thine, O Lord, is the greatness, and the power [*gᵉḇûrâ*], and the victory, and the majesty . . ." (1 Ch. 29:11f.).

*2. Human Power.* Many OT passages express admiration for human power (e.g., *gibbôr,* Gen. 6:4) and particularly celebrate the "mighty power" (*kō[a]ḥ ḥayil*) of warriors (2 Ch. 26:13) and rulers (e.g., *gibbôr,* Ps. 89:19) who further God's purposes. Human power is also criticized, however, from three perspectives. First, it can obscure reliance on God's power. Individuals (e.g., 2 Ch. 26:15f.) and nations as a whole (e.g., Dt. 8:17f.; Ezk. 7:24; 30:6, 18) may become proud and attribute their success to their own power rather than to God, without whom they are powerless (e.g., Lev. 26:18-20; 2 Ch. 25:8). Second, human might may be used for evil purposes such as the oppression of the POOR (e.g., Job 35:9; Ps. 10:10; Eccl. 4:1; *see also* OPPRESS). In response the OT proclaims that God protects the poor and weak and punishes the mighty (e.g., 1 S. 2:4, 9f.; Job 5:15). Third, the OT — especially wisdom literature — warns that might must not overshadow other virtues, for "wisdom is better than might" (*gᵉḇûrâ,* Eccl. 9:16; cf. Ps. 147:10f.; Prov. 16:32; Jer. 9:23f. [MT 22f.]). Thus the OT always views human power in the light of God's sovereignty. Its message is summarized in Zec. 4:6: "Not by might (*ḥayil*), nor by power (*kō[a]ḥ*), but by my Spirit, says the Lord of hosts."

***II. In the NT.**–A. Greek Terms.* In the RSV NT "power" is predominantly the translation of Gk. *dýnamis,* which is derived from *dýnamai* ("be able") and is used frequently by the LXX to render Heb. *ḥayil* and other terms. *Dýnamis* most often denotes the ability to carry out an action, but it can also refer to an act expressing power (RSV "mighty work" or "miracle") or to a supernatural being with great power (often pl., RSV "powers"). The adjective *dynatós* can be rendered "mighty" (Lk. 1:49; 24:19; Acts 7:22), "powerful" (1 Cor. 1:26), "have power" (Rom. 11:23; 2 Cor. 10:4), or (as a substantive) "power" (Rom. 9:22). The noun *dynástēs* (pl.) is rendered "the mighty" in Lk. 1:52.

Another term frequently rendered "power" by the RSV NT is *exousía* (most often rendered "authority"). Whereas *dýnamis* denotes the ability to act (often based on inherent strength or capability), *exousía* stresses authorization to act, i.e., the right, freedom, and power to act by virtue of a position of authority. *Dýnamis* is often linked with anointing by the Holy Spirit (cf. Lk. 1:35; 4:14; 24:49; Acts 1:8; 10:38; Rom. 15:13, 19; 1 Cor. 2:4; etc.), while *exousía* presupposes a commissioning by God, who alone possesses absolute authority and power (cf. Lk. 12:5; Jn. 1:12; 10:18; 17:2; 19:10f.; Rev. 2:26; 6:8; etc.). *Exousía* can also be used to designate one who has authority, i.e., a ruler in either the human or spiritual realm. *See also* AUTHORITY I, II.

In the RSV "might" is seldom used to translate *dýnamis* and is never used for *exousía.* It usually represents *ischýs* (lit. "strength"; e.g., 2 Thess. 1:9) or *krátos* (lit. "power, rule"; e.g., Rev. 5:13). "Power" (*dýnamis*) and "might" (*ischýs* or *krátos*) are used in combination in several passages (Eph. 1:19; Col. 1:11; 2 Pet. 2:11; Rev. 5:12; 7:12). Apart from the use of "mighty work" to render *dýnamis,* "mighty" and "mightier" usually represent the adjective *ischýros* (Mt. 3:11 par.; He. 11:34; Rev. 10:1; 18:2, 8, 10; etc.).

*B. Bearers of Power. 1. God.* In regard to power the basic affirmation of both the OT and NT is the same: God is the source of all *dýnamis* and *exousía* (cf. Jesus' reference to God as "the Power" [*hē dýnamis,* Mt. 26:64 par.], a rabbinic metonym for the Deity), and He employs His supreme power for the salvation of His people (cf. Rev. 12:10; 19:1). While the NT affirms the power of God as shown in creation (e.g., Rom. 1:20; cf. Rev. 6:8; 16:9), this fact is overshadowed by God's new acts of redemption, which are centered in Jesus Christ; e.g., Mary refers to God as *ho dynatós* because of the manifestation of His saving power in the Incarnation (Lk. 1:49). In the NT it is impossible to separate the power of the Father, Son, and Holy Spirit, since God the Father empowers Jesus at every point (cf. *dýnatai,* Jn. 3:2; 5:19, 30), the Son by nature shares the power of God (He. 1:3), and the Holy Spirit is closely identified with the Father and the Son (e.g., Acts 10:38; Rom. 1:4). It is not surprising, then, that the power displayed in the followers of Christ may alternately be attributed to God, Christ, and the Holy Spirit (cf. Rom. 15:13, 19; 1 Cor. 5:4; 2 Cor. 12:9; 13:4; 2 Tim. 1:7f.). The following paragraphs will serve as a discussion of the power of God as displayed through and in relationship to spiritual beings, Jesus Christ, and human beings.

*2. Other Spiritual Beings and Forces.* The NT references to good and evil angelic beings reflect postexilic developments in Jewish angelology (*see* ANGEL; DEMON). As in the OT, angels play a significant role as instruments of God's will (cf. 2 Pet. 2:11, where they are described as "greater in might and power" than human beings; cf. also Rev. 10:1; 14:18; 18:21); but demonic beings who oppose God and His people have a larger role in the NT than in the OT. Although the terms for "power" are seldom applied specifically to Satan and the demons (e.g., *dýnamis,* Lk. 10:19; *exousía,* Acts 26:18; *krátos,* He. 2:14), these beings are clearly depicted as powerful (cf. Lk. 22:53; Rev. 13:2; 18:10). At Jesus' temptation Satan claims without contradiction to have received authority (*exousía*) over all the kingdoms of the world (Lk. 4:6 par. Mt. 4:9). Some of the Epistles — especially those of Paul — refer also to "powers" (along with "principalities," "angels," "authorities," etc.) that oppose the rule of God. These "powers" (*dynámeis,* Rom. 8:38; 1 Pet. 3:22; *exousíai,* Eph. 3:10; 6:12; Col. 2:15) include not only angelic beings (e.g., Satan and the demons) but also human authorities, human traditions, the "elemental spirits of the universe" (Gal. 4:3), etc. (*see* PRINCIPALITIES AND POWERS).

The spiritual struggle between the forces of God and those that oppose Him forms a central theme in the NT. The mission of Jesus — and that of His disciples (Lk.

10:17-20) and Paul (Acts 26:18) — is to liberate people from Satan's power. Through His earthly ministry, death, resurrection, and ascension, Christ has subjected these opposing spiritual powers to Himself (e.g., cf. Lk. 4:36; Col. 2:15; 1 Pet. 3:22); and although Christians continue to do battle against these forces (Eph. 6:12; cf. Rom. 8:38), they do so in the assurance that in the end Christ's victory will be complete, and all His enemies will be destroyed (cf. 1 Cor. 15:24f.). Because the NT, compared with the concreteness of the OT, tends to spiritualize and broaden the concept of power, it sometimes attributes "power" to abstract or symbolic entities on both sides of the conflict, e.g., death (Gk. *pýlai hą́dou,* lit. "gates of Hades," Mt. 16:18), sin (1 Cor. 15:56), the gospel (Rom. 1:16), the cross of Christ (1 Cor. 1:17, contextual translation), two symbolic witnesses (Rev. 11:3, 6), locusts (9:3, 10), horses (v. 19), the dragon (13:2), etc.

*3. Jesus Christ.* From the perspective of the OT and Judaism, the biggest surprise about the NT view of power is the type of power exhibited by the Messiah. Under the domination of Rome, the covenant people looked for an heir of David who would deliver them through a display of military and political might (cf. Lk. 1:33, 71). But Jesus marshalled no troops and attained no recognized political office (cf. Jn. 6:15; 18:36). This does not mean that Jesus was apolitical, but that He transformed politics (for one perspective, see J. H. Yoder, *Politics of Jesus* [1972]). The full, public manifestation of Jesus' power awaits His second coming.

Nonetheless, the NT sees power (both *exousía* and *dýnamis*) revealed in all aspects of Jesus' life and ministry. Jesus' conception and birth are described as a miracle of incarnation through the power of the Holy Spirit, uniquely qualifying Him to be called the "Son of God" (Lk. 1:35). His public ministry begins when He returns to Galilee "in the power [*dýnamis*] of the Spirit" (4:14). Jesus is recognized as "a prophet mighty [*dynatós*] in deed and word" (24:19; cf. Acts 7:22). He exhibits divine power and authority by performing "mighty works" (*dynámeis*) such as healing the sick (e.g., Lk. 5:17; cf. 6:19; 8:46 par. Mk. 5:30, where the power to heal is described as an almost tangible force residing in Jesus) and casting out unclean spirits (e.g., Lk. 4:36; *see also* EXORCISM V). These "mighty works" (e.g., Mt. 11:20-23) parallel the "mighty deeds" of God in the OT and thus confirm that Jesus is of God (Acts 2:22). *See* MIRACLE.

Above all, the power of God in Jesus is demonstrated in the Resurrection (cf. *exousía,* Jn. 10:18). After Jesus had voluntarily submitted Himself to the weakness and humiliation of the cross (2 Cor. 13:4; cf. Phil. 2:5-8), God showed His great "might" (*krátos*) by raising Him from the dead and placing Him above every other power (Eph. 1:19-23; cf. Rev. 5:12f.; see also II.B.2 above). Likewise, Jesus has received from His Father "*exousía* over all flesh, to give eternal life to all whom thou hast given him" (Jn. 17:2). At the end of the age Jesus Christ will return "with power and great glory" (Mt. 24:30 par.; cf. 26:64 par.). At that time of final judgment the enemies of God will be destroyed (cf. 1 Cor. 15:24f.; Rev. 18:8, 10), and Christ will enter upon His eternal reign with a great display of power (Rev. 11:15-17; 12:10). In terms reminiscent of the OT, the great doxology will resound: "Hallelujah! Salvation and glory and power belong to our God . . ." (19:1).

*See also* KINGDOM OF GOD V.

*4. Human Beings.* In contrast to the OT, the NT rarely speaks of military might (cf. "mighty in war," He. 11:34, referring to OT heroes). It is more concerned with the spiritual power needed by those who are joined to Jesus Christ and share in His mission. During Jesus' earthly ministry He authorized His disciples to heal and cast out demons (*dýnamis,* Lk. 9:1). Beginning at Pentecost, the Spirit empowered the disciples and other believers to testify boldly about Jesus (Acts 1:8; 4:33) and to perform miracles (cf. 3:12; 4:7; 6:8). In 2 Cor. 12:12 Paul points to his power to perform "mighty works" as one of the signs of his apostleship (see also Rom. 15:19; cf. Acts 2:43); but elsewhere he refers to this power as one of the gifts of the Spirit that are present in the Christian community and therefore not limited to the apostles (1 Cor. 12:10; cf. Gal. 3:5; He. 2:4). *See also* SPIRITUAL GIFTS.

Bold witnessing and miraculous deeds are not the only signs of God's power. According to Paul religion without power is false (2 Tim. 3:5), for the kingdom of God consists not in pretentious talk but in the power of the Spirit (1 Cor. 2:4f.; 4:19f.). Although apostles are equipped by God's power in special ways (e.g., 1 Cor. 5:4; 2 Cor. 6:7; Eph. 3:7; 1 Thess. 1:5), this power is at work in all believers (Eph. 1:19; 3:20), producing inward strengthening (3:16), knowledge and experience of the love of Christ (vv. 17-19), "endurance and patience with joy" (Col. 1:11), willingness to suffer for the gospel (2 Tim. 1:8), good works (2 Thess. 1:11), godliness (2 Pet. 1:3), and hope (Rom. 15:13). Eph. 6:10-17 admonishes believers to "be strong" (*endýnamai*) in the "strength" (*krátos*) of God's "might" (*ischýs*) by putting on "the whole armor of God." Here the military warfare sometimes celebrated in the OT is fully transformed into spiritual warfare; the weapons used by Christians have "divine power" (cf. 2 Cor. 10:4). Since Jesus' first coming inaugurated the eschatological era, His followers already experience "the powers [*dynámeis,* i.e., mighty works] of the age to come" (He. 6:5). When that age is fulfilled, by God's power they will be raised from the dead (1 Cor. 6:14; cf. 15:42f.) and experience total salvation (1 Pet. 1:5).

In the NT power is not confined to true followers of Christ. Simon Magnus performed magic (Acts 8:10f.). The eschatological "lawless one" will come with power (2 Thess. 2:8; cf. Rev. 13:2; 17:13). Even some who call Jesus "Lord" and perform "mighty works" in His name will come under judgment because they have not done God's will (Mt. 7:21–23). In the NT as well as the OT, human power is viewed positively only when it is exercised in obedience to God.

*C. Power and Weakness.* Although the Gospels never call Jesus "weak," He. 4:15 and 5:2 state that He is able to sympathize with human weaknesses because "he himself is beset with weakness." It is especially Paul, however, who explores the relationship between weakness and power in his letters to the Corinthian Christians, who were neither wise nor powerful by worldly standards (1 Cor. 1:26). In 1 Cor. 1:17–2:16 he contrasts the power of the gospel with the power of worldly wisdom. Compared with the miraculous signs demanded by the Jews and the wisdom sought by the Greeks, a crucified Christ seems to be weakness and folly (1:22f.); but "the weakness of God is stronger than men" (v. 25). Likewise, Paul is not ashamed to conduct his apostleship in the same kind of "weakness" as the crucified — but now risen — Christ; i.e., he comes not with the power of human wisdom but with the power of the Spirit of God (2:1-4; cf. 4:10; 2 Cor. 11:29f.; 13:3f.), for the transcendent power of God is "made perfect" in human weakness (2 Cor. 12:9f.). In these passages Paul proclaims the heart of the Christian gospel: that Jesus the Christ (1 Cor. 1:24), the cross of Christ (v. 17), and the word of the cross (v. 18) are the very power of God.

***Bibliography.***–C. K. Barrett, *Comm. on the First Epistle to the Corinthians* (*HNTC*, 1968), pp. 51-61; H. Berkhof, *Christ and the Powers* (Eng. tr., 2nd ed. 1977); *DNTT,* II, 601-615; III, 711-16;

W. Eichrodt, *Theology of the OT*, I (Eng. tr. 1961), 228-232; C. H. Powell, *Biblical Concept of Power* (1961); *TDNT*, I, *s.v.* βασιλεύς κτλ. (H. Kleinknecht, G. von Rad, K. G. Kuhn, K. L. Schmidt); II, *s.v.* δύναμαι κτλ. (W. Grundmann), ἔξεστιν κτλ.: ἐξουσία (W. Foerster); *TDOT*, II, *s.v.* "gābhar" (H. Kosmala); IV, *s.v.* "zᵉrôaʿ" (F. J. Helfmeyer), "chāzaq" (F. Hesse), "chayil" (H. Eising).

E. LAARMAN

**POWER OF THE KEYS.** *See* KEYS, POWER OF THE.

**PRAETORIUM** prē-tôr'ē-əm, prī-tôr'ē-əm; **PRAETORIAN GUARD** prē-tôr'ē-ən, prī-tôr'ē-ən [Gk. *praitṓrion*, Lat. *praetorium*]; AV also COMMON HALL (Mt. 27:27), HALL OF JUDGMENT (Jn. 18:28), JUDGMENT HALL (Jn. 18:28, 33; 19:9; Acts 23:35), PALACE (Phil. 1:13); NEB (GOVERNOR'S) HEADQUARTERS. The term praetorium (a Latin loanword in Greek) originally designated the commander's (praetor's) tent in camp and later was applied to the official residence of the Roman governors in various cities in the provinces. Such a residence could also have barracks for soldiers and guardrooms for the keeping of prisoners. In Acts 23:35 the term refers to Herod's residence in Caesarea, where Felix placed Paul under custody following his removal from Jerusalem by Claudius Lysias.

The references in the Gospels relate to the trial of Jesus before Pilate. Following the judgment by the Sanhedrin, Jesus was taken to the praetorium (Jn. 18:28a), but for fear of defilement the Jews did not enter the place (v. 28b). Hence, the ensuing conversations between Pilate and the Jews were outside the praetorium, while Pilate's discussions with Jesus were inside the building. Mt. 27:27 and Mk. 15:16 indicate that the soldiers' mocking of Jesus took place in the praetorium shortly before the crucifixion. Mark uses the term *aulḗ* ("hall, palace") to identify the praetorium. Jn. 19:13 states that outside the praetorium proper was an area known as The Pavement (Gk. *lithóstrōton*) and in Aramaic GABBATHA. In this area was located the JUDGMENT SEAT (Gk. *bēma*) where Pilate was seated when he conversed with the Jews.

Two locations have been proposed for the praetorium in Jerusalem. One is the Fortress or Tower Antonia, located just NW of the temple area on the prominent elevation along the southern slope of Mt. Bezetha. In honor of Mark Antony, Herod the Great erected the fortress upon an enlarged platform originally built by the Hasmoneans (Josephus *Ant.* xv.11.4 [403-409]). This structure was a feat of engineering excellence and architectural magnificence, with unusual and elaborate appointments. Functionally, it was an effective military stronghold, with impregnable walls and high towers allowing surveillance over the city, and especially over the temple, by the Roman legion permanently stationed there (Josephus *BJ* v.5.8. [238-247]).

The other suggested location for the praetorium of the Gospels is the palace of Herod near the Jaffa Gate at the westernmost part of the old city of Jerusalem. Among those making this identification are P. Benoit (*RB*, 59 [1952], 531-550; *HTR*, 64 [1971], 137-167; "Archaeological Reconstruction of the Antonia Fortress," in Y. Yadin, ed., *Jerusalem Revealed* [1976]), J. Blinzler (*Trial of Jesus* [1959], pp. 173-76), and P. Maier (*Pontius Pilate* [1968], pp. 215-240). Support for this view includes the use of Gk. *aulḗ* in Mk. 15:16, because Josephus uses this term frequently for the palace of Herod but never for the Antonia (cf. R. E. Brown, comm. on John, II [*AB*, 1970], 845). The palace, surrounded by three magnificent towers, was one of the most elaborate and beautiful structures in Jerusalem, according to Josephus (*BJ* v.4.3. [156-171]). The Roman procurators, e.g., Florus, frequently used this building for their residence and administrative office while in Jerusalem (*BJ* ii.15.5 [325-29]). If this is the praetorium of the Gospels the traditional "way of the cross" will have to be relocated.

Archeological excavations at the apparent site of the Antonia were carried on intermittently from the early 1930's to the middle 1950's. This work, under the direction of L.-H. Vincent and personnel of the Convent of the Dames de Sion, indicates that the fortress was at least 140 m. (450 ft.) long and about 100 m. (325 ft.) wide. Its courtyard, dating from the Roman period, was over 1500 sq. m. (16,000 sq. ft.) in size and was paved with large stone blocks in which striations and drainage gutters are still visible (*see* PAVEMENT, THE). Architectural remains evince the beauty of the fortress (cf. Aline de Sion, *La Forteresse Antonia* [1955], pp. 39-172). The Franciscans of the Convent of the Flagellation have also uncovered evidence of the fortress on their property. That the fortress had a commanding view of the temple area is clearly implied in Acts 21:31-36. A large double pool under and integrated with the pavement provided an adequate water supply for the fortress. A careful study of the archeological remains leaves little doubt that this is Fortress Antonia.

Scholars who have identified the Antonia with the praetorium of the Gospels have suggested that "The Pavement" of Jn. 19:13 is the stone pavement uncovered in the courtyard of the fortress and that this pavement would be where Pilate conducted the public trial of Jesus. Defenders of this identification include de Sion, L. -H. Vincent (*RB*, 59 [1952], 513-530), W. F. Albright (*AP*, p. 245), and J. Finegan *Archeology of the NT* [1969], pp. 156-161).

Early pilgrims to Jerusalem generally identified the praetorium with the Fortress Antonia (summary in Finegan, pp. 157f.). Moreover, the traditional Via Dolorosa begins at this location. These factors, along with the archeological evidence (*pace* Benoit, who dated the Antonia ruins in the 2nd cent. A.D.) and the tense situation requiring Pilate to be near the temple, the center of activity at the time of Passover, favor locating Pilate at the Fortress Antonia for his trial of Jesus. *See also* JERUSALEM III.H.10.

In Phil. 1:13 the use of "and to all the rest" after *praitṓrion* implies that *praitṓrion* here refers to persons associated with a praetorium and not to a place itself. The meaning depends partly on the city from which Paul was writing. If he wrote from Rome it is possible, though very unlikely, that he applied this term (incorrectly) to the imperial residence. Used in Rome itself, the term would normally apply to the praetorian guards, a group of elite soldiers stationed near the city. This meaning is attested in other literature (e.g., Tacitus *Hist.* iv.46; Suetonius *Tiberius* 37; *Hero* 9). If Paul was writing from Ephesus or Caesarea it is much more probable that this term refers to (persons at) the residence of the Roman administrator; but it could also refer to the group of soldiers associated with the provincial capital. *See* PHILIPPIANS, EPISTLE TO THE.

B. VANELDEREN

**PRAISE.** A word derived from Lat. *pretium*, "price" or "value"; thus it may be defined generally as an ascription of value or worth. It is typified by the doxologies to God and to the Lamb in Rev. 4:11; 5:9f., 12, which are inspired by a sense of their worthiness to be adored. Praise of God is a prominent theme throughout the Scriptures, for it is the appropriate response of God's creatures to His majesty and His saving deeds.

*I. Terms.*–The RSV uses "praise" to render a variety

of Hebrew and Greek terms, including both verbs and nouns. In the OT the verb most often represents the piel of Heb. *hālal* (also pual [e.g., Ps. 18:3 (MT 4)] and hithpael [e.g., Prov. 31:30]). The hiphil of *yāḏâ* (lit. "praise," "confess," "give thanks"; cf. noun *tôḏâ*, "thanksgiving") and the piel of *zāmar* (lit. "sing praise [accompanied by stringed instruments]"; e.g., Ps. 7:17 [MT 18]) are also frequently rendered "praise." Other verbs include the piel of *šāḇaḥ* (lit. "praise, glorify"; e.g., Ps. 63:3 [MT 4]; 117:1; 147:12; cf. Aram. *šᵉḇaḥ*, Dnl. 2:23; etc.) and the piel of *rānan* (lit. "shout with joy"; e.g., "joyously praise," Ps. 89:12 [MT 13]). The noun "praise" most often represents *tᵉhillâ* ("praise," "song of praise"), which is derived from *hālal* (cf. also *hillûlîm*, Lev. 19:24); *zāmîr* ("song of praise"; e.g., Ps. 95:2) is derived from *zāmar*.

In the NT "praise" translates the Greek verbs *ainéō* (lit. "extol, glorify"; e.g., Lk. 2:13, 20; 19:37; Acts 2:47; 3:8f.; Rom. 15:11), *doxázō* (lit. "extol, honor"; Mt. 6:2; Lk. 13:13; 17:15; 23:47; Acts 4:21), *epainéō* (lit. "approve, praise"; Rom. 15:11), *exomologéomai* (lit. "confess, praise"; Rom. 14:11; 15:9), *hymnéō* (lit. "sing hymns of praise"; He. 2:12), and *psállō* (lit. "play a stringed instrument," "sing to a harp"; RSV "sing praise," Jas. 5:13). It also renders the nouns *épainos* (lit. "approval, praise"; Rom. 2:29; Eph. 1:6, 12, 14; etc.), *dóxa* (lit. "glory"; Lk. 17:18; Jn. 9:24; 12:43), *aínos* (Mt. 21:16; Lk. 18:43), and *aínēsis* (He. 13:15).

***II. With Human Beings as Object.***–Although the Scriptures direct praise overwhelmingly toward God rather than mankind, there are occasional references to human beings as an object of praise. Such praise may be given either by God or by other persons. Praise that comes from God is inevitably just and is greatly to be desired (cf. Rom. 2:29; 1 Cor. 4:5; 1 Pet. 1:7). Human praise can be a blessing and a mark of divine favor (cf. Gen. 49:8; Dt. 26:19; 32:43; Zeph. 3:19f.). It has value only when it coincides with divine approval. Praise is appropriate when it is a natural response to beauty (e.g., Gen. 12:15; 2 S. 14:25; Cant. 6:9), to good deeds (e.g., Prov. 31:28f., 31), to fear of the Lord (v. 30), or to right action (1 Pet. 2:14; cf. Rom. 13:3). On the other hand, only lawbreakers praise the wicked (Prov. 28:4; cf. Ps. 73:10), and there is a praise that is itself a condemnation (cf. Prov. 27:21; Lk. 6:26). Jesus warned His followers against loving "the praise of men" more than "the praise of God" (Jn. 12:43; cf. Mt. 6:2; Gal. 1:10; 1 Thess. 2:4-6).

***III. With God as Object.***–The praise of God is a characteristic feature of biblical piety. Its importance in Hebrew worship is nowhere more evident than in the book of Psalms, a late Hebrew title of which is *tᵉhillîm*, "praises." The Hebrew term *mizmôr*, a derivative of *zāmar*, occurs in fifty-seven Psalm titles (LXX *psalmós*, lit. "song sung to the accompaniment of a stringed instrument"; RSV "psalm"); the expression *halᵉlû-yāh* (RSV "Praise the Lord!"; *see* HALLELUJAH) occurs twenty-four times in the Psalter as a call to praise. The NT, likewise, resounds with outbursts of praise, e.g., in the doxologies of the book of Revelation (cf. 4:8, 11; 5:9-14; 15:3f.; 19:1-8).

*A. Those Who Render Praise.* The Bible declares that the whole earth praises God (e.g., Ps. 48:10 [MT 11]; 89:12 [MT 13]; cf. 19:1-4 [MT 2-5]; Rev. 5:11-14), and it summons all creatures in heaven and earth to praise Him (cf. Ps. 69:34 [MT 35]; 89:5 [MT 6]), including the angels (e.g., 89:5 [MT 6]; 148:1f.; cf. 103:20), the animals (e.g., 148:10), and inanimate beings such as the heavenly bodies (vv. 3f.), the seas (v. 7), and the mountains and trees (v. 9). But the Scriptures are principally concerned with the praise rendered to God by human beings. They summon not only God's own people (cf. Ps. 22:22-25 [MT 23-26]; 30:4 [MT 5]; 113:1; 135:1f.; etc.; cf. Isa. 12:5f.; Rev. 19:5), but all peoples and nations (Ps. 66:1-4, 8; 67:3-5 [MT 4-6]; 117:1; etc.; cf. Isa. 42:10-12), to praise Him.

*B. Grounds for Praise.* The Scriptures declare God's greatness as manifested both in nature and in history. The OT praises God as the Creator, Sustainer, and Ruler of the world (e.g., 1 Ch. 16:25-34; Ps. 47:6f. [MT 7f.]; 95:1-5; 99:1-5; 104; 148). Above all, it praises Him for His faithfulness, righteousness, and steadfast love displayed in mighty acts of salvation on behalf of His people (e.g., 1 Ch. 16:9; Ps. 9:1f., 11, 14 [MT 2f., 12, 15]; 71:14-16; 106:1f.; Isa. 63:7; Jer. 31:7; Joel 2:26). God is praised because He is a Fortress and Savior to those in distress (Ps. 59:16f. [MT 17f.]; 71:7f., 23; Jer. 20:13), e.g., to the imprisoned (Ps. 102:18-20 [MT 19-21]; Isa. 61:1-3) and the poor (e.g., Ps. 113; Isa. 25:1, 4).

In the NT praise resounds at Jesus' birth (Lk. 2:13, 20), entrance into Jerusalem (19:37; Mt. 21:16), and death (Lk. 23:47). Many of those who experience healing through the mighty works of Jesus and His disciples burst into spontaneous praise of God (Lk. 13:13; 17:15-18; 18:43; Acts 3:8f.; 4:21; etc.). The authors of the Epistles likewise praise God for His salvation and, with the psalmists, summon believers and all peoples to praise God with their voices and lives (cf. Rom. 4:11; 15:9, 11; Eph. 1:6, 12, 14; Phil. 1:11; He. 2:12; 13:15; Jas. 5:13).

*C. Modes of Praise.* True praise of God, as distinguished from false praise (Isa. 29:13; cf. Mt. 15:8), is first of all an inward emotion of JOY (cf. 2 Ch. 29:30; Ps. 4:7 [MT 8]; 33:1f.; 63:5 [MT 6]; 67:3-5 [MT 4-6]; 71:23; 95:1f.; etc.), a gladness that no language can adequately express (Ps. 106:2; cf. 2 Cor. 9:15). But it is natural to give expression to such emotion and to call upon others — e.g., the whole congregation of worshipers — to join in praising God. Thus the mouth expresses the praise of the heart (cf. Ps. 51:15 [MT 17]; 71:8) by telling about the great things that God has done (Ps. 22:22-25 [MT 23-26]; 34:1-3; 107:32; Lk. 18:43; 19:37f.; etc.; cf. Ps. 40:9f. [MT 10f.]), by shouting for joy (cf. Ps. 81:1 [MT 2]; Isa. 42:11f.; 44:23; 48:20), and by singing joyful songs of praise (e.g., 2 S. 22:50; 1 Ch. 16:9; Ps. 7:17 [MT 18]; 9:2, 11 [MT 3, 12]; 18:49 [MT 50]; 30:4 [MT 5]; 40:3 [MT 4]; 147:1 [MT 2]; Jas. 5:13). New acts of salvation call for new songs of praise (Ps. 33:3; 96:1; 98:1; 144:9; 149:1; Rev. 14:3; cf. also Ex. 15:1-18, 21; Jgs. 5; Lk. 1:46-55; Rev. 5:9f.; etc.). Praise is also commonly expressed through dance and the playing of musical instruments (e.g., cf. Ex. 15:20; 2 S. 6:14; Ps. 33:28; 43:4; 71:22; 149:3; 150).

Although music and song always played an important role in Israel's worship, the Chronicler reports that it was King David who first appointed Levites and priests to "minister continually before the ark" with song and musical instruments (cf. 1 Ch. 16:4-42; 23:5, 30; 25:1-8). David also contributed to a fixed order of cultic praise through his considerable influence on the development of the Psalter (*see* PSALMS III.C). David's instructions were followed by Solomon after the completion of the temple (2 Ch. 5:11-13; 7:6; 8:14; cf. 20:19, 21f.), by Hezekiah's reform movement (29:27-30; 30:21; 31:2), and by the post-exilic community (Ezr. 3:10f.; Neh. 12:24, 45f.).

In the NT singing continued to be an important means of expressing praise (cf. Mt. 26:30; the "hymn" sung by Jesus and His disciples was probably from the HALLEL). The earliest Christians worshiped with their fellow Jews at the temple and synagogue (cf. Acts 2:46f.; 3:1; 13:14f.; etc.). Even after they were expelled by the Jews and forced to make their own provisions for worship, they continued to draw upon their Jewish inheritance — especially the Psalter — for forms of praise. But their new experience of

God's grace in Jesus Christ also required the composition of new songs of praise (cf. 1 Cor. 14:26; Eph. 5:19; Col. 3:16; Rev. 5:9f.; etc.), and the text of the NT contains several examples of hymns that were probably used in the formal worship of the early Church (*see* HYMNS IN THE NT).

*See also* MUSIC; PSALMS; SONG; WORSHIP.

***Bibliography.***–A. A. Anderson, *Book of Psalms*, I (*NCBC*, repr. 1981), 32-36; *DNTT*, III, 816-19; *NBD, s.v.* (R. S. Wallace); G. von Rad, *OT Theology*, I (Eng. tr. 1962), 356-370; *TDNT*, I, *s.v.* αἰνέω, αἶνος (H. Schlier); II, *s.v.* ἔπαινος (H. Preisker); VII, *s.v.* ὕμνος, ὑμνέω, φάλλω, ψαλμός (G. Delling); *TDOT*, III, *s.v.* "hll I and II" (H. Ringgren); IV, *s.v.* "zmr" (C. Barth).

J. C. LAMBERT B. L. MARTIN

**PRAY** [Heb. *nā'* (Gen. 19:2; 24:12, 14; etc.), *'ānâ* (Jonah 4:2), *bî* (Jgs. 6:13, 15)]; AV also BESEECH, "oh," "now"; NEB also PLEASE, BEG, ASK, BESEECH, "indeed." A polite, somewhat archaic entreaty or exhortation.

The origin of this use of the Hebrew terms is uncertain (cf. BDB, pp. 58, 106, 609; A. M. Honeyman, *JAOS*, 64 [1944], 81f.; P. Joüon, *Grammaire de l'hébreu biblique* [1947], p. 287 n. 2). The terms seem to have different nuances. *Bî* is always followed by *'ᵃḏōnāy* ("Lord") or *'ᵃḏōnî* ("[my] lord"), in contexts that imply that one of inferior status is politely contradicting a superior (e.g., Jgs. 6:13, 15). Thus it is perhaps best translated "pardon me" (so R. Boling, *Judges* [*AB*, 1975], pp. 128, 131; cf. JB "forgive me"). *Nā'* and *'ānâ* convey the more usual sense of "please" or "for mercy's sake." In Ps. 118:25 Heb. *hôšî'â(-n)nā'*, "save us, we beseech thee," was perhaps the origin of the NT expression HOSANNA. G. A. L.

**PRAYER.** Communion with God, usually comprising petition, adoration, praise, confession, and thanksgiving. The ultimate object of prayer in both OT and NT is not merely the good of the petitioner but the honor of God's name.

- I. Terminology
  - A. Hebrew
  - B. Greek
- II. Prayer in the OT
  - A. Patriarchal Period
  - B. Preexilic Period
  - C. Exilic and Postexilic Periods
- III. Intertestamental Period
  - A. Judaism
  - B. Hellenism
- IV. Prayer in the NT
  - A. Teaching of Jesus
  - B. Life of Jesus
  - C. Luke-Acts
  - D. Pauline Epistles
  - E. Hebrews, James, and 1 Peter
  - F. Epistles of John and Revelation
- V. Theology
  - A. Basis and Purpose
  - B. Aspects
  - C. Conditions
  - D. Unanswered Prayer
  - E. Other Issues
- VI. Summary and Conclusion

***I. Terminology.***–*A. Hebrew.* The vocabulary of prayer is rich. *'Āṯar* specifically means "entreat." It does not have broader frames of reference than prayer, as do the other words below; it is also less common than many of the following terms (e.g., Gen. 25:21; Job 33:26; "make a prayer," Job 22:27; "entreat," Ex. 8:8f., 28-30 [MT 4f., 24-26]; Jgs. 13:8). The hithpael of *pālal* is translated simply "pray," and the related noun is *tᵉpillâ*, "prayer." Although the etymology is debated (*see* MEDIATE), the meaning is clear in context. Usually intercessory prayer is indicated.

*Qārā'* (+*lᵉ*, *'el*, "to") is translated variously, e.g., "call," "call (upon)," "cry (unto)." Typical uses are in Ps. 89:26 (MT 27); 119:146; 130:1; 141:1. *Ṣā'aq* means "cry out," usually for help (e.g., Ex. 17:4; Ps. 107:6, 28; Isa. 46:7; cf. the related noun *ṣᵉ'āqâ*, "cry," Ex. 3:7). *Zā'aq* also means "cry out," but it is used less often than *ṣā'aq* (e.g., "cry for help," Jgs. 6:6; "cry," v. 7; "call," Lam. 3:8). *Šāwa'* means cry out in an intense manner, e.g., "call," Ps. 72:12; "cry for help," Lam. 3:8; Hab. 1:2. The noun *rinnâ* describes a ringing cry, as in Ps. 17:1.

Two frequently-used verbs are usually translated "seek": *dāraš* (e.g., 1 Ch. 16:11a; 2 Ch. 15:2, 12f.; Ps. 105:4a; "search," Dt. 4:29b) and *bāqaš* (e.g., Dt. 4:29a; 1 Ch. 16:11b; Ps. 27:8; 105:3, 4b). *Dāraš* is often also translated "inquire." Another verb signifying inquiry is *šā'al*, often translated "ask" (e.g., Ps. 105:40), sometimes "inquire" (e.g., 1 S. 23:2), and in Ps. 122:6 "pray." The verb *ḥānan*, "be gracious," "pity," is used in the hithpael to mean "beseech" or "implore" (e.g., Dt. 3:23).

Several verbs convey the idea of waiting on, or for, God: *ḥāḵâ* (e.g., Ps. 33:20; Isa. 8:17); *ḥîl* (e.g., Ps. 37:7); *yāḥal* (e.g., Mic. 7:7); *qāwâ* (e.g., Ps. 25:3, 5; 27:14; 37:9, 34; 40:1 [MT 2]; 130:5; Isa. 40:31; "hope," Ps. 69:6 [MT 7]); *śāḇar* (e.g., "hope," Ps. 119:166; Isa. 38:18).

*B. Greek.* Several terms are used with distinctive but overlapping meanings. The most general verb is *proseúchomai* (noun *proseuchḗ*), which in the LXX usually translates Heb. *pālal* (noun *tᵉpillâ*). This terminology occurs in such familiar passages as Mt. 6:5-7, 9 (the Lord's Prayer); Lk. 18:1; Acts 2:42; Eph. 6:18; Jas. 5:17. *Eúchomai* and *euchḗ*, from which the previous words are derived, occur much less frequently in the NT and not at all in the Gospels. The verb and noun appear in Jas. 5:15f., and the verb in Rom. 9:3; 3 Jn. 2.

*Aitéō* (noun *aítēma*) means "want," "ask for," and even "demand something." It translates Heb. *šā'al* in the LXX when a specific request is in mind (e.g., 1 S. 1:17). Some of the NT occurrences of this verb and noun are Mt. 7:7-11 (cf. Lk. 11:9-13); Mt. 21:22 (cf. Mk. 11:24); Jn. 14:13f.; 15:7, 16; 16:23f., 26; Phil. 4:6; Jas. 1:5f.; 1 Jn. 3:22; 5:14-16. *Déomai* is less frequent, though the noun *déēsis* is more common than *aítēma*. *Déomai* and *déēsis* translate several Hebrew words whose idea is beseech, beg, or bring a need (one's own, or another's) to God. These two Greek terms are relatively frequent in Luke-Acts (e.g., Lk. 1:13; 5:12; 9:38, 40; Acts 8:22, 24). *Erōtáō* and *eperōtáō* (the noun *eperṓtēma* occurs only in 1 Pet. 3:21) also convey the idea of asking a question or making a request. The verb naturally translates Heb. *šā'al*. It is often used without reference to prayer but does designate that activity in some passages, especially in the Johannine writings (e.g., Jn. 17:9, 15, 20; 1 Jn. 5:16).

The RSV also translates *epikaléō* "pray" in Acts 7:59. In the LXX this term often renders Heb. *qārā'*. In 1 Tim. 4:5 the RSV translates *énteuxis* "prayer"; in the only other NT occurrence (1 Tim. 2:1) the RSV has "intercession."

Some passages use more than one term for prayer (e.g., Mk. 11:24f.; Phil. 4:6). A broader vocabulary includes words such as *boáō* (Lk. 18:7) and *krázō* (Rom. 8:15), "cry," and *proskynéō*, "worship" (Acts 24:11).

*See also* ASK; CALL; ENTREAT; HOPE; INQUIRE; SEARCH, SEEK.

***II. Prayer in the OT.***–*A. Patriarchal Period.* Although Adam, Eve, and Cain converse with God in Gen. 3 and 4, the first apparent mention of prayer is in 4:26. After saying that Seth named his son Enosh, the writer concluded, "At that time men began to call upon the name of the Lord [*liqrō' bᵉšēm YHWH*]." The point seems to be that at the same time people were being named, they learned and publicly invoked the true name of the Lord (Yahweh). But Gen. 4:26 probably goes beyond the mere act of praying to lay the foundation for all true prayer: acknowledgment of the divine name (see 12:8; 21:33; Ps. 80:18b [MT 19b]; 86:12; 145:1f.; Dnl. 9:19; cf. Mt. 6:9 par. Lk. 11:2).

Those who "call on" the name of the Lord in Genesis sometimes do so in connection with sacrifice, specifically at the erection of an altar or pillar (e.g., 12:8; 26:25; 28:20-22). But other prayers are simply personal petitions, much like those offered by pious individuals in subsequent ages. Thus Abraham prayed for his wife Sarah to have a child (15:1-4) and later for Abimelech's infertile wives and slaves to bear children (20:17). Isaac made the same request of God for his own wife (25:21). Abraham's prayer on behalf of righteous people in Sodom, while historically unique, provides a model of intercession (18:16-33). Hagar and her child cried in the desert, and God heard (21:16-18). Abraham's servant prayed for guidance in finding a wife for Isaac (24:12-14) and praised God when that guidance was given (vv. 26f.). Jacob prayed for protection from Esau (32:9-12).

Prayer in this period was far beyond any primitive magical petitioning of fearsome deities. It was personal and based on God's revelation of Himself. One major example, often overlooked, is that of Enoch, whose walk with God must be considered an ideal expansion of prayer into continuous communion with God (Gen. 5:22-24). The variety of prayers in Genesis and throughout the Pentateuch should be seen as characteristic of the rich and complex nature of prayer rather than as merely characteristic of diverse literary sources.

*B. Preexilic Period.* Exodus records the cry of the people when they were in bondage in Egypt (3:7) and when the Egyptians pursued them (14:10), Moses' dialogue with God over his call to lead the people (3:1–4:17), and his intercession for Pharaoh (8:28-32; 9:27-30; 10:16-18). Moses made an exasperated cry for guidance when the people grumbled in the desert (15:25; 17:4). Exodus also shows Moses interceding for Israel (32:11-13, 31-34; cf. 34:9; Dt. 9:18-21; 10:10; Nu. 11:2); in Israel's case God "repented" (NEB, NIV, "relented," Ex. 32:14).

The record of Moses' conversation with God in Ex. 33:12–34:28, while perhaps not a model of normal prayer because of the extraordinary revelation of God that Moses received, is nevertheless significant because it shows the essential elements of communion with God. These include God's "favor" (33:12f.), His "presence" (vv. 14f.), knowledge of the name Yahweh (33:19; 34:5), assurance that God knows us "by name" (33:12, 17), and the desire to see God's faithfulness to His own covenant (34:10, 27f.).

Leviticus does not specify any prayers for recitation when the various sacrifices are offered, nor is a prayer recorded at the ordination of Aaron and his sons. Although prayers may have been offered, the Levitical emphasis is on the sacrifices.

In Nu. 11:11-15 when the people were complaining, Moses again turned to God, this time in an outburst of frustration. He prayed for Miriam in 12:13. His prayer of intercession for the rebellious people in 14:13-19 appealed to God's reputation, which, he said, would be ruined if God destroyed them in the desert. He founded his plea on the loving, forgiving character of God.

This concern for God's reputation (elsewhere called God's "name") and the appeal to the gracious character of God are elements in petitions throughout Scripture. Moses prayed on the occasion of Korah's rebellion (16:15, 22). He prayed for the people who were dying from the bite of snakes sent in judgment (21:4-9), for wisdom to help people in need (27:5), and for a successor (27:15-17).

While Deuteronomy is primarily a book of legislation, it does have some prayers (e.g., 3:23-25; 9:18-20, 26-29; 10:10). The only liturgy provided is that for the offering of the first fruits and the tithe (26:1-15). It is notable that this last book of the Pentateuch closes with prayer: the Song of Moses, in praise of God's mighty deeds (Dt. 32), and his benedictory prayer for the tribes (ch. 33). Prayer in the Pentateuch arises mainly out of the people's physical needs and the recurring need for intercession because of their rebelliousness (e.g., ch. 33). The basis of prayer is a response to God's revealed character and a desire to uphold His reputation among the nations (e.g., ch. 32).

Three incidents in Joshua provide vivid teaching on prayer. After the defeat at Ai, Joshua prayed along lines that are now familiar: if Israel failed, God's reputation would be ruined (Josh. 7:6-9). In this case, God stopped Joshua's prayer, telling him that Israel had sinned and therefore action, not prayer, was necessary (vv. 10-15). Teaching by negative example is found in Josh. 9. When the people of Gibeon asked for a treaty, pretending to have come from a distance, the people of Israel "did not ask direction from the Lord" (v. 14). In contrast, a dramatic example of prayer occurs in 10:12-14. Joshua's command to the sun to stand still was actually said "to the Lord" (v. 12). Verse 14 says there was never such a time, before or since, when the Lord listened to a man.

Judges opens with a prayer for guidance (1:1). During times of oppression the people cried to the Lord for help (3:15; 4:3; 6:6-8; 10:10-16), and God raised up judges to deliver them. The Song of Deborah and Barak is a form of prayer (ch. 5). Gideon conversed with God about the fleece (6:36-40). Jephthah's vow in 11:30f. is actually a prayer. Samson's father sought guidance (13:8); Samson prayed for aid in 15:18; 16:28. Following the sordid incidents described in ch. 19, the Israelites prayed to God for guidance in their fight against the Benjaminites (20:18-28).

1 Samuel opens with Hannah's moving vow and prayer for a child (1:10f.). Her praise to God after her request was granted (2:1-10) provided a model for Mary's Magnificat (Lk. 1:46-55). During the transition to the monarchy, Samuel was the great intercessor. 1 S. 7:5-9 records two cycles of Samuel's intercession and the people's confession (cf. 12:6-25, esp. v. 23, where Samuel indicated that failure to intercede would be a sin against the Lord). Samuel prayed also in 8:6, 21; 12:18f. and with the tribes in 10:22. King Saul prayed in 14:37, 41. Several prayers of David are included in 1 and 2 Samuel (1 S. 23:2, 4; 30:8; 2 S. 2:1; 5:19, 23; 7:18-29 [David's magnificent prayer acknowledging God's sovereignty after God denied his wish to build the temple]; 21:1 [for guidance]; ch. 22 [cf. Ps. 18]; 24:17 [confession]).

Solomon's prayer for wisdom (1 K. 3:5-9) was probably recorded to serve not so much as a model prayer as a background for the subsequent narrative of his reign. The king's prayer of dedication for the temple, along with the opening blessing and the benediction (1 K. 8:12-61; 2 Ch. 6:1-42), provides a magnificent statement of the role of both temple and people.

The lives of Elijah and Elisha seem to have been particularly characterized by prayer (see esp. 1 K. 17:19-22, Elijah's prayer to bring a boy back to life; 18:20-40, the prayer contest with the prophets of Baal on Mt. Carmel; 19:2-18; cf. Jas. 5:17f.). Elisha, like Elijah, prayed for one who had died (2 K. 4:32-35). He surprised Naaman the leper by not offering public prayer (5:11).

Other prayers in Kings and Chronicles are 1 K. 13:6; 2 K. 13:4; 22:18f.; 1 Ch. 4:10; 5:18-20; 16:7-36 (cf. Ps. 105); 29:10-20; 2 Ch. 14:11; 15:3f.; 20:3-12; 33:10-13.

Hezekiah offered two prayers of great significance. First, he brought a written threat from the Assyrians before the

Lord along with a prayer that emphasized God's royal sovereignty over all nations and sought the defeat of Assyria so that all nations would acknowledge Yahweh as God (2 K. 19:15-19). Hezekiah's other recorded prayer was for the lengthening of his life, in spite of God's word that he would die (2 K. 20:1-7). The granting of his request had serious effects (see V.E.1 below).

The writing prophets frequently prayed (e.g., Am. 7:1-6; Hab. 1, 3; Jonah 2:1-9 [MT 2-10]; 4:1-3, 8-11). The most numerous references to prayer are in Jeremiah (e.g., 1:6; 4:10; 7:16; 11:5, 14; 12:1-17; 18:19-23; 20:7-18; 32:16-25; 33:3). These include Jeremiah's protestations at God's call, his intercession for Israel (and God's negative answers), his prayer for vindication of himself, as well as a complaint before God. At two points (7:16; 11:14) God told Jeremiah not to pray for the people, in strong contrast to His willingness to hear Moses' intercessions. The difference is clearly due to the accumulated years of rebellion. The inclusion of Jeremiah's outburst of frustration (20:7-18) in the canonical Scriptures is an encouragement to honesty with God. In contrast, his prayer of confidence as he purchased a field to symbolize the certainty of Israel's return to the land after captivity (32:16-25) and God's response in vv. 26f. (cf. 33:3) encourage faith in God's word.

The Psalms were collected over a period of time, the selection including, for the most part, Psalms suitable for public use. The majority of the Psalms are songs of praise, many seeking vindication of God's name among unbelievers. This fact is instructive for the shape and balance of our prayers. Only five Psalms (17, 86, 90, 102, 142) are actually called prayers (Heb. *t^e^pillâ*) in the surviving superscriptions. One of these, Ps. 86, may be singled out as especially instructive in prayer because of its structure and emphasis. In the first strophe, vv. 1-4, four petitions alternate with four supporting clauses, each beginning with Heb. *kî* ("for"), that provide the reasons for David's confidence in prayer. Verses 5-10 then provide support by referring to the nature and attributes of God. Here *kî* ("for") occurs at the beginning (v. 5), middle (v. 7), and end (v. 10) of the section. Verses 11-13 are the heart of the prayer, David's request for guidance in order to give whole-hearted devotion to God and to glorify His name. It is only in the final strophe (vv. 14-17) that David articulates his problem, his godless enemies. It is significant that his petition occupies far less space than the preceding expressions of devotion to God (vv. 1-13). This appeal to God for help against one's enemies, introduced by a recollection of God's power among the nations (esp. vv. 8-10), is somewhat similar to the prayer of the apostles for boldness in Acts 4:24-30.

The Psalms contain petitions reflecting a wide variety of needs, including deliverance from enemies (Pss. 3, 7, 13, 17, 26, 37, 143, 144), deliverance from slander (4, 5), deliverance from sickness (102), and deliverance from sin (32, 51).

The book of Job (date unknown) provides the most extreme example of need. Job's experience is important in connection with prayer, which often contains an element of theodicy or of despair (as the petitioner wrestles with the problem of evil, in particular the prosperity of the wicked and the suffering of the righteous). The spirit of prayer pervades the book, even if only by inference or allusion ("O that I might have my request, and that God would grant my desire" [6:8]; "My eye pours out tears to God" [16:20b]). The dialogue between the Lord and Job (38:1–42:6), which forms the climax of the book, concludes with a new vision and awe of God — a desirable result of any prayer.

*C. Exilic and Postexilic Periods.* The Exile brought a great change in both circumstances and mood. The place where God had "put His name" was gone, the sacrifices and regular intercession of the priests had ended, and God's protecting hand had been withdrawn in judgment. It was difficult to sing the songs of the Lord in a foreign land (Ps. 137:4); there was little to do but sit overwhelmed (Ezk. 3:15) and pray repentantly. Eventually new institutions developed, such as the synagogue and the scribal office. The synagogue became primarily a place of study and prayer.

During the exile in Babylon, it was apparently the custom of the Jews to pray three times a day (Dnl. 6:10 [MT 11]; cf. Ps. 55:17 [MT 18]). The book of Daniel contains several outstanding prayers. After the meaning of Nebuchadnezzar's dream was revealed to him, Daniel offered a prayer praising God for His wisdom and sovereignty in history (2:20-23). Nebuchadnezzar, after his restoration, expressed the model confession that pious Jews wanted Gentiles to pray, acknowledging the true God and His kingdom (4:34f. [MT 31f.]; cf. v. 3 [MT 3:33]; cf. also the hope of Zeph. 3:9; Isa. 11:9b; 60:3; 62:2a; Mal. 1:11; etc.). After Daniel's rescue from the den of lions, Darius also prayed an ideal Gentile prayer (6:26f. [MT 27f.]).

The most exemplary prayer in the book of Daniel and one of the most significant in all Scripture is the confession in 9:4-19. Among the elements to be noted are (1) the description of God as righteous, merciful, and forgiving; (2) the contrasting description of the petitioner and his people as shamefully sinful; (3) their disobedience to the revealed laws of God; (4) a concern for the reputation of God (see esp. vv. 16-19, where God is asked for His own sake and because of His great mercy to deliver His people and holy city Jerusalem, which are called by His name). Prayer is thus seen as a means of vindicating God and bringing honor to His name.

After the return to Jerusalem, Ezra pursued his work in an atmosphere of prayer (Ezr. 7:27; 8:22f.; 9:6-15). Nehemiah began with prayer (Neh. 1:5-11) and continued in a prayerful attitude (2:4; 4:4f., 9 [MT 3:36f.; 4:3]). The confession of sin in 9:5-37 is actually a recitation of Jewish history. Nehemiah's prayers are a plea partly for divine recognition of his efforts and partly for retribution against the enemy (5:19; 6:14; 13:14, 22, 29, 31).

***III. Intertestamental Period.–A. Judaism.*** Prayer is frequent in the Apocrypha. The passages with the greatest effect on subsequent theology are 2 Macc. 12:44f.; 15:12-14. The former passage refers to prayer for the dead, "that they might be delivered from their sin," and the latter passage shows the dead, specifically the high priest Onias and the prophet Jeremiah, interceding for the Jewish people. Other prayers include the Prayer of Manasseh, purportedly the confession of that evil king (*see* MANASSEH, PRAYER OF), the Prayer of Azariah and the Song of the Three Young Men, and the prayers of Mordecai and Esther in the Additions to the Book of Esther. The pious legends of Tobit and of Judith also contain prayers (e.g., Tob. 3:1-6; Jth. 9:1-14; 16:1-17).

Prayer was also significant at Qumrân, as the Dead Sea Scrolls testify. Many of the *Hôdāyôt* (Thanksgiving Hymns) express both the theology of the community and the piety of the individual. The community enjoined prayer twice during the daytime, in the morning and at evening (1QS 10:1-3a), and at other times on certain days (10:3b-8a). Specific prayers were to be offered during the eschatological battle and after victory (1QM, *passim*).

Some ideas from this period may be found later in the Talmud. T.B. *Berakoth* 16b-17b has prayers to be delivered from sin, to be occupied with the Torah, to have a long and good life, to have peace, and to be forgiven. Prayer, the "service of the heart," was highly regarded by the rabbis (e.g., T.B. *Taanith* 2a; T.B. *Berakoth* 6b, 32b). The Talmud shows that they debated whether prayer or the

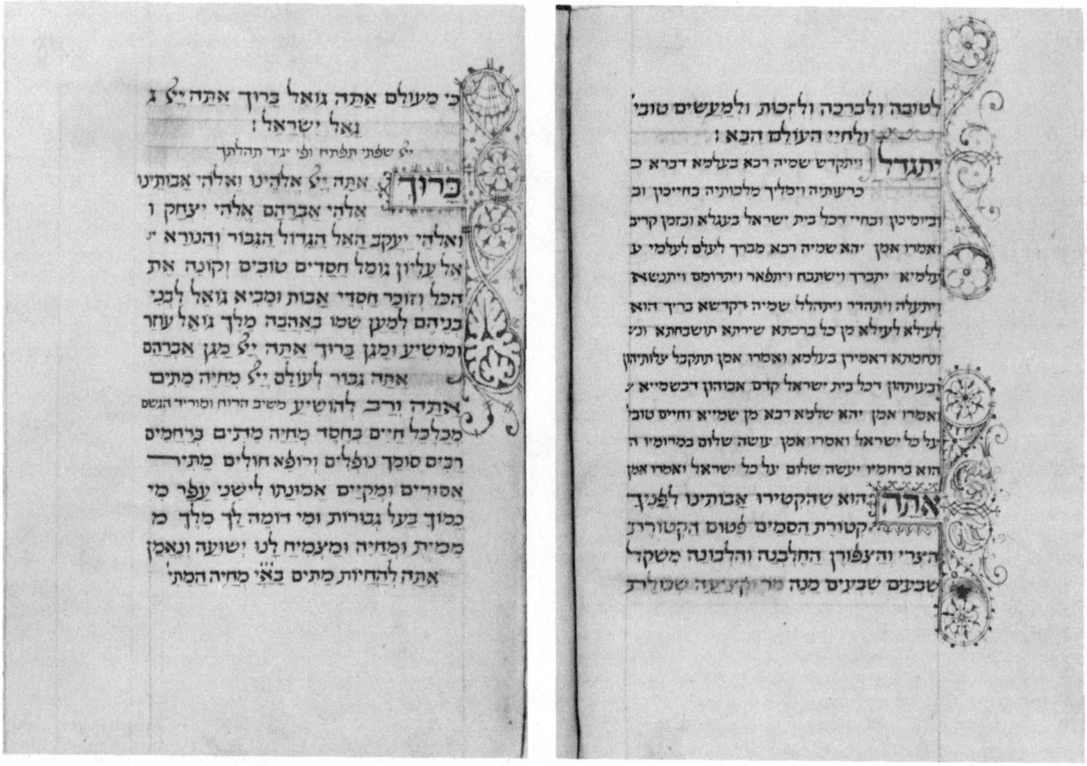

Two pages from a prayer book: the first page of the Eighteen Benedictions (left), and a Kaddish. The Benedictions begin with Ps. 51:15 (MT 17) (in smaller letters) before the characteristic opening "Blessed art thou, O Lord our God," and continues with praises. The Kaddish begins "Magnified and sanctified be his greatness" and continues with praises and requests for peace (Royal Library, Copenhagen)

study of the Torah was more important; since the importance of the latter was widely acknowledged, this debate shows a high regard for prayer.

Liturgical prayer was developed for the synagogue, but the forms were also followed at home. The rabbis were aware of the problem of mere rote praying (T.P. *Berakoth* 4:3, 8a). Prayers were to be recited three times a day (Mish. *Berakoth* iv.1), beginning at the time of the morning sacrifice. If a person could not pray at the temple or the synagogue, he could still identify with the community by praying at the time of the morning and evening sacrifices and at the time that the temple gates were usually closed. The recitation of the Shema was to be accompanied by benedictions, two before and one following the morning recitation and four accompanying the evening recitation. The main prayer, the Tefillah ($t^e$*pillâ*), developed into the present Eighteen Benedictions, the Shemoneh Esreh. The Tefillah is also commonly known now as the Amidah, the standing prayer. It includes a broad range of petitions. Another prayer used over the centuries is the Kaddish, an expression of worship and a petition for messianic deliverance. The biblical Psalms were also used in synagogue worship in Jesus' day, particularly the Hallel (Pss. 113–118) at special times, such as Passover (*see also* HALLEL).

*B. Hellenism.* Since Greco-Roman religion was extremely varied, prayers ranged from simple pleas for help to the literary magnificence of Cleanthes' Hymn to Zeus. Earlier literary evidence includes the so-called Homeric Hymns, celebrating the gods, and the prayers found in Homer's *Iliad,* often for military victory and other material blessings. The prayers in the *Iliad* typically have three parts: (1) the invocation of the god, (2) the reasons why the petitioner thinks that he deserves to be heard, and (3) the petition itself. Ancient Greek literature is so permeated by religious thought that one can find many different expressions of prayer in it, especially in the dramas.

By the Hellenistic period belief in the Olympian gods had long since dissolved into skepticism, despair, and fatalism. Of the primitive superstitions, some had been forsaken, though others continued at least in custom. The mystery religions, which claimed to provide an intimate experience with the deity, were winning converts rapidly. Devotion was offered appropriate to the god or goddess, such as the popular Isis, although syncretism tended to merge deities together. The paganism faced by the early Christian missionaries should not be dismissed as mere secularism, for it contained many elements of piety. Whether out of religion or superstition (cf. Acts 17:22), people did pray.

***IV. Prayer in the NT.–A.*** ***Teaching of Jesus. 1. Sermon on the Mount.*** Jesus' teaching against religious ostentation includes a model for prayer (Mt. 6:5-15). The effectiveness of prayer does not depend on human effort, e.g., on eloquence or length of prayer. The Father's foreknowledge of human needs, far from discouraging prayer, becomes an incentive for it. Prayer is not informing God of one's needs but expressing one's confidence in Him. The Lord's Prayer carries forward much of what the OT taught by example. The knowledge of God, now not only as Yahweh but also as the heavenly Father, is basic. Concern for the honor of His name continues to be central in prayer, as is the extension of His kingdom in a pagan world. The petitions for personal needs are not introduced until a theological basis is established and the sovereignty and glory of God are acknowledged. These petitions include daily provision, forgiveness of sin, and protection against evil. (The prayer in Lk. 11:2-4, though it has some significant differences in detail, is essentially the same.) A series of exhortations about trusting the heavenly Father for material needs appropriately follows the Lord's Prayer in Mt. 6:19-34. Later in the Sermon on the Mount Jesus gives further assurances regarding answers to prayer (7:7-11).

*2. Parables.* In Lk. 11 the Lord's Prayer is followed by the parable of the friend at midnight (vv. 5-8) and then by assurances that parallel Mt. 7:7-11 (with the substitution in v. 13 of "give the Holy Spirit" for "give good things," which is appropriate to Luke's emphasis on the Spirit). The parable itself (vv. 5-8) has perplexed interpreters, because it seems to teach that one must persist in prayer to persuade God to answer. J. Jeremias (*Parables of Jesus* [Eng. tr., 2nd ed. 1972], p. 158) suggested that Gk. *anaídeia* (v. 8) means "avoidance of shame" rather than "importunity" or "persistence." This is linguistically acceptable and also fits ancient Near Eastern custom. The application then is that God will answer prayer if for no other reason than to guard His own reputation.

The parable in Lk. 18:1-8 is similar, in that it seems to teach that persistence is necessary to persuade God. Here Gk. *hypōpiázē me* can be paraphrased "give me a black eye" (i.e., disgrace me; see J. D. M. Derrett, *NTS,* 18 [1971/72], 189f.) rather than "wear me out." This was a possible meaning in Jesus' day and is significant in the context, showing that God will maintain His reputation for vindicating those who trust in Him. This parable follows the eschatological teaching of 17:20-37, so the problem of waiting for vindication is appropriate in the context.

*3. Other Teachings.* When Jesus cast out a demon that the disciples could not exorcise, He did not attribute His success to His own divine power but to the power of prayer, to which they also had access (Mt. 17:14-20 par. Mk. 9:16-29; cf. Lk. 17:6). The story of the cursing of the fig tree (Mk. 11:12-14, 20-24 par. Mt. 21:18-22) teaches the power of believing prayer.

Further instruction occurs in Jesus' farewell discourse (Jn. 14:13f.; 15:16; 16:23f.). Not even He is necessary as an intermediary, for the disciples can approach the Father directly. But they must approach Him in Jesus' name. This expression is generally understood as indicating dependence on, and submission to, Jesus' authority and emphasizing that only through Christ and His death on the cross does one have access to God. It should also be understood against the background of the frequent mention of God's name in OT prayers. It is essential to know who God is and to seek the honor of His name. Now the Son brings glory to the Father when He answers prayer offered in His name (14:13). Honor thus redounds to the name both of the Father and of the Son.

*B. Life of Jesus.* Jesus prayed at all the important events in His life — e.g., His baptism (Lk. 3:21), the Transfiguration (Lk. 9:29), and His vigil in the Garden of Gethsemane before the Crucifixion (Mt. 26:36-46 par. Mk. 14:32-42; Lk. 22:39-46). Submission to God's will is paramount in the last of these prayers. Before the selection of the twelve disciples Jesus spent the night in prayer (Lk. 6:12).

Some of His prayers are thanksgivings to God (Jn. 6:11; 11:41; Mt. 26:27 par., at the Last Supper). When some rejected the gospel, in contrast to those who accepted it, Jesus thanked the Father for His sovereignty in revelation (Mt. 11:25f. par. Lk. 10:21). Other prayers are intercessions. In the great intercessory prayer of Jn. 17, as in the Lord's Prayer and the OT prayers, are the ideas of glorification of God on earth, protection from evil, and the importance of God's name. Jesus prayed especially for Peter before His passion (Lk. 22:31f.). His prayer was answered; although Peter's faith faltered, it did not fail completely (vv. 54-62). Jesus also interceded for others when He was on the cross (23:34).

The Gospels tell not only why but how Jesus prayed. Sometimes He spoke with God early in the morning (e.g., Mk. 1:35-38; Lk. 4:42f.), at night (Lk. 6:12; Mt. 26:36-46 par.), or in private (e.g., Lk. 5:16). He almost always addressed God as "Abba," an intimate term for "Father." It is now generally recognized that before Jesus Jews did not use this term as a normal address to God (*see* ABBA). The sole exception to Jesus' use of Abba-Father is in the "cry of dereliction" on the cross: "My God, my God, why hast thou forsaken me?" (Mt. 27:46 par. Mk. 15:34).

*C. Luke-Acts.* It has long been recognized that Luke gives a special place to the Holy Spirit and prayer in his Gospel and Acts. Several of the instances of prayer in the life of Jesus listed in IV.B above occur only in Luke: the prayer at His baptism (Lk. 3:21); the prayer all night before choosing the twelve disciples (6:12); prayer alone with the disciples before Peter's confession of Him as the Messiah (9:18); His prayer on the Mount of Transfiguration, during which His appearance was changed (9:29); His prayer for Peter before Peter's denial (22:31f.); and on the cross the prayer for the forgiveness of His enemies (23:34) and the final committal (23:46). Also, whereas Matthew gives the Lord's Prayer in the context of the Sermon on the Mount, in Luke the prayer is Jesus' response to the request of the disciples, who have seen Him at prayer (11:1-4). Finally, one exhortation to pray occurs only in Luke (21:36).

This emphasis on prayer continues in the book of Acts. Prayers are offered in the upper room (1:14), for guidance in the selection of a successor to Judas (1:24f.), as a regular activity of the Church (2:42), in the temple at the time of prayer (3:1), and for boldness when the apostles were told not to speak in the name of Christ (4:23-31). Stephen prayed when he was martyred (7:59f.). Peter and John asked that the Holy Spirit come on the believing Samaritans (8:14-17). The pious Gentile Cornelius "prayed constantly" (10:2). Paul prayed after the Damascus-road experience (9:11), with Jewish people by the river outside Philippi (16:13, 16), and on behalf of the Ephesian elders (20:32, 36).

It has been suggested that Luke associated prayer and the Holy Spirit especially with the proclamation, coming, and spread of the kingdom of God. This is observable at a number of crisis points in both the Gospel and Acts. The association of prayer with the kingdom accords with the opening petitions of the Lord's Prayer and the emphasis of the OT prayers on glorifying God's name among the nations. Luke's narratives also tell about the correspondence between human prayer and God's giving of the Holy Spirit (cf. Lk. 11:13, the giving of the Holy Spirit in answer to prayer, with Mt. 7:11, the more general giving of "good things").

*D. Pauline Epistles.* The Epistles are characterized by an opening expression of thanksgiving (Rom. 1:8f.; 1 Cor. 1:4-9; 2 Cor. 1:3f.; Eph. 1:15f.; Phil. 1:3-10; Col. 1:3-14; 1 Thess. 1:2f.; 2 Thess. 1:3). Of the Pastorals only 2 Timothy follows this pattern (1:3). The thanksgiving, an expansion of a literary convention, allowed Paul to express his concept of what is good and therefore worthy of thanks in the growth of the Christian Church. Such thanksgiving is valuable theologically and provides a model for the prayer of all Christians. Growing out of these thanksgivings often are implicit or explicit prayers for further progress (e.g., Phil. 1:9, "And it is my prayer that your love may abound more and more . . ."), which go far beyond literary convention.

Prayers, indirect prayers (e.g., "may God . . . ," with the third person used), and assurances of prayers ("I pray for you . . .") appear throughout Paul's letters. The prayers vary (thanksgivings, blessings, intercessions, etc.), with intercessions predominating.

A good deal about Paul's practice of prayer is known both from the Epistles and from Acts (Acts 9:11; 20:36; 21:5; 22:17-21; 28:8). Paul's exhortations to others (e.g., Eph. 6:18, "Pray at all times in the Spirit, with all prayer and supplication. . . . Keep alert with all perseverance, making supplication for all the saints . . .") reflect his own comprehensive praying (e.g., Phil. 1:3-5, "I thank my God in all my remembrance of you, always in every prayer . . . for you all making my prayer with joy, thankful . . .").

The following passages about prayer call for special attention.

*1. Rom. 8:26f.* Limited knowledge and wisdom need not hinder Christians from prayer, because the Holy Spirit will intercede. The words *stenagmoís alalḗtois* (lit. "sighs unexpressed"; RSV "sighs too deep for words") are difficult to understand (see E. Käsemann, *Comm. on Romans* [Eng. tr. 1980], pp. 239-242). They may refer to (1) what is expressed by the Holy Spirit (RSV, AV, NIV) or (2) one's own sighs or groans, which the Spirit then interprets on one's behalf (NEB). In the latter case the construction of the phrase can be understood as an instrumental dative (i.e., "through . . .") or even as a dative of reference (i.e., "with reference to . . .").

The next sentence (v. 27) is clear, teaching that God understands one's heart and also the mind of the Spirit, and that the Spirit interprets one's prayers in accordance with God's will. This teaching gives assurance to the believer, who may hesitate to pray without being sure of God's will. God Himself will receive such prayers and answer them appropriately. Thus one can assume that a properly motivated and well-intentioned prayer will not go astray simply because the one who prays does not specify the right things.

*2. Eph. 1:15-23.* This prayer is appropriate in its context — the purpose and plan of God. Verses 3-14 are replete with words such as "chose," "destined," "purpose," "will," "wisdom," and "insight." Verse 10 expresses the ultimate goal of uniting all things in heaven and on earth in Christ. The Christian's hope in this context is not merely to be saved but to bring glory to Christ and to share in His ultimate exaltation. The prayer of vv. 15-23 is therefore essentially a request for a deeper understanding of the meaning of this hope. God, who has raised Christ from the dead and exalted Him above all beings, is able to exercise the same power in mankind and to bring all things to completion. Verse 22 introduces the Church, which the Epistle subsequently emphasizes as the focal point of God's work in this age.

*3. Eph. 3:14-21.* This prayer is addressed to God as Father, before whom Paul kneels. Since kneeling was not the only and probably not the main posture for prayer (see V.E.4 below), this action may indicate strong emotion (*see also* KNEE, KNEEL). Paul has now revealed further God's purposes in bringing Jew and Gentile together in one body and in demonstrating (to whatever supernatural beings exist) His wisdom in so doing. The Church is the arena in which God displays His wisdom in this age. Paul will shortly speak of the importance of unity and mutual love in the Church, which demonstrate the reconciling work of Christ described earlier in ch. 2. Fittingly, the prayer in 3:14-21 is for inner strength and an appropriation of the love of Christ. It concludes with a doxology to the One who can accomplish all that has been promised in a way that surpasses what one expects. Significantly, glory redounds to God not only in Christ Jesus but also in the Church.

*4. Col. 1:9-14.* This Epistle emphasizes the supremacy of Christ over all beings. The Christian's prayer should therefore be to live a life worthy of this supreme Lord. While others are seeking religious fulfillment in the speculations that Paul goes on to refute, a Christian can be thankful for an inheritance in the kingdom of light and for rescue from the power of darkness through God's beloved Son and His redemption.

*5. 1 Tim. 2:1-10.* The first reference to prayer in this chapter is an exhortation to pray for all people but especially for kings and those in authority (vv. 1f.). There seem to be two strands of thought here. One is that prayer for all people accords with God's desire for all to be saved. The other is that prayer for those in authority will help rulers and the ruled to live together peacefully. Peace was important for Christians, who were likely to be held in suspicion by the pagan rulers. It had also been customary for Jewish people to pray for pagan rulers (e.g., Letter of Aristeas 45; Bar. 1:10-13; Mish. *Aboth* 3:2).

A further command (v. 8) is that the men pray with uplifted hands, a common practice. Women did not pray in the synagogue; perhaps Paul had only public leadership in mind, as elsewhere he assumed that women would pray and prophesy (1 Cor. 11:5). But the syntactical structure of v. 9 is unclear. The grammar seems to be straightforward: "I want men . . . to lift up holy hands in prayer" (v. 8, NIV) parallels "I also want women to dress modestly" (v. 9, NIV). It can be argued, however, that dressing modestly is an action not significant enough to be compared with praying. Hence the suggestion has been made that the phrase about praying in v. 8 should also be regarded as the object (though not repeated) of "I also want" in v. 9. In this construction women when they pray are to be characterized by a modest appearance, just as men are to pray "without anger or disputing" (v. 8). Both men and women pray, neither doing anything that nullifies the effect of their prayers. The word order (though not the grammar) supports this interpretation. But since it is difficult to determine here whether Paul let women pray, vv. 11-15 and related passages should be taken into consideration.

In addition to such major sections in the Epistles, Paul makes a number of significant individual statements about prayer. It is to be constant (1 Thess. 5:17); it is part of the spiritual battle (Rom. 15:30, "strive together . . . in your prayers"; cf. Col. 2:1 and 4:12, where the word for striving is often lost in translation; see V.E.11 below); it is important in the spiritual warfare, along with the Christian's armor and the Word of God (Eph. 6:13-18). Paul did not list prayer as one of the gifts of the Spirit, presumably because all Christians can and should pray, though he did mention faith, gifts of healing, and other powers (1 Cor. 12:7-11). In 14:14f., however, he spoke about prayer in connection with the exercise of the spiritual gifts, distinguishing between praying with the spirit (i.e., in tongues) and praying with the mind. Although not forbidding the former, he encouraged the latter. Praying *with* the spirit in this context is probably different from praying *in* the Spirit in Eph. 6:18. In the latter passage Paul spoke of "all prayer and supplication" (NIV "with all kinds of prayers and requests"), the reference probably being to specific petitions that must be expressed in a rational way. Ephesians has to do with the leading, power, and intercession of the Spirit; it does not imply praying in tongues as 1 Cor. 14 does.

*E. Hebrews, James, and 1 Peter.* The great contribution of Hebrews is its teaching on the earthly prayer life and heavenly intercession of Christ. Because of His sympathy as one who Himself was subject to the temptations of life, Christ is an effective high priest (He. 4:14-16). One can therefore pray with confidence. While He was on the earth, Jesus prayed with great emotion, and God was receptive to His prayers. Jesus' death, which occurred in spite of His praying to the One "able to save him from death," obviously does not negate the meaning of the passage, for the author certainly knew of Jesus' crucifixion. The present intercession of Christ at the right hand of God, to which Rom. 8:34 briefly alludes, receives a fuller treatment in He. 7:23-25. Prayer is involved when Christians together "draw near with a true heart and full assurance of faith" (10:19-25, esp. v. 22).

James 1:5-7 encourages prayer for wisdom, provided that one prays with confidence. 4:1-3 deals with unanswered prayer due to one's failing to ask or asking out of wrong motives. 5:13-18 is a major passage on prayer. A person who is sick can call the elders, who will pray over him. They will also anoint him with oil, which can be understood as a sacramental act or as a means of soothing or healing. Faith is essential. The passage does not say that this practice pertains only to a case where sin has been committed, but it does say that if the person has sinned he or she will be forgiven. It can be assumed from the following verse that confession of sin is made in such a case. The Roman Catholic Church has understood this passage sacramentally, as a biblical basis for the last rites ("extreme unction"). The passage goes on to emphasize the effectiveness of prayer by righteous persons, like Elijah.

1 Peter opens with a doxology (1:3-9). A sane and sober prayer life is encouraged in 4:7 because "the end of all things is at hand." A familiar exhortation, "Cast all your anxieties on him, for he cares about you," occurs in 5:7.

*F. Epistles of John and Revelation.* 1 Jn. 3:21f. encourages confidence in God when one prays as a believer who has a clear conscience and who is obedient to God. 5:14-17 is difficult to interpret. Assurance that prayer will be answered is possible for those who pray according to God's will (v. 14). Since the passage is intended to encourage prayer, not to inhibit it, one may assume that the Christian can determine what kind of petitions are most in accord with God's revealed character and purposes. Discernment is necessary in praying for someone who is sinning, because some sins are "mortal" (v. 16; AV "unto death"; NEB "deadly"), i.e., under God's judgment, perhaps obviously so. Except for such cases, which lead to death, the Epistle encourages intercession.

Revelation 4–5 describes prayerful worship of God and of the Lamb in heaven. The bowls of incense held by the four living creatures and the elders symbolize the "prayers of the saints" (5:8). Further thanksgiving is expressed in 11:16-18; 15:3f. (the songs of Moses and the Lamb); 16:5-7; 19:1-8. The book and Scripture itself conclude with a prayer, "Amen. Come, Lord Jesus!" (22:20), and with a benediction (v. 21).

***V. Theology.**–A. Basis and Purpose.* The biblical texts surveyed above make it clear that prayer is based on the revelation of the nature and attributes of God. "And those who know thy name put their trust in thee" (Ps. 9:10 [MT 11]). The initiative in prayer does not lie with people but with God Himself. Prayer is a response to multiple explicit and implicit invitations of God. Confidence is possible because God desires prayer and because it is in the nature and character of God to answer prayer. Although there are certain qualifications or conditions for prayer, the effective power of prayer does not ultimately reside in prayer itself but in the One to whom prayer is made. In the same way, the purpose of prayer is not merely to bring good to people but to bring glory to God. Honoring God always brings blessings to mankind, because God desires the good of those whom He created and especially of those whom He redeemed. Jesus' words, "But seek first his kingdom and his righteousness, and all these things shall be yours as well" (Mt. 6:33), certainly can apply to prayer. This is clear from a survey of the great models of prayer in both the OT and the NT, including the Lord's Prayer. Priority is always given to praise and to the goal of honoring God through the extension of His kingdom and the realization of His will on earth (see esp. the comments above on Ps. 86; Dnl. 9; 2 K. 19:15-19; Acts 4:24-31; Mt. 6:5-15). God will hear a prayer that is offered on the correct basis and with a proper purpose.

If prayer is thus grounded in God Himself, it follows that to pray one must have a proper and vital relationship with God. One must, of course, believe that He exists but also that one's very coming to Him brings its own reward (He. 11:6). The greatest reward is not in the receiving of gifts but in a deeper experience of the Giver. This relationship must be intimate and continuing, a relationship described as "abiding" in Him in Jn. 15:7. One may be driven to prayer because of need, but one remains in prayer because of God Himself. The aspect of human relationship with God that is most important for prayer is that of a child to a father. The Lord's Prayer and the rest of Jesus' teaching make this point strongly. It is true that God hears the prayer of any person, whether Christian or not, simply because He is God. He also brings many blessings, such as rain and sunshine, on all people. But one who is not His child through faith in Christ cannot pray to God as Father. Jesus' apparent unwillingness to answer the request of the Syrophoenician woman (Mt. 15:21-28 par. Mk. 7:24-30) was actually a means of pointing out the importance of a proper relationship with God.

*B. Aspects.* While some, by definition, limit prayer to petition (considering worship, thanksgiving, etc., under other categories), this article considers prayer in a broader sense. Prayer is basically of two kinds: (1) an expression of homage to God, and (2) an expression of a need. Both types properly lead to the glory of God. One aspect of prayer always relates to both major types: thanksgiving. As petition is the expression of dependence upon God for provision of needs, thanksgiving is the expression of gratitude to God for provision (past, present, or future). Thanksgiving honors God (type one) by contemplating fulfilled needs (type two).

Confession relates similarly to the divine glory and human need. In first-century Judaism to confess (Heb. *yāḏâ*) was to "give glory to God." Confession relates to sin and need, but it is also a sacrifice to God (Ps. 51:17 [MT 19]).

Several distinct, though overlapping, aspects of prayer may be identified.

*1. Worship.* In worship one is occupied solely with God, ascribing to Him all the virtues of His attributes and giving Him "the glory of [or "due"] his name" (Ps. 29:2). This is the occupation of heaven (Rev. 4–5).

*2. Praise.* In worship one is occupied with what God is, and in praise one considers what He has done. "Sing to him, sing praises to him, tell of all his wonderful works!" (Ps. 105:2).

*3. Thanksgiving.* This is close to praise, but as noted above, it involves the recollection of what God has done specifically for the one who gives thanks. Some of the offerings of the OT were thank offerings. During the revival under King Hezekiah long-neglected sacrifices were brought to God (2 Ch. 29:31-36). It is this aspect of prayer that is most closely connected with sacrifice (cf. Ps. 50:14, 23; 56:12 [MT 13]; 107:22; 116:17). In some cases it is difficult to tell whether prayer itself is considered a sacrifice. It is clearly so considered in Ps. 141:1f. (cf. He. 13:15f.; Rev. 5:8).

*4. Adoration.* This term is almost synonymous with worship. It introduces a more personal note, however, adding the element of love. "I love thee, O Lord, my strength" (Ps. 18:1 [MT 2]). "Whom have I in heaven but thee? And there is nothing upon earth that I desire besides thee" (Ps. 73:25).

*5. Devotion.* This is close to adoration but involves a sense of commitment or consecration. It is not prayer as such, but it issues in prayer or a vow (cf. 1 S. 1:11).

*6. Communion.* This word can describe the essence of prayer. It also can refer to the aspect of prayer that involves not only speaking to God but being aware of His presence and allowing Him through Scripture and by His Holy Spirit to impress the believer with His thoughts toward him. "When I thought, 'My foot slips,' thy steadfast love, O Lord, held me up. When the cares of my heart are many, thy consolations cheer my soul" (Ps. 94:18f.).

*7. Confession.* This can be either individual or corporate (1 S. 7:6; 2 Ch. 6:26-31; Ezr. 9:6-15; 10:1; Neh. 1:5-11; 9:1-37; Pss. 51; 130; Dnl. 9:3-19; Hos. 5:15; Mt. 6:12 par.). Confession is a prerequisite for approaching God in worship and prayer (cf. V.C.1 below).

*8. Petition or Supplication.* This is not to be considered less worthy than the other aspects of prayer mentioned above, for it is clearly encouraged in Scripture by invitation, commandment, and example. But petition should be accompanied by the above aspects and must always be offered for the glory of God. Many of the relevant passages have already been cited in this article. The most worthy petition is for the coming of God's kingdom and the spread of the gospel, that God's name may be honored throughout the earth.

*9. Intercession.* This is a petition or supplication on behalf of another person. A number of Scriptures have been cited in this regard also. Intercession is the present ministry of Christ at the right hand of God on mankind's behalf and is perhaps the greatest expression of love on the part of Christians for one another. It is also clear throughout Scripture that intercession should not be made only for those who are already believers (cf. V.E.9 below).

*C. Conditions.* A term other than "conditions" may be preferable, since the impression must not be given that prayer is efficacious only if certain things are done or, conversely, that if it is not efficacious one must only search for a breach of the conditions. A more biblical framing of the topic may involve listing the qualities that should mark the person who seeks God. The following are the characteristics, according to Scripture, of the "righteous" person whose prayer has "great power in its effects" (Jas. 5:16):

Moral purity (Ps. 66:18; Isa. 59:2b).

Sincerity; proper motives (Jas. 4:3).

Coming in the name of Christ (Jn. 16:23f.; cf. the comments on these verses in IV.A.3 above).

Faith, probably the most frequently mentioned condition of prayer. It is the petitioner's measure of confidence in God's ability and desire to answer prayer (Mt. 8:10 par. Lk. 7:9; Mt. 9:22 par. Mk. 5:34; Lk. 8:48; Mt. 9:29; 17:20 par. Lk. 17:5f.; cf. Mk. 9:29; Mt. 21:22 par. Mk. 11:24; Jas. 1:5-8; 5:15f.). God also honors faith on behalf of others (cf. Mt. 9:2-8 par. Mk. 2:2-12; Lk. 5:18-26).

Continuing intimate fellowship with Christ (Jn. 15:7; cf. v. 16).

Thanksgiving (Phil. 4:6).

In the Spirit (Eph. 6:18).

Obedience (1 Jn. 3:22; cf. Jn. 15:7).

Praying in God's will (1 Jn. 5:15; see IV.F above). In general, God's will can be known by studying the Scriptures, for they show what He has done and therefore what He is likely to desire in certain circumstances. The phrase that Jesus used in Gethsemane, "Not my will, but thine, be done" (Lk. 22:42 par.), should not, however, be wrongly employed to excuse one's lack of perception or of faith when one prays.

True knowledge of God and fidelity to His truth (Ps. 145:18; Jn. 4:24).

Good spiritual relationship between husband and wife (1 Pet. 3:7).

*D. Unanswered Prayer.* Believers of all ages have on occasion felt that God was not responding to their prayers; see Job 19:7; 30:20; Ps. 18:41 (MT 42); 44 (esp. vv. 17, 20, 23f. [MT 18, 21, 24f.]); 60:1-3 (MT 4-7); 79 (esp. vv. 1-5, 9f., 13); 80 (esp. vv. 4-6, 18 [MT 5-7, 19]); Isa. 40:27; Lam. 3:8. The very chapter in Hebrews that speaks of the triumphs of faith tells also of those who were tortured and killed and who "did not receive what was promised" (He. 11:35b-40). Paul's "thorn in the flesh" was not removed although he prayed for that three times (2 Cor. 12:7-9). Paul's experience is instructive. The answer to his request was not a mere No. God did answer by providing grace, and Paul learned that the "thorn" performed a necessary function, keeping him "from being too elated by the abundance of revelations" (v. 7).

Prayer is not mechanical or magical. It is an appeal to an infinitely wise, loving, and powerful heavenly Father. True prayer, i.e., that in accordance with the biblical teaching discussed in V.A-C above, is always heard by God. When no answer is apparent, it is probably appropriate to speak, not of unanswered prayer, but rather of an answer that is superior to the specific petition expressed, that is delayed by God for good reasons, or that takes a negative form because a positive answer would be inappropriate, second-best, or even harmful.

*E. Other Issues. 1. What Happens If One Asks for the Wrong Thing?* It can be assumed from Rom. 8:26f. that God will interpret prayer in accordance with the intent of the heart and His own infinitely superior knowledge. If one prays out of a wrong motive, however, or in opposition to the previously revealed will of God, God may grant the petition to one's own detriment (e.g., the extension of Hezekiah's life, in spite of God's word that he would die, during which time his evil son Manasseh was born, 2 K. 20:1-11; 21:1-9; cf. also Ps. 106:13-15).

*2. Should One "Wait on God" for an Extended Time?* Various Scriptures speak of waiting on God (e.g., Ps. 25:3, 5; 27:14; 33:20; 37:7, 9, 34; 40:1 [MT 2]; 62:1 [MT 2]; 69:6 [MT 7]; 104:27; 130:5f.; Isa. 40:31). Although "wait" can signify simple dependence on God, it is often used to describe the patient endurance of a person who is suffering or who is awaiting God's vindication and the bringing of justice in an evil world (cf. Lk. 18:1-8). It would be difficult to sustain the idea of a marathon of prayer, persisting until an answer comes, from these verses.

*3. Are There Times When One Should not Pray?* On occasion God has made His will known and should not be pressed in the matter. In addition to the Scriptures listed under V.E.1 above, see Ex. 14:15; Dt. 3:26; Josh. 7:10; Jer. 7:16.

*4. Is There a Preferable Time or Posture for Prayer?* Daniel prayed three times a day (Dnl. 6:10), a custom, as noted above, of Jewish people. Paul said that one should pray constantly (1 Thess. 5:17), i.e., not only at certain times and not merely at whim. "Seven times" in Ps. 119:164 means "frequently," though monastic movements have taken it literally and, combining it with the "midnight" prayer, have developed the eight daily offices. Jesus began praying early in the morning (Mk. 1:35) and, in one instance at least, prayed all night (Lk. 6:12). The heart can always be lifted to God, but a special uninterrupted time of quiet daily is also important.

People often prayed while standing, sometimes while kneeling, and occasionally while prostrate. Some of the OT passages that seem to describe standing may mean just that the person was "stationed" before the Lord. 1 K. 8:22 says that Solomon "stood before the altar of the Lord . . . and spread his hands towards heaven," but v. 54 says that, after he concluded, ". . . he arose from before the altar of the Lord, where he had knelt with hands outstretched toward heaven" (cf. 1 S. 1:26; Mt. 6:5; Lk. 18:11, 13). For other postures see Ezr. 9:5; Dnl. 6:10; Eph. 3:14 (kneeling); Gen. 24:26; Neh. 8:6 (bowing head); Josh. 7:6; Rev. 1:17 (prostrate); 1 K. 8:22, 54; Ps. 28:2; 1 Tim. 2:8 (uplifting hands); 2 S. 7:18 (sitting); 1 K. 18:42 (bowing, with face between knees). *See also* POSTURES. The posture for prayer is therefore optional but should be reverent and appropriate to the mood of the prayer.

*5. If God Is Sovereign and Has Foreknowledge, Why Should One Pray?* The accumulated commands and instances of prayer in the Bible leave no alternative to assuming that God invites prayer and responds to it. Presumably God foreknows whether someone is going to pray. It is His sovereign will that He chooses to answer prayer; this in no way compromises His sovereignty. In Mt. 6:7f. Jesus bases His teaching on prayer on the Father's foreknowledge. The reason for prayer, then, is not to inform God of one's needs. Rather, in prayer one expresses confidence in Him as the Father who will not give a stone to the child who needs bread (Mt. 7:9-11). Scripture does not suggest (except for the special case of 1 Jn. 5:16; cf. V.F above) refraining from prayer lest one pray unwittingly for what is not God's will. By becoming better acquainted with God's "ways" (Ex. 33:13; Ps. 25:4), one can pray more wisely. Moreover, the Scriptures, which contain God's revealed will, can be appropriated in prayer (cf. Acts 4:24-28).

*6. Does Prayer Change God, Circumstances, or Oneself?* Calvin (*Inst.* iii.20.3) and others stressed the effect of prayer on the petitioner. One of the greatest benefits of prayer is being changed by the act, but there are other effects. God Himself is affected in that He welcomes and responds to one's prayers. This is consistent with His revealed sovereign purpose and does not entail any unanticipated or unwelcome change on His part. God's "relenting" as a result of people's intercession (e.g., Ex. 32:14) is clearly a gracious act consistent with God's primary desire to bless His people. Prayer also issues in a change of circumstances, as is evident throughout Scripture.

*7. Does It Make a Difference If One Does Not Pray?* If prayer is never efficacious, then all the biblical teaching on it is hollow. Jas. 4:2 says, "You do not have, because you do not ask." Of course, God in His providence may bestow unrequested blessings.

*8. Is It Wrong to Repeat Petitions?* Jesus warns against piling up empty phrases (Mt. 6:7), i.e., against mechanically repeating prayer phraseology. On occasion the repetition of a prayer may also reflect a lack of confidence in God or may express impatience. Each new day presents a new circumstance or opportunity for God to work in response to one's prayers. This is perhaps especially the case when one intercedes for others. Certainly God welcomes faithful continuing prayers.

*9. Should One Pray for the Unconverted?* Since God "desires all men to be saved and to come to the knowledge of the truth" (1 Tim. 2:4), "not wishing that any should perish" (2 Pet. 3:9), prayers for the unconverted are certainly in accordance with His will.

*10. Is Any Subject Too Small to Bring to God in Prayer?* According to Paul (Phil. 4:6), Christians should pray about everything. Some subjects, however, may occupy one's mind to the displacement of matters that are more important for the kingdom of God and the honor of His great name.

*11. Should One "Wrestle with God?"* Jacob's experience at Peniel (Gen. 32:24-32) was unique, was initiated by the divine figure, and is never used as a model of prayer. The vivid image of "struggling" (*agōnizómenos*) in prayer (RSV "remembering . . ."; AV "labouring fervently"; NEB "[pray] hard") in Col. 4:12 does not imply conflict with God; the struggle is against any forces opposed to God.

*12. Is There an Advantage in Corporate Prayer?* Matthew 18:19, ". . . if two of you agree . . . it will be done . . . ," is in the context of church discipline, so that probably the two who agree are the witnesses to the offense (v. 16). Even if the principle expressed has an application beyond that circumstance, there is certainly no guarantee of an automatic answer simply because "two agree." On the other hand, corporate prayer is taught by example in Acts 1:14; 2:42; 4:24; 12:12. There is mutual encouragement to faith in corporate prayer, and God honors faith in prayer. Praying aloud in the hearing of another implies certain belief that God will answer, a commitment that may not be made as decisively in private.

***VI. Summary and Conclusion.***–Prayer in the Bible includes many kinds of communication with God, both articulate and inarticulate, corporate and private. The nature of prayer derives from the nature of God, who is an omniscient, omnipotent, sovereign, and loving heavenly Father. Prayer should be directed toward the enhancement of the name and reputation of God. When good is recognized as having resulted from prayer, God receives the glory, not man. When prayer that is made in the name of Christ is heard and answered, Christ is honored, as is the Father. Any genuine need for guidance, strength, healing, daily bread, growth in grace, or whatever, can be brought to God. Such petitions are answered not in a magical or mechanical way but in response to the faith of a person whose life and motives honor God.

***Bibliography.***–D. R. Ap-Thomas, *VT,* 6 (1956), 225-241; K. Barth, *CD,* esp. III/3, 264-288; III/4, 47-115; D. G. Bloesch, *Struggle of Prayer* (1980); G. A. Buttrick, *Prayer* (1942); D. Coggan, *Prayers of the NT* (1967); *DNTT,* II, 855-886; J. Ellul, *Prayer and Modern Man* (Eng. tr. 1967); F. L. Fisher, *Prayer in the NT* (1964); P. T. Forsyth, *The Soul of Prayer* (1966); O. F. M. Hammon, *Prayer in the NT* (1971); J. D. Hannah, *Prayer in the NT* (1971); *Bibliotheca Sacra,* 136 (1979), 344-353; J. Hastings, *Great Christian Doctrines: Prayer* (1915); A. J. Heschel, *Man's Quest for God* (1954); J. Jeremias, *Prayers of Jesus* (1967); W. B. Pope, *Prayers of St. Paul* (1896); R. L. Simpson, *Interpretation of Prayer in the Early Church* (1965); S. S. Smalley, *Nov.Test.,* 15 (1973), 59-71; W. Spear, *Theology of Prayer* (1979); *TDNT,* I, *s.v.* αἰτέω κτλ. (Stählin); II, *s.v.* δέομαι κτλ. (Greeven); ἐρωτάω κτλ. (Greeven); εὔχομαι κτλ. (Greeven); A. C. Wieand, *Prayer Life and Teachings of Jesus* (1932); G. P. Wiles, *Paul's Intercessory Prayers* (1974). See also the relevant Hebrew verbs in *TDOT* and in R. L. Harris, *et al.,* eds., *Theological Wordbook of the OT* (2 vols., 1980).

W. L. LIEFELD

**PRAYER, HOURS OF.** *See* HOUR(S) OF PRAYER.

**PRAYER, LORD'S.** *See* LORD'S PRAYER.

**PRAYER OF AZARIAH.** *See* SONG OF THE THREE YOUNG MEN.

**PRAYER OF JOSEPH.** *See* JOSEPH, PRAYER OF.

**PRAYER OF MANASSEH.** *See* MANASSEH, PRAYER OF.

**PRAYER OF NABONIDUS.** *See* DANIEL, BOOK OF VIII.B; NABONIDUS.

**PRAYER, PLACE OF** [Gk. *proseuchḗ* (Acts 16:13, 16)]. Every other use of Gk. *proseuchḗ* in the NT (thirty-five times, including seven in Acts) is translated "prayer." In Acts 16, however, where the text is debated (see below), most recent English versions render "place of prayer." The use of Gk. *proseuchḗ* for a place is first attested in Hellenistic Egypt and is regularly a Jewish term (*Papyrus de Magdola* 35.5 [3rd cent. B.C.]; *Tebtunis Papyrus* I, 86.18 [2nd cent. B.C.]; etc.). Later the word is often equivalent to "synagogue"; thus the synagogues in Rome were termed *proseuchaí* (J. B. Frey on *Corpus Inscriptionum Judaicarum,* no. 531 [p. 391]; cf. Juvenal *Satires* iii.296). In Acts, however, the term probably refers to an informal place or enclosure outside a city that lacked the ten Jewish men traditionally needed for a synagogue service. This lack may be implied by the reference to the assembled women. Not all *proseuchaí* were necessarily synagogues, and Luke may have used the word here to distinguish this meeting place from a regular synagogue, for which he always used Gk. *synagōgḗ*. (Cf. the temple as "house of *proseuchḗ* in Isa. 56:7, LXX, quoted in Mt. 21:13 par.; in rare instances the word is applied to a pagan shrine [*CIG,* 2079, of Olbia in Sarmatia], although Jewish influence has then been suspected.) (See M. Hengel, "Proseuche und Synagoge," in G. Jeremias, H.-W. Kuhn, and H. Stegemann, eds., *Tradition und Glaube* [*Festschrift* K. G. Kuhn, 1971], pp. 157-184.)

The "place of prayer" of Acts 16 was evidently beside the small river Gangites, which flows past the western edge of Philippi.

Although the essential meaning is little affected, the interpretation of Acts 16:13 is complicated by textual variations. The principal variants are: *enomízomen proseuchḗn* A corrector Ψ, cf. C (B *proseuchḗ*); *enomízeto proseuchḗ* E TR etc.; *enómizen proseuchḗn* ℵ ($p^{74}$ *proseuchḗ*); *edókei proseuchḗ* D Vulg. All these variants probably derive from two archetypes: (1) the traditional *enomízeto proseuchḗ,* "prayer was wont (to be made)" and (2) *enomízomen proseuchḗn,* "we supposed (there was) a place of prayer." The reading of D evidently arose from misconstruing *enomízeto* as "was supposed," and in the second group the accusative ending *n* may have dropped through influence of other texts or simply by omission of the horizontal stroke that often represented *n*. The balance of evidence appears to favor the second possible archetype. Although it has limited support in extant MSS, several uncials seem to preserve corrupt forms of it. (See B. M. Metzger, *Textual Comm. on the Greek NT* [1971], p. 447.)

C. J. HEMER

**PREACH** [Heb. hiphil of *nāṭap*] (Ezk. 20:46 [MT 21:2]; 21:2 [MT 7]; Am. 7:16; Mic. 2:6, 11); AV "drop (word)," PROPHESY; NEB "pour out words," "go drivelling on," RANT; [Gk. *euangelízomai*–'bring good news,' *proeuangelízomai* ("preach the gospel beforehand," Gal. 3:8), *kēryssō*–'proclaim,' *prokēryssō* ("preach before," Acts 13:24), *légō*–'say' (Mt. 23:3), *laléō*–'speak' (Mk. 2:2), *parrhēsiázomai* ("preach boldly," Acts 9:27, 29), etc.]; AV also PUBLISH, SAY, etc.; NEB also PROCLAIM, SAY, ANNOUNCE, etc.; **PREACHER** [Heb. *qōheleṯ*] (Eccl. 1:1f., 12; 7:27; 12:8-10); NEB SPEAKER; [hiphil part. of *nāṭap*] (Mic. 2:11); AV PROPHET; NEB RANTING; [Gk. part. of *kēryssō* (Rom. 10:14); *kēryx* (1 Tim. 2:7; 2 Tim. 1:11), *katangeleús*–'one who proclaims' (Acts 17:18)]; AV also SETTER FORTH; NEB PROPAGANDIST, "someone to spread the news," HERALD; **PREACHING** [Gk. *kḗrygma* (Mt. 12:41 par.; Rom. 16:25; 1 Cor. 1:21; 15:14; Tit. 1:3), *lógos*–'word, speech' (Acts 18:5; 1 Tim. 5:17; "preach the word," Acts 6:2), *paráklēsis*–'encouragement, exhortation' (1 Tim. 4:13), *rhēma*–'word, saying' (Rom. 10:17)]; AV also "spirit" (reading *pneúma* instead of *lógos,* Acts 18:5), WORD, EXHORTATION; NEB also PROCLAMATION, GOSPEL, etc. In some passages "preach" (Rom. 15:19; 2 Cor. 2:12) and "preaching" (Acts 6:2; 2 Cor. 8:18) represent no Greek term but are supplied contextually by the RSV. Public, authoritative proclamation.

- I. In the OT
  - A. The Root *nṭp*
  - B. *Qōheleṯ*
- II. In the NT
  - A. *Euangelízomai* and Minor Terms
  - B. *Kēryssō* and Related Terms
    1. Current Approaches
    2. Extrabiblical Literature
    3. The Preacher
    4. The Message

***I. In the OT.***–The RSV OT uses "preach" or "preacher" only to render the hiphil of *nāṭap* (in Ezekiel, Amos, and Micah) and *qōheleṯ* (in Ecclesiastes). The AV occasionally uses "preach" to translate the piel of *bāśar* (RSV "tell the glad news," Ps. 40:9 [MT 10]; "bring good tidings," Isa. 61:1; *see also* GOOD NEWS) and *qārā* (RSV "proclaim," Neh. 6:7; Jonah 3:2; cf. *qᵉrîʾâ,* Jonah 3:2; AV "preaching"; RSV "message").

*A. The Root* nṭp. This root occurs in the OT nine times in the qal form, each time with the meaning "drip" (whether of rain, myrrh, wine, or honey; in Job 29:22 it is metaphorically applied to Job's words, which are compared to the welcome spring rains [v. 23]). The same root occurs nine times in the hiphil form. In Am. 9:13 it means simply "drip" or possibly "let drip," referring to wine (cf. qal, Joel 3:18 [MT 4:18]); but in the other eight occurrences it clearly refers to an act of speech, usually (apart from Mic. 2:11) in synonymous parallelism with "prophesy." Thus the RSV renders it "preach." The use of the verb root in Job 29:22 may suggest that here also it denotes a "dripping" of words. Equally plausible is H. W. Wolff's suggestion (p. 315) that the verb describes impassioned speech by a vivid reference to the accompanying spray of saliva from the speaker's mouth (cf. the English expression "spewing forth"). In any case, this use of *nāṭap* has a range in tone similar to that of Eng. "preach"; e.g., while in Ezk. 20:46; 21:2 (MT 21:2, 7) it refers to speech commanded by the Lord, the tone is just as clearly pejorative in Mic. 2:6, 11 (contra Allen, pp. 294f. n. 57; cf. NEB "rant," "ranting") and possibly in Am. 7:16 (NEB "drivelling on"; cf. Zimmerli, p. 422).

*B.* Qōheleṯ. This term occurs seven times in the OT, all in Ecclesiastes (1:1f., 12; 7:27; 12:8-10), and is traditionally, though somewhat doubtfully, translated "the Preacher" (NEB "the Speaker"). The term is a qal fem. part. of the common root *qhl* ("assemble") — which is curious both because it is feminine and because the verb is elsewhere unattested in the qal. Some have argued plausibly that *qōheleṯ* is the title of a functionary, perhaps best rendered "the Assembler" or "the Gatherer" (see Gordis, pp. 203f.; but Whitley [pp. 4-6] has suggested "the Sceptic"). Kidner (p. 13) has pointed out that, while *qōheleṯ* may refer to the "gathering" of a congregation of people (hence LXX *Ekklēsiastḗs*), the book's climactic passage (12:9-12) suggests that it may instead refer to the "gathering" of wise sayings, so impressively exemplified in the book of Ecclesiastes.

*II. In the NT.*–Of the fourteen Greek terms translated "preach," "preacher," or "preaching" by the RSV, by far the most characteristic are the four members of the *kēr͂yssō* word group (seventy-two times) and the two members of the *euangelízō* word group (forty-two times). The last fifty years have seen a growing scholarly consensus (acknowledged also in the more recent popular manuals; cf. J. E. Adams, *Preaching With Purpose* [1982], pp. 5f.) that "preach" is somewhat infelicitous as a rendering for these two word groups. "Preach" accurately conveys the typically public and authoritative character of the various speech acts intended by these Greek terms; but it is a misleading translation to the extent that common English parlance uses "preach" to refer to formal sermonizing directed to the faithful, while the NT uses both *kēr͂yssō* and *euangelízomai* to refer primarily (though not exclusively) to evangelistic activity directed to non-Christians.

*A.* Euangelízomai *and Minor Terms.* The verb *euangelízomai* is derived from *ángelos* ("messenger") or *angéllō* ("announce"); the prefix *eu-* indicates that what is announced is *good* news that brings joy. The RSV renders it by a variety of words and phrases, including "preach" (e.g., Acts 5:42; 1 Cor. 9:18), "preach the gospel" (e.g., Lk. 9:6; Rom. 1:15), "preach the good news" (e.g., Acts 8:12; Rom. 10:15), and "bring good news" (e.g., Lk. 1:19; 2:10); *see* GOOD NEWS. *Euangelízomai* appears most frequently in the Lukan and Pauline writings. Although *euangelízomai* and *kerýssō* have somewhat different nuances (*euangelízomai* usually emphasizing that it is the good news of divine salvation that is being preached), the two terms are often used synonymously to describe the authoritative proclamation of the divine message (see II.B.4 below). For a more thorough study of *euangelízomai* (and the noun *euangélion,* "good news, gospel"), *see* GOSPEL; see also *DNTT,* II, 107-114; *TDNT,* II, 707-721.

The RSV occasionally uses "preach," "preacher," and "preaching" to render a variety of more general Greek terms for speech, presumably to convey the authoritative and public character of the speech acts in these passages. In most of these instances the RSV departs from the practice of the AV. For example, *légō* (usually "say") in Mt. 23:3 is rendered "preach" by the RSV but "say" by the AV and NEB. *Laléō* (usually "speak"), on the other hand, is rendered "preach" by both the AV and RSV of Mk. 2:2. In several passages the RSV uses "preaching" to translate the nouns *lógos* (cognate of *légō*) and *rhēma,* both of which are usually translated "word." *Katangeleús,* which occurs only in Acts 17:18 (RSV "preacher"; AV "setter forth"; NEB "propagandist"), is derived from the verb *katangéllō,* "proclaim." (See also heading.)

*B.* Kēr͂yssō *and Related Terms.* The RSV characteristically translates the *kēr͂yssō* word group by various appropriate forms of "preach," although it occasionally uses other terms. It usually renders *kēr͂yssō* itself "preach" (forty-nine times; cf. also the one occurrence of *prokēr͂yssō* in Acts 13:24), but it also uses "proclaim" (ten times; e.g., Mt. 10:27; Mk. 5:20; 7:36; Lk. 4:18f.) and "talk" (Mk. 1:45). It renders *kēryx* twice as "preacher" and once as "herald" (2 Pet. 2:5). For *kērygma* it uses "preaching" five times, "message" twice (1 Cor. 2:4; 2 Tim. 4:17), and "what one preaches" once (1 Cor. 1:21).

*1. Current Approaches. a. Existentialist Interpretation.* Analysis of the *kēr͂yssō* word group, which is so determinative for the NT concept of preaching, has been complicated in modern times by the regrettable practice of using "kerygma" as a technical term of twentieth-century biblical theology. Certain existentialist theologians (esp. Bultmann and his school) have posited a radical dichotomy between the Jesus of actual history and the "kerygmatic Christ" who confronts people through the message (kerygma) of the early Church. This use of "kerygma" can give the unwary reader the misimpression that the anglicized Greek term preserves the original NT meaning, and hence that the preaching (*kērygma*) of the earliest Christians was not concerned with historical facts. For a critical analysis of this specialized usage of "kerygma," see *DNTT,* III, 57-60.

*b. C. H. Dodd.* The publication of C. H. Dodd's seminal work, *Apostolic Preaching and Its Developments* (1936), marked a turning point in the modern treatment of *kēr͂yssō* and its cognates. With surprisingly modest argumentation Dodd seemed at first to win the day for two crucial propositions. For convenience these are treated here in reverse order.

Dodd's second thesis was that an analysis of the NT writings yielded a discernible pattern underlying the primitive apostolic proclamation to unbelievers (the "kerygma") — a pattern that followed a six-point outline: (1) The age of fulfillment has arrived. (2) This has occurred through the ministry, death, and resurrection of Christ. (3) In His resurrection Christ was exalted to the right hand of God as messianic head of the new Israel. (4) The Holy Spirit in the Church is the evidence of Christ's present power and glory. (5) The messianic age will be consummated shortly in the return of Christ. (6) The kerygma always closes with the message of repentance, forgiveness of sins, the promise of the Holy Spirit, and eternal life for those who enter the "elect community." (See Dodd, pp. 21-24.)

A half century of almost relentless analysis and criticism seems to have left Dodd's thesis in shambles. M. Green (pp. 60f.) cites a parade of modern scholars who have replaced Dodd's original six-point outline with outlines varying from three points to seven — each scholar equally convinced of having at last recovered the earliest kerygma. The cumulative effect of their varying outlines is to discredit the entire enterprise as overly optimistic. More recent scholars generally prefer to speak not of a primitive "kerygma" but rather of "kerygmata" — plural because of the now-established pluriformity and diversity of the early Church's message, though that message everywhere finds its center in Jesus Christ. (*See also* KERYGMA.)

Dodd's first thesis was that "the NT writers draw a distinction between preaching and teaching. . . . Teaching (*didaskein*) is in a large majority of cases ethical instruction. . . . Preaching, on the other hand, is the public proclamation of Christianity to the non-Christian world" (p. 7). Accordingly, Dodd distinguished preaching from teaching both by its content and by its audience, with the latter distinction ("preaching" being aimed at non-Christians) posing the sharpest possible contrast with modern day preaching — at least as perceived from the pew!

This thesis, too, has had its share of detractors. Numerous scholars have pointed out that Dodd's rigid distinction between preaching and teaching is simply not honored in the NT (nor in the LXX). R. Mounce (pp. 40ff.), e.g., cites various parallel passages in the Synoptic Gospels to demonstrate that what one Gospel terms "preaching" the others will at times term "teaching" (e.g., cf. Mt. 4:23 with Mk. 1:39; Lk. 4:44). Perhaps more compelling is the observation that even within a single Gospel the same activity can be referred to both as "teaching" (Mk. 1:21) and as "preaching" (v. 38).

This evidence can be accommodated, however, if Dodd's thesis is modified to allow for the well-established broad semantic range of *didáskō* in the NT (*see* TEACH). Thus in the NT "teaching" can include "preaching" without these terms being considered merely synonymous. In support of Dodd, it remains striking that in the vast majority of cases (though not every case, contra Dodd) "preaching" in the NT is, in fact, directed to unbelievers.

(See also *DNTT*, III, 60-67; McDonald.)

2. *Extrabiblical Literature*. G. Friedrich (*TDNT*, III, 683-694) has amassed an impressive sampling of evidence to help establish the classical and Hellenistic background for the *kērýssō* word group. The following selective arrangement of that evidence departs somewhat from Friedrich's by placing greater emphasis on *kērýssō*'s distinctly political usage as over against its cultic or philosophical usage. Although superficial parallels can be found between Christianity and the Hellenistic religions or Stoic philosophy, the organizing rubric for the NT's usage of these terms (esp. in the teaching of Jesus) lies clearly in the political sphere, i.e., "preaching the kingdom of God."

Two distinct uses of this word group are readily apparent from the classical and Hellenistic evidence: each of these is attested in biblical usage.

In its broadest and most general (though not the most common) use, *kērýssō* describes the making of a loud, attention-getting noise or of a public oral announcement; hence it can simply be translated "proclaim." A biblical example occurs in Zeph. 3:14, LXX, where Israel is enjoined to "shout aloud" (*kērýssō*) its joyful praise to the Lord (cf. also Ex. 32:5; Hos. 5:8; Joel 2:1; Zec. 9:9; Rev. 5:2).

Far more common is the narrower use of *kērýssō* to refer specifically to the proclaiming of a *kḗryx* ("herald" or "preacher"), i.e., one who speaks as a representative of another. The party represented might be a private individual, in which case the "preacher" was frequently the ancient equivalent of an auctioneer. Or the party represented might be an official of a court, a temple, the Areopagus, or even a deity, as in the case of the Stoic philosophers (cf. Epictetus *Dissertationes* iii.22.69). Interestingly, the noun *kḗryx* occurs in the NT much less frequently than the verb. M. Green (p. 292, n. 98) has suggested that, given the superficial similarities between the early Christians and these self-styled emissaries of the pagan gods who left home, possessions, and family (*Dissertationes* iii.22.46ff.) to bring a supposed divine revelation (iii.1.36ff.) offering a peace purported to surpass even the *pax Romana* (iii.13.9f.), it is not surprising that the NT authors show restraint in appropriating the noun *kḗryx*: presumably they wished to avoid these unwelcome associations.

Typically, however, the party represented was the king himself (esp. in the Homeric period) or, later, the state. While modern scholars have drawn attention to the great variety of menial tasks performed by these "preachers" as members of the royal court — e.g., mixing wine or preparing a bath (cf. *TDNT*, III, 684) — these activities were clearly peripheral to their "preaching."

Acting in his official capacity as an envoy of the king, and so bearing the official insignia of the king, the *kḗryx* was granted the inviolable status of the king he represented. To reject him was to reject the king who commissioned him; to harm him was to harm the king and, worse, to incur the wrath of the gods (cf. Demosthenes *Orationes* xii.4). In contrast to the ambassador (*présbys*), who had the authority to engage in negotiations without explicit instructions, the *kḗryx* was required simply to deliver any message exactly as it was given to him and to return at once (*TDNT*, III, 688).

The Bible offers numerous instances of this more narrow use of the *kērýssō* word group (cf., e.g., LXX Ex. 36:6; 2 K. 10:20; 2 Ch. 36:22; Dnl. 5:29). Yet (apart from Jonah) these occurrences are notably lacking where one would most expect to find them, namely, in descriptions of the prophets as spokesmen for their Lord. To explain this surprising absence, proper account must be given to a third usage of these terms attested in the extrabiblical sources.

The third use of the *kērýssō* word group is really just a special development of the second; but because it refers to the work that made the herald most vital to the state and lent his office its greatest dignity, this special use should not be uncritically lumped with the more general description treated above. Expressed most simply by the tenth-century A.D. Greek lexicographer Suidas, "a herald [*kḗryx*] is in time of war what an ambassador [*présbys*] is in peace." Suidas was referring to the Greek practice of sending a *kḗryx* into enemy territory ahead of an advancing army to warn the enemy of certain destruction unless they accepted the proffered terms for peace. In this situation the *kḗryx* was empowered either to accept surrender on behalf of his king or to declare war if those terms were rejected.

This practice, designed to avoid conflict, is attested throughout the ancient world; cf. Dt. 20:10: "When you draw near to a city to fight against it, offer terms of peace to it" (Josephus rendered the last phrase "send an embassy with heralds [*kḗrykes*]," *Ant*. iv.7.41 [296]; cf. also the *kḗryx* sent by Neco to warn Josiah in x.5.1 [75]). What was new with the Greeks was their practice of choosing for this obviously dangerous job people who were otherwise relative nobodies and were therefore considerably more dispensable than, e.g., the Tartan, the Rabsaris, the Rabshakeh sent by the Assyrians (2 K. 18:17)! Julius Pollux (*Onomasticum* vi.128) can therefore list heralds alongside brothel keepers and other wastrels. This by no means implies, however, that harm to such a *kḗryx* would be taken lightly by his king. The swift and fierce retribution incurred by such acts was more than sufficient to establish the seriousness with which the herald's diplomatic immunity was held and so to inspire almost unimaginable feats of courage among their ranks.

A striking example of this kind of outraged response to the murder of a *kḗryx* occurs in Plutarch *Pericles* 30, which describes how Pericles's *kḗryx* Anthemocritus was murdered by the rival city state of Megara, and how this atrocity resulted in an Athenian decree of irreconcilable and implacable enmity between the Athenians and the Megarians. (For another vivid example, see Herodotus vii.131ff.; cf. also Rengstorf, pp. 106-121.)

Examples of singular bravery among the "preachers" of Greece are plentiful. Thucydides i.29, e.g., relates an incident in which seventy-five Corinthian ships, boarding some two thousand hoplites, set sail to wage war against the Corcyraeans. Incredibly, when their fleet reached Actium "the Corcyraeans had sent out a *kḗryx* in a dinghy to forbid their advance"! When the *kḗryx* returned, having failed to secure peace, the Corcyraeans' amusing strategy had bought them sufficient time to prepare for their ultimately victorious counteroffensive.

3. *The Preacher. a. Among the Prophets.* Against this background, it is not surprising that the LXX (and NT; cf. Mt. 12:41) uses *kērýssō* for none of the OT prophets except Jonah; for of the prophets, Jonah alone was commissioned to bring the demand of unconditional surrender into non-Israelite territory ahead of his Lord's advancing armies. With similar import the NT describes Noah as a "herald" to the hostile world of his day as it awaited the approaching judgment of God (2 Pet. 2:5).

When the NT describes John the Baptist's ministry and later that of Jesus as "preaching [*kērýssō*] . . . 'Repent, for the kingdom of heaven is at hand'" (Mt. 3:1f.; 4:17), it depicts their preaching as a dire warning, marking a drastic change from the OT period when Israel had not yet fully become "enemy territory" (as Nineveh was for Jonah). The "prophetic lawsuit" (*rîḇ*) had reached its dreaded final stage. This interpretation is supported by J. R. Michaels's observation (p. 23) that John's use of baptism — paralleling proselyte baptism — reduced even the most religious "son of Abraham" to the level of an outsider needing the ritual of initiation into Israel.

*b. Authority.* Like the Greek heralds or "preachers," Jesus' preachers possessed no special inherent stature in the eyes of the world (cf. 1 Cor. 1:20-29, esp. v. 26: "not many of you were wise according to worldly standards, not many were powerful, not many were of noble birth"). But when Jesus commissioned His disciples to preach the kingdom (Mt. 10), He invested them with His own authority and the inviolable status of the King of kings they would represent. Distinguishing them with the unmistakable insignia of their Lord — His servant attitude and miracle working power (vv. 8-10), Jesus sent them to proclaim the dire warning and promise, "the kingdom of heaven is at hand" (v. 7). Though He sent them as "sheep among wolves" with the warning that persecution awaited them (vv. 16-39), He comforted them with the promise that "he who receives you receives me" (v. 40), and that "it will be more bearable for Sodom and Gomorrah on the day of judgment than for [the town that rejects them]" (vv. 14f.; cf. also 2 Cor. 5:20).

*c. The "Preacherhood" of All Believers.* While it is true that preachers are not self-appointed ("how can they preach unless they are sent?" Rom. 10:15), it should be noted that Jesus commissioned not merely the Twelve but also the rank and file of His disciples to preach the kingdom of God (cf. the extensive parallels between Mt. 10 and Lk. 10, though the latter lacks the term *kēryssō*). Likewise, in Luke's account of the "Great Commission" (that "repentance and forgiveness of sins should be preached in his name to all nations," Lk. 24:47) Jesus' immediate audience included other disciples (e.g., Cleopas and his unnamed companion; cf. also v. 33) in addition to the apostles.

Acts 8:1-4 stresses that it was not the apostles (v. 1) but all the other believers in Jerusalem who "were scattered" and so "went about preaching the word" (v. 4). Since v. 3 specifically mentions that women were included among the believers who were persecuted, the text does not warrant an interpretation that excludes women from those who fled Jerusalem and "went about preaching the word." Here as elsewhere the NT upholds the principle of the "preacherhood of all believers."

It is therefore not surprising that "preachers" and "preaching" are conspicuously absent from the various lists of offices and gifts in the NT (Rom. 12:6-8; 1 Cor. 12:8-10, 28-30; Eph. 4:11; 1 Pet. 4:10f.). The call to preach is not reserved for some elite few among Jesus' followers or for those with special abilities in public speaking. It is the duty and privilege of every believer — for all who would not be ashamed of Jesus and His words (Mk. 8:38).

(For a discussion of the larger question of the role of women in the Church, *see* WOMAN.)

*4. The Message.* The pervasive NT practice of associating "preaching" specifically with the "kingdom of God/heaven" (e.g., Mt. 4:23; 10:7; Acts 20:25; 28:31) makes sense when preachers are understood as envoys sent into enemy territory ahead of their kingdom's approaching armies, bearing their Lord's terms for peace. Likewise, it is not surprising that the message is so often focused on the summons to "repent" (e.g., Mt. 3:1f. par.; 4:17 par.; Mk. 6:12), with the ultimatum to count the cost of discipleship (cf. Lk. 14:25-33; indeed, discipleship costs the surrender of all to Christ, but the alternative of judgment is unaffordable).

But because Jesus' coming means not merely a threat of well-deserved judgment but most of all a promise to set free those tyrannized by the guilt of sin, the message preached can also be characterized more fully as "the gospel of the kingdom" (cf. *kēryssō tó euangélion tḗs basileías*, Mt. 4:23; 9:35; 24:14). Accordingly, *kēryssō* often has merely *euangélion* ("good news" or "gospel") for its content (Mt. 26:13; Mk. 1:14; 13:10; 14:9; Lk. 8:1; Gal. 2:2; Col. 1:23; 1 Thess. 2:9); cf. the parallels between "preach [*kēryssō*] the word" and "do the work of an evangelist [*euangelistḗs*]" in 2 Tim. 4:2, 5, and between "do all for the sake of the gospel" and "preach" in 1 Cor. 9:23, 27. Reflecting the same emphasis on the good news that is preached, the NT frequently uses *euangelízomai* interchangeably with *kēryssō* in descriptions of the same speech acts (e.g., cf. Lk. 4:43 and 9:6 [*euangelízomai*] with parallels in Mk. 1:38 and 6:12 [*kēryssō*]). Other passages characterize the content of the preaching (*kēryssō* or *kḗrygma*) as "Jesus Christ" (2 Cor. 1:19; 11:4; Phil. 1:15; 1 Tim. 3:16) or Christ's death and resurrection (1 Cor. 1:23; 15:12, 14). It is through the preaching of the crucified and risen Christ that salvation is made available to all who believe the good news (cf. Acts 10:39-42; Rom. 10:14; etc.).

The AV of 1 Cor. 1:21 ("it pleased God by the foolishness of preaching to save them that believe") has at times been misconstrued to mean that Paul was denigrating the act of preaching as foolishness. Such an interpretation may seem to gain support from Paul's admission that his own preaching appeared unimpressive since he lacked eloquence and was with them "in weakness and in much fear and trembling" (2:1-5); but since the Greek word for "preaching" here is not the verb but the noun *kḗrygma* (cf. RSV "what we preach"), Paul's main point is that it is the message (not the method) that appears to be "foolishness" — "to those who are perishing" (v. 18).

*See also* KINGDOM OF GOD V; PROCLAIM.

***Bibliography.–OT:*** L. C. Allen, *Books of Joel, Obadiah, Jonah, and Micah* (*NICOT*, 1976); R. Gordis, *Koheleth — The Man and His World* (repr. 1978); D. Kidner, *A Time to Mourn, and a Time to Dance* (1976); C. F. Whitley, *Koheleth* (1979); H. W. Wolff, *Joel and Amos* (Eng. tr., *Hermeneia*, 1977); W. Zimmerli, *Ezekiel*, I (Eng. tr., *Hermeneia*, 1979).

*NT:* W. Baird, *JBL*, 76 (1957), 181-191; E. P. Clowney, *Preaching and Biblical Theology* (1961); *DNTT*, III, 48-68; C. H. Dodd, *Apostolic Preaching and Its Developments* (1936, repr. 1962); C. A. Evans, *JETS*, 24 (1981), 315-322; K. Goldammer, *ZNW*, 48 (1957), 77-101; M. Green, *Evangelism in the Early Church* (1970); J. I. H. McDonald, *Kerygma and Didache* (1980); J. R. Michaels, *Servant and Son* (1981); C. F. D. Moule, in O. Böcher and K. Haacker, eds., *Verborum Veritas* (*Festschrift* G. Stählin 1970), pp. 15-26; R. H. Mounce, *Essential Nature of NT Preaching* (1960); K. H. Rengstorf, "Die Stadt der Mörder," in W. Eltester, ed., *Judentum, Urchristentum, Kirche* (1960), pp. 106-121; J. R. Stott, *Preacher's Portrait* (1961); R. C. Worley, *Preaching and Teaching in the Earliest Church* (1967).

G. P. HUGENBERGER

**PRECEPT** [Heb. *piqqûḏ*, *ṣaw* (Isa. 28:10, 13), *leqaḥ* (Prov. 4:2), *miṣwâ*–'command' (Jer. 35:8); Gk. *éntalma* (Mt. 15:9 par. Mk. 7:7; Col. 2:22), *dikaíōma* (Rom. 2:26)]; AV also STATUTE (Ps. 19:8 [MT 9]), COMMANDMENT (Ps. 111:7; Mt. 15:9; Mk. 7:7; Col. 2:22), DOCTRINE (Prov. 4:2), "righteousness" (Rom. 2:26); NEB also COMMANDMENT (Mt. 15:9; Mk. 7:7), INJUNCTION (Col. 2:22), INSTRUCTION (Jer. 35:8), "learning" (Prov. 4:2), "harsh cries and raucous shouts" (Isa. 28:10, 13). A command, usually a divine injunction setting forth human obligations.

Hebrew *piqqûḏ* (only in the pl.; < *pqd*, "visit," "appoint"; cf. Ugar. *pqd*, "give orders"; Akk. *paqādu*, "entrust," "supervise," "appoint") occurs most often in Ps. 119 (twenty-one times; vv. 4, 15, 27, etc.). This Psalm, a paean for the Torah, uses several similar terms that all relate to the law (see R. Girdlestone, *Synonyms of the OT* [2nd ed. 1897; repr. 1976], pp. 208-210; cf. *THAT*, II, *s.v.* פקד [W. Schottroff]). Heb. *leqaḥ* is from *lāqaḥ*, "take, receive," and thus means that which is received, i.e., instruction, in Prov. 4:2 (cf. W. McKane, *Proverbs* [*OTL*, 1970], pp. 265f., 303f., who defined it as the "appropriation of the tradition"). In Jer. 35:18 the common Hebrew word for commandment, *miṣwâ*, occurs twice and the related verb *ṣāwâ* once. Many of the modern versions fail to convey this repetition so characteristic of Semitic languages and translate *miṣwâ* "precept" as well as "commandment," perhaps for variety's sake (cf. NAB and NASB).

Isaiah 28:10, 13 are difficult verses; the repetition of *ṣaw* and *qaw* has been variously interpreted. By translating *ṣaw* "precept" the RSV and AV indicate a relation to *ṣāwâ* and *miṣwâ*, but this is doubtful. More likely is the NEB's "harsh cries and raucous shouts," a paraphrase based on the assumption that Isaiah is trying to convey the incoherent sounds of a drunken man (cf. vv. 7f.; see F. I. Andersen and D. N. Freedman, *Hosea* [*AB*, 1980], pp. 409f., who derived *ṣaw* from *ṣw'*, a root meaning "stink," hence "filth [of drunkenness]," i.e., vomit). Another interpretation with some merit has been advocated by, e.g., O. Kaiser (*Isaiah 13–39* [Eng. tr., *OTL*, 1974], pp. 245f.), J. Lindblom (*Prophecy in Ancient Israel* [repr. 1973], p. 201), and R. Clements (*Isaiah 1–39* [*NCBC*, 1980], p. 228), who have seen here Isaiah's enemies mocking his preaching by comparing it to a teacher's "prattling" to little children, perhaps a recital of the alphabet (but cf. the criticisms in G. R. Driver, "'Another Little Drink' — Isaiah 28:1-23," in P. R. Ackroyd and B. Lindars, eds., *Words and Meanings* [*Festschrift* for D. W. Thomas, 1968], pp. 53-56; Driver argued for the sense of the NEB).

In the NT Gk. *éntalma* occurs only three times, always meaning human precepts. Mt. 15:9 par. Mk. 7:7 is a slightly modified quotation of Isa. 29:13, LXX, which Jesus used to denounce the hypocritical Pharisees and scribes. Several commentators have pointed out that Col. 2:22 also alludes to Isa. 29:13 (T. Abbott [*ICC*, 1905], p. 275; E. Lohse [Eng. tr., *Hermeneia*, 1971], p. 124; R. Martin [*NCBC*, 1973; repr. 1981], p. 97). According to C. K. Barrett *Epistle to the Romans* [*HNTC*, 1957], p. 58) Gk. *dikaíōma* (< *dikaióō*, "be righteous"; cf. AV) in Rom. 2:26 means "righteous requirements . . . that which the law requires if a man is to be righteous with God." E. Käsemann (*Comm. on Romans* [Eng. tr., 1980], p. 73) saw here a more general reference to the "whole Torah . . . defined by legal statements."

G. A. L.

**PRECINCT** [Heb. *parwār*] (2 K. 23:11); AV SUBURB; NEB COLONNADE. The meaning of Heb. *parwār* is uncertain. Although scholars have suggested various Persian cognates (e.g., M. Ellenbogen, *Foreign Words in the OT* [1962], pp. 137f., suggested Old Pers. *paruva*, "before"), none is convincing. The NEB may rest its translation on the supposed Persian cognate *frabada*, "court, open pavilion," but this term can hardly be cognate with Heb. *parwār* (hence the conjecture, based on some MSS, of *parbāḏ*; cf. KoB, p. 776). *Parwār* is usually equated with the equally obscure *parbār* (1 Ch. 26:18; *see* PARBAR), which in a Lydian Aramaic inscription apparently means "vestibule" (cf. *KAI*, II, 306f.). Some scholars have attempted to link *parbār* (and thus *parwār*) to Sum. E-barbar, "shining house," used of the sun temple in ancient Mesopotamia and thus quite appropriate to the context of 2 K. 23 (cf. also LXX *pharourím*). Another possible cognate is Egyp. *pr wr*, "great house." Despite the links that these last two possibilities might have with *parwār*, neither seems to meet the sense required or to explain the later meanings of the word. *Parwār* is perhaps best understood as "court" or "courtyard," a meaning that both fits the context and corresponds to the later mishnaic and targumic sense.

See also J. Gray, *I & II Kings* (2nd ed., *OTL*, 1970).

G. A. L.

**PRECIOUS** [Heb. *yāqar* ("be precious," 1 S. 26:21; 2 K. 1:13f.; Ps. 72:14; 139:17; Isa. 43:4), *yāqār* (Job 28:16; Ps. 36:7 [MT 8]; 116:15; Prov. 1:13; 3:15; 12:27; 24:4; Isa. 28:16; Jer. 15:19; Lam. 4:2), *yᵉqār* (Prov. 20:15; "precious thing," Job 28:10; Ezk. 22:25), *ḥāmaḏ*–'to desire' (niphal, Prov. 21:20), *ḥemdâ* (2 Ch. 36:10; Dnl. 11:8; Nah. 2:9 [MT 10]; "precious thing," Hos. 13:15), *ḥᵃmûḏâ* (2 Ch. 20:25; Ezr. 8:27; "precious thing," Dnl. 11:43), *maḥmāḏ* (2 Ch. 36:19; "precious thing," Lam. 1:10; Hos. 9:6), *maḥmōḏ* (Lam. 1:7), *ṭôḇ*–'good' (Ps. 133:2; Eccl. 7:1; 2 K. 20:13 par. Isa. 39:2), *migdānâ* ("precious gifts," 2 Ch. 32:23), *tôʿāpâ* (Job 22:25), *ṣāpûn* (Ezk. 7:22), *meḵer* (Prov. 31:10), *gāḏal*–'become great' ("be precious," 1 S. 26:24); Gk. *timḗ*–'honor' (1 Pet. 2:7), *tímios* (Acts 20:24; Jas. 5:7; 1 Pet. 1:19; 2 Pet. 1:4), *polýtimos* (1 Pet. 1:7), *polytelḗs* ("very precious," 1 Pet. 3:4), *éntimos* (1 Pet. 2:4, 6)]; AV also GOODLY, DEAR, "plenty," etc.; NEB also CHOICEST, HIGH VALUE, NOBLE, etc.

Two passages are problematic. In Prov. 12:27b the MT syntax is difficult (lit. "wealth of a man precious diligent"); thus *BHS* suggested rearranging the text to read "precious is the wealth of a diligent man" (cf. RSV, AV). In Hos. 9:6 the MT is obscure. The RSV offers perhaps the most sensible reading (cf. AV). The NEB emends the text substantially in an effort to make sense of it; unfortunately there is little support for the emendation. See the comms., esp. F. I. Andersen and D. N. Freedman (*AB*, 1980), p. 531.

Something is considered precious when it has either intrinsic value or is desirable and rare; some items combine the two ideas. The produce of the earth is counted precious because of its deliciousness and its life-giving value (Jas. 5:7; cf. AV, NEB, Dt. 33:13-16). Good oil is called "precious" (RSV) or "fragrant" (NEB) in 2 K. 20:13; Ps. 133:2; Isa. 39:2. The wisdom school finds wisdom (Prov. 3:15) and a good wife (31:10) "more precious than jewels." Jewels are frequently called precious stones; *see* STONES, PRECIOUS. The vessels of the temple were considered precious because of their metals, their uniqueness, and their holiness. Consequently a conquering king sought them first as his prize spoil (2 Ch. 36:10; Lam. 1:10).

Words are cheap, but if uttered correctly they become precious and health giving (Jer. 15:19). This is especially true of God's word. During the days of Eli the word of God was called precious (1 S. 3:1, AV; Heb. *yāqār*; RSV "rare") because there was no message from Him through a prophet. God's thoughts are viewed as precious because of their inexhaustible wonder (Ps. 139:17). Peter called His promises precious, for through them believers partake of the divine nature (2 Pet. 1:4).

Life is considered to be precious, no doubt because of its intrinsic value (Ps. 72:14). The value placed on the person makes his redemption from death very costly (Ps. 49:8); no man can pay it. David spared the life of his enemy Saul because he valued it, even though he had ample opportunity to kill him (1 S. 26:24). Yahweh watches His people, especially the poor, and their life is precious to Him (Isa. 43:4); also precious is the death of His "saints" (Ps. 116:15). The value of God's people resides in their obedience to and worship of Him; they are "worth their weight in fine gold" (Lam. 4:2). But when they rebel against Him and are punished in captivity, their worth is compared to earthen pots (v. 2).

God's work of salvation is particularly regarded as precious. Jesus becomes the precious CORNERSTONE (Isa. 28:16; 1 Pet. 2:6). People have rejected Him, but God, seeing His value, has chosen Him and accepted His life of obedience (1 Pet. 2:4). Those who believe this also value Jesus Himself as precious, for He paid the costly price of their redemption by giving His precious blood (1:19). Precious, too, is the faith that produces such results (2 Pet. 1:1, AV); more precious than gold is faith that endures testing (1 Pet. 1:7). Those who let Christ work in their hidden heart are gaining a meek and quiet spirit, an "imperishable jewel" that is of great price to God (3:4). This inner quality enhances the value already placed on life and makes it very precious.

In conclusion, a statement in Job reveals that all value ultimately resides in God Himself: "and if the Almighty is your gold, and your precious silver; then you will delight yourself in the Almighty, and lift up your face to God" (Job 22:25f.).

*See also* RICHES; TREASURE. J. E. HARTLEY

**PRECIOUS STONES.** *See* STONES, PRECIOUS.

**PREDESTINATION.**

I. Vocabulary
II. Biblical Doctrine
  A. In the OT
  B. In the NT
III. History of the Doctrine
  A. Early Church
  B. Medieval Church
  C. Reformation Church
  D. Modern Church

***I. Vocabulary.***–In the RSV "predestined" renders Gk. *proorízō* in Acts 4:28; Rom. 8:29f. (NEB "foreordained"). The same word in Eph. 1:5, 11f. is translated "destined." The AV has "predestinate," and in Acts 4:28 "determined before." These passages contain other words that are equally important to the idea of predestination: *boulḗ* (plan, counsel), *thélēma* (will), *eudokía* (purpose, "pleasure"), *próthesis* (purpose), *oikonomía* (plan), *proginṓskō* (foreknow), *eklégomai* (choose), *kaléō* (call). Cf. Rom. 9:11; 11:2; Eph. 3:11; 2 Tim. 1:9; 1 Pet. 1:2, 20; and also *títhēmi*, "destine," in 1 Thess. 5:9; 1 Pet. 2:8.

In the OT a number of words indicate the divine plan and purpose, e.g., Heb. *ʿēṣâ* (plan, AV "counsel," Jer. 49:20; 50:45; Mic. 4:12), *yāʿaṣ* (purpose, Isa. 14:24, 26f.; 19:12; 23:9), and the important word *bāḥar* (choose).

The Eng. "predestination" derives from Lat. *prae destinatio,* which in the Vulgate translates Gk. *proorízō.*

*See also* PLAN; PURPOSE; WILL.

***II. Biblical Doctrine.***–The doctrine of predestination lies at the heart of all Reformed doctrine. Yet this teaching is not merely mysterious but also repulsive unless one goes behind it to the sovereignty of the triune God. The biblical revelation concerning God is that He possesses all power and authority in heaven and earth, and this means that He rules and reigns over all things (Gen. 1:1ff.; Job 38:1–41:34; Isa. 45:12f.; Eph. 1:11). If one believes that the triune God is sovereign, the doctrine of predestination presents no fundamental problem, and is full of comfort; whereas the opposite idea — ultimate chance — is problematic and frightening.

*A. In the OT.* From the earliest chapters of Genesis the concept of predestination takes an important place in the teaching of the Scriptures. The whole idea of creation implies a predetermined operation which God followed in His creative activity. Indeed, many have felt that Gen. 1 has as its primary purpose the setting forth of a rhythmical pattern by which man would understand that God's creative work followed a divinely determined plan (cf. N. H. Ridderbos, *Is There a Conflict Between Gen. 1 and Natural Science?* [Eng. tr. 1957]). Even more clearly predestination appears in the divine promises given to the patriarchs such as Noah and Abraham (Gen. 6:13ff.; 12:1ff.). Little value would attach to the promises of a god who had neither the power nor the wisdom to bring to pass that which he promised. Similarly, the Flood, the destruction of Sodom and Gomorrah, and the fortunes of Joseph are referred by the writer of Genesis to the foreordained purpose of God (Gen. 6:17; 7:1ff.; 18:1–19:26; 45:7ff.). As far back as one may go in the OT records, predestination undergirds the whole historical development.

The core of the OT doctrine of predestination, however, consists in God's choice of Israel to be a peculiar people devoted to Him, through whom He would speak unto men. Israel forms the elect people of the OT, a point that became perfectly clear in the Exodus which God had predestined (Gen. 15:13ff.; Ex. 3:7ff.; 12:41). Moreover, God's plan and purpose included not merely Israel but Egypt as well, for God hardened Pharaoh's heart so that he refused to allow Israel's departure, bringing destruction upon himself and his people (Ex. 3:19ff.; 7:13; 14:13ff.). Thus for the OT from the beginning of time history is the predestined plan of God for the redemption of His people.

As one follows the history of Israel down through the ages, one discovers that to the OT writers all that happened to the nation was the result of the sovereign foreordination and predestination of God. The whole concept of prophecy rests upon this foundation. If God did not foreordain whatever comes to pass, how could He give a predictive message to His representatives? The passages referring to this doctrine are too many to cite, but one may indicate in general some of the areas in which it appears. The historical books in particular teach that God predestines whatever comes to pass, and the prophetic books such as Isaiah, Daniel, Jonah, and the postexilic writers set forth the same point of view.

Yet in no sense do the Scriptures imply that Israel or any of the other nations were merely puppets or automatons in the hand of God. All nations as well as all individuals possess genuine responsibility, for when they act they do so according to their own wills and by their own decisions. When Israel turned away from God, such a turning was Israel's own act (Isa. 1:2ff.; 29:13ff.; Ezk. 18:2; 33:2ff.; Hos. 1:3ff.), just as the Assyrian attack upon Israel came out of the economic and moral condition of the people (Isa. 11:12; 36:1ff.). At the same time, behind all this stands the predestination of God, and yet never does the OT attempt to offer an explanation of the relationship between the two apparently contradictory views.

A large part of the OT deals with God's punishment of Israel's unfaithfulness, stressing that Israel's disobedience to God brought retribution even though that sinfulness and unfaithfulness had already been foretold. The punishment God inflicted upon the recalcitrant nation first brought division between the north and south, then captivity in Assyria and Babylon. Finally, out of this apparent disaster God brought forth redemption through the favor of the Medo-Persian kings such as Cyrus. In all of this one never finds the view that God had merely revealed what He had already foreseen, but rather He had foreordained, predestined, what would and did come to pass (e.g., Isa. 45). Thus the OT sees the whole of Israel's history bound up in God's plan with that of the other nations of the earth.

This divine plan and purpose were centered upon God's purpose of the salvation of sinners from every race, tribe, and tongue. The election of the remnant (Isa. 1:9; 6:13) which would remain faithful to God's law and promises formed part of this plan (*see* ELECTION), as did the divine dealings with Israel as a whole (Isa. 2; Hos. 1:9ff.). Thus in the fulness of time (Gal. 4:4) God sent forth from the believing Jewish remnant the central figure of history, Jesus Christ, to accomplish His redemptive purpose for all.

*B. In the NT.* The NT differs in no way from the OT in its doctrines of God's sovereignty and predestination. The coming of Christ, His life, death, resurrection, and ascension into heaven all fulfilled God's eternal plan and purpose to redeem His elect whom He had predestined unto eternal life (Eph. 1:4; 1 Pet. 1:20). Moreover, the spread of the gospel and the growth of the Church in all nations until the end, when Christ returns once again for His own, are all part of the plan and purpose of God which He hid as a mystery in OT times, but in the last days has, through Jesus Christ, made known to His own (Col. 1:26f.; Eph. 3:5ff.).

In the Synoptic Gospels predestination forms the continuous thread that connects everything, for God has prepared a kingdom, a new life, for those who are His "from the beginning" (Mt. 24:34; Mk. 2:17; Lk. 14:23). Moreover, God's predestination consists not in mere foresight, but in His foreordaining the effectual calling of those whom He has chosen (Mk. 4:11; 13:20; Mt. 20:1-16). Predestination is directed as a concentrated beam of light primarily on the salvation of the elect, though it includes also God's predestination of all things according to His sovereign will (cf. Mt. 6:25ff.; 10:29f.; 24), even man's free actions (Mt. 25).

In the corpus of apostolic teaching one finds the same point of view. According to Peter on the day of Pentecost, Christ's crucifixion was part of God's predestination; but at the same time it was the result of human lawlessness (Acts 2:23). Stephen and others also speak in these terms. 1 Pet. 1 depends upon the doctrine of predestination for its foundation, while the Gospel, Epistles, and Revelation of John either overtly or by implication state the doctrine repeatedly (Jn. 6:35ff.; 8:12ff.; 10:22ff.; ch. 17; 1 Jn. 5:1ff.; Rev. 1:10ff.; 4:1ff.).

Although the doctrine underlies all the apostle Paul's writings, particularly such passages as Phil. 2:5ff. and Col. 1:13ff., he sums up the whole matter, bringing together the teaching of the OT and of the other writers of the NT, in three great passages: Rom. 8:29f.; 9–11; Eph. 1:1-12. In these Paul states absolutely and clearly that God foreordains whatever comes to pass, even, as in the case of Pharaoh, sinful human acts. Central, however, to God's plan and purpose is the redemption of His elect people, chosen in Christ before the foundation of the world (Eph. 1:4), a redemption which has its origin solely in the sovereign determination of God (Rom. 9:11). Thus to the apostle everything exists and acts only in obedience to the will and purpose of God (Eph. 1:11), who has predestined all things according to the counsel of His own will.

Yet Paul's Epistles, like other parts of the Scriptures, express no mechanistic determinism. The apostle insists in all his writings that man is responsible for his acts, since it is he that performs them even though they are all part of God's plan, i.e., predestined by God. At the same time, he also emphasizes that man cannot understand the relationship between God's predestination and man's responsibility, for that relationship involves a joining of time and eternity that is incomprehensible to a being conditioned by space and time (Rom. 9:19–26). Here Paul leaves the mystery before which man must always stand in awe.

No one can explain the relationship of God's predestination to history, nor unravel how God works in and through history, except as God has revealed this in the Scriptures. Nor can the historian, on the basis of historical studies, declare the nature of God's plan in history. The ultimate explanation of all such matters must derive from the divine Word itself. Yet at the same time Christians walk with assurance and confidence, for they believe that God is sovereign and that He has foreordained all things in order that He may show forth His glory to endless ages.

W. S. REID

***III. History of the Doctrine.–A.** Early Church.* In spite of the relevant statements in the NT, the earliest authors seem not to have devoted any particular attention to the doctrine of predestination or election. In fact, it is only for the most part in relation to free will that the topic arises at all. Justin Martyr, for example, argued strongly for freedom in *Apol.* i.10.41; the real opposite here, of course, is Stoic determinism. Tertullian, too, contended for freedom, though he saw a bias toward evil as a result of the fall (*Adv. Marc.* i.22; ii.5f.). Clement of Alexandria naturally upheld freedom (*Protrepticus* [*Exhortatio*] 6.68). In Origen it is indeed the real key to salvation through successive cycles of existence (*De prin.* iii.1.2-4). If all are ultimately to be saved, as Origen inclined to think, there is little room for election; the most one can say is that all are elect.

At a later stage Athanasius in his *De incarnatione Verbi* had a kind of supralapsarianism. Even when God made the world He foresaw its ruin and hence provided for the fulfillment of His basic plan in spite of sin. In the West Ambrose presented a fuller doctrine of original sin: "Adam perished, and in him all perished" (*Expositio evangelii secundum Lucam* vii.234). If he demanded human effort (ii.84), he also said that grace is simply by the will of the giver (*Exhortatio virginitatis* iv.3). Ambrosiaster, too, referred to Adam as him "in whom" all sinned (*In Rom.* 5.12). In his view the consequence is bondage rather than guilt; this causes us all to commit our own sins.

From this it is but a step to the Pelagian crisis, which produced the first developed doctrine of predestination in Augustine. Pelagius, the British monk with a zeal for moral improvement, saw an obstacle in Augustine's cry: "Give what thou commandest, and command what thou wilt" (*Conf.* x.40). This implied, he thought, that God may not choose to give, that if He does not His commands are impossible, that if so God is unjust to command and man is under no genuine responsibility to obey. In contrast, Pelagius argued that man, though weak and needing help, is able to do God's will. "God has not willed to command anything impossible, for he is righteous; and he will not condemn a man for what he could not help, for he is holy" (*Epistula ad Demetriadem* 16).

Fuller analysis shows why Pelagius did not think he denied the doctrine of grace. In any act he saw three things: *posse, velle,* and *esse*. *Posse* (ability), which is the presupposition of the other two, is given by God alone. Everyone has it at birth as Adam did. Hence "everything good or evil is done by us, not born with us" (*Pro libero arbitrio*). Any person is able to live without sin, even if few do. *Velle* (will) and *esse* (reality), however, are man's work. For them there is no need of special help beyond the ability given at creation. If, in fact, most people do need help, this is given by the gospel (*ibid.*).

If Pelagius had stopped there, or had candidly admitted that naural *posse* is no longer adequate, or had seen that a new *posse* is given with conversion, the controversy might well have been avoided. Unfortunately, with the more doctrinaire Celestius and Julian of Ectanum, he became identified with some logical but hardly defensible inferences, e.g., that Adam injured himself alone, or that there were people without sin before Christ, or that infants are as Adam before the fall (Augustine *De gestis Pelagii* 23). Indeed, Julian boasted that "man is emancipated from God" (Augustine *Opus imperfectum contra Julian* i.78). The Pelagians also taught that predestination is simply according to the foreseen quality of a person's life (Augustine *In Rom.* 9.10).

Augustine was the chief opponent of this view. As regards fulfilling the law, he distinguished between external and internal fulfillment; the latter is possible only when the Holy Spirit is present in the heart (*De spiritu et littera* 5). The question of *posse* drove him to his famous distinctions. *Posse non peccare* (ability not to sin) is true of Adam; *non posse non peccare* (inability not to sin) is true of fallen man; *non posse peccare* (inability to sin) will be true of the children of God in their full and final freedom (*Civ. Dei* x.30). Implied is a distinction in freedom. Augustine did not deny freedom of choice, for he, too, rejected philosophical determinism. But this freedom, always limited, now stands under the moral limit of not being a freedom not to sin. There is now "a cruel necessity of sinning" (*De perfectione iusticiae hominis* 9). In this area freedom is simply choice within the general bondage. Even if there were freedom not to sin, this would still fall short of full and authentic freedom such as God Himself enjoys, the freedom of inability to sin. Theologically defined, freedom is freedom from sin. This is what fallen man completely lacks.

Since mankind is in bondage as a result of the fall, it can be described by Augustine as a "mass of sin" or "lump of perdition" (*Ad Simplicianum* i.2.16). From this mass there is no escape except by liberation. This is where grace comes in. Grace is of different kinds, but prevenient grace (grace as initiative) must obviously come first (*Ep.* 217). Then comes cooperating grace. Grace may be either sufficient (*sine quo*) or efficient (*quo*). The former is that without which one could not be free, while the latter is that by which one is free. This distinction is an important one for predestination, both in Augustine and later, for while grace is sufficient for all, it is efficacious only in the elect.

Augustine's doctrine of predestination springs from this need of grace to liberate man. Man has free choice, but his choices are always in some degree bad. Grace puts good choices for bad ones (*De gratia et libero arbitrio* 31). Now grace, although irresistible, is accommodated to us, so that we may accept or reject it (*De spiritu et littera* 60). Grace alone, however, can confer real freedom (*De gratia et libero arbitrio* 31). But since grace must precede, and mankind is a *massa damnata,* God determines (from eternity) who receives it or not (*De correptione et gratia* 12.16). The number of those chosen is limited; they are to fill the gaps left by the fallen angels (*Civ. Dei* xxii.12). Augustine did not see a general decree to save, nor did he think that the selection is based on foreseen merits. God foreknows, but predestination is "the foreknowledge and planning . . . by which they are most surely determined whoever are delivered" (*De dono perseverantiae* 35). The choice is according to "a secret and inscrutable justice" (*Ad Simplicianum* i.2.14-16). To the elect the final grace of perseverance is given, and this is irresistible; they cannot but persevere (*De correptia et gratia* 34ff.). Those to whom it is not granted to believe (even though they might have done so) are left in the "mass of ruin" like the men of Sodom or Tyre (*De dono perseverantiae* 35). This mass includes many Christians lacking the final grace of perseverance even though enjoying grace in other forms. For Augustine, grace is not constraint. It implies that people can and will. "Their will is so kindled by the Holy Spirit that they can, just because they will, and they will just because God works in them so to will" (*De correptione et gratia* 37).

The strong doctrine of election taught by Augustine met with resistance, especially in south Gaul. Here John Cassian argued that the beginnings may be traced in man's volition (*Ep.* xiii.12.2). Man's will is sick, not dead (iii.12.3-5). Grace restores and assists (xiii.13.1). God wills the salvation of all, so that predestination is based on prevision of those who will be saved. This view was close to that of the Eastern Church represented by Theodoret, for whom the vitiation due to the fall was a bias to sin (*In Ps.* 50.7). Theodoret, too, argued for the will's continuing freedom (*In Ps.* 38.6), though grace is needed for eternal life (*In Rom.* 11.15). "There is need of both our efforts and the divine succor. The grace of the Spirit is not vouchsafed to those who make no effort, and without that grace our efforts cannot collect the prize of virtue" (*In Phil.* 1.29f.). If in the long run effort is God's gift, this does not cancel out freedom. It simply implies the inability of freedom without grace.

The south Gaul reaction, in which Cassian was supported by Vincent of Lerins and Faustus of Rhegium, found conciliar expression at Arles in 473. This council condemned the theses that human obedience is not also needed, that the fall extinguished free choice, that Christ did not die for all, and that foreknowledge can impel to death. More positively, it stated "Man's effort . . . is to be united with God's grace; man's freedom of will is not extinct but alienated and weakened; he that is saved is in danger, and he that has perished could have been saved." Yet this was not the final word, for at Orange in 529 we find a new compromise with stronger Augustinian leanings. Anathemas are now passed on the views that the fall did not affect the whole man, that Adam's fall injured himself alone, that the beginning of faith is in us by nature, that there is mercy for those who believe, will, and desire apart from grace, and that by nature a man can think and choose the good. Prevenient grace is strongly affirmed along with the power and duty, after baptism, to perform all things that pertain to the soul's salvation. There is, however, a sharp condemnation of the idea "that some have been predestined to evil by the divine power."

*B. Medieval Church.* If the decisions at Orange became the established orthodoxy of the West, the Gottschalk incident shows that consistent Augustinianism was rejected no less than consistent Pelagianism. Gottschalk (9th cent.) tried to revive the concept of double predestination, i.e., to both life and death. He did, however, make a linguistic distinction, using *praedestinare* ("to predestine") only for the elect and *praescire* ("to know beforehand") for the reprobate. Both elect and reprobate are in God's plan, but He does not will and decree in the same way for the two groups. Election is direct and positive, reprobation permissive. Gottschalk was supported by Ratramn, but the more resolute opposition of Hincmar and Erigina led to his condemnation.

The related question of original sin occupied the lively and powerful mind of Anselm in the 11th century. Anselm pointed out that the word "original" here refers not to creation, but to participation in our common nature (*De origine peccati* 1). Original or natural sin is thus a condition; it is the violation of created nature and entails the guilt of our not being what we should be (ch. 2). It is necessary (even in infants) since Adam passes on fallen nature to us. Individuals are generically or seminally in Adam, and they derive from him the *non posse non peccare* rather

PREDESTINATION

than the *posse non peccare*. As regards freedom, Anselm agreed with Augustine that the power of choice (between sinning and not sinning) is not real freedom. Far from being essential to freedom, this power weakens it. If Adam's sin was an act of weakness, it missed authentic freedom. His sin, though not a sin by compulsion, was really in spite of freedom. The position is still the same today, for the voluntary faculty remains; but by creation the will has only one choice in true freedom, the free self-election of the good. Man cannot originate goodness; he can only will to maintain it (in which is no merit). After the fall he still cannot originate it — hence the need of grace. Yet nothing compelled or compels man to sin. Whether he chooses good or bad, his will is voluntary, but only if he chooses good is it authentically free. Temptation does not force people to sin. Yielding to temptation is by decision, but it brings a moral and guilty necessity of sinning. Anselm distinguished here between faculty as instrument and act as use (of the instrument). Bondage arises in use; through wrong use we cannot turn to God. God does not cause a wrong use, for this would involve the illogicality of His willing that we will what He does not will. In relation to the fall His will is permissive; He does not stop the fall. Yet how can the will be both free and in bondage? The point is that the will is still the same as that which could have chosen righteousness but cannot originate righteousness. As regards the race, if not individuals, the whole process of sin is voluntary, but in neither race nor individuals can the will reverse the process. In this sense Anselm saw no salvation except by electing grace. Essentially he was thus a strong Augustinian, though he avoided the concept of predestination to evil. Man is responsible for his own sin and fall; God predestines to salvation.

Although Scholasticism is associated with semi-Pelagianism, Aquinas, like Anselm, is more Augustinian in his treatment of predestination (*Summa Theol.* i.23). Aquinas not only claimed that God predestines (as a special function within providence) but he was prepared to say that God rejects some men: "Providence permits some of them [men] to fail to attain the end [eternal life]" (art. 3). Rejection, which is more than foreknowledge of man's unbelief, is not contrary to God's love for people, for "he does not will the good of eternal life" for all, but "wills some good" for all (*loc. cit.*). Like Anselm, Aquinas thought that guilt is "due to the free will of him who is rejected" (*loc. cit.*). He also dismissed the idea that foreknowledge of merits might be a reason for predestination. The real reason is the divine goodness, which "God willed to show forth in men by mercifully sparing some of them, whom he predestines, and by justly punishing others, whom he rejects" (art. 5). Predestination is certain (art. 6), and the number of the predestined is certain, both formally in the sense of a general number, and also materially in the sense that the predestined are all known to God (art. 7). If there is a concession to semi-Pelagianism it is more in the analysis of grace as this accomplishes the work of predestination; but with his stress on prevenient grace and the rejection of any merit of condignity unless a work proceeds already from grace, Aquinas could in no sense be regarded as a semi-Pelagian.

The real movement of Scholasticism in a semi-Pelagian direction came with Duns Scotus, who laid such emphasis on the will as to call it "the sole cause of its own acts" (*Sent.* ii.25.2). Yet even this could cut two ways, for the freedom and sovereignty of God's will demanded that He be acknowledged as the ultimate cause of all things. It is not surprising, then, to find a vigorous Augustinianism in the later Middle Ages, e.g., in Thomas Bradwardine, who attacked Pelagianism, or John Wycliffe, who equated the true Church with the number of predestined rather than the members of the external institution (*De ecclesia* 1). Wycliffe in particular prepared the way for the Reformation at this point as at so many others.

*C. Reformation Church.* While the Council of Trent maintained traditional semi-Augustinianism, although with a slightly stronger Pelagian thrust in answer to Luther (Sess. VI on Justification, 4ff.), the Reformers put a new stress on grace that led them back to a full Augustinianism. Zwingli, it is true, had a weak doctrine of original sin as a condition and not sin, yet his concept of God's sovereignty was so strong that the possible Pelagian implications of this were completely lost. Luther even at Leipzig was comparing man to a saw in the worker's hand; and in *The Bondage of the Will,* written in answer to Erasmus, he advanced the full teaching that man has no power of his own to turn to God. God alone, then, can and does provide both the basis of justification in Christ's atoning work and also its means in justifying faith. Calvin, of course, gave the doctrine its most systematic presentation at this period. As he saw it, original sin is a "hereditary depravity and corruption of our nature" (*Inst.* ii.1). Though God is not the author of sin, His activity in the reprobate is more than mere permission. For if He leaves them in sin by withdrawing His Spirit, He also "directs their councils and excites their wills . . . through the agency of Satan, the minister of his wrath" (ii.4). As regards predestination, Calvin dismissed any equation with foreknowledge. Foreknowledge is God's general seeing of all things as present; predestination is His eternal decree "by which he has decided in his own mind what he wishes to happen in the case of each individual. For all men are not created on an equal footing, but for some eternal life is preordained, for others eternal damnation . . ." (iii.21).

That these were not just individual views may be seen from the Reformation confessions. That of Augsburg taught freedom only for civil righteousness, not spiritual (art. XVIII). The First Helvetic said that we can do bad of ourselves, but not good (ch. IX). The Heidelberg Catechism called man "wholly incapable of doing any good" (I, qq. 8-10). The Belgic Confession found God merciful in election, and "just in leaving others in the same fall and perdition wherein they have involved themselves" (art. XVI). The Gallican said of election that "God according to his eternal . . . and immutable counsel calleth all those whom he has chosen by his mercy and goodness alone in Jesus Christ . . . leaving the rest . . . to show in them his justice" (art. XII). The Scots linked the election firmly to the Mediator and the Incarnation and focused more on the election of grace than on reprobation (art. VIII). The Second Helvetic also turned attention to election in Christ, while the Anglican had a doctrine only of predestination to life, i.e., "the everlasting purpose of God . . . to deliver those whom he hath chosen in Christ" (ch. XVII). The English Lambeth Articles (1595) attempted a fuller statement, including reprobation in art. I, God's good pleasure as the efficient cause in II, and "a certain number of predestinate" in III. Though these were not passed, their influence may be seen in the Irish Articles (1615), which also asserted double predestination and a fixed number of elect (no. 12), and found the cause in "God's wise good-pleasure to manifest his glory in mercy and justice" (no. 13).

Already in these later statements one may detect a reply to Socinianism and Arminianism, and this is even more explicit in the teaching of Dort and Westminster and the dogmatics they embody. Dort plainly advocated total depravity, unconditional election, limited atonement (as regards efficacy), irresistible grace, and perseverance of the elect. Westminster denied predestination's equation with prevision (III, 2), saw both predestination to life and foreordination to death (III, 3), taught a fixed number of elect (III, 4), and found God's mercy exalted in election and His justice in reprobation (III, 5, 7). Limited atonement was taught in VIII, 5, bondage of the will in IX, 3, effectual calling in ch. X, and perseverance in ch. XVII. Similar teaching is given in the Shorter Catechism, qq. 7ff.; cf. q. 20 on God's election of some to life "out of his mere good pleasure."

For elaboration, however, one must turn to the dogmatic treatises. Here special predestination (a branch of general providence) is the foreordination of some to life and others to death (Riissen, VI, 19). Its aim is to display God's glory in the exercise of His righteousness and mercy (Braun, *Doct. Foed.* I, 11, 9). God is the primary efficient cause; then His will or decree (Polanus, IV, 7). "In first intent the decree is absolute, in the ultimate it is ordinate or respective" (Wendelin, *Theol. syst. maius*, 298). It is also eternal and immutable (Bucanus, XXXVI, 12). The object in a supralapsarian view is man yet to be created and to fall, for "what is first in intention is last in execution"; in the infralapsarian view the object created and fallen man, for man yet to be created and to fall does not exist (*est non ens,* Riissen, VI, 19, 1) and hence cannot be either "eligible" or "reprobable." This dispute has no chronological reference, since predestination in any case belongs to God's eternity.

Election is positive predestination manifesting God's mercy. The cause is the triune God: "To the Father particularly belongs the election in and by itself, to the Son the *sponsio* [solemn promise], to the Holy Spirit the *obsignatio* [seal, witness]" (Heidegger, V, 28). The impulsive cause is the triune love and mutual glorifying (V, 29). Hence election is not arbitrary; it finds its moral ground in God's essentiality (Walaeus, 385). One is not to seek the ground in man's will, his use of the means of grace, or foreseen faith (Polanus, IV, 9). "A man is not elected because he is going to believe; he believes because he is elect" (Wollebius, 29). Christ's person is the foundation and in a sense the sole object, others being elect in him. As Mastricht said (III/3, 8f.): "The object of election is the whole mystical Christ, i.e., Christ with all his own." Walaeus (380f.) refuted the idea that "in Christ" means that "Christ is held to be elected only after our election." Rather, he said, "Christ as our head was first elected and then his members in him." In this sense, according to Heidegger, "Christ is the cause and the means of eternal election" (V, 31). If His merit is not the cause, "our election was not accomplished without regard to Christ's future merit" (Leiden, *Syn.*, XXIV, 29). In general, however, Christ's work ranks as the cause of salvation rather than election; election is to salvation and also to the means thereto (Heidegger, V, 48). The means are six, three as causes (Christ, effectual calling, and faith), and three as effects (justification, sanctification, and glorification) (Bucanus, XXXVI, 30). Since God wills as well as knows the elect, the number separated from the sin-corrupted mass is fixed (Heidegger, V, 43). God's special saving love differs from His general love. Hence there is no universal election (Riissen, VI, 18, 2). This was asserted in opposition to "the giddy Sam Huber," who replaced this "botched election" with a few elect nominally and all eligible participially, and also in opposition to the Lutherans, who, adopting a distinction in Aquinas, taught universal election by antecedent will and particular election by consequent will. Three final points are made: the elect cannot perish (Riissen, VI, 19, 4); though known only to God they display marks (Polanus, IV, 9: four benefits and four testimonies); and their assurance lies in looking to the gospel or to Christ.

Reprobation is the negative side: the decree "to leave fixed men . . . in the mass of corruption" (Heidegger, V, 54). "He who elects some passes over those whom he does not elect" (V, 55). In reprobation there are two elements, "the denial of grace not due, called *praeteritio,* and the appointment of due punishment, called *praedamnatio*" (Wollebius, 23). Negatively this means that God "did not resolve to pity the rest whom he did not elect," and positively that "he resolved to impose upon the same men, justly left in the lump of perdition . . . the punishment they had earned" (Leiden, *Syn.*, XXIV, 46). Unbelief is not the cause of reprobation, only of damnation (Wollebius, 23). Praeterition does not deprive of common grace (Leiden, *Syn.*, XXIV, 54f.). The reprobate, however, are predestined to continue in sin: "The action and penalty are ordained, not the sin" (Heidegger, V, 66). "The supreme end of reprobation is the glory of God reprobatory; the subordinate end is the righteous condemnation of the reprobated to death for their sins" (V, 64). Various means are discerned, e.g., unbelief, aversion from God (Bucanus, XXXVI, 39), and also various signs, e.g., denial of divine benefits and induration in evil (Polanus, IV, 10). The great sign is "sin against the Holy Spirit and final impenitence" (Cocceius, *Aphor. prol. Op.*, VI, 11, 21, 27). Yet one should not try to judge one's own reprobation or that of others before life ends (Heidegger, V, 67). As regards the whole doctrine, its difficulty is commonly admitted. A mean should thus be observed between silence and the inquisitive pride of those who "attach to God himself the concatenation of the divine decrees which they have designed in their own brains." "With all sobriety . . . it must be dealt with out of Holy Scripture" (Leiden, *Syn.*, XXIV, 61).

For a compilation of the views in III.C see Heppe, pp. 150-189.

*D. Modern Church.* The prevailing modern temper has been one of revolt against a stricter teaching of predestination. Thus in Roman Catholicism the Jansenist attempt (17th cent.) to revive pure Augustinianism met with official resistance, and, if Jesuit Pelagianism failed to carry the day against semi-Augustinian orthodoxy, it exercised a wide and powerful influence. In the Protestant world dissatisfaction with the Reformation statements manifested itself even before the end of the 16th cent., and in spite of the codification at Dort and Westminster it quickly gathered force.

In the Reformed Church Arminius played a leading part here. His position found crisp expression in the Remonstrant Articles (1610), which contained five basic propositions: (1) God predestines those who shall believe and persevere; (2) Jesus died for all; (3) man of himself does not have saving grace, nor can the energy of free will save him; (4) grace is not irresistible; and (5) there is no final assurance of salvation. The aim of these articles was to avoid the problems of strict predestinarianism, e.g., caprice in God, or the sham of general calling. But they obviously equated predestination with foreknowledge and suspended salvation ultimately on the liberated will. High Church Anglicanism, followed in the 18th cent. by John Wesley, espoused Arminianism, first in opposition to the Puritans and then to Anglican Evangelicals like Toplady.

The Lutheran world moved in a similar direction. Melanchthon in his *Loci* had already found three agents in election rather than the more common two, namely, the Word, the Spirit, and man's will accepting the Word. The latter was a feeble seeking and striving brought to perfection by the Word and Spirit. The tendency represented by Melanchthon vanquished the stricter teaching of Luther.

This may be seen in the Formula of Concord (1576), which allowed general foreknowledge (XI, 1) but limited predestination "to the good and beloved children of God" (XI, 4). We go to Christ to learn of it (XI, 6). God has a general will to save, and He issues a general call (XI, 6-9). The cause of damnation is refusal to hear and accept God's Word (XI, 9). God has decreed to save only in Christ (XI, 12). Negatively, the Reformed view that "some men are destined to destruction, not on account of their sins, but by the mere counsel, will and purpose of God," was repudiated (XI, 3). Even more specifically anti-Reformed were the Saxon Visitation Articles (1592). Art. IV said, "God created no man for condemnation." Among the false and thus condemned doctrines are "Christ did not die for all men, but only for the elect," and "God created the greater part of men for eternal damnation."

Perhaps the easiest way to trace the swing of Protestants to Arminianism, which was naturally favored by Liberalism, is through the various confessions of the modern period. The Quakers adopted this line already in propositions 4-6 of the 1675 Confession. Anglicanism did not revise the article on predestination but introduced under Charles I a statement prohibiting nonliteral (i.e., Puritan) interpretation. Wesley, of course, dropped this article from his version of the Anglican Articles in 1784, though he retained the article on the limitation of free will. The small Reformed Episcopal group in America took the different course of emphasizing "man's free agency and responsibility" and the free offer of salvation to all through Christ (1875).

The Baptist (Philadelphia) and Congregationalist churches at first stayed close to Westminster, but with the breakup of the older tradition in the early 19th cent. changes inevitably came in these denominations. The New Hampshire Baptist Confession (1833) found election "perfectly coexistent with the free agency of man" (art. IX), while the Free Will Baptists (1834) stated, "Salvation is rendered equally possible to all" (ch. VIII). Simultaneously the English Congregational Union (1833) reduced predestination to "God's design to redeem fallen man." In Congregationalism the confessional move came later in America, but by 1833 the American Congregational statement equated predestination with God's general will that all repent (art. IV). When the United Church of Canada came into being in 1925, an emphasis on the free offer of all-sufficient salvation became one of the distinguishing marks of the basic confession.

Resistance in the Reformed or Presbyterian world was more stubborn. In the period of Liberal insurgence in the early 19th cent. the Cumberland Confession (1829) included some loosening of Westminster (ch. III) and put in the explanatory statement: "We believe that both Calvinists and Arminians have egregiously erred on this point . . . . We think the intermediate plan on this subject is nearest the whole truth." The Auburn Declaration (1837), while refusing to ground election on foresight, and insisting on man's inability to comply with God's commands apart from the "reviving influence or almighty energy of the Holy Spirit," stated plainly that predestination is "to salvation alone."

By 1848 an Evangelical Free Church had been set up in Geneva with much less rigid articles on election (X, XI, XII), and the next decades saw further changes in British and American Presbyterianism. Thus the English Presbyterian Church in 1890 spoke of "God's high design," but only in such a way as to include in it human freedom and response (art. VI). Then in 1903 the American Presbyterian Church published a declaratory statement to the effect that God's eternal decree is consistent with His love to save all men and with a free offer of the gospel. Finally in 1925 the United Presbyterian Church of North America held out hope for all infants and for those beyond the outward means of grace (art. X). The relativizing of Westminster in 1967 was undoubtedly due in part to problems associated with the stern orthodox doctrine of election and (more particularly) reprobation.

The shift in the confessions naturally met with powerful opposition from orthodox groups, especially in the Presbyterian world. The Princetonian orthodoxy put up staunch, scholarly, and effective resistance in the United States, and this was maintained even to the point of small disruptions in the 20th century. Moreover, smaller Reformed churches have been much slower to abandon or modify their formularies; and the same applies to the Church of Scotland, where the confession is clearly a subsidiary standard, and the Church of England, where discontent has been allayed partly by cavalier treatment of all the articles and partly by the absence of a specific reference to reprobation.

Nevertheless, the movement has been decidedly against a more developed doctrine of predestination. Roman Catholicism was never wholeheartedly Augustinian. Lutheranism after Luther produced its own compromise. Arminianism began its work before the 16th cent. was out and grew in spite of Dort and Westminster. The early Anabaptists had a semi-Pelagian trend, and for all their Calvinist beginnings Baptists quickly found this more congenial to their distinctive teachings. Evangelistic Pietism also fitted easily into this structure. There were notable exceptions, like Edwards, Whitefield, and many Anglican and Scottish preachers. But the Wesleys were unabashedly Arminian; and Finney with his new measures and call for decision waged open war on the older doctrine and helped to make American Evangelicalism (in the main) as Pelagian in practice as almost any group in Christian history. Liberalism, of course, added its own powerful and persuasive voice to the modern chorus. Rationalism has little time for the idea of decree, humanitarianism recoils from the idea of rejection, while subjectivism contends for the autonomy of the thinking and willing ego. The only election that remains in Liberalism is either the election of all men to salvation or the election which man himself makes at the rational, moral, emotional, volitional, or existential level.

The Cumberland Confession of 1829 suggested, as we have seen, that an intermediate plan would be nearest the whole truth. With this many Christians would probably concur. They admit that the crass Pelagianism of much theology and practice fails to do justice to biblical teaching, and yet the serious, weighty, and consistent Calvinism of Protestant orthodoxy does not quite convince the majority, especially in relation to reprobation. Unfortunately the 1829 Confession omitted to tell us precisely what the "intermediate plan" is, and subsequent theology has proved far more adept at repeating old arguments than attempting or even desiring new answers.

The one valiant attempt to break the impasse that history will surely record was that of Karl Barth in his *Church Dogmatics*, II/2. Strictly Barth did not offer an intermediate plan. In his own mind he was Reformed, not Arminian. His aim was a reconstruction of the Reformed doctrine that would enable it to express new and more biblical insights and avoid the offensive features. Some of the critical and constructive points he made are thus worthy of brief analysis and appraisal.

While wishing to present a strong doctrine of election Barth argued that a modern statement cannot merely be a repetition of the older presentation, for this is open to criticism at many points. Thus it uses utility and experience as criteria in addition to Scripture. It also confuses predestination with providence. It replaces the living God with His own fixed decree in such a way as to verge on deism. It tends to make Christ and His work mere instruments by which the decree is executed. Hence true justice is not done to Christ as Himself God. At this point the criticisms converge into the basic thesis that a biblical account of the doctrine will necessarily be christological.

Positively Barth believed that the doctrine is essentially that of the election of grace, not of a predestination that bifurcates into election and reprobation. As the election of grace it is the sum of the gospel. This means that both ontically and noetically it stands in the closest possible relation to Jesus Christ, who is the subject, theme, and center of the gospel. With this focus on Christ Barth picked up hints in Calvin and the Second Helvetic Confession. He also borrowed from the seventeenth-century theologians the two points (1) that the whole trinity is the cause of election, and (2) that Christ is the foundation and even the sole object of election, all others being elect in Him. This twofold line of thought led Barth to his own primary insight that Christ as Son of God is electing God and Christ as Son of man is also elect man.

From this two conclusions follow. First, election is part of the doctrine of God rather than primarily of man. It is thus dealt with in this field; and, since election is covenantal, the basis of ethics, i.e., the command accompanying the promise, also belongs here. Second, supralapsarianism is in principle right. The subject of election is not man already created and fallen. It is the eternal Son in whom man, yet to be created and to fall, is already elected. As Barth put it, the election is the beginning of all God's ways, words, and works. Man's restoration in Christ is simply the fulfillment of the original purpose of election served by creation and, in its own episodic way, the fall.

Barth saw, of course, that a place has to be found for reprobation. God's justice is displayed and enacted as well as His grace. Justice for the sinner means rejection. The point is, however, that as elected man Jesus Christ takes the place of the rejected. In one sense He is elected to rejection, i.e., to the vicarious rejection which is the ground of the inclusion of sinners in His (positive) election. Hence God's justice is worked out, not in the damnation of the wicked, but in the vicarious death of the One elect, which is also and at the same time the execution and expression of God's mercy.

Secondarily, the election is that of the Church, and thirdly that of the individual, as well as Christ. As regards the Church Barth suggested that the first, passing, prophetic form, Israel, corresponds in the first instance to the rejection of Christ, while the second, final, apostolic form, the Christian Church, corresponds to His election. As regards individuals there is a similar twofold "ordination," that of the elect and that of the rejected. The former see that they cannot be elected in themselves but find their election in Christ, their specific ordination being that of witness to Him. The latter resist this, but their ordination is also that of witnessing to Christ in their own negative way, just as Judas fulfilled his apostolic calling by "handing over" Jesus — the very thing the true apostle also does in preaching. Under God, therefore, all are caught up in the one election, both Israel and the Christian Church, both the elect and the rejected. If some men never come to fulfil their ordination in a positive mode, they will still have to do so in a negative mode. There is, however, no reason why they should have to do this in exhibition of the divine justice, since, with God's mercy, this has been enacted already in the one election and vicarious rejection of Christ Himself.

Thus far Barth seemed to offer a reconstruction that avoids the problem of double predestination while not relapsing into Arminianism. The focus on Christ and the interrelation with vicarious atonement (cf. *CD*, IV/1) are particularly valuable features. Nevertheless, certain problems remain. Thus universalism seems to be a logical inference from this view. If Christ is the elect of God, and if He has vicariously suffered the rejection of sinful man, all are elect in Him. Objectively Barth certainly taught this. One might say, then, that if some go to hell it is in spite of predestination rather than on account of it. The ordination of the rejected arises only in the context of the election of grace. But why then should there be any such rejection at all?

At this point Barth steadfastly resisted an Arminian solution, namely, that men are free to choose election in Christ or to reject it themselves and thus go to hell in spite of it. He referred rather to the sovereignty of the Spirit in calling. But if this is so, one seems to be moving back to the discarded teaching. God, even as electing and elect Christ, summons some to faith and leaves others in resistance and rejection according to His inscrutable freedom. Barth did insist, however, that the Spirit, like Christ, is not just the executor of a prior, fixed decree. He is the living God present and active in and with the ministry of calling. He is the God who changes even though He does not ultimately repent. Effectual calling is not the enforced fulfillment of a given fiat. It is personal interaction with the called. If a final mystery remains it is perhaps the paradox of unbelief. The man who elects God does so in the freedom conferred on him by God's election of him. The man who does not remains in bondage, which is all the more nonsensical because it is rejection of his election worked out in the vicarious rejection of Christ. The saint can praise God for his election, but the sinner cannot blame God for his reprobation. He can only bear witness to election in it.

A certain obscurity, undoubtedly, remains in this area. It is easy enough to see why, under the bondage of ignorance and sin, all might resist it. Not so easy to see is why some should respond and some should resist. The alternative explanations—that either God sovereignly ordains it thus or God leaves the choice at this point to men—brings us back either to Augustinianism or Arminianism. Perhaps the only final truth is that no solution is possible because sin itself, being irrational, involves irrationality. Thus both Augustinianism and Arminianism break down because they are too logical for an illogical subject, and there is no intermediate ground except to cling to the fact, contradictory though it may appear, that the saved are saved only by God's election, and the lost are lost only by their own fault in defiance of God's election and in inverse witness to it.

*See also* ELECTION.

***Bibliography.***–H. Heppe, *Reformed Dogmatics* (1950); P. Schaff, *Creeds of Christendom*, III: *Evangelical Protestant Creeds* (4th rev. ed. 1919); J. Calvin, *Eternal Predestination of God*; M. Luther, *On the Bondage of the Will*; H. Bettenson, *Documents of the Christian Church* (1963); A. Plantinga, *God, Freedom, and Evil* (1974).

G. W. BROMILEY

**PRE-EMINENCE** [Heb. hiphil of *yāṯar*–'excel'] ("have pre-eminence," Gen. 49:4); AV, NEB, EXCEL; [*nō(a)h*] (Ezk. 7:11); AV "wailing"; NEB "restless ways"; **PRE-EMINENT** [Heb. *yeṯer*–'abundantly'] (Gen. 49:3); AV EXCELLENCY; NEB EXCELLING; [Gk. *prōteúō*–'be first'] ("be pre-eminent," Col. 1:18); AV HAVE PRE-EMINENCE; NEB BE SUPREME. Superiority in excellence, power, authority, or status.

These words, which in the Bible are used only of persons, mean in the simplest sense to be first, but in particular contexts they take on more specific meanings. In Gen. 49:3f. (Jacob's blessing of his sons) the words are applied to Reuben. Despite the advantage of being the "first-born," which enables him to be "pre-eminent in pride and pre-eminent in power," Reuben "shall not have pre-eminence." It is Judah instead who shall be first in status among the tribes of Israel (v. 10) and from whom shall come the messianic ruler. The preeminence in view here thus entails the fulfillment of Israel's destiny. The meaning of Heb. *nō(a)h* in Ezk. 7:11 is unknown. The text of the verse is corrupt, and the AV, RSV, and NEB reconstructions are conjectural.

The noun occurs also in the AV of Eccl. 3:19, where Qoheleth laments that, inasmuch as both are subject to death, a human being has no "preeminence" (Heb. *môṯār*; RSV, NEB, "advantage") over a beast. The AV of 3 Jn. 9 describes the otherwise unknown Diotrephes as one "who loveth to have preeminence" (Gk. *philoprōteúō*; cf. RSV "likes to put himself first"). Diotrephes' love for pre-eminence apparently involved an arrogant denial of the authority of "the elder" and a refusal to welcome "the brethren" (cf. v. 10).

Undoubtedly the most important occurrence of "pre-eminent" is in Col. 1:18, which describes Christ in phrases that were apparently once part of a hymn (vv. 15-20). Whereas vv. 15-17 describe Christ's priority (both in time and in rank; see *TDNT*, VI, 877-79) over the created order, which was made through Him and for Him, v. 18 describes Christ as the head of the new creation, the Church, by virtue of His resurrection as "first-born from the dead" (cf. v. 15). Having thus become the head of both creations, Christ fulfils God's will "that in everything he might be pre-eminent." This comprehensive preeminence of Christ is possible because "in him all the fulness of God was pleased to dwell" (v. 19; cf. 2:9). It is noteworthy that in Col. 1:18 (cf. v. 15) as well as in Gen. 49:3f. "pre-eminence" occurs together with "first-born." Both terms refer not only to temporal priority but also to priority in status or rank.

*See also* FIRST-BORN.

***Bibliography.***–Comms. on Colossians; *TDNT*, VI, *s.v.* πρῶτος κτλ.: πρωτότοκος, πρωτεύω (W. Michaelis). D. A. HAGNER

**PREEXISTENCE OF SOULS.** The concept that souls have existence before their union with or incarnation in a human body. Such preexistent souls are considered immortal: they are eternally existing entities, emanations from the divine, or entities created by God. The idea of the soul's preexistence is sometimes linked to various views of transmigration and reincarnation. (The preexistence of the divine nature of Jesus Christ as the second person of the TRINITY is an entirely different subject.)

The origin of the belief in the soul's preexistence is obscure, although it was widespread in the ancient world and is still common in non-Christian religions, particularly animistic types. Appearing early in Greek religion, the idea became an important part of Greek philosophy, especially through Plato's *Phaedo* and *Meno*. The belief is common in the religions of India, notably Hinduism. Outside of India it is also part of Buddhism but not of Islam. The idea entered postexilic Judaism through Persian and Greek influences, was prominent in Alexandrian Christianity through Origen, and reappeared in the pantheistic philosophical thought of Germany. It also occurred in some English literary writers (Vaughan, Wordsworth, Rossetti, Browning, Tennyson), is common among modern theosophists, and is an important dogma of the Mormon faith.

Scripture does not present a single clear reference to the idea of the preexistence of human souls. The whole person, "a living being," was created a unity by God's dual action (Gen. 2:7; cf. 1:26f.); no distinction is made here between body and soul and certainly no indication of a preexistent soul. Distinctions between body and soul occur only after the fall and are occasioned by death's disruption of the created unity, which occurred as punishment of human sin. In support of the soul's preexistence some have appealed to various OT passages, including Dt. 29:14f.; 1 S. 2:6; Job 1:21; Ps. 139:15. Only if one approaches Scripture with the presupposition of an initial dichotomy between soul and body do such passages seem to support the idea of the soul as a distinct preexistent entity. Such views did not arise among Jewish interpreters of the OT until after the Exile, under Greek and Persian influences.

Greek influence was especially strong at Alexandria; the preexistence of the soul was held by Philo (*De mutatione nominum* 39 [223]; *De opificio mundi* 51 [145f.]; *De cherubim* 32 [113f.]) and is taught in some apocryphal writings (esp. Wisd. 8:19f.; 15:3). Allusions to the doctrine are also found in the Jewish Talmud and Midrash. Josephus (*BJ* ii.8.11 [154-58]) refers to it as a teaching of the Essenes, but the accuracy of his claim is questioned.

The idea of the soul's preexistence also entered Christian theology from foreign sources. The only NT passage that has relevance for the question is Jn. 9:2, where the disciples ask Jesus: "Rabbi, who sinned, this man or his parents, that he was born blind?" Although belief in the soul's preexistence may have been assumed in this question, the passage does not endorse that idea. The main issue, as in the case of Job's friends (Job 4:7f.), is an implied direct correlation between some specific sin and suffering as its punishment. Jesus' reply rejects that assumption. (The claim that John the Baptist is the prophesied Elijah [Mt. 17:12f.; cf. Mal. 4:5 (MT 3:23)] is figurative, typological language and involves no belief in the soul's preexistence. Likewise, the suggestion that Jesus is a reappearance of John the Baptist, Elijah, or Jeremiah [Mt. 16:14] — which reflects the failure to recognize the Messiah — in no way implies preexistence of the soul.)

The doctrine of the soul's preexistence was held by some Christian sects, e.g., the first-century Palestinian Mandeans, the second-century Gnostics, and the third-century Manichaeans. Under Platonic and Neo-Platonic influence the view appeared in Justin Martyr (*Dial.* 4–5) and especially in Origen of Alexandria, who linked it to a pretemporal fall of the soul (*De prin.* i.7; ii.8; iv.1). Through Origen's influence the doctrine gained wider acceptance, including Rufinus, John of Jerusalem, and the Priscillianists, but it was opposed by Methodius and Gregory of Nyssa. Justinian condemned it in 543, as did a provincial council of Constantinople the same year (cf. H. J. D. Denzinger, *Enchiridion symbolorum* [30th ed. 1954; Eng. tr. *Sources of Catholic Dogma*, 1957], §§ 203-205; cf. 223, 235).

In subsequent history the idea of the preexistence of the soul had few Christian supporters. It never became part of a Christian creed or confession. It was supported in the 9th cent. by John Scotus Erigena (*De divisione naturae* ii) and in the 19th by F. Schleiermacher (cf. *Christian Faith* [Eng. tr. 1928], §§ 59-61) as well as the Lutheran J. Müller, who defended it in his major study, *The Christian Doctrine of Sin*. Variations of the idea are found in some pantheistically oriented philosophies, e.g., those of Spinoza, Leibniz, Kant, Hegel, Schopenhauer, and I. H. Fichte.

Most textbooks in systematic theology discuss preexistentism as one of three historical answers to the question of the origin of the human soul. Under the influence of Greek metaphysical dualism of spirit and matter, many theologians embraced dichotomy (body and soul) or trichotomy (body, soul, and spirit) in explanation of the constitutional nature of man (*see* ANTHROPOLOGY III.E). Those positions then led to the question of the origin of the soul. Most chose either creationism (the theory that God creates a new soul at the conception or birth of each individual) or traducianism (the theory that the human soul is transmitted to the child by the parents) rather than preexistentism. Recent theology has reached a wide consensus on the wholeness and unity of the human person and hence regards as illegitimate the question of the soul's origin. Thus the idea of the preexistence of the soul finds little support in contemporary Christian theology.

*Bibliography*.–L. Berkhof, *Systematic Theology* (2nd ed. 1941, repr. 1982), pp. 196f.; G. C. Berkouwer, *Man: The Image of God* (Eng. tr. 1962, repr. 1981), pp. 194-309; J. F. Bruch, *Die Lehre von der Präexistenz der menschlichen Seelen* (1895); *ERE*, X, *s.v.* "Pre-existence" (R. Moore); R. G. Hamerton-Kelley, *Pre-existence, Wisdom, and the Son of Man* (1973); A. von Harnack, *History of Dogma*, I (Eng. tr. 1896), 318-332; J. Müller, *Christian Doctrine of Sin* (Eng. tr. 1876); J. M. E. McTaggart, *Human Immortality and Pre-existence* (1916, repr. 1970).

F. H. KLOOSTER

**PREFECT** [Aram. *s^e han*] (Dnl. 2:48; 3:2f., 27; 6:7 [MT 8]); AV GOVERNOR. *S^e han* derives from Akk. *šaknu*, which designates the governor of a conquered city or province. Daniel was placed at the head of all the prefects over the wise men in Nebuchadrezzar's court.

For the Roman office of prefect *see* PROCURATOR.

**PREFER.** A term generally used today in the sense of "choose or esteem above another," but used by the AV in the archaic sense of "advance to a rank or position" in Est. 2:9 (Heb. piel of *šānâ*, "change, transfer"; RSV "advance"). The term is possibly used in this same sense by the AV in Jn. 1:15, 30 to translate Gk. *emprosthén mou gégonen* (AV "is preferred before me"; RSV "ranks before me" [cf. NEB]; see Bauer, rev., p. 257; B. F. Westcott, *Gospel According to St. John* [repr. 1971], p. 13; the phrase appears also in the AV of v. 27 but is omitted by the RSV and NEB, which follow a more ancient textual tradition). In Dnl. 6:3, AV, "was preferred" is an inaccurate translation of the Aram. hithpaal of *n^e ṣaḥ* ("distinguish onseself"; RSV "became distinguished"; NEB "outshone"). N. J. O.

**PREPARATION, DAY OF.** The Gk. *hē paraskeuḗ*, "the preparation," is a technical term for the day before the sabbath (Mt. 27:62; Mk. 15:42; Lk. 23:54; Jn. 19:14, 31, 42). Josephus used it in this manner (*Ant.* xvi.6.2 [163]), though Friday was also called *hē pró toú sabbátou* (Jth. 8:6; 2 Macc. 8:26; *Ant.* iii.10.7 [255]). It was a day of intense activity in anticipation of the sabbath observance. To avoid all risk of infraction, the hours from mid-afternoon to sunset were thought to have almost the sanctity of the sabbath itself, and to be unsuitable for normal activity (cf. the "ninth hour" of *Ant.* xvi.6.2 [163]).

All the Gospel passages where *paraskeuḗ* occurs identify the Jewish day of Preparation as the day of the crucifixion of Our Lord. But inasmuch as the sabbath mentioned in the narratives of the crucifixion is evidently the Passover sabbath of that year (Mk. 15:42; Lk. 23:54, 56: Jn. 19:31), and the Fourth Gospel expressly calls the preparation day in question "the Preparation of the Passover" (Jn. 19:14), the determination of the exact day for "the Preparation" during which Christ was crucified depends on the time when the Passover was celebrated that year. Passover takes place on the 14th of the Jewish lunar month Nisan (*Ant.* iii.10.5 [248]), and is the greatest of the "special sabbaths" in the Jewish year. It often coincided with the normal sabbath of the seventh day. But as a fixed date in a lunar month, its relation to the days of the week varied. We know that the correlation of lunar "high days" with the weekly cycle of seven days was a problem within Judaism, at least for sectarian or nonconformist Jews, who argued for a solar reckoning of the festivals (cf. Jub. 6:29-38; 1 En. 82:4-6). And the curious reference to "that sabbath" (Gk. *ekeínou toú sabbátou*) of Jn. 19:31 may have this problem and phenomenon in view. Thus, while Friday is the usual day of Preparation for the normal weekly sabbath, the precise dating of the preparation for the Passover sabbath mentioned in the Gospels depends on the dating of the Passover for that year. And this further depends on establishing the precise year in question.

Also of relevance to the time of the preparation mentioned in the Gospels, and the concomitant issue of the day of crucifixion, is the question of the dating of the Lord's Supper. The Gospels are clear that the Last Supper took place before the Passover (Jesus' death before the Jewish Passover makes this obvious), yet the Synoptics equate the Lord's Supper with the paschal supper of the first part (at night) of Passover (Mt. 26:17; Mk. 14:12; Lk. 22:7f.). Many consider this equation a secondary development. Others believe that the Last Supper was an anticipated Passover in view of the impossibility of Jesus' celebration with His disciples on the proper day. But with the discovery that the Qumrân community followed a solar calendar (1QS 10:1-8), the old theory of two ways of determining Passover has been revived. On the basis of a solar reckoning, 14 Nisan always fell on the Jewish day that corresponds to our Tuesday at sunset to Wednesday at sunset. We know of the existence of such a calendar, and we know that it was highly respected in some quarters (Jub. 6:29-38; 1 En. 82:4-6; 1QS 10:1-7). What we do not have is explicit evidence from the Gospels of Jesus' or the disciples' attitude toward it. Yet Jesus *could have* used this unofficial reckoning in this instance, and such a hypothesis would go far toward solving many apparent discrepancies in the narrative. Perhaps His reason for using it here, though not necessarily following it in His ministry, was His desire to observe the ancient ritual of Passover on a legal day (solar calendar) before accomplishing it by His death on the day of Preparation for the official Passover (lunar calendar).

Combining this hypothesis with the aforementioned issue of the date of the Passover sabbath, the chronology of Passion week may be as follows: (1) the Last Supper on our Tuesday evening, the nonconformist Passover as per a the solar reckoning being from Tuesday sunset to Wednesday sunset; (2) the official day of Preparation on a lunar calculation being from Wednesday sunset to Thursday sunset, with the crucifixion taking place during Thursday; (3) the special sabbath of the Passover occurring on the Jewish day of Thursday sunset to Friday sunset; (4) the sabbath of the seventh day from Friday sunset to Saturday sunset; and (5) the resurrection of Our Lord on Sunday. The difficulty with the above scheme is that it must posit a double set of references to Passover and sabbath in the Gospels. Thus Jesus' activity before the Last Supper is related temporally to the lunar Passover sabbath of official Judaism (Mt. 26:2; Mk. 14:1; Lk. 22:1; Jn. 12:1; 13:1, 29), while the Synoptics are seen as justifying the ascription of paschal significance to the Supper on the basis of veiled allusions to a sectarian solar calendar (Mt. 26:17; Mk. 14:12; Lk. 22:7f.); and the sabbath referred to in the resurrection narratives is the normal sabbath of the seventh day, which in this case followed the special Passover sabbath (Mt. 28:1; Mk. 16:1, Lk 23:56). But such a complex of designations may be justified in view of the existence of two calendars at that time and Jesus' desire both to celebrate the Passover with His disciples and to be Himself the paschal offering.

*See also* PASSOVER.

***Bibliography.***–H. Schauss, *Guide to Jewish Holy Days* (1962); A. Jaubert, *Date of the Last Supper* (Eng. tr. 1965); J. Jeremias, *Eucharistic Words of Jesus* (Eng. tr. 1964); I. H. Marshall, *Last Supper and Lord's Supper* (1980). R. N. LONGENECKER

**PRESBYTER** prez'bə-tər, pres'bə-tər, [Gk. *presbýteros*]. A leader in Jewish society or a church officer. The term "presbyter" has now been replaced by "elder" in the RSV and in most Presbyterian and Reformed churches. The masc. pl. *presbýteroi* is often used to denote elders acting in concert (e.g., the Jewish elders in Mt. 27:1; Acts 4:5, 8; etc.), and the Christian elders, either generally, as in Acts 15:2, 4, or locally, as in 14:23; 1 Tim. 5:17; etc. The related Greek word *presbytérion* (Eng. "presbytery") designates a group of such elders, as in Lk. 22:66, "assembly of the elders"; Acts 22:5, "council of elders"; 1 Tim. 4:14, "elders." Elders were clearly distinguished from the OT priests, although later sacerdotalism introduced confusion into the English word "priest," which is really a contraction of "presbyter" but has also been made to do duty for the OT priests and for Christ in His high-priestly office.

The development of the Christian eldership is much debated. In spite of differences and the testimony of Epiphanius it seems to have been patterned initially after the "elders" of the synagogue (Lk. 7:3). Thus there soon were elders in the church at Jerusalem (Acts 11:30), and the apostles set up elders in other cities to supervise the new Christian communities (14:23; Tit. 1:5). The mode of appointment is not known, although quite possibly the elders were elected as in the synagogue and then ordained or instituted, first by the apostles (Acts 14:23; 2 Tim. 1:6) and later by the apostles' helpers (Tit. 1:5). Teaching and ruling, the latter naturally including the ordering of worship, seem to have been their functions.

There is no clear evidence in the NT of a wider organization than that of the local church. Yet the forces of evangelism and multiplication make such organization a natural and legitimate development. The necessary formation of new congregations in one place did not break local unity but led to a wider exercise of the ministry of the one presbytery. Similarly, missionary work in surrounding areas might result either in further expansion of the presbytery or in the formation of new presbyteries, which naturally felt a kinship with the neighboring center and which thus met occasionally in a local council or synod for matters of common concern.

The relation of the elders to the bishops poses a peculiar problem. In the NT and later it is hard to see any true distinction between the uses of these terms. Yet the practice of a single bishop supported by elders was undoubtedly early. Various forces probably combined to produce the practice, e.g., the special authority vested in men like Timothy, the OT order of the high priest, priests, and Levites, and the need of a presiding elder who might easily become a permanent president. The attractive notion that the pastor is the bishop supported by ruling elders and deacons is a possible interpretation of second-century practice, but even this has no solid NT support. In sum, although the early literature gives no basis for a doctrinaire Episcopalianism that sees in bishops alone the successors of the apostolic ministry, it also gives no basis for a doctrinaire Presbyterianism that excludes, e.g., a presiding bishop as completely contrary to Scripture.

In Revelation the twenty-four elders have a conspicuous place in the Church (Rev. 4:4, 10; 5:5; etc.). They probably represent the combined patriarchs and apostles as the representative founders of Israel in the OT and the new Israel in the NT (cf. Mt. 19:28).

E. MACK G. W. BROMILEY

CLASSICAL ANGLICAN VIEW

As with its ministry generally, Anglicanism has inherited the threefold structure of bishops, priests, and deacons. Strictly, the priests are elders or presbyters, as shown by the underlying Latin term (*presbyter*) in the *Book of Common Prayer*. The doctrinal formularies indicate no dogmatic Episcopalianism, so that the distinction of bishops and presbyters is simply one of order. No specific ministry is conferred on the bishop at his consecration, the particular functions being only matters of order rather than of intrinsic prerogative. The ancient discussion whether the presbyter acts merely as the bishop's delegate or in virtue of his own office is settled along the lines of medieval teaching, which regarded bishops and presbyters as together constituting the final order of ministry. Thus presbyters are vested with the full rights and responsibilities of ministry and maintain their part in ordinations to the presbyterate, thus fulfilling the NT precedent of the laying on of hands by the presbytery. Indeed, in spite of the tendency to parochialism inseparable from too large dioceses, a minimal presbyterian structure is preserved in the rural deaneries or their equivalents.

A candidate for presbyter must be a deacon, at least twenty-four years old, and adequately prepared in learning and character. Although there is no popular election, opportunity is given both locally and in the final service to lodge serious objections, so that popular consent is maintained in a negative form. Searching questions are publicly addressed to the candidate concerning his inward call, acceptance of Scripture, devotion to his task, readiness to dispel error, consecration to theological study, zeal to set a good example, and peaceable and obedient spirit.

The duties of the presbyter are plainly stated during the 1662 ordination service in NT readings and also in the bishop's charge. The office is primarily pastoral, although it includes searching for Christ's sheep scattered abroad. In the ordination itself the saying in Jn. 20:23 is repeated, and the elder is enjoined to be a faithful dispenser of the Word of God and of His holy sacraments. A Bible is given, with the accompanying words: "Take thou authority to preach the Word of God and to minister the holy sacraments in the congregation, where thou shalt be lawfully appointed thereunto."

Four final points may be made. First, there is no suggestion in the ordination service or other formularies that the elder has a sacerdotal function. On this ground, i.e., a supposed lack of full intention, Anglican orders must appear deficient to the Roman Catholic world. Second, ordination itself is not accepted as a sacrament of the gospel. Although 1 Tim. 4:14 is cited in the consecration of bishops, there is no doctrine of an automatically transmitted grace of orders essential to the exercise of a valid ministry. Third, the underlying doctrine of ministry, while it insists on regular calling of church office-bearers and defends Anglican practice as good, does not contend for a single mode of ordination, asking only that there should be calling by those who have public authority given to them in the congregation for this purpose. Fourth, the saying in Jn. 20:23 concerning the remission and retention of sin is divorced from the rejected sacrament of penance and is to be regarded as a proclamation of the gospel promises, as in the various penitential exercises of the *Book of Common Prayer*.

*Bibliography*.–*Book of Common Prayer*, The Thirty-Nine Articles and Ordinal; N. Sykes, *Old Priest and New Presbyter* (1956).

G. W. BROMILEY

REFORMED VIEW

According to John Calvin, presbyter, bishop, pastor, and minister are synonymous and interchangeable terms (*Inst.* iv.3.8). The presbyter is the bishop to whom has been committed the ministry of the word and sacraments, and leadership in pastoral care and discipline. The presbyters of the Church include also its teachers, or doctors, who are not put in charge of discipline or of administering the sacraments, but whose function is to keep doctrine whole and pure among believers and to watch over scriptural interpretation (*Inst.* iv.3.4.).

The pastor (presbyter-bishop) holds an office "not of human devising" (as was the case with the "bishops" of the Roman Church) but ordained by God Himself. A person must be called to such an office. He is normally called to the office in one particular place, from which it is a serious matter to wish to be removed. He is therefore bound to one particular parish, or church, though he can aid others (*Inst.* iv.3.7). His calling involved election by the people (or at least the consent of the people) and appointment by "his colleagues and the elders" as forming a "presbytery" (3.15). He is ordained by the laying on of hands, for which there is "no set precept" but which has been in continual use since the apostles, being an important sign "useful for the dignity of the ministry" and established within the Church by the Spirit of God (3.15).

According to one tradition in the Reformed Church the word presbyter can be used also to designate the "elder" appointed and ordained within the local congregation as a member of the church Session to rule the congregation and to be responsible for its pastoral care. It is argued that such eldership is "an office indistinguishable from the presbyterate except in function." Scriptural basis for this thesis is found in 1 Tim. 5:17, which seems to imply that there are two kinds of presbyter, the one a "teaching elder" and the other a "ruling elder." Calvin gave some encouragement to this view (*Inst.* iv.4.1).

But many have argued against regarding the lay elder as different from the minister-presbyter only in function. They have seen the elder in the Reformed Church more aptly analogous to the NT deacon than to the presbyter. The Westminister Confession of Faith recognized the eldership as a spiritual office to which laymen were called and set apart to help in the government and discipline of the Church, analogous to the "elder of the people" in OT (*see* ELDER IN THE OT).

Certain elders, however, are presbyters in that they are members of the local presbytery, which consists of all the ministers of a delimited area and an equal number of elders. This presbytery may appoint some members as its representatives to higher courts of the Church. In the Church of Scotland these elders do not take part in the laying on of hands in the ordination of ministers.

R. S. WALLACE

**PRESENCE.** In the OT usually the translation of Heb. *pānîm,* "face" (e.g., Gen. 3:8; Ex. 33:14f.; Lev. 22:3; Dt. 4:37; 1 S. 19:7; Neh. 2:1; Job 23:15; Ps. 16:11; 31:20 [MT 21]; 51:11 [MT 13]; 105:4; 139:7; Isa. 64:1-3 [MT 63:19–64:2]; Jonah 1:3 [AV also "face," "countenance," "sight," etc.]). Occasionally it is the translation of *ʿayin,* "eye" (e.g., Gen. 23:11, 18; Ps. 101:7; Jer. 28:1, 5, 11; 32:12f.; Jonah 2:4 [MT 5] [AV also "sight," etc.]), *negeḏ,* "before" (e.g., Gen. 31:32; 1 K. 8:22; Prov. 14:7 [AV also "before"]). Sometimes "presence" represents no particular term but is supplied to suit the context.

In the NT "presence" frequently renders Gk. *prósōpon,* "face," the usual LXX translation of Heb. *pānîm* (e.g., Lk. 2:31; Acts 2:28; 2 Cor. 2:10; 2 Thess. 1:9; He. 9:24; Rev. 20:11 [AV also "face"]). More often it translates *enṓpion,* "before" (e.g., Lk. 1:19; 13:26; Jn. 2:30; Acts 27:35; 1 Tim. 5:20; 6:12f.; 2 Tim. 4:1; Rev. 13:12 [AV also "before"]). Other terms are *katenṓpion,* "before" (Jude 24), *enantíon* (Lk. 20:26 [AV "before"]), *katénanti* (Rom. 4:17 [AV "before"]), *apénanti* (Acts 3:16), and *parousía,* "presence," "coming" (2 Cor. 10:10; Phil. 2:12; *see* PAROUSIA). In Jn. 17:5; 2 Cor. 4:14; Rev. 7:15 the RSV supplies "presence" contextually.

*See* FACE; COUNTENANCE; PRESENCE OF GOD.

N. J. O.

**PRESENCE, BREAD OF THE** [Heb. *leḥem happānîm*–'bread of the face'] (Ex. 25:30; 35:13; 39:36; 1 S. 21:6 [MT 7]; 1 K. 7:48; 2 Ch. 4:19); AV SHEWBREAD; [*šulḥan happānîm*–'table of the face'] ("table of the bread of the presence," Nu. 4:7); AV TABLE OF SHEWBREAD; NEB TABLE OF THE PRESENCE; [Gk. *ártoi tḗs prothéseōs*–'loaves to set before (God)'] (Mt. 12:4; Mk. 2:26; Lk. 6:4); AV SHEWBREAD; NEB SACRED BREAD; [*próthesis* (*tṓn ártōn*)–'a setting forth of the loaves'] (1 Macc. 1:22; 2 Macc. 10:3; He. 9:2); AV SHEWBREAD; **CONTINUAL BREAD** [Heb. *leḥem hattāmîḏ*–'bread of continuity'] (Nu. 4:7); **SHOWBREAD** [Heb. *leḥem hammaʿareḵeṯ*–'bread of the arrangement' 1 Ch. 9:32; 23:29; 2 Ch. 13:11; Neh. 10:33 [MT 34]), *maʿareḵeṯ*–'arrangement' (1 Ch. 28:16; 2 Ch. 2:4 [MT 3]); 29:18)]; AV SHEWBREAD; NEB BREAD OF THE PRESENCE.

***I. Terms***.–The seven Hebrew and Greek expressions listed above, although variously translated, all refer to the twelve loaves of consecrated bread placed on the golden table in the holy place. The older translation "shewbread" or "showbread" came into English through Tyndale's translation (A.D. 1530), which adopted Luther's German rendering *Schaubrot* (Ger. *Schau,* "show, sight, exhibition"). Most scholars accept "bread of the Presence" as an appropriate translation of Heb. *leḥem happānîm.* P. A. H. de Boer has argued that the phrase should be translated literally "bread of the face" or "facial bread," and that *pānîm* indicates that the loaves were "stamped with an image of the deity" (p. 35). But the prohibition of images of Yahweh (Ex. 20:4) makes this theory untenable (see *THAT,* II, 460).

One additional passage not listed in the heading, Lev. 24:5-9, uses none of these combinations but simply calls it the "bread" (Heb. *leḥem,* v. 7) or the twelve "cakes" (*ḥallôṯ,* v. 5). Some commentators link "memorial" (Heb. *'azkārā*) in v. 7 with the bread of Presence, but a careful examination of that text reveals that the "memorial" is the frankincense placed with the bread, not the bread itself.

***II. Preparation and Arrangement***.–Each sabbath the priests replaced the twelve loaves with freshly baked loaves; they themselves ate the week-old loaves in a "holy place" (Lev. 24:5-9). The loaves may have been unleavened (see Josephus *Ant.* iii.6.6 [142]), although this is not stated in Scripture. Frankincense was placed in small dishes with the bread (RSV Lev. 24:7; not sprinkled on the bread, as suggested by the AV and NEB; cf. Nu. 4:7; also *Ant.* iii.6.6 [143]). During the tabernacle period the preparation of the loaves was apparently the responsibility of Aaron and his sons (Lev. 24:5-9). In a later period this work devolved upon the Kohathites (1 Ch. 9:32; cf. 23:29; Nu. 4:7, 15).

The precise arrangement of the loaves on the table is

not certain. Most translators and commentators suggest that the loaves were placed in two "rows" (*maʿarākôt*, Lev. 24:6) of six loaves each (cf. *Ant.* iii.6.6 [142]). But the verbal root *ʿrk* means simply "arrange" with no specific form of arrangement implied (cf. *leḥem hammaʿareḵeṯ*, 1 Ch. 9:32; etc.). Moreover, the size of the loaves even if they were unleavened (each loaf was to contain "two-tenths of an ephah [about 4.4 liters or 18 cups] of fine flour," Lev. 24:5), makes this interpretation practically impossible. Twelves loaves of this size would require more surface area than that provided by the table (Ex. 25:23 indicates that the table's surface area was two cubits by one cubit [91 cm. by 46 cm., or 36 in. by 18 in.]). Most likely the bread was arranged in two "piles" of six loaves each. Such was, in fact, the arrangement in the later period, and the rabbinic tradition indicates that gold spacer-tubes were used to keep the loaves separated so that they would not mold (see Edersheim, pp. 184f.).

*III. History.*–The first mention of the bread of the Presence occurs in the instructions concerning the furniture for the TABERNACLE (II.C.2); the twelve loaves were to be exhibited continually on a golden table in the holy place (e.g., Ex. 25:30). The earliest reference to the practice in the historical books occurs in 1 S. 21:4-6, which tells of Ahimelech the priest giving "holy bread" to David and his men as they were fleeing from Saul. Ahimelech violated the law that only the priests were allowed to eat the bread (Lev. 24:9), but he was concerned that David's men at least be in a state of ritual purity before partaking of the bread. This incident was later cited by Jesus as an example of an excusable violation of a cultic regulation (Mt. 12:3f. par.).

The practice of exhibiting the loaves continued in Solomon's temple (1 K. 7:48). Some passages suggest that Solomon made ten tables for the bread of the Presence (cf. 1 Ch. 28:16; 2 Ch. 4:8, 19), but apparently only one table was used at a time. After the Exile the people of Israel again pledged themselves to provide for the "showbread" (Neh. 10:33). Antiochus IV Epiphanes removed the table of the bread of the Presence from the second temple (1 Macc. 1:22). When Judas Maccabeus cleansed the temple he brought in a new table and restored the bread (1 Macc. 4:49-51; 2 Macc. 10:3). It was probably this table that is portrayed in the Arch of Titus as one of the Jewish treasures carried to Rome after the destruction of Jerusalem in A.D. 70.

*IV. Significance.*–Very similar practices of presenting bread to the deity have been discovered in other ancient Near Eastern countries. In Babylon, e.g., part of the sacrificial rite included the laying of loaves, in a set of twelve or multiple of twelve, before the deity. Some OT passages allude to the practice of preparing food for other gods (e.g., Isa. 65:11; Jer. 7:18; 44:15-19; cf. also Bel and the Dragon). On the basis of these parallels, some scholars have concluded that the original intention of the bread of the Presence was to provide food for the deity (see *HDB*).

Such external similarities do not necessarily indicate common origin or purpose, however. In fact, the OT provides no evidence that the bread of the Presence was ever understood as a sacrifice (contra de Boer). Rather, the twelve loaves are presented as a pledge of the eternal covenant between God and the twelve tribes of Israel (Lev. 24:8; see de Vaux, p. 422). As a symbol of all that nourishes and sustains life, the bread was a constant reminder that Israel's life depended upon God's sustaining presence. The eating of the loaves by the priests (rather than by the deity) symbolized the communion between God and the people to whom He was continually present.

*Bibliography.*–P. A. H. de Boer, "An Aspect of Sacrifice," in G. W. Anderson, *et al.*, eds., *Studies in the Religion of Ancient Israel* (*SVT*, 23; 1972), pp. 27-36; B. S. Childs, *Exodus* (*OTL*, 1974), p. 524; A. Edersheim, *The Temple* (1881, repr. 1978), pp. 181-87; M. Haran, *Scripta Hierosolymitana*, 8 (1961), 272-302; *HDB* (rev. one-vol. ed. 1963), *s.v.* "Showbread" (P. R. Ackroyd); *THAT*, II, *s.v.* פָּנִים (A. S. van der Woude); R. de Vaux, *Ancient Israel* (Eng. tr. 1961, repr. 1965), II, 422; G. J. Wenham, *Leviticus* (*NICOT*, 1979), pp. 309f.

G. L. CARR N. J. O.

**PRESENCE OF GOD.** When referring to God, "presence" in the English versions most often represents Heb. *pānîm* ("face"; Ex. 33:14), Gk. *prósōpon* ("face"; e.g., He. 9:24), or *enṓpion* ("in the face of"; e.g., 1 Cor. 1:29).

*I. In the OT.*–According to Scripture, God's relationship with mankind began with creation (Gen. 2:15-17), but the immediacy of this relationship was soon affected by the disobedience of the human race (3:8, 24). Thereafter, contact was maintained through various means, most of which involved some veiling of the Deity. One such means was a vision leading to communication (e.g., Gen. 15:1). It is significant that Abraham became known as the friend of God (Isa. 41:8), attesting a close relationship. Another method involved the assumption of human form (Gen. 18:1f.; cf. 19:1). Jacob's night of wrestling disclosed such a visitation (Gen. 32:24-30; cf. Josh. 5:13-15; Dnl. 3:24f.). At times God used the dream as a means of self-disclosure (e.g., Gen. 28:12f.). This method was used also for making contact with those outside the covenant relationship (Dnl. 2:1ff.).

A burning bush in the desert arrested Moses' attention and led to his encounter with the angel of the Lord (Ex. 3:2); this in turn brought him into dialogue with the God of Abraham, Isaac, and Jacob. Moses' close relationship with God continued throughout his life, so that he was given the encomium that the Lord knew him "face to face" (Dt. 34:10). This rich fellowship enabled him to assure Israel just before his death that God would go with them and would never leave them nor forsake them (31:6).

The TABERNACLE was erected as the God-appointed means for Israel's worship. Its structure emphasized that the recognition of God's presence in the most holy place was the very essence and climax of the nation's worship. Its movable character underscored that the divine presence was not restricted to one location but continued with the people on their journey. The PILLAR OF CLOUD AND PILLAR OF FIRE symbolized that presence. When it rose from the tabernacle it signaled the beginning of the journey toward the Promised Land. Its stopping was the signal to make camp.

The presence of God was even more significantly symbolized by the ARK OF THE COVENANT, the chest containing the two stone tablets on which were inscribed the Ten Commandments, God's covenant law, which could also be called the "testimony." The ark, then, derived its sacredness from its contents. When the Israelites crossed the Jordan into Canaan, the ark led the way, symbolizing in a dramatic way the presence of the Lord whose aid was essential for the conquest (Josh. 3:1-4). Reverence for the ark as the token of God's presence diminished appreciably in some quarters until it became little more than a fetish. Israelites felt secure fighting the Philistines as long as the ark went with them into battle (1 S. 4:3). God rebuked this travesty by allowing the ark to be captured by the enemy. Restored to Israel, the ark was later given the same place in the temple that it had in the tabernacle — the most holy place, where it continued to represent the presence of God.

To be sure, the Almighty was always free to manifest

Himself in other places and in other ways. E.g., He entered the contest set up between Elijah and the prophets of Baal by sending fire to consume the sacrifice (1 K. 18). Perhaps this prophet came to associate the God of Israel too readily with fire and force; for shortly after the Baal contest, when Elijah was mired in despondency, God again granted him a fiery display, but He was not in the fire. Instead, God manifested Himself in a gentle whisper (1 K. 19:12). One of the most notable self-disclosures of God was granted to another prophet. Isaiah received a vision of the Lord, seated on a throne and exalted, with the surrounding seraphim proclaiming His holiness and glory (Isa. 6:1-3). This vision set the tone for his message to the nation.

The devout Israelite recognized that God's presence was not limited to the temple. God was with His people individually as well as in the congregation. In the throes of anguish over his great sin, David pleaded, "Cast me not away from thy presence, and take not thy holy Spirit from me" (Ps. 51:11 [MT 12]). The godly are assured of God's presence and aid (16:11).

Evidently some Israelites had a limited view of the extent of God's presence. After Yahweh had appeared to Jacob at Bethel, he awoke and exclaimed, "Surely the Lord is in this place; and I did not know it" (Gen. 28:16). When Yahweh directed Jonah to go to Nineveh and call it to repentance, he went in the opposite direction "from the presence of the Lord" (Jonah 1:3). His subsequent experience no doubt enlarged his conception of God.

***II. In the NT.***–In the OT and even more in Judaism God's transcendence so dominated the thinking of His people that they believed He must necessarily make His presence known through intermediate agents (cf. Stewart, p. 180). But the situation of the Christian community was greatly different, since God had now revealed Himself in the person of His Son (He. 1:1f.): in a new sense God now dwelt in the midst of His people. (*See* PERSON OF CHRIST.) Furthermore, the Spirit of God became much more active than under the old covenant, especially in applying the benefits of Christ's redemptive work to His people. Even so, the use of physical phenomena to represent the divine presence was not entirely superseded (Lk. 9:34; Acts 2:1-4).

As the Son of God, Jesus bore the title Immanuel, "God with us" (Mt. 1:23). He was also identified as the Word by whom God revealed Himself as He became flesh and dwelt among men (Jn. 1:14). He explained mighty works by the fact that God was working with Him (Jn. 5:17).

Christ's presence with His people did not end with His ascension. After returning to the Father, having completed His work of redemption (Jn. 20:17), Jesus continued to minister to His people by representing them before the Father (He. 9:24). He also appeared to Saul of Tarsus and set him apart as an apostle (Acts 26:13-18; Gal. 1:1) that through him the gospel might be widely proclaimed (Rom. 15:18f.). Thus Jesus fulfilled His promise that by means of the Holy Spirit He would continue to be with His disciples (Jn. 15:26f.). In John's apocalyptic vision Christ knocks at the door of the heart, promising that anyone who admits Him will enjoy blessed fellowship with Him (Rev. 3:20). Near the end of Paul's life, at his final trial before the Roman authorities, he confessed that "the Lord stood by me and gave me strength to proclaim the message fully . . ." (2 Tim. 4:17).

God's people wait in hope for the end of the present age, when Christ will reappear to gather the saints to glory and conform them fully to His own likeness (He. 9:28; 1 Jn. 3:2f.). In the day of the new heaven and new earth, God Himself will dwell with His people forever (Rev. 21, esp. v. 3). The new Jerusalem will have no temple, "for its temple is the Lord God the Almighty and the Lamb. And the city has no need of sun or moon to shine upon it, for the glory of God is its light, and its lamp is the Lamb" (vv. 22f.).

For further discussion of the concept of God's presence in the OT, NT, Targums, and rabbinic literature, *see* SHEKINAH.

***Bibliography.***–E. Barbotin, *Humanity of God* (1976); T. W. Mann, *Divine Presence and Guidance in Israelite Traditions* (1977); W. J. Phythian-Adams, *The People and the Presence* (1942); R. A. Stewart, *Rabbinic Theology* (1961); S. Terrien, *The Elusive Presence* (1978); M. H. Woudstra, *Ark of the Covenant from Conquest to Kingship* (1965).

E. F. HARRISON

**PRESENT** (vb.) [Heb. hiphil of *qāraḇ*–'bring near' (Lev. 1:5; 16:9, 11, 20, etc.), hiphil of *rûm*–'contribute, offer' (Nu. 15:19f.; 18:19, 24, 26: etc.), hithpael of *yāṣaḇ* (Dt. 31:14; Josh. 24:1; Job 1:6; 2:1, etc.), hiphil of *nāp̱al*–'cause to fall' (Jer. 42:9; Dnl. 9:18, 20), *bô'*–'come, come in, go, go in' (Jer. 41:15; Zec. 14:18), hiphil of *nāg̱aš*–'cause to approach, bring near' (Jgs. 6:19; Isa. 45:21), hiphil of *ʿālâ*–'cause to ascend' (1 Ch. 21:26; Isa. 66:3), *ʿāmaḏ* (Hos. 13:13; hophal, Lev. 16:10), *ʿāśâ*–'do, make' (Lev. 22:23), niphal of *nāṣaḇ*–'take one's stand' (Ex. 34:2), hiphil of *yāṣag̱* (Gen. 47:2), *nāṯan*–'give, put, set,' niphal of *rā'â* (Gen. 46:29); Gk. *parístēmi* (Lk. 2:22; Acts 1:3; 9:41; Eph. 5:17; 2 Tim. 2:15; etc.), *hístēmi*–'put, place, set' (Jude 24), *paragínomai* (Acts 21:18), *prosphérō*–'bring, offer' (Acts 21:26), *laléō*–'speak' (Acts 17:19), *timáō*–'honor' (Acts 28:10)] AV also BRING (NEAR), SHOW, OFFER (UP), STANDING (Zec. 6:5), STAY LONG (Hos. 13:13); NEB also BRING (FORWARD), SHOW, HAND OVER, SET ASIDE, COME AND STAND (Dt. 31:14), TAKE, ENTER, URGE, STAND AND WAIT (Ex. 34:2), etc.; (noun) [Heb. *minḥâ*–'gift, tribute, offering,' *mōhar* (Gen. 34:12; Ex. 22:17 [MT 16]; 1 S. 18:25), *b$^{e}$rāḵâ*–'blessing' (1 S. 25:27; 30:26; 2 K. 5:15), *šōḥaḏ, maś'ēṯ*–'portion' (2 S. 11:8; Jer. 40:5), *t$^{e}$šûrâ*–'gift' (1 S. 9:7); Gk. *dṓron* (Rev. 11:10)]; AV also DOWRY, BLESSING, REWARD, "mess of meat" (2 S. 11:8), GIFT; NEB also GIFT, BRIDE-PRICE, FAVOUR, TOKEN OF GRATITUDE, BRIBE (2 K. 16:8); **PRESENTABLE** [Gk. *euschḗmōn*–'proper, presentable'] (1 Cor. 12:24); AV COMELY; NEB SEEMLY. The act of giving something to someone or the object that is given.

***I. In the OT.***–A number of Hebrew terms when translated "present" by the RSV refer almost exclusively to the offering of sacrifices by the Israelites. Included are *bô'* (Jer. 41:5), *nāṯan* (Ezk. 20:28), *ʿāśâ* (Lev. 22:23), the hophal of *ʿāmaḏ* (Lev. 16:10), and the hiphil of *qāraḇ, rûm, nāg̱aš,* and *ʿālâ*.

Hebrew *qāraḇ* appears in the contexts of the ritual offerings associated with the Day of Atonement (Lev. 16:9, 11, 20), the feasts of the Lord (ch. 23), the Nazirite laws (Nu. 6:16), and the purification of the Levites (8:9f.). The hiphil of *rûm* is used in regard to coarse grain offerings (15:19f.) and other miscellaneous offerings (18:19, 24, 26, 28f.). The offerings of Gideon (Jgs. 6:19) and David (1 Ch. 21:26) were given to the living God of Israel, while others blasphemed the Lord by their sacrifices to inanimate idols (e.g., Ezk. 20:28). Malachi states that the Lord will purify and refine the sons of Levi "till they present right offerings to the Lord" (Mal. 3:3; cf. the hiphil of *nāg̱aš* in 1:7f.; 2:12; and the hophal in 1:11).

The other significant Hebrew verbs are *nāp̱al* and *yāṣaḇ*. The hiphil of *nāp̱al* refers to the offering of supplications to the Lord (Jer. 42:9; Dnl. 9:18, 20). The same verb occurs in Jer. 38:26 with reference to special pleading before a king (RSV "make a plea," lit. "let a supplication fall"). "Presenting oneself" (hithpael of *yāṣaḇ*) before the Lord is often related to the concept of service. In Josh. 24:1, e.g., the people dispose themselves to serve the Lord. In Job 1:6 and 2:1 the sons of God come before the Lord ready for service. Similarly, Moses and Joshua take their places before the Lord for the commissioning of Joshua (Dt. 31:14).

The noun generally used for "gift" or "present" is Heb. *minḥâ* (Jgs. 6:18; 1 S. 10:27; 1 K. 10:25; etc.). This is the term used for Jacob's gifts to Esau (Gen. 32:13, 18, 20f. [MT 14, 19, 21f.]) and for those received by Joseph from his family (43:11, 15, 26). In some cases gifts were a courtesy offered in approaching a person of rank (cf. 1 S. 16:20; 17:18).

A special type of gift in the OT was the *mōhar* (RSV "marriage present"; AV "dowry"; NEB "bride price"). The term represents the sum of money paid to the bride's family, not as a purchase price but as compensation for the loss of a family member (*see* MARRIAGE IV.B.2). Related to this is Heb. *b^erāḵâ*, which is generally translated "blessing" but in Josh. 15:19 and Jgs. 1:15 is a technical term for a groom's gift to his bride (cf. F. I. Andersen and D. N. Freedman, *Hosea* [*AB*, 1980], pp. 272-75).

The NEB "bribe" correctly translates Heb. *šōḥaḏ*. Although bribes were prohibited by law (Ex. 23:8; Dt. 16:19) and were contrary to God's character (Dt. 10:17), they were accepted by Samuel's sons (1 S. 8:3) and were used by Kings Asa and Ahaz (1 K. 15:19; 2 K. 16:8).

The noun *maś'ēṯ* (<*nāśā'*, "lift, carry, take") refers to something that is carried to someone. Heb. *t^ešûrâ* is a hapax legomenon related to Akk. *tāmartu* (<*amāru*, "see") and therefore is a "gift of greeting" given upon seeing someone (cf. P. K. McCarter, *1 Samuel* [*AB*, 1980], p. 176).

***II. In the NT.–*** Greek *parístēmi* is used in several special senses in the NT. In Rom. 12:1, Paul's exhortation to "present your bodies as a living sacrifice . . . to God," *parístēmi* has its extrabiblical sense as a technical term for offering of sacrifices (C. E. B. Cranfield, *Romans*, II [*ICC*, 1979], 598). True worshipers will therefore offer up their entire selves to God. *Parístēmi* has a sacrificial sense also in Col. 1:22, which states that on the basis of Christ's sacrificial death believers may be accepted approvingly by God. A different sense of the word occurs in 2 Cor. 11:2, which refers to "the solemn presentation of a royal bride" to the groom, as in Ps. 45 (see *TDNT*, V, 840; *see also* BRIDE OF CHRIST).

The verb *prosphérō* in Acts 21:26 also reflects a sacrificial sense, referring to the giving of offerings associated with Nazirite vows (cf. Nu. 6:1-21; Mish. *Nazir* vi.6f.).

The only use of the noun "present" in the RSV NT is in Rev. 11:10, where Gk. *dṓron* refers to the gifts exchanged among those celebrating the martyrdom of the two witnesses (cf. Est. 9:19, 22).

*See also* GIFT.

G. L. KNAPP

**PRESENTLY.** A term used by the AV in the original but now obsolete sense of "at once, immediately." The RSV has replaced it with "at once" (Prov. 12:16; Mt. 21:19; 26:53) and "as soon as" (Phil. 2:23).

**PRESIDENT** [Aram. *sāraḵ*] (Dnl. 6:2-4, 6f. [MT 3-5, 7f.]); NEB MINISTER, CHIEF MINISTER. The title of three high officials, one of whom was Daniel, appointed by Darius the Mede to oversee his empire; the one hundred twenty satraps were to "give account," especially of revenues, to these three. When Daniel distinguished himself in this office, Darius "planned to set him over the whole kingdom." His colleagues then became envious and plotted his downfall. Their plot resulted in the incident of the lions' den (vv. 3-28).

Aramaic *sāraḵ* is a loanword from Pers. *saraka* (Avestan *sāra*, "head") and several times in the Targums translates Heb. *šōṭēr*, "officer."

G. A. L.

**PRESS.** The AV translation of Gk. *óchlos* in Mk. 2:4; 5:27, 30; Lk. 8:19; 19:3 (RSV "crowd"; *see* CROWD; MULTITUDE). On "wine press," *see* VINE; WINE PRESS.

The verb occurs in the RSV with at least four different meanings: (1) to squeeze, push down on or against: e.g., Gen. 40:11 (Heb. *śāḥaṭ*); Ezk. 23:3 (pual of *māʿaḵ*); Mk. 5:31 (Gk. *synthlíbō*; AV "throng"); Lk. 8:45 (*apothlíbō*); (2) to constrain, exert influence on: e.g., Gen. 19:3, 9 (Heb. *pāṣar*, "urge strongly"); Jer. 17:16 (hiphil of *'ûṣ*, "urge"; AV "hasten"); (3) to harass, afflict, oppress: e.g., Jgs. 14:17; 16:16 (hiphil of *ṣûq*; AV also "lay sore upon"); Lk. 11:53 (Gk. *enéchō*, "be very hostile"; AV "urge"); cf. Phil. 1:23 (pass. of *synéchō*), where the torment is internal; (4) to pursue, follow through: e.g., Hos. 6:3 (Heb. *rāḏap̄*, "pursue"; AV "follow on"); Phil. 3:12, 14 (Gk. *diṓkō*, "pursue"; AV also "follow after").

N. J. O.

**PRESSFAT.** *See* WINE PRESS.

**PRESUME; PRESUMPTION; PRESUMPTUOUS; PRESUMPTUOUSLY** [Heb. hiphil of *zîḏ*–'act arrogantly or rebelliously' (Dt. 1:43; 17:13; 18:20; Neh. 9:16, 29), *zēḏ*–'arrogant' (Ps. 19:13 [MT 14]), *zāḏôn*–'arrogance' (Dt. 17:12; 18:22; 1 S. 17:28), hiphil of *ʿāpal*–'have the audacity (to)' (Nu. 14:44), *mālē' lēḇ*–'heart has filled,' 'have the audacity (to)' (Est. 7:5); Gk. *dokéō*–'think, suppose' (Mt. 3:9), *axióō heautón*–'think oneself worthy' (Lk. 7:7), *kataphronéō*–'look down upon' (Rom. 2:4), *tolmáō*–'dare' (Jude 9)]; AV also DEAL PROUDLY, PROUD, THINK, "think oneself worthy," DESPISE, DARE; NEB also BE ARROGANT, BE DEFIANT, GO RECKLESSLY, OF SELF-WILL, etc. To speak or act proudly or without warrant.

In the OT these terms refer to those who overstep their bounds or dare to act in a disobedient manner. Disaster befell the Israelites in the hill country because they were "reckless" or "headstrong" (Heb. hiphil of *ʿāpal*; Rashi: "insolent") in presuming they could gain a victory despite Moses' express command not to fight (Nu. 14:44). A similar calamitous fate awaits the prophet who "presumes to speak a word in my name which I have not commanded him to speak" (Dt. 18:20). Haman, too, met an unsavory end when Esther identified him as "he that would presume" to destroy her people (Est. 7:5).

In the NT, John the Baptist warned his audiences not to imagine they have the right to claim Abraham as their father and thus to escape God's coming judgment (Mt. 3:9). By contrast, the centurion who sought Jesus' healing for his slave did not consider himself worthy to meet Jesus (Lk. 7:7).

Paul sternly warned the Roman Christians not to think lightly about God's kindness, forbearance, and patience, for those who treat with contempt these riches of God's goodness are storing up wrath for themselves (Rom. 2:4). According to Jude, the archangel Michael had such respect for God and God's creatures that he dared not "presume to pronounce a reviling judgment" even against the devil (v. 9).

D. K. MCKIM

**PREVENT.** A verb used by the AV only in the archaic sense of "go before, precede," "meet in advance." In the OT it is the translation of the piel and hiphil of Heb. *qādam* ("be in front," "be beforehand"). The RSV replaces "prevent" with "meet" (Ps. 21:3 [MT 4]; 59:10 [MT 11]; Isa. 21:14; Am. 9:10), "come to meet" (Job 30:27; Ps. 79:8), "confront" (2 S. 22:6, 19; Ps. 18:5 [MT 6]), "come before" (88:13 [MT 14]), "rise before" (119:147), etc. In the AV NT "prevent" represents Gk. *phthánō* (1 Thess. 4:15; RSV "precede") and *prophthánō* (Mt. 17:25; RSV "speak first"). "Prevent" occurs in this same sense in the AV of Wisd. 6:13 (RSV "hasten"); 16:28 (RSV "rise before").

**PREY** [Heb. *'ōkel*–'food' (Job 9:26; 39:29; Ps. 104:21), *bāzaz*–'plunder' ("make [or become] prey," Gen. 34:29; Isa. 10:2; 42:22; Jer. 30:16), *ṭerep*–'prey (of wild animals)' (Gen. 49:9; Nu. 23:24; Job 4:11; 24:5; etc.), *baz*–'spoil' (Nu. 14:3, 31; Dt. 1:39; 2 K. 21:14; Isa. 33:23; etc.), *malqô(a)ḥ*–'booty' (Isa. 49:24f.), *m^e^nat*–'portion' (Ps. 63:10 [MT 11]), *m^e^ṣûdâ*–'hunter's bag' (Ezk. 13:21), *'aḏ* (Gen. 49:27), *'ayiṭ*–'birds of prey' (Gen. 15:11; Job. 28:7; Isa. 18:6; 46:11; Jer. 12:9; Ezk. 39:4), *ṣayiḏ*–'food, prey' (Job 38:41; Prov. 12:27), hithpael part. of *šālal*–'plundered' ("make oneself prey," Isa. 59:15), *šālāl*–'booty' (Ezk. 7:21); Gk. *katesthíō*–'devour' (2 Cor. 11:20), *sylagogéō*–'carry off as booty' ("make prey," Col. 2:8), *thēríon*–'wild animal' ("beast of prey," Acts 11:6)]; AV also SPOIL, RAVENOUS FOWL, FOOD, PORTION, HUNTING, DEVOUR, etc.; NEB also KILL, SPOILS OF WAR, CARRION, FOOD, QUARRY, PILLAGE, PLUNDER, EXPLOIT, etc. In the literal sense, an animal seized and devoured by a predator, or (as a verb) the predator's seizing and devouring a weaker animal.

The imagery of ferocious animals or birds devouring their prey is used often in the OT, sometimes in a literal sense but more often in a figurative sense, e.g., to depict the ruthlessness of a powerful people and the helplessness of those whom they oppress. The lion is frequently portrayed as a predator (Gen. 49:9; Nah. 2:11, 13 [MT 12, 14]) that roars (Ps. 104:21; Isa. 5:29; Am. 3:4) and catches its prey (Ezk. 19:3, 6), then growls over it (Isa. 31:4), strangles it, and tears it (Ezk. 22:25; Nah. 2:12 [MT 13]) before devouring it (Nu. 23:24). Demonstrating the contrast between divine wisdom and power and human ignorance and frailty, God asks Job rhetorically, "Can you hunt the prey for the lion, or satisfy the appetite of the young lions?" (Job 38:39; cf. 4:11). Other powerful beasts portrayed as seeking prey to devour include wolves (Gen. 49:27; Ezk. 22:27), wild asses (Job 24:5), and jackals (Ps. 63:10 [MT 11]). Among BIRDS OF PREY are ravens (Job 38:41) and eagles (9:26; 39:29).

People, like animals, are sometimes described as taking prey. In Gen. 34:29 Simeon and Levi avenge the defilement of their sister Dinah by capturing a city and taking everything in it, including women and children, as their "prey" (lit. "plunder"). Traditional wisdom dictated that "a slothful man will not catch his prey, but the diligent man will get precious wealth" (Prov. 12:29). Job proclaims in 29:17, "I broke the fangs of the unrighteous, and made him drop his prey from his teeth."

People are also portrayed as becoming the prey of their enemies (2 K. 21:14; Ps. 124:6; Jer. 2:14). Defenseless "little ones" are particularly vulnerable (Nu. 14:3, 31; Dt. 1:39). Ezekiel prophesied that God's "sheep" had "become a prey" for all the wild beasts (Ezk. 34:8); yet God would save them so they would no longer be prey to the nations (vv. 22, 28; cf. 13:21). Isaiah also used this image to depict the helplessness of the Israelites, who had "become a prey with none to rescue" (Isa. 42:22). Similarly, Hosea referred to "Ephraim's sons" as those "destined for a prey" (Hos. 9:13). Isaiah prophesied woe to the powerful in Israel who made the utterly powerless, the "fatherless," their "prey" (Isa. 10:2); in the wicked nation those who departed from evil made themselves a "prey" (59:15). The prophets saw hope for deliverance only with God, who can rescue the prey of mighty tyrants (49:24f.) and "make a prey" of the oppressors (Jer. 30:16; cf. Ezk. 7:21). When God saves His people, "prey and spoil in abundance will be divided; even the lame will take the prey" (Isa. 33:23). Ezekiel prophesied that on that day the land of Israel, which had "become a prey and derision to the rest of the nations," would be vindicated (Ezk. 36:4).

In the NT "prey" is twice used figuratively. In 2 Cor. 11:20 Paul warns the Corinthians against the false apostles who "prey upon" (*katesthíō*, lit. "devour"; cf. NEB "exploit") them by living at their expense. Col. 2:8 warns the Christians at Colossae to beware that "no one makes a prey of you by philosophy and empty deceit. . . ." The rare verb *sylagōgéō*, which occurs only here in the NT, means "snare" or "capture and carry off booty." The term thus points not only to seduction but also to the evil intentions of those seeking to influence this Christian community (see E. Lohse, *Colossians and Philemon* [Eng. tr., *Hermeneia*, 1971], p. 94). D. K. MCKIM

**PRICE** [Heb. *m^e^ḥîr* (2 S. 24:24; 1 K. 10:28; 2 Ch. 1:16; Job 28:15; Ps. 44:12 [MT 13]; Prov. 17:16; 27:26; Isa. 45:13; 55:1; Dnl. 11:39), *kesep*–'silver,' 'money' (Gen. 23:9, 13; Ex. 21:35; Lev. 25:50f.; 1 Ch. 21:22, 24), *miqnâ* (Lev. 25:16), *g^e^'ullâ* ("price for redemption," v. 51), pass. part. of *pāḏâ*–'redeem' ("redemption price," Nu. 18:16), *kōper*–'ransom' ("price of [his] life," Ps. 49:7 [MT 8]), *mešeḵ*–'pouch, bag' (Job 28:18), *y^e^qār*–'costliness' (Zec. 11:13); Gk. *timḗ* (Mt. 27:9; 1 Cor. 6:20; 7:23), *timáō* ("set a price," Mt. 27:9), *dōreán* ("without price," Rev. 21:6; 22:17)]; AV also MONEY, RANSOM, GAIN, FREELY (Rev. 22:17), etc.; NEB also SUM, PURCHASE, PARCEL (Job 28:18), MONEY, FREE GIFT (Rev. 22:17), etc. In Lev. 5:18; 6:6 (MT 5:25); 2 S. 3:14 the RSV supplies "at the price." In Jer. 17:3 the RSV emends the MT (*bāmōṯeyḵā*, lit. "your high places" [so AV]) to read Heb. *bimḥîr* ("as the price"), following the Syriac and Targums; the NEB reads *lō' bimḥîr* ("for no payment") from 15:13 (it considers 15:13f. an intrusion into the text and 17:3f. to be the proper place of these verses). On Nu. 18:16 see G. B. Gray, comm. on Numbers (*ICC*, 1903), pp. 31, 231.

The quotation in Mt. 27:9f. (referring to the sum that the Jewish leaders paid to Judas for his betrayal of Jesus) is not from Jeremiah but is rather a free paraphrase of Zec. 11:13 with slight allusions to Jer. 18:2f.; 32:6-15 (see comms.). In 1 Cor. 6:20; 7:23 Paul uses the metaphor of the redemption price to describe Christ's saving death and the believer's consequent obligation to serve Christ alone.

*See* BUYING; RANSOM; REDEEMER. N. J. O.

**PRICK.** The noun denotes a slender, pointed object such as a thorn. It occurs in its literal sense in Nu. 33:55, translating Heb. *śēḵ*, "thorn," "splinter" (NEB "barbed hook"). In the AV of Acts 9:5; 26:14 it represents Gk. *kéntron*, "sting," "goad," for urging on a balking animal (cf. RSV, NEB, "goad" in 26:14). The expression "to kick against the pricks" figuratively describes a person resisting the call of God. In 9:5 the RSV and NEB omit the clause, following the earliest MSS (*see* GOAD).

The verb, meaning to pierce with something pointed, occurs in its literal sense in Ezk. 28:24 ("a brier to prick"), translating the hiphil part. of Heb. *mā'ar,* "hurtful." In Ps. 73:21 it renders the hithpolel of *šānan,* "feel sharply stabbed" (cf. NEB "feel the pangs"), figuratively describing the psalmist's intense emotional distress when he doubted the goodness of God. Sharp emotional pain of another sort (Gk. *katanýssomai,* "be stabbed") was experienced by those who heard Peter's Pentecost sermon and recognized their guilt for Jesus' crucifixion (Acts 2:37; AV "pricked in heart"; RSV, NEB, "cut to the heart").

N. J. O.

**PRIDE; PROUD** [Heb. *gē'â* (Prov. 8:13), *gē'eh*–'haughty,' *gē'* (Isa. 16:6), *ga'ᵃwâ, gā'ôn, gē'ûṯ, ga'ᵃyôn* (*K* Ps. 123:4), *gēwâ, gāḇah*–'be high,' *gōḇah*–'height,' *gāḇō(a)h, dāšēn*–'fat' (Ps. 22:29 [MT 30]), *hôḏ*–'splendor, majesty' (Zec. 10:3), *zîḏ* ("proudly defy," Jer. 50:29), *zēḏ, zāḏôn, maḥmaḏ*–'desire' (Lam. 2:4), *mārôm* ("proudly," Ps. 56:2 [MT 3]), *'ālas* ("wave proudly," Job 39:13), *rāhāḇ*–'defiant' (Ps. 40:4 [MT 5]), *rûm, rāḥāḇ* (Prov. 21:4), *śᵉ'ēṯ*–'dignity' (Gen. 49:3), *šaḥaṣ* (Job 28:8; 41:34 [MT 26]); Aram. *gēwâ, zûḏ*]; AV also ARROGANCY, DIGNITY, EXCELLENCY, FAT (Ps. 22:29 [MT 30]), GOODLY (Zec. 10:3), HAUGHTINESS, HIGH, LIFTED UP, "O thou most High" (Ps. 56:2 [MT 3]), POMP, etc.; NEB also ARROGANCE, BOAST, BRUTAL, "buried" (Ps. 22:29 [MT 30]; based on an emendation), CONCEIT, INSOLENCE, LOFTINESS, PRESUMPTUOUS, ROYAL (Zec. 10:3), SURGING, etc.; [Gk. *alazoneía*–'pretension' (1 Jn. 2:16), *alazṓn* (2 Tim. 3:2), *dóxa*–'glory' (1 Cor. 11:15), *kaucháomai*–'boast,' *kaúchēma* (noun)–'boast,' *kaúchēsis*–'boasting,' *hyperēphanía* (Mk. 7:22), *hyperḗphanos, hypsēlá phronéō* (Rom. 11:20), *hýpsōma*–'height' (2 Cor. 10:5)]; AV also BOAST, BOASTER, GLORY, HIGH MINDED, HIGH THING (2 Cor. 10:5), REJOICING; NEB also ARROGANT, GLAMOUR (1 Jn. 2:16), GLORY, HIGH (He. 3:6).

Many of the Hebrew and Greek words, as well as the AV and NEB variant readings, point to the root of pride: being lifted up high, whether literally or figuratively (*see* EXALT). Pride can be attributed metaphorically to natural phenomena that are literally high. Thus the waves of the sea are said in the RSV and AV to be proud (Job 38:11, *gā'ôn*) because they are high and majestic. When attributed to human beings, this sense of exaltation may be either positive or negative, depending on the relative height attributed to God.

Paul insisted that there is a positive kind of pride among Christians. He was proud (*kaucháomai* and related nouns) of the churches he had founded and wanted them to be proud of him as well (Rom. 15:17; 1 Cor. 15:31; 2 Cor. 1:14; 5:12; 7:4, 14; Phil. 2:16); but he was careful to explain that his success was entirely due to God's gifts (e.g., cf. Rom. 15:15-19; 2 Cor. 1:12; 5:11-15). Thus his boasting "in Christ" was tantamount to thanking God (cf. 2 Th. 1:3f.). In a different context he warned against considering oneself so lofty (*hypsēlá*) that one fails to feel awe at the mystery of God's working (Rom. 11:20; cf. vv. 17f., 25-27, 33-36). Pride is legitimate only when it remembers to attribute all honor to God (this may also be inferred from Ps. 47:4 [MT 5] and Isa. 4:2; cf. also 1 Cor. 11:15). *See also* BOAST.

Elsewhere in Scripture, however, pride is almost uniformly censured, precisely because it refuses to thank God but instead cherishes an exalted opinion of the self (2 Ch. 26:16; 32:24f.; see esp. NEB). In relationship to God pride is lofty self-sufficiency; in relationship to other persons pride is haughty lack of concern for their well-being.

The prophets denounced the foreign nations for proudly supposing that they had achieved their military conquests or economic prosperity by their own strength (Isa. 10:12-15; 23:8f.; 25:11; Ezk. 28:2-10, 17). Their loftiness showed itself in arrogance, haughtiness, insolence, false boasts and deeds (Jer. 48:29f.), in defiance of Yahweh (50:29), and in scoffing and boasting against Yahweh's people (Zeph. 2:10). But the prophets also attacked Israel and Judah themselves for relying on their own military power rather than trusting in Yahweh's protection. In Am. 6:8 "the pride of Jacob" and "his strongholds" (a symbol of national self-confidence) are parallel objects of Yahweh's abhorrence and judgment (cf. Ezk. 24:21, where even the temple has become a symbol of human self-sufficiency). Pride is equated with rebelling against Yahweh (Zeph. 3:11). It refuses to listen when Yahweh speaks (Jer. 13:9f., 15-17 [NEB emends in v. 17 to "anguish"]; Lev. 26:18f.; cf. 2 Cor. 10:5) and is unwilling to learn from God's chastening (Isa. 9:8-10, 13). *See* ARROGANCE.

The Psalms and wisdom literature picked up these themes as well: pride tries to ignore God (Ps. 10:4) and prefers to trust in what is deceptive and empty (40:4 [MT 5]). But here the focus is more often on pride in relationship to other people. Pride is associated with wickedness and injustice (Ps. 94:2-7; Prov. 21:3f.; Job 40:11f.) and is antithetical to wisdom (Prov. 8:12f.), patience (Eccl. 7:8), and humility (Prov. 11:2; cf. Jas. 4:6; 1 Pet. 5:5). The proud tell contemptuous lies against the righteous (Ps. 31:18 [MT 19]; 59:12 [MT 13]). At ease in their riches (123:4), they represent the antithesis of the lowly poor (Job 22:29; Prov. 15:25; 16:19; 29:23; cf. Ezk. 16:49, which identifies the sin of Sodom as pride and a complacent prosperity that ignores the needy; cf. also Ps. 73:3-9).

As in the OT, so also in the NT, pride is associated with other vices. In Mk. 7:22 haughtiness (*hyperēphanía*) is listed with the sins of envy, slander, and foolishness; in 2 Tim. 3:2 bragging (*alazṓn*) is mentioned with love of self, love of money, arrogance, and abusiveness. 1 Jn. 2:16 links *alazoneía toú bíou* (which may refer to ostentatious pride in possessions or status, or to overconfidence inflated by possessions or status) with lust (cf. *bíos* [RSV "goods"] in 3:17; see R. E. Brown, *Epistles of John* [*AB*, 1982], pp. 311f.).

Thus the proud person offends against God by self-exaltation, against other people by self-preoccupation, and against the self by self-deception. The delusion increases until one fancies oneself so high as to be invulnerable (Ob. 3). "Though you soar aloft like the eagle, though your nest is set among the stars, thence I will bring you down, says the Lord" (v. 4; cf. Isa. 2:10-17).

*See also* HUMBLE.

***Bibliography.**–DNTT,* III, 27-32; *TDNT,* I, *s.v.* ἀλαζών, ἀλαζονεία (G. Delling); III, *s.v.* καυχάομαι κτλ. (R. Bultmann); VIII, *s.v.* ὑπερήφανος, ὑπερηφανία (G. Bertram); *s.v.* ὕψος κτλ.: ὕψωμα (G. Bertram); *TDOT,* II, *s.v.* "gā'āh" (D. Kellermann); *s.v.* "gābhah" (R. Hentschke); IV, *s.v.* "zûdh" (J. Scharbert).

J. E. SANDERSON

**PRIEST.** *See* PRIESTS AND LEVITES.

**PRIEST, CHRIST AS.** *See* CHRIST, OFFICES OF III; PRIESTHOOD IN THE NT II.

**PRIEST, HIGH** [Heb. *hakkōhēn haggāḏōl*–'the great priest'; Gk. *archiereús*]; **CHIEF PRIEST** [Heb. *hakkōhēn hārō'š*–'the head priest'; Gk. *archiereús*].

I. Background
II. Dress
III. Origin and Importance
IV. Responsibilities
V. Postexilic Development
VI. Greco-Roman Period

*I. Background.*–Sacrificial temples were important religious institutions in the ancient world that usually accommodated the activities of a special group in the society — the priests. The larger temples and the centers with the sizable populations very often had priests of significant status who could be referred to as high priests. For centuries the high priest of Amon at Thebes stood next to the king in power and influence. In fact, in the ancient period the king and the chief priest appear to have had a close relationship. The temple service in Egypt was conducted by and for the king in order that he might have long life, health, and power. Since the high priest was appointed by the king, he emphasized the needs and desires of the king. In Mesopotamia the offices of king and high priest were often united in the same person (cf. Wright and Freedman, eds., *BA Reader,* I, 145-200). In the early Babylonian period the king appointed a high priest to administer a highly developed, extensive bureaucracy that would gather royal taxes and issue charters through the city temples. The Hittite temples, or more precisely "palaces," were the domain of the deity and the upper classes. The rites of worship were carried out by specially ordained priests, led by a chief priest, and they generally excluded involvement by the ordinary citizen. Ugaritic and Phoenician inscriptions refer to a chief priest at the top of a structured priesthood (cf. Cody, p. 21). Thus it seems that a chief priest heading a priestly hierarchy was a fairly common phenomenon in the ancient Near Eastern world, with close if not blurred lines between the king and the high priest.

Some have suggested that Moses' father-in-law was possibly the chief priest of Midian, and thus in the founding and establishing of an ecclesiastical system for ancient Israel it would have been natural and proper to institute a priestly system with a high priest at the head. The chronology of this division and the traditions that surround the high priest are difficult to determine in the early history of ancient Israel. The title "high priest" *(hakkōhēn haggāḏōl)* occurs only twice in the Pentateuch (Nu. 35:25, 28) and once in Joshua (20:6), although there are variant references to this position, such as "the priest who is chief among his brethren" (*hakkōhēn haggāḏôl,* Lev. 21:10) and the "anointed priest" (*hakkōhēn hammāšî[a]ḥ,* Lev. 4:3, 5, 16; 6:22 [MT 15]); cf. the later title "chief priest" (*kōhēn hārō'š,* 2 K. 25:18 par. Jer. 52:24; 2 Ch. 19:11; 24:11; 26:20; 31:10; Ezr. 7:5). Even though ordinary priests were anointed it would appear that the ritual was different for the high priest, since it designated his place at the head of the priestly caste. The anointing of the high priest had similarities to that of royalty, including the pouring of oil on the head of the priest (1 S. 10:1; 2 K. 9:6). Cody (p. 103) has commented that since the king was the highest authority in the sacrificial system of the early stages of ancient Judaism, the absence of the title "high priest" in authentic preexilic texts is not surprising.

*II. Dress.*–The high priest wore a mitre (Heb. *miṣnep̱eṯ*) or elaborate headdress that showed his special status (Ex. 28:36-39; 29:6; 39:30; Lev. 8:9). He also wore the robe of the ephod, the EPHOD, and the breastplate (Lev. 8:7-9). The robe of the ephod seems to have been a sleeveless tunic, made of blue material, fringed with alternate bells and pomegranates (Ex. 28:31-35; 39:22-26). The ephod was a variegated dress of the four colors of the sanctuary: blue, purple, scarlet, and fine linen interwoven with gold (Ex. 28:6-8; 39:2-5; *see* GARMENTS VIII). The breastplate must have contained a pocket of some kind inside, for in it were deposited the URIM AND THUMMIM, which seem to have been tangible objects (Ex. 28:15-30; 39:8-21). The mitre or headdress was of fine linen, the plate of the crown of pure gold, and inscribed upon it were the words "Holy to Yahweh" (Ex. 28:36-38; 39:30f.). When entering the holy of holies the high priest had to dress entirely in linen, but in his ordinary duties he wore the dress of the priests; only when acting as high priest must he wear his special robes.

*III. Origin and Importance.*–Aaron, the brother of Moses, had been traditionally called the first high priest (Lev. 21:10; Nu. 35:25, 28; Ezr. 7:1-5). Only those of the line of the eldest descendants of Aaron could serve as high priest, and a man's position in the hierarchy of holiness and cult was determined from birth. In Nu. 25:10-13 the descendants of Phinehas (Aaron's grandson) are promised a "covenant of eternal priesthood," which apparently refers to a right to the office of high prist.

The importance of the high priest's office was manifest from the first. The high priest Eleazar (Aaron's son) is named in the first rank with Joshua, the prince of the tribes and successor of Moses (Nu. 34:17f.; Josh. 14:1). With others he officiated in the distribution of the spoils of the Midianites (Nu. 31:21, 26). He acted with Moses in important matters (26:1; 31:29). The whole congregation had to go or come according to his word (27:20ff.). The high priest's death was a national event, for then the manslayer was free to leave the city of refuge (35:25, 28; *see* REFUGE, CITIES OF). Six cities had been designated as refuge places for those who had committed unpremeditated manslaughter (35:12f.; Dt. 19:9). The individual would be immune from persecution by the blood avenger and he was free to live a normal life under the restricted context of the city limits. The individual seeking such refuge had to remain there until the death of the officiating high priest. The later rabbis interpreted the death of the high priest as atonement for the injustice of manslaughter (T.B. *Makkoth* 11b). A murderer defiled the earth and caused the presence of God to be withdrawn, while the high priest caused the presence of God to abide with humanity. He was a mainstay of the community. His strength came from the fact that he was the person around whom a holy office gathered (i.e., the priesthood), and through the cultus he represented a strength for the people (cf. *ILC,* III-IV, 196f.).

Because of the diversity within the biblical sources the stipulation that only the firstborn son of the high priest could be high priest is a debated issue. Many scholars view the high priest as a late creation of the second temple period. The power and significance of the priesthood increased in the postexilic period, and it found its supreme expression in the position of the high priest. When the king did not materialize to establish a distinctive nation in the pattern of David's and Solomon's kingdoms, the high priest acquired more and more importance as the person who gave definition to the Israelite community (cf. Tcherikover, pp. 119-142).

Others hold that the hierarchy within the priesthood dates back to a very ancient period of Israel. Eli, in the temple of Shiloh (1 S. 1–3), may be an example of the high priest from the very early period. Deuteronomy offers little about the high priesthood (20:2 may be a reference). The traditional view that Deuteronomy was created under Mosaic authorship implies that the book is a unit and it assumes the division of priest and high priest. Some modern literary critics see different layers of tradition in the text that were brought together *ca.* the 7th cent. B.C. (see Nicholson, pp. 18-36, for a survey of views). Those who hold the latter view usually side with the proposal that the high priest is a somewhat later development in the priestly system. But the lack of reference to a high priest in Deuteronomy may be due to its subject matter; the text does not deal with priestly matters in any detail and thus has no need to describe the office of high priest.

*IV. Responsibilities.*–The primary function of the high priest was to administer and direct the sacrificial system. He alone was allowed to go behind the veil of the holy of holies on the Day of Atonement (Lev. 16:2). He dealt with the sin offerings whose blood was brought into the sanctuary of the temple (Lev. 4:3-21). The high priest's responsibilities included all the sacrificial activities that took place inside the temple, either with his direct involvement or under his supervision.

The restrictions on the high priest were more pronounced than those applying to the ordinary priest. He was to take more care in issues of ritual purity and marriage. For example, in regard to marriage all the restrictions of the priests applied but with the further requirements that he was not to marry a widow and he was admonished only to "take to wife a virgin of his own people" (i.e., Israel, Lev. 21:13-15). He could not observe the external signs of mourning (i.e., letting hair grow, rending clothes) for any person, and he could not leave the sanctuary when news came of death even of a parent. He could not defile himself by contact with any dead body, including a parent (vv.10-12). If he should bring guilt upon the people, he had to present a special offering (Lev. 4:3ff.). Sins affecting the priesthood in general had to be expiated by the other priests as well as himself (Nu. 18:1). He had to wash his feet and hands when he went to the tabernacle of the congregation and when he came near to the altar to minister (Ex. 30:19-21). He had to abstain from holy things during his uncleanness (Lev. 22:1-3) or if he should become leprous (vv. 4, 7). He was to eat the people's meat offering with the priests in the holy place (Lev. 6:16). He had to help to determine whether the leprosy was present in the human body and in garments (Lev. 13:2-59), and to adjudicate legal questions (Dt. 17:12).

*V. Postexilic Development.*–The profile of the high priest increased substantially in the second temple period, after the return from the Babylonian Exile. From this time on the high priest became more prominent. The monarchy was gone, the civil authority was in the hands of the Persians, the Jews were no longer independent, and hence the chief power tended to center in the high priesthood.

He was distinctly known as high priest *(hakkōhēn haggāḏōl)*. He took a leading part in establishing the ecclesiastico-civil system, particularly the building of the temple. The office passed from father to son (Nu. 25:11-13), and if this was not possible a member of the family was appointed. The high priest served in the office until death (Nu. 35:25, 28; this custom ended during the period of Antiochus IV Epiphanes, 174-163 B.C.). He represented the people to the foreign powers that controlled the homeland, caring for the security of Jerusalem and its water supply, and he was responsible for the collection of taxes as well as the supervision of the temple service. Both spiritual and cultural responsibilities were placed on him, e.g., the high priest Simeon, son of Onias II, who traditionally has been referred to as Simeon the Just, exercised great influence upon the religious and spiritual development of Israel.

This exaltation of the high priest is very different from the state of affairs presented by Ezekiel. The high priest is generally regarded as a purely postexilic figure because there is no mention of such a figure in the book of Ezekiel. The "prince" seems to be the chief personage in the ecclesiastical system, and it is extremely difficult to equate this figure with that of the high priest. Since many scholars view Ezekiel as the shift to a special category within the Levites, with a separate category for the sons of Zadok as officials of the cultus, it has been argued that further "refinement" of the office of high priest was unknown to Ezekiel. Therefore the designation of a high priest in the religious system of Israel was a postexilic creation. The description of the high priestly functions, his installation, and his robes of office outlined in the so-called priestly document (P) are understood to be a later reading from a postexilic perspective.

But scholars are increasingly doubtful that the silence of Ezekiel on the high priesthood means that the position was not known. His silence on kingship does not imply that there was no king before his time. Rather, the writer was drawing freely on a familiar institution of the priesthood, and his modification (including the lack of specific references to an office such as high priest) has more to do with the system that he was proposing than a direct correspondence to offices and institutions that may not have existed in his society. Further, Ezekiel appears to be well acquainted with parts of the priestly code and especially the section in Lev. 17–26, which includes a discussion of the high priest (21:10-15).

The book of Chronicles reflects a period when the high priest was a well-established office in the priestly system. He is referred to as the "head" or "chief priest" (2 Ch. 19:11), the "great priest" (2 Ch. 34:9), and the "prince of the house of God" (1 Ch. 9:11). In the sketching of the history of Israel the Chronicler emphasizes the authority of the high priest and the considerable power vested in him. Azariah drove King Uzziah out of the temple for interfering with the priestly responsibilities (2 Ch. 26:16-20), and in Jerusalem during the reign of Jehoshaphat the high priest shared in administrative control with the governor of the house of Judah (2 Ch. 19:8-11; cf. chs. 23–24).

*VI. Greco-Roman Period.*–During the Hellenistic period the high priests varied in their allegiance to Jewish ideals and in their attractions to the Greek culture. Both Simeon II and Onias III continued the reforms of Ezra and Nehemiah while it is probable that Jason, one of the leaders of the Hellenist party, turned Jerusalem into a model of the Greek polis. During the Hasmonean period (165-75 B.C.) the high priest was a national leader, and eventually the positions of high priest and king of Israel were represented by the same person. This practice came to an abrupt end in the Roman period; under the regime of Herod the Great the high priest was an appointment of his choosing from among the priests. This loosened the link of the high priesthood with a particular family. The custom of a high priest holding the position for life was abolished, and although a high status was given to the office it was confined to the religious activities at the temple. After the death of Herod and the removal of Archelaus, the appointment of the high priest became the responsibility of the Roman governors.

In the 1st cent. A.D. the appointment came from the family of Herod (i.e., Agrippa I, Herod of Chalcis, and Agrippa II) and resulted in a group of well-placed, wealthy priestly families being given the office on a regular basis (i.e., the Boethus family, the Phiabi family, and the family of Anan). According to the Talmud (T. B. *Yoma* 18a; *Yebomoth* 61a) the high priest bought the office from the government and the position was changed every year. Since an ex-high priest kept his rights to the dignity of the office, a kind of oligarchy of high priesthood was established with many of the privileges being shared by members of his family. A distinguished and wealthy noble group of families emerged and took advantage of society in social, economic, and religious matters. Thus such groups as the Pharisees and the Dead Sea community severely criticized the high priesthood.

In NT times the high priest was the chief civil and ecclesiastical dignitary among the Jews. He was chairman of the Sanhedrin and head of the political relations with the Roman government. It is not clear just how far he participated in the ceremonies of the temple. No doubt he alone entered the holy of holies once a year on the Day of Atonement, and also offered the daily offerings during that week. What other part he took in the work was according to his pleasure. Josephus indicated that the high priest officiated at the Sabbath, the New Moon, and yearly festivals (Josephus *Ant.* iii. 10 [237-257]). The daily *minḥâ* (Lev. 6:12ff.) that he was required to offer was not always offered by the high priest in person, but he was required to defray the expense of it. This was a duty which, according to Ezekiel's vision, was to be performed by the "prince." The Jews had many contentions with the Romans as to who should keep the garments of the high priest. When Jerusalem fell into the hands of the Romans, the robe of state also fell into their hands.

The general dislike of the high priest was demonstrated during the war of A.D. 66-70 when the Zealots controlled Jerusalem. Many members of the family of the high priest were expelled from Jerusalem and some were killed before they could escape. A high priest was chosen from among the ordinary priests — Phinehas ben Samuel, a stonemason by profession and a relative by marriage to the family of Rabbi Hillel. He was the last high priest; the destruction of the temple at Jerusalem in A.D. 70 ended the necessity of such a figure.

On Christ as high priest, *see* CHRIST, OFFICES OF III; PRIESTHOOD IN THE NT II.

***Bibliography.***–A. Cody, *History of OT Priesthood* (1969); R. de Vaux, *Ancient Israel* (Eng. tr. 1961), II; D. W. Gooding, *Account of the Tabernacle* (1959); J. M. Grintz, "Aspects of the History of the High Priesthood," *Zion,* 23-24 (1958-59), 124-130, 134f. (Hebrew); M. Haran, "The Complex of Ritual Acts Performed Inside the Tabernacle," *Scripta Hierosolymitana,* 8 (1961), 271-302; *ILC,* III-IV; J. Jeremias, *Jerusalem in the Time of Jesus* (Eng. tr. 1969), pp. 147-182; H. J. Katzenstein, *JBL,* 81 (1962), 379-382; E. W. Nicholson, *Deuteronomy and Tradition* (1967); J. B. Segal, *The Hebrew Passover from the Earliest Times to A.D. 70* (1963); V. Tcherikover, *Hellenistic Civilization and the Jews* (1970); G. E. Wright and D. N. Freedman, eds., *BA Reader,* I (1961).

W. O. MCCREADY

**PRIESTHOOD IN THE NT.** Consideration of priesthood in the NT falls readily into three categories: (1) the Jewish priesthood in NT times, (2) the priesthood of Jesus Christ, and (3) the priesthood of believers.

***I. The Jewish Priesthood in NT Times.***–References to Jewish priests occur most frequently in the gospels, where priests are involved in the life, ministry, death, and resurrection of Jesus; in Acts, where they interact (usually negatively) with the apostles as they proclaim the gospel message; and finally in Hebrews, where the author discusses the priesthood of Jesus vis-à-vis the Jewish priesthood. A variety of titles appears in these texts, including Gk. *archiereús* ("high priest," "chief priest"), *hiereús* ("priest"), and *Levítēs* ("Levite"). (See Jeremias, pp. 147-221, for an excellent discussion of the priestly hierarchy.)

Since at the time of Jesus Israel was a theocracy (at least theoretically, for a discussion of the influence of a theocratic view on the author of Hebrews, see Horbury, pp. 44-49) without a king, the high priest was the most important official. The eminence of the high priest was due to his consecration for life to an office in which he might atone for the sins of the whole nation. His death was viewed as having special atoning value, bringing release to those who had fled to cities of refuge. His magnificent vestments were of such importance to the Jews that the Romans effectively contained Jewish rebellion by keeping these splendid garments in their custody. Strict laws governed the ritual purity that the high priest had to maintain for his office, especially on the Day of Atonement. These laws often led to the total isolation of the high priest for the days preceding an important cultic function so as to prevent contamination. Titles, authority, and cultic power were retained even after deposal or retirement (e.g., Annas, high priest A.D. 6-15, though retired, played a part in the trial of Jesus). The traditional prestige of the office, which extended even to the high-priestly families (*HJP,* II, 205), and its lifetime character were seriously weakened, however, by growing political influence on the office, influence that led eventually to substitution of investiture for the prescribed anointing and to frequent ignoring of other prescriptions for the office by the political authorities (the Herods) who appointed the high priest. Pharisaic influence was also replacing traditional Sadducean power (the high priests were Sadducees, Acts 5:17; cf. Denney, p. 98), and abuses by the high priests brought further reduction in the prestige of the office. The high priest remained the most important official in the nation, both because his position put him at the head of negotiations with the Romans and more importantly because, whatever the changing historical circumstances, he alone could atone for the nation's sins. John's observation of Caiaphas emphasizes the indelible nature of the role of this office (Jn. 11:49-53). Though of questionable character, Caiaphas spoke better than he knew when he urged the sacrifice of Jesus as expedient for the nation and thereby accomplished (paradoxically) God's redemptive purposes.

In rank an anointed high priest preceded one simply invested. The high priests were followed by ranks of chief priests and chief Levites: first, captain of the temple, then, in order, director of the weekly course, director of the daily course, temple overseer, treasurer, ordinary priest, and finally Levite. The captain of the temple (Acts 4:1; 5:24, 26) was of course permanently fixed in Jerusalem where he served as right-hand man to the high priest, customarily being chosen as deputy to the high priest on the Day of Atonement. Indeed, a qualification for the office of high priest was prior holding of the office of temple captain. The twenty-four directors of weekly courses and approximately 156 directors of daily courses were spread throughout Judea and Galilee except during their week of duty in Jerusalem and on the three pilgrim festivals. The seven temple overseers (including four chief Levites) supervised the temple and its functions. The

Jerusalem Model of Caiaphas's palace (W. S. LaSor)

temple treasurer administered temple income (offerings in the form of money, objects, property, etc.). The NT, as well as Josephus, sometimes (64 times in the Gospels and Acts) calls this whole body of priests of various ranks Gk. *archiereús* (cf. Heb. *kōhēn gāḏôl,* the talmudic equivalent), which Jeremias (pp. 173-180) shows to mean not "high priest" or retired high priest or family of high priest (so Schürer) but rather "chief priest" — those priests who were in a position over other priests and who formed a definite body of priests permanently stationed at the temple and voting on the Sanhedrin.

The majority of priests, though descendants of Aaron and heirs of the priestly office, did not belong to the priestly aristocracy. Traditionally they were grouped into clans, twenty-one of them at the time of Nehemiah (Neh. 10:3-9), forming twenty-four weekly courses (doing service for 1 week twice a year; cf. Lk. 1:8) by the time of Jesus. Jeremias (pp. 200f.) estimates the number of priests in 100 B.C. to have been about eighteen thousand. From these more than fifty were chosen by lot to carry out the daily services at the temple, thus involving three hundred priests per week plus about four hundred Levites. Many more were needed to officiate on sabbaths and festivals and at private sacrifices, which were apparently offered in very great numbers. For all but the two weeks in the year when their cultic duties called them to Jerusalem they lived at their homes in Judea and Galilee. Here they seldom performed any priestly duty but rather worked mostly in manual trades such as carpentry and masonry (many were scribes) to supplement their priests' income. Thus in many ways these ordinary priests differed from their lordly seniors, including the fact that the rank and file were less prejudiced; thus it was mostly these ordinary priests who became "obedient to the faith" (Acts 6:7; cf. Denney, p. 98).

Last of all came the Levites, of whom there were about ten thousand. According to some scholars (e.g., Jeremias, pp. 207f.; cf. *HJP*², II, 250-54), the Levites were descendants of priests deposed by the Deuteronomic code. Their duties consisted primarily in making music at the temple and performing subordinate duties, such as helping the priests vest, preparing books for reading, cleaning and policing the temple. Like the laity, they were strictly forbidden by the law to enter the temple building.

In the NT priests of various ranks appear in a number of connections. Zechariah, father of John the Baptist, was apparently an ordinary priest who was in Jerusalem for his term at the weekly courses (Lk. 1:8) when an angel appeared to him announcing the end of Elizabeth's barrenness. Both an ordinary priest and a Levite passed by the robbery victim later helped by the good Samaritan (Lk. 10:31f.), though by virtue of their offices compassion might have been expected of them. Jesus sent those healed of diseases (esp. leprosy) that had made them ritually unclean to the priest to receive the prescribed ceremonial cleansing "as a proof to the people" (Mk. 1:44 par.).

The priest as seen in the Gospels is an important agent in bringing about Jesus' death. The high priest's servants were sent to arrest Jesus, and Peter struck one and cut off his ear (Mk. 14:47). At Jesus' trial the high priest questioned Him and condemned Him for blasphemy (Mk. 14:53-65). In his role as high priest Caiaphas "sacrificed" Jesus, speaking prophetically (not of his own accord but by virtue of his office) of Jesus' death on behalf of the nation and all children of God (Jn. 11:49-52). (The incident is reminiscent of rabbinic accounts reporting visions and heavenly voices experienced by the high priest on the day of atonement [*DNTT,* III, 39; T.B. *Sotah* 33a; *Yoma* 53b].) One of the disciples known by the priest was able to enter the court at Jesus' trial and arrange for Peter to be let in as well (Jn. 18:12-16).

As the priests stood against Jesus in the Gospels, so they stood against His disciples in Acts. The priests, captain of the temple, high priest, and the Sadducees opposed and imprisoned Peter and John for healing and preaching "in Jesus the resurrection of the dead" (Acts 4:1-22; 5:17-42), though Gamaliel, a Pharisee on the council and a priest, suggested a more tolerant course. The high priest questioned Stephen on the charges of speaking against the holy place and the law (Acts 6:13-14).The high priest commissioned Saul to find, arrest, and bring to Jerusalem "any belonging to the Way" (Acts 9:1; 22:5). When the tables had turned and Paul had become a persecuted Christian, he unknowingly (because of failing eyesight or a change of office or even because of the priestly behavior; *DNTT,* III, 40) reviled the high priest, who commanded that Paul be struck on the mouth (Acts 23:1-5). Subsequently the high priest presented the case against Paul before the governor (Acts 24:1), assisted later by the chief priests (25:2), who urged that Paul be sent to Jerusalem for trial so they might kill him en route.

*See also* PRIESTS AND LEVITES.

***II. The Priesthood of Christ.***–The conflict between the Jewish priests and Jesus and His followers was due in part to the threat posed to priestly institutions and privileges by Jesus' teaching ("something greater than the temple is here," Mt. 12:6; "destroy this temple and in three days I will raise it up," Jn. 2:19) and mission ("The Son of man came not to be served but to serve, and to give his life a ransom for many," Mk. 10:45). Nevertheless, only the letter to the Hebrews *develops* the motif of Jesus' priesthood.

In He. 2:17 the author's essentially sacerdotal Christology leads him to the conception that as a faithful and merciful high priest (cf. the Targumic description of Aaron in Tg. Pseudo-Jonathan on Dt. 33:8; Horbury, p. 61) He must be like His brethren (Vanhoye, p. 451). Because He was tempted like all men (4:15), He can be sympathetic. Indeed, He learned obedience through suffering so that being thereby perfected He might be a priest after the order of Melchizedek (5:6-10; see Horbury, pp. 59-66, on all these passages on priestly mercy).

The Melchizedek priesthood of Christ is shown to be superior to the Levitical priesthood in four ways: (1) it is forever, unbroken by genealogical beginning or end, 7:1-3 (on this analogy cf. Ladd, pp. 579f.; the author certainly knew Jesus had human parents; cf. 7:14); (2) Levi (in Abraham's loins offered sacrifice to Melchizedek, the lesser to the greater, 7:4-10 (see Horbury, pp. 52-59, on the difficulties of v. 5); (3) the promise (Ps. 110:4) of another order to supersede the Levitical makes clear its imperfection, 7:11-14; and (4) the Melchizedek priesthood was attained, not by "the law of a fleshly commandment" (7:16, lit. tr.), but by the power of an endless life, 7:15-19.

Jesus' better priesthood is also accompanied by an oath (something the old Levitical priests did not have), making Jesus the surety of a better covenant, 7:20-22. The former priests were many because of death, but His priesthood is uninterrupted because He lives forever, 7:23-25. Furthermore, He is a *blameless* high priest (7:26-28) who enters a better sanctuary to offer better sacrifices and perform better rites, 8:1-13 (vv. 8-12 cite Jer. 31:31-34 as scriptural evidence of the inadequacy of the old system).

In contrast to the imperfect sanctuary of the old covenant (9:1-5) and its repeated and imperfect rituals (9:6-10; cf. Young, p. 210, on the typology of the Levitical aspersions), Christ entered a more perfect tent, once for all to offer the perfect sacrifice of himself (9:11-14). As a result Christ is mediator of a new and better covenant ratified by His blood (9:15-22). His once-for-all offering of himself has put away sin forever (9:23-28). The incompleteness of the old offerings, which needed continually to be offered and which could not perfect the offerers (10:1-4), is surpassed by Christ's perfect, obedient offering (10:5-10) made once for all (10:11-18).

Running throughout Hebrews is a duality of the heavenly and the earthly (Ladd, pp. 572f., 580; cf. Young, on *tá hágia*). There is also the paradox of Christ as both priest and offering (9:14, 26): "It was on the cross, in fact, that our Lord became a priest" (Scott, p. 402).

Besides Hebrews, the Johannine literature speaks of Christ's priesthood: this motif runs throughout the Fourth Gospel (cf. esp. chs. 6, 14–16, and the prayer of ch. 17), is pictured in the Apocalypse (chs. 5, 19, 21f.), and is taught in 1 Jn. 1–2.

These motifs are brought together in the words of the hymn:

Thou within the veil hast entered,
  Robed in flesh, our great High Priest;
Thou on earth both Priest and Victim
  In the eucharistic feast.

*See also* CHRIST, OFFICES OF.

***III. The Priesthood of Believers.***–The words of God to Israel in Ex. 19:6, "You shall be to me a kingdom of priests and a holy nation," are applied to the Church in the NT (1 Pet. 2:5, 9; Rev. 1:6; 5:10, 20:6; cf. Isa. 61:6). Best (p. 299) suggested that this universal priesthood can be traced back into Judaism and OT times when Levitical sacrifices were less important than spiritual sacrifices, which any Israelite could offer, though an ordinary Israelite could not be called a priest while the Levitical priesthood remained. In 1 Peter, believers as priests are to worship God, "to offer spiritual sacrifices acceptable to God through Jesus Christ", 2:5 (cf. "access" of Eph. 2:17 and Rom. 5:2; "draw near," He. 5:17; "bring us to God," 1 Pet. 3:18; Denney, p. 99) and to witness to His salvation ("that you may declare the wonderful deeds of him who called you out of darkness into his marvelous light," 2:9; according to G. Fee, *Zondervan's Pictorial Encyclopedia of the Bible,* IV [repr. 1978], 852, this is the only sense in which the NT speaks of a priesthood of believers).

The book of Revelation emphasizes the ruling aspect of this royal priesthood (cf. 1 Pet. 2:9): "they shall be priests and shall reign with him a thousand years," 20:6 (a present experience according to Congar).

It is more in a corporate than an individual sense that the Church exercises its priesthood; the NT does not mention a priestly office in the Church (but cf. Rom. 15:16 and Phil. 2:17; see Schlier, p. 164; Denney, p. 100). But Clement, writing in the last decade of the 1st cent., speaks of the Christian ministry as high priest, priest, and Levite (1 Clem. 40–44); the Didache (13:3) calls Christian prophets "your high priests" and refers to the Eucharist as a sacrifice, "the pure offering among the nations" of Mal. 1:11 (Shepherd, *IDB*, III, p. 890). About A.D. 200 Tertullian (*De baptismo* 17) and Hippolytus (Preface to *Refutatio omnium haeresium*) in the West called Christian ministers "priests" and "high priests," developments that grew out of theological presuppositions about the nature of the Church (Stylianopoulos, pp. 125f.).

***Bibliography.***–E. Best, *Interp.*, 14 (1960), 273-299; F. F. Bruce, *Epistle to the Hebrews* (*NICNT,* 1964); Y. Congar, *Revue de Science, Philosophie, et Théologie,* 67 (1983), 97-115; *DNTT,* III, 32-44; J. H. Elliot, *The Elect and the Holy* (*Nov. Test. Supp.*, 12, 1966); *HDB*, IV, *s.v.* "Priest in NT" (J. Denney); *HJP,* II, 193-305; *HJP*², 237-313; W. Horbury, *Journal for the Study of the NT,* 19 (1983), 43-71; J. Jeremias, *Jerusalem in the Time of Jesus* (Eng. tr. 1969); G. Ladd, *Theology of the NT* (1974); M. Mees, *BZ*, N.F., 22 (1978), 115-124; H. Schlier, *Theologie und Philosophie,* 44 (1969), 161-180; *TDNT,* III, *s.v.* ἱερός κτλ.: ἱεράτευμα, ἱερεύς, ἀρχιερεύς (Schrenk); W. F. M. Scott, *SJT,* 10 (1957), 399-415; T. G. Stylianopoulos, *Greek Orthodox Theological Review,* 23 (1978), 113-130; A. Vanhoye, *Nouvelle Revue Theologique,* 91 (1969), 449-474; N. H. Young, *NTS*, 22 (1980), 198-120.

W. J. MOULDER

**PRIESTS AND LEVITES.**

I. Background
II. Early Stages
III. Levites
IV. Family of Aaron and Levites
V. Priests and Levites
VI. Levitical Duties and Responsibilities
VII. Priestly Duties and Responsibilities
VIII. Postexilic Priesthood
IX. Modern Critical Analysis

***I. Background.***–One of the basic theological principles of ancient Israel was that the Hebrews were in a covenantal relationship with their God. Since their God was viewed as being holy, the people were also to be holy (Lev. 11:44f.). The corporate responsibility of maintaining the unique relationship with God was vested in prophet, priest, and king. The Israelite priesthood survived in this capacity for the whole of the biblical period, outlasting both prophet and king.

The Heb. *kōmer* is used of "idolatrous priests" in 2 K. 23:5; Hos. 10:5; Zeph. 1:4 (AV also Chermarim, Zeph. 1:4; NEB "heathen priest," "priestling"). But the usual Hebrew term for priest is *kōhēn,* which has cognates in Ugaritic, Phoenician-Punic, and Aramaic. *Kōhēn* was not limited to Hebrew priests only; the Hebrew Bible uses the same term to refer to Melchizedek, a Canaanite priest (Gen. 12:18), Egyptian priests (Gen. 41:45, 50; 46:20; 47:26), Philistine priests (1 S. 6:2), priests of Dagon (1 S. 5:5), priests of Baal (2 K. 10:19), priests of Chemosh (Jer. 48:7), and priests of Baalim and Asherim (2 Ch. 34:5). *Kōhēn* has no feminine form; the "daughter of a priest" *(baṯ-kōhēn)* refers to a woman of a priestly family (cf. Lev. 21:9; 22:12f.).

Some scholars see parallels between early Hebrew priests and the ancient Near Eastern custom of the *sadin,* the "guardian" of the temple (de Vaux, II, 348). The guardian looked after the sanctuary and the sacrifices, receiving the worshipers and assisting them with their offerings. Frequently the *sadin* became attached to the place of sacrifice; when his fellow clansmen moved on in their nomadic patterns the *sadin* would remain behind to serve in the sanctuary. The responsibility of the *sadin* would be passed on to his sons and a hereditary line would be established (cf. Jgs. 17–18; 1 S. 1–2).

The priest's involvement in the cultic or sacrificial system must be set within the context of the ancient world, where sacrifices were conceived as a service to the deity. The sacrificial activities were carried out in the temple that was the special abode of the deity. The sacrifice was a means of access to the deity; in the earliest records it may have been a means of appeasing the gods or gaining their attention. By the period of the early Hebrews, however, sacrifices were sophisticated symbols that commemorated past activities of God and anticipated further encounters with Him (cf. G. von Rad, *OT Theology,* I [Eng. tr. 1962], 242; Eichrodt, p. 433).

In the early period of the Hebrew religion the priest's main responsibility was to determine whether a sacrifice was appropriate, i.e., whether the offering itself was correct and whether the attitude of the offerer was proper (cf.

Limestone plaque of a nude priest pouring out a libation to a goddess. From Tello, *ca.* 2500 B.C. (Louvre)

Dt. 33:8-11, which assigns to Levi the three functions of discerning oracles [v. 8], teaching [v. 10a], and sacrificing [v. 10b]). Both these features reflect an assessment of the ethical and moral disposition of the person offering the sacrifice. The priest was recompensed for his services by taking a portion of the sacrifice (cf. de Vaux, II, 347, for such activities recorded at Mari during the period of Hammurabi). As guardian of the proper method of sacrifice the priest eventually became master of sacred knowledge and ultimately exercised that knowledge on the behalf of the community; thus the *kōhēn* was a force to be reckoned with in political, social, and religious areas.

*II. Early Stages.*–In the early patriarchal period the heads of the clans offered sacrifices (Gen. 22; 31:54; 46:1). There were multiple shrines (Gen. 12:7f.; 13:18; 28:18-22; 33:20; cf. Jgs. 8:24; 18:14), and later various families were located at important temple centers (e.g., the family of Eli at Shiloh, 1 S. 1–14; the family of Ahimelech at Nob, 1 S. 22:11-19; and at Jerusalem, David's sons, 2 S. 8:18; Ira of the family of Jair, 2 S. 20:26; and Zadok son of Ahitub, 2 S. 8:17).

It is worthwhile in the context of multiple shrines and priestly families to distinguish between altars (*see* ALTAR) and TEMPLES in the ancient world. Altars consisted of any type of structure (they were usually open structures) where the sacrifices could be made by anyone. Such sites are numerous from the ancient periods and they seem to have been centers of activity for priests and nonpriests. In contrast to altars, the temples were closed structures and they were understood to be the place of priestly sacrifices. Every temple had an adjoining altar but not every altar was attached to a temple. The crucial difference between the two institutions was reflected in the scope and nature of cultic activity: the place of the priests, in Israel as well as other nations, was confined to the temple and the cultic activity carried on there.

As one would expect from a nomadic community, during the early patriarchal period the Hebrews would appear not to have had temples. Thus the Hebrew Bible lacks reference to a priesthood in the early stages of the Hebrew religion (Genesis does not mention priests except in reference to foreign nations, e.g., Egyptian priests, 41:45; 47:42; and Melchizedek, the king-priest of Salem 14:18). This lack of references does not necessarily exclude the presence of a priesthood, but the period of the temples in Israel began after the conquest of Canaan (*ca.* 1250 B.C.), and the profile of the Israelite priesthood emerged at the same time.

*III. Levites.*–The traditional reconstruction of the priesthood goes back to the Israelite wanderings in the desert under the leadership of Moses. From the earliest times the priesthood was tied to the tribe of Levi, and although some evidence points to priests from other families (e.g., Jgs. 17:5), it is clear that a priest who was a Levite was preferred (17:7-13). During the wilderness wanderings the Levites distinguished themselves as loyal followers of Moses in the episode of the golden calf. They supported Moses, and as a reward for their faithfulness to him and to God they were authorized to the priesthood (Ex. 32:26-29; cf.Dt. 10:8f.).

It is probably incorrect to conclude from the account in Ex. 32 that the office of priest is a new phenomenon. Rather, it is the imposition of the Levites as the exclusive members of the priesthood that is new. A great deal of the source material that presents the faithfulness of the Levites is probably from a later period when they had sustained a prominent position for a long time. Part of the basis for their exclusive claim to the priesthood was that their authority and right of privilege came through their practice of a sacrificial system that excluded foreign elements, particularly the Canaanite religious practices. Although the opposition by the Levites to foreign cult practices varied in different parts of Israel and at different times, eventually the biblical tradition presents them as the priestly dynasty that resisted foreign intrusions. The wilderness account serves to highlight this tradition, which gave a sense of authority to the priestly office and the priestly duties.

The Hebrew term for Levite (*lēwî*) denotes a descendant of LEVI, the third son of Jacob by Leah. Nu. 18:2, 4 seems to have a play on words suggesting that the tribe of Levi was to be "attached" or "joined" (Heb. *lāwâ*) to the family of Aaron. It is possible that the Levites were originally foreigners who joined the Israelites during the wilderness wanderings and helped support and define the emerging priestly order within the religion of ancient Israel. But this theory seems to conflict with early biblical references that Levi was one of the original tribes of Israel engaged in war long before it was given cultic responsibilities (Gen. 34:25-30; 49:5).

Levi was the smallest tribe in the clan confederation, and during the wilderness wanderings it was singled out for service of the tabernacle that included carrying the ark of the covenant and attending to the duties of the portable sanctuary (Nu. 8:24-26; Dt. 10:8). It was chosen for this service "instead of all the first-born among the people of Israel," since the number of firstborn was practically identical with that of the Levites (Nu. 3:40-43). As mentioned earlier, Levi stood out as a tribe that was committed to the leadership of Moses and Joshua, and it was apparently thought to have a close relationship to the tribe of Judah (cf. Dt. 33:7-9). At the settlement of Canaan the Levites were not given a fixed territory; as "ministers of God" it would appear that they wandered without possessing any permanent land of their own. At the time of the monarchy the Levites were at the gates of the cities; thus they still did not possess their own territory. The sources explain this lack of land possession as a sign of superior status — "the Lord is their portion" (Dt. 10:9; 18:2). But this special status may have been obvious to every one; many times the Levites are categorized with other disenfranchised groups — such as the stranger, the orphan, and the widow — that needed the support of the community in order to survive (Dt. 14:29; 16:11, 14; 26:11-13). According to Nu. 35:1-8, the Israelites were commanded to set aside forty-eight towns from their territory for the Levites (cf. Josh. 21:4, 13-19). It would appear that these LEVITICAL CITIES were not exclusively inhabited by Levites, but were cities that contained Levitical families.

*IV. Family of Aaron and Levites.*–All biblical sources agree that the priesthood was originally given to the tribe of Levi. The sources disagree, however, as to how the priesthood was constituted within the tribe. One possibility is that the priesthood was made up exclusively of one family within the Levite tribe, the family of Aaron (Ex. 28:1; 30:26-30; 49:9-15). The rest of the tribe was subordinate to the Aaronic priests; only descendants of Aaron could become priests. Even if the rest of the Levite tribe were resident at the place of sacrifice they could not participate in any direct way in the cultic part of the religion. The sacrificial responsibility of ancient Israel was exclusively the right and privilege of the descendants of Aaron. The Levites as a group, however, were given a certain sanctity below the priestly group but distinct from other Israelites. Within the family of priests the firstborn was set apart and given the rank of high priest (*see* PRIEST, HIGH).

*V. Priests and Levites.*–Another view of the priests and Levites was that the entire Levitical tribe (not just the family of Aaron) was appointed to serve in the priesthood, or more precisely, those Levites were appointed who resided in the chosen city (usually identified with Jerusalem; eventually the Jews believed that Jerusalem was the only place where cultic service was permitted). Levites who did not attach themselves to the temple were devoid of any degree of sanctity and in this respect did not differ from ordinary Israelites. Those Levites who lived in provincial towns were not to participate in the sacrificial system. They were encouraged to join well-to-do families to take part in sacrificial meals (Dt. 12:12, 18f.; 16:11-4). This view maintained that every Levite had the right to go to the chosen city and serve God there (Dt. 18:6f.). The entire tribe of Levites would be better off if they went to the chosen place. This possibility was tempered with the reality that if all Levites went to the chosen place the sacrificial system would probably be overstaffed, and the chosen place could not economically support such a situation.

A notable shift in the importance of the priesthood occurred at the beginning of the monarchical period. The family of Eli lost its importance and its place was taken by the family of Zadok. This family served as the priesthood in the central temple in Jerusalem. A further change in the situation of the priests took place in the time of Josiah. After Josiah introduced the cultic reforms a substantial endorsement of the Jerusalem priesthood meant a major purging of idolatry that included the destroying of high places and altars outside the central Jerusalem temple. All the priests in the towns of Judah were brought to Jerusalem, and this probably indicates the beginning of the view that sacrifices were to be made only at the central temple of Jerusalem (2 K. 23:8).

Ezekiel shared the view that the priesthood was made up exclusively of one family within the Levitical tribe, but he substituted the sons of Zadok (a priest during David's reign whose descendants gained control of the priesthood of the Jerusalem temple) for the sons of Aaron (Ezk. 40:46; 43:19; 44:15f.; 48:11). He stipulated that the priests were obligated to refrain from touching ordinary people while officiating in the temple (Ezk. 42:13f.; 44:19; 46:2, 19f.). Although the Levites could never attain the office of priest they served as an important barrier between the priestly family and the congregation (Ezk. 44:13).

The Levites may have become state officials during the reigns of David and Solomon. Chronicles indicates that the Levites enjoyed a high status under David, even in the administration of the government (1 Ch. 23–27). It is possible that the Levites were among those who helped make the transfer of the monarchy to David at Hebron (1 Ch. 12:27), and their loyalty was rewarded when the cult itself was transformed into an instrument of the state at the establishment of Jerusalem as the political and religious center of David's empire. The Levitical loyalty to the kings of the dynasty of David continued until the destruction of the temple in 587 B.C. (2 Ch. 23:2-9, 18f.; 24:5-15). Some of the sources indicate that there was a migration of the Levites from the northern kingdom of Israel to Judah after the division of the old empire of David and Solomon (1 K. 12:31; 13:33; cf. 2 Ch. 11:13-17; 13:9-12). Once the temple was built at Jerusalem the Levites functioned as overseers in the house of the Lord (1 Ch. 23:4). They were choristers, musicians, gatekeepers, judges, craftsmen for the temple, supervisors of chambers and courts, overseers of the temple treasuries and officers in charge of the royal service (1 Ch. 9:22, 26f.; 23:2-4, 28). During the reign of Jehoshaphat the Levites were teachers of Torah and judges in the towns of Judah, including Jerusalem (2 Ch. 19:8, 11). It is possible that in the temple at Jerusalem the lines of demarcation between priests and Levites were not always clearly preserved; some passages indicate that the Levites ministered alongside the priests (1 Ch. 6:13; 23:27-32). Possibly the Levitical family had a ranking system at this time.

*VI. Levitical Duties and Responsibilities.*–The Levites had duties connected with the service in the tabernacle (Nu. 3–4). They were to assist the priests (Nu. 1:50; 3:6, 8; 16:9; 1 Ch. 23:28; Ezr. 3:8f.), prepare the cereal offerings (1 Ch. 23:28-32), and care for the courts and the chambers of the sanctuary. Later the Levites were apparently involved in interpreting the law and thus functioned as teachers (Neh. 8:7, 9; 2 Ch. 17:7-9; 35:3).

The Levites were explicitly permitted to go near the sacred furniture, and this special privilege distinguished them from ordinary Israelites (Nu. 8:19; 16:9f.; 18:22f.). By virtue of this responsibility they were charged with the "work" (*ʿᵃḇōḏâ*) of the tent of meeting (the tabernacle) that included its dismantling, transportation, and reassembling at a new site (Nu. 1:48-54; 4:3-15; 18:6). This was a requirement of all Levites between the ages of twenty-five and fifty (Lev. 8:24-26). In regard to the accessibility to the sacred furniture, the Levites were allowed to approach the furniture only when it was covered (Nu. 18:3). A drastic and clearcut distinction was made between the sphere of the cult and the rest of the community. The realm of the sacred grew stronger as one proceeded through the inside of the tabernacle, until one reached the area that was taboo even for the priests themselves, the holy of holies. The holiness of the area of sacrifice was conceived as being tangible, a physical entity that could be sensorially perceived. The "realm of contact with God" (the sacrificial places) had limited access and demanded skilled entrance. Only one group of people was permitted, by the grace and appointment of God, to come into contact with the holy areas — the priests.

The Levites were inducted into their special role through a series of ceremonies that included lustrations, shaving the body, sacrifice, the laying on of hands, and a solemn presentation to God (Nu. 8:5-13). They were to be supported by the tithe of the people (Lev. 27:32f; Nu. 18:21, 24), but a tenth of this tithe was to be given to the priests (Nu. 18:26-28).

*VII. Priestly Duties and Responsibilities.*–The anointing of

Aaron and his sons with the same oil as the tabernacle furniture implied that the priesthood shared the holiness of the tabernacle (Ex. 30:22-29; 40:9-11; Lev. 8:10f.; Nu. 7:1). It follows that a nonpriest must not come into contact with a priest while he was anointed with holy oil or was officiating in sacrificial duties. The holiness of the priesthood was equated with the holiness of the house of God itself. Both were put on the same level of sanctity and this implied that the sacrifical activities of the priesthood were of the highest rank in the ancient Israelite forms of worship. The biblical sources frequently indicate that during the ordination ceremonies of the priests, and especially of the high priest, they were not to leave the entrance of the tent of meeting (Lev. 8:33) or go out of the *miqdaš,* "the sacred area" of the tabernacle, for fear of contaminating themselves (Lev. 21:10-12).

In order to maintain this holiness, especially during the cultic services, the priests were subject to special obligations and restrictions. A blemished priest could not approach the altar or enter the temple in order to serve in a sacrificial duty (Lev. 21:17-23). He must make special preparations to avoid contamination of either place or act (Lev. 10:9; 22:18-25; Ex. 30:18-21; Ezk. 44:21). This preparation included such stipulations as not defiling himself by contact with the dead, except in cases of the closest of family ties (Lev. 21:1-4; Ezk. 44:25), as well as restrictions of marriage (Lev. 21:7 prohibits a priest from marrying a harlot or a woman who had been defiled; it further stipulates that he could not marry a divorced woman).

The function of the priests was primarily concerned with offering sacrifices on the altar in the temples. This included the sprinkling of blood and burning portions of sacrifices (Lev. 1). Although this form of religious expression may be difficult for the modern person to comprehend, it should be recognized as an essential part of religious life in the ancient world. The priests also blessed the people in the name of God (Dt. 10:8; 21:5). Such responsibilities were an important part of the covenantal relationship between God and Israel. The blessing of God was a guarantee of reward and a validation of God's concern for Israel if they were faithful to the covenantal requirements. Prior to the settlement in Canaan the priests were also responsible for the unique function of carrying the ark of the covenant (Dt. 10:8; 31:9, 25), and during the Conquest the priests were part of the ark processional that led the people to victory (Josh. 3:3-17; 4:3, 9f.; 8:33).

The priests were involved in the treatment and assessment of impurity. In the ancient Near Eastern world disease was often viewed as an external and tangible embodiment of an impure spirit. The response to the presence of this impurity was both to wait until it left the body and to direct its departure through specific acts of purification. The priests dealt with impurities and diseases as a regular part of their profession, for the continued presence of impurity would eventually undermine their sacrificial system and the status of their holiness as representatives of the people. For example, Dt. 24:8 admonishes the people to follow carefully the instructions of the priests in the case of leprosy (cf. Ezk. 44:23). This kind of activity eventually grew into a highly sophisticated system of judging and anticipating impurities of animals and carcasses, bodily disorders, etc., as well as impurity of corpses (Lev. 11; 15; Nu. 19).

The priestly activities also included oracles given for a variety of purposes, from military advice to judging and instructing the people on matters of tribal customs and behavior (Jgs. 18:5; 1 S. 14:18, 41; 22:15; 23:16). The priests became experts on advising the people of God's will as expressed in Israelite customs *(mišpāṭ)* and eventually expressed in Torah. Very frequently the priestly oracle supplemented or interpreted Israelite custom and law (Dt. 17:11; 33:8, 10). Dt. 33:8-11 mentions the sacrificial ministry of the priesthood only after the responsibilities of teaching Israel the law (cf. Eichrodt, p. 396). One of the points of conflict that eventually arose between priest and prophet was that the latter accused the former of not teaching and practicing Torah (Hos. 4:4-10; cf. Mic. 3:11; Zeph. 3:4; Jer. 2:8; Ezk. 7:26). Both prophet and priest disliked any foreign intrusion into the life-style of Israel, and the priests were frequently involved as judges of acceptable beliefs and practices (Dt. 17:8-13; 24:8; Lev. 10:10; 13:1-59). Their function as oracle givers eventually gave way and was replaced by that of teacher and judge.

In the early stages of Hebrew history the priest probably functioned as the king's assistant in the sacrificial system, with the king taking a fairly active and predominant role (2 S. 6:14; 1 K. 8; 9:25; 2 K. 12:5, 9; 16:14; 2 Ch. 4:1; cf. *ILC,* III-IV, 163). As the temples multiplied and the king's concerns became more diversified the priests took over more of the responsibilities for the sanctuary. They managed the property of the temple and maintained the buildings and the necessary organization of the sanctuary system. In some cases they acquired considerable political power because of their close connections with the government and established such an order and character that despite the disappearance of the king in 587 B.C. the priests survived and continued to influence the life of Israel in a very concrete way for another seven hundred years.

***VIII. Postexilic Priesthood.***–After the Babylonian Exile a decisive action took place to rebuild the temple at Jerusalem as a sign of the reaffirmation of national and religious identity for ancient Judaism. This meant a rebirth of the supremacy of the priesthood, and it would appear that during this period it was clearly established that only those who were considered to be descendants of Aaron could serve in the priesthood. The Levites served beside them as a lower class in the priestly structure. The numbers of the priests increased, and in some cases the priests worked various parts of the land (Neh. 13:10f.; 10:35). This allowed for a decreased dependence on the priestly gifts. It is probably at this period that the priestly services and divisions became regulated (1 Ch. 24:3-19).

After the return from the Babylonian Exile the lines between the priests and Levites were firmly established. The Levites acquired an honored status (although the Bible does not refer to any particular robe of the office of the Levites, Josephus relates that Agrippa II granted the Levitical singers the privilege of wearing priestly linen robes, *Ant.* xx.9.6 [216-18]) and their small numbers in comparison to the priests added to their importance (Ezr. 2:40-42). In the period of Ezra and Nehemiah it was necessary to bring Levites from the rural areas of Palestine and from the Exile to have enough staff for the temple of Jerusalem.

During the Hellenistic period the priesthood was the class with the highest status among the people and the high priest functioned as the main representative of the Jews during the late Persian and the Greek regimes (*see* PRIEST, HIGH). It would appear that most of the people in administrative positions were also priests. The temple at Jerusalem overshadowed all other institutions in Judea.

The priesthood seems to have reached its zenith during the Hasmonean period (*ca.* 165-60 B.C.) when it could be legitimately categorized as a part of the Jewish aristocracy with far-reaching influence and position in society. In the late Maccabean era the priests were members in a number of the parties and sects within Judaism. It would

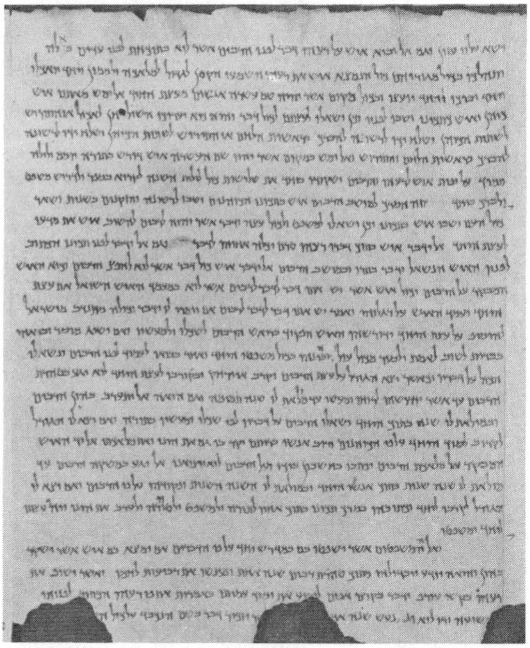

The Manual of Discipline from Qumrân (1QS), col. 6, which mentions the primacy of the priest in the community (J. C. Trever)

seem that the priests were a substantial part of the leadership of the Sadducees, and their membership in the Sanhedrin made them influential powers in both civic and religious matters. Priests also were part of the leadership in the separatist sect of the Essenes. Some of their writings (e.g., the Manual of Discipline) indicate that the priesthood was a vital part of the hierarchy.

With destruction of the Jerusalem temple in A.D. 70 the priesthood lost its main religious base in society; in their role as teachers the priests were replaced by the Pharisees and the rabbis in the synagogues.

In the modern period the prevailing opinion is that to claim to be an Aaronide, of priestly descent, is mainly presumptive because of the lack of reliable registers. In Orthodox Judaism the rights and privileges of the priest, as well as the prohibitions, are in full force. The privileges include the right to be called up first for the reading of the law and the invocation of the Priestly Blessing in the synagogue. Prohibitions are very often directed to avoiding impurities such as contact with the dead. Special arrangements are made in some hospitals to enable the priest to visit the sick without compromising his sanctity as priest. Marriage restrictions include the prohibition of marrying a divorcee. Reform Judaism disregards the laws applying to a priest.

*IX. Modern Critical Analysis.*–As indicated above, the characterization of the Hebrew priesthood based on the biblical sources is not an easy matter. The modern critical analysis of the Hebrew Bible led by Graf and Wellhausen (cf. Harrison, pp. 19-61) has demanded a reassessment of the history of the Hebrew priesthood. In the decades since the original proposals the view of the priesthood and its construction has frequently caused more disagreement than consensus. The critical reconstruction of the Levitical priesthood is closely linked with the Graf-Wellhausen literary analysis of the Pentateuch into four chronological documentary sources (J, E, D, P). Although this hypothesis has had great influence on the estimation of the Hebrew Bible, it is not without challenge; scholars have modified the basic four-source analysis. The greatest liability of the Wellhausen school is that it has oversimplified the religious life of Israel and assumed that belief and institutions were developmental, with simple and sometimes unrefined ideas being designated as early and more advanced concepts being late. Very frequently these presuppositions have shaped the interpretation of the Hebrew Bible, and ideas and institutions have been judged according to this evolutionary process.

The critical reconstruction of the priesthood is usually stated in the following manner. In the earliest period of Hebrew history the priesthood was not limited to the Levitical clan and sacrifices were not the exclusive prerogative of priests. In the period of the judges two official Levitical priestly families had emerged. The one resident at Dan had been established by Micah's Levite, Jonathan, the grandson of Moses (Jgs. 18:1-4, 14-20; 1 Ch. 23:24f), and the other was at Shiloh under Eli and his family (1 S. 1–4; 22:20; 2 S. 8:17). The house of Eli eventually was replaced by the house of Zadok, and the Zadokite priesthood continued in Jerusalem until the destruction of the city in 587 B.C. (2 S. 8:17; 15:24-29, 35; 19:11; 2 Ch. 6:8-11).

The sources are somewhat divided over whether the king should participate in the sacrificial system. 1 S. 13:8-13 and 2 Ch. 26:16-20 reflect opposition to the king's participation in priestly duties (Saul and Uzziah) while both David and Solomon sacrificed and blessed the people in the capacity of priest (2 S. 6:12-19; 1 K. 8:22-53; 9:25). By the end of the 7th cent. the priesthood had narrowed exclusively to the Levites. The reforms of Josiah (*ca.* 621 B.C.) had put an end to local sanctuaries in every town by centralizing worship at Jerusalem. The book of the law, generally regarded as an early edition of Deuteronomy, stipulated that sacrifices could only be offered at Jerusalem (Dt. 12:5-7, 11, 13f.) and all priests were referred to as "sons of Levi" (Dt. 10:8; 18:1; 21:5; 33:8).

By the 5th. cent. the "development" of the priesthood was such that a special group within the Levitical clan had emerged to hold the exclusive position of priest. Ezekiel is viewed as the link between the period when all priests were Levites (preexilic) and the subsequent phase (postexilic) when they were restricted to a particular section of the Levite clan. According to Ezk. 44:15f., the Zadokite priests were responsible for the actual sacrificial service because of their faithfulness when Israel went astray. The general clan of Levites had not proven faithful and as a consequence was given a lower status and confined mainly to menial tasks in the temple service (Ezk. 44:9-14). The critical assessment is that the more "refined" stage of the priesthood is being given theological and historical support (cf. Haran, pp. 103-111). The actual reorganization of the priesthood after the Exile indicates that the priesthood was not restricted to the Zadokite line (as proposed by Ezekiel), for an Aaronic heritage was the criterion for the priesthood (1 Ch. 15:4; 23:28-32; Ps. 115:10, 12; 118:3; 135:9, Sir. 45:6-24; 50:13, 16).

The Priestly Code (P, generally assigned to the 6th or 5th cent.) makes an absolute distinction between the priests and the Levites (Nu. 18:2-7; cf. Lev. 8) with the priests restricted to the house of Aaron (Ex. 28:1, 43; Nu. 3:10; 8:1, 7). If one follows the source hypothesis it is really the Priestly Code, not Ezekiel, that provides the pattern for the postexilic Jerusalem priesthood with its emphasis on the Aaronic hereditary line (cf. Ezr. 2:61-63 and Neh. 7:63-65 where all who claimed to belong to the priesthood were required to prove their descent from Aaron).

Chronicles has frequently been viewed as a supplement to the Priestly Code, and it does affirm the primacy of the Aaronic priesthood. At the same time it gives special prominence to the Levites' importance in the religious system (1 Ch. 15:2-15; 16:4; 2 Ch. 5:4; 35:3). The priesthood is set up into twenty-four "courses" or groups, each of which came up to the temple in turn for its appointed period (1 Ch. 24).

The reconstruction from the earliest Hebrew period depicts the development from a Levitical priesthood competing with heads of clans and other priestly dynasties to a phase where the priesthood is set within a segment of the tribe of Levi with a multiple and complex structure of "assistants" represented in the rest of the priestly family. One of the cardinal doctrines of the Wellhausen school is that the distinction between priests and Levites that is predominant in the Priestly Code was not known in the preexilic period. In the literature representing this earlier period all priests were Levites and all Levites were priests. Thus, Deuteronomy is read as not distinguishing between priest and Levite, a distinction that began with Ezekiel. Ezk. 40:45f.; 44:6-8; 48:13, however, suggest that the writer knew of various divisions in the Levitical family structure before his schema of reorganization. In Deuteronomy the distinction between priest and Levite is not as sharp as in the Priestly Code, but it should not be presupposed that such a distinction may not be detected (Dt. 18:3-8 seems to make allowance for priests ministering at the sanctuary in contrast to those unattached to a specific place; the latter may reflect the Levites). Further, the Priestly Code seems to relate to a later period than Deuteronomy, but it is possible that the priestly material does preserve much earlier material. In fact, it seems quite legitimate to use the Priestly Code, with care, as a substantial source for the preexilic period (i.e., traditions about the Day of Atonement).

The convenient division between "early" and "late" materials is far too simplistic, and it does disservice to the sources and the Hebrew religion. The literary sources of the Hebrew Bible are not as well identified as the earlier proposals may have suggested. The one major and common feature of all the sources is that the priesthood was not granted to common Israelites but only to certain families, that at some point the tribe of Levi emerged as the main base of priestly activity, and that the descendants of Aaron ultimately were in exclusive possession of the office by the postexilic period.

On priestly garments *see* GARMENTS VIII.

*See also* PRIESTHOOD IN THE NT.

***Bibliography.***–G. C. Aalders, *Short Intro. to the Pentateuch* (Eng. tr. 1949), pp. 66-71; N. Avigad, *Bulletin of the Israel Exploration Society*, 22 (1958), 3-10; J. R. Brown, *Temple and Sacrifice in Rabbinic Judaism* (1963); R. E. Clements, *God and Temple* (1965); *Transactions of the Glasgow University Oriental Society*, 19 (1963), 16-28; A. Cody, *History of the OT Priesthood* (1969); F. M. Cross, *JBL*, 94 (1975), 4-18; *Canaanite Myth and Hebrew Epic* (1973), pp. 195-215; R. de Vaux, *Ancient Israel* (Eng. tr. 1961), II; W. Eichrodt, *Theology of the OT*, I (Eng. tr. 1961); G. B. Gray, *Sacrifice in the OT* (1925), pp. 179-270; M. Haran, *Temples and Temple-Service in Ancient Judaism* (Eng. tr. 1978); R. K. Harrison, *Intro. to the OT* (1969); *ILC*, III-IV; E. Jacob, *Theology of the OT* (Eng. tr. 1958), pp. 246-250; E. O. James, *Nature and Function of Priesthood* (1955); J. Jeremias, *Jerusalem in the Time of Jesus* (Eng. tr. 1969); B. Mazar, "The Cities of the Priests and the Levites," in *SVT*, 7 (1960), 193-205; S. Sauneron, *Priests of Ancient Egypt* (1960); J. Strong, *Tabernacle of Israel in the Desert* (1952); A. C. Welch, *Prophet and Priest in Old Israel* (1953); *Post-Exilic Judaism* (1935), pp. 172-184, 217-244; S. Yeivin, *VT*, 3 (1953), 149-166.

W. O. MCCREADY

**PRIMEVAL RUINS** [Heb. *ḥ<sup>o</sup>rāḇôṯ mēʿôlām*] (Ezk. 26:20); AV "places desolate of old"; NEB "places long desolate." The AV and NEB translate literally this figurative detail of the desolation that God would bring upon Tyre. Cf. the use of *ḥorbâ* in Isa. 58:12; Jer. 25:9 (AV, RSV mg.); 49:13. For a good discussion of the thought of Ezk. 26:20 in its ancient Near Eastern context, see W. Eichrodt, *Ezekiel* (Eng. tr., *OTL*, 1970), pp. 373-78.

**PRIMITIVE.** A term used often in biblical studies to designate a very early period in the development of a group or institution, e.g., the Church. In such uses the term is merely chronological; it does not imply "uncivilized" or any other negative judgment on the quality of whatever it designates.

**PRIMOGENITURE** prī-mō-jen'ə-chər. *See* BIRTHRIGHT; HEIR; INHERIT.

**PRINCE** [Heb. *nāśî'*, *nāgîḏ*, *nāḏîḇ*, *śar*, part. of *rāzan*, *rāzôn*, *nāsîḵ*; Gk. *árchōn*]; AV also CAPTAIN, RULER, CHIEF RULER, LEADER, CHIEF GOVERNOR, NOBLE, CHIEF, PRINCIPAL MAN, etc.; NEB also OFFICER, CHIEF, WARRIOR, NOBLE, NOBLEMAN, CAPTAIN, COURTIER, EMBASSY, etc. The RSV translation of numerous terms indicating a position of authority or power to rule. The terms do not refer specifically to the direct male heir to the throne or to a king's physical male descendant.

Hebrew *nāśî'* (lit. "one lifted up") perhaps originally designated a tribal leader or representative elevated by his community to a position of power and importance. The Hittites of Hebron applied the term to Abraham (Gen. 23:6; cf. LXX *basileús*, "king"); it was also applied to leaders in Shechem (34:2) and Midian (Nu. 25:18). Ishmael is said to have become "the father of twelve princes" (Gen. 17:20; 25:16). The term is used of Israel's tribal leaders (1 Ch. 4:38; 7:40; cf. Ezk. 21:12 [MT 17]; 22:6; 45:8f.) as well as other "princes of the earth" (39:18) who have attained preeminence (e.g., 26:16; 27:21; cf. 7:27). In Ezekiel's time, with the decline in power of the kings of Israel and Judah, the term is used frequently (e.g., 38:2f.; 45:7). In his vision of Israel's future restoration and glory, Ezekiel gives special prominence to the role of the prince (esp. chs. 46 and 48), who as the civil leader supports the religious community by providing sanctuaries and upholding law and order (see 45:7–46:13 on the duties of the princes).

Royal and military overtones belong also to *nāgîḏ*. King Hezekiah is called "the prince of my people" (e.g., 2 K. 20:5), Abijah is called a "chief prince" (2 Ch. 11:22), the "Prince of Tyre" is referred to in Ezk. 28:2, and the "prince who is to come" (Antiochus Epiphanes) is mentioned in Dnl. 9:26 (cf. v. 25). Various military officers are also designated by this term (e.g., 1 Ch. 12:27 [MT 28]; 2 Ch. 32:31). In Hebrew poetry the term can indicate a person of wide, general influence (Job 31:37; Ps. 76:12 [MT 13]). The divinely appointed king of Israel is also called a *nāgîḏ* (e.g., in 1 S. 9:16; cf. 10:1; 13:14; 2 S. 6:21; 7:8; Solomon in 1 Ch. 29:22).

*Nāḏîḇ* is associated with nobility and honor, having at its root (cf. *nāḏaḇ*, "make willing, prompt") the notion of voluntary service. It is translated "princes" in 1 S. 2:8; Job. 12:21; Ps. 107:40; 113:8; 118:9; 146:3. In Ps. 47:9 (MT 10) the term designates the leaders of the world.

Hebrew *śar* (cf. Akk. *šarru*) can signify a leader or official in a variety of civil, military, and religious functions. Thus the term denotes various types of rulers and high officials in Egypt (Jer. 25:19; cf. Ex. 2:14), Moab (Nu. 22:8, 13-15; 23:6), Ammon (2 S. 10:3; Am. 1:15), Philistia (1 S. 18:30), Babylon (Jer. 38:17f., 22), and Persia (Est. 1:3, 11, 14, 16; 2:18; etc.). Tribal leaders in Israel are designated by this term (Jgs. 5:15; Nu. 21:18), as are other national leaders (2 K. 24:12; Isa. 1:23; Jer. 1:18; 2:26; 24:1, 8; 26:10-12, etc.; Ezk. 11:1; 17:12; Hos. 3:4; 5:10; 7:3, 5, 16; Mic. 7:3), ambassadors (Jer. 36:14), and priests (Isa. 43:28). In Dnl. 10:13, 20f.; 12:1 *śar* designates a patron-angel assigned to a particular nation (*see* ANGEL II.B; see also comms., e.g., *IB,* VI, 506f.); but the titles "Prince of the host" (8:11) and "Prince of princes" (v. 25) refer to God. Isa. 9:6 prophesies the birth of a messianic king who will be called "Prince of Peace." The title, which was later applied to Jesus, reflects the king's role in securing the peace and prosperity of his people.

Other Hebrew terms rendered by "prince" include the part. of *rāzan,* "dignitary" (Jgs. 5:3; Isa. 40:23; cf. *rāzôn,* Prov. 14:28), and *nāsîḵ,* "tribal leader"(Ps. 83:11 [MT 12]; Ezk. 32:30; Mic. 5:5 [MT 4]).

In the NT Gk. *árchōn* is a general term for RULER. The RSV renders it "prince" in five passages that refer to the ruler or commander of the supernatural forces of evil. In Mt. 9:34 Jesus' opponents claim that His power to cast out demons comes from the "prince of demons," who in 12:24-32 (par. Mk. 3:22-30; Lk. 11:15-23) is identified with BEELZEBUL and with SATAN. In response, Jesus points out the absurdity of imagining that the chief ruler of demons would take sides against his own subordinates; if he did so, his kingdom would collapse. The author of Ephesians refers to the same ruling evil being as "the prince of the power of the air, the spirit that is now at work in the sons of disobedience" (2:2; *see also* AIR; cf. 6:11-17, which refers to the "devil" and the "evil one"). Similarly, the Gospel of John refers to Satan as "the ruler [*árchōn*] of this world" (12:31; 14:30; 16:11) who is about to be thrown out and judged. (See *TDNT,* I, *s.v.* ἄρχω κτλ.: ἄρχων [G. Delling].)

*See also* CHIEF; COMMANDER; GOVERNMENT; LEADER; NOBLE; OFFICER. D. K. MCKIM

**PRINCES, THE SEVEN.** Seven princes named in Est. 1:14: Carshena, Shethar, Admatha, Tarshish, Meres, Marsena, and Memucan (cf. the LXX, which has only 3 names). Memucan is the spokesman for the group. These names seem to be Persian in origin, but they are difficult to identify and bear little resemblance to known Persian names (cf. comms. by C. A. Moore [*AB,* 1971], pp. XLII-XLIII, 9f.; L. B. Paton [*ICC,* 1908], pp. 68f.). Rawlinson has suggestd that Marsena may be Mardonius, and Admatha may be Artabanus, the uncle of Xerxes.

These seven are said to be advisers to the king, perhaps each of them the head of one of the leading families of Persia. They are next in line of succession to the king's family, and have special access to the king. Herodotus (iii.68-84) relates that Darius and the other six conspirators against Pseudo-Smerdis (Gaumata) agreed (before any one of them was chosen as king) to grant permission "for any of the seven to enter the palace unannounced, except when the king was in bed with a woman," and that "the king should not marry outside the families of the seven confederates." Herodotus gives the names of the seven: Darius, Otanes (Utana), Intaphrenes (Vindafarna), Gobryas (Gaubaruva), Hydarnes (Vidarna), Megabyzus (Bagabukhsha), and Aspathines (Aspachana). These agree with the list given by Darius on the BEHISTUN inscription, except for the last name, which Darius gives as Ardumanish. Aspathines appears on the Behistun inscription and on the tomb relief of Darius as the bearer of the battle-ax.

Seven advisers also are mentioned in Ezr. 7:14. The "seven advisers" could easily have their origin in the "seven conspirators," but R. Ghirshman (p. 128) suggested that the college of seven princes may date from the time of Cyrus. These seven formed the royal council of the Persians, and the king was the first among the seven.

*Bibliography.*–A. T. Olmstead, *History of the Persian Empire* (1948); R. Ghirshman, *Iran* (1954). R. E. HAYDEN

**PRINCESS.** A word used four times by the RSV to render two different Hebrew terms or phrases. Heb. *baṯ meleḵ* (lit. "daughter of a king"; cf. AV, NEB, "king's daughter") occurs in Ps. 45:13 (MT 14) and Jer. 43:6. Ps. 45 describes a royal wedding of the king of Israel to a princess of Tyre (cf. v. 12). Following the Targums, which sometimes interpreted this Psalm as referring to the Messiah and Israel, the early Church understood the Psalm as depicting the relationship between Christ and the Church (see Anderson, pp. 346f.; Weiser, p. 365). Jer. 43:6 lists the king's daughters among the refugees from Judah who fled to Egypt under the leadership of Johanan son of Kareah.

Hebrew *śārâ,* the feminine equivalent of *śar* (*see* PRINCE), generally denotes a royal lady of the court (cf. RSV "lady" in Jgs. 5:29; Est. 1:18; "queen" in Isa. 49:23). In 1 K. 11:3 the term is applied to Solomon's seven hundred wives in distinction from the three hundred concubines who also made up part of his harem. In Lam. 1:1 *śārâ* (AV, RSV, "princess"; NEB "queen") figuratively depicts the prominence and glory of Jerusalem before it was devastated by the Babylonians.

*Bibliography.*–A. A. Anderson, *Book of Psalms,* I (*NCBC,* repr. 1981); A. Weiser, *Psalms* (Eng. tr., *OTL,* 1962, repr. 1976).

D. K. MCKIM
N. J. O.

**PRINCIPAL** [Gk. *prṓtos*–'first' (Lk. 19:47; Acts 25:2)]; AV CHIEF; NEB LEADING, LEADER. Both references are to leaders (cf. Acts 28:17; RSV "local leaders") of the Jews. In Lk. 19:47 they are linked with the chief priests and scribes; according to I. H. Marshall (*Gospel of Luke* [*NIGTC,* 1978], p. 722) they are the "lay elders of the people," part of the Sanhedrin. In Acts 25:2 "the principal men of the Jews" are again linked with chief priests.

The AV uses "principal" several times in quite misleading, inaccurate ways. In 1 K. 4:5 the AV translates Heb. *kōhēn* ("priest"; so RSV) as "principal officer" (the NEB, NAB, and JB omit, following LXX B and Lucian). In 2 K. 25:19 par. Jer. 52:25 the AV "principal scribe" (Heb. [*has*]*sōpēr śar*) seems better translated in the RSV ("secretary of the commander"; see KD *in loc.*; but cf. J. Gray, *I & II Kings* [2nd ed., *OTL,* 1970], p. 769). In 1 Ch. 24:31 the AV "principal fathers" gives a wrong sense; cf. the RSV "the head of each father's house."

G. A. L.

**PRINCIPALITIES AND POWERS.** [Primarily the translation of Gk. *archaí* and *exousíai* in the AV and RSV]. The RSV translates *archaí* as either "principalities" (Rom. 8:38; Eph. 3:10; 6:12; Col. 1:16; 2:15) or "rulers" (Lk. 12:11; Tit. 3:1; cf. *pása archḗ,* "every/all rule," 1 Cor. 15:24; Eph. 1:21; Col. 2:10) and *exousíai* as either "powers" (Eph. 3:10; 6:12; Col. 2:15) or "authorities" (Lk. 12:11; Rom. 13:1; Col. 1:16; Tit. 3:1; 1 Pet. 3:22; cf. *pása exousía,* "every/all authority," 1 Cor. 15:24; Eph. 1:21; Col. 2:10). The RSV also uses "rulers" to translate *árchontes* (e.g., 1 Cor. 2:6, 8) and "powers" to translate *dynámeis* (e.g., Rom. 8:38; Eph. 1:21). There is no obvious explanation for the RSV's use of different translations for the same terms. Most modern versions employ a similar range of translations, although some (e.g., NEB and NIV) do not use "principalities." Consideration is here given to only those uses of *archḗ* and *exousía* that are plural (or the plural is implied through the generalizing *pása*) and refer to personal powers.

In some NT passages *archaí* and *exousíai* refer to

human political rulers (e.g., "rulers and authorities," Lk. 12:11; Tit 3:1), following the normal Greek usage. The sense of "superhuman powers" is not found in Hellenism or pagan Gnosticism (see *TDNT,* II, 571). Some scholars (e.g., Dibelius, pp. 189, 193ff.; Cullmann, pp. 55-70, 95-114) have contended that *exousíai hyperéchontes* (RSV "governing authorities") in Rom. 13:1 refers both to the state and to the angelic powers that in Judaism were held to stand behind the state. Support for this interpretation is sought in the use of the plural in Rom. 13:1 (which elsewhere in Paul's writings always refers to superhuman powers) and in the prevailing interpretation of *árchontes tou aiṓnos toútou* (RSV "rulers of this age") in 1 Cor. 2:6, 8. Many interpret "the rulers of this age" as referring either to the demonic forces or to the human and superhuman powers who crucified Jesus; but because of the emphasis on human wisdom in the context, the phrase probably refers to human rulers (cf. Carr, pp. 118-120). As to the first argument when *exousíai* means "superhuman rulers" elsewhere in Paul's writings, it is always accompanied by other terms that clearly indicate this meaning (e.g., *archaí, dynámeis*). In Rom. 13:1, therefore, *exousíai hyperéchontes* probably refers to civil authorities.

Most frequently, however, *archaí* and *exousíai* refer to personal, superhuman powers belonging to the angelic order. Angelology, with its divisions of angels into various classes, underwent extensive development in Judaism, and it is possible that *exousíai* was already being used to denote angelic beings, intermediary between God and mankind, in Dnl. 7:27 (LXX). Here the more immediate reference of *exousíai* (RSV "dominions") is to the kingdoms of this earth; but in ch. 10 it is clear that these kingdoms are associated with powers of the superterrestrial sphere (10:13, 20). In Rom. 8:38 and 1 Pet. 3:22 *archaí* ("principalities"), *exousíai* ("authorities"), and *dynámeis* ("powers") are specifically associated with angels. Some have contended that Paul does not think of these powers as "personal beings," since in Rom. 8:38 he associates them with such nonpersonal entities as "present and future" and "height and depth" (see Berkhof, pp. 17-20). But since these terms did refer to personal beings in Jewish apocalyptic, there is no reason to doubt that Paul also used them in this sense (cf. H. Kakes, pp. 145-47).

The NT writers do not distinguish between the *archaí, exousíai,* etc.; these seem to be different terms for much the same thing (see *TDNT,* II, 573). Nor do the NT writers speculate about these powers, but they always mention them in connection with Christ's work. Their role can best be elucidated, therefore, in connection with creation, redemption, the Church, and the final consummation.

(1) Creation. In Rom. 8:38 the "principalities" (*exousíai*) and "powers" (*dynámeis*), along with the "angels," belong to the created order. Paul indicates this when he adds to the list of personal beings and quasi-personal forces "or anything else in all creation." Angels, principalities, and powers thus stand with mankind on this side of the great divide that separates the Creator from the creature. More specifically the hymn in Col. 1:16 states that the "principalities and authorities" (*archaí* and *exousíai*), along with "thrones" (*thrónoi*), "dominions" (*kyriótētes*), and all things visible and invisible in heaven and on earth, were created "through" (*diá*) and "unto" (*eis*) Christ. Originally, therefore, they were a part of God's good creation.

(2) Redemption. Those principalities and powers created through and unto Christ (Col. 1:20) were among the "all things" reconciled to God through Christ's death on the cross (v.20). Through Christ's crucifixion, resurrection, and enthronement, all "angels, authorities, and powers" have become subject to Him (1 Pet. 3:22). Christ now sits enthroned above every *archḗ* and *exousía* and *dýnamis* and *kyriótētes* ("rule and authority and power and dominion," Eph. 1:21). He is the "head" of every *archḗ* and *exousía* ("rule and authority," Col. 2:10); He is the "head" over all things for the sake of the Church (Eph. 1:22).

Two passages in particular suggest that Christ's victory over the powers was juridical. Col. 2:14 refers to the "certificate of indebtedness" that God cancelled by nailing it to the cross. The image is perhaps taken from an anonymous Jewish apocalyptic work in which the "certificate of indebtedness" is a book of works held by an accusing angel (see Bandstra, pp. 158-162). By "putting off" (*apekdýomai,* lit. "strip off"; RSV "disarm") His body of flesh, Christ openly "exposed" (*deigmatízō*; RSV "make a public example") the principalities and powers, triumphing over them in the cross (for this interpretation of Col. 2:14f., see Bandstra, pp. 162-64; see also J. A. T. Robinson, *The Body* [*SBT,* 1/5, 1952], pp. 41f.). Drawing upon the imagery of Zec. 3:1-5 this passage apparently depicts the principalities and powers in the role of "accuser" (cf. Rev. 12:10-12); thus Christ's work on the cross "exposed" the nonvalidity of their case against believers.

A similar juridical context is present in Rom. 8:31-38, which raises the questions, "Who is against us?" "Who shall bring any charge against God's elect?" "It is God who justifies, who is to condemn?" The passage then declares that nothing can separate us from the love of God in Christ Jesus, neither "angels," nor "principalities," nor "powers." The "angels" here may refer to those angels who stand behind the law (cf. Acts 7:53; Gal. 3:19; He. 2:2). Even angels bent on the justice of the law cannot bring a valid charge against God's elect whom He has justified in Christ. The "principalities" and "powers" may refer, as in Col. 2:14f., to the more demonic accusers of God's people; they too are powerless to separate the justified believer in Christ from God and His love.

Are the principalities and powers good forces or evil forces? In the light of what has been said above, it would seem that they participate in both the positive and the negative aspects of the created world. On the one hand, they were created through and unto Christ; on the other, they have been "reconciled," "exposed," and "subjected" to Christ. Certainly in Eph. 6:12 they represent part of the demonic opposition to the community of believers. The distinctive feature of the NT statements is that the powers represent the tension of the created order: on the one side the carnal aspect of the fallen creation, and on the other the created structure as it comes from God through Christ (see *TDNT,* II, 573). Even though they are fallen, the powers can represent both the positive and negative sides of the creation, for God can use even the fallenness of creation for a positive end (cf. Kakes, pp. 147-150). Certainly the positive contributions of the powers in the creation order, e.g., their maintenance of law and order through fallen institutions, must not be overlooked (see Berkhof, pp. 45-54). On the other hand, when these powers assume a role beyond that intended by God, these become a threat to the well-being of the Church.

This depiction of the powers as both good and evil has been challenged by W. Carr (pp. 45-114), who has argued that in Paul, as in the Jewish sources of these terms, the "principalities" and "powers" are only good "angels" who give homage and worship to Christ the Lord. According to this view Col. 2:14f. should be read not as a victory by Christ over the powers but as a public declaration of Christ's lordship as witnessed to by the worship of His hosts. It is conceded that Eph. 6:12 does not fit into this interpretation; thus it is argued that this verse is a second-century addition to the text. This challenge must be seriously considered, but it does not seem to fit the data. Eph. 6:12 must be allowed to stand as an authentic part of the text of the Ephesians. In Col. 2:15 *deigmatízō* does not mean simply "publicly parade" but has the more negative connotation of "publicly expose," as both Mt. 1:19 and Asc. Isa. 3:13 suggest. The hostile role of the angels, principalities, and powers in Rom. 8:38 cannot simply be dismissed as a "hyperbolic paradox" (Carr, p. 113) but must be seen as a real threat to the believer — a threat that has been overcome by Christ.

(3) The Church. Though Christ has exposed, triumphed over, and made the principalities and powers subject to Himself (Col. 2:15; 1 Pet. 3:22), the Church must continue to fight against these demonic powers by putting on the whole armor of God (Eph. 6:12f.). Because these powers stand behind threats to faith, they must be resisted in the name of Christ. Yet they cannot decisively affect the relationship between the Church and God, since neither angels, nor principalities, nor powers can separate the believing community from the love of God in Christ Jesus (Rom. 8:38). Furthermore, the Church is called to make known the manifold wisdom of God "to the principalities and powers in the heavenly places" (Eph. 3:10). Although the text does not state exactly how the Church is to fulfil this assignment, the context suggests that this will happen through the deeds of the Church (as itself the reconciled community of Greeks and Jews) and its words (as the proclamation in all creation of this mystery of Christ).

(4) The final consummation. At His first coming, by His death and resurrection Christ has publicly exposed and subjected the principalities and powers to Himself. But their power has not yet been completely destroyed. Christ must reign until every "rule" (*arché̄*) and "authority" (*exousía*) and "power" (*dýnamis*) has been completely annulled (1 Cor. 15:24). Then the end shall come.

*See also* ANGEL.

***Bibliography.***–A. J. Bandstra, *The Law and the Elements of the World* (1964); H. Berkhof, *Christ and the Powers* (Eng. tr. 1962); G. B. Caird, *Principalities and Powers* (1956); W. Carr, *Angels and Principalities* (1981); O. Cullmann, *The State in the NT* (Eng. tr. 1957); M. Dibelius, *Die Geisterwelt im Glauben des Paulus* (1909); *DNTT,* II, 601-611; O. Everling, *Die paulinische Angelologie und Dämonologie* (1888); H. Kakes, *Waar zijn de engelen nu?* (1976); G. H. C. Macgregor, *NTS,* 1 (1954/55), 17-28; H. Schlier, *Principalities and Powers in the NT* (Eng. tr. 1961); J. S. Steward, *SJT,* 4 (1951), 292-301; *TDNT,* I, *s.v.* ἄρχω: ἀρχή (G. Delling); II, *s.v.* ἔξεστιν: ἐξουσία (W. Foerster).

A. J. BANDSTRA

**PRINCIPLES.** In He. 5:12 "the first principles of God's word" renders the unusual Greek construction *tá stoicheía tḗs archḗs tṓn logíōn toú theoú* (AV "the first principles of the oracles of God"; NEB "the ABC of God's oracles"). In Greek literature *tá stoicheía* has a variety of meanings (*see* ELEMENT I); among these, it can refer to the rudimentary elements of musical or mathematical instruction or, by extension, to the rudiments of any field of knowledge. In He. 5:12 it refers to the elementary teachings of the Christian faith — teachings beyond which, the author laments, the readers have not progressed.

A parallel phrase occurs in 6:1, where the author continues this theme with an exhortation to "leave *ho tḗs archḗs toú Christoú lógos* and go on to maturity." The syntax of the Greek phrase (RSV "the elementary doctrines of Christ") strongly suggests that in 5:12 *tḗs archḗs tṓn logíōn toú theoú* functions as a genitive of apposition defining *tá stoicheía* more explicitly as the elementary teachings of divine revelation (*see also* ELEMENTARY DOCTRINE OF CHRIST). A list of these elementary teachings appears in 6:1b-2: "repentance from dead works . . . faith toward God . . . ablutions, the laying on of hands, the resurrection of the dead, and eternal judgment." It is remarkable that none of these doctrines transcends the beliefs and practices of Judaism. This may lend support to the traditional view that the Epistle was addressed to a Jewish-Christian community, which, not fully appreciating the finality of the work of Christ, was tempted to avoid persecution by reverting to Judaism.

*See also* ELEMENT II.

***Bibliography.***–Comms., esp. F. F. Bruce, *Epistle to the Hebrews* (*NICNT,* repr. 1981), pp. 107-117; B. F. Westcott, *Epistle to the Hebrews* (1909), pp. 134f., 144.

T. L. DONALDSON

**PRINTING.** *See* WRITING.

**PRISCA** pris'kə [Gk. *Priska*], also the diminutive form **PRISCILLA** pri-sil'ə [Gk. *Priskilla*]. A Christian woman who with her husband AQUILA labored alongside Paul at Corinth. They came to Corinth after Claudius had expelled all the Jews from Rome (Acts 18:2). They were Paul's co-workers at Ephesus also, where they ministered effectively, especially to Apollos (Acts 18:18-26). Priscilla is named before her husband in the majority of passages, which may indicate her strength of character and/or her exceptional usefulness in Christian work (cf. Acts 18:26). After the death of Claudius the couple returned to Rome (Rom. 16:3).

B. R. and P. C. PATTEN

**PRISON** (noun) [Heb. *bêṯ (hak)kele'*–'house of confinement' (1 K. 22:27 par. 2 Ch. 18:26; 2 K. 17:4; 25:27; Isa. 42:7, 22; Jer. 37:4, 15, 18; 52:31), *bêṯ hassōhar*–'house of roundness' (Gen. 39:20-23; 40:3, 5), *masgēr*–'dungeon' (Ps. 142:7 [MT 8]; Isa. 24:22), *mišmār*–'jail, prison' (Gen. 42:17, 19), *bêṯ hā'*$^a$*sîrîm*–'house of the prisoners' (Jgs. 16:21, 25), *bêṯ hāsûrîm*–'house of the prisoners' (Eccl. 4:14), *bêṯ happ*$^e$*quddâ*–'house of custody' (Jer. 52:11), *bêṯ hammahpeḵeṯ*–'house of the stocks' (2 Ch. 16:10), *p*$^e$*qaḥ-qô(a)ḥ*–'opening (of eyes)' ("opening of the prison," Isa. 61:1); Gk. *phylakḗ*–'watch, guard' (Mt. 5:25; 25:36; Lk. 23:19; etc.), *desmōtḗrion*–'prison, jail' (Mt. 11:2; Acts 5:21, 23; 16:26), *tḗrēsis*–'custody, imprisonment,' 'prison' (Acts 5:18), *désmios*–'prisoner' (He. 13:3)]; AV also WARD, BONDS; NEB GAOL, DUNGEONS, ROUND TOWER, "release" (Isa. 61:1), etc.; (vb.) [Heb. niphal of *'āsar*–'be bound,' 'be imprisoned' (Gen. 42:16); Gk. *déō*–'bind, tie' (Mt. 15:7; Acts 24:27; Col. 4:3), *syndéō*–'bind together' (He. 13:3)]; AV also BOND, BOUND; NEB also CUSTODY, etc.; **PRISONER** (noun) [Heb. *'āsîr*–'bondman, prisoner' (Gen. 39:20, 22; Job 3:18; Ps. 68:6 [MT 7]; 79:11; 102:20 [MT 21]; 107:10; Isa. 14:17; Lam. 3:34; Zec. 9:12), *'assîr*–'prisoner' (Isa. 10:4; 24:22; 42:7); Gk. *désmios*–'prisoner' (Acts 16:25; Philem. 1, 9; Eph. 4:1; etc.), *desmṓtēs*–'prisoner' (Acts 27:1, 42), *synaichmálōtos*–'fellow prisoner' (Rom. 16:7; Col. 4:10; Philem. 23)]; AV also IN BONDS, etc.; NEB also IN CUSTODY, COMRADES IN CAPTIVITY, etc.; (vb.) [Heb. part. of *'āsar*–'tie, bind,' 'imprison' (Ps. 146:7; Isa. 49:9), *lāqaḥ*–'take' ("took . . . prisoner," 2 K. 24:12)]; AV also TAKE; NEB also TAKE PRISONER; **PRISON GARMENTS** [Heb. *bigḏê kil'ô*–'garments of imprisonment' (2 K. 25:29 par. Jer. 52:33)]; NEB PRISON CLOTHES; **DUNGEON** [Heb. *bôr*–'pit,' 'cistern, well' (Gen. 40:15; 41:14), *bêṯ habbôr*–'house of the pit' (Ex. 12:29; Jer. 37:16), *masgēr*–'dungeon' (Isa. 42:7)]; AV also PRISON; NEB also PRISON, etc.; **IMPRISON** [Heb. *kālā'*–'shut up,' 'restrain,' 'withhold' (Jer. 32:3), hiphil of *sāgar*–'shut, close' (Job 11:10), *nāṯan bêṯ hā'ēsûr*–'put (in) a house of the bond' ("imprisoned," Jer. 37:15); Gk. *déō*–'bind, tie' (Acts 21:13), *phylakízō*–'imprison' (Acts 22:19)]; AV also SHUT UP, PUT IN PRISON, BOUND; NEB also BOUND, etc.; **IMPRISONMENT** [Aram. *'esûr*–'bond, fetter' (Ezr. 7:26); Gk. *desmós*–'bond, fetter' (Acts 20:23; 23:29; 26:31; Phil. 1:7, 13f., 17; Philem. 10, 13), *phylakḗ*–'watch, guard' (2 Cor. 6:5; 11:23; He. 11:36)]; AV also BOND; NEB also IMPRISONED, PRISON, etc.; **JAILER** [Gk. *basanistḗs*–'torturer,' 'jailer' (Mt. 18:34)]; AV TORMENTERS; NEB "to torture"; [*desmophýlax*–'keeper of the prison' (Acts 16:23, 27, 36)]; AV also KEEPER OF THE PRISON.

***I. In the OT.***–Various places are mentioned in the OT as used for confining prisoners. Only in Ezr. 7:26 does imprisonment function as a legal form of punishment, and in this case it is merely authorized by the Persian king Artaxerxes. Imprisonment functioned as a means to retain a person until the time of trial, sentencing, or execution of the sentence.

The two most common terms for prison are *bêṯ kele'* and *bêṯ hassōhar*. The latter term in Gen. 39 may refer to a fortified structure, which is suggested both by Heb. *sōhar* and by its LXX translation *ochýrōma* (lit. "stronghold, fortress"). The RSV "dungeon" translates three Hebrew terms. Heb. *bôr* indicates the place of Joseph's confinement (Gen. 40:15; 41:14), which may be synonymous with *bêṯ hassōhar* (Gen. 39:20-23; 40:3, 5). Heb. *bôr*, however, usually refers to a cistern (Gen. 37:24; 38:6; Jer. 38:6-11, 13; Zec. 9:11) rather than a special prison structure. In Jer. 37:16 "dungeon cells" translates Heb. *bêṯ habbôr wehaḥanuyôṯ*, lit. "the house of the pit and the cells." This probably refers to an underground prison that was subdivided into smaller individual cells. Jeremiah feared returning to these cells, thinking that he might ultimately die in them; consequently, he appealed to King Zedekiah for another place of confinement, and the appeal was granted (Jer. 37:16-21). In Isa. 42:7 Heb. *masgēr* (< Heb. *sāgar*, "shut, close"; cf. Isa. 24:22) is a place from which prisoners are released by the Servant of the Lord (v. 1). The NT interprets this passage as fulfilled by Messiah and the eschatological people of God (Mt. 11:5; Lk. 1:79; Acts 26:18).

The common OT terms for "prisoner" in the RSV are Heb. *'āsîr* (< *'āsar*, "tie, bind") and its cognate *'āssîr*. Joseph is called an *'āsir* (Gen. 39:20, 22), a term often used for captives in a foreign land (Ps. 68:6 [MT 7]; 69:33 [MT 34]; etc.; cf. A. A. Anderson, *Psalms* [*NCBC*, repr. 1981], I, 486). In 2 K. 24:12 Heb. *lāqaḥ* has the sense of "carry off" or "take" as a prisoner, which is a sense found elsewhere (e.g., Gen. 14:12; 2 K. 18:32 par. Isa. 36:16; 2 K. 23:34 par. 2 Ch. 36:4).

In the OT several important persons were imprisoned. Among these is Joseph, who was incarcerated by Potiphar for alleged indiscretions with Potiphar's wife (Gen. 39). Providentially, Joseph received compassionate treatment from the keeper (Heb. *śar*, "chief") of the prison (vv. 21-23). King Zedekiah imprisoned Jeremiah for prophetic utterances that predicted Zedekiah's defeat and exile (Jer. 32:2-5). Suspected of treason, Jeremiah was placed in prison in the house of Jonathan the secretary (37:15; cf. vv. 4, 18). He was lowered into a deep, muddy cistern (38:6). Removed from there, he was allowed to stay near the palace in the "court of the guard" (38:28).

Other persons who were imprisoned include: Samson, who, bound in chains, performed menial labor in prison (Jgs. 16:21, 25); Micaiah the prophet, whom King Ahab put in prison with only bread and water (1 K. 22:27; 2 Ch. 18:26); King Hoshea, who was incarcerated by Shalmaneser king of Assyria after Hoshea attempted to form an alliance with So king of Egypt (2 K. 17:4); Hanani the seer, who was confined after he confronted King Asa (2 Ch. 16:1-10); King Jehoiakin of Judah, imprisoned by Nebuchadrezzar (2 K. 24:15) but later released by Evil-merodach (2 K. 25:27-30 par. Jer. 52:31-34); King Zedekiah, who, after an attempt to escape, was captured by the Chaldeans, sentenced by Nebuchadrezzar, and confined to prison for the rest of his life (2 K. 25:2-7; Jer. 39:1-7; 52:3-11).

Prisoners, including Libyans and Syrians, on an Egyptian relief from the temple of Sahu-Re at Abusir (*ca.* 2500 B.C.). The second and third men have ropes tied around their elbows, and all are attached by ropes to gods, who present them to Pharaoh (Staatliche Museen zu Berlin, DDR)

Several figurative expressions related to prison occur in Job. In Job. 3:18 "prisoners" are probably prisoners of war who have been enslaved (cf. vv. 18b, 19); but like all the dead in Sheol, they have found rest. The term for "imprison" in Job 11:10 probably means "arrest" (*CHAL*, p. 253). According to Zophar, this act of imprisonment precedes the call to judgment; neither imprisonment nor judgment may be hindered by man if initiated by God.

In Ps. 142:7 the writer appeals to Yahweh for release from a "dungeon," which refers either metaphorically to the distress of a persecuted person or literally to actual confinement (A. A. Anderson, *Psalms* [*NCBC*, repr. 1981], II, 922, 924f.). In Ps. 79:11 "prisoners" refers either to exiles in general or to prisoners of war (Anderson, p. 580; cf. Ps. 102:20, 107:10).

Isaiah describes the cosmic, eschatological judgment of the Lord as a day when the judged "will be gathered together as prisoners in a pit; they will be shut up in a prison" (Isa. 24:22). Isa. 42:7 describes the release of "prisoners" from the "dungeon" or "prison," which refers to release either from spiritual captivity or from the

Relief from Nimrûd showing captives, with their possessions in bags over their shoulders, from the town Astartu (biblical Ashtaroth?), which the Assyrians under Tiglath-pileser III had captured (Trustees of the British Museum)

Babylonian captivity (cf. 49:9; Ps. 146:7). Both the form and the meaning of the unique expression Heb. *p^eqaḥ-qô(a)ḥ* (< *pāqaḥ,* "open") in Isa. 61:1 present difficulties. This term's form may be due to dittography (GKC, §84^bn), and the term may represent a figurative expression for the opening of a prisoner's eyes after release from a dark prison.

***II. In the NT.***–During the period of Roman occupation in Palestine the public prison (Lat. *carcer, publica vincula*) functioned only for short durations of incarceration. It served as a place to detain both suspects awaiting trial and convicted criminals awaiting sentencing and punishment. Imprisonment itself was not considered a form of punishment under the Roman legal system (cf. *Oxford Classical Dictionary* [2nd ed. 1970], p. 879).

"Prison" most frequently renders Gk. *phylakḗ*. The Greek term may refer to the action of guarding, the person who guards, a period of time for guarding (i.e., guard duty), or the place of guarding (the primary NT use). Also translated as "prison" are Gk. *desmōtḗrion* and *tḗrēsis*. The former refers to a place of confinement, such as the places used for John the Baptist (Mt. 11:2), the apostles (Acts 5:21, 23), and Paul and Silas (16:26). The latter term (which is synonymous with *desmōtḗrion* in Acts 5:21, 23) occurs in Acts 5:18 in the phrase *en tērḗsei dēmosía,* which the RSV and AV render "in the common prison" (NEB "in official custody"). Gk. *dēmosía* may be either an adverb or an adjective; consequently, the apostles were either put in prison publicly or they were put into a public prison (i.e., a prison belonging to the government). In Col. 4:3 the AV "in bonds" for Gk. *déō* is perhaps more distinct and preferable to the RSV "in prison," since Paul in Col. 4:18 leaves no doubt that he is actually in chains (R. P. Martin, *Colossians and Philemon* [*NCBC,* repr. 1981], p. 126). The part. of *syndéō* in He. 13:3, rendered "in prison with them," implies a sharing in the sufferings of those in prison even if only by "exercising imaginative sympathy" (F. F. Bruce, *Epistle to the Hebrews* [*NICNT,* 1964], p. 392).

"Prisoner" most often translates Gk. *désmios,* which refers to persons either bound by chains or confined by walls. It applies to prisoners in general (e.g., Acts 16:25, 27; He. 10:34), to Paul in particular (Acts 23:18; 25:14, 27; 28:17), and also to Paul when he designates himself a prisoner of Jesus Christ (Eph. 3:1; Philem. 1, 9; cf. 2 Tim. 1:8; also M. Barth, *Ephesians* [*AB,* 1974], I, 359-362).

"Fellow prisoner" (Gk. *synaichmálōtos*), a term derived from military imagery, may at times reflect a nonliteral meaning (*TDNT,* I, 196f.); Philem. 23, however, in the light of Philem. 1, 9, and 10, probably refers to actual confinement. Thus Epaphras would have shared in Paul's prison experience (cf. Col. 4:12), as did Aristarchus (4:10). Andronicus and Junias are also referred to as Paul's fellow prisoners (Rom. 16:7), but this does not necessitate their being prisoners with Paul at the same time and place (C. E. B. Cranfield, *Romans,* II [*ICC,* 1979], 788f.).

Though the NT mentions groups who were imprisoned (e.g., the apostles in Acts 5:19, 22, 25), certain individuals appear to be more significant. Included here are John the Baptist, Peter, and Paul.

According to Mk. 6:17f. John the Baptist was imprisoned on account of his accusations regarding Herod's unlawful marriage to Herodias. Josephus suggests that John's imprisonment at Machaerus was also due to Herod's fear of John's political activism and its possible repercussions (*Ant.* xviii.5.2 [116-19]).

Acts 4:2f. records how the Sadducees, annoyed at the apostles' teachings, arrested and confined Peter and John (cf. 5:18). Acts 12:1-5 relates the events of Herod's violence toward the Church and subsequent imprisonment of Peter. Significantly, Acts 5:19-26 and 12:6-11 also describe the miraculous release of the apostles and Peter from prison.

In the NT Paul is probably the most renowned figure who experienced incarceration. As a servant of God, Paul endured, among other things, numerous imprisonments (2 Cor. 6:4f.; 11:23-28). The book of Acts records at least three, while early tradition attests to as many as seven confinements (1 Clem. 5:6). In Philippi both Paul and Silas were imprisoned under the care of a jailer (Gk. *desmophýlax,* Acts 16:23, 27, 36; cf. LXX Gen. 39:21; T. Jos. 2:3; *Ant.* ii.5.1 [61]) who subsequently converted to the faith (Acts 16:30-34). To avoid a Jewish ambush, Paul was escorted by a Roman tribune to Caesarea, where he was confined while awaiting his appearance before Felix the procurator of Judea (23:12-35). But in order to win favor with the Jews, Felix left Paul in prison (24:27). Later Paul's appeal to Caesar before Festus destined him for Rome (25:12). After arriving at Rome Paul was guarded by a soldier (28:16) and was bound by a light chain (v. 20; cf. *SPT,* p. 349). He remained in this condition for two years, but enjoyed relative freedom (v. 30). Paul's own prison experiences are ironic in view of his former activities as Saul, "persecutor of the church" (Phil. 3:6; cf. Acts 8:3; 21:1-21).

G. L. KNAPP

**PRISON, THE SPIRITS IN** [Gk. *tá en phylakȩ̄́ pneúmata*]; NEB "the imprisoned spirits." Those to whom Christ preached after His death (1 Pet. 3:19).

Scholars consider 1 Pet. 3:18-22 either a traditional hymn (e.g., Windisch, p. 70; R. P. Martin, *NT Foundations,* II [1978], 260f., 264), a creedal summary (Martin, p. 274), or kerygmatic formulas (H. Koester, *Intro. to the NT* [Eng. tr. 1982], II, 294). These proposals are agreed, however, in emphasizing the redemptive work of Christ. In this context 1 Pet. 3:19 records Christ's proclamation to the spirits.

According to L. Goppelt (p. 246) the understanding of this difficult passage depends on the answers to two questions: (1) what is the referent of *en hǭ́* in v.19, and (2) who are the spirits in prison? (See the comms. for questions on the time, place, and content of Christ's preachings; cf. also *TDNT*, III, 707f.)

Several options exist for clarifying the antecedent of *en hǭ́*. Reicke suggested that *en hǭ́* be understood as a temporal conjunction translated "on which occasion" and identified that occasion as the death and resurrection of Christ mentioned in v.18 (cf. Reicke's comm., p. 138, n. 37; cf. also his *Disobedient Spirits and Christian Baptism* [1946], pp. 108-115). Selwyn took *en hǭ* as "in which state" or "in which circumstance," the "state" being the process of dying and being made alive in the spirit (p. 197). W. J. Dalton suggested that *en hǭ* means "in this sphere" or "under the influence" (i.e., of the Spirit; cf. *Christ's Proclamation to the Spirits* [*Analecta Biblica*, 23, 1965], pp. 137-143; cf. also Kelly, pp. 151f.). Thus the options pertain either to Christ's mode of existence when he preached or to the circumstance or occasion of His preaching.

Regarding the second question scholars generally identify the spirits as either deceased human beings or supernatural beings. Some find support for the former alternative in the NT (He. 12:23), the Pseudepigrapha (e.g., 1 En. 22:3f., 9; 41:8), the Apostolic Fathers (Shep. Herm. Vis. 1:1:8; Sim. 9:28:7), and patristic writers (cf. Kelly, p. 153). Elsewhere in the NT, however, when Gk. *pneúmata* occurs alone and unqualified, it never refers to human beings (cf. Goppelt, p. 247). Thus He. 12:23 affords little support for this view, since in this verse *pneúmata* is qualified and has an unequivocal human reference. Also, 1 Pet. 3:20 uses Gk. *psychḗ,* not *pneúma,* for human beings. The latter view finds extensive support in both the NT (e.g., Mk. 1:23, 26f.; 3:11; 5:2, 8; etc.) and intertestamental literature (e.g., Tob. 6:6; 2 Macc. 3:24; Jub. 10; 15:31; 1 En. 14:8; 19:1; 21:10; T. Naph. 3:3; T. Dan. 1:7; 5:5f.; etc.). Though often qualified by "evil" or "unclean," these "spirits" are nevertheless supernatural beings. The latter view appears to be more probable.

As an alternative, Reicke, following Windisch, identified the *pneúmata* as the beings mentioned in Gen. 6:1-4 but added to them the persons who perished in the flood, whom he identified as "the descendants of the fallen angels" (comm., p. 109; cf. Bigg, p. 162).

*See also* DESCENT INTO HELL (HADES).

***Bibliography.***–Comms. on 1 Peter by E. Best (*NCBC*, repr. 1982); C. A. Bigg (*ICC*, 2nd ed. 1902); L. Goppelt (*KEK*, 1978); J. N. D. Kelly (*HNTC*, 1969); B. Reicke (*AB*, 1964); E. G. Selwyn (2nd ed. 1947); A. M. Stibbs (*TNTC*, 1959); H. Windisch (*HNT*, 2nd ed. 1930).

G. L. K.

**PRIVY** priv'ē; **PRIVILY.** Obsolete terms used by the AV. The RSV equivalent is sometimes "secretly" (Ps. 101:5; Mt. 2:7; Acts 16:37; 2 Pet. 2:1), "stealthily" (2 S. 24:4), or "quietly" (Mt. 1:19). In some texts the RSV translation is quite different from the AV's. In Ps. 11:2 (MT 3) the RSV "in the dark" is more literal. In Jgs. 9:31 the RSV emends Heb. *tormâ* to *'ᵃrûmâ,* "Arumah" (cf. v. 41); but the AV (cf. NEB "he resorted to a ruse") is perhaps correct in understanding *tormâ* as referring to a secret action (an interpretation supported by Tg., LXX B, and Vulg.). According to S. Gevirtz (*JNES*, 17 [1958], 59f.) *tormâ* could be a *qutlat* form from *trm,* "remove, set apart" (cf. Heb. *tarmîṯ,* "deceit"), hence "secret." He appealed to Akk. *turmum,* "treachery," for support (but cf. G. R. Driver, *Annual of the Leeds Oriental Society,* 4 [1962/63], 15). In Ezk. 21:14 (MT 19) the AV "which entereth their privy chamber" translates Heb. *haḥōḏereṯ,* the only OT occurrence of the verb *ḥdr.* The RSV relies on the established sense of the verb *ḥdr* in rabbinical Hebrew and Aramaic, "encircle." In Dt. 23:1 the AV translates Heb. *šop̱kâ,* "penis," by "privy member" (RSV "male member").

G. A. L

**PRIZE.** The translation of three Hebrew terms and one Greek term, with a variety of meanings.

(1) "Prize highly" in Prov. 4:8 (AV "exalt"; NEB "cherish") probably translates a form of Heb. *sālal,* "lift up" (cf. BDB), but the meaning of the unusual term is uncertain, as indicated by the RSV footnote. The idea that the form (*salsᵉlehā*) is from another root meaning "tendril" ("branch" in Jer. 6:9), here meaning "that which twines" and by extension "embrace," has some value but is not convincing (W. McKane, *Proverbs* [*OTL*, 1970], p. 306).

(2) "Prized belongings" in Jer. 20:5 (AV "precious things"; NEB "riches") translates Heb. *yᵉqār* (lit. "preciousness" < *yāqar,* "be precious").

(3) "Prize of war" in Jer. 21:9; 38:2; 39:18; 45:5 (AV "prey"; NEB "nothing more") translates Heb. *šālāl,* "booty," "spoil" (*see* SPOIL). The meaning in all four passages is that the persons addressed could expect no victors' spoil; life itself would be all they could keep (see NEB), and that only by obedient acceptance of God's mercy.

(4) "Prize" in 1 Cor. 9:24; Phil. 3:14 represents Gk. *brabeíon,* the reward received by a victorious athlete. The Greek term refers to that which is given by the athletic official (*brabeús*), so is related to *brabeúō,* "rule," "control," in Col. 3:15 and *katabrabeúō,* "decide against," "disqualify," in 2:18. The use of athletic terms would have been readily understood, for winners of the Olympic and other games became famous. According to 1 Cor. 9:24, however, even their great fame was inconsequential in comparison with what the Christian had to gain (*see also* WREATH). The emphasis in this passage is on striving or self-discipline, running in such a way as to receive the prize. (The mention of the single victor is not an appropriate prooftext for limited atonement, and the metaphor as a whole should not be taken as support for salvation by works.)

In Phil. 3:14 the striving for the prize (or the goal that results in the prize) is combined with the idea of leaving what is behind and pressing onward (Gk. *skopós,* "goal," is what is looked at or for). The "upward call" is probably to be understood as the divine calling that leads to the prize, not as an identification of the prize.

E. W. S.

**PROCESSION** [Heb. *tahᵃluḵōṯ*] ("went in procession," Neh. 12:31); AV WENT; [*hᵃlîḵâ*] (Ps. 68:24 [MT 25]); AV GOINGS; [*dāḏâ*] ("led in procession," Ps. 42:4 [MT 5]); AV "went"; NEB "the great"; [*ḥāg*] ("festal procession," Ps. 118:27); AV SACRIFICE; NEB ORDERED LINE; [*nāhag*–'lead,' 'conduct'] ("led in procession," Isa. 60:11); AV BROUGHT; NEB "under escort."

The RSV interprets Heb. *tahᵃluḵōṯ,* a term that occurs only in Neh. 12:31, as referring to a ritual procession of thanksgiving. The formal organization (vv. 32-36; 40-42) and the direction taken by the two groups of people (vv. 31, 38f.) tend to bear out that conclusion. Some, e.g., *BH* and *BHS,* have suggested that this term is a corruption of *hā'ahaṯ hôleḵeṯ,* "one went" (cf. v. 38). Ps. 68:24f. provides interesting details about such ceremonial processions entering the sanctuary. The AV and RSV interpret *'eddaddēm* in Ps. 42:4 to be a form of the verb *dāḏâ,* literally "lead slowly," as in a procession. The NEB emends to *'addirîm,* "people of rank" (cf. the comms.).

Psalm 118:27 is problematic. Is the *ḥag* to be bound with "branches" or with "cords"? Either is a possible meaning of *'ᵃḇōṯîm.* Is the *ḥag* itself a festal procession, or the sacrificial animal bound to the altar? Taking his cue from the Mish. *Sukkah* iv.5, Mowinckel understood the Psalm to relate to the Feast of Tabernacles, so that the *ḥag* is a procession wending its way through the gates of righteousness (vv. 19f.) and encircling the altar in a festal dance (*Psalms in Israel's Worship* [Eng. tr. 1962] I, 120, 181). Cf. the RSV.

The RSV and NEB renderings of Isa. 60:11 reflect the

MT *neḥûḡîm*; the kings are led in procession. But are they captives or willing servants of Israel? *BH* and *BHS* suggest an emendation to an active participle *nôhaḡîm,* so that the verse reads "with their kings leading them." Cf. Rev. 21:24-27. G. WYPER

**PROCHORUS** prok'ə-rəs [Gk. *Prochoros*]. One of the Seven chosen by the Jerusalem community to supervise the daily distribution to the poor (Acts 6:5). The name is Greek, indicating that he was a Hellenistic Jew. According to tradition he was John the Evangelist's amanuensis, became bishop of Nicomedia, and died a martyr at Antioch. The fifth-century apocryphal Acts of John (not to be confused with the earlier Gnostic work of that name by Lucius), was written under his name.

*See* SEVEN, THE.

**PROCLAIM; (MAKE) PROCLAMATION** (vbs.) [Heb. *qārāʾ*–'call' (Ex. 32:5; 34:5f.; Dt. 15:2; Isa. 61:1f.; etc.), hiphil of *šāmaʿ*–'cause to hear' (1 K. 15:22; Isa. 43:12; Jer. 46:14; Nah. 1:15 [MT 2:11]; etc.), niphal of *šāmaʿ*–'be heard' (Est. 1:20; 2:8), hiphil of *nāgaḏ*–'make known, report, tell' (Ps. 19:1 [MT 2]; 71:17f.; 97:6; Isa. 48:20; etc.), *ʾāmar*–'say' (2 K. 9:13; Ps. 145:6), part. of *gālâ*–'uncover, reveal' (Est. 3:14; 8:13), hiphil of *mālaḵ*–'make or install as king' (2 K. 11:12 par. 2 Ch. 23:11), piel of *bāśar*–'bring news' (Isa. 60:6), hiphil of *zāḵar*–'mention,' 'make known' (Isa. 12:4), hiphil of *zāʿaq*–'have proclamation made' (Jonah 3:7), hiphil of *yāḏaʿ*–'make known' (Ps. 89:1 [MT 2]), piel of *qāwâ*–'collect' (Ps. 52:9 [MT 11]); Aram. haphel of *keraz* (Dnl. 5:29), peal part. of *qerāʾ*–'shout' (Dnl. 3:4); Gk. *katangéllō*–'proclaim' (Acts 3:24; Rom. 1:8; 1 Cor. 11:26; Phil. 1:17f.; etc.), *kērýssō*–'preach, proclaim' (Mt. 10:27; Mk. 5:20 par. Lk. 8:39; Acts 9:20; Rev. 5:2; etc.), *apangéllō* (Mt. 12:18; He. 2:12; 1 Jn. 1:2f.), *diangéllō* (Lk. 9:60; Rom. 9:17), *krázō*–'call, call out, cry' (Jn. 7:28, 37), *anangéllō*–'proclaim,' 'teach' (1 Jn. 1:15), *apodeíknymi* (2 Thess. 2:4), *euangelízō*–'bring or announce good news' (Rev. 14:6), *gínomai*–'come to be, become' (Acts 10:37), *gnōrízō*–'make known, reveal' (Eph. 6:19), *plērophoréō*–'fill (completely), fulfil' ("proclaim . . . fully," 2 Tim. 4:17)]; AV also FORETELL, PUBLISH, PREACH, SPEAK, DECLARE, CRY, etc.; NEB also PREDICT, DECLARE, ANNOUNCE, SHOUT, "spread the news" (Mk. 5:20), etc.; (nouns) [Heb. *qôl*–'voice' (2 Ch. 24:9), *terûʿâ*–'blowing alarm' ("proclaimed with blast of trumpets," Lev. 23:24)]; AV also "blowing of trumpets" (Lev. 23:24); NEB also ACCLAMATION (Lev. 23:24). Occasionally the RSV has "proclaim" (Ex. 36:6; Neh. 8:15) or "make (a) proclamation" (2 Ch. 30:5; 36:22; Ezr. 1:1; 10:7) for the construction of the hiphil of *ʿāḇar* with *qôl*, which together literally means "cause a voice to pass over." The RSV NT has "proclamation" only in a variant ending of Mark's Gospel.

***I. In the OT.***–The term most frequently translated "proclaim" is Heb. *qārāʾ*. Various items that are "proclaimed" include fasts (1 K. 21:9, 12; 2 Ch. 20:3; Ezr. 8:21; Jer. 36:9; Jonah 3:5), holy convocations (Lev. 23:2, 4, 21, 24, 37; cf. 2 K. 10:20), liberty (Lev. 25:10; Jer. 34:8, 15, 17; Isa. 61:1), the year of the Lord's favor (Isa. 61:2), and the name of the Lord (Ex. 33:19; 34:5f.; Dt. 32:3). When convocations (Heb. *miqrāʾ*, "convocation, sacred assembly," <*qārāʾ*) are "proclaimed" the sense of *qārāʾ* is "summon." When the name of the Lord is proclaimed (e.g., Ex. 33:19 and Dt. 32:3) a recitation of God's attributes and/or works follows. And in Ex. 34:5-7 it is the Lord Himself who "proclaims" His attributes (cf. B. Childs, *Book of Exodus* [*OTL,* 1974], p. 603). "Proclaim" also functions as a technical term for prophetic preaching in numerous passages (e.g., 2 K. 23:16; Jer. 2:2; 3:12; 7:2; 11:6; 19:2; Jonah 3:2; cf. *THAT,* II, 669). "Proclaim" may also have the sense of "announce," e.g., a call to battle (Joel 3:9 [MT 4:9]), or a herald who "proclaims" the approach of the royal chariot (Est. 6:9, 11).

Where the prophets function as divine harbingers in the books of Isaiah (41:26; 43:12; 62:11) and Jeremiah (4:5, 15; 5:20; 23:22; 31:7; 46:14; 50:2) the hiphil of *šāmaʿ* is associated with solemn prophetic preaching (*THAT,* II, 979; cf. also Am. 3:9; Nah. 1:15 [MT 2:11]). Est. 1:20 and 2:8 use the niphal of *šāmaʿ* for the public announcement of a royal edict.

The theological significance of the hiphil of *nāgaḏ* is evidenced in contexts of divine praise and worship. For those who worship the Lord the focus of praise centers upon, e.g., the Lord's creative work (Ps. 19:1 [MT 2]), redemptive work (22:31 [MT 32]; cf. Isa. 48:20), and other wonderful works and deeds that He performs on behalf of His people (Ps. 40:5 [MT 6]; cf. 9:11 [MT 12]; 71:17f.; also *THAT,* II, 36). Also Ps. 89:1 (MT 2) refers to the public praising (hiphil of *yāḏaʿ*, lit. "cause to make known"; cf. Ps. 105:1; 145:12; Isa. 12:4) of God for His faithfulness.

In 2 K. 11:12 (par. 2 Ch. 23:11) the RSV "proclaimed him king" suggests a verbal declaration; this nuance, however, is not inherent in the hiphil of *mālaḵ* (lit. "make king, cause to reign" <*mālaḵ*, "be king, reign"). Perhaps the AV rendering "make him king," which is the RSV translation elsewhere for the hiphil of *mālaḵ*, is more accurate.

Several other Hebrew terms also merit brief mention. According to Isa. 60:6 heathen nations will come to Zion to publish the praise of the Lord (cf. *TDOT,* II, 313-16). In Isa. 12:4 the redeemed community is exhorted to "proclaim" (lit. "cause to remember," from the hiphil of *zāḵar*) to others the person of the exalted Lord. Ps. 52:9 (MT 11) also refers to praising God's name (cf. M. Dahood, *Psalms I* [*AB*, repr. 1973], 121f., for the semantic relationships among Heb. *qôl,* "voice," *qāhal,* "to gather," and *qārāʾ*, "to call").

Distressful crying, which perhaps was intended to evoke "communal lament" (*TDOT,* IV, 120), appears to be the import of the hiphil of Heb. *zāʿaq* (<*zaʿaq,* "cry, cry out") in Jonah 3:7.

***II. In the NT.***–A number of Greek verbs rendered "proclaim" are compound forms of Gk. *angéllō,* which according to classical definition means "bear a message," "announce," or "report" (LSJ, p. 7). Although Gk. *angéllō* rarely occurs in the NT (only Jn. 20:28; 4:51 var.), compound verbs including Gk. *anangéllō, apangéllō, diangéllō, exangéllō, katangéllō,* and *parangéllō* occur more frequently. In classical usage several of these terms "often indicate the elevated, ceremonious style of proclamation" (*DNTT,* III, 45). In the NT this word-group usually refers to "proclamation in a special, technical sense: the making known of God's activity, his will to save" (*ibid.*, p. 46; cf. R. Brown, *Epistles of John* [*AB,* 1982], pp. 167f.).

"Proclaim" translates Gk. *katangéllō* (only in Acts and Paul) seventeen times in the NT. This term reflects the "language of mission" (*TDNT,* I, 71f.) and relates to the redemptive purposes of God. Individuals who announce the salvific message include Peter (Acts 3:24), John (4:2), Barnabas (13:5), and Paul ("Saul" in 13:5; cf. 13:38; Rom. 1:8; 1 Cor. 9:14; Phil. 1:17f.; etc.). The content of the proclamation varies, but includes the fulfillment of OT expectations in Jesus' ministry (Acts 3:24; 26:23), the resurrection of Jesus Christ (4:2; cf. v. 33), the Word of God (13:5; 17:13; cf. 15:36), the forgiveness of sins (13:38; cf. 10:43), the way of salvation (16:17), Jesus as Messiah

(17:3), the mystery of God (1 Cor. 2:1), the gospel (1 Cor. 9:14), the Lord's death (11:26), and Christ (Phil. 1:17; Col. 1:28). When Paul proclaimed the "mystery of God" (1 Cor. 2:1; some MSS have Gk. *martýrion,* "witness," a reading defended by H. Conzelmann, *1 Corinthians* [Eng. tr., *Hermeneia,* 1975], p. 53 n. 6; but cf. *TDNT,* IV, 819 n. 141) he announced the secret of God that was unknown to the world until Christ appeared, which was "the revelation of the justification of people by the crucifixion of Christ and the conquest of death by his ressurrection" (W. F. Orr and J. A. Walther, *1 Corinthians* [*AB,* 1976], p. 162). In 1 Cor. 11:26 Paul states that the Lord's death is proclaimed each time the Lord's Supper is celebrated. This probably refers to a verbal recapitulation of Christ's Passion similar to that found in the Passion narratives of the Gospels and patterned after the rehearsal of the Exodus in the Jewish Passover Haggadah (cf. C. K. Barrett, *Comm. on the First Epistle to the Corinthians* [*HNTC,* 1968], p. 270). Gk. *katangéllō* in Phil. 1:17 seems interchangeable with Gk. *kērýssō* in v. 15 (*TDNT,* I, 71), and according to J. -F. Collange the content of "preaching Christ" (v. 15) is His death and resurrection (*Epistle of Saint Paul to the Philippians* [Eng. tr. 1979], p. 56). The proclamation of Christ (Col. 1:28) was not a facile, shallow presentation of salvation, for it was effected by exhortation and instruction concerning Christ, who is "the sum and substance of Paul's message" (P. T. O'Brien, *Colossians, Philemon* [*Word Biblical Comm.,* 1982], p. 87).

The RSV NT renders Gk. *apangéllō* "proclaim" four times. According to Mt. 12:18-21 the actions of Jesus fulfil the prophecies of Isa. 42:1-4. The OT citation follows neither the MT nor the LXX, but is perhaps dependent upon a targumized text or a community understanding of the text that is consonant with "the evangelist's purpose and understanding of the prophecy" (K. Stendahl, *School of St. Matthew* [1954], p. 111; cf. p. 198). The Matthean passage draws attention to the Servant's salvific activity among Gentiles. The OT quotation of Ps. 22:22 (MT 23) used in He. 2:12 expresses Jesus' solidarity with the redeemed people of God (F. F. Bruce, *Hebrews* [*NICNT,* repr. 1977], pp. 45f.). In 1 Jn. 1:2f. the subject of the proclamation is the historical reality of Christ's incarnation, while the purpose of the declaration is to announce the availability of a qualitatively new existence, namely, fellowship with God.

A similar, and perhaps synonymous, term is Gk. *anangéllō,* found in 1 Jn. 1:5, which contains a statement regarding the nature of God, namely, "He is light." The purpose of this "message" (or "command"; <Gk. *angelía,* v. 5) was twofold: to correct heretical beliefs and to encourage ethical behavior.

The Gk. *diangéllō* occurs in Lk. 9:60 within a context dealing with discipleship, a familiar Lukan theme. The Kingdom and its proclamation must occupy a preeminent position in the lives of all true disciples, for the Kingdom is the central theme of Jesus' public proclamation (cf. J. Jeremias, *NT Theology* [Eng. tr. 1971], pp. 96f.). Gk. *diangéllō* also occurs in Rom. 9:17, which illustrates God's sovereign control even with respect of the means by which His redemptive purposes are realized.

In the RSV NT "proclaim" also translates Gk. *kērýssō* ten times. This Greek term and its cognate *kḗrygma* have been the subject of extensive scholarly discussion in recent decades (*see* PREACH II.B). An examination of related terms in the NT reveals that the main emphasis is not given to the person who proclaims (Gk. *kḗryx,* 3 times in the NT), or to the content of the proclamation (Gk. *kḗrygma,* 9 times in the NT), but to the act or the event of proclamation (Gk. *kērýssō,* 61 times in the NT); this, however, is not to suggest that the act of proclamation is void of content.

The account of the healed Gerasene demoniac records not only the fact of proclamation, but its content, for the healed demoniac proclaimed throughout the Decapolis "how much Jesus had done for him" (Mk. 5:20 par. Lk. 8:39). Mk. 7:36 also relates how witnesses "zealously . . . proclaimed" Jesus' healing of a deaf-mute. Lk. 4:18f. states how Jesus' ministry as an anointed prophet fulfilled the prophecies recorded in Isa. 61:1f. The saying found in Mt. 10:27 exhorts the disciples to the fearless public proclamation of what they have been taught; however, this same saying, as adapted in Lk. 12:3, presents a promise of the public pronouncement of the hypocrisy of false religious leaders. A christological emphasis is apparent in Acts 8:5 when Philip announces the Messiah to the Samaritans, and in 9:20 when Paul announces in a Damascus synagogue that Jesus is the Son of God (cf. 13:33; Rom. 1:4; etc.).

In Jn. 7:28, 37 Gk. *krázō* reflects a specialized nuance of meaning. Bultmann's suggestion that it refers to "inspired speech" (*Gospel of John* [Eng. tr. 1971], p. 75 n. 1) is debatable, however. Equally debatable is C. H. Dodd's notion that John supplied Gk. *krázein* for the customary Gk. *kērýssein,* and with the same sense (*Interpretation of the Fourth Gospel* [repr. 1978], p. 382 n. 1). It is more likely that *krázō* in Johannine use (cf. 1:15; 12:44) indicates a solemn public pronouncement that is spoken despite open unbelief and opposition. It is also possible that John avoids using Gk. *kērýssō* since it does not correspond well with his particular eschatological perspective (cf. *DNTT,* III, 46f.).

The three terms Gk. *euangelízō* (Rev. 14:6), *gínomai* (Acts 10:37; cf. vv. 36, 38), and *gnōrízō* (Eph. 6:19) all refer to the proclamation of the gospel. In Rev. 14:6 an "eternal gospel" is announced (cf. *TDNT,* II, 735). The precise nature of this "gospel" is uncertain, but v. 7 indicates that it is a "a summons to fear, honor, and worship the Creator"(R. H. Mounce, *Book of Revelation* [*NICNT,* 1977], p. 273; cf. n. 19). In Eph. 6:19 Paul requests that he may freely "proclaim the mystery of the gospel, " in which case the "mystery" is the gospel (F. F. Bruce, comm. on Ephesians [*NICNT,* 1984], p. 412 n. 94).

***Bibliography.*–*DNTT,*** III, 44-68; R. H. Mounce, *Essential Nature of NT Preaching* (1960); *TDNT,* I, *s.v.* αγγελία κτλ. (Schniewind); II, *s.v.* εὐαγγελίζομαι κτλ. (Friedrich); III, *s.v.* κήρυξ κτλ. (Friedrich); III, *s.v.* κράζω κτλ. (Grundmann).

G. L. KNAPP

**PROCONSUL** prō′kon-səl [Gk. *anthýpatos* (Acts 13:7f., 12; 18:12; 19:38)]; AV DEPUTY; NEB also GOVERNOR. A Roman governmental official. The Roman proconsuls were officers invested with consular power over a district outside Rome, e.g., Gaul or Syria, usually for one year. Originally they were retired consuls, but after Augustus the title was given to governors of senatorial provinces whether or not they had been consuls. The proconsul exercised judicial as well as military power in his province, and his authority was absolute, except that he might be held accountable at the expiration of his office. *See also* GOVERNOR; PROVINCES, ROMAN; PAULUS, SERGIUS.

W. A. HEIDEL

**PROCURATOR** prok′yə-rāt-ər. Probably the office referred to by Gk. *hēgemṓn* in Mt. 27:2, 11, 14f., 21, 27; 28:14; Lk. 20:20; Acts 23:24, 26, 33; 24:1, 10; 26:30, and by participles of the verb *hēgemoneúō* in Lk. 2:2; 3:1.

***I. Terminology.***–The term procurator, "agent," in ordinary Latin refers to a person, usually a free citizen, who managed the estates and business affairs of a wealthy

Roman. Procurators were not connected with public service until the emperor Augustus began to use men of equestrian status to manage the public finances of his own provinces and his extensive private estates throughout the empire. No distinction was made between ordinary procurators and these *procuratores Augusti*. They acted as private agents and had no official power to enforce their personal authority by judicial process, having to depend upon the tribunal of provincial governors, until the emperor Claudius in A.D. 50 secured for them the power of jurisdiction in disputes arising from their duties.

Augustus also employed equestrians in another role, as *praefecti provinciarum*. These were army officers whom Augustus "placed in charge" (*praefecit*) of difficult or isolated districts within his great military provinces,such as Syria or northern Gaul. They acted at first under the authority of the imperial governors (*legati Augusto*, "legates of Augustus") of their provinces but later became largely independent governors of their regions. When Claudius appointed equestrian governors for the new provinces of Mauretania and Thrace they received the title *procurator pro legato*, "procurator acting as legate." Henceforth *procurator* replaced *praefectus* in all the equestrian provinces except Egypt. So the early governors of western and southern Judea, after it became a Roman province in A.D. 6, were officially entitled *praefecti*. Later writers, however, usually referred to them anachronistically as *procuratores* or the Greek equivalent *epítropoi*, although Josephus sometimes used the correct Greek term *éparchos* (*Ant.* xviii.2.2 [33]).

*II. Tenure.*–Procurators of all types were men of equestrian standing who had held commissions as staff officers of Roman legions (*tribuni militum*, "army tribunes") and as commanders of provincial regiments (*praefectus cohortis*, "prefect of a cohort") and had also served as local magistrates. A number were men of humbler origin who had been promoted from the legionary centurionate to commissions in the praetorian guard. Hence all were men of mature years with some experience of practical administration. Their annual salaries, which ranged from fifteen to fifty thousand silver denarii according to the grade of their appointment, were remarkably large in comparison with the annual wage of a common soldier, 275 denarii. A procurator's tenure depended upon the emperor's will. Three or four years were normal, but under Tiberius (A.D. 14-37) much longer tenures were frequent.

Selection usually depended upon the recommendation of senior officials, to whom the procurator might continue to feel a political obligation. Able men could secure three or four procuratorships in succession, but lifelong careers were not possible until the number of posts increased, with the creation of ever more specialized functionaries. Only about twenty-five posts existed throughout the empire until the death of Tiberius, and fifty to sixty under Claudius and Nero (54-68). The NT writers mentioned only the equestrian governors of Judea, PILATE, FELIX (Acts 23:24-26; etc.), and FESTUS (24:27; 25:1-12).

*III. Functions.*–Procuratorial governors held power equivalent to the absolute imperium of a legate or proconsul (*see* PROVINCES, ROMAN). Hence Josephus rightly stated that the first prefect of Judea was given the power of life and death over his provincial subjects (*Ant.* xviii.1.1 [2]; *BJ* ii.8.1 [1]). Unlike the senatorial governors, they were responsible not only for civil administration and defense but also for the financial management of their provinces. Their armed forces were composed not of Roman legions (except in Egypt) but of provincial regiments of five hundred or a thousand men each.

In procuratorial provinces the forms of local self-government that the governor supervised did not differ from those of other regions except in Egypt and Judea. In Egypt instead of municipal autonomy there was a complex bureaucratic system of centralized administration, taken over by Augustus when he annexed Egypt in 30 B.C. In Judea, where city governments were rare, the largely rural townships were grouped for fiscal purposes into administrative districts (toparchies) managed by intermediary officials — zone commanders and village clerks — but were left to manage their internal affairs through traditional councils of elders. The high priest, appointed by the Roman governor, and the Sanhedrin were the local government of Jerusalem and could act as an advisory council on Jewish affairs if the procurator so wished. They exercised traditional jurisdiction in the sphere of the Mosaic law. But it is widely disputed to what extent they were allowed to inflict capital punishment according to Mosaic law, since the universal rule of the Roman empire limited this punishment strictly to the tribunal of the Roman governor. Judaic sources claimed the ancient privilege for the Jewish hierarchy, and probably high priests did exercise the capital power covertly in the absence of the procurators or with their occasional connivance. But the political risk of allowing local officials to eliminate other local leaders or pro-Roman partisans was too great to allow the high priests to usurp this function generally.

*IV. Jurisdiction.*–The procurator's primary responsibility was to maintain public order; otherwise he supervised rather than managed the government as an executive (*see* PROVINCES, ROMAN). In times of insurrection he restored order by direct action and summary punishment. In peaceful times civil order was maintained through the governor's regular jurisdiction (*cognitio*), which is amply illustrated by the accounts in Acts of Paul's trials before the proconsul of Achaia and before the procurators of Judea (18:12-17; 23:1–26:32). These accounts correspond precisely to what is known of Roman provincial jurisdiction from other sources. (The outlines of the same system can be discerned clearly in the Gospel stories of the trial of Jesus; *see* JESUS CHRIST, ARREST AND TRIAL OF; PILATE.) The governor, seated on his tribunal, heard the prosecution, which was conducted not by Roman officials but by provincial individuals who acted as private accusers (*delatores*). He was assisted by an informal body of advisors (*consilium*), whom he consulted before delivering his decision, though he was not bound to take their advice (Acts 25:12). He was free to propose any form of punishment at his own discretion — death by decapitation, fire, crucifixion, or exposure to wild beasts; a term of hard labor in state mines or quarries; or, for persons of high social rank, exile. If a provincial was also a Roman citizen he had a conditional right, if accused of a capital crime, to demand trial at Rome by the formula "I appeal to Caesar," which Paul eventually used (25:11f., 25). By this means he could secure a trial free from local pressure or prejudice.

*Bibliography.*–*HJP*², I, 357-381; A. H. M. Jones, *Studies in Roman Government and Law* (1960), pp. 117-125; *Oxford Classical Dictionary, s.v.*; E. G. Pflaum, *Les Procurateurs éqestres sous le haut-empire romain* (1950); A. N. Sherwin-White, *Papers of the British School at Rome*, N.S., 2 (1939), 1-28.

A. N. SHERWIN-WHITE

**PROFANE** [Heb. *ḥālal*] (Ex. 20:25; 31:14; Lev. 18:21; 19:8, 12, 29; etc.); AV also POLLUTE, DEFILE, PROSTITUTE (Lev. 19:29), etc.; NEB also PROSTITUTE, DEFILE, etc.; [*nāḵar*] (Jer. 19:4); AV ESTRANGE; NEB "treat . . . as if it were not mine"; [*tāpaś*–'seize'] (Prov. 30:9); AV "take . . . in vain"; NEB BLACKEN; [*ḥānap*] (Mic. 4:11); AV BE DEFILED; NEB SUFFER OUTRAGE; [Gk. *bebēlóō*] (Mt. 12:5; Acts 24:6); NEB also

BREAK; [*hēgéomai koinón*] (He. 10:29); AV "count . . . an unholy thing." To defile or make common that which is holy.

To violate or ignore any of the laws governing holy things was regarded in Israel as profanation. In this sense "profane" is similar in meaning to "defile" or "pollute." To profane a holy thing is to make it "common" (used here as the opposite of "holy," but not necessarily meaning "ritually unclean"). The biblical references show a concern for avoiding the profaning of altars (Ex. 20:25), of the sabbath (Neh. 13:17f.; Mt. 12:5), of the sanctuary (Ezk. 23:39), of holy things (Ezk. 22:26), of the covenant (Mal. 2:10), of offerings (Mal. 1:12), and of the priests and their families (Lev. 21:4, 9).

The covenant people were commanded to live as a kingdom of priests and a holy nation (Ex. 19:6), a stipulation that required them to be in a unique relationship of holiness in the sight of God (Lev. 11:44). This holiness represented His supreme ethical and moral character as it was to be reflected in individual and communal life alike. Anything alien to divine holiness that was introduced into Israel's national life profaned the covenantal idea of holiness. Levitical law in particular was adamant that nothing should be allowed to pollute the sanctuary or in any other manner profane the divine name (Lev. 21:6, 12, 23; 22:2, 32, etc.).

The concept that God's name could also be profaned by improper use is found in the Decalogue in the admonition regarding taking the sacred name "in vain" (NEB "make wrong use of," Ex. 20:7). The emphasis is upon prohibiting that gross inversion of spiritual values whereby the name of the one and only true God can be used deliberately in an oath to affirm or substantiate what is patently untrue. Whatever dragged down the name, i.e., the essential being of God, to the level of corrupt ancient Near Eastern society profaned that holy name, and brought the danger alike of pollution and its punishment to the community.

For Israel, to treat the holy as if it were common was ultimately to profane the holy name of God Himself (Lev. 18:21; 22:32; Isa. 48:11; Ezk. 36:20). The seriousness of such offenses is indicated by the threat of death in Nu. 18:32. Since Israel itself was God's holy people, any sinful act could be regarded as profaning God's name (Prov. 30:9), and God could judge Israel by profaning it, i.e., by treating it as common among the nations (Isa. 43:28; 47:6). Ezekiel proclaimed that God would recompense Judah's idolatrous behavior by allowing wicked foreigners to commit the unmentionable act of profaning His house (Ezk. 7:21-23). The covenant people had themselves profaned God's name and holy temple by indulging in idol worship and immediately afterward presenting themselves at the divine sanctuary to participate in the same sort of gross idolatrous and licentious observances (23:39-43). Because of their utter lack of spiritual discernment, they could expect nothing less than for God Himself to profane His own sanctuary (24:21) and cast out all that was unholy (28:16).

In the NT the concern for the profaning of sacred things was early applied to emerging Christian institutions (e.g., communion in 1 Cor. 11:27, where "profaning" is supplied by the RSV). Jesus taught His disciples the dangers inherent in treating some holy occasion as though it were of no significance by dismissing it casually (Mt. 22:1-7). In the same manner Peter was introduced to some of the new theological concepts of the age of grace by being warned not to regard as common something that God had cleansed (Acts 10:14f.).

*See also* COMMON; DEFILE; HOLINESS; POLLUTE.

B. C. BIRCH    R. K. H.

**PROFESS.** To declare openly; often, specifically, to confess or declare one's faith. "Profess" occurs once in the AV OT as a translation of the hiphil of Heb. *nāgad*, "announce, tell," in Dt. 26:3 (RSV, NEB, "declare"). Both the AV and RSV render "profess" for Gk. *epangéllomai*, "announce, proclaim," in 1 Tim. 2:10; 6:21 (NEB "claim") and for *homologéō*, "declare," "confess faith," in Tit. 1:16 (AV also in Mt. 7:23 and 1 Tim. 6:12; RSV "declare," "make [confession]"); NEB "tell to [their] face," "confess"). In Rom. 1:22, AV, "profess" represents *pháskō*, "assert, claim" (RSV "claim"; NEB "boast"). The AV uses the noun "profession" to translate *homología* in 1 Tim. 6:12; He. 3:1; 4:14; 10:23 (RSV "confession"; NEB "confess faith," "the religion we profess," "confession").

*See also* CONFESS.

N. J. O.

**PROFIT** [(noun) Heb. *beṣa'* (Gen. 37:26; Ps. 30:9 [MT 10], *marbîṯ*–'increase' (Lev. 25:37), part. of *šāwâ*–'be equal, suitable' (Est. 3:8), *ḥayil*–'wealth, property' (Job 20:18), *tᵉḇû'â*–'yield, gain' (Prov. 3:14), *môṯār* (Prov. 14:23), hiphil inf. of *yā'al* (Hab. 2:18); Gk. *óphelos* (Jas. 2:14, 16); (verb) hiphil of Heb. *yā'al* ("get profit," 1 S. 12:21; Job 21:15; Prov. 10:2; 11:4; Isa. 30:5f.; 44:9; 48:17; Jer. 2:8, 11; 12:13; 16:19; 23:32), *sāḵan*–'be of use' (Job 34:9); Gk. *ōpheléō* (Mt. 16:26 par.)]; AV also GAIN, INCREASE, "substance," etc.; NEB also BENEFIT, GAIN, HELP, etc.; **(BE) PROFITABLE** [Heb. *sāḵan* (Job 22:2), *ṭôḇ*–'good' (Prov. 31:18), hiphil inf. of *yā'al* (Isa. 44:10); Gk. *ōphélimos* (2 Tim. 3:16; Tit. 3:8), *symphérō* (Acts 20:20)]; AV also GOOD; NEB BENEFIT, "goes well," GOOD, etc.; **UNPROFITABLE** [Heb. *lō' yiskôn* (Job 15:3); Gk. *anōphelḗs* (Tit. 3:9)]. In Ezk. 13:18 the RSV supplies "profit"(cf. AV, NEB).

The Bible refers to profit of various kinds. In Prov. 31:18 economic profit is in view: a good wife works hard and produces profitable merchandise (cf. 14:23). Lev. 25:37 forbids profiting from the poor; rather, the Israelites should follow God's gracious and generous example (v. 38; cf. Job 20:18f.). Some passages warn against the spiritual risks entailed in seeking political and economic profit. In 1 S. 12:20-25 Samuel rebukes the people for wanting a king; he warns them not to "turn aside after vain things which cannot profit or save," but to follow the Lord (cf. also Isa. 30:5f.). Ezekiel denounced false prophetesses for their economic motives (13:18). Twice in Proverbs the clause "righteousness delivers from death" is contrasted with seeking economic gain (10:2; 11:4; see 3:13f., which contrasts the desire for wisdom with the desire for gold; cf. also Jer. 12:13). Jesus stated this idea most pointedly: "What will it profit a man, if he gains the whole world and forfeits his life?" (Mt. 16:26 par. ; cf. Job 21:14-16; 34:9).

A number of texts warn against practices that are spiritually unprofitable. Thus idolatry is frequently denounced as being unprofitable (Isa. 44:9f.; Jer. 2:11; 16:19; Hab. 2:18; cf. Job 21:15), as is false prophecy (Jer. 2:8; 23:32). In Tit. 3:9 the author exhorts Titus to avoid various dissensions because they are unprofitable (cf. also 1 Tim. 1:4); apparently the churches on Crete were beset by controversies (see Tit. 1:10-14; cf. Job 15:2f.). On the other hand, spiritual profit could be gained from the Scriptures (2 Tim. 3:16), good deeds (Tit. 3:8; Jas. 2:14-16), and Paul's preaching and teaching (Acts 20:20). Ultimately, of course, God teaches us what is profitable (Isa. 48:17).

Many scholars interpret the psalmist's prayer for deliverance in Ps. 30:9f. (MT 10f.) as a reflection of the OT ignorance of afterlife (see, e.g., KD; A. A. Anderson, *Psalms*, I [*NCBC*, repr. 1981], 244), but such an interpretation demeans the psalmist into one who in his self-interest begs for life. It seems preferable to see the psalmist's motivation as the result of his recent experience of restoration, i.e., he wants to go on living so he can testify to what the Lord has done (see A. Weiser, *Psalms* [Eng. tr., *OTL,* 1962], pp. 271f.; cf. Calvin *in loc.*).

Several texts in Job discuss whether it is profitable for a person to serve God; indeed, the entire book may be interpreted as a discussion of this issue (Job 1:19-11; 21:14-16; see *CD,* IV/3/1, 387f.; W. Vischer, *Interp.,* 15 [1961], 131-146). Thus in 34:9 Elihu summarizes Job's position: "It profits a man nothing that he should take delight in God" (see the comms. for the difficulties of the translation of this verse). As Job discovers, his faith does not ensure blessing (indeed, as we know from the prologue [Job 1–2], Job's tragedies occur because of his faith), nor does it rule out blessing (42:10-17). The issue of faith transcends such human circumstances — we do serve God for nought.

G. A. L.

**PROGNOSTICATORS, MONTHLY.** The AV translation of Heb. *môḏîʿim* (part. of *yāḏaʿ,* "know") *leḥᵒḏāšîm* (pl. of *ḥōḏeš,* "new moon") in Isa. 47:13 (RSV "who at the new moons predict"; NEB "who foretell your future month by month"). *See* ASTROLOGY IV.

**PROMISE** [Heb. *ʾāmar*–'say,' piel of *dāḇar*–'speak,' niphal of *šāḇaʿ*–'swear,' etc.; Gk. *epangéllomai, proepangéllomai, epangelía, epángelma, homologéō*–'confess' (Mt. 14:7)]; AV also PROFESS, MESSAGE, etc.; NEB also SWEAR, BE RESOLVED, WORD, etc.

I. General Considerations
II. In the OT
III. In the NT
  A. In Greek Literature
  B. Vocabulary
  C. In the Gospels
  D. In Luke-Acts
  E. In Paul
  F. In Hebrews
  G. In Other NT Writings

***I. General Considerations.***–The concept of promise is present throughout the canonical Scriptures. Although the OT essentially lacks technical terms for promise, the concept is nonetheless a decisive reality in it, and the NT writers consistently refer to the OT in terms of fulfilled promise (*see* FULFIL). The Scriptures depict God as the One who alone is true and powerful in effecting the fulfillment of promises. The NT points to Jesus Christ as the great fulfillment of God's promise: "For all the promises of God find their Yes in him" (2 Cor. 1:20).

So comprehensive is the theological category of promise that it can be understood fully only in relationship to a rich array of other terms in both Testaments (e.g., covenant, eternal life, faith, grace, hope, inheritance, kingdom, law, life, rest, righteousness, sonship). The very breadth of its meaning has made the concept difficult for biblical scholarship to define. Among the unresolved questions are the relationship of the OT to the NT and the place of Jesus Christ in the OT. Nonetheless, Scripture shows how God's people are to be sustained by His promises. As the word of promise, Scripture calls and recalls God's people to the God who makes and keeps great promises (2 Pet. 1:4).

***II. In the OT.***–The God of the OT is a God who speaks. He speaks and creation comes into being. He speaks, making covenant with His people and declaring how they may live before Him and prosper. He speaks through His servants the prophets. In all of this God is known and worshiped as the God of promise. Although the OT has no special term for promise, the idea is conveyed by a range of Hebrew terms, including those ordinarily translated by "speak," "speech," "say," "swear," etc. Because God is the faithful one, His words are hope-filled and move toward certain fulfillment.

The OT promises evolve from a number of nodal points. Standing near the beginning of the canonical Scriptures, two moments of promising are critical in the history of salvation: (1) what is known as the *protevangelium* (the promise that the seed of the woman will ultimately be victorious over the seed of the serpent) in Gen. 3:15; and (2) God's promise to Noah that He will never again curse the ground but will sustain the earth with its appointed times and seasons (Gen. 8:21–9:17). The promise of continued providential care provides a framework within which humankind may be sustained in hope as it lives toward the promised salvation.

Of all the OT promises, God's promise to Abraham is preeminent. God swore to Abraham that He would give him a son, that He would give him a land (Canaan), that his posterity would be blessed (Gen. 12:2f.; 13:14-17; 15:8; 17:4-8; 22:17f.; cf. 26:3-5; 28:13-15), and that all the nations of the earth would find blessing in him (Gen. 18:19; 21:1; 22:15-18; 26:1-5; Dt. 1:11; 1 Ch. 16:16). The rite of circumcision was established as a sign of God's promise to Abraham and his posterity (Gen. 17).

God's covenant with Israel at Sinai is the next great center of divine promise. By way of confirming His intent to create a great people out of Abraham, God called Moses to lead His people out of Egyptian bondage to the promised land of Canaan (Gen. 50:22-25; Ex. 3:17; 12:25; 32:13; Nu. 10:29; 14:16f.; Dt. 6:3-23; 9:3-5, 28; 15:6; 19:8; 26:3-18; 29:13; *see* LAND). Leading His people to deliverance, God made covenant with them at Sinai, promising that the people of Israel would be His own favored possession if they would but obey His voice and keep His covenant (Ex. 19:5). God's covenant promise and command at Sinai served as the benchmark for the utterances of God's later messengers, the prophets (Jer. 7:23; Ezk. 16:8; Am. 3:1f.). However disobedient Israel might be, God remained faithful in keeping His promises. His promises were as firm as God Himself.

God continued both to make and to keep promises in His dealings with David, the prototype of the Messiah who would deliver God's people from all their enemies (2 S. 7:12, 16; 23:5; Ps. 89:3f. [MT 4f.]; 132:11). With David God made an everlasting covenant, establishing his throne in perpetuity. Thus God's promises to David carried on the earlier promises to Abraham and also pointed forward to promises that would be given to future generations (1 K. 2:24; 5:12; 8:15-25; 9:5; 2 Ch. 1:9; 6:4-20). The Abrahamic and Davidic promises are connected in Jer. 23:5-8 and Ezk. 37:24-28.

Because God is the holy Promiser and His word is firm, holding fast to His promise is as imperative for Israel as is obedience to His law. Failure to trust in God's promise is one of Israel's cardinal sins (Ps. 106:24; Nu. 14:1-35), for trust in (the promise of) God is the pattern expected of the true servant of God. Ironically, in Matthew's crucifixion narrative, which presents Jesus as the fulfillment of the OT ideal of true righteousness, the accusation spoken against Him is: "He trusts in God" (Mt. 27:43). In the OT, as later in the NT, true fidelity to God is depicted as life lived out in hope in God's promise — despite His apparent absence and the present invisibility of His salvation.

The basic message of the OT is that God makes and keeps promises in spite of the failure and disobedience of His people. Thus, Jer. 31:31-34 promises a "new covenant" in which God will write His word on the heart of His erring people. Anticipating the gift of the Spirit in the NT (cf. esp. Rom. 8:9-13), human responsiveness to God's will is attributed to the efficacy of God's promise rather than to human achievement.

*III. In the NT.*–The NT writers understand their own time as the time of fulfillment and regularly use the language of "promise" and "fulfillment" to proclaim God's great work in Jesus Christ. The rich variety of emphases in the NT makes it profitable to examine both the specific emphases of individual documents and also the general message of the NT as a whole. Although the explication that follows will focus especially on the technical terms for promise, the concept is far richer than a simple word study of these terms can disclose.

*A. In Greek Literature.* The concept of promise was familiar enough in Greek literature, but in all stages of this literature it is human beings who make promises to gods, not gods to human beings. Schniewind and Friedrich report that there is only one known example of the promise of a god to a man (*TDNT,* II, 579). Hence the biblical pattern represents a radical departure, a new revelation of God's relation to creation.

*B. Vocabulary.* The two Greek terms in the NT most frequently represented by "promise" are the verb *epangéllomai* and the noun *epangelía. Epangéllomai* appears fifteen times in the NT. In eleven of these instances it refers to divine promises; interestingly, three of the four examples of human promising have negative connotations: the promise of money to Judas the betrayer (Mk. 14:11), the profession of false teaching (1 Tim. 6:21), and the false freedom promised by false prophets (2 Pet. 2:19). A cognate verb, *proepangéllomai* (lit. "announce beforehand"), is twice rendered "promise" (Rom. 1:2; 2 Cor. 9:5). The noun *epangelía* occurs fifty-two times in the NT (it has no direct OT counterpart and is lacking in the LXX of our canonical OT), primarily in the Pauline corpus and in Hebrews. It may refer either to the words of promise or to the thing promised. The noun *epángelma* is used twice in 2 Peter (1:4; 3:13) as a synonym of *epangelía.*

*C. In the Gospels.* Although the specific vocabulary of promise appears but rarely in the Gospels (only in Mk. 14:11; Lk. 24:49), the Gospels reflect explicitly or implicitly the realization of promise throughout the unfolding narrative. The appearance of Jesus is persistently described as the fulfillment of OT promises (*see* FULFIL). Jesus' own sense of mission arose from His awareness of being in a unique sense the fulfillment of God's great promise of salvation (see Lk. 4:16-21; cf. Isa. 61:1). It fell to Paul to underline the full reality of Christ as the Gospel event that fulfills all the promises of God.

*D. In Luke-Acts.* Luke-Acts makes an especially strong connection between God's promising and the Holy Spirit, as is suggested by the Lukan expression, "the promise of the Spirit" (Acts 2:33, 39; cf. 1:4; Lk. 24:49). The use of promissory language reveals a clear, formal pattern that parallels other NT material. God the Father makes and keeps promises (Lk. 24:49; Acts 1:4; 7:5, 17; 26:6). Objectively, God fulfills His promise to bring salvation; belief in Christ, the God-ordained mediator, is the means by which the promised salvation may be received (Acts 13:23; cf. v. 48). The apostolic proclamation of the *euangélion* ("good news") is declared as fulfillment of (the cognate) *epangelía* ("promise," Acts 13:32f.) — but also the vehicle by which the promise comes to fulfillment again and again. Those who experience salvation in Christ receive the eschatological gift of the Holy Spirit, promised for the last days (2:38f.; cf. 1:4f.; 2:16-21, 33-36), just as Jesus received the anointing of the Spirit in fulfillment of God's promise through Isaiah (Lk. 4:17-19, 21; cf. Isa. 61:1f.).

*E. In Paul.* The Pauline corpus provides the most prominent witness to the centrality of the concept of promise in earliest Christianity. In Rom. 4 (esp. vv. 13f., 16, 20f.) and 9 and Gal. 3 (esp. vv. 14, 16-22, 28) and 4, Paul reflects at length on the fulfillment of God's promise in Christ and the gospel. Essentially, God's offer of salvation in Christ is to be grasped by faith and not by works of the law (Rom. 4:13f., 16, 20f.). By definition, God's promise is a wholly gracious matter and precedes the law (Rom. 4:10-13; Gal. 3:16-19). Works of the law in themselves, rather than meriting the promise, obviate the very presupposition and intent of promise (Gal. 5:2). Abraham is the great prototype of faith in that he allowed his life and destiny to be determined totally by the promise of God (Rom. 4; Gal. 3–4).

The remaining occurrences of "promise" in Paul's writings extend and deepen the teaching of these chapters. In Rom. 1:1-6 Paul speaks of "the gospel of God which he promised beforehand through his prophets in the holy scriptures, the gospel concerning his Son. . . ." This passage presents an important conjunction of (1) the Promiser, (2) the promise (of the gospel), (3) the Promised One (Jesus Christ), and (4) the fulfillment of the promise as declared in the gospel. Before the gospel came to them Gentiles were "strangers to the covenants of the promise" (Eph. 2:12); but now they have become participants in the promise through the gospel (3:6). The gospel brings the promise of life in Christ (2 Tim. 1:1; Tit. 1:2). Those who believe in Christ are sealed with the promised Holy Spirit (Eph. 1:13). Paul calls on those who have received God's promises to cleanse themselves from all defilement and to strive after holiness (2 Cor. 7:1; cf. 6:16-18).

*F. In Hebrews.* Promise occupies a decisive place in the Epistle to the Hebrews. In the first main section the author warns against "drifting away from" (2:1) faith in God's supreme revelation in His Son (cf. ch. 1), for to "neglect such a great salvation" (2:3) would be far more serious than the Israelites' rejection of God's revelation through the law (2:2f.) and through Moses (ch. 3). The author summarizes the readers' situation: "Therefore, while the promise of entering his rest remains, let us fear lest any of you be judged to have failed to reach it. For good news came to us just as to them; but the message which they heard did not benefit them, because it did not meet with faith in the hearers" (4:1f.). The concepts found here — promise, rest, endurance, the gospel, and faith — represent major concerns of the epistle.

Chapter 11, with its gallery of saints, establishes living by faith in God's promise as the distinctive Christian life-style (11:9, 11, 13, 17, 39; cf. 6:12-17; 7:6; 10:36; 11:17). Although the Hebrew Christians had received the promise anticipated by the OT saints (11:39), the necessity of enduring suffering (see esp. 10:32-39; 12:3-11; cf. 2:9f., 14-18; 5:7f.; 11:24-26, 35-38) meant that their own lives had to be oriented anew to promise. Thus the author urges them to exercise mutual exhortation to living by God's promise (10:23-25). For encouragement, believers can look to the veritable "cloud of witnesses" (12:1; cf. ch. 11) who have now inherited the promises through patient endurance (6:12-15; 11:9, 13). They can look forward to entering the "rest" promised to those who went before them (4:1-11). The new covenant mediated by Christ is enacted on even greater promises than those of the old covenant (8:6) — including the promise of an "eternal inheritance" (9:15) and a "kingdom that cannot be shaken" (12:28). The one who promises speaks as the Righteous Judge (vv. 26-29). His oath is unbreakable (cf. 6:13), and His promises stand as the Day draws near (10:23-25).

*G. In Other NT Writings.* The specific vocabulary of promise occurs in only a few passages outside of Luke-Acts, the Pauline corpus, and Hebrews. These texts focus on the reward or inheritance of faith. James speaks of the crown (1:12) and the kingdom (2:5) that "God has promised to those who love him." 2 Pet. 1:4 speaks of the "very great promises" through which Christians may "become partakers of the divine nature," while 1 Jn. 2:25 points to the promise of eternal life. 2 Peter addresses a situation in which scoffers call into question the promise of Christ's return (3:4). The author asserts that the faithful will continue to wait for the promise (v. 13), persuaded that "the Lord is not slow about his promise" (v. 9). This patient waiting for the realization of God's promise — a waiting that allows God to be God and to work out His salvation in His way and time — is one of the chief characteristics of biblical faith.

***Bibliography.***–B. W. Anderson, ed., *OT and Christian Faith* (1969); D. Baker, *Two Testaments: One Bible* (1977); F. Baumgärtel, *Verheissung; Zur Frage des evangelischen Verständnisses des AT* (1952); J. Bright, *Covenant and Promise* (1977); F. F. Bruce, ed., *Promise and Fulfillment* (*Festschrift* for S. H. Hooke; 1963); W. D. Davies, *Gospel and the Land* (1974); *DNTT,* III, 68-74; L. Goppelt, *Typos* (Eng. tr. 1982); J. Jeremias, *Jesus' Promise to the Nations* (Eng. tr., *SBT,* 1/24, 1956); W. Kaiser, *Toward an OT Theology* (1978); W. G. Kümmel, *Promise and Fulfillment* (Eng. tr., *SBT,* 1/23, 1945); J. Moltmann, *Theology of Hope* (Eng. tr. 1967); *TDNT,* II, *s.v.* ἐπαγγέλω κτλ. (J. Schniewind and G. Friedrich); G. von Rad, *OT Theology* (2 vols., Eng. tr. 1962-1965); W. Vischer, *Witness of the OT to Christ* (Eng. tr. 1949); C. Westermann, ed., *Essays on OT Hermeneutics* (Eng. tr. 1963).

R. P. MEYE

**PROOF; PROVE.** The noun "proof" is used by the RSV in two different senses. (1) It means "compelling evidence" in Isa. 41:21 (Heb. *ʿaṣṣumôṯ,* lit. "strong [words]"; AV "strong reasons"; NEB "case"); Mt. 8:4 par. (Gk. *martýrion*; AV "testimony"; NEB "certify"); Acts 1:3 (*tekmḗrion*); 2 Cor. 8:24 (*éndeixis*; NEB "clear expression"); 13:3 (*dokimḗ*). (2) It means "test" in the expression "put to the proof," the RSV translation of Heb. piel of *nāsâ* in contexts where the Israelites, showing a sinful lack of faith, TEST Yahweh's promise to provide for them by asking: "Is the Lord among us or not?" (Ex. 17:7; also v. 2; Nu. 14:22; Ps. 95:9; AV "tempt," "prove"; NEB "challenge"; *see also* MASSAH AND MERIBAH). In contexts where Yahweh tests Israel the RSV usually renders the same Hebrew form "prove" (see below) or "test."

The verb "prove" has three meanings in the RSV. (1) In the OT it several times means "establish by evidence," e.g., in Ezr. 2:59 par. Neh. 7:61 for the Heb. hiphil of *nāgaḏ* (lit. "report," "explain"; AV "show"; NEB "establish"); it has a similar meaning in the expressions "prove [one] perverse" (hiphil of *ʿāqaš,* lit. "declare crooked," Job 9:20), "prove [one] a liar" (hiphil of *kāzaḇ,* lit. "label [one] a liar," 24:25), and "be proved right" (*ṣāḏaq,* Isa. 43:26; AV "be justified"). NT terms rendered in this way are Gk. *parístēmi* (Acts 24:13; NEB "make good"), *apodeíknymi* (25:7), *éndeixis* (Rom. 3:26; AV "declare"; NEB "demonstrate"), *synístēmi* (2 Cor. 7:11; Gal. 2:18), *symbibázō* (Acts 9:22), and *paratíthēmi* (17:3; AV "allege"; NEB "apply to show").

(2) The verb means "test," "try," in passages where it translates Heb. *bāḥan* (Ps. 26:2; AV "examine"; NEB "test"; cf. AV Ps. 17:3; 66:10; 81:7 [MT 8]; Mal. 3:10), the piel of *nāsâ* (Ex. 15:25; 16:4; 20:20; NEB "put to the test"; cf. AV Dt. 8:2, 16, and fifteen additional passages), the pass. part. of *ṣārap* (lit. "refine"; RSV "prove true," 2 S. 22:31; Ps. 18:30 [MT 31]; Prov. 30:5; AV "is tried," "is pure"; NEB "has stood the test"); Gk. *peirasmós* (1 Pet. 4:12; AV "try"; NEB omits) and *dokimázō,* which is rendered "prove" frequently by the AV (e.g., Lk. 14:19; 2 Cor. 8:22; 13:5; Gal. 6:4; Eph. 5:10; 1 Thess. 5:21; 1 Tim. 3:10; He. 3:9; RSV usually "test") but only twice by the RSV (Rom. 12:2; 2 Cor. 8:8; NEB "discern," "put to the test"); in both passages "prove" means APPROVE (cf. RSV Rom. 2:18; 14:22; Phil. 1:10; 1 Thess. 2:4) or "accept as proved" (see Bauer, rev., p. 202). *See also* TEST.

(3) It means "turn out to be," "be shown to be," when it translates Heb. *hāyâ* (lit. "be," 1 K. 1:52; AV "show"); Gk. *gínomai* (lit. "be," "become," Mt. 13:22 par. Mk. 4:19; Lk. 10:36; Jn. 15:8; 2 Cor. 7:14; 1 Thess. 1:5), pass. of *heurískō* (lit. "be found," Rom. 7:10; AV "find"), pass. of *kenóō* (lit. "be emptied [of its justification]," 2 Cor. 9:3; RSV "prove vain"), and *pseúdomai* (lit. "lie," He. 6:18; RSV "prove false").

N. J. O.

**PROPER** [Heb. *$d^e$ḇar-yôm $b^e$yômô*] ("proper day," Lev. 23:37); AV "its own day"; NEB "its day"; [*maṯkōneṯ*] ("proper condition," 2 Ch. 24:13); AV "its state"; NEB "its original design"; [*nismān*] ("proper place," Isa. 28:25); AV "appointed place"; NEB omits; [Gk. *ídios*] (Jude 1:6); AV "own"; [*prépon*] (1 Cor. 11:13); AV "seemly"; NEB "fitting"; **PROPER TIME** [Heb. *$b^e$* + *ʿēṯ*–'in time'] (Eccl. 10:17); AV "due season"; NEB "right time of day"; [Gk. *en kairṓ̜*] (Mt. 24:45; Lk. 12:42); AV "due season"; [*kairoís idíois*] (1 Tim. 2:6; 6:15; Tit. 1:3); AV "its own times," "his own seasons"; NEB "fitting time," "his own good time"; **PROPERLY** [Gk. *en métrō̜*] (Eph. 4:16); AV "in due measure"; NEB "due"; [Gk. *aschēmonéō*] ("not behaving properly," 1 Cor. 7:36); AV "behaveth unseemly."

***I. Proper Place or Condition.***–Isaiah 28:25 refers to sowing barley "in its proper place" (Heb. *nismān*). Although the precise meaning of *nismān* is uncertain, the context requires a meaning related to the agriculturally beneficial arrangement of the crop. Dill and cummin are scattered, wheat is carefully put in rows to prevent the crop from choking itself, and barley, a less favored crop, is put in the less fertile field, its "proper place," with spelt at its border. The standard for propriety here may be simply good husbandry, but those instincts, skills, and knowledge are themselves finally given by God (v. 26). The NEB omits this phrase, following many versions (see *BHS*), apparently taking it as a scribal error, a dittography based on spelt (Heb. *kussemeṯ*).

Jude 6 refers to the disobedient angels who left "their proper dwelling," Gk. *ídion oikētḗrion.* Gk. *ídios* very clearly parallels the previous *heautṓn* and is used in a possessive sense. The standard for propriety is simply proprietorship, but again God's assignments and gifts stand behind such a standard. The angels left "their own" (AV) dwelling because of disobedient lust (Jude 6; cf. Gen. 6:1-4; 1 En. 6–11) and were punished. Jude used that legend as an example and warning for his readers.

In 2 Ch. 24:13 the temple is repaired and restored to its "proper condition." Heb. *maṯkōneṯ* entails some standard (cf. Ezk. 45:11, the standards for the ephah and bath; Ex. 30:32, the standards for the composition of holy oil). In 2 Ch. 24:13 the standard is less obvious; the NEB presumes it to be the temple's "original design." Perhaps Ezk. 43:10 (Heb. *tāḵnîṯ*) refers to the sorts of standards used. This concern of the Chronicler for the "proper condition" of the temple does not occur in the par. 2 K. 12. The Chronicler was of course a good deal more interested in the cultic institutions of Jerusalem than the Deuteronomic historians. His special presentation of history gives legitimacy to the pure worship of God in Jerusalem in postexilic times; the reference to "proper condition" reinforces this concern for worship as prescribed.

***II. Proper Time.***–The appointed feasts are to be celebrated and the offerings made "each on its proper day," *$d^e$ḇar-yôm $b^e$yômô* (Lev. 23:37). This Hebrew phrase in Ex. 5:13, 19 refers to the daily quota of bricks to be produced by the Hebrew slaves, a standard that had been set rationally, according to the straw supply and time, but later was set arbitrarily by the pharaoh. In Ex. 16:4 the phrase indicates the daily quota of manna. In 1 K. 8:59 Solomon prays at the dedication of the temple that God will maintain the cause of His servant and people "as each day requires." Among other uses of the phrase (2 K. 25:30; Jer. 52:34; Neh. 11:23; 12:47; Dnl. 1:5) the most relevant seem to be Ezr. 3:4 and 1 Ch. 16:37, both of which refer to daily ministry at the altar. The standard for propriety at such ministry is the ordinance of God. Similarly, in Lev. 23:37 the standard is explicitly the appointment of God; this verse picks up the heading of v. 4. There are times fixed by God for His people to gather and to offer sacrifices. The propriety is not based on the rhythm of agricultural life, whatever the origin of some of the feasts, but is rather based on the command of God. The agricultural feasts are incorporated and subordinated into the historical focus of Israel's cult (cf. vv. 42f.).

Ecclesiastes 10:17 mentions the "proper time" for princely feasting. The text uses the word for "time," Heb. *ʿēṯ*, with the preposition *bᵉ*; the construction is not unusual. The "proper time" for princes to feast stands in antithetical parallelism to the previous couplet's reference to princes' feasting "in the morning" (v. 16). At the "proper time" they feast "for strength, and not for drunkenness." The next proverb (v. 18) reinforces the judgment against sloth and indolence. The standard for propriety in this mirror for princes is the service to the people, and the standard for impropriety is sloth and gluttony.

In Mt. 24:45; Lk. 12:42 the steward's responsibility is to give the household their food "at the proper time." The Greek phrase *en kairṓi* parallels Heb. *bāʿēṯ* or *bᵉʿittô* (cf. Eccl. 10:17). This parable may also reflect the declaration in Ps. 104:27 that God gives all His creatures their food "in due season." The master has set the steward over the household, and the standard for propriety is the master's will and the vocation of caring for the household for him. Providing "food at the proper time" is a synecdoche for such care.

Three times in the Pastoral Epistles the Greek adjective *ídios* is joined to the noun *kairós* (1 Tim. 2:6; 6:15; Tit. 1:3). In each case the phrase is plural but translated as singular, "proper time" (but cf. the AV). O. Cullmann (*Christ and Time* [Eng. tr., 3rd ed., 1962], pp. 40f.) made these passages refer to the entire *Heilsgeschichte* and assumed that the standard for propriety is the plan of salvation. But such an interpretation seems unwarranted. The most straightforward reading of the cryptic phrase *tó martýrion kairoís idíois* in 1 Tim. 2:6 takes *martýrion* (RSV "testimony") as synonymous with *kḗrygma* or *euangélion, idioís* as a possessive without any particular contrast, and the phrase itself as in apposition to the preceeding confessional statements. Thus the confessional statements "There is one God, and there is one mediator between God and men, the man Christ Jesus, who gave himself as a ransom for all" (vv. 5-6a) are described as "the gospel for your own times." The standard of propriety, if it is accurate to speak of "proper" at all here, is simply proprietorship. Cullmann's assumption of a reference to eschatological events seems unnecessary and ill-fitting to the context. Such a reading of Gk. *kairoís idíois* fits Tit. 1:3 exactly, for it is through Paul's preaching that the Word is made manifest in "your own times."

1 Timothy 6:15, however, has indeed a future reference. The sovereign God will show (Gk. *deíchei*) the "appearing [*epiphaneía*] of our Lord Jesus Christ . . . at the proper time [*kairoís idíois*]." *Kairoís idíois* could be taken as a dative controlled by the verb; the meaning would then be that God will show the appearance to "your own times." But the author of the Pastorals seems more typically to minimize the imminence of the Parousia. (The use of *epiphaneía* rather than *parousía* itself demonstrates a subtle shift in eschatology.) The author emphasizes the sovereignty of God (note the beautiful doxology of vv. 15f.) rather than the imminence of the appearance. The appearance will surely occur, but the author does not want to overemphasize it. It will happen at "the proper time," i.e., in God's own times (NEB "in his own good time").

In all these Pastoral contexts, then, "proper" does not serve so much to make a judgment according to some standard provided by *Heilsgeschichte* as simply to identify the possessor, the one to whom the times belong, whether "our own times" or "God's own times."

***III. Proper Behavior.***–Proper behavior is mentioned in 1 Cor. 11:13, "Is it proper [Gk. *prépon estín*] for a woman to pray to God with her head uncovered?" *To prépon* has Stoic associations (M. Pohlenz, *Nachrichten der Gesellschaft der Wissenschaften in Göttingen,* 33 [1927], 53-92) and suggests not so much something lawful (cf. the preceding argument in vv. 2-12) as something seemly (cf. AV "comely") or "fitting" (NEB). Moreover, the Stoic associations suggest that the standard for propriety may well be provided by nature, so that the question in v. 13, "Is it proper?" is formally very similar to the question of v. 14, "Does not nature itself teach you. . . ?"

1 Corinthians 7:36 uses Gk. *aschēmonéō,* "not behaving properly." The word occurs once elsewhere in the NT, 13:5, where it is translated "is . . . rude." *Aschēmonéō* is the antonym of Gk. *euschēmonéō* and so might be translated "not to act like a gentleman." The standard here is convention and propriety. Love does not tread upon accepted manners and customs (v. 5). Love is not without a sense of propriety, but, it may be added, a sense of propriety without love is less than a "noisy gong." The forms and rules and institutions that order life are prized by love and by Paul. Thus in 7:36 Paul insisted against the Corinthians, who so highly prized self-control, that one may yet pursue the gentlemanly path and marry, as manners would dictate, "his betrothed."

In Eph. 4:16 the RSV renders Gk. *en métrōi* as "properly." The phrase means literally "in measure" (cf. the AV) and recalls vv. 7, 13. "Grace was given to each of us according to the measure of Christ's gift" (v. 7). Those many gifts are all to build up the Church so that "we all attain . . . to the measure of the stature of the fulness of Christ" (vv. 12f.). In v. 16 the repeated reference to "measure" may effectively be translated "properly," but the standard of Christ's gift and fulness may not be elided. The propriety is determined not so much by the congruence of bodily functions as by the gift and pattern of Jesus Christ, the Lord of the Church. The gifts may and must be used — they are the gifts of Christ, after all (v. 7) — but they must and may be used in the service of the Church, for Christ the giver is the pattern and measure, the standard for propriety, as well.

A. D. VERHEY

**PROPER NAMES.** *See* NAMES, PROPER.

**PROPERTY.** *See* AGRARIAN LAWS; HEIR; INHERIT; JUBILEE, YEAR OF; POSSESS; WEALTH.

**PROPHECY, FALSE.** The prophetic literature describes the existence of groups and individuals who delivered messages which were in conflict with the messages of the true prophets of Israel. These false prophets claimed that God or some other god has sent them, but their professions of orthodoxy were negated because their messages contradicted God's revelation. At times even the true prophets were labeled false prophets because the Israelites did not accept the true message of God which they spoke.

*I. Terms for False Prophecy.*–The title "false prophet" was not a well-defined concept among the Hebrews; instead they preferred to talk about false prophecy. The LXX translators employed the term *pseudoprophḗtēs* ("false prophet") to describe the prophets who lied (Jer. 6:13), denied the words of the true prophets (Jer. 27:9 = LXX 34:9; Jer. 28:1 = LXX 35:1), tried to kill the true prophets (Jer. 26:7 = LXX 33:7), and deceived the people with their dreams (Jer. 29:8 = LXX 36:8). The Hebrew writers used several terms to define false prophecy. It was deceitful, a lie or falsehood (*šeqer*: Jer. 8:10; 14:14; 23:25, 32; 27:10, 14, 16; 28:15; 29:9, 21), contained words of peace when there was no peace (Jer. 6:14; 8:11; 14:3; 23:17; 28:2, 11; Ezk. 13:10; Mic. 3:5), was not based on the decisions of the council of Yahweh (Jer. 23:18), included visions out of the prophet's own heart (Jer. 14:14; 23:16; Ezk. 13:2f.; 22:28), was derived from Baal (Jer. 2:8; 23:13), and was sometimes caused by a deceptive spirit from God (1 K. 22:19-23). False prophets from other nations worshiped other gods (*see* PROPHECY II) and practiced divination, witchcraft, sorcery, magic, and necromancy. The Hebrew law demanded that any prophet who tried to persuade the people to follow another god must be killed (Dt. 13:1-5; 18:20). Divination, soothsaying, witchcraft, necromancy, and trust in mediums or the interpretation of omens were expressly forbidden (Lev. 19:26; Dt. 18:10f.). Balaam was a diviner (*qesem*) who worked for a fee (Nu. 22:7; Josh. 13:22), and some Israelite prophets were classified in the same category (Jer. 14:14; 27:9; 29:8; Ezk. 13:6-9; Mic. 3:6f.; Zec. 10:2) because they used magic (Ezk. 13:17-23) to deceive their listeners. Other false prophets called sorcerers (from the verbs *ʿānan* or *kāšap*) were prominent in Egypt (Ex. 7:11), Babylon (Dnl. 2:2; Isa. 47:9, 12), and Israel (Isa. 2:6; 57:3; Mic. 5:12; Mal. 3:5; 2 Ch. 33:6).

*II. The Interpretation of False Prophecy.*–One method of identifying a false prophet was to find out if his prophecy remained unfulfilled. The destruction of Jerusalem proved that the prophets who predicted peace were false prophets (Jer. 6:14f.; 8:11f.; 14:13f.). The application of this yardstick presented two problems. First, the predicted event might not take place for several years, and second, the contingent nature of many prophecies caused the fulfillment of the message to depend on the response of the listeners. Jonah's prophecy of doom for Nineveh was never fulfilled because it was conditionally dependent on a negative response to the prophet's warnings, not because he was a false prophet.

J. Hempel maintained that all prophecy was contingent; therefore, it was impossible to use fulfillment or nonfulfillment to judge the authenticity of any prophecy. R. P. Carroll applied the psychological theory of cognitive dissonance to the prophetic traditions in order to demonstrate how the prophets transformed unfulfilled threats or promises to avoid the dissonance of unfulfilled predictions and the stigma of being labeled a false prophet. G. von Rad approached the issue of false prophecy from the perspective of its social location and its theological perspective and concluded that the false prophets were the cultic prophets who always predicted salvation. The false prophets in Jeremiah's time centered their hope on God's positive promises and the existence of the temple in Jerusalem. He maintained that even Deuteronomy, which based Israel's relationship on God's love for the nation, was strongly influenced by the false institutional prophets who were the heirs of the Mosaic office (Dt. 18:18). (*See* PROPHECY III.A.) Although von Rad was correct in observing that most false prophets preached messages of hope, so did many of the true prophets. This solution reduced a very complex issue down to a simple formula.

The truth of a prophet's message depended on the historical context of the people who received the message. T. W. Overholt concluded that if a true prophecy was applied at the wrong time and to the wrong audience, it passed over into the category of false prophecy. He believed that Jonah's rebellion before and after his faithful ministry at Nineveh brought him close to being a false prophet. The man of God from Judah (1 K. 13) faithfully pronounced the word of the Lord and then was deceived by a false prophet. Later the false prophet functioned as a true prophet when he faithfully delivered God's message of doom (1 K. 13:20-22) on the man of God who had disobeyed God's command. K. Harms surmised that all a genuine prophet of God had to do to become a false prophet was to misapply one prophecy. He believed that the true prophet received his message from the divine council and was exact in delivering that message to its intended recipients.

A complicating factor for this quite valid approach was the few known examples where God sent an enticing spirit to misdirect the prophets (1 K. 22:19-23; Ezk. 14:7-11). But most prophets were seduced into false prophecy by their own desires for recognition and acceptance by the masses, their political leanings which supported nationalistic interests, and their blind application of traditional teaching about the temple and the messianic age to the temporal problems of their day (E. Jacob). S. Blank saw that the only way for the public to discover if a prophet had spoken the truth was for them to listen to the positive affirmations of authenticity given by the prophet: his calling, the contrast between his message and popular thinking, his claim to divine words, his conformity with God's nature, and the fulfillment of his predictions. G. Quell studied the various criteria usually associated with distinguishing true from false prophecy and was forced to the position that only another divinely inspired prophet could determine who stood in the council of God. H. J. Kraus's examination of various crisis situations between prophets led him to propose that the true prophet had direct and immediate access to God and His council while the false prophets were dependent on various lesser modes of revelation. He also drew attention to the misuse of covenant promises by the false prophets and their refusal to expose the sinfulness of the nation (Mic. 3:8; Lam. 2:14). A. S. van der Woude's study of Micah discovered a focus within false prophecy on the Zion and Sinai covenants which promised God's defeat of those who would attack Yahweh's covenant people. His method of identifying quotations of false prophets in Micah was used by J. Crenshaw to create an overview of popular religious beliefs which the false prophets followed. Crenshaw's analysis of the criteria for identifying false prophecy caused him to deny that there was any valid means of separating the genuine from the fake message.

*III. Tests of a False Prophet.*–False prophets who worshiped or prophesied in the name of other gods were easy to distinguish (Jer. 2:8; 23:13; 26:27; 32:32-35), but Jer. 23:17, 25 recorded that these prophets actually used the name Yahweh in their prophecies. The moral character of the prophet himself (Jer. 23:14) provided another checkpoint, but it too had limitations, for none of the true prophets was perfectly sinless (except Jesus). Certainly the alert Israelite must have cast a questioning eye at Hosea's marriage to a prostitute, and Jeremiah (Jer. 38:14-28) and Elisha (2 K. 8:7-15) were not always completely truthful. The false prophets could fake a call experience, claim inspiration, and borrow approved covenant traditions to support their prophecies. Many OT prophecies have still not been fulfilled, so the use of the fulfillment criteria was possible only when specific and immediate predictions were made. The main criterion used in evaluating false prophecy was the degree to which that prophecy was consistent with the message of other divinely inspired prophets who spoke about the same event. Even when the prophets themselves were inspired they were not always able to pick out false prophecy (1 K. 13).

*IV. False Prophets in the NT.*–The presence of the false prophets who denied the truth and deceived believers was a formidable danger for the NT Church. Jesus warned His disciples to expect persecution and beware when people speak only positively, for this was the way that people treated the false prophets in the OT (Lk. 6:26). 2 Pet. 2:1-22 gives an extended warning about the characteristics of false prophets and teachers. They secretly introduce destructive heresies, deny Christ as Master (2:1), follow sensual pleasures (vv. 2, 10-13, 18), are full of greed like the false prophet Balaam (vv. 3, 13f.), and full of arrogant and undisciplined talk and behavior (v. 18). Although not calling them false prophets, Jude seems to describe a similar group of ungodly persons who have secretly crept into the Church. They deny Christ (Jude 4), are licentious and grossly immoral (vv. 2, 7f., 17f.), follow the error of Balaam (v. 11), speak arrogantly and flatter people (v. 16), and cause division (v. 19). These, as well as those described by Jesus in Mt. 7:15-23, appear to be involved Christians who are actively working in the name of Christ. The reality is different, however, for they are "ravenous wolves" who do not know Christ. Some have suggested that these are Gnostics, Pharisees, Zealots, or charismatics, but a specific identification seems impossible (cf. Aune, p. 223).

1 Jn. 4:1-3 encourages believers to test persons who claim to have prophetic gifts to see if they will confess that Christ has come in the flesh from God. A similar test will identify those called "antichrists" (1 Jn. 2:18, 22f.), but these two warnings may not be directed against identical groups. Such exhortations were often given to insure the purity of teachings in the Church (1 Cor. 14:29; 1 Thess. 5:20-22). When Paul and Barnabas met the Jewish magician Bar-Jesus on the island of Paphos, Paul, being full of the Holy Spirit, discerned that he was a false prophet, full of deceit, a son of the devil, and an enemy of righteousness (Acts. 13:6-10). The prophetess Jezebel from the church of Thyatira was also in the line of false prophets (Rev. 2:20).

The danger of false prophets at the end of time is predicted by Jesus in His Mt. Olivet discourse (Mt. 24:1, 24; Mk. 13:22). These persons will perform miraculous signs and wonders to deceive people into following the beast (Rev. 16:13f., 19:20). The false prophet, the beast, and the devil will ultimately be destroyed by Christ when He comes in glory to set up His kingdom (Rev. 19:20; 20:10).

***Bibliography.***–D. E. Aune, *Prophecy in Early Christianity and the Ancient Mediterranean World* (1983); H. Bacht, *Bibl.*, 32 (1951), 237-262; S. H. Blank, *Of a Truth the Lord Hath Sent Me: An Inquiry into the Source of the Prophet's Authority* (1955); J. L. Crenshaw, *Prophetic Conflict* (*BZAW*, 124, 1971); R. P. Carroll, *When Prophecy Failed* (1979); K. Harms, *Die Falschen Propheten: Eine Biblische Untersuchung* (1947); J. Hempel, *Zeitschrift für systematische Theologie*, 7 (1930), 631-660, repr. *Apoxysmata* (1961), pp. 174-197; E. Jacob, *Theologische Zeitschrift*, 13 (1957), 479-486; H. J. Kraus, *Prophetie in der Krisis* (1964); E. Osswald, *False Prophetie im AT* (1962); T. W. Overholt, *Journal of the American Academy of Religion*, 35 (1967), 241-49; *Threat of Falsehood* (*SBT*, 2/16, 1970); G. Quell, *Wahre und False Propheten. Versuch einer Interpretation* (1952); J. A. Sanders, "Hermeneutics in True and False Prophecy," in G. W. Coats and B. O. Long, eds., *Canon and Authority* (1977), pp. 21-41; D. E. Stevenson, *False Prophet* (1965); G. von Rad, *ZAW*, 51 (1933), 109-120; A. S. van der Woude, *VT*, 19 (1969), 244-260.

G. V. SMITH

**PROPHECY, GIFT OF.** *See* SPIRITUAL GIFTS.

**PROPHET; PROPHECY.** A wide range of persons with diverse associations were called prophets because each in some way claimed to be communicating a divine message. The broad usage of the term explains why the patriarch Abram (Gen. 20:7), the priest Aaron (Ex. 7:1), and the singer Jeduthun (1 Ch. 25:3) were all called prophets even though the Scriptures contain no record of their call to a prophetic office. A narrower definition focuses on individuals such as Jeremiah, Isaiah, and Samuel, who received a call to be a prophet and spent their time conveying God's message in an oral, dramatic, or written form.

I. Titles of the Hebrew Prophets
   A. General Designations
   B. Specific Titles and Derived Terms
   C. Related Titles
   D. Distinctions and Relationships Among Titles
II. Prophets in the Ancient Near East
   A. Egypt
   B. Canaan and Syria
   C. Mesopotamia
III. The Prophet's Connection with Israel's Culture
   A. Temple Worship
   B. The Monarchy
   C. Wisdom
   D. Ecstatic Behavior
   E. Covenant Law
   F. Apocalyptic
IV. Message of the Prophets
   A. Reception
   B. Delivery
   C. Content
V. Interpretation of Prophecy
   A. Methodological Approaches
   B. Hermeneutical Principles
VI. Prophecy in the NT

***I. Titles of the Hebrew Prophets.***–The Hebrews used many descriptive terms to designate prophets. Some were considered the Lord's prophets (1 K. 18:13), while many were linked to the Canaanite god Baal (1 K. 18:19; Jer. 2:8). Others were associated with cities (e.g., Jerusalem or Samaria, Jer. 23:13f.) or a nation (e.g., Israel, Ezk. 13:2). But most designations reflected the character or function of the prophet. A careful look at the general terms and the specific titles applied to the prophets will provide some initial insights into the Hebrew concept of a prophet.

*A. General Designations.* Two of the most important general titles were "his (God's) servant" (Heb. *ʿeḇeḏ*) and "man of God" (*ʾîš hāʾᵉlōhîm*). A servant was a humble subject whose goal was to accomplish the tasks assigned by his master. The possessive pronoun recognized the claim of God upon "his servant the prophet" (1 K. 14:18; 2 K. 17:23; 21:10; 24:2). When God warned the Israelites by reminding them of earlier messages given by "my servants the prophets" (2 K. 9:7; 17:13; Jer. 7:25; 29:19; Zec. 1:6), He confirmed the devotion and obedience of those who faithfully declared His word.

"Man of God" was a title of honor used in reference to only a few prophets who had an especially close relationship to God and exercised a particularly strong prophetic gift. Moses was called a "man of God" in contexts that refer to God speaking the law through him (Dt. 33:1; Josh. 14:6; 1 Ch. 23:14; 2 Ch. 30:16; Ezr. 3:2). The title is found primarily in 1 Samuel and 1 and 2 Kings. It was applied to the prophet who announced God's message of judgment upon Eli and his sons (1 S. 2:27). Samuel was identified as a "seer" (1 S. 9:11, 18f.), a "prophet" (cf. v. 9; 19:20), and a "man of God" (9:6-10) who inquired of God and predicted what would happen. Shemaiah (1 K. 12:22; 2 Ch. 11:2), the unknown prophet (not Amos, as proposed by J. L. Crenshaw, *Prophetic Conflict* [1971], pp. 41f.) who went from Judah to Bethel (1 K. 13), and the prophet who warned Amaziah (2 Ch. 25:7-9), were all "men of God" who delivered God's word. The widow whose son was restored to life called Elijah a "man of God" because "the word of the Lord in your mouth is true" (1 K. 17:18, 24; cf. 2 K. 1:6-13). Elisha was called a "man of God" about thirty-five times (4:7-27; 5:8-20; 6:6-15; 7:17–8:11; 23:16f.) because of his miraculous deeds as well as his delivery of God's messages. An angel of the Lord was once confused with a man of God (Jgs. 13:6).

Other general designations applied to prophets include *mēlîṣ* (hiphil part. of *lîṣ*; RSV "mediator," Isa. 43:27), *ṣōpeh* (part. of *ṣāpâ*; RSV "watchman," Isa. 56:10; Jer. 6:17; Ezk. 3:17; 33:7f.), and *mal'āḵ* (RSV "messenger," 2 Ch. 36:15f.; Isa. 44:26; Hag. 1:13).

*B. Specific Titles and Derived Terms.* The concept of prophecy is connected with three Hebrew roots: *r'h, ḥzh,* and *nb'*. These three roots and their derivatives were sometimes used synonymously, but each had its own semantic field and history of application.

The verb *rā'â* has the basic meaning "see, perceive, understand." When it refers to a prophet, the participle *rō'eh* has traditionally been translated "seer." 1 S. 9:9 indicates that the *rō'eh* was a person who revealed secrets by inquiring of God for an answer. Some have concluded on the basis of etymology that the seer's revelation always came in visual form. But in the twelve places where *rō'eh* occurs (most referring to Samuel), there is little or no indication that the seer's answer came in the form of a dream or vision. The verb *rā'â* is used in numerous cases to describe the visual part of a theophany, dream, or vision (e.g., Gen. 16:13; 1 S. 28:13; 1 K. 22:17, 19; 1 Ch. 21:16, 20; Isa. 6:1, 5; Jer. 1:11-13; Ezk. 1:1, 27f.; Dnl. 8:2-7, 15, 20; Am. 7:8; 8:2; Zec. 1:8, 18), but these occurrences do not coincide with the use of the participle *rō'eh*. The derived nouns *mar'eh* and *mar'â*, appearing predominantly in the late books of Ezekiel and Daniel, describe the "visions" that these prophets saw. This evidence does not, however, support the view that the seer was primarily a visionary or a dreamer of dreams. The essence of the idea is that God allowed certain people to "see" (i.e., understand) — or receive a divine communication that contained insight into — past, present, or future events.

The participle *ḥōzeh*, "seer," is applied to three musicians (Heman, 1 Ch. 25:5; Asaph, 2 Ch. 29:30; Jeduthun, 35:15) who were appointed by King David to direct the singing, playing of instruments, and prophesying in the temple worship (cf. 1 Ch. 25:1-7). Elsewhere the title is applied to royal court "seers" during the reigns of David (Gad, 2 S. 24:11; 1 Ch. 21:9; 2 Ch. 29:25), Solomon and Rehoboam (Iddo, 2 Ch. 9:29; 12:15), Jehoshaphat (Hanani, 2 Ch. 19:2), and Manasseh (2 Ch. 33:18f.). These "seers" spoke God's words to the king and recorded them in their chronicles. In these contexts the *ḥōzeh* was the king's advisor who gave him insight into God's will.

The verb from this root, *ḥāzâ* ("see, perceive"), is used in the superscriptions to several books of prophecy (Isa. 1:1; 2:1; Am. 1:1; Mic. 1:1; Hab. 1:1) to indicate that the prophet "saw" or "perceived" the oracle by revelation from God. Ezekiel used the verb to describe what the false prophets "saw" (13:8f., 16, 23; 21:29 [MT 34]; 22:28) from their imaginations and false hopes. Balaam's oracles were derived from words he heard and a vision that he "saw" (Nu. 24:4, 16). But the strong connection of the verb with visionary experience occurs primarily in the Aramaic portions of Daniel. Here *ḥᵃzâ* refers to what Daniel "saw" in dreams and night visions (Dnl. 2, 4, 7).

The nouns derived from *ḥāzâ* (*ḥāzôn, ḥᵃzôṯ, ḥizzāyôn, maḥᵃzeh*, etc.) denote the revelation that is "seen." They frequently refer to a dream or night vision (esp. in Daniel); but the use of *ḥāzôn* in the superscriptions to Isaiah, Obadiah, and Nahum, as well as in titles to the written records of certain prophets (2 Ch. 9:29; 32:32), indicates that it could also refer to the total "revelation" that these prophets perceived through inspiration.

The main term used in the OT to refer to a prophet is *nāḇî'* (or fem. *nᵉḇî'â*). Various theories concerning its etymology have been proposed. Gesenius, Kuenen (p. 42), and von Orelli (pp. 11f.) connected it with *nāḇā'* ("bubble forth"), thus understanding the prophets as ecstatics who bubbled forth words with great fervor. Arnold (p. 93) and Pfeiffer (p. 83) regarded the term as a passive (niphal) participle from *bô'* ("enter"), describing one who was entered by a spirit. Cornill (pp. 9f.), Eiselen (p. 23), and König (p. 260) traced the term to an Arabic root meaning "announce"; thus the prophet was an announcer or spokesman of God's words. Meek (pp. 150f.), Johnson (pp. 24f.), Haldar (p. 109), and Scott (p. 45) favored an Akkadian etymology meaning "speaking or proclaiming." Albright (p. 303), Rowley (pp. 103-05), and Lindblom (p. 102) preferred a passive interpretation, "the one who is called by God." These differences of interpretation indicate the necessity of caution in using an etymological approach to determine the meaning of *nāḇî'*. The exact historical origin of the root may remain uncertain, but a careful study of the usage of its verbal and noun forms can reveal its semantic range.

The verb *nāḇā'*, "prophesy," appears in the niphal and hithpael forms about 115 times in the OT. It occurs in the Pentateuch in only one passage (Nu. 11:25-27). This early text refers to the ability to prophesy as a gift given to the seventy elders of Israel "when the spirit rested upon them." The text does not describe the content of their prophecy, but the context indicates that this new ability enabled the elders to share with Moses the burden of caring for the Israelites. In 1 Samuel the verb describes at least part of the activity of a band of prophets and of Saul (10:5-13; 19:21-24; cf. "rave," 18:10). The first mention of one of these early prophetic bands occurs when Saul meets one coming down from a place of worship, prophesying (probably "singing"; see M. Buber, p. 63; E. J. Young, p. 70) to the sound of musical instruments (10:5, 10). Saul's prophesying was brought on by the Spirit of the Lord and resulted in his being "turned into another man" (v. 6). The direct connection between prophesying and Saul's unusual behavior (cf. 10:6; 18:10; 19:24) is capable of diverse explanations (see III.D below). The choice of *nāḇā'* to describe the "ravings," "prophesying," or "singing" of the prophets of Baal (1 K. 18:29) supports the view that strange behavior sometimes accompanied the expression of the prophetic gift in the ancient Near East; but these prophets' behavior on this occasion cannot be used as a key to determine a normative description of Israelite prophetic behavior.

*Nāḇā'* is frequently associated with speaking a message. Micaiah explained the false message spoken to Ahab by four hundred prophets as having come from a "lying spirit in the mouth of all [Ahab's] prophets" (1 K. 22:22f.) — a clear indication that prophesying meant giving a message. Amos likewise identified prophesying with giving the word of the Lord (Am. 3:8), and this emphasis occurs in the numerous uses of *nāḇā'* in Jeremiah and Ezekiel. Although "prophesying" could refer to the words of both true and false prophets, the false prophets were not sent by God, nor did He command them to speak (Jer. 14:14). Ezekiel repeatedly uses "prophesy" as a parallel to "say" (Ezk. 21:9, 28 [MT 14, 33]; 30:2; 36:3; 37:12; 38:14). In 1 Ch. 25 the verb is applied to the activity of the temple musicians who sang and played for the services in the temple. This use may be related to the "singing, prophesying" of the group of musicians met by Saul (1 S. 10:5). (Cf. also the association between prophesying and music making in Ex. 15:20f., which refers to Miriam as a *n^e^bî'â*, "prophetess," and describes how she led the women in singing, music making, and dancing.) A. Jepsen (pp. 5-11) and R. Rendtorff (*TDNT,* VI, 797-99) held that the hithpael forms of *nāḇā'* (mostly in earlier texts, but also of false prophecy in Jer. 14:14; 23:13) expressed ecstatic behavior while the niphal denoted the prophet's speech. But these tendencies do not occur with enough consistency to permit such a generalization.

The noun *nāḇî'* is the most common designation of a male prophet; the feminine form *n^e^ḇî'â* is sometimes used of a female prophet (e.g., Ex. 15:20; 2 K. 22:14; Neh. 6:14; Isa. 8:3; *see also* PROPHETESS). The plural *n^e^ḇî'îm* is used to describe groups of prophets, true and false prophets, or male and female prophets operating individually. Deborah, the Israelite judge, diviner, charismatic leader, and singer, is called a *n^e^ḇî'â* in Jgs. 4:4. The "sons of the prophets" (*b^e^nê-hann^e^ḇî'îm*) were primarily associated with Elisha (except in 1 K. 20:35). These prophets considered themselves servants of Elisha (2 K. 2:16; 4:1; 6:1-3; 9:1-4), and although some were married and had children (cf. 4:1), they seem to have lived together as a group some of the time (4:38-44; 6:1). Elisha taught them (2 K. 4:38), and they delivered messages that God gave him (9:1-4). At least one received a prophecy directly from God (1 K. 20:35). The function of these prophets — and that of the "bands of prophets" that existed two hundred years earlier in Samuel's time — is not very clear. Because so little is known about these prophetic groups, much hypothetical reconstruction has developed concerning the nature of their prophetic gifts (see III.D below).

The role of the *nāḇî'* is clarified in the relationship between Moses and Aaron. Because Moses refused to speak to Pharaoh, Yahweh appointed Aaron to be his *nāḇî'* (Ex. 6:28–7:2). Moses himself is called a *nāḇî'* because God spoke through him (cf. Nu. 12:1f., 6-8). The prophets were persons who spoke the words that God put in their mouths (Dt. 18:18-22); they were messengers (see C. Westermann, pp. 98-128) who reported God's words, often saying, "Thus says the Lord, the God of Israel" (Jgs. 6:8; 1 K. 11:29-31; 2 Ch. 34:23), or "Thus says the Lord" (2 S. 24:11f.; 1 K. 20:13; 2 K. 20:1; 2 Ch. 12:5; 21:12). Other texts speak of the word of the Lord coming to a prophet (1 K. 16:7, 12; 2 K. 14:25; 2 K. 24:2; 2 Ch. 29:25). The prophetic books record the oracles that God revealed to some of the prophets.

Some prophets wrote books (1 Ch. 29:29; 2 Ch. 9:29; 12:15; 13:22; 26:22; 32:32; Jer. 36:1-6), while others were counselors to kings (1 S. 22:5; 2 S. 24:11; 1 K. 1:8; 22:5-9; 2 K. 22:12-20; 2 Ch. 25:15f.; 32:20; 34:22-28; Jer. 37:17). God is said to have spoken His word to most of the prophets, but to some He gave dreams and visions (cf. Nu. 12:6; Dt. 13:1-5 [MT 2-6]; Ezk. 1; Jer. 23:25; Dnl. 7:1f.). The prophets delivered both positive and negative messages, and some (e.g., Ezekiel) used drama to make their message understood.

*C. Related Titles.* The prophet was not the only messenger or spokesman with a supernatural message, so it is important to distinguish between the prophet and those involved in related but distinct professions. Balaam was considered a diviner or "soothsayer" (Heb. *qôsēm,* Josh. 13:22) and was offered money for his "divination" (*qesem,* Nu. 22:7), which was intended to bring a curse on Israel. Although Balaam in the end did function as a prophet by speaking the words that God put in his mouth (Nu. 22:35, 38; 23:5, 16, 26), this was a supernatural transformation of his usual methods. His methods were probably similar to those of the diviners who advised the Philistines about how to rid themselves of the plague that came upon them after they captured the ark (1 S. 6:2f.). The prophets sometimes classified the false prophets of Israel as "diviners" (Jer. 27:9; 29:8; Ezk. 13:6-9, 23; Mic. 3:6f.; Zec. 10:2). These diviners did not speak God's words but prophesied lies in God's name (Jer. 29:8f.). They offered the message that the inquirer wanted to hear (Jer. 28:9; Ezk. 13:9f.) and used magical methods to achieve their ends (13:17-23). It is clear that many Israelites listened to the diviners and considered them true prophets.

Other groups include the "astrologers" (Aram. part. of *g^e^zar*) who served as advisors to King Nebuchadrezzar (Dnl. 2:27; 4:7 [MT 4]; 5:7, 11), as well as the "soothsayers" who advised the Israelites (Heb. poel part. of *'ānan,* Isa. 2:6; Mic. 5:12 [MT 11]; "sorceress" in Isa. 57:3). "Sorcerers" (piel part. of *kašāp*) were condemned (Ex. 22:18 [MT 17]; Dt. 18:10), but they were common in Israel (2 Ch. 33:6; Mic. 5:12; Mal. 3:5) as well as in Egypt (Ex. 7:11) and Babylon (Dnl. 2:2; Isa. 47:9, 12). The biblical text does not describe in detail the methods used by these and other false prophets, but it does make clear that they continued to be a threat to the nation and to the true prophets who spoke only the words of God (see II below).

*D. Distinctions and Relationships Among Titles.* Most scholars make no distinction between the *ḥōzeh* and *rō'eh* (both "seer"), but the continuity or contrast between the "prophet" (*nāḇî'*) and the "seer" is still a matter of great debate. G. Fohrer (*Intro. to the OT* [Eng. tr. 1968], p. 345) associated the seer with Israel's nomadic heritage and the prophet with Israel's traditions during their settlement in the land. O. S. Rankin (*RTWB,* p. 180) understood "seer" to be a broad title given to almost anyone who could understand signs, explain dreams, have visions, or give oracles; the distinctively ecstatic behavior of the prophets marked them off as a separate group. G. Hölscher (p. 125) and many who followed him emphasized the ecstatic nature of all prophets, both the early groups and the major writing prophets. This resulted in a strong distinction between the ecstatic prophets and the nonecstatic seers, who received their insight through visions, dreams, omens, and spirits. This hypothesis has been strongly criticized by scholars such as H. H. Rowley (*Servant of the Lord,* pp. 98-106) and A. Heschel (pp. 344-350) on several grounds: its interpretation of the classical prophets as ecstatics, its overdependence on etymological theories for the meanings of the terms, its insensitivity to biblical evidence identifying various persons as both *nāḇî'* and *rō'eh* (1 S. 9:9) or *ḥōzeh* (e.g., 2 S. 24:11; Isa. 29:10), its assumption of continuity between the heathen Canaanite ecstatic prophets and the Israelite prophets, and its undue reliance on psychological analysis that is not really accessible from present records. The complexity and dynamic development of the prophetic movement argue against any clearcut distinction between the inspiration and central function of the *nāḇî'* and that of the *rō'eh* or *ḥōzeh*. *Rō'eh* was a more popular title during the early history of Israel while *nāḇîʾ* became the preferred title at a later date (1 S. 9:9). "Seer" appears to be the usual title for certain court prophets (1 Ch. 21:9; 25:5; 29:29; 2 Ch. 9:29; 12:15; 19:2), but it is never used of the "sons of the prophets."

In the end, more insight into the prophetic movement is gained by examining the characteristics and functioning of the prophets than by analyzing their titles. The problem of interpreting the various titles is complicated by the later writers' (Kings, Chronicles) use of older, anachronistic texts as sources. Certain titles preserved through tradition remained firm (Nathan was a "prophet," not a "seer"; Samuel was a "seer") but at other times distinctions were blurred. Gad was called "the *nāḇîʾ* Gad, David's *ḥōzeh*" (2 S. 24:11; cf. 1 S. 22:5); Iddo usually had the title *ḥōzeh* (2 Ch. 9:29; 12:15), but *nāḇîʾ* is also used (13:22); and Jehu was described as both a *nāḇîʾ* (1 K. 16:7, 12) and a *ḥōzeh* (2 Ch. 19:2). During the early monarchy there may have been a distinction between a "prophet" and a "seer," but the nature of this difference is not clearly preserved in the canonical text.

***II. Prophets in the Ancient Near East.***–The biblical references to the "sorcerers" (*meḵaššᵉpîm*) of Egypt (Ex. 7:11) and Babylon (Dnl. 2:2), the "prophets" (*neḇîʾîm*) of Baal (1 K. 18:19), the "soothsayers" (*ʿōnᵉnîm*, Isa. 2:6) and "diviners" (*qōsᵉmîm*, 1 S. 6:2) of the Philistines, and the "medium" (*baʿᵃlaṯ-ʾôḇ*) from Endor (1 S. 28:7-9) signal the existence of individuals who fulfilled functions similar to those of some of Israel's prophets. Since Israel conquered, traded with, and had political relationships with surrounding nations, it is not surprising that these foreign counterparts had a major influence on Israel's false prophets and exerted tremendous pressure on its true prophets. Some have concluded that there was a direct relationship between all of Israel's prophets and their Canaanite counterparts (see G. Hölscher, p. 140), but others have maintained that a broad gulf existed between the method and message of these two very different classes of prophets (A. Heschel, p. 472). A comparative study of the evidence from each of Israel's neighbors reveals both significant differences and important similarities. The similarities explain why the Israelites were so easily led astray by false prophets, while the differences point to the uniqueness and importance of the true prophets who faithfully delivered God's messages.

*A. Egypt.* Center stage in the Egyptian religion was filled primarily by the pharaoh and the priests who served in the nation's many temples. The Egyptians did not distinguish between prophets and priests, but Egyptologists have traditionally identified the activities of certain priests with prophetic functions. The classes of Egyptian priests included the *ueʾb,* who were in charge of drink-offerings and the examination of animal sacrifices for purity; the *cherḥeb,* who recited magical liturgies at temple ceremonies; and the largest class, the *ḥemu neter* ("servants of the god"), who were in charge of the temples and who also gave oracles. The Greeks called the last class of priests "prophets"; although in most respects the term is inappropriate, its use continues in modern literature (see A. Erman, *Life in Ancient Egypt* [Eng. tr. 1894], p. 289).

The oracles given by the "servants of the god" were normally derived from the manipulation of objects or the interpretation of signs. For example, the nodding of the head of the statue of a god might indicate a positive answer to a request (*ANET,* p. 448). The interpretation of dreams was another important means of predicting the future. A dream including the observation of the moon meant that the gods would forgive the dreamer's sins (*ANET,* p. 495). Thutmose IV received a message in a dream that he was to clear the sand away from the sphinx (*ANET,* p. 449). Egyptian interest in dreams is reflected in the significance given to the dream of Pharaoh (Gen. 41) that the diviners (RSV "magician"; Heb. *ḥarṭôm*) could not interpret. These Egyptian divination practices and other magical arts described in the biblical text (Ex. 7:11f., 22; 8:7, 18f. [MT 3, 14f.]; cf. Gen. 44:5, 15) may have influenced the false prophets in Israel. Such practices were strictly forbidden by the Hebrew law and prophets (Lev. 19:26, 31; Dt. 18:10f.; 2 K. 17:17; 21:6; Jer. 27:9). (*See also* DIVINATION II, III.A.)

Only a few Egyptian literary texts come close to fitting the category of prophecy. In the story of "King Cheops and the Magician," the king's son tells his father about Dedi, an old man who seemed to have prophetic insight into the future. Dedi predicted the end of the king's dynasty, and at the end of the text this prediction is verified. This 12th-Dynasty text (Papyrus Westcar) is probably a legend to justify the increased power of the priesthood of Re at Heliopolis rather than a prophecy made in the 4th Dynasty (A. Erman, ed., *Ancient Egyptians* [Eng. tr. 1966], pp. 36-49).

A 20th-Dynasty copy (Leyden Papyrus) of the Middle Kingdom "Admonitions of Ipuwer" condemns Egyptian social conditions in terms reminiscent of the Hebrew prophets, e.g., "Robbery is everywhere. . . . many dead are buried in the river. . . . the desert is spread throughout the land" (*ANET,* p. 441). Ipuwer denounces the kings for permitting such lawlessness and looks forward to the reinstitution of justice and social order. This hope for the future has points of similarity with Hebrew prophetic expectations (justice, joy, an end to fighting, a ruler who cares for his people; see *LAP,* I, 89f.); but it differs in that the Hebrew prophets saw such social evils as rebellion against God and believed that their hope would be brought about through repentance and a divine intervention. There is no indication that Ipuwer's message was inspired by a god; most likely it was composed to praise a new king and criticize his predecessor.

The "Prophecy of Nefer-rohu" purports to tell how Pharaoh Snefru of the 4th Dynasty was entertained by a prophet who predicted that chaos would soon overtake Egypt, but that order and justice would be reestablished when Ameni of Nubia (a reference to Amen-em-hep I, the first king of the 12th Dynasty) became king (*ANET,* pp. 444-46). The so-called prophecy undoubtedly was written as political propaganda to support the rule of Amen-em-hep I (see W. K. Simpson, ed., *Literature of Ancient Egypt* [1973], pp. 234-240). The "Divine Nomination of an Ethiopian King" (*ANET,* pp. 447f.) and the "Prophecy of the Lamb" follow a similar pattern. One text predicts social upheaval followed by a time of peace and stability, and in the other a new king is appointed. Both texts probably functioned as propaganda to support a new king's rise to power (L. Kakosy, *Acta Orientalia,* 19 [1966], 334-356). The late Ptolemaic period produced the "Oracle of the Potter," the "Demotic Chronicle," and other texts that follow the same pattern (C. McCown, *HTR,* 18 [1925], 357-411). All these examples appear to have been created primarily to solidify the power of the pharaoh and to maintain traditional social values. Since only a few texts even claim to be messages from the gods, it appears that divination was the most popular means by which the Egyptians obtained knowledge of the future. These features stand in strong contrast to the Hebrew prophets' frequent condemnation of the contemporary king and their claim to direct revelation from God.

The biblical text (Gen. 41:25, 28, 32, 39) presents Pharaoh's dream as a revelation that God had spoken to him. When Pharaoh Neco marched to Carchemish, he claimed that God had ordered him to go to war (2 Ch. 35:20f.); and the Chronicler confirms that God was the source of the message (v. 22). In these instances God spoke directly to the pharaoh without using a prophet or priestly intermediary.

Although some scholars (e.g., H. Gressman, *JTS,* 27 [1925/26], 241-254) have observed parallels between Egyptian and Israelite prophecy, and J. H. Breasted (*Dawn of Conscience* [1933], p. 336) attempted to derive Hebrew messianic expectations from Egypt, there is little evidence for significant Egyptian influence on Israelite prophecy. Although the prophets accused the Israelites of playing the harlot with Egypt (Ezk. 16:26; 23:19), of defiling themselves with the idols of Egypt (20:7f.), and of depending on the military strength of Egypt (Hos. 7:11), there is no sign of prophetic interdependence unless it is in the divination methods used by the false prophets. Similarities of vocabulary in descriptions of chaotic times and of future times of peace are a testimony to the common hopes for security that all people share.

*B. Canaan and Syria.* Evidence for Canaanite prophetic activity comes from several archeological texts and from the biblical condemnations of Canaanite prophets.

The Egyptian story of "The Journey of Wen-Amon to Phoenicia" (*ANET,* pp. 26-29) contains one of the earliest (1100 B.C.) references to prophetic activity on Canaanite soil. During Wen-Amon's stay in Byblos, where he had journeyed to obtain lumber for the construction of a barge for the god Amon-Re, Zakar-Baal king of Byblos offered a sacrifice to his gods; but during the ceremony the Egyptian god Amon seized control of a young boy and spoke to the king through the boy. This story — an Egyptian story about a Canaanite boy seized by an Egyptian god at a Canaanite temple — may reveal very little about Canaanite prophecy; on the other hand, the frenzy that the boy experienced may in some way be related to the behavior of the prophets of Baal described in 1 K. 18.

An Aramaic inscription of Zakir king of Hamath from the 8th or 9th cent. B.C. (*ANET,* pp. 655f.) describes how the king prayed to Beʿelshamayn and was answered through "seers" and "prophets." The message was that the god would save the king from attack by a Syrian coalition. The term for "seer," Aram. *ḥzyn,* comes from the same root as Heb. *ḥōzeh* ("seer"). The term translated "prophet" (Aram. *ʿddn*) may mean "answer, give a message," or it may bear some relationship to the family line of Iddo the Israelite seer (2 Ch. 12:15; Zec. 1:1; see J. F. Ross, *HTR,* 63 [1970], 1-28).

The Deir ʿallā inscription, although poorly preserved, can be reconstructed to refer to Balaam the son of Beor, a "seer" (Aram. *ḥzn*) of the gods (A. Coquot and A. Lemair, *Syria,* 54 [1977], 193-202). The general tenor of this text agrees with the biblical story of Balaam (Nu. 22–24), but the text's fragmentary nature does not allow for a complete understanding of this seer's functions.

In his inscription, Idrimi of Alalakh reports that during his exile in Emar he used divination through the interpretation of the flight of birds and the inspection of the entrails of lambs (*ANET,* pp. 557f.). Present evidence is insufficient to verify the existence of prophets at Ugarit (A. van Selms, *Ugarit-Forschungen,* 3 [1971], 235-248), but from Ebla comes evidence of *nabiʾūtum*, a class of prophets (G. Pettinato, *BA*, 39 [1976], 49).

The strongest Palestinian influence on Israelite prophecy was apparently the worship of Baal. The praying, dancing, and self-mutilation of the prophets of Baal and Asherah are well-known from the Mt. Carmel contest (1 K. 18), but the biblical text does not present a full explanation of their responsibilities and prophetic role. Jeremiah specifically refers to the prophets of Baal prophesying by Baal (Jer. 2:8; 23:13) but does not indicate the content of their prophecies. Severely injured in a fall, Ahaziah sent to Ekron to inquire of Baal-zebub concerning the possibility of his recovery; but it is not known whether he expected an answer through a prophet of Baal (2 K. 1:2-6, 16). When the Philistines suffered a plague after capturing the ark of God, they approached only the priests (of Dagon) and diviners for advice (1 S. 6:2).

The Balaam oracles in Nu. 22–24 include a mixture of divination and true prophetic activity. Balaam was known to the Moabites and Israelites as a "soothsayer" (*qôsēm,* Josh. 13:22) who could pronounce curses for a fee. He used omens and the sacrifice of animals on a high place of Baal (Nu. 22:7f., 40–23:5, 23, 28–24:1), but in spite of these divination rituals God put His words in Balaam's mouth (22:20, 25; 23:5, 12, 16, 26; 24:13). His message was called an "oracle of him who hears the words of God, who sees the vision of the Almighty" (Nu. 24:4; cf. v. 16); thus his vocabulary and source of information were identical to those of the Hebrew prophets.

In contrast to the meager evidence for parallels between Israelite and Egyptian prophetic activity, the Canaanite and Syrian prophets present many similarities to Israelite prophets. Unlike their Egyptian counterparts (who were actually priests), the Canaanite and Syrian prophets are sometimes called *nᵉḇîʾîm* in the OT, and corresponding titles are used in their own literature. They saw themselves as messengers of the gods, used vocabulary that is often identical to that of the Hebrew prophets, and sometimes deceived the Israelites by their messages. Many Israelite prophets were negatively influenced by Canaanite prophets; but the rejection of the religious practices of the surrounding nation by the Hebrew law and prophets prevented these practices from becoming a normative part of Hebrew prophetic tradition (Lev. 18:3, 24-30; 20:23; Dt. 12:30f.; 13:1-5 [MT 2-6]; 18:9-15; Ezk. 11:12).

G. Hölscher held that the ecstatic characteristics of Israelite prophecy (which he viewed as its essential ingredient) were borrowed from Canaanite neighbors in Syria and Asia Minor because he found no evidence of ecstatic experience in Assyria or Babylon. Following Hölscher, A. Jepsen proposed that a group of ecstatic prophets arose in Israel under Canaanite influence because the temple personnel had limited the oracular use of the ephod to themselves. T. J. Meek and H. Knight adopted similar positions. The discovery of the Mari Letters, however, has shown that Mesopotamian "prophets" had much in common with Israelite prophets, including ecstatic experience of a less uncontrolled type than that found in Canaan. Thus Hölscher's position that Israelite prophecy was borrowed from a Canaanite source is seriously undermined.

*C. Mesopotamia.* The Mesopotamian scribal practice of recording all types of omens and signs has enabled archeologists to recover a sizable quantity of tablets that explain how the Mesopotamian diviners and prophets from the Old Babylonian period (1894-1595 B.C.) made their predictions. Three groups of over a hundred tablets each, known as the *šumma ālu, šumma izbu,* and the *enūma Anu Enlil,* record omens explaining the significance of the actions of animals and humans and the meaning of malformed births (R. R. Wilson, pp. 91-97). The will of the gods could also be learned by interpreting the design of oil drops on water, the patterns of rising smoke from an incense burner, the arrangement of the entrails of animals, the movement and interrelationship of the stars (E. Reiner, *Babylonian Planetary Omens* [1975]), and dreams (A. L. Oppenheim, *Interpretation of Dreams in the Ancient Near*

*East* [1956]). These divination rituals, which were the common method of communicating with the divine powers in the world, were performed by the *bārû* priests. The *bārû* ("the one who sees") priest inquired of the gods and asked them to write their answer on the oil, the smoke, or the entrails of an animal so that the message could be understood and communicated by the priest. These diviners gave the king advice on the affairs of state and particularly on matters of military significance.

The excavation of Mari (Tell el-Ḥarîrī) resulted in the discovery of about twenty-eight "prophetic letters" in the palace of the Amorite dynasty (18th cent. B.C.). The early texts, published before 1967, are concerned primarily with the king's responsibility toward certain temples; but texts published later are concerned with the impending threat of defeat by Hammurabi king of Babylon (*ANET,* pp. 623-632). The "prophets" who speak in the Mari Letters include both men and women who claim to have received a divine message from Adad or Dagon; frequently they quote what the god said. In some instances their messages were public, but many appear to have been private communications. Professional "prophets," as well as laymen who had no cultic function, received divine messages instructing the king about what he should do, warning him of imminent doom, and promising blessing if he performed the will of the gods (H. B. Huffmon, "Prophecy in the Mari Letters," in E. F. Campbell and D. N. Freedman, eds., *Biblical Archaeologist Reader,* III [1970], 199-223).

Among the oracular speakers in the Mari Letters are the *āpilu* (or *āpiltu*), "the one who answers." While the etymology suggests that the *āpilu* gave answers to questions asked of the gods, there is no evidence that they functioned in this way. Some letters relate to a cultic context, but the *āpilu* do not appear to have been temple officials. Several came from outside Mari (Aleppo, Sippar), and their concern was primarily to obtain the king's support for their own local temples or to speak a judgment against a foe of the king. These oracles against foreign nations function as an assurance of salvation for the king of Mari in a setting somewhat similar to that found in the OT.

Three Mari texts refer to *assinnu,* temple personnel who danced, sang, and sometimes played the role of the opposite sex during festivals (it is unlikely that they were homosexuals or cult prostitutes). The Era Epic and texts much later than those from Mari connect the *assinnu* with the worship of Ishtar (Annunitum). Their oracles related to the security of the king of Mari.

A third group was the *muḫḫû* (*muḫḫūtu*), who are frequently interpreted to have been ecstatics. The coherent messages that the *muḫḫû* spoke in their trances cannot be reconciled with the view that they were some sort of delirious frenzied mantics (W. L. Moran, *Bibl.,* 50 [1969], 27). The *muḫḫû* were peripheral temple officials in the cult of Ishtar in Mari or were related to Dagon temples outside Mari. Their oracles dealt primarily with gaining the favor of the king.

Thirteen of the "prophetic letters" do not identify the speaker of the oracle. Many of these were private citizens (eight were women, others servants) who received visions or dreams concerned with a personal request for the king's blessing. A few of the letters relate to battle plans and the building of temples. To test and control spontaneous "prophetic" pronouncements, particularly those made in public, divination on the hair and the fringe of a garment was required of all except persons of established social status.

C. Westermann (pp. 115-128) called attention to the similarities between the messenger function of the Mari and Israelite prophets. F. Ellermeier (*Prophetie in Mari und Israel* [1968], pp. 190-93) criticized Westermann's messenger interpretation by pointing out that many Mari texts do not explicitly state that a god sent the prophet. Nevertheless, the prophets of Mari, like those of Israel (cf. Ex. 7:16; Isa. 6:8; Jer. 26:12), frequently claimed that a god had sent them and began their oracles with words such as "This is what Shamash said," or "Dagon spoke to me saying." In both settings the affairs of the king and state policy were a subject of oracles, and both nations had professional prophets, temple personnel, and private individuals who spoke the word of a god. M. Noth (*Laws in the Pentateuch* [1966], pp. 185-88) concluded that the Mari prophets were actually part of the prehistory of Israelite prophecy, and A. Haldar (pp. 108-126) identified the "seer" with the *bārû* and the prophet with the *muḫḫû*. According to this view, the primary difference between the prophets of the two nations lay in the content of their messages. The Israelite prophets' demands for ethical responsibility and theological purity were totally foreign to the prophetic messages in the Mari Letters. Westermann held that one distinction between these groups was that the Mari texts, unlike the Hebrew prophecies, had no unconditional statements of blessing or judgment. This conclusion must now be tempered by the absolute statement, "I shall put an end to his city" (*ANET,* p. 632), which has been found in a more recently translated text (see J. F. Craghan, *Biblical Theology Bulletin,* 5 [1975], 46).

During the Neo-Assyrian period of Esarhaddon (680-669 B.C.) and Ashurbanipal (668-633 B.C.), certain past forms of divination and "prophecy" continued while new prophetlike individuals were introduced (*ANET,* pp. 605-607). Inscriptions refer to the *maḫḫû* who gave omens, dreams, and positive oracles to both these kings. J. R. Kupper (*ARM,* III, 116) identified the *maḫḫû* with the earlier *muḫḫû,* but A. Malamat ("Prophetic Revelations in New Documents from Mari and the Bible," in *SVT,* 15 [1966], 210) distinguished between these groups. The *maḫḫû* of the Neo-Assyrian period appear to have been more influential both in the royal court and in the temple worship than were the *muḫḫû* at Mari.

New figures included the *raggintû,* women who delivered divine messages for the goddess Ishtar or Ninlil, the *šabrû* (probably closely related to the *bārû*-priest), who in a dream received a vision from Ishtar of Arbela instructing Ashurbanipal about military matters (A. Haldar, pp. 17-21; *ANET,* p. 606), and the *šēlūtu,* women who had a cultic function but also received oracles from Ishtar of Arbela giving assurances to Esarhaddon (*ANET,* p. 605).

The title "prophecies" has sometimes been applied to a group of Akkadian texts that were not given orally, including the Marduk, Shulgi, Uruk, and Dynastic apocalypses (W. W. Hallo, *IEJ,* 16 [1966], 231-242). These texts "predict" the appearance of a new king much like several of the Egyptian prophecies. They were likely produced "after the fact" as propaganda to support the political and religious policies of a new monarch (R. R. Wilson, pp. 119-123).

This survey has pointed out several parallels between the prophetic activity of Israel and that of its neighbors. These parallels have led some scholars to interpret Israelite prophecy as heavily dependent on the influence of Egyptian, Canaanite, or Mesopotamian prophecy. Both Israelite and non-Israelite prophets were messengers of the gods, spoke to political and social issues of their day, used many similar terms and concepts (see A. Malamat, "A Mari Prophecy and Nathan's Dynastic Oracle," in J. A. Emerton, ed., *Prophecy* [*Festschrift* G. Fohrer; *BZAW,* 150, 1980], pp. 68-82), and performed many comparable functions. But despite the general similarities, an investigation into details makes apparent the vast gulf between Israelite and non-Israelite prophecy. In contrast to foreign prophecies, divination was not the approved method of prophetic communication in Israel, and the prophets' function was not focused on preserving or supporting cultic or royal institutions. Foreign prophecies did not use God's holiness and justice as their criteria for measuring society; nor was Israel's privileged covenant relationship with God paralleled in other nations.

***III. The Prophet's Connection with Israel's Culture.***– The Israelites who received and delivered the prophetic word of God functioned in a variety of social contexts. Some were priests as well as prophets; others appeared before the royal court and gave advice to the king but had no official responsibilities in the temple. A few wrote structured literary pieces in magnificent style, while others seemed to behave like madmen with no self-control. Even the messages of the prophets varied tremendously; one argued on the basis of the covenant and the law, while another ignored these and spoke in language much closer to wisdom literature. The variety of prophetic roles within Israel's culture has complicated attempts to fit the prophets into any category that would limit their activity to one institution, method, or message.

*A. Temple Worship.* In the late 19th and early 20th cents. it was commonly held that the prophets acted in direct opposition to the priests (see J. A. Bewer, *Literature of the OT in Its Historical Development* [1922], p. 267). J. Wellhausen (p. 423) used this basic antithesis between the moral teachings of the prophets and the ritual of the priests as a major key for interpreting the evolutionary development of Israel's religion. This view was widely accepted on the basis of several prophets' criticisms of Israelite temple worship (cf. Am. 5:21-25; Isa. 1:10-15; Hos. 6:6; Mic. 6:6-8; 1 S. 15:22; Jer. 6:20; 7:22f.). Nevertheless, this interpretation has undergone considerable criticism and modification. Various scholars have demonstrated that the prophets were not primarily against the sacrificial system or the priests; rather they opposed a false reliance on ritual that was devoid of any concern for moral or spiritual vitality (see C. F. Whitely, pp. 65-67; H. H. Rowley, *From Moses to Qumran* [1963], pp. 116f.). Isaiah condemned those who came to sacrifice with "their hands full of blood" (Isa. 1:15), and Jeremiah demanded that the worshipers at the temple "amend their ways" (Jer. 7:5). The prophets opposed the cult because it no longer represented the ethical nature of true worship required by God. Sacrificial ritual had replaced the fear of God; ignorant ceremonialism had obscured a true knowledge of Yahweh (see R. E. Clements, *Prophecy and Covenant*, pp. 93-102). The prophets did not call for the abolition of the temple worship, nor did they claim to be creating a new system of spiritual values. Instead they called their people back to the traditions upon which the cultic practices were based — traditions that God had instituted early in the nation's history.

Later studies of the relationship of the prophets to temple worship and personnel have reversed the earlier trends, and some scholars have attempted to tie the prophets directly to the temple staff. This movement was initiated by G. Hölscher, who concluded that the early bands of prophets (1 S. 10:5-12) were part of the cultic staff at the high places (p. 143). S. Mowinckel introduced the idea that the classical writing prophets were also part of the temple personnel (*Psalmenstudien III: Die Kultprophetie und prophetische Psalmen* [1923]). He based this conclusion on the theory that the first-person speeches by Yahweh in several Psalms (e.g., Pss. 82, 110) were divine answers — given by a cultic official who had the gift of prophecy — to requests made in the temple worship. Mowinckel's theory was derived in part from his comparative analysis of the role of the "prophets" in Mesopotamia and Greece. A. R. Johnson agreed with Mowinckel's position on the prophet's role as a spokesman for God within the temple. He constructed the following history of the temple prophets: first they were criticized by the writing prophets for misuse of sacrifices; later they were downgraded to temple singers because they had misled the people to believe that Jerusalem was secure from Babylonian attack (pp. 60-75).

The OT evidence that was marshalled to support this general view of the cultic prophets included the following events: Samuel received the word of Yahweh at the tabernacle at Shiloh (1 S. 3:1-14, 19-21); he officiated at a meal at a high place at Ramah (9:6-24); the company of prophets came from a high place of worship (10:5); Nathan was consulted about building the temple (2 S. 7:4-17); God advised David to build an altar at the threshing floor of Araunah (24:18-25); Elijah offered sacrifices on Mt. Carmel (1 K. 18:25-40); Amos prophesied at the altar at Bethel (Am. 7:10-17); and Jeremiah preached in the temple (Jer. 7; 26). Additional evidence was derived from passages that mention the prophets and priests together (2 K. 23:2; Isa. 28:7; Jer. 2:26; 5:31; 8:10; 13:13; 23:11; Lam. 2:20), that refer to the prophets as having rooms in the temple (Jer. 35:4), and that imply a custom of consulting a prophet on the sabbath (2 K. 4:23).

Supporting and building upon these conclusions, A. Haldar (p. 124) equated the Mesopotamian *bārû* diviner-priests with the Israelite seers, and the *muḫḫû* ecstatic oracular speakers with the Hebrew prophets. This extreme position was supported from biblical passages indicating that the prophets used divination (Mic. 3:11; Jer. 14:14; Ezk. 13:9). But other scholars have recognized that these texts deny rather than confirm Haldar's position, for they condemn the false prophets for the use of divination. Haldar's theory actually reduced all prophets to the status of diviners, and even Mowinckel rejected Haldar's attempt to force Israelite prophecy into the mold of Mesopotamian categories. A more common approach that avoided Haldar's excesses was to draw a sharp distinction between the classical writing prophets and the popular bands of prophets who were classified as cultic prophets (see A. Neher, p. 206). Unfortunately, this simple division was an oversimplification of the complex prophetic movement. Another solution was to connect the false prophets with the cultic prophets and to divorce the true prophets from the temple worship (see J. Jocz, *Spiritual History of Israel* [1961], p. 69). But if this were the criterion for defining false prophets, it is surprising that Deuteronomy, Kings, and Ezekiel never mention it as the key factor. Micaiah claimed that the false prophets were misled by a lying spirit sent from God (1 K. 22:19-23), and Jeremiah concluded that they spoke out of their own imagination (Jer. 23); neither points to an illegitimate connection to the cult (*see* PROPHECY, FALSE).

It is clear from the OT that some prophets were present at temple events, but this does not mean that they had responsibilities within the system of temple worship. Samuel exercised the priestly function of sacrificing because he was a priest as well as a prophet, but Amos's negative prophecy at Bethel does not imply that he was a temple official. Isaiah was called while he was at the temple (Isa. 6:1-6), and Jeremiah prophesied the destruction of the nation at the temple (Jer. 7; 26), but there is no evidence that either belonged to the temple staff. Josiah sent Hilkiah the priest to consult Huldah (2 K. 22:14-20), but as Lindblom (p. 210) noted, she was apparently independent of the temple. G. Reventlow's conclusions about the cultic associations within Jeremiah seem to go far beyond the textual support (*Liturgie und prophetisches Ich bei Jeremia* [1963], pp. 24-77). Jeremiah's reference to the quarters for the prophets in the temple (Jer. 35:4) does not mean that they were cultic prophets, for similar quarters were provided for the princes, who clearly were not temple personnel.

Some scholars have concluded that there were no cultic prophets in Israel (B. D. Eerdmans, *Religion of Israel* [1947], p. 141; L. J. Wood, *Prophets of Israel* [1979], p. 78). This position ignores the fact that the temple singers were appointed by David to prophesy by singing (1 Ch. 25:1-5; 2 Ch. 35:15) and that Jahaziel, a Levite, prophesied at the temple in answer to Jehoshaphat's prayer (2 Ch. 20:14-17). Since the superscriptions to certain OT Psalms ascribe their composition to Asaph, Jeduthun, or Heman (cf. Pss. 50, 39, 62, 73–83, 88), it is difficult to deny some prophetic activity in the temple. Heman is called "the king's seer" (1 Ch. 25:5), and Jeduthun (or all three singers, if the plural of the LXX is accepted) is also called a "seer" (2 Ch. 35:15). The Chronicler also substituted "Levites" (34:30) for the "prophets" (2 K. 23:2) who participated in Josiah's reform. D. L. Petersen (pp. 55-87) demonstrated the importance of the Levitical prophets in Chronicles; he concluded that the Chronicler had depicted the Levitical singers of the monarchic period as prophets in order to enhance the position of the Levitical singers in the second temple period. H. H. Rowley suggested that the earlier temple prophets had been reduced in status to the rank of Levitical singers in the exilic era (*Worship in Ancient Israel* [1967], p. 174). But if the Chronicler's report that David instituted the Levitical singers (1 Ch. 15:1-22; 25:1-6; 2 Ch. 29:25-28) is historically accurate, then they could hardly be identical to a late group of demoted cultic prophets. It is probably best to understand cultic prophecy by temple officials as having been limited to the temple singers who functioned throughout the temple era. Since the band of prophets that came down from the high place (1 S. 10:5) were playing music and prophesying (probably singing praises to God), it is possible that these early prophets performed the duties of the Levitical singers before the time of David.

A related issue is the question of whether certain OT books were used as temple liturgies. Some scholars (Balla, Eaton, Hentschke, Humbert, Mowinckel, and Lindblom) have proposed that Habakkuk was used in temple ceremonies. Similar claims have been made for Joel (Engnell, Kapelrud, and Mowinckel), for Nahum (Eaton, Hentschke, Humbert, and Mowinckel); and for Zephaniah (Eaton and Gerlemann); see H. H. Rowley, *From Moses to Qumran* (1963), pp. 132-38. Others connect Obadiah, Isa. 24–27, Malachi, and other prophetic texts to temple ceremonies. The passages frequently show a close connection with the Psalms, and some may have been modeled after these earlier compositions. It is methodologically unsound, however, to conclude that all similar forms have identical cultic functions. It appears unlikely that many of these books were ever used as liturgies in the temple for enthronement festivals or other covenant renewal ceremonies.

*B. The Monarchy.* Although some prophets delivered their messages in the temple, others spent far more time delivering God's word to the kings of Israel. Traditionally, scholars have given the negative prophetic statements about kings a major role in defining the relationship between prophets and kings. Much significance has been attached to the "antimonarchial" texts that describe Samuel's opposition to Saul's kingship (cf. 1 S. 8; 10:17-27; 11:12-14). The conflict between the positive and negative attitudes displayed in the text has often been resolved either by assigning an early date to the positive texts and a late date to the negative texts (Wellhausen, p. 245), or by subsuming Samuel's grudging acceptance of the monarchy under his predominantly negative attitude. An antagonistic relationship between prophets and the monarchy is evident throughout the nation's history: the very request for a king displeased Samuel (1 S. 8:6); Nathan judged David for his sin against Uriah and Bathsheba (2 S. 12:1-14); Ahijah announced that the kingdom would be torn from Solomon (1 K. 11:29-39) and from Jeroboam (14:5-16); Jehu prophesied the fall of Baasha's reign (16:1-4); Jezebel killed the prophets of God (18:4; 19:2); Elijah predicted the end of Ahab's rule (21:17-24); Micaiah was hated by Ahab (22:8, 17f.); Amos foretold the approaching end of Jeroboam II (Am. 7:10-17); Hosea spoke out against kings (Hos. 1:4f.; 7:16; 8:4); Isaiah announced God's judgment on Ahaz (Isa. 7:10, 17), the king of Assyria (10:12), the king of Babylon (14:4-23), and Hezekiah (39:5-7); and Jeremiah predicted God's judgment on Zedekiah (Jer. 21:3-7; 27:12-15; 32:1-5; 34:1-5) and Jehoiakim (22:18-23; 36:10-23, 27-31). From this sampling it is clear that the prophets had much to do with kings, but that this association was often antagonistic. The royal court does not appear to have been the social location or the home of most of the prophets.

Comparative studies of the social setting of the prophets in other nations have led some scholars to reevaluate the prophets' relationship to the royal court. A. Haldar observed that in Mesopotamia the sacred king was the leader of an association of court prophets, and he hypothesized a similarly close relationship between the Israelite prophets and kings (pp. 51, 74, 137-140). Comparisons have also been made between Israelite prophecy and the Mari prophecies, which were addressed to kings. W. Holladay showed how the manner of speaking used by royal messengers in the king's court influenced both Israelite and non-Israelite prophets (*HTR,* 63 [1970], 31), while K. Baltzer argued that the Hebrew prophets' relationships to their kings was analogous to the relationship between the Egyptian vizier and the pharaoh (*HTR,* 61 [1968], 574). H. B. Huffmon theorized that the role of the judge in premonarchial Israel was redistributed into the roles of the prophet, the charismatic leader, and the king, the leader of the army ("The Origins of Prophecy," in F. M. Cross, *et al.,* eds., *Magnalia Dei: The Mighty Acts of God* [*Festschrift* G. E. Wright; 1976], p. 178); thus the roles of prophet and king were closely related from the beginning. D. L. Petersen (pp. 2f.) followed the views of F. M. Cross (*Journal for Theology and the Church,* 6 [1969], 157-165) and P. Hanson (pp. 17f.), who concluded that prophecy emerged as an office with the rise of the monarchy and ended with the final removal of the Davidic house from the throne. The locus of classical prophecy was thus tied directly to the political institution of the monarchy. Within this political-religious setting the prophets had a dual role: to be a messenger for God and a messenger for the king.

Biblical evidence that has been cited as support for placing Hebrew prophets within the royal court includes the following: the prophet Samuel anointed Saul (1 S. 10:1) and proclaimed him king (v. 24; 11:14f.); Elijah anointed Jehu and Hazael (1 K. 19:15f.); Nathan confirmed God's choice of the Davidic dynasty (2 S. 7:1-17) and anointed Solomon (1 K. 1:32-34); Gad and Heman were described as King David's seers (2 S. 24:11; 1 Ch. 21:9; 25:5; 2 Ch. 29:25), and Asaph prophesied "under the direction of the king" (1 Ch. 25:2). Some believe that the four hundred prophets of Ahab were court prophets (1 K. 22:6). Furthermore, the messianic prophecies of a future king from the line of David presuppose a positive attitude toward kingship (Jer. 23:5f.; 33:14-16; Ezk. 37:15-28). In fact, even the negative prophecies against evil kings demonstrate the close association between the prophets and the kings.

Although these more recent studies have drawn attention to one of the significant roles of the prophets, the proposed reconstruction of Israelite prophecy on the basis of comparative evidence is not totally acceptable. The Mari correspondence, e.g., does not show as close a relationship between prophets and kings as has been claimed, for only one text was written by a court prophet. Most of the Mari prophecies dealing with political-religious affairs came from individuals who were not members of the royal court.

The biblical evidence points to a more complex relationship between Israelite prophets and kings. The Israelite prophets primarily represented the sovereign rule of Yahweh rather than the authority of an earthly king (see G. Mendenhall, *Tenth Generation* [1973], pp. 70, 87). The establishment of a sovereign state with its earthly king threatened the concept of the kingship of Yahweh, the true judge, warrior, and ruler of the nation (G. V. Smith, *Trinity Journal,* 3 [1982], 18-38). The conflict within the pro- and antimonarchial texts in Samuel recall the divergent ideological streams within the nation at that time (T. Ishida, *Royal Dynasties in Ancient Israel* [1977], pp. 26-54). The recognition of Yahweh's rule — which was the interest of the prophets — limited the earthly king's power by requiring that he be chosen and anointed by God through a prophet, by granting dynastic appointment on the basis of obedience, and by regulating the king's military efforts through divine oracles.

When the earthly king operated within the divine will, the prophet functioned as an intercessor or as a messenger of God to the king. The Davidic prophets and record keepers, Nathan and Gad, fall into the category of true court prophets (1 Ch. 9:29); Iddo, Shemaiah (2 Ch. 12:15), Hanani (16:7), and Jehu (19:2) may have been of the same type. But direct textual evidence for a social setting in the royal court is lacking for most of the classical prophets. Isaiah went to the Upper Pool to speak to Ahaz (Isa. 7:3), Elijah and Elisha spent most of their time traveling all over the nation, and Josiah sent messengers to consult Huldah at her home (2 K. 22:12-14 par. 2 Ch. 34:20-22). Kings who desired to know God's will often went to visit the prophets (cf. 2 K. 3:11f.), summoned prophets to appear before them at the royal court (cf. 1 K. 22:6-9), or used messengers to carry messages between them and the prophets (cf. 2 K. 19:2, 20). Prophets frequently spoke at public meetings or to individuals without having any direct association with the king's court. W. Brueggemann (pp. 28-43) has demonstrated how radically the prophets reacted against the imperial economic and political oppression initiated by Solomon. The prophets pointed out the despair within the monarchial system and energized the people's imagination concerning God's message of hope and freedom for mankind. The message was primarily directed to the people of the nation, but it included strong criticism of the monarchy. The variety of settings in which the prophets functioned indicates the complexity of the prophets' relationship to the monarchy. Although David and a few other kings used court prophets to guide them in submission to God's kingship, most prophets cannot be classified as court prophets.

*C. Wisdom.* Prior to 1950 little significance was placed on the relationship between wisdom and the prophets. Some thematic continuity was recognized; but since wisdom literature was dated to the postexilic period, it was assumed that the teachings of the prophets were used by the wisdom writers (see W. O. E. Oesterley, *Book of Proverbs* [*WC,* 1929], p. lxi). Although O. S. Rankin (*Israel's Wisdom Literature* [1936]) had earlier maintained that wisdom influenced the prophets, the archeological discoveries of new wisdom texts and the pivotal study of J. Lindblom ("Wisdom in the OT Prophets," in M. Noth and D. W. Thomas, eds., *Wisdom in Israel and in the Ancient Near East* [*SVT,* 3; 1955], pp. 192-204) introduced a new understanding of the relationship between prophecy and wisdom.

The publication of Mesopotamian and Egyptian wisdom texts prompted a spate of comparative studies. The biblical text itself made the comparative judgment that Solomon's wisdom surpassed that of all the peoples in the East and all of Egypt (1 K. 4:30 [MT 5:10]; cf. 5:12 [MT 26]; 10:1-24). Scholars gave special attention to several parallels between Egyptian and Israelite wisdom literature: the similarity of Egyp. *maʿat* ("order, justice") to God's justice and order described in Proverbs, nearly identical wisdom metaphors about gods and human beings, similarities between the sayings of Amenemope and Prov. 22–24, and a multitude of less exact comparisons (see E. Würthwein, "Egyptian Wisdom and the OT," in J. Crenshaw, ed., *Studies in Israelite Wisdom* [1976], pp. 113-133). Since Solomon had friendly relations with the Egyptian royalty (cf. 1 K. 3:1), Egyptian educational and administrative practices were viewed as a likely source of wisdom contact with Israel. The sophisticated language of many Hebrew sayings, the positive statements about the monarchy, and the identification of some collections of proverbs with royal figures all supported the position that Hebrew wisdom literature was the product of a royal "Wisdom School" in Jerusalem that was designed to train scribes and officials to administer the empire.

Against this background, Lindblom proposed that Israel's prophets as well as its sages were aware of foreign wisdom writings. He found little evidence of wisdom in the prophets except in Jeremiah, which uses various literary forms (parable, proverbs, similes, metaphors) common in wisdom texts. J. Fichtner ("Isaiah Among the Wise," in J. Crenshaw, ed., *Studies in Israelite Wisdom,* pp. 429-438) observed that wisdom and prophecy shared the same positive admonitions for righteous living, had similar condemnations of disrespect for elders and the use of false weights, were both critical of the cult, and used similar literary styles of expression. Fichtner did not find wisdom material in pre-Isaiah books, but he pointed out numerous examples of proverbial wisdom in Habakkuk, Jeremiah, and particularly Isaiah. He pointed to Isaiah's use of metaphors (5:1; 28:23), proverbs (1:3; 7:22; 10:15), phrases like "wise in his own eyes" (5:21), and sayings about fools (28:8). He called attention to Isaiah's concern for the poor (11:4) and to the fact that Hezekiah's scribes (cf. Prov. 25–29) collected proverbs during Isaiah's lifetime. He also identified a strong conflict between the prophets and the secular wisdom of the political courtiers who claimed to be wise themselves (e.g., Isa. 5:21; 29:14) instead of recognizing God as the source of true wisdom (cf. 28:29; 31:2). J. W. Whedbee (*Isaiah and Wisdom* [1971]) expanded Fichtner's analysis of Isaiah's use of wisdom forms of speech, and S. Terrien ("Amos and Wisdom," in B. W. Anderson and W. Harrelson, eds., *Israel's Prophetic Heritage,* pp. 108-115) made a similar study of Amos's use of numerical sayings (1:3, 6, 9, 11, 13), rhetorical questions (5:25; 6:2, 12), cause-and-effect sequences (3:3-8), and vocabulary associated with wisdom literature.

Fichtner's insight into the conflict between secular wisdom and prophecy was developed by W. McKane, who drew a sharp distinction between the early wisdom of the royal court officials who were primarily concerned with political affairs and the ethical wisdom taught by the prophets. He saw a fundamental conflict between the word of God that the prophets received and the secular anthropocentric insight of the nation's politicians. He argued that the prophets used wisdom vocabulary and style to denounce secular wisdom. R. E. Clements (*Prophecy and Tradition,* pp. 75f.), on the other hand, rejected McKane's denial of an ethical base to Israel's wisdom tradition and opposed his claim that wisdom and prophecy were necessarily conflicting institutions.

H. W. Wolff concluded from his study of wisdom in Amos and Micah (*Amos, the Prophet: the Man and His Background* [Eng. tr. 1973], p. 37; "Micah the Moreshite — The Prophet and His Background," in J. G. Gammie *et al.*, eds., *Israelite Wisdom* [*Festschrift* S. Terrien; 1978], pp. 77-84) that the roots of Israelite wisdom were to be found in the folk ethos that developed in tribal society well before a wisdom school was establshed in the royal court. This clan wisdom was largely ethical and derived from family life. Wolff pointed to Joab's use of a wise woman from Tekoa (2 S. 14:1f.) and references to Edom's reputation for wisdom (e.g., 1 K. 4:31 [MT 5:11]; Job 2:11; Jer. 49:7; Ob. 8) as evidence of wisdom traditions outside the royal court. He held that Amos's use of numerical sayings (Am. 1:3–2:6), logical reasoning (3:3-8), woe speeches (5:18; 6:1), and wisdom vocabulary indicate his contact with the clan wisdom at Tekoa. J. Crenshaw (*ZAW,* 79 [1967], 42-52) dismissed most of Wolff's evidence for clan wisdom in Amos, contending that almost all of it can be found in other, nonwisdom settings. Crenshaw suggested that the theophany motif in the doxologies (4:13; 5:7-9; 9:5f.) may represent a more significant sign of wisdom influence, but held that this motif likewise was not predominantly or exclusively related to wisdom literature.

One of the problems that have prevented a more exact understanding of the relationship between prophecy and wisdom is the lack of distinctive criteria for identifying wisdom traditions. R. B. Y. Scott's attempt to produce a list of wisdom vocabulary (*Way of Wisdom in the OT* [1971], pp. 121f.) proved unsuccessful because many of the words he listed appear outside the context of wisdom. The methodological criteria set forth by J. Crenshaw (*JBL,* 88 [1969], 129-142) were more realistic and suggested principles that could be applied to prophetic texts. Studies revealing the complexity of Israel's wisdom movement, including the growth of the varied traditions of clan wisdom, court wisdom, and scribal wisdom, have produced a more concrete understanding of the stylistic and ideological relationship between wisdom and prophecy, and these studies have resulted in a greater appreciation of the rich literary and cultural background upon which the prophets drew in order to communicate the word of God effectively to the various strata within Israelite society.

*D. Ecstatic Behavior.* Ecstasy has often been associated with the unusual behavior of the early bands of prophets and the abnormal experiences of the classical prophets (i.e., those from the 8th cent. B.C. onward, whose prophecies were written down). G. Hölscher's psychological analysis of prophetic consciousness concluded that all prophets experienced ecstasy. Following Hölscher's lead, many scholars supported and developed the theory that ecstasy was a fundamental part of prophetic experience. The attempt to define ecstasy, however, resulted in sharp differences of opinion concerning the origin of ecstatic experience, the extent to which all prophets experienced the same type of ecstasy, and the effect of ecstasy on the prophets.

The biblical evidence for ecstatic behavior includes the strange behavior of Saul: his being "turned into another man" (1 S. 10:6) when he "prophesied" (hithpael of *nāḇā'*) among the band of prophets (cf. vv. 9-13), his prophesying while lying naked on the ground (19:18-24), and his irrational attempt, while prophesying (RSV "rave," hithpael of *nāḇā'*), to kill David (18:10). The same Hebrew term is used to refer to the leaping, crying, and self-mutilating actions of the prophets of Baal on Mt. Carmel (AV "prophesy"; RSV "rave"; 1 K. 18:29). The evidence also includes Elisha's use of music as a setting for his prophesying (2 K. 3:15), references to prophets as madmen (*mᵉšûgaʿ*) or fools (2 K. 9:11; Jer. 29:26; Hos. 9:7), and the fact that the writing prophets saw visions and performed a variety of strange symbolic acts to communicate God's word.

The source of prophetic ecstatic experiences was usually traced to Canaanite influences, although some scholars believed the phenomenon was of Greek origin.The discovery of the *muḫḫû* prophets in Mari led Haldar to suggest that Israel's ecstatic prophets were related to the Mesopotamian *muḫḫû* ecstatics (see II.C above). J. Lindblom (pp. 1-46) surveyed both modern and ancient prophetic experiences of ecstasy and concluded that ecstasy has been a normative part of prophecy throughout the world for many centuries. The degree of similarity between various ecstatic experiences suggested a common origin for all prophetic activity; e.g., W. R. Smith (pp. 392) observed that the use of music to induce ecstasy was common among the Arabs as well as in Israel (cf. 2 K. 3:15). T. H. Robinson (pp. 40-45) concluded that the writing prophets were ecstatics like the early popular prophets, since both were called *nāḇî'*.

It is true that the writing prophets as well as the early prophets had visionary trances (Isa. 6; Am. 7–8; Ezk. 1:8-10; Jer. 1:11-14), and both types used ecstasy as a sign that they were possessed by the Spirit of God. But the prophetic movement is far too complex to reduce all prophetic experience to one single pattern. One prophet could experience varying degrees of ecstatic possession at different times (e.g., cf. 1 S. 10:6-11 and 19:20-23; Ezk. 1-3 and 20). The Hebrew prophets were individuals, each with a distinct psychological makeup; they were not carbon copies of Canaanite or Mesopotamian prophets or even of other Hebrew prophets. The title *nāḇî'* refers not to the ecstatic behavior that sometimes accompanied inspiration, but to the fact that one was a messenger of God's words (see I.B above). Many prophetic speeches contain no evidence of an ecstatic experience nor any claim that the prophet had received anything but the word of God. This is the objective criterion that identified the prophets, not some stylized behavior pattern. Very few prophets report convulsive seizures or trances; in fact, the phenomenon appears to have been equally rare among both the writing prophets and the early seers and bands of prophets.

S. Mowinckel drew a sharp distinction between the early ecstatic prophets who received the Spirit of God and the later nonecstatic writing prophets who received the word of God (*JBL,* 53 [1934], 199-227). This distinction is unacceptable, however, since Micah (3:8), Ezekiel (11:5), Isaiah (48:16), and Joel (2:28 [MT 3:1]) all recognized the importance of the Spirit's activity in inspiration. It is likewise inaccurate to classify the ecstatics as false prophets (H. Obbink, *HUCA,* 14 [1939], 23-28); for the canonical prophets never condemned the false prophets for their ecstasy but rather for preaching peace and prosperity from their own imagination instead of the repentance that God commanded (cf. Jer. 23).

Among the scholars who have distinguished sharply between the wild, involuntary speech and behavior of Saul and the artistic, clearly reasoned moral judgments of the writing prophets, some have held that the latter group of prophets achieved a much higher mystical union with God (H. W. Hines, *AJSL,* 40 [1923/24], 37-71) — a union in which the prophet's consciousness was so absorbed into the divine that the two become one corporate personality (see A. R. Johnson, *The One and the Many in the Israelite Conception of God* [1942], pp. 36-38). In its attempt to account for the prophets' overpowering consciousness of being infused with the very thoughts of God Himself, this psychological interpretation has tended to extinguish the individual personalities of the prophets that are so clearly evident in their writings. J. Lindblom, on the other hand, contrasted absorption ecstasy (the "so-called *unio mystica*"), which eradicates the personality of the individual, with "concentration ecstasy," which maintains a distinction between the human and the divine (pp. 106, 299-311). The latter type of ecstasy seems closer to what the Hebrew prophets experienced.

Although the Hebrew prophets were described as "ecstatics" by Philo, some of the rabbis, and the early church fathers (see A. Heschel, pp. 324-350), the assumption that the ecstasy of the writing prophets was analogous to the irrational frenzied ecstasy of the foreign prophets is largely inadmissible. The closest example of comparable phenomena among the Hebrews is the peculiar behavior of Saul when he was among the band of prophets associated with Samuel (1 S. 10:1-13; 19:18-24). Since the semantic field of *nāḇā'* can mean "sing, praise," as well as "prophesy" (1 Ch. 25:1-6), it seems most natural to interpret the prophesying of Saul and the group of prophets as singing praises to God. The second instance of Saul's prophesying among the prophets with uncontrolled ecstatic behavior is left unexplained by the text (1 S. 19:24). According to 18:10f.; 19:9 an evil spirit controlled Saul. Thus it seems most likely that Saul was not one of the prophets (cf. 10:11f.; 19:24); rather he was a man possessed and driven mad by conflicting spiritual powers (J. Sturdy, *VT,* 20 [1970], 210f.).

The ecstasy of the true prophets did not usually display itself in peculiar behavior, for their ecstasy was basically a private experience of the conscious reality of God's presence. Ecstasy as a psychological state was concurrent with but distinct from the reception of God's message. Its importance lay in assuring the prophet that God had spoken. There is no indication, however, that all the prophets' messages resulted directly from ecstatic experiences. Once God's Spirit entered the prophets and filled them with His words, they became messengers of God. The prophets' profound spiritual experiences should not, therefore, be confused with mystical experience, nor with the frenzied and irrational behavior of heathen prophets.

*See also* ECSTASY.

*E. Covenant Law.* The authority of the prophets rested on the word of God that they received. God's message was revealed through unusual means in visions and dreams, but later prophets could also depend on earlier pronouncements, well-known wisdom sayings, hymnic material, and legal traditions. Scholars have raised the question whether the prophets were dependent on inherited ideas of covenant and law or were the originators of these concepts. J. Wellhausen and his followers claimed that the prophets were the first teachers of ethical monotheism. This picture of the prophets raised them out of the context of earlier Israelite tradition and set them up to be the creators of Israel's faith. They did not look back to a forgotten Moses who mediated the covenant laws to Israel at Sinai, but derived their knowledge of God from their own human understanding. Wellhausen (pp. 418-420) believed that the law and covenant ideas were not introduced until the reform of Josiah in 621 B.C. Since according to this view the early prophets before 621 B.C. had no knowledge of the law or covenant (see R. H. Pfeiffer, *JBL,* 70 [1951], 2), the classical prophets were the real pioneers of the nation's faith.

These conclusions have been opposed by other scholars (e.g., N. W. Porteous, "The Basis of the Ethical Teachings of the Prophets," in H. H. Rowley, ed., *Studies in OT Prophecy,* pp. 143-156), who have claimed that the prophets inherited their religious traditions rather than creating them. G. Mendenhall (*Law and Covenant in Israel and the Ancient Near East* [1955], p. 19) found little originality in the prophets and a great deal of dependence on an established covenant concept that contained the stipulations and laws of the nation. These scholars have argued that there is no indication that the prophets thought they were introducing a new doctrine of God or understanding of the covenant relationship between God and His people. Instead, the prophets claimed to be calling the nation to turn from its unrighteous acts, which were contrary to God's will. Had the laws that the prophets accused the people of breaking been unknown, their accusations would have been groundless. When the prophets accused the Israelites of failing to keep what was known to be God's will, they were reminding them of enacted stipulations, not creating innovative traditions.

In his earlier work, *Prophecy and Covenant* (pp. 15-17, 23), R. E. Clements concluded that the prophets built their messages on an inherited tradition of the nation's covenant relationship with Yahweh. But in a later study, *Prophecy and Tradition* (pp. 21-23, 41-49), he reversed his opinion and rejected the idea that Israel had a relatively uniform covenant theology, based on the pattern of the so-called suzerainty treaties, from the time of Moses. Instead, he and other scholars assigned to the so-called Deuteronomic movement an important role in developing Israel's covenant ideology. The covenantal themes in Amos and Hosea were assigned to a Deuteronomic redaction that took place some time after the books were originally written (cf. H. W. Wolff, *Joel and Amos* [Eng. tr., *Hermeneia,* 1977], pp. 106-113). The theory of a Deuteronomic redaction of Amos and Hosea has gained wide acceptance, but this conclusion leaves the early prophets without any standard on which to base their accusations. R. V. Bergren (*Prophets and the Law* [1974], pp. 62-67, 78) surveyed the prophetic accusations and demonstrated how Elijah's condemnation of Ahab (1 K. 21:13) presupposes Ex. 22:28 (MT 27), Amos's reproaches correspond to early apodictic and casuistic laws, and Micah's judgment speeches relate to the legal formulations of his day. The prophets believed that the law was authoritative and binding even on kings, priests, and the rich. This was so because it was ultimately God Himself who spoke through the prophets to enforce the laws that He had enacted. In the prophetic lawsuit God was the plaintiff (Isa. 3:13-15; Mic. 2:1-4), and His accusations were founded on the people's disregard for the laws that governed the covenant relationship between God and Israel.

*F. Apocalyptic.* The approach of Wellhausen and most early literary critics was to make a major division between the rich heritage of Israel's prophets and the impoverished legalism and apocalypticism of postexilic Judaism. The apocalyptic writers (*see* APOCALYPTIC LITERATURE) were considered poor imitators of the prophets. They were interested only in bizzare fantasies, having been influenced by the syncretistic tendencies of the Persian period and the persecution of the Maccabean age. In fact, apocalyptic was largely ignored, since it came out of a period of religious decay.

In opposition to these interpretations, H. H. Rowley (*Relevance of Apocalyptic* [2nd ed. 1952]) hypothesized a fundamental unity between prophecy and apocalyptic thinking. Apocalyptic literature borrowed heavily from the language of the OT; its heroes were Enoch, Abraham, Baruch, and other Jews; its message came from God or one of His angels; and its traditions and stories were those of the OT. Many years earlier R. H. Charles had seen a connection between apocalyptic and Pharisaic thinking, and this conclusion was later confirmed by W. D. Davies (*Christian Origins and Judaism* [1962], pp. 25-29). A variation of this basic position was proposed by O. Plöger (*Theocracy and Eschatology* [Eng. tr. 1968], pp. 35-52), who found two major opposing groups within Judaism. One group was antieschatological (based on his interpretation of Chronicles), made up of the priestly elite, and believed that prophecy was already fulfilled in the established theocratic community of Jews. On the other side was a smaller, less influential group that looked forward to the fulfillment of prophecy in the future, maintained a high regard for eschatology, and accepted certain Iranian influences in the development of their apocalyptic hopes; their thinking can be found in the Isaiah apocalypse (chs. 24–27), the end of Zechariah (chs. 12–14), and Daniel. This highly hypothetical reconstruction drove a wedge between prophetic expectations that are mingled together without conflict in the OT. D. S. Russell (pp. 21-28) also saw two streams of tradition in the late Israelite community: the apocalyptic group was closely connected to the prophets, while the rabbinical group centered its attention on the law and the oral Torah. R. T. Herford (*Pharisees* [1924], p. 188) denied any relationship between normative Pharisaic Judaism and apocalyptic; instead he believed that apocalyptic was part of the Zealot movement.

Various sources have been proposed for the origin of apocalyptic. In addition to Jewish prophecy, H. D. Betz (*Journal for Theology and the Church,* 6 [1969], 134-154) proposed a heavy influence of Hellenistic syncretism. W. Schmithals (*Apocalyptic Movement* [Eng. tr. 1975], pp. 89-126) evaluated the evidence for a connection with Gnosticism as well as the frequently suggested (even by H. H. Rowley) influence of Iranian Zoroastrianism. Each of these sources had some degree of similarity with apocalyptic thinking, but none provided a solid basis for the origin of the movement. Taking a different track, H. G. Hamerton-Kelly (*VT,* 20 [1970], 1-15) derived apocalyptic ideas from a group of Jews who were very concerned about the temple worship but strongly critical of those responsible for its maintenance. G. von Rad boldly proposed that the roots of apocalyptic were to be found in Israel's wisdom literature, because both were pseudonymous, held a deterministic view of history, were influenced by non-Israelite universalistic and individualistic thinking, and used the same literary images (*Theology of the OT,* II [Eng. tr. 1965], 301-313). Von Rad objected strongly to deriving apocalyptic ideas from prophecy; but the presence of eschatological interests in prophecy rather than in wisdom made this hypothesis unconvincing (see P. von der Osten-Sacken, *Die Apocalyptik in ihrem Verhältnis zu Prophetie und Weisheit* [1969]). In spite of these many innovative suggestions, the preponderance of evidence supports the view that apocalyptic writings were most closely related to the eschatological thought patterns in prophetic literature.

Both apocalyptic and prophetic books claimed to be the result of revelation by dreams, visions, or direct speech; both used symbolism and had a pessimistic view of the world situation apart from God; both were universalistic in outlook and saw history as the outworking of God's determined plan; and both looked forward to the Day of Yahweh when God would miraculously redeem His people and judge the evil nations. According to P. Hanson (pp. 11f.) and many others, a distinguishing feature that sets apocalyptic apart from prophecy is the apocalyptic search for a solution to the world's problems through a divine intervention outside of history in another aeon. Nevertheless, Hanson saw a basic continuity between the eschatology in both prophecy and apocalyptic and spoke of these as an unbroken strand. W. Schmithals (*Apocalyptic Movement,* pp. 68-88, 135-150) reconstructed a break between prophecy and apocalyptic. In doing so he essentially claimed that postexilic biblical apocalyptic literature was not part of the stream of eschatological expectation flowing out of the preexilic prophets in the OT. The OT preexilic prophets — unlike the apocalyptic writers — dealt with creation as the beginning of history, with redemption as a part of present and future history, and eschatology as the final acts of history. Each of these events in its own way was an extrahistorical intervention by God into history; each presupposed mankind's limited ability to resolve problems within history; and each was an example of God's cosmic determination to bring about His transcendent purpose in history. There was no radical break into events outside of history.

Following F. Cross (*Canaanite Myth and Hebrew Epic* [1973]), P. Hanson concluded that the dawn of apocalyptic occurred when the later prophets (e.g., Third Isaiah, Zechariah), faced with a contradiction between glorious prophetic promises and the bitter realities of the postexilic period, gradually abdicated the prophetic responsibility of translating the cosmic vision into historical, this-worldly terms and instead used mythical imagery to express their hope for a fulfillment of promises in the cosmic realm (pp. 23-29). Similarly, W. R. Millar (*Isaiah 24–27 and the Origin of Apocalyptic* [1976]) used Canaanite myth to explain the rise of apocalyptic. These "myths," however, can hardly be considered extrahistorical or late inventions, since they are already present in the Psalms, in wisdom literature, and in Israel's record of its military history. The prophets integrated these themes into history; they did not make prophecy nonhistorical or apocalyptic.

When the features of prophetic eschatology are compared with so-called apocalyptic texts in the OT, the formal literary features and the deep theological themes are not appreciably different. As defined by OT texts, therefore, a line of continuity runs through prophecy, prophetic eschatology, and prophetic apocalyptic. On the other hand, Jewish apocryphal literature did contain some full-blown nonprophetic apocalyptic texts that were nonethical, nonhistorical, and largely nontheological (viewing God as having withdrawn from this evil world). Study of these late apocalyptic texts reveals major contrasts between these texts and the OT prophetic apocalyptic texts. These late apocalyptic texts have no bearing on the OT prophetic texts, although they may have influenced NT apocalyptic writings.

*See also* ESCHATOLOGY II, III.A.

***IV. Message of the Prophets.***–The significance of the Israelite prophets must be judged on the basis of what they said, not by the results of their efforts to transform various aspects of Israel's culture. Their consciousness of having met with God revolutionized their thoughts and gave them a burning message of truth for an audience in need of a divine revelation. Their messages included scathing denunciations as well as lofty promises. Sometimes they addressed their audiences orally, but at other times they acted out their message or wrote it on a scroll. Regardless of the medium of delivery, the prophet's responsibility was to apply God's message to the audience's situation. The theological underpinnings of the prophet's message were Yahweh's character and His sovereign rule in history: Yahweh alone was God, and in divine justice and mercy He gave order and meaning to the experience of mankind.

*A. Reception.* The process by which the prophets received their messages has always been hidden in the mystery of divine revelation. The event was reported in words such as "the word of the Lord came. . . ," but this recorded only the source of the prophet's authority and the results of the revelatory event. Some prophets described their initial "call experience" with great vividness (e.g., Jer. 1:1-10), while others recorded no "call" and did not carry on a prolonged prophetic ministry. Kings, priests, and laymen sometimes performed the prophetic function of speaking God's words, but their role can be distinguished from those called to be prophets throughout their lifetime. God spoke to King David on a number of occasions, but He usually spoke to David through the prophets Nathan and Gad. David can be considered a prophet (cf. Acts 2:29f.), but he was called to be a king.

Ezekiel, on the other hand, received in exile an inaugural vision of the glories of God's presence (Ezk. 1). God commanded him to eat the scroll handed to him (2:8–3:4) and to deliver its contents to the rebellious Israelites in exile. God promised Ezekiel strength to face the task (3:7-9), sent His Spirit to empower him (2:2), and warned him that while the people might refuse to receive the message, it was important that they know they had been warned by a prophet (2:5; 3:18f.). The impact of this experience on Ezekiel was a clear sense of God's power and glory, a deep understanding of his prophetic responsibility, a stubborn determination to carry out the purpose of his rather contradictory role, and an inner spiritual awakening. The "call experience" was beyond description, but it was a pivotal point in every prophet's life. The staggering force of such an overwhelming divine encounter and the sense of union with the divine pathos (cf. A. Heschel, pp. 221-231) stretched the limits of rational language.

An essential ingredient of prophetic inspiration was the activity of God's Spirit. The OT describes God as giving His Spirit to His people (Neh. 9:20) and as pouring out His Spirit to enable men and women to prophesy (Joel 2:28 [MT 3:1]). Of most prophets it is said that the Spirit came upon them at the time that they prophesied (cf. 2 Ch. 15:1; 20:14; 24:20). Ezekiel reported that the Spirit entered him when God spoke to him (Ezk. 2:2); later he received a message when the Spirit transported him to Jerusalem in a vision (8:3). Micah declared to Israel its rebellious acts because he was filled with the Spirit of the Lord (Mic. 3:8), and Zechariah condemned the people for rejecting the word that the Lord had revealed to them through the former prophets by His Spirit (Zec. 7:12). David's last words included the claim that the Spirit of Yahweh had spoken through him (2 S. 23:2), and "Deutero-Isaiah" claimed to have been anointed by the Spirit of Yahweh to declare God's good news to the afflicted (Isa. 61:1). In Hos. 9:7 the prophet is called "the man of the spirit."

Through the Spirit's work the prophet received a communication from God in the form of words, a dream, or a vision. Dreamers and prophets were sometimes classified together (e.g., Dt. 13:1, 5; 1 S. 28:6), for God frequently revealed His will to Israelite prophets through dreams and visions (cf. Nu. 12:6; 1 K. 3:5; Dnl. 7:1; 8:2; 10:1). Jeremiah did not deny the possibility of God's revealing Himself through dreams (23:28); his criticism was of those who prophesied "lying dreams" out of their own imaginations (cf. vv. 25-27, 32). Whatever mode was used, the essential factor in revelation was the prophet's understanding of the divine will. The frequent use of the messenger formula may indicate a significant dependence on direct or indirect verbal communication within the prophet's mind.

Although the insight and truth of the prophet's message was based on the Spirit's inspiration, its production in human terms was molded by the framework of the human mind. Many factors, including past traditions, previous and present history, cultural patterns, individual background, and personal style of speech, influenced the shape of the prophet's message. It is unknown to what extent God revealed Himself to the prophets in terms of their finite ability to express themselves in cultural and historical forms. Did the prophets translate the impulses of the Spirit into conceptualized cultural equivalents that mirrored the mind of God, or did God Himself translate the message into human words? Neither solution entirely explains the individual character of each prophetic message; but the employment of the law and covenant traditions, temple hymns, wisdom sayings, and contemporary speech forms demonstrates an important degree of human involvement in formulating the divine message.

*B. Delivery.* Many prophets spoke their messages orally before individuals or groups. Isaiah spoke directly to Ahaz (Isa. 7:3) and Hezekiah (39:5-8), and Jeremiah preached to all the people of Judah in the temple (Jer. 7:2) as well as privately to King Zedekiah (34:1f.). On many occasions the specific audience is not identified. Ezekiel prophesied against the shepherds of Israel (Ezk. 34), against Mt. Seir, and to the mountains of Israel (ch. 35), but the people he addressed in exile are not identified. These oral messages included sharp rebukes (1 S. 2:27-36), words of encouragement (2 Ch. 15:1f.), mourning songs (Am. 5:1-3), riddles (Ezk. 18:2), and quotations from all types of literature. Rhetorical devices such as repetition, wordplays, contrasts, and questions were used in these oral communications. Many spoke in exalted poetic style using imaginative and bold figures of speech, while others used very literal and simple prose (1 K. 13:21f.). There is no evidence that the prophets' original sayings were limited to short, poetic statements, as some critics have held (see V below).

Several prophets illustrated their words with symbolic object lessons. Ahijah ripped his new garment in twelve pieces and gave Jeroboam ten to symbolize the division of the kingdom (1 K. 11:30f.). Jeremiah buried his linen waistcloth by the Euphrates (Jer. 13:1-11), went to the potter's house to observe an illustration of God's sovereignty over the nations (18:1-10), and broke a clay pot to depict God's destruction of Jerusalem (ch. 19). Ezekiel drew a picture of Jerusalem and carried out a mock siege of the city (Ezk. 4:1-3), cut off his hair to depict what would happen to Jerusalem's inhabitants (5:1-12), and packed his baggage and dug a hole through the wall to picture the people's journey into exile (12:1-16). Many of these symbolic acts were designed to capture the attention of a hardened audience that refused to listen to the prophets' words.

Some of the prophets' utterances were selected, arranged, and edited for publication in a written form; cf. the dialogue format of Malachi and the clusters of oracles against the foreign nations in Jeremiah (chs. 46–51), Isaiah (chs. 13–23), and Ezekiel (chs. 25–32). The books themselves do not record who edited and arranged the available literature, but some prophets stated that they had written their messages on tablets or books (Isa. 30:8), in letters (2 Ch. 21:12; Jer. 29:1, 29f.), or on scrolls (Jer. 30:2; 36:2, 32). Baruch wrote the words that Jeremiah dictated to him, and the disciples of other prophets probably did the same (cf. Isa. 8:16). This evidence suggests that the prophets had much to do with the preservation of their words in written form. Disciples may have memorized and recorded the prophets' teachings and assisted in editing the divine messages, but the nature and extent of their role can only be hypothetically reconstructed. Introductory formulas, historical introductions, and explanatory transitions were apparently added to oracles to assist the reader. Some critics have attributed an undue amount of creativity to the process of oral transmission by later disciples. Although parallel passages (Isa. 2:2-4 and Mic. 4:1-4; Jer. 49:14-16 and Ob. 1-4) evidence some fluidity within the material ascribed to the various prophetic oracles, these parallels demonstrate a conservative respect for the original formulation as well as a freedom to recast the truth of God's revelation. (See V below.)

The prophets' messages were called the "word" (Heb. *dāḇār*) of God, an "oracle" or "utterance" (*n$^e$'um*) of Yahweh, or a "burden" (*maśśā'*) from God. God's word delivered by the prophets revealed the divine personality and will; it was creative and authoritative because of the sovereign wisdom and power of God. The phrase *way$^e$hî ḏ$^e$ḇar-yhwh 'ēlay* ("the word of the Lord came to me") occurs over two hundred times in the OT as a technical formula for prophetic revelation. Events foretold by God's word happened according to that word (1 K. 6:12; 13:26); His word did not return without accomplishing its intended purpose (Isa. 55:11). It brought judgment like a fire to those who opposed God (Jer. 23:29), but it brought peace and hope to those who received God's steadfast love (Mic. 7:18-20).

Hebrew *n$^e$'um* (a noun patterned after the qal pass. part. of *nā'am*, "speak," and used in formulas reporting divine speech) has been inconsistently translated in all the versions. Translators have sometimes rendered it as a verb ("say, declare") and sometimes as a noun ("utterance, oracle"). The term, which occurs 167 times in Jeremiah, eighty-three times in Ezekiel, and twenty-three times in Amos, often defines the limits of literary units (see F. S. North, *JBL*, 71 [1952], 10; F. Baumgartel, *ZAW*, 73 [1961], 277-290). It frequently functioned as a concluding formula, but it was also used to introduce prophetic messages. Imitating the true prophets, the false prophets repeated this formula to authenticate their message (Jer. 23:31). The use of *n$^e$'um yhwh* ("oracle of Yahweh"), sometimes in conjunction with a divine oath ("as I live," Ezk. 20:3, 31; see also Gen. 22:16), stressed the finality and authority of God's oracles.

Another term sometimes rendered "oracle" by the RSV is *maśśā'* (lit. "burden"; cf. Jer. 23:33-38), which occurs twenty-five times in prophetic sayings containing threats against foreign nations (Isa. 13:1; 14:28; 15:1; 17:1; 19:1; 21:1, 11, 13; 22:1; 23:1; Nah. 1:1; Hab. 1:1; Zec. 9:1) as well as against wicked people in Israel (2 K. 9:25; 2 Ch. 24:27; Zec. 12:1; Mal. 1:1). P. A. H. de Boer (*Inquiry into the Meaning of the Term Maśśā'* [1948]) concluded that *n$^e$'um* and *maśśā'* had no distinction in meaning; it does appear, however, that *maśśā'*, "burden," contained connotations not found in the rather neutral *n$^e$'um*, "oracle."

The Greek translators of the OT primarily translated these Hebrew terms for the message of God with *lógos* or *rhēma*, "word." The NT authors borrowed the same words when they described the words of Jesus, introduced quotations from the OT, or made general references to what God had said. There seems to be little distinction between the meaning of these two Greek terms. The RSV uses "oracle" to translate *lógion*, which occurs four times in the NT (approximately 50 times in the LXX). The oracle refers to the spoken words of God to Moses and other inspired authors, words that are authoritative for the believer (Acts 7:38; Rom. 3:2; cf. He. 5:12, AV). The preaching of the gospel by those having the special gift is compared to the power and authority of the very sayings ("oracles") of God (1 Pet. 4:11).

Thus the titles that the prophets gave to their messages called attention to the distinctive aspects that the prophets wished to emphasize. Each term or formula demanded respect for the authority behind the message, and each described the divine message as some form of verbal communication. The reception and delivery of God's prophetic word were powerful influences on the personality and morality of Israelite faith, because it was God who spoke, and because His divine will universally controlled the dynamic forces of history as well as each individual's destiny.

*C. Content.* Because the prophetic movement covered several centuries of diverse political, social, and religious circumstances, the messages of the prophets varied tremendously. A prophet's social location (the royal court, the temple singers, at a capital city in Israel or Judah, or among a group of prophets) limited his or her associations and area of influence within Israelite society. But in the last analysis, the revelation of God's word was the primary factor in determining the content of the prophet's message.

Among the individual prophets, Amos condemned the northern nation of Israel for the social injustice that the rich and powerful perpetrated on the weak and predicted the destruction of the nation. Using the figure of the marriage/covenant relationship, Hosea reminded the Israelites of God's hatred of Baalism; he foresaw that the absence of knowledge of God (Hos. 4:6) would soon lead to military defeat, but he also foresaw a later renewal of positive relationships on the basis of God's undying love. Obadiah condemned Edom for its pride and its sins against Judah, while Joel described the day of the Lord in terms of both its negative and positive effects for Israel. Each prophet was unique, and each had a specific message that applied the principles of God's rule to particular situations. Yet each prophet's message was based on a common understanding of God's character and relationship to mankind, each condemned apostasy and demanded a return to God and His covenant, and each believed in a future hope for the nation. A brief analysis of these three theological motifs will provide an overview of the content of the prophets' message.

The prophets knew about God's law and grace through the traditions that had been handed down over the centuries. They were neither the creators of monotheism nor the innovators of a new understanding of God (see III.E above). The fundamental elements of the nation's faith were established early in the nation's experience with God. Israel's election, its redemption from Egypt, and its establishment in an exclusive covenant with Yahweh were the foundation blocks that the prophets called the nation to remember. These traditions are unmistakably present behind the prophetic preaching concerning the social, cultic, and moral obligations of the people of God. The analogies of father and son (Hos. 11), potter and clay (Jer. 18; Isa. 64:8 [MT 7]), shepherd and sheep (Ezk. 34), and husband and wife (Hos. 1–3; Isa. 54:1-8; Jer. 2:2; 3:1-11; Ezk. 16:23) illustrated the prophets' conception of God's relationship to the people. The events that brought about the election, redemption, and covenant traditions established that Yahweh was God and that He was in sovereign control of all people and nations. The gods of the nations were worthless (Jer. 2:5); they could not speak, walk, or do anything (10:5). They were the product of human hands (Isa. 41:7; 44:9-17) and thus were a delusion, nothing but empty wind (41:29). Yahweh alone was God; there was no other God beside Him (44:8; 45:5, 18, 21;

47:8; cf. Ex. 20:3). The prophets insisted that the nation must worship only Yahweh and reject idols (e.g., Isa. 45:5f., 21f.; Jer. 10:1-16; Ezk. 8:5-18; cf. Ex. 20:4f., 23; Lev. 19:4; etc.), for the blessings of the covenant were available only to those who loved, feared, honored, and served Yahweh according to the covenant stipulations (e.g., Dnl. 9:4-19). Because He was holy, they were required to be holy if they wanted Him to dwell in their midst (e.g., Ezk. 20:38-43; 43:7-9; cf. Lev. 11:44f.).

But the Israelites ignored these basic tenets of their faith. They rebelled against God's authority and His covenant, ceased to demonstrate a heart of love and fear, and followed other gods. Many prophetic messages castigated the Israelites for their sins, and some brought words of judgment against foreign nations that refused to honor God. The prophets declared God's hatred for the Israelites' worship of Baal and other gods (Jer. 2:23-28; Ezk. 8:5-18; Hos. 2:13 [MT 15]; 4:13; 1 K. 18:39f.), for their empty ritualistic worship in the temple (Am. 5:21-27; Isa. 1:10-17), for their social injustices against the poor and helpless (Am. 2:6-8; 4:1; 5:10-13; 8:4-6; Mic. 3:1-4, 9-11), and for their rejection of God's law and of the warnings of the true prophets (Am. 2:4; 2 K. 17:7-20). The prophets warned that Israel would receive the curse of the covenant (cf. Dt. 27:15-26; Lev. 26:14-39), instead of its blessing, as punishment for its rebellion; the nation would suffer military defeat and exile if it did not repent (Jer. 3:12-14). The prophets challenged the nation to avoid this judgment, to seek God and live (Am. 5:4, 6, 14). But the people trusted instead in the promises of peace given by the false prophets (Jer. 8:11; Ezk. 13:10), in the eternal promises to David (2 S. 7:12-16), and in the temple (Jer. 7:1-15). God demonstrated His justice by humbling the powerful who oppressed the poor (see J. Limburg, *Prophets and the Powerless* [1977]) and making the land a reproach and a warning to the nations round about (Ezk. 5:15).

The prophets did not preach only doom; they also acknowledged the compassion of God. They foretold the existence of a REMNANT (Isa. 6:13; 7:3; see also G. Hasel, *The Remnant* [1975]) who would return to the land from the nations where they had been scattered (Jer. 3:18; 23:8; Ezk. 11:17; Hos. 1:11 [MT 2:2]; Mic. 2:12; Zec. 10:6-10). They foresaw that God would strengthen His people and turn away His anger (Jer. 3:12; Isa. 54:7f.) because of His everlasting love (Jer. 31:3). For His own name's sake God would redeem His people (Isa. 48:11; Ezk. 36:22-25), make them His people again, and renew the covenant and its promises (Hos. 1:10 [MT 2:1]; Jer. 30–31; Joel 2:21-29 [MT 2:21–3:2]; Ezk. 34:25-31). Then the people would be glad and rejoice, the Spirit of God would be poured out on mankind, and God's people would multiply and rest securely. The righteous seed from David, the suffering servant bearing the sins of many (Isa. 53:1-12), would reign as king in Jerusalem (Isa. 2:1-4; 9:1-7 [MT 8:23–9:6]; Jer. 23:5-7; Ezk. 34:23-31; Hos. 2:18-23 [MT 2:20-25]; 3:5; Am. 9:11-15; Zec. 14:9). Then the nations would come to Jerusalem to hear the law of the Lord, and war would end forever (Mic. 4:1-8). The kingdom of God would be established and His dominion would be everlasting (Dnl. 2:44; 7:13f.). All nations and the earth itself would be laid waste (Isa. 24), and a new heaven and a new earth would be created (65:17; 66:22). Then the departed spirits would rise to life (Isa. 25:8; 26:19) — the wicked to everlasting contempt and the righteous to everlasting life (Dnl. 12:1f.).

***V. Interpretation of Prophecy.***–The various treatments of prophecy range from several so-called orthodox interpretations to sectarian and fanatical extremes. More objective criteria are needed to guide the interpretation of prophecy in order for the prophetic word to maintain the respect that it is due. This goal requires a careful analysis of the different methodological approaches that have been employed in the past as well as a critical evaluation of the hermeneutical principles that have served as the foundation for prophetic interpretation.

*A. Methodological Approaches.* The era when source criticism reigned as the leading method of biblical research was marked by a preoccupation with the initial composition and the subsequent redaction of the text. On the basis of repetitions, contradictions, distinctive vocabulary, and contrasting political and theological viewpoints discovered in the text, the critical scholar tried to identify different sources that had been joined by a later redactor. Since the earliest sources of the Pentateuch were judged to be products of the 8th and 7th cents. B.C., and the laws within them were thought not to precede the prophetic writings (see III.E above), many concluded that the combined redaction of "J" and "E" was a prophetic work (see H. F. Hahn, *OT in Modern Research* [rev. ed. 1966], p. 6). The prophetic point of view, which tied prosperity to righteousness and curses to sinfulness, was particularly prominent in "J," the Yahwistic document. (*See also* CRITICISM II.D.5.)

Applied to the book of Isaiah, this method produced the conclusion that Isa. 40–66 was not written by the same person who wrote most of chs. 1–39. Evidence included the references to the ruined city of Jerusalem that contradicted the perspective of the first half of Isaiah, differences in the literary style and vocabulary, and radically distinct theological ideas of God, the future of the nation, and the messianic king (S. R. Driver, *Intro. to the Literature of the OT* [repr. 1956], pp. 236-243). Similarly, source critics considered the promise in Mic. 2:12f. of a remnant returning to the land to be contradictory to the message of impending doom in the rest of the chapter; thus these verses were assigned to a later exilic or postexilic source. G. Hölscher (*Hesekiel* [1924]) limited Ezekiel's influence to the prophecies of doom that were in poetic style; prose predictions of disaster and the salvation oracles he dated to later generations of redactors. B. Duhm (*Das Buch Jeremia* [1907]) attributed only 280 poetic verses (plus the prose letter in Jer. 29) to Jeremiah, claiming that the biographical narratives were written by Baruch and the rest of the book by exilic and postexilic redactors who emphasized the theology of Deuteronomy.

Although this approach is still used in limited ways at the present time, it has been surpassed by other methods that have yielded more significant results. Few scholars now believe it is possible to limit a prophet's words to poetic utterances, or to deny that a prophet could speak both positive and negative messages. A change in Ezekiel's historical situation could easily have caused him to change his message of doom to a promise of hope (Ezk. 34 is positive after the fall of Jerusalem in 33:21). The results of source-critical research frequently contradicted one another and paid more and more attention to minor details of little importance. Thus the method ceased to be a constructive tool for exegeting the meaning of the text, and on the whole it was impotent to explain the significance of God's revelation to mankind.

Because of the inadequacy of source criticism, H. Gunkel introduced form criticism as a new method of studying prophetic texts. This method focused on the oral stage in the development of the text and sought to determine the specific situation in the life of the people (*Sitz im Leben*) that gave rise to a piece of literature. By analyzing comparative religious literature from other cultures and discovering their settings, and by classifying prophetic texts according to their literary form, Gunkel hoped to discover the meaning of the various types of prophetic texts in their original setting. He believed that the prophets were orators, not authors of books. He saw them as preachers who first threatened the people with a word from God and later expanded on these short "threats" by adding the reason why God was sending judgment (the "reproach"). In addition, Gunkel found within the prophetic books exhortations, disputations, lawsuits, allegories, and historical reviews; poetic literature in the prophets included borrowed secular laments, hymns, songs, liturgies, and torah readings (H. Gunkel, "The Israelite Prophecy from the Time of Amos," in J. Pelikan, ed., *Twentieth Century in the Making* [Eng. tr. 1969], pp. 73f.).

According to Gunkel, the prophetic books developed in three stages. The initial stage was the proclamation of short sayings that were orally transmitted by the prophet's disciples. This corpus included the prophet's first-person accounts as well as third-person stories about the prophet that were added by disciples. In the second stage the sayings were arranged on the basis of subject matter (e.g., woes, oracles against foreign nations), catchwords, or some other similarity. An oracle of salvation was often placed at the end of a series of threats during this stage in order to soften the blow of these strong punishment oracles. The final stage involved the organization of smaller collections into full-length books, along with other redactional alterations and additions.

Gunkel's theory that the "reproach" was a second-stage addition to the original prophetic "threats" was abandoned in later form-critical studies. C. Westermann's comparison of prophetic speech forms with the Mari Letters demonstrated that the prophets used messenger speech patterns (Westermann, pp. 98-128). He proposed two basic speech forms: the judgment speech to individuals and the announcement of judgment against Israel. The second form he considered an expansion of the simple judgment speech to individuals, which was made up of a summons to hear, an accusation, an introduction to the announcement of judgment (which usually began with "therefore" and the messenger formula "thus says the Lord"), and finally the announcement of judgment. Westermann's work was based on good comparative and biblical examples and has done much to clarify some of the terminology used by form critics. K. Koch (*Growth of Biblical Tradition* [Eng. tr. 1969], p. 193) suggested that the title "prediction of disaster" be used in place of Westermann's "announcement of judgment," because the latter title implied that the prophets were declaring the results of a legal decision. Koch's observations have been helpful, but the *Sitz im Leben* of prophecy is still not a settled question.

R. Bach (*Die Aufforderungen zur Flucht und zum Kampf im alttestamentlichen Prophetenspruch* [1962]) concluded that the *Sitz im Leben* of prophetic pronouncements was to be found in the holy war traditions that the classical prophets had inherited from early charismatic leaders of the judges period, while H. G. Reventlow (*Das Amt des Propheten bei Amos* [1962], p. 265) proposed that the prophet was a covenant mediator who officiated at the cultic ritual of the covenant-renewal ceremonies. E. Würthwein (*Wort und Existenz* [1970], pp. 111-126) and Jörg Jeremias (*Kultprophetie und Gerichtsverkündigung in der späten Königszeit Israels* [1970]) also believed that prophecy had a cultic background. But H. J. Boecker (*EvTh,* 20 [1960], 398-412) and several scholars who studied the covenant lawsuit (e.g., H. B. Huffmon, *JBL,* 78 [1959], 285-295; J. Harvey, *Bibl.,* 43 [1962], 172-196) focused on the legal setting that seems to stand behind many prophecies. Other prophetic speech forms that have received considerable analysis include the oracles of salvation, proclamations of salvation, woe oracles, disputation speeches, call narratives, and vision reports (see W. E. March, pp. 141-177). The goal has been to define the structure, discover the *Sitz im Leben,* and trace the development of each form.

The form-critical method has contributed to a better understanding of the relationship between prophetic oracles the basic structure of the oracles, and the way that different types of oracles developed. The attempts to define the setting of prophetic oracles have been less fruitful and conclusive, particularly when they have depended heavily on ambiguous comparative material.

Gunkel's emphasis on oral tradition was developed further by a group of Scandinavian scholars using the traditio-historical method. The goal of this approach was to discover details about the oral development of the text as it was influenced by many different traditions and life situations within the nation's history. Both the scope and the method of tradition criticism remained imprecisely defined for years (see D. A. Knight, *Rediscovering the Traditions of Israel* [rev. ed. 1975], pp. 21-31), but the general focus has been on factors that influenced the transmission of tradition in the oral stage (e.g., reinterpretation, schools of tradition, geography, sociology, politics, and redactional techniques) and on the characteristics of traditional material itself (e.g., vocabulary, plot, theme, problem, motif, and notion). H. S. Nyberg, H. Birkeland, I. Engnell, E. Nielsen, and S. Mowinckel were among the influential tradition critics. Most concluded that it was futile to attempt to find the prophet's original words, since these words were repeatedly changed and refocused during oral transmission as later schools of disciples reinterpreted them in relationship to new events (W. E. Rast, *Tradition History and the OT* [1972], pp. 60f.).

The lack of objective criteria for traditio-historical research has resulted in a considerable amount of intuitive conjecturing by those who have followed this approach. A depreciation of historical studies and a tendency to hypothesize transmissional developments that go beyond objective data have limited the value of many conclusions. Nevertheless, some of the tradition studies that have located the kerygmatic thrust of traditional material have reached significant results (see W. Brueggemann and H. W. Wolff, *Vitality of OT Traditions* [1975]).

Well aware of the limitations of form criticism, J. Muilenburg proposed a new approach to prophetic literature called rhetorical criticism (*JBL,* 88 [1969], 1-18). Form criticism had stressed the typical way in which various forms were used but failed to emphasize the unique features of each individual prophet's use of that form. Rhetorical criticism filled this gap by investigating the structural patterns and particularly the literary devices that marked off units, indicated shifts in the development of compositions, and signified contrasts or emphases. Repetition, vocatives, questions, refrains, and key particles were found to be important signposts to the author's thought patterns (J. Muilenburg, *HUCA,* 32 [1961], 135-160; W. Brueggemann, *JBL,* 92 [1973], 358-374).

Rhetorical criticism has made several solid contributions to the study of the prophets Isaiah (J. Muilenburg, *IB,* V [1956]) and Jeremiah (J. R. Lundbom, *Jeremiah: A Study in Ancient Hebrew Rhetoric* [1975]), although some studies have focused almost entirely on noting rhetorical indicators without demonstrating how these reveal the author's persuasive intent. Nevertheless, this method is based on observable data in the text rather than on hypothetical reconstructions; therefore it has the potential of making a significant contribution to understanding the prophets' message.

Other methods of interpreting the prophets drew their stimulus from sociological or anthropological principles. Scholars such as M. Weber, A. Lods, S. Baron, and N. Gottwald studied the prophets' involvement in the sociological conflicts between the poor and the powerful, the tribal and monarchial forms of government, and the nomadic and urban ideals (see H. F. Hahn, *OT in Modern Research* [rev. ed. 1966], pp. 157-184). Anthropological studies have usually focused on subjects such as primitive mentality, mana and sacrifices, or myth and sacred kingship; more recent studies have analyzed the prophets using comparative anthropological field studies from other cultures (see Hahn, pp. 44-82; R. C. Culley and T. W. Overholt, eds., *Anthropological Perspective on OT Prophecy* [*Semeia* 21, 1982]). These studies are not designed to give a literary understanding of the text but rather to provide a comparative analysis of cultural patterns that influenced the development of the prophetic movement.

Each of these critical approaches has offered its own unique perspective on the prophets, and each has attempted to provide a tool that would open up a few new insights into the development of prophetic literature. No one approach was designed to be used to the exclusion of all others. Subjective reconstructions abound within each area of research, and contradictory results demonstrate that the methodology to interpret prophetic literature is still in the process of development. Careful attention must be given to refining definitions of goals, procedures, and principles of evaluation. Methods that prove less fruitful will necessarily be discarded or de-emphasized, but the interpretative task will continue to be built upon investigation into the historical, cultural, social, political, and religious context of each prophetic text, as well as on an understanding of the semantic, grammatical, syntactical, and literary clues within the text itself. Comparative studies from other cultures and disciplines must remain servants rather than masters of prophetic interpretation. Nevertheless, the result of all these studies, each offering the interpreter a fuller appreciation of prophecy, should be a firmer hermeneutical base for developing a biblical theology of the prophets.

*B. Hermeneutical Principles.* Sound hermeneutical guidelines are needed in order to limit undue speculation and to secure an understanding of prophecy consistent with the original intention of the author. In many cases these principles will coincide with the same exegetical rules that apply to most other narrative or poetic texts. The OT's understanding of its own prophecies and the NT's interpretation of fulfilled prophecies provide initial guidelines for principles of interpretation, but in spite of these examples considerable disagreement still exists over how to interpret prophecy. Many of the early church fathers used allegorical principles of interpretation in order to apply the OT to Christians, but this led to many spiritual senses that were obviously not the intention of the prophets themselves. Most scholars reject these principles today, but the rationalistic approach that denies the possibility of supernatural prediction by the prophets is hardly any closer to the truth.

As with every other type of literature, the interpretation of prophecy requires an understanding of the text's historical background, context, purpose, and language. Thus, e.g., the accounts of Baalism within the northern kingdom of Israel during the time of Jeroboam II and his successors (2 K. 14:24; 15:9, 18, etc.; 17:6-18) provide information concerning the background of Hosea's condemnation of the nation for Baal-worship. Before the meaning of Am. 6:2 can be defined, the interpreter must understand the historical situation at Calneh, Hamath the Great, and Gath of the Philistines. A knowledge of the geography of Petra/Sela makes the imagery of Ob. 3f. more understandable. The literary context of Jeremiah's lament in 15:10-21 (a rejection of his calling, placed just after the Lord's command that Jeremiah was not to pray for the people of Judah because He was utterly rejecting them [14:11f.; cf. v. 19; 15:1]) makes it understandable as a somewhat natural human response (see G. V. Smith, *VT*, 29 [1978], 229-231).

Ultimately, the meaning of an oracle cannot be determined solely by either historical or literary context, but by the purpose of the author. The purpose of a rebuke of a foreign nation may be to bring assurance of salvation to Israel (Isa. 46–47), to prick the conscience of God's people who have committed worse sins (Am. 1–2), or to bring that foreign nation to its knees (Jonah 3:4f.).

Prophetic pronouncements frequently employ figurative language; thus words and syntactical constructions must be analyzed to determine the correct meaning. A shepherd and a horn could symbolize kingship (e.g., 2 S. 5:2; Dnl. 7:24); illogical or hyperbolic statements were characteristic of irony (Am. 4:4f.); figurative expressions such as "cows of Bashan" were used for negative images (4:1); the personification of singing hills could express the total revitalization of joy within the land (Isa. 44:23); and to "go to one's wife" was sometimes a euphemism for sexual relations (8:3).

Many problems in the interpretation of prophecy are connected with the meanings of words and symbols, but prophecies that were fulfilled in the OT provide some clues as to how prophecies should be interpreted. Ahijah's symbolic action and direct prophecy to Jeroboam concerning the immediate division of the kingdom was straightforward (1 K. 11:29-32), and it was literally fulfilled (12:15, 20). When Elisha predicted cheap food in the midst of a severe siege of Samaria, he did not know the details as to how this would happen; but he did know precisely when it would occur, and it happened as he said (2 K. 7:1f., 16-20). Elijah's terrible prophecy about the death of Jezebel (1 K. 21:23) was fulfilled during the reign of Jehu when the dogs ate her body (2 K. 9:31-37); in this case no date nor details about the manner of her death were predicted. Isaiah's message to Hezekiah promised that God would save Jerusalem from Sennacherib (2 K. 19:20-34), but it included nothing about how or when this deliverance would happen (cf. 2 K. 19:35).

As can be seen from these examples, most prophecies did not predict the time when God would act but focused simply on the fact that His judgment or salvation was coming. Prophecy was given to persuade the listeners to act in ways that would avoid God's judgment and bring enjoyment of His blessings. The prophets revealed the character of the sovereign God to convince their listeners to bow before His majestic power and thus receive His lovingkindness and grace. Many prophetic oracles contained conditional elements based on the people's response to God (e.g., Jonah 3:4–4:2; Jer. 26:1-6; 36:1-7; cf. the background of covenantal blessings and curses, Lev. 26; Dt. 27–28). Other prophecies contained no conditional phraseology and included promises of everlasting significance (Nu. 25:12f.; Ps. 106:30f.; Jer. 33:20-22; Ezk. 37:24-28); nevertheless, a positive relationship with God was always a prerequisite for enjoying the blessings of God's everlasting prophecies. Prophecy was therefore not just information about future events, but God's method of changing human thinking and behavior through a deeper understanding of His mighty acts in the past, present, and future.

Particular difficulties surround the optimistic eschatological prophecies that looked forward to a new act of salvation by God. These oracles described what would happen on the "day of the Lord" (cf. Am. 5:18-20; Zec. 14) or on "that day" (Isa. 2:11f.; Jer. 3:16-18) when the messianic kingdom would be established (see L. Černý, *The Day of Yahweh and Some Relevant Problems* [1948]). In various forms, this hope included the regathering of the remnant of Judah and Israel back to the land of Palestine, the renewal of prosperity, peace, and worship in Jerusalem, a spiritual revival and new covenant with God, and the appearance of the suffering servant, the righteous branch and the son of man (cf. Isa. 9, 11, 42, 49, 53; Jer. 23:3-6; 30–31; 33; Ezk. 34:25-31; 37; Hos. 2:14-25; Dnl. 7).

In interpreting these prophecies one must remember that God revealed more and more about this future hope in each successive period. If one accepts the hermeneutical principle that meanings must be based on the intentions of the original author, then interpretations of prophecy must be based on the analogy of earlier Scripture that the writer understood, not on clarifications that appear in later texts. This problem has led some (e.g., Marcion, Schleiermacher, Harnack) to reject the OT prophecies because the fuller revelation in the NT is far superior. Although few would accept this extreme position, some approaches use the allegorical and typological methods of interpretation, which usually make very little of the author's original intention and focus primarily on the NT or "spiritual" meaning. Other scholars, however, have endorsed a *sensus plenior* ("fuller sense") hermeneutical principle for prophecy that goes beyond what the prophets themselves understood. This "fuller sense" was intended by God in the OT but was not revealed until NT times; thus new meaning is read back into OT prophecy, even though one cannot discover this meaning from a grammatical-historical examination of the OT text (R. E. Brown, *The Sensus Plenior of Sacred Scripture* [1955]). Those who have used a double fulfillment or double reference method of interpretation have also rejected the principle of basing one's interpretation solely on the grammatical-historical intentions of the original author; each of these methods has in some way failed to distinguish between the original author's meaning and the new significance that could be drawn out of the text when it was applied to an analogous situation. On the other hand, the phenomenon of prophetic telescoping occurs throughout the prophetic books. Although the prophets sometimes knew the order of events (cf. Dnl. 2, 7–8), their time perspective was restricted because their orientation to future events was incomplete.

At least three reasons can be given for the existence of widely differing views on the interpretation of prophecy: (1) interpreters do not agree on how to interpret visions and other oracles that contain poetic and symbolic images; (2) there is a temptation to read back into earlier prophecies NT fulfillment or even present-day events; and (3) the philosophical or theological biases of present interpreters exert an influence on the way they understand the data. Formulations of more moderate positions that recognize these pitfalls have created a positive outlook for future studies (see K. L. Barker, *JETS*, 25 [1982], 3-16).

*See also* FULFIL.

***VI. Prophecy in the NT.***–During the intertestamental period the Jews recognized that prophecy had ceased, but they did look forward to a revival of prophecy during the future messianic age (cf. 1 Macc. 4:46; 9:27; 14:41). Josephus stated that the period of the prophets ended about the time of Artaxerxes king of Persia (*CAp* i.8 [40]); but he reported that John Hyrcanus had the gift of prophecy (*BJ* i.2.8 [68f.]) and that Theudas (*Ant.* xx.5.1 [97]) and a certain Egyptian (*Ant.* xx.8.6 [169f.]) falsely claimed to be prophets.

The Greek noun *prophḗtēs* (the LXX translation of Heb. *nāḇî'*) and its related verbal, adjectival, and nominal forms were used by the NT to describe the proclamation of God's word through the influence of the Holy Spirit (e.g., Lk. 1:67; 2 Pet. 1:20). The NT's use of *prophḗtēs* to refer to contemporary prophets as well as OT prophets demonstrates that the NT authors saw a continuity between these two eras of prophecy. The NT identified Isaiah as a prophet and quoted him twenty times (e.g., Mt. 1:22; 3:3; 4:14; 8:17; 12:17; 13:14; 15:7), named Samuel as one of the earliest prophets (Acts 3:24), and referred to David (1:16-19; 2:25-32), Elisha (Lk. 4:27), Jeremiah (Mt. 2:17), Daniel (24:15), Joel (Acts 2:16), and Jonah (Mt. 12:39) as prophets. Other prophetic books were quoted but not named: Hosea (Mt. 2:15), Amos (Acts 15:15), Micah (Mt. 2:5), and Habakkuk (Acts 13:40). The NT authors believed that the words of the prophets contained in the holy Scriptures (cf. Rom. 1:2) were the words of God (e.g., Mt. 1:22; 2:15; Acts 3:18, 21; He. 1:1). The NT understood OT prophecy to be filled with predictions about Christ: His virgin birth (Mt. 1:23) in Bethlehem (2:5), His ministry in Zebulun and Naphtali (4:12-16), His entry into Jerusalem (21:4), and His death and resurrection (26:56; Lk. 18:31; 24:25-27, 44; Acts 2:30; 3:18; 26:22). The NT authors frequently referred to the whole body of OT prophetic literature collectively as "the prophets" (e.g., Mt. 26:56; Jn. 6:45; Rom. 1:2), often together with the Law (Mt. 5:17; 7:12; 22:40; Lk. 16:16; 24:44; Jn. 1:45; Acts 13:15; 26:22).

The first instances of NT prophecy occur in the Lukan birth narratives. Filled with the Holy Spirit (cf. Lk. 1:15), Elizabeth prophesied concerning Mary and her unborn child (1:41-45), Zechariah prophesied at John the Baptist's naming (vv. 67-79), and Simeon prophesied at Jesus' purification (2:25-35); at the latter event Jesus was also recognized and proclaimed by Anna the prophetess (vv. 36-38). The Jews and Jesus Himself considered John the Baptist to be a prophet (Mt. 11:9-14; 14:5; 21:26; Mk. 11:32; Lk. 20:6; cf. 1:15); but John denied that he was "the prophet" (Jn. 1:21; cf. Dt. 18:15, 18).

The people of Palestine thought that Jesus was a prophet (Mt. 16:14; 21:46; Mk. 8:27), based on the miracles He performed, e.g., healing the blind man (Jn. 9:17), raising a man from the dead (Lk. 7:15f.), and telling the Samaritan woman about her past life of sin (Jn. 4:19). Some saw Him as "the prophet" (Jn. 6:14; 7:40), i.e., the fulfillment of the promise that God would raise up another great prophet like Moses (Dt. 18:15, 18). Jesus referred to Himself as a prophet at two different times (Mt. 13:57; Mk. 6:4; Lk. 4:24; 13:33). Both Peter and Stephen preached that Jesus was the fulfillment of Moses' promise in Dt. 18 (Acts 3:22; 7:37). When Jesus expounded the Scriptures He taught with authority and not like the scribes (Mt. 7:29 par.). That He spoke the word of God with power caused Him to be associated with the OT prophets (Jn. 7:40). Jesus related His own death to the persecution of the prophets (Lk. 13:33f.); His predictions about His later coming as the Son of man (e.g., Mt. 24:27-31) identified Him with the important eschatological events that the prophets announced (cf. Dnl. 7:13f.).

The early Church had its own prophets. The NT mentions several prophets from Antioch, including Agabus, who predicted a famine in Jerusalem through the inspiration of the Holy Spirit (Acts 11:27f.; 13:1; 21:10); Judas and Silas, who encouraged the congregation at Antioch (15:32); and the four daughters of Philip (21:9). As a result of Paul's ministry at Ephesus, the Holy Spirit came upon the believers, and they spoke in tongues and prophesied (19:6). At Pentecost the whole company of Jesus' disciples (about 120 persons; see 1:15) were filled with the Holy

Spirit and spoke in other tongues (2:4); this was interpreted as a fulfillment of Joel's prophecy that God would pour out His Spirit and sons and daughters would prophesy (Acts 2:17f.; cf. Joel 2:28f. [MT 3:1f.]). Because this prophesying was in recognizable languages (Acts 2:6-11), the author may have held to Paul's distinction between prophecy, which upbuilds, encourages, and edifies the Church, and speaking in tongues, which was for private edification unless there was an interpreter (1 Cor. 14:1-5, 39).

Prophets and apostles were the pillars of the early Church (Eph. 2:20), and the gift of prophecy was listed immediately after the gift of apostleship (1 Cor. 12:28; Eph. 3:5; 4:11). Paul never called himself a prophet, although he did claim to be an apostle. In the Pauline epistles a prophet was one who called mankind to repentance (1 Cor. 14:24). Prophecy was a gift through which God revealed mysteries and knowledge (13:2; cf. 14:30). It involved more than just teaching God's word (cf. 1 Tim. 1:18; 4:14), for the gifts of prophecy and teaching are often distinguished (Acts 13:1; 1 Cor. 12:28; Eph. 4:11). Prophets were not limited to known traditions and doctrines, for they received new revelations about the present and future as well as the past. The prophets were exhorted to examine one another's works to make sure that no false teaching would arise (1 Cor. 14:29; 1 Thess. 5:20-22; 1 Jn. 4:1). (*See also* SPIRITUAL GIFTS.)

*See also* PROPHECY, FALSE.

***Bibliography.***–W. F. Albright, *FSAC*; B. W. Anderson and W. Harrelson, eds., *Israel's Prophetic Heritage* (*Festschrift* J. Muilenburg; 1962); W. R. Arnold, *Ephod and Ark* (1917, repr. 1969); D. Aune, *Prophecy in Early Christianity and the Ancient Mediterranean World* (1983); W. J. Beecher, *Prophets and the Promise* (1905); W. Brueggemann, *Prophetic Imagination* (1978); M. Buber, *Prophetic Faith* (Eng. tr. 1949); R. E. Clements, *Prophecy and Covenant* (*SBT*, 1/43, 1965); *Prophecy and Tradition* (1975); C. H. Cornill, *Prophets of Israel* (Eng. tr. 10th ed. 1913); A. B. Davidson, *OT Prophecy* (1903); B. Duhm, *Israels Propheten* (1922); F. C. Eiselin, *Prophecy and the Prophets* (1909); G. Fohrer, *Studien zur alttestamentlichen Prophetie* (1967); W. Gesenius, *Thesaurus Linguae Hebraeae et Chaldaeae Veteris Testamenti*, II/2 (1840), 838a; R. B. Girdlestone, *Grammar of Prophecy* (1901); N. Gottwald, *All the Kingdoms of the Earth* (1964); A. Guillaume, *Prophecy and Divination Among the Hebrews and Other Semites* (1938); H. Gunkel, *Die Propheten* (1917); H. A. Guy, *NT Prophecy: Its Origin and Significance* (1947); A. Haldar, *Associations of Cult Prophets Among the Ancient Semites* (1945); P. Hanson, *Dawn of Apocalyptic* (rev. ed. 1979); A. Heschel, *The Prophets* (Eng. tr. 1962); G. Hölscher, *Die Profeten: Untersuchungen zur Religionsgeschichte Israels* (1914); J. P. Hyatt, *Prophetic Religion* (1947); A. Jepsen, *Nabi* (1934); A. R. Johnson, *Cultic Prophet in Ancient Israel* (2nd ed. 1962); H. Knight, *Hebrew Prophetic Consciousness* (1947); K. Koch, *Rediscovery of Apocalyptic* (Eng. tr. 1972); *The Prophets* (Eng. tr. 1982); E. König, *Hebräisches und aramäisches Wörterbuch zum AT* (1936); A. Kuenen, *Prophets and Prophecy in Israel* (Eng. tr. 1877); J. Lindblom, *Prophecy in Ancient Israel* (1962); W. E. March, "Prophecy," in J. H. Hayes, ed., *OT Form Criticism* (1974), pp. 141-177; W. McKane, *Prophets and Wise Men* (*SBT*, 1/44, 1965); T. J. Meek, *Hebrew Origins* (rev. ed. 1960), pp. 148-183; S. Mowinckel, *Prophecy and Tradition* (1946); *He That Cometh* (Eng. tr. 1956); B. D. Napier, *Prophets in Perspective* (1963); A. Neher, *Prophetic Existence* (Eng. tr. 1969); C. von Orelli, *OT Prophecy and the Consummation of God's Kingdom* (Eng. tr. 1885); D. L. Petersen, *Late Israelite Prophecy* (1977); R. H. Pfeiffer, *Religion in the OT* (1961); G. von Rad, *Message of the Prophets* (Eng. tr. 1968); T. H. Robinson, *Prophecy and Prophets in Ancient Israel* (2nd ed. 1953); H. H. Rowley, ed., *Studies in OT Prophecy* (*Festschrift* T. H. Robinson; 1950); *Servant of the Lord* (rev. ed. 1965); D. S. Russell, *Method and Message of Jewish Apocalyptic* (1964); S. J. Schultz, *The Prophets Speak* (1968); R. B. Y. Scott, *Relevance of the Prophets* (1947); W. R. Smith, *Prophets of Israel* (1882); *TDNT*, VI, *s.v.* προφήτης κτλ. (Krämer, Rendtorff, Meyer, Friedrich); *THAT*, II, *s.v.* נָבִיא (Jörg Jeremias); J. Wellhausen, *Prolegomena to the History of Israel* (Eng. tr. 1885); C. Westermann, *Basic Forms of Prophetic Speech* (Eng. tr. 1967); C. F. Whitley, *Prophetic Achievement* (1963); R. R. Wilson, *Prophecy and Society in Ancient Israel* (1980); E. J. Young, *My Servants, the Prophets* (repr. 1955); W. Zimmerli, *The Law and the Prophets* (Eng. tr. 1965).

G. V. SMITH

**PROPHET, CHRIST AS.** *See* CHRIST, OFFICES OF II.

**PROPHET, OLD.** *See* OLD PROPHET.

**PROPHETESS** [Heb. *n^eḇîʾâ*; Gk. *prophḗtis*]. A female prophet; in one instance possibly the wife of a prophet (Isa. 8:3).

In the OT the title is applied to five women: to Miriam the sister of Moses and Aaron (Ex. 15:20), to Deborah the charismatic judge (Jgs. 4:4), to the wife of Isaiah (Isa. 8:3), to Huldah, who was consulted by King Josiah (2 K. 22:14; 2 Ch. 34:22), and to No-adiah, a false prophetess who opposed Nehemiah (Neh. 6:14). Rabbinical tradition recognized seven prophetesses who prophesied to Israel: Sarah, Miriam, Deborah, Hannah, Abigail, Huldah, and Esther (T.B. *Megilloth* 14a).

In the NT the term appears only twice, referring to Anna, who recognized and proclaimed Jesus as the Messiah (Lk. 2:36-38), and to the temptress Jezebel, "who calls herself a prophetess" (Rev. 2:20). Other women who prophesied in the early Church are referred to in Acts 21:9 (the four daughters of Philip) and 1 Cor. 11:5. One of the signs of the messianic age is that men and women will prophesy (Acts 2:17f.).

*See also* PROPHECY. N. J. O.

**PROPHETS, FALSE.** *See* PROPHECY, FALSE.

**PROPITIATE; PROPITIATION.** The removal of wrath by the offering of a gift. This may be a crude process of appeasement or bribery, or it may denote something much more refined and spiritual.

In modern times there is a widespread disinclination to use this word of Christ's saving work. Two main points are to be taken into consideration. One is the meaning of the Greek verb *hiláskomai*, which with its cognates translates a number of OT words, notably Heb. *kipper*. In nonbiblical usage there is not the slightest doubt that *hiláskomai*, etc., means "propitiate." The terms are used frequently, always in the sense of averting anger.

Some scholars, such as C. H. Dodd, have argued that in the Bible the word-group means "expiation" rather than propitiation. Although rather complicated, the argument depends largely on translation from Hebrew to the Greek of the LXX. Dodd examined the words that *exiláskomai* renders and found that they do not have meanings like "appease." He also looked at other words used to translate *kipper*, with a like result. He concluded that in the Bible the words of the *hiláskomai* group do not mean "propitiate" but rather "expiate." The examination certainly shows that pagan ideas of bribing the deity are absent from the Bible, but it is doubtful that it shows more. Dodd did not examine the contexts of the passags he chose; the idea of wrath is plainly there, and the *hiláskomai* words clearly denote the removal of this wrath.

For example, the LXX translates Heb. *sālaḥ*, "forgive," by *hiláskomai* in Lam. 3:42f. It might be assumed that *hiláskomai* here means no more than "forgive," but when read in its context the word plainly indicates a forgiveness that involves putting away wrath: "We have transgressed and rebelled, and thou hast not forgiven. Thou hast wrapped thyself with anger and pursued us . . . ." The putting away of wrath appears to be the meaning of these words elsewhere in the Bible and in nonbiblical literature.

The other significant point is that both the OT and NT speak often of the wrath of God. This fact does not depend on the linguistics of *hiláskomai*. If God's wrath is exercised toward sinners, then it must be taken into account in the process whereby forgiveness is secured. Dodd and others have attempted to show that by "wrath" the Bible means nothing other than an impersonal process of cause and effect. A person sins, and disaster follows, which is described as God's wrath coming upon the person. It is hard to see, however, how anger could be more forthrightly expressed as personal than in Ps. 60:1-3 (MT 3-5); Isa. 30:27-31; Jer. 23:20; Ezk. 7:8f.; etc. The Bible writers repeatedly use the language of wrath to bring out the vigorous nature of God's opposition to evil.

It may be granted that words like propitiation and wrath are not ideal words to use of God's activities, but no better words seem to be available. In particular, "expiation," which is favored by most today (including the RSV) as a replacement for "propitiation," simply will not do (see *DNTT,* III, 151-160). It is an impersonal word (one expiates a thing, a sin or a crime), whereas a personal term is needed to describe what Christ has done for His people. Also, "expiation" does not bring out the settled opposition of God's holy nature to everything that is evil. Propitiation does not mean that God is bribed to be gracious; the removal of His wrath is due to Himself alone (cf. Lev. 17:11; Ps. 78:38). But it is really wrath that is removed.

There are four important NT passages. Rom. 3:25, RV, tells of Christ Jesus "whom God set forth to be a propitiation, through faith, in his blood, to show his righteousness because of the passing over of the sins done aforetime." According to He. 2:17, RV, "it behooved him [Christ] in all things to be made like unto his brethren, that he might become a merciful and faithful high priest in things pertaining to God, to make propitiation for the sins of the people." In 1 Jn. 2:22; 4:10, RV, Christ is called "the propitiation for our sins." Each of these passages puts forward the thought that God's opposition to sin is more than token. His wrath is exercised toward those who sin. But in that situation Christ is the answer; He provides the means of averting the divine wrath. It is this that the NT writers have in mind when they speak of propitiation. And this is an element in Christianity that we dare not surrender.

*See also* EXPIATE; ATONE.

***Bibliography.***–*DNTT,* III, 148-166; C. H. Dodd, *Bible and the Greeks* (2nd ed. 1954); *Romans* (*MNTC,* 1932); R. Nicole, *WTJ,* 17 (1954/55), 117-157; L. Morris, *NTS*, 2 (1955), 33-43; *APC*; *TDNT*, III, *s.v.* ἵλεως κτλ. (Hermann, Büchsel). L. MORRIS

**PROPORTION.** A term used by the RSV to denote a "correspondence" with respect to quantity (of land, Nu. 35:8; Heb. *k^epî,* lit. "according to the mouth of"; cf. AV) or degree (of wrongdoing, Dt. 25:2; *k^edê,* lit. "according to the sufficiency of," "corresponding to" [cf. NEB]; AV "according to"). It is employed in the latter sense by the AV, RSV, and NEB to render Gk. *analogía* in Rom. 12:6. The meaning of the phrase *katá tḗn analogían tḗs písteōs* (AV "according to the proportion of faith") has been hotly debated. The interpretation hinges on the meaning of *analogía* (used only here in the NT; in classical Greek it can denote "correspondence," "agreement" [cf. Eng. "analogy"], "right relationship," "standard," or "proportion" — even "mathematical proportion") and of *pístis* (*see* FAITH IV, V). Thus, while some scholars interpret the phrase to mean that the gift of prophecy must be exercised within the limits of one's own gift of faith (e.g., Kittel, Taylor, Barrett, Murray), others read it as instructing that the prophetic gift be exercised in conformity with "the faith" — i.e., the objective faith (or doctrine) they had been taught (e.g., Calvin, Hodge, Bultmann [p. 213], Käsemann).

In the AV "proportion" also translates Heb. *maʿar* (lit. "nakedness," "empty space"; cf. RSV "space"; NEB "blank space") in 1 K. 7:36 and *ʿēreḵ* (lit. "arrangement"; RSV "frame") in Job 41:12 (MT 4).

***Bibliography.***–Comms. on Romans *in loc.* by C. K. Barrett (*HNTC,* 1957), J. Calvin (Eng. tr. 1960), C. Hodge (rev. ed. 1886), E. Käsemann (Eng. tr. 1980), J. Murray (*NICNT,* 1965), and V. Taylor (1955); also *TDNT,* I, *s.v.* ἀναλογία (G. Kittel); IV, *s.v.* πιστεύω κτλ. (R. Bultmann). N. J. O.

**PROSELYTE.**

I. The Term
II. *Gēr* in the OT
III. *Prosḗlytos* in the LXX
IV. Extent of Jewish Proselytism
  A. OT Background
  B. Impact of the Diaspora
  C. Intertestamental Period
  D. Roman Reaction
  E. In the NT
  F. Tannaitic Period
V. Entry Requirements
  A. Circumcision
  B. Baptism
VI. Proselytes and God-Fearers
VII. In Rabbinic Literature
VIII. Conclusion

***I. The Term.***–Our word "proselyte" derives from Gk. *prosḗlytos.* This term, not used in classical Greek, was first introduced in the Septuagint (LXX) in the 2nd cent. B.C. as a translation of Heb. *gēr.* In the OT *gēr* usually designated a "sojourner" or "immigrant" in the land, but by the time of the Mishnah (*ca.* A.D. 200) *gēr* always referred to a convert to Judaism. Similarly, in the NT *prosḗlytos* means "convert." Thus an examination of the word *prosḗlytos* casts light on the history of both Judaism and Christianity.

Other classical Greek words were available to express the same idea that *prosḗlytos* conveyed; *métoikos* for "resident alien"; *épēlys, epḗlytos*, and *epēlýtēs* for "convert" or "newcomer." J. A. Loader thought that *prosḗlytos* derived from the *qrb* ("come near") terminology of the OT, which refers to drawing near to the holy sphere. This terminology was used as "a technical term for the acceptance of proselytes in Israel." The Greek verb *proserchomai* ("come near"), the LXX translation of *qrb*, with its related stem *elyth-* was the origin of the Greek noun *prosḗlytos*. The evolution of *prosḗlytos* from OT terminology, according to Loader, explains why "proselyte" is found only in Jewish literature.

Two cautions need to be raised about Loader's view. First, *prosḗlytos* may not have meant "convert" originally since it was a translation of *gēr.* But if *prosḗlytos* did not mean "convert" from the beginning, then it is unlikely that its origin stems from OT terminology that refers to the acceptance of converts. Second, Loader relies heavily on rabbinic literature to prove his case, but this literature is obviously later and is not decisive for establishing the origin of *prosḗlytos*. Thus more evidence is needed from the OT to establish his thesis, though a line of development from the *qrb* terminology to *prosḗlytos* is possible.

***II.* Gēr *in the OT.***–The *gēr* in the OT was a sojourner or stranger who was not a native resident of a town or region, i.e., he was an immigrant or resident alien. Sometimes *gēr* designated Israel's alien status in a foreign land. When Abraham wanted to buy a burial site in Canaan from the Hittites, he described himself as a *gēr* (Gen. 23:4). Moses lamented that he was a *gēr* in the land of Midian (Ex. 2:22; 18:3), and the Israelites are characterized as *gērîm* in the land of Egypt (Ex. 22:21; 23:9; Lev. 19:34; Dt. 10:19; cf. Dt. 23:7). In the OT *gēr* refers most often to the sojourner who resided in the land of Israel. For further discussion of the OT texts *see* SOJOURNER.

A number of texts, especially in the so-called priestly traditions, allow for a *gēr* to participate in the Israelite religious community. The *gēr,* in contrast to the "foreigner" (*nokrî*), may eat the Passover (Ex. 12:43, 48f.). But this eating is not automatic; the *gēr* must be circumcised to partake in the feast (Ex. 12:48f.; cf. Nu. 9:14; 2 Ch. 30:25). The acceptance of circumcision by a *gēr* implies that he has become a convert (cf. Gen. 17:9-14). So too a *gēr* must bring his burnt offering to the tent of meeting; otherwise, he "shall be cut off from his people" (Lev. 17:8f; cf. Lev. 22:17-19; Nu. 15:14-16). Clearly, a *gēr* must be united with the people of God before he can be cut off from them. The *gēr,* like the native Israelite, was expected to refrain from eating meat with blood or meat that was torn by animals (Lev. 17:10-15). Yahweh Himself would cut off any person who violated this injunction (Lev. 17:10). Curiously, Dt. 14:21 permits a *gēr* to eat animals that have died a natural death. Such permission does not necessarily contradict Lev. 17:10-15, for Dt. 14:21 probably refers to a *gēr* who was uncircumcised and thus not a part of the covenant community (cf. the parallelism of *gēr* with "foreigner" in Dt. 14:21, and the LXX use of *pároikos* rather than *prosēlytos* to translate *gēr*). In Lev. 17, on the other hand, the *gēr* is assumed to be part of the covenant community.

The vital involvement of the *gērîm* with Israel is also indicated by their participation in the feasts that Israel celebrated (Dt. 16:11, 14; 26:11). Such participation was not merely theoretical. In 29:11 the *gērîm* are assembled with the rest of the people before Yahweh, and they are ready to enter into covenant with Him. In Josh. 8:33, 35 the *gērîm* were present when the covenant renewal ceremony was held on Mts. Ebal and Gerizim. Indeed, the *gērîm* were assumed to be present every seven years on the Feast of Booths when the Torah was read (Dt. 31:12).

Ezekiel also believed that the *gēr* was essentially a part of the nation of Israel. Any native Israelite or *gēr* who set up an idol in his heart would be punished by Yahweh (Ezk. 14:7). But any *gēr* who resided in the land was to be treated like a native. Indeed, he would even receive an inheritance of land from the tribe in which he chose to live (Ezk. 47:22f.).

To sum up, the *gēr* in Israel was a resident alien. Even if a *gēr* did not join the poeple of God he was to be treated justly and fairly. But if a *gēr* submitted to circumcision, at least in theory and sometimes in practice he was a recipient of the same covenant privileges as the native Israelite. Thus the OT used *gēr* of the sojourner in Israel in at least two distinct ways: sometimes *gēr* refers to the immigrant who chose to live in the land of Israel, and in other passages *gēr* is a convert.

***III.* Prosēlytos *in the LXX.*–**The LXX used *prosēlytos* over seventy-five times to translate Heb. *gēr*. W. C. Allen argued that this translation designated a convert. Other scholars have argued that *prosēlytos* does not denote "convert" until the 1st cent. A.D.

It is interesting that the LXX used *pároikos* ("sojourner") to designate Israel's alien status in a foreign land (Gen. 15:13; 23:4; Ex. 2:22; Dt. 23:7), and in a theological sense to indicate that God's people were sojourners and aliens on earth (Ps. 39:12 [MT 13]; 119:19; 1 Ch. 29:15). Indeed, *pároikos* is used of God Himself (Jer. 14:8). *Pároikos* seems to have been carefully selected by the LXX translators because it would obviously be inappropriate to call the patriarchs *prosēlytos* in Egypt if the latter word meant "convert." The LXX translators apparently used *pároikos,* then, to express the ideas of one being a sojourner or a resident alien.

The study of *gēr* above has shown that even in the OT *gēr* is often used of Gentiles who had transferred their allegiance to Yahweh the God of Israel. Thus, *prosēlytos* in the LXX would sometimes describe a convert to Judaism. As was pointed out above, W. C. Allen concluded that the LXX almost always used *prosēlytos* to denote a convert. He said that the translators used *pároikos* where *gēr* could mean only "resident alien," and they used *prosēlytos* where *gēr* could possibly mean "convert." Allen was probably right that the LXX translators usually intended *prosēlytos* to be understood as "convert." But the idea that *prosēlytos* always means "convert" in the LXX is hardly convincing. The Israelites are called *prosēlytoi* during their sojourn in Egypt (Ex. 22:21; 23:9; Lev. 19:34; Dt. 10:19), and as K. Lake pointed out, in this context *prosēlytoi* surely does not mean "convert." The translation "alien" or "sojourner" is more fitting. Indeed, even in the land of Israel the native Israelites are described as *prosēlytoi* ("sojourners," Lev. 25:23) because the land belonged to Yahweh.

In addition, at least two passages in the LXX clearly use *prosēlytos* to refer to Gentiles who were not converts but resident aliens in the land. In Dt. 28:43 the *prosēlytos* will become superior to the native if Israel falls into sin and goes into captivity. In 1 Ch. 22:2 David's employment of *prosēlytoi* for forced labor is best understood as the employment of resident aliens instead of converts to Yahwism (cf. 1 K. 9:20-22).

In conclusion, Allen's careful study demonstrated that the primary meaning of *prosēlytos* in the LXX is "convert." Nevertheless, in some LXX passages *prosēlytos* clearly does not mean "convert." The word was sometimes used to describe the resident alien, and in these passages it drew on the original meaning of *gēr*. Thus in the LXX the term *prosēlytos* is in a process of evolution. Like *gēr, prosēlytos* probably meant "immigrant" originally and gradually came to mean "convert."

***IV. Extent of Jewish Proselytism.*–*A. OT Background.*** From the beginning the OT had a universal focus, at least in theory (cf. Gen. 12:3). We have already seen that the Israelites were receiving sojourners (see II-III above). The attitude of Israel toward foreigners was mixed, however. In Dt. 23:1-3 eunuchs, bastards, Ammonites, and Moabites were excluded forever from the asembly of Yahweh. Intermarriage with non-Israelites was frowned upon because such pluralism would lead Israel into idolatry (Dt. 7:1-5). This problem flared up again in the time of Ezra and Nehemiah, and the stern measure of putting away foreign wives was adopted (Ezr. 9:2; 10:1-43; Neh. 10:30; 13:23-27). The prohibition against Ammonites and Moabites was recalled in Nehemiah's time, and Tobiah the Ammonite was expelled from the chambers of the temple (Neh. 13:1-9; cf. Ezk. 44:7-9).

Other OT traditions reflect a positive attitude toward foreigners. The book of Ruth is the story of a Moabite woman who courageously chose to be part of the people of Yahweh. The universalistic emphasis of OT theology is particularly predominant in the Prophets. The book of Jonah is a notable example of Yahweh's love for all nations. Isa. 19:18-24 looks forward to the day when Egypt and Assyria will worship Yahweh together with Israel. Zeph. 3:9f. forecasts a day when all peoples will serve Yahweh (cf. Mal. 1:11). One of the more striking universalistic passages is Isa. 56:3-8. Isaiah promises that the eunuch and foreigner who hold fast to Yahweh's covenant will not be excluded from the people of God. Yahweh's temple is not for Israel alone (cf. Dt. 23:1); it is "a house of prayer for all peoples" (Isa. 56:7). See also 1 K. 8:41-43; Ps. 86:8-10; Isa. 2:2-4; 11:9f.; 49:6; Jer. 3:17; 4:2; 12:14-17; Zec. 8:20-23; 14:16-19.

It is difficult to determine from the OT itself how many foreigners were converted to Yahweh, although the number was probably never large. 2 K. 17:24-34 relates that the Samaritans began to fear Yahweh after an attack of lions, but their religion was consciously syncretistic (cf. the conversion of Naaman, 2 K. 5:15-19a). Est. 8:17 indicates that many embraced Judaism because they were afraid of the Jews. These passages are hardly inspiring examples of success in proselytizing.

*B. Impact of the Diaspora.* Two low points in Hebrew history were the conquest of northern Israel by the Assyrians (722 B.C.) and the capture and destruction of Jerusalem by the Babylonians (586 B.C.). Both the Assyrians and the Babylonians transplanted some of the Jewish people so that a revolt would not arise in Palestine. Indeed, as the time passed, more and more Jews began to live outside Palestine.

The influence of the Jews in the Persian empire is apparent in both Daniel and Esther. Indeed, Est. 8–10 suggests that Jews were scattered throughout all the provinces of Ahasuerus (486-464 B.C.). Numerous OT passages speak of a regathering of dispersed Jews from all over the Mediterranean world (Isa. 11:12; 43:5f.; 56:8; Jer. 23:3; 29:14; 31:8; 32:37; Ezk. 11:17; 20:34, 41; 28:25; 34:13; 36:24; Zeph. 3:10; Zec. 10:10). Thus the OT offers considerable evidence that a large number of dispersed Jews was spread over a large geographical area.

Evidence from the intertestamental period also points to the increasing number of dispersed Jews. In the 5th cent. B.C. a colony of Jewish mercenaries built a temple to Yahweh at Elephantine in southern Egypt. When the Ptolemies and Seleucids fought over the land of Palestine, a large number of Jews decided to live in more peaceful foreign environments. Jews lived in Rome by at least the 2nd cent. B.C. In fact, the Romans were provoked to expel some Jews who were ardent missionaries for Judaism in 139 B.C. The number of Jews in Rome increased after 63 B.C. because Pompey brought many Jews to Rome after capturing Jerusalem.

Josephus quotes Strabo to indicate the extent of the Jewish dispersion: "It is not easy to find any place in the habitable world which has not received this nation and in which it has not made its power felt" (*Ant.* xiv.7.2 [115]). In his letter to Caligula, Agrippa I also noted that there were Jews worldwide: in Egypt, Syria, Phoenicia, Asia Minor, the Greek islands, Europe, and beyond the Euphrates (Philo *De legatione ad Gaium* 281f.). Indeed, Josephus says that in every city the sabbath and Jewish customs were widely observed (*CAp* ii.39 [282]).

The universal extent of Judaism is also acknowledged in the NT. In Acts 15:21 James says: "For from early generations Moses has had in every city those who preach him, for he is read every sabbath in the synagogues." That Paul entered synagogues at almost every stop on his missionary journey is further support for the idea that Jews lived in every part of the Roman empire. On the day of Pentecost Jews were present in Jerusalem from the regions of Mesopotamia, Asia Minor, northern Africa, Arabia, Crete, and Rome (Acts 2:9-11). It is clear from a variety of sources, therefore, that Judaism was well represented in the Roman empire and even outside it.

The significance of the Dispersion for Jewish proselytism should not be overlooked. Numerous Gentiles were exposed for the first time to the God of Israel. They were particularly attracted by the monotheism and high ethical ideals of the Jews. The origin of the SYNAGOGUE should also be sought in the Diaspora. It is difficult to date precisely when the synagogue originated, but that it was a significant force in the proselytizing of the Gentiles in the Diaspora cannot be denied (cf. Acts 15:21). The synagogue was a place where foreigners could hear God's word explained and applied. Such a place of worship may have particularly appealed to Greeks because such a mode of worship was similar in some ways to Greek philosophical schools.

*C. Intertestamental Period.* The success of Jewish proselytism in the intertestamental period was considerable. Even instances of questionable or forced conversions show the impact of Jewish religion. In a legendary account Antiochus Epiphanes promised to become a Jew on his deathbed (2 Macc. 9:17). Hasmonean nationalism was evident in several Jewish leaders. Josephus recounts that both John Hyrcanus (134-104 B.C.) and Aristobolus I (104-103 B.C.) extended the borders of Judaism by forcing circumcision and thus conversion on neighboring regions (Hyrcanus on the Idumeans and Aristobolus on the Ituraeans; *Ant.* xiii.9.1 [257f.]; 11.3 [318]). Alexander Janneus (103-76 B.C.) destroyed Pella because the inhabitants refused to submit to the Jewish law (*Ant.* xiii.15.4 [397]). Metilius, a Roman officer at the beginning of the Jewish revolt, saved his life by promising to become a Jew (*BJ* ii.17.10 [454]). Josephus made it clear that he did not believe in such compulsion (*Vita* 2.3 [113]). The rabbis also insisted that it was wrong to compel someone to be converted (T. B. *Yebamoth* 48b). Interestingly, Josephus never used the word *prosēlytos* to refer to a convert, probably because the word was not familiar to Greek readers.

The family of Herod, which was itself composed of Edomite converts, would not intermarry with anyone from other cultures if the other party would not convert to Judaism. Herod the Great would not give his sister Salome to Syllaeus of Arabia because the latter refused to be circumcised (*Ant.* xvi.7.6 [225]). Epiphanes of Commagene would not marry Drusilla, the daughter of Herod Agrippa, because he did not want to adopt the Jewish religion. Drusilla then married Azizus king of Emesa because he agreed to circumcision (*Ant.* xx.7.1 [139]). Berenice, Drusilla's sister, persuaded Polemo king of Cilicia to be circumcised and marry her, but upon divorce Polemo abandoned the Jewish religion (*Ant.* xx.7.3 [145f.]). The Herods probably required circumcision not because of their devotion to Judaism but because it was politically advantageous to insist on it.

Not all conversions to Judaism were for the sake of expedience. Judith's victory over Holofernes demonstrated the superiority of the Jewish people and the Jewish God to Achior the Ammonite (Jth. 14:10). The most notable example of a genuine conversion is Izates king of Adiabene (*Ant.* xx.2.4 [38-48]). Influenced by his mother Helena who had already been converted to Judaism, Izates was won over to Judaism by a Jew from the Diaspora named Ananias, who recommended that Izates bypass circumcision because such an act would be politically inflammatory. A short time later Eleazar, who held a stricter view on the observance of the law, persuaded Izates that he could not be a true Jew without being circumcised. Izates consented with enthusiasm and motivated his brother Monobazus and the latter's kinsmen to adopt the Jewish religion as well (*Ant.* xx.4.1 [75]).

The success of Jewish proselytism was evident in the ancient world. Apparently a considerable number of the Damascene women had adopted the Jewish religion (*BJ* ii.20.2 [560]). Fulvia, a woman of high social standing and the wife of Senator Saturninus, converted to Judaism (*Ant.* xviii.3.5 [82f.]). Judaism was also popular in Syrian Antioch, for the Jews "were constantly attracting to their religious ceremonies multitudes of Greeks" (*BJ* vii.3.3 [45]). Josephus also claims with reference to the Greeks that "many of them have agreed to adopt our laws" (*CAp* ii.10 [123]). Indeed, Josephus asserts that the Jewish religion had a universal appeal, and that many were anxious to adopt the Jewish law (*CAp* ii.39 [280-84]). Clearly, women were more apt to become proselytes than men because men did not want to undergo the painful operation of circumcision.

Philo also testifies to the success of Jewish proselytism. His writings were aimed at a cultured Greek audience, and he attempted to show that Greek philosophy was consistent with, and even derived from, Judaism. Again and again Philo praised the nobility and beauty of the Jewish religion. Apparently a significant number were converted in Alexandria, for Philo lauds their courage and dedication to their new-found faith. Of course, other Jewish writings were particularly attractive to Greeks, e.g., the LXX, the Letter of Aristeas, the Sibylline Oracles, and the Wisdom of Solomon.

*D. Roman Reaction.* The hostile reaction that the Jews sometimes received from the ancient world testifies to the breadth of the Jewish dispersion and the success of Jewish proselytism. Cicero charged that the Jewish religion was a "barbaric superstition" (*Pro Flacco* 28 [67]). Tacitus was especially disturbed with proselytes because the Jews taught them to be antisocial. Proselytes ended up despising their old gods, abandoning their country, and scorning family members (*Hist.* v.4f.). Juvenal also complained about the Jewish religion. Like Tacitus, he charged that Jews were partial to fellow believers. He also condemned those who were attracted to Judaism. The father would begin by observing the sabbath and other Jewish customs, and the son would go a step further and submit to circumcision (*Satires* xiv.96-106).

Josephus wrote an apologetic work (*Contra Apion*) to counteract the calumnies of an Egyptian named Apion. Apion promulgated the rumor that every year the Jews captured a Greek, sacrificed him, ate his entrails, and promised always to despise Greeks. Josephus showed that the Jewish people had a long and honored antiquity, that their laws were humane and civilized, and that Moses had already anticipated the things of value in Greek culture.

There were other examples of discrimination against Jews in the ancient world. In A.D. 38 the local government in Alexandria propagated an attack on Jewish residents. Philo was sent to Caligula to lodge an official complaint against the perpetrators (Philo *In Flaccum*; *Ad Gaius*). The negative response engendered by Judaism in the Roman world demonstrates the significant impact of Jewish religion in NT times.

*E. In the NT.* The word "proselyte" is mentioned only four times in the NT. In every case it clearly refers to a convert to Judaism. Mt. 23 contains Jesus' blistering exposé of hypocrisy among the Jewish religious leaders: "Woe to you, scribes and Pharisees, hypocrites! for you traverse sea and land to make a single proselyte, and when he becomes a proselyte, you make him twice as much a child of hell as yourselves" (v. 15). Jesus implicitly acknowledged the intensity of Jewish missionary zeal; geographical obstacles did not stop the Jews from pursuing their goal. The verse must be carefully interpreted, for Jesus was not condemning the *fact* of proselytizing; He was criticizing the *result*. The convert becomes twice as bad as the person who converted him.

On the day of Pentecost a great number of Jews from the Diaspora were present for the festival (Act 2:9-11; cf. Dt. 16:11). In Acts 2:10 Luke notes that "both Jews and proselytes" were in the audience, i.e., both Jews and Gentile converts to Judaism were at the feast. In v.11 Luke also notes the presence of Cretans and Arabians. At least three views have been suggested on the placement of "Jews and proselytes" in the list. (1) Luke originally closed out the list with the terms "Jews and proselytes," and the inclusion of Cretans and Arabians was a later gloss. The way the text stands now the words "Jews and proselytes" interrupt the geographical character of Luke's list. But if the words "Cretans and Arabians" were a later gloss, then Luke placed "Jews and proselytes" at the end of his list, indicating that every geographical region had representatives from both classes. The problem with this interpretation is the lack of manuscript evidence for a gloss in v.11. (2) Luke simply inserted "Jews and proselytes" into the middle of the list to indicate that every geographical region listed had representatives from both groups. He added the regions of Crete and Arabia as an afterthought. This interpretation is also possible, but its weakness is that Luke's listing is fairly well organized geographically. Thus the idea that "Cretans and Arabians" is an afterthought is improbable. (3) It seems most likely that Luke included the phrase "both Jews and proselytes" after the phrase "visitors from Rome" for a specific reason. Luke was not saying that every region was represented by both ethnic Jews and proselytes (although such a diverse representation was possible); instead, he was making the specific point that both ethnic Jews and proselytes were represented from Rome. Perhaps he mentioned this because Rome was the ultimate destination of Paul's mission to the Gentiles in the book of Acts (chs. 21–28).

In Acts 6:1-6 the Seven are appointed by the church in Jerusalem to administer the food in such a way that the Hellenistic widows are not treated unfairly. One of the Seven, Nicolaus, is described as "a proselyte of Antioch" (v. 5). Such a description of Nicolaus implies that the other six appointees were ethnic Jews; only Nicolaus was a convert to Judaism.

To sum up, all three of the verses where "proselyte" is mentioned in the NT provide further evidence that the Jews made converts all over the Roman world. (For a discussion of "proselytes" in Acts 13:43, see VI below.)

*F. Tannaitic Period.* The number of proselytes probably declined in the tannaitic period due to several factors. (1) The rabbis had mixed feelings toward proselytes. Some, like Hillel, were disposed to welcome proselytes and were even inclined to relax the requirements a bit at the outset so that the newcomer could perceive the true spirit of Judaism (Mish. *Aboth* i.12; T.B. *Shabbath* 31a). On the other hand, Shammai viewed proselytes with some suspicion and demanded that they be thoroughly examined before admittance. In addition, some Jews feared that proselytes would return to the idolatry whence they came (T.B. *Abodah Zarah* 24a) and that they did not observe the ceremonial law properly (Mish. *Niddah* vii.3). Indeed, some rabbis argued that proselytes were like a scab that adhered to the Jewish people (T.B. *Yebamoth* 47b, 109b; *Kiddushin* 70b). Some scholars suggest, however, that the above description was meant only as a joke and should not be interpreted as a negative attitude toward proselytes. (2) The period around the time of the Bar Cochba revolt (A.D. 132-135) was a time of intense persecution of Judaism. Hadrian (A.D. 117-138) forbade the practice of castration, and circumcision was apparently viewed as an equivalent operation. The restriction against circumcision obviously lessened the chances that any Gentile would turn to Judaism. Antoninus Pius (A.D. 138-161) relaxed the restrictions against circumcision, but conversion to Judaism was still forbidden. (3) Christianity was more attractive to Gentiles than Judaism. The Christian faith did not require circumcision, and it had a more universal appeal. Of course not all proselytizing activity ceased after A.D. 70, but the age of vigorous Jewish missionary effort had ended.

*V. Entry Requirements.*–The OT clearly states that circumcision is the only required initiation rite for entrance into the covenant community (Gen. 17:9-14; Ex. 12:48). From 200 B.C. on, however, two major issues became the focus of controversy. (1) Was circumcision considered unnecessary for conversion to Judaism by a significant number of Jews? (2) When was baptism added as a requirement for proselytes?

*A. Circumcision.* A number of scholars (McEleney, Kuhn, Borgen) maintain that a considerable portion of Judaism, especially in the Diaspora, did not require the circumcision of proselytes. McEleney claimed that Philo apparently did not think circumcision was crucial for a proselyte: "(Scripture) first makes it clearly apparent and demonstrable that in reality the sojourner [Gk. *prosḗlytos*] is one who circumcises not his uncircumcision but his desires and sensual pleasures and the other passions of the soul" (*Quaestiones et Solutiones in Exodum* ii.2). This passage seems to indicate that Philo was not interested in the physical circumcision of proselytes; instead, he demanded that a proselyte be circumcised in heart. Philo proceeds in the same passage to define a proselyte as one who abandons polytheism and worships one God. Indeed, when Philo describes a proselyte he usually focuses on three things: forsaking the fables and ignorance of false gods, cleaving to the truth, and recognizing the validity of monotheism (*De Specialibus legibus* i.56f. [307-309]; iv.34 [177-178]; *De virtutibus* 20 [102-104], 39f. [219-221]).

The incident of King Izates is also used to show that circumcision was not always required of a proselyte (*Ant.* xx.2.4 [38-46]). After all, Ananias, who was a Jew from the Diaspora, did not require circumcision of Izates (*Ant.* xx.2.4 [41]). Izates submitted to circumcision only when Eleazar, a strict Jew from Palestine, convinced him of its necessity. Nevertheless, the view of Ananias, according to some scholars, shows that there was some laxity in requiring circumcision among Diaspora Jews.

McEleney said that rabbinic literature also indicated that circumcision was sometimes waived. The most famous example was the dispute between Rabbi Eliezer and Rabbi Joshua (A.D. 90-130) over whether both circumcision and ritual baptism were required for conversion to Judaism (T.B. *Yebamoth* 46a). Rabbi Eliezer argued that circumcision without baptism sufficed to make one a proselyte, but Rabbi Joshua said that baptism without circumcision was sufficient to be initiated into Judaism, arguing from the fact that women are baptized but not circumcised. The position of Rabbi Joshua seems to show that some circles in Judaism did not require circumcision as an initiation rite.

On the other hand, strong arguments support the idea that circumcision was almost always required of proselytes. J. Nolland maintained that McEleney and others misconstrued the nature of the evidence. Philo did say that a proselyte is not one who is physically circumcised but one who is spiritually circumcised. Yet such a statement from Philo need not imply that he discounted the necessity of circumcision. Elsewhere Philo criticized those who rejected the outward observance of circumcision, even though they were devoted to the spiritual significance of the rite (*Migratione de Abraham* 89-93). Philo thought one should be devoted to both the outward sign and the inward meaning of the rite. In the passage where Philo emphasized spiritual circumcision, he may have been criticizing the notion that physical circumcision alone classifies one as a proselyte. An emphasis on the spiritual significance of the rite fits with Philo's interest in the allegorical or spiritual meaning of outward observances. Nevertheless, Philo's insistance on the necessity of physical circumcision in *Migratione de Abraham* shows that he did not consider the outward rite optional.

The waiver of circumcision by Ananias in the case of King Izates should not be pressed too far. Ananias counseled against circumcision because he was afraid that the king would suffer harm, and also because Ananias was fearful that he himself would be punished. It seems fair to conclude that Ananias's conviction sprang more from expedience than from theological integrity. Moreover, even Ananias said that because of the present danger God would forgive the omission of circumcision. Such a statement makes it plain that Ananias believed that circumcision was necessary and right; otherwise, an assurance of divine forgiveness would be superfluous.

Rabbi Joshua's claim that circumcision should not be required seems to be clear evidence that the necessity of the rite was disputed. But one should be careful about drawing this conclusion too quickly. Often the other side is presented in a rabbinic debate simply for the sake of discussion, not because the issue was really being debated in practice. Furthermore, the heart of the debate between Rabbi Joshua and Rabbi Eleazar seems to have been on the necessity of baptism, rather than on the necessity of circumcision. The requirement of ritual ablutions is treated at length in the text, but the obligation to submit to circumcision is dropped. This lack of discussion on circumcision would be unthinkable if it were seriously being considered as an optional rite. But scant attention is paid to the circumcision issue probably because all Rabbi Joshua wanted to prove was that baptism was necessary. He made a dogmatic statement at the beginning about circumcision as a polemical point to further his argument, not because he was seriously thinking of dispensing with circumcision.

In a few cases circumcision may have been considered unnecessary for conversion, but most of the evidence links circumcision with conversion to Judaism. Even the evidence that is used to suggest that circumcision was unnecessary for conversion in the Diaspora is not very convincing. Indeed, some scholars who think circumcision was optional see a parallel to Paul's claim that circumcision was unnecessary for Gentiles. But the alleged parallel is illusory. For reasons of expedience some Jews may have argued that circumcision was unnecessary for proselytes (e.g., Ananias), but Paul argued for the dissolution of circumcision for Gentiles not for reasons of expedience, but from a theological conviction that the new age had dawned in Christ Jesus (Gal. 5:2-6; 6:12-14; Phil. 3:2-11).

*B. Baptism.* No documentary evidence for the initiation rite of baptism can be certainly dated before the 1st cent. A.D. (Epictetus *Discourses* ii.9.19-21; Sib. Or. 4:162-170). A controversy between the schools of Shammai and Hillel may reveal one of the oldest testimonies to proselyte baptism (Mish. *Pesahim* viii.8; cf. *Eduyoth* v.2), but the text may also refer to a required purification for uncleanness before one participated in the Passover meal. The saying of Rabbi Joshua (T.B. *Yebamoth* 46a) that was examined earlier is another reference to the rite in the 1st cent. A.D. The context of the discussion between Rabbi Joshua and

Rabbi Eliezer suggests that the real controversy was over the validity of baptism as an initiation rite. A controversy over the legitimacy of baptism may imply that baptism was not universally recognized as an appropriate initiation rite. If this is the case, the beginnings of proselyte baptism could have been relatively recent, and this would explain the intensity of the controversy between Rabbi Eliezer and Rabbi Joshua. Scholars who posit such a late date emphasize that Jewish sources reveal no trace of the rite before the 1st cent. A.D. Mostly the advocates of this position would place the origin of proselyte baptism after the destruction of the temple (A.D. 70).

On the other hand most scholars claim that proselyte baptism was much earlier. They suggest that the attestation of proselyte baptism in the 1st cent. A.D. indicates that the rite was practiced some time before it was mentioned in the sources. But the assumption that proselyte baptism was required from the beginning is insupportable (contra M. Pope, *IDB*, III, *s.v.*). After all, there were converts to Yahweh in the OT, and the OT clearly indicates that proselyte baptism was not a requirement for those entering the covenant community. The date of the start of such a practice must be deduced from the available evidence. Since the documentary evidence for the origin of proselyte baptism is not until late in the 1st cent. A.D., the date of the origin of the practice is uncertain. It is entirely possible that the rite started prior to the 1st cent. A.D. and that none of the extant Jewish sources mentions it. One should not, however, build a hypothesis on a hypothesis and claim that John's baptism of repentance was influenced by Jewish proselyte baptism, for this cannot be conclusively demonstrated from the evidence. By the time of the rabbinic period proselytes had to be circumcised, baptized, and present an offering (T.B. *Kerithoth* 9a).

*VI. Proselytes and God-Fearers.*–Many scholars see a parallel between the "God-fearers" in rabbinic literature and the "God-fearers" in the NT. In rabbinic literature the *gēr tôšāḇ* was a Gentile who observed the Noachian commandments but was not considered a convert to Judaism because he did not agree to circumcision. As Moore pointed out, some scholars have made the mistake of calling the *gēr tôšāḇ* a "proselyte" or "semiproselyte." But the *gēr tôšāḇ* was really a resident alien in Israel. He was not considered a convert to Judaism, for he was permitted to eat the meat of animals who were slaughtered incorrectly, and an Israelite could take usury from him. Such practices were forbidden in dealings with fellow Jews.

Some scholars have claimed that the term "those who fear God" (*yir'ê 'ᵉlōhîm/šāmayim*) was used in rabbinic literature to denote Gentiles who were on the fringe of the synagogue. They were not converts to Judaism, although they were attracted to the Jewish religion and observed part of the law. But M. Wilcox argued that the terms "fearers of heaven" and "fearers of God" did not designate a Gentile fringe in the synagogues in rabbinic literature. If this is true one cannot depend on the rabbinic usage in positing a difference between "God fearers" and "proselytes" in Acts. In any case in the OT and other Jewish literature the phrase "those who fear Yahweh" (*yir'ê YHWH*) was a common designation for pious Israelites (Ps. 15:4; 22:23 [MT 24]; 25:12; 115:11, 13; 118:4; 135:20; Mal. 3:16; 4:2 [MT 3:20]; Sir. 2:7-17; 6:16f.; 34:13-15; Ps. Sol. 2:37; 3:16; 4:26; 1QSb 1:1; CD 10:2; 20:19f.), and thus the phrase was not a technical term to designate Gentiles who were adherents of the synagogue in the OT and the intertestamental period, although the status of the term in the rabbinic period is still open to question.

The precise status of "God-fearers" in the book of Acts is also disputed. It is generally agreed that Luke used *phoboúmenos/sebómenos tón theón* to express the same idea. But two different interpretations have been proposed to explain what that idea was. (Interestingly, the word *phobéomai* is used in the first part of Acts [10:2, 22; 13:16, 26, 43], and *sébomai* is used in the second part of the book [13:43, 50; 16:14; 17:4, 17; 18:7].)

The term "God-fearers" in Acts has traditionally been described as a technical term to designate Gentiles who attended the synagogue and were attracted by Jewish monotheism. They were not converts, however, because they did not submit to circumcision. Thus when Paul visited Jewish synagogues he found three groups of people: Jews, proselytes, and God-fearers. Paul was especially successful among God-fearers because the latter were reluctant to undergo the painful operation of circumcision, and they enthusiastically embraced Christianity because Paul contended that the rite was unnecessary.

Peter's encounter with Cornelius is used to defend the traditional view. Cornelius is described as one who fears God (Acts 10:2, 22), and he seems devoted to the Jewish religion (10:2). But it is clear that Cornelius was not a proselyte because he was considered unclean both by Peter (10:28) and by the Jews in Jerusalem (11:2f.). Thus Cornelius seems to belong in the category of Gentiles who were devoted adherents of the synagogue, although he was not a member of the Jewish religion (cf. Lk. 7:1-10).

The above distinction is also found in other places in Acts. At the beginning of his speech in the synagogue at Pisidian Antioch Paul says: "Men of Israel, and you that fear God, listen" (Acts 13:16). A clear distinction between Jews and God-fearers seems to be implied here, and since proselytes are considered part of Israel the term "God-fearers" in the speech must refer to Gentiles who were attracted to the Jewish religion but had not yet been converted. Paul's words later on in the speech are interpreted in the much same way. "Brethren, sons of the family of Abraham, and those among you that fear God" (13:26). Again native Israelites and God-fearers seem to be clearly distinguished. Acts 13:43, which describes the aftermath of Paul's speech at Pisidian Antioch, poses a problem for this interpretation. Luke says that when the meeting ended "many Jews and devout converts [*sebomenōn prosēlýtōn*] to Judaism followed Paul and Barnabas." The word "devout" (*sebomenōn*) describes God-fearers elsewhere, but here that word precedes the word "proselytes," and yet God-fearers and proselytes are supposed to refer to two distinct groups. This problem is solved by those who hold the traditional view in two ways: either the verse is textually corrupt, or Luke is using "proselyte" inaccurately.

The rest of the passages in Acts could also fit with the traditional explanation. In Thessalonica Paul's preaching was particularly effective among the God-fearers in the synagogue (Acts 17:4), and in Athens Paul argued in the synagogue with both Jews and God-fearers (v. 17). Paul departed from the synagogue in Corinth and began to teach in the house of Titius Justus, who was "a worshiper of God" (Acts 18:7). So too, Lydia, who was converted in Philippi, is described as "a worshiper of God" (16:14). In Pisidian Antioch the Jews aroused "the devout women of high standing," and Paul and Barnabas were ejected from the city (13:50).

This traditional interpretation has been the object of trenchant criticism, especially from K. Lake and M. Wilcox. They both claimed that "God-fearers" was not a technical term for Gentiles who attended the synagogue but never took the final step of becoming Jews. Such an interpretation does not necessarily imply that all Gentiles in the synagogues were full converts. It simply means that the terms "God-fearers" and "worshipers of God" were not technical terms. These terms were used to denote the piety of the people being described, whether they were Jews, proselytes, or Gentiles who were attracted to Judaism.

When one looks at the use of the terms in Acts it seems unlikely that *phoboúmenos/sebómenos tón theón* are technical terms. As we have already seen, those who maintain a traditional interpretation of Acts 13:43 claim that "proselytes" in this verse is either a gloss or a Lukan inaccuracy. But it seems clear that such solutions are adopted because the combination "devout proselytes" (*sebomén̄on prosēlýtōn*) confounds the theory that God-fearers are distinct from proselytes. It is better to admit that "God-fearer" is not used technically in Acts. After all, there is no evidence that "proselytes" is a gloss in v. 43. Furthermore, Luke uses "proselyte" accurately elsewhere (Acts 2:10; 6:5). When Luke speaks of "devout proselytes" in Acts 13:43 he is merely saying that these proselytes were pious.

In addition, if Paul distinguished between Jews and proselytes in Acts 13:43, then it is possible that the distinction he draws between "Jews" and "God-fearers" in 13:16, 26 was a distinction between Jews and proselytes rather than between Jews and uncircumcised Gentiles in the synagogue. This interpretation would be consistent with v. 43, and vv. 16 and 26 refer to the same event in Pisidian Antioch.

The references to "devout women" (13:50) and Lydia "a worshiper of God" (16:14) may also suggest that the term *sébomai* is not used as a technical term for Gentile adherents to the synagogue. After all, women did not need to be circumcised to be initiated into Judaism. Thus most women who were attracted to Judaism probably became converts.

If it is true that "God-fearers" was not always a technical term, then one has to determine from context whether the term refers to a proselyte or a Gentile who attended the synagogue. Both Acts 17:17 and 18:7 do not give enough information to decide conclusively. The example of Cornelius shows clearly that some pious Gentiles were attracted to Judaism but had not consented to circumcision (cf. Juvenal *Satires* xiv.96-100). It is possible that the Gentiles described in Acts 17:17 and 18:7 fall into the same category as Cornelius.

Nevertheless, the notion that "God-fearer" was used as a technical term cannot be adequately supported by the evidence. The word simply relates that one is a pious person. Thus Jews, proselytes, and Gentiles who were attracted to Judaism were all described as "pious." The meaning of "God-fearer" in any particular passage must be determined from the context.

In conclusion, Paul may have won the greatest number of converts from the Gentile fringe in the synagogue, but there is simply not enough evidence in Acts to prove this traditional opinion. It cannot be doubted, however, that many of Paul's converts were uncircumcised Gentiles. Otherwise, the need for the Apostolic Council in Acts 15 would be inexplicable. But this still does not prove that a significant number of uncircumcised converts were on the fringes of the synagogues, although it is possible that this was the case.

***VII. In Rabbinic Literature.***–Different facets of the rabbinic view of proselytes have been explored thus far, but at this point it is necessary to examine briefly the rabbinic attitude toward proselytes and the status of proselytes. The rabbis recognized that some people became proselytes from unworthy motives and they were labeled "false proselytes." Those who converted out of fear were called "lion proselytes" (cf. 2 K. 17:25f.). Some turned to Judaism as a result of dreams and were called "dream proselytes." The rabbis also recognized that many became proselytes from deep religious conviction, and these were called "righteous proselytes" or "true proselytes."

In theory at least the status of a proselyte was such that the proselyte was considered a newborn child (T.B. *Yebamoth* 62a). Only children born after a proselyte's conversion could be counted as heirs. Since a woman proselyte was suspected of being a harlot in her Gentile days, she could not marry a priest. But the rabbis did allow a proselyte to enter the courtyard in the Jerusalem temple. This was quite different from the Qumrân community, for the latter forbade proselytes to enter the temple of the Lord. All the verses of the OT that refer to *gēr* were applied to the proselyte in rabbinic literature, so the rabbis strongly emphasized tender concern and care for the proselyte.

***VIII. Conclusion.***–The difference between Paul and Judaism on the requirements for proselytism was a major reason why Christianity and Judaism diverged. Paul claimed that since Jesus the Messiah died on the cross the rite of circumcision was irrelevant (Gal. 5:6; 6:12-14). Such a view was naturally unacceptable to those who held that Gen. 17:9-14 taught that the rite was indissoluble.

***Bibliography.***–Books: A. Bertholet, *Die Stellung der Israeliten und der Juden zu den Fremden* (1896); B. J. Bamberger, *Proselytism in the Talmudic Period* (1939); P. Borgen, "Observations on the Theme 'Paul and Philo,'" in S. Pedersen, ed., *Pauline Literature and Theology* (1980), pp. 85-102; F. M. Derwachter, *Preparing the Way for Paul: The Proselyte Movement in Later Judaism* (1930); J. Jeremias, *Infant Baptism in the First Four Centuries* (Eng. tr. 1960); *Origins of Infant Baptism* (Eng. tr. 1965); J. Juster, *Les Juifs dans l'empire romain,* I (1914), 253-288; K. Lake, "Proselytes and God-Fearers," in *BC,* V (1933), 74-96; G. F. Moore, *Judaism in the First Centuries of the Christian Era* (3 vols., 1927-1930).

Articles: W. C. Allen, *Expos.* 4th ser., 10 (1894), 264-275; J. M. Baumgarten, *JJS,* 33 (1982), 215-225; *RQ,* 8 (1972), 87-96; N. Levison, *SJT,* 10 (1957), 45-56; J. A. Loader, *Nov.Test.*, 15 (1973), 270-77; N. J. McEleney, *NTS,* 20 (1973/74), 319-341; J. Neusner, *JBL,* 83 (1964), 60-66; J. Nolland, *Journal for the Study of Judaism,* 12 (1981), 173-194; K. Pusey, *Expos.T.*, 95 (1984), 141-45; K. Romaniuk, *Aegyptus,* 44 (1964), 66-91; H. H. Rowley, *HUCA,* 15 (1940), 313-334; F. Siegert, *Journal for the Study of Judaism,* 4 (1973), 109-164; D. Smith, *Restoration Quarterly,* 25 (1982), 13-32; T. M. Taylor, *NTS,* 2 (1956/57), 193-98; *TDNT,* VI, *s.v.* προσήλυτος (Kuhn); T. F. Torrance, *NTS,* 1 (1954/55), 150-54; M. Wilcox, *Journal for the Study of the NT,* 13 (1981), 102-122; S. Zeitlin, *JQR,* 49 (1958/59), 241-270.

T. R. SCHREINER

**PROSPER; PROSPEROUS** [Heb. *bānâ*–'build' (Mal. 3:15, hiphil of *ṭôḇ*–'be good' (Jgs. 17:13; "make prosperous," Dt. 30:5), *māṣā' ṭôḇ*–'find good' (Prov. 16:20; 17:20; 19:8), *hāyâ ṭôḇ*–'be good' (Jer. 44:17), hiphil of *yāṯar* + *ṭôḇâ*–'good remains' ("make prosperous," Dt. 30:9), *kāšēr*–'succeed' (Eccl. 11:6), hiphil of *nāśag*–'afford' (Lev. 25:26), hiphil of *ṣālaḥ*–'succeed' (Gen. 24:21; Prov. 28:13; Isa. 48:15; etc.), hiphil of *ṣāmaḥ*–'sprout' (2 S. 23:5), *šālâ*–'have peace and quiet' (Ps. 122:6; Lam. 1:5), hiphil of *śāḵal*–'understand,' 'have success' (Dt. 29:9 [MT 8]; 1 K. 2:3; Isa. 52:13), *'āśâ ḥayil*–'make wealth' (Ruth 4:11), *šalwâ*–'ease' (Ezk. 16:49); Aram. *ra'$^{a}$nan*–'flourish' (Dnl. 4:4 [MT 1]), haphel of *ṣ$^{e}$laḥ* (Ezr. 5:8; Dnl. 6:28 [MT 29]); Gk. *euodóō*–'gain' (1 Cor. 16:2), *ploutéō*–'be rich' (Rev. 3:17)]; **PROSPERITY** [Heb. *ṭôḇ* (1 K. 10:7; Job 21:13; 36:11; etc.), *ṭûḇ* (Job 20:21; 21:16; Ps. 128:5), *ṭôḇâ* (Dt. 23:6 [MT 7]; 28:11; Ezr. 9:12; etc.), *tôm*–'perfection' (Job 21:23), *šālôm*–'peace' (Job 15:21; Ps. 37:11; 72:3; etc.), *y$^{e}$šû'â*–'salvation' (Job 30:15), *šālû*–'ease' (Ps. 30:6 [MT 7]), *šalwâ* (Jer. 22:21), *šālēw*–'be at ease' (Zec. 7:7), *kôšārâ* (Ps. 68:6 [MT 7]), *ṣ$^{e}$ḏāqâ*–'righteousness' (Prov. 8:18)];

AV also PLENTEOUS, MULTIPLY, PEACE, etc.; NEB also SUCCESS, GOOD, LUXURY, etc. In Ps. 10:5 the RSV apparently emends *yāḥîlû* (<*ḥîl,* "be firm, strong") to *yaṣlî(a)ḥ* (hiphil of *ṣālaḥ*); see the comms.; *BH*; KoB, p. 295. In Ezk. 34:29 the RSV emends MT *lᵉšēm,* "for a name," to *šālôm* (see *BHS*). The expression *ʿᵃśê-ḥayil* in Ruth 4:11 is an idiom for gaining wealth (Dt. 8:18; cf. Gen. 34:29). In Job 30:15, *yᵉšûʿâ,* rendered "prosperity" in the RSV, is better translated "safety, deliverance" or "victory" (cf. JB, NEB, NIV). The RSV (and NIV) misunderstand *ṣᵉḏāqâ* in Prov. 8:18. The larger context and the poetic structure of the verse demand a translation like "integrity, virtue" or "justice," instead of "prosperity" (i.e., "riches"/"honor," "wealth"/"integrity"; cf. JB, NEB).

Prosperity in the OT connotes the realization of goals (Gen. 24:21, 40, 42, 56), success in labor (Gen. 39:3, 23; 2 Ch. 32:30), living in peace and safety (Dt. 23:6; 1 Ch. 14:7; cf. Heb. *ṭôḇâ,* "happiness," in Lam. 3:17; AV, NEB, "prosperity"), enjoying the benefits of familial relationships (Ruth 4:11; cf. Job 1:1-5), as well as acquiring and possessing material goods (Dt. 28:11; 1 K. 10:7; 1 Ch. 29:23; Job 21:23f.).

More important to the Hebrews were the spiritual and ethical dimensions of prosperity. True prosperity was linked to the blessings of covenantal obedience before God (Dt. 28:29; 29:9; 1 K. 2:3; 1 Ch. 22:13; etc.). It is God who bestows prosperity on those who keep and do the words of the Mosaic (and subsequent) covenants (Dt. 29:9; 30:9; cf. 28:11; Neh. 2:20; Ps. 68:6 [MT 7]). The material and spiritual blessings tied to covenant-keeping are rewards for the righteous, those who fear the Lord (Ps. 1:3; 25:13; 37:11). In the same vein, prosperity is one of the rewards of godly wisdom, that is, the wise "receive effective instruction" (so McKane, p. 265) and practice righteousness, justice, and equity (Prov. 13:21; 19:8; cf. 1:3-5, 33; 2:8; 3:2-4). Those who refuse to acknowledge God in their prosperity (Jer. 10:21; 22:21) and to share their abundance with the poor and needy (Ezk. 16:49) forfeit the blessings associated with covenant-keeping; instead they are subject to the curses connected with covenant-breaking (Dt. 28:11, 29; 29:9; 30:9; etc.; cf. Prov. 3:9f.).

God's word also prospers and accomplishes His intended purposes (contextually, His word prospers among those who thirst, come, hearken, incline, and seek; cf. Isa. 55:1-11). Prosperity is one of the fruits of the revival and restoration prompted by the implementation of the new covenant in the eschaton (Ps. 106:5; Isa. 48:15; 66:12; Jer. 33:6, 9; 44:17; Zec. 1:17; 8:12). Isaiah prophesies that the Servant of God will prosper, be exalted, and prolong His days, and that the will of God shall prosper in His hand (Isa. 52:13; 53:10). Jewish scholars ascribe these oracles to a messiah yet to come, or find their fulfillment in the fortunes of the nation of Israel during the Exile and the period of postexilic restoration. Christian scholars see the fulfillment of Isaiah's prophecies in the life and ministry of Jesus of Nazareth, called the Christ. As the Servant-Messiah, Jesus prospers in that He always does the will of the Father (Jn. 6:35-40; 10:1-18, 31-39), He reconciled Israel and the gentile nations to God through His redemptive work (Rom. 11:11-32; cf. 5:1-11, 15-17; 2 Cor. 5:16-21), He has been exalted highly and now sits at the right hand of God (Phil. 2:9-11; He. 8:1-7), and He will come again with power and great glory (Mt. 24:29-31).

The Gk. *euodóō* means "be led down a good path," hence "prosper" or "succeed." Paul instructed the Corinthians to give to the Jerusalem church in proportion to their measure of prosperity (1 Cor. 16:2). Prosperity may prove to be a snare to spiritual development because it fosters an attitude of self-sufficiency (Rev. 3:17; cf. Mt. 6:24; 19:23-26; Lk. 12:13-21; 18:18-30; 1 Tim. 6:8-10).

*See also* PEACE; SUCCEED; WEALTH.

***Bibliography.***–W. McKane, *Proverbs* (*OTL,* 1970); *TDNT,* V, *s.v.* ὁδός κτλ.: εὐοδόω (Michaelis); *THAT,* II, *s.v.* צלח (M. Saebø); *s.v.* צמח (S. Amsler); *TWOT,* II, 766, 927.

A. E. HILL

**PROSTITUTION.** *See* CRIME; CULT PROSTITUTE; HARLOT.

**PROSTRATION.** *See* ADORATION II.A; OBEISANCE; POSTURES.

**PROTEVANGELIUM** prə-tē-van-jel′i-əm, prō′tə-van-jel′-i-əm **OF JAMES.** *See* APOCRYPHAL GOSPELS II.B.

**PROTO-LUKE.** *See* GOSPELS, SYNOPTIC V.C.; LUKE, GOSPEL ACCORDING TO III.A.2.

**PROUD.** *See* PRIDE.

**PROVE.** *See* PROOF, PROVE.

**PROVENDER** [Heb. *mispō'* (Gen. 24:25, 32; 42:27; 43:24; Jgs. 19:19), *bᵉlîl* (Isa. 30:24), *bālal* ("give provender," Jgs. 19:21)]; NEB also FODDER; **FODDER** [Heb. *bᵉlîl*] (Job 6:5; 24:6); AV also CORN; NEB also "what is not theirs" (24:6; reading *bᵉlî lô* instead of MT *bᵉlîlô*; cf. LXX). Coarse food given to domestic animals. *Mispō'* seems to be related to an original root *sp'* ("feed"), while *bᵉlîl* is a cognate of *bālal* (usually "mix," but in Jgs. 19:21 "give provender") and may denote a mash that has been fermented by means of soaking (KoB, p. 129). The basic provender was probably the chopped straw or chaff still used today in Palestine. With this were often mixed grasses and grains (including esp. BARLEY, also millet and wheat). Isa. 30:24 prophesies of a time of such abundance that beasts of burden will be fed a seasoned mash made from winnowed grain.

***Bibliography.***–*HGHL,* p. 83; *MPB,* pp. 29, 112, 231f., 254.

N. J. O.

**PROVERB** [Heb. *māšāl, māšal* ("use [as] a proverb," Ezk. 12:33; 16:44); Gk. *parabolḗ* (Lk. 4:23), *paroimía* (2 Pet. 2:22)]; AV also "like" (Job 13:12); NEB also BYWORD, SAYING, MAXIM, MORAL OF THE STORY, "dust." A saying, usually brief, stating observations from experience so arrestingly that it gains popularity. The purpose is to warn against dangerous conduct, while encouraging behavior that promotes personal and social well-being. The book of Proverbs contains the largest biblical collection, although proverbs also served psalmists, prophets, Jesus, and the apostles.

- I. Meaning of Biblical Terms
  - A. OT
  - B. NT
- II. Forms
  - A. Popular Sentences
  - B. Sayings
    - 1. Juxtaposition
    - 2. Comparison
    - 3. Numerical
    - 4. Admonitions
- III. Use of Proverbs
  - A. OT
    - 1. Wisdom Literature
    - 2. Psalms
    - 3. Prophets

- B. Apocrypha
  - 1. Sirach
  - 2. Wisdom of Solomon
- C. NT
  - 1. Sayings of Jesus
  - 2. Epistles
- IV. Sources of Proverbs
  - A. Clan
  - B. Court
  - C. School

***I. Meaning of Biblical Terms.***–*A. OT.* Hebrew writers used *māšāl* to identify forms covering a wide range of English meanings: (1) "mocking saying, taunt" (Dt. 28:37; 1 S. 10:12; 1 K. 9:7; 2 Ch. 7:20; Isa. 14:4; Jer. 24:9; Mic. 2:4; Ps. 69:11 [MT 12]; Ezk. 14:8); frequently the biting force for *māšāl* is disclosed in its association with *šᵉnînâ,* "by-word," "taunt"; (2) "discourse" (Job 27:1; 29:1; Balaam's speeches, Nu. 23:7, 18; 24:3, 15, 20f., 23); (3) "instruction" (substantial lectures, Prov. 1:1-19; 2:1-22; 3:1-12; 3:21-35; 4:1-9, 10-19, 20-27; 5:1-23; 6:20-35; 7:1-27); (4) "wisdom speech" (Prov. 1:20-33; 8:1-36; 9:1-6); (5) "brief words of warning or instruction, based on experience" (1 K. 4:32 [MT 5:12]; Ezk. 12:22f.; 18:2f.; Prov. 1:1, 6; 10:1; 25:1; 26:7, 9; Eccl. 12:9) — the category closest to our understanding of "proverb." The debate on the root meaning of *māšāl* — "rule" or "compare" — has reached an impasse. If these uses have a common core, it has to do with teaching — even a taunt conveys a negative lesson. But context, not etymology, is the key to meaning: *māšāl*'s nuances must be discerned from its use. (See Crenshaw, "Wisdom"; Johnson; Landes.)

*B. NT.* The LXX regularly translates *māšāl* as *parabolḗ,* which, accordingly, means "proverb" in Lk. 4:23, where it is barbed like a taunt: "Physician, heal yourself." *Paroimía* (2 Pet. 2:22) is drawn from classical Greek and intertestamental literature (e.g., Sir. 6:35). In the Fourth Gospel (10:6; 16:25, 29) *paroimía* is a figure used to conceal meaning from all but the most perceptive (in Sir. 39:3 it parallels "riddle"), a role opposite to that of ordinary proverbs.

***II. Forms.***–The variety of shorter proverbial forms invites detailed analysis, not only to put them in categories but, more importantly, to discern their intent and use. (For the longer instructions and wisdom speeches in Prov. 1–9, *see* PROVERBS, BOOK OF I.A.)

*A. Popular Sentences.* These are usually one line without poetic parallelism. They often disclose their beginnings: Nimrod set the pace for later hunters — "Like Nimrod a mighty hunter before the Lord" (Gen. 10:9); Saul's venture into prophecy became a warning against dabbling in it — "Is Saul also among the prophets?" (1 S. 10:12; 19:24); the role of Abel of Beth-maacah in settling disputes made that city a proverb — "Let them ask counsel at Abel" (2 S. 20:18); David's banter with the Jebusites who claimed to defend Jerusalem with their lame and blind spawned the saying — "The blind and the lame shall not come into the house" (2 S. 5:8).

Elsewhere, common sense was the origin: "Out of the wicked comes forth wickedness" (1 S. 24:13); "Let not him that girds on his armor boast himself as he that puts it off" (1 K. 20:11); for other popular proverbs, see Jer. 13:12; 23:28; Hos. 4:11, 14e (cf. Fontaine). NT counterparts are: "Can anything good come out of Nazareth?" (Jn. 1:46); perhaps "Cretans are always liars, evil beasts, lazy gluttons" (Tit. 1:12); and "A prophet is not without honor . . ." (Mt. 13:57; Mk. 6:4; cf. Lk. 4:24).

*B. Sayings.* The typical saying has two lines of Hebrew parallelism, which, according to traditional analysis, takes three forms (for a critique of this traditional analysis, see J. Kugel, *Idea of Biblical Poetry* [1981]; *see also* POETRY, HEBREW). In *synonymous* parallelism the second line restates and underscores the first: "A fool's mouth is his ruin, and his lips are a snare to himself" (Prov. 18:6). (Cf. many other examples in chs. 18–19.)

*Antithetic* parallelism, dominant in Prov. 10-15 and frequent elsewhere in Proverbs, depicts the contrast between wise and foolish ways of life and their consequences: "He who guards his mouth preserves his life; he who opens wide his lips comes to ruin" (Prov. 13:3). This focus on opposites reflects the wisdom teaching of the two ways: the diametrical difference between obedience to God and rebellion against Him — the difference between a flourishing tree and scattered chaff (Ps. 1). These antithetical structures produce an apt union of form and content.

*Synthetic* parallelism uses the second line to advance and complete the thought of the first (e.g., "The words of a whisperer are like delicious morsels; they go down into the inner parts of the body," Prov. 18:8).

The saying's grammar is indicative, not imperative. It generalizes the wisdom of experience and expresses it compellingly. Its power rests not in the teacher's authority, respected though that may be (Prov. 1:8), but in the truth of experience that it retrieves and compresses. The variety of experiences made knowing when to apply which saying one mark of the wise (Prov. 25:11). Another mark was the poetic finesse that shaped the sounds, figures of speech, and variety of types. Israel's wise practiced their art with the care credited to Qoheleth (Eccl. 12:9f.; cf. Prov. 15:23).

*1. Juxtaposition* places elements or whole lines side by side without verbal sign of comparison: "Hope deferred — a sick heart; and a tree of life — desire fulfilled" (Prov. 13:12; cf. RSV, AV, NEB, etc., which supply verbs for smoother reading). The point is that certain things go hand in hand; each type of conduct carries its inevitable result. (Other examples of juxtaposition are Prov. 11:8; 12:1; 14:2, 11; 16:17; 17:19; 21:23; 25:3.)

*2. Comparison* may be conveyed in several ways. It is implied in two juxtaposed lines that compare a desired spiritual experience to a physical one: "[Like] cold water to a thirsty soul, [so is] good news from a far country" (Prov. 25:25). (See Prov. 25:12, 14, 28; 26:7, 9f., 14.) Similes that explicitly employ "like" are common: "Like one who binds the stone in the sling is he who gives honor to a fool" (Prov. 26:8). (See Prov. 26:1f., 11, 18; 27:8, 19.) The similes often focus on the absurd — a vivid technique to expose the utter inanity of a fool's behavior.

"Better" sayings show that wise conduct is infinitely more valuable, even in humble circumstances, than power or affluence without it: "Better is a dinner of herbs where love is than a fatted ox and hatred with it" (Prov. 15:17). Love is not just slightly preferable to hatred; it is so much better that it reverses the values of the things — the herbs and the fatted calf — that go with it (cf. 12:9; 15:16; 16:8, 19; 17:1; 19:1; 27:5, 10b). See G. S. Ogden, *JBL,* 96 (1977), 489-505; 98 (1979), 339-350.

*3. Numerical* sayings reflect the ancients' use of lists of comparable items to comprehend the universe's order. (For proverbs' role in finding and establishing order, *see* PROVERBS, BOOK OF IV.B.) Probably derived from games or riddles, these sayings follow an x, x + 1 pattern, i.e., the second number is one digit higher than the first: "Three things are too wonderful for me; four I do not understand . . ." (Prov. 30:18). (See 30:15b-16, 21-23, 24-28, 29-31.) The second number (x + 1) determines the list's length and serves to spotlight the final item listed — the proverb cited (30:18f.) is about the mysteries of human attraction, not eagles, serpents, or ships. This helps to interpret the x, x + 1 pattern of the seven deadly sins

(6:16-19): the focus is on the "man who sows discord" more than the first six sins. Amos, who seems to have been influenced by the wisdom traditions, uses the x, x + 1, pattern (1:3–2:6), as does Job 5:19. (Cf. H. W. Wolff, *Amos the Prophet: The Man and His Background* [Eng. tr. 1973], pp. 34-44; W. Roth, *Numerical Sayings in the OT* [*SVT,* 13; 1965].)

*4. Admonitions.* In contrast to the sayings, the admonitions teach good behavior by commands and prohibitions. The grammar is imperative or jussive. The *command* is positive: "Listen to advice and accept instruction, that you may gain wisdom for the future" (Prov. 19:20). (Cf. 14:7; 19:27; 20:16; 22:6, 10, 17; 23:1f., 19; and many in Prov. 1–9.) The *prohibition* is negative: "Do not rob the poor because he is poor, or crush the afflicted at the gate; for the Lord will plead their cause and despoil of life those who despoil them" (22:22f.). (Cf. 22:24f., 26f., 28f.; 23:3, 4f., 6-8, 9, 10f., 13f., 17f., 20f., and many in Prov. 1–9.)

Typically, admonitions conclude with a motivation for obeying them, usually introduced by "for" (Heb. *kî*). The imperative was reinforced by a sound reason stating the results. The admonitions resemble certain apodictic laws where the command is followed by its reason (e.g., Dt. 5:8-10, 11, 16). See Nel, Gerstenberger.

*III. Use of Proverbs.–A. OT. 1. Wisdom literature* teems with proverbs. Job's friends press home their call to repentance with them (e.g., Job 4:8; 5:2, 6f.; 11:12, 20; 15:34); Job uses them to counter this call (e.g., 6:14; 12:6, 11f.) and scorns his comforters' sayings (13:12). Job quotes a proverb to refute it, "How forceful are honest words! [proverb] But what does reproof from you reprove?" (6:25), and uses proverb to counter proverb (e.g., 12:12f.).

Ecclesiastes' use of proverbs is similar (e.g., 5:10 [MT 9], saying; 7:9; 11:1, admonitions; 4:6, 9, 13; 5:5 [MT 4]; 7:1-3, 5, 8; 9:17f., "better" sayings). Proverbs reinforce or summarize the Preacher's conclusions (e.g., Eccl. 1:15, 18; 4:5f., 9-12 — almost a numerical proverb), and they are clustered as words of advice (5:1-12 [MT 4:17–5:11]; 7:1–8:9; 9:13–12:8), supporting the counsel to make the best of life despite threats of futility. Like Job, Ecclesiastes cites conventional proverbs to correct them (e.g., 2:14f.; 4:5f.; he also coins "antiproverbs," couching in traditional proverbial form a message questioning the tradition (1:18; contrast with Prov. 2:10; 3:13; 8:34-36). (See Williams, pp. 47-63.)

*2. Psalms.* The Psalter includes entire wisdom psalms (e.g., 1, 32, 34, 37, 49, 73, 112, 127–128, 133) and psalms partly composed of wisdom themes and forms (e.g., 25:8-10, 12-14; 31:23f. [MT 24f.]; 39:4f. [MT 5f.]; 40:4f. [MT 5f.]; 62:8-10 [MT 9-11]; 92:6-8; 94:8-15. Proverbs are imbedded in most of these (e.g., 1:6; 32:8-10; 34:13-15), while others (e.g., 37, a collection of admonitions; 112, 127–128, collections of sayings and promises of happiness) are composed entirely of proverbs. The Psalter's proverbs indicate connections between the wise and the temple staffs; overlaps in activities among the offices of Israel — prophets, priests, singers, scribes, wise men; and links between instruction and prayer in Israel's worship, especially in thanksgiving songs (e.g., 32, 73, 78). (See L. G. Perdue, *Wisdom and Cult* [1977].)

*3. Prophets.* The prophets used wisdom sayings, often in judgment speeches (Isa. 1:3; 10:15; 28:27; Jer. 17:7f., 11; 23:28), to show that disobedience to God's will was a violation of common sense as well as a breach of covenant. Hosea's book concludes with a wisdom admonition (14:9). (Cf. J. W. Whedbee, *Isaiah and Wisdom* [1971]; Thompson, esp. pp. 96-110; for wisdom's relationship to other OT strands, see Morgan.)

*B. Apocrypha. 1. Sirach.* Though Sirach extended his lessons to cover topics more thoroughly than simple proverbs would do and though he reinterpreted Israel's history (chs. 44–50) as a catalog of heroes, he nevertheless used proverbial forms: sayings (e.g., 20:1, 5, 7f.), admonitions (e.g., chs. 7–9; 18:30, 32f.), numerical patterns (e.g., 23:16; 25:7-11; 26:5-8, 28), "better" sayings (e.g., 19:24; 30:14, 17), comparisons (e.g., 21:16; 26:12, 17f.), juxtaposition (e.g., 27:4).

*2. Wisdom of Solomon* virtually buried the proverbial style in the elaborate, closely argued essays. Yet traces of the admonition (e.g., 1:1f.; 6:1-3) and the saying (e.g., 6:6f., 12; 14:2) remain.

*C. NT. 1. Sayings of Jesus.* More than one hundred Synoptic sayings of Jesus reflect wisdom's influence (cf. Crossan); they occur in all four sources (Mark, Q, M, L), indicating how deeply imbedded in apostolic memory was Jesus' use of proverbs. Most of the conventional forms are found: antithetical parallelism (e.g., Mt. 7:13f., 17f., 24-27), admonitions (e.g., Mt. 6:34; 7:13), sayings (e.g., Mt. 6:21, 24; 10:24; 12:25, 33; 24:28), and "better" sayings (e.g., Mk. 9:43-47). While Jesus taught in forms and subjects akin to those in the curricula of other wise men, including classical and Hellenistic sources, He frequently used paradoxical antitheses (Mk. 2:27; 8:35; Mt. 25:29) to highlight the radical nature of the Kingdom (cf. Williams, pp. 60-63) in both its present and future expressions (cf. C. E. Carlston, *JBL,* 99 [1980], 87-105).

*2. The Epistles* employ proverbs—admonitions more than sayings—in passages urging believers to righteous living: (1) Rom. 12:9-21, a chain of admonitions; (2) the "house tables," rules for responsible behavior in Christian households, Eph. 5:21–6:9; Col. 3:18–4:1; cf. 1 Pet. 2:18–3:7; (3) closing exhortations like Gal. 6:7-11, with its prohibitions supported by motivations and illustrated by analogies from nature; cf. 1 Pet. 5:6-10 and He. 12:1-13; 13:1-7, 17f. James's use of Jesus' wisdom sayings and other proverbs marks him as an NT sage: note the admonition in 3:1, a prohibition with motivation (cf. also 4:7-10), but more common are sayings that summarize one section and, sometimes, provide a transition to the next (e.g., 2:13, 26; 3:18; 4:17; 5:20; cf. P. H. Davids, *Epistle of James* [*NIGTC,* 1982], p. 23).

*IV. Sources of Proverbs.*–Sapiential maxims are so ancient and widespread (Egyptian and Sumerian examples hark back to the beginnings of literature in the 3rd millennium B.C.) that their origins are virtually untraceable (see W. G. Lambert, *Babylonian Wisdom Literature* [1960]; E. Gordon, *Sumerian Proverbs* [1959]).

*A. Clan.* Many sayings seem to stem from the family and tribe. Training the young in clan mores and practices — ethics of work, respect for persons and property, bases for sound choices — called for learnable summaries of honorable behavior, especially in cultures stable and largely oral, e.g., Proverbs's emphasis on respect for parents' teaching (cf. 7:1-5; 31:26) and children's responsibility to hear (cf. 1:8; 2:1f.; 3:1f.; 4:1-9; see Gerstenberger).

*B. Court.* The association of OT proverbs with Solomon (1 K. 4:32 [MT 5:12]; Prov. 1:1; 10:1; 25:1) and Hezekiah (Prov. 25:1) suggests the royal court's hand in their cultivation. Solomon's contacts with Egypt acquainted him with Egyptian court practices, especially the role of scribes and other learned administrators. Wisdom materials may have served as guides for Israel's decisions as they did for Egypt's. For Isaiah (e.g., 29:13f.; 30:1-5) and Jeremiah (e.g., 8:3-12; 9:12; 18:18) such wise men were mixed blessings: they helped to preserve the sapiential traditions, but their wisdom also led to counsel contrary to God's plans. (See W. McKane, *Prophets and Wise Men* [*SBT,* 1/44, 1965], for political activities of the wise.)

PROVERBS, BOOK OF

*C. School.* There is no firm evidence of schools in Israel before Sirach's mention of "my house of learning" (51:23) *ca.* 180 B.C. (cf. R. N. Whybray, *Intellectual Tradition in the OT* [*BZAW,* 135, 1974], pp. 33-43). Yet how could life and learning have been carried on without them? Tribal schools were posited by W. Richter (*Recht und Ethos: Versuch einer Ortung des weisheitlichen Mahnspruches* [1966]). A stronger case has been made for court schools, patterned after the Egyptian, which trained nobility, administrators, and scribes (R. E. Murphy, *Wisdom Literature* [*FOTL,* 13, 1981], pp. 6-9). Probably all three entities contributed to shaping and transmitting the sayings, many of which were (1) born in the clan with its need to rear its young; (2) collected and polished in the court where the means of writing and preserving were available; (3) taught to the leaders in the school, in whatever form it existed (cf. Morgan, pp. 141f.).

*See also* WISDOM.

***Bibliography.***–J. Crenshaw, ed., *Studies in Ancient Israelite Wisdom* (1976); "Wisdom," in J. H. Hayes, *OT Form Criticism* (1974), pp. 229-239; J. D. Crossan, *In Fragments: The Aphorisms of Jesus* (1983); C. R. Fontaine, *Traditional Sayings in the OT* (1982); E. Gerstenberger, *Wesen und Herkunft des "apodiktischen Rechts" im AT* (*WMANT,* 20, 1965); A. R. Johnson, "מָשָׁל," in M. Noth and D. W. Thomas, eds., *Wisdom in Israel and in the Ancient Near East* (*SVT,* 3; 1955), pp. 162-69; G. M. Landes, "Jonah: A *Māšāl*?" in J. G. Gammie, *et al., Israelite Wisdom* (*Festschrift* S. Terrien; 1978), pp. 137-158; W. McKane, *Proverbs* (*OTL,* 1970), pp. 10-33; D. F. Morgan, *Wisdom in the OT Traditions* (1981); P. J. Nel, *Structure and Ethos of the Wisdom Admonitions in Proverbs* (*BZAW,* 158, 1982); G. von Rad, *Wisdom in Israel* (Eng. tr. 1972); J. M. Thompson, *Form and Function of Proverbs in Ancient Israel* (1974); J. G. Williams, *Those who Ponder Proverbs* (1981).

D. A. HUBBARD

**PROVERBS, BOOK OF.** The largest biblical compendium of wisdom sayings, Proverbs takes its English name from the Vulg. *Liber Proverbiorum* (on the Hebrew title *mišlê* and the LXX title *Paroimiai see* PROVERB I). In the Hebrew canon Proverbs usually follows Psalms and Job in the third section (Writings or Hagiographa); in some lists Proverbs is between Psalms and Job. English versions place Proverbs after Psalms and before Ecclesiastes in the "poetic" section. If Hebrew wisdom teaches the art of success, Proverbs is a handbook for successful living. If the laws of love (Lev. 19:18; Dt. 6:5) are pivotal OT themes, Proverbs is an extended commentary on them. If other parts of the OT center in Israel's covenant relationship, Proverbs spells indelibly and succinctly the impact of this relationship. All life is ordered by Yahweh, to be lived in dependence on His provision and in response to His demands, i.e., in the fear of Yahweh, which is the beginning of wisdom (Prov. 1:7, 29).

- I. Contents
  - A. Instructions to Seek Wisdom, 1:1–9:18
  - B. Proverbs of Solomon, 10:1–22:16
  - C. Words of the Wise, 22:17–24:22
  - D. More Words of the Wise, 24:23–34
  - E. More Proverbs of Solomon, 25:1–29:27
  - F. Words of Agur, 30:1-33
  - G. Words of Lemuel, 31:1-9
  - H. Acrostic Description of a Virtuous Wife, 31:10-31
- II. Date of Collection
- III. Role in Israel's Life
  - A. Cultural Background
  - B. Canonical Character
- IV. Theological Significance
  - A. Experience as a Means of Revelation
  - B. Creation as the Basis of Order
  - C. Social Responsibility
  - D. Covenant Loyalty
- V. Proverbs and the NT
  - A. Quotations
  - B. Allusions
  - C. Christology
    1. Synoptic Gospels
    2. Fourth Gospel and Epistles

***I. Contents.***–Proverbs is actually a collection of collections, whose various parts are distinguishable by separate headings (e.g., 10:1; 25:1; 30:1; 31:1) or by changes in form (e.g., the acrostic of 31:10-31).

*A. Instructions to Seek Wisdom, 1:1–9:18.* The title and purpose are combined in 1:1-6, which (1) links the collection to Solomon, patron of Israel's wisdom movement (1 K. 4:29-34 [MT 5:9-14]); (2) highlights wisdom's many facets by an array of synonyms (instruction, insight, wise dealing, prudence, knowledge, discretion, learning, understanding, skill); (3) pinpoints wisdom's moral character (e.g., righteousness, justice, equity; v. 3); (4) describes the breadth of its audience (simple, youth, wise man); (5) catalogs its techniques (proverb, figure, sayings of the wise, riddles; v. 6).

Two basic literary forms dominate chs. 1–9: *instructions* — extended admonitions, usually addressed to "my son," which either commend wisdom's virtues (2:1-22; 3:1-20; 4:1-9, 20-27; 9:7-12) or warn against folly's various forms (companionship with sinners, 1:8-19; 4:10-19; conflicts with neighbors, 3:28-35; crooked speech, 4:20-27; sexual immorality, 5:1-23; 6:20-35; 7:1-27; foolish pledges, 6:1-5; laziness, 6:6-11; deceit, 6:12-15; clan discord, 6:16-19); *wisdom speeches* — extended poems in which Wisdom issues her own call to discipleship (1:20-33; 8:1-36; 9:1-6). This is "poetic personification," not "hypostatization," since any view that Wisdom actually existed independently of Yahweh would be unthinkable to OT faith.

Folly is similarly personified in 9:13-18, bribing the foolish with "stolen water" and "bread eaten in secret." The description of Folly as a harlot can be read as a literal warning against fornication, but it may also have a religious connotation: Israel's idolatry was compared to harlotry, especially where idolatry entailed religious prostitution (cf. Hosea and Jeremiah). Wisdom, in her intimate contact with Yahweh, offers life that stems from the fear of Yahweh (8:35f.); Folly, with her worship of false gods, offers only death (9:18).

This section's longer speeches are graced with varied forms (they would otherwise be chains of admonitions): sayings (e.g., 1:17; 6:10f.); rhetorical or disputation questions (6:27f.); numerical sayings (6:16-19); accounts of personal observations (7:6-23); reflections on experiences (4:3-9); beatitudes (3:13f.); antithetical sayings (4:18f.); allegories or extended metaphors (5:15-23) with interpretation.

The closest parallels to chs. 1–9 are Egyptian instructions (*Sebayit*) with a similar mixture of admonitions, prohibitions, motivations, and rhetorical questions. Some scholars liken the wisdom speeches, which have no OT counterpart, to the descriptions of *Maʿat,* Egyptian deity of order or justice. Those who propose an Egyptian influence disagree about how that influence took place and how many instruction speeches are in Proverbs (see Murphy, *Wisdom Literature,* pp. 49-53, for a summary of the work of C. Kayatz, B. Lang, W. McKane, R. N. Whybray). W. F. Albright ("Some Canaanite-Phoenician Sources of Hebrew Wisdom," in M. Noth and D. W. Thomas, eds., *Wisdom in Israel and in the Ancient Near East* [*SVT,* 3; 1955], pp. 1-15) focused on the West Semitic background of chs. 8–9.

The profoundly religious tone, keen concern for social and moral conduct, and hortatory homiletical style of these chapters resemble the speeches in Deuteronomy.

M. Weinfeld (*JBL*, 80 [1961], 241-47; *Deuteronomy and the Deuteronomic School* [1972], pp. 244-370) suggested that Hezekiah's wise men and their successors helped to shape Deuteronomy.

These instructions and wisdom speeches are not necessarily to be dated later than their shorter proverbial counterparts, as though wisdom material developed gradually from shorter to longer forms (cf. von Rad, *Wisdom*, p. 27). Egyptian instructions of Ptahhotep (*ca.* 2450 B.C.) and Merikare (*ca.* 2100 B.C.) were ancient volumes by Solomon's time.

*B. Proverbs of Solomon, 10:1–22:16.* The title (10:1) salutes Solomon's reputation as patron of Israel's wisdom movement (cf. 1 K. 4:29-34 [MT 5:9-14]). Scholarship has tended to validate this tradition (and also the place of the Solomonic era in the development of history writing; cf. *NHI* [Eng. tr., 2nd ed. 1960], pp. 216-224) due to Solomon's relationships with Egypt, his wide-ranging mercantile contacts (e.g., the queen of Sheba's visit and Hiram of Tyre's transportation service, 1 K. 10:1-25), the need of a well-trained administrative bureaucracy, and the opportunity for religious, cultural, and intellectual pursuits that vast wealth and relief from war afforded. The editor may have coded the great king's name into this collection. The number of proverbs, 375, equals the numerical value of Solomon's name in Hebrew, just as the sayings attributed to Hezekiah's men in chs. 25–29 number about 130, the numerical value of Hezekiah's name.

This collection may have combined two earlier ones: 10:1–15:33 and 16:1–22:16. One clue is the poetic parallelism: almost 90 percent of the sayings in 10:1–15:33 are antithetic, the second line stating the opposite of the first: in 16:1–22:16 the synonymous forms slightly outnumber the antithetic, with the so-called synthetic running a close third. P. Skehan has argued that 14:26–16:15 is a bridge or a "suture" to tie together the two longer sections and to increase the total number of proverbs to 375; hence the cryptic clue to Solomon's name (see Murphy, *Wisdom Literature*, pp. 64f., for the details of this argument). The first verses of ch. 10 may be tailored to fit chs. 1–9: the references to "son" (10:1, 5) hark back to the "my son" of the introductory section; the contrast of "righteous" and "wicked" (10:2f., 6f.) continues an emphasis of chs. 1–9 (2:20-22; 3:32-34; 4:14-19; 5:21-23).

The collectors have given very few other clues as to arrangement. Each saying is an independent statement, two lines long (three in 19:7). Catchwords repeated from verse to verse or section to section may suggest a deliberate grouping (O. Plöger, "Zur Auslegung der Sentenzensammlungen des Proverbienbuches," in H. W. Wolff, ed., *Probleme biblischer Theologie* [*Festschrift* G. von Rad; 1971], pp. 402-416, has found topical or thematic clusters in 11:3-8, 9-14, 18-20, 30f.). Four consecutive verses begin with the letter *bēth* — are they so grouped as an aid to memory? Sayings in 15:13-17 are linked by the words "heart" and "good."

W. McKane (pp. 11, 415) attempted to catalog the individual sayings: old wisdom sayings aimed at personal education; old wisdom sayings, largely negative, describing the effect on the community of antisocial behavior; sayings which use God-language to express Yahwistic piety. But these distinctions are foreign to the outlook of Hebrew wisdom.

The proverbs in 10:1–22:16, therefore, are best studied as self-contained units, each designed for an appropriate context. True wisdom knew the right occasion for each saying.

A number of these sayings reflect explicitly Israel's trust in Yahweh and His governance (10:3, 22, 27, 29; 11:1, 20; 12:2, 22; 14:2, 9, 26, 27, 31; 15:3, 8f., 11, 16, 25f., 29, 33; 16:1-7, 9, 11, 20, 33; 17:3, 5, 15; 18:10, 22; 19:3, 14, 17, 21, 23; 20:10, 12, 22f., 27; 21:1-3, 30f.; 22:2, 4, 12). Such proverbs reminded Yahweh's people that they were accountable to Him and prospered most by following His ways. These sayings cast a religious light on other proverbs, even on those which make no note of Israel's faith. Experiences in the proverbs take place in a world ruled by Yahweh; His presence in judgment and blessing is assumed even where it is not mentioned.

Those who believe that one should fear God for who He is rather than to gain reward or avert punishment criticize Proverbs' emphasis on finding happiness ("eudaemonism"). It is shortsighted to fault Proverbs for this, when it occurs frequently throughout the Bible. The Gospels portray Jesus teaching a doctrine of rewards (e.g., Mt. 10:40-42; Mk. 10:29f.) at a time when doctrines of afterlife and final judgment had been disclosed. Why should not the scribes of Israel clarify the life-and-death issues of wisdom and folly by showing the benefits and drawback of the two ways of living?

The catalog of virtues extolled and vices condemned is extensive: respect for parents (e.g., 10:1); true not false witness (12:17; 14:25); honest business practices (11:1; 16:11); love not hatred (10:12); diligent work (10:5, 26; 19:15); valuing righteousness not wealth (11:4); generosity (11:24f.); discipline of children (13:24; 22:6); control of temper (14:17); kindness to the poor (14:31; 17:5; 19:17); restraint in speech (15:1, 4, 18); cheerful disposition (15:13); trusting plans to Yahweh (16:1, 3); humility (16:18f.); rejection of hedonism (21:17); avoiding seductive charms of foreign women (22:14). Many of these concerns parallel the Decalogue, while they range widely into issues that make for personal well-being and social stability. (For the forms and use of the proverbs, *see* PROVERB.)

*C. Words of the Wise, 22:17–24:22.* The title of this section is embedded in 22:17: "Incline your ear, and hear the words of the wise. . . ." The beginning boundaries are marked by the hidden title and the distinct change in form from the sayings (indicative mood) of 10:1–22:16 to the admonitions (imperative or jussive mood) of 22:17–24:23 (*see* PROVERB II.C for a detailed description); the terminal boundary is the title of the brief collection in 24:23-34, which begins: "These also are sayings of the wise."

The admonitions with their motivations result in longer, connected clusters of proverbs, rather than the detached two-line sentences of the previous section. Figures of speech mark it as poetry of grace and power: the fickleness of wealth "flying like an eagle toward heaven" (23:5); "a harlot is a deep pit" (23:27); a drunk as tipsy as a sailor in a storm (23:34).

The topics are varied: concern for the poor (22:22f.); avoidance of angry persons (22:24f.); caution in guaranteeing a payment for someone else (22:26f.); regard for property boundaries (22:28; 23:10f.); caution before kings (23:1-3; 24:21f.); avoidance of greed (23:4f.); danger of accepting generosity from the stingy (23:6-8); discipline of children (23:13f.); shunning of gluttony and drunkenness (23:19-21, 29-35); perils of harlotry (23:27); avoidance of envy (24:1f.); encouragement to wisdom (22:17-21, 29; 23:12, 15-19, 22-25; 24:3-7, 13f.). Are these the curriculum of a single teacher with a single pupil (23:15)?

The beginning of this section resembles the Egyptian instructions of Amenemope (see *ANET*, pp. 421-24), dating from 1000 B.C. or earlier. The debate continues as to which version influenced the other. Parallels noted are the admonitions against robbing the poor (Prov. 22:22f.; Amenemope ch. 2), removing boundary markers (Prov.

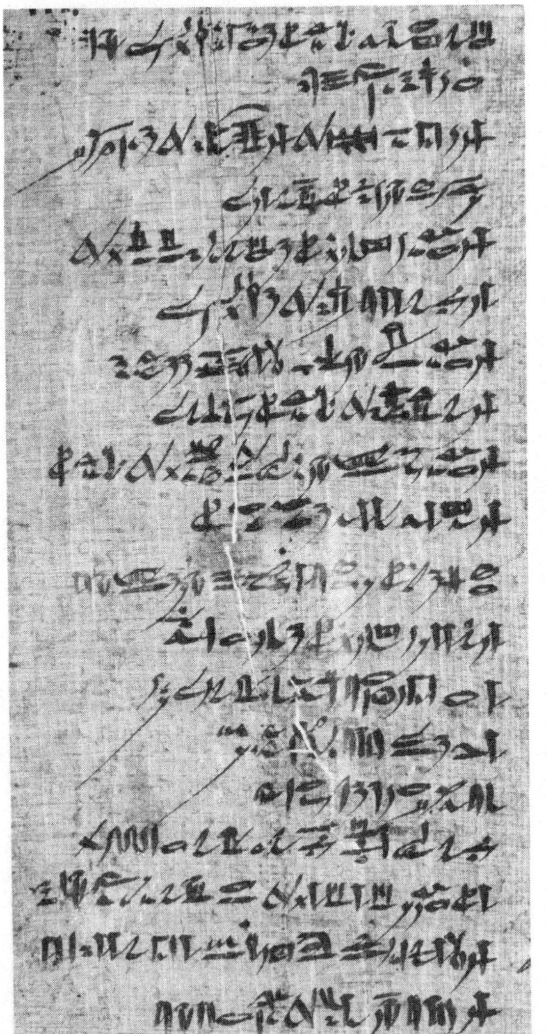

Papyrus containing col. 12 of the Instruction of Amenemope (*ca.* 1000 B.C.), which talks about the destructive speech of an angry man (Trustees of the British Museum)

23:10; Amenemope ch. 6), eating with a king (Prov. 23:1-3; Amenemope ch. 23), and banking on wealth (Prov. 23:5b; Amenemope ch. 8). The call to hear in 22:17f. resembles Amenemope ch. 1, and the MT *šilšôm* (22:20) may be repointed *šᵉlōšîm*, "thirty," to match the thirty chapters of Amenemope, although attempts to identify thirty separate sayings in 22:17–24:22 have not been uniformly accepted. Similarities are noted between 23:12-14 and the Instructions of Ahikar, preserved in Aramaic from the 5th or 4th cent. B.C. (cf. McKane, pp. 385f., for Ahikar; cf. G. E. Bryce, *Legacy of Wisdom* [1979], for Amenemope).

The connections between Proverbs and other ancient wisdom must not be overplayed: (1) the material in Proverbs has not been slavishly copied but has been artistically incorporated into its present contexts; (2) only 22:17–23:11 resemble Amenemope — about one-third of this section; (3) even these parallels are cast to reflect biblical faith, e.g., the injunction against robbing the poor has a Yahwistic reason in Proverbs: "for the Lord will plead their cause" (22:23a).

*D. More Words of the Wise, 24:23-34.* This section, an appendix to the previous (cf. the title, v. 23), is alive with social responsibility. Its contents include an expanded saying against judges who show partiality (vv. 23b-26), an admonition to preparedness (v. 27), a double admonition against using false witness to gain revenge (vv. 28f.), and a personal observation with a summarizing proverb decrying laziness (vv. 30-34; cf. 6:10f.).

*E. More Proverbs of Solomon, 25:1–29:27.* The heading (25:1) testifies to the role of Judah's kings from Solomon to Hezekiah in the garnering, editing, and preserving of wisdom literature. Jewish tradition (T.B. *Baba Bathra* 15), taking its cue here, attributes Proverbs' final authorship to Hezekiah. The Chronicler's description of his restoring of the Davidic patterns of worship, including the psalms of Asaph and David (2 Ch. 29:25-30), is parallel evidence of Hezekiah's literary activities. His scribes undoubtedly added their own sayings, in Solomon's name and spirit, to the earlier collections in their charge.

These proverbs are more varied in form and length (e.g., the instruction in 27:23-27) than the earlier Solomonic ones (10:1–22:16). Particularly prominent are the comparisons, with "like" (e.g., 25:11-14) or "better" (e.g., 25:24; 27:5; 28:6) or simply with lines juxtaposed (e.g., 26:20; 27:3, 20). In these comparisons, vivid poetic imagery abounds.

In form and content chs. 25–27 differ sufficiently from chs. 28–29 to suggest the possibility of two separate collections (so U. Skladny, *Die ältesten Spruchsammlungen in Israel* [1962], pp. 46-67). Chs. 25–27 are replete with comparisons and sprinkled with negative admonitions (prohibitions); chs. 28–29 are largely antithetical. Chs. 25–27 center in the creation, drawing illustrations from flora, fauna, weather, etc., as though designed for farmers and laborers; chs. 28–29 focus on the doctrine of the two ways with its summons to personal and social righteousness, including the obligation of rulers to judge with integrity and to care for the poor. Possibly chs. 25–27 are examples of *clan wisdom,* equipping the young to read wisdom's lessons in all that surrounds them, while chs. 28–29 are *court wisdom,* coaching the nobility and bureaucracy: clan wisdom teaches tact before royalty (e.g., 25:2f., 6f., 15); court wisdom instructs rulers in righteousness (e.g., 28:15f.; 29:2, 4, 12, 14).

The first section's tone is more pragmatic, stressing the common sense that separates wisdom from folly (e.g., 26:1, 4-12); the second section's thrust is more overtly religious: (1) the fear of Yahweh is lauded (28:14; 29:25); (2) Yahweh is the source of justice (29:26); (3) life's choices are righteousness and wickedness more than wisdom and folly; (4) the law (*tôrâ*) is prominent (28:4, 7, 9; 29:18), in contexts that point to the Mosaic instructions (e.g., with prayer in 28:9; with prophecy in 29:18) rather than wisdom teachings (cf. 1:8; 3:1; 4:2).

*F. Words of Agur, 30:1-33.* This section bristles with questions: Who is Agur? Where do his words end? How do we read the Hebrew text of v. 1? Are vv. 1-6 dialogue or soliloquy?

Agur is probably a desert chief or sage from the tribe of Massa in North Arabia (cf. Massa son of Ishmael, Gen. 25:14), an area celebrated for its wisom (1 K. 4:29-34 [MT 5:9-14]). An alternative identification translates Agur "I am a sojourner" (from Heb. *gûr*), referring to Jacob and therefore all Israel (see Gen. 47:9; cf. Ps. 39:12 [MT 13]). This interpretation links the ascending and descending of v. 4 with Jacob's ladder (Gen. 28:12f.) and reads Jakeh (v.1) as an abbreviation of *YHWH qāḏôš hûʾ*, "Yahweh is the holy one" (cf. Skehan, pp. 42f.).

The LXX did not consider ch. 30 a unity, since it placed 30:1-14 immediately after 22:17–24:22 and 30:1-15 after 24:23f. This means that Agur's words do not go beyond

v. 14, but they undoubtedly end earlier, at v. 4, v. 6, or v. 9, depending on whether we treat them as (1) a *riddle* (Skehan, p. 42) ending in v. 4 with the questions of "his name" and "his son's name" and answered in v. 1 in the names of Agur (Jacob) and Jakeh (Yahweh); (2) a *statement* by Agur closing at v. 4, expressing an unrelieved skepticism (McKane, pp. 646f.); (3) a *dialogue,* reaching to v. 6, in which a pious sage rebukes Agur for misinterpreting God's words (in v. 4) and using them to support Agur's conviction that human beings cannot have sure knowledge of God (vv. 5f.; R. B. Y. Scott, *Way of Wisdom in the OT* [1971], pp. 165-69); (4) a *dialogue* (as above) that closes with the sage's prayer that God guard his integrity and adequately, but not lavishly, supply his needs to shield him from twin temptations: stealing and self-sufficiency (vv. 7-9).

The interpretation of v. 1 hinges on the translation of *'îṯî'ēl* and *'uḵāl.* Are they proper names (so JB, NASB, NIV, RSV) or Hebrew (perhaps Aramaic) terms connoting weariness (NEB) or despair (Scott, p. 175) in the quest for true knowledge of God? The second option suits the context better as preparation for vv. 2f., and removes the problem of identifying Ithiel and Ucal.

The passage, then, is a *debate,* with Agur's words ending at v. 4 in his ironic cluster of divine questions (cf. Job 38:2ff.) that explain his despair. Vv. 5f. are an opponent's rebuttal, which, in an integrity formula (cf. Rev. 22:18) comprising the language of Ps. 18:30 (MT 31) and Dt. 4:2, affirms God's trustworthiness and warns against adding to His words.

The prayer in vv. 7-9, beginning with the number two, seems not to be the climax of the Agur portion but a bridge to the numerical sayings (*see* PROVERB II.B.3) that dominate the rest of ch. 30, placed here because of the mention of falsehood (vv. 8; cf. v. 6) and the plea for rescue from the skepticism or blasphemy (v. 9) with which Agur's words flirt (vv. 1-4).

Whether vv. 11-14 were originally a numerical saying (so C. F. Kent and M. Burrows, *Proverbs and Didactic Poems* [1927], p. 109; W. M. W. Roth, *Numerical Sayings in the OT* [*SVT,* 13; 1965], pp. 38ff.) with an introductory rubric like "There are three kinds of men whom Yahweh hates, four that he loathes" is uncertain. They are probably a collection of instructions in social behavior chained together by the catchword *dôr,* "generation."

*G. Words of Lemuel, 31:1-9.* If Massa is the Arabian tribe (cf. 30:1; Gen. 25:14), this section is another foreign contribution (cf. the Aramaic words in vv. 2f.). Though royal instruction is well documented in Egypt (e.g., Instructions of Amenemhet and Merikare in *ANET,* pp. 414-19) and Babylonia (e.g., Advice to a Prince in W. Lambert, *Babylonian Wisdom Literature,* pp. 110f.), the biblical text uniquely makes the king's *mother* teach her son (v. 1; cf. 1:8) in a series of admonitions and instructions about sexual morality (v. 3), sobriety (vv. 4-7), and justice (vv. 8f.). This trio of kingly virtues, by its inclusion in Proverbs and its use long after the close of the monarchy, becomes an account of conduct commendable to all who would be wise (cf. Murphy, *Wisdom Literature,* p. 82).

*H. Acrostic Description of a Virtuous Wife, 31:10-31.* Each successive verse begins with the next letter of the Hebrew alphabet, *'aleph* through *taw,* clearly marking this as a separate poem, whose purposes are to advise women in seemly behavior and men in selecting a wife. The acrostic is an aid to memory, but especially it is an expression of completeness listing gracefully and systematically womanly virtues: diligence, generosity, perspicacity, loyalty, and piety. The poem fittingly closes a book that pictures wisdom as a grand woman enriching her followers (cf. 1:20-33; 8:1-36) and that depicts wise women nurturing their young and, consequently, stabilizing the whole society (cf. 1:8; 31:1).

*II. Date of Collection.*–The following conclusions about the collection may be drawn: (1) only the roughest approximations of dates are possible in Proverbs because of the absence of historical materials apart from references to Solomon (1:1; 10:1; 25:1) and Hezekiah (25:1); (2) the various sections could not have been finally assembled prior to Hezekiah's time (716-687 B.C.; Prov. 25:1); (3) they probably were firmly in place for centuries before Sirach was composed (*ca.* 180 B.C.), because Proverbs does not equate wisdom with Torah as does Sirach; (4) the bulk of assembling must have been completed before the Exile, possible exceptions being the acrostic of 31:10-31 and the words of Agur and Lemuel in 30:1–31:9; (5) the present order of the collection has been determined more by literary form and content than by date of composition; (6) no explanation based on theories of development can be accepted: shorter forms are not necessarily older than longer forms, and sayings with overt concern for religious matters are not necessarily younger than so-called secular ones.

An intriguing approach to Proverbs' structure comes from P. W. Skehan (pp. 27-45). Skehan compares the three major sections (1:1–9:18; 10:1–22:16; 22:17–31:31) to the three parts of a house — porch, nave or main chamber, and rear private room. Thus he credits the book to one editor who meticulously arranged the columns to depict the parts of the house and compiled the lines of each section to fix the total number at 930, a number equal to the letter values (Hebrew letters bore fixed numerical values) of the names in 1:1 — Solomon (375), David (14), Israel (541). The proportions of the three parts are said to resemble those of Solomon's temple, while at the same time constituting the house built by wisdom (9:1; cf. also Wisd. 9:8-11). As radical as Skehan's approach is, it is based in the structure of the text itself, not in the subjective judgments on the dates of the content that have characterized much discussion of Proverbs' composition.

*III. Role in Israel's Life.–A. Cultural Background.* Considerable evidence can be mustered to support the view that Proverbs (along with Job and Ecclesiastes) reflects the life of the land-owning upper classes: (1) the luxurious home of the seductive temptress (7:16-20); (2) precious stones as a ground of comparison to wise conduct (3:15; 8:11; 20:15; 31:10); (3) lavish diets with meat and wine (17:1; 23:1f., 20f., 29-35; 30:8-10); (4) access to royalty (14:35; 22:29; 23:1); (5) power to oppress the poor (22:22); (6) capability of lending and assuming other financial responsibility (11:15); (7) economic prosperity as a desired value (3:16; 10:15; 13:18); (8) the affluence in the portrait of the ideal woman (31:15f., 18, 22). R. Gordis (*HUCA,* 18 [1944], 77-118 [repr. in *Poets, Prophets, and Sages* (1971), pp. 160-197]) argues that the upper class "wisdom academies" that produced and used Proverbs contrast with the pharisaic schools for poor children and anticipate the learning centers of the Sadducees.

The social setting that underlies Proverbs reflects the stable "circumstances of the preexilic monarchical period" and "of an urban cultural milieu" (von Rad, *Wisdom,* p. 76). This picture of changelessness, unruffled by military threats or social upheavals that the prophets depict, mirrors both the sages' conservatism in their quest for order and the nature of a proverb whose task is to capture life's unchanging truths that are not altered by daily social problems.

Not much help is gained from Proverbs in understanding more precisely who Israel's wise men were. Did they hold official positions like scribes (Jer. 8:8-10) or even prophets and priests (Jer. 18:18), or political counselors (W. McKane,

*Prophets and Wise Men* [*SBT,* 1/44, 1965]), or teachers in wisdom academies (R. Gordis, *HUCA,* 18 [1944], 77-118)? Against those who view them as office holders, R. N. Whybray (*Intellectual Tradition in the OT* [*BZAW,* 135, 1974]) has argued that the OT wise were intellectuals from many walks of life, officers of neither court nor school. Indeed, Whybray has questioned the very existence of the wisdom schools to which much importance has been assigned by prevalent scholarly opinion (e.g., H. J. Hermisson, *Studien zur israelitischen Spruchweisheit* [*WMANT,* 28, 1968], pp. 113-136; B. Lang, *Frau Weisheit* [1975]). For discussion on sources of the proverbs, *see* PROVERB IV.

*B. Canonical Character.* Whatever the background of the various collections, it is clear that Proverbs, completed, views itself as a unified entity bearing the word of God to the people of God. Its link to Solomon, announced in the heading, is an important claim to antiquity as well as a reminder that it is a unique part of God's revelation parallel in age and validity to the Law and the Prophets. The refusal of Proverbs' editors to subsume wisdom to Torah or to link wisdom consciously with Israel's national history distinguishes Proverbs from Sirach and affirms its independent worth and its right to be considered canonical on its own merits. The ease with which passages from 2 S. 22:31 (cf. Ps. 18:30 [MT 31]) and Dt. 4:2 are incorporated into Prov. 30:5f. is further evidence that proverbs that sprang from human reflection have been received as Scripture by the believing community. For Proverbs' role as canonical literature, see B. S. Childs, *Intro. to the OT as Scripture* (1979), pp. 551-59.

*IV. Theological Significance.–A. Experience as a Means of Revelation.* The way in which the word of God is conveyed in Proverbs is very different from revelation through the law at Sinai, prophetic oracles, or apocalyptic visions. In the latter instances divine information breaks into human consciousness from beyond, usually bringing a command or an insight not obtainable any other way. In Proverbs the basis of the knowledge gained is personal and social experience — often painful experience: "In every proverb the stable door is only locked after the horse has been stolen" (G. von Rad, *OT Theology,* I, 421).

Such knowledge is considered to have divine authority and to be worthy of inclusion in Scripture because it is received within a world view that sees Yahweh at work in the whole of creation and human endeavor. Beyond that, the covenant faith that forms the context of Proverbs knows that every area of Israel's life is accountable to Yahweh, even those areas not specifically controlled by the Law.

Not that experience alone can lead to true knowledge of God. But when life is perceived as subject to the will of the Creator-Redeemer-King, experience can be an accurate teacher. But that perception of Yahweh's saving sovereignty is not obtainable from observation alone. His historical acts of redemption, interpreted by the prophets and apprehended through the Spirit, are necessary frameworks. Without this special revelation, the creation's more general revelation falls on blind eyes. Certainly anyone can learn from experience, but only those who see Yahweh at work in it fear Him and gain knowledge of the Holy One — requisites of true wisdom (Prov. 9:10).

*B. Creation as the Basis of Order.* Proverbs' silence on matters of salvation-history, public worship (though cf. 15:8), or divine covenant must not be interpreted as secularity. Chs. 1–9, abounding with references to Yahweh and His creation, set the tone for the entire book, which has a primary purpose to discern and display the order that holds all of life together. That order underlies a number of prominent features in Proverbs: (1) the use of analogies, comparisons, and numerical lists of similarities point to an overarching order in which seemingly dissimilar things are related to each other; (2) the cause-effect pattern of blessing and retribution is based on an order that when heeded brings weal; when violated, woe (10:16, 29; cf. R. L. Hubbard, *ZAW,* 94 [1982], 267-280); (3) the emphasis on speaking or doing the right thing at the proper time is built on the reality of order in the universe. (See von Rad, *Wisdom,* pp. 113-143.)

This order stems from a view of creation that is assumed but only rarely expressed (Prov. 8; Job 38ff.) in wisdom literature. Prov. 8:22-31 parades the fact that Wisdom's origins go back to the creation where she, a creature of Yahweh, delighted like a playful child in divine order (cf. 3:19f.). Wisdom, which has been described as "the primeval world order" or "the mystery behind the creation of the world" (von Rad, *Wisdom,* p. 161), is not pictured as an abstract ideal but as a personal entity calling people to submit to the created order that she expresses (8:1-4). Beyond that she declares her love for those who respond to the call and seek to live by the Creator's orders (8:17) — thus affirming that the creation both declares God's ways and calls the human family to be at home in His world (von Rad, *Wisdom,* pp. 166-176), searching for its intelligible principles of order, including the all-important principle of justice (J. L. Crenshaw, "Prolegomena," in *Studies in Ancient Israelite Wisdom* [1976], pp. 31-35).

The search for order needs always to reckon with the mysteries of Yahweh's sovereignty; it needs to leave room for His surprises. However intelligible is the Creator's work, human beings are still creatures who must yield to His divine plans (16:1-4, 9, 33; 19:21; 21:30f.).

*C. Social Responsibility.* The created order calls for a harmonious society where the rights of all, even the poor, are guarded. Since Yahweh is their maker, all are accountable to Him for their treatment of each other (17:5; 19:17; 21:13; 22:2). This accountability expresses itself in an array of demands that match those of the law and prophets: respect for parents (10:1), diligence in labor (10:4), love for others (10:12), just weights and measures (11:1), avoidance of gossip (11:13), kindness (11:17), generosity (11:25), truthfulness (12:19), openness to counsel (13:10), reliable witnessing in court (14:5), patience (14:17), control of temper (14:29), refusal of bribes (15:27), humility (16:18), rejection of violence (16:29), cheerfulness (17:22), just processes of law (17:26), discipline of children (19:18), loyalty (19:22), temperance (20:1), refusal of vengeance (20:22), confession of wrongs (28:13). This understanding of order carries the conviction that not just the individual but the larger society, whether the city or the nation, will pay the price for injustice among the citizenry (11:10f., 14).

*D. Covenant Loyalty.* Behind the call to responsible living lies the quiet influence of covenant obligations. Israel's life is misread wherever too sharp a distinction is made between the beliefs and ministries of prophets, priests, and wise men: (1) wisdom collections are found in the chief literature of the temple — the Psalms; (2) wisdom passages and Psalms have been imbedded in the prophetic oracles; (3) Psalmlike complaints and hymns dominated the speeches of the wise man Job; (4) wise men may have had links with the temple and court scribes. Whatever their differences in function, the various leaders shared a common faith in Yahweh as Creator, in Israel's special calling, and in the obligations of obedience that stemmed from that calling.

As displayed in Proverbs, wisdom is derived from neither prophecy nor law. The three traditions are related in interdependence — not dependence nor independence. There were not three faiths in the covenant Lord but one. The wise men showed how Yahweh's created order reinforced and complemented the ethical commands of the other two traditions. The strong similarities between wisdom, Torah, and prophecy are remarkable evidence of the sages' conviction that Yahweh was indeed Lord of all and everything. For further discussion, see D. A. Hubbard, *Tyndale Bulletin,* 17 (1966), 3ff.; cf. J. Blenkinsopp, *Wisdom and Law in the OT: The Ordering of Life in Israel and Early Judaism* (1983).

***V. Proverbs and the NT.***–*A. Quotations.* The direct quotations (cf. *United Bible Societies' Greek NT* [3rd ed. 1975], p. 899) used in the NT argue for a view of Scripture's continuity, since the sayings and exhortations of Proverbs found in the apostolic writings are employed in virtually the same ways as in their original OT settings: admonition to accept discipline (3:11f. — He. 12:5f.); motivation to humility (3:34 — Jas. 4:6; 1 Pet. 5:5); argument for the necessity of judgment (11:31 — 1 Pet. 4:18); admonition against vengeance (25:21f. — Rom. 12:20); comparative saying against returning to folly (26:11 — 2 Pet. 2:22). The recognition of Proverbs' authority as Scripture is implied in the language used to introduce several of the quotations: "exhortation" (He. 12:5); "scripture" (Jas. 4:6); "it is written" (Rom. 12:19); "true proverb" (2 Pet. 2:22).

*B. Allusions.* In a number of instances the NT writers seize on the language of Proverbs and incorporate it in their sayings without the more formal process of full quotation: 2:4 — Col. 2:3; 3:1-4 — Lk. 2:52; 3:7a — Rom. 12:16; 4:26 — He. 12:13a; 10:12 — Jas. 5:20 and 1 Pet. 4:8; 12:7 — Mt. 7:24-27. These verbal echoes demonstrate how thoroughly the OT book had salted the speech of the apostles who, in turn, expected their hearers to catch the precise flavor of the phrases from Proverbs.

*C. Christology.* The NT portraits of Jesus take some of their colors from the palette of Proverbs, especially the personification of wisdom in Prov. 8 (cf. R. G. Hamerton-Kelly, *Pre-existence, Wisdom, and the Son of Man* [1973]).

*1. Synoptic Gospels.* Luke closely associates Jesus with wisdom: the summary statement on Jesus' growth centers on wisdom as the principal attribute (Lk. 2:52; cf. Prov. 3:1-4); in Jesus' words, wisdom is personified (cf. Prov. 1, 8) and described as having children (Lk. 7:35) or speaking a divine word (Lk. 11:49-51). While Luke views Jesus as wisdom's envoy in whom wisdom found a permanent home (cf. I. H. Marshall, *Gospel of Luke* [*NIGTC,* 1978], pp. 301-304, 502-506), Matthew seems to equate Jesus with the divine wisdom (Mt. 23:34; 12:42). The background of these Synoptic sayings is complex and may indicate the possible influence of Sirach, Wisdom of Solomon, and 1 Enoch, all of which have picked up the motif of personified wisdom from Proverbs and Job 28, and transmitted it with the additions and modifications appropriate to their purposes.

*2. Fourth Gospel and Epistles.* It is in the NT language used to express the preexistence of the Son that Proverbs' contribution to Christology becomes most apparent. The prologue to John's Gospel has drawn from many sources; alongside the doctrine of the creative word from Gen. 1 and Ps. 33, the prophetic word from Isaiah and Jeremiah, the use of *mêmrā'* in the Targums, and the *logos* teachings of Alexandrian Judaism, stands the wisdom emphasis of Proverbs and its apocryphal heirs: like wisdom the Word was with God in the beginning (Jn. 1:1f.; Prov. 8:22-31); like wisdom the Word was present at the creation, although wisdom's participation in that creation is far less clear (Jn. 1:3; Prov. 8:30f. — RSV "master workman," Heb. *'āmôn,* is probably better translated "playful child"); like wisdom the Word is the source of life (Jn. 1:4; Prov. 8:35; cf. L. Morris, *Gospel According to John* [*NICNT,* 1971], pp. 115-126).

Similarly the NT hymns that celebrate the unique role of the Son in creation, revelation, and redemption draw from the language of Proverbs: He. 1:1-3 does so indirectly, being more dependent on Wisdom of Solomon than on Proverbs for its actual wording; Col. 1:15-20 sounds the familiar notes of preexistence and presence at creation, applying them to the Son in terms that reflect also the idea of the Second Adam. This contribution of Proverbs to NT Christology must neither be overlooked nor overplayed. It is clear that the poems of Lady Wisdom from Proverbs furnished part of the language through which the early Christians expressed their understanding of Christ's uniqueness and preexistence, though that language was transmitted and adopted by Judaism, especially in its Hellenistic forms. It is equally clear that no single literary source, nor any assembly of sources, can entirely account for the lofty ascriptions of lordship to Jesus, which the Church knew to be the only appropriate response to His marvelous words and deeds (cf. P. T. O'Brien, *Colossians, Philemon* [*Word Biblical Comm.* 44, 1982], pp. 37-40).

*See also* WISDOM.

***Bibliography.***–A. Barucq, *Le livre des Proverbes* (1964); J. Crenshaw, ed., *Studies in Ancient Israelite Wisdom* (1976); *OT Wisdom* (1981); J. G. Gammie, *et al.,* eds., *Israelite Wisdom* (*Festschrift* S. Terrien, 1978); C. Kayatz, *Studien zu Proverbien 1–9* (1966); D. Kidner, *Proverbs* (*Tyndale OT Comm.,* 1964); G. Kuhn, *Beiträge zur Erklärung des Salomonischen Spruchbuches* (1931); W. McKane, *Proverbs* (*OTL,* 1970); R. E. Murphy, *Interp.,* 20 (1966), 3-14; *Wisdom Literature* (*FOTL,* 13, 1981); P. J. Nel, *Structure and Ethos of the Wisdom Admonitions in Proverbs* (*BZAW,* 158, 1982); G. von Rad, *OT Theology,* I (Eng. tr. 1962), 418-453; *Wisdom in Israel* (Eng. tr. 1972); H. Ranston, *OT Wisdom Books and Their Teaching* (1930); H. Ringgren, *Word and Wisdom* (1947); R. B. Y. Scott, *Proverbs. Ecclesiastes* (*AB,* 1965); P. Skehan, *Studies in Israelite Poetry and Wisdom* (1971); R. N. Whybray, *Wisdom in Proverbs* (*SBT,* 1/45, 1965).

D. A. HUBBARD

## PROVIDENCE.

I. Definition
II. Spheres
III. In the OT
IV. In the NT
V. The Doctrine

***I. Definition.***–The word "provide" (Lat. *providere*) means etymologically "to foresee." The corresponding Greek word is *prónoia,* meaning "forethought." The noun is used in the NT of human foresight (Acts 24:2; Rom. 13:14; cf. also the verb in Rom. 12:17; 2 Cor. 8:21; 1 Tim. 5:8). Foresight, however, implies more than seeing in advance. It also implies anticipation, so that steps are taken either to meet a need which is seen or to lead to a result which is envisaged or planned. It is in this sense that pre-vision becomes pro-vision. The provident person is the one who makes arrangements to deal with contingencies or to reach established goals. Applied to God, providence obviously includes the divine foreseeing, but in God foreseeing has an even fuller and broader reference in view of the divine overruling. Providence, then, is the preservation, superintendence, and teleological direction of all things by God. It is the divine governance whereby all possible events are woven into a coherent pattern and all possible developments are shaped to accomplish the divinely instituted goal.

***II. Spheres.***–Since providence is a comprehensive term, it is sometimes useful to subdivide it according to the different spheres of operation. Thus there is first the divine providence in nature. All creation, i.e., the whole cosmos, falls under the providential disposition of God. The patterns and movements of nature may all be subsumed under this concept. Science itself is a tracing of the ways of providence (cf. the great passages in Job 38–41). It should be remembered, however, that this is not a separate area of providence, which might give rise to a form of natural theology. For one thing, the ways of God are not always easy to see in nature if nature is studied in abstraction. For another, nature does not constitute an autonomous sphere of providence. The cosmos is the setting of God's dealings with man. If there is any particular goal for nature as such, it is necessarily beyond our comprehension. What we do know is that the world is teleologically directed to serve the outworking of God's relationship with humanity.

This leads us to the second sphere of providence, namely, that of human history. However tangled the story of people and nations, it stands always under the moral judgment and the teleological direction of God. Man proposes, God disposes. God's purpose is fulfilled in and through man, and in spite of the confusion of man. Yet here again one can hardly speak of a general purpose, which may make of providence a locus of natural theology. Taken alone, the history of the race seems to stand only under the sign of futility. Even the vaunted hope of progress has little solid basis. The general overruling of history is designed to serve a more special purpose within history, the special history which is often called salvation-history.

This leads us to a further sphere of providence in which it stands in close proximity to the divine election and predestination. This is the sphere of the divine overruling of the special people whom God raises up in His own revealing and reconciling action. Providence here is the providential oversight by which God leads, preserves, controls, and overrules the patriarchs, the prophets, the nation Israel, individual Israelites, the incarnate Son, the Church, and individual Christians in pursuance of His special purpose of calling and salvation. The interweaving of salvation-history into general history, the shaping of general history to serve salvation-history, is providence par excellence. It is to be noted at this point that providence is not a general category of which predestination is a special instance (*contra* Thomas Aquinas). To say this is to reverse the relationship, for in fact providence serves the divine election. Yet it is certainly true that God's general providence in nature and history is to be seen in the light of this particular disclosure of providence in the biblical story and the ensuing story of the Church. For this reason providence, too, has a christological reference, for it is by and for and to Christ that all things consist, and it is toward the consummation of all things in Him that nature and history finally move.

A last sphere of providence, which is already included in what has gone before but which still calls for special mention, is providence in individual lives. As the whole sweep of history stands under the providential ordering of God, so the individual life within history is also brought under the divine overruling. In this sense it is quite right to speak of the singular providences of God, whether in terms of ordinary events or of outstanding circumstances. Here again the providence of God serves the fulfillment of His basic purpose, so that the actions of individuals (e.g., Abraham or Cyrus) serve also to advance the whole. But the purpose itself has an individual reference, namely, the calling of people to faith and their upbuilding in discipleship and service, so that providence may here again serve the end of election and edification. By the providential disposing of God, events in the lives of individuals are woven into the story of their individual relationship with God in Christ, and of the service that they then render in the further advancement of His word and work.

***III. In the OT.***–The divine superintendence of all aspects of the cosmos is plainly disclosed in the OT. The world as God created it gives evidence of purposeful planning, according to Gen. 1. An appropriate setting is provided for the story of God and man; and as herbs and fruits are divinely provided to sustain man, man himself is to exercise dominion over other creatures, not in selfish tyranny, but for the wise and orderly integration of the whole (Gen. 1:28f.). After the deluge, flesh, fish, and fowl are also provided for man's sustenance (Gen. 9:3), and the promise is given that "seedtime and harvest, cold and heat, summer and winter, day and night, shall not cease" (8:22). The order of the sun, moon, and stars is established and maintained by God (1:14ff.); not one can fail (Isa. 40:26). God has also separated the sea and the land, and He has set for the ocean boundaries which it cannot pass (Job 38:8). All the detailed ways of all the creatures, even the most mysterious and the most powerful, are known to Him (Job 38–41). He provides food and drink for animals and man according to the ordered course which He has established and which He maintains (Ps. 104:5ff.). The dependence of living creatures on God is plainly seen, for when He withdraws His hand death supervenes, and when God's breath goes forth again, life is renewed (Ps. 104:29f.). Man in particular is under the providential direction of God. God knows him in all his being. God also accompanies him on his way, compassing his path, besetting him behind and before (Ps. 139:5). This thought of the divine concursus is a particularly rich one. God is above time, and yet He is not just a transcendent traffic-director. He is with the creature in its course, with man in his temporal life. He is the past from which man comes and the future to which he goes. He is also the present in which he lives and moves. If sometimes the divine concursus can have a daunting aspect — even if he wished, the psalmist could not escape God's presence — it has also a supremely comforting aspect. For it means that man has a sustaining power on which to rely (Ps. 91), a higher direction to overrule even his mistakes and to keep him from ultimate evil (cf. Gen. 45:5), and a final teleology to make sense of what seems to be only confusion and futility (cf. the higher ways and thoughts of God in Isa. 55).

Mention of the divine concursus is a reminder that much more is included in the providence of God than the superintendence of the natural order and provision for the material preservation of people. God is Lord of history as well as of nature. He directs the movements of the nations. This is seen on a global scale in the early chapters of Genesis, particularly in the confusion of languages and scattering of the peoples after Babel. But the main illustration is in the nations around Israel, for after all the story of the Bible is primarily the story of salvation-history, of providence as it serves this particular history. God is behind the story of the Ethiopians, and the movements of the Philistines from Caphtor and the Syrians from Kir (Am. 9:7). God brings moral judgments upon Damascus, Gaza, Tyre, Edom, and Ammon (Am. 1). God raises up the Assyrians to punish Israel (Isa. 10:5), the Babylonians to overthrow Assyria, and Cyrus both to destroy Babylon and to redeem Judah (Isa. 45:1). Before God all nations are as a drop from a bucket (v. 15). God sends both evil and good (v. 7) as the situation demands. He knows the end as well as the beginning, so that everything serves His sovereign purpose (41:21ff.). The plans that even the most powerful nations form against God will be frustrated: "The kings of the earth set themselves, and the rulers take counsel together . . . [but] he who sits in the heavens laughs; the Lord has them in derision" (Ps. 2:2, 4). The gods of the nations are not rival powers; they are idols, things of nought, which are nothing in themselves and can accomplish nothing (Ps. 96:5). "The Most High rules the kingdom of men, and gives it to whom he will" (Dnl. 4:25 [MT 22]). To His prophets God sometimes grants visions of the future, whether in general or in detail (cf. esp. Dnl. 4ff., but also Isa. 48:3). These visions take into account that there is conflict due to people's sin. People form their own plans which conflict with each other and with the divine purpose. But in and through all the conflict and the resultant affliction, God fulfils His own purpose and causes His rule to triumph. People do wrong things, but God works even these for good (Gen. 45:5ff.). Hence in the last resort it is always God who "changes times and seasons; he removes kings and sets up kings" (Dnl. 2:21). The ultimate goal is that every knee shall bow to Him and every tongue shall swear (Isa. 45:23). All nations and tongues will be gathered, and they shall come and see God's glory (Isa. 66:18).

The general providence of God in history clearly serves His special providence in salvation-history, for He has chosen that in and through Israel His special purpose shall be worked out, and nothing in heaven or earth is to thwart this. Hence within the historical providence of God there is a particular shaping of history to fulfil the goal of election and redemption. As noted, we have here an overlapping between election and providence, for the election and salvation of God are worked out in history, and the special history of God's people from Israel through Jesus Christ to the new Israel is interwoven into the general history of the race. This may be seen clearly throughout the OT narrative. Abraham's move from Ur to Canaan is in answer to a special call, but it also involves new historical relationships; so, too, does the promising of Canaan to the seed of Abraham. The stay in Egypt, which is brought about by internal division and external famine, serves a purpose of temporary preservation and also provides the occasion for the final mighty deliverance of the Exodus. The story of the judges and the early monarchy provides an illustration of moral judgment in the dealings with the nations and also an example of preservation and molding with a view to the future. Foreign relations continue right up to the time of Christ and on into the history of the Church, with its mission of preaching the reconciling Word; and there are also inner events within Israel, the disruption of the kingdoms, the fratricidal wars, the destruction of the kingdoms, the preservation of a remnant, the scattering among the nations. The story is often complicated and perplexing even as we now follow it under the guidance of the biblical interpretation. But the point is that the hand of God is upon it all, not only to preserve His people but also to shape their history to the accomplishment of the promised salvation for all peoples.

This is how the OT itself interprets the story for us. From first to last God is at work either indirectly or directly. He is behind the migration of Abraham, the going down to Egypt and the deliverance from it, the entry into the Promised Land. Although He punishes Israel, He also causes the stars in their courses to fight against Sisera (Jgs. 5:20). Ps. 105 especially traces out the particular providence of God in relation to Israel (cf. also Pss. 44, 66, 88, etc.). The general principle behind it all is that "the lot is cast into the lap, but the decision is wholly from the Lord" (Prov. 16:33; cf. also 16:9; 21:31). Applied to Israel, this means that the men of Israel may seem to be working out their own plans and following their own desires and seeking their own goals; but God finally controls the ongoing story of the nation, and it is what He does, not what man does, that counts. This is why the achievements of, e.g., Omri can be dismissed so summarily. Unlike the events of Ahab's reign, with its great conflict between Ahab and Elijah, they are of little significance in terms of the divine purpose.

From the standpoint of the NT, of course, the final goal of the OT story is Jesus Christ, the true Israelite, in whom the covenantal, prophetic, and messianic promises are fulfilled. All history, and particularly OT history, converges on Him, and then widens out again from Him to all nations.

In addition to providence in nature, in general history, and in the history of Israel, the OT also depicts the providential ordering of the lives of individuals. This overlaps, of course, with the providential story of the superintendence of the nations, especially of Israel, for the story of the race or nation is often pivotally the story of individuals, of Adam and Noah, of Abraham and Joseph, of Moses and David, of Naaman and Cyrus, of Jonah and Esther, and supremely of Jesus Christ. Yet the individual application is also brought out plainly, both in the narratives and in explicit statements, particularly in Psalms and Proverbs. Thus we read, "The steps of a good man are ordered by the Lord, and he delighteth in his way" (Ps. 37:23, AV). Or again, "in all thy ways acknowledge him, and he shall direct thy paths" (Prov. 3:6, AV). Or again, "The righteous and the wise and their deeds are in the hand of God" (Eccl. 9:1). In the first instance this means, no doubt, that God extends (or in the case of the wicked withholds) protection, and turns things to material advantage (or disadvantage), as in the case of Joseph on the one side or Saul on the other. But already in the OT it is recognized that the ultimate advantage will be spiritual in nature rather than material (cf. Ps. 16:11; 17:15; 73:26), and that in any case it will often come only through affliction.

In the world of sin, of opposition to the will of God, it is natural (albeit intrinsically most unnatural) that there should be suffering. As it falls on the wicked, this is a demonstration of the providence of God's moral judgment. The book of Job warns us, however, that while there is a general moral order in the universe, individual sufferings cannot be providentially related to individual sins. The righteous suffer as well as the wicked. It is true that they are only relatively righteous. Yet they often suffer, not because they are relatively wicked, but because they are righteous. Joseph comes to his glory in Egypt only through betrayal and imprisonment. David, too, attains to the crown only through banishment and harassment even to the point of feigning madness and making alliance with the Philistines. Job finds his supreme prosperity only after he is stripped of everything and reduced to abject misery. The prophets render their service only in face of determined opposition which leads them to flight, imprisonment, obloquy, and even death. In fact, it often seems as though God's providential care is not to be seen where one would most expect it, namely, in the lives of the choicest of His people.

Yet the final issue makes it plain that God's purpose is in fact being worked out even for them as individuals, so that what seems to be evil is really for good. It is good for three main reasons. First, it points indirectly to the moral judgment on the sin of the race, which cannot be suspended. Second, and more deeply, it serves the greater spiritual profit of those who thus suffer. Third, and most profoundly of all, it is for the wider benefit of others. For if the involvement of the righteous in a sinful world necessarily means their involvement in its judgment and affliction, the greatness of God's providential overruling is, not that He preserves them from this, but that He keeps them through it and turns it vicariously to their profit and to that of the wicked. This leads to the great statements of confidence and of faith which are so abundant in the OT. "I know, O Lord . . . that in faithfulness thou hast afflicted me" (Ps. 119:75). "Though he [the good man] fall, he shall not be utterly cast down" (Ps. 37:24, AV). "Why art thou cast down, O my soul . . . ? I shall yet praise him, who is the health of my countenance, and my God" (Ps. 42:11, AV). And with a figurative as well as a literal application, He "turns the rock into a pool of water, the flint into a spring of water" (Ps. 114:8). Thus the doctrine of providence again moves toward that of the NT, in which the providence of God finds its culmination in the vicarious suffering of the one righteous Servant — a suffering which is itself the means of the divine triumph and which is crowned by the glorious victory of the resurrection and the awaited manifestation of glory at the Parousia.

*IV. In the NT.*–As in the OT, so also in the NT, the general providence of God is discerned (1) in nature. God causes His rain to fall and His sun to shine both on the just and on the unjust (Mt. 5:45). He feeds the fowls of the air and clothes the lilies of the field (Mt. 6:26ff.). Not one sparrow falls to the ground without the Father (Mt. 10:29). In particular, God is the one who in fatherly providence cares for man. He has always borne witness to Himself by doing good and giving us rain from heaven and fruitful seasons (Acts 14:17). "He giveth life to all, and breath, and all things. . . . for in him we live, and move, and have our being" (Acts 17:25, 27). As in the OT, God sustains the world He has created, maintaining its orderly course, upholding it as the setting for His special dealings with people.

God is also portrayed no less vividly in the NT (2) as Lord of history. This element is not perhaps quite so prominent in the general sense, but it is equally definite. As Paul says in Athens, the God who made of one blood all the nations of men "hath determined the times before appointed, and the bounds of their habitation" (Acts 17:26, AV). Similarly, the Lord just before His ascension speaks of the times and seasons which the Father has put in His own power (Acts 1:7). In His apocalyptic discourse Jesus also refers to the times of the Gentiles (Lk. 21:28), and a basis theme of this whole address is the divine direction of history to its appointed goal and consummation. The same is true in the book of Revelation. While history seems to pursue its own erratic course, it is in fact superintended by God, not merely in that His moral judgments are operative in it (cf. the collapse of Babylon), but also in that He works out His own purpose, so that all the plans and mistakes of men, all the complications of their acts, both individual and corporate, will finally serve the fulfillment of this purpose. An interesting emphasis in Paul is on the providential significance of law or government. Quite apart from the judgments of events, God has also instituted human law as an instrument of providence (Rom. 13). By means of it the violence of man is held in restraint, and human life is historically preserved against anarchy and self-destruction. (Is this the meaning of 2 Thess. 2:7?) Paul himself sees no reason why this providential instrument of law should not also serve the gospel and its proclamation. This is why he can appeal to his rights as a citizen at Philippi. This is why he can appeal to Caesar as a means of gaining access to imperial circles at Rome. Paul's actions display clearly his belief that law is providentially ordered both generally to make human life tolerable and specifically to create conditions for the more effective propagation of the Christian message and edification of the Christian community.

The specific aspect here leads us to the further point that in the NT general providence is again oriented to God's special providence. This may be seen above all in the providential ordering of history in relation (3) to the coming and the coming again of Christ. In the light of the NT even the history of Israel in the OT is shown to point to the coming of Christ. In the NT record itself the general events of history, which might have seemed to be so important in themselves, e.g., the reigns of Herods and Caesars, serve only as the background for the outworking of the event that is one of the two great foci of history, namely, the human life of the incarnate Son of God. And all that follows in the time of the Church, both in the NT record and beyond, is simply a setting for the mission of the Church and a movement toward the final focus of the human story, the coming again of the risen Lord. In other words, it is now apparent that the central concern of God's providence is that Jesus should come, and come again, to fulfil the divine work of revelation, reconciliation, and final restitution.

The providence of God is displayed in a special way (4) in the life of Jesus. His genealogy is prepared. He comes in the fulness of time (Gal. 4:4). His mother, and nominal father, are specially chosen and informed, and it is foreordained that He be of Davidic descent and be born in Bethlehem. He is revealed to the wise men and yet also protected against the jealous cruelty of Herod. He is brought up in comparative obscurity and yet in a place where He can first bring His light to the tribes of Isa. 9:1, in Galilee of the nations. His ministry moves on irresistibly through its various stages to the right time and place of its fulfillment in the apparent tragedy of the cross. Representatives of both the Jewish and the gentile world are assembled, along with the false apostle, to secure His condemnation and execution. But in this supreme suffering of the supreme Servant, God is supremely present. Jesus was delivered by the determinate counsel and foreknowledge of God (Acts 2:23). God fulfilled in Him the things He had foretold (Acts 3:18). The kings of the earth stood up against Jesus "to do whatever thy hand and thy plan had predestined to take place" (Acts 4:28). God did not lose control of history when this unmerited suffering fell on the Holy One. He was in total command. All nature and history moved to His hour of passion, death, and resurrection. The supreme power of God was here displayed in the shaping of history to bring about the vicarious death and the ensuing resurrection of the incarnate Son. And now all history flows from this event to bring about the calling out of the Church and the final consummation when the kingdoms of this world will be the kingdoms of Our Lord and of His Christ (Rev. 11:15). In this way the NT sheds a whole flood of light on the divine providence. It is providence with a view to salvation and new creation. It is providence that finds its center in Christ, for and to whom are all things, and in whom all nature and history find their meaning and goal.

Also evident in the NT is the providence of God (5) in the life of the Christian. Christ Himself told His disciples that the very hairs of their heads were numbered (Mt. 10:30). The early Church under threat committed itself confidently to God (Acts 4:29f.). The careers of the apostles were plainly guided and overruled by God (cf. Acts 21:11). Paul could affirm with complete certainty, "All things work together for good to them that love God" (Rom. 8:28, AV). Peter could repeat the OT assurance that "the eyes of the Lord are upon the righteous" (1 Pet. 3:12 = Ps. 34:15 [MT 16]). This does not mean in the least that Christians were or are assured of a life of tranquillity, prosperity, ease, or material security. It does not mean that the Church's story is to be one of unbroken success. The lesson of righteous suffering in the OT has been illuminated in a new way by the suffering of Christ. Through suffering, salvation has been wrought. Through suffering, obedience is learned (He. 5:8). By way of suffering, glory comes (He. 12:2). The Christian, then, can expect to suffer under the fatherly providence of God (He. 12:5ff.). In the world he will have tribulation (Jn. 16:33). Afflictions have a constructive part to play both in cutting off the old man and in upbuilding the new in Christian life and character. They are also an integral part of the ministry of the servants of the Suffering Servant. Paul has sufferings which he must fill up on behalf of the Church (Col. 1:24), for under God's providence the vicissitudes of life serve the good of others as well as our own good, and the true boasting of the Christian is in God's strength, not in exemption from affliction but in deliverance and triumph through it (2 Cor. 11:23ff.). The final purpose of God for His children is one of joy and glory. Like Joseph and David, the people of God are to be brought through their suffering to this fulfillment of God's perfect plan for them. Like their Savior and Master, they are to come to Easter Day by way of Good Friday, identified with Christ in His death as well as His resurrection. Hence they are to view their life under the providence of God with the eyes of faith, as did the psalmist when he said: "Weeping may tarry for the night, but joy comes with the morning" (Ps. 30:5 [MT 6]), or the poet Cowper in "Light Shining out of Darkness":

Blind unbelief is sure to err
And scan his work in vain,
God is his own interpreter
And he will make it plain.

The dealings of God are not always evident on the surface, but there is always a purpose of grace which time or eternity will reveal:

Behind a frowning providence,
He hides a smiling face.

*V. The Doctrine.*–The essential elements in the doctrine of providence have naturally emerged already in the presentation of the biblical teaching. It remains only to draw out some of the implications in the face of contrary views and to answer the various questions that are raised about providence, and especially about what might seem to be conflicting data.

The doctrine of providence maintains that there is a purpose behind not merely the existence but also the course of the world. The world is not just a chance event. Its story both in nature and history is no meaningless muddle on which at best a meaning has to be imposed. Its happenings and developments do not simply occur, following no plan and leading to no goal. The world was from the very first planned for a purpose; and although the fall and sin of man have introduced a disruptive element, what takes place still serves this overruling purpose.

The doctrine of providence also makes it plain that this is not just an immanent purpose. The world is not an eternal entity which carries its own providence within itself. It is not itself God, so that the divine purpose is identical with the immanent. Indeed, the world is not just a divinely created mechanism which can now function apart from the One who made it, and which bears an immanent purpose given along with its creation. God Himself, the Creator and Lord of all things, imposes His own purpose on the world and overrules, accompanies, and preserves it on its course with a view to the fulfillment of this purpose. This does not mean, of course, that God is immanent in the world and its events in the sense of full identification. He is certainly immanent insofar as nothing takes place without Him. But He is also personal. God is Himself personally at work. The laws of nature are neither independent of Him nor identical with Him. The movement of history neither takes place without Him nor gives essential expression to Him. He is immanent, yet not in the sense of absorption. Providence is no mechanical or biological process. It is overruling in the strict sense, even though it be overruling in and through planned and orderly events. For the planned and orderly events of creation serve a purpose that is above creation, i.e., the purpose of the Creator. The plan that is worked out is an eternal and transcendent plan. Although its outworking is in time, its roots reach back to pretemporal eternity and its consummation will be in posttemporal eternity. Even in time it comes to its critical fulfillment in the intervention of the eternal God in time.

This leads us to the further point that the doctrine of providence teaches a christological interpretation of history. In the fallen world, no satisfactory philosophy of nature or of history can be read off from events. What is needed is a theology of nature and history, or, in terms of the NT revelation, a Christology. Arrogant though it may sound to non-Christians, all the movements of nature and all dramatic events of history find their center in Christ, for it is in Him that God in the dispensation of the fulness of time plans to gather all things in one (Eph. 1:10). Many aspects of providence are evident enough, but they can only degenerate into pious and rather empty platitudes when divorced from the true purpose of God in Jesus Christ. The incarnate Son is the unifying focus which gives content and meaning to all God's providential dealings, and hence to all the processes and events providentially ordered and controlled.

The Christian interpretation of history sheds a light on the most stubborn problems relating to providence, namely, the problems of choice, of evil, of suffering, of events even in the lives of the righteous that seem to show little sign of the beneficent power of God. It is to be noted that all these problems are fundamentally related, and that they are all to be brought under the christological understanding. If they are isolated from one another, they necessarily become more difficult to understand. If they are made into abstract philosophical problems, they inevitably become insoluble and can lead only to absurd notions or pathetic pleas. It is only in relation to the fundamental purpose of God, not to the detailed operations of providence, that these problems can find their true answer — an answer that, once perceived, is quickly seen again in the detailed operations.

The overruling purpose of God in Christ is man in fellowship with God and with fellow men. The supreme story of the world is the attainment of this purpose in spite of its original frustration. The task of providence is the shaping of natural and historical events in such a way that the purpose is fulfilled. Its fulfillment is in and by the special work of God, which reaches its culmination in the vicarious life and death and resurrection of Jesus Christ, in the application of this work in individual lives, and in the final establishment of His kingdom at the Parousia.

Fellowship, however, is more than automatic obedience. It carries with it the possibility of choice. Providence is not a fixing of the will in advance. Secondary causes are given full play. These include the individual choices of people. The divine providence directs all these in such a way that the purpose of God will still be fulfilled. Only a shallow view of providence can confuse it with determinism. The greatness of the divine providence is that it takes into account all the innumerable possibilities and yet weaves them all into the one predetermined pattern, not with a view to the obliteration of freedom, but with a view to its true establishment.

Evil arises out of the possibility of choice. The Bible seems to leave little doubt that had man chosen to obey God he could and would have controlled even natural evils, quite apart from prevention of all the monstrous injustice and carnage of history. The awaited kingdom is to bring peace among animals as well as among people (Isa. 11:1ff.). The possibility of evil is thus one of the implications of choice, though once evil is present it also becomes a powerful factor in the influencing of choice. Evil could be stamped out altogether only by depriving man of choice, or by winding up history in judgment. The present task of providence is to overrule evil so that, far from frustrating the fulfillment of God's purpose, it will finally serve it. Thus even the wrath of man is turned to God's praise (Ps. 76:10 [MT 11]). A man can be blind that the works of God should be made manifest in him (Jn. 9:2f.). This is not just a shallow view of the best of all possible worlds which unfortunately has to include a little unavoidable evil. Far from being an essential ingredient in the best possible world, evil is an ugly and disruptive thing which will finally be destroyed. On the other hand, there is no room for the skepticism and unbelief of pessimism. God is not struggling against odds that are too much for Him. He is neither a malevolent despot nor a well-meaning blunderer. Evil is indeed a real thing. It is not to be taken lightly. It is not an essential instrument of good. Man's wrath does not on its own account work the righteousness of God (Jas. 1:20). Nevertheless, in the hands of God, for whom no problem is too hard, even this ugly thing can be and is woven into the pattern, so that even the weakness of Pilate, the treachery of Judas, the fickleness of the mob, and the misplaced zeal of the religious leaders can set in train the events by which God accomplishes the reconciliation of man.

Suffering is the consequence of evil. In the general sense, it is thus a true judgment on sin, and its place in the divine providence is easily discerned. It both judges sin and in the form of death helps to contain it. Yet already in the OT there is a recognition that suffering cannot be wholly explained in this way. If righteous children suffer, this may be in part due to their fathers' sins, but it can hardly be regarded as a punishment. Joseph's imprisonment in Egypt might be traced back to a whole series of faults including the deceptions of Jacob and Laban, the partiality of Jacob for the son of Rachel, the envy of the other brothers, and perhaps even some sense of self-importance in the young Joseph; but it is obviously out of all proportion if we try to see in it a direct punishment of Joseph for his own sin. So, too, the sufferings of Job and Jeremiah and the psalmist cannot be directly related to sins in the sense of immediate judgment. The following question thus arises: we may admit that suffering is a consequence of sin and that it bears in general the aspect of judgment; yet how is the often exorbitant suffering of the comparatively righteous to be reconciled with the wise, omnipotent, and righteous providence of God?

Raised in every age, this question has found in Scripture, and supremely in Jesus Christ the true theme of Scripture, its one convincing answer. This answer can be summarized as follows. First, God overrules suffering not merely as an instrument of judgment but also as a means of discipline and mortification (Ps. 119:67). Second, He shows that even suffering can be overruled to a greater and final blessing (Ps. 66:10ff.). Third, God uses suffering, the consequence of sin, as the very weapon by which to make atonement for sin (Isa. 53; 2 Cor. 5:14ff.). In the strict sense, this takes place only in Christ Himself, for He alone is perfectly righteous, and His passion alone avails for the remission of sin. Yet in Christ, in the power of His one perfect and all-sufficient sacrifice, believers may legitimately see a sacrificial value in their own sufferings in Christ's name, for His sake, and for His cause. The people of God are never more powerful in their ministry than when they suffer and even die in their work. Suffering, too, is incorporated into the great ministry of reconciliation.

Against this background the Christian can hardly expect that all events in his life will display God's providence in the sense of prosperity, calm, and security. Believers as well as others can be struck down by disease and accident, by poverty and bereavement, by disappointment and disaster. God does not deliberately send these, but He does not specifically withhold them. In some cases they may come as the result of the Christian's own mistakes. In others they may take the form of a corporate judgment in which Christians, too, are involved. In others they are just part of the ordinary nexus of life in this aeon. The great point is, however, that under the fatherly providence of God they can all finally be blessings, and can be seen as blessings, both to believers themselves and through them to others. But those who fail to see them thus will miss the blessing, just as those who fail to see the crucified Christ as the Savior of the world will never know the reconciliation of God, and will never be able to make any real sense of the world. The all-important thing is to set sufferings too in the light of God's supreme work in Jesus Christ (cf. esp. Rom. 5:3ff.; Jas. 1:12; 1 Pet. 3:14ff.; also Jn. 16:33; Acts 5:41).

This leads us to a final point of great importance. In the long run, providence has to be believed. There are many evident signs of providence in nature and history, but it cannot be finally demonstrated in such a way as to rule out all ignorance or opposition. If providence serves the fulfillment of reconciliation, it does so as a fact, not as an apologetic argument. In an unfallen world God's providence would, of course, be absolutely plain to see. In the new heaven and the new earth there will be no mistaking it. But in a fallen world, in which the fulfillment of God's providence takes the form of reconciliation, regeneration, and ultimate restitution, it can take some curious paths both in history at large and particularly in individual lives. Even believers will often be at a loss to explain individual events as they take place. Moreover, the general providences of God in nature and history, which might seem evident enough, can also be ascribed to immanent causes or questioned in the light of such natural disasters as earthquake or drought. To see God's providential hand with true certainty it is necessary first to know God Himself, to know Him in the outworking of His revealing and reconciling purpose in Jesus Christ, to know Him at the focus and center in the light of which His ways in providence may be discerned. The "smiling face" of God is in the first instance the face unveiled at the cross and the empty tomb, where the God who seems to have averted His face from the sin-bearing Savior is the very God who is well pleased with the Son (Mt. 3:17), who is well pleased with us in Him (Eph. 1:5f.), and who has here worked out, in spite of all appearances to the contrary, the good pleasure of His grace. This God is also the God who preserves and overrules all creation with a view to the fulfillment of His gracious purpose. Hence we may be confident that even if providence is frowning, behind it is the smiling face of God.

***Bibliography.–ERE***; *HDB*; *BDTh.*; *TDNT*, IV, *s.v.* νοέω κτλ.: προνοέω (Behm); K. Barth, *CD*, III/3; A. B. Bruce, *Providential Order of the World* (1897); Calvin *Inst.* i.16-18; H. Heppe, *Reformed Dogmatics* (Eng. tr., rev. ed. 1950), ch. 12; J. Orr, *Christian View of God and the World* (1893; 7th ed. 1904); A. Plantinga, *God, Freedom, and Evil* (repr. 1977).

G. W. BROMILEY

**PROVINCE** [Heb. *m^e^dînâ*–'district of jurisdiction, administration satrapy'] (Ezr. 2:1; Neh. 1:3; Est. 1:1, 3, 16, 22; etc.); NEB also PROVINCIAL (Est. 1:3); [Aram. *m^e^dînâ*] (Ezr. 4:15; 5:8, 6:2; 7:16; Dnl. 2:48f.; 3:1-3, 12,

30). [Gk. *eparcheía*] (Acts 23:34; 25:1); NEB also APPOINTMENT (Acts 25:1). In Ezra and Nehemiah the RSV supplies the word "province" nearly twenty times in the phrase "province Beyond the River" (e.g., Ezr. 4:10f., 16; 5:3, 6; 8:36; Neh. 2:7, 9; 3:7; AV "on this side the river," etc.).

The English word "province" derives from the Lat. *provincia,* which was "originally the sphere of action of a magistrate with *imperium,*" i.e., the highest administrative power, which involved "command in war and the interpretation and execution of law" (*Oxford Classical Dictionary,* pp. 542, 891). The traditional sense of the term, which indicated in an abstract sense the rule of the administrative official, gradually acquired the more concrete sense of a specific region entrusted to an official's care.

With few exceptions the RSV translates the noun *m*$^{e}$*ḏînâ* with "province." Heb. *m*$^{e}$*ḏînâ* (<Heb. *dîn,* "plead one's cause," "contend," or "execute judgment"; KoB, p. 208; cf. *TDOT,* III, *s.v.* "dîn" [Hamp, Botterweck]) "means literally a judicial district, i.e., a province," and "is used frequently in the book of Esther as a technical term for the Persian satrapies" (*ibid.,* p. 190). In other texts it acquires the more general meaning of "district" or "land" (Eccl. 2:8; 5:7 [MT 8]; Dnl. 11:24). It is also used in referring to Judah (Ezr. 2:1; Neh. 7:6) and to Elam (Dnl. 8:2). In the Aramaic texts of Ezra and Daniel *m*$^{e}$*ḏînâ* refers either to an administrative district that has a court of justice (Ezr. 4:15; 5:8;; 6:2; Dnl. 3:2f.) or to a town (Ezr. 7:16; Dnl. 2:48f.; 3:1, 12, 30; KoB, p. 1092); but this latter, narrower meaning has been challenged (*TDOT,* III, 190).

The RSV term "Beyond the River" (Heb. *ʿēḇer hannāhār*; Aram. *ʿ*$^{a}$*ḇar nah*$^{a}$*râ*) must be understood from the perspective of persons dwelling in Persia or Babylon; the region "beyond the river," therefore, was a politico-geographical technical term that referred to the land W of the Euphrates River (*THAT,* II, 203).

In the NT "province" occurs twice in the RSV. In Acts 23:34 Felix asked Paul in what province (Vulg. *provincia*) he had originally resided. This procedural method of questioning the accused helped Felix to determine whether he would hear Paul's case. After learning that Paul was from Cilicia, Felix had a choice either to hear the case himself or to defer it to the legate of Syria (cf. A. N. Sherwin-White, *Roman Society and Roman Law in the NT* [1963], pp. 28-31, 55f.; also E. Haenchen, *Acts of the Apostles* [Eng. tr. 1971], p. 649 n. 1). Acts 25:1 records Festus's accession to administrative office (Gk. *epárcheios*; MSS $p^{74}$, א*, B have *eparcheíǭ,* but cf. BDF, § 23, pp. 13f.) following the removal of Felix (Josephus *Ant.* xx.8.9 [182]).

G. L. KNAPP

**PROVINCES, ROMAN.**

I. Republican Period
II. Imperial Period
  A. Governors
  B. Military Forces
  C. Administration
  D. Municipal Government
  E. Roman Citizenship
  F. Clubs
  G. Cities and State Services
  H. Law
  I. Imperial Control

***I. Republican Period.***–In the later 2nd cent. B.C., when the Romans first made contact with Judaism, there were no provinces — areas permanently controlled by Roman officials — east of the Aegean. The Attalid kingdom in western Turkey was annexed as the province of Asia in 133-128 B.C. and was extended to include Pisidia, Pamphylia, and Lycaonia in the south to the borders of Cappadocia by 100 B.C. After the first wars against Mithridates king of Pontus, this southern zone became a separate province known misleadingly as Cilicia. Bithynia in northwestern Turkey became a Roman province at the death of its last king in 74 B.C. It was extended to include most of Pontus in northeastern Turkey after the final conquest of King Mithridates by the proconsul Gnaeus Pompeius (Pompey) in 67 B.C. Pompey's annexation of Syria in 64-63 led to the submission of the Maccabean princes of Judea, which remained as a tributary principality, despite periodic rebellions, to the end of the Republican period. The generally peaceful provinces of Asia and, later, Bithynia-Pontus were managed by proconsuls who were ex-praetors. But Cilicia and Syria were held from 57 B.C. onward by ex-consuls with extensive military forces aimed against Parthia beyond the Euphrates frontier. Cappadocia, Galatia, and minor districts such as Armenia Minor and Commagene remained, like Judea, under their kings or dynasts. Great Armenia beyond the upper Euphrates yielded to Pompey in 67 B.C. and remained a dependent ally until the defeat of Mark Antony by the Parthians in 36 B.C.

***II. Imperial Period.***–From the principate of Augustus (27 B.C.–A.D. 14) onward, provinces were either "public," governed by proconsuls of either consular or praetorian standing under the immediate authority of the Senate, or imperial, managed by legates (*legati propraetore*) appointed by the emperor. In the earlier empire, beyond the Adriatic only Asia was consular, while the remainder — Macedonia, Achaia, Bithynia-Pontus, Crete, and Cyprus-with-Cyrenaica — were praetorian proconsulships; the northern districts in Europe to the Danube — Dalmatia, Pannonia, and Moesia — were under consular legates of the emperor. Of the imperial provinces in the east, Syria, which now included lowland Cilicia, was the senior command, held by a consular legate with an army of three legions. Galatia, together with Lycaonia (annexed in 23 B.C.) was managed, from about A.D. 14 onward, by a legate of praetorian rank. Cappadocia, annexed in A.D. 17, was left to an official of equestrian rank. But after A.D. 70 Galatia was combined with Cappadocia, eastern Pontus, and certain minor regions to form a great consular legateship with an army of two legions that guarded the Armenian frontier, while the legate of Syria was left in control of the middle Euphrates against Parthia. Judea after the collapse of the dynasty of Herod in A.D. 6 became a Roman province under an equestrian prefect, subordinate to the legate of Syria, but after the great rebellion of A.D. 66-72 it was transferred to an imperial legate as an independent province with a legionary garrison based in Caesarea.

*A. Governors.* The provinces were ruled by governors drawn from the Roman upper classes. There was a distinction between proconsuls of "public" provinces, who were nominally appointed by the senate and responsible to it as the Roman council of state, and the legates of the emperor (Lat. *legati Augusti propraetore*), who were appointed directly by him and governed the imperial provinces. The emperor, however, gradually secured direct control over the proconsuls also. Both types of governors were members of the senate. A third class of officials, known as procurators and prefects, was drawn from the second, or "equestrian," class of Roman society. Some of these were governors of minor provinces such as Judea; others were financial administrators within provinces (*see* PROCURATOR).

These technical differences among provincial officials

meant little to their subjects. All governors had unfettered administrative, military, and judicial power, called *imperium*. Although the emperor gave them general instructions, *mandata Caesaris,* at their appointment, and they could consult him by the imperial postal service (*vehiculatio, cursus publicus*), if some new situation arose for which they lacked the means or money, they were expected to manage their provinces by themselves. Their normal activities required neither previous sanction nor later ratification. They did not send regular reports about the details of their administration to Rome; military commanders, however, gave annual accounts of their campaigns. The management of public revenues and financial expenditure was left to the procurators, or in "public" provinces to the senatorial "quaestors," but the governors were formally responsible for the submission of accounts to the Roman treasury.

*B. Military Forces.* In the prosperous central provinces in which Christianity spread, Roman soldiers were extremely rare. The governors were given small contingents of troops, seldom exceeding a single battalion (*cohors*), for maintaining order in provinces the size of modern Portugal (Lusitania) or western Turkey (Asia). Thus Paul in Acts wanders through the provinces of modern Turkey and Greece without meeting a single Roman soldier. Far from these peaceful provinces, along the outer frontiers of the empire, were stationed the legionary armies under the most senior of the imperial legates. Northern Syria regularly held a strong force of three or four legions that guarded the Euphrates frontier against the great Parthian empire to the east, although an almost unbroken peace existed between the two powers until A.D. 113. In Judea, although it was not a frontier province, several battalions of provincial troops were stationed to control the unruly inhabitants.

*C. Administration.* Outside the military zones provincial government was supervisory rather than executive, detailed administration being in the hands of the municipal authorities. Hence Roman officials were few. The senatorial governors had two or three senatorial assistants (*legati*), and the financial procurators were no more numerous. Secretarial bureaus and archives, manned by a small staff of imperial slaves and freedmen or soldiers, were maintained only at the provincial capital. There the governors spent their time, except for an annual or biennial tour of selected cities where judicial courts (*conventus*) were held. Their courts were frequented by major criminals and tax defaulters or by magnates involved in great lawsuits. The mass of minor jurisdiction was left to the municipal magistrates. A basic rule reserved all capital crimes for the jurisdiction of the governor, who alone could inflict the death sentence, except in the rare "free cities" that had unlimited jurisdiction. In Roman law death was the penalty for a wide range of political and criminal offenses, but so long as the provincials did not seriously misbehave they and their communes were seldom subject to governmental interference.

*D. Municipal Government.* The executive management of the Roman empire depended upon local self-government through a varied pattern of urban and rural or tribal communities (*municipia, poleis, civitates, gentes*). The economy of the ancient world was primarily agricultural and pastoral. The land produced not only food and drink but also the raw materials for clothing, housing, and shipping, and many luxury goods. Products were processed and distributed through townships and cities, which were the seat of local government and the residential centers of the landowning aristocrats, who in the Mediterranean area seldom lived on their estates. Hence a complex system of town life evolved. In the civilized lands such as Syria and Asia, where Christianity developed, public and social life, including dramatic, musical, and athletic festivals, religious celebrations, and the activity of local government, was concentrated in the Hellenistic townships. Power was in the hands of annual officers or magistrates, elected by an assembly of the free inhabitants of the commune, and of a civic council composed either of ex-magistrates and aldermen, holding office for life, or else annually elected councilors. Only the wealthy could hold office, and the councils and magistrates were generally the only ones possessing effective power. In some Greek cities, however, the assemblies of the people retained a limited power of decision, but no popular demonstrations could carry much weight. The magistrates not only managed the secular life of the city and its local jurisdiction, but also held the local priesthoods and maintained the public worship of the civic gods, an integral part of city life.

In Judea the pattern was different. Hellenized cities were rare. Large villages or rural townships, managed informally by councils of elders — "the rulers of the synagogue" — were the basic units (cf. Mk. 13:9; Mt. 5:21f.; 10:17; Lk. 8:41; 11:43; 20:46). These were grouped into "toparchies" administered by commandants (Gk. *stragēgoí*) and village scribes for purposes of provincial government.

Civic life occupied the attention and controlled the activities of the vast majority of provincial inhabitants. The adventures of Paul in the cities of Greece and Asia Minor shows this in some detail. Paul was regularly arrested, imprisoned, put on trial, or expelled by city magistrates (Acts 14:4-6; 16:19-24; 17:6-9). When a riot occurred at Ephesus the chief magistrate reminded the enemies of Paul that they must proceed by due process of law, either before the city court or before the tribunal of the proconsul (19:29-41). The civic magistrates had authority over all the local inhabitants within the civic territory, but only native citizens possessed local political rights. Large immigrant groups, such as Jews, might be allowed a restricted form of communal organization among themselves, but there was no effective inter-city jurisdiction.

Political disputes within or between cities were settled by the intervention of the governor, who conducted relations with the cities through the city magistrates. The cities were, however, brought together in provincial "leagues" or "councils." These consisted of delegates from the provincial communes, two or three per city — known in Asia as "the Asiarchs" (Acts 19:31). Their original function was to celebrate the cult of the emperor as a deified ruler at certain great festivals. Later they acquired some functions of petition and complaint, but they never became provincial parliaments. The delegates elected their own presidents, who acted as high priests of the imperial cult: these posts ranked as the only dignities open to a wellborn and wealthy provincial outside his municipality.

*E. Roman Citizenship.* A provincial could not enter the public service of the Roman empire unless he was a Roman citizen. The upper classes of the eastern provinces increasingly acquired citizenship as individuals through influential connections with Roman officials. The working peasantry could also acquire it by enlistment in the provincial regiments of the Roman army (*cohortes, alae*), which, unlike the legions, were entirely recruited from provincial subjects. After twenty-five years of service the discharged soldier acquired Roman status for himself and for his sons, who were then qualified to enlist for the legionary service. This could open the door to promotion, ultimately to the procuratorial service. The able son of an enlisted provincial might rise to govern a Roman province or to become the prefect of the praetorian guard at Rome. The tribune Claudius Lysias exemplified that process (Acts 22:27f.), but Paul derived his citizenship from his father.

*F. Clubs.* The common man who could not hold office found an outlet in a wide variety of private associations or "clubs" (*collegia*, "guilds," "societies"; Gk. *sýnodoi*, "assemblies," *hetairíai*, "select societies"). Some of these associations were based on crafts, trades, and professions (e.g., the guild of silversmiths in Ephesus that acted effectively against Paul [Acts 19:24-27]), while others centered on a religious cult; all were organized to provide social benefits in the form of regular festivities or dinners. They were managed democratically by the annual election of officers and by business meetings of their corporate members. The Roman government regarded the associations as a possible source of civic disturbances but generally tolerated them. Thus they provided a pattern for the development of early Christian congregations.

*G. Cities and State Services.* The cities not only managed their complex internal life, involving social services, public works, jurisdiction, and administration, but also provided the framework of provincial government. The Roman governors acted through the cities. Their criminal jurisdiction depended upon the arrest of major criminals by the civic police and their dispatch to the provincial courts by the municipal magistrates.

Imperial taxes were collected by a system of tax farming, but the publicans who leased the collection treated the local communes as units and struck bargains with the local authorities. In the later empire the city council members were made liable for collection and held responsible for any deficit. The imperial posting service for the transport of messengers and officials between the provinces and Rome depended entirely upon the communes along the highways; the local townships and villages provided the packhorses, carriages, and wagons at the request of the officials. There was a scale of charges, which the imperial treasury paid, but the duty was severe and was an uneven burden on provincial communities. The rates of direct taxation are not well known, but indirect taxes (sales duty, manumission tax, customs duties) were low, ranging from 2 to 5 percent. The impact of customs duties was not great because they were not collected at each provincial boundary. Instead the empire was divided into extensive zones comprising several provinces.

*H. Law.* The eastern provinces had various native systems of local law; principally the systems were Greek or, in Syria, either Greek or an Aramaic system. In Egypt, where the system is well known from papyri, the Roman governors continued to apply Hellenistic law, with modifications. Governors in other provinces also endeavored to apply the local codes of civil law in the suits of provincial subjects but tended to amend these codes by their knowledge of Roman law. In criminal cases they largely followed Roman usage, but also enforced local custom.

Governors were responsible for civil jurisdiction between Roman citizens in their provinces according to the Roman code. This code dealt with the rules of private property and contracts, inheritance, and the civic status of persons. It regulated the private transactions of Roman citizens in Italy and the provinces, but it did not apply to noncitizens. Hence it was not the law of the mass of the inhabitants of the empire until the *Constitutio Antoniniana* granted Roman citizenship to all provincials in A.D. 212. Roman criminal law was more restricted in scope. Certain statutes defined crimes and penalties in the sphere of murder, forgery, adultery and other sexual offenses, while others dealt with various political offenses, including treason and extortion. The governors applied these as they saw fit to Romans and non-Romans alike, giving judgment by a system of personal jurisdiction that allowed them great latitude (*see* PROCURATOR).

*I. Imperial Control.* The emperors seldom interfered with the activity of their governors unless the latter referred specific problems to them or provincial communes or individuals addressed a petition to them. Petitioning was not uncommon for the provincials, although it was expensive because they did not have access to the imperial postal service. After their term of office, governors could be prosecuted by their subjects for certain abuses of power before a senatorial court at Rome. Prosecutions for extortion were mostly initiated by the provincial councils (see D above). But the relevant "law of recovery" limited such prosecutions to the wrongful enrichment of Roman officials and to excessive cruelty in the execution of their duties. Governors could also be prosecuted by politicians at Rome for dereliction of duty under the so-called law of treason (*maiestas minuta*, neglect of the security of the state). But this procedure was not directly available to the provincial councils.

***Bibliography.***–*CAH*, X (1934), ch. 7/4; XI (1936), chs. 10, 14; J. Crook, *Law and Life of Rome* (1967); P. M. Garnsey, *Social Status and Legal Privilege in the Roman Empire* (1970), ch. 3; A. H. M. Jones, *Criminal Courts of the Roman Republic and Principate* (1972), pp. 113f.; *The Greek City* (1940), chs. 8, 11; *Studies in Roman Government and Roman Law* (1960), pp. 1117-1125; F. de Martino, *Storia della costituzione romana* (1975), IV, chs. 30–32; F. Millar, *The Emperor in the Roman World* (1977), chs. 6–7; F. de Robertis, *Il Diritto associative romano* (1938); A. N. Sherwin-White, *Roman Society and Roman Law in the NT* (1963); *Roman Citizenship* (2nd ed. 1973), chs. 9–13.

A. N. SHERWIN-WHITE

**PROVOCATION; PROVOKE** [Heb. hiphil of *kā'as*–'offend,' 'grieve' (e.g., 1 S. 1:7; 1 K. 16:2, 7, etc.), piel of *kā'as* (1 S. 1:6), *ka'as*–'vexation' (Dt. 32:19, 27; 2 K. 23:26; Prov. 27:3; Ezk. 20:28), hiphil of *qāṣap* ("provoke to wrath," Dt. 9:7f., 22; Zec. 8:14), hithpael of *gārâ*–'engage in strife' (2 K. 14:10; 2 Ch. 25:19), piel and hiphil of *qānā'*–'arouse jealousy' ("provoke to jealousy," 1 K. 14:22; Ezk. 8:33), hiphil of *rāgaz*–'agitate' (Job 12:6), hiphil of *māraṣ*–'irritate, provoke' (Job 16:3), hithpael of *'āḇar*–'become angry' ("provoke to anger," Prov. 20:2), hiphil of *tāwâ*–'trouble' (Ps. 78:41), hiphil inf. of *mārâ*–'behave obstinately' (Job 17:2); Gk. *erethízō*–'arouse to anger' (Col. 3:21), *paraxýnomai*–'become aroused' ("be provoked," Acts 17:16), *prokaléomai*–'call forth, provoke' (Gal. 5:26), *parorgízō*–'make angry' ("provoke to anger," Eph. 6:4), *parazēlóō*–'make jealous' ("provoke to jealousy," 1 Cor. 10:22), *apostomatízō*–'interrogate' ("provoke to speak," Lk. 11:53), *prosochthízō*–'be angry, offended' ("be provoked," He. 3:10, 17)]; AV also MEDDLE (2 K. 14:10; 2 Ch. 25:19), LIMIT (Ps. 78:41), BE GRIEVED, WRATH, etc.; NEB also TORMENT, HURT, ROUSE TO ANGER, EXASPERATE, BE INDIGNANT, etc. To incite to a (usually negative) feeling or action, e.g., anger, jealousy, grief, bitterness, "trouble" (e.g., 2 K. 14:10), or imprudent speech (Job 16:3; cf. Lk. 11:53).

In the OT the RSV uses "provoke" about forty-five times to render the causative form of Heb. *kā'as*. The primary idea expressed by this verb and the cognate noun *ka'as* is not anger but rather the kind of vexation that is caused by unmerited ill treatment (see Driver, p. 72). Occasionally this verb is used of human beings vexing one another (e.g., Peninnah vexing Hannah, 1 S. 1:6f.; cf. the noun in Prov. 27:3). Most often, however, it is used anthropomorphically to describe God's response to human rebellion or unfaithfulness. The word resonates with divine pathos, for it describes God's deep pain when His people, upon whom He has graciously lavished His favor, desert Him to serve other gods. Because such unfaithfulness grievously offends against God's HOLINESS and jealous love (cf. piel of *qānāʾ*, 1 K. 14:22; *see* JEALOUS; on Ezk. 8:3, *see* IDOL I), it evokes not only His anguish but also His WRATH (cf. hiphil of *qāṣap̱*, Dt. 9:7f., 22; Zec. 8:14).

The hiphil of *kāʿas* is used often by the Deuteronomic writers (and less often by other OT writers) to explain Yahweh's judgment upon His covenant people. When Aaron led the Israelites in worshiping a golden calf at Mt. Sinai, Yahweh was so deeply offended that He might have destroyed them all had Moses not interceded for them (Dt. 9:18). Moses warned the Israelites that if, after settling in the Promised Land, they provoked Yahweh by worshiping images, He would destroy them as a nation (4:25-27; cf. 31:29; 32:16, 19, 21). Despite the repeated warnings of Moses and the prophets, however, the Israelites persisted in grieving Yahweh by devoting themselves to idolatrous practices (e.g., Jgs. 2:12; 1 K. 15:30; 16:33; 21:22; 22:53; 2 K. 21:6; 22:17). Eventually the judgment of which they had been forewarned came upon both the northern and southern kingdoms (1 K. 14:15; 2 K. 17:11, 17f.; 21:14f.; 23:26f.; Jer. 7:18f.; 8:19; 11:17; 25:6f.; 32:28-32; 44:3, 8; cf. Ps. 78:56-59).

The NT refers to Israel's provocation of God as a warning to Christians. In 1 Cor. 10 Paul warns the Corinthian Christians against participating in idolatrous feasts as the Israelites did (e.g., v. 7; cf. Ex. 32:6), reminding them that it is sheer madness to provoke the Lord to jealousy (v. 22). He. 3:7-19 uses a quotation from Ps. 95:7b-11 to admonish readers against repeating the tragic folly of the Israelites in the wilderness. The Psalm refers to an event described in Ex. 17:1-7, when the Israelites provoked God by their hard-hearted rebelliousness at a place that Moses named Meribah (Heb. *m$^e$rîḇâ*, lit. "contention") and Massah (*māssâ*, lit. "testing"). The LXX, quoted by He. 3, renders *m$^e$rîḇâ* by Gk. *parapikrasmós* (lit. "embitterment"; RSV "rebellion"; AV "provocation," He. 3:8; cf. also v. 15) and *māssâ* by Gk. *peirasmós* (RSV "testing"; AV "temptation"; cf. also AV "provocation" and "temptation" in Ps. 95:8). The AV uses "provoke" also to translate the verb *parapikraínō* (lit. "embitter"; RSV "be rebellious") in He. 3:16, while the RSV uses "be provoked" to render *prosochthízō* in vv. 10, 17 (AV "be grieved"; cf. RSV "loathe" in Ps. 95:10, rendering Heb. *qûṭ*). The author of Hebrews warns that if Christians commit apostasy as the Israelites did, they too will fail to enter the promised rest (cf. He. 4:1).

Paul's Epistles contain several warnings against behavior that provokes other Christians. In Gal. 5:26 he urges the Galatian Christians to avoid challenging one another, and in Eph. 6:4 and Col. 3:21 he specifically instructs fathers not to abuse their parental authority in a way that irritates and exasperates their children.

The meaning of Gk. *apostomatízō* in Lk. 11:53 is uncertain. Its meaning in classical Greek, "teach by dictation" or "repeat from memory," does not fit the context. Ancient commentators usually rendered it "catch (Him) in something He says" (cf. v. 54); today it is usually translated "question closely" or "interrogate" (cf. NEB "ply him with a host of questions"). Perhaps the best translation is "watch (His) utterances closely" (see Bauer, rev., p. 100).

***Bibliography.***–F. F. Bruce, *Epistle to the Hebrews* (*NICNT*, 1964), pp. 62-69; S. R. Driver, comm. on Deuteronomy (*ICC*, repr. 1973); P. E. Hughes, *Comm. on the Epistle to the Hebrews* (1977), pp. 140-155; *TWOT*, I, 451. N. J. O.

**PRUDENCE; PRUDENT.** The RSV translation primarily of the Hebrew verb *ʿārōm* (Prov. 15:5; 19:25), the cognate adjective *ʿārûm* (12:16, 23; 13:16; 14:8, 15, 18; 22:3; 27:12), and the cognate noun *ʿormâ* (1:4; 8:5, 12). This word-group sometimes has the negative connotations of CRAFTY or CUNNING (cf. Ex. 21:14; RSV "treacherously"). But in Proverbs, where these terms occur most frequently, they always denote the kind of intelligence that manifests itself in wise behavior (cf., e.g., 13:16). As such, prudence was considered one of the highest virtues by oriental wisdom literature, which frequently contrasted it with the senseless, destructive behavior of the FOOL. The hiphil part. of *śāḵal*, which occurs primarily in Psalms and Proverbs, describes those whose behavior is wise and circumspect (Prov. 10:5, 19 [AV "wise"]; 19:14; Am. 5:13). A common synonym, the part. of *bîn* (lit. "discerning, understanding"), is frequently coupled with *ḥāḵām* ("wise") or *ḥoḵmâ* ("wisdom"; cf. Jer. 49:7). The niphal part. of *bîn* (RSV "prudent") characterizes the speech of David (1 S. 16:18); cf. its use in the descriptions of Joseph (RSV "discreet," Gen. 41:33, 39) and Solomon (RSV "discerning," 1 K. 3:12). Similarly, "prudence" (Aram. *ʿēṭāʾ*, lit. "counsel" [so AV]; NEB "cautiously") marks the character of Daniel's speech (Dnl. 2:14).

Earlier editions of the RSV render "prudence" for Gk. *poiéō phronímōs* in Jesus' parable of the dishonest steward (Lk. 16:8), but later editions replace it with "shrewdness" (cf. AV "do wisely"; NEB "act so astutely").

*See also* WISDOM. N. J. O.

**PRUNING HOOK.** *See* HOOK; VINE.

**PSALMS.**

- I. The Book
  - A. Name
  - B. Origin
  - C. Division
  - D. Number of Psalms
  - E. Arrangement
- II. Headings and Other Additions
  - A. General Observations
  - B. Ancient Versions
  - C. Technical Terms
- III. Authors and Dates
  - A. Reversal of Opinion
  - B. General Observations
  - C. Hebrew *l$^e$ḏāwiḏ*
  - D. Sons of Korah, Asaph, etc.
  - E. Conclusions
- IV. Psalms and Cultus
  - A. Psalms in the Life of the People
  - B. Israel's Psalmody and the Cultus
  - C. Are the Psalms Genuine Songs of the Cultus?
- V. Types and Structure
  - A. General Observations
  - B. Various Types
  - C. Deliberate Structure of the Psalms
- VI. Other Questions of Interpretation
  - A. Enemies
  - B. Royal Psalms
  - C. Psalms of Sickness
  - D. Power of the Word
  - E. Democratization
  - F. The Collective Use of "I"
- VII. Poetic Form of the Psalms
  - A. Poetry and Function
  - B. Poetry and Meaning
  - C. Poetry and Music

VIII. Message
- A. In General
- B. The Righteous and the Wicked
- C. The Messiah in the Psalms
- D. The Religion of the Psalms

IX. The Psalms and Ugaritic Studies
- A. The Near Eastern Context
- B. Ugaritic Studies

***I. The Book.**–A. Name.* The word *psalm* in the English title of this book is an anglicized version of the Greek word (*psalmós*), which is used in the LXX to translate Heb. *mizmôr,* meaning either "song" or "instrumental music." The word *mizmôr* occurs in the titles of some fifty-seven Psalms and is thus a general description of the contents of the book. In the rabbinic literature the book is called *tᵉhillîm,* "songs of praise," though this word is used only once in the Psalm titles (in Ps. 145). Both titles for the book indicate central aspects of its character. The title *Psalms* is a reminder that the book contains not merely poetry, but also the songs and hymns sung to musical setting in Israel's worship. The rabbinic title of the book is a reminder that the primary purpose of the book is the *praise* of God.

*B. Origin.* The exact process by which the book of Psalms came into being is not known; nevertheless, it is possible to detect some stages in the process. First, the individual Psalms were composed. Next, a number of relatively small collections of Psalms came into existence. Some Psalms were incorporated into more than one collection, the evidence of which has survived in duplications in the book of Psalms: compare Pss. 14 and 53, 40:13-17 (MT 14-18) and 70, 57:7-11 (MT 8-12) plus 60:5-12 (MT 7-14) and 108. Further evidence of early collections is to be found in Ps. 72:20, which appears to be a conclusion to a collection of David's prayers. Other collections can be identified by the use of particular expressions employed in the Psalm titles; thus there was a "Sons of Korah" collection (Pss. 42–49, 84, 85, 87, 88), an "Asaph" collection (Pss. 50, 73–83), and a collection of "Songs of Ascent" (Pss. 120–134).

The next stage in the development of the Psalter involved bringing together the smaller collections to form larger collections; from this stage in the development, only limited evidence has survived. The most clearly discernible collection of collections is the so-called Elohistic Psalter, Pss. 42–83; these Psalms are distinguished from other Psalms by the much more frequent use of *'Elohim* (God) and the rare usage of *Yahweh* (Lord). (In Pss. 1–41, *Yahweh* is used 272 times and *'Elohim* 15 times. In the so-called Elohistic Psalter, *Yahweh* is used 46 times, but *'Elohim* appears 204 times. Then, in Pss. 84–150, *Yahweh* occurs 362 times, but *'Elohim* only 13 times. The numbers are tentative, given the existence of text-critical problems.) This collection of collections contains a smaller collection of "Korah" Psalms (42–49), a collection of "Asaph" Psalms (50, 73–83), a Davidic collection (51–65 and 68–72), and other miscellaneous Psalms. The existence of this larger collection may also explain the duplications; thus Pss. 14 and 40:13-17, both external to the "Elohistic Psalter," are duplicated within it (Pss. 53 and 70 respectively).

Finally the book of Psalms came into its present form — a compilation of smaller collections, large collections such as the Elohistic Psalter, and various other Psalms added by the editor(s). The date at which the book of Psalms reached its present form is not known. It used to be held that the book was completed *ca.* 100 B.C. or even later, but such a view is most unlikely. Perhaps the most that can be affirmed is that the book of Psalms assumed its present form after the Exile, which in turn is reflected in certain Psalms (e.g., Pss. 102, 126, 137).

*C. Division.* In its present form, the book of Psalms is subdivided into five "books": (1) Pss. 1–41, (2) 42–72, (3) 73–89, (4) 90–106, (5) 107–150. This division of the whole is somewhat artificial and is based primarily on the existence of doxologies at the ends of Pss. 41, 72, 89, and 106. Whether these doxologies were inserted to mark the divisions in the Psalter, or simply occurred as integral parts of the Psalms in question but were interpreted as the conclusions of separate "books," cannot be known with certainty. Ps. 150 certainly serves, by editorial intention, as a doxology to the book of Psalms as a whole. The division of the Psalms into five separate "books" is probably not of great significance; at least with respect to unity of theme, there is nothing of great unifying significance within each of the divisions. It is probable that the whole was divided into five simply on the basis of the analogy with the five books of Moses (the Pentateuch). An old Jewish tradition states: "Moses gave to the Israelites the five books of the *Torah,* and coordinate therewith David gave them the five books of the Psalms" (Midr. *Ps.* 1:1).

*D. Number of Psalms.* The MT and the versions are in agreement that there are 150 Psalms; they differ, however, with respect to the numbering of various Psalms. Thus Pss. 9–10 in Hebrew are a single Psalm (9) in LXX, and Pss. 114–15 in Hebrew are a single Psalm (113) in LXX; but MT Ps. 116 is divided into two in the LXX (114–15), as is MT Ps. 147 (in LXX, 146–47). Thus the total of 150 would appear to be a round number that the editors sought to achieve. The LXX also has a Ps. 151, though it is explicitly identified in the text as being "outside the number." A Hebrew version of LXX's Ps. 151 has been found among the Dead Sea Scrolls at Qumrân in Cave 11 (see Sanders). In addition, several Psalms MSS and fragments have been found at Qumrân (esp. in Cave 4), establishing to a large extent the reliability of the medieval MSS of the book of Psalms on which modern English translations are based. A number of nonbiblical psalms were also found at Qumrân.

*E. Arrangement.* The sequence in which the Psalms have been arranged raises a number of difficulties, some of which may be insoluble. On the one hand, it is clear that the Psalms were not arranged haphazardly; on the other hand, the principles according to which they were arranged are not always clear. To some extent the arrangement is determined by the smaller collections within the Psalter as a whole; these collections may have been brought together for various reasons, e.g., common authorship, common usage in particular acts of worship, or perhaps common theme. Both within and outside the collections it is sometimes possible to detect a reason for the placing together of two or more Psalms. Thus Ps. 17 may follow Ps. 16 because the concluding verses of the two Psalms exhibit affinity. Pss. 34 and 35 may occur together because the "angel of the Lord" is mentioned only in these two Psalms in the Psalter. Pss. 1 and 2 were placed together because they form a proper introduction to the Psalter, describing the beauty of the law and the glory of Zion's king; indeed, in ancient Jewish tradition they were recognized as a single Psalm (T.B. *Berakoth* 9b). Again, Ps. 3 would appear to be a morning prayer, Ps. 4 an evening prayer, and Ps. 5 another morning prayer; their arrangement side by side can hardly be accidental. But for all the clues that have survived concerning the sequence of the Psalms in the Psalter, in many cases it is impossible to infer the significance of some Psalms from their immediate literary context.

*II. Headings and Other Additions.–A. General Observations.* Most Psalms have either long or short titles, or superscriptions, preceding the body of the Psalm as such. Of the 150 Psalms that constitute the Psalter, only 34 do not have a heading or title verse (the MT includes the heading in its versification, but the English versions do not). The majority of the headings probably do not originate with the author of the Psalm; thus a Psalm entitled "Song of Ascent" (e.g., Ps. 120) was probably given this heading when it was incorporated within the collection of such Psalms (Pss. 120–134). In other cases (e.g., Ps. 18) the heading may be integral to the original Psalm. A clay tablet discovered at ancient Ugarit contained not only the words of an ancient Hurrian psalm, but also information parallel to that contained in the headings to the biblical Psalms. Thus in studying the Psalm headings one must attempt to discern between that information which is original and peculiar to the Psalm, and that which pertains to the editorial process by which the Psalm became incorporated in the Psalter. The headings of the Psalms are important, even if they are not always easy to interpret; their substance is worthy of study, forming an integral part of the Hebrew text of the OT. It is thus regrettable that some modern translations of the Bible (e.g., NEB) do not include the substance of the headings in their translation of the text.

*B. Ancient Versions.* The headings in the MT of the Psalter were included in the earliest translations of the OT (e.g., the LXX, translated during the 3rd and 2nd cents. B.C.). In many places the translation in the early versions corresponds to the MT, though it is clear that the translators often had difficulty in knowing how to render some of the words in the headings. This lack of understanding, especially on the part of the translators of the LXX, may point to the antiquity of the Psalm headings, the passage of time having obscured the meaning of some of their words in the later period of the translators. In other cases, it is possible that the technical Hebrew terms in the headings had no equivalent in Greek, and hence apparent discrepancies arose in the versions. (A similar difficulty can be observed in English Bibles, where transliterated words appear in the headings of the Psalms: e.g., MUTH-LABBEN in Ps. 9.)

In many cases the headings in the LXX differ quite substantially from those in the Hebrew Psalter. The following are examples of such deviation. (1) The LXX contains the heading "of David" in Pss. 33, 43, 71, 91, 93-99, 104, and 137, even though the expression is not used in the MT. (2) The headings of Pss. 146–48 in the LXX contain the words "of Haggai and Zechariah," though these words do not appear in the MT. (3) Conversely, where the expression "of David" is used in the MT of Pss. 122 and 124, it is missing in the LXX in these texts. It is not always easy to determine the significance of discrepancies such as these, especially since in the majority of cases the MT and LXX essentially agree. It is probable that the Greek variations reflect different usage of the Psalms in worship, in the context of the Jewish community in Egypt (where the LXX was translated). The headings in the LXX may thus be of more value for studying the history of the Psalms individually, in Jewish worship, than they are in every case a witness to the earliest Hebrew text.

*C. Technical Terms.* The headings of the Psalms contain essentially five categories of information. Within these five categories various words are employed; some are clear and are technical terms, some are names, and some words are of uncertain meaning (they may be technical terms or simply names of tunes or musical arrangements).

(1) Many headings identify the Psalm with a person or groups of persons, either by name (e.g., David, Solomon, Asaph) or by title (e.g., the "choirmaster" [AV "chief musician"]).

(2) Some headings contain what purports to be historical information (e.g., Pss. 18, 34), in which technical terms are rarely employed.

(3) Some headings contain musical information, in which difficult technical terms are employed. Thus Ps. 5 indicates the Psalm was to be sung "to flute music," as the expression NEHILOTH appears to mean. Pss. 6 and 12 contain the expression SHEMINITH, which probably means "octave" and may refer to the manner in which the Psalm was to be sung. Pss. 8, 81, 84 were to be sung "according to the Gittith," which may be a reference to some type of musical instrument employed in accompaniment. This musical accompaniment is clearly indicated in Psalms that have the heading "with stringed instruments" (AV NEGINAH, NEGINOTH, e.g., Pss. 4, 61). The mysterious word SELAH (Heb. *selâ*) should probably also be understood in the context of the musical performance of the Psalms, although its meaning is uncertain: it may refer either to a pause in the singing or to an increase in volume. It is used more than seventy times in the Psalms and occurs also in Hab. 3 (three times). The meaning of many such musical terms in the headings continues to elude biblical scholars; they do serve as a useful reminder, however, that the book of Psalms is not merely a collection of poetry, but contains the hymns and songs employed in Israel's worship.

(4) The fourth category contains liturgical information, shedding light on the usage of the Psalms in particular parts of Israel's worship. Thus the expression "to bring to remembrance" (Pss. 38, 70) may indicate that the Psalms to which the heading was attached were employed in a liturgical activity associated with the memorial offering. Ps. 100 has a heading associating it with a liturgy of thank offering. Likewise, Ps. 30 may have been employed in some kind of dedication liturgy.

(5) The final category of information pertains to the literary *type* of the Psalm. The most common designation of types is the word *mizmôr,* "psalm" (used more than fifty times in the Psalter).

Numerous other expressions employed in the Psalm headings are difficult to classify simply because their meaning is uncertain; such words include SHIGGAION (Ps. 7), MASKIL (Pss. 32, 42, 44, etc.), LILIES (Pss. 45, 60, 69, 80; AV Shoshanim), ALAMOTH (Ps. 46), Do Not Destroy (Pss. 57–59, 75; AV AL-TASCHITH), Dove on Far-off Terebinths Ps. 56; AV JONATH-ELEM-RECHOKIM), Testimony (Ps. 80; AV EDUTH).

*III. Authors and Dates.*– There is considerable variety with respect to the dates at which the individual Psalms were composed. A few may date from the very early period of Israel's history, many come from the time of the monarchy, and some were composed during and after the Exile. For practical purposes the possibility of dating the Psalms, either generally or specifically, can only be determined in the context of a detailed study of the individual Psalms. Nevertheless, it is possible to make some general observations pertaining to the dating.

*A. Reversal of Opinion.* At the beginning of the 20th cent. one of the most commonly held opinions was that the majority of the Psalms were composed in the postexilic period. At the present time, however, that earlier consensus of opinion has changed for the most part; it is commonly recognized now that much of the OT literature, including the major part of the book of Psalms, may have been composed at an earlier date, principally during the time of the monarchy or the Exile. While a few of the Psalms almost certainly come from the postexilic period, the majority reflect earlier periods in the history of Israel's religion.

There is a variety of reasons for this general reversal in scholarly opinion. In part the change is a consequence of the form-critical study of psalms in the context of Israel's cult (see IV below). In part it is a consequence of the fruits of archeological discovery; over the last century the poetry and psalmody of the Egyptians, Babylonians, Assyrians, and other Near Eastern peoples have been rediscovered, thus providing a wider basis for comparison with the Hebrew Psalms. And in part opinions have changed as a result of studying the Psalms in the light of Ugaritic studies (see IX below).

*B. General Observations.* In the attempt to date any particular Psalm one must take some general considerations into account. First, if a connection between a Psalm and the cult can be determined (see IV below), it may have general implications with respect to date. Thus a royal Psalm, e.g., Ps. 20, while it may be difficult to date with precision, can at least be set within the general historical framework of the Hebrew monarchy. Second, grammatical, lexical, and stylistic considerations may have implications with respect to date; thus the distinctive forms and style of Ps. 29 suggest that it comes from the earliest period of Israel's psalmody. Third, if an argument may be sustained in some cases for Davidic authorship, on the basis of the Psalm title, clearly that information is pertinent to the dating of the Psalm, though it leaves open the possibility of the internal modification of the Psalm for its use in later periods of worship. Sometimes the content may be relevant to the dating; thus Ps. 137, on the basis of content alone, would appear to be exilic or postexilic.

It is clear from these general observations that it is not easy to assign a specific date to the majority of the Psalms. Some may be dated to a general period in Israel's history; some cannot be dated with any confidence at all. Very few Psalms can be dated with precision, even after a close analysis of language, form, and content. But while recognizing the difficulty of dating the individual Psalms, one must also see the difficulty in perspective; for the most part the interpretation and appreciation of a particular Psalm does not presuppose its accurate dating. The Psalms have a certain timeless quality; their insight and expression of the praise of God are not restricted to, or by, the period of their composition. Thus, while the attempt to date each Psalm is a worthwhile enterprise, the failure to come to a firm conclusion in many cases need not be a setback in the process of interpretation.

*C. Hebrew* $l^e$ḏāwiḏ. In the attempt both to date and to interpret the Psalms, some attention must be given to the content of the Psalm titles (see further II above). The Hebrew expression *$l^e$ḏāwiḏ* ("to/for David") occurs in the titles of some seventy-three Psalms (Pss. 3–9, 11–32, 34–41, 51–65, 68–70, 86, 101, 103, 108–110, 122, 124, 131, 133, 138–145). In thirteen instances the title provides in addition some information pertaining to an incident in the life of David (Pss. 3, 7, 18, 34, 51, 52, 54, 56, 57, 59, 60, 63, 142; see also Ps. 30). The expression *$l^e$ḏāwiḏ* may in some cases be intended to designate David as author; this is especially probable in those titles providing additional information about in incident in David's life (e.g., Pss. 7 and 18, with which compare Isa. 38:9 and Hab. 3:1). Furthermore, this approach to the interpretation of the titles, with respect to authorship, is very ancient; compare Ps. 110 with Mt. 22:43-45; Ps. 41 with Acts 1:16; Pss. 16 and 110 with Acts 2:25-28; Ps. 32 with Rom. 4:6; Ps. 69 with Rom. 11:9; Ps. 21 with Acts 4:25; and Ps. 95 with He. 4:7. Nevertheless, the interpretation of the phrase *$l^e$ḏāwiḏ* is not without difficulty, and simply from the perspective of language and translation various possibilities remain open.

(1) As already stated, the preposition *$l^e$* may indicate authorship, so that the phrase means "by David" (as author). Such a translation and interpretation are probable with respect to several Psalms (see GKC, §129 a-c). (2) A natural translation of the phrase would be "to David" or "for David," perhaps implying "dedicated to David." (3) The phrase could be translated "concerning/about David." The difficulty in determining the meaning of the phrase *$l^e$ḏāwiḏ* does not lie simply in deciding which of the above possibilities is correct; each possibility must be weighed in each instance that the phrase is employed in a Psalm title. Thus, while sometimes it may mean "by David," in many cases (perhaps the majority) it may mean "for David" (viz., Davidic); that is, the phrase may indicate that the Psalm in question is a royal Psalm, belonging to an early collection of Davidic Psalms. And in a few cases *$l^e$ḏāwiḏ* may mean "about David"; the usage of the same preposition in Ugaritic, a language slightly older than Biblical Hebrew and closely related to it, suggests such a nuance. Thus *lbʿl* in the title of an Ugaritic text means "about/concerning Baal."

While Davidic authorship cannot always be assumed on the basis of the phrase *$l^e$ḏāwiḏ* in the title, it is nevertheless clear that David's influence was very considerable in the development of the tradition of Israel's psalmody. In addition to actually composing Psalms, David's influence is recognized in many parts of the OT. He is described as the "sweet psalmist of Israel" (2 S. 23:1). He was influential in the invention of musical instruments (Am. 6:5) and in the development of Israel's music and musicians (1 Ch. 15:16-24; 16:7, 31), and various historical writers associate him with particular compositions (e.g., 2 S. 1:19-27; 23:3-7). Thus uncertainty as to David's role in the composition of specific Psalms should not detract from the recognition of his central importance in the tradition that ultimately produced the book of Psalms.

There are difficulties associated with the interpretation of the NT references to David and the Psalms. Many would argue that a statement such as that contained in Rom. 4:6 is not intended to assert anything with respect to the authorship of the Psalm in question. On the other hand, the reference to Ps. 110 in Mt. 22:43-45 is more difficult to interpret; the argument of Jesus clearly seems to imply that the words of Ps. 110 were either written by David, or at least spoken by David. This observation opens the door to weighty theological issues that cannot be resolved in this context. Some would say that the reference in Mt. 22:43-45 settles the issue of authorship. Others would argue that with reference to His manner of speech, Jesus spoke out of the perspective of the thought world of His contemporaries. The contemporary perspective was reflected in Jesus' words, for in His time the entire book of Psalms was commonly referred to as "the Psalms of David" (thus including those Psalms with no titles and those with superscriptions indicating other persons, e.g., Ps. 90).

*D. Sons of Korah, Asaph, etc.* The Psalm titles mention other persons and groups of persons in addition to David. They include the following: (1) Solomon (Pss. 72, 127), (2) Moses (Ps. 90), (3) Asaph (twelve times), (4) Heman (Ps. 88), (5) Ethan (Ps. 89), (6) the musical director (more than fifty times; RSV "choirmaster"; AV "chief musician"), and (7) the "Sons of Korah" (eleven times). As with the expression *$l^e$ḏāwiḏ*, the references to persons are subject to difficulties of interpretation. In many cases, however, the references are to early collections of Psalms that preceded the compilation of the book of Psalms, e.g., a "Sons of Korah" collection (see I.B above). Authorship is not necessarily implied by all these references to persons and groups in the Psalm titles; some titles refer to more than one person (e.g., Ps. 88).

*E. Conclusions.* It is clear that it is rarely possible to come to firm conclusions with respect to the date and authorship of the individual Psalms. In a few cases it is possible to propose David as the author of a particular Psalm; in the majority of cases it is safest simply to recognize that the Psalms are, for practical purposes, anonymous, though they may be representative of the praise and worship of Israel as a whole. Many of the Psalms can be dated to general periods (e.g., the time of the monarchy, or the Exile), a few can be dated specifically, and others are essentially undatable (within the confines of the OT period). Nevertheless, the attempt to determine date and authorship should be an important part of the process of studying the individual Psalms.

***IV. Psalms and Cultus.–A.*** *Psalms in the Life of the People.* In the modern Western world poetry has become essentially a literary phenomenon; for the most part it is not rooted in daily life. But in other societies, and especially in other historical periods, poetry has had a quite different role and significance; it is not simply an artistic form of literature, but is rooted in the daily events that constitute the life of a people. Poetry was spoken and recited in human life-settings; its recording in writing was principally for purposes of preservation. Thus poetry played a role in worship, in events such as marriages and funerals, and simply in entertainment (antedating the modern books and movies). In the 19th cent. it was the common practice for biblical scholars to study the Psalms purely as literature; while there was value in this approach, it failed to appreciate the vitality of the Psalms in Israel's daily life and worship. In the 20th cent. a new trend developed in the study of the Psalms, pioneered by Hermann Gunkel; he perceived that a full appreciation of the Psalms would never be gained unless an attempt was made to study them in their original life-settings (or *Sitze im Leben*). Gunkel's was a functional approach to the study of the Psalms; recognizing that the Psalms had been *used* in the life of Israel, he sought to determine not only the social situation in which they were used, but also their function within that setting.

*B. Israel's Psalmody and the Cultus.* Though a few Psalms might originally have functioned within a general social context (e.g., a wedding, see Ps. 45), the majority of Israel's Psalms would have been utilized within the cultus or the formal settings of worship within the temple (and later, perhaps, within the synagogue). The following points provide some general perspectives.

(1) From the earliest period of Israel's history music and song were integral to the activities of worship; in this, the practice of the Israelites was no different from practices known to have existed in such ancient societies as Egypt, Babylon, and Ugarit. Thus long before David's time music and song formed a central part of the worship in Israel's cult. What took place during David's reign, and then later in King Solomon's time, was simply a renewal and growth of the more ancient Israelite traditions of poetry and music; that renewal was to continue to be the practice in the subsequent history of worship.

(2) Many of the Psalms are characterized by a distinctive style that might be described as a "cultic style"; it is not a specifically literary style, for its characteristics appear to have been determined primarily by the influences of cultic usage. The style is such that the Psalms lack concrete and specific points of reference, but are thereby more easily used in various contexts of worship. Many Psalms and songs which were initially composed for a specific occasion are nevertheless written in such a style that they could continue in use beyond the confines of that original occasion. Thus when one reads such ancient songs as the "Song of the Sea" (Ex. 15:1-18), the "Song of Deborah" (Jgs. 5), or David's Lament (2 S. 1), one is struck by the stereotyped forms of expression and lack of specificity; this style probably originated within a circle of cultic singers, being suitable for use in varying ceremonies and forms of worship.

(3) Not only the style, but also the structure of many of the Psalms is very distinctive. For example, several Psalms have one or more changes in subject. In Ps. 2 it is clear that the speaker in vv. 7-9 is different from the speaker in the rest of the Psalm; probably the congregation declared the words of vv. 1-6 and 10-12, while the king may have responded with the words of vv. 7-9. A Psalm of this kind may have been recited in an act of worship in the temple, with different persons and groups of persons participating in the spoken part of the worship. In other examples, a change of subject may introduce a speaker who, in prophetic manner, declares the words of God (see esp. Ps. 12:5 [MT 6]; 20:6 [MT 7]; 28:5; 31:24 [MT 25]; *et al.*).

(4) It used to be a common practice in the study of the Psalms to conclude that many Psalms were composite works, drawn from two or more ancient sources; such a conclusion would be based upon the observation that different parts of a Psalm were characterized by a totally different mood and atmosphere. Fluctuation of this kind was noticed particularly in many of the Psalms of lament, which begin with mournful melancholy, but end with a jubilant expression of thanksgiving (e.g., Ps. 3:7 [MT 8]; 4:7ff. [MT 8ff.]; 5:11f. [MT 12f.]; 6:8-10 [MT 9-11]; 7:10-17 [MT 11-18]; 10:16-18). It is too simple, however, to explain this fluctuation and change as a consequence of antecedent sources. And while it may sometimes be explained psychologically, or in terms of the psalmist's spiritual progress, such explanations are not always satisfactory. In most instances the fluctuating and changing character of particular Psalms can be understood only in the context of the cultic rituals in which they were employed. Thus a person in trouble might come to the temple to take part in a cultic ritual, either private or public. He would begin by stating his case, the lament, which may have been accompanied by the offering of sacrifices. Then a priest or prophetic servant of the temple would declare a word to the supplicant from God; such divine words are sometimes stated in the Psalms explicitly and sometimes only implied. In response to the divine word the supplicant would then conclude his participation in the ritual (sometimes accompanied by fellow worshipers) with the declaration of praise and thanksgiving. Many Psalms of a very uneven character from a strictly literary perspective have a finely rounded wholeness when perceived from a cultic perspective in the setting of Israel's acts of worship.

(5) Other items of more isolated data point to the usage of many of the Psalms in Israel's cultic life. In some cases the psalmist explicitly states that he is present at the sanctuary (e.g., Ps. 5:3, 7 [MT 4, 8]; 9:14 [MT 15]; 22:22-31 [MT 23-32]; 23:5f.; 28:2). In other cases the psalmist makes reference to being absent from the sanctuary (e.g., Pss. 3, 42, 43, 61, 63); in these instances the act of worship is distinctive by virtue of not being in the sanctuary, though the Psalms in question were probably utilized later within the formal acts of worship (see Pss. 102 and 120).

In summary, while a few Psalms were no doubt straightforward literary compositions and can be studied as such, the majority had a more vital role to play in the living context of Israel's worship. While one cannot always determine the specific cultic setting of each Psalm, given the lack of sufficient evidence, the attempt to study the Psalms in a cultic setting is an important step toward correct and illuminating interpretation.

*C. Are the Psalms Genuine Songs of the Cultus?* Gunkel's pioneering work on the relationship between the Psalms and the cult has found a large degree of acceptance in principle among biblical scholars. His views have been developed in a number of different directions, however, and the extent to which the book of Psalms as a whole can be tied to Israel's cultic life has been the source of considerable debate.

Two of the most distinguished scholars to develop Gunkel's initial insights are Sigmund Mowinckel and Artur Weiser. Mowinckel pursued more rigorously than had Gunkel the cult-historical investigation of the Psalms; in particular he closely identified a large number of the Psalms with a proposed Israelite New Year Festival, which he argued was a central act of worship celebrating God's kingship and creation. Weiser, on the other hand, tended to see the covenant festival as Israel's central act of worship, and this provided for him the cultic context in which the majority of the Psalms were to be interpreted. For all the splendid insights of these two scholars, they have probably gone too far in their cult-oriented interpretation of the book of Psalms. A more balanced perspective, still in the tradition of Gunkel, is to be found in the major two-volume commentary by H.-J. Kraus.

As the work of these distinguished scholars of the 20th cent. is assimilated and evaluated, it is becoming clear that many, indeed perhaps the majority, of the Psalms in the Psalter are the genuine songs of Israel's cultus, composed and used in the context of Israel's formal worship. Other Psalms, which may have started as private and literary compositions, came to be used over the passage of time in worship, thus becoming the songs of the cultus at a secondary stage in their development. Still other Psalms, notably the wisdom Psalms (see V below), may have had an initial life-setting in a context quite separate from the cult (e.g., a didactic or educational setting); whether their incorporation in the Psalter implies adaptation for use in worship cannot be known with certainty. And some Psalms may be not only literary compositions, but their survival may also have occurred on literary grounds; thus Ps. 1 appears to be a wisdom Psalm, placed at the head of the Psalter as an appropriate introduction to the literary collection, but probably not utilized in the cult as such. In summary, while it is an important principle in general interpretation to recognize the majority of the Psalms as cultic compositions, sufficient flexibility must be maintained by the interpreter to recognize also the presence of some noncultic material in the Psalter.

*V. Types and Structure.*–One of the significant aspects of the pioneering work of Gunkel was the development of a method of study called *Gattungsforschung,* or a close study of the *forms* in which the Psalms were structured (*Einl. in die Psalmen*). By examining the form of a particular Psalm, Gunkel attempted to determine the literary species or genre to which that Psalm belonged. The examination of form and genre was closely related to the study of the life-setting of the Psalm (see IV above); thus the knowledge that the life-setting of a Psalm was in some activity in Israel's cult or formal worship was of assistance in determining the genre to which a Psalm belonged. A knowledge of the Psalm's function would help in the determination of form, and vice versa, though inevitably this whole process is in danger of circular reasoning.

*A. General Observations.* While the general value of studying the form of a Psalm and attempting to determine its genre is clear, certain limitations are inherent in this method of study that indicate the necessity of caution. Thus, to use an example from English, if one were to take a church hymnal and study the genre "hymn of praise," one could determine several common characteristics, but one would also be impressed by the variety and differences of detail within the genre as a whole. The same is true with respect to the Psalter; many Psalms can be classified as belonging to a particular species or genre; many examples of the genre will have a certain commonality of structure, but variety and difference will also be observed. And sometimes a similar form, or a part thereof, may be common to more than one genre. Thus in the final analysis it is not always possible to determine the purpose and meaning of a Psalm only on the basis of an examination of the characteristics of form; the evidence of content is just as significant as form.

A preliminary step in the approach to the examination of a Psalm's form is to observe the grammatical *person* and *number* employed in the Psalm. On this basis a division can be made between *communal Psalms* (employing, e.g., "we") and *individual Psalms* (employing "I"). The communal Psalms may reflect some kind of communal worship. The individual Psalms may reflect various backgrounds, from individual worship or meditation to the words of an (individual) king in a communal context of worship. It should also be noted that several Psalms fluctuate between individual and communal forms of expression, indicating perhaps a liturgical context with alternating speakers (see IV above).

*B. Various Types.* Gunkel specified various major types (viz., types to which a large number of Psalms belonged) and several minor types whose presence could be determined in the Psalter. The following summaries contain brief characterizations of some of the more important types. Although Gunkel's work remains foundational in the study of the Psalm types, there has been considerable progress and refinement since his time in both the description and classification of the types.

(1) *The Psalm of Praise, or Hymn* (e.g., Pss. 8, 29, 33, 104, 111, 113). The life-setting in which the hymn was employed was some occasion associated with the worship in the temple. Though the majority of hymns may have been for general usage in worship, a few may have been associated with particular festivals. With respect to structure a hymn would normally contain the following component parts: (a) An introduction, containing an invitation to praise. The invitation may be addressed to the congregation gathered in the sanctuary, to the choirs, or to some other person or group. Its object is to direct the praise of Israel toward the Lord, His word, His virtues, or His mighty acts. (b) A central portion, further elaborating the occasion of the praise. In general this section of the Psalm consists of short sentences expressing praise for the Lord's character or actions; dominant themes include God's acts of salvation on behalf of Israel and God's role in creation. (c) A formal conclusion, though the substance of the conclusions varies enormously.

(2) *The Individual Song of Thanksgiving* (e.g., Pss. 30, 34[?], 66, 116, 138). The majority of these individual songs of thanksgiving were probably related to some formal act of worship, though a few may be noncultic. When employed in a formal setting the Psalm would be used by a person who received some specific blessing from God and who had come to the sanctuary to offer thanks, probably in the company of relatives or friends. Principal elements in the structure of these Psalms include: (a) an introduction; (b) a narrative description of the background events leading

to the offering of thanksgiving; (c) other elements, such as a reference to an offering or sacrifice and an invitation to others present to participate in the thanksgiving.

(3) *The Individual Lament* (e.g., Pss. 6, 13, 31, 39). In general terms this genre has been said to be the most common in the Psalter; while the observation is generally correct, it should be noted that in the modern study of the Psalms the individual laments are frequently classified into more precise subcategories (e.g., Psalms of sickness, Ps. 6). The elements of form that may be present in the individual lament include: (a) an initial calling upon the Lord; (b) a complaint, specifying the occasion giving rise to the lament; (c) a prayer, requesting the Lord to hear and respond with respect to the source of the lament; (d) the expression of wishes or desires concerning the fate of friends and enemies; (e) the grounds upon which the appeal to God is based; (f) a concluding expression of confidence that the appeal will be heard, and responded to, by God.

(4) *The Communal Lament* (e.g., Pss. 12, 44, 74, 79). The communal laments were employed within some formal act of worship; they were occasioned normally by some external crisis threatening the health or survival of the nation of Israel. In general the elements of form are similar to those of the individual lament; they differ with respect to the nature of the crisis, in this context threatening the community as a whole, and the plural form of the people's address to God.

(5) *Royal Psalms* (e.g., Pss. 2, 18, 20, 35, 40, 45). The genre of royal Psalms is not so much distinctive in literary terms as it is in functional terms. The royal Psalms were employed within a variety of royal contexts, though in precisely literary terms they may overlap with the categories already described (e.g., some royal Psalms are, in effect, individual laments employed by a king). Thus the royal Psalms can be subclassified into various categories, sometimes on the basis of form, but more commonly on the basis of function. To provide some examples, (a) Ps. 2 is a coronation Psalm; (b) Ps. 18 is a royal (individual) Psalm of thanksgiving; (c) Ps. 20 is a royal liturgy (to be used, perhaps, in an act of worship employed prior to the king's departing for war); (d) Ps. 45 is a royal wedding Psalm. The determination of royal Psalms, given the variety of forms, is a delicate business; they are usually determined on the basis of distinctive terminology and general substance.

(6) *Wisdom Psalms* (e.g., Pss. 1, 32[?], 37, 49, 119). Of the various smaller categories of Psalms, the wisdom Psalms are of particular importance. They reflect the general characteristics of the biblical wisdom literature and probably served a didactic function in ancient Israel, prior to being drawn into the general resources of Israel's worship. Many Psalms reflect a mixed character, in which there is the appearance of a more ancient text being developed in the reflective mode of the wise men in ancient Israel. Thus Ps. 19 has many of the characteristics of a hymn (esp. vv. 1-6), but the Psalm as a whole has the character of a wisdom poem, in which the original hymn celebrating God's glory in creation has been developed in a meditation on the glory of God's law (vv. 7-14). Ps. 1, serving as an introduction to the Psalter as a whole, is a useful reminder of the importance of the tradition of wisdom, perhaps in the compilation of the book of Psalms and certainly in the substance of many of the individual Psalms.

*C. Deliberate Structure of the Psalms.* The study of the Psalms' structure requires sensitivity not only to the structure's literary significance, but also to its religious or functional significance. Two examples will illustrate this point. (1) "A man should always first set forth his praise of the Holy One, blessed be He, and then offer his prayer" (T.P. *Berakoth* 32a); this statement of principle from the Talmud of later Judaism is frequently exemplified in the Psalms. For example, Ps. 40 has been interpreted by many scholars as a composite Psalm, having two principal parts: (a) vv. 1-10 (individual thanksgiving), and (b) vv. 11-17 (individual lament). Such an analysis, however, fails to recognize the coherence of the Psalm as a whole, both with respect to the uniformity of its language and the deliberate nature of its structure. The Psalm deliberately begins by laying a foundation of thanksgiving; only then does it move on to lament and prayer (and the progress within the Psalm may in turn reflect the progress within the formal, liturgical act of worship within which it was employed). (2) A quite different example of deliberate structure may be observed in the collection of alphabetic ACROSTIC Psalms in the Psalter (Pss. 9–10, 25, 34, 37, 111, 112, 119, 145). In these Psalms the structure is based upon the sequence of the letters of the Hebrew alphabet. Although various reasons have been proposed for the acrostic structure, a principal reason may have been didactic; a student thus learned a Psalm "from A to Z," the deliberate structure being an aid to the learning process.

*VI. Other Questions of Interpretation.–A. Enemies.* Frequent reference is made in many of the Psalms to the enemies of the psalmist. In earlier scholarship on the Psalms (notably the works of Mowinckel) several attempts were made to elucidate the identity of these enemies. Mowinckel, e.g., noted the frequent association between sickness and enemies, and concluded that the enemies were sorcerers or magicians who had brought about the sickness and thus were prominent in the psalmist's words. Various scholars made other attempts to elaborate general hypotheses that would enable them to interpret the references to enemies in the Psalter as a whole. Contemporary scholars, however, increasingly recognize the importance of limiting the interpretation of enemies to the context of the particular Psalm under examination. In Psalms of sickness enemies are probably real persons who threaten the psalmist, precisely because they hope to benefit from his weakened physical condition; in other cases, they may be no more than the paranoid projections of the distressed mind of the sick person. In many royal Psalms the enemies are frequently the real enemies of the state (foreign nations) whose actions threaten the welfare and peace of the kingdom. In laments enemies are often unjust persons whose actions or accusations have undermined the stability and peace of mind of the accused person. In each case a knowledge of the function and life-setting of the Psalm will be of considerable assistance in determining the identity of the enemies.

*B. Royal Psalms.* The category of royal Psalms has been recognized since the time of Gunkel; especially since the 1950's, however, these Psalms have become the focus of detailed scrutiny. J. H. Eaton (*Kingship*) and other scholars have recognized that there may be considerably more Psalms in this category within the Psalter than was generally supposed in the past. This trend in contemporary scholarship is a very positive one, though it is beset by a number of difficulties. The principal difficulty concerns the definition of precise criteria by which royal Psalms can be identified. It is clear that such Psalms do not necessarily have a distinctive literary structure and may belong to several literary genres (see V above). The use of criteria such as content and language (e.g., formulaic expressions and royal allusions) is helpful, but frequently difficult, given the vagueness and ambiguity of much of the evidence. Thus, although it is becoming evident that a large number of the Psalms were probably royal Psalms with respect to their initial function, the nature of the surviving evidence is such that the precise identity of all royal Psalms may be beyond recovery. And the difficulty is exacerbated by recognition that many royal Psalms probably continued to be used in worship long after the end of the monarchy; they may have been adapted slightly to this subsequent nonroyal usage, thus rendering still more difficult their identification as royal Psalms.

*C. Psalms of Sickness.* In the modern study of the Psalms, especially of the individual laments, the association between many such Psalms and the human experience of sickness has been recognized. As with the royal Psalms, the Psalms of sickness have a functional unity, but do not necessarily belong to a single literary type. Thus Pss. 22 and 41 may be classified as parts of liturgies for sick persons, reflecting the life-setting of an act of worship in the temple. Pss. 6 and 38, on the other hand, may more appropriately be classified as the prayers of sick persons; their usage may have been personal and private, rather than cultic and public. The language of the Psalms of sickness is for the most part general rather than specific; while such Psalms may in the first instance have reflected the particular sickness of an individual, their general language makes them suitable for use by any person who encounters sickness and disease. The detailed study of the Psalms of sickness, though much remains to be done in this area, illuminates one of several aspects of the perpetual relevance of the Psalms.

*D. Power of the Word.* Many of the Psalms contain frequent references to the words and speech of other persons, notably of the psalmist's enemies. The references to such speech are frequently negative in character; the psalmists refer to evil speech, flattery, false accusations, slander, cursing, and intrigue. It is clear from the many references to speech, especially evil speech, that its power was recognized in a particularly striking fashion in ancient Israel. The lament of Ps. 12 is precipitated by the pervasiveness of evil speech, but hope is to be found in the contrast between human speech in its vanity and the integrity of the divine speech. But while many of the Psalms contain general reflections on speech, care must be taken to note that many references to the speech of enemies may have legal and contractual overtones. Thus the lament in Ps. 7 reflects the experience of false accusation; it is probably not false accusation of a general kind, but an accusation or charge laid against the psalmist in the context of a contractual (or covenantal) relationship. And inasmuch as contractual arrangements between two persons or parties commonly involved the formal invocation of curses on a party of the contract if its stipulations were broken, the Psalms referring to the speech of enemies frequently also contain references to curses. These are not general references to curses, but quite specific references to treaty curses, which in turn threaten to come into effect on the basis of the laying of (false) accusations. Sensitivity to the possibility of a covenantal or contractual background to a Psalm is of considerable assistance in the interpretation of the references to curses in the Psalter as a whole.

*E. Democratization.* A number of scholars have noted that a process of "democratization" has taken place in the history of Israel's psalmody. It may have taken a variety of forms. For example, a Psalm that began its life as a private and poetic composition could later have been incorporated into Israel's hymnbook for public and general use. Or a Psalm that was in the first instance a royal Psalm, specifically for the king's use, could in later times have passed into general and public usage, especially in the period following the demise of Israel's monarchy. What is difficult to determine is whether this process of change with respect to usage and function took place with, or without, modification to the form and substance of the individual Psalms. It could certainly have taken place without any changes to the Psalms in question; thus many Psalms that can clearly be identified as royal Psalms continued to be used (apparently unchanged) long after there ceased to be a monarchy in Israel. Some scholars (particularly French scholars) have attempted to distinguish *relectures* (re-readings), i.e., the additions or modifications in the substance of a Psalm that indicate this changing context of usage. This approach to the Psalms is not without positive prospects, though the nature of the evidence is such that inevitably the process tends to be subjective. Sometimes the Psalm titles (in either the MT or the versions) may provide a clue to the process of change. Thus the Greek title of Ps. 29 explicitly associates the Psalm with the celebration of the Feast of Tabernacles; with respect to its original usage, however, the Psalm was probably a general hymn of victory employed within the worship of the temple.

*F. The Collective Use of "I."* Earlier in the 20th cent. one trend of OT scholarship stressed the "corporate" nature of Israel's thought and downplayed any notions of "individualism." One of the consequences of this approach to OT studies was to stress that apparently "individualistic" texts, e.g., the individual Psalms (employing "I," "me," etc.), were to be interpreted not in terms of an individual person, but rather in terms of a corporate community to which all individuals belonged. Thus it was supposed that the "I" of the Psalms was an expression of the corporate identity of the nation of Israel. But this line of research is no longer pursued in detail. It had a certain value in reminding us that many aspects of the notion of individualism are indeed modern phenomena, and that the psalmists (and those who employed the Psalms) were members of a larger community. It was, nevertheless, a line of research that tended to go too far in virtually denying the genuinely individual aspects of many of the Psalms. (Thus the Psalms of sickness are highly individual, though they are frequently set in a communal context.)

***VII. Poetic Form of the Psalms.***–The Psalms as a whole are written in poetry; for a general discussion, *see* POETRY, HEBREW. A number of aspects of the poetic form of the Psalms deserve particular attention here.

*A. Poetry and Function.* Though the Psalms are written in the form of Hebrew poetry, notably parallelism, they should not always be viewed as poems. While some Psalms are certainly poems, many reflect liturgy and the formalities of worship (see IV above). Thus, while the lines of a Psalm are poetic in form, the Psalm as a whole may not always be viewed as a literary piece of poetry. The approach to the Psalms in nineteenth-century scholarship was principally in the context of examining them as poetic compositions, and this was one of the greatest weaknesses of that approach. It resulted in very negative assessments of many Psalms (perceiving them, e.g., as composite structures), for it approached them from a wrong perspective. Many Psalms, viewed as a whole, are not fine poems, nor were they ever intended to be; rather, they are the poetic words that accompanied an act of worship in the temple, and only in that context may their wholeness and integrity be perceived. In the study of individual Psalms an attempt must be made to grasp the structure and function of the whole before proceeding to an evaluation of the Psalm as a work of art (poetry in the full sense, e.g., Ps. 19) or as a work of liturgy (e.g., Ps. 40, which is very uneven in literary terms, but perfectly balanced when perceived in its liturgical context).

*B. Poetry and Meaning.* The Psalms as a whole address the relationship between Israel (individually and collectively) and God. And yet by its very nature the relationship with God is not easily expressed within the limitations of human speech. Poetry (rather than prose) is used in the Psalms, for it is a form of human language that seeks to transcend the limitations inherent in prosaic speech and to give expression to that which is ultimately inexpressible. The student of the Psalms should be sensitive to the use of poetic language; it may be studied from a literary and scientific perspective, but ultimately it must be appreciated. And the appreciation of the poetry of the Psalms involves such familiarity with it that one may eventually go beyond the words to grasp the living Reality to which they point.

*C. Poetry and Music.* It is clear from various fragments of evidence, and especially the substance of some of the Psalm titles, that many of the Psalms are not only poetic in form, but were also to be sung or recited to musical accompaniment. MUSIC adds still further to the transcendent nature of language that may be conveyed by poetry, so that both the words and the manner of their articulation seek to break through the restrictions integral to all forms of human speech. Unfortunately, however, while a certain amount is known about the usage of choirs and orchestras in Israel's worship, nothing is known in detail about the tunes and musical settings to which certain Psalms were sung. It is nevertheless important to bear in mind the musical context of many Psalms in the progress toward interpretation and appreciation.

*VIII. Message.–A. In General.* Martin Luther's words are an appropriate introduction to the message of the Psalter: "In the Psalms one looks into the hearts of all the saints" (preface to the German Psalter, 1528). His words capture the essence of the book, for in its pages cogent expression is given to the diversity of the life of faith and of the response to the revelation of God. The Psalms reflect the faith not only of ordinary individuals, but also of the kings and of the nation of Israel as a whole. And the use of the Psalms down through the centuries of Israel's history was such that in reading their words, we are hearing what became the normative expression of Israel's faith and piety. And for all the diversity of expression in the book of Psalms, a deep underlying unity permeates the whole.

It may be misleading to view the Psalter as giving expression only to the dimensions of strictly personal faith. While many of the Psalms are profoundly personal and intimate in their expression of the relationship with God, they are concerned nevertheless with the common experiences of human life. What happens to an individual touches the community, frequently the entire nation; in some cases this fact is expressly stated, and in others it is implied by the communal context of worship. Thus even the most individualistic of the psalmists are in a sense the spokesmen of the community as a whole, giving expression in words to the variety of experiences shared by the community.

Some of the Psalms reflect the response of Israel to the revelation and experience of God; others are characterized by a "prophetic" element, in which the Lord's prophetic word may be heard, declared in the context of Israel's worship. Thus prophetic declarations, in which a servant of the temple proclaims the divine word, may be observed in such passages as Ps. 2:6-9; 12:5 (MT 6); and 32:8. In some cases the entire Psalm has a prophetic character; Ps. 50 appears to have served as a prophetic liturgy in the context of a ceremony of covenant renewal. This prophetic background to certain Psalms is given fuller expression outside the Psalter; e.g., the activity of the temple singers is described as prophesying (1 Ch. 25:2f.; see further 2 Ch. 29:30; 35:15; Ex. 15:20; Lk. 1:67). Conversely, certain passages in the prophetic books appear to have a degree of relationship and similarity to the Psalms (see Isa. 12; Hab. 3; *et al.*).

*B. The Righteous and the Wicked.* On reading the Psalms one quickly gains the impression (beginning with Ps. 1!) that all persons can be classified into two categories, the righteous and the wicked. The psalmists, together with their friends and supporters, are the righteous; all their enemies are the wicked. While the prosperity of the righteous is frequently affirmed, an untimely death and other calamities are anticipated for the wicked. When, on the other hand, the righteous suffer calamities, they search for the cause of their distress in past sins they have committed; their adversity is normally for a short time only, for in humbling themselves before God they seek a return to the state of prosperity. The psalmists give vent to expressions against their enemies that seem to be spiteful and vindictive; they desire their undoing. Such is the general impression that may emerge from a reading of many of the Psalms (especially the so-called imprecatory Psalms); it seems at first sight to be somewhat self-righteous and lacking in charity toward enemies. It is, however, too superficial a view to capture the essential meaning of the Psalms in question.

It is true that the Psalms distinguish people into just these two categories. The categories, however, do not designate primarily moral characteristics, in which clearly there would need to be greater variety of differentiation; rather, they separate persons into two groups with respect to their relationship with God. The righteous are those in relationship to God (who thereby experience God's mercy and forgiveness), whereas the wicked are those who, by their actions and speech, have separated themselves from the relationship to God. This differentiation can be seen in the activities of Israel's formal worship, in which the righteous may legitimately participate (see Pss. 15, 24).

The righteousness of which the psalmists speak is thus a religious quality, imputed as a consequence of faith in the Lord. While it undoubtedly has implications with respect to moral behavior, the term righteous does not signify sinless persons. Rather, it points to persons who have experienced mercy and forgiveness and who as a consequence have sought to lead a moral life. The protestations and affirmations of the righteous are thus not the proud exclamations of the self-righteous, but rather the faithful statements of those who have striven to maintain their lives within the merciful context of the covenant relationship with God. The statements concerning righteousness are balanced by the frequent statements in which sin is confessed and mercy and forgiveness are sought.

Nevertheless, while recognizing that the designation "righteous" does not imply self-righteousness and arrogance, the reader may still find many of the psalmists' statements concerning the wicked to be particularly harsh and vindictive. In part this is so because the Psalms contain the reflections of immediate human response to the experience of suffering and persecution. They are a window on the souls of those who suffer, and thus show not only faith and fear, but also anger and the desire for retribution to fall on those who persecute them. (The problem is treated with particular sensitivity in Lewis, *Reflections on the Psalms,* pp. 9-33). Yet there is more to the harsh language of the psalmists than at first appears on the surface; the background is to be found in the context of covenant or treaty.

Israel was bound to God in a relationship of covenant; the commitment to covenant relationship, on Israel's part, involved the recognition that obedience would result in blessing, disobedience in cursing (Dt. 27–28). A similar structure is found in international treaties; the persons binding themselves in a treaty invite curses on their own heads if they should break the conditions of the treaty. And similar conditions applied to personal contracts; two persons bound themselves together in a contractual relationship and agreed upon the "divine curses" that should be invoked in the event that one or other party to the treaty should break its stipulations. It is this context of covenant (or personal contract or national treaty) that forms the background to much of the harsh language employed in the Psalms. In royal Psalms the expression of such harsh sentiments against an enemy is in effect the calling down of the curses of the treaty upon the enemy's head; if the enemy had broken the terms of the treaty, its harsh curses *should* befall him, for he had agreed to such conditions in the formation of the treaty in the first place. A clear example of the covenant context of the harsh language of the Psalms can be seen in Ps. 7, which has the general characteristics of an individual lament. The psalmist prays for his vindication and asks that wicked persons might die (v. 9); yet it is clear that the language of the Psalm as a whole is a reflection of the language of treaty or contract curses. Thus the psalmist invites the same curses to fall on him, *if* he has been guilty of breaking the terms of the treaty or contract (vv. 4f. [MT 5f.]; cf. J. H. Tigay, *JBL,* 89 [1970], 178-186). It becomes clear that the apparently vindictive and harsh nature of much of the language of the Psalms should be interpreted in a legal context, rather than being interpreted as an expression of personal hatred. The enemy of the psalmist has broken the stipulations of an agreement, but seeks to bring discredit on the psalmist, as if he were the guilty party. The psalmist, in turn, calls for the curses of the treaty to fall on the head of the enemy, in part to establish his own innocence of the charges laid against him, and in part because the enemy had agreed that he should suffer the curses if he broke the contractual stipulations. This general context of treaty curses provides not only a perspective for understanding harsh language against enemies, but also for interpreting statements concerning the death of enemies' children. Thus the desire expressed for the destruction of children in Ps. 17:10 must be seen in the context of a national treaty between nations; the Psalm is a royal liturgy, with a treaty background, and its language reflects not personal hatred, but the invocation of treaty curses (agreed to by the enemy) upon all the nation's foes (cf. F. C. Fensham, *ZAW,* 77 [1965], 195-202).

Finally, often in the Psalms the condition of the righteous and the wicked appears to be viewed with a degree of naiveté not matched to the realities of human existence. Thus the way of the righteous is thought to lead always to prosperity, while the way of the wicked culminates always in ruin. Such a perspective is particularly evident in many of the wisdom Psalms, e.g., Ps. 1. The difficulty with this perspective is its lack of nuance; e.g., it appears to be more akin to the theology of Job's friends than to the theology which Job himself eventually espoused.

The principal cause of this difficulty arises as a consequence of viewing the substance of individual Psalms in isolation from a larger context. Thus Ps. 1 sets down certain of the fundamental assumptions of the wisdom tradition with respect to righteous persons and wicked persons; its theology is akin to that of Proverbs, but it cannot encompass within the scope of a few verses the balancing factors (e.g., those of Job and Ecclesiastes), which are essential to a fully rounded wisdom theology. The balance can be achieved, however, by reading a Psalm such as Ps. 1 in the context of other Psalms. Ps. 1, while it may appear naive, is an expression of fundamental faith and confidence; the walk through life may be pursued in two basic ways. Ps. 39, which also has certain characteristics of the wisdom literature, presents a very different perspective; it is a meditation on the transitory nature of human life, marked not by idealism, but by the cold-eyed realism of one who, over a long life, has experienced many of the harsher realities of human existence. The reader of the Psalms should take care not to focus on the substance of a single Psalm in isolation from other Psalms; the Psalms as a whole reflect a fully rounded wisdom on the nature of human life in relation to God, whereas the individual Psalms may contain only a part of the larger picture.

*C. The Messiah in the Psalms.* From the perspective of the NT writers it is clear that many of the Psalms were interpreted within early Christianity as messianic Psalms; their words and verses are quoted with specific reference to Jesus the *Messiah* (or the *Christ*). Pss. 2 and 110 are among the most frequently quoted Psalms in the NT; and, not without good reason, Ps. 22 has been called "The Fifth Gospel" (S. Frost, *Canadian Journal of Theology,* 8 [1962], 102-115). From the perspective of interpretation, however, it is important to ask whether these Psalms are technically messianic Psalms (viz., whether they were considered as such within ancient Israel) or simply came to be considered as messianic Psalms in later Judaism and early Christianity.

Although the question of the messianic character of the Psalms is the subject of continuing debate, it may be best to take the view that none of the Psalms, in the first instance, was messianic; i.e., with respect to their initial usage and interpretation, they were not viewed within ancient Israel as referring, directly or indirectly, to the Messiah. The Psalms that were later viewed as messianic were, for the most part, royal Psalms in the first instance; they referred to the king, who was the Lord's "anointed" (or messiah, Ps. 2:2) and the Lord's "son" (Ps. 2:7). With the end of the monarchy in Israel and Judah (586 B.C.), the Psalms in question continued to be used in the context of worship, but clearly a transformation in their meaning must have begun. A Psalm such as Ps. 2, used initially in the coronation of a Davidic king, could not retain its original meaning in worship in a time when the monarchy no longer existed. The kingdom of Israel, with its human king, had ceased to exist; within Judaism new notions of the kingdom of God began to emerge, sometimes in association with the word messiah, which had originally referred to human kings. In the NT the message of Jesus concerned the "kingdom of God" (Mk. 1:13f.), and the faith of the early Church perceived Jesus to be the King (or Messiah) within that kingdom. Thus in the context of this newly emerging faith Christianity perceived a new, yet latent, meaning in the royal Psalms; they had spoken originally of the Davidic king, but their words applied equally to Jesus the Messiah. Thus the so-called messianic Psalms, though originally royal in character, reflect the development of faith from OT times to NT times, and the understanding that Jesus was the Messiah within the newly proclaimed kingdom of God.

Not all Psalms with a messianic character were royal Psalms, however; Psalms that reflected initially simply the dimensions of human experience were reinterpreted in a new and meaningful way with respect to Jesus. Thus Ps. 22, the "Fifth Gospel," was probably not a royal Psalm; it was rather a *liturgy for the dying,* reflecting a life-setting in a temple ritual. The frequent quotations from and allusions to Ps. 22, both in the words of Jesus and in the narrative of the Evangelists, transform the sense of the original narrative in a remarkable fashion; the ancient liturgy for the dying becomes the framework within which the passion and dying of Jesus are given expression in the Gospels. In summary, the Psalms are not so much messianic in any anticipatory or predictive sense as they are ancient Psalms that have come to take on new and deeper meaning within the revelation of God in Jesus Christ.

*D. The Religion of the Psalms.* The message of the Psalter can be drawn in part from the religion of the Psalms, or more specifically from the larger religious context within which the Psalms were utilized. This religious context had both a theological perspective and a setting in religious practice (or the actual activities of worship). The religious context of the Psalms was not different from the religion of Israel as a whole; rather, it was one particular aspect of the larger whole, on which the substance of the Psalms sheds particular illumination.

The theological dimension of the religion of the Psalter has its primary focus on the centrality of *relationship.* The covenant, which provided the basis for all relationships in ancient Israel, indicates clearly that a person's first relationship is with God, which relationship in turn determines the character of all relationships with other people. While many parts of the OT literature illuminate the various aspects of the Israelite covenant, the Psalms lie close to the heart of the covenant; they are the vehicles through which the members of the covenant community express their relationship to God, and indeed the means by which they communicate with God, whether in public worship or private devotion.

The variety of Psalms, with respect to substance and purpose, illustrates the manifold character of the relationship with God. It may be a relation of joy, expressed in the hymns of praise and thanksgiving; it may be the experience of grief, fear, persecution, or some other trouble, which results in the psalmist's search for God. What is clear from the Psalter as a whole is that no aspect of life, no area of human experience, is excluded from the relationship with God.

Although some of the Psalms express private and individual devotion, the majority functioned within the context of Israel's cult; in public worship, special festivals, or in particular rituals (e.g., for the sick or dying), the concerns of the individual became the concerns of the community, and vice versa. And the formal context of most worship provided a check against the growth of too casual an attitude to worship and the relationship with God. Although God could be known personally and intimately, the approach to God must be undertaken with care and introspection, as is reflected so clearly in such Psalms as Pss. 15 and 26.

The setting of the relationship with God which is given expression in the Psalms is *this life* and *this world.* Some scholars claim that the psalmists' theology has an eschatological perspective, that they view the relationship with God as extending beyond the grave. This tendency is particularly evident in the writings of Mitchell Dahood, whose new translations of the Psalms appear to give some support to this view. In general, however, this trend in the study of the theology of the Psalms is probably not soundly based, resting on highly dubious translations of many parts of the Psalter (see IX below). The OT as a whole (with the exception of a few of the latest writings) does not contain a developed eschatology; the theology of the Psalms, for the most part, shares the noneschatological perspective of the remainder of the OT, focusing upon the relationship with God in the present life. It should be added, of course, that it is appropriate to "re-read" the Psalms from the perspective of NT eschatology and see new significance in their words. All that is stressed here is that the Psalms in their original sense are generally not eschatological in character.

The second dimension of the religious context of the Psalms is the cultic context in which they were, for the most part, employed. As has been noted above, we miss much of the significance of the Psalms if they are viewed solely as literature. They were employed in the cultus, in the formal activities of Israel's religion; they were part of a larger environment characterized by such features as ritual acts, the offering of sacrifices, the coming of pilgrims to the temple during great festivals, and the formal activities of the priests and other servants of the temple. The interpretation of the Psalms should attempt to take into account the ritual setting, for a knowledge of the context contributes to their proper interpretation.

***IX. The Psalms and Ugaritic Studies.***–*A. The Near Eastern Context.* The Hebrew Psalms, viewed as a whole, were not unique in the environment of ancient Near Eastern religions. Most of the known religions of the ancient world employed hymns and prayers of various kinds. The fruits of archeology have included, e.g., the texts of Assyrian, Babylonian, and Egyptian hymns of praise. As might be expected, these ancient hymns have general similarities to the Hebrew hymns, though they differ from them with respect to the details of theology and substance. Scholars who were studying the Psalms at the beginning of the century tended to be too quickly impressed by the similarities between Hebrew and Near Eastern psalms, without taking sufficient account of the considerable dissimilarities. Thus it was noted that there were remarkable parallels between the ancient Egyptian "Hymn to Aten" and Ps. 104. Observations of this kind led to various hypotheses of interrelationship; frequently it was claimed that the Hebrew Psalms had been borrowed or adapted from the resources of ancient Near Eastern psalmody. But as further discoveries were made, greater recognition was given not only to the commonality of Near Eastern psalmody, but also to the distinctive features which separated Hebrew Psalms from Egyptian psalms, Egyptian psalms from Assyrian psalms, and so on. Most of the hypotheses of direct interrelationship between Hebrew and Near Eastern psalms have now been abandoned. Nevertheless, the study of Near Eastern psalmody is of immense value in the study of the Psalter; it provides some of the data needed to reconstruct both the literary and cultic milieu within which the Hebrew Psalms must be studied.

*B. Ugaritic Studies.* Since the discovery of the ancient city of UGARIT (modern Râs Shamrah, Syria) in 1929, much new material has become available for the study of the Psalms. The archeological excavations at Râs Shamrah, still continuing in the 1980's, resulted in the recovery of many ancient texts from the site; the texts (written on clay tablets) are in the Ugaritic language, a close linguistic relative of Biblical Hebrew, and the majority date from the 14th to the early 12th cents. B.C. Many of the Ugaritic texts are poetic in form. These discoveries have had a number of implications for the study of the Psalms.

(1) The discovery of the Ugaritic language has added to the knowledge of Northwest Semitic languages in general. Thus, as a consequence of the study of the Ugaritic texts, more light has been brought to bear on the meaning of certain obscure terms and unusual grammatical forms in the Psalter; there is now greater potential for the accurate translation and interpretation of the Psalms than was available half a century ago.

(2) The study of Ugaritic poetic texts has provided an

improved awareness of the nature, forms, and language of Northwest Semitic poetry. The comparison of Hebrew and Ugaritic poetry has thus made possible more informed evaluations of the Psalms, recognizing what is common and what is distinctive in the poetry of particular Psalms. On the other hand, none of the poetry in the Ugaritic language appears actually in the form of a *psalm*, but is utilized in mythological and literary (narrative) texts; hence, no comparison is possible between the two bodies of poetry with respect to form and function.

(3) The mythological texts, in poetic form, from Ugarit have increased our knowledge of the religious literature available in Northwest Semitic languages. The Ugaritic resources contain extensive mythological texts dealing with gods 'El and Baal. The examination of these texts reveals how the Hebrew psalmists have utilized mythological imagery, especially that associated with Baal, in giving expression to their own faith in the God of Israel. For example, Ps. 29, while clearly Hebrew in its substance and theology, has drawn heavily on language and imagery which is striking in its similarity to the mythological language employed of the god Baal.

(4) One text, reconstructed from fragments found at Râs Shamrah, contained the words of a Hurrian hymn (Hurrian being one of several languages employed in Ugarit); on the same tablet as the hymn were the notations for the musical score to be utilized in the singing of the hymn. The tablet also contained a colophon, the substance of which was of essentially the same nature as that contained in the titles of the biblical Psalms. In addition to being the oldest known example of words and music on the same text, this Hurrian text may provide a parallel to the nature of some of the biblical Psalms prior to their incorporation within the Psalter. And the musical accompaniment for the hymn, though representing Hurrian culture, may perhaps illustrate the kind of musical setting to which many of the biblical Psalms were sung.

(5) For all the values and benefits of the Ugaritic texts, their information has in some cases been applied too radically and without due caution in the translation and interpretation of the Psalms. Perhaps the most important example of the excessive use of the Ugaritic resources in Psalms study is the three-volume commentary on the Psalms by Mitchell Dahood. His commentary contains many brilliant insights, but it is also characterized by a marked lack of methodological control in the application of Ugaritic data to the study of the Hebrew texts. Gradually a number of scholars are submitting to a critical and cautious evaluation the multitude of Dahood's Hebrew-Ugaritic proposals. Eventually it may be possible to distinguish between his lasting contributions to the study of the Psalms and the more fragile hypotheses constructed upon uncertain foundations; in the meantime Dahood's commentary should be employed with caution by those who are not specialists in Ugaritic.

***Bibliography.**–Comms.:* A. A. Anderson (*NCBC*, 1972); E. Beaucamp (*SB*, 1976); C. A. and E. G. Briggs (*ICC*, 1906); P. C. Craigie (*Word Biblical Comm.*, 1983); M. Dahood (*AB*, 1966-1970); J. I. Durham (*Broadman Bible Comm.*, 1972); H. Gunkel (*Handkommentar zum AT*, 4th ed. 1926); D. Kidner (*Tyndale OT Comms.*, 1973); H.-J. Kraus (*BKAT*, 1978); H. Lamparter (*Botschaft des AT*, 1977); J. W. Rogerson and J. W. McKay (*CBC*, 1977); A. Weiser (Eng. tr., *OTL*, 1962).

*Surveys of Scholarship and Bibliography:* J. Becker, *Wege der Psalmenexegese* (1975); B. Childs, *Intro. to the OT* (1979), pp. 504-525; D. J. A. Clines, *Tyndale Bulletin*, 18 (1967), 103-126; 20 (1969), 105-126; J. H. Eaton, "The Psalms and Israelite Worship," in G. W. Anderson, ed., *Tradition and Interpretation* (1979), pp. 238-273; E. Gerstenberger, "Psalms," in J. H. Hayes, ed., *OT Form Criticism* (1974), pp. 179-223; A. R. Johnson, "Psalms," in *OTMS*, pp. 162-209; P. H. A. Neumann, *Zur neueren Psalmenforschung* (1976); J. Schildenberger, *Bibel und Leben*, 8 (1967), 220-231.

*Other Studies:* W. Beyerlin, *Die Rettung der Bedrängten in den Feindpsalmen der Einzelnen auf institutionelle Zusammenhänge untersucht* (*FRLANT*, 99, 1970); R. C. Culley, *Oral Formulaic Language in the Biblical Psalms* (1967); J. H. Eaton, *Kingship and the Psalms* (1976); H. Gunkel and J. Begrich, *Einl. in die Psalmen* (1933); H. Gunkel, *The Psalms: A Form-Critical Introduction* (Eng. tr. 1967); A. R. Johnson, *Cultic Prophet and Israel's Psalmody* (1979); S. Mowinckel, *Psalms in Israel's Worship* (Eng. tr. 1967); N. H. Ridderbos, *Die Psalmen* (*BZAW*, 117, 1972); H. Ringgren, *Faith of the Psalmists* (Eng. tr. 1963); L. Sabourin, *Psalms: Their Origin and Meaning* (rev. ed. 1974); J. A. Sanders, *Psalms Scroll of Qumran Cave 11* (1965); M. Tsevat, *Study of the Language of the Biblical Psalms* (1955); C. Westermann, *Praise of God in the Psalms* (Eng. tr. 1965); G. Widengren, *Accadian and Hebrew Psalms of Lamentation as Religious Documents* (1937).

*General Intros. and Popular Guides:* P. R. Ackroyd, *Doors of Perception: A Guide to Reading the Psalms* (1978); B. W. Anderson, *Out of the Depths. The Psalms Speak for Us Today* (2nd ed. 1974); C. F. Barth, *Intro. to the Psalms* (3 vols.; Eng. tr. 1966); J. H. Hayes, *Understanding the Psalms* (1976); C. S. Lewis, *Reflections on the Psalms* (1958); E. Routley, *Exploring the Psalms* (1975); M. H. Shepherd, *Psalms in Christian Worship: A Practical Guide* (1976); D. W. Vogel, *Psalms for Worship* (1974).

N. H. RIDDERBOS P. C. CRAIGIE

**PSALMS, IMPRECATORY.** *See* PSALMS VIII.B.

**PSALMS OF SOLOMON.** *See* APOCALYPTIC LITERATURE III.D.

**PSALTERY.** A frequent AV translation of Heb. *nēḇel* (or *neḇel*). *See* HARP (the usual RSV translation); MUSIC II.B.

**PSEUDEPIGRAPHA** so͞o-də-pig′rə-fə.

I. Introduction
II. Letter of Aristeas
III. Third Maccabees
IV. Fourth Maccabees
V. Minor Pseudepigrapha
   A. Martyrdom of Isaiah
   B. Apocalypse of Abraham
   C. Testament of Abraham
   D. Third Baruch
   E. Joseph and Asenath
   F. Sibylline Oracles
   G. Lives of the Prophets
   H. Life of Adam and Eve
   I. Fifth Maccabees

***I. Introduction.***–The word "pseudepigrapha" literally means "false writings," i.e., writings attributed to someone who did not write them. J. H. Charlesworth states that "rather than being spurious the documents considered as belonging to the Pseudepigrapha are works written in honor of and inspired by Old Testament heroes" (*Pseudepigrapha and Modern Research* [1976], p. 25). The term is applied to a number of extant Jewish writings that are as important as the APOCRYPHA for understanding the history of first-century Judaism. Some of these are true pseudepigraphs in that they are written in the name of an ancient OT saint. Thus 1 Enoch, Jubilees, the Apocalypse of Baruch, and the Testament of the Twelve Patriarchs are true pseudepigraphs. It should be noted that several books of the Apocrypha are also pseudepigraphical: Wisdom of Solomon, 2 Esdras or 4 Ezra, Letter of Jeremiah. On the other hand, not all of the books usually included in the Pseudepigrapha are pseudepigraphs, notably 3 and 4 Maccabees. In the 17th cent., J. A. Fabricius made a complete collection of the Apocrypha and included two volumes which bore the name *Codex Pseudepigraphicus Vetus Testamenti.* Thus it has become customary to designate the second collection as Pseudepigrapha. Many contemporary scholars, unhappy with both terms since they are artificial, suggest that we should call the entire body of literature the Jewish intertestamental literature.

Several of the books which are usually grouped with the Pseudepigrapha are discussed elsewhere under the heading Apocalyptic Literature: 1 and 2 Enoch, Jubilees, Testaments of the Twelve Patriarchs, Psalms of Solomon, the Apocalypse of Ezra (4 Ezra), and the Apocalypse of Baruch. R. H. Charles's great collection of the Pseudepigrapha includes the Pirkē Aboth, which is a tractate of the Mishnah, and the Zadokite Work, which appears to belong to the Qumrân literature. These will not be discussed here (for criteria used in determining pseudepigraphical books, cf. Charlesworth, *Pseudepigrapha and Modern Research,* pp. 17-25). In addition to the pseudepigraphical books included in Charles's work, we are including reference to other extant pseudepigraphical literature.

*II. Letter of Aristeas.*–This Greek writing is allegedly a letter written by Aristeas, who was a high official in the court of Ptolemy II in Alexandria. It was sent to Jerusalem in order to secure a copy of the Jewish Law together with a group of seventy-two scholars who would translate the Law from Hebrew to Greek. The recipient is Philocrates, about whom nothing is said except that he was a brother of Aristeas. The alleged purpose of the book is to tell the story of the translation of the SEPTUAGINT.

The book contains a delightful story. Demetrius of Phalerum, head of the great library in Alexandria, suggests to the king that a translation be made of the Hebrew Law. The king writes to the high priest Eleazar in Jerusalem requesting him to send seventy-two scribes to perform the work of translation. He sends rich gifts for the temple in Jerusalem. The story includes a description of the Holy City. Eleazar delivers an apologetic for the Law. When the translators come to Alexandria, they are feted in a series of royal banquets. The king plies the scribes with philosophical questions, and they answer with amazing wisdom. Then they are taken to the island of Pharos in the harbor of Alexandria where they set to work. Demetrius compares their work every day and writes down a consensus. They complete the work in seventy-two days. It is then read to the Jews, who laud it. When it is read to the king, he is greatly impressed and expresses wonder as to why it has not been mentioned in earlier Greek literature. Demetrius says that earlier authors were divinely restrained from mentioning it. Finally the translators are sent home bearing rich gifts.

It is obvious that this beautiful story is fictional, although it has a core of reliable information. Aristeas and Philocrates are not known in other historical literature. Furthermore, the Letter of Aristeas itself reflects a knowledge and usage of the LXX. The work also bears obvious unhistorical traits. For example, an Egyptian king would not attribute his throne to the Jewish God (37). The author, however, seems to be thoroughly familiar with the technical and official language of the court and of Alexandrian life and customs.

The purpose of the book is fairly obvious. It is a piece of Hellenistic Jewish apologetic writing designed to commend the Jewish religion and law to the Gentile world. The book emphasizes the honors showered on the seventy by the Greek king. High praise is accorded to Jewish wisdom by heathen philosophers. It explains the failure of Greek historians and poets to mention the Jewish law. The apology of Eleazar on the inner meaning of the law tries to interpret in meaningful categories the Jewish distinction between clean and unclean things. The Jews are said to worship the same god as the Greeks but under a different name. Zeus is really the same as God (16).

The book is really not a true letter but belongs to the genre that may be called belles lettres. It falls in the Greek literary and artistic traditions rather than in the Semitic pattern. This governs its purpose, which is not to impart sound historical information but to produce a general ethical effect. The book is therefore far more important as a reflection of Jewish life and culture in the 2nd cent. B.C. than as an account of the formation of the LXX. Thus very little attention is actually given to the work done on the LXX. We know that in the 2nd cent. B.C., before anti-Semitism had raised its head, a large colony of Jews lived in Alexandria, and the work reflects the fact that they were enthusiastically embracing Hellenistic culture, social usages, literary forms, and philosophical beliefs so far as they did not directly oppose their central religious tenets.

The date of the book is an almost insoluble problem. Scholars date it variously from 200 B.C. to 63 B.C. Perhaps an estimate of about 100 B.C. will suffice. While some scholars think that the LXX involved a protracted development, this letter may reflect the fact that at some time an official translation was made.

*III. Third Maccabees.*–This book has nothing in common with 1 and 2 Maccabees, except that it tells a story of Jewish persecution by a foreign king. The form of the book is that of a historical narrative relating a supposed episode in later Jewish history. In reality it is a palpable piece of fiction.

Ptolemy IV Philopator (221-204 B.C.) won a victory over Antiochus III the Great at Raphia (217 B.C.). On his way back to Egypt, passing through Jerusalem, he expressed an intention to enter the sanctuary of the temple; when he refused to be dissuaded by the Jews, they pleaded to God, and Ptolemy was struck to the ground, stunned.

Returning to Egypt, Ptolemy set out upon a course of revenge. He deprived all Alexandrian Jews of their civil rights. He ordered all Jews in Egypt to be bound and brought to Alexandria where they were confined in a racecourse. Clerks were set up to register all the Jews but they were so numerous that the clerks ceased work after forty days when they ran out of writing materials.

Thereupon Ptolemy ordered five hundred elephants to be made drunk and turned loose in the racecourse to trample the Jews. The execution of this order was delayed because on the first day the king slept too late. On the second day God made him forget. On the third day the king and his troops were approaching the racecourse when two angels appeared, paralyzing the troops with fear. Then the elephants turned and trampled the king's troops.

Finally the king released the Jews and entertained them for seven days. The Jews decided to make this a perpetual festival. The king issued a decree to the governors of the provinces protecting the Jews and permitting faithful Jews to kill their brethren who apostatized. This they did, and then returned home joyfully.

Although written in Greek, the book shows little trace of Hellenistic influence. The author belonged to the strict conservative side of Judaism, utterly devoted to the Law, and bitterly opposed to Hellenistic influences. He represented the uncompromising orthodoxy which had no sympathy with the Hellenistic influences at work in Diaspora Judaism.

The purpose of the book is clearly to exalt Judaism, to make Jews more steadfast in their obedience to the Law, and to warn all would-be persecutors that they risked the judgment of God. The Jews are represented as loyal citizens who have always supported the Egyptian government.

They are protected, however, by the divine providence of God (6:15), who is the eternal Savior of Israel (7:16).

There are no clear indications by which to date the book, and suggestions range from the 1st cent. B.C. to the 1st cent. A.D.

*IV. Fourth Maccabees.*–This book illustrates better than any other book of the Pseudepigrapha the fusion of Hebrew and Greek culture. The text is contained in two Greek manuscripts, Alexandrinus and Sinaiticus. Eusebius knew the book with the title "On the Sovereignty of Reason," but he says that some call it Maccabees (*HE* iii.10.6). It is so called because it relates in great detail the sufferings and martyrdom of Jewish heroes in the Maccabean times.

The form of the book is a synagogue sermon or a diatribe. In the opening words the author speaks of himself in the first person and of his hearers in the second person, and he resumes this idiom in the conclusion. In 18:1 he addresses his hearers in the vocative case, "Men of Israel."

The content of the book includes a narration of events leading up to the Maccabean rebellion, a detailed account of the martyrdom of Eleazar, and a recital of the heroism and sufferings of a mother and her seven sons (2 Macc. 6–7). Their tortures are pictured in lurid detail.

These martyrdoms are not written or spoken merely out of historical interest but to illustrate the purpose of the book that is stated in the opening words: "Thoroughly philosophical is the subject I purpose to discuss, namely, whether religious reason is sovereign over the emotions" (1:1; Hadas's translation). "Reason, then, is the intellect choosing with correct judgment the life of wisdom; and wisdom is knowledge of things human and divine and of their cause" (1:15). There are four types of wisdom: prudence, justice, courage, and temperance. These control the emotions or passions. In defining reason in these terms, the author reflects a knowledge of Stoic philosophy, for prudence, justice, courage, and temperance were the four cardinal Stoic virtues, and they were to be achieved by the rule of reason. Our author differs from the Stoics, however, in that Stoicism taught that right reason extirpates the passions, while Maccabees teaches that reason can control the passions. The author is Jewish in his idea that the emotions are divinely implanted in mankind (2:21) and therefore ineradicable (1:6; 3:2, 5), even though they are controllable.

Again, our author differs from Stoicism in his concept of right reason. Stoicism viewed it as intrinsically human, while Maccabees views it as given by God. It is not reason as such that controls the passions, but "religious reason" — i.e., reason given by God. "Such wisdom is education in the Law through which we learn things divine reverently and things human advantageously" (1:17). The divine wisdom given in the Law expresses itself in the Stoic virtues.

Here is expressed the author's real purpose: to show that the Jewish belief in the divinely given Law was not incompatible with Greek philosophy but was in fact the way the goals of philosophy could be realized. In fact, only Judaism embodied the true philosophy (5:22). Those who "take thought for religion with their whole heart . . . alone are able to dominate the passions of the flesh" (7:18).

The author is thoroughly Jewish in his attitude toward the law. "We do not eat unclean foods. We believe that God has established the Law, and we know that the Creator of the world, in giving us the Law, has conformed it to our nature. That which will be appropriate to our souls He has bidden us eat, and that food which is contrary He has prevented us from eating" (5:25f.).

In one very important point, Greek thought has colored the author's theology. There is no idea of resurrection as in 2 Maccabees. Instead, 4 Maccabees teaches the doctrine of the immortality of the spirit (14:5; 16:13). The righteous will receive "souls pure and deathless from God" (18:23). "Those who die for God will live with God, as do Abraham and Isaac and Jacob and all the patriarchs" (16:25). But this is not an innate possession of human nature, as in Plato; it is a gift of God. The martyrs "loved religion the better, which preserves to eternal life according to God's promise" (15:3). But the fate of the wicked will be eternal torments (9:9; 10:11, 15; 12:12; 13:15).

Fourth Maccabees is also of interest to students of the NT because of its idea of vicarious suffering. The death of the martyrs somehow is to have efficacious value. Dying, Eleazar prays, "Make my blood an expiation for them, and take my life as a ransom for theirs" (6:29). The death of the martyrs is said to have "become as it were for the sin of the nation. It was through the blood of these righteous ones, and through the expiation [Gk. *hilastḗrion*] of their death, that divine providence preserved Israel" (17:21f.).

It is impossible to give definitive answers as to the author, date, and provenance of the work. The author writes excellent Greek, and his familiarity with Greek philosophy clearly suggests a city in the Diaspora, of which Alexandria is most likely, although Antioch has also been suggested. The 1st cent. B.C. is a good estimate for its date, although some have dated it in the 1st or early 2nd cent. A.D. The book is designed to "eulogize those stalwarts who at this season died with their mother" (1:10). This suggests that it is, perhaps, a memorial day address honoring the Maccabean martyrs.

*V. Minor Pseudepigrapha.*–*A. Martyrdom of Isaiah.* This is a hypothetical work, postulated by R. H. Charles and R. Pfeiffer, which is found as chs. 1–5 in the Christian work, the Ascension of Isaiah (possibly 3rd cent. A.D.). C. C. Torrey denied that such a separate Jewish book ever existed. These chapters contain the legend of the death of Isaiah, who was sawn in two by a wood saw (*see* APOCRYPHAL APOCALYPSES II. A).

*B. Apocalypse of Abraham.* This book, preserved in a Slavonic version, was probably written in Hebrew some time after the fall of Jerusalem in A.D. 70. The first part tells of Abraham's conversion from idolatry. The second part is an apocalypse to Abraham of the future of his race. Abraham ascends to heaven, where God gives him a vision of the world, the fall of humanity, and the final division of people into Jews and heathens. Abraham is shown the troubles which will precede the messianic age, and the coming of Messiah, who is called the Elect One, to gather Israel into the Kingdom and to destroy the heathen with fire.

*C. Testament of Abraham.*The Testament of Abraham exists in Greek and was written probably in Hebrew in the 1st or 2nd cent. A.D. Scholars differ as to whether it is a Christian work or a Jewish work with some Christian interpolations. It tells a story of Michael's dispatch to announce to Abraham his approaching death. Abraham begs to be shown the world and all created things before he dies. Then Michael conducts him to heaven where he sees both Hell and Paradise, and the souls of men being judged to determine which way they will go. This is only a preliminary judgment conducted by Abel; at the last day God will judge men. There is no Messiah, no resurrection, and no messianic kingdom.

*D. Third Baruch.* This book has been preserved in Greek and is also called the Greek Baruch. There is also extant a version in Slavonic. It was probably written in the 2nd cent. A.D. in Greek, but was later edited by a Christian writer. The apocalypse relates the journey of Baruch through the five heavens.

*E. Joseph and Asenath.* In the book of Genesis, Asenath is mentioned three times (41:45, 50; 46:20) as the daughter of Potiphera, the priest of On, who became Joseph's wife. This book is a piece of Hellenistic Jewish fiction, written in the early centuries of our era, about the romance between these two. References to the eucharist and confirmation show that it has been reworked by a Christian editor.

*F. Sibylline Oracles.* The Sibyl was a Greek prophetess, the pagan counterpart of the Hebrew prophets, to whom the Greeks and Romans resorted for oracles of guidance in affairs both private and public. There were several of them, having their residences in various places in Greece and Italy.

Written records came into existence that contained these supposed oracles. A collection was made and installed at Rome in 6 B.C. These oracles, in charge of the priests, were constantly studied and were consulted to find the will of the gods on special occasions.

The Jews took over this form of literature (Greek hexameter) to commend their religion to their pagan neighbors. Pfeiffer (p. 226) thought that a Hellenistic Jew composed our collection in Alexandria about 140 B.C. The example of this Jew was followed by both Jewish and Christian writers in later times — between the 2nd cent. B.C. and the 5th cent. A.D.

Our present collection contains pagan, Jewish, and Christian elements. It consisted of fifteen books, twelve of which are extant. Books 3-5 (printed by Charles in *APOT*) are generally regarded as Jewish (cf. Charlesworth, *OT Pseudepigrapha,* I, 317-472).

The Jewish writer makes the Greek Sibyl commend monotheism, the Mosaic ordinances, and important features of Hebrew history. By casting these prophecies in the form of pagan sibylline oracles, the Jews hoped to gain a sympathetic hearing for their religion.

*G. Lives of the Prophets.* This is a legendary work originally written in Hebrew in the 1st cent. A.D. and preserved in Greek and several other languages. It records legends about Isaiah, Jeremiah, Ezekiel, and Daniel, the twelve Minor Prophets, and, in addition, legends about Nathan, Ahijah, Joed, Azariah, Zechariah, Elijah, and Elisha.

*H. Life of Adam and Eve.* This is a hypothetical Jewish book reconstructed from the Latin *Vita Adae et Evae* and a Greek book closely parallel to it. It tells the story of the repentance of Adam and Eve for their sin, and some of their experiences after expulsion from the Garden. Adam, after eating the fruit of knowledge, beheld the vicissitudes of the Jews until the postexilic times and the Last Judgment. The book was probably written in Aramaic in the 1st cent. A.D.

*I. Fifth Maccabees.* *See* MACCABEES, BOOKS OF

*See also* APOCALYPTIC LITERATURE.

***Bibliography.***–E. Schürer, *HJP* (1890), II/3; R. H. Charles, *Ascension of Isaiah* (1900); *APOT*; G. H. Box, *Apocalypse of Abraham* (1918); W. F. Ferrar, *Uncanonical Jewish Books* (1918); E. W. Brooks, *Joseph and Asenath* (1918); G. H. Box, *Testament of Abraham* (1927); C. C. Torrey, *Apocryphal Literature* (1945); *Lives of the Prophets* (1946); R. H. Pfeiffer, *History of NT Times* (1949); M. Hadas, *Aristeas to Philocrates* (1951); *Third and Fourth Books of the Maccabees* (1953); D. S. Russell, *Method and Message of Jewish Apocalyptic* (*OTL,* 1964); O. Eissfeldt, *The OT: An Intro.* (Eng. tr. 1965), esp. pp. 603-636; G. Delling, *Bibliographie zur jüdisch-hellenistischen und intertestamentarischen Literature 1900-1970* (1975); J. H. Charlesworth, *Pseudepigrapha and Modern Research* (1976); L. Rost, *Judaism Outside the Hebrew Canon* (Eng. tr. 1976), pp. 100-190; G. W. E. Nickelsburg, *Jewish Literature Between the Bible and the Mishnah* (1981); J. H. Charlesworth, *OT Pseudepigrapha,* I (1983).

G. E. LADD

**PSEUDO-MATTHEW.** *See* APOCRYPHAL GOSPELS II. D.

**PSYCHOLOGY.**


I. Nature of Biblical Psychology
II. Theological and Scientific Psychology
III. Theological Psychology and Psychology of Religion
IV. Origin of the Soul
V. Constitution of Man
VI. Fall of Man
VII. Destiny of Man


The term "psychology" derives from Gk. *psychḗ* and *lógos,* and denotes the study of the soul or the psychical part of or aspect of man. While the word "psychology" is not found in the Bible, *psychḗ* occurs more than a hundred times in the NT. It is not used, however, in a precise sense, though one should remember that even today strict definition is still very difficult. Hence many Hebrew words have to be taken into account under the general heading of psychology.

***I. Nature of Biblical Psychology.***–It must be grasped at the outset that biblical psychology does not consist, and does not purport to consist, in a scientific investigation of the psychical aspect of man. Anthropology in the Bible is always theological, and this is no less true of psychology. Man is an object of presentation, not in and for himself as an isolated object, nor as one creaturely object among others, but in his relation to God. The purpose of biblical psychology is not to reveal supernaturally data that can then be rediscovered or confirmed by empirical research. The Bible sets forth data regarding God and His dealings with man and the cosmos. In the field of psychology as in all others the facts revealed in Holy Scripture have a primarily theological reference.

***II. Theological and Scientific Psychology.***–This means that a distinction is to be made between biblical and scientific psychology. Within its own terms of reference, scientific psychology is a justifiable pursuit. It can bring to light facts concerning the psyche and can make a valuable contribution in some areas of human activity, especially in the healing of mental disorders. Into the complexities of this ongoing investigation it is not here necessary to go. The main point is that intrinsically scientific psychology is valid and useful as one of the many investigations of creaturely phenomena considered in and for themselves.

In contrast, theological psychology introduces the fact that must always lie beyond the horizon of scientific investigation as such. This is the fact of the Creator Himself in His self-revelation. The bearing of this self-revelation on man is that it sets his origin, constitution, nature, and destiny in the light of his relation to the Creator and Lord of life. Psychology is not now presented for its own sake. It is not now studied within the limited context of creation. It is not approached from an anthropocentric or cosmocentric position. The subject is not just the psyche, or the psyche in relation to the body, to other psyches, or to the world. The subject is not even the psyche in relation to God. It is God in relation to the psyche.

The distinction between theological and scientific psychology is not absolute. The psyche itself is an obvious connecting point. Insofar as there is description of the psyche in both studies, even if from different angles and ultimately for different purposes, there is necessarily a degree of overlapping. Many aspects, e.g., of the constitution of man, will be seen in both studies; and the sinister data regarding the psyche that recent analysis has brought to light, even if they are couched in an esoteric or idiosyncratic jargon and perhaps explained in a highly speculative manner, are no surprise to those acquainted with the biblical account of the fallen psyche. The difference here does not lie in the sphere of data; it is to be found in the terms of reference.

Again, the distinction is not in itself antithetical. Much scientific psychology has in fact taken an anti-Christian or non-Christian turn, largely under the influence of materialism, which explains the soul in terms of physiology and religion in terms of inventions of the soul. At this point we see the familiar circle of much scientific thought. For its own purpose science has to adopt the working principle that all things are to be studied only within the observable context of creation, and it is then in danger of exalting this working principle into a supposedly demonstrated philosophical conclusion. Selecting the object of study, it then claims that this is the only object. But scientific research does not have to make this arrogant, ill-grounded, and obscurantist claim. In terms of psychology, it can study and describe soul and body in their mutual relation and interaction without necessarily explaining one in terms of the other. It can be content simply to do its proper job, i.e., to present the data. It can even admit that the data include things that are not readily explicable in terms of a self-enclosed cosmos. It can be prepared to allow that there may be other data which introduce a completely new factor, the objective reality of God, and which thus throw a whole new light even on the data. It cannot of itself investigate these data, but it can at least be prepared to receive them from those who do. When this happens, there is no conflict between biblical and scientific psychology. Each respects the purpose, the terms of reference, the validity, and the findings of the other. Each uses the other insofar as the other is relevant. Each can see that, if the whole picture does in fact include the Creator and His self-revelation, then it is into this picture that the findings of scientific psychology must finally be fitted, though the scientist qua scientist cannot himself be responsible for this task.

***III. Theological Psychology and Psychology of Religion.***– From the human or creaturely standpoint religion is an activity of the psyche. This is no less true of the subjective or human aspects of Christianity. Faith, repentance, conversion, prayer, ideas, and practices — all these can be studied from the standpoint of scientific psychology. The problems of Christians, e.g., in the internal or external outworking of the Christian life, can be approached from a similar angle. Psychological explanations can be found for these difficulties, and psychological help given toward their solution. This may be done in a purely objective clinical manner by non-Christians, or more sympathetically, and on what is finally a sounder basis, by Christians trained in psychology. When studies or therapeutic practices of this kind are in the hands of Christians who also accept a theological or biblical psychology, no difficulty need arise at this point. In basic principle, however, the question must still be asked whether theological psychology is, or can be, the same thing as religious psychology, or the psychology of religion. To this question only a negative answer can be given.

It was the genius of the theologian Schleiermacher to subsume Christianity under religious psychology. In so doing he had an apologetic interest. Kantian metaphysics seemed to have destroyed all possibility of knowing true reality, rationalism was attacking the credibility of the historical data of Scripture, and empirical science was already threatening to explain the phenomenal world in terms of itself. In this apparent impasse Schleiermacher suggested that the phenomenal world itself contains a religious sphere, the sphere of religious inwardness or experience, whose reality cannot be denied but whose explanation in materialistic terms is at least hazardous. In this subjectivity of Christianity Schleiermacher believed that he had found a citadel which could shelter believers and at the same time could be a home for the cultured of his day who had hitherto been despisers. He was not entirely disappointed in this hope, but his success was dearly won. For one thing, he surrendered the primary objectivity of God. For another, he made man and his religion the true object of Christian faith and proclamation. He thus brought the Christian wholly within the sphere of religious psychology and all its various possibilities from William James to Jung and beyond. He also made possible the final, and to many people the decisive, onslaught on Christianity in terms of the materialistic conceptions of Freud and his successors.

The subjectivist experiment of Schleiermacher is particularly relevant here because it shows very plainly the danger of dissolving theological psychology into the psychology of religion. By its very nature a psychology of religion has to be a scientific psychology. As such it can be for the Christian a tool, but only a tool. The problem is, however, that religious psychology has a particularly strong tendency to usurp the place of theological psychology, to become bad theological psychology, theological psychology that denies itself by being anthropocentric rather than theocentric, in other words, pseudotheological psychology. There is no danger of this in the case of a pronounced opponent like Freud, for the only theology he affirms is a-theology, and hence the distinction between theological and religious psychology is plain to see. On the other hand, the danger is virtually inescapable in the case of the Christian psychologists of a Liberal Protestant background; for the fundamental principle here is that God is reached through valid religious experience, and therefore religious psychology, which helps to this end, is the same thing as theological psychology. The possibility of genuine theological psychology is thus cut at the very root. In practice, religious psychologists of an orthodox background are unfortunately very much exposed to the danger of a similar confusion, for it is only too easy to maintain a theoretical orthodoxy and yet to act as though the psychology of religion were in fact the same thing as theological psychology, to endorse therewith the aberration of Schleiermacher, and even perhaps to try to defend his thesis against the materialistic attack.

In fact, for all the points of overlapping, the two psychologies are not at all the same thing. The psychology of religion examines religious aspects of the psyche, which include the phenomena or manifestations of Christian faith and life. This is a valid and valuable study. In particular, it can help to check spurious, distorted, and unhealthy developments which are no real part of the work of the Holy Spirit but which fit into observable patterns of religious behavior. Along the same lines it can help in the solution of technical psychological problems, e.g., false guilt, which might be confused with other elements in the spiritual life. It can also throw its own light on the profundity of sin and the need of a corresponding profundity in the work of penitence and renewal, especially at the level of motivation. Yet the fact remains that it is not in itself theological psychology, nor is it a stepping-stone to it. Theological psychology begins with God, not with man. Its theme is God in relation to the psyche, God the Father, the Son, and the Holy Spirit. It develops basic themes of psychology, the origin, nature, and destiny of the psyche, against the eternal background of the world and purpose of God. Its knowledge is derived not from clinical data but from the data of the divine self-revelation. Its terms of reference include a study of the Creator as well as the creature. It is based not on inexplicable longings or insecure interpretations, but on the unshakable and eternal truth of the divine self-declaration. It finds the goal of man not in self-realization or in the contribution that he may make to the evolution of the cosmos, but in the divine achievement of the divine purpose. It is read off not from scientific textbooks, but from the divinely given record of Holy Scripture.

*IV. Origin of the Soul.*–The Bible tells us plainly that the soul is from God. It was breathed into man by God (Heb. *wayyippah*; LXX Gk. *enephýsēsen*; Vulg. *inspiravit*). The human being thus "inspired" is a living soul (Heb. *nepes ḥayyâ*) because the breath of life (*nišmaṯ ḥayyîm*) is imparted (Gen. 2:7). It is the breath of the Almighty which gives man life (Job 33:4). The living soul (LXX Gk. *psychḗ zṓsa*) derives from the breath of life (*pnoḗ zoḗs*). The breath characterizes man; it is only seldom applied to animals. In man's nostrils is but a breath (Isa. 2:22). This breath is God's breath (Job 32:8). Paul in the NT has this in view when he says that the first man was made a living soul (1 Cor. 14:45). Possibly Jn. 6:33 also includes an allusion to the general life-giving function.

This teaching rules out all ideas of an emanation of the soul. It also excludes the concept of a preexistence of souls. Advanced by Plato and Vergil, this concept found its way into the Talmud and cabala and was also espoused by some of the early Christian fathers (Justin Martyr, Origen, Theodoret). It was condemned by the Synod of Constantinople in the 6th century. Finally, the biblical teaching is firmly opposed to materialism. The soul is not a development from the body, nor is it merely a psychological function of the body. That it has a close and necessary connection with the body is not to be denied. But like the body, and like the union of soul and body, it derives from God. The body is formed from the dust of the ground, but man becomes a living soul when God breathes into him the breath of life.

Does this mean that each soul is a new creation of God? Or is the soul derived from the parents? This has been a much debated issue in the Church; and both the first view, creationism, and the second, traducianism, have found staunch supporters. The Eastern theologians tended to creationism, and so, too, did Jerome, the Scholastics, the Reformers, and Roman Catholics in the West. Tertullian and Leo advocated traducianism, and Augustine inclined in this direction, though he would not commit himself: "I do not venture to affirm or deny that of which I am ignorant." (On this whole matter cf. W. Shedd, *History of Dogma,* II, 11ff.)

From the theological standpoint both views involve difficulties. Creationism does not accord easily with the doctrines of original sin and the solidarity of the race. Traducianism, however, verges on materialism and seems to leave little place for individuality and individual responsibility (cf. H. Bavinck, *Gereformeerde Dogmatiek* [1895-1901]). The *dictum* of Peter Lombard has often been quoted as a possible interpretation: *creando infundit eas Deus, et infundendo creat* ("in creating God infused the soul, and in infusing He creates"). But this does not seem to have any very clear bearing on the problem except insofar as it points to a twofold element in the divine work.

The basic difficulty is that, while Scripture leaves us in no doubt that both body and soul are divinely created at the first, it gives no precise information on the position with regard to individuals. Such Scriptures as are relevant seem to incline more in the direction of creationism. Thus we read that God "formed the spirit of man within him" (Zec. 12:1), or that He "fashions the hearts of them all" (Ps. 33:15), or that "the spirit returns to God who gave it" (Eccl. 12:7; cf. Nu. 16:22; He. 12:9), or that God is "the God of the spirits of all flesh" (Nu. 27:16). On the other hand, it is plain that children are procreated by their parents, and to this degree there is surely an element of truth in traducianism. The psyche undoubtedly has its origin in God even to the point that God is active in the formation of all psyches. But this does not rule out a genuine unity and continuity of parents and children both in body and also in soul. God acts, yet after the first creation He acts in and with secondary causes. There is solidarity, yet not to the exclusion of individuality; individuality, yet not to the exclusion of solidarity. In the larger sense one need not decide in favor of either view, for elements of truth are emphasized in both.

*V. Constitution of Man.*–It has been noted already that the soul, like the body, derives from God. This implies that man is composed of soul and body, and the Bible makes it plain that this is so. The soul and the body belong together, so that without either the one or the other there is no true man. Disembodied existence in Sheol is unreal. Paul does not seek a life outside the body, but wants to be clothed with a new and spiritual body (1 Cor. 15; 2 Cor. 5). Yet soul and body are also distinct in their unity, and in this distinction the soul takes precedence of the body as heaven takes precedence of earth. In his acute discussion in *CD,* III/2, K. Barth has suggested that the best way to speak of man is as an embodied soul, or a besouled body, or more particularly as the soul of his body. This brings out more precisely what is implied in the common biblical references to the soul and the body of man in their unity and distinction. The proper relationship of soul and body is essential to living a true human life. If the soul merely serves and expresses the body, order is disrupted and there can be no proper relationship with God, with others, with the self, or with the world. On the other hand, the soul is not to try to abstract itself from the body in an unreal world of domination. The proper relation is that the body should serve and express the soul. A formal preservation of this order is the necessary prerequisite of true humanity, though it cannot in itself guarantee it, since the soul may seek and decide what is wrong as well as the body.

This teaching of Scripture on man as soul and body in unity, distinction, and order excludes many erroneous conceptions of the constitution of man. It rules out from the very first all forms of monism. Man is not, as it were, a "doublefaced unity" (Bain). The soul and body are not just two aspects of the same reality. Neither the idealism which would subsume body under soul nor the materialism which would subsume soul under body is tenable. Nor is any place left for dualism. Soul and body are not separate entities which are able to work in concert by virtue of a preestablished harmony (Leibniz). Nor is the soul a pure entity which is imprisoned in, and awaits redemption from, an imperfect and evil body (Gnosticism). The Christian cannot be concerned only with the saving of the soul on the one side or the achieving of bodily well-being on the other. His concern is with the whole man, not as a self-contained and self-explicable entity, but as the creation of God, who has made man both soul and body in distinction and unity.

Is man spirit as well as soul? The Bible often uses the term "spirit" (also "heart") where it seems to be interchangeable, though not wholly synonymous, with "soul." Thus dying is the yielding up of the soul (Gen. 35:18;

Job 11:20), but also of the spirit (Ps. 31:5 [MT 6]; 146:4). The dead are called souls (Rev. 6:9; 20:4) and also spirits (He. 12:23; 1 Pet. 3:19). The living may be grieved in soul (Jgs. 10:16), or vexed (Jgs. 16:16), or discouraged (Nu. 21:4), or weary (Zec. 11:8), but also in anguish of spirit (Ex. 6:9), impatient in spirit (Job 21:4), or straitened in spirit (Mic. 2:7). The soul departs in death (Gen. 35:18), but so, too, does the spirit (Ps. 146:4). In the NT the soul of Jesus was "very sorrowful" (Mt. 26:38), but He was also "troubled in spirit" (Jn. 13:21). *See* SPIRIT; SOUL; HEART. From this it would appear that there is no fundamental distinction between soul and spirit. Man is a living soul because God breathes spirit into him, because he has breath or spirit from the Spirit of God. One cannot strictly say that man is spirit except insofar as spirit and soul are interchangeable. The truth is that he has spirit from the Spirit of God, and is thus soul. It is in this sense that the withdrawal of the spirit brings death (Ps. 104:29) and God is the "God of the spirits of all flesh" (Nu. 16:22; 27:16).

Against this attempts have been made to argue for a tripartite composition of man as body, soul, and spirit. This teaching was common in the early Church, but it came into some discredit when Apollinaris of Laodicea, under Platonic influence, seems to have suggested that in Christ only the body and soul were truly human, while the rational soul or spirit was replaced by the divine Logos. A consideration often advanced for trichotomy is that man shares the soul with the brutes (animal soul), and that only in terms of spirit can a distinction be made. In the battle against modern materialism, with its explanation of (animal) soul in terms of body, this has taken on a new importance. The Bible, however, seems to display little concern for distinctions of this kind. Though it may be wounding to human pride, the Bible is as frank as any scientist as to the elements of kinship between people and animals (cf. Eccl. 3:19f.). If the spirit of man goes upward and that of the beast downward, this is due to the content rather than the form. Certainly spirit is no more peculiar to man than soul, for the breath of life is given to animals, too (cf. Gen. 1:21; Ps. 104:29; Eccl. 3:19). A tripartite distinction does not seem, then, to be of great relevance in this connection. What matters is the kind of psyche, not the addition of a third element.

Some passages of Scripture do suggest a distinction between soul and spirit. In the OT the soul departs at death and returns if there is a restoration to life (1 K. 17:22), but "spirit" is used for the return of consciousness or power to one not dead (Gen. 45:27; Jgs. 15:19; 1 S. 30:12; 1 K. 10:5). In the NT Mary says that her soul magnifies the Lord and her spirit rejoices in God her Savior (Lk. 1:46f., or is this parallelism?). The Master is "very sorrowful" in soul (Mt. 26:38), but it is said of the disciples that the spirit is willing and the flesh is weak (Mt. 26:41). Passages of this kind, however, are rather too imprecise to serve as a basis for trichotomy.

More important are the many Pauline passages in which there is plain reference to spirit either along with soul or in a way that does not allow of explanation in terms of parallelism or interchangeability. Thus in 1 Thess. 5:23 Paul prays quite definitely that "spirit and soul and body be kept sound and blameless." Elsewhere he tells Christians to "stand fast in one spirit [Gk. *pneúma*], with one soul [*psychḗ*] striving together for the faith" (Phil. 1:27, AV). He also tells them to be of the same mind (*sýmpsychoi*, 2:2), and he hopes to be of good comfort (*eupsychṓ*, 2:19). Moreover, he distinguishes between the psychical man and the spiritual (pneumatic) man. The first Adam was a living soul (*psychḗ*); the second is a quickening spirit (*pneúma*). Does not this seem to suggest that in the last resort man has to be distinguished into body, soul, and spirit?

Three points are to be noted in this connection. First, there are other passages in the NT that continue the more common line of OT teaching. In addition to those already quoted, one might mention that Jesus gives His soul for the sheep in Jn. 10:11 but commends His spirit to the Father in Lk. 23:46. Indeed, the more common Pauline formula is simply body and soul rather than spirit and soul and body. If there is apparent distinction in Phil. 1:27, this passage is not speaking of the constitution of man but is an emphatic exhortation to unity, and the further distinction between "in" one spirit and "with" one soul is important.

Second, commentators are by no means agreed that the key passage 1 Thess. 5:23 is really designed to teach trichotomy. One suggestion is that Paul is here heaping up words to drive home the point of entirety. A. Kuyper (*Work of the Holy Spirit* [Eng. tr. 1900; repr. 1975], p. 491) points out that the reference is not to parts but to *télos* or aim. Calvin (comm., *in loc.*) thinks that spirit and soul are here used to denote different aspects of the one soul. F. W. Robertson (*Sermons*) accepts a distinction, but interprets it in terms not of man's natural constitution, but of the new life in the Spirit which is proper to Christians alone.

Third, it would seem that the NT uses spirit in a special sense which is not wholly strange to the OT (cf. Ps. 51:10 [MT 12]) but which is more strictly proper to the NT. For the Christian life is itself a new life, a new creation, in and by the Spirit. To be a Christian is to be born of the Spirit (Jn. 3:8). The Spirit comes to the disciples and dwells in them (Jn. 14:16f.). The spiritual man is the one who has received the Spirit which is of God (1 Cor. 2:10ff.). The spiritual body is that which is raised up by the spirit at the resurrection (1 Cor. 15:44). The Second Adam is a life-giving Spirit because He brings new life in the Spirit. If, then, the soul of the Christian can also be called the spirit, or if there can be reference to spirit in addition to soul, this is because the Christian is directed by the Holy Spirit, the Spirit of life, of God, of Christ, of Him that raised up Jesus, of indwelling, adoption, and witness (Rom. 8:1-16). In other words, as man is a living soul because He has spirit, the Christian is a pneumatic soul because he has spirit in the new sense of regenerate life in the Holy Spirit. The spirit of Christians is the Holy Spirit, or their new life in the Holy Spirit.

This means that spirit is not a part of man's constitution in the same way as body or what is generally denoted by soul. It cannot be isolated by scientific analysis or made the object of psychological presentation. The most that scientific psychology can do is to say that in terms of full human life the data leave a blank, an $x$, which cannot be wholly explained in terms of body, or of soul, or of both together. How this $x$ is found will then depend on other factors. The theoretical empiricist might try to find it somewhere in the known data. The Christian will realize that he is in the sphere of theological psychology and that the $x$ is not so much the spirit of man as the Spirit of God.

Even in the first creation it is God's Spirit that makes man a living soul. Hence the man who tries to live only in terms of body and soul is a defective man. Man must have spirit to be full man. It is true that every person must have spirit even to be able to live at all. But all try to live without spirit, and this is what condemns them both to deficient life and to ineluctable death. The Christian, however, is the person to whom and upon whom, in virtue of the saving power of Christ, the Spirit comes in a new act of regenerating power. He has the spirit of new life as well as that of the old. As there is an $x$ in the life of every person, there is, as it were, an $x^1$ in the life of the Christian.

Only theology, however, can tell us what this *x* or $x^1$ is. For it is not a constituent factor in the empirically accessible constitution of man. It is the Holy Spirit, God.

*VI. Fall of Man.*–Reference to the twofold sense in which the Christian has spirit, i.e., both by creation and by new creation, is a reminder that man in his present state is fallen and sinful man. While it is objectively true that man cannot live without the Spirit, nevertheless the whole attempt of fallen man is to do so, to be self-sufficient, to exist simply as body and soul without spirit, to explain himself simply in terms of the creaturely world, to fill the resultant vacuum with his own ideas of God. It is because of this attempt that man is subject to death (Gen. 2:17). The Spirit is finally to be withdrawn. Body and soul, ceasing to be spiritual, are subject to corruption. It is also because of this attempt that man, if he is to be saved and to have eternal life and fellowship with God, must be the recipient of the Spirit in a new way, i.e., in regeneration and resurrection. In and by himself he is no longer spiritual man in the true sense. He is carnal or psychical man.

The evidences of the fall are patent in all psychological inquiry and practice. Indeed, the main practical application of scientific psychology is in the sphere of the therapy that owes its final necessity to the fall. Psychologists may attempt all kinds of other explanations of the data, whether in terms of psychological or psychosomatic sickness, of the imbalance of psychical, physical, or psychophysical factors, of heredity, environment, or educational and sociological influences, or even of evolution from the material to the psychical. But the data themselves are beyond dispute. Man is at odds with himself. He lives his life in neurotic fear and illusion. He is capable of the greatest nobility but also of the greatest depths of ignorance, viciousness, and cruelty. Even when surface standards are achieved, below are murky depths which it may be helpful to bring to light but which seem to defy all attempts at ultimate purification.

The data do not prove the fall. Indeed, they invite alternative explanations which may very well contain elements of truth. It is in biblical psychology, however, that they find the true explanation. The explanation of human nature as it is now is that man is fundamentally at odds with God. In an act of disobedient self-assertion he is the man who sets his own will and desires against those of God. The effects of this are incalculable, for man hereby entraps himself in a vicious circle. The man who is at odds with God is the man who is also at odds with his fellows, with himself, and with his world. The primary sin brings with it a complicated series of consequences affecting both body and soul, both from without and from within. It initiates a train of hereditary and environmental evils. It enmeshes man in a nexus of sociological, political, cultural, and intellectual disorders. It introduces the factor of death which finally seems to rob life of meaning and which hangs like a sword of Damocles over all human enterprise and achievement. The fall puts all the other data into perspective. The empirically disclosed disorder of man is primarily and fundamentally due to the wrong relation with God. Even perverted religious experiences and illusions bear witness to this. Even scientific psychology, when it steps out of its terms of reference and advances its self-sufficient hypotheses, or even when it fails to see the final inadequacy of its own techniques, bears the same witness.

*VII. Destiny of Man.*–The destiny of man without God is to die (Gen. 2:17). This does not imply only physical death. Indeed, it is at least arguable that apart from the fall man would still have died physically, although it is perhaps more fitting to suppose that he would have been translated from the present earth to God. Be that as it may, the death introduced by sin is also, and more radically, spiritual death. Even as they live, sinners are dead in trespasses and sin (Eph. 2:1). Their life stands under the sign of corruptibility (1 Cor. 15:50). They are liable to be destroyed both body and soul in hell (Mt. 10:28). Beyond the death of the body is the second death (Rev. 20), the Gehenna of Jesus, the place of weeping and wailing, the infinite paradox of life in self-separation from God (2 Thess. 1:9).

The factuality of death is beyond all question. Nor is it genuinely possible to conceive of the continuation or restoration of life apart from God. Yet death is still a mystery, a problem, a threat. It presents in the acutest possible form the self-contradiction of man. Human life cannot achieve its destiny in terms of this life. Man cannot be content to think that his memory may endure for a generation or two, that his influence will outlive him, that the race persists even if the individual perishes. Even the hope of an immortality of the soul apart from the body has a hollow ring, for without the body what is the soul but a ghost, a shade, a wraith? Acceptance of the finality of death brings little relief. For it means acceptance of the futility, not merely of the individual life, but of all human endeavor. In many cases, indeed, it will be achieved only at the price of the worst repressions, relieved at the last only in the empty sham of elaborate obsequies. When it comes to human destiny, to the destiny of fallen man, empirical research can only confirm the comfortless message that man has to die, that rationally or irrationally he does not feel that he should die, and that in a great number of cases he is afraid to die.

It is here that the final invalidity of science apart from God is displayed. This is the invalidity not of necessary error, but of necessary inadequacy. Neither the world nor man can in fact be studied in abstraction from God. Such abstracted study does have a limited validity. It can amass information and bring this information under a valid arrangement. It can also make practical application of its data. But when all the data are assembled, even if all possible data concerning all aspects of the cosmos are included, they are still like naughts with no digit, or figures enclosed by a great minus, or by an unknown and unknowable *x*. Hence they present only a final riddle to which neither the subject not the object of knowledge has the key. The closer this knowledge is to man personally, the more intolerable the riddle becomes, the more empty the data which cannot include the answer, the more powerful the temptation to leave the way of objectivity and to supply by speculation a possible digit, a plus sign, a figure for the *x*. Scientific psychology, to be true to its own terms of reference, has to leave out the true, objective, living God who alone has the key. And when it stands face to face with death, its final invalidity on this account is starkly revealed. It can present the data; the keys of hell and of death are in other hands (Rev. 1:18).

The Bible does not dispute the data. Indeed, it realistically demands that man should face up to his mortality and that he should not seek refuge in illusory immortalities. Yet the Bible can do more. Adding the unknown *x*, it can show why man has to die, and also why death is for man such an intolerable contradiction. In terms of the original plan and purpose of God the violent reaction of man against death is not baseless presumption. It is wholly justifiable in the sense that man was not destined for death but brought death upon himself by his own revolt against God. Death in its final sense is natural only to unnatural, i.e., fallen, man. In other words, it is not natural to man as God created him. The life-giving breath of God is intrinsic to him. Though he has incurred it himself, its withdrawal is an intolerable paradox which involves life in death and death in life.

Yet this is not all that the Bible has to say. The Bible can also show how death can give way to life, not by pretending that the psyche is exempt from death, but by a new act of creation. For God has not abandoned His original will and purpose. He has sent the second man, the Lord from heaven, to die and to rise again both body and soul from the grave. Thus soteriological and eschatological data belong also to psychology. They are to be found in Jesus Christ, incarnate and exalted. By the life-giving Spirit a new life, a life in Christ, an eternal life, is breathed into man, and will come to its consummation in the new great act of the resurrection of man both body and soul from the dead. For those who are in Christ the psyche is already being fashioned into new fulfillment, and new harmony with the body, in the life that is a walk after the Spirit.

The achievement here and now, however, is only imperfect and provisional. Death must be worked out in terms of literal death as well as repentance and mortification. Life must be worked out in terms of resurrection as well as regeneration and renewal. Christians await the new house which will replace the present tent of mortality (2 Cor. 5:1), the fulness of the Spirit (and spirit) beyond the first installment. Then, in the life of the world to come, the renewed soul and body will enter into the fulness of life in the Spirit. Then, in the new heaven and the new earth, man will be physiologically and psychologically transformed into the likeness of the risen Lord. Then the psyche of man will know even as it is known, not in an empiricism apart from God, but in the empiricism of God Himself.

***Bibliography.***–*BDTh*; *TDNT*, IX, *s.v.* ψυχή κτλ. (Bertram, Dihle, Jacob, Lohse, Schweizer, Tröger); Pauly-Wissowa; F. J. Delitzsch *System of Biblical Psychology* (Eng. tr., repr. 1977); J. Laidlaw, *Bible Doctrine of Man* (1879; rev. ed. 1905); J. Orr, *God's Image in Man* (1906). The vast literature of scientific psychology may be consulted for interest and reference, but it has only limited relevance for the purpose of biblical psychology.

G.W. BROMILEY

**PTOLEMAIS** tōl-ə-mā'əs [Gk. *Ptolemais*] (1 Macc. 5:15, 22, 55; 10:1, 39, 56-58, 60; 11:22, 24; 12:45, 48; 13:12; 2 Macc. 13:24f.; Acts 21:7). A town on the northern coast of Palestine, also called ACCO. Paul stopped there on his return from his third missionary journey (Acts 21:1-7).

**PTOLEMY** tol'ə-mi [Gk. *Ptolemaios*]. The dynastic name of the Hellenistic kings reigning in Egypt 323-30 B.C.; also a rather common name during that period.

**1.** Ptolemy I Soter (savior) (367-283 B.C.); son of the Macedonian nobleman Lagos; satrap of Egypt (323-305) and king (305-283). One of Alexander's most trusted generals, Ptolemy I fought with distinction in all of Alexander's campaigns, especially in the conquest of Asia. Upon Alexander's death (323 B.C.), Ptolemy I became the satrap or governor of Egypt. When Perdiccas (another general of Alexander who had become regent) was bringing the body of Alexander from Babylon to Macedonia, Ptolemy met the retinue in Syria and seized the body, taking it to Egypt for burial (Diodorus xviii.26-28; Strabo xvii.1.8). Consequently Perdiccas attacked Egypt, but was killed in 321 by his generals, among whom was Seleucus (Diodorus xviii.36-39). Antipater was now elected regent and the satrapies were redistributed, with Seleucus gaining Babylonia, Laomedon obtaining Syria, and Ptolemy retaining Egypt. In 320, feeling temporarily safe from Babylonian attack, Ptolemy claimed Syrian Palestine as a part of Egypt and deposed Laomedon (Diodorus xviii.43; Appian

Ptolemy I offering a sacrifice to the god Horus. Painted limestone relief from a chapel of Ptolemy at Hermopolis, *ca.* 300 B.C. (Roemer-Pelizaeus Museum, Hildesheim, West Germany)

*Syr.* 52). When Antipater died (319), his general Antigonus tried to unite Alexander's empire by removing those who opposed him. Unable to defend himself against Antigonus, Seleucus fled to Ptolemy in 316 (Diodorus xix.55; Appian *Syr.* 53).

Seleucus's warning to Ptolemy of Antigonus's threat resulted in Ptolemy, Lysimachus, Cassander, and Seleucus forming an alliance against Antigonus. In 315 Antigonus invaded Syria and Palestine and occupied all the country down to Gaza (Diodorus xix.56-62; Appian *Syr.* 53; Polybius v.67). But soon Ptolemy and Seleucus attacked and defeated Demetrius son of Antigonus, who was in charge of Gaza. This decisive victory gave Seleucus rule of Babylonia, and Ptolemy seized Jerusalem with no resistance because it was the sabbath (Appian *Syr.* 54; Josephus *Ant.* xii.1.1 [4f.]; *CAp* 1.22 [186, 209f.]). After an indecisive battle, Antigonus and Ptolemy signed a peace treaty in 311 whereby Ptolemy lost control of Syria and Palestine (Diodorus xix.105). In 309, however, Ptolemy resumed hostilities by attacking the coasts of Lycia and Caria, and in 308 he extended his opposition to the mainland of Greece by seizing Corinth, Sicyon, and Megara, though later he had to abandon these territories. In 306 Demetrius attacked and captured Cyprus, a possession of Ptolemy since 313, in a decisive naval battle at Salamis. In their victory Antigonus and Demetrius assumed the title of kings, and Ptolemy, Seleucus, Cassander, and Lysimachus retaliated by also assuming the title, probably in 305. In the winter of 306-305 Antigonus invaded Egypt unsuccessfully. When Demetrius besieged the Rhodians in 305-304, Ptolemy came to their aid and forced the siege to be lifted; thus the Rhodians conferred on him the honorific title *Soter* ("savior") by which he later was commonly acknowledged.

In 303 Ptolemy, Seleucus, Lysimachus, and Cassander made a pact to overthrow Antigonus, and Ptolemy was promised Coelesyria and Palestine. Ptolemy withdrew from battle when he heard the rumor that Antigonus had defeated Lysimachus. When Antigonus was killed in the decisive battle at Ipsus in Phrygia (301), the other members of the pact decided to give Palestine and Coelesyria to Seleucus since Ptolemy had deserted them. Ptolemy forestalled Seleucus and took possession of Lower Syria (south of Lebanon and of Damascus) and Palestine, and Phoenicia south of the river Eleutherus (Diodorus xx.113-xxi.5; Appian *Syr.*55). This action was the bone of contention between the Seleucidian and Ptolemaic houses for decades to come. The empire of Alexander was divided into four areas: Egypt and Palestine to Ptolemy, Phrygia (up to the Indus, including Syria) to Seleucus, Thrace and Bithynia to Lysimachus, and Macedonia to Cassander (Dnl. 11:4; cf. also 7:6; 8:8, 22).

In 285 Ptolemy virtually abdicated his throne to Ptolemy II Philadelphus, the son of his favorite wife Bernice. Two years later Ptolemy died (283). He had ruled his realm well. The legal and military organization of the Ptolemaic empire was his accomplishment. He founded the library and museum in his capital, Alexandria, and was the originator of the religious cult of the Greco-Egyptian god Serapis. While king he wrote a straightforward history of Alexander's campaigns, which although now lost, can be largely reconstructed because of the historian Arrian's extensive use of it.

**2.** Ptolemy II Philadelphus (brother-loving — a surname properly belonging to his sister-wife, Arsinoe II, but used to distinguish him) (308-246), son of Ptolemy I and Bernice I. *Ca.* 289-288 he married Arisone I, daughter of Lysimachus king of Thrace, and they had three children: Ptolemy III, Lysimachus, and Bernice. Ptolemy II was made joint ruler with his father in 285, and became sole king at the time of his father's death in 283. Ca. 278 Arsinoe was accused of conspiracy and was banished to Coptos in Upper Egypt. Soon after Ptolemy II married his sister Arsinoe II, who became very dominant in Egyptian affairs.

Ptolemy II fought wars with the Seleucid king Antiochus I (280-279 and 276-271) that left Egypt as the dominant naval power in the eastern Mediterranean. Antiochus II, who succeeded his father Antiochus I in 261, fought a war with Ptolemy, the Second Syrian War (260-255), and regained some territories. Nevertheless, this war ended somewhat inconclusively, except that Ptolemy II accomplished a diplomatic master stroke whereby Antiochus II agreed to get rid of his wife Laodice and marry Ptolemy II's daughter Bernice, with the understanding that the kingdom was to go to Bernice's son (Appian *Syr.* 65; Dnl. 11:6). This marriage was consummated in 252.

Ptolemy II devoted much time to the internal administration of Egypt. He continued the interests of his father in the museum and Alexandrian library and was a patron of the arts, sciences, and literature. According to tradition (Letter of Aristeas; see *APOT,* II, 83-122) his persuasion resulted in the Hebrew Scriptures being translated into Greek, though probably only the Pentateuch was translated during his reign. *See* SEPTUAGINT II. A.

**3.** Ptolemy III Euergetes (benefactor), son of Ptolemy II and Arsinoe I; king 246-221 B.C. The diplomatic masterstroke of his father mentioned above failed. Antiochus II returned to his first wife Laodice only to be poisoned by her. She then named her son, Seleucus II, king. Bernice asked her brother Ptolemy III to rescue her and support her son's claim to the throne, but Laodice murdered Bernice and her infant son, causing Ptolemy III to initiate the Third Syrian War or Laodicean War (246-241) by invading Syria, with little or no opposition from the residents (Dnl. 11:7f; 1 Macc. 11:8). In fact, Ptolemy III was very successful, for he overran not only Syria but also plundered Susa and Babylonia and went as far as the borders of India (cf. Appian *Syr.* 66). His fleets recovered territories in the Aegean and made new advances as far as Thrace. This marked the apex of the Ptolemaic power.

After Ptolemy III's return to Egypt, Seleucus II won control of Syria (Dnl. 11:9), but Ptolemy retained the naval prominence in the Aegean. A treaty in 241 established peace between the two houses for about two decades. But Ptolemy II continued with intrigues against Greece, trying to disrupt Macedonian power. He may have been murdered by his son Ptolemy IV (Justinus xxix.1), though more probably he died a natural death (Polybius ii.71).

**4.** Ptolemy IV Philopator (father-loving) (b. 238), son of Ptolemy III and Bernice II; husband of Arsinoe III; king 221-203 B.C. His debauched life of wine and women (Polybius v.87; xiv.12) marked the beginning of the Ptolemaic decline. The Fourth Syrian War (219-217) commenced when Antiochus III invaded Lebanon in an attempt to take Palestine from Ptolemy IV. In 219 Antiochus III captured Seleucia (near Antioch), in 218 he captured Tyre and Ptolemais (Acco) as well as the inland cities all the way from Philoteria to Philadelphia, and in 217 he pushed southward as far as Raphia (near Gaza), where he was utterly defeated, leaving Ptolemy IV in undisputed control of Coelesyria and Phoenicia (Polybius v.51-57; Dnl. 11:11f.; 3 Macc. 1:1-5). For this battle Ptolemy IV enlisted native Egyptians into the army, which had the effect of gaining Egyptian self-respect. Egyptians were not allowed independence, however, and were excluded from high executive positions (limited to Greeks). This resulted in resentment that led to revolts later in his reign and in the reigns of his successors. He crushed the revolt in Upper Egypt late in his reign.

**5.** Ptolemy V Epiphanes (the manifest god; illustrious) (b. 210), son of Ptolemy IV and his sister Arsinoe III; king 203-181 B.C. Because Ptolemy V was only seven years old when he began to rule, Antiochus III saw an opportunity to take Coelesyria from Egypt. In 202 Antiochus made a pact with Philip V of Macedon to divide Egypt between them (Livy xxxi.14.5). In 201 Antiochus invaded Palestine and after great difficulty captured Gaza. Having secured Palestine, Antiochus invaded the dominions of Attalus king of Pergamos (who was pro-Roman against Philip V), in the winter of 199/98. Scopas, an Egyptian general, hearing of Antiochus's absence, invaded Palestine and recovered the lost territories. Antiochus returned to oppose Scopas, and at Panias (NT Caesarea Philippi) Ptolemy V was decisively defeated in 198 (Josephus *Ant.* xii.3.3 [129-33]; Polybius xvi.18f.; 28.1; Dnl. 11:14-16). Seeing the new threat of Rome, in 193 Antiochus made a treaty with Ptolemy V in which Ptolemy married Antiochus's daughter Cleopatra, with the idea that her son/his grandson would become king (Polybius xxviii.20; Appian *Syr.* 5; Josephus *Ant.* xii.4.1 [154]; Dnl. 11:17).

The ROSETTA STONE comes from his reign.

**6.** Ptolemy VI Philometor (mother-loving) (b. 186 or 184/183), elder son of Ptolemy V and older brother of Ptolemy VIII. Ptolemy VI began his infancy rule in 181/180 under the regency of his mother Cleopatra I (daughter of Antiochus III). His mother died in 176 and he married his sister Cleopatra II in 175/174. In 170 the amateur regents Eulaeus and Lenaeus advised Ptolemy VI to avenge Panias and recover Coelesyria. But Antiochus IV heard of the plan, invaded Egypt with a large army in 170/169, defeated Ptolemy VI, and then made peace with him. In the midst of the confusion the Alexandrians made the younger brother Ptolemy VIII their king, thus weakening the Ptolemaic threat toward Antiochus IV. When Antiochus IV withdrew from Egypt, the two brothers and their sister Cleopatra II (also Ptolemy IV's wife) ruled jointly until 164. This alliance displeased Antiochus IV, who marched against Alexandria; but when he was within 6 km. (4 mi.) of the city the Romans ordered him to evacuate Egypt at once (cf. Polybius xxix.2.1-4; 27.1-8; Livy xlv.12.1-6; Appian *Syr.* 66; Justinus xxiv.3; Dnl. 11:28-30). With the help of Rome, Ptolemy VI became sole ruler in 164/163, but the strife between the two brothers continued for another decade.

In 152 Ptolemy VI became involved with Syrian politics in the conflict between Alexander Balas and DEMETRIUS. First, in 150 he sided with Alexander Balas, and after Demetrius was slain in battle, Balas married Ptolemy VI's daughter Cleopatra III. In 47, upon learning of Balas's plot to kill him, Ptolemy retrieved his daughter and gave her to Demetrius's son, Demetrius II Nicator. Finally, in 145 Demetrius II defeated Balas; both Balas and Ptolemy VI were killed in the battle (1 Macc. 10:22-66; 11:1-10; Josephus *Ant.* xiii.2.3 [46-61]; 4.1f. [80-85]; Diodorus xxxii.27.9c; Livy *Epit.* lii). Ptolemy VI seems to have been friendly to the Jews, for when Onias IV, son of Onias III and high priest in Jerusalem, fled to Egypt, Ptolemy allowed him to build a Jewish temple modeled after the Jerusalem temple at Leontopolis in the Delta, *ca.* 154 (Josephus *Ant.* xiii.3.1-3 [62-73]; xx.10.3 [235f.]; *BJ* vii.10.2f. [420-432]).

**7.** Ptolemy VIII Euergetes II (benefactor) (182-116), younger son of Ptolemy V. He was joint ruler with Ptolemy VI and Cleopatra II in 170-164, sole ruler 164-163; the Romans made him king of the separate kingdom of Cyrene. In 145 he returned to Egypt and seized the throne; in 144 he killed his nephew Ptolemy VII and married his sister, the former wife of his brother, Cleopatra II. In 142 he married Cleopatra II's daughter, Cleopatra III, without being able to divorce Cleopatra II. In 132/131 Cleopatra II forced Ptolemy VIII to leave Alexandria and he took refuge in Cyprus. He returned to Alexandria in 127 after Cleopatra II fled to Syria (129/128) and finally made peace with her in 124. Upon his death he bequeathed Cyrene, as a separate kingdom, to his illegitimate son Ptolemy Apion (d. 96), while he gave Egypt and Cyprus to Cleopatra III and to whichever of his two sons by her, Ptolemy IX Soter II and Ptolemy X Alexander, she might choose as her co-regent (Justinus xxxix.3.1; 5.2). The exclusion from the will of Cleopatra II led to further domestic strife.

The reference in the prologue of Sirach to "the thirty-eighth year of Euergetes" is to 132 B.C., since Euergetes dated his reign from his joint rule with his brother and sister.

**8.** Ptolemy IX Soter II (savior) (141-80), eldest son of Ptolemy VIII and Cleopatra III; king 116-110, 109/108, 88-80 B.C. Before his father's death he was married to his sister Cleopatra IV. From 116 to 108 he reigned in Egypt with his mother, though there was much strife between them while her favorite son Ptolemy X ruled Cyprus. In 110 he was ousted from Egypt by his brother Ptolemy X. He was able to return for a short time in 109-108 until his mother called Ptolemy X to Egypt and together they expelled Ptolemy IX to Cyprus. In 89 the Egyptians revolted against Ptolemy X; Ptolemy IX returned to Egypt in 88 and was sole ruler of Egypt and Cyprus until his death. Later internal revolts resulted in the destruction of Thebes in 85.

**9.** Ptolemy XII Philopator Philadelphius Neos Dionysus, nicknamed Auletes (flute-player) (116[?]-51), illegitimate son of Ptolemy IX. He became ruler in 80 and married his sister, Cleopatra V Tryphaeana, in 80/79. His friendship with the Romans resulted in the Alexandrians expelling him in 58, but with the help of the Syrian proconsul Gabinius he was restored in 55. He killed Bernice; when he died in 51 he bequeathed his kingdom to his oldest son (who was 12), who was to marry his seventeen-year-old sister Cleopatra VII.

**10.** Cleopatra VII (69-30), daughter of Ptolemy XII and sister of Ptolemy XIII and XIV. She is probably the best known of the Ptolemies; she was an ambitious and clever politician. She ruled successively with her brothers Ptolemy XIII (51-47) and Ptolemy XIV (47-44) and with her son Ptolemy XV (44-30). Antony summoned her to Tarsus in 41 and subsequently he followed her to Alexandria. They met again in 37 and possibly married at that time. In 32 Octavian warred with Antony and Cleopatra, defeating them at Actium in September, 31. In August, 30 B.C., Cleopatra took her own life rather than be a spectacle in the Roman triumphal procession. Thus Egypt finally came under Roman domination.

Several other Ptolemies are mentioned in the Apocrypha:

**11.** Ptolemy Macron. *See* MACRON.

**12.** Ptolemy son of Abudus; son-in-law of Simon Maccabeus; a governor in Judea. His ambition led him to deceive, trap, and murder Simon and two of his sons at Dok near Jericho (1 Macc. 16:11-17).

**13.** Ptolemy son of Dositheus and father of Lysimachus. Ptolemy was a priest and a Levite who, with his father, brought to Egypt "the Letter of Purim" (perhaps the entire book of Esther), which Lysimachus had translated into Greek (Ad. Est. 11:1).

***Bibliography.***–E. R. Bevan, *History of Egypt under the Ptolemaic Dynasty* (1927); *CAH*, VII (1928), 109-154 (M. Rostovtzeff); *Enc. Brit.* XVIII (1972), *s.v.* "Ptolemies" (R. H. Simpson); P. M. Fraser, *Ptolemaic Alexandria* (3 vols., 1972); M. Hengel, *Jews, Greeks and Barbarians* (Eng. tr. 1980); *Oxford Classical Dictionary* (2nd ed. 1970), *s.v.* (H. H. Scullard); A. E. Samuel, *Ptolemaic Chronology* (1962); W. W. Tarn and G. T. Griffith, *Hellenistic Civilization* (3rd ed. 1961).

H. W. HOEHNER

**PUA** pū'ə.

**1.** (AV, NEB, Nu. 26:23; NEB Gen. 46:13; 1 Ch. 7:1). *See* PUVAH.

**2.** (Jgs. 10:1, NEB). *See* PUAH **3.**

**PUAH** pū'ə.

**1.** [Heb. *pû'â*] (1 Ch. 7:1); NEB PUA. The second son of Issachar, called PUVAH in Gen. 46:13; Nu. 26:23.

**2.** [Heb. *pû'â*–'splendid one,' or possibly < Ugar. *pǵt*–'girl'] (Ex. 1:15). One of the two Hebrew midwives commanded by the Egyptian pharaoh to kill all the male infants of the Hebrews (v.16). Puah and SHIPHRAH disobeyed this command, pretending that the Hebrew infants were born before they arrived (vv.17-19). Because of this daring action, the Israelites continued to multiply and God rewarded the midwives with families of their own (vv. 20f.). In later Jewish tradition Puah was identified with Miriam and Shiphrah with Jochebed (Midr. *Ex. Rabbah*). *See also* MIDWIFE.

**3.** [Heb. *pû'â*] (Jgs. 10:1); NEB PUA. A member of the tribe of Issachar; son of Dodo and father of Tola the judge.

**PUBLICAN.** The AV translation of Gk. *telṓnēs* (RSV "tax collector"; NEB "tax gatherer"). *See* TAX COLLECTOR.

**PUBLIUS** pub'li-əs, po͞ob'li-əs [Gk. *Poplios* < Lat. *Publius*–'popular']. The name might be derived from the Greek rendering of the Roman title Popilus since inscriptions have been found near Malta using it to designate leading citizens of the island. Luke uses it as the name of the chief man of Malta who received Paul and gave him lodging for three days following a shipwreck (Acts 28:7f.). As the leading man of the island, a Roman official, he was responsible for the prisoners, but he extended hospitality to Paul and was richly rewarded by Paul's action in healing his father of a fever. Jerome says that Publius was martyred (*De vir. ill.* xix). B. R. AND P. C. PATTEN

**PUDENS** po͞o'dənz [Gk. *poudēs* < Lat. *Pudens*–'modest']. One of the Christians who sent greeting to Timothy in 2 Tim. 4:21. Some commentators have regarded the Latin name as evidence that the Epistle was written from Rome. Apart from this reference, the Bible tells nothing about Pudens, but tradition and speculation have filled the gap with many intriguing possibilities. The most generally accepted suggestion is that Pudens was a converted Roman senator, later martyred under Nero. He was the son of a certain Priscilla (not the one mentioned in Acts 18) and the father of Praxedis and Pudentiana. He gave his house, where Peter had lodged as his guest, for use as the church later known as the Pudentiana. Excavations under this church have unearthed the ruins of Roman houses, one of them near the Baths of Novatus over which the church was extended when rebuilt, probably in the time of Siricius (A.D. 384-399). Another theory is that the grandson of Pudens, another Pudens, gave the house for use as a church in the time of Pius I, A.D. 140-155.

Mention of Pudens along with Linus and Claudia in 2 Tim. 4:21 has led some scholars to develop a different hypothesis, that Pudens was the husband of Claudia and father of Linus, the first Roman bishop after Peter according to ancient listings. An attempt has also been made to identify this Pudens as the centurion friend of the poet Martial (*Epigrams* i.31), particularly since Martial in iv.13 referred to the wedding of "his own Pudens" to a Claudia Peregrina, thought to have been from Britain. Martial's mention of a Linus in i.76 has also been noted. Attractive though this suggestion is, it is not backed by solid evidence. The name Pudens was common (an inscription mentions even another Pudens and Claudia; cf. *CIL*, VI, 15066), and equating Martial's Pudens with the senatorial Pudens of tradition is virtually impossible. Hence commentators who have accepted the common tradition either have treated the names of 2 Tim. 4:21 as unrelated or, like A. Cousineau (*in loc.*), have regarded Linus as the son of Claudia but not of Pudens. Pudens the senator was canonized in the 6th cent. and is commemorated in the East on April 14 and in the West on May 19.

***Bibliography.***–Comms. on 2 Timothy; Alf. III, 104; *Catholic Encyclopedia*, *s.v.*; R. Lanciani, *Pagan and Christian Rome* (1895), pp. 10ff.; J. B. Lightfoot, *Clement of Rome*, I (rev. ed. 1890), 76ff.; *LTK*; MSt; T. Zahn, *Einl.*, V. (1960), §33, n. 2. G. W. B.

**PUHITES** pū'hīts (AV, NEB, 1 Ch. 2:53). *See* PUTHITES.

**PUITE** pū'īt (Nu. 26:23, NEB). *See* PUNITES.

**PUL** pool [Heb. *pûl*] (2 K. 15:19; 1 Ch. 5:26). Another name for the Assyrian king TIGLATH-PILESER III. This name is known from a Babylonian king list (see *ANET*, p. 272). Although some (e.g., A. T. Olmstead, *History of Assyria* [repr. 1964], p. 181) think that when he took over Babylon Tiglath-pileser apparently used Pul(u) as a throne-name, and others (e.g., H. W. F. Saggs, *The Greatness that was Babylon* [1962], pp. 114f.) say that Tiglath-pileser was the throne-name, J. A. Brinkman (*Political History of the Post-Kassite Babylonia* [1968], pp. 61f., 240-43) has pointed out that no contemporary references use the name Pul(u), and thus it is no doubt just a later name given to Tiglath-pileser III.

The AV also uses Pul for PUT in Isa. 66:19. G. A. L.

**PULPIT** [Heb. *migdāl*–'tower'] (Neh. 8:4); NEB PLATFORM. Although the use of *migdāl* in this sense is unique, it is not inappropriate to the basic sense of *migdāl*, that of an elevated structure (hence the LXX *bēma*; see Bauer, rev., p. 140). The context clearly indicates that a raised wooden platform (stairs led up to it, 9:4) was built for Ezra on this special occasion of the reading of the law. L. H. Brockington (*Ezra, Nehemiah and Esther* [*NCBC*, repr. 1977], p. 131) suggests a connection with the later synagogue situation. G. A. L.

**PULSE.** *See* VEGETABLE.

**PUNISH** [(verbs) Heb. *pāqaḏ*–'attend to,' 'visit,' 'appoint' (Lev. 18:25; Ps. 59:5 [MT 6]; Isa. 10:12; niphal, Isa. 24:22; hophal, Jer. 6:6; etc.), *nāṯan*–'give' (Ezk. 7:3f., 8f.), *nāqam*–'avenge, take vengeance' (niphal, Ex. 21:20; hophal, 21:21), *ḥāśaḵ*–'withhold, refrain' (Ezr. 9:13), *ʿānaš*–'fine, pay a penalty' (Prov. 21:11), *šāpaṭ*–'judge, govern' (1 S. 3:13); Gk. *timōréō* (Acts 22:5; 26:11), *dichotoméō*–'cut in two' (Mt. 24:51 par. Lk. 12:46), part. of *eléncho*–'punish, discipline' (He. 12:5), *ekdikéō*–'take vengeance' (2 Cor. 10:6), *kolázō* (Acts 4:21), part. of *paideúō*–'discipline' (2 Cor. 6:9); (nouns) Heb. *pᵉquddâ*–'vengeance,' 'visitation' (Jer. 8:12); Gk. *ekdíkēsis*–'vengeance,' 'punishment' (1 Pet. 2:14)]; AV also VISIT, RECOMPENSE, JUDGE, CUT ASUNDER, etc.; NEB also DEAL, "visit with punishment" (Zec. 10:3), MAKE SUFFER, "cut in pieces" (Mt. 25:41); **PUNISHMENT** [(nouns) Heb. *ʿāwōn*–'iniquity,' 'guilt,' 'punishment of iniquity' (Gen. 4:13; Ps. 69:27 [MT 28]; Ezk. 4:5; etc.), *pᵉquddâ*–'vengeance,' 'visitation' (Isa. 10:3; Jer. 10:15; Hos. 9:7; etc.), *ḥaṭṭāʾṯ*–'sin,' 'sin offering' (Lam. 4:6; Zec. 14:19), *ḥēṭʾ*–'sin' (Lam. 3:39), *mûsār*–'correction, chastisement' (Jer. 30:14), *tôḵēḥâ*–'punishment, chastisement' (Hos. 5:9); Gk. *díkē*–'penalty, punishment' (2 Thess. 1:9; Jude 7), *kólasis* (Mt. 25:46; 1 Jn. 4:18), *ekdíkēsis*–'vengeance,' 'punishment' (2 Cor. 7:11), *epitimía* (2 Cor. 2:6), *timōría* (He. 10:29); (verbs) Heb. *pāqaḏ*–'attend to,' 'visit,' 'appoint' (Jer. 46:25; 50:18), hiphil of *šûḇ*–'reverse, revoke' (Am. 1:3, 6, 9, 11, 13; 2:1, 4, 6); Gk. *kolázō*–'punish' (2 Pet. 2:9)]; AV also INIQUITY, MISCHIEF, CHASTISEMENT, TORMENT, etc.; NEB also HARM, SIN, "called to account' (Isa. 10:3), RECKONING, PENALTY, etc.; **PUNISHABLE** [Heb. *mišpaṭ*–'judgment' (Dt. 21:22; cf. 22:26)]. In Nu. 12:11 the RSV gives "punish" for Heb. *šîṯ ḥaṭṭāʾṯ ʿal* (lit. "put the blame on"; *CHAL*, p. 368). In Job 31:11 the RSV "iniquity to be punished by the judges" renders Heb. *ʿāwōn pᵉlîlîm* (lit. "iniquity for the judges"; cf. 31:28 and M. H. Pope, *Job* [*AB*, 3rd ed. repr. 1983], p. 232 n. 116). Several MSS that read Heb. *mûsārōh* (< *mûsār*, "correction, punishment"), rather than the MT Heb. *mûsāḏâ* (lit. "foundation," "appointment"), support the RSV "punishment" in Isa. 30:32.

*I. **Terminology**.–A. OT.* "Punish" most frequently renders Heb. *pāqaḏ*. The OT prophets often use this term in reference to divine punishment (Hos. 1:4; 2:13 [MT 15]; 4:9; 12:2 [MT 3]; etc.), e.g., the Lord's punishment of nations (Ps. 59:5 [MT 6]; Jer. 9:25; 46:25; 49:7f.; 50:18, 31), transgressors (Ps. 89:32 [MT 33]; Lam. 4:22; Hos. 4:9; 9:9; 12:2 [MT 3]; Amos 3:2, 14), arrogant human kings (Isa. 10:14; Jer. 25:12; 36:31), faithless Jews (Jer. 44:13, 29), Jerusalem (Jer. 5:9; 6:15; 21:14), the Lord's people (Jer. 5:29; 14:10), and false prophets (Jer. 29:32). Divine punishment also extends to a universal eschatological judgment (Isa. 24:21; cf. v. 22; 26:21). The cognate noun Heb. *pᵉquddâ* also refers to the divine punishment of nations, e.g., Israel (Isa. 10:3; Hos. 9:7; Mic. 7:4), Judah (Jer. 8:12), Egypt (46:21), Moab (48:44), and Babylon (50:27; 51:18). Jer. 10:15 uses this term in reference to the punishment of idols.

Several other OT terms also require discussion. In Ezk. 7 Heb. *nāṯan* has the nuance of requite, namely, for the abominations (vv. 3, 8) and ways (vv. 4, 9) of Israel (cf. Ezk. 23:49). According to Ex. 21:20f. a slave owner who beats his slave will be punished (Heb. *nāqōm yinnāqēm*, lit. "he shall surely be punished"; so AV) in the event of the immediate death of his slave. Though the nature of the punishment is uncertain, both Jewish interpreters and the reading of the Sam. Pent. (*môṯ yûmāṯ*, "he shall be put to death") affirm capital punishment (cf. B. S. Childs, *Book of Exodus* [*OTL,* 1974], p. 471); if, however, the slave should survive for several days, then the owner receives no punishment, which suggests that the loss of the slave was considered sufficient punishment (Ex. 21:21). Heb. *ḥāśaḵ* in Ezr. 9:13 refers to punishment that the Lord held back from Israel, though Ezra acknowledged that it was fully deserved. Heb. *šāpaṭ* in 1 S. 3:13 (used elsewhere of divine punishment; cf. Ezk. 11:10f.; 21:30 [MT 35]; 35:11; etc.) refers to judgment upon the house of Eli due in part for Eli's inadequate discipline of his sons (cf. 1 S. 2:22-25; 4:10f.).

The OT prophets repeatedly address the subject of punishment. The term most frequently rendered "punishment" is Heb. *ʿāwōn.* Often it refers to a consequence of sin; thus it is used of the destruction of Sodom (Gen. 19:15), possible chastisement for necromancy (1 S. 28:10), and Yahweh's judgment upon Babylon (Jer. 51:6), Israel (Ezk. 4:4-6, 17; 14:10; 21:25 [MT 30]), Ammon (21:29 [MT 34]), Edom (35:5), and the idolatrous Levites (44:10, 12). But the OT does not clearly separate the notion of sin as an act (cf. "punishment" for Heb. *ʿāwōn* in Ezk. 4:5; Job 19:29) from its consequences, which may consist of either personal inner guilt or actual physical punishment (cf. G. von Rad, *OT Theology*, I [Eng. tr. 1962], 262-68).

The cognate nouns Heb. *ḥaṭṭa'ṯ* and *ḥēṭ'* are also significant. In Lam. 4:6 the former term may refer to the consequence of sin ("punishment"; so RSV, AV) or to the act of sin (so RSV mg., NEB mg.; cf. Zec. 14:19; also *TDOT,* IV, 312). In Lam. 3:39 the latter term refers to the consequence of the act of sin, i.e., "punishment of... sins" (RSV, AV). Related to this is the concept of "bearing one's sin," which results in the death of the offender (cf. Lev. 19:17; 20:20; 22:9; Ezk. 23:49; Isa. 53:12; etc.; also *TDOT,* IV, 315f.).

In Jer. 30:14 Heb. *mûsār* should possibly be revocalized as the absolute form of the noun, which would alter "the punishment of a merciless foe" (RSV) to "a cruel punishment" (J. A. Thompson, *Book of Jeremiah* [*NICOT,* 1980], p. 558 n. 2). That Heb. *tôḵēḥâ* in Hos. 5:9 is best understood as divine punishment is indicated by other occurrences of the term (e.g., 2 K. 19:3 par. Isa. 37:3; Ps. 149:7; "accusation" is a weakened translation given by F. I. Andersen and D. N. Freedman, *Hosea* [*AB,* 1983], p. 408). In Amos's oracles the hiphil of Heb. *šûḇ* (lit. "reverse, return") occurs in the phrase "I will not revoke the punishment ..." (Heb. *lō' 'ᵃšîḇennû,* Am. 1:3, 6, 9, 11, 13; 2:1, 4, 6). Here "punishment" is supplied by the context.

In the OT "punishable" occurs twice. In Dt. 21:22 the RSV has "a crime punishable by death" for Heb. *ḥēṭ' mišpaṭ-māweṯ,* a "decision leading to capital punishment" (KoB, p. 579). Similarly, Dt. 22:26 has an "offense punishable by death" for Heb. *ḥēṭ' māweṯ,* a "sin deserving death warrant" (KoB, p. 19).

*B. NT.* The RSV translates six verbs and one noun as "punish." Both Acts 22:5 and 26:11 refer to the punishment (Gk. *timōréō*) of Christians in the early Church (cf. Gk. *kolázō* in Acts 4:21). Haenchen suggested a punishment by whipping in 26:11 (*Acts of the Apostles* [Eng. tr. 1971], p. 684), which finds support in other sources (e.g., T. Jos. 13:9–14:1; Josephus *Ant.* iv.8.21 [238]; cf. Mish. *Makkoth* iii.10-15). In 2 Cor. 6:9 "punished" (part. of Gk. *paideúō*) may refer to corporeal punishment (contra Bauer, rev., p. 604; cf. Lk. 23:16, 22; He. 12:7, 10; cf. also 2 Cor. 6:5; 11:23-25). Gk. *elénchō* in He. 12:5 (Prov. 3:11, LXX) concerns divine discipline intended for corrective purposes, which corresponds to the well-intended discipline of a father for his son (vv. 7-11). Gk. *dichotoméō* literally means "cut in pieces" (e.g., 3 Bar. 16:3), but in Mt. 24:51 (par. Lk. 12:46) it may refer to excommunication (cf. D. Hill, *Gospel of Matthew* [*NCBC*, repr. 1981], p. 325; cf. also 1QS 2:16, which uses the terms Heb. *kāraṯ,* "cut off," and *bāḏal,* "separate, divide," to indicate expulsion). In 2 Cor. 10:6 Gk. *ekdikéō* relates to the discipline of persons who, perhaps in violation of an apostolic decision (Gal. 2:9), intruded into Paul's missionary work in Corinth (C. K. Barrett, *Second Epistle to the Corinthians* [*HNTC,* 1973], pp. 253f.). The cognate noun Gk. *ekdíkēsis* in 1 Pet. 2:14 (RSV "to punish") refers to the state's duty to maintain civil justice.

In the NT "punishment" generally refers to chastisement associated with eternal judgment. According to 2 Thess. 1:9 eternal destruction is the penalty that awaits those who persecuted the Thessalonian believers. In classical Greek "pay the penalty" (Gk. *díkēn tísousin,* 2 Thess. 1:9) indicated the punishment meted out as a result of a legal process (I. H. Marshall, *1 and 2 Thessalonians* [*NCBC,* 1983], p. 178). In Jude 7 "undergo punishment" (Gk. *díkēn hypéchein*) is also a technical legal expression. Here the penalty for the wicked persons of Sodom and Gomorrah is "eternal fire."

The NT hapax legomenon Gk. *timōría* in He. 10:29 concerns a punishment much worse than physical death (v. 28) that meets those who repudiate the Son of God. In Mt. 25:46 "eternal punishment" (Gk. *kólasin aiṓnion*) refers to divine retribution meted out at the end of the age (cf. 2 Clem. 6:7; T. Reub. 5:5; T. Gad 7:5; M. Polyc. 11:2; some MSS 2:3). Gk. *kólasis* occurs elsewhere in the NT only in 1 Jn. 4:18, where, in view of the reference to the "day of judgment" in v. 17, it has an eschatological cast. R. E. Brown noted that "fear involves not only the absence of love but also the presence of the punishment it anticipates," namely, eternal punishment (*Epistles of John* [*AB,* 1982], p. 531). *See* ETERNAL; JUDGMENT, LAST.

In 2 Cor. 7:11 Gk. *ekdíkēsis* probably pertains to the disciplinary action taken by the Corinthian congregation toward one of its members (cf. Gk. *epitimía* in 2 Cor. 2:6).

***II. Offenses Requiring Capital Punishment.***–Capital offenses in the OT included: (1) striking or cursing a parent (Ex. 21:15, 17); (2) blasphemy (Lev. 24:14, 16, 23; 1 K. 21:13; Mt. 26:65f.); (3) sabbath breaking (Ex. 31:14f.; 35:2; Nu. 15:32-36); (4) witchcraft and false pretention to prophecy (Ex. 22:18; Lev. 20:27; Dt. 13:1-5; 18:20; 1 S. 28:3, 9); (5) adultery (Lev. 20:10-12; Dt. 22:22); (6) unchastity: (a) before marriage, but detected afterward (Dt. 22:20f. — penalty designated for the woman); (b) due to relations with someone other than one's betrothed (22:23 — penalty designated for the man and the betrothed woman); (c) of a priest's daughter (Lev. 21:9); (7) rape (Dt. 22:25 — penalty for the rapist and the woman if she did not cry for help); (8) incest, homosexuality, and bestiality (Ex. 22:19; Lev. 20:11-17); (9) abducting people for slavery (Ex. 21:16; Dt. 24:7); (10) idolatry (Lev. 20:1-5;

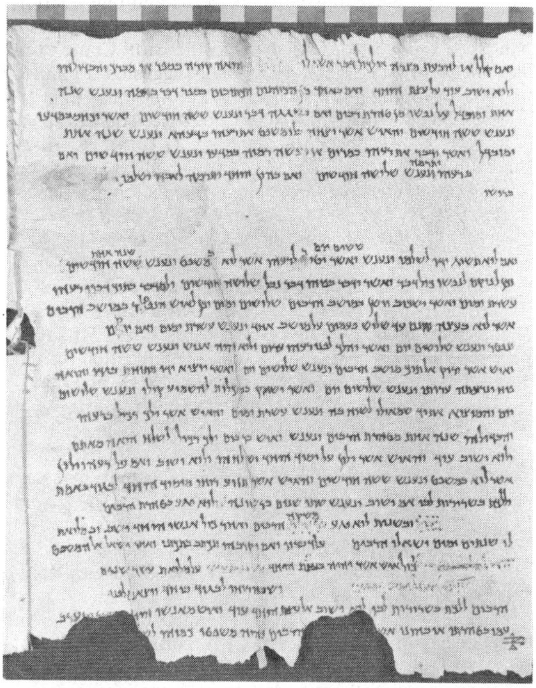

The Manual of Discipline from Qumrân, col. 7, listing fines (or penance) for various infractions as well as the penalty of expulsion for cursing God or apostasy (J. C. Trever)

Dt. 13:2-19; 17:2-7); (11) false witnessing in capital cases (Dt. 19:16, 19); and (12) intentional homicide (Ex. 21:12; Lev. 24:17; Nu. 35:16-21).

"Cutting off from the people" was the OT penalty for a number of offenses. The meaning of this expression has been debated; it may signify excommunication or death (cf. G. J. Wenham, *Book of Leviticus* [*NICOT,* 1979], pp. 241f.). It occurs in connection with the following offenses: (1) breach of morals such as wilful sin in general (Nu. 15:30f.) or incestuous relations (Lev. 18:6-23, 29); (2) breach of covenant effected by uncircumcision (Gen. 17:14), neglect of Passover (Nu. 9:13), sabbath breaking (Ex. 31:14), improper observance of the Day of Atonement (Lev. 23:26-30), the offering of children to Molech (20:3), witchcraft (20:6), anointment of an outsider with holy oil (Ex. 30:31-33); (3) breach of ritual, committed by eating leavened bread during Passover (Ex. 12:15, 19), eating the fat of sacrifices (Lev. 7:25), eating blood (7:27; 17:14), eating sacrifices when the eater is unclean (7:20f.; 22:3-6), eating a sacrifice late (19:5-8), generally neglecting purification (Nu. 19:13, 20), and other improper sacrificial procedures (Lev. 17:3f.; 17:8f.).

***III. Methods of Capital Punishment.***–The various methods of capital punishment included the following.

*A. Stoning.* This was the ordinary mode of execution (e.g., Ex. 19:13; Lev. 20:27; Dt. 22:24; Josh. 7:25; Lk. 20:3-6; Acts 7:58; Mish. *Sanhedrin* vii.4). At least two witnesses were required to substantiate a charge, and they had to cast the first stones (Dt. 17:6f.; cf. Jn. 8:7).

*B. Burning.* Burning was the punishment for unchastity (Gen. 38:24), for incest (Lev. 20:4), and for harlotry by a priest's daughter (Lev. 21:9; cf. Josephus *Ant.* iv.8.23 [249]; Mish. *Sanhedrin* vii.2; ix.1).

*C. Sword.* The sword was another tool of execution (Ex. 32:27; Dt. 13:15), along with the spear (Nu. 25:7f.) and the arrow (Ex. 19:13).

*D. Beheading.* This method was reserved especially for those who affronted royalty (2 S. 16:9; 2 K. 6:31f.). In later times beheading was one of four methods of capital punishment sanctioned by the Jewish court (Mish. *Sanhedrin* vii.1, 3). Accused murderers were executed by this means (Mish. *Sanhedrin* ix.1; cf. *Makkoth* ii.6).

***IV. Secondary Methods of Punishment.***–Other modes of punishment did not result in the death of the offender.

*A. Flogging.* Inflicted upon an offender's back, this common method of punishment usually numbered no more than thirty-nine strokes (Dt. 25:2f.; 2 Cor. 11:24f.). A rod or a switch was used (Prov. 10:13), or sometimes a "scorpion" (1 K. 12:11, 14; 2 Ch. 10:11, 14), which consisted of pointed and knotty rods or of whips embedded with sharp iron points (cf. Jgs. 8:7, 16; Prov. 26:3; *see* FLOG).

*B. Fining.* The modern practice of an offender's putting money into the community coffers is unknown in Scripture, unless Lev. 5:6-19 is an instance. Instead the injured party might receive an amount more than the value of the item in question (Ex. 21:22; Dt. 22:19; Prov. 17:26; Am. 2:8; *see* FINES).

*C. Blinding or Gouging of Eyes.* Blinding someone functioned as a punishment for various unrighteous deeds (cf. Gen. 19:11; 2 K. 6:18; Acts 13:11), while gouging, or putting out someone's eyes, served as a punishment of captives (cf. Jgs. 16:21; 2 K. 25:7).

*D. Chaining.* Manacles or fetters of copper or iron similar to modern handcuffs were sometimes fastened onto the wrists and ankles of a prisoner of war (Jgs. 16:21; 2 K. 25:7). Chaining was also a means of detaining prisoners awaiting trial and sentencing (Acts 12:6; 28:20).

*E. Confiscating Property.* Property was seized if it had fallen under the ban, i.e., had been singled out for destruction by special decrees of Yahweh (e.g., Nu. 21:2; Josh. 6:17), had been reserved for the army (Dt. 2:35; 20:14; Josh. 22:8), or had been given to the priesthood (Josh. 6:19).

*F. Enslaving. See* SLAVERY.

*G. Flaying.* The stripping off of a victim's skin was practiced in Assyria and Persia (*HDB,* I, 525). The OT mentions it figuratively in Mic. 3:2f., where it symbolizes the unjust treatment received by God's people from the corrupt leaders.

*H. Scourging. See* SCOURGE.

*I. Imprisonment.* The OT and NT references to imprisonment indicate that it was a common practice, though prisons functioned primarily for detention rather than punishment. *See* PRISON.

*J. Inflicting Indignities.* Captors, prison guards in charge of prisoners, and even bystanders sometimes humiliated a prisoner with vengeful or pain-inflicting acts (Mt. 26:67f. par. Mk. 14:65; Jn. 18:22; Acts 23:2).

*K. Mutilating.* The law forbade this treatment for any Israelite. It was a barbarous custom of the East (Jgs. 1:6f.; Ezk. 23:25; *see* EUNUCH; POLYGAMY), evidently regarded by the Hebrews as heinous (Dt. 23:1). The only act authorizing mutilation (except in retaliation; see below) is cited in Dt. 25:11f. (see A. D. H. Mayes, *Deuteronomy* [*NCBC,* repr. 1981], p. 330).

*L. Plucking out Hair.* In Neh. 13:25 this measure served as a punishent for those who had entered mixed marriages. According to Isa. 50:6 this method of punishment was particularly humiliating (cf. G. A. F. Knight, *Comm. on the Book of Isaiah 40–55* [*International Theological Comm.,* 1984], p. 145).

*M. Making Restitution.* Various OT laws governed making restitution for physical harm to a family member, a slave, an ox, etc. (cf. Ex. 22:1, 5f., 11-15; Lev. 5:16; Nu. 5:7f.).

*N. Retaliation.* Several passages in the Pentateuch record the so-called *lex talionis* (Ex. 21:23-25; Lev.

24:19-22; Dt. 19:21), which rendered punishment proportionate to the offense (cf. G. J. Wenham, *Book of Leviticus* [*NICOT*, 1979], p. 313).

***Bibliography.***–*ANET*, pp. 159-198; *DNTT*, III, 92-100; W. Eichrodt, *Theology of the OT*, II (Eng. tr. 1967), 423-433; A. N. Sherwin-White, *Roman Society and Roman Law in the NT* (repr. 1978); R. de Vaux, *Ancient Israel* (Eng. tr. repr. 1965), I, 143-163.

J. K. GRIDER G. L. KNAPP

**PUNITES** pū'nīts [Heb. *pûnî*] (Nu. 26:23); NEB PUITE. The family (Heb. *mišpāḥâ*) of PUVAH, one of Issachar's sons (cf. Gen. 46:13).

**PUNON** pū'non, po͞o'nōn [Heb. *pûnōn*]. A place of encampment for the Israelites, located between Zalmonah and Oboth, mentioned in the itinerary of Nu. 33. Punon, the Gr. *Phainōn,* has been identified with modern Feinân, a large copper-smelting site on the eastern edge of the Arabah. Punon was in ancient Edom; one of the tribal chieftains descended from Esau bore the name Pinon (Gen. 36:41; 1 Ch. 1:52), sometimes emended to Punon.

Punon was in an area noted historically for the mining and smelting of copper ore. Numerous smelting sites and mines have been located in surveys in and around Feinân. The available evidence indicates that the first substantial occupation at Feinân was during the last phase of the Early Bronze Age. Little evidence exists for any occupation during most of the Middle Bronze and Late Bronze Ages. From the beginning of the Iron Age (*ca.* 1200) to *ca.* 700, however, Feinân again functioned as an important center for mining and smelting. After a hiatus, activity began again during the Nabatean period and continued until the Arabic period. The favorable location in one of a series of wadis connecting the Arabah with the Edomite plateau (possibly at the junction of Wâdī el-Gheweir and Wâdī esh-Sheger) and the presence of a significant amount of water assured Feinân of regional importance.

Some traditions place the incident of Moses and the bronze serpent (Nu. 21:4-9) at or near Punon. The availability of ore and the fact that Oboth is mentioned as the place of encampment after the incident strengthen the tradition. Later, Eusebius (*Onom.* 123.9; 299.85) reported that Christians and condemned criminals were sent by the Romans to work the mines and smelters of Punon.

***Bibliography.***–*GP*, II, 410f.; N. Glueck, *Explorations in Eastern Palestine*, II (*AASOR*, 15, 1934-35), pp. 32-35.

T. V. BRISCO

**PUR** po͞or. *See* PURIM.

**PURAH** pū'rə [Heb. *purâ*] (Jgs. 7:10f.); AV PHURAH. Gideon's "servant" (Heb. *naʿar*) who accompanied him on his night visit to the Midianite camp. As the study of J. Macdonald (*JNES,* 35 [1976], 147-170, esp. pp. 157f.) has shown, *naʿar* can mean "squire" or "armor-bearer," and it probably does here. Thus it was natural for Gideon to take Purah with him. G. A. L.

**PURCHASE** [Heb. *miqnâ*–'acquisition (by purchase)' (Jer. 32:11f., 14, 16), *miqneh*–'property' (Gen. 49:32), *qānâ*–'acquire' (Gen. 25:10; Ex. 15:16; Jer. 32:7), *šāḇar*–'buy grain' ("purchase food," Dt. 2:6)]; AV also BUY; NEB also BUY, MAKE ONE'S OWN (Ex. 15:16). Apart from Ex. 15:16, the RSV uses "purchase" only in contexts referring to a payment of money for property or food. The verb *qānâ* does not necessarily imply payment of money, however, and in Ex. 15:16 it probably means simply to "acquire as one's own possession" (cf. NEB); cf. Ps. 74:2 (RSV "get"; AV "purchase"); 78:54 (RSV "win"; AV "purchase"). The AV also uses "purchase" to render two NT terms that have the general meaning of "obtain," "gain for oneself": Gk. *ktáomai* (Acts 1:18; 8:20) and *peripoéomai* (Acts 20:28; 1 Tim. 3:13).

*See* BUYING. N. J. O.

**PURE; PURIFICATION; PURITY.**

*I. Terminology.*–*A. OT.* More than half of the uses of "pure" in the RSV OT have to do with GOLD. Usually the Hebrew term is *ṭāhôr*. (In Lev. 24:4, 6 and 2 Ch. 13:11, RSV, *ṭāhôr* ["pure"] modifies "gold," which was apparently added on the basis of Ex. 25:31, 23f., while in the AV ["pure"] and NEB ["ritually clean"] it modifies the lampstand or table itself.) The noun *sāgûr,* "pure gold," is used in conjunction with *zāhāḇ,* "gold," in 1 K. 6:20f.; 7:49f.; 10:21; 2 Ch. 4:20, 22; 9:20 (NEB "red gold"). In 2 Ch. 4:21 "purest" is an attempt to make a smooth rendering of the awkward Hebrew expression *miḵlôṯ zāhāḇ,* lit. "perfection of gold" (AV "perfect gold"; NEB "solid gold"). In Lam. 4:1 the common adjective *ṭôḇ,* "good," is translated "pure" in connection with gold (AV, NEB, "fine"; cf. 2 Ch. 3:5, 8).

"Pure" in the RSV also often represents Heb. *ṭāhôr* when used for something other than gold: salt (Ex. 30:35), lampstand (31:8), incense (37:29), table (2 Ch. 13:11; NEB "ritually clean"), promises (Ps. 12:6 [MT 7]), persons (Prov. 15:26; 30:12), eyes (Hab. 1:13), and offering (Mal. 1:11). Twice "pure" represents a form of the verb *ṭāhēr,* "be clean, pure": Job 4:17 (man); Prov. 20:9 (person — pure [NEB "purged"] from sin).

Hebrew *zaḵ* is also common. In the Pentateuch it is used only for oil (Ex. 27:20; Lev. 24:2) or frankincense (Ex. 30:34; Lev. 24:7). In the Wisdom Literature it is applied to persons (Job 8:6; 33:9; AV, NEB, also "innocent," "blameless"), doctrine (11:4 [NEB "sound"]), prayer (16:17 [NEB "sincere"]), and conduct (Prov. 16:2 [AV "clean"]; 20:11 [NEB "innocent"]; 21:8). The related verbs *zāḵaḵ* and *zāḵâ* are used for a way (conduct) in Ps. 119:9 (AV "cleanse") and of a prince in Lam. 4:7.

Hebrew *bar,* "pure," appears in Ps. 19:8 (MT 9; NEB "shines clear"); 24:4; 73:1. Related forms are the verb *bārar,* used in 2 S. 22:27 par. Ps. 18:26 (MT 27) and the adjective *bārûr* in Zeph. 3:9.

Other Hebrew terms are: *'ĕmeṯ,* "reliability," in the expression *zeraʿ 'ĕmeṯ,* lit. "seed of reliability" (Jer. 2:21; AV "right"; NEB "true"); *niqqāyōn,* "cleanness" (Hos. 8:5; AV "innocency"; NEB "innocent"); and the related Aram. *neqē'* (Dnl. 7:9; NEB "cleanest").

The *ṭhr* root also predominates among Hebrew terms translated "purify" (piel and hithpael of *ṭāhēr,* "be clean, be pure": Gen. 35:2; Ezr. 6:20; Neh. 12:30; 13:22; Isa. 66:17; Ezk. 43:26; Mal. 3:3; AV also "be clean, cleanse oneself"; NEB also "pronounce ritually clean"), "purity" (*ṭāhôr*: Prov. 22:11), (the act of) "purifying" (*ṭōhar*: Lev. 12:4, 6), and (the state of) "purification" (*ṭohºrâ*: Lev. 12:4f.; Neh. 12:45). Other Hebrew terms translated "purify" are the niphal (Isa. 52:11; AV "be clean") and hithpael (Dnl. 12:10) of *bārar*; the piel (Lev. 8:15) and hithpael (Nu. 8:21; 31:19f., 23) of *ḥāṭā'*, "make free from (effect of) sin"; the pual of *zāqaq,* "filter, refine" (Ps. 12:6); and the hithpael of *qādaš,* "make oneself cultically pure" (2 S. 11:4). Cf. Mish. *Tohoroth.*

"Impurity" in the RSV OT always represents Heb. *niddâ*. Cf. Mish. *Niddah.*

*B. NT.* In the NT the most common words for "pure," etc. have the Greek root *kathar-,* "clean": *katharós* ("pure," used esp. of hearts [Mt. 5:8; 1 Tim. 1:5; 2 Tim. 2:22] and linen [Rev. 15:6; 19:8, 14; AV, NEB, "clean"]), *katharízō* ("purify" [Tit. 2:14; He. 9:14, 22f.]) and *ekkathaírō* ("purify" [2 Tim. 2:21; AV "purge"; NEB "cleanse"]), *katharótēs* ("purification" [He. 9:13]), and *katharismós* ("purification, purifying" [Lk. 2:22; Jn. 2:6;

3:25; He. 1:3; AV also "purged"; NEB also "purgation"]). This follows the common LXX use of *katharós* for Heb. *ṭâhôr, bar, zāḵaḵ,* and *ḥāṭāʾ*. Thus this word-group carries the ideas of innocence from sin, freedom from guilt, and cultic cleanness.

Seventeen uses of "pure" in the RSV NT represent the *hagn-* word-group: *hagnós* ("pure": 2 Cor. 11:2 [NEB "chaste"]; Phil. 4:8; 1 Tim. 5:22; Jas. 3:17; 1 Jn. 3:3), *hagnízō* ("purify"; Jn. 11:55; Acts 21:24, 26; 24:18; Jas. 4:8; 1 Pet. 1:22; 1 Jn. 3:3), *hagneía* ("purity": 1 Tim. 4:12; 5:22), *hagnótēs* ("purity": 2 Cor. 6:6 [NEB "innocence"]; 11:3), and *hagnismós* ("purification": Acts 21:26).

In Mk. 7:4 *rhantízō,* the reading of two of the best older MSS (א and B), was accepted by the RSV translators. (The alternative reading *baptízō* has been accepted in the latest editions of the most common texts of the Greek NT.) The only other NT uses of *rhantízō* are in He. 9:19, 21; 10:22 ("sprinkle"). Since in these passages the sprinkling clearly has to do with a rite of purification, the derived sense "purify" is used in Mk. 7:4 (cf. AV, NEB, "wash").

In Phil. 1:10 the Greek term is *eilikrinḗs* (NEB "flawless"). This term and the noun *eilikríneia* generally mean "sincere," "sincerity" in the NT (cf. AV; also RSV in 1 Cor. 5:8; 2 Cor. 1:12; 2:17; 2 Pet. 3:1).

The basic meaning of Gk. *ádolos* in 1 Pet. 2:2 (AV "sincere") is "unadulterated."

The use of *pistikós,* only in Mk. 14:3 and Jn. 12:3 of the nard, is problematical. In later writings the word is used in the sense of "faithful," "trustworthy." This has led to interpretation of its NT use as "genuine," "unadulterated." More probably, however, *pistikós* refers to some kind of name, perhaps derived from Lat. *spicatum,* from the Greek word for the pistachio tree, or from the East-Indian name of a nard plant (cf. Bauer, rev., p. 662).

"Impure" and "impurity" in the RSV NT always represent Gk. *akatharsía* and *akáthartos,* except for *porneía* in Rev. 14:8; 18:3.

***II. OT Meanings.***–Although each of these word-groups has its own origins and nuances, in biblical uses almost all of them have the same range of meaning as English "pure": (1) compositional flawlessness or uniformity; (2) ritual or ceremonial purity; (3) moral or ethical purity. Sometimes more than one of these meanings is intended. Heb. *ṭhr* may have "gleaming" as its basic meaning. In the OT it is usually used of cultic purity. Heb. *zkh* has the nuance of "upright" and *brr* of "clean."

*A. Compositional Flawlessness or Uniformity.* This is surely the basic meaning of the references to pure gold. But since all of the OT references to pure gold except 1 K. 10:21 par. 2 Ch. 9:20; Job 28:19 have to do with furnishings and accessories of the tabernacle (and later the temple) and the garments of the priests, an element of cultic purity may also be present. In Job 28:19 pure gold is a metaphor for wisdom, with an emphasis on value. It is similar to Ps. 12:6, which compares God's pure (*ṭâhôr*) promises with silver that has been "purified" (Heb. *zāqaq,* the second word for "refine" in this verse). The image of refining is also used in Mal. 3:3: God as purifier (*meṭahēr*) purifies (*ṭāhēr*) and refines (*zāqaq*) the sons of Levi. Lack of mixture, with overtones of cultic purity, is also the meaning of "pure" with reference to salt (Ex. 30:35), olive oil (27:20; Lev. 24:2), and frankincense (Ex. 30:34; Lev. 24:7) used in the tabernacle. The pure wool of Dnl. 7:9 is not simply unmixed with other materials but clean and therefore dazzlingly white. The context shows that physical appearance (probably "light-colored, fair") is intended in the expression "purer than snow" in Lam. 4:7.

*B. Ceremonial Purity.* The predominant meaning of "pure" in the OT is cultically or ceremonially pure. This is purity in the sense of being free from defect that would disqualify someone or something from holy uses or holy acts, i.e., from being in the presence or service of God. It is presumed that anything that is of God is pure: His promises (Ps. 12:6) are pure, like refined silver, and His commandment is pure (Ps. 19:8). In anthropomorphic language, Hab. 1:13 assumes that His eyes are too pure to look at evil. It follows that anyone or anything that is to come into His presence or service ought to be pure. The RSV translates most of the *ṭhr* words, and many of their synonyms (e.g., *brr, zkh*), with "clean," etc. *See* CLEAN AND UNCLEAN.

Thus the Levites had to purify themselves for service in the tabernacle (Nu. 8:12). (The practice was used in foreign cults, too; Isa. 66:17 refers to apostate Israelites purifying themselves for worship of a foreign god.) The altar of burnt offering was purified (Lev. 8:15; cf. Ex. 29:36), as would also be done for the altar of Ezekiel's vision (Ezk. 43:26). The objects of "pure gold" used in the tabernacle and temple were probably considered pure in this sense, too. The incense of Ex. 37:29, although a mixture, can thus be called "pure"; it is made according to a specific recipe because of its sacred use. Mal. 1:11 contrasts "pure" offerings to God by Gentiles with the unworthy offerings that His own people were bringing, thus making necessary a new purifying of the Levites (3:3).

Purification in the OT usually has to do not simply with dedication to holy use but with removal of ceremonial uncleanness (or ritual impurity), which occurred in several ways. One was association with foreign gods, especially idols (cf. Gen. 35:2). Therefore contact with foreign peoples, who worshiped the false gods, rendered God's people impure. Isa. 52:11 mentions purification in a passage that anticipates return from Exile. This need for purification, along with the usual purification for holy service, was probably in mind as the priests and Levites purified first themselves (Ezr. 6:20) and then the people and the rebuilt city gates (Neh. 12:30) after the Exile (cf. 12:45; 13:22).

Ceremonial impurity also occurred as a result of bodily emissions: semen, menstrual flow, and other discharges (Lev. 15). Purification in such cases came as a result of bathing, lapse of a prescribed time, and sometimes an offering. (The ceremonial aspect of this kind of "uncleanness," i.e., that it was not simply physical uncleanness, is shown by the fact that bathing alone did not remove it.) The rules regarding the menstrual period found in vv. 19-24 are referred to in 2 S. 11:4; Ezk. 18:6; 22:10; 36:17. Similar rules of purification applied to childbirth (Lev. 12; cf. Lk. 2:22-24), probably because of the discharge of blood that accompanied it.

Another source of ceremonial impurity was contact with a corpse. Nu. 19 describes the "red heifer ceremony," which included the "water for impurity" (vv. 9, 13, 20f.) as part of the purification process. Association with warfare also rendered unclean, so that the garments of soldiers, the captives, and the booty had to be purified in the same way (31:19f., 23).

*C. Ethical Purity.* Associated with the concept of ritual purity is the idea that thought and conduct appropriate for a people chosen by God may also be considered "pure," i.e., there is moral or ethical purity. Sometimes it is difficult to know whether cultic purity or ethical purity is meant in a particular text, and in fact both meanings are probably intended in some texts. Hos. 8:5 has to do with cultic impurity (worship of idols), but a strong moral element is probably involved, too.

This moral purity is expressed especially in the Psalms and Wisdom Literature. Persons themselves may be considered pure (Job 8:6; 33:9; Prov. 15:26; 30:12). Purity of "heart" is mentioned in Ps. 24:4; 73:1; Prov. 22:11. Such purity of the inner life should result in conduct acceptable to the Lord, which can also be considered pure (Job 4:17; Ps. 119:9; Prov. 16:2; 20:9, 11; 21:8). God is seen as good by those who are good, just as He opposes those who do evil (2 S. 22:27 par. Ps. 18:26). Related to pure thought and intention are the pure doctrine of Job 11:41, the pure prayer of 16:17, and the pure speech of Zeph. 3:9.

The purifying of Dnl. 12:10 probably has several levels of meaning: being refined (perhaps through persecution) into a select kind of person, maintaining ceremonial purity (esp. with regard to food and worship of false gods), and ethical conduct.

***III. NT Meanings.***–Compositional flawlessness or uniformity may be the meaning of the purity of the nard in Mk. 14:3; Jn. 12:3 (see I above). In Revelation both the gold of the heavenly city (21:18, 21) and the linen garments of the angels (15:6; 19:8, 14) are pure in both this sense and the sense of religious purity. The same is true of the pure water of He. 10:22. In 1 Pet. 2:2 milk that is pure in this sense is used in a metaphor for what is religiously correct.

The Jewish sacrificial system, with its acts of ceremonial purification, is mentioned in the NT in Mk. 7:4; Lk. 2:22; Jn. 2:6; 3:25; 11:55; Acts 21:24, 26; 24:18.

The concept of purification through sacrifice is applied to Christ's death, which can be seen as a sacrifice that purifies on a higher level than the OT sacrifices (Tit. 2:14; He. 1:3; 9:13f., 22f.). Christ's act puts the believer in a state of purification, acceptable to God.

In 2 Tim. 2:21 the language of ceremonial purity is used in an ethical context. Often in the NT the concept of purity includes both acceptability to God and the ethical deeds that should result from the purified state. This is probably the case in Tit. 1:15 and the references to a pure heart (Mt. 5:8; 1 Tim. 1:5; 2 Tim. 2:22; Jas. 4:8) or soul (1 Pet. 1:22). Cf. the pure conscience of He. 9:14. The loving (Phil. 1:10) or hoping (1 Jn. 3:3) that Christian faith makes possible results in purity.

A definite emphasis on the ethical sense of purity also occurs (1 Tim. 5:2, 22; Jas. 1:27; 3:17), esp. when "pure" or "purity" is used in a list of virtues (2 Cor. 6:6; Phil. 4:8; 1 Tim. 4:12). All uses of "impure" or "impurity" in the RSV NT have this emphasis.

In the figure of the "pure [*hagnós*] bride" of 2 Cor. 11:2f. both ceremonial and ethical purity are involved, as well as the idea of exclusive relationship. The last aspect is expresed in v. 3 by translating Gk. *haplótēs* and *hagnótēs* (lit. "sincerity and purity") as "sincere and pure devotion."

***Bibliography.***–*TDOT*, V, *s.v.* "ṭāhar" (H. Ringgren); *TDNT*, III, *s.v.* καθαρός κτλ. (R. Meyer, F. Hauck).

R. F. YOUNGBLOOD E. W. S.

**PURGE** [Heb. piel of *bāʿar*] (Dt. 13:5 [MT 6]; 17:7, 12; etc.); AV PUT . . . AWAY; [piel of *ṭāhēr*–'cleanse'] (2 Ch. 34:3, 5, 8); NEB also PURIFY; [piel of *ḥāṭā'*] (Ps. 51:7 [MT 9]); NEB "sprinkle"; [*bārar*–'purify'] (Ezk. 20:38); NEB "rid." To eliminate, usually with the idea of cleansing or purifying. Many uses of "purge" in the AV have been displaced by "cleanse" or "purify," since the modern emphatic and medical senses of "purge" are not justified by the Hebrew and Greek originals.

The basic meaning of *bāʿar* is "burn," an intensive force in the piel. Thus the meaning of "purge" in Deuteronomy is probably "destroy completely." The RSV translation of *ṭāhēr* in 2 Ch. 34 probably follows the AV tradition; the RSV has "cleanse" for similar uses of *ṭāhēr* (e.g., 29:15f., 18; Neh. 13:9, 30). With either translation an underlying concept is the goal of purification (cf. NEB). In Ps. 51:7 the meaning of the Hebrew term is derived from the concept of making a sin offering, which results in purification from sin (cf. ASV "purify"). Purification with hyssop refers to the use of hyssop for sprinkling (cf. NEB) in the rites of purification described in Lev. 14 and Nu. 19. In Ezk. 20:38 the driving out of rebels is seen as establishing not only order but also purification.

*See also* PURE; CLEAN AND UNCLEAN.

E. MACK E. W. S.

**PURIFICATION.** *See* PURE.

**PURIM** pōōr'im, pū'rim [Heb. *pûrîm*–'lots' < Akk. *pūrû* (cf. KoB, p. 756a) (Est. 9:26, 28f., 31f.); Gk. *Phrourai*, *Phrourim* (Ad. Est. 11:1)]; AV Apoc. PHURIM; **PUR** pōōr [Heb. *pûr*–'lot'] (Est. 3:7; 9:24, 26). A Jewish festival celebrated one month before Passover on 14 and 15 Adar, the final month of the biblical year, usually corresponding to February/March.

***I. Early References.***–The institution of Purim and the events that led to it are recorded in Esther (esp. 3:7; 9:20-32); it was also mentioned in the apocryphal additions to that book (Ad. Est. 10:10-13). Purim was commemorated as early as the Maccabean period, the first day of the feast (14 Adar) being called "Mordecai's day" (2 Macc. 15:36), and was continuously and widely observed down to Josephus's time (*Ant.* xi.6.13 [284-296]). The NT never mentions Purim (although some scholars had suggested that the unnamed feast in Jn. 5:1 was Purim, this theory has generally been rejected; see the comms.); it was celebrated locally and is therefore not to be connected with any of the festal pilgrimages to Jerusalem.

***II. Institution.***–The book of Esther describes how Haman, who had been made the foremost prince of Persia by King Ahasuerus (probably Xerxes I, 485-465 B.C.), hated the Jews bitterly, some of whom, e.g., Mordecai, were rising to prominence. Haman had the lot *(pûr)* cast to find an opportune day to work his hate upon them. That day turned out to be the 13th of the 12th month (Adar), the last month tried (Est. 3:7-11). But the wisdom of Mordecai, the heroism of Esther the Jewish queen, and the Jews' fasting and praying foiled Haman's dastardly scheme to have all of them slain by royal decree. Haman was hanged on the gallows that he had prepared for Mordecai (7:10; 8:1f.), and Mordecai was honored. The Jews were allowed to defend themselves against their attackers (8:9-14; 9:11-15). Mordecai informed all the Jews in the king's provinces of their great deliverance and enjoined them to keep 14 and 15 Adar as an annual feast (9:20-22). *See also* ESTHER, BOOK OF.

***III. Later Celebration.***–As the Jews passed from one civilization or empire to another, so many causes arose to remind them of the persecutions of Haman that the festival of a triumph over such persecutions was attractive and most significant. The 13th day is observed by fasting in commemoration of Esther's prayer and fasting before she approached the king. In the evening, at the beginning of the 14th day, the book of Esther is read in the synagogues with interpretations; the listeners shout, shake rattles, stamp their feet when Haman's name is read. Other persecutors and foes also sometimes are execrated. The names of Mordecai and Esther receive blessings. On the morning of 14th synagogue services are again held and presents are given to the poor and to friends. The rest of the day and the 15th are spent feasting and rejoicing; even certain excesses are condoned in the exuberance of national spirit. See also Mish. *Megillah*.

***IV. Theories about Its Origin.***–Many attempts have been made to trace the origin of Purim to pagan festivals or to events in Jewish history other than those described in Esther (for surveys see C. A. Moore, pp. xlvi-xlix; and esp. Paton, pp. 77-94). (1) It has been identified with the Assyrian New Year, when officials entered their term of service. (2) The Babylonian *puḫru*, New year festival, is another association; Mordecai then becomes Marduk, Esther is Ishtar, and Haman, Vashti, and Zeresh are Median gods (see Zimmern). (3) The most popular identifications are with Persian festivals; Pur is said to derive from *bahr*, "lot," from *purdighân*, "new year," or from *farwardighan*, the feast of departed souls (see Lewy, *HUCA*). (4) Origin has been sought also in a Greek bacchanalian occasion. (5) Others have linked it with Jewish experiences other than that recorded in Esther, such as a captivity in Edom, a persecution under the Ptolemies in Egypt, or the victory of Judas Maccabeus over Nicanor in 161 B.C. (1 Macc. 7:39-50; 2 Macc. 15:20-36). (6) Twentieth-century thought has tended to discount both mythological and historical experience for the explanation of Purim. R. H. Pfeiffer insisted that the whole book of Esther is fiction, that *pûrîm* has no sensible etymology, and that the feast as well as its name must have been simply invented by the author of the tale (*PIOT*, p. 745). None of these theories, however, squares with the teaching of Scripture or possesses sufficient probability even to have secured for itself geneal acceptance. Esther remains the most reasonable account; the term *pûrîm* is now well authenticated from Akkadian as meaning just what Scripture says it means, namely, "lots" (see Hallo). When excavating the royal city ("Shushan the palace") in 1884-86, M. Dieulafoy found among the debris of the "King's Gate" near the ruined apadana (throne room) a quadrangular prism or die engraved with the numbers 1, 2, 5, and 6, and with this "die" (*pūr*) the lots were cast (cf. M. Unger, *Archaeology and the OT* [1954], p. 309). The difficulties met in Esther are clearly not as great as those presented by other explanations.

*See also* LOTS.

***Bibliography.***–B. W. Anderson, *IB*, III, 824f.; W. W. Hallo, *BA*, 46 (1983), 19-29; *Jew.Enc.*, X, *s.v.* (Malter); J. Lewy, *HUCA*, 14 (1939), 127-151; *Revue hittite et asianique*, 5 (1939), 117-124; C. A. Moore, *Esther* (*AB*, 1971); G. F. Moore, *Judaism* (1927-30), II, 51-54; L. B. Paton, Comm. on Esther (*ICC*, repr. 1951); H. Schauss, *Jewish Festivals* (1938), pp. 237-271; R. de Vaux, *Ancient Israel* (Eng. tr. 1961), II, 514-17; H. Zimmern, *ZAW*, 11 (1891), 157-169.

E. MACK

**PURITY.** *See* PURE.

**PURLOIN.** To misappropriate or steal. The term is the AV translation of Gk. *nosphízomai*, "put aside for oneself, misappropriate" (Bauer, rev., pp. 543f.), in Tit. 2:10 (RSV, NEB, "pilfer"; cf. Acts 5:2f.; AV, RSV, NEB, "keep back"). Embezzlement of a master's property was a common temptation among slaves.

**PURPLE** [Heb. *'argāman* (Ex. 25:4; etc.), *t$^e$ḵēleṯ*–'blue, blue-violet' (Ex. 23:6), *tôlā'*–'scarlet, crimson' (Lam. 4:15); Aram. *'arg$^e$wān* (Dnl. 5:7, 16, 29); Gk. *porphýra* (Mk. 15:17, 20; etc.), *porphyroús* (Jn. 19:2, 5; Rev. 18:16)]; AV also BLUE, SCARLET; NEB also BLUE; **SELLER OF PURPLE GOODS** [Gk. *porphyrópōlis*] (Acts 16:14); NEB "dealer in purple fabric." The most highly prized dye in the ancient world obtained from the secretions of four molluscs native to the eastern Mediterranean: *helix ianthina, murex brandaris, murex trunculus,* and *purpura lapillus.* Various shades could be produced by mixing secretions from different species, by adding salt or other substances, or by using procedures such as double dyeing. Purple-dyeing establishments were located, of course, along the seacoast. A number of references to purple-dyed cloth (*Ugargmn*), sold by weight, have been found in the Ugaritic texts (15th cent. B.C.). Tyre and Sidon were well known as sources of purple, as is attested also by heaps of discarded shells found there. Recent excavations at Ashdod Harbor (Tell Ḥēḏar) have exposed shell heaps as well as dye vats. (*See also* DYE.) Pliny the Elder describes the production of purple in *Nat. hist.* ix.61-64. The importance of this industry can be seen in the name Phoenicia, which derives from *phoinikoús*, "red-purple"; the theory that "Canaan" is derived from a word for purple dye in the Nuzi texts (*kinaḫḫu*) has been seriously questioned (*see* CANAAN I).

Since approximately eight thousand molluscs were required to produce one gram of purple dye, purple cloth was extremely expensive, and the Bible refers to it almost exclusively as used by kings or for cultic purposes. Heb. *'argāmān*, (LXX *porphýra*) occurs repeatedly in the descriptions of the tabernacle curtains, veil, and screen (Ex. 26:1, 31, 36; 27:16; 35:5, 23, 25 35; 36:8; 38:18, 23), of the priestly vestments for Aaron and his sons (28:5, 8, 15, 33; 39:1f., 5, 8, 24, 29), and of the hangings of the Solomonic temple (2 Ch. 2:7 [*'arg$^e$wān*], 14; 3:14). It frequently occurs in a list with *t$^e$ḵēleṯ* (RSV usually "blue"), *tôlā'* (RSV usually "scarlet"), and other rich fabrics, embroidery, gold and silver, etc. It indicated the awe-inspiring luxury of King Solomon's palanquin (Cant. 3:10) and of the hangings in the palace of King Ahasuerus (Est. 1:6). Garments of purple could be a kingly reward (8:15; Aram. *'arg$^e$wān*, Dnl. 5:7, 16, 29); they could also be a sign of well-deserved prosperity (Prov. 31:22).

In other passages, however, reference to the unnecessary expense and luxury of purple carries overtones of the pride that goes before a fall. Purple is the clothing of idols doomed to perish (Jer. 10:9); it is the ship's awning in Ezekiel's oracle against Tyre (Ezk. 27:7); it is the dress of the frightening Assyrian warrior (23:6), who had already been overpowered by Babylon when Ezekiel's prophecy was written. Jesus uses it in this way in the story of the rich man dressed in purple (Gk. *porphýra*) who scorned Lazarus (Lk. 16:19). Likewise, Revelation speaks of the purple clothing of the personified wicked city Babylon (Rev. 17:4; 18:16) and also refers to purple as an article of the city's prosperous but doomed trade (18:12).

In Mk. 15:17, 20 *porphýra* denotes the "purple cloak" with which the soldiers dressed Jesus when they mocked Him; the parallel passage in Jn. 19:2, 5 uses *himátion porphyroún* ("purple robe").

Acts 16 reports that Lydia from Thyatira, who was converted by the apostle Paul when he visited a women's prayer meeting outside Philippi, after her baptism put her house at the disposal of the early Church (vv. 14f., 40). This represented a generous deed by a woman of substantial wealth, since she was a merchant of purple goods (*porphyrópōlis*).

***Bibliography.***–M. C. Astour, *JNES*, 24 (1965), 346-350; *Christian News from Israel*, 11/1 (1960), 16-19, plate 4:3; G. Dalman, *Arbeit und Sitte in Palästina* (1928-1942), II, 300ff.; R. J. Forbes, *Studies in Ancient Technology*, IV (repr. 1965), 98-122; R. Gradwohl, *Die Farben im AT* (*BZAW*, 83, 1963); L. B. Jensen, *JNES*, 22 (1963), 104-118; N. Jedejian, *Tyre Through the Ages* (1969), pp. 143-159.

D. IRVIN

**PURPOSE** (vbs.) [Heb. *yā'aṣ*–'advise, counsel' (Isa. 14:24, 26f.; 19:12, 17; etc.), *zāmam*–'consider, purpose, devise' (Jer. 4:28; Lam. 2:17; Zec. 1:6; 8:14f.), *yāṣar*–'form, fashion' (Isa. 46:11), *ḥāpēṣ*–'delight in' (Isa. 55:11), *'āmar*–'utter, say' (1 K. 5:5 [MT 19]; 2 Ch. 2:1 [MT 1:18])]; AV also DETERMINE, TAKE COUNSEL, THINK, PLEASE; NEB also DESIGN, PREPARE, RESOLVE, PLAN, etc.; (nouns) [Heb. *'ēṣâ*–'counsel, advice' (Ezr. 4:5; Ps. 106:43; Prov. 19:21; 20:15; Isa. 5:19; etc.), *yēṣer*–'form, framing,' 'purpose' (Dt. 31:21; 1 Ch. 29:18), *ḥēpeṣ*–'delight, pleasure' (Isa. 44:28; 46:10; 48:14), *maḥᵃšāḇâ*/*maḥᵃšeḇet*–'thought, plan, device' (Jer. 49:20, 30; 50:45; 51:29), *zimmâ*–'plan, device,' 'wickedness' (Ps. 119:150), *mᵉzimmâ*–'plan, plot' (Job 42:2; Jer. 51:11), *dāḇār*–'speech, word' (Neh. 8:4; Ps. 64:5 [MT 6]), *rā'â*–'evil,' 'misery, distress' ("evil purpose," Ex. 10:10), *ma'ᵃneh*–'answer, response' (Prov. 16:4), *ma'ᵃseh*–'deed, work' (Isa. 54:16); Gk. *próthesis*–'plan, purpose, resolve, will' (Acts 11:23; 27:13; Rom. 8:28; Eph. 1:11; 3:11; 2 Tim. 1:9), *boulḗ*–'counsel,' 'resolution, decision' (Lk. 7:30; 23:51; 1 Cor. 4:5; He. 6:17), *boúlēma*–'intention, purpose' (Acts 27:43), *gnṓmē*–'decision, declaration' (Rev. 17:17), *eudokía*–'favor, good pleasure' (Eph. 1:5, 9), *télos*–'end' (Jas. 5:11]; AV also COUNSEL, IMAGINATION, THOUGHT, PLEASURE, etc.; NEB also PLAN, THOUGHT, WILL, POLICY, PLEASURE, etc. In eight OT passages either contextual considerations or idiomatic expressions account for the RSV rendering "purpose" (Ex. 9:16; Lev. 11:32; 1 Ch. 12:33; Neh. 6:13; Job 10:13; Ps. 57:2 [MT 3]; 138:8; Jer. 6:20). In the NT the RSV "for this purpose" translates the demonstrative *hoútos* when it occurs with the prepositions *epí* (Lk. 4:43), *diá* (Jn. 12:27), or *eis* (Acts 9:21; 26:16). Similar is Gk. *eis autó toúto,* which is rendered "for the very purpose" (Rom. 9:17) and "for this very purpose" (Eph. 6:22; Col. 4:8). The RSV translates the articular infinitive Gk. *eis tó eínai* "the purpose was to make" (Rom. 4:11; AV "that . . . might be"; NEB "consequently"; cf. BDF, § 402 [2]). In Gal. 2:21 the RSV translates Gk. *dōreán* (lit. "freely," "as a gift") "to no purpose" (AV "in vain"; NEB "for nothing"). The RSV translates Gk. *ou kalṓs* "for no good purpose" (Gal. 4:17; AV "not well"; NEB "not with an honest envy"; NEB mg. "not with honest intentions"). In Gal. 4:18 it translates Gk. *en kalǭ* "for a good purpose" (AV "in a good thing").

In prophecies against Assyria (Isa. 14:24-27), Egypt (19:1-15), and Tyre (23:1-12) it is evident that judgment shall come according to that which Yahweh plans (Heb. *yā'aṣ,* Isa. 14:24, 26f.; 19:12, 17; 23:8f.). The cognate noun Heb. *'ēṣâ* reflects similar ideas. On occasion Yahweh's detractors may mock His plan (Isa. 5:19); but His plans supersede those of the most powerful nation (14:26f.). And in spite of what people may plan, only the plans of the Lord shall stand (Prov. 19:21).

Human agents also devise plans. For example Israel's enemies thwarted plans to rebuild the temple in Ezra's time (Ezr. 4:5). Also, Ps. 106 rehearses Israel's deliberate acts of rebellion and ingratitude in the wilderness. Accordingly "they were rebellious in their purposes" (v. 43) despite the Lord's repeated acts of deliverance; however, Heb. *'ēṣâ* has a more positive nuance in Prov. 20:5, where the "purpose" of a person, or profundity of thought, remains hidden and latent until it is elicited by another, namely, "a man of understanding" (cf. W. McKane, *Proverbs* [*OTL,* 1977], pp. 536f.).

When translated by "purpose" in the RSV Heb. *zāmam* most frequently refers to divine punishment (Jer. 4:28; Lam. 2:17; Zec. 1:6; 8:14), but it may also refer to divine blessing (Zec. 8:15). The cognate noun Heb. *mᵉzimmâ* in Jer. 51:11 refers to the punishment of Babylon as Yahweh's plan (cf. 23:20; 30:24). This latter term occurs in Job 42:2 where Job affirms that no one is able to thwart God's plans. Elsewhere in the OT *mᵉzimmâ* is used of human plans. Used almost exclusively with a negative sense is a second cognate noun Heb. *zimmâ* found in Ps. 119:150 where it connotes an evil plan or device (cf. Ps. 26:10; Prov. 24:9; Isa. 32:7; cf. also *TDOT,* IV, 87-90).

In several instances Heb. *yāṣar* means "form" or 'fashion," e.g., as a potter who fashions clay (Isa. 29:16; Jer. 18:2, 4, 6); but when reference is made to God's previously determined plans, as in Isa. 46:11 (cf. 2 K. 19:25 par. Isa. 37:26; Ps. 139:16 [pual]; Isa. 22:11), it has a figurative sense of "frame" or "pre-ordain." The cognate noun Heb. *yēṣer* occurs in Dt. 31:21 and 1 Ch. 29:18. As a noun it pertains to the inclinations or intentions in a person's heart, which in Dt. 31:21 tend toward evil (cf. Gen. 6:5; 8:21).

According to Isa. 55:11 the Lord's word accomplishes that which He "purposes" or desires (Heb. *ḥāpēṣ*), i.e., "nothing can prevent its effective operation" (R. N. Whybray, *Isaiah* [*NCBC,* repr. 1981], II, 193). Heb. *ḥēpeṣ*, a cognate noun, also occurs in Isaiah and refers to the good pleasure or will of Yahweh (Isa. 44:28; 46:10; 48:14; cf. Jgs. 13:23).

In 1 K. 5:5 (MT 19) and 2 Ch. 2:1 (MT 1:18) Heb. *'āmar* with the preposition *lᵉ* and an infinitive has the sense of "intend," thus the RSV "purpose" (cf. Ex. 2:14; 2 S. 21:6; 2 Ch. 28:10, 13).

Also, Jeremiah's oracles against the nations (Jer. 46:1–51:64) include a plan (Heb. *maḥᵃšāḇâ* / *maḥᵃšeḇeṯ* [ < *ḥāšaḇ*, "think, account"]) for judgment of Edom (49:20), of various Arab tribes (49:30), and of Babylon (50:45; 51:29).

In the NT Gk. *próthesis* pertains to human resolving, undertaking, or purposing when the RSV translates it by "purpose" (Acts 11:23; 27:13; *TDNT,* VIII, 166). Also, in Rom. 8:28 this term does not refer to a person's "free act of choice," but rather to "God's eternal purpose of mercy" (C. E. B. Cranfield, *Romans,* I [*ICC,* 1975], 492f.), which is integrally related to His effectual calling (cf. vv. 29f.; also 9:11). Likewise, the plan of reconciliation in Christ was according to God's "eternal purpose" (Eph. 3:11; cf. 1:11; also 2 Tim. 1:9).

When translated "purpose" Gk. *boulḗ* may be roughly divided into two categories: divine will (Lk. 7:30; He. 6:17) and human will (Lk. 23:51; 1 Cor. 4:5). Lk. 7:30 refers to the rejection of God's redemptive plan (Gk. *boulḗ*) by the Pharisees and the lawyers. In He. 6:17 this term pertains to the unchangable character of God's plan, namely, His plan of universal scope that He promised to realize in Abraham's seed (v. 14; cf. Gen. 22:16-18). 1 Cor. 4:5 uses this term in the sense of inner deliberations (*TDNT,* I, 635). Similar to this term is the cognate Gk. *boúlēma* found in Acts 27:43, which relates the plans or intentions of the soldiers to kill the shipwrecked prisoners (cf. Gk. *boulḗ,* v. 42).

In Eph. 1:5, 9 Gk. *eudokía* refers to God's free good pleasure, and specifically to "His resolution to save" (*TDNT,* II, 747; cf. M. Barth, *Ephesians* [*AB,* 1974], I, 105-109).

The precise nuance of Gk. *gnṓmē* in Rev. 17:17 is difficult to ascertain. It may refer to a royal decree similar to the edicts of the Persian kings (cf. J. M. Ford, *Revelation* [*AB,* repr. 1981], p. 292), or it may simply refer to the "decision" or "purpose" of God. Also, it should be noted that "purpose" and "mind" in 17:17 translate the same Greek term, which makes possible the rendering "God has put it into their hearts to carry out his mind by being of one mind . . . " (G. R. Beasley-Murray, *Revelation* [*NCBC,* repr. 1981], p. 260).

Though Gk. *télos* may mean "cessation" or "death" it does not, as is often assumed, have this sense in Jas. 5:11. Rather it has the sense of "outcome," i.e., the outcome of